E.M...
HANDBO...

BUTTERWORTHS EMPLOYMENT LAW HANDBOOK

Twenty-seventh edition

Editor

PETER WALLINGTON QC

LexisNexis®

Members of the LexisNexis® Group worldwide

United Kingdom — RELX (UK) Limited trading as LexisNexis®, 1–3 Strand, London WC2N 5JR and 9–10 St Andrew Square, Edinburgh EH2 2AF

LNUK Global Partners — LexisNexis® encompasses authoritative legal publishing brands dating back to the 19th century including: Butterworths® in the United Kingdom, Canada and the Asia-Pacific region; Les Editions du Juris Classeur in France; and Matthew Bender® worldwide. Details of LexisNexis® locations worldwide can be found at **www.lexisnexis.com**

Published by LexisNexis®

This is a Butterworths® title

A CIP Catalogue record for this book is available from the British Library.

ISBN for this volume: 978 1 4743 1127 4

Printed and bound by CPI Group (UK) Ltd, Croydon, CR0 4YY.

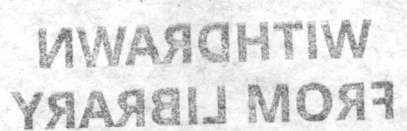

Visit LexisNexis at www.lexisnexis.co.uk

EDITOR'S INTRODUCTION TO THE TWENTY-SEVENTH EDITION

It has been a recurring editorial problem, over the 40 years since this *Handbook* was first published, that it has not been possible to know with any certainty whether particular new legislation would complete its (often tortuous) path through Parliament in time for inclusion in the particular edition under preparation. This was perhaps most dramatically felt with the Equality Act 2010, which finally made it to Royal Assent on the very day Parliament was dissolved in April 2010 for a general election; only then was it possible to start to finalise the contents of that year's edition.

This year the problem faced in preparing this edition of the *Handbook* has been very different but no less difficult: the uncertainty over when, and indeed whether, the UK will leave the European Union. This has meant that a battery of statutory instruments, amending a wide range of statutes, have been passed by Parliament that may, or may not, come into effect at 11pm on 31 October 2019 ('exit day', as it stands at the time of writing) – or at all. The prospective changes made by these EU Exit Regulations, most significantly to the Data Protection Act 2018, and to the General Data Protection Regulation it complements, are, together with the most relevant parts of the European Union (Withdrawal) Act 2018, at least potentially the most significant changes in the material in this edition.

Whatever one's views on the desirability of the UK leaving the EU, there can be little dispute that the process has consumed so much of Parliamentarians', Ministers' and civil servants' time that the usual flow of new legislation has been more of a trickle in the past year. Nevertheless, there have been important developments which are incorporated in the text. These include:

- The Parental Bereavement (Leave and Pay) Act 2018 (but not yet the Regulations needed to flesh out the statutory framework)
- Amendments to the Employment Rights Act 1996 Part I, and to the Working Time Regulations 1998, made by the Employment Rights (Employment Particulars and Paid Annual Leave) (Amendment) Regulations 2018
- The Employment Rights (Miscellaneous Amendments) Regulations 2019, which amongst other provisions also amend Part I of the 1996 Act
- The Agency Workers (Amendment) Regulations 2019, which amend the 2010 Regulations by removing the so-called 'Swedish Derogation'
- The Merchant Shipping (Work in Fishing Convention) Regulations 2018, which give effect to the ILO Work in Fishing Convention
- A new Employment Appeal Tribunal Practice Direction
- A revised Home Office Code of Practice on the Civil Penalty Scheme for Preventing Illegal Working
- Directive 2018/957/EU, which amends the Posted Workers Directive 1996, and which may be the last EU Directive in the field of employment law which the UK is required to implement.

The text in this edition is fully up to date to 15 May 2019, though later developments have been noted where possible.

The format of the *Handbook* is as in previous editions. Amendments are indicated as follows: repeals and revocations are indicated by an ellipsis; insertions and substitutions are in square brackets; and prospective repeals and substitutions are in italics, with the text to be substituted set out in the notes. Details of the provenance of changes are given in the notes, together with the effective date (unless this was before 15 May 2014 and, where still relevant, details of any savings and transitional provisions in the implementing legislation. Paragraphs are numbered consecutively within each Part: so paragraphs in Part 1 begin **[1.1]** and in Part 2 **[2.1]**.

Part 1 contains statutes, in chronological order and printed as amended and in force on 15 May 2019. Part 2 contains statutory instruments, in similar format and with similar annotations. Part 3 is European material, covering relevant Treaty provisions and EU Regulations and Directives, with any amendments annotated. Part 4 contains statutory and some non-statutory Codes of Practice, and relevant Guidance. Part 5 (Miscellaneous materials) includes international materials; Employment Appeal Tribunal Practice Directions; Employment Tribunal Presidential Directions and Guidance; Early Conciliation, Claim and Response Forms; and a list of useful addresses and contact details.

All the materials in this Handbook apply equally to England and Wales and Scotland unless otherwise stated. However, no attempt is made to cover Northern Ireland, and this book is not suitable for researching Northern Ireland domestic legislation; nor does it necessarily indicate whether particular legislation applies in Northern Ireland.

I am grateful to those, sadly too numerous to name individually, who have contributed, wittingly or otherwise, to the development of the Handbook over the past 40 years of its publication, and to this edition in particular. I include those who have drawn my attention to materials or supplied copies and those who have helpfully commented on coverage and format (even those whose suggestions on content have not been adopted). I am particularly grateful to LexisNexis for its organisational support and commitment, and especially to its editorial staff for their efficiency and forbearance in the face of what this year has been a particularly demanding schedule for publication. Responsibility for the selection of contents is mine.

Peter Wallington QC

North Berwick, East Lothian

7 June 2019

pwallington@btinternet.com

CONTENTS

Alphabetical list

PART 2 STATUTORY INSTRUMENTS

Chronological list

Alphabetical list

PART 3 EUROPEAN UNION MATERIALS

A. CONSTITUTIONAL MATERIALS

B. REGULATIONS & DIRECTIVES

Complete chronological list

Alphabetical list of common names of principal Regulations & Directives

G. SECRETARY OF STATE

H. CODES MADE BY BODIES REPLACED BY THE EHRC

I. CABINET OFFICE

J. EMPLOYMENT TRIBUNALS

PART 5 MISCELLANEOUS MATERIALS

A. INTERNATIONAL LAW MATERIALS

B. EMPLOYMENT TRIBUNAL & EAT PRACTICE DIRECTIONS & PRACTICE STATEMENTS, ETC

1. EAT PRACTICE DIRECTIONS

2. EAT PRACTICE STATEMENTS

C. FORMS FOR EMPLOYMENT TRIBUNAL CLAIMS

D. CABINET OFFICE AND GOVERNMENT EQUALITIES OFFICE MATERIALS

E. USEFUL ADDRESSES

PART 1
STATUTES

APPORTIONMENT ACT 1870

(1870 c 35)

An Act for the better Apportionment of Rents and other periodical Payments

[1 August 1870]

NOTES

See *Harvey* BI(1)(B).

[1.1]

1 Short title

This Act may be cited for all purposes as "The Apportionment Act 1870".

[1.2]

2 Rents, etc to be apportionable in respect of time

. . . All rents, annuities, dividends, and other periodical payments in the nature of income (whether reserved or made payable under an instrument in writing or otherwise) shall, like interest on money lent, be considered as accruing from day to day, and shall be apportionable in respect of time accordingly.

NOTES

Words omitted repealed by the Statute Law Revision (No 2) Act 1893.

3, 4 *(Outside the scope of this work.)*

[1.3]

5 Interpretation

In the construction of this Act—

The word "rents" includes rent service, rentcharge, and rent seck, and also tithes and all periodical payments or renderings in lieu of or in the nature of rent or tithe.

The word "annuities" includes salaries and pensions.

The word "dividends" includes (besides dividends strictly so called) all payments made by the name of dividend, bonus or otherwise out of the revenue of trading or other public companies, divisible between all or any of the members of such respective companies, whether such payments shall be usually made or declared, at any fixed times or otherwise; and all such divisible revenue shall, for the purposes of this Act, be deemed to have accrued by equal daily increment during or within the period for or in respect of which the payment of the same revenue shall be declared or expressed to be made, but the said word "dividend" does not include payments in the nature of a return or reimbursement of capital.

6 *(Outside the scope of this work.)*

[1.4]

7 Nor where stipulation made to the contrary

The provisions of this Act shall not extend to any case in which it is or shall be expressly stipulated that no apportionment shall take place.

EQUAL PAY ACT 1970 (NOTE)

(1970 c 41)

[1.5]

NOTES

The whole of this Act was repealed by the Equality Act 2010, s 211(2), Sch 27, Pt 1, as from 1 October 2010. The Equality Act 2010 (Commencement No 4, Savings, Consequential, Transitional, Transitory and Incidental Provisions and Revocation) Order 2010, SI 2010/2317 provides for various transitional provisions and savings in connection with the commencement of the 2010 Act and the repeal of this Act. See, in particular, art 15 (saving where the act complained of occurs wholly before 1 October 2010), and Schs 3, 4 (savings in relation to work on ships, hovercraft and in relation to seafarers).

SUPERANNUATION ACT 1972

(1972 c 11)

ARRANGEMENT OF SECTIONS

Persons employed in the civil service, etc

An Act to amend the law relating to pensions and other similar benefits payable to or in respect of persons in certain employment; to provide for distribution without proof of title of certain sums due to or in respect of certain deceased persons; to abolish the Civil Service Committee for Northern Ireland; to repeal section 6 of the Appropriation Act 1957; and for purposes connected with the matters aforesaid

[1 March 1972]

NOTES

Only sections of this Act relevant to employment law are reproduced here. For reasons of space, the subject matter of sections not printed is not annotated. All the provisions reproduced here apply to Great Britain – see s 30 (Short title, construction of references, commencement and extent) (not reproduced).

See *Harvey* BI(9).

Persons employed in the civil service, etc

[1.6]

1 Superannuation schemes as respects civil servants, etc

(1) The Minister for the Civil Service (in this Act referred to as "the Minister")—

(a) may make, maintain, and administer schemes (whether contributory or not) whereby provision is made with respect to the pensions, allowances or gratuities which, subject to the fulfilment of such requirements and conditions as may be prescribed by the scheme, are to be paid, or may be paid, by the Minister to or in respect of such of the persons to whom this section applies as he may determine;

(b) may, in relation to such persons as any such scheme may provide, pay or receive transfer values;

(c) may make, in such circumstances as any such scheme may provide, payments by way of a return of contributions, with or without interest; and

(d) may make such payments as he thinks fit towards the provision, otherwise than by virtue of such a scheme, of superannuation benefits for or in respect of the persons to whom this section applies as he may determine.

[(1A) Subsection (1) is subject to sections 18 and 19 of the Public Service Pensions Act 2013 (restrictions on benefits provided under existing schemes).]

(2) The Minister may, to such extent and subject to such conditions as he thinks fit, delegate to any other Minister or officer of the Crown any functions exercisable by him by virtue of this section or any scheme made thereunder.

[(2A) Where a money purchase scheme under this section includes provision enabling a member to elect for the benefits which are to be provided to or in respect of him to be purchased from any authorised provider whom he may specify, then—

(a) notwithstanding subsection (1)(a) above, the scheme may make provision for the making of such an election to have the effect, in such cases as the scheme may specify, of discharging any liability of the Treasury to pay those benefits to or in respect of that member; but

(b) the scheme shall not be so framed as to have the effect that benefits under it may only be provided in a manner which discharges that liability of the Treasury.]

[(2B) The Minister may, to such extent and subject to such conditions as he thinks fit, delegate to the Scottish Parliamentary Corporate Body any function exercisable by him by virtue of this section or any scheme made thereunder so far as that function or scheme relates to any employees of that Body.]

(3) Before making any scheme under this section the Minister, or, if the Minister so directs in relation to a particular scheme [(other than a scheme mentioned in subsection (3A) below)], another Minister of the Crown specified in the direction, shall consult with persons appearing to the Minister or that other Minister, as the case may be, to represent persons likely to be affected by the proposed scheme or with the last-mentioned persons.

[(3A) Before making any scheme under this section relating to any employees of the Scottish Parliamentary Corporate Body (referred to as "the Parliamentary corporation") the Minister, or, if the Minister so directs, the Parliamentary corporation, shall consult with—

(a) persons appearing to the Minister or the Parliamentary corporation, as the case may be, to represent persons likely to be affected by the proposed scheme, or

(b) the last-mentioned persons.]

(4) This section applies to persons serving—

(a) in employment in the civil service of the State; or
(b) in employment of any of the kinds listed in Schedule 1 to this Act; or
(c) in an office so listed.

[(4A) This section also applies to persons serving in employment or in an office, not being service in employment or in an office of a kind mentioned in subsection (4), where the employment or office is specified in a list produced for the purposes of this subsection (see section 1A).]

(5) Subject to subsection (6) below, the Minister may by order—
(a) add any employment to those listed in the said Schedule 1, being employment by a body or in an institution specified in the order,
(b) add any office so specified to the offices so listed, or
(c) remove any employment or office from the employments or offices so listed.

(6) No employment or office shall be added to those listed in the said Schedule 1 unless [at the date from which the addition has effect] the remuneration of persons serving in that employment or office is paid out of moneys provided by Parliament [the Consolidated Fund or the Scottish Consolidated Fund].

(7) Notwithstanding subsection (6) above, the Minister may by order provide that this section shall apply to persons serving in employment which is remunerated out of a fund specified in the order, being a fund established by or under an Act of Parliament.

(8) An order under subsection (5) or (7) above—
(a) may be made so as to have effect as from a date before the making of the order;
(b) may include transitional and other supplemental provisions;
(c) may vary or revoke a previous order made under that subsection; and
(d) shall be made by statutory instrument, which shall be subject to annulment in pursuance of a resolution of either House of Parliament.

[(9) In this section—

["authorised provider", in relation to the investment of any sums paid by way of voluntary contributions or the provision of any benefit, means—
(a) a person who has permission under [Part 4A] of the Financial Services and Markets Act 2000 to invest such sums or, as the case may be, to provide that benefit;
(b) an EEA firm of a kind mentioned in paragraph 5(a), (b) or (c) of Schedule 3 to that Act, which has permission under paragraph 15 of that Schedule (as a result of qualifying for authorisation under paragraph 12 of that Schedule) to invest such sums or, as the case may be, to provide that benefit and which satisfies the conditions applicable to it which are specified in subsection (9B), (9C) or (9D); or
(c) an EEA firm of a kind mentioned in paragraph 5(d) of Schedule 3 to that Act, which has permission under paragraph 15 of that Schedule (as a result of qualifying for authorisation under paragraph 12 of that Schedule) to invest such sums or, as the case may be, to provide that benefit;]

"money purchase scheme" [has the meaning given by section 181(1) of the Pension Schemes Act 1993].]

[(9A) In subsection (9), the definition of "authorised provider" must be read with—
(a) section 22 of the Financial Services and Markets Act 2000;
(b) any relevant order under that section; and
(c) Schedule 2 to that Act.

(9B) If the EEA firm concerned is of the kind mentioned in paragraph 5(a) of Schedule 3 to the Financial Services and Markets Act 2000, the conditions are—
(a) that, in investing of the sums in question, or in providing the benefit in question, the firm is carrying on a service falling within section A or [B of Annex I to the markets in financial instruments directive]; and
(b) that the firm is authorised by its home state authorisation to carry on that service.

(9C) If the EEA firm concerned is of the kind mentioned in paragraph 5(b) of that Schedule, the conditions are—
(a) that, in investing of the sums in question, or in providing the benefit in question, the firm is carrying on an activity falling within Annex 1 to the [capital requirements directive]; and
(b) that the activity in question is one in relation to which an authority in the firm's home State has regulatory functions.

(9D) If the EEA firm concerned is of the kind mentioned in paragraph 5(c) of that Schedule, the conditions are—
(a) that, in investing of the sums in question, or in providing the benefit in question, the firm is carrying on an activity falling within Annex 1 to the [capital requirements directive];
(b) that the activity in question is one in relation to which an authority in the firm's home State has regulatory functions; and
(c) that the firm also carries on the activity in question in its home State.

(9E) Expressions used in subsections (9B) to (9D) which are also used in Schedule 3 to the Financial Services and Markets Act 2000 have the same meaning in those subsections as they have in that Schedule.]

NOTES

Sub-s (1A): inserted by the Public Service Pensions Act 2013, s 27, Sch 8, paras 6, 7.

Sub-s (2A): inserted by the Pensions (Miscellaneous Provisions) Act 1990, s 8(1).

Sub-s (2B), (3A): inserted by the Scotland Act 1998 (Consequential Modifications) Order 2000, SI 2000/2040, art 2(1), Schedule, Pt I, para 5(1), (2), (4).

Sub-s (3): words in square brackets inserted by SI 2000/2040, art 2(1), Schedule, Pt I, para 5(1), (3).

Sub-s (4A): inserted by the Public Service Pensions Act 2013, s 29, Sch 9, paras 1, 2.

Sub-s (6): words in first pair of square brackets inserted by the Public Bodies Act 2011, s 34; words in second pair of square brackets substituted by the Scotland Act 1998, s 125, Sch 8, para 14.

Sub-s (9): inserted by the Pensions (Miscellaneous Provisions) Act 1990, s 8(2); definition "authorised provider" substituted by the Financial Services and Markets Act 2000 (Consequential Amendments and Repeals) Order 2001, SI 2001/3649, art 106(1), (2); words in square brackets in para (a) of the definition "authorised provider" substituted by the Financial Services Act 2012, s 114(1), Sch 18, Pt 2, para 35; words in square brackets in the definition "money purchase scheme" substituted by the Pension Schemes Act 1993, s 190, Sch 8, para 6.

Sub-ss (9A)–(9E): inserted by SI 2001/3649, art 106(1), (3); words in square brackets in sub-s (9B)(a) substituted by the Financial Services and Markets Act 2000 (Markets in Financial Instruments) Regulations 2007, SI 2007/126, reg 3(6), Sch 6, Pt 1, para 4; words in square brackets in sub-ss (9C)(a) and (9D)(a) substituted by the Capital Requirements Regulations 2013, SI 2013/3115, reg 46(1), Sch 2, Pt 2, para 31.

Modifications: various enactments modify this section so that (i) references to a Minister of the Crown include the Scottish Ministers and the Welsh Ministers, and (ii) references to an officer of the Crown other than a Minister include (for example) the Electoral Commission's chief executive and the chief executive of the Local Government Boundary Commission. These enactments are considered outside the scope of this work.

Orders: a large number of Orders have been made under this section in relation to the admission of various categories of persons and office-holders to Sch 1 to this Act. The list of Orders has been omitted for reasons of space.

[1.7]

[1A List of employments and offices for purposes of section 1(4A)

(1) The Minister may specify an employment or office in a list produced for the purposes of section 1(4A) if subsection (2), (3) or (4) applies in relation to the employment or office.

(2) This subsection applies to an employment or office if—

(a) at any time on or after the commencement of this section, the employment or office ceases to be of a kind mentioned in section 1(4), and

(b) immediately before that time, persons serving in the employment or office are, or are eligible to be, members of a scheme under section 1 by virtue of section 1(4).

(3) This subsection applies to an employment or office if—

(a) at any time before the commencement of this section, the employment or office ceased to be of a kind mentioned in section 1(4), and

(b) at that time, persons serving in the employment or office ceased to be members of a scheme under section 1 or to be eligible for membership of such a scheme.

(4) This subsection applies to an employment or office if—

(a) it is of a description prescribed by regulations, and

(b) the Minister determines that it is appropriate for it to be specified for the purposes of section 1(4A).

(5) The power to specify an employment or office in reliance on subsection (4) may be exercised so as to have retrospective effect.

(6) The Minister—

(a) may at any time amend a list produced under this section, and

(b) must publish the list (and any amendments to it).

(7) The published list must comply with such requirements, and contain such information, as may be prescribed by regulations.

(8) Regulations made under this section must be made by the Minister by statutory instrument; and an instrument containing such regulations is subject to annulment in pursuance of a resolution of either House of Parliament.]

NOTES

Inserted by the Public Service Pensions Act 2013, s 29, Sch 9, paras 1, 3.

[1.8]

2 Further provisions relating to schemes under s 1

(1) A scheme under section 1 of this Act which makes provision with respect to the pensions, allowances or gratuities which are to be, or may be, paid to or in respect of a person to whom that section applies and who is incapacitated or dies as a result of an injury sustained, or disease contracted, in circumstances prescribed by the scheme may make the like provision in relation to any other person, being a person who is employed in a civil capacity for the purposes of Her Majesty's Government in the United Kingdom, whether temporarily or permanently and whether for reward or not, or is a person holding office in that Government and who is incapacitated or dies as a result of an injury or disease so sustained or contracted.

(2) Any scheme under the said section 1 may make provision for the payment by the Minister of pensions, allowances or gratuities by way of compensation to or in respect of persons—

(a) to whom that section applies; and

(b) who suffer loss of office or employment, or loss or diminution of emoluments, in such circumstances, or by reason of the happening of such an event, as may be prescribed by the scheme.

[(3) [Subject to subsection (3A) below,] no scheme under the said section 1 shall make any provision which would have the effect of reducing the amount of any pension, allowance or gratuity, in so far as that amount is directly or indirectly referable to rights which have accrued (whether by virtue of service rendered, contributions paid or any other thing done) before the coming into operation of the scheme, unless the persons consulted in accordance with section 1(3) of this Act have agreed to the inclusion of that provision.]

[(3A) Subsection (3) above does not apply to a provision which would have the effect of reducing the amount of a compensation benefit except in so far as the compensation benefit is one provided in respect of a loss of office or employment which is the consequence of—

(a) a notice of dismissal given before the coming into operation of the scheme which would have that effect, or

(b) an agreement made before the coming into operation of that scheme.

(3B) In this section—

"compensation benefit" means so much of any pension, allowance or gratuity as is provided under the civil service compensation scheme by way of compensation to or in respect of a person by reason only of the person's having suffered loss of office or employment;

"the civil service compensation scheme" means so much of any scheme under the said section 1 (whenever made) as provides by virtue of subsection (2) above for benefits to be provided by way of compensation to or in respect of persons who suffer loss of office or employment.

(3C) In subsection (3B) above a reference to suffering loss of office or employment includes a reference to suffering loss or diminution of emoluments as a consequence of suffering loss of office or employment.]

[(3D) So far as it relates to a provision of a scheme under the said section 1 which would have the effect of reducing the amount of a compensation benefit, the duty to consult in section 1(3) of this Act is a duty to consult with a view to reaching agreement with the persons consulted.]

(4) Subject to subsection (3) above, any scheme under the said section 1, or any provision thereof, may be framed—

(a) so as to have effect as from a date earlier than the date on which the scheme is made; or

(b) so as to apply in relation to the pensions, allowances or gratuities paid or payable to or in respect of persons who, having been persons to whom the said section 1 applies, have died or ceased to be persons to whom that section applies before the scheme comes into operation; or

(c) so as to require or authorise the payment of pensions, allowances or gratuities to or in respect of such persons.

(5) Where an order has been made under section 1 (7) of this Act, any scheme under that section may provide for the payment to the Minister out of the fund specified in the order of benefits or other sums paid by him in accordance with the scheme to or in respect of persons to whom that section applies by virtue of the order, together with any administrative expenses incurred in connection with the payment of those sums, and for the payment into that fund of contributions paid in accordance with the scheme by or in respect of those persons and of any transfer values received in respect of them.

(6) Any scheme under the said section 1 may provide for the determination by the Minister of questions arising under the scheme and may provide that the decision of the Minister on any such question shall be final.

(7) Where under any such scheme any question falls to be determined by the Minister, then, at any time before the question is determined, the Minister may (and if so directed by any of the Courts hereinafter mentioned shall) state in the form of a special case for determination by the High Court, the Court of Session or the Court of Appeal in Northern Ireland any question of law arising out of the question which falls to be determined by him.

(8) Where such a case is stated for determination by the High Court, an appeal to the Court of Appeal from the determination by the High Court shall lie only with the leave of the High Court or of the Court of Appeal; and where such a case is stated for determination by the Court of Session then, subject to any rules of court, the Minister shall be entitled to appear and be heard when the case is being considered by that Court.

(9) Any scheme under the said section 1 may amend or revoke any previous scheme made thereunder.

(10) Different schemes may be made under the said section 1 in relation to different classes of persons to whom that section applies, and in this section "the principal civil service pension scheme" means the principal scheme so made relating to persons serving in employment in the [civil service of the State].

(11) Before a scheme made under the said section 1, being the principal civil service scheme or a scheme amending or revoking that scheme, comes into operation the Minister shall lay a copy of the scheme before Parliament.

[(11A) Subsection (11B) below applies if a scheme made under the said section 1 makes any provision which would have the effect of reducing the amount of a compensation benefit.

(11B) Before the scheme comes into operation, the Minister must have laid before Parliament a report providing information about—

(a) the consultation that took place for the purposes of section 1(3) of this Act, so far as relating to the provision,

(b) the steps taken in connection with that consultation with a view to reaching agreement in relation to the provision with the persons consulted, and

(c) whether such agreement has been reached.]

(12) Notwithstanding any repeal made by this Act, the existing civil service superannuation provisions, that is to say, the enactments and instruments listed in Schedule 2 to this Act, shall, with the necessary adaptations and modifications, have effect as from the commencement of this Act as if they constituted a scheme made under the said section 1 in relation to the persons to whom that section applies, being the principal civil service pension scheme, and coming into operation on the said commencement and may be revoked or amended accordingly.

NOTES

Sub-s (3): substituted by the Pensions (Miscellaneous Provisions) Act 1990, s 9; words in square brackets inserted by the Superannuation Act 2010, s 1(1), (2).

Sub-ss (3A)–(3C): inserted by the Superannuation Act 2010, s 1(1), (3).

Sub-ss (3D), (11A), (11B): inserted by the Superannuation Act 2010, s 2(1)–(3).

Sub-s (10): words in square brackets substituted by the Constitutional Reform and Governance Act 2010, s 19, Sch 2, Pt 1, para 2.

Rules, etc: various Rules and Regulations relating to the Principal Civil Service Pension Scheme which were made under the Superannuation Act 1965 (repealed by this Act) now have effect under this section. They are omitted as outside the scope of this work.

[1.9]

5 Benefits under civil service superannuation on schemes not assignable

(1) Any assignment (or, in Scotland, assignation) of or charge on, and any agreement to assign or charge, any benefit payable under a scheme made under section 1 of this Act shall be void.

(2) Nothing in subsection (1) above shall affect the powers of any court under [section 310 of the Insolvency Act 1986] . . . (bankrupt's salary, pension, etc may be ordered to be paid to the trustee in bankruptcy) or under any enactment applying to Northern Ireland (including an enactment of the Parliament of Northern Ireland) and corresponding to [section 51(2) of the Bankruptcy Act 1914 or [the said section 310]] [or the powers of any person under section 90 or 95 of the Bankruptcy (Scotland) Act 2016].

NOTES

Sub-s (2): words "section 310 of the Insolvency Act 1986" and "the said section 310" in square brackets substituted by the Insolvency Act 1986, s 439(2), Sch 14; words omitted repealed, and words in final pair of square brackets inserted, by the Bankruptcy (Scotland) Act 2016 (Consequential Provisions and Modifications) Order 2016, SI 2016/1034, art 7(1), Sch 1, Pt 1, para 1, as from 30 November 2016; words in second (outer) pair of square brackets substituted by the Insolvency Act 1985, s 235(1), Sch 8, para 19.

Persons employed in local government service, etc

[1.10]

7 Superannuation of persons employed in local government service, etc

(1) The Secretary of State may by regulations make provision with respect to the pensions, allowances or gratuities which, subject to the fulfilment of such requirements and conditions as may be prescribed by the regulations, are to be, or may be, paid to or in respect of such persons, or classes of persons, as may be so prescribed, being—

(a) persons, or classes of persons, employed in local government service; and
(b) other persons, or classes of persons, for whom it is appropriate, in the opinion of the Secretary of State, to provide pensions, allowances or gratuities under the regulations.

[(1A) Subsection (1) is subject to sections 18 and 19 of the Public Service Pensions Act 2013 (restrictions on benefits provided under existing schemes).]

(2) Without prejudice to the generality of subsection (1) above, regulations under this section—

(a) may include all or any of the provisions referred to in Schedule 3 to this Act; and
(b) may make different provision as respects different classes of persons and different circumstances.

(3) Notwithstanding anything in the Pensions (Increase) Act 1971, regulations under this section may provide—

(a) that increases under that Act of such of the pensions, allowances or gratuities payable under the regulations as may be prescribed by the regulations, or such part of those increases as may be so prescribed, shall be paid out of such of the superannuation funds established under the regulations as the regulations may provide; and
(b) that the cost of those increases or that part thereof, as the case may be, shall be defrayed by contributions from the persons to whom any services in respect of which the pensions, allowances or gratuities are or may become payable were or are being rendered or by such of those persons as may be so prescribed;

and any provisions of the said Act of 1971, or of regulations made under section 5 thereof, relating to liability for the cost of increases under that Act of pensions, allowances or gratuities payable under the regulations shall have effect subject to the provisions of any regulations made by virtue of this subsection and for the time being in force.

(4) Without prejudice to subsection (2) above, regulations made by virtue of subsection (3) above may make different provision as respects different classes of pensions, allowances or gratuities.

(5) Before making any regulations under this section the Secretary of State shall consult with—

(a) such associations of local authorities as appear to him to be concerned;
(b) any local authority with whom consultation appears to him to be desirable; and
(c) such representatives of other persons likely to be affected by the proposed regulations as appear to him to be appropriate.

NOTES

Sub-s (1A): inserted by the Public Service Pensions Act 2013, s 27, Sch 8, paras 6, 8.

Transfer of Functions: functions under this section are transferred, in so far as they are exercisable in or as regards Scotland, to the Scottish Ministers, by the Scotland Act 1998 (Transfer of Functions to the Scottish Ministers etc) Order 1999, SI 1999/1750, art 2, Sch 1.

Regulations: a large number of Regulations have been made under this section constituting and amending what is now the Local Government Pension Scheme. The principal Regulations for England and Wales are the Local Government Pension Scheme Regulations 2013, SI 2013/2356 (as amended). The equivalent Regulations applying to Scotland (with effect from 1 June 2018) are the Local Government Pension Scheme (Scotland) Regulations 2018, SSI 2018/141 which were made under the powers conferred by the Public Services Pensions Act 2013.

Teachers

[1.11]

9 Superannuation of teachers

(1) The Secretary of State may, by regulations made with the consent of the Minister, make provision with respect to the pensions, allowances or gratuities which, subject to the fulfilment of such requirements and conditions as may be prescribed by the regulations, are to be, or may be, paid [to or in respect of teachers by the Secretary of State or, in the case of injury benefit, by the Secretary of State, an employer of teachers or such other person as the Secretary of State may consider appropriate and may specify in the regulations].

[(1A) Subsection (1) is subject to sections 18 and 19 of the Public Service Pensions Act 2013 (restrictions on benefits provided under existing schemes).]

(2) Without prejudice to the generality of subsection (1) above, regulations under this section—

(a) may include all or any of the provisions referred to in Schedule 3 to this Act; and

(b) may make different provision as respects different classes of persons and different circumstances.

[(2A) Where regulations under this section make provision with respect to money purchase benefits, they may also—

(a) include provision enabling a person to elect for such money purchase benefits as are to be provided to or in respect of him under the regulations to be purchased from any authorised provider whom he may specify; and

(b) notwithstanding subsection (1) above, provide that the making of such an election shall have the effect, in such cases as may be specified in the regulations, of discharging any liability of the Secretary of State to pay those benefits to or in respect of that person;

but no regulations under this section shall be so framed as to have the effect that any money purchase benefits to be provided under them may only be provided in a manner which discharges that liability of the Secretary of State.]

(3) Where the regulations provide for the making of any such payment as is referred to in paragraph 3, 5 or 6 of the said Schedule 3, they may also provide for the payment to be made by the Secretary of State.

[(3A) Notwithstanding anything in the Pensions (Increase) Act 1971, regulations under this section may provide that the cost of increases under that Act of such of the pensions, allowances or gratuities payable under the regulations as may be prescribed by the regulations, or such part of those increases as may be so prescribed, shall be defrayed—

(a) by contributions from employers of teachers or from such other persons or classes of person (apart from teachers) as the Secretary of State may consider appropriate and may specify in the regulations; or

(b) by contributions from such of those employers or other persons as may be so specified;

and any provisions of the said Act of 1971, or of regulations made under section 5 thereof, relating to liability for the cost of increases under that Act of pensions, allowances or gratuities payable under the regulations shall have effect subject to the provisions of any regulations made by virtue of this subsection and for the time being in force.]

(4) Where regulations under this section provide for the establishment of a superannuation fund, the regulations may also provide for the payment by the Secretary of State—

(a) of the administrative expenses of the persons by whom, in accordance with the regulations, the fund is to be administered; and

(b) of such travelling, subsistence and other allowances to those persons as the Secretary of State may, with the consent of the Minister, determine.

(5) Before making any such regulations the Secretary of State shall consult with representatives of [local authorities, or, in Scotland, education authorities] and of teachers and with such representatives of other persons likely to be affected by the proposed regulations as appear to him to be appropriate.

[(5A) The powers exercisable by a [local authority] or, in Scotland, an education authority, by virtue of—

(a) section 111 of the Local Government Act 1972 (subsidiary powers of local authorities), or

(b) section 69 of the Local Government (Scotland) Act 1973 (similar provision for Scotland),

shall be taken to include, and to have at all times included, power to pay, or arrange for the payment of, injury benefit to or in respect of teachers; but that section shall cease to confer any such power on an authority in either part of Great Britain as from the coming into force of the first regulations under this section which make provision for the payment of injury benefit by such an authority to or in respect of teachers in that part.]

(6) In this section

["authorised provider" has the meaning given in section 1;]

["injury benefit" means a pension, allowance or gratuity payable under the regulations to or in respect of a teacher in consequence of any injury sustained, or disease contracted, by him in the course of his employment in that capacity;]

["local authority" has the meaning given by section 579(1) of the Education Act 1996;]

"money purchase benefits" has the meaning given by [section 181(1) of the Pension Schemes Act 1993];]

"teachers" includes such persons as may be prescribed by regulations made under this section, being persons employed otherwise than as teachers—

(a) in a capacity connected with education which to a substantial extent involves the control or supervision of teachers; or

(b) in employment which involves the performance of duties in connection with the provision of education or services ancillary to education.

(7) . . .

NOTES

Sub-s (1): words in square brackets substituted by the Pensions (Miscellaneous Provisions) Act 1990, s 11(1).

Sub-s (1A): inserted by the Public Service Pensions Act 2013, s 27, Sch 8, paras 6, 9.

Sub-ss (2A), (3A), (5A): inserted by the Pensions (Miscellaneous Provisions) Act 1990, ss 4(1), 8(3), 11(2).

Sub-s (6) is amended as follows:

Definition "authorised provider" inserted by the Pensions (Miscellaneous Provisions) Act 1990, s 8(4), and subsequently substituted by the Financial Services and Markets Act 2000 (Consequential Amendments and Repeals) Order 2001, SI 2001/3649, art 107.

Definition "injury benefit" inserted by the Pensions (Miscellaneous Provisions) Act 1990, s 11(3).

Definition "local authority" inserted by SI 2010/1158, art 5(1), Sch 2, Pt 2, para 27(1), (4).

Definition "money purchase benefits" inserted by the Pensions (Miscellaneous Provisions) Act 1990, s 8(4).

Words in square brackets in the definition "money purchase benefits" substituted by the Pension Schemes Act 1993, s 190, Sch 8, para 7.

Sub-s (7): repealed by SI 2010/1158, art 5(1), (2), Sch 2, Pt 2, para 27(1), (5), Sch 3, Pt 2.

Transfer of Functions: functions under this section are transferred, in so far as they are exercisable in or as regards Scotland, to the Scottish Ministers, by the Scotland Act 1998 (Transfer of Functions to the Scottish Ministers etc) Order 1999, SI 1999/1750, art 2, Sch 1.

Regulations: with effect from 1 April 2015, the principal Regulations for England and Wales are the Teachers' Pensions Scheme Regulations 2014, SI 2014/512, which were made under the powers conferred by the Public Services Pensions Act 2013. Note that the Teachers' Pensions Regulations 2010, SI 2010/990 (which were made under this section) are still in force. For Scotland, the principal Regulations are the Teachers' Superannuation (Scotland) Regulations 2005, SSI 2005/393 (as amended). Other Regulations are omitted for reasons of space.

Persons engaged in health services, etc

[1.12]

10 Superannuation of persons engaged in health services, etc

(1) The Secretary of State may, by regulations made with the consent of the Minister, make provision with respect to the pensions, allowances or gratuities which, subject to the fulfilment of such requirements and conditions as may be prescribed by the regulations, are to be, or may be, paid by the Secretary of State to or in respect of such persons, or classes of persons, as may be so prescribed [(in this section referred to as "health staff")], being—

(a) persons, or classes of persons, engaged in health services other than services provided by a . . . local authority; and

(b) other persons, or classes of persons, for whom it is appropriate, in the opinion of the Secretary of State, to provide pensions, allowances or gratuities under the regulations.

[(1A) Subsection (1) is subject to sections 18 and 19 of the Public Service Pensions Act 2013 (restrictions on benefits provided under existing schemes).]

(2) Without prejudice to the generality of subsection (1) above, regulations under this section—

(a) may include all or any of the provisions referred to in Schedule 3 to this Act; and

(b) may make different provision as respects different classes of persons and different circumstances.

[(2A) Where regulations under this section make provision with respect to money purchase benefits, they may also—

(a) include provision enabling a person to elect for such money purchase benefits as are to be provided to or in respect of him under the regulations to be purchased from any authorised provider whom he may specify; and

(b) notwithstanding subsection (1) above, provide that the making of such an election shall have the effect, in such cases as may be specified in the regulations, of discharging any liability of the Secretary of State to pay those benefits to or in respect of that person;

but no regulations under this section shall be so framed as to have the effect that any money purchase benefits to be provided under them may only be provided in a manner which discharges that liability of the Secretary of State.]

(3) Where the regulations provide for the making of any such payment as is referred to in paragraph 3, 5 or 6 of the said Schedule 3, they may also provide for the payment to be made by the Secretary of State.

[(3A) Notwithstanding anything in the Pensions (Increase) Act 1971, regulations under this section may provide that the cost of increases under that Act of such of the pensions, allowances or gratuities payable under the regulations as may be prescribed by the regulations, or such part of those increases as may be so prescribed, shall be defrayed—

(a) by contributions from employers of health staff or from such other persons or classes of person (apart from health staff) as the Secretary of State may consider appropriate and may specify in the regulations; or

(b) by contributions from such of those employers or other persons as may be so specified;

and any provisions of the said Act of 1971, or of regulations made under section 5 thereof, relating to liability for the cost of increases under that Act of pensions, allowances or gratuities payable under the regulations shall have effect subject to the provisions of any regulations made by virtue of this subsection and for the time being in force.]

(4) Before making any such regulations the Secretary of State shall consult with such representatives of persons likely to be affected by the proposed regulations as appear to him to be appropriate.

(5) *(Amends the Superannuation (Miscellaneous Provisions) Act 1967, s 7).*

[(6) In this section—

["authorised provider" has the meaning given in section 1;]

"money purchase benefits" has the meaning given by [section 181(1) of the Pension Schemes Act 1993].]

NOTES

Sub-s (1): words in square brackets inserted by the Pensions (Miscellaneous Provisions) Act 1990, s 4(2); words omitted repealed by the National Health Service Reorganisation Act 1973, ss 57, 58, Sch 5.

Sub-s (1A): inserted by the Public Service Pensions Act 2013, s 27, Sch 8, paras 6, 10.

Sub-ss (2A), (3A): inserted by the Pensions (Miscellaneous Provisions) Act 1990, ss 4(2), 8(5).

Sub-s (6): added by the Pensions (Miscellaneous Provisions) Act 1990, s 8(6); definition "authorised provider" substituted by the Financial Services and Markets Act 2000 (Consequential Amendments and Repeals) Order 2001, SI 2001/3649, art 108; words in square brackets in the definition "money purchase benefits" substituted by the Pension Schemes Act 1993, s 190, Sch 8, para 7.

Transfer of Functions: functions under this section are transferred, in so far as they are exercisable in or as regards Scotland, to the Scottish Ministers, by the Scotland Act 1998 (Transfer of Functions to the Scottish Ministers etc) Order 1999, SI 1999/1750, art 2, Sch 1.

Regulations: with effect from 1 April 2015, the principal Regulations for England and Wales are the National Health Service Pension Scheme Regulations 2015, SI 2015/94, which were made under the powers conferred by the Public Services Pensions Act 2013. Note that the National Health Service Pension Scheme Regulations 1995, SI 1995/300 and the National Health Service Pension Scheme Regulations 2008, SI 2008/653 (both of which were made under this section) are still in force. For transitional provisions and savings in relation to the NHS Pension Scheme contained in the 1995 Regulations and the 2008 Regulations, see the National Health Service Pension Scheme (Transitional and Consequential Provisions) Regulations 2015, SI 2015/95 (which were made under this section). With effect from 1 April 2015, the principal Regulations for Scotland are the National Health Service Pension Scheme (Scotland) Regulations 2015, SSI 2015/94, which were also made under the powers conferred by the Public Services Pensions Act 2013. Note that the National Health Service Superannuation Scheme (Scotland) Regulations 2011, SSI 2011/117 and the National Health Service Superannuation Scheme (2008 Section) (Scotland) Regulations 2013, SSI 2013/174 (both of which were made under this section) are still in force. For transitional provisions and savings in relation to the NHS Pension Scheme contained in the 2011 Regulations and 2013 Regulations, see the National Health Service Pension Scheme (Transitional and Consequential Provisions) (Scotland) Regulations 2015, SSI 2015/95. Other Regulations are omitted for reasons of space.

Miscellaneous and Supplemental

[1.13]

24 Compensation for loss of office, etc

(1) Subject to subsection (2) below, the Secretary of State may, with the consent of the Minister, by regulations provide for the payment by such person as may be prescribed by or determined under regulations of pensions, allowances or gratuities by way of compensation to or in respect of the following persons, that is to say, persons—

(a) in relation to whom regulations may be made under section 7, section 9 or section 10 of this Act or section 1 of the [Police Pensions Act 1976] or [in respect of whose service payments may be made under a scheme brought into operation under section 34 of the Fire and Rescue Services Act 2004]; and

(b) who suffer loss of office or employment, or loss or diminution of emoluments, in such circumstances, or by reason of the happening of such an event, as may be prescribed by the regulations.

[(1A) Subsection (1) is subject to section 19 of the Public Service Pensions Act 2013 (restrictions on benefits provided under existing schemes).]

(2) Regulations under this section relating to persons in relation to whom regulations may be made under section 7 of this Act may be made without the consent of the Minister.

(3) Regulations under this section may—

(a) include provision as to the manner in which and the person to whom any claim for compensation is to be made, and for the determination of all questions arising under the regulations;

(b) make different provision as respects different classes of persons and different circumstances and make or authorise the Secretary of State to make exceptions and conditions; and

(c) be framed so as to have effect from a date earlier than the making of the regulations,

but so that regulations having effect from a date earlier than the date of their making shall not place any individual who is qualified to participate in the benefits for which the regulations provide in a worse position than he would have been in if the regulations had been so framed as to have effect only from the date of their making.

(4) Regulations under this section may include all or any of the provisions referred to in paragraphs 8, 9 and 13 of Schedule 3 to this Act.

(5) Regulations under this section shall be made by statutory instrument, which shall be subject to annulment in pursuance of a resolution of either House of Parliament.

NOTES

Sub-s (1): words in first pair of square brackets substituted by the Police Pensions Act 1976, s 13(1), Sch 2, para 10; words in second pair of square brackets substituted by the Fire and Rescue Services Act 2004, s 53(1), Sch 1, para 37 (for transitional provisions in relation to the Firefighters' Pension Scheme, see the Fire and Rescue Services Act 2004 (Firefighters' Pension Scheme) (Wales) Order 2004, SI 2004/2918 and the Firefighters' Pension Scheme (England and Scotland) Order 2004, SI 2004/2306).

Sub-s (1A): inserted by the Public Service Pensions Act 2013, s 27, Sch 8, paras 6, 11.

Transfer of Functions: functions under this section are transferred, in so far as they are exercisable in or as regards Scotland, to the Scottish Ministers, by the Scotland Act 1998 (Transfer of Functions to the Scottish Ministers etc) Order 1999, SI 1999/1750, art 2, Sch 1.

Regulations: Regulations made under this section include the National Health Service (Compensation for Premature Retirement) Regulations 2002, SI 2002/1311, the Local Government (Early Termination of Employment) (Discretionary Compensation) (England and Wales) Regulations 2006, SI 2006/2914 at **[2.919]**, the Teachers' Pensions Regulations 2010, SI 2010/990, and the Local Government (Discretionary Payments) (Injury Allowances) Regulations 2011, SI 2011/2954. Other Regulations are omitted for reasons of space.

EUROPEAN COMMUNITIES ACT 1972

(1972 c 68)

ARRANGEMENT OF SECTIONS

PART I
GENERAL PROVISIONS

SCHEDULES

An Act to make provision in connection with the enlargement of the European Communities to include the United Kingdom, together with (for certain purposes) the Channel Islands, the Isle of Man and Gibraltar

[17 October 1972]

NOTES

The whole of this Act is repealed by the European Union (Withdrawal) Act 2018, s 1, as from exit day (as defined in s 20 of that Act).

The Parts of this Act which have been reproduced here are those which govern the status in UK law of the European Union Treaties and legislation, and empower the incorporation of EU legislation into UK law.

See *Harvey* PII.

PART I
GENERAL PROVISIONS

[1.14]

1 Short title and interpretation

(1) This Act may be cited as the European Communities Act 1972.

(2) In this Act . . . —

["the EU" means the European Union, being the Union established by the Treaty on European Union signed at Maastricht on 7th February 1992 (as amended by any later Treaty),]

"the Communities" means the European Economic Community, the European Coal and Steel Community and the European Atomic Energy Community;

"the Treaties" or "[the EU Treaties]" means, subject to subsection (3) below, the pre-accession treaties, that is to say, those described in Part I of Schedule 1 to this Act, taken with—

(a) the treaty relating to the accession of the United Kingdom to the European Economic Community and to the European Atomic Energy Community, signed at Brussels on the 22nd January 1972; and

(b) the decision, of the same date, of the Council of the European Communities relating to the accession of the United Kingdom to the European Coal and Steel Community; [and

(c) the treaty relating to the accession of the Hellenic Republic to the European Economic Community and to the European Atomic Energy Community, signed at Athens on 28th May 1979; and

(d) the decision, of 24th May 1979, of the Council relating to the accession of the Hellenic Republic to the European Coal and Steel Community;] [and

[(e) the decisions of the Council of 7 May 1985, 24 June 1988, 31 October 1994, 29 September 2000 and 7 June 2007 on the Communities' system of own resources, and the decision of the Council of 26 May 2014 on the EU's system of own resources;]]

[(g) the treaty relating to the accession of the Kingdom of Spain and the Portuguese Republic to the European Economic Community and to the European Atomic Energy Community, signed at Lisbon and Madrid on 12th June 1985; and

(h) the decision, of 11th June 1985, of the Council relating to the accession of the Kingdom of Spain and the Portuguese Republic to the European Coal and Steel Community;] [and

(j) the following provisions of the Single European Act signed at Luxembourg and The Hague on 17th and 28th February 1986, namely Title II (amendment of the treaties

establishing the Communities) and, so far as they relate to any of the Communities or any Community institution, the preamble and Titles I (common provisions) and IV (general and final provisions);] [and

(k) *Titles II, III and IV of the Treaty on European Union signed at Maastricht on 7th February 1992, together with the other provisions of the Treaty so far as they relate to those Titles, and the Protocols adopted at Maastricht on that date and annexed to the Treaty establishing the European Community with the exception of the Protocol on Social Policy on page 117 of Cm 1934] [and*

(l) *the decision, of 1st February 1993, of the Council amending the Act concerning the election of the representatives of the European Parliament by direct universal suffrage annexed to Council Decision 76/787/ECSC, EEC, Euratom of 20th September 1976] [and*

(m) *the Agreement on the European Economic Area signed at Oporto on 2nd May 1992 together with the Protocol adjusting that Agreement signed at Brussels on 17th March 1993] [and*

(n) *the treaty concerning the accession of the Kingdom of Norway, the Republic of Austria, the Republic of Finland and the United Kingdom of Sweden to the European Union, signed at Corfu on 24th June 1994;] [and*

(o) *the following provisions of the Treaty signed at Amsterdam on 2nd October 1997 amending the Treaty on European Union, the Treaties establishing the European Communities and certain related Acts—*

(i) *Articles 2 to 9,*

(ii) *Article 12, and*

(iii) *the other provisions of the Treaty so far as they relate to those Articles,*

and the Protocols adopted on that occasion other than the Protocol on Article J.7 of the Treaty on European Union;] [and

(p) *the following provisions of the Treaty signed at Nice on 26th February 2001 amending the Treaty on European Union, the Treaties establishing the European Communities and certain related Acts—*

(i) *Articles 2 to 10, and*

(ii) *the other provisions of the Treaty so far as they relate to those Articles,*

and the Protocols adopted on that occasion;] [and

(q) *the treaty concerning the accession of the Czech Republic, the Republic of Estonia, the Republic of Cyprus, the Republic of Latvia, the Republic of Lithuania, the Republic of Hungary, the Republic of Malta, the Republic of Poland, the Republic of Slovenia and the Slovak Republic to the European Union, signed at Athens on 16th April 2003;] [and*

(r) *the treaty concerning the accession of the Republic of Bulgaria and Romania to the European Union, signed at Luxembourg on 25th April 2005;] [and*

(s) *the Treaty of Lisbon Amending the Treaty on European Union and the Treaty Establishing the European Community signed at Lisbon on 13th December 2007 (together with its Annex and protocols), excluding any provision that relates to, or in so far as it relates to or could be applied in relation to, the Common Foreign and Security Policy;] [and*

(t) *the Protocol amending the Protocol (No 36) on transitional provisions annexed to the Treaty on European Union, to the Treaty on the Functioning of the European Union and to the Treaty establishing the European Atomic Energy Community, signed at Brussels on 23 June 2010;] [and*

(u) *the treaty concerning the accession of the Republic of Croatia to the European Union, signed at Brussels on 9 December 2011; and*

(v) *the Protocol on the concerns of the Irish people on the Treaty of Lisbon, adopted at Brussels on 16 May 2012;]*

and [any other treaty entered into by the EU (except in so far as it relates to, or could be applied in relation to, the Common Foreign and Security Policy)], with or without any of the member States, or entered into, as a treaty ancillary to any of the Treaties, by the United Kingdom;

and any expression defined in Schedule 1 to this Act has the meaning there given to it.

(3) If Her Majesty by Order in Council declares that a treaty specified in the Order is to be regarded as one of [the EU Treaties] as herein defined, the Order shall be conclusive that it is to be so regarded; but a treaty entered into by the United Kingdom after the 22nd January 1972, other than a pre-accession treaty to which the United Kingdom accedes on terms settled on or before that date, shall not be so regarded unless it is so specified, nor be so specified unless a draft of the Order in Council has been approved by resolution of each House of Parliament.

(4) For purposes of subsections (2) and (3) above, "treaty" includes any international agreement, and any protocol or annex to a treaty or international agreement.

NOTES

Repealed as noted at the beginning of this Act.

Sub-s (2) is amended as follows:

Words omitted repealed by the Interpretation Act 1978, s 25(1), Sch 3.

Definition "the EU" inserted by the European Union (Amendment) Act 2008, s 3(1).

In the definitions "the Treaties" or "the EU Treaties" (originally the "the Treaties" or "the Community Treaties") words "the EU Treaties" substituted by the European Union (Amendment) Act 2008, s 3(3), Schedule, Pt 1; paras (c), (d) and the word immediately preceding para (c), inserted by the European Communities (Greek Accession) Act 1979, s 1; para (e) and the word immediately preceding it originally inserted (together with para (f)) by the European Communities (Finance) Act 1985, s 1, and substituted, together with the word immediately preceding it, (for paras (e), (f)) by the European Communities (Finance) Act 2001, s 1; para (e) further substituted by the European Union (Finance) Act 2015, s 1(2), as from 21 September 2015; para (g) and the word immediately preceding it and para (h) inserted by the European Communities (Spanish and Portuguese Accession) Act 1985, s 1; para (j) and the word immediately preceding it inserted by the European Communities (Amendment) Act 1986, s 1; para (k) and the word immediately preceding it inserted by the European Communities (Amendment) Act 1993, s 1(1); para (l) and the word immediately preceding it inserted by the European Parliamentary Elections Act 1993, s 3(2); para (m) and the word immediately preceding it inserted by the European Economic Area Act 1993, s 1; para (n) and the word immediately preceding it added by the European Union (Accessions) Act 1994, s 1; para (o) and the word immediately preceding it added by the European Communities (Amendment) Act 1998, s 1; para (p) and the word immediately preceding it added by the European Communities (Amendment) Act 2002, s 1(1); words "any other treaty entered into by the EU (except in so far as it relates to, or could be applied in relation to, the Common Foreign and Security Policy)" in square brackets substituted by the European Union (Amendment) Act 2008, s 3(3), Schedule, Pt 1; para (q) and the word immediately preceding it added by the European Union (Accessions) Act 2003, s 1(1); para (r) and the word immediately preceding it added by the European Union (Accessions) Act 2006, s 1(1); para (s) and the word immediately preceding it added by the European Union (Amendment) Act 2008, s 2; para (t) and the word immediately preceding it added by the European Union Act 2011, s 15(2); paras (u), (v) and the word immediately preceding para (u) inserted by the European Union (Croatian Accession and Irish Protocol) Act 2013, s 3.

Sub-s (3): words in square brackets substituted by the European Union (Amendment) Act 2008, s 3(3), Schedule, Pt 1.

The reference in sub-s (2)(n) to Norway was superseded by the subsequent decision of Norway not to accede to the Union.

Orders in Council made under this section: omitted as outside the scope of this work.

[1.15]

2 General implementation of Treaties

(1) All such rights, powers, liabilities, obligations and restrictions from time to time created or arising by or under the Treaties, and all such remedies and procedures from time to time provided for by or under the Treaties, as in accordance with the Treaties are without further enactment to be given legal effect or used in the United Kingdom shall be recognised and available in law, and be enforced, allowed and followed accordingly; and the expression ["enforceable EU right"] and similar expressions shall be read as referring to one to which this subsection applies.

(2) Subject to Schedule 2 to this Act, at any time after its passing Her Majesty may by Order in Council, and any designated Minister or department may [by order, rules, regulations or scheme], make provision—

(a) for the purpose of implementing any [EU obligation] of the United Kingdom, or enabling any such obligation to be implemented, or of enabling any rights enjoyed or to be enjoyed by the United Kingdom under or by virtue of the Treaties to be exercised; or

(b) for the purpose of dealing with matters arising out of or related to any such obligation or rights or the coming into force, or the operation from time to time, of subsection (1) above;

and in the exercise of any statutory power or duty, including any power to give directions or to legislate by means of orders, rules, regulations or other subordinate instrument, the person entrusted with the power or duty may have regard to the [objects of the EU] and to any such obligation or rights as aforesaid.

In this subsection "designated Minister or department" means such Minister of the Crown or government department as may from time to time be designated by Order in Council in relation to any matter or for any purpose, but subject to such restrictions or conditions (if any) as may be specified by the Order in Council.

(3) There shall be charged on and issued out of the Consolidated Fund or, if so determined by the Treasury, the National Loans Fund the amounts required to meet any [EU obligation] to make payments to [the EU or a member State], or any [EU obligation] in respect of contributions to the capital or reserves of the European Investment Bank or in respect of loans to the Bank, or to redeem any notes or obligations issued or created in respect of any such [EU obligation]; and, except as otherwise provided by or under any enactment,—

(a) any other expenses incurred under or by virtue of the Treaties or this Act by any Minister of the Crown or government department may be paid out of moneys provided by Parliament; and

(b) any sums received under or by virtue of the Treaties or this Act by any Minister of the Crown or government department, save for such sums as may be required for disbursements permitted by any other enactment, shall be paid into the Consolidated Fund or, if so determined by the Treasury, the National Loans Fund.

(4) The provision that may be made under subsection (2) above includes, subject to Schedule 2 to this Act, any such provision (of any such extent) as might be made by Act of Parliament, and any enactment passed or to be passed, other than one contained in this Part of this Act, shall be construed and have effect subject to the foregoing provisions of this section; but, except as may be provided by any Act passed after this Act, Schedule 2 shall have effect in connection with the powers conferred by this and the following sections of this Act to make Orders in Council [or orders, rules, regulations or schemes].

(5), (6) (Relate to Northern Ireland, the Channel Islands and the Isle of Man.)

NOTES

Repealed as noted at the beginning of this Act.

The words in the first pair of square brackets in sub-s (2), and the words in square brackets in sub-s (4), were substituted by the Legislative and Regulatory Reform Act 2006, s 27(1).

All the other words in square brackets were substituted by the European Union (Amendment) Act 2008, s 3(3), Schedule, Pt 1.

Transfer of functions and modification in relation to Scotland: various functions under this section are, in so far as exercisable in or as regards Scotland, transferred to the Scottish Ministers by the Scotland Act 1998 (Transfer of Functions to the Scottish Ministers etc) Order 1999, SI 1999/1750, the Scotland Act 1998 (Transfer of Functions to the Scottish Ministers etc) Order 2005, SI 2005/849, and the Scotland Act 1998 (Transfer of Functions to the Scottish Ministers etc) Order 2006, SI 2006/304.

References in this section to a statutory power or duty include a power or duty conferred by an Act of the Scottish Parliament or an instrument made under such an Act, and references to an enactment include an enactment within the meaning of the Scotland Act 1998: see the Scotland Act 1998, s 125, Sch 8, para 15(1), (2). In relation to any order, rules, regulations or scheme made by the Scottish Ministers, or an Order in Council made on the recommendation of the First Minister, the word "designated" in the first sentence of sub-s (2), and the second sentence of that subsection, are to be disregarded, and references to an Act of Parliament are to be read as references to an Act of the Scottish Parliament: see the Scotland Act 1998, s 125, Sch 8, para 15(1), (3) (as amended by the Legislative and Regulatory Reform Act 2006, s 27(4)).

See also the Government of Wales Act 2006, s 59(1) which provides that the power to designate a Minister of the Crown or government department under this section may be exercised to so designate the Welsh Ministers.

The number of Orders and Regulations made under this section is so numerous that references are omitted for reasons of space.

[1.16]

3 Decisions on, and proof of, Treaties and [EU instruments], etc

(1) For the purposes of all legal proceedings any question as to the meaning or effect of any of the Treaties, or as to the validity, meaning or effect of any [EU instrument], shall be treated as a question of law (and, if not referred to the European Court, be for determination as such in accordance with the principles laid down by and any relevant [decision of the [the European Court]]).

(2) Judicial notice shall be taken of the Treaties, of the [Official Journal of the European Union] and of any decision of, or expression of opinion by, [the European Court] on any such question as aforesaid; and the Official Journal shall be admissible as evidence of any instrument or other act thereby communicated of [the EU] or of any [EU institution].

(3) Evidence of any instrument issued by an [EU institution], including any judgment or order of [the European Court], or of any document in the custody of an [EU institution], or any entry in or extract from such a document, may be given in any legal proceedings by production of a copy certified as a true copy by an official of that institution; and any document purporting to be such a copy shall be received in evidence without proof of the official position or handwriting of the person signing the certificate.

(4) Evidence of any [EU instrument] may also be given in any legal proceedings—

(a) by production of a copy purporting to be printed by the Queen's Printer;

(b) where the instrument is in the custody of a government department (including a department of the Government of Northern Ireland), by production of a copy certified on behalf of the department to be a true copy by an officer of the department generally or specially authorised so to do;

and any document purporting to be such a copy as is mentioned in paragraph (b) above of an instrument in the custody of a department shall be received in evidence without proof of the official position or handwriting of the person signing the certificate, or of his authority to do so, or of the document being in the custody of the department.

(5) In any legal proceedings in Scotland evidence of any matter given in a manner authorised by this section shall be sufficient evidence of it.

NOTES

Repealed as noted at the beginning of this Act.

The words in the second (outer) pair of square brackets in sub-s (1) were substituted by the European Communities (Amendment) Act 1986, s 2.

All the other words in square brackets (including those in the section heading) were substituted by the European Union (Amendment) Act 2008, s 3(3), Schedule, Pt 1.

Modification in relation to Scotland: references in sub-s (4) to a government department include any part of the Scottish Administration: see the Scotland Act 1998, s 125, Sch 8, para 15(1), (4).

4–12 *(Outside the scope of this work.)*

SCHEDULES

SCHEDULE 1
DEFINITIONS RELATING TO [EU]

NOTES

Repealed as noted at the beginning of this Act.

The abbreviation "EU" was substituted by the European Union (Amendment) Act 2008, s 3(3), Schedule, Pt 1.

Section 1

PART I
THE PRE-ACCESSION TREATIES

[1.17]

1. *The "ECSC Treaty", that is to say, the Treaty establishing the European Coal and Steel Community, signed at Paris on the 18th April 1951.*

2. *The "EEC Treaty", that is to say, the Treaty establishing the European Economic Community, signed at Rome on the 25th March 1957.*

3. *The "Euratom Treaty", that is to say, the Treaty establishing the European Atomic Energy Community, signed at Rome on the 25th March 1957.*

4. The Convention on certain Institutions common to the European Communities, signed at Rome on the 25th March 1957.

5. The Treaty establishing a single Council and a single Commission of the European Communities, signed at Brussels on the 8th April 1965.

6. The Treaty amending certain Budgetary Provisions of the Treaties establishing the European Communities and of the Treaty establishing a single Council and a single Commission of the European Communities, signed at Luxembourg on the 22nd April 1970.

7. Any treaty entered into before the 22nd January 1972 by any of the Communities (with or without any of the member States) or, as a treaty ancillary to any treaty included in this Part of this Schedule, by the member States (with or without any other country).

PART II
OTHER DEFINITIONS

[1.18]
"Economic Community", "Coal and Steel Community" and "Euratom" mean respectively the European Economic Community, the European Coal and Steel Community and the European Atomic Energy Community.

["EU customs duty"] means, in relation to any goods, such duty of customs as may from time to time be fixed for those goods by directly applicable [EU provision] as the duty chargeable on importation into member States.

["EU institution" means any institution of the EU.]

["EU instrument"] means any instrument [issued by an EU institution].

["EU obligation"] means any obligation created or arising by or under the Treaties, whether an [enforceable EU obligation] or not.

["Enforceable EU right"] and similar expressions shall be construed in accordance with section 2(1) of this Act.

"Entry date" means the date on which the United Kingdom becomes a member of the Communities.

["European Court" means the Court of Justice of the European Union.]

"Member", in the expression "member State", refers to [membership of the EU].

NOTES

Repealed as noted at the beginning of this Act.
All words in square brackets were substituted by the European Union (Amendment) Act 2008, s 3(3), Schedule, Pt 1.

SCHEDULE 2
PROVISIONS AS TO SUBORDINATE LEGISLATION
Section 2

[1.19]
1. (1) The powers conferred by section 2(2) of this Act to make provision for the purposes mentioned in section 2(2)(a) and (b) shall not include power—
- *(a) to make any provision imposing or increasing taxation; or*
- *(b) to make any provision taking effect from a date earlier than that of the making of the instrument containing the provision; or*
- *(c) to confer any power to legislate by means of orders, rules, regulations or other subordinate instrument, other than rules of procedure for any court or tribunal; or*
- *(d) to create any new criminal offence punishable with imprisonment for more than two years or punishable on summary conviction with imprisonment for more than three months or with a fine of more than [level 5 on the standard scale] (if not calculated on a daily basis) or with a fine of more than [£100 a day].*

(2) Sub-paragraph (1)(c) above shall not be taken to preclude the modification of a power to legislate conferred otherwise than under section 2(2), or the extension of any such power to purposes of the like nature as those for which it was conferred; and a power to give directions as to matters of administration is not to be regarded as a power to legislate within the meaning of sub-paragraph (1)(c).

[(3) In sub-paragraph (1)(d), "the prescribed term" means—
- *(a) in relation to England and Wales, where the offence is a summary offence, 51 weeks;*
- *(b) in relation to England and Wales, where the offence is triable either way, twelve months;*
- *(c) in relation to Scotland and Northern Ireland, three months.]*

[1A. (1) Where—
- *(a) subordinate legislation makes provision for a purpose mentioned in section 2(2) of this Act,*
- *(b) the legislation contains a reference to an [EU instrument] or any provision of an [EU instrument], and*

(c) it appears to the person making the legislation that it is necessary or expedient for the reference to be construed as a reference to that instrument or that provision as amended from time to time,

the subordinate legislation may make express provision to that effect.

(2) In this paragraph "subordinate legislation" means any Order in Council, order, rules, regulations, scheme, warrant, byelaws or other instrument made after the coming into force of this paragraph under any Act, Act of the Scottish Parliament[, Measure or Act of the National Assembly for Wales] or Northern Ireland legislation passed or made before or after the coming into force of this paragraph.]

2. *(1) Subject to paragraph 3 below, where a provision contained in any section of this Act confers power to make [any order, rules, regulations or scheme] (otherwise than by modification or extension of an existing power), the power shall be exercisable by statutory instrument.*

(2) Any statutory instrument containing an Order in Council or [any order, rules, regulations or scheme] made in the exercise of a power so conferred, if made without a draft having been approved by resolution of each House of Parliament, shall be subject to annulment in pursuance of a resolution of either House.

[2A. *(1) This paragraph applies where, pursuant to paragraph 2(2) above, a draft of a statutory instrument containing provision made in exercise of the power conferred by section 2(2) of this Act is laid before Parliament for approval by resolution of each House of Parliament and—*

(a) the instrument also contains provision made in exercise of a power conferred by any other enactment; and

(b) apart from this paragraph, any of the conditions in sub-paragraph (2) below applies in relation to the instrument so far as containing that provision.

(2) The conditions referred to in sub-paragraph (1)(b) above are that—

(a) the instrument, so far as containing the provision referred to in sub-paragraph (1)(a) above, is by virtue of any enactment subject to annulment in pursuance of a resolution of either House of Parliament;

(b) the instrument so far as containing that provision is by virtue of any enactment required to be laid before Parliament after being made and to be approved by resolution of each House of Parliament in order to come into or remain in force;

(c) in a case not falling within paragraph (a) or (b) above, the instrument so far as containing that provision is by virtue of any enactment required to be laid before Parliament after being made;

(d) the instrument or a draft of the instrument so far as containing that provision is not by virtue of any enactment required at any time to be laid before Parliament.

(3) Where this paragraph applies in relation to the draft of a statutory instrument—

(a) the instrument, so far as containing the provision referred to in sub-paragraph (1)(a) above, may not be made unless the draft is approved by a resolution of each House of Parliament;

(b) in a case where the condition in sub-paragraph (2)(a) above is satisfied, the instrument so far as containing that provision is not subject to annulment in pursuance of a resolution of either House of Parliament;

(c) in a case where the condition in sub-paragraph (2)(b) above is satisfied, the instrument is not required to be laid before Parliament after being made (and accordingly any requirement that the instrument be approved by each House of Parliament in order for it to come into or remain in force does not apply); and

(d) in a case where the condition in sub paragraph (2)(c) above is satisfied, the instrument so far as containing that provision is not required to be laid before Parliament after being made.

(4) In this paragraph, references to an enactment are to an enactment passed or made before or after the coming into force of this paragraph.

2B. *(1) This paragraph applies where, pursuant to paragraph 2(2) above, a statutory instrument containing provision made in exercise of the power conferred by section 2(2) of this Act is laid before Parliament under section 5 of the Statutory Instruments Act 1946 (instruments subject to annulment) and—*

(a) the instrument also contains provision made in exercise of a power conferred by any other enactment; and

(b) apart from this paragraph, either of the conditions in sub-paragraph (2) below applies in relation to the instrument so far as containing that provision.

(2) The conditions referred to in sub-paragraph (1)(b) above are that—

(a) the instrument so far as containing the provision referred to in sub-paragraph (1)(a) above is by virtue of any enactment required to be laid before Parliament after being made but—

(i) is not subject to annulment in pursuance of a resolution of either House of Parliament; and

(ii) is not by virtue of any enactment required to be approved by resolution of each House of Parliament in order to come into or remain in force;

(b) the instrument or a draft of the instrument so far as containing that provision is not by virtue of any enactment required at any time to be laid before Parliament.

(3) Where this paragraph applies in relation to a statutory instrument, the instrument, so far as containing the provision referred to in sub-paragraph (1)(a) above, is subject to annulment in pursuance of a resolution of either House of Parliament.

(4) In this paragraph, references to an enactment are to an enactment passed or made before or after the coming into force of this paragraph.

2C. Paragraphs 2A and 2B above apply to a Scottish statutory instrument containing provision made in the exercise of the power conferred by section 2(2) of this Act (and a draft of any such instrument) as they apply to any other statutory instrument containing such provision (or, as the case may be, any draft of such an instrument), but subject to the following modifications—

(a) references to Parliament and to each or either House of Parliament are to be read as references to the Scottish Parliament;

(b) references to an enactment include an enactment comprised in, or in an instrument made under, an Act of the Scottish Parliament; and

(c) the reference in paragraph 2B(1) to section 5 of the Statutory Instruments Act 1946 is to be read as a reference to [section 28 of the Interpretation and Legislative Reform (Scotland) Act 2010 (asp 10)].]

3. Nothing in paragraph 2 above shall apply to any Order in Council made by the Governor of Northern Ireland or to any [any order, rules, regulations or scheme] made by a Minister or department of the Government of Northern Ireland; but where a provision contained in any section of this Act confers power to make such an Order in Council or [any order, rules, regulations or scheme], then any Order in Council or [any order, rules, regulations or scheme] made in the exercise of that power, if made without a draft having been approved by resolution of each House of the Parliament of Northern Ireland, shall be subject to negative resolution within the meaning of section 41(6) of the Interpretation Act (Northern Ireland) 1954 as if the Order or [any order, rules, regulations or scheme] were a statutory instrument within the meaning of that Act.

4, 5. (Outside the scope of this work.)

NOTES

Repealed as noted at the beginning of this Act.

Para 1: for the words "three months" in sub-para (1)(d) there are substituted the words "the prescribed term", and sub-para (3) is added, by the Criminal Justice Act 2003, s 283, Sch 27, para 3, as from a day to be appointed; first-mentioned maximum fine in sub-para (1)(d) increased and converted to a level on the standard scale by the Criminal Justice Act 1982, ss 37, 40, 46; words in second pair of square brackets in sub-para (1)(d) substituted by the Criminal Law Act 1977, s 32(3).

Paras 1A, 2A–2C: inserted by the Legislative and Regulatory Reform Act 2006, ss 28, 29; words in square brackets in sub-para 1A(1)(b) substituted by the European Union (Amendment) Act 2008, s 3(3), Schedule, Pt 1; words in square brackets in sub-para 1A(2) inserted by the Government of Wales Act 2006 (Consequential Modifications and Transitional Provisions) Order 2007, SI 2007/1388, art 3, Sch 1, para 1; words in square brackets in sub-para 2C(c) substituted by the Interpretation and Legislative Reform (Scotland) Act 2010 (Consequential, Savings and Transitional Provisions) Order 2011, SSI 2011/396, art 11.

Paras 2, 3: words in square brackets substituted by the Legislative and Regulatory Reform Act 2006, s 27(2).

Modification in relation to Scotland: para 2(2) has effect in relation to any order, rules, regulations or scheme made by Scottish Ministers, or an Order in Council made on the recommendation of the First Minister, under s 2 of this Act, as if the references to each, or either, House of Parliament were to the Scottish Parliament: see the Scotland Act 1998, s 125, Sch 8, para 15(3)(c).

Welsh Ministers: see the note to s 2 at **[1.15]** with regard to the Government of Wales Act 2006, s 59(1). Note also s 59(4) of the 2006 Act which disapplies para 2(2) above in relation to any statutory instrument made by the Welsh Ministers in certain circumstances.

EMPLOYMENT AGENCIES ACT 1973

(1973 c 35)

ARRANGEMENT OF SECTIONS

Prohibition orders

An Act to regulate employment agencies and businesses; and for connected purposes

[18 July 1973]

NOTES

Disapplication of Act: this Act does not apply to an employment agency or an employment business in so far as its activities consist of activities for which a licence is required under the Gangmasters (Licensing) Act 2004; see s 27 of that Act at **[1.1412]**.

Regulatory functions: the regulatory functions conferred by, or under, this Act are subject to the Legislative and Regulatory Reform Act 2006, ss 21, 22; see the Legislative and Regulatory Reform (Regulatory Functions) Order 2007, SI 2007/3544 (made under s 24(2) of the 2006 Act) for details.

See *Harvey* AI(4).

1–3 *(Repealed by the Deregulation and Contracting Out Act 1994, ss 35, 81(1), Sch 10, para 1(1), (2), Sch 17.)*

[Prohibition orders

[1.20]

3A Power to make orders

(1) On application by the Secretary of State, an [employment tribunal] may by order prohibit a person from carrying on, or being concerned with the carrying on of—

(a) any employment agency or employment business; or

(b) any specified description of employment agency or employment business.

(2) An order under subsection (1) of this section (in this Act referred to as "a prohibition order") may either prohibit a person from engaging in an activity altogether or prohibit him from doing so otherwise than in accordance with specified conditions.

(3) A prohibition order shall be made for a period beginning with the date of the order and ending—

(a) on a specified date, or

(b) on the happening of a specified event,

in either case, not more than ten years later.

(4) Subject to subsections (5) and (6) of this section, an [employment tribunal] shall not make a prohibition order in relation to any person unless it is satisfied that he is, on account of his misconduct or for any other sufficient reason, unsuitable to do what the order prohibits.

(5) An [employment tribunal] may make a prohibition order in relation to a body corporate if it is satisfied that—

(a) any director, secretary, manager or similar officer of the body corporate,

(b) any person who performs on behalf of the body corporate the functions of a director, secretary, manager or similar officer, or

(c) any person in accordance with whose directions or instructions the directors of the body corporate are accustomed to act,

is unsuitable, on account of his misconduct or for any other sufficient reason, to do what the order prohibits.

(6) An [employment tribunal] may make a prohibition order in relation to a partnership if it is satisfied that any member of the partnership, or any manager employed by the partnership, is unsuitable, on account of his misconduct or for any other sufficient reason, to do what the order prohibits.

(7) For the purposes of subsection (4) of this section, where an employment agency or employment business has been improperly conducted, each person who was carrying on, or concerned with the carrying on of, the agency or business at the time, shall be deemed to have been responsible for what happened unless he can show that it happened without his connivance or consent and was not attributable to any neglect on his part.

(8) A person shall not be deemed to fall within subsection (5)(c) of this section by reason only that the directors act on advice given by him in a professional capacity.

(9) In this section—

"director", in relation to a body corporate whose affairs are controlled by its members, means a member of the body corporate; and

"specified", in relation to a prohibition order, means specified in the order.]

NOTES

Inserted, together with ss 3B–3D, by the Deregulation and Contracting Out Act 1994, s 35, Sch 10, para 1(1), (3).

Sub-ss (1), (4)–(6): words in square brackets substituted by the Employment Rights (Dispute Resolution) Act 1998, s 1(2)(a).

[1.21]

[3B Enforcement

Any person who, without reasonable excuse, fails to comply with a prohibition order shall be guilty of an offence and liable—

[(a) on conviction on indictment, to a fine;

(b) on summary conviction, to a fine not exceeding the statutory maximum].]

NOTES

Inserted as noted to s 3A at **[1.20]**.

Words in square brackets substituted by the Employment Act 2008, s 15.

[1.22]
[3C Variation and revocation of orders

(1) On application by the person to whom a prohibition order applies, an [employment tribunal] may vary or revoke the order if the tribunal is satisfied that there has been a material change of circumstances since the order was last considered.

(2) An [employment tribunal] may not, on an application under this section, so vary a prohibition order as to make it more restrictive.

(3) The Secretary of State shall be a party to any proceedings before an [employment tribunal] with respect to an application under this section, and be entitled to appear and be heard accordingly.

(4) When making a prohibition order or disposing of an application under this section, an [employment tribunal] may, with a view to preventing the making of vexatious or frivolous applications, by order prohibit the making of an application, or further application, under this section in relation to the prohibition order before such date as the tribunal may specify in the order under this subsection.]

NOTES

Inserted as noted to s 3A at **[1.20]**.

Words in square brackets substituted by the Employment Rights (Dispute Resolution) Act 1998, s 1(2)(a).

[1.23]
[3D Appeals

(1) An appeal shall lie to the Employment Appeal Tribunal on a question of law arising from any decision of, or arising in proceedings before, an [employment tribunal] under section 3A or 3C of this Act.

(2) No other appeal shall lie from a decision of an [employment tribunal] under section 3A or 3C of this Act; and section 11 of the Tribunals and Inquiries Act 1992 (appeals from certain tribunals to High Court or Court of Session) shall not apply to proceedings before an [employment tribunal] under section 3A or 3C of this Act.]

NOTES

Inserted as noted to s 3A at **[1.20]**.

Words in square brackets substituted by the Employment Rights (Dispute Resolution) Act 1998, s 1(2)(a).

4 *(S 4 was substituted (together with s 3) by a new s 3 only by the Employment Protection Act 1975, s 114, Sch 13, para 4 (s 3 was subsequently repealed as noted ante).)*

Conduct of employment agencies and employment businesses

[1.24]
5 General regulations

(1) The Secretary of State may make regulations to secure the proper conduct of employment agencies and employment businesses and to protect the interests of persons availing themselves of the services of such agencies and businesses, and such regulations may in particular make provision—

(a) requiring persons carrying on such agencies and businesses to keep records;
(b) prescribing the form of such records and the entries to be made in them;
(c) prescribing qualifications appropriate for persons carrying on such agencies and businesses;
(d) regulating advertising by persons carrying on such agencies and businesses;
(e) safeguarding client's money deposited with or otherwise received by persons carrying on such agencies and businesses;
[(ea) restricting the services which may be provided by persons carrying on such agencies and businesses;
(eb) regulating the way in which and the terms on which services may be provided by persons carrying on such agencies and businesses;
(ec) restricting or regulating the charging of fees by persons carrying on such agencies and businesses].

[(1A) A reference in subsection (1)(ea) to (ec) of this section to services includes a reference to services in respect of—

(a) persons seeking employment outside the United Kingdom;
(b) persons normally resident outside the United Kingdom seeking employment in the United Kingdom.]

(2) Any person who contravenes or fails to comply with any regulation made under this section shall be guilty of an offence and liable—

[(a) on conviction on indictment, to a fine;
(b) on summary conviction, to a fine not exceeding the statutory maximum].

NOTES

Sub-s (1): paras (ea)–(ec) substituted, for the original paras (f), (g) and the subsequent proviso, by the Employment Relations Act 1999, s 31, Sch 7, paras 1, 2(1), (2).

Sub-s (1A): inserted by the Employment Relations Act 1999, s 31, Sch 7, paras 1, 2(1), (3).

Sub-s (2): words in square brackets substituted by the Employment Act 2008, s 15.

Regulations: the Conduct of Employment Agencies and Employment Businesses Regulations 2003, SI 2003/3319 at **[2.690]**; the Conduct of Employment Agencies and Employment Businesses (Amendment) Regulations 2007, SI 2007/3575; the Conduct of Employment Agencies and Employment Businesses (Amendment) Regulations 2010, SI 2010/1782; the Conduct of Employment Agencies and Employment Businesses (Amendment) Regulations 2014, SI 2014/3351; the Conduct of Employment Agencies and Employment Businesses (Amendment) Regulations 2016, SI 2016/510; the Employment Rights

(Amendment) (EU Exit) (No 2) Regulations 2019, SI 2019/536 at **[2.2183]**; the Conduct of Employment Agencies and Employment Businesses (Amendment) Regulations 2019, SI 2019/725 at **[2.2193]**.

[1.25]

6 Restriction on charging persons seeking employment, etc

[(1) Except in such cases or classes of case as the Secretary of State may prescribe—

(a) a person carrying on an employment agency shall not request or directly or indirectly receive any fee from any person for providing services (whether by the provision of information or otherwise) for the purpose of finding him employment or seeking to find him employment;

(b) a person carrying on an employment business shall not request or directly or indirectly receive any fee from an employee for providing services (whether by the provision of information or otherwise) for the purpose of finding or seeking to find another person, with a view to the employee acting for and under the control of that other person;

(c) a person carrying on an employment business shall not request or directly or indirectly receive any fee from a second person for providing services (whether by the provision of information or otherwise) for the purpose of finding or seeking to find a third person, with a view to the second person becoming employed by the first person and acting for and under the control of the third person.]

(2) Any person who contravenes this section shall be guilty of an offence and liable

[(a) on conviction on indictment, to a fine;

(b) on summary conviction, to a fine not exceeding the statutory maximum].

NOTES

Sub-s (1): substituted by the Employment Relations Act 1999, s 31, Sch 7, paras 1, 3.

Sub-s (2): words in square brackets substituted by the Employment Act 2008, s 15.

Regulations: the Conduct of Employment Agencies and Employment Businesses Regulations 2003, SI 2003/3319 at **[2.690]**; the Conduct of Employment Agencies and Employment Businesses (Amendment) Regulations 2007, SI 2007/3575; the Conduct of Employment Agencies and Employment Businesses (Amendment) Regulations 2010, SI 2010/1782.

7 *(Repealed by the Deregulation and Contracting Out Act 1994, s 81(1), Sch 17.)*

Supplementary provisions

8 *(S 8 repealed by the Employment Protection Act 1975, ss 114, 125(3), Sch 13, para 5, Sch 18.)*

[1.26]

[8A Appointment of officers

(1) The Secretary of State may—

(a) appoint officers to act for the purposes of this Act, and

(b) instead of or in addition to appointing any officers under this section, arrange with any relevant authority for officers of that authority to act for those purposes.

(2) The following are relevant authorities—

(a) any Minister of the Crown or government department;

(b) any body performing functions on behalf of the Crown;

(c) the Gangmasters and Labour Abuse Authority.]

NOTES

Commencement: 12 July 2016.

Inserted by the Immigration Act 2016, s 11, Sch 2, paras 1, 2, as from 12 July 2016.

9–11B *(Ss 9–11, 11A, 11B outside the scope of this work.)*

[1.27]

12 Regulations and orders

(1) Subject to the next following subsection, the Secretary of State shall have power to make regulations for prescribing anything which under this Act is to be prescribed.

(2) The Secretary of State shall not make any regulations under this Act except after consultation with such bodies as appear to him to be representative of the interests concerned.

(3) Regulations under this Act may make different provision in relation to different cases or classes of case.

(4) The power of the Secretary of State to make regulations and orders under this Act shall be exercisable by statutory instrument.

[(5) Regulations under section 5(1) or 6(1) of this Act shall not be made unless a draft has been laid before, and approved by resolution of, each House of Parliament.

(6) Regulations under section 13(7)(i) of this Act or an order under section 14(3) shall be subject to annulment in pursuance of a resolution of either House of Parliament.]

NOTES

Sub-ss (5), (6): substituted, for the original sub-s (5), by the Employment Relations Act 1999, s 31, Sch 7, paras 1, 6.

Regulations: the Conduct of Employment Agencies and Employment Businesses (Amendment) Regulations 2019, SI 2019/725 at **[2.2193]**.

[1.28]

13 Interpretation

(1) In this Act—

. . .

"employment" includes—

(a) employment by way of a professional engagement or otherwise under a contract for services;

(b) the reception in a private household of a person under an arrangement whereby that person is to assist in the domestic work of the household in consideration of receiving hospitality and pocket money or hospitality only;

and "worker" and "employer" shall be construed accordingly;

"employment agency" has the meaning assigned by subsection (2) of this section but does not include any arrangements, services, functions or business to which this Act does not apply by virtue of subsection (7) of this section;

"employment business" has the meaning assigned by subsection (3) of this section but does not include any arrangements, services, functions or business to which this Act does not apply by virtue of subsection (7) of this section;

"fee" includes any charge however described;

. . .

. . .

"local authority", in relation to England . . . , means a county council, . . . , the Common Council of the City of London, a district council or a London borough council [and in relation to Wales, means a county council or a county borough council,] and, in relation to Scotland means a [council constituted under section 2 of the Local Government etc (Scotland) Act 1994];

"organisation" includes an association of organisations;

"organisation of employers" means an organisation which consists wholly or mainly of employers and whose principal objects include the regulation of relations between employers and workers or organisations of workers

"organisation of workers" means an organisation which consists wholly or mainly of workers and whose principal objects include the regulation of relations between workers and employers or organisations of employers;

"prescribed" means prescribed by regulations made under this Act by the Secretary of State;

["prohibition order" has the meaning given by section 3A(2) of this Act;]

. . .

(2) For the purposes of this Act "employment agency" means the business (whether or not carried on with a view to profit and whether or not carried on in conjunction with any other business) of providing services (whether by the provision of information or otherwise) for the purpose of finding [persons] employment with employers or of supplying employers with [persons] for employment by them.

(3) For the purposes of this Act "employment business" means the business (whether or not carried on with a view to profit and whether or not carried on in conjunction with any other business) of supplying persons in the employment of the person carrying on the business, to act for, and under the control of, other persons in any capacity.

(4) The reference in subsection (2) of this section to providing services does not include a reference—

(a) to publishing a newspaper or other publication unless it is published wholly or mainly for the purpose mentioned in that subsection;

(b) to the display by any person of advertisements on premises occupied by him otherwise than for the said purpose; [or

(c) to providing a programme service (within the meaning of the Broadcasting Act 1990)].

(5) For the purposes of section 269 of the Local Government Act 1972, this Act shall be deemed to have been passed after 1st April 1974.

(6) In this Act, except where the context otherwise requires, references to any enactment shall be construed as references to that enactment as amended, extended or applied by or under any other enactment.

(7) This Act does not apply to—

(a) any business which is carried on exclusively for the purpose of obtaining employment for—

(i) persons formerly members of Her Majesty's naval, military or air forces; or

(ii) persons released from a [custodial sentence passed by a criminal court in the United Kingdom, the Channel Islands or the Isle of Man;]

and which is certified annually by or on behalf of the Admiralty Board of the Defence Council, the Army Board of the Defence Council or the Air Force Board of the Defence Council or by the Secretary of State (as the case may be) to be properly conducted;

(b) *any agency for the supply of nurses as defined in section 8 of the Nurses Agencies Act 1957 or section 32 of the Nurses (Scotland) Act 1951;*

(c) *the business carried on by any county or district nursing association or other similar organisation, being an association or organisation established and existing wholly or mainly for the purpose of providing patients with the services of a nurse to visit them in their own homes without herself taking up residence there;*

[(ca) an early years childminder agency or a later years childminder agency (as defined in section 98 of the Childcare Act 2006);]

(d) services which are ancillary to the letting upon hire of any aircraft, vessel, vehicle, plant or equipment;

(e) . . .

(f) the exercise by a local authority . . . [or a joint authority established by Part IV of the Local Government Act 1985] of any of their functions;

[(fza) . . .]

[(fzb) the exercise by an economic prosperity board established under section 88 of the Local Democracy, Economic Development and Construction Act 2009 of any of its functions;

(fzc) the exercise by a combined authority established under section 103 of that Act of any of its functions;]

[(fa) the exercise by a police and crime commissioner of any of the commissioner's functions;

(fb) the exercise by the Mayor's Office for Policing and Crime of any of that Office's functions;

(fc) the exercise by a chief constable established under section 2 of the Police Reform and Social Responsibility Act 2011 of any of the chief constable's functions;

(fd) the exercise by the Commissioner of Police of the Metropolis of any of the Commissioner's functions;]

[(ff) the exercise by the Broads Authority of any of its functions;]

[(fg) the exercise by a National Park authority of any of its functions;]

[(fh) the exercise by the London Fire Commissioner of any of the Commissioner's functions;]

[(fi) the exercise by a fire and rescue authority created by an order under section 4A of the Fire and Rescue Services Act 2004 of any of its functions;]

(g) services provided by any organisation of employers or organisation of workers for its members;

[(ga) services provided in pursuance of arrangements made, or a direction given, under section 10 of the Employment and Training Act 1973;]

(h) services provided by an appointments board or service controlled by—

(i) one or more universities;

(ii) a central institution as defined in section 145 of the Education (Scotland) Act 1962 or a college of education as defined in the said section 145;

[(i) any prescribed business or service, or prescribed class of business or service or business or service carried on or provided by prescribed persons or classes of person]:

Provided that paragraph (b) of this subsection shall not be taken as exempting from the provisions of this Act any other business carried on in conjunction with an agency for the supply of nurses.

(8) Subsection (7)(c) of this section shall have effect in its application to Scotland as if at the end there were added the words "or mainly or substantially supported by voluntary subscriptions and providing patients with the services of a nurse whether or not the nurse takes up residence in the patient's house".

NOTES

Sub-s (1) is amended as follows:

First, second and final definitions omitted repealed, and definition "prohibition order" inserted, by the Deregulation and Contracting Out Act 1994, ss 35, 81, Sch 10, para 1(5), Sch 17.

Third definition omitted repealed by the Employment Protection Act 1975, ss 114, 125(3), Sch 13, para 7, Sch 18.

In definition "local authority" first words omitted repealed, and words in first pair of square brackets inserted, by the Local Government (Wales) Act 1994, s 66(6), (8), Sch 16, para 41, Sch 18; second words omitted repealed by the Local Government Act 1985, s 102, Sch 17; words in second pair of square brackets substituted by the Local Government etc (Scotland) Act 1994, s 180(1), Sch 13, para 90.

Sub-s (2): words in square brackets substituted by the Employment Relations Act 1999, s 31, Sch 7, paras 1, 7.

Sub-s (4): words in square brackets substituted by the Broadcasting Act 1990, s 203(1), Sch 20, para 18.

Sub-s (7) is amended as follows:

Words in square brackets in sub-para (a)(ii) substituted by the Criminal Justice Act 1988, s 123(6), Sch 8, para 7.

Paras (b), (c) and the proviso (following para (i)) repealed by the Care Standards Act 2000, ss 111(2), 117(2), Sch 6, in relation to England and Wales (the italicised paragraphs remain in force for Scotland, though note that the Nurses Agencies Act 1957 and the Nurses (Scotland) Act 1951 have both been repealed).

Para (ca) inserted by the Children and Families Act 2014, s 84, Sch 4, Pt 6, para 64, as from 1 September 2014.

Para (e) repealed by the Deregulation and Contracting Out Act 1994, ss 35, 81, Sch 10, para 4, Sch 17.

In para (f), words omitted repealed by a combination of the Police Reform and Social Responsibility Act 2011, s 99, Sch 16, Pt 3, para 118(a), the Serious Organised Crime and Police Act 2005, ss 59, 174(2), Sch 4, para 19, Sch 17, Pt 2, and the Education Reform Act 1988, s 237, Sch 13, Pt I; words in square brackets inserted by the Local Government Act 1985, s 84, Sch 14, para 50.

Para (fza) inserted by the Local Government and Public Involvement in Health Act 2007, s 209(2), Sch 13, Pt 2, para 30; subsequently repealed by the Deregulation Act 2015, s 59, Sch 13, Pt 3, para 6(1), (8), as from 26 May 2015.

Paras (fzb), (fzc) inserted by the Local Democracy, Economic Development and Construction Act 2009, s 119, Sch 6, para 40.

Paras (fa)–(fd) substituted for the original para (fa) (as inserted by the Greater London Authority Act 1999, s 325, Sch 27, para 37) by the Police Reform and Social Responsibility Act 2011, s 99, Sch 16, Pt 3, para 188(b).

Para (ff) inserted by the Norfolk and Suffolk Broads Act 1988, s 21, Sch 6.

Para (fg) inserted by the Environment Act 1995, s 78, Sch 10, para 11.

Para (fh) inserted by the Greater London Authority Act 1999, ss 325, 328, Sch 27, para 37, Sch 29, Pt I, para 22; subsequently substituted by the Policing and Crime Act 2017, s 9(3)(c), Sch 2, Pt 2, para 48, as from 1 April 2018.

Para (fi) inserted by the Policing and Crime Act 2017, s 6, Sch 1, Pt 2, para 3, as from 3 April 2017.

Para (ga) inserted by the Trade Union Reform and Employment Rights Act 1993, s 49(2), Sch 8, para 4.

Para (i) substituted by the Employment Relations Act 1999, s 31, Sch 7, paras 1, 8.

Sub-s (8): substituted by the Care Standards Act 2000, s 111(2), as from a day to be appointed, as follows (note that the substituted subsection was amended by the Regulation of Care (Scotland) Act 2001, s 79, Sch 3, para 6)—

"(8) This Act, in its application to Scotland, does not apply to—

(a) [a nurse agency as defined in section 2(6) of the Regulation of Care (Scotland) Act 2001 (asp 8)] (but excluding any other business carried on in conjunction with such an agency);

(b) the business carried on by any county or district nursing association or other similar organisation, being an association or organisation within paragraph (a) or (b) of that definition.".

Regulations: the Employment Agencies Act 1973 (Exemption) Regulations 1976, SI 1976/710; the Employment Agencies Act 1973 (Exemption) (No 2) Regulations 1979, SI 1979/1741; the Employment Agencies Act 1973 (Exemption) (No 2) Regulations 1984, SI 1984/978 (all made under sub-s (7)(i)).

[1.29]

14 Short title, repeals, commencement and extent

(1) This Act may be cited as the Employment Agencies Act 1973.

(2) The enactments specified in the Schedule to this Act are hereby repealed to the extent specified in the third column of that Schedule.

(3) The Secretary of State may, after consultation with such bodies as appear to him to be concerned, by order repeal any provision of any local Act, being a provision which is not specified in Part II of the said Schedule and which appears to him to be unnecessary having regard to the provisions of this Act, or to be inconsistent with the provisions of this Act, and may by that order make such amendments of that or any other local Act as appear to him to be necessary in consequence of the repeal and such transitional provision as appears to him to be necessary or expedient in connection with the matter.

(4) This Act shall come into force on such date as the Secretary of State may by order appoint, and different dates may be appointed for different provisions and for different purposes.

(5) This Act does not extend to Northern Ireland.

NOTES

Orders: the Employment Agencies Act 1973 (Commencement) Order 1976, SI 1976/709.

SCHEDULE

(Schedule (repeals) outside the scope of this work.)

HEALTH AND SAFETY AT WORK ETC ACT 1974

(1974 c 37)

ARRANGEMENT OF SECTIONS

PART I

HEALTH, SAFETY AND WELFARE IN CONNECTION WITH WORK, AND CONTROL OF DANGEROUS SUBSTANCES AND CERTAIN EMISSIONS INTO THE ATMOSPHERE

An Act to make further provision for securing the health, safety and welfare of persons at work, for protecting others against risks to health or safety in connection with the activities of persons at work, for controlling the keeping and use and preventing the unlawful acquisition, possession and use of dangerous substances, and for controlling certain emissions into the atmosphere; to make further provision with respect to the employment medical advisory service; to amend the law relating to building regulations, and the Building (Scotland) Act 1959; and for connected purposes

[31 July 1974]

NOTES

The Act confers extensive powers to make subordinate legislation. Considerations of space preclude reference to all Orders made under the Act, for details of which specialist works on Health and Safety should be consulted.

As to the transfer of railway safety functions to the Office of Road and Rail (formerly the Office of Rail Regulation) and for transitional provisions in connection with the transfer, see the Railways Act 2005, s 2, Schs 1, 3. See also the Health and Safety (Enforcing Authority for Railways and Other Guided Transport Systems) Regulations 2006, SI 2006/557, which provide that the ORR shall be responsible for the enforcement of the relevant statutory provisions (within the meaning of s 53) to the extent that they relate to the operation of a railway, the operation of a tramway, and the operation of any other system of guided transport.

Disapplication: as to the disapplication of this Act (subject to certain exceptions) in relation to premises to which the Regulatory Reform (Fire Safety) Order 2005, SI 2005/1541 applies, see art 47 of the 2005 Order. See also the Fire (Scotland) Act 2005, s 70 (Consequential restriction of application of Part I of the Health and Safety at Work etc Act 1974).

As to the transfer of the functions of the Minister for the Civil Service to the Treasury, see the Transfer of Functions (Minister for the Civil Service and Treasury) Order 1981, SI 1981/1670.

Regulatory functions: the regulatory functions conferred by, or under, this Act are subject to the Legislative and Regulatory Reform Act 2006, ss 21, 22; see the Legislative and Regulatory Reform (Regulatory Functions) Order 2007, SI 2007/3544 (made under s 24(2) of the 2006 Act) for details.

See *Harvey* NIII.

PART I
HEALTH, SAFETY AND WELFARE IN CONNECTION WITH WORK, AND CONTROL OF DANGEROUS SUBSTANCES AND CERTAIN EMISSIONS INTO THE ATMOSPHERE

NOTES

The general purposes of this Part of this Act are extended by the Offshore Safety Act 1992, ss 1(1), 2(1), the Consumer Protection Act 1987, s 36, and the Railways Act 1993, s 117(2), (6), (7).

For the power of the Secretary of State to exempt, by order, a contractor, in relation to premises used by the contractor for the purposes of, or for purposes which include, providing defence procurement services to the Secretary of State, from any provision of this Part of this Act or any provision of regulations made under this Part, see the Defence Reform Act 2014, s 4, Sch 1, paras 1, 4.

Preliminary

[1.30]

1 Preliminary

(1) The provisions of this Part shall have effect with a view to—

(a) securing the health, safety and welfare of persons at work;

(b) protecting persons other than persons at work against risks to health or safety arising out of or in connection with the activities of persons at work;

(c) controlling the keeping and use of explosive or highly flammable or otherwise dangerous substances, and generally preventing the unlawful acquisition, possession and use of such substances; . . .

(d) . . .

(2) The provisions of this Part relating to the making of health and safety regulations . . . and the preparation and approval of codes of practice shall in particular have effect with a view to enabling the enactments specified in the third column of Schedule 1 and the regulations, orders and other instruments in force under those enactments to be progressively replaced by a system of regulations and approved codes of practice operating in combination with the other provisions of this Part and designed to maintain or improve the standards of health, safety and welfare established by or under those enactments.

(3) For the purposes of this Part risks arising out of or in connection with the activities of persons at work shall be treated as including risks attributable to the manner of conducting an undertaking, the plant or substances used for the purposes of an undertaking and the condition of premises so used or any part of them.

(4) References in this Part to the general purposes of this Part are references to the purposes mentioned in subsection (1) above.

NOTES

Sub-s (1): words omitted repealed by the Environmental Protection Act 1990, s 162(2), Sch 16, Pt I.

Sub-s (2): words omitted repealed by the Employment Protection Act 1975, ss 116, 125(3), Sch 15, para 1, Sch 18.

Dangerous substances: for certain purposes, the reference to dangerous substances in sub-s (1)(c) above is extended to include environmentally hazardous substances; see the Health and Safety at Work etc Act 1974 (Application to Environmentally Hazardous Substances) Regulations 2002, SI 2002/282.

Regulations: the Control of Asbestos in the Air Regulations 1990, SI 1990/556 (revoked in relation to England and Wales by the Environmental Permitting (England and Wales) (Amendment) Regulations 2013, SI 2013/390).

General duties

[1.31]

2 General duties of employers to their employees

(1) It shall be the duty of every employer to ensure, so far as is reasonably practicable, the health, safety and welfare at work of all his employees.

(2) Without prejudice to the generality of an employer's duty under the preceding subsection, the matters to which that duty extends include in particular—

(a) the provision and maintenance of plant and systems of work that are, so far as is reasonably practicable, safe and without risks to health;

(b) arrangements for ensuring, so far as is reasonably practicable, safety and absence of risks to health in connection with the use, handling, storage and transport of articles and substances;

(c) the provision of such information, instruction, training and supervision as is necessary to ensure, so far as is reasonably practicable, the health and safety at work of his employees;

(d) so far as is reasonably practicable as regards any place of work under the employer's control, the maintenance of it in a condition that is safe and without risks to health and the provision and maintenance of means of access to and egress from it that are safe and without such risks;

(e) the provision and maintenance of a working environment for his employees that is, so far as is reasonably practicable, safe, without risks to health, and adequate as regards facilities and arrangements for their welfare at work.

(3) Except in such cases as may be prescribed, it shall be the duty of every employer to prepare and as often as may be appropriate revise a written statement of his general policy with respect to the health and safety at work of his employees and the organisation and arrangements for the time being in force for carrying out that policy, and to bring the statement and any revision of it to the notice of all his employees.

(4) Regulations made by the Secretary of State may provide for the appointment in prescribed cases by recognised trade unions (within the meaning of the regulations) of safety representatives from amongst the employees, and those representatives shall represent the employees in consultations with the employers under subsection (6) below and shall have such other functions as may be prescribed.

(5) . . .

(6) It shall be the duty of every employer to consult any such representatives with a view to the making and maintenance of arrangements which will enable him and his employees to co-operate effectively in promoting and developing measures to ensure the health and safety at work of the employees, and in checking the effectiveness of such measures.

(7) In such cases as may be prescribed it shall be the duty of every employer, if requested to do so by the safety representatives mentioned in [subsection (4)] above, to establish, in accordance with regulations made by the Secretary of State, a safety committee having the function of keeping under review the measures taken to ensure the health and safety at work of his employees and such other functions as may be prescribed.

NOTES

Sub-s (5): repealed by the Employment Protection Act 1975, ss 116, 125(3), Sch 15, para 2, Sch 18.

Sub-s (7): words in square brackets substituted by the Employment Protection Act 1975, ss 116, 125(3), Sch 15, para 2, Sch 18.

Exclusion or modification: see s 15(3)(b) and (6)(c) at **[1.43]**.

Regulations: the Employers' Health and Safety Policy Statements (Exceptions) Regulations 1975, SI 1975/1584 (which exempt employers with fewer than 5 employees from the requirements of sub-s (3)); the Safety Representatives and Safety Committees Regulations 1977, SI 1977/500 at **[2.30]**; the Police (Health and Safety) Regulations 1999, SI 1999/860 at **[2.407]**.

[1.32]

3 General duties of employers and self-employed to persons other than their employees

(1) It shall be the duty of every employer to conduct his undertaking in such a way as to ensure, so far as is reasonably practicable, that persons not in his employment who may be affected thereby are not thereby exposed to risks to their health or safety.

(2) It shall be the duty of every self-employed person [who conducts an undertaking of a prescribed description] to conduct [the undertaking] in such a way as to ensure, so far as is reasonably practicable, that he and other persons (not being his employees) who may be affected thereby are not thereby exposed to risks to their health or safety.

[(2A) A description of undertaking included in regulations under subsection (2) may be framed by reference to—

- (a) the type of activities carried out by the undertaking, where those activities are carried out or any other feature of the undertaking;
- (b) whether persons who may be affected by the conduct of the undertaking, other than the self-employed person (or his employees), may thereby be exposed to risks to their health or safety.]

(3) In such cases as may be prescribed, it shall be the duty of every employer and every self-employed person, in the prescribed circumstances and in the prescribed manner, to give to persons (not being his employees) who may be affected by the way in which he conducts his undertaking the prescribed information about such aspects of the way in which he conducts his undertaking as might affect their health or safety.

NOTES

Words in first pair of square brackets in sub-s (2) inserted, words in seconds pair of square brackets in that subsection substituted, and sub-s (2A) inserted, by the Deregulation Act 2015, s 1(1)–(3), as from 26 March 2015 (in so far as is necessary for enabling the exercise on or after that day of any power to make provision by an order or regulations made by statutory instrument), and as from 1 October 2015 (otherwise).

Exclusion or modification: see s 15(3)(b) and (6)(c) at **[1.43]**.

Regulations: the Health and Safety at Work etc Act 1974 (General Duties of Self-Employed Persons) (Prescribed Undertakings) Regulations 2015, SI 2015/1583 at **[2.1921]**.

[1.33]

4 General duties of persons concerned with premises to persons other than their employees

(1) This section has effect for imposing on persons duties in relation to those who—

- (a) are not their employees; but
- (b) use non-domestic premises made available to them as a place of work or as a place where they may use plant or substances provided for their use there,

and applies to premises so made available and other non-domestic premises used in connection with them.

(2) It shall be the duty of each person who has, to any extent, control of premises to which this section applies or of the means of access thereto or egress therefrom or of any plant or substance in such premises to take such measures as it is reasonable for a person in his position to take to ensure, so far as

is reasonably practicable, that the premises, all means of access thereto or egress therefrom available for use by persons using the premises, and any plant or substance in the premises or, as the case may be, provided for use there, is or are safe and without risks to health.

(3) Where a person has, by virtue of any contract or tenancy, an obligation of any extent in relation to—

(a) the maintenance or repair of any premises to which this section applies or any means of access thereto or egress therefrom; or

(b) the safety of or the absence of risks to health arising from plant or substances in any such premises;

that person shall be treated, for the purposes of subsection (2) above, as being a person who has control of the matters to which his obligation extends.

(4) Any reference in this section to a person having control of any premises or matter is a reference to a person having control of the premises or matter in connection with the carrying on by him of a trade, business or other undertaking (whether for profit or not).

NOTES

Exclusion or modification: see s 15(3)(b) and (6)(c) at **[1.43]**.

5 *(Repealed by the Environmental Protection Act 1990, ss 162(2), 164(3), Sch 16, Pt I.)*

[1.34]

6 General duties of manufacturers etc as regards articles and substances for use at work

[(1) It shall be the duty of any person who designs, manufactures, imports or supplies any article for use at work or any article of fairground equipment—

(a) to ensure, so far as is reasonably practicable, that the article is so designed and constructed that it will be safe and without risks to health at all times when it is being set, used, cleaned or maintained by a person at work;

(b) to carry out or arrange for the carrying out of such testing and examination as may be necessary for the performance of the duty imposed on him by the preceding paragraph;

(c) to take such steps as are necessary to secure that persons supplied by that person with the article are provided with adequate information about the use for which the article is designed or has been tested and about any conditions necessary to ensure that it will be safe and without risks to health at all such times as are mentioned in paragraph (a) above and when it is being dismantled or disposed of; and

(d) to take such steps as are necessary to secure, so far as is reasonably practicable, that persons so supplied are provided with all such revisions of information provided to them by virtue of the preceding paragraph as are necessary by reason of its becoming known that anything gives rise to a serious risk to health or safety.

(1A) It shall be the duty of any person who designs, manufactures, imports or supplies any article of fairground equipment—

(a) to ensure, so far as is reasonably practicable, that the article is so designed and constructed that it will be safe and without risks to health at all times when it is being used for or in connection with the entertainment of members of the public;

(b) to carry out or arrange for the carrying out of such testing and examination as may be necessary for the performance of the duty imposed on him by the preceding paragraph;

(c) to take such steps as are necessary to secure that persons supplied by that person with the article are provided with adequate information about the use for which the article is designed or has been tested and about any conditions necessary to ensure that it will be safe and without risks to health at all times when it is being used for or in connection with the entertainment of members of the public; and

(d) to take such steps as are necessary to secure, so far as is reasonably practicable, that persons so supplied are provided with all such revisions of information provided to them by virtue of the preceding paragraph as are necessary by reason of its becoming known that anything gives rise to a serious risk to health or safety.]

(2) It shall be the duty of any person who undertakes the design or manufacture of any article for use at work [or of any article of fairground equipment] to carry out or arrange for the carrying out of any necessary research with a view to the discovery and, so far as is reasonably practicable, the elimination or minimisation of any risks to health or safety to which the design or article may give rise.

(3) It shall be the duty of any person who erects or installs any article for use at work in any premises where that article is to be used by persons at work [or who erects or installs any article of fairground equipment] to ensure, so far as is reasonably practicable, that nothing about the way in which [the article is erected or installed makes it unsafe or a risk to health at any such time as is mentioned in paragraph (a) of subsection (1) or, as the case may be, in paragraph (a) of subsection (1) or (1A) above].

[(4) It shall be the duty of any person who manufactures, imports or supplies any substance—

(a) to ensure, so far as is reasonably practicable, that the substance will be safe and without risks to health at all times when it is being used, handled, processed, stored or transported by a person at work or in premises to which section 4 above applies;

(b) to carry out or arrange for the carrying out of such testing and examination as may be necessary for the performance of the duty imposed on him by the preceding paragraph;

(c) to take such steps as are necessary to secure that persons supplied by that person with the substance are provided with adequate information about any risks to health or safety to which the inherent properties of the substance may give rise, about the results of any relevant tests which have been carried out on or in connection with the substance and about any conditions necessary to ensure that the substance will be safe and without risks to health at all such times as are mentioned in paragraph (a) above and when the substance is being disposed of; and

(d) to take such steps as are necessary to secure, so far as is reasonably practicable, that persons so supplied are provided with all such revisions of information provided to them by virtue of the preceding paragraph as are necessary by reason of its becoming known that anything gives rise to a serious risk to health or safety.]

(5) It shall be the duty of any person who undertakes the manufacture of any [substance] to carry out or arrange for the carrying out of any necessary research with a view to the discovery and, so far as is reasonably practicable, the elimination or minimisation of any risks to health or safety to which the substance may give rise [at all such times as are mentioned in paragraph (a) of subsection (4) above].

(6) Nothing in the preceding provisions of this section shall be taken to require a person to repeat any testing, examination or research which has been carried out otherwise than by him or at his instance, in so far as it is reasonable for him to rely on the results thereof for the purposes of those provisions.

(7) Any duty imposed on any person by any of the preceding provisions of this section shall extend only to things done in the course of a trade, business or other undertaking carried on by him (whether for profit or not) and to matters within his control.

(8) Where a person designs, manufactures, imports or supplies an article [for use at work or an article of fairground equipment and does so for or to another] on the basis of a written undertaking by that other to take specified steps sufficient to ensure, so far as is reasonably practicable, that the article will be safe and without risks to health [at all such times as are mentioned in paragraph (a) of subsection (1) or, as the case may be, in paragraph (a) of subsection (1) or (1A) above], the undertaking shall have the effect of relieving the first-mentioned person from the duty imposed [by virtue of that paragraph] above to such extent as is reasonable having regard to the terms of the undertaking.

[(8A) Nothing in subsection (7) or (8) above shall relieve any person who imports any article or substance from any duty in respect of anything which—

(a) in the case of an article designed outside the United Kingdom, was done by and in the course of any trade, profession or other undertaking carried on by, or was within the control of, the person who designed the article; or

(b) in the case of an article or substance manufactured outside the United Kingdom, was done by and in the course of any trade, profession or other undertaking carried on by, or was within the control of, the person who manufactured the article or substance.]

(9) Where a person ("the ostensible supplier") supplies any [article or substance] to another ("the customer") under a hire-purchase agreement, conditional sale agreement or credit-sale agreement, and the ostensible supplier—

(a) carries on the business of financing the acquisition of goods by others by means of such agreements; and

(b) in the course of that business acquired his interest in the article or substance supplied to the customer as a means of financing its acquisition by the customer from a third person ("the effective supplier"),

the effective supplier and not the ostensible supplier shall be treated for the purposes of this section as supplying the article or substance to the customer, and any duty imposed by the preceding provisions of this section on suppliers shall accordingly fall on the effective supplier and not on the ostensible supplier.

[(10) For the purposes of this section an absence of safety or a risk to health shall be disregarded in so far as the case in or in relation to which it would arise is shown to be one the occurrence of which could not reasonably be foreseen; and in determining whether any duty imposed by virtue of paragraph (a) of subsection (1), (1A) or (4) above has been performed regard shall be had to any relevant information or advice which has been provided to any person by the person by whom the article has been designed, manufactured, imported or supplied or, as the case may be, by the person by whom the substance has been manufactured, imported or supplied.]

NOTES

Sub-ss (1), (1A): substituted, for the original sub-s (1), by the Consumer Protection Act 1987, s 36, Sch 3, para 1(1), (2).

Sub-ss (2), (3), (5), (8), (9): words in square brackets inserted or substituted by the Consumer Protection Act 1987, s 36, Sch 3, para 1(1), (3), (4), (6), (7), (9).

Sub-ss (4), (10): substituted by the Consumer Protection Act 1987, s 36, Sch 3, para 1(1), (5), (10).

Sub-s (8A): inserted by the Consumer Protection Act 1987, s 36, Sch 3, para 1(1), (8).

Exclusion or modification: see s 15(3)(b) and (6)(c) at **[1.43]**.

Enforcing authority: the Office of Road and Rail (formerly the Office of Rail Regulation) is the enforcing authority for the purposes of this section in so far as it relates to articles designed, manufactured, imported or supplied (or substances manufactured, imported or supplied), to be used exclusively or primarily in the operation of railways, tramways and certain other systems of guided transport (or, in the case of sub-s (3), in so far as it relates to the erection or installation of articles for use at work in the operation of such systems of transport); see the Health and Safety (Enforcing Authority for Railways and Other Guided Transport Systems) Regulations 2006, SI 2006/557.

[1.35]

7 General duties of employees at work

It shall be the duty of every employee while at work—

(a) to take reasonable care for the health and safety of himself and of other persons who may be affected by his acts or omissions at work; and

(b) as regards any duty or requirement imposed on his employer or any other person by or under any of the relevant statutory provisions, to co-operate with him so far as is necessary to enable that duty or requirement to be performed or complied with.

NOTES

Exclusion or modification: see s 15(3)(b) and (6)(c) at **[1.43]**.

[1.36]

8 Duty not to interfere with or misuse things provided pursuant to certain provisions

No person shall intentionally or recklessly interfere with or misuse anything provided in the interests of health, safety or welfare in pursuance of any of the relevant statutory provisions.

NOTES

Exclusion or modification: see s 15(3)(b) and (6)(c) at **[1.43]**.

[1.37]

9 Duty not to charge employees for things done or provided pursuant to certain specific requirements

No employer shall levy or permit to be levied on any employee of his any charge in respect of anything done or provided in pursuance of any specific requirement of the relevant statutory provisions.

NOTES

Exclusion or modification: see s 15(3)(b) and (6)(c) at **[1.43]**.

[The Health and Safety Executive]

[1.38]

[10 Establishment of the Executive

(1) There shall be a body corporate to be known as the Health and Safety Executive (in this Act referred to as "the Executive").

(2) The provisions of Schedule 2 shall have effect with respect to the Executive.

(3) The functions of the Executive and of its officers and servants shall be performed on behalf of the Crown.

(4) For the purpose of any civil proceedings arising out of those functions—

(a) in England and Wales and Northern Ireland, the Crown Proceedings Act 1947 shall apply to the Executive as if it were a government department within the meaning of that Act, and

(b) in Scotland, the Crown Suits (Scotland) Act 1857 shall apply to the Executive as if it were a public department within the meaning of that Act.]

NOTES

Substituted by the Legislative Reform (Health and Safety Executive) Order 2008, SI 2008/960, arts 3, 4.

Note: the Legislative Reform (Health and Safety Executive) Order 2008, SI 2008/960 does not amend the heading immediately before this section. However, in light of the other amendments made by that Order, and in light of the abolition of the HSC by art 2 of that Order, the heading has been changed from "The Health and Safety Commission and the Health and Safety Executive" to "The Health and Safety Executive".

[1.39]

[11 Functions of the Executive

(1) It shall be the general duty of the Executive to do such things and make such arrangements as it considers appropriate for the general purposes of this Part.

(2) In connection with the general purposes of this Part, the Executive shall—

(a) assist and encourage persons concerned with matters relevant to those purposes to further those purposes;

(b) make such arrangements as it considers appropriate for the carrying out of research and the publication of the results of research and the provision of training and information, and encourage research and the provision of training and information by others;

(c) make such arrangements as it considers appropriate to secure that the following persons are provided with an information and advisory service on matters relevant to those purposes and are kept informed of and are adequately advised on such matters—

(i) government departments,

(ii) local authorities,

(iii) employers,

(iv) employees,

(v) organisations representing employers or employees, and

(vi) other persons concerned with matters relevant to the general purposes of this Part.

(3) The Executive shall submit from time to time to the Secretary of State such proposals as the Executive considers appropriate for the making of regulations under any of the relevant statutory provisions.

(4) In subsections (1) to (3)—

(a) references to the general purposes of this Part do not include references to [any of the transferred purposes]; and

(b) the reference to the making of regulations under the relevant statutory provisions does not include a reference so far as the regulations are made[—

(i) for any of the transferred purposes, or

(ii) under section 43 and concern fees relating to nuclear site regulation].

[(4A) In subsection (4)—

(a) "the transferred purposes" means—

(i) the railway safety purposes;
(ii) the nuclear safety purposes;
(iii) the nuclear security purposes;
(iv) the nuclear safeguards purposes;
(v) the radioactive material transport purposes;

(b) "fees relating to nuclear site regulation" means fees payable for or in connection with the performance of a function by or on behalf of—
(i) the Office for Nuclear Regulation, or
(ii) any inspector appointed by the Office for Nuclear Regulation.

[(4AA) Subsection (4)(b)(i) does not apply in relation to the making of regulations under section 3(2) for the railway safety purposes (and, accordingly, the Executive shall submit under subsection (3) such proposals as the Executive considers appropriate for the making of regulations under section 3(2) for those purposes).]

(4B) The Executive may submit to the Secretary of State any proposal submitted to it by the Office for Nuclear Regulation under section 81 of the Energy Act 2013 (proposals about orders and regulations).]

(5) It shall be the duty of the Executive—
(a) to submit to the Secretary of State from time to time particulars of what it proposes to do for the purpose of performing of its functions;
(b) to ensure that its activities are in accordance with proposals approved by the Secretary of State; and
(c) to give effect to any directions given to it by the Secretary of State.

(6) The Executive shall provide a Minister of the Crown on request—
(a) with information about its activities in connection with any matter with which the Minister is concerned; and
(b) with advice on any matter with which he is concerned, where relevant expert advice is obtainable from any of the officers or servants of the Executive, but which is not relevant to the general purposes of this Part.]

NOTES

Ss 11–13 substituted by the Legislative Reform (Health and Safety Executive) Order 2008, SI 2008/960, arts 3, 5.

The words in square brackets in sub-s (4) were substituted, and sub-ss (4A), (4B) were inserted, by the Energy Act 2013, s 116, Sch 12, Pt 1, paras 1, 2.

Sub-s (4AA) was inserted by the Deregulation Act 2015, s 1(1), (4), as from 26 March 2015 (in so far as is necessary for enabling the exercise on or after that day of any power to make provision by an order or regulations made by statutory instrument), and as from 1 October 2015 (otherwise).

[1.40]

[12 Control of the Executive by the Secretary of State

(1) The Secretary of State may approve any proposals submitted to him under section 11(5)(a) with or without modifications.

(2) The Secretary of State may at any time give to the Executive—
(a) such directions as he thinks fit with respect to its functions, or
(b) such directions as appear to him requisite or expedient to give in the interests of the safety of the State.

(3) The Secretary of State may not under subsection (2) give any directions with regard to the enforcement of the relevant statutory provisions in any particular case.

(4) The reference to directions in subsection (2)(a)—
(a) includes directions modifying the Executive's functions, but
(b) does not include directions conferring functions on the Executive other than any functions of which it was deprived by previous directions given under subsection (2)(a).]

NOTES

Substituted as noted to s 11 at **[1.39]**.

[1.41]

[13 Powers of the Executive

(1) Subject to subsection (2), the Executive shall have power to do anything which is calculated to facilitate, or is conducive or incidental to, the performance of its functions, including a function conferred on it under this subsection.

(2) The power in subsection (1) shall not include the power to borrow money.

(3) The Executive may make agreements with a government department or other person for that department or person to perform any of its functions, with or without payment.

(4) Subject to subsections (5) and (6), the Executive may make agreements with a Minister of the Crown, with a government department or with a public authority to perform functions exercisable by that Minister, department or authority, with or without payment.

(5) The functions referred to in subsection (4)—
(a) in the case of a Minister of the Crown, include functions not conferred by an enactment;
(b) shall be functions which the Secretary of State considers can be appropriately performed by the Executive; and
(c) do not include any power to make regulations or other instruments of a legislative character.

(6) The Executive may provide services or facilities, with or without payment, otherwise than for the general purposes of this Part, to a government department or public authority in connection with the exercise of that department's or authority's functions.

[(6A) The reference in subsection (6) to the general purposes of this Part does not include a reference to any of the following—

(a) the nuclear safety purposes;
(b) the nuclear security purposes;
(c) the nuclear safeguards purposes;
(d) the radioactive material transport purposes.]

(7) The Executive may appoint persons or committees of persons to provide it with advice in connection with any of its functions and, without prejudice to subsection (8), it may remunerate these persons.

(8) The Executive may, in connection with the performance of its functions, pay to any person—

(a) travelling and subsistence allowances, and
(b) compensation for loss of remunerative time.

(9) Any amounts paid under subsections (7) and (8) shall be such as may be determined by the Secretary of State, with the approval of the Minister for the Civil Service.

(10) The Executive may—

(a) carry out, arrange for, or make payments for the carrying out of, research into any matter connected with its functions, and
(b) disseminate or arrange for or make payments for the dissemination of information derived from this research.

(11) The Executive may include, in any arrangements made for the provision of services or facilities under subsection (6), provision for the making of payments to the Executive, or any person acting on its behalf, by other parties to the arrangements and by persons using those services or facilities.]

NOTES

Substituted as noted to s 11 at **[1.39]**.
Sub-s (6A): inserted by the Energy Act 2013, s 116, Sch 12, Pt 1, paras 1, 3.

[1.42]

14 Power of [the Executive] to direct investigations and inquiries

(1) This section applies to the following matters, that is to say any accident, occurrence, situation or other matter whatsoever which [the Executive] thinks it necessary or expedient to investigate for any of the general purposes of this Part or with a view to the making of regulations for those purposes; and for the purposes of this subsection—

[(a) those general purposes shall be treated as not including the railway safety purposes [or the ONR's purposes]; but
(b) it is otherwise]

immaterial whether the Executive is or is not responsible for securing the enforcement of such (if any) of the relevant statutory provisions as relate to the matter in question.

[(2) The Executive may at any time—

(a) investigate and make a special report on any matter to which this section applies; or
(b) authorise another person to investigate and make a special report into any such matter.

(2A) The Executive may at any time, with the consent of the Secretary of State, direct an inquiry to be held into any matter to which this section applies.]

(3) Any inquiry held by virtue of [subsection (2A)] above shall be held in accordance with regulations made for the purposes of this subsection by the Secretary of State, and shall be held in public except where or to the extent that the regulations provide otherwise.

(4) Regulations made for the purposes of subsection (3) above may in particular include provision—

(a) conferring on the person holding any such inquiry, and any person assisting him in the inquiry, powers of entry and inspection;
(b) conferring on any such person powers of summoning witnesses to give evidence or produce documents and power to take evidence on oath and administer oaths or require the making of declarations;
(c) requiring any such inquiry to be held otherwise than in public where or to the extent that a Minister of the Crown so directs.

[(4A) Provision that may be made by virtue of subsection (4)(a) includes, in particular, provision conferring functions on the Office for Nuclear Regulation in relation to powers of entry and inspection in relation to any premises for which it is an enforcing authority.]

[(5) In the case of a special report made by virtue of subsection (2), or a report made by the person holding an inquiry by virtue of subsection (2A), the Executive may cause the report, or so much of it as the Executive thinks fit, to be made public at such time and in such manner as it thinks fit.]

(6) [The Executive]—

(a) in the case of an investigation and special report made by virtue of [subsection (2)] above (otherwise than by an officer or servant of the Executive), may pay to the person making it such remuneration and expenses as the Secretary of State may, with the approval of the Minister for the Civil Service, determine;
(b) in the case of an inquiry held by virtue of [subsection (2A)] above, may pay to the person holding it and to any assessor appointed to assist him such remuneration and expenses, and to persons attending the inquiry as witnesses such expenses, as the Secretary of State may, with the like approval, determine; and
(c) may, to such extent as the Secretary of State may determine, defray the other costs, if any, of any such investigation and special report or inquiry.

(7) . . .

NOTES

Sub-s (1): words in first pair of square brackets substituted by the Legislative Reform (Health and Safety Executive) Order 2008, SI 2008/960, arts 3, 6(1), (2); paras (a), (b) substituted by the Railways 2005, s 2, Sch 3, para 4(5); words in square brackets in para (a) inserted by the Energy Act 2013, s 116, Sch 12, Pt 1, paras 1, 4(1), (2).

Sub-ss (2), (2A): substituted, for the original sub-s (2), by SI 2008/960, arts 3, 6(1), (3).

Sub-ss (3), (6): words in square brackets substituted by SI 2008/960, arts 3, 6(1), (4), (6).

Sub-s (4A): inserted by the Energy Act 2013, s 116, Sch 12, Pt 1, paras 1, 4(1), (3).

Sub-s (5): substituted by SI 2008/960, arts 3, 6(1), (5).

Sub-s (7): repealed, in relation to Scotland, by the Inquiries into Fatal Accidents and Sudden Deaths etc (Scotland) Act 2016, s 39(2), Sch 2, para 2(1), (2), as from 15 June 2017, and, in relation to England and Wales, by the Inquiries into Fatal Accidents and Sudden Deaths etc (Scotland) Act 2016 (Consequential Provisions and Modifications) Order 2016, SI 2016/1142, art 7(1), Schedule, Pt 2, para 3(1), (2), as from 15 June 2017.

'The ONR's purposes': see the definition in s 53(1); the ONR is the Office for Nuclear Regulation.

Note: the Legislative Reform (Health and Safety Executive) Order 2008, SI 2008/960 does not amend the title of this section. However, in light of the other amendments made by that Order, and in light of the abolition of the HSC by art 2 of that Order, the title of this section has been changed from "Power of the Commission to direct investigations and inquiries" to "Power of the Executive to direct investigations and inquiries".

Regulations: the Health and Safety Inquiries (Procedure) Regulations 1975, SI 1975/335; the Health and Safety Inquiries (Procedure) (Amendment) Regulations 1976, SI 1976/1246.

Health and safety regulations and approved codes of practice

[1.43]

15 Health and safety regulations

[(1) Subject to the provisions of section 50, the Secretary of State . . . shall have power to make regulations under this section for any of the general purposes of this Part (and regulations so made are in this Part referred to as "health and safety regulations").]

[(1A) In subsection (1), the reference to the general purposes of this Part does not include a reference to any of the following—

(a) the nuclear safety purposes;
(b) the nuclear security purposes;
(c) the nuclear safeguards purposes;
(d) the radioactive material transport purposes.

(1B) Subsection (1A) does not preclude health and safety regulations from including provision merely because the provision could be made for any of the purposes mentioned in paragraphs (a) to (d) of that subsection.]

(2) Without prejudice to the generality of [subsection (1)], health and safety regulations may for any of the general purposes of this Part make provision for any of the purposes mentioned in Schedule 3.

(3) Health and safety regulations—

(a) may repeal or modify any of the existing statutory provisions;
(b) may exclude or modify in relation to any specified class of case any of the provisions of sections 2 to 9 or any of the existing statutory provisions;
(c) may make a specified authority or class of authorities responsible, to such extent as may[, subject to subsection (3A),] be specified, for the enforcement of any of the relevant statutory provisions.

[(3A) Nothing in this section is to be taken to permit health and safety regulations to make provision about responsibility for the enforcement of any of the relevant statutory provisions as they apply in relation to any GB nuclear site.

(3B) Subsection (3A) does not prevent health and safety regulations providing for [the Office of Rail and Road] to be responsible for the enforcement, in relation to GB nuclear sites, of any of the relevant statutory provisions that are made for the railway safety purposes.

(3C) In subsections (3A) and (3B), "GB nuclear site" has the same meaning as in section 68 of the Energy Act 2013 (nuclear safety purposes).]

(4) Health and safety regulations—

(a) may impose requirements by reference to the approval of [the Executive] or any other specified body or person;
(b) may provide for references in the regulations to any specified document to operate as references to that document as revised or re-issued from time to time.

(5) Health and safety regulations—

(a) may provide (either unconditionally or subject to conditions, and with or without limit of time) for exemptions from any requirement or prohibition imposed by or under any of the relevant statutory provisions;
(b) may enable exemptions from any requirement or prohibition imposed by or under any of the relevant statutory provisions to be granted (either unconditionally or subject to conditions, and with or without limit of time) by any specified person or by any person authorised in that behalf by a specified authority.

(6) Health and safety regulations—

(a) may specify the persons or classes of persons who, in the event of a contravention of a requirement or prohibition imposed by or under the regulations, are to be guilty of an offence, whether in addition to or to the exclusion of other persons or classes of persons;
(b) may provide for any specified defence to be available in proceedings for any offence under the relevant statutory provisions either generally or in specified circumstances;

(c) may exclude proceedings on indictment in relation to offences consisting of a contravention of a requirement or prohibition imposed by or under any of the existing statutory provisions, sections 2 to 9 or health and safety regulations;

(d) may restrict the punishments [(other than the maximum fine on conviction on indictment)] which can be imposed in respect of any such offence as is mentioned in paragraph (c) above.

[(e) . . .]

(7) Without prejudice to section 35, health and safety regulations may make provision for enabling offences under any of the relevant statutory provisions to be treated as having been committed at any specified place for the purpose of bringing any such offence within the field of responsibility of any enforcing authority or conferring jurisdiction on any court to entertain proceedings for any such offence.

(8) Health and safety regulations may take the form of regulations applying to particular circumstances only or to a particular case only (for example, regulations applying to particular premises only).

(9) If an Order in Council is made under section 84(3) providing that this section shall apply to or in relation to persons, premises or work outside Great Britain then, notwithstanding the Order, health and safety regulations shall not apply to or in relation to aircraft in flight, vessels, hovercraft or offshore installations outside Great Britain or persons at work outside Great Britain in connection with submarine cables or submarine pipelines except in so far as the regulations expressly so provide.

(10) In this section "specified" means specified in health and safety regulations.

NOTES

Sub-s (1): substituted by the Employment Protection Act 1975, s 116, Sch 15, para 6; words omitted repealed by the Ministry of Agriculture, Fisheries and Food (Dissolution) Order 2002, SI 2002/794, art 5(2), Sch 2.

Sub-ss (1A), (1B), (3A)–(3C): inserted by the Energy Act 2013, s 116, Sch 12, Pt 1, paras 1, 5(1), (2), (5); words in square brackets in sub-s (3B) substituted by the Office of Rail Regulation (Change of Name) Regulations 2015, SI 2015/1682, reg 2(2), Schedule, Pt 1, para 4(c)(i), as from 16 October 2015.

Sub-s (2): words in square brackets substituted by the Energy Act 2013, s 116, Sch 12, Pt 1, paras 1, 5(1), (3).

Sub-s (3): words in square brackets inserted by the Energy Act 2013, s 116, Sch 12, Pt 1, paras 1, 5(1), (4).

Sub-s (4): words in square brackets substituted by the Legislative Reform (Health and Safety Executive) Order 2008, SI 2008/960, arts 3, 7.

Sub-s (6): words in square brackets in para (d) inserted by the Criminal Law Act 1977, s 65(4), Sch 12; para (e) originally added by the Offshore Safety Act 1992, s 4(1), (6), and subsequently repealed by the Health and Safety (Offences) Act 2008, ss 2(1), 3(3), Sch 3, para 2(1), Sch 4.

"May repeal or modify any of the existing statutory provisions" (sub-s (3)): the scope of regulations under this section is extended by: (a) the Offshore Safety Act 1992, ss 1(2), (3), 2(2), (3); (b) the Railways Act 1993, s 117(3), (4); and (c) the Energy Act 2008, s 99(2). As to the power of the Secretary of State to revoke any provision of regulations under this section which has effect in place of a provision which was an existing statutory provision for the purposes of this Part of this Act, see the Deregulation and Contracting Out Act 1994, s 37(1)(b).

Regulations: a very large number of regulations has been made under this section, and specialist Health and Safety publications should be consulted for a full list. Among the most important currently in force (many as subsequently amended) are: the Safety Representatives and Safety Committees Regulations 1977, SI 1977/500 at **[2.30]**; the Health and Safety (First-Aid) Regulations 1981, SI 1981/917; the Electricity at Work Regulations 1989, SI 1989/635; the Health and Safety Information for Employees Regulations 1989, SI 1989/682 at **[2.113]**; the Health and Safety (Display Screen Equipment) Regulations 1992, SI 1992/2792; the Manual Handling Operations Regulations 1992, SI 1992/2793; the Personal Protective Equipment at Work Regulations 1992, SI 1992/2966; the Workplace (Health, Safety and Welfare) Regulations 1992, SI 1992/3004; the Health and Safety (Enforcing Authority) Regulations 1998, SI 1998/494; the Provision and Use of Work Equipment Regulations 1998, SI 1998/2306; the Lifting Operations and Lifting Equipment Regulations 1998, SI 1998/2307; the Police (Health and Safety) Regulations 1999, SI 1999/860 at **[2.407]**; the Railway Safety Regulations 1999, SI 1999/2244; the Management of Health and Safety at Work Regulations 1999, SI 1999/3242 at **[2.417]**; the Control of Lead at Work Regulations 2002, SI 2002/2676; the Control of Substances Hazardous to Health Regulations 2002, SI 2002/2677; the Work at Height Regulations 2005, SI 2005/735; the Control of Vibration at Work Regulations 2005, SI 2005/1093; the Control of Noise at Work Regulations 2005, SI 2005/1643; the Health and Safety (Enforcing Authority for Railways and Other Guided Transport Systems) Regulations 2006, SI 2006/557; the Carriage of Dangerous Goods and Use of Transportable Pressure Equipment Regulations 2009, SI 2009/1348; the Agency Workers Regulations 2010, SI 2010/93 at **[2.1085]**; the Control of Artificial Optical Radiation at Work Regulations 2010, SI 2010/1140; the Control of Asbestos Regulations 2012, SI 2012/632; the Health and Safety (Sharp Instruments in Healthcare) Regulations 2013, SI 2013/645; the Reporting of Injuries, Diseases and Dangerous Occurrences Regulations 2013, SI 2013/1471; the Biocidal Products and Chemicals (Appointment of Authorities and Enforcement) Regulations 2013, SI 2013/1506; the Health and Safety at Work etc Act 1974 (Civil Liability) (Exceptions) Regulations 2013, SI 2013/1667 at **[2.1449]**; the Petroleum (Consolidation) Regulations 2014, SI 2014/1637; the Explosives Regulations 2014, SI 2014/1638; the Acetylene Safety (England and Wales and Scotland) Regulations 2014, SI 2014/1639; the Genetically Modified Organisms (Contained Use) Regulations 2014, SI 2014/1663; the Mines Regulations 2014, SI 2014/3248; the Construction (Design and Management) Regulations 2015, SI 2015/51; the Offshore Installations (Offshore Safety Directive) (Safety Case etc) Regulations 2015, SI 2015/398; the Control of Major Accident Hazards Regulations 2015, SI 2015/483; the Control of Electromagnetic Fields at Work Regulations 2016, SI 2016/588; the Dangerous Goods in Harbour Areas Regulations 2016, SI 2016/721; the Freight Containers (Safety Convention) Regulations 2017, SI 2017/325; the Ionising Radiations Regulations 2017, SI 2017/1075. Note that many of the Regulations made under this section are amended (as from exit day) by the Health and Safety (Amendment) (EU Exit) Regulations 2018, SI 2018/1370 (made under the European Union (Withdrawal) Act 2018).

[1.44]

16 Approval of codes of practice by [the Executive]

(1) For the purpose of providing practical guidance with respect to the requirements of any provision of [any of the enactments or instruments mentioned in subsection (1A) below], [the Executive] may, subject to the following subsection . . . —

(a) approve and issue such codes of practice (whether prepared by it or not) as in its opinion are suitable for that purpose;

(b) approve such codes of practice issued or proposed to be issued otherwise than by [the Executive] as in its opinion are suitable for that purpose.

[(1A) Those enactments and instruments are—

(a) sections 2 to 7 above;

(b) health and safety regulations, except so far as they make provision exclusively in relation to transport systems falling within paragraph 1(3) of Schedule 3 to the Railways Act 2005; and

(c) the existing statutory provisions that are not such provisions by virtue of section 117(4) of the Railways Act 1993.]

(2) [The Executive] shall not approve a code of practice under subsection (1) above without the consent of the Secretary of State, and shall, before seeking his consent, consult—

(a) any government department or other body that appears to [the Executive] to be appropriate . . . ; and

(b) such government departments and other bodies, if any, as in relation to any matter dealt with in the code, [the Executive] is required to consult under this section by virtue of directions given to it by the Secretary of State.

(3) Where a code of practice is approved by [the Executive] under subsection (1) above, [the Executive] shall issue a notice in writing—

(a) identifying the code in question and stating the date on which its approval by [the Executive] is to take effect; and

(b) specifying for which of the provisions mentioned in subsection (1) above the code is approved.

(4) [The Executive] may—

(a) from time to time revise the whole or any part of any code of practice prepared by it in pursuance of this section;

(b) approve any revision or proposed revision of the whole or any part of any code of practice for the time being approved under this section;

and the provisions of subsections (2) and (3) above shall, with the necessary modifications, apply in relation to the approval of any revision under this subsection as they apply in relation to the approval of a code of practice under subsection (1) above.

(5) [The Executive] may at any time with the consent of the Secretary of State withdraw its approval from any code of practice approved under this section, but before seeking his consent shall consult the same government departments and other bodies as it would be required to consult under subsection (2) above if it were proposing to approve the code.

(6) Where under the preceding subsection [the Executive] withdraws its approval from a code of practice approved under this section, [the Executive] shall issue a notice in writing identifying the code in question and stating the date on which its approval of it is to cease to have effect.

(7) References in this part to an approved code of practice are references to that code as it has effect for the time being by virtue of any revision of the whole or any part of it approved under this section.

(8) The power of [the Executive] under subsection (1)(b) above to approve a code of practice issued or proposed to be issued otherwise than by [the Executive] shall include power to approve a part of such a code of practice; and accordingly in this Part "code of practice" may be read as including a part of such a code of practice.

NOTES

Words "the Executive" in square brackets in each place they occur substituted by the Legislative Reform (Health and Safety Executive) Order 2008, SI 2008/960, arts 3, 8.

Other amendments to this section are as follows.

Sub-s (1): words in first pair of square brackets substituted by the Railways Act 2005, s 2, Sch 3, para 9(1); words omitted repealed by the Employment Protection Act 1975, ss 116, 125(3), Sch 15, para 7, Sch 18.

Sub-s (1A): inserted by the Railways Act 2005, s 2, Sch 3, para 9(2).

Sub-s (2): words omitted repealed by the Health and Social Care Act 2012, s 56(4), Sch 7, paras 4, 5.

For reasons of space, the only Codes of Practice made under this section which are reproduced in this work are Safety Representatives and Safety Committees (1978) at **[4.163]** and Time off for the Training of Safety Representatives (1978) at **[4.165]**.

[1.45]

17 Use of approved codes of practice in criminal proceedings

(1) A failure on the part of any person to observe any provision of an approved code of practice shall not of itself render him liable to any civil or criminal proceedings; but where in any criminal proceedings a party is alleged to have committed an offence by reason of a contravention of any requirement or prohibition imposed by or under any such provision as is mentioned in section 16(1) being a provision for which there was an approved code of practice at the time of the alleged contravention, the following subsection shall have effect with respect to that code in relation to those proceedings.

(2) Any provision of the code of practice which appears to the court to be relevant to the requirement or prohibition alleged to have been contravened shall be admissible in evidence in the proceedings; and if it is proved that there was at any material time a failure to observe any provision of the code which appears to the court to be relevant to any matter which it is necessary for the prosecution to prove in order to establish a contravention of that requirement or prohibition, that matter shall be taken as proved unless the court is satisfied that the requirement or prohibition was in respect of that matter complied with otherwise than by way of observance of that provision of the code.

(3) In any criminal proceedings—

(a) a document purporting to be a notice issued by [the Executive] under section 16 shall be taken to be such a notice unless the contrary is proved; and

(b) a code of practice which appears to the court to be the subject of such a notice shall be taken to be the subject of that notice unless the contrary is proved.

NOTES

Sub-s (3): words in square brackets substituted by the Legislative Reform (Health and Safety Executive) Order 2008, SI 2008/960, arts 3, 9.

Enforcement

[1.46]

18 Authorities responsible for enforcement of the relevant statutory provisions

(1) It shall be the duty of the Executive to make adequate arrangements for the enforcement of the relevant statutory provisions except to the extent that some other authority or class of authorities is by any of those provisions or by regulations under subsection (2) below made responsible for their enforcement.

[(1A) The Office for Nuclear Regulation is responsible for the enforcement of the relevant statutory provisions as they apply in relation to GB nuclear sites (within the meaning given in section 68 of the Energy Act 2013 (nuclear safety purposes)).

(1B) Subsection (1A) is subject to any provision of health and safety regulations making the [Office of Rail and Road] responsible for the enforcement of any of the relevant statutory provisions to any extent in relation to such sites.]

(2) The Secretary of State may by regulations—

[(za) make the Office for Nuclear Regulation responsible for the enforcement of the relevant statutory provisions to such extent as may be prescribed (and may in particular provide for any site or matter in relation to which the Office for Nuclear Regulation is made so responsible to be determined by the Secretary of State or the Office for Nuclear Regulation under the regulations);]

(a) make local authorities responsible for the enforcement of the relevant statutory provisions to such extent as may be prescribed;

(b) make provision for enabling responsibility for enforcing any of the relevant statutory provisions to be, to such extent as may be determined under the regulations—

[(zi) transferred from the Executive or local authorities to the Office for Nuclear Regulation, or from the Office for Nuclear Regulation to the Executive or local authorities;]

(i) transferred from the Executive to local authorities or from local authorities to the Executive; or

(ii) assigned to the Executive[, to the Office for Nuclear Regulation] or to local authorities for the purpose of removing any uncertainty as to what are by virtue of [subsection (1A) or] this subsection their respective responsibilities for the enforcement of those provisions;

[(iii) assigned to the [Office of Rail and Road] or the Office for Nuclear Regulation for the purpose of removing any uncertainty as to what are by virtue of any of the relevant statutory provisions their respective responsibilities for the enforcement of any of those provisions;]

and any regulations made in pursuance of paragraph (b) above shall include provision for securing that any transfer or assignment effected under the regulations is brought to the notice of persons affected by it.

(3) Any provision made by regulations under the preceding subsection shall have effect subject to any provision made by health and safety regulations . . . in pursuance of section 15(3)(c).

[(3A) Regulations under subsection (2)(a) may not make local authorities enforcing authorities in relation to any site in relation to which the Office for Nuclear Regulation is an enforcing authority.

(3B) Where the Office for Nuclear Regulation is, by or under subsection (1A) or (2), made responsible for the enforcement of any of the relevant statutory provisions to any extent, it must make adequate arrangements for the enforcement of those provisions to that extent.]

(4) It shall be the duty of every local authority—

(a) to make adequate arrangements for the enforcement within their area of the relevant statutory provisions to the extent that they are by any of those provisions or by regulations under subsection (2) above made responsible for their enforcement; and

(b) to perform the duty imposed on them by the preceding paragraph and any other functions conferred on them by any of the relevant statutory provisions in accordance with such guidance as [the Executive] may give them.

[(4A) Before the Executive gives guidance under subsection (4)(b) it shall consult the local authorities.

(4B) It shall be the duty of the Executive and the local authorities—

(a) to work together to establish best practice and consistency in the enforcement of the relevant statutory provisions;

(b) to enter into arrangements with each other for securing cooperation and the exchange of information in connection with the carrying out of their functions with regard to the relevant statutory provisions; and

(c) from time to time to review those arrangements and to revise them when they consider it appropriate to do so.]

(5) Where any authority other than . . . the Executive[, the Office for Nuclear Regulation] or a local authority is by any of the relevant statutory provisions . . . made responsible for the enforcement of any of those provisions to any extent, it shall be the duty of that authority—

(a) to make adequate arrangements for the enforcement of those provisions to that extent; and

(b) [except where that authority is the [Office of Rail and Road],] to perform the duty imposed on the authority by the preceding paragraph and any other functions conferred on the authority by any of the relevant statutory provisions in accordance with such guidance as [the Executive] may give to the authority.

(6) Nothing in the provisions of this Act or of any regulations made thereunder charging any person in Scotland with the enforcement of any of the relevant statutory provisions shall be construed as authorising that person to institute proceedings for any offence.

(7) In this Part—

(a) "enforcing authority" means the Executive or any other authority which is by any of the relevant statutory provisions or by regulations under subsection (2) above made responsible for the enforcement of any of those provisions to any extent; and

(b) any reference to an enforcing authority's field of responsibility is a reference to the field over which that authority's responsibility for the enforcement of those provisions extends for the time being;

but where by virtue of [subsection (3) of section 13] [of this Act or section 95 of the Energy Act 2013 (power for Office for Nuclear Regulation to arrange for exercise of functions by others)] the performance of any function of . . . the Executive [or the Office for Nuclear Regulation] is delegated to a government department or person, references to . . . the Executive [or the Office for Nuclear Regulation (as the case may be)] (or to an enforcing authority where that authority is the Executive [or the Office for Nuclear Regulation]) in any provision of this Part which relates to that function shall, so far as may be necessary to give effect to any agreement [or arrangements under the provision in question], be construed as references to that department or person; and accordingly any reference to the field of responsibility of an enforcing authority shall be construed as a reference to the field over which that department or person for the time being performs such a function.

NOTES

Sub-ss (1A), (1B), (3A), (3B): inserted by the Energy Act 2013, s 116, Sch 12, Pt 1, paras 1, 6(1), (2), (4); words in square brackets in sub-s (1B) substituted by the Office of Rail Regulation (Change of Name) Regulations 2015, SI 2015/1682, reg 2(2), Schedule, Pt 1, para 4(c)(ii), as from 16 October 2015.

Sub-s (2): words "Office of Rail and Road" in square brackets in sub-para (b)(iii) substituted by SI 2015/1682, reg 2(2), Schedule, Pt 1, para 4(c)(ii), as from 16 October 2015; other words in square brackets inserted by the Energy Act 2013, s 116, Sch 12, Pt 1, paras 1, 6(1), (3).

Sub-s (3): words omitted repealed by the Employment Protection Act 1975, ss 116, 125(3), Sch 15, para 8, Sch 18.

Sub-s (4): words in square brackets substituted by the Legislative Reform (Health and Safety Executive) Order 2008, SI 2008/960, arts 3, 10(1), (2).

Sub-ss (4A), (4B): inserted by SI 2008/960, arts 3, 10(1), (3).

Sub-s (5): first words omitted repealed by the Employment Protection Act 1975, ss 116, 125(3), Sch 15, para 8, Sch 18; words in first pair of square brackets inserted by the Energy Act 2013, s 116, Sch 12, Pt 1, paras 1, 6(1), (5); second words omitted repealed by the Railways Act 2005, s 59(6), Sch 13, Pt 1; words in first (outer) pair of square brackets in para (b) inserted by the Railways Act 2005, s 2, Sch 3, para 10(3); words in second (inner) pair of square brackets in para (b) substituted by SI 2015/1682, reg 2(2), Schedule, Pt 1, para 4(c)(ii), as from 16 October 2015; words in final pair of square brackets in para (b) substituted by SI 2008/960, arts 3, 10(1), (4).

Sub-s (7): words omitted repealed, and words "subsection (3) of section 13" in square brackets substituted, by SI 2008/960, arts 3, 10(1), (5); other words in square brackets inserted or substituted by the Energy Act 2013, s 116, Sch 12, Pt 1, paras 1, 6(1), (6).

See also the Health and Safety (Enforcing Authority for Railways and Other Guided Transport Systems) Regulations 2006, SI 2006/557, which provides that the Office of Rail and Road shall be responsible for the enforcement of the relevant statutory provisions to the extent that they relate to the operation of a railway, the operation of a tramway, and the operation of any other system of guided transport.

Regulations: the Railway Safety (Miscellaneous Provisions) Regulations 1997, SI 1997/553; the Health and Safety (Enforcing Authority) Regulations 1998, SI 1998/494; the Ammonium Nitrate Materials (High Nitrogen Content) Safety Regulations 2003, SI 2003/1082; the Adventure Activities (Enforcing Authority) Regulations 2004, SI 2004/1359; the Railways and Other Guided Transport Systems (Safety) Regulations 2006, SI 2006/599; the Health and Safety (Miscellaneous Amendments and Revocations) Regulations 2009, SI 2009/693; the Major Accident Off-Site Emergency Plan (Management of Waste from Extractive Industries) (England and Wales) Regulations 2009, SI 2009/1927; the Local Policing Bodies (Consequential Amendments) Regulations 2011, SI 2011/3058; the Control of Asbestos Regulations 2012, SI 2012/632; the Petroleum (Consolidation) Regulations 2014, SI 2014/1637; the Explosives Regulations 2014, SI 2014/1638; the Mines Regulations 2014, SI 2014/3248; the Ionising Radiations Regulations 2017, SI 2017/1075.

[1.47]

19 Appointment of inspectors

(1) Every enforcing authority may appoint as inspectors (under whatever title it may from time to time determine) such persons having suitable qualifications as it thinks necessary for carrying into effect the relevant statutory provisions within its field of responsibility, and may terminate any appointment made under this section.

(2) Every appointment of a person as an inspector under this section shall be made by an instrument in writing specifying which of the powers conferred on inspectors by the relevant statutory provisions are to be exercisable by the person appointed; and an inspector shall in right of his appointment under this section—

(a) be entitled to exercise only such of those powers as are so specified; and

(b) be entitled to exercise the powers so specified only within the field of responsibility of the authority which appointed him.

(3) So much of an inspector's instrument of appointment as specifies the powers which he is entitled to exercise may be varied by the enforcing authority which appointed him.

(4) An inspector shall, if so required when exercising or seeking to exercise any power conferred on him by any of the relevant statutory provisions, produce his instrument of appointment or a duly authenticated copy thereof.

[1.48]

20 Powers of inspectors

(1) Subject to the provisions of section 19 and this section, an inspector may, for the purpose of carrying into effect any of the relevant statutory provisions within the field of responsibility of the enforcing authority which appointed him, exercise the powers set out in subsection (2) below.

(2) The powers of an inspector referred to in the preceding subsection are the following, namely—

(a) at any reasonable time (or, in a situation which in his opinion is or may be dangerous, at any time) to enter any premises which he has reason to believe it is necessary for him to enter for the purpose mentioned in subsection (1) above;

(b) to take with him a constable if he has reasonable cause to apprehend any serious obstruction in the execution of his duty;

(c) without prejudice to the preceding paragraph, on entering any premises by virtue of paragraph (a) above to take with him—

(i) any other person duly authorised by his (the inspector's) enforcing authority; and

(ii) any equipment or materials required for any purpose for which the power of entry is being exercised;

(d) to make such examination and investigation as may in any circumstances be necessary for the purpose mentioned in subsection (1) above;

(e) as regards any premises which he has power to enter, to direct that those premises or any part of them, or anything therein, shall be left undisturbed (whether generally or in particular respects) for so long as is reasonably necessary for the purpose of any examination or investigation under paragraph (d) above;

(f) to take such measurements and photographs and make such recordings as he considers necessary for the purpose of any examination or investigation under paragraph (d) above;

(g) to take samples of any articles or substances found in any premises which he has power to enter, and of the atmosphere in or in the vicinity of any such premises;

(h) in the case of any article or substance found in any premises which he has power to enter, being an article or substance which appears to him to have caused or to be likely to cause danger to health or safety, to cause it to be dismantled or subjected to any process or test (but not so as to damage or destroy it unless this is in the circumstances necessary for the purpose mentioned in subsection (1) above);

(i) in the case of any such article or substance as is mentioned in the preceding paragraph, to take possession of it and detain it for so long as is necessary for all or any of the following purposes, namely—

(i) to examine it and do to it anything which he has power to do under that paragraph;

(ii) to ensure that it is not tampered with before his examination of it is completed;

(iii) to ensure that it is available for use as evidence in any proceedings for an offence under any of the relevant statutory provisions or any proceedings relating to a notice under section 21 or 22;

(j) to require any person whom he has reasonable cause to believe to be able to give any information relevant to any examination or investigation under paragraph (d) above to answer (in the absence of persons other than a person nominated by him to be present and any persons whom the inspector may allow to be present) such questions as the inspector thinks fit to ask and to sign a declaration of the truth of his answers;

(k) to require the production of, inspect, and take copies of or of any entry in—

(i) any books or documents which by virtue of any of the relevant statutory provisions are required to be kept; and

(ii) any other books or documents which it is necessary for him to see for the purposes of any examination or investigation under paragraph (d) above;

(l) to require any person to afford him such facilities and assistance with respect to any matters or things within that person's control or in relation to which that person has responsibilities as are necessary to enable the inspector to exercise any of the powers conferred on him by this section;

(m) any other power which is necessary for the purpose mentioned in subsection (1) above.

(3) The Secretary of State may by regulations make provision as to the procedure to be followed in connection with the taking of samples under subsection (2)(g) above (including provision as to the way in which samples that have been so taken are to be dealt with).

(4) Where an inspector proposes to exercise the power conferred by subsection (2)(h) above in the case of an article or substance found in any premises, he shall, if so requested by a person who at the time is present in and has responsibilities in relation to those premises, cause anything which is to be done by virtue of that power to be done in the presence of that person unless the inspector considers that its being done in that person's presence would be prejudicial to the safety of the State.

(5) Before exercising the power conferred by subsection (2)(h) above in the case of any article or substance, an inspector shall consult such persons as appear to him appropriate for the purpose of ascertaining what dangers, if any, there may be in doing anything which he proposes to do under that power.

(6) Where under the power conferred by subsection (2)(i) above an inspector takes possession of any article or substance found in any premises, he shall leave there, either with a responsible person or, if that is impracticable, fixed in a conspicuous position, a notice giving particulars of that article or substance

sufficient to identify it and stating that he has taken possession of it under that power; and before taking possession of any such substance under that power an inspector shall, if it is practicable for him to do so, take a sample thereof and give to a responsible person at the premises a portion of the sample marked in a manner sufficient to identify it.

(7) No answer given by a person in pursuance of a requirement imposed under subsection (2)(j) above shall be admissible in evidence against that person or the [spouse or civil partner] of that person in any proceedings.

(8) Nothing in this section shall be taken to compel the production by any person of a document of which he would on grounds of legal professional privilege be entitled to withhold production on an order for discovery in an action in the High Court or, as the case may be, on an order for the production of documents in an action in the Court of Session.

[(9) Nothing in this section is to be read as enabling an inspector to secure the disclosure by a telecommunications operator or postal operator of communications data without the consent of the operator.

(10) In subsection (9) "communications data", "postal operator" and "telecommunications operator" have the same meanings as in the Investigatory Powers Act 2016 (see sections 261 and 262 of that Act).]

NOTES

Sub-s (7): words in square brackets substituted by the Civil Partnership Act 2004, s 261(1), Sch 27, para 49.

Sub-ss (9), (10): added by the Investigatory Powers Act 2016, s 12(1), Sch 2, para 1, as from a day to be appointed.

Regulations: the Ammonium Nitrate Materials (High Nitrogen Content) Safety Regulations 2003, SI 2003/1082.

Fees: see the Health and Safety and Nuclear (Fees) Regulations 2016, SI 2016/253 at **[2.1931]** which introduce fees for breaches of the statutory provisions leading to enforcement action under this Act.

[1.49]

21 Improvement notices

If an inspector is of the opinion that a person—

(a) is contravening one or more of the relevant statutory provisions; or

(b) has contravened one or more of those provisions in circumstances that make it likely that the contravention will continue or be repeated,

he may serve on him a notice (in this Part referred to as "an improvement notice") stating that he is of that opinion, specifying the provision or provisions as to which he is of that opinion, giving particulars of the reasons why he is of that opinion, and requiring that person to remedy the contravention or, as the case may be, the matters occasioning it within such period (ending not earlier than the period within which an appeal against the notice can be brought under section 24) as may be specified in the notice.

NOTES

Fees: see the note to s 20 at **[1.48]**.

[1.50]

22 Prohibition notices

(1) This section applies to any activities which are being or are [likely] to be carried on by or under the control of any person, being activities to or in relation to which any of the relevant statutory provisions apply or will, if the activities are so carried on, apply.

(2) If as regards any activities to which this section applies an inspector is of the opinion that, as carried on or [likely] to be carried on by or under the control of the person in question, the activities involve or, as the case may be, will involve a risk of serious personal injury, the inspector may serve on that person a notice (in this Part referred to as "a prohibition notice").

(3) A prohibition notice shall—

(a) state that the inspector is of the said opinion;

(b) specify the matters which in his opinion give or, as the case may be, will give rise to the said risk;

(c) where in his opinion any of those matters involves or, as the case may be, will involve a contravention of any of the relevant statutory provisions, state that he is of that opinion, specify the provision or provisions as to which he is of that opinion, and give particulars of the reasons why he is of that opinion; and

(d) direct that the activities to which the notice relates shall not be carried on by or under the control of the person on whom the notice is served unless the matters specified in the notice in pursuance of paragraph (b) above and any associated contraventions of provisions so specified in pursuance of paragraph (c) above have been remedied.

[(4) A direction contained in a prohibition notice in pursuance of subsection (3)(d) above shall take effect—

(a) at the end of the period specified in the notice; or

(b) if the notice so declares, immediately.]

NOTES

Sub-ss (1), (2): words in square brackets substituted by the Consumer Protection Act 1987, s 36, Sch 3, para 2(a).

Sub-s (4): substituted by the Consumer Protection Act 1987, s 36, Sch 3, para 2(b).

Fees: see the note to s 20 at **[1.48]**.

[1.51]

23 Provisions supplementary to ss 21 and 22

(1) In this section "a notice" means an improvement notice or a prohibition notice.

(2) A notice may (but need not) include directions as to the measures to be taken to remedy any contravention or matter to which the notice relates; and any such directions—

(a) may be framed to any extent by reference to any approved code of practice; and

(b) may be framed so as to afford the person on whom the notice is served a choice between different ways of remedying the contravention or matter.

(3) Where any of the relevant statutory provisions applies to a building or any matter connected with a building and an inspector proposes to serve an improvement notice relating to a contravention of that provision in connection with that building or matter, the notice shall not direct any measures to be taken to remedy the contravention of that provision which are more onerous than those necessary to secure conformity with the requirements of any building regulations for the time being in force to which that building or matter would be required to conform if the relevant building were being newly erected unless the provision in question imposes specific requirements more onerous than the requirements of any such building regulations to which the building or matter would be required to conform as aforesaid.

In this subsection "the relevant building", in the case of a building, means that building, and, in the case of a matter connected with a building, means the building with which the matter is connected.

(4) Before an inspector serves in connection with any premises used or about to be used as a place of work a notice requiring or likely to lead to the taking of measures affecting the means of escape in case of fire with which the premises are or ought to be provided, he shall consult the [fire and rescue authority].

In this subsection "[fire and rescue authority]"[, in relation to premises, means—

(a) where the Regulatory Reform (Fire Safety) Order 2005 applies to the premises, the enforcing authority within the meaning given by article 25 of that Order;

(b) in any other case, the fire and rescue authority under the Fire and Rescue Services Act 2004 for the area where the premises are (or are to be) situated].

(5) Where an improvement notice or a prohibition notice which is not to take immediate effect has been served—

(a) the notice may be withdrawn by an inspector at any time before the end of the period specified therein in pursuance of section 21 or section 22(4) as the case may be; and

(b) the period so specified may be extended or further extended by an inspector at any time when an appeal against the notice is not pending.

(6) In the application of this section to Scotland—

(a) in subsection (3) for the words from "with the requirements" to "aforesaid" there shall be substituted the words—

"(a) to any provisions of the building standards regulations to which that building or matter would be required to conform if the relevant building were being newly erected; or

(b) where the sheriff, on an appeal to him under section 16 of the Building (Scotland) Act 1959—

(i) against an order under section 10 of that Act requiring the execution of operations necessary to make the building or matter conform to the building standards regulations, or

(ii) against an order under section 11 of that Act requiring the building or matter to conform to a provision of such regulations,

has varied the order, to any provisions of the building standards regulations referred to in paragraph (a) above as affected by the order as so varied,

unless the relevant statutory provision imposes specific requirements more onerous than the requirements of any provisions of building standards regulations as aforesaid or, as the case may be, than the requirements of the order as varied by the sheriff.";

(b) after subsection (5) there shall be inserted the following subsection—

"(5A) In subsection (3) above "building standards regulations" has the same meaning as in section 3 of the Building (Scotland) Act 1959.".

NOTES

Sub-s (4): words in first and second pairs of square brackets substituted, in relation to England and Wales only, by the Fire and Rescue Services Act 2004, s 53(1), Sch 1, para 44; words in third pair of square brackets substituted, in relation to England and Wales only, by the Regulatory Reform (Fire Safety) Order 2005, SI 2005/1541, art 53(1), Sch 2, para 9. Note that this subsection has also been amended, in relation to Scotland only, by the Fire (Scotland) Act 2005 (Consequential Modifications and Savings) Order 2006, SSI 2006/475, art 2(1), Sch 1, para 6, and the Police and Fire Reform (Scotland) Act 2012, s 128(1), Sch 7, Pt 2, para 49 (other amendments made to sub-s (4) have been superseded by the amendments noted above). In relation to Scotland, this subsection reads as follows—

"(4) Before an inspector serves in connection with any premises used or about to be used as a place of work a notice requiring or likely to lead to the taking of measures affecting the means of escape in case of fire with which the premises are or ought to be provided, he shall consult—

(a) where Part 3 of the Fire (Scotland) Act 2005 (asp 5) applies in relation to the premises, the enforcing authority (as defined in section 61(9) of that Act);

(b) in any other case, the [Scottish Fire and Rescue Service].".

Fees: see the note to s 20 at **[1.48]**.

[1.52]

24 Appeal against improvement or prohibition notice

(1) In this section "a notice" means an improvement notice or a prohibition notice.

(2) A person on whom a notice is served may within such period from the date of its service as may be prescribed appeal to an [employment tribunal]; and on such an appeal the tribunal may either cancel or affirm the notice and, if it affirms it, may do so either in its original form or with such modifications as the tribunal may in the circumstances think fit.

(3) Where an appeal under this section is brought against a notice within the period allowed under the preceding subsection, then—

(a) in the case of an improvement notice, the bringing of the appeal shall have the effect of suspending the operation of the notice until the appeal is finally disposed of or, if the appeal is withdrawn, until the withdrawal of the appeal;

(b) in the case of a prohibition notice, the bringing of the appeal shall have the like effect if, but only if, on the application of the appellant the tribunal so directs (and then only from the giving of the direction).

(4) One or more assessors may be appointed for the purposes of any proceedings brought before an [employment tribunal] under this section.

NOTES

Sub-ss (2), (4): words in square brackets substituted by the Employment Rights (Dispute Resolution) Act 1998, s 1(2)(a).

Fees: see the note to s 20 at **[1.48]**.

Regulations: the Employment Tribunals (Constitution and Rules of Procedure) Regulations 2013, SI 2013/1237 at **[2.1323]**.

[1.53]

25 Power to deal with cause of imminent danger

(1) Where, in the case of any article or substance found by him in any premises which he has power to enter, an inspector has reasonable cause to believe that, in the circumstances in which he finds it, the article or substance is a cause of imminent danger of serious personal injury, he may seize it and cause it to be rendered harmless (whether by destruction or otherwise).

(2) Before there is rendered harmless under this section—

(a) any article that forms part of a batch of similar articles; or

(b) any substance,

the inspector shall, if it is practicable for him to do so, take a sample thereof and give to a responsible person at the premises where the article or substance was found by him a portion of the sample marked in a manner sufficient to identify it.

(3) As soon as may be after any article or substance has been seized and rendered harmless under this section, the inspector shall prepare and sign a written report giving particulars of the circumstances in which the article or substance was seized and so dealt with by him, and shall—

(a) give a signed copy of the report to a responsible person at the premises where the article or substance was found by him; and

(b) unless that person is the owner of the article or substance, also serve a signed copy of the report on the owner;

and if, where paragraph (b) above applies, the inspector cannot after reasonable enquiry ascertain the name or address of the owner, the copy may be served on him by giving it to the person to whom a copy was given under the preceding paragraph.

NOTES

Fees: see the note to s 20 at **[1.48]**.

[1.54]

[25A Power of customs officer to detain articles and substances

(1) A customs officer may, for the purpose of facilitating the exercise or performance by any enforcing authority or inspector of any of the powers or duties of the authority or inspector under any of the relevant statutory provisions, seize any imported article or imported substance and detain it for not more than two working days.

(2) Anything seized and detained under this section shall be dealt with during the period of its detention in such manner as the Commissioners of Customs and Excise may direct.

(3) In subsection (1) above the reference to two working days is a reference to a period of forty-eight hours calculated from the time when the goods in question are seized but disregarding so much of any period as falls on a Saturday or Sunday or on Christmas Day, Good Friday or a day which is a bank holiday under the Banking and Financial Dealings Act 1971 in the part of Great Britain where the goods are seized.]

NOTES

Inserted by the Consumer Protection Act 1987, s 36, Sch 3, para 3.

Commissioners of Customs and Excise: a reference to the Commissioners of Customs and Excise is now to be taken as a reference to the Commissioners for Her Majesty's Revenue and Customs; see the Commissioners for Revenue and Customs Act 2005, s 50(1), (7).

[1.55]

26 Power of enforcing authorities to indemnify their inspectors

Where an action has been brought against an inspector in respect of an act done in the execution or purported execution of any of the relevant statutory provisions and the circumstances are such that he is not legally entitled to require the enforcing authority which appointed him to indemnify him, that authority may, nevertheless, indemnify him against the whole or part of any damages and costs or expenses which he may have been ordered to pay or may have incurred, if the authority is satisfied that he honestly believed that the act complained of was within his powers and that his duty as an inspector required or entitled him to do it.

Obtaining and disclosure of information

[1.56]

27 Obtaining of information by . . . the Executive, enforcing authorities etc

(1) For the purpose of obtaining—

(a) any information which [the Executive] needs for the discharge of its functions; or

(b) any information which an enforcing authority [other than the Office for Nuclear Regulation] needs for the discharge of the authority's functions,

[the Executive] may, with the consent of the Secretary of State, serve on any person a notice requiring that person to furnish to [the Executive] or, as the case may be, to the enforcing authority in question such information about such matters as may be specified in the notice, and to do so in such form and manner and within such time as may be so specified.

In this subsection "consent" includes a general consent extending to cases of any stated description.

(2) Nothing in section 9 of the Statistics of Trade Act 1947 (which restricts the disclosure of information obtained under that Act) shall prevent or penalise—

(a) the disclosure by a Minister of the Crown to . . . the Executive of information obtained under that Act about any undertaking within the meaning of that Act, being information consisting of the names and addresses of the persons carrying on the undertaking, the nature of the undertaking's activities, the numbers of persons of different descriptions who work in the undertaking, the addresses or places where activities of the undertaking are or were carried on, the nature of the activities carried on there, or the numbers of persons of different descriptions who work or worked in the undertaking there; . . .

(b) . . .

[(3) In the preceding subsection, any reference to a Minister of the Crown or the Executive includes respectively a reference to an officer of that person or of that body and also, in the case of a reference to the Executive, includes a reference to—

(a) a person performing any functions of the Executive on its behalf by virtue of section 13(3);

(b) an officer of a body which is so performing any such functions; and

(c) an adviser appointed under section 13(7).]

(4) A person to whom information is disclosed in pursuance of subsection (2) above shall not use the information for a purpose other than a purpose . . . of the Executive.

NOTES

Sub-s (1): words "the Executive" in square brackets substituted by the Legislative Reform (Health and Safety Executive) Order 2008, SI 2008/960, arts 3, 11(1), (2); words "other than the Office for Nuclear Regulation" in square brackets inserted by the Energy Act 2013, s 116, Sch 12, Pt 1, paras 1, 7.

Sub-s (2): first words omitted repealed by SI 2008/960, arts 3, 11(1), (3); other words omitted repealed by the Employment Act 1989, s 29(3), (4), Sch 6, para 10, Sch 7, Pt I.

Sub-s (3): substituted by SI 2008/960, arts 3, 11(1), (4).

Sub-s (4): words omitted repealed by SI 2008/960, arts 3, 11(1), (5).

Note: the Legislative Reform (Health and Safety Executive) Order 2008, SI 2008/960 does not amend the title of this section. However, in light of the other amendments made by that Order, and in light of the abolition of the HSC by art 2 of that Order, the title of this section has been changed from "Obtaining of information by the Commission, the Executive, enforcing authorities etc" to "Obtaining of information by the Executive, enforcing authorities etc".

[1.57]

[27A [Information communicated by Commissioners for Revenue and Customs]

(1) If they think it appropriate to do so for the purpose of facilitating the exercise or performance by any person to whom subsection (2) below applies of any of that person's powers or duties under any of the relevant statutory provisions, [the Commissioners for Her Majesty's Revenue and Custom] may authorise the disclosure to that person of any information obtained [or held] for the purposes of the exercise [by Her Majesty's Revenue and Customs] of their functions in relation to imports.

(2) This subsection applies to an enforcing authority and to an inspector[, other than the Office for Nuclear Regulation or an inspector appointed by the Office for Nuclear Regulation].

(3) A disclosure of information made to any person under subsection (1) above shall be made in such manner as may be directed by [the Commissioners for Her Majesty's Revenue and Customs] and may be made through such persons acting on behalf of that person as may be so directed.

(4) Information may be disclosed to a person under subsection (1) above whether or not the disclosure of the information has been requested by or on behalf of that person.]

NOTES

Inserted by the Consumer Protection Act 1987, s 36, Sch 3, para 4.

Section heading: substituted by the Commissioners for Revenue and Customs Act 2005, s 50(6), Sch 4, para 18(1), (4).

Sub-s (1): words in first and third pairs of square brackets substituted, and words in second pair of square brackets inserted, by the Commissioners for Revenue and Customs Act 2005, s 50(6), Sch 4, para 18(1), (2).

Sub-s (2): words in square brackets inserted by the Energy Act 2013, s 116, Sch 12, Pt 1, paras 1, 8.

Sub-s (3): words in square brackets substituted by the Commissioners for Revenue and Customs Act 2005, s 50(6), Sch 4, para 18(1), (3).

[1.58]

28 Restrictions on disclosure of information

(1) In this and the two following subsections—

(a) "relevant information" means information obtained by a person under section 27(1) or furnished to any person[, other than the Office for Nuclear Regulation (or an inspector appointed by it),] [under section 27A above[, by virtue of section 43A(6) below] or] in pursuance of a requirement imposed by any of the relevant statutory provisions; and

(b) "the recipient", in relation to any relevant information, means the person by whom that information was so obtained or to whom that information was so furnished, as the case may be.

(2) Subject to the following subsection, no relevant information shall be disclosed without the consent of the person by whom it was furnished.

(3) The preceding subsection shall not apply to—

(a) disclosure of information to . . . the Executive[, the Office for Nuclear Regulation], [the Environment Agency, [the Natural Resources Body for Wales,] the Scottish Environment Protection Agency,] a government department or any enforcing authority;

(b) without prejudice to paragraph (a) above, disclosure by the recipient of information to any person for the purpose of any function conferred on the recipient by or under any of the relevant statutory provisions;

(c) without prejudice to paragraph (a) above, disclosure by the recipient of information to—

(i) an officer of a local authority who is authorised by that authority to receive it,

[(ii) an officer . . . of a water undertaker, sewerage undertaker, water authority or water development board who is authorised by that . . . undertaker, authority or board to receive it,]

(iii) . . .

(iv) a constable authorised by a chief officer of police to receive it;

(d) disclosure by the recipient of information in a form calculated to prevent it from being identified as relating to a particular person or case;

(e) disclosure of information for the purposes of any legal proceedings or any investigation or inquiry held by virtue of [section 14(2) or (2A)], or for the purposes of a report of any such proceedings or inquiry or of a special report made by virtue of [section 14(2) or (2A)];

[(f) any other disclosure of information by the recipient, if—

(i) the recipient is, or is acting on behalf of a person who is, a public authority for the purposes of the Freedom of Information Act 2000 [or a Scottish public authority for the purposes of the Freedom of Information (Scotland) Act 2002], and

(ii) the information is not held by the authority on behalf of another person].

[(4) In the preceding subsection, any reference to the Executive[, the Office for Nuclear Regulation], the Environment Agency, [the Natural Resources Body for Wales,] the Scottish Environment Protection Agency, a government department or an enforcing authority includes respectively a reference to an officer of that body or authority (including, in the case of an enforcing authority, any inspector appointed by it), and also, in the case of a reference to the Executive [or the Office for Nuclear Regulation], includes a reference to—

(a) a person performing any functions of the Executive [or Office for Nuclear Regulation] on its behalf by virtue of section 13(3) [of this Act or, as the case may be, section 95 of the Energy Act 2013];

(b) an officer of a body which is so performing any such functions; and

(c) an adviser appointed under section 13(7) [or, in the case of the Office for Nuclear Regulation, a person providing advice to that body].]

(5) A person to whom information is disclosed in pursuance of [any of paragraphs (a) to (e) of] subsection (3) above shall not use the information for a purpose other than—

(a) in a case falling within paragraph (a) of that subsection, a purpose . . . of the Executive[, of the Office for Nuclear Regulation] or [of the Environment Agency [or of the Natural Resources Body for Wales] or of the Scottish Environment Protection Agency or] of the government department in question, or the purposes of the enforcing authority in question in connection with the relevant statutory provisions, as the case may be;

(b) in the case of information given to an officer of a [body which is a local authority, . . . a water undertaker, a sewerage undertaker, a water authority, a river purification board or a water development board, the purposes of the body] in connection with the relevant statutory provisions or any enactment whatsoever relating to public health, public safety or the protection of the environment;

(c) in the case of information given to a constable, the purposes of the police in connection with the relevant statutory provisions or any enactment whatsoever relating to public health, public safety or the safety of the State.

[(6) References in subsections (3) and (5) above to a local authority include . . . a joint authority established by Part IV of the Local Government Act 1985, [an economic prosperity board established under section 88 of the Local Democracy, Economic Development and Construction Act 2009, a combined authority established under section 103 of that Act,] [a fire and rescue authority created by an order under section 4A of the Fire and Rescue Services Act 2004] . . . [and the London Fire Commissioner].]

(7) A person shall not disclose any information obtained by him as a result of the exercise of any power conferred by section 14(4)(a) or 20 (including, in particular, any information with respect to any trade secret obtained by him in any premises entered by him by virtue of any such power) except—

(a) for the purposes of his functions; or

(b) for the purposes of any legal proceedings or any investigation or inquiry held by virtue of [section 14(2) or (2A)] or for the purposes of a report of any such proceedings or inquiry or of a special report made by virtue of [section 14(2) or (2A)]; or

(c) with the relevant consent.

In this subsection "the relevant consent" means, in the case of information furnished in pursuance of a requirement imposed under section 20, the consent of the person who furnished it, and, in any other case, the consent of a person having responsibilities in relation to the premises where the information was obtained.

(8) Notwithstanding anything in the preceding subsection an inspector shall, in circumstances in which it is necessary to do so for the purpose of assisting in keeping persons (or the representatives of persons) employed at any premises adequately informed about matters affecting their health, safety and welfare, give to such persons or their representatives the following descriptions of information, that is to say—

(a) factual information obtained by him as mentioned in that subsection which relates to those premises or anything which was or is therein or was or is being done therein; and

(b) information with respect to any action which he has taken or proposes to take in or in connection with those premises in the performance of his functions;

and, where an inspector does as aforesaid, he shall give the like information to the employer of the first-mentioned persons.

[(9) Notwithstanding anything in subsection (7) above, a person who has obtained such information as is referred to in that subsection may furnish to a person who appears to him to be likely to be a party to any civil proceedings arising out of any accident, occurrence, situation or other matter, a written statement of relevant facts observed by him in the course of exercising any of the powers referred to in that subsection.]

[(9A) Subsection (7) above does not apply if—

(a) the person who has obtained any such information as is referred to in that subsection is, or is acting on behalf of a person who is, a public authority for the purposes of the Freedom of Information Act 2000 [or a Scottish public authority for the purposes of the Freedom of Information (Scotland) Act 2002], and

(b) the information is not held by the authority on behalf of another person.]

[(9B) Nothing in subsection (7) or (9) applies to a person appointed as an inspector by the Office for Nuclear Regulation in relation to functions which the person has by virtue of that appointment.]

[(10) The Broads Authority and every National Park authority shall be deemed to be local authorities for the purposes of this section.]

NOTES

Sub-s (1): words in first pair of square brackets inserted by the Energy Act 2013, s 116, Sch 12, Pt 1, paras 1, 9(1), (2); words in second (outer) pair of square brackets inserted by the Consumer Protection Act 1987, s 36, Sch 3, para 5; words in third (inner) pair of square brackets inserted by the Railways and Transport Safety Act 2003, s 105(2).

Sub-s (3) is amended as follows:

Words omitted from para (a) repealed by the Legislative Reform (Health and Safety Executive) Order 2008, SI 2008/960, arts 3, 12(1), (2)(a).

Words in first pair of square brackets in para (a) inserted by the Energy Act 2013, s 116, Sch 12, Pt 1, paras 1, 9(1), (3).

Words in second (outer) pair of square brackets in para (a) inserted by the Environment Act 1995, s 120(1), (3), Sch 22, para 30(1), (6)(a).

Words in third (inner) pair of square brackets in para (a) inserted by the Natural Resources Body for Wales (Functions) Order 2013, SI 2013/755, art 4(1), Sch 2, paras 111, 112(1), (2).

Sub-para (c)(ii) substituted by the Water Act 1989, s 190, Sch 25, para 46, in relation to England and Wales only; words omitted from that paragraph repealed by the Environment Act 1995, s 120(1), (3), Sch 22, para 30(1), (6)(b).

Sub-para (c)(ii), as it applies to Scotland, was substituted by the Environment Act 1995, s 120(1), (3), Sch 22, para 30(1), (6)(c), and further amended by the Water Industry (Scotland) Act 2002 (Consequential Modifications) Order 2004, SI 2004/1822, art 2, Schedule, Pt 1, para 8(a), and now reads as follows—

> "(ii) an officer of a water undertaker, sewerage undertaker [or Scottish Water] who is authorised by [that undertaker or, as the case may be, Scottish Water] to receive it,".

Sub-para (c)(iii) repealed by the Environment Act 1995, s 120(1), (3), Sch 22, para 30(1), (6)(d).

Words in square brackets in para (e) substituted by SI 2008/960, arts 3, 12(1), (2)(b).

Para (f) added by the Freedom of Information (Removal and Relaxation of Statutory Prohibitions on Disclosure of Information) Order 2004, SI 2004/3363, art 5(1), (2); words in square brackets inserted by the Freedom of Information (Relaxation of Statutory Prohibitions on Disclosure of Information) (Scotland) Order 2008, SSI 2008/339, art 5(1), (2).

Sub-s (4): substituted by SI 2008/960, arts 3, 12(1), (3); words "the Natural Resources Body for Wales," in square brackets inserted by SI 2013/755, art 4(1), Sch 2, paras 111, 112(1), (3); all other words in square brackets inserted by the Energy Act 2013, s 116, Sch 12, Pt 1, paras 1, 9(1), (4).

Sub-s (5) is amended as follows:

Words in first pair of square brackets inserted by SI 2004/3363, art 5(1), (3).

Words omitted from para (a) repealed by SI 2008/960, arts 3, 12(1), (4).

Words in first pair of square brackets in para (a) inserted by inserted by the Energy Act 2013, s 116, Sch 12, Pt 1, paras 1, 9(1), (4).

Words in second (outer) square brackets in para (a) inserted by the Environment Act 1995, s 120(1), (3), Sch 22, para 30(1), (6)(f).

Words in third (inner) pair of square brackets in para (a) inserted by SI 2013/755, art 4(1), Sch 2, paras 111, 112(1), (4).

Words in square brackets in para (b) substituted by the Water Act 1989, s 190, Sch 25, para 46; words omitted from that paragraph repealed by the Environment Act 1995, s 120(1), (3), Sch 22, para 30(6)(f).

The words from the beginning of para (b) to "in connection" were substituted by the Environment Act 1995, s 120(1), (3), Sch 22, para 30(1), (6)(f), in relation to Scotland only, and that paragraph was further amended (in relation to Scotland only) by SI 2004/1822, art 2, Schedule, Pt 1, para 8(b). Para (b), as it applies to Scotland, now reads as follows—

"(b) [in the case of information given to an officer of a body which is a local authority, a water undertaker [or a sewerage undertaker or to an officer of Scottish Water,] the purposes of the [authority, undertaker or, as the case may be, Scottish Water] in connection] with the relevant statutory provisions or any enactment whatsoever relating to public health, public safety or the protection of the environment;".

Sub-s (6) was substituted by the Local Government Act 1985, s 84, Sch 14, para 52, and is further amended as follows:
First words omitted repealed by the Education Reform Act 1988, s 237, Sch 13, Pt I.
Words in first pair of square brackets inserted by the Local Democracy, Economic Development and Construction Act 2009, s 119, Sch 6, para 42.
Words in second pair of square brackets inserted by the Policing and Crime Act 2017, s 6, Sch 1, Pt 2, para 35, as from 3 April 2017.
Second words omitted repealed by the Deregulation Act 2015, s 59, Sch 13, Pt 3, para 6(1), (10), as from 26 May 2015.
Words in final pair of square brackets substituted by the Policing and Crime Act 2017, s 9(3)(c), Sch 2, Pt 2, para 50, as from 1 April 2018.
Sub-s (7): words in square brackets substituted by SI 2008/960, arts 3, 12(1), (5).
Sub-s (9): added by the Employment Protection Act 1975, s 116, Sch 15, para 9.
Sub-s (9A): inserted by SI 2004/3363, art 5(1), (4); words in square brackets inserted by SSI 2008/339, art 5(1), (3).
Sub-s (9B): inserted by the Energy Act 2013, art 4(2), Sch 12, Pt 1, paras 1, 9(1), (6).
Sub-s (10): added by the Norfolk and Suffolk Broads Act 1988, s 21, Sch 6, para 13; substituted by the Environment Act 1995, s 78, Sch 10, para 12.
Disclosure: sub-s (7) has effect in relation to the disclosure of information by or on behalf of a public authority as if the purposes for which disclosure is authorised included the purposes mentioned in the Anti-terrorism, Crime and Security Act 2001, s 17; see Sch 4, Pt 1 to that Act.

29–32 *(Repealed by the Employment Protection Act 1975, ss 116, 125(3), Sch 15, para 10, Sch 18.)*

Provisions as to offences

[1.59]

33 Offences

(1) It is an offence for a person—

(a) to fail to discharge a duty to which he is subject by virtue of sections 2 to 7;
(b) to contravene section 8 or 9;
(c) to contravene any health and safety regulations . . . or any requirement or prohibition imposed under any such regulations (including any requirement or prohibition to which he is subject by virtue of the terms of or any condition or restriction attached to any licence, approval, exemption or other authority issued, given or granted under the regulations);
(d) to contravene any requirement imposed by or under regulations under section 14 or intentionally to obstruct any person in the exercise of his powers under that section;
(e) to contravene any requirement imposed by an inspector under section 20 or 25;
(f) to prevent or attempt to prevent any other person from appearing before an inspector or from answering any question to which an inspector may by virtue of section 20(2) require an answer;
(g) to contravene any requirement or prohibition imposed by an improvement notice or a prohibition notice (including any such notice as modified on appeal);
(h) intentionally to obstruct an inspector in the exercise or performance of his powers or duties [or to obstruct a customs officer in the exercise of his powers under section 25A];
(i) to contravene any requirement imposed by a notice under section 27(1);
(j) to use or disclose any information in contravention of section 27(4) or 28;
(k) to make a statement which he knows to be false or recklessly to make a statement which is false where the statement is made—
  (i) in purported compliance with a requirement to furnish any information imposed by or under any of the relevant statutory provisions; or
  (ii) for the purpose of obtaining the issue of a document under any of the relevant statutory provisions to himself or another person;
(l) intentionally to make a false entry in any register, book, notice or other document required by or under any of the relevant statutory provisions to be kept, served or given or, with intent to deceive, to made use of any such entry which he knows to be false;
(m) with intent to deceive, to . . . use a document issued or authorised to be issued under any of the relevant statutory provisions or required for any purpose thereunder or to make or have in his possession a document so closely resembling any such document as to be calculated to deceive;
(n) falsely to pretend to be an inspector;
(o) to fail to comply with an order made by a court under section 42.

[(2) Schedule 3A (which specifies the mode of trial and maximum penalty applicable to offences under this section and the existing statutory provisions) has effect.

(3) Schedule 3A is subject to any provision made by virtue of section 15(6)(c) or (d).]

(5), (6) . . .

NOTES

Sub-s (1): words omitted from para (c) repealed by the Employment Protection Act 1975, ss 116, 125(3), Sch 15, para 11, Sch 18; words in square brackets in para (h) added by the Consumer Protection Act 1987, s 36, Sch 3, para 6; words omitted from para (m) repealed by the Forgery and Counterfeiting Act 1981, s 30, Schedule, Pt I.
Sub-ss (2), (3): substituted (for sub-ss (1A), (2), (2A)–(4)) by the Health and Safety (Offences) Act 2008, s 1(1). Note that sub-ss (1A) and (2A) were originally inserted by the Offshore Safety Act 1992, s 4(2), (3), (6).
Sub-s (5): repealed by the Offshore Safety Act 1992, ss 4(5), (6), 7(2), Sch 2.

Sub-s (6): repealed by the Forgery and Counterfeiting Act 1981, s 30, Schedule, Pt I.

[1.60]

34 Extension of time for bringing summary proceedings

(1) Where—

(a) a special report on any matter to which section 14 of this Act applies is made by virtue of subsection [(2)] of that section; or

(b) a report is made by the person holding an inquiry into any such matter by virtue of subsection [(2A)]) of that section; or

(c) [an investigation under Part 1 of the Coroners and Justice Act 2009 is conducted into] the death of any person whose death may have been caused by an accident which happened while he was at work or by a disease which he contracted or probably contracted at work or by any accident, act or omission which occurred in connection with the work of any person whatsoever; or

[(d) an inquiry into any death that may have been so caused is held under the Inquiries into Fatal Accidents and Sudden Deaths etc (Scotland) Act 2016;]

and it appears [from the report or investigation or, in a case falling within paragraph (d) above, from the proceedings at the] inquiry, that any of the relevant statutory provisions was contravened at a time which is material in relation to the subject-matter of the [report, investigation or inquiry], summary proceedings against any person liable to be proceeded against in respect of the contravention may be commenced at any time within three months of the making of the report or, in a case falling within paragraph (c) or (d) above, within three months of the [conclusion of the investigation] or inquiry.

(2) Where an offence under any of the relevant statutory provisions is committed by reason of a failure to do something at or within a time fixed by or under any of those provisions, the offence shall be deemed to continue until that thing is done.

(3) Summary proceedings for an offence to which this subsection applies may be commenced at any time within six months from the date on which there comes to the knowledge of a responsible enforcing authority evidence sufficient in the opinion of that authority to justify a prosecution for that offence; and for the purposes of this subsection—

(a) a certificate of an enforcing authority stating that such evidence came to its knowledge on a specified date shall be conclusive evidence of that fact; and

(b) a document purporting to be such a certificate and to be signed by or on behalf of the enforcing authority in question shall be presumed to be such a certificate unless the contrary is proved.

(4) The preceding subsection applies to any offence under any of the relevant statutory provisions which a person commits by virtue of any provision or requirement to which he is subject as the designer, manufacturer, importer or supplier of any thing; and in that subsection "responsible enforcing authority" means an enforcing authority within whose field of responsibility the offence in question lies, whether by virtue of section 35 or otherwise.

(5) In the application of subsection (3) above to Scotland—

(a) for the words from "there comes" to "that offence" there shall be substituted the words "evidence, sufficient in the opinion of the enforcing authority to justify a report to the Lord Advocate with a view to consideration of the question of prosecution, comes to the knowledge of the authority";

(b) at the end of paragraph (b) there shall be added the words

"and

(c) [section 331(3) of the Criminal Procedure (Scotland) Act 1975] (date of commencement of proceedings) shall have effect as it has effect for the purposes of that section".

[(6) In the application of subsection (4) above to Scotland, after the words "applies to" there shall be inserted the words "any offence under section 33(1)(c) above where the health and safety regulations concerned were made for the general purpose mentioned in section 18(1) of the Gas Act 1986 and".]

NOTES

Sub-s (1): the figures "(2)" in para (a) and "(2A)" in para (b) were substituted by the Legislative Reform (Health and Safety Executive) Order 2008, SI 2008/960, arts 3, 13. Para (d) substituted by the Inquiries into Fatal Accidents and Sudden Deaths etc (Scotland) Act 2016, s 39(2), Sch 2, para 2(1), (3), as from 15 June 2017 (for transitional provisions in relation to inquiries applied for before that date, see SSI 2017/155, regs 4, 5). All other words in square brackets were substituted by the Coroners and Justice Act 2009, s 177(1), Sch 21, Pt 1, para 25.

Sub-s (5): words in square brackets in para (b) substituted by the Criminal Procedure (Scotland) Act 1975, s 461(1), Sch 9, para 51.

Sub-s (6): added by the Gas Act 1986, s 67(1), Sch 7, para 18.

Criminal Procedure (Scotland) Act 1975: repealed by Criminal Procedure (Consequential Provisions) (Scotland) Act 1995, s 6, Sch 5. Section 331 of the 1975 Act was replaced by s 136 of the Criminal Procedure (Scotland) Act 1995.

Gas Act 1986, s 18(1): repealed by the Offshore Safety Act 1992, ss 3(3)(a), 7(2), Sch 2.

[1.61]

35 Venue

An offence under any of the relevant statutory provisions committed in connection with any plant or substance may, if necessary for the purpose of bringing the offence within the field of responsibility of any enforcing authority or conferring jurisdiction on any court to entertain proceedings for the offence, be treated as having been committed at the place where that plant or substance is for the time being.

[1.62]

36 Offences due to fault of other person

(1) Where the commission by any person of an offence under any of the relevant statutory provisions is due to the act or default of some other person, that other person shall be guilty of the offence, and a person may be charged with and convicted of the offence by virtue of this subsection whether or not proceedings are taken against the first-mentioned person.

(2) Where there would be or have been the commission of an offence under section 33 by the Crown but for the circumstance that that section does not bind the Crown, and that fact is due to the act or default of a person other than the Crown, that person shall be guilty of the offence which, but for that circumstance, the Crown would be committing or would have committed, and may be charged with and convicted of that offence accordingly.

(3) The preceding provisions of this section are subject to any provision made by virtue of section 15(6).

NOTES

The Crown: references to the Crown in this section shall be treated as including the Assembly Commission; see the National Assembly for Wales Commission (Crown Status) (No 2) Order 2007, SI 2007/1353, art 2.

[1.63]

37 Offences by bodies corporate

(1) Where an offence under any of the relevant statutory provisions committed by a body corporate is proved to have been committed with the consent or connivance of, or to have been attributable to any neglect on the part of, any director, manager, secretary or other similar officer of the body corporate or a person who was purporting to act in any such capacity, he as well as the body corporate shall be guilty of that offence and shall be liable to be proceeded against and punished accordingly.

(2) Where the affairs of a body corporate are managed by its members, the preceding subsection shall apply in relation to the acts and defaults of a member in connection with his functions of management as if he were a director of the body corporate.

[1.64]

38 Restriction on institution of proceedings in England and Wales

Proceedings for an offence under any of the relevant statutory provisions shall not, in England and Wales, be instituted except by an inspector[, the Environment Agency or the Natural Resources Body for Wales] [or] by or with the consent of the Director of Public Prosecutions.

NOTES

Words in first pair of square brackets substituted by the Natural Resources Body for Wales (Functions) Order 2013, SI 2013/755, art 4(1), Sch 2, paras 111, 113; word in second pair of square brackets inserted by the Environment Act 1995, s 120(1), Sch 22, para 30(1), (7).

[1.65]

39 Prosecutions by inspectors

(1) An inspector, if authorised in that behalf by the enforcing authority which appointed him, may, although not of counsel or a solicitor, prosecute before a magistrates' court proceedings for an offence under any of the relevant statutory provisions.

(2) This section shall not apply to Scotland.

[1.66]

40 Onus of proving limits of what is practicable etc

In any proceedings for an offence under any of the relevant statutory provisions consisting of a failure to comply with a duty or requirement to do something so far as is practicable or so far as is reasonably practicable, or to use the best practicable means to do something, it shall be for the accused to prove (as the case may be) that it was not practicable or not reasonably practicable to do more than was in fact done to satisfy the duty or requirement, or that there was no better practicable means than was in fact used to satisfy the duty or requirement.

[1.67]

41 Evidence

(1) Where an entry is required by any of the relevant statutory provisions to be made in any register or other record, the entry, if made, shall, as against the person by or on whose behalf it was made, be admissible as evidence or in Scotland sufficient evidence of the facts stated therein.

(2) Where an entry which is so required to be so made with respect to the observance of any of the relevant statutory provisions has not been made, that fact shall be admissible as evidence or in Scotland sufficient evidence that that provision has not been observed.

[1.68]

42 Power of court to order cause of offence to be remedied or, in certain cases, forfeiture

(1) Where a person is convicted of an offence under any of the relevant statutory provisions in respect of any matters which appear to the court to be matters which it is in his power to remedy, the court may, in addition to or instead of imposing any punishment, order him, within such time as may be fixed by the order, to take such steps as may be specified in the order for remedying the said matters.

(2) The time fixed by an order under subsection (1) above may be extended or further extended by order of the court on an application made before the end of that time as originally fixed or as extended under this subsection, as the case may be.

(3) Where a person is ordered under subsection (1) above to remedy any matters, that person shall not be liable under any of the relevant statutory provisions in respect of those matters in so far as they continue during the time fixed by the order or any further time allowed under subsection (2) above.
[(3A) Subsection (4) applies where a person is convicted of an offence consisting of acquiring or attempting to acquire, possessing or using an explosive article or substance (within the meaning of any of the relevant statutory provisions) in contravention of any of the relevant statutory provisions.]
(4) Subject to the following subsection, the court by or before which [the person is convicted of the offence] may order the article or substance in question to be forfeited and either destroyed or dealt with in such other manner as the court may order.
(5) The court shall not order anything to be forfeited under the preceding subsection where a person claiming to be the owner of or otherwise interested in it applies to be heard by the court, unless an opportunity has been given to him to show cause why the order should not be made.

NOTES

Sub-s (3A): inserted by the Health and Safety (Offences) Act 2008, s 2(1), Sch 3, para 2(2).
Sub-s (4): words in square brackets substituted by the Health and Safety (Offences) Act 2008, s 2(1), Sch 3, para 2(3).

Financial provisions

[1.69]
43 Financial provisions
(1) It shall be the duty of the Secretary of State to pay to [the Executive] such sums as are approved by the Treasury and as he considers appropriate for the purpose of enabling [the Executive] to perform its functions; . . .
(2) Regulations may provide for such fees as may be fixed by or determined under the regulations to be payable for or in connection with the performance by or on behalf of any authority to which this subsection applies of any function conferred on that authority by or under any of the relevant statutory provisions.
(3) Subsection (2) above applies to the following authorities, namely . . . the Executive, the Secretary of State, . . . every enforcing authority, and any other person on whom any function is conferred by or under any of the relevant statutory provisions.
(4) Regulations under this section may specify the person by whom any fee payable under the regulations is to be paid; but no such fee shall be made payable by a person in any of the following capacities, namely an employee, a person seeking employment, a person training for employment, and a person seeking training for employment.
(5) Without prejudice to section 82(3), regulations under this section may fix or provide for the determination of different fees in relation to different functions, or in relation to the same function in different circumstances.
[(6) The power to make regulations under this section shall be exercisable by the Secretary of State . . .]
(7) . . .
(8) In subsection (4) above the references to a person training for employment and a person seeking training for employment shall include respectively a person attending an industrial rehabilitation course provided by virtue of the Employment and Training Act 1973 and a person seeking to attend such a course.
(9) For the purposes of this section the performance by an inspector of his functions shall be treated as the performance by the enforcing authority which appointed him of functions conferred on that authority by or under any of the relevant statutory provisions.

NOTES

Sub-s (1): words in square brackets substituted, and words omitted repealed, by the Legislative Reform (Health and Safety Executive) Order 2008, SI 2008/960, arts 3, 14(a).
Sub-s (3): first words omitted repealed by SI 2008/960, arts 3, 14(b); second words omitted repealed by the Employment Protection Act 1975, ss 116, 125(3), Sch 15, para 12, Sch 18.
Sub-s (6): substituted, for the original sub-ss (6), (7), by the Employment Protection Act 1975, s 116, Sch 15, para 12; words omitted repealed by the Ministry of Agriculture, Fisheries and Food (Dissolution) Order 2002, SI 2002/794, art 5(2), Sch 2.
Fees: the current Regulations prescribing fees are the Health and Safety and Nuclear (Fees) Regulations 2016, SI 2016/253 at **[2.1931]**.
Regulations: other Regulations made under this section are considered to be outside the scope of this work (see further the introductory notes to this Act *ante*).

43A *(S 43A (Railway safety levy) outside the scope of this work.)*

Miscellaneous and supplementary

44, 45 *(S 44 (Appeals in connection with licensing provisions in the relevant statutory provisions), s 45 (Default powers) outside the scope of this work.)*

[1.70]
46 Service of notices
(1) Any notice required or authorised by any of the relevant statutory provisions to be served on or given to an inspector may be served or given by delivering it to him or by leaving it at, or sending it by post to, his office.
(2) Any such notice required or authorised to be served on or given to a person other than an inspector may be served or given by delivering it to him, or by leaving it at his proper address, or by sending it by post to him at that address.

(3) Any such notice may—

(a) in the case of a body corporate, be served on or given to the secretary or clerk of that body;

(b) in the case of a partnership, be served on or given to a partner or a person having the control or management of the partnership business or, in Scotland, the firm.

(4) For the purposes of this section and of section 26 of the Interpretation Act 1889 (service of documents by post) in its application to this section, the proper address of any person on or to whom any such notice is to be served or given shall be his last known address, except that—

(a) in the case of a body corporate or their secretary or clerk, it shall be the address of the registered or principal office of that body;

(b) in the case of a partnership or a person having the control or the management of the partnership business, it shall be the principal office of the partnership;

and for the purposes of this subsection the principal office of a company registered outside the United Kingdom or of a partnership carrying on business outside the United Kingdom shall be their principal office within the United Kingdom.

(5) If the person to be served with or given any such notice has specified an address within the United Kingdom other than his proper address within the meaning of subsection (4) above as the one at which he or someone on his behalf will accept notices of the same description as that notice, that address shall also be treated for the purposes of this section and section 26 of the Interpretation Act 1889 as his proper address.

(6) Without prejudice to any other provision of this section, any such notice required or authorised to be served on or given to the owner or occupier of any premises (whether a body corporate or not) may be served or given by sending it by post to him at those premises, or by addressing it by name to the person on or to whom it is to be served or given and delivering it to some responsible person who is or appears to be resident or employed in the premises.

(7) If the name or the address of any owner or occupier of premises on or to whom any such notice as aforesaid is to be served or given cannot after reasonable inquiry be ascertained, the notice may be served or given by addressing it to the person on or to whom it is to be served or given by the description of "owner" or "occupier" of the premises (describing them) to which the notice relates, and by delivering it to some responsible person who is or appears to be resident or employed in the premises, or, if there is no such person to whom it can be delivered, by affixing it or a copy of it to some conspicuous part of the premises.

(8) The preceding provisions of this section shall apply to the sending or giving of a document as they apply to the giving of a notice.

NOTES

Interpretation Act 1889, s 26: see now the Interpretation Act 1978, s 7, Sch 2, para 3.

[1.71]

47 Civil Liability

(1) Nothing in this Part shall be construed—

(a) as conferring a right of action in any civil proceedings in respect of any failure to comply with any duty imposed by sections 2 to 7 or any contravention of section 8; or

(b) . . .

(c) as affecting the operation of section 12 of the Nuclear Installations Act 1965 (right to compensation by virtue of certain provisions of that Act).

[(2) Breach of a duty imposed by a statutory instrument containing (whether alone or with other provision) health and safety regulations shall not be actionable except to the extent that regulations under this section so provide.

(2A) Breach of a duty imposed by an existing statutory provision shall not be actionable except to the extent that regulations under this section so provide (including by modifying any of the existing statutory provisions).

(2B) Regulations under this section may include provision for—

(a) a defence to be available in any action for breach of the duty mentioned in subsection (2) or (2A);

(b) any term of an agreement which purports to exclude or restrict any liability for such a breach to be void.]

(3) No provision made by virtue of section 15(6)(b) shall afford a defence in any civil proceedings . . .

(4) Subsections (1)(a)[, (2) and (2A)] above are without prejudice to any right of action which exists apart from the provisions of this Act, and subsection [(2B)(a)] above is without prejudice to any defence which may be available apart from the provisions of the regulations there mentioned.

(5), (6) . . .

[(7) The power to make regulations under this section shall be exercisable by the Secretary of State.]

NOTES

Sub-s (1): para (b) repealed by the Enterprise and Regulatory Reform Act 2013, s 69(1), (2).

Sub-ss (2), (2A), (2B): substituted, for the original sub-s (2), by the Enterprise and Regulatory Reform Act 2013, s 69(1), (3).

Sub-s (3): words omitted repealed by the Enterprise and Regulatory Reform Act 2013, s 69(1), (4).

Sub-s (4): words in square brackets substituted by the Enterprise and Regulatory Reform Act 2013, s 69(1), (5).

Sub-ss (5), (6): repealed by the Enterprise and Regulatory Reform Act 2013, s 69(1), (6).

Sub-s (7): added by the Enterprise and Regulatory Reform Act 2013, s 69(1), (7).

Regulations: the Health and Safety at Work etc Act 1974 (Civil Liability) (Exceptions) Regulations 2013, SI 2013/1667 at **[2.1449]**. Other Regulations made under this section are considered to be outside the scope of this work (see further the introductory notes to this Act *ante*).

[1.72]

48 Application to Crown

(1) Subject to the provisions of this section, the provisions of this Part, except sections 21 to 25 and 33 to 42, and of regulations made under this Part shall bind the Crown.

(2) Although they do not bind the Crown, sections 33 to 42 shall apply to persons in the public service of the Crown as they apply to other persons.

(3) For the purposes of this Part and regulations made thereunder persons in the service of the Crown shall be treated as employees of the Crown whether or not they would be so treated apart from this subsection.

(4) Without prejudice to section 15(5), the Secretary of State may, to the extent that it appears to him requisite or expedient to do so in the interests of the safety of the State or the safe custody of persons lawfully detained, by order exempt the Crown either generally or in particular respects from all or any of the provisions of this Part which would, by virtue of subsection (1) above, bind the Crown.

(5) The power to make orders under this section shall be exercisable by statutory instrument, and any such order may be varied or revoked by a subsequent order.

(6) Nothing in this section shall authorise proceedings to be brought against Her Majesty in her private capacity, and this subsection shall be construed as if section 38(3) of the Crown Proceedings Act 1947 (interpretation of references in that Act to Her Majesty in her private capacity) were contained in this Act.

NOTES

The Crown: references to the Crown in sub-ss (1)–(4) shall be treated as including the Assembly Commission; see the National Assembly for Wales Commission (Crown Status) (No 2) Order 2007, SI 2007/1353, art 2.

Secretary of State: the power of the Secretary of State under sub-s (4) above includes power to provide for exemptions in relation to designated premises within the meaning of the Atomic Weapons Establishment Act 1991, or activities carried on by a contractor at such premises; see s 3(1) of, and the Schedule, paras 1, 7(1) to, that Act.

Orders: as of 15 May 2019, no Orders had been made under this section.

49 *(S 49 (Adaptation of enactments to metric units or appropriate metric units) outside the scope of this work.)*

[1.73]

50 Regulations under the relevant statutory provisions

[(1) Where any power to make regulations under any of the relevant statutory provisions is exercisable by the Secretary of State, that power may be exercised either—

(a) so as to give effect (with or without modifications) to proposals submitted by the Executive under section 11(3); or

(b) subject to subsection (1AA), independently of such proposals.

(1AA) The Secretary of State shall not exercise the power referred to in subsection (1) independently of proposals from the Executive unless [the Secretary of State has consulted—

(a) the Executive,

(b) the Office for Nuclear Regulation, and

(c) such other bodies as appear to the Secretary of State to be appropriate].]

[(1A) Subsection (1) does not apply to the exercise of a power to make regulations so far as it is exercised—

(a) for giving effect (with or without modifications) to proposals submitted by [the Office of Rail and Road] under paragraph 2(5) of Schedule 3 to the Railways Act 2005; or

(b) otherwise for or in connection with the railway safety purposes.]

(2) Where the [authority who is to exercise any such power as is mentioned in subsection (1) above proposes to exercise that power] so as to give effect to any such proposals as are there mentioned with modifications, he shall, before making the regulations, consult[—

(a) the Executive, and

(b) the Office for Nuclear Regulation].

(3) Where [the Executive] proposes to submit [under section [11(3)]] any such proposals as are mentioned in subsection (1) above except proposals for the making of regulations under section 43(2), it shall, before so submitting them, consult—

[(za) the Office for Nuclear Regulation;]

(a) any government department or other body that appears to [the Executive] to be appropriate (and, in particular, in the case of proposals for the making of regulations under section 18(2), any body representing local authorities that so appears . . .);

(b) such government departments and other bodies, if any, as, in relation to any matter dealt with in the proposals, [the Executive] is required to consult under this subsection by virtue of directions given to it by the Secretary of State.

[(4) If the Executive has consulted the Office for Nuclear Regulation under subsection (3) in relation to a proposal under section 11(3) for regulations under any of the relevant statutory provisions, it must, when it submits the proposal (with or without modification) to the Secretary of State, also submit—

(a) any representations made by the Office for Nuclear Regulation in response to the consultation, and

(b) any response to those representations given by the Executive to the Office for Nuclear Regulation.

(5) The preceding provisions of this section do not apply to the exercise of the power in section 43 to make ONR fees regulations, but the Secretary of State must consult the Office for Nuclear Regulation before—

(a) making ONR fees regulations independently of any proposals submitted by the Office for Nuclear Regulation under section 81(1) of the Energy Act 2013, or

(b) making ONR fees regulations which give effect to such proposals but with modifications.

(6) In subsection (5) "ONR fees regulations" means regulations under section 43 so far as they make provision in relation to fees payable for or in connection with the performance of a function by or on behalf of—

(a) the Office for Nuclear Regulation, or

(b) any inspector appointed by the Office for Nuclear Regulation.]

NOTES

Sub-ss (1), (1AA): substituted, for the original sub-s (1), by the Legislative Reform (Health and Safety Executive) Order 2008, SI 2008/960, arts 3, 16(1), (2); words in square brackets in sub-s (1AA) substituted by the Energy Act 2013, s 116, Sch 12, Pt 1, paras 1, 11(1), (2).

Sub-s (1A): inserted by the Railways Act 2005, s 2, Sch 3, para 13; words in square brackets substituted by the Office of Rail Regulation (Change of Name) Regulations 2015, SI 2015/1682, reg 2(2), Schedule, Pt 1, para 4(c)(iv), as from 16 October 2015.

Sub-s (2): words in first pair of square brackets substituted by the Employment Protection Act 1975, s 116, Sch 15, para 16(2); words in second pair of square brackets substituted by the Energy Act 2013, s 116, Sch 12, Pt 1, paras 1, 11(1), (3).

Sub-s (3): words "the Executive" in square brackets (in each place they occur) and the figure "11(3)" in square brackets substituted by SI 2008/960, arts 3, 16(1), (4); words in second (outer) pair of square brackets substituted by the Employment Protection Act 1975, s 116, Sch 15, para 16(3); para (za) inserted by the Energy Act 2013, s 116, Sch 12, Pt 1, paras 1, 11(1), (4); words omitted repealed by the Health and Social Care Act 2012, s 56(4), Sch 7, paras 4, 6.

Sub-ss (4)–(6): added by the Energy Act 2013, s 116, Sch 12, Pt 1, paras 1, 11(1), (5). Note that the original sub-ss (4) and (5) of this section were repealed by the Employment Protection Act 1975, ss 116, 125(3), Sch 15, para 16(4), Sch 18.

[1.74]

51 Exclusion of application to domestic employment

Nothing in this Part shall apply in relation to a person by reason only that he employs another, or is himself employed, as a domestic servant in a private household.

[1.75]

[51A Application of Part to police

(1) For the purposes of this Part, a person who, otherwise than under a contract of employment, holds the office of constable or an appointment as police cadet shall be treated as an employee of the relevant officer.

(2) In this section "the relevant officer"—

(a) in relation to a member of a police force or a special constable or police cadet appointed for a police area, [means—

(i) the chief officer of police of that force, or

(ii) in the case of a member of the force or a special constable who is, by virtue of a collaboration agreement under section 22A of the Police Act 1996, under the direction and control of a chief officer (within the meaning given by section 23I of that Act), that chief officer,]

[(b) in relation to a member of a police force seconded to the [National Crime Agency to serve as a National Crime Agency officer], means that Agency, and]

(c) in relation to any other person holding the office of constable or an appointment as police cadet, [means—

(i) the person who has the direction and control of the body of constables or cadets in question, or

(ii) in the case of a constable who is, by virtue of a collaboration agreement under section 22A of the Police Act 1996, under the direction and control of a chief officer (within the meaning given by section 23I of that Act), that chief officer.]

[(2A) For the purposes of this Part the relevant officer, as defined by subsection (2)(a) or (c) above, shall[, if not a corporation sole,] be treated as a corporation sole.

(2B) Where, in a case in which the relevant officer, as so defined, is guilty of an offence by virtue of this section, it is proved—

(a) that the officer-holder personally consented to the commission of the offence,

(b) that he personally connived in its commission, or

(c) that the commission of the offence was attributable to personal neglect on his part,

the office-holder (as well as the corporation sole) shall be guilty of the offence and shall be liable to be proceeded against and punished accordingly.

(2C) In subsection (2B) above "the office-holder", in relation to the relevant officer, means an individual who, at the time of the consent, connivance or neglect—

(a) held the office or other position mentioned in subsection (2) above as the office or position of that officer; or

(b) was for the time being responsible for exercising and performing the powers and duties of that office or position.

(2D) The provisions mentioned in subsection (2E) below (which impose the same liability for unlawful conduct of constables on persons having their direction or control as would arise if the constables were employees of those persons) do not apply to any liability by virtue of this Part.

(2E) Those provisions are—

[(a) section 24 of the Police and Fire Reform (Scotland) Act 2012 (asp 8);]

(b) section 88(1) of the Police Act 1996;
(c), (d) . . .
(e) paragraph 14(1) of Schedule 3 to the Criminal Justice and Police Act 2001;
[(f) paragraph 2 of Schedule 4 to the Crime and Courts Act 2013;]
[(g) paragraph 20 of Schedule 1 to the Police and Justice Act 2006].

(2F) In the application of this section to Scotland—
(a) subsection (2A) shall have effect as if for the words "corporation sole" there were substituted "distinct juristic person (that is to say, as a juristic person distinct from the individual who for the time being is the office-holder)";
(b) subsection (2B) shall have effect as if for the words "corporation sole" there were substituted "juristic person"; and
(c) subsection (2C) shall have effect as if for the words "subsection (2B)" there were substituted "subsections (2A) and (2B)".]

(3) For the purposes of regulations under section 2(4) above—
(a) the Police Federation for England and Wales shall be treated as a recognised trade union recognised by each chief officer of police in England and Wales,
(b) the Police Federation for Scotland shall be treated as a recognised trade union recognised by [the chief constable of the Police Service of Scotland], and
(c) any body recognised by the Secretary of State for the purposes of section 64 of the Police Act 1996 shall be treated as a recognised trade union recognised by each chief officer of police in England, Wales and Scotland.

(4) Regulations under section 2(4) above may provide, in relation to persons falling within subsection (2)(b) or (c) above, that a body specified in the regulations is to be treated as a recognised trade union recognised by such person as may be specified.]

NOTES

Inserted by the Police (Health and Safety) Act 1997, s 1.

Sub-s (2): words in square brackets in paras (a), (c) substituted by the Police Reform and Social Responsibility Act 2011, s 99, Sch 16, Pt 3, para 119(1), (2); para (b) substituted by the Serious Organised Crime and Police Act 2005, s 59, Sch 4, para 20; words in square brackets in para (b) substituted by the Crime and Courts Act 2013, s 15(3), Sch 8, Pt 2, para 21(1), (2).

Sub-ss (2A)–(2F): inserted by the Serious Organised Crime and Police Act 2005, s 158(1), (5); words in square brackets in sub-s (2A) substituted by the Police Reform and Social Responsibility Act 2011, s 99, Sch 16, Pt 3, para 119(1), (3); in sub-s (2E), para (a) substituted (in relation to Scotland) by the Police and Fire Reform (Scotland) Act 2012, s 128(1), Sch 7, Pt 1, para 2(a), and (in relation to England and Wales) by the Police and Fire Reform (Scotland) Act 2012 (Consequential Provisions and Modifications) Order 2013, SI 2013/602, art 25, Sch 1, para 2(a); in sub-s (2E), paras (c), (d) repealed, and para (g) added, by the Police and Justice Act 2006, ss 1(3), 52, Sch 1, Pt 7, para 54, Sch 15, Pt 1; in sub-s (2E) para (f) substituted by the Crime and Courts Act 2013, s 15(3), Sch 8, Pt 2, para 21(1), (3).

Sub-s (3): words in square brackets in para (b) substituted (in relation to Scotland) by the Police and Fire Reform (Scotland) Act 2012, s 128(1), Sch 7, Pt 1, para 2(b), and (in relation to England and Wales) by SI 2013/602, art 25, Sch 1, para 2(b).

Criminal Justice and Police Act 2001, Sch 3: repealed by the Police and Justice Act 2006, s 52, Sch 15.

Police and Justice Act 2006: Sch 1 to that Act was repealed by the Crime and Courts Act 2013, s 15(3), Sch 8, Pt 2, paras 167, 170.

Regulations under section 2(4): see the Police (Health and Safety) Regulations 1999, SI 1999/860 at **[2.407]**.

[1.76]

52 Meaning of work and at work

(1) For the purposes of this Part—
(a) "work" means work as an employee or as a self-employed person;
(b) an employee is at work throughout the time when he is in the course of his employment, but not otherwise;
[(bb) a person holding the office of constable is at work throughout the time when he is on duty, but not otherwise; and]
(c) a self-employed person is at work throughout such time as he devotes to work as a self-employed person;

and, subject to the following subsection, the expressions "work" and "at work", in whatever context, shall be construed accordingly.

(2) Regulations made under this subsection may—
(a) extend the meaning of "work" and "at work" for the purposes of this Part; and
(b) in that connection provide for any of the relevant statutory provisions to have effect subject to such adaptations as may be specified in the regulations.

[(3) The power to make regulations under subsection (2) above shall be exercisable by the Secretary of State . . .]

NOTES

Sub-s (1): para (bb) substituted for the original word "and" following para (b) by the Police (Health and Safety) Act 1997, s 2.

Sub-s (3): substituted, for the original sub-ss (3), (4), by the Employment Protection Act 1975, s 116, Sch 15, para 17; words omitted repealed by the Ministry of Agriculture, Fisheries and Food (Dissolution) Order 2002, SI 2002/794, art 5(2), Sch 2.

Modifications: in accordance with sub-s (2) above, the definitions "work" and "at work" are modified, inter alia, by the Health and Safety (Training for Employment) Regulations 1990, SI 1990/1380, which extend the definitions of "work" and "at work" to cover persons engaged in specified training.

Regulations: see the note above; other Regulations made under this section are considered to be outside the scope of this work (see further the introductory notes to this Act *ante*).

[1.77]

53 General interpretation of Part I

(1) In this Part, unless the context otherwise requires—

. . .

"article for use at work" means—

(a) any plant designed for use or operation (whether exclusively or not) by persons at work, and

(b) any article designed for use as a component in any such plant;

["article of fairground equipment" means any fairground equipment or any article designed for use as a component in any such equipment;]

"code of practice" (without prejudice to section 16(8)) includes a standard, a specification and any other documentary form of practical guidance;

. . .

"conditional sale agreement" means an agreement for the sale of goods under which the purchase price or part of it is payable by instalments, and the property in the goods is to remain in the seller (notwithstanding that the buyer is to be in possession of the goods) until such conditions as to the payment of instalments or otherwise as may be specified in the agreement are fulfilled;

"contract of employment" means a contract of employment or apprenticeship (whether express or implied and, if express, whether oral or in writing);

"credit-sale agreement" means an agreement for the sale of goods, under which the purchase price or part of it is payable by instalments, but which is not a conditional sale agreement;

["customs officer" means an officer within the meaning of the Customs and Excise Management Act 1979;]

"domestic premises" means premises occupied as a private dwelling (including any garden, yard, garage, outhouse or other appurtenance of such premises which is not used in common by the occupants of more than one such dwelling), and "non-domestic premises" shall be construed accordingly;

"employee" means an individual who works under a contract of employment [or is treated by section 51A as being an employee], and related expressions shall be construed accordingly;

"enforcing authority" has the meaning assigned by section 18(7);

"the Executive" has the meaning assigned by section [10(1)];

"the existing statutory provisions" means the following provisions while and to the extent that they remain in force, namely the provisions of the Acts mentioned in Schedule 1 which are specified in the third column of that Schedule and of the regulations, orders or other instruments of a legislative character made or having effect under any provision so specified;

. . .

["fairground equipment" means any fairground ride, any similar plant which is designed to be in motion for entertainment purposes with members of the public on or inside it or any plant which is designed to be used by members of the public for entertainment purposes either as a slide or for bouncing upon, and in this definition the reference to plant which is designed to be in motion with members of the public on or inside it includes a reference to swings, dodgems and other plant which is designed to be in motion wholly or partly under the control of, or to be put in motion by, a member of the public;]

"the general purposes of this Part" has the meaning assigned by section 1;

"health and safety regulations" has the meaning assigned by section 15(1);

"hire-purchase agreement" means an agreement other than a conditional sale agreement, under which—

(a) goods are bailed or (in Scotland) hired in return for periodical payments by the person to whom they are bailed or hired; and

(b) the property in the goods will pass to that person if the terms of the agreement are complied with and one or more of the following occurs—

(i) the exercise of an option to purchase by that person;

(ii) the doing of any other specified act by any party to the agreement;

(iii) the happening of any other event;

and "hire-purchase" shall be construed accordingly;

"improvement notice" means a notice under section 21;

"inspector" means an inspector appointed under section 19;

. . .

"local authority" means—

(a) in relation to England . . . , a county council, . . . , a district council, a London borough council, the Common Council of the City of London, the Sub-Treasurer of the Inner Temple or the Under-Treasurer of the Middle Temple,

[(aa) in relation to Wales, a county council or a county borough council,]

(b) in relation to Scotland, a [council constituted under section 2 of the Local Government etc (Scotland) Act 1994] except that before 16th May 1975 it means a town council or county council;

["micro-organism" includes any microscopic biological entity which is capable of replication;]

["nuclear safeguards purposes" has the same meaning as in Part 3 of the Energy Act 2013 (nuclear regulation etc) (see section 72 of that Act);]

["nuclear safety purposes" has the same meaning as in that Part of that Act (see section 68 of that Act);]

["nuclear security purposes" has the same meaning as in that Part of that Act (see section 70 of that Act);]

"offshore installation" means any installation which is intended for underwater exploitation of mineral resources or exploration with a view to such exploitation;

["the ONR's purposes" has the same meaning as in Part 3 of the Energy Act 2013 (see section 67 of that Act);"]

"personal injury" includes any disease and any impairment of a person's physical or mental condition;

"plant" includes any machinery, equipment or appliance;

"premises" includes any place and, in particular, includes—

(a) any vehicle, vessel, aircraft or hovercraft,

(b) any installation on land (including the foreshore and other land intermittently covered by water), any offshore installation, and any other installation (whether floating, or resting on the seabed or the subsoil thereof, or resting on other land covered with water or the subsoil thereof), and

(c) any tent or movable structure;

"prescribed" means prescribed by regulations made by the Secretary of State;

"prohibition notice" means a notice under section 22;

["the radioactive material transport purposes" means the transport purposes within the meaning of Part 3 of the Energy Act 2013 (see section 73 of that Act);]

["railway safety purposes" has the same meaning as in Schedule 3 to the Railways Act 2005;]

. . .

"the relevant statutory provisions" means—

(a) the provisions of this Part and of any health and safety regulations . . . ; and

(b) the existing statutory provisions;

"self-employed person" means an individual who works for gain or reward otherwise than under a contract of employment, whether or not he himself employs others;

"substance" means any natural or artificial substance [(including micro-organisms)], whether in solid or liquid form or in the form of a gas or vapour;

. . .

"supply", where the reference is to supplying articles or substances, means supplying them by way of sale, lease, hire or hire-purchase, whether as principal or agent for another.

(2)–(6) . . .

NOTES

Sub-s (1): definitions "article of fairground equipment", "customs officer", "fairground equipment" and "micro-organism" inserted by the Consumer Protection Act 1987, s 36, Sch 3, para 7; definition "the Commission" (omitted) repealed, and figure in square brackets in definition "the Executive" substituted, by the Legislative Reform (Health and Safety Executive) Order 2008, SI 2008/960, arts 3, 17; words in square brackets in the definition "employee" inserted by the Police (Health and Safety) Act 1997, s 6(1); in the definition "local authority", second words omitted repealed by the Local Government Act 1985, s 102, Sch 17, first words omitted from that definition repealed, and para (aa) inserted, by the Local Government (Wales) Act 1994, ss 22(3), 66(8), Sch 9, para 9, Sch 18, and words in square brackets in para (b) of that definition substituted by the Local Government etc (Scotland) Act 1994, s 180(1), Sch 13, para 93(3); definitions "nuclear safeguards purposes", "nuclear safety purposes", "nuclear security purposes", "the ONR's purposes", and "the radioactive material transport purposes" inserted by the Energy Act 2013, s 116, Sch 12, Pt 1, paras 1, 12; definition "railway safety purposes" inserted by the Railways Act 2005, s 2, Sch 3, para 15(3); in definition "substance", words in square brackets inserted by the Consumer Protection Act 1987, s 36, Sch 3, para 7; definition "substance for use at work" (omitted) repealed by the Consumer Protection Act 1987, s 48, Sch 5; other words and definitions omitted repealed by the Employment Protection Act 1975, ss 116, 125(3), Sch 15, para 18, Sch 18.

Sub-ss (2)–(6): repealed by the Employment Protection Act 1975, ss 116, 125(3), Sch 15, para 18, Sch 18.

[1.78]

54 Application of Part I to Isles of Scilly

This Part, in its application to the Isles of Scilly, shall apply as if those Isles were a local government area and the Council of those Isles were a local authority.

55–76 *(Ss 55–60 (Pt II: Employment Medical Advisory Service) outside the scope of this work; Pt III (ss 61–76) repealed as follows: ss 61–74, 76 repealed by the Building Act 1984, s 133(2), Sch 7; s 75 repealed by the Building (Scotland) Act 2003, s 58, Sch 6, para 9.)*

PART IV
MISCELLANEOUS AND GENERAL

77–79 *(S 77 repealed by the Health Protection Agency Act 2004, s 11(2), Sch 4; s 78 repealed by the Regulatory Reform (Fire Safety) Order 2005, SI 2005/1541 and the Fire (Scotland) Act 2005 (Consequential Modifications and Savings) Order 2006, SSI 2006/475; s 79 repealed by the Companies Consolidation (Consequential Provisions) Act 1985, s 29, Sch 1.)*

[1.79]

80 General power to repeal or modify Acts and instruments

(1) Regulations made under this subsection may repeal or modify any provision to which this subsection applies if it appears to the authority making the regulations that the repeal or, as the case may be, the modification of that provision is expedient in consequence of or in connection with any provision made by or under Part I.

(2) Subsection (1) above applies to any provision, not being among the relevant statutory provisions, which—

(a) is contained in this Act or in any other Act passed before or in the same Session as this Act; or
(b) is contained in any regulations, order or other instrument of a legislative character which was made under an Act before the passing of this Act; or
(c) applies, excludes or for any other purpose refers to any of the relevant statutory provisions and is contained in any Act not falling within paragraph (a) above or in any regulations, order or other instrument of a legislative character which is made under an Act but does not fall within paragraph (b) above.

[(2A) Subsection (1) above shall apply to provisions in [the Employment Rights Act 1996 or the Trade Union and Labour Relations (Consolidation) Act 1992 which derive from provisions of the Employment Protection (Consolidation) Act 1978 which re-enacted] provisions previously contained in the Redundancy Payments Act 1965, the Contracts of Employment Act 1972 and the Trade Union and Labour Relations Act 1974 as it applies to provisions contained in Acts passed before or in the same session as this Act.]

(3) Without prejudice to the generality of subsection (1) above, the modifications which may be made by regulations thereunder include modifications relating to the enforcement of provisions to which this section applies (including the appointment of persons for the purpose of such enforcement, and the powers of persons so appointed).

[(4) The power to make regulations under subsection (1) above shall be exercisable by the Secretary of State . . . ; but the authority who is to exercise the power shall, before exercising it, consult such bodies as appear to him to be appropriate.

(5) In this section "the relevant statutory provisions" has the same meaning as in Part I.]

NOTES

Sub-s (2A): inserted by the Employment Protection (Consolidation) Act 1978, s 159(2), Sch 16, para 17; words in square brackets substituted by the Employment Rights Act 1996, s 240, Sch 1, para 5.

Sub-ss (4), (5): substituted, for the original sub-ss (4)–(6), by the Employment Protection Act 1975, s 116, Sch 15, para 19; words omitted from sub-s (4) repealed by the Ministry of Agriculture, Fisheries and Food (Dissolution) Order 2002, SI 2002/794, art 5(2), Sch 2.

Employment Protection (Consolidation) Act 1978: repealed by the Trade Union and Labour Relations (Consolidation) Act 1992, s 300(1), Sch 1, and the Employment Rights Act 1996, s 242, Sch 3, Pt I.

Redundancy Payments Act 1965; Contracts of Employment Act 1972; Trade Union and Labour Relations Act 1974: the relevant provisions previously contained in those Acts were repealed by the Employment Protection (Consolidation) Act 1978, s 159(3), Sch 17.

Regulations: Regulations made under this section are considered to be outside the scope of this work (see further the introductory notes to this Act *ante*).

[1.80]

81 Expenses and receipts

There shall be paid out of money provided by Parliament—

(a) any expenses incurred by a Minister of the Crown or government department for the purposes of this Act; and
(b) any increase attributable to the provisions of this Act in the sums payable under any other Act out of money so provided;

and any sums received by a Minister of the Crown or government department by virtue of this Act shall be paid into the Consolidated Fund.

[1.81]

82 General provisions as to interpretation and regulations

(1) In this Act—

(a) "Act" includes a provisional order confirmed by an Act;
(b) "contravention" includes failure to comply, and "contravene" has a corresponding meaning;
(c) "modifications" includes additions, omissions and amendments, and related expressions shall be construed accordingly;
(d) any reference to a Part, section or Schedule not otherwise identified is a reference to that Part or section of, or Schedule to, this Act.

(2) Except in so far as the context otherwise requires, any reference in this Act to an enactment is a reference to it as amended, and includes a reference to it as applied, by or under any other enactment, including this Act.

(3) Any power conferred by Part I or II or this Part to make regulations—

(a) includes power to make different provision by the regulations for different circumstances or cases and to include in the regulations such incidental, supplemental and transitional provisions as the authority making the regulations considers appropriate in connection with the regulations; and
(b) shall be exercisable by statutory instrument, which [(unless [subsection (3A), (3B) or (4)] applies)] shall be subject to annulment in pursuance of a resolution of either House of Parliament.

[(3A) In the case of a statutory instrument which also contains regulations under section 74 of the Energy Act 2013 (nuclear regulations), subsection (3) is subject to section 113 of that Act (subordinate legislation).]

[(3B) Regulations under section 3(2) shall not be made unless a draft has been laid before and approved by resolution of each House of Parliament.]

[(4) The first regulations under section 43A(1) shall not be made unless a draft has been laid before and approved by resolution of each House of Parliament.]

NOTES

Words in first (outer) pair of square brackets in sub-s (3)(b) inserted, and sub-s (4) added, by the Railways and Transport Safety Act 2003, s 105(3).

Words in second (inner) pair of square brackets in sub-s (3)(b) substituted, and sub-s (3B) inserted, by the Deregulation Act 2015, s 1(1), (5), as from 26 March 2015.

Sub-s (3A): inserted by the Energy Act 2013, s 116, Sch 12, Pt 1, paras 1, 13.

83 *(Repealed by the Statute Law (Repeals) Act 1993.)*

[1.82]

84 Extent, and application of Act

(1) This Act, except—

(a) Part I and this Part so far as may be necessary to enable regulations under section 15 . . . to be made and operate for the purpose mentioned in paragraph 2 of Schedule 3; and

(b) paragraph . . . 3 of Schedule 9,

does not extend to Northern Ireland.

(2) Part III, except section 75 and Schedule 7, does not extend to Scotland.

(3) Her Majesty may by order in Council provide that the provisions of Parts I and II and this Part shall, to such extent and for such purposes as may be specified in the Order, apply (with or without modification) to or in relation to persons, premises, work, articles, substances and other matters (of whatever kind) outside Great Britain as those provisions apply within Great Britain or within a part of Great Britain so specified.

For the purposes of this subsection "premises", "work" and "substance" have the same meanings as they have for the purposes of Part I.

(4) An Order in Council under subsection (3) above—

(a) may make different provision for different circumstances or cases;

(b) may (notwithstanding that this may affect individuals or bodies corporate outside the United Kingdom) provide for any of the provisions mentioned in that subsection, as applied by such an Order, to apply to individuals whether or not they are British subjects and to bodies corporate whether or not they are incorporated under the law of any part of the United Kingdom;

(c) may make provision for conferring jurisdiction on any court or class of courts specified in the Order with respect to offences under Part I committed outside Great Britain or with respect to causes of action arising by virtue of section 47(2) in respect of acts or omissions taking place outside Great Britain, and for the determination, in accordance with the law in force in such part of Great Britain as may be specified in the Order, of questions arising out of such acts or omissions;

(d) may exclude from the operation of section 3 of the Territorial Waters Jurisdiction Act 1878 (consents required for prosecutions) proceedings for offences under any provision of Part I committed outside Great Britain;

(e) may be varied or revoked by a subsequent Order in Council under this section;

and any such Order shall be subject to annulment in pursuance of a resolution of either House of Parliament.

(5) . . .

(6) Any jurisdiction conferred on any court under this section shall be without prejudice to any jurisdiction exercisable apart from this section by that or any other court.

NOTES

Sub-s (1): words omitted from para (a) repealed by the Employment Protection Act 1975, ss 116, 125(3), Sch 15, para 20; words omitted from para (b) repealed by the House of Commons Disqualification Act 1975, s 10(2), Sch 3.

Sub-s (5): repealed by the Offshore Safety Act 1992, ss 3(1)(b), 7(2), Sch 2.

Orders: the Health and Safety at Work etc Act 1974 (Application outside Great Britain) Order 2013, SI 2013/240 (which applies provisions of the Act, with appropriate modifications, to various offshore activities); the Freight Containers (Safety Convention) Regulations 2017, SI 2017/325.

[1.83]

85 Short title and commencement

(1) This Act may be cited as the Health and Safety at Work etc Act 1974.

(2) This Act shall come into operation on such day as the Secretary of State may by order made by statutory instrument appoint, and different days may be appointed under this subsection for different purposes.

(3) An order under this section may contain such transitional provisions and savings as appear to the Secretary of State to be necessary or expedient in connection with the provisions thereby brought into force, including such adaptations of those provisions or any provision of this Act then in force as appear to him to be necessary or expedient in consequence of the partial operation of this Act (whether before or after the day appointed by the order).

NOTES

Orders: six commencement orders have been made under this section. The combined effect of the Orders is that the unrepealed provisions of this Act were brought into force on various dates between 1 October 1974 and 17 March 1980.

SCHEDULES

SCHEDULE 1
EXISTING ENACTMENTS WHICH ARE RELEVANT STATUTORY PROVISIONS

Sections 1, 53

[1.84]

Chapter	*Short title*	*Provisions which are relevant statutory provisions*
1875 c 17	The Explosives Act 1875	The whole Act except sections *30 to 32, 80 and* 116 to 121.
1882 c 22	The Boiler Explosions Act 1882	The whole Act.
1890 c 35	The Boiler Explosions Act 1890	The whole Act.
1906 c 14	The Alkali, &c Works Regulation Act 1906	The whole Act.
1909 c 43	The Revenue Act 1909	Section 11.
. . .	. . .	. . .
1920 c 65	The Employment of Women, Young Persons and Children Act 1920	The whole Act.
. . .	. . .	. . .
. . .	. . .	. . .
1926 c 43	The Public Health (Smoke Abatement) Act 1926	The whole Act.
1928 c 32	The Petroleum (Consolidation) Act 1928	The whole Act.
1936 c 22	The Hours of Employment (Conventions) Act 1936	The whole Act except section 5.
1936 c 27	The Petroleum (Transfer of Licences) Act 1936	The whole Act.
1937 c 45	The Hydrogen Cyanide (Fumigation) Act 1937	The whole Act.
1945 c 19	The Ministry of Fuel and Power Act 1945	Section 1(1) so far as it relates to maintaining and improving the safety, health and welfare of persons employed in or about mines and quarries in Great Britain.
1946 c 59	The Coal Industry Nationalisation Act 1946	Section 42(1) and (2).
1948 c 37	The Radioactive Substances Act 1948	Section 5(1)(a).
1951 c 21	The Alkali, &c Works Regulations (Scotland) Act 1951	The whole Act.
. . .	. . .	. . .
1952 c 60	The Agriculture (Poisonous Substances) Act 1952	The whole Act.
. . .	. . .	. . .
[. . .	. . .	. . .]
1954 c 70	The Mines and Quarries Act 1954	The whole Act except section 151.
1956 c 49	The Agriculture (Safety, Health and Welfare Provisions) Act 1956	The whole Act.
1961 c 34	The Factories Act 1961	The whole Act except section 135.
1961 c 64	The Public Health Act 1961	Section 73.
1962 c 58	The Pipe-lines Act 1962	Sections 20 to 26, 33, 34 and 42, Schedule 5.
1963 c 41	The Offices, Shops and Railway Premises Act 1963	The whole Act.
. . .	. . .	. . .
. . .	. . .	. . .
1971 c 20	The Mines Management Act 1971	The whole Act.
1972 c 28	The Employment Medical Advisory Service Act 1972	The whole Act except sections 1 and 6 and Schedule 1.

NOTES

Words in italics in the entry relating to the Explosives Act 1875 repealed by the Fireworks Act 2003, s 15, Schedule, as from a day to be appointed.

Entry relating to "The Anthrax Prevention Act 1919" (omitted) repealed by the Anthrax Prevention Order 1971 etc (Revocation) Regulations 2005, SI 2005/228, reg 2(2).

Entry relating to "The Celluloid and Cinematograph Film Act 1922" (omitted) repealed by the Health and Safety (Miscellaneous Repeals, Revocations and Amendments) Regulations 2013, SI 2013/448, reg 2(1), Schedule.

Entries relating to "The Explosives Act 1923", "The Fireworks Act 1951" and "The Emergency Laws (Miscellaneous Provisions) Act 1953" (omitted) repealed by the Manufacture and Storage of Explosives Regulations 2005, SI 2005/1082, reg 28(1), (2), Sch 5, Pt 1, para 14, Sch 6, Pt 1.

Entry relating to the "Baking Industry (Hours of Work) Act 1954" (omitted) originally inserted by the Sex Discrimination Act 1975, s 23(3), Sch 5, para 3, and repealed by the Sex Discrimination Act 1986, s 9, Schedule, Pt III.

Entry relating to the Nuclear Installations Act 1965 (omitted) repealed by the Energy Act 2013, s 116, Sch 12, Pt 1, paras 1, 14.

Entry relating to "The Mines and Quarries (Tips) Act 1969" (omitted) repealed by the Mines Regulations 2014, SI 2014/3248, reg 74(1), Sch 3, Pt 1, as from 6 April 2015.

Existing enactments which are relevant statutory provisions: the term "the relevant statutory provisions" is defined by s 53(1) of this Act as the provisions of Part I and of any health and safety regulations and the existing statutory provisions. The provisions of the Acts mentioned in this Schedule which are specified in the third column and of the regulations, orders or other instruments of a legislative character made or having effect under any provision so specified (while and to the extent that they remain in force) are the "existing statutory provisions"; see s 53(1) *ante*.

The "existing statutory provisions" also include the enactments and regulations specified by: (a) the Gas Act 1986, Sch 8, para 6(3); (b) the Energy Act 2008, s 99(1); (c) the Offshore Safety Act 1992, ss 1(1), (3), 2(1), (3); (d) Railways Act 1993, ss 117(1), (4); (e) the Gas Act 1995, Sch 4, para 10.

As to the power of the Secretary of State to repeal or revoke any provision which is an existing statutory provision for the purposes of Part I of this Act, see the Deregulation and Contracting Out Act 1994, s 37(1)(a).

Boiler Explosions Act 1882; Boiler Explosions Act 1890; Alkali, &c Works Regulation Act 1906; Revenue Act 1909, s 11; Public Health (Smoke Abatement) Act 1926; Petroleum (Consolidation) Act 1928; Hours of Employment (Conventions) Act 1936; Petroleum (Transfer of Licences) Act 1936; Hydrogen Cyanide (Fumigation) Act 1937; Coal Industry Nationalisation Act 1946, s 42; Radioactive Substances Act 1948, s 5(1)(a); Alkali, &c Works Regulations (Scotland) Act 1951; Agriculture (Poisonous Substances) Act 1952; Pipe-lines Act 1962, ss 20–26, 33, 34, 42, Sch 5; Mines Management Act 1971: all repealed.

Ministry of Fuel and Power Act 1945, s 1(1): repealed, in so far as it is a relevant statutory provision.

[SCHEDULE 2
ADDITIONAL PROVISIONS RELATING TO THE CONSTITUTION ETC OF THE HEALTH AND SAFETY EXECUTIVE

Section 10

The Health and Safety Executive

[1.85]

1. The Executive shall consist of—
- (a) the Chair of the Executive, and
- (b) at least seven and no more than [twelve] other members (referred to in this Schedule as "members").

2. (1) The Secretary of State shall appoint the Chair of the Executive.

(2) [Subject to sub-paragraph (3A),] the Secretary of State shall appoint the other members of the Executive according to sub-paragraph (3).

(3) The Secretary of State—
- (a) shall appoint three members after consulting such organisations representing employers as he considers appropriate;
- (b) shall appoint three members after consulting such organisations representing employees as he considers appropriate;
- (c) shall appoint one member after consulting such organisations representing local authorities as he considers appropriate; and
- (d) may appoint up to four other members after consulting, as he considers appropriate—
  - (i) the Scottish Ministers,
  - (ii) the Welsh Ministers, or
  - (iii) such organisations as he considers appropriate, including professional bodies, whose activities are concerned with matters relating to the general purposes of this Part.

[(3A) The Office for Nuclear Regulation may appoint a member from among the non-executive members of the Office for Nuclear Regulation ("an ONR member").

(3B) The Office for Nuclear Regulation must notify the Executive and the Secretary of State whenever it appoints an ONR member.]

(4) Service as the Chair or as another member of the Executive is not service in the civil service of the State.

(5) The Secretary of State, with the approval of the Chair, may appoint one of the other members appointed under sub-paragraph (2) to be the deputy chair of the Executive.

Terms of Appointment of the Executive

3. Subject to paragraphs 4[, 4A] and 5, a person shall hold and vacate office as the Chair or as another member according to the terms of the instrument appointing him to that office.

4. The Chair or any other member of the Executive[, other than an ONR member,] may at any time resign his office by giving notice in writing to the Secretary of State.

[**4A.** (1) An ONR member may at any time resign from office by giving notice in writing to the Office for Nuclear Regulation.

(2) An ONR member ceases to be a member of the Executive upon ceasing to be a non-executive member of the Office for Nuclear Regulation.

(3) The Office for Nuclear Regulation may remove an ONR member from office by giving notice in writing.

(4) The Office for Nuclear Regulation must notify the Executive and the Secretary of State whenever an ONR member—

(a) resigns from office,
(b) ceases to be a non-executive member of the Office for Nuclear Regulation, or
(c) is removed from office.]

5. The Secretary of State may remove a Chair or other member[, other than an ONR member,] who—

(a) has been absent from meetings of the Executive for a period longer than six months without the permission of the Executive;
(b) has become bankrupt or [has had a debt relief order (under Part 7A of the Insolvency Act 1986) made in respect of him or] has made an arrangement with his creditors;
(c) in Scotland, has had his estate sequestrated or has made a trust deed for creditors or a composition contract;
(d) has become incapacitated by physical or mental illness; or
(e) is otherwise, in the opinion of the Secretary of State, unable or unfit to carry out his functions.

Remuneration of Members

6. (1) The Executive shall pay[—

(a) to each member, other than an ONR member, such remuneration, and
(b) to each member such travelling and other allowances,

as may be determined by the Secretary of State].

(2) The Executive shall pay to, or in respect of, any member [other than an ONR member], such sums by way of pension, superannuation allowances and gratuities as the Secretary of State may determine.

(3) Where a person ceases to be a member [other than an ONR member] otherwise than on the expiry of his term of office, and the Secretary of State determines that there are special circumstances which make it right that he should receive compensation, the Executive shall pay to him such amount by way of compensation as the Secretary of State may determine.

[(4) Where—

(a) a member appointed under paragraph 4(4)(a) of Schedule 7 to the Energy Act 2013 to be a member of the Office for Nuclear Regulation (the "HSE member of the ONR")—
  (i) ceases to be the HSE member of the ONR otherwise than on the expiry of his or her term of office as HSE member of the ONR, but
  (ii) does not cease to be a member of the Executive, and
(b) it appears to the Executive that there are special circumstances that make it right for that person to receive compensation,

the Executive may pay the member such amount by way of compensation as the Secretary of State may determine.]

Proceedings of the Executive

7. (1) The Executive may regulate its own procedure.

(2) The validity of any proceedings of the Executive shall not be affected by any vacancy among the members or by any defect in the appointment of a member.

(3) The Executive shall consult with the Secretary of State before making or revising its rules and procedures for dealing with conflicts of interest.

(4) The Executive shall from time to time publish a summary of its rules and procedures.

Staff

8. (1) The Executive shall, with the consent of the Secretary of State, appoint a person to act as Chief Executive on such terms and conditions as the Secretary of State may determine.

(2) The Executive shall appoint such other staff to the service of the Executive as it may determine, with the consent of the Secretary of State as to numbers of persons appointed and as to the terms and conditions of their service.

(3) The Executive shall pay to the Minister for the Civil Service at such times as that Minister may direct, such sums as the Minister may determine in respect of any increase attributable to this paragraph in the sums payable out of monies provided by Parliament under the Superannuation Act 1972.

(4) A person appointed to the staff of the Executive may not at the same time be a member of the Executive.

(5) Service as a member of staff of the Executive is service in the civil service of the State.

Performance of functions

9. (1) Subject to sub-paragraphs (2) to (4), anything authorised or required to be done by the Executive (including exercising the powers under this paragraph) may be done by—

(a) such members of the Executive or members of staff of the Executive as the Executive considers fit to authorise for that purpose, whether generally or specifically; or

(b) any committee of the Executive which has been so authorised.

(2) Sub-paragraph (1)(b) does not apply to a committee whose members include a person who is neither a member of the Executive nor a member of staff of the Executive.

(3) The Executive—

(a) shall authorise such of its members of staff as it considers fit to authorise for that purpose, to perform on its behalf those of its functions which consist of the enforcement of the relevant statutory provisions in any particular case; but

(b) shall not authorise any member or committee of the Executive to make decisions concerning the enforcement of the relevant statutory provisions in any particular case.

(4) The Executive shall not authorise any person to legislate by subordinate instrument.

(5) The Executive shall publish any authorisations which it makes under this paragraph.

Accounts and Reports

10. (1) It shall be the duty of the Chief Executive—

(a) to keep proper accounts and proper records in relation to the accounts;

(b) to prepare in respect of each accounting year a statement of accounts in such form as the Secretary of State may direct with the approval of the Treasury; and

(c) to send copies of the statement to the Secretary of State and the Comptroller and Auditor General before the end of November next following the accounting year to which the statement relates.

(2) The Comptroller and the Auditor General shall examine, certify and report on each statement referred to in sub-paragraph (1)(c) and shall lay copies of each statement and his report before each House of Parliament.

(3) As soon as possible after the end of the accounting year, the Executive shall make to the Secretary of State a report on the performance of the Executive's functions during the year.

(4) The Secretary of State shall lay the report referred to in sub-paragraph (3) before each House of Parliament.

(5) In this paragraph, "accounting year" means the period of 12 months ending with 31st March in any year; but the first accounting year of the Executive shall, if the Secretary of State so directs, be of such other period not exceeding 2 years as may be specified in the direction.

Supplemental

11. The Secretary of State shall not make any determination or give his consent under paragraph 6 or 8 of this Schedule except with the approval of the Minister for the Civil Service.

12. (1) The fixing of the common seal of the Executive shall be authenticated by the signature of the Chair or some other person authorised by the Executive to act for that purpose.

(2) A document purporting to be duly executed under the seal of the Executive shall be received in evidence and shall be deemed to be so executed unless the contrary is proved.

(3) This paragraph does not apply to Scotland.]

NOTES

Substituted by the Legislative Reform (Health and Safety Executive) Order 2008, SI 2008/960, arts 3, 16(1), (2).

The words in square brackets in para 5(b) were inserted by the Tribunals, Courts and Enforcement Act 2007 (Consequential Amendments) Order 2012, SI 2012/2404, art 3(2), Sch 2, para 6. All other words in square brackets in this Schedule were inserted or substituted by the Energy Act 2013, s 116, Sch 12, Pt 1, paras 1, 15.

SCHEDULE 3
SUBJECT-MATTER OF HEALTH AND SAFETY REGULATIONS

Section 15

[1.86]

1. (1) Regulating or prohibiting—

(a) the manufacture, supply or use of any plant;

(b) the manufacture, supply, keeping or use of any substance;

(c) the carrying on of any process or the carrying out of any operation.

(2) Imposing requirements with respect to the design, construction, guarding, siting, installation, commissioning, examination, repair, maintenance, alteration, adjustment, dismantling, testing or inspection of any plant.

(3) Imposing requirements with respect to the marking of any plant or of any articles used or designed for use as components in any plant, and in that connection regulating or restricting the use of specified markings.

(4) Imposing requirements with respect to the testing, labelling or examination of any substance.

(5) Imposing requirements with respect to the carrying out of research in connection with any activity mentioned in sub-paragraphs (1) to (4) above.

2. (1) Prohibiting the importation into the United Kingdom or the landing or unloading there of articles or substances of any specified description, whether absolutely or unless conditions imposed by or under the regulations are complied with.

(2) Specifying, in a case where an act or omission in relation to such an importation, landing or unloading as is mentioned in the preceding sub-paragraph constitutes an offence under a provision of this Act and of [the Customs and Excise Acts 1979], the Act under which the offence is to be punished.

3. (1) Prohibiting or regulating the transport of articles or substances of any specified description.

(2) Imposing requirements with respect to the manner and means of transporting articles or substances of any specified description, including requirements with respect to the construction, testing and marking of containers and means of transport and the packaging and labelling of articles or substances in connection with their transport.

4. (1) Prohibiting the carrying on of any specified activity or the doing of any specified thing except under the authority and in accordance with the terms and conditions of a licence, or except with the consent or approval of specified authority.

(2) Providing for the grant, renewal, variation, transfer and revocation of licences (including the variation and revocation of conditions attached to licences).

5. Requiring any person, premises or thing to be registered in any specified circumstances or as a condition of the carrying on of any specified activity or the doing of any specified thing.

6. (1) Requiring, in specified circumstances, the appointment (whether in a specified capacity or not) of persons (or persons with specified qualifications or experience, or both) to perform specified functions, and imposing duties or conferring powers on persons appointed (whether in pursuance of the regulations or not) to perform specified functions.

(2) Restricting the performance of specified functions to persons possessing specified qualifications or experience.

7. Regulating or prohibiting the employment in specified circumstances of all persons or any class of persons.

8. (1) Requiring the making of arrangements for securing the health of persons at work or other persons, including arrangements for medical examinations and health surveys.

(2) Requiring the making of arrangements for monitoring the atmospheric or other conditions in which persons work.

9. Imposing requirements with respect to any matter affecting the conditions in which persons work, including in particular such matters as the structural condition and stability of premises, the means of access to and egress from premises, cleanliness, temperature, lighting, ventilation, overcrowding, noise, vibrations, ionising and other radiations, dust and fumes.

10. Securing the provision of specified welfare facilities for persons at work, including in particular such things as an adequate water supply, sanitary conveniences, washing and bathing facilities, ambulance and first-aid arrangements, cloakroom accommodation, sitting facilities and refreshment facilities.

11. Imposing requirements with respect to the provision and use in specified circumstances of protective clothing or equipment, including affording protection against the weather.

12. Requiring in specified circumstances the taking of specified precautions in connection with the risk of fire.

13. (1) Prohibiting or imposing requirements in connection with the emission into the atmosphere of any specified gas, smoke or dust or any other specified substance whatsoever.

(2) Prohibiting or imposing requirements in connection with the emission of noise, vibrations or any ionising or other radiations.

(3) Imposing requirements with respect to the monitoring of any such emission as is mentioned in the preceding sub-paragraphs.

14. Imposing requirements with respect to the instruction, training and supervision of persons at work.

15. (1) Requiring, in specified circumstances, specified matters to be notified in a specified manner to specified persons.

(2) Empowering inspectors in specified circumstances to require persons to submit written particulars of measures proposed to be taken to achieve compliance with any of the relevant statutory provisions.

16. Imposing requirements with respect to the keeping and preservation of records and other documents, including plans and maps.

17. Imposing requirements with respect to the management of animals.

18. The following purposes as regards premises of any specified description where persons work, namely—

(a) requiring precautions to be taken against dangers to which the premises or persons therein are or may be exposed by reason of conditions (including natural conditions) existing in the vicinity;

(b) securing that persons in the premises leave them in specified circumstances.

19. Conferring, in specified circumstances involving a risk of fire or explosion, power to search a person or any article which a person has with him for the purpose of ascertaining whether he has in his possession any article of a specified kind likely in those circumstances to cause a fire or explosion, and power to seize and dispose of any article of that kind found on such a search.

20. Restricting, prohibiting or requiring the doing of any specified thing where any accident or other occurrence of a specified kind has occurred.

21. As regards cases of any specified class, being a class such that the variety in the circumstances of particular cases within it calls for the making of special provision for particular cases, any of the following purposes, namely—

(a) conferring on employers or other persons power to make rules or give directions with respect to matters affecting health or safety;

(b) requiring employers or other persons to make rules with respect to any such matters;

(c) empowering specified persons to require employers or other persons either to make rules with respect to any such matters or to modify any such rules previously made by virtue of this paragraph; and

(d) making admissible in evidence without further proof, in such circumstances and subject to such conditions as may be specified, documents which purport to be copies of rules or rules of any specified class made under this paragraph.

22. Conferring on any local or public authority power to make byelaws with respect to any specified matter, specifying the authority or person by whom any byelaws made in the exercise of that power need to be confirmed, and generally providing for the procedure to be followed in connection with the making of any such byelaws.

Interpretation

23. (1) In this Schedule "specified" means specified in health and safety regulations.

(2) It is hereby declared that the mention in this Schedule of a purpose that falls within any more general purpose mentioned therein is without prejudice to the generality of the more general purpose.

NOTES

Para 2: words in square brackets in sub-para (2) substituted by the Customs and Excise Management Act 1979, s 177(1), Sch 4, para 12, Table, Pt I.

Regulations: see the note to s 15 at **[1.35]**.

[SCHEDULE 3A
OFFENCES: MODE OF TRIAL AND MAXIMUM PENALTY

[1.87]

1. The mode of trial and maximum penalty applicable to each offence listed in the first column of the following table are as set out opposite that offence in the subsequent columns of the table.

Offence	Mode of trial	Penalty on summary conviction	Penalty on conviction on indictment
An offence under section 33(1)(a) consisting of a failure to discharge a duty to which a person is subject by virtue of sections 2 to 6.	Summarily or on indictment.	Imprisonment for a term not exceeding 12 months, or a [fine], or both.	Imprisonment for a term not exceeding two years, or a fine, or both.
An offence under section 33(1)(a) consisting of a failure to discharge a duty to which a person is subject by virtue of section 7.	Summarily or on indictment.	Imprisonment for a term not exceeding 12 months, or a [fine], or both.	Imprisonment for a term not exceeding two years, or a fine, or both.
An offence under section 33(1)(b) consisting of a contravention of section 8.	Summarily or on indictment.	Imprisonment for a term not exceeding 12 months, or [fine], or both.	Imprisonment for a term not exceeding two years, or a fine, or both.
An offence under section 33(1)(b) consisting of a contravention of section 9.	Summarily or on indictment.	A [fine].	A fine.

Offence	Mode of trial	Penalty on summary conviction	Penalty on conviction on indictment
An offence under section 33(1)(c).	Summarily or on indictment.	Imprisonment for a term not exceeding 12 months, or a [fine], or both.	Imprisonment for a term not exceeding two years, or a fine, or both.
An offence under section 33(1)(d).	Summarily only.	A [fine].	
An offence under section 33(1)(e), (f) or (g).	Summarily or on indictment.	Imprisonment for a term not exceeding 12 months, or a [fine], or both.	Imprisonment for a term not exceeding two years, or a fine, or both.
An offence under section 33(1)(h).	Summarily only.	Imprisonment for a term not exceeding 51 weeks (in England and Wales) or 12 months (in Scotland), or a [fine], or both.	
An offence under section 33(1)(i).	Summarily or on indictment.	A [fine]	A fine.
An offence under section 33(1)(j).	Summarily or on indictment.	Imprisonment for a term not exceeding 12 months, or a [fine], or both.	Imprisonment for a term not exceeding two years, or a fine, or both.
An offence under section 33(1)(k), (l) or (m).	Summarily or on indictment.	Imprisonment for a term not exceeding 12 months, or a [fine], or both.	Imprisonment for a term not exceeding two years, or a fine, or both.
An offence under section 33(1)(n).	Summarily only.	A [fine].	
An offence under section 33(1)(o).	Summarily or on indictment.	Imprisonment for a term not exceeding 12 months, or a [fine], or both.	Imprisonment for a term not exceeding two years, or a fine, or both.
An offence under the existing statutory provisions for which no other penalty is specified.	Summarily or on indictment.	Imprisonment for a term not exceeding 12 months, or a [fine], or both.	Imprisonment for a term not exceeding two years, or a fine, or both.

2. (1) This paragraph makes transitional modifications of the table as it applies to England and Wales.

(2) In relation to an offence committed before the commencement of section 154(1) of the Criminal Justice Act 2003 (general limit on magistrates' court's powers to imprison), a reference to imprisonment for a term not exceeding 12 months is to be read as a reference to imprisonment for a term not exceeding six months.

(3) In relation to an offence committed before the commencement of section 281(5) of that Act (alteration of penalties for summary offences), a reference to imprisonment for a term not exceeding 51 weeks is to be read as a reference to imprisonment for a term not exceeding six months]

NOTES

Inserted by the Health and Safety (Offences) Act 2008, s 1(2), Sch 1.

Para 1 is amended as follows:

In rows 1, 3, 4, 5, 7, 11, 13 and 14 of the table, the word "fine" in square brackets was substituted (for the original words "fine not exceeding £20,000") by the Legal Aid, Sentencing and Punishment of Offenders Act 2012 (Fines on Summary Conviction) Regulations 2015, SI 2015/664, reg 4(1), Sch 4, Pt 1, para 7(a), in relation to England and Wales only, as from 12 March 2015 (for transitional provisions, see the final note below).

In rows 2, 9 and 10 of the table, the word "fine" in square brackets was substituted (for the original words "fine not exceeding the statutory maximum") by SI 2015/664, reg 4(1), Sch 4, Pt 1, para 7(b), in relation to England and Wales only, as from 12 March 2015 (for transitional provisions, see the final note below).

In rows 6, 8 and 12 of the table, the word "fine" in square brackets was substituted (for the original words "fine not exceeding level 5 on the standard scale") by SI 2015/664, reg 4(1), Sch 4, Pt 1, para 7(c), in relation to England and Wales only, as from 12 March 2015 (for transitional provisions, see the final note below).

The provisions of the Criminal Justice Act 2003 mentioned in paras 2(2), (3) above have not, as of 15 May 2019, come into force.

Transitional provisions: the Legal Aid, Sentencing and Punishment of Offenders Act 2012 (Fines on Summary Conviction) Regulations 2015, SI 2015/664, reg 5 provides that the 2015 Regulations do not affect (a) fines for offences committed before 12 March 2015, (b) the operation of restrictions on fines that may be imposed on a person aged under 18, or (c) fines that may be imposed on a person convicted by a magistrates' court who is to be sentenced as if convicted on indictment.

SCHEDULES 4–10

(Sch 4 repealed by the Employment Protection Act 1975, ss 116, 125(3), Sch 15, para 21, Sch 18; Schs 5, 6 repealed by the Building Act 1984, s 133(2), Sch 7; Sch 7 repealed by the Building (Scotland) Act 2003, s 58, Sch 6, para 9; Sch 8 repealed by the Regulatory Reform (Fire Safety) Order 2005, SI 2005/1541 and the Fire (Scotland) Act 2005 (Consequential Modifications and Savings) Order 2006, SSI 2006/475; Schs 9, 10 repealed by the Statute Law (Repeals) Act 1993.)

REHABILITATION OF OFFENDERS ACT 1974

(1974 c 53)

ARRANGEMENT OF SECTIONS

SCHEDULES

An Act to rehabilitate offenders who have not been reconvicted of any serious offence for periods of years, to penalise the unauthorised disclosure of their previous convictions, to amend the law of defamation, and for purposes connected therewith

[31 July 1974]

NOTES

See *Harvey* DI(9)(B)(5).

[1.88]

1 Rehabilitated persons and spent convictions

(1) Subject to [subsections (2), (5) and (6)] below, where an individual has been convicted, whether before or after the commencement of this Act, of any offence or offences, and the following conditions are satisfied, that is to say—

(a) he did not have imposed on him in respect of that conviction a sentence which is excluded from rehabilitation under this Act; and

(b) he has not had imposed on him in respect of a subsequent conviction during the rehabilitation period applicable to the first-mentioned conviction in accordance with section 6 below a sentence which is excluded from rehabilitation under this Act;

then, after the end of the rehabilitation period so applicable (including, where appropriate, any extension under section 6(4) below of the period originally applicable to the first-mentioned conviction) or, where that rehabilitation period ended before the commencement of this Act, after the commencement of this Act, that individual shall for the purposes of this Act be treated as a rehabilitated person in respect of the first-mentioned conviction and that conviction shall for those purposes be treated as spent.

(2) A person shall not become a rehabilitated person for the purposes of this Act in respect of a conviction unless he has served or otherwise undergone or complied with any sentence imposed on him in respect of that conviction; but the following shall not, by virtue of this subsection, prevent a person from becoming a rehabilitated person for those purposes—

(a) failure to pay a fine or other sum adjudged to be paid by or imposed on a conviction, or breach of a condition of a recognizance or of a bond of caution to keep the peace or be of good behaviour;

(b) breach of any condition or requirement applicable in relation to a sentence which renders the person to whom it applies liable to be dealt with for the offence for which the sentence was imposed, or, where the sentence was a suspended sentence of imprisonment, liable to be dealt with in respect of that sentence (whether or not, in any case, he is in fact so dealt with);

(c) failure to comply with any requirement of a suspended sentence supervision order;

[(2A) Where in respect of a conviction a person has been sentenced to imprisonment with an order under section 47(1) of the Criminal Law Act 1977, he is to be treated for the purposes of subsection (2) above as having served the sentence as soon as he completes service of so much of the sentence as was by that order required to be served in prison.]

[(2B) In subsection (2)(a) above the reference to a fine or other sum adjudged to be paid by or imposed on a conviction does not include a reference to an amount payable under a confiscation order made under Part 2 or 3 of the Proceeds of Crime Act 2002.]

(3) In this Act "sentence" includes any order made by a court in dealing with a person in respect of his conviction of any offence or offences, other than—

[(za) a surcharge imposed under section 161A of the Criminal Justice Act 2003;]

(a) an order for committal or any other order made in default of payment of any fine or other sum adjudged to be paid by or imposed on a conviction, or for want of sufficient distress to satisfy any such fine or other sum;

(b) an order dealing with a person in respect of a suspended sentence of imprisonment;

[(c) an order under section 21A of the Prosecution of Offences Act 1985 (criminal courts charge)].

[(3A) In subsection (3)(a), the reference to want of sufficient distress to satisfy a fine or other sum includes a reference to circumstances where—

(a) there is power to use the procedure in Schedule 12 to the Tribunals, Courts and Enforcement Act 2007 to recover the fine or other sum from a person, but

(b) it appears, after an attempt has been made to exercise the power, that the person's goods are insufficient to pay the amount outstanding (as defined by paragraph 50(3) of that Schedule).]

(4) In this Act, references to a conviction, however expressed, include references—

(a) to a conviction by or before a court outside [England, Wales and Scotland]; and

(b) to any finding (other than a finding linked with a finding of insanity [or, as the case may be, a finding that a person is not criminally responsible under section 51A of the Criminal Procedure (Scotland) Act 1995 (c 46)]) in any criminal proceedings . . . that a person has committed an offence or done the act or made the omission charged;

and notwithstanding anything in [section 247 of the Criminal Procedure (Scotland) Act 1995 (c 46)] or [section 14 of the Powers of Criminal Courts (Sentencing) Act 2000] [or section 187 of the Armed Forces Act 2006] (conviction of a person . . . discharged to be deemed not to be a conviction) a conviction in respect of which an order is made [discharging the person concerned] absolutely or conditionally shall be treated as a conviction for the purposes of this Act and the person in question may become a rehabilitated person in respect of that conviction and the conviction a spent conviction for those purposes accordingly.

[(5) This Act does not apply to any disregarded conviction or caution within the meaning of Chapter 4 of Part 5 of the Protection of Freedoms Act 2012.

(6) Accordingly, references in this Act to a conviction or caution do not include references to any such disregarded conviction or caution.]

NOTES

Sub-s (1): words in square brackets substituted by the Protection of Freedoms Act 2012, s 115(1), Sch 9, Pt 9, para 134(1), (2).

Sub-s (2A): inserted by the Criminal Law Act 1977, s 47, Sch 9, para 11.

Sub-s (2B): inserted by the Proceeds of Crime Act 2002, s 456, Sch 11, paras 1, 7.

Sub-s (3): para (za) inserted by the Domestic Violence, Crime and Victims Act 2004, s 58(1), Sch 10, para 9; para (c) added by the Criminal Justice and Courts Act 2015, s 54(3), Sch 12, para 1, as from 13 April 2015.

Sub-s (3A): inserted by the Tribunals, Courts and Enforcement Act 2007, s 62(3), Sch 13, para 38.

Sub-s (4) is amended as follows:

The words in square brackets in para (a) were substituted by virtue of the Legal Aid, Sentencing and Punishment of Offenders Act 2012, s 141(10), Sch 25, Pt 1, paras 1, 2, 12, 13.

Words in second pair of square brackets inserted by the Criminal Justice and Licensing (Scotland) Act 2010, s 203, Sch 7, paras 7, 8.

First words omitted repealed by the Children Act 1989, s 108(7), Sch 15.

Words in third pair of square brackets substituted by the Criminal Justice and Licensing (Scotland) Act 2010, s 24(1).

Words in fourth pair of square brackets substituted by the Powers of Criminal Courts (Sentencing) Act 2000, s 165(1), Sch 9, para 47.

Words in fifth pair of square brackets inserted by the Armed Forces Act 2006, s 378(1), Sch 16, para 63.

Second words omitted repealed, and words in final pair of square brackets substituted, by the Criminal Justice Act 1991, ss 100, 101(2), Sch 11, para 20, Sch 13.

Sub-ss (5), (6): added by the Protection of Freedoms Act 2012, s 115(1), Sch 9, Pt 9, para 134(1), (3).

Criminal Law Act 1977, s 47(1): repealed by the Criminal Justice Act 1991.

2, 3 *(S 2 (Rehabilitation of persons dealt with in service disciplinary proceedings), s 3 (Special provision with respect to certain disposals by children's hearings under the Social Work (Scotland) Act 1968) outside the scope of this work.)*

[1.89]

4 Effect of rehabilitation

(1) Subject to sections 7 and 8 below, a person who has become a rehabilitated person for the purposes of this Act in respect of a conviction shall be treated for all purposes in law as a person who has not committed or been charged with or prosecuted for or convicted of or sentenced for the offence or offences which were the subject of that conviction; and, notwithstanding the provisions of any other enactment or rule of law to the contrary, but subject as aforesaid—

(a) no evidence shall be admissible in any proceedings before a judicial authority exercising its jurisdiction or functions in [England, Wales or Scotland] to prove that any such person has committed or been charged with or prosecuted for or convicted of or sentenced for any offence which was the subject of a spent conviction; and

(b) a person shall not, in any such proceedings, be asked, and, if asked, shall not be required to answer, any question relating to his past which cannot be answered without acknowledging or referring to a spent conviction or spent convictions or any circumstances ancillary thereto.

(2) Subject to the provisions of any order made under subsection (4) below, where a question seeking information with respect to a person's previous convictions, offences, conduct or circumstances is put to him or to any other person otherwise than in proceedings before a judicial authority—

(a) the question shall be treated as not relating to spent convictions or to any circumstances ancillary to spent convictions, and the answer thereto may be framed accordingly; and

(b) the person questioned shall not be subjected to any liability or otherwise prejudiced in law by reason of any failure to acknowledge or disclose a spent conviction or any circumstances ancillary to a spent conviction in his answer to the question.

(3) Subject to the provisions of any order made under subsection (4) below,—

(a) any obligation imposed on any person by any rule of law or by the provisions of any agreement or arrangement to disclose any matters to any other person shall not extend to requiring him to disclose a spent conviction or any circumstances ancillary to a spent conviction (whether the conviction is his own or another's); and

(b) a conviction which has become spent or any circumstances ancillary thereto, or any failure to disclose a spent conviction or any such circumstances, shall not be a proper ground for dismissing or excluding a person from any office, profession, occupation or employment, or for prejudicing him in any way in any occupation or employment.

(4) The Secretary of State may by order—

(a) make such provision as seems to him appropriate for excluding or modifying the application of either or both of paragraphs (a) and (b) of subsection (2) above in relation to questions put in such circumstances as may be specified in the order;

(b) provide for such exceptions from the provisions of subsection (3) above as seem to him appropriate, in such cases or classes of case, and in relation to convictions of such a description, as may be specified in the order.

(5) For the purposes of this section and section 7 below any of the following are circumstances ancillary to a conviction, that is to say—

(a) the offence or offences which were the subject of that conviction;

(b) the conduct constituting that offence or those offences; and

(c) any process or proceedings preliminary to that conviction, any sentence imposed in respect of that conviction, any proceedings (whether by way of appeal or otherwise) for reviewing that conviction or any such sentence, and anything done in pursuance of or undergone in compliance with any such sentence.

(6) For the purposes of this section and section 7 below "proceedings before a judicial authority" includes, in addition to proceedings before any of the ordinary courts of law, proceedings before any tribunal, body or person having power—

(a) by virtue of any enactment, law, custom or practice;

(b) under the rules governing any association, institution, profession, occupation or employment; or

(c) under any provision of an agreement providing for arbitration with respect to questions arising thereunder;

to determine any question affecting the rights, privileges, obligations or liabilities of any person, or to receive evidence affecting the determination of any such question.

NOTES

Sub-s (1): the words in square brackets in para (a) were substituted by virtue of the Legal Aid, Sentencing and Punishment of Offenders Act 2012, s 141(10), Sch 25, Pt 1, paras 1, 5, 12, 15.

Exceptions: for exceptions to this section, see ss 7, 8 and note sub-s (4) above and the Orders listed below. See also, for restrictions on the operation of this section, the National Lottery etc Act 1993, s 19 (repealed by the Police Act 1997, ss 133(d), 134(2), Sch 10, as from a day to be appointed), the Criminal Justice Act 2003, s 327B(8), the Gambling Act 2005, s 125, and the UK Borders Act 2007, s 56A.

Secretary of State: the functions conferred by sub-s (4) are, in so far as exercisable in relation to Scotland, transferred to the Scottish Ministers, by the Scotland Act 1998 (Transfer of Functions to the Scottish Ministers etc) Order 2003, SI 2003/415, art 2, Schedule.

Orders: the main Orders made under this section are the Rehabilitation of Offenders Act 1974 (Exceptions) Order 1975, SI 1975/1023 at **[2.15]**, as amended, and the Rehabilitation of Offenders Act 1974 (Exclusions and Exceptions) (Scotland) Order 2013, SSI 2013/50 at **[2.1310]**, as amended.

[1.90]

5 Rehabilitation periods for particular sentences

(1) The sentences excluded from rehabilitation under this Act are—

(a) a sentence of imprisonment for life;

(b) a sentence of imprisonment[, youth custody] [detention in a young offender institution] or corrective training for a term exceeding [forty-eight months];

(c) a sentence of preventive detention; . . .

(d) a sentence of detention during Her Majesty's pleasure or for life [under section 90 or 91 of the Powers of Criminal Courts (Sentencing) Act 2000], [or under section 209 or 218 of the Armed Forces Act 2006,] [or under section 205(2) or (3) of the Criminal Procedure (Scotland) Act

1975,] [or a sentence of detention for a term exceeding [forty-eight months] passed under section 91 of the said Act of 2000] [or section 209 of the said Act of 2006] [(young offenders convicted of grave crimes) or under section 206 of the said Act of 1975 (detention of children convicted on indictment)] [. . .];

[(e) a sentence of custody for life][; and

(f) a sentence of imprisonment for public protection under section 225 of the Criminal Justice Act 2003, a sentence of detention for public protection under section 226 of that Act or an extended sentence under section [226A, 226B,] 227 or 228 of that Act [(including any sentence within this paragraph passed as a result of any of sections 219 to 222 of the Armed Forces Act 2006)]];

and any other sentence is a sentence subject to rehabilitation under this Act.

[(1A) In [this section]—

(a) references to section 209 of the Armed Forces Act 2006 include references to section 71A(4) of the Army Act 1955 or Air Force Act 1955 or section 43A(4) of the Naval Discipline Act 1957;

(b) the reference to section 218 of the Armed Forces Act 2006 includes a reference to section 71A(3) of the Army Act 1955 or Air Force Act 1955 or section 43A(3) of the Naval Discipline Act 1957.]

[(2) For the purposes of this Act and subject to subsections (3) and (4), the rehabilitation period for a sentence is the period—

(a) beginning with the date of the conviction in respect of which the sentence is imposed, and

(b) ending at the time listed in the following Table in relation to that sentence:

Sentence	*End of rehabilitation period for adult offenders*	*End of rehabilitation period for offenders under 18 at date of conviction*
A custodial sentence of more than 30 months and up to, or consisting of, 48 months	The end of the period of 7 years beginning with the day on which the sentence (including any licence period) is completed	The end of the period of 42 months beginning with the day on which the sentence (including any licence period) is completed
A custodial sentence of more than 6 months and up to, or consisting of, 30 months	The end of the period of 48 months beginning with the day on which the sentence (including any licence period) is completed	The end of the period of 24 months beginning with the day on which the sentence (including any licence period) is completed
A custodial sentence of 6 months or less	The end of the period of 24 months beginning with the day on which the sentence (including any licence period) is completed	The end of the period of 18 months beginning with the day on which the sentence (including any licence period) is completed
Removal from Her Majesty's service	The end of the period of 12 months beginning with the date of the conviction in respect of which the sentence is imposed	The end of the period of 6 months beginning with the date of the conviction in respect of which the sentence is imposed
A sentence of service detention	The end of the period of 12 months beginning with the day on which the sentence is completed	The end of the period of 6 months beginning with the day on which the sentence is completed
A fine	The end of the period of 12 months beginning with the date of the conviction in respect of which the sentence is imposed	The end of the period of 6 months beginning with the date of the conviction in respect of which the sentence is imposed
A compensation order	The date on which the payment is made in full	The date on which the payment is made in full
A community or youth rehabilitation order	The end of the period of 12 months beginning with the day provided for by or under the order as the last day on which the order is to have effect	The end of the period of 6 months beginning with the day provided for by or under the order as the last day on which the order is to have effect
A relevant order	The day provided for by or under the order as the last day on which the order is to have effect	The day provided for by or under the order as the last day on which the order is to have effect

(3) Where no provision is made by or under a community or youth rehabilitation order or a relevant order for the last day on which the order is to have effect, the rehabilitation period for the order is to be the period of 24 months beginning with the date of conviction.

(4) There is no rehabilitation period for—

(a) an order discharging a person absolutely for an offence, or

(b) any other sentence in respect of a conviction where the sentence is not dealt with in the Table or under subsection (3),

and, in such cases, references in this Act to any rehabilitation period are to be read as if the period of time were nil.

(5) See also—

(a) section 8AA (protection afforded to spent alternatives to prosecution), and

(b) Schedule 2 (protection for spent cautions).

(6) The Secretary of State may by order amend column 2 or 3 of the Table or the number of months for the time being specified in subsection (3).

(7) For the purposes of this section—

(a) consecutive terms of imprisonment or other custodial sentences are to be treated as a single term,

(b) terms of imprisonment or other custodial sentences which are wholly or partly concurrent (that is terms of imprisonment or other custodial sentences imposed in respect of offences of which a person was convicted in the same proceedings) are to be treated as a single term,

(c) no account is to be taken of any subsequent variation, made by a court dealing with a person in respect of a suspended sentence of imprisonment, of the term originally imposed,

(d) no account is to be taken of any subsequent variation of the day originally provided for by or under an order as the last day on which the order is to have effect,

(e) no account is to be taken of any detention or supervision ordered by a court under section 104(3) of the Powers of Criminal Courts (Sentencing) Act 2000,

(f) a sentence imposed by a court outside England and Wales is to be treated as the sentence mentioned in this section to which it most closely corresponds.

(8) In this section—

"community or youth rehabilitation order" means—

(a) a community order under section 177 of the Criminal Justice Act 2003,

(b) a service community order or overseas community order under the Armed Forces Act 2006,

(c) a youth rehabilitation order under Part 1 of the Criminal Justice and Immigration Act 2008, or

(d) any order of a kind superseded (whether directly or indirectly) by an order mentioned in paragraph (a), (b) or (c),

"custodial sentence" means—

(a) a sentence of imprisonment,

(b) a sentence of detention in a young offender institution,

(c) a sentence of Borstal training,

(d) a sentence of youth custody,

(e) a sentence of corrective training,

(f) a sentence of detention under section 91 of the Powers of Criminal Courts (Sentencing) Act 2000 or section 209 of the Armed Forces Act 2006,

(g) a detention and training order under section 100 of the Powers of Criminal Courts (Sentencing) Act 2000 or an order under section 211 of the Armed Forces Act 2006,

(h) any sentence of a kind superseded (whether directly or indirectly) by a sentence mentioned in paragraph (f) or (g),

"earlier statutory order" means—

(a) an order under section 54 of the Children and Young Persons Act 1933 committing the person convicted to custody in a remand home,

(b) an approved school order under section 57 of that Act, or

(c) any order of a kind superseded (whether directly or indirectly) by an order mentioned in any of paragraphs (c) to (e) of the definition of "relevant order" or in paragraph (a) or (b) above,

"relevant order" means—

(a) an order discharging a person conditionally for an offence,

(b) an order binding a person over to keep the peace or be of good behaviour,

(c) an order under section 1(2A) of the Street Offences Act 1959,

(d) a hospital order under Part 3 of the Mental Health Act 1983 (with or without a restriction order),

(e) a referral order under section 16 of the Powers of Criminal Courts (Sentencing) Act 2000,

(f) an earlier statutory order, or

(g) any order which imposes a disqualification, disability, prohibition or other penalty and is not otherwise dealt with in the Table or under subsection (3),

but does not include a reparation order under section 73 of the Powers of Criminal Courts (Sentencing) Act 2000,

"removal from Her Majesty's service" means a sentence of dismissal with disgrace from Her Majesty's service, a sentence of dismissal from Her Majesty's service or a sentence of cashiering or discharge with ignominy,

"sentence of imprisonment" includes a sentence of penal servitude (and "term of imprisonment" is to be read accordingly),

"sentence of service detention" means—

(a) a sentence of service detention (within the meaning given by section 374 of the Armed Forces Act 2006), or a sentence of detention corresponding to such a sentence, in respect of a conviction in service disciplinary proceedings, or

(b) any sentence of a kind superseded (whether directly or indirectly) by a sentence mentioned in paragraph (a).]

NOTES

Sub-s (1): words in first pair of square brackets in para (b) inserted by the Criminal Justice Act 1982, ss 77, 78, Sch 14, para 36; words in second pair of square brackets in para (b) inserted by the Criminal Justice Act 1988, s 123(6), Sch 8, para 9(a); words "forty eight months" in paras (b) and (d) substituted (for the original words "thirty months"), in relation to England and Wales, by the Legal Aid, Sentencing and Punishment of Offenders Act 2012, s 139(1), (2), subject to transitional provisions in s 141 thereof (as noted below); word omitted from para (c) repealed, and para (e) added, by the Criminal Justice Act 1982, ss 77, 78, Sch 14, para 36, Sch 16; words in first pair of square brackets in para (d) inserted, and words in fourth (outer) pair of square brackets substituted, by the Powers of Criminal Courts (Sentencing) Act 2000, s 165(1), Sch 9, para 48(1), (2); words in second and sixth pairs of square brackets inserted by the Armed Forces Act 2006, s 378(1), Sch 16, para 65(1), (2)(a)(i), (ii); words in third pair of square brackets in para (d) inserted, and words in seventh pair of square brackets substituted, by the Criminal Justice (Scotland) Act 1980, s 83(2), Sch 7, para 24; the words omitted from para (d) were originally inserted by the Armed Forces Act 1976, s 22, Sch 9, para 20(4), and repealed by the Armed Forces Act 2006, s 378(1), Sch 16, para 65(1), (2)(a)(iii), Sch 17; para (f) and the word immediately preceding it added by the Criminal Justice Act 2003, s 304, Sch 32, Pt 1, para 18(1), (2)(b); references in first pair of square brackets in para (f) inserted by the Legal Aid, Sentencing and Punishment of Offenders Act 2012, s 126, Sch 21, Pt 1, para 2; words in second pair of square brackets in para (f) added by the Armed Forces Act 2006, s 378(1), Sch 16, para 65(1), (2)(b).

Sub-s (1A): inserted by the Armed Forces Act 1976, s 22, Sch 9, para 20(5); substituted by the Armed Forces Act 2006, s 378(1), Sch 16, para 65(1), (3); words in square brackets substituted (for the original words "subsection (1)(d)"), in relation to England and Wales, by the Legal Aid, Sentencing and Punishment of Offenders Act 2012, s 139(1), (3), subject to transitional provisions in s 141 thereof (as noted below).

Sub-ss (2)–(8): substituted (for the original sub-ss (2), (2A), (3), (4), (4A)–(4D), (5), (6), (6A), (7)–(10), (10A), (11)), in relation to England and Wales, by the Legal Aid, Sentencing and Punishment of Offenders Act 2012, s 139(1), (4), subject to transitional provisions in s 141 thereof (as noted below). The original text (along with the amendment notes relating to the text) remains in force for Scotland, and accordingly, is set out below:

(2) For the purposes of this Act—

(a) the rehabilitation period applicable to a sentence specified in the first column of Table A below is the period specified in the second column of that Table in relation to that sentence, or, where the sentence was imposed on a person who was under [eighteen years of age] at the date of his conviction, half that period; and

(b) the rehabilitation period applicable to a sentence specified in the first column of Table B below is the period specified in the second column of that Table in relation to that sentence;

reckoned in either case from the date of the conviction in respect of which the sentence was imposed.

Table A

Rehabilitation periods subject to reduction by half for persons [under 18]

Sentence	*Rehabilitation period*
A sentence of imprisonment [detention in a young offender institution] [or youth custody] or corrective training for a term exceeding six months but not exceeding thirty months.	Ten years
A sentence of cashiering, discharge with ignominy or dismissal with disgrace from Her Majesty's service.	Ten years
A sentence of imprisonment [detention in a young offender institution] [or youth custody] for a term not exceeding six months.	Seven years
A sentence of dismissal from Her Majesty's service.	Seven years
[Any sentence of service detention within the meaning of the Armed Forces Act 2006, or any sentence of detention corresponding to such a sentence,] in respect of a conviction in service disciplinary proceedings.	Five years
A fine or any other sentence subject to rehabilitation under this Act, not being a sentence to which Table B below or any of subsections (3) [to (8)] below applies.	Five years

Table B

Rehabilitation periods for certain sentences confined to young offenders

Sentence	*Rehabilitation period*
A sentence of Borstal training.	Seven years
[A custodial order under Schedule 5A to the Army Act 1955 or the Air Force Act 1955, or under Schedule 4A to the Naval Discipline Act 1957, where the maximum period of detention specified in the order is more than six months.	Seven years]
[A custodial order under section 71AA of the Army Act 1955 or the Air Force Act 1955, or under section 43AA of the Naval Discipline Act 1957, where the maximum period of detention specified in the order is more than six months.	Seven years]
A sentence of detention for a term exceeding six months but not exceeding thirty months passed under [section 91 of the Powers of Criminal Courts (Sentencing) Act 2000] [or under section 209 of the Armed Forces Act 2006] or under section [206 of the Criminal Procedure (Scotland) Act 1975.]	Five years
A sentence of detention for a term not exceeding six months passed under [any provision mentioned in the fourth entry in this Table].	Three years
An order for detention in a detention centre made under [section 4 of the Criminal Justice Act 1982,] section 4 of the Criminal Justice Act 1961 . . .	Three years

Sentence	Rehabilitation period
[A custodial order under any of the Schedules to the said Acts of 1955 and 1957 mentioned above, where the maximum period of detention specified in the order is six months or less.	Three years]
[A custodial order under section 71AA of the said Acts of 1955, or section 43AA of the said Act of 1957, where the maximum period of detention specified in the order is six months or less.	Three years]

[(2A) Table B applies in relation to a sentence under section 71A(4) of the Army Act 1955 or Air Force Act 1955 or section 43A(4) of the Naval Discipline Act 1957 as it applies in relation to one under section 209 of the Armed Forces Act 2006.]

(3) The rehabilitation period applicable—

(a) to an order discharging a person absolutely for an offence; *and*

(b) to the discharge by a children's hearing under section [69(1)(b) and (12) of the Children (Scotland) Act 1995] of the referral of a child's case;

shall be six months from the date of conviction.

(4) Where in respect of a conviction a person was conditionally discharged, bound over to keep the peace or be of good behaviour, . . . the rehabilitation period applicable to the sentence shall be one year from the date of conviction or a period beginning with that date and ending when the order for conditional discharge . . . or (as the case may be) the recognisance or bond of caution to keep the peace or be of good behaviour ceases or ceased to have effect, whichever is the longer.

[(4A) Where in respect of a conviction [. . . [. . . a community order under section 177 of the Criminal Justice Act 2003] was made], the rehabilitation period applicable to the sentence shall be—

(a) in the case of a person aged eighteen years or over at the date of his conviction, five years from the date of conviction;

(b) in the case of a person aged under the age of eighteen years at the date of his conviction, two and a half years from the date of conviction or a period beginning with the date of conviction and ending when the [order in question] ceases or ceased to have effect, whichever is the longer.]

[(4B) Where in respect of a conviction a referral order (within the meaning of [the Powers of Criminal Courts (Sentencing) Act 2000]) is made in respect of the person convicted, the rehabilitation period applicable to the sentence shall be—

(a) if a youth offender contract takes effect under [section 23] of that Act between him and a youth offender panel, the period beginning with the date of conviction and ending on the date when (in accordance with [section 24] of that Act) the contract ceases to have effect;

(b) if no such contract so takes effect, the period beginning with the date of conviction and having the same length as the period for which such a contract would (ignoring any order under paragraph 11 or 12 of Schedule 1 to that Act) have had effect had one so taken effect.

(4C) Where in respect of a conviction an order is made in respect of the person convicted under paragraph 11 or 12 of Schedule 1 to [the Powers of Criminal Courts (Sentencing) Act 2000] (extension of period for which youth offender contract has effect), the rehabilitation period applicable to the sentence shall be—

(a) if a youth offender contract takes effect under [section 23] of that Act between the offender and a youth offender panel, the period beginning with the date of conviction and ending on the date when (in accordance with [section 24] of that Act) the contract ceases to have effect;

(b) if no such contract so takes effect, the period beginning with the date of conviction and having the same length as the period for which, in accordance with the order, such a contract would have had effect had one so taken effect.]

[(4D) The rehabilitation period applicable to an order under section 1(2A) of the Street Offences Act 1959 shall be six months from the date of conviction for the offence in respect of which the order is made.]

(5) Where in respect of a conviction any of the following sentences was imposed, that is to say—

(a) an order under section 57 of the Children and Young Persons Act 1933 or section 61 of the Children and Young Persons (Scotland) Act 1937 committing the person convicted to the care of a fit person;

(b) a supervision order under any provision of either of those Acts or of the Children and Young Persons Act 1963;

[(c) an order under section 413 of the Criminal Procedure (Scotland) Act 1975 committing a child for the purpose of his undergoing residential training;]

(d) an approved school order under section 61 of the said Act of 1937;

[(da) a youth rehabilitation order under Part 1 of the Criminal Justice and Immigration Act 2008;]

(e) . . . a supervision order under [section 63(1) of the Powers of Criminal Courts (Sentencing) Act 2000]; or

(f) a supervision requirement under any provision of the [Children (Scotland) Act 1995];

[(g) a community supervision order under Schedule 5A to the Army Act 1955 or the Air Force Act 1955, or under Schedule 4A to the Naval Discipline Act 1957;

(h) . . .]

the rehabilitation period applicable to the sentence shall be one year from the date of conviction or a period beginning with that date and ending when the order or requirement ceases or ceased to have effect, whichever is the longer.

(6) Where in respect of a conviction any of the following orders was made, that is to say—

(a) an order under section 54 of the said Act of 1933 committing the person convicted to custody in a remand home;

(b) an approved school order under section 57 of the said Act of 1933; or

(c) an attendance centre order under [section 60 of the Powers of Criminal Courts (Sentencing) Act 2000]; [or

(d) a secure training order under section 1 of the Criminal Justice and Public Order Act 1994;]

the rehabilitation period applicable to the sentence shall be a period beginning with the date of conviction and ending one year after the date on which the order ceases or ceased to have effect.

[(6A) Where in respect of a conviction a detention and training order was made under [section 100 of the Powers of Criminal Courts (Sentencing) Act 2000][, or an order under section 211 of the Armed Forces Act 2006 was made], the rehabilitation period applicable to the sentence shall be—

(a) in the case of a person aged fifteen years or over at the date of his conviction, five years if the order was, and three and a half years if the order was not, for a term exceeding six months;

(b) in the case of a person aged under fifteen years at the date of his conviction, a period beginning with that date and ending one year after the date on which the order ceases to have effect.]

(7) Where in respect of a conviction a hospital order under [Part III of the Mental Health Act 1983] or under [Part VI of the Criminal Procedure (Scotland) Act 1995] (with or without [a restriction order]) was made, the rehabilitation period applicable to the sentence shall be the period of five years from the date of conviction or a period beginning with that date and ending two years after the date on which the hospital order ceases or ceased to have effect, whichever is the longer.

(8) Where in respect of a conviction an order was made imposing on the person convicted any disqualification, disability, prohibition or other penalty, the rehabilitation period applicable to the sentence shall be a period beginning with the date of conviction and ending on the date on which the disqualification, disability, prohibition or penalty (as the case may be) ceases or ceased to have effect.

(9) For the purposes of this section—

(a) "sentence of imprisonment" includes a sentence of detention [under section 207 or 415 of the Criminal Procedure (Scotland) Act 1975] and a sentence of penal servitude, and "term of imprisonment" shall be construed accordingly;

(b) consecutive terms of imprisonment or of detention under [section 91 of the Powers of Criminal Courts (Sentencing) Act 2000] or [section 206 of the said Act of 1975] and terms which are wholly or partly concurrent (being terms of imprisonment or detention imposed in respect of offences of which a person was convicted in the same proceedings) shall be treated as a single term;

(c) no account shall be taken of any subsequent variation, made by a court in dealing with a person in respect of a suspended sentence of imprisonment, of the term originally imposed; and

(d) a sentence imposed by a court outside Great Britain shall be treated as a sentence of that one of the descriptions mentioned in this section which most nearly corresponds to the sentence imposed.

(10) References in this section to the period during which a probation order, or a . . . supervision order under [the Powers of Criminal Courts (Sentencing) Act 2000], *or a supervision requirement under the [Children (Scotland) Act 1995]*, is or was in force include references to any period during which any order or requirement to which this subsection applies, being an order or requirement made or imposed directly or indirectly in substitution for the first-mentioned order or requirement, is or was in force.

This subsection applies—

(a) to any such order or requirement as is mentioned above in this subsection;

(b) to any order having effect under section 25(2) of [the Children and Young Persons Act 1969] as if it were a training school order in Northern Ireland; and

(c) to any supervision order made under section 72(2) of the said Act of 1968 and having effect as a supervision order under the Children and Young Persons Act (Northern Ireland) 1950.

[(10A) . . .]

(11) The Secretary of State may by order—

(a) substitute different periods or terms for any of the periods or terms mentioned in subsections (1) to (8) above; and

(b) substitute a different age for the age mentioned in subsection (2)(a) above.

Sub-ss (2)–(11) as set out above were amended as follows:

Sub-s (2): words in square brackets in para (a) and in the heading to Table A substituted by the Criminal Justice Act 1991, ss 68, 101(1), Sch 8, para 5, Sch 12, para 22 (with additional effect in relation to any sentence imposed on any person who was convicted before 1 October 1992 and was aged 17 at the date of his conviction).

In Table A: words in first and third pairs of pairs of square brackets inserted by the Criminal Justice Act 1988, s 123(6), Sch 8, para 9(b); words in second and fourth pairs of square brackets inserted by the Criminal Justice Act 1982, s 77, Sch 14, para 37; words in fifth pair of square brackets substituted by the Armed Forces Act 2006, s 378(1), Sch 16, para 65(1), (4)(a); words in final pair of square brackets originally inserted by the Criminal Justice and Public Order Act 1994, s 168(1), (3), Sch 9, para 11, and substituted by the Youth Justice and Criminal Evidence Act 1999, s 67, Sch 4, para 6(1), (2).

Table B has been amended as follows—

Entry beginning with the words "A custodial order under Schedule 5A" inserted by the Armed Forces Act 1976, s 22, Sch 9, para 21(1).

Entry beginning with the words "A custodial order under section 71AA" inserted by the Armed Forces Act 1981, s 28, Sch 4, para 2.

In the entry beginning with the words "A sentence of detention for a term exceeding six months" words "section 91 of the Powers of Criminal Courts (Sentencing) Act 2000" in square brackets substituted by the Powers of Criminal Courts (Sentencing) Act 2000, s 165(1), Sch 9, para 48(1), (3); in that entry the words "or under section 209 of the Armed Forces Act 2006" in square brackets inserted by the Armed Forces Act 2006, s 378(1), Sch 16, para 65(1), (4)(b)(i); in that entry the words "206 of the Criminal Procedure (Scotland) Act 1975" in square brackets substituted by the Criminal Justice (Scotland) Act 1980, s 83(2), Sch 7, para 24.

In the entry beginning with the words "A sentence of detention for a term not exceeding six months" words in square brackets substituted by the Armed Forces Act 2006, s 378(1), Sch 16, para 65(1), (4)(b)(ii).

In the entry beginning "An order for detention in a detention centre" words "section 4 of the Criminal Justice Act 1982" in square brackets inserted by the Criminal Justice Act 1982, s 77, Sch 14, para 37; words omitted from that entry repealed by the Criminal Justice (Scotland) Act 1980, s 83(2), Sch 7, para 24.

Penultimate entry in square brackets inserted by the Armed Forces Act 1976, s 22, Sch 9, para 21(1).

Final entry in square brackets inserted by the Armed Forces Act 1981, s 28, Sch 4, para 2.

Sub-s (2A): inserted by the Armed Forces Act 2006, s 378(1), Sch 16, para 65(1), (5).

Sub-s (3): para (b) and the word immediately preceding it repealed by the Children's Hearings (Scotland) Act 2011, s 203(2), Sch 6, as from a day to be appointed; words in square brackets in para (b) substituted by the Children (Scotland) Act 1995, s 105(4), (5), Sch 4, para 23(1), (3).

Sub-s (4): words omitted repealed by the Criminal Justice and Public Order Act 1994, s 168(1), (3), Sch 9, para 11(1)(b), (2), Sch 11.

Sub-s (4A): inserted by the Criminal Justice and Public Order Act 1994, s 168(1), (3), Sch 9, para 11(1)(c), (2); words in first (outer) and fourth pairs of square brackets substituted by the Criminal Justice and Court Services Act 2000, s 74, Sch 7, Pt II, paras 48, 49; words omitted repealed by the Criminal Justice and Licensing (Scotland) Act 2010, s 1(2), Sch 2, Pt 2, para 32(1), (2) (see also SSI 2010/413, art 3 which provides that this amendment is of no effect in relation to an offence committed before 1 February 2011 or in relation to any probation order, supervised attendance order or community service order made under the

Criminal Procedure (Scotland) Act 1995); words in second (inner) pair of square brackets inserted by the Criminal Justice Act 2003, s 304, Sch 32, Pt 1, para 18(1), (3); words in third (inner) pair of square brackets inserted by the Armed Forces Act 2006, s 378(1), Sch 16, para 65(1), (6).

Sub-s (4B): inserted, together with sub-s (4C), by the Youth Justice and Criminal Evidence Act 1999, s 67, Sch 4, para 6(1), (3); words in square brackets substituted by the Powers of Criminal Courts (Sentencing) Act 2000, s 165(1), Sch 9, para 48(1), (4).

Sub-s (4C): inserted as noted above; words in square brackets substituted by the Powers of Criminal Courts (Sentencing) Act 2000, s 165(1), Sch 9, para 48(1), (5).

Sub-s (4D): inserted by the Policing and Crime Act 2009, s 18(1), (2).

Sub-s (5): para (c) substituted by the Criminal Justice (Scotland) Act 1980, s 83(2), Sch 7, para 24; para (da) inserted by the Criminal Justice and Immigration Act 2008, s 6(2), Sch 4, Pt 1, paras 20, 21; words omitted from para (e) repealed by the Children Act 1989, s 108(7), Sch 15; words in square brackets in para (e) substituted by the Powers of Criminal Courts (Sentencing) Act 2000, s 165(1), Sch 9, para 48(1), (6); para (f) repealed by the Children's Hearings (Scotland) Act 2011, s 203(2), Sch 6, as from a day to be appointed; words in square brackets in para (f) substituted by the Children (Scotland) Act 1995, s 105(4), (5), Sch 4, para 23(1), (3); paras (g), (h) added by the Armed Forces Act 1976, s 22, Sch 9, para 21(2); para (h) repealed by the Armed Forces Act 1991, s 26, Sch 3.

Sub-s (6): words in square brackets in para (c) substituted by the Powers of Criminal Courts (Sentencing) Act 2000, s 165(1), Sch 9, para 48(1), (7); para (d) and the word immediately preceding it added by the Criminal Justice and Public Order Act 1994, s 168(2), Sch 10, para 30.

Sub-s (6A): inserted by the Crime and Disorder Act 1998, s 119, Sch 8, para 35; words in first pair of square brackets substituted by the Powers of Criminal Courts (Sentencing) Act 2000, s 165(1), Sch 9, para 48(1), (8); words in second pair of square brackets inserted by the Armed Forces Act 2006, s 378(1), Sch 16, para 65(1), (7).

Sub-s (7): words in first pair of square brackets substituted by the Mental Health Act 1983, s 148, Sch 4, para 39; words in second pair of square brackets substituted by the Mental Health (Care and Treatment) (Scotland) Act 2003 (Modification of Enactments) Order 2005, SSI 2005/465, art 2, Sch 1, para 6; words in third pair of square brackets substituted by the Mental Health (Amendment) Act 1982, s 65(1), Sch 3, para 49.

Sub-s (9): words in first and fourth pairs of square brackets substituted by the Criminal Justice (Scotland) Act 1980, s 83(2), Sch 7, para 24; words in second pair of square brackets substituted by the Powers of Criminal Courts (Sentencing) Act 2000, s 165(1), Sch 9, para 48(1), (9); words in third pair of square brackets inserted by the Armed Forces Act 2006, s 378(1), Sch 16, para 65(1), (8).

Sub-s (10): words omitted repealed by the Children Act 1989, s 108(7), Sch 15; words in first and third pairs of square brackets substituted by the Powers of Criminal Courts (Sentencing) Act 2000, s 165(1), Sch 9, para 48(1), (10); words in second pair of square brackets substituted by the Children (Scotland) Act 1995, s 105(4), (5), Sch 4, para 23(1), (3), Sch 5; words in italics repealed by the Children's Hearings (Scotland) Act 2011, s 203(2), Sch 6, as from a day to be appointed.

Sub-s (10A): inserted by the Armed Forces Act 1976, s 22, Sch 9, para 21(3); repealed by the Children (Scotland) Act 1995, s 105(4), (5), Sch 4, para 23(1), (3), Sch 5.

Transitional Provisions: the Legal Aid, Sentencing and Punishment of Offenders Act 2012, s 141 provides as follows:

"141 Transitional and consequential provision

(1) Section 139 applies in relation to convictions or (as the case may be) cautions before the commencement date (as well as in relation to convictions or cautions on or after that date).

(2) The Rehabilitation of Offenders Act 1974 ("the 1974 Act") applies in relation to convictions or cautions before the commencement date as if the amendments and repeals made by section 139 had always had effect.

(3) Where by virtue of subsection (2)—

(a) a person would, before the commencement date, have been treated for the purposes of the 1974 Act as a rehabilitated person in respect of a conviction, or

(b) a conviction would, before that date, have been treated for the purposes of that Act as spent,

the person or conviction concerned is (subject to any order made by virtue of section 4(4) or 7(4) of that Act) to be so treated on and after that date.

(4) Where by virtue of subsection (2)—

(a) a person would, before the commencement date, have been treated as mentioned in paragraph 3(1) of Schedule 2 to the 1974 Act in respect of a caution, or

(b) a caution would, before that date, have been treated for the purposes of that Act as spent,

the person or caution concerned is (subject to any order made by virtue of paragraph 4 or 6(1) and (4) of that Schedule to that Act) to be so treated on and after that date.

(5) But—

(a) no person who, immediately before the commencement date—

(i) is treated as a rehabilitated person for the purposes of the 1974 Act in respect of a conviction, or

(ii) is treated as mentioned in paragraph 3(1) of Schedule 2 to that Act in respect of a caution, and

(b) no conviction or caution which, immediately before the commencement date, is treated for the purposes of that Act as spent,

is to cease to be so treated merely because of section 139.

(6) Section 139 does not apply in relation to alternatives to prosecution given before the commencement date.

(7)–(11) *(Outside the scope of this work.)*

(12) In this section "the commencement date" means such day as may be specified by order of the Secretary of State made by statutory instrument; and different days may be specified for different purposes.".

Youth custody; detention in a young offender institution: detention centre orders and youth custody sentences were amalgamated into a single custodial sentence of detention in a young offender institution by the Criminal Justice Act 1982, s 1A (repealed). As to detention in a young offender institution, see the Powers of Criminal Courts (Sentencing) Act 2000, ss 96–98 (repealed by the Criminal Justice and Court Services Act 2000, ss 74, 75, Sch 7, Pt II, paras 160, 182, Sch 8, as from a day to be appointed), and as to the abolition of this sentence, see s 61 of that Act.

Corrective training; preventive detention: these sentences were authorised in certain cases by the Criminal Justice Act 1948, s 21 (repealed) but were abolished by the Criminal Justice Act 1967, s 37(1) (repealed).

Custody for life: as to custody for life, see the Powers of Criminal Courts (Sentencing) Act 2000, ss 93–95 (repealed by the Criminal Justice and Court Services Act 2000, ss 74, 75, Sch 7, Pt II, paras 160, 182, Sch 8, as from a day to be appointed), and as to the abolition of this sentence, see s 61 of that Act.

Borstal training: borstal training was replaced by youth custody (as to which, see the note above).

Order for detention in a detention centre: see the note "Youth custody; detention in a young offender institution" above.

Probation orders: renamed community rehabilitation orders in accordance with the Criminal Justice and Court Services Act 2000, s 43. The power to make community rehabilitation orders was given by the Powers of Criminal Courts (Sentencing) Act 2000, ss 41–45 (repealed subject to savings).

Penal Servitude: the courts no longer have the power to sentence a person to penal servitude (see the Criminal Justice Act 1948, s 1(1), (2)). That section also provides that every enactment conferring power on a court to pass such sentence is to be construed as conferring the power to pass a sentence of imprisonment for a similar term.

Air Force Act 1955, Army Act 1955, Naval Discipline Act 1957: repealed by the Armed Forces Act 2006, s 378, Sch 17.

Children and Young Persons Act 1933: ss 54, 57 repealed by the Children and Young Persons Act 1969, ss 7(6), 72(4), Sch 6.

Criminal Justice Act 1961, s 4: repealed by the Criminal Justice Act 1982, s 78, Sch 16.

Criminal Justice Act 1982, s 4: repealed by the Criminal Justice Act 1988, s 170(2), Sch 16.

Criminal Justice and Public Order Act 1994, s 1: repealed by the Crime and Disorder Act 1998, ss 73(7)(b), 120(2), Sch 10.

Criminal Procedure (Scotland) Act 1975: repealed, subject to transitional provisions and savings, by the Criminal Procedure (Consequential Provisions) Act 1995, ss 4, 6, Schs 3, 5, 6.

Orders: as of 15 May 2019, no Orders had been made under this section.

[1.91]

6 The rehabilitation period applicable to a conviction

(1) Where only one sentence is imposed in respect of a conviction (not being a sentence excluded from rehabilitation under this Act) the rehabilitation period applicable to the conviction is, subject to the following provisions of this section, the period applicable to the sentence in accordance with section 5 above.

(2) Where more than one sentence is imposed in respect of a conviction (whether or not in the same proceedings) and none of the sentences imposed is excluded from rehabilitation under this Act, then, subject to the following provisions of this section, if the periods applicable to those sentences in accordance with section 5 above differ, the rehabilitation period applicable to the conviction shall be the longer or the longest (as the case may be) of those periods.

(3) Without prejudice to subsection (2) above, where in respect of a conviction a person was conditionally discharged *or [a probation order was made]* and after the end of the rehabilitation period applicable to the conviction in accordance with subsection (1) or (2) above he is dealt with, in consequence of a breach of conditional discharge *[or a breach of the order]*, for the offence for which the order for conditional discharge *or probation order* was made, then, if the rehabilitation period applicable to the conviction in accordance with subsection (2) above (taking into account any sentence imposed when he is so dealt with) ends later than the rehabilitation period previously applicable to the conviction, he shall be treated for the purposes of this Act as not having become a rehabilitated person in respect of that conviction, and the conviction shall for those purposes be treated as not having become spent, in relation to any period falling before the end of the new rehabilitation period.

[(3A) Without prejudice to subsection (2), where—

(a) an order is made under section 1(2A) of the Street Offences Act 1959 in respect of a conviction,

(b) after the end of the rehabilitation period applicable to the conviction the offender is dealt with again for the offence for which that order was made, and

(c) the rehabilitation period applicable to the conviction in accordance with subsection (2) (taking into account any sentence imposed when so dealing with the offender) ends later than the rehabilitation period previously applicable to the conviction,

the offender shall be treated for the purposes of this Act as not having become a rehabilitated person in respect of that conviction, and that conviction shall for those purposes be treated as not having become spent, in relation to any period falling before the end of the new rehabilitation period.]

(4) Subject to subsection (5) below, where during the rehabilitation period applicable to a conviction—

(a) the person convicted is convicted of a further offence; and

(b) no sentence excluded from rehabilitation under this Act is imposed on him in respect of the later conviction;

if the rehabilitation period applicable in accordance with this section to either of the convictions would end earlier than the period so applicable in relation to the other, the rehabilitation period which would (apart from this subsection) end the earlier shall be extended so as to end at the same time as the other rehabilitation period.

(5) Where the rehabilitation period applicable to a conviction is the rehabilitation period applicable [by virtue of paragraph (g) of the definition of "relevant order" in section 5(8) above] to an order imposing on a person any disqualification, disability, prohibition or other penalty, the rehabilitation period applicable to another conviction shall not by virtue of subsection (4) above be extended by reference to that period; but if any other sentence is imposed in respect of the first-mentioned conviction for which a rehabilitation period is prescribed by any other provision of section 5 above, the rehabilitation period applicable to another conviction shall, where appropriate, be extended under subsection (4) above by reference to the rehabilitation period applicable in accordance with that section to that sentence or, where more than one such sentence is imposed, by reference to the longer or longest of the periods so applicable to those sentences, as if the period in question were the rehabilitation period applicable to the first-mentioned conviction.

(6) . . . , for the purposes of subsection (4)(a) above there shall be disregarded—

(a) any conviction in England and Wales of [a summary offence or of a scheduled offence (within the meaning of [section 22 of the Magistrates' Courts Act 1980] tried summarily in pursuance of subsection (2) of that section (summary trial where value involved is small),] [or of an offence under section 17 of the Crime (Sentences) Act 1997 (breach of conditions of release supervision order);]

(b) *any conviction in Scotland of an offence which is not excluded from the jurisdiction of inferior courts of summary jurisdiction by virtue of section 4 of the Summary Jurisdiction (Scotland) Act 1954 (certain crimes not to be tried in inferior courts of summary jurisdiction);*

[(bb) *any conviction in service disciplinary proceedings for an offence listed in [Schedule 1] to this Act;] and*

(c) *any conviction by or before a court outside Great Britain of an offence in respect of conduct which, if it had taken place in any part of Great Britain, would not have constituted an offence under the law in force in that part of Great Britain.*

(7) . . .

NOTES

Sub-s (3): words in square brackets substituted by the Criminal Justice and Court Services Act 2000, s 74, Sch 7, Pt II, paras 48, 50; words in italics repealed, in relation to Scotland, by the Criminal Justice and Licensing (Scotland) Act 2010, s 1(2), Sch 2, Pt 2, para 32(1), (3) (see also SSI 2010/413, art 3 which provides that these amendments are of no effect in relation to an offence committed before 1 February 2011 or in relation to any probation order, supervised attendance order or community service order made under the Criminal Procedure (Scotland) Act 1995).

Sub-s (3A): inserted by the Policing and Crime Act 2009, s 18(1), (3).

Sub-s (5): words in square brackets substituted (for the original words "in accordance with section 5(8) above"), in relation to England and Wales, by the Legal Aid, Sentencing and Punishment of Offenders Act 2012, s 139(1), (5)(a). For transitional provisions see the note "Transitional Provisions" to s 5 of this Act at **[1.90]**.

Sub-s (6): repealed, in relation to England and Wales, by the Legal Aid, Sentencing and Punishment of Offenders Act 2012, s 139(1), (5)(b). For transitional provisions see the note "Transitional Provisions" to s 5 of this Act at **[1.90]**. See also SI 2014/423, art 3 which confirms that this repeal has effect in relation to a road traffic endorsement. Sub-s (6) remains in force in relation to Scotland. It was previously amended as follows:

Words omitted repealed, and para (bb) inserted, by the Armed Forces Act 1996, ss 13(1), (3)(a), (b), 35(2), Sch 7, Pt III; words in first (outer) pair of square brackets in para (a) substituted by the Criminal Law Act 1977, s 65(4), Sch 12, words in second (inner) square brackets in para (a) substituted by the Magistrates' Courts Act 1980, s 154, Sch 7, para 134, words in final pair of square brackets in that paragraph inserted by the Crime (Sentences) Act 1997, s 55, Sch 4, para 9(2); words in square brackets in para (bb) substituted by the Criminal Justice and Immigration Act 2008, s 49, Sch 10, paras 1, 2 (in relation to England and Wales), and by the Criminal Justice and Licensing (Scotland) Act 2010, s 203, Sch 7, paras 7, 9 (in relation to Scotland).

Sub-s (7): repealed by the Armed Forces Act 1996, s 35(2), Sch 7, Pt III.

Probation orders: see the note to s 5 at **[1.90]**.

Summary Jurisdiction (Scotland) Act 1954: repealed by the Criminal Procedure (Scotland) Act 1975, s 461(2), Sch 10, Pt I.

[1.92]

7 Limitations on rehabilitation under this Act, etc

(1) Nothing in section 4(1) above shall affect—

(a) any right of Her Majesty, by virtue of Her Royal prerogative or otherwise, to grant a free pardon, to quash any conviction or sentence, or to commute any sentence;

(b) the enforcement by any process or proceedings of any fine or other sum adjudged to be paid by or imposed on a spent conviction;

(c) the issue of any process for the purpose of proceedings in respect of any breach of a condition or requirement applicable to a sentence imposed in respect of a spent conviction; or

(d) the operation of any enactment by virtue of which, in consequence of any conviction, a person is subject, otherwise than by way of sentence, to any disqualification, disability, prohibition or other penalty the period of which extends beyond the rehabilitation period applicable in accordance with section 6 above to the conviction.

(2) Nothing in section 4(1) above shall affect the determination of any issue, or prevent the admission or requirement of any evidence, relating to a person's previous convictions or to circumstances ancillary thereto—

(a) in any criminal proceedings before a court in [England, Wales or Scotland] (including any appeal or reference in a criminal matter);

(b) in any service disciplinary proceedings or in any proceedings on appeal from any service disciplinary proceedings;

[(bb) in any proceedings under Part 2 of the Sexual Offences Act 2003, or on appeal from any such proceedings;]

[(bc) in any proceedings on an application under section 2, 4 or 5 of the Protection of Children and Prevention of Sexual Offences (Scotland) Act 2005 (asp 9) or in any appeal under section 6 of that Act;]

[(c) in any proceedings relating to adoption, the marriage of any minor, [or the formation of a civil partnership by any minor,] the exercise of the inherent jurisdiction of the High Court with respect to minors or the provision by any person of accommodation, care or schooling for minors;

(cc) in any proceedings brought under the Children Act 1989;]

[(d) in any proceedings relating to the variation or discharge of a youth rehabilitation order under Part 1 of the Criminal Justice and Immigration Act 2008, or on appeal from any such proceedings;]

(e) . . .

(f) in any proceedings in which he is a party or a witness, provided that, on the occasion when the issue or the admission or requirement of the evidence falls to be determined, he consents to the determination of the issue or, as the case may be, the admission or requirement of the evidence notwithstanding the provisions of section 4(1); [. . .

(g) . . .] [or

(h) in any proceedings brought under Part 7 of the Coroners and Justice Act 2009 (criminal memoirs etc).]

. . .

(3) If at any stage in any proceedings before a judicial authority in [England, Wales or Scotland] (not being proceedings to which, by virtue of any of paragraphs (a) to (e) of subsection (2) above or of any order for the time being in force under subsection (4) below, section 4(1) above has no application, or proceedings to which section 8 below applies) the authority is satisfied, in the light of any considerations which appear to it to be relevant (including any evidence which has been or may thereafter be put before it), that justice cannot be done in the case except by admitting or requiring evidence relating to a person's spent convictions or to circumstances ancillary thereto, that authority may admit or, as the case may be, require the evidence in question notwithstanding the provisions of subsection (1) of section 4 above, and may determine any issue to which the evidence relates in disregard, so far as necessary, of those provisions.

(4) The Secretary of State may by order exclude the application of section 4(1) above in relation to any proceedings specified in the order (other than proceedings to which section 8 below applies) to such extent and for such purposes as may be so specified.

(5) No order made by a court with respect to any person otherwise than on a conviction shall be included in any list or statement of that person's previous convictions given or made to any court which is considering how to deal with him in respect of any offence.

NOTES

Sub-s (2) is amended as follows:

Words in square brackets in para (a) substituted by virtue of the Legal Aid, Sentencing and Punishment of Offenders Act 2012, s 141(10), Sch 25, Pt 1, paras 1, 6(1), (2), 12, 16(1), (2).

Para (bb) inserted by the Crime and Disorder Act 1998, s 119, Sch 8, para 36, and substituted by the Sexual Offences Act 2003, s 139, Sch 6, para 19.

Para (bc) inserted, in relation to Scotland, by the Criminal Justice and Licensing (Scotland) Act 2010, s 104.

Paras (c), (cc) substituted, for the original para (c), in relation to England and Wales only, by the Children Act 1989, s 108(5), Sch 13, para 35(1), (2); words in square brackets in para (c) inserted by the Civil Partnership Act 2004, s 261(1), Sch 27, para 53.

Para (c) also substituted, in relation to Scotland only, by the Children (Scotland) Act 1995, s 105(4), Sch 4, para 23(1), (4)(a), as follows—

"(c) in any proceedings relating to parental responsibilities or parental rights (within the meaning of section 1(3) and section 2(4) respectively of the Children (Scotland) Act 1995), guardianship, adoption or the provision by any person of accommodation, care or schooling for children under the age of 18 years;

(cc) in any proceedings under Part II of the Children (Scotland) Act 1995;".

Para (d) substituted by the Criminal Justice and Immigration Act 2008, s 6(2), Sch 4, Pt 1, paras 20, 22.

Para (e) and final words omitted repealed by the Children (Scotland) Act 1995, s 105(4), (5), Sch 4, para 23(1), (4)(b), (c), Sch 5.

Para (g) repealed by the Banking Act 1987, s 108(2), Sch 7, Pt I.

Para (h) and the word immediately preceding it inserted, in relation to England and Wales, by the Coroners and Justice Act 2009, s 158(1).

Sub-s (3): words in square brackets substituted by virtue of the Legal Aid, Sentencing and Punishment of Offenders Act 2012, s 141(10), Sch 25, Pt 1, paras 1, 6(1), (3), 12, 16(1), (3).

Secretary of State: the functions conferred by sub-s (4) are, in so far as exercisable in relation to Scotland, transferred to the Scottish Ministers, by the Scotland Act 1998 (Transfer of Functions to the Scottish Ministers etc) Order 2003, SI 2003/415, art 2, Schedule.

Orders: the main Orders made under this section are the Rehabilitation of Offenders Act 1974 (Exceptions) Order 1975, SI 1975/1023 at **[2.15]**, as amended, and the Rehabilitation of Offenders Act 1974 (Exclusions and Exceptions) (Scotland) Order 2013, SSI 2013/50 at **[2.1310]**, as amended.

8 *((Defamation actions) outside the scope of this work.)*

[1.93]

[8A Protection afforded to spent cautions

(1) Schedule 2 to this Act (protection for spent cautions) shall have effect.

(2) In this Act "caution" means—

(a) a conditional caution, that is to say, a caution given under section 22 of the Criminal Justice Act 2003 (c 44) (conditional cautions for adults) or under section 66A of the Crime and Disorder Act 1998 (c 37) (conditional cautions for children and young persons);

(b) any other caution given to a person in England and Wales in respect of an offence which, at the time the caution is given, that person has admitted;

(c) . . .

(d) anything corresponding to a caution . . . falling within [paragraph (a) or (b)] (however described) which is given to a person in respect of an offence under the law of a country outside England and Wales [and which is not an alternative to prosecution (within the meaning of section 8AA)].]

NOTES

Inserted by the Criminal Justice and Immigration Act 2008, s 49, Sch 10, paras 1, 3.

Sub-s (2)(c) repealed, words omitted from sub-s (2)(d) repealed, and words in the first pair of square brackets in sub-s (2)(d) substituted, by the Legal Aid, Sentencing and Punishment of Offenders Act 2012, s 135(3), Sch 24, paras 1, 2.

Words in second pair of square brackets in sub-s (2)(d) inserted, in relation to England and Wales, by the Legal Aid, Sentencing and Punishment of Offenders Act 2012, s 141(10), Sch 25, Pt 1, paras 1, 8 (subject to transitional provisions as noted in the "Transitional Provisions" note to s 5 of this Act at **[1.90]**).

[1.94]
[8AA Protection afforded to spent alternatives to prosecution

(1) The following provisions of this Act apply, with the modifications specified in subsection (3), to a spent alternative to prosecution as they apply to a spent caution—

(a) section 9A (unauthorised disclosure of spent cautions), and

(b) paragraphs 2 to 6 of Schedule 2 (protection relating to spent cautions and ancillary circumstances).

(2) An alternative to prosecution becomes spent for the purposes of this Act when it becomes spent under the law of Scotland.

(3) The modifications mentioned in subsection (1) are—

(a) references to cautions are to be read as references to alternatives to prosecution (and references to cautioned are to be read accordingly),

(b) references to the offence which was the subject of the caution are to be read as references to the offence in respect of which the alternative to prosecution was given,

(c) paragraphs (e) and (f) of paragraph 2(1) of Schedule 2 are to be read as if they were—

"(e) anything done or undergone in pursuance of the terms of the alternative to prosecution,",

(d) references to cautions for an offence are to be read as references to alternatives to prosecution in respect of an offence, and

(e) the reference in paragraph 5 of Schedule 2 to the rehabilitation period applicable to the caution is to be read as a reference to the time at which the alternative to prosecution becomes spent.

(4) In this section "alternative to prosecution" has the same meaning as in section 8B as that section has effect in the law of Scotland but disregarding subsection (1)(f) of that section.]

NOTES

Inserted, in relation to England and Wales, by the Legal Aid, Sentencing and Punishment of Offenders Act 2012, s 139(1), (6) (subject to transitional provisions as noted in the "Transitional Provisions" note to s 5 of this Act at **[1.90]**).

[1.95]
[8B Protection afforded to spent alternatives to prosecution: Scotland

(1) For the purposes of this Act, a person has been given an alternative to prosecution in respect of an offence if the person (whether before or after the commencement of this section)—

(a) has been given a warning in respect of the offence by—

(i) a constable in Scotland, or

(ii) a procurator fiscal,

(b) has accepted, or is deemed to have accepted—

(i) a conditional offer issued in respect of the offence under section 302 of the Criminal Procedure (Scotland) Act 1995 (c 46), or

(ii) a compensation offer issued in respect of the offence under section 302A of that Act,

(c) has had a work order made against the person in respect of the offence under section 303ZA of that Act,

[(ca) has, under subsection (5) of section 20A of the Nature Conservation (Scotland) Act 2004 (asp 6), given notice of intention to comply with a restoration notice given under subsection (4) of that section,]]

(d) has been given a fixed penalty notice in respect of the offence under section 129 of the Antisocial Behaviour etc (Scotland) Act 2004 (asp 8),

(e) has accepted an offer made by a procurator fiscal in respect of the offence to undertake an activity or treatment or to receive services or do any other thing as an alternative to prosecution, or

(f) in respect of an offence under the law of a country or territory outside Scotland, has been given, or has accepted or is deemed to have accepted, anything corresponding to a warning, offer, order or notice falling within paragraphs (a) to (e) under the law of that country or territory.

[(1A) For the purposes of this Act, a person has also been given an alternative to prosecution in respect of an offence if (whether before or after the commencement of this section) in proceedings before a children's hearing to which subsection (1B) applies—

(a) a compulsory supervision order (as defined in section 83 of the 2011 Act) has been made or, as the case may be, varied or continued in relation to the person, or

(b) the referral to the children's hearing has been discharged (whether wholly or in relation to the ground that the person committed the offence).

(1B) This subsection applies to proceedings if the proceedings were taken in relation to the person on the ground (whether alone or with other grounds) that the person had committed the offence and—

(a) the ground was accepted for the purposes of the 2011 Act by—

(i) the person, and

(ii) any person who was a relevant person as respects those proceedings, or

(b) the ground was established or treated as established for the purposes of the 2011 Act.

(1C) In subsections (1A) and (1B)—

"the 2011 Act" means the Children's Hearings (Scotland) Act 2011, "relevant person"—

(a) has the meaning given by section 200 of the 2011 Act, and

(b) includes a person who was deemed to be a relevant person by virtue of section 81(3), 160(4)(b) or 164(6) of that Act.

(1D) For the purposes of this Act, a person has also been given an alternative to prosecution in respect of an offence if (whether before or after the commencement of this section) in proceedings before a children's hearing to which subsection (1E) applies—

(a) a supervision requirement has been made or, as the case may be, varied or continued under the Children (Scotland) Act 1995 ("the 1995 Act") in relation to the person, or

(b) the referral to the children's hearing has been discharged (whether wholly or in relation to the ground that the person committed the offence).

(1E) This subsection applies to proceedings if the proceedings were taken in relation to the person on the ground (whether alone or with other grounds) that the person had committed the offence and—

(a) the ground was accepted for the purposes of the 1995 Act by the person and, where necessary, the relevant person (as defined in section 93(2) of that Act), or

(b) the ground was established, or deemed to have been established, for the purposes of that Act.]

(2) In this Act, references to an "alternative to prosecution" are to be read in accordance with *subsection (1)*.

(3) Schedule 3 to this Act (protection for spent alternatives to prosecution: Scotland) has effect.]

NOTES

Inserted, in relation to Scotland, by the Criminal Justice and Licensing (Scotland) Act 2010, s 109(1), (2).

Sub-s (1): para (ca) inserted by the Wildlife and Natural Environment (Scotland) Act 2011, s 40(2).

Sub-ss (1A)–(1E): inserted by the Children's Hearings (Scotland) Act 2011, s 187(1), (2)(a), as from a day to be appointed.

Sub-s (2): for the words in italics there are substituted the words "subsections (1), (1A) and (1D)" by the Children's Hearings (Scotland) Act 2011, s 187(1), (2)(b), as from a day to be appointed.

[1.96]

9 Unauthorised disclosure of spent convictions

(1) In this section—

"official record" means a record kept for the purposes of its functions by any court, police force, Government department, local or other public authority in Great Britain, or a record kept, in Great Britain or elsewhere, for the purposes of any of Her Majesty's forces, being in either case a record containing information about persons convicted of offences; and

"specified information" means information imputing that a named or otherwise identifiable rehabilitated living person has committed or been charged with or prosecuted for or convicted of or sentenced for any offence which is the subject of a spent conviction.

(2) Subject to the provisions of any order made under subsection (5) below, any person who, in the course of his official duties, has or at any time has had custody of or access to any official record or the information contained therein, shall be guilty of an offence if, knowing or having reasonable cause to suspect that any specified information he has obtained in the course of those duties is specified information, he discloses it, otherwise than in the course of those duties, to another person.

(3) In any proceedings for an offence under subsection (2) above it shall be a defence for the defendant . . . to show that the disclosure was made—

(a) to the rehabilitated person or to another person at the express request of the rehabilitated person; or

(b) to a person whom he reasonably believed to be the rehabilitated person or to another person at the express request of a person whom he reasonably believed to be the rehabilitated person.

(4) Any person who obtains any specified information from any official record by means of any fraud, dishonesty or bribe shall be guilty of an offence.

(5) The Secretary of State may by order make such provision as appears to him to be appropriate for excepting the disclosure of specified information derived from an official record from the provisions of subsection (2) above in such cases or classes of case as may be specified in the order.

(6) Any person guilty of an offence under subsection (2) above shall be liable on summary conviction to a fine not exceeding [level 4 on the standard scale].

(7) Any person guilty of an offence under subsection (4) above shall be liable on summary conviction to a fine not exceeding [level 5 on the standard scale] or to imprisonment for a term not exceeding six months, or to both.

(8) Proceedings for an offence under subsection (2) above shall not . . . be instituted except by or on behalf of the Director of Public Prosecutions.

NOTES

Sub-s (3): words omitted repealed, in relation to England and Wales, by the Legal Aid, Sentencing and Punishment of Offenders Act 2012, s 141(10), Sch 25, Pt 1, paras 1, 9(1), (2) (subject to transitional provisions as noted in the "Transitional Provisions" note to s 5 of this Act at **[1.90]**).

As it applies in relation to Scotland (and as amended by the Legal Aid, Sentencing and Punishment of Offenders Act 2012, s 141(10), Sch 25, Pt 1, paras 12, 17(1), (2)), sub-s (3) is set out below:

"(3) In any proceedings for an offence under subsection (2) above it shall be a defence for the [accused person] to show that the disclosure was made—

(a) to the rehabilitated person or to another person at the express request of the rehabilitated person; or

(b) to a person whom he reasonably believed to be the rehabilitated person or to another person at the express request of a person whom he reasonably believed to be the rehabilitated person.".

Sub-ss (6), (7): maximum fines increased and converted to levels on the standard scale by the Criminal Justice Act 1982, ss 37, 38, 46.

Sub-s (8): words omitted repealed, in relation to England and Wales, by the Legal Aid, Sentencing and Punishment of Offenders Act 2012, s 141(10), Sch 25, Pt 1, paras 1, 9(1), (3) (subject to transitional provisions as noted in the "Transitional Provisions" note to s 5 of this Act at **[1.90]**). In relation to Scotland, the whole of sub-s (8) was repealed by the Legal Aid, Sentencing and Punishment of Offenders Act 2012, s 141(10), Sch 25, Pt 1, paras 12, 17(1), (3).

Orders: as of 15 May 2019, no Orders had been made under this section.

[1.97]

[9A Unauthorised disclosure of spent cautions

(1) In this section—

(a) "official record" means a record which—

(i) contains information about persons given a caution for any offence or offences; and

(ii) is kept for the purposes of its functions by any court, police force, Government department or other public authority in England and Wales;

(b) "caution information" means information imputing that a named or otherwise identifiable living person ("the named person") has committed, been charged with or prosecuted or cautioned for any offence which is the subject of a spent caution; and

(c) "relevant person" means any person who, in the course of his official duties (anywhere in the United Kingdom), has or at any time has had custody of or access to any official record or the information contained in it.

(2) Subject to the terms of any order made under subsection (5), a relevant person shall be guilty of an offence if, knowing or having reasonable cause to suspect that any caution information he has obtained in the course of his official duties is caution information, he discloses it, otherwise than in the course of those duties, to another person.

(3) In any proceedings for an offence under subsection (2) it shall be a defence for the defendant to show that the disclosure was made—

(a) to the named person or to another person at the express request of the named person;

(b) to a person whom he reasonably believed to be the named person or to another person at the express request of a person whom he reasonably believed to be the named person.

(4) Any person who obtains any caution information from any official record by means of any fraud, dishonesty or bribe shall be guilty of an offence.

(5) The Secretary of State may by order make such provision as appears to him to be appropriate for excepting the disclosure of caution information derived from an official record from the provisions of subsection (2) in such cases or classes of case as may be specified in the order.

(6) A person guilty of an offence under subsection (2) is liable on summary conviction to a fine not exceeding level 4 on the standard scale.

(7) A person guilty of an offence under subsection (4) is liable on summary conviction to a fine not exceeding level 5 on the standard scale, or to imprisonment for a term not exceeding 51 weeks, or to both.

(8) Proceedings for an offence under subsection (2) shall not be instituted except by or on behalf of the Director of Public Prosecutions.]

NOTES

Inserted, in relation to England and Wales only, by the Criminal Justice and Immigration Act 2008, s 49, Sch 10, paras 1, 4; for transitional provisions see the note below.

Transitional provisions: Sch 27, Pt 4, para 20 to the Criminal Justice and Immigration Act 2008 provides that in the application of sub-s (7) above to offences committed before the commencement of section 281(5) of the Criminal Justice Act 2003, the reference to 51 weeks is to be read as a reference to 6 months. Note that as of 15 May 2019, s 281(5) of the 2003 Act had not been brought into force.

Orders: as of 15 May 2019, no Orders had been made under this section.

[1.98]

[9B Unauthorised disclosure of spent alternatives to prosecution: Scotland

(1) In this section—

(a) "official record" means a record that—

(i) contains information about persons given an alternative to prosecution in respect of an offence, and

(ii) is kept for the purposes of its functions by a court, [the Police Service of Scotland or another] police force, Government department, part of the Scottish Administration or other local or public authority in Scotland,

(b) "relevant information" means information imputing that a named or otherwise identifiable living person has committed, been charged with, prosecuted for or given an alternative to prosecution in respect of an offence which is the subject of an alternative to prosecution which has become spent,

(c) "subject of the information", in relation to relevant information, means the named or otherwise identifiable living person to whom the information relates.

(2) Subsection (3) applies to a person who, in the course of the person's official duties (anywhere in the United Kingdom), has or has had custody of or access to an official record or the information contained in an official record.

(3) The person commits an offence if the person—

(a) obtains relevant information in the course of the person's official duties,

(b) knows or has reasonable cause to suspect that the information is relevant information, and

(c) discloses the information to another person otherwise than in the course of the person's official duties.

(4) Subsection (3) is subject to the terms of an order under subsection (6).

(5) In proceedings for an offence under subsection (3), it is a defence for the accused to show that the disclosure was made—

(a) to the subject of the information or to a person whom the accused reasonably believed to be the subject of the information, or

(b) to another person at the express request of the subject of the information or of a person whom the accused reasonably believed to be the subject of the information.

(6) The Scottish Ministers may by order provide for the disclosure of relevant information derived from an official record to be excepted from the provisions of subsection (3) in cases or classes of cases specified in the order.

(7) A person guilty of an offence under subsection (3) is liable on summary conviction to a fine not exceeding level 4 on the standard scale.

(8) A person commits an offence if the person obtains relevant information from an official record by means of fraud, dishonesty or bribery.

(9) A person guilty of an offence under subsection (8) is liable on summary conviction to a fine not exceeding level 5 on the standard scale, or to imprisonment for a term not exceeding 6 months, or to both.]

NOTES

Inserted, in relation to Scotland, by the Criminal Justice and Licensing (Scotland) Act 2010, s 109(1), (3).

Sub-s (1): words in square brackets in para (a)(ii) inserted by the Police and Fire Reform (Scotland) Act 2012, s 128(1), Sch 7, Pt 1, para 3.

Orders: as of 15 May 2019, no Orders had been made under this section.

[1.99]

10 Orders

(1) Any power of the Secretary of State to make an order under any provision of this Act shall be exercisable by statutory instrument, and an order made under any provision of this Act except section 11 below may be varied or revoked by a subsequent order made under that provision.

[(1A) Any power of the Secretary of State to make an order under any provision of this Act includes power—

(a) to make different provision for different purposes, and

(b) to make incidental, consequential, supplementary, transitional, transitory or saving provision.

(1B) The power of the Secretary of State to make an order under section 5(6) includes power to make consequential provision which amends or repeals any provision of this Act or any other enactment.]

(2) No order shall be made by the Secretary of State under any provision of this Act other than section 11 below unless a draft of it has been laid before, and approved by resolution of, each House of Parliament.

NOTES

Sub-ss (1A), (1B): inserted, in relation to England and Wales, by the Legal Aid, Sentencing and Punishment of Offenders Act 2012, s 141(10), Sch 25, Pt 1, paras 1, 10 (subject to transitional provisions as noted in the "Transitional Provisions" note to s 5 of this Act at **[1.90]**).

[1.100]

11 Citation, commencement and extent

(1) This Act may be cited as the Rehabilitation of Offenders Act 1974.

(2) This Act shall come into force on 1st July 1975 or such earlier day as the Secretary of State may by order appoint.

(3) This Act shall not apply to Northern Ireland.

SCHEDULES

[SCHEDULE [1]
SERVICE DISCIPLINARY CONVICTIONS

Section 6(4)

[1.101]

1. Any conviction for an offence mentioned in this Schedule is a conviction referred to in section 6(6)(bb) of this Act (convictions to be disregarded for the purposes of extending a period of rehabilitation following subsequent conviction).

Provisions of the Army Act 1955 and the Air Force Act 1955

2. Any offence under any of the provisions of the Army Act 1955 or the Air Force Act 1955 listed in the first column of the following table—

Provision	*Subject-matter*
Section 29	*Offences by or in relation to sentries, persons on watch etc.*
Section 29A	*Failure to attend for duty, neglect of duty etc.*
Section 33	*Insubordinate behaviour.*

Provision	*Subject-matter*
Section 34	*Disobedience to lawful commands.*
Section 34A	*Failure to provide a sample for drug testing.*
Section 35	*Obstruction of provost officers.*
Section 36	*Disobedience to standing orders.*
Section 38	*Absence without leave.*
Section 39	*Failure to report or apprehend deserters or absentees.*
Section 42	*Malingering.*
Section 43	*Drunkenness.*
Section 43A	*Fighting, threatening words etc.*
Section 44	*Damage to, and loss of, public or service property etc.*
Section 44A	*Damage to, and loss of, Her Majesty's aircraft or aircraft material.*
Section 44B	*Interference etc with equipment, messages or signals.*
Section 45	*Misapplication and waste of public or service property.*
Section 46	*Offences relating to issues and decorations.*
Section 47	*Billeting offences.*
Section 48	*Offences in relation to requisitioning of vehicles.*
Section 50	*Inaccurate certification.*
Section 51	*Low flying.*
Section 52	*Annoyance by flying.*
Section 54	*Permitting escape, and unlawful release of prisoners.*
Section 55	*Resistance to arrest.*
Section 56	*Escape from confinement.*
Section 57	*Offences in relation to courts-martial.*
Section 61	*Making of false statements on enlistment.*
Section 62	*Making of false documents.*
Section 63	*Offences against civilian population.*
Section 69	*Conduct to prejudice of military discipline or air-force discipline.*

3. *Any offence under section 68 (attempt to commit military offence) or 68A (aiding and abetting etc, and inciting, military offence) of the Army Act 1955 in relation to an offence under any of the provisions of that Act listed in paragraph 2.*

4. *Any offence under section 68 (attempt to commit air-force offence) or 68A (aiding and abetting etc, and inciting, air-force offence) of the Air Force Act 1955 in relation to an offence under any of the provisions of that Act listed in paragraph 2.*

Provisions of the Naval Discipline Act 1957

5. *Any offence under any of the provisions of the Naval Discipline Act 1957 listed in the first column of the following table:—*

Provision	*Subject-matter*
Section 6	*Offences by or in relation to sentries, persons on watch etc.*
Section 7	*Failure to attend for duty, neglect of duty etc.*
Section 11	*Insubordinate behaviour.*
Section 12	*Disobedience to lawful commands.*
Section 12A	*Failure to provide a sample for drug testing.*
Section 13	*Fighting, threatening words etc.*
Section 14	*Obstruction of provost officers.*
Section 14A	*Disobedience to standing orders.*
Section 17	*Absence without leave etc.*
Section 18	*Failure to report deserters and absentees.*
Section 21	*Low flying.*
Section 22	*Annoyance by flying.*
Section 25	*Inaccurate certification.*
Section 27	*Malingering.*
Section 28	*Drunkenness.*

Provision	*Subject-matter*
Section 29	*Damage to, and loss of, public or service property etc.*
Section 29A	*Damage to, and loss of, Her Majesty's aircraft or aircraft material.*
Section 29B	*Interference etc with equipment, messages or signals.*
Section 30	*Misapplication and waste of public or service property.*
Section 31	*Offences relating to issues and decorations.*
Section 32	*Billeting offences.*
Section 33	*Offences in relation to the requisitioning of vehicles etc.*
Section 33A	*Permitting escape, and unlawful release of prisoners.*
Section 33B	*Resistance to arrest.*
Section 33C	*Escape from confinement.*
Section 34A	*False statements on entry.*
Section 35	*Falsification of documents.*
Section 35A	*Offences against civilian population.*
Section 38	*Offences in relation to courts-martial.*
Section 39	*Conduct to the prejudice of naval discipline.*

6. Any offence under section 40 (attempt to commit naval offence) or 41 (aiding and abetting etc, and inciting, naval offence) of the Naval Discipline Act 1957 in relation to an offence under any of the provisions of that Act listed in paragraph 5.

[Provisions of the Armed Forces Act 2006

7. Any service offence within the meaning of the Armed Forces Act 2006 except one punishable in the case of an offender aged 18 or over with imprisonment for more than two years.]]

NOTES

Added by the Armed Forces Act 1996, s 13(1), (4), Sch 4.

Numbered as Schedule 1 by the Criminal Justice and Licensing (Scotland) Act 2010, s 203, Sch 7, paras 7, 10 (in relation to Scotland). Note that this Schedule was also numbered as Schedule 1, in relation to England and Wales, by the Criminal Justice and Immigration Act 2008, s 49, Sch 10, paras 1, 5.

This Schedule was repealed, in relation to England and Wales, by the Legal Aid, Sentencing and Punishment of Offenders Act 2012, s 141(10), Sch 25, Pt 1, paras 1, 11 (subject to transitional provisions as noted in the "Transitional Provisions" note to s 5 of this Act at **[1.90]**), but remains in force for Scotland.

Para 7: added by the Armed Forces Act 2006, s 378(1), Sch 16, para 66.

Note that Sch 4 to the Armed Forces Act 1996 indicated that s 6(4) of this Act is the enabling provision for this Schedule. However, that provision makes no reference to this Schedule and it is assumed that s 6(6)(bb) is actually the enabling provision of this Schedule.

Air Force Act 1955, Army Act 1955, Naval Discipline Act 1957: repealed by the Armed Forces Act 2006, s 378, Sch 17.

[SCHEDULE 2
PROTECTION FOR SPENT CAUTIONS

Preliminary

[1.102]

1. (1) For the purposes of this Schedule a caution shall be regarded as a spent caution—

(a) in the case of a conditional caution (as defined in section 8A(2)(a))[—

(i) at the end of the period of three months from the date on which the caution is given, or

(ii) if earlier, when the caution ceases to have effect; and]

(b) in any other case, at the time the caution is given.

(2), (3) . . .

2. (1) In this Schedule "ancillary circumstances", in relation to a caution, means any circumstances of the following—

(a) the offence which was the subject of the caution or the conduct constituting that offence;

(b) any process preliminary to the caution (including consideration by any person of how to deal with that offence and the procedure for giving the caution);

(c) any proceedings for that offence which take place before the caution is given (including anything which happens after that time for the purpose of bringing the proceedings to an end);

(d) any judicial review proceedings relating to the caution;

(e) in the case of a [youth caution given under section 66ZA] of the Crime and Disorder Act 1998 (c 37), anything done in pursuance of or undergone in compliance with a requirement to participate in a rehabilitation programme under section [66ZB(2) or (3)] of that Act;

(f) in the case of a conditional caution, any conditions attached to the caution or anything done in pursuance of or undergone in compliance with those conditions.

(2) Where the caution relates to two or more offences, references in sub-paragraph (1) to the offence which was the subject of the caution include a reference to each of the offences concerned.

(3) In this Schedule "proceedings before a judicial authority" has the same meaning as in section 4.

Protection relating to spent cautions and ancillary circumstances

3. (1) A person who is given a caution for an offence shall, from the time the caution is spent, be treated for all purposes in law as a person who has not committed, been charged with or prosecuted for, or been given a caution for the offence; and notwithstanding the provisions of any other enactment or rule of law to the contrary—

(a) no evidence shall be admissible in any proceedings before a judicial authority exercising its jurisdiction or functions in England and Wales to prove that any such person has committed, been charged with or prosecuted for, or been given a caution for the offence; and

(b) a person shall not, in any such proceedings, be asked and, if asked, shall not be required to answer, any question relating to his past which cannot be answered without acknowledging or referring to a spent caution or any ancillary circumstances.

(2) Nothing in sub-paragraph (1) applies in relation to any proceedings for the offence which are not part of the ancillary circumstances relating to the caution.

(3) Where a question seeking information with respect to a person's previous cautions, offences, conduct or circumstances is put to him or to any other person otherwise than in proceedings before a judicial authority—

(a) the question shall be treated as not relating to spent cautions or to any ancillary circumstances, and the answer may be framed accordingly; and

(b) the person questioned shall not be subjected to any liability or otherwise prejudiced in law by reason of any failure to acknowledge or disclose a spent caution or any ancillary circumstances in his answer to the question.

(4) Any obligation imposed on any person by any rule of law or by the provisions of any agreement or arrangement to disclose any matters to any other person shall not extend to requiring him to disclose a spent caution or any ancillary circumstances (whether the caution is his own or another's).

(5) A caution which has become spent or any ancillary circumstances, or any failure to disclose such a caution or any such circumstances, shall not be a proper ground for dismissing or excluding a person from any office, profession, occupation or employment, or for prejudicing him in any way in any occupation or employment.

(6) This paragraph has effect subject to paragraphs 4 to 6.

4. The Secretary of State may by order—

(a) make provision for excluding or modifying the application of either or both of paragraphs (a) or (b) of paragraph 3(3) in relation to questions put in such circumstances as may be specified in the order;

(b) provide for exceptions from the provisions of sub-paragraphs (4) and (5) of paragraph 3, in such cases or classes of case, and in relation to cautions of such a description, as may be specified in the order.

5. Nothing in paragraph 3 affects—

(a) the operation of the caution in question; or

(b) the operation of any enactment by virtue of which, in consequence of any caution, a person is subject to any disqualification, disability, prohibition or other restriction or effect, the period of which extends beyond the rehabilitation period applicable to the caution.

6. (1) Section 7(2), (3) and (4) apply for the purposes of this Schedule as follows.

(2) Subsection (2) (apart from paragraphs (b) and (d)) applies to the determination of any issue, and the admission or requirement of any evidence, relating to a person's previous cautions or to ancillary circumstances as it applies to matters relating to a person's previous convictions and circumstances ancillary thereto.

(3) Subsection (3) applies to evidence of a person's previous cautions and ancillary circumstances as it applies to evidence of a person's convictions and the circumstances ancillary thereto; and for this purpose subsection (3) shall have effect as if—

(a) any reference to subsection (2) or (4) of section 7 were a reference to that subsection as applied by this paragraph; and

(b) the words "or proceedings to which section 8 below applies" were omitted.

(4) Subsection (4) applies for the purpose of excluding the application of paragraph 3(1); and for that purpose subsection (4) shall have effect as if the words " (other than proceedings to which section 8 below applies)" were omitted.

(5) References in the provisions applied by this paragraph to section 4(1) are to be read as references to paragraph 3(1).]

NOTES

Inserted, in relation to England and Wales only, by the Criminal Justice and Immigration Act 2008, s 49, Sch 10, paras 1, 6.

Para 1 is amended as follows:

Words in square brackets in sub-para (1)(a) substituted by the Legal Aid, Sentencing and Punishment of Offenders Act 2012, s 139(1), (7)(a) (subject to transitional provisions as noted in the "Transitional Provisions" note to s 5 of this Act at **[1.90]**).

Sub-paras (2), (3), repealed by the Legal Aid, Sentencing and Punishment of Offenders Act 2012, s 139(1), (7)(b) (subject to transitional provisions as noted in the "Transitional Provisions" note to s 5 of this Act at **[1.90]**).

Para 2: words in square brackets in sub-para (1)(e) substituted by the Legal Aid, Sentencing and Punishment of Offenders Act 2012, s 135(3), Sch 24, paras 1, 3.

Orders: Orders made under this Schedule amend the Rehabilitation of Offenders Act 1974 (Exceptions) Order 1975, SI 1975/1023 at **[2.15]**.

[SCHEDULE 3
PROTECTION FOR SPENT ALTERNATIVES TO PROSECUTION: SCOTLAND

(introduced by section 8B(3))

Preliminary

[1.103]

1. (1) For the purposes of this Act, an alternative to prosecution given to any person (whether before or after the commencement of this Schedule) becomes spent—

(a) in the case of—

(i) a warning referred to in paragraph (a) of subsection (1) of section 8B, or

(ii) a fixed penalty notice referred to in paragraph (d) of that subsection,

at the time the warning or notice is given,

[(aa) in the case of—

(i) a compulsory supervision order referred to in paragraph (a) of subsection (1A) of that section, the period of 3 months beginning on the day the compulsory supervision order is made or, as the case may be, varied or continued, or

(ii) a discharge referred to in paragraph (b) of subsection (1A) of that section, the period of 3 months beginning on the day of the discharge,

(ab) in the case of—

(i) a supervision requirement referred to in paragraph (a) of subsection (1D) of that section, the period of 3 months beginning on the day the supervision requirement is made or, as the case may be, varied or continued, or

(ii) a discharge referred to in paragraph (b) of subsection (1D) of that section, the period of 3 months beginning on the day of the discharge,]

(b) in any other case, at the end of the relevant period.

(2) The relevant period in relation to an alternative to prosecution is the period of 3 months beginning on the day on which the alternative to prosecution is given.

(3) Sub-paragraph (1)(a) is subject to sub-paragraph (5).

(4) Sub-paragraph (2) is subject to sub-paragraph (6).

(5) If a person who is given a fixed penalty notice referred to in section 8B(1)(d) in respect of an offence is subsequently prosecuted and convicted of the offence, the notice—

(a) becomes spent at the end of the rehabilitation period for the offence, and

(b) is to be treated as not having become spent in relation to any period before the end of that rehabilitation period.

(6) If a person who is given an alternative to prosecution (other than one to which sub-paragraph (1)(a) applies) in respect of an offence is subsequently prosecuted and convicted of the offence—

(a) the relevant period in relation to the alternative to prosecution ends at the same time as the rehabilitation period for the offence ends, and

(b) if the conviction occurs after the end of the period referred to in sub-paragraph (2), the alternative to prosecution is to be treated as not having become spent in relation to any period before the end of the rehabilitation period for the offence.

2. (1) In this Schedule, "ancillary circumstances", in relation to an alternative to prosecution, means any circumstances of the following—

(a) the offence in respect of which the alternative to prosecution is given or the conduct constituting the offence,

(b) any process preliminary to the alternative to prosecution being given (including consideration by any person of how to deal with the offence and the procedure for giving the alternative to prosecution),

(c) any proceedings for the offence which took place before the alternative to prosecution was given (including anything that happens after that time for the purpose of bringing the proceedings to an end),

(d) any judicial review proceedings relating to the alternative to prosecution,

(e) anything done or undergone in pursuance of the terms of the alternative to prosecution.

(2) Where an alternative to prosecution is given in respect of two or more offences, references in sub-paragraph (1) to the offence in respect of which the alternative to prosecution is given includes a reference to each of the offences.

(3) In this Schedule, "proceedings before a judicial authority" has the same meaning as in section 4.

Protection for spent alternatives to prosecution and ancillary circumstances

3. (1) A person who is given an alternative to prosecution in respect of an offence is, from the time the alternative to prosecution becomes spent, to be treated for all purposes in law as a person who has not committed, been charged with or prosecuted for, or been given an alternative to prosecution in respect of, the offence.

(2) Despite any enactment or rule of law to the contrary—

(a) where an alternative to prosecution given to a person in respect of an offence has become spent, evidence is not admissible in any proceedings before a judicial authority exercising its jurisdiction or functions in Scotland to prove that the person has committed, been charged with or prosecuted for, or been given an alternative to prosecution in respect of, the offence,

(b) a person must not, in any such proceedings, be asked any question relating to the person's past which cannot be answered without acknowledging or referring to an alternative to prosecution that has become spent or any ancillary circumstances, and

(c) if a person is asked such a question in any such proceedings, the person is not required to answer it.

(3) Sub-paragraphs (1) and (2) do not apply in relation to any proceedings—

(a) for the offence in respect of which the alternative to prosecution was given, and

(b) which are not part of the ancillary circumstances.

4. (1) This paragraph applies where a person ("A") is asked a question, otherwise than in proceedings before a judicial authority, seeking information about—

(a) A's or another person's previous conduct or circumstances,

(b) offences previously committed by A or the other person, or

(c) alternatives to prosecution previously given to A or the other person.

(2) The question is to be treated as not relating to alternatives to prosecution that have become spent or to any ancillary circumstances and may be answered accordingly.

(3) A is not to be subjected to any liability or otherwise prejudiced in law because of a failure to acknowledge or disclose an alternative to prosecution that has become spent or any ancillary circumstances in answering the question.

5. (1) An obligation imposed on a person ("A") by a rule of law or by the provisions of an agreement or arrangement to disclose any matter to another person does not extend to requiring A to disclose an alternative to prosecution (whether one given to A or another person) that has become spent or any ancillary circumstances.

(2) An alternative to prosecution that has become spent or any ancillary circumstances, or any failure to disclose an alternative to prosecution that has become spent or any ancillary circumstances, is not a ground for dismissing or excluding a person from any office, profession, occupation or employment, or for prejudicing the person in any way in any occupation or employment.

6. The Scottish Ministers may by order—

(a) exclude or modify the application of either or both of sub-paragraphs (2) and (3) of paragraph 4 in relation to questions put in such circumstances as may be specified in the order,

(b) provide for exceptions from any of the provisions of paragraph 5 in such cases or classes of case, or in relation to alternatives to prosecution of such descriptions, as may be specified in the order

7. Paragraphs 3 to 5 do not affect—

(a) the operation of an alternative to prosecution, or

(b) the operation of an enactment by virtue of which, because of an alternative to prosecution, a person is subject to a disqualification, disability, prohibition or other restriction or effect for a period extending beyond the time at which the alternative to prosecution becomes spent

8. (1) Section 7(2), (3) and (4) apply for the purpose of this Schedule as follows.

(2) Subsection (2), apart from paragraphs (b) and (d), applies to the determination of any issue, and the admission or requirement of evidence, relating to alternatives to prosecution previously given to a person and to ancillary circumstances as it applies to matters relating to a person's previous convictions and circumstances ancillary thereto.

(3) Subsection (3) applies to evidence of alternatives to prosecution previously given to a person and ancillary circumstances as it applies to evidence of a person's previous convictions and the circumstances ancillary thereto.

(4) For that purpose, subsection (3) has effect as if—

(a) a reference to subsection (2) or (4) of section 7 were a reference to that subsection as applied by this paragraph, and

(b) the words "or proceedings to which section 8 below applies" were omitted.

(5) Subsection (4) applies for the purpose of excluding the application of paragraph 3.

(6) For that purpose, subsection (4) has effect as if the words "(other than proceedings to which section 8 below applies)" were omitted.

(7) References in the provisions applied by this paragraph to section 4(1) are to be read as references to paragraph 3.]

[**9.** (1) The powers conferred on the Scottish Ministers by—

(a) paragraph 6, and

(b) section 7(4), as applied by paragraph 8,

may be exercised to make provision relating to reserved matters and are not subject to the restrictions imposed by section 29(2)(b) or (c) of, or Schedule 4 to, the Scotland Act 1998.

(2) In this paragraph, "reserved matters" has the same meaning as in the Scotland Act 1998.]

NOTES

Inserted, in relation to Scotland, by the Criminal Justice and Licensing (Scotland) Act 2010, s 109(1), (4).

Para 1: sub-paras (aa), (ab) inserted by the Children's Hearings (Scotland) Act 2011, s 187(1), (3), as from a day to be appointed.

Para 9: added by the Criminal Justice and Courts Act 2015, s 19, as from 13 April 2015.

SEX DISCRIMINATION ACT 1975 (NOTE)

(1975 c 65)

[1.104]

NOTES

In so far as this Act was still in force, the vast majority of it was repealed by the Equality Act 2010, s 211(2), Sch 27, Pt 1, as from 1 October 2010 (see Equality Act 2010 (Commencement No 4, Savings, Consequential, Transitional, Transitory and Incidental Provisions and Revocation) Order 2010, SI 2010/2317). Sections 76A–76C, and s 81 (in so far as relating to those sections) were also repealed by the 2010 Act, as from 5 April 2011 (see the Equality Act 2010 (Commencement No 6) Order, SI 2011/1066). The commencement of the repeal of this Act by the 2010 Act on 1 October 2010 was provided for by SI 2010/2317 as noted above. That Order provides for numerous transitional provisions and savings in connection with the commencement of the 2010 Act and the repeal of this Act. See, in particular, art 15 (saving where the act complained of occurs wholly before 1 October 2010), Schs 1, 2 (savings in relation to shipping matters), Schs 3, 4 (savings in relation to work on ships, hovercraft and in relation to seafarers), and Schs 5, 6 (savings in relation to existing insurance policies).

RACE RELATIONS ACT 1976 (NOTE)

(1976 c 74)

[1.105]

NOTES

In so far as this Act was still in force, the vast majority of it was repealed by the Equality Act 2010, s 211(2), Sch 27, Pt 1, as from 1 October 2010 (see Equality Act 2010 (Commencement No 4, Savings, Consequential, Transitional, Transitory and Incidental Provisions and Revocation) Order 2010, SI 2010/2317). Sections 71, 71A, 71B and Sch 1A were also repealed by the 2010 Act, as from 5 April 2011 (see the Equality Act 2010 (Commencement No 6) Order, SI 2011/1066). The commencement of the repeal of this Act by the 2010 Act on 1 October 2010 was provided for by SI 2010/2317 as noted above. That Order provides for numerous transitional provisions and savings in connection with the commencement of the 2010 Act and the repeal of this Act. See, in particular, art 15 (saving where the act complained of occurs wholly before 1 October 2010), Schs 1, 2 (savings in relation to shipping matters), Schs 3, 4 (savings in relation to work on ships, hovercraft and in relation to seafarers), and Schs 5, 6 (savings in relation to existing insurance policies).

PATENTS ACT 1977

(1977 c 37)

ARRANGEMENT OF SECTIONS

PART I
NEW DOMESTIC LAW

Employees' inventions

PART III
MISCELLANEOUS AND GENERAL

Supplemental

An Act to establish a new law of patents applicable to future patents and applications for patents; to amend the law of patents applicable to existing patents and applications for patents; to give effect to certain international conventions on patents; and for connected purposes

[29 July 1977]

NOTES

Only those sections of this Act concerned with inventions made by employees are reproduced here, ie ss 39–43 (and s 132 which makes provision as to the extent, etc of the Act). For definitions within the Act see s 130 (not reproduced). For reasons of space, the subject matter of sections, etc, not printed is not annotated.

PART I
NEW DOMESTIC LAW

Employees' inventions

[1.106]

39 Right to employees' inventions

(1) Notwithstanding anything in any rule of law, an invention made by an employee shall, as between him and his employer, be taken to belong to his employer for the purposes of this Act and all other purposes if—

(a) it was made in the course of the normal duties of the employee or in the course of duties falling outside his normal duties, but specifically assigned to him, and the circumstances in either case were such that an invention might reasonably be expected to result from the carrying out of his duties; or

(b) the invention was made in the course of the duties of the employee and, at the time of making the invention, because of the nature of his duties and the particular responsibilities arising from the nature of his duties he had a special obligation to further the interests of the employer's undertaking.

(2) Any other invention made by an employee shall, as between him and his employer, be taken for those purposes to belong to the employee.

[(3) Where by virtue of this section an invention belongs, as between him and his employer, to an employee, nothing done—

(a) by or on behalf of the employee or any person claiming under him for the purposes of pursuing an application for a patent, or

(b) by any person for the purpose of performing or working the invention,

shall be taken to infringe any copyright or design right to which, as between him and his employer, his employer is entitled in any model or document relating to the invention.]

NOTES

Sub-s (3): added by the Copyright, Designs and Patents Act 1988, s 295, Sch 5, para 11(1).

[1.107]

40 Compensation of employees for certain inventions

[(1) Where it appears to the court or the comptroller on an application made by an employee within the prescribed period that—

(a) the employee has made an invention belonging to the employer for which a patent has been granted,

(b) having regard among other things to the size and nature of the employer's undertaking, the invention or the patent for it (or the combination of both) is of outstanding benefit to the employer, and

(c) by reason of those facts it is just that the employee should be awarded compensation to be paid by the employer,

the court or the comptroller may award him such compensation of an amount determined under section 41 below.]

(2) Where it appears to the court or the comptroller on an application made by an employee within the prescribed period that—

(a) a patent has been granted for an invention made by and belonging to the employee;

(b) his rights in the invention, or in any patent or application for a patent for the invention, have since the appointed day been assigned to the employer or an exclusive licence under the patent or application has since the appointed day been granted to the employer;

(c) the benefit derived by the employee from the contract of assignment, assignation or grant or any ancillary contract ("the relevant contract") is inadequate in relation to the benefit derived by the employer from [the invention or the patent for it (or both)]; and

(d) by reason of those facts it is just that the employee should be awarded compensation to be paid by the employer in addition to the benefit derived from the relevant contract;

the court or the comptroller may award him such compensation of an amount determined under section 41 below.

(3) Subsections (1) and (2) above shall not apply to the invention of an employee where a relevant collective agreement provides for the payment of compensation in respect of inventions of the same description as that invention to employees of the same description as that employee.

(4) Subsection (2) above shall have effect notwithstanding anything in the relevant contract or any agreement applicable to the invention (other than any such collective agreement).

(5) If it appears to the comptroller on an application under this section that the application involves matters which would more properly be determined by the court, he may decline to deal with it.

(6) In this section—

"the prescribed period", in relation to proceedings before the court, means the period prescribed by rules of court, and

"relevant collective agreement" means a collective agreement within the meaning of [the Trade Union and Labour Relations (Consolidation) Act 1992], made by or on behalf of a trade union to which the employee belongs, and by the employer or an employers' association to which the employer belongs which is in force at the time of the making of the invention.

(7) References in this section to an invention belonging to an employer or employee are references to it so belonging as between the employer and the employee.

NOTES

Sub-s (1): substituted by the Patents Act 2004, s 10(1).

Sub-s (2): words in square brackets in para (c) substituted by the Patents Act 2004, s 10(2).

Sub-s (6): words in square brackets substituted by the Trade Union and Labour Relations (Consolidation) Act 1992, s 300(2), Sch 2, para 9.

Rules of court: the Patents Rules 2007, SI 2007/3291 (made under ss 14(6), 25(5), 32, 74B, 77(9), 92, 123, 125A and 130(2) of this Act). See r 91 of the 2007 Rules (period prescribed for applications by employee for compensation for the purposes of sub-ss (1), (2)). See also r 73 of, and Sch 3 to, the 2007 Rules in relation to applications under this section and s 41(8) post.

[1.108]

41 Amount of compensation

[(1) An award of compensation to an employee under section 40(1) or (2) above shall be such as will secure for the employee a fair share (having regard to all the circumstances) of the benefit which the employer has derived, or may reasonably be expected to derive, from any of the following—

(a) the invention in question;

(b) the patent for the invention;

(c) the assignment, assignation or grant of—

(i) the property or any right in the invention, or

(ii) the property in, or any right in or under, an application for the patent,

to a person connected with the employer.]

(2) For the purposes of subsection (1) above the amount of any benefit derived or expected to be derived by an employer from the assignment, assignation or grant of—

(a) the property in, or any right in or under, a patent for the invention or an application for such a patent; or

(b) the property or any right in the invention;

to a person connected with him shall be taken to be the amount which could reasonably be expected to be so derived by the employer if that person had not been connected with him.

(3) Where the Crown[, United Kingdom Research and Innovation] or a Research Council in its capacity as employer assigns or grants the property in, or any right in or under, an invention, patent or application for a patent to a body having among its functions that of developing or exploiting inventions resulting from public research and does so for no consideration or only a nominal consideration, any benefit derived from the invention, patent or application by that body shall be treated for the purposes of the foregoing provisions of this section as so derived by the Crown[, United Kingdom Research and Innovation or the Research Council (as the case may be)].

In this subsection "Research Council" means a body which is a Research Council for the purposes of the Science and Technology Act 1965 [. . .].

(4) In determining the fair share of the benefit to be secured for an employee in respect of . . . an invention which has always belonged to an employer, the court or the comptroller shall, among other things, take the following matters into account, that is to say—

(a) the nature of the employee's duties, his remuneration and the other advantages he derives or has derived from his employment or has derived in relation to the invention under this Act;

(b) the effort and skill which the employee has devoted to making the invention;

(c) the effort and skill which any other person has devoted to making the invention jointly with the employee concerned, and the advice and other assistance contributed by any other employee who is not a joint inventor of the invention; and

(d) the contribution made by the employer to the making, developing and working of the invention by the provision of advice, facilities and other assistance, by the provision of opportunities and by his managerial and commercial skill and activities.

(5) In determining the fair share of the benefit to be secured for an employee in respect of . . . an invention which originally belonged to him, the court or the comptroller shall, among other things, take the following matters into account, that is to say—

(a) any conditions in a licence or licences granted under this Act or otherwise in respect of the invention or the patent [for it];

(b) the extent to which the invention was made jointly by the employee with any other person; and

(c) the contribution made by the employer to the making, developing and working of the invention as mentioned in subsection (4)(d) above.

(6) Any order for the payment of compensation under section 40 above may be an order for the payment of a lump sum or for periodical payment, or both.

(7) Without prejudice to section 32 of the Interpretation Act 1889 (which provides that a statutory power may in general be exercised from time to time), the refusal of the court or the comptroller to make any such order on an application made by an employee under section 40 above shall not prevent a further application being made under that section by him or any successor in title of his.
(8) Where the court or the comptroller has made any such order, the court or he may on the application of either the employer or the employee vary or discharge it or suspend any provision of the order and revive any provision so suspended, and section 40(5) above shall apply to the application as it applies to an application under that section.
(9) In England and Wales any sums awarded by the comptroller under section 40 above shall, if [the county court] so orders, be recoverable [under section 85 of the County Courts Act 1984] or otherwise as if they were payable under an order of that court.
(10) In Scotland an order made under section 40 above by the comptroller for the payment of any sums may be enforced in like manner as [an extract registered decree arbitral bearing a warrant for execution issued by the sheriff court of any sheriffdom in Scotland].
(11) In Northern Ireland an order made under section 40 above by the comptroller for the payment of any sums may be enforced as if it were a money judgment.

NOTES

Sub-s (1): substituted by the Patents Act 2004, s 10(3).

Sub-s (3): words in first pair of square brackets inserted, words in second pair of square brackets substituted, and words omitted repealed, by the Higher Education and Research Act 2017, s 122, Sch 12, para 13, as from 1 April 2018 (the repealed words were originally inserted by the Higher Education Act 2004, s 49, Sch 6, para 5).

Sub-s (4): words omitted repealed by the Patents Act 2004, ss 10(4), 16(2), Sch 3.

Sub-s (5): words omitted repealed, and words in square brackets inserted, by the Patents Act 2004, ss 10(4), (5), 16(2), Sch 3.

Sub-s (9): words in first pair of square brackets substituted by the Crime and Courts Act 2013, s 17(5), Sch 9, Pt 3, para 52; words in second pair of square brackets substituted by the Tribunals, Courts and Enforcement Act 2007, s 62(3), Sch 13, paras 39, 40.

Sub-s (10): words in square brackets substituted by the Patents Act 2004, s 16(1), Sch 2, paras 1(1), 11.

Applications under sub-s (8): see the note "Rules" to s 40 at **[1.107]**.

Interpretation Act 1889, s 32: repealed and replaced by the Interpretation Act 1978.

[1.109]
42 Enforceability of contracts relating to employees' inventions

(1) This section applies to any contract (whenever made) relating to inventions made by an employee, being a contract entered into by him—
- (a) with the employer (alone or with another); or
- (b) with some other person at the request of the employer or in pursuance of the employee's contract of employment.

(2) Any term in a contract to which this section applies which diminishes the employee's rights in inventions of any description made by him after the appointed day and the date of the contract, or in or under patents for those inventions or applications for such patents, shall be unenforceable against him to the extent that it diminishes his rights in an invention of that description so made, or in or under a patent for such an invention or an application for any such patent.
(3) Subsection (2) above shall not be construed as derogating from any duty of confidentiality owed to his employer by an employee by virtue of any rule of law or otherwise.
(4) This section applies to any arrangement made with a Crown employee by or on behalf of the Crown as his employer as it applies to any contract made between an employee and an employer other than the Crown, and for the purposes of this section "Crown employee" means a person employed under or for the purposes of a government department or any officer or body exercising on behalf of the Crown functions conferred by any enactment [or a person serving in the naval, military or air forces of the Crown].

NOTES

Words in square brackets added with retrospective effect by the Armed Forces Act 1981, s 22(1), (2).

[1.110]
43 Supplementary

(1) Sections 39 to 42 above shall not apply to an invention made before the appointed day.
(2) Sections 39 to 42 above shall not apply to an invention made by an employee unless at the time he made the invention one of the following conditions was satisfied in his case, that is to say—
- (a) he was mainly employed in the United Kingdom; or
- (b) he was not mainly employed anywhere or his place of employment could not be determined, but his employer had a place of business in the United Kingdom to which the employee was attached, whether or not he was also attached elsewhere.

(3) In section 39 to 42 above and this section, except so far as the context otherwise requires, references to the making of an invention by an employee are references to his making it alone or jointly with any other person, but do not include references to his merely contributing advice or other assistance in the making of an invention by another employee.
(4) Any references [in sections 39 to 42] above to a patent and to a patent being granted are respectively references to a patent or other protection and to its being granted whether under the law of the United Kingdom or the law in force in any other country or under any treaty or international convention.

(5) For the purposes of sections 40 and 41 above the benefit derived or expected to be derived by an employer from [an invention or patent] shall, where he dies before any award is made under section 40 above in respect of [it], include any benefit derived or expected to be derived from [it] by his personal representatives or by any person in whom it was vested by their assent.
[(5A) For the purposes of sections 40 and 41 above the benefit derived or expected to be derived by an employer from an invention shall not include any benefit derived or expected to be derived from the invention after the patent for it has expired or has been surrendered or revoked.]
(6) Where an employee dies before an award is made under section 40 above in respect of a patented invention made by him, his personal representatives or their successors in title may exercise his right to make or proceed with an application for compensation under subsection (1) or (2) of that section.
(7) In sections 40 and 41 above and this section "benefit" means benefit in money or money's worth.
(8) Section 533 of the Income and Corporation Taxes Act 1970 (definition of connected persons) shall apply for determining for the purposes of section 41(2) above whether one person is connected with another as it applies for determining that question for the purposes of the Tax Acts.

NOTES

Sub-s (4): words in square brackets substituted by the Copyright, Designs and Patents Act 1988, s 295, Sch 5, para 11(2).

Sub-s (5): words in square brackets substituted by the Patents Act 2004, s 10(6).

Sub-s (5A): inserted by the Patents Act 2004, s 10(7).

Income and Corporation Taxes Act 1970: repealed and originally replaced by the Income and Corporation Taxes Act 1988, s 839 (also repealed). See now the Corporation Tax Act 2010, s 1122. There has been no amendment to this section to reflect the change.

PART III
MISCELLANEOUS AND GENERAL

Supplemental

[1.111]

132 Short title, extent, commencement, consequential amendments and repeals

(1) This Act may be cited as the Patents Act 1977.
(2) This Act shall extend to the Isle of Man, subject to any modifications contained in an Order made by Her Majesty in Council, and accordingly, subject to any such order, references in this Act to the United Kingdom shall be construed as including references to the Isle of Man.
(3) For the purposes of this Act the territorial waters of the United Kingdom shall be treated as part of the United Kingdom.
(4) This Act applies to acts done in an area designated by order under section 1(7) of the Continental Shelf Act 1964, [or specified by Order under [section 10(8) of the Petroleum Act 1998] in connection with any activity falling within [section 11(2)] of that Act], as it applies to acts done in the United Kingdom.
(5) This Act (except sections 77(6), (7) and (9), 78(7) and (8), this subsection and the repeal of section 41 of the 1949 Act) shall come into operation on such day as may be appointed by the Secretary of State by order, and different days may be appointed under this subsection for different purposes.
(6), (7) (*Outside the scope of this work.*)

NOTES

Sub-s (4): words in first (outer) pair of square brackets substituted by the Oil and Gas (Enterprise) Act 1982, s 37(1), Sch 3, para 39; words in second and third (inner) pairs of square brackets substituted by the Petroleum Act 1998, s 50, Sch 4, para 14.

Orders: the Patents Act 1977 (Commencement No 1) Order 1977, SI 1977/2090; the Patents Act 1977 (Commencement No 2) Order 1978, SI 1978/586; the Patents (Isle of Man) Order 2013, SI 2013/2602 (which modifies this Act in its application to the Isle of Man, and which has been amended by subsequent Orders made under this section).

STATE IMMUNITY ACT 1978

(1978 c 33)

ARRANGEMENT OF SECTIONS

PART I
PROCEEDINGS IN UNITED KINGDOM BY OR AGAINST OTHER STATES

Immunity from jurisdiction

Exceptions from immunity

Procedure

Supplementary provisions

PART III
MISCELLANEOUS AND SUPPLEMENTARY

An Act to make new provision with respect to proceedings in the United Kingdom by or against other States; to provide for the effect of judgments given against the United Kingdom in the courts of States parties to the European Convention on State Immunity; to make new provision with respect to the immunities and privileges of heads of State; and for connected purposes

[20 July 1978]

NOTES

Only sections of this Act relevant to employment law are reproduced here. For reasons of space, the subject matter of sections not printed is not annotated.

See *Harvey* DI(1)(C), PI(C)(4).

PART I
PROCEEDINGS IN UNITED KINGDOM BY OR AGAINST OTHER STATES

Immunity from jurisdiction

[1.112]

1 General immunity from jurisdiction

(1) A State is immune from the jurisdiction of the courts of the United Kingdom except as provided in the following provisions of this Part of this Act.

(2) A court shall give effect to the immunity conferred by this section even though the State does not appear in the proceedings in question.

Exceptions from immunity

[1.113]

2 Submission to jurisdiction

(1) A State is not immune as respects proceedings in respect of which it has submitted to the jurisdiction of the courts of the United Kingdom.

(2) A State may submit after the dispute giving rise to the proceedings has arisen or by a prior written agreement; but a provision in any agreement that it is to be governed by the law of the United Kingdom is not to be regarded as a submission.

(3) A State is deemed to have submitted—

(a) if it has instituted the proceedings; or

(b) subject to subsections (4) and (5) below, if it has intervened or taken any step in the proceedings.

(4) Subsection (3)(b) above does not apply to intervention or any step taken for the purpose only of—

(a) claiming immunity; or

(b) asserting an interest in property in circumstances such that the State would have been entitled to immunity if the proceedings had been brought against it.

(5) Subsection (3)(b) above does not apply to any step taken by the State in ignorance of facts entitling it to immunity if those facts could not reasonably have been ascertained and immunity is claimed as soon as reasonably practicable.

(6) A submission in respect of any proceedings extends to any appeal but not to any counter-claim unless it arises out of the same legal relationship or facts as the claim.

(7) The head of a State's diplomatic mission in the United Kingdom, or the person for the time being performing his functions, shall be deemed to have authority to submit on behalf of the State in respect of any proceedings; and any person who has entered into a contract on behalf of and with the authority of a State shall be deemed to have authority to submit on its behalf in respect of proceedings arising out of the contract.

[1.114]
4 Contracts of employment
(1) A State is not immune as respects proceedings relating to a contract of employment between the State and an individual where the contract was made in the United Kingdom or the work is to be wholly or partly performed there.
(2) Subject to subsections (3) and (4) below, this section does not apply if—
- (a) at the time when the proceedings are brought the individual is a national of the State concerned; or
- (b) at the time when the contract was made the individual was neither a national of the United Kingdom nor habitually resident there; or
- (c) the parties to the contract have otherwise agreed in writing.

(3) Where the work is for an office, agency or establishment maintained by the State in the United Kingdom for commercial purposes, subsection (2) (a) and (b) above do not exclude the application of this section unless the individual was, at the time when the contract was made, habitually resident in that State.
(4) Subsection (2)(c) above does not exclude the application of this section where the law of the United Kingdom requires the proceedings to be brought before a court of the United Kingdom.
(5) In subsection (2)(b) above "national of the United Kingdom" [means—
- (a) a British citizen, a [British overseas territories citizen][, a British National (Overseas)] or a British Overseas citizen; or
- (b) a person who under the British Nationality Act 1981 is a British subject; or
- (c) a British protected person (within the meaning of that Act)].

(6) In this section "proceedings relating to a contract of employment" includes proceedings between the parties to such a contract in respect of any statutory rights or duties to which they are entitled or subject as employer or employee.

NOTES
Sub-s (5): words in first (outer) pair of square brackets substituted by the British Nationality Act 1981, s 52(6), Sch 7; words in second (inner) pair of square brackets substituted by virtue of the British Overseas Territories Act 2002, s 2(3); words in third (inner) pair of square brackets inserted by the Hong Kong (British Nationality) Order 1986, SI 1986/948, art 8, Schedule.

Procedure

[1.115]
12 Service of process and judgements in default of appearance
(1) Any writ or other document required to be served for instituting proceedings against a State shall be served by being transmitted through the Foreign and Commonwealth Office to the Ministry of Foreign Affairs of the State and service shall be deemed to have been effected when the writ or document is received at the Ministry.
(2) Any time for entering an appearance (whether prescribed by rules of court or otherwise) shall begin to run two months after the date on which the writ or document is received as aforesaid.
(3) A State which appears in proceedings cannot thereafter object that subsection (1) above has not been complied with in the case of those proceedings.
(4) No judgment in default of appearance shall be given against a State except on proof that subsection (1) above has been complied with and that the time for entering an appearance as extended by subsection (2) above has expired.
(5) A copy of any judgment given against a State in default of appearance shall be transmitted through the Foreign and Commonwealth Office to the Ministry of Foreign Affairs of that State and any time for applying to have the judgment set aside (whether prescribed by rules of court or otherwise) shall begin to run two months after the date on which the copy of the judgment is received at the Ministry.
(6) Subsection (1) above does not prevent the service of a writ or other document in any manner to which the State has agreed and subsections (2) and (4) above do not apply where service is effected in any such manner.
(7) This section shall not be construed as applying to proceedings against a State by way of counter-claim or to an action in rem; and subsection (1) above shall not be construed as affecting any rules of court whereby leave is required for the service of process outside the jurisdiction.

Supplementary provisions

[1.116]
16 Excluded matters
(1) This Part of this Act does not affect any immunity or privilege conferred by the Diplomatic Privileges Act 1964 or the Consular Relations Act 1968; and—
- (a) section 4 above does not apply to proceedings concerning the employment of the members of a mission within the meaning of the Convention scheduled to the said Act of 1964 or of the members of a consular post within the meaning of the Convention scheduled to the said Act of 1968;
- (b) section 6(1) above does not apply to proceedings concerning a State's title to or its possession of property used for the purposes of a diplomatic mission.

(2) This Part of this Act does not apply to proceedings relating to anything done by or in relation to the armed forces of a State while present in the United Kingdom and, in particular, has effect subject to the Visiting Forces Act 1952.
(3) This Part of this Act does not apply to proceedings to which section 17(6) of the Nuclear Installations Act 1965 applies.
(4) This Part of this Act does not apply to criminal proceedings.
(5) This Part of this Act does not apply to any proceedings relating to taxation other than those mentioned in section 11 above.

[1.117]
17 Interpretation of Part I
(1) In this Part of this Act—
"the Brussels Convention" means the International Convention for the Unification of Certain Rules Concerning the Immunity of State-owned Ships signed in Brussels on 10th April 1926;
"commercial purposes" means purposes of such transactions or activities as are mentioned in section 3(3) above;
"ship" includes hovercraft.
(2) In sections 2(2) and 13(3) above references to an agreement include references to a treaty, convention or other international agreement.
(3) For the purposes of sections 3 to 8 above the territory of the United Kingdom shall be deemed to include any [British overseas territory] in respect of which the United Kingdom is a party to the European Convention on State Immunity.
(4) In sections 3(1), 4(1), 5 and 16(2) above references to the United Kingdom include references to its territorial waters and any area designated under section 1(7) of the Continental Shelf Act 1964.
(5) In relation to Scotland in this Part of this Act "action in rem" means such an action only in relation to Admiralty proceedings.

NOTES
Sub-s (3): words in square brackets substituted by virtue of the British Overseas Territories Act 2002, s 1(2).
Brussels Convention: the text of the Brussels Convention is set out in Cmd 5672.

PART III
MISCELLANEOUS AND SUPPLEMENTARY

[1.118]
23 Short title, repeals commencement and extent
(1) This Act may be cited as the State Immunity Act 1978.
(2) . . .
(3) Subject to subsection (4) below, Parts I and II of this Act do not apply to proceedings in respect of matters that occurred before the date of the coming into force of this Act and, in particular—
(a) sections 2(2) and 13(3) do not apply to any prior agreement, and
(b) sections 3, 4 and 9 do not apply to any transaction, contract or arbitration agreement,
entered into before that date.
(4) Section 12 above applies to any proceedings instituted after the coming into force of this Act.
(5) This Act shall come into force on such date as may be specified by an order made by the Lord Chancellor by statutory instrument.
(6) This Act extends to Northern Ireland.
(7) Her Majesty may by Order in Council extend any of the provisions of this Act, with or without modification, to any [British overseas territory].

NOTES
Sub-s (2): repeals the Administration of Justice (Miscellaneous Provisions) Act 1938, s 13, and the Law Reform (Miscellaneous Provisions) (Scotland) Act 1940, s 7.
Sub-s (7): words in square brackets substituted by virtue of the British Overseas Territories Act 2002, s 1(2).
Orders: the State Immunity Act 1978 (Commencement) Order 1978, SI 1978/1572 (bringing this Act into force on 22 November 1978); the State Immunity (Overseas Territories) Order 1979, SI 1979/458; the State Immunity (Guernsey) Order 1980, SI 1980/871; the State Immunity (Isle of Man) Order 1981, SI 1981/1112; the State Immunity (Jersey) Order 1985, SI 1985/1642.

LIMITATION ACT 1980

(1980 c 58)

ARRANGEMENT OF SECTIONS

PART I
ORDINARY TIME LIMITS FOR DIFFERENT CLASSES OF ACTION

An Act to consolidate the Limitation Acts 1939 to 1980

[13 November 1980]

NOTES

Only certain sections of this Act are relevant to employment law, and accordingly, only those sections of most relevance have been included in this work. For reasons of space, the subject matter of the sections and Schedules omitted is not annotated. This Act extends to England and Wales only (subject to a minor exception that is outside the scope of this work). This Act, except s 35, came into force on 1 May 1981.

Application to arbitral proceedings: this Act applies to arbitral proceedings as it applies to legal proceedings; see the Arbitration Act 1996, s 13(1). As to the commencement of arbitral proceedings for the purposes of this Act, see ss 12 (in particular sub-s (5)), 13(2), (4), 14 of the 1996 Act, and as to when a cause of action accrued, see s 13(3), (4) of the 1996 Act.

PART I
ORDINARY TIME LIMITS FOR DIFFERENT CLASSES OF ACTION

Time limits under Part I subject to extension or exclusion under Part II

[1.119]

1 Time limits under Part I subject to extension or exclusion under Part II

(1) This Part of this Act gives the ordinary time limits for bringing actions of the various classes mentioned in the following provisions of this Part.

(2) The ordinary time limits given in this Part of this Act are subject to extension or exclusion in accordance with the provisions of Part II of this Act.

Actions founded on tort

[1.120]

2 Time limit for actions founded on tort

An action founded on tort shall not be brought after the expiration of six years from the date on which the cause of action accrued.

[1.121]

[4A Time limit for actions for defamation or malicious falsehood

The time limit under section 2 of this Act shall not apply to an action for—

(a) libel or slander, or malicious falsehood.

(b) slander of title, slander of goods or other malicious falsehood,

but no such action shall be brought after the expiration of one year from the date on which the cause of action accrued.]

NOTES

Inserted by the Administration of Justice Act 1985, s 57(2), and substituted by the Defamation Act 1996, s 5(2), (6).

Actions founded on simple contract

[1.122]

5 Time limit for actions founded on simple contract

An action founded on simple contract shall not be brought after the expiration of six years from the date on which the cause of action accrued.

Actions for sums recoverable by statute

[1.123]

9 Time limit for actions for sums recoverable by statute

(1) An action to recover any sum recoverable by virtue of any enactment shall not be brought after the expiration of six years from the date on which the cause of action accrued.

(2) Subsection (1) above shall not affect any action to which section 10 [or 10A] of this Act applies.

NOTES

Sub-s (2): words in square brackets inserted by the Automated and Electric Vehicles Act 2018, s 20(1), Schedule, para 8, as from a day to be appointed.

[1.124]

10 Special time limit for claiming contribution

(1) Where under section 1 of the Civil Liability (Contribution) Act 1978 any person becomes entitled to a right to recover contribution in respect of any damage from any other person, no action to recover contribution by virtue of that right shall be brought after the expiration of two years from the date on which that right accrued.

(2) For the purposes of this section the date on which a right to recover contribution in respect of any damage accrues to any person (referred to below in this section as "the relevant date") shall be ascertained as provided in subsections (3) and (4) below.

(3) If the person in question is held liable in respect of that damage—

(a) by a judgment given in any civil proceedings; or

(b) by an award made on any arbitration;

the relevant date shall be the date on which the judgment is given, or the date of the award (as the case may be).

For the purposes of this subsection no account shall be taken of any judgment or award given or made on appeal in so far as it varies the amount of damages awarded against the person in question.

(4) If, in any case not within subsection (3) above, the person in question makes or agrees to make any payment to one or more persons in compensation for that damage (whether he admits any liability in respect of the damage or not), the relevant date shall be the earliest date on which the amount to be paid by him is agreed between him (or his representative) and the person (or each of the persons, as the case may be) to whom the payment is to be made.

(5) An action to recover contribution shall be one to which sections 28, 32[, *33A*] and 35 of this Act apply, but otherwise Parts II and III of this Act (except sections 34, 37 and 38) shall not apply for the purposes of this section.

NOTES

Sub-s (5): number in square brackets and italics inserted by the Cross-Border Mediation (EU Directive) Regulations 2011, SI 2011/1133, regs 22, 23 and subsequently repealed by the Cross-Border Mediation (EU Directive) (EU Exit) Regulations 2019, SI 2019/469, reg 4, Sch 1, Pt 1, para 7(1), (2), as from exit day (as defined in the European Union (Withdrawal) Act 2018, s 20).

Actions in respect of wrongs causing personal injuries or death

[1.125]

11 Special time limit for actions in respect of personal injuries

(1) This section applies to any action for damages for negligence, nuisance or breach of duty (whether the duty exists by virtue of a contract or of provision made by or under a statute or independently of any contract or any such provision) where the damages claimed by the plaintiff for the negligence, nuisance or breach of duty consist of or include damages in respect of personal injuries to the plaintiff or any other person.

[(1A) This section does not apply to any action brought for damages under section 3 of the Protection from Harassment Act 1997.]

(2) None of the time limits given in the preceding provisions of this Act shall apply to an action to which this section applies.

(3) An action to which this section applies shall not be brought after the expiration of the period applicable in accordance with subsection (4) or (5) below.

(4) Except where subsection (5) below applies, the period applicable is three years from—

(a) the date on which the cause of action accrued; or

(b) the date of knowledge (if later) of the person injured.

(5) If the person injured dies before the expiration of the period mentioned in subsection (4) above, the period applicable as respects the cause of action surviving for the benefit of his estate by virtue of section 1 of the Law Reform (Miscellaneous Provisions) Act 1934 shall be three years from—

(a) the date of death; or

(b) the date of the personal representative's knowledge;

whichever is the later.

(6) For the purposes of this section "personal representative" includes any person who is or has been a personal representative of the deceased, including an executor who has not proved the will (whether or not he has renounced probate) but not anyone appointed only as a special personal representative in relation to settled land; and regard shall be had to any knowledge acquired by any such person while a personal representative or previously.

(7) If there is more than one personal representative, and their dates of knowledge are different, subsection (5)(b) above shall be read as referring to the earliest of those dates.

NOTES

Sub-s (1A): inserted by the Protection from Harassment Act 1997, s 6.

[1.126]

14 Definition of date of knowledge for purposes of *sections 11 and 12*

(1) [Subject to *subsection (1A)* below,] In sections 11 and 12 of this Act references to a person's date of knowledge are references to the date on which he first had knowledge of the following facts—

(a) that the injury in question was significant; and

(b) that the injury was attributable in whole or in part to the act or omission which is alleged to constitute negligence, nuisance or breach of duty; and

(c) the identity of the defendant; and

(d) if it is alleged that the act or omission was that of a person other than the defendant, the identity of that person and the additional facts supporting the bringing of an action against the defendant;

and knowledge that any acts or omissions did or did not, as a matter of law, involve negligence, nuisance or breach of duty is irrelevant.

[(1A)], [(1B)] (*Outside the scope of this work.*)

(2) For the purposes of this section an injury is significant if the person whose date of knowledge is in question would reasonably have considered it sufficiently serious to justify his instituting proceedings for damages against a defendant who did not dispute liability and was able to satisfy a judgment.

(3) For the purposes of this section a person's knowledge includes knowledge which he might reasonably have been expected to acquire—

(a) from facts observable or ascertainable by him; or

(b) from facts ascertainable by him with the help of medical or other appropriate expert advice which it is reasonable for him to seek;

but a person shall not be fixed under this subsection with knowledge of a fact ascertainable only with the help of expert advice so long as he has taken all reasonable steps to obtain (and, where appropriate, to act on) that advice.

NOTES

Words in square brackets in sub-s (1) inserted, and sub-s (1A) inserted, by the Consumer Protection Act 1987, s 6, Sch 1, Pt I, para 3.

For the words in italics in the section heading there are substituted the words "sections 11 to 12", for the words in italics in sub-s (1) there are substituted the words "subsections (1A) and (1B)", and sub-s (1B) is inserted, by the Automated and Electric Vehicles Act 2018, s 20(1), Schedule, para 13, as from a day to be appointed.

Note: sub-s (1A) concerns actions in relation to death caused by defective products (Consumer Protection Act 1987, s 6(1)(a)), and sub-s (1B) concerns death caused by automated vehicles (Automated and Electric Vehicles Act 2018, s 6(1)(a)); both subsections are outside the scope of this work.

[Actions in respect of latent damage not involving personal injuries

[1.127]
14A Special time limit for negligence actions where facts relevant to cause of action are not known at date of accrual

(1) This section applies to any action for damages for negligence, other than one to which section 11 of this Act applies, where the starting date for reckoning the period of limitation under subsection (4)(b) below falls after the date on which the cause of action accrued.

(2) Section 2 of this Act shall not apply to an action to which this section applies.

(3) An action to which this section applies shall not be brought after the expiration of the period applicable in accordance with subsection (4) below.

(4) That period is either—

(a) six years from the date on which the cause of action accrued; or

(b) three years from the starting date as defined by subsection (5) below, if that period expires later than the period mentioned in paragraph (a) above.

(5) For the purposes of this section, the starting date for reckoning the period of limitation under subsection (4)(b) above is the earliest date on which the plaintiff or any person in whom the cause of action was vested before him first had both the knowledge required for bringing an action for damages in respect of the relevant damage and a right to bring such an action.

(6) In subsection (5) above "the knowledge required for bringing an action for damages in respect of the relevant damage" means knowledge both—

(a) of the material facts about the damage in respect of which damages are claimed; and

(b) of the other facts relevant to the current action mentioned in subsection (8) below.

(7) For the purposes of subsection (6)(a) above, the material facts about the damage are such facts about the damage as would lead a reasonable person who had suffered such damage to consider it sufficiently serious to justify his instituting proceedings for damages against a defendant who did not dispute liability and was able to satisfy a judgment.

(8) The other facts referred to in subsection (6)(b) above are—

(a) that the damage was attributable in whole or in part to the act or omission which is alleged to constitute negligence; and

(b) the identity of the defendant; and

(c) if it is alleged that the act or omission was that of a person other than the defendant, the identity of that person and the additional facts supporting the bringing of an action against the defendant.

(9) Knowledge that any acts or omissions did or did not, as a matter of law, involve negligence is irrelevant for the purposes of subsection (5) above.

(10) For the purposes of this section a person's knowledge includes knowledge which he might reasonably have been expected to acquire—

(a) from facts observable or ascertainable by him; or

(b) from facts ascertainable by him with the help of appropriate expert advice which it is reasonable for him to seek;

but a person shall not be taken by virtue of this subsection to have knowledge of a fact ascertainable only with the help of expert advice so long as he has taken all reasonable steps to obtain (and, where appropriate, to act on) that advice.]

NOTES

Inserted, together with the preceding heading and s 14B, by the Latent Damage Act 1986, s 1.

[1.128]
[14B Overriding time limit for negligence actions not involving personal injuries

(1) An action for damages for negligence, other than one to which section 11 of this Act applies, shall not be brought after the expiration of fifteen years from the date (or, if more than one, from the last of the dates) on which there occurred any act or omission—

(a) which is alleged to constitute negligence; and

(b) to which the damage in respect of which damages are claimed is alleged to be attributable (in whole or in part).

(2) This section bars the right of action in a case to which subsection (1) above applies notwithstanding that—

(a) the cause of action has not yet accrued; or

(b) where section 14A of this Act applies to the action, the date which is for the purposes of that section the starting date for reckoning the period mentioned in subsection (4)(b) of that section has not yet occurred;

before the end of the period of limitation prescribed by this section.]

NOTES

Inserted as noted to s 14A at **[1.127]**.

PART II
EXTENSION OR EXCLUSION OF ORDINARY TIME LIMITS

Disability

[1.129]

28 Extension of limitation period in case of disability

(1) Subject to the following provisions of this section, if on the date when any right of action accrued for which a period of limitation is prescribed by this Act, the person to whom it accrued was under a disability, the action may be brought at any time before the expiration of six years from the date when he ceased to be under a disability or died (whichever first occurred) notwithstanding that the period of limitation has expired.

(2) This section shall not affect any case where the right of action first accrued to some person (not under a disability) through whom the person under a disability claims.

(3) When a right of action which has accrued to a person under a disability accrues, on the death of that person while still under a disability, to another person under a disability, no further extension of time shall be allowed by reason of the disability of the second person.

(4) No action to recover land or money charged on land shall be brought by virtue of this section by any person after the expiration of thirty years from the date on which the right of action accrued to that person or some person through whom he claims.

[(4A) If the action is one to which section 4A of this Act applies, subsection (1) above shall have effect—

(a) in the case of an action for libel or slander, as if for the words from "at any time" to "occurred)" there were substituted the words "by him at any time before the expiration of one year from the date on which he ceased to be under a disability"; and

(b) in the case of an action for slander of title, slander of goods or other malicious falsehood, as if for the words "six years" there were substituted the words "one year".]

(5) If the action is one to which section 10 of this Act applies, subsection (1) above shall have effect as if for the words "six years" there were substituted the words "two years".

(6) If the action is one to which section 11[, 11B] or 12(2) of this Act applies, subsection (1) above shall have effect as if for the words "six years" there were substituted the words "three years".

[(7) If the action is one to which section 11A of this Act applies or one by virtue of section 6(1)(a) of the Consumer Protection Act 1987 (death caused by defective product), subsection (1) above—

(a) shall not apply to the time limit prescribed by subsection (3) of the said section 11A or to that time limit as applied by virtue of section 12(1) of this Act; and

(b) in relation to any other time limit prescribed by this Act shall have effect as if for the word "six years" there were substituted the words "three years".]

NOTES

Sub-s (4A): inserted by the Administration of Justice Act 1985, ss 57(3), 69(5), Sch 9, para 14; substituted by the Defamation Act 1996, s 5(3), (6).

Sub-s (6): figure in square brackets inserted by the Automated and Electric Vehicles Act 2018, s 20(1), Schedule, para 14, as from a day to be appointed.

Sub-s (7): added by the Consumer Protection Act 1987, s 6, Sch 1, Pt I, para 4.

[1.130]

[28A Extension for cases where the limitation period is the period under section 14A(4)(b)

(1) Subject to subsection (2) below, if in the case of any action for which a period of limitation is prescribed by section 14A of this Act—

(a) the period applicable in accordance with subsection (4) of that section is the period mentioned in paragraph (b) of that subsection;

(b) on the date which is for the purposes of that section the starting date for reckoning that period the person by reference to whose knowledge that date fell to be determined under subsection (5) of that section was under a disability; and

(c) section 28 of this Act does not apply to the action;

the action may be brought at any time before the expiration of three years from the date when he ceased to be under a disability or died (whichever first occurred) notwithstanding that the period mentioned above has expired.

(2) An action may not be brought by virtue of subsection (1) above after the end of the period of limitation prescribed by section 14B of this Act.]

NOTES

Inserted by the Latent Damage Act 1986, s 2(1).

Fraud, concealment and mistake

[1.131]

32 Postponement of limitation period in case of fraud, concealment and mistake

(1) Subject to [subsections (3) *and (4A)*] below, where in the case of any action for which a period of limitation is prescribed by this Act, either—

(a) the action is based upon the fraud of the defendant; or

(b) any fact relevant to the plaintiff's right of action has been deliberately concealed from him by the defendant; or

(c) the action is for relief from the consequences of a mistake;

the period of limitation shall not begin to run until the plaintiff has discovered the fraud, concealment or mistake (as the case may be) or could with reasonable diligence have discovered it.

References in this subsection to the defendant include references to the defendant's agent and to any person through whom the defendant claims and his agent.

(2) For the purposes of subsection (1) above, deliberate commission of a breach of duty in circumstances in which it is unlikely to be discovered for some time amounts to deliberate concealment of the facts involved in that breach of duty.

(3) Nothing in this section shall enable any action—

(a) to recover, or recover the value of, any property; or

(b) to enforce any charge against, or set aside any transaction affecting, any property;

to be brought against the purchaser of the property or any person claiming through him in any case where the property has been purchased for valuable consideration by an innocent third party since the fraud or concealment or (as the case may be) the transaction in which the mistake was made took place.

(4) A purchaser is an innocent third party for the purposes of this section—

(a) in the case of fraud or concealment of any fact relevant to the plaintiff's right of action, if he was not a party to the fraud or (as the case may be) to the concealment of that fact and did not at the time of the purchase know or have reason to believe that the fraud or concealment had taken place; and

(b) in the case of mistake, if he did not at the time of the purchase know or have reason to believe that the mistake had been made.

[(4A) Subsection (1) above shall not apply in relation to the time limit prescribed by section 11A(3) of this Act or in relation to that time limit as applied by virtue of section 12(1) of this Act.]

[(4B) Subsection (1) above shall not apply in relation to the time limit prescribed by section 11B(2) or (4) of this Act or in relation to that time limit as applied by virtue of section 12(1) of this Act.]

[(5) Sections 14A and 14B of this Act shall not apply to any action to which subsection (1)(b) above applies (and accordingly the period of limitation referred to in that subsection, in any case to which either of those sections would otherwise apply, is the period applicable under section 2 of this Act).]

NOTES

Sub-s (1): words in square brackets substituted by the Consumer Protection Act 1987, s 6, Sch 1, Pt I, para 5(a); for the words in italics there are substituted the words ", (4A) and (4B)" by the Automated and Electric Vehicles Act 2018, s 20(1), Schedule, para 15(1), (2), as from a day to be appointed.

Sub-s (4A): inserted by the Consumer Protection Act 1987, s 6, Sch 1, Pt I, para 5(b).

Sub-s (4B): inserted by the Automated and Electric Vehicles Act 2018, s 20(1), Schedule, para 15(1), (3), as from a day to be appointed.

Sub-s (5): added by the Latent Damage Act 1986, s 2(2).

Discretionary exclusion of time limit for actions in respect of personal injuries or death

[1.132]

33 Discretionary exclusion of time limit for actions in respect of personal injuries or death

(1) If it appears to the court that it would be equitable to allow an action to proceed having regard to the degree to which—

(a) the provisions of section 11 [*or 11A*] or 12 of this Act prejudice the plaintiff or any person whom he represents; and

(b) any decision of the court under this subsection would prejudice the defendant or any person whom he represents;

the court may direct that those provisions shall not apply to the action, or shall not apply to any specified cause of action to which the action relates.

[(1A) The court shall not under this section disapply—

(a) subsection (3) of section 11A; or

(b) where the damages claimed by the plaintiff are confined to damages for loss of or damage to any property, any other provision in its application to an action by virtue of Part I of the Consumer Protection Act 1987.]

[(1B) Where the damages claimed are confined to damages for loss of or damage to any property, the court shall not under this section disapply any provision in its application to an action under section 2 of the Automated and Electric Vehicles Act 2018.]

(2) The court shall not under this section disapply section 12(1) except where the reason why the person injured could no longer maintain an action was because of the time limit in section 11 [*or subsection (4) of section 11A*].

If, for example, the person injured could at his death no longer maintain an action under the Fatal Accidents Act 1976 because of the time limit in Article 29 in Schedule 1 to the Carriage by Air Act 1961, the court has no power to direct that section 12(1) shall not apply.

(3) In acting under this section the court shall have regard to all the circumstances of the case and in particular to—

(a) the length of, and the reasons for, the delay on the part of the plaintiff;

(b) the extent to which, having regard to the delay, the evidence adduced or likely to be adduced by the plaintiff or the defendant is or is likely to be less cogent than if the action had been brought within the time allowed by section 11[, by section 11A][, by section 11B] or (as the case may be) by section 12;

(c) the conduct of the defendant after the cause of action arose, including the extent (if any) to which he responded to requests reasonably made by the plaintiff for information or inspection for the purpose of ascertaining facts which were or might be relevant to the plaintiff's cause of action against the defendant;

(d) the duration of any disability of the plaintiff arising after the date of the accrual of the cause of action;
(e) the extent to which the plaintiff acted promptly and reasonably once he knew whether or not the act or omission of the defendant, to which the injury was attributable, might be capable at that time of giving rise to an action for damages;
(f) the steps, if any, taken by the plaintiff to obtain medical, legal or other expert advice and the nature of any such advice he may have received.

(4) In a case where the person injured died when, because of section 11 [*or subsection (4) of section 11A*], he could no longer maintain an action and recover damages in respect of the injury, the court shall have regard in particular to the length of, and the reasons for, the delay on the part of the deceased.

(5) In a case under subsection (4) above, or any other case where the time limit, or one of the time limits, depends on the date of knowledge of a person other than the plaintiff, subsection (3) above shall have effect with appropriate modifications, and shall have effect in particular as if references to the plaintiff included references to any person whose date of knowledge is or was relevant in determining a time limit.

(6) A direction by the court disapplying the provisions of section 12(1) shall operate to disapply the provisions to the same effect in section 1(1) of the Fatal Accidents Act 1976.

(7) In this section "the court" means the court in which the action has been brought.

(8) References in this section to section 11 [*or 11A*] include references to that section as extended by any of the [provisions of this Part of this Act other than this section] or by any provision of Part III of this Act.

NOTES

Sub-s (1): words in square brackets substituted by the Consumer Protection Act 1987, s 6, Sch 1, Pt I, para 6(a). Those words are further substituted (by the figures ", 11A, 11B") by the Automated and Electric Vehicles Act 2018, s 20(1), Schedule, para 16(1), (2), as from a day to be appointed.

Sub-s (1A): inserted by the Consumer Protection Act 1987, s 6, Sch 1, Pt I, para 6(b).

Sub-s (1B): inserted by the Automated and Electric Vehicles Act 2018, s 20(1), Schedule, para 16(1), (3), as from a day to be appointed.

Sub-s (2): words in square brackets substituted by the Consumer Protection Act 1987, s 6, Sch 1, Pt I, para 6(c). Those words are further substituted (by the words ", 11A(4) or 11B(2) or (4)") by the Automated and Electric Vehicles Act 2018, s 20(1), Schedule, para 16(1), (4), as from a day to be appointed.

Sub-s (3): words in first pair of square brackets in para (b) inserted by the Consumer Protection Act 1987, s 6, Sch 1, Pt I, para 6(d). Words in second pair of square brackets inserted by the Automated and Electric Vehicles Act 2018, s 20(1), Schedule, para 16(1), (5), as from a day to be appointed.

Sub-s (4): words in square brackets substituted by the Consumer Protection Act 1987, s 6, Sch 1, Pt I, para 6(c). Those words are further substituted (by the words ", 11A(4) or 11B(2) or (4)") by the Automated and Electric Vehicles Act 2018, s 20(1), Schedule, para 16(1), (4), as from a day to be appointed.

Sub-s (8): words in first pair of square brackets substituted by the Consumer Protection Act 1987, s 6, Sch 1, Pt I, para 6(c). Those words are further substituted (by the words ", 11A or 11B") by the Automated and Electric Vehicles Act 2018, s 20(1), Schedule, para 16(1), (6), as from a day to be appointed. Words in second pair of square brackets substituted by the Cross-Border Mediation (EU Directive) Regulations 2011, SI 2011/1133, regs 22, 251.

[Mediation in certain cross-border disputes

[1.133]

33A Extension of time limits because of mediation in certain cross-border disputes

(1) In this section—
(a) "Mediation Directive" means Directive 2008/52/EC of the European Parliament and of the Council of 21 May 2008 on certain aspects of mediation in civil and commercial matters,
(b) "mediation" has the meaning given by article 3(a) of the Mediation Directive,
(c) "mediator" has the meaning given by article 3(b) of the Mediation Directive, and
(d) "relevant dispute" means a dispute to which article 8(1) of the Mediation Directive applies (certain cross-border disputes).

(2) Subsection (3) applies where—
(a) a time limit under this Act relates to the subject of the whole or part of a relevant dispute,
(b) a mediation in relation to the relevant dispute starts before the time limit expires, and
(c) if not extended by this section, the time limit would expire before the mediation ends or less than eight weeks after it ends.

(3) For the purposes of initiating judicial proceedings or arbitration, the time limit expires instead at the end of eight weeks after the mediation ends (subject to subsection (4)).

(4) If a time limit has been extended by this section, subsections (2) and (3) apply to the extended time limit as they apply to a time limit mentioned in subsection (2)(a).

(5) Where more than one time limit applies in relation to a relevant dispute, the extension by subsection (3) of one of those time limits does not affect the others.

(6) For the purposes of this section, a mediation starts on the date of the agreement to mediate that is entered into by the parties and the mediator.

(7) For the purposes of this section, a mediation ends on the date of the first of these to occur—
(a) the parties reach an agreement in resolution of the relevant dispute,
(b) a party completes the notification of the other parties that it has withdrawn from the mediation,
(c) a party to whom a qualifying request is made fails to give a response reaching the other parties within 14 days of the request,

(d) *after the parties are notified that the mediator's appointment has ended (by death, resignation or otherwise), they fail to agree within 14 days to seek to appoint a replacement mediator,*

(e) *the mediation otherwise comes to an end pursuant to the terms of the agreement to mediate.*

(8) For the purpose of subsection (7), a qualifying request is a request by a party that another (A) confirm to all parties that A is continuing with the mediation.

(9) In the case of any relevant dispute, references in this section to a mediation are references to the mediation so far as it relates to that dispute, and references to a party are to be read accordingly.]

NOTES

Inserted, together with the preceding heading, by the Cross-Border Mediation (EU Directive) Regulations 2011, SI 2011/1133, regs 22, 26 (revoked by the Cross-Border Mediation (EU Directive) (EU Exit) Regulations 2019, SI 2019/469, reg 2(1), as from exit day (as defined in the European Union (Withdrawal) Act 2018, s 20)).

Repealed by SI 2019/469, reg 4, Sch 1, Pt 1, para 7(1), (4), as from exit day (as defined in the European Union (Withdrawal) Act 2018, s 20) and subject to the modifications specified in Sch 2 to the 2019 Regulations for any mediation to which this section applies, issued before exit day (see reg 5, Sch 2, Pt 1, para 8 at **[2.2131]**, **[2.2132]**).

PART III
MISCELLANEOUS AND GENERAL

[1.134]

39 Saving for other limitation enactments

This Act shall not apply to any action or arbitration for which a period of limitation is prescribed by or under any other enactment (whether passed before or after the passing of this Act) or to any action or arbitration to which the Crown is a party and for which, if it were between subjects, a period of limitation would be prescribed by or under any such other enactment.

CIVIL JURISDICTION AND JUDGMENTS ACT 1982

(1982 c 27)

An Act to make further provision about the jurisdiction of courts and tribunals in the United Kingdom and certain other territories and about the recognition and enforcement of judgments given in the United Kingdom or elsewhere; to provide for the modification of certain provisions relating to legal aid; and for connected purposes

[13 July 1982]

NOTES

Only those sections of this Act within the scope of this work are reproduced here; other sections are not annotated.

PART I
IMPLEMENTATION OF THE CONVENTIONS

Main implementing provisions

NOTES

For the words "Main implementing provisions" in the heading above there is substituted the word "Interpretation", by the Civil Jurisdiction and Judgments (Amendment) (EU Exit) Regulations 2019, SI 2019/479, regs 4, 5, as from exit day (as defined in the European Union (Withdrawal) Act 2018, s 20).

[1.135]

1 Interpretation of references to the Conventions and Contracting States

(1) In this Act—

"the 1968 Convention" means the Convention on jurisdiction and the enforcement of judgments in civil and commercial matters (including the Protocol annexed to that Convention), signed at Brussels on 27th September 1968;

"the 1971 Protocol" means the Protocol on the interpretation of the 1968 Convention by the European Court, signed at Luxembourg on 3rd June 1971;

"the Accession Convention" means the Convention on the accession to the 1968 Convention and the 1971 Protocol of Denmark, the Republic of Ireland and the United Kingdom, signed at Luxembourg on 9th October 1978;

["the 1982 Accession Convention" means the Convention on the accession of the Hellenic Republic to the 1968 Convention and the 1971 Protocol, with the adjustments made to them by the Accession Convention, signed at Luxembourg on 25th October 1982;]

["the 1989 Accession Convention" means the Convention on the accession of the Kingdom of Spain and the Portuguese Republic to the 1968 Convention and the 1971 Protocol, with the adjustments made to them by the Accession Convention and the 1982 Accession Convention, signed at Donostia — San Sebastián on 26th May 1989;]

["the 1996 Accession Convention" means the Convention on the accession of the Republic of Austria, the Republic of Finland and the Kingdom of Sweden to the 1968 Convention and the 1971 Protocol, with the adjustments made to them by the Accession Convention, the 1982 Accession Convention and the 1989 Accession Convention, signed at Brussels on 29th November 1996,]

["the 2005 Hague Convention" means the Convention on Choice of Court Agreements concluded on 30th June 2005 at the Hague;]

["the 2007 Hague Convention" means the Convention on the International Recovery of Child Support and other forms of Family Maintenance done at The Hague on 23 November 2007;]

[["the Brussels Conventions"] means the 1968 Convention, the 1971 Protocol, the Accession Convention, the 1982 Accession Convention[, the 1989 Accession Convention and the 1996 Accession Convention]]

["the Lugano Convention" means the Convention on jurisdiction and the recognition and enforcement of judgments in civil and commercial matters, between the European Community and the Republic of Iceland, the Kingdom of Norway, the Swiss Confederation and the Kingdom of Denmark signed on behalf of the European Community on 30th October 2007;]

["the Maintenance Regulation" means Council Regulation (EC) No 4/2009 including as applied in relation to Denmark by virtue of the Agreement made on 19th October 2005 between the European Community and the Kingdom of Denmark;]

["the Regulation" means Regulation (EU) No 1215/2012 of the European Parliament and of the Council of 12 December 2012 on jurisdiction and the recognition and enforcement of judgments in civil and commercial matters (recast) *as amended from time to time* and as applied by virtue of the Agreement made on 19 October 2005 between the European Community and the Kingdom of Denmark on jurisdiction and the recognition and enforcement of judgments in civil and commercial matters (OJ No L 299, 16.11.2005, p 62; OJ No L79, 21.3.2013, p 4) [as that Regulation had effect and was applied immediately before exit day]].

(2) In this Act, unless the context otherwise requires—

[(a) references to, or to any provision of, the 1968 Convention or the 1971 Protocol are references to that Convention, Protocol or provision as amended by the Accession Convention, the 1982 Accession Convention[, the 1989 Accession Convention and the 1996 Accession Convention]; and]

[(aa) . . .]

[(b) any reference in any provision to a numbered Article without more is a reference—

(i) to the Article so numbered of the 1968 Convention, in so far as the provision applies in relation to that Convention, and

(ii) to the Article so numbered of the Lugano Convention, in so far as the provision applies in relation to that Convention,

and any reference to a sub-division of a numbered Article shall be construed accordingly].

[(3) [In this Act—

["2005 Hague Convention State", in any provision, in the application of that provision in relation to the 2005 Hague Convention, means a State bound by that Convention;]

["2007 Hague Convention State", in any provision, in the application of that provision in relation to the 2007 Hague Convention, means a State bound by that Convention;]

["Brussels Contracting State" means a state which is one of the original parties to the 1968 Convention or one of the parties acceding to that Convention under the Accession Convention, or under the 1982 Accession Convention, or under the 1989 Accession Convention, but only with respect to any territory—

(a) to which the Brussels Conventions apply; and

(b) which is excluded from the scope of the Regulation pursuant to [Articles 349 and 355 of the Treaty on the Functioning of the European Union];]

"Contracting State", without more, in any provision means—

(a) in the application of the provision in relation to the Brussels Conventions, a Brussels Contracting State; . . .

(b) in the application of the provision in relation to the Lugano Convention, a [State bound by the Lugano Convention];] [and

(c) in the application of the provision in relation to the 2005 Hague Convention, a 2005 Hague Convention State;]

["Maintenance Regulation State", in any provision, in the application of that provision in relation to the Maintenance Regulation means a Member State;]

["State bound by the Lugano Convention" in any provision, in the application of that provision in relation to the Lugano Convention has the same meaning as in Article 1(3) of that Convention;]

["Regulation State" in any provision, in the application of that provision in relation to the Regulation, means a Member State].]

[(4) Any question arising as to whether it is the Regulation, any of [the Brussels Conventions, the Lugano Convention, or the 2005 Hague Convention] which applies in the circumstances of a particular case shall be determined as follows—

(a) in accordance with [Article 64] of the Lugano Convention (which determines the relationship between the Brussels Conventions and the Lugano Convention); . . .

(b) in accordance with Article 68 of the Regulation (which determines the relationship between the Brussels Conventions and the Regulation)[; and

(c) in accordance with Article 26 of the 2005 Hague Convention (which determines the relationship between the Brussels Conventions, the Lugano Convention, the Regulation and the 2005 Hague Convention)].]

NOTES

Sub-s (1) is amended as follows:

Definition "the 1982 Accession Convention" inserted by the Civil Jurisdiction and Judgments Act 1982 (Amendment) Order 1989, SI 1989/1346, art 3.

Definition "the 1989 Accession Convention" inserted by the Civil Jurisdiction and Judgments Act 1982 (Amendment) Order 1990, SI 1990/2591, art 3.

Definition "the 1996 Accession Convention" inserted by the Civil Jurisdiction and Judgments Act 1982 (Amendment) Order 2000, SI 2000/1824, art 3(a) and repealed by the Civil Jurisdiction and Judgments (Amendment) (EU Exit) Regulations 2019, SI 2019/479, regs 4, 6(1), (2)(a)(i), as from exit day (as defined in the European Union (Withdrawal) Act 2018, s 20).

Definition "the 2005 Hague Convention" inserted by the Civil Jurisdiction and Judgments (Hague Convention on Choice of Court Agreements 2005) Regulations 2015, SI 2015/1644, regs 2, 3(1), (2), as from 1 October 2015.

Definition "the 2007 Hague Convention" inserted by the International Recovery of Maintenance (Hague Convention 2007) (Rules of Court) Regulations 2012, SI 2012/1770, regs 3, 4(a).

Definition "the Brussels Convention" repealed by SI 2019/479, regs 4, 6(1), (2)(a)(ii), as from exit day (as defined in the European Union (Withdrawal) Act 2018, s 20); words in square brackets therein substituted by SI 2000/1824, art 3(b).

Definition "the Lugano Convention" (as inserted by the Civil Jurisdiction and Judgments Act 1991, s 2(3)) substituted by the Civil Jurisdiction and Judgments Regulations 2009, SI 2009/3131, regs 2, 3(1), (2) and repealed by SI 2019/479, regs 4, 6(1), (2)(a)(iii), as from exit day (as defined in the European Union (Withdrawal) Act 2018, s 20)

Definition "the Maintenance Regulation" inserted by the Civil Jurisdiction and Judgments (Maintenance) (Rules of Court) Regulations 2011, SI 2011/1215, regs 3, 4(1), (2).

Definition "the Regulation" (as inserted by SI 2001/3929, art 4, Sch 2, Pt I, para 1(a)) substituted by the Civil Jurisdiction and Judgments (Amendment) Regulations 2014, SI 2014/2947, reg 2, Sch 1, paras 1, 2, as from 10 January 2015; words in italics repealed and words in square brackets inserted, by SI 2019/479, regs 4, 6(1), (2)(b), as from exit day (as defined in the European Union (Withdrawal) Act 2018, s 20).

Sub-s (2): repealed by SI 2019/479, regs 4, 6(1), (3), as from exit day (as defined in the European Union (Withdrawal) Act 2018, s 20); words in square brackets in para (a) substituted by SI 2000/1824, art 4; para (aa) inserted by SI 2000/1824, art 9 and repealed by SI 2009/3131, regs 2, 3(1), (3).

Sub-s (3) is substituted by SI 1990/2591, art 6 and subsequently amended as follows:

Words in square brackets beginning with the words "In this Act" substituted by the Civil Jurisdiction and Judgments Act 1991, s 2(5), (6).

Definition "2005 Hague Convention State" inserted by SI 2015/1644, regs 2, 3(1), (3)(a), as from 1 October 2015.

Definition "2007 Hague Convention State" inserted by SI 2012/1770, regs 3, 4(b).

Definition "Brussels Contracting State" substituted by SI 2007/1655, reg 2(1), (3)(a); words in square brackets substituted by SI 2012/1809, art 3(1), Schedule, Pt 1; repealed by SI 2019/479, regs 4, 6(1), (4)(b), as from exit day (as defined in the European Union (Withdrawal) Act 2018, s 20).

In definition "Contracting State" word omitted from para (a) repealed, and para (c) and word "and" immediately preceding it inserted, by SI 2015/1644, regs 2, 3(1), (3)(b), as from 1 October 2015; words in square brackets in para (b) substituted by SI 2009/3131, regs 2, 3(1), (4)(a); paras (a), (b) repealed by SI 2019/479, regs 4, 6(1), (4)(a), as from exit day (as defined in the European Union (Withdrawal) Act 2018, s 20).

Definition "Maintenance Regulation State" inserted by SI 2011/1215, regs 3, 4(1), (3).

Definition "State bound by the Lugano Convention" substituted, for definition "Lugano Contracting State" (as inserted by the Civil Jurisdiction and Judgments Act 1991, s 2(5), (6)), by SI 2009/3131, regs 2, 3(1), (4)(b); repealed by SI 2019/479, regs 4, 6(1), (4)(c)(i), as from exit day (as defined in the European Union (Withdrawal) Act 2018, s 20)

Definition "Regulation State" (as inserted by SI 2001/3929, art 4, Sch 2, Pt I, para 1(b)(ii)) substituted by SI 2007/1655, reg 2(1), (3)(b); repealed by SI 2019/479, regs 4, 6(1), (4)(c)(ii), as from exit day (as defined in the European Union (Withdrawal) Act 2018, s 20)

Sub-s (4): inserted by SI 2001/3929, art 4, Sch 2, Pt I, para 1(c); words in first pair of square brackets substituted, word omitted from para (a) repealed, and para (c) inserted together with word immediately preceding it, by SI 2015/1644, regs 2, 3(1), (4), as from 1 October 2015; words in square brackets in para (a) substituted by SI 2009/3131, regs 2, 3(1), (5); repealed by SI 2019/479, regs 4, 6(1), (5), as from exit day (as defined in the European Union (Withdrawal) Act 2018, s 20)

PART II
JURISDICTION, AND RECOGNITION AND ENFORCEMENT OF JUDGMENTS, WITHIN UNITED KINGDOM

[Jurisdiction in consumer and employment matters

[1.136]
15A Scope of sections 15B to 15E

(1) Sections 15B to 15E make provision about the jurisdiction of courts in the United Kingdom—

(a) in matters relating to consumer contracts where the consumer is domiciled in the United Kingdom;

(b) in matters relating to individual contracts of employment.

(2) Sections 15B and 15C apply only if the subject-matter of the proceedings and the nature of the proceedings are within the scope of the Regulation as determined by Article 1 of the Regulation (whether or not the Regulation would have had effect before exit day in relation to the proceedings).

(3) Sections 15B to 15E do not apply to proceedings of a description listed in Schedule 5 or to proceedings in Scotland under an enactment which confers jurisdiction on a Scottish court in respect of a specific subject-matter on specific grounds.]

NOTES

Commencement: exit day (as defined in the European Union (Withdrawal) Act 2018, s 20).

Inserted, together with preceding heading, by the Civil Jurisdiction and Judgments (Amendment) (EU Exit) Regulations 2019, SI 2019/479, regs 4, 26, as from exit day (as defined in the European Union (Withdrawal) Act 2018, s 20).

[1.137]
[15C Jurisdiction in relation to individual contracts of employment

(1) This section applies in relation to proceedings whose subject-matter is a matter relating to an individual contract of employment.

(2) The employer may be sued by the employee—

(a) where the employer is domiciled in the United Kingdom, in the courts for the part of the United Kingdom in which the employer is domiciled,

(b) in the courts for the place in the United Kingdom where or from where the employee habitually carries out the employee's work or last did so (regardless of the domicile of the employer), or

(c) if the employee does not or did not habitually carry out the employee's work in any one part of the United Kingdom, in the courts for the place in the United Kingdom where the business which engaged the employee is situated (regardless of the domicile of the employer).

(3) If the employee is domiciled in the United Kingdom, the employer may only sue the employee in the part of the United Kingdom in which the employee is domiciled (regardless of the domicile of the employer).

(4) Subsections (2) and (3) are subject to rule 11 of Schedule 4 (and rule 14 of Schedule 4 has effect accordingly).

(5) Subsections (2) and (3) do not affect—

(a) the right (under rule 5(c) of Schedule 4 or otherwise) to bring a counterclaim in the court in which, in accordance with subsection (2) or (3), the original claim is pending,

(b) the operation of rule 3(e) of Schedule 4,

(c) the operation of rule 5(a) of Schedule 4 so far as it permits an employer to be sued by an employee, or

(d) the operation of any other rule of law which permits a person not domiciled in the United Kingdom to be sued in the courts of a part of the United Kingdom.

(6) Subsections (2) and (3) may be departed from only by an agreement which—

(a) is entered into after the dispute has arisen, or

(b) allows the employee to bring proceedings in courts other than those indicated in this section.

(7) For the purposes of this section, where an employee enters into an individual contract of employment with an employer who is not domiciled in the United Kingdom, the employer is deemed to be domiciled in the relevant part of the United Kingdom if the employer has a branch, agency or other establishment in that part of the United Kingdom and the dispute arose from the operation of that branch, agency or establishment.]

NOTES

Commencement: exit day (as defined in the European Union (Withdrawal) Act 2018, s 20).

Inserted by the Civil Jurisdiction and Judgments (Amendment) (EU Exit) Regulations 2019, SI 2019/479, regs 4, 26, as from exit day (as defined in the European Union (Withdrawal) Act 2018, s 20).

[1.138]

[15D Further provision as to jurisdiction

(1) Agreements or provisions of a trust instrument conferring jurisdiction shall have no legal force if they are contrary to the provisions of section 15B(6) or 15C(6).

(2) Even if it would not otherwise have jurisdiction under section 15B or 15C, a court of a part of the United Kingdom before which a defendant enters an appearance has jurisdiction in those proceedings.

(3) Subsection (2) does not apply where —

(a) appearance was entered to contest the jurisdiction, or

(b) another court in the United Kingdom has exclusive jurisdiction by virtue of rule 11 of Schedule 4.

(4) Subsection (2) does not apply if the defendant is the consumer or employee in relation to the subject-matter of the proceedings, unless the defendant is informed by the court of—

(a) the defendant's right to contest the jurisdiction, and

(b) the consequences of entering or not entering an appearance.

(5) Subsection (6) applies where—

(a) a defendant domiciled in the United Kingdom is sued in a court of a part of the United Kingdom other than the part in which the defendant is domiciled and does not enter an appearance, and

(b) the subject-matter of the proceedings is a matter in relation to which section 15B or 15C applies.

(6) The court must—

(a) declare of its own motion that it has no jurisdiction, unless it has jurisdiction by virtue of section 15B or 15C or a rule referred to in section 15B(4) or (5) or 15C(4) or (5);

(b) stay the proceedings so long as it is not shown that—

(i) the defendant has been able to receive the document instituting the proceedings or an equivalent document in sufficient time to enable the defendant to arrange for the defendant's defence, or

(ii) all necessary steps have been taken to this end.

(7) Application may be made to the courts of a part of the United Kingdom for such provisional, including protective, measures as may be available under the law of that part, even if, by virtue of section 15B or 15C or this section, the courts of another part of the United Kingdom have jurisdiction as to the substance of the matter.]

NOTES

Commencement: exit day (as defined in the European Union (Withdrawal) Act 2018, s 20).

Inserted by the Civil Jurisdiction and Judgments (Amendment) (EU Exit) Regulations 2019, SI 2019/479, regs 4, 26, as from exit day (as defined in the European Union (Withdrawal) Act 2018, s 20).

[1.139]

[15E Interpretation

(1) In sections 15A to 15D and this section—

"consumer", in relation to a consumer contract, means a person who concludes the contract for a purpose which can be regarded as being outside the person's trade or profession;

"consumer contract" means—

(a) a contract for the sale of goods on instalment credit terms,

(b) a contract for a loan repayable by instalments, or for any other form of credit, made to finance the sale of goods, or

(c) a contract which has been concluded with a person who—

but it does not include a contract of transport other than a contract which, for an inclusive price, provides for a combination of travel and accommodation or a contract of insurance,

(i) pursues commercial or professional activities in the part of the United Kingdom in which the consumer is domiciled, or

(ii) by any means, directs such activities to that part or to other parts of the United Kingdom including that part,

and which falls within the scope of such activities,

"defendant" includes defender.

(2) In determining any question as to the meaning or effect of any provision contained in sections 15A to 15D and this section—

(a) regard is to be had to any relevant principles laid down before exit day by the European Court in connection with Title II of the 1968 Convention or Chapter 2 of the Regulation and to any relevant decision of that court before exit day as to the meaning or effect of any provision of that Title or Chapter, and

(b) without prejudice to the generality of paragraph (a), the expert reports relating to the 1968 Convention may be considered and are, so far as relevant, to be given such weight as is appropriate in the circumstances.]

NOTES

Commencement: exit day (as defined in the European Union (Withdrawal) Act 2018, s 20).

Inserted by the Civil Jurisdiction and Judgments (Amendment) (EU Exit) Regulations 2019, SI 2019/479, regs 4, 26, as from exit day (as defined in the European Union (Withdrawal) Act 2018, s 20).

[Jurisdiction in other civil proceedings]

NOTES

Heading inserted by the Civil Jurisdiction and Judgments (Amendment) (EU Exit) Regulations 2019, SI 2019/479, regs 4, 27, as from exit day (as defined in the European Union (Withdrawal) Act 2018, s 20).

[1.140]

16 Allocation within UK of jurisdiction in certain civil proceedings

(1) The provisions set out in Schedule 4 (which contains a modified version of [Chapter II of the Regulation]) shall have effect for determining, for each part of the United Kingdom, whether the courts of law of that part, or any particular court of law in that part, have or has jurisdiction in proceedings where—

[(a) the subject-matter of the proceedings is within the scope of the Regulation as determined by Article 1 of the Regulation (whether or not the Regulation *has effect* in relation to the proceedings); and]

(b) the defendant or defender is domiciled in the United Kingdom or the proceedings are of a kind mentioned in [[Article 24] of the Regulation] (exclusive jurisdiction regardless of domicile).

[(1A) This section and Schedule 4 do not apply for the purposes of determining jurisdiction in proceedings in relation to which section 15B, 15C or 15D(2) applies, except as specified in those sections.]

(2) . . .

(3) In determining any question as to the meaning or effect of any provision contained in Schedule 4—

(a) regard shall be had to any relevant principles laid down by the European Court in connection with Title II of the 1968 Convention [or Chapter II of the Regulation] and to any relevant decision of that court as to the meaning or effect of any provision of that Title [or that Chapter]; and

(b) without prejudice to the generality of paragraph (a), *the reports mentioned in section 3(3)* may be considered and shall, so far as relevant, be given such weight as is appropriate in the circumstances.

[(3A) The requirement in subsection (3)(a) applies only in relation to principles laid down, or decisions made, by the European Court before exit day.]

(4) The provisions of this section and Schedule 4 shall have effect subject to [*the Regulation*[, Schedule 6 to the Civil Jurisdiction and Judgments (Maintenance) Regulations 2011],] *the 1968 Convention*[*, the Lugano Convention* and the 2005 Hague Convention] and to the provisions of *section 17*.

(5) . . .

NOTES

Sub-s (1): words in first pair of square brackets, para (a), and words in first (outer) pair of square brackets in para (b) substituted by the Civil Jurisdiction and Judgments Order 2001, SI 2001/3929, art 4, Sch 2, Pt II, para 3(a); words in second (inner) pair of square brackets in para (b) substituted by the Civil Jurisdiction and Judgments (Amendment) Regulations 2014, SI 2014/2947, reg 2, Sch 1, paras 1, 3; for the words in italics in para (a) there are substituted the words "would have had effect before exit day", by the Civil Jurisdiction and Judgments (Amendment) (EU Exit) Regulations 2019, SI 2019/479, regs 4, 28(1), (2), as from exit day (as defined in the European Union (Withdrawal) Act 2018, s 20).

Sub-s (1A): inserted by SI 2019/479, regs 4, 28(1), (3), as from exit day (as defined in the European Union (Withdrawal) Act 2018, s 20).

Sub-s (2): repealed by SI 2001/3929, art 4, Sch 2, Pt II, para 3(b).

Sub-s (3): words in square brackets in para (a) inserted by SI 2001/3929, art 4, Sch 2, Pt II, para 3(c); for the words in italics in para (b) there are substituted the words "the expert reports relating to the 1968 Convention", by SI 2019/479, regs 4, 28(1), (4), as from exit day (as defined in the European Union (Withdrawal) Act 2018, s 20).

Sub-s (3A): inserted by SI 2019/479, regs 4, 28(1), (5), as from exit day (as defined in the European Union (Withdrawal) Act 2018, s 20).

Sub-s (4): words in first (outer) pair of square brackets inserted by SI 2001/3929, art 4, Sch 2, Pt II, para 3(d); words in second (inner) pair of square brackets inserted by the Civil Jurisdiction and Judgments (Maintenance) Regulations 2011, SI 2011/1484, reg 6, Sch 4, paras 1, 2; words in third pair of square brackets substituted by the Civil Jurisdiction and Judgments (Hague Convention on Choice of Court Agreements 2005) Regulations 2015, SI 2015/1644, regs 2, 11; words in italics in the first and second places repealed and for the words in italics in the third place there are substituted the words "sections 15B, 15C, 15D and 17", by SI 2019/479, regs 4, 28(1), (6), as from exit day (as defined in the European Union (Withdrawal) Act 2018, s 20).

Sub-s (5): amends the Maintenance Orders Act 1950, s 15(1)(a).

[Recognition of judgments]

NOTES

Heading inserted by the Civil Jurisdiction and Judgments (Amendment) (EU Exit) Regulations 2019, SI 2019/479, regs 4, 29, as from exit day (as defined in the European Union (Withdrawal) Act 2018, s 20).

[1.141]

18 Enforcement of UK judgments in other parts of UK

(1) In relation to any judgment to which this section applies—

(a) Schedule 6 shall have effect for the purpose of enabling any money provisions contained in the judgment to be enforced in a part of the United Kingdom other than the part in which the judgment was given; and

(b) Schedule 7 shall have effect for the purpose of enabling any non-money provisions so contained to be so enforced.

(2) In this section "judgment" means any of the following (references to the giving of a judgment being construed accordingly)—

(a) any judgment or order (by whatever name called) given or made by a court of law in the United Kingdom;

(b) any judgment or order not within paragraph (a) which has been entered in England and Wales [in the High Court or the county court or in] Northern Ireland in the High Court or a county court;

(c) any document which in Scotland has been registered for execution in the Books of Council and Session or in the sheriff court books kept for any sheriffdom;

(d) any award or order made by a tribunal in any part of the United Kingdom which is enforceable in that part without an order of a court of law;

(e) an arbitration award which has become enforceable in the part of the United Kingdom in which it was given in the same manner as a judgment given by a court of law in that part;

[(f) an order made, or a warrant issued, under Part 8 of the Proceeds of Crime Act 2002 for the purposes of a civil recovery investigation [. . .] within the [meaning] given by section 341 of that Act [or an unexplained wealth order made under that Part (see sections 362A and 396A of that Act)];]

[(g) an order made, or a warrant issued, under Chapter 3 of Part 8 of the Proceeds of Crime Act 2002 for the purposes of a detained cash investigation[, a detained property investigation or a frozen funds investigation] within the [meanings] given by section 341 of that Act;]

and, subject to the following provisions of this section, this section applies to all such judgments.

(3) Subject to [subsections (4)][, (4ZA) and (4ZB)], this section does not apply to—

(a) a judgment given in proceedings in a magistrates' court in England and Wales or Northern Ireland;

(b) a judgment given in proceedings other than civil proceedings;

[(ba) a judgment given in the exercise of jurisdiction in relation to insolvency law, within the meaning of section [426 of the Insolvency Act 1986];]

(c) a judgment given in proceedings relating to—

(i) . . .

(ii) . . .

(iii) the obtaining of title to administer the estate of a deceased person;

[(d) an order made under Part 2, 3 or 4 of the Proceeds of Crime Act 2002 (confiscation)].

(4) This section applies, whatever the nature of the proceedings in which it is made, to—

(a) a decree issued under section 13 of the Court of Exchequer (Scotland) Act 1856 (recovery of certain rentcharges and penalties by process of the Court of Session);

(b) an order which is enforceable in the same manner as a judgment of the High Court in England and Wales by virtue of section 16 of the Contempt of Court Act 1981 or section 140 of the [Senior Courts Act 1981] (which relate to fines for contempt of court and forfeiture of recognisances).

[(4ZA) This section applies to a freezing order made under section 40D of the Immigration Act 2014 by a magistrates' court in England and Wales or a court of summary jurisdiction in Northern Ireland.]

[(4ZB) This section applies to the following orders made by a magistrates' court in England and Wales or Northern Ireland—

(a) an account freezing order made under section 303Z3 of the Proceeds of Crime Act 2002;

(b) an order for the forfeiture of money made under section 303Z14 of that Act;

(c) an account freezing order made under paragraph 10S of Schedule 1 to the Anti-terrorism, Crime and Security Act 2001;

(d) an order for the forfeiture of money made under paragraph 10Z2 of that Schedule.]

[(4A) This section does not apply as respects—

(a) the enforcement in Scotland of orders made by the High Court or [the county court] in England and Wales under or for the purposes of Part VI of the Criminal Justice Act 1988 or the Drug Trafficking Act 1994 (confiscation of the proceeds of certain offences or of drug trafficking); or

(b) the enforcement in England and Wales of orders made by the Court of Session [or by the sheriff] under or for the purposes of [the Proceeds of Crime (Scotland) Act 1995].]

(5) This section does not apply to so much of any judgment as—

(a) is an order to which section 16 of the Maintenance Orders Act 1950 applies (and is therefore an order for whose enforcement in another part of the United Kingdom provision is made by Part II of that Act);

(b) concerns the status or legal capacity of an individual;

(c) relates to the management of the affairs of a person not capable of managing his own affairs;

(d) is a provisional (including protective) measure [other than an order of any of the following kinds—

(i) a freezing order of the kind mentioned in paragraph (a) or (c) of subsection (4ZB) made (in Scotland) by the sheriff (in addition to such orders made by a magistrates' court in England and Wales or Northern Ireland);

(ii) an order for the making of an interim payment;
(iii) an interim order made in connection with the civil recovery of proceeds of unlawful conduct;
(iv) an interim freezing order under section 362J of the Proceeds of Crime Act 2002;
(v) an interim freezing order under section 396J of that Act];

and except where otherwise stated references to a judgment to which this section applies are to such a judgment exclusive of any such provisions.

(6) The following are within subsection (5)(b), but without prejudice to the generality of that provision—

(a) a decree of judicial separation or of separation;
[(b) any order which is a Part I order for the purposes of the Family Law Act 1986.]

[(6A) In subsection (5)(d), "an interim order made in connection with the civil recovery of proceeds of unlawful conduct" means any of the following made under Chapter 2 of Part 5 of the Proceeds of Crime Act 2002—

(a) a property freezing order or prohibitory property order;
(b) an order under section 245E or 245F of that Act (order relating to receivers in connection with property freezing order);
(c) an interim receiving order or interim administration order;
[(d) an order under section 255G or 255H of that Act (order relating to PPO receivers in connection with prohibitory property order)].]

(7) This section does not apply to a judgment of a court outside the United Kingdom which falls to be treated for the purposes of its enforcement as a judgment of a court of law in the United Kingdom by virtue of registration under Part II of the Administration of Justice Act 1920, Part I of the Foreign Judgments (Reciprocal Enforcement) Act 1933, Part I of the Maintenance Orders (Reciprocal Enforcement) Act 1972[, the International Recovery of Maintenance (Hague Convention 2007) Regulations 2012] *or section 4 or 5 of this Act* [or by virtue of the Civil Jurisdiction and Judgments (Maintenance) Regulations 2011].

(8) A judgment to which this section applies, other than a judgment within paragraph (e) of subsection (2), shall not be enforced in another part of the United Kingdom except by way of registration under Schedule 6 or 7.

NOTES

Sub-s (2) is amended as follows:

In para (b) words in square brackets substituted by the Crime and Courts Act 2013, s 17(5), Sch 9, Pt 3, para 66.

Para (f) inserted by the Proceeds of Crime Act 2002 (Investigations in different parts of the United Kingdom) Order 2003, SI 2003/425, art 34; words omitted from first pair of square brackets inserted by the Serious Crime Act 2007, s 77, Sch 10, para 26(a) and repealed by the Policing and Crime Act 2009, s 112(1), (2), Sch 7, Pt 8, para 114, Sch 8, Pt 5, as from 1 June 2015; word in second pair of square brackets substituted by the Policing and Crime Act 2009, s 112(1), Sch 7, Pt 8, para 114(a)(ii), as from 1 June 2015; words in third pair of square brackets inserted by the Criminal Finances Act 2017, s 53, Sch 5, para 3(1), (2), as from 16 April 2018.

Para (g) inserted by the Policing and Crime Act 2009, s 112(1), Sch 7, Pt 8, para 114(b), as from 1 June 2015; words in first pair of square brackets inserted by the Criminal Finances Act 2017, s 53, Sch 5, para 3(1), (3)(a), as from 16 April 2018; word in second pair of square brackets substituted by the Criminal Finances Act 2017, s 53, Sch 5, para 3(1), (3)(b), as from 16 April 2018.

Sub-s (3): words in first pair of square brackets substituted by the Immigration Act 2016, s 45, Sch 7, para 7(1), (2), as from 30 October 2017; words in second pair of square brackets substituted by the Criminal Finances Act 2017, s 53, Sch 5, para 3(1), (4), as from 16 April 2018; para (ba) inserted by the Insolvency Act 1985, s 235, Sch 8, para 36 and words in square brackets therein substituted by the Insolvency Act 1986, s 439(2), Sch 14; para (c)(i), (ii) repealed by the Insolvency Act 1986, s 437, Sch 11; para (d) inserted by the Proceeds of Crime Act 2002, s 456, Sch 11, paras 1, 11.

Sub-s (4): words in square brackets in para (b) substituted by the Constitutional Reform Act 2005, s 59(5), Sch 11, Pt 1, para 1(2).

Sub-s (4ZA): inserted by the Immigration Act 2016, s 45, Sch 7, para 7(1), (3), as from 30 October 2017.

Sub-s (4ZB): inserted by the Criminal Finances Act 2017, s 53, Sch 5, para 3(1), (5), as from 16 April 2018.

Sub-s (4A): inserted by the Drug Trafficking Offences Act 1986, s 39(4) and substituted by the Drug Trafficking Act 1994, s 65, Sch 1, para 6; words in square brackets in para (a) substituted by the Crime and Courts Act 2013, s 17(5), Sch 9, Pt 3, para 52(1)(b), (2); in para (b), first words in square brackets inserted by the Criminal Justice (Scotland) Act 1995, s 117, Sch 6, para 183 and second words in square brackets substituted by the Criminal Procedure (Consequential Provisions) (Scotland) Act 1995, s 5, Sch 4, para 42.

Sub-s (5): in para (d) words in square brackets substituted by the Criminal Finances Act 2017, s 53, Sch 5, para 3(1), (6), as from 16 April 2018.

Sub-s (6): para (b) substituted by the Courts and Legal Services Act 1990, s 116, Sch 16, para 41.

Sub-s (6A): inserted by the Crime and Courts Act 2013, s 48(6)(a), Sch 18, Pt 1, paras 1, 3, as from 1 June 2015; para (d) inserted by the Serious Crime Act 2015, s 85(1), Sch 4, para 6, as from 1 June 2015.

Sub-s (7): words in first pair of square brackets inserted by SI 2012/2814, reg 8, Sch 4, para 5(1), (2), as from a day to be appointed; words in second pair of square brackets inserted by the Civil Jurisdiction and Judgments (Maintenance) Regulations 2011, SI 2011/1484, reg 6, Sch 4, paras 1, 3; words in italics repealed by the Civil Jurisdiction and Judgments (Amendment) (EU Exit) Regulations 2019, SI 2019/479, regs 4, 30, as from exit day (as defined in the European Union (Withdrawal) Act 2018, s 20).

Regulations: the Employment Tribunals (Enforcement of Orders in Other Jurisdictions) (Scotland) Regulations 2002, SI 2002/2972 at **[2.676]**.

[1.142]
19 Recognition of UK judgments in other parts of UK
(1) A judgment to which this section applies given in one part of the United Kingdom shall not be refused recognition in another part of the United Kingdom solely on the ground that, in relation to that judgment, the court which gave it was not a court of competent jurisdiction according to the rules of private international law in force in that other part.
(2) Subject to subsection (3), this section applies to any judgment to which section 18 applies.
(3) This section does not apply to—
(a) the documents mentioned in paragraph (c) of the definition of "judgment" in section 18(2);
(b) the awards and orders mentioned in paragraphs (d) and (e) of that definition;
(c) the decrees and orders referred to in section 18(4).

PART III
JURISDICTION IN SCOTLAND

[1.143]
20 Rules as to jurisdiction in Scotland
(1) Subject to [*the Regulation, to*] Parts I and II and to the following provisions of this Part, Schedule 8 has effect to determine in what circumstances a person may be sued in civil proceedings in the Court of Session or in a sheriff court.
(2) Nothing in Schedule 8 affects the competence as respects subject-matter or value of the Court of Session or of the sheriff court.
(3) [Section 43 of the Courts Reform (Scotland) Act 2014 does not apply—]
[(a)] . . . in relation to any matter to which Schedule 8 applies[; and
(b) to the extent that it relates to any matter where jurisdiction falls to be determined by reference to the jurisdictional requirements of the Maintenance Regulation and Schedule 6 to the Civil Jurisdiction and Judgments (Maintenance) Regulations 2011].
(4) . . .
(5) In determining any question as to the meaning or effect of any provision contained in Schedule 8 . . . —
(a) regard shall be had to any relevant principles laid down by the European Court in connection with Title II of the 1968 Convention [or Chapter II of the Regulation] and to any relevant decision of that court as to the meaning or effect of any provision of that Title [or that Chapter]; and
(b) without prejudice to the generality of paragraph (a), *the reports mentioned in section 3(3)* may be considered and shall, so far as relevant, be given such weight as is appropriate in the circumstances.
[(6) The requirement in subsection (5)(a) applies only in relation to principles laid down, or decisions made, by the European Court before exit day.]

NOTES
Sub-s (1): words in square brackets inserted by the Civil Jurisdiction and Judgments Order 2001, SI 2001/3929, art 4, Sch 2, Pt III, para 6(a) and repealed by the Civil Jurisdiction and Judgments (Amendment) (EU Exit) Regulations 2019, SI 2019/479, regs 4, 31(1), (2), as from exit day (as defined in the European Union (Withdrawal) Act 2018, s 20).
Sub-s (3): words in first pair of square brackets substituted and words omitted repealed in relation to Scotland by the Courts Reform (Scotland) Act 2014, s 132, Sch 5, Pt 1, para 7 and in relation to England and Wales by the Courts Reform (Scotland) Act 2014 (Consequential Provisions and Modifications) Order 2015, SI 2015/700, art 2, Schedule, para 11(1), (2), as from 1 April 2015; para (a) numbered as such, and para (b) and word "; and" immediately preceding it inserted, by the Civil Jurisdiction and Judgments (Maintenance) Regulations 2011, SI 2011/1484, reg 6, Sch 4, paras 1, 4; words omitted repealed in relation to Scotland by the Courts Reform (Scotland) Act 2014, s 132, Sch 5, Pt 1, para 7 and in relation to England and Wales by SI 2015/700, art 10, Schedule, para 11(1), (2)(b), as from 1 April 2015.
Sub-s (4): repealed by SI 2001/3929, art 4, Sch 2, Pt III, para 6(b).
Sub-s (5): words omitted repealed, and words in square brackets inserted, by SI 2001/3929, art 4, Sch 2, Pt III, para 6(c); for the words in italics there are substituted the words "the expert reports relating to the 1968 Convention", by SI 2019/479, regs 4, 31(1), (3), as from exit day (as defined in the European Union (Withdrawal) Act 2018, s 20).
Sub-s (6): added by SI 2019/479, regs 4, 31(1), (4), as from exit day (as defined in the European Union (Withdrawal) Act 2018, s 20).

PART V
SUPPLEMENTARY AND GENERAL PROVISIONS

Domicile

[1.144]
[42A Domicile of corporation or association for purposes of certain civil proceedings
(1) This section determines whether a corporation or association is domiciled in the United Kingdom for the purposes of—
(a) sections 15A to 15E, and
(b) section 16(1)(b).
(2) A corporation or association has its domicile in the United Kingdom if and only if—
(a) its registered office is at a place in the United Kingdom,
(b) its place of incorporation is in the United Kingdom (in a case where it has no registered office),
(c) the place under the law of which its formation took place is a place in the United Kingdom (in a case where it has no registered office or place of incorporation),
(d) its central administration is in the United Kingdom, or

(e) its principal place of business is in the United Kingdom.]

NOTES

Commencement: exit day (as defined in the European Union (Withdrawal) Act 2018, s 20).

Inserted by the Civil Jurisdiction and Judgments (Amendment) (EU Exit) Regulations 2019, SI 2019/479, regs 4, 42, as from exit day (as defined in the European Union (Withdrawal) Act 2018, s 20).

General

[1.145]

50 Interpretation: general

In this Act, unless the context otherwise requires—

["the Accession Convention", ["the 1982 Accession Convention", *"the 1989 Accession Convention" and "the 1996 Accession Convention"*] have the meaning given by section 1(1);]

"Article" and references to sub-divisions of numbered Articles are to be construed in accordance with section 1(2)(b);

"association" means an unincorporated body of persons;

["Brussels Contracting State" has the meaning given by section 1(3);

"the Brussels Conventions" has the meaning given by section 1(1);]

"Contracting State" has the meaning given by section 1(3);

"the 1968 Convention" has the meaning given by section 1(1), and references to that Convention and to provisions of it are to be construed in accordance with section 1(2)(a);

["the 2005 Hague Convention" has the meaning given by section 1(1);

"2005 Hague Convention State" has the meaning given by section 1(3);]

. . .

"corporation" means a body corporate, and includes a partnership subsisting under the law of Scotland;

"court", without more, includes a tribunal;

"court of law", in relation to the United Kingdom, means any of the following courts, namely—

[(a) the Supreme Court,]

[(aa) in England and Wales, the Court of Appeal, the High Court, the Crown Court, the family court, the county court and a magistrates' court,]

(b) in . . . Northern Ireland, the Court of Appeal, the High Court, the Crown Court, a county court and a magistrates' court,

(c) in Scotland, the Court of Session[, the Sheriff Appeal Court] and a sheriff court;

"the Crown" is to be construed in accordance with section 51(2);

"enactment" includes an enactment comprised in Northern Ireland legislation;

["the expert reports relating to the 1968 Convention" means—

(a) the reports by Mr P Jenard on the 1968 Convention and the 1971 Protocol;

(b) the report by Professor Peter Schlosser on the Accession Convention;

(c) the report by Professor Demetrios I Evrigenis and Professor K D Kerameus on the 1982 Accession Convention; and

(d) the report by Mr Martinho de Almeida Cruz, Mr Manuel Desantes Real and Mr P Jenard on the 1989 Accession Convention;]

["the 2007 Hague Convention" has the meaning given by section 1(1);

"2007 Hague Convention State" has the meaning given by section 1(3);]

"judgment", subject to sections 15(1) and 18(2) and to paragraph 1 of Schedules 6 and 7, means any judgment or order (by whatever name called) given or made by a court in any civil proceedings;

[. . .

"the Lugano Convention" has the meaning given by section 1(1);]

"magistrates' court", in relation to Northern Ireland, means a court of summary jurisdiction;

["the Maintenance Regulation" has the meaning given by section 1(1);

"Maintenance Regulation State" has the meaning given by section 1(3);]

"modifications" includes additions, omissions and alterations;

"overseas country" means any country or territory outside the United Kingdom;

"part of the United Kingdom" means England and Wales, Scotland or Northern Ireland;

"the 1971 Protocol" has the meaning given by section 1(1), and references to that Protocol and to provisions of it are to be construed in accordance with section 1(2)(a);

["the Regulation" has the meaning given by section 1(1);]

["Regulation State" has the meaning given by section 1(3);]

"rules of court", in relation to any court, means rules, orders or regulations made by the authority having power to make rules, orders or regulations regulating the procedure of that court, and includes—

(a) in Scotland, Acts of Sederunt;

(b) in Northern Ireland, Judgment Enforcement Rules;

["State bound by the Lugano Convention" has the meaning given by section 1(3);]

"statutory provision" means any provision contained in an Act, or in any Northern Ireland legislation, or in—

(a) subordinate legislation (as defined in section 21(1) of the Interpretation Act 1978); or

(b) any instrument of a legislative character made under any Northern Ireland legislation;

"tribunal"—

(a) means a tribunal of any description other than a court of law;

(b) *in relation to an overseas country, includes, as regards matters relating to maintenance within the meaning of the 1968 Convention, any authority having power to give, enforce, vary or revoke a maintenance order.*

NOTES

Definition "the Accession Convention" substituted by the Civil Jurisdiction and Judgments Act 1982 (Amendment) Order 1990, SI 1990/2591, art 9; words in square brackets substituted by the Civil Jurisdiction and Judgments Act 1982 (Amendment) Order 2000, SI 2000/1824, art 7; for the words in italics there are substituted the words "and "the 1989 Accession Convention"", by the Civil Jurisdiction and Judgments (Amendment) (EU Exit) Regulations 2019, SI 2019/479, regs 4, 52(1), (2), as from exit day (as defined in the European Union (Withdrawal) Act 2018, s 20).

Definition "Article" repealed by SI 2019/479, regs 4, 52(1), (4)(a), as from exit day (as defined in the European Union (Withdrawal) Act 2018, s 20).

Definitions "Brussels Contracting State" and "the Brussels Conventions" inserted by the Civil Jurisdiction and Judgments Act 1991, s 3, Sch 2, para 25 and repealed by SI 2019/479, regs 4, 52(1), (4)(b), (c), as from exit day (as defined in the European Union (Withdrawal) Act 2018, s 20).

Definitions "the 2005 Hague Convention" and "2005 Hague Convention State" inserted by the Civil Jurisdiction and Judgments (Hague Convention on Choice of Court Agreements 2005) Regulations 2015, SI 2015/1644, regs 2, 20, as from 1 October 2015.

Definition "the Conventions" repealed by the Civil Jurisdiction and Judgments Act 1991, s 3, Sch 2, para 25.]

In definition "court of law" para (a) substituted by the Constitutional Reform Act 2005, s 145, Sch 17, Pt 2, para 23, para (aa) inserted and words omitted from para (b) repealed by the Crime and Courts Act 2013, s 17(6), Sch 11, Pt 1, para 86(1), (17), words in square brackets in para (c) inserted in relation to Scotland by the Courts Reform (Scotland) Act 2014, s 132, Sch 5, Pt 2, para 13 and in relation to England and Wales by the Courts Reform (Scotland) Act 2014 (Consequential Provisions and Modifications) Order 2015, SI 2015/700, art 10, Schedule, para 11(1), (3), as from 1 January 2016.

Definition "the expert reports relating to the 1968 Convention" inserted by the Civil Jurisdiction and Judgments (Amendment) (EU Exit) Regulations 2019, SI 2019/479, regs 4, 52(1), (3), as from exit day (as defined in the European Union (Withdrawal) Act 2018, s 20).

Definition "the 2007 Hague Convention" and "2007 Hague Convention State" inserted by SI 2012/1770, regs 3, 6.

Definition "Lugano Contracting State" (omitted) inserted by the Civil Jurisdiction and Judgments Act 1991, s 3, Sch 2, para 25 and repealed by the Civil Jurisdiction and Judgments Regulations 2009, SI 2009/3131, regs 2, 24(a).

Definition "the Lugano Convention" inserted by the Civil Jurisdiction and Judgments Act 1991, s 3, Sch 2, para 25; repealed by SI 2019/479, regs 4, 52(1), (4)(d), as from exit day (as defined in the European Union (Withdrawal) Act 2018, s 20).

Definitions "the Maintenance Regulation" and "Maintenance Regulation State" inserted by the Civil Jurisdiction and Judgments (Maintenance) (Rules of Court) Regulations 2011, SI 2011/1215, regs 3, 6.

Definition "the Regulation" inserted by the Civil Jurisdiction and Judgments Order 2001, SI 2001/3929, art 4, Sch 2, Pt V, para 18.

Definition "Regulation State" inserted by SI 2001/3929, art 4, Sch 2, Pt V, para 18 and repealed by SI 2019/479, regs 4, 52(1), (4)(e), as from exit day (as defined in the European Union (Withdrawal) Act 2018, s 20).

Definition "State bound by the Lugano Convention" inserted by SI 2009/3131, regs 2, 24(b) and repealed by SI 2019/479, regs 4, 52(1), (4)(f), as from exit day (as defined in the European Union (Withdrawal) Act 2018, s 20).

In definition "tribunal", para (b) repealed by SI 2019/479, regs 4, 52(1), (5), as from exit day (as defined in the European Union (Withdrawal) Act 2018, s 20).

[1.146]

51 Application to Crown

(1) This Act binds the Crown.

(2) In this section and elsewhere in this Act references to the Crown do not include references to Her Majesty in Her private capacity or to Her Majesty in right of Her Duchy of Lancaster or to the Duke of Cornwall.

[1.147]

55 Short title

This Act may be cited as the Civil Jurisdiction and Judgments Act 1982.

[SCHEDULE 8
RULES AS TO JURISDICTION IN SCOTLAND

Section 20

General

[1.148]

1 Subject to the following rules, persons shall be sued in the courts for the place where they are domiciled.

Special jurisdiction

2 Subject to rules 3 (jurisdiction over consumer contracts), 4 (jurisdiction over individual contracts of employment), 5 (exclusive jurisdiction) and 6 (prorogation), a person may also be sued—

(a) where he has no fixed residence, in a court within whose jurisdiction he is personally cited;
(b) in matters relating to a contract, in the courts for the place of performance of the obligation in question;
(c) in matters relating to delict or quasi-delict, in the courts for the place where the harmful event occurred or may occur;
(d) as regards a civil claim for damages or restitution which is based on an act giving rise to criminal proceedings, in the court seised of those proceedings to the extent that the court has jurisdiction to entertain civil proceedings;
(e) . . .

(f) as regards a dispute arising out of the operations of a branch, agency or other establishment, in the courts for the place in which the branch, agency or other establishment is situated;
(g) in his capacity as settlor, trustee or beneficiary of a trust domiciled in Scotland created by the operation of a statute, or by a written instrument, or created orally and evidenced in writing, in the Court of Session, or the appropriate sheriff court within the meaning of section 24A of the Trusts (Scotland) Act 1921;
[(ga) in the person's capacity as an executor (where confirmation has been obtained in Scotland)—
(i) in the Court of Session, or
(ii) before a sheriff of the sheriffdom in which confirmation was obtained;]
(h) where he is not domiciled in the United Kingdom, in the courts for any place where—
(i) any movable property belonging to him has been arrested; or
(ii) any immovable property in which he has any beneficial interest is situated;
(i) in proceedings which are brought to assert, declare or determine proprietary or possessory rights, or rights of security, in or over movable property, or to obtain authority to dispose of movable property, in the courts for the place where the property is situated;
(j) in proceedings for interdict, in the courts for the place where it is alleged that the wrong is likely to be committed;
(k) in proceedings concerning a debt secured over immovable property, in the courts for the place where the property is situated;
(l) in proceedings which have as their object a decision of an organ of a company or other legal person or of an association of natural or legal persons, in the courts for the place where that company, legal person or association has its seat;
(m) in proceedings concerning an arbitration which is conducted in Scotland or in which the procedure is governed by Scots law, in the Court of Session;
(n) in proceedings principally concerned with the registration in the United Kingdom or the validity in the United Kingdom of patents, trade marks, designs or other similar rights required to be deposited or registered, in the Court of Session;
(o)
(i) where he is one of a number of defenders, in the courts for the place where any one of them is domiciled, provided the claims are so closely connected that it is expedient to hear and determine them together to avoid the risk of irreconcilable judgments resulting from separate proceedings;
(ii) as a third party in an action on a warranty or guarantee or in any other third party proceedings, in the court seised of the original proceedings, unless these were instituted solely with the object of removing him from the jurisdiction of the court which would be competent in his case;
(iii) on a counterclaim arising from the same contract or facts on which the original claim was based, in the court in which the original claim is pending;
(p) in matters relating to a contract, if the action may be combined with an action against the same defender in matters relating to rights in rem in immovable property, in the courts for the place where the property is situated;
(q) as regards a claim for limitation of liability arising from the use or operation of a ship, in the court having jurisdiction in the action relating to such liability.

3 (*Jurisdiction over consumer contracts: outside the scope of this work.*)

Jurisdiction over individual contracts of employment

4 (1) In matters relating to individual contracts of employment, jurisdiction shall be determined by this rule, without prejudice to rule 2(f).

(2) An employer may be sued—
(a) in the courts for the place where he is domiciled; or
(b) in the courts for the place where the employee habitually carries out his work or in the courts for the last place where he did so; or
(c) if the employee does not or did not habitually carry out his work in any one place, in the courts for the place where the business which engaged the employee is or was situated.

(3) An employer may bring proceedings only in the courts for the place in which the employee is domiciled.

(4) The provisions of this rule shall not affect the right to bring a counter-claim in the court in which, in accordance with this rule, the original claim is pending.

(5) The provisions of this rule may be departed from only by an agreement on jurisdiction—
(a) which is entered into after the dispute has arisen; or
(b) which allows the employee to bring proceedings in courts other than those indicated in this rule.

Exclusive jurisdiction

5 (1) Notwithstanding anything contained in any of rules 1 to 4 above or 6 to 9 below but subject to paragraph (3) below, the following courts shall have exclusive jurisdiction:—
(a) in proceedings which have as their object rights *in rem* in, or tenancies of, immovable property, the courts for the place where the property is situated;
(b) in proceedings which have as their object the validity of the constitution, the nullity or the dissolution of companies or other legal persons or associations of natural or legal persons, the courts for the place where the company, legal person or association has its seat;

(c) in proceedings which have as their object the validity of entries in public registers, the courts for the place where the register is kept;

(d) in proceedings concerned with the enforcement of judgments, the courts for the place where the judgment has been or is to be enforced.

(2) No court shall exercise jurisdiction in a case where immovable property, the seat of a body mentioned in paragraph (1)(b) above, a public register or the place where a judgment has been or is to be enforced is situated outside Scotland and where paragraph (1) would apply if the property, seat, register or, as the case may be, place of enforcement were situated in Scotland.

(3) In proceedings which have as their object tenancies of immovable property concluded for temporary private use for a maximum period of six consecutive months, the courts for the place in which the defender is domiciled shall also have jurisdiction, provided that the tenant is a natural person and that the landlord and tenant are domiciled in Scotland.

Prorogation of jurisdiction

6 (1) If the parties have agreed that a court is to have jurisdiction to settle any disputes which have arisen or which may arise in connection with a particular legal relationship, that court shall have jurisdiction.

(2) Such an agreement conferring jurisdiction shall be either—

(a) in writing or evidenced in writing; or

(b) in a form which accords with practices which the parties have established between themselves; or

(c) in international trade or commerce, in a form which accords with a usage of which the parties are or ought to have been aware and which in such trade or commerce is widely known to, and regularly observed by, parties to contracts of the type involved in the particular trade or commerce concerned.

(3) Any communication by electronic means which provides a durable record of the agreement shall be equivalent to "writing".

(4) The court on which a trust instrument has conferred jurisdiction shall have exclusive jurisdiction in any proceedings brought against a settlor, trustee or beneficiary, if relations between these persons or their rights or obligations under the trust are involved.

(5) Where an agreement or a trust instrument confers jurisdiction on the courts of the United Kingdom or of Scotland, proceedings to which paragraph (1) or, as the case may be, (4) above applies may be brought in any court in Scotland.

(6) Agreements or provisions of a trust instrument conferring jurisdiction shall have no legal force if the courts whose jurisdiction they purport to exclude have exclusive jurisdiction by virtue of rule 5 or where rule 5(2) applies.

7 (1) Apart from jurisdiction derived from other provisions of this Schedule, a court before whom a defender enters an appearance shall have jurisdiction.

(2) This rule shall not apply where appearance was entered to contest jurisdiction, or where another court has exclusive jurisdiction by virtue of rule 5 or where rule 5(2) applies.

Examination as to jurisdiction and admissibility

8 Where a court is seised of a claim which is principally concerned with a matter over which another court has exclusive jurisdiction by virtue of rule 5, or where it is precluded from exercising jurisdiction by rule 5(2), it shall declare of its own motion that it has no jurisdiction.

9 Where in any case a court has no jurisdiction which is compatible with this Schedule, and the defender does not enter an appearance, the court shall declare of its own motion that it has no jurisdiction.]

NOTES

Schedule substituted by the Civil Jurisdiction and Judgments Order 2001, SI 2001/3929, art 4, Sch 2, Pt III, para 7.

Para 2: sub-para (e) repealed by the Civil Jurisdiction and Judgments (Maintenance) Regulations 2011, SI 2011/1484, reg 6, Sch 4, paras 1, 13; sub-para (ga) inserted by the Succession (Scotland) Act 2016, s 27, as from 1 November 2016.

INSOLVENCY ACT 1986

(1986 c 45)

ARRANGEMENT OF SECTIONS

THE FIRST GROUP OF PARTS
COMPANY INSOLVENCY; COMPANIES WINDING UP

PART I
COMPANY VOLUNTARY ARRANGEMENTS

The Proposal

PART II
ADMINISTRATION

PART III
RECEIVERSHIP

CHAPTER I
RECEIVERS AND MANAGERS (ENGLAND AND WALES)

Receivers and managers appointed out of court

Administrative receivers: general

CHAPTER II
RECEIVERS (SCOTLAND)

PART IV
WINDING UP OF COMPANIES REGISTERED UNDER THE COMPANIES ACTS

CHAPTER VI
WINDING UP BY THE COURT

Commencement of winding up

THE SECOND GROUP OF PARTS
INSOLVENCY OF INDIVIDUALS; BANKRUPTCY

PART VIII
INDIVIDUAL VOLUNTARY ARRANGEMENTS

Moratorium for insolvent debtor

Consideration and implementation of debtor's proposal

PART IX
BANKRUPTCY

CHAPTER II
PROTECTION OF BANKRUPT'S ESTATE AND INVESTIGATION OF HIS AFFAIRS

THE THIRD GROUP OF PARTS
MISCELLANEOUS MATTERS BEARING ON BOTH COMPANY AND INDIVIDUAL INSOLVENCY;
GENERAL INTERPRETATION;
FINAL PROVISIONS

PART XII
PREFERENTIAL DEBTS IN COMPANY AND INDIVIDUAL INSOLVENCY

PART XIX
FINAL PROVISIONS

SCHEDULES

An Act to consolidate the enactments relating to company insolvency and winding up (including the winding up of companies that are not insolvent, and of unregistered companies); enactments relating to the insolvency and bankruptcy of individuals; and other enactments bearing on those two subject matters, including the functions and qualification of insolvency practitioners, the public administration of insolvency, the penalisation and redress of malpractice and wrongdoing, and the avoidance of certain transactions at an undervalue

[25 July 1986]

NOTES

Most of this Act covers matters outside the scope of this work, and only those provisions most directly relevant to employment law are printed. For reasons of space, the subject matter of sections, etc, not printed is not annotated. All provisions of the Act printed here except ss 37, 44, 57, and the provisions in the Second Group of Parts (ss 252, 254, 260, 285) apply to England, Wales and Scotland. Sections 37 and 44 apply only to England and Wales (by virtue of s 28) and s 57 applies only to Scotland (by virtue of s 50). None of the provisions in the Second Group of Parts (insolvency of individuals) apply to Scotland (by virtue of s 440). For provisions relating to individual insolvency in Scotland, see the Bankruptcy (Scotland) Act 2016 (outside the scope of this work).

For the application of this Act to limited liability partnerships, see the Limited Liability Partnerships Act 2000, the Limited Liability Partnerships Regulations 2001, SI 2001/1090 and the Limited Liability Partnerships (Scotland) Regulations 2001, SSI 2001/128. This Act has also been applied to the insolvency of various types of company and institutions, including the following: (i) special administration regimes (see the note to s 8 at **[1.150]**); (ii) banks (see the Banking (Special Provisions) Act 2008 and the Banking Act 2009 and the Orders and Regulations made under those Acts); (iii) open-ended investment companies (see the Open-Ended Investment Companies Regulations 2001, SI 2001/1228); (iv) insurers (see the Financial Services and Markets Act 2000 (Administration Orders Relating to Insurers) Order 2010, SI 2010/3023, and the Insurers (Reorganisation and Winding Up) Regulations 2004, SI 2004/353); (v) European public limited-liability companies (see the European Public Limited-Liability Company Regulations 2004, SI 2004/2326); (vi) NHS foundation trusts (see the National Health Service Act 2006); (vii) energy companies (see the Energy Act 2004); (viii) partnerships (see the Insolvent Partnerships Order 1994, SI 1994/2421); (ix) the Royal Mail (see the Postal Services Act 2011, ss 68–88); (x) bodies that hold a licence issued by the Law Society which is in force under Part 5 of the Legal Services Act 2007 (see the Legal Services Act 2007 (Designation as a Licensing Authority) (No 2) Order 2011, SI 2011/2866); (xi) charities and charitable incorporated organisations etc in England and Wales (see the Charities Act 2011 and the Charitable Incorporated Organisations (Insolvency and Dissolution) Regulations 2012, SI 2012/3013). See also the Enterprise Act 2002, ss 254, 255 (power of the Secretary of State and the Treasury to extend the application of this Act to companies incorporated outside Great Britain and to non-companies respectively).

See *Harvey* G.

THE FIRST GROUP OF PARTS
COMPANY INSOLVENCY; COMPANIES WINDING UP

PART I COMPANY VOLUNTARY ARRANGEMENTS

The Proposal

[1.149]
[1A Moratorium

(1) Where the directors of an eligible company intend to make a proposal for a voluntary arrangement, they may take steps to obtain a moratorium for the company.

(2) The provisions of Schedule A1 to this Act have effect with respect to—

(a) companies eligible for a moratorium under this section,
(b) the procedure for obtaining such a moratorium,
(c) the effects of such a moratorium, and
(d) the procedure applicable (in place of sections 1 to 6 and 7) in relation to the approval and implementation of a voluntary arrangement where such a moratorium is or has been in force.]

NOTES

Inserted by the Insolvency Act 2000, s 1, Sch 1, paras 1, 2.

[PART II ADMINISTRATION

[1.150]
8 Administration

Schedule B1 to this Act (which makes provision about the administration of companies) shall have effect.]

NOTES

This section was substituted for Pt II of this Act (ss 8–27) by the Enterprise Act 2002, s 248(1), subject to savings in relation to special administration regimes (as to which see s 249(1), (2) of the 2002 Act).

PART III RECEIVERSHIP

CHAPTER I
RECEIVERS AND MANAGERS (ENGLAND AND WALES)

Receivers and managers appointed out of court

[1.151]
37 Liability for contracts, etc

(1) A receiver or manager appointed under powers conferred in an instrument (other than an administrative receiver) is, to the same extent as if he had been appointed by order of the court—

(a) personally liable on any contract entered into by him in the performance of his functions (except in so far as the contract otherwise provides) and on any contract of employment adopted by him in the performance of those functions, and

(b) entitled in respect of that liability to indemnity out of the assets.

(2) For the purposes of subsection (1)(a), the receiver or manager is not to be taken to have adopted a contract of employment by reason of anything done or omitted to be done within 14 days after his appointment.

(3) Subsection (1) does not limit any right to indemnity which the receiver or manager would have apart from it, nor limit his liability on contracts entered into without authority, nor confer any right to indemnity in respect of that liability.

(4) Where at any time the receiver or manager so appointed vacates office—

(a) his remuneration and any expenses properly incurred by him, and

(b) any indemnity to which he is entitled out of the assets of the company,

shall be charged on and paid out of any property of the company which is in his custody or under his control at that time in priority to any charge or other security held by the person by or on whose behalf he was appointed.

Administrative receivers: general

[1.152]
44 Agency and liability for contracts

(1) The administrative receiver of a company—

(a) is deemed to be the company's agent, unless and until the company goes into liquidation;

(b) is personally liable on any contract entered into by him in the carrying out of his functions (except in so far as the contract otherwise provides) and[, to the extent of any qualifying liability,] on any contract of employment adopted by him in the carrying out of those functions; and

(c) is entitled in respect of that liability to an indemnity out of the assets of the company.

(2) For the purposes of subsection (1)(b) the administrative receiver is not to be taken to have adopted a contract of employment by reason of anything done or omitted to be done within 14 days after his appointment.

[(2A) For the purposes of subsection (1)(b), a liability under a contract of employment is a qualifying liability if—

(a) it is a liability to pay a sum by way of wages or salary or contribution to an occupational pension scheme,

(b) it is incurred while the administrative receiver is in office, and

(c) it is in respect of services rendered wholly or partly after the adoption of the contract.

(2B) Where a sum payable in respect of a liability which is a qualifying liability for the purposes of subsection (1)(b) is payable in respect of services rendered partly before and partly after the adoption of the contract, liability under subsection (1)(b) shall only extend to so much of the sum as is payable in respect of services rendered after the adoption of the contract.

(2C) For the purposes of subsections (2A) and (2B)—

(a) wages or salary payable in respect of a period of holiday or absence from work through sickness or other good cause are deemed to be wages or (as the case may be) salary in respect of services rendered in that period, and

(b) a sum payable in lieu of holiday is deemed to be wages or (as the case may be) salary in respect of services rendered in the period by reference to which the holiday entitlement arose.

(2D) . . .]

(3) This section does not limit any right to indemnity which the administrative receiver would have apart from it, nor limit his liability on contracts entered into or adopted without authority, nor confer any right to indemnity in respect of that liability.

NOTES

Words in square brackets in sub-s (1) inserted, and sub-ss (2A)–(2D) inserted, by the Insolvency Act 1994, s 2.

Sub-s (2D): repealed by the Deregulation Act 2015, s 19, Sch 6, Pt 7, paras 24, 26, as from 26 May 2015.

CHAPTER II
RECEIVERS (SCOTLAND)

[1.153]
57 Agency and liability of receiver for contracts

(1) A receiver is deemed to be the agent of the company in relation to such property of the company as is attached by the floating charge by virtue of which he was appointed.

[(1A) Without prejudice to subsection (1), a receiver is deemed to be the agent of the company in relation to any contract of employment adopted by him in the carrying out of his functions.]
(2) A receiver (including a receiver whose powers are subsequently suspended under section 56) is personally liable on any contract entered into by him in the performance of his functions, except in so far as the contract otherwise provides, and[, to the extent of any qualifying liability,] on any contract of employment adopted by him in the carrying out of those functions.
[(2A) For the purposes of subsection (2), a liability under a contract of employment is a qualifying liability if—
(a) it is a liability to pay a sum by way of wages or salary or contribution to an occupational pension scheme,
(b) it is incurred while the receiver is in office, and
(c) it is in respect of services rendered wholly or partly after the adoption of the contract.
(2B) Where a sum payable in respect of a liability which is a qualifying liability for the purposes of subsection (2) is payable in respect of services rendered partly before and partly after the adoption of the contract, liability under that subsection shall only extend to so much of the sum as is payable in respect of services rendered after the adoption of the contract.
(2C) For the purposes of subsections (2A) and (2B)—
(a) wages or salary payable in respect of a period of holiday or absence from work through sickness or other good cause are deemed to be wages or (as the case may be) salary in respect of services rendered in that period, and
(b) a sum payable in lieu of holiday is deemed to be wages or (as the case may be) salary in respect of services rendered in the period by reference to which the holiday entitlement arose.
(2D) . . .]
(3) A receiver who is personally liable by virtue of subsection (2) is entitled to be indemnified out of the property in respect of which he was appointed.
(4) Any contract entered into by or on behalf of the company prior to the appointment of a receiver continues in force (subject to its terms) notwithstanding that appointment, but the receiver does not by virtue only of his appointment incur any personal liability on any such contract.
(5) For the purposes of subsection (2), a receiver is not to be taken to have adopted a contract of employment by reason of anything done or omitted to be done within 14 days after his appointment.
(6) This section does not limit any right to indemnity which the receiver would have apart from it, nor limit his liability on contracts entered into or adopted without authority, nor confer any right to indemnity in respect of that liability.
(7) Any contract entered into by a receiver in the performance of his functions continues in force (subject to its terms) although the powers of the receiver are subsequently suspended under section 56.

NOTES

Words in square brackets in sub-s (2) inserted, and sub-ss (1A), (2A)–(2D) inserted, by the Insolvency Act 1994, s 3.

Sub-s (2D) repealed by the Public Services Reform (Insolvency) (Scotland) Order 2016, SSI 2016/141, art 3, as from 1 April 2016.

PART IV WINDING UP OF COMPANIES REGISTERED UNDER THE COMPANIES ACTS

CHAPTER VI

Winding Up by the Court

Commencement of winding up

[1.154]

130 Consequences of winding-up order

(1) On the making of a winding-up order, a copy of the order must forthwith be forwarded by the company (or otherwise as may be prescribed) to the registrar of companies, who shall enter it in his records relating to the company.
(2) When a winding-up order has been made or a provisional liquidator has been appointed, no action or proceeding shall be proceeded with or commenced against the company or its property, except by leave of the court and subject to such terms as the court may impose.
(3) When an order has been made for winding up a company [registered but not formed under the Companies Act 2006], no action or proceeding shall be commenced or proceeded with against the company or its property or any contributory of the company, in respect of any debt of the company, except by leave of the court, and subject to such terms as the court may impose.
[(3A) In subsections (2) and (3), the reference to an action or proceeding includes action in respect of the company under Part 1 of Schedule 8 to the Finance (No 2) Act 2015 (enforcement by deduction from accounts).]
(4) An order for winding up a company operates in favour of all the creditors and of all contributories of the company as if made on the joint petition of a creditor and of a contributory.

NOTES

Sub-s (3): words in square brackets substituted by the Companies Act 2006 (Consequential Amendments, Transitional Provisions and Savings) Order 2009, SI 2009/1941, art 2(1), Sch 1, para 75(1), (15).

Sub-s (3A): inserted by the Finance (No 2) Act 2015, s 51, Sch 8, Pt 2, paras 26, 29, as from 18 November 2015.

Application to Scotland: by virtue of the Scotland Act 1998, s 125, Sch 8, para 23, anything directed to be done, or which may be done, to or by the registrar of companies in Scotland by virtue of sub-s (1) above in relation to friendly societies, industrial and provident societies or building societies, shall, or (as the case may be) may, also be done to or by the Accountant in Bankruptcy.

THE SECOND GROUP OF PARTS
INSOLVENCY OF INDIVIDUALS; BANKRUPTCY

PART VIII INDIVIDUAL VOLUNTARY ARRANGEMENTS

Moratorium for insolvent debtor

[1.155]
252 Interim order of court
(1) In the circumstances specified below, the court may in the case of a debtor (being an individual) make an interim order under this section.
(2) An interim order has the effect that, during the period for which it is in force—
(a) no bankruptcy petition relating to the debtor may be presented or proceeded with,
[(aa) no landlord or other person to whom rent is payable may exercise any right of forfeiture by peaceable re-entry in relation to premises let to the debtor in respect of a failure by the debtor to comply with any term or condition of his tenancy of such premises, except with the leave of the court] and
(b) no other proceedings, and no execution or other legal process, may be commenced or continued [and no distress may be levied] against the debtor or his property except with the leave of the court.

NOTES
Sub-s (2): para (aa), and words in square brackets in para (b), inserted by the Insolvency Act 2000, s 3, Sch 3, paras 1, 2.

[1.156]
254 Effect of application
(1) At any time when an application under section 253 for an interim order is pending,
[(a) no landlord or other person to whom rent is payable may exercise any right of forfeiture by peaceable re-entry in relation to premises let to the debtor in respect of a failure by the debtor to comply with any term or condition of his tenancy of such premises, except with the leave of the court, and
(b)] the court may [forbid the levying of any distress on the debtor's property or its subsequent sale, or both, and] stay any action, execution or other legal process against the property or person of the debtor.
(2) Any court in which proceedings are pending against an individual may, on proof that an application under that section has been made in respect of that individual, either stay the proceedings or allow them to continue on such terms as it thinks fit.

NOTES
Sub-s (1): words in square brackets inserted by the Insolvency Act 2000, s 3, Sch 3, paras 1, 4.

Consideration and implementation of debtor's proposal

[1.157]
260 Effect of approval
(1) This section has effect where [pursuant to section 257 the debtor's creditors decide to approve] the proposed voluntary arrangement (with or without modifications).
(2) The approved arrangement—
(a) takes effect as if made by the debtor [at the time the creditors decided to approve the proposal], and
[(b) binds every person who in accordance with the rules—
(i) was entitled to vote [in the creditors' decision procedure by which the decision to approve the proposal was made], or
(ii) would have been so entitled if he had had notice of it, as if he were a party to the arrangement.
(2A) If—
(a) when the arrangement ceases to have effect any amount payable under the arrangement to a person bound by virtue of subsection (2)(b)(ii) has not been paid, and
(b) the arrangement did not come to an end prematurely,
the debtor shall at that time become liable to pay to that person the amount payable under the arrangement.]
(3) . . .
(4) Any interim order in force in relation to the debtor immediately before the end of the period of 28 days beginning with the day on which the report with respect to the creditors' [decision] was made to the court under section 259 ceases to have effect at the end of that period.
This subsection applies except to such extent as the court may direct for the purposes of any application under section 262 below.
(5) Where proceedings on a bankruptcy petition have been stayed by an interim order which ceases to have effect under subsection (4), the petition is deemed, unless the court otherwise orders, to have been dismissed.

NOTES
Sub-ss (1), (4): words in square brackets substituted by the Small Business, Enterprise and Employment Act 2015, s 126, Sch 9, Pt 2, paras 60, 67(1), (2), (4), as from 6 April 2017 (subject to transitional and savings provisions in relation to meetings

to be held consequential on notices, statements (etc) issued before that date: see the Small Business, Enterprise and Employment Act 2015 (Commencement No 6 and Transitional and Savings Provisions) Regulations 2016, SI 2016/1020, reg 5, as amended).

Sub-s (2): words in square brackets substituted by the Small Business, Enterprise and Employment Act 2015, s 126, Sch 9, Pt 2, paras 60, 67(1), (3), as from 6 April 2017 (subject to transitional and savings provisions as noted to the sub-s (1) note above).

Para (b) was substituted, together with sub-s (2A), by the Insolvency Act 2000, s 3, Sch 3, paras 1, 10.

Sub-s (2A): substituted as noted above

Sub-s (3): repealed by the Deregulation Act 2015, s 19, Sch 6, Pt 1, paras 2(1), (11)(a), 3, except in relation to a deed of arrangement registered under the Deeds of Arrangement Act 1914, s 5 before 1 October 2015, if, immediately before that date, the estate of the debtor who executed the deed of arrangement has not been finally wound up.

PART IX BANKRUPTCY

CHAPTER II
PROTECTION OF BANKRUPT'S ESTATE AND INVESTIGATION OF HIS AFFAIRS

[1.158]
285 Restriction on proceedings and remedies

(1) At any time when [proceedings on a bankruptcy application are ongoing or] proceedings on a bankruptcy petition are pending or an individual has been [made] bankrupt the court may stay any action, execution or other legal process against the property or person of the debtor or, as the case may be, of the bankrupt.

(2) Any court in which proceedings are pending against any individual may, on proof that [a bankruptcy application has been made or] a bankruptcy petition has been presented in respect of that individual or that he is an undischarged bankrupt, either stay the proceedings or allow them to continue on such terms as it thinks fit.

(3) After the making of a bankruptcy order no person who is a creditor of the bankrupt in respect of a debt provable in the bankruptcy shall—

(a) have any remedy against the property or person of the bankrupt in respect of that debt, or

(b) before the discharge of the bankrupt, commence any action or other legal proceedings against the bankrupt except with the leave of the court and on such terms as the court may impose.

This is subject to sections 346 (enforcement procedures) and 347 (limited right to distress).

(4) Subject as follows, subsection (3) does not affect the right of a secured creditor of the bankrupt to enforce his security.

(5) Where any goods of an undischarged bankrupt are held by any person by way of pledge, pawn or other security, the official receiver may, after giving notice in writing of his intention to do so, inspect the goods.

Where such a notice has been given to any person, that person is not entitled, without leave of the court, to realise his security unless he has given the trustee of the bankrupt's estate a reasonable opportunity of inspecting the goods and of exercising the bankrupt's right of redemption.

(6) References in this section to the property or goods of the bankrupt are to any of his property or goods, whether or not comprised in his estate.

NOTES

Sub-s (1): words in first pair of square brackets inserted, and word in second pair of square brackets substituted, by the Enterprise and Regulatory Reform Act 2013, s 71(3), Sch 19, paras 1, 16(1), (2), as from 6 April 2016, except in respect of a petition for a bankruptcy order presented to the court by a debtor before that date.

Sub-s (2): words in square brackets inserted by the Enterprise and Regulatory Reform Act 2013, s 71(3), Sch 19, paras 1, 16(1), (3), as from 6 April 2016, except in respect of a petition for a bankruptcy order presented to the court by a debtor before that date.

THE THIRD GROUP OF PARTS
MISCELLANEOUS MATTERS BEARING ON BOTH COMPANY AND INDIVIDUAL INSOLVENCY; GENERAL INTERPRETATION; FINAL PROVISIONS

PART XII PREFERENTIAL DEBTS IN COMPANY AND INDIVIDUAL INSOLVENCY

[1.159]
386 Categories of preferential debts

(1) A reference in this Act to the preferential debts of a company or an individual is to the debts listed in Schedule 6 to this Act [(contributions to occupational pension schemes; remuneration, &c. of employees; levies on coal and steel production)][; debts owed to the Financial Services Compensation Scheme][; deposits covered by Financial Services Compensation Scheme][; other deposits]; and references to preferential creditors are to be read accordingly.

[(1A) A reference in this Act to the "ordinary preferential debts" of a company or an individual is to the preferential debts listed in any of paragraphs 8 to 15B of Schedule 6 to this Act.

(1B) A reference in this Act to the "secondary preferential debts" of a company or an individual is to the preferential debts listed in paragraph 15BA or 15BB of Schedule 6 to this Act.]

(2) In [Schedule 6] "the debtor" means the company or the individual concerned.

(3) Schedule 6 is to be read with [Schedule 4 to the Pension Schemes Act 1993] (occupational pension scheme contributions).

NOTES

Sub-s (1): words in first pair of square brackets substituted by the Enterprise Act 2002, s 251(3); words in second pair of square brackets inserted by the Deposit Guarantee Scheme Regulations 2015, SI 2015/486, reg 14(1), (2), as from 26 March 2015; words in third pair of square brackets inserted by the Financial Services (Banking Reform) Act 2013, s 13(2), as from 31 December 2014; words in final pair of square brackets inserted by the Banks and Building Societies (Depositor Preference and Priorities) Order 2014, SI 2014/3486, arts 3, 8(1), (2), as from 1 January 2015, except in relation to any insolvency proceedings commenced before that date.

Sub-ss (1A), (1B): inserted by SI 2014/3486, arts 3, 8(1), (3), as from 1 January 2015, except in relation to any insolvency proceedings commenced before that date.

Sub-s (2): words in square brackets substituted by SI 2014/3486, arts 3, 8(1), (4), as from 1 January 2015, except in relation to any insolvency proceedings commenced before that date.

Sub-s (3): words in square brackets substituted by the Pension Schemes Act 1993, s 190, Sch 8, para 8.

PART XIX FINAL PROVISIONS

[1.160]

443 Commencement

This Act comes into force on the day appointed under section 236(2) of the Insolvency Act 1985 for the coming into force of Part III of that Act (individual insolvency and bankruptcy), immediately after that Part of that Act comes into force for England and Wales.

[1.161]

444 Citation

This Act may be cited as the Insolvency Act 1986.

SCHEDULES

[SCHEDULE A1
MORATORIUM WHERE DIRECTORS PROPOSE VOLUNTARY ARRANGEMENT

NOTES

Only the provisions of this Schedule most directly relevant to employment law are printed; omitted paragraphs are not annotated.

Section 1A

PART I
INTRODUCTORY

Interpretation

[1.162]

1. In this Schedule—

"the beginning of the moratorium" has the meaning given by paragraph 8(1),

"the date of filing" means the date on which the documents for the time being referred to in paragraph 7(1) are filed or lodged with the court,

"hire-purchase agreement" includes a conditional sale agreement, a chattel leasing agreement and a retention of title agreement,

"market contract" and "market charge" have the meanings given by Part VII of the Companies Act 1989,

. . .

"moratorium" means a moratorium under section 1A,

"the nominee" includes any person for the time being carrying out the functions of a nominee under this Schedule,

"the settlement finality regulations" means the Financial Markets and Insolvency (Settlement Finality) Regulations 1999,

"system-charge" has the meaning given by the Financial Markets and Insolvency Regulations 1996.

Eligible companies

2. (1) A company is eligible for a moratorium if it meets the requirements of paragraph 3, unless—

(a) it is excluded from being eligible by virtue of paragraph 4, or

(b) it falls within sub-paragraph (2).

(2) A company falls within this sub-paragraph if—

[(a) it effects or carries out contracts of insurance, but is not exempt from the general prohibition, within the meaning of section 19 of the Financial Services and Markets Act 2000, in relation to that activity,

(b) it has permission under Part IV of that Act to accept deposits,

(bb) it has a liability in respect of a deposit which it accepted in accordance with the Banking Act 1979 (c 37) or 1987 (c 22),]

(c) it is a party to a market contract . . . or any of its property is subject to a market charge . . . or a system-charge, or

(d) it is a participant (within the meaning of the settlement finality regulations) or any of its property is subject to a collateral security charge (within the meaning of those regulations).

[(3) Paragraphs (a), (b) and (bb) of sub-paragraph (2) must be read with—

(a) section 22 of the Financial Services and Markets Act 2000;

(b) any relevant order under that section; and

(c) Schedule 2 to that Act.]

3. (1) A company meets the requirements of this paragraph if the qualifying conditions are met—

(a) in the year ending with the date of filing, or

(b) in the financial year of the company which ended last before that date.

(2) For the purposes of sub-paragraph (1)—

(a) the qualifying conditions are met by a company in a period if, in that period, it satisfies two or more of the requirements for being a small company specified for the time being in [section 382(3) of the Companies Act 2006], and

(b) a company's financial year is to be determined in accordance with that Act.

(3) [Section 382(4), (5) and (6)] of that Act apply for the purposes of this paragraph as they apply for the purposes of that section.

[(4) A company does not meet the requirements of this paragraph if it is a [parent company] of a group of companies which does not qualify as a small group or a medium-sized group [in relation to] the financial year of the company which ended last before the date of filing.

[(5) For the purposes of sub-paragraph (4)—

(a) "group" has the same meaning as in Part 15 of the Companies Act 2006 (see section 474(1) of that Act); and

(b) a group qualifies as small in relation to a financial year if it so qualifies under section 383(2) to (7) of that Act, and qualifies as medium-sized in relation to a financial year if it so qualifies under section 466(2) to (7) of that Act.]]

[(6) Expressions used in this paragraph that are defined expressions in Part 15 of the Companies Act 2006 (accounts and reports) have the same meaning in this paragraph as in that Part.]

4. (1) A company is excluded from being eligible for a moratorium if, on the date of filing—

[(a) the company is in administration,]

(b) the company is being wound up,

(c) there is an administrative receiver of the company,

(d) a voluntary arrangement has effect in relation to the company,

(e) there is a provisional liquidator of the company,

(f) a moratorium has been in force for the company at any time during the period of 12 months ending with the date of filing and—

(i) no voluntary arrangement had effect at the time at which the moratorium came to an end, or

(ii) a voluntary arrangement which had effect at any time in that period has come to an end prematurely,

[(fa) an administrator appointed under paragraph 22 of Schedule B1 has held office in the period of 12 months ending with the date of filing,] or

(g) a voluntary arrangement in relation to the company which had effect in pursuance of a proposal under section 1(3) has come to an end prematurely and, during the period of 12 months ending with the date of filing, an order under section 5(3)(a) has been made.

(2) Sub-paragraph (1)(b) does not apply to a company which, by reason of a winding-up order made after the date of filing, is treated as being wound up on that date.

5. The Secretary of State may by regulations modify the qualifications for eligibility of a company for a moratorium.]

NOTES

This Schedule was inserted by the Insolvency Act 2000, s 1, Sch 1, paras 1, 4.

Para 1: definitions omitted repealed by virtue of the Financial Services and Markets Act 2000 (Consequential Amendments) Order 2002, SI 2002/1555, art 28(1), (2).

Para 2: sub-paras (2)(a)–(bb) substituted (for the original sub-paras (2)(a), (b)), words omitted from sub-para (2)(c) repealed, and sub-para (3) added, by virtue of SI 2002/1555, arts 28(1), (3), 29.

Para 3 is amended as follows:

Words in square brackets in sub-paras (2), (3) substituted by the Companies Act 2006 (Consequential Amendments etc) Order 2008, SI 2008/948, art 3(1), Sch 1, Pt 2, para 99(1)–(3).

Sub-paras (4), (5) added by the Insolvency Act 1986 (Amendment) (No 3) Regulations 2002, SI 2002/1990, reg 3(1), (2).

Words in square brackets in sub-para (4) substituted by SI 2008/948, art 3(1), Sch 1, Pt 2, para 99(1), (4).

Sub-para (5) substituted by SI 2008/948, art 3(1), Sch 1, Pt 2, para 99(1), (5).

Sub-para (6) added by the Companies Act 2006 (Consequential Amendments, Transitional Provisions and Savings) Order 2009, SI 2009/1941, art 2(1), Sch 1, para 71(1), (4)(a).

Para 4: sub-para (1)(a) substituted, and sub-para (1)(fa) inserted, by the Enterprise Act 2002, s 248(3), Sch 17, paras 9, 37(1) subject to savings in relation to special administration regimes as noted to s 8 of this Act at **[1.150]**.

Banking Act 1987, Insurance Companies Act 1982: repealed by the Financial Services and Markets Act 2000 (Consequential Amendments and Repeals) Order 2001, SI 2001/3649, art 3(1)(b), (d).

Financial Services and Markets Act 2000 (Financial Promotion) Order 2001, SI 2001/1335: revoked and replaced by the Financial Services and Markets Act 2000 (Financial Promotion) Order 2005, SI 2005/1529.

Regulations: the Insolvency Act 1986 (Amendment) (No 3) Regulations 2002, SI 2002/1990.

[PART II
OBTAINING A MORATORIUM

Nominee's statement

[1.163]

6. (1) Where the directors of a company wish to obtain a moratorium, they shall submit to the nominee—

(a) a document setting out the terms of the proposed voluntary arrangement,
(b) a statement of the company's affairs containing—
 (i) such particulars of its creditors and of its debts and other liabilities and of its assets as may be prescribed, and
 (ii) such other information as may be prescribed, and
(c) any other information necessary to enable the nominee to comply with sub-paragraph (2) which he requests from them.

(2) The nominee shall submit to the directors a statement in the prescribed form indicating whether or not, in his opinion—

(a) the proposed voluntary arrangement has a reasonable prospect of being approved and implemented,
(b) the company is likely to have sufficient funds available to it during the proposed moratorium to enable it to carry on its business, and
[(c) the proposed voluntary arrangement should be considered by a meeting of the company and by the company's creditors.]

(3) In forming his opinion on the matters mentioned in sub-paragraph (2), the nominee is entitled to rely on the information submitted to him under sub-paragraph (1) unless he has reason to doubt its accuracy.

(4) The reference in sub-paragraph (2)(b) to the company's business is to that business as the company proposes to carry it on during the moratorium.

Documents to be submitted to court

7. (1) To obtain a moratorium the directors of a company must file (in Scotland, lodge) with the court—

(a) a document setting out the terms of the proposed voluntary arrangement,
(b) a statement of the company's affairs containing—
 (i) such particulars of its creditors and of its debts and other liabilities and of its assets as may be prescribed, and
 (ii) such other information as may be prescribed,
(c) a statement that the company is eligible for a moratorium,
(d) a statement from the nominee that he has given his consent to act, and
(e) a statement from the nominee that, in his opinion—
 (i) the proposed voluntary arrangement has a reasonable prospect of being approved and implemented,
 (ii) the company is likely to have sufficient funds available to it during the proposed moratorium to enable it to carry on its business, and
 [(iii) the proposed voluntary arrangement should be considered by a meeting of the company and by the company's creditors.]

(2) Each of the statements mentioned in sub-paragraph (1)(b) to (e), except so far as it contains the particulars referred to in paragraph (b)(i), must be in the prescribed form.

(3) The reference in sub-paragraph (1)(e)(ii) to the company's business is to that business as the company proposes to carry it on during the moratorium.

(4) The Secretary of State may by regulations modify the requirements of this paragraph as to the documents required to be filed (in Scotland, lodged) with the court in order to obtain a moratorium.

Duration of moratorium

8. (1) A moratorium comes into force when the documents for the time being referred to in paragraph 7(1) are filed or lodged with the court and references in this Schedule to "the beginning of the moratorium" shall be construed accordingly.

[(2) A moratorium ends with the later of—

(a) the day on which the company meeting summoned under paragraph 29 is first held, and
(b) the day on which the company's creditors decide whether to approve the proposed voluntary arrangement,

unless it is extended under paragraph 32; but this is subject to the rest of this paragraph.

(3) In this paragraph the "initial period" means the period of 28 days beginning with the day on which the moratorium comes into force.

(3A) If the company meeting has not first met before the end of the initial period the moratorium ends at the end of that period, unless before the end of that period it is extended under paragraph 32.

(3B) If the company's creditors have not decided whether to approve the proposed voluntary arrangement before the end of the initial period the moratorium ends at the end of that period, unless before the end of that period—

(a) the moratorium is extended under paragraph 32, or
(b) a meeting of the company's creditors is summoned in accordance with section 246ZE.

(3C) Where sub-paragraph (3B)(b) applies, the moratorium ends with the day on which the meeting of the company's creditors is first held, unless it is extended under paragraph 32.

(4) The moratorium ends at the end of the initial period if the nominee has not before the end of that period—

(a) summoned a meeting of the company, and
(b) sought a decision from the company's creditors,

as required by paragraph 29(1).]

(5) If the moratorium is extended (or further extended) under paragraph 32, it ends at the end of the day to which it is extended (or further extended).

(6) Sub-paragraphs (2) to (5) do not apply if the moratorium comes to an end before the time concerned by virtue of—

(a) paragraph 25(4) (effect of withdrawal by nominee of consent to act),
(b) an order under paragraph 26(3), 27(3) or 40 (challenge of actions of nominee or directors), or
[(c) a decision of one or both of—
 (i) the meeting of the company summoned under paragraph 29, or
 (ii) the company's creditors.]

(7) If the moratorium has not previously come to an end in accordance with sub-paragraphs (2) to (6), it ends at the end of the day on which a decision under paragraph 31 to approve a voluntary arrangement takes effect under paragraph 36.

(8) The Secretary of State may by order increase or reduce the period for the time being specified in sub-paragraph (3).

Notification of beginning of moratorium

9. (1) When a moratorium comes into force, the directors shall notify the nominee of that fact forthwith.

(2) If the directors without reasonable excuse fail to comply with sub-paragraph (1), each of them is liable to imprisonment or a fine, or both.

10. (1) When a moratorium comes into force, the nominee shall, in accordance with the rules—

(a) advertise that fact forthwith, and
(b) notify the registrar of companies, the company and any petitioning creditor of the company of whose claim he is aware of that fact.

(2) In sub-paragraph (1)(b), "petitioning creditor" means a creditor by whom a winding-up petition has been presented before the beginning of the moratorium, as long as the petition has not been dismissed or withdrawn.

(3) If the nominee without reasonable excuse fails to comply with sub-paragraph (1)(a) or (b), he is liable to a fine.

Notification of end of moratorium

11. (1) When a moratorium comes to an end, the nominee shall, in accordance with the rules—

(a) advertise that fact forthwith, and
(b) notify the court, the registrar of companies, the company and any creditor of the company of whose claim he is aware of that fact.

(2) If the nominee without reasonable excuse fails to comply with sub-paragraph (1)(a) or (b), he is liable to a fine.]

NOTES

Inserted as noted to Pt I of this Schedule at **[1.162]**.

Para 6: sub-para (2)(c) substituted by the Small Business, Enterprise and Employment Act 2015, s 126, Sch 9, Pt 1, paras 1, 9(1), (2), as from 6 April 2017 (in relation to England and Wales (subject to transitional and savings provisions in relation to meetings to be held consequential on notices, statements (etc) issued before that date: see the Small Business, Enterprise and Employment Act 2015 (Commencement No 6 and Transitional and Savings Provisions) Regulations 2016, SI 2016/1020, reg 5, as amended)), and as from 6 April 2019 (in relation to Scotland (subject to transitional and savings provisions in relation to meetings taking place on or after that date: see the Small Business, Enterprise and Employment Act 2015 (Commencement No 7, Consequential, Transitional and Savings Provisions) Regulations 2019, SI 2019/816, reg 5)).

Para 7: sub-para (1)(e)(iii) substituted by the Small Business, Enterprise and Employment Act 2015, s 126, Sch 9, Pt 1, paras 1, 9(1), (3), as from the dates noted above and subject to the transitional and savings provisions noted above.

Para 8 is amended as follows:

Sub-paras (2), (3), (3A)–(3C), (4) substituted (for the original sub-paras (2), (3), (4)), by the Small Business, Enterprise and Employment Act 2015, s 126, Sch 9, Pt 1, paras 1, 9(1), (4), as from the dates noted above and subject to the transitional and savings provisions noted above.

Sub-para (6)(c) substituted by the Small Business, Enterprise and Employment Act 2015, s 126, Sch 9, Pt 1, paras 1, 9(1), (5), as from the dates noted above and subject to the transitional and savings provisions noted above.

[PART III
EFFECTS OF MORATORIUM

Effect on creditors, etc

[1.164]

12. (1) During the period for which a moratorium is in force for a company—

(a) no petition may be presented for the winding up of the company,

(b) no meeting of the company may be called or requisitioned except with the consent of the nominee or the leave of the court and subject (where the court gives leave) to such terms as the court may impose,

(c) no resolution may be passed or order made for the winding up of the company,

[(d) no administration application may be made in respect of the company,

(da) no administrator of the company may be appointed under paragraph 14 or 22 of Schedule B1,]

(e) no administrative receiver of the company may be appointed,

(f) no landlord or other person to whom rent is payable may exercise any right of forfeiture by peaceable re-entry in relation to premises let to the company in respect of a failure by the company to comply with any term or condition of its tenancy of such premises, except with the leave of the court and subject to such terms as the court may impose,

(g) no other steps may be taken to enforce any security over the company's property, or to repossess goods in the company's possession under any hire-purchase agreement, except with the leave of the court and subject to such terms as the court may impose, and

(h) no other proceedings and no execution or other legal process may be commenced or continued, and no distress may be levied, against the company or its property except with the leave of the court and subject to such terms as the court may impose.

(2) Where a petition, other than an excepted petition, for the winding up of the company has been presented before the beginning of the moratorium, section 127 shall not apply in relation to any disposition of property, transfer of shares or alteration in status made during the moratorium or at a time mentioned in paragraph 37(5)(a).

(3) In the application of sub-paragraph (1)(h) to Scotland, the reference to execution being commenced or continued includes a reference to diligence being carried out or continued, and the reference to distress being levied is omitted.

(4) Paragraph (a) of sub-paragraph (1) does not apply to an excepted petition and, where such a petition has been presented before the beginning of the moratorium or is presented during the moratorium, paragraphs (b) and (c) of that sub-paragraph do not apply in relation to proceedings on the petition.

(5) For the purposes of this paragraph, "excepted petition" means a petition under—

(a) section 124A [or 124B] of this Act,

(b) section 72 of the Financial Services Act 1986 on the ground mentioned in subsection (1)(b) of that section, or

(c) section 92 of the Banking Act 1987 on the ground mentioned in subsection (1)(b) of that section,

[(d) section 367 of the Financial Services and Markets Act 2000 on the ground mentioned in subsection (3)(b) of that section.]

Effect on company

15. (1) Paragraphs 16 to 23 apply in relation to a company for which a moratorium is in force.

(2) The fact that a company enters into a transaction in contravention of any of paragraphs 16 to 22 does not—

(a) make the transaction void, or

(b) make it to any extent unenforceable against the company.

Company invoices, etc

16. [(1) Every invoice, order for goods or services, business letter or order form (whether in hard copy, electronic or any other form) issued by or on behalf of the company, and all the company's websites, must also contain the nominee's name and a statement that the moratorium is in force for the company.]

(2) If default is made in complying with sub-paragraph (1), the company and (subject to sub-paragraph (3)) any officer of the company is liable to a fine.

(3) An officer of the company is only liable under sub-paragraph (2) if, without reasonable excuse, he authorises or permits the default.

NOTES

Inserted as noted to Pt I of this Schedule at **[1.162]**.

Para 12: sub-paras (1)(d), (da) substituted, for the original sub-para (1)(d), by the Enterprise Act 2002, s 248(3), Sch 17, paras 9, 37(1), (3) subject to savings in relation to special administration regimes as noted to s 8 of this Act at **[1.150]**; words in square brackets in sub-para (5)(a) inserted by the European Public Limited-Liability Company Regulations 2004, SI 2004/2326, reg 73(4)(b); sub-para (5)(d) inserted by virtue of the Financial Services and Markets Act 2000 (Consequential Amendments) Order 2002, SI 2002/1555.

Para 16: sub-para (1) substituted by the Companies (Trading Disclosures) (Insolvency) Regulations 2008, SI 2008/1897, reg 3(1).

Banking Act 1987, Financial Services Act 1986: repealed by the Financial Services and Markets Act 2000 (Consequential Amendments and Repeals) Order 2001, SI 2001/3649, art 3(1)(c), (d).

[PART V
CONSIDERATION AND IMPLEMENTATION OF VOLUNTARY ARRANGEMENT

[Duty to summon company meeting and seek creditors' decision]

[1.165]

29. (1) Where a moratorium is in force, the nominee [shall—

(a) summon a meeting of the company to consider the proposed voluntary arrangement for such a time, date (within the period of time for the time being specified in paragraph 8(3)) and place as he thinks fit, and

(b) seek a decision from the company's creditors as to whether they approve the proposed voluntary arrangement.]

[(2) The decision of the company's creditors is to be made by a qualifying decision procedure.

(3) Notice of the qualifying decision procedure must be given to every creditor of the company of whose claim the nominee is aware.]

Extension of moratorium

32. (1) Subject to sub-paragraph (2), a [company] meeting summoned under paragraph 29 which resolves that it be adjourned (or further adjourned) may resolve that the moratorium be extended (or further extended), with or without conditions.

[(1A) Subject to sub-paragraph (2) the company's creditors may, by a qualifying decision procedure, decide to extend (or further extend) the moratorium, with or without conditions.]

[(2) The moratorium may not be extended (or further extended) to a day later than the end of the period of two months beginning with the day after the last day of the period mentioned in paragraph 8(3).]

(3) [Where] it is proposed to extend (or further extend) the moratorium, before a decision is taken with respect to that proposal, the nominee shall inform the meeting [of the company or (as the case may be) inform the company's creditors]—

(a) of what he has done in order to comply with his duty under paragraph 24 and the cost of his actions for the company, and

(b) of what he intends to do to continue to comply with that duty if the moratorium is extended (or further extended) and the expected cost of his actions for the company.

(4) Where, in accordance with sub-paragraph (3)(b), the nominee informs a meeting [of the company or informs the company's creditors,] of the expected cost of his intended actions, the meeting shall resolve[, or (as the case may be) the creditors by a qualifying decision procedure shall decide,] whether or not to approve that expected cost.

(5) If a decision not to approve the expected cost of the nominee's intended actions has effect under paragraph 36, the moratorium comes to an end.

(6) A meeting [of the company may resolve, and the creditors by a qualifying decision procedure may decide,] that a moratorium which has been extended (or further extended) be brought to an end before the end of the period of the extension (or further extension).

(7) The Secretary of State may by order increase or reduce the period for the time being specified in sub-paragraph (2).

NOTES

Inserted by the Insolvency Act 2000, s 1, Sch 1, paras 1, 4.

Para 29 is amended as follows:

The heading preceding para 29 was substituted (for original heading "Summoning of meetings") by the Small Business, Enterprise and Employment Act 2015, s 126, Sch 9, Pt 1, paras 1, 9(1), (6), as from 6 April 2017 (in relation to England and Wales (subject to transitional and savings provisions in relation meetings to be held consequential on notices, statements (etc) issued before that date: see the Small Business, Enterprise and Employment Act 2015 (Commencement No 6 and Transitional and Savings Provisions) Regulations 2016, SI 2016/1020, reg 5, as amended)), and as from 6 April 2019 (in relation to Scotland (subject to transitional and savings provisions in relation to meetings taking place on or after that date: see the Small Business, Enterprise and Employment Act 2015 (Commencement No 7, Consequential, Transitional and Savings Provisions) Regulations 2019, SI 2019/816, reg 5)).

Words in square brackets in sub-para (1) substituted by the Small Business, Enterprise and Employment Act 2015, s 126, Sch 9, Pt 1, paras 1, 9(1), (7), as from the dates noted above and subject to the transitional and savings provisions noted above.

Sub-paras (2), (3) substituted (for the original sub-para (2)) by the Small Business, Enterprise and Employment Act 2015, s 126, Sch 9, Pt 1, paras 1, 9(1), (8), as from the dates noted above and subject to the transitional and savings provisions noted above.

Para 32: all words in square brackets were substituted or inserted by the Small Business, Enterprise and Employment Act 2015, s 126, Sch 9, Pt 1, paras 1, 9(1), (20)–(25), as from the dates noted above and subject to the transitional and savings provisions noted above.

[SCHEDULE B1
ADMINISTRATION

Section 8

NOTES

Only the provisions of this Schedule most directly relevant to employment law are printed; omitted paragraphs are not annotated.

NATURE OF ADMINISTRATION

Administration

[1.166]

1. (1) For the purposes of this Act "administrator" of a company means a person appointed under this Schedule to manage the company's affairs, business and property.

(2) For the purposes of this Act—

(a) a company is "in administration" while the appointment of an administrator of the company has effect,
(b) a company "enters administration" when the appointment of an administrator takes effect,
(c) a company ceases to be in administration when the appointment of an administrator of the company ceases to have effect in accordance with this Schedule, and
(d) a company does not cease to be in administration merely because an administrator vacates office (by reason of resignation, death or otherwise) or is removed from office.

2. A person may be appointed as administrator of a company—
(a) by administration order of the court under paragraph 10,
(b) by the holder of a floating charge under paragraph 14, or
(c) by the company or its directors under paragraph 22.

Purpose of administration

3. (1) The administrator of a company must perform his functions with the objective of—
(a) rescuing the company as a going concern, or
(b) achieving a better result for the company's creditors as a whole than would be likely if the company were wound up (without first being in administration), or
(c) realising property in order to make a distribution to one or more secured or preferential creditors.

(2) Subject to sub-paragraph (4), the administrator of a company must perform his functions in the interests of the company's creditors as a whole.

(3) The administrator must perform his functions with the objective specified in sub-paragraph (1)(a) unless he thinks either—
(a) that it is not reasonably practicable to achieve that objective, or
(b) that the objective specified in sub-paragraph (1)(b) would achieve a better result for the company's creditors as a whole.

(4) The administrator may perform his functions with the objective specified in sub-paragraph (1)(c) only if—
(a) he thinks that it is not reasonably practicable to achieve either of the objectives specified in sub-paragraph (1)(a) and (b), and
(b) he does not unnecessarily harm the interests of the creditors of the company as a whole.

4. The administrator of a company must perform his functions as quickly and efficiently as is reasonably practicable.

Status of administrator

5. An administrator is an officer of the court (whether or not he is appointed by the court).

EFFECT OF ADMINISTRATION

Moratorium on other legal process

43. (1) This paragraph applies to a company in administration.

(2) No step may be taken to enforce security over the company's property except—
(a) with the consent of the administrator, or
(b) with the permission of the court.

(3) No step may be taken to repossess goods in the company's possession under a hire-purchase agreement except—
(a) with the consent of the administrator, or
(b) with the permission of the court.

(4) A landlord may not exercise a right of forfeiture by peaceable re-entry in relation to premises let to the company except—
(a) with the consent of the administrator, or
(b) with the permission of the court.

(5) In Scotland, a landlord may not exercise a right of irritancy in relation to premises let to the company except—
(a) with the consent of the administrator, or
(b) with the permission of the court.

(6) No legal process (including legal proceedings, execution, distress and diligence) may be instituted or continued against the company or property of the company except—
(a) with the consent of the administrator, or
(b) with the permission of the court.

[(6A) An administrative receiver of the company may not be appointed.]

(7) Where the court gives permission for a transaction under this paragraph it may impose a condition on or a requirement in connection with the transaction.

(8) In this paragraph "landlord" includes a person to whom rent is payable.

Interim moratorium

44. (1) This paragraph applies where an administration application in respect of a company has been made and—

(a) the application has not yet been granted or dismissed, or
(b) the application has been granted but the administration order has not yet taken effect.

(2) This paragraph also applies from the time when a copy of notice of intention to appoint an administrator under paragraph 14 is filed with the court until—
(a) the appointment of the administrator takes effect, or
(b) the period of five business days beginning with the date of filing expires without an administrator having been appointed.

(3) Sub-paragraph (2) has effect in relation to a notice of intention to appoint only if it is in the prescribed form.

(4) This paragraph also applies from the time when a copy of notice of intention to appoint an administrator is filed with the court under paragraph 27(1) until—
(a) the appointment of the administrator takes effect, or
(b) the period specified in paragraph 28(2) expires without an administrator having been appointed.

(5) The provisions of paragraphs 42 and 43 shall apply (ignoring any reference to the consent of the administrator).

(6) If there is an administrative receiver of the company when the administration application is made, the provisions of paragraphs 42 and 43 shall not begin to apply by virtue of this paragraph until the person by or on behalf of whom the receiver was appointed consents to the making of the administration order.

(7) This paragraph does not prevent or require the permission of the court for—
(a) the presentation of a petition for the winding up of the company under a provision mentioned in paragraph 42(4),
(b) the appointment of an administrator under paragraph 14,
(c) the appointment of an administrative receiver of the company, or
(d) the carrying out by an administrative receiver (whenever appointed) of his functions.

REPLACING ADMINISTRATOR

Vacation of office: charges and liabilities

99. (1) This paragraph applies where a person ceases to be the administrator of a company (whether because he vacates office by reason of resignation, death or otherwise, because he is removed from office or because his appointment ceases to have effect).

(2) In this paragraph—
"the former administrator" means the person referred to in sub-paragraph (1), and
"cessation" means the time when he ceases to be the company's administrator.

(3) The former administrator's remuneration and expenses shall be—
(a) charged on and payable out of property of which he had custody or control immediately before cessation, and
(b) payable in priority to any security to which paragraph 70 applies.

(4) A sum payable in respect of a debt or liability arising out of a contract entered into by the former administrator or a predecessor before cessation shall be—
(a) charged on and payable out of property of which the former administrator had custody or control immediately before cessation, and
(b) payable in priority to any charge arising under sub-paragraph (3).

(5) Sub-paragraph (4) shall apply to a liability arising under a contract of employment which was adopted by the former administrator or a predecessor before cessation; and for that purpose—
(a) action taken within the period of 14 days after an administrator's appointment shall not be taken to amount or contribute to the adoption of a contract,
(b) no account shall be taken of a liability which arises, or in so far as it arises, by reference to anything which is done or which occurs before the adoption of the contract of employment, and
(c) no account shall be taken of a liability to make a payment other than wages or salary.

(6) In sub-paragraph (5)(c) "wages or salary" includes—
(a) a sum payable in respect of a period of holiday (for which purpose the sum shall be treated as relating to the period by reference to which the entitlement to holiday accrued),
(b) a sum payable in respect of a period of absence through illness or other good cause,
(c) a sum payable in lieu of holiday,
(d) . . . and
(e) a contribution to an occupational pension scheme.]

NOTES

Inserted by the Enterprise Act 2002, s 248(2), Sch 16 subject to savings in relation to special administration regimes (within the meaning of s 249 of the 2002 Act).

Para 43: sub-para (6A) inserted by the Enterprise Act 2002 (Insolvency) Order 2003, SI 2003/2096, art 2(1), (3).

Para 99: words omitted from sub-para (6)(d) repealed by the Deregulation Act 2015, s 19, Sch 6, Pt 7, paras 24, 27, as from 26 May 2015.

SCHEDULE 6
THE CATEGORIES OF PREFERENTIAL DEBTS

Section 386

[1.167]

1–7. . . .

Category 4: Contributions to occupational pension schemes, etc

8. Any sum which is owed by the debtor and is a sum to which [Schedule 4 to the Pension Schemes Act 1993] applies (contributions to occupational pension schemes and state scheme premiums).

Category 5: Remuneration, etc, of employees

9. So much of any amount which—

(a) is owed by the debtor to a person who is or has been an employee of the debtor, and

(b) is payable by way of remuneration in respect of the whole or any part of the period of 4 months next before the relevant date,

as does not exceed so much as may be prescribed by order made by the Secretary of State.

10. An amount owed by way of accrued holiday remuneration, in respect of any period of employment before the relevant date, to a person whose employment by the debtor has been terminated, whether before, on or after that date.

11. So much of any sum owed in respect of money advanced for the purpose as has been applied for the payment of a debt which, if it had not been paid, would have been a debt falling within paragraph 9 or 10.

12. So much of any amount which—

(a) is ordered (whether before or after the relevant date) to be paid by the debtor under the Reserve Forces (Safeguard of Employment) Act 1985, and

(b) is so ordered in respect of a default made by the debtor before that date in the discharge of his obligations under that Act,

as does not exceed such amount as may be prescribed by order made by the Secretary of State.

Interpretation for Category 5

13. (1) For the purposes of paragraphs 9 to 12, a sum is payable by the debtor to a person by way of remuneration in respect of any period if—

(a) it is paid as wages or salary (whether payable for time or for piece work or earned wholly or partly by way of commission) in respect of services rendered to the debtor in that period, or

(b) it is an amount falling within the following sub-paragraph and is payable by the debtor in respect of that period.

[(2) An amount falls within this sub-paragraph if it is—

(a) a guarantee payment under Part III of the Employment Rights Act 1996 (employee without work to do);

(b) any payment for time off under section 53 (time off to look for work or arrange training) or section 56 (time off for ante-natal care) of that Act or under section 169 of the Trade Union and Labour Relations (Consolidation) Act 1992 (time off for carrying out trade union duties etc);

(c) remuneration on suspension on medical grounds, or on maternity grounds, under Part VII of the Employment Rights Act 1996; or

(d) remuneration under a protective award under section 189 of the Trade Union and Labour Relations (Consolidation) Act 1992 (redundancy dismissal with compensation).]

14. (1) This paragraph relates to a case in which a person's employment has been terminated by or in consequence of his employer going into liquidation or being [made] bankrupt or (his employer being a company not in liquidation) by or in consequence of—

(a) a receiver being appointed as mentioned in section 40 of this Act (debenture-holders secured by floating charge), or

(b) the appointment of a receiver under section 53(6) or 54(5) of this Act (Scottish company with property subject to floating charge), or

(c) the taking of possession by debenture-holders (so secured), as mentioned in [section 754 of the Companies Act 2006].

(2) For the purposes of paragraphs 9 to 12, holiday remuneration is deemed to have accrued to that person in respect of any period of employment if, by virtue of his contract of employment or of any enactment that remuneration would have accrued in respect of that period if his employment had continued until he became entitled to be allowed the holiday.

(3) The reference in sub-paragraph (2) to any enactment includes an order or direction made under an enactment.

15. Without prejudice to paragraphs 13 and 14—

(a) any remuneration payable by the debtor to a person in respect of a period of holiday or of absence from work through sickness or other good cause is deemed to be wages or (as the case may be) salary in respect of services rendered to the debtor in that period, . . .

(b) . . .

15A, 15AA, 15B, 15BA, 15BB, 15C *(Paras 15A (Levies on coal and steel production), 15AA (Debts owed to the Financial Services Compensation Scheme), 15B (Deposits covered by Financial Services Compensation Scheme), 15BA, 15BB (Other deposits) and 15C (interpretation of those paragraphs) are outside the scope of this work.)*

Orders

16. An order under paragraph 9 or 12—

(a) may contain such transitional provisions as may appear to the Secretary of State necessary or expedient;

(b) shall be made by statutory instrument subject to annulment in pursuance of a resolution of either House of Parliament.

NOTES

Paras 1–7: repealed by the Enterprise Act 2002, ss 251(1), 278(2), Sch 26.

Para 8: words in square brackets substituted by the Pension Schemes Act 1993, s 190, Sch 8, para 18.

Para 13: sub-para (2) substituted by the Employment Rights Act 1996, s 240, Sch 1, para 29.

Para 14: word in first pair of square brackets substituted (for the original word "adjudged"), in relation to England and Wales, by the Enterprise and Regulatory Reform Act 2013, s 71(3), Sch 19, paras 1, 64, as from 6 April 2016, except in respect of a petition for a bankruptcy order presented to the court by a debtor before that date; words in square brackets in sub-para (1)(c) substituted by the Companies Act 2006 (Consequential Amendments etc) Order 2008, SI 2008/948, art 3(1), Sch 1, Pt 2, para 104.

Para 15: sub-para (b) (and the preceding word) repealed by the Deregulation Act 2015, s 19, Sch 6, Pt 7, paras 24, 28, as from 26 May 2015.

Orders: the Insolvency Proceedings (Monetary Limits) Order 1986, SI 1986/1996 (art 4 of which prescribes £800 for the purposes of paras 9, 12 above).

EMPLOYMENT ACT 1988

(1988 c 19)

An Act to make provision with respect to trade unions, their members and their property, to things done for the purpose of enforcing membership of a trade union, to trade union ballots and elections and to proceedings involving trade unions; to provide for the Manpower Services Commission to be known as the Training Commission; to amend the law with respect to the constitution and functions of that Commission and with respect to persons to whom facilities for work-experience and training for employment are made available; to enable additional members to be appointed to industrial training boards and to the Agricultural Training Board; and to provide that the terms on which certain persons hold office or employment under the Crown are to be treated for certain purposes as contained in contracts of employment

[26 May 1988]

NOTES

Most of this Act has been repealed by, and re-enacted in, the Trade Union and Labour Relations (Consolidation) Act 1992 at **[1.268]** et seq. The provisions so affected are ss 1–23, 30, Sch 1 and parts of Sch 3. Various other provisions have also been repealed, as noted below. Remaining provisions of the Act are printed in full except as noted below.

1–23 *((Pt I) repealed by the Trade Union and Labour Relations (Consolidation) Act 1992, s 300(1), Sch 1.)*

PART II
EMPLOYMENT AND TRAINING

24, 25 *(S 24 repealed by the Employment Act 1989, s 29(4), Sch 7, Pt I; s 25 substitutes the Employment and Training Act 1973, ss 2, 3 and introduces Sch 2 (further amendments, etc, to the 1973 Act).)*

[1.168]

26 Status of trainees etc

(1) Where it appears to the Secretary of State that provision has been made under section 2 of the 1973 Act[, or under section 2(3) [or section 14A] of the Enterprise and New Towns (Scotland) Act 1990,] for persons using facilities provided in pursuance of arrangements under [any of those three sections] to receive payments from any person in connection with their use of those facilities, the Secretary of State may by order provide—

(a) that those persons are, for the purposes and in the cases specified or described in or determined under the order, to be treated in respect of their use of those facilities as being or as not being employed;

(b) that where those persons are treated as being employed they are to be treated as being the employees of the persons so specified, described or determined and of no others;

(c) that where those persons are treated as not being employed they are to be treated as being trained, or are to be treated in such other manner as may be so specified, described or determined; and

(d) that those payments are to be treated for the purposes of such enactments and subordinate legislation as may be so specified, described or determined in such manner as may be so specified, described or determined.

[(1A) The Secretary of State may make an order under subsection (1B) where it appears to the Secretary of State that provision has been made for trainees to receive payments—

(a) from the Secretary of State under section 14 of the Education Act 2002,

(b) . . .

(c) from the Welsh Ministers under section 34(1)(c) of the Learning and Skills Act 2000.

(1B) An order under this subsection may provide—

(a) that the trainees are, for the purposes and in the cases specified or described in or determined under the order, to be treated in respect of the training as being or as not being employed;

(b) that where the trainees are treated as being employed they are to be treated as being the employees of the persons so specified, described or determined and of no others;

(c) that where the trainees are treated as not being employed, they are to be treated in such other manner as may be so specified, described or determined; and

(d) that the payments are to be treated for the purposes of such enactments and subordinate legislation as may be so specified, described or determined in such manner as may be so specified, described or determined.

For the purposes of subsection (1A) and this subsection, trainees are persons receiving or proposing to receive training.]

(2) The power to make an order under this section shall be exercisable by statutory instrument subject to annulment in pursuance of a resolution of either House of Parliament; and such an order may—

(a) modify any enactment or subordinate legislation;

(b) make different provision for different purposes and for different cases; and

(c) contain such incidental, consequential and transitional provision as appears to the Secretary of State to be appropriate.

(3) The consent of the Treasury shall be required for the making of any order under this section which contains provision for the manner in which any payment is to be treated for the purposes of the Income Tax Acts.

(4) In this section—

"enactment" includes an enactment contained in this Act or in any Act passed after this Act; and

"subordinate legislation" has the same meaning as in the Interpretation Act 1978.

NOTES

Sub-s (1): words in first (outer) pair of square brackets inserted by the Enterprise and New Towns (Scotland) Act 1990, s 38(1), Sch 4, para 16; words in second (inner) pair of square brackets inserted, and words in third pair of square brackets substituted, by the Trade Union Reform and Employment Rights Act 1993, s 49(2), Sch 8, para 38.

Sub-ss (1A), (1B): substituted, for sub-s (1A) (as inserted by the Learning and Skills Act 2000, s 149, Sch 9, paras 1, 14), by the Education Act 2011, s 67(1), Sch 16, para 7; sub-s (1A)(b) repealed by the Deregulation Act 2015, s 64(3), Sch 14, Pt 2, para 34, as from 26 May 2015.

Orders: the Social Security (Employment Training: Payments) Order 1988, SI 1988/1409; the Employment Action (Miscellaneous Provisions) Order 1991, SI 1991/1995; the North Norfolk Action (Miscellaneous Provisions) Order 1993, SI 1993/1065; the Community Action (Miscellaneous Provisions) Order 1993, SI 1993/1621; the Learning for Work (Miscellaneous Provisions) Order 1993, SI 1993/1949; the Training for Work (Miscellaneous Provisions) Order 1995, SI 1995/1780; the Project Work (Miscellaneous Provisions) Order 1996, SI 1996/1623; the New Deal (Miscellaneous Provisions) Order 1998, SI 1998/217; the New Deal (Miscellaneous Provisions) (Amendment) Order 1998, SI 1998/1425; the Training for Work (Miscellaneous Provisions) (Amendment) Order 1998, SI 1998/1426; the New Deal (25 plus) (Miscellaneous Provisions) Order 1999, SI 1999/779; the New Deal (Miscellaneous Provisions) Order 2001, SI 2001/970; the New Deal (Lone Parents) (Miscellaneous Provisions) Order 2001, SI 2001/2915; the Flexible New Deal (Miscellaneous Provisions) Order 2009, SI 2009/1562; the Community Task Force (Miscellaneous Provisions) Order 2010, SI 2010/349.

27–29 *(S 27 repealed by the Social Security (Consequential Provisions) Act 1992, s 3(1), Sch 1; s 28 amends the Employment and Training Act 1973, s 4(3), (5); s 29 (membership of training boards) outside the scope of this work.)*

PART III
MISCELLANEOUS AND SUPPLEMENTAL

30 *(Repealed by the Trade Union and Labour Relations (Consolidation) Act 1992, s 300(1), Sch 1.)*

Supplemental

[1.169]
31 Financial provisions

There shall be paid out of money provided by Parliament any increases attributable to this Act in the sums payable under any other Act out of money so provided.

[1.170]
32 Interpretation

(1) In this Act, except in so far as the context otherwise requires—

. . .

"the 1973 Act" means the Employment and Training Act 1973;

. . .

"modifications" includes additions, alterations and omissions, and cognate expressions shall be construed accordingly;

. . .
(2) . . .

NOTES

Sub-s (1): definitions omitted repealed by the Trade Union and Labour Relations (Consolidation) Act 1992, s 300(1), Sch 1.
Sub-s (2): repealed by the Trade Union and Labour Relations (Consolidation) Act 1992, s 300(1), Sch 1.

33 *(Introduces Schs 3 and 4 (minor and consequential amendments, and repeals) outside the scope of this work.)*

[1.171]
34 Short title, commencement and extent

(1) This Act may be cited as the Employment Act 1988.
(2), (3) . . .
(4)–(6) *(Application to Northern Ireland; outside the scope of this work.)*

NOTES

Sub-ss (2), (3): repealed by the Trade Union and Labour Relations (Consolidation) Act 1992, s 300(1), Sch 1.

SCHEDULES

(Sch 1, Sch 3, Pt I repealed by the Trade Union and Labour Relations (Consolidation) Act 1992, s 300(1), Sch 1; Sch 2 repealed in part by the Employment Act 1989, s 29(4), Sch 7, Pt I, the remainder amends the Employment and Training Act 1973, ss 11(3), 12; Sch 3, Pt II contains minor and consequential amendments with regard to employment and training; Sch 4 contains various repeals.)

ACCESS TO MEDICAL REPORTS ACT 1988

(1988 c 28)

ARRANGEMENT OF SECTIONS

An Act to establish a right of access by individuals to reports relating to themselves provided by medical practitioners for employment or insurance purposes and to make provision for related matters

[29 July 1988]

[1.172]
1 Right of access

It shall be the right of an individual to have access, in accordance with the provisions of this Act, to any medical report relating to the individual which is to be, or has been, supplied by a medical practitioner for employment purposes or insurance purposes.

[1.173]
2 Interpretation

(1) In this Act—

"the applicant" means the person referred to in section 3(1) below;

"care" includes examination, investigation or diagnosis for the purposes of, or in connection with, any form of medical treatment;

"employment purposes", in the case of any individual, means the purposes in relation to the individual of any person by whom he is or has been, or is seeking to be, employed (whether under a contract of service or otherwise);

["health professional" has the same meaning as in the Data Protection Act 2018 (see section 204 of that Act);]

["insurance purposes", in a case of any individual who has entered into, or is seeking to enter into, a contract of insurance with an insurer, means the purposes of that insurer in relation to that individual;

"insurer" means—

(a) a person who has permission under [Part 4A] of the Financial Services and Markets Act 2000 to effect or carry out contracts of insurance;

(b) an EEA firm of the kind mentioned in paragraph 5(d) of Schedule 3 to that Act, which has permission under paragraph 15 of that Schedule (as a result of qualifying for authorisation under paragraph 12 of that Schedule) to effect or carry out relevant contracts of insurance.]

"medical practitioner" means a person registered under the Medical Act 1983;

"medical report", in the case of an individual, means a report relating to the physical or mental health of the individual prepared by a medical practitioner who is or has been responsible for the clinical care of the individual.

[(1A) The definitions of "insurance purposes" and "insurer" in subsection (1) must be read with—

(a) section 22 of the Financial Services and Markets Act 2000;

(b) any relevant order under that section; and

(c) Schedule 2 to that Act.]

(2) Any reference in this Act to the supply of a medical report for employment or insurance purposes shall be construed—

(a) as a reference to the supply of such a report for employment or insurance purposes which are purposes of the person who is seeking to be supplied with it; or

(b) (in the case of a report that has already been supplied) as a reference to the supply of such a report for employment or insurance purposes which, at the time of its being supplied, were purposes of the person to whom it was supplied.

NOTES

Sub-s (1): definition "health professional" substituted by the Data Protection Act 2018, s 211, Sch 19, Pt 1, para 34, as from 25 May 2018 (for transitional provisions and savings relating to the repeal of the Data Protection Act 1998, see Sch 20 to the 2018 Act at **[1.2232]**); definitions "insurance purposes" and "insurer" substituted (for the original definition "insurance purposes") by the Financial Services and Markets Act 2000 (Consequential Amendments and Repeals) Order 2001, SI 2001/3649, art 311(1), (2); words in square brackets in definition "insurer" substituted by the Financial Services Act 2012, s 114(1), Sch 18, Pt 2, para 59; in definition "insurer", para (b) repealed by the EEA Passport Rights (Amendment, etc, and Transitional Provisions) (EU Exit) Regulations 2018, SI 2018/1149, reg 3, Schedule, para 30, as from exit day (as defined in the European Union (Withdrawal) Act 2018, s 20).

Sub-s (1A): inserted by SI 2001/3649, art 311(1), (3).

[1.174]

3 Consent to applications for medical reports for employment or insurance purposes

(1) A person shall not apply to a medical practitioner for a medical report relating to any individual to be supplied to him for employment or insurance purposes unless—

(a) that person ("the applicant") has notified the individual that he proposes to make the application; and

(b) the individual has notified the applicant that he consents to the making of the application.

(2) Any notification given under subsection (1)(a) above must inform the individual of his right to withhold his consent to the making of the application, and of the following rights under this Act, namely—

(a) the rights arising under sections 4(1) to (3) and 6(2) below with respect to access to the report before or after it is supplied,

(b) the right to withhold consent under subsection (1) of section 5 below, and

(c) the right to request the amendment of the report under subsection (2) of that section,

as well as of the effect of section 7 below.

[1.175]

4 Access to reports before they are supplied

(1) An individual who gives his consent under section 3 above to the making of an application shall be entitled, when giving his consent, to state that he wishes to have access to the report to be supplied in response to the application before it is so supplied; and, if he does so, the applicant shall—

(a) notify the medical practitioner of that fact at the time when the application is made, and

(b) at the same time notify the individual of the making of the application;

and each such notification shall contain a statement of the effect of subsection (2) below.

(2) Where a medical practitioner is notified by the applicant under subsection (1) above that the individual in question wishes to have access to the report before it is supplied, the practitioner shall not supply the report unless—

(a) he has given the individual access to it and any requirements of section 5 below have been complied with, or

(b) the period of 21 days beginning with the date of the making of the application has elapsed without his having received any communication from the individual concerning arrangements for the individual to have access to it.

(3) Where a medical practitioner—

(a) receives an application for a medical report to be supplied for employment or insurance purposes without being notified by the applicant as mentioned in subsection (1) above, but

(b) before supplying the report receives a notification from the individual that he wishes to have access to the report before it is supplied,

the practitioner shall not supply the report unless—

(i) he has given the individual access to it and any requirements of section 5 below have been complied with, or

(ii) the period of 21 days beginning with the date of that notification has elapsed without his having received (either with that notification or otherwise) any communication from the individual concerning arrangements for the individual to have access to it.

(4) References in this section and section 5 below to giving an individual access to a medical report are references to—

(a) making the report or a copy of it available for his inspection; or

(b) supplying him with a copy of it;

and where a copy is supplied at the request, or otherwise with the consent, of the individual the practitioner may charge a reasonable fee to cover the costs of supplying it.

[1.176]

5 Consent to supplying of report and correction of errors

(1) Where an individual has been given access to a report under section 4 above the report shall not be supplied in response to the application in question unless the individual has notified the medical practitioner that he consents to its being so supplied.

(2) The individual shall be entitled, before giving his consent under subsection (1) above, to request the medical practitioner to amend any part of the report which the individual considers to be incorrect or misleading; and, if the individual does so, the practitioner—

(a) if he is to any extent prepared to accede to the individual's request, shall amend the report accordingly;

(b) if he is to any extent not prepared to accede to it but the individual requests him to attach to the report a statement of the individual's views in respect of any part of the report which he is declining to amend, shall attach such a statement to the report.

(3) Any request made by an individual under subsection (2) above shall be made in writing.

[1.177]

6 Retention of reports

(1) A copy of any medical report which a medical practitioner has supplied for employment or insurance purposes shall be retained by him for at least six months from the date on which it was supplied.

(2) A medical practitioner shall, if so requested by an individual, give the individual access to any medical report relating to him which the practitioner has supplied for employment or insurance purposes in the previous six months.

(3) The reference in subsection (2) above to giving an individual access to a medical report is a reference to—

(a) making a copy of the report available for his inspection; or

(b) supplying him with a copy of it;

and where a copy is supplied at the request, or otherwise with the consent, of the individual the practitioner may charge a reasonable fee to cover the costs of supplying it.

[1.178]

7 Exemptions

(1) A medical practitioner shall not be obliged to give an individual access, in accordance with the provisions of section 4(4) or 6(3) above, to any part of a medical report whose disclosure would in the opinion of the practitioner be likely to cause serious harm to the physical or mental health of the individual or others or would indicate the intentions of the practitioner in respect of the individual.

(2) A medical practitioner shall not be obliged to give an individual access, in accordance with those provisions, to any part of a medical report whose disclosure would be likely to reveal information about another person, or to reveal the identity of another person who has supplied information to the practitioner about the individual, unless—

(a) that person has consented; or

(b) that person is a health professional who has been involved in the care of the individual and the information relates to or has been provided by the professional in that capacity.

(3) Where it appears to a medical practitioner that subsection (1) or (2) above is applicable to any part (but not the whole) of a medical report—

(a) he shall notify the individual of that fact; and

(b) references in the preceding sections of this Act to the individual being given access to the report shall be construed as references to his being given access to the remainder of it;

and other references to the report in sections 4(4), 5(2) and 6(3) above shall similarly be construed as references to the remainder of the report.

(4) Where it appears to a medical practitioner that subsection (1) or (2) above is applicable to the whole of a medical report—

(a) he shall notify the individual of that fact; but

(b) he shall not supply the report unless he is notified by the individual that the individual consents to its being supplied;

and accordingly, if he is so notified by the individual, the restrictions imposed by section 4(2) and (3) above on the supply of the report shall not have effect in relation to it.

[1.179]

8 Application to the court

(1) If a court is satisfied on the application of an individual that any person, in connection with a medical report relating to that individual, has failed or is likely to fail to comply with any requirement of this Act, the court may order that person to comply with that requirement.

(2) The jurisdiction conferred by this section shall be exercisable by [the county court] or, in Scotland, by the sheriff.

NOTES

Sub-s (2): words in square brackets substituted by the Crime and Courts Act 2013, s 17(5), Sch 9, Pt 3, para 52.

[1.180]
9 Notifications under this Act

Any notification required or authorised to be given under this Act—
- (a) shall be given in writing; and
- (b) may be given by post.

[1.181]
10 Short title, commencement and extent

(1) This Act may be cited as the Access to Medical Reports Act 1988.
(2) This Act shall come into force on 1st January 1989.
(3) Nothing in this Act applies to a medical report prepared before the coming into force of this Act.
(4) This Act does not extend to Northern Ireland.

EDUCATION REFORM ACT 1988

(1988 c 40)

An Act to amend the law relating to education

[29 July 1988]

NOTES

Most of the provisions of this Act that were within the scope of this work were repealed and re-enacted by the Education Act 1996. Those provisions have in turn been repealed and re-enacted with (relatively minor) amendments by the School Standards and Framework Act 1998. Only s 221 of this Act is now relevant and, for reasons of space, the subject matter of sections, etc, not printed is not annotated. By virtue of s 238 (Citation, extent etc) (not printed), s 221 applies to England and Wales only.

PART IV
MISCELLANEOUS AND GENERAL

Miscellaneous provisions

[1.182]
221 Avoidance of certain contractual terms

[(1) This section applies to any contract made after 20th November 1987—
- (a) for purposes connected with a local authority's education functions, between the authority and a person employed by the authority; or
- (b) between a governing body of a foundation, voluntary aided or foundation special school and a person employed by the governing body,

other than a contract made in contemplation of the employee's pending dismissal by reason of redundancy.]

(2) In so far as a contract to which this section applies provides that the employee—
- (a) shall not be dismissed by reason of redundancy; or
- (b) if he is so dismissed, shall be paid a sum in excess of the sum which the employer is liable to pay him under [section 135 of the Employment Rights Act 1996],

the contract shall be void and of no effect.

(3) In this section—

"governing body, in relation to an institution, includes a body corporate established for the purpose of conducting that institution;

. . .

NOTES

Sub-s (1): substituted by the Local Education Authorities and Children's Services Authorities (Integration of Functions) Order 2010, SI 2010/1158, art 5, Sch 2, Pt 1, para 4(1), (4).

Sub-s (2): words in square brackets substituted by the Employment Rights Act 1996, s 240, Sch 1, paras 37(1), (4).

Sub-s (3): definition omitted repealed by the Further and Higher Education Act 1992, s 93, Sch 8, Pt I, paras 27, 52, Sch 9.

SOCIAL SECURITY ACT 1989

(1989 c 24)

An Act to amend the law relating to social security and occupational and personal pension schemes; to make provision with respect to certain employment-related benefit schemes; to provide for the recovery, out of certain compensation payments, of amounts determined by reference to payments of benefit; to make fresh provision with respect to the constitution and functions of war pensions committees; and for connected purposes

[21 July 1989]

NOTES

Only s 23 and Sch 5, which implemented Council Directive 86/378/EEC, and s 33 (short title, etc) are printed here. The Directive itself required implementation by 1 January 1993, but as of 15 May 2019, only those parts of Sch 5 relating to (i) unfair maternity and parental leave provisions, (ii) unfair paternity leave provisions, (iii) unfair shared parental leave provisions, and (iv) non-compliance – compulsory levelling up (in respect of unfair paternity leave provisions and unfair adoption leave provisions) have been brought into force (as from 23 June 1994, 6 April 2005, 1 December 2014, and 24 August 2007, respectively); see the first note to Sch 5 for details. Note that the 1986 Directive was repealed and replaced as from 15 August 2009 by the Directive of the European Parliament and of the Council on the implementation of the principle of equal opportunities and equal treatment of men and women in matters of employment and occupation (recast) (Directive 2006/54/EC at **[3.363]** et seq). No provisions of Sch 5, Pt II have been brought into effect, and all have been repealed. The provisions relating to paternity and adoption leave were inserted into Sch 5 by the Pensions Act 2004, s 265(1), and those relating to unfair shared parental leave were inserted by the Children and Families Act 2014, as noted below.

See *Harvey* BI(11), J(3)(A), L(2).

Occupational and personal pensions etc

[1.183]

23 Equal treatment for men and women

Schedule 5 to this Act shall have effect for the purpose of implementing the directive of the Council of the European Communities, dated 24th July 1986, relating to the principle of equal treatment for men and women in occupational social security schemes, and of making additional, supplemental and consequential provision.

NOTES

Commencement: 23 June 1994 and 24 August 2007, in so far as relating to those original provisions of Sch 5 which came into force on those dates (see the note to Sch 5 at **[1.185]** for details); to be appointed (otherwise).

[1.184]

33 Short title, commencement and extent

(1) This Act may be cited as the Social Security Act 1989; and this Act, other than section 25, and the Social Security Acts 1975 to 1988 may be cited together as the Social Security Acts 1975 to 1989.

(2) Apart from the provisions specified in subsection (3) below, this Act shall come into force on such day as the Secretary of State may by order appoint; and different days may be so appointed for different provisions or different purposes of the same provision.

(3)–(7) (*Outside the scope of this work.*)

NOTES

Orders: the commencement orders relevant to the provisions printed here are the Social Security Act 1989 (Commencement No 5) Order 1994, SI 1994/1661 and the Social Security Act 1989 (Commencement No 6) Order 2007, SI 2007/2445.

SCHEDULES

SCHEDULE 5
EMPLOYMENT-RELATED SCHEMES FOR PENSIONS OR OTHER BENEFITS: EQUAL TREATMENT FOR MEN AND WOMEN

Section 23

PART I
COMPLIANCE BY SCHEMES

Schemes to comply with the principle of equal treatment

[1.185]

1. Every employment-related benefit scheme shall comply with the principle of equal treatment.

The principle

2. (1) The principle of equal treatment is that persons of the one sex shall not, on the basis of sex, be treated less favourably than persons of the other sex in any respect relating to an employment-related benefit scheme.

(2) Sub-paragraphs (3) to (6) below have effect, where applicable, for the purpose of determining whether a scheme complies with the principle of equal treatment.

(3) Where any provision of the scheme imposes on both male and female members a requirement or condition—

- (a) which is such that the proportion of persons of the one sex ("the sex affected") who can comply with it is considerably smaller than the proportion of persons of the other sex who can do so, and
- (b) which is not justifiable irrespective of the sex of the members,

the imposition of that requirement or condition shall be regarded as less favourable treatment of persons of the sex affected.

(4) No account shall be taken of—

(a) any difference, on the basis of the sex of members, in the levels of contributions—

(i) . . .

(ii) which the employer makes, to the extent that the difference is for the purpose of removing or limiting differences, as between men and women, in the amount or value of money purchase benefits;

(b) any difference, on the basis of sex, in the amount or value of money purchase benefits, to the extent that the difference is justifiable on actuarial grounds;

(c) any special treatment for the benefit of women in connection with pregnancy or childbirth;

(d) any permitted age-related differences;

(e) any difference of treatment in relation to benefits for a deceased member's surviving husband, wife or other dependants;

(f) any difference of treatment in relation to any optional provisions available; or

(g) any provisions of a scheme to the extent that they have been specially arranged for the benefit of one particular member of the scheme;

. . .

(5) Where the scheme treats persons of the one sex differently according to their marital or family status, that treatment is to be compared with the scheme's treatment of persons of the other sex who have the same status.

(6) The principle of equal treatment applies in relation to members' dependants as it applies in relation to members.

(7) If any question arises whether a condition or requirement falling within sub-paragraph (3)(a) above is or is not justifiable irrespective of the sex of the members, it shall be for those who assert that it is so justifiable to prove that fact.

(8) In this paragraph—

"money purchase benefits" has the meaning given by *section 84(1) of the 1986 Act*, but with the substitution for references to a personal or occupational pension scheme of references to an employment-related benefit scheme;

"optional provisions available" means those provisions of a scheme—

(a) which apply only in the case of members who elect for them to do so; and

(b) whose purpose is to secure for those members—

(i) benefits in addition to those otherwise provided under the scheme; or

(ii) a choice with respect to the date on which benefits under the scheme are to commence; or

(iii) a choice between any two or more benefits;

"permitted age-related difference" means any difference, on the basis of sex, in the age—

(a) at which a service-related benefit in respect of old age or retirement commences; or

(b) at which, in consequence of the commencement of such a benefit, any other service-related benefit either ceases to be payable or becomes payable at a reduced rate calculated by reference to the amount of the benefit so commencing.

(9) For the purposes of this paragraph—

(a) any reference to a person's family status is a reference to his having an unmarried partner or any dependants; and

(b) a person "has an unmarried partner" if that person and some other person to whom he is not married live together as husband and wife.

Non-compliance: compulsory levelling up

3. (1) To the extent that any provision of an employment-related benefit scheme does not comply with the principle of equal treatment, it shall be overridden by this Schedule and the more favourable treatment accorded to persons of the one sex shall also be accorded to persons of the other sex.

(2) Where more favourable treatment is accorded to any persons by virtue of sub-paragraph (1) above, that sub-paragraph requires them, in accordance with the principle of equal treatment—

(a) to pay contributions at a level appropriate to the treatment so accorded; and

(b) to bear any other burden which is an incident of that treatment;

but persons of either sex may instead elect to receive the less favourable treatment and, in accordance with the principle of equal treatment, pay contributions at the level appropriate to that treatment and bear the other burdens incidental to it.

(3) Where any provision of a scheme is overridden by sub-paragraph (1) above, nothing in this Schedule shall affect any rights accrued or obligations incurred during the period before the date on which that provision is so overridden.

(4) Sub-paragraph (1) above is without prejudice to the exercise, in compliance with the principle of equal treatment, of any power to amend the scheme.

4. . . .

Unfair maternity provisions

5. . . .

[Unfair paternity leave provisions

5A. (1) Where an employment-related benefit scheme includes any unfair paternity leave provisions (irrespective of any differences on the basis of sex in the treatment accorded to members under those provisions), then—

(a) the scheme shall be regarded to that extent as not complying with the principle of equal treatment; and

(b) subject to sub-paragraph (3), this Schedule shall apply accordingly.

(2) In this paragraph "unfair paternity leave provisions", in relation to an employment-related benefit scheme, means any provision—

(a) which relates to continuing membership of, or the accrual of rights under, the scheme during any period of paid paternity leave in the case of any member who is (or who, immediately before the commencement of such a period, was) an employed earner and which treats such a member otherwise than in accordance with the normal employment requirement; or

(b) which requires the amount of any benefit payable under the scheme to or in respect of any such member, to the extent that it falls to be determined by reference to earnings during a period which included a period of paid paternity leave, to be determined otherwise than in accordance with the normal employment requirement.

(3) In the case of any unfair paternity leave provision—

(a) the more favourable treatment required by paragraph 3(1) is treatment no less favourable than would be accorded to the member in accordance with the normal employment requirement; and

(b) paragraph 3(2) does not authorise the making of any such election as is there mentioned;

but, in respect of any period of paid paternity leave, a member shall only be required to pay contributions on the amount of contractual remuneration [or statutory paternity pay] actually paid to or for him in respect of that period.

(4) In this paragraph—

"period of paid paternity leave", in the case of a member, means a period—

(a) throughout which the member is absent from work in circumstances where sub-paragraph (5), (6)[, (7)[, (7A) or (7B)] . . .] applies, and

(b) for which the employer (or if he is no longer in his employment, his former employer) pays him any contractual remuneration [or statutory paternity pay]; and

"the normal employment requirement" is the requirement that any period of paid paternity leave shall be treated as if it were a period throughout which the member in question works normally and receives the remuneration likely to be paid for doing so.

(5) This sub-paragraph applies if—

(a) the member's absence from work is due to the birth or expected birth of a child, and

(b) the member satisfies the conditions prescribed under section 171ZA(2)(a)(i) and (ii) of the Social Security Contributions and Benefits Act 1992 in relation to that child.

(6) This sub-paragraph applies if—

(a) the member's absence from work is due to the placement or expected placement of a child for adoption under the law of any part of the United Kingdom, and

(b) the member satisfies the conditions prescribed under section 171ZB(2)(a)(i) and (ii) of that Act in relation to that child.

(7) This sub-paragraph applies if—

(a) the member's absence from work is due to the adoption or expected adoption of a child who has entered the United Kingdom in connection with or for the purposes of adoption which does not involve the placement of the child for adoption under the law of any part of the United Kingdom, and

(b) the member satisfies the conditions prescribed under section 171ZB(2)(a)(i) and (ii) of that Act (as applied by virtue of [section 171ZK(1)] of that Act (adoption cases not involving placement under the law of the United Kingdom)) in relation to that child.

[(7A) This sub-paragraph applies if—

(a) the member's absence from work is due to the placement or expected placement of a child under section 22C of the Children Act 1989 [or section 81 of the Social Services and Well-being (Wales) Act 2014], and

[(b) in relation to that child, the member satisfies the conditions prescribed under section 171ZB(2)(a)(i) and (ii) of the Social Security Contributions and Benefits Act 1992, as modified—

(i) in relation to a local authority in England, by section 171ZB(8) of that Act (cases involving the placing of a child by a local authority in England with a local authority foster parent who has been approved as a prospective adopter);

(ii) in relation to a local authority in Wales, by section 171ZB(10) of that Act (cases involving the placing of a child by a local authority in Wales with a local authority foster parent who has been approved as a prospective adopter).]

(7B) This sub-paragraph applies if—

(a) the member's absence from work is due to the birth or expected birth of a child, and

(b) in relation to that child, the member satisfies the conditions prescribed under section 171ZB(2)(a)(i) and (ii) of the Social Security Contributions and Benefits Act 1992, as applied by virtue of section 171ZK(2) of that Act (cases involving applicants for parental orders under section 54 of the Human Fertilisation and Embryology Act 2008).]

[(8) . . .]

Unfair adoption leave provisions

5B. (1) Where an employment-related benefit scheme includes any unfair adoption leave provisions (irrespective of any differences on the basis of sex in the treatment accorded to members under those provisions), then—

(a) the scheme shall be regarded to that extent as not complying with the principle of equal treatment; and

(b) subject to sub-paragraph (3), this Schedule shall apply accordingly.

(2) In this paragraph "unfair adoption leave provisions", in relation to an employment-related benefit scheme, means any provision—

(a) which relates to continuing membership of, or the accrual of rights under, the scheme during any period of paid adoption leave in the case of any member who is (or who, immediately before the commencement of such a period, was) an employed earner and which treats such a member otherwise than in accordance with the normal employment requirement; or

(b) which requires the amount of any benefit payable under the scheme to or in respect of any such member, to the extent that it falls to be determined by reference to earnings during a period which included a period of paid adoption leave, to be determined otherwise than in accordance with the normal employment requirement.

(3) In the case of any unfair adoption leave provision—

(a) the more favourable treatment required by paragraph 3(1) is treatment no less favourable than would be accorded to the member in accordance with the normal employment requirement; and

(b) paragraph 3(2) does not authorise the making of any such election as is there mentioned;

but, in respect of any period of paid adoption leave, a member shall only be required to pay contributions on the amount of contractual remuneration or statutory adoption pay actually paid to or for him in respect of that period.

(4) In this paragraph—

"period of paid adoption leave", in the case of a member, means a period—

(a) throughout which the member is absent from work in circumstances where sub-paragraph (5)[, (6), (7) or (8)] applies, and

(b) for which the employer (or, if he is no longer in his employment, his former employer) pays him any contractual remuneration or statutory adoption pay; and

"the normal employment requirement" is the requirement that any period of paid adoption leave shall be treated as if it were a period throughout which the member in question works normally and receives the remuneration likely to be paid for doing so.

(5) This sub-paragraph applies if—

(a) the member's absence from work is due to the placement, or expected placement, of a child for adoption under the law of any part of the United Kingdom, and

(b) the member is a person with whom the child is, or is expected to be, placed for such adoption.

(6) This sub-paragraph applies if—

(a) the member's absence from work is due to the adoption or expected adoption of a child who has entered the United Kingdom in connection with or for the purposes of adoption which does not involve the placement of the child for adoption under the law of any part of the United Kingdom, and

(b) the member is a person by whom the child has been or is expected to be adopted.

[(7) This sub-paragraph applies if—

(a) the member's absence from work is due to the placement or expected placement of a child under section 22C of the Children Act 1989 [or section 81 of the Social Services and Well-being (Wales) Act 2014], and

[(b) in relation to that child, the member satisfies the condition in section 171ZL(2)(a) of the Social Security Contributions and Benefits Act 1992, as modified—

(i) in relation to a local authority in England, by section 171ZL(9) of that Act (cases involving the placing of a child by a local authority in England with a local authority foster parent who has been approved as a prospective adopter);

(ii) in relation to a local authority in Wales, by section 171ZL(11) of that Act (cases involving the placing of a child by a local authority in Wales with a local authority foster parent who has been approved as a prospective adopter).]

(8) This sub-paragraph applies if—

(a) the member's absence from work is due to the birth or expected birth of a child, and

(b) in relation to that child, the member satisfies the condition in section 171ZL(2)(a) of the Social Security Contributions and Benefits Act 1992, as applied by virtue of section 171ZT(2) of that Act (cases involving applicants for parental orders under section 54 of the Human Fertilisation and Embryology Act 2008).]]

[Unfair shared parental leave provisions

5C. (1) Where an employment-related benefit scheme includes any unfair shared parental leave provisions (irrespective of any differences on the basis of sex in the treatment accorded to members under those provisions), then—

(a) the scheme shall be regarded to that extent as not complying with the principle of equal treatment; and

(b) subject to sub-paragraph (3), this Schedule shall apply accordingly.

(2) In this paragraph "unfair shared parental leave provisions", in relation to an employment-related benefit scheme, means any provision—

(a) which relates to continuing membership of, or the accrual of rights under, the scheme during any period of paid shared parental leave in the case of any member who is (or who, immediately before the commencement of such a period, was) an employed earner and which treats such a member otherwise than in accordance with the normal employment requirement; or

(b) which requires the amount of any benefit payable under the scheme to or in respect of any such member, to the extent that it falls to be determined by reference to earnings during a period which included a period of paid shared parental leave, to be determined otherwise than in accordance with the normal employment requirement.

(3) In the case of any unfair shared parental leave provision—

(a) the more favourable treatment required by paragraph 3(1) is treatment no less favourable than would be accorded to the member in accordance with the normal employment requirement; and

(b) paragraph 3(2) does not authorise the making of any such election as is there mentioned;

but, in respect of any period of paid shared parental leave, a member shall only be required to pay contributions on the amount of contractual remuneration or statutory shared parental pay actually paid to or for the member in respect of that period.

(4) In this paragraph—

"the normal employment requirement" is the requirement that any period of paid shared parental leave shall be treated as if it were a period throughout which the member in question works normally and receives the remuneration likely to be paid for doing so;

"period of paid adoption leave" has the same meaning as in paragraph 5B;

"period of paid paternity leave" has the same meaning as in paragraph 5A;

"period of paid shared parental leave", in the case of a member, means a period—

(a) throughout which the member is absent from work in circumstances where sub-paragraph (5), (6), (7), (8), (9) or (10) applies, and

(b) for which the employer (or if the member is no longer in that person's employment, his former employer) pays the member any contractual remuneration or statutory shared parental pay.

(5) This sub-paragraph applies if—

(a) the member's absence from work is due to the birth of a child,

(b) the member is the mother of the child, and

(c) the absence from work is not absence on maternity leave (within the meaning of the Equality Act 2010).

(6) This sub-paragraph applies if—

(a) the member's absence from work is due to the birth of a child,

(b) the member is a person who satisfies the conditions prescribed under section 171ZU(4)(b)(i) or (ii) of the Social Security Contributions and Benefits Act 1992 in relation to the child, and

(c) the member's absence from work is not absence during a period of paid paternity leave.

(7) This sub-paragraph applies if—

(a) the member's absence from work is due to the placement of a child for adoption under the law of any part of the United Kingdom,

(b) the member is—

(i) a person with whom a child is placed for adoption under the law of any part of the United Kingdom, or

(ii) a person who satisfies the conditions prescribed under section 171ZV(4)(b)(i) or (ii) of the Social Security Contributions and Benefits Act 1992 in relation to the child, and

(c) the member's absence from work is not absence during—

(i) a period of paid paternity leave, or

(ii) a period of paid adoption leave.

(8) This sub-paragraph applies if—

[(a) the member's absence from work is due to the placement of a child under—

(i) section 22C of the Children Act 1989 by a local authority in England, or

(ii) section 81 of the Social Services and Well-being (Wales) Act 2014 by a local authority in Wales,

with a local authority foster parent who has been approved as a prospective adopter,]

(b) the member is—

(i) the local authority foster parent with whom the child in question is placed under section 22C of the Children Act 1989 [or section 81 of the Social Services and Well-being (Wales) Act 2014], or

(ii) a person who satisfies the conditions prescribed under section 171ZV(4)(b)(i) or (ii) of the Social Security Contributions and Benefits Act 1992, as modified by section 171ZV(18) of that Act (cases involving the placing of a child by a local authority in England [or Wales] with a local authority foster parent who has been approved as a prospective adopter), in relation to the child, and

(c) the member's absence from work is not absence during—

(i) a period of paid paternity leave, or

(ii) a period of paid adoption leave.

(9) This sub-paragraph applies if—

(a) the member's absence from work is due to the adoption or expected adoption of a child who has entered the United Kingdom in connection with or for the purposes of adoption which does not involve placement of the child for adoption under the law of any part of the United Kingdom,
(b) the member is—
(i) the person who has adopted or expects to adopt the child in question, or
(ii) a person who satisfies the conditions prescribed under section 171ZV(4)(b)(i) or (ii) of the Social Security Contributions and Benefits Act 1992, as applied by virtue of section 171ZZ5(1) of that Act (adoption cases not involving placement under the law of the United Kingdom), in relation to the child, and
(c) the member's absence from work is not absence during—
(i) a period of paid paternity leave, or
(ii) a period of paid adoption leave.

(10) This sub-paragraph applies if—
(a) the member's absence from work is due to the birth of a child,
(b) the member is a person who has applied, or intends to apply, for a parental order under section 54 of the Human Fertilisation and Embryology Act 2008 in relation to the child, and
(c) the member's absence from work is not absence during—
(i) a period of paid paternity leave, or
(ii) a period of paid adoption leave.]

[Unfair parental bereavement leave provisions

5D. (1) Where an employment-related benefit scheme includes any unfair parental bereavement leave provisions (irrespective of any differences on the basis of sex in the treatment accorded to members under those provisions), then—
(a) the scheme is to be regarded to that extent as not complying with the principle of equal treatment; and
(b) subject to sub-paragraph (3), this Schedule is to apply accordingly.

(2) In this paragraph "unfair parental bereavement leave provisions", in relation to an employment-related benefit scheme, means any provision—
(a) which relates to continuing membership of, or the accrual of rights under, the scheme during any period of paid parental bereavement leave in the case of any member who is (or who, immediately before the commencement of such a period, was) an employed earner and which treats such a member otherwise than in accordance with the normal employment requirement; or
(b) which requires the amount of any benefit payable under the scheme to or in respect of any such member, to the extent that it falls to be determined by reference to earnings during a period which included a period of paid parental bereavement leave, to be determined otherwise than in accordance with the normal employment requirement.

(3) In the case of any unfair parental bereavement leave provision—
(a) the more favourable treatment required by paragraph 3(1) is treatment no less favourable than would be accorded to the member in accordance with the normal employment requirement; and
(b) paragraph 3(2) does not authorise the making of any such election as is there mentioned;

but, in respect of any period of paid parental bereavement leave, a member is only required to pay contributions on the amount of contractual remuneration or statutory parental bereavement pay actually paid to or for the member in respect of that period.

(4) In this paragraph—
"the normal employment requirement" is the requirement that any period of paid parental bereavement leave is to be treated as if it were a period throughout which the member in question works normally and receives the remuneration likely to be paid for doing so;
"period of paid parental bereavement leave", in the case of a member, means any period—
(a) throughout which a member who is a bereaved parent (within the meaning given by section 171ZZ6(3) of the Social Security Contributions and Benefits Act 1992) is absent from work due to the death of a child, otherwise than by virtue of a period of leave mentioned in sub-paragraph (5); and
(b) for which the employer (or if the member is no longer in that person's employment, his former employer) pays the member any contractual remuneration or statutory parental bereavement pay.

(5) The periods of leave referred to in paragraph (a) of the definition of "period of paid parental bereavement leave" are—
(a) a period of paid paternity leave (within the meaning of paragraph 5A),
(b) a period of maternity leave (within the meaning of the Equality Act 2010),
(c) a period of paid adoption leave (within the meaning of paragraph 5B), or
(d) a period of shared parental leave (within the meaning of paragraph 5C).]

Unfair family leave provisions

6. (1) Where an employment-related benefit scheme includes any unfair family leave provisions (irrespective of any differences on the basis of sex in the treatment accorded to members under those provisions), then—
(a) the scheme shall be regarded to that extent as not complying with the principle of equal treatment; and
(b) subject to sub-paragraph (3) below, this Schedule shall apply accordingly.

(2) In this Schedule "unfair family leave provisions" means any provision—

(a) which relates to continuing membership of, or the accrual of rights under, the scheme during any period of paid family leave in the case of any member who is an employed earner and which treats such a member otherwise than in accordance with the normal leave requirement; or

(b) which requires the amount of any benefit payable under the scheme to or in respect of any such member to the extent that it falls to be determined by reference to earnings during a period which included a period of paid family leave, to be determined otherwise than in accordance with the normal leave requirement.

(3) In the case of any unfair family leave provision—

(a) the more favourable treatment required by paragraph 3(1) above is treatment no less favourable than would be accorded to the members in accordance with the normal leave requirement;

(b) paragraph 3(2) above does not authorise the making of any such election as is there mentioned; and

(c) paragraph 4(1)(a) above does not authorise the making of any modification which does not satisfy the requirements of paragraph (a) above;

but, in respect of a period of paid family leave, a member shall only be required to pay contributions on the amount of contractual remuneration actually paid to or for him in respect of that period.

(4) In this paragraph—

(a) "period of paid family leave" means any period—

(i) throughout which a member is absent from work for family reasons; and

(ii) for which the employer pays him any contractual remuneration;

(b) "the normal leave requirement" is the requirement that any period of paid family leave shall be treated as if it were a period throughout which the member in question works normally but only receives the remuneration in fact paid to him for that period.

Meaning of "employment-related benefit scheme" etc

7. In this Schedule—

(a) "employment-related benefit scheme" means any scheme or arrangement which is comprised in one or more instruments or agreements and which has, or is capable of having, effect in relation to one or more descriptions or categories of employments so as to provide service-related benefits to or in respect of employed or self-employed earners—

(i) who have qualifying service in an employment of any such description or category, or

(ii) who have made arrangements with the trustees or managers of the scheme to enable them to become members of the scheme,

but does not include a limited scheme;

(b) "limited scheme" means—

(i) any personal scheme for employed earners to which the employer does not contribute;

(ii) any scheme which has only one member, other than a personal scheme for an employed earner to which his employer contributes;

(iii) any contract of insurance which is made for the benefit of employed earners only and to which the employer is not a party;

(c) "personal scheme" means any scheme or arrangement which falls within paragraph (a) above by virtue of sub-paragraph (ii) of that paragraph (or which would so fall apart from paragraph (b) above);

(d) "public service scheme" has *the meaning given by section 51(3)(b) of the 1973 Act*;

(e) "service-related benefits" means benefits, in the form of pensions or otherwise, payable in money or money's worth in respect of—

(i) termination of service;

(ii) retirement, old age or death;

(iii) interruptions of service by reason of sickness or invalidity;

(iv) accidents, injuries or diseases connected with employment;

(v) unemployment; or

(vi) expenses incurred in connection with children or other dependants;

and includes, in the case of a member who is an employed earner, any other benefit so payable to or in respect of the member in consequence of his employment.

Extension of ban on compulsory membership

8. *Section 15(1) of the 1986 Act* (which renders void any provision making membership of a pension scheme compulsory for an employed earner) shall apply in relation to a self-employed earner as it applies in relation to an employed earner, but with the substitution for references to a personal pension scheme of references to an employment-related benefit scheme which would be such a pension scheme if self-employed earners were regarded as employed earners.

Jurisdiction

9. (1) The court, on the application of any person interested, shall have jurisdiction to determine any question arising as to—

(a) whether any provision of an employment-related benefit scheme does or does not comply with the principle of equal treatment; or

(b) whether, and with what effect, any such provision is overridden by paragraph 3 above.

(2) In sub-paragraph (1) above "the court" means—

(a) in England and Wales, the High Court or [the county court]; and

(b) in Scotland, the Court of Session or the sheriff court.

(3) An application under sub-paragraph (1) above may be commenced in [the county court] notwithstanding—

(a) any financial limit otherwise imposed on the jurisdiction of [that] court; or

(b) that the only relief claimed is a declaration or an injunction.

Interpretation

10. Expressions other than "benefit" which are used in this Part of this Schedule and in the principal Act have the same meaning in this Part of this Schedule as they have in that Act.

Supplemental

11. . . .

Future repeal of actuarial provisions

12. The Secretary of State may by order repeal paragraph 2(4)(a)(i) above; and if and to the extent that he has not done so before 30th July 1999 it shall cease to have effect on that date.

NOTES

Commencement: this Schedule has been brought into force as follows (and is not in force otherwise)—

(i) on 23 June 1994 in so far as relating to paras 5 (except sub-para (2)(b) and (c)) and 6 (except sub-para (3)(b) and (c)); also paras 1, 2(1), (2), (4)(c), (5), (9), 3 (except sub-para (2)), 7 (except sub-para (d)), 9 and 10, but for the purposes only of giving effect to the provisions of paras 5 and 6 brought into force from that date: see SI 1994/1661, art 2(a), (b), Schedule, Pts I, II.

(ii) on 24 August 2007 in so far as relating to para 3 (except sub-paragraph (2)) for the purposes of paras 5A, 5B: see SI 2007/2445, art 2.

Note that paras 5A, 5B (as inserted by the Pensions Act 2004) came into force on 6 April 2005 (see below); and para 5C (as inserted by Children and Families Act 2014) came into force on 1 December 2014.

Para 2: sub-para (4)(a)(i) repealed by para 12 (qv; no order was made under para 12 prior to the date of its repeal (30 July 1999)); final words omitted from sub-para (4) repealed by the Equality Act 2010, s 211(2), Sch 27, Pt 1; for the words in italics in sub-para (8) there are substituted the words "section 181(1) of the Pension Schemes Act 1993" by the Pension Schemes Act 1993, s 190, Sch 7, para 2(a), as from a day to be appointed.

Para 4: repealed by the Pensions Act 1995, ss 151, 177, Sch 5, para 13(2), Sch 7, Pt III.

Para 5: repealed by the Equality Act 2010, s 211(2), Sch 27, Pt 1.

Para 5A: inserted, together with para 5B, by the Pensions Act 2004, s 265(1); and subsequently amended as follows:

Words in first (outer) pair of square brackets in the definition "period of paid paternity leave" in sub-para (4) substituted by the Work and Families Act 2006, s 11(1), Sch 1, para 1(1), (3)(a).

Words in square brackets in sub-para (3) substituted by the Children and Families Act 2014, s 126(1), Sch 7, paras 1, 2(1), (2), as from 5 April 2015 (note that this amendment does not have effect in relation to (a) children whose expected week of birth ends on or before 4 April 2015, and (b) children placed for adoption on or before that date: see the Children and Families Act 2014 (Commencement No 3, Transitional Provisions and Savings) Order 2014, SI 2014/1640, art 16).

Words ", (7A) or (7B)" in square brackets in para (a) of the definition "period of paid paternity leave" in sub-para (4) inserted by the Children and Families Act 2014, s 126(1), Sch 7, paras 1, 2(1), (3)(a), as from 1 December 2014.

Words omitted from para (a) of the definition "period of paid paternity leave" in sub-para (4) repealed, and words in square brackets in para (b) of that definition substituted, by the Children and Families Act 2014, s 126(1), Sch 7, paras 1, 2(1), (3)(b), (c), as from 5 April 2015 (note that these amendments do not have effect in relation to (a) children whose expected week of birth ends on or before 4 April 2015, and (b) children placed for adoption on or before that date: see SI 2014/1640, art 16).

Words in square brackets in sub-para (7) substituted by the Children and Families Act 2014, s 126(1), Sch 7, paras 1, 2(1), (4), as from 30 June 2014.

Sub-paras (7A), (7B) inserted by the Children and Families Act 2014, s 126(1), Sch 7, paras 1, 2(1), (5), as from 1 December 2014 (in so far as relating to sub-para (7B)), and as from 5 April 2015 (in so far as relating to sub-para (7A)) (note that sub-para (7A) does not have effect in relation to (a) children whose expected week of birth ends on or before 4 April 2015, and (b) children placed for adoption on or before that date: see SI 2014/1640, art 16). Words in square brackets in sub-para (7A)(a) inserted, and sub-para (7A)(b) substituted, by the Social Services and Well-being (Wales) Act 2014 (Consequential Amendments) Regulations 2016, SI 2016/413, regs 53, 54(a), (b), as from 6 April 2016.

Sub-para (8) originally added by the Work and Families Act 2006, s 11(1), Sch 1, para 1(1), (4); repealed by the Children and Families Act 2014, s 126(1), Sch 7, paras 1, 2(1), (6), as from 5 April 2015 (note that this repeal does not have effect in relation to (a) children whose expected week of birth ends on or before 4 April 2015, and (b) children placed for adoption on or before that date: see SI 2014/1640, art 16).

Para 5B: inserted as noted above. Words in square brackets in para (a) of the definition "period of paid adoption leave" in sub-para (4) substituted, and sub-paras (7), (8) added, by the Children and Families Act 2014, s 126(1), Sch 7, paras 1, 3, as from 1 December 2014 (in so far as relating to the amendment to sub-para (4) and the addition of sub-para (8)), and as from 5 April 2015 (in so far as relating to the addition of sub-para (7)) (note that the addition of sub-para (7) does not have effect in relation to (a) children whose expected week of birth ends on or before 4 April 2015, and (b) children placed for adoption on or before that date: see SI 2014/1640, art 16). Words in square brackets in sub-para (7)(a) inserted, and sub-para (7)(b) substituted, by the Social Services and Well-being (Wales) Act 2014 (Consequential Amendments) Regulations 2016, SI 2016/413, regs 53, 54(c), (d), as from 6 April 2016.

Para 5C: inserted by the Children and Families Act 2014, s 126(1), Sch 7, paras 1, 4, as from 1 December 2014. Sub-para (8)(a) substituted, and words in square brackets in sub-para (8)(b) inserted, by the Social Services and Well-being (Wales) Act 2014 (Consequential Amendments) Regulations 2016, SI 2016/413, regs 53, 54(e)–(g), as from 6 April 2016.

Para 5D: inserted by the Parental Bereavement (Leave and Pay) Act 2018, s 1(c), Schedule, Pt 3, para 7, as from a day to be appointed.

Para 7: for the words in italics in sub-para (d) there are substituted the words "the same meaning as "public service pension scheme" in section 1 of the Pension Schemes Act 1993" by the Pension Schemes Act 1993, s 190, Sch 7, para 2(b), as from a day to be appointed.

Para 8: for the words in italics there are substituted the words "section 160(1) of the Pension Schemes Act 1993" by the Pension Schemes Act 1993, s 190, Sch 7, para 2(c), as from a day to be appointed.

Para 9: words in square brackets substituted by the Crime and Courts Act 2013, s 17(5), Sch 9, Pt 3, paras 52, 128.
Para 11: repealed by the Pension Schemes Act 1993, s 188(1), Sch 5, Pt I.
Statutory paternity pay: as to the meaning of this, see the Children and Families Act 2014, s 126 at **[1.1894]**.
1986 Act: ie, the Social Security Act 1986. Section 15(1) and the definition "money purchase benefits" in s 84(1) were repealed and replaced by the Pension Schemes Act 1993 (see now s 160(1) and s 181(1) of that Act respectively).
1973 Act: ie, the Social Security Act 1973. Section 51(3)(b) was repealed by the Pension Schemes Act 1993. The definition "public service scheme" is now replaced by the definition "public service pension scheme" in s 1 of that Act.
Principal Act: ie, the Social Security Act 1975. Repealed by the Social Security (Consequential Provisions) Act 1992 and replaced by the Social Security Administration Act 1992 and the Social Security Contributions and Benefits Act 1992.

(Sch 5, Pt II: para 13 repealed by the Pension Schemes Act 1993, s 188(1), Sch 5, Pt II; para 14 repealed by the Pensions Act 1995, s 177, Sch 7, Pt I; Sch 5, Pt II, para 15 repealed by the Trade Union Reform and Employment Rights Act 1993, s 51, Sch 10.)

EMPLOYMENT ACT 1989

(1989 c 38)

ARRANGEMENT OF SECTIONS

Discrimination as respects training

An Act to amend the Sex Discrimination Act 1975 in pursuance of the Directive of the Council of the European Communities, dated 9th February 1976, (No 76/207/EEC) on the implementation of the principle of equal treatment for men and women as regards access to employment, vocational training and promotion, and working conditions; to repeal or amend prohibitions or requirements relating to the employment of young persons and other categories of employees; to make other amendments of the law relating to employment and training; to repeal section 1(1)(a) of the Celluloid and Cinematograph Film Act 1922; to dissolve the Training Commission; to make further provision with respect to industrial training boards; to make provision with respect to the transfer of staff employed in the Skills Training Agency; and for connected purposes

[16 November 1989]

NOTES

Transfer of functions in relation to Wales: as to the transfer of functions under this Act from Ministers of the Crown to the National Assembly for Wales, see the National Assembly for Wales (Transfer of Functions) Order 1999, SI 1999/672.
See *Harvey* L2(E), (F), (G).

1–6 *(Ss 1–6 repealed by the Equality Act 2010, s 211(2), Sch 27, Pt 1.)*

Discrimination as respects training

7 *(Repealed by the Equality Act 2010, s 211(2), Sch 27, Pt 1.)*

[1.186]

8 Power to exempt discrimination in favour of lone parents in connection with training

(1) The Secretary of State may by order provide with respect to—

(a) any specified arrangements made under section 2 of the Employment and Training Act 1973 (functions of the Secretary of State as respects employment and training) [or under section 2(3) of the Enterprise and New Towns (Scotland) Act 1990 (arrangements by Scottish Enterprise and Highlands and Islands Enterprise in connection with training etc)], or

(b) any specified class or description of training for employment provided otherwise than in pursuance of [either of those sections], . . .

(c) . . .

that this section shall apply to such special treatment afforded to or in respect of lone parents in connection with their participation in those arrangements, or in that training or scheme, as is specified or referred to in the order.

(2) Where this section applies to any treatment afforded to or in respect of lone parents, neither the treatment so afforded nor any act done in the implementation of any such treatment shall be regarded [for the purposes of the Equality Act 2010 as giving rise to any contravention of Part 5 of that Act, so far as relating to marriage and civil partnership discrimination (within the meaning of that Act)]

(3) An order under subsection (1) above may specify or refer to special treatment afforded as mentioned in that subsection—

(a) whether it is afforded by the making of any payment or by the fixing of special conditions for participation in the arrangements, training or scheme in question, or otherwise, and

(b) whether it is afforded by the Secretary of State or by some other person;

and, without prejudice to the generality of paragraph (b) of that subsection, any class or description of training for employment specified in such an order by virtue of that paragraph may be framed by reference to the person, or the class or description of persons, by whom the training is provided.

(4) In this section—

(a) "employment" and "training" have the same meaning as in the Employment and Training Act 1973; and

[(b) "couple" has the meaning given by section 39(1) of the Welfare Reform Act 2012; and

(c) "lone parent" means a person who—

(i) is not a member of a couple, and

(ii) is responsible for, and a member of the same household as, a child.]

NOTES

Sub-s (1): words in square brackets in para (a) inserted, and words in square brackets in para (b) substituted, by the Enterprise and New Towns (Scotland) Act 1990, s 38(1), Sch 4, para 18; para (c) (and the word immediately preceding it) repealed by the Statute Law (Repeals) Act 2004.

Sub-s (2): words in square brackets substituted by the Equality Act 2010, s 211(1), Sch 26, Pt 1, paras 13, 14.

Sub-s (4): paras (b), (c) substituted (for the original para (b)) by the Universal Credit (Consequential, Supplementary, Incidental and Miscellaneous Provisions) Regulations 2013, SI 2013/630, reg 7.

Orders: the Sex Discrimination Act (Exemption of Special Treatment for Lone Parents) Order 1989, SI 1989/2140 at **[2.120]**; the Sex Discrimination Act (Exemption of Special Treatment for Lone Parents) Order 1991, SI 1991/2813 at **[2.135]**.

Removal of restrictions and other requirements relating to employment

9, 10 *(S 9 repealed by the Equality Act 2010, s 211(2), Sch 27, Pt 1; s 10 (Removal of restrictions relating to employment of young persons) outside the scope of this work.)*

[1.187]

11 Exemption of Sikhs from requirements as to wearing of safety helmets [at workplaces]

(1) Any requirement to wear a safety helmet which (apart from this section) would, by virtue of any statutory provision or rule of law, be imposed on a Sikh who is [at a workplace] shall not apply to him at any time when he is wearing a turban.

(2) Accordingly, where—

(a) a Sikh who is [at a workplace] is for the time being wearing a turban, and

(b) (apart from this section) any associated requirement would, by virtue of any statutory provision or rule of law, be imposed—

(i) on the Sikh, or

(ii) on any other person,

in connection with the wearing by the Sikh of a safety helmet, that requirement shall not apply to the Sikh or (as the case may be) to that other person.

(3) In subsection (2) "associated requirement" means any requirement (other than one falling within subsection (1)) which is related to or connected with the wearing, provision or maintenance of safety helmets.

(4) It is hereby declared that, where a person does not comply with any requirement, being a requirement which for the time being does not apply to him by virtue of subsection (1) or (2)—

(a) he shall not be liable in tort to any person in respect of any injury, loss or damage caused by his failure to comply with that requirement; and

(b) in Scotland no action for reparation shall be brought against him by any person in respect of any such injury, loss or damage.

(5) If a Sikh who is [at a workplace]—

(a) does not comply with any requirement to wear a safety helmet, being a requirement which for the time being does not apply to him by virtue of subsection (1), and

(b) in consequence of any act or omission of some other person sustains any injury, loss or damage which is to any extent attributable to the fact that he is not wearing a safety helmet in compliance with the requirement,

that other person shall, if liable to the Sikh in tort (or, in Scotland, in an action for reparation), be so liable only to the extent that injury, loss or damage would have been sustained by the Sikh even if he had been wearing a safety helmet in compliance with the requirement.

(6) Where—

(a) the act or omission referred to in subsection (5) causes the death of the Sikh, and

(b) the Sikh would have sustained some injury (other than loss of life) in consequence of the act or omission even if he had been wearing a safety helmet in compliance with the requirement in question,

the amount of any damages which, by virtue of that subsection, are recoverable in tort (or, in Scotland, in an action for reparation) in respect of that injury shall not exceed the amount of any damages which would (apart from that subsection) be so recoverable in respect of the Sikh's death.

[(6A) This section does not apply to a Sikh who—

(a) works, or is training to work, in an occupation that involves (to any extent) providing an urgent response to fire, riot or other hazardous situations, and

(b) is at the workplace—

(i) to provide such a response in circumstances where the wearing of a safety helmet is necessary to protect the Sikh from a risk of injury, or

(ii) to receive training in how to provide such a response in circumstances of that kind.

(6B) This section also does not apply to a Sikh who—

(a) is a member of Her Majesty's forces or a person providing support to Her Majesty's forces, and

(b) is at the workplace—

(i) to take part in a military operation in circumstances where the wearing of a safety helmet is necessary to protect the Sikh from a risk of injury, or

(ii) to receive training in how to take part in such an operation in circumstances of that kind.]

(7) In this section—

. . .

. . .

["Her Majesty's forces" has the same meaning as in the Armed Forces Act 2006;]

"injury" includes loss of life, any impairment of a person's physical or mental condition and any disease;

"safety helmet" means any form of protective headgear;

"statutory provision" means a provision of an Act or of subordinate legislation; and

["workplace" means any premises where work is being undertaken, including premises occupied or normally occupied as a private dwelling; and "premises" includes any place and, in particular, includes—

(a) any vehicle, vessel, aircraft or hovercraft,

(b) any installation (including a floating installation or one resting on the seabed or its subsoil or on other land covered with water or its subsoil), and

(c) any tent or moveable structure].

(8) In this section—

(a) any reference to a Sikh is a reference to a follower of the Sikh religion; and

(b) any reference to a Sikh being [at a workplace] is a reference to his being there whether while at work or otherwise.

(9) This section shall have effect in relation to any [relevant workplace] within the territorial sea adjacent to Great Britain as it has effect in relation to any [workplace] within Great Britain.

(10) In subsection (9) ["relevant workplace" means any workplace where work is being undertaken if the premises and the activities being undertaken there are premises and activities to which the Health and Safety at Work etc Act 1974 applies by virtue of the Health and Safety at Work etc Act 1974 (Application outside Great Britain) Order 2013].

NOTES

Section heading: words in square brackets substituted by the Deregulation Act 2015, s 6(1), (10), as from 1 October 2015 (for a savings provision see the note below).

Sub-ss (1), (2), (5), (8)–(10): words in square brackets substituted by the Deregulation Act 2015, s 6(1)–(4), (7)–(9), as from 1 October 2015 (for a savings provision see the note below).

Sub-ss (6A), (6B): inserted by the Deregulation Act 2015, s 6(1), (5), as from 1 October 2015 (for a savings provision see the note below).

Sub-s (7): definitions "building operations", "works of engineering construction" and "construction site" (omitted) repealed, and definitions in square brackets inserted, by the Deregulation Act 2015, s 6(1), (6), as from 1 October 2015 (for a savings provision see the note below).

Savings: the Deregulation Act 2015 (Commencement No 1 and Transitional and Saving Provisions) Order 2015, SI 2015/994, art 12(1) provides that the coming into force of s 6(1)–(10) of the Deregulation Act 2015 does not affect: (a) any right, privilege, obligation or liability acquired, accrued or incurred immediately before 1 October 2015; (b) any penalty, forfeiture or punishment incurred in respect of any offence committed before that date; or (c) any investigation, legal proceeding or remedy in respect of (a) or (b) above. Accordingly, any such investigation, legal proceeding or remedy may be instituted, continued or enforced, and any such penalty, forfeiture or punishment may be imposed as if those provisions of the 2015 Act had not been commenced.

[1.188]

12 Protection of Sikhs from racial discrimination in connection with requirements as to wearing of safety helmets

(1) Where—

(a) any person applies to a Sikh any [provision, criterion or practice] relating to the wearing by him of a safety helmet while he is [at a workplace], and

(b) at the time when he so applies the [provision, criterion or practice] that person has no reasonable grounds for believing that the Sikh would not wear a turban at all times when [at such a workplace],

then, for the purpose of determining whether the application of the [provision, criterion or practice] to the Sikh constitutes an act of discrimination falling within [section 19 of the Equality Act 2010 (indirect discrimination), the provision, criterion or practice is to be taken as one in relation to which the condition in subsection (2)(d) of that section (proportionate means of achieving a legitimate aim) is satisfied].

(2) Any special treatment afforded to a Sikh in consequence of section 11(1) or (2) above shall not be regarded for the purposes of [section 13 of the Equality Act 2010 as giving rise to discrimination against any other person].

(3) [Subsections (6A) to (10)] of section 11 above shall apply for the purposes of this section as they apply for the purposes of that section.

NOTES

Sub-s (1): words in first, third, fifth and final pairs of square brackets substituted by the Equality Act 2010, s 211(1), Sch 26, para 15(1)–(3); other words in square brackets substituted by the Deregulation Act 2015, s 6(11), (12), as from 1 October 2015 (for a savings provision see the final note below).

Sub-s (2): words in square brackets substituted by the Equality Act 2010, s 211(1), Sch 26, para 15(1), (4).

Sub-s (3): words in square brackets substituted by the Deregulation Act 2015, s 6(11), (13), as from 1 October 2015 (for a savings provision see the final note below).

Savings: the Deregulation Act 2015 (Commencement No 1 and Transitional and Saving Provisions) Order 2015, SI 2015/994, art 12(2) provides that the coming into force of s 6(11)–(13) of the Deregulation Act 2015 does not affect the application of this section in relation to: (a) any provision, criterion or practice applied to a Sikh before 1 October 2015; or (b) any special treatment afforded to a Sikh before that date.

13–26 *(Ss 13–20 amended the Employment Protection (Consolidation) Act 1978, and are repealed as follows: s 13 repealed by the Trade Union Reform and Employment Rights Act 1993, s 51, Sch 10; s 14 repealed by the Trade Union and Labour Relations (Consolidation) Act 1992, s 300(1), Sch 1; ss 15–18 repealed by the Employment Rights Act 1996, s 242, Sch 3, Pt I; s 19 repealed by the Pension Schemes Act 1993, s 188(1), Sch 5, Pt I and the Employment Rights Act 1996, s 242, Sch 3, Pt I; s 20 repealed by the Employment Tribunals Act 1996, s 45, Sch 3, Pt I; s 21 repealed by the Statute Law (Repeals) Act 2004; ss 22 (dissolution of Training Commission), 23–25 (Industrial Training Boards) outside the scope of this work; s 26 repealed by the Education and Inspections Act 2006, s 184, Sch 18, Pt 2.)*

General

27 *((Power to legislate for Northern Ireland) outside the scope of this work.)*

[1.189]
28 Orders

(1) Any power to make an order under this Act shall be exercisable by statutory instrument.

(2), (3) . . .

(4) Any statutory instrument containing an order under this Act other than—

(a), (b) . . .

(c) an order under section 30,

shall be subject to annulment in pursuance of a resolution of either House of Parliament.

(5) An order under this Act may contain such consequential or transitional provisions or savings as appear to the Secretary of State to be necessary or expedient.

NOTES

Sub-ss (2), (3): repealed by the Equality Act 2010, s 211, Sch 26, Pt 1, paras 13, 16, Sch 27, Pt 1.

Sub-s (4): para (a) repealed by the Equality Act 2010, s 211, Sch 26, Pt 1, paras 13, 16, Sch 27, Pt 1; para (b) repealed by the Education and Inspections Act 2006, s 184, Sch 18, Pt 2.

[1.190]
29 Interpretation, minor and consequential amendments, repeals, etc

(1) In this Act—

. . .

. . .

"act" includes a deliberate omission;

"subordinate legislation" has the same meaning as in the Interpretation Act 1978;

"vocational training" includes advanced vocational training and retraining.

(2) Any reference in this Act to vocational training shall be construed as including a reference to vocational guidance.

(3)–(6) *(Introduce Schs 6–9 (minor and consequential amendments, repeals, revocations and transitional provisions).)*

NOTES

Sub-s (1): definition "the 1975 Act" (omitted) repealed by the Equality Act 2010, s 211, Sch 26, Pt 1, paras 13, 17, Sch 27, Pt 1. Definition "the 1978 Act" (omitted) repealed by the Employment Rights Act 1996, s 242, Sch 3, Pt I.

[1.191]
30 Short title, commencement and extent

(1) This Act may be cited as the Employment Act 1989.

(2)–(4) . . .

(5), (6) *(Application to Northern Ireland (outside the scope of this work).)*

NOTES

Sub-ss (2)–(4): repealed by the Statute Law (Repeals) Act 2004.

Orders: the Employment Act 1989 (Commencement and Transitional Provisions) Order 1990, SI 1990/189; the Employment Act 1989 (Commencement No 2) Order 1997, SI 1997/134.

SCHEDULES 1–9

(Sch 1 (Provisions Concerned with Protection of Women at Work) was not specifically repealed by the

Equality Act 2010 but it effectively lapsed following the repeal of its enabling provision (ie, s 4 of this Act); Sch 2 (Revocation etc of subordinate legislation requiring different treatment of certain employees); Sch 3 (Removal of restrictions relating to employment of young persons); Schs 4, 5 (dissolution of Training Commission), 6–8 (minor and consequential amendments, repeals and revocations); Sch 9 (transitional provisions and savings): in so far as these provisions are still in force, they are outside the scope of this work.)

CONTRACTS (APPLICABLE LAW) ACT 1990

(1990 c 36)

ARRANGEMENT OF SECTIONS

SCHEDULES

An Act to make provision as to the law applicable to contractual obligations in the case of conflict of laws

[26 July 1990]

NOTES

This Act is included for its provisions as to the applicable law of contracts of employment only, and other provisions of the Act and of the Rome Convention are omitted. So far as relevant and except as indicated in the notes below, the Act came into force on 1 April 1991. Note that this Act is disapplied by the effect of s 4A at **[1.195]** (for England and Wales) and by s 4B at **[1.196]** (for Scotland), in cases where the Rome I Regulation of the EU applies, namely, contracts entered into on or after 17 December 2009 (see Article 28 at **[3.453]**).

See *Harvey* H(3)(B).

[1.192]

1 Meaning of "the Conventions"

In this Act—

(a) "the Rome Convention" means the Convention on the law applicable to contractual obligations opened for signature in Rome on 19th June 1980 and signed by the United Kingdom on 7th December 1981;

(b) "the Luxembourg Convention" means the Convention on the accession of the Hellenic Republic to the Rome Convention signed by the United Kingdom in Luxembourg on 10th April 1984; and

(c) "the Brussels Protocol" means the first Protocol on the interpretation of the Rome Convention by the European Court signed by the United Kingdom in Brussels on 19th December 1988;

[(d) "the Funchal Convention" means the Convention on the accession of the Kingdom of Spain and the Portuguese Republic to the Rome Convention and the Brussels Protocol, with adjustments made to the Rome Convention by the Luxembourg Convention, signed by the United Kingdom in Funchal on 18th May 1992;]

[(e) "the 1996 Accession Convention" means the Convention on the accession of the Republic of Austria, the Republic of Finland and the Kingdom of Sweden to the Rome Convention and the Brussels Protocol, with the adjustments made to the Rome Convention by the Luxembourg Convention and the Funchal Convention, signed by the United Kingdom in Brussels on 29th November 1996;]

and [these Conventions and this Protocol] are together referred to as "the Conventions".

NOTES

Substituted by the Law Applicable to Contractual Obligations and Non-Contractual Obligations (Amendment etc) (EU Exit) Regulations 2019, SI 2019/834, reg 3(1), (2), as from exit day (as defined in the European Union (Withdrawal) Act 2018, s 20), as follows—

> **"1 Meaning of "the Rome Convention"**
>
> In this Act, a reference to the Rome Convention is a reference to the provisions contained in Schedule 1 (which is derived from the Convention on the law applicable to contractual obligations opened for signature in Rome on 19th June 1980).".

Para (d) added, and words in final pair of square brackets substituted, by the Contracts (Applicable Law) Act 1990 (Amendment) Order 1994, SI 1994/1900, arts 3, 4; para (e) added by the Contracts (Applicable Law) Act 1990 (Amendment) Order 2000, SI 2000/1825, art 3.

[1.193]

2 *Conventions to have force of law*

(1) Subject to subsections (2) and (3) below, the Conventions shall have the force of law in the United Kingdom.

[(1A) The internal law for the purposes of Article 1(3) of the Rome Convention is the provisions of the regulations for the time being in force under section 424(3) of the Financial Services and Markets Act 2000.]

(2) Articles 7(1) and 10(1)(e) of the Rome Convention shall not have the force of law in the United Kingdom.

(3) *Notwithstanding Article 19(2) of the Rome Convention, the Conventions* shall apply in the case of conflicts between the laws of different parts of the United Kingdom.

(4) For ease of reference there are set out in [Schedules 1, 2, 3[, 3A and 3B]] to this Act respectively the English texts of—

(a) the Rome Convention;

(b) the Luxembourg Convention; . . .

(c) the Brussels Protocol[, and

[(d) the Funchal Convention; and

(e) the 1996 Accession Convention.]]

NOTES

Commencement: 1 April 1991 (sub-s (1) in so far as relating to the Rome Convention and Luxembourg Convention, and sub-ss (2)–(4)); 1 March 2005 (sub-s (1) in so far as relating to the Brussels Protocol); to be appointed (sub-s (1) otherwise).

Heading: words in italics substituted by the words "Application of the Rome Convention", by the Law Applicable to Contractual Obligations and Non-Contractual Obligations (Amendment etc) (EU Exit) Regulations 2019, SI 2019/834, reg 3(1), (3)(a), as from exit day (as defined in the European Union (Withdrawal) Act 2018, s 20).

Sub-s (1): substituted by SI 2019/834, reg 3(1), (3)(b), as from exit day (as defined in the European Union (Withdrawal) Act 2018, s 20), as follows—

"(1) The Rome Convention applies to contracts made on or after 1st April 1991.".

Sub-s (1A): inserted by the Insurance Companies (Amendment) Regulations 1993, SI 1993/174, reg 9; subsequently substituted by the Financial Services and Markets Act 2000 (Consequential Amendments and Repeals) Order 2001, SI 2001/3649, art 320; repealed by SI 2019/834, reg 3(1), (3)(c), as from exit day (as defined in the European Union (Withdrawal) Act 2018, s 20).

Sub-s (2): repealed by SI 2019/834, reg 3(1), (3)(c), as from exit day (as defined in the European Union (Withdrawal) Act 2018, s 20).

Sub-s (3): for the words in italics there are substituted the words "The Rome Convention", by SI 2019/834, reg 3(1), (3)(d), as from exit day (as defined in the European Union (Withdrawal) Act 2018, s 20).

Sub-s (4): words in first (outer) pair of square brackets substituted, word omitted repealed, and original para (d) and the word immediately preceding it added, by the Contracts (Applicable Law) Act 1990 (Amendment) Order 1994, SI 1994/1900, arts 5, 6; words in second (inner) pair of square brackets substituted, and paras (d), (e) substituted (for para (d) as added as noted above), by the Contracts (Applicable Law) Act 1990 (Amendment) Order 2000, SI 2000/1825, art 4; repealed by SI 2019/834, reg 3(1), (3)(c), as from exit day (as defined in the European Union (Withdrawal) Act 2018, s 20).

[1.194]

3 Interpretation of *Conventions*

(1) Any question as to the meaning or effect of any provision of the Conventions shall, if not referred to the European Court in accordance with the Brussels Protocol, be determined in accordance with the principles laid down by, and any relevant decision of, the European Court.

(2) Judicial notice shall be taken of any decision of, or expression of opinion by, the European Court on any such question.

(3) Without prejudice to any practice of the courts as to the matters which may be considered apart from this subsection—

(a) the report on the *Rome Convention* by Professor Mario Giuliano and Professor Paul Lagarde which is reproduced in the Official Journal of the Communities of 31st October 1980 may be considered in ascertaining the meaning or effect of any provision of *that Convention*; *and*

(b) any report on the Brussels Protocol which is reproduced in the Official Journal of the [European Union] may be considered in ascertaining the meaning or effect of any provision of that Protocol.

NOTES

Heading: for the word in italics there are substituted the words "the Rome Convention", by the Law Applicable to Contractual Obligations and Non-Contractual Obligations (Amendment etc) (EU Exit) Regulations 2019, SI 2019/834, reg 3(1), (4)(a), as from exit day (as defined in the European Union (Withdrawal) Act 2018, s 20).

Sub-s (1): substituted by SI 2019/834, reg 3(1), (4)(b), as from exit day (as defined in the European Union (Withdrawal) Act 2018, s 20), as follows—

"(1) Any question as to the meaning or effect of any provision of the Rome Convention is to be decided in accordance with section 6 of the European Union (Withdrawal) Act 2018 (interpretation of retained EU law).".

Sub-s (2): repealed by SI 2019/834, reg 3(1), (4)(c), as from exit day (as defined in the European Union (Withdrawal) Act 2018, s 20).

Sub-s (3): for the words in italics in the first and second places in para (a) there are substituted the words "Convention on the law applicable to contractual obligations" and "the Rome Convention" respectively, and para (b) is repealed together with the word immediately preceding it, by SI 2019/834, reg 3(1), (4)(d), (e), as from exit day (as defined in the European Union

(Withdrawal) Act 2018, s 20); final words in square brackets substituted by the Treaty of Lisbon (Changes in Terminology) Order 2011, SI 2011/1043, art 4(1).

4 *(S 4 (Revision of Conventions etc) outside the scope of this work.)*

[1.195]

[4A Disapplication where the rules in the Rome I Regulations apply: England and Wales and Northern Ireland

(1) Nothing in this Act applies to affect the determination of issues relating to contractual obligations which fall to be determined under the Rome I Regulation.

(2) In this section the "Rome I Regulation" means Regulation (EC) No 593/2008 of the European Parliament and of the Council on the law applicable to contractual obligations, including that Regulation as applied by regulation 3 of the Law Applicable to Contractual Obligations (England and Wales and Northern Ireland) Regulations 2009 (*conflicts falling within Article 22(2)* of Regulation (EC) No 593/2008).

(3) This section extends to England and Wales and Northern Ireland only.]

NOTES

Inserted by the Law Applicable to Contractual Obligations (England and Wales and Northern Ireland) Regulations 2009, SI 2009/3064, reg 2. Note that the Rome I Regulation applies to contracts concluded on or after 17 December 2009 (see Article 28 at **[3.453]**)

Sub-s (2): for the words in italics there is substituted the word "application", by the Law Applicable to Contractual Obligations and Non-Contractual Obligations (Amendment etc) (EU Exit) Regulations 2019, SI 2019/834, reg 3(1), (6), as from exit day (as defined in the European Union (Withdrawal) Act 2018, s 20).

[1.196]

[4B Disapplication where the rules in the Rome I Regulation apply: Scotland

(1) Nothing in this Act applies to affect the determination of issues relating to contractual obligations which fall to be determined by the Rome I Regulation.

(2) In this section "the Rome I Regulation" means Regulation (EC) No 593/2008 of the European Parliament and of the Council on the law applicable to contractual obligations (Rome I), including that Regulation as applied by regulation 4 of the Law Applicable to Contractual Obligations (Scotland) Regulations 2009 (*conflicts falling within Article 22(2)* of Regulation (EC) No 593/2008).

(3) This section extends to Scotland only.]

NOTES

Inserted by the Law Applicable to Contractual Obligations (Scotland) Regulations 2009, SSI 2009/410, reg 2(a). Note that the Rome I Regulation applies to contracts concluded on or after 17 December 2009 (see Article 28 at **[3.453]**).

Sub-s (2): for the words in italics there is substituted the word "application", by the Law Applicable to Contractual Obligations and Non-Contractual Obligations (Amendment etc) (EU Exit) Regulations 2019, SI 2019/834, reg 3(1), (7), as from exit day (as defined in the European Union (Withdrawal) Act 2018, s 20).

5, 6 *(S 5 (Consequential amendments) outside the scope of this work; s 6 provides that this Act binds the Crown.)*

[1.197]

7 Commencement

This Act shall come into force on such day as the Lord Chancellor and the Lord Advocate may by order made by statutory instrument appoint; and different days may be appointed for different provisions or different purposes.

NOTES

Orders: the Contracts (Applicable Law) Act 1990 (Commencement No 1) Order 1991, SI 1991/707; the Contracts (Applicable Law) Act 1990 (Commencement No 2) Order 2004, SI 2004/3448.

By virtue of the Scotland Act 1998, s 44(1)(c), the Lord Advocate ceased, on 20 May 1999, to be a Minister of the Crown and became a member of the Scottish Executive. Accordingly, certain functions of the Lord Advocate were transferred to the Secretary of State (or as the case may be the Secretary of State for Scotland), or the Advocate General for Scotland: see the Transfer of Functions (Lord Advocate and Secretary of State) Order 1999, SI 1999/678 and the Transfer of Functions (Lord Advocate and Advocate General for Scotland) Order 1999, SI 1999/679.

8 *(S 8 (extent) provides, inter alia, that except as provided by virtue of s 4B(3), this Act applies to the whole of the UK (see also s 4A(3) though).)*

[1.198]

9 Short title

This Act may be cited as the Contracts (Applicable Law) Act 1990.

SCHEDULES

SCHEDULE 1
THE ROME CONVENTION

Section 2

NOTES

Only provisions relevant to employment law are reproduced. Provisions omitted are outside the scope of this work. Article 27 of the Convention has been rescinded and, as included in this Schedule, was repealed by the Contracts (Applicable Law) Act 1990 (Amendment) Order 1994, SI 1994/1900. Articles 22, 30, 31 were also amended by the 1994 Order. The Protocol to the Convention (not reproduced) was substituted by the Contracts (Applicable Law) Act 1990 (Amendment) Order 2000, SI 2000/1825, art 5. The Convention has not otherwise been amended. Note further that the Rome Convention is disapplied, and the Rome I Regulation (at **[3.430]**) applied to contracts concluded on or after 17 December 2009, by s 4A (at **[1.195]**) for England and Wales, and s 4B (at **[1.196]**) for Scotland (but subject to the effects of amendments to be made to this Act by the Law Applicable to Contractual Obligations and Non-Contractual Obligations (Amendment etc) (EU Exit) Regulations 2019, SI 2019/834, as from exit day (as defined in the European Union (Withdrawal) Act 2018, s 20), as noted to the provisions of this Act *ante*).

[1.199]

The High Contracting Parties to the Treaty establishing the European Economic Community,

Anxious to continue in the field of private international law the work of unification of law which has already been done within the Community, in particular in the field of jurisdiction and enforcement of judgments,

Wishing to establish uniform rules concerning the law applicable to contractual obligations,

Have agreed as follows:

TITLE I SCOPE OF THE CONVENTION

Article 1

Scope of the Convention

1. The rules of this Convention shall apply to contractual obligations in any situation involving a choice between the laws of different countries.

2–4. . . .

Article 2

Application of law of non-contracting States

Any law specified by this Convention shall be applied whether or not it is the law of *a Contracting State*.

TITLE II UNIFORM RULES

Article 3

Freedom of choice

1. A contract shall be governed by the law chosen by the parties. The choice must be express or demonstrated with reasonable certainty by the terms of the contract or the circumstances of the case. By their choice the parties can select the law applicable to the whole or a part only of the contract.

2. The parties may at any time agree to subject the contract to a law other than that which previously governed it, whether as a result of an earlier choice under this Article or of other provisions of this Convention. Any variation by the parties of the law to be applied made after the conclusion of the contract shall not prejudice its formal validity under Article 9 or adversely affect the rights of third parties.

3. The fact that the parties have chosen a foreign law, whether or not accompanied by the choice of a foreign tribunal, shall not, where all the other elements relevant to the situation at the time of the choice are connected with one country only, prejudice the application of rules of the law of that country which cannot be derogated from by contract, hereinafter called "mandatory rules".

4. The existence and validity of the consent of the parties as to the choice of the applicable law shall be determined in accordance with the provisions of Articles 8, 9 and 11.

Article 4

Applicable law in the absence of choice

1. To the extent that the law applicable to the contract has not been chosen in accordance with Article 3, the contract shall be governed by the law of the country with which it is most closely connected. Nevertheless, a severable part of the contract which has a closer connection with another country may by way of exception be governed by the law of that other country.

2. Subject to the provisions of paragraph 5 of this Article, it shall be presumed that the contract is most closely connected with the country where the party who is to effect the performance which is characteristic of the contract has, at the time of conclusion of the contract, his habitual residence, or, in the case of a body corporate or unincorporate, its central administration. However, if the contract is entered into in the course of that party's trade or profession, that country shall be the country in which the principal place of business is situated or, where under the terms of the contract the performance is to be effected through a place of business other than the principal place of business, the country in which that other place of business is situated.

3, 4. . . .

5. Paragraph 2 shall not apply if the characteristic performance cannot be determined, and the presumptions in paragraphs 2, 3 and 4 shall be disregarded if it appears from the circumstances as a whole that the contract is more closely connected with another country.

Article 6

Individual employment contracts

1. Notwithstanding the provisions of Article 3, in a contract of employment a choice of law made by the parties shall not have the result of depriving the employee of the protection afforded to him by the mandatory rules of the law which would be applicable under paragraph 2 in the absence of choice.

2. Notwithstanding the provisions of Article 4, a contract of employment shall, in the absence of choice in accordance with Article 3, be governed:

(a) by the law of the country in which the employee habitually carries out his work in performance of the contract, even if he is temporarily employed in another country; or

(b) if the employee does not habitually carry out his work in any one country, by the law of the country in which the place of business through which he was engaged is situated;

unless it appears from the circumstances as a whole that the contract is more closely connected with another country, in which case the contract shall be governed by the law of that country.

Article 7

Mandatory rules

1. When applying under this Convention the law of a country, effect may be given to the mandatory rules of the law of another country with which the situation has a close connection, if and in so far as, under the law of the latter country, those rules must be applied whatever the law applicable to the contract. In considering whether to give effect to these mandatory rules, regard shall be had to their nature and purpose and to the consequences of their application or non-application.

2. Nothing in this Convention shall restrict the application of the rules of the law of the forum in a situation where they are mandatory irrespective of the law otherwise applicable to the contract.

Article 9

Formal validity

1. A contract concluded between persons who are in the same country is formally valid if it satisfies the formal requirements of the law which governs it under this Convention or of the law of the country where it is concluded.

2. A contract concluded between persons who are in different countries is formally valid if it satisfies the formal requirements of the law which governs it under this Convention or of the law of one of those countries.

3–6. . . .

Article 10

Scope of the applicable law

1. The law applicable to a contract by virtue of Articles 3 to 6 and 12 of this Convention shall govern in particular:

(a) interpretation;

(b) performance;

(c) within the limits of the powers conferred on the court by its procedural law, the consequences of breach, including the assessment of damages in so far as it is governed by rules of law;

(d) the various ways of extinguishing obligations, and prescription and limitation of actions;

(e) the consequences of nullity of the contract.

2. In relation to the manner of performance and the steps to be taken in the event of defective performance regard shall be had to the law of the country in which performance takes place.

Article 14

Burden of proof, etc

1. The law governing the contract under this Convention applies to the extent that it contains, in the law of contract, rules which raise presumptions of law or determine the burden of proof.

2. A contract or an act intended to have legal effect may be proved by any mode of proof recognised by the law of the forum or by any of the laws referred to in Article 9 under which that contract or act is formally valid, provided that such mode of proof can be administered by the forum.

Article 17

No retrospective effect

This Convention shall apply in a Contracting State to contracts made after the date on which this Convention has entered into force with respect to that State.

Article 18

Uniform interpretation

In the interpretation and application of the preceding uniform rules, regard shall be had to their international character and to the desirability of achieving uniformity in their interpretation and application.

Article 19

States with more than one legal system

1. Where a State comprises several territorial units each of which has its own rules of law in respect of contractual obligations, each territorial unit shall be considered as a country for the purposes of identifying the law applicable under this Convention.

2. A State within which different territorial units have their own rules of law in respect of contractual obligations shall not be bound to apply this Convention to conflicts solely between the laws of such units.

NOTES

Opening words in italics repealed by the Law Applicable to Contractual Obligations and Non-Contractual Obligations (Amendment etc) (EU Exit) Regulations 2019, SI 2019/834, reg 3(1), (9)(a), as from exit day (as defined in the European Union (Withdrawal) Act 2018, s 20).

In Article 2, for the words in italics in the first and second places there are substituted the words "Application of law of a country outside of the United Kingdom" and "the United Kingdom or a part of the United Kingdom" respectively, by SI 2019/834, reg 3(1), (9)(c), as from exit day (as defined in the European Union (Withdrawal) Act 2018, s 20).

Articles 7(1), 10(1)(e), 17, 19(2) are repealed by SI 2019/834, reg 3(1), (9)(d)–(g), as from exit day (as defined in the European Union (Withdrawal) Act 2018, s 20).

SCHEDULES 2–4

(Schs 2–4 outside the scope of this work.)

SOCIAL SECURITY CONTRIBUTIONS AND BENEFITS ACT 1992

(1992 c 4)

ARRANGEMENT OF SECTIONS

PART XI
STATUTORY SICK PAY

Employer's liability

The qualifying conditions

Limitations on entitlement etc

Rates of payment, etc

PART XIII
GENERAL

Short title, commencement and extent

SCHEDULES

An Act to consolidate certain enactments relating to social security contributions and benefits with amendments to give effect to recommendations of the Law Commission and the Scottish Law Commission

[13 February 1992]

NOTES

This consolidating Act re-enacts the statutory provisions as to statutory sick pay (Pt XI) and statutory maternity pay (Pt XII) previously in the Social Security and Housing Benefits Act 1982 and the Social Security Act 1986 respectively. By virtue of the Social Security (Consequential Provisions) Act 1992, s 2 (Continuity of the law), Regulations made under the repealed Acts continue to have effect as if made under the corresponding provision of the consolidating Acts (ie, this Act, the Social Security Administration Act 1992, and the Social Security (Consequential Provisions) Act 1992). Pre-1992 Regulations that continue to have effect (and which are amended by Regulations made under this Act) are noted to the appropriate section/Schedule below. Parts XIIZA and XIIZB, providing respectively for statutory paternity pay and statutory adoption pay, were inserted by the Employment Act 2002, ss 2 and 4 respectively. Sections 171ZEA–171ZEE (additional statutory paternity pay: birth and adoption) were originally inserted therein by the Work and Families Act 2006, ss 6–10, and were repealed (as from 6 April 2015) by the Children and Families Act 2014, s 125(2), subject to transitional provisions as detailed below. Part 12ZC (statutory shared parental pay) was inserted by the Children and Families Act 2014, s 119, as from 1 June 2014. These are reproduced here, together with the associated Schedules. Other provisions not printed here are not annotated.

See *Harvey* BI(2)(B), J(2), (8).

PART XI
STATUTORY SICK PAY

Employer's liability

[1.200]

151 Employer's liability

(1) Where an employee has a day of incapacity for work in relation to his contract of service with an employer, that employer shall, if the conditions set out in sections 152 to 154 below are satisfied, be liable to make him, in accordance with the following provisions of this Part of this Act, a payment (to be known as "statutory sick pay") in respect of that day.

(2) Any agreement shall be void to the extent that it purports—
- (a) to exclude, limit or otherwise modify any provision of this Part of this Act, or
- (b) to require an employee to contribute (whether directly or indirectly) towards any costs incurred by his employer under this Part of this Act.

(3) For the avoidance of doubt, any agreement between an employer and an employee authorising any deductions from statutory sick pay which the employer is liable to pay to the employee in respect of any period shall not be void by virtue of subsection (2)(a) above if the employer—
- (a) is authorised by that or another agreement to make the same deductions from any contractual remuneration which he is liable to pay in respect of the same period, or
- (b) would be so authorised if he were liable to pay contractual remuneration in respect of that period.

(4) For the purposes of this Part of this Act [a day of incapacity for work in relation to a contract of service means a day on which] the employee concerned is, or is deemed in accordance with regulations to be, incapable by reason of some specific disease or bodily or mental disablement of doing work which he can reasonably be expected to do under that contract.

(5) In any case where an employee has more than one contract of service with the same employer the provisions of this Part of this Act shall, except in such cases as may be prescribed and subject to the following provisions of this Part of this Act, have effect as if the employer were a different employer in relation to each contract of service.

(6) Circumstances may be prescribed in which, notwithstanding the provisions of subsections (1) to (5) above, the liability to make payments of statutory sick pay is to be a liability of the [Commissioners of Inland Revenue].

[(7) Regulations under subsection (6) above must be made with the concurrence of the Commissioners of Inland Revenue.]

NOTES

Sub-s (4): words in square brackets substituted by the Social Security (Incapacity for Work) Act 1994, s 11(1), Sch 1, Pt I, para 34.

Sub-s (6): words in square brackets substituted by the Social Security Contributions (Transfer of Functions, etc) Act 1999, s 1(1), Sch 1, para 9.

Sub-s (7): added by the Social Security Contributions (Transfer of Functions, etc) Act 1999, s 1(1), Sch 1, para 9.

Commissioners of Inland Revenue: a reference to the Commissioners of Inland Revenue is now to be taken as a reference to the Commissioners for Her Majesty's Revenue and Customs; see the Commissioners for Revenue and Customs Act 2005, s 50(1), (7).

Regulations: the Statutory Sick Pay (General) Regulations 1982, SI 1982/894 at **[2.44]**, have effect as if made under this section by virtue of the Social Security (Consequential Provisions) Act 1992, s 2(2); the Statutory Sick Pay (General) Amendment Regulations 2006, SI 2006/799; the Social Security (Miscellaneous Amendments) (No 3) Regulations 2011, SI 2011/2425.

The qualifying conditions

[1.201]

152 Period of incapacity for work

(1) The first condition is that the day in question forms part of a period of incapacity for work.

(2) In this Part of this Act "period of incapacity for work" means any period of four or more consecutive days, each of which is a day of incapacity for work in relation to the contract of service in question.

(3) Any two periods of incapacity for work which are separated by a period of not more than 8 weeks shall be treated as a single period of incapacity for work.

(4) The Secretary of State may by regulations direct that a larger number of weeks specified in the regulations shall be substituted for the number of weeks for the time being specified in subsection (3) above.

(5) No day of the week shall be disregarded in calculating any period of consecutive days for the purposes of this section.

(6) A day may be a day of incapacity for work in relation to a contract of service, and so form part of a period of incapacity for work, notwithstanding that—

(a) it falls before the making of the contract or after the contract expires or is brought to an end; or

(b) it is not a day on which the employee concerned would be required by that contract to be available for work.

NOTES

Regulations: as of 15 May 2019, no Regulations had been made under sub-s (4).

[1.202]

153 Period of entitlement

(1) The second condition is that the day in question falls within a period which is, as between the employee and his employer, a period of entitlement.

(2) For the purposes of this Part of this Act a period of entitlement, as between an employee and his employer, is a period beginning with the commencement of a period of incapacity for work and ending with whichever of the following first occurs—

(a) the termination of that period of incapacity for work;

(b) the day on which the employee reaches, as against the employer concerned, his maximum entitlement to statutory sick pay (determined in accordance with section 155 below);

(c) the day on which the employee's contract of service with the employer concerned expires or is brought to an end;

(d) in the case of an employee who is, or has been, pregnant, the day immediately preceding the beginning of the disqualifying period.

(3) Schedule 11 to this Act has effect for the purpose of specifying circumstances in which a period of entitlement does not arise in relation to a particular period of incapacity for work.

(4) A period of entitlement as between an employee and an employer of his may also be, or form part of, a period of entitlement as between him and another employer of his.

(5) The Secretary of State may by regulations—

(a) specify circumstances in which, for the purpose of determining whether an employee's maximum entitlement to statutory sick pay has been reached in a period of entitlement as between him and an employer of his, days falling within a previous period of entitlement as between the employee and any person who is or has in the past been an employer of his are to be counted; and

(b) direct that in prescribed circumstances an employer shall provide a person who is about to leave his employment, or who has been employed by him in the past, with a statement in the prescribed form containing such information as may be prescribed in relation to any entitlement of the employee to statutory sick pay.

(6) Regulations may provide, in relation to prescribed cases, for a period of entitlement to end otherwise than in accordance with subsection (2) above.

(7) In a case where the employee's contract of service first takes effect on a day which falls within a period of incapacity for work, the period of entitlement begins with that day.

(8) In a case where the employee's contract of service first takes effect between two periods of incapacity for work which by virtue of section 152(3) above are treated as one, the period of entitlement begins with the first day of the second of those periods.

(9) In any case where, otherwise than by virtue of section 6(1)(b) above, an employee's earnings under a contract of service in respect of the day on which the contract takes effect do not attract a liability to pay secondary Class 1 contributions, subsections (7) and (8) above shall have effect as if for any reference to the contract first taking effect there were substituted a reference to the first day in respect of which the employee's earnings attract such a liability.
(10) Regulations shall make provision as to an employer's liability under this Part of this Act to pay statutory sick pay to an employee in any case where the employer's contract of service with that employee has been brought to an end by the employer solely, or mainly, for the purpose of avoiding liability for statutory sick pay.
(11) Subsection (2)(d) above does not apply in relation to an employee who has been pregnant if her pregnancy terminated, before the beginning of the disqualifying period, otherwise than by confinement.
(12) In this section—
"confinement" is to be construed in accordance with section 171(1) below;
"disqualifying period" means—
(a) in relation to a woman entitled to statutory maternity pay, the maternity pay period; and
(b) in relation to a woman entitled to maternity allowance, the maternity allowance period;
"maternity allowance period" has the meaning assigned to it by section 35(2) above, and
"maternity pay period" has the meaning assigned to it by section 165(1) below.

NOTES

Regulations: the Statutory Sick Pay (General) Regulations 1982, SI 1982/894 at **[2.44]**, and the Statutory Sick Pay (Mariners, Airmen and Persons Abroad) Regulations 1982, SI 1982/1349, have effect as if made under this section by virtue of the Social Security (Consequential Provisions) Act 1992, s 2(2); the Social Security Maternity Benefits and Statutory Sick Pay (Amendment) Regulations 1994, SI 1994/1367; the Social Security Contributions, Statutory Maternity Pay and Statutory Sick Pay (Miscellaneous Amendments) Regulations 1996, SI 1996/777; the Social Security, Statutory Maternity Pay and Statutory Sick Pay (Miscellaneous Amendments) Regulations 2002, SI 2002/2690; the Statutory Sick Pay (General) (Amendment) Regulations 2008, SI 2008/1735.

[1.203]
154 Qualifying days

(1) The third condition is that the day in question is a qualifying day.
(2) The days which are for the purposes of this Part of this Act to be qualifying days as between an employee and an employer of his (that is to say, those days of the week on which he is required by his contract of service with that employer to be available for work or which are chosen to reflect the terms of that contract) shall be such day or days as may, subject to regulations, be agreed between the employee and his employer or, failing such agreement, determined in accordance with regulations.
(3) In any case where qualifying days are determined by agreement between an employee and his employer there shall, in each week (beginning with Sunday), be at least one qualifying day.
(4) A day which is a qualifying day as between an employee and an employer of his may also be a qualifying day as between him and another employer of his.

NOTES

Regulations: the Statutory Sick Pay (General) Regulations 1982, SI 1982/894 at **[2.44]**, have effect as if made under this section by virtue of the Social Security (Consequential Provisions) Act 1992, s 2(2).

Limitations on entitlement, etc

[1.204]
155 Limitations on entitlement

(1) Statutory sick pay shall not be payable for the first three qualifying days in any period of entitlement.
(2) An employee shall not be entitled, as against any one employer, to an aggregate amount of statutory sick pay in respect of any one period of entitlement which exceeds his maximum entitlement.
(3) The maximum entitlement as against any one employer is reached on the day on which the amount to which the employee has become entitled by way of statutory sick pay during the period of entitlement in question first reaches or passes the entitlement limit.
(4) The entitlement limit is an amount equal to 28 times [the weekly rate applicable in accordance with] section 157 below.
(5) Regulations may make provision for calculating the entitlement limit in any case where an employee's entitlement to statutory sick pay is calculated by reference to different weekly rates in the same period of entitlement.

NOTES

Sub-s (4): words in square brackets substituted by the Social Security (Incapacity for Work) Act 1994, s 8(4).

Regulations: the Statutory Sick Pay (General) Regulations 1982, SI 1982/894 at **[2.44]**, have effect as if made under this section by virtue of the Social Security (Consequential Provisions) Act 1992, s 2(2).

[1.205]
156 Notification of incapacity for work

(1) Regulations shall prescribe the manner in which, and the time within which, notice of any day of incapacity for work is to be given by or on behalf of an employee to his employer.
(2) An employer who would, apart from this section, be liable to pay an amount of statutory sick pay to an employee in respect of a qualifying day (the "day in question") shall be entitled to withhold payment of that amount if—

(a) the day in question is one in respect of which he has not been duly notified in accordance with regulations under subsection (1) above; or

(b) he has not been so notified in respect of any of the first three qualifying days in a period of entitlement (a "waiting day") and the day in question is the first qualifying day in that period of entitlement in respect of which the employer is not entitled to withhold payment—

(i) by virtue of paragraph (a) above; or

(ii) in respect of an earlier waiting day by virtue of this paragraph.

(3) Where an employer withholds any amount of statutory sick pay under this section—

(a) the period of entitlement in question shall not be affected; and

(b) for the purposes of calculating his maximum entitlement in accordance with section 155 above the employee shall not be taken to have become entitled to the amount so withheld.

NOTES

Regulations: the Statutory Sick Pay (General) Regulations 1982, SI 1982/894 at **[2.44]**, have effect as if made under this section by virtue of the Social Security (Consequential Provisions) Act 1992, s 2(2).

Rates of payment, etc

[1.206]

157 Rates of payment

(1) Statutory sick pay shall be payable by an employer at the weekly rate of [£94.25].

(2) The Secretary of State may by order—

[(a) amend subsection (1) above so as to substitute different provision as to weekly rate or rates of statutory sick pay; and]

(b) make such consequential amendments as appear to him to be required of any provision contained in this Part of this Act.

(3) The amount of statutory sick pay payable by any one employer in respect of any day shall be the weekly rate applicable on that day divided by the number of days which are, in the week (beginning with Sunday) in which that day falls, qualifying days as between that employer and the employee concerned.

NOTES

Sub-s (1): sum in square brackets substituted by the Social Security Benefits Up-rating Order 2019, SI 2019/480, art 9, as from 6 April 2019.

Previous amounts were: £92.05 (as from 6 April 2018, see the Social Security Benefits Up-rating Order 2018, SI 2018/281, art 9); £89.35 (as from 6 April 2017, see the Social Security Benefits Up-rating Order 2017, SI 2017/460, art 9); £88.45 (as from 6 April 2015, see the Welfare Benefits Up-rating Order 2015, SI 2015/30, art 3); £87.55 (as from 6 April 2014, see the Welfare Benefits Up-rating Order 2014, SI 2014/147, art 3); £86.70 (as from 6 April 2013, see the Social Security Benefits Up-rating Order 2013, SI 2013/574, art 8); £85.85 (as from 6 April 2012, see the Social Security Benefits Up-rating Order 2012, SI 2012/780, art 9). Note that there was no increase in the weekly rate in 2016.

Sub-s (2): para (a) substituted by the Social Security (Incapacity for Work) Act 1994, s 8(3).

Orders: as of 15 May 2019, no Order had been made under sub-s (2).

158, 159 *(Repealed by the Statutory Sick Pay Percentage Threshold Order 1995, SI 1995/512, art 5(a).)*

[1.207]

[159A Power to provide for recovery by employers of sums paid by way of statutory sick pay

(1) The Secretary of State may by order provide for the recovery by employers, in accordance with the order, of the amount (if any) by which their payments of, or liability incurred for, statutory sick pay in any period exceeds the specified percentage of the amount of their liability for contributions payments in respect of the corresponding period.

(2) An order under subsection (1) above may include provision—

(a) as to the periods by reference to which the calculation referred to above is to be made,

(b) for amounts which would otherwise be recoverable but which do not exceed the specified minimum for recovery not to be recoverable,

(c) for the rounding up or down of any fraction of a pound which would otherwise result from a calculation made in accordance with the order, and

(d) for any deduction from contributions payments made in accordance with the order to be disregarded for such purposes as may be specified,

and may repeal sections 158 and 159 above and make any amendments of other enactments which are consequential on the repeal of those sections.

(3) In this section—

"contributions payments" means payments which a person is required by or under any enactment to make in discharge of any liability of his as an employer in respect of primary or secondary Class 1 contributions; and

"specified" means specified in or determined in accordance with an order under subsection (1).

(4) The Secretary of State may by regulations make such transitional and consequential provision, and such savings, as he considers necessary or expedient for or in connection with the coming into force of any order under subsection (1) above.]

NOTES

Inserted by the Statutory Sick Pay Act 1994, s 3(1).

Orders: the Statutory Sick Pay Percentage Threshold (Revocations, Transitional and Saving Provisions) (Great Britain and Northern Ireland) Order 2014, SI 2014/897.

Regulations: the Statutory Sick Pay Percentage Threshold Order 1995 (Consequential) Regulations 1995, SI 1995/513.

Miscellaneous

[1.208]
160 Relationship with benefits and other payments, etc
Schedule 12 to this Act has effect with respect to the relationship between statutory sick pay and certain benefits and payments.

[1.209]
161 Crown employment—Part XI
(1) Subject to subsection (2) below, the provisions of this Part of this Act apply in relation to persons employed by or under the Crown as they apply in relation to persons employed otherwise than by or under the Crown.
(2) The provisions of this Part of this Act do not apply in relation to persons serving as members of Her Majesty's forces, in their capacity as such.
(3) For the purposes of this section Her Majesty's forces shall be taken to consist of such establishments and organisations as may be prescribed [by regulations made by the Secretary of State with the concurrence of the Treasury], being establishments and organisations in which persons serve under the control of the Defence Council.

NOTES

Sub-s (3): words in square brackets inserted by the Social Security Contributions (Transfer of Functions, etc) Act 1999, s 1(1), Sch 1, para 10.

Regulations: as of 15 May 2019, no Regulations had been made under this section.

[1.210]
162 Special classes of persons
(1) The Secretary of State may [with the concurrence of the Treasury] make regulations modifying this Part of this Act in such manner as he thinks proper in their application to any person who is, has been or is to be—
- (a) employed on board any ship, vessel, hovercraft or aircraft;
- (b) outside Great Britain at any prescribed time or in any prescribed circumstances; or
- (c) in prescribed employment in connection with continental shelf operations, as defined in section 120(2) above.

(2) Regulations under subsection (1) above may in particular provide—
- (a) for any provision of this Part of this Act to apply to any such person, notwithstanding that it would not otherwise apply;
- (b) for any such provision not to apply to any such person, notwithstanding that it would otherwise apply;
- (c) for excepting any such person from the application of any such provision where he neither is domiciled nor has a place of residence in any part of Great Britain;
- (d) for the taking of evidence, for the purposes of the determination of any question arising under any such provision, in a country or territory outside Great Britain, by a British consular official or such other person as may be determined in accordance with the regulations.

NOTES

Sub-s (1): words in square brackets inserted by the Social Security Contributions (Transfer of Functions, etc) Act 1999, s 1(1), Sch 1, para 11.

Regulations: the Statutory Sick Pay (Mariners, Airmen and Persons Abroad) Regulations 1982, SI 1982/1349, have effect as if made under this section by virtue of the Social Security (Consequential Provisions) Act 1992, s 2(2); the Social Security Contributions, Statutory Maternity Pay and Statutory Sick Pay (Miscellaneous Amendments) Regulations 1996, SI 1996/777.

[1.211]
163 Interpretation of Part XI and supplementary provisions
(1) In this Part of this Act—

"contract of service" (except in paragraph (a) of the definition below of "employee") includes any arrangement providing for the terms of appointment of an employee;

"employee" means a person who is—
- (a) gainfully employed in Great Britain either under a contract of service or in an office (including elective office) with [earnings (within the meaning of Parts 1 to 5 above)]; . . .
- (b) . . .

but subject to regulations, which may provide for cases where any such person is not to be treated as an employee for the purposes of this Part of this Act and for cases where any person who would not otherwise be an employee for those purposes is to be treated as an employee for those purposes;

["employer", in relation to an employee and a contract of service of his, means a person who—
- (a) under section 6 above is liable to pay secondary Class 1 contributions in relation to any earnings of the employee under the contract, or
- (b) would be liable to pay such contributions but for—
  - (i) the condition in section 6(1)(b), or
  - (ii) the employee being under the age of 16;]

"period of entitlement" has the meaning given by section 153 above;

"period of incapacity for work" has the meaning given by section 152 above;

. . .

"prescribed" means prescribed by regulations;

"qualifying day" has the meaning given by section 154 above;

"week" means any period of 7 days.

(2) For the purposes of this Part of this Act an employee's normal weekly earnings shall, subject to subsection (4) below, be taken to be the average weekly earnings which in the relevant period have been paid to him or paid for his benefit under his contract of service with the employer in question.

(3) For the purposes of subsection (2) above, the expressions "earnings" and "relevant period" shall have the meaning given to them by regulations.

(4) In such cases as may be prescribed an employee's normal weekly earnings shall be calculated in accordance with regulations.

(5) Without prejudice to any other power to make regulations under this Part of this Act, regulations may specify cases in which, for the purposes of this Part of this Act or such of its provisions as may be prescribed—

(a) two or more employers are to be treated as one;

(b) two or more contracts of service in respect of which the same person is an employee are to be treated as one.

(6) Where, in consequence of the establishment of one or more National Health Service trusts under [*the National Health Service Act 2006,* the National Health Service (Wales) Act 2006] or the National Health Service (Scotland) Act 1978, a person's contract of employment is treated by a scheme under [any of those Acts] as divided so as to constitute two or more contracts, [or where an order under [paragraph 26(1) of Schedule 3 to the National Health Service Act 2006] provides that a person's contract of employment is so divided,] regulations may make provision enabling him to elect for all of those contracts to be treated as one contract for the purposes of this Part of this Act or of such provisions of this Part of this Act as may be prescribed; and any such regulations may prescribe—

(a) the conditions that must be satisfied if a person is to be entitled to make such an election;

(b) the manner in which, and the time within which, such an election is to be made;

(c) the persons to whom, and the manner in which, notice of such an election is to be given;

(d) the information which a person who makes such an election is to provide, and the persons to whom, and the time within which, he is to provide it;

(e) the time for which such an election is to have effect;

(f) which one of the person's employers under the two or more contracts is to be regarded for the purposes of statutory sick pay as his employer under the one contract;

and the powers conferred by this subsection are without prejudice to any other power to make regulations under this Part of this Act.

(7) Regulations may provide for periods of work which begin on one day and finish on the following day to be treated, for the purposes of this Part of this Act, as falling solely within one or other of those days.

NOTES

Sub-s (1) is amended as follows:

Words in square brackets in definition "employee" substituted by the National Insurance Contributions Act 2014, s 15(3), Sch 2, paras 1, 3.

Para (b) of the definition "employee" (and the word immediately preceding it) repealed by the Employment Equality (Age) Regulations 2006, SI 2006/1031, reg 49(1), Sch 8, Pt 1, paras 8, 9(1), (2).

Definition "employer" substituted by SI 2006/1031, reg 49(1), Sch 8, Pt 1, paras 8, 9(1), (3).

Definition omitted repealed by the Jobseekers Act 1995, s 41(5), Sch 3.

Sub-s (6): words in first, second and fourth (inner) pairs of square brackets substituted by the National Health Service (Consequential Provisions) Act 2006, s 2, Sch 1, paras 142, 147; words in third (outer) pair of square brackets inserted by the Health Act 1999 (Supplementary, Consequential etc Provisions) Order 2000, SI 2000/90, art 3(1), Sch 1, para 27(1), (2); words in italics repealed by the Health and Social Care Act 2012, s 179, Sch 14, Pt 2, paras 58, 59, as from a day to be appointed.

Regulations: the Statutory Sick Pay Percentage Threshold Order 1995 (Consequential) Regulations 1995, SI 1995/513; the Social Security Contributions, Statutory Maternity Pay and Statutory Sick Pay (Miscellaneous Amendments) Regulations 1996, SI 1996/777; the Social Security Contributions, Statutory Maternity Pay and Statutory Sick Pay (Miscellaneous Amendments) Regulations 1999, SI 1999/567; the Social Security, Statutory Maternity Pay and Statutory Sick Pay (Miscellaneous Amendments) Regulations 2002, SI 2002/2690. Also, by virtue of the Social Security (Consequential Provisions) Act 1992, s 2(2), the Statutory Sick Pay (General) Regulations 1982, SI 1982/894 at **[2.44]**, the Statutory Sick Pay (Mariners, Airmen and Persons Abroad) Regulations 1982, SI 1982/1349, and the Statutory Sick Pay (National Health Service Employees) Regulations 1991, SI 1991/589, have effect as if made under this section. As of 15 May 2019, no Regulations had been made under sub-s (7).

PART XII
STATUTORY MATERNITY PAY

[1.212]

164 Statutory maternity pay—entitlement and liability to pay

(1) Where a woman who is or has been an employee satisfies the conditions set out in this section, she shall be entitled, in accordance with the following provisions of this Part of this Act, to payments to be known as "statutory maternity pay".

(2) The conditions mentioned in subsection (1) above are—

(a) that she has been in employed earner's employment with an employer for a continuous period of at least 26 weeks ending with the week immediately preceding the 14th week before the expected week of confinement but has ceased to work for him . . . ;

[(aa) that at the end of the week immediately preceding that 14th week she was entitled to be in that employment;]

(b) that her normal weekly earnings for the period of 8 weeks ending with the week immediately preceding the 14th week before the expected week of confinement are not less than the lower earnings limit in force under section 5(1)(a) above immediately before the commencement of the 14th week before the expected week of confinement; and

(c) that she has become pregnant and has reached, or been confined before reaching, the commencement of the 11th week before the expected week of confinement.

(3) The liability to make payments of statutory maternity pay to a woman is a liability of any person of whom she has been an employee as mentioned in subsection (2)(a) above.

[(4) A woman shall be entitled to payments of statutory maternity pay only if—

(a) she gives the person who will be liable to pay it notice of the date from which she expects his liability to pay her statutory maternity pay to begin; and

(b) the notice is given at least 28 days before that date or, if that is not reasonably practicable, as soon as is reasonably practicable.]

(5) The notice shall be in writing if the person who is liable to pay the woman statutory maternity pay so requests.

(6) Any agreement shall be void to the extent that it purports—

(a) to exclude, limit or otherwise modify any provision of this Part of this Act; or

(b) to require an employee or former employee to contribute (whether directly or indirectly) towards any costs incurred by her employer or former employer under this Part of this Act.

(7) For the avoidance of doubt, any agreement between an employer and an employee authorising any deductions from statutory maternity pay which the employer is liable to pay to the employee in respect of any period shall not be void by virtue of subsection (6)(a) above if the employer—

(a) is authorised by that or another agreement to make the same deductions from any contractual remuneration which he is liable to pay in respect of the same period, or

(b) would be so authorised if he were liable to pay contractual remuneration in respect of that period.

(8) Regulations shall make provision as to a former employer's liability to pay statutory maternity pay to a woman in any case where the former employer's contract of service with her has been brought to an end by the former employer solely, or mainly, for the purpose of avoiding liability for statutory maternity pay.

(9) The Secretary of State may by regulations—

(a) specify circumstances in which, notwithstanding subsections (1) to (8) above, there is to be no liability to pay statutory maternity pay in respect of a week;

(b) specify circumstances in which, notwithstanding subsections (1) to (8) above, the liability to make payments of statutory maternity pay is to be a liability [of the Commissioners of Inland Revenue];

(c) specify in what circumstances employment is to be treated as continuous for the purposes of this Part of this Act;

(d) provide that a woman is to be treated as being employed for a continuous period of at least 26 weeks where—

(i) she has been employed by the same employer for at least 26 weeks under two or more separate contracts of service; and

(ii) those contracts were not continuous;

[(da) provide for circumstances in which subsection (2)(aa) above does not apply;]

(e) provide that any of the provisions specified in subsection (10) below shall have effect subject to prescribed modifications [in such cases as may be prescribed]—

[(ea) provide that subsection (4) above shall not have effect, or shall have effect subject to prescribed modifications, in such cases as may be prescribed;]

(f) provide for amounts earned by a woman under separate contracts of service with the same employer to be aggregated for the purposes of this Part of this Act; and

(g) provide that—

(i) the amount of a woman's earnings for any period, or

(ii) the amount of her earnings to be treated as comprised in any payment made to her or for her benefit,

shall be calculated or estimated in such manner and on such basis as may be prescribed and that for that purpose payments of a particular class or description made or falling to be made to or by a woman shall, to such extent as may be prescribed, be disregarded or, as the case may be, be deducted from the amount of her earnings.

(10) The provisions mentioned in subsection (9)(e) above are—

(a) subsection (2)(a) and (b) above; and

(b) [section 166(1) and (2)], . . . below.

[(11) Any regulations under subsection (9) above which are made by virtue of paragraph (b) of that subsection must be made with the concurrence of the Commissioners of Inland Revenue.]

NOTES

Sub-s (2): words omitted repealed by the Employment Act 2002, ss 20(a), 54, Sch 8; para (aa) inserted by the Welfare Reform Act 2012, s 63(1), (3)(a), as from a day to be appointed.

Sub-s (4): substituted by the Employment Act 2002, s 20(b).

Sub-s (9): words in square brackets in para (b) substituted by the Social Security Contributions (Transfer of Functions, etc) Act 1999, s 1(1), Sch 1, para 12(1), (2); para (da) inserted by the Welfare Reform Act 2012, s 63(1), (3)(b), as from a day to be appointed; words in square brackets in para (e) substituted, and para (ea) added, by the Employment Act 2002, s 20(c), (d).

Sub-s (10): words in square brackets substituted by the Employment Act 2002, s 53, Sch 7, paras 2, 6; words omitted repealed by the Maternity Allowance and Statutory Maternity Pay Regulations 1994, SI 1994/1230, regs 1(2), 6(1).

Sub-s (11): added by the Social Security Contributions (Transfer of Functions, etc) Act 1999, s 1(1), Sch 1, para 12(1), (3).

Commissioners of Inland Revenue: a reference to the Commissioners of Inland Revenue is now to be taken as a reference to the Commissioners for Her Majesty's Revenue and Customs; see the Commissioners for Revenue and Customs Act 2005, s 50(1), (7).

Regulations: the Statutory Maternity Pay (General) Regulations 1986, SI 1986/1960 at **[2.73]**, have effect as if made under this section by virtue of the Social Security (Consequential Provisions) Act 1992, s 2(2); the Social Security Maternity Benefits and Statutory Sick Pay (Amendment) Regulations 1994, SI 1994/1367; the Statutory Maternity Pay (General) Amendment Regulations 1996, SI 1996/1335; the Statutory Maternity Pay (General) (Modification and Amendment) Regulations 2000, SI 2000/2883; the Social Security, Statutory Maternity Pay and Statutory Sick Pay (Miscellaneous Amendments) Regulations 2002, SI 2002/2690; the Statutory Maternity Pay (General) and the Statutory Paternity Pay and Statutory Adoption Pay (General) (Amendment) Regulations 2005, SI 2005/358; the Statutory Maternity Pay (General) (Amendment) Regulations 2005 SI 2005/729.

[1.213]

165 The maternity pay period

(1) Statutory maternity pay shall be payable, subject to the provisions of this Part of this Act, in respect of each week during a prescribed period ("the maternity pay period") of a duration not exceeding [52 weeks].

[(2) Subject to subsections (3) and (7), the maternity pay period shall begin with the 11th week before the expected week of confinement.

(3) Cases may be prescribed in which the first day of the period is to be a prescribed day after the beginning of the 11th week before the expected week of confinement, but not later than the day immediately following the day on which she is confined.]

[(3A) Regulations may provide for the duration of the maternity pay period as it applies to a woman to be reduced, subject to prescribed restrictions and conditions.

(3B) Regulations under subsection (3A) are to secure that the reduced period ends at a time—

- (a) after a prescribed period beginning with the day on which the woman is confined, and
- (b) when at least a prescribed part of the maternity pay period remains unexpired.

(3C) Regulations under subsection (3A) may, in particular, prescribe restrictions and conditions relating to—

- (a) the end of the woman's entitlement to maternity leave;
- (b) the doing of work by the woman;
- (c) the taking of prescribed steps by the woman or another person as regards leave under section 75E of the Employment Rights Act 1996 in respect of the child;
- (d) the taking of prescribed steps by the woman or another person as regards statutory shared parental pay in respect of the child.

(3D) Regulations may provide for a reduction in the duration of the maternity pay period as it applies to a woman to be revoked, or to be treated as revoked, subject to prescribed restrictions and conditions.]

(4) [Except in such cases as may be prescribed,] statutory maternity pay shall not be payable to a woman by a person in respect of any week during any part of which she works under a contract of service with him.

(5) It is immaterial for the purposes of subsection (4) above whether the work referred to in that subsection is work under a contract of service which existed immediately before the maternity pay period or a contract of service which did not so exist.

(6) Except in such cases as may be prescribed, statutory maternity pay shall not be payable to a woman in respect of any week after she has been confined and during any part of which she works for any employer who is not liable to pay her statutory maternity pay.

(7) Regulations may provide that this section shall have effect subject to prescribed modifications in relation—

- (a) to cases in which a woman has been confined before the 11th week before the expected week of confinement; and
- (b) to cases in which—
  - (i) a woman is confined [at any time after the end of the week immediately preceding the 11th week] before the expected week of confinement; and
  - (ii) the maternity pay period has not then commenced for her.

[(8) In subsections (1), (4) and (6) "week" means a period of seven days beginning with the day of the week on which the maternity pay period begins.]

NOTES

Sub-s (1): words in square brackets substituted by the Work and Families Act 2006, s 1.

Sub-ss (2), (3): substituted by the Work and Families Act 2006, s 11(1), Sch 1, para 7(1), (2).

Sub-ss (3A)–(3D): inserted by the Children and Families Act 2014, s 120(1), (4), as from 30 June 2014.

Sub-s (4): words in square brackets inserted by the Work and Families Act 2006, s 11(1), Sch 1, para 7(1), (3).

Sub-s (7): words in square brackets substituted by the Maternity Allowance and Statutory Maternity Pay Regulations 1994, SI 1994/1230, regs 1(2), 3.

Sub-s (8): inserted by the Work and Families Act 2006, s 11(1), Sch 1, para 7(1), (4).

Regulations: the Statutory Maternity Pay (General) Regulations 1986, SI 1986/1960 at **[2.73]**, have effect as if made under this section by virtue of the Social Security (Consequential Provisions) Act 1992, s 2(2); the Social Security Maternity Benefits and Statutory Sick Pay (Amendment) Regulations 1994, SI 1994/1367; the Statutory Maternity Pay (General) (Modification and Amendment) Regulations 2000, SI 2000/2883; the Social Security, Statutory Maternity Pay and Statutory Sick Pay (Miscellaneous Amendments) Regulations 2002, SI 2002/2690; the Statutory Maternity Pay, Social Security (Maternity

Allowance) and Social Security (Overlapping Benefits) (Amendment) Regulations 2006, SI 2006/2379; the Statutory Maternity Pay and Statutory Adoption Pay (Curtailment) Regulations 2014, SI 2014/3054 at **[2.1688]**.

[1.214]

[166 Rate of statutory maternity pay

(1) Statutory maternity pay shall be payable to a woman—

(a) at the earnings-related rate, in respect of the first 6 weeks in respect of which it is payable; and

(b) at whichever is the lower of the earnings-related rate and such weekly rate as may be prescribed, in respect of the remaining portion of the maternity pay period.

[(1A) In subsection (1) "week" means any period of seven days.]

(2) The earnings-related rate is a weekly rate equivalent to 90 per cent of a woman's normal weekly earnings for the period of 8 weeks immediately preceding the 14th week before the expected week of confinement.

(3) The weekly rate prescribed under subsection (1)(b) above must not be less than the weekly rate of statutory sick pay for the time being specified in section 157(1) above or, if two or more such rates are for the time being so specified, the higher or highest of those rates.

[(4) Where for any purpose of this Part of this Act or of regulations it is necessary to calculate the daily rate of statutory maternity pay, the amount payable by way of statutory maternity pay for any day shall be taken as one seventh of the weekly rate.]]

NOTES

Substituted by the Employment Act 2002, s 19.

Sub-ss (1A), (4): inserted and added respectively by the Work and Families Act 2006, s 11(1), Sch 1, para 8.

The rate prescribed under sub-s (1)(b) is £148.68 (see the Statutory Maternity Pay (General) Regulations 1986, SI 1986/1960, reg 6, as amended by the Social Security Benefits Up-rating Order 2019, SI 2019/480, art 10, and note that this has effect as from 7 April 2019, except for the purpose of determining the rate of maternity allowance in accordance with s 35A(1) of this Act, for which purpose it comes into force on 8 April 2019).

Previous prescribed rates were: £145.18 (as from 1 and 9 April 2018, see SI 2018/281, art 10); £140.98 (as from 2 and 10 April 2017, see SI 2017/460, art 10); £139.58 (as from 5 and 6 April 2015, see SI 2015/30, art 4); £138.18 (as from 6 and 7 April 2014, see SI 2014/147, art 4); £136.78 (as from 7 and 8 April 2013, see SI 2013/574, art 9); £135.45 (as from 1 and 9 April 2012, see SI 2012/780, art 10). Note that there was no increase in the prescribed rate in April 2016.

Regulations: the Statutory Maternity Pay (General) Regulations 1986, SI 1986/1960 at **[2.73]**, have effect as if made under this section by virtue of the Social Security (Consequential Provisions) Act 1992, s 2(2); the Social Security Maternity Benefits and Statutory Sick Pay (Amendment) Regulations 1994, SI 1994/1367; the Social Security, Statutory Maternity Pay and Statutory Sick Pay (Miscellaneous Amendments) Regulations 2002, SI 2002/2690.

[1.215]

[167 Funding of employers' liabilities in respect of statutory maternity pay

(1) Regulations shall make provision for the payment by employers of statutory maternity pay to be funded by the Commissioners of Inland Revenue to such extent as may be prescribed.

(2) Regulations under subsection (1) shall—

(a) make provision for a person who has made a payment of statutory maternity pay to be entitled, except in prescribed circumstances, to recover an amount equal to the sum of—

(i) the aggregate of such of those payments as qualify for small employers' relief; and

(ii) an amount equal to 92 per cent of the aggregate of such of those payments as do not so qualify; and

(b) include provision for a person who has made a payment of statutory maternity pay qualifying for small employers' relief to be entitled, except in prescribed circumstances, to recover an additional amount, determined in such manner as may be prescribed—

(i) by reference to secondary Class 1 contributions paid in respect of statutory maternity pay;

(ii) by reference to secondary Class 1 contributions paid in respect of statutory sick pay; or

(iii) by reference to the aggregate of secondary Class 1 contributions paid in respect of statutory maternity pay and secondary Class 1 contributions paid in respect of statutory sick pay.

(3) For the purposes of this section a payment of statutory maternity pay which a person is liable to make to a woman qualifies for small employers' relief if, in relation to that woman's maternity pay period, the person liable to make the payment is a small employer.

(4) For the purposes of this section "small employer", in relation to a woman's maternity pay period, shall have the meaning assigned to it by regulations, and, without prejudice to the generality of the foregoing, any such regulations—

(a) may define that expression by reference to the amount of a person's contributions payments for any prescribed period; and

(b) if they do so, may in that connection make provision for the amount of those payments for that prescribed period—

(i) to be determined without regard to any deductions that may be made from them under this section or under any other enactment or instrument; and

(ii) in prescribed circumstances, to be adjusted, estimated or otherwise attributed to him by reference to their amount in any other prescribed period.

(5) Regulations under subsection (1) may, in particular, make provision—

(a) for funding in advance as well as in arrear;

(b) for funding, or the recovery of amounts due under provision made by virtue of subsection (2)(b), by means of deductions from such amounts for which employers are accountable to the Commissioners of Inland Revenue as may be prescribed, or otherwise;

(c) for the recovery by the Commissioners of Inland Revenue of any sums overpaid to employers under the regulations.

(6) Where in accordance with any provision of regulations under subsection (1) an amount has been deducted from an employer's contributions payments, the amount so deducted shall (except in such cases as may be prescribed) be treated for the purposes of any provision made by or under any enactment in relation to primary or secondary Class 1 contributions—

(a) as having been paid (on such date as may be determined in accordance with the regulations), and

(b) as having been received by the Commissioners of Inland Revenue,

towards discharging the employer's liability in respect of such contributions.

(7) Regulations under this section must be made with the concurrence of the Commissioners of Inland Revenue.

(8) In this section "contributions payments", in relation to an employer, means any payments which the employer is required, by or under any enactment, to make in discharge of any liability in respect of primary or secondary Class 1 contributions.]

NOTES

Substituted by the Employment Act 2002, s 21(1).

Commissioners of Inland Revenue: a reference to the Commissioners of Inland Revenue is now to be taken as a reference to the Commissioners for Her Majesty's Revenue and Customs; see the Commissioners for Revenue and Customs Act 2005, s 50(1), (7).

Regulations: the Statutory Maternity Pay (Compensation of Employers) and Miscellaneous Amendment Regulations 1994, SI 1994/1882; the Statutory Maternity Pay (Compensation of Employers) Amendment Regulations 1995, SI 1995/566; the Statutory Maternity Pay (Compensation of Employers) Amendment Regulations 1999, SI 1999/363; the Statutory Maternity Pay (Compensation of Employers) Amendment Regulations 2003, SI 2003/672; the Statutory Maternity Pay (Compensation of Employers) Amendment Regulations 2004, SI 2004/698; the Statutory Maternity Pay (Compensation of Employers) Amendment Regulations 2011, SI 2011/725.

[1.216]

168 Relationship with benefits and other payments etc

Schedule 13 to this Act has effect with respect to the relationship between statutory maternity pay and certain benefits and payments.

[1.217]

169 Crown employment—Part XII

The provisions of this Part of this Act apply in relation to women employed by or under the Crown as they apply in relation to women employed otherwise than by or under the Crown.

[1.218]

170 Special classes of person

(1) The Secretary of State may [with the concurrence of the Treasury] make regulations modifying this Part of this Act in such manner as he thinks proper in their application to any person who is, has been or is to be—

(a) employed on board any ship, vessel, hovercraft or aircraft;

(b) outside Great Britain at any prescribed time or in any prescribed circumstances; or

(c) in prescribed employment in connection with continental shelf operations, as defined in section 120(2) above.

(2) Regulations under subsection (1) above may in particular provide—

(a) for any provision of this Part of this Act to apply to any such person, notwithstanding that it would not otherwise apply;

(b) for any such provision not to apply to any such person, notwithstanding that it would otherwise apply;

(c) for excepting any such person from the application of any such provision where he neither is domiciled nor has a place of residence in any part of Great Britain;

(d) for the taking of evidence, for the purposes of the determination of any question arising under any such provision, in a country or territory outside Great Britain, by a British consular official or such other person as may be determined in accordance with the regulations.

NOTES

Sub-s (1): words in square brackets inserted by the Social Security Contributions (Transfer of Functions, etc) Act 1999, s 1(1), Sch 1, para 14.

Regulations: the Statutory Maternity Pay (Persons Abroad and Mariners) Regulations 1987, SI 1987/418, have effect as if made under this section by virtue of the Social Security (Consequential Provisions) Act 1992, s 2(2); the Social Security Contributions, Statutory Maternity Pay and Statutory Sick Pay (Miscellaneous Amendments) Regulations 1996, SI 1996/777.

[1.219]

171 Interpretation of Part XII and supplementary provisions

(1) In this Part of this Act—

"confinement" means—

(a) labour resulting in the issue of a living child, or

(b) labour after [24 weeks] of pregnancy resulting in the issue of a child whether alive or dead,

and "confined" shall be construed accordingly; and where a woman's labour begun on one day results in the issue of a child on another day she shall be taken to be confined on the day of the issue of the child or, if labour results in the issue of twins or a greater number of children, she shall be taken to be confined on the day of the issue of the last of them;

"dismissed" is to be construed in accordance with [Part X of the Employment Rights Act 1996];

"employee" means a woman who is—

(a) gainfully employed in Great Britain either under a contract of service or in an office (including elective office) with [earnings (within the meaning of Parts 1 to 5 above)]; . . .

(b) . . .

but subject to regulations [made with the concurrence of [Her Majesty's Revenue and Customs]] which may provide for cases where any such woman is not to be treated as an employee for the purposes of this Part of this Act and for cases where a woman who would not otherwise be an employee for those purposes is to be treated as an employee for those purposes;

["employer", in relation to a woman who is an employee, means a person who—

(a) under section 6 above is liable to pay secondary Class 1 contributions in relation to any of her earnings; or

(b) would be liable to pay such contributions but for—

(i) the condition in section 6(1)(b), or

(ii) the employee being under the age of 16;]

"maternity pay period" has the meaning assigned to it by section 165(1) above;

"modifications" includes additions, omissions and amendments, and related expressions shall be construed accordingly;

"prescribed" means specified in or determined in accordance with regulations;

. . .

[(1A) In this Part, except section 165(1), (4) and (6), section 166(1) and paragraph 3(2) of Schedule 13, "week" means a period of 7 days beginning with Sunday or such other period as may be prescribed in relation to any particular case or class of case.]

(2) Without prejudice to any other power to make regulations under this Part of this Act, regulations may specify cases in which, for the purposes of this Part of this Act or of such provisions of this Part of this Act as may be prescribed—

(a) two or more employers are to be treated as one;

(b) two or more contracts of service in respect of which the same woman is an employee are to be treated as one.

(3) Where, in consequence of the establishment of one or more National Health Service trusts under [*the National Health Service Act 2006*, the National Health Service (Wales) Act 2006] or the National Health Service (Scotland) Act 1978, a woman's contract of employment is treated by a scheme under [any of those Acts] as divided so as to constitute two or more contracts, [or where an order under [paragraph 26(1) of Schedule 3 to the National Health Service Act 2006] provides that a woman's contract of employment is so divided,] regulations may make provision enabling her to elect for all of those contracts to be treated as one contract for the purposes of this Part of this Act or of such provisions of this Part of this Act as may be prescribed; and any such regulations may prescribe—

(a) the conditions that must be satisfied if a woman is to be entitled to make such an election;

(b) the manner in which, and the time within which, such an election is to be made;

(c) the persons to whom, and the manner in which, notice of such an election is to be given;

(d) the information which a woman who makes such an election is to provide, and the persons to whom, and the time within which, she is to provide it;

(e) the time for which such an election is to have effect;

(f) which one of the woman's employers under the two or more contracts is to be regarded for the purposes of statutory maternity pay as her employer under the one contract;

and the powers conferred by this subsection are without prejudice to any other power to make regulations under this Part of this Act.

(4) For the purposes of this Part of this Act a woman's normal weekly earnings shall, subject to subsection (6) below, be taken to be the average weekly earnings which in the relevant period have been paid to her or paid for her benefit under the contract of service with the employer in question.

(5) For the purposes of subsection (4) above "earnings" and "relevant period" shall have the meanings given to them by regulations.

(6) In such cases as may be prescribed a woman's normal weekly earnings shall be calculated in accordance with regulations.

[(7) Regulations under any of subsections (2) to (6) above must be made with the concurrence of the Commissioners of Inland Revenue.]

NOTES

Sub-s (1) is amended as follows:

Words in square brackets in definition "confinement" substituted by the Still-Birth (Definition) Act 1992, ss 2(1), 4(2).

Words in square brackets in definition "dismissed" substituted by the Employment Rights Act 1996, s 240, Sch 1, para 51.

Words in first pair of square brackets in definition "employee" substituted by the National Insurance Contributions Act 2014, s 15(3), Sch 2, paras 1, 4.

Para (b) of the definition "employee" (and the word omitted immediately preceding it) repealed by the Employment Equality (Age) Regulations 2006, SI 2006/1031, reg 49(1), Sch 8, Pt 1, paras 8, 10(1), (2).

Words in second (outer) pair of square brackets in definition "employee" inserted by the Social Security Contributions (Transfer of Functions, etc) Act 1999, s 1(1), Sch 1, para 15(1), (2).

Words in third (inner) pair of square brackets in definition "employee" substituted by the Commissioners for Revenue and Customs Act 2005, s 50(6), Sch 4, para 43.

Definition "employer" substituted by SI 2006/1031, reg 49(1), Sch 8, Pt 1, paras 8, 10(1), (3).

Definition "week" (omitted) repealed by the Work and Families Act 2006, ss 11(1), 15, Sch 1, para 9(1), (2), Sch 2.

Sub-s (1A): inserted by the Work and Families Act 2006, s 11(1), Sch 1, para 9(1), (3).

Sub-s (3): words in first, second and fourth (inner) pairs of square brackets substituted by the National Health Service (Consequential Provisions) Act 2006, s 2, Sch 1, paras 142, 148; words in third (outer) pair of square brackets inserted by the Health Act 1999 (Supplementary, Consequential etc Provisions) Order 2000, SI 2000/90, art 3(1), Sch 1, para 27(1), (3); words in italics repealed by the Health and Social Care Act 2012, s 179, Sch 14, Pt 2, paras 58, 60, as from a day to be appointed.

Sub-s (7): added by the Social Security Contributions (Transfer of Functions, etc) Act 1999, s 1(1), Sch 1, para 15(1), (3).

Commissioners of Inland Revenue: a reference to the Commissioners of Inland Revenue is now to be taken as a reference to the Commissioners for Her Majesty's Revenue and Customs; see the Commissioners for Revenue and Customs Act 2005, s 50(1), (7).

Regulations: the Statutory Maternity Pay (General) Regulations 1986, SI 1986/1960 (as amended) at **[2.73]**, and the Statutory Maternity Pay (National Health Service Employees) Regulations 1991, SI 1991/590 have effect as if made under this section by virtue of the Social Security (Consequential Provisions) Act 1992, s 2(2).

[PART XIIZA
[. . . STATUTORY PATERNITY PAY]

NOTES

Part XIIZA was inserted by the Employment Act 2002, s 2. Sections 171ZEA–171ZEE were inserted into this Part by the Work and Families Act 2006, ss 6–10, and were repealed by the Children and Families Act 2014, s 125(2), as from 5 April 2015 (subject to transitional provisions).

The Part heading (above) was substituted by the Work and Families Act 2006, s 11(1), Sch 1, para 10. The words omitted were repealed by the Children and Families Act 2014, s 126(1), Sch 7, paras 6, 10, as from 5 April 2015 (note that this repeal does not have effect in relation to (a) children whose expected week of birth ends on or before 4 April 2015, and (b) children placed for adoption on or before that date: see the Children and Families Act 2014 (Commencement No 3, Transitional Provisions and Savings) Order 2014, SI 2014/1640, art 16).

Application to parental order parents: this Part is applied, subject to certain modifications, to parental order parents by the Social Security Contributions and Benefits Act 1992 (Application of Parts 12ZA, 12ZB and 12ZC to Parental Order Cases) Regulations 2014, SI 2014/2866, reg 3, Sch 1 at **[2.1531]**, **[2.1534]**.

Application to adoptions from overseas: this Part is applied, subject to certain modifications, to adoptions from overseas by the Social Security Contributions and Benefits Act 1992 (Application of Parts 12ZA, 12ZB and 12ZC to Adoptions from Overseas) Regulations 2003, SI 2003/499, Sch 1.

Statutory paternity pay: as to the meaning of this, see the Children and Families Act 2014, s 126 at **[1.1894]**

[. . .]

NOTES

The above heading was inserted by the Work and Families Act 2006, s 11(1), Sch 1, para 11, and was repealed by the Children and Families Act 2014, s 126(1), Sch 7, paras 6, 11, as from 5 April 2015 (note that this repeal does not have effect in relation to (a) children whose expected week of birth ends on or before 4 April 2015, and (b) children placed for adoption on or before that date: see the Children and Families Act 2014 (Commencement No 3, Transitional Provisions and Savings) Order 2014, SI 2014/1640, art 16).

[1.220]

171ZA Entitlement: birth

(1) Where a person satisfies the conditions in subsection (2) below, he shall be entitled in accordance with the following provisions of this Part to payments to be known as "[statutory paternity pay]".

(2) The conditions are—

- (a) that he satisfies prescribed conditions—
  - (i) as to relationship with a newborn child, and
  - (ii) as to relationship with the child's mother;
- (b) that he has been in employed earner's employment with an employer for a continuous period of at least 26 weeks ending with the relevant week;
- [(ba) that at the end of the relevant week he was entitled to be in that employment;]
- (c) that his normal weekly earnings for the period of 8 weeks ending with the relevant week are not less than the lower earnings limit in force under section 5(1)(a) above at the end of the relevant week; and
- (d) that he has been in employed earner's employment with the employer by reference to whom the condition in paragraph (b) above is satisfied for a continuous period beginning with the end of the relevant week and ending with the day on which the child is born.

(3) The references in subsection (2) above to the relevant week are to the week immediately preceding the 14th week before the expected week of the child's birth.

[(3A) Regulations may provide for circumstances in which subsection (2)(ba) above does not apply.]

(4) A person's entitlement to [. . . statutory paternity pay] under this section shall not be affected by the birth, or expected birth, of more than one child as a result of the same pregnancy.

(5) In this section, "newborn child" includes a child stillborn after twenty-four weeks of pregnancy.]

NOTES

Inserted as noted at the beginning of this Part.

Sub-s (1): words in square brackets substituted by the Children and Families Act 2014, s 126(1), Sch 7, paras 6, 12(1), (2), as from 5 April 2015 (note that this amendment does not have effect in relation to (a) children whose expected week of birth ends on or before 4 April 2015, and (b) children placed for adoption on or before that date: see the Children and Families Act 2014 (Commencement No 3, Transitional Provisions and Savings) Order 2014, SI 2014/1640, art 16.

Sub-s (2): para (ba) inserted by the Welfare Reform Act 2012, s 63(1), (4)(a), as from a day to be appointed.

Sub-s (3A): inserted by the Welfare Reform Act 2012, s 63(1), (4)(b), as from a day to be appointed.

Sub-s (4): words in square brackets substituted by the Work and Families Act 2006, s 11(1), Sch 1, para 12; word omitted repealed by the Children and Families Act 2014, s 126(1), Sch 7, paras 6, 12(1), (3), as from 5 April 2015 (for effect see the sub-s (1) note above).

Application to parental order parents and to adoptions from overseas: see the introductory notes to this Part.

Regulations: the Statutory Paternity Pay and Statutory Adoption Pay (General) Regulations 2002, SI 2002/2822 at **[2.625]**.

[1.221]

[171ZB Entitlement: adoption

(1) Where a person satisfies the conditions in subsection (2) below, he shall be entitled in accordance with the following provisions of this Part to payments to be known as "[statutory paternity pay]".

(2) The conditions are—

(a) that he satisfies prescribed conditions—

(i) as to relationship with a child who is placed for adoption under the law of any part of the United Kingdom, and

(ii) as to relationship with a person with whom the child is so placed for adoption;

(b) that he has been in employed earner's employment with an employer for a continuous period of at least 26 weeks ending with the relevant week;

[(ba) that at the end of the relevant week he was entitled to be in that employment;]

(c) that his normal weekly earnings for the period of 8 weeks ending with the relevant week are not less than the lower earnings limit in force under section 5(1)(a) at the end of the relevant week;

(d) that he has been in employed earner's employment with the employer by reference to whom the condition in paragraph (b) above is satisfied for a continuous period beginning with the end of the relevant week and ending with the day on which the child is placed for adoption; and

(e) where he is a person with whom the child is placed for adoption, that he has elected to receive statutory paternity pay.

(3) The references in subsection (2) to the relevant week are to the week in which the adopter is notified of being matched with the child for the purposes of adoption.

[(3A) Regulations may provide for circumstances in which subsection (2)(ba) above does not apply.]

(4) A person may not elect to receive [. . . statutory paternity pay] if he has elected in accordance with section 171ZL below to receive statutory adoption pay.

(5) Regulations may make provision about elections for the purposes of subsection (2)(e) above.

(6) A person's entitlement to [. . . statutory paternity pay] under this section shall not be affected by the placement for adoption of more than one child as part of the same arrangement.

(7) In this section, "adopter", in relation to a person who satisfies the condition under subsection (2)(a)(ii) above, means the person by reference to whom he satisfies that condition.

[(8) This section has effect in a case involving a child placed under section 22C of the Children Act 1989 by a local authority in England with a local authority foster parent who has been approved as a prospective adopter with the following modifications—

(a) the references in subsection (2) to a child being placed for adoption under the law of any part of the United Kingdom are to be treated as references to a child being placed under section 22C in that manner;

(b) the reference in subsection (3) to the week in which the adopter is notified of being matched with the child for the purposes of adoption is to be treated as a reference to the week in which the prospective adopter is notified that the child is to be, or is expected to be, placed with the prospective adopter under section 22C;

(c) the reference in subsection (6) to placement for adoption is to be treated as a reference to placement under section 22C;

(d) the definition in subsection (7) is to be treated as if it were a definition of "prospective adopter".

(9) Where, by virtue of subsection (8), a person becomes entitled to statutory paternity pay in connection with the placement of a child under section 22C of the Children Act 1989, the person may not become entitled to payments of statutory paternity pay in connection with the placement of the child for adoption.]

[(10) This section has effect in a case involving a child placed under section 81 of the Social Services and Well-being (Wales) Act 2014 by a local authority in Wales with a local authority foster parent who has been approved as a prospective adopter with the following modifications—

(a) the references in subsection (2) to a child being placed for adoption under the law of any part of the United Kingdom are to be treated as references to a child being placed under section 81 in that manner;

(b) the reference in subsection (3) to the week in which the adopter is notified of being matched with the child for the purposes of adoption is to be treated as a reference to the week in which the prospective adopter is notified that the child is to be, or is expected to be, placed with the prospective adopter under section 81;

(c) the reference in subsection (6) to placement for adoption is to be treated as a reference to placement under section 81;

(d) the definition in subsection (7) is to be treated as if it were a definition of "prospective adopter".

(11) Where, by virtue of subsection (10), a person becomes entitled to statutory paternity pay in connection with the placement of a child under section 81 of the Social Services and Well-being (Wales) Act 2014, the person may not become entitled to payments of statutory paternity pay in connection with the placement of the child for adoption.]]

NOTES

Inserted as noted at the beginning of this Part.

Sub-s (1): words in square brackets substituted by the Children and Families Act 2014, s 126(1), Sch 7, paras 6, 13(1), (2), as from 5 April 2015 (note that this amendment does not have effect in relation to (a) children whose expected week of birth ends on or before 4 April 2015, and (b) children placed for adoption on or before that date: see the Children and Families Act 2014 (Commencement No 3, Transitional Provisions and Savings) Order 2014, SI 2014/1640, art 16).

Sub-s (2): para (ba) inserted by the Welfare Reform Act 2012, s 63(1), (5)(a), as from a day to be appointed.

Sub-s (3A): inserted by the Welfare Reform Act 2012, s 63(1), (5)(b), as from a day to be appointed.

Sub-ss (4), (6): words in square brackets substituted by the Work and Families Act 2006, s 11(1), Sch 1, para 13; words omitted repealed by the Children and Families Act 2014, s 126(1), Sch 7, paras 6, 13, as from 5 April 2015 (for effect see the sub-s (1) note above).

Sub-ss (8), (9): added by the Children and Families Act 2014, s 121(3), as from 30 June 2014.

Sub-ss (10), (11): added by the Social Services and Well-being (Wales) Act 2014 (Consequential Amendments) Regulations 2016, SI 2016/413, regs 130, 132, as from 6 April 2016.

Application to parental order parents and to adoptions from overseas: see the introductory notes to this Part.

Regulations: the Statutory Paternity Pay and Statutory Adoption Pay (General) Regulations 2002, SI 2002/2822 at **[2.625]**; the Statutory Paternity Pay (Adoption) and Statutory Adoption Pay (Adoptions from Overseas) (No 2) Regulation 2003, SI 2003/1194; the Statutory Paternity Pay and Statutory Adoption Pay (Amendment) Regulations 2004, SI 2004/488; the Statutory Paternity Pay and Statutory Adoption Pay (Parental Orders and Prospective Adopters) Regulations 2014, SI 2014/2934 at **[2.1551]**.

[1.222]

[171ZC Entitlement: general

(1) A person shall be entitled to payments of [. . . statutory paternity pay] in respect of any period [only if he gives the person who will be liable to pay it notice of the week or weeks in respect of which he expects there to be liability to pay him statutory paternity pay].

[(1A) Regulations may provide for the time by which notice under subsection (1) is to be given.]

(2) The notice shall be in writing if the person who is liable to pay the [. . . statutory paternity pay] so requests.

(3) The Secretary of State may by regulations—

(a) provide that subsection (2)(b), (c) or (d) of section 171ZA or 171ZB above shall have effect subject to prescribed modifications in such cases as may be prescribed;

(b) provide that subsection (1) above shall not have effect, or shall have effect subject to prescribed modifications, in such cases as may be prescribed;

(c) impose requirements about evidence of entitlement;

(d) specify in what circumstances employment is to be treated as continuous for the purposes of section 171ZA or 171ZB above;

(e) provide that a person is to be treated for the purposes of section 171ZA or 171ZB above as being employed for a continuous period of at least 26 weeks where—

(i) he has been employed by the same employer for at least 26 weeks under two or more separate contracts of service; and

(ii) those contracts were not continuous;

(f) provide for amounts earned by a person under separate contracts of service with the same employer to be aggregated for the purposes of section 171ZA or 171ZB above;

(g) provide that—

(i) the amount of a person's earnings for any period, or

(ii) the amount of his earnings to be treated as comprised in any payment made to him or for his benefit,

shall be calculated or estimated for the purposes of section 171ZA or 171ZB above in such manner and on such basis as may be prescribed and that for that purpose payments of a particular class or description made or falling to be made to or by a person shall, to such extent as may be prescribed, be disregarded or, as the case may be, be deducted from the amount of his earnings.]

NOTES

Inserted as noted at the beginning of this Part.

Sub-s (1): words in first pair of square brackets substituted by the Work and Families Act 2006, s 11(1), Sch 1, para 14; word omitted repealed by the Children and Families Act 2014, s 126(1), Sch 7, paras 6, 14(1), (2), as from 5 April 2015 (note that this amendment does not have effect in relation to (a) children whose expected week of birth ends on or before 4 April 2015, and (b) children placed for adoption on or before that date: see the Children and Families Act 2014 (Commencement No 3, Transitional Provisions and Savings) Order 2014, SI 2014/1640, art 16); words in second pair of square brackets substituted by s 123(1), (2)(a) of the 2014 Act, as from 30 June 2014 (except in relation to (a) children whose expected week of birth ends on or before 4 April 2015; (b) children placed for adoption on or before that date).

Sub-s (1A): inserted by the Children and Families Act 2014, s 123(1), (2)(b), as from 30 June 2014 (except in relation to (a) children whose expected week of birth ends on or before 4 April 2015; (b) children placed for adoption on or before that date: see SI 2014/1640, art 9).

Sub-s (2): words in square brackets substituted by the Work and Families Act 2006, s 11(1), Sch 1, para 14; word omitted repealed by the Children and Families Act 2014, s 126(1), Sch 7, paras 6, 14(1), (2), as from 5 April 2015 (note that this amendment does not have effect in relation to (a) children whose expected week of birth ends on or before 4 April 2015, and (b) children placed for adoption on or before that date: see SI 2014/1640, art 16).

Application to parental order parents and to adoptions from overseas: see the introductory notes to this Part.

Regulations: the Statutory Paternity Pay and Statutory Adoption Pay (General) Regulations 2002, SI 2002/2822 at **[2.625]**; the Statutory Paternity Pay (Adoption) and Statutory Adoption Pay (Adoptions from Overseas) (No 2) Regulations 2003, SI 2003/1194; the Statutory Maternity Pay (General) and the Statutory Paternity Pay and Statutory Adoption Pay (General) (Amendment) Regulations 2005, SI 2005/358; the Statutory Paternity Pay and Statutory Adoption Pay (General) (Amendment)

Regulations 2014, SI 2014/2862; the Statutory Paternity Pay and Statutory Adoption Pay (Parental Orders and Prospective Adopters) Regulations 2014, SI 2014/2934 at **[2.1551]**.

[1.223]

[171ZD Liability to make payments

(1) The liability to make payments of [. . .] statutory paternity pay under section 171ZA or 171ZB above is a liability of any person of whom the person entitled to the payments has been an employee as mentioned in subsection (2)(b) and (d) of that section.

(2) Regulations shall make provision as to a former employer's liability to pay [. . . statutory paternity pay] to a person in any case where the former employee's contract of service with him has been brought to an end by the former employer solely, or mainly, for the purpose of avoiding [liability for . . . statutory paternity pay . . .].

(3) The Secretary of State may, with the concurrence of the Board, by regulations specify circumstances in which, notwithstanding this section, liability to make payments of statutory paternity pay is to be a liability of the Board.]

NOTES

Inserted as noted at the beginning of this Part.

Sub-ss (1), (2): words in square brackets inserted by the Work and Families Act 2006, s 11(1), Sch 1, para 15; words omitted repealed by the Children and Families Act 2014, s 126(1), Sch 7, paras 6, 15, as from 5 April 2015 (note that this amendment does not have effect in relation to (a) children whose expected week of birth ends on or before 4 April 2015, and (b) children placed for adoption on or before that date: see the Children and Families Act 2014 (Commencement No 3, Transitional Provisions and Savings) Order 2014, SI 2014/1640, art 16).

Application to parental order parents and to adoptions from overseas: see the introductory notes to this Part.

Regulations: the Statutory Paternity Pay and Statutory Adoption Pay (General) Regulations 2002, SI 2002/2822 at **[2.625]**; the Statutory Paternity Pay (Adoption) and Statutory Adoption Pay (Adoptions from Overseas) (No 2) Regulations 2003, SI 2003/1194; the Statutory Paternity Pay and Statutory Adoption Pay (Parental Orders and Prospective Adopters) Regulations 2014, SI 2014/2934 at **[2.1551]**.

[1.224]

[171ZE Rate and period of pay

(1) [. . . statutory paternity pay] shall be payable at such fixed or earnings-related weekly rate as may be prescribed by regulations, which may prescribe different kinds of rate for different cases.

(2) [. . . statutory paternity pay] shall *be payable in respect of—*

(a) a period of two consecutive weeks within the qualifying period beginning on such date within that period as the person entitled may choose in accordance with regulations, or

(b) if regulations permit the person entitled to choose to receive [. . . statutory paternity pay] in respect of—

(i) a period of a week, or

(ii) two non-consecutive periods of a week,

such week or weeks within the qualifying period as he may choose in accordance with regulations.

[(2A) Provision under subsection (2)(b) is to secure that the prescribed number of weeks is not less than two.]

[(2B) Regulations under subsection (2) may permit a person entitled to receive statutory paternity pay to choose to receive such pay in respect of non-consecutive periods each of which is a week or a number of weeks.]

(3) For the purposes of subsection (2) above, the qualifying period shall be determined in accordance with regulations, which shall secure that it is a period of at least 56 days beginning—

(a) in the case of a person to whom the conditions in section 171ZA(2) above apply, with the date of the child's birth, and

(b) in the case of a person to whom the conditions in section 171ZB(2) above apply, with the date of the child's placement for adoption.

[(3A) Statutory paternity pay is not payable to a person in respect of a statutory pay week if—

(a) statutory shared parental pay is payable to that person in respect of any part of that week or that person takes shared parental leave in any part of that week, or

(b) statutory shared parental pay was payable to that person or that person has taken shared parental leave in respect of the child before that week.]

(4) [. . . statutory paternity pay] shall not be payable to a person in respect of a statutory pay week if it is not his purpose at the beginning of the week—

(a) to care for the child by reference to whom he satisfies the condition in sub-paragraph (i) of section 171ZA(2)(a) or 171ZB(2)(a) above, or

(b) to support the person by reference to whom he satisfies the condition in sub-paragraph (ii) of that provision.

(5) A person shall not be liable to pay [. . . statutory paternity pay] to another in respect of a statutory pay week during any part of which the other works under a contract of service with him.

(6) It is immaterial for the purposes of subsection (5) above whether the work referred to in that subsection is work under a contract of service which existed immediately before the statutory pay week or a contract of service which did not so exist.

(7) Except in such cases as may be prescribed, [. . . statutory paternity pay] shall not be payable to a person in respect of a statutory pay week during any part of which he works for any employer who is not liable to pay him [*ordinary* statutory paternity pay].

(8) The Secretary of State may by regulations specify circumstances in which there is to be no liability to pay [. . . statutory paternity pay] in respect of a statutory pay week.

(9) Where more than one child is born as a result of the same pregnancy, the reference in subsection (3)(a) to the date of the child's birth shall be read as a reference to the date of birth of the first child born as a result of the pregnancy.

(10) Where more than one child is placed for adoption as part of the same arrangement, the reference in subsection (3)(b) to the date of the child's placement shall be read as a reference to the date of placement of the first child to be placed as part of the arrangement.

[(10A) Where for any purpose of this Part of this Act or of regulations it is necessary to calculate the daily rate of . . . statutory paternity pay, the amount payable by way of . . . statutory paternity pay for any day shall be taken as one seventh of the weekly rate.]

(11) In this section—

"statutory pay week", in relation to a person entitled to [. . . statutory paternity pay], means a week chosen by him as a week in respect of which [. . . statutory paternity pay] shall be payable;

"week" means any period of seven days.

[(12) Where statutory paternity pay is payable to a person by virtue of section 171ZB(8), this section has effect as if—

(a) the references in subsections (3)(b) and (10) to placement for adoption were references to placement under section 22C of the Children Act 1989;

(b) the references in subsection (10) to being placed for adoption were references to being placed under section 22C.]]

[(13) Where statutory paternity pay is payable to a person by virtue of section 171ZB(10), this section has effect as if—

(a) the references in subsections (3)(b) and (10) to placement for adoption were references to placement under section 81 of the Social Services and Well-being (Wales) Act 2014;

(b) the references in subsection (10) to being placed for adoption were references to being placed under section 81.]]

NOTES

Inserted as noted at the beginning of this Part.

Sub-ss (1), (4), (5), (7), (8), (11): words in square brackets substituted by the Work and Families Act 2006, s 11(1), Sch 1, para 16(1), (2); words omitted repealed by the Children and Families Act 2014, s 126(1), Sch 7, paras 6, 16(1), (2), (4)–(7), (9), as from 5 April 2015 (note that these amendments do not have effect in relation to (a) children whose expected week of birth ends on or before 4 April 2015, and (b) children placed for adoption on or before that date: see the Children and Families Act 2014 (Commencement No 3, Transitional Provisions and Savings) Order 2014, SI 2014/1640, art 16).

Sub-s (2): words in square brackets substituted by the Work and Families Act 2006, s 11(1), Sch 1, para 16(1), (2); words omitted repealed by the Children and Families Act 2014, s 126(1), Sch 7, paras 6, 16(1), (3)(a), as from 5 April 2015 (for effect see the sub-s (1) (etc) note above); for the words in italics there are substituted the following words by s 123(1), (3)(a) of the 2014 Act, as from a day to be appointed—

"be payable in respect of—

(a) such week within the qualifying period, or

(b) such number of weeks, not exceeding the prescribed number of weeks, within the qualifying period,

as he may choose in accordance with regulations.".

Sub-ss (2A), (2B): inserted by the Children and Families Act 2014, s 123(1), (3)(b), (c), as from a day to be appointed.

Sub-s (3A): inserted by the Children and Families Act 2014, s 120(1), (5), as from 30 June 2014.

Sub-s (10A): inserted by the Work and Families Act 2006, s 11(1), Sch 1, para 16(1), (3); words omitted repealed by the Children and Families Act 2014, s 126(1), Sch 7, paras 6, 16(1), (8), as from 5 April 2015 (for effect see the sub-s (1) (etc) note above).

Sub-s (12): added by the Children and Families Act 2014, s 121(4), as from 30 June 2014.

Sub-s (13): added by the Social Services and Well-being (Wales) Act 2014 (Consequential Amendments) Regulations 2016, SI 2016/413, regs 130, 133, as from 6 April 2016.

Note that the Children and Families Act 2014, s 126(1), Sch 7, paras 6, 16(1), (3) provides that the word "ordinary" should be repealed in both places that it occurs in sub-s (2) above. However, the second occurrence of the word (ie, in para (b)) is in text that is also prospectively substituted by s 123(1), (3)(a) of the 2014 Act.

The fixed rate, as from 7 April 2019, is £148.68 per week (see the Statutory Paternity Pay and Statutory Adoption Pay (Weekly Rates) Regulations, SI 2002/2818, reg 2 at **[2.608]**, as amended by the Social Security Benefits Up-rating Order 2019, SI 2019/480, art 11(1)(a). Previous rates were: £145.18 (as from 1 April 2018, see SI 2018/281, art 11(1)(a)); £140.98 (as from 2 April 2017, see SI 2017/260, art 11(1)(a); £139.58 (as from 5 April 2015, see SI 2015/30, art 5(1)(a); £138.18 (as from 6 April 2014, see SI 2014/147, art 5(1)(a); £136.78 (as from 7 April 2013, see SI 2013/574, art 10(1)(a)); £135.45 (as from 1 April 2012, see SI 2012/780, art 11(1)(a)). Note that there was no increase in April 2016.

Application to parental order parents and to adoptions from overseas: see the introductory notes to this Part.

Regulations: the Statutory Paternity Pay and Statutory Adoption Pay (Weekly Rates) Regulations 2002, SI 2002/2818 at **[2.607]**; the Statutory Paternity Pay and Statutory Adoption Pay (General) Regulations 2002, SI 2002/2822 at **[2.625]**; the Statutory Paternity Pay (Adoption) and Statutory Adoption Pay (Adoptions from Overseas) (No 2) Regulations 2003, SI 2003/1194; the Statutory Paternity Pay and Statutory Adoption Pay (Weekly Rates) (Amendment) Regulations 2004, SI 2004/925; the Statutory Paternity Pay and Statutory Adoption Pay (Parental Orders and Prospective Adopters) Regulations 2014, SI 2014/2934 at **[2.1551]**.

. . .

171ZEA–171ZEE *(Inserted by the Work and Families Act 2006, s 6, and repealed (together with the preceding heading) by the Children and Families Act 2014, s 125(2), as from 5 April 2015 (note that this repeal does not have effect in relation to (a) children whose expected week of birth ends on or before 4 April 2015; (b) children placed for adoption on or before that date: see the Children and Families Act 2014 (Commencement No 3, Transitional Provisions and Savings) Order 2014, SI 2014/1640, art 14).)*

[. . .]

NOTES

The above heading was inserted by the Work and Families Act 2006, s 11(1), Sch 1, para 17, and was repealed by the Children and Families Act 2014, s 126(1), Sch 7, paras 6, 18, as from 5 April 2015 (note that this repeal does not have effect in relation to (a) children whose expected week of birth ends on or before 4 April 2015, and (b) children placed for adoption on or before that date: see the Children and Families Act 2014 (Commencement No 3, Transitional Provisions and Savings) Order 2014, SI 2014/1640, art 16).

[1.225]

[171ZF Restrictions on contracting out

(1) Any agreement shall be void to the extent that it purports—

(a) to exclude, limit or otherwise modify any provision of this Part of this Act, or

(b) to require an employee or former employee to contribute (whether directly or indirectly) towards any costs incurred by his employer or former employer under this Part of this Act.

(2) For the avoidance of doubt, any agreement between an employer and an employee authorising any deductions from [statutory paternity pay] which the employer is liable to pay to the employee in respect of any period shall not be void by virtue of subsection (1)(a) above if the employer—

(a) is authorised by that or another agreement to make the same deductions from any contractual remuneration which he is liable to pay in respect of the same period, or

(b) would be so authorised if he were liable to pay contractual remuneration in respect of that period.]

NOTES

Inserted as noted at the beginning of this Part.

Sub-s (2): words in square brackets substituted by the Children and Families Act 2014, s 126(1), Sch 7, paras 6, 19, as from 5 April 2015 (note that this amendment does not have effect in relation to (a) children whose expected week of birth ends on or before 4 April 2015, and (b) children placed for adoption on or before that date: see the Children and Families Act 2014 (Commencement No 3, Transitional Provisions and Savings) Order 2014, SI 2014/1640, art 16).

Application to parental order parents and to adoptions from overseas: see the introductory notes to this Part.

[1.226]

[171ZG Relationship with contractual remuneration

(1) Subject to subsections (2) and (3) below, any entitlement to statutory paternity pay shall not affect any right of a person in relation to remuneration under any contract of service ("contractual remuneration").

(2) Subject to subsection (3) below—

(a) any contractual remuneration paid to a person by an employer of his in respect of any period shall go towards discharging any liability of that employer to pay statutory paternity pay to him in respect of that period; and

(b) any statutory paternity pay paid by an employer to a person who is an employee of his in respect of any period shall go towards discharging any liability of that employer to pay contractual remuneration to him in respect of that period.

(3) Regulations may make provision as to payments which are, and those which are not, to be treated as contractual remuneration for the purposes of subsections (1) and (2) above.

[(4) . . .]]

NOTES

Inserted as noted at the beginning of this Part.

Sub-s (4): added by the Work and Families Act 2006, s 11(1), Sch 1, para 19, and repealed by the Children and Families Act 2014, s 126(1), Sch 7, paras 6, 20, as from 5 April 2015 (note that this repeal does not have effect in relation to (a) children whose expected week of birth ends on or before 4 April 2015, and (b) children placed for adoption on or before that date: see the Children and Families Act 2014 (Commencement No 3, Transitional Provisions and Savings) Order 2014, SI 2014/1640, art 16).

Application to parental order parents and to adoptions from overseas: see the introductory notes to this Part.

Regulations: the Statutory Paternity Pay and Statutory Adoption Pay (General) Regulations 2002, SI 2002/2822 at **[2.625]**; the Statutory Paternity Pay (Adoption) and Statutory Adoption Pay (Adoptions from Overseas) (No 2) Regulations 2003, SI 2003/1194; the Additional Statutory Paternity Pay (General) Regulations 2010, SI 2010/1056; the Additional Statutory Paternity Pay (Adoptions from Overseas) Regulations 2010, SI 2010/1057; the Statutory Paternity Pay and Statutory Adoption Pay (Parental Orders and Prospective Adopters) Regulations 2014, SI 2014/2934 at **[2.1551]**.

[1.227]

[171ZH Crown employment—Part 12ZA

The provisions of this Part of this Act apply in relation to persons employed by or under the Crown as they apply in relation to persons employed otherwise than by or under the Crown.]

NOTES

Inserted as noted at the beginning of this Part.

Application to parental order parents and to adoptions from overseas: see the introductory notes to this Part.

[1.228]

[171ZI Special classes of person

(1) The Secretary of State may with the concurrence of the Treasury make regulations modifying any provision of this Part of this Act in such manner as he thinks proper in its application to any person who is, has been or is to be—

(a) employed on board any ship, vessel, hovercraft or aircraft;
(b) outside Great Britain at any prescribed time or in any prescribed circumstances; or
(c) in prescribed employment in connection with continental shelf operations, as defined in section 120(2) above.

(2) Regulations under subsection (1) above may, in particular, provide—
(a) for any provision of this Part of this Act to apply to any such person, notwithstanding that it would not otherwise apply;
(b) for any such provision not to apply to any such person, notwithstanding that it would otherwise apply;
(c) for excepting any such person from the application of any such provision where he neither is domiciled nor has a place of residence in any part of Great Britain;
(d) for the taking of evidence, for the purposes of the determination of any question arising under any such provision, in a country or territory outside Great Britain, by a British consular official or such other person as may be determined in accordance with the regulations.]

NOTES

Inserted as noted at the beginning of this Part.

Application to parental order parents and to adoptions from overseas: see the introductory notes to this Part.

Regulations: the Statutory Paternity Pay and Statutory Adoption Pay (Persons Abroad and Mariners) Regulations 2002, SI 2002/2821; the Ordinary Statutory Paternity Pay (Adoption), Additional Statutory Paternity Pay (Adoption) and Statutory Adoption Pay (Adoptions from Overseas) (Persons Abroad and Mariners) Regulations 2010, SI 2010/150; the Statutory Paternity Pay and Statutory Adoption Pay (Persons Abroad and Mariners) Regulations 2002 (Amendment) Regulations 2010, SI 2010/151.

[1.229]
[171ZJ Part 12ZA: supplementary

(1) In this Part of this Act—

"the Board" means the Commissioners of Inland Revenue;

["employer", in relation to a person who is an employee, means a person who—
(a) under section 6 above is, liable to pay secondary Class 1 contributions in relation to any of the earnings of the person who is an employee; or
(b) would be liable to pay such contributions but for—
(i) the condition in section 6(1)(b), or
(ii) the employee being under the age of 16;]

["local authority" has the same meaning as in the Children Act 1989 (see section 105(1) of that Act);

"local authority foster parent" has the same meaning as in the Children Act 1989 (see [section 105(1)] of that Act);]

"modifications" includes additions, omissions and amendments, and related expressions are to be read accordingly;

"prescribed" means prescribed by regulations.

(2) In this Part of this Act, "employee" means a person who is—
(a) gainfully employed in Great Britain either under a contract of service or in an office (including elective office) with [earnings (within the meaning of Parts 1 to 5 above)]; . . .
(b) . . .

(3) Regulations may provide—
(a) for cases where a person who falls within the definition in subsection (2) above is not to be treated as an employee for the purposes of this Part of this Act, and
(b) for cases where a person who would not otherwise be an employee for the purposes of this Part of this Act is to be treated as an employee for those purposes.

(4) Without prejudice to any other power to make regulations under this Part of this Act, regulations may specify cases in which, for the purposes of this Part of this Act or of such provisions of this Part of this Act as may be prescribed—
(a) two or more employers are to be treated as one;
(b) two or more contracts of service in respect of which the same person is an employee are to be treated as one.

(5) In this Part, except [section 171ZE], "week" means a period of 7 days beginning with Sunday or such other period as may be prescribed in relation to any particular case or class of cases.

(6) For the purposes of this Part of this Act, a person's normal weekly earnings shall, subject to subsection (8) below, be taken to be the average weekly earnings which in the relevant period have been paid to him or paid for his benefit under the contract of service with the employer in question.

(7) For the purposes of subsection (6) above, "earnings" and "relevant period" shall have the meanings given to them by regulations.

(8) In such cases as may be prescribed, a person's normal weekly earnings shall be calculated in accordance with regulations.

(9) Where—
(a) in consequence of the establishment of one or more National Health Service trusts under [*the National Health Service Act 2006,* the National Health Service (Wales) Act 2006] or the National Health Service (Scotland) Act 1978 (c 29), a person's contract of employment is treated by a scheme under [any of those Acts] as divided so as to constitute two or more contracts, or
(b) an order under [paragraph 26(1) of Schedule 3 to the National Health Service Act 2006] provides that a person's contract of employment is so divided,

regulations may make provision enabling the person to elect for all of those contracts to be treated as one contract for the purposes of this Part of this Act or such provisions of this Part of this Act as may be prescribed.

(10) Regulations under subsection (9) above may prescribe—

(a) the conditions that must be satisfied if a person is to be entitled to make such an election;

(b) the manner in which, and the time within which, such an election is to be made;

(c) the persons to whom, and the manner in which, notice of such an election is to be given;

(d) the information which a person who makes such an election is to provide, and the persons to whom, and the time within which, he is to provide it;

(e) the time for which such an election is to have effect;

(f) which one of the person's employers under two or more contracts is to be regarded for the purposes of [statutory paternity pay] as his employer under the contract.

(11) The powers under subsections (9) and (10) are without prejudice to any other power to make regulations under this Part of this Act.

(12) Regulations under any of subsections (4) to (10) above must be made with the concurrence of the Board.]

NOTES

Inserted as noted at the beginning of this Part.

Sub-s (1): definition "employer" substituted by the Employment Equality (Age) Regulations 2006, SI 2006/1031, reg 49(1), Sch 8, Pt 1, paras 8, 11(1), (2), (4); definitions "local authority" and "local authority foster parent" inserted by the Children and Families Act 2014, s 121(7)(a), as from 30 June 2014; words in square brackets in definition "local authority foster parent" substituted by the Social Services and Well-being (Wales) Act 2014 (Consequential Amendments) Regulations 2016, SI 2016/413, regs 130, 134, as from 6 April 2016.

Sub-s (2): words in square brackets in para (a) substituted by the National Insurance Contributions Act 2014, s 15(3), Sch 2, paras 1, 5; para (b) (and the word omitted immediately preceding it) repealed by SI 2006/1031, reg 49(1), Sch 8, Pt 1, paras 8, 11(1), (3), (4).

Sub-ss (5), (10): words in square brackets substituted by the Children and Families Act 2014, s 126(1), Sch 7, paras 6, 21, as from 5 April 2015 (note that this amendment does not have effect in relation to (a) children whose expected week of birth ends on or before 4 April 2015, and (b) children placed for adoption on or before that date: see the Children and Families Act 2014 (Commencement No 3, Transitional Provisions and Savings) Order 2014, SI 2014/1640, art 16).

Sub-s (9): words in square brackets substituted by the National Health Service (Consequential Provisions) Act 2006, s 2, Sch 1, paras 142, 149; words in italics repealed by the Health and Social Care Act 2012, s 179, Sch 14, Pt 2, paras 58, 61, as from a day to be appointed.

Application to parental order parents and to adoptions from overseas: see the introductory notes to this Part.

Commissioners of Inland Revenue: a reference to the Commissioners of Inland Revenue is now to be taken as a reference to the Commissioners for Her Majesty's Revenue and Customs; see the Commissioners for Revenue and Customs Act 2005, s 50(1), (7).

Regulations: the Statutory Paternity Pay and Statutory Adoption Pay (National Health Service Employees) Regulations 2002, SI 2002/2819; the Statutory Paternity Pay and Statutory Adoption Pay (General) Regulations 2002, SI 2002/2822 at **[2.625]**; the Statutory Paternity Pay (Adoption) and Statutory Adoption Pay (Adoptions from Overseas) (No 2) Regulations 2003, SI 2003/1194; the Statutory Paternity Pay and Statutory Adoption Pay (Amendment) Regulations 2004, SI 2004/488; the Ordinary Statutory Paternity Pay (Adoption), Additional Statutory Paternity Pay (Adoption) and Statutory Adoption Pay (Adoptions from Overseas) (Persons Abroad and Mariners) Regulations 2010, SI 2010/150; the Additional Statutory Paternity Pay (National Health Service Employees) Regulations 2010, SI 2010/152; the Additional Statutory Paternity Pay (General) Regulations 2010, SI 2010/1056; the Additional Statutory Paternity Pay (Adoptions from Overseas) Regulations 2010, SI 2010/1057; the Statutory Paternity Pay and Statutory Adoption Pay (Parental Orders and Prospective Adopters) Regulations 2014, SI 2014/2934 at **[2.1551]**; the Statutory Paternity Pay, Statutory Adoption Pay and Statutory Shared Parental Pay (Amendment) Regulations 2015, SI 2015/2065.

[1.230]

[171ZK Power to apply Part 12ZA . . .

[(1)] The Secretary of State may by regulations provide for this Part to have effect in relation to cases which involve adoption, but not the placement of a child for adoption under the law of any part of the United Kingdom, with such modifications as the regulations may prescribe.

[(2) The Secretary of State may by regulations provide for this Part to have effect in relation to cases which involve a person who has applied, or intends to apply, with another person for a parental order under section 54 of the Human Fertilisation and Embryology Act 2008 and a child who is, or will be, the subject of the order, with such modifications as the regulations may prescribe.]]

NOTES

Inserted as noted at the beginning of this Part.

The words omitted from the section heading were repealed, sub-s (1) was numbered as such, and sub-s (2) was added, by the Children and Families Act 2014, s 122(5), as from 30 June 2014.

Application to parental order parents and to adoptions from overseas: see the introductory notes to this Part.

Regulations: the Social Security Contributions and Benefits Act 1992 (Application of Parts 12ZA and 12ZB to Adoptions from Overseas) Regulations 2003, SI 2003/499; the Statutory Paternity Pay and Statutory Adoption Pay (Amendment) Regulations 2004, SI 2004/488; the Social Security Contributions and Benefits Act 1992 (Application of Parts 12ZA and 12ZB to Adoptions from Overseas) Regulations 2003 (Amendment) Regulations 2010, SI 2010/153; the Social Security Contributions and Benefits Act 1992 (Application of Parts 12ZA, 12ZB and 12ZC to Parental Order Cases) Regulations 2014, SI 2014/2866 at **[2.1529]**.

[PART XIIZB
STATUTORY ADOPTION PAY

NOTES

Part XIIZB was inserted by the Employment Act 2002, s 4, in relation to a person with whom a child is, or is expected to be placed for adoption on or after 6 April 2003.

Statutory paternity pay: as to the meaning of this, see the Children and Families Act 2014, s 126 at **[1.1894]**

Application to parental order parents: this Part is applied, subject to certain modifications, to parental order parents by the Social Security Contributions and Benefits Act 1992 (Application of Parts 12ZA, 12ZB and 12ZC to Parental Order Cases) Regulations 2014, SI 2014/2866, reg 4, Sch 2 at **[2.1532]**, **[2.1535]**.

Application to adoptions from overseas: this Part is applied, subject to certain modifications, to adoptions from overseas by the Social Security Contributions and Benefits Act 1992 (Application of Parts 12ZA, 12ZB and 12ZC to Adoptions from Overseas) Regulations 2003, SI 2003/499, Sch 2.

[1.231]

171ZL Entitlement

(1) Where a person who is, or has been, an employee satisfies the conditions in subsection (2) below, he shall be entitled in accordance with the following provisions of this Part to payments to be known as "statutory adoption pay".

(2) The conditions are—

(a) that he is a person with whom a child is, or is expected to be, placed for adoption under the law of any part of the United Kingdom;

(b) that he has been in employed earner's employment with an employer for a continuous period of at least 26 weeks ending with the relevant week;

[(ba) that at the end of the relevant week he was entitled to be in that employment;]

(c) that he has ceased to work for the employer;

(d) that his normal weekly earnings for the period of 8 weeks ending with the relevant week are not less than the lower earnings limit in force under section 5(1)(a) at the end of the relevant week; and

(e) that he has elected to receive statutory adoption pay.

(3) The references in subsection (2)(b)[, (ba)] and (d) above to the relevant week are to the week in which the person is notified that he has been matched with the child for the purposes of adoption.

(4) A person may not elect to receive statutory adoption pay if—

(a) he has elected in accordance with section 171ZB above to receive statutory paternity pay, or

[(b) he falls within subsection (4A)].

[(4A) A person falls within this subsection if—

(a) the child is, or is expected to be, placed for adoption with him as a member of a couple;

(b) the other member of the couple is a person to whom the conditions in subsection (2) above apply; and

(c) the other member of the couple has elected to receive statutory adoption pay.

(4B) For the purposes of subsection (4A), a person is a member of a couple if—

(a) in the case of an adoption or expected adoption under the law of England and Wales, he is a member of a couple within the meaning of section 144(4) of the Adoption and Children Act 2002;

(b) in the case of an adoption or an expected adoption under the law . . . of Northern Ireland, he is a member of a married couple.;

[(c) in the case of an adoption or expected adoption under the law of Scotland he is a member of a relevant couple within the meaning of section 29(3) of the Adoption and Children (Scotland) Act 2007].]

(5) A person's entitlement to statutory adoption pay shall not be affected by the placement, or expected placement, for adoption of more than one child as part of the same arrangement.

(6) A person shall be entitled to payments of statutory adoption pay only if—

(a) he gives the person who will be liable to pay it notice of the date from which he expects the liability to pay him statutory adoption pay to begin; and

(b) the notice is given at least 28 days before that date or, if that is not reasonably practicable, as soon as is reasonably practicable.

(7) The notice shall be in writing if the person who is liable to pay the statutory adoption pay so requests.

(8) The Secretary of State may by regulations—

[(za) exclude the application of subsection (2)(ba) above in prescribed circumstances;]

(a) provide that subsection (2)(b), (c) or (d) above shall have effect subject to prescribed modifications in such cases as may be prescribed;

(b) provide that subsection (6) above shall not have effect, or shall have effect subject to prescribed modifications, in such cases as may be prescribed;

(c) impose requirements about evidence of entitlement;

(d) specify in what circumstances employment is to be treated as continuous for the purposes of this section;

(e) provide that a person is to be treated for the purposes of this section as being employed for a continuous period of at least 26 weeks where—

(i) he has been employed by the same employer for at least 26 weeks under two or more separate contracts of service; and

(ii) those contracts were not continuous;

(f) provide for amounts earned by a person under separate contracts of service with the same employer to be aggregated for the purposes of this section;

(g) provide that—

(i) the amount of a person's earnings for any period, or

(ii) the amount of his earnings to be treated as comprised in any payment made to him or for his benefit,

shall be calculated or estimated for the purposes of this section in such manner and on such basis as may be prescribed and that for that purpose payments of a particular class or description made or falling to be made to or by a person shall, to such extent as may be prescribed, be disregarded or, as the case may be, be deducted from the amount of his earnings;

(h) make provision about elections for statutory adoption pay.

[(9) This section has effect in a case involving a child who is, or is expected to be, placed under section 22C of the Children Act 1989 by a local authority in England with a local authority foster parent who has been approved as a prospective adopter with the following modifications—

(a) the references in subsections (2)(a) and (4A)(a) to a child being placed for adoption under the law of any part of the United Kingdom are to be treated as references to a child being placed under section 22C in that manner;

(b) the reference in subsection (3) to the week in which the person is notified that he has been matched with the child for the purposes of adoption is to be treated as a reference to the week in which the person is notified that the child is to be, or is expected to be, placed with him under section 22C;

(c) the references in subsection (4B)(a) to adoption are to be treated as references to placement under section 22C;

(d) the reference in subsection (5) to placement, or expected placement, for adoption is to be treated as a reference to placement, or expected placement, under section 22C.

(10) Where, by virtue of subsection (9), a person becomes entitled to statutory adoption pay in respect of a child who is, or is expected to be, placed under section 22C of the Children Act 1989, the person may not become entitled to payments of statutory adoption pay as a result of the child being, or being expected to be, placed for adoption.]

(11) This section has effect in a case involving a child who is, or is expected to be, placed under section 81 of the Social Services and Well-being (Wales) Act 2014 by a local authority in Wales with a local authority foster parent who has been approved as a prospective adopter with the following modifications—

(a) the references in subsections (2)(a) and (4A)(a) to a child being placed for adoption under the law of any part of the United kingdom are to be treated as references to a child being placed under section 81 in that manner;

(b) the reference in subsection (3) to the week in which the person is notified that he has been matched with the child for the purposes of adoption is to be treated as a reference to the week in which the person is notified that the child is to be, or is expected to be placed with him under section 8;

(c) the references in subsection (4B)(a) to adoption are to be treated as references to placement under section 81;

(d) the reference in subsection (5) to placement, or expected placement, for adoption is to be treated as a reference to placement, or expected placement under section 81.

(12) Where, by virtue of subsection (11), a person becomes entitled to statutory adoption pay in respect of a child who is, or is expected to be, placed under section 81 of the Social Services and Well-being (Wales) Act 2014, the person may not become entitled to payments of statutory adoption pay as a result of the child being, or being expected to be, placed for adoption.]]

NOTES

Inserted as noted at the beginning of this Part.

Sub-s (2): para (ba) inserted by the Welfare Reform Act 2012, s 63(1), (8)(a), as from a day to be appointed.

Sub-s (3): reference in square brackets inserted by the Welfare Reform Act 2012, s 63(1), (8)(b), as from a day to be appointed.

Sub-s (4): para (b) substituted by the Adoption and Children Act 2002 (Consequential Amendment to Statutory Adoption Pay) Order 2006, SI 2006/2012, art 3(a).

Sub-ss (4A), (4B): inserted by SI 2006/2012, art 3(b); words omitted from sub-s (4B)(b) repealed, and sub-s (4B)(c) inserted, by the Adoption and Children (Scotland) Act 2007 (Consequential Modifications) Order 2011, SI 2011/1740, art 2, Sch 1, Pt 1, para 4, Sch 1, Pt 3.

Sub-s (8): para (za) inserted by the Welfare Reform Act 2012, s 63(1), (8)(c), as from a day to be appointed.

Sub-ss (9), (10): added by the Children and Families Act 2014, s 121(5), as from 30 June 2014.

Sub-ss (11), (12): added by the Social Services and Well-being (Wales) Act 2014 (Consequential Amendments) Regulations 2016, SI 2016/413, regs 130, 135, as from 6 April 2016.

Application to parental order parents and to adoptions from overseas: see the introductory notes to this Part.

Regulations: the Statutory Paternity Pay and Statutory Adoption Pay (General) Regulations 2002, SI 2002/2822 at **[2.625]**; the Statutory Paternity Pay (Adoption) and Statutory Adoption Pay (Adoptions from Overseas) (No 2) Regulations 2003, SI 2003/1194; the Statutory Maternity Pay (General) and the Statutory Paternity Pay and Statutory Adoption Pay (General) (Amendment) Regulations 2005, SI 2005/358; the Statutory Paternity Pay and Statutory Adoption Pay (Parental Orders and Prospective Adopters) Regulations 2014, SI 2014/2934 at **[2.1551]**.

[1.232]

[171ZM Liability to make payments

(1) The liability to make payments of statutory adoption pay is a liability of any person of whom the person entitled to the payments has been an employee as mentioned in section 171ZL(2)(b) above.

(2) Regulations shall make provision as to a former employer's liability to pay statutory adoption pay to a person in any case where the former employee's contract of service with him has been brought to an end by the former employer solely, or mainly, for the purpose of avoiding liability for statutory adoption pay.

(3) The Secretary of State may, with the concurrence of the Board, by regulations specify circumstances in which, notwithstanding this section, liability to make payments of statutory adoption pay is to be a liability of the Board.]

NOTES

Inserted as noted at the beginning of this Part.

Application to parental order parents and to adoptions from overseas: see the introductory notes to this Part.

Regulations: the Statutory Paternity Pay and Statutory Adoption Pay (General) Regulations 2002, SI 2002/2822 at **[2.625]**; the Statutory Paternity Pay (Adoption) and Statutory Adoption Pay (Adoptions from Overseas) (No 2) Regulations 2003, SI 2003/1194; the Statutory Paternity Pay and Statutory Adoption Pay (Parental Orders and Prospective Adopters) Regulations 2014, SI 2014/2934 at **[2.1551]**.

[1.233]

[171ZN Rate and period of pay

(1) . . .

(2) Statutory adoption pay shall be payable, subject to the provisions of this Part of this Act, in respect of each week during a prescribed period ("the adoption pay period") of a duration not exceeding [52 weeks].

[(2A) Regulations may provide for the duration of the adoption pay period as it applies to a person ("A") to be reduced, subject to prescribed restrictions and conditions.

(2B) Regulations under subsection (2A) are to secure that the reduced period ends at a time—

(a) after a prescribed part of the adoption pay period has expired, and

(b) when at least a prescribed part of the adoption pay period remains unexpired.

(2C) Regulations under subsection (2A) may, in particular, prescribe restrictions and conditions relating to—

(a) the end of A's entitlement to adoption leave;

(b) the doing of work by A;

(c) the taking of prescribed steps by A or another person as regards leave under section 75G of the Employment Rights Act 1996 in respect of the child;

(d) the taking of prescribed steps by A or another person as regards statutory shared parental pay in respect of the child.

(2D) Regulations may provide for a reduction in the duration of the adoption pay period as it applies to a person to be revoked, or to be treated as revoked, subject to prescribed restrictions and conditions.]

[(2E) Statutory adoption pay shall be payable to a person—

(a) at the earnings-related rate, in respect of the first 6 weeks in respect of which it is payable; and

(b) at whichever is the lower of the earnings-related rate and such weekly rate as may be prescribed, in respect of the remaining portion of the adoption pay period.

(2F) The earnings-related rate is a weekly rate equivalent to 90 per cent of a person's normal weekly earnings for the period of 8 weeks ending with the week in which the person is notified that the person has been matched with a child for the purposes of adoption.

(2G) The weekly rate prescribed under subsection (2E)(b) must not be less than the weekly rate of statutory sick pay for the time being specified in section 157(1) or, if two or more such rates are for the time being so specified, the higher or highest of those rates.]

(3) [Except in such cases as may be prescribed,] a person shall not be liable to pay statutory adoption pay to another in respect of any week during any part of which the other works under a contract of service with him.

(4) It is immaterial for the purposes of subsection (3) above whether the work referred to in that subsection is work under a contract of service which existed immediately before the adoption pay period or a contract of service which did not so exist.

(5) Except in such cases as may be prescribed, statutory adoption pay shall not be payable to a person in respect of any week during any part of which he works for any employer who is not liable to pay him statutory adoption pay.

(6) The Secretary of State may by regulations specify circumstances in which there is to be no liability to pay statutory adoption pay in respect of a week.

[(6A) Where for any purpose of this Part of this Act or of regulations it is necessary to calculate the daily rate of statutory adoption pay, the amount payable by way of statutory adoption pay for any day shall be taken as one seventh of the weekly rate.]

(7) In [subsections (2) and (2E)] above, "week" means any period of seven days.

(8) In subsections (3), (5) and (6) above, "week" means a period of seven days beginning with the day of the week on which the adoption pay period begins.

[(9) Where statutory adoption pay is payable to a person by virtue of section 171ZL(9), this section has effect as if the reference in subsection (2F) to the week in which the person is notified that he has been matched with a child for the purposes of adoption were a reference to the week in which the person is notified that a child is to be, or is expected to be, placed with him under section 22C of the Children Act 1989.]

[(10) Where statutory adoption pay is payable to a person by virtue of section 171ZL(11), this section has effect as if the reference in subsection (2F) to the week in which the person is notified that he has been matched with a child for the purposes of adoption were a reference to the week in which the person is notified that a child is to be, or is expected to be, placed with him under section 81 of the Social Services and Well-being (Wales) Act 2014.]]

NOTES

Inserted as noted at the beginning of this Part.

Sub-ss (1): repealed by the Children and Families Act 2014, s 124(1)(a), as from 5 April 2015, in relation to any adoption pay period which begins on or after that date (see the Children and Families Act 2014 (Commencement No 3, Transitional Provisions and Savings) Order 2014, SI 2014/1640, art 13).

Sub-s (2): words in square brackets substituted by the Work and Families Act 2006, s 2.

Sub-ss (2A)–(2D): inserted by the Children and Families Act 2014, s 120(1), (6), as from 30 June 2014.

Sub-ss (2E)–(2G): inserted by the Children and Families Act 2014, s 124(1)(b), as from 5 April 2015, in relation to any adoption pay period which begins on or after that date (see SI 2014/1640, art 13).

Sub-s (3): words in square brackets inserted by the Work and Families Act 2006, s 11(1), Sch 1, para 21(1), (2).

Sub-s (6A): inserted by the Work and Families Act 2006, s 11(1), Sch 1, para 21(1), (3).

Sub-s (7): words in square brackets substituted by the Children and Families Act 2014, s 124(1)(a), as from 5 April 2015, in relation to any adoption pay period which begins on or after that date (see SI 2014/1640, art 13).

Sub-s (9): added by the Children and Families Act 2014, s 121(6), as from 30 June 2014.

Sub-s (10): added by the Social Services and Well-being (Wales) Act 2014 (Consequential Amendments) Regulations 2016, SI 2016/413, regs 130, 136, as from 6 April 2016.

The fixed rate, as from 7 April 2019, is £148.68 per week (see the Statutory Paternity Pay and Statutory Adoption Pay (Weekly Rates) Regulations, SI 2002/2818, reg 3 at **[2.609]**, as amended by the Social Security Benefits Up-rating Order 2019, SI 2019/480, art 11(1)(b)). Previous rates were: £145.18 (as from 1 April 2018, see SI 2018/281, art 11(1)(b)); £140.98 (as from 2 April 2017, see SI 2017/260); £139.58 (as from 5 April 2015, see SI 2015/30); £138.18 (as from 6 April 2014, see SI 2014/147); £136.78 (as from 7 April 2013, see SI 2013/574); £135.45 (as from 1 April 2012, see SI 2012/780). Note that there was no increase in April 2016.

Application to parental order parents and to adoptions from overseas: see the introductory notes to this Part.

Regulations: the Statutory Paternity Pay and Statutory Adoption Pay (Weekly Rates) Regulations 2002, SI 2002/2818 at **[2.607]**; the Statutory Paternity Pay and Statutory Adoption Pay (General) Regulations 2002, SI 2002/2822 at **[2.625]**; the Statutory Paternity Pay (Adoption) and Statutory Adoption Pay (Adoptions from Overseas) (No 2) Regulations 2003, SI 2003/1194; the Statutory Paternity Pay and Statutory Adoption Pay (General) and the Statutory Paternity Pay and Statutory Adoption Pay (Weekly Rates) (Amendment) Regulations 2006, SI 2006/2236; the Statutory Paternity Pay and Statutory Adoption Pay (Parental Orders and Prospective Adopters) Regulations 2014, SI 2014/2934 at **[2.1551]**; the Statutory Maternity Pay and Statutory Adoption Pay (Curtailment) Regulations 2014, SI 2014/3054 at **[2.1688]**.

[1.234]

[171ZO Restrictions on contracting out

(1) Any agreement shall be void to the extent that it purports—

(a) to exclude, limit or otherwise modify any provision of this Part of this Act, or

(b) to require an employee or former employee to contribute (whether directly or indirectly) towards any costs incurred by his employer or former employer under this Part of this Act.

(2) For the avoidance of doubt, any agreement between an employer and an employee authorising any deductions from statutory adoption pay which the employer is liable to pay to the employee in respect of any period shall not be void by virtue of subsection (1)(a) above if the employer—

(a) is authorised by that or another agreement to make the same deductions from any contractual remuneration which he is liable to pay in respect of the same period, or

(b) would be so authorised if he were liable to pay contractual remuneration in respect of that period.]

NOTES

Inserted as noted at the beginning of this Part.

Application to parental order parents and to adoptions from overseas: see the introductory notes to this Part.

[1.235]

[171ZP Relationship with benefits and other payments etc

(1) Except as may be prescribed, a day which falls within the adoption pay period shall not be treated as a day of incapacity for work for the purposes of determining, for this Act, whether it forms part of a period of incapacity for work for the purposes of incapacity benefit.

(2) Regulations may provide that in prescribed circumstances a day which falls within the adoption pay period shall be treated as a day of incapacity for work for the purposes of determining entitlement to the higher rate of short-term incapacity benefit or to long-term incapacity benefit.

(3) Regulations may provide that an amount equal to a person's statutory adoption pay for a period shall be deducted from any such benefit in respect of the same period and a person shall be entitled to such benefit only if there is a balance after the deduction and, if there is such a balance, at a weekly rate equal to it.

(4) Subject to subsections (5) and (6) below, any entitlement to statutory adoption pay shall not affect any right of a person in relation to remuneration under any contract of service ("contractual remuneration").

(5) Subject to subsection (6) below—

(a) any contractual remuneration paid to a person by an employer of his in respect of a week in the adoption pay period shall go towards discharging any liability of that employer to pay statutory adoption pay to him in respect of that week; and

(b) any statutory adoption pay paid by an employer to a person who is an employee of his in respect of a week in the adoption pay period shall go towards discharging any liability of that employer to pay contractual remuneration to him in respect of that week.

(6) Regulations may make provision as to payments which are, and those which are not, to be treated as contractual remuneration for the purposes of subsections (4) and (5) above.

(7) In subsection (5) above, "week" means a period of seven days beginning with the day of the week on which the adoption pay period begins.]

NOTES

Inserted as noted at the beginning of this Part.

Sub-ss (1)–(3): repealed by the Welfare Reform Act 2007, s 67, Sch 8, as from a day to be appointed.

Application to parental order parents and to adoptions from overseas: see the introductory notes to this Part.

Regulations: the Social Security, Statutory Maternity Pay and Statutory Sick Pay (Miscellaneous Amendments) Regulations 2002, SI 2002/2690; the Statutory Paternity Pay and Statutory Adoption Pay (General) Regulations 2002, SI 2002/2822 at **[2.625]**; the Statutory Paternity Pay (Adoption) and Statutory Adoption Pay (Adoptions from Overseas) (No 2) Regulations 2003, SI 2003/1194; the Statutory Paternity Pay and Statutory Adoption Pay (Parental Orders and Prospective Adopters) Regulations 2014, SI 2014/2934 at **[2.1551]**.

[1.236]

[171ZQ Crown employment—Part 12ZB

The provisions of this Part of this Act apply in relation to persons employed by or under the Crown as they apply in relation to persons employed otherwise than by or under the Crown.]

NOTES

Inserted as noted at the beginning of this Part.

Application to parental order parents and to adoptions from overseas: see the introductory notes to this Part.

[1.237]

[171ZR Special classes of person

(1) The Secretary of State may with the concurrence of the Treasury make regulations modifying any provision of this Part of this Act in such manner as he thinks proper in its application to any person who is, has been or is to be—

(a) employed on board any ship, vessel, hovercraft or aircraft;

(b) outside Great Britain at any prescribed time or in any prescribed circumstances; or

(c) in prescribed employment in connection with continental shelf operations, as defined in section 120(2) above.

(2) Regulations under subsection (1) above may, in particular, provide—

(a) for any provision of this Part of this Act to apply to any such person, notwithstanding that it would not otherwise apply;

(b) for any such provision not to apply to any such person, notwithstanding that it would otherwise apply;

(c) for excepting any such person from the application of any such provision where he neither is domiciled nor has a place of residence in any part of Great Britain;

(d) for the taking of evidence, for the purposes of the determination of any question arising under any such provision, in a country or territory outside Great Britain, by a British consular official or such other person as may be determined in accordance with the regulations.]

NOTES

Inserted as noted at the beginning of this Part.

Application to parental order parents and to adoptions from overseas: see the introductory notes to this Part.

Regulations: the Statutory Paternity Pay and Statutory Adoption Pay (Persons Abroad and Mariners) Regulations 2002, SI 2002/2821; the Ordinary Statutory Paternity Pay (Adoption), Additional Statutory Paternity Pay (Adoption) and Statutory Adoption Pay (Adoptions from Overseas) (Persons Abroad and Mariners) Regulations 2010, SI 2010/150; the Statutory Paternity Pay and Statutory Adoption Pay (Persons Abroad and Mariners) Regulations 2002 (Amendment) Regulations 2010, SI 2010/151.

[1.238]

[171ZS Part 12ZB: supplementary

(1) In this Part of this Act—

"adoption pay period" has the meaning given by section 171ZN(2) above;

"the Board" means the Commissioners of Inland Revenue;

["employer", in relation to a person who is an employee, means a person who—

(a) under section 6 above is liable to pay secondary Class 1 contributions in relation to any of the earnings of the person who is an employee; or

(b) would be liable to pay such contributions but for—

(i) the condition in section 6(1)(b), or

(ii) the employee being under the age of 16;]

["local authority" has the same meaning as in the Children Act 1989 (see section 105(1) of that Act);

"local authority foster parent" has the same meaning as in the Children Act 1989 (see [section 105(1)] of that Act);]

"modifications" includes additions, omissions and amendments, and related expressions are to be read accordingly;

"prescribed" means prescribed by regulations.

(2) In this Part of this Act, "employee" means a person who is—

(a) gainfully employed in Great Britain either under a contract of service or in an office (including elective office) with [earnings (within the meaning of Parts 1 to 5 above)]; . . .

(b) . . .

(3) Regulations may provide—

(a) for cases where a person who falls within the definition in subsection (2) above is not to be treated as an employee for the purposes of this Part of this Act, and

(b) for cases where a person who would not otherwise be an employee for the purposes of this Part of this Act is to be treated as an employee for those purposes.

(4) Without prejudice to any other power to make regulations under this Part of this Act, regulations may specify cases in which, for the purposes of this Part of this Act or of such provisions of this Part of this Act as may be prescribed—

(a) two or more employers are to be treated as one;

(b) two or more contracts of service in respect of which the same person is an employee are to be treated as one.

(5) In this Part, except sections 171ZN and 171ZP, "week" means a period of 7 days beginning with Sunday or such other period as may be prescribed in relation to any particular case or class of cases.

(6) For the purposes of this Part of this Act, a person's normal weekly earnings shall, subject to subsection (8) below, be taken to be the average weekly earnings which in the relevant period have been paid to him or paid for his benefit under the contract of service with the employer in question.

(7) For the purposes of subsection (6) above, "earnings" and "relevant period" shall have the meanings given to them by regulations.

(8) In such cases as may be prescribed, a person's normal weekly earnings shall be calculated in accordance with regulations.

(9) Where—

(a) in consequence of the establishment of one or more National Health Service trusts under [*the National Health Service Act 2006,* the National Health Service (Wales) Act 2006] or the National Health Service (Scotland) Act 1978 (c 29), a person's contract of employment is treated by a scheme under [any of those Acts] as divided so as to constitute two or more contracts, or

(b) an order under [paragraph 26(1) of Schedule 3 to the National Health Service Act 2006] provides that a person's contract of employment is so divided,

regulations may make provision enabling the person to elect for all of those contracts to be treated as one contract for the purposes of this Part of this Act or such provisions of this Part of this Act as may be prescribed.

(10) Regulations under subsection (9) above may prescribe—

(a) the conditions that must be satisfied if a person is to be entitled to make such an election;

(b) the manner in which, and the time within which, such an election is to be made;

(c) the persons to whom, and the manner in which, notice of such an election is to be given;

(d) the information which a person who makes such an election is to provide, and the persons to whom, and the time within which, he is to provide it;

(e) the time for which such an election is to have effect;

(f) which one of the person's employers under two or more contracts is to be regarded for the purposes of statutory adoption pay as his employer under the contract.

(11) The powers under subsections (9) and (10) are without prejudice to any other power to make regulations under this Part of this Act.

(12) Regulations under any of subsections (4) to (10) above must be made with the concurrence of the Board.]

NOTES

Inserted as noted at the beginning of this Part.

Sub-s (1): definition "employer" substituted by the Employment Equality (Age) Regulations 2006, SI 2006/1031, reg 49(1), Sch 8, Pt 1, paras 8, 12(1), (2); definitions "local authority" and "local authority foster parent" inserted by the Children and Families Act 2014, s 121(7)(b), as from 30 June 2014; words in square brackets in definition "local authority foster parent" substituted by the Social Services and Well-being (Wales) Act 2014 (Consequential Amendments) Regulations 2016, SI 2016/413, regs 130, 137, as from 6 April 2016.

Sub-s (2): words in square brackets in para (a) substituted by the National Insurance Contributions Act 2014, s 15(3), Sch 2, paras 1, 6; para (b) (and the word omitted immediately preceding it) repealed by SI 2006/1031, reg 49(1), Sch 8, Pt 1, paras 8, 12(1), (3), (4).

Sub-s (9): words in square brackets substituted by the National Health Service (Consequential Provisions) Act 2006, s 2, Sch 1, paras 142, 150; words in italics repealed by the Health and Social Care Act 2012, s 179, Sch 14, Pt 2, paras 58, 62, as from a day to be appointed.

Application to parental order parents and to adoptions from overseas: see the introductory notes to this Part.

Commissioners of Inland Revenue: a reference to the Commissioners of Inland Revenue is now to be taken as a reference to the Commissioners for Her Majesty's Revenue and Customs; see the Commissioners for Revenue and Customs Act 2005, s 50(1), (7).

Regulations: the Statutory Paternity Pay and Statutory Adoption Pay (National Health Service Employees) Regulations 2002, SI 2002/2819; the Statutory Paternity Pay and Statutory Adoption Pay (General) Regulations 2002, SI 2002/2822 at **[2.625]**; the Statutory Paternity Pay (Adoption) and Statutory Adoption Pay (Adoptions from Overseas) (No 2) Regulations 2003, SI 2003/1194; the Statutory Paternity Pay and Statutory Adoption Pay (Amendment) Regulations 2004, SI 2004/488; the Ordinary Statutory Paternity Pay (Adoption), Additional Statutory Paternity Pay (Adoption) and Statutory Adoption Pay (Adoptions from Overseas) (Persons Abroad and Mariners) Regulations 2010, SI 2010/150; the Statutory Paternity Pay and Statutory Adoption Pay (Parental Orders and Prospective Adopters) Regulations 2014, SI 2014/2934 at **[2.1551]**;

the Statutory Paternity Pay, Statutory Adoption Pay and Statutory Shared Parental Pay (Amendment) Regulations 2015, SI 2015/2065.

[1.239]
[171ZT Power to apply Part 12ZB . . .

[(1)] The Secretary of State may by regulations provide for this Part to have effect in relation to cases which involve adoption, but not the placement of a child for adoption under the law of any part of the United Kingdom, with such modifications as the regulations may prescribe.

[[(2) The Secretary of State may by regulations provide for this Part to have effect, with such modifications as the regulations may prescribe, in relation to—

(a) cases which involve a person who has applied, or intends to apply, with another person for a parental order under section 54 of the Human Fertilisation and Embryology Act 2008 and a child who is, or will be, the subject of the order,

(b) cases which involve a person who has applied, or intends to apply, for a parental order under section 54A of that Act and a child who is, or will be, the subject of the order.]

(3) Regulations under subsection (2) may modify section 171ZL(8)(c) so as to enable regulations to impose requirements to make statutory declarations as to—

(a) eligibility to apply for a parental order [under section 54 or 54A of the Human Fertilisation and Embryology Act 2008];

(b) intention to apply for such an order.]

NOTES

Inserted as noted at the beginning of this Part.

The words omitted from the section heading were repealed, sub-s (1) was numbered as such, and sub-ss (2), (3) were added, by the Children and Families Act 2014, s 122(6), as from 30 June 2014.

Sub-s (2) was substituted, and the words in square brackets in sub-s (3) were inserted, by the Human Fertilisation and Embryology Act 2008 (Remedial) Order 2018, SI 2018/1413, art 3(1), Sch 1, para 7, as from 3 January 2019.

Application to parental order parents and to adoptions from overseas: see the introductory notes to this Part.

Regulations: the Social Security Contributions and Benefits Act 1992 (Application of Parts 12ZA and 12ZB to Adoptions from Overseas) Regulations 2003, SI 2003/499; the Statutory Paternity Pay and Statutory Adoption Pay (Amendment) Regulations 2004, SI 2004/488; the Social Security Contributions and Benefits Act 1992 (Application of Parts 12ZA, 12ZB and 12ZC to Parental Order Cases) Regulations 2014, SI 2014/2866 at **[2.1529]**.

[PART 12ZC
STATUTORY SHARED PARENTAL PAY

NOTES

Part 12ZC was inserted by the Children and Families Act 2014, s 119(1), as from 30 June 2014.

Application to parental order parents: this Part is applied, subject to certain modifications, to parental order parents by the Social Security Contributions and Benefits Act 1992 (Application of Parts 12ZA, 12ZB and 12ZC to Parental Order Cases) Regulations 2014, SI 2014/2866, reg 5, Sch 3 at **[2.1533]**, **[2.1536]**.

Application to adoptions from overseas: this Part is applied, subject to certain modifications, to adoptions from overseas by the Social Security Contributions and Benefits Act 1992 (Application of Parts 12ZA, 12ZB and 12ZC to Adoptions from Overseas) Regulations 2003, SI 2003/499 (as amended by the Social Security Contributions and Benefits Act 1992 (Application of Parts 12ZA and 12ZB to Adoptions from Overseas) (Amendment) Regulations 2014, SI 2014/2857).

[1.240]
171ZU Entitlement: birth

(1) Regulations may provide that, where all the conditions in subsection (2) are satisfied in relation to a person who is the mother of a child ("the claimant mother"), the claimant mother is to be entitled in accordance with the following provisions of this Part to payments to be known as "statutory shared parental pay".

(2) The conditions are—

(a) that the claimant mother and another person ("P") satisfy prescribed conditions as to caring or intending to care for the child;

(b) that P satisfies prescribed conditions—

(i) as to employment or self-employment,

(ii) as to having earnings of a prescribed amount for a prescribed period, and

(iii) as to relationship either with the child or with the claimant mother;

(c) that the claimant mother has been in employed earner's employment with an employer for a continuous period of at least the prescribed length ending with a prescribed week;

(d) that at the end of that prescribed week the claimant mother was entitled to be in that employment;

(e) that the claimant mother's normal weekly earnings for a prescribed period ending with a prescribed week are not less than the lower earnings limit in force under section 5(1)(a) at the end of that week;

(f) if regulations so provide, that the claimant mother continues in employed earner's employment (whether or not with the employer by reference to whom the condition in paragraph (c) is satisfied) until a prescribed time;

(g) that the claimant mother became entitled to statutory maternity pay by reference to the birth of the child;

(h) that the claimant mother satisfies prescribed conditions as to the reduction of the duration of the maternity pay period;

(i) that the claimant mother has given the person who will be liable to pay statutory shared parental pay to her notice of—
  (i) the number of weeks in respect of which she would be entitled to claim statutory shared parental pay in respect of the child if the entitlement were fully exercised (disregarding for these purposes any intention of P to claim statutory shared parental pay in respect of the child),
  (ii) the number of weeks in respect of which she intends to claim statutory shared parental pay, and
  (iii) the number of weeks in respect of which P intends to claim statutory shared parental pay;
(j) that the claimant mother has given the person who will be liable to pay statutory shared parental pay to her notice of the period or periods during which she intends to claim statutory shared parental pay in respect of the child;
(k) that a notice under paragraph (i) or (j)—
  (i) is given by such time as may be prescribed, and
  (ii) satisfies prescribed conditions as to form and content;
(l) that P consents to the extent of the claimant mother's intended claim for statutory shared parental pay;
(m) that it is the claimant mother's intention to care for the child during each week in respect of which statutory shared parental pay is paid to her;
(n) that the claimant mother is absent from work during each week in respect of which statutory shared parental pay is paid to her;
(o) that, where she is an employee within the meaning of the Employment Rights Act 1996, the claimant mother's absence from work during each such week is absence on shared parental leave.

(3) Regulations may provide that, where all the conditions in subsection (4) are satisfied in relation to a person ("the claimant"), the claimant is to be entitled in accordance with the following provisions of this Part to payments to be known as "statutory shared parental pay".

(4) The conditions are—
(a) that the claimant and another person ("M") who is the mother of a child satisfy prescribed conditions as to caring or intending to care for the child;
(b) that the claimant satisfies—
  (i) prescribed conditions as to relationship with the child, or
  (ii) prescribed conditions as to relationship with M;
(c) that M satisfies prescribed conditions—
  (i) as to employment or self-employment, and
  (ii) as to having earnings of a prescribed amount for a prescribed period;
(d) that the claimant has been in employed earner's employment with an employer for a continuous period of at least the prescribed length ending with a prescribed week;
(e) that at the end of that prescribed week the claimant was entitled to be in that employment;
(f) that the claimant's normal weekly earnings for a prescribed period ending with a prescribed week are not less than the lower earnings limit in force under section 5(1)(a) at the end of that week;
(g) if regulations so provide, that the claimant continues in employed earner's employment (whether or not with the employer by reference to whom the condition in paragraph (d) is satisfied) until a prescribed time;
(h) that M became entitled, by reference to the birth of the child, to—
  (i) a maternity allowance, or
  (ii) statutory maternity pay;
(i) that M satisfies prescribed conditions as to—
  (i) the reduction of the duration of the maternity allowance period, or
  (ii) the reduction of the duration of the maternity pay period, as the case may be;
(j) that the claimant has given the person who will be liable to pay statutory shared parental pay to the claimant notice of—
  (i) the number of weeks in respect of which the claimant would be entitled to claim statutory shared parental pay in respect of the child if the entitlement were fully exercised (disregarding for these purposes any intention of M to claim statutory shared parental pay in respect of the child),
  (ii) the number of weeks in respect of which the claimant intends to claim statutory shared parental pay, and
  (iii) the number of weeks in respect of which M intends to claim statutory shared parental pay;
(k) that the claimant has given the person who will be liable to pay statutory shared parental pay to the claimant notice of the period or periods during which the claimant intends to claim statutory shared parental pay in respect of the child;
(l) that a notice under paragraph (j) or (k)—
  (i) is given by such time as may be prescribed, and
  (ii) satisfies prescribed conditions as to form and content;
(m) that M consents to the extent of the claimant's intended claim for statutory shared parental pay;
(n) that it is the claimant's intention to care for the child during each week in respect of which statutory shared parental pay is paid to the claimant;
(o) that the claimant is absent from work during each week in respect of which statutory shared parental pay is paid to the claimant;

(p) that, where the claimant is an employee within the meaning of the Employment Rights Act 1996, the claimant's absence from work during each such week is absence on shared parental leave.

(5) Regulations may provide for—

(a) the determination of the extent of a person's entitlement to statutory shared parental pay in respect of a child;

(b) when statutory shared parental pay is to be payable.

(6) Provision under subsection (5)(a) is to secure that the number of weeks in respect of which a person is entitled to payments of statutory shared parental pay in respect of a child does not exceed the number of weeks of the maternity pay period reduced by—

(a) where the mother of the child takes action that is treated by regulations as constituting for the purposes of this section her return to work without satisfying conditions prescribed under subsection (2)(h) or, as the case may be, subsection (4)(i)—

(i) the number of relevant weeks in respect of which maternity allowance or statutory maternity pay is payable to the mother, or

(ii) if that number of relevant weeks is less than a number prescribed by regulations, that prescribed number of weeks, or

(b) except where paragraph (a) applies, the number of weeks to which the maternity allowance period is reduced by virtue of section 35(3A) or, as the case may be, the maternity pay period is reduced by virtue of section 165(3A).

(7) In subsection (6)(a) "relevant week" means—

(a) where maternity allowance is payable to a mother, a week or part of a week falling before the time at which the mother takes action that is treated by regulations as constituting for the purposes of this section her return to work;

(b) where statutory maternity pay is payable to a mother, a week falling before the week in which the mother takes action that is so treated.

For these purposes "week" has the meaning given by section 122(1), in relation to maternity allowance, or the meaning given by section 165(8), in relation to statutory maternity pay.

(8) In determining the number of weeks for the purposes of subsection (6)(b)—

(a) "week" has the same meaning as in subsection (7), and

(b) a part of a week is to be treated as a week.

(9) Provision under subsection (5)(a) is to secure that, where two persons are entitled to payments of statutory shared parental pay in respect of a child, the extent of one's entitlement and the extent of the other's entitlement do not, taken together, exceed what would be available to one person (see subsection (6)).

(10) Provision under subsection (5)(b) is to secure that no payment of statutory shared parental pay may be made to a person in respect of a child after the end of such period as may be prescribed.

(11) Provision under subsection (5)(b) is to secure that no payment of statutory shared parental pay in respect of a child may be made to a person who is the mother of the child before the end of the mother's maternity pay period.

(12) Regulations may provide that, where the conditions in subsection (13) are satisfied in relation to a person who is entitled to statutory shared parental pay under subsection (1) or (3) ("V"), V may vary the period or periods during which V intends to claim statutory shared parental pay in respect of the child in question, subject to complying with provision under subsection (14) where that is relevant.

(13) The conditions are—

(a) that V has given the person who will be liable to pay statutory shared parental pay to V notice of an intention to vary the period or periods during which V intends to claim statutory shared parental pay;

(b) that a notice under paragraph (a)—

(i) is given by such time as may be prescribed, and

(ii) satisfies prescribed conditions as to form and content.

(14) Regulations may provide that, where the conditions in subsection (15) are satisfied in relation to a person who is entitled to statutory shared parental pay under subsection (1) or (3) ("V"), V may vary the number of weeks in respect of which V intends to claim statutory shared parental pay.

(15) The conditions are—

(a) that V has given the person who will be liable to pay statutory shared parental pay to V notice of—

(i) the extent to which V has exercised an entitlement to statutory shared parental pay in respect of the child,

(ii) the extent to which V intends to claim statutory shared parental pay in respect of the child,

(iii) the extent to which another person has exercised an entitlement to statutory shared parental pay in respect of the child, and

(iv) the extent to which another person intends to claim statutory shared parental pay in respect of the child;

(b) that a notice under paragraph (a)—

(i) is given by such time as may be prescribed, and

(ii) satisfies prescribed conditions as to form and content;

(c) that the person who is P or, as the case may be, M in relation to V consents to that variation.

(16) A person's entitlement to statutory shared parental pay under this section is not affected by the birth of more than one child as a result of the same pregnancy.[

NOTES

Commencement: 30 June 2014.

Inserted as noted at the beginning of this Part.

Application to parental order parents and to adoptions from overseas: see the introductory notes to this Part.

Regulations: the Statutory Shared Parental Pay (General) Regulations 2014, SI 2014/3051 at **[2.1625]**; the Statutory Shared Parental Pay (General) (Amendment) Regulations 2015, SI 2015/189.

[1.241]

[171ZV Entitlement: adoption

(1) Regulations may provide that, where all the conditions in subsection (2) are satisfied in relation to a person with whom a child is, or is expected to be, placed for adoption under the law of any part of the United Kingdom ("claimant A"), claimant A is to be entitled in accordance with the following provisions of this Part to payments to be known as "statutory shared parental pay".

(2) The conditions are—

(a) that claimant A and another person ("X") satisfy prescribed conditions as to caring or intending to care for the child;

(b) that X satisfies prescribed conditions—

(i) as to employment or self-employment,

(ii) as to having earnings of a prescribed amount for a prescribed period, and

(iii) as to relationship either with the child or with claimant A;

(c) that claimant A has been in employed earner's employment with an employer for a continuous period of at least the prescribed length ending with a prescribed week;

(d) that at the end of that prescribed week claimant A was entitled to be in that employment;

(e) that claimant A's normal weekly earnings for a prescribed period ending with a prescribed week are not less than the lower earnings limit in force under section 5(1)(a) at the end of that week;

(f) if regulations so provide, that claimant A continues in employed earner's employment (whether or not with the employer by reference to whom the condition in paragraph (c) is satisfied) until a prescribed time;

(g) that claimant A became entitled to statutory adoption pay by reference to the placement for adoption of the child;

(h) that claimant A satisfies prescribed conditions as to the reduction of the duration of the adoption pay period;

(i) that claimant A has given the person who will be liable to pay statutory shared parental pay to claimant A notice of—

(i) the number of weeks in respect of which claimant A would be entitled to claim statutory shared parental pay in respect of the child if the entitlement were fully exercised (disregarding for these purposes any intention of X to claim statutory shared parental pay in respect of the child),

(ii) the number of weeks in respect of which claimant A intends to claim statutory shared parental pay, and

(iii) the number of weeks in respect of which X intends to claim statutory shared parental pay;

(j) that claimant A has given the person who will be liable to pay statutory shared parental pay to claimant A notice of the period or periods during which claimant A intends to claim statutory shared parental pay in respect of the child;

(k) that a notice under paragraph (i) or (j)—

(i) is given by such time as may be prescribed, and

(ii) satisfies prescribed conditions as to form and content;

(l) that X consents to the extent of claimant A's intended claim for statutory shared parental pay;

(m) that it is claimant A's intention to care for the child during each week in respect of which statutory shared parental pay is paid to claimant A;

(n) that claimant A is absent from work during each week in respect of which statutory shared parental pay is paid to claimant A;

(o) that, where claimant A is an employee within the meaning of the Employment Rights Act 1996, claimant A's absence from work during each such week is absence on shared parental leave.

(3) Regulations may provide that, where all the conditions in subsection (4) are satisfied in relation to a person ("claimant B"), claimant B is to be entitled in accordance with the following provisions of this Part to payments to be known as "statutory shared parental pay".

(4) The conditions are—

(a) that claimant B and another person ("Y") who is a person with whom a child is, or is expected to be, placed for adoption under the law of any part of the United Kingdom satisfy prescribed conditions as to caring or intending to care for the child;

(b) that claimant B satisfies—

(i) prescribed conditions as to relationship with the child, or

(ii) prescribed conditions as to relationship with Y;

(c) that Y satisfies prescribed conditions—

(i) as to employment or self-employment, and

(ii) as to having earnings of a prescribed amount for a prescribed period;

(d) that claimant B has been in employed earner's employment with an employer for a continuous period of at least the prescribed length ending with a prescribed week;

(e) that at the end of that prescribed week claimant B was entitled to be in that employment;

(f) that claimant B's normal weekly earnings for a prescribed period ending with a prescribed week are not less than the lower earnings limit in force under section 5(1)(a) at the end of that week;
(g) if regulations so provide, that claimant B continues in employed earner's employment (whether or not with the employer by reference to whom the condition in paragraph (d) is satisfied) until a prescribed time;
(h) that Y became entitled to statutory adoption pay by reference to the placement for adoption of the child;
(i) that Y satisfies prescribed conditions as to the reduction of the duration of the adoption pay period;
(j) that claimant B has given the person who will be liable to pay statutory shared parental pay to claimant B notice of—
(i) the number of weeks in respect of which claimant B would be entitled to claim statutory shared parental pay in respect of the child if the entitlement were fully exercised (disregarding for these purposes any intention of Y to claim statutory shared parental pay in respect of the child),
(ii) the number of weeks in respect of which claimant B intends to claim statutory shared parental pay, and
(iii) the number of weeks in respect of which Y intends to claim statutory shared parental pay;
(k) that claimant B has given the person who will be liable to pay statutory shared parental pay to claimant B notice of the period or periods during which claimant B intends to claim statutory shared parental pay in respect of the child;
(l) that a notice under paragraph (j) or (k)—
(i) is given by such time as may be prescribed, and
(ii) satisfies prescribed conditions as to form and content;
(m) that Y consents to the extent of claimant B's intended claim for statutory shared parental pay;
(n) that it is claimant B's intention to care for the child during each week in respect of which statutory shared parental pay is paid to claimant B;
(o) that claimant B is absent from work during each week in respect of which statutory shared parental pay is paid to claimant B;
(p) that, where claimant B is an employee within the meaning of the Employment Rights Act 1996, claimant B's absence from work during each such week is absence on shared parental leave.

(5) Regulations may provide for—
(a) the determination of the extent of a person's entitlement to statutory shared parental pay in respect of a child;
(b) when statutory shared parental pay is to be payable.

(6) Provision under subsection (5)(a) is to secure that the number of weeks in respect of which a person is entitled to payments of statutory shared parental pay in respect of a child does not exceed the number of weeks of the adoption pay period reduced by—
(a) where the person who became entitled to receive statutory adoption pay takes action that is treated by regulations as constituting for the purposes of this section the person's return to work without satisfying conditions prescribed under subsection (2)(h) or, as the case may be, subsection (4)(i)—
(i) the number of relevant weeks in respect of which statutory adoption pay is payable to the person, or
(ii) if that number of relevant weeks is less than a number prescribed by regulations, that prescribed number of weeks, or
(b) except where paragraph (a) applies, the number of weeks to which the adoption pay period has been reduced by virtue of section 171ZN(2A).

(7) In subsection (6)(a) "relevant week" means a week falling before the week in which a person takes action that is treated by regulations as constituting for the purposes of this section the person's return to work, and for these purposes "week" has the meaning given by section 171ZN(8).

(8) In determining the number of weeks for the purposes of subsection (6)(b)—
(a) "week" has the same meaning as in subsection (7), and
(b) a part of a week is to be treated as a week.

(9) Provision under subsection (5)(a) is to secure that, where two persons are entitled to payments of statutory shared parental pay in respect of a child, the extent of one's entitlement and the extent of the other's entitlement do not, taken together, exceed what would be available to one person (see subsection (6)).

(10) Provision under subsection (5)(b) is to secure that no payment of statutory shared parental pay may be made to a person in respect of a child after the end of such period as may be prescribed.

(11) Provision under subsection (5)(b) is to secure that no payment of statutory shared parental pay in respect of a child may be made to a person who became entitled to receive statutory adoption pay in respect of the child before the end of the person's adoption pay period.

(12) Regulations may provide that, where the conditions in subsection (13) are satisfied in relation to a person who is entitled to statutory shared parental pay under subsection (1) or (3) ("V"), V may vary the period or periods during which V intends to claim statutory shared parental pay in respect of the child in question, subject to complying with provision under subsection (14) where that is relevant.

(13) The conditions are—
(a) that V has given the person who will be liable to pay statutory shared parental pay to V notice of an intention to vary the period or periods during which V intends to claim statutory shared parental pay;
(b) that a notice under paragraph (a)—

(i) is given by such time as may be prescribed, and
(ii) satisfies prescribed conditions as to form and content.

(14) Regulations may provide that, where the conditions in subsection (15) are satisfied in relation to a person who is entitled to statutory shared parental pay under subsection (1) or (3) ("V"), V may vary the number of weeks in respect of which V intends to claim statutory shared parental pay.

(15) The conditions are—

(a) that V has given the person who will be liable to pay statutory shared parental pay to V notice of—
(i) the extent to which V has exercised an entitlement to statutory shared parental pay in respect of the child,
(ii) the extent to which V intends to claim statutory shared parental pay in respect of the child,
(iii) the extent to which another person has exercised an entitlement to statutory shared parental pay in respect of the child, and
(iv) the extent to which another person intends to claim statutory shared parental pay in respect of the child;
(b) that a notice under paragraph (a)—
(i) is given by such time as may be prescribed, and
(ii) satisfies prescribed conditions as to form and content;
(c) that the person who is X or, as the case may be, Y in relation to V consents to that variation.

(16) A person's entitlement to statutory shared parental pay under this section is not affected by the placement for adoption of more than one child as part of the same arrangement.

[(17) Regulations are to provide for entitlement to statutory shared parental pay in respect of a child placed, or expected to be placed—

(a) under section 22C of the Children Act 1989 by a local authority in England, or
(b) under section 81 of the Social Services and Well-being (Wales) Act 2014 by a local authority in Wales,

with a local authority foster parent who has been approved as a prospective adopter.

(18) This section has effect in relation to regulations made by virtue of subsection (17) as if—

(a) references to a child being placed for adoption under the law of any part of the United Kingdom were references to being placed under section 22C of the Children Act 1989 or section 81 of the Social Services and Well-being (Wales) Act 2014 with a local authority foster parent who has been approved as a prospective adopter;
(b) references to a placement for adoption were references to placement under section 22C of the Children Act 1989 or section 81 of the Social Services and Well-being (Wales) Act 2014 with such a person.]]

NOTES

Commencement: 30 June 2014.

Inserted as noted at the beginning of this Part.

Sub-s (17), (18): substituted by the Social Services and Well-being (Wales) Act 2014 (Consequential Amendments) Regulations 2016, SI 2016/413, regs 130, 138, as from 6 April 2016.

Application to parental order parents and to adoptions from overseas: see the introductory notes to this Part.

Regulations: the Statutory Shared Parental Pay (General) Regulations 2014, SI 2014/3051 at **[2.1625]**; the Statutory Shared Parental Pay (Adoption from Overseas) Regulations 2014, SI 2014/3093 at **[2.1725]**; the Statutory Shared Parental Pay (Parental Order Cases) Regulations 2014, SI 2014/3097 at **[2.1784]**; the Statutory Shared Parental Pay (General) (Amendment) Regulations 2015, SI 2015/189.

[1.242]

[171ZW Entitlement: general

(1) Regulations may—

(a) provide that the following do not have effect, or have effect subject to prescribed modifications, in such cases as may be prescribed—
(i) section 171ZU(2)(a) to (o),
(ii) section 171ZU(4)(a) to (p),
(iii) section 171ZU(13)(a) and (b),
(iv) section 171ZU(15)(a) to (c),
(v) section 171ZV(2)(a) to (o),
(vi) section 171ZV(4)(a) to (p),
(vii) section 171ZV(13)(a) and (b), and
(viii) section 171ZV(15)(a) to (c);
(b) impose requirements about evidence of entitlement and procedures to be followed;
(c) specify in what circumstances employment is to be treated as continuous for the purposes of section 171ZU or 171ZV;
(d) provide that a person is to be treated for the purposes of section 171ZU or 171ZV as being employed for a continuous period of at least the prescribed period where—
(i) the person has been employed by the same employer for at least the prescribed period under two or more separate contracts of service, and
(ii) those contracts were not continuous;
(e) provide for amounts earned by a person under separate contracts of service with the same employer to be aggregated for the purposes of section 171ZU or 171ZV;
(f) provide that—
(i) the amount of a person's earnings for any period, or

(ii) the amount of the person's earnings to be treated as comprised in any payment made to the person or for the person's benefit,

are to be calculated or estimated for the purposes of section 171ZU or 171ZV in such manner and on such basis as may be prescribed and that for that purpose payments of a particular class or description made or falling to be made to or by a person are, to such extent as may be prescribed, to be disregarded or, as the case may be, to be deducted from the amount of the person's earnings.

(2) The persons upon whom requirements may be imposed by virtue of subsection (1)(b) include—

(a) a person who, in connection with another person's claim to be paid statutory shared parental pay, is required to satisfy conditions prescribed under section 171ZU(2)(b) or (4)(c) or 171ZV(2)(b) or (4)(c);

(b) an employer or former employer of such a person.

(3) In subsection (1)(d) "the prescribed period" means the period of the length prescribed by regulations under section 171ZU(2)(c) or (4)(d) or 171ZV(2)(c) or (4)(d), as the case may be.]

NOTES

Commencement: 30 June 2014.

Inserted as noted at the beginning of this Part.

Application to parental order parents and to adoptions from overseas: see the introductory notes to this Part.

Regulations: the Statutory Shared Parental Pay (General) Regulations 2014, SI 2014/3051 at **[2.1625]**; the Statutory Shared Parental Pay (Adoption from Overseas) Regulations 2014, SI 2014/3093 at **[2.1725]**; the Statutory Shared Parental Pay (Parental Order Cases) Regulations 2014, SI 2014/3097 at **[2.1784]**; the Statutory Shared Parental Pay (General) (Amendment) Regulations 2015, SI 2015/189.

[1.243]

[171ZX Liability to make payments

(1) The liability to make payments of statutory shared parental pay under section 171ZU or 171ZV is a liability of any person of whom the person entitled to the payments has been an employee as mentioned in section 171ZU(2)(c) or (4)(d) or 171ZV(2)(c) or (4)(d), as the case may be.

(2) Regulations must make provision as to a former employer's liability to pay statutory shared parental pay to a person in any case where the former employee's contract of service with the person has been brought to an end by the former employer solely, or mainly, for the purpose of avoiding liability for statutory shared parental pay.

(3) The Secretary of State may, with the concurrence of the Commissioners for Her Majesty's Revenue and Customs, by regulations specify circumstances in which, notwithstanding this section, liability to make payments of statutory shared parental pay is to be a liability of the Commissioners.]

NOTES

Commencement: 30 June 2014.

Inserted as noted at the beginning of this Part.

Application to parental order parents and to adoptions from overseas: see the introductory notes to this Part.

Regulations: the Statutory Shared Parental Pay (General) Regulations 2014, SI 2014/3051 at **[2.1625]**; the Statutory Shared Parental Pay (Adoption from Overseas) Regulations 2014, SI 2014/3093 at **[2.1725]**; the Statutory Shared Parental Pay (Parental Order Cases) Regulations 2014, SI 2014/3097 at **[2.1784]**.

[1.244]

[171ZY Rate and period of pay

(1) Statutory shared parental pay is payable at such fixed or earnings-related weekly rate as may be prescribed by regulations, which may prescribe different kinds of rate for different cases.

(2) Subject to the following provisions of this section, statutory shared parental pay is payable to a person in respect of each week falling within a relevant period, up to the number of weeks determined in the case of that person in accordance with regulations under section 171ZU(5) or 171ZV(5).

(3) Except in such cases as may be prescribed, statutory shared parental pay is not payable to a person in respect of a week falling within a relevant period if it is not the person's intention at the beginning of the week to care for the child by reference to whom the person satisfies—

(a) the condition in section 171ZU(2)(a) or (4)(a), or

(b) the condition in section 171ZV(2)(a) or (4)(a).

(4) Except in such cases as may be prescribed, statutory shared parental pay is not payable to a person in respect of a week falling within a relevant period during any part of which week the person works for any employer.

(5) The Secretary of State may by regulations specify circumstances in which there is to be no liability to pay statutory shared parental pay in respect of a week falling within a relevant period.

(6) Where for any purpose of this Part or of regulations it is necessary to calculate the daily rate of statutory shared parental pay, the amount payable by way of statutory shared parental pay for any day shall be taken as one seventh of the weekly rate.

(7) For the purposes of this section a week falls within a relevant period if it falls within a period specified in a notice under—

(a) section 171ZU(2)(j), (4)(k) or (13)(a), or

(b) section 171ZV(2)(j), (4)(k) or (13)(a),

and is not afterwards excluded from such a period by a variation of the period or periods during which the person in question intends to claim statutory shared parental pay.

(8) In this section "week", in relation to a relevant period, means a period of seven days beginning with the day of the week on which the relevant period starts.]

NOTES

Commencement: 30 June 2014.

Inserted as noted at the beginning of this Part.

Application to parental order parents and to adoptions from overseas: see the introductory notes to this Part.

Regulations: the Statutory Shared Parental Pay (General) Regulations 2014, SI 2014/3051 at **[2.1625]**; the Statutory Shared Parental Pay (Adoption from Overseas) Regulations 2014, SI 2014/3093 at **[2.1725]**; the Statutory Shared Parental Pay (Parental Order Cases) Regulations 2014, SI 2014/3097 at **[2.1784]**.

[1.245]
[171ZZ Restrictions on contracting out

(1) An agreement is void to the extent that it purports—

(a) to exclude, limit or otherwise modify any provision of this Part, or

(b) to require a person to contribute (whether directly or indirectly) towards any costs incurred by that person's employer or former employer under this Part.

(2) For the avoidance of doubt, an agreement between an employer and an employee, authorising deductions from statutory shared parental pay which the employer is liable to pay to the employee in respect of any period, is not void by virtue of subsection (1)(a) if the employer—

(a) is authorised by that or another agreement to make the same deductions from any contractual remuneration which the employer is liable to pay in respect of the same period, or

(b) would be so authorised if the employer were liable to pay contractual remuneration in respect of that period.]

NOTES

Commencement: 30 June 2014.

Inserted as noted at the beginning of this Part.

Application to parental order parents and to adoptions from overseas: see the introductory notes to this Part.

[1.246]
[171ZZ1 Relationship with contractual remuneration

(1) Subject to subsections (2) and (3), any entitlement to statutory shared parental pay is not to affect any right of a person in relation to remuneration under any contract of service ("contractual remuneration").

(2) Subject to subsection (3)—

(a) any contractual remuneration paid to a person by an employer of that person in respect of any period is to go towards discharging any liability of that employer to pay statutory shared parental pay to that person in respect of that period; and

(b) any statutory shared parental pay paid by an employer to a person who is an employee of that employer in respect of any period is to go towards discharging any liability of that employer to pay contractual remuneration to that person in respect of that period.

(3) Regulations may make provision as to payments which are, and those which are not, to be treated as contractual remuneration for the purposes of subsections (1) and (2).]

NOTES

Commencement: 30 June 2014.

Inserted as noted at the beginning of this Part.

Application to parental order parents and to adoptions from overseas: see the introductory notes to this Part.

Regulations: the Statutory Shared Parental Pay (General) Regulations 2014, SI 2014/3051 at **[2.1625]**; the Statutory Shared Parental Pay (Adoption from Overseas) Regulations 2014, SI 2014/3093 at **[2.1725]**; the Statutory Shared Parental Pay (Parental Order Cases) Regulations 2014, SI 2014/3097 at **[2.1784]**.

[1.247]
[171ZZ2 Crown employment

The provisions of this Part apply in relation to persons employed by or under the Crown as they apply in relation to persons employed otherwise than by or under the Crown.]

NOTES

Commencement: 30 June 2014.

Inserted as noted at the beginning of this Part.

Application to parental order parents and to adoptions from overseas: see the introductory notes to this Part.

[1.248]
[171ZZ3 Special classes of person

(1) The Secretary of State may with the concurrence of the Treasury make regulations modifying any provision of this Part in such manner as the Secretary of State thinks proper in its application to any person who is, has been or is to be—

(a) employed on board any ship, vessel, hovercraft or aircraft;

(b) outside Great Britain at any prescribed time or in any prescribed circumstances; or

(c) in prescribed employment in connection with continental shelf operations, as defined in section 120(2).

(2) Regulations under subsection (1) may, in particular, provide—

(a) for any provision of this Part to apply to any such person, notwithstanding that it would not otherwise apply;

(b) for any such provision not to apply to any such person, notwithstanding that it would otherwise apply;
(c) for excepting any such person from the application of any such provision where the person neither is domiciled nor has a place of residence in any part of Great Britain;
(d) for the taking of evidence, for the purposes of the determination of any question arising under any such provision, in a country or territory outside Great Britain, by a British consular official or such other person as may be determined in accordance with the regulations.]

NOTES

Commencement: 30 June 2014.
Inserted as noted at the beginning of this Part.
Application to parental order parents and to adoptions from overseas: see the introductory notes to this Part.
Regulations: the Statutory Shared Parental Pay (Persons Abroad and Mariners) Regulations 2014, SI 2014/3134 at **[2.1800]**.

[1.249]
[171ZZ4 Part 12ZC: supplementary

(1) In this Part—
"adoption pay period" has the meaning given in section 171ZN(2);
"employer", in relation to a person who is an employee, means a person who—
(a) under section 6 is liable to pay secondary Class 1 contributions in relation to any of the earnings of the person who is an employee, or
(b) would be liable to pay such contributions but for—
(i) the condition in section 6(1)(b), or
(ii) the employee being under the age of 16;
"local authority" has the same meaning as in the Children Act 1989 (see section 105(1) of that Act);
"local authority foster parent" has the same meaning as in the Children Act 1989 (see [section 105(1)] of that Act);
"maternity allowance period" has the meaning given in section 35(2);
"maternity pay period" has the meaning given in section 165(1);
"modifications" includes additions, omissions and amendments, and related expressions are to be read accordingly;
"prescribed" means prescribed by regulations.

(2) In this Part "employee" means a person who is gainfully employed in Great Britain either under a contract of service or in an office (including elective office) with general earnings (as defined by section 7 of the Income Tax (Earnings and Pensions) Act 2003).

(3) Regulations may provide—
(a) for cases where a person who falls within the definition in subsection (2) is not to be treated as an employee for the purposes of this Part, and
(b) for cases where a person who would not otherwise be an employee for the purposes of this Part is to be treated as an employee for those purposes.

(4) Without prejudice to any other power to make regulations under this Part, regulations may specify cases in which, for the purposes of this Part or of such provisions of this Part as may be prescribed—
(a) two or more employers are to be treated as one;
(b) two or more contracts of service in respect of which the same person is an employee are to be treated as one.

(5) In this Part, except where otherwise provided, "week" means a period of seven days beginning with Sunday or such other period as may be prescribed in relation to any particular case or class of cases.

(6) For the purposes of this Part, a person's normal weekly earnings are, subject to subsection (8), to be taken to be the average weekly earnings which in the relevant period have been paid to the person or paid for the person's benefit under the contract of service with the employer in question.

(7) For the purposes of subsection (6) "earnings" and "relevant period" have the meanings given to them by regulations.

(8) In such cases as may be prescribed, a person's normal weekly earnings are to be calculated in accordance with regulations.

(9) Where—
(a) in consequence of the establishment of one or more National Health Service trusts under the National Health Service Act 2006, the National Health Service (Wales) Act 2006 or the National Health Service (Scotland) Act 1978, a person's contract of employment is treated by a scheme under any of those Acts as divided so as to constitute two or more contracts, or
(b) an order under paragraph 26(1) of Schedule 3 to the National Health Service Act 2006 provides that a person's contract of employment is so divided,

regulations may make provision enabling the person to elect for all of those contracts to be treated as one contract for the purposes of this Part or such provisions of this Part as may be prescribed.

(10) Regulations under subsection (9) may prescribe—
(a) the conditions that must be satisfied if a person is to be entitled to make such an election;
(b) the manner in which, and the time within which, such an election is to be made;
(c) the persons to whom, and the manner in which, notice of such an election is to be given;
(d) the information which a person who makes such an election is to provide, and the persons to whom, and the time within which, the person is to provide it;
(e) the time for which such an election is to have effect;
(f) which one of the person's employers under two or more contracts is to be regarded for the purposes of statutory shared parental pay as the person's employer under the contract.

(11) The powers under subsections (9) and (10) are without prejudice to any other power to make regulations under this Part.
(12) Regulations under any of subsections (4) to (10) must be made with the concurrence of the Commissioners for Her Majesty's Revenue and Customs.]

NOTES

Commencement: 30 June 2014.

Inserted as noted at the beginning of this Part.

Sub-s (1): words in square brackets in definition "local authority foster parent" substituted by the Social Services and Well-being (Wales) Act 2014 (Consequential Amendments) Regulations 2016, SI 2016/413, regs 130, 139, as from 6 April 2016.

Application to parental order parents and to adoptions from overseas: see the introductory notes to this Part.

Regulations: the Statutory Shared Parental Pay (General) Regulations 2014, SI 2014/3051 at **[2.1625]**; the Statutory Shared Parental Pay (Adoption from Overseas) Regulations 2014, SI 2014/3093 at **[2.1725]**; the Statutory Shared Parental Pay (Parental Order Cases) Regulations 2014, SI 2014/3097 at **[2.1784]**; the Statutory Shared Parental Pay (Persons Abroad and Mariners) Regulations 2014, SI 2014/3134 at **[2.1800]**; the Statutory Paternity Pay, Statutory Adoption Pay and Statutory Shared Parental Pay (Amendment) Regulations 2015, SI 2015/2065.

[1.250]

[171ZZ5 Power to apply Part 12ZC

(1) The Secretary of State may by regulations provide for this Part to have effect in relation to cases which involve adoption, but not the placement of a child for adoption under the law of any part of the United Kingdom, with such modifications as the regulations may prescribe.
(2) The Secretary of State may by regulations provide for this Part to have effect in relation to cases which involve a person who has applied, or intends to apply, with another person for a parental order under section 54 of the Human Fertilisation and Embryology Act 2008 and a child who is, or will be, the subject of the order, with such modifications as the regulations may prescribe.
(3) Where section 171ZW(1)(b) has effect in relation to such cases as are described in subsection (2), regulations under section 171ZW(1)(b) may impose requirements to make statutory declarations as to—
 (a) eligibility to apply for a parental order;
 (b) intention to apply for such an order.]

NOTES

Commencement: 30 June 2014.

Inserted as noted at the beginning of this Part.

Application to parental order parents and to adoptions from overseas: see the introductory notes to this Part.

Regulations: the Social Security Contributions and Benefits Act 1992 (Application of Parts 12ZA and 12ZB to Adoptions from Overseas) (Amendment) Regulations 2014, SI 2014/2857; the Social Security Contributions and Benefits Act 1992 (Application of Parts 12ZA, 12ZB and 12ZC to Parental Order Cases) Regulations 2014, SI 2014/2866 at **[2.1529]**.

[PART 12ZD
STATUTORY PARENTAL BEREAVEMENT PAY

NOTES

Commencement: to be appointed.

Part 12ZD (ss 171ZZ6–171ZZ15) is inserted by the Parental Bereavement (Leave and Pay) Act 2018, s 1(b), Schedule, Pt 2, para 5, as from a day to be appointed.

[1.251]

171ZZ6 Entitlement

(1) A person who satisfies the conditions in subsection (2) is entitled in accordance with the following provisions of this Part to payments to be known as "statutory parental bereavement pay".
(2) The conditions are—
 (a) that the person is a bereaved parent,
 (b) that the person has been in employed earner's employment with an employer for a continuous period of at least 26 weeks ending with the relevant week,
 (c) that at the end of the relevant week the person was entitled to be in that employment (but see subsection (7)),
 (d) that the person's normal weekly earnings for the period of 8 weeks ending with the relevant week are not less than the lower earnings limit in force under section 5(1)(a) at the end of the relevant week, and
 (e) that the person has been in employed earner's employment with the employer by reference to whom the condition in paragraph (b) is satisfied for a continuous period beginning with the end of the relevant week and ending with the day on which the child dies.
(3) For the purposes of subsection (2) an employee is a "bereaved parent" if the employee satisfies prescribed conditions as to relationship with a child who has died.
(4) The conditions prescribed under subsection (3) may be framed, in whole or in part, by reference to the employee's care of the child before the child's death.
(5) In subsection (2) "relevant week" means the week immediately before the one in which the child dies.
(6) Where a person satisfies the conditions in subsection (2) as a result of the death of more than one child, the person is entitled to statutory parental bereavement pay in respect of each child.

(7) In relation to a bereaved parent whose child dies before the day on which section 63(3) of the Welfare Reform Act 2012 comes fully into force, subsection (2) above is to be read as if paragraph (c) were omitted.]

NOTES

Commencement: to be appointed.

Part 12ZD (this section and ss 171ZZ7–171ZZ15) is inserted by the Parental Bereavement (Leave and Pay) Act 2018, s 1(b), Schedule, Pt 2, para 5, as from a day to be appointed.

[1.252]

[171ZZ7 Entitlement: supplementary

(1) A person is entitled to payments of statutory parental bereavement pay in respect of any period only if the person gives notice to whoever is liable to make the payments stating the week or weeks in respect of which they are to be made.

(2) Regulations may provide for the time by which notice under subsection (1) must be given.

(3) The notice must be in writing if the person who is liable to pay the statutory parental bereavement pay so requests.

(4) The Secretary of State may by regulations—

(a) provide that section 171ZZ6(2)(b), (d) or (e) has effect subject to prescribed modifications in such cases as may be prescribed;

(b) provide for circumstances in which section 171ZZ6(2)(c) does not have effect;

(c) provide that subsection (1) of this section does not have effect, or has effect subject to prescribed modifications, in such cases as may be prescribed;

(d) impose requirements about evidence of entitlement;

(e) specify in what circumstances employment is to be treated as continuous for the purposes of section 171ZZ6;

(f) provide that a person is to be treated for the purposes of section 171ZZ6 as being employed for a continuous period of at least 26 weeks where—

(i) the person has been employed by the same employer for at least 26 weeks under two or more separate con-tracts of service, and

(ii) those contracts were not continuous;

(g) provide for amounts earned by a person under separate contracts of service with the same employer to be aggregated for the purposes of section 171ZZ6;

(h) provide that—

(i) the amount of a person's earnings for any period, or

(ii) the amount of the person's earnings to be treated as comprised in any payment made to the person or for the person's benefit,

is to be calculated or estimated for the purposes of section 171ZZ6 in such manner and on such basis as may be prescribed and that for that purpose payments of a particular class or description made or falling to be made to or by a person shall, to such extent as may be prescribed, be disregarded or, as the case may be, be deducted from the amount of the person's earnings.]

NOTES

Commencement: to be appointed.

Inserted as noted to s 171ZZ6 at **[1.251]**.

[1.253]

[171ZZ8 Liability to make payments

(1) The liability to make payments of statutory parental bereavement pay under section 171ZZ6 is a liability of any person of whom the person entitled to the payments has been an employee as mentioned in subsection (2)(b) and (e) of that section.

(2) The Secretary of State must by regulations make provision as to a former employer's liability to pay statutory parental bereavement pay to a former employee in any case where the employee's contract of service with the employer has been brought to an end by the employer solely, or mainly, for the purpose of avoiding liability for statutory parental bereavement pay.

(3) The Secretary of State may, with the concurrence of the Commissioners for Her Majesty's Revenue and Customs, by regulations specify circumstances in which, notwithstanding this section, liability to make payments of statutory parental bereavement pay is to be a liability of the Commissioners.]

NOTES

Commencement: to be appointed.

Inserted as noted to s 171ZZ6 at **[1.251]**.

[1.254]

[171ZZ9 Rate and period of pay

(1) Statutory parental bereavement pay is payable at such fixed or earnings-related weekly rate as may be prescribed by regulations, which may prescribe different kinds of rate for different cases.

(2) Statutory parental bereavement pay is payable in respect of—

(a) such week within the qualifying period, or

(b) such number of weeks, not exceeding the prescribed number of weeks, within the qualifying period,

as the person entitled may choose in accordance with regulations.

(3) Provision under subsection (2)(b) must secure that the prescribed number of weeks is not less than two.
(4) Regulations under subsection (2)(b) may permit a person entitled to receive statutory parental bereavement pay to choose to receive such pay in respect of non-consecutive periods each of which is a week or a number of weeks.
(5) For the purposes of subsection (2), the qualifying period is to be determined in accordance with regulations, which must secure that it is a period of at least 56 days beginning with the date of the child's death.
(6) A person is not liable to pay statutory parental bereavement pay to another in respect of any statutory pay week during any part of which the other works under a contract of service with the person.
(7) It is immaterial for the purposes of subsection (6) whether the work referred to in that subsection is work under a contract of service which existed immediately before the statutory pay week or a contract of service which did not so exist.
(8) Except in such cases as may be prescribed, statutory parental bereavement pay is not payable to a person in respect of a statutory pay week during any part of which the person works for any employer who is not liable to pay the person statutory parental bereavement pay.
(9) The Secretary of State may by regulations specify circumstances in which there is to be no liability to pay statutory parental bereavement pay in respect of a statutory pay week.
(10) Where for any purpose of this Part or of regulations it is necessary to calculate the daily rate of statutory parental bereavement pay, the amount payable by way of statutory parental bereavement pay for any day is to be taken as one seventh of the weekly rate.
(11) In this section—

"statutory pay week", in relation to a person entitled to statutory parental bereavement pay, means a week chosen by the person as a week in respect of which statutory parental bereavement pay is to be payable;

"week" means any period of seven days.]

NOTES

Commencement: to be appointed.
Inserted as noted to s 171ZZ6 at **[1.251]**.

[1.255]
[171ZZ10 Restrictions on contracting out

(1) An agreement is void to the extent that it purports—
- (a) to exclude, limit or otherwise modify any provision of this Part, or
- (b) to require a person to contribute (whether directly or indirectly) towards any costs incurred by that person's employer or former employer under this Part.

(2) An agreement between an employer and an employee, authorising any deductions from statutory parental bereavement pay which the employer is liable to pay to the employee in respect of any period, is not void by virtue of subsection (1)(a) if the employer—
- (a) is authorised by that or another agreement to make the same deductions from any contractual remuneration which the employer is liable to pay in respect of the same period, or
- (b) would be so authorised if the employer were liable to pay contractual remuneration in respect of that period.]

NOTES

Commencement: to be appointed.
Inserted as noted to s 171ZZ6 at **[1.251]**.

[1.256]
[171ZZ11 Relationship with contractual remuneration

(1) Subject to subsections (2) and (3), any entitlement to statutory parental bereavement pay does not affect any right of a person in relation to remuneration under any contract of service ("contractual remuneration").
(2) Subject to subsection (3)—
- (a) any contractual remuneration paid to a person by an employer of that person in respect of any period is to go towards discharging any liability of that employer to pay statutory parental bereavement pay to that person in respect of that period; and
- (b) any statutory parental bereavement pay paid by an employer to a person who is an employee of that employer in respect of any period is to go towards discharging any liability of that employer to pay contractual remuneration to that person in respect of that period.

(3) Regulations may make provision as to payments which are, and those which are not, to be treated as contractual remuneration for the purposes of subsections (1) and (2).]

NOTES

Commencement: to be appointed.
Inserted as noted to s 171ZZ6 at **[1.251]**.

[1.257]
[171ZZ12 Crown employment

The provisions of this Part apply in relation to persons employed by or under the Crown as they apply in relation to persons employed otherwise than by or under the Crown.]

NOTES

Commencement: to be appointed.
Inserted as noted to s 171ZZ6 at [1.251].

[1.258]

[171ZZ13 Special classes of person

(1) The Secretary of State may with the concurrence of the Treasury make regulations modifying any provision of this Part in such manner as the Secretary of State thinks proper in its application to any person who is, has been or is to be—

(a) employed on board any ship, vessel, hovercraft or aircraft;

(b) outside Great Britain at any prescribed time or in any prescribed circumstances; or

(c) in prescribed employment in connection with continental shelf operations, as defined in section 120(2).

(2) Regulations under subsection (1) may, in particular, provide—

(a) for any provision of this Part to apply to any such person, notwithstanding that it would not otherwise apply;

(b) for any such provision not to apply to any such person, notwithstanding that it would otherwise apply;

(c) for excepting any such person from the application of any such provision where the person neither is domiciled nor has a place of residence in any part of Great Britain;

(d) for the taking of evidence, for the purposes of the determination of any question arising under any such provision, in a country or territory outside Great Britain, by a British consular official or such other person as may be determined in accordance with the regulations.]

NOTES

Commencement: to be appointed.
Inserted as noted to s 171ZZ6 at [1.251].

[1.259]

[171ZZ14 Supplementary

(1) In this Part—

"child" means a person under the age of 18 (see also section 171ZZ15 for the application of this Part in relation to stillbirths);

"employer", in relation to a person who is an employee, means a person who—

(a) under section 6 is liable to pay secondary Class 1 contributions in relation to any of the earnings of the person who is an employee, or

(b) would be liable to pay such contributions but for—

(i) the condition in section 6(1)(b), or

(ii) the employee being under the age of 16;

"modifications" includes additions, omissions and amendments, and related expressions are to be read accordingly;

"prescribed" means prescribed by regulations.

(2) In this Part, "employee" means a person who is gainfully employed in Great Britain either under a contract of service or in an office (including elective office) with earnings (within the meaning of Parts 1 to 5).

(3) Regulations may provide—

(a) for cases where a person who falls within the definition in subsection (2) is not to be treated as an employee for the purposes of this Part, and

(b) for cases where a person who would not otherwise be an employee for the purposes of this Part is to be treated as an employee for those purposes.

(4) Without prejudice to any other power to make regulations under this Part, regulations may specify cases in which, for the purposes of this Part or of such provisions of this Part as may be prescribed—

(a) two or more employers are to be treated as one;

(b) two or more contracts of service in respect of which the same person is an employee are to be treated as one.

(5) In this Part, except section 171ZZ9, "week" means a period of 7 days beginning with Sunday or such other period as may be prescribed in relation to any particular case or class of cases.

(6) For the purposes of this Part, a person's normal weekly earnings are, subject to subsection (8), to be taken to be the average weekly earnings which in the relevant period have been paid to the person or paid for the person's benefit under the contract of service with the employer in question.

(7) For the purposes of subsection (6), "earnings" and "relevant period" have the meanings given to them by regulations.

(8) In such cases as may be prescribed, a person's normal weekly earnings are to be calculated in accordance with regulations.

(9) Where in consequence of the establishment of one or more National Health Service trusts under the National Health Service (Wales) Act 2006, a person's contract of employment is treated by a scheme under that Act as divided so as to constitute two or more contracts, regulations may make provision enabling the person to elect for all of those contracts to be treated as one contract for the purposes of this Part or such provisions of this Part as may be prescribed.

(10) Regulations under subsection (9) may prescribe—

(a) the conditions that must be satisfied if a person is to be entitled to make such an election;

(b) the manner in which, and the time within which, such an election is to be made;
(c) the persons to whom, and the manner in which, notice of such an election is to be given;
(d) the information which a person who makes such an election is to provide, and the persons to whom, and the time within which, the person is to provide it;
(e) the time for which such an election is to have effect;
(f) which one of the person's employers under two or more contracts is to be regarded for the purposes of statutory parental bereavement pay as the person's employer under the contract.

(11) The powers under subsections (9) and (10) are without prejudice to any other power to make regulations under this Part.

(12) Regulations under any of subsections (4) to (10) must be made with the concurrence of the Commissioners for Her Majesty's Revenue and Customs.]

NOTES

Commencement: to be appointed.
Inserted as noted to s 171ZZ6 at **[1.251]**.

[1.260]

[171ZZ15 Application in relation to stillbirths

In this Part—

(a) references to a child include a child stillborn after twenty-four weeks of pregnancy, and
(b) references to the death of a child are to be read, in relation to a stillborn child, as references to the birth of the child.]

NOTES

Commencement: to be appointed.
Inserted as noted to s 171ZZ6 at **[1.251]**.

PART XIII
GENERAL

Short title, commencement and extent

[1.261]

177 Short title, commencement and extent

(1) This Act may be cited as the Social Security Contributions and Benefits Act 1992.
(2) *(Outside the scope of this work.)*
(3) The enactments consolidated by this Act are repealed, in consequence of the consolidation, by the Consequential Provisions Act.
(4) Except as provided in Schedule 4 to the Consequential Provisions Act, this Act shall come into force on 1st July 1992.
(5), (6) *(Outside the scope of this work.)*

SCHEDULES

SCHEDULE 11
CIRCUMSTANCES IN WHICH PERIODS OF ENTITLEMENT TO STATUTORY SICK PAY DO NOT ARISE

Section 153(3)

[1.262]

1. A period of entitlement does not arise in relation to a particular period of incapacity for work in any of the circumstances set out in paragraph 2 below or in such other circumstances as may be prescribed.

[**1A.** Regulations under paragraph 1 above must be made with the concurrence of the Treasury.]

2. The circumstances are that—

(a), (b) . . .
(c) at the relevant date the employee's normal weekly earnings are less than the lower earnings limit then in force under section 5(1)(a) above;
[(d) in the period of 57 days ending immediately before the relevant date the employee had at least one day on which—
  (i) he was entitled to incapacity benefit (or would have been so entitled had he satisfied the contribution conditions mentioned in section 30A(2)(a) above), . . .
  (ii), (iii). . .]
[(dd) in the period of 85 days ending immediately before the relevant date the employee had at least one day on which he was entitled to an employment and support allowance (or would have been so entitled had he satisfied the requirements in section 1(2) of the Welfare Reform Act 2007;]
(f) the employee has done no work for his employer under his contract of service;
(g) on the relevant date there is . . . a stoppage of work due to a trade dispute at the employee's place of employment;
(h) the employee is, or has been, pregnant and the relevant date falls within the disqualifying period (within the meaning of section 153(12) above);
[(i) the employee is not entitled to be in his employment on the relevant date].

3. In this Schedule "relevant date" means the date on which a period of entitlement would begin in accordance with section 153 above if this Schedule did not prevent it arising.

4, 5. . . .

[5A. (1) Paragraph 2(d)(i) above does not apply if, at the relevant date, the employee is over pensionable age and is not entitled to incapacity benefit.

(2) Paragraph 2(d)(i) above ceases to apply if, at any time after the relevant date, the employee is over pensionable age and is not entitled to incapacity benefit.

(3) In this paragraph "pensionable age" has the meaning given by the rules in paragraph 1 of Schedule 4 to the Pensions Act 1995.]

6. For the purposes of paragraph 2(f) above, if an employee enters into a contract of service which is to take effect not more than 8 weeks after the date on which a previous contract of service entered into by him with the same employer ceased to have effect, the two contracts shall be treated as one.

7. Paragraph 2(g) above does not apply in the case of an employee who proves that at no time on or before the relevant date did he have a direct interest in the trade dispute in question.

8. Paragraph 2(h) above does not apply in relation to an employee who has been pregnant if her pregnancy terminated, before the beginning of the disqualifying period, otherwise than by confinement (as defined for the purposes of statutory maternity pay in section 171(1) above).

[9. Paragraph 2(i) above does not apply in prescribed circumstances.]

NOTES

Para 1A: inserted by the Social Security Contributions (Transfer of Functions, etc) Act 1999, s 1(1), Sch 1, para 20.

Para 2: sub-para (a) repealed by the Employment Equality (Age) Regulations 2006, SI 2006/1031, reg 49(1), Sch 8, Pt 1, paras 8, 13(1); sub-para (b) repealed by the Fixed-term Employees (Prevention of Less Favourable Treatment) Regulations 2002, SI 2002/2034, reg 11, Sch 2, Pt 1, para 1(a); sub-para (d) substituted (for the original sub-paras (d), (e)) by the Social Security (Incapacity for Work) Act 1994, s 11, Sch 1, Pt I, para 43, Sch 2; sub-para (d)(i) repealed by the Welfare Reform Act 2007, s 67, Sch 8, as from a day to be appointed; word omitted from sub-para (d)(i), and sub-para (d)(iii), repealed by the Welfare Reform and Pensions Act 1999, s 88, Sch 13, Pt IV; sub-para (d)(ii) repealed by the Social Security Act 1998, ss 73, 86(2), Sch 8; sub-para (dd) inserted by the Employment and Support Allowance (Consequential Provisions) (No 2) Regulations 2008, SI 2008/1554, reg 44; words omitted from sub-para (g) repealed by the Jobseekers Act 1995, s 41(5), Sch 3; sub-para (i) added by the Welfare Reform Act 2012, s 63(1), (10)(a), as from a day to be appointed.

Para 4: repealed by SI 2002/2034, reg 11, Sch 2, Pt 1, para 1(b).

Para 5: repealed by the Social Security (Incapacity for Work) Act 1994, s 11, Sch 1, Pt I, para 43, Sch 2.

Para 5A: inserted by the Employment Equality (Age) (Consequential Amendments) Regulations 2007, SI 2007/825, reg 2.

Para 9: added by the Welfare Reform Act 2012, s 63(1), (10)(b), as from a day to be appointed.

Regulations: the Statutory Sick Pay (General) Regulations 1982, SI 1982/894 at **[2.44]**, and the Statutory Sick Pay (Mariners, Airmen and Persons Abroad) Regulations 1982, SI 1982/1349, have effect as if made under this Schedule by virtue of the Social Security (Consequential Provisions) Act 1992, s 2(2); the Social Security (Welfare to Work) Regulations 1998, SI 1998/2231; the Social Security, Statutory Maternity Pay and Statutory Sick Pay (Miscellaneous Amendments) Regulations 2002, SI 2002/2690.

SCHEDULE 12
RELATIONSHIP OF STATUTORY SICK PAY WITH BENEFITS AND OTHER PAYMENTS, ETC

Section 160

The general principle

[1.263]

1. Any day which—

(a) is a day of incapacity for work in relation to any contract of service; and

(b) falls within a period of entitlement (whether or not it is also a qualifying day),

shall not be treated for the purposes of this Act as a day of incapacity for work for the purposes of determining whether a period is . . . a period of incapacity for work for the purposes of incapacity benefit].

Contractual remuneration

2. (1) Subject to sub-paragraphs (2) and (3) below, any entitlement to statutory sick pay shall not affect any right of an employee in relation to remuneration under any contract of service ("contractual remuneration").

(2) Subject to sub-paragraph (3) below—

(a) any contractual remuneration paid to an employee by an employer of his in respect of a day of incapacity for work shall go towards discharging any liability of that employer to pay statutory sick pay to that employee in respect of that day; and

(b) any statutory sick pay paid by an employer to an employee of his in respect of a day of incapacity for work shall go towards discharging any liability of that employer to pay contractual remuneration to that employee in respect of that day.

(3) Regulations may make provision as to payments which are, and those which are not, to be treated as contractual remuneration for the purposes of sub-paragraph (1) or (2) above.

[Incapacity benefit

3. (1) This paragraph and paragraph 4 below have effect to exclude, where a period of entitlement as between an employee and an employer of his comes to an end, the provisions by virtue of which short-term incapacity benefit is not paid for the first three days.

(2) If the first day immediately following the day on which the period of entitlement came to an end—

(a) is the day of incapacity for work in relation to that employee, and

(b) is not a day in relation to which paragraph 1 above applies by reason of any entitlement as between the employee and another employer,

that day shall, except in prescribed cases, be or form part of a period of incapacity for work notwithstanding section 30C(1)(b) above (by virtue of which a period of incapacity for work must be at least 4 days long).

(3) Where each of the first two consecutive days, or the first three consecutive days, following the day on which the period of entitlement came to an end is a day to which paragraphs (a) and (b) of sub-paragraph (2) above apply, that sub-paragraph has effect in relation to the second day or, as the case may be, in relation to the second and third days, as it has effect in relation to the first.

4. (1) Where a period of entitlement as between an employee and an employer of his comes to an end, section 30A(3) above (exclusion of benefit for first 3 days of period) does not apply in relation to any day which—

(a) is or forms part of a period of incapacity for work (whether by virtue of paragraph 3 above or otherwise), and

(b) falls within the period of 57 days immediately following the day on which the period of entitlement came to an end.

(2) Where sub-paragraph (1) above applies in relation to a day, section 30A(3) above does not apply in relation to any later day in the same period of incapacity for work.

Incapacity benefit for widows and widowers

5. Paragraph 1 above does not apply for the purpose of determining whether the conditions specified in section 40(3) or (4) or 41(2) or (3) above are satisfied.]

Unemployability supplement

6. Paragraph 1 above does not apply in relation to paragraph 3 of Schedule 7 to this Act and accordingly the references in paragraph 3 of that Schedule to a period of interruption of employment shall be construed as if the provisions re-enacted in this Part of this Act had not been enacted.

NOTES

Para 1: repealed by the Welfare Reform Act 2007, s 67, Sch 8, as from a day to be appointed; words in square brackets inserted by the Social Security (Incapacity for Work) Act 1994, s 11, Sch 1, Pt I, para 44; words omitted repealed by the Jobseekers Act 1995, s 41(5), Sch 3.

Paras 3–5: substituted by the Social Security (Incapacity for Work) Act 1994, s 11, Sch 1, Pt I, para 44; repealed by the Welfare Reform Act 2007, s 67, Sch 8, as from a day to be appointed.

Para 6: repealed by the Welfare Reform Act 2007, s 67, Sch 8, as from a day to be appointed.

Regulations: the Statutory Sick Pay (General) Regulations 1982, SI 1982/894 at **[2.44]** have effect as if made under this Schedule by virtue of the Social Security (Consequential Provisions) Act 1992, s 2(2).

SCHEDULE 13
RELATIONSHIP OF STATUTORY MATERNITY PAY WITH BENEFITS AND OTHER PAYMENTS, ETC

Section 168

The general principle

[1.264]

[1. Except as may be prescribed, a day which falls within the maternity pay period shall not be treated as a day of incapacity for work for the purposes of determining, for this Act, whether it forms part of a period of incapacity for work for the purposes of incapacity benefit.]

[Incapacity benefit

2. (1) Regulations may provide that in prescribed circumstances a day which falls within the maternity pay period shall be treated as a day of incapacity for work for the purpose of determining entitlement to the higher rate of short-term incapacity benefit or to long-term incapacity benefit.

(2) Regulations may provide that an amount equal to a woman's statutory maternity pay for a period shall be deducted from any such benefit in respect of the same period and a woman shall be entitled to such benefit only if there is a balance after the deduction and, if there is such a balance, at a weekly rate equal to it.]

Contractual remuneration

3. (1) Subject to sub-paragraphs (2) and (3) below, any entitlement to statutory maternity pay shall not affect any right of a woman in relation to remuneration under any contract of service ("contractual remuneration").

(2) Subject to sub-paragraph (3) below—

(a) any contractual remuneration paid to a woman by an employer of hers in respect of a week in the maternity pay period shall go towards discharging any liability of that employer to pay statutory maternity pay to her in respect of that week; and

(b) any statutory maternity pay paid by an employer to a woman who is an employee of his in respect of a week in the maternity pay period shall go towards discharging any liability of that employer to pay contractual remuneration to her in respect of that week.

[(2A) In sub-paragraph (2) "week" means a period of seven days beginning with the day of the week on which the maternity pay period begins.]

(3) Regulations may make provision as to payments which are, and those which are not, to be treated as contractual remuneration for the purposes of sub-paragraphs (1) and (2) above.

NOTES

Para 1: substituted by the Jobseekers Act 1995, s 41(4), Sch 2, para 37; repealed by the Welfare Reform Act 2007, s 67, Sch 8, as from a day to be appointed.

Para 2: substituted by the Social Security (Incapacity for Work) Act 1994, s 11(1), Sch 1, Pt I, para 45(1), (3); repealed by the Welfare Reform Act 2007, s 67, Sch 8, as from a day to be appointed.

Para 3: sub-para (2A) inserted by the Work and Families Act 2006, s 11(1), Sch 1, para 23.

Regulations: the Statutory Maternity Pay (General) Regulations 1986, SI 1986/1960 at **[2.73]** have effect as if made under this Schedule by virtue of the Social Security (Consequential Provisions) Act 1992, s 2(2); the Social Security, Statutory Maternity Pay and Statutory Sick Pay (Miscellaneous Amendments) Regulations 2002, SI 2002/2690.

OFFSHORE SAFETY ACT 1992

(1992 c 15)

An Act to extend the application of Part I of the Health and Safety at Work etc Act 1974; to increase the penalties for certain offences under that Part; to confer powers for preserving the security of supplies of petroleum and petroleum products; and for connected purposes

[6 March 1992]

NOTES

Regulatory functions: the regulatory functions conferred by, or under, this Act are subject to the Legislative and Regulatory Reform Act 2006, ss 21, 22; see the Legislative and Regulatory Reform (Regulatory Functions) Order 2007, SI 2007/3544 (made under s 24(2) of the 2006 Act) for details.

[1.265]

1 Application of Part I of 1974 Act for offshore purposes

(1) The general purposes of Part I of the Health and Safety at Work etc Act 1974 ("the 1974 Act") shall include—

(a) securing the safety, health and welfare of persons on offshore installations or engaged on pipe-line works;

(b) securing the safety of such installations and preventing accidents on or near them;

(c) securing the proper construction and safe operation of pipe-lines and preventing damage to them; and

(d) securing the safe dismantling, removal and disposal of offshore installations and pipe-lines;

and that Part shall have effect as if the provisions mentioned in subsection (3) below were existing statutory provisions within the meaning of that Part and, in the case of the enactments there mentioned, were specified in the third column of Schedule 1 to that Act.

(2) Without prejudice to the generality of subsection (1) of section 15 of the 1974 Act (health and safety regulations), regulations under that section may—

(a) repeal or modify any of the provisions mentioned in subsection (3) below; and

(b) make any provision which, but for any such repeal or modification, could be made by regulations or orders made under any enactment there mentioned.

(3) The provisions referred to in subsections (1) and (2) above are—

(a) the Mineral Workings (Offshore Installations) Act 1971;

[(b) sections 10 and 25 of the Petroleum Act 1998;]

(c) in the Petroleum Act 1987, . . . sections 11 to 24 (safety zones); and

(d) the provisions of any regulations or orders made or having effect under any enactment mentioned in the foregoing paragraphs.

(4) In this section—

"offshore installation" means any installation which is an offshore installation within the meaning of the Mineral Workings (Offshore Installations) Act 1971, or is to be taken to be an installation for the purposes of sections 11 to 23 of the Petroleum Act 1987;

["pipe-line" means, subject to subsection (4A), a controlled pipeline within the meaning of Part III of the Petroleum Act 1998; and

"pipe-line works" means works of any of the following kinds, namely—

(a) assembling or placing a pipe-line or length of pipe-line;

(b) inspecting, testing, maintaining, adjusting, repairing, altering or renewing a pipe-line or length of pipe-line;

(c) changing the position of or dismantling or removing a pipe-line or length of pipe-line;

(d) opening the bed of the sea for the purposes of works mentioned in paragraphs (a) to (c), tunnelling or boring for those purposes and other works needed for or incidental to those purposes;

(e) works for the purpose of determining whether a place is suitable as part of the site of a proposed pipe-line and the carrying out of surveying operations for the purpose of settling the route of a proposed pipe-line.]

[(4A) In this section "pipe-line" does not include—

(a) any pipe-line so far as it forms part of the equipment of a vessel or vehicle; or

(b) any apparatus and works associated with a pipe or system of pipes and prescribed for the purpose of this paragraph by regulations made by the Secretary of State.

(4B) A statutory instrument containing regulations made by virtue of subsection (4A) shall be subject to annulment in pursuance of a resolution of either House of Parliament; and section 25 of the Petroleum Act 1998 shall apply in relation to any such regulations as it applies in relation to regulations under section 20 of that Act.]

(5) The provisions mentioned in subsection (3) above and the definitions in subsection (4) above shall have effect as if any reference in—

(a) section 1(4) of the Mineral Workings (Offshore Installations) Act 1971;

(b) . . .

(c) section . . . 21(7) of the Petroleum Act 1987[; or

(d) section 14(2) or 45 of the Petroleum Act 1998,]

to tidal waters and parts of the sea in or adjacent to the United Kingdom, or to the territorial sea adjacent to the United Kingdom, were a reference to tidal waters and parts of the sea in or adjacent to Great Britain, or to the territorial sea adjacent to Great Britain.

NOTES

Sub-s (3): para (b) substituted, and words omitted from para (c) repealed, by the Petroleum Act 1998, ss 50, 51(1), Sch 4, para 33(1), (2)(a), Sch 5, Pt I.

Sub-s (4): definitions "pipe-line" and "pipe-line works" substituted by the Petroleum Act 1998, s 50, Sch 4, para 33(1), (2)(b).

Sub-ss (4A), (4B): inserted by the Petroleum Act 1998, s 50, Sch 4, para 33(1), (2)(c).

Sub-s (5): para (b) and words omitted from para (c) repealed, and para (d) and word immediately preceding it inserted, by the Petroleum Act 1998, ss 50, 51(1), Sch 4, para 33(1), (2)(d), Sch 5, Pt I.

Regulations: the Offshore Safety (Repeals and Modifications) Regulations 1993, SI 1993/1823; the Offshore Safety (Miscellaneous Amendments) Regulations 2002, SI 2002/2175; the Offshore Installations (Safety Case) Regulations 2005, SI 2005/3117.

[1.266]

2 Application of Part I for other purposes

(1) The general purposes of Part I of the 1974 Act shall include—

(a) securing the proper construction and safe operation of pipe-lines and preventing damage to them;

(b) securing that, in the event of the accidental escape or ignition of anything in a pipe-line, immediate notice of the event is given to persons who will or may have to discharge duties or take steps in consequence of the happening of the event; and

(c) protecting the public from personal injury, fire, explosions and other dangers arising from the transmission, distribution, supply or use of gas;

and that Part shall have effect as if the provisions mentioned in subsection (3) below were existing statutory provisions within the meaning of that Part and, in the case of the enactments there mentioned, were specified in the third column of Schedule 1 to that Act.

(2) Without prejudice to the generality of subsection (1) of section 15 of the 1974 Act (health and safety regulations), regulations under that section may—

(a) repeal or modify any of the provisions mentioned in subsection (3) below; and

(b) make any provision which, but for any such repeal or modification, could be made by regulations made under any enactment mentioned in paragraph (b) of that subsection.

(3) The provisions referred to in subsections (1) and (2) above are—

(a) sections 17 to 32 and 37 (avoidance of damage to pipe-lines and notification of accidents etc) of the Pipe-lines Act 1962;

(b) . . .

(c) the provisions of any regulations made or having effect under any enactment mentioned in paragraph (b) above.

(4) In this section—

"gas" means any substance which is or (if it were in a gaseous state) would be gas within the meaning of Part I of the Gas Act 1986;

"pipe-line" has the same meaning as in the Pipe-lines Act 1962.

NOTES

Sub-s (3): para (b) repealed by the Utilities Act 2000, s 108, Sch 8.

Regulations: the Offshore Safety (Repeals and Modifications) Regulations 1993, SI 1993/182.

3–6 *(S 3 (Provisions consequential on ss 1, 2) outside the scope of this work; s 4 (Increased penalties under Part I) repealed by the Health and Safety (Offences) Act 2008, s 2(1), Sch 4; s 5 (directions by the Secretary of State for preserving the security of petroleum and petroleum products), s 6 (corresponding provisions for Northern Ireland) both outside the scope of this work.)*

[1.267]
7 Short title, repeals, commencement and extent
(1) This Act may be cited as the Offshore Safety Act 1992.
(2) The enactments mentioned in Schedule 2 to this Act are hereby repealed to the extent specified in the third column of that Schedule.
(3) The following provisions of this Act, namely—
(a) section 2(3)(b) and (c);
(b) section 3(1)(a) and (e), (2) and (3)(b); and
(c) subsection (2) above so far as relating to the repeal in the Continental Shelf Act 1964 and the second repeal in the Gas Act 1986,

shall not come into force until such day as the Secretary of State may by order made by statutory instrument appoint, and different days may be appointed for different provisions or for different purposes.
(4) This Act, except section 6 above, does not extend to Northern Ireland.

NOTES

Orders: the Offshore Safety Act 1992 (Commencement No 1) Order 1993, SI 1993/2406; the Offshore Safety Act 1992 (Commencement No 2) Order 1996, SI 1996/487.

SCHEDULES 1 AND 2

(Sch 1 (model clauses), Sch 2 (repeals) outside the scope of this work.)

TRADE UNION AND LABOUR RELATIONS (CONSOLIDATION) ACT 1992

(1992 c 52)

ARRANGEMENT OF SECTIONS

PART I
TRADE UNIONS
CHAPTER I
INTRODUCTORY

Meaning of "trade union"

The list of trade unions

Certification as independent trade union

Supplementary

CHAPTER II
STATUS AND PROPERTY OF TRADE UNIONS

General

Property of trade union

Liability of trade unions in proceedings in tort

Restriction on enforcement against certain property

CHAPTER III
TRADE UNION ADMINISTRATION

Register of members' names and addresses

Duty to supply copy of rules

Accounting records

Annual return, accounts and audit

Investigation of financial affairs

Members' superannuation schemes

Supplementary

CHAPTER IV
ELECTIONS FOR CERTAIN POSITIONS

Duty to hold elections

Requirements to be satisfied with respect to elections

Remedy for failure to comply with requirements

Supplementary

CHAPTER V
RIGHTS OF TRADE UNION MEMBERS

Right to a ballot before industrial action

Right not to be denied access to the courts

Right not to be unjustifiably disciplined

Right not to suffer deduction of unauthorised or excessive union subscriptions

Right to terminate membership of union

Supplementary

CHAPTER VA
COLLECTIVE BARGAINING: RECOGNITION

CHAPTER VI
APPLICATION OF FUNDS FOR POLITICAL OBJECTS

Restriction on use of funds for certain political objects

Political resolution

The political fund

Duties of employer who deducts union contributions

Position where political resolution ceases to have effect

Supplementary

CHAPTER VII
AMALGAMATIONS AND SIMILAR MATTERS

Amalgamation or transfer of engagements

Change of name

Supplementary

CHAPTER VIIA
BREACH OF RULES

CHAPTER IX
MISCELLANEOUS AND GENERAL PROVISIONS

Final provisions

SCHEDULES

An Act to consolidate the enactments relating to collective labour relations, that is to say, to trade unions, employers' associations, industrial relations and industrial action

[16 July 1992]

NOTES

This Act consolidates the legislation relating to trade unions and industrial relations. It came into force on 16 October 1992.

The Act is printed in full except for provisions relating to Northern Ireland (ss 294, 301(2), (3), Sch 3, para 12) and repealing and amending provisions (s 300(1), (2), Schs 1, 2), and provisions subsequently repealed. The Act was substantially amended by, inter alia, the Trade Union Reform and Employment Rights Act 1993, the Employment Relations Act 1999, the Employment Act 2002, the Employment Relations Act 2004, the Transparency of Lobbying, Non-Party Campaigning and Trade Union Administration Act 2014, and the Trade Union Act 2016 (details are given in notes to each section affected). As to the further power to amend, repeal or modify this Act, see the Employment Relations Act 2004, s 42(1), (4)(d) at **[1.1415]**, the Health and Safety at Work etc Act 1974, s 80 at **[1.79]**, and the Pensions Act 2004, ss 259, 260 at **[1.1424]**, **[1.1425]**.

Employment Appeal Tribunal: an appeal lies to the Employment Appeal Tribunal on any question of law arising from any decision of, or in any proceedings before, an employment tribunal under or by virtue of this Act; see the Employment Tribunals Act 1996, s 21(1)(d) at **[1.764]**.

Ballots or elections under this Act: as to the power of the Secretary of State to provide that any ballot or election authorised or required by this Act should be conducted in a specified permissible manner, see the Employment Relations Act 2004, s 54 at **[1.1416]**.

See *Harvey* DI(15), DII(9), E(17), M, NI, NII.

PART I
TRADE UNIONS

CHAPTER I INTRODUCTORY

Meaning of "trade union"

[1.268]

1 Meaning of "trade union"

In this Act a "trade union" means an organisation (whether temporary or permanent)—

(a) which consists wholly or mainly of workers of one or more descriptions and whose principal purposes include the regulation of relations between workers of that description or those descriptions and employers or employers' associations; or

(b) which consists wholly or mainly of—

(i) constituent or affiliated organisations which fulfil the conditions in paragraph (a) (or themselves consist wholly or mainly of constituent or affiliated organisations which fulfil those conditions), or

(ii) representatives of such constituent or affiliated organisations,

and whose principal purposes include the regulation of relations between workers and employers or between workers and employers' associations, or the regulation of relations between its constituent or affiliated organisations.

The list of trade unions

[1.269]

2 The list of trade unions

(1) The Certification Officer shall keep a list of trade unions containing the names of—

(a) the organisations whose names were, immediately before the commencement of this Act, duly entered in the list of trade unions kept by him under section 8 of the Trade Union and Labour Relations Act 1974, and
(b) the names of the organisations entitled to have their names entered in the list in accordance with this Part.

(2) The Certification Officer shall keep copies of the list of trade unions, as for the time being in force, available for public inspection at all reasonable hours free of charge.
(3) A copy of the list shall be included in his annual report.
(4) The fact that the name of an organisation is included in the list of trade unions is evidence (in Scotland, sufficient evidence) that the organisation is a trade union.
(5) On the application of an organisation whose name is included in the list, the Certification Officer shall issue it with a certificate to that effect.
(6) A document purporting to be such a certificate is evidence (in Scotland, sufficient evidence) that the name of the organisation is entered in the list.

NOTES

Trade Union and Labour Relations Act 1974, s 8: repealed by this Act.

[1.270]
3 Application to have name entered on list

(1) An organisation of workers, whenever formed, whose name is not entered in the list of trade unions may apply to the Certification Officer to have its name entered in the list.
(2) The application shall be made in such form and manner as the Certification Officer may require and shall be accompanied by—
(a) a copy of the rules of the organisation,
(b) a list of its officers,
(c) the address of its head or main office, and
(d) the name under which it is or is to be known,
and by the prescribed fee.
(3) If the Certification Officer is satisfied—
(a) that the organisation is a trade union,
(b) that subsection (2) has been complied with, and
(c) that entry of the name in the list is not prohibited by subsection (4),
he shall enter the name of the organisation in the list of trade unions.
(4) The Certification Officer shall not enter the name of an organisation in the list of trade unions if the name is the same as that under which another organisation—
(a) was on 30th September 1971 registered as a trade union under the Trade Union Acts 1871 to 1964,
(b) was at any time registered as a trade union or employers' association under the Industrial Relations Act 1971, or
(c) is for the time being entered in the list of trade unions or in the list of employers' associations kept under Part II of this Act,
or if the name is one so nearly resembling any such name as to be likely to deceive the public.

NOTES

Prescribed fee: the current fee is £150 (see the Certification Officer (Amendment of Fees) Regulations 2005, SI 2005/713, reg 5).

Trade Union Acts 1871 to 1964: the Acts which were cited together under this collective title were: the Trade Union Act 1871 (repealed); the Trade Union Act Amendment Act 1876 (repealed); the Trade Disputes Act 1906 (repealed); the Trade Union Act 1913 (repealed, with a saving, by this Act); the Trade Union (Amalgamation) Act 1917 (repealed); the Trade Disputes and Trade Unions Act 1927 (repealed); the Societies (Miscellaneous Provisions) Act 1940, s 6 (repealed); and the Trade Union (Amalgamations, etc) Act 1964 (repealed by this Act).

Industrial Relations Act 1971: repealed by the Trade Union and Labour Relations Act 1974, ss 1, 25(3), Sch 5.

[1.271]
4 Removal of name from the list

(1) If it appears to the Certification Officer, on application made to him or otherwise, that an organisation whose name is entered in the list of trade unions is not a trade union, he may remove its name from the list.
(2) He shall not do so without giving the organisation notice of his intention and considering any representations made to him by the organisation within such period (of not less than 28 days beginning with the date of the notice) as may be specified in the notice.
(3) The Certification Officer shall remove the name of an organisation from the list of trade unions if—
(a) he is requested by the organisation to do so, or
(b) he is satisfied that the organisation has ceased to exist.

Certification as independent trade union

[1.272]
5 Meaning of "independent trade union"

In this Act an "independent trade union" means a trade union which—
(a) is not under the domination or control of an employer or group of employers or of one or more employers' associations, and

(b) is not liable to interference by an employer or any such group or association (arising out of the provision of financial or material support or by any other means whatsoever) tending towards such control;

and references to "independence", in relation to a trade union, shall be construed accordingly.

[1.273]
6 Application for certificate of independence

(1) A trade union whose name is entered on the list of trade unions may apply to the Certification Officer for a certificate that it is independent.

The application shall be made in such form and manner as the Certification Officer may require and shall be accompanied by the prescribed fee.

(2) The Certification Officer shall maintain a record showing details of all applications made to him under this section and shall keep it available for public inspection (free of charge) at all reasonable hours.

(3) If an application is made by a trade union whose name is not entered on the list of trade unions, the Certification Officer shall refuse a certificate of independence and shall enter that refusal on the record.

(4) In any other case, he shall not come to a decision on the application before the end of the period of one month after it has been entered on the record; and before coming to his decision he shall make such enquiries as he thinks fit and shall take into account any relevant information submitted to him by any person.

(5) He shall then decide whether the applicant trade union is independent and shall enter his decision and the date of his decision on the record.

(6) If he decides that the trade union is independent he shall issue a certificate accordingly; and if he decides that it is not, he shall give reasons for his decision.

NOTES

Prescribed fee: the current fee is £4,066 (see the Certification Officer (Amendment of Fees) Regulations 2005, SI 2005/713, reg 7).

[1.274]
7 Withdrawal or cancellation of certificate

(1) The Certification Officer may withdraw a trade union's certificate of independence if he is of the opinion that the union is no longer independent.

(2) Where he proposes to do so he shall notify the trade union and enter notice of the proposal in the record.

(3) He shall not come to a decision on the proposal before the end of the period of one month after notice of it was entered on the record; and before coming to his decision he shall make such enquiries as he thinks fit and shall take into account any relevant information submitted to him by any person.

(4) He shall then decide whether the trade union is independent and shall enter his decision and the date of his decision on the record.

(5) He shall confirm or withdraw the certificate accordingly; and if he decides to withdraw it, he shall give reasons for his decision.

(6) Where the name of an organisation is removed from the list of trade unions, the Certification Officer shall cancel any certificate of independence in force in respect of that organisation by entering on the record the fact that the organisation's name has been removed from that list and that the certificate is accordingly cancelled.

[1.275]
8 Conclusive effect of Certification Officer's decision

(1) A certificate of independence which is in force is conclusive evidence for all purposes that a trade union is independent; and a refusal, withdrawal or cancellation of a certificate of independence, entered on the record, is conclusive evidence for all purposes that a trade union is not independent.

(2) A document purporting to be a certificate of independence and to be signed by the Certification Officer, or by a person authorised to act on his behalf, shall be taken to be such a certificate unless the contrary is proved.

(3) A document purporting to be a certified copy of an entry on the record and to be signed by the Certification Officer, or by a person authorised to act on his behalf, shall be taken to be a true copy of such an entry unless the contrary is proved.

(4) If in any proceedings before a court, the Employment Appeal Tribunal, the Central Arbitration Committee, ACAS or an [employment tribunal] a question arises whether a trade union is independent and there is no certificate of independence in force and no refusal, withdrawal or cancellation of a certificate recorded in relation to that trade union—

(a) that question shall not be decided in those proceedings, and

(b) the proceedings shall instead be stayed or sisted until a certificate of independence has been issued or refused by the Certification Officer.

(5) The body before whom the proceedings are stayed or sisted may refer the question of the independence of the trade union to the Certificate Officer who shall proceed in accordance with section 6 as on an application by that trade union.

NOTES

Sub-s (4): words in square brackets substituted by the Employment Rights (Dispute Resolution) Act 1998, s 1(2)(a).

Supplementary

[1.276]

9 Appeal against decision of Certification Officer

(1) An organisation aggrieved by the refusal of the Certification Officer to enter its name in the list of trade unions, or by a decision of his to remove its name from the list, may appeal to the Employment Appeal Tribunal [on any appealable question].

(2) A trade union aggrieved by the refusal of the Certification Officer to issue it with a certificate of independence, or by a decision of his to withdraw its certificate, may appeal to the Employment Appeal Tribunal [on any appealable question].

(3) . . .

(4) [For the purposes of this section, an appealable question is any question of law] arising in the proceedings before, or arising from the decision of, the Certification Officer.

NOTES

Sub-ss (1), (2): words in square brackets added by the Employment Relations Act 2004, s 51(1)(a).
Sub-s (3): repealed by the Employment Relations Act 2004, ss 51(1)(b), 57(2), Sch 2.
Sub-s (4): words in square brackets substituted by the Employment Relations Act 2004, s 51(1)(c).

CHAPTER II STATUS AND PROPERTY OF TRADE UNIONS

General

[1.277]

10 Quasi-corporate status of trade unions

(1) A trade union is not a body corporate but—

(a) it is capable of making contracts;

(b) it is capable of suing and being sued in its own name, whether in proceedings relating to property or founded on contract or tort or any other cause of action; and

(c) proceedings for an offence alleged to have been committed by it or on its behalf may be brought against it in its own name.

(2) A trade union shall not be treated as if it were a body corporate except to the extent authorised by the provisions of this Part.

(3) A trade union shall not be registered—

(a) as a company under [the Companies Act 2006], or

(b) under the Friendly Societies Act 1974 or [the Co-operative and Community Benefit Societies Act 2014];

and any such registration of a trade union (whenever effected) is void.

NOTES

Sub-s (3): words in square brackets in para (a) substituted by the Companies Act 2006 (Consequential Amendments, Transitional Provisions and Savings) Order 2009, SI 2009/1941, art 2(1), Sch 1, para 134(1), (2); words in square brackets in para (b) substituted by the Co-operative and Community Benefit Societies Act 2014, s 151, Sch 4, Pt 2, para 54, as from 1 August 2014.

[1.278]

11 Exclusion of common law rules as to restraint of trade

(1) The purposes of a trade union are not, by reason only that they are in restraint of trade, unlawful so as—

(a) to make any member of the trade union liable to criminal proceedings for conspiracy or otherwise, or

(b) to make any agreement or trust void or voidable.

(2) No rule of a trade union is unlawful or unenforceable by reason only that it is in restraint of trade.

Property of trade union

[1.279]

12 Property to be vested in trustees

(1) All property belonging to a trade union shall be vested in trustees in trust for it.

(2) A judgment, order or award made in proceedings of any description brought against a trade union is enforceable, by way of execution, diligence, punishment for contempt or otherwise, against any property held in trust for it to the same extent and in the same manner as if it were a body corporate.

(3) Subsection (2) has effect subject to section 23 (restriction on enforcement of awards against certain property).

[1.280]

13 Vesting of property in new trustees

(1) The provisions of this section apply in relation to the appointment or discharge of trustees in whom any property is vested in trust for a trade union whose name is entered in the list of trade unions.

(2) In the following sections as they apply to such trustees references to a deed shall be construed as references to an instrument in writing—

(a) section 39 of the Trustee Act 1925 and section 38 of the Trustee Act (Northern Ireland) 1958 (retirement of trustee without a new appointment), and

(b) section 40 of the Trustee Act 1925 and section 39 of the Trustee Act (Northern Ireland) 1958 (vesting of trust property in new or continuing trustees).

(3) Where such a trustee is appointed or discharged by a resolution taken by or on behalf of the union, the written record of the resolution shall be treated for the purposes of those sections as an instrument in writing appointing or discharging the trustee.

(4) In section 40 of the Trustee Act 1925 and section 39 of the Trustee Act (Northern Ireland) 1958 as they apply to such trustees, paragraphs (a) and (c) of subsection (4) (which exclude certain property from the section) shall be omitted.

[1.281]

14 Transfer of securities held in trust for trade union

(1) In this section—

"instrument of appointment" means an instrument in writing appointing a new trustee of a trade union whose name is entered in the list of trade unions, and

"instrument of discharge" means an instrument in writing discharging a trustee of such a trade union; and for the purposes of this section where a trustee is appointed or discharged by a resolution taken by or on behalf of such a trade union, the written record of the resolution shall be treated as an instrument in writing appointing or discharging the trustee.

(2) Where by any enactment or instrument the transfer of securities of any description is required to be effected or recorded by means of entries in a register, then if—

(a) there is produced to the person authorised or required to keep the register a copy of an instrument of appointment or discharge which contains or has attached to it a list identifying the securities of that description held in trust for the union at the date of the appointment or discharge, and

(b) it appears to that person that any of the securities so identified are included in the register kept by him,

he shall make such entries as may be necessary to give effect to the instrument of appointment or discharge.

This subsection has effect notwithstanding anything in any enactment or instrument regulating the keeping of the register.

(3) A document which purports to be a copy of an instrument of appointment or discharge containing or having attached to it such a list, and to be certified in accordance with the following subsection to be a copy of such an instrument, shall be taken to be a copy of such an instrument unless the contrary is proved.

(4) The certificate shall be given by the president and general secretary of the union and, in the case of an instrument to which a list of securities is attached, shall appear both on the instrument and on the list.

(5) Nothing done for the purposes of or in pursuance of this section shall be taken to affect any person with notice of any trust or to impose on any person a duty to inquire into any matter.

(6) In relation to a Scottish trust, references in this section to the appointment and discharge of a trustee shall be construed as including references to, respectively, the assumption and resignation of a trustee; and references to an instrument appointing or discharging a trustee shall be construed accordingly.

[1.282]

15 Prohibition on use of funds to indemnify unlawful conduct

(1) It is unlawful for property of a trade union to be applied in or towards—

(a) the payment for an individual of a penalty which has been or may be imposed on him for an offence or for contempt of court,

(b) the securing of any such payment, or

(c) the provision of anything for indemnifying an individual in respect of such a penalty.

(2) Where any property of a trade union is so applied for the benefit of an individual on whom a penalty has been or may be imposed, then—

(a) in the case of a payment, an amount equal to the payment is recoverable by the union from him, and

(b) in any other case, he is liable to account to the union for the value of the property applied.

(3) If a trade union fails to bring or continue proceedings which it is entitled to bring by virtue of subsection (2), a member of the union who claims that the failure is unreasonable may apply to the court on that ground for an order authorising him to bring or continue the proceedings on the union's behalf and at the union's expense.

(4) In this section "penalty", in relation to an offence, includes an order to pay compensation and an order for the forfeiture of any property; and references to the imposition of a penalty for an offence shall be construed accordingly.

(5) The Secretary of State may by order designate offences in relation to which the provisions of this section do not apply.

Any such order shall be made by statutory instrument which shall be subject to annulment in pursuance of a resolution of either House of Parliament.

(6) This section does not affect—

(a) any other enactment, any rule of law or any provision of the rules of a trade union which makes it unlawful for the property of a trade union to be applied in a particular way; or

(b) any other remedy available to a trade union, the trustees of its property or any of its members in respect of an unlawful application of the union's property.

(7) In this section "member", in relation to a trade union consisting wholly or partly of, or of representatives of, constituent or affiliated organisations, includes a member of any of the constituent or affiliated organisations.

NOTES

Orders: as of 15 May 2019, no Orders had been made under this section.

[1.283]

16 Remedy against trustees for unlawful use of union property

(1) A member of a trade union who claims that the trustees of the union's property—

(a) have so carried out their functions, or are proposing so to carry out their functions, as to cause or permit an unlawful application of the union's property, or

(b) have complied, or are proposing to comply, with an unlawful direction which has been or may be given, or purportedly given, to them under the rules of the union,

may apply to the court for an order under this section.

(2) In a case relating to property which has already been unlawfully applied, or to an unlawful direction that has already been complied with, an application under this section may be made only by a person who was a member of the union at the time when the property was applied or, as the case may be, the direction complied with.

(3) Where the court is satisfied that the claim is well-founded, it shall make such order as it considers appropriate.

The court may in particular—

(a) require the trustees (if necessary, on behalf of the union) to take all such steps as may be specified in the order for protecting or recovering the property of the union;

(b) appoint a receiver of, or in Scotland a judicial factor on, the property of the union;

(c) remove one or more of the trustees.

(4) Where the court makes an order under this section in a case in which—

(a) property of the union has been applied in contravention of an order of any court, or in compliance with a direction given in contravention of such an order, or

(b) the trustees were proposing to apply property in contravention of such an order or to comply with any such direction,

the court shall by its order remove all the trustees except any trustee who satisfies the court that there is a good reason for allowing him to remain a trustee.

(5) Without prejudice to any other power of the court, the court may on an application for an order under this section grant such interlocutory relief (in Scotland, such interim order) as it considers appropriate.

(6) This section does not affect any other remedy available in respect of a breach of trust by the trustees of a trade union's property.

(7) In this section "member", in relation to a trade union consisting wholly or partly of, or of representatives of, constituent or affiliated organisations, includes a member of any of the constituent or affiliated organisations.

[1.284]

17 Nomination by members of trade unions

(1) The Secretary of State may make provision by regulations for enabling members of trade unions who are not under 16 years of age to nominate a person or persons to become entitled, on the death of the person making the nomination, to the whole or part of any money payable on his death out of the funds of the trade union.

(2) The regulations may include provision as to the manner in which nominations may be made and as to the manner in which nominations may be varied or revoked.

(3) The regulations may provide that, subject to such exceptions as may be prescribed, no nomination made by a member of a trade union shall be valid if at the date of the nomination the person nominated is an officer or employee of the trade union or is otherwise connected with the trade union in such manner as may be prescribed by the regulations.

(4) The regulations may include such incidental, transitional or supplementary provisions as the Secretary of State may consider appropriate.

(5) They may, in particular, include provision for securing, to such extent and subject to such conditions as may be prescribed in the regulations, that nominations made under the Trade Union Act 1871 Amendment Act 1876 have effect as if made under the regulations and may be varied or revoked accordingly.

(6) Regulations under this section shall be made by statutory instrument which shall be subject to annulment in pursuance of a resolution of either House of Parliament.

NOTES

Trade Union Act 1871 Amendment Act 1876: repealed by the Industrial Relations Act 1971.

Regulations: as of 15 May 2019, no Regulations had been made under this section. However, the Trade Union (Nominations) Regulations 1977, SI 1977/789, have effect as if so made by virtue of s 300(3) of, and Sch 3, para 1(2) to, this Act, and the Interpretation Act 1978, s 17(2)(b).

[1.285]

18 Payments out of union funds on death of member

(1) The Secretary of State may make provision by regulations for enabling money payable out of the funds of a trade union on the death of a member, to an amount not exceeding £5,000, to be paid or distributed on his death without letters of administration, probate of any will or confirmation.

(2) The regulations may include such incidental, transitional and supplementary provisions as the Secretary of State may consider appropriate.

(3) Regulations under this section shall be made by statutory instrument which shall be subject to annulment in pursuance of a resolution of either House of Parliament.
(4) The Treasury may by order under section 6(1) of the Administration of Estates (Small Payments) Act 1965 direct that subsection (1) above shall have effect with the substitution for the reference to £5,000 of a reference to such higher amount as may be specified in the order.

NOTES

Regulations: as of 15 May 2019, no Regulations had been made under this section. However, the Trade Union (Nominations) Regulations 1977, SI 1977/789, have effect as if so made by virtue of s 300(3) of, and Sch 3, para 1(2) to, this Act, and the Interpretation Act 1978, s 17(2)(b).

[1.286]
19 Application of certain provisions relating to industrial assurance or friendly societies
[(1) Section 99 of the Friendly Societies Act 1992 (insurance of lives of children under 10) applies to a trade union as to [a friendly society].]
(2) . . .
(3) Section 52 of the Friendly Societies Act 1974 (charitable subscriptions and contributions to other registered societies) extends to a trade union, or branch of a trade union, as regards contributing to the funds and taking part in the government of a medical society, that is, a society for the purpose of relief in sickness by providing medical attendance and medicine.

A trade union, or branch of a trade union, shall not withdraw from contributing to the funds of such a society except on three months' notice to the society and on payment of all contributions accrued or accruing due to the date of the expiry of the notice.
[(4) . . .]

NOTES

Sub-s (1): substituted by the Friendly Societies Act 1992 (Transitional and Consequential Provisions) Regulations 1993, SI 1993/3084, reg 7; words in square brackets substituted by the Financial Services and Markets Act 2000 (Consequential Amendments and Repeals) Order 2001, SI 2001/3649, art 332.

Sub-s (2): repealed by SI 1993/3084, reg 8.

Sub-s (4): added by the Financial Services and Markets Act 2000 (Consequential Amendments and Savings) (Industrial Assurance) Order 2001, SI 2001/3647, art 5, Sch 3, Pt I, para 14; repealed by the Employment Relations Act 2004, s 57, Sch 1, para 3, Sch 2.

Liability of trade unions in proceedings in tort

[1.287]
20 Liability of trade union in certain proceedings in tort
(1) Where proceedings in tort are brought against a trade union—
(a) on the ground that an act—
(i) induces another person to break a contract or interferes or induces another person to interfere with its performance, or
(ii) consists in threatening that a contract (whether one to which the union is a party or not) will be broken or its performance interfered with, or that the union will induce another person to break a contract or interfere with its performance, or
(b) in respect of an agreement or combination by two or more persons to do or to procure the doing of an act which, if it were done without any such agreement or combination, would be actionable in tort on such a ground,

then, for the purpose of determining in those proceedings whether the union is liable in respect of the act in question, that act shall be taken to have been done by the union if, but only if, it is to be taken to have been authorised or endorsed by the trade union in accordance with the following provisions.
(2) An act shall be taken to have been authorised or endorsed by a trade union if it was done, or was authorised or endorsed—
(a) by any person empowered by the rules to do, authorise or endorse acts of the kind in question, or
(b) by the principal executive committee or the president or general secretary, or
(c) by any other committee of the union or any other official of the union (whether employed by it or not).
(3) For the purposes of paragraph (c) of subsection (2)—
(a) any group of persons constituted in accordance with the rules of the union is a committee of the union; and
(b) an act shall be taken to have been done, authorised or endorsed by an official if it was done, authorised or endorsed by, or by any member of, any group of persons of which he was at the material time a member, the purposes of which included organising or co-ordinating industrial action.
(4) The provisions of paragraphs (b) and (c) of subsection (2) apply notwithstanding anything in the rules of the union, or in any contract or rule of law, but subject to the provisions of section 21 (repudiation by union of certain acts).
(5) Where for the purposes of any proceedings an act is by virtue of this section taken to have been done by a trade union, nothing in this section shall affect the liability of any other person, in those or any other proceedings, in respect of that act.
(6) In proceedings arising out of an act which is by virtue of this section taken to have been done by a trade union, the power of the court to grant an injunction or interdict includes power to require the union to take such steps as the court considers appropriate for ensuring—

(a) that there is no, or no further, inducement of persons to take part or to continue to take part in industrial action, and
(b) that no person engages in any conduct after the granting of the injunction or interdict by virtue of having been induced before it was granted to take part or to continue to take part in industrial action.

The provisions of subsections (2) to (4) above apply in relation to proceedings for failure to comply with any such injunction or interdict as they apply in relation to the original proceedings.
(7) In this section "rules", in relation to a trade union, means the written rules of the union and any other written provision forming part of the contract between a member and the other members.

[1.288]
21 Repudiation by union of certain acts
(1) An act shall not be taken to have been authorised or endorsed by a trade union by virtue only of paragraph (c) of section 20(2) if it was repudiated by the executive, president or general secretary as soon as reasonably practicable after coming to the knowledge of any of them.
(2) Where an act is repudiated—
(a) written notice of the repudiation must be given to the committee or official in question, without delay, and
(b) the union must do its best to give individual written notice of the fact and date of repudiation, without delay—
(i) to every member of the union who the union has reason to believe is taking part, or might otherwise take part, in industrial action as a result of the act, and
(ii) to the employer of every such member.
(3) The notice given to members in accordance with paragraph (b)(i) of subsection (2) must contain the following statement—

"Your union has repudiated the call (or calls) for industrial action to which this notice relates and will give no support to unofficial industrial action taken in response to it (or them). If you are dismissed while taking unofficial industrial action, you will have no right to complain of unfair dismissal."

(4) If subsection (2) or (3) is not complied with, the repudiation shall be treated as ineffective.
(5) An act shall not be treated as repudiated if at any time after the union concerned purported to repudiate it the executive, president or general secretary has behaved in a manner which is inconsistent with the purported repudiation.
(6) The executive, president or general secretary shall be treated as so behaving if, on a request made to any of them within [three months] of the purported repudiation by a person who—
(a) is a party to a commercial contract whose performance has been or may be interfered with as a result of the act in question, and
(b) has not been given written notice by the union of the repudiation,
it is not forthwith confirmed in writing that the act has been repudiated.
(7) In this section "commercial contract" means any contract other than—
(a) a contract of employment, or
(b) any other contract under which a person agrees personally to do work or perform services for another.

NOTES
Sub-s (6): words in square brackets substituted by the Trade Union Reform and Employment Rights Act 1993, s 49(1), Sch 7, para 17.

[1.289]
22 Limit on damages awarded against trade unions in actions in tort
(1) This section applies to any proceedings in tort brought against a trade union, except—
(a) proceedings for personal injury as a result of negligence, nuisance or breach of duty;
(b) proceedings for breach of duty in connection with the ownership, occupation, possession, control or use of property;
(c) proceedings brought by virtue of Part I of the Consumer Protection Act 1987 (product liability).
(2) In any proceedings in tort to which this section applies the amount which may be awarded against the union by way of damages shall not exceed the following limit—

Number of members of union	*Maximum award of damages*
Less than 5,000	£10,000
5,000 or more but less than 25,000	£50,000
25,000 or more but less than 100,000	£125,000
100,000 or more	£250,000

(3) The Secretary of State may by order amend subsection (2) so as to vary any of the sums specified; and the order may make such transitional provision as the Secretary of State considers appropriate.
(4) Any such order shall be made by statutory instrument which shall be subject to annulment in pursuance of a resolution of either House of Parliament.
(5) In this section—
"breach of duty" means breach of a duty imposed by any rule of law or by or under any enactment;

"personal injury" includes any disease and any impairment of a person's physical or mental condition; and

"property" means any property, whether real or personal (or in Scotland, heritable or moveable).

NOTES

Orders: as of 15 May 2019, no Orders had been made under this section.

Restriction on enforcement against certain property

[1.290]

23 Restriction on enforcement of awards against certain property

(1) Where in any proceedings an amount is awarded by way of damages, costs or expenses—

(a) against a trade union,

(b) against trustees in whom property is vested in trust for a trade union, in their capacity as such (and otherwise than in respect of a breach of trust on their part), or

(c) against members or officials of a trade union on behalf of themselves and all of the members of the union,

no part of that amount is recoverable by enforcement against any protected property.

(2) The following is protected property—

(a) property belonging to the trustees otherwise than in their capacity as such;

(b) property belonging to any member of the union otherwise than jointly or in common with the other members;

(c) property belonging to an official of the union who is neither a member nor a trustee;

(d) property comprised in the union's political fund where that fund—

(i) is subject to rules of the union which prevent property which is or has been comprised in the fund from being used for financing strikes or other industrial action, and

(ii) was so subject at the time when the act in respect of which the proceedings are brought was done;

(e) property comprised in a separate fund maintained in accordance with the rules of the union for the purpose only of providing provident benefits.

(3) For this purpose "provident benefits" includes—

(a) any payment expressly authorised by the rules of the union which is made—

(i) to a member during sickness or incapacity from personal injury or while out of work, or

(ii) to an aged member by way of superannuation, or

(iii) to a member who has met with an accident or has lost his tools by fire or theft;

(b) a payment in discharge or aid of funeral expenses on the death of a member or [the spouse or civil partner] of a member or as provision for the children of a deceased member.

NOTES

Sub-s (3): words in square brackets in para (b) substituted by the Civil Partnership Act 2004, s 261(1), Sch 27, para 144.

CHAPTER III TRADE UNION ADMINISTRATION

Register of members' names and addresses

[1.291]

24 Duty to maintain register of members' names and addresses

(1) A trade union shall compile and maintain a register of the names and addresses of its members, and shall secure, so far as is reasonably practicable, that the entries in the register are accurate and are kept up-to-date.

(2) The register may be kept by means of a computer.

(3) A trade union shall—

(a) allow any member, upon reasonable notice, to ascertain from the register, free of charge and at any reasonable time, whether there is an entry on it relating to him; and

(b) if requested to do so by any member, supply him as soon as reasonably practicable, either free of charge or on payment of a reasonable fee, with a copy of any entry on the register relating to him.

(4) . . .

(5) For the purposes of this section a member's address means either his home address or another address which he has requested the union in writing to treat as his postal address.

(6) The remedy for failure to comply with the requirements of this section is by way of application under section 25 (to the Certification Officer) or section 26 (to the court)[; see also the powers of the Certification Officer under section 24B to make a declaration and an enforcement order].

. . .

NOTES

Sub-s (4): repealed by the Trade Union Reform and Employment Rights Act 1993, s 51, Sch 10.

Sub-s (6): words in square brackets inserted by the Transparency of Lobbying, Non-Party Campaigning and Trade Union Administration Act 2014, s 43(1), (3), as from 1 June 2016; words omitted repealed by the Employment Relations Act 1999, ss 29, 44, Sch 6, paras 1, 2, Sch 9(7).

[1.292]

[24ZA Duty to provide membership audit certificate

[(1) A trade union required to maintain a register of the names and addresses of its members by section 24 must send to the Certification Officer a membership audit certificate in relation to each reporting period.

(2) In this section and in sections 24ZB to 24ZF, a "reporting period" means a period in relation to which the union is required by section 32 to send an annual return to the Certification Officer.

(3) The union must send the membership audit certificate in relation to a reporting period to the Certification Officer at the same time as it sends to the Officer its annual return under section 32 in relation to that period.

(4) In the case of a trade union required by section 24ZB to appoint an assurer in relation to a reporting period, the "membership audit certificate" in relation to that period is the certificate which the assurer is required to provide to the union in relation to that period pursuant to that appointment.

(5) In any other case, the "membership audit certificate" in relation to a reporting period is a certificate which—

(a) must be signed by an officer of the trade union who is authorised to sign on its behalf,

(b) must state the officer's name, and

(c) must state whether, to the best of the officer's knowledge and belief, the union has complied with its duties under section 24(1) throughout the reporting period.

(6) A trade union must, at a person's request, supply the person with a copy of its most recent membership audit certificate either free of charge or on payment of a reasonable charge.

(7) The Certification Officer must at all reasonable hours keep available for public inspection, either free of charge or on payment of a reasonable charge, copies of all membership audit certificates sent to the Officer under this section.]

NOTES

Commencement: 6 April 2015.

Inserted by the Transparency of Lobbying, Non-Party Campaigning and Trade Union Administration Act 2014, s 40(1), (2), as from 6 April 2015, in relation to a reporting period which commences on or after that date.

[1.293]

[24ZB Duty to appoint an assurer

[(1) A trade union required to maintain a register of the names and addresses of its members by section 24 must, in relation to each reporting period, appoint a qualified independent person to be an assurer in relation to that period.

(2) There is incorporated in the assurer's appointment a duty which the assurer owes to the trade union—

(a) to provide to the union a membership audit certificate in relation to the reporting period which accords with the requirements of section 24ZD, and

(b) to carry out such enquiries as the assurer considers necessary to enable the assurer to provide that certificate.

(3) A person is a "qualified independent person" if—

(a) the person either satisfies such conditions as may be specified for the purposes of this section by order of the Secretary of State or is specified by name in such an order, and

(b) the trade union has no grounds for believing that—

(i) the person will carry out an assurer's functions otherwise than competently, or

(ii) the person's independence in relation to the union might reasonably be called into question.

(4) None of the following may act as an assurer—

(a) an officer or employee of the trade union or of any of its branches or sections;

(b) a person who is a partner of, or in the employment of, or who employs, such an officer or employee.

(5) This section does not apply to a trade union in relation to a reporting period if the number of its members at the end of the preceding reporting period did not exceed 10,000.

(6) Any order under this section is to be made by statutory instrument and is to be subject to annulment in pursuance of a resolution of either House of Parliament.]

NOTES

Commencement: 30 January 2014 (for the purposes of making Orders under sub-s (3)); 6 April 2015 (otherwise).

Inserted by the Transparency of Lobbying, Non-Party Campaigning and Trade Union Administration Act 2014, s 41(1), (2), as from 30 January 2014 (for the purposes of making Orders under sub-s (3)), and as from 6 April 2015 (otherwise), in relation to a reporting period which commences on or after that date.

Orders: the Membership Audit Certificate (Qualified Independent Person) (Specified Conditions) Order 2015, SI 2015/716. This Order provides that a qualified independent person for the purposes of this section must satisfy one or more of the conditions specified in arts 3, 4 and 5 of the Order. These are: (i) that the person has in force a practising certificate issued by the Law Society of England and Wales or the Law Society of Scotland (art 3); (ii) that the person is eligible for appointment as a statutory auditor under Part 42 of the Companies Act 2006 (art 4); (iii) that the person is specified by art 7 of the Trade Union Ballots and Elections (Independent Scrutineer Qualifications) Order 1993, SI 1993/1909 (at **[2.138]**) (art 5).

[1.294]

[24ZC Appointment and removal of an assurer

[(1) The rules of every trade union to which section 24ZB applies must contain provision for the appointment and removal of an assurer.

But the following provisions have effect notwithstanding anything in the rules.

(2) An assurer must not be removed from office except by resolution passed at a general meeting of the members of the union or of delegates of its members.

(3) A person duly appointed as an assurer in relation to a reporting period must be reappointed as assurer in relation to the following reporting period, unless—

(a) a resolution has been passed at a general meeting of the trade union appointing somebody else instead or providing expressly that the person is not to be re-appointed,

(b) the person has given notice to the union in writing of the person's unwillingness to be re-appointed,

(c) the person is not qualified for the appointment in accordance with section 24ZB, or

(d) the person has ceased to act as assurer by reason of incapacity.

(4) But a person need not automatically be re-appointed where—

(a) the person is retiring,

(b) notice has been given of an intended resolution to appoint somebody else instead, and

(c) that resolution cannot be proceeded with at the meeting because of the death or incapacity of the proposed replacement.]

NOTES

Commencement: 6 April 2015.

Inserted by the Transparency of Lobbying, Non-Party Campaigning and Trade Union Administration Act 2014, s 41(1), (2), as from 6 April 2015, in relation to a reporting period which commences on or after that date.

Transitional provisions: the Transparency of Lobbying, Non-Party Campaigning and Trade Union Administration Act 2014 (Commencement No 2 and Transitional Provision) Order 2015, SI 2015/717, art 3(2) provides that the first sentence of sub-s (1) does not apply to a trade union before the last day of that trade union's first reporting period which commences on or after 6 April 2015.

[1.295]

[24ZD Requirements of assurer's membership audit certificate

[(1) For the purposes of section 24ZB(2)(a) the requirements of a membership audit certificate in relation to a reporting period provided by an assurer are as follows.

(2) The certificate must state the name of, and be signed by, the assurer.

(3) The certificate must state—

(a) whether, in the assurer's opinion, the trade union's system for compiling and maintaining the register of the names and addresses of its members was satisfactory for the purposes of complying with the union's duties under section 24(1) throughout the reporting period, and

(b) whether, in the assurer's opinion, the assurer has obtained the information and explanations which the assurer considers necessary for the performance of the assurer's functions.

(4) If the certificate states that—

(a) in the assurer's opinion, the trade union's system for compiling and maintaining the register was not satisfactory for the purposes of complying with the union's duties under section 24(1) throughout the reporting period, or

(b) in the assurer's opinion, the assurer has failed to obtain the information and explanations which the assurer considers necessary for the performance of the assurer's functions,

the certificate must state the assurer's reasons for making that statement.

(5) In the case of a failure to obtain information or explanations as described in subsection (4)(b), the certificate must also—

(a) provide a description of the information or explanations requested or required which have not been obtained, and

(b) state whether the assurer required that information or those explanations from the union's officers, or officers of any of its branches or sections, under section 24ZE.

(6) The reference in subsection (2) to signature by the assurer is, where that office is held by a body corporate or partnership, to signature in the name of the body corporate or partnership by an individual authorised to sign on its behalf.]

NOTES

Commencement: 6 April 2015.

Inserted by the Transparency of Lobbying, Non-Party Campaigning and Trade Union Administration Act 2014, s 41(1), (2), as from 6 April 2015, in relation to a reporting period which commences on or after that date.

[1.296]

[24ZE Rights of assurer

[(1) An assurer appointed by a trade union under section 24ZB—

(a) has a right of access at all reasonable times to the register of the names and addresses of the union's members and to all other documents which the assurer considers may be relevant to whether the union has complied with any of the requirements of section 24(1), and

(b) is entitled to require from the union's officers, or the officers of any of its branches or sections, such information and explanations as the assurer considers necessary for the performance of the assurer's functions.

(2) In subsection (1) references to documents include information recorded in any form.]

NOTES

Commencement: 6 April 2015.

Inserted by the Transparency of Lobbying, Non-Party Campaigning and Trade Union Administration Act 2014, s 41(1), (2), as from 6 April 2015, in relation to a reporting period which commences on or after that date.

[1.297]
[24ZF Duty to inform the Certification Officer
[If an assurer provides a membership audit certificate in relation to a reporting period to a trade union which states that, in the assurer's opinion—
- (a) the union's system for compiling and maintaining the register was not satisfactory for the purposes of complying with the union's duties under section 24(1) throughout that period, or
- (b) the assurer has failed to obtain the information and explanations which the assurer considers necessary for the performance of the assurer's functions,

the assurer must send a copy of the certificate to the Certification Officer as soon as is reasonably practicable after it is provided to the union.]

NOTES
Commencement: 6 April 2015.
Inserted by the Transparency of Lobbying, Non-Party Campaigning and Trade Union Administration Act 2014, s 41(1), (2), as from 6 April 2015, in relation to a reporting period which commences on or after that date.

[1.298]
[24ZG Duty of confidentiality
[(1) The duty of confidentiality as respects the register is incorporated in an assurer's appointment by a trade union under section 24ZB.
(2) The duty of confidentiality as respects the register is a duty which the assurer owes to the union—
- (a) not to disclose any name or address in the register of the names and addresses of the union's members except in permitted circumstances, and
- (b) to take all reasonable steps to secure that there is no disclosure of any such name or address by another person except in permitted circumstances.

(3) The circumstances in which disclosure of a member's name or address is permitted are—
- (a) where the member consents,
- (b) where it is required or requested by the Certification Officer for the purposes of the discharge of any of the Officer's functions,
- (c) where it is required for the purposes of the discharge of any of the functions of an inspector appointed by the Officer,
- (d) where it is required for the purposes of the discharge of any of the functions of the assurer, or
- (e) where it is required for the purposes of the investigation of crime or criminal proceedings.]

NOTES
Commencement: 6 April 2015.
Inserted by the Transparency of Lobbying, Non-Party Campaigning and Trade Union Administration Act 2014, s 41(1), (2), as from 6 April 2015, in relation to a reporting period which commences on or after that date.

[1.299]
[24ZH Power of Certification Officer to require production of documents etc
[(1) If the Certification Officer thinks there is good reason to do so, the Officer—
- *(a) may give directions to a trade union, or a branch or section of a trade union, requiring it to produce such relevant documents as are specified in the directions;*
- *(b) may authorise a member of the Officer's staff or any other person ("an authorised person"), on producing (if so required) evidence of that authority, to require a trade union, or a branch or section of a trade union, to produce immediately to the authorised person such relevant documents as that person specifies.*

(2) "Relevant documents", in relation to a trade union or a branch or section of a trade union, means—
- *(a) the register of the names and addresses of the trade union's members, and*
- *(b) documents of any other description which the Certification Officer or authorised person considers may be relevant to whether the union has failed to comply with any of the requirements of section 24(1) (duties regarding the register of members).*

(3) Directions under subsection (1)(a) must specify the time and place at which the documents are to be produced.
(4) Where the Certification Officer, or an authorised person, has power to require the production of documents by virtue of subsection (1), the Officer or authorised person has the like power to require production of those documents from any person who appears to the Officer or authorised person to be in possession of them.
(5) The power under this section to require the production of documents includes the power—
- *(a) if the documents are produced—*
  - *(i) to take copies of them or extracts from them;*
  - *(ii) to require the person by whom they are produced to provide an explanation of any of them;*
  - *(iii) to require any person who is or has been an official or agent of the trade union to provide an explanation of any of them;*
- *(b) if the documents are not produced, to require the person who was required to produce them to state, to the best of the person's knowledge and belief, where they are.*

(6) For the purposes of subsection (5)(a)(iii), "agent" includes an assurer appointed by the trade union under section 24ZB.
(7) For supplementary provision, see section 24ZK.]

NOTES
Commencement: 6 June 2016.
Inserted by the Transparency of Lobbying, Non-Party Campaigning and Trade Union Administration Act 2014, s 42(1), (2), as from 6 June 2016.
Repealed by the Trade Union Act 2016, s 22, Sch 4, para 1, as from a day to be appointed.

[1.300]
[24ZI Investigations by inspectors
[(1) The Certification Officer may appoint one or more members of the Officer's staff or other persons as an inspector or inspectors to—
(a) investigate whether a trade union has failed to comply with any of the requirements of section 24(1) (duties regarding the register of members), and
(b) report to the Officer in such manner as the Officer may direct.
(2) The Certification Officer may only make such an appointment if it appears to the Officer that there are circumstances suggesting that the union has failed to comply with a requirement of section 24(1), 24ZA or 24ZB (duties etc relating to the register of members).
(3) Where any person appears to the inspector or inspectors to be in possession of information relating to a matter considered by the inspector or inspectors to be relevant to the investigation, the inspector or inspectors may require the person—
(a) to produce to the inspector or inspectors any relevant documents relating to that matter,
(b) to attend before the inspector or inspectors, and
(c) otherwise to give the inspector or inspectors all assistance in connection with the investigation which the person is reasonably able to give.
(4) "Relevant documents" means—
(a) the register of the names and addresses of the trade union's members, and
(b) documents of any other description which the inspector or inspectors consider may be relevant to whether the union has failed to comply with any of the requirements of section 24(1).
(5) Where a person who is not a member of the Certification Officer's staff is appointed as an inspector under this section, there is incorporated in the appointment the duty of confidentiality as respects the register of the names and addresses of the trade union's members.
(6) The duty of confidentiality as respects that register is a duty which the inspector owes to the Certification Officer—
(a) not to disclose any name or address in the register of the names and addresses of the union's members except in permitted circumstances, and
(b) to take all reasonable steps to secure that there is no disclosure of any such name or address by another person except in permitted circumstances.
(7) The circumstances in which disclosure of a member's name or address is permitted are—
(a) where the member consents,
(b) where it is required or requested by the Certification Officer for the purposes of the discharge of any of the Officer's functions,
(c) where it is required for the purposes of the discharge of any of the functions of the inspector or any other inspector appointed by the Officer,
(d) where it is required for the purposes of the discharge of any of the functions of an assurer appointed under section 24ZB, or
(e) where it is required for the purposes of the investigation of crime or criminal proceedings.
(8) For supplementary provision, see section 24ZK.]

NOTES
Commencement: 6 June 2016.
Inserted by the Transparency of Lobbying, Non-Party Campaigning and Trade Union Administration Act 2014, s 42(1), (2), as from 6 June 2016.
Repealed by the Trade Union Act 2016, s 22, Sch 4, para 1, as from a day to be appointed.

[1.301]
[24ZJ Inspectors' reports etc
[(1) An inspector or inspectors appointed under section 24ZI—
(a) may make interim reports to the Certification Officer,
(b) must make such reports if so directed by the Officer, and
(c) on the conclusion of the investigation, must make a final report to the Officer.
(2) A report under subsection (1) must be in writing.
(3) An inspector or inspectors—
(a) may at any time inform the Certification Officer of any matters coming to their knowledge as a result of the investigation, and
(b) must do so if the Officer so directs.
(4) The Certification Officer may direct an inspector or inspectors—
(a) to take no further steps in the investigation, or
(b) to take only such further steps as are specified in the direction.
(5) Where such a direction is made, the inspector or inspectors are not required under subsection (1)(c) to make a final report to the Certification Officer unless the Officer so directs.]

NOTES

Commencement: 6 June 2016.

Inserted by the Transparency of Lobbying, Non-Party Campaigning and Trade Union Administration Act 2014, s 42(1), (2), as from 6 June 2016.

Repealed by the Trade Union Act 2016, s 22, Sch 4, para 1, as from a day to be appointed.

[1.302]

[24ZK Sections 24ZH and 24ZI: supplementary

[(1) Nothing in section 24ZH or 24ZI requires or authorises anyone to require—

(a) the disclosure by a person of information which the person would in an action in the court be entitled to refuse to disclose on grounds of legal professional privilege, or

(b) the production by a person of a document which the person would in such an action be entitled to refuse to produce on such grounds.

(2) But a lawyer may be required under section 24ZH or 24ZI to disclose the name and address of the lawyer's client.

(3) A person is not excused from providing an explanation or making a statement in compliance with a requirement imposed under section 24ZH(5) or 24ZI(3) on the ground that to do so would tend to expose the person to proceedings for an offence.

(4) But an explanation so provided or a statement so made may only be used in evidence against the person by whom it is provided or made on a prosecution for an offence where, in giving evidence, the person makes a statement inconsistent with it.

(5) In this section and in sections 24ZH and 24ZI—

(a) references to documents include information recorded in any form, and

(b) in relation to information recorded otherwise than in legible form, references to its production are to the production of a copy of the information in legible form.]

NOTES

Commencement: 6 June 2016.

Inserted by the Transparency of Lobbying, Non-Party Campaigning and Trade Union Administration Act 2014, s 42(1), (2), as from 6 June 2016.

Repealed by the Trade Union Act 2016, s 22, Sch 4, para 1, as from a day to be appointed.

[1.303]

[24A Securing confidentiality of register during ballots

(1) This section applies in relation to a ballot of the members of a trade union on—

(a) an election under Chapter IV for a position to which that Chapter applies,

(b) a political resolution under Chapter VI, and

(c) a resolution to approve an instrument of amalgamation or transfer under Chapter VII.

(2) Where this section applies in relation to a ballot the trade union shall impose the duty of confidentiality in relation to the register of members' names and addresses on the scrutineer appointed by the union for the purposes of the ballot and on any person appointed by the union as the independent person for the purposes of the ballot.

(3) The duty of confidentiality[, in the context of a scrutineer or independent person,] in relation to the register of members' names and addresses is, when imposed on a scrutineer or on an independent person, a duty—

(a) not to disclose any name or address in the register except in permitted circumstances; and

(b) to take all reasonable steps to secure that there is no disclosure of any such name or address by any other person except in permitted circumstances;

and any reference in this Act to "the duty of confidentiality" is a reference to the duty prescribed in this subsection.

(4) The circumstances in which disclosure of a member's name and address is permitted are—

(a) where the member consents;

(b) where it is [required or] requested by the Certification Officer for the purposes of the discharge of any of his functions or it is required for the purposes of the discharge of any of the functions of an inspector appointed by him;

(c) where it is required for the purposes of the discharge of any of the functions of the scrutineer or independent person, as the case may be, under the terms of his appointment;

(d) where it is required for the purposes of the investigation of crime or of criminal proceedings.

(5) Any provision of this Part which incorporates the duty of confidentiality as respects the register into the appointment of a scrutineer or an independent person has the effect of imposing that duty on the scrutineer or independent person as a duty owed by him to the trade union.

(6) The remedy for failure to comply with the requirements of this section is by way of application under section 25 (to the Certification Officer) or section 26 (to the court).

. . .

NOTES

Inserted by the Trade Union Reform and Employment Rights Act 1993, s 6.

Sub-ss (3), (4): words in square brackets inserted by the Transparency of Lobbying, Non-Party Campaigning and Trade Union Administration Act 2014, ss 41(1), (3), 42(1), (3), as from 6 April 2015, in relation to a reporting period which commences on or after that date (in relation to the sub-s (3) amendment), and as from 1 June 2016 (in relation to the sub-s (4) amendment).

Sub-s (6): words omitted repealed by the Employment Relations Act 1999, ss 29, 44, Sch 6, paras 1, 3, Sch 9(7).

[1.304]

[24B Enforcement of sections 24 to 24ZC by Certification Officer

(1) Where the Certification Officer is satisfied that a trade union has failed to comply with any of the requirements of section 24, 24ZA, 24ZB or 24ZC (duties etc relating to the register of members), the Officer may make a declaration to that effect.

(2) Before making such a declaration, the Certification Officer—

(a) may make such enquiries as the Officer thinks fit,

(b) must give the union an opportunity to make written representations, and

(c) may give the union an opportunity to make oral representations.

(3) If the Certification Officer makes a declaration it must specify the provisions with which the union has failed to comply.

(4) Where the Certification Officer makes a declaration and is satisfied—

(a) that steps have been taken by the union with a view to remedying the declared failure or securing that a failure of the same or any similar kind does not occur in future, or

(b) that the union has agreed to take such steps,

the Officer must specify those steps in the declaration.

(5) Where a declaration is made, the Certification Officer must give reasons in writing for making the declaration.

(6) Where a declaration is made, the Certification Officer must also make an enforcement order unless the Officer considers that to do so would be inappropriate.

(7) An "enforcement order" is an order imposing on the union one or both of the following requirements—

(a) to take such steps to remedy the declared failure, within such period, as may be specified in the order;

(b) to abstain from such acts as may be so specified with a view to securing that a failure of the same or a similar kind does not occur in future.

(8) Where, having given the union an opportunity to make written representations under subsection (2)(b), the Certification Officer determines not to make a declaration under subsection (1), the Officer must give the union notice in writing of that determination.

(9) Where the Certification Officer requests a person to provide information to the Officer in connection with enquiries under this section, the Officer must specify the date by which that information is to be provided.

(10) Where the information is not provided by the specified date, the Certification Officer must proceed with determining whether to make a declaration under subsection (1) unless the Officer considers that it would be inappropriate to do so.

(11) A declaration made by the Certification Officer under this section may be relied on as if it were a declaration made by the court.

(12) An enforcement order made by the Certification Officer under this section may be enforced [by the Officer] in the same way as an order of the court.

(13) Where an enforcement order has been made, a person who is a member of the union and was a member at the time it was made is entitled to enforce obedience to the order as if the order had been made on an application by that person.]

NOTES

Commencement: 1 June 2016.

Inserted by the Transparency of Lobbying, Non-Party Campaigning and Trade Union Administration Act 2014, s 43(1), (2), as from 1 June 2016.

Sub-s (12): words in square brackets inserted by the Trade Union Act 2016, s 19(4), as from a day to be appointed.

[1.305]

[24C Enforcement of sections 24ZH and 24ZI by Certification Officer

(1) Where the Certification Officer is satisfied that a trade union or any other person has failed to comply with any requirement imposed under—

(a) section 24ZH (power of Certification Officer to require production of documents etc), or

(b) section 24ZI (investigations by inspectors),

the Officer may make an order requiring the trade union or person to comply with the requirement.

(2) Before making such an order, the Certification Officer must give the trade union or person an opportunity to be heard.

(3) In the case of a failure to comply with a requirement imposed under section 24ZH or 24ZI to produce a document, the Certification Officer may make an order only if the Officer is satisfied that—

(a) the document is in the possession of the union or person, and

(b) it is reasonably practicable for the union or person to comply with the requirement.

(4) In the case of a failure to comply with any other requirement imposed under section 24ZH or 24ZI, the Certification Officer may make an order only if the Officer is satisfied that it is reasonably practicable for the union or person to comply with the requirement.

(5) The order must specify—

(a) the requirement with which the trade union or person has failed to comply, and

(b) the date by which the trade union or person must comply.

(6) An order made by the Certification Officer under this section may be enforced in the same way as an order of the court.]

NOTES

Commencement: 1 June 2016.

Inserted by the Transparency of Lobbying, Non-Party Campaigning and Trade Union Administration Act 2014, s 43(1), (2), as from 1 June 2016.

Repealed by the Trade Union Act 2016, s 22, Sch 4, para 1, as from a day to be appointed.

[1.306]

25 Remedy for failure: application to Certification Officer

(1) A member of a trade union who claims that the union has failed to comply with any of the requirements of section 24 [or 24A] (duties with respect to register of members' names and addresses) may apply to the Certification Officer for a declaration to that effect.

(2) On an application being made to him, the Certification Officer shall—

(a) make such enquiries as he thinks fit, and

(b) . . . give the applicant and the trade union an opportunity to be heard,

and may make or refuse the declaration asked for.

(3) If he makes a declaration he shall specify in it the provisions with which the trade union has failed to comply.

(4) Where he makes a declaration and is satisfied that steps have been taken by the union with a view to remedying the declared failure, or securing that a failure of the same or any similar kind does not occur in future, or that the union has agreed to take such steps, he shall specify those steps in the declaration.

(5) Whether he makes or refuses a declaration, he shall give reasons for his decision in writing; and the reasons may be accompanied by written observations on any matter arising from, or connected with, the proceedings.

[(5A) Where the Certification Officer makes a declaration he shall also, unless he considers that to do so would be inappropriate, make an enforcement order, that is, an order imposing on the union one or both of the following requirements—

(a) to take such steps to remedy the declared failure, within such period, as may be specified in the order;

(b) to abstain from such acts as may be so specified with a view to securing that a failure of the same or a similar kind does not occur in future.

(5B) Where an enforcement order has been made, any person who is a member of the union and was a member at the time it was made is entitled to enforce obedience to the order as if he had made the application on which the order was made.]

(6) In exercising his functions under this section the Certification Officer shall ensure that, so far as is reasonably practicable, an application made to him is determined within six months of being made.

[(6A) For the purposes of subsection (6) the circumstances in which it is not reasonably practicable to determine an application within that time frame may include, in particular, where delay is caused by the exercise of the powers under *section 24ZH or 24ZI* (powers to require production of documents etc and to appoint inspectors).]

(7) Where he requests a person to furnish information to him in connection with enquiries made by him under this section, he shall specify the date by which that information is to be furnished and, unless he considers that it would be inappropriate to do so, shall proceed with his determination of the application notwithstanding that the information has not been furnished to him by the specified date.

[(8) The Certification Officer shall not entertain an application for a declaration as respects an alleged failure to comply with the requirements of section 24A in relation to a ballot to which that section applies unless the application is made before the end of the period of one year beginning with the last day on which votes could be cast in the ballot.]

[(9) A declaration made by the Certification Officer under this section may be relied on as if it were a declaration made by the court.

(10) An enforcement order made by the Certification Officer under this section may be enforced [(by the Certification Officer, the applicant or a person mentioned in subsection (5B))] in the same way as an order of the court.

(11) The following paragraphs have effect if a person applies under section 26 in relation to an alleged failure—

(a) that person may not apply under this section in relation to that failure;

(b) on an application by a different person under this section in relation to that failure, the Certification Officer shall have due regard to any declaration, order, observations or reasons made or given by the court regarding that failure and brought to the Certification Officer's notice.]

NOTES

Sub-s (1): words in square brackets inserted by the Trade Union Reform and Employment Rights Act 1993, s 49(2), Sch 8, para 40(a).

Sub-s (2): words omitted repealed by the Employment Relations Act 1999, ss 29, 44, Sch 6, paras 1, 4(1), (2), Sch 9(7).

Sub-ss (5A), (5B), (9)–(11): inserted and added respectively by the Employment Relations Act 1999, s 29, Sch 6, paras 1, 4(1), (3), (4); words in square brackets in sub-s (10) inserted by the Trade Union Act 2016, s 19(4), as from a day to be appointed.

Sub-s (6A): inserted by the Transparency of Lobbying, Non-Party Campaigning and Trade Union Administration Act 2014, s 43(1), (4), as from 1 June 2016; for the words in italics there are substituted the words "paragraph 2 or 3 of Schedule A3" by the Trade Union Act 2016, s 22, Sch 4, para 2, as from a day to be appointed.

Sub-s (8): added by the Trade Union Reform and Employment Rights Act 1993, s 49(2), Sch 8, para 40(b).

[1.307]

26 Remedy for failure: application to court

(1) A member of a trade union who claims that the union has failed to comply with any of the requirements of section 24 [or 24A] (duties with respect to register of members' names and addresses) may apply to the court for a declaration to that effect.

(2) . . .

(3) If the court makes a declaration it shall specify in it the provisions with which the trade union has failed to comply.

(4) Where the court makes a declaration it shall also, unless it considers that to do so would be inappropriate, make an enforcement order, that is, an order imposing on the union one or both of the following requirements—

(a) to take such steps to remedy the declared failure, within such period, as may be specified in the order;

(b) to abstain from such acts as may be so specified with a view to securing that a failure of the same or a similar kind does not occur in future.

(5) Where an enforcement order has been made, any person who is a member of the union and was a member at the time it was made, is entitled to enforce obedience to the order as if he had made the application on which the order was made.

(6) Without prejudice to any other power of the court, the court may on an application under this section grant such interlocutory relief (in Scotland, such interim order) as it considers appropriate.

[(7) The court shall not entertain an application for a declaration as respects an alleged failure to comply with the requirements of section 24A in relation to a ballot to which that section applies unless the application is made before the end of the period of one year beginning with the last day on which votes could be cast in the ballot.]

[(8) The following paragraphs have effect if a person applies under section 25 in relation to an alleged failure—

(a) that person may not apply under this section in relation to that failure;

(b) on an application by a different person under this section in relation to that failure, the court shall have due regard to any declaration, order, observations or reasons made or given by the Certification Officer regarding that failure and brought to the court's notice.]

[(9) Where a person applies under this section in relation to an alleged failure and the Certification Officer has made a declaration regarding that failure under section 24B, the court must have due regard to the declaration and any order, observations or reasons made or given by the Officer under that section regarding that failure and brought to the court's notice.]

NOTES

Sub-s (1): words in square brackets inserted by the Trade Union Reform and Employment Rights Act 1993, s 49(2), Sch 8, para 41(a).

Sub-s (2): repealed by the Employment Relations Act 1999, ss 29, 44, Sch 6, paras 1, 5(1), (2), Sch 9(7).

Sub-s (7): added by the Trade Union Reform and Employment Rights Act 1993, s 49(2), Sch 8, para 41(b).

Sub-s (8): added by the Employment Relations Act 1999, s 29, Sch 6, paras 1, 5(1), (3).

Sub-s (9): added by the Transparency of Lobbying, Non-Party Campaigning and Trade Union Administration Act 2014, s 43(1), (5), as from 1 June 2016.

Duty to supply copy of rules

[1.308]

27 Duty to supply copy of rules

A trade union shall at the request of any person supply him with a copy of its rules either free of charge or on payment of a reasonable charge.

Accounting records

[1.309]

28 Duty to keep accounting records

(1) A trade union shall—

(a) cause to be kept proper accounting records with respect to its transactions and its assets and liabilities, and

(b) establish and maintain a satisfactory system of control of its accounting records, its cash holdings and all its receipts and remittances.

(2) Proper accounting records shall not be taken to be kept with respect to the matters mentioned in subsection (1)(a) unless there are kept such records as are necessary to give a true and fair view of the state of the affairs of the trade union and to explain its transactions.

[1.310]

29 Duty to keep records available for inspection

(1) A trade union shall keep available for inspection from their creation until the end of the period of six years beginning with the 1st January following the end of the period to which they relate such of the records of the union, or of any branch or section of the union, as are, or purport to be, records required to be kept by the union under section 28.

This does not apply to records relating to periods before 1st January 1988.

(2) In section 30 (right of member to access to accounting records)—

(a) references to a union's accounting records are to any such records as are mentioned in subsection (1) above, and

(b) references to records available for inspection are to records which the union is required by that subsection to keep available for inspection.

(3) The expiry of the period mentioned in subsection (1) above does not affect the duty of a trade union to comply with a request for access made under section 30 before the end of that period.

[1.311]

30 Right of access to accounting records

(1) A member of a trade union has a right to request access to any accounting records of the union which are available for inspection and relate to periods including a time when he was a member of the union.

In the case of records relating to a branch or section of the union, it is immaterial whether he was a member of that branch or section.

(2) Where such access is requested the union shall—

(a) make arrangements with the member for him to be allowed to inspect the records requested before the end of the period of twenty-eight days beginning with the day the request was made,

(b) allow him and any accountant accompanying him for the purpose to inspect the records at the time and place arranged, and

(c) secure that at the time of the inspection he is allowed to take, or is supplied with, any copies of, or of extracts from, records inspected by him which he requires.

(3) The inspection shall be at a reasonable hour and at the place where the records are normally kept, unless the parties to the arrangements agree otherwise.

(4) An "accountant" means a person who is eligible for appointment as a [statutory auditor under Part 42 of the Companies Act 2006].

(5) The union need not allow the member to be accompanied by an accountant if the accountant fails to enter into such agreement as the union may reasonably require for protecting the confidentiality of the records.

(6) Where a member who makes a request for access to a union's accounting records is informed by the union, before any arrangements are made in pursuance of the request—

(a) of the union's intention to charge for allowing him to inspect the records to which the request relates, for allowing him to take copies of, or extracts from, those records or for supplying any such copies, and

(b) of the principles in accordance with which its charges will be determined,

then, where the union complies with the request, he is liable to pay the union on demand such amount, not exceeding the reasonable administrative expenses incurred by the union in complying with the request, as is determined in accordance with those principles.

(7) In this section "member", in relation to a trade union consisting wholly or partly of, or of representatives of, constituent or affiliated organisations, includes a member of any of the constituent or affiliated organisations.

NOTES

Sub-s (4): words in square brackets substituted by the Companies Act 2006 (Consequential Amendments etc) Order 2008, SI 2008/948, art 3(1)(a), Sch 1, Pt 1, para 1(qq)(i).

[1.312]

31 Remedy for failure to comply with request for access

(1) A person who claims that a trade union has failed in any respect to comply with a request made by him under section 30 may apply to the court [or to the Certification Officer].

(2) Where [on an application to it] the court is satisfied that the claim is well-founded, it shall make such order as it considers appropriate for ensuring that [the applicant]—

(a) is allowed to inspect the records requested,

(b) is allowed to be accompanied by an accountant when making the inspection of those records, and

(c) is allowed to take, or is supplied with, such copies of, or of extracts from, the records as he may require.

[(2A) On an application to him the Certification Officer shall—

(a) make such enquiries as he thinks fit, and

(b) give the applicant and the trade union an opportunity to be heard.

(2B) Where the Certification Officer is satisfied that the claim is well-founded he shall make such order as he considers appropriate for ensuring that the applicant—

(a) is allowed to inspect the records requested,

(b) is allowed to be accompanied by an accountant when making the inspection of those records, and

(c) is allowed to take, or is supplied with, such copies of, or of extracts from, the records as he may require.

(2C) In exercising his functions under this section the Certification Officer shall ensure that, so far as is reasonably practicable, an application made to him is determined within six months of being made.]

(3) Without prejudice to any other power of the court, the court may on an application [to it] under this section grant such interlocutory relief (in Scotland, such interim order) as it considers appropriate.

[(4) Where the Certification Officer requests a person to furnish information to him in connection with enquiries made by him under this section, he shall specify the date by which that information is to be furnished and, unless he considers that it would be inappropriate to do so, shall proceed with his determination of the application notwithstanding that the information has not been furnished to him by the specified date.

(5) An order made by the Certification Officer under this section may be enforced [(by the Certification Officer or the applicant)] in the same way as an order of the court.
(6) If a person applies to the court under this section in relation to an alleged failure he may not apply to the Certification Officer under this section in relation to that failure.
(7) If a person applies to the Certification Officer under this section in relation to an alleged failure he may not apply to the court under this section in relation to that failure.]

NOTES

Sub-ss (1), (3): words in square brackets inserted by the Employment Relations Act 1999, s 29, Sch 6, paras 1, 6(1), (2), (5).
Sub-s (2): words in first pair of square brackets inserted, and words in second pair of square brackets substituted, by the Employment Relations Act 1999, s 29, Sch 6, paras 1, 6(1), (3).
Sub-ss (2A)–(2C), (4)–(7): inserted and added respectively by the Employment Relations Act 1999, s 29, Sch 6, paras 1, 6(1), (4), (6); words in square brackets in sub-s (5) inserted by the Trade Union Act 2016, s 19(4), as from a day to be appointed.

Annual return, accounts and audit

[1.313]
32 Annual return

(1) A trade union shall send to the Certification Officer as respects each calendar year a return relating to its affairs.
(2) The annual return shall be in such form and be signed by such persons as the Certification Officer may require and shall be sent to him before 1st June in the calendar year following that to which it relates.
(3) The annual return shall contain—
(a) the following accounts—
(i) revenue accounts indicating the income and expenditure of the trade union for the period to which the return relates,
(ii) a balance sheet as at the end of that period, and
(iii) such other accounts as the Certification Officer may require,
each of which must give a true and fair view of the matters to which it relates,
[(aa) details of the salary paid to and other benefits provided to or in respect of—
(i) each member of the executive,
(ii) the president, and
(iii) the general secretary,
by the trade union during the period to which the return relates,]
(b) a copy of the report made by the auditor or auditors of the trade union on those accounts and such other documents relating to those accounts and such further particulars as the Certification Officer may require, . . .
(c) a copy of the rules of the trade union as in force at the end of the period to which the return relates[, and
(d) in the case of a trade union required to maintain a register by section 24, a statement of the number of names on the register as at the end of the period to which the return relates and the number of those names which were not accompanied by an address which is a member's address for the purposes of that section;]
and shall have attached to it a note of all the changes in the officers of the union and of any change in the address of the head or main office of the union during the period to which the return relates.
(4) The Certification Officer may, if in any particular case he considers it appropriate to do so—
(a) direct that the period for which a return is to be sent to him shall be a period other than the calendar year last preceding the date on which the return is sent;
(b) direct that the date before which a return is to be sent to him shall be such date (whether before or after 1st June) as may be specified in the direction.
(5) A trade union shall at the request of any person supply him with a copy of its most recent return either free of charge or on payment of a reasonable charge.
(6) The Certification Officer shall at all reasonable hours keep available for public inspection either free of charge or on payment of a reasonable charge, copies of all annual returns sent to him under this section.
[(7) For the purposes of this section and section 32A "member of the executive" includes any person who, under the rules or practice of the union, may attend and speak at some or all of the meetings of the executive, otherwise than for the purpose of providing the committee with factual information or with technical or professional advice with respect to matters taken into account by the executive in carrying out its functions.]

NOTES

Sub-s (3): para (aa) inserted, word omitted from para (b) repealed, and para (d) and the word immediately preceding it inserted, by the Trade Union Reform and Employment Rights Act 1993, ss 8, 51, Sch 10.
Sub-s (7): added by the Trade Union Reform and Employment Rights Act 1993, s 49(2), Sch 8, para 42.

[1.314]
[32ZA Details of industrial action etc to be included in annual return

(1) If industrial action was taken during any return period in response to any inducement on the part of a trade union, the union's return under section 32 for that period shall set out—
(a) the nature of the trade dispute to which the industrial action related;
(b) the nature of the industrial action;
(c) when the industrial action was taken.

(2) If a trade union held a ballot during any return period in respect of industrial action, the union's return under section 32 for that period shall contain the information mentioned in section 231 (information as to result of ballot).
(3) In this section "return period" means a period for which a trade union is required to send a return to the Certification Officer under section 32.]

NOTES

Commencement: 1 March 2017.

Inserted by the Trade Union Act 2016, s 7, as from 1 March 2017 (in relation to returns for periods that begin after that date (see **[1.2005]**)).

[1.315]

[32ZB Details of political expenditure to be included in annual return

(1) This section applies where the expenditure of a trade union paid out of its political fund in any calendar year exceeds £2,000 in total.
(2) The union's return for that year under section 32 must give the required information (see subsections (3) to (7)) for each category of expenditure paid out of its political fund; and for this purpose—
- (a) expenditure falling within paragraph (a) of section 72(1) is one category of expenditure, expenditure falling within paragraph (b) of section 72(1) is another, and so on;
- (b) expenditure not falling within section 72(1) is a further category of expenditure.

(3) For expenditure falling within section 72(1)(a), (b) or (e) the required information is—
- (a) the name of each political party in relation to which money was expended;
- (b) the total amount expended in relation to each one.

(4) For expenditure falling within section 72(1)(c) the required information is—
- (a) each election to a political office in relation to which money was expended;
- (b) in relation to each election—
  - (i) the name of each political party to which money was paid, and the total amount paid to each one;
  - (ii) the name of each other organisation to which money was paid, and the total amount paid to each one;
  - (iii) the name of each candidate in relation to whom money was expended (or, where money was expended in relation to candidates in general of a particular political party, the name of the party), and the total amount expended in relation to each one (excluding expenditure within sub-paragraph (i) or (ii));
  - (iv) the total amount of all other expenditure incurred.

(5) For expenditure falling within section 72(1)(d) the required information is—
- (a) the name of each holder of a political office on whose maintenance money was expended;
- (b) the total amount expended in relation to each one.

(6) For expenditure falling within section 72(1)(f) the required information is—
- (a) the name of each organisation to which money was paid, and the total amount paid to each one;
- (b) the name of each political party or candidate that people were intended to be persuaded to vote for, or not to vote for, and the total amount expended in relation to each one (excluding expenditure within paragraph (a)).

(7) For expenditure not falling within section 72(1) the required information is—
- (a) the nature of each cause or campaign for which money was expended, and the total amount expended in relation to each one;
- (b) the name of each organisation to which money was paid (otherwise than for a particular cause or campaign), and the total amount paid to each one;
- (c) the total amount of all other money expended.

(8) The Secretary of State may by regulations made by statutory instrument amend subsection (1) by substituting a different amount, which may not be less than £2,000, for the amount for the time being specified in that subsection.
(9) Regulations under subsection (8) that substitute a higher amount shall be subject to annulment in pursuance of a resolution of either House of Parliament.
(10) No regulations under subsection (8) that substitute a lower amount shall be made unless a draft of them has been laid before Parliament and approved by a resolution of each House of Parliament.
(11) Where, because of a direction under section 32(4)(a), a trade union is required to send a return for a period other than a calendar year—
- (a) this section has effect as if references to a calendar year were references to that period; and
- (b) if that period is more or less than a year, subsection (1) has effect as if the amount specified in it were proportionately increased or reduced.

(12) In this section "candidate", "electors" and "political office" have the same meaning as in section 72.]

NOTES

Commencement: 1 March 2017.

Inserted by the Trade Union Act 2016, s 12(1), as from 1 March 2017 (in relation to returns for periods that begin after that date (see **[1.2010]**)).

Regulations: as of 15 May 2019, no Regulations had been made under this section.

[1.316]

[32ZC Enforcement of sections 32ZA and 32ZB by Certification Officer

(1) Where the Certification Officer is satisfied that a trade union has failed to comply with any of the requirements of section 32ZA or 32ZB, the Officer may make a declaration to that effect.

(2) Before making such a declaration, the Certification Officer—

- (a) may make such enquiries as the Officer thinks fit,
- (b) must give the union an opportunity to make written representations, and
- (c) may give the union an opportunity to make oral representations.

(3) If the Certification Officer makes a declaration it must specify the provisions with which the union has failed to comply.

(4) Where the Certification Officer makes a declaration and is satisfied—

- (a) that steps have been taken by the union with a view to remedying the declared failure or securing that a failure of the same or any similar kind does not occur in future, or
- (b) that the union has agreed to take such steps,

the Officer must specify those steps in the declaration.

(5) Where a declaration is made, the Certification Officer must give reasons in writing for making the declaration.

(6) Where a declaration is made, the Certification Officer must also make an enforcement order unless the Officer considers that to do so would be inappropriate.

(7) An "enforcement order" is an order requiring the union to take such steps to remedy the declared failure, within such period, as may be specified in the order.

(8) Where, having given the union an opportunity to make written representations under subsection (2)(b), the Certification Officer determines not to make a declaration under subsection (1), the Officer must give the union notice in writing of that determination.

(9) Where the Certification Officer requests a person to provide information to the Officer in connection with enquiries under this section, the Officer must specify the date by which that information is to be provided.

(10) Where the information is not provided by the specified date, the Certification Officer must proceed with determining whether to make a declaration under subsection (1) unless the Officer considers that it would be inappropriate to do so.

(11) A declaration made by the Certification Officer under this section may be relied on as if it were a declaration made by the court.

(12) An enforcement order made by the Certification Officer under this section may be enforced by the Officer in the same way as an order of the court.

(13) Where an enforcement order has been made, a person who is a member of the union and was a member at the time it was made is entitled to enforce obedience to the order as if the order had been made on an application by that person.]

NOTES

Commencement: 1 March 2017.

Inserted by the Trade Union Act 2016, s 18(1), as from 1 March 2017 (in relation to returns for periods that begin after that date (see **[1.2016]**)).

[1.317]

[32A Statement to members following annual return

(1) A trade union shall take all reasonable steps to secure that, not later than the end of the period of eight weeks beginning with the day on which the annual return of the union is sent to the Certification Officer, all the members of the union are provided with the statement required by this section by any of the methods allowed by subsection (2).

(2) Those methods are—

- (a) the sending of individual copies of the statement to members; or
- (b) any other means (whether by including the statement in a publication of the union or otherwise) which it is the practice of the union to use when information of general interest to all its members needs to be provided to them.

(3) The statement required by this section shall specify—

- (a) the total income and expenditure of the trade union for the period to which the return relates,
- (b) how much of the income of the union for that period consisted of payments in respect of membership,
- (c) the total income and expenditure for that period of any political fund of the union, and
- (d) the salary paid to and other benefits provided to or in respect of—
  - (i) each member of the executive,
  - (ii) the president, and
  - (iii) the general secretary,

  by the trade union during that period.

(4) The requirement imposed by this section is not satisfied if the statement specifies anything inconsistent with the contents of the return.

(5) The statement—

- (a) shall also set out in full the report made by the auditor or auditors of the union on the accounts contained in the return and state the name and address of that auditor or of each of those auditors, and
- (b) may include any other matter which the union considers may give a member significant assistance in making an informed judgment about the financial activities of the union in the period to which the return relates.

(6) The statement—

(a) shall also include the following statement—

"A member who is concerned that some irregularity may be occurring, or have occurred, in the conduct of the financial affairs of the union may take steps with a view to investigating further, obtaining clarification and, if necessary, securing regularisation of that conduct.

The member may raise any such concern with such one or more of the following as it seems appropriate to raise it with: the officials of the union, the trustees of the property of the union, the auditor or auditors of the union, the Certification Officer (who is an independent officer appointed by the Secretary of State) and the police.

Where a member believes that the financial affairs of the union have been or are being conducted in breach of the law or in breach of rules of the union and contemplates bringing civil proceedings against the union or responsible officials or trustees, he [should] consider obtaining independent legal advice."; and

(b) may include such other details of the steps which a member may take for the purpose mentioned in the statement set out above as the trade union considers appropriate.

(7) A trade union shall send to the Certification Officer a copy of the statement which is provided to its members in pursuance of this section as soon as is reasonably practicable after it is so provided.

(8) Where the same form of statement is not provided to all the members of a trade union, the union shall send to the Certification Officer in accordance with subsection (7) a copy of each form of statement provided to any of them.

(9) If at any time during the period of two years beginning with the day referred to in subsection (1) any member of the trade union requests a copy of the statement required by this section, the union shall, as soon as practicable, furnish him with such a copy free of charge.]

NOTES

Inserted by the Trade Union Reform and Employment Rights Act 1993, s 9.

Sub-s (6): word in square brackets substituted by the Employment Relations Act 1999, s 28(3).

[1.318]

33 Duty to appoint auditors

(1) A trade union shall in respect of each accounting period appoint an auditor or auditors to audit the accounts contained in its annual return.

(2) An "accounting period" means any period in relation to which it is required to send a return to the Certification Officer.

[1.319]

34 Eligibility for appointment as auditor

(1) A person is not qualified to be the auditor or one of the auditors of a trade union unless he is eligible for appointment as a [statutory auditor under Part 42 of the Companies Act 2006].

(2) Two or more persons who are not so qualified may act as auditors of a trade union in respect of an accounting period if—

(a) the receipts and payments in respect of the union's last preceding accounting period did not in the aggregate exceed £5,000,

(b) the number of its members at the end of that period did not exceed 500, and

(c) the value of its assets at the end of that period did not in the aggregate exceed £5,000.

(3) Where by virtue of subsection (2) persons who are not qualified as mentioned in subsection (1) act as auditors of a trade union in respect of an accounting period, the Certification Officer may (during that period or after it comes to an end) direct the union to appoint a person who is so qualified to audit its accounts for that period.

(4) The Secretary of State may by regulations—

(a) substitute for any sum or number specified in subsection (2) such sum or number as may be specified in the regulations; and

(b) prescribe what receipts and payments are to be taken into account for the purposes of that subsection.

Any such regulations shall be made by statutory instrument which shall be subject to annulment in pursuance of a resolution of either House of Parliament.

(5) None of the following shall act as auditor of a trade union—

(a) an officer or employee of the trade union or of any of its branches or sections;

(b) a person who is a partner of, or in the employment of, or who employs, such an officer or employee;

(c) . . .

. . .

NOTES

Sub-s (1): words in square brackets substituted by the Companies Act 2006 (Consequential Amendments etc) Order 2008, SI 2008/948, art 3(1)(a), Sch 1, Pt 1, para 1(qq)(ii).

Sub-s (5): para (c) repealed by the Employment Relations Act 2004, s 53(1), 57(2), Sch 2; final words omitted repealed by the Trade Union Reform and Employment Rights Act 1993, ss 49(1), 51, Sch 7, para 18, Sch 10.

Regulations: as of 15 May 2019, no Regulations had been made under this section.

[1.320]
35 Appointment and removal of auditors

(1) The rules of every trade union shall contain provision for the appointment and removal of auditors.

But the following provisions have effect notwithstanding anything in the rules.

(2) An auditor of a trade union shall not be removed from office except by resolution passed at a general meeting of its members or of delegates of its members.

(3) An auditor duly appointed to audit the accounts of a trade union shall be re-appointed as auditor for the following accounting period, unless—

(a) a resolution has been passed at a general meeting of the trade union appointing somebody instead of him or providing expressly that he shall not be re-appointed, or
(b) he has given notice to the trade union in writing of his unwillingness to be re-appointed, or
(c) he is ineligible for re-appointment, or
(d) he has ceased to act as auditor by reason of incapacity.

(4) Where notice has been given of an intended resolution to appoint somebody in place of a retiring auditor but the resolution cannot be proceeded with at the meeting because of the death or incapacity of that person, or because he is ineligible for the appointment, the retiring auditor need not automatically be re-appointed.

(5) The references above to a person being ineligible for appointment as auditor of a trade union are to his not being qualified for the appointment in accordance with [subsections (1) to (4)] of section 34 or being precluded by [subsection (5)] of that section from acting as its auditor.

(6) The Secretary of State may make provision by regulations as to the procedure to be followed when it is intended to move a resolution—

(a) appointing another auditor in place of a retiring auditor, or
(b) providing expressly that a retiring auditor shall not be reappointed,

and as to the rights of auditors and members of the trade union in relation to such a motion.

Any such regulations shall be made by statutory instrument which shall be subject to annulment in pursuance of a resolution of either House of Parliament.

(7) Where regulations under subsection (6)—

(a) require copies of any representations made by a retiring auditor to be sent out, or
(b) require any such representations to be read out at a meeting,

the court, on the application of the trade union or of any other person, may dispense with the requirement if satisfied that the rights conferred on the retiring auditor by the regulations are being abused to secure needless publicity for defamatory matter.

(8) On such an application the court may order the costs or expenses of the trade union to be paid, in whole or in part, by the retiring auditor, whether he is a party to the application or not.

NOTES

Sub-s (5): words in square brackets substituted by the Trade Union Reform and Employment Rights Act 1993, s 49(1), Sch 7, para 19.

Regulations: as of 15 May 2019, no Regulations had been made under this section.

[1.321]
36 Auditor's report

(1) The auditor or auditors of a trade union shall make a report to it on the accounts audited by him or them and contained in its annual return.

[(1A) The report shall state the names of, and be signed by, the auditor or auditors.]

(2) The report shall state whether, in the opinion of the auditor or auditors, the accounts give a true and fair view of the matters to which they relate.

(3) It is the duty of the auditor or auditors in preparing their report to carry out such investigations as will enable them to form an opinion as to—

(a) whether the trade union has kept proper accounting records in accordance with the requirements of section 28,
(b) whether it has maintained a satisfactory system of control over its transactions in accordance with the requirements of that section, and
(c) whether the accounts to which the report relates agree with the accounting records.

(4) If in the opinion of the auditor or auditors the trade union has failed to comply with section 28, or if the accounts do not agree with the accounting records, the auditor or auditors shall state that fact in the report.

[(5) Any reference in this section to signature by an auditor is, where the office of auditor is held by a body corporate or partnership, to signature in the name of the body corporate or partnership by an individual authorised to sign on its behalf.]

NOTES

Sub-ss (1A), (5): inserted and added respectively by the Employment Relations Act 2004, s 53(2), (3).

[1.322]
37 Rights of auditors

(1) Every auditor of a trade union—

(a) has a right of access at all times to its accounting records and to all other documents relating to its affairs, and
(b) is entitled to require from its officers, or the officers of any of its branches or sections, such information and explanations as he thinks necessary for the performance of his duties as auditor.

(2) If an auditor fails to obtain all the information and explanations which, to the best of his knowledge and belief, are necessary for the purposes of an audit, he shall state that fact in his report.

(3) Every auditor of a trade union is entitled—

(a) to attend any general meeting of its members, or of delegates of its members, and to receive all notices of and other communications relating to any general meeting which any such member or delegate is entitled to receive, and

(b) to be heard at any meeting which he attends on any part of the business of the meeting which concerns him as auditor.

[(4) In the case of an auditor which is a body corporate or partnership, its right to attend or be heard at a meeting is exercisable by an individual authorised by it to act as its representative at the meeting.]

NOTES

Sub-s (4): added by the Employment Relations Act 2004, s 53(4).

[Investigation of financial affairs

[1.323]

37A Power of Certification Officer to require production of documents etc

(1) The Certification Officer may at any time, if he thinks there is good reason to do so, give directions to a trade union, or a branch or section of a trade union, requiring it to produce such relevant documents as may be specified in the directions; and the documents shall be produced at such time and place as may be so specified.

(2) The Certification Officer may at any time, if he thinks there is good reason to do so, authorise a member of his staff or any other person, on producing (if so required) evidence of his authority, to require a trade union, or a branch or section of a trade union, to produce forthwith to the member of staff or other person such relevant documents as the member of staff or other person may specify.

(3) Where the Certification Officer, or a member of his staff or any other person, has power to require the production of documents by virtue of subsection (1) or (2), the Certification Officer, member of staff or other person has the like power to require production of those documents from any person who appears to the Certification Officer, member of staff or other person to be in possession of them.

(4) Where such a person claims a lien on documents produced by him, the production is without prejudice to the lien.

(5) The power under this section to require the production of documents includes power—

(a) if the documents are produced—

(i) to take copies of them or extracts from them, and

(ii) to require the person by whom they are produced, or any person who is or has been an official or agent of the trade union, to provide an explanation of any of them; and

(b) if the documents are not produced, to require the person who was required to produce them to state, to the best of his knowledge and belief, where they are.

(6) In subsections (1) and (2) "relevant documents", in relation to a trade union or a branch or section of a trade union, means accounting documents, and documents of any other description, which may be relevant in considering the financial affairs of the trade union.

(7) A person shall not be excused from providing an explanation or making a statement in compliance with a requirement imposed under subsection (5) on the ground that to do so would tend to expose him to proceedings for an offence; but an explanation so provided or statement so made may only be used in evidence against the person by whom it is made or provided—

(a) on a prosecution for an offence under section 45(9) (false explanations and statements), or

(b) on a prosecution for some other offence where in giving evidence the person makes a statement inconsistent with it.]

NOTES

Inserted, together with the preceding heading, and ss 37B–37E, by the Trade Union Reform and Employment Rights Act 1993, s 10.

[1.324]

[37B Investigations by inspectors

(1) The Certification Officer may appoint one or more members of his staff or other persons as an inspector or inspectors to investigate the financial affairs of a trade union and to report on them in such manner as he may direct.

(2) The Certification Officer may only make such an appointment if it appears to him that there are circumstances suggesting—

(a) that the financial affairs of the trade union are being or have been conducted for a fraudulent or unlawful purpose,

(b) that persons concerned with the management of those financial affairs have, in connection with that management, been guilty of fraud, misfeasance or other misconduct,

(c) that the trade union has failed to comply with any duty imposed on it by this Act in relation to its financial affairs, or

(d) that a rule of the union relating to its financial affairs has not been complied with.

(3) Where an inspector is, or inspectors are, appointed under this section it is the duty of all persons who are or have been officials or agents of the trade union—

(a) to produce to the inspector or inspectors all relevant documents which are in their possession,

(b) to attend before the inspector or inspectors when required to do so, and

(c) otherwise to give the inspector or inspectors all assistance in connection with the investigation which they are reasonably able to give.

(4) Where any person (whether or not within subsection (3)) appears to the inspector or inspectors to be in possession of information relating to a matter which he considers, or they consider, to be relevant to the investigation, the inspector or inspectors may require him—

(a) to produce to the inspector or inspectors any relevant documents relating to that matter,
(b) to attend before the inspector or inspectors, and
(c) otherwise to give the inspector or inspectors all assistance in connection with the investigation which he is reasonably able to give;

and it is the duty of the person to comply with the requirement.

(5) In subsections (3) and (4) "relevant documents", in relation to an investigation of the financial affairs of a trade union, means accounting documents, and documents of any other description, which may be relevant to the investigation.

(6) A person shall not be excused from providing an explanation or making a statement in compliance with subsection (3) or a requirement imposed under subsection (4) on the ground that to do so would tend to expose him to proceedings for an offence; but an explanation so provided or statement so made may only be used in evidence against the person by whom it is provided or made—

(a) on a prosecution for an offence under section 45(9) (false explanations and statements), or
(b) on a prosecution for some other offence where in giving evidence the person makes a statement inconsistent with it.]

NOTES

Inserted as noted to s 37A at **[1.323]**.

[1.325]

[37C Inspectors' reports etc

(1) An inspector or inspectors appointed under section 37B—

(a) may, and if so directed by the Certification Officer shall, make interim reports, and
(b) on the conclusion of their investigation shall make a final report,

to the Certification Officer.

(2) Any report under subsection (1) shall be written or printed, as the Certification Officer directs.

(3) An inspector or inspectors appointed under section 37B may at any time, and if so directed by the Certification Officer shall, inform the Certification Officer of any matters coming to his or their knowledge as a result of the investigation.

(4) The Certification Officer may direct an inspector or inspectors appointed under section 37B to take no further steps in the investigation, or to take only such further steps as are specified in the direction, if—

(a) it appears to the Certification Officer that matters have come to light in the course of the investigation which suggest that a criminal offence has been committed and those matters have been referred to the appropriate prosecuting authority, or
(b) it appears to the Certification Officer appropriate to do so in any other circumstances.

(5) Where an investigation is the subject of a direction under subsection (4), the inspector or inspectors shall make a final report to the Certification Officer only where the Certification Officer directs him or them to do so at the time of the direction under that subsection or subsequently.

(6) The Certification Officer shall publish a final report made to him under this section.

(7) The Certification Officer shall furnish a copy of such a report free of charge—

(a) to the trade union which is the subject of the report,
(b) to any auditor of that trade union or of any branch or section of the union, if he requests a copy before the end of the period of three years beginning with the day on which the report is published, and
(c) to any member of the trade union if—
    (i) he has complained to the Certification Officer that there are circumstances suggesting any of the states of affairs specified in section 37B(2)(a) to (d),
    (ii) the Certification Officer considers that the report contains findings which are relevant to the complaint, and
    (iii) the member requests a copy before the end of the period of three years beginning with the day on which the report is published.

(8) A copy of any report under this section, certified by the Certification Officer to be a true copy, is admissible in any legal proceedings as evidence of the opinion of the inspector or inspectors in relation to any matter contained in the report; and a document purporting to be a certificate of the Certification Officer under this subsection shall be received in evidence and be deemed to be such a certificate unless the contrary is proved.]

NOTES

Inserted as noted to s 37A at **[1.323]**.

[1.326]

[37D Expenses of investigations

(1) The expenses of an investigation under section 37B shall be defrayed in the first instance by the Certification Officer.

(2) For the purposes of this section there shall be treated as expenses of an investigation, in particular, such reasonable sums as the Certification Officer may determine in respect of general staff costs and overheads.

(3) A person who is convicted on a prosecution instituted as a result of the investigation may in the same proceedings be ordered to pay the expenses of the investigation to such extent as may be specified in the order.]

NOTES

Inserted as noted to s 37A at **[1.323]**.

[1.327]

[37E Sections 37A and 37B: supplementary

(1) Where—

(a) a report of the auditor or auditors of a trade union, or a branch or section of a trade union, on the accounts audited by him or them and contained in the annual return of the union, or branch or section—

(i) does not state without qualification that the accounts give a true and fair view of the matters to which they relate, or

(ii) includes a statement in compliance with section 36(4), or

(b) a member of a trade union has complained to the Certification Officer that there are circumstances suggesting any of the states of affairs specified in section 37B(2)(a) to (d),

the Certification Officer shall consider whether it is appropriate for him to exercise any of the powers conferred on him by sections 37A and 37B.

(2) If in a case where a member of a trade union has complained as mentioned in subsection (1)(b) the Certification Officer decides not to exercise any of the powers conferred by those sections he shall, as soon as reasonably practicable after making a decision not to do so, notify the member of his decision and, if he thinks fit, of the reasons for it.

(3) Nothing in section 37A or 37B—

(a) requires or authorises anyone to require the disclosure by a person of information which he would in an action in the High Court or the Court of Session be entitled to refuse to disclose on grounds of legal professional privilege except, if he is a lawyer, the name and address of his client, or

(b) requires or authorises anyone to require the production by a person of a document which he would in such an action be entitled to refuse to produce on such grounds.

(4) Nothing in section 37A or 37B requires or authorises anyone to require the disclosure of information or the production of documents in respect of which the person to whom the requirement would relate owes an obligation of confidence by virtue of carrying on the business of banking unless—

(a) the person to whom the obligation is owed is the trade union, or any branch or section of the union, concerned or a trustee of any fund concerned, or

(b) the person to whom the obligation of confidence is owed consents to the disclosure or production.

(5) In sections 37A and 37B and this section—

(a) references to documents include information recorded in any form, and

(b) in relation to information recorded otherwise than in legible form, references to its production are to the production of a copy of the information in legible form.]

NOTES

Inserted as noted to s 37A at **[1.323]**.

Members' superannuation schemes

[1.328]

38 Members' superannuation schemes: separate fund to be maintained

(1) In the following provisions a "members' superannuation scheme" means any scheme or arrangement made by or on behalf of a trade union (including a scheme or arrangement shown in the rules of the union) in so far as it provides—

(a) for benefits to be paid by way of pension (including any widows'[, widowers', surviving civil partners'] or children's pensions or dependants' pensions) to or in respect of members or former members of the trade union, and

(b) for those benefits to be so paid either out of the funds of the union or under an insurance scheme maintained out of those funds.

(2) A trade union shall not maintain a members' superannuation scheme unless it maintains a separate fund for the payment of benefits in accordance with the scheme.

A "separate fund" means a fund separate from the general funds of the trade union.

NOTES

Sub-s (1): words in square brackets in para (a) inserted, in relation to England and Wales, by the Marriage (Same Sex Couples) Act 2013 (Consequential and Contrary Provisions and Scotland) Order 2014, SI 2014/560, art 2, Sch 1, para 24, as from 13 March 2014 and, in relation to Scotland, by the Marriage and Civil Partnership (Scotland) Act 2014 and Civil Partnership Act 2004 (Consequential Provisions and Modifications) Order 2014, SI 2014/3229, art 29, Sch 5, para 10, as from 16 December 2014.

[1.329]

39 Examination of proposals for new scheme

(1) A trade union shall not begin to maintain a members' superannuation scheme unless, before the date on which the scheme begins to be maintained—

(a) the proposals for the scheme have been examined by an appropriately qualified actuary, and

(b) a copy of a report made to the trade union by the actuary on the results of his examination of the proposals, signed by the actuary, has been sent to the Certification Officer.

(2) The actuary's report shall state—

(a) whether in his opinion the premium or contribution rates will be adequate,

(b) whether the accounting or funding arrangements are suitable, and

(c) whether in his opinion the fund for the payment of benefits will be adequate.

(3) A copy of the actuary's report shall, on the application of any of the union's members, be supplied to him free of charge.

[1.330]

40 Periodical re-examination of existing schemes

(1) Where a trade union maintains a members' superannuation scheme, it shall arrange for the scheme to be examined periodically by an appropriately qualified actuary and for a report to be made to it by the actuary on the result of his examination.

(2) The examination shall be of the scheme as it has effect at such date as the trade union may determine, not being more than five years after the date by reference to which the last examination or, as the case may be, the examination of the proposals for the scheme was carried out.

(3) The examination shall include a valuation (as at the date by reference to which the examination is carried out) of the assets comprised in the fund maintained for the payment of benefits and of the liabilities falling to be discharged out of it.

(4) The actuary's report shall state—

(a) whether in his opinion the premium or contribution rates are adequate,

(b) whether the accounting or funding arrangements are suitable, and

(c) whether in his opinion the fund for the payment of benefits is adequate.

(5) A copy of the report, signed by the actuary, shall be sent to the Certification Officer.

(6) The trade union shall make such arrangements as will enable the report to be sent to the Certification Officer within a year of the date by reference to which the examination was carried out.

(7) A copy of the actuary's report shall, on the application of any of the union's members, be supplied to him free of charge.

[1.331]

41 Powers of the Certification Officer

(1) The Certification Officer may, on the application of a trade union—

(a) exempt a members' superannuation scheme which the union proposes to maintain from the requirements of section 39 (examination of proposals for new scheme), or

(b) exempt a members' superannuation scheme which the union maintains from the requirements of section 40 (periodical re–examination of scheme),

if he is satisfied that, by reason of the small number of members to which the scheme is applicable or for any other special reasons, it is unnecessary for the scheme to be examined in accordance with those provisions.

(2) An exemption may be revoked if it appears to the Certification Officer that the circumstances by reason of which it was granted have ceased to exist.

(3) Where an exemption is revoked under subsection [(2)], the date as at which the next periodical examination is to be carried out under section 40 shall be such as the Certification Officer may direct.

(4) The Certification Officer may in any case direct that section 40 (periodical re-examination of schemes) shall apply to a trade union with the substitution for the reference to five years of a reference to such shorter period as may be specified in the direction.

NOTES

Sub-s (3): number in square brackets substituted by the Employment Relations Act 2004, s 57(1), Sch 1, para 4.

[1.332]

42 Meaning of "appropriately qualified actuary"

In sections 39 and 40 an "appropriately qualified actuary" means a person who is either—

(a) a Fellow of the Institute of Actuaries, or

(b) a Fellow of the Faculty of Actuaries,

or is approved by the Certification Officer on the application of the trade union as a person having actuarial knowledge.

Supplementary

[1.333]

43 Newly-formed trade unions

(1) The following provisions of this Chapter do not apply to a trade union which has been in existence for less than twelve months—

(a) section 27 (duty to supply copy of rules),

(b) sections 32 to 37 (annual return, [statement for members,] accounts and audit), . . .

[(ba) sections 37A to 37E (investigation of financial affairs), and]

(c) sections 38 to 42 (members' superannuation schemes).

(2) Sections 24 to 26 (register of members' names and addresses) do not apply to a trade union until more than one year has elapsed since its formation (by amalgamation or otherwise).

For this purpose the date of formation of a trade union formed otherwise than by amalgamation shall be taken to be the date on which the first members of the executive of the union are first appointed or elected.

NOTES

Sub-s (1): words in square brackets in para (b) inserted, word omitted repealed, and para (ba) inserted, by the Trade Union Reform and Employment Rights Act 1993, ss 49(2), 51, Sch 8, para 43, Sch 10.

[1.334]

44 Discharge of duties in case of union having branches or sections

(1) The following provisions apply where a trade union consists of or includes branches or sections.

(2) Any duty falling upon the union in relation to a branch or section under the provisions of—

section 28 (duty to keep accounting records),

[sections 32 and 33 to 37] (annual return, accounts and audit), or

sections 38 to 42 (members' superannuation schemes),

shall be treated as discharged to the extent to which a branch or section discharges it instead of the union.

(3) In sections 29 to 31 (right of member to access to accounting records) references to a branch or section do not include a branch or section which is itself a trade union.

(4) Any duty falling upon a branch or section by reason of its being a trade union under—

section 24 (register of members' names and addresses),

[section 24ZA (duty to provide membership audit certificate),]

[sections 24ZB and 24ZC (duty to appoint an assurer etc),]

section 28 (duty to keep accounting records),

[sections 32 and 33 to 37] (annual return, accounts and audit), or

sections 38 to 42 (members' superannuation schemes),

shall be treated as discharged to the extent to which the union of which it is a branch or section discharges the duty instead of it.

[(5) Where the duty falling on a trade union under section 32 to send to the Certification Officer a return relating to its affairs is treated as discharged by the union by virtue of subsection (2) or (4) of this section, the duties imposed by section 32A in relation to the return shall be treated as duties of the branch or section of the union, or the trade union of which it is a branch or section, by which that duty is in fact discharged.]

NOTES

Sub-s (2): words in square brackets substituted by the Trade Union Reform and Employment Rights Act 1993, s 49(2), Sch 8, para 44(a).

Sub-s (4): words in first and second pairs of square brackets inserted by the Transparency of Lobbying, Non-Party Campaigning and Trade Union Administration Act 2014, ss 40(1), (3), 41(1), (4), as from 6 April 2015, in relation to a reporting period which commences on or after that date; words in third pair of square brackets substituted by the Trade Union Reform and Employment Rights Act 1993, s 49(2), Sch 8, para 44(a).

Sub-s (5): added by the Trade Union Reform and Employment Rights Act 1993, s 49(2), Sch 8, para 44(b).

[1.335]

45 Offences

(1) If a trade union refuses or wilfully neglects to perform a duty imposed on it by or under any of the provisions of—

section 27 (duty to supply copy of rules),

sections 28 to 30 (accounting records),

[section 32 (but not sections 32ZA and 32ZB) and sections 32A] to 37 (annual return, [statement for members,] accounts and audit), or

sections 38 to 42 (members' superannuation schemes),

it commits an offence.

(2) The offence shall be deemed to have been also committed by—

(a) every officer of the trade union who is bound by the rules of the union to discharge on its behalf the duty breach of which constitutes the offence, or

(b) if there is no such officer, every member of the general committee of management of the union.

(3) In any proceedings brought against an officer or member by virtue of subsection (2) in respect of a breach of duty, it is a defence for him to prove that he had reasonable cause to believe, and did believe, that some other person who was competent to discharge that duty was authorised to discharge it instead of him and had discharged it or would do so.

(4) A person who wilfully alters or causes to be altered a document which is required for the purposes of any of the provisions mentioned in subsection (1), with intent to falsify the document or to enable a trade union to evade any of those provisions, commits an offence.

[(5) If a person contravenes any duty, or requirement imposed, under section 37A (power of Certification officer to require production of documents etc) or 37B (investigations by inspectors) he commits an offence.

(6) In any proceedings brought against a person in respect of a contravention of a requirement imposed under section 37A(3) or 37B(4) to produce documents it is a defence for him to prove—

(a) that the documents were not in his possession, and

(b) that it was not reasonably practicable for him to comply with the requirement.

(7) If an official or agent of a trade union—

(a) destroys, mutilates or falsifies, or is privy to the destruction, mutilation or falsification of, a document relating to the financial affairs of the trade union, or

(b) makes, or is privy to the making of, a false entry in any such document,

he commits an offence unless he proves that he had no intention to conceal the financial affairs of the trade union or to defeat the law.

(8) If such a person fraudulently—
(a) parts with, alters or deletes anything in any such document, or
(b) is privy to the fraudulent parting with, fraudulent alteration of or fraudulent deletion in, any such document,
he commits an offence.
(9) If a person in purported compliance with a duty, or requirement imposed, under section 37A or 37B to provide an explanation or make a statement—
(a) provides or makes an explanation or statement which he knows to be false in a material particular, or
(b) recklessly provides or makes an explanation or statement which is false in a material particular,
he commits an offence.]

NOTES

Sub-s (1): words in first pair of square brackets substituted by the Trade Union Act 2016, s 18(3), as from 1 March 2017; words in second pair of square brackets inserted by the Trade Union Reform and Employment Rights Act 1993, s 49(2), Sch 8, para 45.

Sub-ss (5)–(9): substituted, for the original sub-s (5), by the Trade Union Reform and Employment Rights Act 1993, s 11(1).

[1.336]

[45A Penalties and prosecution time limits

(1) A person guilty of an offence under section 45 is liable on summary conviction—
(a) in the case of an offence under subsection (1) or (5), to a fine not exceeding level 5 on the standard scale;
(b) in the case of an offence under subsection (4), (7), (8) or (9), to imprisonment for a term not exceeding six months or to a fine not exceeding level 5 on the standard scale or to both.
(2) Proceedings for an offence under section 45(1) relating to the duty imposed by section 32 (duty to send annual return to Certification Officer) may be commenced at any time before the end of the period of three years beginning with the date when the offence was committed.
(3) Proceedings for any other offence under section 45(1) may be commenced—
(a) at any time before the end of the period of six months beginning with the date when the offence was committed, or
(b) at any time after the end of that period but before the end of the period of twelve months beginning with the date when evidence sufficient in the opinion of the Certification Officer or, in Scotland, the procurator fiscal, to justify the proceedings came to his knowledge;
but no proceedings may be commenced by virtue of paragraph (b) after the end of the period of three years beginning with the date when the offence was committed.
(4) For the purposes of subsection (3)(b), a certificate signed by or on behalf of the Certification Officer or the procurator fiscal which states the date on which evidence sufficient in his opinion to justify the proceedings came to his knowledge shall be conclusive evidence of that fact.
(5) A certificate stating that matter and purporting to be so signed shall be deemed to be so signed unless the contrary is proved.
(6) For the purposes of this section—
(a) in England and Wales, proceedings are commenced when an information is laid, and
(b) in Scotland, subsection (3) of [section 136 of the Criminal Procedure (Scotland) Act 1995] (date of commencement of proceedings) applies as it applies for the purposes of that section.]

NOTES

Inserted by the Trade Union Reform and Employment Rights Act 1993, s 11(2).

Sub-s (6): words in square brackets substituted by the Criminal Procedure (Consequential Provisions) (Scotland) Act 1995, s 5, Sch 4, para 85.

[1.337]

[45B Duty to secure positions not held by certain offenders

(1) A trade union shall secure that a person does not at any time hold a position in the union to which this section applies if—
(a) within the period of five years immediately preceding that time he has been convicted of an offence under subsection (1) or (5) of section 45, or
(b) within the period of ten years immediately preceding that time he has been convicted of an offence under subsection (4), (7), (8) or (9) of that section.
(2) Subject to subsection (4), the positions to which this section applies are—
(a) member of the executive,
(b) any position by virtue of which a person is a member of the executive,
(c) president, and
(d) general secretary.
(3) For the purposes of subsection (2)(a) "member of the executive" includes any person who, under the rules or practice of the union, may attend and speak at some or all of the meetings of the executive, otherwise than for the purpose of providing the committee with factual information or with technical or professional advice with respect to matters taken into account by the executive in carrying out its functions.
(4) This section does not apply to the position of president or general secretary if the holder of that position—
(a) is not, in respect of that position, either a voting member of the executive or an employee of the union,

(b) holds that position for a period which under the rules of the union cannot end more than thirteen months after he took it up, and

(c) has not held either position at any time in the period of twelve months ending with the day before he took up that position.

(5) In subsection (4)(a) "a voting member of the executive" means a person entitled in his own right to attend meetings of the executive and to vote on matters on which votes are taken by the executive (whether or not he is entitled to attend all such meetings or to vote on all such matters or in all circumstances).]

NOTES

Inserted, together with s 45C, by the Trade Union Reform and Employment Rights Act 1993, s 12.

[1.338]

[45C Remedies and enforcement

(1) A member of a trade union who claims that the union has failed to comply with the requirement of section 45B may apply to the Certification Officer or to the court for a declaration to that *effect*.

[(1A) Where an application is made to the Certification Officer under this section, the Officer must ensure that, so far as is reasonably practicable, it is determined within six months of being made.]

(2) On an application being made to him, the Certification Officer—

[(aa) shall make such enquiries as he thinks fit,]

(a) shall . . . give the applicant and the trade union an opportunity to be heard,

(b) shall ensure that, so far as is reasonably practicable, the application is determined within six months of being made,

(c) may make or refuse the declaration asked for, and

(d) shall, whether he makes or refuses the declaration, give reasons for his decision in writing.

(3), (4) . . .

(5) Where the court makes a declaration it shall also, unless it considers that it would be inappropriate, make an order imposing on the trade union a requirement to take within such period as may be specified in the order such steps to remedy the declared failure as may be so specified.

[(5A) Where the Certification Officer makes a declaration he shall also, unless he considers that it would be inappropriate, make an order imposing on the trade union a requirement to take within such period as may be specified in the order such steps to remedy the declared failure as may be so specified.

(5B) The following paragraphs have effect if a person applies to the Certification Officer under this section in relation to an alleged failure—

(a) that person may not apply to the court under this section in relation to that failure;

(b) on an application by a different person to the court under this section in relation to that failure, the court shall have due regard to any declaration, order, observations or reasons made or given by the Certification Officer regarding that failure and brought to the court's notice.

(5C) The following paragraphs have effect if a person applies to the court under this section in relation to an alleged failure—

(a) that person may not apply to the Certification Officer under this section in relation to that failure;

(b) on an application by a different person to the Certification Officer under this section in relation to that failure, the Certification Officer shall have regard to any declaration, order, observations or reasons made or given by the court regarding that failure and brought to the Certification Officer's notice.]

(6) Where an order has been made [under subsection (5) or (5A)], any person who is a member of the trade union and was a member at the time the order was made is entitled to enforce the order as if he had made *the application on which the order was made*.

[(7) Where the Certification Officer requests a person to furnish information to him in connection with enquiries made by him under this section, he shall specify the date by which that information is to be furnished and, unless he considers that it would be inappropriate to do so, shall proceed with his determination *of the application* notwithstanding that the information has not been furnished to him by the specified date.

(8) A declaration made by the Certification Officer under this section may be relied on as if it were a declaration made by the court.

(9) An order made by the Certification Officer under this section may be enforced [(by the Certification Officer, the applicant or a person mentioned in subsection (6))] in the same way as an order of the court.]]

NOTES

Inserted as noted to s 45B at **[1.337]**.

Sub-s (1): for the word in italics there is substituted "effect; but the Certification Officer may also exercise the powers under this section where no application is made under this section" by the Trade Union Act 2016, s 17(3), Sch 2, para 1(1), (2), as from a day to be appointed.

Sub-s (1A): inserted by the Trade Union Act 2016, s 17(3), Sch 2, para 1(1), (3), as from a day to be appointed.

Sub-s (2): para (aa) inserted, and words omitted from para (a) repealed, by the Employment Relations Act 1999, ss 29, 44, Sch 6, paras 1, 7(1)–(3), Sch 9(7). This subsection is substituted by the Trade Union Act 2016, s 17(3), Sch 2, para 1(1), (4), as from a day to be appointed, as follows—

"(2) Where the Certification Officer is satisfied that a trade union has failed to comply with the requirement of section 45B, the Officer may make a declaration to that effect.

(2A) Before deciding the matter the Certification Officer—

(a) may make such enquiries as the Officer thinks fit,

(b) must give the union and the applicant (if any) an opportunity to make written representations, and

(c) may give the union and the applicant (if any) an opportunity to make oral representations.

(2B) The Certification Officer must give reasons for the Officer's decision in writing.".

Sub-ss (3), (4): repealed by the Employment Relations Act 1999, ss 29, 44, Sch 6, paras 1, 7(1), (4), Sch 9(7).

Sub-ss (5A)–(5C), (7)–(9): inserted and added respectively by the Employment Relations Act 1999, s 29, Sch 6, paras 1, 7(1), (5), (7); words in square brackets in sub-s (9) inserted by the Trade Union Act 2016, s 19(4), as from a day to be appointed.

Sub-s (6): words in square brackets inserted by the Employment Relations Act 1999, s 29, Sch 6, paras 1, 7(1), (6); for the words in italics there are substituted the words "an application under this section" by the Trade Union Act 2016, s 17(3), Sch 2, para 1(1), (5), as from a day to be appointed.

Sub-s (7): words in italics repealed by the Trade Union Act 2016, s 17(3), Sch 2, para 1(1), (6), as from a day to be appointed.

[1.339]

[45D Appeals from Certification Officer

An appeal lies to the Employment Appeal Tribunal *on any question of law arising* in proceedings before or arising from any decision of the Certification Officer under section [24B, *24C*,] 25, 31[, 32ZC] or 45C [or paragraph 5 of Schedule A3].]

NOTES

Inserted by the Employment Relations Act 1999, s 29, Sch 6, paras 1, 8.

For the words in italics there are substituted the words "on any question arising" by the Trade Union Act 2016, s 21(a), as from a day to be appointed.

Figures in first pair of square brackets inserted by the Transparency of Lobbying, Non-Party Campaigning and Trade Union Administration Act 2014, s 43(1), (6), as from 1 June 2016.

The figure "24C," in italics is repealed, and the words "or paragraph 5 of Schedule A3" in square brackets are inserted, by the Trade Union Act 2016, s 22, Sch 4, para 3, as from a day to be appointed.

Figure ", 32ZC" in square brackets inserted by the Trade Union Act 2016, s 18(4), as from 1 March 2017.

CHAPTER IV ELECTIONS FOR CERTAIN POSITIONS

Duty to hold elections

[1.340]

46 Duty to hold elections for certain positions

(1) A trade union shall secure—

(a) that every person who holds a position in the union to which this Chapter applies does so by virtue of having been elected to it at an election satisfying the requirements of this Chapter, and

(b) that no person continues to hold such a position for more than five years without being re-elected at such an election.

(2) The positions to which this Chapter applies (subject as mentioned below) are—

(a) member of the executive,

(b) any position by virtue of which a person is a member of the executive,

(c) president, and

(d) general secretary;

. . .

(3) In this Chapter "member of the executive" includes any person who, under the rules or practice of the union, may attend and speak at some or all of the meetings of the executive, otherwise than for the purpose of providing the committee with factual information or with technical or professional advice with respect to matters taken into account by the executive in carrying out its functions.

(4) This Chapter does not apply to the position of president or general secretary if the holder of that position—

(a) is not, in respect of that position, either a voting member of the executive or an employee of the union,

(b) holds that position for a period which under the rules of the union cannot end more than 13 months after he took it up, and

(c) has not held either position at any time in the period of twelve months ending with the day before he took up that position.

[(4A) This Chapter also does not apply to the position of president if—

(a) the holder of that position was elected or appointed to it in accordance with the rules of the union,

(b) at the time of his election or appointment as president he held a position mentioned in paragraph (a), (b) or (d) of subsection (2) by virtue of having been elected to it at a qualifying election,

(c) it is no more than five years since—

(i) he was elected, or re-elected, to the position mentioned in paragraph (b) which he held at the time of his election or appointment as president, or

(ii) he was elected to another position of a kind mentioned in that paragraph at a qualifying election held after his election or appointment as president of the union, and

(d) he has, at all times since his election or appointment as president, held a position mentioned in paragraph (a), (b) or (d) of subsection (2) by virtue of having been elected to it at a qualifying election.]

(5) [In subsection (4)] a "voting member of the executive" means a person entitled in his own right to attend meetings of the executive and to vote on matters on which votes are taken by the executive (whether or not he is entitled to attend all such meetings or to vote on all such matters or in all circumstances).

[(5A) In subsection (4A) "qualifying election" means an election satisfying the requirements of this Chapter.
(5B) The "requirements of this Chapter" referred to in subsections (1) and (5A) are those set out in sections 47 to 52 below.]
(6) The provisions of this Chapter apply notwithstanding anything in the rules or practice of the union; and the terms and conditions on which a person is employed by the union shall be disregarded in so far as they would prevent the union from complying with the provisions of this Chapter.

NOTES

Sub-s (2): words omitted repealed by the Employment Relations Act 2004, ss 52(1), (2), 57(2), Sch 2.
Sub-ss (4A), (5A), (5B): inserted by the Employment Relations Act 2004, s 52(1), (3), (5).
Sub-s (5): words in square brackets inserted by the Employment Relations Act 2004, s 52(1), (4).

Requirements to be satisfied with respect to elections

[1.341]
47 Candidates

(1) No member of the trade union shall be unreasonably excluded from standing as a candidate.
(2) No candidate shall be required, directly or indirectly, to be a member of a political party.
(3) A member of a trade union shall not be taken to be unreasonably excluded from standing as a candidate if he is excluded on the ground that he belongs to a class of which all the members are excluded by the rules of the union.

But a rule which provides for such a class to be determined by reference to whom the union chooses to exclude shall be disregarded.

[1.342]
48 Election addresses

(1) The trade union shall—
(a) provide every candidate with an opportunity of preparing an election address in his own words and of submitting it to the union to be distributed to the persons accorded entitlement to vote in the election; and
(b) secure that, so far as reasonably practicable, copies of every election address submitted to it in time are distributed to each of those persons by post along with the voting papers for the election.
(2) The trade union may determine the time by which an election address must be submitted to it for distribution; but the time so determined must not be earlier than the latest time at which a person may become a candidate in the election.
(3) The trade union may provide that election addresses submitted to it for distribution—
(a) must not exceed such length, not being less than one hundred words, as may be determined by the union, and
(b) may, as regards photographs and other matter not in words, incorporate only such matter as the union may determine.
(4) The trade union shall secure that no modification of an election address submitted to it is made by any person in any copy of the address to be distributed except—
(a) at the request or with the consent of the candidate, or
(b) where the modification is necessarily incidental to the method adopted for producing that copy.
(5) The trade union shall secure that the same method of producing copies is applied in the same way to every election address submitted and, so far as reasonably practicable, that no such facility or information as would enable a candidate to gain any benefit from—
(a) the method by which copies of the election addresses are produced, or
(b) the modifications which are necessarily incidental to that method,
is provided to any candidate without being provided equally to all the others.
(6) The trade union shall, so far as reasonably practicable, secure that the same facilities and restrictions with respect to the preparation, submission, length or modification of an election address, and with respect to the incorporation of photographs or other matter not in words, are provided or applied equally to each of the candidates.
(7) The arrangements made by the trade union for the production of the copies to be so distributed must be such as to secure that none of the candidates is required to bear any of the expense of producing the copies.
(8) No-one other than the candidate himself shall incur any civil or criminal liability in respect of the publication of a candidate's election address or of any copy required to be made for the purposes of this section.

[1.343]
49 Appointment of independent scrutineer

(1) The trade union shall, before the election is held, appoint a qualified independent person ("the scrutineer") to carry out—
(a) the functions in relation to the election which are required under this section to be contained in his appointment; and
(b) such additional functions in relation to the election as may be specified in his appointment.
(2) A person is a qualified independent person in relation to an election if—
(a) he satisfies such conditions as may be specified for the purposes of this section by order of the Secretary of State or is himself so specified; and

(b) the trade union has no grounds for believing either that he will carry out any functions conferred on him in relation to the election otherwise than competently or that his independence in relation to the union, or in relation to the election, might reasonably be called into question.

An order under paragraph (a) shall be made by statutory instrument which shall be subject to annulment in pursuance of a resolution of either House of Parliament.

(3) The scrutineer's appointment shall require him—

(a) to be the person who supervises the production [of the voting papers and (unless he is appointed under section 51A to undertake the distribution of the voting papers) their distribution] and to whom the voting papers are returned by those voting;

[(aa) to—

(i) inspect the register of names and addresses of the members of the trade union, or

(ii) examine the copy of the register as at the relevant date which is supplied to him in accordance with subsection (5A)(a),

whenever it appears to him appropriate to do so and, in particular, when the conditions specified in subsection (3A) are satisfied;]

(b) to take such steps as appear to him to be appropriate for the purpose of enabling him to make his report (see section 52);

(c) to make his report to the trade union as soon as reasonably practicable after the last date for the return of voting papers; and

(d) to retain custody of all voting papers returned for the purposes of the election [and the copy of the register supplied to him in accordance with subsection (5A)(a)]—

(i) until the end of the period of one year beginning with the announcement by the union of the result of the election; and

(ii) if within that period an application is made under section 54 (complaint of failure to comply with election requirements), until the Certification Officer or the court authorises him to dispose of the papers [or copy].

[(3A) The conditions referred to in subsection (3)(aa) are—

(a) that a request that the scrutineer inspect the register or examine the copy is made to him during the appropriate period by a member of the trade union or candidate who suspects that the register is not, or at the relevant date was not, accurate and up-to-date, and

(b) that the scrutineer does not consider that the suspicion of the member or candidate is ill-founded.

(3B) In subsection (3A) "the appropriate period" means the period—

(a) beginning with the first day on which a person may become a candidate in the election or, if later, the day on which the scrutineer is appointed, and

(b) ending with the day before the day on which the scrutineer makes his report to the trade union.

(3C) The duty of confidentiality as respects the register is incorporated in the scrutineer's appointment.]

(4) The trade union shall ensure that nothing in the terms of the scrutineer's appointment (including any additional functions specified in the appointment) is such as to make it reasonable for any person to call the scrutineer's independence in relation to the union into question.

(5) The trade union shall, before the scrutineer begins to carry out his functions, either—

(a) send a notice stating the name of the scrutineer to every member of the union to whom it is reasonably practicable to send such a notice, or

(b) take all such other steps for notifying members of the name of the scrutineer as it is the practice of the union to take when matters of general interest to all its members need to be brought to their attention.

[(5A) The trade union shall—

(a) supply to the scrutineer as soon as is reasonably practicable after the relevant date a copy of the register of names and addresses of its members as at that date, and

(b) comply with any request made by the scrutineer to inspect the register.

(5B) Where the register is kept by means of a computer the duty imposed on the trade union by subsection (5A)(a) is either to supply a legible printed copy or (if the scrutineer prefers) to supply a copy of the computer data and allow the scrutineer use of the computer to read it at any time during the period when he is required to retain custody of the copy.]

(6) The trade union shall ensure that the scrutineer duly carries out his functions and that there is no interference with his carrying out of those functions which would make it reasonable for any person to call the scrutineer's independence in relation to the union into question.

(7) The trade union shall comply with all reasonable requests made by the scrutineer for the purposes of, or in connection with, the carrying out of his functions.

[(8) In this section "the relevant date" means—

(a) where the trade union has rules determining who is entitled to vote in the election by reference to membership on a particular date, that date, and

(b) otherwise, the date, or the last date, on which voting papers are distributed for the purposes of the election.]

NOTES

Sub-s (3): words in square brackets in para (a) substituted, and para (aa) and the words in square brackets in para (d) inserted, by the Trade Union Reform and Employment Rights Act 1993, ss 1(1)(a), (b), 49(2), Sch 8, para 46.

Sub-ss (3A)–(3C), (5A), (5B), (8): inserted and added respectively by the Trade Union Reform and Employment Rights Act 1993, s 1(1)(c)–(e).

Orders: the Trade Union Ballots and Elections (Independent Scrutineer Qualifications) Order 1993, SI 1993/1909 at **[2.138]**; the Trade Union Ballots and Elections (Independent Scrutineer Qualifications) (Amendment) Order 2010, SI 2010/436; the Trade Union Ballots and Elections (Independent Scrutineer Qualifications) (Amendment) Order 2017, SI 2017/877.

[1.344]
50 Entitlement to vote
(1) Subject to the provisions of this section, entitlement to vote shall be accorded equally to all members of the trade union.
(2) The rules of the union may exclude entitlement to vote in the case of all members belonging to one of the following classes, or to a class falling within one of the following—
(a) members who are not in employment;
(b) members who are in arrears in respect of any subscription or contribution due to the union;
(c) members who are apprentices, trainees or students or new members of the union.
(3) The rules of the union may restrict entitlement to vote to members who fall within—
(a) a class determined by reference to a trade or occupation,
(b) a class determined by reference to a geographical area, or
(c) a class which is by virtue of the rules of the union treated as a separate section within the union,
or to members who fall within a class determined by reference to any combination of the factors mentioned in paragraphs (a), (b) and (c).
The reference in paragraph (c) to a section of a trade union includes a part of the union which is itself a trade union.
(4) Entitlement may not be restricted in accordance with subsection (3) if the effect is that any member of the union is denied entitlement to vote at all elections held for the purposes of this Chapter otherwise than by virtue of belonging to a class excluded in accordance with subsection (2).

[1.345]
51 Voting
(1) The method of voting must be by the marking of a voting paper by the person voting.
(2) Each voting paper must—
(a) state the name of the independent scrutineer and clearly specify the address to which, and the date by which, it is to be returned,
(b) be given one of a series of consecutive whole numbers every one of which is used in giving a different number in that series to each voting paper printed or otherwise produced for the purposes of the election, and
(c) be marked with its number.
(3) Every person who is entitled to vote at the election must—
(a) be allowed to vote without interference from, or constraint imposed by, the union or any of its members, officials or employees, and
(b) so far as is reasonably practicable, be enabled to do so without incurring any direct cost to himself.
(4) So far as is reasonably practicable, every person who is entitled to vote at the election must—
(a) have sent to him by post, at his home address or another address which he has requested the trade union in writing to treat as his postal address, a voting paper which either lists the candidates at the election or is accompanied by a separate list of those candidates; and
(b) be given a convenient opportunity to vote by post.
(5) The ballot shall be conducted so as to secure that—
(a) so far as is reasonably practicable, those voting do so in secret, and
(b) the votes given at the election are fairly and accurately counted.
For the purposes of paragraph (b) an inaccuracy in counting shall be disregarded if it is accidental and on a scale which could not affect the result of the election.
(6) The ballot shall be so conducted as to secure that the result of the election is determined solely by counting the number of votes cast directly for each candidate.
(7) Nothing in subsection (6) shall be taken to prevent the system of voting used for the election being the single transferable vote, that is, a vote capable of being given so as to indicate the voter's order of preference for the candidates and of being transferred to the next choice—
(a) when it is not required to give a prior choice the necessary quota of votes, or
(b) when, owing to the deficiency in the number of votes given for a prior choice, that choice is eliminated from the list of candidates.

[1.346]
[51A Counting of votes etc by independent person
(1) The trade union shall ensure that—
(a) the storage and distribution of the voting papers for the purposes of the election, and
(b) the counting of the votes cast in the election,
are undertaken by one or more independent persons appointed by the union.
(2) A person is an independent person in relation to an election if—
(a) he is the scrutineer, or
(b) he is a person other than the scrutineer and the trade union has no grounds for believing either that he will carry out any functions conferred on him in relation to the election otherwise than competently or that his independence in relation to the union, or in relation to the election, might reasonably be called into question.
(3) An appointment under this section shall require the person appointed to carry out his functions so as to minimise the risk of any contravention of requirements imposed by or under any enactment or the occurrence of any unfairness or malpractice.
(4) The duty of confidentiality as respects the register is incorporated in an appointment under this section.

(5) Where the person appointed to undertake the counting of votes is not the scrutineer, his appointment shall require him to send the voting papers back to the scrutineer as soon as reasonably practicable after the counting has been completed.

(6) The trade union—

(a) shall ensure that nothing in the terms of an appointment under this section is such as to make it reasonable for any person to call into question the independence of the person appointed in relation to the union,

(b) shall ensure that a person appointed under this section duly carries out his functions and that there is no interference with his carrying out of those functions which would make it reasonable for any person to call into question the independence of the person appointed in relation to the union, and

(c) shall comply with all reasonable requests made by a person appointed under this section for the purposes of, or in connection with, the carrying out of his functions.]

NOTES

Inserted by the Trade Union Reform and Employment Rights Act 1993, s 2(1).

[1.347]

52 Scrutineer's report

(1) The scrutineer's report on the election shall state—

(a) the number of voting papers distributed for the purposes of the election,

(b) the number of voting papers returned to the scrutineer,

(c) the number of valid votes cast in the election for each candidate, . . .

(d) the number of spoiled or otherwise invalid voting papers returned[, and

(e) the name of the person (or of each of the persons) appointed under section 51A or, if no person was so appointed, that fact.]

(2) The report shall also state whether the scrutineer is satisfied—

(a) that there are no reasonable grounds for believing that there was any contravention of a requirement imposed by or under any enactment in relation to the election,

(b) that the arrangements made [(whether by him or any other person)] with respect to the production, storage, distribution, return or other handling of the voting papers used in the election, and the arrangements for the counting of the votes, included all such security arrangements as were reasonably practicable for the purpose of minimising the risk that any unfairness or malpractice might occur, and

(c) that he has been able to carry out his functions without such interference as would make it reasonable for any person to call his independence in relation to the union into question;

and if he is not satisfied as to any of those matters, the report shall give particulars of his reasons for not being satisfied as to that matter.

[(2A) The report shall also state—

(a) whether the scrutineer—

(i) has inspected the register of names and addresses of the members of the trade union, or

(ii) has examined the copy of the register as at the relevant date which is supplied to him in accordance with section 49(5A)(a),

(b) if he has, whether in the case of each inspection or examination he was acting on a request by a member of the trade union or candidate or at his own instance,

(c) whether he declined to act on any such request, and

(d) whether any inspection of the register, or any examination of the copy of the register, has revealed any matter which he considers should be drawn to the attention of the trade union in order to assist it in securing that the register is accurate and up-to-date,

but shall not state the name of any member or candidate who has requested such an inspection or examination.]

[(2B) Where one or more persons other than the scrutineer are appointed under section 51A, the statement included in the scrutineer's report in accordance with subsection (2)(b) shall also indicate—

(a) whether he is satisfied with the performance of the person, or each of the persons, so appointed, and

(b) if he is not satisfied with the performance of the person, or any of them, particulars of his reasons for not being so satisfied.]

(3) The trade union shall not publish the result of the election until it has received the scrutineer's report.

(4) The trade union shall within the period of three months after it receives the report either—

(a) send a copy of the report to every member of the union to whom it is reasonably practicable to send such a copy; or

(b) take all such other steps for notifying the contents of the report to the members of the union (whether by publishing the report or otherwise) as it is the practice of the union to take when matters of general interest to all its members need to be brought to their attention.

(5) Any such copy or notification shall be accompanied by a statement that the union will, on request, supply any member of the union with a copy of the report, either free of charge or on payment of such reasonable fee as may be specified in the notification.

(6) The trade union shall so supply any member of the union who makes such a request and pays the fee (if any) notified to him.

NOTES

Sub-s (1): word omitted from para (c) repealed, and para (e) and the word immediately preceding it added, by the Trade Union Reform and Employment Rights Act 1993, ss 2(2)(a), 51, Sch 10.

Sub-s (2): words in square brackets in para (b) inserted by the Trade Union Reform and Employment Rights Act 1993, s 2(2)(b).

Sub-ss (2A), (2B): inserted by the Trade Union Reform and Employment Rights Act 1993, ss 1(2), 2(2)(c).

[1.348]

53 Uncontested elections

Nothing in this Chapter shall be taken to require a ballot to be held at an uncontested election.

Remedy for failure to comply with requirements

[1.349]

54 Remedy for failure to comply with requirements: general

(1) The remedy for a failure on the part of a trade union to comply with the requirements of this Chapter is by way of application under section 55 (to the Certification Officer) or section 56 (to the court).

. . .

(2) *An application under those sections may be made*—

(a) by a person who is a member of the trade union (provided, where the election has been held, he was also a member at the time when it was held), or

(b) by a person who is or was a candidate at the election;

and the references in those sections to a person having a sufficient interest are to such a person.

(3) [Where an election has been held, no application under those sections with respect to that election] may be made after the end of the period of one year beginning with the day on which the union announced the result of the election.

NOTES

Sub-s (1): words omitted repealed by the Employment Relations Act 1999, ss 29, 44, Sch 6, paras 1, 9, Sch 9(7). This subsection is substituted by the Trade Union Act 2016, s 17(3), Sch 2, para 2(1), (2), as from a day to be appointed, as follows—

"(1) A person alleging a failure on the part of a trade union to comply with any of the requirements of this Chapter may apply for—

(a) a declaration under section 55 (by the Certification Officer), or

(b) a declaration under section 56 (by the court);

but the Certification Officer may also exercise the powers under section 55 where no application is made.".

Sub-s (2): for the words in italics there are substituted the words "An application for a declaration under section 55 or 56 may be made only" by the Trade Union Act 2016, s 17(3), Sch 2, para 2(1), (3), as from a day to be appointed

Sub-s (3): words in square brackets substituted by the Employment Relations Act 2004, s 57(1), Sch 1, para 5.

[1.350]

55 *Application to* Certification Officer

(1) A person having a sufficient interest (see section 54(2)) who claims that a trade union has failed to comply with any of the requirements of this Chapter may apply to the Certification Officer for a declaration to that effect.

(2) On an application being made to him, the Certification Officer shall—

(a) make such enquiries as he thinks fit, and

(b) . . . give the applicant and the trade union an opportunity to be heard,

and may make or refuse the declaration asked for.

(3) If he makes a declaration he shall specify in it the provisions with which the trade union has failed to comply.

(4) Where he makes a declaration and is satisfied that steps have been taken by the union with a view to remedying the declared failure, or securing that a failure of the same or any similar kind does not occur in future, or that the union has agreed to take such steps, he shall specify those steps in the declaration.

(5) Whether he makes or refuses a declaration, he shall give reasons for his decision in writing; and the reasons may be accompanied by written observations on any matter arising from, or connected with, the proceedings.

[(5A) Where the Certification Officer makes a declaration he shall also, unless he considers that to do so would be inappropriate, make an enforcement order, that is, an order imposing on the union one or more of the following requirements—

(a) to secure the holding of an election in accordance with the order;

(b) to take such other steps to remedy the declared failure as may be specified in the order;

(c) to abstain from such acts as may be so specified with a view to securing that a failure of the same or a similar kind does not occur in future.

The Certification Officer shall in an order imposing any such requirement as is mentioned in paragraph (a) or (b) specify the period within which the union is to comply with the requirements of the order.

(5B) Where the Certification Officer makes an order requiring the union to hold a fresh election, he shall (unless he considers that it would be inappropriate to do so in the particular circumstances of the case) require the election to be conducted in accordance with the requirements of this Chapter and such other provisions as may be made by the order.

(5C) Where an enforcement order has been made—

(a) any person who is a member of the union and was a member at the time the order was made, or

(b) any person who is or was a candidate in the election in question,

is entitled to enforce obedience to the order as if he had made *the application on which the order was made*.]

(6) In exercising his functions under this section the Certification Officer shall ensure that, so far as is reasonably practicable, an application made to him is determined within six months of being made.

(7) Where he requests a person to furnish information to him in connection with enquiries made by him under this section, he shall specify the date by which that information is to be furnished and, unless he considers that it would be inappropriate to do so, shall proceed with his determination *of the application* notwithstanding that the information has not been furnished to him by the specified date.

[(8) A declaration made by the Certification Officer under this section may be relied on as if it were a declaration made by the court.

(9) An enforcement order made by the Certification Officer under this section may be enforced [(by the Certification Officer, the applicant or a person mentioned in subsection (5C))] in the same way as an order of the court.

(10) The following paragraphs have effect if a person applies under section 56 in relation to an alleged failure—

(a) that person may not apply under this section in relation to that failure;

(b) on an application by a different person under this section in relation to that failure, the Certification Officer shall have due regard to any declaration, order, observations or reasons made or given by the court regarding that failure and brought to the Certification Officer's notice.]

NOTES

Section heading: for the words in italics there are substituted the words "Powers of" by the Trade Union Act 2016, s 17(3), Sch 2, para 3(1), (2), as from a day to be appointed.

Sub-ss (1), (2): substituted by the Trade Union Act 2016, s 17(3), Sch 2, para 3(1), (3), as from a day to be appointed, as follows—

"(1) Where the Certification Officer is satisfied that a trade union has failed to comply with any of the requirements of this Chapter, either—

(a) on an application by a person having a sufficient interest (see section 54(2)), or

(b) without any such application having been made,

the Officer may make a declaration to that effect.

(2) Before deciding the matter the Certification Officer—

(a) may make such enquiries as the Officer thinks fit,

(b) must give the union and the applicant (if any) an opportunity to make written representations, and

(c) may give the union and the applicant (if any) an opportunity to make oral representations.".

The words omitted from sub-s (2)(b) were repealed by the Employment Relations Act 1999, ss 29, 44, Sch 6, paras 1, 10(1), (2), Sch 9(7).

Sub-ss (5A)–(5C): inserted by the Employment Relations Act 1999, s 29, Sch 6, paras 1, 10(1), (3); for the words in italics in sub-s (5C) there are substituted the words "an application under this section" by the Trade Union Act 2016, s 17(3), Sch 2, para 3(1), (4), as from a day to be appointed.

Sub-s (7): words in italics repealed by the Trade Union Act 2016, s 17(3), Sch 2, para 3(1), (5), as from a day to be appointed.

Sub-ss (8)–(10): added by the Employment Relations Act 1999, s 29, Sch 6, paras 1, 10(1), (4); words in square brackets in sub-s (9) inserted by the Trade Union Act 2016, s 19(4), as from a day to be appointed.

[1.351]

56 Application to court

(1) A person having a sufficient interest (see section 54(2)) who claims that a trade union has failed to comply with any of the requirements of this Chapter may apply to the court for a declaration to that effect.

(2) . . .

(3) If the court makes the declaration asked for, it shall specify in the declaration the provisions with which the trade union has failed to comply.

(4) Where the court makes a declaration it shall also, unless it considers that to do so would be inappropriate, make an enforcement order, that is, an order imposing on the union one or more of the following requirements—

(a) to secure the holding of an election in accordance with the order;

(b) to take such other steps to remedy the declared failure as may be specified in the order;

(c) to abstain from such acts as may be so specified with a view to securing that a failure of the same or a similar kind does not occur in future.

The court shall in an order imposing any such requirement as is mentioned in paragraph (a) or (b) specify the period within which the union is to comply with the requirements of the order.

(5) Where the court makes an order requiring the union to hold a fresh election, the court shall (unless it considers that it would be inappropriate to do so in the particular circumstances of the case) require the election to be conducted in accordance with the requirements of this Chapter and such other provisions as may be made by the order.

(6) Where an enforcement order has been made—

(a) any person who is a member of the union and was a member at the time the order was made, or

(b) any person who is or was a candidate in the election in question, is entitled to enforce obedience to the order as if he had made the application on which the order was made.

(7) Without prejudice to any other power of the court, the court may on an application under this section grant such interlocutory relief (in Scotland, such interim order) as it considers appropriate.

[(8) The following paragraphs have effect if a person applies under section 55 in relation to an alleged failure—

(a) that person may not apply under this section in relation to that failure;

(b) on an application by a different person under this section in relation to that failure, the court shall have due regard to any declaration, order, observations or reasons made or given by the Certification Officer regarding that failure and brought to the court's notice.]

NOTES

Sub-s (2): repealed by the Employment Relations Act 1999, ss 29, 44, Sch 6, paras 1, 11(1), (2), Sch 9(7).

Sub-s (8): added by the Employment Relations Act 1999, s 29, Sch 6, paras 1, 11(1), (3).

[1.352]

[56A Appeals from Certification Officer

An appeal lies to the Employment Appeal Tribunal *on any question of law arising* in proceedings before or arising from any decision of the Certification Officer under section 55.]

NOTES

Inserted by the Employment Relations Act 1999, s 29, Sch 6, paras 1, 12.

For the words in italics there are substituted the words "on any question arising" by the Trade Union Act 2016, s 21(b), as from a day to be appointed.

Supplementary

[1.353]

57 Exemption of newly-formed trade unions, &c

(1) The provisions of this Chapter do not apply to a trade union until more than one year has elapsed since its formation (by amalgamation or otherwise).

For this purpose the date of formation of a trade union formed otherwise than by amalgamation shall be taken to be the date on which the first members of the executive of the union are first appointed or elected.

(2) Where a trade union is formed by amalgamation, the provisions of this Chapter do not apply in relation to a person who—

(a) by virtue of an election held a position to which this Chapter applies in one of the amalgamating unions immediately before the amalgamation, and

(b) becomes the holder of a position to which this Chapter applies in the amalgamated union in accordance with the instrument of transfer,

until after the end of the period for which he would have been entitled in accordance with this Chapter to continue to hold the first-mentioned position without being re-elected.

(3) Where a trade union transfers its engagements to another trade union, the provisions of this Chapter do not apply in relation to a person who—

(a) held a position to which this Chapter applies in the transferring union immediately before the transfer, and

(b) becomes the holder of a position to which this Chapter applies in the transferee union in accordance with the instrument of transfer,

until after the end of the period of one year beginning with the date of the transfer or, if he held the first-mentioned position by virtue of an election, any longer period for which he would have been entitled in accordance with this Chapter to continue to hold that position without being re-elected.

[1.354]

58 Exemption of certain persons nearing retirement

(1) Section 46(1)(b) (requirement of re-election) does not apply to a person holding a position to which this Chapter applies if the following conditions are satisfied.

(2) The conditions are that—

(a) he holds the position by virtue of having been elected at an election in relation to which the requirements of this Chapter were satisfied,

(b) he is a full-time employee of the union by virtue of the position,

(c) he will reach retirement age within five years,

(d) he is entitled under the rules of the union to continue as the holder of the position until retirement age without standing for re-election,

(e) he has been a full-time employee of the union for a period (which need not be continuous) of at least ten years, and

(f) the period between the day on which the election referred to in paragraph (a) took place and the day immediately preceding that on which paragraph (c) is first satisfied does not exceed five years.

(3) For the purposes of this section "retirement age", in relation to any person, means the earlier of—

(a) the age fixed by, or in accordance with, the rules of the union for him to retire from the position in question, or

(b) the age which is for the time being pensionable age [within the meaning given by the rules in paragraph 1 of Schedule 4 to the Pensions Act 1995].

NOTES

Sub-s (3): words in square brackets substituted by the Pensions Act 1995, s 126(c), Sch 4, Pt III, para 15.

[1.355]

59 Period for giving effect to election

Where a person holds a position to which this Chapter applies immediately before an election at which he is not re-elected to that position, nothing in this Chapter shall be taken to require the union to prevent him from continuing to hold that position for such period (not exceeding six months) as may reasonably be required for effect to be given to the result of the election.

[1.356]

60 Overseas members

(1) A trade union which has overseas members may choose whether or not to accord any of those members entitlement to vote at an election for a position to which this Chapter applies.

(2) An "overseas member" means a member of the union (other than a merchant seaman or offshore worker) who is outside Great Britain throughout the period during which votes may be cast.

For this purpose—

"merchant seaman" means a person whose employment, or the greater part of it, is carried out on board sea-going ships; and

"offshore worker" means a person in offshore employment, other than one who is in such employment in an area where the law of Northern Ireland applies.

(3) Where the union chooses to accord an overseas member entitlement to vote, section 51 (requirements as to voting) applies in relation to him; but nothing in section 47 (candidates) or section 50 (entitlement to vote) applies in relation to an overseas member or in relation to a vote cast by such a member.

[1.357]

61 Other supplementary provisions

(1) For the purposes of this Chapter the date on which a contested election is held shall be taken, in the case of an election in which votes may be cast on more than one day, to be the last of those days.

(2) Nothing in this Chapter affects the validity of anything done by a person holding a position to which this Chapter applies.

CHAPTER V RIGHTS OF TRADE UNION MEMBERS

Right to a ballot before industrial action

[1.358]

62 Right to ballot before industrial action

(1) A member of a trade union who claims that members of the union, including himself, are likely to be or have been induced by the union to take part or to continue to take part in industrial action which does not have the support of a ballot may apply to the court for an order under this section.

[In this section "the relevant time" means the time when the application is made.]

[(2) For this purpose the question whether industrial action is regarded as having the support of a ballot shall be determined in accordance with section 226(2).]

(3) Where on an application under this section the court is satisfied that the claim is well-founded, it shall make such order as it considers appropriate for requiring the union to take steps for ensuring—

(a) that there is no, or no further, inducement of members of the union to take part or to continue to take part in the industrial action to which the application relates, and

(b) that no member engages in conduct after the making of the order by virtue of having been induced before the making of the order to take part or continue to take part in the action.

(4) Without prejudice to any other power of the court, the court may on an application under this section grant such interlocutory relief (in Scotland, such interim order) as it considers appropriate.

(5) For the purposes of this section an act shall be taken to be done by a trade union if it is authorised or endorsed by the union; and the provisions of section 20(2) to (4) apply for the purpose of determining whether an act is to be taken to be so authorised or endorsed.

Those provisions also apply in relation to proceedings for failure to comply with an order under this section as they apply in relation to the original proceedings.

(6) In this section—

"inducement" includes an inducement which is or would be ineffective, whether because of the member's unwillingness to be influenced by it or for any other reason; and

"industrial action" means a strike or other industrial action by persons employed under contracts of employment.

(7) Where a person holds any office or employment under the Crown on terms which do not constitute a contract of employment between that person and the Crown, those terms shall nevertheless be deemed to constitute such a contract for the purposes of this section.

(8) References in this section to a contract of employment include any contract under which one person personally does work or performs services for another; and related expressions shall be construed accordingly.

(9) Nothing in this section shall be construed as requiring a trade union to hold separate ballots for the purposes of this section and sections 226 to 234 (requirement of ballot before action by trade union).

NOTES

Sub-s (1): words in square brackets added by the Trade Union Reform and Employment Rights Act 1993, s 49(2), Sch 8, para 47(a).

Sub-s (2): substituted by the Trade Union Act 2016, s 22, Sch 4, para 4, as from 1 March 2017.

Right not to be denied access to the courts

[1.359]

63 Right not to be denied access to the courts

(1) This section applies where a matter is under the rules of a trade union required or allowed to be submitted for determination or conciliation in accordance with the rules of the union, but a provision of the rules purporting to provide for that to be a person's only remedy has no effect (or would have no effect if there were one).

(2) Notwithstanding anything in the rules of the union or in the practice of any court, if a member or former member of the union begins proceedings in a court with respect to a matter to which this section applies, then if—

- (a) he has previously made a valid application to the union for the matter to be submitted for determination or conciliation in accordance with the union's rules, and
- (b) the court proceedings are begun after the end of the period of six months beginning with the day on which the union received the application,

the rules requiring or allowing the matter to be so submitted, and the fact that any relevant steps remain to be taken under the rules, shall be regarded for all purposes as irrelevant to any question whether the court proceedings should be dismissed, stayed or sisted, or adjourned.

(3) An application shall be deemed to be valid for the purposes of subsection (2)(a) unless the union informed the applicant, before the end of the period of 28 days beginning with the date on which the union received the application, of the respects in which the application contravened the requirements of the rules.

(4) If the court is satisfied that any delay in the taking of relevant steps under the rules is attributable to unreasonable conduct of the person who commenced the proceedings, it may treat the period specified in subsection (2)(b) as extended by such further period as it considers appropriate.

(5) In this section—

- (a) references to the rules of a trade union include any arbitration or other agreement entered into in pursuance of a requirement imposed by or under the rules; and
- (b) references to the relevant steps under the rules, in relation to any matter, include any steps falling to be taken in accordance with the rules for the purposes of or in connection with the determination or conciliation of the matter, or any appeal, review or reconsideration of any determination or award.

(6) This section does not affect any enactment or rule of law by virtue of which a court would apart from this section disregard any such rules of a trade union or any such fact as is mentioned in subsection (2).

Right not to be unjustifiably disciplined

[1.360]

64 Right not to be unjustifiably disciplined

(1) An individual who is or has been a member of a trade union has the right not to be unjustifiably disciplined by the union.

(2) For this purpose an individual is "disciplined" by a trade union if a determination is made, or purportedly made, under the rules of the union or by an official of the union or a number of persons including an official that—

- (a) he should be expelled from the union or a branch or section of the union,
- (b) he should pay a sum to the union, to a branch or section of the union or to any other person;
- (c) sums tendered by him in respect of an obligation to pay subscriptions or other sums to the union, or to a branch or section of the union, should be treated as unpaid or paid for a different purpose,
- (d) he should be deprived to any extent of, or of access to, any benefits, services or facilities which would otherwise be provided or made available to him by virtue of his membership of the union, or a branch or section of the union,
- (e) another trade union, or a branch or section of it, should be encouraged or advised not to accept him as a member, or
- (f) he should be subjected to some other detriment;

and whether an individual is "unjustifiably disciplined" shall be determined in accordance with section 65.

(3) Where a determination made in infringement of an individual's right under this section requires the payment of a sum or the performance of an obligation, no person is entitled in any proceedings to rely on that determination for the purpose of recovering the sum or enforcing the obligation.

(4) Subject to that, the remedies for infringement of the right conferred by this section are as provided by sections 66 and 67, and not otherwise.

(5) The right not to be unjustifiably disciplined is in addition to (and not in substitution for) any right which exists apart from this section; [and, subject to section 66(4), nothing] in this section or sections 65 to 67 affects any remedy for infringement of any such right.

NOTES

Sub-s (5): words in square brackets substituted by the Trade Union Reform and Employment Rights Act 1993, s 49(2), Sch 8, para 48.

[1.361]

65 Meaning of "unjustifiably disciplined"

(1) An individual is unjustifiably disciplined by a trade union if the actual or supposed conduct which constitutes the reason, or one of the reasons, for disciplining him is—

(a) conduct to which this section applies, or

(b) something which is believed by the union to amount to such conduct;

but subject to subsection (6) (cases of bad faith in relation to assertion of wrongdoing).

(2) This section applies to conduct which consists in—

(a) failing to participate in or support a strike or other industrial action (whether by members of the union or by others), or indicating opposition to or a lack of support for such action;

(b) failing to contravene, for a purpose connected with such a strike or other industrial action, a requirement imposed on him by or under a contract of employment;

(c) asserting (whether by bringing proceedings or otherwise) that the union, any official or representative of it or a trustee of its property has contravened, or is proposing to contravene, a requirement which is, or is thought to be, imposed by or under the rules of the union or any other agreement or by or under any enactment (whenever passed) or any rule of law;

(d) encouraging or assisting a person

(i) to perform an obligation imposed on him by a contract of employment, . . .

(ii) to make or attempt to vindicate any such assertion as is mentioned in paragraph (c); . . .

(e) contravening a requirement imposed by or in consequence of a determination which infringes the individual's or another individual's right not to be unjustifiably disciplined,

[(f) failing to agree, or withdrawing agreement, to the making from his wages (in accordance with arrangements between his employer and the union) of deductions representing payments to the union in respect of his membership,

(g) resigning or proposing to resign from the union or from another union, becoming or proposing to become a member of another union, refusing to become a member of another union, or being a member of another union,

(h) working with, or proposing to work with, individuals who are not members of the union or who are or are not members of another union,

(i) working for, or proposing to work for, an employer who employs or who has employed individuals who are not members of the union or who are or are not members of another union, or

(j) requiring the union to do an act which the union is, by any provision of this Act, required to do on the requisition of a member].

(3) This section applies to conduct which involves . . . the Certification Officer being consulted or asked to provide advice or assistance with respect to any matter whatever, or which involves any person being consulted or asked to provide advice or assistance with respect to a matter which forms, or might form, the subject-matter of any such assertion as is mentioned in subsection (2)(c) above.

(4) This section also applies to conduct which consists in proposing to engage in, or doing anything preparatory or incidental to, conduct falling within subsection (2) or (3).

(5) This section does not apply to an act, omission or statement comprised in conduct falling within subsection (2), (3) or (4) above if it is shown that the act, omission or statement is one in respect of which individuals would be disciplined by the union irrespective of whether their acts, omissions or statements were in connection with conduct within subsection (2) or (3) above.

(6) An individual is not unjustifiably disciplined if it is shown—

(a) that the reason for disciplining him, or one of them, is that he made such an assertion as is mentioned in subsection (2)(c), or encouraged or assisted another person to make or attempt to vindicate such an assertion,

(b) that the assertion was false, and

(c) that he made the assertion, or encouraged or assisted another person to make or attempt to vindicate it, in the belief that it was false or otherwise in bad faith,

and that there was no other reason for disciplining him or that the only other reasons were reasons in respect of which he does not fall to be treated as unjustifiably disciplined.

(7) In this section—

"conduct" includes statements, acts and omissions;

"contract of employment", in relation to an individual, includes any agreement between that individual and a person for whom he works or normally works[, "employer" includes such a person and related expressions shall be construed accordingly;] . . .

"representative", in relation to a union, means a person acting or purporting to act—

(a) in his capacity as a member of the union, or

(b) on the instructions or advice of a person acting or purporting to act in that capacity or in the capacity of an official of the union;

["require" (on the part of an individual) includes request or apply for, and "requisition" shall be construed accordingly; and

"wages" shall be construed in accordance with the definitions of "contract of employment", "employer" and related expressions.]

(8) Where a person holds any office or employment under the Crown on terms which do not constitute a contract of employment between him and the Crown, those terms shall nevertheless be deemed to constitute such a contract for the purposes of this section.

NOTES

Sub-s (2): word omitted from para (d) repealed, and paras (f)–(j) added, by the Trade Union Reform and Employment Rights Act 1993, ss 16(1), 51, Sch 10.

Sub-s (3): words omitted repealed by the Employment Relations Act 1999, s 44, Sch 9(6).

Sub-s (7): in definition "contract of employment", words in square brackets added, and word omitted repealed, and definitions "require" and "wages" added, by the Trade Union Reform and Employment Rights Act 1993, ss 16(2), 49(2), 51, Sch 8, para 49, Sch 10.

[1.362]

66 Complaint of infringement of right

(1) An individual who claims that he has been unjustifiably disciplined by a trade union may present a complaint against the union to an [employment tribunal].

(2) The tribunal shall not entertain such a complaint unless it is presented—

(a) before the end of the period of three months beginning with the date of the making of the determination claimed to infringe the right, or

(b) where the tribunal is satisfied—

(i) that it was not reasonably practicable for the complaint to be presented before the end of that period, or

(ii) that any delay in making the complaint is wholly or partly attributable to a reasonable attempt to appeal against the determination or to have it reconsidered or reviewed,

within such further period as the tribunal considers reasonable.

[(2A) Section 292A (extension of time limits to facilitate conciliation before institution of proceedings) applies for the purposes of subsection (2)(a).]

(3) Where the tribunal finds the complaint well-founded, it shall make a declaration to that effect.

[(4) Where a complaint relating to an expulsion which is presented under this section is declared to be well-founded, no complaint in respect of the expulsion shall be presented or proceeded with under section 174 (right not to be excluded or expelled from trade union).]

NOTES

Sub-s (1): words in square brackets substituted by the Employment Rights (Dispute Resolution) Act 1998, s 1(2)(a).

Sub-s (2A): inserted by the Enterprise and Regulatory Reform Act 2013, s 8, Sch 2, paras 1, 2.

Sub-s (4): substituted by the Trade Union Reform and Employment Rights Act 1993, s 49(2), Sch 8, para 50.

Conciliation: employment tribunal proceedings under this section are "relevant proceedings" for the purposes of the conciliation provisions contained in the Employment Tribunals Act 1996, ss 18–18C; see s 18(1)(a) of the 1996 Act at **[1.757]**.

[1.363]

67 Further remedies for infringement of right

(1) An individual whose complaint under section 66 has been declared to be well-founded may make an application [to an employment tribunal] for one or both of the following—

(a) an award of compensation to be paid to him by the union;

(b) an order that the union pay him an amount equal to any sum which he has paid in pursuance of any such determination as is mentioned in section 64(2)(b).

(2) . . .

(3) An application under this section shall not be entertained if made before the end of the period of four weeks beginning with the date of the declaration or after the end of the period of six months beginning with that date.

(4) . . .

(5) The amount of compensation awarded shall, subject to the following provisions, be such as the . . . [employment tribunal] considers just and equitable in all the circumstances.

(6) In determining the amount of compensation to be awarded, the same rule shall be applied concerning the duty of a person to mitigate his loss as applies to damages recoverable under the common law in England and Wales or Scotland.

(7) Where the . . . [employment tribunal] finds that the infringement complained of was to any extent caused or contributed to by the action of the applicant, it shall reduce the amount of the compensation by such proportion as it considers just and equitable having regard to that finding.

(8) The amount of compensation [calculated in accordance with subsections (5) to (7)] shall not exceed the aggregate of—

(a) an amount equal to 30 times the limit for the time being imposed by [section 227(1)(a) of the Employment Rights Act 1996] (maximum amount of a week's pay for basic award in unfair dismissal cases), and

(b) an amount equal to the limit for the time being imposed by [section 124(1)] of that Act (maximum compensatory award in such cases);

. . .

[(8A) If on the date on which the application was made—

(a) the determination infringing the applicant's right not to be unjustifiably disciplined has not been revoked, or

(b) the union has failed to take all the steps necessary for securing the reversal of anything done for the purpose of giving effect to the determination, the amount of compensation shall be not less than the amount for the time being specified in section 176(6A).]

(9) . . .

NOTES

Sub-s (1): words in square brackets inserted by the Employment Relations Act 2004, s 34(1), (2).

Sub-ss (2), (4): repealed by the Employment Relations Act 2004, ss 34(1), (3), 57(2), Sch 2.

Sub-ss (5), (7): words omitted repealed by the Employment Relations Act 2004, ss 34(1), (4), 57(2), Sch 2; words in square brackets substituted by the Employment Rights (Dispute Resolution) Act 1998, s 1(2)(a).

Sub-s (8): words in first pair of square brackets substituted by the Trade Union Reform and Employment Rights Act 1993, s 49(2), Sch 8, para 51(a); words in second and third pairs of square brackets substituted by the Employment Rights Act 1996, s 240, Sch 1, para 56(1), (2); words omitted repealed by the Employment Relations Act 2004, ss 34(1), (5), 57(2), Sch 2.

Sub-s (8A): inserted by the Employment Relations Act 2004, s 34(1), (6).

Sub-s (9): repealed by the Trade Union Reform and Employment Rights Act 1993, ss 49(2), 51, Sch 8, para 51(b), Sch 10.

[Right not to suffer deduction of unauthorised or excessive union subscriptions

[1.364]

[68 Right not to suffer deduction of unauthorised subscriptions

(1) Where arrangements ("subscription deduction arrangements") exist between the employer of a worker and a trade union relating to the making from workers' wages of deductions representing payments to the union in respect of the workers' membership of the union ("subscription deductions"), the employer shall ensure that no subscription deduction is made from wages payable to the worker on any day unless—

- (a) the worker has authorised in writing the making from his wages of subscription deductions; and
- (b) the worker has not withdrawn the authorisation.

(2) A worker withdraws an authorisation given for the purposes of subsection (1), in relation to a subscription deduction which falls to be made from wages payable to him on any day, if a written notice withdrawing the authorisation has been received by the employer in time for it to be reasonably practicable for the employer to secure that no such deduction is made.

(3) A worker's authorisation of the making of subscription deductions from his wages shall not give rise to any obligation on the part of the employer to the worker to maintain or continue to maintain subscription deduction arrangements.

(4) In this section and section 68A, "employer", "wages" and "worker" have the same meanings as in the Employment Rights Act 1996.]]

NOTES

Substituted, together with the preceding heading and s 68A, for the original s 68, by the Trade Union Reform and Employment Rights Act 1993, s 15; this section was further substituted by the Deregulation (Deduction from Pay of Union Subscriptions) Order 1998, SI 1998/1529, art 2(1).

The rights conferred by this section are "relevant statutory rights" for the purposes of the Employment Rights Act 1996, s 104 (dismissal on grounds of assertion of statutory right); see s 104(4)(c) of that Act at **[1.1015]**.

[1.365]

[68A Complaint of infringement of rights

(1) A worker may present a complaint to an [employment tribunal] that his employer has made a deduction from his wages in contravention of section 68—

- (a) within the period of three months beginning with the date of the payment of the wages from which the deduction, or (if the complaint relates to more than one deduction) the last of the deductions, was made, or
- (b) where the tribunal is satisfied that it was not reasonably practicable for the complaint to be presented within that period, within such further period as the tribunal considers reasonable.

[(1A) Section 292A (extension of time limits to facilitate conciliation before institution of proceedings) applies for the purposes of subsection (1)(a).]

[(2) Where a tribunal finds that a complaint under this section is well founded, it shall make a declaration to that effect and shall order the employer to pay to the worker the whole amount of the deduction, less any such part of the amount as has already been paid to the worker by the employer.]

(3) Where the making of a deduction from the wages of a worker both contravenes section 68(1) and involves one or more of the contraventions specified in subsection (4) of this section, the aggregate amount which may be ordered by an [employment tribunal] or court (whether on the same occasion or on different occasions) to be paid in respect of the contraventions shall not exceed the amount, or (where different amounts may be ordered to be paid in respect of different contraventions) the greatest amount, which may be ordered to be paid in respect of any one of them.

(4) The contraventions referred to in subsection (3) are—

- (a) a contravention of the requirement not to make a deduction without having given the particulars required by section 8 (itemised pay statements) or 9(1) (standing statements of fixed deductions) of [the Employment Rights Act 1996],
- (b) a contravention of [section 13 of that Act] (requirement not to make unauthorised deductions), and
- (c) a contravention of section 86(1) or 90(1) of this Act (requirements not to make deductions of political fund contributions in certain circumstances).]

NOTES

Substituted as noted to s 68 at **[1.364]**.

Sub-ss (1), (3): words in square brackets substituted by the Employment Rights (Dispute Resolution) Act 1998, s 1(2)(a).

Sub-s (1A): inserted by the Enterprise and Regulatory Reform Act 2013, s 8, Sch 2, paras 1, 3.
Sub-s (2): substituted by the Deregulation (Deduction from Pay of Union Subscriptions) Order 1998, SI 1998/1529, art 2(2).
Sub-s (4): words in square brackets substituted by the Employment Rights Act 1996, s 240, Sch 1, para 56(1), (4).
Conciliation: employment tribunal proceedings under this section are "relevant proceedings" for the purposes of the conciliation provisions contained in the Employment Tribunals Act 1996, ss 18–18C; see s 18(1)(a) of the 1996 Act at [**1.757**].

Right to terminate membership of union

[1.366]

69 Right to terminate membership of union

In every contract of membership of a trade union, whether made before or after the passing of this Act, a term conferring a right on the member, on giving reasonable notice and complying with any reasonable conditions, to terminate his membership of the union shall be implied.

Supplementary

[1.367]

70 Membership of constituent or affiliated organisation

In this Chapter "member", in relation to a trade union consisting wholly or partly of, or of representatives of, constituent or affiliated organisations, includes a member of any of the constituent or affiliated organisations.

[CHAPTER VA COLLECTIVE BARGAINING: RECOGNITION

[1.368]

70A Recognition of trade unions

Schedule A1 shall have effect.]

NOTES

Inserted, together with the preceding heading, by the Employment Relations Act 1999, s 1(1), (2).

[1.369]

[70B Training

(1) This section applies where—

(a) a trade union is recognised, in accordance with Schedule A1, as entitled to conduct collective bargaining on behalf of a bargaining unit (within the meaning of Part I of that Schedule), and
(b) a method for the conduct of collective bargaining is specified by the Central Arbitration Committee under paragraph 31(3) of that Schedule (and is not the subject of an agreement under paragraph 31(5)(a) or (b)).

(2) The employer must from time to time invite the trade union to send representatives to a meeting for the purpose of—

(a) consulting about the employer's policy on training for workers within the bargaining unit,
(b) consulting about his plans for training for those workers during the period of six months starting with the day of the meeting, and
(c) reporting about training provided for those workers since the previous meeting.

(3) The date set for a meeting under subsection (2) must not be later than—

(a) in the case of a first meeting, the end of the period of six months starting with the day on which this section first applies in relation to a bargaining unit, and
(b) in the case of each subsequent meeting, the end of the period of six months starting with the day of the previous meeting.

(4) The employer shall, before the period of two weeks ending with the date of a meeting, provide to the trade union any information—

(a) without which the union's representatives would be to a material extent impeded in participating in the meeting, and
(b) which it would be in accordance with good industrial relations practice to disclose for the purposes of the meeting.

[(4A) If the information mentioned in subjection (4) includes information relating to the employment situation the employer must (so far as not required by subsection (4)) also provide at the same time to the trade union the following information—

(a) the number of agency workers working temporarily for and under the supervision and direction of the employer,
(b) the parts of the employer's undertaking in which those agency workers are working, and
(c) the type of work those agency workers are carrying out.]

(5) Section 182(1) shall apply in relation to the provision of information under subsection (4) [or (4A)] as it applies in relation to the disclosure of information under section 181.

(6) The employer shall take account of any written representations about matters raised at a meeting which he receives from the trade union within the period of four weeks starting with the date of the meeting.

(7) Where more than one trade union is recognised as entitled to conduct collective bargaining on behalf of a bargaining unit, a reference in this section to "the trade union" is a reference to each trade union.

(8) Where at a meeting under this section (Meeting 1) an employer indicates his intention to convene a subsequent meeting (Meeting 2) before the expiry of the period of six months beginning with the date of Meeting 1, for the reference to a period of six months in subsection (2)(b) there shall be substituted a reference to the expected period between Meeting 1 and Meeting 2.

(9) The Secretary of State may by order made by statutory instrument amend any of subsections (2) to (6).

(10) No order shall be made under subsection (9) unless a draft has been laid before, and approved by resolution of, each House of Parliament.]

NOTES

Inserted, together with s 70C, by the Employment Relations Act 1999, s 5.

Sub-s (4A): inserted by the Agency Workers Regulations 2010, SI 2010/93, reg 25, Sch 2, Pt 1, paras 1, 2(a).

Sub-s (5): words in square brackets inserted by SI 2010/93, reg 25, Sch 2, Pt 1, paras 1, 2(b).

Orders: as of 15 May 2019, no Orders had been made under this section.

[1.370]

[70C Section 70B: complaint to employment tribunal

(1) A trade union may present a complaint to an employment tribunal that an employer has failed to comply with his obligations under section 70B in relation to a bargaining unit.

(2) An employment tribunal shall not consider a complaint under this section unless it is presented—

(a) before the end of the period of three months beginning with the date of the alleged failure, or

(b) within such further period as the tribunal considers reasonable in a case where it is satisfied that it was not reasonably practicable for the complaint to be presented before the end of that period of three months.

[(2A) Section 292A (extension of time limits to facilitate conciliation before institution of proceedings) applies for the purposes of subsection (2)(a).]

(3) Where an employment tribunal finds a complaint under this section well-founded it—

(a) shall make a declaration to that effect, and

(b) may make an award of compensation to be paid by the employer to each person who was, at the time when the failure occurred, a member of the bargaining unit.

(4) The amount of the award shall not, in relation to each person, exceed two weeks' pay.

(5) For the purpose of subsection (4) a week's pay—

(a) shall be calculated in accordance with Chapter II of Part XIV of the Employment Rights Act 1996 (taking the date of the employer's failure as the calculation date), and

(b) shall be subject to the limit in section 227(1) of that Act.

(6) Proceedings for enforcement of an award of compensation under this section—

(a) may, in relation to each person to whom compensation is payable, be commenced by that person, and

(b) may not be commenced by a trade union.]

NOTES

Inserted as noted to s 70B at **[1.369]**.

Sub-s (2A): inserted by the Enterprise and Regulatory Reform Act 2013, s 8, Sch 2, paras 1, 4.

Conciliation: employment tribunal proceedings under this section are "relevant proceedings" for the purposes of the conciliation provisions contained in the Employment Tribunals Act 1996, ss 18–18C; see s 18(1)(a) of the 1996 Act at **[1.757]**.

CHAPTER VI APPLICATION OF FUNDS FOR POLITICAL OBJECTS

Restriction on use of funds for certain political objects

[1.371]

71 Restriction on use of funds for certain political objects

(1) The funds of a trade union shall not be applied in the furtherance of the political objects to which this Chapter applies unless—

(a) there is in force in accordance with this Chapter a resolution (a "political resolution") approving the furtherance of those objects as an object of the union (see sections 73 to 81), and

(b) there are in force rules of the union as to—

(i) the making of payments in furtherance of those objects out of a separate fund, and

[(ii) the making of contributions to that fund by members,]

which comply with this Chapter (see sections 82, 84 and 85) and have been approved by the Certification Officer.

(2) This applies whether the funds are so applied directly, or in conjunction with another trade union, association or body, or otherwise indirectly.

NOTES

Sub-s (1): sub-para (b)(ii) substituted by the Trade Union Act 2016, s 22, Sch 4, para 5, as from 1 March 2017. Note that this amendment applies only after the end of the transition period of 12 months beginning on 1 March 2017 specified under the Trade Union Act 2016, s 11(6), and only in relation to a person (a) who after the end of that period joins a trade union that has a political fund, or (b) who is a member of a trade union that has a political fund but did not have one immediately before the end of that period (see **[2.1977]**). The original text read as follows—

"(ii) the exemption of any member of the union objecting to contribute to that fund,".

[1.372]

72 Political objects to which restriction applies

(1) The political objects to which this Chapter applies are the expenditure of money—

(a) on any contribution to the funds of, or on the payment of expenses incurred directly or indirectly by, a political party;

(b) on the provision of any service or property for use by or on behalf of any political party;

(c) in connection with the registration of electors, the candidature of any person, the selection of any candidate or the holding of any ballot by the union in connection with any election to a political office;

(d) on the maintenance of any holder of a political office;

(e) on the holding of any conference or meeting by or on behalf of a political party or of any other meeting the main purpose of which is the transaction of business in connection with a political party;

(f) on the production, publication or distribution of any literature, document, film, sound recording or advertisement the main purpose of which is to persuade people to vote for a political party or candidate or to persuade them not to vote for a political party or candidate.

(2) Where a person attends a conference or meeting as a delegate or otherwise as a participator in the proceedings, any expenditure incurred in connection with his attendance as such shall, for the purposes of subsection (1)(e), be taken to be expenditure incurred on the holding of the conference or meeting.

(3) In determining for the purposes of subsection (1) whether a trade union has incurred expenditure of a kind mentioned in that subsection, no account shall be taken of the ordinary administrative expenses of the union.

(4) In this section—

"candidate" means a candidate for election to a political office and includes a prospective candidate;

"contribution", in relation to the funds of a political party, includes any fee payable for affiliation to, or membership of, the party and any loan made to the party;

"electors" means electors at an election to a political office;

"film" includes any record, however made, of a sequence of visual images, which is capable of being used as a means of showing that sequence as a moving picture;

"local authority" means a local authority within the meaning of section 270 of the Local Government Act 1972 or section 235 of the Local Government (Scotland) Act 1973; and

"political office" means the office of member of Parliament, member of the European Parliament or member of a local authority or any position within a political party.

[1.373]

[72A Application of funds in breach of section 71

(1) A person who is a member of a trade union and who claims that it has applied its funds in breach of section 71 may apply to the Certification Officer for a declaration that it has done *so.*

[(1A) Where an application is made under subsection (1), the Certification Officer must ensure that, so far as is reasonably practicable, it is determined within six months of being made.]

(2) On an application under this section the Certification Officer—

(a) shall make such enquiries as he thinks fit,

(b) shall give the applicant and the union an opportunity to be heard,

(c) shall ensure that, so far as is reasonably practicable, the application is determined within six months of being made,

(d) may make or refuse the declaration asked for,

(e) shall, whether he makes or refuses the declaration, give reasons for his decision in writing, and

(f) may make written observations on any matter arising from, or connected with, the proceedings.

(3) If he makes a declaration he shall specify in it—

(a) the provisions of section 71 breached, and

(b) the amount of the funds applied in breach.

(4) If he makes a declaration and is satisfied that the union has taken or agreed to take steps with a view to—

(a) remedying the declared breach, or

(b) securing that a breach of the same or any similar kind does not occur in future,

he shall specify those steps in making the declaration.

(5) If he makes a declaration he may make such order for remedying the breach as he thinks just under the circumstances.

(6) Where the Certification Officer requests a person to furnish information to him in connection with enquiries made by him under this section, he shall specify the date by which that information is to be furnished and, unless he considers that it would be inappropriate to do so, shall proceed with his determination *of the application* notwithstanding that the information has not been furnished to him by the specified date.

(7) A declaration made by the Certification Officer under this section may be relied on as if it were a declaration made by the court.

(8) Where an order has been made under this section, any person who is a member of the union and was a member at the time it was made is entitled to enforce obedience to the order as if he had made *the application on which the order was made.*

(9) An order made by the Certification Officer under this section may be enforced [(by the Certification Officer, the applicant or a person mentioned in subsection (8))] in the same way as an order of the court.

(10) If a person applies to the Certification Officer under this section in relation to an alleged breach he may not apply to the court in relation to the breach; but nothing in this subsection shall prevent such a person from exercising any right to appeal against or challenge the Certification Officer's decision on the application to him.

(11) If—

(a) a person applies to the court in relation to an alleged breach, and

(b) the breach is one in relation to which he could have made an application to the Certification Officer under this section,

he may not apply to the Certification Officer under this section in relation to the breach.]

NOTES

Inserted by the Employment Relations Act 1999, s 29, Sch 6, paras 1, 13.

Sub-s (1): for the word in italics there is substituted "so; but the Certification Officer may also exercise the powers under this section where no application is made" by the Trade Union Act 2016, s 17(3), Sch 2, para 4(1), (2), as from a day to be appointed.

Sub-s (1A): inserted by the Trade Union Act 2016, s 17(3), Sch 2, para 4(1), (3), as from a day to be appointed.

Sub-s (2): substituted by the Trade Union Act 2016, s 17(3), Sch 2, para 4(1), (4), as from a day to be appointed, as follows—

"(2) Where the Certification Officer is satisfied that a trade union has applied its funds in breach of section 71, the Officer may make a declaration to that effect.

(2A) Before deciding the matter the Certification Officer—

(a) may make such enquiries as the Officer thinks fit,

(b) must give the union and the applicant (if any) an opportunity to make written representations, and

(c) may give the union and the applicant (if any) an opportunity to make oral representations.

(2B) The Certification Officer—

(a) must give reasons for the Officer's decision in writing, and

(b) may make written observations on any matter arising from, or connected with, the proceedings.".

Sub-s (6): words in italics repealed by the Trade Union Act 2016, s 17(3), Sch 2, para 4(1), (5), as from a day to be appointed.

Sub-s (8): for the words in italics there are substituted the words "an application under this section" by the Trade Union Act 2016, s 17(3), Sch 2, para 4(1), (6), as from a day to be appointed.

Sub-s (9): words in square brackets inserted by the Trade Union Act 2016, s 19(4), as from a day to be appointed.

Political resolution

[1.374]

73 Passing and effect of political resolution

(1) A political resolution must be passed by a majority of those voting on a ballot of the members of the trade union held in accordance with this Chapter.

(2) A political resolution so passed shall take effect as if it were a rule of the union and may be rescinded in the same manner and subject to the same provisions as such a rule.

(3) If not previously rescinded, a political resolution shall cease to have effect at the end of the period of ten years beginning with the date of the ballot on which it was passed.

(4) Where before the end of that period a ballot is held on a new political resolution, then—

(a) if the new resolution is passed, the old resolution shall be treated as rescinded, and

(b) if it is not passed, the old resolution shall cease to have effect at the end of the period of two weeks beginning with the date of the ballot.

[1.375]

74 Approval of political ballot rules

(1) A ballot on a political resolution must be held in accordance with rules of the trade union (its "political ballot rules") approved by the Certification Officer.

(2) Fresh approval is required for the purposes of each ballot which it is proposed to hold, notwithstanding that the rules have been approved for the purposes of an earlier ballot.

(3) The Certification Officer shall not approve a union's political ballot rules unless he is satisfied that the requirements set out in—

section 75 (appointment of independent scrutineer),
section 76 (entitlement to vote),
section 77 (voting), . . .
[section 77A (counting of votes etc. by independent person), and]
section 78 (scrutineer's report),

would be satisfied in relation to a ballot held by the union in accordance with the rules.

NOTES

Sub-s (3): word omitted repealed, and words in square brackets inserted, by the Trade Union Reform and Employment Rights Act 1993, ss 3, 51, Sch 1, para 1, Sch 10.

[1.376]

75 Appointment of independent scrutineer

(1) The trade union shall, before the ballot is held, appoint a qualified independent person ("the scrutineer") to carry out—

(a) the functions in relation to the ballot which are required under this section to be contained in his appointment; and

(b) such additional functions in relation to the ballot as may be specified in his appointment.

(2) A person is a qualified independent person in relation to a ballot if—

(a) he satisfies such conditions as may be specified for the purposes of this section by order of the Secretary of State or is himself so specified; and

(b) the trade union has no grounds for believing either that he will carry out any functions conferred on him in relation to the ballot otherwise than competently or that his independence in relation to the union, or in relation to the ballot, might reasonably be called into question.

An order under paragraph (a) shall be made by statutory instrument which shall be subject to annulment in pursuance of a resolution of either House of Parliament.

(3) The scrutineer's appointment shall require him—

(a) to be the person who supervises the production [of the voting papers and (unless he is appointed under section 77A to undertake the distribution of the voting papers) their distribution] and to whom the voting papers are returned by those voting;

[(aa) to—

(i) inspect the register of names and addresses of the members of the trade union, or

(ii) examine the copy of the register as at the relevant date which is supplied to him in accordance with subsection (5A)(a),

whenever it appears to him appropriate to do so and, in particular, when the conditions specified in subsection (3A) are satisfied;]

(b) to take such steps as appear to him to be appropriate for the purpose of enabling him to make his report (see section 78);

(c) to make his report to the trade union as soon as reasonably practicable after the last date for the return of voting papers; and

(d) to retain custody of all voting papers returned for the purposes of the ballot [and the copy of the register supplied to him in accordance with subsection (5A)(a)]—

(i) until the end of the period of one year beginning with the announcement by the union of the result of the ballot; and

(ii) if within that period an application is made under section 79 (complaint of failure to comply with ballot rules), until the Certification Officer or the court authorises him to dispose of the papers [or copy].

[(3A) The conditions referred to in subsection (3)(aa) are—

(a) that a request that the scrutineer inspect the register or examine the copy is made to him during the appropriate period by a member of the trade union who suspects that the register is not, or at the relevant date was not, accurate and up-to-date, and

(b) that the scrutineer does not consider that the member's suspicion is ill-founded.

(3B) In subsection (3A) "the appropriate period" means the period—

(a) beginning with the day on which the scrutineer is appointed, and

(b) ending with the day before the day on which the scrutineer makes his report to the trade union.

(3C) The duty of confidentiality as respects the register is incorporated in the scrutineer's appointment.]

(4) The trade union shall ensure that nothing in the terms of the scrutineer's appointment (including any additional functions specified in the appointment) is such as to make it reasonable for any person to call the scrutineer's independence in relation to the union into question.

(5) The trade union shall, before the scrutineer begins to carry out his functions, either—

(a) send a notice stating the name of the scrutineer to every member of the union to whom it is reasonably practicable to send such a notice, or

(b) take all such other steps for notifying members of the name of the scrutineer as it is the practice of the union to take when matters of general interest to all its members need to be brought to their attention.

[(5A) The trade union shall—

(a) supply to the scrutineer as soon as is reasonably practicable after the relevant date a copy of the register of names and addresses of its members as at that date, and

(b) comply with any request made by the scrutineer to inspect the register.

(5B) Where the register is kept by means of a computer the duty imposed on the trade union by subsection (5A)(a) is either to supply a legible printed copy or (if the scrutineer prefers) to supply a copy of the computer data and allow the scrutineer use of the computer to read it at any time during the period when he is required to retain custody of the copy.]

(6) The trade union shall ensure that the scrutineer duly carries out his functions and that there is no interference with his carrying out of those functions which would make it reasonable for any person to call the scrutineer's independence in relation to the union into question.

(7) The trade union shall comply with all reasonable requests made by the scrutineer for the purposes of, or in connection with, the carrying out of his functions.

[(8) In this section "the relevant date" means—

(a) where the trade union has rules determining who is entitled to vote in the ballot by reference to membership on a particular date, that date, and

(b) otherwise, the date, or the last date, on which voting papers are distributed for the purposes of the ballot.]

NOTES

Sub-s (3): words in square brackets in para (a) substituted, para (aa) inserted, and words in square brackets in para (d) inserted, by the Trade Union Reform and Employment Rights Act 1993, s 3, Sch 1, para 2(a)–(c).

Sub-ss (3A)–(3C), (5A), (5B), (8): inserted and added respectively by the Trade Union Reform and Employment Rights Act 1993, s 3, Sch 1, para 2(d)–(f).

Orders: the Trade Union Ballots and Elections (Independent Scrutineer Qualifications) Order 1993, SI 1993/1909 at **[2.138]**; the Trade Union Ballots and Elections (Independent Scrutineer Qualifications) (Amendment) Order 2010, SI 2010/436; the Trade Union Ballots and Elections (Independent Scrutineer Qualifications) (Amendment) Order 2017, SI 2017/877.

[1.377]

76 Entitlement to vote

Entitlement to vote in the ballot shall be accorded equally to all members of the trade union.

[1.378]

77 Voting

(1) The method of voting must be by the marking of a voting paper by the person voting.

(2) Each voting paper must—

(a) state the name of the independent scrutineer and clearly specify the address to which, and the date by which, it is to be returned, and

(b) be given one of a series of consecutive whole numbers every one of which is used in giving a different number in that series to each voting paper printed or otherwise produced for the purposes of the ballot, and

(c) be marked with its number.

(3) Every person who is entitled to vote in the ballot must—

(a) be allowed to vote without interference from, or constraint imposed by, the union or any of its members, officials or employees, and

(b) so far as is reasonably practicable, be enabled to do so without incurring any direct cost to himself.

(4) So far as is reasonably practicable, every person who is entitled to vote in the ballot must—

(a) have a voting paper sent to him by post at his home address or another address which he has requested the trade union in writing to treat as his postal address, and

(b) be given a convenient opportunity to vote by post.

(5) The ballot shall be conducted so as to secure that—

(a) so far as is reasonably practicable, those voting do so in secret, and

(b) the votes given in the ballot are fairly and accurately counted.

For the purposes of paragraph (b) an inaccuracy in counting shall be disregarded if it is accidental and on a scale which could not affect the result of the ballot.

[1.379]

[77A Counting of votes etc by independent person

(1) The trade union shall ensure that—

(a) the storage and distribution of the voting papers for the purposes of the ballot, and

(b) the counting of the votes cast in the ballot,

are undertaken by one or more independent persons appointed by the union.

(2) A person is an independent person in relation to a ballot if—

(a) he is the scrutineer, or

(b) he is a person other than the scrutineer and the trade union has no grounds for believing either that he will carry out any functions conferred on him in relation to the ballot otherwise than competently or that his independence in relation to the union, or in relation to the ballot, might reasonably be called into question.

(3) An appointment under this section shall require the person appointed to carry out his functions so as to minimise the risk of any contravention of requirements imposed by or under any enactment or the occurrence of any unfairness or malpractice.

(4) The duty of confidentiality as respects the register is incorporated in an appointment under this section.

(5) Where the person appointed to undertake the counting of votes is not the scrutineer, his appointment shall require him to send the voting papers back to the scrutineer as soon as reasonably practicable after the counting has been completed.

(6) The trade union—

(a) shall ensure that nothing in the terms of an appointment under this section is such as to make it reasonable for any person to call into question the independence of the person appointed in relation to the union,

(b) shall ensure that a person appointed under this section duly carries out his functions and that there is no interference with his carrying out of those functions which would make it reasonable for any person to call into question the independence of the person appointed in relation to the union, and

(c) shall comply with all reasonable requests made by a person appointed under this section for the purposes of, or in connection with, the carrying out of his functions.]

NOTES

Inserted by the Trade Union Reform and Employment Rights Act 1993, s 3, Sch 1, para 3.

[1.380]

78 Scrutineer's report

(1) The scrutineer's report on the ballot shall state—

(a) the number of voting papers distributed for the purposes of the ballot,

(b) the number of voting papers returned to the scrutineer,

(c) the number of valid votes cast in the ballot for and against the resolution, . . .

(d) the number of spoiled or otherwise invalid voting papers returned[; and

(e) the name of the person (or of each of the persons) appointed under section 77A or, if no person was so appointed, that fact.]

(2) The report shall also state whether the scrutineer is satisfied—

(a) that there are no reasonable grounds for believing that there was any contravention of a requirement imposed by or under any enactment in relation to the ballot,

(b) that the arrangements made [(whether by him or any other person)] with respect to the production, storage, distribution, return or other handling of the voting papers used in the ballot, and the arrangements for the counting of the votes, included all such security arrangements as were reasonably practicable for the purpose of minimising the risk that any unfairness or malpractice might occur, and

(c) that he has been able to carry out his functions without such interference as would make it reasonable for any person to call his independence in relation to the union into question;

and if he is not satisfied as to any of those matters, the report shall give particulars of his reasons for not being satisfied as to that matter.

[(2A) The report shall also state—

(a) whether the scrutineer—

(i) has inspected the register of names and addresses of the members of the trade union, or

(ii) has examined the copy of the register as at the relevant date which is supplied to him in accordance with section 75(5A)(a),

(b) if he has, whether in the case of each inspection or examination he was acting on a request by a member of the trade union or at his own instance,

(c) whether he declined to act on any such request, and

(d) whether any inspection of the register, or any examination of the copy of the register, has revealed any matter which he considers should be drawn to the attention of the trade union in order to assist it in securing that the register is accurate and up-to-date,

but shall not state the name of any member who has requested such an inspection or examination.

(2B) Where one or more persons other than the scrutineer are appointed under section 77A, the statement included in the scrutineer's report in accordance with subsection (2)(b) shall also indicate—

(a) whether he is satisfied with the performance of the person, or each of the persons, so appointed, and

(b) if he is not satisfied with the performance of the person, or any of them, particulars of his reasons for not being so satisfied.]

(3) The trade union shall not publish the result of the ballot until it has received the scrutineer's report.

(4) The trade union shall within the period of three months after it receives the report—

(a) send a copy of the report to every member of the union to whom it is reasonably practicable to send such a copy; or

(b) take all such other steps for notifying the contents of the report to the members of the union (whether by publishing the report or otherwise) as it is the practice of the union to take when matters of general interest to all its members need to be brought to their attention.

(5) Any such copy or notification shall be accompanied by a statement that the union will, on request, supply any member of the union with a copy of the report, either free of charge or on payment of such reasonable fee as may be specified in the notification.

(6) The trade union shall so supply any member of the union who makes such a request and pays the fee (if any) notified to him.

NOTES

Sub-s (1): word omitted from para (c) repealed, and para (e) and the word immediately preceding it added, by the Trade Union Reform and Employment Rights Act 1993, ss 3, 51, Sch 1, para 4(a), Sch 10.

Sub-s (2): words in square brackets inserted by the Trade Union Reform and Employment Rights Act 1993, s 3, Sch 1, para 4(b).

Sub-ss (2A), (2B): inserted by the Trade Union Reform and Employment Rights Act 1993, s 3, Sch 1, para 4(c).

[1.381]

79 Remedy for failure to comply with ballot rules: general

(1) The remedy for—

(a) the taking by a trade union of a ballot on a political resolution otherwise than in accordance with political ballot rules approved by the Certification Officer, or

(b) the failure of a trade union, in relation to a proposed ballot on a political resolution, to comply with the political ballot rules so approved,

is by way of application under section 80 (to the Certification Officer) or 81 (to the court).

. . .

(2) An application under *those sections* may be made only by a person who is a member of the trade union and, where the ballot has been held, was a member at the time when it was held.

References in those sections to a person having a sufficient interest are to such a person.

(3) No such application may be made after the end of the period of one year beginning with the day on which the union announced the result of the ballot.

NOTES

Sub-s (1): words omitted repealed by the Employment Relations Act 1999, ss 29, 44, Sch 6, paras 1, 14, Sch 9(7). This subsection is substituted by the Trade Union Act 2016, s 17(3), Sch 2, para 5(1), (2), as from a day to be appointed, as follows—

"(1) A person alleging that a trade union—

(a) has held a ballot on a political resolution otherwise than in accordance with political ballot rules approved by the Certification Officer, or

(b) has failed in relation to a proposed ballot on a political resolution to comply with political ballot rules so approved,

may apply for a declaration under section 80 (by the Certification Officer) or section 81 (by the court); but the Certification Officer may also exercise the powers under section 80 where no application is made.".

Sub-s (2): for the words in italics there are substituted the words "section 80 or 81" by the Trade Union Act 2016, s 17(3), Sch 2, para 5(1), (3), as from a day to be appointed.

[1.382]

80 *Application to* Certification Officer

(1) A person having a sufficient interest (see section 79(2)) who claims that a trade union—

(a) has held a ballot on a political resolution otherwise than in accordance with political ballot rules approved by the Certification Officer, or

(b) has failed in relation to a proposed ballot on a political resolution to comply with political ballot rules so approved,

may apply to the Certification Officer for a declaration to that effect.

(2) On an application being made to him, the Certification Officer shall—

(a) make such enquiries as he thinks fit, and

(b) . . . give the applicant and the trade union an opportunity to be heard,

and may make or refuse the declaration asked for.

(3) If he makes a declaration he shall specify in it the provisions with which the trade union has failed to comply.

(4) Where he makes a declaration and is satisfied that steps have been taken by the union with a view to remedying the declared failure, or securing that a failure of the same or any similar kind does not occur in future, or that the union has agreed to take such steps, he shall in making the declaration specify those steps.

(5) Whether he makes or refuses a declaration, he shall give reasons for his decision in writing; and the reasons may be accompanied by written observations on any matter arising from, or connected with, the proceedings.

[(5A) Where the Certification Officer makes a declaration he shall also, unless he considers that to do so would be inappropriate, make an enforcement order, that is, an order imposing on the union one or more of the following requirements—

(a) to secure the holding of a ballot in accordance with the order;

(b) to take such other steps to remedy the declared failure as may be specified in the order;

(c) to abstain from such acts as may be so specified with a view to securing that a failure of the same or a similar kind does not occur in future.

The Certification Officer shall in an order imposing any such requirement as is mentioned in paragraph (a) or (b) specify the period within which the union must comply with the requirements of the order.

(5B) Where the Certification Officer makes an order requiring the union to hold a fresh ballot, he shall (unless he considers that it would be inappropriate to do so in the particular circumstances of the case) require the ballot to be conducted in accordance with the union's political ballot rules and such other provisions as may be made by the order.

(5C) Where an enforcement order has been made, any person who is a member of the union and was a member at the time the order was made is entitled to enforce obedience to the order as if he had made *the application on which the order was made*.]

(6) In exercising his functions under this section the Certification Officer shall ensure that, so far as is reasonably practicable, an application made to him is determined within six months of being made.

(7) Where he requests a person to furnish information to him in connection with enquiries made by him under this section, he shall specify the date by which that information is to be furnished and shall, unless he considers that it would be inappropriate to do so, proceed with his determination *of the application* notwithstanding that the information has not been furnished to him by the specified date.

[(8) A declaration made by the Certification Officer under this section may be relied on as if it were a declaration made by the court.

(9) An enforcement order made by the Certification Officer under this section may be enforced [(by the Certification Officer, the applicant or a person mentioned in subsection (5C))] in the same way as an order of the court.

(10) The following paragraphs have effect if a person applies under section 81 in relation to a matter—

(a) that person may not apply under this section in relation to that matter;

(b) on an application by a different person under this section in relation to that matter, the Certification Officer shall have due regard to any declaration, order, observations, or reasons made or given by the court regarding that matter and brought to the Certification Officer's notice.]

NOTES

Section heading: for the words in italics there are substituted the words "Powers of" by the Trade Union Act 2016, s 17(3), Sch 2, para 6(1), (2), as from a day to be appointed.

Sub-ss (1), (2): substituted by the Trade Union Act 2016, s 17(3), Sch 2, para 6(1), (3), as from a day to be appointed, as follows—

"(1) Where the Certification Officer is satisfied, either on an application by a person having a sufficient interest (see section 79(2)) or without any such application having been made, that a trade union—

(a) has held a ballot on a political resolution otherwise than in accordance with political ballot rules approved by the Certification Officer, or

(b) has failed in relation to a proposed ballot on a political resolution to comply with political ballot rules so approved,

the Officer may make a declaration to that effect.

(2) Before deciding the matter the Certification Officer—

(a) may make such enquiries as the Officer thinks fit,

(b) must give the union and the applicant (if any) an opportunity to make written representations, and
(c) may give the union and the applicant (if any) an opportunity to make oral representations.".

The words omitted from sub s (2)(b) were repealed by the Employment Relations Act 1999, ss 29, 44, Sch 6, paras 1, 15(1), (2), Sch 9(7).

Sub-ss (5A)–(5C): inserted by the Employment Relations Act 1999, s 29, Sch 6, paras 1, 15(1), (3); for the words in italics in sub-s (5C) there are substituted the words "an application under this section" by the Trade Union Act 2016, s 17(3), Sch 2, para 6(1), (4), as from a day to be appointed.

Sub-s (7): words in italics repealed by the Trade Union Act 2016, s 17(3), Sch 2, para 6(1), (5), as from a day to be appointed.

Sub-ss (8)–(10): added by the Employment Relations Act 1999, s 29, Sch 6, paras 1, 15(1), (4); words in square brackets in sub-s (9) inserted by the Trade Union Act 2016, s 19(4), as from a day to be appointed.

[1.383]

81 Application to court

(1) A person having a sufficient interest (see section 79(2)) who claims that a trade union—

(a) has held a ballot on a political resolution otherwise than in accordance with political ballot rules approved by the Certification Officer, or

(b) has failed in relation to a proposed ballot on a political resolution to comply with political ballot rules so approved,

may apply to the court for a declaration to that effect.

(2) . . .

(3) If the court makes the declaration asked for, it shall specify in the declaration the provisions with which the trade union has failed to comply.

(4) Where the court makes a declaration it shall also, unless it considers that to do so would be inappropriate, make an enforcement order, that is, an order imposing on the union one or more of the following requirements—

(a) to secure the holding of a ballot in accordance with the order;

(b) to take such other steps to remedy the declared failure as may be specified in the order;

(c) to abstain from such acts as may be so specified with a view to securing that a failure of the same or a similar kind does not occur in future.

The court shall in an order imposing any such requirement as is mentioned in paragraph (a) or (b) specify the period within which the union must comply with the requirements of the order.

(5) Where the court makes an order requiring the union to hold a fresh ballot, the court shall (unless it considers that it would be inappropriate to do so in the particular circumstances of the case) require the ballot to be conducted in accordance with the union's political ballot rules and such other provisions as may be made by the order.

(6) Where an enforcement order has been made, any person who is a member of the union and was a member at the time the order was made is entitled to enforce obedience to the order as if he had made the application on which the order was made.

(7) Without prejudice to any other power of the court, the court may on an application under this section grant such interlocutory relief (in Scotland, such interim order) as it considers appropriate.

[(8) The following paragraphs have effect if a person applies under section 80 in relation to a matter—

(a) that person may not apply under this section in relation to that matter;

(b) on an application by a different person under this section in relation to that matter, the court shall have due regard to any declaration, order, observations or reasons made or given by the Certification Officer regarding that matter and brought to the court's notice.]

NOTES

Sub-s (2): repealed by the Employment Relations Act 1999, ss 29, 44, Sch 6, paras 1, 16(1), (2), Sch 9(7).

Sub-s (8): added by the Employment Relations Act 1999, s 29, Sch 6, paras 1, 16(1), (3).

The political fund

[1.384]

82 Rules as to political fund

(1) The trade union's rules must provide—

(a) that payments in the furtherance of the political objects to which this Chapter applies shall be made out of a separate fund (the "political fund" of the union);

[(b) that a member of the union who is not a contributor (see section 84) shall not be under any obligation to contribute to the political fund;]

(c) that a member shall not by reason of [not being a contributor]—

(i) be excluded from any benefits of the union, or

(ii) be placed in any respect either directly or indirectly under a disability or at a disadvantage as compared with other members of the union (except in relation to the control or management of the political fund);

[(ca) that, if the union has a political fund, any form (including an electronic form) that a person has to complete in order to become a member of the union shall include—

(i) a statement to the effect that the person may opt to be a contributor to the fund, and

(ii) a statement setting out the effect of paragraph (c); and]

(d) that contribution to the political fund shall not be made a condition for admission to the union.

(2) A member of a trade union who claims that he is aggrieved by a breach of any rule made in pursuance of this section may complain to the Certification *Officer.*

[(2A) On a complaint being made to him the Certification Officer shall make such enquiries as he thinks fit.]

(3) Where, after giving the member and a representative of the union an opportunity of being heard, the Certification Officer considers that a breach has been committed, he may make such order for remedying the breach as he thinks just under the circumstances.

[(3A) Where the Certification Officer requests a person to furnish information to him in connection with enquiries made by him under this section, he shall specify the date by which that information is to be furnished and, unless he considers that it would be inappropriate to do so, shall proceed with his determination *of the application* notwithstanding that the information has not been furnished to him by the specified date.]

[(4A) Where an order has been made under this section, any person who is a member of the union and was a member at the time it was made is entitled to enforce obedience to the order as if he had made *the complaint on which it was made*.

(4B) An order made by the Certification Officer under this section may be enforced [(by the Certification Officer, the complainant or a person mentioned in subsection (4A))]—

(a) in England and Wales, in the same way as an order of the county court;

(b) in Scotland, in the same way as an order of the sheriff.]

NOTES

Sub-s (1) is amended as follows:

Para (b) was substituted, and the first words in square brackets in para (c) were substituted (for the original words "being so exempt"), by the Trade Union Act 2016, s 22, Sch 4, para 6, as from 1 March 2017. Note that this amendment applies only after the end of the transition period of 12 months beginning on 1 March 2017 specified under the Trade Union Act 2016, s 11(6), and only in relation to a person (a) who after the end of that period joins a trade union that has a political fund, or (b) who is a member of a trade union that has a political fund but did not have one immediately before the end of that period (see **[2.1977]**). The original para (b) read as follows—

"(b) that a member of the union who gives notice in accordance with section 84 that he objects to contributing to the political fund shall be exempt from any obligation to contribute to it;".

Para (ca) was substituted (for the original word "and" at the end of para (c)) by the Trade Union Act 2016, s 11(4), as from 1 March 2017 (note that this amendment applies only after the end of the transition period (ie, a period of not less than 12 months starting on that date), and only to a person: (a) who after the end of that period joins a trade union that has a political fund, or (b) who is a member of a trade union that has a political fund but did not have one immediately before the end of that period (see **[1.2009]**)).

Sub-s (2): for the word in italics there is substituted "Officer; but the Officer may also exercise the powers under this section where no complaint under this section is made" by the Trade Union Act 2016, s 17(3), Sch 2, para 7(1), (2), as from a day to be appointed.

Sub-s (2A): inserted by the Employment Relations Act 1999, s 29, Sch 6, paras 1, 17. This subsection, together with sub-s (3), is substituted by the Trade Union Act 2016, s 17(3), Sch 2, para 7(1), (3), as from a day to be appointed, as follows—

"(2A) Where the Certification Officer is satisfied that a breach has been committed, the Officer may make such order for remedying the breach as he thinks just under the circumstances.

(3) Before deciding the matter the Certification Officer—

(a) may make such enquiries as the Officer thinks fit,

(b) must give a representative of the union and the complainant (if any) an opportunity to make written representations, and

(c) may give a representative of the union and the complainant (if any) an opportunity to make oral representations.".

Sub-s (3): prospectively substituted as noted above.

Sub-s (3A): inserted by the Employment Relations Act 1999, s 29, Sch 6, paras 1, 17; words in italics repealed by the Trade Union Act 2016, s 17(3), Sch 2, para 7(1), (4), as from a day to be appointed.

Sub-ss (4A), (4B): substituted, for the original sub-s (4), by the Employment Relations Act 2004, s 57(1), Sch 1, para 6; for the words in italics in sub-s (4A) there are substituted the words "a complaint under this section" by the Trade Union Act 2016, s 17(3), Sch 2, para 7(1), (5), as from a day to be appointed; words in square brackets in sub-s (4B) inserted by the Trade Union Act 2016, s 19(4), as from a day to be appointed.

[1.385]

83 Assets and liabilities of political fund

(1) There may be added to a union's political fund only—

(a) sums representing contributions made to the fund by members of the union or by any person other than the union itself, and

(b) property which accrues to the fund in the course of administering the assets of the fund.

(2) The rules of the union shall not be taken to require any member to contribute to the political fund at a time when there is no political resolution in force in relation to the union.

(3) No liability of a union's political fund shall be discharged out of any other fund of the union.

This subsection applies notwithstanding any term or condition on which the liability was incurred or that an asset of the other fund has been charged in connection with the liability.

[1.386]

[84 Contributions to political fund from members of the union

(1) It is unlawful to require a member of a trade union to make a contribution to the political fund of a trade union if—

(a) the member has not given to the union notice of the member's willingness to contribute to that fund (an "opt-in notice"); or

(b) an opt-in notice given by the member has been withdrawn in accordance with subsection (2).

(2) A member of a trade union who has given an opt-in notice may withdraw that notice by giving notice to the union (a "withdrawal notice").

(3) A withdrawal notice takes effect at the end of the period of one month beginning with the day on which it is given.
(4) A member of a trade union may give an opt-in notice or a withdrawal notice—
(a) by delivering it (either personally or by an authorised agent or by post) at the head office or a branch office of the union;
(b) by sending it by e-mail to an address that the union has told its members can be used for sending such notices;
(c) by completing an electronic form provided by the union which sets out the notice, and sending it to the union by electronic means in accordance with instructions given by the union; or
(d) by such other electronic means as may be prescribed.
(5) In this Act "contributor", in relation to the political fund of a trade union, means a member who has given to the union an opt-in notice that has not been withdrawn.]

NOTES

Commencement: 1 March 2017.

Substituted by the Trade Union Act 2016, s 11(1), as from 1 March 2017 (note that this amendment applies only after the end of the transition period (ie, a period of not less than 12 months starting on that date), and only to a person: (a) who after the end of that period joins a trade union that has a political fund, or (b) who is a member of a trade union that has a political fund but did not have one immediately before the end of that period (see **[1.2009]**)). The original text read as follows—

"84 Notice of objection to contributing to political fund

(1) A member of a trade union may give notice in the following form, or in a form to the like effect, that he objects to contribute to the political fund—

Name of Trade Union

POLITICAL FUND (EXEMPTION NOTICE)

I give notice that I object to contributing to the Political Fund of the Union, and am in consequence exempt, in manner provided by Chapter VI of Part I of the Trade Union and Labour Relations (Consolidation) Act 1992, from contributing to that fund.

A. B.

Address. . . . .

day of. . . . . 19. . . . . . .

(2) On the adoption of a political resolution, notice shall be given to members of the union acquainting them—
(a) that each member has a right to be exempted from contributing to the union's political fund, and
(b) that a form of exemption notice can be obtained by or on behalf of a member either by application at or by post from—
(i) the head office or any branch office of the union, or
(ii) the office of the Certification Officer.
(3) The notice to members shall be given in accordance with rules of the union approved for the purpose by the Certification Officer, who shall have regard in each case to the existing practice and character of the union.
(4) On giving an exemption notice in accordance with this section, a member shall be exempt from contributing to the union's political fund—
(a) where the notice is given within one month of the giving of notice to members under subsection (2) following the passing of a political resolution on a ballot held at a time when no such resolution is in force, as from the date on which the exemption notice is given;
(b) in any other case, as from the 1st January next after the exemption notice is given.
(5) An exemption notice continues to have effect until it is withdrawn."

[1.387]

[84A Information to members about contributing to political fund

(1) A trade union shall take all reasonable steps to secure that, not later than the end of the period of eight weeks beginning with the day on which the annual return of the union is sent to the Certification Officer, all the members of the union are notified of their right to give a withdrawal notice under section 84(2).
(2) The notification may be given—
(a) by sending individual copies of it to members; or
(b) by any other means (whether by including the notification in a publication of the union or otherwise) which it is the practice of the union to use when information of general interest to all its members needs to be provided to them;
and, in particular, the notification may be included with the statement required to be given by section 32A.
(3) A trade union shall send to the Certification Officer a copy of the notification which is provided to its members in pursuance of this section as soon as is reasonably practicable after it is so provided.
(4) Where the same form of notification is not provided to all the members of a trade union, the union shall send to the Certification Officer in accordance with subsection (3) a copy of each form of notification provided to any of them.
(5) Where the Certification Officer is satisfied that a trade union has failed to comply with a requirement of this section, the Officer may make such order for remedying the failure as he thinks just under the circumstances.
(6) Before deciding the matter the Certification Officer—
(a) may make such enquiries as the Officer thinks fit;

(b) must give the union, and any member of the union who made a complaint to the Officer regarding the matter, an opportunity to make written representations; and

(c) may give the union, and any such member as is mentioned in paragraph (b), an opportunity to make oral representations.]

NOTES

Commencement: 1 March 2017.

Inserted by the Trade Union Act 2016, s 11(2), as from 1 March 2017 (note that this amendment applies only after the end of the transition period (ie, a period of not less than 12 months starting on that date), and only to a person: (a) who after the end of that period joins a trade union that has a political fund, or (b) who is a member of a trade union that has a political fund but did not have one immediately before the end of that period (see **[1.2009]**)).

[1.388]

[85 Manner of giving effect to section 84

(1) A union that has a political fund must either—

(a) make a separate levy of contributions to that fund from the members who are contributors, or

(b) relieve members who are not contributors from the payment of the appropriate portion of any periodical contribution required from members towards the expenses of the union.

(2) In the latter case, the rules shall provide—

(a) that relief shall be given as far as possible to all members who are not contributors on the occasion of the same periodical payment, and

(b) for enabling each member of the union to know what portion (if any) of any periodical contribution payable by the member is a contribution to the political fund.]

NOTES

Commencement: 1 March 2017.

Substituted by the Trade Union Act 2016, s 11(3), as from 1 March 2017 (note that this section applies only after the end of the transition period (ie, a period of not less than 12 months starting on that date), and only to a person: (a) who after the end of that period joins a trade union that has a political fund, or (b) who is a member of a trade union that has a political fund but did not have one immediately before the end of that period (see **[1.2009]**)). The original text read as follows—

"**85 Manner of giving effect to exemptions**

(1) Effect may be given to the exemption of members from contributing to the political fund of a union either—

(a) by a separate levy of contributions to that fund from the members who are not exempt, or

(b) by relieving members who are exempt from the payment of the whole or part of any periodical contribution required from members towards the expenses of the union.

(2) In the latter case, the rules shall provide—

(a) that relief shall be given as far as possible to all members who are exempt on the occasion of the same periodical payment, and

(b) for enabling each member of the union to know what portion (if any) of any periodical contribution payable by him is a contribution to the political fund.".

Duties of employer who deducts union contributions

[1.389]

86 [Employer not to deduct contributions where member gives certificate]

(1) If a member of a trade union which has a political fund certifies in writing to his employer that, or to the effect that[, he is not a contributor to the fund,] the employer shall ensure that no amount representing a contribution to the political fund is deducted by him from emoluments payable to the member.

(2) The employer's duty under subsection (1) applies from the first day, following the giving of the certificate, on which it is reasonably practicable for him to comply with that subsection, until the certificate is withdrawn.

(3) An employer may not refuse to deduct any union dues from emoluments payable to a person who has given a certificate under this section if he continues to deduct union dues from emoluments payable to other members of the union, unless his refusal is not attributable to the giving of the certificate or otherwise connected with the duty imposed by subsection (1).

NOTES

The section heading was substituted (for the original heading "Certificate of exemption or objection to contributing to political fund"), and the words in square brackets in sub-s (1) were substituted, by the Trade Union Act 2016, s 22, Sch 4, para 7, as from 1 March 2017. Note that these amendments apply only after the end of the transition period of 12 months beginning on 1 March 2017 specified under the Trade Union Act 2016, s 11(6), and only in relation to a person (a) who after the end of that period joins a trade union that has a political fund, or (b) who is a member of a trade union that has a political fund but did not have one immediately before the end of that period (see **[2.1977]**). The original text in sub-s (1) read as follows—

"(a) he is exempt from the obligation to contribute to the fund, or

(b) he has, in accordance with section 84, notified the union in writing of his objection to contributing to the fund,".

No complaint is to be presented under the Employment Rights Act 1996, s 23 in respect of any deduction made in contravention of this section; see sub-s (5) of that section at **[1.837]**.

The rights conferred by this section are "relevant statutory rights" for the purposes of the Employment Rights Act 1996, s 104 (dismissal on grounds of assertion of statutory right); see s 104(4)(c) of that Act at **[1.1015]**.

[1.390]

[87 Complaint in respect of employer's failure

(1) A person who claims his employer has failed to comply with section 86 in deducting or refusing to deduct any amount from emoluments payable to him may present a complaint to an employment tribunal.

(2) A tribunal shall not consider a complaint under subsection (1) unless it is presented—

(a) within the period of three months beginning with the date of the payment of the emoluments or (if the complaint relates to more than one payment) the last of the payments, or

(b) where the tribunal is satisfied that it was not reasonably practicable for the complaint to be presented within that period, within such further period as the tribunal considers reasonable.

[(2A) Section 292A (extension of time limits to facilitate conciliation before institution of proceedings) applies for the purposes of subsection (2)(a).]

(3) Where on a complaint under subsection (1) arising out of subsection (3) (refusal to deduct union dues) of section 86 the question arises whether the employer's refusal to deduct an amount was attributable to the giving of the certificate or was otherwise connected with the duty imposed by subsection (1) of that section, it is for the employer to satisfy the tribunal that it was not.

(4) Where a tribunal finds that a complaint under subsection (1) is well-founded—

(a) it shall make a declaration to that effect and, where the complaint arises out of subsection (1) of section 86, order the employer to pay to the complainant the amount deducted in contravention of that subsection less any part of that amount already paid to him by the employer, and

(b) it may, if it considers it appropriate to do so in order to prevent a repetition of the failure, make an order requiring the employer to take, within a specified time, the steps specified in the order in relation to emoluments payable by him to the complainant.

(5) A person who claims his employer has failed to comply with an order made under subsection (4)(b) on a complaint presented by him may present a further complaint to an employment tribunal; but only one complaint may be presented under this subsection in relation to any order.

(6) A tribunal shall not consider a complaint under subsection (5) unless it is presented—

(a) after the end of the period of four weeks beginning with the date of the order, but

(b) before the end of the period of six months beginning with that date.

(7) Where on a complaint under subsection (5) a tribunal finds that an employer has, without reasonable excuse, failed to comply with an order made under subsection (4)(b), it shall order the employer to pay to the complainant an amount equal to two weeks pay.

(8) Chapter II of Part XIV of the Employment Rights Act 1996 (calculation of a week's pay) applies for the purposes of subsection (7) with the substitution for section 225 of the following—

> "For the purposes of this Chapter in its application to subsection (7) of section 87 of the Trade Union and Labour Relations (Consolidation) Act 1992, the calculation date is the date of the payment, or (if more than one) the last of the payments, to which the complaint related."]

NOTES

Substituted by the Employment Rights (Dispute Resolution) Act 1998, s 6.

Sub-s (2A): inserted by the Enterprise and Regulatory Reform Act 2013, s 8, Sch 2, paras 1, 5.

Conciliation: employment tribunal proceedings under this section are "relevant proceedings" for the purposes of the conciliation provisions contained in the Employment Tribunals Act 1996, ss 18–18C; see s 18(1)(a) of the 1996 Act at **[1.757]**.

88 *((Application of provisions of Wages Act 1986) repealed by the Employment Rights (Dispute Resolution) Act 1998, s 15, Sch 2.)*

Position where political resolution ceases to have effect

[1.391]

89 Administration of political fund where no resolution in force

(1) The following provisions have effect with respect to the political fund of a trade union where there ceases to be any political resolution in force in relation to the union.

(2) If the resolution ceases to have effect by reason of a ballot being held on which a new political resolution is not passed, the union may continue to make payments out of the fund as if the resolution had continued in force for six months beginning with the date of the ballot.

But no payment shall be made which causes the fund to be in deficit or increases a deficit in it.

(3) There may be added to the fund only—

(a) contributions to the fund paid to the union (or to a person on its behalf) before the resolution ceased to have effect, and

(b) property which accrues to the fund in the course of administering the assets of the fund.

(4) The union may, notwithstanding any of its rules or any trusts on which the fund is held, transfer the whole or part of the fund to such other fund of the union as it thinks fit.

(5) If a new political resolution is subsequently passed, no property held immediately before the date of the ballot by or on behalf of the union otherwise than in its political fund, and no sums representing such property, may be added to the fund.

[1.392]

90 Discontinuance of contributions to political fund

(1) Where there ceases to be any political resolution in force in relation to a trade union, the union shall take such steps as are necessary to ensure that the collection of contributions to its political fund is discontinued as soon as is reasonably practicable.

(2) The union may, notwithstanding any of its rules, pay into any of its other funds any such contribution which is received by it after the resolution ceases to have effect.

(3) If the union continues to collect contributions, it shall refund to a member who applies for a refund the contributions made by him collected after the resolution ceased to have effect.

(4) A member of a trade union who claims that the union has failed to comply with subsection (1) may apply to the court for a declaration to that effect.

(5) Where the court is satisfied that the complaint is well-founded, it may, if it considers it appropriate to do so in order to secure that the collection of contributions to the political fund is discontinued, make an order requiring the union to take, within such time as may be specified in the order, such steps as may be so specified.

Such an order may be enforced by a person who is a member of the union and was a member at the time the order was made as if he had made the application.

(6) The remedy for failure to comply with subsection (1) is in accordance with subsections (4) and (5), and not otherwise; but this does not affect any right to recover sums payable to a person under subsection (3).

[1.393]
91 Rules to cease to have effect

(1) If there ceases to be any political resolution in force in relation to a trade union, the rules of the union made for the purpose of complying with this Chapter also cease to have effect, except so far as they are required to enable the political fund to be administered at a time when there is no such resolution in force.

(2) If the resolution ceases to have effect by reason of a ballot being held on which a new political resolution is not passed, the rules cease to have effect at the end of the period of six months beginning with the date of the ballot.

In any other case the rules cease to have effect when the resolution ceases to have effect.

(3) Nothing in this section affects the operation of section 82(2) (complaint to Certification Officer in respect of breach of rules) in relation to a breach of a rule occurring before the rule in question ceased to have effect.

(4) [A member of a trade union who has at any time not been a contributor to its political fund shall not for that reason—]

- (a) be excluded from any benefits of the union, or
- (b) be placed in any respect either directly or indirectly under a disability or at a disadvantage as compared with other members (except in relation to the control or management of the political fund).

NOTES

Sub-s (4): words in square brackets substituted (for the original words "No member of a trade union who has at any time been exempt from the obligation to contribute to its political fund shall by reason of his having been exempt") by the Trade Union Act 2016, s 22, Sch 4, para 8, as from 1 March 2017. Note that this amendment applies only after the end of the transition period of 12 months beginning on 1 March 2017 specified under the Trade Union Act 2016, s 11(6), and only in relation to a person (a) who after the end of that period joins a trade union that has a political fund, or (b) who is a member of a trade union that has a political fund but did not have one immediately before the end of that period (see **[2.1977]**).

Supplementary

[1.394]
92 Manner of making union rules

If the Certification Officer is satisfied, and certifies, that rules of a trade union made for any of the purposes of this Chapter and requiring approval by him have been approved—

- (a) by a majority of the members of the union voting for the purpose, or
- (b) by a majority of delegates of the union at a meeting called for the purpose,

the rules shall have effect as rules of the union notwithstanding that the rules of the union as to the alteration of rules or the making of new rules have not been complied with.

[1.395]
93 Effect of amalgamation

(1) Where on an amalgamation of two or more trade unions—

- (a) there is in force in relation to each of the amalgamating unions a political resolution and such rules as are required by this Chapter, and
- (b) the rules of the amalgamated union in force immediately after the amalgamation include such rules as are required by this Chapter,

the amalgamated union shall be treated for the purposes of this Chapter as having passed a political resolution.

(2) That resolution shall be treated as having been passed on the date of the earliest of the ballots on which the resolutions in force immediately before the amalgamation with respect to the amalgamating unions were passed.

(3) Where one of the amalgamating unions is a Northern Ireland union, the references above to the requirements of this Chapter shall be construed as references to the requirements of the corresponding provisions of the law of Northern Ireland.

[1.396]
94 Overseas members of trade unions

(1) Where a political resolution is in force in relation to the union—

- (a) rules made by the union for the purpose of complying with section 74 (political ballot rules) in relation to a proposed ballot may provide for overseas members of the union not to be accorded entitlement to vote in the ballot, *and*

(b) *rules made by the union for the purpose of complying with section 84 (notice of right to object to contribute to political fund to be given where resolution passed) may provide for notice not to be given by the union to its overseas members.*

(2) Accordingly, where provision is made in accordance with subsection (1)(a), the Certification Officer shall not on that ground withhold his approval of the rules*; and where provision is made in accordance with subsection (1)(b), section 84(2) (duty to give notice) shall not be taken to require notice to be given to overseas members*.

(3) An "overseas member" means a member of the trade union (other than a merchant seaman or offshore worker) who is outside Great Britain throughout the period during which votes may be cast.

For this purpose—

"merchant seaman" means a person whose employment, or the greater part of it, is carried out on board sea-going ships; and

"offshore worker" means a person in offshore employment, other than one who is in such employment in an area where the law of Northern Ireland applies.

NOTES

Sub-ss (1), (2): words in italics repealed by the Trade Union Act 2016, s 22, Sch 4, para 9, as from 1 March 2017. Note that these amendments apply only after the end of the transition period of 12 months beginning on 1 March 2017 specified under the Trade Union Act 2016, s 11(6), and only in relation to a person (a) who after the end of that period joins a trade union that has a political fund, or (b) who is a member of a trade union that has a political fund but did not have one immediately before the end of that period (see **[2.1977]**).

[1.397]

95 Appeals from Certification Officer

An appeal lies to the Employment Appeal Tribunal *on any question of law arising* in proceedings before or arising from any decision of the Certification Officer under this Chapter.

NOTES

For the words in italics there are substituted the words "on any question arising" by the Trade Union Act 2016, s 21(c), as from a day to be appointed.

[1.398]

96 Meaning of "date of the ballot"

In this Chapter the "date of the ballot" means, in the case of a ballot in which votes may be cast on more than one day, the last of those days.

CHAPTER VII AMALGAMATIONS AND SIMILAR MATTERS

NOTES

Regulations: for Regulations supplementing the provisions of this Chapter, see the Trade Unions and Employers' Associations (Amalgamations etc) Regulations 1975, SI 1975/536 at **[2.1]**.

Amalgamation or transfer of engagements

[1.399]

97 Amalgamation or transfer of engagements

(1) Two or more trade unions may amalgamate and become one trade union, with or without a division or dissolution of the funds of any one or more of the amalgamating unions, but shall not do so unless—

(a) the instrument of amalgamation is approved in accordance with section 98, and

(b) the requirements of [section 99 (notice to members) and section 100 (resolution to be passed by required majority in ballot held in accordance with sections 100A to 100E)] are complied with in respect of each of the amalgamating unions.

(2) A trade union may transfer its engagements to another trade union which undertakes to fulfil those engagements, but shall not do so unless—

(a) the instrument of transfer is approved in accordance with section 98, and

(b) the requirements of [section 99 (notice to members) and section 100 (resolution to be passed by required majority in ballot held in accordance with sections 100A to 100E)] are complied with in respect of the transferor union.

(3) An amalgamation or transfer of engagements does not prejudice any right of any creditor of any trade union party to the amalgamation or transfer.

(4) The above provisions apply to every amalgamation or transfer of engagements notwithstanding anything in the rules of any of the trade unions concerned.

NOTES

Sub-ss (1), (2): words in square brackets substituted by the Trade Union Reform and Employment Rights Act 1993, s 49(2), Sch 8, para 52.

[1.400]

98 Approval of instrument of amalgamation or transfer

(1) The instrument of amalgamation or transfer must be approved by the Certification Officer and shall be submitted to him for approval before [a ballot of the members of any amalgamating union, or (as the case may be) of the transferor union, is held on the resolution to approve the instrument].

[(2) If the Certification Officer is satisfied—

(a) that an instrument of amalgamation complies with the requirements of any regulations in force under this Chapter, and

(b) that he is not prevented from approving the instrument of amalgamation by subsection (3),

he shall approve the instrument.

(3) The Certification Officer shall not approve an instrument of amalgamation if it appears to him that the proposed name of the amalgamated union is the same as the name under which another organisation—

(a) was on 30th September 1971 registered as a trade union under the Trade Union Acts 1871 to 1964,

(b) was at any time registered as a trade union or employers' association under the Industrial Relations Act 1971, or

(c) is for the time being entered in the list of trade unions or in the list of employers' associations,

or if the proposed name is one so nearly resembling any such name as to be likely to deceive the public.

(4) Subsection (3) does not apply if the proposed name is the name of one of the amalgamating unions.

(5) If the Certification Officer is satisfied that an instrument of transfer complies with the requirements of any regulations in force under this Chapter, he shall approve the instrument.]

NOTES

Sub-s (1): words in square brackets substituted by the Trade Union Reform and Employment Rights Act 1993, s 49(2), Sch 8, para 53.

Sub-ss (2)–(5): substituted, for the original sub-s (2), by the Employment Relations Act 2004, s 50(1).

Trade Union Acts 1871 to 1964: repealed, see the note to s 3 at **[1.270]**.

Industrial Relations Act 1971: repealed by the Trade Union and Labour Relations Act 1974, ss 1, 25(3), Sch 5.

[1.401]

99 Notice to be given to members

(1) The trade union shall take all reasonable steps to secure [that every voting paper which is supplied for voting in the ballot on the resolution to approve the instrument of amalgamation or transfer is accompanied by] a notice in writing approved for the purpose by the Certification Officer.

(2) The notice shall be in writing and shall either—

(a) set out in full the instrument of amalgamation or transfer to which the resolution relates, or

(b) give an account of it sufficient to enable those receiving the notice to form a reasonable judgment of the main effects of the proposed amalgamation or transfer.

(3) If the notice does not set out the instrument in full it shall state where copies of the instrument may be inspected by those receiving the notice.

[(3A) The notice shall not contain any statement making a recommendation or expressing an opinion about the proposed amalgamation or transfer.]

(4) The notice shall also comply with the requirements of any regulations in force under this Chapter.

(5) The notice proposed to be supplied to members of the union under this section shall be submitted to the Certification Officer for approval; and he shall approve it if he is satisfied that it meets the requirements of this section.

NOTES

Sub-s (1): words in square brackets substituted by the Trade Union Reform and Employment Rights Act 1993, s 49(2), Sch 8, para 54.

Sub-s (3A): inserted by the Trade Union Reform and Employment Rights Act 1993, s 5.

[1.402]

[100 Requirement of ballot on resolution

(1) A resolution approving the instrument of amalgamation or transfer must be passed on a ballot of the members of the trade union held in accordance with sections 100A to 100E.

(2) A simple majority of those voting is sufficient to pass such a resolution unless the rules of the trade union expressly require it to be approved by a greater majority or by a specified proportion of the members of the union.]

NOTES

Substituted, together with ss 100A–100E for the original s 100, by the Trade Union Reform and Employment Rights Act 1993, s 4.

[1.403]

[100A Appointment of independent scrutineer

(1) The trade union shall, before the ballot is held, appoint a qualified independent person ("the scrutineer") to carry out—

(a) the functions in relation to the ballot which are required under this section to be contained in his appointment; and

(b) such additional functions in relation to the ballot as may be specified in his appointment.

(2) A person is a qualified independent person in relation to a ballot if—

(a) he satisfies such conditions as may be specified for the purposes of this section by order of the Secretary of State or is himself so specified; and

(b) the trade union has no grounds for believing either that he will carry out any functions conferred on him in relation to the ballot otherwise than competently or that his independence in relation to the union, or in relation to the ballot, might reasonably be called into question.

An order under paragraph (a) shall be made by statutory instrument which shall be subject to annulment in pursuance of a resolution of either House of Parliament.

(3) The scrutineer's appointment shall require him—

(a) to be the person who supervises the production of the voting papers and (unless he is appointed under section 100D to undertake the distribution of the voting papers) their distribution and to whom the voting papers are returned by those voting;

(b) to—

(i) inspect the register of names and addresses of the members of the trade union, or

(ii) examine the copy of the register as at the relevant date which is supplied to him in accordance with subsection (9)(a),

whenever it appears to him appropriate to do so and, in particular, when the conditions specified in subsection (4) are satisfied;

(c) to take such steps as appear to him to be appropriate for the purpose of enabling him to make his report (see section 100E);

(d) to make his report to the trade union as soon as reasonably practicable after the last date for the return of voting papers; and

(e) to retain custody of all voting papers returned for the purposes of the ballot and the copy of the register supplied to him in accordance with subsection (9)(a)—

(i) until the end of the period of one year beginning with the announcement by the union of the result of the ballot; and

(ii) if within that period a complaint is made under section 103 (complaint as regards passing of resolution), until the Certification Officer or Employment Appeal Tribunal authorises him to dispose of the papers or copy.

(4) The conditions referred to in subsection (3)(b) are—

(a) that a request that the scrutineer inspect the register or examine the copy is made to him during the appropriate period by a member of the trade union who suspects that the register is not, or at the relevant date was not, accurate and up-to-date, and

(b) that the scrutineer does not consider that the member's suspicion is ill-founded.

(5) In subsection (4) "the appropriate period" means the period—

(a) beginning with the day on which the scrutineer is appointed, and

(b) ending with the day before the day on which the scrutineer makes his report to the trade union.

(6) The duty of confidentiality as respects the register is incorporated in the scrutineer's appointment.

(7) The trade union shall ensure that nothing in the terms of the scrutineer's appointment (including any additional functions specified in the appointment) is such as to make it reasonable for any person to call the scrutineer's independence in relation to the union into question.

(8) The trade union shall, before the scrutineer begins to carry out his functions, either—

(a) send a notice stating the name of the scrutineer to every member of the union to whom it is reasonably practicable to send such a notice, or

(b) take all such other steps for notifying members of the name of the scrutineer as it is the practice of the union to take when matters of general interest to all its members need to be brought to their attention.

(9) The trade union shall—

(a) supply to the scrutineer as soon as is reasonably practicable after the relevant date a copy of the register of names and addresses of its members as at that date, and

(b) comply with any request made by the scrutineer to inspect the register.

(10) Where the register is kept by means of a computer the duty imposed on the trade union by subsection (9)(a) is either to supply a legible printed copy or (if the scrutineer prefers) to supply a copy of the computer data and allow the scrutineer use of the computer to read it at any time during the period when he is required to retain custody of the copy.

(11) The trade union shall ensure that the scrutineer duly carries out his functions and that there is no interference with his carrying out of those functions which would make it reasonable for any person to call the scrutineer's independence in relation to the union into question.

(12) The trade union shall comply with all reasonable requests made by the scrutineer for the purposes of, or in connection with, the carrying out of his functions.

(13) In this section "the relevant date" means—

(a) where the trade union has rules determining who is entitled to vote in the ballot by reference to membership on a particular date, that date, and

(b) otherwise, the date, or the last date, on which voting papers are distributed for the purposes of the ballot.]

NOTES

Substituted as noted to s 100 at **[1.402]**.

Orders: the Trade Union Ballots and Elections (Independent Scrutineer Qualifications) Order 1993, SI 1993/1909 at **[2.138]**; the Trade Union Ballots and Elections (Independent Scrutineer Qualifications) (Amendment) Order 2010, SI 2010/436; the Trade Union Ballots and Elections (Independent Scrutineer Qualifications) (Amendment) Order 2017, SI 2017/877.

[1.404]

[100B Entitlement to vote

Entitlement to vote in the ballot shall be accorded equally to all members of the trade union.]

NOTES

Substituted as noted to s 100 at **[1.402]**.

[1.405]
[100C Voting

(1) The method of voting must be by the marking of a voting paper by the person voting.

(2) Each voting paper must—

(a) state the name of the independent scrutineer and clearly specify the address to which, and the date by which, it is to be returned, and

(b) be given one of a series of consecutive whole numbers every one of which is used in giving a different number in that series to each voting paper printed or otherwise produced for the purposes of the ballot, and

(c) be marked with its number.

(3) Every person who is entitled to vote in the ballot must—

(a) be allowed to vote without interference or constraint, and

(b) so far as is reasonably practicable, be enabled to do so without incurring any direct cost to himself.

(4) So far as is reasonably practicable, every person who is entitled to vote in the ballot must—

(a) have a voting paper sent to him by post at his home address or another address which he has requested the trade union in writing to treat as his postal address, and

(b) be given a convenient opportunity to vote by post.

(5) No voting paper which is sent to a person for voting shall have enclosed with it any other document except—

(a) the notice which, under section 99(1), is to accompany the voting paper,

(b) an addressed envelope, and

(c) a document containing instructions for the return of the voting paper,

without any other statement.

(6) The ballot shall be conducted so as to secure that—

(a) so far as is reasonably practicable, those voting do so in secret, and

(b) the votes given in the ballot are fairly and accurately counted.

For the purposes of paragraph (b) an inaccuracy in counting shall be disregarded if it is accidental and on a scale which could not affect the result of the ballot.]

NOTES

Substituted as noted to s 100 at **[1.402]**.

[1.406]
[100D Counting of votes etc by independent person

(1) The trade union shall ensure that—

(a) the storage and distribution of the voting papers for the purposes of the ballot, and

(b) the counting of the votes cast in the ballot,

are undertaken by one or more independent persons appointed by the trade union.

(2) A person is an independent person in relation to a ballot if—

(a) he is the scrutineer, or

(b) he is a person other than the scrutineer and the trade union has no grounds for believing either that he will carry out any functions conferred on him in relation to the ballot otherwise than competently or that his independence in relation to the union, or in relation to the ballot, might reasonably be called into question.

(3) An appointment under this section shall require the person appointed to carry out his functions so as to minimise the risk of any contravention of requirements imposed by or under any enactment or the occurrence of any unfairness or malpractice.

(4) The duty of confidentiality as respects the register is incorporated in the scrutineer's appointment.

(5) Where the person appointed to undertake the counting of votes is not the scrutineer, his appointment shall require him to send the voting papers back to the scrutineer as soon as reasonably practicable after the counting has been completed.

(6) The trade union—

(a) shall ensure that nothing in the terms of an appointment under this section is such as to make it reasonable for any person to call into question the independence of the person appointed in relation to the union,

(b) shall ensure that a person appointed under this section duly carries out his functions and that there is no interference with his carrying out of those functions which would make it reasonable for any person to call into question the independence of the person appointed in relation to the union, and

(c) shall comply with all reasonable requests made by a person appointed under this section for the purposes of, or in connection with, the carrying out of his functions.]

NOTES

Substituted as noted to s 100 at **[1.402]**.

[1.407]
[100E Scrutineer's report

(1) The scrutineer's report on the ballot shall state—

(a) the number of voting papers distributed for the purposes of the ballot,

(b) the number of voting papers returned to the scrutineer,

(c) the number of valid votes cast in the ballot for and against the resolution,

(d) the number of spoiled or otherwise invalid voting papers returned, and

(e) the name of the person (or of each of the persons) appointed under section 100D or, if no person was so appointed, that fact.

(2) The report shall also state whether the scrutineer is satisfied—

(a) that there are no reasonable grounds for believing that there was any contravention of a requirement imposed by or under any enactment in relation to the ballot,

(b) that the arrangements made (whether by him or any other person) with respect to the production, storage, distribution, return or other handling of the voting papers used in the ballot, and the arrangements for the counting of the votes, included all such security arrangements as were reasonably practicable for the purpose of minimising the risk that any unfairness or malpractice might occur, and

(c) that he has been able to carry out his functions without any such interference as would make it reasonable for any person to call his independence in relation to the union into question;

and if he is not satisfied as to any of those matters, the report shall give particulars of his reasons for not being satisfied as to that matter.

(3) The report shall also state—

(a) whether the scrutineer—

(i) has inspected the register of names and addresses of the members of the trade union, or

(ii) has examined the copy of the register as at the relevant date which is supplied to him in accordance with section 100A(9)(a),

(b) if he has, whether in the case of each inspection or examination he was acting on a request by a member of the trade union or at his own instance,

(c) whether he declined to act on any such request, and

(d) whether any inspection of the register, or any examination of the copy of the register, has revealed any matter which he considers should be drawn to the attention of the trade union in order to assist it in securing that the register is accurate and up-to-date,

but shall not state the name of any member who has requested such an inspection or examination.

(4) Where one or more persons other than the scrutineer are appointed under section 100D, the statement included in the scrutineer's report in accordance with subsection (2)(b) shall also indicate—

(a) whether he is satisfied with the performance of the person, or each of the persons, so appointed, and

(b) if he is not satisfied with the performance of the person, or any of them, particulars of his reasons for not being so satisfied.

(5) The trade union shall not publish the result of the ballot until it has received the scrutineer's report.

(6) The trade union shall within the period of three months after it receives the report—

(a) send a copy of the report to every member of the union to whom it is reasonably practicable to send such a copy; or

(b) take all such other steps for notifying the contents of the report to the members of the union (whether by publishing the report or otherwise) as it is the practice of the union to take when matters of general interest to all its members need to be brought to their attention.

(7) Any such copy or notification shall be accompanied by a statement that the union will, on request, supply any member of the trade union with a copy of the report, either free of charge or on payment of such reasonable fee as may be specified in the notification.

(8) The trade union shall so supply any member of the union who makes such a request and pays the fee (if any) notified to him.]

NOTES

Substituted as noted to s 100 at **[1.402]**.

[1.408]

101 Registration of instrument of amalgamation or transfer

(1) An instrument of amalgamation or transfer shall not take effect before it has been registered by the Certification Officer under this Chapter.

(2) It shall not be so registered before the end of the period of six weeks beginning with the date on which an application for its registration is sent to the Certification Officer.

[(3) An application for registration of an instrument of amalgamation or transfer shall not be sent to the Certification Officer until section 100E(6) has been complied with in relation to the scrutineer's report on the ballot held on the resolution to approve the instrument.]

NOTES

Sub-s (3): added by the Trade Union Reform and Employment Rights Act 1993, s 49(2), Sch 8, para 55.

[1.409]

[101A Listing and certification after amalgamation

(1) Subsection (2) applies if when an instrument of amalgamation is registered by the Certification Officer under this Chapter each of the amalgamating unions is entered in the list of trade unions.

(2) The Certification Officer shall—

(a) enter, with effect from the amalgamation date, the name of the amalgamated union in the list of trade unions, and

(b) remove, with effect from that date, the names of the amalgamating unions from that list.

(3) Subsection (4) applies if when an instrument of amalgamation is registered by the Certification Officer under this Chapter each of the amalgamating unions has a certificate of independence which is in force.

(4) The Certification Officer shall issue to the amalgamated trade union, with effect from the amalgamation date, a certificate that the union is independent.

(5) In this section "the amalgamation date" means the date on which the instrument of amalgamation takes effect.]

NOTES

Inserted, together with s 101B, by the Employment Relations Act 2004, s 50(2).

[1.410]

[101B Supply of information by amalgamated union

(1) If an instrument of amalgamation is registered under this Chapter by the Certification Officer and the amalgamated union is entered in the list of trade unions in accordance with section 101A, that union shall send to him, in such manner and form as he may require—

- (a) a copy of the rules of the union,
- (b) a list of its officers, and
- (c) the address of its head or main office.

(2) The information required to be sent under subsection (1) must be accompanied by any fee prescribed for the purpose under section 108.

(3) The information must be sent—

- (a) before the end of the period of six weeks beginning with the date on which the instrument of amalgamation takes effect, or
- (b) if the Certification Officer considers that it is not reasonably practicable for the amalgamated union to send it in that period, before the end of such longer period, beginning with that date, as he may specify to the amalgamated union.

(4) If any of subsections (1) to (3) are not complied with by the amalgamated union, the Certification Officer shall remove its name from the list of trade unions.]

NOTES

Inserted as noted to s 101A at **[1.409]**.

Prescribed fee: the fee of £41 is prescribed for the purposes of sub-s (2) above in circumstances where, at the time the instrument of amalgamation was registered by the Certification Officer, the condition in s 101A(3) was satisfied and the Certification Officer was, accordingly, under the duty in sub-s (4) of that section to issue a certificate of independence to the amalgamated union (see the Certification Officer (Amendment of Fees) Regulations 2005, SI 2005/713, reg 8).

[1.411]

102 Power to alter rules of transferee union for purposes of transfer

(1) Where a trade union proposes to transfer its engagements to another trade union and an alteration of the rules of the transferee union is necessary to give effect to provisions in the instrument of transfer, the committee of management or other governing body of that union may by memorandum in writing alter the rules of that union so far as is necessary to give effect to those provisions.

This subsection does not apply if the rules of the trade union expressly provide that this section is not to apply to that union.

(2) An alteration of the rules of a trade union under subsection (1) shall not take effect unless or until the instrument of transfer takes effect.

(3) The provisions of subsection (1) have effect, where they apply, notwithstanding anything in the rules of the union.

[1.412]

103 *Complaints* as regards passing of resolution

[(1) A member of a trade union who claims that the union—

- (a) has failed to comply with any of the requirements of sections 99 to 100E, or
- (b) has, in connection with a resolution approving an instrument of amalgamation or transfer, failed to comply with any rule of the union relating to the passing of the resolution,

may complain to the Certification *Officer*.]

(2) Any complaint must be made before the end of the period of six weeks beginning with the date on which an application for registration of the instrument of amalgamation or transfer is sent to the Certification Officer.

Where a complaint is made, the Certification Officer shall not register the instrument before the complaint is finally determined or is withdrawn.

[(2A) On a complaint being made to him the Certification Officer shall make such enquiries as he thinks fit].

(3) *If the Certification Officer, after giving the complainant and the trade union an opportunity of being heard, finds the complaint to be justified*—

- (a) he shall make a declaration to that effect, and
- (b) he may make an order specifying the steps which must be taken before he will entertain any application to register the instrument of amalgamation or transfer;

and where he makes such an order, he shall not entertain any application to register the instrument unless he is satisfied that the steps specified in the order have been taken.

An order under this subsection may be varied by the Certification Officer by a further order.

[(3A) Before deciding the matter the Certification Officer—

- (a) may make such enquiries as the Officer thinks fit,
- (b) must give the union and the complainant (if any) an opportunity to make written representations, and

(c) may give the union and the complainant (if any) an opportunity to make oral representations.]
(4) The Certification Officer shall furnish a statement, orally or in writing, of the reasons for his decision *on a complaint* under this section.
(5) The validity of a resolution approving an instrument of amalgamation or transfer shall not be questioned in any legal proceedings whatsoever (except proceedings before the Certification Officer under this section or proceedings arising out of such proceedings) on any ground on which a complaint could be, or could have been, made to the Certification Officer under this section.
[(6) Where the Certification Officer requests a person to furnish information to him in connection with enquiries made by him under this section, he shall specify the date by which that information is to be furnished and, unless he considers that it would be inappropriate to do so, shall proceed with his determination *of the application* notwithstanding that the information has not been furnished to him by the specified date.
(7) A declaration made by the Certification Officer under this section may be relied on as if it were a declaration made by the court.
(8) Where an order has been made under this section, any person who is a member of the union and was a member at the time it was made is entitled to enforce obedience to the order as if he had made *the [complaint] on which the order was made*.
(9) An order made by the Certification Officer under this section may be enforced in the same way as an order of the court].

NOTES

Section heading: for the word in italics there is substituted "Powers of Certification Officer" by the Trade Union Act 2016, s 17(3), Sch 2, para 8(1), (2), as from a day to be appointed.

Sub-s (1): substituted by the Trade Union Reform and Employment Rights Act 1993, s 49(2), Sch 8, para 56; for the word in italics there is substituted "Officer; but the Officer may also exercise the powers under this section where no complaint under this section is made" by the Trade Union Act 2016, s 17(3), Sch 2, para 8(1), (3), as from a day to be appointed.

Sub-s (2A): inserted by the Employment Relations Act 1999, s 29, Sch 6, paras 1, 18; and repealed by the Trade Union Act 2016, s 17(3), Sch 2, para 8(1), (4), as from a day to be appointed.

Sub-s (3): for the words in italics there is substituted "Where the Certification Officer is satisfied that there has been a failure such as is mentioned in paragraph (a) or (b) of subsection (1)" by the Trade Union Act 2016, s 17(3), Sch 2, para 8(1), (5), as from a day to be appointed.

Sub-s (3A): inserted by the Trade Union Act 2016, s 17(3), Sch 2, para 8(1), (6), as from a day to be appointed.

Sub-s (4): words in italics repealed by the Trade Union Act 2016, s 17(3), Sch 2, para 8(1), (7), as from a day to be appointed.

Sub-s (6): added (together with sub-ss (7)–(9)) by the Employment Relations Act 1999, s 29, Sch 6, paras 1, 18; words in italics repealed by the Trade Union Act 2016, s 17(3), Sch 2, para 8(1), (8), as from a day to be appointed.

Sub-s (7): added as noted to sub-s (6) above.

Sub-s (8): added as noted to sub-s (6) above; word in square brackets substituted by the Employment Relations Act 2004, s 57(1), Sch 1, para 7; for the words in italics there are substituted the words "a complaint under this section" by the Trade Union Act 2016, s 17(3), Sch 2, para 8(1), (9), as from a day to be appointed.

Sub-s (9): added as noted to sub-s (6) above.

[1.413]
104 Appeal from decision of Certification Officer
An appeal lies to the Employment Appeal Tribunal, at the instance of the complainant or the trade union, *on any question of law arising* in any proceedings before, or arising from any decision of, the Certification Officer under section 103.

NOTES

For the words in italics there are substituted the words "on any question arising" by the Trade Union Act 2016, s 21(d), as from a day to be appointed.

[1.414]
105 Transfer of property on amalgamation or transfer
(1) Where an instrument of amalgamation or transfer takes effect, the property held—
(a) for the benefit of any of the amalgamating unions, or for the benefit of a branch of any of those unions, by the trustees of the union or branch, or
(b) for the benefit of the transferor trade union, or for the benefit of a branch of the transferor trade union, by the trustees of the union or branch,

shall without any conveyance, assignment or assignation vest, on the instrument taking effect, or on the appointment of the appropriate trustees, whichever is the later, in the appropriate trustees.
(2) In the case of property to be held for the benefit of a branch of the amalgamated union, or of the transferee union, "the appropriate trustees" means the trustees of that branch, unless the rules of the amalgamated or transferee union provide that the property to be so held is to be held by the trustees of the union.
(3) In any other case "the appropriate trustees" means the trustees of the amalgamated or transferee union.
(4) This section does not apply—
(a) to property excepted from the operation of this section by the instrument of amalgamation or transfer, or
(b) to stocks and securities in the public funds of the United Kingdom or Northern Ireland.

[1.415]

106 Amalgamation or transfer involving Northern Ireland

(1) This Chapter has effect subject to the following modifications in the case of an amalgamation or transfer of engagements to which a trade union and a Northern Ireland union are party.

(2) The requirements of sections [98 to 100E and 101(3) (approval of instrument, notice to members and ballot on resolution)] do not apply in relation to the Northern Ireland union; but the Certification Officer shall not register the instrument under section 101 unless he is satisfied that it will be effective under the law of Northern Ireland.

(3) The instrument of amalgamation or transfer submitted to the Certification Officer for his approval under section 98 shall state which of the bodies concerned is a Northern Ireland union and, in the case of an amalgamation, whether the amalgamated body is to be a Northern Ireland union; and the Certification Officer shall withhold his approval if the instrument does not contain that information.

(4) Nothing in section 102 (alteration of rules) or [sections 103 and 104] (complaint as to passing of resolution) applies in relation to the Northern Ireland union.

(5) Subject to the exceptions specified above, the provisions of this Chapter as to amalgamations or transfers of engagements apply in relation to the Northern Ireland union.

NOTES

Sub-ss (2), (4): words in square brackets substituted by the Trade Union Reform and Employment Rights Act 1993, s 49(2), Sch 8, para 57(a), (b).

Change of name

[1.416]

107 Change of name of trade union

(1) A trade union may change its name by any method expressly provided for by its rules or, if its rules do not expressly provide for a method of doing so, by adopting in accordance with its rules an alteration of the provision in them which gives the union its name.

(2) If the name of the trade union is entered in the list of trade unions a change of name shall not take effect until approved by the Certification Officer.

(3) The Certification Officer shall not approve a change of name if it appears to him that the proposed new name—

(a) is the same as one entered in the list as the name of another trade union, or

(b) is the same as one entered in the list of employers' associations kept under Part II of this Act,

or is a name so nearly resembling such a name as to be likely to deceive the public.

(4) A change of name by a trade union does not affect any right or obligation of the union or any of its members; and any pending legal proceedings may be continued by or against the union, the trustees of the union or any other officer of the union who can sue or be sued on its behalf notwithstanding its change of name.

Supplementary

[1.417]

108 General powers to make regulations

(1) The Secretary of State may make regulations as respects—

(a) applications to the Certification Officer under this Chapter,

(b) the registration under this Chapter of any document or matter,

(c) the inspection of documents kept by the Certification Officer under this Chapter,

(d) the charging of fees in respect of such matters, and of such amounts, as may with the approval of the Treasury be prescribed by the regulations,

and generally for carrying this Chapter into effect.

(2) Provision may in particular be made—

(a) requiring an application for the registration of an instrument of amalgamation or transfer, or of a change of name, to be accompanied by such statutory declarations or other documents as may be specified in the regulations;

(b) as to the form or content of any document required by this Chapter, or by the regulations, to be sent or submitted to the Certification Officer and as to the manner in which any such document is to be signed or authenticated;

(c) authorising the Certification Officer to require notice to be given or published in such manner as he may direct of the fact that an application for registration of an instrument of amalgamation or transfer has been or is to be made to him.

(3) Regulations under this section may make different provision for different circumstances.

(4) Regulations under this section shall be made by statutory instrument which shall be subject to annulment in pursuance of a resolution of either House of Parliament.

NOTES

Regulations: the Certification Officer (Amendment of Fees) Regulations 2005, SI 2005/713. By virtue of s 300(3) of, and Sch 3, para 1(2) to, this Act, and the Interpretation Act 1978, s 17(2)(b), the Trade Union and Employers' Associations (Amalgamations, etc) Regulations 1975, SI 1975/536 (at **[2.1]**), have effect as if made under this section.

[CHAPTER VIIA BREACH OF RULES

[1.418]
108A Right to apply to Certification Officer
(1) A person who claims that there has been a breach or threatened breach of the rules of a trade union relating to any of the matters mentioned in subsection (2) may apply to the Certification Officer for a declaration to that effect, subject to subsections (3) to (7).
(2) The matters are—
(a) the appointment or election of a person to, or the removal of a person from, any office;
(b) disciplinary proceedings by the union (including expulsion);
(c) the balloting of members on any issue other than industrial action;
(d) the constitution or proceedings of any executive committee or of any decision-making meeting;
(e) such other matters as may be specified in an order made by the Secretary of State.
(3) The applicant must be a member of the union, or have been one at the time of the alleged breach or threatened breach.
(4) A person may not apply under subsection (1) in relation to a claim if he is entitled to apply under section 80 in relation to the claim.
(5) No application may be made regarding—
(a) the dismissal of an employee of the union;
(b) disciplinary proceedings against an employee of the union.
(6) An application must be made—
(a) within the period of six months starting with the day on which the breach or threatened breach is alleged to have taken place, or
(b) if within that period any internal complaints procedure of the union is invoked to resolve the claim, within the period of six months starting with the earlier of the days specified in subsection (7).
(7) Those days are—
(a) the day on which the procedure is concluded, and
(b) the last day of the period of one year beginning with the day on which the procedure is invoked.
(8) The reference in subsection (1) to the rules of a union includes references to the rules of any branch or section of the union.
(9) In subsection (2)(c) "industrial action" means a strike or other industrial action by persons employed under contracts of employment.
(10) For the purposes of subsection (2)(d) a committee is an executive committee if—
(a) it is a committee of the union concerned and has power to make executive decisions on behalf of the union or on behalf of a constituent body,
(b) it is a committee of a major constituent body and has power to make executive decisions on behalf of that body, or
(c) it is a sub-committee of a committee falling within paragraph (a) or (b).
(11) For the purposes of subsection (2)(d) a decision-making meeting is—
(a) a meeting of members of the union concerned (or the representatives of such members) which has power to make a decision on any matter which, under the rules of the union, is final as regards the union or which, under the rules of the union or a constituent body, is final as regards that body, or
(b) a meeting of members of a major constituent body (or the representatives of such members) which has power to make a decision on any matter which, under the rules of the union or the body, is final as regards that body.
(12) For the purposes of subsections (10) and (11), in relation to the trade union concerned—
(a) a constituent body is any body which forms part of the union, including a branch, group, section or region;
(b) a major constituent body is such a body which has more than 1,000 members.
(13) Any order under subsection (2)(e) shall be made by statutory instrument; and no such order shall be made unless a draft of it has been laid before and approved by resolution of each House of Parliament.
(14) If a person applies to the Certification Officer under this section in relation to an alleged breach or threatened breach he may not apply to the court in relation to the breach or threatened breach; but nothing in this subsection shall prevent such a person from exercising any right to appeal against or challenge the Certification Officer's decision on the application to him.
(15) If—
(a) a person applies to the court in relation to an alleged breach or threatened breach, and
(b) the breach or threatened breach is one in relation to which he could have made an application to the Certification Officer under this section,

he may not apply to the Certification Officer under this section in relation to the breach or threatened breach.]

NOTES

Inserted, together with the preceding heading and ss 108B, 108C, by the Employment Relations Act 1999, s 29, Sch 6, paras 1, 19.

Orders: as of 15 May 2019, no Orders had been made under this section.

[1.419]
[108B Declarations and orders

(1) The Certification Officer may refuse to accept an application under section 108A unless he is satisfied that the applicant has taken all reasonable steps to resolve the claim by the use of any internal complaints procedure of the union.

(2) If he accepts an application under section 108A the Certification Officer—
- (a) shall make such enquiries as he thinks fit,
- (b) shall give the applicant and the union an opportunity to be heard,
- (c) shall ensure that, so far as is reasonably practicable, the application is determined within six months of being made,
- (d) may make or refuse the declaration asked for, and
- (e) shall, whether he makes or refuses the declaration, give reasons for his decision in writing.

(3) Where the Certification Officer makes a declaration he shall also, unless he considers that to do so would be inappropriate, make an enforcement order, that is, an order imposing on the union one or both of the following requirements—
- (a) to take such steps to remedy the breach, or withdraw the threat of a breach, as may be specified in the order;
- (b) to abstain from such acts as may be so specified with a view to securing that a breach or threat of the same or a similar kind does not occur in future.

(4) The Certification Officer shall in an order imposing any such requirement as is mentioned in subsection (3)(a) specify the period within which the union is to comply with the requirement.

(5) Where the Certification Officer requests a person to furnish information to him in connection with enquiries made by him under this section, he shall specify the date by which that information is to be furnished and, unless he considers that it would be inappropriate to do so, shall proceed with his determination of the application notwithstanding that the information has not been furnished to him by the specified date.

(6) A declaration made by the Certification Officer under this section may be relied on as if it were a declaration made by the court.

(7) Where an enforcement order has been made, any person who is a member of the union and was a member at the time it was made is entitled to enforce obedience to the order as if he had made the application on which the order was made.

(8) An enforcement order made by the Certification Officer under this section may be enforced [(by the Certification Officer, the applicant or a person mentioned in subsection (7))] in the same way as an order of the court.

(9) An order under section 108A(2)(e) may provide that, in relation to an application under section 108A with regard to a prescribed matter, the preceding provisions of this section shall apply with such omissions or modifications as may be specified in the order; and a prescribed matter is such matter specified under section 108A(2)(e) as is prescribed under this subsection].

NOTES

Inserted as noted to s 108A at **[1.418]**.

Sub-s (8): words in square brackets inserted by the Trade Union Act 2016, s 19(4), as from a day to be appointed.

[1.420]
[108C Appeals from Certification Officer

An appeal lies to the Employment Appeal Tribunal *on any question of law arising* in proceedings before or arising from any decision of the Certification Officer under this Chapter.]

NOTES

Inserted as noted to s 108A at **[1.418]**.

For the words in italics there are substituted the words "on any question arising" by the Trade Union Act 2016, s 21(e), as from a day to be appointed.

109–114 *((Chapter VIII) repealed by the Employment Relations Act 1999, ss 28(2)(a), 44, Sch 9(6).)*

CHAPTER IX MISCELLANEOUS AND GENERAL PROVISIONS

115, 116 *(Repealed by the Trade Union Reform and Employment Rights Act 1993, ss 7(1), (4), 51, Sch 10.)*

[Union modernisation

[1.421]
116A Provision of money for union modernisation

(1) The Secretary of State may provide money to a trade union to enable or assist it to do any or all of the following—
- (a) improve the carrying out of any of its existing functions;
- (b) prepare to carry out any new function;
- (c) increase the range of services it offers to persons who are or may become members of it;
- (d) prepare for an amalgamation or the transfer of any or all of its engagements;
- (e) ballot its members (whether as a result of a requirement imposed by this Act or otherwise).

(2) No money shall be provided to a trade union under this section unless at the time when the money is provided the union has a certificate of independence.

(3) Money may be provided in such a way as the Secretary of State thinks fit (whether as grants or otherwise) and on such terms as he thinks fit (whether as to repayment or otherwise).

(4) If money is provided to a trade union under this section, the terms on which it is so provided shall be deemed to include a prohibition ("a political fund prohibition") on any of it being added to the political fund of the union.

(5) If a political fund prohibition is contravened, the Secretary of State—

(a) is entitled to recover from the trade union as a debt due to him an amount equal to the amount of money added to the union's political fund in contravention of the prohibition (whether or not that money continues to form part of the political fund); and

(b) must take such steps as are reasonably practicable to recover that amount.

(6) An amount recoverable under subsection (5) is a liability of the trade union's political fund.

(7) Subsection (5) does not prevent money provided to a trade union under this section from being provided on terms containing further sanctions for a contravention of the political fund prohibition.]

NOTES

Inserted, together with the preceding heading, by the Employment Relations Act 2004, s 55(1).

[Deduction of trade union subscriptions from wages

[1.422]

116B Restriction on deduction of union subscriptions from wages in public sector

(1) A relevant public sector employer may make deductions from its workers' wages in respect of trade union subscriptions only if—

(a) those workers have the option to pay their trade union subscriptions by other means, and

(b) arrangements have been made for the union to make reasonable payments to the employer in respect of the making of the deductions.

(2) Payments are "reasonable" for the purposes of subsection (1) if the employer is satisfied that the total amount of the payments is substantially equivalent to the total cost to public funds of making the deductions.

(3) An employer is a relevant public sector employer if the employer is a public authority specified, or of a description specified, in regulations made by a Minister of the Crown.

[(3A) But regulations under subsection (3) may not specify—

(a) a devolved Welsh authority, or

(b) a description of public authority that applies to a devolved Welsh authority.]

(4) A Minister of the Crown may by regulations provide, in relation to a body or other person that is not a public authority but has functions of a public nature and is funded wholly or mainly from public funds, that the body or other person is to be treated as a public authority for the purposes of this section.

(5) Regulations under this section may make provision specifying the person or other entity that is to be treated for the purposes of this section as the employer of a person who is employed by the Crown.

(6) The regulations may—

(a) deem a category of persons holding an office or employment under the Crown (or two or more such categories taken together) to be an entity for the purposes of provision made under subsection (5);

(b) make different provision under subsection (5) for different categories of persons holding an office or employment under the Crown.

(7) Regulations under this section may—

(a) make different provision for different purposes;

(b) make transitional provision in connection with the coming into force of any provision of the regulations;

(c) make consequential provision amending or otherwise modifying contracts of employment or collective agreements.

(8) Regulations under this section are to be made by statutory instrument.

(9) A statutory instrument containing regulations under this section may not be made unless a draft of the instrument has been laid before and approved by a resolution of each House of Parliament.

(10) In this section—

"trade union subscriptions" means payments to a trade union in respect of a worker's membership of the union;

"wages" has the same meaning as in Part 2 of the Employment Rights Act 1996 (see section 27);

"worker" has the same meaning as in that Act.]

NOTES

Commencement: 1 March 2017 (for the purpose of making Regulations); to be appointed (otherwise).

Inserted, together with the preceding heading, by the Trade Union Act 2016, s 15(1), as from 1 March 2017 (for the purpose of making Regulations), and as from a day to be appointed (otherwise).

Sub-s (3A): inserted by the Trade Union (Wales) Act 2017, s 1(1), (2), as from 13 September 2017.

Regulations: as of 15 May 2019, no Regulations had been made under this section.

Exceptions and adaptations for certain bodies

[1.423]

117 Special register bodies

(1) In this section a "special register body" means an organisation whose name appeared in the special register maintained under section 84 of the Industrial Relations Act 1971 immediately before 16 September 1974, and which is a company [registered under the Companies Act 2006] or is incorporated by charter or letters patent.

(2) The provisions of this Part apply to special register bodies as to other trade unions, subject to the following exceptions and adaptations.

(3) In Chapter II (status and property of trade unions)—

(a) in section 10 (quasi-corporate status of trade unions)—

(i) subsections (1) and (2) (prohibition on trade union being incorporated) do not apply, and

(ii) subsection (3) (prohibition on registration under certain Acts) does not apply so far as it relates to registration as a company under [the Companies Act 2006];

(b) section 11 (exclusion of common law rules as to restraint of trade) applies to the purposes or rules of a special register body only so far as they relate to the regulation of relations between employers or employers' associations and workers;

(c) sections 12 to 14 (vesting of property in trustees; transfer of securities) do not apply; and

(d) in section 20 (liability of trade union in certain proceedings in tort) in subsection (7) the reference to the contract between a member and the other members shall be construed as a reference to the contract between a member and the body.

(4) Sections 33 to 35 (appointment and removal of auditors) do not apply to a special register body which is registered as a company under the [Companies Act 2006]; and sections 36 and 37 (rights and duties of auditors) apply to the auditors appointed by such a body under [Chapter 2 of Part 16 of that Act].

(5) [Sections 45B and 45C (disqualification) and Chapter IV (elections) apply only] to—

(a) the position of voting member of the executive, and

(b) any position by virtue of which a person is a voting member of the executive.

In this subsection "voting member of the executive" has the meaning given by section 46(5).

NOTES

Sub-ss (1), (3), (4): words in square brackets substituted by the Companies Act 2006 (Consequential Amendments, Transitional Provisions and Savings) Order 2009, SI 2009/1941, art 2(1), Sch 1, para 134(1), (3).

Sub-s (5): words in square brackets substituted by the Trade Union Reform and Employment Rights Act 1993, s 49(3), Sch 8, para 61.

Industrial Relations Act 1971: repealed by the Trade Union and Labour Relations Act 1974, ss 1, 25(3), Sch 5.

[1.424]

118 Federated trade unions

(1) In this section a "federated trade union" means a trade union which consists wholly or mainly of constituent or affiliated organisations, or representatives or such organisations, as described in paragraph (b) of the definition of "trade union" in section 1.

(2) The provisions of this Part apply to federated trade unions subject to the following exceptions and adaptations.

(3) For the purposes of section 22 (limit on amount of damages) as it applies to a federated trade union, the members of such of its constituent or affiliated organisations as have their head or main office in Great Britain shall be treated as members of the union.

(4) The following provisions of Chapter III (trade union administration) do not apply to a federated trade union which consists wholly or mainly of representatives of constituent or affiliated organisations—

(a) section 27 (duty to supply copy of rules),

(b) section 28 (duty to keep accounting records),

(c) sections 32 to 37 (annual return, [statement for members,] accounts and audit), . . .

[(ca) sections 37A to 37E (investigation of financial affairs), and]

(d) sections 38 to 42 (members' superannuation schemes).

[(4A) In the case of a federated trade union which, by virtue of subsection (4), is not required to send an annual return to the Certification Officer under section 32, section 24ZA (duty to provide membership audit certificate) applies as if section 32 does apply to the union.]

(5) Sections 29 to 31 (right of member to access to accounting records) do not apply to a federated trade union which has no members other than constituent or affiliated organisations or representatives of such organisations.

(6) Sections 24 to 26 (register of members' names and addresses) and Chapter IV (elections for certain trade union positions) do not apply to a federated trade union—

(a) if it has no individual members other than representatives of constituent or affiliated organisations, or

(b) if its individual members (other than such representatives) are all merchant seamen and a majority of them are ordinarily resident outside the United Kingdom.

For this purpose "merchant seaman" means a person whose employment, or the greater part of it, is carried out on board sea-going ships.

(7) The provisions of Chapter VI (application of funds for political objects) apply to a trade union which is in whole or part an association or combination of other unions as if the individual members of the component unions were members of that union and not of the component unions.

But nothing in that Chapter prevents a component union from collecting contributions on behalf of the association or combination from such of its members as are [contributors] to the political fund of the association or combination.

[(8) In the application of section 116A to a federated trade union, subsection (2) of that section shall be omitted.]

NOTES

Sub-s (4): words in square brackets in para (c) inserted, word omitted from that paragraph repealed, and para (ca) inserted, by the Trade Union Reform and Employment Rights Act 1993, ss 49(3), 51, Sch 8, para 62, Sch 10.

Sub-s (4A): inserted by the Transparency of Lobbying, Non-Party Campaigning and Trade Union Administration Act 2014, s 40(1), (4), as from 6 April 2015, in relation to a reporting period which commences on or after that date.

Sub-s (7): word in square brackets substituted (for the original words "not exempt from the obligation to contribute") by the Trade Union Act 2016, s 22, Sch 4, para 10, as from 1 March 2017. Note that this amendment applies only after the end of the transition period of 12 months beginning on 1 March 2017 specified under the Trade Union Act 2016, s 11(6), and only in relation to a person (a) who after the end of that period joins a trade union that has a political fund, or (b) who is a member of a trade union that has a political fund but did not have one immediately before the end of that period (see **[2.1977]**).

Sub-s (8): added by the Employment Relations Act 2004, s 55(2).

Interpretation

[1.425]

119 Expressions relating to trade unions

In this Act, in relation to a trade union—

["agent" means a banker or solicitor of, or any person employed as an auditor by, the union or any branch or section of the union;]

"branch or section", except where the context otherwise requires, includes a branch or section which is itself a trade union;

"executive" means the principal committee of the union exercising executive functions, by whatever name it is called;

["financial affairs" means affairs of the union relating to any fund which is applicable for the purposes of the union (including any fund of a branch or section of the union which is so applicable);]

"general secretary" means the official of the union who holds the office of general secretary or, where there is no such office, holds an office which is equivalent, or (except in section 14(4)) the nearest equivalent, to that of general secretary;

"officer" includes—

(a) any member of the governing body of the union, and

(b) any trustee of any fund applicable for the purposes of the union;

"official" means—

(a) an officer of the union or of a branch or section of the union, or

(b) a person elected or appointed in accordance with the rules of the union to be a representative of its members or of some of them,

and includes a person so elected or appointed who is an employee of the same employer as the members or one or more of the members whom he is to represent;

"president" means the official of the union who holds the office of president or, where there is no such office, who holds an office which is equivalent, or (except in section 14(4) or Chapter IV) the nearest equivalent, to that of president; and

"rules", except where the context otherwise requires, includes the rules of any branch or section of the union.

NOTES

Definitions "agent" and "financial affairs" inserted by the Trade Union Reform and Employment Rights Act 1993, s 49(2), Sch 8, para 63.

[1.426]

120 Northern Ireland unions

In this Part a "Northern Ireland union" means a trade union whose principal office is situated in Northern Ireland.

[1.427]

121 Meaning of "the court"

In this Part "the court" (except where the reference is expressed to be to the county court or sheriff court) means the High Court or the Court of Session.

PART II
EMPLOYERS' ASSOCIATIONS

Introductory

[1.428]

122 Meaning of "employers' association"

(1) In this Act an "employers' association" means an organisation (whether temporary or permanent)—

(a) which consists wholly or mainly of employers or individual owners of undertakings of one or more descriptions and whose principal purposes include the regulation of relations between employers of that description or those descriptions and workers or trade unions; or

(b) which consists wholly or mainly of—

(i) constituent or affiliated organisations which fulfil the conditions in paragraph (a) (or themselves consist wholly or mainly of constituent or affiliated organisations which fulfil those conditions), or

(ii) representatives of such constituent or affiliated organisations,

and whose principal purposes include the regulation of relations between employers and workers or between employers and trade unions, or the regulation of relations between its constituent or affiliated organisations.

(2) References in this Act to employers' associations include combinations of employers and employers' associations.

The list of employers' associations

[1.429]
123 The list of employers' associations

(1) The Certification Officer shall keep a list of employers' associations containing the names of—
- (a) the organisations whose names were, immediately before the commencement of this Act, duly entered in the list of employers' associations kept by him under section 8 of the Trade Union and Labour Relations Act 1974, and
- (b) the names of the organisations entitled to have their names entered in the list in accordance with this Part.

(2) The Certification Officer shall keep copies of the list of employers' associations, as for the time being in force, available for public inspection at all reasonable hours free of charge.

(3) A copy of the list shall be included in his annual report.

(4) The fact that the name of an organisation is included in the list of employers' associations is evidence (in Scotland, sufficient evidence) that the organisation is an employers' association.

(5) On the application of an organisation whose name is included in the list, the Certification Officer shall issue it with a certificate to that effect.

(6) A document purporting to be such a certificate is evidence (in Scotland, sufficient evidence) that the name of the organisation is entered in the list.

NOTES

Trade Union and Labour Relations Act 1974, s 8: repealed by this Act.

[1.430]
124 Application to have name entered in the list

(1) An organisation of employers, whenever formed, whose name is not entered in the list of employers' associations may apply to the Certification Officer to have its name entered in the list.

(2) The application shall be made in such form and manner as the Certification Officer may require and shall be accompanied by—
- (a) a copy of the rules of the organisation,
- (b) a list of its officers,
- (c) the address of its head or main office, and
- (d) the name under which it is or is to be known,

and by the prescribed fee.

(3) If the Certification Officer is satisfied—
- (a) that the organisation is an employers' association,
- (b) that subsection (2) has been complied with, and
- (c) that entry of the name in the list is not prohibited by subsection (4),

he shall enter the name of the organisation in the list of employers' associations.

(4) The Certification Officer shall not enter the name of an organisation in the list of employers' associations if the name is the same as that under which another organisation—
- (a) was on 30th September 1971 registered as a trade union under the Trade Union Acts 1871 to 1964,
- (b) was at any time registered as an employers' association or trade union under the Industrial Relations Act 1971, or
- (c) is for the time being entered in the list of employers' associations or in the list of trade unions kept under Chapter I of Part I of this Act,

or if the name is one so nearly resembling any such name as to be likely to deceive the public.

NOTES

Prescribed fee: the current fee is £150 (see the Certification Officer (Amendment of Fees) Regulations 2005, SI 2005/713, reg 6).

Trade Union Acts 1871 to 1964: repealed, see the note to s 3 at **[1.270]**.

Industrial Relations Act 1971: repealed by the Trade Union and Labour Relations Act 1974, ss 1, 25(3), Sch 5.

[1.431]
125 Removal of name from the list

(1) If it appears to the Certification Officer, on application made to him or otherwise, that an organisation whose name is entered in the list of employers' associations is not an employers' association, he may remove its name from the list.

(2) He shall not do so without giving the organisation notice of his intention and considering any representations made to him by the organisation within such period (of not less than 28 days beginning with the date of the notice) as may be specified in the notice.

(3) The Certification Officer shall remove the name of an organisation from the list of employers' associations if—
- (a) he is requested by the organisation to do so, or
- (b) he is satisfied that the organisation has ceased to exist.

[1.432]
126 Appeal against decision of Certification Officer

(1) An organisation aggrieved by the refusal of the Certification Officer to enter its name in the list of employers' associations, or by a decision of his to remove its name from the list, may appeal to the Employment Appeal Tribunal [on any appealable question].

(2) . . .

(3) [For the purposes of this section, an appealable question is any question of law] arising in the proceedings before, or arising from the decision of, the Certification Officer.

NOTES

Sub-s (1): words in square brackets added by the Employment Relations Act 2004, s 51(2)(a).
Sub-s (2): repealed by the Employment Relations Act 2004, ss 51(2)(b), 57(2), Sch 2.
Sub-s (3): words in square brackets substituted by the Employment Relations Act 2004, s 51(2)(c).

Status and property of employers' associations

[1.433]
127 Corporate or quasi-corporate status of employers' associations

(1) An employers' association may be either a body corporate or an unincorporated association.
(2) Where an employers' association is unincorporated—
(a) it is capable of making contracts;
(b) it is capable of suing and being sued in its own name, whether in proceedings relating to property or founded on contract or tort or any other cause of action; and
(c) proceedings for an offence alleged to have been committed by it or on its behalf may be brought against it in its own name.
(3) . . .

NOTES

Sub-s (3): repealed by the Regulatory Reform (Removal of 20 Member Limit in Partnerships etc) Order 2002, SI 2002/3203, art 4.

[1.434]
128 Exclusion of common law rules as to restraint of trade

(1) The purposes of an unincorporated employers' association and, so far as they relate to the regulation of relations between employers and workers or trade unions, the purposes of an employers' association which is a body corporate are not, by reason only that they are in restraint of trade, unlawful so as—
(a) to make any member of the association liable to criminal proceedings for conspiracy or otherwise, or
(b) to make any agreement or trust void or voidable.
(2) No rule of an unincorporated employers' association or, so far as it relates to the regulation of relations between employers and workers or trade unions, of an employers' association which is a body corporate, is unlawful or unenforceable by reason only that it is in restraint of trade.

[1.435]
129 Property of unincorporated employers' associations, &c

(1) The following provisions of Chapter II of Part I of this Act apply to an unincorporated employers' association as in relation to a trade union—
(a) section 12(1) and (2) (property to be vested in trustees),
(b) section 13 (vesting of property in new trustees), and
(c) section 14 (transfer of securities held in trust for trade union).
(2) In sections 13 and 14 as they apply by virtue of subsection (1) the reference to entry in the list of trade unions shall be construed as a reference to entry in the list of employers' associations.
(3) Section 19 (application of certain provisions relating to . . . friendly societies) applies to any employers' association as in relation to a trade union.

NOTES

Sub-s (3): words omitted repealed by the Financial Services and Markets Act 2000 (Consequential Amendments and Repeals) Order 2001, SI 2001/3649, art 333.

[1.436]
130 Restriction on enforcement of awards against certain property

(1) Where in any proceedings an amount is awarded by way of damages, costs or expenses—
(a) against an employers' association,
(b) against trustees in whom property is vested in trust for an employers' association, in their capacity as such (and otherwise than in respect of a breach of trust on their part), or
(c) against members or officials of an employers' association on behalf of themselves and all of the members of the association,

no part of that amount is recoverable by enforcement against any protected property.
(2) The following is protected property—
(a) property belonging to the trustees otherwise than in their capacity as such;
(b) property belonging to any member of the association otherwise than jointly or in common with the other members;
(c) property belonging to an official of the association who is neither a member nor a trustee.

Administration of employers' associations

[1.437]
131 Administrative provisions applying to employers' associations

(1) The following provisions of Chapter III of Part I of this Act apply to an employers' association as in relation to a trade union—
section 27 (duty to supply copy of rules),

section 28 (duty to keep accounting records),
[section 32(1), (2), (3)(a), (b) and (c) and (4) to (6)[, section 32ZB] and sections 33 to 37] (annual return, accounts and audit),
[sections 37A to 37E (investigation of financial affairs),]
sections 38 to 42 (members' superannuation schemes),
section 43(1) (exemption for newly-formed organisations),
section 44(1), (2) and (4) (discharge of duties in case of organisation having branches or sections), and
[sections 45 and 45A] (offences).

(2) Sections 33 to 35 (appointment and removal of auditors) do not apply to an employers' association which is registered as a company under [the Companies Act 2006]; and sections 36 and 37 (rights and duties of auditors) apply to the auditors appointed by such an association under . . . [. . . Chapter 2 of Part 16 of that Act]].

NOTES

Sub-s (1): words in first (outer) and fourth pairs of square brackets substituted, and words in third pair of square brackets inserted, by the Trade Union Reform and Employment Rights Act 1993, s 49(2), Sch 8, para 64; words in second (inner) pair of square brackets inserted by the Trade Union Act 2016, s 12(2), as from 1 March 2017 (note that this amendment applies only to returns for periods that begin after that date (see **[1.2010]**)).

Sub-s (2): words in first pair and third (inner) pair of square brackets substituted by the Companies Act 2006 (Consequential Amendments, Transitional Provisions and Savings) Order 2009, SI 2009/1941, art 2(1), Sch 1, para 134(1), (4); words omitted repealed by the Companies Act 2006 (Consequential Amendments etc) Order 2008, SI 2008/948, art 3(1)(b), (2), Sch 1, Pt 2, para 188, Sch 2; words in second (outer) pair of square brackets added by the Companies Act 2006 (Commencement No 3, Consequential Amendments, Transitional Provisions and Savings) Order 2007, SI 2007/2194, art 10(1), (2), Sch 4, Pt 3, para 74.

Application of funds for political objects

[1.438]

132 Application of funds for political objects

[(1)] [Subject to subsections (2) to (5), the] provisions of Chapter VI of Part I of this Act (application of funds for political objects) apply to an unincorporated employers' association as in relation to a trade union.

[(2) Subsection (1) does not apply to these provisions—
- (a) section 72A;
- (b) in section 80, subsections (5A) to (5C) and (8) to (10);
- (c) in section 81, subsection (8).

(3) In its application to an unincorporated employers' association, section 79 shall have effect as if at the end of subsection (1) there were inserted—

> "The making of an application to the Certification Officer does not prevent the applicant, or any other person, from making an application to the court in respect of the same matter."

(4) In its application to an unincorporated employers' association, section 80(2)(b) shall have effect as if the words "where he considers it appropriate," were inserted at the beginning.

(5) In its application to an unincorporated employers' association, section 81 shall have effect as if after subsection (1) there were inserted—

> "(2) If an application in respect of the same matter has been made to the Certification Officer, the court shall have due regard to any declaration, reasons or observations of his which are brought to its notice."]

NOTES

Original text of this section numbered sub-s (1), words in square brackets therein substituted, and sub-ss (2)–(5) added by the Employment Relations Act 1999, s 29, Sch 6, paras 1, 20.

Amalgamations and similar matters

[1.439]

[133 Amalgamations and transfers of engagements

(1) Subject to subsection (2), the provisions of Chapter VII of Part I of this Act (amalgamations and similar matters) apply to unincorporated employers' associations as in relation to trade unions.

(2) In its application to such associations that Chapter shall have effect—
- (a) as if in section 99(1) for the words from "that every" to "accompanied by" there were substituted the words "that, not less than seven days before the ballot on the resolution to approve the instrument of amalgamation or transfer is held, every member is supplied with",
- (b) as if the requirements imposed by sections 100A to 100E consisted only of those specified in sections 100B and 100C(1) and (3)(a) together with the requirement that every member must, so far as is reasonably possible, be given a fair opportunity of voting, . . .
- [(ba) as if the references in sections 101A and 101B to the list of trade unions were to the list of employers' associations, and]
- (c) with the omission of sections 101(3)[, 101A(3) and (4)][, 103(2A) and (6) to (9)] and 107.]

NOTES

Substituted by the Trade Union Reform and Employment Rights Act 1993, s 49(2), Sch 8, para 65.

Sub-s (2): word omitted from para (b) repealed, para (ba) inserted, and words in first pair of square brackets in para (c) inserted, by the Employment Relations Act 2004, ss 50(3), 57(2), Sch 2; words in second pair of square brackets in para (c) inserted by the Employment Relations Act 1999, s 29, Sch 6, paras 1, 21.

[1.440]
134 Change of name of employers' association
(1) An unincorporated employers' association may change its name by any method expressly provided for by its rules or, if its rules do not expressly provide for a method of doing so, by adopting in accordance with its rules an alteration of the provision in them which gives the association its name.
(2) If the name of an employers' association, whether incorporated or unincorporated, is entered in the list of employers' associations a change of name shall not take effect until approved by the Certification Officer.
(3) The Certification Officer shall not approve a change of name if it appears to him that the proposed new name—
(a) is the same as one entered in the list as the name of another employers' association, or
(b) is the same as one entered in the list of trade unions kept under Part I of this Act,
or is a name so nearly resembling such a name as to be likely to deceive the public.
(4) A change of name by an unincorporated employers' association does not affect any right or obligation of the association or any of its members; and any pending legal proceedings may be continued by or against the association, the trustees of the association or any other officer of the association who can sue or be sued on its behalf notwithstanding its change of name.
(5) The power conferred by section 108 (power to make regulations for carrying provisions into effect) applies in relation to this section as in relation to a provision of Chapter VII of Part I.

General

[1.441]
135 Federated employers' associations
(1) In this section a "federated employers' association" means an employers' association which consists wholly or mainly of constituent or affiliated organisations, or representatives or such organisations, as described in paragraph (b) of the definition of "employers' association" in section 122.
(2) The provisions of Part I applied by this Part to employers' associations apply to federated employers' associations subject to the following exceptions and adaptations.
(3) The following provisions of Chapter III of Part I (administration) do not apply to a federated employers' association which consists wholly or mainly of representatives of constituent or affiliated organisations—
(a) section 27 (duty to supply copy of rules),
(b) section 28 (duty to keep accounting records),
(c) [section 32(1), (2), (3)(a), (b) and (c) and (4) to (6)[, section 32ZB] and sections 33 to 37] (annual return, accounts and audit), . . .
[(ca) sections 37A to 37E (investigation of financial affairs), and]
(d) sections 38 to 42 (members' superannuation schemes).
(4) The provisions of Chapter VI of Part I (application of funds for political objects) apply to a employers' association which is in whole or part an association or combination of other associations as if the individual members of the component associations were members of that association and not of the component associations.

But nothing in that Chapter prevents a component association from collecting contributions on behalf of the association or combination from such of its members as are [contributors] to the political fund of the association or combination.

NOTES

Sub-s (3): words in first (outer) pair of square brackets in para (c) substituted, word omitted from that paragraph repealed, and para (ca) inserted, by the Trade Union Reform and Employment Rights Act 1993, ss 49(2), 51, Sch 8, para 66, Sch 10; words in second (inner) pair of square brackets in para (c) inserted by the Trade Union Act 2016, s 12(3), as from 1 March 2017 (note that this amendment applies only to returns for periods that begin after that date (see **[1.2010]**)).

Sub-s (4): word in square brackets substituted (for the original words "not exempt from the obligation to contribute") by the Trade Union Act 2016, s 22, Sch 4, para 11, as from 1 March 2017. Note that this amendment applies only after the end of the transition period of 12 months beginning on 1 March 2017 specified under the Trade Union Act 2016, s 11(6), and only in relation to a person (a) who after the end of that period joins a trade union that has a political fund, or (b) who is a member of a trade union that has a political fund but did not have one immediately before the end of that period (see **[2.1977]**).

[1.442]
136 Meaning of "officer" of employers' association
In this Act "officer", in relation to an employers' association, includes—
(a) any member of the governing body of the association, and
(b) any trustee of any fund applicable for the purposes of the association.

PART III
RIGHTS IN RELATION TO UNION MEMBERSHIP AND ACTIVITIES

Access to employment

[1.443]
137 Refusal of employment on grounds related to union membership
(1) It is unlawful to refuse a person employment—
(a) because he is, or is not, a member of a trade union, or

(b) because he is unwilling to accept a requirement—
(i) to take steps to become or cease to be, or to remain or not to become, a member of a trade union, or
(ii) to make payments or suffer deductions in the event of his not being a member of a trade union.

(2) A person who is thus unlawfully refused employment has a right of complaint to an [employment tribunal].

(3) Where an advertisement is published which indicates, or might reasonably be understood as indicating—
(a) that employment to which the advertisement relates is open only to a person who is, or is not, a member of a trade union, or
(b) that any such requirement as is mentioned in subsection (1)(b) will be imposed in relation to employment to which the advertisement relates,

a person who does not satisfy that condition or, as the case may be, is unwilling to accept that requirement, and who seeks and is refused employment to which the advertisement relates, shall be conclusively presumed to have been refused employment for that reason.

(4) Where there is an arrangement or practice under which employment is offered only to persons put forward or approved by a trade union, and the trade union puts forward or approves only persons who are members of the union, a person who is not a member of the union and who is refused employment in pursuance of the arrangement or practice shall be taken to have been refused employment because he is not a member of the trade union.

(5) A person shall be taken to be refused employment if he seeks employment of any description with a person and that person—
(a) refuses or deliberately omits to entertain and process his application or enquiry, or
(b) causes him to withdraw or cease to pursue his application or enquiry, or
(c) refuses or deliberately omits to offer him employment of that description, or
(d) makes him an offer of such employment the terms of which are such as no reasonable employer who wished to fill the post would offer and which is not accepted, or
(e) makes him an offer of such employment but withdraws it or causes him not to accept it.

(6) Where a person is offered employment on terms which include a requirement that he is, or is not, a member of a trade union, or any such requirement as is mentioned in subsection (1)(b), and he does not accept the offer because he does not satisfy or, as the case may be, is unwilling to accept that requirement, he shall be treated as having been refused employment for that reason.

(7) Where a person may not be considered for appointment or election to an office in a trade union unless he is a member of the union, or of a particular branch or section of the union or of one of a number of particular branches or sections of the union, nothing in this section applies to anything done for the purpose of securing compliance with that condition although as holder of the office he would be employed by the union.

For this purpose an "office" means any position—
(a) by virtue of which the holder is an official of the union, or
(b) to which Chapter IV of Part I applies (duty to hold elections).

(8) The provisions of this section apply in relation to an employment agency acting, or purporting to act, on behalf of an employer as in relation to an employer.

NOTES

Sub-s (2): words in square brackets substituted by the Employment Rights (Dispute Resolution) Act 1998, s 1(2)(a).

Conciliation: employment tribunal proceedings under this section are "relevant proceedings" for the purposes of the conciliation provisions contained in the Employment Tribunals Act 1996, ss 18–18C; see s 18(1)(a) of the 1996 Act at **[1.757]**.

[1.444]

138 Refusal of service of employment agency on grounds related to union membership

(1) It is unlawful for an employment agency to refuse a person any of its services—
(a) because he is, or is not, a member of a trade union, or
(b) because he is unwilling to accept a requirement to take steps to become or cease to be, or to remain or not to become, a member of a trade union.

(2) A person who is thus unlawfully refused any service of an employment agency has a right of complaint to an [employment tribunal].

[(2A) Section 12A of the Employment Tribunals Act 1996 (financial penalties) applies in relation to a complaint under this section as it applies in relation to a claim involving an employer and a worker (reading references to an employer as references to the employment agency and references to a worker as references to the complainant).]

(3) Where an advertisement is published which indicates, or might reasonably be understood as indicating—
(a) that any service of an employment agency is available only to a person who is, or is not, a member of a trade union, or
(b) that any such requirement as is mentioned in subsection (1)(b) will be imposed in relation to a service to which the advertisement relates,

a person who does not satisfy that condition or, as the case may be, is unwilling to accept that requirement, and who seeks to avail himself of and is refused that service, shall be conclusively presumed to have been refused it for that reason.

(4) A person shall be taken to be refused a service if he seeks to avail himself of it and the agency—
(a) refuses or deliberately omits to make the service available to him, or
(b) causes him not to avail himself of the service or to cease to avail himself of it, or

(c) does not provide the same service, on the same terms, as is provided to others.

(5) Where a person is offered a service on terms which include a requirement that he is, or is not, a member of a trade union, or any such requirement as is mentioned in subsection (1)(b), and he does not accept the offer because he does not satisfy or, as the case may be, is unwilling to accept that requirement, he shall be treated as having been refused the service for that reason.

NOTES

Sub-s (2): words in square brackets substituted by the Employment Rights (Dispute Resolution) Act 1998, s 1(2)(a).

Sub-s (2A): inserted by the Enterprise and Regulatory Reform Act 2013, s 16(2), Sch 3, para 1.

Conciliation: employment tribunal proceedings under this section are "relevant proceedings" for the purposes of the conciliation provisions contained in the Employment Tribunals Act 1996, ss 18–18C; see s 18(1)(a) of the 1996 Act at **[1.757]**.

[1.445]

139 Time limit for proceedings

(1) An [employment tribunal] shall not consider a complaint under section 137 or 138 unless it is presented to the tribunal—

(a) before the end of the period of three months beginning with the date of the conduct to which the complaint relates, or

(b) where the tribunal is satisfied that it was not reasonably practicable for the complaint to be presented before the end of that period, within such further period as the tribunal considers reasonable.

(2) The date of the conduct to which a complaint under section 137 relates shall be taken to be—

(a) in the case of an actual refusal, the date of the refusal;

(b) in the case of a deliberate omission—

(i) to entertain and process the complainant's application or enquiry, or

(ii) to offer employment,

the end of the period within which it was reasonable to expect the employer to act;

(c) in the case of conduct causing the complainant to withdraw or cease to pursue his application or enquiry, the date of that conduct;

(d) in a case where an offer was made but withdrawn, the date when it was withdrawn;

(e) in any other case where an offer was made but not accepted, the date on which it was made.

(3) The date of the conduct to which a complaint under section 138 relates shall be taken to be—

(a) in the case of an actual refusal, the date of the refusal;

(b) in the case of a deliberate omission to make a service available, the end of the period within which it was reasonable to expect the employment agency to act;

(c) in the case of conduct causing the complainant not to avail himself of a service or to cease to avail himself of it, the date of that conduct;

(d) in the case of failure to provide the same service, on the same terms, as is provided to others, the date or last date on which the service in fact provided was provided.

[(4) Section 292A (extension of time limits to facilitate conciliation before institution of proceedings) applies for the purposes of subsection (1)(a).]

NOTES

Sub-s (1): words in square brackets substituted by the Employment Rights (Dispute Resolution) Act 1998, s 1(2)(a).

Sub-s (4): added by the Enterprise and Regulatory Reform Act 2013, s 8, Sch 2, paras 1, 6.

[1.446]

140 Remedies

(1) Where the [employment tribunal] finds that a complaint under section 137 or 138 is well-founded, it shall make a declaration to that effect and may make such of the following as it considers just and equitable—

(a) an order requiring the respondent to pay compensation to the complainant of such amount as the tribunal may determine;

(b) a recommendation that the respondent take within a specified period action appearing to the tribunal to be practicable for the purpose of obviating or reducing the adverse effect on the complainant of any conduct to which the complaint relates.

(2) Compensation shall be assessed on the same basis as damages for breach of statutory duty and may include compensation for injury to feelings.

(3) If the respondent fails without reasonable justification to comply with a recommendation to take action, the tribunal may increase its award of compensation or, if it has not made such an award, make one.

(4) The total amount of compensation shall not exceed the limit for the time being imposed by [section 124(1) of the Employment Rights Act 1996] (limit on compensation for unfair dismissal).

NOTES

Sub-s (1): words in square brackets substituted by the Employment Rights (Dispute Resolution) Act 1998, s 1(2)(a).

Sub-s (4): words in square brackets substituted by the Employment Rights Act 1996, s 240, Sch 1, para 56(1), (6).

[1.447]

141 Complaint against employer and employment agency

(1) Where a person has a right of complaint against a prospective employer and against an employment agency arising out of the same facts, he may present a complaint against either of them or against them jointly.

(2) If a complaint is brought against one only, he or the complainant may request the tribunal to join or sist the other as a party to the proceedings.

The request shall be granted if it is made before the hearing of the complaint begins, but may be refused if it is made after that time; and no such request may be made after the tribunal has made its decision as to whether the complaint is well-founded.

(3) Where a complaint is brought against an employer and an employment agency jointly, or where it is brought against one and the other is joined or sisted as a party to the proceedings, and the tribunal—

(a) finds that the complaint is well-founded as against the employer and the agency, and

(b) makes an award of compensation,

it may order that the compensation shall be paid by the one or the other, or partly by one and partly by the other, as the tribunal may consider just and equitable in the circumstances.

[1.448]

142 Awards against third parties

(1) If in proceedings on a complaint under section 137 or 138 either the complainant or the respondent claims that the respondent was induced to act in the manner complained of by pressure which a trade union or other person exercised on him by calling, organising, procuring or financing a strike or other industrial action, or by threatening to do so, the complainant or the respondent may request the [employment tribunal] to direct that the person who he claims exercised the pressure be joined or sisted as a party to the proceedings.

(2) The request shall be granted if it is made before the hearing of the complaint begins, but may be refused if it is made after that time; and no such request may be made after the tribunal has made its decision as to whether the complaint is well-founded.

(3) Where a person has been so joined or sisted as a party to the proceedings and the tribunal—

(a) finds that the complaint is well-founded,

(b) makes an award of compensation, and

(c) also finds that the claim in subsection (1) above is well-founded,

it may order that the compensation shall be paid by the person joined instead of by the respondent, or partly by that person and partly by the respondent, as the tribunal may consider just and equitable in the circumstances.

(4) Where by virtue of section 141 (complaint against employer and employment agency) there is more than one respondent, the above provisions apply to either or both of them.

NOTES

Sub-s (1): words in square brackets substituted by the Employment Rights (Dispute Resolution) Act 1998, s 1(2)(a).

[1.449]

143 Interpretation and other supplementary provisions

(1) In sections 137 to 143—

"advertisement" includes every form of advertisement or notice, whether to the public or not, and references to publishing an advertisement shall be construed accordingly;

"employment" means employment under a contract of employment, and related expressions shall be construed accordingly; and

"employment agency" means a person who, for profit or not, provides services for the purpose of finding employment for workers or supplying employers with workers, but subject to subsection (2) below.

(2) For the purposes of sections 137 to 143 as they apply to employment agencies—

(a) services other than those mentioned in the definition of "employment agency" above shall be disregarded, and

(b) a trade union shall not be regarded as an employment agency by reason of services provided by it only for, or in relation to, its members.

(3) References in sections 137 to 143 to being or not being a member of a trade union are to being or not being a member of any trade union, of a particular trade union or of one of a number of particular trade unions.

Any such reference includes a reference to being or not being a member of a particular branch or section of a trade union or of one of a number of particular branches or sections of a trade union.

(4) The remedy of a person for conduct which is unlawful by virtue of section 137 or 138 is by way of a complaint to an [employment tribunal] in accordance with this Part, and not otherwise.

No other legal liability arises by reason that conduct is unlawful by virtue of either of those sections.

NOTES

Sub-s (4): words in square brackets substituted by the Employment Rights (Dispute Resolution) Act 1998, s 1(2)(a).

Contracts for supply of goods or services

[1.450]

144 Union membership requirement in contract for goods or services void

A term or condition of a contract for the supply of goods or services is void in so far as it purports to require that the whole, or some part, of the work done for the purposes of the contract is done only by persons who are, or are not, members of trade unions or of a particular trade union.

[1.451]

145 Refusal to deal on union membership grounds prohibited

(1) A person shall not refuse to deal with a supplier or prospective supplier of goods or services on union membership grounds.

"Refuse to deal" and "union membership grounds" shall be construed as follows.

(2) A person refuses to deal with a person if, where he maintains (in whatever form) a list of approved suppliers of goods or services, or of persons from whom tenders for the supply of goods or services may be invited, he fails to include the name of that person in that list.

He does so on union membership grounds if the ground, or one of the grounds, for failing to include his name is that if that person were to enter into a contract with him for the supply of goods or services, work to be done for the purposes of the contract would, or would be likely to, be done by persons who were, or who were not, members of trade unions or of a particular trade union.

(3) A person refuses to deal with a person if, in relation to a proposed contract for the supply of goods or services—

(a) he excludes that person from the group of persons from whom tenders for the supply of the goods or services are invited, or

(b) he fails to permit that person to submit such a tender, or

(c) he otherwise determines not to enter into a contract with that person for the supply of the goods or services.

He does so on union membership grounds if the ground, or one of the grounds, on which he does so is that if the proposed contract were entered into with that person, work to be done for the purposes of the contract would, or would be likely to, be done by persons who were, or who were not, members of trade unions or of a particular trade union.

(4) A person refuses to deal with a person if he terminates a contract with him for the supply of goods or services.

He does so on union membership grounds if the ground, or one of the grounds, on which he does so is that work done, or to be done, for the purposes of the contract has been, or is likely to be, done by persons who are or are not members of trade unions or of a particular trade union.

(5) The obligation to comply with this section is a duty owed to the person with whom there is a refusal to deal and to any other person who may be adversely affected by its contravention; and a breach of the duty is actionable accordingly (subject to the defences and other incidents applying to actions for breach of statutory duty).

[Inducements

[1.452]

145A Inducements relating to union membership or activities

(1) A worker has the right not to have an offer made to him by his employer for the sole or main purpose of inducing the worker—

(a) not to be or seek to become a member of an independent trade union,

(b) not to take part, at an appropriate time, in the activities of an independent trade union,

(c) not to make use, at an appropriate time, of trade union services, or

(d) to be or become a member of any trade union or of a particular trade union or of one of a number of particular trade unions.

(2) In subsection (1) "an appropriate time" means—

(a) a time outside the worker's working hours, or

(b) a time within his working hours at which, in accordance with arrangements agreed with or consent given by his employer, it is permissible for him to take part in the activities of a trade union or (as the case may be) make use of trade union services.

(3) In subsection (2) "working hours", in relation to a worker, means any time when, in accordance with his contract of employment (or other contract personally to do work or perform services), he is required to be at work.

(4) In subsections (1) and (2)—

(a) "trade union services" means services made available to the worker by an independent trade union by virtue of his membership of the union, and

(b) references to a worker's "making use" of trade union services include his consenting to the raising of a matter on his behalf by an independent trade union of which he is a member.

(5) A worker or former worker may present a complaint to an employment tribunal on the ground that his employer has made him an offer in contravention of this section.]

NOTES

Inserted, together with the preceding heading and ss 145B–145F, by the Employment Relations Act 2004, s 29.

Conciliation: employment tribunal proceedings under this section are "relevant proceedings" for the purposes of the conciliation provisions contained in the Employment Tribunals Act 1996, ss 18–18C; see s 18(1)(a) of the 1996 Act at **[1.757]**.

Tribunal jurisdiction: the Employment Act 2002, s 38 applies to proceedings before the employment tribunal relating to a claim under this section and ss 145B, 146; see s 38(1) of, and Sch 5 to, the 2002 Act at **[1.1279]**, **[1.1287]**. See also s 207A of this Act at **[1.524]** (as inserted by the Employment Act 2008). That section provides that in proceedings before an employment tribunal relating to a claim by an employee under any of the jurisdictions listed in Sch A2 to this Act at **[1.704]** (which includes this section and ss 145B, 146) the tribunal may adjust any award given if the employer or the employee has unreasonably failed to comply with a relevant Code of Practice as defined by s 207A(4). See also the revised Acas Code of Practice 1 – Disciplinary and Grievance Procedures (2015) at **[4.1]**, and the Acas Code of Practice 4 – Settlement Agreements (2013) at **[4.54]**.

National security: for the effect of national security considerations on a complaint under this section and ss 145B, 146, see the Employment Tribunals Act 1996, s 10(1) at **[1.745]**.

Relevant statutory rights: the rights conferred by this section (and ss 145B, 146) are "relevant statutory rights" for the purposes of the Employment Rights Act 1996, s 104 (dismissal on grounds of assertion of statutory right); see s 104(4)(c) of that Act at **[1.1015]**.

[1.453]
[145B Inducements relating to collective bargaining

(1) A worker who is a member of an independent trade union which is recognised, or seeking to be recognised, by his employer has the right not to have an offer made to him by his employer if—

(a) acceptance of the offer, together with other workers' acceptance of offers which the employer also makes to them, would have the prohibited result, and

(b) the employer's sole or main purpose in making the offers is to achieve that result.

(2) The prohibited result is that the workers' terms of employment, or any of those terms, will not (or will no longer) be determined by collective agreement negotiated by or on behalf of the union.

(3) It is immaterial for the purposes of subsection (1) whether the offers are made to the workers simultaneously.

(4) Having terms of employment determined by collective agreement shall not be regarded for the purposes of section 145A (or section 146 or 152) as making use of a trade union service.

(5) A worker or former worker may present a complaint to an employment tribunal on the ground that his employer has made him an offer in contravention of this section.]

NOTES

Inserted as noted to s 145A at **[1.452]**.

Conciliation: see the note to s 145A at **[1.452]**.

Tribunal jurisdiction: see the note to s 145A at **[1.452]**.

National security: see the note to s 145A at **[1.452]**.

Relevant statutory rights: see the note to s 145A at **[1.452]**.

[1.454]
[145C Time limit for proceedings

[(1)] An employment tribunal shall not consider a complaint under section 145A or 145B unless it is presented—

(a) before the end of the period of three months beginning with the date when the offer was made or, where the offer is part of a series of similar offers to the complainant, the date when the last of them was made, or

(b) where the tribunal is satisfied that it was not reasonably practicable for the complaint to be presented before the end of that period, within such further period as it considers reasonable.

[(2) Section 292A (extension of time limits to facilitate conciliation before institution of proceedings) applies for the purposes of subsection (1)(a).]

NOTES

Inserted as noted to s 145A at **[1.452]**.

The existing provision was numbered as sub-s (1), and sub-s (2) was added, by the Enterprise and Regulatory Reform Act 2013, s 8, Sch 2, paras 1, 7.

[1.455]
[145D Consideration of complaint

(1) On a complaint under section 145A it shall be for the employer to show what was his sole or main purpose in making the offer.

(2) On a complaint under section 145B it shall be for the employer to show what was his sole or main purpose in making the offers.

(3) On a complaint under section 145A or 145B, in determining any question whether the employer made the offer (or offers) or the purpose for which he did so, no account shall be taken of any pressure which was exercised on him by calling, organising, procuring or financing a strike or other industrial action, or by threatening to do so; and that question shall be determined as if no such pressure had been exercised.

(4) In determining whether an employer's sole or main purpose in making offers was the purpose mentioned in section 145B(1), the matters taken into account must include any evidence—

(a) that when the offers were made the employer had recently changed or sought to change, or did not wish to use, arrangements agreed with the union for collective bargaining,

(b) that when the offers were made the employer did not wish to enter into arrangements proposed by the union for collective bargaining, or

(c) that the offers were made only to particular workers, and were made with the sole or main purpose of rewarding those particular workers for their high level of performance or of retaining them because of their special value to the employer.]

NOTES

Inserted as noted to s 145A at **[1.452]**.

[1.456]
[145E Remedies

(1) Subsections (2) and (3) apply where the employment tribunal finds that a complaint under section 145A or 145B is well-founded.

(2) The tribunal—

(a) shall make a declaration to that effect, and
(b) shall make an award to be paid by the employer to the complainant in respect of the offer complained of.

(3) The amount of the award shall be [£4,193] (subject to any adjustment of the award that may fall to be made under Part 3 of the Employment Act 2002).

(4) Where an offer made in contravention of section 145A or 145B is accepted—
(a) if the acceptance results in the worker's agreeing to vary his terms of employment, the employer cannot enforce the agreement to vary, or recover any sum paid or other asset transferred by him under the agreement to vary;
(b) if as a result of the acceptance the worker's terms of employment are varied, nothing in section 145A or 145B makes the variation unenforceable by either party.

(5) Nothing in this section or sections 145A and 145B prejudices any right conferred by section 146 or 149.

(6) In ascertaining any amount of compensation under section 149, no reduction shall be made on the ground—
(a) that the complainant caused or contributed to his loss, or to the act or failure complained of, by accepting or not accepting an offer made in contravention of section 145A or 145B, or
(b) that the complainant has received or is entitled to an award under this section.]

NOTES

Inserted as noted to s 145A at **[1.452]**.

Sub-s (3): sum in square brackets substituted by the Employment Rights (Increase of Limits) Order 2019, SI 2019/324, art 3, Schedule, as from 6 April 2019, in relation to any case where the appropriate date (as defined in the order) falls on or after that date (see SI 2019/324, art 4 at **[2.2117]**). The previous sums were: £4,059, as from 6 April 2018 (see SI 2018/194 (revoked)); £3,907, as from 6 April 2017 (see SI 2017/175 (revoked)); and £3,830, as from 6 April 2016 (see SI 2016/288 (revoked)). This sum may be further varied by the Secretary of State, see the Employment Relations Act 1999, s 34(1)(ea) at **[1.1258]**.

[1.457]
[145F Interpretation and other supplementary provisions

(1) References in sections 145A to 145E to being or becoming a member of a trade union include references—
(a) to being or becoming a member of a particular branch or section of that union, and
(b) to being or becoming a member of one of a number of particular branches or sections of that union.

(2) References in those sections—
(a) to taking part in the activities of a trade union, and
(b) to services made available by a trade union by virtue of membership of the union,
shall be construed in accordance with subsection (1).

(3) In sections 145A to 145E—
"worker" means an individual who works, or normally works, as mentioned in paragraphs (a) to (c) of section 296(1), and
"employer" means—
(a) in relation to a worker, the person for whom he works;
(b) in relation to a former worker, the person for whom he worked.

(4) The remedy of a person for infringement of the right conferred on him by section 145A or 145B is by way of a complaint to an employment tribunal in accordance with this Part, and not otherwise.]

NOTES

Inserted as noted to s 145A at **[1.452]**.

[Detriment]

[1.458]
146 [Detriment] on grounds related to union membership or activities

(1) [A worker] has the right not to [be subjected to any detriment as an individual by any act, or any deliberate failure to act, by his employer if the act or failure takes place] for [the sole or main purpose] of—
(a) preventing or deterring him from being or seeking to become a member of an independent trade union, or penalising him for doing so,
(b) preventing or deterring him from taking part in the activities of an independent trade union at an appropriate time, or penalising him for doing so, . . .
[(ba) preventing or deterring him from making use of trade union services at an appropriate time, or penalising him for doing so, or]
(c) compelling him to be or become a member of any trade union or of a particular trade union or of one of a number of particular trade unions.

(2) In subsection [(1)] "an appropriate time" means—
(a) a time outside the [worker's] working hours, or
(b) a time within his working hours at which, in accordance with arrangements agreed with or consent given by his employer, it is permissible for him to take part in the activities of a trade union [or (as the case may be) make use of trade union services];
and for this purpose "working hours", in relation to [a worker], means any time when, in accordance with his contract of employment [(or other contract personally to do work or perform services)], he is required to be at work.

[(2A) In this section—

(a) "trade union services" means services made available to the worker by an independent trade union by virtue of his membership of the union, and

(b) references to a worker's "making use" of trade union services include his consenting to the raising of a matter on his behalf by an independent trade union of which he is a member.

(2B) If an independent trade union of which a worker is a member raises a matter on his behalf (with or without his consent), penalising the worker for that is to be treated as penalising him as mentioned in subsection (1)(ba).

(2C) A worker also has the right not to be subjected to any detriment as an individual by any act, or any deliberate failure to act, by his employer if the act or failure takes place because of the worker's failure to accept an offer made in contravention of section 145A or 145B.

(2D) For the purposes of subsection (2C), not conferring a benefit that, if the offer had been accepted by the worker, would have been conferred on him under the resulting agreement shall be taken to be subjecting him to a detriment as an individual (and to be a deliberate failure to act).]

(3) [A worker] also has the right not to [be subjected to any detriment as an individual by any act, or any deliberate failure to act, by his employer if the act or failure takes place] for [the sole or main purpose] of enforcing a requirement (whether or not imposed by [a contract of employment] or in writing) that, in the event of his not being a member of any trade union or of a particular trade union or of one of a number of particular trade unions, he must make one or more payments.

(4) For the purposes of subsection (3) any deduction made by an employer from the remuneration payable to [a worker] in respect of his employment shall, if it is attributable to his not being a member of any trade union or of a particular trade union or of one of a number of particular trade unions, be treated as [a detriment to which he has been subjected as an individual by an act of his employer taking place] for [the sole or main purpose] of enforcing a requirement of a kind mentioned in that subsection.

(5) [A worker or former worker] may present a complaint to an [employment tribunal] on the ground that [he has been subjected to a detriment] by his employer in contravention of this section.

[(5A) This section does not apply where—

(a) the worker is an employee; and

(b) the detriment in question amounts to dismissal.]

NOTES

The heading preceding this section and the words in square brackets in the section heading were substituted by the Employment Relations Act 2004, s 30(7).

Sub-s (1): words in first and third pairs of square brackets substituted, word omitted from para (b) repealed, and para (ba) inserted, by the Employment Relations Act 2004, ss 30(1), (2), 31(1), (2), 57, Sch 1, para 8, Sch 2; words in second pair of square brackets substituted by the Employment Relations Act 1999, s 2, Sch 2, paras 1, 2(1), (2).

Sub-s (2): words in first, second and fourth pairs of square brackets substituted, and words in third and fifth pairs of square brackets inserted, by the Employment Relations Act 2004, ss 30(1)–(3), 31(1), (3).

Sub-ss (2A)–(2D): inserted by the Employment Relations Act 2004, s 31(1), (4).

Sub-s (3): words in first, third and fourth pairs of square brackets substituted by the Employment Relations Act 2004, ss 30(1), (2), (4), 57(1), Sch 1, para 8; words in second pair of square brackets substituted by the Employment Relations Act 1999, s 2, Sch 2, paras 1, 2(1), (3).

Sub-s (4): words in first and third pairs of square brackets substituted by the Employment Relations Act 2004, ss 30(1), (2), 57(1), Sch 1, para 8; words in second pair of square brackets substituted by the Employment Relations Act 1999, s 2, Sch 2, paras 1, 2(1), (4).

Sub-s (5): words in first pair of square brackets substituted by the Employment Relations Act 2004, s 30(1), (5); words in second pair of square brackets substituted by the Employment Rights (Dispute Resolution) Act 1998, s 1(2)(a); words in third pair of square brackets substituted by the Employment Relations Act 1999, s 2, Sch 2, paras 1, 2(1), (5).

Sub-s (5A): added (as sub-s (6)) by the Employment Relations Act 1999, s 2, Sch 2, paras 1, 2(1), (6); substituted (and renumbered) by the Employment Relations Act 2004, s 30(1), (6).

This section and ss 147, 152–154 and 181–185 are modified, in relation to governing bodies with delegated budgets, by the Education (Modification of Enactments Relating to Employment) (England) Order 2003, SI 2003/1964, art 3, Schedule at **[2.685]**, **[2.689]** and the Education (Modification of Enactments Relating to Employment) (Wales) Order 2006, SI 2006/1073, art 3, Schedule at **[2.915]**, **[2.918]**.

Conciliation: see the note to s 145A at **[1.452]**.

Tribunal jurisdiction: see the note to s 145A at **[1.452]**.

National security: see the note to s 145A at **[1.452]**.

Relevant statutory rights: see the note to s 145A at **[1.452]**.

[1.459]

147 Time limit for proceedings

[(1)] An [employment tribunal] shall not consider a complaint under section 146 unless it is presented—

(a) before the end of the period of three months beginning with the date of the [act or failure to which the complaint relates or, where that act or failure is part of a series of similar acts or failures (or both) the last of them], or

(b) where the tribunal is satisfied that it was not reasonably practicable for the complaint to be presented before the end of that period, within such further period as it considers reasonable.

[(2) For the purposes of subsection (1)—

(a) where an act extends over a period, the reference to the date of the act is a reference to the last day of that period;

(b) a failure to act shall be treated as done when it was decided on.

(3) For the purposes of subsection (2), in the absence of evidence establishing the contrary an employer shall be taken to decide on a failure to act—

(a) when he does an act inconsistent with doing the failed act, or

(b) if he has done no such inconsistent act, when the period expires within which he might reasonably have been expected to do the failed act if it was to be done.]

[(4) Section 292A (extension of time limits to facilitate conciliation before institution of proceedings) applies for the purposes of subsection (1)(a).]

NOTES

Sub-s (1): original text renumbered as sub-s (1) and words in second pair of square brackets substituted by the Employment Relations Act 1999, s 2, Sch 2, paras 1, 3(1)–(3); words in first pair of square brackets substituted by the Employment Rights (Dispute Resolution) Act 1998, s 1(2)(a).

Sub-ss (2), (3): added by the Employment Relations Act 1999, s 2, Sch 2, paras 1, 3(1), (4).

Sub-s (4): added by the Enterprise and Regulatory Reform Act 2013, s 8, Sch 2, paras 1, 8.

Modified as noted to s 146 at **[1.458]**.

[1.460]

148 Consideration of complaint

(1) On a complaint under section 146 it shall be for the employer to show [what was the sole or main purpose] for which [he acted or failed to act].

(2) In determining any question whether [the employer acted or failed to act, or the purpose for which he did so], no account shall be taken of any pressure which was exercised on him by calling, organising, procuring or financing a strike or other industrial action, or by threatening to do so; and that question shall be determined as if no such pressure had been exercised.

[(3)–(5) . . .]

NOTES

Sub-s (1): words in first pair of square brackets substituted by the Employment Relations Act 2004, s 57(1), Sch 1, para 9; words in second pair of square brackets substituted by the Employment Relations Act 1999, s 2, Sch 2, paras 1, 4(1), (2).

Sub-s (2): words in square brackets substituted by the Employment Relations Act 1999, s 2, Sch 2, paras 1, 4(1), (3).

Sub-ss (3)–(5): added by the Trade Union Reform and Employment Rights Act 1993, s 13; repealed by the Employment Relations Act 2004, ss 31, 57(2), Sch 2.

[1.461]

149 Remedies

(1) Where the [employment tribunal] finds that a complaint under section 146 is well-founded, it shall make a declaration to that effect and may make an award of compensation to be paid by the employer to the complainant in respect of the [act or failure] complained of.

(2) The amount of the compensation awarded shall be such as the tribunal considers just and equitable in all the circumstances having regard to the infringement complained of and to any loss sustained by the complainant which is attributable to the [act or failure] which infringed his right.

(3) The loss shall be taken to include—

(a) any expenses reasonably incurred by the complainant in consequence of the [act or failure] complained of, and

(b) loss of any benefit which he might reasonably be expected to have had but for that [act or failure].

(4) In ascertaining the loss, the tribunal shall apply the same rule concerning the duty of a person to mitigate his loss as applies to damages recoverable under the common law of England and Wales or Scotland.

(5) In determining the amount of compensation to be awarded no account shall be taken of any pressure which was exercised on the employer by calling, organising, procuring or financing a strike or other industrial action, or by threatening to do so; and that question shall be determined as if no such pressure had been exercised.

(6) Where the tribunal finds that the [act or failure] complained of was to any extent caused or contributed to by action of the complainant, it shall reduce the amount of the compensation by such proportion as it considers just and equitable having regard to that finding.

NOTES

Sub-s (1): words in first pair of square brackets substituted by the Employment Rights (Dispute Resolution) Act 1998, s 1(2)(a); words in second pair of square brackets substituted by the Employment Relations Act 1999, s 2, Sch 2, paras 1, 5(a).

Sub-ss (2), (3), (6): words in square brackets substituted by the Employment Relations Act 1999, s 2, Sch 2, paras 1, 5(a), (b).

[1.462]

150 Awards against third parties

(1) If in proceedings on a complaint under section 146—

(a) the complaint is made on the ground that [the complainant has been subjected to detriment by an act or failure by his employer taking place] for [the sole or main purpose] of compelling him to be or become a member of any trade union or of a particular trade union or of one of a number of particular trade unions, and

(b) either the complainant or the employer claims in proceedings before the tribunal that the employer was induced to [act or fail to act in the way] complained of by pressure which a trade union or other person exercised on him by calling, organising, procuring or financing a strike or other industrial action, or by threatening to do so,

the complainant or the employer may request the tribunal to direct that the person who he claims exercised the pressure be joined or sisted as a party to the proceedings.

(2) The request shall be granted if it is made before the hearing of the complaint begins, but may be refused if it is made after that time; and no such request may be made after the tribunal has made a declaration that the complaint is well-founded.

(3) Where a person has been so joined or sisted as a party to proceedings and the tribunal—

(a) makes an award of compensation, and

(b) finds that the claim mentioned in subsection (1)(b) is well-founded,

it may order that the compensation shall be paid by the person joined instead of by the employer, or partly by that person and partly by the employer, as the tribunal may consider just and equitable in the circumstances.

NOTES

Sub-s (1): words in first pair of square brackets in para (a) and words in square brackets in para (b) substituted by the Employment Relations Act 1999, s 2, Sch 2, paras 1, 6; words in second pair of square brackets in para (a) substituted by the Employment Relations Act 2004, s 57(1), Sch 1, para 10.

[1.463]

151 Interpretation and other supplementary provisions

(1) References in sections 146 to 150 to being, becoming or ceasing to remain a member of a trade union include references to being, becoming or ceasing to remain a member of a particular branch or section of that union and to being, becoming or ceasing to remain a member of one of a number of particular branches or sections of that union . . .

[(1A) References in those sections—

(a) to taking part in the activities of a trade union, and

(b) to services made available by a trade union by virtue of membership of the union,

shall be construed in accordance with subsection (1).]

[(1B) In sections 146 to 150—

"worker" means an individual who works, or normally works, as mentioned in paragraphs (a) to (c) of section 296(1), and

"employer" means—

(a) in relation to a worker, the person for whom he works;

(b) in relation to a former worker, the person for whom he worked.]

(2) The remedy of [a person] for infringement of the right conferred on him by section 146 is by way of a complaint to an [employment tribunal] in accordance with this Part, and not otherwise.

NOTES

Sub-s (1): words omitted repealed by the Employment Relations Act 2004, ss 31(6), 57(2), Sch 2.

Sub-ss (1A), (1B): inserted by the Employment Relations Act 2004, s 31(7), (8).

Sub-s (2): words in first pair of square brackets substituted by the Employment Relations Act 2004, s 30(9); words in second pair of square brackets substituted by the Employment Rights (Dispute Resolution) Act 1998, s 1(2)(a).

Dismissal [of employee]

[1.464]

152 Dismissal [of employee] on grounds related to union membership or activities

(1) For purposes of [Part X of the Employment Rights Act 1996] (unfair dismissal) the dismissal of an employee shall be regarded as unfair if the reason for it (or, if more than one, the principal reason) was that the employee—

(a) was, or proposed to become, a member of an independent trade union, . . .

(b) had taken part, or proposed to take part, in the activities of an independent trade union at an appropriate time, . . .

[(ba) had made use, or proposed to make use, of trade union services at an appropriate time,

(bb) had failed to accept an offer made in contravention of section 145A or 145B, or]

(c) was not a member of any trade union, or of a particular trade union, or of one of a number of particular trade unions, or had refused, or proposed to refuse, to become or remain a member.

(2) In subsection [(1)] "an appropriate time" means—

(a) a time outside the employee's working hours, or

(b) a time within his working hours at which, in accordance with arrangements agreed with or consent given by his employer, it is permissible for him to take part in the activities of a trade union [or (as the case may be) make use of trade union services];

and for this purpose "working hours", in relation to an employee, means any time when, in accordance with his contract of employment, he is required to be at work.

[(2A) In this section—

(a) "trade union services" means services made available to the employee by an independent trade union by virtue of his membership of the union, and

(b) references to an employee's "making use" of trade union services include his consenting to the raising of a matter on his behalf by an independent trade union of which he is a member.

(2B) Where the reason or one of the reasons for the dismissal was that an independent trade union (with or without the employee's consent) raised a matter on behalf of the employee as one of its members, the reason shall be treated as falling within subsection (1)(ba).]

(3) Where the reason, or one of the reasons, for the dismissal was—

(a) the employee's refusal, or proposed refusal, to comply with a requirement (whether or not imposed by his contract of employment or in writing) that, in the event of his not being a member of any trade union, or of a particular trade union, or of one of a number of particular trade unions, he must make one or more payments, or

(b) his objection, or proposed objection, (however expressed) to the operation of a provision (whether or not forming part of his contract of employment or in writing) under which, in the event mentioned in paragraph (a), his employer is entitled to deduct one or more sums from the remuneration payable to him in respect of his employment,

the reason shall be treated as falling within subsection (1)(c).

(4) References in this section to being, becoming or ceasing to remain a member of a trade union include references to being, becoming or ceasing to remain a member of a particular branch or section of that union or of one of a number of particular branches or sections of that trade union . . .

[(5) References in this section—

(a) to taking part in the activities of a trade union, and

(b) to services made available by a trade union by virtue of membership of the union,

shall be construed in accordance with subsection (4).]

NOTES

The words in square brackets in the heading preceding this section and in the section heading were substituted by the Employment Relations Act 2004, s 30(10).

Sub-s (1): words in first pair of square brackets substituted by the Employment Rights Act 1996, s 240, Sch 1, para 56(1), (7); words omitted from paras (a), (b) repealed, and paras (ba), (bb) inserted, by the Employment Relations Act 2004, ss 32(1), (2), 57(2), Sch 2.

Sub-s (2): number in square brackets substituted, and words in square brackets inserted, by the Employment Relations Act 2004, s 32(1), (3).

Sub-ss (2A), (2B), (5): inserted and added respectively by the Employment Relations Act 2004, s 32(1), (4), (6).

Sub-s (4): words omitted repealed by the Employment Relations Act 2004, ss 32(1), (5), 57(2), Sch 2.

Modified as noted to s 146 at **[1.458]**.

[1.465]

153 Selection for redundancy on grounds related to union membership or activities

Where the reason or principal reason for the dismissal of an employee was that he was redundant, but it is shown—

(a) that the circumstances constituting the redundancy applied equally to one or more other employees in the same undertaking who held positions similar to that held by him and who have not been dismissed by the employer, and

(b) that the reason (or, if more than one, the principal reason) why he was selected for dismissal was one of those specified in section 152(1),

the dismissal shall be regarded as unfair for the purposes of [Part X of the Employment Rights Act 1996] (unfair dismissal).

NOTES

Words in square brackets substituted by the Employment Rights Act 1996, s 240, Sch 1, para 56(1), (7).

Modified as noted to s 146 at **[1.458]**.

[1.466]

[154 Disapplication of qualifying period and upper age limit for unfair dismissal

Sections 108(1) and 109(1) of the Employment Rights Act 1996 (qualifying period and upper age limit for unfair dismissal protection) do not apply to a dismissal which by virtue of section 152 or 153 is regarded as unfair for the purposes of Part 10 of that Act.]

NOTES

Substituted by the Employment Relations Act 2004, s 35.

Modified as noted to s 146 at **[1.458]**.

Section 109 of the Employment Rights Act 1996 was repealed by the Employment Equality (Age) Regulations 2006, SI 2006/1031, reg 49(1), Sch 8, Pt 1, paras 21, 25, but there has been no corresponding amendment to this section.

[1.467]

155 Matters to be disregarded in assessing contributory fault

(1) Where an [employment tribunal] makes an award of compensation for unfair dismissal in a case where the dismissal is unfair by virtue of section 152 or 153, the tribunal shall disregard, in considering whether it would be just and equitable to reduce, or further reduce, the amount of any part of the award, any such conduct or action of the complainant as is specified below.

(2) Conduct or action of the complainant shall be disregarded in so far as it constitutes a breach or proposed breach of a requirement—

(a) to be or become a member of any trade union or of a particular trade union or of one of a number of particular trade unions,

(b) to cease to be, or refrain from becoming, a member of any trade union or of a particular trade union or of one of a number of particular trade unions, . . .

(c) not to take part in the activities of any trade union or of a particular trade union or of one of a number of particular trade unions[, or

(d) not to make use of services made available by any trade union or by a particular trade union or by one of a number of particular trade unions].

For the purposes of this subsection a requirement means a requirement imposed on the complainant by or under an arrangement or contract of employment or other agreement.

[(2A) Conduct or action of the complainant shall be disregarded in so far as it constitutes acceptance of or failure to accept an offer made in contravention of section 145A or 145B.]

(3) Conduct or action of the complainant shall be disregarded in so far as it constitutes a refusal, or proposed refusal, to comply with a requirement of a kind mentioned in section 152(3)(a) (payments in lieu of membership) or an objection, or proposed, objection, (however expressed) to the operation of a provision of a kind mentioned in section 152(3)(b) (deductions in lieu of membership).

NOTES

Sub-s (1): words in square brackets substituted by the Employment Rights (Dispute Resolution) Act 1998, s 1(2)(a).

Sub-s (2): word omitted from para (b) repealed, and para (d) and the word immediately preceding it inserted, by the Employment Relations Act 2004, s 57, Sch 1, para 11(1), (2), Sch 2.

Sub-s (2A): inserted by the Employment Relations Act 2004, s 57(1), Sch 1, para 11(1), (3).

[1.468]

156 Minimum basic award

(1) Where a dismissal is unfair by virtue of section 152(1) or 153, the amount of the basic award of compensation, before any reduction is made under [section 122 of the Employment Rights Act 1996], shall be not less than [£6,408].

(2) But where the dismissal is unfair by virtue of section 153, [subsection (2)] of that section (reduction for contributory fault) applies in relation to so much of the basic award as is payable because of subsection (1) above.

NOTES

Sub-s (1): words in first pair of square brackets substituted by the Employment Rights Act 1996, s 240, Sch 1, para 56(1), (9); sum in second pair of square brackets substituted by the Employment Rights (Increase of Limits) Order 2019, SI 2019/324, art 3, Schedule, as from 6 April 2019, in relation to any case where the appropriate date (as defined in the order) falls on or after that date (see SI 2019/324, art 4 at **[2.2117]**). The previous sums were: £6,203 (as from 6 April 2018 (see SI 2018/194 (revoked)); £5,970, as from 6 April 2017 (see SI 2017/175 (revoked)); and £5,853, as from 6 April 2016 (see SI 2016/288 (revoked)). This sum may be further varied by the Secretary of State, see the Employment Relations Act 1999, s 34(1)(f) at **[1.1258]**.

Sub-s (2): words in square brackets substituted by the Employment Rights Act 1996, s 240, Sch 1, para 56(1), (9).

157–159 *(Ss 157, 158 repealed by the Employment Relations Act 1999, ss 33(1)(b), 36(1)(b), 44, Sch 9(10); s 159 repealed by the Employment Relations Act 1999, ss 36(1)(b), (3), 44, Sch 9(10).)*

[1.469]

160 Awards against third parties

(1) If in proceedings before an [employment tribunal] on a complaint of unfair dismissal either the employer or the complainant claims—

(a) that the employer was induced to dismiss the complainant by pressure which a trade union or other person exercised on the employer by calling, organising, procuring or financing a strike or other industrial action, or by threatening to do so, and

(b) that the pressure was exercised because the complainant was not a member of any trade union or of a particular trade union or of one of a number of particular trade unions,

the employer or the complainant may request the tribunal to direct that the person who he claims exercised the pressure be joined or sisted as a party to the proceedings.

(2) The request shall be granted if it is made before the hearing of the complaint begins, but may be refused after that time; and no such request may be made after the tribunal has made an award of compensation for unfair dismissal or an order for reinstatement or re-engagement.

(3) Where a person has been so joined or sisted as a party to the proceedings and the tribunal—

(a) makes an award of compensation for unfair dismissal, and

(b) finds that the claim mentioned in subsection (1) is well-founded,

the tribunal may order that the compensation shall be paid by that person instead of the employer, or partly by that person and partly by the employer, as the tribunal may consider just and equitable.

NOTES

Sub-s (1): words in square brackets substituted by the Employment Rights (Dispute Resolution) Act 1998, s 1(2)(a).

[1.470]

161 Application for interim relief

(1) An employee who presents a complaint of unfair dismissal alleging that the dismissal is unfair by virtue of section 152 may apply to the tribunal for interim relief.

(2) The tribunal shall not entertain an application for interim relief unless it is presented to the tribunal before the end of the period of seven days immediately following the effective date of termination (whether before, on or after that date).

(3) In a case where the employee relies on [section 152(1)(a), (b) or (ba), or on section 152(1)(bb) otherwise than in relation to an offer made in contravention of section 145A(1)(d),] the tribunal shall not entertain an application for interim relief unless before the end of that period there is also so presented a certificate in writing signed by an authorised official of the independent trade union of which the employee was or proposed to become a member stating—

(a) that on the date of the dismissal the employee was or proposed to become a member of the union, and

(b) that there appear to be reasonable grounds for supposing that the reason for his dismissal (or, if more than one, the principal reason) was one alleged in the complaint.

(4) An "authorised official" means an official of the trade union authorised by it to act for the purposes of this section.

(5) A document purporting to be an authorisation of an official by a trade union to act for the purposes of this section and to be signed on behalf of the union shall be taken to be such an authorisation unless the contrary is proved; and a document purporting to be a certificate signed by such an official shall be taken to be signed by him unless the contrary is proved.

(6) For the purposes of subsection (3) the date of dismissal shall be taken to be—

(a) where the employee's contract of employment was terminated by notice (whether given by his employer or by him), the date on which the employer's notice was given, and

(b) in any other case, the effective date of termination.

NOTES

Sub-s (3): words in square brackets substituted by the Employment Relations Act 2004, s 57(1), Sch 1, para 12.

[1.471]
162 Application to be promptly determined

(1) An [employment tribunal] shall determine an application for interim relief as soon as practicable after receiving the application and, where appropriate, the requisite certificate.

(2) The tribunal shall give to the employer, not later than seven days before the hearing, a copy of the application and of any certificate, together with notice of the date, time and place of the hearing.

(3) If a request under section 160 (awards against third parties) is made three days or more before the date of the hearing, the tribunal shall also give to the person to whom the request relates, as soon as reasonably practicable, a copy of the application and of any certificate, together with notice of the date, time and place of the hearing.

(4) The tribunal shall not exercise any power it has of postponing the hearing of an application for interim relief except where it is satisfied that special circumstances exist which justify it in doing so.

NOTES

Sub-s (1): words in square brackets substituted by the Employment Rights (Dispute Resolution) Act 1998, s 1(2)(a).

[1.472]
163 Procedure on hearing of application and making of order

(1) If on hearing an application for interim relief it appears to the tribunal that it is likely that on determining the complaint to which the application relates that it will find that, by virtue of section 152, the complainant has been unfairly dismissed, the following provisions apply.

(2) The tribunal shall announce its findings and explain to both parties (if present) what powers the tribunal may exercise on the application and in what circumstances it will exercise them, and shall ask the employer (if present) whether he is willing, pending the determination or settlement of the complaint—

(a) to reinstate the employee, that is to say, to treat him in all respects as if he had not been dismissed, or

(b) if not, to re-engage him in another job on terms and conditions not less favourable than those which would have been applicable to him if he had not been dismissed.

(3) For this purpose "terms and conditions not less favourable than those which would have been applicable to him if he had not been dismissed" means as regards seniority, pension rights and other similar rights that the period prior to the dismissal shall be regarded as continuous with his employment following the dismissal.

(4) If the employer states that he is willing to reinstate the employee, the tribunal shall make an order to that effect.

(5) If the employer states that he is willing to re-engage the employee in another job, and specifies the terms and conditions on which he is willing to do so, the tribunal shall ask the employee whether he is willing to accept the job on those terms and conditions; and—

(a) if the employee is willing to accept the job on those terms and conditions, the tribunal shall make an order to that effect, and

(b) if he is not, then, if the tribunal is of the opinion that the refusal is reasonable, the tribunal shall make an order for the continuation of his contract of employment, and otherwise the tribunal shall make no order.

(6) If on the hearing of an application for interim relief the employer fails to attend before the tribunal, or states that he is unwilling either to reinstate the employee or re-engage him as mentioned in subsection (2), the tribunal shall make an order for the continuation of the employee's contract of employment.

[1.473]
164 Order for continuation of contract of employment

(1) An order under section 163 for the continuation of a contract of employment is an order that the contract of employment continue in force—

(a) for the purposes of pay or [any other benefit] derived from the employment, seniority, pension rights and other similar matters, and

(b) for the purpose of determining for any purpose the period for which the employee has been continuously employed,

from the date of its termination (whether before or after the making of the order) until the determination or settlement of the complaint.

(2) Where the tribunal makes such an order it shall specify in the order the amount which is to be paid by the employer to the employee by way of pay in respect of each normal pay period, or part of any such period, falling between the date of dismissal and the determination or settlement of the complaint.

(3) Subject as follows, the amount so specified shall be that which the employee could reasonably have been expected to earn during that period, or part, and shall be paid—

(a) in the case of payment for any such period falling wholly or partly after the making of the order, on the normal pay day for that period, and

(b) in the case of a payment for any past period, within such time as may be specified in the order.

(4) If an amount is payable in respect only of part of a normal pay period, the amount shall be calculated by reference to the whole period and reduced proportionately.

(5) Any payment made to an employee by an employer under his contract of employment, or by way of damages for breach of that contract, in respect of a normal pay period or part of any such period shall go towards discharging the employer's liability in respect of that period under subsection (2); and conversely any payment under that subsection in respect of a period shall go towards discharging any liability of the employer under, or in respect of the breach of, the contract of employment in respect of that period.

(6) If an employee, on or after being dismissed by his employer, receives a lump sum which, or part of which, is in lieu of wages but is not referable to any normal pay period, the tribunal shall take the payment into account in determining the amount of pay to be payable in pursuance of any such order.

(7) For the purposes of this section the amount which an employee could reasonably have been expected to earn, his normal pay period and the normal pay day for each such period shall be determined as if he had not been dismissed.

NOTES

Sub-s (1): words in square brackets substituted by the Trade Union Reform and Employment Rights Act 1993, s 49(2), Sch 8, para 69.

[1.474]

165 Application for variation or revocation of order

(1) At any time between the making of an order under section 163 and the determination or settlement of the complaint, the employer or the employee may apply to an [employment tribunal] for the revocation or variation of the order on the ground of a relevant change of circumstances since the making of the order.

(2) Sections 161 to 163 apply in relation to such an application as in relation to an original application for interim relief, except that—

(a) no certificate need be presented to the tribunal under section 161(3), and

(b) in the case of an application by the employer, section 162(2) (service of copy of application and notice of hearing) has effect with the substitution of a reference to the employee for the reference to the employer.

NOTES

Sub-s (1): words in square brackets substituted by the Employment Rights (Dispute Resolution) Act 1998, s 1(2)(a).

[1.475]

166 Consequences of failure to comply with order

(1) If on the application of an employee an [employment tribunal] is satisfied that the employer has not complied with the terms of an order for the reinstatement or re-engagement of the employee under section 163(4) or [(5)], the tribunal shall—

(a) make an order for the continuation of the employee's contract of employment, and

(b) order the employer to pay the employee such compensation as the tribunal considers just and equitable in all the circumstances having regard—

(i) to the infringement of the employee's right to be reinstated or re-engaged in pursuance of the order, and

(ii) to any loss suffered by the employee in consequence of the non-compliance.

(2) Section 164 applies to an order under subsection (1)(a) as in relation to an order under section 163.

(3) If on the application of an employee an [employment tribunal] is satisfied that the employer has not complied with the terms of an order for the continuation of a contract of employment, the following provisions apply.

(4) If the non-compliance consists of a failure to pay an amount by way of pay specified in the order, the tribunal shall determine the amount owed by the employer on the date of the determination.

If on that date the tribunal also determines the employee's complaint that he has been unfairly dismissed, it shall specify that amount separately from any other sum awarded to the employee.

(5) In any other case, the tribunal shall order the employer to pay the employee such compensation as the tribunal considers just and equitable in all the circumstances having regard to any loss suffered by the employee in consequence of the non-compliance.

NOTES

Sub-s (1): words in first pair of square brackets substituted by the Employment Rights (Dispute Resolution) Act 1998, s 1(2)(a); number in second pair of square brackets substituted by the Trade Union Reform and Employment Rights Act 1993, s 49(1), Sch 7, para 22.

Sub-s (3): words in square brackets substituted by the Employment Rights (Dispute Resolution) Act 1998, s 1(2)(a).

[1.476]

167 Interpretation and other supplementary provisions

(1) [Part X of the Employment Rights Act 1996] (unfair dismissal) has effect subject to the provisi of sections 152 to 166 above.

(2) Those sections shall be construed as one with that Part; and in those sections—

"complaint of unfair dismissal" means a complaint under [section 111 of the Employment Rights Act 1996];

"award of compensation for unfair dismissal" means an award of compensation for unfair dismissal under [section 112(4) or 117(3)(a)] of that Act; and

"order for reinstatement or re-engagement" means an order for reinstatement or re-engagement under [section 113] of that Act.

(3) Nothing in those sections shall be construed as conferring a right to complain of unfair dismissal from employment of a description to which that Part does not otherwise apply.

NOTES

Sub-ss (1), (2): words in square brackets substituted by the Employment Rights Act 1996, s 240, Sch 1, para 56(1), (12).

Time off for trade union duties and activities

[1.477]

168 Time off for carrying out trade union duties

(1) An employer shall permit an employee of his who is an official of an independent trade union recognised by the employer to take time off during his working hours for the purpose of carrying out any duties of his, as such an official, concerned with—

(a) negotiations with the employer related to or connected with matters falling within section 178(2) (collective bargaining) in relation to which the trade union is recognised by the employer, or

(b) the performance on behalf of employees of the employer of functions related to or connected with matters falling within that provision which the employer has agreed may be so performed by the trade union[, or

(c) receipt of information from the employer and consultation by the employer under section 188 (redundancies) or under the [Transfer of Undertakings (Protection of Employment) Regulations 2006]][, or

(d) negotiations with a view to entering into an agreement under regulation 9 of the Transfer of Undertakings (Protection of Employment) Regulations 2006 that applies to employees of the employer, or

(e) the performance on behalf of employees of the employer of functions related to or connected with the making of an agreement under that regulation.]

(2) He shall also permit such an employee to take time off during his working hours for the purpose of undergoing training in aspects of industrial relations—

(a) relevant to the carrying out of such duties as are mentioned in subsection (1), and

(b) approved by the Trades Union Congress or by the independent trade union of which he is an official.

(3) The amount of time off which an employee is to be permitted to take under this section and the purposes for which, the occasions on which and any conditions subject to which time off may be so taken are those that are reasonable in all the circumstances having regard to any relevant provisions of a Code of Practice issued by ACAS.

(4) An employee may present a complaint to an [employment tribunal] that his employer has failed to permit him to take time off as required by this section.

NOTES

Sub-s (1): para (c) and the word immediately preceding it added by the Collective Redundancies and Transfer of Undertakings (Protection of Employment) (Amendment) Regulations 1999, SI 1999/1925, reg 14; words in square brackets in para (c) substituted, and paras (d), (e) and the word immediately preceding them added, by the Transfer of Undertakings (Protection of Employment) Regulations 2006, SI 2006/246, regs 9(4), 20, Sch 2, para 1(e).

Sub-s (4): words in square brackets substituted by the Employment Rights (Dispute Resolution) Act 1998, s 1(2)(a).

Conciliation: employment tribunal proceedings under this section are "relevant proceedings" for the purposes of the conciliation provisions contained in the Employment Tribunals Act 1996, ss 18–18C; see s 18(1)(a) of the 1996 Act at **[1.757]**.

The relevant code is ACAS Code of Practice 3: Time off for Trade Union Duties and Activities (2010) at **[4.45]**.

Relevant statutory rights: the rights conferred by this section are "relevant statutory rights" for the purposes of the Employment Rights Act 1996, s 104 (dismissal on grounds of assertion of statutory right); see s 104(4)(c) of that Act at **[1.1015]**.

[1.478]

[168A Time off for union learning representatives

(1) An employer shall permit an employee of his who is—

(a) a member of an independent trade union recognised by the employer, and

(b) a learning representative of the trade union,

to take time off during his working hours for any of the following purposes.

(2) The purposes are—

(a) carrying on any of the following activities in relation to qualifying members of the trade union—

(i) analysing learning or training needs,

(ii) providing information and advice about learning or training matters,

(iii) arranging learning or training, and

(iv) promoting the value of learning or training,

(b) consulting the employer about carrying on any such activities in relation to such members of the trade union,

(c) preparing for any of the things mentioned in paragraphs (a) and (b).

(3) Subsection (1) only applies if—

(a) the trade union has given the employer notice in writing that the employee is a learning representative of the trade union, and

(b) the training condition is met in relation to him.

(4) The training condition is met if—

(a) the employee has undergone sufficient training to enable him to carry on the activities mentioned in subsection (2), and the trade union has given the employer notice in writing of that fact,

(b) the trade union has in the last six months given the employer notice in writing that the employee will be undergoing such training, or

(c) within six months of the trade union giving the employer notice in writing that the employee will be undergoing such training, the employee has done so, and the trade union has given the employer notice of that fact.

(5) Only one notice under subsection (4)(b) may be given in respect of any one employee.

(6) References in subsection (4) to sufficient training to carry out the activities mentioned in subsection (2) are to training that is sufficient for those purposes having regard to any relevant provision of a Code of Practice issued by ACAS or the Secretary of State.

(7) If an employer is required to permit an employee to take time off under subsection (1), he shall also permit the employee to take time off during his working hours for the following purposes—

(a) undergoing training which is relevant to his functions as a learning representative, and

(b) where the trade union has in the last six months given the employer notice under subsection (4)(b) in relation to the employee, undergoing such training as is mentioned in subsection (4)(a).

(8) The amount of time off which an employee is to be permitted to take under this section and the purposes for which, the occasions on which and any conditions subject to which time off may be so taken are those that are reasonable in all the circumstances having regard to any relevant provision of a Code of Practice issued by ACAS or the Secretary of State.

(9) An employee may present a complaint to an employment tribunal that his employer has failed to permit him to take time off as required by this section.

(10) In subsection (2)(a), the reference to qualifying members of the trade union is to members of the trade union—

(a) who are employees of the employer of a description in respect of which the union is recognised by the employer, and

(b) in relation to whom it is the function of the union learning representative to act as such.

(11) For the purposes of this section, a person is a learning representative of a trade union if he is appointed or elected as such in accordance with its rules.]

NOTES

Inserted by the Employment Act 2002, s 43(1), (2).

Conciliation: employment tribunal proceedings under this section are "relevant proceedings" for the purposes of the conciliation provisions contained in the Employment Tribunals Act 1996, ss 18–18C; see s 18(1)(a) of the 1996 Act at **[1.757]**.

The relevant code is ACAS Code of Practice 3: Time off for Trade Union Duties and Activities (2010) at **[4.45]**.

Relevant statutory rights: the rights conferred by this section are "relevant statutory rights" for the purposes of the Employment Rights Act 1996, s 104 (dismissal on grounds of assertion of statutory right); see s 104(4)(c) of that Act at **[1.1015]**.

Note: the Employment Act 2002 (Commencement No 4 and Transitional Provisions) Order 2003, SI 2003/1190, art 3 provides that the requirements of sub-s (3) above shall be treated as being satisfied in relation to an employee if (a) immediately before 27 April 2003 he has the function of carrying on any or all of the activities mentioned in sub-s (2) above in relation to qualifying members of the union and has had that function for a continuous period of six months or more, and (b) he acquired that function by reason of being appointed or elected, in accordance with the rules of the union, to carry it on.

[1.479]

169 Payment for time off under section 168

(1) An employer who permits an employee to take time off under section 168 [or 168A] shall pay him for the time taken off pursuant to the permission.

(2) Where the employee's remuneration for the work he would ordinarily have been doing during that time does not vary with the amount of work done, he shall be paid as if he had worked at that work for the whole of that time.

(3) Where the employee's remuneration for the work he would ordinarily have been doing during that time varies with the amount of work done, he shall be paid an amount calculated by reference to the average hourly earnings for that work.

The average hourly earnings shall be those of the employee concerned or, if no fair estimate can be made of those earnings, the average hourly earnings for work of that description of persons in comparable employment with the same employer or, if there are no such persons, a figure of average hourly earnings which is reasonable in the circumstances.

(4) A right to be paid an amount under this section does not affect any right of an employee in relation to remuneration under his contract of employment, but—

(a) any contractual remuneration paid to an employee in respect of a period of time off to which this section applies shall go towards discharging any liability of the employer under this section in respect of that period, and

(b) any payment under this section in respect of a period shall go towards discharging any liability of the employer to pay contractual remuneration in respect of that period.

(5) An employee may present a complaint to an [employment tribunal] that his employer has failed to pay him in accordance with this section.

NOTES

Sub-s (1): words in square brackets inserted by the Employment Act 2002, s 43(1), (3).

Sub-s (5): words in square brackets substituted by the Employment Rights (Dispute Resolution) Act 1998, s 1(2)(a).

Conciliation: employment tribunal proceedings under this section are "relevant proceedings" for the purposes of the conciliation provisions contained in the Employment Tribunals Act 1996, ss 18–18C; see s 18(1)(a) of the 1996 Act at **[1.757]**.

Relevant statutory rights: the rights conferred by this section are "relevant statutory rights" for the purposes of the Employment Rights Act 1996, s 104 (dismissal on grounds of assertion of statutory right); see s 104(4)(c) of that Act at **[1.1015]**.

[1.480]

170 Time off for trade union activities

(1) An employer shall permit an employee of his who is a member of an independent trade union recognised by the employer in respect of that description of employee to take time off during his working hours for the purpose of taking part in—

(a) any activities of the union, and

(b) any activities in relation to which the employee is acting as a representative of the union.

(2) The right conferred by subsection (1) does not extent to activities which themselves consist of industrial action, whether or not in contemplation or furtherance of a trade dispute.

[(2A) The right conferred by subsection (1) does not extend to time off for the purpose of acting as, or having access to services provided by, a learning representative of a trade union.

(2B) An employer shall permit an employee of his who is a member of an independent trade union recognised by the employer in respect of that description of employee to take time off during his working hours for the purpose of having access to services provided by a person in his capacity as a learning representative of the trade union.

(2C) Subsection (2B) only applies if the learning representative would be entitled to time off under subsection (1) of section 168A for the purpose of carrying on in relation to the employee activities of the kind mentioned in subsection (2) of that section.]

(3) The amount of time off which an employee is to be permitted to take under this section and the purposes for which, the occasions on which and any conditions subject to which time off may be so taken are those that are reasonable in all the circumstances having regard to any relevant provisions of a Code of Practice issued by ACAS.

(4) An employee may present a complaint to an [employment tribunal] that his employer has failed to permit him to take time off as required by this section.

[(5) For the purposes of this section—

(a) a person is a learning representative of a trade union if he is appointed or elected as such in accordance with its rules, and

(b) a person who is a learning representative of a trade union acts as such if he carries on the activities mentioned in section 168A(2) in that capacity.]

NOTES

Sub-ss (2A)–(2C), (5): inserted and added respectively by the Employment Act 2002, s 43(1), (4), (5).

Sub-s (4): words in square brackets substituted by the Employment Rights (Dispute Resolution) Act 1998, s 1(2)(a).

Code of Practice under sub-s (3): the code under the provisions contained in this subsection is ACAS Code of Practice 3: Time off for Trade Union Duties and Activities (2010) at **[4.45]**.

Conciliation: employment tribunal proceedings under this section are "relevant proceedings" for the purposes of the conciliation provisions contained in the Employment Tribunals Act 1996, ss 18–18C; see s 18(1)(a) of the 1996 Act at **[1.757]**.

Relevant statutory rights: the rights conferred by this section are "relevant statutory rights" for the purposes of the Employment Rights Act 1996, s 104 (dismissal on grounds of assertion of statutory right); see s 104(4)(c) of that Act at **[1.1015]**.

[1.481]

171 Time limit for proceedings

[(1)] An [employment tribunal] shall not consider a complaint under section 168, [168A,] 169 or 170 unless it is presented to the tribunal—

(a) within three months of the date when the failure occurred, or

(b) where the tribunal is satisfied that it was not reasonably practicable for the complaint to be presented within that period, within such further period as the tribunal considers reasonable.

[(2) Section 292A (extension of time limits to facilitate conciliation before institution of proceedings) applies for the purposes of subsection (1)(a).]

NOTES

The existing provision was numbered as sub-s (1) and sub-s (2) was added, by the Enterprise and Regulatory Reform Act 2013, s 8, Sch 2, paras 1, 9.

In sub-s (1), the words in the first pair of square brackets were substituted by the Employment Rights (Dispute Resolution) Act 1998, s 1(2)(a), and the number in the second pair of square brackets was inserted by the Employment Act 2002, s 53, Sch 7, paras 18, 19.

[1.482]
172 Remedies
(1) Where the tribunal finds a complaint under section 168[, 168A] or 170 is well-founded, it shall make a declaration to that effect and may make an award of compensation to be paid by the employer to the employee.
(2) The amount of the compensation shall be such as the tribunal considers just and equitable in all the circumstances having regard to the employer's default in failing to permit time off to be taken by the employee and to any loss sustained by the employee which is attributable to the matters complained of.
(3) Where on a complaint under section 169 the tribunal finds that the employer has failed to pay the employee in accordance with that section, it shall order him to pay the amount which it finds to be due.

NOTES
Sub-s (1): number in square brackets inserted by the Employment Act 2002, s 53, Sch 7, paras 18, 20.

[1.483]
[172A Publication requirements in relation to facility time
(1) A Minister of the Crown may by regulations made by statutory instrument require relevant public sector employers to publish any information within subsection (3).
(2) An employer is a relevant public sector employer if the employer—
(a) is a public authority specified, or of a description specified, in the regulations, and
(b) has at least one employee who is a relevant union official.
[(2A) But regulations under subsection (1) may not specify—
(a) a devolved Welsh authority, or
(b) a description of public authority that applies to a devolved Welsh authority.]
(3) The information that is within this subsection is information relating to facility time for relevant union officials including, in particular—
(a) how many of an employer's employees are relevant union officials, or relevant union officials within specified categories;
(b) the total amount spent by an employer in a specified period on paying relevant union officials for facility time, or for specified categories of facility time;
(c) the percentage of an employer's total pay bill for a specified period spent on paying relevant union officials for facility time, or for specified categories of facility time;
(d) the percentage of the aggregate amount of facility time taken by an employer's relevant union officials in a specified period that was attributable to specified categories of duties or activities;
(e) information relating to facilities provided by an employer for use by relevant union officials in connection with facility time.
(4) In subsection (3) "specified" means specified in the regulations.
(5) The regulations may make provision—
(a) as to the times or intervals at which the information is to be published;
(b) as to the form in which the information is to be published.
(6) The regulations may make different provision for different employers or different categories of employer.
(7) In this section a "relevant union official" means—
(a) a trade union official;
(b) a learning representative of a trade union, within the meaning given by section 168A(11);
(c) a safety representative appointed under regulations made under section 2(4) of the Health and Safety at Work etc Act 1974.
(8) In this section "facility time" means time off taken by a relevant union official that is permitted by the official's employer under—
(a) section 168, section 168A or section 170(1)(b);
(b) section 10(6) of the Employment Relations Act 1999;
(c) regulations made under section 2(4) of the Health and Safety at Work etc Act 1974.
(9) The regulations may provide, in relation to a body or other person that is not a public authority but has functions of a public nature and is funded wholly or mainly from public funds, that the body or other person is to be treated as a public authority for the purposes of subsection (2).
(10) The regulations may make provision specifying the person or other entity that is to be treated for the purposes of this section as the employer of a relevant union official who is employed by the Crown.
(11) The regulations may—
(a) deem a category of persons holding an office or employment under the Crown (or two or more such categories taken together) to be an entity for the purposes of provision made under subsection (10);
(b) make different provision under subsection (10) for different categories of persons holding an office or employment under the Crown.
(12) No regulations containing provision made by virtue of subsection (9) shall be made unless a draft of the statutory instrument containing them has been laid before Parliament and approved by a resolution of each House.
(13) Regulations under this section to which subsection (12) does not apply shall be subject to annulment in pursuance of a resolution of either House of Parliament.]

NOTES
Commencement: 1 March 2017.
Inserted by the Trade Union Act 2016, s 13, as from 1 March 2017.
Sub-s (2A): inserted by the Trade Union (Wales) Act 2017, s 1(1), (3), as from 13 September 2017.

Regulations: Trade Union (Facility Time Publication Requirements) Regulations 2017, SI 2017/328 at **[2.1994]**.

[1.484]

[172B Reserve powers in relation to facility time

(1) After the end of the period of three years beginning with the day on which the first regulations under section 172A come into force, a Minister of the Crown may exercise the reserve powers (see subsection (3)) if the Minister considers it appropriate to do so having regard to—

(a) information published by employers in accordance with publication requirements;

(b) the cost to public funds of facility time in relation to each of those employers;

(c) the nature of the various undertakings carried on by those employers;

(d) any particular features of those undertakings that are relevant to the reasonableness of the amount of facility time;

(e) any other matters that the Minister thinks relevant.

(2) The reserve powers may not be exercised so as to apply to any particular employer unless—

(a) a Minister of the Crown has given notice in writing to the employer—

(i) setting out the Minister's concerns about the amount of facility time in the employer's case, and

(ii) informing the employer that the Minister is considering exercising the reserve powers in relation to that employer;

(b) the employer has had a reasonable opportunity to respond to the notice under paragraph (a) and to take any action that may be appropriate in view of the concerns set out in it;

and the powers may not be exercised until after the end of the period of 12 months beginning with the day on which the notice under paragraph (a) was given.

(3) The reserve powers are powers to make regulations—

(a) applying to relevant public sector employers on whom the publication requirements were imposed, and

(b) containing any provision that the Minister considers appropriate for the purpose of ensuring that, in each period specified by the regulations, the percentage of an employer's total pay bill spent on paying relevant union officials for facility time does not exceed a percentage that is so specified.

(4) The regulations may, in particular, make provision restricting rights of relevant union officials to facility time by amending or otherwise modifying any of the following—

(a) section 168 or 168A;

(b) section 10 of the Employment Relations Act 1999;

(c) regulations made under section 2(4) of the Health and Safety at Work etc Act 1974.

(5) The regulations may make provision as to the calculation of working time, of paid facility time, or of an employer's total pay bill.

(6) The regulations may impose requirements on employers in relation to whom the reserve powers are exercised to publish any further information that the Minister considers appropriate.

(7) Where requirements are imposed under subsection (6) the regulations may make provision—

(a) as to the times or intervals at which the further information is to be published;

(b) as to the form in which the further information is to be published.

(8) The regulations may provide that some or all of their provisions do not apply—

(a) in cases specified by the regulations, or

(b) if a person specified in the regulations is satisfied that conditions that are so specified are met.

(9) The regulations may confer power on a Minister of the Crown, by notice in writing to a particular employer, to suspend the application of the regulations to that employer for such period and to such extent as the Minister may specify in the notice.

(10) The regulations may—

(a) make provision in relation to any or all of the employers in relation to which the reserve powers are exercisable;

(b) make different provision for different employers or different categories of employer;

(c) make transitional provision in connection with the coming into force of any provision of the regulations;

(d) make consequential provision amending or otherwise modifying section 170, contracts of employment or collective agreements.

(11) In this section—

(a) "publication requirements" means requirements imposed under section 172A or subsection (6);

(b) "relevant public sector employer" has the same meaning as in section 172A, read with any regulations made under subsection (9) of that section;

(c) "relevant union official" and "facility time" have the same meaning as in section 172A.

(12) Subsections (10) and (11) of section 172A apply for the purposes of this section as they apply for the purposes of that section.

(13) Regulations under this section shall be made by statutory instrument.

(14) No regulations under this section shall be made unless a draft of them has been laid before Parliament and approved by a resolution of each House of Parliament.]

NOTES

Commencement: to be appointed.

Inserted by the Trade Union Act 2016, s 14, as from a day to be appointed.

Regulations: as of 15 May 2019, no Regulations had been made under this section.

[1.485]
173 Interpretation and other supplementary provisions
(1) For the purposes of sections 168[, 168A] and 170 the working hours of an employee shall be taken to be any time when in accordance with his contract of employment he is required to be at work.
(2) The remedy of an employee for infringement of the rights conferred on him by section 168, [168A,] 169 or 170 is by way of complaint to an [employment tribunal] in accordance with this Part, and not otherwise.
[(3) The Secretary of State may by order made by statutory instrument amend section 168A for the purpose of changing the purposes for which an employee may take time off under that section.
(4) No order may be made under subsection (3) unless a draft of the order has been laid before and approved by resolution of each House of Parliament.]

NOTES

Sub-s (1): number in square brackets inserted by the Employment Act 2002, s 53, Sch 7, paras 18, 21(a).

Sub-s (2): number in first pair of square brackets inserted by the Employment Act 2002, s 53, Sch 7, paras 18, 21(b); words in second pair of square brackets substituted by the Employment Rights (Dispute Resolution) Act 1998, s 1(2)(a).

Sub-ss (3), (4): added by the Employment Act 2002, s 43(1), (6).

Orders: as of 15 May 2019, no Orders had been made under this section.

[Right to membership of trade union

[1.486]
174 Right not to be excluded or expelled from union
(1) An individual shall not be excluded or expelled from a trade union unless the exclusion or expulsion is permitted by this section.
(2) The exclusion or expulsion of an individual from a trade union is permitted by this section if (and only if)—
- (a) he does not satisfy, or no longer satisfies, an enforceable membership requirement contained in the rules of the union,
- (b) he does not qualify, or no longer qualifies, for membership of the union by reason of the union operating only in a particular part or particular parts of Great Britain,
- (c) in the case of a union whose purpose is the regulation of relations between its members and one particular employer or a number of particular employers who are associated, he is not, or is no longer, employed by that employer or one of those employers, or
- (d) the exclusion or expulsion is entirely attributable to [conduct of his (other than excluded conduct) and the conduct to which it is wholly or mainly attributable is not protected conduct].

(3) A requirement in relation to membership of a union is "enforceable" for the purposes of subsection (2)(a) if it restricts membership solely by reference to one or more of the following criteria—
- (a) employment in a specified trade, industry or profession,
- (b) occupational description (including grade, level or category of appointment), and
- (c) possession of specified trade, industrial or professional qualifications or work experience.

[(4) For the purposes of subsection (2)(d) "excluded conduct", in relation to an individual, means—
- (a) conduct which consists in his being or ceasing to be, or having been or ceased to be, a member of another trade union,
- (b) conduct which consists in his being or ceasing to be, or having been or ceased to be, employed by a particular employer or at a particular place, or
- (c) conduct to which section 65 (conduct for which an individual may not be disciplined by a union) applies or would apply if the references in that section to the trade union which is relevant for the purposes of that section were references to any trade union.

(4A) For the purposes of subsection (2)(d) "protected conduct" is conduct which consists in the individual's being or ceasing to be, or having been or ceased to be, a member of a political party.
(4B) Conduct which consists of activities undertaken by an individual as a member of a political party is not conduct falling within subsection (4A).]
[(4C) Conduct which consists in an individual's being or having been a member of a political party is not conduct falling within subsection (4A) if membership of that political party is contrary to—
- (a) a rule of the trade union, or
- (b) an objective of the trade union.

(4D) For the purposes of subsection (4C)(b) in the case of conduct consisting in an individual's being a member of a political party, an objective is to be disregarded—
- (a) in relation to an exclusion, if it is not reasonably practicable for the objective to be ascertained by a person working in the same trade, industry or profession as the individual;
- (b) in relation to an expulsion, if it is not reasonably practicable for the objective to be ascertained by a member of the union.

(4E) For the purposes of subsection (4C)(b) in the case of conduct consisting in an individual's having been a member of a political party, an objective is to be disregarded—
- (a) in relation to an exclusion, if at the time of the conduct it was not reasonably practicable for the objective to be ascertained by a person working in the same trade, industry or profession as the individual;
- (b) in relation to an expulsion, if at the time of the conduct it was not reasonably practicable for the objective to be ascertained by a member of the union.

(4F) Where the exclusion or expulsion of an individual from a trade union is wholly or mainly attributable to conduct which consists of an individual's being or having been a member of a political party but which by virtue of subsection (4C) is not conduct falling within subsection (4A), the exclusion or expulsion is not permitted by virtue of subsection (2)(d) if any one or more of the conditions in subsection (4G) apply.

(4G) Those conditions are—

(a) the decision to exclude or expel is taken otherwise than in accordance with the union's rules;

(b) the decision to exclude or expel is taken unfairly;

(c) the individual would lose his livelihood or suffer other exceptional hardship by reason of not being, or ceasing to be, a member of the union.

(4H) For the purposes of subsection (4G)(b) a decision to exclude or expel an individual is taken unfairly if (and only if)—

(a) before the decision is taken the individual is not given—

(i) notice of the proposal to exclude or expel him and the reasons for that proposal, and

(ii) a fair opportunity to make representations in respect of that proposal, or

(b) representations made by the individual in respect of that proposal are not considered fairly.]

(5) An individual who claims that he has been excluded or expelled from a trade union in contravention of this section may present a complaint to an [employment tribunal].]

NOTES

Substituted, together with the preceding heading, by the Trade Union Reform and Employment Rights Act 1993, s 14.

Sub-s (2): words in square brackets in para (d) substituted by the Employment Relations Act 2004, s 33(1), (2), (7).

Sub-ss (4), (4A), (4B): substituted, for the original sub-s (4), by the Employment Relations Act 2004, s 33(1), (3), (7).

Sub-ss (4C)–(4H): inserted by the Employment Act 2008, s 19(1), (2).

Sub-s (5): words in square brackets substituted by the Employment Rights (Dispute Resolution) Act 1998, s 1(2)(a).

Conciliation: employment tribunal proceedings under this section are "relevant proceedings" for the purposes of the conciliation provisions contained in the Employment Tribunals Act 1996, ss 18–18C; see s 18(1)(a) of the 1996 Act at **[1.757]**.

[1.487]

[175 Time limit for proceedings

[(1)] An [employment tribunal] shall not entertain a complaint under section 174 unless it is presented—

(a) before the end of the period of six months beginning with the date of the exclusion or expulsion, or

(b) where the tribunal is satisfied that it was not reasonably practicable for the complaint to be presented before the end of that period, within such further period as the tribunal considers reasonable.

[(2) Section 292A (extension of time limits to facilitate conciliation before institution of proceedings) applies for the purposes of subsection (1)(a).]]

NOTES

Substituted by the Trade Union Reform and Employment Rights Act 1993, s 14.

The existing provision was numbered as sub-s (1) and sub-s (2) was added, by the Enterprise and Regulatory Reform Act 2013, s 8, Sch 2, paras 1, 10.

The words in square brackets in sub-s (1) were substituted by the Employment Rights (Dispute Resolution) Act 1998, s 1(2)(a).

[1.488]

[176 Remedies

(1) Where the [employment tribunal] finds a complaint under section 174 is well-founded, it shall make a declaration to that effect.

[(1A) If a tribunal makes a declaration under subsection (1) and it appears to the tribunal that the exclusion or expulsion was mainly attributable to conduct falling within section 174(4A) it shall make a declaration to that effect.

(1B) If a tribunal makes a declaration under subsection (1A) and it appears to the tribunal that the other conduct to which the exclusion or expulsion was attributable consisted wholly or mainly of conduct of the complainant which was contrary to—

(a) a rule of the union, or

(b) an objective of the union,

it shall make a declaration to that effect.

(1C) For the purposes of subsection (1B), it is immaterial whether the complainant was a member of the union at the time of the conduct contrary to the rule or objective.

(1D) A declaration by virtue of subsection (1B)(b) shall not be made unless the union shows that, at the time of the conduct of the complainant which was contrary to the objective in question, it was reasonably practicable for that objective to be ascertained—

(a) if the complainant was not at that time a member of the union, by [a person working in the same trade, industry or profession as the complainant], and

(b) if he was at that time a member of the union, by a member of the union.]

(2) An individual whose complaint has been declared to be well-founded may make an application [to an employment tribunal] for an award of compensation to be paid to him by the union.

. . .

(3) The application shall not be entertained if made—

(a) before the end of the period of four weeks beginning with the date of the declaration [under subsection (1)], or
(b) after the end of the period of six months beginning with that date.

(4) The amount of compensation awarded shall, subject to the following provisions, be such as the [employment tribunal] . . . considers just and equitable in all the circumstances.

(5) Where the [employment tribunal] . . . finds that the exclusion or expulsion complained of was to any extent caused or contributed to by the action of the applicant, it shall reduce the amount of the compensation by such proportion as it considers just and equitable having regard to that finding.

(6) The amount of compensation calculated in accordance with subsections (4) and (5) shall not exceed the aggregate of—
(a) an amount equal to thirty times the limit for the time being imposed by [section 227(1)(a) of the Employment Rights Act 1996] (maximum amount of a week's pay for basic award in unfair dismissal cases), and
(b) an amount equal to the limit for the time being imposed by [section 113] of that Act (maximum compensatory award in such cases);

. . .

[(6A) If on the date on which the application was made the applicant had not been admitted or re-admitted to the union, the award shall not be less than [£9,787].

(6B) Subsection (6A) does not apply in a case where the tribunal which made the declaration under subsection (1) also made declarations under subsections (1A) and (1B).]

(7), (8) . . .]

NOTES

Substituted by the Trade Union Reform and Employment Rights Act 1993, s 14.

Sub-s (1): words in square brackets substituted by the Employment Rights (Dispute Resolution) Act 1998, s 1(2)(a).

Sub-ss (1A)–(1C): inserted, together with sub-s (1D), by the Employment Relations Act 2004, s 33(1), (4), (7).

Sub-s (1D): inserted as noted above; words in square brackets in para (a) substituted by the Employment Act 2008, s 19(1), (3).

Sub-s (2): words in square brackets inserted, and words omitted repealed, by the Employment Relations Act 2004, ss 34(7), (8)(b), 57(2), Sch 2.

Sub-s (3): words in square brackets in para (a) inserted by the Employment Relations Act 2004, s 33(1), (5), (7).

Sub-ss (4), (5): words in square brackets substituted by the Employment Rights (Dispute Resolution) Act 1998, s 1(2)(a); words omitted repealed by the Employment Relations Act 2004, ss 34(7), (9), (10), 57(2).

Sub-s (6): words in square brackets substituted by the Employment Rights Act 1996, s 240, Sch 1, para 56(1), (13); words omitted repealed by the Employment Relations Act 2004, ss 34(7), (11), 57(2), Sch 2.

Sub-s (6A): inserted, together with sub-s (6B), by the Employment Relations Act 2004, s 33(1), (6), (7); sum in square brackets substituted by the Employment Rights (Increase of Limits) Order 2019, SI 2019/324, art 3, Schedule, as from 6 April 2019, in relation to any case where the appropriate date (as defined in the order) falls on or after that date (see SI 2019/324, art 4 at **[2.2117]**). The previous sums were: £9,474 (as from 6 April 2018 (see SI 2018/194 (revoked)); £9,118, as from 6 April 2017 (see SI 2017/175 (revoked)); and £8,939, as from 6 April 2016 (see SI 2016/288 (revoked)). This sum may be further varied by the Secretary of State, see the Employment Relations Act 1999, s 34(1)(g) at **[1.1258]**.

Sub-s (6B): inserted as noted above.

Sub-ss (7), (8): repealed by the Employment Relations Act 1999, ss 36(1)(b), 44, Sch 9(10).

[1.489]

[177 Interpretation and other supplementary provisions

(1) For the purposes of section 174—
(a) "trade union" does not include an organisation falling within paragraph (b) of section 1,
(b) "conduct" includes statements, acts and omissions, and
(c) "employment" includes any relationship whereby an individual personally does work or performs services for another person (related expressions being construed accordingly).

(2) For the purposes of sections 174 to 176—
(a) if an individual's application for membership of a trade union is neither granted nor rejected before the end of the period within which it might reasonably have been expected to be granted if it was to be granted, he shall be treated as having been excluded from the union on the last day of that period, and
(b) an individual who under the rules of a trade union ceases to be a member of the union on the happening of an event specified in the rules shall be treated as having been expelled from the union.

(3) The remedy of an individual for infringement of the rights conferred by section 174 is by way of a complaint to an [employment tribunal] in accordance with that section, sections 175 and 176 and this section, and not otherwise.

(4) Where a complaint relating to an expulsion which is presented under section 174 is declared to be well-founded, no complaint in respect of the expulsion shall be presented or proceeded with under section 66 (complaint of infringement of right not to be unjustifiably disciplined).

(5) The rights conferred by section 174 are in addition to, and not in substitution for, any right which exists apart from that section; and, subject to subsection (4), nothing in that section, section 175 or 176 or this section affects any remedy for infringement of any such right.]

NOTES

Substituted by the Trade Union Reform and Employment Rights Act 1993, s 14.

Sub-s (3): words in square brackets substituted by the Employment Rights (Dispute Resolution) Act 1998, s 1(2)(a).

PART IV
INDUSTRIAL RELATIONS
CHAPTER I COLLECTIVE BARGAINING

Introductory

[1.490]

178 Collective agreements and collective bargaining

(1) In this Act "collective agreement" means any agreement or arrangement made by or on behalf of one or more trade unions and one or more employers or employers' associations and relating to one or more of the matters specified below; and "collective bargaining" means negotiations relating to or connected with one or more of those matters.

(2) The matters referred to above are—

(a) terms and conditions of employment, or the physical conditions in which any workers are required to work;

(b) engagement or non-engagement, or termination or suspension of employment or the duties of employment, of one or more workers;

(c) allocation of work or the duties of employment between workers or groups of workers;

(d) matters of discipline;

(e) a worker's membership or non-membership of a trade union;

(f) facilities for officials of trade unions; and

(g) machinery for negotiation or consultation, and other procedures, relating to any of the above matters, including the recognition by employers or employers' associations of the right of a trade union to represent workers in such negotiation or consultation or in the carrying out of such procedures.

(3) In this Act "recognition", in relation to a trade union, means the recognition of the union by an employer, or two or more associated employers, to any extent, for the purpose of collective bargaining; and "recognised" and other related expressions shall be construed accordingly.

Enforceability of collective agreements

[1.491]

179 Whether agreement intended to be a legally enforceable contract

(1) A collective agreement shall be conclusively presumed not to have been intended by the parties to be a legally enforceable contract unless the agreement—

(a) is in writing, and

(b) contains a provision which (however expressed) states that the parties intend that the agreement shall be a legally enforceable contract.

(2) A collective agreement which does satisfy those conditions shall be conclusively presumed to have been intended by the parties to be a legally enforceable contract.

(3) If a collective agreement is in writing and contains a provision which (however expressed) states that the parties intend that one or more parts of the agreement specified in that provision, but not the whole of the agreement, shall be a legally enforceable contract, then—

(a) the specified part or parts shall be conclusively presumed to have been intended by the parties to be a legally enforceable contract, and

(b) the remainder of the agreement shall be conclusively presumed not to have been intended by the parties to be such a contract.

(4) A part of a collective agreement which by virtue of subsection (3)(b) is not a legally enforceable contract may be referred to for the purpose of interpreting a party of the agreement which is such a contract.

[1.492]

180 Effect of provisions restricting right to take industrial action

(1) Any terms of a collective agreement which prohibit or restrict the right of workers to engage in a strike or other industrial action, or have the effect of prohibiting or restricting that right, shall not form part of any contract between a worker and the person for whom he works unless the following conditions are met.

(2) The conditions are that the collective agreement—

(a) is in writing,

(b) contains a provision expressly stating that those terms shall or may be incorporated in such a contract,

(c) is reasonably accessible at his place of work to the worker to whom it applies and is available for him to consult during working hours, and

(d) is one where each trade union which is a party to the agreement is an independent trade union;

and that the contract with the worker expressly or impliedly incorporates those terms in the contract.

(3) The above provisions have effect notwithstanding anything in section 179 and notwithstanding any provision to the contrary in any agreement (including a collective agreement or a contract with any worker).

Disclosure of information for purposes of collective bargaining

[1.493]

181 General duty of employers to disclose information

(1) An employer who recognises an independent trade union shall, for the purposes of all stages of collective bargaining about matters, and in relation to descriptions of workers, in respect of which the union is recognised by him, disclose to representatives of the union, on request, the information required by this section.

In this section and sections 182 to 185 "representative", in relation to a trade union, means an official or other person authorised by the union to carry on such collective bargaining.

(2) The information to be disclosed is all information relating to the employer's undertaking [(including information relating to use of agency workers in that undertaking)] which is in his possession, or that of an associated employer, and is information—

(a) without which the trade union representatives would be to a material extent impeded in carrying on collective bargaining with him, and

(b) which it would be in accordance with good industrial relations practice that he should disclose to them for the purposes of collective bargaining.

(3) A request by trade union representatives for information under this section shall, if the employer so requests, be in writing or be confirmed in writing.

(4) In determining what would be in accordance with good industrial relations practice, regard shall be had to the relevant provisions of any Code of Practice issued by ACAS, but not so as to exclude any other evidence of what that practice is.

(5) Information which an employer is required by virtue of this section to disclose to trade union representatives shall, if they so request, be disclosed or confirmed in writing.

NOTES

Sub-s (2): words in square brackets inserted by the Agency Workers Regulations 2010, SI 2010/93, reg 25, Sch 2, Pt 1, paras 1, 3.

Code of Practice for the purposes of sub-s (4): see ACAS Code of Practice 2: Disclosure of Information to Trade Unions for Collective Bargaining Purposes (1998) at **[4.37]**.

Modified as noted to s 146 at **[1.458]**.

[1.494]

182 Restrictions on general duty

(1) An employer is not required by section 181 to disclose information—

(a) the disclosure of which would be against the interests of national security, or

(b) which he could not disclose without contravening a prohibition imposed by or under an enactment, or

(c) which has been communicated to him in confidence, or which he has otherwise obtained in consequence of the confidence reposed in him by another person, or

(d) which relates specifically to an individual (unless that individual has consented to its being disclosed), or

(e) the disclosure of which would cause substantial injury to his undertaking for reasons other than its effect on collective bargaining, or

(f) obtained by him for the purpose of bringing, prosecuting or defending any legal proceedings.

In formulating the provisions of any Code of Practice relating to the disclosure of information, ACAS shall have regard to the provisions of this subsection.

(2) In the performance of his duty under section 181 an employer is not required—

(a) to produce, or allow inspection of, any document (other than a document prepared for the purpose of conveying or confirming the information) or to make a copy of or extracts from any document, or

(b) to compile or assemble any information where the compilation or assembly would involve an amount of work or expenditure out of reasonable proportion to the value of the information in the conduct of collective bargaining.

NOTES

Modified as noted to s 146 at **[1.458]**.

[1.495]

183 Complaint of failure to disclose information

(1) A trade union may present a complaint to the Central Arbitration Committee that an employer has failed—

(a) to disclose to representatives of the union information which he was required to disclose to them by section 181, or

(b) to confirm such information in writing in accordance with that section.

The complaint must be in writing and in such form as the Committee may require.

(2) If on receipt of a complaint the Committee is of the opinion that it is reasonably likely to be settled by conciliation, it shall refer the complaint to ACAS and shall notify the trade union and employer accordingly, whereupon ACAS shall seek to promote a settlement of the matter.

If a complaint so referred is not settled or withdrawn and ACAS is of the opinion that further attempts at conciliation are unlikely to result in a settlement, it shall inform the Committee of its opinion.

(3) If the complaint is not referred to ACAS or, if it is so referred, on ACAS informing the Committee of its opinion that further attempts at conciliation are unlikely to result in a settlement, the Committee shall proceed to hear and determine the complaint and shall make a declaration stating whether it finds the complaint well-founded, wholly or in part, and stating the reasons for its findings.
(4) On the hearing of a complaint any person who the Committee considers has a proper interest in the complaint is entitled to be heard by the Committee, but a failure to accord a hearing to a person other than the trade union and employer directly concerned does not affect the validity of any decision of the Committee in those proceedings.
(5) If the Committee finds the complaint wholly or partly well founded, the declaration shall specify—
(a) the information in respect of which the Committee finds that the complaint is well founded,
(b) the date (or, if more than one, the earliest date) on which the employer refused or failed to disclose or, as the case may be, to confirm in writing, any of the information in question, and
(c) a period (not being less than one week from the date of the declaration) within which the employer ought to disclose that information, or, as the case may be, to confirm it in writing.
(6) On a hearing of a complaint under this section a certificate signed by or on behalf of a Minister of the Crown and certifying that a particular request for information could not be complied with except by disclosing information the disclosure of which would have been against the interests of national security shall be conclusive evidence of that fact.

A document which purports to be such a certificate shall be taken to be such a certificate unless the contrary is proved.

NOTES

Modified as noted to s 146 at **[1.458]**.

[1.496]

184 Further complaint of failure to comply with declaration

(1) After the expiration of the period specified in a declaration under section 183(5)(c) the trade union may present a further complaint to the Central Arbitration Committee that the employer has failed to disclose or, as the case may be, to confirm in writing to representatives of the union information specified in the declaration.

The complaint must be in writing and in such form as the Committee may require.
(2) On receipt of a further complaint the Committee shall proceed to hear and determine the complaint and shall make a declaration stating whether they find the complaint well-founded, wholly or in part, and stating the reasons for their finding.
(3) On the hearing of a further complaint any person who the Committee consider has a proper interest in that complaint shall be entitled to be heard by the Committee, but a failure to accord a hearing to a person other than the trade union and employer directly concerned shall not affect the validity of any decision of the Committee in those proceedings.
(4) If the Committee find the further complaint wholly or partly well-founded the declaration shall specify the information in respect of which the Committee find that that complaint is well-founded.

NOTES

Modified as noted to s 146 at **[1.458]**.

[1.497]

185 Determination of claim and award

(1) On or after presenting a further complaint under section 184 the trade union may present to the Central Arbitration Committee a claim, in writing, in respect of one or more descriptions of employees (but not workers who are not employees) specified in the claim that their contracts should include the terms and conditions specified in the claim.
(2) The right to present a claim expires if the employer discloses or, as the case may be, confirms in writing, to representatives of the trade union the information specified in the declaration under section 183(5) or 184(4); and a claim presented shall be treated as withdrawn if the employer does so before the Committee make an award on the claim.
(3) If the Committee find, or have found, the further complaint wholly or partly well-founded, they may, after hearing the parties, make an award that in respect of any description of employees specified in the claim the employer shall, from a specified date, observe either—
(a) the terms and conditions specified in the claim; or
(b) other terms and conditions which the Committee consider appropriate.

The date specified may be earlier than that on which the award is made but not earlier than the date specified in accordance with section 183(5)(b) in the declaration made by the Committee on the original complaint.
(4) An award shall be made only in respect of a description of employees, and shall comprise only terms and conditions relating to matters in respect of which the trade union making the claim is recognised by the employer.
(5) Terms and conditions which by an award under this section an employer is required to observe in respect of an employee have effect as part of the employee's contract of employment as from the date specified in the award, except in so far as they are superseded or varied—
(a) by a subsequent award under this section,
(b) by a collective agreement between the employer and the union for the time being representing that employee, or
(c) by express or implied agreement between the employee and the employer so far as that agreement effects an improvement in terms and conditions having effect by virtue of the award.

(6) Where—
- (a) by virtue of any enactment, other than one contained in this section, providing for minimum remuneration or terms and conditions, a contract of employment is to have effect as modified by an award, order or other instrument under that enactment, and
- (b) by virtue of an award under this section any terms and conditions are to have effect as part of that contract,

that contract shall have effect in accordance with that award, order or other instrument or in accordance with the award under this section, whichever is the more favourable, in respect of any terms and conditions of that contract, to the employee.

(7) No award may be made under this section in respect of terms and conditions of employment which are fixed by virtue of any enactment.

NOTES

Modified as noted to s 146 at **[1.458]**.

Prohibition of union recognition requirements

[1.498]

186 Recognition requirement in contract for goods or services void

A term or condition of a contract for the supply of goods or services is void in so far as it purports to require a party to the contract—
- (a) to recognise one or more trade unions (whether or not named in the contract) for the purpose of negotiating on behalf of workers, or any class of worker, employed by him, or
- (b) to negotiate or consult with, or with an official of, one or more trade unions (whether or not so named).

[1.499]

187 Refusal to deal on grounds of union exclusion prohibited

(1) A person shall not refuse to deal with a supplier or prospective supplier of goods or services if the ground or one of the grounds for his action is that the person against whom it is taken does not, or is not likely to—
- (a) recognise one or more trade unions for the purpose of negotiating on behalf of workers, or any class of worker, employed by him, or
- (b) negotiate or consult with, or with an official of, one or more trade unions.

(2) A person refuses to deal with a person if—
- (a) where he maintains (in whatever form) a list of approved suppliers of goods or services, or of persons from whom tenders for the supply of goods or services may be invited, he fails to include the name of that person in that list; or
- (b) in relation to a proposed contract for the supply of goods or services—
  - (i) he excludes that person from the group of persons from whom tenders for the supply of the goods or services are invited, or
  - (ii) he fails to permit that person to submit such a tender; or
  - [(iii)] he otherwise determines not to enter into a contract with that person for the supply of the goods or services [or
- (c) he terminates a contract with that person for the supply of goods or services.]

(3) The obligation to comply with this section is a duty owed to the person with whom there is a refusal to deal and to any other person who may be adversely affected by its contravention; and a breach of the duty is actionable accordingly (subject to the defences and other incidents applying to actions for breach of statutory duty).

NOTES

Sub-s (2): original para (c) renumbered as sub-para (iii) of para (b), and new para (c) and the word immediately preceding it added, by the Trade Union Reform and Employment Rights Act 1993, s 49(1), Sch 7, para 23.

CHAPTER II PROCEDURE FOR HANDLING REDUNDANCIES

Duty of employer to consult . . . representatives

[1.500]

188 Duty of employer to consult . . . representatives

[(1) Where an employer is proposing to dismiss as redundant 20 or more employees at one establishment within a period of 90 days or less, the employer shall consult about the dismissals all the persons who are appropriate representatives of any of the employees who may be [affected by the proposed dismissals or may be affected by measures taken in connection with those dismissals.]

(1A) The consultation shall begin in good time and in any event—
- (a) where the employer is proposing to dismiss 100 or more employees as mentioned in subsection (1), at least [45 days], and
- (b) otherwise, at least 30 days,

before the first of the dismissals takes effect.

[(1B) For the purposes of this section the appropriate representatives of any affected employees are—
- (a) if the employees are of a description in respect of which an independent trade union is recognised by their employer, representatives of the trade union, or
- (b) in any other case, whichever of the following employee representatives the employer chooses:—

(i) employee representatives appointed or elected by the affected employees otherwise than for the purposes of this section, who (having regard to the purposes for and the method by which they were appointed or elected) have authority from those employees to receive information and to be consulted about the proposed dismissals on their behalf;

(ii) employee representatives elected by the affected employees, for the purposes of this section, in an election satisfying the requirements of section 188A(1).]

(2) The consultation shall include consultation about ways of—

(a) avoiding the dismissals,

(b) reducing the numbers of employees to be dismissed, and

(c) mitigating the consequences of the dismissals,

and shall be undertaken by the employer with a view to reaching agreement with the appropriate representatives.]

(3) In determining how many employees an employer is proposing to dismiss as redundant no account shall be taken of employees in respect of whose proposed dismissals consultation has already begun.

(4) For the purposes of the consultation the employer shall disclose in writing to the [appropriate] representatives—

(a) the reasons for his proposals,

(b) the numbers and descriptions of employees whom it is proposed to dismiss as redundant,

(c) the total number of employees of any such description employed by the employer at the establishment in question,

(d) the proposed method of selecting the employees who may be dismissed, . . .

(e) the proposed method of carrying out the dismissals, with due regard to any agreed procedure, including the period over which the dismissals are to take effect [. . .

(f) the proposed method of calculating the amount of any redundancy payments to be made (otherwise than in compliance with an obligation imposed by or by virtue of any enactment) to employees who may be dismissed],

[(g) the number of agency workers working temporarily for and under the supervision and direction of the employer,

(h) the parts of the employer's undertaking in which those agency workers are working, and

(i) the type of work those agency workers are carrying out].

(5) That information shall be [given to each of the appropriate representatives by being delivered to them], or sent by post to an address notified by them to the employer, or [in the case of representatives of a trade union)] sent by post to the union at the address of its head or main office.

[(5A) The employer shall allow the appropriate representatives access to [the affected employees] and shall afford to those representatives such accommodation and other facilities as may be appropriate.]

(6) . . .

(7) If in any case there are special circumstances which render it not reasonably practicable for the employer to comply with a requirement of subsection [(1A), (2) or (4)], the employer shall take all such steps towards compliance with that requirement as are reasonably practicable in those circumstances.

[Where the decision leading to the proposed dismissals is that of a person controlling the employer (directly or indirectly), a failure on the part of that person to provide information to the employer shall not constitute special circumstances rendering it not reasonably practicable for the employer to comply with such a requirement.]

[(7A) Where—

[(a) the employer has invited any of the affected employees to elect employee representatives, and]

(b) the invitation was issued long enough before the time when the consultation is required by subsection (1A)(a) or (b) to begin to allow them to elect representatives by that time,

the employer shall be treated as complying with the requirements of this section in relation to those employees if he complies with those requirements as soon as is reasonably practicable after the election of the representatives.]

[(7B) If, after the employer has invited affected employees to elect representatives, the affected employees fail to do so within a reasonable time, he shall give to each affected employee the information set out in subsection (4).]

(8) This section does not confer any rights on a trade union[, a representative] or an employee except as provided by sections 189 to 192 below.

NOTES

In the section-heading and the heading preceding this section, words omitted repealed by the Collective Redundancies and Transfer of Undertakings (Protection of Employment) (Amendment) Regulations 1995, SI 1995/2587, reg 3(1), (10).

Sub-s (1): substituted, together with sub-ss (1A), (1B), (2), for the original sub-ss (1), (2), by SI 1995/2587, reg 3(1), (2); words in square brackets substituted by the Collective Redundancies and Transfer of Undertakings (Protection of Employment) (Amendment) Regulations 1999, SI 1999/1925, regs 2(1), (2), 3(1), (2).

Sub-s (1A): substituted as noted above; words in square brackets substituted by the Trade Union and Labour Relations (Consolidation) Act 1992 (Amendment) Order 2013, SI 2013/763, art 3(1), (2).

Sub-s (1B): substituted as noted above; further substituted by SI 1999/1925, regs 2(1), (2), 3(1), (3).

Sub-s (2): substituted as noted above.

Sub-s (4): word in first pair of square brackets substituted by SI 1995/2587, reg 3(1), (3); word omitted from para (d) repealed, and para (f) and the word immediately preceding it added, by the Trade Union Reform and Employment Rights Act 1993, ss 34(1), (2)(a), 51, Sch 10; word omitted from para (e) repealed, and paras (g)–(i) added, by the Agency Workers Regulations 2010, SI 2010/93, reg 25, Sch 2, Pt 1, paras 1, 4(1), (3).

Sub-s (5): words in square brackets substituted or inserted by SI 1995/2587, reg 3(1), (4).

Sub-s (5A): inserted by SI 1995/2587, reg 3(1), (5); words in square brackets substituted by SI 1999/1925, regs 2(1), (2), 3(1), (4).

Sub-s (6): repealed by SI 1995/2587, reg 3(1), (6).

Sub-s (7): words in first pair of square brackets substituted by SI 1995/2587, reg 3(1), (7); words in second pair of square brackets added by the Trade Union Reform and Employment Rights Act 1993, s 34(1), (2)(c).

Sub-s (7A): inserted by SI 1995/2587, reg 3(1), (8); para (a) substituted by SI 1999/1925, regs 2(1), (2), 3(1), (5).

Sub-s (7B): inserted by SI 1999/1925, regs 2(1), (2), 3(1), (6).

Sub-s (8): words in square brackets inserted by SI 1995/2587, reg 3(1), (9).

[1.501]
[188A

(1) The requirements for the election of employee representatives under section 188(1B)(b)(ii) are that—

(a) the employer shall make such arrangements as are reasonably practical to ensure that the election is fair;

(b) the employer shall determine the number of representatives to be elected so that there are sufficient representatives to represent the interests of all the affected employees having regard to the number and classes of those employees;

(c) the employer shall determine whether the affected employees should be represented either by representatives of all the affected employees or by representatives of particular classes of those employees;

(d) before the election the employer shall determine the term of office as employee representatives so that it is of sufficient length to enable information to be given and consultations under section 188 to be completed;

(e) the candidates for election as employee representatives are affected employees on the date of the election;

(f) no affected employee is unreasonably excluded from standing for election;

(g) all affected employees on the date of the election are entitled to vote for employee representatives;

(h) the employees entitled to vote may vote for as many candidates as there are representatives to be elected to represent them or, if there are to be representatives for particular classes of employees, may vote for as many candidates as there are representatives to be elected to represent their particular class of employee;

(i) the election is conducted so as to secure that—

(i) so far as is reasonably practicable, those voting do so in secret, and

(ii) the votes given at the election are accurately counted.

(2) Where, after an election of employee representatives satisfying the requirements of subsection (1) has been held, one of those elected ceases to act as an employee representative and any of those employees are no longer represented, they shall elect another representative by an election satisfying the requirements of subsection (1)(a), (e), (f) and (i).]

NOTES

Inserted by the Collective Redundancies and Transfer of Undertakings (Protection of Employment) (Amendment) Regulations 1999, SI 1999/1925, regs 2(1), (2), 4.

[1.502]
189 Complaint . . . and protective award

[(1) Where an employer has failed to comply with a requirement of section 188 or section 188A, a complaint may be presented to an employment tribunal on that ground—

(a) in the case of a failure relating to the election of employee representatives, by any of the affected employees or by any of the employees who have been dismissed as redundant;

(b) in the case of any other failure relating to employee representatives, by any of the employee representatives to whom the failure related,

(c) in the case of failure relating to representatives of a trade union, by the trade union, and

(d) in any other case, by any of the affected employees or by any of the employees who have been dismissed as redundant.]

[(1A) If on a complaint under subsection (1) a question arises as to whether or not any employee representative was an appropriate representative for the purposes of section 188, it shall be for the employer to show that the employee representative had the authority to represent the affected employees.

(1B) On a complaint under subsection (1)(a) it shall be for the employer to show that the requirements in section 188A have been satisfied.]

(2) If the tribunal finds the complaint well-founded it shall make a declaration to that effect and may also make a protective award.

(3) A protective award is an award in respect of one or more descriptions of employees—

(a) who have been dismissed as redundant, or whom it is proposed to dismiss as redundant, and

(b) in respect of whose dismissal or proposed dismissal the employer has failed to comply with a requirement of section 188,

ordering the employer to pay remuneration for the protected period.

(4) The protected period—

(a) begins with the date on which the first of the dismissals to which the complaint relates takes effect, or the date of the award, whichever is the earlier, and

(b) is of such length as the tribunal determines to be just and equitable in all the circumstances having regard to the seriousness of the employer's default in complying with any requirement of section 188;

but shall not exceed 90 days . . .

(5) An [employment tribunal] shall not consider a complaint under this section unless it is presented to the tribunal—

(a) before the [date on which the last of the dismissals to which the complaint relates] takes effect, or

(b) [during] the period of three months beginning with [that date], or

(c) where the tribunal is satisfied that it was not reasonably practicable for the complaint to be presented [during the] period of three months, within such further period as it considers reasonable.

[(5A) Where the complaint concerns a failure to comply with a requirement of section 188 [or 188A], section 292A (extension of time limits to facilitate conciliation before institution of proceedings) applies for the purposes of subsection (5)(b).]

(6) If on a complaint under this section a question arises—

(a) whether there were special circumstances which rendered it not reasonably practicable for the employer to comply with any requirement of section 188, or

(b) whether he took all such steps towards compliance with that requirement as were reasonably practicable in those circumstances,

it is for the employer to show that there were and that he did.

NOTES

Section heading: words omitted repealed by the Collective Redundancies and Transfer of Undertakings (Protection of Employment) (Amendment) Regulations 1995, SI 1995/2587, reg 4(1), (5).

Sub-s (1): substituted by the Collective Redundancies and Transfer of Undertakings (Protection of Employment) (Amendment) Regulations 1999, SI 1999/1925, regs 2(1), (2), 5(1), (2).

Sub-ss (1A), (1B): inserted by SI 1999/1925, regs 2(1), (2), 5(1), (3).

Sub-s (4): words omitted repealed by SI 1999/1925, regs 2(1), (2), 5(1), (4).

Sub-s (5): words in first pair of square brackets substituted by the Employment Rights (Dispute Resolution) Act 1998, s 1(2)(a); other words in square brackets substituted by SI 1995/2587, reg 4(1), (4).

Sub-s (5A): inserted by the Enterprise and Regulatory Reform Act 2013, s 8, Sch 2, paras 1, 11; words in square brackets inserted by the Employment Tribunals Act 1996 (Application of Conciliation Provisions) Order 2014, SI 2014/431, art 3, Schedule, para 1.

Conciliation: employment tribunal proceedings under this section are "relevant proceedings" for the purposes of the conciliation provisions contained in the Employment Tribunals Act 1996, ss 18–18C; see s 18(1)(a) of the 1996 Act at **[1.757]**.

[1.503]

190 Entitlement under protective award

(1) Where an [employment tribunal] has made a protective award, every employee of a description to which the award relates is entitled, subject to the following provisions and to section 191, to be paid remuneration by his employer for the protected period.

(2) The rate of remuneration payable is a week's pay for each week of the period; and remuneration in respect of a period less than one week shall be calculated by reducing proportionately the amount of a week's pay.

(3) . . .

(4) An employee is not entitled to remuneration under a protective award in respect of a period during which he is employed by the employer unless he would be entitled to be paid by the employer in respect of that period—

(a) by virtue of his contract of employment, or

(b) by virtue of [sections 87 to 91 of the Employment Rights Act 1996] (rights of employee in period of notice),

if that period fell within the period of notice required to be given by [section 86(1)] of that Act.

(5) [Chapter II of Part XIV of the Employment Rights Act 1996] applies with respect to the calculation of a week's pay for the purposes of this section.

The calculation date for the purposes of [that Chapter] is the date on which the protective award was made or, in the case of an employee who was dismissed before the date on which the protective award was made, the date which by virtue of [section 226(5)] is the calculation date for the purpose of computing the amount of a redundancy payment in relation to that dismissal (whether or not the employee concerned is entitled to any such payment).

(6) If an employee of a description to which a protective award relates dies during the protected period, the award has effect in his case as if the protected period ended on his death.

NOTES

Sub-s (1): words in square brackets substituted by the Employment Rights (Dispute Resolution) Act 1998, s 1(2)(a).

Sub-s (3): repealed by the Trade Union Reform and Employment Rights Act 1993, ss 34(1), (3), 51, Sch 10.

Sub-ss (4), (5): words in square brackets substituted by the Employment Rights Act 1996, s 240, Sch 1, para 56(1), (14).

[1.504]

191 Termination of employment during protected period

(1) Where the employee is employed by the employer during the protected period and—

(a) he is fairly dismissed by his employer [otherwise than as redundant], or

(b) he unreasonably terminates the contract of employment,

then, subject to the following provisions, he is not entitled to remuneration under the protective award in respect of any period during which but for that dismissal or termination he would have been employed.

(2) If an employer makes an employee an offer (whether in writing or not and whether before or after the ending of his employment under the previous contract) to renew his contract of employment, or to re-engage him under a new contract, so that the renewal or re-engagement would take effect before or during the protected period, and either—

(a) the provisions of the contract as renewed, or of the new contract, as to the capacity and place in which he would be employed, and as to the other terms and conditions of his employment, would not differ from the corresponding provisions of the previous contract, or

(b) the offer constitutes an offer of suitable employment in relation to the employee,

the following subsections have effect.

(3) If the employee unreasonably refuses the offer, he is not entitled to remuneration under the protective award in respect of a period during which but for that refusal he would have been employed.

(4) If the employee's contract of employment is renewed, or he is re-engaged under a new contract of employment, in pursuance of such an offer as is referred to in subsection (2)(b), there shall be a trial period in relation to the contract as renewed, or the new contract (whether or not there has been a previous trial period under this section).

(5) The trial period begins with the ending of his employment under the previous contract and ends with the expiration of the period of four weeks beginning with the date on which he starts work under the contract as renewed, or the new contract, or such longer period as may be agreed in accordance with subsection (6) for the purpose of retraining the employee for employment under that contract.

(6) Any such agreement—

(a) shall be made between the employer and the employee or his representative before the employee starts work under the contract as renewed or, as the case may be, the new contract,

(b) shall be in writing,

(c) shall specify the date of the end of the trial period, and

(d) shall specify the terms and conditions of employment which will apply in the employee's case after the end of that period.

(7) If during the trial period—

(a) the employee, for whatever reason, terminates the contract, or gives notice to terminate it and the contract is thereafter, in consequence, terminated, or

(b) the employer, for a reason connected with or arising out of the change to the renewed, or new, employment, terminates the contract, or gives notice to terminate it and the contract is thereafter, in consequence, terminated,

the employee remains entitled under the protective award unless, in a case falling within paragraph (a), he acted unreasonably in terminating or giving notice to terminate the contract.

NOTES

Sub-s (1): words in square brackets substituted by the Trade Union Reform and Employment Rights Act 1993, s 49(2), Sch 8, para 70.

[1.505]

192 Complaint by employee to [employment tribunal]

(1) An employee may present a complaint to an [employment tribunal] on the ground that he is an employee of a description to which a protective award relates and that his employer has failed, wholly or in part, to pay him remuneration under the award.

(2) An [employment tribunal] shall not entertain a complaint under this section unless it is presented to the tribunal—

(a) before the end of the period of three months beginning with the day (or, if the complaint relates to more than one day, the last of the days) in respect of which the complaint is made of failure to pay remuneration, or

(b) where the tribunal is satisfied that it was not reasonably practicable for the complaint to be presented within the period of three months, within such further period as it may consider reasonable.

[(2A) Section 292A (extension of time limits to facilitate conciliation before institution of proceedings) applies for the purposes of subsection (2)(a).]

(3) Where the tribunal finds a complaint under this section well founded it shall order the employer to pay the complainant the amount of remuneration which it finds is due to him.

(4) The remedy of an employee for infringement of his right to remuneration under a protective award is by way of complaint under this section, and not otherwise.

NOTES

Section heading, sub-ss (1), (2): words in square brackets substituted by the Employment Rights (Dispute Resolution) Act 1998, s 1(2)(a).

Sub-s (2A): inserted by the Enterprise and Regulatory Reform Act 2013, s 8, Sch 2, paras 1, 12.

Conciliation: employment tribunal proceedings under this section are "relevant proceedings" for the purposes of the conciliation provisions contained in the Employment Tribunals Act 1996, ss 18–18C; see s 18(1)(a) of the 1996 Act at **[1.757]**.

Duty of employer to notify Secretary of State

[1.506]

193 Duty of employer to notify Secretary of State of certain redundancies

(1) An employer proposing to dismiss as redundant 100 or more employees at one establishment within a period of 90 days or less shall notify the Secretary of State, in writing, of his proposal[—

(a) before giving notice to terminate an employee's contract of employment in respect of any of those dismissals, and (b)] at least [45 days] before the first of those dismissals takes effect.

(2) An employer proposing to dismiss as redundant [20] or more employees at one establishment within [such a period] shall notify the Secretary of State, in writing, of his proposal[—

(a) before giving notice to terminate an employee's contract of employment in respect of any of those dismissals, and

(b)] at least 30 days before the first of those dismissals takes effect.

(3) In determining how many employees an employer is proposing to dismiss as redundant within the period mentioned in subsection (1) or (2), no account shall be taken of employees in respect of whose proposed dismissal notice has already been given to the Secretary of State.

(4) A notice under this section shall—

(a) be given to the Secretary of State by delivery to him or by sending it by post to him, at such address as the Secretary of State may direct in relation to the establishment where the employees proposed to be dismissed are employed,

[(b) where there are representatives to be consulted under section 188, identify them and state the date when consultation with them under that section began,] and

(c) be in such form and contain such particulars, in addition to those required by paragraph (b), as the Secretary of State may direct.

(5) After receiving a notice under this section from an employer the Secretary of State may by written notice require the employer to give him such further information as may be specified in the notice.

(6) [Where there are representatives to be consulted under section 188 the employer shall give to each of them a copy of any notice given under section (1) or (2).]

The copy shall be delivered to them or sent by post to an address notified by them to the employer, or [(in the case of representatives of a trade union)] sent by post to the union at the address of its head or main office.

(7) If in any case there are special circumstances rendering it not reasonably practicable for the employer to comply with any of the requirements of subsections (1) to (6), he shall take all such steps towards compliance with that requirement as are reasonably practicable in the circumstances.

[Where the decision leading to the proposed dismissals is that of a person controlling the employer (directly or indirectly), a failure on the part of that person to provide information to the employer shall not constitute special circumstances rendering it not reasonably practicable for the employer to comply with any of those requirements.]

NOTES

Sub-s (1): words in first pair of square brackets inserted by the Collective Redundancies (Amendment) Regulations 2006, SI 2006/2387, reg 3; words in square brackets in para (b) substituted by the Trade Union and Labour Relations (Consolidation) Act 1992 (Amendment) Order 2013, SI 2013/763, art 3(1), (3).

Sub-s (2): number and words in first and second pairs of square brackets substituted by the Collective Redundancies and Transfer of Undertakings (Protection of Employment) (Amendment) Regulations 1995, SI 1995/2587, reg 5(1), (2); final words in square brackets inserted by SI 2006/2387, reg 3.

Sub-s (4): para (b) substituted by SI 1995/2587, regs 2(2), 5(1), (3).

Sub-s (6): words in first pair of square brackets substituted, and words in second pair of square brackets added, by SI 1995/2587, reg 5(1), (4).

Sub-s (7): words in square brackets added by the Trade Union Reform and Employment Rights Act 1993, s 34(1), (4).

[1.507]

[193A Duty of employer to notify competent authority of a vessel's flag State of certain redundancies

(1) Section 193 has effect subject to this section if—

(a) the duty under section 193(1) or 193(2) applies to a proposal to dismiss employees as redundant, and

(b) the employees concerned are members of the crew of a seagoing vessel which is registered at a port outside Great Britain.

(2) The employer shall give the notification required by section 193(1) or (2) to the competent authority of the state where the vessel is registered (instead of to the Secretary of State).]

NOTES

Commencement: 6 February 2018.

Inserted by the Seafarers (Transnational Information and Consultation, Collective Redundancies and Insolvency Miscellaneous Amendments) Regulations 2018, SI 2018/26, reg 3(1), (2), as from 6 February 2018, in relation to dismissals which are first proposed by an employer on or after that date (see reg 3(4)).

[1.508]

194 Offence of failure to notify

(1) An employer who fails to give notice to the Secretary of State in accordance with section 193 commits an offence and is liable on summary conviction to a fine not exceeding level 5 on the standard scale.

(2) Proceedings in England or Wales for such an offence shall be instituted only by or with the consent of the Secretary of State or by an officer authorised for that purpose by special or general directions of the Secretary of State.

An officer so authorised may . . . prosecute or conduct proceedings for such an offence before a magistrates' court.

(3) Where an offence under this section committed by a body corporate is proved to have been committed with the consent or connivance of, or to be attributable to neglect on the part of, any director, manager, secretary or other similar officer of the body corporate, or any person purporting to act in any such capacity, he as well as the body corporate is guilty of the offence and liable to be proceeded against and punished accordingly.

(4) Where the affairs of a body corporate are managed by its members, subsection (3) applies in relation to the acts and defaults of a member in connection with his functions of management as if he were a director of the body corporate.

NOTES

Sub-s (2): words omitted repealed by the Legal Services Act 2007, ss 208(1), 210, Sch 21, paras 104, 105, Sch 23.

Supplementary provisions

[1.509]

[195 Construction of references to dismissal as redundant etc

(1) In this Chapter references to dismissal as redundant are references to dismissal for a reason not related to the individual concerned or for a number of reasons all of which are not so related.

(2) For the purposes of any proceedings under this Chapter, where an employee is or is proposed to be dismissed it shall be presumed, unless the contrary is proved, that he is or is proposed to be dismissed as redundant.]

NOTES

Substituted by the Trade Union Reform and Employment Rights Act 1993, s 34(1), (5).

[1.510]

[196 Construction of references to representatives

(1) For the purposes of this Chapter persons are employee representatives if—

(a) they have been elected by employees for the specific purpose of being consulted by their employer about dismissals proposed by him, or

(b) having been elected [or appointed] by employees (whether before or after dismissals have been proposed by their employer) otherwise than for that specific purpose, it is appropriate (having regard to the purposes for which they were elected) for the employer to consult them about dismissals proposed by him,

and (in either case) they are employed by the employer at the time when they are elected [or appointed].

(2) References in this Chapter to representatives of a trade union, in relation to an employer, are to officials or other persons authorised by the trade union to carry on collective bargaining with the employer.]

[(3) References in this Chapter to affected employees are to employees who may be affected by the proposed dismissals or who may be affected by measures taken in connection with such dismissals.]

NOTES

Substituted by the Collective Redundancies and Transfer of Undertakings (Protection of Employment) (Amendment) Regulations 1995, SI 1995/2587, reg 6.

Sub-s (1): words in square brackets inserted by the Collective Redundancies and Transfer of Undertakings (Protection of Employment) (Amendment) Regulations 1999, SI 1999/1925, regs 2(1), (2), 6(1)–(3).

Sub-s (3): added by SI 1999/1925, regs 2(1), (2), 6(1), (4).

[1.511]

197 Power to vary provisions

(1) The Secretary of State may by order made by statutory instrument vary—

(a) the provisions of sections 188(2) and 193(1) (requirements as to consultation and notification), and

(b) the periods referred to at the end of section 189(4) (maximum protected period);

but no such order shall be made which has the effect of reducing to less than 30 days the periods referred to in sections 188(2) and 193(1) as the periods which must elapse before the first of the dismissals takes effect.

(2) No such order shall be made unless a draft of the order has been laid before Parliament and approved by a resolution of each House of Parliament.

NOTES

"The periods referred to in sections 188(2) and 193(1)": the provisions referred to in s 188(2) as originally enacted now appear in s 188(1A), but there has been no corresponding amendment to the reference to s 188(2) here.

Orders: the Trade Union and Labour Relations (Consolidation) Act 1992 (Amendment) Order 2013, SI 2013/763.

[1.512]

198 Power to adapt provisions in case of collective agreement

(1) This section applies where there is in force a collective agreement which establishes—

(a) arrangements for providing alternative employment for employees to whom the agreement relates if they are dismissed as redundant by an employer to whom it relates, or

(b) arrangements for [handling the dismissal of employees as redundant].

(2) On the application of all the parties to the agreement the Secretary of State may, if he is satisfied having regard to the provisions of the agreement that the arrangements are on the whole at least as favourable to those employees as the foregoing provisions of this Chapter, by order made by statutory instrument adapt, modify or exclude any of those provisions both in their application to all or any of those employees and in their application to any other employees of any such employer.

(3) The Secretary of State shall not make such an order unless the agreement—

(a) provides for procedures to be followed (whether by arbitration or otherwise) in cases where an employee to whom the agreement relates claims that any employer or other person to whom it relates has not complied with the provisions of the agreement, and

(b) provides that those procedures include a right to arbitration or adjudication by an independent referee or body in cases where (by reason of an equality of votes or otherwise) a decision cannot otherwise be reached,

or indicates that any such employee may present a complaint to an [employment tribunal] that any such employer or other person has not complied with those provisions.

(4) An order under this section may confer on an [employment tribunal] to whom a complaint is presented as mentioned in subsection (3) such powers and duties as the Secretary of State considers appropriate.

(5) An order under this section may be varied or revoked by a subsequent order thereunder either in pursuance of an application made by all or any of the parties to the agreement in question or without any such application.

NOTES

Sub-s (1): words in square brackets in para (b) substituted by the Trade Union Reform and Employment Rights Act 1993, s 49(2), Sch 8, para 71.

Sub-ss (3), (4): words in square brackets substituted by the Employment Rights (Dispute Resolution) Act 1998, s 1(2)(a).

Orders: as of 15 May 2019, no Orders had been made under this section.

[1.513]

[198A Employees being transferred to the employer from another undertaking

(1) This section applies where the following conditions are met—

(a) there is to be, or is likely to be, a relevant transfer,

(b) the transferee is proposing to dismiss as redundant 20 or more employees at one establishment within a period of 90 days or less, and

(c) the individuals who work for the transferor and who are to be (or are likely to be) transferred to the transferee's employment under the transfer ("transferring individuals") include one or more individuals who may be affected by the proposed dismissals or by measures taken in connection with the proposed dismissals.

(2) Where this section applies, the transferee may elect to consult, or to start to consult, representatives of affected transferring individuals about the proposed dismissals before the transfer takes place ("pre-transfer consultation").

(3) Any such election—

(a) may be made only if the transferor agrees to it, and

(b) must be made by way of written notice to the transferor.

(4) If the transferee elects to carry out pre-transfer consultation—

(a) sections 188 to 198 apply from the time of the election (and continue to apply after the transfer) as if the transferee were already the transferring individuals' employer and as if any transferring individuals who may be affected by the proposed dismissals were already employed at the establishment mentioned in subsection (1)(b) (but this is subject to section 198B), and

(b) the transferor may provide information or other assistance to the transferee to help the transferee meet the requirements of this Chapter.

(5) A transferee who elects to carry out pre-transfer consultation may cancel that election at any time by written notice to the transferor.

(6) If the transferee cancels an election to carry out pre-transfer consultation—

(a) sections 188 to 198 no longer apply as mentioned in subsection (4)(a),

(b) anything done under those sections has no effect so far as it was done in reliance on the election,

(c) if the transferee notified an appropriate representative, a transferring individual or the Secretary of State of the election or the proposed dismissals, the transferee must notify him or her of the cancellation as soon as reasonably practicable, and

(d) the transferee may not make another election under subsection (2) in relation to the proposed dismissals.

(7) For the purposes of this section and section 198B—

"affected transferring individual" means a transferring individual who may be affected by the proposed dismissals or who may be affected by measures taken in connection with the proposed dismissals;

"pre-transfer consultation" has the meaning given in subsection (2);

"relevant transfer" means—

(a) a relevant transfer under the Transfer of Undertakings (Protection of Employment) Regulations 2006,

(b) anything else regarded, by virtue of an enactment, as a relevant transfer for the purposes of those Regulations, or

(c) where an enactment provides a power to make provision which is the same as or similar to those Regulations, any other novation of a contract of employment effected in the exercise of that power,

and "transferor" and "transferee" are to be construed accordingly;

"transferring individual" has the meaning given in subsection (1)(c).]

NOTES

Inserted by the Collective Redundancies and Transfer of Undertakings (Protection of Employment) (Amendment) Regulations 2014, SI 2014/16, reg 3(1).

[1.514]

[198B Section 198A: supplementary

(1) Where section 198A applies and the transferee elects to carry out pre-transfer consultation (and has not cancelled the election), the application under section 198A(4)(a) of sections 188 to 198 is (both before and after the transfer) subject to the following modifications—

(a) for section 188(1B)(a) substitute—

"(a) for transferring individuals of a description in respect of which an independent trade union is recognised by the transferor, representatives of that trade union,

(aa) for employees, other than transferring individuals, of a description in respect of which an independent trade union is recognised by the transferee, representatives of that trade union, or";

(b) in section 188(5), for "the employer" substitute "the transferor or transferee";

(c) in section 188(5A), for "shall allow the appropriate representatives access to the affected employees and shall afford to those representatives such accommodation and other facilities as may be appropriate" substitute "shall ensure that the appropriate representatives are allowed access to the affected transferring individuals and that such accommodation and other facilities as may be appropriate are afforded to those representatives";

(d) in section 188(7), at the end insert—

"A failure on the part of the transferor to provide information or other assistance to the transferee does not constitute special circumstances rendering it not reasonably practicable for the transferee to comply with such a requirement.";

(e) where an employment tribunal makes a protective award under section 189 ordering the transferee to pay remuneration for a protected period in respect of a transferring individual, then, so far as the protected period falls before the relevant transfer, the individual's employer before the transfer is to be treated as the employer for the purpose of determining under sections 190(2) to (6) and 191 the period (if any) in respect of which, and the rate at which, the individual is entitled to be paid remuneration by the transferee under section 190(1);

(f) in section 189, at the end insert—

"(7) If on a complaint under this section a question arises whether the transferor agreed to an election or the transferee gave notice of an election as required under section 198A(3), it is for the transferee to show that the agreement or notice was given as required.";

(g) in section 192, at the end insert—

"(5) If on a complaint under this section a question arises whether the transferor agreed to an election or the transferee gave notice of an election as required under section 198A(3), it is for the transferee to show that the agreement or notice was given as required.";

(h) in section 193(6), for "the employer" the second time it appears substitute "the transferor or transferee";

(i) in section 193(7), at the end insert—

"A failure on the part of the transferor to provide information or other assistance to the transferee does not constitute special circumstances rendering it not reasonably practicable for the transferee to comply with any of those requirements.";

(j) in section 196(1), in the closing words, for "employed by the employer" substitute "employed by the transferor or transferee";

(k) for section 196(2) substitute—

"(2) References in this Chapter to representatives of a trade union are to officials or other persons authorised by the trade union to carry on collective bargaining with the transferee.".

(2) Where section 198A applies and the transferee elects to carry out pre-transfer consultation (and has not cancelled the election), both before and after the transfer section 168(1)(c) applies as follows in relation to an official of an independent trade union who, as such an official, is an affected transferring individual's appropriate representative under section 188(1B)(a)—

(a) in relation to the official's duties as such a representative, the reference in the opening words of section 168(1) to an independent trade union being recognised by the employer is to be read as a reference to an independent trade union being recognised by the transferor;

(b) the references in section 168(1)(c) to the employer in relation to section 188 are to be read as references to the transferee.]

NOTES

Inserted by the Collective Redundancies and Transfer of Undertakings (Protection of Employment) (Amendment) Regulations 2014, SI 2014/16, reg 3(1).

CHAPTER III CODES OF PRACTICE

Codes of Practice issued by ACAS

[1.515]

199 Issue of Codes of Practice by ACAS

(1) ACAS may issue Codes of Practice containing such practical guidance as it thinks fit for the purpose of promoting the improvement of industrial relations [or for purposes connected with trade union learning representatives].

(2) In particular, ACAS shall in one or more Codes of Practice provide practical guidance on the following matters—

(a) the time off to be permitted by an employer to a trade union official in accordance with section 168 (time off for carrying out trade union duties);

(b) the time off to be permitted by an employer to a trade union member in accordance with section 170 (time off for trade union activities); and

(c) the information to be disclosed by employers to trade union representatives in accordance with sections 181 and 182 (disclosure of information for purposes of collective bargaining).

(3) The guidance mentioned in subsection (2)(a) shall include guidance on the circumstances in which a trade union official is to be permitted to take time off under section 168 in respect of duties connected with industrial action; and the guidance mentioned in subsection (2)(b) shall include guidance on the question whether, and the circumstances in which, a trade union member is to be permitted to take time off under section 170 for trade union activities connected with industrial action.

(4) ACAS may from time to time revise the whole or any part of a Code of Practice issued by it and issue that revised Code.

NOTES

Sub-s (1): words in square brackets added by the Employment Act 2002, s 43(1), (7).

Codes made under this section: the current codes are: ACAS Code of Practice 1–Disciplinary and Grievance Procedures (2015) at **[4.1]**; ACAS Code of Practice 2–Disclosure of information to trade unions for collective bargaining purposes (1998) at **[4.37]**; ACAS Code of Practice 3–Time off for trade union duties and activities (2010) at **[4.45]**; ACAS Code of Practice 4–Settlement Agreements (2013) at **[4.54]**; ACAS Code of Practice 5–Handling in a Reasonable Manner Requests to Work Flexibly (2014) at **[4.63]**.

[1.516]

200 Procedure for issue of Code by ACAS

(1) Where ACAS proposes to issue a Code of Practice, or a revised Code, it shall prepare and publish a draft of the Code, shall consider any representations made to it about the draft and may modify the draft accordingly.

(2) If ACAS determines to proceed with the draft, it shall transmit the draft to the Secretary of State who—

(a) if he approves of it, shall lay it before both Houses of Parliament, and

(b) if he does not approve of it, shall publish details of his reasons for withholding approval.

[(3) A Code containing practical guidance—

(a) on the time off to be permitted to a trade union learning representative in accordance with section 168A (time off for training and carrying out functions as a learning representative),

(b) on the training that is sufficient to enable a trade union learning representative to carry on the activities mentioned in section 168A(2) (activities for which time off is to be permitted), or

(c) on any of the matters referred to in section 199(2),

shall not be issued unless the draft has been approved by a resolution of each House of Parliament; and if it is so approved, ACAS shall issue the Code in the form of the draft.]

(4) In any other case the following procedure applies—

(a) if, within the period of 40 days beginning with the day on which the draft is laid before Parliament, (or, if copies are laid before the two Houses on different days, with the later of the two days) either House so resolves, no further proceedings shall be taken thereon, but without prejudice to the laying before Parliament of a new draft;

(b) if no such resolution is passed, ACAS shall issue the Code in the form of the draft.

In reckoning the period of 40 days no account shall be taken of any period during which Parliament is dissolved or prorogued or during which both Houses are adjourned for more than four days.

(5) A Code issued in accordance with this section shall come into effect on such day as the Secretary of State may appoint by order made by statutory instrument.

The order may contain such transitional provisions or savings as appear to him to be necessary or expedient.

NOTES

Sub-s (3): substituted by the Employment Act 2002, s 43(1), (8).

The current codes are as noted to s 199 at **[1.515]**.

Orders: the Employment Protection Code of Practice (Time Off for Trade Union Duties and Activities) Order 2009, SI 2009/3223; the Employment Code of Practice (Settlement Agreements) Order 2013, SI 2013/1665; the Code of Practice (Handling in a Reasonable Manner Requests to Work Flexibly) Order 2014, SI 2014/1665; the Code of Practice (Disciplinary and Grievance Procedures) Order 2015, SI 2015/649. Note that new Orders made under this section (upon the revision of an existing Code of Practice) effectively supersede previous Orders.

[1.517]

201 Consequential revision of Code issued by ACAS

(1) A Code of Practice issued by ACAS may be revised by it in accordance with this section for the purpose of bringing it into conformity with subsequent statutory provisions by the making of consequential amendments and the omission of obsolete passages.

"Subsequent statutory provisions" means provisions made by or under an Act of Parliament and coming into force after the Code was issued (whether before or after the commencement of this Act).

(2) Where ACAS proposes to revise a Code under this section, it shall transmit a draft of the revised Code to the Secretary of State who—

(a) if he approves of it, shall lay the draft before each House of Parliament, and

(b) if he does not approve of it, shall publish details of his reasons for withholding approval.

(3) If within the period of 40 days beginning with the day on which the draft is laid before Parliament, (or, if copies are laid before the two Houses on different days, with the later of the two days) either House so resolves, no further proceedings shall be taken thereon, but without prejudice to the laying before Parliament of a new draft.

In reckoning the period of 40 days no account shall be taken of any period during which Parliament is dissolved or prorogued or during which both Houses are adjourned for more than four days.

(4) If no such resolution is passed ACAS shall issue the Code in the form of the draft and it shall come into effect on such day as the Secretary of State may appoint by order made by statutory instrument.

The order may contain such transitional provisions or savings as appear to the Secretary of State to be necessary or expedient.

NOTES

Orders: the Employment Protection Code of Practice (Disclosure of Information) Order 1998, SI 1998/45.

[1.518]

202 Revocation of Code issued by ACAS

(1) A Code of Practice issued by ACAS may, at the request of ACAS, be revoked by the Secretary of State by order made by statutory instrument.

The order may contain such transitional provisions and savings as appear to him to be appropriate.

(2) If ACAS requests the Secretary of State to revoke a Code and he decides not to do so, he shall publish details of his reasons for his decision.

(3) An order shall not be made under this section unless a draft of it has been laid before and approved by resolution of each House of Parliament.

NOTES

Orders: as of 15 May 2019, no Orders had been made under this section, but by virtue of s 300(3) of, and Sch 3, para 1(2) to, this Act, and the Interpretation Act 1978, s 17(2)(b), the Employment Codes of Practice (Revocation) Order 1991, SI 1991/1264 has effect as if made under this section.

Codes of Practice issued by the Secretary of State

[1.519]

203 Issue of Codes of Practice by the Secretary of State

(1) The Secretary of State may issue Codes of Practice containing such practical guidance as he thinks fit for the purpose—

(a) of promoting the improvement of industrial relations, or

(b) of promoting what appear to him to be to be desirable practices in relation to the conduct by trade unions of ballots and elections [or for purposes connected with trade union learning representatives].

(2) The Secretary of State may from time to time revise the whole or any part of a Code of Practice issued by him and issue that revised Code.

NOTES

Sub-s (1): words in square brackets in para (b) added by the Employment Act 2002, s 43(1), (7).

Codes issued under this section: Access and unfair practices during recognition and derecognition ballots (2005) at **[4.266]**; Industrial Action Ballots and Notice to Employers (2017) at **[4.293]**; Code of Practice on Picketing (2017) at **[4.284]**.

Orders: the Code of Practice (Industrial Action Ballots and Notice to Employers) Order 2017, SI 2017/233, and the Code of Practice (Picketing) Order 2017, SI 2017/237 are purportedly made under this section (and s 205 *post*). However, this section does not contain Order making powers and previous codes were made under s 204 of this Act.

[1.520]

204 Procedure for issue of Code by Secretary of State

(1) When the Secretary of State proposes to issue a Code of Practice, or a revised Code, he shall after consultation with ACAS prepare and publish a draft of the Code, shall consider any representations made to him about the draft and may modify the draft accordingly.

(2) If he determines to proceed with the draft, he shall lay it before both Houses of Parliament and, if it is approved by resolution of each House, shall issue the Code in the form of the draft.

(3) A Code issued under this section shall come into effect on such day as the Secretary of State may by order appoint.

The order may contain such transitional provisions or savings as appear to him to be necessary or expedient.
(4) An order under subsection (3) shall be made by statutory instrument, which shall be subject to annulment in pursuance of a resolution of either House of Parliament.

NOTES
Orders: the Employment Code of Practice (Industrial Action Ballots and Notice to Employers) Order 2005, SI 2005/2420; the Employment Code of Practice (Access and Unfair Practices during Recognition and Derecognition Ballots) Order 2005, SI 2005/2421. Note that new Orders made under this section (upon the revision of an existing Code of Practice) effectively supersede previous Orders. The 2005 Orders have not been revoked but are effectively superseded by the two 2017 Orders noted to s 203 *ante*. Also, by virtue of s 300(3) of, and Sch 3, para 1(2) to, this Act, and the Interpretation Act 1978, s 17(2)(b), the Employment Code of Practice (Picketing) Order 1992, SI 1992/476, had effect as if made under this section.

[1.521]
205 Consequential revision of Code issued by Secretary of State
(1) A Code of Practice issued by the Secretary of State may be revised by him in accordance with this section for the purpose of bringing it into conformity with subsequent statutory provisions by the making of consequential amendments and the omission of obsolete passages.
"Subsequent statutory provisions" means provisions made by or under an Act of Parliament and coming into force after the Code was issued (whether before or after the commencement of this Act).
(2) Where the Secretary of State proposes to revise a Code under this section, he shall lay a draft of the revised Code before each House of Parliament.
(3) If within the period of 40 days beginning with the day on which the draft is laid before Parliament, or, if copies are laid before the two Houses on different days, with the later of the two days, either House so resolves, no further proceedings shall be taken thereon, but without prejudice to the laying before Parliament of a new draft.
In reckoning the period of 40 days no account shall be taken of any period during which Parliament is dissolved or prorogued or during which both Houses are adjourned for more than four days.
(4) If no such resolution is passed the Secretary of State shall issue the Code in the form of the draft and it shall come into effect on such day as he may appoint by order made by statutory instrument.
The order may contain such transitional provisions and savings as appear to him to be appropriate.

NOTES
Orders: see the note to s 203 *ante*.

[1.522]
206 Revocation of Code issued by Secretary of State
(1) A Code of Practice issued by the Secretary of State may be revoked by him by order made by statutory instrument.
The order may contain such transitional provisions and savings as appear to him to be appropriate.
(2) An order shall not be made under this section unless a draft of it has been laid before and approved by resolution of each House of Parliament.

Supplementary provisions

[1.523]
207 Effect of failure to comply with Code
(1) A failure on the part of any person to observe any provision of a Code of Practice issued under this Chapter shall not of itself render him liable to any proceedings.
(2) In any proceedings before an [employment tribunal] or the Central Arbitration Committee any Code of Practice issued under this Chapter by ACAS shall be admissible in evidence, and any provision of the Code which appears to the tribunal or Committee to be relevant to any question arising in the proceedings shall be taken into account in determining that question.
(3) In any proceedings before a court or [employment tribunal] or the Central Arbitration Committee any Code of Practice issued under this Chapter by the Secretary of State shall be admissible in evidence, and any provision of the Code which appears to the court, tribunal or Committee to be relevant to any question arising in the proceedings shall be taken into account in determining that question.

NOTES
Sub-ss (2), (3): words in square brackets substituted by the Employment Rights (Dispute Resolution) Act 1998, s 1(2)(a).

[1.524]
[207A Effect of failure to comply with Code: adjustment of awards
(1) This section applies to proceedings before an employment tribunal relating to a claim by an employee under any of the jurisdictions listed in Schedule A2.
(2) If, in the case of proceedings to which this section applies, it appears to the employment tribunal that—
(a) the claim to which the proceedings relate concerns a matter to which a relevant Code of Practice applies,
(b) the employer has failed to comply with that Code in relation to that matter, and
(c) that failure was unreasonable,
the employment tribunal may, if it considers it just and equitable in all the circumstances to do so, increase any award it makes to the employee by no more than 25%.

(3) If, in the case of proceedings to which this section applies, it appears to the employment tribunal that—

(a) the claim to which the proceedings relate concerns a matter to which a relevant Code of Practice applies,

(b) the employee has failed to comply with that Code in relation to that matter, and

(c) that failure was unreasonable,

the employment tribunal may, if it considers it just and equitable in all the circumstances to do so, reduce any award it makes to the employee by no more than 25%.

(4) In subsections (2) and (3), "relevant Code of Practice" means a Code of Practice issued under this Chapter which relates exclusively or primarily to procedure for the resolution of disputes.

(5) Where an award falls to be adjusted under this section and under section 38 of the Employment Act 2002, the adjustment under this section shall be made before the adjustment under that section.

(6) The Secretary of State may by order amend Schedule A2 for the purpose of—

(a) adding a jurisdiction to the list in that Schedule, or

(b) removing a jurisdiction from that list.

(7) The power of the Secretary of State to make an order under subsection (6) includes power to make such incidental, supplementary, consequential or transitional provision as the Secretary of State thinks fit.

(8) An order under subsection (6) shall be made by statutory instrument.

(9) No order shall be made under subsection (6) unless a draft of the statutory instrument containing it has been laid before Parliament and approved by a resolution of each House.]

NOTES

Inserted by the Employment Act 2008, s 3(1), (2).

"A relevant Code": see ACAS Code of Practice 1: Disciplinary and grievance Procedures (2015) at **[4.1]** and ACAS Code of Practice 4: Settlement Agreements (2013) at **[4.54]**.

Orders: as of 15 May 2019, no Orders had been made under this section.

Where an award of compensation for unfair dismissal falls to be reduced or increased under this section, the adjustment is to be in the amount awarded under the Employment Rights Act 1996, s 118(1)(b), and is to be applied immediately before any reduction under s 123(6), (7) of that Act; see s 124A of the 1996 Act at **[1.1043]**.

[1.525]

208 Provisions of earlier Code superseded by later

(1) If ACAS is of the opinion that the provisions of a Code of Practice to be issued by it under this Chapter will supersede the whole or part of a Code previously issued under this Chapter, by it or by the Secretary of State, it shall in the new Code state that on the day on which the new Code comes into effect the old Code or a specified part of it shall cease to have effect.

(2) If the Secretary of State is of the opinion that the provisions of a Code of Practice to be issued by him under this Chapter will supersede the whole or part of a Code previously issued under this Chapter by him or by ACAS, he shall in the new Code state that on the day on which the new Code comes into effect the old Code or a specified part of it shall cease to have effect.

(3) The above provisions do not affect any transitional provisions or savings made by the order bringing the new Code into effect.

CHAPTER IV GENERAL

Functions of ACAS

[1.526]

209 General duty to promote improvement of industrial relations

It is the general duty of ACAS to promote the improvement of industrial relations . . .

NOTES

Words omitted repealed by the Employment Relations Act 1999, ss 26, 44, Sch 9(5).

[1.527]

210 Conciliation

(1) Where a trade dispute exists or is apprehended ACAS may, at the request of one or more parties to the dispute or otherwise, offer the parties to the dispute its assistance with a view to bringing about a settlement.

(2) The assistance may be by way of conciliation or by other means, and may include the appointment of a person other than an officer or servant of ACAS to offer assistance to the parties to the dispute with a view to bringing about a settlement.

(3) In exercising its functions under this section ACAS shall have regard to the desirability of encouraging the parties to a dispute to use any appropriate agreed procedures for negotiation or the settlement of disputes.

[1.528]

[210A Information required by ACAS for purpose of settling recognition disputes

(1) This section applies where ACAS is exercising its functions under section 210 with a view to bringing about a settlement of a recognition dispute.

(2) The parties to the recognition dispute may jointly request ACAS or a person nominated by ACAS to do either or both of the following—

(a) hold a ballot of the workers involved in the dispute;

(b) ascertain the union membership of the workers involved in the dispute.

(3) In the following provisions of this section references to ACAS include references to a person nominated by ACAS, and anything done by such a person under this section shall be regarded as done in the exercise of the functions of ACAS mentioned in subsection (1).
(4) At any time after ACAS has received a request under subsection (2), it may require any party to the recognition dispute—
- (a) to supply ACAS with specified information concerning the workers involved in the dispute, and
- (b) to do so within such period as it may specify.

(5) ACAS may impose a requirement under subsection (4) only if it considers that it is necessary to do so—
- (a) for the exercise of the functions mentioned in subsection (1); and
- (b) in order to enable or assist it to comply with the request.

(6) The recipient of a requirement under this section must, within the specified period, supply ACAS with such of the specified information as is in the recipient's possession.
(7) A request under subsection (2) may be withdrawn by any party to the recognition dispute at any time and, if it is withdrawn, ACAS shall take no further steps to hold the ballot or to ascertain the union membership of the workers involved in the dispute.
(8) If a party to a recognition dispute fails to comply with subsection (6), ACAS shall take no further steps to hold the ballot or to ascertain the union membership of the workers involved in the dispute.
(9) Nothing in this section requires ACAS to comply with a request under subsection (2).
(10) In this section—

"party", in relation to a recognition dispute, means each of the employers, employers' associations and trade unions involved in the dispute;

"a recognition dispute" means a trade dispute between employers and workers which is connected wholly or partly with the recognition by employers or employers' associations of the right of a trade union to represent workers in negotiations, consultations or other procedures relating to any of the matters mentioned in paragraphs (a) to (f) of section 218(1);

"specified" means specified in a requirement under this section; and

"workers" has the meaning given in section 218(5).]

NOTES

Inserted by the Employment Relations Act 2004, s 21.

[1.529]
211 Conciliation officers

(1) ACAS shall designate some of its officers to perform the functions of conciliation officers under any enactment (whenever passed) relating to matters which are or could be the subject of proceedings before an [employment tribunal].
(2) References in any such enactment to a conciliation officer are to an officer designated under this section.

NOTES

Sub-s (1): words in square brackets substituted by the Employment Rights (Dispute Resolution) Act 1998, s 1(2)(a).

[1.530]
212 Arbitration

(1) Where a trade dispute exists or is apprehended ACAS may, at the request of one or more of the parties to the dispute and with the consent of all the parties to the dispute, refer all or any of the matters to which the dispute relates for settlement to the arbitration of—
- (a) one or more persons appointed by ACAS for that purpose (not being officers or employees of ACAS), or
- (b) the Central Arbitration Committee.

(2) In exercising its functions under this section ACAS shall consider the likelihood of the dispute being settled by conciliation.
(3) Where there exist appropriate agreed procedures for negotiation or the settlement of disputes, ACAS shall not refer a matter for settlement to arbitration under this section unless—
- (a) those procedures have been used and have failed to result in a settlement, or
- (b) there is, in ACAS's opinion, a special reason which justifies arbitration under this section as an alternative to those procedures.

(4) Where a matter is referred to arbitration under subsection (1)(a)—
- (a) if more than one arbitrator or arbiter is appointed, ACAS shall appoint one of them to act as chairman; and
- (b) the award may be published if ACAS so decides and all the parties consent.

(5) [Nothing in any of sections 1 to 15 of and schedule 1 to the Arbitration (Scotland) Act 2010 or] [Part I of the Arbitration Act 1996] (general provisions as to arbitration) [applies] to an arbitration under this section.

NOTES

Sub-s (5): words in first pair of square brackets inserted, and word in final pair of square brackets substituted, by the Arbitration (Scotland) Act 2010 (Consequential Amendments) Order 2010, SSI 2010/220, art 2, Schedule, para 6(1), (2); words in second pair of square brackets substituted by the Arbitration Act 1996, s 107(1), Sch 3, para 56.

[1.531]

[212A Arbitration scheme for unfair dismissal cases etc

(1) ACAS may prepare a scheme providing for arbitration in the case of disputes involving proceedings, or claims which could be the subject of proceedings, before an employment tribunal [under, or] arising out of a contravention or alleged contravention of—

[(zza) section 63F(4), (5) or (6) or 63I(1)(b) of the Employment Rights Act 1996 (study and training);]

[(za) section 80G(1) or 80H(1)(b) of *the Employment Rights Act 1996* (flexible working),]

(a) Part X of [that Act] (unfair dismissal), or

(b) any enactment specified in an order made by the Secretary of State.

(2) When ACAS has prepared such a scheme it shall submit a draft of the scheme to the Secretary of State who, if he approves it, shall make an order—

(a) setting out the scheme, and

(b) making provision for it to come into effect.

(3) ACAS may from time to time prepare a revised version of such a scheme and, when it has done so, shall submit a draft of the revised scheme to the Secretary of State who, if he approves it, shall make an order—

(a) setting out the revised scheme, and

(b) making provision for it to come into effect.

(4) ACAS may take any steps appropriate for promoting awareness of a scheme prepared under this section.

(5) Where the parties to any dispute within subsection (1) agree in writing to submit the dispute to arbitration in accordance with a scheme having effect by virtue of an order under this section, ACAS shall refer the dispute to the arbitration of a person appointed by ACAS for the purpose (not being an officer or employee of ACAS).

(6) Nothing in the Arbitration Act 1996 shall apply to an arbitration conducted in accordance with a scheme having effect by virtue of an order under this section except to the extent that the order provides for any provision of Part I of that Act so to apply; and the order may provide for any such provision so to apply subject to modifications.

(7) A scheme set out in an order under this section may, in relation to an arbitration conducted in accordance with the law of Scotland, make provision—

(a) that a reference on a preliminary point may be made, or

(b) conferring a right of appeal which shall lie,

to the relevant court on such grounds and in respect of such matters as may be specified in the scheme; and in this subsection "relevant court" means such court, being the Court of Session or the Employment Appeal Tribunal, as may be specified in the scheme, and a different court may be specified as regards different grounds or matters.

(8) Where a scheme set out in an order under this section includes provision for the making of re-employment orders in arbitrations conducted in accordance with the scheme, the order setting out the scheme may require employment tribunals to enforce such orders—

(a) in accordance with section 117 of the Employment Rights Act 1996 (enforcement by award of compensation), or

(b) in accordance with that section as modified by the order.

For this purpose "re-employment orders" means orders requiring that persons found to have been unfairly dismissed be reinstated, re-engaged or otherwise re-employed.

(9) An order under this section setting out a scheme may provide that, in the case of disputes within subsection (1)(a), such part of an award made in accordance with the scheme as is specified by the order shall be treated as a basic award of compensation for unfair dismissal for the purposes of section 184(1)(d) of the Employment Rights Act 1996 (which specifies such an award as a debt which the Secretary of State must satisfy if the employer has become insolvent).

(10) An order under this section shall be made by statutory instrument.

(11) No order shall be made under subsection (1)(b) unless a draft of the statutory instrument containing it has been laid before Parliament and approved by a resolution of each House.

(12) A statutory instrument containing an order under this section (other than one of which a draft has been approved by resolution of each House of Parliament) shall be subject to annulment in pursuance of a resolution of either House of Parliament.]

NOTES

Inserted by the Employment Rights (Dispute Resolution) Act 1998, s 7.

Sub-s (1) is amended as follows:

The words in the first pair of square brackets were inserted, para (za) was inserted, and the words in square brackets in para (a) were substituted, by the Employment Act 2002, s 53, Sch 7, paras 18, 22.

Para (zza) inserted, and for the words in italics in para (za) there are substituted the words "that Act", by the Apprenticeships, Skills, Children and Learning Act 2009, s 40(5), Sch 1, paras 12, 13, as from 6 April 2010 (except in relation to small employers and their employees), and as from a day to be appointed (otherwise) (as to the meaning of "small employers" etc, see further the notes at **[1.937]**).

Orders: the ACAS Arbitration Scheme (Great Britain) Order 2004, SI 2004/753 at **[2.717]**; the ACAS (Flexible Working) Arbitration Scheme (Great Britain) Order 2004, SI 2004/2333.

[1.532]
[212B Dismissal procedures agreements
ACAS may, in accordance with any dismissal procedures agreement (within the meaning of the Employment Rights Act 1996), refer any matter to the arbitration of a person appointed by ACAS for the purpose (not being an officer or employee of ACAS).]

NOTES
Inserted by the Employment Rights (Dispute Resolution) Act 1998, s 15, Sch 1, para 7.

[1.533]
[213 Advice
(1) ACAS may, on request or otherwise, give employers, employers' associations, workers and trade unions such advice as it thinks appropriate on matters concerned with or affecting or likely to affect industrial relations.
(2) ACAS may also publish general advice on matters concerned with or affecting or likely to affect industrial relations.]

NOTES
Substituted by the Trade Union Reform and Employment Rights Act 1993, s 43(2).

[1.534]
214 Inquiry
(1) ACAS may, if it thinks fit, inquire into any question relating to industrial relations generally or to industrial relations in any particular industry or in any particular undertaking or part of an undertaking.
(2) The findings of an inquiry under this section, together with any advice given by ACAS in connection with those findings, may be published by ACAS if—
(a) it appears to ACAS that publication is desirable for the improvement of industrial relations, either generally or in relation to the specific question inquired into, and
(b) after sending a draft of the findings to all parties appearing to be concerned and taking account of their views, it thinks fit.

Courts of inquiry

[1.535]
215 Inquiry and report by court of inquiry
(1) Where a trade dispute exists or is apprehended, the Secretary of State may inquire into the causes and circumstances of the dispute, and, if he thinks fit, appoint a court of inquiry and refer to it any matters appearing to him to be connected with or relevant to the dispute.
(2) The court shall inquire into the matters referred to it and report on them to the Secretary of State; and it may make interim reports if it thinks fit.
(3) Any report of the court, and any minority report, shall be laid before both Houses of Parliament as soon as possible.
(4) The Secretary of State may, before or after the report has been laid before Parliament, publish or cause to be published from time to time, in such manner as he thinks fit, any information obtained or conclusions arrived at by the court as the result or in the course of its inquiry.
(5) No report or publication made or authorised by the court or the Secretary of State shall include any information obtained by the court of inquiry in the course of its inquiry—
(a) as to any trade union, or
(b) as to any individual business (whether carried on by a person, firm, or company),
which is not available otherwise than through evidence given at the inquiry, except with the consent of the secretary of the trade union or of the person, firm, or company in question.
Nor shall any individual member of the court or any person concerned in the inquiry disclose such information without such consent.
(6) The Secretary of State shall from time to time present to Parliament a report of his proceedings under this section.

[1.536]
216 Constitution and proceedings of court of inquiry
(1) A court of inquiry shall consist of—
(a) a chairman and such other persons as the Secretary of State thinks fit to appoint, or
(b) one person appointed by the Secretary of State,
as the Secretary of State thinks fit.
(2) A court may act notwithstanding any vacancy in its number.
(3) A court may conduct its inquiry in public or. in private, at its discretion.
(4) The Secretary of State may make rules regulating the procedure of a court of inquiry, including rules as to summoning of witnesses, quorum, and the appointment of committees and enabling the court to call for such documents as the court may determine to be relevant to the subject matter of the inquiry.
(5) A court of inquiry may, if and to such extent as may be authorised by rules under this section, by order require any person who appears to the court to have knowledge of the subject-matter of the inquiry—
(a) to supply (in writing or otherwise) such particulars in relation thereto as the court may require, and
(b) where necessary, to attend before the court and give evidence on oath;
and the court may administer or authorise any person to administer an oath for that purpose.

(6) Provision shall be made by rules under this section with respect to the cases in which persons may appear by [a relevant lawyer] in proceedings before a court of inquiry, and except as provided by those rules no person shall be entitled to appear in any such proceedings by [a relevant lawyer].

[(7) In subsection (6) "relevant lawyer" means—

(a) a person who, for the purposes of the Legal Services Act 2007, is an authorised person in relation to an activity which constitutes the exercise of a right of audience or the conduct of litigation within the meaning of that Act, or

(b) an advocate or solicitor in Scotland.]

NOTES

Sub-s (6): words in square brackets substituted by the Legal Services Act 2007, s 208(1), Sch 21, paras 104, 106(a).

Sub-s (7): added by the Legal Services Act 2007, s 208(1), Sch 21, paras 104, 106(b).

Rules: as of 15 May 2019, no Rules had been made under this section.

Supplementary provisions

[1.537]

217 Exclusion of power of arbiter to state case to Court of Session

Section 3 of the Administration of Justice (Scotland) Act 1972 (power of arbiter to state case for opinion of Court of Session) does not apply to—

(a) any form of arbitration relating to a trade dispute, or

(b) any other arbitration arising from a collective agreement.

[1.538]

218 Meaning of "trade dispute" in Part IV

(1) In this Part "trade dispute" means a dispute between employers and workers, or between workers and workers, which is connected with one or more of the following matters—

(a) terms and conditions of employment, or the physical conditions in which any workers are required to work;

(b) engagement or non-engagement, or termination or suspension of employment or the duties of employment, of one or more workers;

(c) allocation of work or the duties of employment as between workers or groups of workers;

(d) matters of discipline;

(e) the membership or non-membership of a trade union on the part of a worker;

(f) facilities for officials of trade unions; and

(g) machinery for negotiation or consultation, and other procedures, relating to any of the foregoing matters, including the recognition by employers or employers' associations of the right of a trade union to represent workers in any such negotiation or consultation or in the carrying out of such procedures.

(2) A dispute between a Minister of the Crown and any workers shall, notwithstanding that he is not the employer of those workers, be treated for the purposes of this Part as a dispute between an employer and those workers if the dispute relates—

(a) to matters which have been referred for consideration by a joint body on which, by virtue of any provision made by or under any enactment, that Minister is represented, or

(b) to matters which cannot be settled without that Minister exercising a power conferred on him by or under an enactment.

(3) There is a trade dispute for the purpose of this Part even though it relates to matters occurring outside Great Britain.

(4) A dispute to which a trade union or employer's association is a party shall be treated for the purposes of this Part as a dispute to which workers or, as the case may be, employers are parties.

(5) In this section—

"employment" includes any relationship whereby one person personally does work or performs services for another; and

"worker", in relation to a dispute to which an employer is a party, includes any worker even if not employed by that employer.

PART V
INDUSTRIAL ACTION

Protection of acts in contemplation or furtherance of trade dispute

[1.539]

219 Protection from certain tort liabilities

(1) An act done by a person in contemplation or furtherance of a trade dispute is not actionable in tort on the ground only—

(a) that it induces another person to break a contract or interferes or induces another person to interfere with its performance, or

(b) that it consists in his threatening that a contract (whether one to which he is a party or not) will be broken or its performance interfered with, or that he will induce another person to break a contract or interfere with its performance.

(2) An agreement or combination by two or more persons to do or procure the doing of an act in contemplation or furtherance of a trade dispute is not actionable in tort if the act is one which if done without any such agreement or combination would not be actionable in tort.

(3) Nothing in subsections (1) and (2) prevents an act done in the course of picketing from being actionable in tort [unless—

(a) it is done in the course of attendance declared lawful by section 220 (peaceful picketing), and
(b) in the case of picketing to which section 220A applies, the requirements in that section (union supervision of picketing) are complied with.]

(4) Subsections (1) and (2) have effect subject to sections 222 to 225 (action excluded from protection) and [to sections 226 (requirement of ballot before action by trade union) and 234A (requirement of notice to employer of industrial action); and in those sections "not protected" means excluded from the protection afforded by this section or, where the expression is used with reference to a particular person, excluded from that protection as respects that person.]

NOTES

Sub-s (3): words in square brackets substituted (for the original words "unless it is done in the course of attendance declared lawful by section 220 (peaceful picketing)") by the Trade Union Act 2016, s 10(1), as from 1 March 2017. Note that this amendment applies in relation to a trade union organising or encouraging members after 1 March 2017 to take part in picketing (in accordance with s 220A(1) of this Act). See **[2.1976]**.

Sub-s (4): words in square brackets substituted by the Trade Union Reform and Employment Rights Act 1993, s 49(2), Sch 8, para 72.

[1.540]
220 Peaceful picketing

(1) It is lawful for a person in contemplation or furtherance of a trade dispute to attend—
(a) at or near his own place of work, or
(b) if he is an official of a trade union, at or near the place of work of a member of the union whom he is accompanying and whom he represents,

for the purpose only of peacefully obtaining or communicating information, or peacefully persuading any person to work or abstain from working.

(2) If a person works or normally works—
(a) otherwise than at any one place, or
(b) at a place the location of which is such that attendance there for a purpose mentioned in subsection (1) is impracticable,

his place of work for the purposes of that subsection shall be any premises of his employer from which he works or from which his work is administered.

(3) In the case of a worker not in employment where—
(a) his last employment was terminated in connection with a trade dispute, or
(b) the termination of his employment was one of the circumstances giving rise to a trade dispute,

in relation to that dispute his former place of work shall be treated for the purposes of subsection (1) as being his place of work.

(4) A person who is an official of a trade union by virtue only of having been elected or appointed to be a representative of some of the members of the union shall be regarded for the purposes of subsection (1) as representing only those members; but otherwise an official of a union shall be regarded for those purposes as representing all its members.

[1.541]
[220A Union supervision of picketing

(1) Section 220 does not make lawful any picketing that a trade union organises, or encourages its members to take part in, unless the requirements in subsections (2) to (8) are complied with.

(2) The union must appoint a person to supervise the picketing.

(3) That person ("the picket supervisor") must be an official or other member of the union who is familiar with any provisions of a Code of Practice issued under section 203 that deal with picketing.

(4) The union or picket supervisor must take reasonable steps to tell the police—
(a) the picket supervisor's name;
(b) where the picketing will be taking place;
(c) how to contact the picket supervisor.

(5) The union must provide the picket supervisor with a letter stating that the picketing is approved by the union.

(6) If an individual who is, or is acting on behalf of, the employer asks the picket supervisor for sight of the approval letter, the picket supervisor must show it to that individual as soon as reasonably practicable.

(7) While the picketing is taking place, the picket supervisor must—
(a) be present where it is taking place, or
(b) be readily contactable by the union and the police, and able to attend at short notice.

(8) While present where the picketing is taking place, the picket supervisor must wear something that readily identifies the picket supervisor as such.

(9) In this section—
"approval letter" means the letter referred to in subsection (5);
"employer" means the employer to which the trade dispute relates;
"picketing" means attendance at or near a place of work, in contemplation or furtherance of a trade dispute, for the purpose of—
(a) obtaining or communicating information, or
(b) persuading any person to work or abstain from working.

(10) In relation to picketing that two or more unions organise or encourage members to take part in—
(a) in subsection (2) "the union" means any one of those unions, and
(b) other references in this section to "the union" are to that union.]

NOTES

Commencement: 1 March 2017.

Inserted by the Trade Union Act 2016, s 10(2), as from 1 March 2017. Note that this section applies in relation to a trade union organising or encouraging members after 1 March 2017 to take part in picketing (in accordance with sub-s (1) of this section). See **[2.1976]**.

[1.542]

221 Restrictions on grant of injunctions and interdicts

(1) Where—

(a) an application for an injunction or interdict is made to a court in the absence of the party against whom it is sought or any in representative of his, and

(b) he claims, or in the opinion of the court would be likely to claim, that he acted in contemplation or furtherance of a trade dispute,

the court shall not grant the injunction or interdict unless satisfied that all steps which in the circumstances were reasonable have been taken with a view to securing that notice of the application and an opportunity of being heard with respect to the application have been given to him.

(2) Where—

(a) an application for an interlocutory injunction is made to a court pending the trial of an action, and

(b) the party against whom it is sought claims that he acted in contemplation or furtherance of a trade dispute,

the court shall, in exercising its discretion whether or not to grant the injunction, have regard to the likelihood of that party's succeeding at the trial of the action in establishing any matter which would afford a defence to the action under section 219 (protection from certain tort liabilities) or section 220 (peaceful picketing).

This subsection does not extend to Scotland.

Action excluded from protection

[1.543]

222 Action to enforce trade union membership

(1) An act is not protected if the reason, or one of the reasons, for which it is done is the fact or belief that a particular employer—

(a) is employing, has employed or might employ a person who is not a member of a trade union, or

(b) is failing, has failed or might fail to discriminate against such a person.

(2) For the purposes of subsection (1)(b) an employer discriminates against a person if, but only if, he ensures that his conduct in relation to—

(a) persons, or persons of any description, employed by him, or who apply to be, or are, considered by him for employment, or

(b) the provision of employment for such persons,

is different, in some or all cases, according to whether or not they are members of a trade union, and is more favourable to those who are.

(3) An act is not protected if it constitutes, or is one of a number of acts which together constitute, an inducement or attempted inducement of a person—

(a) to incorporate in a contract to which that person is a party, or a proposed contract to which he intends to be a party, a term or condition which is or would be void by virtue of section 144 (union membership requirement in contract for goods or services), or

(b) to contravene section 145 (refusal to deal with person on grounds relating to union membership).

(4) References in this section to an employer employing a person are to a person acting in the capacity of the person for whom a worker works or normally works.

(5) References in this section to not being a member of a trade union are to not being a member of any trade union, of a particular trade union or of one of a number of particular trade unions.

Any such reference includes a reference to not being a member of a particular branch or section of a trade union or of one of a number of particular branches or sections of a trade union.

[1.544]

223 Action taken because of dismissal for taking unofficial action

An act is not protected if the reason, or one of the reasons, for doing it is the fact or belief that an employer has dismissed one or more employees in circumstances such that by virtue of section 237 (dismissal in connection with unofficial action) they have no right to complain of unfair dismissal.

[1.545]

224 Secondary action

(1) An act is not protected if one of the facts relied on for the purpose of establishing liability is that there has been secondary action which is not lawful picketing.

(2) There is secondary action in relation to a trade dispute when, and only when, a person—

(a) induces another to break a contract of employment or interferes or induces another to interfere with its performance, or

(b) threatens that a contract of employment under which he or another is employed will be broken or its performance interfered with, or that he will induce another to break a contract of employment or to interfere with its performance, and the employer under the contract of employment is not the employer party to the dispute.

(3) Lawful picketing means acts done in the course of such attendance as is declared lawful by section 220 (peaceful picketing)—

(a) by a worker employed (or, in the case of a worker not in employment, last employed) by the employer party to the dispute, or

(b) by a trade union official whose attendance is lawful by virtue of subsection (1)(b) of that section.

(4) For the purposes of this section an employer shall not be treated as party to a dispute between another employer and workers of that employer; and where more than one employer is in dispute with his workers, the dispute between each employer and his workers shall be treated as a separate dispute.

In this subsection "worker" has the same meaning as in section 244 (meaning of "trade dispute").

(5) An act in contemplation or furtherance of a trade dispute which is primary action in relation to that dispute may not be relied on as secondary action in relation to another trade dispute.

Primary action means such action as is mentioned in paragraph (a) or (b) of subsection (2) where the employer under the contract of employment is the employer party to the dispute.

(6) In this section "contract of employment" includes any contract under which one person personally does work or performs services for another, and related expressions shall be construed accordingly.

[1.546]
225 Pressure to impose union recognition requirement

(1) An act is not protected if it constitutes, or is one of a number of acts which together constitute, an inducement or attempted inducement of a person—

(a) to incorporate in a contract to which that person is a party, or a proposed contract to which he intends to be a party, a term or condition which is or would be void by virtue of section 186 (recognition requirement in contract for goods or services), or

(b) to contravene section 187 (refusal to deal with person on grounds of union exclusion).

(2) An act is not protected if—

(a) it interferes with the supply (whether or not under a contract) of goods or services, or can reasonably be expected to have that effect, and

(b) one of the facts relied upon for the purpose of establishing liability is that a person has—

(i) induced another to break a contract of employment or interfered or induced another to interfere with its performance, or

(ii) threatened that a contract of employment under which he or another is employed will be broken or its performance interfered with, or that he will induce another to break a contract of employment or to interfere with its performance, and

(c) the reason, or one of the reasons, for doing the act is the fact or belief that the supplier (not being the employer under the contract of employment mentioned in paragraph (b)) does not, or might not—

(i) recognise one or more trade unions for the purpose of negotiating on behalf of workers, or any class of worker, employed by him, or

(ii) negotiate or consult with, or with an official of, one or more trade unions.

Requirement of ballot before action by trade union

[1.547]
226 Requirement of ballot before action by trade union

(1) An act done by a trade union to induce a person to take part, or continue to take part, in industrial action—

[(a) is not protected unless the industrial action has the support of a ballot, and

(b) where section 226A falls to be complied with in relation to the person's employer, is not protected as respects the employer unless the trade union has complied with section 226A in relation to him.]

[In this section "the relevant time", in relation to an act by a trade union to induce a person to take part, or continue to take part, in industrial action, means the time at which proceedings are commenced in respect of the act.]

(2) Industrial action shall be regarded as having the support of a ballot only if—

[(a) the union has held a ballot in respect of the action—

(i) in relation to which the requirements of section 226B so far as applicable before and during the holding of the ballot were satisfied,

(ii) in relation to which the requirements of sections 227 to [231] were satisfied, . . .

[(iia) in which at least 50% of those who were entitled to vote in the ballot did so, and].

(iii) in which [the required number of persons (see subsections (2A) to (2C))] answered "Yes" to the question applicable in accordance with section 229(2) to industrial action of the kind to which the act of inducement relates;

(b) such of the requirements of the following sections as have fallen to be satisfied at the relevant time have been satisfied, namely—

(i) section 226B so far as applicable after the holding of the ballot, and

(ii) section 231B; . . .

[(bb) section 232A does not prevent the industrial action from being regarded as having the support of the ballot; and]

(c) the requirements of section 233 (calling of industrial action with support of ballot) are satisfied.

Any reference in this subsection to a requirement of a provision which is disapplied or modified by section 232 has effect subject to that section.]

[(2A) In all cases, the required number of persons for the purposes of subsection (2)(a)(iii) is the majority voting in the ballot.

(2B) There is an additional requirement where the majority of those who were entitled to vote in the ballot are at the relevant time normally engaged in the provision of important public services, unless at that time the union reasonably believes this not to be the case.

(2C) The additional requirement is that at least 40% of those who were entitled to vote in the ballot answered "Yes" to the question.

(2D) In subsection (2B) "important public services" has the meaning given by regulations made by statutory instrument by the Secretary of State.

(2E) Regulations under subsection (2D) may specify only services that fall within any of the following categories—

- (a) health services;
- (b) education of those aged under 17;
- (c) fire services;
- (d) transport services;
- (e) decommissioning of nuclear installations and management of radioactive waste and spent fuel;
- (f) border security.

[(2EA) But regulations under subsection (2D) may not specify services provided by a devolved Welsh authority.]

(2F) No regulations shall be made under subsection (2D) unless a draft of them has been laid before Parliament and approved by a resolution of each House of Parliament.]

(3) Where separate workplace ballots are held by virtue of [section 228(1)—

- (a) industrial action shall be regarded as having the support of a ballot if the conditions specified in subsection (2) are satisfied, and
- (b) the trade union shall be taken to have complied with the requirements relating to a ballot imposed by section 226A if those requirements are complied with,

in relation] to the ballot for the place of work of the person induced to take part, or continue to take part, in the industrial action.

[(3A) If the requirements of section 231A fall to be satisfied in relation to an employer, as respects that employer industrial action shall not be regarded as having the support of a ballot unless those requirements are satisfied in relation to that employer.]

(4) For the purposes of this section an inducement, in relation to a person, includes an inducement which is or would be ineffective, whether because of his unwillingness to be influenced by it or for any other reason.

NOTES

Sub-s (1): words in first pair of square brackets substituted, and words in second pair of square brackets added, by the Trade Union Reform and Employment Rights Act 1993, ss 18(1), 49(2), Sch 8, para 73(a).

Sub-s (2) is amended as follows:

Paras (a)–(c) substituted by the Trade Union Reform and Employment Rights Act 1993, s 49(2), Sch 8, para 73(b).

Figure in square brackets in sub-para (a)(ii) substituted, word omitted from para (b) repealed, and para (bb) inserted, by the Employment Relations Act 1999, ss 4, 44, Sch 3, paras 1, 2(1), (2), Sch 9(1).

The word omitted from sub-para (a)(ii) was repealed by the Trade Union Act 2016, s 22, Sch 4, para 12, as from 1 March 2017.

Sub-para (a)(iia) inserted by the Trade Union Act 2016, s 2, as from 1 March 2017 (note that this amendment does not apply to any ballot opened before that date (see **[1.2000]**)).

Words in square brackets in sub-para (a)(iii) substituted (for the original words "the majority voting in the ballot") by the Trade Union Act 2016, s 3(1), as from 1 March 2017 (note that this amendment does not apply to any ballot opened before that date (see **[1.2001]**)).

Sub-ss (2A)–(2E), (2F): inserted by the Trade Union Act 2016, s 3(2), as from 1 March 2017 (note that this amendment does not apply to any ballot opened before that date (see **[1.2001]**)).

Sub-s (2EA): inserted by the Trade Union (Wales) Act 2017, s 1(1), (4), as from 13 September 2017.

Sub-s (3): words in square brackets substituted by the Trade Union Reform and Employment Rights Act 1993, s 49(2), Sch 8, para 73(c).

Sub-s (3A): inserted by the Employment Relations Act 1999, s 4, Sch 3, paras 1, 2(1), (3).

Orders: the Important Public Services (Health) Regulations 2017, SI 2017/132 at **[2.1964]**; the Important Public Services (Education) Regulations 2017, SI 2017/133 at **[2.1966]**; the Important Public Services (Fire) Regulations 2017, SI 2017/134 at **[2.1968]**; the Important Public Services (Transport) Regulations 2017, SI 2017/135 at **[2.1970]**; the Important Public Services (Border Security) Regulations 2017, SI 2017/136 at **[2.1972]**.

[1.548]

[226A Notice of ballot and sample voting paper for employers

[(1) The trade union must take such steps as are reasonably necessary to ensure that—

- (a) not later than the seventh day before the opening day of the ballot, the notice specified in subsection (2), and
- (b) not later than the third day before the opening day of the ballot, the sample voting paper specified in [subsection (2F)],

is received by every person who it is reasonable for the union to believe (at the latest time when steps could be taken to comply with paragraph (a)) will be the employer of persons who will be entitled to vote in the ballot.

(2) The notice referred to in paragraph (a) of subsection (1) is a notice in writing—

- (a) stating that the union intends to hold the ballot,
- (b) specifying the date which the union reasonably believes will be the opening day of the ballot, and

[(c) containing—
(i) the lists mentioned in subsection (2A) and the figures mentioned in subsection (2B), together with an explanation of how those figures were arrived at, or
(ii) where some or all of the employees concerned are employees from whose wages the employer makes deductions representing payments to the union, either those lists and figures and that explanation or the information mentioned in subsection (2C)].

[(2A) The lists are—
(a) a list of the categories of employee to which the employees concerned belong, and
(b) a list of the workplaces at which the employees concerned work.

(2B) The figures are—
(a) the total number of employees concerned,
(b) the number of the employees concerned in each of the categories in the list mentioned in subsection (2A)(a), and
(c) the number of the employees concerned who work at each workplace in the list mentioned in subsection (2A)(b).

(2C) The information referred to in subsection (2)(c)(ii) is such information as will enable the employer readily to deduce—
(a) the total number of employees concerned,
(b) the categories of employee to which the employees concerned belong and the number of the employees concerned in each of those categories, and
(c) the workplaces at which the employees concerned work and the number of them who work at each of those workplaces.

(2D) The lists and figures supplied under this section, or the information mentioned in subsection (2C) that is so supplied, must be as accurate as is reasonably practicable in the light of the information in the possession of the union at the time when it complies with subsection (1)(a).

(2E) For the purposes of subsection (2D) information is in the possession of the union if it is held, for union purposes—
(a) in a document, whether in electronic form or any other form, and
(b) in the possession or under the control of an officer or employee of the union.

(2F) The sample voting paper referred to in paragraph (b) of subsection (1) is—
(a) a sample of the form of voting paper which is to be sent to the employees concerned, or
(b) where the employees concerned are not all to be sent the same form of voting paper, a sample of each form of voting paper which is to be sent to any of them.

(2G) Nothing in this section requires a union to supply an employer with the names of the employees concerned.

(2H) In this section references to the "employees concerned" are references to those employees of the employer in question who the union reasonably believes will be entitled to vote in the ballot.

(2I) For the purposes of this section, the workplace at which an employee works is—
(a) in relation to an employee who works at or from a single set of premises, those premises, and
(b) in relation to any other employee, the premises with which his employment has the closest connection.]

(3), [(3A), (3B)] . . .

(4) In this section references to the opening day of the ballot are references to the first day when a voting paper is sent to any person entitled to vote in the ballot.

(5) This section, in its application to a ballot in which merchant seamen to whom section 230(2A) applies are entitled to vote, shall have effect with the substitution in [subsection (2F)], for references to the voting paper which is to be sent to the employees, of references to the voting paper which is to be sent or otherwise provided to them.]

NOTES

Inserted by the Trade Union Reform and Employment Rights Act 1993, s 18(2).

Sub-ss (1), (5): words in square brackets substituted by the Employment Relations Act 2004, s 22(1), (2), (6).

Sub-s (2): para (c) substituted by the Employment Relations Act 2004, s 22(1), (3).

Sub-ss (2A)–(2I): inserted by the Employment Relations Act 2004, s 22(1), (4).

Sub-s (3): repealed by the Employment Relations Act 2004, ss 22(1), (5), 57(2), Sch 2.

Sub-ss (3A), (3B): inserted by the Employment Relations Act 1999, s 4, Sch 3, paras 1, 3(1), (3), and repealed by the Employment Relations Act 2004, ss 22(1), (5), 57(2), Sch 2.

[1.549]

[226B Appointment of scrutineer

(1) The trade union shall, before the ballot in respect of the industrial action is held, appoint a qualified person ("the scrutineer") whose terms of appointment shall require him to carry out in relation to the ballot the functions of—
(a) taking such steps as appear to him to be appropriate for the purpose of enabling him to make a report to the trade union (see section 231B); and
(b) making the report as soon as reasonably practicable after the date of the ballot and, in any event, not later than the end of the period of four weeks beginning with that date.

(2) A person is a qualified person in relation to a ballot if—
(a) he satisfies such conditions as may be specified for the purposes of this section by order of the Secretary of State or is himself so specified; and
(b) the trade union has no grounds for believing either that he will carry out the functions conferred on him under subsection (1) otherwise than competently or that his independence in relation to the union, or in relation to the ballot, might reasonably be called into question.

An order under paragraph (a) shall be made by statutory instrument which shall be subject to annulment in pursuance of a resolution of either House of Parliament.

(3) The trade union shall ensure that the scrutineer duly carries out the functions conferred on him under subsection (1) and that there is no interference with the carrying out of those functions from the union or any of its members, officials or employees.

(4) The trade union shall comply with all reasonable requests made by the scrutineer for the purposes of, or in connection with, the carrying out of those functions.]

NOTES

Inserted by the Trade Union Reform and Employment Rights Act 1993, s 20(1).

Orders: the Trade Union Ballots and Elections (Independent Scrutineer Qualifications) Order 1993, SI 1993/1909 at **[2.138]**; the Trade Union Ballots and Elections (Independent Scrutineer Qualifications) (Amendment) Order 2010, SI 2010/436; the Trade Union Ballots and Elections (Independent Scrutineer Qualifications) (Amendment) Order 2017, SI 2017/877.

[1.550]

[226C Exclusion for small ballots

Nothing in section 226B, section 229(1A)(a) or section 231B shall impose a requirement on a trade union unless—

(a) the number of members entitled to vote in the ballot, or

(b) where separate workplace ballots are held in accordance with section 228(1), the aggregate of the number of members entitled to vote in each of them,

exceeds 50.]

NOTES

Inserted by the Trade Union Reform and Employment Rights Act 1993, s 20(4).

[1.551]

227 Entitlement to vote in ballot

(1) Entitlement to vote in the ballot must be accorded equally to all the members of the trade union who it is reasonable at the time of the ballot for the union to believe will be induced [by the union] to take part or, as the case may be, to continue to take part in the industrial action in question, and to no others.

(2) . . .

NOTES

Sub-s (1): words in square brackets inserted by the Employment Relations Act 2004, s 23.

Sub-s (2): repealed by the Employment Relations Act 1999, ss 4, 44, Sch 3, paras 1, 4, Sch 9(1).

[1.552]

[228 Separate workplace ballots

(1) Subject to subsection (2), this section applies if the members entitled to vote in a ballot by virtue of section 227 do not all have the same workplace.

(2) This section does not apply if the union reasonably believes that all those members have the same workplace.

(3) Subject to section 228A, a separate ballot shall be held for each workplace; and entitlement to vote in each ballot shall be accorded equally to, and restricted to, members of the union who—

(a) are entitled to vote by virtue of section 227, and

(b) have that workplace.

(4) In this section and section 228A "workplace" in relation to a person who is employed means—

(a) if the person works at or from a single set of premises, those premises, and

(b) in any other case, the premises with which the person's employment has the closest connection.]

NOTES

Substituted, together with s 228A for the original s 228, by the Employment Relations Act 1999, s 4, Sch 3, paras 1, 5.

[1.553]

[228A Separate workplaces: single and aggregate ballots

(1) Where section 228(3) would require separate ballots to be held for each workplace, a ballot may be held in place of some or all of the separate ballots if one of subsections (2) to (4) is satisfied in relation to it.

(2) This subsection is satisfied in relation to a ballot if the workplace of each member entitled to vote in the ballot is the workplace of at least one member of the union who is affected by the dispute.

(3) This subsection is satisfied in relation to a ballot if entitlement to vote is accorded to, and limited to, all the members of the union who—

(a) according to the union's reasonable belief have an occupation of a particular kind or have any of a number of particular kinds of occupation, and

(b) are employed by a particular employer, or by any of a number of particular employers, with whom the union is in dispute.

(4) This subsection is satisfied in relation to a ballot if entitlement to vote is accorded to, and limited to, all the members of the union who are employed by a particular employer, or by any of a number of particular employers, with whom the union is in dispute.

(5) For the purposes of subsection (2) the following are members of the union affected by a dispute—

(a) if the dispute relates (wholly or partly) to a decision which the union reasonably believes the employer has made or will make concerning a matter specified in subsection (1)(a), (b) or (c) of section 244 (meaning of "trade dispute"), members whom the decision directly affects,
(b) if the dispute relates (wholly or partly) to a matter specified in subsection (1)(d) of that section, members whom the matter directly affects,
(c) if the dispute relates (wholly or partly) to a matter specified in subsection (1)(e) of that section, persons whose membership or non-membership is in dispute,
(d) if the dispute relates (wholly or partly) to a matter specified in subsection (1)(f) of that section, officials of the union who have used or would use the facilities concerned in the dispute.]

NOTES

Substituted as noted to s 228 at **[1.552]**.

[1.554]
229 Voting paper

(1) The method of voting in a ballot must be by the marking of a voting paper by the person voting.
[(1A) Each voting paper must—
(a) state the name of the independent scrutineer,
(b) clearly specify the address to which, and the date by which, it is to be returned,
(c) be given one of a series of consecutive whole numbers every one of which is used in giving a different number in that series to each voting paper printed or otherwise produced for the purposes of the ballot, and
(d) be marked with its number.

This subsection, in its application to a ballot in which merchant seamen to whom section 230(2A) applies are entitled to vote, shall have effect with the substitution, for the reference to the address to which the voting paper is to be returned, of a reference to the ship to which the seamen belong.]
(2) The voting paper must contain at least one of the following questions—
(a) a question (however framed) which requires the person answering it to say, by answering "Yes" or "No", whether he is prepared to take part or, as the case may be, to continue to take part in a strike;
(b) a question (however framed) which requires the person answering it to say, by answering "Yes" or "No", whether he is prepared to take part or, as the case may be, to continue to take part in industrial action short of a strike.

[(2A) For the purposes of subsection (2) an overtime ban and a call-out ban constitute industrial action short of a strike.]
[(2B) The voting paper must include a summary of the matter or matters in issue in the trade dispute to which the proposed industrial action relates.
(2C) Where the voting paper contains a question about taking part in industrial action short of a strike, the type or types of industrial action must be specified (either in the question itself or elsewhere on the voting paper).
(2D) The voting paper must indicate the period or periods within which the industrial action or, as the case may be, each type of industrial action is expected to take place.]
(3) The voting paper must specify who, in the event of a vote in favour of industrial action, is authorised for the purposes of section 233 to call upon members to take part or continue to take part in the industrial action.

The person or description of persons so specified need not be authorised under the rules of the union but must be within section [20(2)] (persons for whose acts the union is taken to be responsible).
(4) The following statement must (without being qualified or commented upon by anything else on the voting paper) appear on every voting paper—

> "If you take part in a strike or other industrial action, you may be in breach of your contract of employment.
> [However, if you are dismissed for taking part in strike or other industrial action which is called officially and is otherwise lawful, the dismissal will be unfair if it takes place fewer than [twelve] weeks after you started taking part in the action, and depending on the circumstances may be unfair if it takes place later.]".

NOTES

Sub-s (1A): inserted by the Trade Union Reform and Employment Rights Act 1993, s 20(2).

Sub-s (2A): inserted by the Employment Relations Act 1999, s 4, Sch 3, paras 1, 6(1), (2).

Sub-ss (2B)–(2D): inserted by the Trade Union Act 2016, s 5, as from 1 March 2017 (note that this amendment does not apply to any ballot opened before that date (see **[1.2003]**)).

Sub-s (3): number in square brackets substituted by the Trade Union Reform and Employment Rights Act 1993, s 49(1), Sch 7, para 25.

Sub-s (4): words in first (outer) pair of square brackets added by the Employment Relations Act 1999, s 4, Sch 3, paras 1, 6(1), (3); word in second (inner) pair of square brackets substituted by the Employment Relations Act 2004, s 57(1), Sch 1, para 13.

[1.555]
230 Conduct of ballot

(1) Every person who is entitled to vote in the ballot must—
(a) be allowed to vote without interference from, or constraint imposed by, the union or any of its members, officials or employees, and

(b) so far as is reasonably practicable, be enabled to do so without incurring any direct cost to himself.

[(2) Except as regards persons falling within subsection (2A), so far as is reasonably practicable, every person who is entitled to vote in the ballot must—

(a) have a voting paper sent to him by post at his home address or any other address which he has requested the trade union in writing to treat as his postal address; and

(b) be given a convenient opportunity to vote by post.]

[(2A) Subsection (2B) applies to a merchant seaman if the trade union reasonably believes that—

(a) he will be employed in a ship either at sea or at a place outside Great Britain at some time in the period during which votes may be cast, and

(b) it will be convenient for him to receive a voting paper and to vote while on the ship or while at a place where the ship is rather than in accordance with subsection (2).

(2B) Where this subsection applies to a merchant seaman he shall, if it is reasonably practicable—

(a) have a voting paper made available to him while on the ship or while at a place where the ship is, and

(b) be given an opportunity to vote while on the ship or while at a place where the ship is.]

[(2C) In subsections (2A) and (2B) "merchant seaman" means a person whose employment, or the greater part of it, is carried out on board sea-going ships.]

(4) A ballot shall be conducted so as to secure that—

(a) so far as is reasonably practicable, those voting do so in secret, and

(b) the votes given in the ballot are fairly and accurately counted.

For the purposes of paragraph (b) an inaccuracy in counting shall be disregarded if it is accidental and on a scale which could not affect the result of the ballot.

NOTES

Sub-ss (2)–(2C): substituted, for the original sub-ss (2), (3), by the Trade Union Reform and Employment Rights Act 1993, s 17; sub-ss (2A), (2B) further substituted by the Employment Relations Act 1999, s 4, Sch 3, paras 1, 7.

[1.556]

231 Information as to result of ballot

As soon as is reasonably practicable after the holding of the ballot, the trade union shall take such steps as are reasonably necessary to ensure that all persons entitled to vote in the ballot [are told—

(a) the number of individuals who were entitled to vote in the ballot,

(b) the number of votes cast in the ballot,

(c) the number of individuals answering "Yes" to the question, or as the case may be, to each question,

(d) the number of individuals answering "No" to the question, or as the case may be, to each question,

(e) the number of spoiled or otherwise invalid voting papers returned,

(f) whether or not the number of votes cast in the ballot is at least 50% of the number of individuals who were entitled to vote in the ballot, and

(g) where section 226(2B) applies, whether or not the number of individuals answering "Yes" to the question (or each question) is at least 40% of the number of individuals who were entitled to vote in the ballot.]

NOTES

Sub-s (1): words in square brackets substituted by the Trade Union Act 2016, s 6, as from 1 March 2017 (note that this amendment does not apply to any ballot opened before that date **[1.2004]**)).

[1.557]

[231A Employers to be informed of ballot result

(1) As soon as reasonably practicable after the holding of the ballot, the trade union shall take such steps as are reasonably necessary to ensure that every relevant employer is informed of the matters mentioned in section 231.

(2) In subsection (1) "relevant employer" means a person who it is reasonable for the trade union to believe (at the time when the steps are taken) was at the time of the ballot the employer of any persons entitled to vote.]

NOTES

Inserted by the Trade Union Reform and Employment Rights Act 1993, s 19.

[1.558]

[231B Scrutineer's report

(1) The scrutineer's report on the ballot shall state whether the scrutineer is satisfied—

(a) that there are no reasonable grounds for believing that there was any contravention of a requirement imposed by or under any enactment in relation to the ballot,

(b) that the arrangements made with respect to the production, storage, distribution, return or other handling of the voting papers used in the ballot, and the arrangements for the counting of the votes, included all such security arrangements as were reasonably practicable for the purpose of minimising the risk that any unfairness or malpractice might occur, and

(c) that he has been able to carry out the functions conferred on him under section 226B(1) without any interference from the trade union or any of its members, officials or employees;

and if he is not satisfied as to any of those matters, the report shall give particulars of his reason for not being satisfied as to that matter.

(2) If at any time within six months from the date of the ballot—

(a) any person entitled to vote in the ballot, or

(b) the employer of any such person,

requests a copy of the scrutineer's report, the trade union must, as soon as practicable, provide him with one either free of charge or on payment of such reasonable fee as may be specified by the trade union.]

NOTES

Inserted by the Trade Union Reform and Employment Rights Act 1993, s 20(3).

[1.559]

232 Balloting of overseas members

(1) A trade union which has overseas members may choose whether or not to accord any of those members entitlement to vote in a ballot; and nothing in section [226B to 230 and 231B] applies in relation to an overseas member or a vote cast by such a member.

[(2) Where overseas members have voted in the ballot—

(a) the references in sections 231 and 231A to persons entitled to vote in the ballot do not include overseas members, and

(b) those sections shall be read as requiring the information mentioned in section 231 to distinguish between overseas members and other members.]

(3) An "overseas member" of a trade union means a member (other than a merchant seaman or offshore worker) who is outside Great Britain throughout the period during which votes may be cast.

For this purpose—

"merchant seaman" means a person whose employment, or the greater part of it, is carried out on board sea-going ships; and

"offshore worker" means a person in offshore employment, other than one who is in such employment in an area where the law of Northern Ireland applies.

(4) A member who throughout the period during which votes may be cast is in Northern Ireland shall not be treated as an overseas member—

(a) where the ballot is one to which section 228(1) or (2) applies (workplace ballots) and his place of work is in Great Britain, or

(b) where the ballot is one to which section 228(3) applies (general ballots) and relates to industrial action involving members both in Great Britain and in Northern Ireland.

(5) In relation to offshore employment the references in subsection (4) to Northern Ireland include any area where the law of Northern Ireland applies and the references to Great Britain include any area where the law of England and Wales or Scotland applies.

NOTES

Sub-s (1): words in square brackets substituted by the Trade Union Reform and Employment Rights Act 1993, s 49(2), Sch 8, para 74(a).

Sub-s (2): substituted by the Trade Union Reform and Employment Rights Act 1993, s 49(2), Sch 8, para 74(b).

[1.560]

[232A Inducement of member denied entitlement to vote

Industrial action shall not be regarded as having the support of a ballot if the following conditions apply in the case of any person—

(a) he was a member of the trade union at the time when the ballot was held,

(b) it was reasonable at that time for the trade union to believe he would be induced to take part or, as the case may be, to continue to take part in the industrial action,

(c) he was not accorded entitlement to vote in the ballot, and

(d) he was induced by the trade union to take part or, as the case may be, to continue to take part in the industrial action.]

NOTES

Inserted by the Employment Relations Act 1999, s 4, Sch 3, paras 1, 8.

[1.561]

[232B Small accidental failures to be disregarded

(1) If—

(a) in relation to a ballot there is a failure (or there are failures) to comply with a provision mentioned in subsection (2) or with more than one of those provisions, and

(b) the failure is accidental and on a scale which is unlikely to affect the result of the ballot or, as the case may be, the failures are accidental and taken together are on a scale which is unlikely to affect the result of the ballot,

the failure (or failures) shall be disregarded [for all purposes (including, in particular, those of section 232A(c))].

(2) The provisions are section 227(1), section 230(2) and section [230(2B)].]

NOTES

Inserted by the Employment Relations Act 1999, s 4, Sch 3, paras 1, 9.

Words in square brackets inserted by the Employment Relations Act 2004, s 24(1).

[1.562]
233 Calling of industrial action with support of ballot
[(1) Industrial action shall be regarded as having the support of a ballot only if—
(a) it is called by a person specified or of a description specified in the voting paper for the ballot in accordance with section 229(3), and
(b) there was no call by the trade union to take part or continue to take part in industrial action to which the ballot relates, or any authorisation or endorsement by the union of any such industrial action, before the date of the ballot.]
(4) For the purposes of this section a call shall be taken to have been made by a trade union if it was authorised or endorsed by the union; and the provisions of section 20(2) to (4) apply for the purpose of determining whether a call, or industrial action, is to be taken to have been so authorised or endorsed.

NOTES
Sub-s (1): substituted (for the original sub-ss (1)–(3)) by the Trade Union Act 2016, s 22, Sch 4, para 13, as from 1 March 2017. Note that this amendment does not apply to any industrial action the ballot for which opened before that date (see **[1.2007]**)).

[1.563]
234 Period after which ballot ceases to be effective
[(1) Industrial action that is regarded as having the support of a ballot shall cease to be so regarded at the end of the period, beginning with the date of the ballot—
(a) of six months, or
(b) of such longer duration not exceeding nine months as is agreed between the union and the members' employer.
(1A) Subsection (1) has effect—
(a) without prejudice to the possibility of the industrial action getting the support of a fresh ballot; and
(b) subject to the following provisions.]
(2) Where for the whole or part of that period the calling or organising of industrial action is prohibited—
(a) by virtue of a court order which subsequently lapses or is discharged, recalled or set aside, or
(b) by virtue of an undertaking given to a court by any person from which he is subsequently released or by which he ceases to be bound,
the trade union may apply to the court for an order that the period during which the prohibition had effect shall not count towards the period referred to in subsection (1).
(3) The application must be made forthwith upon the prohibition ceasing to have effect—
(a) to the court by virtue of whose decision it ceases to have effect, or
(b) where an order lapses or an undertaking ceases to bind without any such decision, to the court by which the order was made or to which the undertaking was given;
. . .
(4) The court shall not make an order if it appears to the court—
(a) that the result of the ballot no longer represents the views of the union members concerned, or
(b) that an event is likely to occur as a result of which those members would vote against industrial action if another ballot were to be held.
(5) No appeal lies from the decision of the court to make or refuse an order under this section.
(6) The period between the making of an application under this section and its determination does not count towards the period referred to in subsection (1).
. . .

NOTES
Sub-ss (1), (1A): substituted (for the original sub-s (1)) by the Trade Union Act 2016, s 9, as from 1 March 2017.
Sub-ss (3), (6): words omitted repealed by the Trade Union Act 2016, s 22, Sch 4, para 14, as from 1 March 2017. Note that these amendments do not apply to any industrial action the ballot for which opened before that date (see **[1.2007]**)).

[Requirement on trade union to give notice of industrial action

[1.564]
234A Notice to employers of industrial action
(1) An act done by a trade union to induce a person to take part, or continue to take part, in industrial action is not protected as respects his employer unless the union has taken or takes such steps as are reasonably necessary to ensure that the employer receives within the appropriate period a relevant notice covering the act.
(2) Subsection (1) imposes a requirement in the case of an employer only if it is reasonable for the union to believe, at the latest time when steps could be taken to ensure that he receives such a notice, that he is the employer of persons who will be or have been induced to take part, or continue to take part, in the industrial action.
(3) For the purposes of this section a relevant notice is a notice in writing which—
[(a) contains—
(i) the lists mentioned in subsection (3A) and the figures mentioned in subsection (3B), together with an explanation of how those figures were arrived at, or
(ii) where some or all of the affected employees are employees from whose wages the employer makes deductions representing payments to the union, either those lists and figures and that explanation or the information mentioned in subsection (3C), and]
(b) states whether industrial action is intended to be continuous or discontinuous and specifies—

(i) where it is to be continuous, the intended date for any of the affected employees to begin to take part in the action,

(ii) where it is to be discontinuous, the intended dates for any of the affected employees to take part in the action, . . .

(c) . . .

[(3A) The lists referred to in subsection (3)(a) are—

(a) a list of the categories of employee to which the affected employees belong, and

(b) a list of the workplaces at which the affected employees work.

(3B) The figures referred to in subsection (3)(a) are—

(a) the total number of the affected employees,

(b) the number of the affected employees in each of the categories in the list mentioned in subsection (3A)(a), and

(c) the number of the affected employees who work at each workplace in the list mentioned in subsection (3A)(b).

(3C) The information referred to in subsection (3)(a)(ii) is such information as will enable the employer readily to deduce—

(a) the total number of the affected employees,

(b) the categories of employee to which the affected employees belong and the number of the affected employees in each of those categories, and

(c) the workplaces at which the affected employees work and the number of them who work at each of those workplaces.

(3D) The lists and figures supplied under this section, or the information mentioned in subsection (3C) that is so supplied, must be as accurate as is reasonably practicable in the light of the information in the possession of the union at the time when it complies with subsection (1).

(3E) For the purposes of subsection (3D) information is in the possession of the union if it is held, for union purposes—

(a) in a document, whether in electronic form or any other form, and

(b) in the possession or under the control of an officer or employee of the union.

(3F) Nothing in this section requires a union to supply an employer with the names of the affected employees.]

(4) For the purposes of subsection (1) the appropriate period is the period—

(a) beginning with the day when the union satisfies the requirement of section 231A in relation to the ballot in respect of the industrial action, and

[(b) ending with the 14th day before the starting date, or the seventh day before that date if the union and the employer so agree.

In paragraph (b) "starting date" means the day, or the first of the days, specified in the relevant notice.]

(5) For the purposes of subsection (1) a relevant notice covers an act done by the union if the person induced [falls within a notified category of employee and the workplace at which he works is a notified workplace] and—

(a) where he is induced to take part or continue to take part in industrial action which the union intends to be continuous, if—

(i) the notice states that the union intends the industrial action to be continuous, and

(ii) there is no participation by him in the industrial action before the date specified in the notice in consequence of any inducement by the union not covered by a relevant notice; and

(b) where he is induced to take part or continue to take part in industrial action which the union intends to be discontinuous, if there is no participation by him in the industrial action on a day not so specified in consequence of any inducement by the union not covered by a relevant notice.

[(5B) In subsection (5)—

(a) a "notified category of employee" means—

(i) a category of employee that is listed in the notice, or

(ii) where the notice contains the information mentioned in subsection (3C), a category of employee that the employer (at the time he receives the notice) can readily deduce from the notice is a category of employee to which some or all of the affected employees belong, and

(b) a "notified workplace" means—

(i) a workplace that is listed in the notice, or

(ii) where the notice contains the information mentioned in subsection (3C), a workplace that the employer (at the time he receives the notice) can readily deduce from the notice is the workplace at which some or all of the affected employees work.

(5C) In this section references to the "affected employees" are references to those employees of the employer who the union reasonably believes will be induced by the union, or have been so induced, to take part or continue to take part in the industrial action.

(5D) For the purposes of this section, the workplace at which an employee works is—

(a) in relation to an employee who works at or from a single set of premises, those premises, and

(b) in relation to any other employee, the premises with which his employment has the closest connection.]

(6) For the purposes of this section—

(a) a union intends industrial action to be discontinuous if it intends it to take place only on some days on which there is an opportunity to take the action, and

(b) a union intends industrial action to be continuous if it intends it to be not so restricted.

(7) [Subject to subsections (7A) and (7B),] where—
- (a) continuous industrial action which has been authorised or endorsed by a union ceases to be so authorised or endorsed . . ., and
- (b) the industrial action has at a later date again been authorised or endorsed by the union (whether as continuous or discontinuous action),

no relevant notice covering acts done to induce persons to take part in the earlier action shall operate to cover acts done to induce persons to take part in the action authorised or endorsed at the later date and this section shall apply in relation to an act to induce a person to take part, or continue to take part, in the industrial action after that date as if the references in subsection (3)(b)(i) to the industrial action were to the industrial action taking place after that date.

[(7A) Subsection (7) shall not apply where industrial action ceases to be authorised or endorsed in order to enable the union to comply with a court order or an undertaking given to a court.

(7B) Subsection (7) shall not apply where—
- (a) a union agrees with an employer, before industrial action ceases to be authorised or endorsed, that it will cease to be authorised or endorsed with effect from a date specified in the agreement ("the suspension date") and that it may again be authorised or endorsed with effect from a date not earlier than a date specified in the agreement ("the resumption date"),
- (b) the action ceases to be authorised or endorsed with effect from the suspension date, and
- (c) the action is again authorised or endorsed with effect from a date which is not earlier than the resumption date or such later date as may be agreed between the union and the employer.]

(8) The requirement imposed on a trade union by subsection (1) shall be treated as having been complied with if the steps were taken by other relevant persons or committees whose acts were authorised or endorsed by the union and references to the belief or intention of the union in subsection (2) or, as the case may be, subsections (3), (5)[, (5C)] and (6) shall be construed as references to the belief or the intention of the person or committee taking the steps.

(9) The provisions of section 20(2) to (4) apply for the purpose of determining for the purposes of subsection (1) who are relevant persons or committees and whether the trade union is to be taken to have authorised or endorsed the steps the person or committee took and for the purposes of [subsections (7) to (7B)] whether the trade union is to be taken to have authorised or endorsed the industrial action.]

NOTES

Inserted, together with the preceding heading, by the Trade Union Reform and Employment Rights Act 1993, s 21.

Sub-s (3): para (a) substituted, and para (c) and the word immediately preceding it repealed, by the Employment Relations Act 2004, ss 25(1), (2), 57(2), Sch 2.

Sub-ss (3A)–(3F): inserted by the Employment Relations Act 2004, s 25(1), (3).

Sub-s (4): para (b), and the words that follow it, substituted (for the original para (b)) by the Trade Union Act 2016, s 8, as from 1 March 2017. Note that this amendment does not apply to any industrial action in relation to which the employer receives a relevant notice before that date (see **[1.2006]**).

Sub-s (5): words in square brackets substituted by the Employment Relations Act 2004, s 25(1), (4).

Sub-ss (5B)–(5D): substituted (for the original sub-s (5A) as inserted by the Employment Relations Act 1999, s 4, Sch 3, paras 1, 11(1), (3)) by the Employment Relations Act 2004, s 25(1), (5).

Sub-s (7): words in square brackets inserted, and words omitted repealed, by the Employment Relations Act 1999, ss 4, 44, Sch 3, paras 1, 11(1), (4), Sch 9(1).

Sub-ss (7A), (7B): inserted by the Employment Relations Act 1999, s 4, Sch 3, paras 1, 11(1), (5).

Sub-s (8): number in square brackets inserted by the Employment Relations Act 2004, s 25(1), (6).

Sub-s (9): words in square brackets substituted by the Employment Relations Act 1999, s 4, Sch 3, paras 1, 11(1), (6).

[1.565]

235 Construction of references to contract of employment

In sections 226 to [234A] (requirement of ballot before action by trade union) references to a contract of employment include any contract under which one person personally does work or performs services for another; [and "employer" and other related expressions] shall be construed accordingly.

NOTES

Number and words in square brackets substituted by the Trade Union Reform and Employment Rights Act 1993, s 49(2), Sch 8, para 75.

[Industrial action affecting supply of goods or services to an individual

[1.566]

235A Industrial action affecting supply of goods or services to an individual

(1) Where an individual claims that—
- (a) any trade union or other person has done, or is likely to do, an unlawful act to induce any person to take part, or to continue to take part, in industrial action, and
- (b) an effect, or a likely effect, of the industrial action is or will be to—
  - (i) prevent or delay the supply of goods or services, or
  - (ii) reduce the quality of goods or services supplied,

  to the individual making the claim,

he may apply to the High Court or the Court of Session for an order under this section.

(2) For the purposes of this section an act to induce any person to take part, or to continue to take part, in industrial action is unlawful—
- (a) if it is actionable in tort by any one or more persons, or
- (b) (where it is or would be the act of a trade union) if it could form the basis of an application by a member under section 62.

(3) In determining whether an individual may make an application under this section it is immaterial whether or not the individual is entitled to be supplied with the goods or services in question.

(4) Where on an application under this section the court is satisfied that the claim is well-founded, it shall make such order as it considers appropriate for requiring the person by whom the act of inducement has been, or is likely to be, done to take steps for ensuring—

(a) that no, or no further, act is done by him to induce any persons to take part or to continue to take part in the industrial action, and

(b) that no person engages in conduct after the making of the order by virtue of having been induced by him before the making of the order to take part or continue to take part in the industrial action.

(5) Without prejudice to any other power of the court, the court may on an application under this section grant such interlocutory relief (in Scotland, such interim order) as it considers appropriate.

(6) For the purposes of this section an act of inducement shall be taken to be done by a trade union if it is authorised or endorsed by the union; and the provisions of section 20(2) to (4) apply for the purposes of determining whether such an act is to be taken to be so authorised or endorsed.

Those provisions also apply in relation to proceedings for failure to comply with an order under this section as they apply in relation to the original proceedings.]

NOTES

Inserted, together with the preceding heading and ss 235B, 235C, by the Trade Union Reform and Employment Rights Act 1993, s 22.

235B, 235C (*Inserted by the Trade Union Reform and Employment Rights Act 1993, s 22; repealed by the Employment Relations Act 1999, ss 28(2)(b), 44, Sch 9(6).*)

No compulsion to work

[1.567]

236 No compulsion to work

No court shall, whether by way of—

(a) an order for specific performance or specific implement of a contract of employment, or

(b) an injunction or interdict restraining a breach or threatened breach of such a contract,

compel an employee to do any work or attend at any place for the doing of any work.

Loss of unfair dismissal protection

[1.568]

237 Dismissal of those taking part in unofficial industrial action

(1) An employee has no right to complain of unfair dismissal if at the time of dismissal he was taking part in an unofficial strike or other unofficial industrial action.

[(1A) Subsection (1) does not apply to the dismissal of the employee if it is shown that the reason (or, if more than one, the principal reason) for the dismissal or, in a redundancy case, for selecting the employee for dismissal was one of those specified in [or under—

(a) section [98B,] 99, 100, 101A(d), 103[, 103A, 104C *or 104D*] of the Employment Rights Act 1996 (dismissal in [jury service,] family, health and safety, working time, employee representative, [protected disclosure, flexible working *and pension scheme membership*] cases),

(b) section 104 of that Act in its application in relation to time off under section 57A of that Act (dependants)].]

In this subsection "redundancy case" has the meaning given in [section 105(9)] of that Act[; and a reference to a specified reason for dismissal includes a reference to specified circumstances of dismissal].]

(2) A strike or other industrial action is unofficial in relation to an employee unless—

(a) he is a member of a trade union and the action is authorised or endorsed by that union, or

(b) he is not a member of a trade union but there are among those taking part in the industrial action members of a trade union by which the action has been authorised or endorsed.

Provided that, a strike or other industrial action shall not be regarded as unofficial if none of those taking part in it are members of a trade union.

(3) The provisions of section 20(2) apply for the purpose of determining whether industrial action is to be taken to have been authorised or endorsed by a trade union.

(4) The question whether industrial action is to be so taken in any case shall be determined by reference to the facts as at the time of dismissal.

Provided that, where an act is repudiated as mentioned in section 21, industrial action shall not thereby be treated as unofficial before the end of the next working day after the day on which the repudiation takes place.

(5) In this section the "time of dismissal" means—

(a) where the employee's contract of employment is terminated by notice, when the notice is given,

(b) where the employee's contract of employment is terminated without notice, when the termination takes effect, and

(c) where the employee is employed under a contract for a fixed term which expires without being renewed under the same contract, when that term expires;

and a "working day" means any day which is not a Saturday or Sunday, Christmas Day, Good Friday or a bank holiday under the Banking and Financial Dealings Act 1971.

(6) For the purposes of this section membership of a trade union for purposes unconnected with the employment in question shall be disregarded; but an employee who was a member of a trade union when he began to take part in industrial action shall continue to be treated as a member for the purpose of determining whether that action is unofficial in relation to him or another notwithstanding that he may in fact have ceased to be a member.

NOTES

Sub-s (1A): inserted by the Trade Union Reform and Employment Rights Act 1993, s 49(2), Sch 8, para 76, and subsequently amended as follows—

Words in first (outer) pair of square brackets substituted by the Employment Relations Act 1999, s 9, Sch 4, Pt III, paras 1, 2(a).

Number "98B," in square brackets inserted by the Employment Relations Act 2004, s 40(8)(a).

Words ", 103A, 104C or 104D" in square brackets substituted by the Pensions Act 2008, s 57(1), (6)(a), and for the words "or 104D" in italics there is substituted ", 104D or 104E", by the Apprenticeships, Skills, Children and Learning Act 2009, s 40(5), Sch 1, paras 12, 14(a), as from 6 April 2010 (except in relation to small employers and their employees), and as from a day to be appointed (otherwise). As to the meaning of "small employers" see the note at **[1.937]**.

Words "jury service," in square brackets inserted by the Employment Relations Act 2004, s 40(8)(b).

Words "protected disclosure, flexible working and pension scheme membership" in square brackets substituted by the Pensions Act 2008, s 57(1), (6)(b), and for the words in italics within those square brackets there are substituted the words ", pension scheme membership, and study and training", by the Apprenticeships, Skills, Children and Learning Act 2009, s 40(5), Sch 1, paras 12, 14(b), as from 6 April 2010 (except in relation to small employers and their employees), and as from a day to be appointed (otherwise). As to the meaning of "small employers" see the note at **[1.937]**.

Words "section 105(9)" in square brackets substituted by the Employment Rights Act 1996, s 240, Sch 1, para 56(1), (15).

Words "; and a reference to a specified reason for dismissal includes a reference to specified circumstances of dismissal" in square brackets inserted by the Employment Relations Act 1999, s 9, Sch 4, Pt III, paras 1, 2(b).

[1.569]

238 Dismissals in connection with other industrial action

(1) This section applies in relation to an employee who has a right to complain of unfair dismissal (the "complainant") and who claims to have been unfairly dismissed, where at the date of the dismissal—

(a) the employer was conducting or instituting a lock-out, or

(b) the complainant was taking part in a strike or other industrial action.

(2) In such a case an [employment tribunal] shall not determine whether the dismissal was fair or unfair unless it is shown—

(a) that one or more relevant employees of the same employer have not been dismissed, or

(b) that a relevant employee has before the expiry of the period of three months beginning with the date of his dismissal been offered re-engagement and that the complainant has not been offered re-engagement.

[(2A) Subsection (2) does not apply to the dismissal of the employee if it is shown that the reason (or, if more than one, the principal reason) for the dismissal or, in a redundancy case, for selecting the employee for dismissal was one of those specified in [or under—

(a) section [98B,] 99, 100, 101A(d)[, 103, 104C *or 104D*] of the Employment Rights Act 1996 (dismissal in [jury service,] family, health and safety, working time[, employee representative, flexible working *and pension scheme membership*] cases),

(b) section 104 of that Act in its application in relation to time off under section 57A of that Act (dependants);]

In this subsection "redundancy case" has the meaning given in [section 105(9)] of that Act[; and a reference to a specified reason for dismissal includes a reference to specified circumstances of dismissal].]

[(2B) Subsection (2) does not apply in relation to an employee who is regarded as unfairly dismissed by virtue of section 238A below.]

(3) For this purpose "relevant employees" means—

(a) in relation to a lock-out, employees who were directly interested in the dispute in contemplation or furtherance of which the lock-out occurred, and

(b) in relation to a strike or other industrial action, those employees at the establishment of the employer at or from which the complainant works who at the date of his dismissal were taking part in the action.

Nothing in section 237 (dismissal of those taking part in unofficial industrial action) affects the question who are relevant employees for the purposes of this section.

(4) An offer of re-engagement means an offer (made either by the original employer or by a successor of that employer or an associated employer) to re-engage an employee, either in the job which he held immediately before the date of dismissal or in a different job which would be reasonably suitable in his case.

(5) In this section "date of dismissal" means—

(a) where the employee's contract of employment was terminated by notice, the date on which the employer's notice was given, and

(b) in any other case, the effective date of termination.

NOTES

Sub-s (2): words in square brackets substituted by the Employment Rights (Dispute Resolution) Act 1998, s 1(2)(a).

Sub-s (2A): inserted by the Trade Union Reform and Employment Rights Act 1993, s 49(2), Sch 8, para 77, and subsequently amended as follows—

Words in first (outer) pair of square brackets substituted by the Employment Relations Act 1999, s 9, Sch 4, Pt III, paras 1, 3(a).

Number "98B," in square brackets inserted by the Employment Relations Act 2004, s 40(9)(a).
Words ", 103, 104C or 104D" in square brackets substituted by the Pensions Act 2008, s 57(1), (7)(a), and for the words "or 104D" in italics there are substituted the words ", 104D or 104E" by the Apprenticeships, Skills, Children and Learning Act 2009, s 40(5), Sch 1, paras 12, 15(a), as from 6 April 2010 (except in relation to small employers and their employees), and as from a day to be appointed (otherwise). As to the meaning of "small employers" see the note at **[1.937]**.
Words "jury service," in square brackets inserted by the Employment Relations Act 2004, s 40(9)(b).
Words ", employee representative, flexible working and pension scheme membership" in square brackets substituted by the Pensions Act 2008, s 57(1), (7)(b), and for the words in italics within those square brackets there are substituted the words ", pension scheme membership, and study and training", by the Apprenticeships, Skills, Children and Learning Act 2009, s 40(5), Sch 1, paras 12, 15(b), as from 6 April 2010 (except in relation to small employers and their employees), and as from a day to be appointed (otherwise). As to the meaning of "small employers" see the note at **[1.937]**.
Words "section 105(9)" in square brackets substituted by the Employment Rights Act 1996, s 240, Sch 1, para 56(1), (15).
Words "; and a reference to a specified reason for dismissal includes a reference to specified circumstances of dismissal" in square brackets inserted by the Employment Relations Act 1999, s 9, Sch 4, Pt III, paras 1, 3(b).
Sub-s (2B): inserted by the Employment Relations Act 1999, s 16, Sch 5, paras 1, 2.

[1.570]
[238A Participation in official industrial action

(1) For the purposes of this section an employee takes protected industrial action if he commits an act which, or a series of acts each of which, he is induced to commit by an act which by virtue of section 219 is not actionable in tort.

(2) An employee who is dismissed shall be regarded for the purposes of Part X of the Employment Rights Act 1996 (unfair dismissal) as unfairly dismissed if—

(a) the reason (or, if more than one, the principal reason) for the dismissal is that the employee took protected industrial action, and
(b) subsection (3), (4) or (5) applies to the dismissal.

(3) This subsection applies to a dismissal if [the date of the dismissal is] [within the protected period].

(4) This subsection applies to a dismissal if—

(a) [the date of the dismissal is] after the end of that period, and
(b) the employee had stopped taking protected industrial action before the end of that period.

(5) This subsection applies to a dismissal if—

(a) [the date of the dismissal is] after the end of that period,
(b) the employee had not stopped taking protected industrial action before the end of that period, and
(c) the employer had not taken such procedural steps as would have been reasonable for the purposes of resolving the dispute to which the protected industrial action relates.

(6) In determining whether an employer has taken those steps regard shall be had, in particular, to—

(a) whether the employer or a union had complied with procedures established by any applicable collective or other agreement;
(b) whether the employer or a union offered or agreed to commence or resume negotiations after the start of the protected industrial action;
(c) whether the employer or a union unreasonably refused, after the start of the protected industrial action, a request that conciliation services be used;
(d) whether the employer or a union unreasonably refused, after the start of the protected industrial action, a request that mediation services be used in relation to procedures to be adopted for the purposes of resolving the dispute;
[(e) where there was agreement to use either of the services mentioned in paragraphs (c) and (d), the matters specified in section 238B].

(7) In determining whether an employer has taken those steps no regard shall be had to the merits of the dispute.

[(7A) For the purposes of this section "the protected period", in relation to the dismissal of an employee, is the sum of the basic period and any extension period in relation to that employee.

(7B) The basic period is twelve weeks beginning with the first day of protected industrial action.

(7C) An extension period in relation to an employee is a period equal to the number of days falling on or after the first day of protected industrial action (but before the protected period ends) during the whole or any part of which the employee is locked out by his employer.

(7D) In subsections (7B) and (7C), the "first day of protected industrial action" means the day on which the employee starts to take protected industrial action (even if on that day he is locked out by his employer).]

(8) For the purposes of this section no account shall be taken of the repudiation of any act by a trade union as mentioned in section 21 in relation to anything which occurs before the end of the next working day (within the meaning of section 237) after the day on which the repudiation takes place.

[(9) In this section "date of dismissal" has the meaning given by section 238(5).]]

NOTES

Inserted by the Employment Relations Act 1999, s 16, Sch 5, paras 1, 3.
Sub-ss (3)–(5): words in square brackets substituted by the Employment Relations Act 2004, ss 26(1), (2), 27(1)–(4).
Sub-s (6): para (e) inserted by the Employment Relations Act 2004, s 28(1).
Sub-ss (7A)–(7D), (9): inserted and added respectively by the Employment Relations Act 2004, ss 26(1), (3), 27(1), (5)).
"Locked out": this expression is not defined for the purposes of this Act, but for a definition of "lock-out" see the Employment Rights Act 1996, s 235(4) at **[1.1150]**.

[1.571]

[238B Conciliation and mediation: supplementary provisions

(1) The matters referred to in subsection (6)(e) of section 238A are those specified in subsections (2) to (5); and references in this section to "the service provider" are to any person who provided a service mentioned in subsection (6)(c) or (d) of that section.

(2) The first matter is: whether, at meetings arranged by the service provider, the employer or, as the case may be, a union was represented by an appropriate person.

(3) The second matter is: whether the employer or a union, so far as requested to do so, co-operated in the making of arrangements for meetings to be held with the service provider.

(4) The third matter is: whether the employer or a union fulfilled any commitment given by it during the provision of the service to take particular action.

(5) The fourth matter is: whether, at meetings arranged by the service provider between the parties making use of the service, the representatives of the employer or a union answered any reasonable question put to them concerning the matter subject to conciliation or mediation.

(6) For the purposes of subsection (2) an "appropriate person" is—

(a) in relation to the employer—

(i) a person with the authority to settle the matter subject to conciliation or mediation on behalf of the employer, or

(ii) a person authorised by a person of that type to make recommendations to him with regard to the settlement of that matter, and

(b) in relation to a union, a person who is responsible for handling on the union's behalf the matter subject to conciliation or mediation.

(7) For the purposes of subsection (4) regard may be had to any timetable which was agreed for the taking of the action in question or, if no timetable was agreed, to how long it was before the action was taken.

(8) In any proceedings in which regard must be had to the matters referred to in section 238A(6)(e)—

(a) notes taken by or on behalf of the service provider shall not be admissible in evidence;

(b) the service provider must refuse to give evidence as to anything communicated to him in connection with the performance of his functions as a conciliator or mediator if, in his opinion, to give the evidence would involve his making a damaging disclosure; and

(c) the service provider may refuse to give evidence as to whether, for the purposes of subsection (5), a particular question was or was not a reasonable one.

(9) For the purposes of subsection (8)(b) a "damaging disclosure" is—

(a) a disclosure of information which is commercially sensitive, or

(b) a disclosure of information that has not previously been disclosed which relates to a position taken by a party using the conciliation or mediation service on the settlement of the matter subject to conciliation or mediation,

to which the person who communicated the information to the service provider has not consented.]

NOTES

Inserted by the Employment Relations Act 2004, s 28(2).

[1.572]

239 Supplementary provisions relating to unfair dismissal

(1) [Sections 237 to 238A] (loss of unfair dismissal protection in connection with industrial action) shall be construed as one with [Part X of the Employment Rights Act 1996][; but sections 108 and 109 of that Act (qualifying period and age limit) shall not apply in relation to section 238A of this Act].

(2) In relation to a complaint to which section 238 [or 238A] applies, [section 111(2)] of that Act (time limit for complaint) does not apply, but an [employment tribunal] shall not consider the complaint unless it is presented to the tribunal—

(a) before the end of the period of six months beginning with the date of the complainant's dismissal (as defined by section 238(5)), or

(b) where the tribunal is satisfied that it was not reasonably practicable for the complaint to be presented before the end of that period, within such further period as the tribunal considers reasonable.

(3) Where it is shown that the condition referred to in section 238(2)(b) is fulfilled (discriminatory re-engagement), the references in—

(a) [sections 98 to 106 of the Employment Rights Act 1996], and

(b) sections 152 and 153 of this Act,

to the reason or principal reason for which the complainant was dismissed shall be read as references to the reason or principal reason he has not been offered re-engagement.

[(4) In relation to a complaint under section 111 of the 1996 Act (unfair dismissal: complaint to employment tribunal) that a dismissal was unfair by virtue of section 238A of this Act—

(a) no order shall be made under section 113 of the 1996 Act (reinstatement or re-engagement) until after the conclusion of protected industrial action by any employee in relation to the relevant dispute,

(b) regulations under section 7 of the Employment Tribunals Act 1996 may make provision about the adjournment and renewal of applications (including provision requiring adjournment in specified circumstances), and

(c) regulations under section 9 of that Act may require a pre-hearing review to be carried out in specified circumstances.]

NOTES

Sub-s (1): words in first pair of square brackets substituted, and words in third pair of square brackets added, by the Employment Relations Act 1999, s 16, Sch 5, paras 1, 4(1)–(3); words in second pair of square brackets substituted by the Employment Rights Act 1996, s 240, Sch 1, para 56(1), (16).

Sub-s (2): words in first pair of square brackets inserted by the Employment Relations Act 1999, s 16, Sch 5, paras 1, 4(1), (4); words in second pair of square brackets substituted by the Employment Rights Act 1996, s 240, Sch 1, para 56(1), (16); words in final pair of square brackets substituted by the Employment Rights (Dispute Resolution) Act 1998, s 1(2)(a).

Sub-s (3): words in square brackets substituted by the Employment Rights Act 1996, s 240, Sch 1, para 56(1), (16).

Sub-s (4): added by the Employment Relations Act 1999, s 16, Sch 5, paras 1, 4(1), (5).

Criminal offences

[1.573]

240 Breach of contract involving injury to persons or property

(1) A person commits an offence who wilfully and maliciously breaks a contract of service or hiring, knowing or having reasonable cause to believe that the probable consequences of his so doing, either alone or in combination with others, will be—

(a) to endanger human life or cause serious bodily injury, or

(b) to expose valuable property, whether real or personal, to destruction or serious injury.

(2) Subsection (1) applies equally whether the offence is committed from malice conceived against the person endangered or injured or, as the case may be, the owner of the property destroyed or injured, or otherwise.

(3) A person guilty of an offence under this section is liable on summary conviction *to imprisonment for a term not exceeding three months or* to a fine not exceeding level 2 on the standard scale *or both*.

(4) This section does not apply to seamen.

NOTES

Sub-s (3): words in italics repealed by the Criminal Justice Act 2003, s 332, Sch 37, Pt 9, in relation to England and Wales, as from a day to be appointed.

By virtue of the Criminal Justice Act 2003, s 280(1), Sch 25, para 95, a summary offence under this section is not punishable with imprisonment. As of 15 May 2019, Sch 25 to the 2003 Act had not been brought into force.

[1.574]

241 Intimidation or annoyance by violence or otherwise

(1) A person commits an offence who, with a view to compelling another person to abstain from doing or to do any act which that person has a legal right to do or abstain from doing, wrongfully and without legal authority—

(a) uses violence to or intimidates that person or his [spouse or civil partner] or children, or injures his property,

(b) persistently follows that person about from place to place,

(c) hides any tools, clothes or other property owned or used by that person, or deprives him of or hinders him in the use thereof,

(d) watches or besets the house or other place where that person resides, works, carries on business or happens to be, or the approach to any such house or place, or

(e) follows that person with two or more other persons in a disorderly manner in or through any street or road.

(2) A person guilty of an offence under this section is liable on summary conviction to imprisonment for a term not exceeding six months or a fine not exceeding level 5 on the standard scale, or both.

(3) . . .

NOTES

Sub-s (1): words in square brackets substituted by the Civil Partnership Act 2004, s 261(1), Sch 27, para 145.

Sub-s (3): repealed by the Serious Organised Crime and Police Act 2005, ss 111, 174(2), Sch 7, Pt 1, para 30, Sch 17, Pt 2.

[1.575]

242 Restriction of offence of conspiracy: England and Wales

(1) Where in pursuance of any such agreement as is mentioned in section 1(1) of the Criminal Law Act 1977 (which provides for the offence of conspiracy) the acts in question in relation to an offence are to be done in contemplation or furtherance of a trade dispute, the offence shall be disregarded for the purposes of that subsection if it is a summary offence which is not punishable with imprisonment.

(2) This section extends to England and Wales only.

[1.576]

243 Restriction of offence of conspiracy: Scotland

(1) An agreement or combination by two or more persons to do or procure to be done an act in contemplation or furtherance of a trade dispute is not indictable as a conspiracy if that act committed by one person would not be punishable as a crime.

(2) A crime for this purpose means an offence punishable on indictment, or an offence punishable on summary conviction, and for the commission of which the offender is liable under the statute making the offence punishable to be imprisoned either absolutely or at the discretion of the court as an alternative for some other punishment.

(3) Where a person is convicted of any such agreement or combination as is mentioned above to do or procure to be done an act which is punishable only on summary conviction, and is sentenced to imprisonment, the imprisonment shall not exceed three months or such longer time as may be prescribed by the statute for the punishment of the act when committed by one person.

(4) Nothing in this section—

(a) exempts from punishment a person guilty of a conspiracy for which a punishment is awarded by an Act of Parliament, or

(b) affects the law relating to riot, unlawful assembly, breach of the peace, . . . or any offence against the State or the Sovereign.

(5) This section extends to Scotland only.

NOTES

Sub-s (4): words omitted from para (b) repealed by the Criminal Justice and Licensing (Scotland) Act 2010, s 203, Sch 7, para 19.

Supplementary

[1.577]

244 Meaning of "trade dispute" in Part V

(1) In this Part a "trade dispute" means a dispute between workers and their employer which relates wholly or mainly to one or more of the following—

(a) terms and conditions of employment, or the physical conditions in which any workers are required to work;

(b) engagement or non-engagement, or termination or suspension of employment or the duties of employment, of one or more workers;

(c) allocation of work or the duties of employment between workers or groups of workers;

(d) matters of discipline;

(e) a worker's membership or non-membership of a trade union;

(f) facilities for officials of trade unions; and

(g) machinery for negotiation or consultation, and other procedures, relating to any of the above matters, including the recognition by employers or employers' associations of the right of a trade union to represent workers in such negotiation or consultation or in the carrying out of such procedures.

(2) A dispute between a Minister of the Crown and any workers shall, notwithstanding that he is not the employer of those workers, be treated as a dispute between those workers and their employer if the dispute relates to matters which—

(a) have been referred for consideration by a joint body on which, by virtue of provision made by or under any enactment, he is represented, or

(b) cannot be settled without him exercising a power conferred on him by or under an enactment.

(3) There is a trade dispute even though it relates to matters occurring outside the United Kingdom, so long as the person or persons whose actions in the United Kingdom are said to be in contemplation or furtherance of a trade dispute relating to matters occurring outside the United Kingdom are likely to be affected in respect of one or more of the matters specified in subsection (1) by the outcome of the dispute.

(4) An act, threat or demand done or made by one person or organisation against another which, if resisted, would have led to a trade dispute with that other, shall be treated as being done or made in contemplation of a trade dispute with that other, notwithstanding that because that other submits to the act or threat or accedes to the demand no dispute arises.

(5) In this section—

"employment" includes any relationship whereby one person personally does work or performs services for another; and

"worker", in relation to a dispute with an employer, means—

(a) a worker employed by that employer; or

(b) a person who has ceased to be so employed if his employment was terminated in connection with the dispute or if the termination of his employment was one of the circumstances giving rise to the dispute.

[1.578]

245 Crown employees and contracts

Where a person holds any office or employment under the Crown on terms which do not constitute a contract of employment between that person and the Crown, those terms shall nevertheless be deemed to constitute such a contract for the purposes of—

(a) the law relating to liability in tort of a person who commits an act which—

(i) induces another person to break a contract, interferes with the performance of a contract or induces another person to interfere with its performance, or

(ii) consists in a threat that a contract will be broken or its performance interfered with, or that any person will be induced to break a contract or interfere with its performance, and

(b) the provisions of this or any other Act which refer (whether in relation to contracts generally or only in relation to contracts of employment) to such an act.

[1.579]

246 Minor definitions

In this Part—

"date of the ballot" means, in the case of a ballot in which votes may be cast on more than one day, the last of those days;

. . .

"strike" means [(except for the purposes of section 229(2))] any concerted stoppage of work;

"working hours", in relation to a person, means any time when under his contract of employment, or other contract personally to do work or perform services, he is required to be at work.

NOTES

Definition "place of work" (omitted) repealed by the Trade Union Reform and Employment Rights Act 1993, ss 49(1), 51, Sch 7, para 26, Sch 10; words in square brackets in definition "strike" inserted by the Employment Relations Act 1999, s 4, Sch 3, paras 1, 6(4).

PART VI
ADMINISTRATIVE PROVISIONS

ACAS

[1.580]

247 ACAS

(1) There shall continue to be a body called the Advisory, Conciliation and Arbitration Service (referred to in this Act as "ACAS").

(2) ACAS is a body corporate of which the corporators are the members of its Council.

(3) Its functions, and those of its officers and servants, shall be performed on behalf of the Crown, but not so as to make it subject to directions of any kind from any Minister of the Crown as to the manner in which it is to exercise its functions under any enactment.

(4) For the purposes of civil proceedings arising out of those functions the Crown Proceedings Act 1947 applies to ACAS as if it were a government department and the Crown Suits (Scotland) Act 1857 applies to it as if it were a public department.

(5) Nothing in section 9 of the Statistics of Trade Act 1947 (restriction on disclosure of information obtained under that Act) shall prevent or penalise the disclosure to ACAS, for the purposes of the exercise of any of its functions, of information obtained under that Act by a government department.

(6) ACAS shall maintain offices in such of the major centres of employment in Great Britain as it thinks fit for the purposes of discharging its functions under any enactment.

[1.581]

248 The Council of ACAS

(1) ACAS shall be directed by a Council which, subject to the following provisions, shall consist of a chairman and nine ordinary members appointed by the Secretary of State.

(2) Before appointing those ordinary members of the Council, the Secretary of State shall—
- (a) as to three of them, consult such organisations representing employers as he considers appropriate, and
- (b) as to three of them, consult such organisations representing workers as he considers appropriate.

(3) The Secretary of State may, if he thinks fit, appoint a further two ordinary members of the Council (who shall be appointed so as to take office at the same time); and before making those appointments he shall—
- (a) as to one of them, consult such organisations representing employers as he considers appropriate, and
- (b) as to one of them, consult such organisations representing workers as he considers appropriate.

(4) The Secretary of State may appoint up to three deputy chairman who may be appointed from the ordinary members, or in addition to those members.

(5) The Council shall determine its own procedure, including the quorum necessary for its meetings.

(6) If the Secretary of State has not appointed a deputy chairman, the Council may choose a member to act as chairman in the absence or incapacity of the chairman.

(7) The validity of proceedings of the Council is not affected by any vacancy among the members of the Council or by any defect in the appointment of any of them.

[1.582]

249 Terms of appointment of members of Council

(1) The members of the Council shall hold and vacate office in accordance with their terms of appointment, subject to the following provisions.

(2) . . .

Appointment as [chairman, or as] deputy chairman, or as an ordinary member of the Council, may be a full-time or part-time appointment; and the Secretary of State may, with the consent of the member concerned, vary the terms of his appointment as to whether his appointment is full-time or part-time.

(3) A person shall not be appointed to the Council for a term exceeding five years, but previous membership does not affect eligibility for re-appointment.

(4) A member may at any time resign his membership, and the chairman or a deputy chairman may at any time resign his office as such, by notice in writing to the Secretary of State.

A deputy chairman appointed in addition to the ordinary members of the Council shall on resigning his office as deputy chairman cease to be a member of the Council.

(5) If the Secretary of State is satisfied that a member—
- (a) has been absent from meetings of the Council for a period longer than six consecutive months without the permission of the Council, or

(b) has become bankrupt or [has had a debt relief order (under Part 7A of the Insolvency Act 1986) made in respect of him or has] made an arrangement with his creditors (or, in Scotland, has had his estate sequestrated or has made a trust deed for his creditors or has made and had accepted a composition contract), or

(c) is incapacitated by physical or mental illness, or

(d) is otherwise unable or unfit to discharge the functions of a member,

the Secretary of State may declare his office as a member to be vacant and shall notify the declaration in such manner as he thinks fit, whereupon the office shall become vacant.

If the chairman or a deputy chairman ceases to be a member of the Council, he shall also cease to be chairman or, as the case may be, a deputy chairman.

NOTES

Sub-s (2): words omitted repealed, and words in square brackets inserted, by the Trade Union Reform and Employment Rights Act 1993, ss 43(3), 51, Sch 10.

Sub-s (5): words in square brackets in para (b) inserted by the Tribunals, Courts and Enforcement Act 2007 (Consequential Amendments) Order 2012, SI 2012/2404, art 3(2), Sch 2, para 28(1), (2).

[1.583]

250 Remuneration, &c of members of Council

(1) ACAS shall pay to the members of its Council such remuneration and travelling and other allowances as may be determined by the Secretary of State.

(2) The Secretary of State may pay, or make provision for payment, to or in respect of a member of the Council such pension, allowance or gratuity on death or retirement as he may determine.

(3) Where a person ceases to be the holder of the Council otherwise than on the expiry of his term of office and it appears to the Secretary of State that there are special circumstances which make it right for him to receive compensation, he may make him a payment of such amount he may determine.

(4) The approval of the Treasury is required for any determination by the Secretary of State under this section.

NOTES

Transfer of Functions: by the Transfer of Functions (Treasury and Minister for the Civil Service) Order 1995, SI 1995/269, arts 3, 5(2), Schedule, para 21, the function of the Treasury under this section was transferred to the Minister for the Civil Service, and accordingly the reference to the Treasury in sub-s (4) above is to be read as if it were a reference to the Minister for the Civil Service.

[1.584]

251 Secretary, officers and staff of ACAS

(1) ACAS may, with the approval of the Secretary of State, appoint a secretary.

The consent of the Secretary of State is required as to his terms and conditions of service.

(2) ACAS may appoint such other officers and staff as it may determine.

The consent of the Secretary of State is required as to their numbers, manner of appointment and terms and conditions of service.

(3) The Secretary of State shall not give his consent under subsection (1) or (2) without the approval of the Treasury.

(4) ACAS shall pay to the Treasury, at such times in each accounting year as may be determined by the Treasury, sums of such amounts as may be so determined as being equivalent to the increase in that year of such liabilities of his as are attributable to the provision of pensions, allowances or gratuities to or in respect of persons who are or have been in the service of ACAS in so far as that increase results from the service of those persons during that accounting year and to the expense to be incurred in administering those pensions, allowances or gratuities.

(5) The fixing of the common seal of ACAS shall be authenticated by the signature of the secretary of ACAS or some other person authorised by ACAS to act for that purpose.

A document purporting to be duly executed under the seal of ACAS shall be received in evidence and shall, unless the contrary is proved, be deemed to be so executed.

[1.585]

[251A Fees for exercise of functions by ACAS

(1) ACAS may, in any case in which it thinks it appropriate to do so, but subject to any directions under subsection (2) below, charge a fee for exercising a function in relation to any person.

(2) The Secretary of State may direct ACAS to charge fees, in accordance with the direction, for exercising any function specified in the direction, but the Secretary of State shall not give a direction under this subsection without consulting ACAS.

(3) A direction under subsection (2) above may require ACAS to charge fees in respect of the exercise of a function only in specified descriptions of case.

(4) A direction under subsection (2) above shall specify whether fees are to be charged in respect of the exercise of any specified function—

(a) at the full economic cost level, or

(b) at a level less than the full economic cost but not less than a specified proportion or percentage of the full economic cost.

(5) Where a direction requires fees to be charged at the full economic cost level ACAS shall fix the fee for the case at an amount estimated to be sufficient to cover the administrative costs of ACAS of exercising the function including an appropriate sum in respect of general staff costs and overheads.

(6) Where a direction requires fees to be charged at a level less than the full economic cost ACAS shall fix the fee for the case at such amount, not being less than the proportion or percentage of the full economic cost specified under subsection (4)(b) above, as it thinks appropriate (computing that cost in the same way as under subsection (5) above).

(7) No liability to pay a fee charged under this section shall arise on the part of any person unless ACAS has notified that person that a fee may or will be charged.

(8) For the purposes of this section—

(a) a function is exercised "in relation to" a person who avails himself of the benefit of its exercise, whether or not he requested its exercise and whether the function is such as to be exercisable in relation to particular persons only or in relation to persons generally; and

(b) where a function is exercised in relation to two or more persons the fee chargeable for its exercise shall be apportioned among them as ACAS thinks appropriate.]

NOTES

Inserted by the Trade Union Reform and Employment Rights Act 1993, s 44.

[1.586]

[251B Prohibition on disclosure of information

(1) Information held by ACAS shall not be disclosed if the information—

(a) relates to a worker, an employer of a worker or a trade union (a "relevant person"), and

(b) is held by ACAS in connection with the provision of a service by ACAS or its officers.

This is subject to subsection (2).

(2) Subsection (1) does not prohibit the disclosure of information if—

(a) the disclosure is made for the purpose of enabling or assisting ACAS to carry out any of its functions under this Act,

(b) the disclosure is made for the purpose of enabling or assisting an officer of ACAS to carry out the functions of a conciliation officer under any enactment,

(c) the disclosure is made for the purpose of enabling or assisting—

(i) a person appointed by ACAS under section 210(2), or

(ii) an arbitrator or arbiter appointed by ACAS under any enactment,

to carry out functions specified in the appointment,

[(ca) the disclosure is made for the purpose of enabling or assisting an enforcement officer within the meaning of Part 2A of the Employment Tribunals Act 1996 to carry out the officer's functions under that Part,]

(d) the disclosure is made for the purposes of a criminal investigation or criminal proceedings (whether or not within the United Kingdom),

(e) the disclosure is made in order to comply with a court order,

(f) the disclosure is made in a manner that ensures that no relevant person to whom the information relates can be identified, or

(g) the disclosure is made with the consent of each relevant person to whom the information relates.

(3) Subsection (2) does not authorise the making of a disclosure which contravenes [the data protection legislation].

(4) A person who discloses information in contravention of this section commits an offence and is liable on summary conviction to a fine not exceeding level 5 on the standard scale.

(5) Proceedings in England and Wales for an offence under this section may be instituted only with the consent of the Director of Public Prosecutions.

(6) For the purposes of this section information held by—

(a) a person appointed by ACAS under section 210(2) in connection with functions specified in the appointment, or

(b) an arbitrator or arbiter appointed by ACAS under any enactment in connection with functions specified in the appointment,

is information that is held by ACAS in connection with the provision of a service by ACAS.

[(7) In this section, "the data protection legislation" has the same meaning as in the Data Protection Act 2018 (see section 3 of that Act).]]

NOTES

Inserted by the Enterprise and Regulatory Reform Act 2013, s 10.

Sub-s (2): para (ca) inserted by the Small Business, Enterprise and Employment Act 2015, s 150(7), as from 6 April 2016. By virtue of s 150(8) of the 2015 Act, this amendment has effect only in relation to relevant sums where (a) in the case of a financial award, the decision of the employment tribunal on the claim to which the financial award relates is made on or after the day on which this section comes into force; (b) in the case of a settlement sum, the certificate under the Employment Tribunals Act 1996, s 19A(1) in respect of the settlement under whose terms it is payable is issued on or after that day.

Sub-s (3): words in square brackets substituted by the Data Protection Act 2018, s 211, Sch 19, Pt 1, para 40(1), (2), as from 25 May 2018 (for transitional provisions and savings relating to the repeal of the Data Protection Act 1998, see Sch 20 to the 2018 Act at **[1.2232]**).

Sub-s (7): added by the Data Protection Act 2018, s 211, Sch 19, Pt 1, para 40(1), (3), as from 25 May 2018 (for transitional provisions and savings relating to the repeal of the Data Protection Act 1998, see Sch 20 to the 2018 Act at **[1.2232]**).

[1.587]

252 General financial provisions

(1) The Secretary of State shall pay to ACAS such sums as are approved by the Treasury and as he considers appropriate for the purpose of enabling ACAS to perform its functions.

(2) ACAS may pay to—

(a) persons appointed under section 210(2) (conciliation) who are not officers or servants of ACAS, and

(b) arbitrators or arbiters appointed by ACAS under any enactment,

such fees and travelling and other allowances as may be determined by the Secretary of State with the approval of the Treasury.

[1.588]
253 Annual report and accounts

(1) ACAS shall as soon as practicable after the end of each [financial year] make a report to the Secretary of State on its activities during that year.

The Secretary of State shall lay a copy of the report before each House of Parliament and arrange for it to be published.

(2) ACAS shall keep proper accounts and proper records in relation to the accounts and shall prepare in respect of each financial year a statement of accounts, in such form as the Secretary of State may, with the approval of the Treasury, direct.

(3) ACAS shall not later than 30th November following the end of the financial year to which the statement relates, send copies of the statement to the Secretary of State and to the Comptroller and Auditor General.

(4) The Comptroller and Auditor General shall examine, certify and report on each such statement and shall lay a copy of the statement and of his report before each House of Parliament.

NOTES

Sub-s (1): words in square brackets substituted by the Employment Relations Act 1999, s 27(1).

The Certification Officer

[1.589]
254 The Certification Officer

(1) There shall continue to be an officer called the Certification Officer.

(2) The Certification Officer shall be appointed by the Secretary of State after consultation with ACAS [(but is not subject to directions of any kind from any Minister of the Crown as to the manner in which he is to exercise his functions)].

(3) The Certification Officer may appoint one or more assistant certification officers and shall appoint an assistant certification officer for Scotland.

(4) The Certification Officer may delegate to an assistant certification officer such functions as he thinks appropriate, and in particular may delegate to the assistant certification officer for Scotland such functions as he thinks appropriate in relation to organisations whose principal office is in Scotland.

References to the Certification Officer in enactments relating to his functions shall be construed accordingly.

(5) ACAS shall provide for the Certification Officer the requisite staff (from among the officers and servants of ACAS) and the requisite accommodation, equipment and other facilities.

[(5A) *Subject to subsection (6),* ACAS shall pay to the Certification Officer such sums as he may require for the performance of any of his functions.]

(6) The Secretary of State shall pay to the Certification Officer such sums as he may require for making payments under the scheme under section 115 (payments towards expenditure in connection with secret ballots).

NOTES

Sub-s (2): words in square brackets inserted by the Trade Union Act 2016, s 16, as from a day to be appointed.

Sub-s (5A): inserted by the Trade Union Reform and Employment Rights Act 1993, s 49(2), Sch 8, para 78; words in italics repealed by the Trade Union Act 2016, s 22, Sch 4, para 15(a), as from a day to be appointed.

Sub-s (6): repealed by the Trade Union Act 2016, s 22, Sch 4, para 15(b), as from a day to be appointed.

[1.590]
255 Remuneration, &c of Certification Officer and assistants

(1) ACAS shall pay to the Certification Officer and any assistant certification officer such remuneration and travelling and other allowances as may be determined by the Secretary of State.

(2) The Secretary of State may pay, or make provision for payment, to or in respect of the Certification Officer and any assistant certification officer such pension, allowance or gratuity on death or retirement as he may determine.

(3) Where a person ceases to be the Certification Officer or an assistant certification officer otherwise than on the expiry of his term of office and it appears to the Secretary of State that there are special circumstances which make it right for him to receive compensation, he may make him a payment of such amount as he may determine.

(4) The approval of the Treasury is required for any determination by the Secretary of State under this section.

[1.591]
256 Procedure before the Certification Officer

(1) Except in relation to matters as to which express provision is made by or under an enactment, the Certification Officer may regulate the procedure to be followed—

(a) on any application or complaint made to him, . . .

(b) where his approval is sought with respect to any matter[, or

(c) determining whether to make a declaration or *enforcement order under section 24B or an order under section 24C*].

[(2) He shall in particular make provision about the disclosure, and restriction of the disclosure, of the identity of an individual who has made or is proposing to make any such application or complaint.

(2A) Provision under subsection (2) shall be such that if the application or complaint relates to a trade union—

(a) the individual's identity is disclosed to the union unless the Certification Officer thinks the circumstances are such that it should not be so disclosed;

(b) the individual's identity is disclosed to such other persons (if any) as the Certification Officer thinks fit.]

(3) The Secretary of State may, with the consent of the Treasury, make a scheme providing for the payment by the Certification Officer to persons of such sums as may be specified in or determined under the scheme in respect of expenses incurred by them for the purposes of, or in connection with, their attendance at hearings held by him in the course of carrying out his functions.

(4) . . .

NOTES

Sub-s (1): word omitted from para (a) repealed, and para (c) (and the preceding word) inserted, by the Transparency of Lobbying, Non-Party Campaigning and Trade Union Administration Act 2014, s 43(1), (7), as from 1 June 2016; for the words in italics in para (c) there are substituted the words "order under section 24B, 32ZC, 45C, 55, 72A, 80, 82 or 103 or under paragraph 5 of Schedule A3" by the Trade Union Act 2016, s 22, Sch 4, para 16, as from a day to be appointed.

Sub-ss (2), (2A): substituted, for the original sub-s (2), by the Employment Relations Act 1999, s 29, Sch 6, paras 1, 22.

Sub-s (4): repealed by the Trade Union Reform and Employment Rights Act 1993, s 51, Sch 10.

[1.592]

[256ZA Striking out

(1) At any stage of proceedings on an application or complaint made to the Certification Officer, he may—

(a) order the application or complaint, or any response, to be struck out on the grounds that it is scandalous, vexatious, has no reasonable prospect of success or is otherwise misconceived,

(b) order anything in the application or complaint, or in any response, to be amended or struck out on those grounds, or

(c) order the application or complaint, or any response, to be struck out on the grounds that the manner in which the proceedings have been conducted by or on behalf of the applicant or complainant or (as the case may be) respondent has been scandalous, vexatious, or unreasonable.

(2) The Certification Officer may order an application or complaint made to him to be struck out for excessive delay in proceeding with it.

(3) An order under this section may be made on the Certification Officer's own initiative and may also be made—

(a) if the order sought is to strike out an application or complaint, or to amend or strike out anything in an application or complaint, on an application by the respondent, or

(b) if the order sought is to strike out any response, or to amend or strike out anything in any response, on an application by the person who made the application or complaint mentioned in subsection (1).

(4) Before making an order under this section, the Certification Officer shall send notice to the party against whom it is proposed that the order should be made giving him an opportunity to show cause why the order should not be made.

(5) Subsection (4) shall not be taken to require the Certification Officer to send a notice under that subsection if the party against whom it is proposed that the order under this section should be made has been given an opportunity to show cause orally why the order should not be made.

(6) Nothing in this section prevents the Certification Officer from making further provision under section 256(1) about the striking out of proceedings on any application or complaint made to him.

(7) An appeal lies to the Employment Appeal Tribunal on any question of law arising from a decision of the Certification Officer under this section.

(8) In this section—

"response" means any response made by a trade union or other body in the exercise of a right to be heard, or to make representations, in response to the application or complaint;

"respondent" means any trade union, or other body, that has such a right.]

NOTES

Inserted by the Employment Relations Act 2004, s 48.

[1.593]

[256A Vexatious litigants

(1) The Certification Officer may refuse to entertain any application or complaint made to him under a provision of Chapters III to VIIA of Part I by a vexatious litigant.

(2) The Certification Officer must give reasons for such a refusal.

(3) Subsection (1) does not apply to a complaint under section 37E(1)(b) or to an application under section 41.

(4) For the purposes of subsection (1) a vexatious litigant is a person who is the subject of—

(a) . . .

(b) a civil proceedings order or an all proceedings order which is made under section 42(1) of the [Senior Courts Act 1981] and which remains in force,
(c) an order which is made under section 1 of the Vexatious Actions (Scotland) Act 1898 [or a vexatious litigation order made under section 100 of the Courts Reform (Scotland) Act 2014], or
(d) an order which is made under section 32 of the Judicature (Northern Ireland) Act 1978.]

NOTES

Inserted by the Employment Relations Act 1999, s 29, Sch 6, paras 1, 23.

Sub-s (4): para (a) repealed by the Employment Relations Act 2004, ss 49(1), (9), 57(2), Sch 2; words in square brackets in para (b) substituted by the Constitutional Reform Act 2005, s 59(5), Sch 11, Pt 1, para 1(2); words in square brackets in para (c) inserted by the Courts Reform (Scotland) Act 2014 (Relevant Officer and Consequential Provisions) Order 2016, SSI 2016/387, art 3, Sch 2, Pt 1, para 2, as from 28 November 2016.

[1.594]

[256B Vexatious litigants: applications disregarded

(1) For the purposes of a relevant enactment an application to the Certification Officer shall be disregarded if—
(a) it was made under a provision mentioned in the relevant enactment, and
(b) it was refused by the Certification Officer under section 256A(1).

(2) The relevant enactments are sections 26(8), 31(7), 45C(5B), 56(8), 72A(10), 81(8) and 108A(13).]

NOTES

Inserted by the Employment Relations Act 1999, s 29, Sch 6, paras 1, 23.

[1.595]

[256C Investigatory powers

Schedule A3 (Certification Officer: investigatory powers) shall have effect.]

NOTES

Commencement: to be appointed.

Inserted by the Trade Union Act 2016, s 17(1), as from a day to be appointed.

[1.596]

[256D Power to impose financial penalties

Schedule A4 (Certification Officer: power to impose financial penalties) shall have effect.]

NOTES

Commencement: to be appointed.

Inserted by the Trade Union Act 2016, s 19(1), as from a day to be appointed (note that this amendment does not apply in relation to any acts or omissions of a trade union or other person occurring before s 19 of the 2016 Act comes into force (see **[1.2017]**)).

[1.597]

257 Custody of documents submitted under earlier legislation

(1) The Certification Officer shall continue to have custody of the annual returns, accounts, copies of rules and other documents submitted for the purposes of—
(a) the Trade Union Acts 1871 to 1964,
(b) the Industrial Relations Act 1971, or
(c) the Trade Union and Labour Relations Act 1974,

of which he took custody under section 9 of the Employment Protection Act 1975.

(2) He shall keep available for public inspection (either free of charge or on payment of a reasonable charge) at all reasonable hours such of those documents as were available for public inspection in pursuance of any of those Acts.

NOTES

Trade Union Acts 1871 to 1964: repealed, see the note to s 3 at **[1.270]**.

Industrial Relations Act 1971: repealed by the Trade Union and Labour Relations Act 1974, ss 1, 25(3), Sch 5.

Trade Union and Labour Relations Act 1974; Employment Protection Act 1975, s 9: repealed by this Act.

[1.598]

[257A Levy payable to Certification Officer

(1) The Secretary of State may by regulations make provision for the Certification Officer to require trade unions and employers' associations ("relevant organisations") to pay a levy to the Officer.

(2) The regulations must require the Certification Officer, in determining the amounts to be levied, to aim to ensure that the total amount levied over any period of three years does not exceed the total amount of the Officers's expenses over that period that are referable to specified functions of the Officer.

(3) The regulations may make provision for determining what things count as expenses of the Certification Officer for the purposes of provision made by virtue of subsection (2), and may in particular provide for the expenses to be treated as including—
(a) expenses incurred by ACAS in providing staff, accommodation, equipment and other facilities under section 254(5), or
(b) expenses in respect of which payments are made under section 255(1) or (2).

(4) The regulations may provide for the Certification Officer to determine the amount of levy payable by a relevant organisation by reference to specified criteria, which may include—

(a) the number of members or the amount of income that the organisation has;

(b) whether the organisation is—

(i) a federated trade union,

(ii) a trade union that is not a federated trade union,

(iii) a federated employers' association, or

(iv) an employers' association that is not a federated employers' association;

(c) the different proportions of the Officer's expenses that are referable to—

(i) functions in relation to federated trade unions,

(ii) functions in relation to trade unions that are not federated trade unions,

(iii) functions in relation to federated employers' associations, and

(iv) functions in relation to employers' associations that are not federated employers' associations.

(5) The regulations may provide—

(a) for the levy not to be payable, or for a reduced amount to be payable, in specified cases or in cases determined by the Certification Officer in accordance with the regulations;

(b) for the intervals at which the levy is to be paid;

(c) for interest to be payable where a payment is not made by the required date;

(d) for an amount levied to be recoverable by the Certification Officer as a debt.

(6) The regulations may contain such incidental, supplementary or transitional provisions as appear to the Secretary of State to be necessary or expedient.

(7) In this section—

"federated employers' association" has the same meaning as in section 135;

"federated trade union" has the same meaning as in section 118;

"specified" means specified in the regulations.

(8) Before making regulations under this section the Secretary of State must consult relevant organisations and ACAS.

(9) No regulations under this section shall be made unless a draft of them has been laid before Parliament and approved by a resolution of each House of Parliament.

(10) The Certification Officer shall pay into the Consolidated Fund amounts received by virtue of this section.]

NOTES

Commencement: to be appointed.

Inserted by the Trade Union Act 2016, s 20(1), as from a day to be appointed.

Regulations: as of 15 May 2019, no regulations had been made under this section.

[1.599]

258 Annual report and accounts

(1) The Certification Officer shall, as soon as practicable after the end of each [financial year], make a report of his activities during that year to ACAS and to the Secretary of State.

The Secretary of State shall lay a copy of the report before each House of Parliament and arrange for it to be published.

[(1A) A report under this section shall include details of—

(a) amounts levied by the Certification Officer by virtue of section 257A in the year in question, and

(b) how the amounts were determined.]

(2) The accounts prepared by ACAS in respect of any financial year shall show separately any sums disbursed to or on behalf of the Certification Officer in consequence of the provisions of this Part.

NOTES

Sub-s (1): words in square brackets substituted by the Employment Relations Act 1999, s 29, Sch 6, paras 1, 24.

Sub-s (1A): inserted by the Trade Union Act 2016, s 20(2), as from a day to be appointed.

Central Arbitration Committee

[1.600]

259 The Central Arbitration Committee

(1) There shall continue to be a body called the Central Arbitration Committee.

(2) The functions of the Committee shall be performed on behalf of the Crown, but not so as to make it subject to directions of any kind from any Minister of the Crown as to the manner in which it is to exercise its functions.

(3) ACAS shall provide for the Committee the requisite staff (from among the officers and servants of ACAS) and the requisite accommodation, equipment and other facilities.

[1.601]

260 The members of the Committee

[(1) The Central Arbitration Committee shall consist of members appointed by the Secretary of State.

(2) The Secretary of State shall appoint a member as chairman, and may appoint a member as deputy chairman or members as deputy chairmen.

(3) The Secretary of State may appoint as members only persons experienced in industrial relations, and they shall include some persons whose experience is as representatives of employers and some whose experience is as representatives of workers.

(3A) Before making an appointment under subsection (1) or (2) the Secretary of State shall consult ACAS and may consult other persons.]

(4) At any time when the chairman of the Committee is absent or otherwise incapable of acting, or there is a vacancy in the office of chairman, and the Committee has a deputy chairman or deputy chairmen—

(a) the deputy chairman, if there is only one, or

(b) if there is more than one, such of the deputy chairmen as they may agree or in default of agreement as the Secretary of State may direct,

may perform any of the functions of chairman of the Committee.

(5) At any time when every person who is chairman or deputy chairman is absent or otherwise incapable of acting, or there is no such person, such member of the Committee as the Secretary of State may direct may perform any of the functions of the chairman of the Committee.

(6) The validity of any proceedings of the Committee shall not be affected by any vacancy among the members of the Committee or by any defect in the appointment of a member of the Committee.

NOTES

Sub-ss (1)–(3A): substituted, for the original sub-ss (1)–(3), by the Employment Relations Act 1999, s 24.

[1.602]

261 Terms of appointment of members of Committee

(1) The members of the Central Arbitration Committee shall hold and vacate office in accordance with their terms of appointment, subject to the following provisions.

(2) A person shall not be appointed to the Committee for a term exceeding five years, but previous membership does not affect eligibility for re-appointment.

(3) The Secretary of State may, with the consent of the member concerned, vary the terms of his appointment as to whether he is a full-time or part-time member.

(4) A member may at any time resign his membership, and the chairman or a deputy chairman may at any time resign his office as such, by notice in writing to the Secretary of State.

(5) If the Secretary of State is satisfied that a member—

(a) has become bankrupt or [has had a debt relief order (under Part 7A of the Insolvency Act 1986) made in respect of him or has] made an arrangement with his creditors (or, in Scotland, has had his estate sequestrated or has made a trust deed for his creditors or has made and had accepted a composition contract), or

(b) is incapacitated by physical or mental illness, or

(c) is otherwise unable or unfit to discharge the functions of a member,

the Secretary of State may declare his office as a member to be vacant and shall notify the declaration in such manner as he thinks fit, whereupon the office shall become vacant.

(6) If the chairman or a deputy chairman ceases to be a member of the Committee, he shall also cease to be chairman or, as the case may be, a deputy chairman.

NOTES

Sub-s (5): words in square brackets in para (a) inserted by the Tribunals, Courts and Enforcement Act 2007 (Consequential Amendments) Order 2012, SI 2012/2404, art 3(2), Sch 2, para 28(1), (3).

[1.603]

262 Remuneration, &c of members of Committee

(1) ACAS shall pay to the members of the Central Arbitration Committee such remuneration and travelling and other allowances as may be determined by the Secretary of State.

(2) The Secretary of State may pay, or make provision for payment, to or in respect of a member of the Committee such pension, allowance or gratuity on death or retirement as he may determine.

(3) Where a person ceases to be the holder of the Committee otherwise than on the expiry of his term of office and it appears to the Secretary of State that there are special circumstances which make it right for him to receive compensation, he may make him a payment of such amount he may determine.

(4) The approval of the Treasury is required for any determination by the Secretary of State under this section.

[1.604]

263 Proceedings of the Committee

(1) For the purpose of discharging its functions in any particular case the Central Arbitration Committee shall consist of the chairman and such other members as the chairman may direct:

Provided that, it may sit in two or more divisions constituted of such members as the chairman may direct, and in a division in which the chairman does not sit the functions of the chairman shall be performed by a deputy chairman.

(2) The Committee may, at the discretion of the chairman, where it appears expedient to do so, call in the aid of one or more assessors, and may settle the matter wholly or partly with their assistance.

(3) The Committee may at the discretion of the chairman sit in private where it appears expedient to do so.

(4) If in any case the Committee cannot reach a unanimous decision on its award, the chairman shall decide the matter acting with the full powers of an umpire or, in Scotland, an oversman.

(5) Subject to the above provisions, the Committee shall determine its own procedure.

(6) [Part I of the Arbitration Act 1996] (general provisions as to arbitration) and [sections 1 to 15 of and schedule 1 to the Arbitration (Scotland) Act 2010] do not apply to proceedings before the Committee.

[(7) In relation to the discharge of the Committee's functions under Schedule A1—

(a) section 263A and subsection (6) above shall apply, and
(b) subsections (1) to (5) above shall not apply.]

NOTES

Sub-s (6): words in first pair of square brackets substituted by the Arbitration Act 1996, s 107(1), Sch 3, para 6; words in second pair of square brackets substituted by the Arbitration (Scotland) Act 2010 (Consequential Amendments) Order 2010, SSI 2010/220, art 2, Schedule, para 6(1), (3).

Sub-s (7): added by the Employment Relations Act 1999, s 25(1), (2).

[1.605]

[263A Proceedings of the Committee under Schedule A1

(1) For the purpose of discharging its functions under Schedule A1 in any particular case, the Central Arbitration Committee shall consist of a panel established under this section.

(2) The chairman of the Committee shall establish a panel or panels, and a panel shall consist of these three persons appointed by him—

(a) the chairman or a deputy chairman of the Committee, who shall be chairman of the panel;
(b) a member of the Committee whose experience is as a representative of employers;
(c) a member of the Committee whose experience is as a representative of workers.

(3) The chairman of the Committee shall decide which panel is to deal with a particular case.

(4) A panel may at the discretion of its chairman sit in private where it appears expedient to do so.

(5) If—

(a) a panel cannot reach a unanimous decision on a question arising before it, and
(b) a majority of the panel have the same opinion,

the question shall be decided according to that opinion.

(6) If—

(a) a panel cannot reach a unanimous decision on a question arising before it, and
(b) a majority of the panel do not have the same opinion,

the chairman of the panel shall decide the question acting with the full powers of an umpire or, in Scotland, an oversman.

(7) Subject to the above provisions, a panel shall determine its own procedure.

[(8) The reference in subsection (1) to the Committee's functions under Schedule A1 does not include a reference to its functions under paragraph 166 of that Schedule.]]

NOTES

Inserted by the Employment Relations Act 1999, s 25(1), (3).

Sub-s (8): added by the Employment Relations Act 2004, s 57(1), Sch 1, para 15.

[1.606]

264 Awards of the Committee

(1) The Central Arbitration Committee may correct in any award[, or in any decision or declaration of the Committee under Schedule A1] any clerical mistake or error arising from an accidental slip or omission.

(2) If a question arises as to the interpretation of an award of the Committee, [or of a decision or declaration of the Committee under Schedule A1] any party may apply to the Committee for a decision; and the Committee shall decide the question after hearing the parties or, if the parties consent, without a hearing, and shall notify the parties.

(3) Decisions of the Committee in the exercise of any of its functions shall be published.

NOTES

Sub-ss (1), (2): words in square brackets inserted by the Employment Relations Act 1999, s 25(1), (4).

[1.607]

265 Annual report and accounts

(1) ACAS shall, as soon as practicable after the end of each [financial year], make a report to the Secretary of State on the activities of the Central Arbitration Committee during that year.

For that purpose the Committee shall, as soon as practicable after the end of each [financial year], transmit to ACAS an account of its activities during that year.

(2) The accounts prepared by ACAS in respect of any financial year shall show separately any sums disbursed to or on behalf of the Committee in consequence of the provisions of this Part.

NOTES

Sub-s (1): words in square brackets substituted by the Employment Relations Act 1999, s 27(2).

266–271 *(Repealed by the Employment Relations Act 1999, ss 28(2)(c), 44, Sch 9(6).)*

Supplementary

[1.608]

272 Meaning of "financial year"

In this Part "financial year" means the twelve months ending with 31st March.

PART VII
MISCELLANEOUS AND GENERAL

Crown employment, etc

[1.609]
273 Crown employment

(1) The provisions of this Act have effect (except as mentioned below) in relation to Crown employment and persons in Crown employment as in relation to other employment and other workers or employees.

(2) The following provisions are excepted from subsection (1)—

[section 87(4)(b) (power of tribunal] to make order in respect of employer's failure to comply with duties as to union contributions);

sections 184 and 185 (remedy for failure to comply with declaration as to disclosure of information);

Chapter II of Part IV (procedure for handling redundancies).

(3) In this section "Crown employment" means employment under or for the purposes of a government department or any officer or body exercising on behalf of the Crown functions conferred by an enactment.

(4) For the purposes of the provisions of this Act as they apply in relation to Crown employment or persons in Crown employment—

(a) "employee" and "contract of employment" mean a person in Crown employment and the terms of employment of such a person (but subject to subsection (5) below);

(b) "dismissal" means the termination of Crown employment;

(c) . . .

(d) the reference in 182(1)(e) (disclosure of information for collective bargaining: restrictions on general duty) to the employer's undertaking shall be construed as a reference to the national interest; and

(e) any other reference to an undertaking shall be construed, in relation to a Minister of the Crown, as a reference to his functions or (as the context may require) to the department of which he is in charge, and in relation to a government department, officer or body shall be construed as a reference to the functions of the department, officer or body or (as the context may require) to the department, officer or body.

(5) Sections 137 to 143 (rights in relation to trade union membership: access to employment) apply in relation to Crown employment otherwise than under a contract only where the terms of employment correspond to those of a contract of employment.

(6) This section has effect subject to section 274 (armed forces) and section 275 (exemption on grounds of national security).

NOTES

Sub-s (2): words in square brackets substituted by the Employment Rights (Dispute Resolution) Act 1998, s 15, Sch 1, para 8.

Sub-s (4): para (c) repealed by the Trade Union Reform and Employment Rights Act 1993, s 51, Sch 10.

Note: Employment by the Office for Nuclear Regulation is not Crown employment for the purposes of this Act; see the Energy Act 2013, Sch 7, para 14(4).

[1.610]
274 Armed forces

(1) Section 273 (application of Act to Crown employment) does not apply to service as a member of the naval, military or air forces of the Crown.

(2) But that section applies to employment by an association established for the purposes of [Part XI of the Reserve Forces Act 1996] (territorial, auxiliary and reserve forces associations) as it applies to employment for the purposes of a government department.

NOTES

Sub-s (2): words in square brackets substituted by the Reserve Forces Act 1996, s 131(1), Sch 10, para 24.

[1.611]
275 Exemption on grounds of national security

(1) Section 273 (application of Act to Crown employment) does not apply to employment in respect of which there is in force a certificate issued by or on behalf of a Minister of the Crown certifying that employment of a description specified in the certificate, or the employment of a particular person so specified, is (or, at a time specified in the certificate, was) required to be excepted from that section for the purpose of safeguarding national security.

(2) A document purporting to be such a certificate shall, unless the contrary is proved, be deemed to be such a certificate.

[1.612]
276 Further provision as to Crown application

(1) Section 138 (refusal of service of employment agency on grounds related to union membership), and the other provisions of Part III applying in relation to that section, bind the Crown so far as they relate to the activities of an employment agency in relation to employment to which those provisions apply.

This does not affect the operation of those provisions in relation to Crown employment by virtue of section 273.

(2) Sections 144 and 145 (prohibition of union membership requirements) and sections 186 and 187 (prohibition of union recognition requirements) bind the Crown.

House of Lords and House of Commons staff

[1.613]

277 House of Lords staff

(1) [The provisions of this Act (except those specified below)] apply in relation to employment as a relevant member of the House of Lords staff as in relation to other employment.

[(1A) The following provisions are excepted from subsection (1)—

sections 184 and 185 (remedy for failure to comply with declaration as to disclosure of information),
Chapter II of Part IV (procedure for handling redundancies).]

(2) Nothing in any rule of law or the law or practice of Parliament prevents a person from bringing [a civil employment claim before the court or from bringing] before an [employment tribunal] proceedings of any description . . . which could be brought before such a tribunal in relation to other employment.

[(2A) For the purposes of the application of the other provisions of this Act as they apply by virtue of this section—

(a) the reference in section 182(1)(e) (disclosure of information for collective bargaining: restrictions) to a person's undertaking shall be construed as a reference to the national interest or, if the case so requires, the interests of the House of Lords; and

(b) any other reference to an undertaking shall be construed as a reference to the House of Lords.]

[(3) In this section—

"relevant member of the House of Lords staff" means any person who is employed under a contract of employment with the Corporate Officer of the House of Lords;

"civil employment claim" means a claim arising out of or relating to a contract of employment or any other contract connected with employment, or a claim in tort arising in connection with a person's employment; and

"the court" means the High Court or [the county court].]

NOTES

Sub-s (1): words in square brackets substituted by the Trade Union Reform and Employment Rights Act 1993, s 49(1), Sch 7, para 12(a).

Sub-s (1A): inserted by the Trade Union Reform and Employment Rights Act 1993, s 49(1), Sch 7, para 12(b).

Sub-s (2): words in first pair of square brackets inserted, and words omitted repealed, by the Trade Union Reform and Employment Rights Act 1993, ss 49(1), 51, Sch 7, para 12(c), Sch 10; words in second pair of square brackets substituted by the Employment Rights (Dispute Resolution) Act 1998, s 1(2)(a).

Sub-s (2A): inserted by the Trade Union Reform and Employment Rights Act 1993, s 49(1), Sch 7, para 12(d).

Sub-s (3): substituted, for the original sub-ss (3)–(6), by the Trade Union Reform and Employment Rights Act 1993, s 49(1), Sch 7, para 12(e); words in square brackets in the definition "the court" substituted by the Crime and Courts Act 2013, s 17(5), Sch 9, Pt 3, para 52.

[1.614]

278 House of Commons staff

(1) The provisions of this Act (except those specified below) apply in relation to employment as a relevant member of the House of Commons staff as in relation to other employment.

(2) The following provisions are excepted from subsection (1)—

sections 184 and 185 (remedy for failure to comply with declaration as to disclosure of information),
Chapter II of Part IV (procedure for handling redundancies).

[(2A) Nothing in any rule of law or the law or practice of Parliament prevents a relevant member of the House of Commons staff from bringing a civil employment claim before the court or from bringing before an [employment tribunal] proceedings of any description which could be brought before such a tribunal by any person who is not such a member.]

(3) In this section "relevant member of the House of Commons staff" has the same meaning as in section 139 of the Employment Protection (Consolidation) Act 1978.

["civil employment claim" means a claim arising out of or relating to a contract of employment or any other contract connected with employment, or a claim in tort arising in connection with a person's employment; and

"the court" means the High Court or the county court.]

(4) For the purposes of the other provisions of this Act as they apply by virtue of this section—

(a) "employee" and "contract of employment" include a relevant member of the House of Commons staff and the terms of employment of any such member (but subject to subsection (5) below);

(b) "dismissal" includes the termination of any such member's employment;

(c) the reference in [section] 182(1)(e) (disclosure of information for collective bargaining: restrictions on general duty) to the employer's undertaking shall be construed as a reference to the national interest or, if the case so requires, the interests of the House of Commons; and

(d) any other reference to an undertaking shall be construed as a reference to the House of Commons.

(5) Sections 137 to 143 (access to employment) apply by virtue of this section in relation to employment otherwise than under a contract only where the terms of employment correspond to those of a contract of employment.

(6) [Subsections (6) to (12) of section 195 of the Employment Rights Act 1996] (person to be treated as employer of House of Commons staff) apply, with any necessary modifications, for the purposes of this section.

NOTES

Sub-s (2A): inserted by the Trade Union Reform and Employment Rights Act 1993, s 49(2), Sch 8, para 85(a); words in square brackets substituted by the Employment Rights (Dispute Resolution) Act 1998, s 1(2)(a).

Sub-s (3): definitions "civil employment claim" and "the court" inserted by the Trade Union Reform and Employment Rights Act 1993, s 49(2), Sch 8, para 85(b). See further note to sub-s (6) below.

Sub-s (4): word in square brackets in para (c) inserted by the Trade Union Reform and Employment Rights Act 1993, s 49(1), Sch 7, para 27.

Sub-s (6): words in square brackets substituted by the Employment Rights Act 1996, s 240, Sch 1, para 56(1), (17). The 1996 Act does not provide for the equivalent substitution of a reference to s 195 for the reference to s 139 of the 1978 Act in sub-s (3) of this section; this is presumably a drafting error.

Employment Protection (Consolidation) Act 1978, s 139: repealed so far as relevant by the Employment Rights Act 1996, s 242, Sch 3, Pt I; for the meaning of "relevant member of the House of Commons staff", see now s 195(5) of the 1996 Act at **[1.1110]**.

Health service practitioners

[1.615]

279 Health service practitioners

[(1)] In this Act "worker" includes an individual regarded in his capacity as one who works or normally works or seeks to work as a person [performing . . . personal dental services or] providing . . . general dental services, general ophthalmic services or pharmaceutical services in accordance with arrangements made—

(a) by [the National Health Service Commissioning Board] [[under section 126 of the National Health Service Act 2006] or] [a] [Local Health Board] under section [. . .] . . . , [71 or 80 of the National Health Service (Wales) Act 2006] of the National Health Service Act 1977, or

(b) by a Health Board under section [17C,] . . . , 25, *26, or 27* of the National Health Service (Scotland) Act 1978 [or as a person providing local pharmaceutical services under a pilot scheme [established under section 134 of the National Health Service Act 2006 or section 92 of the National Health Service (Wales) Act 2006, or under an LPS scheme established under Schedule 12 to the National Health Service Act 2006 or Schedule 7 to the National Health Service (Wales) Act 2006]];

and "employer", in relation to such an individual, regarded in that capacity, means that . . . board.

[(2) In this Act "worker" also includes an individual regarded in his capacity as one who works or normally works or seeks to work as a person performing primary medical services *or primary dental services*—

(a) in accordance with arrangements made by [the National Health Service Commissioning Board or a] Local Health Board under [section 92 or 107 of the National Health Service Act 2006, or section 50 or 64 of the National Health Service (Wales) Act 2006]; or

(b) under a contract under [section 84 or 100 of the National Health Service Act 2006 or section 42 or 57 of the National Health Service (Wales) Act 2006] entered into by him with [the National Health Service Commissioning Board or a] Local Health Board, [or under a contract under section 117 of the National Health Service Act 2006 [entered into by him with the National Health Service Commissioning Board],]

and "employer" in relation to such an individual, regarded in that capacity, means that Trust, . . . Board.]

[(3) In this Act "worker" also includes an individual regarded in his capacity as one who works or normally works or seeks to work as a person performing primary medical services—

(a) in accordance with arrangements made by a Health Board under section 17C of the National Health Service (Scotland) Act 1978; or

(b) under a contract under section 17J of that Act entered into by him with a Health Board,

and "employer" in relation to such an individual, regarded in that capacity, means that Health Board.]

[(4) In this Act—

(a) "worker" also includes an individual regarded in his capacity as one who works or normally works or seeks to work as a person performing pharmaceutical care services under a contract entered into by him with a Health Board under section 17Q of the National Health Service (Scotland) Act 1978; and

(b) "employer" in relation to such a person, regarded in that capacity, means that Health Board.]

NOTES

This section has been amended as follows:

Sub-s (1): numbered as such by the Health and Social Care (Community Health and Standards) Act 2003, s 184, Sch 11, para 59(1), (3).

Sub-s (1) (opening paragraph): words in square brackets inserted by the National Health Service (Primary Care) Act 1997, s 41(10), Sch 2, Pt I, para 67(a); words omitted repealed by the Primary Medical Services (Scotland) Act 2004 (Consequential Modifications) Order 2004, SI 2004/957, art 2, Schedule, para 7(a)(i).

Sub-s (1)(a): words in first pair of square brackets substituted, and word in fourth pair of square brackets inserted, by the Health and Social Care Act 2012, s 55(2), Sch 5, para 66(a), (b); words in second (outer) pair of square brackets inserted by the National Health Service Reform and Health Care Professions Act 2002, s 2(5), Sch 2, Pt 2, para 60; words in third (inner) pair of square brackets inserted by the National Health Service (Consequential Provisions) Act 2006, s 2, Sch 1, paras 153, 154(a)(ii); words in fifth pair of square brackets substituted by the References to Health Authorities Order 2007, SI 2007/961, art 3, Schedule, para 22; the figure omitted from the sixth pair of square brackets was originally inserted by the National Health Service (Primary Care) Act 1997, s 41(10), Sch 2, Pt I, para 67(b), and repealed by the Health and Social Care (Community Health and Standards) Act 2003, ss 184, 196, Sch 11, para 59(1), (2), Sch 14, Pt 4; second figure omitted repealed by the Health and Social Care (Community Health and Standards) Act 2003, ss 184, 196, Sch 11, para 59(1), (2), Sch 14, Pt 4; final words in square brackets substituted by the National Health Service (Consequential Provisions) Act 2006, s 2, Sch 1, paras 153, 154(a)(iii) (it is assumed that a drafting error has occurred in this paragraph, as references to specific provisions of the National Health Service Act 1977 have been repealed, but the (redundant) reference to that Act has not been repealed).

Sub-s (1)(b): figure in first pair of square brackets inserted by the National Health Service (Primary Care) Act 1997, s 41(10), Sch 2, Pt I, para 67(c); figure omitted repealed by the Primary Medical Services (Scotland) Act 2004 (Consequential Modifications) Order 2004, SI 2004/957, art 2, Schedule, para 7(a)(ii); for the words in italics there are substituted the words "or 26" by the Smoking, Health and Social Care (Scotland) Act 2005 (Consequential Modifications) (England, Wales and Northern Ireland) Order 2006, SI 2006/1056, art 2, Schedule, Pt 1, para 6(a), as from a day to be appointed; words in second (outer) pair of square brackets inserted by the Health and Social Care Act 2001, s 67(1), Sch 5, Pt I, para 9; words in third (inner) pair of square brackets substituted by the National Health Service (Consequential Provisions) Act 2006, s 2, Sch 1, paras 153, 154(b); final words omitted repealed by the Health and Social Care Act 2012, s 55(2), Sch 5, para 66(c).

Sub-s (2): added by the Health and Social Care (Community Health and Standards) Act 2003, s 184, Sch 11, para 59(1), (4); for the words in italics in the opening paragraph there are substituted the words ", primary dental services or primary ophthalmic services" by the Health Act 2006, s 80(1), Sch 8, para 30(a), as from a day to be appointed; words in first pair of square brackets in para (a) substituted by the Health and Social Care Act 2012, s 55(2), Sch 5, para 66(d); words in second pair of square brackets in para (a) and words in first pair of square brackets in para (b) substituted by the National Health Service (Consequential Provisions) Act 2006, s 2, Sch 1, paras 153, 155; words in second and fourth (inner) pairs of square brackets in para (b) substituted, and final words omitted repealed by the Health and Social Care Act 2012, s 55(2), Sch 5, para 66(e)–(g); words in third (outer) pair of square brackets in para (b) inserted by the Health Act 2006, s 80(1), Sch 8, para 30(b) (as amended by the National Health Service (Consequential Provisions) Act 2006, s 2, Sch 1, paras 281, 291), as from a day to be appointed.

Sub-s (3): added by the Primary Medical Services (Scotland) Act 2004 (Consequential Modifications) Order 2004, SI 2004/957, art 2, Schedule, para 7(b).

Sub-s (4): added by SI 2006/1056, art 2, Schedule, Pt 1, para 6(b), as from a day to be appointed.

Transitional provisions and miscellaneous:

The General Medical Services Transitional and Consequential Provisions (Wales) (No 2) Order 2004, SI 2004/1016, art 85(1), (2)(d) (made under the Health and Social Care (Community Health and Standards) Act 2003, ss 176, 195(1), 200, 201) provides that until such time as default contracts entered into pursuant to s 176(3) of the 2003 Act cease to exist, any reference to a general medical services contract or to a contract under the National Health Service Act 1977, s 28Q includes a reference to a default contract. Note that the General Medical Services and Personal Medical Services Transitional and Consequential Provisions Order 2004, SI 2004/865, art 109(1), (2)(d) (which made similar provision in relation to England) was revoked by the National Health Service (General Medical Services Contracts) Regulations 2015, SI 2015/1862, as from 7 December 2015. See also the General Medical Services and Section 17C Agreements (Transitional and other Ancillary Provisions) (Scotland) Order 2004, SSI 2004/163 which provides that for as long as default contracts entered into pursuant to article 13 of the General Medical Services (Transitional and other Ancillary Provisions) (Scotland) Order 2004 continue to exist, the reference in this section to a general medical services contract or to a contract under section 17J of the 1978 Act shall be deemed to include a reference to a default contract.

Police service

[1.616]

280 Police service

(1) In this Act "employee" or "worker" does not include a person in police service; and the provisions of sections 137 and 138 (rights in relation to trade union membership: access to employment) do not apply in relation to police service.

(2) "Police service" means service as a member of any constabulary maintained by virtue of an enactment, or in any other capacity by virtue of which a person has the powers or privileges of a constable.

NOTES

Meaning of "police service":

An individual who as a member of the prison service acts in a capacity in which he has the powers or privileges of a constable is not, by virtue of his having those powers or privileges, to be regarded as in police service for the purposes of any provision of this Act; see the Criminal Justice and Public Order Act 1994, s 126(1), (2) at **[1.726]**.

A member of the Independent Office for Police Conduct's staff, who is not a constable, is not treated as being in police service for the purposes of this section; see the Police Reform Act 2002, s 13, Sch 3, Pt 3, para 19(5).

A constable or cadet of the British Transport Police Force may not be a member of a trade union, except for the British Transport Police Federation, although the Chief Constable of the British Transport Police Force may allow an officer to continue membership of a trade union acquired before joining the Force; see the Railways and Transport Safety Act 2003, s 30.

A National Crime Agency officer who is designated as having the powers and privileges of a constable is not to be regarded, by virtue of having those powers and privileges, as in police service for the purposes of any provision of this Act; see the Crime and Courts Act 2013, Sch 5, Pt 4, para 15.

Excluded classes of employment

281 *(Repealed by the Employment Protection (Part-time Employees) Regulations 1995, SI 1995/31, regs 5, 6, Schedule.)*

[1.617]

[282 Fixed term employment

(1) In this section, "fixed term contract" means a contract of employment that, under its provisions determining how it will terminate in the normal course, will terminate—

(a) on the expiry of a specific term,
(b) on the completion of a particular task, or
(c) on the occurrence or non-occurrence of any other specific event other than the attainment by the employee of any normal and bona fide retiring age in the establishment for an employee holding the position held by him.

(2) The provisions of Chapter II of Part IV (procedure for handling redundancies) do not apply to employment under a fixed term contract unless—

(a) the employer is proposing to dismiss the employee as redundant; and

(b) the dismissal will take effect before the expiry of the specific term, the completion of the particular task or the occurrence or non-occurrence of the specific event (as the case may be).]

NOTES

Substituted by the Trade Union and Labour Relations (Consolidation) Act 1992 (Amendment) Order 2013, SI 2013/763, art 3(1), (4).

283 *(Repealed by the Trade Union Reform and Employment Rights Act 1993, ss 34(1), (6), 51, Sch 10.)*

[1.618]

284 Share fishermen

The following provisions of this Act do not apply to employment as master or as member of the crew of a fishing vessel where the employee [(or, in the case of sections 145A to 151, the worker)] is remunerated only by a share in the profits or gross earnings of the vessel—

In Part III (rights in relation to trade union membership and activities)—
sections 137 to 143 (access to employment),
[sections 145A to 151 (inducements and detriment)], and
sections 168 to 173 (time off for trade union duties and activities);
In Part IV, Chapter II (procedure for handling redundancies).

NOTES

Words in first pair of square brackets inserted, and words in second pair of square brackets substituted, by the Employment Relations Act 2004, s 57(1), Sch 1, para 16.

Words in italics repealed by the Seafarers (Insolvency, Collective Redundancies and Information and Consultation Miscellaneous Amendments) Regulations 2018, SI 2018/407, reg 3(1), (2), as from 13 April 2018. Note that by virtue of reg 3(3) of those Regulations, this amendment only has effect in relation to dismissals which are first proposed by an employer on or after that date (see **[2.2052]**).

[1.619]

285 Employment outside Great Britain

(1) The following provisions of this Act do not apply to employment where under his contract of employment an employee works, or in the case of a prospective employee would ordinarily work, outside Great Britain—

In Part III (rights in relation to trade union membership and activities)—
sections 137 to 143 (access to employment),
[sections 145A to 151 (inducements and detriment)], and
sections 168 to 173 (time off for trade union duties and activities);
In Part IV, [sections [193 to 194] (duty to notify Secretary of State of certain redundancies)].

[(1A) Sections 145A to 151 do not apply to employment where under his contract personally to do work or perform services a worker who is not an employee works outside Great Britain.]

[(1B) For the purposes of subsection (1) as it relates to sections 193 to 194, employment on board a ship registered in the United Kingdom shall be treated as employment where under his contract a person ordinarily works in Great Britain.]

(2) For the [other purposes of subsection (1) and the purposes of subsection (1A)] employment on board a ship registered in the United Kingdom shall be treated as employment where under his contract a person ordinarily works in Great Britain unless—

(a) the ship is registered at a port outside Great Britain, or

(b) the employment is wholly outside Great Britain, or

(c) the employee or, as the case may be, [the worker or] the person seeking employment or seeking to avail himself of a service of an employment agency, is not ordinarily resident in Great Britain.

NOTES

Sub-s (1): words in first pair of square brackets substituted by the Employment Relations Act 2004, s 57(1), Sch 1, para 17(1), (2); words in second (outer) pair of square brackets substituted by the Employment Relations Act 1999, s 32(1); words in third (inner) pair of square brackets substituted by the Seafarers (Transnational Information and Consultation, Collective Redundancies and Insolvency Miscellaneous Amendments) Regulations 2018, SI 2018/26, reg 3(1), (3)(a), as from 6 February 2018, in relation to dismissals which are first proposed by an employer on or after that date (see reg 3(4)).

Sub-s (1A): inserted by the Employment Relations Act 2004, s 57(1), Sch 1, para 17(1), (3).

Sub-s (1B): inserted by SI 2018/26, reg 3(1), (3)(b), as from 6 February 2018, in relation to dismissals which are first proposed by an employer on or after that date (see reg 3(4)).

Sub-s (2): words in first pair of square brackets substituted by SI 2018/26, reg 3(1), (3)(c), as from 6 February 2018, in relation to dismissals which are first proposed by an employer on or after that date (see reg 3(4)); words in square brackets in para (c) inserted by the Employment Relations Act 2004, s 57(1), Sch 1, para 17(1), (4).

[1.620]

286 Power to make further provision as to excluded classes of employment

(1) This section applies in relation to the following provisions—

In Part III (rights in relation to trade union membership and activities), [sections 145A to 151 (inducements and detriment)],
In Part IV, Chapter II (procedure for handling redundancies), and

In Part V (industrial action), section 237 (dismissal of those taking part in unofficial industrial action).

(2) The Secretary of State may by order made by statutory instrument provide that any of those provisions—

(a) shall not apply to persons or to employment of such classes as may be prescribed by the order, or

(b) shall apply to persons or employments of such classes as may be prescribed by the order subject to such exceptions and modifications as may be so prescribed,

and may vary or revoke any of the provisions of sections 281 to 285 above (excluded classes of employment) so far as they relate to any such provision.

(3) Any such order shall be made by statutory instrument and may contains such incidental, supplementary or transitional provisions as appear to the Secretary of State to be necessary or expedient.

(4) No such order shall be made unless a draft of the order has been laid before Parliament and approved by a resolution of each House of Parliament.

NOTES

Sub-s (1): words in square brackets substituted by the Employment Relations Act 2004, s 57(1), Sch 1, para 18.

Orders: the Trade Union and Labour Relations (Consolidation) Act 1992 (Amendment) Order 2013, SI 2013/763; the Seafarers (Insolvency, Collective Redundancies and Information and Consultation Miscellaneous Amendments) Regulations 2018, SI 2018/407.

Offshore employment

[1.621]

287 Offshore employment

(1) In this Act "offshore employment" means employment for the purposes of activities—

(a) in the territorial waters of the United Kingdom, or

(b) connected with the exploration of the sea-bed or subsoil, or the exploitation of their natural resources, in the United Kingdom sector of the continental shelf, or

(c) connected with the exploration or exploitation, in a foreign sector of the continental shelf, of a cross-boundary petroleum field.

(2) Her Majesty may by Order in Council provide that—

(a) the provisions of this Act, and

(b) any Northern Ireland legislation making provision for purposes corresponding to any of the purposes of this Act,

apply, to such extent and for such purposes as may be specified in the Order and with or without modification, to or in relation to a person in offshore employment or, in relation to sections 137 to 143 (access to employment), a person seeking such employment.

(3) An Order in Council under this section—

(a) may make different provision for different cases;

(b) may provide that the enactments to which this section applies, as applied, apply—

(i) to individuals whether or not they are British subjects, and

(ii) to bodies corporate whether or not they are incorporated under the law of a part of the United Kingdom,

and apply notwithstanding that the application may affect the activities of such an individual or body outside the United Kingdom;

(c) may make provision for conferring jurisdiction on any court or class of court specified in the Order, or on [employment tribunals], in respect of offences, causes of action or other matters arising in connection with offshore employment;

(d) may provide that the enactments to which this section applies apply in relation to a person in offshore employment in a part of the areas referred to in subsection (1)(a) and (b);

(e) may exclude from the operation of section 3 of the Territorial Waters Jurisdiction Act 1878 (consents required for prosecutions) proceedings for offences under the enactments to which this section applies in connection with offshore employment;

(f) may provide that such proceedings shall not be brought without such consent as may be required by the Order;

(g) may modify or exclude any of sections 281 to 285 (excluded classes of employment) or any corresponding provision of Northern Ireland legislation.

[(3A) An Order in Council under this section shall be subject to annulment in pursuance of a resolution of either House of Parliament.]

(4) Any jurisdiction conferred on a court or tribunal under this section is without prejudice to jurisdiction exercisable apart from this section, by that or any other court or tribunal.

(5) In this section—

"cross-boundary petroleum field" means a petroleum field that extends across the boundary between the United Kingdom sector of the continental shelf and a foreign sector;

"foreign sector of the continental shelf" means an area outside the territorial waters of any state, within which rights with respect to the sea-bed and subsoil and their natural resources are exercisable by a state other than the United Kingdom;

"petroleum field" means a geological structure identified as an oil or gas field by the Order in Council concerned; and

"United Kingdom sector of the continental shelf" means the areas designated under section 1(7) of the Continental Shelf Act 1964.

NOTES

Sub-s (1): substituted by the Petroleum Act 1998, s 50, Sch 4, para 34(2), as from a day to be appointed, as follows—

"(1) In this Act "offshore employment" means employment for the purposes of—
(a) any activities in the territorial sea adjacent to the United Kingdom, and
(b) any such activities as are mentioned in section 11(2) of the Petroleum Act 1998 in waters within subsection (8)(b) or (c) of that section.".

Sub-s (3): words in square brackets in para (c) substituted by the Employment Rights (Dispute Resolution) Act 1998, s 1(2)(a).

Sub-s (3A): inserted by the Employment Relations Act 1999, s 32(2).

Sub-s (5): repealed by the Petroleum Act 1998, ss 50, 51, Sch 4, para 34(3), Sch 5, Pt I, as from a day to be appointed.

Orders: the Employment Relations (Offshore Employment) Order 2000, SI 2000/1828. Also, by virtue of s 300(3) of, and Sch 3, para 1(2) to, this Act, and the Interpretation Act 1978, s 17(2)(b), the Employment Protection (Offshore Employment) Order 1976, SI 1976/766, has effect as if made under this section.

Contracting out, &c

[1.622]

288 Restriction on contracting out

(1) Any provision in an agreement (whether a contract of employment or not) is void in so far as it purports—
(a) to exclude or limit the operation of any provision of this Act, or
(b) to preclude a person from bringing—
(i) proceedings before an [employment tribunal] or the Central Arbitration Committee under any provision of this Act, . . .
(ii) . . .

(2) Subsection (1) does not apply to an agreement to refrain from instituting or continuing proceedings where a conciliation officer has taken action under [[any of sections 18A to 18C] of [the Employment Tribunals Act 1996] (conciliation).]

[(2A) Subsection (1) does not apply to an agreement to refrain from instituting or continuing any proceedings, other than excepted proceedings, specified in [subsection (1)(b) of that section] before an [employment tribunal] if the conditions regulating [settlement] agreements under this Act are satisfied in relation to the agreement.

(2B) The conditions regulating [settlement] agreements under this Act are that—
(a) the agreement must be in writing;
(b) the agreement must relate to the particular [proceedings];
(c) the complainant must have received [advice from a relevant independent adviser] as to the terms and effect of the proposed agreement and in particular its effect on his ability to pursue his rights before an [employment tribunal];
(d) there must be in force, when the adviser gives the advice, a [contract of insurance, or an indemnity provided for members of a professional body] covering the risk of a claim by the complainant in respect of loss arising in consequence of the advice;
(e) the agreement must identify the adviser; and
(f) the agreement must state that the conditions regulating [settlement] agreements under this Act are satisfied.

(2C) The proceedings excepted from subsection (2A) are proceedings on a complaint of non-compliance with section 188.]

(3) Subsection (1) does not apply—
(a) to such an agreement as is referred to in section 185(5)(b) or (c) to the extent that it varies or supersedes an award under that section;
(b) to any provision in a collective agreement excluding rights under Chapter II of Part IV (procedure for handling redundancies), if an order under section 198 is in force in respect of it.

[(4) A person is a relevant independent adviser for the purposes of subsection (2B)(c)—
(a) if he is a qualified lawyer,
(b) if he is an officer, official, employee or member of an independent trade union who has been certified in writing by the trade union as competent to give advice and as authorised to do so on behalf of the trade union,
(c) if he works at an advice centre (whether as an employee or a volunteer) and has been certified in writing by the centre as competent to give advice and as authorised to do so on behalf of the centre, or
(d) if he is a person of a description specified in an order made by the Secretary of State.

(4A) But a person is not a relevant independent adviser for the purposes of subsection (2B)(c) in relation to the complainant—
(a) if he is, is employed by or is acting in the matter for the other party or a person who is connected with the other party,
(b) in the case of a person within subsection (4)(b) or (c), if the trade union or advice centre is the other party or a person who is connected with the other party,
(c) in the case of a person within subsection (4)(c), if the complainant makes a payment for the advice received from him, or
(d) in the case of a person of a description specified in an order under subsection (4)(d), if any condition specified in the order in relation to the giving of advice by persons of that description is not satisfied.

(4B) In subsection (4)(a) "qualified lawyer" means—

(a) as respects England and Wales, a [a person who, for the purposes of the Legal Services Act 2007, is an authorised person in relation to an activity which constitutes the exercise of a right of audience or the conduct of litigation (within the meaning of that Act), and]

(b) as respects Scotland, an advocate (whether in practice as such or employed to give legal advice), or a solicitor who holds a practising certificate.

(4C) An order under subsection (4)(d) shall be made by statutory instrument which shall be subject to annulment in pursuance of a resolution of either House of Parliament.

(5) For the purposes of subsection (4A) any two persons are to be treated as connected—

(a) if one is a company of which the other (directly or indirectly) has control, or

(b) if both are companies of which a third person (directly or indirectly) has control.]

[(6) An agreement under which the parties agree to submit a dispute to arbitration—

(a) shall be regarded for the purposes of subsections (2) and (2A) as being an agreement to refrain from instituting or continuing proceedings if—

(i) the dispute is covered by a scheme having effect by virtue of an order under section 212A, and

(ii) the agreement is to submit it to arbitration in accordance with the scheme, but

(b) shall be regarded for those purposes as neither being nor including such an agreement in any other case.]

NOTES

Sub-s (1): words in square brackets in sub-para (b)(i) substituted by the Employment Rights (Dispute Resolution) Act 1998, s 1(2)(a); sub-para (b)(ii) and the word immediately preceding it repealed by the Employment Relations Act 2004, s 57, Sch 1, para 19, Sch 2.

Sub-s (2): words in first (outer) pair of square brackets substituted by the Employment Tribunals Act 1996, s 43, Sch 1, para 8(a); words "any of sections 18A to 18C" in square brackets substituted by the Enterprise and Regulatory Reform Act 2013, s 7(2), Sch 1, para 1; words "the Employment Tribunals Act 1996" in square brackets substituted by the Employment Rights (Dispute Resolution) Act 1998, s 1(2)(c).

Sub-s (2A): inserted, together with sub-ss (2B), (2C), by the Trade Union Reform and Employment Rights Act 1993, s 39(2), Sch 6, para 4(a); words in first pair of square brackets substituted by the Employment Tribunals Act 1996, s 43, Sch 1, para 8(b); words in second pair of square brackets substituted by the Employment Rights (Dispute Resolution) Act 1998, s 1(2)(a); word in third pair of square brackets substituted by the Enterprise and Regulatory Reform Act 2013, s 23(1)(a). See further the penultimate note below.

Sub-s (2B): inserted as noted above; word "settlement" in square brackets (in both places it occurs) substituted by the Enterprise and Regulatory Reform Act 2013, s 23(1)(a); other words in square brackets substituted by the Employment Rights (Dispute Resolution) Act 1998, ss 1(2)(a), 9(1), (2)(c), 10(1), (2)(c), 15, Sch 1, para 9(1), (2).

Sub-s (2C): inserted as noted above.

Sub-ss (4), (4A)–(4C), (5): substituted, for the original sub-ss (4), (5) (as added by the Trade Union Reform and Employment Rights Act 1993, s 39(2), Sch 6, para 4(b)), by the Employment Rights (Dispute Resolution) Act 1998, s 15, Sch 1, para 9(1), (3).

Sub-s (4B): substituted as noted above; words square brackets substituted by the Legal Services Act 2007, s 208(1), Sch 21, paras 104, 107.

Sub-s (6): added by the Employment Rights (Dispute Resolution) Act 1998, s 8(3).

Note: prior to its amendment by the Enterprise and Regulatory Reform Act 2013, s 7(2), Sch 1, para 1, sub s (2) above contained a reference to s 18 of the Employment Tribunals Act 1996. It would appear that sub-s (2A) has not been amended to take account of the amendment to sub-s (2) above, nor the amendment to s 18 of the 1996 Act made by the Employment Tribunals Act 1996 (Application of Conciliation Provisions) Order 2014, SI 2014/431, art 2. It is believed that the words "subsection (1)(b) of that section" in sub-s (2A) should now be read as "subsection (1)(a) of section 18 of that Act".

Orders: the Settlement Agreements (Description of Person) Order 2004, SI 2004/754 at **[2.725]**; the Compromise Agreements (Description of Person) Order 2004 (Amendment) Order 2004, SI 2004/2515. Note that the title of SI 2004/754 was amended by SI 2013/1956, art 2, Schedule, para 10(a) (ie, the word "Settlement" was substituted for the word "Compromise"). No corresponding change was made to SI 2004/2515.

[1.623]

289 Employment governed by foreign law

For the purposes of this Act it is immaterial whether the law which (apart from this Act) governs any person's employment is the law of the United Kingdom, or of a part of the United Kingdom, or not.

290, 291 *(Repealed by the Employment Tribunals Act 1996, s 45, Sch 3, Pt I. S 291(1) had been repealed by the Trade Union Reform and Employment Rights Act 1993. S 290 and s 291(2) and (3) are re-enacted respectively as ss 18(1) and 21(1) and (2) of the 1996 Act, at* **[1.757]**, **[1.764]**.)

Other supplementary provisions

[1.624]

292 Death of employee or employer

(1) This section has effect in relation to the following provisions so far as they confer rights on employees or make provision in connection therewith—

(a) . . .

(b) sections 168 to 173 (time off for trade union duties and activities);

(c) sections 188 to 198 (procedure for handling redundancies).

[(1A) This section also has effect in relation to sections 145A to 151 so far as those sections confer rights on workers or make provision in connection therewith.]

(2) Where the employee [or worker] or employer dies, tribunal proceedings may be instituted or continued by a personal representative of the deceased employee [or worker] or, as the case may be, defended by a personal representative of the deceased employer.

(3) If there is no personal representative of a deceased employee [or worker], tribunal proceedings or proceedings to enforce a tribunal award may be instituted or continued on behalf of his estate by such other person as the [employment tribunal] may appoint, being either—

(a) a person authorised by the employee [or worker] to act in connection with the proceedings before his death, or

(b) the widower, widow, [surviving civil partner,] child, father, mother, brother or sister of the employee [or worker].

In such a case any award made by the [employment tribunal] shall be in such terms and shall be enforceable in such manner as may be prescribed.

(4) Any right arising under any of the provisions mentioned in subsection (1) [or (1A)] which by virtue of this section accrues after the death of the employee [or worker] in question shall devolve as if it had accrued before his death.

(5) Any liability arising under any of those provisions which by virtue of this section accrues after the death of the employer in question shall be treated for all purposes as if it had accrued immediately before his death.

NOTES

Sub-s (1): para (a) repealed by the Employment Relations Act 2004, s 57, Sch 1, para 20(1), (2), Sch 2.

Sub-s (1A): inserted by the Employment Relations Act 2004, s 57(1), Sch 1, para 20(1), (3).

Sub-ss (2), (4): words in square brackets inserted by the Employment Relations Act 2004, s 57(1), Sch 1, para 20(1), (4), (5).

Sub-s (3): words in first, third and fifth pairs of square brackets inserted by the Employment Relations Act 2004, s 57(1), Sch 1, para 20(1), (4); words in second and final pairs of square brackets substituted by the Employment Rights (Dispute Resolution) Act 1998, s 1(1), (2)(a); words in fourth pair of square brackets inserted by the Civil Partnership Act 2004, s 261(1), Sch 27, para 146.

Regulations: as of 15 May 2019, no Regulations have been made under this section but, by virtue of s 300(3) of, and Sch 3, para 1(2) to, this Act, and the Interpretation Act 1978, s 17(2)(b), the Employment Tribunal Awards (Enforcement in case of death) Regulations 1976, SI 1976/663, have effect as if made under this section.

[1.625]

[292A Extension of time limits to facilitate conciliation before institution of proceedings

(1) This section applies where this Act provides for it to apply for the purposes of a provision of this Act (a "relevant provision").

(2) In this section—

(a) Day A is the day on which the complainant concerned complies with the requirement in subsection (1) of section 18A of the Employment Tribunals Act 1996 (requirement to contact ACAS before instituting proceedings) in relation to the matter in respect of which the proceedings are brought, and

(b) Day B is the day on which the complainant concerned receives or, if earlier, is treated as receiving (by virtue of regulations made under subsection (11) of that section) the certificate issued under subsection (4) of that section.

(3) In working out when a time limit set by a relevant provision expires the period beginning with the day after Day A and ending with Day B is not to be counted.

(4) If a time limit set by a relevant provision would (if not extended by this subsection) expire during the period beginning with Day A and ending one month after Day B, the time limit expires instead at the end of that period.

(5) Where an employment tribunal has power under this Act to extend a time limit set by a relevant provision, the power is exercisable in relation to the time limit as extended by this section.]

NOTES

Inserted by the Enterprise and Regulatory Reform Act 2013, s 8, Sch 2, paras 1, 13.

[1.626]

293 Regulations

(1) The Secretary of State may by regulations prescribe anything authorised or required to be prescribed for the purposes of this Act.

(2) The regulations may contain such incidental, supplementary or transitional provisions as appear to the Secretary of State to be necessary or expedient.

(3) Regulations under this section shall be made by statutory instrument which shall be subject to annulment in pursuance of a resolution of either House of Parliament.

294 *(Reciprocal arrangements with Northern Ireland: outside the scope of this work.)*

Interpretation

[1.627]

295 Meaning of "employee" and related expressions

(1) In this Act—

"contract of employment" means a contract of service or of apprenticeship,

"employee" means an individual who has entered into or works under (or, where the employment has ceased, worked under) a contract of employment, and

"employer", in relation to an employee, means the person by whom the employee is (or, where the employment has ceased, was) employed.

(2) Subsection (1) has effect subject to section 235 and other provisions conferring a wider meaning on "contract of employment" or related expressions.

[1.628]
296 Meaning of "worker" and related expressions

(1) In this Act "worker" means an individual who works, or normally works or seeks to work—

(a) under a contract of employment, or

(b) under any other contract whereby he undertakes to do or perform personally any work or services for another party to the contract who is not a professional client of his, or

(c) in employment under or for the purposes of a government department (otherwise than as a member of the naval, military or air forces of the Crown) in so far as such employment does not fall within paragraph (a) or (b) above.

(2) In this Act "employer", in relation to a worker, means a person for whom one or more workers work, or have worked or normally work or seek to work.

[(3) This section has effect subject to [sections 68(4), [116B(10),] 145F(3) and 151(1B)].]

NOTES

Sub-s (3): added by the Trade Union Reform and Employment Rights Act 1993, s 49(2), Sch 8, para 88; words in square brackets substituted by the Employment Relations Act 2004, s 57(1), Sch 1, para 21; figure in square brackets inserted by the Trade Union Act 2016, s 15(2), as from a day to be appointed.

[1.629]
297 Associated employers

For the purposes of this Act any two employers shall be treated as associated if—

(a) one is a company of which the other (directly or indirectly) has control, or

(b) both are companies of which a third person (directly or indirectly) has control;

and "associated employer" shall be construed accordingly.

[1.630]
[297A Meaning of "voting"

For the purposes of this Act, the number of persons voting in a ballot includes those who return ballot papers that are spoiled or otherwise invalid.]

NOTES

Commencement: 1 March 2017.

Inserted by the Trade Union Act 2016, s 22, Sch 4, para 17, as from 1 March 2017.

[1.631]
[297B Devolved Welsh authorities

For the purposes of this Act a "devolved Welsh authority" has the same meaning as in section 157A of the Government of Wales Act 2006 (c 32).]

NOTES

Commencement: 13 September 2017.

Inserted by the Trade Union (Wales) Act 2017, s 1(1), (5), as from 13 September 2017.

[1.632]
298 Minor definitions: general

In this Act, unless the context otherwise requires—

"act" and "action" each includes omission, and references to doing an act or taking action shall be construed accordingly;

["agency worker" has the meaning given in regulation 3 of the Agency Workers Regulations 2010;]

["certificate of independence" means a certificate issued under—

(a) section 6(6), or

(b) section 101A(4);]

"contravention" includes a failure to comply, and cognate expressions shall be construed accordingly;

"dismiss", "dismissal" and "effective date of termination", in relation to an employee, shall be construed in accordance with [Part X of the Employment Rights Act 1996];

["legal professional privilege", as respects Scotland, means confidentiality of communications;]

. . .

"tort", as respects Scotland, means delict, and cognate expressions shall be construed accordingly.

NOTES

Definition "agency worker" inserted by the Agency Workers Regulations 2010, SI 2010/93, reg 25, Sch 2, Pt 1, paras 1, 5; definition "certificate of independence" inserted by the Employment Relations Act 2004, s 50(4); words in square brackets in definitions "dismiss", "dismissal", and "effective date of termination" substituted by the Employment Rights Act 1996, s 240, Sch 1, para 56(1), (19); definition "legal professional privilege" inserted by the Trade Union Act 2016, s 22, Sch 4, para 18, as from 1 March 2017; definition "post" (omitted) repealed by the Postal Services Act 2000 (Consequential Modifications No 1) Order 2001, SI 2001/1149, art 3(2), Sch 2.

[1.633]
299 Index of defined expressions

In this Act the expressions listed below are defined by or otherwise fall to be construed in accordance with the provisions indicated—

ACAS	section 247(1)

act and action	section 298
advertisement (in sections 137 to 143)	section 143(1)
[affected employees (in Part IV, Chapter II)	section 196(3)]
[affected transferring individual (in sections 198A and 198B)	section 198A(7)]
[agency worker	section 298]
[agent (of trade union)	section 119]
appropriately qualified actuary (in sections 38 to 41)	section 42
associated employer	section 297
branch or section (of trade union)	section 119
[certificate of independence	section 298]
collective agreement and collective bargaining	section 178(1)
. . .	
contract of employment	
—generally	section 295(1)
—in sections 226 to 234	section 235
—in relation to Crown employment	section 273(4)(a)
—in relation to House of Lords or House of Commons staff	section 277(4) and 278(4)(a)
contravention	section 298
[contributor (in relation to the political fund of a trade union)	section 84(5)]
the court (in Part I)	section 121
date of the ballot (in Part V)	section 246
[devolved Welsh authority	section 297B]
dismiss and dismissal	
—generally	section 298
—in relation to Crown employment	section 273(4)(c)
—in relation to House of Commons staff	section 278(4)(b)
[the duty of confidentiality[, in the context of a scrutineer or independent person]	section 24A(3)]
effective date of termination	section 298
employee	
—generally	section 295(1)
—in relation to Crown employment	section 273(4)(a)
—in relation to House of Commons staff	section 278(4)(a)
—excludes police service	section 280
[employee representatives (in Part IV, Chapter II)	section 196(1)]
employer	
—in relation to an employee	section 295(1)
—in relation to a worker	section 296(2)
—in relation to health service practitioners	section 279
employment and employment agency (in sections 137 to 143)	section 143(1)
executive (of trade union)	section 119
[financial affairs (of trade union)	section 119]
financial year (in Part VI)	section 72
general secretary	section 119
independent trade union (and related expressions)	section 5
[legal professional privilege (as respects Scotland)	section 298]
list	
—of trade unions	section 2
—of employers' associations	section 123
Northern Ireland union (in Part I)	section 120

not protected (in sections 222 to 226)	section 219(4)
officer —of trade union —of employers' association	 section 119 section 136
official (of trade union)	section 119
offshore employment	section 287
. . .	. . .
political fund	section 82(1)(a)
political resolution	section 82(1)(a)
. . .	. . .
prescribed	section 293(1)
president	section 119
[pre-transfer consultation (in sections 198A and 198B)	section 198A(7)]
recognised, recognition and related expressions	section 178(3)
. . .	. . .
[relevant transfer (in sections 198A and 198B)	section 198(7)]
[representatives of a trade union (in Part IV, Chapter II)	section 196(2)]
rules (of trade union)	section 119
strike (in Part V)	section 246
tort (as respects Scotland)	section 298
trade dispute —in Part IV —in Part V	 section 218 section 244
trade union	section 1
[transferee and transferor (in sections 198A and 198B)	section 198A(7)
transferring individual (in section 198A and 198B)	section 198A(7)]
undertaking (of employer) —in relation to Crown employment —in relation to House of Commons staff	 section 273(4)(e) and (f) section 278(4)(c) and (d)
[voting	section 297A]
worker —generally —includes health service practitioners —excludes police service	 section 296(1) section 279 section 280
working hours (in Part V)	section 246

NOTES

Entry "affected employees (in Part IV, Chapter II)" inserted by the Collective Redundancies and Transfer of Undertakings (Protection of Employment) (Amendment) Regulations 1999, SI 1999/1925, regs 2(1), (2), 7.

Entries "affected transferring individual (in sections 198A and 198B)", "pre-transfer consultation (in sections 198A and 198B)", "relevant transfer (in sections 198A and 198B)", "transferee and transferor (in sections 198A and 198B)" and "transferring individual (in sections 198A and 198B)" inserted by the Collective Redundancies and Transfer of Undertakings (Protection of Employment) (Amendment) Regulations 2014, SI 2014/16, reg 3(2).

Entry "agency worker" inserted by the Agency Workers Regulations 2010, SI 2010/93, reg 25, Sch 2, Pt 1, paras 1, 6.

Entries "agent (of trade union)" and "financial affairs (of trade union)" inserted by the Trade Union Reform and Employment Rights Act 1993, s 49(2), Sch 8, para 89.

Entries "contributor (in relation to the political fund of a trade union)", "legal professional privilege (as respects Scotland)", and "voting" inserted by the Trade Union Act 2016, s 22, Sch 4, para 19, as from 1 March 2017.

Entry beginning "the duty of confidentiality" inserted by the Trade Union Reform and Employment Rights Act 1993, s 49(2), Sch 8, para 89; words in square brackets in that entry inserted by the Transparency of Lobbying, Non-Party Campaigning and Trade Union Administration Act 2014, s 41(1), (5), as from 6 April 2015, in relation to a reporting period which commences on or after that date.

Entry "certificate of independence" inserted by the Employment Relations Act 2004, s 50(5).

Entries "the Commissioner" and "redundancy" (omitted) repealed by the Trade Union Reform and Employment Rights Act 1993, s 51, Sch 10.

Entry "devolved Welsh authority" inserted by the Trade Union (Wales) Act 2017, s 1(1), (6), as from 13 September 2017.

Entry "employee representatives" inserted, and entry "representatives of a trade union" substituted, by the Collective Redundancies and Transfer of Undertakings (Protection of Employment) (Amendment) Regulations 1995, SI 1995/2587, reg 7.

Entry relating to "place of work (in Part V)" (omitted) repealed by the Employment Relations Act 2004, s 57, Sch 1, para 22, Sch 2.

Entry "post" (omitted) repealed by the Postal Services Act 2000 (Consequential Modifications No 1) 2001, SI 2001/1149, art 3(2), Sch 2.

Final provisions

[1.634]
300 Repeals, consequential amendments, transitional provisions and savings
(1), (2) (*Introduce Sch 1 (repeals), and Sch 2 (amendments) respectively.*)
(3) Schedule 3 contains transitional provisions and savings.

[1.635]
301 Extent
(1) This Act extends to England and Wales and [(apart from section 212A(6)) to] Scotland.
(2), (3) (*Application to Northern Ireland (outside the scope of this work).*)

NOTES
Sub-s (1): words in square brackets inserted by the Employment Rights (Dispute Resolution) Act 1998, s 15, Sch 1, para 10.

[1.636]
302 Commencement
This Act comes into force at the end of the period of three months beginning with the day on which it is passed.

[1.637]
303 Short title
This Act may be cited as the Trade Union and Labour Relations (Consolidation) Act 1992.

SCHEDULES

[SCHEDULE A1
COLLECTIVE BARGAINING: RECOGNITION

Section 70A

NOTES

This Schedule was inserted by the Employment Relations Act 1999, s 1(1), (3), Sch 1.

PART I
RECOGNITION

Introduction

[1.638]

1. A trade union (or trade unions) seeking recognition to be entitled to conduct collective bargaining on behalf of a group or groups of workers may make a request in accordance with this Part of this Schedule.

2. (1) This paragraph applies for the purposes of this Part of this Schedule.

(2) References to the bargaining unit are to the group of workers concerned (or the groups taken together).

(3) References to the proposed bargaining unit are to the bargaining unit proposed in the request for recognition.

[(3A) References to an appropriate bargaining unit's being decided by the CAC are to a bargaining unit's being decided by the CAC to be appropriate under paragraph 19(2) or (3) or 19A(2) or (3).]

(4) References to the employer are to the employer of the workers constituting the bargaining unit concerned.

(5) References to the parties are to the union (or unions) and the employer.

3. (1) This paragraph applies for the purposes of this Part of this Schedule.

(2) The meaning of collective bargaining given by section 178(1) shall not apply.

(3) References to collective bargaining are to negotiations relating to pay, hours and holidays; but this has effect subject to sub-paragraph (4).

(4) If the parties agree matters as the subject of collective bargaining, references to collective bargaining are to negotiations relating to the agreed matters; and this is the case whether the agreement is made before or after the time when the CAC issues a declaration, or the parties agree, that the union is (or unions are) entitled to conduct collective bargaining on behalf of a bargaining unit.

(5) Sub-paragraph (4) does not apply in construing paragraph 31(3).

(6) Sub-paragraphs (2) to (5) do not apply in construing paragraph 35 or 44.

NOTES

Inserted as noted at the beginning of this Schedule.

Para 2: sub-para (3A) inserted by the Employment Relations Act 2004, s 57(1), Sch 1, para 23(1), (2).

Request for recognition

[1.639]

4. (1) The union or unions seeking recognition must make a request for recognition to the employer.

(2) Paragraphs 5 to 9 apply to the request.

5. The request is not valid unless it is received by the employer.

6. The request is not valid unless the union (or each of the unions) has a certificate [of independence].

7. (1) The request is not valid unless the employer, taken with any associated employer or employers, employs—

- (a) at least 21 workers on the day the employer receives the request, or
- (b) an average of at least 21 workers in the 13 weeks ending with that day.

(2) To find the average under sub-paragraph (1)(b)—

- (a) take the number of workers employed in each of the 13 weeks (including workers not employed for the whole of the week);
- (b) aggregate the 13 numbers;
- (c) divide the aggregate by 13.

(3) For the purposes of sub-paragraph (1)(a) any worker employed by an associated company incorporated outside Great Britain must be ignored unless the day the request was made fell within a period during which he ordinarily worked in Great Britain.

(4) For the purposes of sub-paragraph (1)(b) any worker employed by an associated company incorporated outside Great Britain must be ignored in relation to a week unless the whole or any part of that week fell within a period during which he ordinarily worked in Great Britain.

(5) For the purposes of sub-paragraphs (3) and (4) a worker who is employed on board a ship registered in the register maintained under section 8 of the Merchant Shipping Act 1995 shall be treated as ordinarily working in Great Britain unless—

(a) the ship's entry in the register specifies a port outside Great Britain as the port to which the vessel is to be treated as belonging,
(b) the employment is wholly outside Great Britain, or
(c) the worker is not ordinarily resident in Great Britain.

[(5A) Sub-paragraph (5B) applies to an agency worker whose contract within regulation 3(1)(b) of the Agency Workers Regulations 2010 (contract with the temporary work agency) is not a contract of employment.

(5B) For the purposes of sub-paragraphs (1) and (2), the agency worker is to be treated as having a contract of employment with the temporary work agency for the duration of the assignment with the employer (and "assignment" has the same meaning as in those Regulations).]

(6) The Secretary of State may by order—
(a) provide that sub-paragraphs (1) to (5) are not to apply, or are not to apply in specified circumstances, or
(b) vary the number of workers for the time being specified in sub-paragraph (1);
and different provision may be made for different circumstances.

(7) An order under sub-paragraph (6)—
(a) shall be made by statutory instrument, and
(b) may include supplementary, incidental, saving or transitional provisions.

(8) No such order shall be made unless a draft of it has been laid before Parliament and approved by a resolution of each House of Parliament.

8. The request is not valid unless it—
(a) is in writing,
(b) identifies the union or unions and the bargaining unit, and
(c) states that it is made under this Schedule.

9. The Secretary of State may by order made by statutory instrument prescribe the form of requests and the procedure for making them; and if he does so the request is not valid unless it complies with the order.

NOTES

Inserted as noted at the beginning of this Schedule.

Para 6: words in square brackets substituted by the Employment Relations Act 2004, s 50(6).

Para 7: sub-paras (5A), (5B) inserted by the Agency Workers Regulations 2010, SI 2010/93, reg 25, Sch 2, Pt 1, paras 1, 7(1), (2).

Orders: as of 15 May 2019, no Orders had been made under para 7 or 9.

Parties agree

[1.640]

10. (1) If before the end of the first period the parties agree a bargaining unit and that the union is (or unions are) to be recognised as entitled to conduct collective bargaining on behalf of the unit, no further steps are to be taken under this Part of this Schedule.

(2) If before the end of the first period the employer informs the union (or unions) that the employer does not accept the request but is willing to negotiate, sub-paragraph (3) applies.

(3) The parties may conduct negotiations with a view to agreeing a bargaining unit and that the union is (or unions are) to be recognised as entitled to conduct collective bargaining on behalf of the unit.

(4) If such an agreement is made before the end of the second period no further steps are to be taken under this Part of this Schedule.

(5) The employer and the union (or unions) may request ACAS to assist in conducting the negotiations.

(6) The first period is the period of 10 working days starting with the day after that on which the employer receives the request for recognition.

(7) The second period is—
(a) the period of 20 working days starting with the day after that on which the first period ends, or
(b) such longer period (so starting) as the parties may from time to time agree.

NOTES

Inserted as noted at the beginning of this Schedule.

Employer rejects request

[1.641]

11. (1) This paragraph applies if—
(a) before the end of the first period the employer fails to respond to the request, or
(b) before the end of the first period the employer informs the union (or unions) that the employer does not accept the request (without indicating a willingness to negotiate).

(2) The union (or unions) may apply to the CAC to decide both these questions—
[(a) whether the proposed bargaining unit is appropriate;]
(b) whether the union has (or unions have) the support of a majority of the workers constituting the appropriate bargaining unit.

NOTES

Inserted as noted at the beginning of this Schedule.

Para 11: sub-para (2)(a) substituted by the Employment Relations Act 2004, s 1(1).

Negotiations fail

[1.642]
12. (1) Sub-paragraph (2) applies if—
(a) the employer informs the union (or unions) under paragraph 10(2), and
(b) no agreement is made before the end of the second period.
(2) The union (or unions) may apply to the CAC to decide both these questions—
[(a) whether the proposed bargaining unit is appropriate;]
(b) whether the union has (or unions have) the support of a majority of the workers constituting the appropriate bargaining unit.
(3) Sub-paragraph (4) applies if—
(a) the employer informs the union (or unions) under paragraph 10(2), and
(b) before the end of the second period the parties agree a bargaining unit but not that the union is (or unions are) to be recognised as entitled to conduct collective bargaining on behalf of the unit.
(4) The union (or unions) may apply to the CAC to decide the question whether the union has (or unions have) the support of a majority of the workers constituting the bargaining unit.
(5) But no application may be made under this paragraph if within the period of 10 working days starting with the day after that on which the employer informs the union (or unions) under paragraph 10(2) the employer proposes that ACAS be requested to assist in conducting the negotiations and—
(a) the union rejects (or unions reject) the proposal, or
(b) the union fails (or unions fail) to accept the proposal within the period of 10 working days starting with the day after that on which the employer makes the proposal.

NOTES
Inserted as noted at the beginning of this Schedule.
Para 12: sub-para (2)(a) substituted by the Employment Relations Act 2004, s 1(2).

Acceptance of applications

[1.643]
13. The CAC must give notice to the parties of receipt of an application under paragraph 11 or 12.

14. (1) This paragraph applies if—
(a) two or more relevant applications are made,
(b) at least one worker falling within one of the relevant bargaining units also falls within the other relevant bargaining unit (or units), and
(c) the CAC has not accepted any of the applications.
(2) A relevant application is an application under paragraph 11 or 12.
(3) In relation to a relevant application, the relevant bargaining unit is—
(a) the proposed bargaining unit, where the application is under paragraph 11(2) or 12(2);
(b) the agreed bargaining unit, where the application is under paragraph 12(4).
(4) Within the acceptance period the CAC must decide, with regard to each relevant application, whether the 10 per cent test is satisfied.
(5) The 10 per cent test is satisfied if members of the union (or unions) constitute at least 10 per cent of the workers constituting the relevant bargaining unit.
(6) The acceptance period is—
(a) the period of 10 working days starting with the day after that on which the CAC receives the last relevant application, or
(b) such longer period (so starting) as the CAC may specify to the parties by notice containing reasons for the extension.
(7) If the CAC decides that—
(a) the 10 per cent test is satisfied with regard to more than one of the relevant applications, or
(b) the 10 per cent test is satisfied with regard to none of the relevant applications,
the CAC must not accept any of the relevant applications.
(8) If the CAC decides that the 10 per cent test is satisfied with regard to one only of the relevant applications the CAC—
(a) must proceed under paragraph 15 with regard to that application, and
(b) must not accept any of the other relevant applications.
(9) The CAC must give notice of its decision to the parties.
(10) If by virtue of this paragraph the CAC does not accept an application, no further steps are to be taken under this Part of this Schedule in relation to that application.

15. (1) This paragraph applies to these applications—
(a) any application with regard to which no decision has to be made under paragraph 14;
(b) any application with regard to which the CAC must proceed under this paragraph by virtue of paragraph 14.
(2) Within the acceptance period the CAC must decide whether—
(a) the request for recognition to which the application relates is valid within the terms of paragraphs 5 to 9, and

(b) the application is made in accordance with paragraph 11 or 12 and admissible within the terms of paragraphs 33 to 42.

(3) In deciding those questions the CAC must consider any evidence which it has been given by the employer or the union (or unions).

(4) If the CAC decides that the request is not valid or the application is not made in accordance with paragraph 11 or 12 or is not admissible—

(a) the CAC must give notice of its decision to the parties,

(b) the CAC must not accept the application, and

(c) no further steps are to be taken under this Part of this Schedule.

(5) If the CAC decides that the request is valid and the application is made in accordance with paragraph 11 or 12 and is admissible it must—

(a) accept the application, and

(b) give notice of the acceptance to the parties.

(6) The acceptance period is—

(a) the period of 10 working days starting with the day after that on which the CAC receives the application, or

(b) such longer period (so starting) as the CAC may specify to the parties by notice containing reasons for the extension.

NOTES

Inserted as noted at the beginning of this Schedule.

Withdrawal of application

[1.644]

16. (1) If an application under paragraph 11 or 12 is accepted by the CAC, the union (or unions) may not withdraw the application—

(a) after the CAC issues a declaration under paragraph [19F(5) or] 22(2), or

(b) after the union (or the last of the unions) receives notice under paragraph 22(3) or 23(2).

(2) If an application is withdrawn by the union (or unions)—

(a) the CAC must give notice of the withdrawal to the employer, and

(b) no further steps are to be taken under this Part of this Schedule.

NOTES

Inserted as noted at the beginning of this Schedule.

Para 16: words in square brackets in sub-para (1) inserted by the Employment Relations Act 2004, s 57(1), Sch 1, para 23(1), (3).

Notice to cease consideration of application

[1.645]

17. (1) This paragraph applies if the CAC has received an application under paragraph 11 or 12 and—

(a) it has not decided whether the application is admissible, or

(b) it has decided that the application is admissible.

(2) No further steps are to be taken under this Part of this Schedule if, before the final event occurs, the parties give notice to the CAC that they want no further steps to be taken.

(3) The final event occurs when the first of the following occurs—

(a) the CAC issues a declaration under paragraph [19F(5) or] 22(2) in consequence of the application;

(b) the last day of the notification period ends;

and the notification period is that defined by paragraph [24(6)] and arising from the application.

NOTES

Inserted as noted at the beginning of this Schedule.

Para 17: words in square brackets in sub-para (3) inserted, and number in square brackets in that sub-paragraph substituted, by the Employment Relations Act 2004, s 57(1), Sch 1, para 23(1), (4).

Appropriate bargaining unit

[1.646]

18. (1) If the CAC accepts an application under paragraph 11(2) or 12(2) it must try to help the parties to reach within the appropriate period an agreement as to what the appropriate bargaining unit is.

(2) The appropriate period is [(subject to any notice under sub-paragraph (3), (4) or (5))]—

(a) the period of 20 working days starting with the day after that on which the CAC gives notice of acceptance of the application, or

(b) such longer period (so starting) as the CAC may specify to the parties by notice containing reasons for the extension.

[(3) If, during the appropriate period, the CAC concludes that there is no reasonable prospect of the parties' agreeing an appropriate bargaining unit before the time when (apart from this sub-paragraph) the appropriate period would end, the CAC may, by a notice given to the parties, declare that the appropriate period ends with the date of the notice.

(4) If, during the appropriate period, the parties apply to the CAC for a declaration that the appropriate period is to end with a date (specified in the application) which is earlier than the date with which it would otherwise end, the CAC may, by a notice given to the parties, declare that the appropriate period ends with the specified date.

(5) If the CAC has declared under sub-paragraph (4) that the appropriate period ends with a specified date, it may before that date by a notice given to the parties specify a later date with which the appropriate period ends.

(6) A notice under sub-paragraph (3) must contain reasons for reaching the conclusion mentioned in that sub-paragraph.

(7) A notice under sub-paragraph (5) must contain reasons for the extension of the appropriate period.]

[18A. (1) This paragraph applies if the CAC accepts an application under paragraph 11(2) or 12(2).

(2) Within 5 working days starting with the day after that on which the CAC gives the employer notice of acceptance of the application, the employer must supply the following information to the union (or unions) and the CAC—

(a) a list of the categories of worker in the proposed bargaining unit,
(b) a list of the workplaces at which the workers in the proposed bargaining unit work, and
(c) the number of workers the employer reasonably believes to be in each category at each workplace.

(3) The lists and numbers supplied under this paragraph must be as accurate as is reasonably practicable in the light of the information in the possession of the employer at the time when he complies with sub-paragraph (2).

(4) The lists and numbers supplied to the union (or unions) and to the CAC must be the same.

(5) For the purposes of this paragraph, the workplace at which a worker works is—

(a) if the person works at or from a single set of premises, those premises, and
(b) in any other case, the premises with which the worker's employment has the closest connection.]

[19. (1) This paragraph applies if—

(a) the CAC accepts an application under paragraph 11(2) or 12(2),
(b) the parties have not agreed an appropriate bargaining unit at the end of the appropriate period (defined by paragraph 18), and
(c) at the end of that period either no request under paragraph 19A(1)(b) has been made or such a request has been made but the condition in paragraph 19A(1)(c) has not been met.

(2) Within the decision period, the CAC must decide whether the proposed bargaining unit is appropriate.

(3) If the CAC decides that the proposed bargaining unit is not appropriate, it must also decide within the decision period a bargaining unit which is appropriate.

(4) The decision period is—

(a) the period of 10 working days starting with the day after that with which the appropriate period ends, or
(b) such longer period (so starting) as the CAC may specify to the parties by notice containing reasons for the extension.

19A. (1) This paragraph applies if—

(a) the CAC accepts an application under paragraph 11(2) or 12(2),
(b) during the appropriate period (defined by paragraph 18), the CAC is requested by the union (or unions) to make a decision under this paragraph, and
(c) the CAC is, either at the time the request is made or at a later time during the appropriate period, of the opinion that the employer has failed to comply with the duty imposed by paragraph 18A.

(2) Within the decision period, the CAC must decide whether the proposed bargaining unit is appropriate.

(3) If the CAC decides that the proposed bargaining unit is not appropriate, it must also decide within the decision period a bargaining unit which is appropriate.

(4) The decision period is—

(a) the period of 10 working days starting with the day after the day on which the request is made, or
(b) such longer period (so starting) as the CAC may specify to the parties by notice containing reasons for the extension.

19B. (1) This paragraph applies if the CAC has to decide whether a bargaining unit is appropriate for the purposes of paragraph 19(2) or (3) or 19A(2) or (3).

(2) The CAC must take these matters into account—

(a) the need for the unit to be compatible with effective management;
(b) the matters listed in sub-paragraph (3), so far as they do not conflict with that need.

(3) The matters are—

(a) the views of the employer and of the union (or unions);
(b) existing national and local bargaining arrangements;
(c) the desirability of avoiding small fragmented bargaining units within an undertaking;

(d) the characteristics of workers falling within the bargaining unit under consideration and of any other employees of the employer whom the CAC considers relevant;

(e) the location of workers.

(4) In taking an employer's views into account for the purpose of deciding whether the proposed bargaining unit is appropriate, the CAC must take into account any view the employer has about any other bargaining unit that he considers would be appropriate.

(5) The CAC must give notice of its decision to the parties.]

NOTES

Inserted as noted at the beginning of this Schedule.

Para 18: words in square brackets in sub-para (2) inserted, and sub-paras (3)–(7) added, by the Employment Relations Act 2004, s 2(1), (2).

Para 18A: inserted by the Employment Relations Act 2004, s 3.

Paras 19, 19A, 19B: substituted, for the original para 19, by the Employment Relations Act 2004, s 4.

[Union communications with workers after acceptance of application

[1.647]

19C. (1) This paragraph applies if the CAC accepts an application under paragraph 11(2) or 12(2) or (4).

(2) The union (or unions) may apply to the CAC for the appointment of a suitable independent person to handle communications during the initial period between the union (or unions) and the relevant workers.

(3) In the case of an application under paragraph 11(2) or 12(2), the relevant workers are—

(a) in relation to any time before an appropriate bargaining unit is agreed by the parties or decided by the CAC, those falling within the proposed bargaining unit, and

(b) in relation to any time after an appropriate bargaining unit is so agreed or decided, those falling within the bargaining unit agreed or decided upon.

(4) In the case of an application under paragraph 12(4), the relevant workers are those falling within the bargaining unit agreed by the parties.

(5) The initial period is the period starting with the day on which the CAC informs the parties under sub-paragraph (7)(b) and ending with the first day on which any of the following occurs—

(a) the application under paragraph 11 or 12 is withdrawn;

(b) the CAC gives notice to the union (or unions) of a decision under paragraph 20 that the application is invalid;

(c) the CAC notifies the union (or unions) of a declaration issued under paragraph 19F(5) or 22(2);

(d) the CAC informs the union (or unions) under paragraph 25(9) of the name of the person appointed to conduct a ballot.

(6) A person is a suitable independent person if—

(a) he satisfies such conditions as may be specified for the purposes of paragraph 25(7)(a) by an order under that provision, or is himself specified for those purposes by such an order, and

(b) there are no grounds for believing either that he will carry out any functions arising from his appointment otherwise than competently or that his independence in relation to those functions might reasonably be called into question.

(7) On an application under sub-paragraph (2) the CAC must as soon as reasonably practicable—

(a) make such an appointment as is mentioned in that sub-paragraph, and

(b) inform the parties of the name of the person appointed and the date of his appointment.

(8) The person appointed by the CAC is referred to in paragraphs 19D and 19E as "the appointed person".

19D. (1) An employer who is informed by the CAC under paragraph 19C(7)(b) must comply with the following duties (so far as it is reasonable to expect him to do so).

(2) The duties are—

(a) to give to the CAC, within the period of 10 working days starting with the day after that on which the employer is informed under paragraph 19C(7)(b), the names and home addresses of the relevant workers;

(b) if the relevant workers change as a result of an appropriate bargaining unit being agreed by the parties or decided by the CAC, to give to the CAC, within the period of 10 working days starting with the day after that on which the bargaining unit is agreed or the CAC's decision is notified to the employer, the names and home addresses of those who are now the relevant workers;

(c) to give to the CAC, as soon as reasonably practicable, the name and home address of any worker who joins the bargaining unit after the employer has complied with paragraph (a) or (b);

(d) to inform the CAC, as soon as reasonably practicable, of any worker whose name has been given to the CAC under paragraph (a), (b) or (c) and who ceases to be a relevant worker (otherwise than by reason of a change mentioned in paragraph (b)).

(3) Nothing in sub-paragraph (2) requires the employer to give information to the CAC after the end of the initial period.

(4) As soon as reasonably practicable after the CAC receives any information under sub-paragraph (2), it must pass it on to the appointed person.

19E. (1) During the initial period, the appointed person must if asked to do so by the union (or unions) send to any worker—
- (a) whose name and home address have been passed on to him under paragraph 19D(4), and
- (b) who is (so far as the appointed person is aware) still a relevant worker,

any information supplied by the union (or unions) to the appointed person.

(2) The costs of the appointed person shall be borne—
- (a) if the application under paragraph 19C was made by one union, by the union, and
- (b) if that application was made by more than one union, by the unions in such proportions as they jointly indicate to the appointed person or, in the absence of such an indication, in equal shares.

(3) The appointed person may send to the union (or each of the unions) a demand stating his costs and the amount of those costs to be borne by the recipient.

(4) In such a case the recipient must pay the amount stated to the person sending the demand and must do so within the period of 15 working days starting with the day after that on which the demand is received.

(5) In England and Wales, if the amount stated is not paid in accordance with sub-paragraph (4) it shall, if [the county court] so orders, be recoverable [under section 85 of the County Courts Act 1984] or otherwise as if it were payable under an order of that court.

(6) [Where a warrant of control is issued under section 85 of the 1984 Act to recover an amount in accordance with sub-paragraph (5), the power conferred by the warrant is exercisable], to the same extent and in the same manner as if the union were a body corporate, against any property held in trust for the union other than protected property as defined in section 23(2).

(7) References to the costs of the appointed person are to—
- (a) the costs wholly, exclusively and necessarily incurred by the appointed person in connection with handling during the initial period communications between the union (or unions) and the relevant workers,
- (b) such reasonable amount as the appointed person charges for his services, and
- (c) such other costs as the union (or unions) agree.

19F. (1) If the CAC is satisfied that the employer has failed to fulfil a duty mentioned in paragraph 19D(2), and the initial period has not yet ended, the CAC may order the employer—
- (a) to take such steps to remedy the failure as the CAC considers reasonable and specifies in the order, and
- (b) to do so within such period as the CAC considers reasonable and specifies in the order;

and in this paragraph a "remedial order" means an order under this sub-paragraph.

(2) If the CAC is satisfied that the employer has failed to comply with a remedial order and the initial period has not yet ended, the CAC must as soon as reasonably practicable notify the employer and the union (or unions) that it is satisfied that the employer has failed to comply.

(3) A remedial order and a notice under sub-paragraph (2) must draw the recipient's attention to the effect of sub-paragraphs (4) and (5).

(4) Sub-paragraph (5) applies if—
- (a) the CAC is satisfied that the employer has failed to comply with a remedial order,
- (b) the parties have agreed an appropriate bargaining unit or the CAC has decided an appropriate bargaining unit,
- (c) in the case of an application under paragraph 11(2) or 12(2), the CAC, if required to do so, has decided under paragraph 20 that the application is not invalid, and
- (d) the initial period has not yet ended.

(5) The CAC may issue a declaration that the union is (or unions are) recognised as entitled to conduct collective bargaining on behalf of the workers constituting the bargaining unit.]

NOTES

This Schedule was inserted as noted at the beginning of this Schedule.

Paras 19C, 19D, 19F: inserted, together with para 19E, by the Employment Relations Act 2004, s 5(1).

Para 19E: inserted as noted above; words in first pair of square brackets in sub-para (5) substituted by the Crime and Courts Act 2013, s 17(5), Sch 9, Pt 3, para 52; words in second pair of square brackets in sub-para (5) substituted, and words in square brackets in sub-para (6) substituted, by the Tribunals, Courts and Enforcement Act 2007, s 62(3), Sch 13, paras 108, 109.

Union recognition

[1.648]

20. (1) This paragraph applies if—
- (a) the CAC accepts an application under paragraph 11(2) or 12(2),
- (b) the parties have agreed an appropriate bargaining unit at the end of the appropriate period [(defined by paragraph 18)], or the CAC has decided an appropriate bargaining unit, and
- (c) that bargaining unit differs from the proposed bargaining unit.

(2) Within the decision period the CAC must decide whether the application is invalid within the terms of paragraphs 43 to 50.

(3) In deciding whether the application is invalid, the CAC must consider any evidence which it has been given by the employer or the union (or unions).

(4) If the CAC decides that the application is invalid—
- (a) the CAC must give notice of its decision to the parties,
- (b) the CAC must not proceed with the application, and

(c) no further steps are to be taken under this Part of this Schedule.

(5) If the CAC decides that the application is not invalid it must—

(a) proceed with the application, and

(b) give notice to the parties that it is so proceeding.

(6) The decision period is—

(a) the period of 10 working days starting with the day after that on which the parties agree an appropriate bargaining unit or the CAC decides an appropriate bargaining unit, or

(b) such longer period (so starting) as the CAC may specify to the parties by notice containing reasons for the extension.

21. (1) This paragraph applies if—

(a) the CAC accepts an application under paragraph 11(2) or 12(2),

(b) the parties have agreed an appropriate bargaining unit at the end of the appropriate period [(defined by paragraph 18)], or the CAC has decided an appropriate bargaining unit, and

(c) that bargaining unit is the same as the proposed bargaining unit.

(2) This paragraph also applies if the CAC accepts an application under paragraph 12(4).

(3) The CAC must proceed with the application.

22. (1) This paragraph applies if—

(a) the CAC proceeds with an application in accordance with paragraph 20 or 21 [(and makes no declaration under paragraph 19F(5))], and

(b) the CAC is satisfied that a majority of the workers constituting the bargaining unit are members of the union (or unions).

(2) The CAC must issue a declaration that the union is (or unions are) recognised as entitled to conduct collective bargaining on behalf of the workers constituting the bargaining unit.

(3) But if any of the three qualifying conditions is fulfilled, instead of issuing a declaration under sub-paragraph (2) the CAC must give notice to the parties that it intends to arrange for the holding of a secret ballot in which the workers constituting the bargaining unit are asked whether they want the union (or unions) to conduct collective bargaining on their behalf.

(4) These are the three qualifying conditions—

(a) the CAC is satisfied that a ballot should be held in the interests of good industrial relations;

[(b) the CAC has evidence, which it considers to be credible, from a significant number of the union members within the bargaining unit that they do not want the union (or unions) to conduct collective bargaining on their behalf;]

(c) membership evidence is produced which leads the CAC to conclude that there are doubts whether a significant number of the union members within the bargaining unit want the union (or unions) to conduct collective bargaining on their behalf.

(5) For the purposes of sub-paragraph (4)(c) membership evidence is—

(a) evidence about the circumstances in which union members became members;

(b) evidence about the length of time for which union members have been members, in a case where the CAC is satisfied that such evidence should be taken into account.

23. (1) This paragraph applies if—

(a) the CAC proceeds with an application in accordance with paragraph 20 or 21 [(and makes no declaration under paragraph 19F(5))], and

(b) the CAC is not satisfied that a majority of the workers constituting the bargaining unit are members of the union (or unions).

(2) The CAC must give notice to the parties that it intends to arrange for the holding of a secret ballot in which the workers constituting the bargaining unit are asked whether they want the union (or unions) to conduct collective bargaining on their behalf.

24. (1) This paragraph applies if the CAC gives notice under paragraph 22(3) or 23(2).

(2) Within the notification period—

(a) the union (or unions), or

(b) the union (or unions) and the employer,

may notify the CAC that the party making the notification does not (or the parties making the notification do not) want the CAC to arrange for the holding of the ballot.

(3) If the CAC is so notified—

(a) it must not arrange for the holding of the ballot,

(b) it must inform the parties that it will not arrange for the holding of the ballot, and why, and

(c) no further steps are to be taken under this Part of this Schedule.

(4) If the CAC is not so notified it must arrange for the holding of the ballot.

[(5) The notification period is, in relation to notification by the union (or unions)—

(a) the period of 10 working days starting with the day on which the union (or last of the unions) receives the CAC's notice under paragraph 22(3) or 23(2), or

(b) such longer period so starting as the CAC may specify to the parties by notice.

(6) The notification period is, in relation to notification by the union (or unions) and the employer—

(a) the period of 10 working days starting with the day on which the last of the parties receives the CAC's notice under paragraph 22(3) or 23(2), or

(b) such longer period so starting as the CAC may specify to the parties by notice.

(7) The CAC may give a notice under sub-paragraph (5)(b) or (6)(b) only if the parties have applied jointly to it for the giving of such a notice.]

25. (1) This paragraph applies if the CAC arranges under paragraph 24 for the holding of a ballot.

(2) The ballot must be conducted by a qualified independent person appointed by the CAC.

(3) The ballot must be conducted within—

(a) the period of 20 working days starting with the day after that on which the qualified independent person is appointed, or

(b) such longer period (so starting) as the CAC may decide.

(4) The ballot must be conducted—

(a) at a workplace or workplaces decided by the CAC,

(b) by post, or

(c) by a combination of the methods described in sub-paragraphs (a) and (b),

depending on the CAC's preference.

(5) In deciding how the ballot is to be conducted the CAC must take into account—

(a) the likelihood of the ballot being affected by unfairness or malpractice if it were conducted at a workplace or workplaces;

(b) costs and practicality;

(c) such other matters as the CAC considers appropriate.

(6) The CAC may not decide that the ballot is to be conducted as mentioned in sub-paragraph (4)(c) unless there are special factors making such a decision appropriate; and special factors include—

(a) factors arising from the location of workers or the nature of their employment;

(b) factors put to the CAC by the employer or the union (or unions).

[(6A) If the CAC decides that the ballot must (in whole or in part) be conducted at a workplace (or workplaces), it may require arrangements to be made for workers—

(a) who (but for the arrangements) would be prevented by the CAC's decision from voting by post, and

(b) who are unable, for reasons relating to those workers as individuals, to cast their votes in the ballot at the workplace (or at any of them),

to be given the opportunity (if they request it far enough in advance of the ballot for this to be practicable) to vote by post; and the CAC's imposing such a requirement is not to be treated for the purposes of sub-paragraph (6) as a decision that the ballot be conducted as mentioned in sub-paragraph (4)(c).]

(7) A person is a qualified independent person if—

(a) he satisfies such conditions as may be specified for the purposes of this paragraph by order of the Secretary of State or is himself so specified, and

(b) there are no grounds for believing either that he will carry out any functions conferred on him in relation to the ballot otherwise than competently or that his independence in relation to the ballot might reasonably be called into question.

(8) An order under sub-paragraph (7)(a) shall be made by statutory instrument subject to annulment in pursuance of a resolution of either House of Parliament.

(9) As soon as is reasonably practicable after the CAC is required under paragraph 24 to arrange for the holding of a ballot it must inform the parties—

(a) that it is so required;

(b) of the name of the person appointed to conduct the ballot and the date of his appointment;

(c) of the period within which the ballot must be conducted;

(d) whether the ballot is to be conducted by post or at a workplace or workplaces;

(e) of the workplace or workplaces concerned (if the ballot is to be conducted at a workplace or workplaces).

26. (1) An employer who is informed by the CAC under paragraph 25(9) must comply with the following [five] duties.

(2) The first duty is to co-operate generally, in connection with the ballot, with the union (or unions) and the person appointed to conduct the ballot; and the second and third duties are not to prejudice the generality of this.

(3) The second duty is to give to the union (or unions) such access to the workers constituting the bargaining unit as is reasonable to enable the union (or unions) to inform the workers of the object of the ballot and to seek their support and their opinions on the issues involved.

(4) The third duty is to do the following (so far as it is reasonable to expect the employer to do so)—

(a) to give to the CAC, within the period of 10 working days starting with the day after that on which the employer is informed under paragraph 25(9), the names and home addresses of the workers constituting the bargaining unit;

(b) to give to the CAC, as soon as is reasonably practicable, the name and home address of any worker who joins the unit after the employer has complied with paragraph (a);

(c) to inform the CAC, as soon as is reasonably practicable, of any worker whose name has been given to the CAC under paragraph [19D or paragraph (a) or (b) of this sub-paragraph and] who ceases to be within the unit.

[(4A) The fourth duty is to refrain from making any offer to any or all of the workers constituting the bargaining unit which—

(a) has or is likely to have the effect of inducing any or all of them not to attend any relevant meeting between the union (or unions) and the workers constituting the bargaining unit, and

(b) is not reasonable in the circumstances.

(4B) The fifth duty is to refrain from taking or threatening to take any action against a worker solely or mainly on the grounds that he—

(a) attended or took part in any relevant meeting between the union (or unions) and the workers constituting the bargaining unit, or

(b) indicated his intention to attend or take part in such a meeting.

(4C) A meeting is a relevant meeting in relation to a worker for the purposes of sub-paragraphs (4A) and (4B) if—

(a) it is organised in accordance with any agreement reached concerning the second duty or as a result of a step ordered to be taken under paragraph 27 to remedy a failure to comply with that duty, and

(b) it is one which the employer is, by such an agreement or order as is mentioned in paragraph (a), required to permit the worker to attend.

(4D) Without prejudice to the generality of the second duty imposed by this paragraph, an employer is to be taken to have failed to comply with that duty if—

(a) he refuses a request for a meeting between the union (or unions) and any or all of the workers constituting the bargaining unit to be held in the absence of the employer or any representative of his (other than one who has been invited to attend the meeting) and it is not reasonable in the circumstances for him to do so,

(b) he or a representative of his attends such a meeting without having been invited to do so,

(c) he seeks to record or otherwise be informed of the proceedings at any such meeting and it is not reasonable in the circumstances for him to do so, or

(d) he refuses to give an undertaking that he will not seek to record or otherwise be informed of the proceedings at any such meeting unless it is reasonable in the circumstances for him to do either of those things.

(4E) The fourth and fifth duties do not confer any rights on a worker; but that does not affect any other right which a worker may have.]

[(4F) Sub-paragraph (4)(a) does not apply to names and addresses that the employer has already given to the CAC under paragraph 19D.

(4G) Where (because of sub-paragraph (4F)) the employer does not have to comply with sub-paragraph (4)(a), the reference in sub-paragraph (4)(b) to the time when the employer complied with sub-paragraph (4)(a) is to be read as a reference to the time when the employer is informed under paragraph 25(9).

(4H) If—

(a) a person was appointed on an application under paragraph 19C, and

(b) the person appointed to conduct the ballot is not that person,

the CAC must, as soon as is reasonably practicable, pass on to the person appointed to conduct the ballot the names and addresses given to it under paragraph 19D.]

(5) As soon as is reasonably practicable after the CAC receives any information under sub-paragraph (4) it must pass it on to the person appointed to conduct the ballot.

(6) If asked to do so by the union (or unions) the person appointed to conduct the ballot must send to any worker—

(a) whose name and home address have been [passed on to him under paragraph 19D or this paragraph], and

(b) who is still within the unit (so far as the person so appointed is aware),

any information supplied by the union (or unions) to the person so appointed.

(7) The duty under sub-paragraph (6) does not apply unless the union bears (or unions bear) the cost of sending the information.

[(8) Each of the powers specified in sub-paragraph (9) shall be taken to include power to issue Codes of Practice—

(a) about reasonable access for the purposes of sub-paragraph (3), and

(b) about the fourth duty imposed by this paragraph.

(9) The powers are—

(a) the power of ACAS under section 199(1);

(b) the power of the Secretary of State under section 203(1)(a).]

27. (1) If the CAC is satisfied that the employer has failed to fulfil any of the [duties imposed on him] by paragraph 26, and the ballot has not been held, the CAC may order the employer—

(a) to take such steps to remedy the failure as the CAC considers reasonable and specifies in the order, and

(b) to do so within such period as the CAC considers reasonable and specifies in the order.

(2) If the CAC is satisfied that the employer has failed to comply with an order under sub-paragraph (1), and the ballot has not been held, the CAC may issue a declaration that the union is (or unions are) recognised as entitled to conduct collective bargaining on behalf of the bargaining unit.

(3) If the CAC issues a declaration under sub-paragraph (2) it shall take steps to cancel the holding of the ballot; and if the ballot is held it shall have no effect.

[27A. (1) Each of the parties informed by the CAC under paragraph 25(9) must refrain from using any unfair practice.

(2) A party uses an unfair practice if, with a view to influencing the result of the ballot, the party—

(a) offers to pay money or give money's worth to a worker entitled to vote in the ballot in return for the worker's agreement to vote in a particular way or to abstain from voting,
(b) makes an outcome-specific offer to a worker entitled to vote in the ballot,
(c) coerces or attempts to coerce a worker entitled to vote in the ballot to disclose—
 (i) whether he intends to vote or to abstain from voting in the ballot, or
 (ii) how he intends to vote, or how he has voted, in the ballot,
(d) dismisses or threatens to dismiss a worker,
(e) takes or threatens to take disciplinary action against a worker,
(f) subjects or threatens to subject a worker to any other detriment, or
(g) uses or attempts to use undue influence on a worker entitled to vote in the ballot.

(3) For the purposes of sub-paragraph (2)(b) an "outcome-specific offer" is an offer to pay money or give money's worth which—
(a) is conditional on the issuing by the CAC of a declaration that—
 (i) the union is (or unions are) recognised as entitled to conduct collective bargaining on behalf of the bargaining unit, or
 (ii) the union is (or unions are) not entitled to be so recognised, and
(b) is not conditional on anything which is done or occurs as a result of the declaration in question.

(4) The duty imposed by this paragraph does not confer any rights on a worker; but that does not affect any other right which a worker may have.

(5) Each of the following powers shall be taken to include power to issue Codes of Practice about unfair practices for the purposes of this paragraph—
(a) the power of ACAS under section 199(1);
(b) the power of the Secretary of State under section 203(1)(a).

27B. (1) A party may complain to the CAC that another party has failed to comply with paragraph 27A.

(2) A complaint under sub-paragraph (1) must be made on or before the first working day after—
(a) the date of the ballot, or
(b) if votes may be cast in the ballot on more than one day, the last of those days.

(3) Within the decision period the CAC must decide whether the complaint is well-founded.

(4) A complaint is well-founded if—
(a) the CAC finds that the party complained against used an unfair practice, and
(b) the CAC is satisfied that the use of that practice changed or was likely to change, in the case of a worker entitled to vote in the ballot—
 (i) his intention to vote or to abstain from voting,
 (ii) his intention to vote in a particular way, or
 (iii) how he voted.

(5) The decision period is—
(a) the period of 10 working days starting with the day after that on which the complaint under sub-paragraph (1) was received by the CAC, or
(b) such longer period (so starting) as the CAC may specify to the parties by a notice containing reasons for the extension.

(6) If, at the beginning of the decision period, the ballot has not begun, the CAC may by notice to the parties and the qualified independent person postpone the date on which it is to begin until a date which falls after the end of the decision period.

27C. (1) This paragraph applies if the CAC decides that a complaint under paragraph 27B is well-founded.

(2) The CAC must, as soon as is reasonably practicable, issue a declaration to that effect.

(3) The CAC may do either or both of the following—
(a) order the party concerned to take any action specified in the order within such period as may be so specified, or
(b) give notice to the employer and to the union (or unions) that it intends to arrange for the holding of a secret ballot in which the workers constituting the bargaining unit are asked whether they want the union (or unions) to conduct collective bargaining on their behalf.

(4) The CAC may give an order or a notice under sub-paragraph (3) either at the same time as it issues the declaration under sub-paragraph (2) or at any other time before it acts under paragraph 29.

(5) The action specified in an order under sub-paragraph (3)(a) shall be such as the CAC considers reasonable in order to mitigate the effect of the failure of the party concerned to comply with the duty imposed by paragraph 27A.

(6) The CAC may give more than one order under sub-paragraph (3)(a).

27D. (1) This paragraph applies if the CAC issues a declaration under paragraph 27C(2) and the declaration states that the unfair practice used consisted of or included—
(a) the use of violence, or
(b) the dismissal of a union official.

(2) This paragraph also applies if the CAC has made an order under paragraph 27C(3)(a) and—
(a) it is satisfied that the party subject to the order has failed to comply with it, or
(b) it makes another declaration under paragraph 27C(2) in relation to a complaint against that party.

(3) If the party concerned is the employer, the CAC may issue a declaration that the union is (or unions are) recognised as entitled to conduct collective bargaining on behalf of the bargaining unit.

(4) If the party concerned is a union, the CAC may issue a declaration that the union is (or unions are) not entitled to be so recognised.

(5) The powers conferred by this paragraph are in addition to those conferred by paragraph 27C(3).

27E. (1) This paragraph applies if the CAC issues a declaration that a complaint under paragraph 27B is well-founded and—

- (a) gives a notice under paragraph 27C(3)(b), or
- (b) issues a declaration under paragraph 27D.

(2) If the ballot in connection with which the complaint was made has not been held, the CAC shall take steps to cancel it.

(3) If that ballot is held, it shall have no effect.

27F. (1) This paragraph applies if the CAC gives a notice under paragraph 27C(3)(b).

(2) Paragraphs 24 to 29 apply in relation to that notice as they apply in relation to a notice given under paragraph 22(3) or 23(2) but with the modifications specified in sub-paragraphs (3) to (6).

(3) In each of sub-paragraphs (5)(a) and (6)(a) of paragraph 24 for "10 working days" substitute "5 working days".

(4) An employer's duty under paragraph (a) of paragraph 26(4) is limited to—

- (a) giving the CAC the names and home addresses of any workers in the bargaining unit which have not previously been given to it in accordance with that duty;
- (b) giving the CAC the names and home addresses of those workers who have joined the bargaining unit since he last gave the CAC information in accordance with that duty;
- (c) informing the CAC of any change to the name or home address of a worker whose name and home address have previously been given to the CAC in accordance with that duty; and
- (d) informing the CAC of any worker whose name had previously been given to it in accordance with that duty who has ceased to be within the bargaining unit.

(5) Any order given under paragraph 27(1) or 27C(3)(a) for the purposes of the cancelled or ineffectual ballot shall have effect (to the extent that the CAC specifies in a notice to the parties) as if it were made for the purposes of the ballot to which the notice under paragraph 27C(3)(b) relates.

(6) The gross costs of the ballot shall be borne by such of the parties and in such proportions as the CAC may determine and, accordingly, sub-paragraphs (2) and (3) of paragraph 28 shall be omitted and the reference in sub-paragraph (4) of that paragraph to the employer and the union (or each of the unions) shall be construed as a reference to the party or parties which bear the costs in accordance with the CAC's determination.]

28. (1) This paragraph applies if the holding of a ballot has been arranged under paragraph 24 whether or not it has been cancelled.

(2) The gross costs of the ballot shall be borne—

- (a) as to half, by the employer, and
- (b) as to half, by the union (or unions).

(3) If there is more than one union they shall bear their half of the gross costs—

- (a) in such proportions as they jointly indicate to the person appointed to conduct the ballot, or
- (b) in the absence of such an indication, in equal shares.

(4) The person appointed to conduct the ballot may send to the employer and the union (or each of the unions) a demand stating—

- (a) the gross costs of the ballot, and
- (b) the amount of the gross costs to be borne by the recipient.

(5) In such a case the recipient must pay the amount stated to the person sending the demand, and must do so within the period of 15 working days starting with the day after that on which the demand is received.

(6) In England and Wales, if the amount stated is not paid in accordance with sub-paragraph (5) it shall, if [the county court] so orders, be recoverable [under section 85 of the County Courts Act 1984] or otherwise as if it were payable under an order of that court.

[(6A) [Where a warrant of control is issued under section 85 of the 1984 Act to recover an amount in accordance with sub-paragraph (6), the power conferred by the warrant is exercisable], to the same extent and in the same manner as if the union were a body corporate, against any property held in trust for the union other than protected property as defined in section 23(2).]

(7) References to the costs of the ballot are to—

- (a) the costs wholly, exclusively and necessarily incurred in connection with the ballot by the person appointed to conduct it,
- (b) such reasonable amount as the person appointed to conduct the ballot charges for his services, and
- (c) such other costs as the employer and the union (or unions) agree.

29. (1) As soon as is reasonably practicable after the CAC is informed of the result of a ballot by the person conducting it, the CAC must act under this paragraph.

[(1A) The duty in sub-paragraph (1) does not apply if the CAC gives a notice under paragraph 27C(3)(b).]

(2) The CAC must inform the employer and the union (or unions) of the result of the ballot.

(3) If the result is that the union is (or unions are) supported by—

(a) a majority of the workers voting, and

(b) at least 40 per cent of the workers constituting the bargaining unit,

the CAC must issue a declaration that the union is (or unions are) recognised as entitled to conduct collective bargaining on behalf of the bargaining unit.

(4) If the result is otherwise the CAC must issue a declaration that the union is (or unions are) not entitled to be so recognised.

(5) The Secretary of State may by order amend sub-paragraph (3) so as to specify a different degree of support; and different provision may be made for different circumstances.

(6) An order under sub-paragraph (5) shall be made by statutory instrument.

(7) No such order shall be made unless a draft of it has been laid before Parliament and approved by a resolution of each House of Parliament.

NOTES

Inserted as noted at the beginning of this Schedule.

Paras 20, 21: words in square brackets inserted by the Employment Relations Act 2004, s 57(1), Sch 1, para 23(1), (5).

Para 22: words in square brackets in sub-para (1)(a) inserted, and sub-para (4)(b) substituted, by the Employment Relations Act 2004, ss 5(2), 6(1).

Para 23: words in square brackets in sub-para (1)(a) inserted by the Employment Relations Act 2004, s 5(2).

Para 24: sub-paras (5)–(7) substituted, for the original sub-para (5), by the Employment Relations Act 2004, s 7.

Para 25: sub-para (6A) inserted by the Employment Relations Act 2004, s 8(1).

Para 26: word in square brackets in sub-para (1) substituted, sub-paras (4A)–(4E) inserted, and sub-paras (8), (9) substituted (for the original sub-para (8)), by the Employment Relations Act 2004, s 9(1)–(4); words in square brackets in sub-paras (4)(c), (6)(a) substituted, and sub-paras (4F)–(4H) inserted, by s 5(3)–(5) of the 2004 Act.

Para 27: words in square brackets substituted by the Employment Relations Act 2004, s 9(5).

Paras 27A–27F: inserted by the Employment Relations Act 2004, s 10(1).

Para 28: words in first pair of square brackets in sub-para (6) substituted by the Crime and Courts Act 2013, s 17(5), Sch 9, Pt 3, para 52; words in second pair of square brackets in sub-para (6) substituted by the Tribunals, Courts and Enforcement Act 2007, s 62(3), Sch 13, paras 108, 110(1), (2); sub-para (6A) inserted by the Employment Relations Act 2004, s 57(1), Sch 1, para 23(1), (6); words in square brackets in sub-para (6A) substituted by the Tribunals, Courts and Enforcement Act 2007, s 62(3), Sch 13, paras 108, 110(1), (3).

Para 29: sub-para (1A) inserted by the Employment Relations Act 2004, s 10(2).

Orders: the Recognition and Derecognition Ballots (Qualified Persons) Order 2000, SI 2000/1306 at **[2.531]**; the Recognition and Derecognition Ballots (Qualified Persons) (Amendment) Order 2010, SI 2010/437; the Recognition and Derecognition Ballots (Qualified Persons) (Amendment) Order 2017, SI 2017/878 (all made under para 25). As of 15 May 2019, no Orders had been made under para 29.

Consequences of recognition

[1.649]

30. (1) This paragraph applies if the CAC issues a declaration under this Part of this Schedule that the union is (or unions are) recognised as entitled to conduct collective bargaining on behalf of a bargaining unit.

(2) The parties may in the negotiation period conduct negotiations with a view to agreeing a method by which they will conduct collective bargaining.

(3) If no agreement is made in the negotiation period the employer or the union (or unions) may apply to the CAC for assistance.

(4) The negotiation period is—

(a) the period of 30 working days starting with the start day, or

(b) such longer period (so starting) as the parties may from time to time agree.

(5) The start day is the day after that on which the parties are notified of the declaration.

31. (1) This paragraph applies if an application for assistance is made to the CAC under paragraph 30.

(2) The CAC must try to help the parties to reach in the agreement period an agreement on a method by which they will conduct collective bargaining.

(3) If at the end of the agreement period the parties have not made such an agreement the CAC must specify to the parties the method by which they are to conduct collective bargaining.

(4) Any method specified under sub-paragraph (3) is to have effect as if it were contained in a legally enforceable contract made by the parties.

(5) But if the parties agree in writing—

(a) that sub-paragraph (4) shall not apply, or shall not apply to particular parts of the method specified by the CAC, or

(b) to vary or replace the method specified by the CAC,

the written agreement shall have effect as a legally enforceable contract made by the parties.

(6) Specific performance shall be the only remedy available for breach of anything which is a legally enforceable contract by virtue of this paragraph.

(7) If at any time before a specification is made under sub-paragraph (3) the parties jointly apply to the CAC requesting it to stop taking steps under this paragraph, the CAC must comply with the request.

(8) The agreement period is—

(a) the period of 20 working days starting with the day after that on which the CAC receives the application under paragraph 30, or
(b) such longer period (so starting) as the CAC may decide with the consent of the parties.

NOTES

Inserted as noted at the beginning of this Schedule.

Method not carried out

[1.650]

32. (1) This paragraph applies if—
(a) the CAC issues a declaration under this Part of this Schedule that the union is (or unions are) recognised as entitled to conduct collective bargaining on behalf of a bargaining unit,
(b) the parties agree a method by which they will conduct collective bargaining, and
(c) one or more of the parties fails to carry out the agreement.

(2) The [employer or the union (or unions)] may apply to the CAC for assistance.

(3) Paragraph 31 applies as if "paragraph 30" (in each place) read "paragraph 30 or paragraph 32".

NOTES

Inserted as noted at the beginning of this Schedule.

Para 32: words in square brackets in sub-para (2) substituted by the Employment Relations Act 2004, s 57(1), Sch 1, para 23(1), (7).

General provisions about admissibility

[1.651]

33. An application under paragraph 11 or 12 is not admissible unless—
(a) it is made in such form as the CAC specifies, and
(b) it is supported by such documents as the CAC specifies.

34. An application under paragraph 11 or 12 is not admissible unless the union gives (or unions give) to the employer—
(a) notice of the application, and
(b) a copy of the application and any documents supporting it.

35. (1) An application under paragraph 11 or 12 is not admissible if the CAC is satisfied that there is already in force a collective agreement under which a union is (or unions are) recognised as entitled to conduct collective bargaining on behalf of any workers falling within the relevant bargaining unit.

(2) But sub-paragraph (1) does not apply to an application under paragraph 11 or 12 if—
(a) the union (or unions) recognised under the collective agreement and the union (or unions) making the application under paragraph 11 or 12 are the same, and
(b) the matters in respect of which the union is (or unions are) entitled to conduct collective bargaining do not include [all of the following: pay, hours and holidays ("the core topics")].

(3) A declaration of recognition which is the subject of a declaration under paragraph 83(2) must for the purposes of sub-paragraph (1) be treated as ceasing to have effect to the extent specified in paragraph 83(2) on the making of the declaration under paragraph 83(2).

(4) In applying sub-paragraph (1) an agreement for recognition (the agreement in question) must be ignored if—
(a) the union does not have (or none of the unions has) a certificate [of independence],
(b) at some time there was an agreement (the old agreement) between the employer and the union under which the union (whether alone or with other unions) was recognised as entitled to conduct collective bargaining on behalf of a group of workers which was the same or substantially the same as the group covered by the agreement in question, and
(c) the old agreement ceased to have effect in the period of three years ending with the date of the agreement in question.

(5) It is for the CAC to decide whether one group of workers is the same or substantially the same as another, but in deciding the CAC may take account of the views of any person it believes has an interest in the matter.

(6) The relevant bargaining unit is—
(a) the proposed bargaining unit, where the application is under paragraph 11(2) or 12(2);
(b) the agreed bargaining unit, where the application is under paragraph 12(4).

36. (1) An application under paragraph 11 or 12 is not admissible unless the CAC decides that—
(a) members of the union (or unions) constitute at least 10 per cent of the workers constituting the relevant bargaining unit, and
(b) a majority of the workers constituting the relevant bargaining unit would be likely to favour recognition of the union (or unions) as entitled to conduct collective bargaining on behalf of the bargaining unit.

(2) The relevant bargaining unit is—
(a) the proposed bargaining unit, where the application is under paragraph 11(2) or 12(2);
(b) the agreed bargaining unit, where the application is under paragraph 12(4).

(3) The CAC must give reasons for the decision.

37. (1) This paragraph applies to an application made by more than one union under paragraph 11 or 12.

(2) The application is not admissible unless—

(a) the unions show that they will co-operate with each other in a manner likely to secure and maintain stable and effective collective bargaining arrangements, and

(b) the unions show that, if the employer wishes, they will enter into arrangements under which collective bargaining is conducted by the unions acting together on behalf of the workers constituting the relevant bargaining unit.

(3) The relevant bargaining unit is—

(a) the proposed bargaining unit, where the application is under paragraph 11(2) or 12(2);

(b) the agreed bargaining unit, where the application is under paragraph [12(4)].

38. (1) This paragraph applies if—

(a) the CAC accepts a relevant application relating to a bargaining unit or proceeds under paragraph 20 with an application relating to a bargaining unit,

(b) the application has not been withdrawn,

(c) no notice has been given under paragraph 17(2),

(d) the CAC has not issued a declaration under paragraph [19F(5), 22(2), 27(2), 27D(3), 27D(4),] 29(3) or 29(4) in relation to that bargaining unit, and

(e) no notification has been made under paragraph 24(2).

(2) Another relevant application is not admissible if—

(a) at least one worker falling within the relevant bargaining unit also falls within the bargaining unit referred to in sub-paragraph (1), and

(b) the application is made by a union (or unions) other than the union (or unions) which made the application referred to in sub-paragraph (1).

(3) A relevant application is an application under paragraph 11 or 12.

(4) The relevant bargaining unit is—

(a) the proposed bargaining unit, where the application is under paragraph 11(2) or 12(2);

(b) the agreed bargaining unit, where the application is under paragraph 12(4).

39. (1) This paragraph applies if the CAC accepts a relevant application relating to a bargaining unit or proceeds under paragraph 20 with an application relating to a bargaining unit.

(2) Another relevant application is not admissible if—

(a) the application is made within the period of 3 years starting with the day after that on which the CAC gave notice of acceptance of the application mentioned in sub-paragraph (1),

(b) the relevant bargaining unit is the same or substantially the same as the bargaining unit mentioned in sub-paragraph (1), and

(c) the application is made by the union (or unions) which made the application mentioned in sub-paragraph (1).

(3) A relevant application is an application under paragraph 11 or 12.

(4) The relevant bargaining unit is—

(a) the proposed bargaining unit, where the application is under paragraph 11(2) or 12(2);

(b) the agreed bargaining unit, where the application is under paragraph 12(4).

(5) This paragraph does not apply if paragraph 40 or 41 applies.

40. (1) This paragraph applies if the CAC issues a declaration under paragraph [27D(4) or] 29(4) that a union is (or unions are) not entitled to be recognised as entitled to conduct collective bargaining on behalf of a bargaining unit; and this is so whether the ballot concerned is [arranged] under this Part or Part III of this Schedule.

(2) An application under paragraph 11 or 12 is not admissible if—

(a) the application is made within the period of 3 years starting with the day after that on which the declaration was issued,

(b) the relevant bargaining unit is the same or substantially the same as the bargaining unit mentioned in sub-paragraph (1), and

(c) the application is made by the union (or unions) which made the application leading to the declaration.

(3) The relevant bargaining unit is—

(a) the proposed bargaining unit, where the application is under paragraph 11(2) or 12(2);

(b) the agreed bargaining unit, where the application is under paragraph 12(4).

41. (1) This paragraph applies if the CAC issues a declaration under paragraph [119D(4), 119H(5) or] 121(3) that bargaining arrangements are to cease to have effect; and this is so whether the ballot concerned is [arranged] under Part IV or Part V of this Schedule.

(2) An application under paragraph 11 or 12 is not admissible if—

(a) the application is made within the period of 3 years starting with the day after that on which the declaration was issued,

(b) the relevant bargaining unit is the same or substantially the same as the bargaining unit to which the bargaining arrangements mentioned in sub-paragraph (1) relate, and

(c) the application is made by the union which was a party (or unions which were parties) to the proceedings leading to the declaration.

(3) The relevant bargaining unit is—

(a) the proposed bargaining unit, where the application is under paragraph 11(2) or 12(2);
(b) the agreed bargaining unit, where the application is under paragraph 12(4).

42. (1) This paragraph applies for the purposes of paragraphs 39 to 41.

(2) It is for the CAC to decide whether one bargaining unit is the same or substantially the same as another, but in deciding the CAC may take account of the views of any person it believes has an interest in the matter.

NOTES

Inserted as noted at the beginning of this Schedule.

Para 35: words in square brackets in sub-para (2)(b) substituted by the Employment Relations Act 2004, s 11; words in square brackets in sub-para (4)(a) substituted by s 50(6) of the 2004 Act.

Paras 37, 38: numbers in square brackets substituted by the Employment Relations Act 2004, s 57(1), Sch 1, para 23(1), (8), (9).

Paras 40, 41: words in first pair of square brackets in sub-para (1) inserted, and word in second pair of square brackets in that sub-paragraph substituted, by the Employment Relations Act 2004, s 57(1), Sch 1, para 23(1), (10), (11).

General provisions about validity

[1.652]

43. (1) Paragraphs 44 to 50 apply if the CAC has to decide under paragraph 20 whether an application is valid.

(2) In those paragraphs—
(a) references to the application in question are to that application, and
(b) references to the relevant bargaining unit are to the bargaining unit agreed by the parties or decided by the CAC.

44. (1) The application in question is invalid if the CAC is satisfied that there is already in force a collective agreement under which a union is (or unions are) recognised as entitled to conduct collective bargaining on behalf of any workers falling within the relevant bargaining unit.

(2) But sub-paragraph (1) does not apply to the application in question if—
(a) the union (or unions) recognised under the collective agreement and the union (or unions) making the application in question are the same, and
(b) the matters in respect of which the union is (or unions are) entitled to conduct collective bargaining do not include [all of the following: pay, hours and holidays ("the core topics")].

(3) A declaration of recognition which is the subject of a declaration under paragraph 83(2) must for the purposes of sub-paragraph (1) be treated as ceasing to have effect to the extent specified in paragraph 83(2) on the making of the declaration under paragraph 83(2).

(4) In applying sub-paragraph (1) an agreement for recognition (the agreement in question) must be ignored if—
(a) the union does not have (or none of the unions has) a certificate [of independence],
(b) at some time there was an agreement (the old agreement) between the employer and the union under which the union (whether alone or with other unions) was recognised as entitled to conduct collective bargaining on behalf of a group of workers which was the same or substantially the same as the group covered by the agreement in question, and
(c) the old agreement ceased to have effect in the period of three years ending with the date of the agreement in question.

(5) It is for the CAC to decide whether one group of workers is the same or substantially the same as another, but in deciding the CAC may take account of the views of any person it believes has an interest in the matter.

45. The application in question is invalid unless the CAC decides that—
(a) members of the union (or unions) constitute at least 10 per cent of the workers constituting the relevant bargaining unit, and
(b) a majority of the workers constituting the relevant bargaining unit would be likely to favour recognition of the union (or unions) as entitled to conduct collective bargaining on behalf of the bargaining unit.

46. (1) This paragraph applies if—
(a) the CAC accepts an application under paragraph 11 or 12 relating to a bargaining unit or proceeds under paragraph 20 with an application relating to a bargaining unit,
(b) the application has not been withdrawn,
(c) no notice has been given under paragraph 17(2),
(d) the CAC has not issued a declaration under paragraph [19F(5), 22(2), 27(2), 27D(3), 27D(4),] 29(3) or 29(4) in relation to that bargaining unit, and
(e) no notification has been made under paragraph 24(2).

(2) The application in question is invalid if—
(a) at least one worker falling within the relevant bargaining unit also falls within the bargaining unit referred to in sub-paragraph (1), and
(b) the application in question is made by a union (or unions) other than the union (or unions) which made the application referred to in sub-paragraph (1).

47. (1) This paragraph applies if the CAC accepts an application under paragraph 11 or 12 relating to a bargaining unit or proceeds under paragraph 20 with an application relating to a bargaining unit.

(2) The application in question is invalid if—

(a) the application is made within the period of 3 years starting with the day after that on which the CAC gave notice of acceptance of the application mentioned in sub-paragraph (1),

(b) the relevant bargaining unit is the same or substantially the same as the bargaining unit mentioned in sub-paragraph (1), and

(c) the application is made by the union (or unions) which made the application mentioned in sub-paragraph (1).

(3) This paragraph does not apply if paragraph 48 or 49 applies.

48. (1) This paragraph applies if the CAC issues a declaration under paragraph [27D(4) or] 29(4) that a union is (or unions are) not entitled to be recognised as entitled to conduct collective bargaining on behalf of a bargaining unit; and this is so whether the ballot concerned is [arranged] under this Part or Part III of this Schedule.

(2) The application in question is invalid if—

(a) the application is made within the period of 3 years starting with the date of the declaration,

(b) the relevant bargaining unit is the same or substantially the same as the bargaining unit mentioned in sub-paragraph (1), and

(c) the application is made by the union (or unions) which made the application leading to the declaration.

49. (1) This paragraph applies if the CAC issues a declaration under paragraph [119D(4), 119H(5) or] 121(3) that bargaining arrangements are to cease to have effect; and this is so whether the ballot concerned is [arranged] under Part IV or Part V of this Schedule.

(2) The application in question is invalid if—

(a) the application is made within the period of 3 years starting with the day after that on which the declaration was issued,

(b) the relevant bargaining unit is the same or substantially the same as the bargaining unit to which the bargaining arrangements mentioned in sub-paragraph (1) relate, and

(c) the application is made by the union which was a party (or unions which were parties) to the proceedings leading to the declaration.

50. (1) This paragraph applies for the purposes of paragraphs 47 to 49.

(2) It is for the CAC to decide whether one bargaining unit is the same or substantially the same as another, but in deciding the CAC may take account of the views of any person it believes has an interest in the matter.

NOTES

Inserted as noted at the beginning of this Schedule.

Para 44: words in square brackets in sub-para (2)(b) substituted by the Employment Relations Act 2004, s 11; words in square brackets in sub-para (4)(a) substituted by s 50(6) of the 2004 Act.

Para 46: numbers in square brackets substituted by the Employment Relations Act 2004, s 57(1), Sch 1, para 23(1), (12).

Paras 48, 49: words in first pair of square brackets in sub-para (1) inserted, and word in second pair of square brackets in that sub-paragraph substituted, by the Employment Relations Act 2004, s 57(1), Sch 1, para 23(1), (13), (14).

Competing applications

[1.653]

51. (1) For the purposes of this paragraph—

(a) the original application is the application referred to in paragraph 38(1) or 46(1), and

(b) the competing application is the other application referred to in paragraph 38(2) or the application in question referred to in paragraph 46(2);

but an application cannot be an original application unless it was made under paragraph 11(2) or 12(2).

(2) This paragraph applies if—

(a) the CAC decides that the competing application is not admissible by reason of paragraph 38 or is invalid by reason of paragraph 46,

(b) at the time the decision is made the parties to the original application have not agreed the appropriate bargaining unit under paragraph 18, and the CAC has not decided the appropriate bargaining unit under paragraph 19 [or 19A], in relation to the application, and

(c) the 10 per cent test (within the meaning given by paragraph 14) is satisfied with regard to the competing application.

(3) In such a case—

(a) the CAC must cancel the original application,

(b) the CAC must give notice to the parties to the application that it has been cancelled,

(c) no further steps are to be taken under this Part of this Schedule in relation to the application, and

(d) the application shall be treated as if it had never been admissible.

NOTES

Inserted as noted at the beginning of this Schedule.

Para 51: words in square brackets in sub-para (2)(b) inserted by the Employment Relations Act 2004, s 57(1), Sch 1, para 23(1), (15).

PART II
VOLUNTARY RECOGNITION

Agreements for recognition

[1.654]
52. (1) This paragraph applies for the purposes of this Part of this Schedule.

(2) An agreement is an agreement for recognition if the following conditions are fulfilled in relation to it—

(a) the agreement is made in the permitted period between a union (or unions) and an employer in consequence of a request made under paragraph 4 and valid within the terms of paragraphs 5 to 9;
(b) under the agreement the union is (or unions are) recognised as entitled to conduct collective bargaining on behalf of a group or groups of workers employed by the employer;
(c) if sub-paragraph (5) applies to the agreement, it is satisfied.

(3) The permitted period is the period which begins with the day on which the employer receives the request and ends when the first of the following occurs—

(a) the union withdraws (or unions withdraw) the request;
(b) the union withdraws (or unions withdraw) any application under paragraph 11 or 12 made in consequence of the request;
(c) the CAC gives notice of a decision under paragraph 14(7) which precludes it from accepting such an application under paragraph 11 or 12;
(d) the CAC gives notice under paragraph 15(4)(a) or 20(4)(a) in relation to such an application under paragraph 11 or 12;
(e) the parties give notice to the CAC under paragraph 17(2) in relation to such an application under paragraph 11 or 12;
(f) the CAC issues a declaration under paragraph [19F(5) or] 22(2) in consequence of such an application under paragraph 11 or 12;
(g) the CAC is notified under paragraph 24(2) in relation to such an application under paragraph 11 or 12;
(h) the last day of the notification period ends (the notification period being that defined by paragraph [24(6)]) and arising from such an application under paragraph 11 or 12);
(i) the CAC is required under paragraph 51(3) to cancel such an application under paragraph 11 or 12.

(4) Sub-paragraph (5) applies to an agreement if—

(a) at the time it is made the CAC has received an application under paragraph 11 or 12 in consequence of the request mentioned in sub-paragraph (2), and
(b) the CAC has not decided whether the application is admissible or it has decided that it is admissible.

(5) This sub-paragraph is satisfied if, in relation to the application under paragraph 11 or 12, the parties give notice to the CAC under paragraph 17 before the final event (as defined in paragraph 17) occurs.

NOTES

Inserted as noted at the beginning of this Schedule.

Para 52: words in square brackets in sub-para (3)(f) inserted, and number in square brackets in sub-para (3)(h) substituted, by the Employment Relations Act 2004, s 57(1), Sch 1, para 23(1), (16).

Other interpretation

[1.655]
53. (1) This paragraph applies for the purposes of this Part of this Schedule.

(2) In relation to an agreement for recognition, references to the bargaining unit are to the group of workers (or the groups taken together) to which the agreement for recognition relates.

(3) In relation to an agreement for recognition, references to the parties are to the union (or unions) and the employer who are parties to the agreement.

54. (1) This paragraph applies for the purposes of this Part of this Schedule.

(2) The meaning of collective bargaining given by section 178(1) shall not apply.

(3) Except in paragraph 63(2), in relation to an agreement for recognition references to collective bargaining are to negotiations relating to the matters in respect of which the union is (or unions are) recognised as entitled to conduct negotiations under the agreement for recognition.

(4) In paragraph 63(2) the reference to collective bargaining is to negotiations relating to pay, hours and holidays.

NOTES

Inserted as noted at the beginning of this Schedule.

Determination of type of agreement

[1.656]
55. (1) This paragraph applies if one or more of the parties to an agreement applies to the CAC for a decision whether or not the agreement is an agreement for recognition.

(2) The CAC must give notice of receipt of an application under sub-paragraph (1) to any parties to the agreement who are not parties to the application.

(3) The CAC must within the decision period decide whether the agreement is an agreement for recognition.

(4) If the CAC decides that the agreement is an agreement for recognition it must issue a declaration to that effect.

(5) If the CAC decides that the agreement is not an agreement for recognition it must issue a declaration to that effect.

(6) The decision period is—

(a) the period of 10 working days starting with the day after that on which the CAC receives the application under sub-paragraph (1), or

(b) such longer period (so starting) as the CAC may specify to the parties to the agreement by notice containing reasons for the extension.

NOTES

Inserted as noted at the beginning of this Schedule.

Termination of agreement for recognition

[1.657]

56. (1) The employer may not terminate an agreement for recognition before the relevant period ends.

(2) After that period ends the employer may terminate the agreement, with or without the consent of the union (or unions).

(3) The union (or unions) may terminate an agreement for recognition at any time, with or without the consent of the employer.

(4) Sub-paragraphs (1) to (3) have effect subject to the terms of the agreement or any other agreement of the parties.

(5) The relevant period is the period of three years starting with the day after the date of the agreement.

57. (1) If an agreement for recognition is terminated, as from the termination the agreement and any provisions relating to the collective bargaining method shall cease to have effect.

(2) For this purpose provisions relating to the collective bargaining method are—

(a) any agreement between the parties as to the method by which collective bargaining is to be conducted with regard to the bargaining unit, or

(b) anything effective as, or as if contained in, a legally enforceable contract and relating to the method by which collective bargaining is to be conducted with regard to the bargaining unit.

NOTES

Inserted as noted at the beginning of this Schedule.

Application to CAC to specify method

[1.658]

58. (1) This paragraph applies if the parties make an agreement for recognition.

(2) The parties may in the negotiation period conduct negotiations with a view to agreeing a method by which they will conduct collective bargaining.

(3) If no agreement is made in the negotiation period the employer or the union (or unions) may apply to the CAC for assistance.

(4) The negotiation period is—

(a) the period of 30 working days starting with the start day, or

(b) such longer period (so starting) as the parties may from time to time agree.

(5) The start day is the day after that on which the agreement is made.

59. (1) This paragraph applies if—

(a) the parties to an agreement for recognition agree a method by which they will conduct collective bargaining, and

(b) one or more of the parties fails to carry out the agreement as to a method.

(2) The employer or the union (or unions) may apply to the CAC for assistance.

60. (1) This paragraph applies if an application for assistance is made to the CAC under paragraph 58 or 59.

(2) The application is not admissible unless the conditions in sub-paragraphs (3) and (4) are satisfied.

(3) The condition is that the employer, taken with any associated employer or employers, must—

(a) employ at least 21 workers on the day the application is made, or

(b) employ an average of at least 21 workers in the 13 weeks ending with that day.

(4) The condition is that the union (or every union) has a certificate [of independence].

(5) To find the average under sub-paragraph (3)(b)—

(a) take the number of workers employed in each of the 13 weeks (including workers not employed for the whole of the week);

(b) aggregate the 13 numbers;

(c) divide the aggregate by 13.

(6) For the purposes of sub-paragraph (3)(a) any worker employed by an associated company incorporated outside Great Britain must be ignored unless the day the application was made fell within a period during which he ordinarily worked in Great Britain.

(7) For the purposes of sub-paragraph (3)(b) any worker employed by an associated company incorporated outside Great Britain must be ignored in relation to a week unless the whole or any part of that week fell within a period during which he ordinarily worked in Great Britain.

(8) For the purposes of sub-paragraphs (6) and (7) a worker who is employed on board a ship registered in the register maintained under section 8 of the Merchant Shipping Act 1995 shall be treated as ordinarily working in Great Britain unless—

(a) the ship's entry in the register specifies a port outside Great Britain as the port to which the vessel is to be treated as belonging,
(b) the employment is wholly outside Great Britain, or
(c) the worker is not ordinarily resident in Great Britain.

(9) An order made under paragraph 7(6) may also—

(a) provide that sub-paragraphs (2), (3) and (5) to (8) of this paragraph are not to apply, or are not to apply in specified circumstances, or
(b) vary the number of workers for the time being specified in sub-paragraph (3).

61. (1) An application to the CAC is not admissible unless—

(a) it is made in such form as the CAC specifies, and
(b) it is supported by such documents as the CAC specifies.

(2) An application which is made by a union (or unions) to the CAC is not admissible unless the union gives (or unions give) to the employer—

(a) notice of the application, and
(b) a copy of the application and any documents supporting it.

(3) An application which is made by an employer to the CAC is not admissible unless the employer gives to the union (or each of the unions)—

(a) notice of the application, and
(b) a copy of the application and any documents supporting it.

NOTES

Inserted as noted at the beginning of this Schedule.

Para 60: words in square brackets in sub-para (4) substituted by the Employment Relations Act 2004, s 50(6).

CAC's response to application

[1.659]

62. (1) The CAC must give notice to the parties of receipt of an application under paragraph 58 or 59.

(2) Within the acceptance period the CAC must decide whether the application is admissible within the terms of paragraphs 60 and 61.

(3) In deciding whether an application is admissible the CAC must consider any evidence which it has been given by the employer or the union (or unions).

(4) If the CAC decides that the application is not admissible—

(a) the CAC must give notice of its decision to the parties,
(b) the CAC must not accept the application, and
(c) no further steps are to be taken under this Part of this Schedule.

(5) If the CAC decides that the application is admissible it must—

(a) accept the application, and
(b) give notice of the acceptance to the parties.

(6) The acceptance period is—

(a) the period of 10 working days starting with the day after that on which the CAC receives the application, or
(b) such longer period (so starting) as the CAC may specify to the parties by notice containing reasons for the extension.

63. (1) If the CAC accepts an application it must try to help the parties to reach in the agreement period an agreement on a method by which they will conduct collective bargaining.

(2) If at the end of the agreement period the parties have not made such an agreement the CAC must specify to the parties the method by which they are to conduct collective bargaining.

(3) Any method specified under sub-paragraph (2) is to have effect as if it were contained in a legally enforceable contract made by the parties.

(4) But if the parties agree in writing—

(a) that sub-paragraph (3) shall not apply, or shall not apply to particular parts of the method specified by the CAC, or
(b) to vary or replace the method specified by the CAC,

the written agreement shall have effect as a legally enforceable contract made by the parties.

(5) Specific performance shall be the only remedy available for breach of anything which is a legally enforceable contract by virtue of this paragraph.

(6) If the CAC accepts an application, the applicant may not withdraw it after the end of the agreement period.

(7) If at any time before a specification is made under sub-paragraph (2) the parties jointly apply to the CAC requesting it to stop taking steps under this paragraph, the CAC must comply with the request.

(8) The agreement period is—

(a) the period of 20 working days starting with the day after that on which the CAC gives notice of acceptance of the application, or

(b) such longer period (so starting) as the parties may from time to time agree.

NOTES

Inserted as noted at the beginning of this Schedule.

PART III
CHANGES AFFECTING BARGAINING UNIT

Introduction

[1.660]

64. (1) This Part of this Schedule applies if—

(a) the CAC has issued a declaration that a union is (or unions are) recognised as entitled to conduct collective bargaining on behalf of a bargaining unit, and

(b) provisions relating to the collective bargaining method apply in relation to the unit.

(2) In such a case, in this Part of this Schedule—

(a) references to the original unit are to the bargaining unit on whose behalf the union is (or unions are) recognised as entitled to conduct collective bargaining, and

(b) references to the bargaining arrangements are to the declaration and to the provisions relating to the collective bargaining method which apply in relation to the original unit.

(3) For this purpose provisions relating to the collective bargaining method are—

(a) the parties' agreement as to the method by which collective bargaining is to be conducted with regard to the original unit,

(b) anything effective as, or as if contained in, a legally enforceable contract and relating to the method by which collective bargaining is to be conducted with regard to the original unit, or

(c) any provision of this Part of this Schedule that a method of collective bargaining is to have effect with regard to the original unit.

65. References in this Part of this Schedule to the parties are to the employer and the union (or unions) concerned.

NOTES

Inserted as noted at the beginning of this Schedule.

Either party believes unit no longer appropriate

[1.661]

66. (1) This paragraph applies if the employer believes or the union believes (or unions believe) that the original unit is no longer an appropriate bargaining unit.

(2) The employer or union (or unions) may apply to the CAC to make a decision as to what is an appropriate bargaining unit.

67. (1) An application under paragraph 66 is not admissible unless the CAC decides that it is likely that the original unit is no longer appropriate by reason of any of the matters specified in sub-paragraph (2).

(2) The matters are—

(a) a change in the organisation or structure of the business carried on by the employer;

(b) a change in the activities pursued by the employer in the course of the business carried on by him;

(c) a substantial change in the number of workers employed in the original unit.

68. (1) The CAC must give notice to the parties of receipt of an application under paragraph 66.

(2) Within the acceptance period the CAC must decide whether the application is admissible within the terms of paragraphs 67 and 92.

(3) In deciding whether the application is admissible the CAC must consider any evidence which it has been given by the employer or the union (or unions).

(4) If the CAC decides that the application is not admissible—

(a) the CAC must give notice of its decision to the parties,

(b) the CAC must not accept the application, and

(c) no further steps are to be taken under this Part of this Schedule.

(5) If the CAC decides that the application is admissible it must—

(a) accept the application, and

(b) give notice of the acceptance to the parties.

(6) The acceptance period is—

(a) the period of 10 working days starting with the day after that on which the CAC receives the application, or

(b) such longer period (so starting) as the CAC may specify to the parties by notice containing reasons for the extension.

69. (1) This paragraph applies if—
(a) the CAC gives notice of acceptance of the application, and
(b) before the end of the first period the parties agree a bargaining unit or units (the new unit or units) differing from the original unit and inform the CAC of their agreement.

(2) If in the CAC's opinion the new unit (or any of the new units) contains at least one worker falling within an outside bargaining unit no further steps are to be taken under this Part of this Schedule.

(3) If sub-paragraph (2) does not apply—
(a) the CAC must issue a declaration that the union is (or unions are) recognised as entitled to conduct collective bargaining on behalf of the new unit or units;
(b) so far as it affects workers in the new unit (or units) who fall within the original unit, the declaration shall have effect in place of any declaration that the union is (or unions are) recognised as entitled to conduct collective bargaining on behalf of the original unit;
(c) the method of collective bargaining relating to the original unit shall have effect in relation to the new unit or units, with any modifications which the CAC considers necessary to take account of the change of bargaining unit and specifies in the declaration.

(4) The first period is—
(a) the period of 10 working days starting with the day after that on which the CAC gives notice of acceptance of the application, or
(b) such longer period (so starting) as the parties may from time to time agree and notify to the CAC.

(5) An outside bargaining unit is a bargaining unit which fulfils these conditions—
(a) it is not the original unit;
(b) a union is (or unions are) recognised as entitled to conduct collective bargaining on its behalf;
(c) the union (or at least one of the unions) is not a party referred to in paragraph 64.

70. (1) This paragraph applies if—
(a) the CAC gives notice of acceptance of the application, and
(b) the parties do not inform the CAC before the end of the first period that they have agreed a bargaining unit or units differing from the original unit.

(2) During the second period—
(a) the CAC must decide whether or not the original unit continues to be an appropriate bargaining unit;
(b) if the CAC decides that the original unit does not so continue, it must decide what other bargaining unit is or units are appropriate;
(c) the CAC must give notice to the parties of its decision or decisions under paragraphs (a) and (b).

(3) In deciding whether or not the original unit continues to be an appropriate bargaining unit the CAC must take into account only these matters—
(a) any change in the organisation or structure of the business carried on by the employer;
(b) any change in the activities pursued by the employer in the course of the business carried on by him;
(c) any substantial change in the number of workers employed in the original unit.

(4) In deciding what other bargaining unit is or units are appropriate the CAC must take these matters into account—
(a) the need for the unit or units to be compatible with effective management;
(b) the matters listed in sub-paragraph (5), so far as they do not conflict with that need.

(5) The matters are—
(a) the views of the employer and of the union (or unions);
(b) existing national and local bargaining arrangements;
(c) the desirability of avoiding small fragmented bargaining units within an undertaking;
(d) the characteristics of workers falling within the original unit and of any other employees of the employer whom the CAC considers relevant;
(e) the location of workers.

(6) If the CAC decides that two or more bargaining units are appropriate its decision must be such that no worker falls within more than one of them.

(7) The second period is—
(a) the period of 10 working days starting with the day after that on which the first period ends, or
(b) such longer period (so starting) as the CAC may specify to the parties by notice containing reasons for the extension.

71. If the CAC gives notice under paragraph 70 of a decision that the original unit continues to be an appropriate bargaining unit no further steps are to be taken under this Part of this Schedule.

72. Paragraph 82 applies if the CAC gives notice under paragraph 70 of—
(a) a decision that the original unit is no longer an appropriate bargaining unit, and
(b) a decision as to the bargaining unit which is (or units which are) appropriate.

73. (1) This paragraph applies if—
(a) the parties agree under paragraph 69 a bargaining unit or units differing from the original unit,
(b) paragraph 69(2) does not apply, and

(c) at least one worker falling within the original unit does not fall within the new unit (or any of the new units).

(2) In such a case—

(a) the CAC must issue a declaration that the bargaining arrangements, so far as relating to the worker or workers mentioned in sub-paragraph (1)(c), are to cease to have effect on a date specified by the CAC in the declaration, and

(b) the bargaining arrangements shall cease to have effect accordingly.

NOTES

Inserted as noted at the beginning of this Schedule.

Employer believes unit has ceased to exist

[1.662]

74. (1) If the employer—

(a) believes that the original unit has ceased to exist, and

(b) wishes the bargaining arrangements to cease to have effect,

he must give the union (or each of the unions) a notice complying with sub-paragraph (2) and must give a copy of the notice to the CAC.

(2) A notice complies with this sub-paragraph if it—

(a) identifies the unit and the bargaining arrangements,

(b) states the date on which the notice is given,

(c) states that the unit has ceased to exist, and

(d) states that the bargaining arrangements are to cease to have effect on a date which is specified in the notice and which falls after the end of the period of 35 working days starting with the day after that on which the notice is given.

(3) Within the validation period the CAC must decide whether the notice complies with sub-paragraph (2).

(4) If the CAC decides that the notice does not comply with sub-paragraph (2)—

(a) the CAC must give the parties notice of its decision, and

(b) the employer's notice shall be treated as not having been given.

(5) If the CAC decides that the notice complies with sub-paragraph (2) it must give the parties notice of the decision.

(6) The bargaining arrangements shall cease to have effect on the date specified under sub-paragraph (2)(d) if—

(a) the CAC gives notice under sub-paragraph (5), and

(b) the union does not (or unions do not) apply to the CAC under paragraph 75.

(7) The validation period is—

(a) the period of 10 working days starting with the day after that on which the CAC receives the copy of the notice, or

(b) such longer period (so starting) as the CAC may specify to the parties by notice containing reasons for the extension.

75. (1) Paragraph 76 applies if—

(a) the CAC gives notice under paragraph 74(5), and

(b) within the period of 10 working days starting with the day after that on which the notice is given the union makes (or unions make) an application to the CAC for a decision on the questions specified in sub-paragraph (2).

(2) The questions are—

(a) whether the original unit has ceased to exist;

(b) whether the original unit is no longer appropriate by reason of any of the matters specified in sub-paragraph (3).

(3) The matters are—

(a) a change in the organisation or structure of the business carried on by the employer;

(b) a change in the activities pursued by the employer in the course of the business carried on by him;

(c) a substantial change in the number of workers employed in the original unit.

76. (1) The CAC must give notice to the parties of receipt of an application under paragraph 75.

(2) Within the acceptance period the CAC must decide whether the application is admissible within the terms of paragraph 92.

(3) In deciding whether the application is admissible the CAC must consider any evidence which it has been given by the employer or the union (or unions).

(4) If the CAC decides that the application is not admissible—

(a) the CAC must give notice of its decision to the parties,

(b) the CAC must not accept the application, and

(c) no further steps are to be taken under this Part of this Schedule.

(5) If the CAC decides that the application is admissible it must—

(a) accept the application, and

(b) give notice of the acceptance to the parties.

(6) The acceptance period is—

(a) the period of 10 working days starting with the day after that on which the CAC receives the application, or
(b) such longer period (so starting) as the CAC may specify to the parties by notice containing reasons for the extension.

77. (1) If the CAC accepts an application it—
(a) must give the employer and the union (or unions) an opportunity to put their views on the questions in relation to which the application was made;
(b) must decide the questions before the end of the decision period.

(2) If the CAC decides that the original unit has ceased to exist—
(a) the CAC must give the parties notice of its decision, and
(b) the bargaining arrangements shall cease to have effect on the termination date.

(3) If the CAC decides that the original unit has not ceased to exist, and that it is not the case that the original unit is no longer appropriate by reason of any of the matters specified in paragraph 75(3)—
(a) the CAC must give the parties notice of its decision, and
(b) the employer's notice shall be treated as not having been given.

(4) If the CAC decides that the original unit has not ceased to exist, and that the original unit is no longer appropriate by reason of any of the matters specified in paragraph 75(3), the CAC must give the parties notice of its decision.

(5) The decision period is—
(a) the period of 10 working days starting with the day after that on which the CAC gives notice of acceptance of the application, or
(b) such longer period (so starting) as the CAC may specify to the parties by notice containing reasons for the extension.

(6) The termination date is the later of—
(a) the date specified under paragraph 74(2)(d), and
(b) the day after the last day of the decision period.

78. (1) This paragraph applies if—
(a) the CAC gives notice under paragraph 77(4), and
(b) before the end of the first period the parties agree a bargaining unit or units (the new unit or units) differing from the original unit and inform the CAC of their agreement.

(2) If in the CAC's opinion the new unit (or any of the new units) contains at least one worker falling within an outside bargaining unit no further steps are to be taken under this Part of this Schedule.

(3) If sub-paragraph (2) does not apply—
(a) the CAC must issue a declaration that the union is (or unions are) recognised as entitled to conduct collective bargaining on behalf of the new unit or units;
(b) so far as it affects workers in the new unit (or units) who fall within the original unit, the declaration shall have effect in place of any declaration that the union is (or unions are) recognised as entitled to conduct collective bargaining on behalf of the original unit;
(c) the method of collective bargaining relating to the original unit shall have effect in relation to the new unit or units, with any modifications which the CAC considers necessary to take account of the change of bargaining unit and specifies in the declaration.

(4) The first period is—
(a) the period of 10 working days starting with the day after that on which the CAC gives notice under paragraph 77(4), or
(b) such longer period (so starting) as the parties may from time to time agree and notify to the CAC.

(5) An outside bargaining unit is a bargaining unit which fulfils these conditions—
(a) it is not the original unit;
(b) a union is (or unions are) recognised as entitled to conduct collective bargaining on its behalf;
(c) the union (or at least one of the unions) is not a party referred to in paragraph 64.

79. (1) This paragraph applies if—
(a) the CAC gives notice under paragraph 77(4), and
(b) the parties do not inform the CAC before the end of the first period that they have agreed a bargaining unit or units differing from the original unit.

(2) During the second period the CAC—
(a) must decide what other bargaining unit is or units are appropriate;
(b) must give notice of its decision to the parties.

(3) In deciding what other bargaining unit is or units are appropriate, the CAC must take these matters into account—
(a) the need for the unit or units to be compatible with effective management;
(b) the matters listed in sub-paragraph (4), so far as they do not conflict with that need.

(4) The matters are—
(a) the views of the employer and of the union (or unions);
(b) existing national and local bargaining arrangements;
(c) the desirability of avoiding small fragmented bargaining units within an undertaking;
(d) the characteristics of workers falling within the original unit and of any other employees of the employer whom the CAC considers relevant;
(e) the location of workers.

(5) If the CAC decides that two or more bargaining units are appropriate its decision must be such that no worker falls within more than one of them.

(6) The second period is—

(a) the period of 10 working days starting with the day after that on which the first period ends, or

(b) such longer period (so starting) as the CAC may specify to the parties by notice containing reasons for the extension.

80. Paragraph 82 applies if the CAC gives notice under paragraph 79 of a decision as to the bargaining unit which is (or units which are) appropriate.

81. (1) This paragraph applies if—

(a) the parties agree under paragraph 78 a bargaining unit or units differing from the original unit,

(b) paragraph 78(2) does not apply, and

(c) at least one worker falling within the original unit does not fall within the new unit (or any of the new units).

(2) In such a case—

(a) the CAC must issue a declaration that the bargaining arrangements, so far as relating to the worker or workers mentioned in sub-paragraph (1)(c), are to cease to have effect on a date specified by the CAC in the declaration, and

(b) the bargaining arrangements shall cease to have effect accordingly.

NOTES

Inserted as noted at the beginning of this Schedule.

Position where CAC decides new unit

[1.663]

82. (1) This paragraph applies if the CAC gives notice under paragraph 70 of—

(a) a decision that the original unit is no longer an appropriate bargaining unit, and

(b) a decision as to the bargaining unit which is (or units which are) appropriate.

(2) This paragraph also applies if the CAC gives notice under paragraph 79 of a decision as to the bargaining unit which is (or units which are) appropriate.

(3) The CAC—

(a) must proceed as stated in paragraphs 83 to 89 with regard to the appropriate unit (if there is one only), or

(b) must proceed as stated in paragraphs 83 to 89 with regard to each appropriate unit separately (if there are two or more).

(4) References in those paragraphs to the new unit are to the appropriate unit under consideration.

83. (1) This paragraph applies if in the CAC's opinion the new unit contains at least one worker falling within a statutory outside bargaining unit.

(2) In such a case—

(a) the CAC must issue a declaration that the relevant bargaining arrangements, so far as relating to workers falling within the new unit, are to cease to have effect on a date specified by the CAC in the declaration, and

(b) the relevant bargaining arrangements shall cease to have effect accordingly.

(3) The relevant bargaining arrangements are—

(a) the bargaining arrangements relating to the original unit, and

(b) the bargaining arrangements relating to each statutory outside bargaining unit containing workers who fall within the new unit.

(4) The bargaining arrangements relating to the original unit are the bargaining arrangements as defined in paragraph 64.

(5) The bargaining arrangements relating to an outside unit are—

(a) the declaration recognising a union (or unions) as entitled to conduct collective bargaining on behalf of the workers constituting the outside unit, and

(b) the provisions relating to the collective bargaining method.

(6) For this purpose the provisions relating to the collective bargaining method are—

(a) any agreement by the employer and the union (or unions) as to the method by which collective bargaining is to be conducted with regard to the outside unit,

(b) anything effective as, or as if contained in, a legally enforceable contract and relating to the method by which collective bargaining is to be conducted with regard to the outside unit, or

(c) any provision of this Part of this Schedule that a method of collective bargaining is to have effect with regard to the outside unit.

(7) A statutory outside bargaining unit is a bargaining unit which fulfils these conditions—

(a) it is not the original unit;

(b) a union is (or unions are) recognised as entitled to conduct collective bargaining on its behalf by virtue of a declaration of the CAC;

(c) the union (or at least one of the unions) is not a party referred to in paragraph 64.

(8) The date specified under sub-paragraph [(2)(a)] must be—

(a) the date on which the relevant period expires, or

(b) if the CAC believes that to maintain the relevant bargaining arrangements would be impracticable or contrary to the interests of good industrial relations, the date after the date on which the declaration is issued;

and the relevant period is the period of 65 working days starting with the day after that on which the declaration is issued.

84. (1) This paragraph applies if in the CAC's opinion the new unit contains—

(a) at least one worker falling within a voluntary outside bargaining unit, but

(b) no worker falling within a statutory outside bargaining unit.

(2) In such a case—

(a) the CAC must issue a declaration that the original bargaining arrangements, so far as relating to workers falling within the new unit, are to cease to have effect on a date specified by the CAC in the declaration, and

(b) the original bargaining arrangements shall cease to have effect accordingly.

(3) The original bargaining arrangements are the bargaining arrangements as defined in paragraph 64.

(4) A voluntary outside bargaining unit is a bargaining unit which fulfils these conditions—

(a) it is not the original unit;

(b) a union is (or unions are) recognised as entitled to conduct collective bargaining on its behalf by virtue of an agreement with the employer;

(c) the union (or at least one of the unions) is not a party referred to in paragraph 64.

(5) The date specified under sub-paragraph (2)(a) must be—

(a) the date on which the relevant period expires, or

(b) if the CAC believes that to maintain the original bargaining arrangements would be impracticable or contrary to the interests of good industrial relations, the date after the date on which the declaration is issued;

and the relevant period is the period of 65 working days starting with the day after that on which the declaration is issued.

85. (1) If the CAC's opinion is not that mentioned in paragraph 83(1) or 84(1) it must—

(a) decide whether the difference between the original unit and the new unit is such that the support of the union (or unions) within the new unit needs to be assessed, and

(b) inform the parties of its decision.

(2) If the CAC's decision is that such support does not need to be assessed—

(a) the CAC must issue a declaration that the union is (or unions are) recognised as entitled to conduct collective bargaining on behalf of the new unit;

(b) so far as it affects workers in the new unit who fall within the original unit, the declaration shall have effect in place of any declaration that the union is (or unions are) recognised as entitled to conduct collective bargaining on behalf of the original unit;

(c) the method of collective bargaining relating to the original unit shall have effect in relation to the new unit, with any modifications which the CAC considers necessary to take account of the change of bargaining unit and specifies in the declaration.

86. (1) This paragraph applies if the CAC decides under paragraph 85(1) that the support of the union (or unions) within the new unit needs to be assessed.

(2) The CAC must decide these questions—

(a) whether members of the union (or unions) constitute at least 10 per cent of the workers constituting the new unit;

(b) whether a majority of the workers constituting the new unit would be likely to favour recognition of the union (or unions) as entitled to conduct collective bargaining on behalf of the new unit.

(3) If the CAC decides one or both of the questions in the negative—

(a) the CAC must issue a declaration that the bargaining arrangements, so far as relating to workers falling within the new unit, are to cease to have effect on a date specified by the CAC in the declaration, and

(b) the bargaining arrangements shall cease to have effect accordingly.

87. (1) This paragraph applies if—

(a) the CAC decides both the questions in paragraph 86(2) in the affirmative, and

(b) the CAC is satisfied that a majority of the workers constituting the new unit are members of the union (or unions).

(2) The CAC must issue a declaration that the union is (or unions are) recognised as entitled to conduct collective bargaining on behalf of the workers constituting the new unit.

(3) But if any of the three qualifying conditions is fulfilled, instead of issuing a declaration under sub-paragraph (2) the CAC must give notice to the parties that it intends to arrange for the holding of a secret ballot in which the workers constituting the new unit are asked whether they want the union (or unions) to conduct collective bargaining on their behalf.

(4) These are the three qualifying conditions—

(a) the CAC is satisfied that a ballot should be held in the interests of good industrial relations;

[(b) the CAC has evidence, which it considers to be credible, from a significant number of the union members within the new bargaining unit that they do not want the union (or unions) to conduct collective bargaining on their behalf;]

(c) membership evidence is produced which leads the CAC to conclude that there are doubts whether a significant number of the union members within the new unit want the union (or unions) to conduct collective bargaining on their behalf.

(5) For the purposes of sub-paragraph (4)(c) membership evidence is—

(a) evidence about the circumstances in which union members became members;

(b) evidence about the length of time for which union members have been members, in a case where the CAC is satisfied that such evidence should be taken into account.

(6) If the CAC issues a declaration under sub-paragraph (2)—

(a) so far as it affects workers in the new unit who fall within the original unit, the declaration shall have effect in place of any declaration that the union is (or unions are) recognised as entitled to conduct collective bargaining on behalf of the original unit;

(b) the method of collective bargaining relating to the original unit shall have effect in relation to the new unit, with any modifications which the CAC considers necessary to take account of the change of bargaining unit and specifies in the declaration.

88. (1) This paragraph applies if—

(a) the CAC decides both the questions in paragraph 86(2) in the affirmative, and

(b) the CAC is not satisfied that a majority of the workers constituting the new unit are members of the union (or unions).

(2) The CAC must give notice to the parties that it intends to arrange for the holding of a secret ballot in which the workers constituting the new unit are asked whether they want the union (or unions) to conduct collective bargaining on their behalf.

89. (1) If the CAC gives notice under paragraph 87(3) or 88(2) the union (or unions) may within the notification period notify the CAC that the union does not (or unions do not) want the CAC to arrange for the holding of the ballot; and the notification period is the period of 10 working days starting with the day after that on which the union (or last of the unions) receives the CAC's notice.

(2) If the CAC is so notified—

(a) it must not arrange for the holding of the ballot,

(b) it must inform the parties that it will not arrange for the holding of the ballot, and why,

(c) it must issue a declaration that the bargaining arrangements, so far as relating to workers falling within the new unit, are to cease to have effect on a date specified by it in the declaration, and

(d) the bargaining arrangements shall cease to have effect accordingly.

(3) If the CAC is not so notified it must arrange for the holding of the ballot.

(4) Paragraph 25 applies if the CAC arranges under this paragraph for the holding of a ballot (as well as if the CAC arranges under paragraph 24 for the holding of a ballot).

(5) Paragraphs 26 to 29 apply accordingly, [but as if—

(a) references to the bargaining unit were references to the new unit, and

(b) paragraph 26(4F) to (4H), and the references in paragraph 26(4) and (6) to paragraph 19D, were omitted].

(6) If as a result of the ballot the CAC issues a declaration that the union is (or unions are) recognised as entitled to conduct collective bargaining on behalf of the new unit—

(a) so far as it affects workers in the new unit who fall within the original unit, the declaration shall have effect in place of any declaration that the union is (or unions are) recognised as entitled to conduct collective bargaining on behalf of the original unit;

(b) the method of collective bargaining relating to the original unit shall have effect in relation to the new unit, with any modifications which the CAC considers necessary to take account of the change of bargaining unit and specifies in the declaration.

(7) If as a result of the ballot the CAC issues a declaration that the union is (or unions are) not entitled to be recognised as entitled to conduct collective bargaining on behalf of the new unit—

(a) the CAC must state in the declaration the date on which the bargaining arrangements, so far as relating to workers falling within the new unit, are to cease to have effect, and

(b) the bargaining arrangements shall cease to have effect accordingly.

(8) Paragraphs (a) and (b) of sub-paragraph (6) also apply if the CAC issues a declaration under paragraph 27(2) [or 27D(3)].

[(9) Paragraphs (a) and (b) of sub-paragraph (7) also apply if the CAC issues a declaration under paragraph 27D(4).]

NOTES

Inserted as noted at the beginning of this Schedule.

Para 83: number in square brackets substituted by the Employment Relations Act 2004, s 57(1), Sch 1, para 23(1), (17).

Para 87: sub-para (4)(b) substituted by the Employment Relations Act 2004, s 6(2).

Para 89: words in square brackets in sub-para (5) substituted, words in square brackets in sub-para (8) inserted, and sub-para (9) added, by the Employment Relations Act 2004, s 57(1), Sch 1, para 23(1), (18)–(20).

Residual workers

[1.664]

90. (1) This paragraph applies if—

(a) the CAC decides an appropriate bargaining unit or units under paragraph 70 or 79, and

(b) at least one worker falling within the original unit does not fall within the new unit (or any of the new units).

(2) In such a case—

(a) the CAC must issue a declaration that the bargaining arrangements, so far as relating to the worker or workers mentioned in sub-paragraph (1)(b), are to cease to have effect on a date specified by the CAC in the declaration, and

(b) the bargaining arrangements shall cease to have effect accordingly.

91. (1) This paragraph applies if—

(a) the CAC has proceeded as stated in paragraphs 83 to 89 with regard to the new unit (if there is one only) or with regard to each new unit (if there are two or more), and

(b) in so doing the CAC has issued one or more declarations under paragraph 83.

(2) The CAC must—

(a) consider each declaration issued under paragraph 83, and

(b) in relation to each declaration, identify each statutory outside bargaining unit which contains at least one worker who also falls within the new unit to which the declaration relates;

and in this paragraph each statutory outside bargaining unit so identified is referred to as a parent unit.

(3) The CAC must then—

(a) consider each parent unit, and

(b) in relation to each parent unit, identify any workers who fall within the parent unit but who do not fall within the new unit (or any of the new units);

and in this paragraph the workers so identified in relation to a parent unit are referred to as a residual unit.

(4) In relation to each residual unit, the CAC must issue a declaration that the outside union is (or outside unions are) recognised as entitled to conduct collective bargaining on its behalf.

(5) But no such declaration shall be issued in relation to a residual unit if the CAC has received an application under paragraph 66 or 75 in relation to its parent unit.

(6) In this paragraph references to the outside union (or to outside unions) in relation to a residual unit are to the union which is (or unions which are) recognised as entitled to conduct collective bargaining on behalf of its parent unit.

(7) If the CAC issues a declaration under sub-paragraph (4)—

(a) the declaration shall have effect in place of the existing declaration that the outside union is (or outside unions are) recognised as entitled to conduct collective bargaining on behalf of the parent unit, so far as the existing declaration relates to the residual unit;

(b) if there is a method of collective bargaining relating to the parent unit, it shall have effect in relation to the residual unit with any modifications which the CAC considers necessary to take account of the change of bargaining unit and specifies in the declaration.

NOTES

Inserted as noted at the beginning of this Schedule.

Applications under this Part

[1.665]

92. (1) An application to the CAC under this Part of this Schedule is not admissible unless—

(a) it is made in such form as the CAC specifies, and

(b) it is supported by such documents as the CAC specifies.

(2) An application which is made by a union (or unions) to the CAC under this Part of this Schedule is not admissible unless the union gives (or unions give) to the employer—

(a) notice of the application, and

(b) a copy of the application and any documents supporting it.

(3) An application which is made by an employer to the CAC under this Part of this Schedule is not admissible unless the employer gives to the union (or each of the unions)—

(a) notice of the application, and

(b) a copy of the application and any documents supporting it.

NOTES

Inserted as noted at the beginning of this Schedule.

Withdrawal of application

[1.666]

93. (1) If an application under paragraph 66 or 75 is accepted by the CAC, the applicant (or applicants) may not withdraw the application—

(a) after the CAC issues a declaration under paragraph 69(3) or 78(3),

(b) after the CAC decides under paragraph 77(2) or 77(3),

(c) after the CAC issues a declaration under paragraph [83(2)], 85(2), 86(3) or 87(2) in relation to the new unit (where there is only one) or a declaration under any of those paragraphs in relation to any of the new units (where there is more than one),

(d) after the union has (or unions have) notified the CAC under paragraph 89(1) in relation to the new unit (where there is only one) or any of the new units (where there is more than one), or

(e) after the end of the notification period referred to in paragraph 89(1) and relating to the new unit (where there is only one) or any of the new units (where there is more than one).

(2) If an application is withdrawn by the applicant (or applicants)—

(a) the CAC must give notice of the withdrawal to the other party (or parties), and

(b) no further steps are to be taken under this Part of this Schedule.

NOTES

Inserted as noted at the beginning of this Schedule.

Para 93: number in square brackets in sub-para (1)(c) substituted by the Employment Relations Act 2004, s 57(1), Sch 1, para 23(1), (21).

Meaning of collective bargaining

[1.667]

94. (1) This paragraph applies for the purposes of this Part of this Schedule.

(2) Except in relation to paragraphs 69(5), 78(5) and 83(6), the meaning of collective bargaining given by section 178(1) shall not apply.

(3) In relation to a new unit references to collective bargaining are to negotiations relating to the matters which were the subject of collective bargaining in relation to the corresponding original unit; and the corresponding original unit is the unit which was the subject of an application under paragraph 66 or 75 in consequence of which the new unit was agreed by the parties or decided by the CAC.

(4) But if the parties agree matters as the subject of collective bargaining in relation to the new unit, references to collective bargaining in relation to that unit are to negotiations relating to the agreed matters; and this is the case whether the agreement is made before or after the time when the CAC issues a declaration that the union is (or unions are) recognised as entitled to conduct collective bargaining on behalf of the new unit.

(5) In relation to a residual unit in relation to which a declaration is issued under paragraph 91, references to collective bargaining are to negotiations relating to the matters which were the subject of collective bargaining in relation to the corresponding parent unit.

(6) In construing paragraphs 69(3)(c), 78(3)(c), 85(2)(c), 87(6)(b) and 89(6)(b)—

(a) sub-paragraphs (3) and (4) do not apply, and

(b) references to collective bargaining are to negotiations relating to pay, hours and holidays.

NOTES

Inserted as noted at the beginning of this Schedule.

Method of collective bargaining

[1.668]

95. (1) This paragraph applies for the purposes of this Part of this Schedule.

(2) Where a method of collective bargaining has effect in relation to a new unit, that method shall have effect as if it were contained in a legally enforceable contract made by the parties.

(3) But if the parties agree in writing—

(a) that sub-paragraph (2) shall not apply, or shall not apply to particular parts of the method, or

(b) to vary or replace the method,

the written agreement shall have effect as a legally enforceable contract made by the parties.

(4) Specific performance shall be the only remedy available for breach of anything which is a legally enforceable contract by virtue of this paragraph.

NOTES

Inserted as noted at the beginning of this Schedule.

PART IV
DERECOGNITION: GENERAL

Introduction

[1.669]

96. (1) This Part of this Schedule applies if the CAC has issued a declaration that a union is (or unions are) recognised as entitled to conduct collective bargaining on behalf of a bargaining unit.

(2) In such a case references in this Part of this Schedule to the bargaining arrangements are to the declaration and to the provisions relating to the collective bargaining method.

(3) For this purpose the provisions relating to the collective bargaining method are—

(a) the parties' agreement as to the method by which collective bargaining is to be conducted,

(b) anything effective as, or as if contained in, a legally enforceable contract and relating to the method by which collective bargaining is to be conducted, or

(c) any provision of Part III of this Schedule that a method of collective bargaining is to have effect.

97. For the purposes of this Part of this Schedule the relevant date is the date of the expiry of the period of 3 years starting with the date of the CAC's declaration.

98. References in this Part of this Schedule to the parties are to the employer and the union (or unions) concerned.

NOTES

Inserted as noted at the beginning of this Schedule.

Employer employs fewer than 21 workers

[1.670]

99. (1) This paragraph applies if—

(a) the employer believes that he, taken with any associated employer or employers, employed an average of fewer than 21 workers in any period of 13 weeks, and

(b) that period ends on or after the relevant date.

(2) If the employer wishes the bargaining arrangements to cease to have effect, he must give the union (or each of the unions) a notice complying with sub-paragraph (3) and must give a copy of the notice to the CAC.

(3) A notice complies with this sub-paragraph if it—

[(za) is not invalidated by paragraph 99A,]

(a) identifies the bargaining arrangements,

(b) specifies the period of 13 weeks in question,

(c) states the date on which the notice is given,

(d) is given within the period of 5 working days starting with the day after the last day of the specified period of 13 weeks,

(e) states that the employer, taken with any associated employer or employers, employed an average of fewer than 21 workers in the specified period of 13 weeks, and

(f) states that the bargaining arrangements are to cease to have effect on a date which is specified in the notice and which falls after the end of the period of 35 working days starting with the day after that on which the notice is given.

(4) To find the average number of workers employed by the employer, taken with any associated employer or employers, in the specified period of 13 weeks—

(a) take the number of workers employed in each of the 13 weeks (including workers not employed for the whole of the week);

(b) aggregate the 13 numbers;

(c) divide the aggregate by 13.

(5) For the purposes of sub-paragraph (1)(a) any worker employed by an associated company incorporated outside Great Britain must be ignored in relation to a week unless the whole or any part of that week fell within a period during which he ordinarily worked in Great Britain.

[(5A) Sub-paragraph (5B) applies to an agency worker whose contract within regulation 3(1)(b) of the Agency Workers Regulations 2010 (contract with the temporary work agency) is not a contract of employment.

(5B) For the purposes of sub-paragraphs (1) and (4), the agency worker is to be treated as having a contract of employment with the temporary work agency for the duration of the assignment with the employer (and "assignment" has the same meaning as in those Regulations).]

(6) For the purposes of sub-paragraph (5) a worker who is employed on board a ship registered in the register maintained under section 8 of the Merchant Shipping Act 1995 shall be treated as ordinarily working in Great Britain unless—

(a) the ship's entry in the register specifies a port outside Great Britain as the port to which the vessel is to be treated as belonging,

(b) the employment is wholly outside Great Britain, or

(c) the worker is not ordinarily resident in Great Britain.

(7) An order made under paragraph 7(6) may also—

(a) provide that sub-paragraphs (1) to (6) of this paragraph and paragraphs [99A] to 103 are not to apply, or are not to apply in specified circumstances, or

(b) vary the number of workers for the time being specified in sub-paragraphs (1)(a) and (3)(e).

[99A. (1) A notice given for the purposes of paragraph 99(2) ("the notice in question") is invalidated by this paragraph if—

(a) a relevant application was made, or an earlier notice under paragraph 99(2) was given, within the period of 3 years prior to the date when the notice in question was given,

(b) the relevant application, or that earlier notice, and the notice in question relate to the same bargaining unit, and

(c) the CAC accepted the relevant application or (as the case may be) decided under paragraph 100 that the earlier notice under paragraph 99(2) complied with paragraph 99(3).

(2) A relevant application is an application made to the CAC—

(a) by the employer under paragraph 106, 107 or 128, or

(b) by a worker (or workers) under paragraph 112.]

100. (1) [If an employer gives notice for the purposes of paragraph 99(2),] within the validation period the CAC must decide whether the notice complies with paragraph 99(3).

(2) If the CAC decides that the notice does not comply with paragraph 99(3)—

(a) the CAC must give the parties notice of its decision, and

(b) the employer's notice shall be treated as not having been given.

(3) If the CAC decides that the notice complies with paragraph 99(3) it must give the parties notice of the decision.

(4) The bargaining arrangements shall cease to have effect on the date specified under paragraph 99(3)(f) if—

(a) the CAC gives notice under sub-paragraph (3), and

(b) the union does not (or unions do not) apply to the CAC under paragraph 101.

(5) The validation period is—

(a) the period of 10 working days starting with the day after that on which the CAC receives the copy of the notice, or

(b) such longer period (so starting) as the CAC may specify to the parties by notice containing reasons for the extension.

101. (1) This paragraph applies if—

(a) the CAC gives notice under paragraph 100(3), and

(b) within the period of 10 working days starting with the day after that on which the notice is given, the union makes (or unions make) an application to the CAC for a decision whether the period of 13 weeks specified under paragraph 99(3)(b) ends on or after the relevant date and whether the statement made under paragraph 99(3)(e) is correct.

(2) An application is not admissible unless—

(a) it is made in such form as the CAC specifies, and

(b) it is supported by such documents as the CAC specifies.

(3) An application is not admissible unless the union gives (or unions give) to the employer—

(a) notice of the application, and

(b) a copy of the application and any documents supporting it.

(4), (5) . . .

102. (1) The CAC must give notice to the parties of receipt of an application under paragraph 101.

(2) Within the acceptance period the CAC must decide whether the application is admissible within the terms of paragraph 101.

(3) In deciding whether an application is admissible the CAC must consider any evidence which it has been given by the employer or the union (or unions).

(4) If the CAC decides that the application is not admissible—

(a) the CAC must give notice of its decision to the parties,

(b) the CAC must not accept the application,

(c) no further steps are to be taken under this Part of this Schedule, and

(d) the bargaining arrangements shall cease to have effect on the date specified under paragraph 99(3)(f).

(5) If the CAC decides that the application is admissible it must—

(a) accept the application, and

(b) give notice of the acceptance to the parties.

(6) The acceptance period is—

(a) the period of 10 working days starting with the day after that on which the CAC receives the application, or

(b) such longer period (so starting) as the CAC may specify to the parties by notice containing reasons for the extension.

103. (1) If the CAC accepts an application it—

(a) must give the employer and the union (or unions) an opportunity to put their views on the questions whether the period of 13 weeks specified under paragraph 99(3)(b) ends on or after the relevant date and whether the statement made under paragraph 99(3)(e) is correct;

(b) must decide the questions within the decision period and must give reasons for the decision.

(2) If the CAC decides that the period of 13 weeks specified under paragraph 99(3)(b) ends on or after the relevant date and that the statement made under paragraph 99(3)(e) is correct the bargaining arrangements shall cease to have effect on the termination date.

(3) If the CAC decides that the period of 13 weeks specified under paragraph 99(3)(b) does not end on or after the relevant date or that the statement made under paragraph 99(3)(e) is not correct, the notice under paragraph 99 shall be treated as not having been given.

[(3A) Sub-paragraph (3) does not prevent the notice from being treated for the purposes of the provisions mentioned in sub-paragraph (3B) as having been given.

(3B) Those provisions are—

(a) paragraphs 109(1), 113(1) and 130(1);

(b) paragraph 99A(1) in its application to a later notice given for the purposes of paragraph 99(2).]

(4) The decision period is—

(a) the period of 10 working days starting with the day after that on which the CAC gives notice of acceptance of the application, or

(b) such longer period (so starting) as the CAC may specify to the parties by notice containing reasons for the extension.

(5) The termination date is the later of—

(a) the date specified under paragraph 99(3)(f), and

(b) the day after the last day of the decision period.

NOTES

Inserted as noted at the beginning of this Schedule.

Para 99: sub-para (3)(za) inserted, and number in square brackets in sub-para (7)(a) substituted, by the Employment Relations Act 2004, s 12(1)–(3); sub-paras (5A), (5B) inserted by the Agency Workers Regulations 2010, SI 2010/93, reg 25, Sch 2, Pt 1, paras 1, 7(1), (3).

Part 1 Statutes

Para 99A: inserted by the Employment Relations Act 2004, s 12(4).
Para 100: words in square brackets in sub-para (1) inserted by the Employment Relations Act 2004, s 12(5).
Para 101: sub-paras (4), (5) repealed by the Employment Relations Act 2004, ss 12(6), 57(2), Sch 2.
Para 103: sub-paras (3A), (3B) inserted by the Employment Relations Act 2004, s 12(7).

Employer's request to end arrangements

[1.671]
104. (1) This paragraph and paragraphs 105 to 111 apply if after the relevant date the employer requests the union (or each of the unions) to agree to end the bargaining arrangements.

(2) The request is not valid unless it—
(a) is in writing,
(b) is received by the union (or each of the unions),
(c) identifies the bargaining arrangements, and
(d) states that it is made under this Schedule.

105. (1) If before the end of the first period the parties agree to end the bargaining arrangements no further steps are to be taken under this Part of this Schedule.

(2) Sub-paragraph (3) applies if before the end of the first period—
(a) the union informs the employer that the union does not accept the request but is willing to negotiate, or
(b) the unions inform the employer that the unions do not accept the request but are willing to negotiate.

(3) The parties may conduct negotiations with a view to agreeing to end the bargaining arrangements.

(4) If such an agreement is made before the end of the second period no further steps are to be taken under this Part of this Schedule.

(5) The employer and the union (or unions) may request ACAS to assist in conducting the negotiations.

(6) The first period is the period of 10 working days starting with the day after—
(a) the day on which the union receives the request, or
(b) the last day on which any of the unions receives the request.

(7) The second period is—
(a) the period of 20 working days starting with the day after that on which the first period ends, or
(b) such longer period (so starting) as the parties may from time to time agree.

106. (1) This paragraph applies if—
(a) before the end of the first period the union fails (or unions fail) to respond to the request, or
(b) before the end of the first period the union informs the employer that it does not (or unions inform the employer that they do not) accept the request (without indicating a willingness to negotiate).

(2) The employer may apply to the CAC for the holding of a secret ballot to decide whether the bargaining arrangements should be ended.

107. (1) This paragraph applies if—
(a) the union informs (or unions inform) the employer under paragraph 105(2), and
(b) no agreement is made before the end of the second period.

(2) The employer may apply to the CAC for the holding of a secret ballot to decide whether the bargaining arrangements should be ended.

(3) But no application may be made if within the period of 10 working days starting with the day after that on which the union informs (or unions inform) the employer under paragraph 105(2) the union proposes (or unions propose) that ACAS be requested to assist in conducting the negotiations and—
(a) the employer rejects the proposal, or
(b) the employer fails to accept the proposal within the period of 10 working days starting with the day after that on which the union makes (or unions make) the proposal.

108. (1) An application under paragraph 106 or 107 is not admissible unless—
(a) it is made in such form as the CAC specifies, and
(b) it is supported by such documents as the CAC specifies.

(2) An application under paragraph 106 or 107 is not admissible unless the employer gives to the union (or each of the unions)—
(a) notice of the application, and
(b) a copy of the application and any documents supporting it.

109. (1) An application under paragraph 106 or 107 is not admissible if—
(a) a relevant application was made[, or a notice under paragraph 99(2) was given,] within the period of 3 years prior to the date of the application under paragraph 106 or 107,
(b) the relevant application[, or notice under paragraph 99(2),] and the application under paragraph 106 or 107 relate to the same bargaining unit, and
(c) the CAC accepted the relevant application [or (as the case may be) decided under paragraph 100 that the notice complied with paragraph 99(3)].

(2) A relevant application is an application made to the CAC—
(a) . . .
(b) by the employer under paragraph 106, 107 or 128, or

(c) by a worker (or workers) under paragraph 112.

110. (1) An application under paragraph 106 or 107 is not admissible unless the CAC decides that—
(a) at least 10 per cent of the workers constituting the bargaining unit favour an end of the bargaining arrangements, and
(b) a majority of the workers constituting the bargaining unit would be likely to favour an end of the bargaining arrangements.

(2) The CAC must give reasons for the decision.

111. (1) The CAC must give notice to the parties of receipt of an application under paragraph 106 or 107.

(2) Within the acceptance period the CAC must decide whether—
(a) the request is valid within the terms of paragraph 104, and
(b) the application is made in accordance with paragraph 106 or 107 and admissible within the terms of paragraphs 108 to 110.

(3) In deciding those questions the CAC must consider any evidence which it has been given by the employer or the union (or unions).

(4) If the CAC decides that the request is not valid or the application is not made in accordance with paragraph 106 or 107 or is not admissible—
(a) the CAC must give notice of its decision to the parties,
(b) the CAC must not accept the application, and
(c) no further steps are to be taken under this Part of this Schedule.

(5) If the CAC decides that the request is valid and the application is made in accordance with paragraph 106 or 107 and is admissible it must—
(a) accept the application, and
(b) give notice of the acceptance to the parties.

(6) The acceptance period is—
(a) the period of 10 working days starting with the day after that on which the CAC receives the application, or
(b) such longer period (so starting) as the CAC may specify to the parties by notice containing reasons for the extension.

NOTES

Inserted as noted at the beginning of this Schedule.

Para 109: words in square brackets in sub-para (1) inserted, and sub-para (2)(a) repealed, by the Employment Relations Act 2004, ss 12(8), (9), 57(2).

Workers' application to end arrangements

[1.672]

112. (1) A worker or workers falling within the bargaining unit may after the relevant date apply to the CAC to have the bargaining arrangements ended.

(2) An application is not admissible unless—
(a) it is made in such form as the CAC specifies, and
(b) it is supported by such documents as the CAC specifies.

(3) An application is not admissible unless the worker gives (or workers give) to the employer and to the union (or each of the unions)—
(a) notice of the application, and
(b) a copy of the application and any documents supporting it.

113. (1) An application under paragraph 112 is not admissible if—
(a) a relevant application was made[, or a notice under paragraph 99(2) was given,] within the period of 3 years prior to the date of the application under paragraph 112,
(b) the relevant application[, or notice under paragraph 99(2),] and the application under paragraph 112 relate to the same bargaining unit, and
(c) the CAC accepted the relevant application [or (as the case may be) decided under paragraph 100 that the notice complied with paragraph 99(3)].

(2) A relevant application is an application made to the CAC—
(a) . . .
(b) by the employer under paragraph 106, 107 or 128, or
(c) by a worker (or workers) under paragraph 112.

114. (1) An application under paragraph 112 is not admissible unless the CAC decides that—
(a) at least 10 per cent of the workers constituting the bargaining unit favour an end of the bargaining arrangements, and
(b) a majority of the workers constituting the bargaining unit would be likely to favour an end of the bargaining arrangements.

(2) The CAC must give reasons for the decision.

115. (1) The CAC must give notice to the worker (or workers), the employer and the union (or unions) of receipt of an application under paragraph 112.

(2) Within the acceptance period the CAC must decide whether the application is admissible within the terms of paragraphs 112 to 114.

(3) In deciding whether the application is admissible the CAC must consider any evidence which it has been given by the employer, the union (or unions) or any of the workers falling within the bargaining unit.

(4) If the CAC decides that the application is not admissible—
- (a) the CAC must give notice of its decision to the worker (or workers), the employer and the union (or unions),
- (b) the CAC must not accept the application, and
- (c) no further steps are to be taken under this Part of this Schedule.

(5) If the CAC decides that the application is admissible it must—
- (a) accept the application, and
- (b) give notice of the acceptance to the worker (or workers), the employer and the union (or unions).

(6) The acceptance period is—
- (a) the period of 10 working days starting with the day after that on which the CAC receives the application, or
- (b) such longer period (so starting) as the CAC may specify to the worker (or workers), the employer and the union (or unions) by notice containing reasons for the extension.

116. (1) If the CAC accepts the application, in the negotiation period the CAC must help the employer, the union (or unions) and the worker (or workers) with a view to—
- (a) the employer and the union (or unions) agreeing to end the bargaining arrangements, or
- (b) the worker (or workers) withdrawing the application.

(2) The negotiation period is—
- (a) the period of 20 working days starting with the day after that on which the CAC gives notice of acceptance of the application, or
- (b) such longer period (so starting) as the CAC may decide with the consent of the worker (or workers), the employer and the union (or unions).

NOTES

Inserted as noted at the beginning of this Schedule.

Para 113: words in square brackets in sub-para (1) inserted, and sub-para (2)(a) repealed, by the Employment Relations Act 2004, ss 12(8), (9), 57(2), Sch 2.

Ballot on derecognition

[1.673]

117. (1) This paragraph applies if the CAC accepts an application under paragraph 106 or 107.

(2) This paragraph also applies if—
- (a) the CAC accepts an application under paragraph 112, and
- (b) in the period mentioned in paragraph 116(1) there is no agreement or withdrawal as there described.

(3) The CAC must arrange for the holding of a secret ballot in which the workers constituting the bargaining unit are asked whether the bargaining arrangements should be ended.

(4) The ballot must be conducted by a qualified independent person appointed by the CAC.

(5) The ballot must be conducted within—
- (a) the period of 20 working days starting with the day after that on which the qualified independent person is appointed, or
- (b) such longer period (so starting) as the CAC may decide.

(6) The ballot must be conducted—
- (a) at a workplace or workplaces decided by the CAC,
- (b) by post, or
- (c) by a combination of the methods described in sub-paragraphs (a) and (b),

depending on the CAC's preference.

(7) In deciding how the ballot is to be conducted the CAC must take into account—
- (a) the likelihood of the ballot being affected by unfairness or malpractice if it were conducted at a workplace or workplaces;
- (b) costs and practicality;
- (c) such other matters as the CAC considers appropriate.

(8) The CAC may not decide that the ballot is to be conducted as mentioned in sub-paragraph (6)(c) unless there are special factors making such a decision appropriate; and special factors include—
- (a) factors arising from the location of workers or the nature of their employment;
- (b) factors put to the CAC by the employer or the union (or unions).

[(8A) If the CAC decides that the ballot must (in whole or in part) be conducted at a workplace (or workplaces), it may require arrangements to be made for workers—
- (a) who (but for the arrangements) would be prevented by the CAC's decision from voting by post, and
- (b) who are unable, for reasons relating to those workers as individuals, to cast their votes in the ballot at the workplace (or at any of them),

to be given the opportunity (if they request it far enough in advance of the ballot for this to be practicable) to vote by post; and the CAC's imposing such a requirement is not to be treated for the purposes of sub-paragraph (8) as a decision that the ballot be conducted as mentioned in sub-paragraph (6)(c).]

(9) A person is a qualified independent person if—

(a) he satisfies such conditions as may be specified for the purposes of this paragraph by order of the Secretary of State or is himself so specified, and

(b) there are no grounds for believing either that he will carry out any functions conferred on him in relation to the ballot otherwise than competently or that his independence in relation to the ballot might reasonably be called into question.

(10) An order under sub-paragraph (9)(a) shall be made by statutory instrument subject to annulment in pursuance of a resolution of either House of Parliament.

(11) As soon as is reasonably practicable after the CAC is required under sub-paragraph (3) to arrange for the holding of a ballot it must inform the employer and the union (or unions)—

(a) that it is so required;

(b) of the name of the person appointed to conduct the ballot and the date of his appointment;

(c) of the period within which the ballot must be conducted;

(d) whether the ballot is to be conducted by post or at a workplace or workplaces;

(e) of the workplace or workplaces concerned (if the ballot is to be conducted at a workplace or workplaces).

118. (1) An employer who is informed by the CAC under paragraph 117(11) must comply with the following [five] duties.

(2) The first duty is to co-operate generally, in connection with the ballot, with the union (or unions) and the person appointed to conduct the ballot; and the second and third duties are not to prejudice the generality of this.

(3) The second duty is to give to the union (or unions) such access to the workers constituting the bargaining unit as is reasonable to enable the union (or unions) to inform the workers of the object of the ballot and to seek their support and their opinions on the issues involved.

(4) The third duty is to do the following (so far as it is reasonable to expect the employer to do so)—

(a) to give to the CAC, within the period of 10 working days starting with the day after that on which the employer is informed under paragraph 117(11), the names and home addresses of the workers constituting the bargaining unit;

(b) to give to the CAC, as soon as is reasonably practicable, the name and home address of any worker who joins the unit after the employer has complied with paragraph (a);

(c) to inform the CAC, as soon as is reasonably practicable, of any worker whose name has been given to the CAC under paragraph (a) or (b) but who ceases to be within the unit.

[(4A) The fourth duty is to refrain from making any offer to any or all of the workers constituting the bargaining unit which—

(a) has or is likely to have the effect of inducing any or all of them not to attend any relevant meeting between the union (or unions) and the workers constituting the bargaining unit, and

(b) is not reasonable in the circumstances.

(4B) The fifth duty is to refrain from taking or threatening to take any action against a worker solely or mainly on the grounds that he—

(a) attended or took part in any relevant meeting between the union (or unions) and the workers constituting the bargaining unit, or

(b) indicated his intention to attend or take part in such a meeting.

(4C) A meeting is a relevant meeting in relation to a worker for the purposes of sub-paragraph (4A) and (4B) if—

(a) it is organised in accordance with any agreement reached concerning the second duty or as a result of a step ordered to be taken under paragraph 119 to remedy a failure to comply with that duty, and

(b) it is one which the employer is, by such an agreement or order as is mentioned in paragraph (a), required to permit the worker to attend.

(4D) Without prejudice to the generality of the second duty imposed by this paragraph, an employer is to be taken to have failed to comply with that duty if—

(a) he refuses a request for a meeting between the union (or unions) and any or all of the workers constituting the bargaining unit to be held in the absence of the employer or any representative of his (other than one who has been invited to attend the meeting) and it is not reasonable in the circumstances for him to do so,

(b) he or a representative of his attends such a meeting without having been invited to do so,

(c) he seeks to record or otherwise be informed of the proceedings at any such meeting and it is not reasonable in the circumstances for him to do so, or

(d) he refuses to give an undertaking that he will not seek to record or otherwise be informed of the proceedings at any such meeting unless it is reasonable in the circumstances for him to do either of those things.

(4E) The fourth and fifth duties do not confer any rights on a worker; but that does not affect any other right which a worker may have.]

(5) As soon as is reasonably practicable after the CAC receives any information under sub-paragraph (4) it must pass it on to the person appointed to conduct the ballot.

(6) If asked to do so by the union (or unions) the person appointed to conduct the ballot must send to any worker—

(a) whose name and home address have been given under sub-paragraph (5), and

(b) who is still within the unit (so far as the person so appointed is aware), any information supplied by the union (or unions) to the person so appointed.

(7) The duty under sub-paragraph (6) does not apply unless the union bears (or unions bear) the cost of sending the information.

[(8) Each of the powers specified in sub-paragraph (9) shall be taken to include power to issue Codes of Practice—

(a) about reasonable access for the purposes of sub-paragraph (3), and
(b) about the fourth duty imposed by this paragraph.

(9) The powers are—

(a) the power of ACAS under section 199(1);
(b) the power of the Secretary of State under section 203(1)(a).]

119. (1) If the CAC is satisfied that the employer has failed to fulfil any of the [duties imposed on him] by paragraph 118, and the ballot has not been held, the CAC may order the employer—

(a) to take such steps to remedy the failure as the CAC considers reasonable and specifies in the order, and
(b) to do so within such period as the CAC considers reasonable and specifies in the order.

(2) If—

(a) the ballot has been arranged in consequence of an application under paragraph 106 or 107,
(b) the CAC is satisfied that the employer has failed to comply with an order under sub-paragraph (1), and
(c) the ballot has not been held,

the CAC may refuse the application.

(3) . . .

(4) If the CAC refuses an application under sub-paragraph (2) it shall take steps to cancel the holding of the ballot; and if the ballot is held it shall have no effect.

[119A. (1) Each of the parties informed by the CAC under paragraph 117(11) must refrain from using any unfair practice.

(2) A party uses an unfair practice if, with a view to influencing the result of the ballot, the party—

(a) offers to pay money or give money's worth to a worker entitled to vote in the ballot in return for the worker's agreement to vote in a particular way or to abstain from voting,
(b) makes an outcome-specific offer to a worker entitled to vote in the ballot,
(c) coerces or attempts to coerce a worker entitled to vote in the ballot to disclose—
  (i) whether he intends to vote or to abstain from voting in the ballot, or
  (ii) how he intends to vote, or how he has voted, in the ballot,
(d) dismisses or threatens to dismiss a worker,
(e) takes or threatens to take disciplinary action against a worker,
(f) subjects or threatens to subject a worker to any other detriment, or
(g) uses or attempts to use undue influence on a worker entitled to vote in the ballot.

(3) For the purposes of sub-paragraph (2)(b) an "outcome-specific offer" is an offer to pay money or give money's worth which—

(a) is conditional on—
  (i) the issuing by the CAC of a declaration that the bargaining arrangements are to cease to have effect, or
  (ii) the refusal by the CAC of an application under paragraph 106, 107 or 112, and
(b) is not conditional on anything which is done or occurs as a result of that declaration or, as the case may be, of that refusal.

(4) The duty imposed by this paragraph does not confer any rights on a worker; but that does not affect any other right which a worker may have.

(5) Each of the following powers shall be taken to include power to issue Codes of Practice about unfair practices for the purposes of this paragraph—

(a) the power of ACAS under section 199(1);
(b) the power of the Secretary of State under section 203(1)(a).

119B. (1) A party may complain to the CAC that another party has failed to comply with paragraph 119A.

(2) A complaint under sub-paragraph (1) must be made on or before the first working day after—

(a) the date of the ballot, or
(b) if votes may be cast in the ballot on more than one day, the last of those days.

(3) Within the decision period the CAC must decide whether the complaint is well-founded.

(4) A complaint is well-founded if—

(a) the CAC finds that the party complained against used an unfair practice, and
(b) the CAC is satisfied that the use of that practice changed or was likely to change, in the case of a worker entitled to vote in the ballot—
  (i) his intention to vote or to abstain from voting,
  (ii) his intention to vote in a particular way, or
  (iii) how he voted.

(5) The decision period is—

(a) the period of 10 working days starting with the day after that on which the complaint under sub-paragraph (1) was received by the CAC, or

(b) such longer period (so starting) as the CAC may specify to the parties by a notice containing reasons for the extension.

(6) If, at the beginning of the decision period, the ballot has not begun, the CAC may by notice to the parties and the qualified independent person postpone the date on which it is to begin until a date which falls after the end of the decision period.

119C. (1) This paragraph applies if the CAC decides that a complaint under paragraph 119B is well-founded.

(2) The CAC must, as soon as is reasonably practicable, issue a declaration to that effect.

(3) The CAC may do either or both of the following—

(a) order the party concerned to take any action specified in the order within such period as may be so specified, or

(b) make arrangements for the holding of a secret ballot in which the workers constituting the bargaining unit are asked whether the bargaining arrangements should be ended.

(4) The CAC may give an order or make arrangements under sub-paragraph (3) either at the same time as it issues the declaration under sub-paragraph (2) or at any other time before it acts under paragraph 121.

(5) The action specified in an order under sub-paragraph (3)(a) shall be such as the CAC considers reasonable in order to mitigate the effect of the failure of the party complained against to comply with the duty imposed by paragraph 119A.

(6) The CAC may give more than one order under sub-paragraph (3)(a).

119D. (1) This paragraph applies if the CAC issues a declaration under paragraph 119C(2) and the declaration states that the unfair practice used consisted of or included—

(a) the use of violence, or

(b) the dismissal of a union official.

(2) This paragraph also applies if the CAC has made an order under paragraph 119C(3)(a) and—

(a) it is satisfied that the party subject to the order has failed to comply with it, or

(b) it makes another declaration under paragraph 119C(2) in relation to a complaint against that party.

(3) If the party concerned is the employer, the CAC may refuse the employer's application under paragraph 106 or 107.

(4) If the party concerned is a union, the CAC may issue a declaration that the bargaining arrangements are to cease to have effect on a date specified by the CAC in the declaration.

(5) If a declaration is issued under sub-paragraph (4) the bargaining arrangements shall cease to have effect accordingly.

(6) The powers conferred by this paragraph are in addition to those conferred by paragraph 119C(3).

119E. (1) This paragraph applies if the CAC issues a declaration that a complaint under paragraph 119B is well-founded and—

(a) makes arrangements under paragraph 119C(3)(b),

(b) refuses under paragraph 119D(3) or 119H(6) an application under paragraph 106, 107 or 112, or

(c) issues a declaration under paragraph 119D(4) or 119H(5).

(2) If the ballot in connection with which the complaint was made has not been held, the CAC shall take steps to cancel it.

(3) If that ballot is held, it shall have no effect.

119F. (1) This paragraph applies if the CAC makes arrangements under paragraph 119C(3)(b).

(2) Paragraphs 117(4) to (11) and 118 to 121 apply in relation to those arrangements as they apply in relation to arrangements made under paragraph 117(3) but with the modifications specified in sub-paragraphs (3) to (5).

(3) An employer's duty under paragraph (a) of paragraph 118(4) is limited to—

(a) giving the CAC the names and home addresses of any workers in the bargaining unit which have not previously been given to it in accordance with that duty;

(b) giving the CAC the names and home addresses of those workers who have joined the bargaining unit since he last gave the CAC information in accordance with that duty;

(c) informing the CAC of any change to the name or home address of a worker whose name and home address have previously been given to the CAC in accordance with that duty; and

(d) informing the CAC of any worker whose name had previously been given to it in accordance with that duty who has ceased to be within the bargaining unit.

(4) Any order given under paragraph 119(1) or 119C(3)(a) for the purposes of the cancelled or ineffectual ballot shall have effect (to the extent that the CAC specifies in a notice to the parties) as if it were made for the purposes of the ballot for which arrangements are made under paragraph 119C(3)(b).

(5) The gross costs of the ballot shall be borne by such of the parties and in such proportions as the CAC may determine and, accordingly, sub-paragraphs (2) and (3) of paragraph 120 shall be omitted and the reference in sub-paragraph (4) of that paragraph to the employer and the union (or each of the unions) shall be construed as a reference to the party or parties which bear the costs in accordance with the CAC's determination.

119G. (1) Paragraphs 119A to 119C, 119E and 119F apply in relation to an application under paragraph 112 as they apply in relation to an application under paragraph 106 or 107 but with the modifications specified in this paragraph.

(2) References in those paragraphs (and, accordingly, in paragraph 119H(3)) to a party shall be read as including references to the applicant worker or workers; but this is subject to sub-paragraph (3).

(3) The reference in paragraph 119A(1) to a party informed under paragraph 117(11) shall be read as including a reference to the applicant worker or workers.

119H. (1) This paragraph applies in relation to an application under paragraph 112 in the cases specified in sub-paragraphs (2) and (3).

(2) The first case is where the CAC issues a declaration under paragraph 119C(2) and the declaration states that the unfair practice used consisted of or included—

(a) the use of violence, or

(b) the dismissal of a union official.

(3) The second case is where the CAC has made an order under paragraph 119C(3)(a) and—

(a) it is satisfied that the party subject to the order has failed to comply with it, or

(b) it makes another declaration under paragraph 119C(2) in relation to a complaint against that party.

(4) If the party concerned is the employer, the CAC may order him to refrain from further campaigning in relation to the ballot.

(5) If the party concerned is a union, the CAC may issue a declaration that the bargaining arrangements are to cease to have effect on a date specified by the CAC in the declaration.

(6) If the party concerned is the applicant worker (or any of the applicant workers), the CAC may refuse the application under paragraph 112.

(7) If a declaration is issued under sub-paragraph (5) the bargaining arrangements shall cease to have effect accordingly.

(8) The powers conferred by this paragraph are in addition to those conferred by paragraph 119C(3).

119I. (1) This paragraph applies if—

(a) a ballot has been arranged in consequence of an application under paragraph 112,

(b) the CAC has given the employer an order under paragraph 119(1), 119C(3) or 119H(4), and

(c) the ballot for the purposes of which the order was made (or any other ballot for the purposes of which it has effect) has not been held.

(2) The applicant worker (or each of the applicant workers) and the union (or each of the unions) is entitled to enforce obedience to the order.

(3) The order may be enforced—

(a) in England and Wales, in the same way as an order of the county court;

(b) in Scotland, in the same way as an order of the sheriff.]

120. (1) This paragraph applies if the holding of a ballot has been arranged under paragraph 117(3), whether or not it has been cancelled.

(2) The gross costs of the ballot shall be borne—

(a) as to half, by the employer, and

(b) as to half, by the union (or unions).

(3) If there is more than one union they shall bear their half of the gross costs—

(a) in such proportions as they jointly indicate to the person appointed to conduct the ballot, or

(b) in the absence of such an indication, in equal shares.

(4) The person appointed to conduct the ballot may send to the employer and the union (or each of the unions) a demand stating—

(a) the gross costs of the ballot, and

(b) the amount of the gross costs to be borne by the recipient.

(5) In such a case the recipient must pay the amount stated to the person sending the demand, and must do so within the period of 15 working days starting with the day after that on which the demand is received.

(6) In England and Wales, if the amount stated is not paid in accordance with sub-paragraph (5) it shall, if [the county court] so orders, be recoverable [under section 85 of the County Courts Act 1984] or otherwise as if it were payable under an order of that court.

[(6A) [Where a warrant of control is issued under section 85 of the 1984 Act to recover an amount in accordance with sub-paragraph (6), the power conferred by the warrant is exercisable], to the same extent and in the same manner as if the union were a body corporate, against any property held in trust for the union other than protected property as defined in section 23(2).]

(7) References to the costs of the ballot are to—

(a) the costs wholly, exclusively and necessarily incurred in connection with the ballot by the person appointed to conduct it,

(b) such reasonable amount as the person appointed to conduct the ballot charges for his services, and

(c) such other costs as the employer and the union (or unions) agree.

121. (1) As soon as is reasonably practicable after the CAC is informed of the result of a ballot by the person conducting it, the CAC must act under this paragraph.

[(1A) The duty in sub-paragraph (1) does not apply if the CAC makes arrangements under paragraph 119C(3)(b).]

(2) The CAC must inform the employer and the union (or unions) of the result of the ballot.

(3) If the result is that the proposition that the bargaining arrangements should be ended is supported by—

(a) a majority of the workers voting, and

(b) at least 40 per cent of the workers constituting the bargaining unit,

the CAC must issue a declaration that the bargaining arrangements are to cease to have effect on a date specified by the CAC in the declaration.

(4) If the result is otherwise the CAC must refuse the application under paragraph 106, 107 or 112.

(5) If a declaration is issued under sub-paragraph (3) the bargaining arrangements shall cease to have effect accordingly.

(6) The Secretary of State may by order amend sub-paragraph (3) so as to specify a different degree of support; and different provision may be made for different circumstances.

(7) An order under sub-paragraph (6) shall be made by statutory instrument.

(8) No such order shall be made unless a draft of it has been laid before Parliament and approved by a resolution of each House of Parliament.

NOTES

Inserted as noted at the beginning of this Schedule.

Para 117: sub-para (8A) inserted by the Employment Relations Act 2004, s 8(2).

Para 118: word in square brackets in sub-para (1) substituted, sub-paras (4A)–(4E) inserted, and sub-paras (8), (9) substituted (for the original sub-para (8)), by the Employment Relations Act 2004, s 9(6)–(9).

Para 119: words in square brackets in sub-para (1) substituted, and sub-para (3) repealed, by the Employment Relations Act 2004, ss 9(10), 57, Sch 1, paras 23(1), (22), Sch 2.

Paras 119A–119I: inserted by the Employment Relations Act 2004, s 13(1).

Para 120: words in first pair of square brackets in sub-para (6) substituted by the Crime and Courts Act 2013, s 17(5), Sch 9, Pt 3, para 52; words in second pair of square brackets in sub-para (6) substituted by the Tribunals, Courts and Enforcement Act 2007, s 62(3), Sch 13, paras 108, 111(1), (2); sub-para (6A) inserted by the Employment Relations Act 2004, s 57(1), Sch 1, para 23(1), (23); words in square brackets in sub-para (6A) substituted by the Tribunals, Courts and Enforcement Act 2007, s 62(3), Sch 13, paras 108, 111(1), (3).

Para 121: sub-para (1A) inserted by the Employment Relations Act 2004, s 13(2).

Code of Practice: Access and unfair practices during recognition and derecognition ballots (2005) at **[4.266]**.

Orders: the Recognition and Derecognition Ballots (Qualified Persons) Order 2000, SI 2000/1306 at **[2.531]**; the Recognition and Derecognition Ballots (Qualified Persons) (Amendment) Order 2010, SI 2010/437; the Recognition and Derecognition Ballots (Qualified Persons) (Amendment) Order 2017, SI 2017/878.

PART V
DERECOGNITION WHERE RECOGNITION AUTOMATIC

Introduction

[1.674]

122. (1) This Part of this Schedule applies if—

(a) the CAC has issued a declaration under paragraph [19F(5), 22(2), 27(2) or 27D(3)] that a union is (or unions are) recognised as entitled to conduct collective bargaining on behalf of a bargaining unit, and

(b) the parties have agreed under paragraph 30 or 31 a method by which they will conduct collective bargaining.

(2) In such a case references in this Part of this Schedule to the bargaining arrangements are to—

(a) the declaration, and

(b) the parties' agreement.

123. (1) This Part of this Schedule also applies if—

(a) the CAC has issued a declaration under paragraph [19F(5), 22(2), 27(2) or 27D(3)] that a union is (or unions are) recognised as entitled to conduct collective bargaining on behalf of a bargaining unit, and

(b) the CAC has specified to the parties under paragraph 31(3) the method by which they are to conduct collective bargaining.

(2) In such a case references in this Part of this Schedule to the bargaining arrangements are to—

(a) the declaration, and

(b) anything effective as, or as if contained in, a legally enforceable contract by virtue of paragraph 31.

124. (1) This Part of this Schedule also applies if the CAC has issued a declaration under paragraph 87(2) that a union is (or unions are) recognised as entitled to conduct collective bargaining on behalf of a bargaining unit.

(2) In such a case references in this Part of this Schedule to the bargaining arrangements are to—

(a) the declaration, and

(b) paragraph 87(6)(b).

125. For the purposes of this Part of this Schedule the relevant date is the date of the expiry of the period of 3 years starting with the date of the CAC's declaration.

126. References in this Part of this Schedule to the parties are to the employer and the union (or unions) concerned.

NOTES

Inserted as noted at the beginning of this Schedule.

Paras 122, 123: words in square brackets substituted by the Employment Relations Act 2004, s 57(1), Sch 1, para 23(1), (24), (25).

Employer's request to end arrangements

[1.675]

127. (1) The employer may after the relevant date request the union (or each of the unions) to agree to end the bargaining arrangements.

(2) The request is not valid unless it—

(a) is in writing,

(b) is received by the union (or each of the unions),

(c) identifies the bargaining arrangements,

(d) states that it is made under this Schedule, and

(e) states that fewer than half of the workers constituting the bargaining unit are members of the union (or unions).

128. (1) If before the end of the negotiation period the parties agree to end the bargaining arrangements no further steps are to be taken under this Part of this Schedule.

(2) If no such agreement is made before the end of the negotiation period, the employer may apply to the CAC for the holding of a secret ballot to decide whether the bargaining arrangements should be ended.

(3) The negotiation period is the period of 10 working days starting with the day after—

(a) the day on which the union receives the request, or

(b) the last day on which any of the unions receives the request;

or such longer period (so starting) as the parties may from time to time agree.

129. (1) An application under paragraph 128 is not admissible unless—

(a) it is made in such form as the CAC specifies, and

(b) it is supported by such documents as the CAC specifies.

(2) An application under paragraph 128 is not admissible unless the employer gives to the union (or each of the unions)—

(a) notice of the application, and

(b) a copy of the application and any documents supporting it.

130. (1) An application under paragraph 128 is not admissible if—

(a) a relevant application was made[, or a notice under paragraph 99(2) was given,] within the period of 3 years prior to the date of the application under paragraph 128,

(b) the relevant application[, or notice under paragraph 99(2),] and the application under paragraph 128 relate to the same bargaining unit, and

(c) the CAC accepted the relevant application [or (as the case may be) decided under paragraph 100 that the notice complied with paragraph 99(3)].

(2) A relevant application is an application made to the CAC—

(a) . . .

(b) by the employer under paragraph 106, 107 or 128, or

(c) by a worker (or workers) under paragraph 112.

131. (1) An application under paragraph 128 is not admissible unless the CAC is satisfied that fewer than half of the workers constituting the bargaining unit are members of the union (or unions).

(2) The CAC must give reasons for the decision.

132. (1) The CAC must give notice to the parties of receipt of an application under paragraph 128.

(2) Within the acceptance period the CAC must decide whether—

(a) the request is valid within the terms of paragraph 127, and

(b) the application is admissible within the terms of paragraphs 129 to 131.

(3) In deciding those questions the CAC must consider any evidence which it has been given by the parties.

(4) If the CAC decides that the request is not valid or the application is not admissible—

(a) the CAC must give notice of its decision to the parties,

(b) the CAC must not accept the application, and

(c) no further steps are to be taken under this Part of this Schedule.

(5) If the CAC decides that the request is valid and the application is admissible it must—

(a) accept the application, and

(b) give notice of the acceptance to the parties.

(6) The acceptance period is—

(a) the period of 10 working days starting with the day after that on which the CAC receives the application, or

(b) such longer period (so starting) as the CAC may specify to the parties by notice containing reasons for the extension.

NOTES

Inserted as noted at the beginning of this Schedule.

Para 130: words in square brackets in sub-para (1) inserted, and sub-para (2)(a) repealed, by the Employment Relations Act 2004, ss 12(8), (9), 57(2), Sch 2.

Ballot on derecognition

[1.676]

133. (1) Paragraph 117 applies if the CAC accepts an application under paragraph 128 (as well as in the cases mentioned in paragraph 117(1) and (2)).

(2) Paragraphs 118 to 121 apply accordingly, but as if—

(a) the [references in paragraphs 119(2)(a) and 119D(3)] to paragraph 106 or 107 were to paragraph 106, 107 or 128;

(b) the [references in paragraphs 119A(3)(a)(ii), 119E(1)(b) and 121(4)] to paragraph 106, 107 or 112 were to paragraph 106, 107, 112 or 128.

NOTES

Inserted as noted at the beginning of this Schedule.

Para 133: words in square brackets in sub-para (2) substituted by the Employment Relations Act 2004, s 57(1), Sch 1, para 23(1), (26).

PART VI
DERECOGNITION WHERE UNION NOT INDEPENDENT

Introduction

[1.677]

134. (1) This Part of this Schedule applies if—

(a) an employer and a union (or unions) have agreed that the union is (or unions are) recognised as entitled to conduct collective bargaining on behalf of a group or groups of workers, and

(b) the union does not have (or none of the unions has) a certificate [of independence].

(2) In such a case references in this Part of this Schedule to the bargaining arrangements are to—

(a) the parties' agreement mentioned in sub-paragraph (1)(a), and

(b) any agreement between the parties as to the method by which they will conduct collective bargaining.

135. In this Part of this Schedule—

(a) references to the parties are to the employer and the union (or unions);

(b) references to the bargaining unit are to the group of workers referred to in paragraph 134(1)(a) (or the groups taken together).

136. The meaning of collective bargaining given by section 178(1) shall not apply in relation to this Part of this Schedule.

NOTES

Inserted as noted at the beginning of this Schedule.

Para 134: words in square brackets in sub-para (1)(b) substituted by the Employment Relations Act 2004, s 50(6).

Workers' application to end arrangements

[1.678]

137. (1) A worker or workers falling within the bargaining unit may apply to the CAC to have the bargaining arrangements ended.

(2) An application is not admissible unless—

(a) it is made in such form as the CAC specifies, and

(b) it is supported by such documents as the CAC specifies.

(3) An application is not admissible unless the worker gives (or workers give) to the employer and to the union (or each of the unions)—

(a) notice of the application, and

(b) a copy of the application and any documents supporting it.

138. An application under paragraph 137 is not admissible if the CAC is satisfied that any of the unions has a certificate [of independence].

139. (1) An application under paragraph 137 is not admissible unless the CAC decides that—

(a) at least 10 per cent of the workers constituting the bargaining unit favour an end of the bargaining arrangements, and

(b) a majority of the workers constituting the bargaining unit would be likely to favour an end of the bargaining arrangements.

(2) The CAC must give reasons for the decision.

140. An application under paragraph 137 is not admissible if the CAC is satisfied that—

(a) the union (or any of the unions) has made an application to the Certification Officer under section 6 for a certificate that it is independent, and

(b) the Certification Officer has not come to a decision on the application (or each of the applications).

141. (1) The CAC must give notice to the worker (or workers), the employer and the union (or unions) of receipt of an application under paragraph 137.

(2) Within the acceptance period the CAC must decide whether the application is admissible within the terms of paragraphs 137 to 140.

(3) In deciding whether the application is admissible the CAC must consider any evidence which it has been given by the employer, the union (or unions) or any of the workers falling within the bargaining unit.

(4) If the CAC decides that the application is not admissible—

(a) the CAC must give notice of its decision to the worker (or workers), the employer and the union (or unions),

(b) the CAC must not accept the application, and

(c) no further steps are to be taken under this Part of this Schedule.

(5) If the CAC decides that the application is admissible it must—

(a) accept the application, and

(b) give notice of the acceptance to the worker (or workers), the employer and the union (or unions).

(6) The acceptance period is—

(a) the period of 10 working days starting with the day after that on which the CAC receives the application, or

(b) such longer period (so starting) as the CAC may specify to the worker (or workers), the employer and the union (or unions) by notice containing reasons for the extension.

142. (1) If the CAC accepts the application, in the negotiation period the CAC must help the employer, the union (or unions) and the worker (or workers) with a view to—

(a) the employer and the union (or unions) agreeing to end the bargaining arrangements, or

(b) the worker (or workers) withdrawing the application.

(2) The negotiation period is—

(a) the period of 20 working days starting with the day after that on which the CAC gives notice of acceptance of the application, or

(b) such longer period (so starting) as the CAC may decide with the consent of the worker (or workers), the employer and the union (or unions).

143. (1) This paragraph applies if—

(a) the CAC accepts an application under paragraph 137,

(b) during the period mentioned in paragraph 142(1) or 145(3) the CAC is satisfied that the union (or each of the unions) has made an application to the Certification Officer under section 6 for a certificate that it is independent, that the application (or each of the applications) to the Certification Officer was made before the application under paragraph 137 and that the Certification Officer has not come to a decision on the application (or each of the applications), and

(c) at the time the CAC is so satisfied there has been no agreement or withdrawal as described in paragraph 142(1) or 145(3).

(2) In such a case paragraph 142(1) or 145(3) shall cease to apply from the time when the CAC is satisfied as mentioned in sub-paragraph (1)(b).

144. (1) This paragraph applies if the CAC is subsequently satisfied that—

(a) the Certification Officer has come to a decision on the application (or each of the applications) mentioned in paragraph 143(1)(b), and

(b) his decision is that the union (or any of the unions) which made an application under section 6 is independent.

(2) In such a case—

(a) the CAC must give the worker (or workers), the employer and the union (or unions) notice that it is so satisfied, and

(b) the application under paragraph 137 shall be treated as not having been made.

145. (1) This paragraph applies if the CAC is subsequently satisfied that—

(a) the Certification Officer has come to a decision on the application (or each of the applications) mentioned in paragraph 143(1)(b), and

(b) his decision is that the union (or each of the unions) which made an application under section 6 is not independent.

(2) The CAC must give the worker (or workers), the employer and the union (or unions) notice that it is so satisfied.

(3) In the new negotiation period the CAC must help the employer, the union (or unions) and the worker (or workers) with a view to—

(a) the employer and the union (or unions) agreeing to end the bargaining arrangements, or

(b) the worker (or workers) withdrawing the application.

(4) The new negotiation period is—

(a) the period of 20 working days starting with the day after that on which the CAC gives notice under sub-paragraph (2), or

(b) such longer period (so starting) as the CAC may decide with the consent of the worker (or workers), the employer and the union (or unions).

146. (1) This paragraph applies if—

(a) the CAC accepts an application under paragraph 137,

(b) paragraph 143 does not apply, and

(c) during the relevant period the CAC is satisfied that a certificate of independence has been issued to the union (or any of the unions) under section 6.

(2) In such a case the relevant period is the period starting with the first day of the negotiation period (as defined in paragraph 142(2)) and ending with the first of the following to occur—

(a) any agreement by the employer and the union (or unions) to end the bargaining arrangements;

(b) any withdrawal of the application by the worker (or workers);

(c) the CAC being informed of the result of a relevant ballot by the person conducting it;

and a relevant ballot is a ballot held by virtue of this Part of this Schedule.

(3) This paragraph also applies if—

(a) the CAC gives notice under paragraph 145(2), and

(b) during the relevant period the CAC is satisfied that a certificate of independence has been issued to the union (or any of the unions) under section 6.

(4) In such a case, the relevant period is the period starting with the first day of the new negotiation period (as defined in paragraph 145(4)) and ending with the first of the following to occur—

(a) any agreement by the employer and the union (or unions) to end the bargaining arrangements;

(b) any withdrawal of the application by the worker (or workers);

(c) the CAC being informed of the result of a relevant ballot by the person conducting it;

and a relevant ballot is a ballot held by virtue of this Part of this Schedule.

(5) If this paragraph applies—

(a) the CAC must give the worker (or workers), the employer and the union (or unions) notice that it is satisfied as mentioned in sub-paragraph (1)(c) or (3)(b), and

(b) the application under paragraph 137 shall be treated as not having been made.

NOTES

Inserted as noted at the beginning of this Schedule.

Para 138: words in square brackets substituted by the Employment Relations Act 2004, s 50(6).

Ballot on derecognition

[1.679]

147. (1) Paragraph 117 applies if—

(a) the CAC accepts an application under paragraph 137, and

(b) in the period mentioned in paragraph 142(1) or 145(3) there is no agreement or withdrawal as there described,

(as well as in the cases mentioned in paragraph 117(1) and (2)).

(2) Paragraphs 118 to 121 apply accordingly, but as if—

(a) the [references in paragraphs 119H(1) and 119I(1)(a)] to paragraph 112 were to paragraph 112 or 137;

(b) the [references in paragraphs 119A(3)(a)(ii), 119E(1)(b) and 121(4)] to paragraph 106, 107 or 112 were to paragraph 106, 107, 112 or 137;

(c) the reference in paragraph 119(4) to the CAC refusing an application under paragraph 119(2) included a reference to it being required to give notice under paragraph 146(5).

NOTES

Inserted as noted at the beginning of this Schedule.

Para 147: words in square brackets in sub-para (2) substituted by the Employment Relations Act 2004, s 57(1), Sch 1, para 23(1), (27).

Derecognition: other cases

[1.680]

148. (1) This paragraph applies if as a result of a declaration by the CAC another union is (or other unions are) recognised as entitled to conduct collective bargaining on behalf of a group of workers at least one of whom falls within the bargaining unit.

(2) The CAC must issue a declaration that the bargaining arrangements are to cease to have effect on a date specified by the CAC in the declaration.

(3) If a declaration is issued under sub-paragraph (2) the bargaining arrangements shall cease to have effect accordingly.

(4) It is for the CAC to decide whether sub-paragraph (1) is fulfilled, but in deciding the CAC may take account of the views of any person it believes has an interest in the matter.

NOTES

Inserted as noted at the beginning of this Schedule.

PART VII
LOSS OF INDEPENDENCE

Introduction

[1.681]

149. (1) This Part of this Schedule applies if the CAC has issued a declaration that a union is (or unions are) recognised as entitled to conduct collective bargaining on behalf of a bargaining unit.

(2) In such a case references in this Part of this Schedule to the bargaining arrangements are to the declaration and to the provisions relating to the collective bargaining method.

(3) For this purpose the provisions relating to the collective bargaining method are—

(a) the parties' agreement as to the method by which collective bargaining is to be conducted,

(b) anything effective as, or as if contained in, a legally enforceable contract and relating to the method by which collective bargaining is to be conducted, or

(c) any provision of Part III of this Schedule that a method of collective bargaining is to have effect.

150. (1) This Part of this Schedule also applies if—

(a) the parties have agreed that a union is (or unions are) recognised as entitled to conduct collective bargaining on behalf of a bargaining unit,

(b) the CAC has specified to the parties under paragraph 63(2) the method by which they are to conduct collective bargaining, and

(c) the parties have not agreed in writing to replace the method or that paragraph 63(3) shall not apply.

(2) In such a case references in this Part of this Schedule to the bargaining arrangements are to—

(a) the parties' agreement mentioned in sub-paragraph (1)(a), and

(b) anything effective as, or as if contained in, a legally enforceable contract by virtue of paragraph 63.

151. References in this Part of this Schedule to the parties are to the employer and the union (or unions) concerned.

NOTES

Inserted as noted at the beginning of this Schedule.

Loss of certificate

[1.682]

152. (1) This paragraph applies if—

(a) only one union is a party, and

(b) under section 7 the Certification Officer withdraws the union's certificate of independence.

(2) This paragraph also applies if—

(a) more than one union is a party, and

(b) under section 7 the Certification Officer withdraws the certificate of independence of each union (whether different certificates are withdrawn on the same or on different days).

(3) Sub-paragraph (4) shall apply on the day after—

(a) the day on which the Certification Officer informs the union (or unions) of the withdrawal (or withdrawals), or

(b) if there is more than one union, and he informs them on different days, the last of those days.

(4) The bargaining arrangements shall cease to have effect; and the parties shall be taken to agree that the union is (or unions are) recognised as entitled to conduct collective bargaining on behalf of the bargaining unit concerned.

NOTES

Inserted as noted at the beginning of this Schedule.

Certificate re-issued

[1.683]

153. (1) This paragraph applies if—

(a) only one union is a party,

(b) paragraph 152 applies, and

(c) as a result of an appeal under section 9 against the decision to withdraw the certificate, the Certification Officer issues a certificate that the union is independent.

(2) This paragraph also applies if—

(a) more than one union is a party,

(b) paragraph 152 applies, and

(c) as a result of an appeal under section 9 against a decision to withdraw a certificate, the Certification Officer issues a certificate that any of the unions concerned is independent.

(3) Sub-paragraph (4) shall apply, beginning with the day after—

(a) the day on which the Certification Officer issues the certificate, or

(b) if there is more than one union, the day on which he issues the first or only certificate.

(4) The bargaining arrangements shall have effect again; and paragraph 152 shall cease to apply.

NOTES

Inserted as noted at the beginning of this Schedule.

Miscellaneous

[1.684]

154. Parts III to VI of this Schedule shall not apply in the case of the parties at any time when, by virtue of this Part of this Schedule, the bargaining arrangements do not have effect.

155. If—

(a) by virtue of paragraph 153 the bargaining arrangements have effect again beginning with a particular day, and

(b) in consequence section 70B applies in relation to the bargaining unit concerned,

for the purposes of section 70B(3) that day shall be taken to be the day on which section 70B first applies in relation to the unit.

NOTES

Inserted as noted at the beginning of this Schedule.

PART VIII
DETRIMENT

Detriment

[1.685]

156. (1) A worker has a right not to be subjected to any detriment by any act, or any deliberate failure to act, by his employer if the act or failure takes place on any of the grounds set out in sub-paragraph (2).

(2) The grounds are that—

(a) the worker acted with a view to obtaining or preventing recognition of a union (or unions) by the employer under this Schedule;

(b) the worker indicated that he supported or did not support recognition of a union (or unions) by the employer under this Schedule;

(c) the worker acted with a view to securing or preventing the ending under this Schedule of bargaining arrangements;

(d) the worker indicated that he supported or did not support the ending under this Schedule of bargaining arrangements;

(e) the worker influenced or sought to influence the way in which votes were to be cast by other workers in a ballot arranged under this Schedule;

(f) the worker influenced or sought to influence other workers to vote or to abstain from voting in such a ballot;

(g) the worker voted in such a ballot;

(h) the worker proposed to do, failed to do, or proposed to decline to do, any of the things referred to in paragraphs (a) to (g).

(3) A ground does not fall within sub-paragraph (2) if it constitutes an unreasonable act or omission by the worker.

(4) This paragraph does not apply if the worker is an employee and the detriment amounts to dismissal within the meaning of the Employment Rights Act 1996.

(5) A worker may present a complaint to an employment tribunal on the ground that he has been subjected to a detriment in contravention of this paragraph.

(6) Apart from the remedy by way of complaint as mentioned in sub-paragraph (5), a worker has no remedy for infringement of the right conferred on him by this paragraph.

157. (1) An employment tribunal shall not consider a complaint under paragraph 156 unless it is presented—

(a) before the end of the period of 3 months starting with the date of the act or failure to which the complaint relates or, if that act or failure is part of a series of similar acts or failures (or both), the last of them, or

(b) where the tribunal is satisfied that it was not reasonably practicable for the complaint to be presented before the end of that period, within such further period as it considers reasonable.

(2) For the purposes of sub-paragraph (1)—

(a) where an act extends over a period, the reference to the date of the act is a reference to the last day of that period;

(b) a failure to act shall be treated as done when it was decided on.

(3) For the purposes of sub-paragraph (2), in the absence of evidence establishing the contrary an employer must be taken to decide on a failure to act—

(a) when he does an act inconsistent with doing the failed act, or

(b) if he has done no such inconsistent act, when the period expires within which he might reasonably have been expected to do the failed act if it was to be done.

[(4) Section 292A (extension of time limits to facilitate conciliation before institution of proceedings) applies for the purposes of sub-paragraph (1)(a).]

158. On a complaint under paragraph 156 it shall be for the employer to show the ground on which he acted or failed to act.

159. (1) If the employment tribunal finds that a complaint under paragraph 156 is well-founded it shall make a declaration to that effect and may make an award of compensation to be paid by the employer to the complainant in respect of the act or failure complained of.

(2) The amount of the compensation awarded shall be such as the tribunal considers just and equitable in all the circumstances having regard to the infringement complained of and to any loss sustained by the complainant which is attributable to the act or failure which infringed his right.

(3) The loss shall be taken to include—

(a) any expenses reasonably incurred by the complainant in consequence of the act or failure complained of, and

(b) loss of any benefit which he might reasonably be expected to have had but for that act or failure.

(4) In ascertaining the loss, the tribunal shall apply the same rule concerning the duty of a person to mitigate his loss as applies to damages recoverable under the common law of England and Wales or Scotland.

(5) If the tribunal finds that the act or failure complained of was to any extent caused or contributed to by action of the complainant, it shall reduce the amount of the compensation by such proportion as it considers just and equitable having regard to that finding.

160. (1) If the employment tribunal finds that a complaint under paragraph 156 is well-founded and—

(a) the detriment of which the worker has complained is the termination of his worker's contract, but

(b) that contract was not a contract of employment,

any compensation awarded under paragraph 159 must not exceed the limit specified in sub-paragraph (2).

(2) The limit is the total of—

(a) the sum which would be the basic award for unfair dismissal, calculated in accordance with section 119 of the Employment Rights Act 1996, if the worker had been an employee and the contract terminated had been a contract of employment, and

(b) the sum for the time being specified in section 124(1) of that Act which is the limit for a compensatory award to a person calculated in accordance with section 123 of that Act.

NOTES

Inserted as noted at the beginning of this Schedule.

Para 157: sub-para (4) added by the Enterprise and Regulatory Reform Act 2013, s 8, Sch 2, paras 1, 14.

Conciliation: employment tribunal proceedings under para 156 are "relevant proceedings" for the purposes of the conciliation provisions contained in the Employment Tribunals Act 1996, ss 18–18C; see s 18(1)(a) of the 1996 Act at **[1.757]**.

Tribunal jurisdiction: the Employment Act 2002, s 38 applies to proceedings before the employment tribunal relating to a claim under para 156; see s 38(1) of, and Sch 5 to, the 2002 Act at **[1.1279]**, **[1.1287]**. See also s 207A of this Act at **[1.524]** (as inserted by the Employment Act 2008). That section provides that in proceedings before an employment tribunal relating to a claim by an employee under any of the jurisdictions listed in Sch A2 to the 1992 Act at **[1.704]** (which includes para 156) the tribunal may adjust any award given if the employer or the employee has unreasonably failed to comply with a relevant Code of Practice as defined by s 207A(4). See also the revised Acas Code of Practice 1 – Disciplinary and Grievance Procedures (2015) at **[4.1]**, and the Acas Code of Practice 4 – Settlement Agreements (2013) at **[4.54]**.

Dismissal

[1.686]

161. (1) For the purposes of Part X of the Employment Rights Act 1996 (unfair dismissal) the dismissal of an employee shall be regarded as unfair if the dismissal was made—

(a) for a reason set out in sub-paragraph (2), or

(b) for reasons the main one of which is one of those set out in sub-paragraph (2).

(2) The reasons are that—

(a) the employee acted with a view to obtaining or preventing recognition of a union (or unions) by the employer under this Schedule;

(b) the employee indicated that he supported or did not support recognition of a union (or unions) by the employer under this Schedule;

(c) the employee acted with a view to securing or preventing the ending under this Schedule of bargaining arrangements;

(d) the employee indicated that he supported or did not support the ending under this Schedule of bargaining arrangements;

(e) the employee influenced or sought to influence the way in which votes were to be cast by other workers in a ballot arranged under this Schedule;

(f) the employee influenced or sought to influence other workers to vote or to abstain from voting in such a ballot;

(g) the employee voted in such a ballot;

(h) the employee proposed to do, failed to do, or proposed to decline to do, any of the things referred to in paragraphs (a) to (g).

(3) A reason does not fall within sub-paragraph (2) if it constitutes an unreasonable act or omission by the employee.

NOTES

Inserted as noted at the beginning of this Schedule.

Selection for redundancy

[1.687]

162. For the purposes of Part X of the Employment Rights Act 1996 (unfair dismissal) the dismissal of an employee shall be regarded as unfair if the reason or principal reason for the dismissal was that he was redundant but it is shown—

(a) that the circumstances constituting the redundancy applied equally to one or more other employees in the same undertaking who held positions similar to that held by him and who have not been dismissed by the employer, and

(b) that the reason (or, if more than one, the principal reason) why he was selected for dismissal was one falling within paragraph 161(2).

NOTES

Inserted as noted at the beginning of this Schedule.

Employees with fixed-term contracts

[1.688]

163. *Section 197(1) of the Employment Rights Act 1996 (fixed-term contracts) does not prevent Part X of that Act from applying to a dismissal which is regarded as unfair by virtue of paragraph 161 or 162.*

NOTES

Inserted as noted at the beginning of this Schedule.

Para 163: repealed by the Employment Relations Act 1999, s 44, Sch 9(3), as from a day to be appointed.

Note that s 197(1) of the 1996 Act was itself repealed by s 44 of, and Sch 9(3) to, the 1999 Act.

Exclusion of requirement as to qualifying period

[1.689]

164. Sections 108 and 109 of the Employment Rights Act 1996 (qualifying period and upper age limit for unfair dismissal protection) do not apply to a dismissal which by virtue of paragraph 161 or 162 is regarded as unfair for the purposes of Part X of that Act.

NOTES

Inserted as noted at the beginning of this Schedule.

Section 109 of the Employment Rights Act 1996 was repealed by the Employment Equality (Age) Regulations 2006, SI 2006/1031, reg 49(1), Sch 8, Pt 1, paras 21, 25, but there has been no corresponding amendment to this paragraph.

Meaning of worker's contract

[1.690]

165. References in this Part of this Schedule to a worker's contract are to the contract mentioned in paragraph (a) or (b) of section 296(1) or the arrangements for the employment mentioned in paragraph (c) of section 296(1).

NOTES

Inserted as noted at the beginning of this Schedule.

PART IX
GENERAL

[Rights of appeal against demands for costs

[1.691]

165A. (1) This paragraph applies where a demand has been made under paragraph 19E(3), 28(4) or 120(4).

(2) The recipient of the demand may appeal against the demand within 4 weeks starting with the day after receipt of the demand.

(3) An appeal under this paragraph lies to an employment tribunal.

(4) On an appeal under this paragraph against a demand under paragraph 19E(3), the tribunal shall dismiss the appeal unless it is shown that—

(a) the amount specified in the demand as the costs of the appointed person is too great, or

(b) the amount specified in the demand as the amount of those costs to be borne by the recipient is too great.

(5) On an appeal under this paragraph against a demand under paragraph 28(4) or paragraph 120(4), the tribunal shall dismiss the appeal unless it is shown that—

(a) the amount specified in the demand as the gross costs of the ballot is too great, or

(b) the amount specified in the demand as the amount of the gross costs to be borne by the recipient is too great.

(6) If an appeal is allowed, the tribunal shall rectify the demand and the demand shall have effect as if it had originally been made as so rectified.

(7) If a person has appealed under this paragraph against a demand and the appeal has not been withdrawn or finally determined, the demand—

(a) is not enforceable until the appeal has been withdrawn or finally determined, but

(b) as from the withdrawal or final determination of the appeal shall be enforceable as if paragraph (a) had not had effect.]

NOTES

This Schedule was inserted as noted at the beginning of this Schedule.

Para 165A: inserted by the Employment Relations Act 2004, s 14.

Power to amend

[1.692]

166. [(1) This paragraph applies if the CAC represents to the Secretary of State that a provision of this Schedule has an unsatisfactory effect and should be amended.

(2) The Secretary of State, with a view to rectifying the effect—

(a) may amend the provision by exercising (if applicable) any of the powers conferred on him by paragraphs 7(6), 29(5), 121(6), 166A, 166B, 169A, 169B and 171A, or

(b) may amend the provision by order in such other way as he thinks fit.

(2A) The Secretary of State need not proceed in a way proposed by the CAC (if it proposes one).

(2B) Nothing in this paragraph prevents the Secretary of State from exercising any of the powers mentioned in sub-paragraph (2)(a) in the absence of a representation from the CAC.]

(3) An order under [sub-paragraph (2)(b)] shall be made by statutory instrument.

(4) No such order shall be made unless a draft of it has been laid before Parliament and approved by a resolution of each House of Parliament.

[166A. (1) This paragraph applies in relation to any provision of paragraph 19D(2), 26(4) or 118(4) which requires the employer to give to the CAC a worker's home address.

(2) The Secretary of State may by order provide that the employer must give to the CAC (in addition to the worker's home address) an address of a specified kind for the worker.

(3) In this paragraph "address" includes any address or number to which information may be sent by any means.

(4) An order under this paragraph may—

(a) amend this Schedule;

(b) include supplementary or incidental provision (including, in particular, provision amending paragraph 19E(1)(a), 26(6)(a) or 118(6)(a));

(c) make different provision for different cases or circumstances.

(5) An order under this paragraph shall be made by statutory instrument.

(6) No such order shall be made unless a draft of it has been laid before Parliament and approved by a resolution of each House of Parliament.]

[166B. (1) The Secretary of State may by order provide that, during any period beginning and ending with the occurrence of specified events, employers and unions to which the order applies are prohibited from using such practices as are specified as unfair practices in relation to an application under this Schedule of a specified description.

(2) An order under this paragraph may make provision about the consequences of a contravention of any prohibition imposed by the order (including provision modifying the effect of any provision of this Schedule in the event of such a contravention).

(3) An order under this paragraph may confer functions on the CAC

(4) An order under this paragraph may contain provision extending for the purposes of the order either or both of the following powers to issue Codes of Practice—

(a) the power of ACAS under section 199(1);

(b) the power of the Secretary of State under section 203(1)(a).

(5) An order under this paragraph may—

(a) include supplementary or incidental provisions (including provision amending this Schedule), and

(b) make different provision for different cases or circumstances.

(6) An order under this paragraph shall be made by statutory instrument.

(7) No such order shall be made unless a draft of it has been laid before and approved by a resolution of each House of Parliament.

(8) In this paragraph "specified" means specified in an order under this paragraph.]

NOTES

Inserted as noted at the beginning of this Schedule.

Para 166: sub-paras (1), (2), (2A), (2B) substituted, for the original sub-paras (1), (2), and words in square brackets in sub-para (3) substituted, by the Employment Relations Act 2004, s 15.

Paras 166A, 166B: inserted by the Employment Relations Act 2004, ss 16, 17.

Guidance

[1.693]

167. (1) The Secretary of State may issue guidance to the CAC on the way in which it is to exercise its functions under paragraph 22 or 87.

(2) The CAC must take into account any such guidance in exercising those functions.

(3) However, no guidance is to apply with regard to an application made to the CAC before the guidance in question was issued.

(4) The Secretary of State must—
(a) lay before each House of Parliament any guidance issued under this paragraph, and
(b) arrange for any such guidance to be published by such means as appear to him to be most appropriate for drawing it to the attention of persons likely to be affected by it.

NOTES
Inserted as noted at the beginning of this Schedule.

Method of conducting collective bargaining

[1.694]
168. (1) After consulting ACAS the Secretary of State may by order specify for the purposes of paragraphs 31(3) and 63(2) a method by which collective bargaining might be conducted.
(2) If such an order is made the CAC—
(a) must take it into account under paragraphs 31(3) and 63(2), but
(b) may depart from the method specified by the order to such extent as the CAC thinks it is appropriate to do so in the circumstances.
(3) An order under this paragraph shall be made by statutory instrument subject to annulment in pursuance of a resolution of either House of Parliament.

NOTES
Inserted as noted at the beginning of this Schedule.
Orders: the Trade Union Recognition (Method of Collective Bargaining) Order 2000, SI 2000/1300 at **[2.528]**.

Directions about certain applications

[1.695]
169. (1) The Secretary of State may make to the CAC directions as described in sub-paragraph (2) in relation to any case where—
(a) two or more applications are made to the CAC,
(b) each application is a relevant application,
(c) each application relates to the same bargaining unit, and
(d) the CAC has not accepted any of the applications.
(2) The directions are directions as to the order in which the CAC must consider the admissibility of the applications.
(3) The directions may include—
(a) provision to deal with a case where a relevant application is made while the CAC is still considering the admissibility of another one relating to the same bargaining unit;
(b) other incidental provisions.
(4) A relevant application is an application under paragraph 101, 106, 107, 112 or 128.

NOTES
Inserted as noted at the beginning of this Schedule.

[Rights of appeal against demands for costs

[1.696]
169A. (1) The Secretary of State may by order make provision for any case where—
(a) an application has been made, a declaration has been issued, or any other thing has been done under or for the purposes of this Schedule by, to or in relation to a union, or
(b) anything has been done in consequence of anything so done,
and the union amalgamates or transfers all or any of its engagements.
(2) An order under this paragraph may, in particular, make provision for cases where an amalgamated union, or union to which engagements are transferred, does not have a certificate of independence.]

NOTES
This Schedule was inserted as noted at the beginning of this Schedule.
Para 169A: inserted, together with paras 169B, 169C, by the Employment Relations Act 2004, s 18.

[Effect of change of identity of employer

[1.697]
169B. (1) The Secretary of State may by order make provision for any case where—
(a) an application has been made, a declaration has been issued, or any other thing has been done under or for the purposes of this Schedule in relation to a group of workers, or
(b) anything has been done in consequence of anything so done,
and the person who was the employer of the workers constituting that group at the time the thing was done is no longer the employer of all of the workers constituting that group (whether as a result of a transfer of the whole or part of an undertaking or business or otherwise).
(2) In this paragraph "group" includes two or more groups taken together.]

NOTES
This Schedule was inserted as noted at the beginning of this Schedule.
Para 169B: inserted as noted to para 169A at **[1.696]**.

[Orders under paragraphs 169A and 169B: supplementary

[1.698]

169C. (1) An order under paragraph 169A or 169B may—

(a) amend this Schedule;

(b) include supplementary, incidental, saving or transitional provisions;

(c) make different provision for different cases or circumstances.

(2) An order under paragraph 169A or 169B shall be made by statutory instrument.

(3) No such order shall be made unless a draft of it has been laid before Parliament and approved by a resolution of each House of Parliament.]

NOTES

This Schedule was inserted as noted at the beginning of this Schedule.

Para 169C: inserted as noted to para 169A at **[1.696]**.

Notice of declarations

[1.699]

170. (1) If the CAC issues a declaration under this Schedule it must notify the parties of the declaration and its contents.

(2) The reference here to the parties is to—

(a) the union (or unions) concerned and the employer concerned, and

(b) if the declaration is issued in consequence of an application by a worker or workers, the worker or workers making it.

NOTES

Inserted as noted at the beginning of this Schedule.

[Supply of information to CAC

[1.700]

170A. (1) The CAC may, if it considers it necessary to do so to enable or assist it to exercise any of its functions under this Schedule, exercise any or all of the powers conferred in sub-paragraphs (2) to (4).

(2) The CAC may require an employer to supply the CAC case manager, within such period as the CAC may specify, with specified information concerning either or both of the following—

(a) the workers in a specified bargaining unit who work for the employer;

(b) the likelihood of a majority of those workers being in favour of the conduct by a specified union (or specified unions) of collective bargaining on their behalf.

(3) The CAC may require a union to supply the CAC case manager, within such period as the CAC may specify, with specified information concerning either or both of the following—

(a) the workers in a specified bargaining unit who are members of the union;

(b) the likelihood of a majority of the workers in a specified bargaining unit being in favour of the conduct by the union (or by it and other specified unions) of collective bargaining on their behalf.

(4) The CAC may require an applicant worker to supply the CAC case manager, within such period as the CAC may specify, with specified information concerning the likelihood of a majority of the workers in his bargaining unit being in favour of having bargaining arrangements ended.

(5) The recipient of a requirement under this paragraph must, within the specified period, supply the CAC case manager with such of the specified information as is in the recipient's possession.

(6) From the information supplied to him under this paragraph, the CAC case manager must prepare a report and submit it to the CAC.

(7) If an employer, a union or a worker fails to comply with sub-paragraph (5), the report under sub-paragraph (6) must mention that failure; and the CAC may draw an inference against the party concerned.

(8) The CAC must give a copy of the report under sub-paragraph (6) to the employer, to the union (or unions) and, in the case of an application under paragraph 112 or 137, to the applicant worker (or applicant workers).

(9) In this paragraph—

"applicant worker" means a worker who—

(a) falls within a bargaining unit ("his bargaining unit") and

(b) has made an application under paragraph 112 or 137 to have bargaining arrangements ended;

"the CAC case manager" means the member of the staff provided to the CAC by ACAS who is named in the requirement (but the CAC may, by notice given to the recipient of a requirement under this paragraph, change the member of that staff who is to be the CAC case manager for the purposes of that requirement);

"collective bargaining" is to be construed in accordance with paragraph 3; and

"specified" means specified in a requirement under this paragraph.]

NOTES

This Schedule was inserted as noted at the beginning of this Schedule.

Para 170A: inserted by the Employment Relations Act 2004, s 19.

CAC's general duty

[1.701]
171. In exercising functions under this Schedule in any particular case the CAC must have regard to the object of encouraging and promoting fair and efficient practices and arrangements in the workplace, so far as having regard to that object is consistent with applying other provisions of this Schedule in the case concerned.

NOTES
Inserted as noted at the beginning of this Schedule.

["Pay" and other matters subject to collective bargaining

[1.702]
171A. (1) In this Schedule "pay" does not include terms relating to a person's membership of or rights under, or his employer's contributions to—
(a) an occupational pension scheme (as defined by section 1 of the Pension Schemes Act 1993), or
(b) a personal pension scheme (as so defined).
(2) The Secretary of State may by order amend sub-paragraph (1).
(3) The Secretary of State may by order—
(a) amend paragraph 3(3), 54(4) or 94(6)(b) by adding specified matters relating to pensions to the matters there specified to which negotiations may relate;
(b) amend paragraph 35(2)(b) or 44(2)(b) by adding specified matters relating to pensions to the core topics there specified.
(4) An order under this paragraph may—
(a) include supplementary, incidental, saving or transitional provisions including provision amending this Schedule, and
(b) make different provision for different cases.
(5) An order under this paragraph may make provision deeming—
(a) the matters to which any pre-commencement declaration of recognition relates, and
(b) the matters to which any pre-commencement method of collective bargaining relates,
to include matters to which a post-commencement declaration of recognition or method of collective bargaining could relate.
(6) In sub-paragraph (5)—
"pre-commencement declaration of recognition" means a declaration of recognition issued by the CAC before the coming into force of the order,
"pre-commencement method of collective bargaining" means a method of collective bargaining specified by the CAC before the coming into force of the order,
and references to a post-commencement declaration of recognition or method of collective bargaining shall be construed accordingly.
(7) An order under this paragraph shall be made by statutory instrument; and no such order shall be made unless a draft of it has been laid before Parliament and approved by a resolution of each House of Parliament.]

NOTES
This Schedule was inserted as noted at the beginning of this Schedule.
Para 171A: inserted by the Employment Relations Act 2004, s 20.

General interpretation

[1.703]
172. (1) References in this Schedule to the CAC are to the Central Arbitration Committee.
(2) For the purposes of this Schedule in its application to a part of Great Britain a working day is a day other than—
(a) a Saturday or a Sunday,
(b) Christmas day or Good Friday, or
(c) a day which is a bank holiday under the Banking and Financial Dealings Act 1971 in that part of Great Britain.]

NOTES
Inserted as noted at the beginning of this Schedule.

SCHEDULE A2
TRIBUNAL JURISDICTIONS TO WHICH SECTION 207A APPLIES

[1.704]

. . .

. . .

. . .

Section 145A of this Act (inducements relating to union membership or activities)

Section 145B of this Act (inducements relating to collective bargaining)

Section 146 of this Act (detriment in relation to union membership and activities)

Paragraph 156 of Schedule A1 to this Act (detriment in relation to union recognition rights)

. . .

Section 23 of the Employment Rights Act 1996 (c 18) (unauthorised deductions and payments)

Section 48 of that Act (detriment in employment)

Section 111 of that Act (unfair dismissal)

Section 163 of that Act (redundancy payments)

Section 24 of the National Minimum Wage Act 1998 (c 39) (detriment in relation to national minimum wage)

[Sections 120 and 127 of the Equality Act 2010 (discrimination etc in work cases)]

The Employment Tribunals Extension of Jurisdiction (England and Wales) Order 1994 (SI 1994/1623) (breach of employment contract and termination)

The Employment Tribunals Extension of Jurisdiction (Scotland) Order 1994 (SI 1994/1624) (corresponding provision for Scotland)

Regulation 30 of the Working Time Regulations 1998 (SI 1998/1833) (breach of regulations)

Regulation 32 of the Transnational Information and Consultation of Employees Regulations 1999 (SI 1999/3323) (detriment relating to European Works Councils)

. . .

. . .

Regulation 45 of the European Public Limited-Liability Company Regulations 2004 (SI 2004/2326) (detriment in employment)

Regulation 33 of the Information and Consultation of Employees Regulations 2004 (SI 2004/3426) (detriment in employment)

Paragraph 8 of the Schedule to the Occupational and Personal Pension Schemes (Consultation by Employers and Miscellaneous Amendment) Regulations 2006 (SI 2006/349) (detriment in employment)

. . .

Regulation 34 of the European Cooperative Society (Involvement of Employees) Regulations 2006 (SI 2006/2059) (detriment in relation to involvement in a European Cooperative Society)

Regulation 17 of the Cross-border Railway Services (Working Time) Regulations 2008 (SI 2008/1660) (breach of regulations).]

[Regulation 9 of the Employment Relations Act 1999 (Blacklists) Regulations 2010 (SI 2010/493) (detriment connected with prohibited list)].]

NOTES

Inserted by the Employment Act 2008, s 3(1), (3).

Entries relating to "Section 2 of the Equal Pay Act 1970", "Section 63 of the Sex Discrimination Act 1975", "Section 54 of the Race Relation Act 1976", "section 17A of the Disability Discrimination Act 1995", "Regulation 28 of the Employment Equality (Sexual Orientation) Regulations 2003", "Regulation 28 of the Employment Equality (Religion or Belief) Regulations 2003", and "Regulation 36 of the Employment Equality (Age) Regulations 2006" (all omitted) repealed by the Equality Act 2010, s 211, Sch 26, Pt 1, para 24(1), (2), Sch 27, Pt 1.

Entry relating to "Sections 120 and 127 of the Equality Act 2010" inserted by the Equality Act 2010, s 211, Sch 26, Pt 1, paras 24(1), (3) (as to transitional provisions and savings, see the note immediately above).

Entry relating to the Employment Relations Act 1999 (Blacklists) Regulations 2010 inserted by the Employment Relations Act 1999 (Blacklists) Regulations 2010, SI 2010/493, reg 17(1), (6).

Note that there is an error in the Employment Act 2008, s 3 concerning SI 1994/1623 and SI 1994/1624 above. Ie, the original Queen's printer's copy refers to them as the Employment *Tribunal* Extension of Jurisdiction (etc) Orders. This has been corrected above.

[SCHEDULE A3
CERTIFICATION OFFICER: INVESTIGATORY POWERS

Section 256C

Introduction

[1.705]

1. (1) The following are "relevant obligations" for the purposes of this Schedule—
- (a) any of the requirements of section 24(1) (duties regarding the register of members);
- (b) the requirement of section 45B (duty to secure positions not held by certain offenders);
- (c) any of the requirements of Chapter 4 of Part 1 (elections for certain positions);
- (d) the restriction in section 71 on the application of a trade union's funds in the furtherance of political objects;
- (e) any of the requirements of Chapter 6 of Part 1 about compliance with rules as to ballots on political resolutions;
- (f) any of the requirements of a trade union's rules made in pursuance of section 82 (rules as to political fund);
- (g) any of the requirements of sections 99 to 100E (ballots on amalgamations or transfers);
- (h) any requirement of a conditional penalty order made under Schedule A4.

(2) In relation to the relevant obligations listed in sub-paragraph (1)(d) to (g) as they apply to unincorporated employers' associations by virtue of section 132 or 133, this Schedule applies to an unincorporated employers' association as in relation to a trade union.

(3) In its application to an unincorporated employers' association, this Schedule has effect—
- (a) with any necessary modifications, and
- (b) with such modifications as may be prescribed.

Power of Certification Officer to require production of documents etc

2. (1) If the Certification Officer thinks there is good reason to do so, the Officer—
- (a) may give directions to a trade union, or a branch or section of a trade union, requiring it to produce such relevant documents as are specified in the directions;
- (b) may authorise a member of the Officer's staff or any other person ("an authorised person"), on producing (if so required) evidence of that authority, to require a trade union, or a branch or section of a trade union, to produce immediately to the authorised person such relevant documents as that person specifies.

(2) "Relevant documents", in relation to a trade union or a branch or section of a trade union, means documents that in the opinion of the Certification Officer or authorised person may be relevant to whether the trade union has failed to comply with a relevant obligation.
Such documents may in particular include, in the case of a requirement of section 24(1), the register of the names and addresses of the union's members.

(3) Directions under sub-paragraph (1)(a) must specify the time and place at which the documents are to be produced.

(4) Where the Certification Officer, or an authorised person, has power to require the production of documents by virtue of sub-paragraph (1), the Officer or authorised person has the like power to require production of those documents from any person who appears to the Officer or authorised person to be in possession of them.

(5) The power under this paragraph to require the production of documents includes the power—
- (a) if the documents are produced—
  - (i) to take copies of them or extracts from them;
  - (ii) to require the person by whom they are produced to provide an explanation of any of them;
  - (iii) to require any person who is or has been an official or agent of the trade union to provide an explanation of any of them;
- (b) if the documents are not produced, to require the person who was required to produce them to state, to the best of the person's knowledge and belief, where they are.

(6) For the purposes of sub-paragraph (5)(a)(iii), "agent" includes an assurer appointed by the trade union under section 24ZB.

(7) For supplementary provision, see paragraph 6.

Investigation by inspectors

3. (1) If the Certification Officer has reasonable grounds to suspect that a trade union has failed to comply with a relevant obligation, the Officer may appoint one or more members of the Officer's staff or other persons as an inspector or inspectors—
- (a) to investigate whether the union has failed to comply with such an obligation, and
- (b) to report to the Officer in such manner as the Officer may direct.

(2) Where any person appears to the inspector or inspectors to be in possession of information relating to a matter considered by the inspector or inspectors to be relevant to the investigation, the inspector or inspectors may require the person—
- (a) to produce to the inspector or inspectors any relevant documents relating to that matter,
- (b) to attend before the inspector or inspectors, and

(c) otherwise to give the inspector or inspectors all assistance in connection with the investigation which the person is reasonably able to give.

(3) "Relevant documents" means documents that in the opinion of the inspector or inspectors may be relevant to whether the trade union has failed to comply with a relevant obligation.

(4) Where a person who is not a member of the Certification Officer's staff is appointed as an inspector under this paragraph, there is incorporated in the appointment the duty of confidentiality as respects the register of the names and addresses of the trade union's members.

(5) The duty of confidentiality as respects that register is a duty which the inspector owes to the Certification Officer—

(a) not to disclose any name or address in the register of the names and addresses of the union's members except in permitted circumstances, and

(b) to take all reasonable steps to secure that there is no disclosure of any such name or address by another person except in permitted circumstances.

(6) The circumstances in which disclosure of a member's name or address is permitted are—

(a) where the member consents,

(b) where it is required or requested by the Certification Officer for the purposes of the discharge of any of the Officer's functions,

(c) where it is required for the purposes of the discharge of any of the functions of the inspector or any other inspector appointed by the Officer,

(d) where it is required for the purposes of the discharge of any of the functions of an assurer appointed under section 24ZB, or

(e) where it is required for the purposes of the investigation of crime or criminal proceedings.

(7) For supplementary provision, see paragraph 6.

Inspectors' reports etc

4. (1) An inspector or inspectors appointed under paragraph 3—

(a) may make interim reports to the Certification Officer,

(b) must make such reports if so directed by the Officer, and

(c) on the conclusion of the investigation, must make a final report to the Officer.

(2) A report under sub-paragraph (1) must be in writing.

(3) An inspector or inspectors—

(a) may at any time inform the Certification Officer of any matters coming to their knowledge as a result of the investigation, and

(b) must do so if the Officer so directs.

(4) The Certification Officer may direct an inspector or inspectors—

(a) to take no further steps in the investigation, or

(b) to take only such further steps as are specified in the direction.

(5) Where such a direction is made, the inspector or inspectors are not required under sub-paragraph (1)(c) to make a final report to the Certification Officer unless the Officer so directs.

Enforcement of paragraphs 2 and 3 by Certification Officer

5. (1) Where the Certification Officer is satisfied that a trade union or any other person has failed to comply with any requirement imposed under paragraph 2 or 3, the Officer may make an order requiring the trade union or person to comply with the requirement.

(2) Before making such an order, the Certification Officer must give the trade union or person an opportunity to be heard.

(3) In the case of a failure to comply with a requirement imposed under paragraph 2 or 3 to produce a document, the Certification Officer may make an order only if the Officer is satisfied that—

(a) the document is in the possession of the union or person, and

(b) it is reasonably practicable for the union or person to comply with the requirement.

(4) In the case of a failure to comply with any other requirement imposed under paragraph 2 or 3, the Certification Officer may make an order only if the Officer is satisfied that it is reasonably practicable for the union or person to comply with the requirement.

(5) The order must specify—

(a) the requirement with which the trade union or person has failed to comply, and

(b) the date by which the trade union or person must comply.

(6) An order made by the Certification Officer under this paragraph may be enforced by the Officer in the same way as an order of the High Court or the Court of Session.

Supplementary

6. (1) Nothing in this Schedule requires or authorises anyone to require—

(a) the disclosure by a person of information which the person would in an action in the High Court or the Court of Session be entitled to refuse to disclose on grounds of legal professional privilege, or

(b) the production by a person of a document which the person would in such an action be entitled to refuse to produce on such grounds.

(2) But a lawyer may be required under paragraph 2 or 3 to disclose the name and address of the lawyer's client if that information may be relevant to whether a trade union has failed to comply with a requirement of section 24(1).

(3) A person is not excused from providing an explanation or making a statement in compliance with a requirement imposed under paragraph 2(5) or 3(2) on the ground that to do so would tend to expose the person to proceedings for an offence.

(4) But an explanation so provided or a statement so made may be used in evidence against the person by whom it is provided or made on a prosecution for an offence only where, in giving evidence, the person makes a statement inconsistent with it.

(5) In this Schedule—

(a) references to documents include information recorded in any form;

(b) in relation to information recorded otherwise than in legible form, references to its production are to the production of a copy of the information in legible form.]

NOTES

Commencement: to be appointed.

Inserted by the Trade Union Act 2016, s 17(2), Sch 1, as from a day to be appointed.

Regulations: as of 15 May 2019, no Regulations had been made under this Schedule.

[SCHEDULE A4
CERTIFICATION OFFICER: POWER TO IMPOSE FINANCIAL PENALTIES

Section 256D

Introduction

[1.706]

1. (1) In this Schedule "enforcement order" means an order made by the Certification Officer under any of the following provisions of this Act—

(a) section 24B(6) or 25(5A) (order on failure by union to comply with duties regarding the register of members);

(b) section 31(2B) (order on failure by union to comply with member's request for access to accounting records);

(c) section 32ZC(6) (order on failure by union to provide details of industrial action etc, or political expenditure, in annual return);

(d) section 45C(5A) (order on failure by union to comply with duty to secure positions not held by certain offenders);

(e) section 55(5A) (order on failure by union to comply with requirements about elections for certain positions);

(f) section 72A(5) (order on failure by union to comply with restriction on applying union's funds in the furtherance of political objects);

(g) section 80(5A) (order on failure by union to comply with rules as to ballots on political resolutions);

(h) section 82(2A) (order on failure by union to comply with rules as to political fund);

(i) section 84A(5) (order on failure by union to provide required information to members about contributing to political fund);

(j) section 108B(3) (order on breach or threatened breach by union of rules on certain matters);

(k) paragraph 5(1) of Schedule A3 (order on failure by union or other person to comply with investigatory requirements).

(2) In this Schedule "the person in default" means the trade union against which, or other person against whom, an enforcement order is or could be made.

(3) A reference in this Schedule to taking steps includes a reference to abstaining from acts.

Power to impose financial penalties

2. (1) Where the Certification Officer—

(a) makes an enforcement order, or

(b) has power to make an enforcement order but does not do so,

the Officer may make a penalty order or a conditional penalty order against the person in default.

(2) A "penalty order" is an order requiring the person in default to pay a penalty of a specified amount to the Certification Officer by a specified date.

(3) A "conditional penalty order" is an order requiring the person in default to pay a penalty of a specified amount to the Certification Officer by a specified date unless the person takes specified steps by a specified date or within a specified period.

(4) Where the Certification Office makes both an enforcement order and a conditional penalty order, the steps specified in the conditional penalty order may, but need not, be the same as those that the enforcement order requires the person in default to take.

(5) In this paragraph "specified" means specified in the penalty order or conditional penalty order.

Enforcement of conditional penalty order

3. (1) This paragraph applies where the Certification Officer has made a conditional penalty order.

(2) If the Certification Officer is satisfied that the steps specified in the order have been taken by the date or within the period specified, the Officer must notify the person in default that the penalty is not payable.

(3) If the Certification Officer is not so satisfied, and the penalty has not been paid by the required date, the Officer must make a further order requiring payment of—

(a) the amount originally ordered, or

(b) where sub-paragraph (4) applies, a lesser amount specified in the further order.

(4) This sub-paragraph applies where it appears to the Certification Officer that—

(a) steps specified in the conditional penalty order have to some extent been taken, or have been taken (to any extent) but not by the date or within the period specified, and

(b) it would be just to reduce the amount of the penalty for that reason.

(5) An order under this paragraph may require payment immediately or by a specified date.

Representations

4. Before making a penalty order or a conditional penalty order, or an order under paragraph 3, the Certification Officer—

(a) must inform the person in default of the grounds on which the Officer proposes to make the order,

(b) must give that person an opportunity to make written representations, and

(c) may give that person an opportunity to make oral representations.

Appeals

5. A person in default may appeal to the Employment Appeal Tribunal against a decision of the Certification Officer under this Schedule on the ground that—

(a) it was based on an error of fact,

(b) it was wrong in law, or

(c) it was unreasonable,

or on such other grounds as may be prescribed.

Amount of penalty

6. (1) The amount specified in a penalty order or a conditional penalty order—

(a) may not be less than the minimum amount set by regulations, and

(b) may not be more than the maximum amount set by regulations.

(2) Different amounts may be set by regulations—

(a) in relation to different enforcement orders,

(b) by reference to whether the person in default is an individual or an organisation, and

(c) in the case of an organisation, by reference to the number of members that it has.

(3) But—

(a) no minimum amount set by regulations may be less than £200, and

(b) no maximum amount set by regulations may be more than £20,000.

(4) Regulations may amend sub-paragraph (3)(a) or (b) by substituting a different amount.

Early or late payment, and enforcement

7. (1) In relation to orders under this Schedule requiring payment of penalties, regulations may make provision for—

(a) early payment discounts;

(b) the payment of interest or other financial penalties for late payment;

(c) enforcement.

(2) Provision made by virtue of sub-paragraph (1)(b) must secure that the interest or other financial penalties for late payment do not in total exceed the amount of the penalty itself.

(3) Provision made by virtue of sub-paragraph (1)(c) may include—

(a) provision for the Certification Officer to recover the penalty, and any interest or other financial penalty for late payment, as a debt;

(b) provision for the penalty, and any interest or other financial penalty for late payment, to be recoverable, on the order of a court, as if payable under a court order.

Regulations

8. (1) Regulations may make provision that is incidental or supplementary to that made by this Schedule.

(2) Regulations under this Schedule may include transitional or consequential provision.

(3) Regulations under this Schedule shall be made by the Secretary of State by statutory instrument.

(4) No regulations under paragraph 6 or 7 or this paragraph shall be made unless a draft of them has been laid before Parliament and approved by a resolution of each House of Parliament.

Payment of penalties etc into Consolidated Fund

9. The Certification Officer shall pay into the Consolidated Fund amounts received—

(a) under penalty orders and conditional penalty orders (including orders under paragraph 3), and

(b) by way of interest and other financial penalties for late payment in relation to such orders.]

NOTES

Commencement: to be appointed.

Inserted by the Trade Union Act 2016, s 19(2), Sch 3, as from a day to be appointed (note that this Schedule does not apply in relation to any acts or omissions of a trade union or other person occurring before s 19 of the 2016 Act comes into force (see **[1.2017]**)).

Regulations: as of 15 May 2019, no Regulations had been made under this Schedule.

SCHEDULES 1 AND 2

(Schs 1, 2 contain repeals and consequential amendments; in so far as relevant, these have been incorporated at the appropriate place.)

SCHEDULE 3
TRANSITIONAL PROVISIONS AND SAVINGS

Section 300(3)

Continuity of the law

[1.707]

1. (1) The repeal and re-enactment of provisions in this Act does not affect the continuity of the law.

(2) Anything done (including subordinate legislation made), or having effect as done, under a provision reproduced in this Act has effect as if done under the corresponding provision of this Act.

(3) References (express or implied) in this Act or any other enactment, instrument or document to a provision of this Act shall, so far as the context permits, be construed as including, in relation to times, circumstances and purposes before the commencement of this Act, a reference to corresponding earlier provisions.

(4) A reference (express or implied) in any enactment, instrument or other document to a provision reproduced in this Act shall be construed, so far as is required for continuing its effect, and subject to any express amendment made by this Act, as being, or as the case may required including, a reference to the corresponding provision of this Act.

General saving for old transitional provisions and savings

2. (1) The repeal by this Act of a transitional provision or saving relating to the coming into force of a provision reproduced in this Act does not affect the operation of the transitional provision or saving, in so far as it is not specifically reproduced in this Act but remains capable of having effect in relation to the corresponding provision of this Act.

(2) The repeal by this Act of an enactment previously repealed subject to savings does not affect the continued operation of those savings.

(3) The repeal by this Act of a saving on the previous repeal of an enactment does not affect the operation of the saving in so far as it is not specifically reproduced in this Act but remains capable of having effect.

Effect of repeal of 1946 Act

3. The repeal by this Act of the Trade Disputes and Trade Unions Act 1946 shall not be construed as reviving in any respect the effect of the Trade Disputes and Trade Unions Act 1927.

Pre-1974 references to registered trade unions or employers' associations

4. (1) Any reference in an enactment passed, or instrument made under an enactment, before 16th September 1974—

(a) to a trade union or employers' association registered under—

(i) the Trade Union Acts 1871 to 1964, or

(ii) the Industrial Relations Act 1971, or

(b) to an organisation of workers or an organisation of employers within the meaning of the Industrial Relations Act 1971,

shall be construed as a reference to a trade union or employers' association within the meaning of this Act.

(2) Subsection (1) does not apply to any enactment relating to income tax or corporation tax.

Enforceability of collective agreements

5. Section 179 of this Act (enforceability of collective agreements) does not apply to a collective agreement made on or after 1st December 1971 and before 16th September 1974.

Trade unions and employers' associations ceasing to be incorporated by virtue of 1974 Act

6. (1) The repeal by this Act of section 19 of the Trade Union and Labour Relations Act 1974 (transitional provisions for trade unions and employers' associations ceasing to be incorporated) does not affect—

(a) the title to property which by virtue of that section vested on 16th September 1974 in "the appropriate trustees" as defined by that section, or

(b) any liability, obligation or right affecting such property which by virtue of that section became a liability, obligation or right of those trustees.

(2) A certificate given by the persons who on that date were the president and general secretary of a trade union or employers' association, or occupied positions equivalent to that of president and general secretary, that the persons named in the certificate are the appropriate trustees of the union or association for the purposes of section 19(2) of the Trade Union and Labour Relations Act 1974 is conclusive evidence that those persons were the appropriate trustees for those purposes.

(3) A document which purports to be such a certificate shall be taken to be such a certificate unless the contrary is proved.

References to former Industrial Arbitration Board

7. Any reference to the former Industrial Arbitration Board in relation to which section 10(2) of the Employment Protection Act 1975 applied immediately before the commencement of this Act shall continue to be construed as a reference to the Central Arbitration Committee.

Effect of political resolution passed before 1984 amendments

8. A resolution under section 3 of the Trade Union Act 1913, or rule made for the purposes of that section, in relation to which section 17(2) of the Trade Union Act 1984 applied immediately before the commencement of this Act shall continue to have effect as if for any reference to the political objects to which section 3 of the 1913 Act formerly applied there were substituted a reference to the objects to which that section applied as amended by the 1984 Act.

Persons elected to trade union office before 1988 amendments

9, 10. (*Spent.*)

Qualification to act as auditor of trade union or employers' association

11. (1) Nothing in section 34 (eligibility for appointment as auditor) affects the validity of any appointment as auditor of a trade union or employers' association made before 1st October 1991 (when section 389 of the Companies Act 1985 was repealed and replaced by the provisions of Part II of the Companies Act 1989).

(2) A person who is not qualified as mentioned in section 34(1) may act as auditor of a trade union in respect of an accounting period if—

(a) the union was registered under the Trade Union Acts 1871 to 1964 on 30th September 1971,

(b) he acted as its auditor in respect of the last period in relation to which it was required to make an annual return under section 16 of the Trade Union Act 1871,

(c) he has acted as its auditor in respect of every accounting period since that period, and

(d) he retains an authorisation formerly granted by the Board of Trade or the Secretary of State under section 16(1)(b) of the Companies Act 1948 (adequate knowledge and experience, or pre-1947 practice).

12. . . .

Use of existing forms, &c

13. Any document made, served or issued on or after the commencement of this Act which contains a reference to an enactment repealed by this Act shall be construed, except so far as a contrary intention appears, as referring or, as the context may require, including a reference to the corresponding provision of this Act.

Saving for power to vary or revoke

14. The power of the Secretary of State by further order to vary or revoke the Funds for Trade Union Ballots Order 1982 extends to so much of section 115(2)(a) as reproduces the effect of Article 2 of that order.

NOTES

Para 12: applied to Northern Ireland only and was repealed by the Trade Union and Labour Relations (Northern Ireland) Order 1995, SI 1995/1980.

Note: it is assumed that the word "required" in the second place it occurs in para 1 should read "require".

Companies Act 1948: repealed (see now the Companies Act 1985 and the Companies Act 2006). Note that most of the 1985 Act was repealed by the 2006 Act.

Companies Act 1985: see the note above.

Companies Act 1989: Part II of the 1989 Act was repealed by the Companies Act 2006.

Employment Act 1988: ss 12(1), 13–15 of that Act are repealed by s 300(1) of, and Sch 1 to, this Act.

Employment Protection Act 1975: s 10(2) of that Act is repealed by s 300(1) of, and Sch 1 to, this Act.

Industrial Relations Act 1971: repealed by the Trade Union and Labour Relations Act 1974, ss 1, 25(3), Sch 5.

Trade Disputes and Trade Unions Act 1927: repealed by the Trade Disputes and Trade Unions Act 1946, s 1.

Trade Disputes and Trade Unions Act 1946: repealed by s 300(1) of, and Sch 1 to, this Act.

Trade Union Act 1913: s 3 of that Act is repealed by s 300(1) of, and Sch 1 to, this Act.

Trade Union Acts 1871 to 1964: repealed, see the note to s 3 at **[1.270]**.

Trade Union Act 1984: s 3 was repealed by the Employment Act 1988, ss 14(2), 33(2), Sch 4. The whole Act is repealed by s 300(1) of, and Sch 1 to, this Act.

Trade Union and Labour Relations Act 1974: repealed by s 300(1) of, and Sch 1 to, this Act.

TRADE UNION REFORM AND EMPLOYMENT RIGHTS ACT 1993 (NOTE)

(1993 c 19)

An Act to make further reforms of the law relating to trade unions and industrial relations; to make amendments of the law relating to employment rights and to abolish the right to statutory minimum remuneration; to amend the law relating to the constitution and jurisdiction of industrial tribunals and the Employment Appeal Tribunal; to amend section 56A of the Sex Discrimination Act 1975; to provide for the Secretary of State to have functions of securing the provision of careers services; to make further provision about employment and training functions of Scottish Enterprise and of Highlands and Islands Enterprise; and for connected purposes

1 July 1993

[1.708]

NOTES

Almost all of this major Act either amends other legislation (principally the Trade Union and Labour Relations (Consolidation) Act 1992) or has since been repealed and re-enacted by the Employment Tribunals Act 1996 and the Employment Rights Act 1996. It is therefore not necessary to reproduce provisions of the Act here. Instead this note summarises the position under the two major categories indicated above, in the following tables.

1 PROVISIONS AMENDING THE 1992 ACT

Section/Schedule	*Amendments*
1	Amends ss 49, 52
2	Inserts s 51A, amends s 52
3	Introduces Sch 1 (which amends ss 74, 75 and 78 and inserts s 77A)
4	Substitutes s 100 with new ss 100–100E
5	Amends s 99
6	Inserts s 24A
7	Repeals ss 115, 116
8	Amends s 32
9	Inserts s 32A
10	Inserts ss 37A–37E
11	Amends s 45 and inserts s 45A
12	Inserts ss 45B, 45C
13	Amends s 148
14	Substitutes ss 174–177
15	Substitutes s 68 with new ss 68 and 68A
16	Amends s 65
17	Amends s 230
18	Amends s 226 and inserts s 226A
19	Inserts s 231A
20	Amends s 229 and inserts ss 226B, 226C, 231B
21	Inserts s 234A
22	Inserts ss 235A–235C
34	Amends ss 188, 190, 193, substitutes s 195, rep
43	Amends ss 209, 249, substitutes s 213
44	Inserts s 251A
Sch 1	Amends ss 74, 75, 78, inserts s 77A
Sch 6 (part)	Amends s 288

2 PROVISIONS REPEALED BY THE EMPL... NALS ACT 1996

Section/Schedule	*...on*	*Provisions as re-enacted*
36	Amended the Em... (Consolidation) Act 1978, s 128	4(1)–(7), 41(2)
37	Substituted s ...he 1978 Act	28(2)–(5)
38	Amende... 1978 Act	3(1), (3), (5), 8(2), (4)
40	Ame... 8A to the 1978 Act	7(5), 11(1)–(6)
41	... 78 Act	31
42		33, 37(3)

3 PROVISIONS REPEALED BY THE EMPLOYMENT RIGHTS ACT 1996

Section/Schedule	*Effect of provision*	*Provisions as re-enacted*
23	Substituted the Employment Protection (Consolidation) Act 1978, Pt III with ss 33–38A and ss 39–44 (enacted by Sch 2)	71–78, 236(3), 79–83, 85, 236(3)
24	Substituted s 60, amended ss 53, 59, 64 of the 1978 Act	99(1)–(3), 105(1), (2), 108(3), 109(2), 92(4)
25	Introduced Sch 3 (inserted ss 45–47 of the 1978 Act)	66–70, 106(3)
26	Introduced Sch 4 (substituted ss 1–6 of the 1978 Act)	1–7, 198
28	Introduced Sch 5 (inserted ss 22A–C, 57A, 75A, 77–79 and amended ss 57(3), 59(2), 64(4), 71–73 of the 1978 Act)	44, 48, 49, 98(6), 100, 105(3), 108(3), 109(2), 117(3), (4), 118, 119(1), 120, 122(3), 125, 128–132, 236(3).
29	Inserted s 60A, amended ss 59(2), 64(4) of the 1978 Act	104, 105(7), 108(3), 109(2)
30	Amended ss 71, 74, 75 of the 1978 Act	117(2), 123(1), 124(3),(4)
31	Amended s 138, inserted s 138A of the 1978 Act	192(1)–(8), 236(3)
39(1)	Amended s 140 of the 1978 Act	203(2)–(4)
Sch 2	Substituted ss 39–44 of the 1978 Act	79–83, 85, 236(3)
Sch 3	Inserted ss 45–47 of the 1978 Act	66–70, 106(3)
Sch 4	Substituted ss 1–6 of the 1978 Act	1–7, 198
Sch 5	Inserted ss 22A–C, 57A, 75A, 77–79 and amended ss 57(3), 59(2), 64(4), 71–73 of the 1978 Act	44, 48, 49, 98(6), 100, 105(3), 108(3), 109(2), 117(3), (4), 118, 119(1), 120, 122(3), 125, 128–132, 236(3)
Sch 6 (part)	Amended the Wages Act 1986, s 6	203(2)–(4), 231

4 OTHER PROVISIONS NOT REPRODUCED

Section/Schedule	*Effect of provision*	*Status*
27	Inserted the Employment Protection (Consolidation) Act 1978, s146(4A)–(4C)	Repealed by SI 1995/31
32	Inserted the Sex Discrimination Act 1986, s 6(4A)–(4D)	Repealed by the Equality Act 2010
33	Amended SI 1981/1794	Repealed by SI 2006/246
35	Repealed the Wages Act 1986, Pt II	Repealed by the Statute Law (Repeals) Act 2004
39(2)	Introduces Sch 6	See Sch 6 below
45–47	Amend the Employment and Training Act 1973, Enterprise and the New Towns (Scotland) Act 1990	Outside the scope of this work
48	Interpretation	Unnecessary
49	Introduces Schs … 8	See Schs 7 and 8 below
50	Introduces Sch 9	S… Sch 9 below
51	Introduces Sch 10	See …h 10 below
52	Commencement	Unnecessary
53	Final… provision	Unnecessary
54	Applica… to Northern Ireland	Outside the scope of this work
55	Short titl…	Unnecessary
Sch 6 (part)	Amended t… Discrimination Act 1975, s 77 and the Race Relations Ac…	Repealed by the Equality Act 2010
Sch 7	Miscellaneous …72 …ts	Unnecessary (in so far as relevant to this work such amendments have been incorporated)
Schs 8	Consequential amen…	Unnecessary (in so far as relevant to this work such amendments have been incorporated)
Sch 9	Transitional provisions an…	Spent
Sch 10	Repeals	Unnecessary (in so far as relevant to this work such repeals have been incorporated)

PENSION SCHEMES ACT 1993

(1993 c 48)

ARRANGEMENT OF SECTIONS

PART VII
INSOLVENCY OF EMPLOYERS

CHAPTER II
PAYMENT BY SECRETARY OF STATE OF UNPAID SCHEME CONTRIBUTIONS

PART X
INVESTIGATIONS: THE PENSIONS OMBUDSMAN

PART XI
GENERAL AND MISCELLANEOUS PROVISIONS

Avoidance of certain transactions and provisions

PART XII
SUPPLEMENTARY PROVISIONS

Supplemental provisions

An Act to consolidate certain enactments relating to pension schemes with amendments to give effect to recommendations of the Law Commission and the Scottish Law Commission

[5 November 1993]

NOTES

Only certain parts of this Act most relevant to employment law are reproduced. Provisions omitted are not annotated.

Bank insolvency or administration: in so far as any provision of this Act applies to liquidation or administration, it applies with specified modifications in the case of a bank insolvency or administration; see the Banking Act 2009 (Parts 2 and 3 Consequential Amendments) Order 2009, SI 2009/317.

See *Harvey* BI(9), G(1)(E).

PART VII
INSOLVENCY OF EMPLOYERS

CHAPTER II PAYMENT BY SECRETARY OF STATE OF UNPAID SCHEME CONTRIBUTIONS

[1.709]

123 Interpretation of Chapter II

(1) For the purposes of this Chapter, an employer shall be taken to be insolvent if, but only if, in England and Wales—

(a) he has been [made] bankrupt or has made a composition or arrangement with his creditors;

(b) he has died and his estate falls to be administered in accordance with an order under section 421 of the Insolvency Act 1986; . . .

(c) where the employer is a company—

(i) a winding-up order . . . is made or a resolution for voluntary winding up is passed with respect to it [or the company enters administration],

(ii) a receiver or manager of its undertaking is duly appointed,

(iii) possession is taken, by or on behalf of the holders of any debentures secured by a floating charge, of any property of the company comprised in or subject to the charge, or

(iv) a voluntary arrangement proposed for the purpose of Part I of the Insolvency Act 1986 is approved under that Part[; or

(d) where subsection (2A) is satisfied].

(2) For the purposes of this Chapter, an employer shall be taken to be insolvent if, but only if, in Scotland—

(a) sequestration of his estate is awarded or he executes a trust deed for his creditors or enters into a composition contract;

(b) he has died and a judicial factor appointed under section 11A of the Judicial Factors (Scotland) Act 1889 is required by this section to divide his insolvent estate among his creditors; or

(c) where the employer is a company—

(i) a winding-up order . . . is made or a resolution for voluntary winding up is passed with respect to it [or the company enters administration],

(ii) a receiver of its undertaking is duly appointed, or

(iii) a voluntary arrangement proposed for the purpose of Part I of the Insolvency Act 1986 is approved under that Part.

[(2ZA) This subsection is satisfied in the case of an employer if—

(a) the employer is a legal person,

(b) a request has been made for the first opening of collective proceedings—

(i) based on the insolvency of the employer, as provided for under the law of any part of the United Kingdom, and

(ii) involving the partial or total divestment of the employer's assets and the appointment of a liquidator or a person performing a similar task, and

(c) any of the following has decided to open the proceedings—

(i) a court,

(ii) a meeting of creditors, or

(iii) the creditors by a decision procedure.]

[(2A) This subsection is satisfied if—

(a) a request has been made for the first opening of collective proceedings—

(i) based on the insolvency of the employer, as provided for under the laws, regulations and administrative provisions of a member State; and

(ii) involving the partial or total divestment of the employer's assets and the appointment of a liquidator or a person performing a similar task; and

(b) the competent authority has—

(i) decided to open the proceedings; or

(ii) established that the employer's undertaking or business has been definitively closed down and the available assets of the employer are insufficient to warrant the opening of the proceedings.

(2B) For the purposes of *subsection (2A)*—

(a) "liquidator or person performing a similar task" includes the official receiver or an administrator, trustee in bankruptcy, judicial factor, supervisor of a voluntary arrangement, or person performing a similar task,

(b) "competent authority" includes—

(i) a court,

(ii) a meeting of creditors,

(iii) a creditors' committee,

(iv) the creditors by a decision procedure, and

(v) an authority of a member State empowered to open insolvency proceedings, to confirm the opening of such proceedings or to take decisions in the course of such proceedings.

(2C) An application under section 124 may only be made in respect of a worker who worked or habitually worked in Great Britain in that employment to which the application relates.]

(3) In this Chapter—

["employer", "employment", "worker" and "worker's contract" and other expressions which are defined in the Employment Rights Act 1996 have the same meaning as in that Act (see further subsections (3A) and (3B));]

"holiday pay" means—

(a) pay in respect of holiday actually taken; or

(b) any accrued holiday pay which under [the worker's contract] would in the ordinary course have become payable to him in respect of the period of a holiday if his employment with the employer had continued until he became entitled to a holiday;

. . .

[(3A) Section 89 of the Pensions Act 2008 (agency workers) applies for the purposes of this Chapter as it applies for the purposes of Part 1 of that Act.

(3B) References in this Chapter to a worker include references to an individual to whom Part 1 of the Pensions Act 2008 applies as if the individual were a worker because of regulations made under section 98 of that Act; and related expressions are to be read accordingly.]

(4) . . .

(5) Any reference in this Chapter to the resources of a scheme is a reference to the funds out of which the benefits provided by the scheme are from time to time payable.

NOTES

Sub-s (1): word in square brackets in para (a) substituted by the Enterprise and Regulatory Reform Act 2013 (Consequential Amendments) (Bankruptcy) and the Small Business, Enterprise and Employment Act 2015 (Consequential Amendments) Regulations 2016, SI 2016/481, reg 2(1), Sch 1, Pt 2, para 18, as from 6 April 2016. Word omitted from para (b) repealed, and para (d) (and the preceding word) inserted, by the Employment Rights Act 1996 and Pension Schemes Act 1993 (Amendment) Regulations 2017, SI 2017/1205, reg 3(1), (2)(a), as from 26 December 2017. Words omitted from sub-para (c)(i) repealed, and words in square brackets in that sub-paragraph added, by the Enterprise Act 2002 (Insolvency) Order 2003, SI 2003/2096, art 4, Schedule, para 22(a). Para (d) substituted by the Insolvency (Amendment) (EU Exit) Regulations 2019, SI 2019/146, reg 2, Schedule, Pt 11, para 254(1), (2)(a), as from exit day (as defined in the European Union (Withdrawal) Act 2018, s 20) and subject to savings in regs 4, 5 thereof, as follows:

"(d) subsection (2A) or (2ZA) is satisfied.".

Sub-s (2): words omitted from sub-para (c)(i) repealed, and words in square brackets in that sub-paragraph added, by SI 2003/2096, art 4, Schedule, para 22(b).

Sub-s (2ZA): inserted by SI 2019/146, reg 2, Schedule, Pt 11, para 254(1), (2)(b), as from exit day (as defined in the European Union (Withdrawal) Act 2018, s 20) and subject to savings in regs 4, 5 thereof.

Sub-ss (2A)–(2C): inserted by SI 2017/1205, reg 3(1), (2)(b), as from 26 December 2017. For the words in italics in sub-s (2B) there are substituted the words "this section", by SI 2019/146, reg 2, Schedule, Pt 11, para 254(1), (2)(c), as from exit day (as defined in the European Union (Withdrawal) Act 2018, s 20) and subject to savings in regs 4, 5 thereof.

Sub-s (3): definitions ""employer", "employment", "worker" and "worker's contract"" substituted (for the original definitions ""contract of employment", "employee", "employer" and "employment"), and words in square brackets in the definition "holiday pay" substituted, by the Pensions Act 2014, s 42(1), (2)(a), (b), as from 11 September 2014.

Sub-ss (3A), (3B): inserted by the Pensions Act 2014, s 42(1), (2)(c), as from 11 September 2014.

Definition "occupational pension scheme" (omitted) repealed by the Pensions Act 2004, ss 319(1), 320, Sch 12, paras 9, 19(a), Sch 13, Pt 1.

Sub-s (4): repealed by the Pensions Act 2004, ss 319(1), 320, Sch 12, paras 9, 19(b), Sch 13, Pt 1.

[1.710]

124 Duty of Secretary of State to pay unpaid contributions to schemes

(1) If, on an application made to him in writing by the persons competent to act in respect of an occupational pension scheme or a personal pension scheme, the Secretary of State is satisfied—

(a) that an employer has become insolvent; and

(b) that at the time he did so there remained unpaid relevant contributions falling to be paid by him to the scheme,

then, subject to the provisions of this section and section 125, the Secretary of State shall pay into the resources of the scheme the sum which in his opinion is payable in respect of the unpaid relevant contributions.

(2) In this section and section 125 "relevant contributions" means contributions falling to be paid by an employer to an occupational pension scheme or a personal pension scheme, either on his own account or on behalf of [a worker]; and for the purposes of this section a contribution shall not be treated as falling to be paid on behalf of [a worker] unless a sum equal to that amount has been deducted from the pay of [the worker] by way of a contribution from him.

(3) [Subject to subsection (3A),] the sum payable under this section in respect of unpaid contributions of an employer on his own account to an occupational pension scheme or a personal pension scheme shall be the least of the following amounts—

(a) the balance of relevant contributions remaining unpaid on the date when he became insolvent and payable by the employer on his own account to the scheme in respect of the 12 months immediately preceding that date;

(b) the amount certified by an actuary to be necessary for the purpose of meeting the liability of the scheme on dissolution to pay the benefits provided by the scheme to or in respect of the [workers] of the employer;

(c) an amount equal to 10 per cent. of the total amount of remuneration paid or payable to those [workers] in respect of the 12 months immediately preceding the date on which the employer became insolvent.

[*(3A) Where the scheme in question is a money purchase scheme, the sum payable under this section by virtue of subsection (3) shall be the lesser of the amounts mentioned in paragraphs (a) and (c) of that subsection.*]

(4) For the purposes of subsection (3)(c), "remuneration" includes holiday pay, statutory sick pay, statutory maternity pay under Part V of the Social Security Act 1986 or Part XII of the Social Security Contributions and Benefits Act 1992 [and any payment such as is referred to in section 184(2) of the Employment Rights Act 1996].

Any sum payable under this section in respect of unpaid contributions on behalf of [a worker] shall not exceed the amount deducted from the pay of [the worker] in respect of [the worker's] contributions to the scheme during the 12 months immediately preceding the date on which the employer became insolvent.

[(6) In this section "on his own account", in relation to an employer, means on his own account but to fund benefits for, or in respect of, one or more [workers].]

NOTES

Sub-ss (2), (5): words in square brackets substituted by the Pensions Act 2014, s 42(1), (3)(a)–(c), as from 11 September 2014.

Sub-s (3): words in first pair of square brackets inserted by the Pensions Act 1995, s 90. Other words in square brackets substituted by the Pensions Act 2014, s 42(1), (3)(d), as from 11 September 2014.

Sub-s (3A): inserted by the Pensions Act 1995, s 90, and substituted by the Pension Schemes Act 2015, s 46, Sch 2, paras 1, 4, as from a day to be appointed, as follows—

"(3A) The sum payable under this section by virtue of subsection (3) shall be the lesser of the amounts mentioned in paragraphs (a) and (c) of that subsection in any case where the scheme is—

(a) a defined contributions scheme,

(b) a shared risk scheme under which all the benefits that may be provided are money purchase benefits, or

(c) a shared risk scheme under which all the benefits that may be provided are money purchase benefits or collective benefits.".

Sub-s (4): words in square brackets substituted by the Employment Rights Act 1996, s 240, Sch 1, para 61(1), (3).
Sub-s (6): added by the Pensions Act 2004, s 319(1), Sch 12, paras 9, 20; words in square brackets substituted by the Pensions Act 2014, s 42(1), (3)(d), as from 11 September 2014.
Social Security Act 1986, Pt V: repealed by the Social Security (Consequential Provisions) Act 1992. The relevant provisions of that Part relating to maternity pay were re-enacted in the Social Security Contributions and Benefits Act 1992, Pt XII.

[1.711]
125 Certification of amounts payable under s 124 by insolvency officers
(1) This section applies where one of the officers mentioned in subsection (2) ("the relevant officer") has been or is required to be appointed in connection with an employer's insolvency.
(2) The officers referred to in subsection (1) are—
(a) a trustee in bankruptcy;
(b) a liquidator;
(c) an administrator;
(d) a receiver or manager; or
(e) a trustee under a composition or arrangement between the employer and his creditors or under a trust deed for his creditors executed by the employer;
and in this subsection "trustee", in relation to a composition or arrangement, includes the supervisor of a voluntary arrangement proposed for the purposes of and approved under Part I or VIII of the Insolvency Act 1986.
(3) Subject to subsection (5), where this section applies the Secretary of State shall not make any payment under section 124 in respect of unpaid relevant contributions until he has received a statement from the relevant officer of the amount of relevant contributions which appear to have been unpaid on the date on which the employer became insolvent and to remain unpaid; and the relevant officer shall on request by the Secretary of State provide him as soon as reasonably practicable with such a statement.
(4) Subject to subsection (5), an amount shall be taken to be payable, paid or deducted as mentioned in subsection (3)(a) or (c) or (5) of section 124 only if it is so certified by the relevant officer.
(5) If the Secretary of State is satisfied—
(a) that he does not require a statement under subsection (3) in order to determine the amount of relevant contributions that was unpaid on the date on which the employer became insolvent and remains unpaid, or
(b) that he does not require a certificate under subsection (4) in order to determine the amounts payable, paid or deducted as mentioned in subsection (3)(a) or (c) or (5) of section 124,
he may make a payment under that section in respect of the contributions in question without having received such a statement or, as the case may be, such a certificate.

[1.712]
126 Complaint to [employment tribunal]
(1) Any persons who are competent to act in respect of an occupational pension scheme or a personal pension scheme and who have applied for a payment to be made under section 124 into the resources of the scheme may present a complaint to an [employment tribunal] that—
(a) the Secretary of State has failed to make any such payment; or
(b) any such payment made by him is less than the amount which should have been paid.
(2) Such a complaint must be presented within the period of three months beginning with the date on which the decision of the Secretary of State on that application was communicated to the persons presenting it or, if that is not reasonably practicable, within such further period as is reasonable.
(3) Where an [employment tribunal] finds that the Secretary of State ought to make a payment under section 124, it shall make a declaration to that effect and shall also declare the amount of any such payment which it finds that the Secretary of State ought to make.

NOTES
Section heading, sub-ss (1), (3): words in square brackets substituted by the Employment Rights (Dispute Resolution) Act 1998, s 1(2)(a).

[1.713]
127 Transfer to Secretary of State of rights and remedies
(1) Where in pursuance of section 124 the Secretary of State makes any payment into the resources of an occupational pension scheme or a personal pension scheme in respect of any contributions to the scheme, any rights and remedies in respect of those contributions belonging to the persons competent to act in respect of the scheme shall, on the making of the payment, become rights and remedies of the Secretary of State.
(2) Where the Secretary of State makes any such payment as is mentioned in subsection (1) and the sum (or any part of the sum) falling to be paid by the employer on account of the contributions in respect of which the payment is made constitutes—
(a) a preferential debt within the meaning of the Insolvency Act 1986 for the purposes of any provision of that Act (including any such provision as applied by an order made under that Act) or any provision of [the Companies Acts (as defined in section 2(1) of the Companies Act 2006)]; or
(b) a preferred debt within the meaning of the Bankruptcy (Scotland) Act [2016] for the purposes of any provision of that Act (including any such provision as applied by section 11A of the Judicial Factors (Scotland) Act 1889,

then, without prejudice to the generality of subsection (1), there shall be included among the rights and remedies which become rights and remedies of the Secretary of State in accordance with that subsection any right arising under any such provision by reason of the status of that sum (or that part of it) as a preferential or preferred debt.

(3) In computing for the purposes of any provision referred to in subsection (2)(a) or (b) the aggregate amount payable in priority to other creditors of the employer in respect of—

(a) any claim of the Secretary of State to be so paid by virtue of subsection (2); and

(b) any claim by the persons competent to act in respect of the scheme,

any claim falling within paragraph (a) shall be treated as if it were a claim of those persons; but the Secretary of State shall be entitled, as against those persons, to be so paid in respect of any such claim of his (up to the full amount of the claim) before any payment is made to them in respect of any claim falling within paragraph (b).

NOTES

Sub-s (2): words in square brackets in para (a) substituted by the Companies Act 2006 (Consequential Amendments, Transitional Provisions and Savings) Order 2009, SI 2009/1941, art 2(1), Sch 1, para 144(1), (2). Year "2016" in square brackets in para (b) substituted by the Bankruptcy (Scotland) Act 2016 (Consequential Provisions and Modifications) Order 2016, SI 2016/1034, art 7(1), Sch 1, Pt 1, para 11(1), (3), as from 30 November 2016.

PART X
INVESTIGATIONS: THE PENSIONS OMBUDSMAN

[1.714]

145 The Pensions Ombudsman

(1) For the purpose of conducting investigations in accordance with this Part or any corresponding legislation having effect in Northern Ireland there shall be a commissioner to be known as the Pensions Ombudsman.

[(1A) Provisions conferring power on the Pensions Ombudsman to conduct investigations as mentioned in subsection (1) are to be read as conferring power that—

(a) in a case of a prescribed description, or

(b) in a case involving a scheme that is prescribed or is of a prescribed description,

may be exercised whatever the extent of any connections with places outside the United Kingdom.

(1B) In subsection (1A) "scheme" means occupational pension scheme or personal pension scheme.

(1C) Subsection (1A) shall not be taken to prejudice any power of the Pensions Ombudsman apart from that subsection to conduct investigations in a case having connections with places outside the United Kingdom.]

(2) The Pensions Ombudsman shall be appointed by the Secretary of State and shall hold [and vacate] office upon such terms and conditions as the Secretary of State may think fit.

[(3) The Pensions Ombudsman may resign or be removed from office in accordance with those terms and conditions.]

[(4A) The Pensions Ombudsman may (with the approval of the Secretary of State as to numbers) appoint such persons to be employees of his as he thinks fit, on such terms and conditions as to remuneration and other matters as the Pensions Ombudsman may with the approval of the Secretary of State determine.

(4B) The Secretary of State may, on such terms as to payment by the Pensions Ombudsman as the Secretary of State thinks fit, make available to the Pensions Ombudsman such additional staff and such other facilities as he thinks fit.

(4C) Any function of the Pensions Ombudsman, other than the determination of complaints made and disputes referred under this Part, may be performed by any—

(a) employee appointed by the Pensions Ombudsman under subsection (4A), or

(b) member of staff made available to him by the Secretary of State under subsection (4B),

who is authorised for that purpose by the Pensions Ombudsman.]

(5) The Secretary of State may—

(a) pay to or in respect of the Pensions Ombudsman such amounts by way of remuneration, compensation for loss of office, pension, allowances and gratuities, or by way of provision for any such benefits, as the Secretary of State may determine . . . ; and

(b) reimburse him in respect of any expenses incurred by him in the performance of his functions.

(6) The Pensions Ombudsman shall prepare a report on the discharge of his functions for each financial year, and shall submit it to the Secretary of State as soon as practicable afterwards.

(7) The Secretary of State shall arrange for the publication of each report submitted to him under subsection (6).

[(8) As soon as is reasonably practicable, the Pensions Ombudsman shall send to the Comptroller and Auditor General a statement of the Pensions Ombudsman's accounts in respect of a financial year.

(9) The Comptroller and Auditor General shall—

(a) examine, certify and report on a statement received under this section; and

(b) send a copy of the statement and the report to the Secretary of State who shall lay them before Parliament.

(10) In this section "financial year" means a period of 12 months ending with 31st March.]

NOTES

Sub-ss (1A)–(1C): inserted by the Pensions Act 2004, s 319(1), Sch 12, paras 9, 23, as from a day to be appointed.

Sub-s (2): words in square brackets inserted by the Pensions Act 2004, s 274(1).

Sub-s (3): substituted by the Pensions Act 2004, s 274(2).

Sub-ss (4A)–(4C): substituted, for the original sub-s (4), by the Pensions Act 1995, s 156.

Sub-s (5): words omitted repealed by the Pensions Act 1995, ss 173, 177, Sch 6, paras 2, 7, Sch 7, Pt IV.
Sub-ss (8)–(10): added by the Government Resources and Accounts Act 2000 (Audit of Public Bodies) Order 2008, SI 2008/817, arts 9, 10.

[1.715]
[145A Deputy Pensions Ombudsman

(1) The Secretary of State may appoint one or more persons to act as a deputy to the Pensions Ombudsman ("a Deputy Pensions Ombudsman").
(2) Any such appointment is to be upon such terms and conditions as the Secretary of State thinks fit.
(3) A Deputy Pensions Ombudsman—
(a) is to hold and vacate office in accordance with the terms and conditions of his appointment, and
(b) may resign or be removed from office in accordance with those terms and conditions.
(4) A Deputy Pensions Ombudsman may perform the functions of the Pensions Ombudsman—
(a) during any vacancy in that office,
(b) at any time when the Pensions Ombudsman is for any reason unable to discharge his functions, or
(c) at any other time, with the consent of the Secretary of State.
(5) References to the Pensions Ombudsman in relation to the performance of his functions are accordingly to be construed as including references to a Deputy Pensions Ombudsman in relation to the performance of those functions.
(6) The Secretary of State may—
(a) pay to or in respect of a Deputy Pensions Ombudsman such amounts—
(i) by way of remuneration, compensation for loss of office, pension, allowances and gratuities, or
(ii) by way of provision for any such benefits,
as the Secretary of State may determine, and
(b) reimburse the Pensions Ombudsman in respect of any expenses incurred by a Deputy Pensions Ombudsman in the performance of any of the Pensions Ombudsman's functions.]

NOTES
Inserted by the Pensions Act 2004, s 274(3).

[1.716]
146 Functions of the Pensions Ombudsman

[(1) The Pensions Ombudsman may investigate and determine the following [matters]—
(a) a complaint made to him by or on behalf of an actual or potential beneficiary of an occupational or personal pension scheme who alleges that he has sustained injustice in consequence of maladministration in connection with any act or omission of a person responsible for the management of the scheme,
(b) a complaint made to him—
(i) by or on behalf of a person responsible for the management of an occupational pension scheme who in connection with any act or omission of another person responsible for the management of the scheme, alleges maladministration of the scheme, or
(ii) by or on behalf of the trustees or managers or an occupational pension scheme who in connection with any act or omission of any trustee or manager of another such scheme, allege maladministration of the other scheme,
and in any case falling within sub-paragraph (ii) references in this Part to the scheme to which the complaint relates [are references to the other scheme referred to in that sub-paragraph],
[(ba) a complaint made to him by or on behalf of an independent trustee of a trust scheme who, in connection with any act or omission which is an act or omission either—
(i) of trustees of the scheme who are not independent trustees, or
(ii) of former trustees of the scheme who were not independent trustees,
alleges maladministration of the scheme,]
(c) any dispute of fact or law . . . in relation to an occupational or personal pension scheme between—
(i) a person responsible for the management of the scheme, and
(ii) an actual or potential beneficiary,
and which is referred to him by or on behalf of the actual or potential beneficiary, and
(d) any dispute of fact or law . . . between the trustees or managers of an occupational pension scheme and—
(i) another person responsible for the management of the scheme, or
(ii) any trustee or manager of another such scheme, [and in a case falling within sub-paragraph (ii) references in this Part to the scheme to which the reference relates are references to each of the schemes,
(e) any dispute not falling within paragraph (f) between different trustees of the same occupational pension scheme,
[(f) any dispute, in relation to a time while section 22 of the Pensions Act 1995 (circumstances in which Regulatory Authority may appoint an independent trustee) applies in relation to an occupational pension scheme, between an independent trustee of the scheme appointed under section 23(1) of that Act and either—
(i) other trustees of the scheme, or

(ii) former trustees of the scheme who were not independent trustees appointed under section 23(1) of that Act, and]

(g) any question relating, in the case of an occupational pension scheme with a sole trustee, to the carrying out of the functions of that trustee.]

[(1A) The Pensions Ombudsman shall not investigate or determine any dispute or question falling within subsection (1)(c) to (g) unless it is referred to him—

(a) in the case of a dispute falling within subsection (1)(c), by or on behalf of the actual or potential beneficiary who is a party to the dispute,

(b) in the case of a dispute falling within subsection (1)(d), by or on behalf of any of the parties to the dispute,

(c) in the case of a dispute falling within subsection (1)(e), by or on behalf of at least half the trustees of the scheme,

(d) in the case of a dispute falling within subsection (1)(f), by or on behalf of the independent trustee who is a party to the dispute,

(e) in the case of a question falling within subsection (1)(g), by or on behalf of the sole trustee.

(1B) For the purposes of this Part, any reference to or determination by the Pensions Ombudsman of a question falling within subsection (1)(g) shall be taken to be the reference or determination of a dispute.]

(2) Complaints and references made to the Pensions Ombudsman must be made to him in writing.

(3) For the purposes of this Part, the following persons (subject to subsection (4)) are responsible for the management of an occupational pension scheme [or a personal pension scheme]—

(a) the trustees or managers, and

(b) the employer;

but, in relation to a person falling within one of those paragraphs, references in this Part to another person responsible for the management of the same scheme are to a person falling within the other paragraph.

(3A)

(4) Regulations may provide that, subject to any prescribed modifications or exceptions, this Part shall apply in the case of an occupational or personal pension scheme in relation to any prescribed person or body of persons where the person or body—

(a) is not a trustee or manager of employer, but

(b) is concerned with the financing or administration of, or the provision or benefits under, the scheme,

as if for the purposes of this Part he were a person responsible for the management of the scheme.]

[(4A) For the purposes of subsection (4) a person or body of persons is concerned with the administration of an occupational or personal pension scheme where the person or body is responsible for carrying out an act of administration concerned with the scheme.]

(5) The Pensions Ombudsman may investigate a complaint or dispute notwithstanding that it arose, or relates to a matter which arose, before 1st October 1990 (the date on which the provisions under which his office was constituted came into force).

(6) The Pensions Ombudsman shall not investigate or determine a complaint or dispute—

[(a) if, before the making of the complaint or the reference of the dispute—

(i) proceedings in respect of the matters which would be the subject of the investigation have been begun in any court or employment tribunal, and

(ii) those proceedings are proceedings which have not been discontinued or which have been discontinued on the basis of a settlement or compromise binding all the persons by or on whose behalf the complaint or reference is made;]

(b) if the scheme is of a description which is excluded from the jurisdiction of the Pensions Ombudsman by regulations under this subsection; or

(c) if and to the extent that the complaint or dispute, or any matter arising in connection with the complaint or dispute, is of a description which is excluded from the jurisdiction of the Pensions Ombudsman by regulations under this subsection.

[(6A) For the purposes of subsection (6)(c)—

(a) a description of complaint may be framed (in particular) by reference to the person making the complaint or to the scheme concerned (or to both), and

(b) a description of dispute may be framed (in particular) by reference to the person referring the dispute or to the scheme concerned (or to both).]

(7) The persons who, for the purposes of this Part are [actual or potential beneficiaries] in relation to a scheme are—

(a) a member of the scheme,

(b) the [widow, widower or surviving civil partner], or any surviving dependant, of a deceased member of the scheme;

[(ba) a person who is entitled to a pension credit as against the trustees or managers of the scheme;]

[(bb) a person who has given notice in accordance with section 8 of the Pensions Act 2008 (right to opt out of membership of an automatic enrolment scheme);]

(c) where the complaint or dispute relates to the question—

(i) whether a person who claims to be such a person as is mentioned in [paragraph (a), (b)[, (ba) or (bb)]] is such a person, or

(ii) whether a person who claims to be entitled to become a member of the scheme is so entitled,

the person so claiming.

(8) In this Part—

"employer", in relation to a pension scheme, includes a person—

(a) who is or has been an employer in relation to the scheme, or

(b) who is or has been treated under section 181(2) as an employer in relation to the scheme for the purposes of any provision of this Act, or under section 176(2) of the Pension Schemes (Northern Ireland) Act 1993 as an employer in relation to the scheme for the purposes of any provision of that Act;

["independent trustee", in relation to a scheme, means—

(a) a trustee of the scheme appointed under [section 23(1) of the Pensions Act 1995 (appointment of independent trustee by the Regulatory Authority)],

(b) a person appointed under section 7(1) of that Act to replace a trustee falling within paragraph (a) or this paragraph;]

"member", in relation to a pension scheme, includes a person—

(a) who is or has been in pensionable service under the scheme, or

(b) who is or has been treated under section 181(4) as a member in relation to the scheme for the purposes of any provision of this Act or under section 176(3) of the Pension Schemes (Northern Ireland) Act 1993 as a member in relation to the scheme for the purposes of any provision of that Act;

"Northern Ireland public service pension scheme" means a public service pension scheme within the meaning of section 176(1) of that Act;

"pensionable service" in this subsection includes pensionable service as defined in section 176(1) of that Act;

"trustees or managers", in relation to a pension scheme which is a public service pension scheme or a Northern Ireland public service pension scheme, includes the scheme's administrators.

NOTES

Sub-s (1): substituted, together with sub-ss (2), (3), (3A), (4), for the original sub-ss (1)–(4), by the Pensions Act 1995, s 157(1), (2); word in first pair of square brackets and words in square brackets in paras (b), (d) substituted, para (ba) inserted, and words omitted repealed, by the Child Support, Pensions and Social Security Act 2000, s 53(1), (2), (9)(a)–(c), Sch 9, Pt III(3); para (f) substituted by the Pensions Act 2004, s 319(1), Sch 12, paras 9, 24(a).

Sub-ss (1A), (1B): inserted by the Child Support, Pensions and Social Security Act 2000, s 53(1), (4).

Sub-ss (2), (4): substituted as noted above.

Sub-s (3): substituted as noted above; words in square brackets inserted by the Child Support, Pensions and Social Security Act 2000, s 53(1), (5).

Sub-s (3A): substituted as noted above; repealed by the Child Support, Pensions and Social Security Act 2000, s 85, Sch 9, Pt III(3).

Sub-s (4A): inserted by the Pensions Act 2004, s 275.

Sub-s (6): para (a) substituted by the Child Support, Pensions and Social Security Act 2000, s 53(1), (6), (10).

Sub-s (6A): inserted by the Pensions Act 2004, s 319(1), Sch 12, paras 9, 24(b), as from a day to be appointed.

Sub-s (7): words in first pair of square brackets substituted by the Pensions Act 1995, s 157(1), (3); words in square brackets in para (b) substituted by the Civil Partnership (Pensions and Benefit Payments) (Consequential, etc Provisions) Order 2005, SI 2005/2053, art 2, Schedule, Pt 3, para 16; para (ba) inserted, and words in first (outer) pair of square brackets in sub-para (c)(i) substituted, by the Child Support, Pensions and Social Security Act 2000, s 53(1), (7); para (bb) inserted, and words in second (inner) pair of square brackets in sub-para (c)(i) substituted, by the Pensions Act 2008, s 66.

Sub-s (8): definition "independent trustee" inserted by the Child Support, Pensions and Social Security Act 2000, s 53(1), (8); words in square brackets in that definition substituted by the Pensions Act 2004, s 319(1), Sch 12, paras 9, 24(c).

Regulations: the Personal and Occupational Pension Schemes (Pensions Ombudsman) Regulations 1996, SI 1996/2475; the Pension Protection Fund, Occupational and Personal Pension Schemes (Miscellaneous Amendments) Regulations 2013, SI 2013/627.

[1.717]

147 Death, insolvency or disability of authorised complainant

(1) Where an [actual or potential beneficiary] dies or is a minor or is otherwise unable to act for himself, then, unless subsection (3) applies—

(a) any complaint or dispute (whenever arising) which the [actual or potential beneficiary] might otherwise have made or referred under this Part may be made or referred by the appropriate person, and

(b) anything in the process of being done by or in relation to the [actual or potential beneficiary] under or by virtue of this Part may be continued by or in relation to the appropriate person,

and any reference in this Part, except this section, to an [actual or potential beneficiary] shall be construed as including a reference to the appropriate person.

(2) For the purposes of subsection (1) "the appropriate person" means—

(a) where the [actual or potential beneficiary] has died, his personal representatives; or

(b) in any other case, a member of [his] family, or some body or individual suitable to represent him.

(3) Where a person is acting as an insolvency practitioner in relation to [a person by whom, or on whose behalf, a complaint or reference has been made under this Part], investigations under this Part shall be regarded for the purposes of the Insolvency Act 1986 and the Bankruptcy (Scotland) Act [2016] as legal proceedings.

(4) In this section "acting as an insolvency practitioner" shall be construed in accordance with section 388 of the Insolvency Act 1986, but disregarding subsection (5) of that section (exclusion of official receiver).

NOTES

Sub-ss (1), (2): words in square brackets substituted by the Pensions Act 1995, s 157.

Sub-s (3): words in first pair of square brackets substituted by the Pensions Act 1995, s 157. Year "2016" in square brackets substituted by the Bankruptcy (Scotland) Act 2016 (Consequential Provisions and Modifications) Order 2016, SI 2016/1034, art 7(1), Sch 1, Pt 1, para 11(1), (5), as from 30 November 2016.

[1.718]

148 Staying court proceedings where a complaint is made or a dispute is referred

(1) This section applies where—

(a) complaint has been made or a dispute referred to the Pensions Ombudsman; and

(b) any party to the investigation subsequently commences any legal proceedings in any court against any other party to the investigation in respect of any of the matters which are the subject of the complaint or dispute.

(2) In England and Wales, where this section applies any party to the legal proceedings may at any time after acknowledgement of service, and before delivering any pleadings or taking any other step in the proceedings, apply to that court to stay the proceedings.

(3) In Scotland, where this section applies any party to the legal proceedings may—

(a) if the proceedings are in the Court of Session, at any time—

(i) after appearance has been entered but before defences have been lodged or any other step in the proceedings has been taken; or

(ii) (in procedure by petition) after intimation and service but before answers have been lodged or any other step in the proceedings has been taken; and

(b) if the proceedings are in the sheriff court, at any time—

(i) after notice has been given of intention to defend but before defences have been lodged or any other step in the proceedings has been taken; or

(ii) (in summary cause procedure) after appearance has been made, or notice of intention to appear has been lodged, but before any defence has been stated or any other step in the proceedings has been taken,

apply to the court for a sist of process.

(4) On an application under subsection (2) or (3) the court may make an order staying or, in Scotland, sisting the proceedings if it is satisfied—

(a) that there is no sufficient reason why the matter should not be investigated by the Pensions Ombudsman; and

(b) that the applicant was at the time when the legal proceedings were commenced and still remains ready and willing to do all things necessary to the proper conduct of the investigation.

(5) For the purposes of this section the parties to an investigation are—

[(a) to the person by whom, or on whose behalf, the complaint or reference was made, and

(b) to any person (if different) responsible for the management of the scheme to which the complaint or reference relates;]

[(ba), (bb) . . .]

(c) any person against whom allegations are made in the complaint or reference; and

(d) any person claiming under a person falling within paragraphs (a) to (c).

NOTES

Sub-s (5): paras (a), (b) substituted by the Pensions Act 1995, s 157(1), (6); paras (ba), (bb) inserted by the Child Support, Pensions and Social Security Act 2000, s 54(1), (2)(a), and repealed by the Pensions Act 2004, ss 276(2)(a), 320, Sch 13, Pt 1. Note that this amendment was brought into force on 1 March 2002 for the purposes of making rules and regulations only (see SI 2002/437). However, section 54 of the 2000 Act was subsequently repealed by the Pensions Act 2004, ss 276(2)(b), 320, Sch 13, Pt 1 without being brought into force for the remaining purposes

[1.719]

149 Procedure on an investigation

(1) Where the Pensions Ombudsman proposes to conduct an investigation into a complaint made or dispute referred under this Part, he shall give—

(a) [any person (other than the person by whom, or on whose behalf, the complaint or reference was made) responsible for the management of the scheme to which the complaint or reference relates], and

(b) any other person against whom allegations are made in the complaint or reference,

an opportunity to comment on any allegations contained in the complaint or reference.

(2) The Secretary of State may make rules with respect to the procedure which is to be adopted in connection with the making of complaints, the reference of disputes, and the investigation of complaints made and disputes referred, under this Part.

(3) The rules may include provision—

(a) requiring any oral hearing held in connection with such an investigation to take place in public, except in such cases as may be specified in the rules; . . .

(b) as to the persons entitled to appear and be heard on behalf of parties to an investigation, as defined in section 148(5);

[(ba) . . .]

(c) for the payment by the Ombudsman of such travelling and other allowances (including compensation for loss of remunerative time) as the Secretary of State may determine, to—

(i) actual or potential beneficiaries of a scheme to which a complaint or reference relates, or

(ii) person appearing and being heard on behalf of such actual or potential beneficiaries,

who attend at the request of the Ombudsman any oral hearing held in connection with an investigation into the complaint or dispute][; . . .

(d) . . .]

(4) Subject to any provision made by the rules, the procedure for conducting such an investigation shall be such as the Pensions Ombudsman considers appropriate in the circumstances of the case; and he may, in particular, obtain information from such persons and in such manner, and make such inquiries, as he thinks fit.

[(5) The Pensions Ombudsman may disclose any information which he obtains for the purposes of an investigation under this Part to any person to whom subsection (6) applies, if the Ombudsman considers that the disclosure would enable or assist that person to discharge any of his functions.

(6) This subsection applies to the following—

(a) the Regulatory Authority,

[(b) the Board of the Pension Protection Fund,

(ba) the Ombudsman for the Board of the Pension Protection Fund,]

(c) . . .

(d) any department of the Government (including the government of Northern Ireland),

[(e) the Financial Conduct Authority,

(ea) the Prudential Regulation Authority,

(eb) the Bank of England [(acting otherwise than in its capacity as the Prudential Regulation Authority)],]

(f), (g) . . .

[(h) a person appointed under—

(i) Part 14 of the Companies Act 1985,

(ii) section 167 of the Financial Services and Markets Act 2000,

(iii) subsection (3) or (5) of section 168 of that Act, or

(iv) section 284 of that Act,

to conduct an investigation;]

(j) . . .

[(k) a body designated under section 326(1) of the Financial Services and Markets Act 2000; . . .

(l) a recognised investment exchange[, recognised clearing house, *EEA central counterparty*[, third country central counterparty, recognised CSD, *EEA CSD* or third country CSD]] (as defined by section 285 of that Act)];

[(n) a person who, in a member State *other than the United Kingdom*, has functions corresponding to functions of the Pensions Ombudsman]'

[(o) [the body corporate mentioned in paragraph 2] of Schedule 17 to the Financial Services and Markets Act 2000 (the scheme operator of the ombudsman scheme);

(p) an ombudsman as defined in paragraph 1 of that Schedule (interpretation)].

(7) The Secretary of State may by order—

(a) amend subsection (6) by adding any person or removing any person for the time being specified in that subsection, or

(b) restrict the circumstances in which, or impose conditions subject to which, disclosure may be made to any person for the time being specified in that subsection.]

[(8) . . .]

NOTES

Sub-s (1): words in square brackets in para (a) substituted by the Pensions Act 1995, s 157(7). Note that this subsection was substituted (by new sub-ss (1), (1A), (1B)) by the Child Support, Pensions and Social Security Act 2000, s 54(1), (3), (9). This amendment was brought into force on 1 March 2002 for the purposes of making rules and regulations only (see SI 2002/437). However, section 54 of the 2000 Act was subsequently repealed by the Pensions Act 2004, ss 276(2)(b), 320, Sch 13, Pt 1 without being brought into force for the remaining purposes.

Sub-s (3): word omitted from para (a) repealed, and para (c) inserted, by the Pensions Act 1995, ss 158, 177, Sch 7, Pt IV; paras (ba), (d) and the word immediately preceding para (d) inserted, by the Child Support, Pensions and Social Security Act 2000, s 54(1), (4), (5), (9), and repealed by the Pensions Act 2004, ss 276(2)(c), (d), 320, Sch 13, Pt 1.

Sub-ss (5), (7): added, together with sub-s (6), by the Pensions Act 1995, s 159(1).

Sub-s (6): added as noted above and is amended as follows:

Paras (b), (ba) substituted (for the original para (b)), and para (n) added, by the Pensions Act 2004, s 319(1), Sch 12, paras 9, 25.

Para (c) and the word omitted from para (k) repealed by the Pensions Act 2004, s 320, Sch 13, Pt 1.

Paras (e), (ea), (eb) substituted (for the original para (e)), by the Financial Services Act 2012, s 114(1), Sch 18, Pt 2, para 78(1), (2)(a); words in square brackets in para (eb) inserted by the Bank of England and Financial Services (Consequential Amendments) Regulations 2017, SI 2017/80, reg 2, Schedule, Pt 1, para 8(a), as from 1 March 2017.

Paras (f), (g) repealed, para (h) substituted, and paras (k), (l) substituted (for the original paras (k)–(m)), by the Financial Services and Markets Act 2000 (Consequential Amendments and Repeals) Order 2001, SI 2001/3649, art 123.

Para (j) repealed by the Companies Act 2006 (Consequential Amendments, Transitional Provisions and Savings) Order 2009, SI 2009/1941, art 2(1), Sch 1, para 144(1), (3).

Words in square brackets first (outer) pair of square brackets in para (l) substituted by the Financial Services and Markets Act 2000 (Over the Counter Derivatives, Central Counterparties and Trade Repositories) Regulations 2013, SI 2013/504, reg 21. Words in second (inner) pair of square brackets substituted by the Central Securities Depositories Regulations 2017, SI 2017/1064, reg 10, Schedule, Pt 1, para 7(1), (2), as from 28 November 2017.

Words in italics in paras (l), (n) repealed by the Occupational and Personal Pension Schemes (Amendment etc) (EU Exit) Regulations 2019, SI 2019/192, reg 2(1), (4), as from exit day (as defined in the European Union (Withdrawal) Act 2018, s 20).

Paras (o), (p) added by the Pensions Ombudsman (Disclosure of Information) (Amendment of Specified Persons) Order 2005, SI 2005/2743, art 2; words in square brackets in para (o) substituted by the Financial Services Act 2012, s 114(1), Sch 18, Pt 2, para 78(1), (2)(b).

Sub-s (8): added by the Child Support, Pensions and Social Security Act 2000, s 54(1), (6), and repealed by the Pensions Act 2004, ss 276(2)(e), 320, Sch 13, Pt 1 (see further the note to sub-s (1) above).

Rules: the Personal and Occupational Pensions (Pensions Ombudsman) Procedure Rules 1995, SI 1995/1053; the Personal and Occupational Pension Schemes (Pensions Ombudsman) (Procedure) Amendment Rules 1996, SI 1996/2638.

Orders: the Pensions Ombudsman (Disclosure of Information) (Amendment of Specified Persons) Order 2005, SI 2005/2743.

[1.720]
150 Investigations: further provisions
(1) For the purposes of an investigation under this Part or under any corresponding legislation having effect in Northern Ireland, the Pensions Ombudsman may require—

(a) [any person responsible for the management of the scheme to which the complaint or reference relates], or

(b) any other person who, in his opinion is able to furnish information or produce documents relevant to the investigation,

to furnish any such information or produce any such documents.

(2) For the purposes of any such investigation the Pensions Ombudsman shall have the same powers as the court in respect of the attendance and examination of witnesses (including the administration of oaths and affirmations and the examination of witnesses abroad) and in respect of the production of documents.

(3) No person shall be compelled for the purposes of any such investigation to give any evidence or produce any document which he could not be compelled to give or produce in civil proceedings before the court.

(4) If any person without lawful excuse obstructs the Pensions Ombudsman in the performance of his functions or is guilty of any act or omission in relation to an investigation under this Part which, if that investigation were a proceeding in the court, would constitute contempt of court, the Pensions Ombudsman may certify the offence to the court.

(5) Where an offence is certified under subsection (4) the court may inquire into the matter and, after hearing any witnesses who may be produced against or on behalf of the person charged with the offence and hearing any statement that may be offered in defence, deal with him in any manner in which the court could deal with him if he had committed the like offence in relation to the court.

(6) To assist him in an investigation, the Pensions Ombudsman may obtain advice from any person who in his opinion is qualified to give it and may pay to any such person such fees or allowances as he may with the approval of the Treasury determine.

(7) The Pensions Ombudsman may refer any question of law arising for determination in connection with a complaint or dispute to the High Court or, in Scotland, the Court of Session.

(8) In this section "the court" means—

(a) in England and Wales, [the county court];

(b) in Scotland, the sheriff.

(9) Subsections (4) and (5) shall be construed, in their application to Scotland, as if contempt of court were categorised as an offence in Scots law.

NOTES

Sub-s (1): words in square brackets substituted by the Pensions Act 1995, s 157(1), (8).

Sub-s (8): words in square brackets substituted by the Crime and Courts Act 2013, s 17(5), Sch 9, Pt 3, para 52.

[1.721]
151 Determinations of the Pensions Ombudsman
(1) Where the Pensions Ombudsman has conducted an investigation under this Part he shall send a written statement of his determination of the complaint or dispute in question—

[(a) to the person by whom, or on whose behalf, the complaint or reference was made, and

(b) to any person (if different) responsible for the management of the scheme to which the complaint or reference relates][. . .

(c) . . .]

and any such statement shall contain the reasons for his determination.

(2) Where the Pensions Ombudsman makes a determination under this Part or under any corresponding legislation having effect in Northern Ireland, he may direct [any person responsible for the management of the scheme to which the complaint or reference relates] to take, or refrain from taking, such steps as he may specify in the statement referred to in subsection (1) or otherwise in writing.

(3) Subject to subsection (4), the determination by the Pensions Ombudsman of a complaint or dispute, and any direction given by him under subsection (2), shall be final and binding on—

[(a) the person by whom, or on whose behalf, the complaint or reference was made,

(b) any person (if different) responsible for the management of the scheme to which the complaint or reference relates,

[(ba), (bb) . . .]

(c) any person claiming under a person falling within paragraph (a) or (b).]

(4) An appeal on a point of law shall lie to the High Court or, in Scotland, the Court of Session from a determination or direction of the Pensions Ombudsman at the instance of any person falling within paragraphs (a) to (c) of subsection (3).

(5) Any determination or direction of the Pensions Ombudsman shall be enforceable—

(a) in England and Wales, in [the county court] as if it were a judgment or order of that court, and

(b) in Scotland, [in like manner as an extract registered decree arbitral bearing warrant for execution issued by the sheriff court of any sheriffdom in Scotland].

(6) If the Pensions Ombudsman considers it appropriate to do so in any particular case, he may publish in such form and manner as he thinks fit a report of any investigation under this Part and of the result of that investigation.

(7) For the purposes of the law of defamation, the publication of any matter by the Pensions Ombudsman—

(a) in submitting or publishing a report under section 145(6) or subsection (6) of this section, or
[(aa) in disclosing any information under s 149(5)]
(b) in sending to any person a statement under subsection (1) or a direction under subsection (2),
shall be absolutely privileged.

NOTES

Sub-s (1): paras (a), (b) substituted by the Pensions Act 1995, s 157(1), (9); para (c) and the word immediately preceding it inserted by the Child Support, Pensions and Social Security Act 2000, s 54(1), (7), (9), and repealed by the Pensions Act 2004, ss 276(2)(f), 320, Sch 13, Pt 1.

Sub-s (2): words in square brackets substituted by the Pensions Act 1995, s 157(1), (10).

Sub-s (3): paras (a)–(c) originally substituted by the Pensions Act 1995, s 157(1), (11); paras (ba), (bb) substituted for the original word "and" at the end of para (b) by the Child Support, Pensions and Social Security Act 2000, s 54(1), (8), (9), and repealed by the Pensions Act 2004, ss 276(2)(g), 320, Sch 13, Pt 1.

Sub-s (5): words in square brackets in para (a) substituted by the Crime and Courts Act 2013, s 17(5), Sch 9, Pt 3, para 52; words in square brackets in para (b) substituted by the Pensions Act 1995, s 173, Sch 6, paras 2, 8.

Sub-s (7): para (aa) inserted by the Pensions Act 1995, s 159(2).

[1.722]
[151A Interest on late payment of benefit
Where under this Part the Pensions Ombudsman directs a person responsible for the management of an occupational or personal pension scheme to make any payment in respect of benefit under the scheme which, in his opinion, ought to have been paid earlier, his direction may also require the payment of interest at the prescribed rate.]

NOTES

Inserted by the Pensions Act 1995, s 160.

Regulations: the Personal and Occupational Pension Schemes (Pensions Ombudsman) Regulations 1996, SI 1996/2475.

PART XI
GENERAL AND MISCELLANEOUS PROVISIONS

Avoidance of certain transactions and provisions

[1.723]
160 Terms of contracts of service or schemes restricting choice to be void
(1) Subject to such exceptions as may be prescribed—
(a) any term of a contract of service (whenever made) or any rule of a personal or occupational pension scheme to the effect that an employed earner must be a member—
(i) of a personal or occupational pension scheme,
(ii) of a particular personal or occupational pension scheme, or
(iii) of one or other of a number of particular personal or occupational pension schemes,
shall be void; and
(b) any such term or rule to the effect that contributions shall be paid by or in respect of an employed earner—
(i) to a particular personal or occupational pension scheme of which the earner is not a member, or
(ii) to one or other of a number of personal or occupational pension schemes of none of which he is a member,
shall be unenforceable for so long as he is not a member of the scheme or any of the schemes.

(2) Subsection (1) shall not be construed so as to have the effect that an employer is required, when he would not otherwise be—
(a) to make contributions to a personal or occupational pension scheme; or
(b) to increase an employed earner's pay in lieu of making contributions to a personal or occupational pension scheme.

NOTES

Regulations: by virtue of s 189(1) of, and Sch 6, Pt I, para 2(2) to, this Act, the Pension Schemes (Voluntary Contributions Requirements and Voluntary and Compulsory Membership) Regulations 1987, SI 1987/1108 have effect as if made under this section.

[1.724]
161 Provisions excluding Chapter II of Part VII to be void
Any provision in an agreement (whether a [worker's contract] or not) shall be void in so far as it purports—
(a) to exclude or limit the operation of any provision of Chapter II of Part VII of this Act; or
(b) to preclude any person from presenting a complaint to, or bringing any proceedings before, an [employment tribunal] under that Chapter.

NOTES

Words "worker's contract" in square brackets substituted by the Pensions Act 2014, s 42(1), (4), as from 11 September 2014.

Words "employment tribunal" in square brackets substituted by the Employment Rights (Dispute Resolution) Act 1998, s 1(2)(a).

PART XII
SUPPLEMENTARY PROVISIONS

Supplemental provisions

[1.725]

193 Short title and commencement

(1) This Act may be cited as the Pension Schemes Act 1993.

(2) Subject to the provisions of Schedule 9, this Act shall come into force on such day as the Secretary of State may by order appoint.

(3) As respects the coming into force of—

(a) Part II of Schedule 5 and section 188(1) so far as it relates to it; or

(b) Schedule 7 and section 190 so far as it relates to it,

an order under subsection (2) may appoint different days from the day appointed for the other provisions of this Act or different days for different purposes.

NOTES

Orders: the Pension Schemes Act 1993 (Commencement No 1) Order 1994, SI 1994/86.

CRIMINAL JUSTICE AND PUBLIC ORDER ACT 1994

(1994 c 33)

NOTES

Only the provisions of this Act relating to the prison service are relevant to this Handbook. Provisions not reproduced are not annotated. Sections 126 and 127 came into force on the date of Royal assent (3 November 1994), and s 127A was inserted with effect from 8 May 2008. By virtue of s 172 (not reproduced) Chapter IV of Part VIII extends to the whole of the UK.

An Act to make further provision in relation to criminal justice (including employment in the prison service); to amend or extend the criminal law and powers for preventing crime and enforcing that law; to amend the Video Recordings Act 1984; and for purposes connected with those purposes

[3rd November 1994]

PART VIII
PRISON SERVICES AND THE PRISON SERVICE

CHAPTER IV THE PRISON SERVICE

[1.726]

126 Service in England and Wales and Northern Ireland

(1) The relevant employment legislation shall have effect as if an individual who as a member of the prison service acts in a capacity in which he has the powers or privileges of a constable were not, by virtue of his so having those powers or privileges, to be regarded as in police service for the purposes of any provision of that legislation.

(2) In this section "the relevant employment legislation" means—

[(a) the Trade Union and Labour Relations (Consolidation) Act 1992 and the Employment Rights Act 1996;]

[(b) the Trade Union and Labour Relations (Northern Ireland) Order 1995 and the Employment Rights (Northern Ireland) Order 1996.]

(3) For the purposes of this section a person is a member of the prison service if he is an individual holding a post to which he has been appointed for the purposes of section 7 of the Prison Act 1952 or under section 2(2) of the Prison Act (Northern Ireland) 1953 (appointment of prison staff).

(4) Except for the purpose of validating anything that would have been a contravention of section 127(1) below if it had been in force, subsection (1) above, so far as it relates to the question whether an organisation consisting wholly or mainly of members of the prison service is a trade union, shall be deemed always to have had effect and to have applied, in relation to times when provisions of the relevant employment legislation were not in force, to the corresponding legislation then in force.

(5) Subsection (6) below shall apply where—

(a) the certificate of independence of any organisation has been cancelled, at any time before the passing of this Act, in consequence of the removal of the name of that organisation from a list of trade unions kept under provisions of the relevant employment legislation; but

(b) it appears to the Certification Officer that the organisation would have remained on the list, and that the certificate would have remained in force, had that legislation had effect at and after that time in accordance with subsection (1) above.

(6) Where this subsection applies—

(a) the Certification Officer shall restore the name to the list and delete from his records any entry relating to the cancellation of the certificate;

(b) the removal of the name from the list, the making of the deleted entry and the cancellation of the certificate shall be deemed never to have occurred; and

(c) the organisation shall accordingly be deemed, for the purposes for which it is treated by virtue of subsection (4) above as having been a trade union, to have been independent throughout the period between the cancellation of the certificate and the deletion of the entry relating to that cancellation.

NOTES

Sub s (2): para (a) substituted by the Employment Rights Act 1996, s 240, Sch 1, para 65. Para (b) substituted by the Employment Rights (Northern Ireland) Order 1996, SI 1996/1919, art 255, Sch 1.

[1.727]

127 Inducements to withhold services or to indiscipline

(1) A person contravenes this subsection if he induces a prison officer—

[(a) to take (or continue to take) any industrial action;]

(b) to commit a breach of discipline.

[(1A) In subsection (1) "industrial action" means—

(a) the withholding of services as a prison officer; or

(b) any action that would be likely to put at risk the safety of any person (whether a prisoner, a person working at or visiting a prison, a person working with prisoners or a member of the public).]

(2) The obligation not to contravene subsection (1) above shall be a duty owed to the Secretary of State [or, in Scotland, to the Scottish Ministers] [or, in Northern Ireland, to the Department of Justice].

(3) Without prejudice to the right of the Secretary of State [or, in Scotland, to the Scottish Ministers] [or, in Northern Ireland, of the Department of Justice], by virtue of the preceding provisions of this section, to bring civil proceedings in respect of any apprehended contravention of subsection (1) above, any breach of the duty mentioned in subsection (2) above which causes the Secretary of State [or, in Scotland, to the Scottish Ministers] [or, in Northern Ireland, the Department of Justice] to sustain loss or damage shall be actionable, at his suit or instance, against the person in breach.

(4) In this section "prison officer" means any individual who—

(a) holds any post, otherwise than as a chaplain or assistant chaplain or as a medical officer, to which he has been appointed . . . under section 2(2) of the Prison Act (Northern Ireland) 1953 (appointment of prison staff),

[(aa) holds any post, other than as a chaplain or assistant chaplain, to which he has been appointed for the purposes of section 7 of the Prison Act 1952 (appointment of prison staff),]

[(b) holds any post, otherwise than as a medical officer, to which he has been appointed for the purposes of section 3(1A) of the Prisons (Scotland) Act 1989;] or

(c) is a custody officer within the meaning of Part I of this Act or a prisoner custody officer, within the meaning of Part IV of the Criminal Justice Act 1991 or Chapter II or III of this Part.

(5) The reference in subsection (1) above to a breach of discipline by a prison officer is a reference to a failure by a prison officer to perform any duty imposed on him by the prison rules or any code of discipline having effect under those rules or any other contravention by a prison officer of those rules or any such code.

(6) In subsection (5) above "the prison rules" means any rules for the time being in force under section 47 [or 47A] of the Prison Act 1952, section 39 of the Prisons (Scotland) Act 1989 or section 13 of the Prison Act (Northern Ireland) 1953 (prison rules).

(7) This section shall be disregarded in determining for the purposes of any of the relevant employment legislation whether any trade union is an independent trade union.

(8) Nothing in the relevant employment legislation shall affect the rights of the Secretary of State [or in Scotland, the Scottish Ministers] [or, in Northern Ireland, the Department of Justice] by virtue of this section.

(9) In this section "the relevant employment legislation" has the same meaning as in section 126 above.

NOTES

Sub-s (1): para (a) substituted by the Criminal Justice and Immigration Act 2008, s 138(1), (2).

Sub-s (1A): inserted by the Criminal Justice and Immigration Act 2008, s 138(1), (3).

Sub-ss (2), (8): words in first pair of square brackets inserted by the Scotland Act 1998 (Consequential Modifications) (No 2) Order 1999, SI 1999/1820, art 4, Sch 2, Pt I, para 115(1), (10)(a), (c). Words in second pair of square brackets inserted by the Northern Ireland Act 1998 (Devolution of Policing and Justice Functions) Order 2010, SI 2010/976, art 6(4), Sch 7, paras 1, 3(a), (d).

Sub-s (3): words in first and third pairs of square brackets inserted by SI 1999/1820, art 4, Sch 2, Pt I, para 115(1), (10)(b). Words in second and fourth pairs of square brackets inserted by SI 2010/976, art 6(4), Sch 7, paras 1, 3(b), (c).

Sub-s (4): words omitted from para (a) repealed by the Regulatory Reform (Prison Officers) (Industrial Action) Order 2005, SI 2005/908, art 2(a). Para (aa) inserted by the Criminal Justice and Immigration Act 2008, s 138(1), (4). Para (b) inserted by the Criminal Justice and Immigration Act 2008, s 138(1), (5), as from a day to be appointed (note that the original para (b) was repealed by SI 2005/908, art 2(b)).

Sub-s (6): words in square brackets inserted by the Legal Aid, Sentencing and Punishment of Offenders Act 2012, s 129(6), as from a day to be appointed.

[1.728]

[127A Power to suspend the operation of section 127]

[(1) The Secretary of State may make orders suspending, or later reviving, the operation of section 127.

[(1A) In the application of this section to Northern Ireland, in subsection (1) the reference to the Secretary of State is to be read as a reference to the Department of Justice in Northern Ireland.]

(2) An order under this section may make different provision in relation to different descriptions of prison officer.

(3) The power to make orders under this section is exercisable by statutory instrument [(subject to subsection (5))].

(4) A statutory instrument containing an order under this section may not be made unless a draft of the instrument has been laid before, and approved by resolution of, each House of Parliament.]
[(5) The power of the Department of Justice in Northern Ireland to make orders under this section is exercisable by statutory rule for the purposes of the Statutory Rules (Northern Ireland) Order 1979 (and not by statutory instrument).
(6) No order may be made by the Department of Justice under this section unless a draft of the order has been laid before, and approved by a resolution of, the Northern Ireland Assembly.
(7) Section 41(3) of the Interpretation Act (Northern Ireland) 1954 applies for the purposes of subsection (6) in relation to the laying of a draft as it applies in relation to the laying of a statutory document under an enactment.]

NOTES

Inserted by the Criminal Justice and Immigration Act 2008, s 139.

Sub-s (1A): inserted by the Northern Ireland Act 1998 (Devolution of Policing and Justice Functions) Order 2010, SI 2010/976, art 6(4), Sch 7, paras 1, 4(1), (2).

Sub-s (3): words in square brackets inserted by SI 2010/976, art 6(4), Sch 7, paras 1, 4(1), (3).

Sub-ss (5)–(7): added by SI 2010/976, art 6(4), Sch 7, paras 1, 4(1), (4).

[EMPLOYMENT TRIBUNALS ACT 1996]

(1996 c 17)

ARRANGEMENT OF SECTIONS

PART I
EMPLOYMENT TRIBUNALS

Introductory

Jurisdiction

Membership etc

Procedure

Financial penalties

Costs etc, interest and enforcement

Recoupment of social security benefits

Conciliation

PART II
THE EMPLOYMENT APPEAL TRIBUNAL

Introductory

Jurisdiction

Membership etc

Procedure

Decisions and further appeals

PART 2A
FINANCIAL PENALTIES FOR FAILURE TO PAY SUMS ORDERED
TO BE PAID OR SETTLEMENT SUMS

PART III
SUPPLEMENTARY

Crown employment and Parliamentary staff

An Act to consolidate enactments relating to [employment tribunals] and the Employment Appeal Tribunal

[22 May 1996]

NOTES

Title: substituted by the Employment Rights (Dispute Resolution) Act 1998, s 1(2)(c).

Long title: words in square brackets substituted by virtue of the Employment Rights (Dispute Resolution) Act 1998, s 1(2)(b).

This Act is the first separate legislation devoted to the constitution, powers and procedure of Employment Tribunals and the Employment Appeal Tribunal. It consolidates provisions mainly in the Employment Protection (Consolidation) Act 1978 but also widely scattered in other Acts.

As to the further power to amend this Act, see s 40 *post*, the Employment Relations Act 2004, s 42(1), (4)(d) at **[1.1415]**, and the Pensions Act 2004, ss 259, 260.

Employment Appeal Tribunal: an appeal lies to the Employment Appeal Tribunal on any question of law arising from any decision of, or in any proceedings before, an employment tribunal under or by virtue of this Act; see s 21(1)(g) at **[1.764]**.

By the Tribunals, Courts and Enforcement Act 2007, Sch 6, Pt 6, an employment tribunal is a scheduled tribunal for the purposes of s 35 of that Act, under which the Lord Chancellor has powers relating to the transfer of Ministerial responsibilities for scheduled tribunals.

By the Tribunals, Courts and Enforcement Act 2007, Sch 6, Pt 5, the Employment Appeal Tribunal is a scheduled tribunal for the purposes of ss 35, 36 of that Act. For the powers of the Lord Chancellor relating to the transfer of Ministerial responsibilities for scheduled tribunals and the transfer of powers to make procedural rules, see ss 35, 36, respectively of that Act.

For the power of the Lord Chancellor to provide for a function of a scheduled tribunal (as specified in Sch 6, Pts 1–4 to the 2007 Act) to be transferred to an employment tribunal or the Employment Appeal Tribunal, see the Tribunals, Courts and Enforcement Act 2007, s 30.

See *Harvey* PI.

PART I
[EMPLOYMENT TRIBUNALS]

NOTES

The Part heading was substituted by the Employment Rights (Dispute Resolution) Act 1998, s 1(2)(b).

Introductory

[1.729]

1 [Employment tribunals]

(1) The Secretary of State may by regulations make provision for the establishment of tribunals to be known as [employment tribunals].

(2) Regulations made wholly or partly under section 128(1) of the Employment Protection (Consolidation) Act 1978 and in force immediately before this Act comes into force shall, so far as made under that provision, continue to have effect (until revoked) as if made under subsection (1); . . .

NOTES

Section heading, sub-s (1): words in square brackets substituted by the Employment Rights (Dispute Resolution) Act 1998, s 1(2)(b).

Sub-s (2): words omitted repealed by the Employment Rights (Dispute Resolution) Act 1998, s 15, Sch 2.

Employment Protection (Consolidation) Act 1978, s 128(1): repealed by this Act.

Regulations: the Employment Tribunals (Constitution and Rules of Procedure) Regulations 2013, SI 2013/1237 at **[2.1323]**. The 2013 Regulations revoked and replaced the Employment Tribunals (Constitution and Rules of Procedure) Regulations 2004, SI 2004/1861 (for transitional provisions see reg 15 of the 2013 Regulations at **[2.1337]**). The 2004 Regulations revoked and replaced (again, subject to transitional provisions) the Employment Tribunals (Constitution and Rules of Procedure) Regulations 2001, SI 2001/1171, and the Employment Tribunals (Constitution and Rules of Procedure) (Scotland)

Regulations 2001, SI 2001/1170. The Regulations continued in force by sub-s (2) were revoked and replaced by the 2001 Regulations.

Jurisdiction

[1.730]

2 Enactments conferring jurisdiction on [employment tribunals]

[Employment tribunals] shall exercise the jurisdiction conferred on them by or by virtue of this Act or any other Act, whether passed before or after this Act.

NOTES

Words in square brackets substituted by the Employment Rights (Dispute Resolution) Act 1998, s 1(2)(b).

[1.731]

3 Power to confer further jurisdiction on [employment tribunals]

(1) The appropriate Minister may by order provide that proceedings in respect of—

(a) any claim to which this section applies, or

(b) any claim to which this section applies and which is of a description specified in the order,

may, subject to such exceptions (if any) as may be so specified, be brought before an [employment tribunal].

(2) Subject to subsection (3), this section applies to—

(a) a claim for damages for breach of a contract of employment or other contract connected with employment,

(b) a claim for a sum due under such a contract, and

(c) a claim for the recovery of a sum in pursuance of any enactment relating to the terms or performance of such a contract,

if the claim is such that a court in England and Wales or Scotland would under the law for the time being in force have jurisdiction to hear and determine an action in respect of the claim.

(3) This section does not apply to a claim for damages, or for a sum due, in respect of personal injuries.

(4) Any jurisdiction conferred on an [employment tribunal] by virtue of this section in respect of any claim is exercisable concurrently with any court in England and Wales or in Scotland which has jurisdiction to hear and determine an action in respect of the claim.

(5) In this section—

"appropriate Minister", as respects a claim in respect of which an action could be heard and determined by a court in England and Wales, means the Lord Chancellor and, as respects a claim in respect of which an action could be heard and determined by a court in Scotland, means the [Secretary of State], and

"personal injuries" includes any disease and any impairment of a person's physical or mental condition.

(6) In this section a reference to breach of a contract includes a reference to breach of—

(a) a term implied in a contract by or under any enactment or otherwise,

(b) a term of a contract as modified by or under any enactment or otherwise, and

(c) a term which, although not contained in a contract, is incorporated in the contract by another term of the contract.

NOTES

Section heading, sub-ss (1), (4): words in square brackets substituted by the Employment Rights (Dispute Resolution) Act 1998, s 1(2)(a), (b).

Sub-s (5): words in square brackets in definition "appropriate Minister" substituted by virtue of the Transfer of Functions (Lord Advocate and Secretary of State) Order 1999, SI 1999/678, art 2(1), Schedule.

Transfer of functions: functions under this section are transferred, in so far as they are exercisable in or as regards Scotland, to the Scottish Ministers, by the Scotland Act 1998 (Transfer of Functions to the Scottish Ministers etc) Order 1999, SI 1999/1750, art 2, Sch 1.

Orders: as of 15 May 2019, no Orders had been made under this section but, by virtue of s 44 of, and Sch 2, Pt I, paras 1–4 to, this Act, the Employment Tribunals Extension of Jurisdiction (England and Wales) Order 1994, SI 1994/1623 at **[2.215]**, and the Employment Tribunals Extension of Jurisdiction (Scotland) Order 1994, SI 1994/1624 at **[2.227]**, have effect as if made under this section.

[1.732]

[3A Meaning of "Employment Judge"

A person who is a member of a panel of [Employment Judges] which is appointed in accordance with regulations under section 1(1) may be referred to as an Employment Judge.]

NOTES

Inserted by the Tribunals, Courts and Enforcement Act 2007, s 48(1), Sch 8, paras 35, 36.

Words in square brackets substituted by the Crime and Courts Act 2013, s 21(4), Sch 14, Pt 7, para 13(1).

Membership etc

[1.733]

4 Composition of a tribunal

(1) Subject to the following provisions of this section [and to section 7(3A)], proceedings before an [employment tribunal] shall be heard by—

(a) the person who, in accordance with regulations made under section 1(1), is the chairman, and

(b) *two other members, or (with the consent of the parties) one other member, selected as the other members (or member) in accordance with regulations so made.*

(2) Subject to subsection (5), the proceedings specified in subsection (3) shall be heard by the person mentioned in subsection (1)(a) alone [or alone by any Employment Judge who, in accordance with regulations made under section 1(1), is a member of the tribunal].

(3) The proceedings referred to in subsection (2) are—

(a) proceedings [on a complaint under section 68A[, 87] or 192 of the Trade Union and Labour Relations (Consolidation) Act 1992 or] on an application under section 161, 165 or 166 of [that Act],

(b) proceedings on a complaint under section 126 of the Pension Schemes Act 1993,

(c) proceedings [on a reference under section 11, 163 or 170 of the Employment Rights Act 1996,] on a complaint under section 23[, 34][, 111] or 188 of [that Act, on a complaint under section 70(1) of that Act relating to section 64 of that Act,] on an application under section 128, 131 or 132 of that [Act or for an appointment under section 206(4) of that] Act,

[(ca) proceedings on a complaint under [regulation 15(10) of the Transfer of Undertakings (Protection of Employment) Regulations 2006],]

[(cc) proceedings on a complaint under section 11 of the National Minimum Wage Act 1998;

(cd) proceedings on an appeal under [section 19C] of the National Minimum Wage Act 1998;]

[(ce) proceedings on a complaint under regulation 30 of the Working Time Regulations 1998 relating to an amount due under regulation 14(2) or 16(1) of those Regulations,

(cf) proceedings on a complaint under regulation 18 of the Merchant Shipping (Working Time: Inland Waterways) Regulations 2003 relating to an amount due under regulation 11 of those Regulations,

(cg) proceedings on a complaint under regulation 18 of the Civil Aviation (Working Time) Regulations 2004 relating to an amount due under regulation 4 of those Regulations,

(ch) proceedings on a complaint under regulation 19 of the Fishing Vessels (Working Time: Sea-fishermen) Regulations 2004 relating to an amount due under regulation 11 of those Regulations,]

(d) proceedings in respect of which an [employment tribunal] has jurisdiction by virtue of section 3 of this Act,

(e) proceedings in which the parties have given their written consent to the proceedings being heard in accordance with subsection (2) (whether or not they have subsequently withdrawn it),

(f) . . . and

(g) proceedings in which the person (or, where more than one, each of the persons) against whom the proceedings are brought does not, or has ceased to, contest the case.

(4) The Secretary of State [and the Lord Chancellor, acting jointly,] may by order amend the provisions of subsection (3).

(5) Proceedings specified in subsection (3) shall be heard in accordance with subsection (1) if a person who, in accordance with regulations made under section 1(1), may be the chairman of an [employment tribunal], having regard to—

(a) whether there is a likelihood of a dispute arising on the facts which makes it desirable for the proceedings to be heard in accordance with subsection (1),

(b) whether there is a likelihood of an issue of law arising which would make it desirable for the proceedings to be heard in accordance with subsection (2),

(c) any views of any of the parties as to whether or not the proceedings ought to be heard in accordance with either of those subsections, and

(d) whether there are other proceedings which might be heard concurrently but which are not proceedings specified in subsection (3),

decides at any stage of the proceedings that the proceedings are to be heard in accordance with subsection (1).

(6) Where (in accordance with the following provisions of this Part) the Secretary of State makes [employment tribunal] procedure regulations, the regulations may provide that [any act which is required or authorised by the regulations to be done by an employment tribunal and is of a description specified by the regulations for the purposes of this subsection may] be done by the person mentioned in subsection (1)(a) alone [or alone by any Employment Judge who, in accordance with regulations made under section 1(1), is a member of the tribunal].

[(6A) Subsection (6) in particular enables employment tribunal procedure regulations to provide that—

(a) the determination of proceedings in accordance with regulations under section 7(3A), (3B) or (3C)(a),

(b) the carrying-out of pre-hearing reviews in accordance with regulations under subsection (1) of section 9 (including the exercise of powers in connection with such reviews in accordance with regulations under paragraph (b) of that subsection), or

(c) the hearing and determination of a preliminary issue in accordance with regulations under section 9(4) (where it involves hearing witnesses other than the parties or their representatives as well as where, in accordance with regulations under section 7(3C)(b), it does not),

may be done by the person mentioned in subsection (1)(a) alone [or alone by any Employment Judge who, in accordance with regulations made under section 1(1), is a member of the tribunal].]

[(6B) Employment tribunal procedure regulations may (subject to subsection (6C)) also provide that any act which—

(a) by virtue of subsection (6) may be done by the person mentioned in subsection (1)(a) alone [or alone by any Employment Judge who, in accordance with regulations made under section 1(1), is a member of the tribunal], and

(b) is of a description specified by the regulations for the purposes of this subsection, may be done by a person appointed as a legal officer in accordance with regulations under section 1(1); and any act so done shall be treated as done by an employment tribunal.

(6C) But regulations under subsection (6B) may not specify—

(a) the determination of any proceedings, other than proceedings in which the parties have agreed the terms of the determination or in which the person bringing the proceedings has given notice of the withdrawal of the case, or

(b) the carrying-out of pre-hearing reviews in accordance with regulations under section 9(1).]

[(6D) A person appointed as a legal officer in accordance with regulations under section 1(1) may determine proceedings in respect of which an employment tribunal has jurisdiction, or make a decision falling to be made in the course of such proceedings, if—

(a) the proceedings are of a description specified in an order under this subsection made by the Secretary of State and the Lord Chancellor acting jointly, and

(b) all the parties to the proceedings consent in writing;

and any determination or decision made under this subsection shall be treated as made by an employment tribunal.]

(7) . . .

NOTES

Sub-s (1): words in square brackets substituted by the Employment Rights (Dispute Resolution) Act 1998, ss 1(2)(a), 15, Sch 1, para 12(1), (2); para (b) substituted by s 4 of the 1998 Act, as from a day to be appointed, as follows—

"(b) two other members selected as the other members in accordance with regulations so made or, with appropriate consent, one other member selected as the other member in accordance with regulations so made;

and in paragraph (b) "appropriate consent" means either consent given at the beginning of the hearing by such of the parties as are then present in person or represented, or consent given by each of the parties.".

Sub-s (2): words in square brackets inserted by the Tribunals, Courts and Enforcement Act 2007, s 48(1), Sch 8, paras 35, 37.

Sub-s (3) is amended as follows:

All words and numbers in square brackets in paras (a), (c) (with the exception of the number ", 111") were inserted or substituted by the Employment Rights (Dispute Resolution) Act 1998, ss 3(1)–(3), 15, Sch 1, para 12.

Number ", 111" in square brackets in para (c) inserted by the Employment Tribunals Act 1996 (Tribunal Composition) Order 2012, SI 2012/988, art 2.

Para (ca) inserted, words in square brackets in para (d) substituted, and para (f) repealed, by the Employment Rights (Dispute Resolution) Act 1998, ss 1(2)(a), 3(1), (4), (5), 15, Sch 1, para 12, Sch 2.

Words in square brackets in para (ca) substituted by the Transfer of Undertakings (Protection of Employment) Regulations 2006, SI 2006/246, reg 20, Sch 2, para 8.

Paras (cc), (cd) inserted by the National Minimum Wage Act 1998, s 27(1).

Words in square brackets in para (cd) substituted by the Employment Act 2008, s 9(4).

Paras (ce)–(ch) inserted by the Employment Tribunals Act 1996 (Tribunal Composition) Order 2009, SI 2009/789, art 2.

Sub-s (4): words in square brackets inserted by the Tribunals, Courts and Enforcement Act 2007, s 48(1), Sch 8, paras 35, 38.

Sub-s (5): words in square brackets substituted by the Employment Rights (Dispute Resolution) Act 1998, ss 1(2)(a), 15, Sch 1, para 12(1), (4).

Sub-s (6): words in first and second pairs of square brackets substituted by the Employment Rights (Dispute Resolution) Act 1998, ss 1(2)(a), 15, Sch 1, para 12(1), (4); words in final pair of square brackets inserted by the Tribunals, Courts and Enforcement Act 2007, s 48(1), Sch 8, paras 35, 37.

Sub-ss (6A)–(6C): inserted by the Employment Rights (Dispute Resolution) Act 1998, ss 3(6), 5; words in square brackets in sub-ss (6A), (6B) inserted by the Tribunals, Courts and Enforcement Act 2007, s 48(1), Sch 8, paras 35, 37.

Sub-s (6D): inserted by the Enterprise and Regulatory Reform Act 2013, s 11(1), as from 25 April 2013 (for enabling the exercise on or after that date of any power to make provision by regulations made by statutory instrument), and as from a day to be appointed (otherwise).

Sub-s (7): repealed by the Employment Relations Act 1999, ss 41, 44, Sch 8, para 2, Sch 9(12).

Regulations: the Employment Tribunals (Constitution and Rules of Procedure) Regulations 2013, SI 2013/1237 at **[2.1323]** (made under sub-ss (6), (6A)). As to previous Regulations made under this section, see further the note to s 1 *ante*, and note that Regulations made under this section which amended the 2004 Regulations are spent.

Orders: the Employment Tribunals Act 1996 (Tribunal Composition) Order 2009, SI 2009/789; the Employment Tribunals Act 1996 (Tribunal Composition) Order 2012, SI 2012/988 (both of which were made under sub-s (4), and amend sub-s (3) above).

[1.734]

5 Remuneration, fees and allowances

(1) The Secretary of State may pay to—

(a) the [President of the Employment Tribunals (England and Wales)],

(b) the [President of the Employment Tribunals (Scotland)], . . .

[(c) any person who is an Employment Judge on a full-time basis, and]

[(d) any person who is a legal officer appointed in accordance with such regulations,]

such remuneration as he may with the consent of the Treasury determine.

(2) The Secretary of State may pay to—

(a) members of [employment tribunals],

(b) any assessors appointed for the purposes of proceedings before [employment tribunals], and

(c) any persons required for the purposes of section [131(2) of the Equality Act 2010] to prepare reports,,

such fees and allowances as he may with the consent of the Treasury determine.

(3) The Secretary of State may pay to any other persons such allowances as he may with the consent of the Treasury determine for the purposes of, or in connection with, their attendance at [employment tribunals].

NOTES

Sub-s (1): words in first and second pairs of square brackets substituted, word omitted from para (b) repealed, and para (d) inserted, by the Employment Rights (Dispute Resolution) Act 1998, ss 1(2)(d), (e), 15, Sch 1, para 13, Sch 2; para (c) substituted by the Tribunals, Courts and Enforcement Act 2007, s 48(1), Sch 8, paras 35, 39.

Sub-s (2): words in square brackets in para (c) substituted by the Equality Act 2010, s 211(1), Sch 26, Pt 1, paras 27, 28; other words in square brackets substituted by the Employment Rights (Dispute Resolution) Act 1998, s 1(2)(b).

Sub-s (3): words in square brackets substituted by the Employment Rights (Dispute Resolution) Act 1998, s 1(2)(b).

[1.735]
[5A Training etc

The Senior President of Tribunals is responsible, within the resources made available by the Lord Chancellor, for the maintenance of appropriate arrangements for the training, guidance and welfare of members of panels of members of employment tribunals (in their capacities as members of such panels, whether or not panels of [Employment Judges]).]

NOTES

Inserted, together with ss 5B–5D, by the Tribunals, Courts and Enforcement Act 2007, s 48(1), Sch 8, paras 35, 40.

Words in square brackets substituted by the Crime and Courts Act 2013, s 21(4), Sch 14, Pt 7, para 13(1).

[1.736]
[5B Members of employment tribunals: removal from office

(1) Any power by which the President of the Employment Tribunals (England and Wales) may be removed from that office may be exercised only with the concurrence of the Lord Chief Justice of England and Wales.

(2) Any power by which the President of the Employment Tribunals (Scotland) may be removed from that office may be exercised only with the concurrence of the Lord President of the Court of Session.

(3) Any power by which a member of a panel may be removed from membership of the panel—

(a) may, if the person exercises functions wholly or mainly in Scotland, be exercised only with the concurrence of the Lord President of the Court of Session;

(b) may, if paragraph (a) does not apply, be exercised only with the concurrence of the Lord Chief Justice of England and Wales.

(4) In subsection (3) "panel" means—

(a) a panel of [Employment Judges], or

(b) any other panel of members of employment tribunals,

which is appointed in accordance with regulations made under section 1(1).

(5) The Lord Chief Justice of England and Wales may nominate a judicial office holder (as defined in section 109(4) of the Constitutional Reform Act 2005) to exercise his functions under this section.

(6) The Lord President of the Court of Session may nominate a judge of the Court of Session who is a member of the First or Second Division of the Inner House of that Court to exercise his functions under this section.]

NOTES

Inserted as noted to s 5A at **[1.735]**.

Sub-s (4): words in square brackets substituted by the Crime and Courts Act 2013, s 21(4), Sch 14, Pt 7, para 13(1).

[1.737]
[5C Oaths

(1) Subsection (2) applies to a person ("the appointee")—

(a) who is appointed—

(i) as President of the Employment Tribunals (England and Wales),

(ii) as President of the Employment Tribunals (Scotland), or

(iii) as a member of a panel (as defined in section 5B(4)), and

(b) who has not previously taken the required oaths after accepting another office.

(2) The appointee must take the required oaths before—

(a) the Senior President of Tribunals, or

(b) an eligible person who is nominated by the Senior President of Tribunals for the purpose of taking the oaths from the appointee.

(3) If the appointee is a President or panel member appointed before the coming into force of this section, the requirement in subsection (2) applies in relation to the appointee from the coming into force of this section.

(4) A person is eligible for the purposes of subsection (2)(b) if one or more of the following paragraphs applies to him—

(a) he holds high judicial office (as defined in section 60(2) of the Constitutional Reform Act 2005);

(b) he holds judicial office (as defined in section 109(4) of that Act);

(c) he holds (in Scotland) the office of sheriff.

(5) In this section "the required oaths" means—

(a) the oath of allegiance, and

(b) the judicial oath,

as set out in the Promissory Oaths Act 1868.]

NOTES

Inserted as noted to s 5A at **[1.735]**.

[1.738]

[5D Judicial assistance

(1) Subsection (2) applies where regulations under section 1(1) make provision for a relevant tribunal judge, or a relevant judge, to be able by virtue of his office to act as a member of a panel of members of employment tribunals.

(2) The provision has effect only if—

(a) the persons in relation to whom the provision operates have to be persons nominated for the purposes of the provision by the Senior President of Tribunals,

(b) its operation in relation to a panel established for England and Wales in any particular case requires the consent of the President of Employment Tribunals (England and Wales),

(c) its operation in relation to a panel established for Scotland in any particular case requires the consent of the President of Employment Tribunals (Scotland),

(d) its operation as respects a particular relevant judge requires—

(i) the consent of the relevant judge, and

(ii) the appropriate consent (see subsection (3)) [except where the relevant judge is the Lord Chief Justice of England and Wales], and

(e) it operates as respects a relevant tribunal judge or a relevant judge only for the purpose of enabling him to act as a member of a panel of [Employment Judges].

(3) In subsection (2)(d)(ii) "the appropriate consent" means—

(a) the consent of the Lord Chief Justice of England and Wales where the relevant judge is—

(i) [the Master of the Rolls or] an ordinary judge of the Court of Appeal in England and Wales,

[(ia) within subsection (4)(b)(ia),]

(ii) a puisne judge of the High Court in England and Wales,

(iii) a circuit judge,

(iv) a district judge in England and Wales, . . .

(v) a District Judge (Magistrates' Courts); [or

(vi) within subsection (4)(b)(x) to (xvi);]

(b) the consent of the Lord President of the Court of Session where the relevant judge is—

(i) a judge of the Court of Session, or

(ii) a sheriff;

(c) the consent of the Lord Chief Justice of Northern Ireland where the relevant judge is—

(i) a Lord Justice of Appeal in Northern Ireland,

(ii) a puisne judge of the High Court in Northern Ireland,

(iii) a county court judge in Northern Ireland, or

(iv) a district judge in Northern Ireland.

(4) In this section—

(a) "relevant tribunal judge" means—

(i) a person who is a judge of the First-tier Tribunal by virtue of appointment under paragraph 1(1) of Schedule 2 to the Tribunals, Courts and Enforcement Act 2007,

(ii) a transferred-in judge of the First-tier Tribunal,

(iii) a person who is a judge of the Upper Tribunal by virtue of appointment under paragraph 1(1) of Schedule 3 to that Act,

(iv) a transferred-in judge of the Upper Tribunal,

(v) a deputy judge of the Upper Tribunal, . . .

(vi) a person who is the Chamber President of a chamber of the First-tier Tribunal, or of a chamber of the Upper Tribunal, and does not fall within any of sub-paragraphs (i) to (v)[, or

(vii) is the Senior President of Tribunals;]

(b) "relevant judge" means a person who—

(i) is [the Lord Chief Justice of England and Wales, the Master of the Rolls or] an ordinary judge of the Court of Appeal in England and Wales (including the vice-president, if any, of either division of that Court),

[(ia) is the President of the Queen's Bench Division or Family Division, or the Chancellor, of the High Court in England and Wales,]

(ii) is a Lord Justice of Appeal in Northern Ireland,

(iii) is a judge of the Court of Session,

(iv) is a puisne judge of the High Court in England and Wales or Northern Ireland,

(v) is a circuit judge,

(vi) is a sheriff in Scotland,

(vii) is a county court judge in Northern Ireland,

(viii) is a district judge in England and Wales or Northern Ireland, . . .

(ix) is a District Judge (Magistrates' Courts),

[(x) is a deputy judge of the High Court in England and Wales,

(xi) is a Recorder,

(xii) is a Deputy District Judge (Magistrates' Courts),

(xiii) is a deputy district judge appointed under section 8 of the County Courts Act 1984 or section 102 of the Senior Courts Act 1981,

(xiv) holds an office listed in the first column of the table in section 89(3C) of the Senior Courts Act 1981 (senior High Court Masters etc),

(xv) holds an office listed in column 1 of Part 2 of Schedule 2 to that Act (High Court Masters etc), or

(xvi) is the Judge Advocate General or a person appointed under section 30(1)(a) or (b) of the Courts-Martial (Appeals) Act 1951 (assistants to the Judge Advocate General).]

(5) References in subsection (4)(b)(iii) to (ix) to office-holders do not include deputies or temporary office-holders.]

NOTES

Inserted as noted to s 5A at **[1.735]**.

Sub-s (2): words in square brackets in sub-para (d)(ii) inserted by the Crime and Courts Act 2013, s 21(4), Sch 14, Pt 6, para 12(1), (2); words in square brackets in para (e) substituted by s 21(4) of, and Sch 14, Pt 7, para 13(1) to, the 2013 Act.

Sub-ss (3), (4): words in square brackets inserted, and word omitted repealed, by the Crime and Courts Act 2013, s 21(4), Sch 14, Pt 6, para 12(1), (3)–(7).

Procedure

[1.739]

6 Conduct of hearings

(1) A person may appear before an [employment tribunal] in person or be represented by—

(a) counsel or a solicitor,

(b) a representative of a trade union or an employers' association, or

(c) any other person whom he desires to represent him.

(2) [Nothing in any of sections 1 to 15 of and schedule 1 to the Arbitration (Scotland) Act 2010 or] [Part I of the Arbitration Act 1996] [applies] to any proceedings before an [employment tribunal].

NOTES

Sub-s (1): words in square brackets substituted by the Employment Rights (Dispute Resolution) Act 1998, s 1(2)(a).

Sub-s (2): words in first pair of square brackets inserted, and word in third pair of square brackets substituted, by the Arbitration (Scotland) Act 2010 (Consequential Amendments) Order 2010, SSI 2010/220, art 2, Schedule, para 7; words in second pair of square brackets substituted by the Arbitration Act 1996, s 107(1), Sch 3, para 62; words in final pair of square brackets substituted by the Employment Rights (Dispute Resolution) Act 1998, s 1(2)(a).

[1.740]

7 [Employment tribunal] procedure regulations

(1) The Secretary of State may by regulations ("[employment tribunal] procedure regulations") make such provision as appears to him to be necessary or expedient with respect to proceedings before [employment tribunals].

(2) Proceedings before [employment tribunals] shall be instituted in accordance with [employment tribunal] procedure regulations.

(3) [Employment tribunal] procedure regulations may, in particular, include provision—

(a) for determining by which tribunal any proceedings are to be determined,

(b) for enabling an [employment tribunal] to hear and determine proceedings brought by virtue of section 3 concurrently with proceedings brought before the tribunal otherwise than by virtue of that section,

(c) for treating the Secretary of State (either generally or in such circumstances as may be prescribed by the regulations) as a party to any proceedings before an [employment tribunal] (where he would not otherwise be a party to them) and entitling him to appear and to be heard accordingly,

(d) for requiring persons to attend to give evidence and produce documents and for authorising the administration of oaths to witnesses,

(e) for enabling an [employment tribunal], on the application of any party to the proceedings before it or of its own motion, to order—

(i) in England and Wales, such discovery or inspection of documents, or the furnishing of such further particulars, as might be ordered by [the county court] on application by a party to proceedings before it, or

(ii) in Scotland, such recovery or inspection of documents as might be ordered by a sheriff,

(f) for prescribing the procedure to be followed in any proceedings before an [employment tribunal], including provision—

(i) . . .

[(ia) for postponing fixing a time and place for a hearing, or postponing a time fixed for a hearing, for such period as may be determined in accordance with the regulations for the purpose of giving an opportunity for the proceedings to be settled by way of conciliation and withdrawn, and]

(ii) for enabling an [employment tribunal] to review its decisions, and revoke or vary its orders and awards, in such circumstances as may be determined in accordance with the regulations,

(g) for the appointment of one or more assessors for the purposes of any proceedings before an [employment tribunal], where the proceedings are brought under an enactment which provides for one or more assessors to be appointed,

(h) for authorising an [employment tribunal] to require persons to furnish information and produce documents to a person required for the purposes of section [131(2) of the Equality Act 2010] to prepare a report, and

(j) for the registration and proof of decisions, orders and awards of [employment tribunals].

[(3ZA) Employment tribunal procedure regulations may—

(a) authorise the Secretary of State to prescribe, or prescribe requirements in relation to, any form which is required by such regulations to be used for the purpose of instituting, or entering an appearance to, proceedings before employment tribunals,
(b) authorise the Secretary of State to prescribe requirements in relation to documents to be supplied with any such form [(including certificates issued under section 18A(4))], and
(c) make provision about the publication of anything prescribed under authority conferred by virtue of this subsection.]

[(3ZB) Provision in employment tribunal procedure regulations about postponement of hearings may include provision for limiting the number of relevant postponements available to a party to proceedings.

(3ZC) For the purposes of subsection (3ZB)—
(a) "relevant postponement", in relation to a party to proceedings, means the postponement of a hearing granted on the application of that party in—,
(i) the proceedings, or
(ii) any other proceedings identified in accordance with the regulations,
except in circumstances determined in accordance with the regulations, and
(b) "postponement" includes adjournment.]

[(3A) Employment tribunal procedure regulations may authorise the determination of proceedings without any hearing in such circumstances as the regulations may prescribe.]

[(3AA) Employment tribunal procedure regulations under subsection (3A) may only authorise the determination of proceedings without any hearing in circumstances where—
(a) all the parties to the proceedings consent in writing to the determination without a hearing, or
(b) the person (or, where more than one, each of the persons) against whom the proceedings are brought—
(i) has presented no response in the proceedings, or
(ii) does not contest the case.

(3AB) For the purposes of subsection (3AA)(b), a person does not present a response in the proceedings if he presents a response but, in accordance with provision made by the regulations, it is not accepted.]

(3B) Employment tribunal procedure regulations may authorise the determination of proceedings without hearing anyone other than the person or persons by whom the proceedings are brought (or his or their representatives) where—
(a) the person (or, where more than one, each of the persons) against whom the proceedings are brought has done nothing to contest the case, or
(b) it appears from the application made by the person (or, where more than one, each of the persons) bringing the proceedings that he is not (or they are not) seeking any relief which an employment tribunal has power to give or that he is not (or they are not) entitled to any such relief.

(3C) Employment tribunal procedure regulations may authorise the determination of proceedings without hearing anyone other than the person or persons by whom, and the person or persons against whom, the proceedings are brought (or his or their representatives) where—
(a) an employment tribunal is on undisputed facts bound by the decision of a court in another case to dismiss the case of the person or persons by whom, or of the person or persons against whom, the proceedings are brought, or
(b) the proceedings relate only to a preliminary issue which may be heard and determined in accordance with regulations under section 9(4).]

(4) A person who without reasonable excuse fails to comply with—
(a) any requirement imposed by virtue of subsection (3)(d) or (h), or
(b) any requirement with respect to the discovery, recovery or inspection of documents imposed by virtue of subsection (3)(e)[, or
(c) any requirement imposed by virtue of employment tribunal procedure regulations to give written answers for the purpose of facilitating the determination of proceedings as mentioned in subsection (3A), (3B) or (3C),]
is guilty of an offence and liable on summary conviction to a fine not exceeding level 3 on the standard scale.

(5) Subject to any regulations under section 11(1)(a), [employment tribunal] procedure regulations may include provision authorising or requiring an [employment tribunal], in circumstances specified in the regulations, to send notice or a copy of—
(a) any document specified in the regulations which relates to any proceedings before the tribunal, or
(b) any decision, order or award of the tribunal,
to any government department or other person or body so specified.

(6) Where in accordance with [employment tribunal] procedure regulations an [employment tribunal] determines in the same proceedings—
(a) a complaint presented under section 111 of the Employment Rights Act 1996, and
(b) a question referred under section 163 of that Act,
subsection (2) of that section has no effect for the purposes of the proceedings in so far as they relate to the complaint under section 111.

NOTES

Section heading, sub-ss (1), (2), (5), (6): words in square brackets substituted by the Employment Rights (Dispute Resolution) Act 1998, s 1(2)(a), (b).

Sub-s (3): words in square brackets in para (e) substituted by the Crime and Courts Act 2013, s 17(5), Sch 9, Pt 3, para 52; sub-para (f)(ia) inserted by the Employment Act 2002, s 24(1); words in square brackets in para (h) substituted by the Equality

Act 2010, s 211(1), Sch 26, Pt 1, paras 27, 29; other words in square brackets substituted, and sub-para (f)(i) repealed, by the Employment Rights (Dispute Resolution) Act 1998, ss 1(2)(a), (b), 15, Sch 1, para 14(1), (2), Sch 2.

Sub-s (3ZA): inserted by the Employment Act 2002, s 25; words in square brackets in para (b) inserted by the Enterprise and Regulatory Reform Act 2013, s 7(2), Sch 1, paras 2, 3.

Sub-ss (3ZB), (3ZC): inserted by the Small Business, Enterprise and Employment Act 2015, s 151(1), (2), as from 26 March 2015.

Sub-ss (3A), (3B): inserted, together with sub-s (3C), by the Employment Rights (Dispute Resolution) Act 1998, s 2.

Sub-ss (3AA), (3AB): inserted by the Employment Act 2008, s 4.

Sub-s (3C): inserted as noted above; substituted by the Employment Act 2002, s 26.

Sub-s (4): para (c) and the word immediately preceding it inserted by the Employment Rights (Dispute Resolution) Act 1998, s 15, Sch 1, para 14(1), (3).

Note: sub-s (3) did not contain a para (i) in the Queen's Printer's copy of this Act.

Regulations: the Employment Tribunals (Enforcement of Orders in Other Jurisdictions) (Scotland) Regulations 2002, SI 2002/2972 at **[2.676]**; the Employment Tribunals (Constitution and Rules of Procedure) Regulations 2013, SI 2013/1237 at **[2.1323]**; the Employment Tribunals (Constitution and Rules of Procedure) (Consequential Amendments) Regulations 2013, SI 2013/1948; the Employment Tribunals (Constitution and Rules of Procedure) (Amendment) Regulations 2014, SI 2014/271; the Employment Tribunals (Constitution and Rules of Procedure) (Amendment) (No 2) Regulations 2014, SI 2014/611; the Employment Tribunals (Constitution and Rules of Procedure) (Amendment) (No 3) Regulations 2014, SI 2014/787; the Employment Tribunals (Constitution and Rules of Procedure) (Amendment) Regulations 2016, SI 2016/271. As to previous Regulations made under this section, see further the note to s 1 *ante*, and note that Regulations made under this section which amended the 2004 Regulations are spent.

[1.741]

[7A Practice directions

[(A1) The Senior President of Tribunals may make directions about the procedure of employment tribunals.]

(1) Employment tribunal procedure regulations may include provision—

(a) enabling the [territorial] President to make directions about the procedure of employment tribunals, including directions about the exercise by tribunals of powers under such regulations,

(b) for securing compliance with [directions under subsection (A1) or paragraph (a)], and

(c) about the publication of [directions under subsection (A1) or paragraph (a)].

(2) Employment tribunal procedure regulations may, instead of providing for any matter, refer to provision made or to be made about that matter by directions made [under subsection (A1) or (1)(a)].

[(2A) The power under subsection (A1) includes—

(a) power to vary or revoke directions made in exercise of the power, and

(b) power to make different provision for different purposes (including different provision for different areas).

(2B) Directions under subsection (A1) may not be made without the approval of the Lord Chancellor.

(2C) Directions under subsection (1)(a) may not be made without the approval of—

(a) the Senior President of Tribunals, and

(b) the Lord Chancellor.

(2D) Subsections (2B) and (2C)(b) do not apply to directions to the extent that they consist of guidance about any of the following—

(a) the application or interpretation of the law;

(b) the making of decisions by members of an employment tribunal.

(2E) Subsections (2B) and (2C)(b) do not apply to directions to the extent that they consist of criteria for determining which members of employment tribunals may be selected to decide particular categories of matter; but the directions may, to that extent, be made only after consulting the Lord Chancellor.]

(3) In this section, references to the [territorial] President are to a person appointed in accordance with regulations under section 1(1) as—

(a) President of the Employment Tribunals (England and Wales), or

(b) President of the Employment Tribunals (Scotland).]

NOTES

Inserted by the Employment Act 2002, s 27.

Sub-ss (A1), (2A)–(2E): inserted by the Tribunals, Courts and Enforcement Act 2007, s 48(1), Sch 8, paras 35, 41(1), (2), (5).

Sub-s (1): word in square brackets in para (a) inserted, and words in square brackets in paras (b), (c) substituted, by the Tribunals, Courts and Enforcement Act 2007, s 48(1), Sch 8, paras 35, 41(1), (3).

Sub-s (2): words in square brackets substituted by the Tribunals, Courts and Enforcement Act 2007, s 48(1), Sch 8, paras 35, 41(1), (4).

Sub-s (3): word in square brackets inserted by the Tribunals, Courts and Enforcement Act 2007, s 48(1), Sch 8, paras 35, 41(1), (6).

Regulations: the Employment Tribunals (Constitution and Rules of Procedure) Regulations 2013, SI 2013/1237 at **[2.1323]**. As to previous Regulations made under this section, see further the note to s 1 *ante*.

Directions under sub-s (A1): as at 15 May 2019, no directions have been made under sub-s (A1).

[1.742]

[7B Mediation

(1) Employment tribunal procedure regulations may include provision enabling practice directions to provide for members to act as mediators in relation to disputed matters in a case that is the subject of proceedings.

(2) The provision that may be included in employment tribunal procedure regulations by virtue of subsection (1) includes provision for enabling practice directions to provide for a member to act as mediator in relation to disputed matters in a case even though the member has been selected to decide matters in the case.

(3) Once a member has begun to act as mediator in relation to a disputed matter in a case that is the subject of proceedings, the member may decide matters in the case only with the consent of the parties.

(4) Staff appointed under section 40(1) of the Tribunals, Courts and Enforcement Act 2007 (staff for employment and other tribunals) may, subject to their terms of appointment, act as mediators in relation to disputed matters in a case that is the subject of proceedings.

(5) Before making a practice direction that makes provision in relation to mediation, the person making the direction must consult [ACAS].

(6) In this section—

"member" means a member of a panel of members of employment tribunals (whether or not a panel of [Employment Judges];

"practice direction" means a direction under section 7A;

"proceedings" means proceedings before an employment tribunal.]

NOTES

Inserted by the Tribunals, Courts and Enforcement Act 2007, s 48(1), Sch 8, paras 35, 42.

Sub-s (5): reference to "ACAS" in square brackets substituted by the Enterprise and Regulatory Reform Act 2013, s 7(2), Sch 1, paras 2, 4.

Sub-s (6): words in square brackets substituted by the Crime and Courts Act 2013, s 21(4), Sch 14, Pt 7, para 13(1).

Regulations: the Employment Tribunals (Constitution and Rules of Procedure) Regulations 2013, SI 2013/1237 at **[2.1323]**.

[1.743]

8 Procedure in contract cases

(1) Where in proceedings brought by virtue of section 3 an [employment tribunal] finds that the whole or part of a sum claimed in the proceedings is due, the tribunal shall order the respondent to the proceedings to pay the amount which it finds due.

(2) An order under section 3 may provide that an [employment tribunal] shall not in proceedings in respect of a claim, or a number of claims relating to the same contract, order the payment of an amount exceeding such sum as may be specified in the order as the maximum amount which an [employment tribunal] may order to be paid in relation to a claim or in relation to a contract.

(3) An order under section 3 may include provisions—

(a) as to the manner in which and time within which proceedings are to be brought by virtue of that section, and

(b) modifying any other enactment.

(4) An order under that section may make different provision in relation to proceedings in respect of different descriptions of claims.

NOTES

Sub-ss (1), (2): words in square brackets substituted by the Employment Rights (Dispute Resolution) Act 1998, s 1(2)(a).

The sum specified for the purposes of sub-s (2) is £25,000, see the Employment Tribunals Extension of Jurisdiction (England and Wales) Order 1994, SI 1994/1623, art 10 at **[2.226]**, and the Employment Tribunals Extension of Jurisdiction (Scotland) Order 1994, SI 1994/1624, art 10 at **[2.238]**.

[1.744]

9 Pre-hearing reviews and preliminary matters

(1) [Employment tribunal] procedure regulations may include provision—

(a) for authorising the carrying-out by an [employment tribunal] of a preliminary consideration of any proceedings before it (a "pre-hearing review"), and

(b) for enabling such powers to be exercised in connection with a pre-hearing review as may be prescribed by the regulations.

(2) Such regulations may in particular include provision—

(a) for authorising any tribunal carrying out a pre-hearing review under the regulations to make, in circumstances specified in the regulations, an order requiring a party to the proceedings in question . . . to pay a deposit of an amount not exceeding [£1,000] [as a condition of

(i) continuing to participate in those proceedings, or

(ii) pursuing any specified allegations or arguments], and

(b) for prescribing—

(i) the manner in which the amount of any such deposit is to be determined in any particular case,

(ii) the consequences of non-payment of any such deposit, and

(iii) the circumstances in which any such deposit, or any part of it, may be refunded to the party who paid it or be paid over to another party to the proceedings.

[(2A) Regulations under subsection (1)(b), so far as relating to striking out, may not provide for striking out on a ground which does not apply outside a pre-hearing review.]

(3) The Secretary of State may from time to time by order substitute for the sum specified in subsection (2)(a) such other sum as is specified in the order.

(4) [Employment tribunal] procedure regulations may also include provision for authorising an [employment tribunal] to hear and determine [separately any preliminary issue of a description prescribed by the regulations which is raised by any case].

NOTES

Sub-s (1): words in square brackets substituted by the Employment Rights (Dispute Resolution) Act 1998, s 1(2)(a); para (a) substituted by the Employment Act 2002, s 28(1), (2), as from a day to be appointed, as follows—

"(a) for authorising an employment tribunal to carry out a review of any proceedings before it at any time before a hearing held for the purpose of determining them (a "pre-hearing review"),".

Sub-s (2): words omitted repealed, and words in second pair of square brackets inserted, by the Enterprise and Regulatory Reform Act 2013, s 21(1), (2); sum in first pair of square brackets in para (a) substituted by the Employment Tribunals (Increase of Maximum Deposit) Order 2012, SI 2012/149, art 2.

Sub-s (2A): inserted by the Employment Act 2002, s 28(1), (3).

Sub-s (4): words in square brackets substituted by the Employment Rights (Dispute Resolution) Act 1998, ss 1(2)(a), 15, Sch 1, para 15.

Regulations: the Employment Tribunals (Constitution and Rules of Procedure) Regulations 2013, SI 2013/1237 at **[2.1323]**. As to previous Regulations made under this section, see further the note to s 1 *ante*, and note that Regulations made under this section which amended the 2004 Regulations are spent.

Orders: the Employment Tribunals (Increase of Maximum Deposit) Order 2012, SI 2012/149 (which supersedes previous Orders made under sub-s (3) above).

[1.745]

[10 National security

(1) If on a complaint under—

[(a) section 145A, 145B or 146 of the Trade Union and Labour Relations (Consolidation) Act 1992 (inducements and detriments in respect of trade union membership etc),] . . .

(b) section 111 of the Employment Rights Act 1996 (unfair dismissal), [. . . .

(c) regulation 9 of the Employment Relations Act 1999 (Blacklists) Regulations 2010 (detriment connected with prohibited list)], [or

(d) regulation 4 of the Employment Rights Act 1996 (NHS Recruitment—Protected Disclosure) Regulations 2018 (complaint to employment tribunal),]

it is shown that the action complained of was taken for the purpose of safeguarding national security, the employment tribunal shall dismiss the complaint.

(2) Employment tribunal procedure regulations may make provision about the composition of the tribunal (including provision disapplying or modifying section 4) for the purposes of proceedings in relation to which—

(a) a direction is given under subsection (3), or

(b) an order is made under subsection (4).

(3) A direction may be given under this subsection by a Minister of the Crown if—

(a) it relates to particular Crown employment proceedings, and

(b) the Minister considers it expedient in the interests of national security.

(4) An order may be made under this subsection by the President or a Regional [Employment Judge] in relation to particular proceedings if he considers it expedient in the interests of national security.

(5) Employment tribunal procedure regulations may make provision enabling a Minister of the Crown, if he considers it expedient in the interests of national security—

(a) to direct a tribunal to sit in private for all or part of particular Crown employment proceedings;

(b) to direct a tribunal to exclude the applicant from all or part of particular Crown employment proceedings;

(c) to direct a tribunal to exclude the applicant's representatives from all or part of particular Crown employment proceedings;

(d) to direct a tribunal to take steps to conceal the identity of a particular witness in particular Crown employment proceedings;

(e) to direct a tribunal to take steps to keep secret all or part of the reasons for its decision in particular Crown employment proceedings.

[(6) Employment tribunal procedure regulations may enable a tribunal, if it considers it expedient in the interests of national security, to do in relation to particular proceedings before it anything of a kind which, by virtue of subsection (5), employment tribunal procedure regulations may enable a Minister of the Crown to direct a tribunal to do in relation to particular Crown employment proceedings.]

(7) In relation to cases where a person has been excluded by virtue of subsection (5)(b) or (c) or (6), employment tribunal procedure regulations may make provision—

(a) for the appointment by the Attorney General, or by the Advocate General for Scotland, of a person to represent the interests of the applicant;

(b) about the publication and registration of reasons for the tribunal's decision;

(c) permitting an excluded person to make a statement to the tribunal before the commencement of the proceedings, or the part of the proceedings, from which he is excluded.

(8) Proceedings are Crown employment proceedings for the purposes of this section if the employment to which the complaint relates—

(a) is Crown employment, or

(b) is connected with the performance of functions on behalf of the Crown.

(9) The reference in subsection (4) to the President or a Regional Chairman is to a person appointed in accordance with regulations under section 1(1) as—

(a) a Regional Chairman,

(b) President of the Employment Tribunals (England and Wales), or

(c) President of the Employment Tribunals (Scotland).]

NOTES

Substituted, together with ss 10A, 10B for the original s 10, by the Employment Relations Act 1999, s 41, Sch 8, para 3.

Sub-s (1): para (a) substituted by the Employment Relations Act 2004, s 57(1), Sch 1, para 24. Word omitted from para (a) repealed, and para (c) (and the word immediately preceding it) inserted, by the Employment Relations Act 1999 (Blacklists) Regulations 2010, SI 2010/493, reg 17(1), (2). Word omitted from para (b) repealed, and para (d) (and the word immediately preceding it) inserted, the Employment Rights Act 1996 (NHS Recruitment—Protected Disclosure) Regulations 2018, SI 2018/579, reg 10(1), (2), as from 23 May 2018.

Sub-s (4): words in square brackets substituted by the Crime and Courts Act 2013, s 21(4), Sch 14, Pt 7, para 13(3).

Sub-s (6): substituted by the Employment Relations Act 2004, s 36.

Attorney General: the functions of the Attorney General may be discharged by the Solicitor General; see the Law Officers Act 1997, s 1.

Regulations: the Employment Tribunals (Constitution and Rules of Procedure) Regulations 2013, SI 2013/1237 at **[2.1323]**. As to previous Regulations made under this section, see further the note to s 1 *ante*, and note that Regulations made under this section which amended the 2004 Regulations are spent.

[1.746]

[10A Confidential information

(1) Employment tribunal procedure regulations may enable an employment tribunal to sit in private for the purpose of hearing evidence from any person which in the opinion of the tribunal is likely to consist of—

- (a) information which he could not disclose without contravening a prohibition imposed by or by virtue of any enactment,
- (b) information which has been communicated to him in confidence or which he has otherwise obtained in consequence of the confidence reposed in him by another person, or
- (c) information the disclosure of which would, for reasons other than its effect on negotiations with respect to any of the matters mentioned in section 178(2) of the Trade Union and Labour Relations (Consolidation) Act 1992, cause substantial injury to any undertaking of his or in which he works.

(2) The reference in subsection (1)(c) to any undertaking of a person or in which he works shall be construed—

- (a) in relation to a person in Crown employment, as a reference to the national interest,
- (b) in relation to a person who is a relevant member of the House of Lords staff, as a reference to the national interest or (if the case so requires) the interests of the House of Lords, and
- (c) in relation to a person who is a relevant member of the House of Commons staff, as a reference to the national interest or (if the case so requires) the interests of the House of Commons.]

NOTES

Substituted as noted to s 10 at **[1.745]**.

Regulations: the Employment Tribunals (Constitution and Rules of Procedure) Regulations 2013, SI 2013/1237 at **[2.1323]**. As to previous Regulations made under this section, see further the note to s 1 *ante*.

[1.747]

[10B Restriction of publicity in cases involving national security

(1) This section applies where a tribunal has been directed under section 10(5) or has determined under section 10(6)—

- (a) to take steps to conceal the identity of a particular witness, or
- (b) to take steps to keep secret all or part of the reasons for its decision.

(2) It is an offence to publish—

- (a) anything likely to lead to the identification of the witness, or
- (b) the reasons for the tribunal's decision or the part of its reasons which it is directed or has determined to keep secret.

(3) A person guilty of an offence under this section is liable on summary conviction to a fine not exceeding level 5 on the standard scale.

(4) Where a person is charged with an offence under this section it is a defence to prove that at the time of the alleged offence he was not aware, and neither suspected nor had reason to suspect, that the publication in question was of, or included, the matter in question.

(5) Where an offence under this section committed by a body corporate is proved to have been committed with the consent or connivance of, or to be attributable to any neglect on the part of—

- (a) a director, manager, secretary or other similar officer of the body corporate, or
- (b) a person purporting to act in any such capacity,

he as well as the body corporate is guilty of the offence and liable to be proceeded against and punished accordingly.

(6) A reference in this section to publication includes a reference to inclusion in a programme which is included in a programme service, within the meaning of the Broadcasting Act 1990.]

NOTES

Substituted as noted to s 10 at **[1.745]**.

[1.748]

11 Restriction of publicity in cases involving sexual misconduct

(1) [Employment tribunal] procedure regulations may include provision—

(a) for cases involving allegations of the commission of sexual offences, for securing that the registration or other making available of documents or decisions shall be so effected as to prevent the identification of any person affected by or making the allegation, and provision—

(b) for cases involving allegations of sexual misconduct, enabling an [employment tribunal], on the application of any party to proceedings before it or of its own motion, to make a restricted reporting order having effect (if not revoked earlier) until the promulgation of the decision of the tribunal.

(2) If any identifying matter is published or included in a relevant programme in contravention of a restricted reporting order—

(a) in the case of publication in a newspaper or periodical, any proprietor, any editor and any publisher of the newspaper or periodical,

(b) in the case of publication in any other form, the person publishing the matter, and

(c) in the case of matter included in a relevant programme—

(i) any body corporate engaged in providing the service in which the programme is included, and

(ii) any person having functions in relation to the programme corresponding to those of an editor of a newspaper,

shall be guilty of an offence and liable on summary conviction to a fine not exceeding level 5 on the standard scale.

(3) Where a person is charged with an offence under subsection (2) it is a defence to prove that at the time of the alleged offence he was not aware, and neither suspected nor had reason to suspect, that the publication or programme in question was of, or included, the matter in question.

(4) Where an offence under subsection (2) committed by a body corporate is proved to have been committed with the consent or connivance of, or to be attributable to any neglect on the part of—

(a) a director, manager, secretary or other similar officer of the body corporate, or

(b) a person purporting to act in any such capacity,

he as well as the body corporate is guilty of the offence and liable to be proceeded against and punished accordingly.

(5) In relation to a body corporate whose affairs are managed by its members "director", in subsection (4), means a member of the body corporate.

(6) In this section—

"identifying matter", in relation to a person, means any matter likely to lead members of the public to identify him as a person affected by, or as the person making, the allegation,

"relevant programme" has the same meaning as in the Sexual Offences (Amendment) Act 1992,

"restricted reporting order" means an order—

(a) made in exercise of a power conferred by regulations made by virtue of this section, and

(b) prohibiting the publication in Great Britain of identifying matter in a written publication available to the public or its inclusion in a relevant programme for reception in Great Britain,

"sexual misconduct" means the commission of a sexual offence, sexual harassment or other adverse conduct (of whatever nature) related to sex, and conduct is related to sex whether the relationship with sex lies in the character of the conduct or in its having reference to the sex or sexual orientation of the person at whom the conduct is directed,

"sexual offence" means any offence to which section 4 of the Sexual Offences (Amendment) Act 1976, the Sexual Offences (Amendment) Act 1992 or section 274(2) of the Criminal Procedure (Scotland) Act 1995 applies (offences under the Sexual Offences Act 1956, Part I of the Criminal Law (Consolidation) (Scotland) Act 1995 and certain other enactments), and

"written publication" has the same meaning as in the Sexual Offences (Amendment) Act 1992.

NOTES

Sub-s (1): words in square brackets substituted by the Employment Rights (Dispute Resolution) Act 1998, s 1(2)(a).

Sexual Offences (Amendment) Act 1976, s 4: repealed by Youth Justice and Criminal Evidence Act 1999, ss 48, 67(3), Sch 2, para 4, Sch 6.

Sexual Offences (Amendment) Act 1992: the definition "written publication" in that Act was repealed by the Youth Justice and Criminal Evidence Act 1999, ss 48, 67(3), Sch 2, paras 6, 12(1), (2), Sch 6.

Regulations: the Employment Tribunals (Constitution and Rules of Procedure) Regulations 2013, SI 2013/1237 at **[2.1323]**. As to previous Regulations made under this section, see further the note to s 1 *ante*.

[1.749]

12 Restriction of publicity in disability cases

(1) This section applies to proceedings on a complaint under [section 120 of the Equality Act 2010, where the complaint relates to disability] in which evidence of a personal nature is likely to be heard by the [employment tribunal] hearing the complaint.

(2) [Employment tribunal] procedure regulations may include provision in relation to proceedings to which this section applies for—

(a) enabling an [employment tribunal], on the application of the complainant or of its own motion, to make a restricted reporting order having effect (if not revoked earlier) until the promulgation of the decision of the tribunal, and

(b) where a restricted reporting order is made in relation to a complaint which is being dealt with by the tribunal together with any other proceedings, enabling the tribunal to direct that the order is to apply also in relation to those other proceedings or such part of them as the tribunal may direct.

(3) If any identifying matter is published or included in a relevant programme in contravention of a restricted reporting order—

(a) in the case of publication in a newspaper or periodical, any proprietor, any editor and any publisher of the newspaper or periodical,

(b) in the case of publication in any other form, the person publishing the matter, and

(c) in the case of matter included in a relevant programme—

(i) any body corporate engaged in providing the service in which the programme is included, and

(ii) any person having functions in relation to the programme corresponding to those of an editor of a newspaper,

shall be guilty of an offence and liable on summary conviction to a fine not exceeding level 5 on the standard scale.

(4) Where a person is charged with an offence under subsection (3), it is a defence to prove that at the time of the alleged offence he was not aware, and neither suspected nor had reason to suspect, that the publication or programme in question was of, or included, the matter in question.

(5) Where an offence under subsection (3) committed by a body corporate is proved to have been committed with the consent or connivance of, or to be attributable to any neglect on the part of—

(a) a director, manager, secretary or other similar officer of the body corporate, or

(b) a person purporting to act in any such capacity,

he as well as the body corporate is guilty of the offence and liable to be proceeded against and punished accordingly.

(6) In relation to a body corporate whose affairs are managed by its members "director", in subsection (5), means a member of the body corporate.

(7) In this section—

"evidence of a personal nature" means any evidence of a medical, or other intimate, nature which might reasonably be assumed to be likely to cause significant embarrassment to the complainant if reported,

"identifying matter" means any matter likely to lead members of the public to identify the complainant or such other persons (if any) as may be named in the order,

"promulgation" has such meaning as may be prescribed by regulations made by virtue of this section,

"relevant programme" means a programme included in a programme service, within the meaning of the Broadcasting Act 1990,

"restricted reporting order" means an order—

(a) made in exercise of a power conferred by regulations made by virtue of this section, and

(b) prohibiting the publication in Great Britain of identifying matter in a written publication available to the public or its inclusion in a relevant programme for reception in Great Britain, and

"written publication" includes a film, a sound track and any other record in permanent form but does not include an indictment or other document prepared for use in particular legal proceedings.

NOTES

Sub-s (1): words in first pair of square brackets substituted by the Equality Act 2010, s 211(1), Sch 26, Pt 1, paras 27, 30; words in second pair of square brackets substituted by the Employment Rights (Dispute Resolution) Act 1998, s 1(2)(a).

Sub-s (2): words in square brackets substituted by the Employment Rights (Dispute Resolution) Act 1998, s 1(2)(a).

Regulations: the Employment Tribunals (Constitution and Rules of Procedure) Regulations 2013, SI 2013/1237 at **[2.1323]**. As to previous Regulations made under this section, see further the note to s 1 *ante*.

[Financial penalties

[1.750]

12A Financial penalties

(1) Where an employment tribunal determining a claim involving an employer and a worker—

(a) concludes that the employer has breached any of the worker's rights to which the claim relates, and

(b) is of the opinion that the breach has one or more aggravating features,

the tribunal may order the employer to pay a penalty to the Secretary of State (whether or not it also makes a financial award against the employer on the claim).

(2) The tribunal shall have regard to an employer's ability to pay—

(a) in deciding whether to order the employer to pay a penalty under this section;

(b) (subject to subsections (3) to (7)) in deciding the amount of a penalty.

(3) The amount of a penalty under this section shall be—

(a) at least £100;

(b) no more than [£20,000].

This subsection does not apply where subsection (5) or (7) applies.

(4) Subsection (5) applies where an employment tribunal—

(a) makes a financial award against an employer on a claim, and

(b) also orders the employer to pay a penalty under this section in respect of the claim.

(5) In such a case, the amount of the penalty under this section shall be 50% of the amount of the award, except that—

(a) if the amount of the financial award is less than £200, the amount of the penalty shall be £100;

(b) if the amount of the financial award is more than [£40,000], the amount of the penalty shall be [£20,000].

(6) Subsection (7) applies, instead of subsection (5), where an employment tribunal—

(a) considers together two or more claims involving different workers but the same employer, and

(b) orders the employer to pay a penalty under this section in respect of any of those claims.

(7) In such a case—

(a) the amount of the penalties in total shall be at least £100;

(b) the amount of a penalty in respect of a particular claim shall be—

(i) no more than [£20,000], and

(ii) where the tribunal makes a financial award against the employer on the claim, no more than 50% of the amount of the award.

But where the tribunal makes a financial award on any of the claims and the amount awarded is less than £200 in total, the amount of the penalties in total shall be £100 (and paragraphs (a) and (b) shall not apply).

(8) Two or more claims in respect of the same act and the same worker shall be treated as a single claim for the purposes of this section.

(9) Subsection (5) or (7) does not require or permit an order under subsection (1) (or a failure to make such an order) to be reviewed where the tribunal subsequently awards compensation under—

(a) section 140(3) of the Trade Union and Labour Relations (Consolidation) Act 1992 (failure to comply with tribunal's recommendation),

(b) section 117 of the Employment Rights Act 1996 (failure to reinstate etc),

(c) section 124(7) of the Equality Act 2010 (failure to comply with tribunal's recommendation), or

(d) any other provision empowering the tribunal to award compensation, or further compensation, for a failure to comply (or to comply fully) with an order or recommendation of the tribunal.

(10) An employer's liability to pay a penalty under this section is discharged if 50% of the amount of the penalty is paid no later than 21 days after the day on which notice of the decision to impose the penalty is sent to the employer.

(11) In this section—

"claim"—

(a) means anything that is referred to in the relevant legislation as a claim, a complaint or a reference, other than a reference made by virtue of section 122(2) or 128(2) of the Equality Act 2010 (reference by court of question about a non-discrimination or equality rule etc), and

(b) also includes an application, under regulations made under section 45 of the Employment Act 2002, for a declaration that a person is a permanent employee;

"employer" has the same meaning as in Part 4A of the Employment Rights Act 1996, and also—

(a) in relation to an individual seeking to be employed by a person as a worker, includes that person;

(b) in relation to a right conferred by section 47A or 63A of the Employment Rights Act 1996 (right to time off for young person for study or training), includes the principal within the meaning of section 63A(3) of that Act;

(c) in relation to a right conferred by the Agency Workers Regulations 2010 (SI 2010/93), includes the hirer within the meaning of those Regulations and (where the worker is not actually employed by the temporary work agency) the temporary work agency within that meaning;

"financial award" means an award of a sum of money, but does not including anything payable by virtue of section 13;

"worker" has the same meaning as in Part 4A of the Employment Rights Act 1996, and also includes an individual seeking to be employed by a person as a worker.

(12) The Secretary of State may by order—

(a) amend subsection (3), (5) or (7) by substituting a different amount;

(b) amend subsection (5), (7) or (10) by substituting a different percentage;

(c) amend this section so as to alter the meaning of "claim".

[(12A) Any provision that could be made by an order under subsection (12) may instead—

(a) in the case of provision that could be made under paragraph (a) or (b) of that subsection, be included in regulations under section 37N;

(b) in the case of provision that could be made under paragraph (c) of that subsection, be included in regulations under section 37Q.]

(13) The Secretary of State shall pay sums received under this section into the Consolidated Fund.]

NOTES

Inserted, together with preceding heading, by the Enterprise and Regulatory Reform Act 2013, s 16(1).

Sub-ss (3), (7): the sum "£20,000" in square brackets was substituted for the original sum "£5,000", by the Employment Rights (Miscellaneous Amendments) Regulations 2019, SI 2019/731, reg 2(1), (2), (4), as from 6 April 2019, in relation to a penalty payable in respect of a breach of a worker's rights which begins on or after that date; see reg 3 of the 2019 Regulations at **[2.2196]**.

Sub-s (5): the sums "£40,000" and £20,000" in square brackets were substituted for the original sums "£10,000" and "£5,000" respectively, by SI 2019/731, reg 2(1), (3), as from 6 April 2019, in relation to a penalty payable in respect of a breach of a worker's rights which begins on or after that date; see reg 3 of the 2019 Regulations at **[2.2196]**.

Sub-s (12A): inserted by the Small Business, Enterprise and Employment Act 2015, s 150(1), (3), as from 6 April 2016, in relation to relevant sums where (a) in the case of a financial award, the decision of the employment tribunal on the claim to which the financial award relates is made on or after the day on which this amendment comes into force; (b) in the case of a settlement sum, the certificate under s 19A(1) of this Act in respect of the settlement under whose terms it is payable is issued on or after that day (see s 150 of the 2015 Act at **[1.1926]**).

Orders: the Employment Rights (Miscellaneous Amendments) Regulations 2019, SI 2019/731 at **[2.2195]**.

[Costs etc, interest and enforcement]

NOTES

Above heading inserted by the Enterprise and Regulatory Reform Act 2013, s 16(2), Sch 3, paras 2, 3.

[1.751]

13 Costs and expenses

[(1) Employment tribunal procedure regulations may include provision—

(a) for the award of costs or expenses;

(b) for the award of any allowances payable under section 5(2)(c) or (3).

(1A) Regulations under subsection (1) may include provision authorising an employment tribunal to have regard to a person's ability to pay when considering the making of an award against him under such regulations.

(1B) Employment tribunal procedure regulations may include provision for authorising an employment tribunal—

(a) to disallow all or part of the costs or expenses of a representative of a party to proceedings before it by reason of that representative's conduct of the proceedings;

(b) to order a representative of a party to proceedings before it to meet all or part of the costs or expenses incurred by a party by reason of the representative's conduct of the proceedings;

(c) to order a representative of a party to proceedings before it to meet all or part of any allowances payable by the Secretary of State under section 5(2)(c) or (3) by reason of the representative's conduct of the proceedings.

(1C) Employment tribunal procedure regulations may also include provision for taxing or otherwise settling the costs or expenses referred to in subsection (1)(a) or (1B)(b) (and, in particular in England and Wales, for enabling the amount of such costs to be assessed by way of detailed assessment in [the county court]).]

(2) In relation to proceedings under section 111 of the Employment Rights Act 1996—

(a) where the employee has expressed a wish to be reinstated or re-engaged which has been communicated to the employer at least seven days before the hearing of the complaint, . . .

(b) . . .

[employment tribunal] procedure regulations shall include provision for requiring the employer to pay the costs or expenses of any postponement or adjournment of the hearing caused by his failure, without a special reason, to adduce reasonable evidence as to the availability of the job from which the complainant was dismissed . . . or of comparable or suitable employment.

[(3) Provision included in employment tribunal procedure regulations under subsection (1) must include provision for requiring an employment tribunal, in any proceedings in which a late postponement application has been granted, to consider whether to make an award against the party who made the application in respect of any costs or expenses connected with the postponement, except in circumstances specified in the regulations.

(4) For the purposes of subsection (3)—

(a) a late postponement application is an application for the postponement of a hearing in the proceedings which is made after a time determined in accordance with the regulations (whether before or after the hearing has begun), and

(b) "postponement" includes adjournment.]

NOTES

Sub-ss (1), (1A)–(1C): substituted, for the original sub-s (1), by the Employment Act 2002, s 22(1); words in square brackets in sub-s (1C) substituted by the Crime and Courts Act 2013, s 17(5), Sch 9, Pt 3, para 52.

Sub-s (2): words in square brackets substituted by the Employment Rights (Dispute Resolution) Act 1998, s 1(2)(a); words omitted repealed by the Employment Relations Act 1999, ss 9, 44, Sch 4, Pt III, paras 1, 4, Sch 9(2).

Sub-ss (3), (4): added by the Small Business, Enterprise and Employment Act 2015, s 151(1), (3), as from 26 March 2015.

Regulations: the Employment Tribunals (Constitution and Rules of Procedure) Regulations 2013, SI 2013/1237 at **[2.1323]**; the Employment Tribunals (Constitution and Rules of Procedure) (Amendment) Regulations 2016, SI 2016/271. As to previous Regulations made under this section, see further the note to s 1 *ante*.

[1.752]

[13A Payments in respect of preparation time

(1) Employment tribunal procedure regulations may include provision for authorising an employment tribunal to order a party to proceedings before it to make a payment to any other party in respect of time spent in preparing that other party's case.

(2) Regulations under subsection (1) may include provision authorising an employment tribunal to have regard to a person's ability to pay when considering the making of an order against him under such regulations.

[(2A) Provision included in employment tribunal procedure regulations under subsection (1) must include provision for requiring an employment tribunal, in any proceedings in which a late postponement application has been granted, to consider whether to make an order of the kind mentioned in subsection (1) against the party who made the application in respect of any time spent in connection with the postponement, except in circumstances specified in the regulations.

(2B) For the purposes of subsection (2A)—

(a) a late postponement application is an application for the postponement of a hearing in the proceedings which is made after a time determined in accordance with the regulations (whether before or after the hearing has begun), and

(b) "postponement" includes adjournment.]

(3) If employment tribunal procedure regulations include—

(a) provision of the kind mentioned in subsection (1), and
(b) provision of the kind mentioned in section 13(1)(a),

they shall also[, subject to subsection (4),] include provision to prevent an employment tribunal exercising its powers under both kinds of provision in favour of the same person in the same proceedings.

[(4) Subsection (3) does not require the regulations to include provision to prevent an employment tribunal from making—
(a) an order of the kind mentioned in subsection (1), and
(b) an award of the kind mentioned in section 13(1)(a) that is limited to witnesses' expenses.]]

NOTES

Inserted by the Employment Act 2002, s 22(2).

Sub-ss (2A), (2B): inserted by the Small Business, Enterprise and Employment Act 2015, s 151(1), (4), as from 26 March 2015.

Words in square brackets in sub-s (3) inserted, and sub-s (4) added, by the Enterprise and Regulatory Reform Act 2013, s 21(1), (3).

Regulations: the Employment Tribunals (Constitution and Rules of Procedure) Regulations 2013, SI 2013/1237 at **[2.1323]**; the Employment Tribunals (Constitution and Rules of Procedure) (Amendment) Regulations 2016, SI 2016/271. As to previous Regulations made under this section, see further the note to s 1 *ante*.

[1.753]
14 Interest

(1) The Secretary of State may by order made with the approval of the Treasury provide that sums payable in pursuance of decisions of [employment tribunals] shall carry interest at such rate and between such times as may be prescribed by the order.

(2) Any interest due by virtue of such an order shall be recoverable as a sum payable in pursuance of the decision.

(3) The power conferred by subsection (1) includes power—
(a) to specify cases or circumstances in which interest is not payable,
(b) to provide that interest is payable only on sums exceeding a specified amount or falling between specified amounts,
(c) to make provision for the manner in which and the periods by reference to which interest is to be calculated and paid,
(d) to provide that any enactment—
 (i) does or does not apply in relation to interest payable by virtue of subsection (1), or
 (ii) applies to it with such modifications as may be specified in the order,
(e) to make provision for cases where sums are payable in pursuance of decisions or awards made on appeal from [employment tribunals],
(f) to make such incidental or supplemental provision as the Secretary of State considers necessary.

(4) In particular, an order under subsection (1) may provide that the rate of interest shall be the rate specified in section 17 of the Judgments Act 1838 as that enactment has effect from time to time.

NOTES

Sub-ss (1), (3): words in square brackets substituted by the Employment Rights (Dispute Resolution) Act 1998, s 1(2)(b).

Orders under sub-s (1): Regulations under the Equality Act 2010, s 139 may modify the operation of an order made under this section in so far as it relates to an award in proceedings under that Act; see s 139(2) of the 2010 Act at **[1.1722]**.

Orders: the Employment Tribunals (Interest) Order (Amendment) Order 2013, SI 2013/1671. Also, by virtue of s 44 of, and Sch 2, Pt I, paras 1–4 to, this Act, the Employment Tribunals (Interest) Order 1990, SI 1990/479 at **[2.123]** has effect as if made under this section.

[1.754]
15 Enforcement

(1) Any sum payable in pursuance of a decision of an [employment tribunal] in England and Wales which has been registered in accordance with [employment tribunal] procedure regulations [shall be recoverable [under section 85 of the County Courts Act 1984] or otherwise as if it were payable under an order of [the county court]].

(2) Any order for the payment of any sum made by an [employment tribunal] in Scotland (or any copy of such an order certified by the Secretary of the Tribunals) may be enforced as if it were an extract registered decree arbitral bearing a warrant for execution issued by the sheriff court of any sheriffdom in Scotland.

(3) In this section a reference to a decision or order of an [employment tribunal]—
(a) does not include a decision or order which, on being reviewed, has been revoked by the tribunal, and
(b) in relation to a decision or order which on being reviewed, has been varied by the tribunal, shall be construed as a reference to the decision or order as so varied.

NOTES

Sub-s (1): words "employment tribunal" in square brackets (in both places that they occur) substituted by the Employment Rights (Dispute Resolution) Act 1998, s 1(2)(a); words in third (outer) pair of square brackets substituted by the Tribunals, Courts and Enforcement Act 2007, s 48(1), Sch 8, paras 35, 43; words "under section 85 of the County Courts Act 1984" in square brackets substituted by the Tribunals, Courts and Enforcement Act 2007, s 62(3), Sch 13, para 125 (as amended by the Crime and Courts Act 2013, s 25(9)(d)); words "the county court" in square brackets substituted by the Crime and Courts Act 2013, s 17(5), Sch 9, Pt 3, para 52.

Sub-ss (2), (3): words in square brackets substituted by the Employment Rights (Dispute Resolution) Act 1998, s 1(2)(a).

Recoupment of social security benefits

[1.755]

16 Power to provide for recoupment of benefits

(1) This section applies to payments which are the subject of proceedings before [employment tribunals] and which are—

(a) payments of wages or compensation for loss of wages,

(b) payments by employers to employees under sections 146 to 151, sections 168 to 173 or section 192 of the Trade Union and Labour Relations (Consolidation) Act 1992,

(c) payments by employers to employees under—

(i) Part III, V, VI or VII,

(ii) section 93, or

(iii) Part X,

of the Employment Rights Act 1996, . . .

(d) payments by employers to employees of a nature similar to, or for a purpose corresponding to the purpose of, payments within paragraph (b) or (c), [. . .

(e) payments by employers to employees under regulation 5, 6 or 9 of the Employment Relations Act 1999 (Blacklists) Regulations 2010,] [or

(f) payments by NHS employers to applicants under regulation 6 of the Employment Rights Act 1996 (NHS Recruitment—Protected Disclosure) Regulations 2018 (remedies),]

and to payments of remuneration under a protective award under section 189 of the Trade Union and Labour Relations (Consolidation) Act 1992.

(2) The Secretary of State may by regulations make with respect to payments to which this section applies provision for any or all of the purposes specified in subsection (3).

(3) The purposes referred to in subsection (2) are—

(a) enabling the Secretary of State to recover from an employer, by way of total or partial recoupment of [universal credit,] jobseeker's allowance, [*income support* or income-related employment and support allowance]—

(i) a sum not exceeding the amount of the prescribed element of the monetary award, or

(ii) in the case of a protective award, the amount of the remuneration,

(b) requiring or authorising an [employment tribunal] to order the payment of such a sum, by way of total or partial recoupment of [universal credit,] [jobseeker's allowance, *income support* or income-related employment and support allowance], to the Secretary of State instead of to an employee, and

(c) requiring an [employment tribunal] to order the payment to an employee of only the excess of the prescribed element of the monetary award over the amount of any [universal credit,] jobseeker's allowance, [*income support* or income-related employment and support allowance] shown to the tribunal to have been paid to the employee and enabling the Secretary of State to recover from the employer, by way of total or partial recoupment of the benefit, a sum not exceeding that amount.

(4) Regulations under this section may be framed—

(a) so as to apply to all payments to which this section applies or to one or more classes of those payments, and

[(b) so as to apply to all or any of the benefits mentioned in subsection (3)].

(5) Regulations under this section may—

(a) confer powers and impose duties on [employment tribunals] or . . . other persons,

(b) impose on an employer to whom a monetary award or protective award relates a duty—

(i) to furnish particulars connected with the award, and

(ii) to suspend payments in pursuance of the award during any period prescribed by the regulations,

(c) provide for an employer who pays a sum to the Secretary of State in pursuance of this section to be relieved from any liability to pay the sum to another person,

[(cc) provide for the determination by the Secretary of State of any issue arising as to the total or partial recoupment in pursuance of the regulations of [universal credit,] a jobseeker's allowance, unemployment benefit, [income support or income-related employment and support allowance],

(d) confer on an employee a right of appeal to an appeal tribunal constituted under Chapter I of Part I of the Social Security Act 1998 against any decision of the Secretary of State on any such issue, and]

(e) provide for the proof in proceedings before [employment tribunals] (whether by certificate or in any other manner) of any amount of [universal credit,] jobseeker's allowance, [*income support* or income-related employment and support allowance] paid to an employee.

(6) Regulations under this section may make different provision for different cases.

NOTES

Sub-s (1): words in first pair of square brackets substituted by the Employment Rights (Dispute Resolution) Act 1998, s 1(2)(b). Word omitted from para (c) repealed, and para (e) (and the word immediately preceding it) inserted, by the Employment Relations Act 1999 (Blacklists) Regulations 2010, SI 2010/493, reg 17(1), (3). Word omitted from para (d) repealed, and para (f) (and the word immediately preceding it) inserted, the Employment Rights Act 1996 (NHS Recruitment—Protected Disclosure) Regulations 2018, SI 2018/579, reg 10(1), (3), as from 23 May 2018.

Sub-s (3): words "employment tribunal" in square brackets substituted by the Employment Rights (Dispute Resolution) Act 1998, s 1(2)(a); words "universal credit," in square brackets in paras (a), (b) and (c) inserted by the Universal Credit (Consequential, Supplementary, Incidental and Miscellaneous Provisions) Regulations 2013, SI 2013/630, reg 11(1), (2)(a); other words in square brackets substituted by the Welfare Reform Act 2007, s 28, Sch 3, Pt 1, para 15(1), (2)(a), (b); the words

"*, income support*" in italics in paras (a), (b), (c) are repealed by the Welfare Reform Act 2009, ss 9(3)(b), 58(1), Sch 7, Pt 1, as from a day to be appointed (for further provisions in relation to the abolition of income support, see s 9 of that Act).

Sub-s (4): para (b) substituted by the Welfare Reform Act 2007, s 28, Sch 3, Pt 1, para 15(1), (2)(c).

Sub-s (5): words in square brackets in para (a), and words in first pair of square brackets in para (e), substituted by the Employment Rights (Dispute Resolution) Act 1998, s 1(2)(b); words omitted from para (a) repealed, and paras (cc), (d) substituted (for the original para (d)), by the Social Security Act 1998, s 86, Sch 7, para 147, Sch 8; words in second pair of square brackets in para (cc), and words in third pair of square brackets in para (e), substituted by the Welfare Reform Act 2007, s 28, Sch 3, Pt 1, para 15(1), (2)(a); words in first pair of square brackets in para (cc) and words in second pair of square brackets in para (e) inserted by SI 2013/630, reg 11(1), (2)(b), (3); the words "*, income support*" in italics in para (e) are repealed by the Welfare Reform Act 2009, ss 9(3)(b), 58(1), Sch 7, Pt 1, as from a day to be appointed (for further provisions in relation to the abolition of income support, see s 9 of that Act, and note that the 2009 Act does not provide for the repeal of these words in para (cc) of this subsection).

Regulations: the Employment Protection (Recoupment of Benefits) Regulations 1996, SI 1996/2349 at **[2.252]**.

[1.756]

17 Recoupment: further provisions

(1) Where in pursuance of any regulations under section 16 a sum has been recovered by or paid to the Secretary of State by way of total or partial recoupment of [universal credit,] jobseeker's allowance[, *income support* or income-related employment and support allowance]—

- (a) no sum shall be recoverable under Part III *or V* of the Social Security Administration Act 1992, and
- (b) no abatement, payment or reduction shall be made by reference to the [universal credit,] jobseeker's allowance[, *income support* or income-related employment and support allowance] recouped.

(2) Any amount found to have been duly recovered by or paid to the Secretary of State in pursuance of regulations under section 16 by way of total or partial recoupment of jobseeker's allowance shall be paid into the National Insurance Fund.

(3) In section 16—

"monetary award" means the amount which is awarded, or ordered to be paid, to the employee by the tribunal or would be so awarded or ordered apart from any provision of regulations under that section, and

"the prescribed element", in relation to any monetary award, means so much of that award as is attributable to such matters as may be prescribed by regulations under that section.

(4) In section 16 "income-based jobseeker's allowance" has the same meaning as in the Jobseekers Act 1995.

[(5) In this section and section 16 "income-related employment and support allowance" means an income-related allowance under Part 1 of the Welfare Reform Act 2007 (employment and support allowance).]

NOTES

Sub-s (1): words "universal credit," in square brackets (in both places in which they occur) inserted by the Universal Credit (Consequential, Supplementary, Incidental and Miscellaneous Provisions) Regulations 2013, SI 2013/630, reg 11(1), (4); other words in square brackets substituted by the Welfare Reform Act 2007, s 28, Sch 3, Pt 1, para 15(1), (3); words "*, income support*" in italics (in both places in which they occur) and words "*or V*" in italics repealed by the Welfare Reform Act 2009, ss 9(3)(b), 58(1), Sch 7, Pt 1, as from a day to be appointed (for further provisions in relation to the abolition of income support, see s 9 of that Act).

Sub-s (5): added by the Welfare Reform Act 2007, s 28, Sch 3, Pt 1, para 15(1), (4).

Conciliation

[1.757]

18 Conciliation[: relevant proceedings etc]

(1) [In this section and sections 18A to 18C "relevant proceedings" means employment tribunal proceedings—]

- [(a) under section 66, 68A, 70C, 87, 137, 138, 145A, 145B, 146, 168, 168A, 169, 170, 174, 189 or 192 of, or paragraph 156 of Schedule A1 to, the Trade Union and Labour Relations (Consolidation) Act 1992,
- (b) under section 11, 23, 34, 63I, 70, 70A, 80(1), 80H, 93, 111, 163 or 177 of the Employment Rights Act 1996, or under Part 5 or 6 of that Act,
- (c) under section 11, 19D(1)(a) or 24 of the National Minimum Wage Act 1998,
- (d) under section 56 of the Pensions Act 2008,
- (e) under section 120 or 127 of the Equality Act 2010,
- (f) under regulation 11 of the Safety Representatives and Safety Committees Regulations 1977,
- (g) under article 6 of the Employment Tribunals Extension of Jurisdiction (England and Wales) Order 1994,
- (h) under article 6 of the Employment Tribunals Extension of Jurisdiction (Scotland) Order 1994,
- (i) under paragraph 2 of Schedule 2 to the Health and Safety (Consultation with Employees) Regulations 1996,
- (j) under regulation 30 of the Working Time Regulations 1998,
- (k) under regulation 27 or 32 of the Transnational Information and Consultation of Employees Regulation 1999,
- (l) under regulation 8 of the Part-time Workers (Prevention of Less Favourable Treatment) Regulations 2000,

(m) under regulation 7 or 9 of the Fixed-term Employees (Prevention of Less Favourable Treatment) Regulations 2002,

[(n) under regulation 26 of the Merchant Shipping (Maritime Labour Convention) (Hours of Work) Regulations 2018 (SI 2018/58),]

(o) under regulation 15 of the Flexible Working (Procedural Requirements) Regulations 2002,

(p) under regulation 18 of the Merchant Shipping (Working Time: Inland Waterways) Regulations 2003,

(q) under regulation 18 of the Civil Aviation (Working Time) Regulations 2004,

(r) under regulation 19 of the Fishing Vessels (Working Time: Sea-fishermen) Regulations 2004,

(s) under regulation 29 or 33 of the Information and Consultation of Employees Regulations 2004,

(t) under paragraphs 4 or 8 of the Schedule to the Occupational and Personal Pension Schemes (Consultation by Employers and Miscellaneous Amendment) Regulations 2006,

(u) under regulation 30 or 34 of the European Cooperative Society (Involvement of Employees) Regulations 2006,

(v) under regulation 45 or 51 of the Companies (Cross-Border Mergers) Regulations 2007,

(w) under regulation 17 of the Cross-border Railway Services (Working Time) Regulations 2008,

(x) under regulation 9 of Ecclesiastical Offices (Terms of Service) Regulations 2009,

(y) under regulation 28 or 32 of the European Public Limited-Liability Company (Employee Involvement) (Great Britain) Regulations 2009,

(z) under regulation 18 of the Agency Workers Regulations 2010,

(z1) under regulation 17 of the Employee Study and Training (Procedural Requirements) Regulations 2010, . . .

(z2) under regulation 5, 6 or 9 of the Employment Relations Act 1999 (Blacklists) Regulations 2010][, . . .

(z3) under regulation 3 of the Exclusivity Terms in Zero Hours Contracts (Redress) Regulations 2015][, . . .

(z4) under regulation 6 of the Posted Workers (Enforcement of Employment Rights) Regulations 2016], [*or*

(z5) under regulation 4 of the Employment Rights Act 1996 (NHS Recruitment—Protected Disclosure) Regulations 2018][, or

(z6) under paragraph (3) of regulation 4 or paragraph (6) of regulation 5 of the Agency Workers (Amendment) Regulations 2019.]

[(1A) Sections 18A and 18B apply in the case of matters which could be the subject of relevant proceedings, and section 18C applies in the case of relevant proceedings themselves.]

(2), [(2A)] . . .

(3)–(5) . . .

(6) In proceeding under [any of sections 18A to 18C] a conciliation officer shall, where appropriate, have regard to the desirability of encouraging the use of other procedures available for the settlement of grievances.

(7) Anything communicated to a conciliation officer in connection with the performance of his functions under [any of sections 18A to 18C] shall not be admissible in evidence in any proceedings before an [employment tribunal], except with the consent of the person who communicated it to that officer.

(8) The Secretary of State [and the Lord Chancellor, acting jointly,] may by order [amend the definition of "relevant proceedings" in subsection (1) by adding to or removing from the list in that subsection particular types of employment tribunal proceedings].

[(9) An order under subsection (8) that adds employment tribunal proceedings to the list in subsection (1) may amend an enactment so as to extend the time limit for instituting those proceedings in such a way as appears necessary or expedient in order to facilitate the conciliation process provided for by section 18A.

(10) An order under subsection (8) that removes employment tribunal proceedings from the list in subsection (1) may—

(a) repeal or revoke any provision of an enactment that, for the purpose mentioned in subsection (9), extends the time limit for instituting those proceedings;

(b) make further amendments which are consequential on that repeal or revocation.]

NOTES

Section heading: words in square brackets inserted by the Enterprise and Regulatory Reform Act 2013, s 7(2), Sch 1, paras 2, 5(1), (2).

Sub-s (1) is amended as follows:

Words in first pair of square brackets substituted by the Enterprise and Regulatory Reform Act 2013, s 7(2), Sch 1, paras 2, 5(1), (3).

Paras (a)–(z2) substituted (for the original paras (a)–(y)) by the Employment Tribunals Act 1996 (Application of Conciliation Provisions) Order 2014, SI 2014/431, art 2.

Para (n) substituted by the Merchant Shipping (Maritime Labour Convention) (Hours of Work) Regulations 2018, SI 2018/58, reg 31, Sch 2, para 1(a), as from 6 April 2018.

Para (v) repealed by the Companies, Limited Liability Partnerships and Partnerships (Amendment etc) (EU Exit) Regulations 2019, SI 2019/348, reg 8, Sch 3, paras 2, 3, as from exit day (as defined in the European Union (Withdrawal) Act 2018, s 20).

Word omitted from para (z1) repealed, and para (z3) (and the word immediately preceding it) inserted, by the Employment Tribunals Act 1996 (Application of Conciliation Provisions) Order 2015, SI 2015/2054, art 2, as from 11 January 2016.

Word omitted from para (z2) repealed, and para (z4) (and the word immediately preceding it) inserted, by the Posted Workers (Enforcement of Employment Rights) Regulations 2016, SI 2016/539, reg 10, as from 18 June 2016.

Word omitted from para (z3) repealed, and para (z5) (and the word immediately preceding it) inserted, by the Employment Rights Act 1996 (NHS Recruitment—Protected Disclosure) Regulations 2018, SI 2018/579, reg 10(1), (4), as from 23 May 2018.

Word in italics in para (z4) repealed, and para (z6) (and the word immediately preceding it) inserted, by the Agency Workers (Amendment) Regulations 2019, SI 2019/724, reg 8(3), (4), as from 6 April 2020.

Sub-s (1A): inserted by the Enterprise and Regulatory Reform Act 2013, s 7(2), Sch 1, paras 2, 5(1), (7).

Sub-ss (2), (4): repealed by the Enterprise and Regulatory Reform Act 2013, s 7(2), Sch 1, paras 2, 5(1), (8).

Sub-s (2A): originally inserted by the Employment Act 2002, s 24(2), and repealed by the Employment Act 2008, ss 6(1), 20, Schedule, Pt 1.

Sub-s (3), (5): repealed by the Enterprise and Regulatory Reform Act 2013, s 7(2), Sch 1, paras 2, 5(1), (8).

Sub-s (6): words in square brackets substituted by the Enterprise and Regulatory Reform Act 2013, s 7(2), Sch 1, paras 2, 5(1), (9).

Sub-s (7): words in first pair of square brackets substituted by the Enterprise and Regulatory Reform Act 2013, s 7(2), Sch 1, paras 2, 5(1), (9); words in second pair of square brackets substituted by the Employment Rights (Dispute Resolution) Act 1998, s 1(2)(a).

Sub-s (8): words in first pair of square brackets inserted by the Tribunals, Courts and Enforcement Act 2007, s 48(1), Sch 8, paras 35, 38; words in second pair of square brackets substituted by the Enterprise and Regulatory Reform Act 2013, s 9(1), (2).

Sub-ss (9), (10): added by the Enterprise and Regulatory Reform Act 2013, s 9(1), (3).

Note: the Employment Relations Act 1999, ss 10–13, are to be treated as provisions of the Employment Rights Act 1996, Pt V, for the purposes of sub-s (1)(b) above; see s 14 of the 1999 Act at **[1.1251]** (as amended by the Employment Tribunals Act 1996 (Application of Conciliation Provisions) Order 2014, SI 2014/431, art 3, Schedule, para 6).

Restriction on contracting out, etc: various provisions do not apply to an agreement to refrain from instituting or continuing proceedings where a conciliation officer has taken action under this section or ss 18A, 18B; see the Trade Union and Labour Relations (Consolidation) Act 1992, s 288 at **[1.622]**, the Employment Rights Act 1996, s 203 at **[1.1116]**, the National Minimum Wage Act 1998, s 49 at **[1.1219]**, and the Pensions Act 2008, s 58 at **[1.1605]**. See also the Equality Act 2010, s 144 at **[1.1731]**, which makes equivalent provision for agreements in respect of claims or potential claims under that Act, but without specific reference to this Act.

Orders: the Employment Tribunals Act (Application of Conciliation Provisions) Order 2000, SI 2000/1299 (revoked by SI 2000/1336 without coming into force); the Employment Tribunals Act (Application of Conciliation Provisions) Order 2000 (Revocation) Order 2000, SI 2000/1336; the Employment Tribunals Act 1996 (Application of Conciliation Provisions) Order 2000, SI 2000/1337; the Employment Tribunals Act 1996 (Application of Conciliation Provisions) Order 2014, SI 2014/431; the Employment Tribunals Act 1996 (Application of Conciliation Provisions) Order 2015, SI 2015/2054. Note that SI 2000/1337 (which was made under sub-s (8)(a), (b) of this section prior to the amendment to sub-s (8) as noted above) amended sub-s (1)(d) of this section (prior to its substitution as noted above), and specified that the Trade Union and Labour Relations (Consolidation) Act 1992, s 70B and Sch 1, para 156 are provisions to which sub-s (1)(f) of this section applied (prior to its substitution as noted above). Note also that Sch A1, para 156 to the 1992 Act is now included in sub-s (1)(a) above, as is s 70C of that Act (right to present a complaint to an employment tribunal that an employer has failed to comply with his obligations under s 70B). It is therefore assumed that SI 2000/1337 is effectively spent and has also lapsed.

[1.758]

[18A Requirement to contact ACAS before instituting proceedings

(1) Before a person ("the prospective claimant") presents an application to institute relevant proceedings relating to any matter, the prospective claimant must provide to ACAS prescribed information, in the prescribed manner, about that matter.

This is subject to subsection (7).

(2) On receiving the prescribed information in the prescribed manner, ACAS shall send a copy of it to a conciliation officer.

(3) The conciliation officer shall, during the prescribed period, endeavour to promote a settlement between the persons who would be parties to the proceedings.

(4) If—

(a) during the prescribed period the conciliation officer concludes that a settlement is not possible, or

(b) the prescribed period expires without a settlement having been reached,

the conciliation officer shall issue a certificate to that effect, in the prescribed manner, to the prospective claimant.

(5) The conciliation officer may continue to endeavour to promote a settlement after the expiry of the prescribed period.

(6) In subsections (3) to (5) "settlement" means a settlement that avoids proceedings being instituted.

(7) A person may institute relevant proceedings without complying with the requirement in subsection (1) in prescribed cases.

The cases that may be prescribed include (in particular)—

cases where the requirement is complied with by another person instituting relevant proceedings relating to the same matter;

cases where proceedings that are not relevant proceedings are instituted by means of the same form as proceedings that are;

cases where section 18B applies because ACAS has been contacted by a person against whom relevant proceedings are being instituted.

(8) A person who is subject to the requirement in subsection (1) may not present an application to institute relevant proceedings without a certificate under subsection (4).

(9) Where a conciliation officer acts under this section in a case where the prospective claimant has ceased to be employed by the employer and the proposed proceedings are proceedings under section 111 of the Employment Rights Act 1996, the conciliation officer may in particular—

(a) seek to promote the reinstatement or re-engagement of the prospective claimant by the employer, or by a successor of the employer or by an associated employer, on terms appearing to the conciliation officer to be equitable, or

(b) where the prospective claimant does not wish to be reinstated or re-engaged, or where reinstatement or re-engagement is not practicable, seek to promote agreement between them as to a sum by way of compensation to be paid by the employer to the prospective claimant.

(10) In subsections (1) to (7) "prescribed" means prescribed in employment tribunal procedure regulations.

(11) The Secretary of State may by employment tribunal procedure regulations make such further provision as appears to the Secretary of State to be necessary or expedient with respect to the conciliation process provided for by subsections (1) to (8).

(12) Employment tribunal procedure regulations may (in particular) make provision—

(a) authorising the Secretary of State to prescribe, or prescribe requirements in relation to, any form which is required by such regulations to be used for the purpose of providing information to ACAS under subsection (1) or issuing a certificate under subsection (4);

(b) requiring ACAS to give a person any necessary assistance to comply with the requirement in subsection (1);

(c) for the extension of the period prescribed for the purposes of subsection (3);

(d) treating the requirement in subsection (1) as complied with, for the purposes of any provision extending the time limit for instituting relevant proceedings, by a person who is relieved of that requirement by virtue of subsection (7)(a).]

NOTES

Inserted, together with s 18B, by the Enterprise and Regulatory Reform Act 2013, s 7(1).

Time limits: as to the extension of certain time limits in connection with the operation of this section, see, inter alia, (a) the Trade Union and Labour Relations (Consolidation) Act 1992, s 292A at **[1.625]**; (b) the Employment Rights Act 1996, s 207B at **[1.1123]**; (c) the National Minimum Wage Act 1998, s 11A at **[1.1178]**; (d) the Equality Act 2010, s 140B at **[1.1727]**; and (e) s 18(9), (10) of this Act at **[1.757]**.

Restriction on contracting out, etc: see the note to s 18 at **[1.757]**.

Regulations: the Employment Tribunals (Early Conciliation: Exemptions and Rules of Procedure) Regulations 2014, SI 2014/254 at **[2.1474]**; the Employment Tribunals (Early Conciliation: Exemptions and Rules of Procedure) (Amendment) Regulations 2014, SI 2014/847.

[1.759]

[18B Conciliation before institution of proceedings: other ACAS duties

(1) This section applies where—

(a) a person contacts ACAS requesting the services of a conciliation officer in relation to a matter that (if not settled) is likely to give rise to relevant proceedings against that person, and

(b) ACAS has not received information from the prospective claimant under section 18A(1).

(2) This section also applies where—

(a) a person contacts ACAS requesting the services of a conciliation officer in relation to a matter that (if not settled) is likely to give rise to relevant proceedings by that person, and

(b) the requirement in section 18A(1) would apply to that person but for section 18A(7).

(3) Where this section applies a conciliation officer shall endeavour to promote a settlement between the persons who would be parties to the proceedings.

(4) If at any time—

(a) the conciliation officer concludes that a settlement is not possible, or

(b) a conciliation officer comes under the duty in section 18A(3) to promote a settlement between the persons who would be parties to the proceedings,

the duty in subsection (3) ceases to apply at that time.

(5) In subsections (3) and (4) "settlement" means a settlement that avoids proceedings being instituted.

(6) Subsection (9) of section 18A applies for the purposes of this section as it applies for the purposes of that section.]

NOTES

Inserted as noted to s 18A at **[1.758]**.

Restriction on contracting out, etc: see the note to s 18 at **[1.757]**.

[1.760]

[18C Conciliation after institution of proceedings

(1) Where an application instituting relevant proceedings has been presented to an employment tribunal, and a copy of it has been sent to a conciliation officer, the conciliation officer shall endeavour to promote a settlement—

(a) if requested to do so by the person by whom and the person against whom the proceedings are brought, or

(b) if, in the absence of any such request, the conciliation officer considers that the officer could act under this section with a reasonable prospect of success.

(2) Where a person who has presented a complaint to an employment tribunal under section 111 of the Employment Rights Act 1996 has ceased to be employed by the employer against whom the complaint was made, the conciliation officer may in particular—

(a) seek to promote the reinstatement or re-engagement of the complainant by the employer, or by a successor of the employer or by an associated employer, on terms appearing to the conciliation officer to be equitable, or

(b) where the complainant does not wish to be reinstated or re-engaged, or where reinstatement or re-engagement is not practicable, and the parties desire the conciliation officer to act, seek to promote agreement between them as to a sum by way of compensation to be paid by the employer to the complainant.

(3) In subsection (1) "settlement" means a settlement that brings proceedings to an end without their being determined by an employment tribunal.]

NOTES

Inserted by the Enterprise and Regulatory Reform Act 2013, s 7(2), Sch 1, paras 2, 6.

[1.761]

19 Conciliation procedure

[(1)] [Employment tribunal] procedure regulations shall include in relation to [employment tribunal] proceedings in the case of which any enactment makes provision for conciliation—

(a) provisions requiring a copy of the application by which the proceedings are instituted, and a copy of any notice relating to it which is lodged by or on behalf of the person against whom the proceedings are brought, to be sent to a conciliation officer, [and]

(b) provisions securing that the applicant and the person against whom the proceedings are brought are notified that the services of a conciliation officer are available to them, . . .

(c) . . .

[(2) . . .]

NOTES

Sub-s (1): numbered as such by the Employment Act 2002, s 24(4); word omitted from para (b) and the whole of para (c) repealed by ss 24(3), 54 of, and Sch 8 to, the 2002 Act; word "and" in square brackets inserted by s 53 of, and Sch 7, para 23(1), (3) to, the 2002 Act; other words in square brackets substituted by the Employment Rights (Dispute Resolution) Act 1998, s 1(2)(a).

Sub-s (2): originally added by the Employment Act 2002, s 24(4), and repealed by the Employment Act 2008, ss 6(2), 20, Schedule, Pt 1.

Regulations: the Employment Tribunals (Constitution and Rules of Procedure) Regulations 2013, SI 2013/1237 at **[2.1323]**. As to previous Regulations made under this section, see further the note to s 1 *ante*.

[1.762]

[19A Conciliation: recovery of sums payable under [settlements]

(1) Subsections (3) to (6) apply if—

(a) a conciliation officer—

(i) has taken action under [any of sections 18A to 18C] in a case, and

(ii) issues a certificate in writing stating that a [settlement] has been reached in the case, and

(b) all of the terms of the [settlement] are set out—

(i) in a single relevant document, or

(ii) in a combination of two or more relevant documents.

(2) A document is a "relevant document" for the purposes of subsection (1) if—

(a) it is the certificate, or

(b) it is a document that is referred to in the certificate or that is referred to in a document that is within this paragraph.

(3) Any sum payable by a person under the terms of the [settlement] (a "[settlement] sum") shall, subject to subsections (4) to (7), be recoverable—

(a) in England and Wales, by execution issued from [the county court] or otherwise as if the sum were payable under an order of that court;

(b) in Scotland, by diligence as if the certificate were an extract registered decree arbitral bearing a warrant for execution issued by the sheriff court of any sheriffdom in Scotland.

(4) A [settlement] sum is not recoverable under subsection (3) if—

(a) the person by whom it is payable applies for a declaration that the sum would not be recoverable from him under the general law of contract, and

(b) that declaration is made.

(5) If rules of court so provide, a [settlement] sum is not recoverable under subsection (3) during the period—

(a) beginning with the issue of the certificate, and

(b) ending at such time as may be specified in, or determined under, rules of court.

(6) If the terms of the [settlement] provide for the person to whom a [settlement] sum is payable to do anything in addition to discontinuing or not starting proceedings, that sum is recoverable by him under subsection (3)—

(a) in England and Wales, only if [the county court] so orders;

(b) in Scotland, only if the sheriff so orders.

(7) Once an application has been made for a declaration under subsection (4) in relation to a sum, no further reliance may be placed on subsection (3) for the recovery of the sum while the application is pending.

(8) An application for a declaration under subsection (4) may be made to an employment tribunal, [the county court] or the sheriff.

(9) Employment tribunal procedure regulations may (in particular) make provision as to the time within which an application to an employment tribunal for a declaration under subsection (4) is to be made.

(10) Rules of court may make provision as to—

(a) the time within which an application to [the county court] for a declaration under subsection (4) is to be made;
(b) the time within which an application to the sheriff for a declaration under subsection (4) is to be made;
(c) when an application (whether made to [the county court], the sheriff or an employment tribunal) for a declaration under subsection (4) is pending for the purposes of subsection (7).

[(10A) A term of any document which is a relevant document for the purposes of subsection (1) is void to the extent that it purports to prevent the disclosure of any provision of any such document to a person appointed or authorised to act under section 37M.]

(11) Nothing in this section shall be taken to prejudice any rights or remedies that a person has apart from this section.

(12) In this section "[settlement]" (except in the phrase "[settlement] sum") means a settlement . . . to avoid proceedings or bring proceedings to an end.]

NOTES

Inserted by the Tribunals, Courts and Enforcement Act 2007, s 142.

The words "settlements" and "settlement" in square brackets (in each place that they occur) were substituted, and the words omitted from sub-s (12) were repealed, by the Enterprise and Regulatory Reform Act 2013, s 23(2).

The words "any of sections 18A to 18C" in square brackets in sub-s (1) were substituted by the Enterprise and Regulatory Reform Act 2013, s 7(2), Sch 1, paras 2, 7.

The words "the county court" in square brackets (in each place that they occur) were substituted by the Crime and Courts Act 2013, s 17(5), Sch 9, Pt 3, para 52.

Sub-s (10A): inserted by the Small Business, Enterprise and Employment Act 2015, s 150(4), as from 6 April 2016, in relation to relevant sums where (a) in the case of a financial award, the decision of the employment tribunal on the claim to which the financial award relates is made on or after the day on which this amendment comes into force; (b) in the case of a settlement sum, the certificate under s 19A(1) of this Act in respect of the settlement under whose terms it is payable is issued on or after that day (see s 150(8) of the 2015 Act at **[1.1926]**).

Subordinate Legislation: the Act of Sederunt (Summary Applications, Statutory Applications and Appeals etc Rules) Amendment (Employment Tribunals Act 1996) 2009, SSI 2009/109.

PART II
THE EMPLOYMENT APPEAL TRIBUNAL

Introductory

[1.763]
20 The Appeal Tribunal

(1) The Employment Appeal Tribunal ("the Appeal Tribunal") shall continue in existence.

(2) The Appeal Tribunal shall have a central office in London but may sit at any time and in any place in Great Britain.

(3) The Appeal Tribunal shall be a superior court of record and shall have an official seal which shall be judicially noticed.

[(4) Subsection (2) is subject to regulation 34 of the Transnational Information and Consultation of Employees Regulations [1999,] [regulation 46(1) of the European Public Limited-Liability Company Regulations] [2004,] [regulation 36(1) of the Information and Consultation of Employees Regulations] [2004,] [regulation 37(1) of the European Cooperative Society (Involvement of Employees) Regulations] [2006,] [regulation 58(1) of the Companies (Cross-Border Mergers) Regulations 2007] [and regulation 33(1) of the European Public Limited-Liability Company (Employee Involvement) (Great Britain) Regulations 2009 (SI 2009/2401)].]

NOTES

Sub-s (4): added by the Transnational Information and Consultation of Employees Regulations 1999, SI 1999/3323, reg 35(1), (2), and subsequently amended as follows:

Entry relating to the European Public Limited-Liability Company Regulations inserted by the European Public Limited-Liability Company Regulations 2004, SI 2004/2326, reg 48(2).

Entry relating to the Information and Consultation of Employees Regulations inserted by the Information and Consultation of Employees Regulations 2004, SI 2004/3426, reg 36(2) at **[2.805]**.

Entry relating to the European Cooperative Society (Involvement of Employees) Regulations inserted by the European Cooperative Society (Involvement of Employees) Regulations 2006, SI 2006/2059, reg 37.

Entry relating to the Companies (Cross-Border Mergers) Regulations inserted by the Companies (Cross-Border Mergers) Regulations 2007, SI 2007/2974, reg 58(2)(b).

Entry relating to the European Public Limited-Liability Company (Employee Involvement) (Great Britain) Regulations 2009 inserted by the European Public Limited-Liability Company (Employee Involvement) (Great Britain) Regulations 2009, SI 2009/2401, reg 35(2)(b).

The other amendments in sub-s (4) are purely grammatical changes made by the same Regulations noted above, ie, the substitution of a particular year and the word "and", with the same year and a comma.

Jurisdiction

[1.764]
21 Jurisdiction of Appeal Tribunal

(1) An appeal lies to the Appeal Tribunal on any question of law arising from any decision of, or arising in any proceedings before, an [employment tribunal] under or by virtue of—
(a)–(c) . . .
(d) the Trade Union and Labour Relations (Consolidation) Act 1992,
(e) . . .

(f) the Employment Rights Act 1996, [. . .
[(ff) . . .]
[(fg) . . .]
[(g) this Act,
(ga) the National Minimum Wage Act 1998,
(gb) the Employment Relations Act 1999],
[(gc) the Equality Act 2006,]
[(gd) the Pensions Act 2008,]
[(ge) the Equality Act 2010,]]
[(h) the Working Time Regulations 1998, . . .
(i) the Transnational Information and Consultation of Employees Regulations 1999]; [. . .
(j) the Part-time Workers (Prevention of Less Favourable Treatment) Regulations 2000,][. . .
(k) the Fixed-term Employees (Prevention of Less Favourable Treatment) Regulations 2002,][. . .
(l) . . .][. . .
(m) . . .],
[(n) the Merchant Shipping (Working Time: Inland Waterways) Regulations 2003], [. . .
(o) the European Public Limited-Liability Company Regulations 2004],
[[(p)] the Fishing Vessels (Working Time: Sea-fishermen) Regulations 2004], [. . .
(q) the Information and Consultation of Employees Regulations 2004], [. . .
(r) the Schedule to the Occupational and Personal Pension Schemes (Consultation by Employers and Miscellaneous Amendment) Regulations 2006], [. . .
(s) . . .][, . . .
(t) the European Cooperative Society (Involvement of Employees) Regulations 2006], [. . .
(u) the Companies (Cross-Border Mergers) Regulations 2007][, . . .
(v) the Cross-border Railway Services (Working Time) Regulations 2008][, . . .
(w) the European Public Limited-Liability Company (Employee Involvement) (Great Britain) Regulations 2009 (SI 2009/2401)][, . . .
(x) the Employment Relations Act 1999 (Blacklists) Regulations 2010][, . . .
(y) the Agency Workers Regulations 2010], [or]
[(z) the Merchant Shipping (Maritime Labour Convention) (Hours of Work) Regulations 2018 (SI 2018/58)].

(2) No appeal shall lie except to the Appeal Tribunal from any decision of an [employment tribunal] under or by virtue of the Acts listed [or the Regulations referred to] in subsection (1).

(3) Subsection (1) does not affect any provision contained in, or made under, any Act which provides for an appeal to lie to the Appeal Tribunal (whether from an [employment tribunal], the Certification Officer or any other person or body) otherwise than on a question to which that subsection applies.

[(4) The Appeal Tribunal also has any jurisdiction in respect of matters other than appeals which is conferred on it by or under—
(a) the Trade Union and Labour Relations (Consolidation) Act 1992,
(b) this Act, or
(c) any other Act].

NOTES

Sub-s (1) has been amended as follows:

Words in first pair of square brackets substituted by the Employment Rights (Dispute Resolution) Act 1998, s 1(2)(a).

Paras (a)–(c), (e) repealed by the Equality Act 2010, s 211, Sch 26, Pt 1, paras 27, 32(a), Sch 27, Pt 1 (see further the savings note below).

Word omitted from para (f) repealed by the National Minimum Wage Act 1998, s 53, Sch 3.

Para (ff) originally inserted by the National Minimum Wage Act 1998, s 29 (see further the notes below).

Para (fg) originally inserted by the Tax Credits Act 1999, s 7, Sch 3, para 5, and repealed by the Tax Credits Act 2002, s 60, Sch 6.

Para (g) added by the Employment Rights (Dispute Resolution) Act 1998, s 15, Sch 1, para 17(1), (2) (see further the notes below).

Paras (g), (ga), (gb) substituted, for the original para (ff) (as inserted as noted above) and the original para (g) (as inserted as noted above), by the Employment Relations Act 2004, s 38.

Para (gc) inserted by the Equality Act 2006, s 40, Sch 3, para 57.

Para (gd) inserted by the Pensions Act 2008, s 59.

Para (ge) inserted by the Equality Act 2010, s 211(1), Sch 26, Pt 1, paras 27, 32(b).

Paras (h), (i) substituted (for words that appeared in the original para (g) (as inserted as noted above)) by the Transnational Information and Consultation of Employees Regulations 1999, SI 1999/3323, reg 35(1), (3).

Word omitted from para (h) repealed, and para (j) and the word immediately preceding it added, by the Part-time Workers (Prevention of Less Favourable Treatment) Regulations 2000, SI 2000/1551, reg 10, Schedule, para 1(b).

Word omitted from para (i) repealed, and para (k) and the word immediately preceding it added, by the Fixed-term Employees (Prevention of Less Favourable Treatment) Regulations 2002, SI 2002/2034, reg 11, Sch 2, Pt 1, para 2(b).

Word omitted from para (j) repealed, and para (l) and the word immediately preceding it added, by the Employment Equality (Sexual Orientation) Regulations 2003, SI 2003/1661, reg 39, Sch 5, para 1(b); para (l) subsequently repealed by the Equality Act 2010, s 211, Sch 26, Pt 1, paras 27, 32(a), Sch 27, Pt 1 (see further the savings note below).

Word omitted from para (k) repealed, and para (m) and the word immediately preceding it added, by the Employment Equality (Religion or Belief) Regulations 2003, SI 2003/1660, reg 39(2), Sch 5, para 1(b); para (m) subsequently repealed by the Equality Act 2010, s 211, Sch 26, Pt 1, paras 27, 32(a), Sch 27, Pt 1 (see further the savings note below).

Word omitted from para (l) repealed, and para (n) added, by the Merchant Shipping (Working Time: Inland Waterways) Regulations 2003, SI 2003/3049, reg 20, Sch 2, para 2(1), (3).

Word omitted from para (n) repealed by the Information and Consultation of Employees Regulations 2004, SI 2004/3426, reg 37(a).

Para (o) and the word immediately preceding it added by the European Public Limited-Liability Company Regulations 2004, SI 2004/2326, reg 49.

Para (p) inserted by the Fishing Vessels (Working Time: Sea fishermen) Regulations 2004, SI 2004/1713, reg 21, Sch 2, para 1(1), (3). Note that this paragraph was originally added as para (o) and was redesignated as para (p) by SI 2004/3426, reg 37(b).

Para (q) and the word immediately preceding it added by SI 2004/3426, reg 37(c).

Para (r) and the word immediately preceding it added, and word omitted from para (p) repealed, by the Occupational and Personal Pension Schemes (Consultation by Employers and Miscellaneous Amendment) Regulations 2006, SI 2006/349, reg 17, Schedule, para 10.

Para (s) and the word immediately preceding it added, and word omitted from para (q) repealed, by the Employment Equality (Age) Regulations 2006, SI 2006/1031, reg 49(1), Sch 8, Pt 1, paras 18, 20; para (s) subsequently repealed by the Equality Act 2010, s 211, Sch 26, Pt 1, paras 27, 32(a), Sch 27, Pt 1 (see further the savings note below).

Para (t) and the word immediately preceding it added, and word omitted from para (r) repealed, by the European Cooperative Society (Involvement of Employees) Regulations 2006, SI 2006/2059, reg 38.

Para (u) and the word immediately preceding it added, and word omitted from para (s) repealed, by the Companies (Cross-Border Mergers) Regulations 2007, SI 2007/2974, reg 59.

Para (u) repealed by the Companies, Limited Liability Partnerships and Partnerships (Amendment etc) (EU Exit) Regulations 2019, SI 2019/348, reg 8, Sch 3, paras 2, 4, as from exit day (as defined in the European Union (Withdrawal) Act 2018, s 20).

Para (v) and the word immediately preceding it added, and word omitted from para (t) repealed, by the Cross-border Railway Services (Working Time) Regulations 2008, SI 2008/1660, reg 19, Sch 3, para 1(b).

Para (w) and the word immediately preceding it added, and word omitted from para (u) repealed, by the European Public Limited-Liability Company (Employee Involvement) (Great Britain) Regulations 2009, SI 2009/2401, reg 36.

Para (x) and the word immediately preceding it added, and word omitted from para (v) repealed, by the Employment Relations Act 1999 (Blacklists) Regulations 2010, SI 2010/493, reg 17(1), (5).

Para (y) and the word immediately preceding it added, and word omitted from para (w) repealed, by the Agency Workers Regulations 2010, SI 2010/93, reg 25, Sch 2, Pt 1, para 8(b)(i).

Para (z) and the word immediately preceding it added, and word omitted from para (x) repealed, by the Merchant Shipping (Maritime Labour Convention) (Hours of Work) (Amendment) Regulations 2014, SI 2014/308, reg 3, Schedule, para 1(1), (3)(a). Para (z) subsequently substituted by the Merchant Shipping (Maritime Labour Convention) (Hours of Work) Regulations 2018, SI 2018/58, reg 31, Sch 2, para 1(b), as from 6 April 2018.

Sub-s (2): words in first pair of square brackets substituted by the Employment Rights (Dispute Resolution) Act 1998, s 1(2)(a); words in second pair of square brackets inserted by SI 1998/1833, reg 34(b).

Sub-s (3): words square brackets substituted by the Employment Rights (Dispute Resolution) Act 1998, s 1(2)(a).

Sub-s (4): added by the Employment Rights (Dispute Resolution) Act 1998, s 15, Sch 1, para 17(1), (3).

Savings: sub-s (1)(a)–(c), (e), (l), (m) and (s) related to the EAT's jurisdiction under the Equal Pay Act 1970, the Sex Discrimination Act 1975, the Race Relations Act 1976, the Disability Discrimination Act 1995, the Employment Equality (Sexual Orientation) Regulations 2003, the Employment Equality (Religion or Belief) Regulations 2003, and the Employment Equality (Age) Regulations 2006 respectively (all of which were repealed or revoked by the Equality Act 2010). The Equality Act 2010 (Commencement No 4, Savings, Consequential, Transitional, Transitory and Incidental Provisions and Revocation) Order 2010, SI 2010/2317, art 15 provides that the 2010 Act does not apply where the act complained of occurs wholly before 1 October 2010 so that (a) nothing in the 2010 Act affects (i) the operation of a previous enactment or anything duly done or suffered under a previous enactment; (ii) any right, obligation or liability acquired or incurred under a previous enactment; (iii) any penalty incurred in relation to any unlawful act under a previous enactment; (iv) any investigation, legal proceeding or remedy in respect of any such right, obligation, liability or penalty; and (b) any such investigation, legal proceeding or remedy may be instituted, continued or enforced, and any such penalty may be imposed, as if the 2010 Act had not been commenced. By art 1 of the 2010 Order "previous enactment" includes the six enactments listed *ante*.

Appeal Tribunal: the Tribunals and Inquiries Act 1992, s 11 (appeals from certain tribunals) does not apply in relation to proceedings before employment tribunals which arise under or by virtue of any of the enactments mentioned in sub-s (1) above; see s 11(2) of the 1992 Act.

See also as a source of authority to hear appeals, the Transfer of Undertakings (Protection of Employment) Regulations 2006, SI 2006/246, reg 16(2) at **[2.884]**.

Membership etc

[1.765]

22 Membership of Appeal Tribunal

(1) The Appeal Tribunal shall consist of—

(a) such number of judges as may be nominated from time to time [by the Lord Chief Justice, after consulting the Lord Chancellor,] from the judges . . . of the High Court and the Court of Appeal [and the judges within subsection (2A)],

(b) at least one judge of the Court of Session nominated from time to time by the Lord President of the Court of Session, and

(c) such number of other members as may be appointed from time to time by Her Majesty on the joint recommendation of the Lord Chancellor and the Secretary of State ("appointed members").

(2) The appointed members shall be persons who appear to the Lord Chancellor and the Secretary of State to have special knowledge or experience of industrial relations either—

(a) as representatives of employers, or

(b) as representatives of workers (within the meaning of the Trade Union and Labour Relations (Consolidation) Act 1992).

[(2A) A person is a judge within this subsection if the person—

(a) is the Senior President of Tribunals,

(b) is a deputy judge of the High Court,

(c) is the Judge Advocate General,

(d) is a Circuit judge,

(e) is a Chamber President, or a Deputy Chamber President, of a chamber of the Upper Tribunal or of a chamber of the First-tier Tribunal,
(f) is a judge of the Upper Tribunal by virtue of appointment under paragraph 1(1) of Schedule 3 to the Tribunals, Courts and Enforcement Act 2007,
(g) is a transferred-in judge of the Upper Tribunal (see section 31(2) of that Act),
(h) is a deputy judge of the Upper Tribunal (whether under paragraph 7 of Schedule 3 to, or section 31(2) of, that Act),
(i) is a district judge, which here does not include a deputy district judge, . . .
(j) is a District Judge (Magistrates' Courts), which here does not include a Deputy District Judge (Magistrates' Courts),
[(k) is the President of Employment Tribunals (England and Wales), or
(l) is the President of Employment Tribunals (Scotland)].]

(3) The [Lord Chief Justice shall] appoint one of the judges nominated under subsection (1) to be the President of the Appeal Tribunal.

[(3A) The Lord Chief Justice must not make an appointment under subsection (3) unless—
(a) he has consulted the Lord Chancellor, and
(b) the Lord President of the Court of Session agrees.]

(4) No judge shall be nominated a member of the Appeal Tribunal [under subsection (1)(b)] except with his consent.

[(5) The Lord Chief Justice may nominate a judicial office holder (as defined in section 109(4) of the Constitutional Reform Act 2005) to exercise his functions under this section.

(6) The Lord President of the Court of Session may nominate a judge of the Court of Session who is a member of the First or Second Division of the Inner House of that Court to exercise his functions under subsection (3A)(b).]

NOTES

Sub-s (1): words in first pair of square brackets substituted, and words omitted repealed, by the Constitutional Reform Act 2005, ss 15, 146, Sch 4, Pt 1, paras 245, 246(1), (2), Sch 18, Pt 2; words in second pair of square brackets inserted by the Crime and Courts Act 2013, s 21(4), Sch 14, Pt 5, para 11(1), (2).

Sub-s (2A): inserted by the Crime and Courts Act 2013, s 21(4), Sch 14, Pt 5, para 11(1), (3); word omitted from para (i) repealed and paras (k), (l) added, by the Courts and Tribunals (Judiciary and Functions of Staff) Act 2018, s 1(5), as from 20 February 2019.

Sub-s (3): words in square brackets substituted by the Constitutional Reform Act 2005, s 15, Sch 4, Pt 1, paras 245, 246(1), (3).

Sub-ss (3A), (5), (6): inserted and added respectively by the Constitutional Reform Act 2005, s 15, Sch 4, Pt 1, paras 245, 246(1), (4), (5).

Sub-s (4): words in square brackets inserted by the Crime and Courts Act 2013, s 21(4), Sch 14, Pt 5, para 11(1), (4).

[1.766]

23 Temporary membership

(1) At any time when—
(a) the office of President of the Appeal Tribunal is vacant, or
(b) the person holding that office is temporarily absent or otherwise unable to act as the President of the Appeal Tribunal,

the [Lord Chief Justice] may nominate another judge nominated under section 22(1)(a) to act temporarily in his place.

(2) At any time when a judge of the Appeal Tribunal nominated under paragraph (a) or (b) of subsection (1) of section 22 is temporarily absent or otherwise unable to act as a member of the Appeal Tribunal—
(a) in the case of a judge nominated under paragraph (a) of that subsection, the [Lord Chief Justice] may nominate another judge who is qualified to be nominated under that paragraph to act temporarily in his place, and
(b) in the case of a judge nominated under paragraph (b) of that subsection, the Lord President of the Court of Session may nominate another judge who is qualified to be nominated under that paragraph to act temporarily in his place.

(3) At any time when an appointed member of the Appeal Tribunal is temporarily absent or otherwise unable to act as a member of the Appeal Tribunal, the Lord Chancellor and the Secretary of State may jointly appoint a person appearing to them to have the qualifications for appointment as an appointed member to act temporarily in his place.

(4) A person nominated or appointed to act temporarily in place of the President or any other member of the Appeal Tribunal, when so acting, has all the functions of the person in whose place he acts.

(5) No judge shall be nominated to act temporarily as a member of the Appeal Tribunal except with his consent.

[(6) The functions conferred on the Lord Chief Justice by the preceding provisions of this section may be exercised only after consulting the Lord Chancellor.

(7) The functions conferred on the Lord Chancellor by subsection (3) may be exercised only after consultation with the Lord Chief Justice.

(8) The Lord Chief Justice may nominate a judicial office holder (as defined in section 109(4) of the Constitutional Reform Act 2005) to exercise his functions under this section.]

NOTES

Sub-ss (1), (2): words in square brackets substituted by the Constitutional Reform Act 2005, s 15, Sch 4, Pt 1, paras 245, 247(1)–(3).

Sub-ss (6)–(8): added by the Constitutional Reform Act 2005, s 15, Sch 4, Pt 1, paras 245, 247(1), (4).

[1.767]
24 Temporary additional judicial membership
[(1) This section applies if both of the following conditions are met—
(a) the Lord Chancellor thinks that it is expedient, after consulting the Lord Chief Justice, for a qualified person to be appointed to be a temporary additional judge of the Appeal Tribunal in order to facilitate in England and Wales the disposal of business in the Appeal Tribunal;
(b) the Lord Chancellor requests the Lord Chief Justice to make such an appointment.
(1A) The Lord Chief Justice may, after consulting the Lord Chancellor, appoint a qualified person as mentioned in subsection (1)(a).
(1B) An appointment under this section is—
(a) for such period, or
(b) on such occasions,
as the Lord Chief Justice determines, after consulting the Lord Chancellor.]
(2) In [this section] "qualified person" means a person who—
(a) is qualified for appointment as a judge of the High Court under section 10 of the [Senior Courts Act 1981], or
(b) has held office as a judge of the High Court or the Court of Appeal.
(3) A person appointed to be a temporary additional judge of the Appeal Tribunal has all the functions of a judge nominated under section 22(1)(a).
[(4) The Lord Chief Justice may nominate a judicial office holder (as defined in section 109(4) of the Constitutional Reform Act 2005) to exercise his functions under this section.]

NOTES
Sub-ss (1), (1A), (1B): substituted, for the original sub-s (1), by the Constitutional Reform Act 2005, s 15, Sch 4, Pt 1, paras 245, 248(1), (2).
Sub-s (2): words in first pair of square brackets substituted by the Constitutional Reform Act 2005, s 15, Sch 4, Pt 1, paras 245, 248(1), (3); words in second pair of square brackets substituted by the Constitutional Reform Act 2005, s 59, Sch 11, Pt 1, para 1(2).
Sub-s (4): added by the Constitutional Reform Act 2005, s 15, Sch 4, Pt 1, paras 245, 248(1), (4).

[1.768]
[24A Training etc of members of Appeal Tribunal
The Senior President of Tribunals is responsible, within the resources made available by the Lord Chancellor, for the maintenance of appropriate arrangements for the training, guidance and welfare of judges, and other members, of the Appeal Tribunal (in their capacities as members of the Appeal Tribunal).]

NOTES
Inserted, together with s 24B, by the Tribunals, Courts and Enforcement Act 2007, s 48(1), Sch 8, paras 35, 44.

[1.769]
[24B Oaths
(1) Subsection (2) applies to a person ("the appointee")—
(a) who is appointed under section 22(1)(c) or 23(3), or
(b) who is appointed under section 24(1A) and—
(i) falls when appointed within paragraph (a), but not paragraph (b), of section 24(2), and
(ii) has not previously taken the required oaths after accepting another office.
(2) The appointee must take the required oaths before—
(a) the Senior President of Tribunals, or
(b) an eligible person who is nominated by the Senior President of Tribunals for the purpose of taking the oaths from the appointee.
(3) If the appointee is a member of the Appeal Tribunal appointed before the coming into force of this section, the requirement in subsection (2) applies in relation to the appointee from the coming into force of this section.
(4) A person is eligible for the purposes of subsection (2)(b) if one or more of the following paragraphs applies to him—
(a) he holds high judicial office (as defined in section 60(2) of the Constitutional Reform Act 2005);
(b) he holds judicial office (as defined in section 109(4) of that Act);
(c) he holds (in Scotland) the office of sheriff.
(5) In this section "the required oaths" means—
(a) the oath of allegiance, and
(b) the judicial oath,
as set out in the Promissory Oaths Act 1868.]

NOTES
Inserted as noted to s 24A at **[1.768]**.

[1.770]
25 Tenure of appointed members
(1) Subject to subsections (2) to (4), an appointed member shall hold and vacate office in accordance with the terms of his appointment.

(2) An appointed member—
(a) may at any time resign his membership by notice in writing addressed to the Lord Chancellor and the Secretary of State, and
(b) shall vacate his office on the day on which he attains the age of seventy.

(3) Subsection (2)(b) is subject to section 26(4) to (6) of the Judicial Pensions and Retirement Act 1993 (Lord Chancellor's power to authorise continuance of office up to the age of seventy-five).

(4) If the Lord Chancellor, after consultation with the Secretary of State, is satisfied that an appointed member—
(a) has been absent from sittings of the Appeal Tribunal for a period longer than six consecutive months without the permission of the President of the Appeal Tribunal,
(b) has become bankrupt or [had a debt relief order (under Part 7A of the Insolvency Act 1986) made in respect of him or has] made an arrangement with his creditors, or has had his estate sequestrated or made a trust deed for behoof of his creditors or a composition contract,
(c) is incapacitated by physical or mental illness, or
(d) is otherwise unable or unfit to discharge the functions of a member,

the Lord Chancellor may declare his office as a member to be vacant and shall notify the declaration in such manner as the Lord Chancellor thinks fit; and when the Lord Chancellor does so, the office becomes vacant.

[(5) The Lord Chancellor may declare an appointed member's office vacant under subsection (4) only with the concurrence of the appropriate senior judge.

(6) The appropriate senior judge is the Lord Chief Justice of England and Wales, unless the member whose office is to be declared vacant exercises functions wholly or mainly in Scotland, in which case it is the Lord President of the Court of Session.]

NOTES

Sub-s (4): words in square brackets in para (b) inserted by the Tribunals, Courts and Enforcement Act 2007 (Consequential Amendments) Order 2012, SI 2012/2404, arts 3(2), 5, Sch 2, para 35, in relation to a debt relief order the application for which is made after 1 October 2012.

Sub-ss (5), (6): added by the Constitutional Reform Act 2005, s 15, Sch 4, Pt 1, paras 245, 249.

26 *(Repealed by the Tribunals, Courts and Enforcement Act 2007, s 146, Sch 23, Pt 1.)*

[1.771]

27 Remuneration, pensions and allowances

(1) The Secretary of State shall pay—
(a) the appointed members, [and]
(b) any person appointed to act temporarily in the place of an appointed member, . . .
(c) . . .

such remuneration and such travelling and other allowances as he may, with the relevant approval, determine; and for this purpose the relevant approval is that of the Treasury in the case of persons within paragraph (a) or (b) . . .

(2) A person appointed to be a temporary additional judge of the Appeal Tribunal shall be paid such remuneration and allowances as the Lord Chancellor may, with the approval of the Treasury, determine.

(3) If the Secretary of State determines, with the approval of the Treasury, that this subsection applies in the case of an appointed member, the Secretary of State shall—
(a) pay such pension, allowance or gratuity to or in respect of that person on his retirement or death, or
(b) make to the member such payments towards the provision of a pension, allowance or gratuity for his retirement or death,

as the Secretary of State may, with the approval of the Treasury, determine.

(4) Where—
(a) a person ceases to be an appointed member otherwise than on his retirement or death, and
(b) it appears to the Secretary of State that there are special circumstances which make it right for him to receive compensation,

the Secretary of State may make to him a payment of such amount as the Secretary of State may, with the approval of the Treasury, determine.

NOTES

Sub-s (1): word in square brackets inserted, and words omitted repealed, by the Tribunals, Courts and Enforcement Act 2007, ss 48(1), 146, Sch 8, paras 35, 45, Sch 23, Pt 1.

[1.772]

28 Composition of Appeal Tribunal

(1) The Appeal Tribunal may sit, in accordance with directions given by the President of the Appeal Tribunal, either as a single tribunal or in two or more divisions concurrently.

[(2) Proceedings before the Appeal Tribunal are to be heard by a judge alone.

This is subject to subsections (3) to (6) and to any provision made by virtue of section 30(2)(f) or (2A).

(3) A judge may direct that proceedings are to be heard by a judge and either two or four appointed members.

(4) A judge may, with the consent of the parties, direct that proceedings are to be heard by a judge and either one or three appointed members.

(5) The Lord Chancellor may by order provide for proceedings of a description specified in the order to be heard by a judge and either two or four appointed members.

(6) In proceedings heard by a judge and two or four appointed members, there shall be an equal number of—
(a) employer-representative members, and
(b) worker-representative members.
(7) In this section—
"employer-representative members" means appointed members whose knowledge or experience of industrial relations is as representatives of employers;
"worker-representative members" means appointed members whose knowledge or experience of industrial relations is as representatives of workers.]

NOTES

Sub-ss (2)–(7): substituted (for the original sub-ss (2)–(4A)) by the Enterprise and Regulatory Reform Act 2013, s 12(1), (2). Note that sub-s (4A) was originally inserted by the Tribunals, Courts and Enforcement Act 2007, s 48(1), Sch 8, paras 35, 46(1), (3), and the original sub-s (5) was repealed by the Employment Relations Act 1999, ss 41, 44, Sch 8, para 4, Sch 9(12).
Orders: as of 15 May 2019, no Orders had been made under this section.

Procedure

[1.773]

29 Conduct of hearings

(1) A person may appear before the Appeal Tribunal in person or be represented by—
(a) counsel or a solicitor,
(b) a representative of a trade union or an employers' association, or
(c) any other person whom he desires to represent him.
(2) The Appeal Tribunal has in relation to—
(a) the attendance and examination of witnesses,
(b) the production and inspection of documents, and
(c) all other matters incidental to its jurisdiction,
the same powers, rights, privileges and authority (in England and Wales) as the High Court and (in Scotland) as the Court of Session.

[1.774]

[29A Practice directions

(1) Directions about the procedure of the Appeal Tribunal may be given—
(a) by the Senior President of Tribunals, or
(b) by the President of the Appeal Tribunal.
(2) A power under subsection (1) includes—
(a) power to vary or revoke directions given in exercise of the power, and
(b) power to make different provision for different purposes.
(3) Directions under subsection (1)(a) may not be given without the approval of the Lord Chancellor.
(4) Directions under subsection (1)(b) may not be given without the approval of—
(a) the Senior President of Tribunals, and
(b) the Lord Chancellor.
(5) Subsection (1) does not prejudice any power apart from that subsection to give directions about the procedure of the Appeal Tribunal.
(6) Directions may not be given in exercise of any such power as is mentioned in subsection (5) without the approval of—
(a) the Senior President of Tribunals, and
(b) the Lord Chancellor.
(7) Subsections (3), (4)(b) and (6)(b) do not apply to directions to the extent that they consist of guidance about any of the following—
(a) the application or interpretation of the law;
(b) the making of decisions by members of the Appeal Tribunal.
(8) Subsections (3), (4)(b) and (6)(b) do not apply to directions to the extent that they consist of criteria for determining which members of the Appeal Tribunal may be chosen to decide particular categories of matter; but the directions may, to that extent, be given only after consulting the Lord Chancellor.
(9) Subsections (4) and (6) do not apply to directions given in a particular case for the purposes of that case only.
(10) Subsection (6) does not apply to directions under section 28(1).]

NOTES

Inserted by the Tribunals, Courts and Enforcement Act 2007, s 48(1), Sch 8, paras 35, 47.
Practice Directions: the current Practice Direction, issued by the President of the EAT on 19 December 2018, is at **[5.29]**.

[1.775]

30 Appeal Tribunal procedure rules

(1) The Lord Chancellor, after consultation with the Lord President of the Court of Session, shall make rules ("Appeal Tribunal procedure rules") with respect to proceedings before the Appeal Tribunal.
(2) Appeal Tribunal procedure rules may, in particular, include provision—
(a) with respect to the manner in which, and the time within which, an appeal may be brought,
(b) with respect to the manner in which any application [or complaint] to the Appeal Tribunal may be made,
(c) for requiring persons to attend to give evidence and produce documents and for authorising the administration of oaths to witnesses,

(d) for requiring or enabling the Appeal Tribunal to sit in private in circumstances in which an [employment tribunal] is required or empowered to sit in private by virtue of [section 10A] of this Act,

(e) . . . and

(f) for interlocutory matters arising on any appeal or application to the Appeal Tribunal to be dealt with [by an officer of the Appeal Tribunal].

[(2A) Appeal Tribunal procedure rules may make provision of a kind which may be made by employment tribunal procedure regulations under section 10(2), (5), (6) or (7).

(2B) For the purposes of subsection (2A)—

(a) the reference in section 10(2) to section 4 shall be treated as a reference to section 28, and

(b) the reference in section 10(4) to the President or a Regional [Employment Judge] shall be treated as a reference to a judge of the Appeal Tribunal.

(2C) Section 10B shall have effect in relation to a direction to or determination of the Appeal Tribunal as it has effect in relation to a direction to or determination of an employment tribunal.]

(3) Subject to Appeal Tribunal procedure rules [and directions under section 28(1) or 29A(1)], the Appeal Tribunal has power to regulate its own procedure.

NOTES

Sub-s (2): words in square brackets in para (b) inserted by the Transnational Information and Consultation of Employees Regulations 1999, SI 1999/3323, reg 35(1), (4); words in first pair of square brackets in para (d) substituted by the Employment Rights (Dispute Resolution) Act 1998, s 1(2)(a), and words in second pair of square brackets substituted by the Employment Relations Act 1999, s 41, Sch 8, para (1), (2); para (e) repealed by the Employment Relations Act 2004, s 57, Sch 1, para 26, Sch 2; words in square brackets in para (f) substituted by the Enterprise and Regulatory Reform Act 2013, s 12(1), (3).

Sub-ss (2A)–(2C): inserted by the Employment Relations Act 1999, s 41, Sch 8, para 5(1), (3); words in square brackets in sub-s (2B) substituted by the Crime and Courts Act 2013, s 21(4), Sch 14, Pt 7, para 13(3).

Sub-s (3): words in square brackets inserted by the Tribunals, Courts and Enforcement Act 2007, s 48(1), Sch 8, paras 35, 48.

Rules: by virtue of s 44 of, and Sch 2, Pt I, paras 1–4 to, this Act, the Employment Appeal Tribunal Rules 1993, SI 1993/2854 at **[2.145]** have effect as if made under this section. These Rules have subsequently been amended by Rules made under this section; ie, the Employment Appeal Tribunal (Amendment) Rules 1996, SI 1996/3216; the Employment Appeal Tribunal (Amendment) Rules 2001, SI 2001/1128; the Employment Appeal Tribunal (Amendment) Rules 2001 (Amendment) Rules 2001, SI 2001/1476; the Employment Appeal Tribunal (Amendment) Rules 2004, SI 2004/2526; the Employment Appeal Tribunal (Amendment) Rules 2005, SI 2005/1871; the Employment Appeal Tribunal (Amendment) Rules 2013, SI 2013/1693.

[1.776]

31 Restriction of publicity in cases involving sexual misconduct

(1) Appeal Tribunal procedure rules may, as respects proceedings to which this section applies, include provision—

(a) for cases involving allegations of the commission of sexual offences, for securing that the registration or other making available of documents or divisions shall be so effected as to prevent the identification of any person affected by or making the allegation, and

(b) for cases involving allegations of sexual misconduct, enabling the Appeal Tribunal, on the application of any party to the proceedings before it or of its own motion, to make a restricted reporting order having effect (if not revoked earlier) until the promulgation of the decision of the Appeal Tribunal.

(2) This section applies to—

(a) proceedings on an appeal against a decision of an [employment tribunal] to make, or not to make, a restricted reporting order, and

(b) proceedings on an appeal against any interlocutory decision of an [employment tribunal] in proceedings in which the [employment tribunal] has made a restricted reporting order which it has not revoked.

(3) If any identifying matter is published or included in a relevant programme in contravention of a restricted reporting order—

(a) in the case of publication in a newspaper or periodical, any proprietor, any editor and any publisher of the newspaper or periodical,

(b) in the case of publication in any other form, the person publishing the matter, and

(c) in the case of matter included in a relevant programme—

(i) any body corporate engaged in providing the service in which the programme is included, and

(ii) any person having functions in relation to the programme corresponding to those of an editor of a newspaper,

shall be guilty of an offence and liable on summary conviction to a fine not exceeding level 5 on the standard scale.

(4) Where a person is charged with an offence under subsection (3) it is a defence to prove that at the time of the alleged offence he was not aware, and neither suspected nor had reason to suspect, that the publication or programme in question was of, or included, the matter in question.

(5) Where an offence under subsection (3) committed by a body corporate is proved to have been committed with the consent or connivance of, or to be attributable to any neglect on the part of—

(a) a director, manager, secretary or other similar officer of the body corporate, or

(b) a person purporting to act in any such capacity,

he as well as the body corporate is guilty of the offence and liable to be proceeded against and punished accordingly.

(6) In relation to a body corporate whose affairs are managed by its members "director", in subsection (5), means a member of the body corporate.

(7) "Restricted reporting order" means—
(a) in subsections (1) and (3), an order—
(i) made in exercise of a power conferred by rules made by virtue of this section, and
(ii) prohibiting the publication in Great Britain of identifying matter in a written publication available to the public or its inclusion in a relevant programme for reception in Great Britain, and
(b) in subsection (2), an order which is a restricted reporting order for the purposes of section 11.
(8) In this section—
"identifying matter", in relation to a person, means any matter likely to lead members of the public to identify him as a person affected by, or as the person making, the allegation,
"relevant programme" has the same meaning as in the Sexual Offences (Amendment) Act 1992,
"sexual misconduct" means the commission of a sexual offence, sexual harassment or other adverse conduct (of whatever nature) related to sex, and conduct is related to sex whether the relationship with sex lies in the character of the conduct or in its having reference to the sex or sexual orientation of the person at whom the conduct is directed,
"sexual offence" means any offence to which section 4 of the Sexual Offences (Amendment) Act 1976, the Sexual Offences (Amendment) Act 1992 or section 274(2) of the Criminal Procedure (Scotland) Act 1995 applies (offences under the Sexual Offences Act 1956, Part I of the Criminal Law (Consolidation) (Scotland) Act 1995 and certain other enactments), and
"written publication" has the same meaning as in the Sexual Offences (Amendment) Act 1992.

NOTES

Sub-s (2): words in square brackets substituted by the Employment Rights (Dispute Resolution) Act 1998, s 1(2)(a).

Sexual Offences (Amendment) Act 1976, s 4: repealed by Youth Justice and Criminal Evidence Act 1999, ss 48, 67(3), Sch 2, para 4, Sch 6.

Sexual Offences (Amendment) Act 1992: the definition "written publication" in that Act was repealed by the Youth Justice and Criminal Evidence Act 1999, ss 48, 67(3), Sch 2, paras 6, 12(1), (2), Sch 6.

Rules: see the note to s 30 at **[1.775]**.

[1.777]

32 Restriction of publicity in disability cases

(1) This section applies to proceedings—
(a) on an appeal against a decision of an [employment tribunal] to make, or not to make, a restricted reporting order, or
(b) on an appeal against any interlocutory decision of an [employment tribunal] in proceedings in which the [employment tribunal] has made a restricted reporting order which it has not revoked.
(2) Appeal Tribunal procedure rules may, as respects proceedings to which this section applies, include provision for—
(a) enabling the Appeal Tribunal, on the application of the complainant or of its own motion, to make a restricted reporting order having effect (if not revoked earlier) until the promulgation of the decision of the Appeal Tribunal, and
(b) where a restricted reporting order is made in relation to an appeal which is being dealt with by the Appeal Tribunal together with any other proceedings, enabling the Appeal Tribunal to direct that the order is to apply also in relation to those other proceedings or such part of them as the Appeal Tribunal may direct.
(3) If any identifying matter is published or included in a relevant programme in contravention of a restricted reporting order—
(a) in the case of publication in a newspaper or periodical, any proprietor, any editor and any publisher of the newspaper or periodical,
(b) in the case of publication in any other form, the person publishing the matter, and
(c) in the case of matter included in a relevant programme—
(i) any body corporate engaged in providing the service in which the programme is included, and
(ii) any person having functions in relation to the programme corresponding to those of an editor of a newspaper,

shall be guilty of an offence and liable on summary conviction to a fine not exceeding level 5 on the standard scale.
(4) Where a person is charged with an offence under subsection (3), it is a defence to prove that at the time of the alleged offence he was not aware, and neither suspected nor had reason to suspect, that the publication or programme in question was of, or included, the matter in question.
(5) Where an offence under subsection (3) committed by a body corporate is proved to have been committed with the consent or connivance of, or to be attributable to any neglect on the part of—
(a) a director, manager, secretary or other similar officer of the body corporate, or
(b) a person purporting to act in any such capacity,

he as well as the body corporate is guilty of the offence and liable to be proceeded against and punished accordingly.
(6) In relation to a body corporate whose affairs are managed by its members "director", in subsection (5), means a member of the body corporate.
(7) "Restricted reporting order" means—
(a) in subsection (1), an order which is a restricted reporting order for the purposes of section 12, and
(b) in subsections (2) and (3), an order—
(i) made in exercise of a power conferred by rules made by virtue of this section, and

(ii) prohibiting the publication in Great Britain of identifying matter in a written publication available to the public or its inclusion in a relevant programme for reception in Great Britain.

(8) In this section—

"complainant" means the person who made the complaint to which the proceedings before the Appeal Tribunal relate,

"identifying matter" means any matter likely to lead members of the public to identify the complainant or such other persons (if any) as may be named in the order,

"promulgation" has such meaning as may be prescribed by rules made by virtue of this section,

"relevant programme" means a programme included in a programme service, within the meaning of the Broadcasting Act 1990, and

"written publication" includes a film, a sound track and any other record in permanent form but does not include an indictment or other document prepared for use in particular legal proceedings.

NOTES

Sub-s (1): words in square brackets substituted by the Employment Rights (Dispute Resolution) Act 1998, s 1(2)(a).

Rules: see the note to s 30 at **[1.775]**.

[1.778]

33 Restriction of vexatious proceedings

(1) If, on an application made by the Attorney General or the Lord Advocate under this section, the Appeal Tribunal is satisfied that a person has habitually and persistently and without any reasonable ground—

(a) instituted vexatious proceedings, whether [before the Certification Officer,] in an [employment tribunal] or before the Appeal Tribunal, and whether against the same person or against different persons, or

(b) made vexatious applications in any proceedings, whether [before the Certification Officer,] in an [employment tribunal] or before the Appeal Tribunal,

the Appeal Tribunal may, after hearing the person or giving him an opportunity of being heard, make a restriction of proceedings order.

(2) A "restriction of proceedings order" is an order that—

(a) no proceedings shall without the leave of the Appeal Tribunal be instituted [before the Certification Officer,] in any [employment tribunal] or before the Appeal Tribunal by the person against whom the order is made,

(b) any proceedings instituted by him [before the Certification Officer,] in any [employment tribunal] or before the Appeal Tribunal before the making of the order shall not be continued by him without the leave of the Appeal Tribunal, and

(c) no application (other than one for leave under this section) is to be made by him in any proceedings [before the Certification Officer,] in any [employment tribunal] or before the Appeal Tribunal without the leave of the Appeal Tribunal.

(3) A restriction of proceedings order may provide that it is to cease to have effect at the end of a specified period, but otherwise it remains in force indefinitely.

(4) Leave for the institution or continuance of, or for the making of an application in, any proceedings [before the Certification Officer,] in an [employment tribunal] or before the Appeal Tribunal by a person who is the subject of a restriction of proceedings order shall not be given unless the Appeal Tribunal is satisfied—

(a) that the proceedings or application are not an abuse of [process], and

(b) that there are reasonable grounds for the proceedings or application.

(5) A copy of a restriction of proceedings order shall be published in the London Gazette and the Edinburgh Gazette.

NOTES

Sub-s (1): words in first pair of square brackets in paras (a), (b) inserted by the Employment Relations Act 2004, s 49(1)–(3); words in second pair of square brackets in those paragraphs substituted by the Employment Rights (Dispute Resolution) Act 1998, s 1(2)(a).

Sub-s (2): words in first pair of square brackets in paras (a)–(c) inserted by the Employment Relations Act 2004, s 49(1), (4)–(6); words in second pair of square brackets in those paragraphs substituted by the Employment Rights (Dispute Resolution) Act 1998, s 1(2)(a).

Sub-s (4): words in first pair of square brackets inserted, and word in third pair of square brackets substituted, by the Employment Relations Act 2004, s 49(1), (7); words in second pair of square brackets substituted by the Employment Rights (Dispute Resolution) Act 1998, s 1(2)(a).

[1.779]

[34 Costs and expenses

(1) Appeal Tribunal procedure rules may include provision for the award of costs or expenses.

(2) Rules under subsection (1) may include provision authorising the Appeal Tribunal to have regard to a person's ability to pay when considering the making of an award against him under such rules.

(3) Appeal Tribunal procedure rules may include provision for authorising the Appeal Tribunal—

(a) to disallow all or part of the costs or expenses of a representative of a party to proceedings before it by reason of that representative's conduct of the proceedings;

(b) to order a representative of a party to proceedings before it to meet all or part of the costs or expenses incurred by a party by reason of the representative's conduct of the proceedings.

(4) Appeal Tribunal procedure rules may also include provision for taxing or otherwise settling the costs or expenses referred to in subsection (1) or (3)(b) (and, in particular in England and Wales, for enabling the amount of such costs to be assessed by way of detailed assessment in the High Court).]

NOTES

Substituted by the Employment Act 2002, s 23.

Rules: see the note to s 30 at **[1.775]**.

Decisions and further appeals

[1.780]

35 Powers of Appeal Tribunal

(1) For the purpose of disposing of an appeal, the Appeal Tribunal may—

(a) exercise any of the powers of the body or officer from whom the appeal was brought, or

(b) remit the case to that body or officer.

(2) Any decision or award of the Appeal Tribunal on an appeal has the same effect, and may be enforced in the same manner, as a decision or award of the body or officer from whom the appeal was brought.

[1.781]

36 Enforcement of decisions etc

(1)–(3) . . .

(4) No person shall be punished for contempt of the Appeal Tribunal except by, or with the consent of, a judge.

(5) A magistrates' court shall not remit the whole or part of a fine imposed by the Appeal Tribunal unless it has the consent of a judge who is a member of the Appeal Tribunal.

NOTES

Sub-ss (1)–(3): repealed by the Employment Relations Act 2004, s 57, Sch 1, para 27, Sch 2.

[1.782]

37 Appeals from Appeal Tribunal

(1) Subject to subsection (3), an appeal on any question of law lies from any decision or order of the Appeal Tribunal to the relevant appeal court with the leave of the Appeal Tribunal or of the relevant appeal court.

(2) In subsection (1) the "relevant appeal court" means—

(a) in the case of proceedings in England and Wales, the Court of Appeal, and

(b) in the case of proceedings in Scotland, the Court of Session.

(3) No appeal lies from a decision of the Appeal Tribunal refusing leave for the institution or continuance of, or for the making of an application in, proceedings by a person who is the subject of a restriction of proceedings order made under section 33.

(4) This section is without prejudice to section 13 of the Administration of Justice Act 1960 (appeal in case of contempt of court).

[1.783]

[37ZA Appeals to Supreme Court: grant of certificate by Appeal Tribunal

(1) If the Appeal Tribunal is satisfied that—

(a) the conditions in subsection (4) or (5) are fulfilled in relation to the Appeal Tribunal's decision or order in any proceedings, and

(b) as regards that decision or order, a sufficient case for an appeal to the Supreme Court has been made out to justify an application under section 37ZB,

the Appeal Tribunal may grant a certificate to that effect.

(2) The Appeal Tribunal may grant a certificate under this section only on an application made by a party to the proceedings.

(3) The Appeal Tribunal may not grant a certificate under this section in the case of proceedings in Scotland.

(4) The conditions in this subsection are that a point of law of general public importance is involved in the decision or order of the Appeal Tribunal and that point of law is—

(a) a point of law that—

(i) relates wholly or mainly to the construction of an enactment or statutory instrument, and

(ii) has been fully argued in the proceedings and fully considered in the judgment of the Appeal Tribunal in the proceedings, or

(b) a point of law—

(i) in respect of which the Appeal Tribunal is bound by a decision of the Court of Appeal or the Supreme Court in previous proceedings, and

(ii) that was fully considered in the judgments given by the Court of Appeal or, as the case may be, the Supreme Court in those previous proceedings.

(5) The conditions in this subsection are that a point of law of general public importance is involved in the decision or order of the Appeal Tribunal and that—

(a) the proceedings entail a decision relating to a matter of national importance or consideration of such a matter,

(b) the result of the proceedings is so significant (whether considered on its own or together with other proceedings or likely proceedings) that, in the opinion of the Appeal Tribunal, a hearing by the Supreme Court is justified, or

(c) the Appeal Tribunal is satisfied that the benefits of earlier consideration by the Supreme Court outweigh the benefits of consideration by the Court of Appeal.

(6) No appeal lies against the grant or refusal of a certificate under subsection (1).]

NOTES

Commencement: 8 August 2016.

Inserted by the Criminal Justice and Courts Act 2015, s 65, as from 8 August 2016, except in relation to a decision or order of the Employment Appeal Tribunal made before that date (see the Criminal Justice and Courts Act 2015 (Commencement No 4 and Transitional Provisions) Order 2016, SI 2016/717, art 5).

Note that this section and ss 37ZB, 37ZC were originally inserted as ss 37A–37C. The Small Business, Enterprise and Employment Act 2015, s 150(1), (2) subsequently inserted a new Part 2A (ss 37A–37Q (see *post*)). The section numbers of the sections inserted by the Criminal Justice and Courts Act 2015 were renumbered as ss 37ZA–37ZC (and internal cross-references were changed) by a correction slip issued in September 2015.

[1.784]

[37ZB Appeals to Supreme Court: permission to appeal

(1) If the Appeal Tribunal grants a certificate under section 37ZA in relation to any proceedings, a party to those proceedings may apply to the Supreme Court for permission to appeal directly to the Supreme Court.

(2) An application under subsection (1) must be made—

(a) within one month from the date on which the certificate is granted, or

(b) within such time as the Supreme Court may allow in a particular case.

(3) If on such an application it appears to the Supreme Court to be expedient to do so, the Supreme Court may grant permission for such an appeal.

(4) If permission is granted under this section—

(a) no appeal from the decision or order to which the certificate relates lies to the Court of Appeal, but

(b) an appeal lies from that decision or order to the Supreme Court.

(5) An application under subsection (1) is to be determined without a hearing.

(6) Subject to subsection (4), no appeal lies to the Court of Appeal from a decision or order of the Appeal Tribunal in respect of which a certificate is granted under section 37ZA until—

(a) the time within which an application can be made under subsection (1) has expired, and

(b) where such an application is made, that application has been determined in accordance with this section.]

NOTES

Commencement: 8 August 2016.

Inserted by the Criminal Justice and Courts Act 2015, s 65, as from 8 August 2016, except in relation to a decision or order of the Employment Appeal Tribunal made before that date (see the Criminal Justice and Courts Act 2015 (Commencement No 4 and Transitional Provisions) Order 2016, SI 2016/717, art 5).

[1.785]

[37ZC Appeals to Supreme Court: exclusions

(1) No certificate may be granted under section 37ZA in respect of a decision or order of the Appeal Tribunal in any proceedings where, by virtue of any enactment (other than sections 37ZA and 37ZB), no appeal would lie from that decision or order of the Appeal Tribunal to the Court of Appeal, with or without the leave or permission of the Appeal Tribunal or the Court of Appeal.

(2) No certificate may be granted under section 37ZA in respect of a decision or order of the Appeal Tribunal in any proceedings where, by virtue of any enactment, no appeal would lie from a decision of the Court of Appeal on that decision or order of the Appeal Tribunal to the Supreme Court, with or without the leave or permission of the Court of Appeal or the Supreme Court.

(3) Where no appeal would lie to the Court of Appeal from the decision or order of the Appeal Tribunal except with the leave or permission of the Appeal Tribunal or the Court of Appeal, no certificate may be granted under section 37ZA in respect of a decision or order of the Appeal Tribunal unless it appears to the Appeal Tribunal that it would be a proper case for granting leave or permission to appeal to the Court of Appeal.

(4) No certificate may be granted under section 37ZA where the decision or order of the Appeal Tribunal is made in the exercise of its jurisdiction to punish for contempt.]

NOTES

Commencement: 8 August 2016.

Inserted by the Criminal Justice and Courts Act 2015, s 65, as from 8 August 2016, except in relation to a decision or order of the Employment Appeal Tribunal made before that date (see the Criminal Justice and Courts Act 2015 (Commencement No 4 and Transitional Provisions) Order 2016, SI 2016/717, art 5).

[PART 2A
FINANCIAL PENALTIES FOR FAILURE TO PAY SUMS ORDERED TO BE PAID OR SETTLEMENT SUMS

[1.786]

37A Sums to which financial penalty can relate

(1) This section has effect for the purposes of this Part.

(2) "Financial award"—

(a) means a sum of money (or, if more than one, the sums of money) ordered by an employment tribunal on a claim involving an employer and a worker, or on a relevant appeal, to be paid by the employer to the worker, and

(b) includes—

(i) any sum (a "costs sum") required to be paid in accordance with an order in respect of costs or expenses which relate to proceedings on, or preparation time relating to, the claim or a relevant appeal, and

(ii) in a case to which section 16 applies, a sum ordered to be paid to the Secretary of State under that section.

(3) Subsection (2)(b)(i) applies irrespective of when the order was made or the amount of the costs sum was determined.

(4) "Settlement sum" means a sum payable by an employer to a worker under the terms of a settlement in respect of which a certificate has been issued under section 19A(1).

(5) "Relevant sum" means—

(a) a financial award, or

(b) a settlement sum.

(6) "Relevant appeal", in relation to a financial award, means an appeal against—

(a) the decision on the claim to which it relates,

(b) a decision to make, or not to make, an order in respect of a financial award (including any costs sum) on the claim,

(c) the amount of any such award, or

(d) any decision made on an appeal within paragraphs (a) to (c) or this paragraph.

(7) Sections 37B to 37D apply for the purposes of calculating the unpaid amount on any day of a relevant sum.]

NOTES

Commencement: 6 April 2016.

Inserted, together with ss 37B–37Q, by the Small Business, Enterprise and Employment Act 2015, s 150(1), (2), as from 6 April 2016, in relation to relevant sums where (a) in the case of a financial award, the decision of the employment tribunal on the claim to which the financial award relates is made on or after the day on which this section comes into force; (b) in the case of a settlement sum, the certificate under s 19A(1) of this Act in respect of the settlement under whose terms it is payable is issued on or after that day (see s 150(8) of the 2015 Act at **[1.1926]**).

[1.787]

[37B Financial award: unpaid amount

(1) In the case of a financial award, the unpaid amount on any day means the amount outstanding immediately before that day in respect of—

(a) the initial amount of the financial award (see subsection (2)), and

(b) interest payable in respect of the financial award by virtue of section 14.

(2) The initial amount of a financial award is—

(a) in a case to which section 16 applies, the monetary award within the meaning of that section (see section 17(3)), together with any costs sum, and

(b) in any other case, the sum or sums of money ordered to be paid (including any costs sum).

(3) An amount in respect of a financial award is not to be regarded as outstanding—

(a) when the worker could make an application for an order for a costs sum in relation to—

(i) proceedings on the claim to which the financial award relates,

(ii) proceedings on a relevant appeal,

(b) when the worker has made such an application but the application has not been withdrawn or finally determined,

(c) when the employer or worker could appeal against—

(i) the decision on the claim to which it relates,

(ii) a decision to make, or not to make, a financial award (including any costs sum) on the claim,

(iii) the amount of any such award, or

(iv) any decision made on an appeal within sub-paragraphs (i) to (iii) or this sub-paragraph,

but has not done so, or

(d) when the employer or worker has made such an appeal but the appeal has not been withdrawn or finally determined.]

NOTES

Commencement: 6 April 2016.

Inserted as noted to s 37A at **[1.786]**; for effect see the note to s 37A at **[1.786]**.

[1.788]

[37C Settlement sum: unpaid amount

(1) In the case of a settlement sum, the unpaid amount on any day means the amount outstanding immediately before that day in respect of—

(a) the settlement sum, and

(b) interest (if any) calculated in accordance with the settlement (within the meaning of section 19A).

(2) Subject to section 37D(2) and (3), an amount in respect of a settlement sum is not to be regarded as outstanding if the settlement sum is not recoverable under section 19A(3).]

NOTES

Commencement: 6 April 2016.

Inserted as noted to s 37A at **[1.786]**; for effect see the note to s 37A at **[1.786]**.

[1.789]

[37D Unpaid amount of relevant sum: further provision

(1) Subsections (2) and (3) apply where—

(a) a relevant sum is to be paid by instalments,

(b) any instalment is not paid on or before the day on which it is due to be paid, and

(c) a warning notice (see section 37E) is given in consequence of the failure to pay that instalment ("the unpaid instalment").

(2) For the purposes of calculating the unpaid amount for—

(a) that warning notice, and

(b) any penalty notice given in respect of that warning notice,

any remaining instalments (whether or not yet due) are to be treated as having been due on the same day as the unpaid instalment.

(3) Accordingly, the amount outstanding in respect of the financial award or settlement sum is to be taken to be—

(a) the aggregate of—

(i) the unpaid instalment, and

(ii) any remaining instalments,

including, in the case of a settlement sum, any amount which is not recoverable under section 19A(3) by reason only of not being due,

(b) interest on those amounts calculated in accordance with section 37B(1)(b) or 37C(1)(b) (and subsection (2)).

(4) Subsections (2) and (3) are not to be taken to affect the time at which any remaining instalment is due to be paid by the employer.

(5) The provisions of this Part apply where a financial award consists of two or more sums (whether or not any of them is a costs sum) which are required to be paid at different times as if—

(a) it were a relevant sum to be paid by instalments, and

(b) those sums were the instalments.

(6) Where a payment by an employer is made, or purported to be made, in respect of a relevant sum, an enforcement officer may determine whether, and to what extent, the payment is to be treated as being—

(a) in respect of that relevant sum or instead in respect of some other amount owed by the employer;

(b) in respect of the initial amount or interest on it, in the case of a payment treated as being in respect of the relevant sum.]

NOTES

Commencement: 6 April 2016.

Inserted as noted to s 37A at **[1.786]**; for effect see the note to s 37A at **[1.786]**.

[1.790]

[37E Warning notice

(1) This section applies where an enforcement officer considers that an employer who is required to pay a relevant sum has failed—

(a) in the case of a relevant sum which is to be paid by instalments, to pay an instalment on or before the day on which it is due to be paid, or

(b) in any other case, to pay the relevant sum in full on or before the day on which it is due to be paid.

(2) The officer may give the employer a notice (a "warning notice") stating the officer's intention to impose a financial penalty in respect of the relevant sum unless before a date specified in the warning notice ("the specified date") the employer has paid in full the amount so specified ("the specified amount").

This is subject to subsection (3).

(3) Where a penalty notice has previously been given in respect of the relevant sum, the officer may not give a warning notice until—

(a) 3 months have elapsed since the end of the relevant period (within the meaning of section 37H) relating to the last penalty notice given in respect of the relevant sum, and

(b) if the relevant sum is to be paid by instalments, the last instalment has become due for payment.

(4) The specified date must be after the end of the period of 28 days beginning with the day on which the warning notice is given.

(5) The specified amount must be the unpaid amount of the relevant sum on the day on which the warning notice is given.

(6) A warning notice must identify the relevant sum and state—

(a) how the specified amount has been calculated;

(b) the grounds on which it is proposed to impose a penalty;

(c) the amount of the financial penalty that would be imposed if no payment were made in respect of the relevant sum before the specified date;

(d) that the employer may before the specified date make representations about the proposal to impose a penalty, including representations—

(i) about payments which the employer makes in respect of the relevant sum after the warning notice is given;

(ii) about the employer's ability to pay both a financial penalty and the relevant sum;

(e) how any such representations may be made.

(7) The statement under subsection (6)(e) must include provision for allowing representations to be made by post (whether or not it also allows them to be made in any other way).

(8) If the employer pays the specified amount before the specified date, the relevant sum is to be treated for the purposes of this Part as having been paid in full.

(9) Subsection (8) is not to be taken to affect the liability of the employer to pay any increase in the unpaid amount between the date of the warning notice and the date of payment.]

NOTES

Commencement: 6 April 2016.

Inserted as noted to s 37A at **[1.786]**; for effect see the note to s 37A at **[1.786]**.

[1.791]

[37F Penalty notice

(1) This section applies where an enforcement officer—

(a) has given a warning notice to an employer, and

(b) is satisfied that the employer has failed to pay the specified amount in full before the specified date.

(2) The officer may give the employer a notice (a "penalty notice") requiring the employer to pay a financial penalty to the Secretary of State.

(3) A penalty notice must identify the relevant sum and state—

(a) the grounds on which the penalty notice is given;

(b) the unpaid amount of the relevant sum on the specified date and how it has been calculated;

(c) the amount of the financial penalty (see subsections (4) to (6));

(d) how the penalty must be paid;

(e) the period within which the penalty must be paid;

(f) how the employer may pay a reduced penalty instead of the financial penalty;

(g) the amount of the reduced penalty (see subsection (8));

(h) how the employer may appeal against the penalty notice;

(i) the consequences of non-payment.

(4) Subject to subsections (5) and (6), the amount of the financial penalty is 50% of the unpaid amount of the relevant sum on the specified date.

(5) If the unpaid amount on the specified date is less than £200, the amount of the penalty is £100.

(6) If the unpaid amount on the specified date is more than £10,000, the amount of the financial penalty is £5,000.

(7) The period specified under subsection (3)(e) must be a period of not less than 28 days beginning with the day on which the penalty notice is given.

(8) The amount of the reduced penalty is 50% of the amount of the financial penalty.

(9) Subsection (10) applies if, within the period of 14 days beginning with the day on which the penalty notice is given, the employer—

(a) pays the unpaid amount of the relevant sum on the specified date (as stated in the notice under subsection (3)(b)), and

(b) pays the reduced penalty to the Secretary of State.

(10) The employer is to be treated—

(a) for the purposes of this Part, as having paid the relevant sum in full, and

(b) by paying the reduced penalty, as having paid the whole of the financial penalty.

(11) Subsection (10)(a) is not to be taken to affect the liability of the employer to pay any increase in the unpaid amount of the relevant sum between the specified date and the date of payment.]

NOTES

Commencement: 6 April 2016.

Inserted as noted to s 37A at **[1.786]**; for effect see the note to s 37A at **[1.786]**.

[1.792]

[37G Appeal against penalty notice

(1) An employer to whom a penalty notice is given may, before the end of the period specified under section 37F(3)(e) (period within which penalty must be paid), appeal against—

(a) the penalty notice; or

(b) the amount of the financial penalty.

(2) An appeal under subsection (1) lies to an employment tribunal.

(3) An appeal under subsection (1) may be made on one or more of the following grounds—

(a) that the grounds stated in the penalty notice under section 37F(3)(a) were incorrect;

(b) that it was unreasonable for the enforcement officer to have given the notice;

(c) that the calculation of an amount stated in the penalty notice was incorrect.

(4) On an appeal under subsection (1), an employment tribunal may—

(a) allow the appeal and cancel the penalty notice;

(b) in the case of an appeal made on the ground that the calculation of an amount stated in the penalty notice was incorrect, allow the appeal and substitute the correct amount for the amount stated in the penalty notice;
(c) dismiss the appeal.

(5) Where an employer has made an appeal under subsection (1), the penalty notice is not enforceable until the appeal has been withdrawn or finally determined.]

NOTES

Commencement: 6 April 2016.

Inserted as noted to s 37A at **[1.786]**; for effect see the note to s 37A at **[1.786]**.

[1.793]

[37H Interest and recovery

(1) This section applies if all or part of a financial penalty which an employer is required by a penalty notice to pay is unpaid at the end of the relevant period.

(2) The relevant period is—
(a) if no appeal is made under section 37G(1) relating to the penalty notice, the period specified in the penalty notice under section 37F(3)(e);
(b) if such an appeal is made, the period ending when the appeal is withdrawn or finally determined.

(3) The outstanding amount of the financial penalty for the time being carries interest—
(a) at the rate that, on the last day of the relevant period, was specified in section 17 of the Judgments Act 1838,
(b) from the end of the relevant period until the time when the amount of interest calculated under this subsection equals the amount of the financial penalty,

(and does not also carry interest as a judgment debt under that section).

(4) The outstanding amount of a penalty and any interest is recoverable—
(a) in England and Wales, if the county court so orders, under section 85 of the County Courts Act 1984 or otherwise as if the sum were payable under an order of the county court;
(b) in Scotland, by diligence as if the penalty notice were an extract registered decree arbitral bearing a warrant for execution issued by the sheriff court of any sheriffdom in Scotland.

(5) Any amount received by the Secretary of State under this Part is to be paid into the Consolidated Fund.]

NOTES

Commencement: 6 April 2016.

Inserted as noted to s 37A at **[1.786]**; for effect see the note to s 37A at **[1.786]**.

[1.794]

[37I Withdrawal of warning notice

(1) Where—
(a) a warning notice has been given (and not already withdrawn),
(b) it appears to an enforcement officer that—
(i) the notice incorrectly omits any statement or is incorrect in any particular, or
(ii) the warning notice was given in contravention of section 37E(3), and
(c) if a penalty notice has been given in relation to the warning notice, any appeal made under section 37G(1) has not been determined,

the officer may withdraw the warning notice by giving notice of withdrawal to the employer.

(2) Where a warning notice is withdrawn, no penalty notice may be given in relation to it.

(3) Where a warning notice is withdrawn after a penalty notice has been given in relation to it—
(a) the penalty notice ceases to have effect;
(b) any sum paid by or recovered from the employer by way of financial penalty payable under the penalty notice must be repaid to the employer with interest at the appropriate rate running from the date when the sum was paid or recovered;
(c) any appeal under section 37G(1) relating to the penalty notice must be dismissed.

(4) In subsection (3)(b), the appropriate rate means the rate that, on the date the sum was paid or recovered, was specified in section 17 of the Judgments Act 1838.

(5) A notice of withdrawal under this section must indicate the effect of the withdrawal (but a failure to do so does not make the notice of withdrawal ineffective).

(6) Withdrawal of a warning notice relating to a relevant sum does not preclude a further warning notice being given in relation to that sum (subject to section 37E(3))].

NOTES

Commencement: 6 April 2016.

Inserted as noted to s 37A at **[1.786]**; for effect see the note to s 37A at **[1.786]**.

[1.795]

[37J Withdrawal of penalty notice

(1) Where—
(a) a penalty notice has been given (and not already withdrawn or cancelled), and
(b) it appears to an enforcement officer that—
(i) the notice incorrectly omits any statement required by section 37F(3), or
(ii) any statement so required is incorrect in any particular,

the officer may withdraw it by giving notice of the withdrawal to the employer.

(2) Where a penalty notice is withdrawn and no replacement penalty notice is given in accordance with section 37K—

(a) any sum paid by or recovered from the employer by way of financial penalty payable under the notice must be repaid to the employer with interest at the appropriate rate running from the date when the sum was paid or recovered;

(b) any appeal under section 37G(1) relating to the penalty notice must be dismissed.

(3) In a case where subsection (2) applies, the notice of withdrawal must indicate the effect of that subsection (but a failure to do so does not make the withdrawal ineffective).

(4) In subsection (2)(a), "the appropriate rate" means the rate that, on the date the sum was paid or recovered, was specified in section 17 of the Judgments Act 1838.]

NOTES

Commencement: 6 April 2016.

Inserted as noted to s 37A at **[1.786]**; for effect see the note to s 37A at **[1.786]**.

[1.796]

37K Replacement penalty notice

(1) Where an enforcement officer—

(a) withdraws a penalty notice ("the original penalty notice") under section 37J, and

(b) is satisfied that the employer failed to pay the specified amount in full before the specified date in accordance with the warning notice in relation to which the original penalty notice was given,

the officer may at the same time give another penalty notice in relation to the warning notice ("the replacement penalty notice").

(2) The replacement penalty notice must—

(a) indicate the differences between it and the original penalty notice that the enforcement officer reasonably considers material, and

(b) indicate the effect of section 37L.

(3) Failure to comply with subsection (2) does not make the replacement penalty notice ineffective.

(4) Where a replacement penalty notice is withdrawn under section 37J, no further replacement penalty notice may be given under subsection (1) pursuant to the withdrawal.

(5) Nothing in this section affects any power that arises apart from this section to give a penalty notice.

NOTES

Commencement: 6 April 2016.

Inserted as noted to s 37A at **[1.786]**; for effect see the note to s 37A at **[1.786]**.

[1.797]

[37L Effect of replacement penalty notice

(1) This section applies where a penalty notice is withdrawn under section 37J and a replacement penalty notice is given in accordance with section 37K.

(2) If an appeal relating to the original penalty notice has been made under section 37G(1) and has not been withdrawn or finally determined before the time when that notice is withdrawn—

(a) the appeal ("the earlier appeal") is to have effect after that time as if it were against the replacement penalty notice, and

(b) the employer may exercise the right under section 37G to appeal against the replacement penalty notice only after withdrawing the earlier appeal.

(3) If a sum was paid by or recovered from the employer by way of financial penalty under the original penalty notice—

(a) an amount equal to that sum (or, if more than one, the total of those sums) is to be treated as having been paid in respect of the replacement penalty notice, and

(b) any amount by which that sum (or total) exceeds the amount of the financial penalty payable under the replacement penalty notice must be repaid to the employer with interest at the appropriate rate running from the date when the sum (or, if more than one, the first of them) was paid or recovered.

(4) In subsection (3)(b) "the appropriate rate" means the rate that, on the date mentioned in that provision, was specified in section 17 of the Judgments Act 1838.]

NOTES

Commencement: 6 April 2016.

Inserted as noted to s 37A at **[1.786]**; for effect see the note to s 37A at **[1.786]**.

[1.798]

[37M Enforcement officers

The Secretary of State may appoint or authorise persons to act as enforcement officers for the purposes of this Part.]

NOTES

Commencement: 6 April 2016.

Inserted as noted to s 37A at **[1.786]**; for effect see the note to s 37A at **[1.786]**.

[1.799]
[37N Power to amend Part 2A
(1) The Secretary of State may by regulations—
 (a) amend subsection (5) or (6) of section 37F by substituting a different amount;
 (b) amend subsection (4) or (8) of that section by substituting a different percentage;
 (c) amend section 37E(4) or 37F(7) or (9) by substituting a different number of days.
(2) Any provision that could be made by regulations under this section may instead be included in an order under section 12A(12).]

NOTES
Commencement: 6 April 2016.
Inserted as noted to s 37A at **[1.786]**; for effect see the note to s 37A at **[1.786]**.

[1.800]
[37O Modification in particular cases
(1) The Secretary of State may by regulations make provision for this Part to apply with modifications in cases where—
 (a) two or more financial awards were made against an employer on claims relating to different workers that were considered together by an employment tribunal, or
 (b) settlement sums are payable by an employer under two or more settlements in cases dealt with together by a conciliation officer.
(2) Regulations under subsection (1) may in particular provide for any provision of this Part to apply as if any such financial awards or settlement sums, taken together, were a single relevant sum.
(3) The Secretary of State may by regulations make provision for this Part to apply with modifications in cases where a financial award has been made against an employer but is not regarded as outstanding by virtue only of the fact that an application for an order for a costs sum has not been finally determined (or any appeal within section 37B(3)(c) so far as relating to the application could still be made or has not been withdrawn or finally determined).
(4) Regulations under subsection (3) may in particular provide—
 (a) for any provision of this Part to apply, or to apply if the enforcement officer so determines, as if the application had not been, and could not be, made;
 (b) for any costs sum the amount of which is subsequently determined, or the order for which is subsequently made, to be treated for the purposes of this Part as a separate relevant sum.]

NOTES
Commencement: 6 April 2016.
Inserted as noted to s 37A at **[1.786]**; for effect see the note to s 37A at **[1.786]**.

[1.801]
[37P Giving of notices
(1) For the purposes of section 7 of the Interpretation Act 1978 in its application to this Part, the proper address of an employer is—
 (a) if the employer has notified an enforcement officer of an address at which the employer is willing to accept notices, that address;
 (b) otherwise—
  (i) in the case of a body corporate, the address of the body's registered or principal office;
  (ii) in the case of a partnership or an unincorporated body or association, the principal office of the partnership, body or association;
  (iii) in any other case, the last known address of the person in question.
(2) In the case of—
 (a) a body corporate registered outside the United Kingdom,
 (b) a partnership carrying on business outside the United Kingdom, or
 (c) an unincorporated body or association with offices outside the United Kingdom,
the references in subsection (1) to its principal office include references to its principal office within the United Kingdom (if any).]

NOTES
Commencement: 6 April 2016.
Inserted as noted to s 37A at **[1.786]**; for effect see the note to s 37A at **[1.786]**.

[1.802]
[37Q Financial penalties for non-payment: interpretation
(1) In this Part, the following terms have the following meanings—
"claim"—
  (a) means anything that is referred to in the relevant legislation as a claim, a complaint or a reference, other than a reference made by virtue of section 122(2) or 128(2) of the Equality Act 2010 (reference by court of question about a non-discrimination or equality rule etc), and
  (b) also includes an application, under regulations made under section 45 of the Employment Act 2002, for a declaration that a person is a permanent employee;
"costs sum" has the meaning given by section 37A;
"employer" has the same meaning as in section 12A;
"enforcement officer" means a person appointed or authorised to act under section 37M;

"financial award" has the meaning given by section 37A;
"penalty notice" has the meaning given by section 37F;
"relevant appeal" has the meaning given by section 37A;
"relevant sum" has the meaning given by section 37A;
"settlement sum" has the meaning given by section 37A;
"specified amount" and "specified date", in relation to a warning notice or a penalty notice given in relation to it, have the meanings given by section 37E(2);
"unpaid amount"—
(a) in relation to a financial award, has the meaning given by section 37B;
(b) in relation to a settlement sum, has the meaning given by section 37C;
subject, in each case, to section 37D;
"warning notice" has the meaning given by section 37E(2);
"worker" has the same meaning as in section 12A.

(2) References in this Part to an employer, in relation to a warning notice or penalty notice, are to the person to whom the notice is given (whether or not the person is an employer at the time in question).
(3) For the purposes of this Part a relevant sum is to be regarded as having been paid in full when the amount unpaid in respect of that sum on the date of payment has been paid.
(4) For the purposes of this Part, a penalty notice is given in relation to a warning notice if it is given as the result of a failure by the employer to pay the specified amount before the specified date.
(5) The Secretary of State may by regulations amend this section so as to alter the meaning of "claim".
(6) Any provision that could be made by regulations under subsection (5) may instead be included in an order under section 12A(12).]

NOTES

Commencement: 6 April 2016.
Inserted as noted to s 37A at **[1.786]**; for effect see the note to s 37A at **[1.786]**.

PART III
SUPPLEMENTARY

Crown employment and Parliamentary staff

[1.803]
38 Crown employment

(1) This Act has effect in relation to Crown employment and persons in Crown employment as it has effect in relation to other employment and other employees.
(2) In this Act "Crown employment" means employment under or for the purposes of a government department or any officer or body exercising on behalf of the Crown functions conferred by a statutory provision.
(3) For the purposes of the application of this Act in relation to Crown employment in accordance with subsection (1)—
(a) references to an employee shall be construed as references to a person in Crown employment, and
(b) references to a contract of employment shall be construed as references to the terms of employment of a person in Crown employment.
(4) Subsection (1) applies to—
(a) service as a member of the naval, military or air forces of the Crown, and
(b) employment by an association established for the purposes of Part XI of the Reserve Forces Act 1996;
but Her Majesty may by Order in Council make any provision of this Act apply to service as a member of the naval, military or air forces of the Crown subject to such exceptions and modifications as may be specified in the Order in Council.

NOTES

Sub-s (4) has effect, by virtue of Sch 2, Pt II, para 9, and until the relevant commencement date as defined in para 9(2), as if the subsection set out in para 9(1) were substituted for sub-s (4) of this section: see Sch 2, Pt II, para 9 at **[1.812]** and the notes thereto.
Orders: as of 15 May 2019, no Orders in Council had been made under this section.

[1.804]
39 Parliamentary staff

(1) This Act has effect in relation to employment as a relevant member of the House of Lords staff or a relevant member of the House of Commons staff as it has effect in relation to other employment.
(2) Nothing in any rule of law or the law or practice of Parliament prevents a relevant member of the House of Lords staff or a relevant member of the House of Commons staff from bringing before an [employment tribunal] proceedings of any description which could be brought before such a tribunal by a person who is not a relevant member of the House of Lords staff or a relevant member of the House of Commons staff.
(3) For the purposes of the application of this Act in relation to a relevant member of the House of Commons staff—
(a) references to an employee shall be construed as references to a relevant member of the House of Commons staff, and
(b) references to a contract of employment shall be construed as including references to the terms of employment of a relevant member of the House of Commons staff.

(4) In this Act "relevant member of the House of Lords staff" means any person who is employed under a contract of employment with the Corporate Officer of the House of Lords.

(5) In this Act "relevant member of the House of Commons staff" has the same meaning as in section 195 of the Employment Rights Act 1996; and (subject to an Order in Council under subsection (12) of that section)—

(a) subsections (6) and (7) of that section have effect for determining who is the employer of a relevant member of the House of Commons staff for the purposes of this Act, and

(b) subsection (8) of that section applies in relation to proceedings brought by virtue of this section.

NOTES

Sub-s (2): words in square brackets substituted by the Employment Rights (Dispute Resolution) Act 1998, s 1(2)(a).

General

[1.805]

40 Power to amend Act

(1) The Secretary of State [and the Lord Chancellor, acting jointly,] may by order—

(a) provide that any provision of this Act to which this section applies and which is specified in the order shall not apply to persons, or to employments, of such classes as may be prescribed in the order, or

(b) provide that any provision of this Act to which this section applies shall apply to persons or employments of such classes as may be prescribed in the order subject to such exceptions and modifications as may be so prescribed.

(2) This section applies to sections 3, 8, 16 and 17 . . .

NOTES

Sub-s (1): words in square brackets inserted by the Tribunals, Courts and Enforcement Act 2007, s 48(1), Sch 8, paras 35, 38.

Sub-s (2): words omitted repealed by the Enterprise and Regulatory Reform Act 2013, s 7(2), Sch 1, paras 2, 8.

Employment Protection (Consolidation) Act 1978: s 133 of that Act is repealed by s 45 of, and Sch 3, Pt I to, this Act.

Orders: as of 15 May 2019, no Orders had been made under this section but, by virtue of s 44 of, and Sch 2, Pt I, paras 1–4 to, this Act, the Redundancy Payments (National Health Service) (Modification) Order 1993, SI 1993/3167, and the Employment Protection (Continuity of Employment of National Health Service Employees) (Modification) Order 1996, SI 1996/1023, have effect as if made under this section.

[1.806]

41 Orders, regulations and rules

(1) Any power conferred by this Act on a Minister of the Crown to make an order, and any power conferred by this Act to make regulations or rules, is exercisable by statutory instrument.

(2) No recommendation shall be made to Her Majesty to make an Order in Council under section 38(4), . . . no order shall be made under section 3, 4(4) [or (6D)][,12A(12)], [28(5)] or 40, [and no regulations are to be made under section 37N, 37O or 37Q(5),] unless a draft of the Order in Council [, order or regulations] has been laid before Parliament and approved by a resolution of each House of Parliament.

(3) A statutory instrument containing—

(a) an order made by a Minister of the Crown under any other provision of this Act except Part II of Schedule 2, or

(b) [any other regulations] or rules made under this Act,

is subject to annulment in pursuance of a resolution of either House of Parliament.

(4) Any power conferred by this Act which is exercisable by statutory instrument includes power to make such incidental, supplementary or transitional provision as appears to the Minister exercising the power to be necessary or expedient.

NOTES

Sub-s (2): the word omitted was repealed, the words "and no regulations are to be made under section 37N, 37O or 37Q(5)," in square brackets were inserted, and the words ", order or regulations" in square brackets were substituted, by the Small Business, Enterprise and Employment Act 2015, s 150(1), (5), as from 6 April 2016, in relation to relevant sums where (a) in the case of a financial award, the decision of the employment tribunal on the claim to which the financial award relates is made on or after the day on which these amendments come into force; (b) in the case of a settlement sum, the certificate under s 19A(1) of this Act in respect of the settlement under whose terms it is payable is issued on or after that day (see s 150 of the 2015 Act at **[1.1926]**). The other words and figures in square brackets were inserted by the Enterprise and Regulatory Reform Act 2013, ss 11(2), 12(1), (4), 16(2), Sch 3, paras 2, 4. In relation to the figure "28(5)" see the savings in s 24(2) of the 2013 Act at **[1.1824]**.

Sub-s (3): words in square brackets substitute by the Small Business, Enterprise and Employment Act 2015, s 150(1), (5), as from 6 April 2016 (for effect see the note above).

[1.807]

42 Interpretation

(1) In this Act [(except where otherwise expressly provided)]—

["ACAS" means the Advisory, Conciliation and Arbitration Service,]

"the Appeal Tribunal" means the Employment Appeal Tribunal,

"Appeal Tribunal procedure rules" shall be construed in accordance with section 30(1),

"appointed member" shall be construed in accordance with section 22(1)(c),

["Certification Officer" shall be construed in accordance with section 254 of the Trade Union and Labour Relations (Consolidation) Act 1992,] "conciliation officer" means an officer designated by [ACAS] under section 211 of the Trade Union and Labour Relations (Consolidation) Act 1992,

"contract of employment" means a contract of service or apprenticeship, whether express or implied, and (if it is express) whether oral or in writing,

"employee" means an individual who has entered into or works under (or, where the employment has ceased, worked under) a contract of employment,

"employer", in relation to an employee, means the person by whom the employee is (or, where the employment has ceased, was) employed,

"employers' association" has the same meaning as in the Trade Union and Labour Relations (Consolidation) Act 1992,

"employment" means employment under a contract of employment and "employed" shall be construed accordingly,

"[employment tribunal] procedure regulations" shall be construed in accordance with section 7(1),

["representative" shall be construed in accordance with section 6(1) (in Part 1) or section 29(1) (in Part 2),]

"statutory provision" means a provision, whether of a general or a special nature, contained in, or in any document made or issued under, any Act, whether of a general or special nature,

"successor", in relation to the employer of an employee, means (subject to subsection (2)) a person who in consequence of a change occurring (whether by virtue of a sale or other disposition or by operation of law) in the ownership of the undertaking, or of the part of the undertaking, for the purposes of which the employee was employed, has become the owner of the undertaking or part, and

"trade union" has the meaning given by section 1 of the Trade Union and Labour Relations (Consolidation) Act 1992.

(2) The definition of "successor" in subsection (1) has effect (subject to the necessary modifications) in relation to a case where—

(a) the person by whom an undertaking or part of an undertaking is owned immediately before a change is one of the persons by whom (whether as partners, trustees or otherwise) it is owned immediately after the change, or

(b) the persons by whom an undertaking or part of an undertaking is owned immediately before a change (whether as partners, trustees or otherwise) include the persons by whom, or include one or more of the persons by whom, it is owned immediately after the change,

as it has effect where the previous owner and the new owner are wholly different persons.

(3) For the purposes of this Act any two employers shall be treated as associated if—

(a) one is a company of which the other (directly or indirectly) has control, or

(b) both are companies of which a third person (directly or indirectly) has control;

and "associated employer" shall be construed accordingly.

NOTES

Sub-s (1): words in first pair of square brackets inserted by the Small Business, Enterprise and Employment Act 2015, s 150(1), (6), as from 6 April 2016, in relation to relevant sums where (a) in the case of a financial award, the decision of the employment tribunal on the claim to which the financial award relates is made on or after the day on which this amendment comes into force, (b) in the case of a settlement sum, the certificate under s 19A(1) of this Act in respect of the settlement under whose terms it is payable is issued on or after that day (see s 150 of the 2015 Act at **[1.1926]**). Definition "ACAS" inserted, and word in square brackets in the definition "conciliation officer" substituted, by the Enterprise and Regulatory Reform Act 2013, s 7(2), Sch 1, paras 2, 9. Definition "Certification Officer" inserted by the Employment Relations Act 2004, s 49(8). In definition "employment tribunal procedure regulations" words in square brackets substituted by the Employment Rights (Dispute Resolution) Act 1998, s 1(2)(a). Definition "representative" inserted by the Enterprise and Regulatory Reform Act 2013, s 21(1), (4).

Final provisions

43–45 *(S 43 introduces Sch 1 (consequential amendments), s 44 introduces Sch 2 (transitional provisions, savings and transitory provisions), s 45 introduces Sch 3 (repeals and revocations).)*

[1.808]

46 Commencement

This Act shall come into force at the end of the period of three months beginning with the day on which it is passed.

[1.809]

47 Extent

This Act does not extend to Northern Ireland.

[1.810]

48 Short title

This Act may be cited as the [Employment Tribunals Act 1996].

NOTES

Words in square brackets substituted by the Employment Rights (Dispute Resolution) Act 1998, s 1(2)(c).

SCHEDULES

SCHEDULE 1

(Sch 1 (Consequential amendments; in so far as relevant to this work, these amendments have been incorporated at the appropriate place).)

SCHEDULE 2
TRANSITIONAL PROVISIONS, SAVINGS AND TRANSITORY PROVISIONS

Section 44

PART I
TRANSITIONAL PROVISIONS AND SAVINGS

[1.811]

1. The substitution of this Act for the provisions repealed or revoked by this Act does not affect the continuity of the law.

2. Anything done, or having effect as done, (including the making of subordinate legislation) under or for the purposes of any provision repealed or revoked by this Act has effect as if done under or for the purposes of any corresponding provision of this Act.

3. Any reference (express or implied) in this Act or any other enactment, or in any instrument or document, to a provision of this Act is (so far as the context permits) to be read as (according to the context) being or including in relation to times, circumstances and purposes before the commencement of this Act a reference to the corresponding provision repealed or revoked by this Act.

4. (1) Any reference (express or implied) in any enactment, or in any instrument or document, to a provision repealed or revoked by this Act is (so far as the context permits) to be read as (according to the context) being or including in relation to times, circumstances and purposes after the commencement of this Act a reference to the corresponding provision of this Act.

(2) In particular, where a power conferred by an Act is expressed to be exercisable in relation to enactments contained in Acts passed before or in the same Session as the Act conferring the power, the power is also exercisable in relation to provisions of this Act which reproduce such enactments.

5. Paragraphs 1 to 4 have effect in place of section 17(2) of the Interpretation Act 1978 (but are without prejudice to any other provision of that Act).

6. The repeal by the Act of section 130 of, and Schedule 10 to, the Employment Protection (Consolidation) Act 1978 (jurisdiction of referees under specified provisions to be exercised by [employment tribunals]) does not affect—

(a) the operation of those provisions in relation to any question which may arise after the commencement of this Act, or

(b) the continued operation of those provisions after the commencement of this Act in relation to any question which has arisen before that commencement.

NOTES

Para 6: words in square brackets substituted by the Employment Rights (Dispute Resolution) Act 1998, s 1(2)(b).

PART II
TRANSITORY PROVISIONS

[1.812]

7, 8. *(Para 7 (transitory provisions – disability discrimination) and para 8 (transitory provisions – jobseeker's allowance) are spent. Note that para 7 was also repealed by the Equality Act 2010, s 211(2), Sch 27, Pt 1.)*

Armed forces

9. (1) If section 31 of the Trade Union Reform and Employment Rights Act 1993 has not come into force before the commencement of this Act, section 38 shall have effect until the relevant commencement date as if for subsection (4) there were substituted—

"(4) Subsection (1)—

(a) does not apply to service as a member of the naval, military or air forces of the Crown, but

(b) does apply to employment by an association established for the purposes of Part XI of the Reserve Forces Act 1996.".

(2) The reference in sub-paragraph (1) to the relevant commencement date is a reference—

(a) if an order has been made before the commencement of this Act appointing a day after that commencement as the day on which section 31 of the Trade Union Reform and Employment Rights Act 1993 is to come into force, to the day so appointed, and

(b) otherwise, to such day as the Secretary of State may by order appoint.

10. *(Para 10 (further transitory provisions – armed forces) is spent.)*

NOTES

Para 9: the Trade Union Reform and Employment Rights Act 1993, s 31 was repealed (never having been brought into force) by the Employment Rights Act 1996, s 242, Sch 3, Pt I, and replaced by s 192 of the 1996 Act at **[1.1107]**. The said s 192 had not been brought into force as of 15 May 2019, and is the subject of transitional provisions as noted to that section.

"Relevant commencement date": no such Order as is mentioned in para 9(2)(a) was made, and as of 15 May 2019 no Order had been made under para 9(2)(b).

SCHEDULE 3

(Sch 3 (repeals and revocations) in so far as relevant to this work, these have been incorporated at the appropriate place.)

EMPLOYMENT RIGHTS ACT 1996

(1996 c 18)

ARRANGEMENT OF SECTIONS

PART I
EMPLOYMENT PARTICULARS

Right to statements of employment particulars

Right to itemised pay statement

Enforcement

PART II
PROTECTION OF WAGES

Deductions by employer

Payments to employer

Cash shortages and stock deficiencies in retail employment

Enforcement

Supplementary

PART 2A
ZERO HOURS WORKERS

PART III
GUARANTEE PAYMENTS

PART IV
SUNDAY WORKING FOR SHOP AND BETTING WORKERS

Protected shop workers and betting workers

Opting-out of Sunday work

PART IVA
PROTECTED DISCLOSURES

PART V
PROTECTION FROM SUFFERING DETRIMENT IN EMPLOYMENT

Rights not to suffer detriment

Enforcement

Application to police of rights relating to health and safety

PART 5A
PROTECTION FOR APPLICANTS FOR EMPLOYMENT ETC IN THE HEALTH SERVICE

PART VI
TIME OFF WORK

Public duties

Looking for work and making arrangements for training

Ante-natal care

Ante-natal care: agency workers

Accompanying to ante-natal appointments

Accompanying to ante-natal appointments: agency workers

Adoption appointments

Adoption appointments: agency workers

Dependants

Occupational pension scheme trustees

Employee representatives

PART 6A
STUDY AND TRAINING

PART VII
SUSPENSION FROM WORK

Suspension on medical grounds

Suspension on maternity grounds

Ending the supply of an agency worker on maternity grounds

General

PART VIII

CHAPTER I
MATERNITY LEAVE

CHAPTER IA
ADOPTION LEAVE

CHAPTER 1B
SHARED PARENTAL LEAVE

CHAPTER II
PARENTAL LEAVE

CHAPTER III
PATERNITY LEAVE

CHAPTER 4
PARENTAL BEREAVEMENT LEAVE

PART VIIIA
FLEXIBLE WORKING

PART IX
TERMINATION OF EMPLOYMENT

Minimum period of notice

Written statement of reasons for dismissal

PART X
UNFAIR DISMISSAL

CHAPTER I
RIGHT NOT TO BE UNFAIRLY DISMISSED

The right

Dismissal

Fairness

Other dismissals

CHAPTER II
WEEK'S PAY

CHAPTER III
OTHER INTERPRETATION PROVISIONS

PART XV
GENERAL AND SUPPLEMENTARY

SCHEDULES

An Act to consolidate enactments relating to employment rights

[22 May 1996]

NOTES

This Act consolidates the individual employment legislation contained principally in the Employment Protection (Consolidation) Act 1978 (as extensively and repeatedly amended) and unrepealed provisions of the Wages Act 1986. Provisions of the 1978 Act relating to employment tribunals and the Employment Appeal Tribunal were separately consolidated into the Employment Tribunals Act 1996 at **[1.729]** et seq.

The Act came into force on 22 August 1996, subject to transitional provisions in Sch 2, Pt II relating to consolidation of legislation not yet in force. Commencement details are not given for individual sections unless affected by Sch 2 or subsequently inserted by other legislation with effect on or after 11 May 2013. The whole of the Act is printed except for ss 238 and 239, which apply to Northern Ireland and the Isle of Man, and Schedules 1 and 3, which enact consequential amendments and repeals, and the sections (240 and 242) introducing them. In so far as within the scope of this work, those amendments, repeals and revocations have been incorporated at the appropriate place. Other provisions omitted are those repealed by subsequent legislation (as noted to each such provision). As to the further power to amend this Act, see s 209 of this Act *post*, the Employment Relations Act 2004, s 42(1), (4)(d) at **[1.1415]**, the Health and Safety at Work etc Act 1974, s 80 at **[1.79]**, and the Pensions Act 2004, ss 259, 260.

Employment Appeal Tribunal: an appeal lies to the Employment Appeal Tribunal on any question of law arising from any decision of, or in any proceedings before, an employment tribunal under or by virtue of this Act; see the Employment Tribunals Act 1996, s 21(1)(f) at **[1.764]**.

See *Harvey* CII, DI, DII, E, G, H, J.

PART I
EMPLOYMENT PARTICULARS

Right to statements of employment particulars

[1.813]

1 Statement of initial employment particulars

(1) Where *an employee* begins employment with an employer, the employer shall give to *the employee* a written statement of particulars of employment.

(2) The statement may (subject to section 2(4)) be given in instalments and (whether or not given in instalments) shall be given not later than two months after the beginning of the employment.

(3) The statement shall contain particulars of—

(a) the names of the employer and *employee*,

(b) the date when the employment began, and

(c) [in the case of a statement given to an employee,] the date on which the employee's period of continuous employment began (taking into account any employment with a previous employer which counts towards that period).

(4) The statement shall also contain particulars, as at a specified date not more than seven days before the statement *(or the instalment containing them)* is given, of—

(a) the scale or rate of remuneration or the method of calculating remuneration,

(b) the intervals at which remuneration is paid (that is, weekly, monthly or other specified intervals),

(c) any terms and conditions relating to hours of work (including any terms and conditions relating to normal working hours),

(d) any terms and conditions relating to any of the following—

(i) entitlement to holidays, including public holidays, and holiday pay (the particulars given being sufficient to enable the *employee's* entitlement, including any entitlement to accrued holiday pay on the termination of employment, to be precisely calculated),

(ii) incapacity for work due to sickness or injury, including any provision for sick pay, *and*

[(iia) any other paid leave, and]

(iii) pensions and pension schemes,

[(da) any other benefits provided by the employer that do not fall within another paragraph of this subsection,]

(e) the length of notice which the *employee* is obliged to give and entitled to receive to terminate his contract of employment [or other worker's contract],

(f) the title of the job which the *employee* is employed to do or a brief description of the work for which he is employed,

(g) where the employment is not intended to be permanent, the period for which it is expected to continue or, if it is for a fixed term, the date when it is to end,

[(ga) any probationary period, including any conditions and its duration,]

(h) either the place of work or, where the *employee* is required or permitted to work at various places, an indication of that and of the address of the employer,

(j) any collective agreements which directly affect the terms and conditions of the employment including, where the employer is not a party, the persons by whom they were made, *and*

(k) where the *employee* is required to work outside the United Kingdom for a period of more than one month—

(i) the period for which he is to work outside the United Kingdom,

(ii) the currency in which remuneration is to be paid while he is working outside the United Kingdom,

(iii) any additional remuneration payable to him, and any benefits to be provided to or in respect of him, by reason of his being required to work outside the United Kingdom, and

(iv) any terms and conditions relating to his return to the United Kingdom;

[(l) any training entitlement provided by the employer,

(m) any part of that training entitlement which the employer requires the worker to complete, and

(n) any other training which the employer requires the worker to complete and which the employer will not bear the cost of.]

(5) Subsection (4)(d)(iii) does not apply to *an employee* of a body or authority if—

(a) the *employee's* pension rights depend on the terms of a pension scheme established under any provision contained in or having effect under any Act, and

(b) any such provision requires the body or authority to give to a new *employee* information concerning the *employee's* pension rights or the determination of questions affecting those rights.

[(6) In this section "probationary period" means a temporary period specified in the contract of employment or other worker's contract between a worker and an employer that—

(a) commences at the beginning of the employment, and

(b) is intended to enable the employer to assess the worker's suitability for the employment.]

NOTES

This section is amended by the Employment Rights (Miscellaneous Amendments) Regulations 2019, SI 2019/731, regs 4, 5, as from 6 April 2020, subject to reg 15 of the 2019 Regulations at **[2.2197]**, as follows—

in sub-s (1), for "an employee" and "the employee" in italics there is substituted "a worker" and "the worker" respectively;

in sub-s (3), for "employee" in italics there is substituted "worker" and words in square brackets are inserted;

in sub-s (4), for "employee's" and "employee" in italics there is substituted "worker's" and "worker" respectively and words in square brackets in para (e) are inserted;

in sub-s (5), for "an employee", "employee's" and "employee" in italics there is substituted "a worker", "worker's" and "worker" respectively.

This section is also amended, as follows, by the Employment Rights (Employment Particulars and Paid Annual Leave) (Amendment) Regulations 2018, SI 2018/1378, regs 2, 3, as from 6 April 2020, in relation to a written statement required by s 1 or 4 of this Act where the worker to whom the statement must be given begins employment with the employer on or after 6 April 2020 (see reg 8 of the 2018 Regulations at **[2.2113]**)—

sub-s (2) is substituted as set out below—

"(2) Subject to sections 2(2) to (4)—

(a) the particulars required by subsections (3) and (4) must be included in a single document; and

(b) the statement must be given not later than the beginning of the employment.";

in sub-s (4), for the words "(or the instalment containing them)" in italics in the first place there are substituted the words "(or the instalment of a statement given under section 2(4) containing them)", para (c) is substituted as set out below, in para (d) word in italics repealed and words in square brackets inserted, paras (da), (ga) inserted, word in italics in para (j) repealed, and paras (l)–(n) inserted, and sub-s (6) is added—

"(c) any terms and conditions relating to hours of work including any terms and conditions relating to—

(i) normal working hours,

(ii) the days of the week the worker is required to work, and

(iii) whether or not such hours or days may be variable, and if they may be how they vary or how that variation is to be determined.".

Failure to give statement: as to penalties for the failure to give a statement of employer particulars under sub-s (1) above or s 4(1) *post*, in relation to proceedings to which the Employment Act 2002, s 38, Sch 5 applies, see s 38 of that Act at **[1.1279]**.

Note: sub-s (4) did not contain a para (i) in the Queen's Printer's copy of this Act.

[1.814]

2 Statement of initial particulars: supplementary

(1) If, in the case of a statement under section 1, there are no particulars to be entered under any of the heads of paragraph (d) or (k) of subsection (4) of that section, or under any of the other paragraphs of subsection (3) or (4) of that section, that fact shall be stated.

(2) A statement under section 1 may refer the *employee* for particulars of any of the matters specified in *subsection (4)(d)(ii) and (iii)* of that section to the provisions of some other document which is reasonably accessible to the *employee*.

(3) A statement under section 1 may refer the *employee* for particulars of either of the matters specified in subsection (4)(e) of that section to the law or to the provisions of any collective agreement directly affecting the terms and conditions of the employment which is reasonably accessible to the *employee*.

(4) The particulars required by section 1(3) and (4)(a) to (c), (d)(i), (f) and (h) shall be included in a single document.

(5) Where before the end of the period of two months after the beginning of *an employee's* employment the *employee* is to begin to work outside the United Kingdom for a period of more than one month, *the statement under section 1* shall be given to him not later than the time when he leaves the United Kingdom in order to begin so to work.

(6) A statement shall be given to a person under section 1 even if his employment ends before the end of the period within which the statement is required to be given.

NOTES

For the word "employee" in each place it appears in italics in sub-ss (2), (3), (5) there is substituted the word "worker", and for the words "an employee's" in italics in sub-s (5) there are substituted the words "a worker's", by the Employment Rights (Miscellaneous Amendments) Regulations 2019, SI 2019/731, regs 4, 6, as from 6 April 2020, subject to reg 15 of the 2019 Regulations at **[2.2197]**.

For the words "subsection (4)(d)(ii) and (iii)" in italics in sub-s (2) there are substituted the words "subsection (4)(d)(ii) to (iii) and (l)", sub-s (4) is substituted as set out below, for the words "the statement under section 1" in italics in sub-s (5) there are substituted the words "any instalment of a statement given under subsection (4)", and sub-s (6) is repealed, by the Employment Rights (Employment Particulars and Paid Annual Leave) (Amendment) Regulations 2018, SI 2018/1378, regs 2, 4, as from 6 April 2020, in relation to a written statement required by s 1 or 4 of this Act where the worker to whom the statement must be given begins employment with the employer on or after 6 April 2020 (see reg 8 of the 2018 Regulations at **[2.2113]**)—

"(4) A statement, insofar as it relates to the particulars required by section1(4)(d)(iii), (j) and (l) and the note required by section 3—

(a) may be given in instalments; and

(b) must be given not later than two months after the beginning of the employment, even where the employment ends before that date. ".

[1.815]

3 Note about disciplinary procedures and pensions

(1) A statement under section 1 shall include a note—

(a) specifying any disciplinary rules applicable to *the employee* or referring the employee to the provisions of a document specifying such rules which is reasonably accessible to *the employee*,

[(aa) specifying any procedure applicable to the taking of disciplinary decisions relating to *the employee*, or to a decision to dismiss *the employee*, or referring *the employee* to the provisions of a document specifying such a procedure which is reasonably accessible to *the employee*,]

(b) specifying (by description or otherwise)—

(i) a person to whom *the employee* can apply if dissatisfied with any disciplinary decision relating to him [or any decision to dismiss him], and

(ii) a person to whom *the employee* can apply for the purpose of seeking redress of any grievance relating to his employment, and the manner in which any such application should be made, and

(c) where there are further steps consequent on any such application, explaining those steps or referring to the provisions of a document explaining them which is reasonably accessible to *the employee*.

(2) Subsection (1) does not apply to rules, disciplinary decisions, [decisions to dismiss,] grievances or procedures relating to health or safety at work.

(3)–(5) . . .

NOTES

Sub-s (1): words in square brackets inserted by the Employment Act 2002, s 35; for the words "the employee" in each place they appear in italics there are substituted the words "the worker", by the Employment Rights (Miscellaneous Amendments) Regulations 2019, SI 2019/731, regs 4, 7, as from 6 April 2020, subject to reg 15 of the 2019 Regulations at **[2.2197]**.

Sub-s (2): words in square brackets inserted by the Employment Act 2002, s 35.

Sub-ss (3), (4): repealed by the Employment Act 2002, ss 36, 54, Sch 8.

Sub-s (5): repealed by the Pensions Act 2014, s 24, Sch 13, Pt 2, paras 66, 67, as from 6 April 2016.

[1.816]

4 Statement of changes

(1) If, after the material date, there is a change in any of the matters particulars of which are required by sections 1 to 3 to be included or referred to in a statement under section 1, the employer shall give to *the employee* a written statement containing particulars of the change.

(2) For the purposes of subsection (1)—

(a) in relation to a matter particulars of which are included or referred to in a statement given under section 1 *otherwise than in instalments*, the material date is the date to which the statement relates,

(b) in relation to a matter particulars of which—

(i) are included or referred to in an instalment of a statement given under *section 1, or*

(ii) are required by section 2(4) to be included in a single document but are not included in an instalment of a statement given under section 1 which does include other particulars to which that provision applies,

the material date is the date to which the instalment relates, and

(c) in relation to any other matter, the material date is the date by which a statement under section 1 is required to be given.

(3) A statement under subsection (1) shall be given at the earliest opportunity and, in any event, not later than—

(a) one month after the change in question, or

(b) where that change results from *the employee* being required to work outside the United Kingdom for a period of more than one month, the time when he leaves the United Kingdom in order to begin so to work, if that is earlier.

(4) A statement under subsection (1) may refer *the employee* to the provisions of some other document which is reasonably accessible to *the employee* for a change in any of the matters specified in *sections 1(4)(d)(ii) and (iii)* and 3(1)(a) and (c).

(5) A statement under subsection (1) may refer *the employee* for a change in either of the matters specified in section 1(4)(e) to the law or to the provisions of any collective agreement directly affecting the terms and conditions of the employment which is reasonably accessible to *the employee*.

(6) Where, after an employer has given to *an employee* a statement under section 1, either—

(a) the name of the employer (whether an individual or a body corporate or partnership) is changed without any change in the identity of the employer, or

(b) [in the case of a statement given to an employee,] the identity of the employer is changed in circumstances in which the continuity of the employee's period of employment is not broken,

and subsection (7) applies in relation to the change, the person who is the employer immediately after the change is not required to give to *the employee* a statement under section 1; but the change shall be treated as a change falling within subsection (1) of this section.

(7) This subsection applies in relation to a change if it does not involve any change in any of the matters (other than the names of the parties) particulars of which are required by sections 1 to 3 to be included or referred to in the statement under section 1.

(8) A statement under subsection (1) which informs an employee of a change such as is referred to in subsection (6)(b) shall specify the date on which the employee's period of continuous employment began.

NOTES

For the words "the employee" in each place they appear in italics there are substituted the words "the worker", for the words "an employee" in italics in sub-s (6) there are substituted the words "a worker", and the words in square brackets in sub-s (6) are inserted, by the Employment Rights (Miscellaneous Amendments) Regulations 2019, SI 2019/731, regs 4, 8, as from 6 April 2020, subject to reg 15 of the 2019 Regulations at **[2.2197]**.

In sub-s (2), the words in italics in para (a) are repealed, for the words in italics in para (b)(i) there are substituted the words "section 2(4)", para (b)(ii) is repealed, and in sub-s (4) for the words "sections 1(4)(d)(ii) and (iii)" in italics there are substituted the words "sections 1(4)(d)(ii) to (iii)", by the Employment Rights (Employment Particulars and Paid Annual Leave) (Amendment) Regulations 2018, SI 2018/1378, regs 2, 5, as from 6 April 2020, in relation to a written statement required by s 1 or 4 of this Act where the worker to whom the statement must be given begins employment with the employer on or after 6 April 2020 (see reg 8 of the 2018 Regulations at **[2.2113]**).

Failure to give statement: see the note to s 1 at **[1.813]**.

[1.817]

5 Exclusion from rights to statements

(1) Sections 1 to 4 apply to *an employee* who at any time comes or ceases to come within the exceptions from those sections provided by [section] 199, and under section 209, as if his employment with his employer terminated or began at that time.

(2) The fact that section 1 is directed by subsection (1) to apply to *an employee* as if his employment began on his ceasing to come within the exceptions referred to in that subsection does not affect the obligation under section 1(3)(b) to specify the date on which his employment actually began.

NOTES

Word in square brackets in sub-s (1) substituted by the Employment Relations Act 1999, s 32(3).

For the words "an employee" in each place they appear in italics there are substituted the words "a worker", by the Employment Rights (Miscellaneous Amendments) Regulations 2019, SI 2019/731, regs 4, 9, as from 6 April 2020, subject to reg 15 of the 2019 Regulations at **[2.2197]**.

[1.818]

6 Reasonably accessible document or collective agreement

In sections 2 to 4 references to a document or collective agreement which is reasonably accessible to *an employee* are references to a document or collective agreement which—

(a) *the employee* has reasonable opportunities of reading in the course of his employment, or

(b) is made reasonably accessible to *the employee* in some other way.

NOTES

For the words "an employee" and "the employee" in italics there are substituted the words "a worker" and "the worker" respectively, by the Employment Rights (Miscellaneous Amendments) Regulations 2019, SI 2019/731, regs 4, 10, as from 6 April 2020, subject to reg 15 of the 2019 Regulations at **[2.2197]**.

[1.819]

7 Power to require particulars of further matters

The Secretary of State may by order provide that section 1 shall have effect as if particulars of such further matters as may be specified in the order were included in the particulars required by that section; and, for that purpose, the order may include such provisions amending that section as appear to the Secretary of State to be expedient.

NOTES

Orders: as of 15 May 2019, no Orders had been made under this section.

[1.820]

[7A Use of alternative documents to give particulars

(1) Subsections (2) and (3) apply where—

(a) an employer gives *an employee* a document in writing in the form of a contract of employment [or other worker's contract] or letter of engagement,

(b) the document contains information which, were the document in the form of a statement under section 1, would meet the employer's obligation under that section in relation to the matters mentioned *in subsections (3) and (4)(a) to (c), (d)(i), (f) and (h) of that section*, and

(c) the document is given after the beginning of the employment and before the end of the period for giving a statement under that section.

(2) The employer's duty under section 1 in relation to any matter shall be treated as met if the document given to the *employee* contains information which, were the document in the form of a statement under that section, would meet the employer's obligation under that section in relation to that matter.

(3) The employer's duty under section 3 shall be treated as met if the document given to the *employee* contains information which, were the document in the form of a statement under section 1 and the information included in the form of a note, would meet the employer's obligation under section 3.

(4) For the purposes of this section a document to which subsection (1)(a) applies shall be treated, in relation to information in respect of any of the matters mentioned in section 1(4), as specifying the date on which the document is given to the *employee* as the date as at which the information applies.

(5) Where subsection (2) applies in relation to any matter, the date on which the document by virtue of which that subsection applies is given to the *employee* shall be the material date in relation to that matter for the purposes of section 4(1).

(6) Where subsection (3) applies, the date on which the document by virtue of which that subsection applies is given to the *employee* shall be the material date for the purposes of section 4(1) in relation to the matters of which particulars are required to be given under section 3.

(7) The reference in section 4(6) to an employer having given a statement under section 1 shall be treated as including his having given a document by virtue of which his duty to give such a statement is treated as met.]

NOTES

Inserted, together with s 7B, by the Employment Act 2002, s 37.

Sub-s (1): for the words "an employee" in italics there are substituted the words "a worker" and the words in square brackets are inserted, by the Employment Rights (Miscellaneous Amendments) Regulations 2019, SI 2019/731, regs 4, 11(a), as from 6 April 2020, subject to reg 15 of the 2019 Regulations at **[2.2197]**; for the words in italics in para (b) there are substituted the words "in that section save for the particulars specified in section 2(4) and", and para (c) is substituted as set out below, by the Employment Rights (Employment Particulars and Paid Annual Leave) (Amendment) Regulations 2018, SI 2018/1378, regs 2,

6, as from 6 April 2020, in relation to a written statement required by s 1 or 4 of this Act where the worker to whom the statement must be given begins employment with the employer on or after 6 April 2020 (see reg 8 of the 2018 Regulations at **[2.2113]**)—

"(c) the document is given not later than the beginning of the employment.".

Sub-ss (2)–(6): for the word "employee" in each place it appears in italics there is substituted the word "worker", by SI 2019/731, regs 4, 11(b), as from 6 April 2020, subject to reg 15 of the 2019 Regulations at **[2.2197]**.

[1.821]

[7B Giving of alternative documents before start of employment

A document in the form of a contract of employment [or other worker's contract] or letter of engagement given by an employer to *an employee* before the beginning of the *employee's* employment with the employer shall, when the employment begins, be treated for the purposes of section 7A as having been given at that time.]

NOTES

Inserted as noted to s 7A at **[1.820]**.

Words in square brackets inserted, and for the words "an employee" and "employee's" in italics there are substituted the words "a worker" and "worker's" respectively, by the Employment Rights (Miscellaneous Amendments) Regulations 2019, SI 2019/731, regs 4, 12, as from 6 April 2020, subject to reg 15 of the 2019 Regulations at **[2.2197]**.

Right to itemised pay statement

[1.822]

8 Itemised pay statement

(1) [A worker] has the right to be given by his employer, at or before the time at which any payment of wages or salary is made to him, a written itemised pay statement.

(2) The statement shall contain particulars of—

(a) the gross amount of the wages or salary,

(b) the amounts of any variable, and (subject to section 9) any fixed, deductions from that gross amount and the purposes for which they are made,

(c) the net amount of wages or salary payable, . . .

(d) where different parts of the net amount are paid in different ways, the amount and method of payment of each part-payment[, and

(e) where the amount of wages or salary varies by reference to time worked, the total number of hours worked in respect of the variable amount of wages or salary either as—

(i) a single aggregate figure, or

(ii) separate figures for different types of work or different rates of pay].

NOTES

Para (1): words in square brackets substituted for original words "An employee" by the Employment Rights Act 1996 (Itemised Pay Statement) (Amendment) (No 2) Order 2018, SI 2018/529, art 2(1), (2), as from 6 April 2019. Note that by virtue of art 3 of that Order (at **[2.2055]**), this amendment does not apply in relation to wages or salary paid in respect of a period of work which commences before that date.

Para (2): the word "and" omitted from sub-para (c) is repealed, and sub-para (e) (and the preceding word) is added, by the Employment Rights Act 1996 (Itemised Pay Statement) (Amendment) Order 2018, SI 2018/147, art 2, as from 6 April 2019. Note that by virtue of art 3 of that Order (at **[2.2049]**), these amendments do not apply in relation to wages or salary paid in respect of a period of work which commences before that date.

National minimum wage statement: a statement required to be given to a worker under the National Minimum Wage Act 1998, s 12 (national minimum wage statement) by his employer may, if the worker is an employee, be included in the written itemised pay statement required to be given to him by his employer under this section; see s 12(3) of the 1998 Act at **[1.1179]**.

Contravention of this section: for restrictions on the amount which may be ordered by an employment tribunal or court to be paid under the Trade Union and Labour Relations (Consolidation) Act 1992, s 68A, where the making of a deduction from the wages of a worker both contravenes s 68(1) of that Act and involves a contravention of the requirement not to make a deduction without having given the particulars required by this section, see s 68A(3), (4) of the 1992 Act at **[1.365]**.

[1.823]

9 Standing statement of fixed deductions

(1) A pay statement given in accordance with section 8 need not contain separate particulars of a fixed deduction if—

(a) it contains instead an aggregate amount of fixed deductions, including that deduction, and

(b) the employer has given to [the worker], at or before the time at which the pay statement is given, a standing statement of fixed deductions which satisfies subsection (2).

(2) A standing statement of fixed deductions satisfies this subsection if—

(a) it is in writing,

(b) it contains, in relation to each deduction comprised in the aggregate amount of deductions, particulars of—

(i) the amount of the deduction,

(ii) the intervals at which the deduction is to be made, and

(iii) the purpose for which it is made, and

(c) it is (in accordance with subsection (5)) effective at the date on which the pay statement is given.

(3) A standing statement of fixed deductions may be amended, whether by—

(a) addition of a new deduction,

(b) a change in the particulars, or

(c) cancellation of an existing deduction,

by notice in writing, containing particulars of the amendment, given by the employer to [the worker].

(4) An employer who has given to [a worker] a standing statement of fixed deductions shall—

(a) within the period of twelve months beginning with the date on which the first standing statement was given, and

(b) at intervals of not more than twelve months afterwards,

re-issue it in a consolidated form incorporating any amendments notified in accordance with subsection (3).

(5) For the purposes of subsection (2)(c) a standing statement of fixed deductions—

(a) becomes effective on the date on which it is given to [the worker], and

(b) ceases to be effective at the end of the period of twelve months beginning with that date or, where it is re-issued in accordance with subsection (4), with the end of the period of twelve months beginning with the date of the last re-issue.

NOTES

Words "the worker" and "a worker" in square brackets in each place they appear substituted for original words "the employee" and "an employee" respectively, by the Employment Rights Act 1996 (Itemised Pay Statement) (Amendment) (No 2) Order 2018, SI 2018/529, art 2(1), (3), as from 6 April 2019. Note that by virtue of art 3 of that Order (at **[2.2055]**), these amendments do not apply in relation to wages or salary paid in respect of a period of work which commences before that date.

Contravention of this section: for restrictions on the amount which may be ordered by an employment tribunal or court to be paid under the Trade Union and Labour Relations (Consolidation) Act 1992, s 68A, where the making of a deduction from the wages of a worker both contravenes s 68(1) of that Act and involves a contravention of the requirement not to make a deduction without having given the particulars required by sub-s (1) above, see s 68A(3), (4) of the 1992 Act at **[1.365]**.

[1.824]

10 Power to amend provisions about pay and standing statements

The Secretary of State may by order—

(a) vary the provisions of sections 8 and 9 as to the particulars which must be included in a pay statement or a standing statement of fixed deductions by adding items to, or removing items from, the particulars listed in those sections or by amending any such particulars, and

(b) vary the provisions of subsections (4) and (5) of section 9 so as to shorten or extend the periods of twelve months referred to in those subsections, or those periods as varied from time to time under this section.

NOTES

Orders: the Employment Rights Act 1996 (Itemised Pay Statement) (Amendment) Order 2018, SI 2018/147.

Enforcement

[1.825]

11 References to [employment tribunals]

[(1) Where an employer does not give—

(a) an employee a statement as required by section 1 or 4, or

(b) a worker a statement as required by section 8,

(either because he gives him no statement or because the statement he gives does not comply with what is required), the employee or the worker may require a reference to be made to an employment tribunal to determine what particulars ought to have been included or referred to in a statement so as to comply with the requirements of the section concerned.]

(2) Where—

(a) *a statement purporting to be a statement under section 1 or 4 [has been given to an employee], or a pay statement or a standing statement of fixed deductions purporting to comply with [section 8 or 9 has been given to a worker], and*

(b) a question arises as to the particulars which ought to have been included or referred to in the statement so as to comply with the requirements of this Part,

either the employer or [*the person to whom the statement has been given*] may require the question to be referred to and determined by an [employment tribunal].

(3) For the purposes of this section—

(a) . . .

(b) a question as to the particulars which ought to have been included in a pay statement or standing statement of fixed deductions does not include a question solely as to the accuracy of an amount stated in any such particulars.

(4) An [employment tribunal] shall not consider a reference under this section in a case where the employment to which the reference relates has ceased unless an application requiring the reference to be made was made—

(a) before the end of the period of three months beginning with the date on which the employment ceased, or

(b) within such further period as the tribunal considers reasonable in a case where it is satisfied that it was not reasonably practicable for the application to be made before the end of that period of three months.

[(5) Section 207A(3) (extension because of mediation in certain European cross-border disputes) applies for the purposes of subsection (4)(a)].

[(6) [Section] 207B (extension of time limits to facilitate conciliation before institution of proceedings) also applies for the purposes of subsection (4)(a).]

NOTES

Section heading: words in square brackets substituted by the Employment Rights (Dispute Resolution) Act 1998, s 1(2)(a), (b).

Sub-s (1): substituted by the Employment Rights Act 1996 (Itemised Pay Statement) (Amendment) (No 2) Order 2018, SI 2018/529, art 2(1), (4)(a), as from 6 April 2019 (note that by virtue of art 3 of that Order (at **[2.2055]**), this substitution does not apply in relation to wages or salary paid in respect of a period of work which commences before that date); sub-s (1) is further substituted by the Employment Rights (Miscellaneous Amendments) Regulations 2019, SI 2019/731, regs 4, 13(a), as from 6 April 2020, subject to reg 15 of the 2019 Regulations at **[2.2197]**, as follows—

"(1) Where an employer does not give a worker a statement as required by section 1, 4 or 8 (either because the employer gives the worker no statement or because the statement the employer gives does not comply with what is required), the worker may require a reference to be made to an employment tribunal to determine what particulars ought to have been included or referred to in a statement so as to comply with the requirements of the section concerned.".

Sub-s (2) is amended as follows:

Words in first pair of square brackets inserted, and words in second and third pairs of square brackets substituted, by SI 2018/529, art 2(1), (4)(b), as from 6 April 2019. Note that by virtue of art 3 of that Order (at **[2.2055]**), these amendments do not apply in relation to wages or salary paid in respect of a period of work which commences before that date.

Words "employment tribunal" in square brackets substituted by the Employment Rights (Dispute Resolution) Act 1998, s 1(2)(a), (b).

Para (a) is substituted as follows, and for the words in italics in para (b) there are substituted the words "the worker", by the Employment Rights (Miscellaneous Amendments) Regulations 2019, SI 2019/731, regs 4, 13(b), (c), as from 6 April 2020, subject to reg 15 of the 2019 Regulations at **[2.2197]**—

"(a) a statement purporting to be a statement under section 1 or 4, or a pay statement or a standing statement of fixed deductions purporting to comply with section 8 or 9, has been given to a worker, and".

Sub-s (3): para (a) repealed by the Pensions Act 2014, s 24, Sch 13, Pt 2, paras 66, 68, as from 6 April 2016.

Sub-s (4): words in square brackets substituted by the Employment Rights (Dispute Resolution) Act 1998, s 1(2)(a), (b).

Sub-s (5): added by the Cross-Border Mediation (EU Directive) Regulations 2011, SI 2011/1133, regs 30, 31 and repealed by the Cross-Border Mediation (EU Directive) (EU Exit) Regulations 2019, SI 2019/469, reg 4, Sch 1, Pt 1, para 12(1), (2), as from exit day (as defined in the European Union (Withdrawal) Act 2018, s 20).

Sub-s (6): added by the Enterprise and Regulatory Reform Act 2013, s 8, Sch 2, paras 15, 16; word in square brackets substituted the Employment Tribunals Act 1996 (Application of Conciliation Provisions) Order 2014, SI 2014/431, art 3, Schedule, paras 2, 3.

Conciliation: employment tribunal proceedings under this section are "relevant proceedings" for the purposes of the conciliation provisions contained in the Employment Tribunals Act 1996, ss 18–18C; see s 18(1)(b) of the 1996 Act at **[1.757]**.

[1.826]

12 Determination of references

(1) Where, on a reference under section 11(1), an [employment tribunal] determines particulars as being those which ought to have been included or referred to in a statement given under section 1 or 4, the employer shall be deemed to have given to the *employee* a statement in which those particulars were included, or referred to, as specified in the decision of the tribunal.

(2) On determining a reference under section 11(2) relating to a statement purporting to be a statement under section 1 or 4, an [employment tribunal] may—

(a) confirm the particulars as included or referred to in the statement given by the employer,

(b) amend those particulars, or

(c) substitute other particulars for them,

as the tribunal may determine to be appropriate; and the statement shall be deemed to have been given by the employer to the *employee* in accordance with the decision of the tribunal.

(3) Where on a reference under section 11 an [employment tribunal] finds—

(a) that an employer has failed to give [a worker] any pay statement in accordance with section 8, or

(b) that a pay statement or standing statement of fixed deductions does not, in relation to a deduction, contain the particulars required to be included in that statement by that section or section 9,

the tribunal shall make a declaration to that effect.

(4) Where on a reference in the case of which subsection (3) applies the tribunal further finds that any unnotified deductions have been made (from the pay of [the worker] during the period of thirteen weeks immediately preceding the date of the application for the reference (whether or not the deductions were made in breach of the contract of employment), the tribunal may order the employer to pay [the worker] a sum not exceeding the aggregate of the unnotified deductions so made.

(5) For the purposes of subsection (4) a deduction is an unnotified deduction if it is made without the employer giving [the worker], in any pay statement or standing statement of fixed deductions, the particulars of the deduction required by section 8 or 9.

NOTES

The words "employment tribunal" in square brackets (in each place that they occur) were substituted by the Employment Rights (Dispute Resolution) Act 1998, s 1(2)(a).

For the word "employee" in italics in sub-ss (1), (2) there is substituted the word "worker", by the Employment Rights (Miscellaneous Amendments) Regulations 2019, SI 2019/731, regs 4, 14, as from 6 April 2020, subject to reg 15 of the 2019 Regulations at **[2.2197]**.

In sub-ss (3)–(5), words "a worker" and "the worker" in square brackets in each place they appear substituted for original words "an employee" and "the employee" respectively, by the Employment Rights Act 1996 (Itemised Pay Statement)

(Amendment) (No 2) Order 2018, SI 2018/529, art 2(1), (5), as from 6 April 2019. Note that by virtue of art 3 of that Order (at **[2.2055]**), these amendments do not apply in relation to wages or salary paid in respect of a period of work which commences before that date.

PART II
PROTECTION OF WAGES

Deductions by employer

[1.827]

13 Right not to suffer unauthorised deductions

(1) An employer shall not make a deduction from wages of a worker employed by him unless—

(a) the deduction is required or authorised to be made by virtue of a statutory provision or a relevant provision of the worker's contract, or

(b) the worker has previously signified in writing his agreement or consent to the making of the deduction.

(2) In this section "relevant provision", in relation to a worker's contract, means a provision of the contract comprised—

(a) in one or more written terms of the contract of which the employer has given the worker a copy on an occasion prior to the employer making the deduction in question, or

(b) in one or more terms of the contract (whether express or implied and, if express, whether oral or in writing) the existence and effect, or combined effect, of which in relation to the worker the employer has notified to the worker in writing on such an occasion.

(3) Where the total amount of wages paid on any occasion by an employer to a worker employed by him is less than the total amount of the wages properly payable by him to the worker on that occasion (after deductions), the amount of the deficiency shall be treated for the purposes of this Part as a deduction made by the employer from the worker's wages on that occasion.

(4) Subsection (3) does not apply in so far as the deficiency is attributable to an error of any description on the part of the employer affecting the computation by him of the gross amount of the wages properly payable by him to the worker on that occasion.

(5) For the purposes of this section a relevant provision of a worker's contract having effect by virtue of a variation of the contract does not operate to authorise the making of a deduction on account of any conduct of the worker, or any other event occurring, before the variation took effect.

(6) For the purposes of this section an agreement or consent signified by a worker does not operate to authorise the making of a deduction on account of any conduct of the worker, or any other event occurring, before the agreement or consent was signified.

(7) This section does not affect any other statutory provision by virtue of which a sum payable to a worker by his employer but not constituting "wages" within the meaning of this Part is not to be subject to a deduction at the instance of the employer.

NOTES

Contravention of this section: for restrictions on the amount which may be ordered by an employment tribunal or court to be paid under the Trade Union and Labour Relations (Consolidation) Act 1992, s 68A, where the making of a deduction from the wages of a worker both contravenes s 68(1) of that Act and involves a contravention of this section, see s 68A(3), (4) of the 1992 Act at **[1.365]**.

[1.828]

14 Excepted deductions

(1) Section 13 does not apply to a deduction from a worker's wages made by his employer where the purpose of the deduction is the reimbursement of the employer in respect of—

(a) an overpayment of wages, or

(b) an overpayment in respect of expenses incurred by the worker in carrying out his employment,

made (for any reason) by the employer to the worker.

(2) Section 13 does not apply to a deduction from a worker's wages made by his employer in consequence of any disciplinary proceedings if those proceedings were held by virtue of a statutory provision.

(3) Section 13 does not apply to a deduction from a worker's wages made by his employer in pursuance of a requirement imposed on the employer by a statutory provision to deduct and pay over to a public authority amounts determined by that authority as being due to it from the worker if the deduction is made in accordance with the relevant determination of that authority.

(4) Section 13 does not apply to a deduction from a worker's wages made by his employer in pursuance of any arrangements which have been established—

(a) in accordance with a relevant provision of his contract to the inclusion of which in the contract the worker has signified his agreement or consent in writing, or

(b) otherwise with the prior agreement or consent of the worker signified in writing,

and under which the employer is to deduct and pay over to a third person amounts notified to the employer by that person as being due to him from the worker, if the deduction is made in accordance with the relevant notification by that person.

(5) Section 13 does not apply to a deduction from a worker's wages made by his employer where the worker has taken part in a strike or other industrial action and the deduction is made by the employer on account of the worker's having taken part in that strike or other action.

(6) Section 13 does not apply to a deduction from a worker's wages made by his employer with his prior agreement or consent signified in writing where the purpose of the deduction is the satisfaction (whether wholly or in part) of an order of a court or tribunal requiring the payment of an amount by the worker to the employer.

Payments to employer

[1.829]
15 Right not to have to make payments to employer

(1) An employer shall not receive a payment from a worker employed by him unless—

(a) the payment is required or authorised to be made by virtue of a statutory provision or a relevant provision of the worker's contract, or

(b) the worker has previously signified in writing his agreement or consent to the making of the payment.

(2) In this section "relevant provision", in relation to a worker's contract, means a provision of the contract comprised—

(a) in one or more written terms of the contract of which the employer has given the worker a copy on an occasion prior to the employer receiving the payment in question, or

(b) in one or more terms of the contract (whether express or implied and, if express, whether oral or in writing) the existence and effect, or combined effect, of which in relation to the worker the employer has notified to the worker in writing on such an occasion.

(3) For the purposes of this section a relevant provision of a worker's contract having effect by virtue of a variation of the contract does not operate to authorise the receipt of a payment on account of any conduct of the worker, or any other event occurring, before the variation took affect.

(4) For the purposes of this section an agreement or consent signified by a worker does not operate to authorise the receipt of a payment on account of any conduct of the worker, or any other event occurring, before the agreement or consent was signified.

(5) Any reference in this Part to an employer receiving a payment from a worker employed by him is a reference to his receiving such a payment in his capacity as the worker's employer.

[1.830]
16 Excepted payments

(1) Section 15 does not apply to a payment received from a worker by his employer where the purpose of the payment is the reimbursement of the employer in respect of—

(a) an overpayment of wages, or

(b) an overpayment in respect of expenses incurred by the worker in carrying out his employment,

made (for any reason) by the employer to the worker.

(2) Section 15 does not apply to a payment received from a worker by his employer in consequence of any disciplinary proceedings if those proceedings were held by virtue of a statutory provision.

(3) Section 15 does not apply to a payment received from a worker by his employer where the worker has taken part in a strike or other industrial action and the payment has been required by the employer on account of the worker's having taken part in that strike or other action.

(4) Section 15 does not apply to a payment received from a worker by his employer where the purpose of the payment is the satisfaction (whether wholly or in part) of an order of a court or tribunal requiring the payment of an amount by the worker to the employer.

Cash shortages and stock deficiencies in retail employment

[1.831]
17 Introductory

(1) In the following provisions of this Part—

"cash shortage" means a deficit arising in relation to amounts received in connection with retail transactions, and

"stock deficiency" means a stock deficiency arising in the course of retail transactions.

(2) In the following provisions of this Part "retail employment", in relation to a worker, means employment involving (whether or not on a regular basis)—

(a) the carrying out by the worker of retail transactions directly with members of the public or with fellow workers or other individuals in their personal capacities, or

(b) the collection by the worker of amounts payable in connection with retail transactions carried out by other persons directly with members of the public or with fellow workers or other individuals in their personal capacities.

(3) References in this section to a "retail transaction" are to the sale or supply of goods or the supply of services (including financial services).

(4) References in the following provisions of this Part to a deduction made from wages of a worker in retail employment, or to a payment received from such a worker by his employer, on account of a cash shortage or stock deficiency include references to a deduction or payment so made or received on account of—

(a) any dishonesty or other conduct on the part of the worker which resulted in any such shortage or deficiency, or

(b) any other event in respect of which he (whether or not together with any other workers) has any contractual liability and which so resulted,

in each case whether or not the amount of the deduction or payment is designed to reflect the exact amount of the shortage or deficiency.

(5) References in the following provisions of this Part to the recovery from a worker of an amount in respect of a cash shortage or stock deficiency accordingly include references to the recovery from him of an amount in respect of any such conduct or event as is mentioned in subsection (4)(a) or (b).
(6) In the following provisions of this Part "pay day", in relation to a worker, means a day on which wages are payable to the worker.

[1.832]
18 Limits on amount and time of deductions
(1) Where (in accordance with section 13) the employer of a worker in retail employment makes, on account of one or more cash shortages or stock deficiencies, a deduction or deductions from wages payable to the worker on a pay day, the amount or aggregate amount of the deduction or deductions shall not exceed one-tenth of the gross amount of the wages payable to the worker on that day.
(2) Where the employer of a worker in retail employment makes a deduction from the worker's wages on account of a cash shortage or stock deficiency, the employer shall not be treated as making the deduction in accordance with section 13 unless (in addition to the requirements of that section being satisfied with respect to the deduction)—
- (a) the deduction is made, or
- (b) in the case of a deduction which is one of a series of deductions relating to the shortage or deficiency, the first deduction in the series was made,

not later than the end of the relevant period.
(3) In subsection (2) "the relevant-period" means the period of twelve months beginning with the date when the employer established the existence of the shortage or deficiency or (if earlier) the date when he ought reasonably to have done so.

[1.833]
19 Wages determined by reference to shortages etc
(1) This section applies where—
- (a) by virtue of an agreement between a worker in retail employment and his employer, the amount of the worker's wages or any part of them is or may be determined by reference to the incidence of cash shortages or stock deficiencies, and
- (b) the gross amount of the wages payable to the worker on any pay day is, on account of any such shortages or deficiencies, less than the gross amount of the wages that would have been payable to him on that day if there had been no such shortages or deficiencies.

(2) The amount representing the difference between the two amounts referred to in subsection (1)(b) shall be treated for the purposes of this Part as a deduction from the wages payable to the worker on that day made by the employer on account of the cash shortages or stock deficiencies in question.
(3) The second of the amounts referred to in subsection (1)(b) shall be treated for the purposes of this Part (except subsection (1)) as the gross amount of the wages payable to him on that day.
(4) Accordingly—
- (a) section 13, and
- (b) if the requirements of section 13 and subsection (2) of section 18 are satisfied, subsection (1) of section 18,

have effect in relation to the amount referred to in subsection (2) of this section.

[1.834]
20 Limits on method and timing of payments
(1) Where the employer of a worker in retail employment receives from the worker a payment on account of a cash shortage or stock deficiency, the employer shall not be treated as receiving the payment in accordance with section 15 unless (in addition to the requirements of that section being satisfied with respect to the payment) he has previously—
- (a) notified the worker in writing of the worker's total liability to him in respect of that shortage or deficiency, and
- (b) required the worker to make the payment by means of a demand for payment made in accordance with the following provisions of this section.

(2) A demand for payment made by the employer of a worker in retail employment in respect of a cash shortage or stock deficiency—
- (a) shall be made in writing, and
- (b) shall be made on one of the worker's pay days.

(3) A demand for payment in respect of a particular cash shortage or stock deficiency, or (in the case of a series of such demands) the first such demand, shall not be made—
- (a) earlier than the first pay day of the worker following the date when he is notified of his total liability in respect of the shortage or deficiency in pursuance of subsection (1)(a) or, where he is so notified on a pay day, earlier than that day, or
- (b) later than the end of the period of twelve months beginning with the date when the employer established the existence of the shortage or deficiency or (if earlier) the date when he ought reasonably to have done so.

(4) For the purposes of this Part a demand for payment shall be treated as made by the employer on one of a worker's pay days if it is given to the worker or posted to, or left at, his last known address—
- (a) on that pay day, or
- (b) in the case of a pay day which is not a working day of the employer's business, on the first such working day following that pay day.

(5) Legal proceedings by the employer of a worker in retail employment for the recovery from the worker of an amount in respect of a cash shortage or stock deficiency shall not be instituted by the employer after the end of the period referred to in subsection (3)(b) unless the employer has within that period made a demand for payment in respect of that amount in accordance with this section.

[1.835]
21 Limit on amount of payments
(1) Where the employer of a worker in retail employment makes on any pay day one or more demands for payment in accordance with section 20, the amount or aggregate amount required to be paid by the worker in pursuance of the demand or demands shall not exceed—
(a) one-tenth of the gross amount of the wages payable to the worker on that day, or
(b) where one or more deductions falling within section 18(1) are made by the employer from those wages, such amount as represents the balance of that one-tenth after subtracting the amount or aggregate amount of the deduction or deductions.
(2) Once an amount has been required to be paid by means of a demand for payment made in accordance with section 20 on any pay day, that amount shall not be taken into account under subsection (1) as it applies to any subsequent pay day, even though the employer is obliged to make further requests for it to be paid.
(3) Where in any legal proceedings the court finds that the employer of a worker in retail employment is (in accordance with section 15 as it applies apart from section 20(1)) entitled to recover an amount from the worker in respect of a cash shortage or stock deficiency, the court shall, in ordering the payment by the worker to the employer of that amount, make such provision as appears to the court to be necessary to ensure that it is paid by the worker at a rate not exceeding that at which it could be recovered from him by the employer in accordance with this section.

[1.836]
22 Final instalments of wages
(1) In this section "final instalment of wages", in relation to a worker, means—
(a) the amount of wages payable to the worker which consists of or includes an amount payable by way of contractual remuneration in respect of the last of the periods for which he is employed under his contract prior to its termination for any reason (but excluding any wages referable to any earlier such period), or
(b) where an amount in lieu of notice is paid to the worker later than the amount referred to in paragraph (a), the amount so paid,

in each case whether the amount in question is paid before or after the termination of the worker's contract.
(2) Section 18(1) does not operate to restrict the amount of any deductions which may (in accordance with section 13(1)) be made by the employer of a worker in retail employment from the worker's final instalment of wages.
(3) Nothing in section 20 or 21 applies to a payment falling within section 20(1) which is made on or after the day on which any such worker's final instalment of wages is paid; but (even if the requirements of section 15 would otherwise be satisfied with respect to it) his employer shall not be treated as receiving any such payment in accordance with that section if the payment was first required to be made after the end of the period referred to in section 20(3)(b).
(4) Section 21(3) does not apply to an amount which is to be paid by a worker on or after the day on which his final instalment of wages is paid.

Enforcement

[1.837]
23 Complaints to [employment tribunals]
(1) A worker may present a complaint to an [employment tribunal]—
(a) that his employer has made a deduction from his wages in contravention of section 13 (including a deduction made in contravention of that section as it applies by virtue of section 18(2)),
(b) that his employer has received from him a payment in contravention of section 15 (including a payment received in contravention of that section as it applies by virtue of section 20(1)),
(c) that his employer has recovered from his wages by means of one or more deductions falling within section 18(1) an amount or aggregate amount exceeding the limit applying to the deduction or deductions under that provision, or
(d) that his employer has received from him in pursuance of one or more demands for payment made (in accordance with section 20) on a particular pay day, a payment or payments of an amount or aggregate amount exceeding the limit applying to the demand or demands under section 21(1).
(2) Subject to subsection (4), an [employment tribunal] shall not consider a complaint under this section unless it is presented before the end of the period of three months beginning with—
(a) in the case of a complaint relating to a deduction by the employer, the date of payment of the wages from which the deduction was made, or
(b) in the case of a complaint relating to a payment received by the employer, the date when the payment was received.
(3) Where a complaint is brought under this section in respect of—
(a) a series of deductions or payments, or

(b) a number of payments falling within subsection (1)(d) and made in pursuance of demands for payment subject to the same limit under section 21(1) but received by the employer on different dates,

the references in subsection (2) to the deduction or payment are to the last deduction or payment in the series or to the last of the payments so received.

[(3A) Section 207A(3) (extension because of mediation in certain European cross-border disputes) [and section 207B (extension of time limits to facilitate conciliation before institution of proceedings) apply] for the purposes of subsection (2).]

(4) Where the [employment tribunal] is satisfied that it was not reasonably practicable for a complaint under this section to be presented before the end of the relevant period of three months, the tribunal may consider the complaint if it is presented within such further period as the tribunal considers reasonable.

[(4A) An employment tribunal is not (despite subsections (3) and (4)) to consider so much of a complaint brought under this section as relates to a deduction where the date of payment of the wages from which the deduction was made was before the period of two years ending with the date of presentation of the complaint.

(4B) Subsection (4A) does not apply so far as a complaint relates to a deduction from wages that are of a kind mentioned in section 27(1)(b) to (j).]

[(5) No complaint shall be presented under this section in respect of any deduction made in contravention of section 86 of the Trade Union and Labour Relations (Consolidation) Act 1992 (deduction of political fund contribution where certificate of exemption or objection has been given).]

NOTES

Section heading, sub-ss (1), (2), (4): words in square brackets substituted by the Employment Rights (Dispute Resolution) Act 1998, s 1(2)(a), (b).

Sub-s (3A): inserted by the Cross-Border Mediation (EU Directive) Regulations 2011, SI 2011/1133, regs 30, 32; words in square brackets substituted by the Enterprise and Regulatory Reform Act 2013, s 8, Sch 2, paras 15, 17; substituted by the Cross-Border Mediation (EU Directive) (EU Exit) Regulations 2019, SI 2019/469, reg 4, Sch 1, Pt 1, para 12(1), (3), as from exit day (as defined in the European Union (Withdrawal) Act 2018, s 20), as follows—

"(3A) Section 207B (extension of time limits to facilitate conciliation before institution of proceedings) applies for the purposes of subsection (2).".

Sub-ss (4A), (4B): inserted by the Deduction from Wages (Limitation) Regulations 2014, SI 2014/3322, regs 2, 4, as from 8 January 2015, in relation to complaints presented to an employment tribunal on or after 1 July 2015.

Sub-s (5): added by the Employment Rights (Dispute Resolution) Act 1998, s 15, Sch 1, para 18.

Conciliation: employment tribunal proceedings under this section are "relevant proceedings" for the purposes of the conciliation provisions contained in the Employment Tribunals Act 1996, ss 18–18C; see s 18(1)(b) of the 1996 Act at **[1.757]**.

Tribunal jurisdiction: the Employment Act 2002, s 38 applies to proceedings before the employment tribunal relating to a claim under this section; see s 38(1) of, and Sch 5 to, the 2002 Act at **[1.1279]**, **[1.1287]**. See also the Trade Union and Labour Relations (Consolidation) Act 1992, s 207A at **[1.524]** (as inserted by the Employment Act 2008). That section provides that in proceedings before an employment tribunal relating to a claim by an employee under any of the jurisdictions listed in Sch A2 to the 1992 Act at **[1.704]** (which includes this section) the tribunal may adjust any award given if the employer or the employee has unreasonably failed to comply with a relevant Code of Practice as defined by s 207A(4). See also the revised Acas Code of Practice 1 – Disciplinary and Grievance Procedures (2015) at **[4.1]**, and the Acas Code of Practice 4 – Settlement Agreements (2013) at **[4.54]**.

As to the power of an officer acting for the purposes of the National Minimum Wage Act 1998 to present a complaint under sub-s (1)(a) above where a notice of underpayment served under s 19 of the 1998 Act has not been complied with, see s 19D(1)(a) of that Act at **[1.1191]**. As to the reversal of the burden of proof where such a complaint is made, see s 28(2) of that Act at **[1.1198]**.

[1.838]

24 Determination of complaints

[(1)] Where a tribunal finds a complaint under section 23 well-founded, it shall make a declaration to that effect and shall order the employer—

(a) in the case of a complaint under section 23(1)(a), to pay to the worker the amount of any deduction made in contravention of section 13,

(b) in the case of a complaint under section 23(1)(b), to repay to the worker the amount of any payment received in contravention of section 15,

(c) in the case of a complaint under section 23(1)(c), to pay to the worker any amount recovered from him in excess of the limit mentioned in that provision, and

(d) in the case of a complaint under section 23(1)(d), to repay to the worker any amount received from him in excess of the limit mentioned in that provision.

[(2) Where a tribunal makes a declaration under subsection (1), it may order the employer to pay to the worker (in addition to any amount ordered to be paid under that subsection) such amount as the tribunal considers appropriate in all the circumstances to compensate the worker for any financial loss sustained by him which is attributable to the matter complained of.]

NOTES

Sub-s (1) numbered as such, and sub-s (2) added, by the Employment Act 2008, s 7(1).

[1.839]
25 Determinations: supplementary
(1) Where, in the case of any complaint under section 23(1)(a), a tribunal finds that, although neither of the conditions set out in section 13(1)(a) and (b) was satisfied with respect to the whole amount of the deduction, one of those conditions was satisfied with respect to any lesser amount, the amount of the deduction shall for the purposes of section 24(a) be treated as reduced by the amount with respect to which that condition was satisfied.
(2) Where, in the case of any complaint under section 23(1)(b), a tribunal finds that, although neither of the conditions set out in section 15(1)(a) and (b) was satisfied with respect to the whole amount of the payment, one of those conditions was satisfied with respect to any lesser amount, the amount of the payment shall for the purposes of section 24(b) be treated as reduced by the amount with respect to which that condition was satisfied.
(3) An employer shall not under section 24 be ordered by a tribunal to pay or repay to a worker any amount in respect of a deduction or payment, or in respect of any combination of deductions or payments, in so far as it appears to the tribunal that he has already paid or repaid any such amount to the worker.
(4) Where a tribunal has under section 24 ordered an employer to pay or repay to a worker any amount in respect of a particular deduction or payment falling within section 23(1)(a) to (d), the amount which the employer is entitled to recover (by whatever means) in respect of the matter in relation to which the deduction or payment was originally made or received shall be treated as reduced by that amount.
(5) Where a tribunal has under section 24 ordered an employer to pay or repay to a worker any amount in respect of any combination of deductions or payments falling within section 23(1)(c) or (d), the aggregate amount which the employer is entitled to recover (by whatever means) in respect of the cash shortages or stock deficiencies in relation to which the deductions or payments were originally made or required to be made shall be treated as reduced by that amount.

[1.840]
26 Complaints and other remedies
Section 23 does not affect the jurisdiction of an [employment tribunal] to consider a reference under section 11 in relation to any deduction from the wages of a worker; but the aggregate of any amounts ordered by an [employment tribunal] to be paid under section 12(4) and under section 24 (whether on the same or different occasions) in respect of a particular deduction shall not exceed the amount of the deduction.

NOTES
Words in square brackets substituted by the Employment Rights (Dispute Resolution) Act 1998, s 1(2)(a).

Supplementary

[1.841]
27 Meaning of "wages" etc
(1) In this Part "wages", in relation to a worker, means any sums payable to the worker in connection with his employment, including—
(a) any fee, bonus, commission, holiday pay or other emolument referable to his employment, whether payable under his contract or otherwise,
(b) statutory sick pay under Part XI of the Social Security Contributions and Benefits Act 1992,
(c) statutory maternity pay under Part XII of that Act,
[(ca) [statutory paternity pay] under Part 12ZA of that Act,
(cb) statutory adoption pay under Part 12ZB of that Act,]
[(cc) statutory shared parental pay under Part 12ZC of that Act,]
[(cd) statutory parental bereavement pay under Part 12ZD of that Act,]
(d) a guarantee payment (under section 28 of this Act),
(e) any payment for time off under Part VI of this Act or section 169 of the Trade Union and Labour Relations (Consolidation) Act 1992 (payment for time off for carrying out trade union duties etc),
(f) remuneration on suspension on medical grounds under section 64 of this Act and remuneration on suspension on maternity grounds under section 68 of this Act,
[(fa) remuneration on ending the supply of an agency worker on maternity grounds under section 68C of this Act,]
(g) any sum payable in pursuance of an order for reinstatement or re-engagement under section 113 of this Act,
(h) any sum payable in pursuance of an order for the continuation of a contract of employment under section 130 of this Act or section 164 of the Trade Union and Labour Relations (Consolidation) Act 1992, and
(j) remuneration under a protective award under section 189 of that Act,
but excluding any payments within subsection (2).
(2) Those payments are—
(a) any payment by way of an advance under an agreement for a loan or by way of an advance of wages (but without prejudice to the application of section 13 to any deduction made from the worker's wages in respect of any such advance),
(b) any payment in respect of expenses incurred by the worker in carrying out his employment,
(c) any payment by way of a pension, allowance or gratuity in connection with the worker's retirement or as compensation for loss of office,
(d) any payment referable to the worker's redundancy, and
(e) any payment to the worker otherwise than in his capacity as a worker.

(3) Where any payment in the nature of a non-contractual bonus is (for any reason) made to a worker by his employer, the amount of the payment shall for the purposes of this Part—

(a) be treated as wages of the worker, and

(b) be treated as payable to him as such on the day on which the payment is made.

(4) In this Part "gross amount", in relation to any wages payable to a worker, means the total amount of those wages before deductions of whatever nature.

(5) For the purposes of this Part any monetary value attaching to any payment or benefit in kind furnished to a worker by his employer shall not be treated as wages of the worker except in the case of any voucher, stamp or similar document which is—

(a) of a fixed value expressed in monetary terms, and

(b) capable of being exchanged (whether on its own or together with other vouchers, stamps or documents, and whether immediately or only after a time) for money, goods or services (or for any combination of two or more of those things).

NOTES

Sub-s (1) is amended as follows:

Paras (ca), (cb) inserted by the Employment Act 2002, s 53, Sch 7, paras 24, 25.

Words in square brackets in para (ca) substituted by the Children and Families Act 2014, s 126, Sch 7, paras 29, 30(a), as from 5 April 2015 (note that this amendment does not have effect in relation to (a) children whose expected week of birth ends on or before 4 April 2015, and (b) children placed for adoption on or before that date: see the Children and Families Act 2014 (Commencement No 3, Transitional Provisions and Savings) Order 2014, SI 2014/1640, art 16).

Para (cc) inserted by the Children and Families Act 2014, s 126, Sch 7, paras 29, 30(b), as from 1 December 2014.

Para (cd) inserted by the Parental Bereavement (Leave and Pay) Act 2018, s 1(c), Schedule, Pt 3, paras 20, 21, as from a day to be appointed.

Para (fa) inserted by the Agency Workers Regulations 2010, SI 2010/93, reg 25, Sch 2, Pt 1, paras 9, 10.

Note: sub-s (1) did not contain a para (i) in the Queen's Printer's copy of this Act.

Statutory paternity pay: as to the meaning of this, see the Children and Families Act 2014, s 126 at **[1.1894]**

[PART 2A
ZERO HOURS WORKERS

[1.842]

27A Exclusivity terms unenforceable in zero hours contracts

(1) In this section "zero hours contract" means a contract of employment or other worker's contract under which—

(a) the undertaking to do or perform work or services is an undertaking to do so conditionally on the employer making work or services available to the worker, and

(b) there is no certainty that any such work or services will be made available to the worker.

(2) For this purpose, an employer makes work or services available to a worker if the employer requests or requires the worker to do the work or perform the services.

(3) Any provision of a zero hours contract which—

(a) prohibits the worker from doing work or performing services under another contract or under any other arrangement, or

(b) prohibits the worker from doing so without the employer's consent,

is unenforceable against the worker.

(4) Subsection (3) is to be disregarded for the purposes of determining any question whether a contract is a contract of employment or other worker's contract.]

NOTES

Commencement: 26 May 2015.

Part 2A (ss 27A, 27B) was inserted by the Small Business, Enterprise and Employment Act 2015, s 153(1), (2), as from 26 May 2015.

[1.843]

[27B Power to make further provision in relation to zero hours workers

(1) The Secretary of State may by regulations make provision for the purpose of securing that zero hours workers, or any description of zero hours workers, are not restricted by any provision or purported provision of their contracts or arrangements with their employers from doing any work otherwise than under those contracts or arrangements.

(2) In this section, "zero hours workers" means—

(a) employees or other workers who work under zero hours contracts;

(b) individuals who work under non-contractual zero hours arrangements;

(c) individuals who work under worker's contracts of a kind specified by the regulations.

(3) The worker's contracts which may be specified by virtue of subsection (2)(c) are those in relation to which the Secretary of State considers it appropriate for provision made by the regulations to apply, having regard, in particular, to provision made by the worker's contracts as to income, rate of pay or working hours.

(4) In this section "non-contractual zero hours arrangement" means an arrangement other than a worker's contract under which—

(a) an employer and an individual agree terms on which the individual will do any work where the employer makes it available to the individual and the individual agrees to do it, but

(b) the employer is not required to make any work available to the individual, nor the individual required to accept it, and in this section "employer", in relation to a non-contractual zero hours arrangement, is to be read accordingly.

(5) Provision that may be made by regulations under subsection (1) includes provision for—

(a) modifying—

(i) zero hours contracts;

(ii) non-contractual zero hours arrangements;

(iii) other worker's contracts;

(b) imposing financial penalties on employers;

(c) requiring employers to pay compensation to zero hours workers;

(d) conferring jurisdiction on employment tribunals;

(e) conferring rights on zero hours workers.

(6) Provision that may be made by virtue of subsection (5)(a) may, in particular, include provision for exclusivity terms in prescribed categories of worker's contracts to be unenforceable, in cases in which section 27A does not apply.

For this purpose an exclusivity term is any term by virtue of which a worker is restricted from doing any work otherwise than under the worker's contract.

(7) Regulations under this section may—

(a) make different provision for different purposes;

(b) make provision subject to exceptions.

(8) For the purposes of this section—

(a) "zero hours contract" has the same meaning as in section 27A;

(b) an employer makes work available to an individual if the employer requests or requires the individual to do it;

(c) references to work and doing work include references to services and performing them.

(9) Nothing in this section is to be taken to affect any worker's contract except so far as any regulations made under this section expressly apply in relation to it.]

NOTES

Commencement: 26 May 2015.

Part 2A (ss 27A, 27B) was inserted by the Small Business, Enterprise and Employment Act 2015, s 153(1), (2), as from 26 May 2015.

Regulations: the Exclusivity Terms in Zero Hours Contracts (Redress) Regulations 2015, SI 2015/2021 at **[2.1925]**.

PART III
GUARANTEE PAYMENTS

NOTES

Recoupment of social security benefits: as to the power to provide for recoupment of social security benefits in relation to payments by employers to employees under this Part, that are the subject of proceedings before employment tribunals, see the Employment Tribunals Act 1996, s 16 at **[1.755]**.

[1.844]

28 Right to guarantee payment

(1) Where throughout a day during any part of which an employee would normally be required to work in accordance with his contract of employment the employee is not provided with work by his employer by reason of—

(a) a diminution in the requirements of the employer's business for work of the kind which the employee is employed to do, or

(b) any other occurrence affecting the normal working of the employer's business in relation to work of the kind which the employee is employed to do,

the employee is entitled to be paid by his employer an amount in respect of that day.

(2) In this Act a payment to which an employee is entitled under subsection (1) is referred to as a guarantee payment.

(3) In this Part—

(a) a day falling within subsection (1) is referred to as a "workless day", and

(b) "workless period" has a corresponding meaning.

(4) In this Part "day" means the period of twenty-four hours from midnight to midnight.

(5) Where a period of employment begun on any day extends, or would normally extend, over midnight into the following day—

(a) if the employment before midnight is, or would normally be, of longer duration than that after midnight, the period of employment shall be treated as falling wholly on the first day, and

(b) in any other case, the period of employment shall be treated as falling wholly on the second day.

[1.845]

29 Exclusions from right to guarantee payment

(1) An employee is not entitled to a guarantee payment unless he has been continuously employed for a period of not less than one month ending with the day before that in respect of which the guarantee payment is claimed.

(2) . . .

(3) An employee is not entitled to a guarantee payment in respect of a workless day if the failure to provide him with work for that day occurs in consequence of a strike, lock-out or other industrial action involving any employee of his employer or of an associated employer.

(4) An employee is not entitled to a guarantee payment in respect of a workless day if—

(a) his employer has offered to provide alternative work for that day which is suitable in all the circumstances (whether or not it is work which the employee is under his contract employed to perform), and
(b) the employee has unreasonably refused that offer.

(5) An employee is not entitled to a guarantee payment if he does not comply with reasonable requirements imposed by his employer with a view to ensuring that his services are available.

NOTES

Sub-s (2): repealed by the Fixed-term Employees (Prevention of Less Favourable Treatment) Regulations 2002, SI 2002/2034, reg 11, Sch 2, Pt 1, para 3(1), (2) (except in relation to Government training schemes, agency workers and apprentices; see regs 18–20 of the 2002 Regulations at **[2.571]** et seq).

[1.846]
30 Calculation of guarantee payment

(1) Subject to section 31, the amount of a guarantee payment payable to an employee in respect of any day is the sum produced by multiplying the number of normal working hours on the day by the guaranteed hourly rate; and, accordingly, no guarantee payment is payable to an employee in whose case there are no normal working hours on the day in question.

(2) The guaranteed hourly rate, in relation to an employee, is the amount of one week's pay divided by the number of normal working hours in a week for that employee when employed under the contract of employment in force on the day in respect of which the guarantee payment is payable.

(3) But where the number of normal working hours differs from week to week or over a longer period, the amount of one week's pay shall be divided instead by—
(a) the average number of normal working hours calculated by dividing by twelve the total number of the employee's normal working hours during the period of twelve weeks ending with the last complete week before the day in respect of which the guarantee payment is payable, or
(b) where the employee has not been employed for a sufficient period to enable the calculation to be made under paragraph (a), a number which fairly represents the number of normal working hours in a week having regard to such of the considerations specified in subsection (4) as are appropriate in the circumstances.

(4) The considerations referred to in subsection (3)(b) are—
(a) the average number of normal working hours in a week which the employee could expect in accordance with the terms of his contract, and
(b) the average number of normal working hours of other employees engaged in relevant comparable employment with the same employer.

(5) If in any case an employee's contract has been varied, or a new contract has been entered into, in connection with a period of short-time working, subsections (2) and (3) have effect as if for the references to the day in respect of which the guarantee payment is payable there were substituted references to the last day on which the original contract was in force.

[1.847]
31 Limits on amount of and entitlement to guarantee payment

(1) The amount of a guarantee payment payable to an employee in respect of any day shall not exceed [£29.00].

(2) An employee is not entitled to guarantee payments in respect of more than the specified number of days in any period of three months.

(3) The specified number of days for the purposes of subsection (2) is the number of days, not exceeding five, on which the employee normally works in a week under the contract of employment in force on the day in respect of which the guarantee payment is claimed.

(4) But where that number of days varies from week to week or over a longer period, the specified number of days is instead—
(a) the average number of such days, not exceeding five, calculated by dividing by twelve the total number of such days during the period of twelve weeks ending with the last complete week before the day in respect of which the guarantee payment is claimed, and rounding up the resulting figure to the next whole number, or
(b) where the employee has not been employed for a sufficient period to enable the calculation to be made under paragraph (a), a number which fairly represents the number of the employee's normal working days in a week, not exceeding five, having regard to such of the considerations specified in subsection (5) as are appropriate in the circumstances.

(5) The considerations referred to in subsection (4)(b) are—
(a) the average number of normal working days in a week which the employee could expect in accordance with the terms of his contract, and
(b) the average number of such days of other employees engaged in relevant comparable employment with the same employer.

(6) If in any case an employee's contract has been varied, or a new contract has been entered into, in connection with a period of short-time working, subsections (3) and (4) have effect as if for the references to the day in respect of which the guarantee payment is claimed there were substituted references to the last day on which the original contract was in force.

[(7) The Secretary of State may by order vary—
(a) the length of the period specified in subsection (2);
(b) a limit specified in subsection (3) or (4).]

NOTES

Sub-s (1): sum in square brackets substituted by the Employment Rights (Increase of Limits) Order 2019, SI 2019/324, art 3, Schedule, as from 6 April 2019, in relation to any case where the appropriate date (as defined in the order) falls on or after that date (see SI 2019/324, art 4 at **[2.2117]**).

The previous sum was £28.00 (see SI 2018/194). The sum may be varied by the Secretary of State, see the Employment Relations Act 1999, s 34(1)(a), (3)(a) at **[1.1258]**.

Sub-s (7): substituted by the Employment Relations Act 1999, s 35.

[1.848]

32 Contractual remuneration

(1) A right to a guarantee payment does not affect any right of an employee in relation to remuneration under his contract of employment ("contractual remuneration").

(2) Any contractual remuneration paid to an employee in respect of a workless day goes towards discharging any liability of the employer to pay a guarantee payment in respect of that day; and, conversely, any guarantee payment paid in respect of a day goes towards discharging any liability of the employer to pay contractual remuneration in respect of that day.

(3) For the purposes of subsection (2), contractual remuneration shall be treated as paid in respect of a workless day—

(a) where it is expressed to be calculated or payable by reference to that day or any part of that day, to the extent that it is so expressed, and

(b) in any other case, to the extent that it represents guaranteed remuneration, rather than remuneration for work actually done, and is referable to that day when apportioned rateably between that day and any other workless period falling within the period in respect of which the remuneration is paid.

[1.849]

33 Power to modify provisions about guarantee payments

The Secretary of State may by order provide that in relation to any description of employees the provisions of—

(a) sections 28(4) and (5), 30, 31(3) to (5) (as originally enacted or as varied under section 31(7)) and 32, and

(b) so far as they apply for the purposes of those provisions, Chapter II of Part XIV and section 234,

shall have effect subject to such modifications and adaptations as may be prescribed by the order.

NOTES

Orders: as of 15 May 2019, no Orders had been made under this section.

[1.850]

34 Complaints to [employment tribunals]

(1) An employee may present a complaint to an [employment tribunal] that his employer has failed to pay the whole or any part of a guarantee payment to which the employee is entitled.

(2) An [employment tribunal] shall not consider a complaint relating to a guarantee payment in respect of any day unless the complaint is presented to the tribunal—

(a) before the end of the period of three months beginning with that day, or

(b) within such further period as the tribunal considers reasonable in a case where it is satisfied that it was not reasonably practicable for the complaint to be presented before the end of that period of three months.

[(2A) Section 207A(3) (extension because of mediation in certain European cross-border disputes) [and section 207B (extension of time limits to facilitate conciliation before institution of proceedings) apply] for the purposes of subsection (2)(a).]

(3) Where an [employment tribunal] finds a complaint under this section well-founded, the tribunal shall order the employer to pay to the employee the amount of guarantee payment which it finds is due to him.

NOTES

Words "employment tribunals" and "employment tribunal" in square brackets substituted by the Employment Rights (Dispute Resolution) Act 1998, s 1(2)(a), (b).

Sub-s (2A): inserted by the Cross-Border Mediation (EU Directive) Regulations 2011, SI 2011/1133, regs 30, 33; words in square brackets substituted by the Enterprise and Regulatory Reform Act 2013, s 8, Sch 2, paras 15, 18; substituted by the Cross-Border Mediation (EU Directive) (EU Exit) Regulations 2019, SI 2019/469, reg 4, Sch 1, Pt 1, para 12(1), (4), as from exit day (as defined in the European Union (Withdrawal) Act 2018, s 20), as follows—

"(2A) Section 207B (extension of time limits to facilitate conciliation before institution of proceedings) applies for the purposes of subsection (2)(a).".

Conciliation: employment tribunal proceedings under this section are "relevant proceedings" for the purposes of the conciliation provisions contained in the Employment Tribunals Act 1996, ss 18–18C; see s 18(1)(b) of the 1996 Act at **[1.757]**.

[1.851]

35 Exemption orders

(1) Where—

(a) at any time there is in force a collective agreement, or an agricultural wages order, under which employees to whom the agreement or order relates have a right to guaranteed remuneration, and

(b) on the application of all the parties to the agreement, or of the Board making the order, the appropriate Minister (having regard to the provisions of the agreement or order) is satisfied that section 28 should not apply to those employees,

he may make an order under this section excluding those employees from the operation of that section.

(2) In subsection (1) "agricultural wages order" means an order made under—

(a) section 3 of the Agricultural Wages Act 1948, or

(b) section 3 of the Agricultural Wages (Scotland) Act 1949.

(3) In subsection (1) "the appropriate Minister" means—

(a) in relation to a collective agreement or to an order such as is referred to in subsection (2)(b), the Secretary of State, *and*

(b) in relation to an order such as is referred to in subsection (2)(a), the [Secretary of State].

(4) The Secretary of State shall not make an order under this section in respect of an agreement unless—

(a) the agreement provides for procedures to be followed (whether by arbitration or otherwise) in cases where an employee claims that his employer has failed to pay the whole or any part of any guaranteed remuneration to which the employee is entitled under the agreement and those procedures include a right to arbitration or adjudication by an independent referee or body in cases where (by reason of an equality of votes or otherwise) a decision cannot otherwise be reached, or

(b) the agreement indicates that an employee to whom the agreement relates may present a complaint to an [employment tribunal] that his employer has failed to pay the whole or any part of any guaranteed remuneration to which the employee is entitled under the agreement.

(5) Where an order under this section is in force in respect of an agreement indicating as described in paragraph (b) of subsection (4) an [employment tribunal] shall have jurisdiction over a complaint such as is mentioned in that paragraph as if it were a complaint falling within section 34.

(6) An order varying or revoking an earlier order under this section may be made in pursuance of an application by all or any of the parties to the agreement in question, or the Board which made the order in question, or in the absence of such an application.

NOTES

Sub-s (2): para (a) repealed by the Enterprise and Regulatory Reform Act 2013, s 72(4), Sch 20, as from 1 October 2013 (in relation to England), and as from a day to be appointed (in relation to Wales). Note that the 1948 Act does not apply to Scotland.

Sub-s (3): words in square brackets in para (b) substituted by the Ministry of Agriculture, Fisheries and Food (Dissolution) Order 2002, SI 2002/794, art 5(1), Sch 1, para 37; para (b) and word immediately preceding it repealed by the Enterprise and Regulatory Reform Act 2013, s 72(4), Sch 20, as from 1 October 2013 (in relation to England), and as from a day to be appointed (in relation to Wales).

Sub-ss (4), (5): words in square brackets substituted by the Employment Rights (Dispute Resolution) Act 1998, s 1(2)(a).

Orders: as of 15 May 2019, no Orders had been made under this section. However, the following Guarantee Payments Exemption Orders in force at the date this section came into force (22 August 1996) and not subsequently revoked have effect as if made hereunder by virtue of s 241 of, and Sch 2, Pt I, paras 1–4 to, this Act: No 1 (SI 1977/156) Federation of Civil Engineering Contractors; No 2 (SI 1977/157) National Federation of Demolition Contractors; No 5 (SI 1977/902) British Footwear Manufacturers' Federation; No 6 (SI 1977/1096) Steeplejacks and Lightning Conductor Engineers; No 7 (SI 1977/1158) Paper and Board Industry; No 8 (SI 1977/1322) Smiths Food Group; No 9 (SI 1977/1349) British Leather Federation; No 10 (SI 1977/1522) Fibreboard Packing Case Industry; No 11 (SI 1977/1523) Henry Wiggin & Co Ltd; No 12 (SI 1977/1583) Refractory Users Federation; No 13 (SI 1977/1601) Multiwall Sack Manufacturers; No 14 (SI 1977/2032) Tudor Food Products; No 15 (SI 1978/153) British Carton Association; No 16 (SI 1978/429) Henry Wiggin & Co; No 17 (SI 1978/737) NJC for Workshops for the Blind; No 18 (SI 1978/826) Employers' Federation of Card Clothing Manufacturers; No 19 (SI 1979/1403) NJC for the Motor Vehicle Repair Industry; No 21 (SI 1981/6) Plant Hire Working Rule Agreement; No 23 (SI 1987/1757) National Agreement for Wire and Wire Rope Industries (revoking No 4); No 24 (SI 1989/1326) Rowntree Mackintosh Confectionery Ltd (revoking No 22 as amended); No 25 (SI 1989/1575) Building and Allied Trades Joint Industrial Council (revoking No 20); No 26 (SI 1989/2163) Airflow Streamlines; No 27 (SI 1990/927) G & G Kynock plc; No 28 (SI 1990/2330) Bridon Ropes Ltd; No 30 (SI 1996/2132) National Joint Council for the Building Industry.

PART IV
SUNDAY WORKING FOR SHOP AND BETTING WORKERS

Protected shop workers and betting workers

[1.852]

36 Protected shop workers and betting workers

(1) Subject to subsection (5), a shop worker or betting worker is to be regarded as "protected" for the purposes of any provision of this Act if (and only if) subsection (2) or (3) applies to him.

(2) This subsection applies to a shop worker or betting worker if—

(a) on the day before the relevant commencement date he was employed as a shop worker or a betting worker but not to work only on Sunday,

(b) he has been continuously employed during the period beginning with that day and ending with the day which, in relation to the provision concerned, is the appropriate date, and

(c) throughout that period, or throughout every part of it during which his relations with his employer were governed by a contract of employment, he was a shop worker or a betting worker.

(3) This subsection applies to any shop worker or betting worker whose contract of employment is such that under it he—

(a) is not, and may not be, required to work on Sunday, and

(b) could not be so required even if the provisions of this Part were disregarded.

(4) Where on the day before the relevant commencement date an employee's relations with his employer had ceased to be governed by a contract of employment, he shall be regarded as satisfying subsection (2)(a) if—

(a) that day fell in a week which counts as a period of employment with that employer under section 212(2) or (3) or under regulations under section 219, and

(b) on the last day before the relevant commencement date on which his relations with his employer were governed by a contract of employment, the employee was employed as a shop worker or a betting worker but not to work only on Sunday.

(5) A shop worker is not a protected shop worker, and a betting worker is not a protected betting worker, if—

(a) he has given his employer an opting-in notice on or after the relevant commencement date, and

(b) after giving the notice, he has expressly agreed with his employer to do shop work, or betting work, on Sunday or on a particular Sunday.

(6) In this Act "opting-in notice", in relation to a shop worker or a betting worker, means written notice, signed and dated by the shop worker or betting worker, in which the shop worker or betting worker expressly states that he wishes to work on Sunday or that he does not object to Sunday working.

(7) [Subject to subsection (8),] in this Act "the relevant commencement date" means—

(a) in relation to a shop worker, 26th August 1994, and

(b) in relation to a betting worker, 3rd January 1995.

[(8) In any provision of this Act which applies to Scotland by virtue of section 1(5) of the Sunday Working (Scotland) Act 2003 (extension to Scotland of provisions which refer to shop workers and betting workers), "the relevant commencement date" means, in relation to Scotland, the date on which that section came into force.]

NOTES

Sub-s (7): words in square brackets inserted by the Sunday Working (Scotland) Act 2003, s 1(1), (2)(a).

Sub-s (8): added by the Sunday Working (Scotland) Act 2003, s 1(1), (2)(b).

Relevant commencement date: the Sunday Working (Scotland) Act 2003, s 1 came into force on 6 April 2004 (see SI 2004/958).

[1.853]

37 Contractual requirements relating to Sunday work

(1) Any contract of employment under which a shop worker or betting worker who satisfies section 36(2)(a) was employed on the day or before the relevant commencement date is unenforceable to the extent that it—

(a) requires the shop worker to do shop work, or the betting worker to do betting work, on Sunday on or after that date, or

(b) requires the employer to provide the shop worker with shop work, or the betting worker with betting work, on Sunday on or after that date.

(2) Subject to subsection (3), any agreement entered into after the relevant commencement date between a protected shop worker, or a protected betting worker, and his employer is unenforceable to the extent that it—

(a) requires the shop worker to do shop work, or the betting worker to do betting work, on Sunday, or

(b) requires the employer to provide the shop worker with shop work, or the betting worker with betting work, on Sunday.

(3) Where, after giving an opting-in notice, a protected shop worker or a protected betting worker expressly agrees with his employer to do shop work or betting work on Sunday or on a particular Sunday (and so ceases to be protected), his contract of employment shall be taken to be varied to the extent necessary to give effect to the terms of the agreement.

(4) . . .

(5) For the purposes of section 36(2)(b), the appropriate date—

(a) in relation to subsections (2) and (3) of this section, is the day on which the agreement is entered into, . . .

(b) . . .

NOTES

Sub-s (4): repealed by the Employment Relations Act 1999, ss 9, 44, Sch 4, Pt III, paras 1, 5, 6(a), Sch 9(2).

Sub-s (5): word omitted from para (a), and para (b), repealed by the Employment Relations Act 1999, ss 9, 44, Sch 4, Pt III, paras 1, 5, 6(b), (c), Sch 9(2).

[1.854]

38 Contracts with guaranteed hours

(1) This section applies where—

(a) under the contract of employment under which a shop worker or betting worker who satisfies section 36(2)(a) was employed on the day before the relevant commencement date, the employer is, or may be, required to provide him with shop work, or betting work, for a specified number of hours each week,

(b) under the contract the shop worker or betting worker was, or might have been, required to work on Sunday before that date, and

(c) the shop worker has done shop work, or the betting worker betting work, on Sunday in that employment (whether or not before that day) but has, on or after that date, ceased to do so.

(2) So long as the shop worker remains a protected shop worker, or the betting worker remains a protected betting worker, the contract shall not be regarded as requiring the employer to provide him with shop work, or betting work, on weekdays in excess of the hours normally worked by the shop worker or betting worker on weekdays before he ceased to do shop work, or betting work, on Sunday.
(3) For the purposes of section 36(2)(b), the appropriate date in relation to this section is any time in relation to which the contract is to be enforced.

[1.855]
39 Reduction of pay etc
(1) This section applies where—
  (a) under the contract of employment under which a shop worker or betting worker who satisfies section 36(2)(a) was employed on the day before the relevant commencement date, the shop worker or betting worker was, or might have been, required to work on Sunday before the relevant commencement date,
  (b) the shop worker has done shop work, or the betting worker has done betting work, on Sunday in that employment (whether or not before that date) but has, on or after that date, ceased to do so, and
  (c) it is not apparent from the contract what part of the remuneration payable, or of any other benefit accruing, to the shop worker or betting worker was intended to be attributable to shop work, or betting work, on Sunday.
(2) So long as the shop worker remains a protected shop worker, or the betting worker remains a protected betting worker, the contract shall be regarded as enabling the employer to reduce the amount of remuneration paid, or the extent of the other benefit provided, to the shop worker or betting worker in respect of any period by the relevant proportion.
(3) In subsection (2) "the relevant proportion" means the proportion which the hours of shop work, or betting work, which (apart from this Part) the shop worker, or betting worker, could have been required to do on Sunday in the period ("the contractual Sunday hours") bears to the aggregate of those hours and the hours of work actually done by the shop worker, or betting worker, in the period.
(4) Where, under the contract of employment, the hours of work actually done on weekdays in any period would be taken into account determining the contractual Sunday hours, they shall be taken into account in determining the contractual Sunday hours for the purposes of subsection (3).
(5) For the purposes of section 36(2)(b), the appropriate date in relation to this section is the end of the period in respect of which the remuneration is paid or the benefit accrues.

Opting-out of Sunday work

[1.856]
40 Notice of objection to Sunday working
(1) A shop worker or betting worker to whom this section applies may at any time give his employer written notice, signed and dated by the shop worker or betting worker, to the effect that he objects to Sunday working.
(2) In this Act "opting-out notice" means a notice given under subsection (1) by a shop worker or betting worker to whom this section applies.
(3) This section applies to any shop worker or betting worker under his contract of employment—
  (a) is or may be required to work on Sunday (whether or not a result of previously giving an opting-in notice), but
  (b) is not employed to work only on Sunday.

[1.857]
41 Opted-out shop workers and betting workers
(1) Subject to subsection (2), a shop worker or betting worker is regarded as "opted-out" for the purposes of any provision of this (and only if)—
  (a) he has given his employer an opting-out notice,
  (b) he has been continuously employed during the period beginning with the day on which the notice was given and ending with the day which, in relation to the provision concerned, is the appropriate date, and
  (c) throughout that period, or throughout every part of it during which his relations with his employer were governed by a contract of employment, he was a shop worker or a betting worker.
(2) A shop worker is not an opted-out shop worker, and a betting worker is not an opted out betting worker, if—
  (a) after giving the opting-out notice concerned, he has given his employer an opting-in notice, and
  (b) after giving the opting-in notice, he has expressly agreed with his employer to do shop work, or betting work, on Sunday or on a particular Sunday.
(3) In this Act "notice period", in relation to an opted-out shop worker or an opted-out betting worker, means, subject to section 42(2), the period of three months beginning with the day on which the opting-out notice concerned was given.

NOTES
Sub-s (3): substituted by the Enterprise Act 2016, s 33, Sch 5, paras 1, 2, as from a day to be appointed, as follows—

"(3) In this Act "notice period", in relation to an opted-out shop worker or an opted-out betting worker, means—
  (a) in the case of an opted-out shop worker who does shop work in or about a large shop, the period of one month beginning with the day on which the opting-out notice concerned was given;
  (b) in any other case, the period of three months beginning with that day.

This subsection is subject to sections 41D(2) and 42(2).".

[1.858]
[41A Notice of objection by shop workers to working additional hours on Sunday

(1) A shop worker may at any time give to his or her employer a written notice, signed and dated by the shop worker, to the effect that he or she objects to doing shop work for additional hours on Sunday.

(2) In this Part—

"additional hours" means any number of hours of shop work that a shop worker is (or could be) required to work under a contract of employment on Sunday that are (or would be) in excess of the shop worker's normal Sunday working hours;

"objection notice" means a notice given under subsection (1).

(3) The "normal Sunday working hours" of a shop worker are to be calculated in accordance with regulations.

(4) Regulations under this section may provide—

(a) for the calculation to be determined (for example) by reference to the average number of hours that the shop worker has worked on Sundays during a period specified or described in the regulations;

(b) for a calculation of the kind mentioned in paragraph (a) to be varied in special cases;

(c) for the right to give an objection notice not to be exercisable in special cases (and subsection (1) is subject to provision made by virtue of this paragraph).

(5) Provision under subsection (4)(b) or (c) may, in particular, include provision—

(a) about how the calculation of normal Sunday working hours is to be made in the case of a shop worker who has not been employed for a sufficient period of time to enable a calculation to be made as otherwise provided for in the regulations;

(b) for the right to give an objection notice not to be exercisable by such a shop worker until he or she has completed a period of employment specified or described in the regulations.

(6) But regulations under this section may not include provision preventing a shop worker who has been continuously employed under a contract of employment for a period of one year or more from giving to the employer an objection notice.

(7) Regulations under this section may make different provision for different purposes.]

NOTES

Commencement: 4 May 2016 (for the purpose of enabling the exercise of any power to make regulations); to be appointed (otherwise).

Inserted by the Enterprise Act 2016, s 33, Sch 5, paras 1, 3, as from 4 May 2016 (for the purpose of enabling the exercise of any power to make regulations), and as from a day to be appointed (otherwise).

Regulations: as of 15 May 2019, no Regulations had been made under this section.

[1.859]
[41B Explanatory statement: persons who become shop workers

(1) This section applies where a person becomes a shop worker who, under a contract of employment, is or may be required to do shop work on Sundays.

(2) The employer must give to the shop worker a written statement informing the shop worker of the following rights—

(a) the right to object to working on Sundays by giving the employer an opting-out notice (if section 40 applies to the shop worker);

(b) the right to object to doing shop work for additional hours on Sundays by giving the employer an objection notice.

(3) The statement must be given before the end of the period of two months beginning with the day on which the person becomes a shop worker as mentioned in subsection (1).

(4) An employer does not fail to comply with subsections (2) and (3) in a case where, before the end of the period referred to in subsection (3), the shop worker has given to the employer an opting-out notice (and that notice has not been withdrawn).

(5) A statement under this section must comply with such requirements as to form and content as regulations may provide.

(6) Regulations under this section may make different provision for different purposes.]

NOTES

Commencement: 4 May 2016 (for the purpose of enabling the exercise of any power to make regulations); to be appointed (otherwise).

Inserted by the Enterprise Act 2016, s 33, Sch 5, paras 1, 3, as from 4 May 2016 (for the purpose of enabling the exercise of any power to make regulations), and as from a day to be appointed (otherwise).

Regulations: as of 15 May 2019, no Regulations had been made under this section.

[1.860]
[41C Explanatory statement: shop workers at commencement date

(1) This section applies where—

(a) under a contract of employment a shop worker is or may be required to do shop work on Sundays, and

(b) the shop worker was employed under that contract on the day before the commencement date.

(2) The shop worker's employer must give to the shop worker a written statement informing the shop worker of the rights mentioned in section 41B(2).

(3) The statement must be given before the end of the period of two months beginning with the commencement date.
(4) An employer does not fail to comply with subsections (2) and (3) in a case where, before the end of the period referred to in subsection (3), the shop worker has given to the employer an opting-out notice (and that notice has not been withdrawn).
(5) A statement under this section must comply with such requirements as to form and content as regulations may provide.
(6) Regulations under this section may make different provision for different purposes.
(7) In this section "commencement date" means the date appointed by regulations under section 44 of the Enterprise Act 2016 for the coming into force of section 33 of, and Schedule 5 to, that Act.]

NOTES

Commencement: 4 May 2016 (for the purpose of enabling the exercise of any power to make regulations); to be appointed (otherwise).

Inserted by the Enterprise Act 2016, s 33, Sch 5, paras 1, 3, as from 4 May 2016 (for the purpose of enabling the exercise of any power to make regulations), and as from a day to be appointed (otherwise).

Regulations: as of 15 May 2019, no Regulations had been made under this section.

[1.861]
[41D Failure to give explanatory statement under section 41B or 41C
(1) This section applies if an employer fails to give to a shop worker a written statement in accordance with—
- (a) section 41B(2) and (3), or
- (b) section 41C(2) and (3).

(2) If the shop worker gives to the employer an opting-out notice, the notice period under section 41(3) that applies in relation to the shop worker is varied as follows—
- (a) if the notice period under that provision would have been one month, it becomes 7 days instead;
- (b) if the notice period under that provision would have been three months, it becomes one month instead.

(3) If the shop worker gives to the employer an objection notice, the relevant period under section 43ZA(2) that applies in relation to the shop worker is varied as follows—
- (a) if the relevant period under that provision would have been one month, it becomes 7 days instead;
- (b) if the relevant period under that provision would have been three months, it becomes one month instead.]

NOTES

Commencement: to be appointed.

Inserted by the Enterprise Act 2016, s 33, Sch 5, paras 1, 3, as from a day to be appointed.

[1.862]
42 Explanatory statement[: betting workers]
(1) Where a person becomes a *shop worker or* betting worker to whom section 40 applies, his employer shall, before the end of the period two months beginning with the day on which that person becomes such worker, give him a written statement in the prescribed form.
(2) If—
- (a) an employer fails to comply with subsection (1) in relation to any *shop worker or* betting worker, and
- (b) the *shop worker or* betting worker, on giving the employer an opting-out notice, becomes *an opted-out shop worker or* an opted-out betting worker,

section 41(3) has effect in relation to the *shop worker or* betting worker with the substitution for "three months" of "one month".
(3) An employer shall not be regarded as failing to comply with subsection (1) in any case where, before the end of the period referred to that subsection, the *shop worker or* betting worker has given him an opting-out notice.
(4) Subject to subsection (6), the prescribed form in the case of a shop worker is as follows—

"STATUTORY RIGHTS IN RELATION TO SUNDAY SHOP WORK

You have become employed as a shop worker and are or can be required under your contract of employment to do the Sunday work your contract provides for.

However, if you wish, you can give a notice, as described in the next paragraph, to your employer and you will then have the right not to work in or about a shop on any Sunday on which the shop is open once three months have passed from the date on which you gave the notice.

Your notice must—
be in writing;
be signed and dated by you;
say that you object to Sunday working.

For three months after you give the notice, your employer can still require you to do all the Sunday work your contract provides for. After the three month period has ended, you have the right to complain to an [employment tribunal] if, because of your refusal to work on Sundays on which the shop is open, your employer—

dismisses you, or

does something else detrimental to you, for example, failing to promote you.

Once you have the rights described, you can surrender them only by giving your employer a further notice, signed and dated by you, saying that you wish to work on Sunday or that you do not object to Sunday working and then agreeing with your employer to work on Sundays or on a particular Sunday.".

(5) Subject to subsection (6), the prescribed form in the case of betting worker is as follows—

"STATUTORY RIGHTS IN RELATION TO SUNDAY BETTING WORK

You have become employed under a contract of employment under which you are or can be required to do Sunday betting work that is to say, work—

at a track on a Sunday on which your employer is taking bets at the track, or

in a licensed betting office on a Sunday on which it is open for business.

However, if you wish, you can give a notice, as described in the next paragraph, to your employer and you will then have the right not to do Sunday betting work once three months have passed from the date on which you gave the notice.

Your notice must—

be in writing;

be signed and dated by you;

say that you object to doing Sunday betting work.

For three months after you give the notice, your employer can still require you to do all the Sunday betting work your contract provides for. After the three month period has ended, you have the right to complain to an [employment tribunal] if, because of your refusal to do Sunday betting work, your employer—

dismisses you, or

does something else detrimental to you, for example, failing to promote you.

Once you have the rights described, you can surrender them only by giving your employer a further notice, signed and dated by you, saying that you wish to do Sunday betting work or that you do not object to doing Sunday betting work and then agreeing with your employer to do such work on Sundays or on a particular Sunday.".

(6) The Secretary of State may by order amend the prescribed *forms* set out in *subsections (4) and (5)*.

NOTES

Section heading: words in square brackets inserted by the Enterprise Act 2016, s 33, Sch 5, paras 1, 4(1), (2), as from a day to be appointed.

Sub-ss (1)–(3): words in italics repealed by the Enterprise Act 2016, s 33, Sch 5, paras 1, 4(1), (3)–(5), as from a day to be appointed.

Sub-s (4): words in square brackets substituted by the Employment Rights (Dispute Resolution) Act 1998, s 1(2)(a); this subsection is repealed by the Enterprise Act 2016, s 33, Sch 5, paras 1, 4(1), (6), as from a day to be appointed.

Sub-s (5): words in square brackets substituted by the Employment Rights (Dispute Resolution) Act 1998, s 1(2)(a).

Sub-s (6): for the first word in italics there is substituted "form", and for the second words in italics there are substituted the words "subsection (5)", by the Enterprise Act 2016, s 33, Sch 5, paras 1, 4(1), (7), as from a day to be appointed.

Orders: as of 15 May 2019, no Orders had been made under this section.

[1.863]

43 Contractual requirements relating to Sunday work[: opting-out notices]

(1) Where a shop worker or betting worker gives his employer an opting-out notice, the contract of employment under which he was employed immediately before he gave that notice becomes unenforceable to the extent that it—

(a) requires the shop worker to do shop work, or the betting worker to do betting work, on Sunday after the end of the notice period, or

(b) requires the employer to provide the shop worker with shop work, or the betting worker with betting work, on Sunday after the end of that period.

(2) Subject to subsection (3), any agreement entered into between an opted-out shop worker, or an opted-out betting worker, and his employer is unenforceable to the extent that it—

(a) requires the shop worker to do shop work, or the betting worker to do betting work, on Sunday after the end of the notice period, or

(b) requires the employer to provide the shop worker with shop work, or the betting worker with betting work, on Sunday after the end of that period.

(3) Where, after giving an opting-in notice, an opted-out shop worker an opted-out betting worker expressly agrees with his employer to do shop work or betting work on Sunday or on a particular Sunday (and so ceases to be opted-out), his contract of employment shall be taken to be varied to the extent necessary to give effect to the terms of the agreement.

(4) . . .

(5) For the purposes of section 41(1)(b), the appropriate date—

(a) in relation to subsections (2) and (3) of this section, is the day on which the agreement is entered into, . . .

(b) . . .

NOTES

Section heading: words in square brackets inserted by the Enterprise Act 2016, s 33, Sch 5, paras 1, 5, as from a day to be appointed.

Sub-s (4): repealed by the Employment Relations Act 1999, ss 9, 44, Sch 4, Pt III, paras 1, 5, 7(a), Sch 9(2).

Sub-s (5): word omitted from para (a), and para (b), repealed by the Employment Relations Act 1999, ss 9, Sch 4, Pt III, paras 1, 5, 7(b), (c), Sch 9(2).

[1.864]

[43ZA Contractual requirements relating to working additional hours on Sundays: objection notices

(1) Where a shop worker gives to his or her employer an objection notice, any agreement entered into between the shop worker and the employer becomes unenforceable to the extent that—

(a) it requires the shop worker to do shop work for additional hours on Sunday after the end of the relevant period, or

(b) it requires the employer to provide the shop worker with shop work for additional hours on Sunday after the end of that period.

(2) The "relevant period" is—

(a) in the case of a shop worker who is or may be required to do shop work in or about a large shop, the period of one month beginning with the day on which the objection notice is given;

(b) in any other case, the period of three months beginning with that day.

This subsection is subject to section 41D(3).

(3) A shop worker who has given an objection notice may revoke the notice by giving a further written notice to the employer.

(4) Where—

(a) a shop worker gives to the employer a notice under subsection (3), and

(b) after giving the notice the shop worker expressly agrees with the employer to do shop work for additional hours on Sunday (whether on Sundays generally or on a particular Sunday),

the contract of employment between the shop worker and the employer is to be taken to be varied to the extent necessary to give effect to the terms of the agreement.

(5) The reference in subsection (1) to any agreement—

(a) includes the contract of employment under which the shop worker is employed immediately before giving the objection notice;

(b) includes an agreement of a kind mentioned in subsection (4), or a contract of employment as taken to be varied under that subsection, only if an objection notice is given in relation to the working of additional hours under that agreement or contract as varied.]

NOTES

Commencement: to be appointed.

Inserted by the Enterprise Act 2016, s 33, Sch 5, paras 1, 6, as from a day to be appointed.

[1.865]

[43ZB Interpretation

(1) In this Part—

"additional hours" has the meaning given in section 41A(2);

"large shop" means a shop which has a relevant floor area exceeding 280 square metres;

"objection notice" has the meaning given in section 41A(2);

"regulations" means regulations made by the Secretary of State.

(2) In the definition of "large shop" in subsection (1)—

(a) "shop" means any premises where there is carried on a trade or business consisting wholly or mainly of the sale of goods;

(b) "relevant floor area" means the internal floor area of so much of the large shop in question as consists of or is comprised in a building.

(3) For the purposes of subsection (2), any part of the shop which is not used for the serving of customers in connection with the sale or display of goods is to be disregarded.

(4) The references in subsections (2) and (3) to the sale of goods does not include—

(a) the sale of meals, refreshments or alcohol (within the meaning of the Licensing Act 2003 or, in relation to Scotland, the Licensing (Scotland) Act 2005 (asp 16)) for consumption on the premises on which they are sold, or

(b) the sale of meals or refreshments prepared to order for immediate consumption off those premises.]

NOTES

Commencement: to be appointed.

Inserted by the Enterprise Act 2016, s 33, Sch 5, paras 1, 6, as from a day to be appointed.

[PART IVA PROTECTED DISCLOSURES

[1.866]

43A Meaning of "protected disclosure"

In this Act a "protected disclosure" means a qualifying disclosure (as defined by section 43B) which is made by a worker in accordance with any of sections 43C to 43H.]

NOTES

Part IVA (originally ss 43A–43L) was inserted by the Public Interest Disclosure Act 1998, s 1.

[1.867]

[43B Disclosures qualifying for protection

(1) In this Part a "qualifying disclosure" means any disclosure of information which, in the reasonable belief of the worker making the disclosure, [is made in the public interest and] tends to show one or more of the following—

- (a) that a criminal offence has been committed, is being committed or is likely to be committed,
- (b) that a person has failed, is failing or is likely to fail to comply with any legal obligation to which he is subject,
- (c) that a miscarriage of justice has occurred, is occurring or is likely to occur,
- (d) that the health or safety of any individual has been, is being or is likely to be endangered,
- (e) that the environment has been, is being or is likely to be damaged, or
- (f) that information tending to show any matter falling within any one of the preceding paragraphs has been, or is likely to be deliberately concealed.

(2) For the purposes of subsection (1), it is immaterial whether the relevant failure occurred, occurs or would occur in the United Kingdom or elsewhere, and whether the law applying to it is that of the United Kingdom or of any other country or territory.

(3) A disclosure of information is not a qualifying disclosure if the person making the disclosure commits an offence by making it.

(4) A disclosure of information in respect of which a claim to legal professional privilege (or, in Scotland, to confidentiality as between client and professional legal adviser) could be maintained in legal proceedings is not a qualifying disclosure if it is made by a person to whom the information had been disclosed in the course of obtaining legal advice.

(5) In this Part "the relevant failure", in relation to a qualifying disclosure, means the matter falling within paragraphs (a) to (f) of subsection (1).]

NOTES

Inserted as noted to s 43A at **[1.866]**.
Sub-s (1): words in square brackets inserted by the Enterprise and Regulatory Reform Act 2013, s 17.

[1.868]

[43C Disclosure to employer or other responsible person

(1) A qualifying disclosure is made in accordance with this section if the worker makes the disclosure . . . —

- (a) to his employer, or
- (b) where the worker reasonably believes that the relevant failure relates solely or mainly to—
  - (i) the conduct of a person other than his employer, or
  - (ii) any other matter for which a person other than his employer has legal responsibility,

  to that other person.

(2) A worker who, in accordance with a procedure whose use by him is authorised by his employer, makes a qualifying disclosure to a person other than his employer, is to be treated for the purposes of this Part as making the qualifying disclosure to his employer.]

NOTES

Inserted as noted to s 43A at **[1.866]**.
Sub-s (1): words omitted repealed by the Enterprise and Regulatory Reform Act 2013, s 18(1)(a).

[1.869]

[43D Disclosure to legal adviser

A qualifying disclosure is made in accordance with this section if it is made in the course of obtaining legal advice.]

NOTES

Inserted as noted to s 43A at **[1.866]**.

[1.870]

[43E Disclosure to Minister of the Crown

A qualifying disclosure is made in accordance with this section if—

- (a) the worker's employer is—
  - (i) an individual appointed under any enactment [(including any enactment comprised in, or in an instrument made under, an Act of the Scottish Parliament)] by a Minister of the Crown [or a member of the Scottish Executive], or
  - (ii) a body any of whose members are so appointed, and

(b) the disclosure is made . . . to a Minister of the Crown [or a member of the Scottish Executive].]

NOTES

Inserted as noted to s 43A at **[1.866]**.

Words in square brackets inserted by the Scotland Act 1998 (Consequential Modifications) Order 2000, SI 2000/2040, arts 1(1), 2(1), Schedule, Pt I, para 19.

Words omitted repealed by the Enterprise and Regulatory Reform Act 2013, s 18(1)(b).

[1.871]

[43F Disclosure to prescribed person

(1) A qualifying disclosure is made in accordance with this section if the worker—

(a) makes the disclosure . . . to a person prescribed by an order made by the Secretary of State for the purposes of this section, and

(b) reasonably believes—

(i) that the relevant failure falls within any description of matters in respect of which that person is so prescribed, and

(ii) that the information disclosed, and any allegation contained in it, are substantially true.

(2) An order prescribing persons for the purposes of this section may specify persons or descriptions of persons, and shall specify the descriptions of matters in respect of which each person, or persons of each description, is or are prescribed.]

NOTES

Inserted as noted to s 43A at **[1.866]**.

Sub-s (1): words omitted repealed by the Enterprise and Regulatory Reform Act 2013, s 18(1)(c).

Orders: the Public Interest Disclosure (Prescribed Persons) Order 2014, SI 2014/2418 at **[2.1513]**; the Public Interest Disclosure (Prescribed Persons) (Amendment) Order 2015, SI 2015/1407; the Public Interest Disclosure (Prescribed Persons) (Amendment) (No 2) Order 2015, SI 2015/1981; the Public Interest Disclosure (Prescribed Persons) (Amendment) Order 2016, SI 2016/968; the Public Interest Disclosure (Prescribed Persons) (Amendment) Order 2017, SI 2017/880; the NHS Counter Fraud Authority (Investigatory Powers and Other Miscellaneous Amendments) Order 2017, SI 2017/960.

[1.872]

[43FA Prescribed persons: duty to report on disclosures of information]

[(1) The Secretary of State may make regulations requiring a person prescribed for the purposes of section 43F to produce an annual report on disclosures of information made to the person by workers.

(2) The regulations must set out the matters that are to be covered in a report, but must not require a report to provide detail that would enable either of the following to be identified—

(a) a worker who has made a disclosure;

(b) an employer or other person in respect of whom a disclosure has been made.

(3) The regulations must make provision about the publication of a report, and such provision may include (but is not limited to) any of the following requirements—

(a) to send the report to the Secretary of State for laying before Parliament;

(b) to include the report in another report or in information required to be published by the prescribed person;

(c) to publish the report on a website.

(4) The regulations may make provision about the time period within which a report must be produced and published.

(5) Regulations under subsections (2) to (4) may make different provision for different prescribed persons.]

NOTES

Commencement: 1 January 2016.

Inserted by the Small Business, Enterprise and Employment Act 2015, s 148(1), (2), as from 1 January 2016.

Regulations: the Prescribed Persons (Reports on Disclosures of Information) Regulations 2017, SI 2017/507 at **[2.2019]**.

[1.873]

[43G Disclosure in other cases

(1) A qualifying disclosure is made in accordance with this section if—

(a) . . .

(b) [the worker] reasonably believes that the information disclosed, and any allegation contained in it, are substantially true,

(c) he does not make the disclosure for purposes of personal gain,

(d) any of the conditions in subsection (2) is met, and

(e) in all the circumstances of the case, it is reasonable for him to make the disclosure.

(2) The conditions referred to in subsection (1)(d) are—

(a) that, at the time he makes the disclosure, the worker reasonably believes that he will be subjected to a detriment by his employer if he makes a disclosure to his employer or in accordance with section 43F,

(b) that, in a case where no person is prescribed for the purposes of section 43F in relation to the relevant failure, the worker reasonably believes that it is likely that evidence relating to the relevant failure will be concealed or destroyed if he makes a disclosure to his employer, or

(c) that the worker has previously made a disclosure of substantially the same information—

(i) to his employer, or

(ii) in accordance with section 43F.

(3) In determining for the purposes of subsection (1)(e) whether it is reasonable for the worker to make the disclosure, regard shall be had, in particular, to—

(a) the identity of the person to whom the disclosure is made,

(b) the seriousness of the relevant failure,

(c) whether the relevant failure is continuing or is likely to occur in the future,

(d) whether the disclosure is made in breach of a duty of confidentiality owed by the employer to any other person,

(e) in a case falling within subsection (2)(c)(i) or (ii), any action which the employer or the person to whom the previous disclosure in accordance with section 43F was made has taken or might reasonably be expected to have taken as a result of the previous disclosure, and

(f) in a case falling within subsection (2)(c)(i), whether in making the disclosure to the employer the worker complied with any procedure whose use by him was authorised by the employer.

(4) For the purposes of this section a subsequent disclosure may be regarded as a disclosure of substantially the same information as that disclosed by a previous disclosure as mentioned in subsection (2)(c) even though the subsequent disclosure extends to information about action taken or not taken by any person as a result of the previous disclosure.]

NOTES

Inserted as noted to s 43A at **[1.866]**.

Sub-s (1): para (a) repealed, and words in square brackets in para (b) substituted, by the Enterprise and Regulatory Reform Act 2013, s 18(2).

[1.874]

[43H Disclosure of exceptionally serious failure

(1) A qualifying disclosure is made in accordance with this section if—

(a) . . .

(b) [the worker] reasonably believes that the information disclosed, and any allegation contained in it, are substantially true,

(c) he does not make the disclosure for purposes of personal gain,

(d) the relevant failure is of an exceptionally serious nature, and

(e) in all the circumstances of the case, it is reasonable for him to make the disclosure.

(2) In determining for the purposes of subsection (1)(e) whether it is reasonable for the worker to make the disclosure, regard shall be had, in particular, to the identity of the person to whom the disclosure is made.]

NOTES

Inserted as noted to s 43A at **[1.866]**.

Sub-s (1): para (a) repealed, and words in square brackets in para (b) substituted, by the Enterprise and Regulatory Reform Act 2013, s 18(3).

[1.875]

[43J Contractual duties of confidentiality

(1) Any provision in an agreement to which this section applies is void in so far as it purports to preclude the worker from making a protected disclosure.

(2) This section applies to any agreement between a worker and his employer (whether a worker's contract or not), including an agreement to refrain from instituting or continuing any proceedings under this Act or any proceedings for breach of contract.]

NOTES

Inserted as noted to s 43A at **[1.866]**.

[1.876]

[43K Extension of meaning of "worker" etc for Part IVA

(1) For the purposes of this Part "worker" includes an individual who is not a worker as defined by section 230(3) but who—

(a) works or worked for a person in circumstances in which—

(i) he is or was introduced or supplied to do that work by a third person, and

(ii) the terms on which he is or was engaged to do the work are or were in practice substantially determined not by him but by the person for whom he works or worked, by the third person or by both of them,

(b) contracts or contracted with a person, for the purposes of that person's business, for the execution of work to be done in a place not under the control or management of that person and would fall within section 230(3)(b) if for "personally" in that provision there were substituted "(whether personally or otherwise)",

[(ba) works or worked as a person performing services under a contract entered into by him with [the National Health Service Commissioning Board] [under [section 83(2), 84, 92, 100, 107, 115(4), 117 or 134 of, or Schedule 12 to,] the National Health Service Act 2006 or with a Local Health Board under [section 41(2)(b), 42, 50, 57, 64 or 92 of, or Schedule 7 to,] the National Health Service (Wales) Act 2006] . . .

[(bb) works or worked as a person performing services under a contract entered into by him with a Health Board under section 17J [or 17Q] of the National Health Service (Scotland) Act 1978,]

(c) [works or worked as a person providing services] in accordance with arrangements made—

(i) by [the National Health Service Commissioning Board] [[under section 126 of the National Health Service Act 2006,] or] [Local Health Board] under [section 71 or 80 of the National Health Service (Wales) Act 2006], or

(ii) by a Health Board under section [2C, 17AA, 17C,] . . . 25, *26 or 27* of the National Health Service (Scotland) Act 1978, . . .

[(ca) . . .]

[(cb) is or was provided with work experience provided pursuant to a course of education or training approved by, or under arrangements with, the Nursing and Midwifery Council in accordance with article 15(6)(a) of the Nursing and Midwifery Order 2001 (SI 2002/253), or]

(d) is or was provided with work experience provided pursuant to a training course or programme or with training for employment (or with both) otherwise than—

(i) under a contract of employment, or

(ii) by an educational establishment on a course run by that establishment;

and any reference to a worker's contract, to employment or to a worker being "employed" shall be construed accordingly.

(2) For the purposes of this Part "employer" includes—

(a) in relation to a worker falling within paragraph (a) of subsection (1), the person who substantially determines or determined the terms on which he is or was engaged,

[(aa) in relation to a worker falling within paragraph (ba) of that subsection, [. . . or the] Local Health Board referred to in that paragraph,]

[(ab) in relation to a worker falling within paragraph (bb) of that subsection, the Health Board referred to in that paragraph,]

(b) in relation to a worker falling within paragraph (c) of that subsection, the authority or board referred to in that paragraph, and

[(ba) . . .]

(c) in relation to a worker falling within paragraph [(cb) or] (d) of that subsection, the person providing the work experience or training.

(3) In this section "educational establishment" includes any university, college, school or other educational establishment.

[(4) The Secretary of State may by order make amendments to this section as to what individuals count as "workers" for the purposes of this Part (despite not being within the definition in section 230(3)).

(5) An order under subsection (4) may not make an amendment that has the effect of removing a category of individual unless the Secretary of State is satisfied that there are no longer any individuals in that category.]]

NOTES

Inserted as noted to s 43A at **[1.866]**.

Sub-s (1) is amended as follows:

Para (ba): inserted by the Health and Social Care (Community Health and Standards) Act 2003, s 184, Sch 11, para 65(1), (2); and subsequently amended as follows:

Words "the National Health Service Commissioning Board" in square brackets substituted by the Health and Social Care Act 2012, s 55(2), Sch 5, paras 72, 73(a).

Words in second (outer) pair of square brackets (ie, beginning with the word "under") substituted by the National Health Service (Consequential Provisions) Act 2006, s 2, Sch 1, paras 177, 178(a).

Words "section 83(2), 84, 92, 100, 107, 115(4), 117 or 134 of, or Schedule 12 to," and "section 41(2)(b), 42, 50, 57, 64 or 92 of, or Schedule 7 to," in square brackets substituted, and words omitted repealed, by the Enterprise and Regulatory Reform Act 2013, s 20(1), (2).

Para (bb): inserted by the Primary Medical Services (Scotland) Act 2004 (Consequential Modifications) Order 2004, SI 2004/957, art 2, Schedule, para 8(a)(i); words in square brackets inserted by the Enterprise and Regulatory Reform Act 2013, s 20(1), (3).

Para (c): words in first pair of square brackets substituted by the Enterprise and Regulatory Reform Act 2013, s 20(1), (4)(a); words "the National Health Service Commissioning Board" in square brackets in sub-para (c)(i) substituted by the Health and Social Care Act 2012, s 55(2), Sch 5, paras 72, 73(b); words in second (outer) pair of square brackets in sub-para (c)(i) (effectively now only the word "or" preceding the words "Local Health Board") inserted by the National Health Service Reform and Health Care Professions Act 2002, s 2(5), Sch 2, Pt 2, para 63; words "under section 126 of the National Health Service Act 2006," and "section 71 or 80 of the National Health Service (Wales) Act 2006" in square brackets in sub-para (c)(i) inserted and substituted respectively, by the National Health Service (Consequential Provisions) Act 2006, s 2, Sch 1, paras 177, 178(b); words "Local Health Board" in square brackets in sub-para (c)(i) substituted by the References to Health Authorities Order 2007, SI 2007/961, art 3, Schedule, para 27(1), (2); figures in square brackets in sub-para (c)(ii) inserted by the Enterprise and Regulatory Reform Act 2013, s 20(1), (4)(b); figure omitted from sub-para (c)(ii) repealed by SI 2004/957, art 2, Schedule, para 8(a)(iii); for the words in italics in sub-para (c)(ii) there are substituted the words "or 26", by the Smoking, Health and Social Care (Scotland) Act 2005 (Consequential Modifications) (England, Wales and Northern Ireland) Order 2006, SI 2006/1056, art 2, Schedule, Pt 1, para 7(a)(i), as from a day to be appointed.

Para (ca): inserted by SI 2006/1056, art 2, Schedule, Pt 1, para 7(a)(ii), as from a day to be appointed, and repealed, together with word immediately preceding it, by the Enterprise and Regulatory Reform Act 2013, s 20(1), (5).

Para (cb) inserted by the Protected Disclosures (Extension of Meaning of Worker) Order 2015, SI 2015/491, art 2(1), (2), as from 6 April 2015.

Sub-s (2) is amended as follows:

Para (aa): inserted by the Health and Social Care (Community Health and Standards) Act 2003, s 184, Sch 11, para 65(1), (3); words in square brackets therein substituted by the Health and Social Care Act 2012, s 55(2), Sch 5, paras 72, 73(c).

Para (ab): inserted by SI 2004/957, art 2, Schedule, para 8(b).

Para (ba): inserted by SI 2006/1056, art 2, Schedule, Pt 1, para 7(b), as from a day to be appointed, and repealed by the Enterprise and Regulatory Reform Act 2013, s 20(1), (6).

Words in square brackets in para (c) inserted by SI 2015/491, art 2(1), (3), as from 6 April 2015.

Sub-ss (4), (5): added by the Enterprise and Regulatory Reform Act 2013, s 20(1), (7).

Transitional provisions and miscellaneous: the General Medical Services Transitional and Consequential Provisions (Wales) (No 2) Order 2004, SI 2004/1016, art 85(1), (2)(d) (made under the Health and Social Care (Community Health and Standards) Act 2003, ss 176, 195(1), 200, 201) provides that until such time as default contracts entered into pursuant to s 176(3) of the 2003 Act cease to exist, any reference to a general medical services contract or to a contract under the National Health Service Act 1977, s 28Q shall include a reference to a default contract. Note that the General Medical Services and Personal Medical Services Transitional and Consequential Provisions Order 2004, SI 2004/865, art 109(1), (2)(d) (which made similar provision in relation to England) was revoked by the National Health Service (General Medical Services Contracts) Regulations 2015, SI 2015/1862, as from 7 December 2015. See also the General Medical Services and Section 17C Agreements (Transitional and other Ancillary Provisions) (Scotland) Order 2004, SSI 2004/163, which provides that for as long as default contracts entered into pursuant to article 13 of the General Medical Services (Transitional and other Ancillary Provisions) (Scotland) Order 2004 continue to exist, the reference in this section to a general medical services contract or to a contract under section 17J of the 1978 Act shall be deemed to include a reference to a default contract.

See further the Enterprise and Regulatory Reform Act 2013, s 20(10) at **[1.1823]** which provides that until the coming into force of the repeal (made by Schedule 3 to the Smoking, Health and Social Care (Scotland) Act 2005) of ss 27 to 28 of the National Health Service (Scotland) Act 1978 ("the 1978 Act"), sub-s (1)(c)(ii) above has effect as if it included a reference to section 27A of the 1978 Act.

Orders: the Protected Disclosures (Extension of Meaning of Worker) Order 2015, SI 2015/491 (which amends this section).

[1.877]

[43KA Application of this Part and related provisions to police

(1) For the purposes of—

(a) this Part,

(b) section 47B and sections 48 and 49 so far as relating to that section, and

(c) section 103A and the other provisions of Part 10 so far as relating to the right not to be unfairly dismissed in a case where the dismissal is unfair by virtue of section 103A,

a person who holds, otherwise than under a contract of employment, the office of constable or an appointment as a police cadet shall be treated as an employee employed by the relevant officer under a contract of employment; and any reference to a worker being "employed" and to his "employer" shall be construed accordingly.

(2) In this section "the relevant officer" means—

(a) in relation to a member of a police force or a special constable appointed for a police area, the chief officer of police;

[(b) in relation to a member of a police force seconded to the [National Crime Agency to serve as a National Crime Agency officer], that Agency; and]

(d) in relation to any other person holding the office of constable or an appointment as police cadet, the person who has the direction and control of the body of constables or cadets in question.]

NOTES

Inserted by the Police Reform Act 2002, s 37(1).

Sub-s (2): para (b) substituted, for the original paras (b), (c), by the Serious Organised Crime and Police Act 2005, s 59, Sch 4, paras 84, 85; words in square brackets in para (b) substituted by the Crime and Courts Act 2013, s 15(3), Sch 8, Pt 2, paras 49, 50.

[1.878]

[43L Other interpretative provisions

(1) In this Part—

"qualifying disclosure" has the meaning given by section 43B;

"the relevant failure", in relation to a qualifying disclosure, has the meaning given by section 43B(5).

(2) In determining for the purposes of this Part whether a person makes a disclosure for purposes of personal gain, there shall be disregarded any reward payable by or under any enactment.

(3) Any reference in this Part to the disclosure of information shall have effect, in relation to any case where the person receiving the information is already aware of it, as a reference to bringing the information to his attention.]

NOTES

Inserted as noted to s 43A at **[1.866]**.

PART V
PROTECTION FROM SUFFERING DETRIMENT IN EMPLOYMENT

NOTES

Conciliation: employment tribunal proceedings under this Part are "relevant proceedings" for the purposes of the conciliation provisions contained in the Employment Tribunals Act 1996, ss 18–18C; see s 18(1)(b) of the 1996 Act at **[1.757]**.

Recoupment of social security benefits: as to the power to provide for recoupment of social security benefits in relation to payments by employers to employees under this Part that are the subject of proceedings before employment tribunals, see the Employment Tribunals Act 1996, s 16 at **[1.755]**.

Rights not to suffer detriment

[1.879]

[43M Jury service

(1) An employee has the right not to be subjected to any detriment by any act, or any deliberate failure to act, by his employer on the ground that the employee—

(a) has been summoned under the Juries Act 1974, [Part 1 of the Coroners and Justice Act 2009], the Court of Session Act 1988 or the Criminal Procedure (Scotland) Act 1995 to attend for service as a juror, or

(b) has been absent from work because he attended at any place in pursuance of being so summoned.

(2) This section does not apply where the detriment in question amounts to dismissal within the meaning of Part 10.

(3) For the purposes of this section, an employee is not to be regarded as having been subjected to a detriment by a failure to pay remuneration in respect of a relevant period unless under his contract of employment he is entitled to be paid that remuneration.

(4) In subsection (3) "a relevant period" means any period during which the employee is absent from work because of his attendance at any place in pursuance of being summoned as mentioned in subsection (1)(a).]

NOTES

Inserted by the Employment Relations Act 2004, s 40(1).

Sub-s (1): words in square brackets in para (a) substituted by the Coroners and Justice Act 2009, s 177(1), Sch 21, Pt 1, para 36(1), (2).

Conciliation: see the note following the Part heading *ante*.

[1.880]

44 Health and safety cases

(1) An employee has the right not to be subjected to any detriment by any act, or any deliberate failure to act, by his employer done on the ground that—

(a) having been designated by the employer to carry out activities in connection with preventing or reducing risks to health and safety at work, the employee carried out (or proposed to carry out) any such activities,

(b) being a representative of workers on matters of health and safety at work or member of a safety committee—

(i) in accordance with arrangements established under or by virtue of any enactment, or

(ii) by reason of being acknowledged as such by the employer,

the employee performed (or proposed to perform) any functions as such a representative or a member of such committee,

[(ba) the employee took part (or proposed to take part) in consultation with the employer pursuant to the Health and Safety (Consultation with Employees) Regulations 1996 or in an election of representatives of employee safety within the meaning of those Regulations (whether as a candidate or otherwise),]

(c) being an employee at a place where—

(i) there was no such representative or safety committee, or

(ii) there was such a representative or safety committee but it was not reasonably practicable for the employee to raise the matter by those means,

he brought to his employer's attention, by reasonable means, circumstances connected with his work which he reasonably believed were harmful or potentially harmful to health or safety,

(d) in circumstances of danger which the employee reasonable believed to be serious and imminent and which he could no reasonably have been expected to avert, he left (or proposed to leave) or (while the danger persisted) refused to return to his place of work or any dangerous part of his place of work, or

(e) in circumstances of danger which the employee reasonably believed to be serious and imminent, he took (or proposed to take) appropriate steps to protect himself or other persons from the danger.

(2) For the purposes of subsection (1)(e) whether steps which employee took (or proposed to take) were appropriate is to be judged by reference to all the circumstances including, in particular, his knowledge and the facilities and advice available to him at the time.

(3) An employee is not to be regarded as having been subjected to a detriment on the ground specified in subsection (1)(e) if the employer shows that it was (or would have been) so negligent for the employee to take the steps which he took (or proposed to take) that a reasonable employer might have treated him as the employer did.

(4) . . . this section does not apply where the detriment in question amounts to dismissal (within the meaning of [Part X]).

NOTES

Sub-s (1): para (ba) inserted by the Health and Safety (Consultation with Employees) Regulations 1996, SI 1996/1513, reg 8.

Sub-s (4): words omitted repealed, and words in square brackets substituted, by the Employment Relations Act 1999, ss 18(2), 44, Sch 9(3).

Conciliation: see the note following the Part heading *ante*.

[1.881]

45 Sunday working for shop and betting workers

(1) An employee who is—

(a) a protected shop worker or an opted-out shop worker, or

(b) a protected betting worker or an opted-out betting worker, has the right not to be subjected to any detriment by any act, or any deliberate failure to act, by his employer done on the ground that he employee refused (or proposed to refuse) to do shop work, or betting work, on Sunday or on a particular Sunday.

(2) Subsection (1) does not apply to anything done in relation to an opted-out shop worker or an opted-out betting worker on the ground that he refused (or proposed to refuse) to do shop work, or betting work, on any Sunday or Sundays falling before the end of the notice period.

(3) An employee who is a shop worker or a betting worker has the right not to be subjected to any detriment by any act, or any deliberate failure to act, by his employer done on the ground that the employee gave (or proposed to give) an opting-out notice to his employer.

(4) Subsections (1) and (3) do not apply where the detriment in question amounts to dismissal (within the meaning of Part X).

(5) For the purposes of this section a shop worker or betting worker who does not work on Sunday or on a particular Sunday is not to be regarded as having been subjected to any detriment by—

- (a) a failure to pay remuneration in respect of shop work, or betting work, on a Sunday which he has not done,
- (b) a failure to provide him with any other benefit, where that failure results from the application (in relation to a Sunday on which the employee has not done shop work, or betting work) of a contractual term under which the extent of that benefit varies according to the number of hours worked by the employee or the remuneration of the employee, or
- (c) a failure to provide him with any work, remuneration or other benefit which by virtue of section 38 or 39 the employer is not obliged to provide.

(6) Where an employer offers to pay a sum specified in the offer to any or more employees—

- (a) who are protected shop workers or opted-out shop workers or protected betting workers or opted-out betting workers, or
- (b) who under their contracts of employment are not obliged to do shop work, or betting work, on Sunday,

if they agree to do shop work, or betting work, on Sunday or on a particular Sunday subsections (7) and (8) apply.

(7) An employee to whom the offer is not made is not to be regarded for the purposes of this section as having been subjected to any detriment by any failure to make the offer to him or to pay him the sum specified in the offer.

(8) An employee who does not accept the offer is not to be regarded for the purposes of this section as having been subjected to any detriment by any failure to pay him the sum specified in the offer.

(9) For the purposes of section 36(2)(b) or 41(1)(b), the appropriate date in relation to this section is the date of the act or failure to act.

(10) For the purposes of subsection (9)—

- (a) where an act extends over a period, the "date of the act" means the first day of that period, and
- (b) a deliberate failure to act shall be treated as done when it was decided on;

and, in the absence of evidence establishing the contrary, an employee shall be taken to decide on a failure to act when he does an act inconsistent with doing the failed act or, if he has done no such inconsistent act, when the period expires within which he might reasonably have been expected to do the failed act if it was to be done.

NOTES

Conciliation: see the note following the Part heading *ante*.

[1.882]

[45ZA Sunday working for shop workers: additional hours

(1) Subsection (2) applies where a shop worker has given an objection notice to his or her employer and the notice has not been withdrawn.

(2) The shop worker has the right not to be subjected to any detriment by any act, or any deliberate failure to act, by the employer done on the ground that the shop worker refused (or proposed to refuse) to do shop work for additional hours on Sunday or on a particular Sunday.

(3) Subsection (2) does not apply to anything done on the ground that the shop worker refused (or proposed to refuse) to do shop work for additional hours on any Sunday or Sundays falling before the end of the relevant period.

(4) A shop worker has the right not to be subjected to any detriment by any act, or any deliberate failure to act, by his or her employer on the ground that the shop worker gave (or proposed to give) an objection notice to the employer.

(5) Subsections (2) and (4) do not apply where the detriment in question amounts to dismissal (within the meaning of Part 10).

(6) For the purposes of this section, a shop worker who does not do shop work for additional hours on Sunday or on a particular Sunday is not to be regarded as having been subjected to any detriment by—

- (a) a failure to pay remuneration in respect of doing shop work for additional hours on Sunday which the shop worker has not done, or
- (b) a failure to provide any other benefit where the failure results from the application (in relation to a Sunday on which the shop worker has not done shop work for additional hours) of a contractual term under which the extent of the benefit varies according to the number of hours worked by, or the remuneration paid to, the shop worker.

(7) Subsections (8) and (9) apply where—

- (a) an employer offers to pay a sum specified in the offer to a shop worker if he or she agrees to do shop work for additional hours on Sunday or on a particular Sunday, and
- (b) the shop worker—

(i) has given an objection notice to the employer that has not been withdrawn, or

(ii) is not obliged under a contract of employment to do shop work for additional hours on Sunday.

(8) A shop worker to whom the offer is not made is not to be regarded for the purposes of this section as having been subjected to any detriment by any failure—

(a) to make the offer to the shop worker, or

(b) to pay the shop worker the sum specified in the offer.

(9) A shop worker who does not accept the offer is not to be regarded for the purposes of this section as having been subjected to any detriment by any failure to pay the shop worker the sum specified in the offer.

(10) In this section—

"additional hours" and "objection notice" have the meanings given by section 41A(2);

"relevant period" means the period determined by section 43ZA(2) (but subject to section 41D(3)).]

NOTES

Commencement: to be appointed.

Inserted by the Enterprise Act 2016, s 33, Sch 5, paras 1, 7, as from a day to be appointed.

Conciliation: see the note following the Part heading *ante*.

[1.883]

[45A Working time cases

(1) A worker has the right not to be subjected to any detriment by any act, or any deliberate failure to act, by his employer done on the ground that the worker—

(a) refused (or proposed to refuse) to comply with a requirement which the employer imposed (or proposed to impose) in contravention of the Working Time Regulations 1998,

(b) refused (or proposed to refuse) to forgo a right conferred on him by those Regulations,

(c) failed to sign a workforce agreement for the purposes of those Regulations, or to enter into, or agree to vary or extend, any other agreement with his employer which is provided for in those Regulations,

(d) being—

(i) a representative of members of the workforce for the purposes of Schedule 1 to those Regulations, or

(ii) a candidate in an election in which any person elected will, on being elected, be such a representative,

performed (or proposed to perform) any functions or activities as such a representative or candidate,

(e) brought proceedings against the employer to enforce a right conferred on him by those Regulations, or

(f) alleged that the employer had infringed such a right.

(2) It is immaterial for the purposes of subsection (1)(e) or (f)—

(a) whether or not the worker has the right, or

(b) whether or not the right has been infringed,

but, for those provisions to apply, the claim to the right and that it has been infringed must be made in good faith.

(3) It is sufficient for subsection (1)(f) to apply that the worker, without specifying the right, made it reasonably clear to the employer what the right claimed to have been infringed was.

(4) This section does not apply where a worker is an employee and the detriment in question amounts to dismissal within the meaning of Part X . . .]

[(5) A reference in this section to the Working Time Regulations 1998 includes a reference to—

[(a)] the Merchant Shipping (Working Time: Inland Waterways) Regulations 2003;

[(b) the Fishing Vessels (Working Time: Sea-fishermen) Regulations 2004];

[(c) the Cross-border Railway Services (Working Time) Regulations 2008];

[(d) the Merchant Shipping (Maritime Labour Convention) (Hours of Work) Regulations 2018 (SI 2018/58)].]]

NOTES

Inserted by the Working Time Regulations 1998, SI 1998/1833, regs 2(1), 31(1).

Sub-s (4): words omitted repealed by the Employment Relations Act 1999, ss 18(3), 44, Sch 9(3).

Sub-s (5): added by the Merchant Shipping (Working Time: Inland Waterways) Regulations 2003, SI 2003/3049, reg 20, Sch 2, para 3(1), (2); the letter "(a)" and para (b) were inserted by the Fishing Vessels (Working Time: Sea-fishermen) Regulations 2004, SI 2004/1713, reg 21, Sch 2, para 2(1), (2)(b); para (c) added by the Cross-border Railway Services (Working Time) Regulations 2008, SI 2008/1660, reg 19, Sch 3, para 2(1), (2); para (d) originally added by the Merchant Shipping (Maritime Labour Convention) (Hours of Work) (Amendment) Regulations 2014, SI 2014/308, reg 3, Schedule, para 2(1), (2), and subsequently substituted by the Merchant Shipping (Maritime Labour Convention) (Hours of Work) Regulations 2018, SI 2018/58, reg 31, Sch 2, para 2(a), as from 6 April 2018.

Conciliation: see the note following the Part heading *ante*.

[1.884]

46 Trustees of occupational pension schemes

(1) An employee has the right not to be subjected to any detriment by any act, or any deliberate failure to act, by his employer done on the ground that, being a trustee of a relevant occupational pension scheme which relates to his employment, the employee performed (or propose to perform) any functions as such a trustee.

(2) . . . this section does not apply where the detriment in question amounts to dismissal (within the meaning of [Part X]).

[(2A) This section applies to an employee who is a director of a company which is a trustee of a relevant occupational pension scheme as it applies to an employee who is a trustee of such a scheme (references to such a trustee being read for this purpose as references to such a director).]

(3) In this section "relevant occupational pension scheme" means an occupational pension scheme (as defined in section 1 of the Pension Schemes Act 1993) established under a trust.

NOTES

Sub-s (2): words omitted repealed, and words in square brackets substituted, by the Employment Relations Act 1999, ss 18(2), 44, Sch 9(3).

Sub-s (2A): inserted by the Welfare Reform and Pensions Act 1999, s 18, Sch 2, para 19(1), (2).

Conciliation: see the note following the Part heading *ante*.

[1.885]

47 Employee representatives

(1) An employee has the right not to be subjected to any detriment by any act, or any deliberate failure to act, by his employer done on the ground that, being—

(a) an employee representative for the purposes of Chapter II of Part IV of the Trade Union and Labour Relation (Consolidation) Act 1992 (redundancies) or [regulations 9, 13 and 15 of the Transfer of Undertakings (Protection of Employment) Regulations 2006], or

(b) a candidate in an election in which any person elected will, on being elected, be such an employee representative,

he performed (or proposed to perform) any functions or activities as such an employee representative or candidate.

[(1A) An employee has the right not to be subjected to any detriment by any act, or by any deliberate failure to act, by his employer done on the ground of his participation in an election of employee representatives for the purposes of Chapter II of Part IV of the Trade Union and Labour Relations (Consolidation) Act 1992 (redundancies) or [regulations 9, 13 and 15 of the Transfer of Undertakings (Protection of Employment) Regulations 2006].]

(2) . . . this section does not apply where the detriment in question amounts to dismissal (within the meaning of [Part X]).

NOTES

Sub-s (1): words in square brackets in para (a) substituted by the Transfer of Undertakings (Protection of Employment) Regulations 2006, SI 2006/246, reg 20, Sch 2, para 10.

Sub-s (1A): inserted by the Collective Redundancies and Transfer of Undertakings (Protection of Employment) (Amendment) Regulations 1999, SI 1999/1925, reg 12; words in square brackets substituted by SI 2006/246, reg 20, Sch 2, para 10.

Sub-s (2): words omitted repealed, and words in square brackets substituted, by the Employment Relations Act 1999, ss 18(2), 44, Sch 9(3).

Conciliation: see the note following the Part heading *ante*.

[1.886]

[47A Employees exercising the right to time off work for study or training

(1) An employee has the right not to be subjected to any detriment by any act, or any deliberate failure to act, by his employer or the principal (within the meaning of section 63A(3)) done on the ground that, being a person entitled to—

(a) time off under section 63A(1) or (3), and

(b) remuneration under section 63B(1) in respect of that time taken off,

the employee exercised (or proposed to exercise) that right or received (or sought to receive) such remuneration.

(2) . . . this section does not apply where the detriment in question amounts to dismissal (within the meaning of [Part X]).]

NOTES

Inserted by the Teaching and Higher Education Act 1998, s 44(1), Sch 3, para 10.

Sub-s (2): words omitted repealed, and words in square brackets substituted, by the Employment Relations Act 1999, ss 18(2), 44, Sch 9(3).

Conciliation: see the note following the Part heading *ante*.

[1.887]

[47AA Employees in England aged 16 or 17 participating in education or training

(1) An employee has the right not to be subjected to any detriment by any act, or any deliberate failure to act, by his employer done on the ground that, being a person entitled to be permitted to participate in education or training by section 27 or 28 of the Education and Skills Act 2008, the employee exercised, or proposed to exercise, that right.

(2) This section does not apply where the detriment in question amounts to dismissal (within the meaning of Part 10).]

NOTES

Commencement: to be appointed.

Inserted by the Education and Skills Act 2008, s 37, as from a day to be appointed.

Corresponding provision for Wales: where a Measure of the National Assembly for Wales includes provision that appears to the Secretary of State to correspond to provision made by the Education and Skills Act 2008, s 2 (duty to participate in education or training), the Secretary of State may make provision, by order, in relation to Wales that corresponds to any provision inserted by ss 37–39 of the 2008 Act; see 67 of the 2008 Act. As of 15 May 2019, no such Order had been made.

Conciliation: see the note following the Part heading *ante*.

[1.888]

[47B Protected disclosures

(1) A worker has the right not to be subjected to any detriment by any act, or any deliberate failure to act, by his employer done on the ground that the worker has made a protected disclosure.

[(1A) A worker ("W") has the right not to be subjected to any detriment by any act, or any deliberate failure to act, done—

(a) by another worker of W's employer in the course of that other worker's employment, or

(b) by an agent of W's employer with the employer's authority,

on the ground that W has made a protected disclosure.

(1B) Where a worker is subjected to detriment by anything done as mentioned in subsection (1A), that thing is treated as also done by the worker's employer.

(1C) For the purposes of subsection (1B), it is immaterial whether the thing is done with the knowledge or approval of the worker's employer.

(1D) In proceedings against W's employer in respect of anything alleged to have been done as mentioned in subsection (1A)(a), it is a defence for the employer to show that the employer took all reasonable steps to prevent the other worker—

(a) from doing that thing, or

(b) from doing anything of that description.

(1E) A worker or agent of W's employer is not liable by reason of subsection (1A) for doing something that subjects W to detriment if—

(a) the worker or agent does that thing in reliance on a statement by the employer that doing it does not contravene this Act, and

(b) it is reasonable for the worker or agent to rely on the statement.

But this does not prevent the employer from being liable by reason of subsection (1B).]

(2) . . . this section does not apply where—

(a) the worker is an employee, and

(b) the detriment in question amounts to dismissal (within the meaning of [Part X]).

(3) For the purposes of this section, and of sections 48 and 49 so far as relating to this section, "worker", "worker's contract", "employment" and "employer" have the extended meaning given by section 43K.]

NOTES

Inserted by the Public Interest Disclosure Act 1998, ss 2, 18(2).

Sub-ss (1A)–(1E): inserted by the Enterprise and Regulatory Reform Act 2013, s 19(1).

Sub-s (2): words omitted repealed, and words in square brackets substituted, by the Employment Relations Act 1999, ss 18(2), Sch 9(3).

Conciliation: see the note following the Part heading *ante*.

[1.889]

[47C Leave for family and domestic reasons

(1) An employee has the right not to be subjected to any detriment by any act, or any deliberate failure to act, by his employer done for a prescribed reason.

(2) A prescribed reason is one which is prescribed by regulations made by the Secretary of State and which relates to—

(a) pregnancy, childbirth or maternity,

[(aa) time off under section 57ZE,]

[(ab) time off under section 57ZJ or 57ZL,]

(b) ordinary, compulsory or additional maternity leave,

[(ba) ordinary or additional adoption leave,]

[(bb) shared parental leave,]

(c) parental leave,

[(ca) . . . paternity leave,]

[(cb) parental bereavement leave,] [or]

(d) time off under section 57A.

(3) A reason prescribed under this section in relation to parental leave may relate to action which an employee takes, agrees to take or refuses to take under or in respect of a collective or workforce agreement.

(4) Regulations under this section may make different provision for different cases or circumstances.

[(5) An agency worker has the right not to be subjected to any detriment by any act, or any deliberate failure to act, by the temporary work agency or the hirer done on the ground that—

(a) being a person entitled to—

(i) time off under section 57ZA, and

(ii) remuneration under section 57ZB in respect of that time off,

the agency worker exercised (or proposed to exercise) that right or received (or sought to receive) that remuneration,

(b) being a person entitled to time off under section 57ZG, the agency worker exercised (or proposed to exercise) that right,

(c) being a person entitled to—
(i) time off under section 57ZN, and
(ii) remuneration under section 57ZO in respect of that time off,
the agency worker exercised (or proposed to exercise) that right or received (or sought to receive) that remuneration, or
(d) being a person entitled to time off under section 57ZP, the agency worker exercised (or proposed to exercise) that right.

(6) Subsection (5) does not apply where the agency worker is an employee.

(7) In this section the following have the same meaning as in the Agency Workers Regulations 2010 (SI 2010/93)—
"agency worker";
"hirer";
"temporary work agency".]]

NOTES

Inserted by the Employment Relations Act 1999, s 9, Sch 4, Pt III, paras 1, 5, 8.

Sub-s (2) is amended as follows:

Paras (aa), (ab) inserted by the Children and Families Act 2014, ss 127(2)(a), 128(2)(a), as from 30 June 2014.

Para (ba) inserted, and para (ca) substituted for the original word "or" at the end of para (c), by the Employment Act 2002, s 53, Sch 7, paras 24, 26.

Para (bb) inserted by the Children and Families Act 2014, s 126, Sch 7, paras 29, 31(a), as from 30 June 2014.

Para (ca) further substituted (together with word following para (cb)) by the Work and Families Act 2006, s 11(1), Sch 1, para 30.

Words omitted from para (ca) repealed by the Children and Families Act 2014, s 126, Sch 7, paras 29, 31(b), as from 5 April 2015 (note that this amendment does not have effect in relation to (a) children whose expected week of birth ends on or before 4 April 2015, and (b) children placed for adoption on or before that date: see the Children and Families Act 2014 (Commencement No 3, Transitional Provisions and Savings) Order 2014, SI 2014/1640, art 16).

Para (cb) inserted by the Parental Bereavement (Leave and Pay) Act 2018, s 1(c), Schedule, Pt 3, paras 20, 22, as from a day to be appointed.

Sub-ss (5)–(7): added by the Children and Families Act 2014, s 129(1), as from 1 October 2014 (in so far as relating to sub-ss (5)(a), (b), (6), (7)), and as from 5 April 2015 (in so far as relating to sub-s (5)(c), (d)).

Regulations: the Maternity and Parental Leave etc Regulations 1999, SI 1999/3312 at **[2.447]**; the Paternity and Adoption Leave Regulations 2002, SI 2002/2788 at **[2.576]**; the Maternity and Parental Leave (Amendment) Regulations 2002, SI 2002/2789; the Paternity and Adoption Leave (Adoptions from Overseas) Regulations 2003, SI 2003/921; the Maternity and Parental Leave etc and the Paternity and Adoption Leave (Amendment) Regulations 2006, SI 2006/2014; the Maternity and Parental Leave etc and the Paternity and Adoption Leave (Amendment) Regulations 2008, SI 2008/1966; the Additional Paternity Leave Regulations 2010, SI 2010/1055; the Additional Paternity Leave (Adoptions from Overseas) Regulations 2010, SI 2010/1059; the Paternity and Adoption Leave (Amendment) Regulations 2014, SI 2014/2112 at **[2.1512]**; the Shared Parental Leave Regulations 2014, SI 2014/3050 at **[2.1577]**; the Shared Parental Leave and Paternity and Adoption Leave (Adoptions from Overseas) Regulations 2014, SI 2014/3092 at **[2.1704]**; the Paternity, Adoption and Shared Parental Leave (Parental Order Cases) Regulations 2014, SI 2014/3096 at **[2.1747]**.

Conciliation: see the note following the Part heading *ante*.

[1.890]
[47D Tax credits

(1) An employee has the right not to be subjected to any detriment by any act, or any deliberate failure to act, by his employer, done on the ground that—
(a) any action was taken, or was proposed to be taken, by or on behalf of the employee with a view to enforcing, or otherwise securing the benefit of, a right conferred on the employee by regulations under section 25 of the Tax Credits Act 2002,
(b) a penalty was imposed on the employer, or proceedings for a penalty were brought against him, under that Act, as a result of action taken by or on behalf of the employee for the purpose of enforcing, or otherwise securing the benefit of, such a right, or
(c) the employee is entitled, or will or may be entitled, to working tax credit.

(2) It is immaterial for the purposes of subsection (1)(a) or (b)—
(a) whether or not the employee has the right, or
(b) whether or not the right has been infringed,
but, for those provisions to apply, the claim to the right and (if applicable) the claim that it has been infringed must be made in good faith.

(3) Subsections (1) and (2) apply to a person who is not an employee within the meaning of this Act but who is an employee within the meaning of section 25 of the Tax Credits Act 2002, with references to his employer in those subsections (and sections 48(2) and (4) and 49(1)) being construed in accordance with that section.

(4) Subsections (1) and (2) do not apply to an employee if the detriment in question amounts to dismissal (within the meaning of Part 10).]

NOTES

Inserted by the Tax Credits Act 2002, s 27, Sch 1, paras 1(1), (2).

Conciliation: see the note following the Part heading *ante*.

[1.891]
[47E Flexible working

(1) An employee has the right not to be subjected to any detriment by any act, or any deliberate failure to act, by his employer done on the ground that the employee—

(a) made (or proposed to make) an application under section 80F,

(b) . . .

(c) brought proceedings against the employer under section 80H, or

(d) alleged the existence of any circumstance which would constitute a ground for bringing such proceedings.

(2) This section does not apply where the detriment in question amounts to dismissal within the meaning of Part 10.]

NOTES

Inserted by the Employment Act 2002, s 47(1), (3).

Sub-s (1): para (b) repealed by the Children and Families Act 2014, s 132(5)(a), as from 30 June 2014, except in relation to any application for a change in terms and conditions which is made on or before 29 June 2014 (see the Children and Families Act 2014 (Commencement No 3, Transitional Provisions and Savings) Order 2014, SI 2014/1640, art 10).

Note: in the Queen's Printer's copy of the Employment Act 2002, this section was originally numbered as s 47D. In a correction slip, issued in December 2002, the section number was changed to s 47E to take account of the fact that a s 47D had already been inserted by the Tax Credits Act 2002.

Conciliation: see the note following the Part heading *ante*.

[1.892]

[47F Study and training

(1) An employee has the right not to be subjected to any detriment by any act, or any deliberate failure to act, by the employee's employer done on the ground that the employee—

(a) made (or proposed to make) a section 63D application,

(b) exercised (or proposed to exercise) a right conferred on the employee under section 63F,

(c) brought proceedings against the employer under section 63I, or

(d) alleged the existence of any circumstance which would constitute a ground for bringing such proceedings.

(2) This section does not apply if the detriment in question amounts to dismissal within the meaning of Part 10.]

NOTES

Commencement: 6 April 2010 (except in relation to small employers and their employees); to be appointed (otherwise).

Inserted by the Apprenticeships, Skills, Children and Learning Act 2009, s 40(1), (3), as from 6 April 2010 (except in relation to small employers and their employees), and as from a day to be appointed (otherwise) (as to the meaning of "small employers" etc, see further the notes at **[1.937]**).

Conciliation: see the note following the Part heading *ante*.

[1.893]

[47G Employee shareholder status

(1) An employee has the right not to be subjected to a detriment by any act, or any deliberate failure to act, by the employee's employer done on the ground that the employee refused to accept an offer by the employer for the employee to become an employee shareholder (within the meaning of section 205A).

(2) This section does not apply if the detriment in question amounts to dismissal within the meaning of Part 10.]

NOTES

Inserted by the Growth and Infrastructure Act 2013, s 31(2).

Enforcement

[1.894]

48 Complaints to [employment tribunals]

(1) An employee may present a complaint to an [employment tribunal] that he has been subjected to a detriment in contravention of section [43M, 44, 45, 46, 47, 47A, 47C(1), 47E, 47F or 47G].

[(1YA) A shop worker may present a complaint to an employment tribunal that he or she has been subjected to a detriment in contravention of section 45ZA.]

[(1ZA) A worker may present a complaint to an employment tribunal that he has been subjected to a detriment in contravention of section 45A.]

[(1A) A worker may present a complaint to an employment tribunal that he has been subjected to a detriment in contravention of section 47B.]

[(1AA) An agency worker may present a complaint to an employment tribunal that the agency worker has been subjected to a detriment in contravention of section 47C(5) by the temporary work agency or the hirer.]

[(1B) A person may present a complaint to an employment tribunal that he has been subjected to a detriment in contravention of section 47D.]

(2) On [a complaint under subsection (1), (1ZA), (1A) or (1B)] it is for the employer to show the ground on which any act, or deliberate failure to act, was done.

[(2A) On a complaint under subsection (1AA) it is for the temporary work agency or (as the case may be) the hirer to show the ground on which any act, or deliberate failure to act, was done.]

(3) An [employment tribunal] shall not consider a complaint under this section unless it is presented—

(a) before the end of the period of three months beginning with the date of the act or failure to act to which the complaint relates or, where that act or failure is part of a series of similar acts or failures, the last of them, or

(b) within such further period as the tribunal considers reasonable in a case where it is satisfied that it was not reasonably practicable for the complaint to be presented before the end of that period of three months.

(4) For the purposes of subsection (3)—

(a) where an act extends over a period, the "date of the act" means the last day of that period, and

(b) a deliberate failure to act shall be treated as done when it was decided on;

and, in the absence of evidence establishing the contrary, an employer[, a temporary work agency or a hirer] shall be taken to decide on a failure to act when he does an act inconsistent with doing the failed act or, if he has done no such inconsistent act, when the period expires within which he might reasonably have been expected do the failed act if it was to be done.

[(4A) Section 207A(3) (extension because of mediation in certain European cross-border disputes) [and section 207B (extension of time limits to facilitate conciliation before institution of proceedings) apply] for the purposes of subsection (3)(a).]

[(5) In this section and section 49 any reference to the employer [includes—

(a) where] a person complains that he has been subjected to a detriment in contravention of section 47A, the principal (within the meaning of section 63A(3));

(b) in the case of proceedings against a worker or agent under section 47B(1A), the worker or agent].]

[(6) In this section and section 49 the following have the same meaning as in the Agency Workers Regulations 2010 (SI 2010/93)—

"agency worker";

"hirer";

"temporary work agency".]

NOTES

Section heading: words in square brackets substituted by the Employment Rights (Dispute Resolution) Act 1998, s 1(2)(b).

Sub-s (1) is amended as follows:

Words in first pair of square brackets substituted by the Employment Rights (Dispute Resolution) Act 1998, s 1(2)(a).

The figures and words in the second pair of square brackets are set out as amended by the Teaching and Higher Education Act 1998, s 44(1), Sch 3, para 11(a); the Employment Relations Act 1999, s 9, Sch 4, Pt III, paras 5, 9; the Employment Act 2002, s 53, Sch 7, paras 24, 27; the Employment Relations Act 2004, ss 40(2), 41(3); the Apprenticeships, Skills, Children and Learning Act 2009, s 40(5), Sch 1, paras 1, 2 (as from 6 April 2010 (except in relation to small employers and their employees), and as from a day to be appointed (otherwise) (as to the meaning of "small employers" etc, see further the notes at **[1.937]**)); the Growth and Infrastructure Act 2013, s 31(3); and the Children and Families Act 2014, s 129(2)(a) (as from 1 October 2014). Note that words ", 47E or 47F" were substituted for original words "or 47E" in relation to small employers and their employees by the Apprenticeships, Skills, Children and Learning Act 2009, s 40(5), Sch 1, paras 1, 2, as from a day to be appointed. However, the subsequent amendment made by the Growth and Infrastructure Act 2013, s 31(3), had the effect of substituting the words "or 47F" with the words ", 47F or 47G".

Sub-s (1YA): inserted by the Enterprise Act 2016, s 33, Sch 5, paras 1, 8, as from a day to be appointed.

Sub-s (1ZA): inserted by the Working Time Regulations 1998, SI 1998/1833, regs 2(1), 31(2).

Sub-s (1A): inserted by the Public Interest Disclosure Act 1998, ss 3, 18(2).

Sub-ss (1AA), (2A), (6): inserted and added respectively by the Children and Families Act 2014, s 129(2)(b), (d), (f), as from 1 October 2014.

Sub-s (1B): inserted by the Tax Credits Act 2002, s 27, Sch 1, para 1(1), (3).

Sub-s (2): words in square brackets substituted by the Children and Families Act 2014, s 129(2)(c), as from 1 October 2014.

Sub-s (3): words in square brackets substituted by the Employment Rights (Dispute Resolution) Act 1998, s 1(2)(a).

Sub-s (4): words in square brackets inserted by the Children and Families Act 2014, s 129(2)(e), as from 1 October 2014.

Sub-s (4A): inserted by the Cross-Border Mediation (EU Directive) Regulations 2011, SI 2011/1133, regs 30, 34; words in square brackets substituted by the Enterprise and Regulatory Reform Act 2013, s 8, Sch 2, paras 15, 19; substituted by the Cross-Border Mediation (EU Directive) (EU Exit) Regulations 2019, SI 2019/469, reg 4, Sch 1, Pt 1, para 12(1), (5), as from exit day (as defined in the European Union (Withdrawal) Act 2018, s 20), as follows—

"(4A) Section 207B (extension of time limits to facilitate conciliation before institution of proceedings) applies for the purposes of subsection (3)(a).".

Sub-s (5): added by the Teaching and Higher Education Act 1998, s 44(1), Sch 3, para 11(b); words in first pair of square brackets substituted, and para (b) added, by the Enterprise and Regulatory Reform Act 2013, s 19(2).

Conciliation: see the note following the Part heading *ante*.

Tribunal jurisdiction: the Employment Act 2002, s 38 applies to proceedings before the employment tribunal relating to a claim under this section; see s 38(1) of, and Sch 5 to, the 2002 Act at **[1.1279]**, **[1.1287]**. See also the Trade Union and Labour Relations (Consolidation) Act 1992, s 207A at **[1.524]** (as inserted by the Employment Act 2008). That section provides that in proceedings before an employment tribunal relating to a claim by an employee under any of the jurisdictions listed in Sch A2 to the 1992 Act at **[1.704]** (which includes this section) the tribunal may adjust any award given if the employer or the employee has unreasonably failed to comply with a relevant Code of Practice as defined by s 207A(4). See also the revised Acas Code of Practice 1 – Disciplinary and Grievance Procedures (2015) at **[4.1]**, and the Acas Code of Practice 4 – Settlement Agreements (2013) at **[4.54]**.

[1.895]

49 Remedies

(1) Where an [employment tribunal] finds a complaint [under section 48(1), (1ZA), (1A) or (1B)] well-founded, the tribunal—

(a) shall make a declaration to that effect, and

(b) may make an award of compensation to be paid by the employer to the complainant in respect of the act or failure to act to which the complaint relates.

[(1A) Where an employment tribunal finds a complaint under section 48(1AA) well-founded, the tribunal—

(a) shall make a declaration to that effect, and
(b) may make an award of compensation to be paid by the temporary work agency or (as the case may be) the hirer to the complainant in respect of the act or failure to act to which the complaint relates.]

(2) [Subject to [subsections (5A) and (6)]] The amount of the compensation awarded shall be such as the tribunal considers just and equitable in all the circumstances having regard to—
(a) the infringement to which the complaint relates, and
(b) any loss which is attributable to the act, or failure to act, which infringed the complainant's right.

(3) The loss shall be taken to include—
(a) any expenses reasonably incurred by the complainant in consequence of the act, or failure to act, to which the complaint relates, and
(b) loss of any benefit which he might reasonably be expected to have had but for that act or failure to act.

(4) In ascertaining the loss the tribunal shall apply the same rule concerning the duty of a person to mitigate his loss as applies to damages recoverable under the common law of England and Wales or (as the case may be) Scotland.

(5) Where the tribunal finds that the act, or failure to act, to which the complaint relates was to any extent caused or contributed to by action of the complainant, it shall reduce the amount of the compensation by such proportion as it considers just and equitable having regard to that finding.

[(5A) Where—
(a) the complaint is made under section 48(1ZA),
(b) the detriment to which the worker is subjected is the termination of his worker's contract, and
(c) that contract is not a contract of employment,

any compensation must not exceed the compensation that would be payable under Chapter II of Part X if the worker had been an employee and had been dismissed for the reason specified in section 101A.]

[(6) Where—
(a) the complaint is made under section 48(1A),
(b) the detriment to which the worker is subjected is the termination of his worker's contract, and
(c) that contract is not a contract of employment,

any compensation must not exceed the compensation that would be payable under Chapter II of Part X if the worker had been an employee and had been dismissed for the reason specified in section 103A.]

[(6A) Where—
(a) the complaint is made under section 48(1A), and
(b) it appears to the tribunal that the protected disclosure was not made in good faith,

the tribunal may, if it considers it just and equitable in all the circumstances to do so, reduce any award it makes to the worker by no more than 25%.]

[(7) Where—
(a) the complaint is made under section 48(1B) by a person who is not an employee, and
(b) the detriment to which he is subjected is the termination of his contract with the person who is his employer for the purposes of section 25 of the Tax Credits Act 2002,

any compensation must not exceed the compensation that would be payable under Chapter 2 of Part 10 if the complainant had been an employee and had been dismissed for the reason specified in section 104B.]

NOTES

Sub-s (1): words in first pair of square brackets substituted by the Employment Rights (Dispute Resolution) Act 1998, s 1(2)(a); words in second pair of square brackets substituted by the Children and Families Act 2014, s 129(3)(a), as from 1 October 2014.

Sub-s (1A): inserted by the Children and Families Act 2014, s 129(3)(b), as from 1 October 2014.

Sub-s (2): words in first (outer) pair of square brackets inserted by the Public Interest Disclosure Act 1998, ss 4(1), (2), 18(2); words in second (inner) pair of square brackets substituted by the Working Time Regulations 1998, SI 1998/1833, regs 2(1), 31(3)(a).

Sub-s (5A): inserted by the Working Time Regulations 1998, SI 1998/1833, regs 2(1), 31(3)(b).

Sub-s (6): added by the Public Interest Disclosure Act 1998, ss 4(1), (3), 18(2).

Sub-s (6A): inserted by the Enterprise and Regulatory Reform Act 2013, s 18(4).

Sub-s (7): added by the Tax Credits Act 2002, s 27, Sch 1, para 1(1), (4).

Conciliation: see the note following the Part heading *ante*.

[Application to police of rights relating to health and safety

[1.896]

49A Application to police of section 44 and related provisions

(1) For the purposes of section 44, and of sections 48 and 49 so far as relating to that section, the holding, otherwise than under a contract of employment, of the office of constable or an appointment as police cadet shall be treated as employment by the relevant officer under a contract of employment.

[(2) In this section "the relevant officer", in relation to—
(a) a person holding the office of constable, or
(b) a person holding an appointment as a police cadet,

means the person who under section 51A of the Health and Safety at Work etc Act 1974 is to be treated as his employer for the purposes of Part 1 of that Act.]

NOTES

Inserted by the Police (Health and Safety) Act 1997, s 3.

Sub-s (2): substituted by the Serious Organised Crime and Police Act 2005, s 158(1), (2)(a), (3), (5).

Conciliation: see the note following the Part heading *ante*.

[PART 5A
PROTECTION FOR APPLICANTS FOR EMPLOYMENT ETC *IN THE HEALTH SERVICE*

NOTES

The words in italics in the Part heading are repealed by the Children and Social Work Act 2017, s 32(1), (2), as from a day to be appointed.

[1.897]

49B [The health service:] Regulations prohibiting discrimination because of protected disclosure

[(1) The Secretary of State may make regulations prohibiting an NHS employer from discriminating against an applicant because it appears to the NHS employer that the applicant has made a protected disclosure.

(2) An "applicant", in relation to an NHS employer, means an individual who applies to the NHS employer for—

- (a) a contract of employment,
- (b) a contract to do work personally, or
- (c) appointment to an office or post.

(3) For the purposes of subsection (1), an NHS employer discriminates against an applicant if the NHS employer refuses the applicant's application or in some other way treats the applicant less favourably than it treats or would treat other applicants in relation to the same contract, office or post.

(4) Regulations under this section may, in particular—

- (a) make provision as to circumstances in which discrimination by a worker or agent of an NHS employer is to be treated, for the purposes of the regulations, as discrimination by the NHS employer;
- (b) confer jurisdiction (including exclusive jurisdiction) on employment tribunals or the Employment Appeal Tribunal;
- (c) make provision for or about the grant or enforcement of specified remedies by a court or tribunal;
- (d) make provision for the making of awards of compensation calculated in accordance with the regulations;
- (e) make different provision for different cases or circumstances;
- (f) make incidental or consequential provision, including incidental or consequential provision amending—
  - (i) an Act of Parliament (including this Act),
  - (ii) an Act of the Scottish Parliament,
  - (iii) a Measure or Act of the National Assembly for Wales, or
  - (iv) an instrument made under an Act or Measure within any of sub-paragraphs (i) to (iii).

(5) Subsection (4)(f) does not affect the application of section 236(5) to the power conferred by this section.

(6) "NHS employer" means an NHS public body prescribed by regulations under this section.

(7) "NHS public body" means—

- (a) the National Health Service Commissioning Board;
- (b) a clinical commissioning group;
- (c) a Special Health Authority;
- (d) an NHS trust;
- (e) an NHS foundation trust;
- (f) the Care Quality Commission;
- (g) Health Education England;
- (h) the Health Research Authority;
- (i) the Health and Social Care Information Centre;
- (j) the National Institute for Health and Care Excellence;
- (k) Monitor;
- (l) a Local Health Board established under section 11 of the National Health Service (Wales) Act 2006;
- (m) the Common Services Agency for the Scottish Health Service;
- (n) Healthcare Improvement Scotland;
- (o) a Health Board constituted under section 2 of the National Health Service (Scotland) Act 1978;
- (p) a Special Health Board constituted under that section.

(8) The Secretary of State must consult the Welsh Ministers before making regulations prescribing any of the following NHS public bodies for the purposes of the definition of "NHS employer"—

- (a) a Special Health Authority established under section 22 of the National Health Service (Wales) Act 2006;
- (b) an NHS trust established under section 18 of that Act;
- (c) a Local Health Board established under section 11 of that Act.

(9) The Secretary of State must consult the Scottish Ministers before making regulations prescribing an NHS public body within any of paragraphs (m) to (p) of subsection (7) for the purposes of the definition of "NHS employer".

(10) For the purposes of subsection (4)(a)—

- (a) "worker" has the extended meaning given by section 43K, and

(b) a person is a worker of an NHS employer if the NHS employer is an employer in relation to the person within the extended meaning given by that section.]

NOTES

Commencement: 26 May 2015.

Part 5A (originally s 49B only) was inserted by the Small Business, Enterprise and Employment Act 2015, s 149(1), (2), as from 26 May 2015.

Section heading: words in square brackets inserted by the Children and Social Work Act 2017, s 32(1), (3), as from a day to be appointed.

Regulations: the Employment Rights Act 1996 (NHS Recruitment—Protected Disclosure) Regulations 2018 SI 2018/579 at **[2.2056]**.

[1.898]

[49C Children's social care: regulations prohibiting discrimination because of protected disclosure

(1) The Secretary of State may make regulations prohibiting a relevant employer from discriminating against a person who applies for a children's social care position (an "applicant") because it appears to the employer that the applicant has made a protected disclosure.

(2) A "position" means a position in which a person works under—

- (a) a contract of employment,
- (b) a contract to do work personally, or
- (c) the terms of an appointment to an office or post.

(3) A position is a "children's social care position" if the work done in it relates to the children's social care functions of a relevant employer.

(4) For the purposes of subsection (1), a relevant employer discriminates against an applicant if the employer refuses the applicant's application or in some other way treats the applicant less favourably than it treats or would treat other applicants for the same position.

(5) Regulations under this section may, in particular—

- (a) make provision as to circumstances in which discrimination by a worker or agent of a relevant employer is to be treated, for the purposes of the regulations, as discrimination by the employer;
- (b) confer jurisdiction (including exclusive jurisdiction) on employment tribunals or the Employment Appeal Tribunal;
- (c) make provision for or about the grant or enforcement of specified remedies by a court or tribunal;
- (d) make provision for the making of awards of compensation calculated in accordance with the regulations;
- (e) make different provision for different cases or circumstances;
- (f) make incidental or consequential provision, including incidental or consequential provision amending—
  - (i) an Act of Parliament (including this Act),
  - (ii) an Act of the Scottish Parliament,
  - (iii) a Measure or Act of the National Assembly for Wales, or
  - (iv) an instrument made under an Act or Measure within any of sub-paragraphs (i) to (iii).

(6) Subsection (5)(f) does not affect the application of section 236(5) to the power conferred by this section.

(7) "Relevant employer" means any of the following that are prescribed by regulations under this section—

- (a) a local authority in England;
- (b) a body corporate that, under arrangements made by a local authority in England under section 1 of the Children and Young Persons Act 2008, exercises children's social care functions;
- (c) a person who, as a result of a direction under section 497A(4) or (4A) of the Education Act 1996 as applied by section 50 of the Children Act 2004 (local authorities in England: intervention by Secretary of State) exercises children's social care functions;
- (d) the council of a county or county borough in Wales;
- (e) a person who, as a result of a direction under any of sections 153 to 157 of the Social Services and Well-being (Wales) Act 2014, exercises children's social care functions;
- (f) a council constituted under section 2 of the Local Government etc (Scotland) Act 1994.

(8) A "local authority in England" means—

- (a) a county council in England;
- (b) a district council;
- (c) a London borough council;
- (d) the Common Council of the City of London (in their capacity as a local authority);
- (e) the Council of the Isles of Scilly;
- (f) a combined authority established under section 103 of the Local Democracy, Economic Development and Construction Act 2009.

(9) "Children's social care functions"—

- (a) in relation to a relevant employer referred to in subsection (7)(a) to (c), means functions of a local authority in England under—
  - (i) any legislation specified in Schedule 1 to the Local Authority Social Services Act 1970 so far as relating to those under the age of 18;
  - (ii) sections 23C to 24D of the Children Act 1989, so far as not within sub-paragraph (i);
  - (iii) the Children Act 2004;

(iv) any subordinate legislation (within the meaning given by section 21(1) of the Interpretation Act 1978) under the legislation mentioned in sub-paragraphs (i) to (iii);

(b) in relation to a relevant employer referred to in subsection (7)(d) or (e), means any functions relating to the social care of children in Wales that are prescribed by regulations under this section;

(c) in relation to a relevant employer referred to in subsection (7)(f), means any functions relating to the social care of children in Scotland that are prescribed by regulations under this section.

(10) The Secretary of State must consult the Welsh Ministers before making regulations under this section in reliance on subsection (7)(d) or (e) or (9)(b).

(11) The Secretary of State must consult the Scottish Ministers before making regulations under this section in reliance on subsection (7)(f) or (9)(c).

(12) For the purposes of subsection (5)(a)—

(a) "worker" has the extended meaning given by section 43K, and

(b) a person is a worker of a relevant employer if the relevant employer is an employer in relation to the person within the extended meaning given by that section.]

NOTES

Commencement: to be appointed.

Inserted by the Children and Social Work Act 2017, s 32(1), (4), as from a day to be appointed.

PART VI
TIME OFF WORK

NOTES

Conciliation: employment tribunal proceedings under this Part are "relevant proceedings" for the purposes of the conciliation provisions contained in the Employment Tribunals Act 1996, ss 18–18C; see s 18(1)(b) of the 1996 Act at **[1.757]**.

Public duties

[1.899]

50 Right to time off for public duties

[(1) An employer shall permit an employee of his who is—

(a) a justice of the peace, or

(b) an independent prison monitor appointed in accordance with section 7B(2) of the Prisons (Scotland) Act 198,

to take time off during the employee's working hours for the purpose of performing any of the duties of the office.]

(2) An employer shall permit an employee of his who is a member of—

(a) a local authority,

(b) a statutory tribunal,

[(c) . . .]

[(ca) . . .]

(d) [an independent monitoring board for a prison] . . . ,

(e) a relevant health body,

(f) a relevant education body, . . .

(g) the Environment Agency or the Scottish Environment Protection Agency, [. . .

[(h) Scottish Water . . . ,]]

[(i) a panel of lay observers appointed in accordance with section 81(1)(b) of the Criminal Justice Act 1991;

(j) a Visiting Committee appointed in accordance with section 152(1) of the Immigration and Asylum Act 1999, or

(k) a Visiting Committee appointed by the Secretary of State for a short-term holding facility (within the meaning given by section 147 of the Immigration and Asylum Act 1999)].

to take time off during the employee's working hours for the purposes specified in subsection (3).

(3) The purposes referred to in subsection (2) are—

(a) attendance at a meeting of the body or any of its committees or sub-committees, and

(b) the doing of any other thing approved by the body, or anything of a class so approved, for the purpose of the discharge of the functions of the body or of any of its committees or sub-committees[, and

(c) in the case of a local authority which are operating executive arrangements—

(i) attendance at a meeting of the executive of that local authority or committee of that executive; and

(ii) the doing of any other thing, by an individual member of that executive, for the purposes of the discharge of any function which is to any extent the responsibility of that executive.]

(4) The amount of time off which an employee is to be permitted to take under this section, and the occasions on which and any condition subject to which time off may be so taken, are those that are reasonable in all the circumstances having regard, in particular, to—

(a) how much time off is required for the performance of the duties of the office or as a member of the body in question, and how much time off is required for the performance of the particular duty,

(b) how much time off the employee has already been permitted under this section or sections 168 and 170 of the Trade Union and Labour Relations (Consolidation) Act 1992 (time off trade union duties and activities), and

(c) the circumstances of the employer's business and the effect of the employee's absence on the running of that business.

(5) In subsection (2)(a) "a local authority" means—

(a) a local authority within the meaning of the Local Government Act 1972,

(b) a council constituted under section 2 of the Local Government etc (Scotland) Act 1994,

(c) the Common Council of the City of London,

(d) a National Park authority, or

(e) the Broads Authority.

(6) . . .

(7) In subsection (2)(d)—

(a) ["independent monitoring board" means a board] appointed under section 6(2) of the Prison Act 1952, and

(b) . . .

(8) In subsection (2)(e) "a relevant health body" means—

[(za) the National Health Service Commissioning Board,

(zb) a clinical commissioning group established under section 14D of the National Health Service Act 2006,]

(a) a National Health Service trust established under [*section 25 of the National Health Service Act 2006,* section 18 of the National Health Service (Wales) Act 2006] or the National Health Service (Scotland) Act 1978,

[(ab) an NHS foundation trust,]

[(ac) the National Institute for Health and Care Excellence,]

[(ad) the Health and Social Care Information Centre,]

(b) a . . . [Local Health Board established under section 11 of the National Health Service (Wales) Act 2006] . . . [, a Special Health Authority established under [section 28 of the National Health Service Act 2006 or section 22 of the National Health Service (Wales) Act 2006] . . .] or

(c) a Health Board constituted under section 2 of the National Health Service (Scotland) Act 1978.

(9) In subsection (2)(f) "a relevant education body" means—

(a) a managing or governing body of an educational establishment maintained by a [local authority (as defined in section 579(1) of the Education Act 1996)],

[(b) a further education corporation, sixth form college corporation or higher education corporation,]

(c) a school council appointed under section 125(1) of the Local Government (Scotland) Act 1973,

[(d) a parent council within the meaning of section 5(2) of the Scottish Schools (Parental Involvement) Act 2006,]

(e) . . .

(f) a board of management of a college of further education within the meaning of section 36(1) of the Further and Higher Education (Scotland) Act 1992,

(g) a governing body of a central institution within the meaning of section 135(1) of the Education (Scotland) Act 1980, . . .

(h) a governing body of a designated institution within the meaning of Part II of the Further and Higher Education (Scotland) Act 1992,

[(i) . . .

(j) the General Teaching Council for Wales.]

[(9A) In subsection (3)(c) of this section "executive" and "executive arrangements" have the same meaning as in Part II of the Local Government Act 2000.]

[(9B) In subsection (9)(b) "further education corporation", "sixth form college corporation" and "higher education corporation" have the same meanings as in the Further and Higher Education Act 1992.]

(10) The Secretary of State may by order—

(a) modify the provisions of subsections (1) and (2) and (5) to (9) by adding any office or body, removing any office or body or altering the description of any office or body, or

(b) modify the provisions of subsection (3).

(11) For the purposes of this section the working hours of an employee shall be taken to be any time when, in accordance with his contract of employment, the employee is required to be at work.

NOTES

Sub-s (1): substituted by the Time Off for Public Duties Order 2018, SI 2018/665, art 2(a), as from 1 October 2018.

Sub-s (2) is amended as follows:

Para (c) substituted by the Police and Justice Act 2006, s 52, Sch 14, para 31, and repealed by the Police Reform and Social Responsibility Act 2011, s 99, Sch 16, Pt 3, para 219.

Para (ca) inserted by the Police Act 1997, s 134(1), Sch 9, para 88, and repealed by the Serious Organised Crime and Police Act 2005, ss 59, 174(2), Sch 4, paras 84, 86, Sch 17, Pt 2.

Words in square brackets in para (d) substituted by the Offender Management Act 2007, s 39, Sch 3, Pt 2, para 8(a); words omitted from para (d) repealed by the Public Services Reform (Inspection and Monitoring of Prisons) (Scotland) Order 2015, SSI 2015/39, art 6, Schedule, Pt 1, para 5(a), as from 31 August 2015.

Word omitted from para (f) repealed, and para (h) and the word immediately preceding it added, by the Time Off for Public Duties Order 2000, SI 2000/1737, art 2.

Word omitted from para (g) repealed, and paras (i)–(k) added, by SI 2018/665, art 2(b), as from 1 October 2018.

Para (h) substituted by the Water Industry (Scotland) Act 2002 (Consequential Modifications) Order 2004, SI 2004/1822, art 2, Schedule, Pt 1, para 18; words omitted from para (h) repealed by Public Services Reform (Scotland) Act 2010 (Consequential Modifications of Enactments) Order 2011, SI 2011/2581, art 2, Sch 3, Pt 1, para 2.

Sub-s (3): para (c) and the word immediately preceding it inserted, in relation to England, by the Local Authorities (Executive and Alternative Arrangements) (Modification of Enactments and Other Provisions) (England) Order 2001,

SI 2001/2237, art 30(a), and in relation to Wales, by the Local Authorities (Executive and Alternative Arrangements) (Modification of Enactments and Other Provisions) (Wales) Order 2002, SI 2002/808, arts 2(o), 29(a).

Sub-s (6): repealed by the Police and Justice Act 2006, s 52, Sch 15, Pt 1.

Sub-s (7): words in square brackets in para (a) substituted by the Offender Management Act 2007, s 39, Sch 3, Pt 2, para 8(b); para (b) repealed by SSI 2015/39, art 6, Schedule, Pt 1, para 5(b), as from 31 August 2015.

Sub-s (8) is amended as follows:

Paras (za), (zb) inserted by the Health and Social Care Act 2012, s 55(2), Sch 5, paras 72, 74(a).

Words in square brackets in para (a) substituted by the National Health Service (Consequential Provisions) Act 2006, s 2, Sch 1, paras 177, 179(a).

Words in italics in para (a) repealed by the Health and Social Care Act 2012, s 179, Sch 14, paras 68, 69, as from a day to be appointed.

Para (ab) inserted by the Health and Social Care (Community Health and Standards) Act 2003, s 34, Sch 4, paras 99, 100.

Para (ac) inserted by the Health and Social Care Act 2012, s 249, Sch 17, para 6(1), (2).

Para (ad) inserted by the Health and Social Care Act 2012, s 277, Sch 19, para 6(1), (2).

First and third words omitted from para (b) repealed by the Health and Social Care Act 2012, s 55(2), Sch 5, paras 72, 74(b)(i), (ii).

Words "Local Health Board established under section 11 of the National Health Service (Wales) Act 2006" in first pair of square brackets in para (b) substituted by the References to Health Authorities Order 2007, SI 2007/961, art 3, Schedule, para 27(1), (3).

Second words omitted from para (b) repealed by the National Health Service (Consequential Provisions) Act 2006, s 2, Sch 1, paras 177, 179(b)(ii).

Words beginning ", a Special Health Authority" in second (outer) pair of square brackets in para (b) substituted by the Health Act 1999 (Supplementary, Consequential etc Provisions) Order 2000, SI 2000/90, art 3(1), Sch 1, para 30(1), (2).

Words "section 28 of the National Health Service Act 2006 or section 22 of the National Health Service (Wales) Act 2006" in third (inner) pair of square brackets in para (b) substituted by the National Health Service (Consequential Provisions) Act 2006, s 2, Sch 1, paras 177, 179(b)(iii).

Sub-s (9): words in square brackets in para (a) substituted by the Local Education Authorities and Children's Services Authorities (Integration of Functions) Order 2010, SI 2010/1158, art 5, Sch 2, Pt 2, para 41(1), (2); para (b) substituted by the Apprenticeships, Skills, Children and Learning Act 2009 (Consequential Amendments) (England and Wales) Order 2010, SI 2010/1080, art 2, Sch 1, Pt 1, para 96(a); para (d) substituted by the Time Off for Public Duties (Parent Councils) Order 2007, SI 2007/1837, art 2; para (e) repealed by the Standards in Scotland's Schools etc Act 2000, s 60(2), Sch 3; word omitted from para (g) repealed, and paras (i), (j) added, by the Time Off for Public Duties (No 2) Order 2000, SI 2000/2463, art 2; para (i) repealed by the Education Act 2011, s 11(1), Sch 2, para 24.

Sub-s (9A): inserted, in relation to England, by SI 2001/2237, art 30(b), and in relation to Wales, by SI 2002/808, arts 2(o), 29(b).

Sub-s (9B): inserted by SI 2010/1080, art 2, Sch 1, Pt 1, para 96(b).

Conciliation: see the note following the Part heading *ante*.

Local Government (Scotland) Act 1973, s 125: repealed by the Self-Governing Schools etc (Scotland) Act 1989, s 82(2), Sch 11.

Orders: the Time Off for Public Duties Order 2000, SI 2000/1737; the Time Off for Public Duties (No 2) Order 2000, SI 2000/2463; the Time Off for Public Duties (Parent Councils) Order 2007, SI 2007/1837; the Time Off for Public Duties Order 2018, SI 2018/665.

[1.900]

51 Complaints to [employment tribunals]

(1) An employee may present a complaint to an [employment tribunal] that his employer has failed to permit him to take time off as required by section 50.

(2) An [employment tribunal] shall not consider a complaint under this section that an employer has failed to permit an employee to take time off unless it is presented—

(a) before the end of the period of three months beginning with the date on which the failure occurred, or

(b) within such further period as the tribunal considers reasonable in a case where it is satisfied that it was not reasonably practicable for the complaint to be presented before the end of that period of three months.

[(2A) Section 207A(3) (extension because of mediation in certain European cross-border disputes) [and section 207B (extension of time limits to facilitate conciliation before institution of proceedings) apply] for the purposes of subsection (2)(a).]

(3) Where an [employment tribunal] finds a complaint under this section well-founded, the tribunal—

(a) shall make a declaration to that effect, and

(b) may make an award of compensation to be paid by the employer to the employee.

(4) The amount of the compensation shall be such as the tribunal considers just and equitable in all the circumstances having regard to—

(a) the employer's default in failing to permit time off to be taken by the employee, and

(b) any loss sustained by the employee which is attributable to the matters to which the complaint relates.

NOTES

Section heading, sub-ss (1)–(3): words in square brackets substituted by the Employment Rights (Dispute Resolution) Act 1998, s 1(2)(a), (b).

Sub-s (2A): inserted by the Cross-Border Mediation (EU Directive) Regulations 2011, SI 2011/1133, regs 30, 35; words in square brackets substituted by the Enterprise and Regulatory Reform Act 2013, s 8, Sch 2, paras 15, 20; substituted by the Cross-Border Mediation (EU Directive) (EU Exit) Regulations 2019, SI 2019/469, reg 4, Sch 1, Pt 1, para 12(1), (6), as from exit day (as defined in the European Union (Withdrawal) Act 2018, s 20), as follows—

"(2A) Section 207B (extension of time limits to facilitate conciliation before institution of proceedings) applies for the purposes of subsection (2)(a).".

Conciliation: see the note following the Part heading *ante*.

Looking for work and making arrangements for training

[1.901]

52 Right to time off to look for work or arrange training

(1) An employee who is given notice of dismissal by reason of redundancy is entitled to be permitted by his employer to take reasonable time off during the employee's working hours before the end of his notice in order to—

(a) look for new employment, or

(b) make arrangements for training for future employment.

(2) An employee is not entitled to take time off under this section unless, on whichever is the later of—

(a) the date on which the notice is due to expire, and

(b) the date on which it would expire were it the notice required to be given by section 86(1),

he will have been (or would have been) continuously employed for period of two years or more.

(3) For the purposes of this section the working hours of an employee shall be taken to be any time when, in accordance with his contract of employment, the employee is required to be at work.

NOTES

Conciliation: see the note following the Part heading *ante*.

[1.902]

53 Right to remuneration for time off under section 52

(1) An employee who is permitted to take time off under section 52 is entitled to be paid remuneration by his employer for the period of absence at the appropriate hourly rate.

(2) The appropriate hourly rate, in relation to an employee, is the amount of one week's pay divided by the number of normal working hours in a week for that employee when employed under the contract of employment in force on the day when the notice of dismissal was given.

(3) But where the number of normal working hours differs from week to week or over a longer period, the amount of one week's pay shall be divided instead by the average number of normal working hours calculated by dividing by twelve the total number of the employee's normal working hours during the period of twelve weeks ending with the last complete week before the day on which the notice was given.

(4) If an employer unreasonably refuses to permit an employee to take time off from work as required by section 52, the employee is entitled to be paid an amount equal to the remuneration to which he would have been entitled under subsection (1) if he had been permitted to take the time off.

(5) The amount of an employer's liability to pay remuneration under subsection (1) shall not exceed, in respect of the notice period of any employee, forty per cent of a week's pay of that employee.

(6) A right to any amount under subsection (1) or (4) does not affect any right of an employee in relation to remuneration under his contract of employment ("contractual remuneration").

(7) Any contractual remuneration paid to an employee in respect of a period of time off under section 52 goes towards discharging any liability of the employer to pay remuneration under subsection (1) in respect of that period; and, conversely, any payment of remuneration under subsection (1) in respect of a period goes towards discharging any liability the employer to pay contractual remuneration in respect of that period.

NOTES

Conciliation: see the note following the Part heading *ante*.

[1.903]

54 Complaints to [employment tribunals]

(1) An employee may present a complaint to an [employment tribunal] that his employer—

(a) has unreasonably refused to permit him to take time off as required by section 52, or

(b) has failed to pay the whole or any part of any amount to which the employee is entitled under section 53(1) or (4).

(2) An [employment tribunal] shall not consider a complaint under this section unless it is presented—

(a) before the end of the period of three months beginning with the date on which it is alleged that the time off should have been permitted, or

(b) within such further period as the tribunal considers reasonable in a case where it is satisfied that it was not reasonably practicable for the complaint to be presented before the end of that period of three months.

[(2A) Section 207A(3) (extension because of mediation in certain European cross-border disputes) [and section 207B (extension of time limits to facilitate conciliation before institution of proceedings) apply] for the purposes of subsection (2)(a).]

(3) Where an [employment tribunal] finds a complaint under this section well-founded, the tribunal shall—

(a) make a declaration to that effect, and

(b) order the employer to pay to the employee the amount which it finds due to him.

(4) The amount which may be ordered by a tribunal to be paid by an employer under subsection (3) (or, where the employer is liable to pay remuneration under section 53, the aggregate of that amount and the amount of that liability) shall not exceed, in respect of the notice period of any employee, forty per cent of a week's pay of that employee.

NOTES

Section heading, sub-ss (1)–(3): words in square brackets substituted by the Employment Rights (Dispute Resolution) Act 1998, s 1(2)(a), (b).

Sub-s (2A): inserted by the Cross-Border Mediation (EU Directive) Regulations 2011, SI 2011/1133, regs 30, 36; words in square brackets substituted by the Enterprise and Regulatory Reform Act 2013, s 8, Sch 2, paras 15, 21; substituted by the Cross-Border Mediation (EU Directive) (EU Exit) Regulations 2019, SI 2019/469, reg 4, Sch 1, Pt 1, para 12(1), (7), as from exit day (as defined in the European Union (Withdrawal) Act 2018, s 20), as follows—

"(2A) Section 207B (extension of time limits to facilitate conciliation before institution of proceedings) applies for the purposes of subsection (2)(a).".

Conciliation: see the note following the Part heading *ante*.

Ante-natal care

[1.904]

55 Right to time off for ante-natal care

(1) An employee who—

(a) is pregnant, and

(b) has, on the advice of a registered medical practitioner, registered midwife or [registered nurse], made an appointment to attend at any place for the purpose of receiving ante-natal care,

is entitled to be permitted by her employer to take time off during the employee's working hours in order to enable her to keep the appointment.

(2) An employee is not entitled to take time off under this section to keep an appointment unless, if her employer requests her to do so, she produces for his inspection—

(a) a certificate from a registered medical practitioner, registered midwife or [registered nurse] stating that the employee is pregnant, and

(b) an appointment card or some other document showing that the appointment has been made.

(3) Subsection (2) does not apply where the employee's appointment is the first appointment during her pregnancy for which she seek permission to take time off in accordance with subsection (1).

(4) For the purposes of this section the working hours of an employee shall be taken to be any time when, in accordance with her contract of employment, the employee is required to be at work.

[(5) References in this section to a registered nurse are to such a nurse—

(a) who is also registered in the Specialist Community Public Health Nurses' Part of the register maintained under article 5 of the Nursing and Midwifery Order 2001, and

(b) whose entry in that Part of the register is annotated to show that he holds a qualification in health visiting.]

NOTES

Sub-ss (1), (2): words in square brackets substituted by the Nursing and Midwifery Order 2001, SI 2002/253, art 54(3), Sch 5, para 13.

Sub-s (5): added by the Health Act 1999 (Consequential Amendments) (Nursing and Midwifery) Order 2004, SI 2004/1771, art 3, Schedule, Pt 1, para 3.

Conciliation: see the note following the Part heading *ante*.

[1.905]

56 Right to remuneration for time off under section 55

(1) An employee who is permitted to take time off under section 55 is entitled to be paid remuneration by her employer for the period of absence at the appropriate hourly rate.

(2) The appropriate hourly rate, in relation to an employee, is the amount of one week's pay divided by the number of normal working hours in a week for that employee when employed under the contract of employment in force on the day when the time off is taken.

(3) But where the number of normal working hours differs from week to week or over a longer period, the amount of one week's pay shall be divided instead by—

(a) the average number of normal working hours calculated by dividing by twelve the total number of the employee's normal working hours during the period of twelve weeks ending with the last complete week before the day on which the time off taken, or

(b) where the employee has not been employed for a sufficient period to enable the calculation to be made under paragraph (a), a number which fairly represents the number of normal working hours in a week having regard to such of the considerations specified in subsection (4) as are appropriate in the circumstances.

(4) The considerations referred to in subsection (3)(b) are—

(a) the average number of normal working hours in a week which the employee could expect in accordance with the terms of her contract, and

(b) the average number of normal working hours of other employees engaged in relevant comparable employment with the same employer.

(5) A right to any amount under subsection (1) does not affect any right of an employee in relation to remuneration under her contract of employment ("contractual remuneration").

(6) Any contractual remuneration paid to an employee in respect of a period of time off under section 55 goes towards discharging any liability of the employer to pay remuneration under subsection (1) in respect of that period; and, conversely, any payment of remuneration under subsection (1) in respect of a period goes towards discharging any liability of the employer to pay contractual remuneration in respect of that period.

Part 1 Statutes

NOTES

Conciliation: see the note following the Part heading *ante*.

[1.906]

57 Complaints to [employment tribunals]

(1) An employee may present a complaint to an [employment tribunal] that her employer—

(a) has unreasonably refused to permit her to take time off as required by section 55, or

(b) has failed to pay the whole or any part of any amount to which the employee is entitled under section 56.

(2) An [employment tribunal] shall not consider a complaint under this action unless it is presented—

(a) before the end of the period of three months beginning with the date of the appointment concerned, or

(b) within such further period as the tribunal considers reasonable in a case where it is satisfied that it was not reasonably practicable for the complaint to be presented before the end of that period of three months.

[(2A) Section 207A(3) (extension because of mediation in certain European cross-border disputes) [and section 207B (extension of time limits to facilitate conciliation before institution of proceedings) apply for the purposes of subsection (2)(a)].]

(3) Where an [employment tribunal] finds a complaint under this section well-founded, the tribunal shall make a declaration to that effect.

(4) If the complaint is that the employer has unreasonably refused to permit the employee to take time off, the tribunal shall also order the employer to pay to the employee [an amount that is twice the amount of] the remuneration to which she would have been entitled under section 56 if the employer had not refused.

(5) If the complaint is that the employer has failed to pay the employee the whole or part of any amount to which she is entitled under section 56, the tribunal shall also order the employer to pay to the employee the amount which it finds due to her.

NOTES

The words "employment tribunals" and "employment tribunal" in square brackets (in each place that they occur) were substituted by the Employment Rights (Dispute Resolution) Act 1998, s 1(2)(a), (b).

Sub-s (2A): inserted by the Cross-Border Mediation (EU Directive) Regulations 2011, SI 2011/1133, regs 30, 37; words in square brackets substituted by the Enterprise and Regulatory Reform Act 2013, s 8, Sch 2, paras 15, 22; substituted by the Cross-Border Mediation (EU Directive) (EU Exit) Regulations 2019, SI 2019/469, reg 4, Sch 1, Pt 1, para 12(1), (8), as from exit day (as defined in the European Union (Withdrawal) Act 2018, s 20), as follows—

"(2A) Section 207B (extension of time limits to facilitate conciliation before institution of proceedings) applies for the purposes of subsection (2)(a).".

Sub-s (4): words in square brackets substituted by the Children and Families Act 2014, s 130(1), as from 1 October 2014, in relation to any refusal to permit time off which is made on or after that date (see the Children and Families Act 2014 (Commencement No 3, Transitional Provisions and Savings) Order 2014, SI 2014/1640, art 11).

Conciliation: see the note following the Part heading *ante*.

[Ante-natal care: agency workers

[1.907]

57ZA Right to time off for ante-natal care (agency workers)

(1) An agency worker who—

(a) is pregnant, and

(b) has, on the advice of a registered medical practitioner, registered midwife or registered nurse, made an appointment to attend at any place for the purpose of receiving ante-natal care,

is entitled to be permitted, by the temporary work agency and the hirer, to take time off during the agency worker's working hours in order to enable her to keep the appointment.

(2) An agency worker is not entitled to be permitted by either of those persons to take time off under this section to keep an appointment unless, if that person requests her to do so, she produces for that person's inspection—

(a) a certificate from a registered medical practitioner, registered midwife or registered nurse stating that the agency worker is pregnant, and

(b) an appointment card or some other document showing that the appointment has been made.

(3) Subsection (2) does not apply where the agency worker's appointment is the first appointment during her pregnancy for which she seeks permission to take time off in accordance with subsection (1).

(4) For the purposes of this section the working hours of an agency worker shall be taken to be any time when, in accordance with the terms under which the agency worker works temporarily for and under the supervision and direction of the hirer, the agency worker is required to be at work.

(5) In this section references to a registered nurse have the same meaning as in section 55.]

NOTES

Inserted, together with the preceding heading and ss 57ZB–57ZD, by the Agency Workers Regulations 2010, SI 2010/93, reg 25, Sch 2, Pt 1, paras 9, 11.

Conciliation: see the note following the Part heading *ante*.

[1.908]

[57ZB Right to remuneration for time off under section 57ZA

(1) An agency worker who is permitted to take time off under section 57ZA is entitled to be paid remuneration by the temporary work agency for the period of absence at the appropriate hourly rate.

(2) The appropriate hourly rate, in relation to an agency worker, is the amount of one week's pay divided by the number of normal working hours in a week for that agency worker in accordance with the terms under which the agency worker works temporarily for and under the supervision and direction of the hirer that are in force on the day when the time off is taken.

(3) But where the number of normal working hours during the assignment differs from week to week or over a longer period, the amount of one week's pay shall be divided instead by the average number of normal working hours calculated by dividing by twelve the total number of the agency worker's normal working hours during the period of twelve weeks ending with the last complete week before the day on which the time off is taken.

(4) A right to any amount under subsection (1) does not affect any right of an agency worker in relation to remuneration under her contract with the temporary work agency ("contractual remuneration").

(5) Any contractual remuneration paid to an agency worker in respect of a period of time off under section 57ZA goes towards discharging any liability of the temporary work agency to pay remuneration under subsection (1) in respect of that period; and, conversely, any payment of remuneration under subsection (1) in respect of a period goes towards discharging any liability of the temporary work agency to pay contractual remuneration in respect of that period.]

NOTES

Inserted as noted to s 57ZA at **[1.907]**.

Conciliation: see the note following the Part heading *ante*.

[1.909]

[57ZC Complaint to employment tribunal: agency workers

(1) An agency worker may present a complaint to an employment tribunal that the temporary work agency—

(a) has unreasonably refused to permit her to take time off as required by section 57ZA, or

(b) has failed to pay the whole or any part of any amount to which she is entitled under section 57ZB.

(2) An agency worker may present a complaint to an employment tribunal that the hirer has unreasonably refused to permit her to take time off as required by section 57ZA.

(3) An employment tribunal shall not consider a complaint under subsection (1) or (2) unless it is presented—

(a) before the end of the period of three months beginning with the date of the appointment concerned, or

(b) within such further period as the tribunal considers reasonable in a case where it is satisfied that it was not reasonably practicable for the complaint to be presented before the end of that period of three months.

[(3A) Section 207A(3) (extension because of mediation in certain European cross-border disputes) and section 207B (extension of time limits to facilitate conciliation before institution of proceedings) apply for the purposes of subsection (3)(a).]

(4) Where an employment tribunal finds a complaint under this section well-founded, the tribunal shall make a declaration to that effect.

(5) If the complaint is that the temporary work agency or hirer has unreasonably refused to permit the agency worker to take time off, the tribunal shall also order payment to the agency worker of [an amount that is twice the amount of] the remuneration to which she would have been entitled under section 57ZB if she had not been refused the time off.

(6) Where the tribunal orders payment under subsection (5), the amount payable by each party shall be such as may be found by the tribunal to be just and equitable having regard to the extent of each respondent's responsibility for the infringement to which the complaint relates.

(7) If the complaint is that the temporary work agency has failed to pay the agency worker the whole or part of any amount to which she is entitled under section 57ZB, the tribunal shall also order the temporary work agency to pay to the agency worker the amount which it finds due to her.]

NOTES

Inserted as noted to s 57ZA at **[1.907]**.

Sub-s (3A): inserted by the Enterprise and Regulatory Reform Act 2013, s 8, Sch 2, paras 15, 23; substituted by the Cross-Border Mediation (EU Directive) (EU Exit) Regulations 2019, SI 2019/469, reg 4, Sch 1, Pt 1, para 12(1), (9), as from exit day (as defined in the European Union (Withdrawal) Act 2018, s 20), as follows—

"(3A) Section 207B (extension of time limits to facilitate conciliation before institution of proceedings) applies for the purposes of subsection (3)(a).".

Sub-s (5): words in square brackets substituted by the Children and Families Act 2014, s 130(2), as from 1 October 2014, in relation to any refusal to permit time off which is made on or after that date (see the Children and Families Act 2014 (Commencement No 3, Transitional Provisions and Savings) Order 2014, SI 2014/1640, art 11).

Conciliation: see the note following the Part heading *ante*.

[1.910]
[57ZD Agency workers: supplementary

(1) Without prejudice to any other duties of the hirer or temporary work agency under any enactment or rule of law sections 57ZA to 57ZC do not apply where the agency worker—

(a) has not completed the qualifying period, or
(b) is no longer entitled to the rights conferred by regulation 5 of the Agency Workers Regulations 2010 pursuant to regulation 8(a) or (b) of those Regulations.

(2) Nothing in those sections imposes a duty on the hirer or temporary work agency beyond the original intended duration, or likely duration of the assignment, whichever is the longer.

(3) Those sections do not apply where sections 55 to 57 apply.

(4) In this section and sections 57ZA to 57ZC the following have the same meaning as in the Agency Workers Regulations 2010—

"agency worker";
"assignment";
"hirer";
"qualifying period";
"temporary work agency".]

NOTES

Inserted as noted to s 57ZA at **[1.907]**.
Conciliation: see the note following the Part heading *ante*.

[Accompanying to ante-natal appointments

[1.911]
57ZE Right to time off to accompany to ante-natal appointment

(1) An employee who has a qualifying relationship with a pregnant woman or her expected child is entitled to be permitted by his or her employer to take time off during the employee's working hours in order that he or she may accompany the woman when she attends by appointment at any place for the purpose of receiving ante-natal care.

(2) In relation to any particular pregnancy, an employee is not entitled to take time off for the purpose specified in subsection (1) on more than two occasions.

(3) On each of those occasions, the maximum time off during working hours to which the employee is entitled is six and a half hours.

(4) An employee is not entitled to take time off for the purpose specified in subsection (1) unless the appointment is made on the advice of a registered medical practitioner, registered midwife or registered nurse.

(5) Where the employer requests the employee to give the employer a declaration signed by the employee, the employee is not entitled to take time off for the purpose specified in subsection (1) unless the employee gives that declaration (which may be given in electronic form).

(6) The employee must state in the declaration—

(a) that the employee has a qualifying relationship with a pregnant woman or her expected child,
(b) that the employee's purpose in taking time off is the purpose specified in subsection (1),
(c) that the appointment in question is made on the advice of a registered medical practitioner, registered midwife or registered nurse, and
(d) the date and time of the appointment.

(7) A person has a qualifying relationship with a pregnant woman or her expected child if—

(a) the person is the husband or civil partner of the pregnant woman,
(b) the person, being of a different sex or the same sex, lives with the woman in an enduring family relationship but is not a relative of the woman,
(c) the person is the father of the expected child,
(d) the person is a parent of the expected child by virtue of section 42 or 43 of the Human Fertilisation and Embryology Act 2008, . . .
(e) the person is a potential applicant for a parental order under section 54 of the Human Fertilisation and Embryology Act 2008 in respect of the expected child,[or
(f) the person is a potential applicant for a parental order under section 54A of the Human Fertilisation and Embryology Act 2008 in respect of the expected child.]

(8) For the purposes of subsection (7) a relative of a person is the person's parent, grandparent, sister, brother, aunt or uncle.

(9) The references to relationships in subsection (8)—

(a) are to relationships of the full blood or half blood or, in the case of an adopted person, such of those relationships as would exist but for the adoption, and
(b) include the relationship of a child with the child's adoptive, or former adoptive, parents,

but do not include any other adoptive relationships.

(10) For the purposes of subsection (7)(e) a person ("A") is a potential applicant for a parental order under section 54 of the Human Fertilisation and Embryology Act 2008 in respect of an expected child only if—

(a) A intends to apply, jointly with another person ("B"), for such an order in respect of the expected child within the time allowed by section 54(3),
(b) the expected child is being carried by the pregnant woman as a result of such procedure as is described in section 54(1)(a),
(c) the requirement in section 54(1)(b) is satisfied by reference to A or B,
(d) A and B would satisfy section 54(2) if they made an application under section 54 at the time that A seeks to exercise the right under this section, and

(e) A expects that A and B will satisfy the conditions in section 54(2), (4), (5) and (8) as regards the intended application.

[(10A) For the purposes of subsection (7)(f) a person is a potential applicant for a parental order under section 54A of the Human Fertilisation and Embryology Act 2008 in respect of an expected child only if—

(a) the person intends to apply for such an order in respect of the expected child within the time allowed by section 54A(2),

(b) the expected child is being carried by the pregnant woman as a result of such procedure as is described in section 54A(1)(a),

(c) the requirement in section 54A(1)(b) is satisfied by reference to the person, and

(d) the person expects that he or she will satisfy the conditions in section 54A(3), (4) and (7) as regards the intended application.]

(11) The references in this section to a registered nurse are references to a registered nurse—

(a) who is also registered in the Specialist Community Public Health Nurses Part of the register maintained under article 5 of the Nursing and Midwifery Order 2001 (SI 2002/253), and

(b) whose entry in that Part of the register is annotated to show that the nurse holds a qualification in health visiting.

(12) For the purposes of this section the working hours of an employee are to be taken to be any time when, in accordance with the employee's contract of employment, the employee is required to be at work.]

NOTES

Commencement: 1 October 2014.

Inserted, together with the preceding heading and s 57ZF–57ZI, by the Children and Families Act 2014, s 127(1), as from 1 October 2014.

Sub-s (7): word omitted from para (d) repealed, and para (f) inserted together with word preceding it, by the Human Fertilisation and Embryology Act 2008 (Remedial) Order 2018, SI 2018/1413, art 3(1), Sch 1, para 11(1)–(4), as from 3 January 2019.

Sub-s (10A): inserted by SI 2018/1413, art 3(1), Sch 1, para 11(1), (2), (5), as from 3 January 2019.

Conciliation: see the note following the Part heading *ante*.

[1.912]

[57ZF Complaint to employment tribunal

(1) An employee may present a complaint to an employment tribunal that his or her employer has unreasonably refused to let him or her take time off as required by section 57ZE.

(2) An employment tribunal may not consider a complaint under this section unless it is presented—

(a) before the end of the period of three months beginning with the day of the appointment in question, or

(b) within such further period as the tribunal considers reasonable in a case where it is satisfied that it was not reasonably practicable for the complaint to be presented before the end of that period of three months.

(3) Sections 207A(3) and 207B apply for the purposes of subsection (2)(a).

(4) Where an employment tribunal finds a complaint under subsection (1) well-founded, it—

(a) must make a declaration to that effect, and

(b) must order the employer to pay to the employee an amount determined in accordance with subsection (5).

(5) The amount payable to the employee is—

$A \times B \times 2$

where—

(a) A is the appropriate hourly rate for the employee, and

(b) B is the number of working hours for which the employee would have been entitled under section 57ZE to be absent if the time off had not been refused.

(6) The appropriate hourly rate, in relation to an employee, is the amount of one week's pay divided by the number of normal working hours in a week for that employee when employed under the contract of employment in force on the day when the time off would have been taken.

(7) But where the number of normal working hours differs from week to week or over a longer period, the amount of one week's pay shall be divided instead by—

(a) the average number of normal working hours calculated by dividing by twelve the total number of the employee's normal working hours during the period of twelve weeks ending with the last complete week before the day on which the time off would have been taken, or

(b) where the employee has not been employed for a sufficient period to enable the calculation to be made under paragraph (a), a number which fairly represents the number of normal working hours in a week having regard to such of the considerations specified in subsection (8) as are appropriate in the circumstances.

(8) The considerations referred to in subsection (7)(b) are—

(a) the average number of normal working hours in a week which the employee could expect in accordance with the terms of the employee's contract, and

(b) the average number of normal working hours of other employees engaged in relevant comparable employment with the same employer.]

NOTES

Commencement: 1 October 2014.

Inserted as noted to s 57ZD at **[1.911]**.

Sub-s (3): substituted by the Cross-Border Mediation (EU Directive) (EU Exit) Regulations 2019, SI 2019/469, reg 4, Sch 1, Pt 1, para 12(1), (10), as from exit day (as defined in the European Union (Withdrawal) Act 2018, s 20), as follows—

"(3) Section 207B applies for the purposes of subsection (2)(a).".

Conciliation: see the note following the Part heading *ante*.

[Accompanying to ante-natal appointments: agency workers

[1.913]

57ZG Right to time off to accompany to ante-natal appointment: agency workers

(1) An agency worker who has a qualifying relationship with a pregnant woman or her expected child is entitled to be permitted, by the temporary work agency and the hirer, to take time off during the agency worker's working hours in order that he or she may accompany the woman when she attends by appointment at any place for the purpose of receiving ante-natal care.

(2) In relation to any particular pregnancy, an agency worker is not entitled to take time off for the purpose specified in subsection (1) on more than two occasions.

(3) On each of those occasions, the maximum time off during working hours to which the agency worker is entitled is six and a half hours.

(4) An agency worker is not entitled to take time off for the purpose specified in subsection (1) unless the appointment is made on the advice of a registered medical practitioner, registered midwife or registered nurse.

(5) Where the temporary work agency or the hirer requests the agency worker to give that person a declaration signed by the agency worker, the agency worker is not entitled to take time off for the purpose specified in subsection (1) unless the agency worker gives that declaration (which may be given in electronic form).

(6) The agency worker must state in the declaration—

(a) that the agency worker has a qualifying relationship with a pregnant woman or her expected child,

(b) that the agency worker's purpose in taking time off is the purpose specified in subsection (1),

(c) that the appointment in question is made on the advice of a registered medical practitioner, registered midwife or registered nurse, and

(d) the date and time of the appointment.

(7) A person has a qualifying relationship with a pregnant woman or her expected child if—

(a) the person is the husband or civil partner of the pregnant woman,

(b) the person, being of a different sex or the same sex, lives with the woman in an enduring family relationship but is not a relative of the woman,

(c) the person is the father of the expected child,

(d) the person is a parent of the expected child by virtue of section 42 or 43 of the Human Fertilisation and Embryology Act 2008, . . .

(e) the person is a potential applicant for a parental order under section 54 of the Human Fertilisation and Embryology Act 2008 in respect of the expected child[, or

(f) the person is a potential applicant for a parental order under section 54A of the Human Fertilisation and Embryology Act 2008 in respect of the expected child.]

(8) For the purposes of subsection (7) a relative of a person is the person's parent, grandparent, sister, brother, aunt or uncle.

(9) The references to relationships in subsection (8)—

(a) are to relationships of the full blood or half blood or, in the case of an adopted person, such of those relationships as would exist but for the adoption, and

(b) include the relationship of a child with the child's adoptive, or former adoptive, parents,

but do not include any other adoptive relationships.

(10) For the purposes of subsection (7)(e) a person ("A") is a potential applicant for a parental order under section 54 of the Human Fertilisation and Embryology Act 2008 in respect of an expected child only if—

(a) A intends to apply, jointly with another person ("B"), for such an order in respect of the expected child within the time allowed by section 54(3),

(b) the expected child is being carried by the pregnant woman as a result of such procedure as is described in section 54(1)(a),

(c) the requirement in section 54(1)(b) is satisfied by reference to A or B,

(d) A and B would satisfy section 54(2) if they made an application under section 54 at the time that A seeks to exercise the right under this section, and

(e) A expects that A and B will satisfy the conditions in section 54(2), (4), (5) and (8) as regards the intended application.

[(10A) For the purposes of subsection (7)(f) a person is a potential applicant for a parental order under section 54A of the Human Fertilisation and Embryology Act 2008 in respect of an expected child only if—

(a) the person intends to apply for such an order in respect of the expected child within the time allowed by section 54A(2),

(b) the expected child is being carried by the pregnant woman as a result of such procedure as is described in section 54A(1)(a),

(c) the requirement in section 54A(1)(b) is satisfied by reference to the person, and

(d) the person expects that he or she will satisfy the conditions in section 54A(3), (4) and (7) as regards the intended application.]

(11) The references in this section to a registered nurse are references to a registered nurse—

(a) who is also registered in the Specialist Community Public Health Nurses Part of the register maintained under article 5 of the Nursing and Midwifery Order 2001 (SI 2002/253), and
(b) whose entry in that Part of the register is annotated to show that the nurse holds a qualification in health visiting.

(12) For the purposes of this section the working hours of an agency worker are to be taken to be any time when, in accordance with the terms under which the agency worker works temporarily for and under the supervision and direction of the hirer, the agency worker is required to be at work.]

NOTES

Commencement: 1 October 2014.

Inserted as noted to s 57ZD at **[1.911]**.

Sub-s (7): word omitted from para (d) repealed, and para (f) inserted together with word preceding it, by the Human Fertilisation and Embryology Act 2008 (Remedial) Order 2018, SI 2018/1413, art 3(1), Sch 1, para 11(1), (6)–(8), as from 3 January 2019.

Sub-s (10A): inserted by SI 2018/1413, art 3(1), Sch 1, para 11(1), (6), (9), as from 3 January 2019.

Conciliation: see the note following the Part heading *ante*.

[1.914]

[57ZH Complaint to employment tribunal: agency workers

(1) An agency worker may present a complaint to an employment tribunal that the temporary work agency has unreasonably refused to let him or her take time off as required by section 57ZG.

(2) An agency worker may present a complaint to an employment tribunal that the hirer has unreasonably refused to let him or her take time off as required by section 57ZG.

(3) An employment tribunal may not consider a complaint under subsection (1) or (2) unless it is presented—

(a) before the end of the period of three months beginning with the day of the appointment in question, or
(b) within such further period as the tribunal considers reasonable in a case where it is satisfied that it was not reasonably practicable for the complaint to be presented before the end of that period of three months.

(4) Sections 207A(3) and 207B apply for the purposes of subsection (3)(a).

(5) Where an employment tribunal finds a complaint under subsection (1) or (2) well-founded, it—

(a) must make a declaration to that effect, and
(b) must order the payment to the agency worker of an amount determined in accordance with subsection (7).

(6) Where the tribunal orders that payment under subsection (5) be made by the temporary work agency and the hirer, the proportion of that amount payable by each respondent is to be such as may be found by the tribunal to be just and equitable having regard to the extent of each respondent's responsibility for the infringement to which the complaint relates.

(7) The amount payable to the agency worker is—

$A \times B \times 2$

where—

(a) A is the appropriate hourly rate for the agency worker, and
(b) B is the number of working hours for which the agency worker would have been entitled under section 57ZG to be absent if the time off had not been refused.

(8) The appropriate hourly rate, in relation to an agency worker, is the amount of one week's pay divided by the number of normal working hours in a week for that agency worker in accordance with the terms under which the agency worker works temporarily for and under the supervision and direction of the hirer that are in force on the day when the time off would have been taken.

(9) But where the number of normal working hours during the assignment differs from week to week or over a longer period, the amount of one week's pay shall be divided instead by the average number of normal working hours calculated by dividing by twelve the total number of the agency worker's normal working hours during the period of twelve weeks ending with the last complete week before the day on which the time off would have been taken.]

NOTES

Commencement: 1 October 2014.

Inserted as noted to s 57ZD at **[1.911]**.

Sub-s (4): substituted by the Cross-Border Mediation (EU Directive) (EU Exit) Regulations 2019, SI 2019/469, reg 4, Sch 1, Pt 1, para 12(1), (11), as from exit day (as defined in the European Union (Withdrawal) Act 2018, s 20), as follows—

"(4) Section 207B applies for the purposes of subsection (3)(a).".

Conciliation: see the note following the Part heading *ante*.

[1.915]

[57ZI Agency workers: supplementary

(1) Without prejudice to any other duties of the hirer or temporary work agency under any enactment or rule of law, sections 57ZG and 57ZH do not apply where the agency worker—

(a) has not completed the qualifying period, or
(b) pursuant to regulation 8(a) or (b) of the Agency Workers Regulations 2010 (SI 2010/93), is no longer entitled to the rights conferred by regulation 5 of those Regulations.

(2) Nothing in sections 57ZG and 57ZH imposes a duty on the hirer or temporary work agency beyond the original intended duration, or likely duration, of the assignment, whichever is the longer.

(3) Sections 57ZG and 57ZH do not apply where sections 57ZE and 57ZF apply.
(4) In this section and sections 57ZG and 57ZH the following have the same meaning as in the Agency Workers Regulations 2010—

"agency worker";
"assignment";
"hirer";
"qualifying period";
"temporary work agency".]

NOTES

Commencement: 1 October 2014.
Inserted as noted to s 57ZD at **[1.911]**.
Conciliation: see the note following the Part heading *ante*.

[Adoption appointments

[1.916]
57ZJ Right to paid time off to attend adoption appointments

(1) An employee who has been notified by an adoption agency that a child is to be, or is expected to be, placed for adoption with the employee alone is entitled to be permitted by his or her employer to take time off during the employee's working hours in order that he or she may attend by appointment at any place for the purpose of having contact with the child or for any other purpose connected with the adoption.

(2) An employee who—
(a) has been notified by an adoption agency that a child is to be, or is expected to be, placed for adoption with the employee and another person jointly, and
(b) has elected to exercise the right to take time off under this section in connection with the adoption,

is entitled to be permitted by his or her employer to take time off during the employee's working hours in order that he or she may attend by appointment at any place for the purpose of having contact with the child or for any other purpose connected with the adoption.

(3) An employee may not make an election for the purposes of subsection (2)(b) if—
(a) the employee has made an election for the purposes of section 57ZL(1)(b) in connection with the adoption, or
(b) the other person with whom the child is to be, or is expected to be, placed for adoption has made an election for the purposes of subsection (2)(b) or section 57ZN(2)(b) in connection with the adoption.

(4) An employee is not entitled to take time off under this section on or after the date of the child's placement for adoption with the employee.

(5) In relation to any particular adoption, an employee is not entitled to take time off under this section on more than five occasions.

(6) On each of those occasions, the maximum time off during working hours to which the employee is entitled is six and a half hours.

(7) An employee is not entitled to take time off under this section unless the appointment has been arranged by or at the request of the adoption agency which made the notification described in subsection (1) or (2)(a).

(8) An employee is not entitled to take time off under subsection (1) unless, if the employer requests it, the employee gives the employer a document showing the date and time of the appointment in question and that it has been arranged as described in subsection (7).

(9) An employee is not entitled to take time off under subsection (2) unless, if the employer requests it, the employee gives the employer—
(a) a declaration signed by the employee stating that the employee has made an election for the purposes of subsection (2)(b) in connection with the adoption, and
(b) a document showing the date and time of the appointment in question and that it has been arranged as described in subsection (7).

(10) A document or declaration requested under subsection (8) or (9) may be given in electronic form.

(11) In cases where more than one child is to be, or is expected to be, placed for adoption with an employee as part of the same arrangement, this section has effect as if—
(a) the purposes specified in subsections (1) and (2) were the purpose of having contact with any one or more of the children and any other purpose connected with any of the adoptions that are part of the arrangement;
(b) the references in subsections (2)(b) and (9)(a) to the adoption were references to all of the adoptions that are part of the arrangement;
(c) the references in subsection (3) to the adoption were references to any of the adoptions that are part of the arrangement;
(d) the reference in subsection (4) to the date of the child's placement for adoption were a reference to the date of placement of the first child to be placed as part of the arrangement;
(e) the reference in subsection (5) to a particular adoption were a reference to the adoptions that are part of a particular arrangement.

(12) For the purposes of this section the working hours of an employee are to be taken to be any time when, in accordance with the employee's contract of employment, the employee is required to be at work.

(13) In this section "adoption agency" means an adoption agency within the meaning of section 2 of the Adoption and Children Act 2002 or as defined in section 119(1)(a) of the Adoption and Children (Scotland) Act 2007.]

NOTES

Commencement: 5 April 2015.

Inserted, together with the preceding heading and ss 57ZK–57ZS, by the Children and Families Act 2014, s 128(1), as from 5 April 2015.

Conciliation: see the note following the Part heading *ante*.

[1.917]

[57ZK Right to remuneration for time off under section 57ZJ

(1) An employee who is permitted to take time off under section 57ZJ is entitled to be paid remuneration by his or her employer for the number of working hours for which the employee is entitled to be absent at the appropriate hourly rate.

(2) The appropriate hourly rate, in relation to an employee, is the amount of one week's pay divided by the number of normal working hours in a week for that employee when employed under the contract of employment in force on the day when the time off is taken.

(3) But where the number of normal working hours differs from week to week or over a longer period, the amount of one week's pay shall be divided instead by—

(a) the average number of normal working hours calculated by dividing by twelve the total number of the employee's normal working hours during the period of twelve weeks ending with the last complete week before the day on which the time off is taken, or

(b) where the employee has not been employed for a sufficient period to enable the calculation to be made under paragraph (a), a number which fairly represents the number of normal working hours in a week having regard to such of the considerations specified in subsection (4) as are appropriate in the circumstances.

(4) The considerations referred to in subsection (3)(b) are—

(a) the average number of normal working hours in a week which the employee could expect in accordance with the terms of the employee's contract, and

(b) the average number of normal working hours of other employees engaged in relevant comparable employment with the same employer.

(5) A right to any amount under subsection (1) does not affect any right of an employee in relation to remuneration under the employee's contract of employment ("contractual remuneration").

(6) Any contractual remuneration paid to an employee in respect of a period of time off under section 57ZJ goes towards discharging any liability of the employer to pay remuneration under subsection (1) in respect of that period.

(7) Any payment of remuneration under subsection (1) in respect of a period of time off under section 57ZJ goes towards discharging any liability of the employer to pay contractual remuneration in respect of that period.]

NOTES

Commencement: 5 April 2015.

Inserted as noted to s 57ZJ at **[1.916]**.

Conciliation: see the note following the Part heading *ante*.

[1.918]

[57ZL Right to unpaid time off to attend adoption appointments

(1) An employee who—

(a) has been notified by an adoption agency that a child is to be, or is expected to be, placed for adoption with the employee and another person jointly, and

(b) has elected to exercise the right to take time off under this section in connection with the adoption,

is entitled to be permitted by his or her employer to take time off during the employee's working hours in order that he or she may attend by appointment at any place for the purpose of having contact with the child or for any other purpose connected with the adoption.

(2) An employee may not make an election for the purposes of subsection (1)(b) if—

(a) the employee has made an election for the purposes of section 57ZJ(2)(b) in connection with the adoption, or

(b) the other person with whom the child is to be, or is expected to be, placed for adoption has made an election for the purposes of subsection (1)(b) or section 57ZP(1)(b) in connection with the adoption.

(3) An employee is not entitled to take time off under this section on or after the date of the child's placement for adoption with the employee.

(4) In relation to any particular adoption, an employee is not entitled to take time off under this section on more than two occasions.

(5) On each of those occasions, the maximum time off during working hours to which the employee is entitled is six and a half hours.

(6) An employee is not entitled to take time off under this section unless the appointment has been arranged by or at the request of the adoption agency which made the notification described in subsection (1)(a).

(7) An employee is not entitled to take time off under this section unless, if the employer requests it, the employee gives the employer—

(a) a declaration signed by the employee stating that the employee has made an election for the purposes of subsection (1)(b) in connection with the adoption, and

(b) a document showing the date and time of the appointment in question and that it has been arranged as described in subsection (6).

(8) A declaration or document requested under subsection (7) may be given in electronic form.

(9) In cases where more than one child is to be, or is expected to be, placed for adoption with an employee and another person jointly as part of the same arrangement, this section has effect as if—

(a) the purposes specified in subsection (1) were the purpose of having contact with any one or more of the children and any other purpose connected with any of the adoptions that are part of the arrangement;

(b) the references in subsections (1)(b) and (7)(a) to the adoption were references to all of the adoptions that are part of the arrangement;

(c) the references in subsection (2) to the adoption were references to any of the adoptions that are part of the arrangement;

(d) the reference in subsection (3) to the date of the child's placement for adoption were a reference to the date of placement of the first child to be placed as part of the arrangement;

(e) the reference in subsection (4) to a particular adoption were a reference to the adoptions that are part of a particular arrangement.

(10) For the purposes of this section the working hours of an employee are to be taken to be any time when, in accordance with the employee's contract of employment, the employee is required to be at work.

(11) In this section "adoption agency" means an adoption agency within the meaning of section 2 of the Adoption and Children Act 2002 or as defined in section 119(1)(a) of the Adoption and Children (Scotland) Act 2007.]

NOTES

Commencement: 5 April 2015.

Inserted as noted to s 57ZJ at **[1.916]**.

Conciliation: see the note following the Part heading *ante*.

[1.919]

[57ZM Complaint to employment tribunal

(1) An employee may present a complaint to an employment tribunal that his or her employer—

(a) has unreasonably refused to let him or her take time off as required by section 57ZJ or 57ZL, or

(b) has failed to pay the whole or any part of any amount to which the employee is entitled under section 57ZK.

(2) An employment tribunal may not consider a complaint under this section unless it is presented—

(a) before the end of the period of three months beginning with the day of the appointment in question, or

(b) within such further period as the tribunal considers reasonable in a case where it is satisfied that it was not reasonably practicable for the complaint to be presented before the end of that period of three months.

(3) Sections 207A(3) and 207B apply for the purposes of subsection (2)(a).

(4) Where an employment tribunal finds a complaint under subsection (1) well-founded, it must make a declaration to that effect.

(5) If the complaint is that the employer has unreasonably refused to let the employee take time off as required by section 57ZJ, the tribunal must also order the employer to pay to the employee an amount that is twice the amount of the remuneration to which the employee would have been entitled under section 57ZK if the employer had not refused.

(6) If the complaint is that the employer has failed to pay the employee the whole or part of any amount to which the employee is entitled under section 57ZK, the tribunal must also order the employer to pay to the employee the amount which it finds due to the employee.

(7) If the complaint is that the employer has unreasonably refused to let the employee take time off as required by section 57ZL, the tribunal must also order the employer to pay to the employee an amount determined in accordance with subsection (8).

(8) The amount payable to the employee is—

$$A \times B \times 2$$

where—

(a) A is the appropriate hourly rate for the employee determined in accordance with section 57ZK(2) to (4), and

(b) B is the number of working hours for which the employee would have been entitled under section 57ZL to be absent if the time off had not been refused.]

NOTES

Commencement: 5 April 2015.

Inserted as noted to s 57ZJ at **[1.916]**.

Sub-s (3): substituted by the Cross-Border Mediation (EU Directive) (EU Exit) Regulations 2019, SI 2019/469, reg 4, Sch 1, Pt 1, para 12(1), (12), as from exit day (as defined in the European Union (Withdrawal) Act 2018, s 20), as follows—

"(3) Section 207B applies for the purposes of subsection (2)(a).".

Conciliation: see the note following the Part heading *ante*.

Adoption appointments: agency workers

[1.920]

[57ZN Right to paid time off to attend adoption appointments: agency workers

(1) An agency worker who has been notified by an adoption agency that a child is to be, or is expected to be, placed for adoption with the agency worker alone is entitled to be permitted by the temporary work agency and the hirer to take time off during the agency worker's working hours in order that he or she may attend by appointment at any place for the purpose of having contact with the child or for any other purpose connected with the adoption.

(2) An agency worker who—

(a) has been notified by an adoption agency that a child is to be, or is expected to be, placed for adoption with the agency worker and another person jointly, and

(b) has elected to exercise the right to take time off under this section in connection with the adoption,

is entitled to be permitted by the temporary work agency and the hirer to take time off during the agency worker's working hours in order that he or she may attend by appointment at any place for the purpose of having contact with the child or for any other purpose connected with the adoption.

(3) An agency worker may not make an election for the purposes of subsection (2)(b) if—

(a) the agency worker has made an election for the purposes of section 57ZP(1)(b) in connection with the adoption, or

(b) the other person with whom the child is to be, or is expected to be, placed for adoption has made an election for the purposes of subsection (2)(b) or section 57ZJ(2)(b) in connection with the adoption.

(4) An agency worker is not entitled to take time off under this section on or after the date of the child's placement for adoption with the agency worker.

(5) In relation to any particular adoption, an agency worker is not entitled to take time off under this section on more than five occasions.

(6) On each of those occasions, the maximum time off during working hours to which the agency worker is entitled is six and a half hours.

(7) An agency worker is not entitled to take time off under this section unless the appointment has been arranged by or at the request of the adoption agency which made the notification described in subsection (1) or (2)(a).

(8) An agency worker is not entitled to take time off under subsection (1) unless, if the temporary work agency or the hirer requests it, the agency worker gives that person a document showing the date and time of the appointment in question and that it has been arranged as described in subsection (7).

(9) An agency worker is not entitled to take time off under subsection (2) unless, if the temporary work agency or the hirer requests it, the agency worker gives that person—

(a) a declaration signed by the agency worker stating that the agency worker has made an election for the purposes of subsection (2)(b) in connection with the adoption, and

(b) a document showing the date and time of the appointment in question and that it has been arranged as described in subsection (7).

(10) A document or declaration requested under subsection (8) or (9) may be given in electronic form.

(11) In cases where more than one child is to be, or is expected to be, placed for adoption with an agency worker as part of the same arrangement, this section has effect as if—

(a) the purposes specified in subsections (1) and (2) were the purpose of having contact with any one or more of the children and any other purpose connected with any of the adoptions that are part of the arrangement;

(b) the references in subsections (2)(b) and (9)(a) to the adoption were references to all of the adoptions that are part of the arrangement;

(c) the references in subsection (3) to the adoption were references to any of the adoptions that are part of the arrangement;

(d) the reference in subsection (4) to the date of the child's placement for adoption were a reference to the date of placement of the first child to be placed as part of the arrangement;

(e) the reference in subsection (5) to a particular adoption were a reference to the adoptions that are part of a particular arrangement.

(12) For the purposes of this section the working hours of an agency worker are to be taken to be any time when, in accordance with the terms under which the agency worker works temporarily for and under the supervision and direction of the hirer, the agency worker is required to be at work.

(13) In this section "adoption agency" means an adoption agency within the meaning of section 2 of the Adoption and Children Act 2002 or as defined in section 119(1)(a) of the Adoption and Children (Scotland) Act 2007.]

NOTES

Commencement: 5 April 2015.

Inserted as noted to s 57ZJ at **[1.916]**.

Conciliation: see the note following the Part heading *ante*.

[1.921]

[57ZO Right to remuneration for time off under section 57ZN

(1) An agency worker who is permitted to take time off under section 57ZN is entitled to be paid remuneration by the temporary work agency for the number of working hours for which the agency worker is entitled to be absent at the appropriate hourly rate.

(2) The appropriate hourly rate, in relation to an agency worker, is the amount of one week's pay divided by the number of normal working hours in a week for that agency worker in accordance with the terms under which the agency worker works temporarily for and under the supervision and direction of the hirer that are in force on the day when the time off is taken.
(3) But where the number of normal working hours during the assignment differs from week to week or over a longer period, the amount of one week's pay shall be divided instead by the average number of normal working hours calculated by dividing by twelve the total number of the agency worker's normal working hours during the period of twelve weeks ending with the last complete week before the day on which the time off is taken.
(4) A right to any amount under subsection (1) does not affect any right of an agency worker in relation to remuneration under the agency worker's contract with the temporary work agency ("contractual remuneration").
(5) Any contractual remuneration paid to an agency worker in respect of a period of time off under section 57ZN goes towards discharging any liability of the temporary work agency to pay remuneration under subsection (1) in respect of that period.
(6) Any payment of remuneration under subsection (1) in respect of a period of time off under section 57ZN goes towards discharging any liability of the temporary work agency to pay contractual remuneration in respect of that period.]

NOTES

Commencement: 5 April 2015.
Inserted as noted to s 57ZJ at **[1.916]**.
Conciliation: see the note following the Part heading *ante*.

[1.922]
[57ZP Right to unpaid time off to attend adoption meetings: agency workers
(1) An agency worker who—
(a) has been notified by an adoption agency that a child is to be, or is expected to be, placed for adoption with the agency worker and another person jointly, and
(b) has elected to exercise the right to take time off under this section in connection with the adoption,

is entitled to be permitted by the temporary work agency and the hirer to take time off during the agency worker's working hours in order that he or she may attend by appointment at any place for the purpose of having contact with the child or for any other purpose connected with the adoption.
(2) An agency worker may not make an election for the purposes of subsection (1)(b) if—
(a) the agency worker has made an election for the purposes of section 57ZN(2)(b) in connection with the adoption, or
(b) the other person with whom the child is to be, or is expected to be, placed for adoption has made an election for the purposes of subsection (1)(b) or section 57ZL(1)(b) in connection with the adoption.

(3) An agency worker is not entitled to take time off under this section on or after the date of the child's placement for adoption with the agency worker.
(4) In relation to any particular adoption, an agency worker is not entitled to take time off under this section on more than two occasions.
(5) On each of those occasions, the maximum time off during working hours to which the agency worker is entitled is six and a half hours.
(6) An agency worker is not entitled to take time off under this section unless the appointment has been arranged by or at the request of the adoption agency which made the notification described in subsection (1)(a).
(7) An agency worker is not entitled to take time off under this section unless, if the temporary work agency or the hirer requests it, the agency worker gives that person—
(a) a declaration signed by the agency worker stating that the agency worker has made an election for the purposes of subsection (1)(b) in connection with the adoption, and
(b) a document showing the date and time of the appointment in question and that it has been arranged as described in subsection (6).

(8) A declaration or document requested under subsection (7) may be given in electronic form.
(9) In cases where more than one child is to be, or is expected to be, placed for adoption with an agency worker and another person jointly as part of the same arrangement, this section has effect as if—
(a) the purposes specified in subsection (1) were the purpose of having contact with any one or more of the children and any other purpose connected with any of the adoptions that are part of the arrangement;
(b) the references in subsections (1)(b) and (7)(a) to the adoption were references to all of the adoptions that are part of the arrangement;
(c) the references in subsection (2) to the adoption were references to any of the adoptions that are part of the arrangement;
(d) the reference in subsection (3) to the date of the child's placement for adoption were a reference to the date of placement of the first child to be placed as part of the arrangement;
(e) the reference in subsection (4) to a particular adoption were a reference to the adoptions that are part of a particular arrangement.

(10) For the purposes of this section the working hours of an agency worker are to be taken to be any time when, in accordance with the terms under which the agency worker works temporarily for and under the supervision and direction of the hirer, the agency worker is required to be at work.

(11) In this section "adoption agency" means an adoption agency within the meaning of section 2 of the Adoption and Children Act 2002 or as defined by section 119(1)(a) of the Adoption and Children (Scotland) Act 2007.]

NOTES

Commencement: 5 April 2015.

Inserted as noted to s 57ZJ at **[1.916]**.

Conciliation: see the note following the Part heading *ante*.

[1.923]

[57ZQ Complaint to employment tribunal: agency workers

(1) An agency worker may present a complaint to an employment tribunal that the temporary work agency—

(a) has unreasonably refused to let him or her take time off as required by section 57ZN or 57ZP, or

(b) has failed to pay the whole or any part of any amount to which the agency worker is entitled under section 57ZO.

(2) An agency worker may present a complaint to an employment tribunal that the hirer has unreasonably refused to let him or her take time off as required by section 57ZN or 57ZP.

(3) An employment tribunal may not consider a complaint under subsection (1) or (2) unless it is presented—

(a) before the end of the period of three months beginning with the day of the appointment in question, or

(b) within such further period as the tribunal considers reasonable in a case where it is satisfied that it was not reasonably practicable for the complaint to be presented before the end of that period of three months.

(4) Sections 207A(3) and 207B apply for the purposes of subsection (3)(a).

(5) Where an employment tribunal finds a complaint under subsection (1) or (2) well-founded, it must make a declaration to that effect.

(6) If the complaint is that the temporary work agency or hirer has unreasonably refused to let the agency worker take time off as required by section 57ZN, the tribunal must also order payment to the agency worker of an amount that is twice the amount of the remuneration to which the agency worker would have been entitled under section 57ZO if the agency worker had not been refused the time off.

(7) If the complaint is that the temporary work agency has failed to pay the agency worker the whole or part of any amount to which the agency worker is entitled under section 57ZO, the tribunal must also order the temporary work agency to pay to the agency worker the amount which it finds due to the agency worker.

(8) If the complaint is that the temporary work agency or hirer has unreasonably refused to let the agency worker take time off as required by section 57ZP, the tribunal must also order payment to the agency worker of an amount determined in accordance with subsection (9).

(9) The amount payable to the agency worker under subsection (8) is—

$A \times B \times 2$

where—

(a) A is the appropriate hourly rate for the agency worker determined in accordance with section 57ZO(2) and (3), and

(b) B is the number of working hours for which the agency worker would have been entitled under section 57ZP to be absent if the time off had not been refused.

(10) Where the tribunal orders that payment under subsection (6) or (8) be made by the temporary work agency and the hirer, the proportion of that amount payable by each respondent is to be such as may be found by the tribunal to be just and equitable having regard to the extent of each respondent's responsibility for the infringement to which the complaint relates.]

NOTES

Commencement: 5 April 2015.

Inserted as noted to s 57ZJ at **[1.916]**.

Sub-s (4): substituted by the Cross-Border Mediation (EU Directive) (EU Exit) Regulations 2019, SI 2019/469, reg 4, Sch 1, Pt 1, para 12(1), (13), as from exit day (as defined in the European Union (Withdrawal) Act 2018, s 20), as follows—

"(4) Section 207B applies for the purposes of subsection (3)(a).".

Conciliation: see the note following the Part heading *ante*.

[1.924]

[57ZR Agency workers: supplementary

(1) Without prejudice to any other duties of the hirer or temporary work agency under any enactment or rule of law, sections 57ZN to 57ZQ do not apply where the agency worker—

(a) has not completed the qualifying period, or

(b) pursuant to regulation 8(a) or (b) of the Agency Workers Regulations 2010 (SI 2010/93), is no longer entitled to the rights conferred by regulation 5 of those Regulations.

(2) Nothing in sections 57ZN to 57ZQ imposes a duty on the hirer or temporary work agency beyond the original intended duration, or likely duration, of the assignment, whichever is the longer.

(3) Sections 57ZN to 57ZQ do not apply where sections 57ZJ to 57ZM apply.

(4) In this section and sections 57ZN to 57ZQ the following have the same meaning as in the Agency Workers Regulations 2010—

"agency worker";
"assignment";
"hirer";
"qualifying period";
"temporary work agency".]

NOTES

Commencement: 5 April 2015.
Inserted as noted to s 57ZJ at **[1.916]**.
Conciliation: see the note following the Part heading *ante*.

[1.925]
[57ZS Placement of looked after children with prospective adopters

(1) Subsection (2) applies where a local authority in England notifies a person—
 (a) who is a local authority foster parent, and
 (b) who has been approved as a prospective adopter,
that a child is to be, or is expected to be, placed with that person under section 22C of the Children Act 1989.

(2) Where this subsection applies, sections 57ZJ, 57ZL, 57ZN and 57ZP have effect as if—
 (a) references to adoption or placement for adoption were references to placement of a child under section 22C of the Children Act 1989 with a local authority foster parent who has been approved as a prospective adopter;
 (b) references to placing for adoption were references to placing a child under section 22C of that Act with a local authority foster parent who has been approved as a prospective adopter;
 (c) references to an adoption agency were references to a local authority in England.

[(2A) Subsection (2B) applies where a local authority in Wales notifies a person—
 (a) who is a local authority foster parent, and
 (b) who has been approved as a prospective adopter,
that a child is to be, or is expected to be, placed with that person under section 81 of the Social Services and Well-being (Wales) Act 2014.

(2B) Where this subsection applies, sections 57ZJ, 57ZL, 57ZN and 57ZP have effect as if—
 (a) references to adoption or placement for adoption were references to placement of a child under section 81 of the Social Services and Well-being (Wales) Act 2014 with a local authority foster parent who has been approved as a prospective adopter;
 (b) references to placing for adoption were references to placing a child under section 81 of that Act with a local authority foster parent who has been approved as a prospective adopter;
 (c) references to an adoption agency were references to a local authority in Wales.]

(3) Where a child is placed under section 22C of the Children Act 1989 [or section 81 of the Social Services and Well-being (Wales) Act 2014] with a local authority foster parent who has been approved as a prospective adopter, notification of that person by an adoption agency during that placement that the child is to be, or is expected to be, placed with that person for adoption is not to give rise to a right to time off under section 57ZJ, 57ZL, 57ZN or 57ZP for that person or another person.]

NOTES

Commencement: 6 April 2015.
Inserted as noted to s 57ZJ at **[1.916]**.
Sub-ss (2A), (2B): inserted by the Social Services and Well-being (Wales) Act 2014 (Consequential Amendments) Regulations 2016, SI 2016/413, regs 143, 144(a), as from 6 April 2016.
Sub-s (3): words in square brackets inserted by SI 2016/413, regs 143, 144(b), as from 6 April 2016.
Conciliation: see the note following the Part heading *ante*.

[Dependants

[1.926]
57A Time off for dependants

(1) An employee is entitled to be permitted by his employer to take a reasonable amount of time off during the employee's working hours in order to take action which is necessary—
 (a) to provide assistance on an occasion when a dependant falls ill, gives birth or is injured or assaulted,
 (b) to make arrangements for the provision of care for a dependant who is ill or injured,
 (c) in consequence of the death of a dependant,
 (d) because of the unexpected disruption or termination of arrangements for the care of a dependant, or
 (e) to deal with an incident which involves a child of the employee and which occurs unexpectedly in a period during which an educational establishment which the child attends is responsible for him.

(2) Subsection (1) does not apply unless the employee—
 (a) tells his employer the reason for his absence as soon as reasonably practicable, and
 (b) except where paragraph (a) cannot be complied with until after the employee has returned to work, tells his employer for how long he expects to be absent.

(3) Subject to subsections (4) and (5), for the purposes of this section "dependant" means, in relation to an employee—
 (a) a spouse [or civil partner],
 (b) a child,

Part 1 Statutes

(c) a parent,
(d) a person who lives in the same household as the employee, otherwise than by reason of being his employee, tenant, lodger or boarder.

(4) For the purposes of subsection (1)(a) or (b) "dependant" includes, in addition to the persons mentioned in subsection (3), any person who reasonably relies on the employee—
(a) for assistance on an occasion when the person falls ill or is injured or assaulted, or
(b) to make arrangements for the provision of care in the event of illness or injury.

(5) For the purposes of subsection (1)(d) "dependant" includes, in addition to the persons mentioned in subsection (3), any person who reasonably relies on the employee to make arrangements for the provision of care.

(6) A reference in this section to illness or injury includes a reference to mental illness or injury.]

NOTES

Inserted, together with preceding heading and s 57B, by the Employment Relations Act 1999, s 8, Sch 4, Pt II.
Sub-s (3): words in square brackets in para (a) inserted by the Civil Partnership Act 2004, s 261(1), Sch 27, para 151.
Conciliation: see the note following the Part heading *ante*.

[1.927]
[57B Complaint to employment tribunal

(1) An employee may present a complaint to an employment tribunal that his employer has unreasonably refused to permit him to take time off as required by section 57A.

(2) An employment tribunal shall not consider a complaint under this section unless it is presented—
(a) before the end of the period of three months beginning with the date when the refusal occurred, or
(b) within such further period as the tribunal considers reasonable in a case where it is satisfied that it was not reasonably practicable for the complaint to be presented before the end of that period of three months.

[(2A) Section 207A(3) (extension because of mediation in certain European cross-border disputes) [and section 207B (extension of time limits to facilitate conciliation before institution of proceedings) apply] for the purposes of subsection (2)(a).]

(3) Where an employment tribunal finds a complaint under subsection (1) well-founded, it—
(a) shall make a declaration to that effect, and
(b) may make an award of compensation to be paid by the employer to the employee.

(4) The amount of compensation shall be such as the tribunal considers just and equitable in all the circumstances having regard to—
(a) the employer's default in refusing to permit time off to be taken by the employee, and
(b) any loss sustained by the employee which is attributable to the matters complained of.]

NOTES

Inserted as noted to s 57A at **[1.926]**.
Sub-s (2A): inserted by the Cross-Border Mediation (EU Directive) Regulations 2011, SI 2011/1133, regs 30, 38; words in square brackets substituted by the Enterprise and Regulatory Reform Act 2013, s 8, Sch 2, paras 15, 24; substituted by the Cross-Border Mediation (EU Directive) (EU Exit) Regulations 2019, SI 2019/469, reg 4, Sch 1, Pt 1, para 12(1), (14), as from exit day (as defined in the European Union (Withdrawal) Act 2018, s 20), as follows—

"(2A) Section 207B (extension of time limits to facilitate conciliation before institution of proceedings) applies for the purposes of subsection (2)(a).".

Conciliation: see the note following the Part heading *ante*.

Occupational pension scheme trustees

[1.928]
58 Right to time off for pension scheme trustees

(1) The employer in relation to a relevant occupational pension scheme shall permit an employee of his who is a trustee of the scheme to the time off during the employee's working hours for the purpose of—
(a) performing any of his duties as such a trustee, or
(b) undergoing training relevant to the performance of those duties.

(2) The amount of time off which an employee is to be permitted to take under this section and the purposes for which, the occasions on which and any conditions subject to which time off may be so taken are those that are reasonable in all the circumstances having regard, in particular, to—
(a) how much time off is required for the performance of the duties of a trustee of the scheme and the undergoing of relevant training, and how much time off is required for performing the particular duty or for undergoing the particular training, and
(b) the circumstances of the employer's business and the effect of the employee's absence on the running of that business.

[(2A) This section applies to an employee who is a director of a company which is a trustee of a relevant occupational pension scheme as it applies to an employee who is a trustee of such a scheme (references to such a trustee being read for this purpose as references to such a director).]

(3) In this section—
(a) "relevant occupational pension scheme" means an occupational pension scheme (as defined in section 1 of the Pension Schemes Act 1993) established under a trust, and
(b) references to the employer, in relation to such a scheme, are to an employer of persons in the description *or category* of employment to which the scheme relates[, and
(c) references to training are to training on the employer's premises or elsewhere.]

(4) For the purposes of this section the working hours of an employee shall be taken to be any time when, in accordance with his contract of employment, the employee is required to be at work.

NOTES

Sub-s (2A): inserted by the Welfare Reform and Pensions Act 1999, s 18, Sch 2, para 19(1), (3).

Sub-s (3): words in italics in para (b) repealed by the Pensions Act 2004, s 320, Sch 13, Pt 1, as from a day to be appointed; para (c) and word immediately preceding it added by the Teaching and Higher Education Act 1998, s 44(1), Sch 3, para 12.

Conciliation: see the note following the Part heading *ante*.

[1.929]

59 Right to payment for time off under section 58

(1) An employer who permits an employee to take time off under section 58 shall pay him for the time taken off pursuant to the permission.

(2) Where the employee's remuneration for the work he would ordinarily have been doing during that time does not vary with the amount of work done, he must be paid as if he had worked at that work for the whole of that time.

(3) Where the employee's remuneration for the work he would ordinarily have been doing during that time varies with the amount of work done, he must be paid an amount calculated by reference to the average hourly earnings for that work.

(4) The average hourly earnings mentioned in subsection (3) are—

(a) those of the employee concerned, or

(b) if no fair estimate can be made of those earnings, the average hourly earnings for work of that description of persons in comparable employment with the same employer or, if there are no such persons, a figure of average hourly earnings which is reasonable in the circumstances.

(5) A right to be paid an amount under subsection (1) does not affect any right of an employee in relation to remuneration under his contract of employment ("contractual remuneration").

(6) Any contractual remuneration paid to an employee in respect of a period of time off under section 58 goes towards discharging any liability of the employer under subsection (1) in respect of that period; and, conversely, any payment under subsection (1) in respect of a period goes towards discharging any liability of the employer to pay contractual remuneration in respect of that period.

NOTES

Conciliation: see the note following the Part heading *ante*.

[1.930]

60 Complaints to [employment tribunals]

(1) An employee may present a complaint to an [employment tribunal] that his employer—

(a) has failed to permit him to take time off as required by section 58, or

(b) has failed to pay him in accordance with section 59.

(2) An [employment tribunal] shall not consider a complaint under this section unless it is presented—

(a) before the end of the period of three months beginning with the date when the failure occurred, or

(b) within such further period as the tribunal considers reasonable in a case where it is satisfied that it was not reasonably practicable for the complaint to be presented before the end of that period of three months.

[(2A) Section 207A(3) (extension because of mediation in certain European cross-border disputes) [and section 207B (extension of time limits to facilitate conciliation before institution of proceedings) apply] for the purposes of subsection (2)(a).]

(3) Where an [employment tribunal] finds a complaint under subsection (1)(a) well-founded, the tribunal—

(a) shall make a declaration to that effect, and

(b) may make an award of compensation to be paid by the employer to the employee.

(4) The amount of the compensation shall be such as the tribunal considers just and equitable in all the circumstances having regard to—

(a) the employer's default in failing to permit time off to be taken by the employee, and

(b) any loss sustained by the employee which is attributable to the matters complained of.

(5) Where on a complaint under subsection (1)(b) an [employment tribunal] finds that an employer has failed to pay an employee in accordance with section 59, it shall order the employer to pay the amount which it finds to be due.

NOTES

Section heading, sub-ss (1)–(3), (5): words in square brackets substituted by the Employment Rights (Dispute Resolution) Act 1998, s 1(2)(a), (b).

Sub-s (2A): inserted by the Cross-Border Mediation (EU Directive) Regulations 2011, SI 2011/1133, regs 30, 39; words in square brackets substituted by the Enterprise and Regulatory Reform Act 2013, s 8, Sch 2, paras 15, 25; substituted by the Cross-Border Mediation (EU Directive) (EU Exit) Regulations 2019, SI 2019/469, reg 4, Sch 1, Pt 1, para 12(1), (15), as from exit day (as defined in the European Union (Withdrawal) Act 2018, s 20), as follows—

"(2A) Section 207B (extension of time limits to facilitate conciliation before institution of proceedings) applies for the purposes of subsection (2)(a).".

Conciliation: see the note following the Part heading *ante*.

Employee representatives

[1.931]

61 Right to time off for employee representatives

(1) An employee who is—

(a) an employee representative for the purposes of Chapter II of Part IV of the Trade Union and Labour Relations (Consolidation) Act 1992 (redundancies) or [regulations 9, 13 and 15 of the Transfer of Undertakings (Protection of Employment) Regulations 2006], or

(b) a candidate in an election in which any person elected will, on being elected, be such an employee representative,

is entitled to be permitted by his employer to take reasonable time off during the employee's working hours in order to perform his functions as such an employee representative or candidate [or in order to undergo training to perform such functions].

(2) For the purposes of this section the working hours of an employee shall be taken to be any time when, in accordance with his contract of employment, the employee is required to be at work.

NOTES

Sub-s (1): words in square brackets in para (a) substituted by the Transfer of Undertakings (Protection of Employment) Regulations 2006, SI 2006/246, reg 20, Sch 2, para 10; words in second pair of square brackets added by the Collective Redundancies and Transfer of Undertakings (Protection of Employment) (Amendment) Regulations 1999, SI 1999/1925, reg 15.

Conciliation: see the note following the Part heading *ante*.

[1.932]

62 Right to remuneration for time off under section 61

(1) An employee who is permitted to take time off under section 61 is entitled to be paid remuneration by his employer for the time taken off at the appropriate hourly rate.

(2) The appropriate hourly rate, in relation to an employee, is the amount of one week's pay divided by the number of normal working hours in a week for that employee when employed under the contract of employment in force on the day when the time off is taken.

(3) But where the number of normal working hours differs from week to week or over a longer period, the amount of one week's pay shall be divided instead by—

(a) the average number of normal working hours calculated by dividing by twelve the total number of the employee's normal working hours during the period of twelve weeks ending with the last complete week before the day on which the time off is taken, or

(b) where the employee has not been employed for a sufficient period to enable the calculation to be made under paragraph (a), a number which fairly represents the number of normal working hours in a week having regard to such of the considerations specified in subsection (4) as are appropriate in the circumstances.

(4) The considerations referred to in subsection (3)(b) are—

(a) the average number of normal working hours in a week which the employee could expect in accordance with the terms of his contract, and

(b) the average number of normal working hours of other employees engaged in relevant comparable employment with the same employer.

(5) A right to any amount under subsection (1) does not affect any right of an employee in relation to remuneration under his contract of employment ("contractual remuneration").

(6) Any contractual remuneration paid to an employee in respect of a period of time off under section 61 goes towards discharging any liability of the employer to pay remuneration under subsection (1) in respect of that period; and, conversely, any payment of remuneration under subsection (1) in respect of a period goes towards discharging any liability of the employer to pay contractual remuneration in respect of that period.

NOTES

Conciliation: see the note following the Part heading *ante*.

[1.933]

63 Complaints to [employment tribunals]

(1) An employee may present a complaint to an [employment tribunal] that his employer—

(a) has unreasonably refused to permit him to take time off as required by section 61, or

(b) has failed to pay the whole or any part of any amount to which the employee is entitled under section 62.

(2) An [employment tribunal] shall not consider a complaint under this section unless it is presented—

(a) before the end of the period of three months beginning with the day on which the time off was taken or on which it is alleged the time off should have been permitted, or

(b) within such further period as the tribunal considers reasonable in a case where it is satisfied that it was not reasonably practicable for the complaint to be presented before the end of that period of three months.

[(2A) Section 207A(3) (extension because of mediation in certain European cross-border disputes) [and section 207B (extension of time limits to facilitate conciliation before institution of proceedings) apply] for the purposes of subsection (2)(a).]

(3) Where an [employment tribunal] finds a complaint under this section well-founded, the tribunal shall make a declaration to that effect.

(4) If the complaint is that the employer has unreasonably refused to permit the employee to take time off, the tribunal shall also order the employer to pay to the employee an amount equal to the remuneration to which he would have been entitled under section 62 if the employer had not refused.

(5) If the complaint is that the employer has failed to pay the employee the whole or part of any amount to which he is entitled under section 62, the tribunal shall also order the employer to pay to the employee the amount which it finds due to him.

NOTES

Section heading, sub-ss (1)–(3): words in square brackets substituted by the Employment Rights (Dispute Resolution) Act 1998, s 1(2)(a), (b).

Sub-s (2A): inserted by the Cross-Border Mediation (EU Directive) Regulations 2011, SI 2011/1133, regs 30, 40; words in square brackets substituted by the Enterprise and Regulatory Reform Act 2013, s 8, Sch 2, paras 15, 26; substituted by the Cross-Border Mediation (EU Directive) (EU Exit) Regulations 2019, SI 2019/469, reg 4, Sch 1, Pt 1, para 12(1), (16), as from exit day (as defined in the European Union (Withdrawal) Act 2018, s 20), as follows—

"(2A) Section 207B (extension of time limits to facilitate conciliation before institution of proceedings) applies for the purposes of subsection (2)(a).".

Conciliation: see the note following the Part heading *ante*.

[1.934]

[63A Right to time off for young person [in Wales or Scotland] for study or training

(1) An employee who—

(a) is aged 16 or 17,

(b) is not receiving full-time secondary or further education, and

(c) has not attained such standard of achievement as is prescribed by regulations made by the Secretary of State,

is entitled to be permitted by his employer to take time off during the employee's working hours in order to undertake study or training leading to a relevant qualification.

(2) In this section—

(a) "secondary education"—

(i) in relation to England and Wales, has the same meaning as in the Education Act 1996, and

(ii) in relation to Scotland, has the same meaning as in section 135(2)(b) of the Education (Scotland) Act 1980;

(b) "further education"—

(i) in relation to England and Wales, [has the same meaning as in the Education Act 1996,] and

(ii) in relation to Scotland, has the same meaning as in section 1(3) of the Further and Higher Education (Scotland) Act 1992; and

(c) "relevant qualification" means an external qualification the attainment of which—

(i) would contribute to the attainment of the standard prescribed for the purposes of subsection (1)(c), and

(ii) would be likely to enhance the employee's employment prospects (whether with his employer or otherwise);

and for the purposes of paragraph (c) "external qualification" means an academic or vocational qualification awarded or authenticated by such person or body as may be specified in or under regulations made by the Secretary of State.

(3) An employee who—

(a) satisfies the requirements of paragraphs (a) to (c) of subsection (1), and

(b) is for the time being supplied by his employer to another person ("the principal") to perform work in accordance with a contract made between the employer and the principal,

is entitled to be permitted by the principal to take time off during the employee's working hours in order to undertake study or training leading to a relevant qualification.

(4) Where an employee—

(a) is aged 18,

(b) is undertaking study or training leading to a relevant qualification, and

(c) began such study or training before attaining that age,

subsections (1) and (3) shall apply to the employee, in relation to that study or training, as if "or 18" were inserted at the end of subsection (1)(a).

(5) The amount of time off which an employee is to be permitted to take under this section, and the occasions on which and any conditions subject to which time off may be so taken, are those that are reasonable in all the circumstances having regard, in particular, to—

(a) the requirements of the employee's study or training, and

(b) the circumstances of the business of the employer or the principal and the effect of the employee's time off on the running of that business.

[(5A) References in this section to an employee do not include a person to whom Part 1 of the Education and Skills Act 2008 (duty to participate in education or training for 16 and 17 year olds in England) applies, or is treated by section 29 of that Act (extension for person reaching 18) as applying.]

(6) Regulations made for the purposes of subsections (1)(c) and (2) may make different provision for different cases, and in particular may make different provision in relation to England, Wales and Scotland respectively.

(7) References in this section to study or training are references to study or training on the premises of the employer or (as the case may be) principal or elsewhere.

(8) For the purposes of this section the working hours of an employee shall be taken to be any time when, in accordance with his contract of employment, the employee is required to be at work.]

NOTES

Inserted by the Teaching and Higher Education Act 1998, s 32.

Section heading: words in square brackets inserted by the Education and Skills Act 2008, s 39(1), (2).

Sub-s (2): words in square brackets substituted by the Learning and Skills Act 2000, s 149, Sch 9, paras 1, 50.

Sub-s (5A): inserted by the Education and Skills Act 2008, s 39(1), (2).

Conciliation: see the note following the Part heading *ante*.

Transfer of functions: functions under sub-ss (1)(c) and (2) are transferred, in so far as they are exercisable in or as regards Scotland, to the Scottish Ministers subject to the requirement that they are exercisable only after consultation with the Secretary of State, by the Scotland Act 1998 (Transfer of Functions to the Scottish Ministers etc) Order 1999, SI 1999/1750, art 2, Sch 1.

Regulations: the Right to Time Off for Study or Training (Scotland) Regulations 1999, SI 1999/1058; the Right to Time Off for Study or Training Regulations 2001, SI 2001/2801; the Right to Time Off for Study or Training (Scotland) Amendment Regulations 2001, SSI 2001/211; the Right to Time Off for Study or Training (Scotland) Amendment (No 2) Regulations 2001, SSI 2001/298.

[1.935]

[63B Right to remuneration for time off under section 63A

(1) An employee who is permitted to take time off under section 63A is entitled to be paid remuneration by his employer for the time taken off at the appropriate hourly rate.

(2) The appropriate hourly rate, in relation to an employee, is the amount of one week's pay divided by the number of normal working hours in a week for that employee when employed under the contract of employment in force on the day when the time off is taken.

(3) But where the number of normal working hours differs from week to week or over a longer period, the amount of one week's pay shall be divided instead by—

(a) the average number of normal working hours calculated by dividing by twelve the total number of the employee's working hours during the period of twelve weeks ending with the last complete week before the day on which the time off is taken, or

(b) where the employee has not been employed for a sufficient period to enable the calculation to be made under paragraph (a), a number which fairly represents the number of normal working hours in a week having regard to such of the considerations specified in subsection (4) as are appropriate in the circumstances.

(4) The considerations referred to in subsection (3)(b) are—

(a) the average number of normal working hours in a week which the employee could expect in accordance with the terms of his contract, and

(b) the average number of normal working hours of other employees engaged in relevant comparable employment with the same employer.

(5) A right to any amount under subsection (1) does not affect any right of an employee in relation to remuneration under his contract of employment ("contractual remuneration").

(6) Any contractual remuneration paid to an employee in respect of a period of time off under section 63A goes towards discharging any liability of the employer to pay remuneration under subsection (1) in respect of that period; and, conversely, any payment of remuneration under subsection (1) in respect of a period goes towards discharging any liability of the employer to pay contractual remuneration in respect of that period.]

NOTES

Inserted, together with s 63C, by the Teaching and Higher Education Act 1998, s 33.

Conciliation: see the note following the Part heading *ante*.

[1.936]

[63C Complaints to employment tribunals

(1) An employee may present a complaint to an employment tribunal that—

(a) his employer, or the principal referred to in subsection (3) of section 63A, has unreasonably refused to permit him to take time off as required by that section, or

(b) his employer has failed to pay the whole or any part of any amount to which the employee is entitled under section 63B.

(2) An employment tribunal shall not consider a complaint under this section unless it is presented—

(a) before the end of the period of three months beginning with the day on which the time off was taken or on which it is alleged the time off should have been permitted, or

(b) within such further period as the tribunal considers reasonable in a case where it is satisfied that it was not reasonably practicable for the complaint to be presented before the end of that period of three months.

[(2A) Section 207A(3) (extension because of mediation in certain European cross-border disputes) [and section 207B (extension of time limits to facilitate conciliation before institution of proceedings) apply] for the purposes of subsection (2)(a).]

(3) Where an employment tribunal finds a complaint under this section well-founded, the tribunal shall make a declaration to that effect.

(4) If the complaint is that the employer or the principal has unreasonably refused to permit the employee to take time off, the tribunal shall also order the employer or the principal, as the case may be, to pay to the employee an amount equal to the remuneration to which he would have been entitled under section 63B if the employer or the principal had not refused.

(5) If the complaint is that the employer has failed to pay the employee the whole or part of any amount to which he is entitled under section 63B, the tribunal shall also order the employer to pay to the employee the amount which it finds due to him.]

NOTES

Inserted as noted to s 63B at **[1.935]**.

Sub-s (2A): inserted by the Cross-Border Mediation (EU Directive) Regulations 2011, SI 2011/1133, regs 30, 41; words in square brackets substituted by the Enterprise and Regulatory Reform Act 2013, s 8, Sch 2, paras 15, 27; substituted by the Cross-Border Mediation (EU Directive) (EU Exit) Regulations 2019, SI 2019/469, reg 4, Sch 1, Pt 1, para 12(1), (17), as from exit day (as defined in the European Union (Withdrawal) Act 2018, s 20), as follows—

"(2A) Section 207B (extension of time limits to facilitate conciliation before institution of proceedings) applies for the purposes of subsection (2)(a).".

Conciliation: see the note following the Part heading *ante*.

[PART 6A
STUDY AND TRAINING

[1.937]

63D Statutory right to make request in relation to study or training

(1) A qualifying employee may make an application under this section to his or her employer.

(2) An application under this section (a "section 63D application") is an application that meets—

(a) the conditions in subsections (3) to (5), and

(b) any further conditions specified by the Secretary of State in regulations.

(3) The application must be made for the purpose of enabling the employee to undertake study or training (or both) within subsection (4).

(4) Study or training is within this subsection if its purpose is to improve—

(a) the employee's effectiveness in the employer's business, and

(b) the performance of the employer's business.

(5) The application must state that it is an application under this section.

(6) An employee is a qualifying employee for the purposes of this section if the employee—

(a) satisfies any conditions about duration of employment specified by the Secretary of State in regulations, and

(b) is not a person within subsection (7).

(7) The following persons are within this subsection—

(a) a person of compulsory school age (or, in Scotland, school age);

(b) a person to whom Part 1 of the Education and Skills Act 2008 (duty to participate in education or training for 16 and 17 year olds) applies;

(c) a person who, by virtue of section 29 of that Act, is treated as a person to whom that Part applies for the purposes specified in that section (extension for person reaching 18);

(d) a person to whom section 63A of this Act (right to time off for young person for study or training) applies;

(e) an agency worker;

(f) a person of a description specified by the Secretary of State in regulations.

(8) Nothing in this Part prevents an employee and an employer from making any other arrangements in relation to study or training.

(9) In this section—

"agency worker" means a worker supplied by a person (the "agent") to do work for another person (the "principal") under a contract or other arrangement between the agent and principal;

"compulsory school age" has the meaning given in section 8 of the Education Act 1996;

"school age" has the meaning given in section 31 of the Education (Scotland) Act 1980.]

NOTES

Commencement: 6 April 2010 (except in relation to small employers and their employees); to be appointed (otherwise).

Part 6A (ss 63D–63K) was inserted by the Apprenticeships, Skills, Children and Learning Act 2009, s 40(1), (2), as from 6 April 2010 (except in relation to small employers and their employees), and as from a day to be appointed (otherwise) (see further the notes below).

Meaning of "small employers", etc: the Apprenticeships, Skills, Children and Learning Act 2009 (Commencement No 2 and Transitional and Saving Provisions) Order 2010, SI 2010/303, Sch 3 provides as follows—

"(1) "small employer" means an employer who employs fewer than 250 employees.

(2) For the purposes of (1) above—

(a) Subject to (3) below, the number of employees employed by an employer at any time shall be determined by ascertaining the average number of employees employed by the employer in the previous twelve months, calculated in accordance with (b).

(b) The average number of employees employed by an employer in a twelve month period is to be ascertained by determining the number of employees employed by the employer in each month in the twelve month period (whether they were employed throughout the month or not), adding together those monthly figures and dividing the number by 12.

(3) If the undertaking has been in existence for less than twelve months, the references to twelve months in (2)(a) and (b) and the divisor of 12 referred to in (2)(b), are to be replaced by the number of months the undertaking has been in existence.".

Note also that by virtue of the Apprenticeships, Skills, Children and Learning Act 2009 (Commencement No 2 and Transitional and Saving Provisions) Order 2010, SI 2010/303, art 7 and Sch 6, section 40 of the 2009 Act was due to come into force for all remaining purposes on 6 April 2011. However, art 7 of, and Sch 6 to, the 2010 Order were revoked by the Apprenticeships, Skills, Children and Learning Act 2009 (Commencement No 2 and Transitional and Saving Provisions) Order

2010 (Amendment) Order 2011, SI 2011/882, art 2, as from 21 March 2011. Therefore, section 40 did not come into force for all remaining purposes on 6 April 2011 and, as at 15 May 2019, has not been commenced for such other purposes.

Regulations: the Employee Study and Training (Qualifying Period of Employment) Regulations 2010, SI 2010/800 at **[2.1178]** (which provide that employees must have 26 weeks' continuous service in order to be a qualifying employee for the purposes of this section).

[1.938]

[63E Section 63D application: supplementary

(1) A section 63D application may—

(a) be made in relation to study or training of any description (subject to section 63D(3) and (4) and regulations under section 63D(2));

(b) relate to more than one description of study or training.

(2) The study or training may (in particular) be study or training that (if undertaken)—

(a) would be undertaken on the employer's premises or elsewhere (including at the employee's home);

(b) would be undertaken by the employee while performing the duties of the employee's employment or separately;

(c) would be provided or supervised by the employer or by someone else;

(d) would be undertaken without supervision;

(e) would be undertaken within or outside the United Kingdom.

(3) The study or training need not be intended to lead to the award of a qualification to the employee.

(4) A section 63D application must—

(a) give the following details of the proposed study or training—

(i) its subject matter;

(ii) where and when it would take place;

(iii) who would provide or supervise it;

(iv) what qualification (if any) it would lead to;

(b) explain how the employee thinks the proposed study or training would improve—

(i) the employee's effectiveness in the employer's business, and

(ii) the performance of the employer's business;

(c) contain information of any other description specified by the Secretary of State in regulations.

(5) The Secretary of State may make regulations about—

(a) the form of a section 63D application;

(b) when a section 63D application is to be taken to be received for the purposes of this Part.]

NOTES

Commencement: 6 April 2010 (except in relation to small employers and their employees); to be appointed (otherwise).

Inserted by the Apprenticeships, Skills, Children and Learning Act 2009, s 40 as noted to s 63D at **[1.937]** (see further the notes to that section regarding the meaning of "small employer" and the delayed commencement of s 40 of the 2009 Act).

Regulations: the Employee Study and Training (Eligibility, Complaints and Remedies) Regulations 2010, SI 2010/156 at **[2.1131]**.

[1.939]

[63F Employer's duties in relation to application

(1) Subsections (4) to (7) apply if—

(a) an employer receives a section 63D application (the "current application") from an employee, and

(b) during the relevant 12 month period the employer has not received another section 63D application (an "earlier application") from the employee.

(2) The "relevant 12 month period" is the 12 month period ending with the day on which the employer receives the current application.

(3) The Secretary of State may make regulations about circumstances in which, at an employee's request, an employer is to be required to ignore an earlier application for the purposes of subsection (1).

(4) The employer must deal with the application in accordance with regulations made by the Secretary of State.

(5) The employer may refuse a section 63D application only if the employer thinks that one or more of the permissible grounds for refusal applies in relation to the application.

(6) The employer may refuse part of a section 63D application only if the employer thinks that one or more of the permissible grounds for refusal applies in relation to that part.

(7) The permissible grounds for refusal are—

(a) that the proposed study or training to which the application, or the part in question, relates would not improve—

(i) the employee's effectiveness in the employer's business, or

(ii) the performance of the employer's business;

(b) the burden of additional costs;

(c) detrimental effect on ability to meet customer demand;

(d) inability to re-organise work among existing staff;

(e) inability to recruit additional staff;

(f) detrimental impact on quality;

(g) detrimental impact on performance;

(h) insufficiency of work during the periods the employee proposes to work;

(i) planned structural changes;

(j) any other grounds specified by the Secretary of State in regulations.]

NOTES

Commencement: 6 April 2010 (except in relation to small employers and their employees); to be appointed (otherwise).

Inserted by the Apprenticeships, Skills, Children and Learning Act 2009, s 40 as noted to s 63D at **[1.937]** (see further the notes to that section regarding the meaning of "small employer" and the delayed commencement of s 40 of the 2009 Act).

Regulations: the Employee Study and Training (Procedural Requirements) Regulations 2010, SI 2010/155 at **[2.1110]**.

[1.940]

[63G Regulations about dealing with applications

(1) Regulations under section 63F(4) may, in particular, include provision—

(a) for the employee to have a right to be accompanied by a person of a specified description when attending meetings held in relation to a section 63D application in accordance with any such regulations;

(b) for the postponement of such a meeting if the employee's companion under paragraph (a) is not available to attend it;

(c) in relation to companions under paragraph (a), corresponding to section 10(6) and (7) of the Employment Relations Act 1999 (right to paid time off to act as companion, etc);

(d) in relation to the rights under paragraphs (a) to (c), for rights to complain to an employment tribunal and not to be subjected to a detriment, and about unfair dismissal;

(e) for section 63D applications to be treated as withdrawn in specified circumstances.

(2) In this section "specified" means specified in the regulations.]

NOTES

Commencement: 6 April 2010 (except in relation to small employers and their employees); to be appointed (otherwise).

Inserted by the Apprenticeships, Skills, Children and Learning Act 2009, s 40 as noted to s 63D at **[1.937]** (see further the notes to that section regarding the meaning of "small employer" and the delayed commencement of s 40 of the 2009 Act).

[1.941]

[63H Employee's duties in relation to agreed study or training

(1) This section applies if an employer has agreed to a section 63D application, or part of a section 63D application, made by an employee in relation to particular study or training (the "agreed study or training").

(2) The employee must inform the employer if the employee—

(a) fails to start the agreed study or training;

(b) fails to complete the agreed study or training;

(c) undertakes, or proposes to undertake, study or training that differs from the agreed study or training in any respect (including those specified in section 63E(4)(a)).

(3) The Secretary of State may make regulations about the way in which the employee is to comply with the duty under subsection (2).]

NOTES

Commencement: 6 April 2010 (except in relation to small employers and their employees); to be appointed (otherwise).

Inserted by the Apprenticeships, Skills, Children and Learning Act 2009, s 40 as noted to s 63D at **[1.937]** (see further the notes to that section regarding the meaning of "small employer" and the delayed commencement of s 40 of the 2009 Act).

Regulations: the Employee Study and Training (Procedural Requirements) Regulations 2010, SI 2010/155 at **[2.1110]**.

[1.942]

[63I Complaints to employment tribunals

(1) An employee who makes a section 63D application may present a complaint to an employment tribunal that—

(a) the employer has failed to comply with section 63F(4), (5) or (6), or

(b) the employer's decision to refuse the application, or part of it, is based on incorrect facts.

This is subject to the following provisions of this section.

(2) No complaint under this section may be made in respect of a section 63D application which has been disposed of by agreement or withdrawn.

(3) In the case of a section 63D application that has not been disposed of by agreement or withdrawn, a complaint under this section may only be made if the employer—

(a) notifies the employee of a decision to refuse the application (or part of it) on appeal, or

(b) commits a breach of regulations under section 63F(4), where the breach is of a description specified by the Secretary of State in regulations.

(4) No complaint under this section may be made in respect of failure to comply with provision included in regulations under section 63F(4) because of—

(a) section 63G(1)(a) or (b), if provision is included in regulations under section 63F(4) by virtue of section 63G(1)(d), or

(b) section 63G(1)(c).

(5) An employment tribunal may not consider a complaint under this section unless the complaint is presented—

(a) before the end of the period of three months beginning with the relevant date, or

(b) within any further period that the tribunal considers reasonable, if the tribunal is satisfied that it was not reasonably practicable for the complaint to be presented before the end of that period of three months.

(6) The relevant date is—

(a) in the case of a complaint permitted by subsection (3)(a), the date on which the employee is notified of the decision on the appeal;

(b) in the case of a complaint permitted by subsection (3)(b), the date on which the breach was committed.

[(7) Section 207A(3) (extension because of mediation in certain European cross-border disputes) [and section 207B (extension of time limits to facilitate conciliation before institution of proceedings) apply] to subsection (5)(a).]]

NOTES

Commencement: 6 April 2010 (except in relation to small employers and their employees); to be appointed (otherwise).

Inserted by the Apprenticeships, Skills, Children and Learning Act 2009, s 40 as noted to s 63D at **[1.937]** (see further the notes to that section regarding the meaning of "small employer" and the delayed commencement of s 40 of the 2009 Act).

Sub-s (7): added by the Cross-Border Mediation (EU Directive) Regulations 2011, SI 2011/1133, regs 30, 42; words in square brackets substituted by the Enterprise and Regulatory Reform Act 2013, s 8, Sch 2, paras 15, 28; substituted by the Cross-Border Mediation (EU Directive) (EU Exit) Regulations 2019, SI 2019/469, reg 4, Sch 1, Pt 1, para 12(1), (18), as from exit day (as defined in the European Union (Withdrawal) Act 2018, s 20), as follows—

"(7) Section 207B (extension of time limits to facilitate conciliation before institution of proceedings) applies to subsection (5)(a).".

Conciliation: employment tribunal proceedings under this section are "relevant proceedings" for the purposes of the conciliation provisions contained in the Employment Tribunals Act 1996, ss 18–18C; see s 18(1)(b) of the 1996 Act at **[1.757]**.

Regulations: the Employee Study and Training (Eligibility, Complaints and Remedies) Regulations 2010, SI 2010/156 at **[2.1131]**.

[1.943]

[63J Remedies

(1) If an employment tribunal finds a complaint under section 63I well-founded it must make a declaration to that effect and may—

(a) make an order for reconsideration of the section 63D application;

(b) make an award of compensation to be paid by the employer to the employee.

(2) The amount of any compensation must be the amount the tribunal considers just and equitable in all the circumstances, but must not exceed the permitted maximum.

(3) The permitted maximum is the number of weeks' pay specified by the Secretary of State in regulations.

(4) If an employment tribunal makes an order under subsection (1)(a), section 63F and regulations under that section apply as if the application had been received on the date of the order (instead of on the date it was actually received).]

NOTES

Commencement: 6 April 2010 (except in relation to small employers and their employees); to be appointed (otherwise).

Inserted by the Apprenticeships, Skills, Children and Learning Act 2009, s 40 as noted to s 63D at **[1.937]** (see further the notes to that section regarding the meaning of "small employer" and the delayed commencement of s 40 of the 2009 Act).

Regulations: the Employee Study and Training (Eligibility, Complaints and Remedies) Regulations 2010, SI 2010/156 at **[2.1131]**.

[1.944]

[63K Supplementary

Regulations under this Part may make different provision for different cases.]

NOTES

Commencement: 6 April 2010 (except in relation to small employers and their employees); to be appointed (otherwise).

Inserted by the Apprenticeships, Skills, Children and Learning Act 2009, s 40 as noted to s 63D at **[1.937]** (see further the notes to that section regarding the meaning of "small employer" and the delayed commencement of s 40 of the 2009 Act).

Regulations: the Employee Study and Training (Eligibility, Complaints and Remedies) Regulations 2010, SI 2010/156 at **[2.1131]**.

PART VII
SUSPENSION FROM WORK

NOTES

Recoupment of social security benefits: as to the power to provide for recoupment of social security benefits in relation to payments by employers to employees under this Part, that are the subject of proceedings before employment tribunals, see the Employment Tribunals Act 1996, s 16 at **[1.755]**.

Suspension on medical grounds

[1.945]

64 Right to remuneration on suspension on medical grounds

(1) An employee who is suspended from work by his employer on medical grounds is entitled to be paid by his employer remuneration while he is so suspended for a period not exceeding twenty-six weeks.

(2) For the purposes of this Part an employee is suspended from work on medical grounds if he is suspended from work in consequence of—

(a) a requirement imposed by or under a provision of an enactment or of an instrument made under an enactment, or

(b) a recommendation in a provision of a code of practice issued or approved under section 16 of the Health and Safety at Work etc Act 1974,

and the provision is for the time being specified in subsection (3).

(3) The provisions referred to in subsection (2) are—

Regulation16 of the Control of Lead at Work Regulations 1980,

[Regulation 25 of the Ionising Radiations Regulation 2017 (SI 2017/1075)], and

Regulation 11 of the Control of Substances Hazardous to Health Regulations 1988.

(4) The Secretary of State may by order add provisions to or remove provisions from the list of provisions specified in subsection (3).

(5) For the purposes of this Part an employee shall be regarded as suspended from work on medical grounds only if and for so long as he—

(a) continues to be employed by his employer, but

(b) is not provided with work or does not perform the work he normally performed before the suspension.

NOTES

Sub-s (3): words in square brackets substituted by the Ionising Radiations Regulations 2017, SI 2017/1075, reg 42(1), Sch 9, para 2, as from 1 January 2018.

Control of Lead at Work Regulations 1980, SI 1980/1248: revoked and replaced by the Control of Lead at Work Regulations 1998, SI 1998/543 (revoked). See now, the Control of Substances Hazardous to Health Regulations 2002, SI 2002/2677.

The reference to the Control of Substances Hazardous to Health Regulations 1988 is an apparent drafting error as these regulations had been revoked and replaced by the (largely consolidating) Control of Substances Hazardous to Health Regulations 1994, SI 1994/3246. See now the Control of Substances Hazardous to Health Regulations 2002, SI 2002/2677.

[1.946]

65 Exclusions from right to remuneration

(1) An employee is not entitled to remuneration under section 64 unless he has been continuously employed for a period of not less than one month ending with the day before that on which the suspension begins.

(2) . . .

(3) An employee is not entitled to remuneration under section 64 in respect of any period during which he is incapable of work by reason of disease or bodily or mental disablement.

(4) An employee is not entitled to remuneration under section 64 in respect of any period if—

(a) his employer has offered to provide him with suitable alternative work during the period (whether or not it is work which the employee is under his contract, or was under the contract in force before the suspension, employed to perform) and the employee has unreasonably refused to perform that work, or

(b) he does not comply with reasonable requirements imposed by his employer with a view to ensuring that his services are available.

NOTES

Sub-s (2): repealed by the Fixed-term Employees (Prevention of Less Favourable Treatment) Regulations 2002, SI 2002/2034, reg 11, Sch 2, Pt 1, para 3(1), (3) (except in relation to Government training schemes, agency workers and apprentices; see regs 18–20 of the 2002 Regulations at **[2.571]** et seq).

Suspension on maternity grounds

[1.947]

66 Meaning of suspension on maternity grounds

(1) For the purposes of this Part an employee is suspended from work on maternity grounds if, in consequence of any relevant requirement or relevant recommendation, she is suspended from work by her employer on the ground that she is pregnant, has recently given birth or is breastfeeding a child.

(2) In subsection (1)—

"relevant requirement" means a requirement imposed by or under a specified provision of an enactment or of an instrument made under an enactment, and

"relevant recommendation" means a recommendation in a specified provision of a code of practice issued or approved under section 16 of the Health and Safety at Work etc Act 1974;

and in this subsection "specified provision" means a provision for the time being specified in an order made by the Secretary of State under this subsection.

(3) For the purposes of this Part an employee shall be regarded as suspended from work on maternity grounds only if and for so long as she—

(a) continues to be employed by her employer, but

(b) is not provided with work or (disregarding alternative work for the purposes of section 67) does not perform the work she normally performed before the suspension.

NOTES

Modified, in relation to governing bodies with delegated budgets, by the Education (Modification of Enactments Relating to Employment) (England) Order 2003, SI 2003/1964, art 3, Schedule at **[2.685]**, **[2.689]** and the Education (Modification of Enactments Relating to Employment) (Wales) Order 2006, SI 2006/1073, art 3, Schedule at **[2.915]**, **[2.918]**.

Orders: the Suspension from Work on Maternity Grounds (Merchant Shipping and Fishing Vessels) Order 1998, SI 1998/587, specifying regs 8(3) and 9(2) of the Merchant Shipping and Fishing Vessels (Health and Safety at Work) Regulations 1997, SI 1997/2962, for the purposes of this section. Also, by virtue of s 241 of, and Sch 2, Pt I, paras 1–4 to, this Act, the Suspension from Work (on Maternity Grounds) Order 1994, SI 1994/2930 has effect as if made under this section. That Order now has the effect of specifying regs 16(3) and 17 of the Management of Health and Safety at Work Regulations 1999, SI 1999/3242 for the purposes of this section.

[1.948]

67 Right to offer of alternative work

(1) Where an employer has available suitable alternative work for an employee, the employee has a right to be offered to be provided with the alternative work before being suspended from work on maternity grounds.

(2) For alternative work to be suitable for an employee for the purposes of this section—

(a) the work must be of a kind which is both suitable in relation to her and appropriate for her to do in the circumstances, and

(b) the terms and conditions applicable to her for performing the work, if they differ from the corresponding terms and conditions applicable to her for performing the work she normally performs under her contract of employment, must not be substantially less favourable to her than those corresponding terms and conditions.

NOTES

Modified as noted to s 66 at **[1.947]**.

[1.949]

68 Right to remuneration

(1) An employee who is suspended from work on maternity grounds is entitled to be paid remuneration by her employer while she is so suspended.

(2) An employee is not entitled to remuneration under this section in respect of any period if—

(a) her employer has offered to provide her during the period with work which is suitable alternative work for her for the purposes of section 67, and

(b) the employee has unreasonably refused to perform that work.

NOTES

Modified as noted to s 66 at **[1.947]**.

[Ending the supply of an agency worker on maternity grounds

[1.950]

68A Meaning of ending the supply of an agency worker on maternity grounds

(1) For the purposes of this Part the supply of an agency worker to a hirer is ended on maternity grounds if, in consequence of action taken pursuant to a provision listed in subsection (2), the supply of the agency worker to the hirer is ended on the ground that she is pregnant, has recently given birth or is breastfeeding a child.

(2) The provisions are—

(a) regulations 8(3) or 9(2) of the Merchant Shipping and Fishing Vessels (Health and Safety at Work) Regulations 1997;

(b) regulation 16A(2) or 17A of the Management of Health and Safety at Work Regulations 1999; or

(c) regulation 20 of the Conduct of Employment Agencies and Employment Businesses Regulations 2003.]

NOTES

Inserted, together with the preceding heading and ss 68B–68D, by the Agency Workers Regulations 2010, SI 2010/93, reg 25, Sch 2, Pt 1, paras 9, 12.

[1.951]

[68B Right to offer of alternative work

(1) Where the supply of an agency worker to a hirer is ended on maternity grounds and the temporary work agency has available suitable alternative work, the agency worker has a right to be offered to be proposed for such alternative work.

(2) For alternative work to be suitable for an agency worker for the purposes of this section—

(a) the work must be of a kind which is both suitable in relation to her and appropriate for her to do in the circumstances, and

(b) the terms and conditions applicable to her whilst performing the work, if they differ from the corresponding terms and conditions which would have applied to her but for the fact that the supply of the agency worker to the hirer was ended on maternity grounds, must not be substantially less favourable to her than those corresponding terms and conditions.

(3) Subsection (1) does not apply—

(a) where the agency worker has confirmed in writing that she no longer requires the work-finding services of the temporary work agency, or

(b) beyond the original intended duration, or likely duration, whichever is the longer, of the assignment which ended when the supply of the agency worker to the hirer was ended on maternity grounds.]

NOTES

Inserted as noted to s 68A at **[1.950]**.

[1.952]
[68C Right to remuneration

(1) Where the supply of an agency worker to a hirer is ended on maternity grounds, that agency worker is entitled to be paid remuneration by the temporary work agency.

(2) An agency worker is not entitled to remuneration under this section in respect of any period if—

(a) the temporary work agency has—

(i) offered to propose the agency worker to a hirer that has alternative work available which is suitable alternative work for her for the purposes of section 68B, or

(ii) proposed the agency worker to a hirer that has such suitable alternative work available, and that hirer has agreed to the supply of that agency worker, and

(b) the agency worker has unreasonably refused that offer or to perform that work.

(3) Nothing in this section imposes a duty on the temporary work agency to pay remuneration beyond the original intended duration, or likely duration, whichever is the longer, of the assignment which ended when the supply of the agency worker to the hirer was ended on maternity grounds.]

NOTES

Inserted as noted to s 68A at **[1.950]**.

[1.953]
[68D Agency workers: supplementary

(1) Without prejudice to any other duties of the hirer or temporary work agency under any enactment or rule of law sections 68A, 68B and 68C do not apply where the agency worker—

(a) has not completed the qualifying period, or

(b) is no longer entitled to the rights conferred by regulation 5 of the Agency Workers Regulations 2010 pursuant to regulation 8(a) or (b) of those Regulations.

(2) Nothing in those sections imposes a duty on the hirer or temporary work agency beyond the original intended duration, or likely duration of the assignment, whichever is the longer.

(3) Those sections do not apply where sections 66 to 68 apply.

(4) In this section and sections 68A to 68C the following have the same meaning as in the Agency Workers Regulations 2010—

"agency worker"
"assignment";
"hirer";
"qualifying period";
"temporary work agency".]

NOTES

Inserted as noted to s 68A at **[1.950]**.

General

[1.954]
69 Calculation of remuneration

(1) The amount of remuneration payable by an employer to an employee under section 64 or 68 is a week's pay in respect of each week of the period of suspension; and if in any week remuneration is payable in respect of only part of that week the amount of a week's pay shall be reduced proportionately.

(2) A right to remuneration under section 64 or 68 does not affect any right of an employee in relation to remuneration under the employee's contract of employment ("contractual remuneration").

(3) Any contractual remuneration paid by an employer to an employee in respect of any period goes towards discharging the employer's liability under section 64 or 68 in respect of that period; and, conversely, any payment of remuneration in discharge of an employer's liability under section 64 or 68 in respect of any period goes towards discharging any obligation of the employer to pay contractual remuneration in respect of that period.

[1.955]
[69A Calculation of remuneration (agency workers)

(1) The amount of remuneration payable by a temporary work agency to an agency worker under section 68C is a week's pay in respect of each week for which remuneration is payable in accordance with section 68C; and if in any week remuneration is payable in respect of only part of that week the amount of a week's pay shall be reduced proportionately.

(2) A right to remuneration under section 68C does not affect any right of the agency worker in relation to remuneration under the contract with the temporary work agency ("contractual remuneration").

(3) Any contractual remuneration paid by the temporary work agency to an agency worker in respect of any period goes towards discharging the temporary work agency's liability under section 68C in respect of that period; and, conversely, any payment of remuneration in discharge of a temporary work agency's liability under section 68C in respect of any period goes towards discharging any obligation of the temporary work agency to pay contractual remuneration in respect of that period.

(4) For the purposes of subsection (1), a week's pay is the weekly amount that would have been payable to the agency worker for performing the work, according to the terms of the contract with the temporary work agency, but for the fact that the supply of the agency worker to the hirer was ended on maternity grounds.

(5) Expressions used in this section and sections 68A to 68C have the same meaning as in those sections (see section 68D).]

NOTES

Inserted by the Agency Workers Regulations 2010, SI 2010/93, reg 25, Sch 2, Pt 1, paras 9, 13.

[1.956]

70 Complaints to [employment tribunals]

(1) An employee may present a complaint to an [employment tribunal] that his or her employer has failed to pay the whole or any part of remuneration to which the employee is entitled under section 64 or 68.

(2) An [employment tribunal] shall not consider a complaint under subsection (1) relating to remuneration in respect of any day unless it is presented—

(a) before the end of the period of three months beginning with that day, or

(b) within such further period as the tribunal considers reasonable in a case where it is satisfied that it was not reasonably practicable for the complaint to be presented within that period of three months.

(3) Where an [employment tribunal] finds a complaint under subsection (1) well-founded, the tribunal shall order the employer to pay the employee the amount of remuneration which it finds is due to him or her.

(4) An employee may present a complaint to an [employment tribunal] that in contravention of section 67 her employer has failed to offer to provide her with work.

(5) An [employment tribunal] shall not consider a complaint under subsection (4) unless it is presented—

(a) before the end of the period of three months beginning with the first day of the suspension, or

(b) within such further period as the tribunal considers reasonable in a case where it is satisfied that it was not reasonably practicable for the complaint to be presented within that period of three months.

(6) Where an [employment tribunal] finds a complaint under subsection (4) well-founded, the tribunal may make an award of compensation to be paid by the employer to the employee.

(7) The amount of the compensation shall be such as the tribunal considers just and equitable in all the circumstances having regard to—

(a) the infringement of the employee's right under section 67 by the failure on the part of the employer to which the complaint relates, and

(b) any loss sustained by the employee which is attributable to that failure.

[(8) Section 207A(3) (extension because of mediation in certain European cross-border disputes) [and section 207B (extension of time limits to facilitate conciliation before institution of proceedings) apply] for the purposes of subsections (2)(a) and (5)(a).]

NOTES

Section heading, sub-ss (1)–(6): words in square brackets substituted by the Employment Rights (Dispute Resolution) Act 1998, s 1(2)(a), (b).

Sub-s (8): added by the Cross-Border Mediation (EU Directive) Regulations 2011, SI 2011/1133, regs 30, 42; words in square brackets substituted by the Enterprise and Regulatory Reform Act 2013, s 8, Sch 2, paras 15, 29; substituted by the Cross-Border Mediation (EU Directive) (EU Exit) Regulations 2019, SI 2019/469, reg 4, Sch 1, Pt 1, para 12(1), (19), as from exit day (as defined in the European Union (Withdrawal) Act 2018, s 20), as follows—

"(8) Section 207B (extension of time limits to facilitate conciliation before institution of proceedings) applies for the purposes of subsections (2)(a) and (5)(a).".

Modified as noted to s 66 at **[1.947]**.

Conciliation: employment tribunal proceedings under this section are "relevant proceedings" for the purposes of the conciliation provisions contained in the Employment Tribunals Act 1996, ss 18–18C; see s 18(1)(b) of the 1996 Act at **[1.757]**.

Recoupment of social security benefits: see the note at the beginning of this Part.

[1.957]

[70A Complaints to employment tribunals: agency workers

(1) An agency worker may present a complaint to an employment tribunal that the temporary work agency has failed to pay the whole or any part of remuneration to which the agency worker is entitled under section 68C.

(2) An employment tribunal shall not consider a complaint under subsection (1) relating to remuneration in respect of any day unless it is presented—

(a) before the end of the period of three months beginning with the day on which the supply of the agency worker to a hirer was ended on maternity grounds, or

(b) within such further period as the tribunal considers reasonable in a case where it is satisfied that it was not reasonably practicable for the complaint to be presented within that period of three months.

(3) Where an employment tribunal finds a complaint under subsection (1) well-founded, the tribunal shall order the temporary work agency to pay the agency worker the amount of remuneration which it finds is due to her.

(4) An agency worker may present a complaint to an employment tribunal that in contravention of section 68B the temporary work agency has failed to offer to propose the agency worker to a hirer that has suitable alternative work available.

(5) An employment tribunal shall not consider a complaint under subsection (4) unless it is presented—

(a) before the end of the period of three months beginning with the day on which the supply of the agency worker to a hirer was ended on maternity grounds, or

(b) within such further period as the tribunal considers reasonable in a case where it is satisfied that it was not reasonably practicable for the complaint to be presented within that period of three months.

(6) Where an employment tribunal finds a complaint under subsection (4) well-founded, the tribunal shall order the temporary work agency to pay the agency worker the amount of compensation which it finds is due to her.

(7) The amount of the compensation shall be such as the tribunal considers just and equitable in all the circumstances having regard to—

(a) the infringement of the agency worker's right under section 68B by the failure on the part of the temporary work agency to which the complaint relates, and

(b) any loss sustained by the agency worker which is attributable to that failure.

[(7A) Section 207A(3) (extension because of mediation in certain European cross-border disputes) and section 207B (extension of time limits to facilitate conciliation before institution of proceedings) apply for the purposes of subsections (2)(a) and (5)(a).]

(8) Expressions used in this section and sections 68A to 68C have the same meaning as in those sections (see section 68D).]

NOTES

Inserted by the Agency Workers Regulations 2010, SI 2010/93, reg 25, Sch 2, Pt 1, paras 9, 14.

Sub-s (7A): inserted by the Enterprise and Regulatory Reform Act 2013, s 8, Sch 2, paras 15, 30; substituted by the Cross-Border Mediation (EU Directive) (EU Exit) Regulations 2019, SI 2019/469, reg 4, Sch 1, Pt 1, para 12(1), (20), as from exit day (as defined in the European Union (Withdrawal) Act 2018, s 20), as follows—

"(7A) Section 207B (extension of time limits to facilitate conciliation before institution of proceedings) applies for the purposes of subsections (2)(a) and (5)(a).".

Conciliation: employment tribunal proceedings under this section are "relevant proceedings" for the purposes of the conciliation provisions contained in the Employment Tribunals Act 1996, ss 18–18C; see s 18(1)(b) of the 1996 Act at **[1.757]**.

Recoupment of social security benefits: see the note at the beginning of this Part.

[PART VIII

CHAPTER I MATERNITY LEAVE]

NOTES

A new Pt VIII (ss 71–75, 76–80) was substituted for the original Pt VIII (ss 71–85) by the Employment Relations Act 1999, s 7, Sch 4, Pt I. Subsequently, various amendments have been made to this Part, including the insertions of ss 75A–75K, 80A–80E, 80EA–80EE and 80F–80I.

[1.958]

[71 Ordinary maternity leave

(1) An employee may, provided that she satisfies any conditions which may be prescribed, be absent from work at any time during an ordinary maternity leave period.

(2) An ordinary maternity leave period is a period calculated in accordance with regulations made by the Secretary of State.

[(3) Regulations under subsection (2)—

(a) shall secure that, where an employee has a right to leave under this section, she is entitled to an ordinary maternity leave period of at least 26 weeks;

(b) may allow an employee to choose, subject to prescribed restrictions, the date on which an ordinary maternity leave period starts;

[(ba) may allow an employee to bring forward the date on which an ordinary maternity leave period ends, subject to prescribed restrictions and subject to satisfying prescribed conditions;

(bb) may allow an employee in prescribed circumstances to revoke, or to be treated as revoking, the bringing forward of that date;]

(c) may specify circumstances in which an employee may work for her employer during an ordinary maternity leave period without bringing the period to an end.]

[(3A) Provision under subsection (3)(ba) is to secure that an employee may bring forward the date on which an ordinary maternity leave period ends only if the employee or another person has taken, or is taking, prescribed steps as regards leave under section 75E or statutory shared parental pay in respect of the child.]

(4) Subject to section 74, an employee who exercises her right under subsection (1)—

(a) is entitled[, for such purposes and to such extent as may be prescribed,] to the benefit of the terms and conditions of employment which would have applied if she had not been absent,

(b) is bound[, for such purposes and to such extent as may be prescribed,] by any obligations arising under those terms and conditions (except in so far as they are inconsistent with subsection (1)), and

[(c) is entitled to return from leave to a job of a prescribed kind].

(5) In subsection (4)(a) "terms and conditions of employment"—

(a) includes matters connected with an employee's employment whether or not they arise under her contract of employment, but

(b) does not include terms and conditions about remuneration.

(6) The Secretary of State may make regulations specifying matters which are, or are not, to be treated as remuneration for the purposes of this section.

[(7) The Secretary of State may make regulations making provision, in relation to the right to return under subsection (4)(c) above, about—

(a) seniority, pension rights and similar rights;

(b) terms and conditions of employment on return.]]

NOTES

Substituted as noted following the Part heading above.

Sub-s (3): substituted by the Work and Families Act 2006, s 11(1), Sch 1, para 31; paras (ba), (bb) inserted by the Children and Families Act 2014, s 118(1), (2)(a), as from 30 June 2014.

Sub-s (3A): inserted by the Children and Families Act 2014, s 118(1), (2)(b), as from 30 June 2014.

Sub-s (4): words in square brackets in paras (a), (b) inserted, and para (c) substituted, by the Employment Act 2002, s 17(1), (2).

Sub-s (7): substituted by the Employment Act 2002, s 17(1), (3).

Modified as noted to s 66 at **[1.947]**.

Regulations: the Maternity and Parental Leave etc Regulations 1999, SI 1999/3312 at **[2.447]**; the Maternity and Parental Leave (Amendment) Regulations 2002, SI 2002/2789; the Maternity and Parental Leave etc and the Paternity and Adoption Leave (Amendment) Regulations 2006, SI 2006/2014; the Maternity and Adoption Leave (Curtailment of Statutory Rights to Leave) Regulations 2014, SI 2014/3052 at **[2.1676]**; the Maternity and Parental Leave etc (Amendment) Regulations 2014, SI 2014/3221.

[1.959]

[72 Compulsory maternity leave

(1) An employer shall not permit an employee who satisfies prescribed conditions to work during a compulsory maternity leave period.

(2) A compulsory maternity leave period is a period calculated in accordance with regulations made by the Secretary of State.

(3) Regulations under subsection (2) shall secure—

(a) that no compulsory leave period is less than two weeks, and

(b) that every compulsory maternity leave period falls within an ordinary maternity leave period.

(4) Subject to subsection (5), any provision of or made under the Health and Safety at Work etc Act 1974 shall apply in relation to the prohibition under subsection (1) as if it were imposed by regulations under section 15 of that Act.

(5) Section 33(1)(c) of the 1974 Act shall not apply in relation to the prohibition under subsection (1); and an employer who contravenes that subsection shall be—

(a) guilty of an offence, and

(b) liable on summary conviction to a fine not exceeding level 2 on the standard scale.]

NOTES

Substituted as noted following the Part heading above.

Regulations: the Maternity and Parental Leave etc Regulations 1999, SI 1999/3312 at **[2.447]**.

[1.960]

[73 Additional maternity leave

(1) An employee who satisfies prescribed conditions may be absent from work at any time during an additional maternity leave period.

(2) An additional maternity leave period is a period calculated in accordance with regulations made by the Secretary of State.

[(3) Regulations under subsection (2)—

(a) may allow an employee [to bring forward the date on which an additional maternity leave period ends, subject to prescribed restrictions and subject to satisfying prescribed conditions];

[(aa) may allow an employee in prescribed circumstances to revoke, or to be treated as revoking, the bringing forward of that date;]

(b) may specify circumstances in which an employee may work for her employer during an additional maternity leave period without bringing the period to an end.]

[(3A) Provision under subsection (3)(a) is to secure that an employee may bring forward the date on which an additional maternity leave period ends only if the employee or another person has taken, or is taking, prescribed steps as regards leave under section 75E or statutory shared parental pay in respect of the child.]

(4) Subject to section 74, an employee who exercises her right under subsection (1)—

(a) is entitled, for such purposes and to such extent as may be prescribed, to the benefit of the terms and conditions of employment which would have applied if she had not been absent,

(b) is bound, for such purposes and to such extent as may be prescribed, by obligations arising under those terms and conditions (except in so far as they are inconsistent with subsection (1)), and

(c) is entitled to return from leave to a job of a prescribed kind.

(5) In subsection (4)(a) "terms and conditions of employment"—

(a) includes matters connected with an employee's employment whether or not they arise under her contract of employment, but

(b) does not include terms and conditions about remuneration.

[(5A) In subsection (4)(c), the reference to return from leave includes, where appropriate, a reference to a continuous period of absence attributable partly to additional maternity leave and partly to ordinary maternity leave.]

(6) The Secretary of State may make regulations specifying matters which are, or are not, to be treated as remuneration for the purposes of this section.

(7) The Secretary of State may make regulations making provision, in relation to the right to return under subsection (4)(c), about—

(a) seniority, pension rights and similar rights;

(b) terms and conditions of employment on return.]

NOTES

Substituted as noted following the Part heading above.

Sub-s (3): substituted by the Work and Families Act 2006, s 11(1), Sch 1, para 32; words in square brackets in para (a) substituted, and para (aa) inserted, by the Children and Families Act 2014, s 118(1), (3)(a), (b), as from 30 June 2014.

Sub-s (3A): inserted by the Children and Families Act 2014, s 118(1), (3)(c), as from 30 June 2014.

Sub-s (5A): inserted by the Employment Act 2002, s 17(1), (4).

Regulations: the Maternity and Parental Leave etc Regulations 1999, SI 1999/3312 at **[2.447]**; the Maternity and Parental Leave (Amendment) Regulations 2002, SI 2002/2689; the Maternity and Parental Leave etc and the Paternity and Adoption Leave (Amendment) Regulations 2006, SI 2006/2014; the Maternity and Parental Leave etc and the Paternity and Adoption Leave (Amendment) Regulations 2008, SI 2008/1966; the Maternity and Adoption Leave (Curtailment of Statutory Rights to Leave) Regulations 2014, SI 2014/3052 at **[2.1676]**.

[1.961]

[74 Redundancy and dismissal

(1) Regulations under section 71 or 73 may make provision about redundancy during an ordinary or additional maternity leave period.

(2) Regulations under section 71 or 73 may make provision about dismissal (other than by reason of redundancy) during an ordinary or additional maternity leave period.

(3) Regulations made by virtue of subsection (1) or (2) may include—

(a) provision requiring an employer to offer alternative employment;

(b) provision for the consequences of failure to comply with the regulations (which may include provision for a dismissal to be treated as unfair for the purposes of Part X).

(4) Regulations under section [71 or] 73 may make provision—

(a) for section [71(4)(c) or] 73(4)(c) not to apply in specified cases, and

(b) about dismissal at the conclusion of an [ordinary or] additional maternity leave period.]

NOTES

Substituted as noted following the Part heading above.

Sub-s (4): words in square brackets inserted by the Employment Act 2002, s 17(1), (5).

[1.962]

[75 Sections 71 to 73: supplemental

(1) Regulations under section 71, 72 or 73 may—

(a) make provision about notices to be given, evidence to be produced and other procedures to be followed by employees and employers;

(b) make provision for the consequences of failure to give notices, to produce evidence or to comply with other procedural requirements;

(c) make provision for the consequences of failure to act in accordance with a notice given by virtue of paragraph (a);

(d) make special provision for cases where an employee has a right which corresponds to a right under this Chapter and which arises under her contract of employment or otherwise;

(e) make provision modifying the effect of Chapter II of Part XIV (calculation of a week's pay) in relation to an employee who is or has been absent from work on ordinary or additional maternity leave;

(f) make provision applying, modifying or excluding an enactment, in such circumstances as may be specified and subject to any conditions specified, in relation to a person entitled to ordinary, compulsory or additional maternity leave;

(g) make different provision for different cases or circumstances.

(2) In sections 71 to 73 "prescribed" means prescribed by regulations made by the Secretary of State.]

NOTES

Substituted as noted following the Part heading above.

[CHAPTER IA ADOPTION LEAVE

[1.963]

75A Ordinary adoption leave

(1) An employee who satisfies prescribed conditions may be absent from work at any time during an ordinary adoption leave period.

[(1A) The conditions that may be prescribed under subsection (1) include conditions as to—

(a) being a local authority foster parent;

(b) being approved as a prospective adopter;

[(c) being notified—

(i) by a local authority in England that a child is to be, or is expected to be, placed with the employee under section 22C of the Children Act 1989;

(ii) by a local authority in Wales that a child is to be, or is expected to be, placed with the employee under section 81 of the Social Services and Well-being (Wales) Act 2014].]

(2) An ordinary adoption leave period is a period calculated in accordance with regulations made by the Secretary of State.

[(2A) Regulations under subsection (2)[—

(a) may allow an employee to bring forward the date on which an ordinary adoption leave period ends, subject to prescribed restrictions and subject to satisfying prescribed conditions;

(b) may allow an employee in prescribed circumstances to revoke, or to be treated as revoking, the bringing forward of that date;]

[(c)] may specify circumstances in which an employee may work for his employer during an ordinary adoption leave period without bringing the period to an end.]

[(2B) Provision under subsection (2A)(a) is to secure that an employee may bring forward the date on which an ordinary adoption leave period ends only if the employee or another person has taken, or is taking, prescribed steps as regards leave under section 75G or statutory shared parental pay in respect of the child.]

(3) Subject to section 75C, an employee who exercises his right under subsection (1)—

(a) is entitled, for such purposes and to such extent as may be prescribed, to the benefit of the terms and conditions of employment which would have applied if he had not been absent,

(b) is bound, for such purposes and to such extent as may be prescribed, by any obligations arising under those terms and conditions (except in so far as they are inconsistent with subsection (1)), and

(c) is entitled to return from leave to a job of a prescribed kind.

(4) In subsection (3)(a) "terms and conditions of employment"—

(a) includes matters connected with an employee's employment whether or not they arise under his contract of employment, but

(b) does not include terms and conditions about remuneration.

(5) In subsection (3)(c), the reference to return from leave includes, where appropriate, a reference to a continuous period of absence attributable partly to ordinary adoption leave and partly to maternity leave.

(6) The Secretary of State may make regulations specifying matters which are, or are not, to be treated as remuneration for the purposes of this section.

(7) The Secretary of State may make regulations making provision, in relation to the right to return under subsection (3)(c), about—

(a) seniority, pension rights and similar rights;

(b) terms and conditions of employment on return.

[(8) The Secretary of State may by regulations provide for this section to have effect, with such modifications as the regulations may prescribe, in relation to—

(a) cases which involve an employee who has applied, or intends to apply, with another person for a parental order under section 54 of the Human Fertilisation and Embryology Act 2008 and a child who is, or will be, the subject of the order,

(b) cases which involve an employee who has applied, or intends to apply, for a parental order under section 54A of that Act and a child who is, or will be, the subject of the order.]]

NOTES

Chapter IA (ss 75A–75D) inserted by the Employment Act 2002, s 3.

Sub-s (1A): inserted by the Children and Families Act 2014, s 121(1), as from 30 June 2014; para (c) substituted by the Social Services and Well-being (Wales) Act 2014 (Consequential Amendments) Regulations 2016, SI 2016/413, regs 143, 145, as from 6 April 2016.

Sub-s (2A): inserted by the Work and Families Act 2006, s 11(1), Sch 1, para 33; words in square brackets inserted by the Children and Families Act 2014, s 118(1), (4)(a), (b), as from 30 June 2014.

Sub-s (2B): inserted by the Children and Families Act 2014, s 118(1), (4)(c), as from 30 June 2014.

Sub-s (8): added by the Children and Families Act 2014, s 122(1), as from 30 June 2014; substituted by the Human Fertilisation and Embryology Act 2008 (Remedial) Order 2018, SI 2018/1413, art 3(1), Sch 1, para 11(1), (10), as from 3 January 2019.

Application: this section applies to parental order parents, see the Employment Rights Act 1996 (Application of Sections 75A, 75B, 75G, 75H, 80A and 80B to Parental Order Cases) Regulations 2014, SI 2014/3095, reg 2 at **[2.1742]**.

Regulations: the Paternity and Adoption Leave Regulations 2002, SI 2002/2788 at **[2.576]**; the Paternity and Adoption Leave (Adoptions from Overseas) Regulations 2003, SI 2003/921; the Paternity and Adoption Leave (Amendment) Regulations 2004, SI 2004/923; the Maternity and Parental Leave etc and the Paternity and Adoption Leave (Amendment) Regulations 2006, SI 2006/2014; the Paternity and Adoption Leave (Amendment) Regulations 2014, SI 2014/2112 at **[2.1512]**; the Maternity and Adoption Leave (Curtailment of Statutory Rights to Leave) Regulations 2014, SI 2014/3052 at **[2.1676]**; the Shared Parental Leave and Paternity and Adoption Leave (Adoptions from Overseas) Regulations 2014, SI 2014/3092 at **[2.1704]**; the Employment Rights Act 1996 (Application of Sections 75A, 75B, 75G, 75H, 80A and 80B to Parental Order Cases) Regulations 2014, SI 2014/3095 at **[2.1741]**; the Paternity, Adoption and Shared Parental Leave (Parental Order Cases) Regulations 2014, SI 2014/3096 at **[2.1747]**; the Paternity and Adoption Leave (Amendment) (No 2) Regulations 2014, SI 2014/3206; the Shared Parental Leave and Leave Curtailment (Amendment) Regulations 2015, SI 2015/552.

[1.964]

[75B Additional adoption leave

(1) An employee who satisfies prescribed conditions may be absent from work at any time during an additional adoption leave period.

(2) An additional adoption leave period is a period calculated in accordance with regulations made by the Secretary of State.

[(3) Regulations under subsection (2)—

(a) may allow an employee [to bring forward the date on which an additional adoption leave period ends, subject to prescribed restrictions and subject to satisfying prescribed conditions];
[(aa) may allow an employee in prescribed circumstances to revoke, or to be treated as revoking, the bringing forward of that date;]
(b) may specify circumstances in which an employee may work for his employer during an additional adoption leave period without bringing the period to an end.]

[(3A) Provision under subsection (3)(a) is to secure that an employee may bring forward the date on which an additional adoption leave period ends only if the employee or another person has taken, or is taking, prescribed steps as regards leave under section 75G or statutory shared parental pay in respect of the child.]

(4) Subject to section 75C, an employee who exercises his right under subsection (1)—
(a) is entitled, for such purposes and to such extent as may be prescribed, to the benefit of the terms and conditions of employment which would have applied if he had not been absent,
(b) is bound, for such purposes and to such extent as may be prescribed, by obligations arising under those terms and conditions (except in so far as they are inconsistent with subsection (1)), and
(c) is entitled to return from leave to a job of a prescribed kind.

(5) In subsection (4)(a) "terms and conditions of employment"—
(a) includes matters connected with an employee's employment whether or not they arise under his contract of employment, but
(b) does not include terms and conditions about remuneration.

(6) In subsection (4)(c), the reference to return from leave includes, where appropriate, a reference to a continuous period of absence attributable partly to additional adoption leave and partly to—
(a) maternity leave, or
(b) ordinary adoption leave,
or to both.

(7) The Secretary of State may make regulations specifying matters which are, or are not, to be treated as remuneration for the purposes of this section.

(8) The Secretary of State may make regulations making provision, in relation to the right to return under subsection (4)(c), about—
(a) seniority, pension rights and similar rights;
(b) terms and conditions of employment on return.

[(9) The Secretary of State may by regulations provide for this section to have effect, with such modifications as the regulations may prescribe, in relation to—
(a) cases which involve an employee who has applied, or intends to apply, with another person for a parental order under section 54 of the Human Fertilisation and Embryology Act 2008 and a child who is, or will be, the subject of the order,
(b) cases which involve an employee who has applied, or intends to apply, for a parental order under section 54A of that Act and a child who is, or will be, the subject of the order.]]

NOTES

Inserted as noted to s 75A at **[1.963]**.

Sub-s (3): substituted by the Work and Families Act 2006, s 11(1), Sch 1, para 34; words in square brackets in para (a) substituted, and para (aa) is inserted, by the Children and Families Act 2014, s 118(1), (5)(a), (b), as from 30 June 2014.

Sub-s (3A): inserted by the Children and Families Act 2014, s 118(1), (5)(c), as from 30 June 2014.

Sub-s (9): added by the Children and Families Act 2014, s 122(2), as from 30 June 2014; substituted by the Human Fertilisation and Embryology Act 2008 (Remedial) Order 2018, SI 2018/1413, art 3(1), Sch 1, para 11(1), (11), as from 3 January 2019.

Application: this section applies to parental order parents, see the Employment Rights Act 1996 (Application of Sections 75A, 75B, 75G, 75H, 80A and 80B to Parental Order Cases) Regulations 2014, SI 2014/3095, reg 2 at **[2.1742]**.

Regulations: the Paternity and Adoption Leave Regulations 2002, SI 2002/2788 at **[2.576]**; the Paternity and Adoption Leave (Adoptions from Overseas) Regulations 2003, SI 2003/921; the Paternity and Adoption Leave (Amendment) Regulations 2004, SI 2004/923; the Maternity and Parental Leave etc and the Paternity and Adoption Leave (Amendment) Regulations 2006, SI 2006/2014; the Maternity and Parental Leave etc and the Paternity and Adoption Leave (Amendment) Regulations 2008, SI 2008/1966; the Maternity and Adoption Leave (Curtailment of Statutory Rights to Leave) Regulations 2014, SI 2014/3052 at **[2.1676]**; the Shared Parental Leave and Paternity and Adoption Leave (Adoptions from Overseas) Regulations 2014, SI 2014/3092 at **[2.1704]**; the Employment Rights Act 1996 (Application of Sections 75A, 75B, 75G, 75H, 80A and 80B to Parental Order Cases) Regulations 2014, SI 2014/3095 at **[2.1741]**; the Paternity, Adoption and Shared Parental Leave (Parental Order Cases) Regulations 2014, SI 2014/3096 at **[2.1747]**; the Shared Parental Leave and Leave Curtailment (Amendment) Regulations 2015, SI 2015/552.

[1.965]

[75C Redundancy and dismissal

(1) Regulations under section 75A or 75B may make provision about—
(a) redundancy, or
(b) dismissal (other than by reason of redundancy),
during an ordinary or additional adoption leave period.

(2) Regulations made by virtue of subsection (1) may include—
(a) provision requiring an employer to offer alternative employment;
(b) provision for the consequences of failure to comply with the regulations (which may include provision for a dismissal to be treated as unfair for the purposes of Part 10).

(3) Regulations under section 75A or 75B may make provision—
(a) for section 75A(3)(c) or 75B(4)(c) not to apply in specified cases, and
(b) about dismissal at the conclusion of an ordinary or additional adoption leave period.]

NOTES

Inserted as noted to s 75A at **[1.963]**.

[1.966]

[75D Chapter 1A: supplemental

(1) Regulations under section 75A or 75B may—

(a) make provision about notices to be given, evidence to be produced and other procedures to be followed by employees and employers;

(b) make provision requiring employers or employees to keep records;

(c) make provision for the consequences of failure to give notices, to produce evidence, to keep records or to comply with other procedural requirements;

(d) make provision for the consequences of failure to act in accordance with a notice given by virtue of paragraph (a);

(e) make special provision for cases where an employee has a right which corresponds to a right under this Chapter and which arises under his contract of employment or otherwise;

(f) make provision modifying the effect of Chapter 2 of Part 14 (calculation of a week's pay) in relation to an employee who is or has been absent from work on ordinary or additional adoption leave;

(g) make provision applying, modifying or excluding an enactment, in such circumstances as may be specified and subject to any conditions specified, in relation to a person entitled to ordinary or additional adoption leave;

(h) make different provision for different cases or circumstances.

[(1A) Where section 75A or 75B has effect in relation to such cases as are described in section 75A(8) or 75B(9), regulations under section 75A or 75B about evidence to be produced may require statutory declarations as to—

(a) eligibility to apply for a parental order [under section 54 or 54A of the Human Fertilisation and Embryology Act 2008];

(b) intention to apply for such an order.]

(2) In sections 75A and 75B "prescribed" means prescribed by regulations made by the Secretary of State.]

NOTES

Inserted as noted to s 75A at **[1.963]**.

Sub-s (1A): inserted by the Children and Families Act 2014, s 122(3), as from 30 June 2014; words in square brackets in para (a) inserted by the Human Fertilisation and Embryology Act 2008 (Remedial) Order 2018, SI 2018/1413, art 3(1), Sch 1, para 11(1), (12), as from 3 January 2019.

[CHAPTER 1B SHARED PARENTAL LEAVE

[1.967]

75E Entitlement to shared parental leave: birth

(1) The Secretary of State may make regulations entitling an employee who satisfies specified conditions—

(a) as to duration of employment,

(b) as to being, or expecting to be, the mother of a child,

(c) as to caring or intending to care, with another person ("P"), for the child,

(d) as to entitlement to maternity leave,

(e) as to the exercise of that entitlement and the extent of any such exercise,

(f) as to giving notice of an intention to exercise an entitlement to leave under this subsection, and

(g) as to the consent of P to the amount of leave under this subsection that the employee intends to take,

to be absent from work on leave under this subsection for the purpose of caring for the child.

(2) Regulations under subsection (1) may provide that the employee's entitlement is subject to the satisfaction by P of specified conditions—

(a) as to employment or self-employment,

(b) as to having earnings of a specified amount for a specified period,

(c) as to caring or intending to care, with the employee, for the child, and

(d) as to relationship with the child or the employee.

(3) Provision under subsection (1)(f) may require the employee to give notice to the employer about—

(a) the amount of leave to which the employee would be entitled if the entitlement were fully exercised (disregarding for these purposes any intention of P to exercise an entitlement to leave under subsection (4) or to statutory shared parental pay);

(b) how much of the entitlement to leave the employee intends to exercise;

(c) the extent to which P intends to exercise an entitlement to leave under subsection (4) or to statutory shared parental pay.

(4) The Secretary of State may make regulations entitling an employee who satisfies specified conditions—

(a) as to duration of employment,

(b) as to relationship with a child or expected child or with the child's mother,

(c) as to caring or intending to care, with the child's mother, for the child,

(d) as to giving notice of an intention to exercise an entitlement to leave under this subsection, and

(e) as to the consent of the child's mother to the amount of leave under this subsection that the employee intends to take,

to be absent from work on leave under this subsection for the purpose of caring for the child.

(5) Regulations under subsection (4) may provide that the employee's entitlement is subject to the satisfaction by the child's mother of specified conditions—

(a) as to employment or self-employment,

(b) as to having earnings of a specified amount for a specified period,

(c) as to caring or intending to care, with the employee, for the child,

(d) as to entitlement (or lack of entitlement) to maternity leave, statutory maternity pay or maternity allowance, and

(e) as to the exercise of any such entitlement and the extent of any such exercise.

(6) Provision under subsection (4)(d) may require the employee to give notice to the employer about—

(a) the amount of leave to which the employee would be entitled if the entitlement were fully exercised (disregarding for these purposes any intention of the child's mother to exercise an entitlement to leave under subsection (1) or to statutory shared parental pay);

(b) how much of the entitlement to leave the employee intends to exercise;

(c) the extent to which the child's mother intends to exercise an entitlement to leave under subsection (1) or to statutory shared parental pay.]

NOTES

Commencement: 30 June 2014.

Inserted, together with the preceding Chapter heading and ss 75F–75K, by the Children and Families Act 2014, s 117(1), as from 30 June 2014.

Regulations: the Shared Parental Leave Regulations 2014, SI 2014/3050 at **[2.1577]**; the Shared Parental Leave and Leave Curtailment (Amendment) Regulations 2015, SI 2015/552.

[1.968]

[75F Entitlement to leave under section 75E: further provision

(1) Regulations under section 75E are to include provision for determining—

(a) the amount of leave under section 75E(1) or (4) to which an employee is entitled in respect of a child;

(b) when leave under section 75E(1) or (4) may be taken.

(2) Provision under subsection (1)(a) is to secure that the amount of leave to which an employee is entitled in respect of a child does not exceed—

(a) in a case where the child's mother became entitled to maternity leave, the relevant amount of time reduced by—

(i) where her maternity leave ends without her ordinary or additional maternity leave period having been curtailed by virtue of section 71(3)(ba) or 73(3)(a), the amount of maternity leave taken by the child's mother, or

(ii) except where sub-paragraph (i) applies, the amount of time between the beginning of her maternity leave and the time when her ordinary or additional maternity leave period, as curtailed by virtue of section 71(3)(ba) or 73(3)(a), comes to an end;

(b) in a case where the child's mother became entitled to statutory maternity pay or maternity allowance but not maternity leave, the relevant amount of time reduced by an amount determined in accordance with paragraph (a) or, as the case may be, paragraph (b) of section 171ZU(6) of the Social Security Contributions and Benefits Act 1992.

(3) In subsection (2) "the relevant amount of time" means an amount of time specified in or determined in accordance with regulations under section 75E.

(4) Provision under subsection (1)(a) is to secure that the amount of leave that an employee is entitled to take in respect of a child takes into account—

(a) in a case where another person is entitled to leave under section 75E in respect of the child, the amount of such leave taken by the other person;

(b) in a case where another person is entitled to statutory shared parental pay in respect of the child but not leave under section 75E, the number of weeks in respect of which such pay is payable to the other person.

(5) In reckoning for the purposes of subsection (2) the amount of maternity leave taken, a part of a week is to be treated as a full week.

(6) In reckoning for the purposes of subsection (4) the amount of leave under section 75E taken during a period of such leave, a part of a week is to be treated as a full week.

(7) Provision under subsection (1)(b) is to secure that leave under section 75E must be taken before the end of such period as may be specified by the regulations.

(8) Regulations under section 75E are to provide for the taking of leave under section 75E in a single period or in non-consecutive periods.

(9) Regulations under section 75E may—

(a) provide for an employer, subject to such restrictions as may be specified, to require an employee who proposes to take non-consecutive periods of leave under section 75E to take that amount of leave as a single period of leave;

(b) provide for a single period of leave that is so imposed on an employee to start with a day proposed by the employee or, if no day is proposed, with the first day of the first period of leave proposed by the employee.

(10) Regulations under section 75E may provide for the variation, subject to such restrictions as may be specified, of—

(a) the period or periods during which an amount of leave under section 75E may be taken;

(b) the amount of leave under section 75E that the employee previously specified in accordance with provision under section 75E(3)(b) or (6)(b) or subsection (13)(b) of this section.

(11) Provision under subsection (10)(a) may provide for variation to be subject to the consent of an employer in circumstances specified by the regulations.

(12) Provision under subsection (10)(b) may require an employee to satisfy specified conditions—

(a) as to giving notice of an intention to vary the amount of leave under section 75E to be taken by the employee;

(b) if the employee proposes to vary the amount of leave under section 75E(1) to be taken by the employee, as to the consent of P to that variation;

(c) if the employee proposes to vary the amount of leave under section 75E(4) to be taken by the employee, as to the consent of the child's mother to that variation.

(13) Provision under subsection (12)(a) may require an employee to give notice to the employer about—

(a) the extent to which the employee has exercised an entitlement to leave under section 75E(1) or (4) in respect of the child;

(b) how much of the entitlement to leave the employee intends to exercise;

(c) the extent to which a person other than the employee has exercised an entitlement to leave under section 75E or to statutory shared parental pay in respect of the child;

(d) the extent to which a person other than the employee intends to exercise such an entitlement.

(14) Regulations under section 75E may—

(a) specify things which are, or are not, to be taken as done for the purpose of caring for a child;

(b) make provision excluding the right to be absent on leave under section 75E in respect of a child where more than one child is born as a result of the same pregnancy;

(c) specify a minimum amount of leave under section 75E which may be taken;

(d) make provision about how leave under section 75E may be taken;

(e) specify circumstances in which an employee may work for the employer during a period of leave under section 75E without bringing the particular period of leave, or the employee's entitlement to leave under section 75E, to an end;

(f) specify circumstances in which an employee may be absent on leave under section 75E otherwise than for the purpose of caring for a child without bringing the person's entitlement to leave under section 75E to an end.

(15) In this section "week" means any period of seven days.

(16) The Secretary of State may by regulations provide that the following do not have effect, or have effect with modifications specified by the regulations, in a case where the mother of a child dies before another person has become entitled to leave under section 75E in respect of the child—

(a) section 75E(4)(b), (c) and (e);

(b) section 75E(5);

(c) section 75E(6)(c);

(d) subsection (12)(c);

(e) subsection (13)(c) and (d).]

NOTES

Commencement: 30 June 2015.

Inserted as noted to s 75E at **[1.967]**.

Regulations; the Shared Parental Leave Regulations 2014, SI 2014/3050 at **[2.1577]** (made, in part, under sub-s (16)).

[1.969]

[75G Entitlement to shared parental leave: adoption

(1) The Secretary of State may make regulations entitling an employee who satisfies specified conditions—

(a) as to duration of employment,

(b) as to being a person with whom a child is, or is expected to be, placed for adoption under the law of any part of the United Kingdom,

(c) as to caring or intending to care, with another person ("P"), for the child,

(d) as to entitlement to adoption leave,

(e) as to the exercise of that entitlement and the extent of any such exercise,

(f) as to giving notice of an intention to exercise an entitlement to leave under this subsection, and

(g) as to the consent of P to the amount of leave under this subsection that the employee intends to take,

to be absent from work on leave under this subsection for the purpose of caring for the child.

(2) Regulations under subsection (1) may provide that the employee's entitlement is subject to the satisfaction by P of specified conditions—

(a) as to employment or self-employment,

(b) as to having earnings of a specified amount for a specified period,

(c) as to caring or intending to care, with the employee, for the child, and

(d) as to relationship with the child or the employee.

(3) Provision under subsection (1)(f) may require the employee to give notice to the employer about—

(a) the amount of leave to which the employee would be entitled if the entitlement were fully exercised (disregarding for these purposes any intention of P to exercise an entitlement to leave under subsection (4) or to statutory shared parental pay);

(b) how much of the entitlement to leave the employee intends to exercise;

(c) the extent to which P intends to exercise an entitlement to leave under subsection (4) or to statutory shared parental pay.

(4) The Secretary of State may make regulations entitling an employee who satisfies specified conditions—
(a) as to duration of employment,
(b) as to relationship with a child placed, or expected to be placed, for adoption under the law of any part of the United Kingdom or with a person ("A") with whom the child is, or is expected to be, so placed,
(c) as to caring or intending to care, with A, for the child,
(d) as to giving notice of an intention to exercise an entitlement to leave under this subsection, and
(e) as to the consent of A to the amount of leave under this subsection that the employee intends to take,

to be absent from work on leave under this subsection for the purpose of caring for the child.

(5) Regulations under subsection (4) may provide that the employee's entitlement is subject to the satisfaction by A of specified conditions—
(a) as to employment or self-employment,
(b) as to having earnings of a specified amount for a specified period,
(c) as to caring or intending to care, with the employee, for the child,
(d) as to entitlement (or lack of entitlement) to adoption leave or statutory adoption pay, and
(e) as to the exercise of any such entitlement and the extent of any such exercise.

(6) Provision under subsection (4)(d) may require the employee to give notice to the employer about—
(a) the amount of leave to which the employee would be entitled if the entitlement were fully exercised (disregarding for these purposes any intention of A to exercise an entitlement to leave under subsection (1) or to statutory shared parental pay);
(b) how much of the entitlement to leave the employee intends to exercise;
(c) the extent to which A intends to exercise an entitlement to leave under subsection (1) or to statutory shared parental pay.

[(7) Regulations under subsections (1) and (4) are to provide for leave in respect of a child placed, or expected to be placed—
(a) under section 22C of the Children Act 1989 by a local authority in England, or
(b) under section 81 of the Social Services and Well-being (Wales) Act 2014 by a local authority in Wales,

with a local authority foster parent who has been approved as a prospective adopter.]

(8) This section and section 75H have effect in relation to regulations made by virtue of subsection (7) as if references to a child being placed for adoption under the law of any part of the United Kingdom were references to being placed under section 22C of the Children Act 1989[, or section 81 of the Social Services and Well-being (Wales) Act 2014] with a local authority foster parent who has been approved as a prospective adopter.]

NOTES

Commencement: 30 June 2014.

Inserted as noted to s 75E at **[1.967]**.

Sub-s (7): substituted by the Social Services and Well-being (Wales) Act 2014 (Consequential Amendments) Regulations 2016, SI 2016/413, regs 143, 146(a), as from 6 April 2016.

Sub-s (8): words in square brackets inserted by SI 2016/413, regs 143, 146(b), as from 6 April 2016.

Application: this section applies to parental order parents subject to certain modifications, see the Employment Rights Act 1996 (Application of Sections 75A, 75B, 75G, 75H, 80A and 80B to Parental Order Cases) Regulations 2014, SI 2014/3095, reg 3 and Sch 1 at **[2.1743]** and **[2.1745]**.

Application: this section applies to adoptions from overseas subject to certain modifications, see the Employment Rights Act 1996 (Application of Sections 75G and 75H to Adoptions from Overseas) Regulations 2014, SI 2014/3091, reg 2 and Schedule at **[2.1702]** and **[2.1703]**.

Regulations: the Shared Parental Leave Regulations 2014, SI 2014/3050 at **[2.1577]**; the Shared Parental Leave and Paternity and Adoption Leave (Adoptions from Overseas) Regulations 2014, SI 2014/3092 at **[2.1704]**; the Paternity, Adoption and Shared Parental Leave (Parental Order Cases) Regulations 2014, SI 2014/3096 at **[2.1747]**; the Shared Parental Leave and Leave Curtailment (Amendment) Regulations 2015, SI 2015/552.

[1.970]

[75H Entitlement to leave under section 75G: further provision

(1) Regulations under section 75G are to include provision for determining—
(a) the amount of leave under section 75G(1) or (4) to which an employee is entitled in respect of a child;
(b) when leave under section 75G(1) or (4) may be taken.

(2) Provision under subsection (1)(a) is to secure that the amount of leave to which an employee is entitled in respect of a child does not exceed—
(a) in a case where a person with whom the child is, or is expected to be, placed for adoption became entitled to adoption leave, the relevant amount of time reduced by—
 (i) where the person's adoption leave ends without the person's ordinary or additional adoption leave period having been curtailed by virtue of section 75A(2A)(a) or 75B(3)(a), the amount of adoption leave taken by that person, or
 (ii) except where sub-paragraph (i) applies, the amount of time between the beginning of the person's adoption leave and the time when the person's ordinary or additional adoption leave period, as curtailed by virtue of section 75A(2A)(a) or 75B(3)(a), comes to an end;

(b) in a case where a person with whom the child is, or is expected to be, placed for adoption became entitled to statutory adoption pay but not adoption leave, the relevant amount of time reduced by an amount determined in accordance with paragraph (a) or, as the case may be, paragraph (b) of section 171ZV(6) of the Social Security Contributions and Benefits Act 1992.

(3) In subsection (2) "the relevant amount of time" means an amount of time specified in or determined in accordance with regulations under section 75G.

(4) Provision under subsection (1)(a) is to secure that the amount of leave that an employee is entitled to take in respect of a child takes into account—

(a) in a case where another person is entitled to leave under section 75G in respect of the child, the amount of such leave taken by the other person;

(b) in a case where another person is entitled to statutory shared parental pay in respect of the child but not leave under section 75G, the number of weeks in respect of which such pay is payable to the other person.

(5) In reckoning for the purposes of subsection (2) the amount of adoption leave taken, a part of a week is to be treated as a full week.

(6) In reckoning for the purposes of subsection (4) the amount of leave under section 75G taken during a period of such leave, a part of a week is to be treated as a full week.

(7) Provision under subsection (1)(b) is to secure that leave under section 75G must be taken before the end of such period as may be prescribed by the regulations.

(8) Regulations under section 75G are to provide for the taking of leave under section 75G in a single period or in non-consecutive periods.

(9) Regulations under section 75G may—

(a) provide for an employer, subject to such restrictions as may be specified, to require an employee who proposes to take non-consecutive periods of leave under section 75G to take that amount of leave as a single period of leave, and

(b) provide for a single period of leave that is so imposed on an employee to start with a day proposed by the employee or, if no day is proposed, with the first day of the first period of leave proposed by the employee.

(10) Regulations under section 75G may provide for the variation, subject to such restrictions as may be specified, of—

(a) the period or periods during which an amount of leave under section 75G is to be taken;

(b) the amount of leave under section 75G that the employee previously specified in accordance with provision under section 75G(3)(b) or (6)(b) or subsection (13)(b) of this section.

(11) Provision under subsection (10)(a) may provide for variation to be subject to the consent of an employer in circumstances specified by the regulations.

(12) Provision under subsection (10)(b) may require an employee to satisfy specified conditions—

(a) as to giving notice of an intention to vary the amount of leave under section 75G to be taken by the employee;

(b) if the employee proposes to vary the amount of leave under section 75G(1) to be taken by the employee, as to the consent of P to that variation;

(c) if the employee proposes to vary the amount of leave under section 75G(4) to be taken by the employee, as to the consent of A to that variation.

(13) Provision under subsection (12)(a) may require an employee to give notice to the employer about—

(a) the extent to which the employee has exercised an entitlement to leave under section 75G(1) or (4) in respect of the child;

(b) how much of the entitlement to leave the employee intends to exercise;

(c) the extent to which a person other than the employee has exercised an entitlement to leave under section 75G or to statutory shared parental pay in respect of the child;

(d) the extent to which a person other than the employee intends to exercise such an entitlement.

(14) Regulations under section 75G may—

(a) specify things which are, or are not, to be taken as done for the purpose of caring for a child;

(b) make provision excluding the right to be absent on leave under section 75G in respect of a child where more than one child is placed for adoption as part of the same arrangement;

(c) specify a minimum amount of leave under section 75G which may be taken;

(d) make provision about how leave under section 75G may be taken;

(e) specify circumstances in which an employee may work for the employer during a period of leave under section 75G without bringing the particular period of leave, or the employee's entitlement to leave under section 75G, to an end;

(f) specify circumstances in which an employee may be absent on leave under section 75G otherwise than for the purpose of caring for a child without bringing the person's entitlement to leave under section 75G to an end.

(15) In this section "week" means any period of seven days.

(16) The Secretary of State may by regulations provide that the following do not have effect, or have effect with modifications specified by the regulations, in a case where a person who is taking adoption leave or is entitled to be paid statutory adoption pay in respect of a child dies before another person has become entitled to leave under section 75G in respect of the child—

(a) section 75G(4)(b), (c) and (e);

(b) section 75G(5);

(c) section 75G(6)(c);

(d) subsection (12)(c);

(e) subsection (13)(c) and (d).

(17) The Secretary of State may by regulations provide for section 75G and this section to have effect in relation to cases which involve adoption, but not the placement of a child for adoption under the law of any part of the United Kingdom, with such modifications as the regulations may prescribe.
(18) The Secretary of State may by regulations provide for section 75G and this section to have effect in relation to cases which involve an employee who has applied, or intends to apply, with another person for a parental order under section 54 of the Human Fertilisation and Embryology Act 2008 and a child who is, or will be, the subject of the order, with such modifications as the regulations may prescribe.]

NOTES

Commencement: 30 June 2015.

Inserted as noted to s 75E at **[1.967]**.

Application: this section applies to parental order parents subject to certain modifications, see the Employment Rights Act 1996 (Application of Sections 75A, 75B, 75G, 75H, 80A and 80B to Parental Order Cases) Regulations 2014, SI 2014/3095, reg 3 and Sch 1 at **[2.1743]** and **[2.1745]**.

Application: this section applies to adoptions from overseas subject to certain modifications, see the Employment Rights Act 1996 (Application of Sections 75G and 75H to Adoptions from Overseas) Regulations 2014, SI 2014/3091, reg 2 and Schedule at **[2.1702]** and **[2.1703]**.

Regulations: the Shared Parental Leave Regulations 2014, SI 2014/3050 at **[2.1577]**; the Employment Rights Act 1996 (Application of Sections 75G and 75H to Adoptions from Overseas) Regulations 2014, SI 2014/3091 at **[2.1701]**; the Shared Parental Leave and Paternity and Adoption Leave (Adoptions from Overseas) Regulations 2014, SI 2014/3092 at **[2.1704]**; the Employment Rights Act 1996 (Application of Sections 75A, 75B, 75G, 75H, 80A and 80B to Parental Order Cases) Regulations 2014, SI 2014/3095 at **[2.1741]**; the Paternity, Adoption and Shared Parental Leave (Parental Order Cases) Regulations 2014, SI 2014/3096 at **[2.1747]** (all made under sub-ss (16), (17) or (18)).

[1.971]
[75I Rights during and after shared parental leave
(1) Regulations under section 75E or 75G are to provide—
(a) that an employee who is absent on leave under that section is entitled, for such purposes and to such extent as the regulations may prescribe, to the benefit of the terms and conditions of employment which would have applied if the employee had not been absent;
(b) that an employee who is absent on leave under that section is bound, for such purposes and to such extent as the regulations may prescribe, by obligations arising under those terms and conditions, except in so far as they are inconsistent with section 75E(1) or (4) or 75G(1) or (4), as the case may be; and
(c) that an employee who is absent on leave under that section is entitled to return from leave to a job of a kind prescribed by the regulations, subject to section 75J(1).
(2) In subsection (1)(a) "terms and conditions of employment"—
(a) includes matters connected with an employee's employment whether or not they arise under the employee's contract of employment, but
(b) does not include terms and conditions about remuneration.
(3) The reference in subsection (1)(c) to absence on leave under section 75E or 75G includes, where appropriate, a reference to a continuous period of absence attributable partly to leave under one of those sections and partly to any one or more of the following—
(a) leave under the other of those sections,
(b) maternity leave,
(c) paternity leave,
(d) adoption leave, *and*
(e) parental leave[, and
(f) parental bereavement leave.]
(4) Regulations under section 75E or 75G may specify matters which are, or are not, to be treated as remuneration for the purposes of this section.
(5) Regulations under section 75E or 75G may make provision, in relation to the right to return mentioned in subsection (1)(c), about—
(a) seniority, pension rights and similar rights;
(b) terms and conditions of employment on return.]

NOTES

Commencement: 30 June 2014.

Inserted as noted to s 75E at **[1.967]**.

Sub-s (3): word in italics in para (d) repealed and para (f) inserted, together with word preceding it, by the Parental Bereavement (Leave and Pay) Act 2018, s 1(c), Schedule, Pt 3, paras 20, 23, as from a day to be appointed.

[1.972]
[75J Redundancy and dismissal
(1) Regulations under section 75E or 75G may make provision about—
(a) redundancy, or
(b) dismissal (other than by reason of redundancy),
during a period of leave under that section.
(2) Provision made by virtue of subsection (1) may include—
(a) provision requiring an employer to offer alternative employment;
(b) provision for the consequences of failure to comply with the regulations (which may include provision for a dismissal to be treated as unfair for the purposes of Part 10).]

NOTES

Commencement: 30 June 2014.

Inserted as noted to s 75E at **[1.967]**.

[1.973]

[75K Chapter 1B: supplemental

(1) Regulations under section 75E or 75G may—

(a) make provision about notices to be given, evidence to be produced and other procedures to be followed by—

(i) employees,

(ii) employers, and

(iii) relevant persons;

(b) make provision requiring such persons to keep records;

(c) make provision for the consequences of failure to give notices, to produce evidence, to keep records or to comply with other procedural requirements;

(d) make provision for the consequences of failure to act in accordance with a notice given by virtue of paragraph (a);

(e) make special provision for cases where an employee has a right which corresponds to a right under section 75E or 75G and which arises under the employee's contract of employment or otherwise;

(f) make provision modifying the effect of Chapter 2 of Part 14 (calculation of a week's pay) in relation to an employee who is or has been absent from work on leave under section 75E or 75G;

(g) make provision applying, modifying or excluding an enactment, in such circumstances as may be specified and subject to any conditions which may be specified, in relation to a person entitled to take leave under section 75E or 75G.

(2) In subsection (1) "relevant person" means—

(a) a person who, in connection with an employee's claim to be entitled to leave under section 75E or 75G, is required to satisfy conditions specified in provision under section 75E(2) or (5) or 75G(2) or (5), or

(b) a person who is an employer or former employer of such a person.

(3) In subsection (2)(b) "employer", in relation to a person falling within subsection (2)(a) who is an employed earner, includes a person who is a secondary contributor as regards that employed earner.

(4) The conditions as to employment or self-employment that may be specified in provision under section 75E(2) or (5) or 75G(2) or (5) include conditions as to being in employed or self-employed earner's employment.

(5) In subsections (3) and (4)—

"employed earner" and "self-employed earner" have the meaning given by section 2 of the Social Security Contributions and Benefits Act 1992, subject for these purposes to the effect of regulations made under section 2(2)(b) of that Act (persons who are to be treated as employed or self-employed earners);

"employment", in the case of employment as an employed or self-employed earner, has the meaning given by section 122 of that Act;

"secondary contributor", as regards an employed earner, means a person who—

(a) is indicated by section 7(1) of that Act, as that subsection has effect subject to section 7(2) of that Act, as being a secondary contributor as regards the earner, or

(b) is indicated by regulations under section 7(2) of that Act as being a person to be treated as a secondary contributor as regards the earner.

(6) Regulations under any of sections 75E to 75H may make different provision for different cases or circumstances.

(7) Where sections 75G and 75H have effect in relation to such cases as are described in section 75H(18), regulations under section 75G about evidence to be produced may require statutory declarations as to—

(a) eligibility to apply for a parental order;

(b) intention to apply for such an order.]

NOTES

Commencement: 30 June 2014.

Inserted as noted to s 75E at **[1.967]**.

[CHAPTER II PARENTAL LEAVE

[1.974]

76 Entitlement to parental leave

(1) The Secretary of State shall make regulations entitling an employee who satisfies specified conditions—

(a) as to duration of employment, and

(b) as to having, or expecting to have, responsibility for a child,

to be absent from work on parental leave for the purpose of caring for a child.

(2) The regulations shall include provision for determining—

(a) the extent of an employee's entitlement to parental leave in respect of a child;

(b) when parental leave may be taken.

(3) Provision under subsection (2)(a) shall secure that where an employee is entitled to parental leave in respect of a child he is entitled to a period or total period of leave of at least three months; but this subsection is without prejudice to any provision which may be made by the regulations for cases in which—

(a) a person ceases to satisfy conditions under subsection (1);

(b) an entitlement to parental leave is transferred.

(4) Provision under subsection (2)(b) may, in particular, refer to—

(a) a child's age, or

(b) a specified period of time starting from a specified event.

(5) Regulations under subsection (1) may—

(a) specify things which are, or are not, to be taken as done for the purpose of caring for a child;

(b) require parental leave to be taken as a single period of absence in all cases or in specified cases;

(c) require parental leave to be taken as a series of periods of absence in all cases or in specified cases;

(d) require all or specified parts of a period of parental leave to be taken at or by specified times;

(e) make provision about the postponement by an employer of a period of parental leave which an employee wishes to take;

(f) specify a minimum or maximum period of absence which may be taken as part of a period of parental leave.

(g) specify a maximum aggregate of periods of parental leave which may be taken during a specified period of time.]

NOTES

Substituted as noted following the Part heading above.

Regulations: the Maternity and Parental Leave etc Regulations 1999, SI 1999/3312 at **[2.447]**; the Maternity and Parental Leave (Amendment) Regulations 2001, SI 2001/4010; the Maternity and Parental Leave (Amendment) Regulations 2002, SI 2002/2789; the Parental Leave (EU Directive) Regulations 2013, SI 2013/283; the Maternity and Parental Leave etc (Amendment) Regulations 2014, SI 2014/3221.

[1.975]

[77 Rights during and after parental leave

(1) Regulations under section 76 shall provide—

(a) that an employee who is absent on parental leave is entitled, for such purposes and to such extent as may be prescribed, to the benefit of the terms and conditions of employment which would have applied if he had not been absent,

(b) that an employee who is absent on parental leave is bound, for such purposes and to such extent as may be prescribed, by any obligations arising under those terms and conditions (except in so far as they are inconsistent with section 76(1)), and

(c) that an employee who is absent on parental leave is entitled, subject to section 78(1), to return from leave to a job of such kind as the regulations may specify.

(2) In subsection (1)(a) "terms and conditions of employment"—

(a) includes matters connected with an employee's employment whether or not they arise under a contract of employment, but

(b) does not include terms and conditions about remuneration.

(3) Regulations under section 76 may specify matters which are, or are not, to be treated as remuneration for the purposes of subsection (2)(b) above.

(4) The regulations may make provision, in relation to the right to return mentioned in subsection (1)(c), about—

(a) seniority, pension rights and similar rights;

(b) terms and conditions of employment on return.]

NOTES

Substituted as noted following the Part heading above.

[1.976]

[78 Special cases

(1) Regulations under section 76 may make provision—

(a) about redundancy during a period of parental leave;

(b) about dismissal (other than by reason of redundancy) during a period of parental leave.

(2) Provision by virtue of subsection (1) may include—

(a) provision requiring an employer to offer alternative employment;

(b) provision for the consequences of failure to comply with the regulations (which may include provision for a dismissal to be treated as unfair for the purposes of Part X).

(3) Regulations under section 76 may provide for an employee to be entitled to choose to exercise all or part of his entitlement to parental leave—

(a) by varying the terms of his contract of employment as to hours of work, or

(b) by varying his normal working practice as to hours of work,

in a way specified in or permitted by the regulations for a period specified in the regulations.

(4) Provision by virtue of subsection (3)—

(a) may restrict an entitlement to specified circumstances;

(b) may make an entitlement subject to specified conditions (which may include conditions relating to obtaining the employer's consent);

(c) may include consequential and incidental provision.

(5) Regulations under section 76 may make provision permitting all or part of an employee's entitlement to parental leave in respect of a child to be transferred to another employee in specified circumstances.

(6) The reference in section 77(1)(c) to absence on parental leave includes, where appropriate, a reference to a continuous period of absence attributable partly [to parental leave and partly to—

(a) maternity leave, or

(b) adoption leave,

or to both].

(7) Regulations under section 76 may provide for specified provisions of the regulations not to apply in relation to an employee if any provision of his contract of employment—

(a) confers an entitlement to absence from work for the purpose of caring for a child, and

(b) incorporates or operates by reference to all or part of a collective agreement, or workforce agreement, of a kind specified in the regulations.]

NOTES

Substituted as noted following the Part heading above.

Sub-s (6): words in square brackets substituted by the Employment Act 2002, s 53, Sch 7, paras 24, 28.

[1.977]

[79 Supplemental

(1) Regulations under section 76 may, in particular—

(a) make provision about notices to be given and evidence to be produced by employees to employers, by employers to employees, and by employers to other employers;

(b) make provision requiring employers or employees to keep records;

(c) make provision about other procedures to be followed by employees and employers;

(d) make provision (including provision creating criminal offences) specifying the consequences of failure to give notices, to produce evidence, to keep records or to comply with other procedural requirements;

(e) make provision specifying the consequences of failure to act in accordance with a notice given by virtue of paragraph (a);

(f) make special provision for cases where an employee has a right which corresponds to a right conferred by the regulations and which arises under his contract of employment or otherwise;

(g) make provision applying, modifying or excluding an enactment, in such circumstances as may be specified and subject to any conditions specified, in relation to a person entitled to parental leave;

(h) make different provision for different cases or circumstances.

(2) The regulations may make provision modifying the effect of Chapter II of Part XIV (calculation of a week's pay) in relation to an employee who is or has been absent from work on parental leave.

(3) Without prejudice to the generality of section 76, the regulations may make any provision which appears to the Secretary of State to be necessary or expedient—

(a) for the purpose of implementing Council Directive 96/34/EC on the framework agreement on parental leave, or

(b) for the purpose of dealing with any matter arising out of or related to the United Kingdom's obligations under that Directive.]

NOTES

Substituted as noted following the Part heading above.

Sub-s (3): repealed by the Employment Rights (Amendment) (EU Exit) Regulations 2019, SI 2019/535, reg 2(1), Sch 1, Pt 1, paras 1, 2, as from exit day (as defined in the European Union (Withdrawal) Act 2018, s 20) and subject to savings in Sch 1, Pt 3, para 22 thereto, which provides that the repeal does not affect the validity of any regulations made under this Act that came into force before exit day.

[1.978]

[80 Complaint to employment tribunal

(1) An employee may present a complaint to an employment tribunal that his employer—

(a) has unreasonably postponed a period of parental leave requested by the employee, or

(b) has prevented or attempted to prevent the employee from taking parental leave.

(2) An employment tribunal shall not consider a complaint under this section unless it is presented—

(a) before the end of the period of three months beginning with the date (or last date) of the matters complained of, or

(b) within such further period as the tribunal considers reasonable in a case where it is satisfied that it was not reasonably practicable for the complaint to be presented before the end of that period of three months.

[(2A) Section 207A(3) (extension because of mediation in certain European cross-border disputes) [and section 207B (extension of time limits to facilitate conciliation before institution of proceedings) apply] for the purposes of subsection (2)(a).]

(3) Where an employment tribunal finds a complaint under this section well-founded it—

(a) shall make a declaration to that effect, and

(b) may make an award of compensation to be paid by the employer to the employee.

(4) The amount of compensation shall be such as the tribunal considers just and equitable in all the circumstances having regard to—

(a) the employer's behaviour, and

(b) any loss sustained by the employee which is attributable to the matters complained of.]

NOTES

Substituted as noted following the Part heading above.

Sub-s (2A): inserted by the Cross-Border Mediation (EU Directive) Regulations 2011, SI 2011/1133, regs 30, 44; words in square brackets substituted by the Enterprise and Regulatory Reform Act 2013, s 8, Sch 2, paras 15, 31; substituted by the Cross-Border Mediation (EU Directive) (EU Exit) Regulations 2019, SI 2019/469, reg 4, Sch 1, Pt 1, para 12(1), (21), as from exit day (as defined in the European Union (Withdrawal) Act 2018, s 20), as follows—

"(2A) Section 207B (extension of time limits to facilitate conciliation before institution of proceedings) applies for the purposes of subsection (2)(a).".

Conciliation: employment tribunal proceedings under this section are "relevant proceedings" for the purposes of the conciliation provisions contained in the Employment Tribunals Act 1996, ss 18–18C; see s 18(1)(b) of the 1996 Act at **[1.757]**.

[CHAPTER III PATERNITY LEAVE

[1.979]

80A Entitlement to [. . .] paternity leave: birth

(1) The Secretary of State shall make regulations entitling an employee who satisfies specified conditions—

(a) as to duration of employment,

(b) as to relationship with a newborn, or expected, child, and

(c) as to relationship with the child's mother,

to be absent from work on leave under this section for the purpose of caring for the child or supporting the mother.

(2) The regulations shall include provision for determining—

(a) the extent of an employee's entitlement to leave under this section in respect of a child;

(b) when leave under this section may be taken.

(3) Provision under subsection (2)(a) shall secure that where an employee is entitled to leave under this section in respect of a child he is entitled to at least two weeks' leave.

(4) Provision under subsection (2)(b) shall secure that leave under this section must be taken before the end of a period of at least 56 days beginning with the date of the child's birth.

[(4A) Provision under subsection (2)(b) must secure that, once an employee takes leave under section 75E in respect of a child, the employee may not take leave under this section in respect of the child.]

(5) Regulations under subsection (1) may—

(a) specify things which are, or are not, to be taken as done for the purpose of caring for a child or supporting the child's mother;

(b) make provision excluding the right to be absent on leave under this section in respect of a child where more than one child is born as a result of the same pregnancy;

(c) make provision about how leave under this section may be taken.

(6) Where more than one child is born as a result of the same pregnancy, the reference in subsection (4) to the date of the child's birth shall be read as a reference to the date of birth of the first child born as a result of the pregnancy.

(7) In this section—

"newborn child" includes a child stillborn after twenty-four weeks of pregnancy;

"week" means any period of seven days.]

NOTES

Chapter III (ss 80A–80E) inserted by the Employment Act 2002, s 1.

Section heading: word omitted originally inserted by the Work and Families Act 2006, s 11(1), Sch 1, para 35, and repealed by the Children and Families Act 2014, s 126, Sch 7, paras 29, 32, as from 5 April 2015 (note that this amendment does not have effect in relation to (a) children whose expected week of birth ends on or before 4 April 2015, and (b) children placed for adoption on or before that date: see the Children and Families Act 2014 (Commencement No 3, Transitional Provisions and Savings) Order 2014, SI 2014/1640, art 16).

Sub-s (4A): inserted by the Children and Families Act 2014, s 118(1), (6), as from 30 June 2014.

Application: this section applies to parental order parents subject to certain modifications, see the Employment Rights Act 1996 (Application of Sections 75A, 75B, 75G, 75H, 80A and 80B to Parental Order Cases) Regulations 2014, SI 2014/3095, reg 4 and Sch 2 at **[2.1744]** and **[2.1746]**.

Regulations: the Paternity and Adoption Leave Regulations 2002, SI 2002/2788 at **[2.576]**; the Paternity and Adoption Leave (Amendment) Regulations 2014, SI 2014/2112 at **[2.1512]**; the Paternity, Adoption and Shared Parental Leave (Parental Order Cases) Regulations 2014, SI 2014/3096 at **[2.1747]**.

80AA *(Inserted by the Work and Families Act 2006, s 3, and repealed by the Children and Families Act 2014, s 125(1), as from 5 April 2015, except in relation to (a) children whose expected week of birth ends on or before 4 April 2015, and (b) children placed for adoption on or before that date (see the Children and Families Act 2014 (Commencement No 3, Transitional Provisions and Savings) Order 2014, SI 2014/1640, art 16).)*

[1.980]

[80B Entitlement to [. . .] paternity leave: adoption

(1) The Secretary of State shall make regulations entitling an employee who satisfies specified conditions—

(a) as to duration of employment,

(b) as to relationship with a child placed, or expected to be placed, for adoption under the law of any part of the United Kingdom, and

(c) as to relationship with a person with whom the child is, or is expected to be, so placed for adoption,

to be absent from work on leave under this section for the purpose of caring for the child or supporting the person by reference to whom he satisfies the condition under paragraph (c).

(2) The regulations shall include provision for determining—

(a) the extent of an employee's entitlement to leave under this section in respect of a child;

(b) when leave under this section may be taken.

(3) Provision under subsection (2)(a) shall secure that where an employee is entitled to leave under this section in respect of a child he is entitled to at least two weeks' leave.

(4) Provision under subsection (2)(b) shall secure that leave under this section must be taken before the end of a period of at least 56 days beginning with the date of the child's placement for adoption.

[(4A) Provision under subsection (2)(b) must secure that, once an employee takes leave under section 75G in respect of a child, the employee may not take leave under this section in respect of the child.]

(5) Regulations under subsection (1) may—

(a) specify things which are, or are not, to be taken as done for the purpose of caring for a child or supporting a person with whom a child is placed for adoption;

[(aa) make provision excluding the right to be absent on leave under this section in the case of an employee who, by virtue of provision under subsection (6A), has already exercised a right to be absent on leave under this section in connection with the same child;]

(b) make provision excluding the right to be absent on leave under this section in the case of an employee who exercises a right to be absent from work on adoption leave;

[(ba) make provision excluding the right to be absent on leave under this section in the case of an employee who has exercised a right to take time off under section 57ZJ;]

(c) make provision excluding the right to be absent on leave under this section in respect of a child where more than one child is placed for adoption as part of the same arrangement;

(d) make provision about how leave under this section may be taken.

(6) Where more than one child is placed for adoption as part of the same arrangement, the reference in subsection (4) to the date of the child's placement shall be read as a reference to the date of placement of the first child to be placed as part of the arrangement.

[(6A) Regulations under subsection (1) shall include provision for leave in respect of a child placed, or expected to be placed—

(a) under section 22C of the Children Act 1989 by a local authority in England, or

(b) under section 81 of the Social Services and Well-being (Wales) Act 2014 by a local authority in Wales,

with a local authority foster parent who has been approved as a prospective adopter.]

(6B) This section has effect in relation to regulations made by virtue of subsection (6A) as if—

(a) references to being placed for adoption were references to being placed under section 22C of the Children Act 1989[, or section 81 of the Social Services and Well-being (Wales) Act 2014] with a local authority foster parent who has been approved as a prospective adopter;

(b) references to placement for adoption were references to placement under section 22C [of the Children Act 1989, or section 81 of the Social Services and Well-being (Wales) Act 2014] with such a person;

(c) paragraph (aa) of subsection (5) were omitted.]

(7) In this section, "week" means any period of seven days.

(8) The Secretary of State may by regulations provide for this section to have effect in relation to cases which involve adoption, but not the placement of a child for adoption under the law of any part of the United Kingdom, with such modifications as the regulations may prescribe.

[(9) The Secretary of State may by regulations provide for this section to have effect in relation to cases which involve an employee who has applied, or intends to apply, with another person for a parental order under section 54 of the Human Fertilisation and Embryology Act 2008 and a child who is, or will be, the subject of the order, with such modifications as the regulations may prescribe.]]

NOTES

Inserted as noted to s 80A at **[1.979]**.

Section heading: word omitted originally inserted by the Work and Families Act 2006, s 11(1), Sch 1, para 36, and repealed by the Children and Families Act 2014, s 126, Sch 7, paras 29, 33, as from 5 April 2015 (note that this amendment does not have effect in relation to (a) children whose expected week of birth ends on or before 4 April 2015, and (b) children placed for adoption on or before that date: see the Children and Families Act 2014 (Commencement No 3, Transitional Provisions and Savings) Order 2014, SI 2014/1640, art 16).

Sub-s (4A): inserted by the Children and Families Act 2014, s 118(1), (7), as from 30 June 2014.

Sub-s (5): paras (aa), (ba) inserted by the Children and Families Act 2014, ss 121(2)(a), 128(2)(b), as from 30 June 2014.

Sub-ss (6A), (6B): inserted by the Children and Families Act 2014, s 121(2)(b), as from 30 June 2014; sub-s (6A) subsequently substituted, and words in square brackets in sub-s (6B) inserted, by the Social Services and Well-being (Wales) Act 2014 (Consequential Amendments) Regulations 2016, SI 2016/413, regs 143, 147, as from 6 April 2016.

Sub-s (9): added by the Children and Families Act 2014, s 122(4), as from 30 June 2014.

Modified, in relation to adoptions from overseas, by the Employment Rights Act 1996 (Application of Section 80B to Adoptions from Overseas) Regulations 2003, SI 2003/920.

Application: this section applies to parental order parents subject to certain modifications, see the Employment Rights Act 1996 (Application of Sections 75A, 75B, 75G, 75H, 80A and 80B to Parental Order Cases) Regulations 2014, SI 2014/3095, reg 4 and Sch 2 at **[2.1744]** and **[2.1746]**.

Regulations: the Paternity and Adoption Leave Regulations 2002, SI 2002/2788 at **[2.576]**; the Employment Rights Act 1996 (Application of Section 80B to Adoptions from Overseas) Regulations 2003, SI 2003/920; the Paternity and Adoption Leave (Adoptions from Overseas) Regulations 2003, SI 2003/921; the Paternity and Adoption Leave (Amendment) Regulations 2014, SI 2014/2112 at **[2.1512]**; the Shared Parental Leave and Paternity and Adoption Leave (Adoptions from Overseas) Regulations 2014, SI 2014/3092 at **[2.1704]**; the Employment Rights Act 1996 (Application of Sections 75A, 75B, 75G, 75H, 80A and 80B to Parental Order Cases) Regulations 2014, SI 2014/3095 at **[2.1741]**; the Paternity, Adoption and Shared Parental Leave (Parental Order Cases) Regulations 2014, SI 2014/3096 at **[2.1747]**; the Paternity and Adoption Leave (Amendment) (No 2) Regulations 2014, SI 2014/3206.

80BB *(Inserted by the Work and Families Act 2006, s 4, and repealed by the Children and Families Act 2014, s 125(1), as from 5 April 2015, except in relation to (a) children whose expected week of birth ends on or before 4 April 2015, and (b) children placed for adoption on or before that date (see the Children and Families Act 2014 (Commencement No 3, Transitional Provisions and Savings) Order 2014, SI 2014/1640, art 16).)*

[1.981]
[80C Rights during and after paternity leave

(1) Regulations under section 80A [. . .] shall provide—
- (a) that an employee who is absent on leave under that section is entitled, for such purposes and to such extent as the regulations may prescribe, to the benefit of the terms and conditions of employment which would have applied if he had not been absent;
- (b) that an employee who is absent on leave under that section is bound, for such purposes and to such extent as the regulations may prescribe, by obligations arising under those terms and conditions (except in so far as they are inconsistent with subsection (1) of that section), and
- (c) that an employee who is absent on leave under that section is entitled to return from leave to a job of a kind prescribed by regulations, subject to section 80D(1).

(2) The reference in subsection (1)(c) to absence on leave under section 80A [. . .] includes, where appropriate, a reference to a continuous period of absence attributable partly to leave under that section and partly to any one or more of the following—
- [(za) . . .]
- (a) maternity leave,
- (b) adoption leave, . . .
- [(ba) shared parental leave,]
- [(bb) parental bereavement leave,] [and]
- (c) parental leave.

(3) Subsection (1) shall apply to regulations under section 80B [. . . as it applies to regulations under section 80A . . .].

(4) In the application of subsection (1)(c) to regulations under section 80B [. . .], the reference to absence on leave under that section includes, where appropriate, a reference to a continuous period of absence attributable partly to leave under that section and partly to any one or more of the following—
- [(za) . . .
- (a) maternity leave,
- (b) adoption leave,
- [(ba) shared parental leave,]
- [(bb) parental bereavement leave,]
- (c) parental leave, and
- (d) leave under section 80A [. . .].

(5) In subsection (1)(a), "terms and conditions of employment"—
- (a) includes matters connected with an employee's employment whether or not they arise under his contract of employment, but
- (b) does not include terms and conditions about remuneration.

(6) Regulations under [section 80A or 80B] may specify matters which are, or are not, to be treated as remuneration for the purposes of this section.

(7) Regulations under [section 80A or 80B] may make provision, in relation to the right to return mentioned in subsection (1)(c), about—
- (a) seniority, pension rights and similar rights;
- (b) terms and conditions of employment on return.]

NOTES

Inserted as noted to s 80A at **[1.979]**.

Sub-s (1): words omitted originally inserted by the Work and Families Act 2006, s 5(1), (2), and repealed by the Children and Families Act 2014, s 126(1), Sch 7, paras 29, 34(1), (2), as from 5 April 2015 (note that this repeal does not have effect in relation to (a) children whose expected week of birth ends on or before 4 April 2015, and (b) children placed for adoption on or before that date: see the Children and Families Act 2014 (Commencement No 3, Transitional Provisions and Savings) Order 2014, SI 2014/1640, art 16).

Sub-s (2) is amended as follows:

First words omitted, and para (za) originally inserted, by the Work and Families Act 2006, s 5(1), (3), and repealed by the Children and Families Act 2014, s 126(1), Sch 7, paras 29, 34(1), (3)(a), (b), as from 5 April 2015 (note that these repeals do not have effect in relation to (a) children whose expected week of birth ends on or before 4 April 2015, and (b) children placed for adoption on or before that date: see SI 2014/1640, art 16).

Word omitted from para (b) repealed, and para (ba) inserted (together with word following para (bb), by the Children and Families Act 2014, s 126(1), Sch 7, paras 29, 34(1), (3)(c), (d), as from 30 June 2014.

Para (bb) inserted by the Parental Bereavement (Leave and Pay) Act 2018, s 1(c), Schedule, Pt 3, paras 20, 24(1), (2), as from a day to be appointed.

Sub-s (3): words in square brackets substituted by the Work and Families Act 2006, s 5(1), (4); words omitted repealed by the Children and Families Act 2014, s 126(1), Sch 7, paras 29, 34(1), (4), as from 5 April 2015 (note that this repeal does not have effect in relation to (a) children whose expected week of birth ends on or before 4 April 2015, and (b) children placed for adoption on or before that date: see SI 2014/1640, art 16).

Sub-s (4) is amended as follows:

First words omitted, and para (za) originally inserted by the Work and Families Act 2006, s 5(1), (5), and repealed by the Children and Families Act 2014, s 126(1), Sch 7, paras 29, 34(1), (5)(a), (b), as from 5 April 2015 (note that these repeals do not have effect in relation to (a) children whose expected week of birth ends on or before 4 April 2015, and (b) children placed for adoption on or before that date: see SI 2014/1640, art 16).

Para (ba) inserted by the Children and Families Act 2014, s 126(1), Sch 7, paras 29, 34(1), (5)(c), as from 30 June 2014.

Para (bb) inserted by the Parental Bereavement (Leave and Pay) Act 2018, s 1(c), Schedule, Pt 3, paras 20, 24(1), (3), as from a day to be appointed.

Words omitted from para (d) originally inserted by the Work and Families Act 2006, s 5(1), (5)(c), and repealed by the Children and Families Act 2014, s 126(1), Sch 7, paras 29, 34(1), (5)(d), as from 5 April 2015 (note that this repeal does not have effect in relation to (a) children whose expected week of birth ends on or before 4 April 2015, and (b) children placed for adoption on or before that date: see SI 2014/1640, art 16).

Sub-ss (6), (7): words in square brackets substituted by the Children and Families Act 2014, s 126(1), Sch 7, paras 29, 34(1), (6), (7), as from 5 April 2015 (note that these amendments do not have effect in relation to (a) children whose expected week of birth ends on or before 4 April 2015, and (b) children placed for adoption on or before that date: see SI 2014/1640, art 16).

[1.982]

[80D Special cases

[(1) Regulations under section [80A [or 80B]] may make provision about—

(a) redundancy, or

(b) dismissal (other than by reason of redundancy),

during a period of leave under that section.

(2) Provision by virtue of subsection (1) may include—

(a) provision requiring an employer to offer alternative employment;

(b) provision for the consequences of failure to comply with the regulations (which may include provision for a dismissal to be treated as unfair for the purposes of Part 10).]

NOTES

Inserted as noted to s 80A at **[1.979]**.

Sub-s (1): figure in first (outer) pair of square brackets substituted by the Work and Families Act 2006, s 11(1), Sch 1, para 37; words in second (inner) pair of square brackets substituted by the Children and Families Act 2014, s 126, Sch 7, paras 29, 35, as from 5 April 2015 (note that this amendment does not have effect in relation to (a) children whose expected week of birth ends on or before 4 April 2015, and (b) children placed for adoption on or before that date: see the Children and Families Act 2014 (Commencement No 3, Transitional Provisions and Savings) Order 2014, SI 2014/1640, art 16).

[1.983]

[80E Chapter 3: supplemental

[(1)] Regulations under [section 80A or 80B] may—

(a) make provision about notices to be given, evidence to be produced and other procedures to be followed by employees and employers;

(b) make provision requiring employers or employees to keep records;

(c) make provision for the consequences of failure to give notices, to produce evidence, to keep records or to comply with other procedural requirements;

(d) make provision for the consequences of failure to act in accordance with a notice given by virtue of paragraph (a);

(e) make special provision for cases where an employee has a right which corresponds to a right under [section 80A or 80B] and which arises under his contract of employment or otherwise;

(f) make provision modifying the effect of Chapter 2 of Part 14 (calculation of a week's pay) in relation to an employee who is or has been absent from work on leave under [section 80A or 80B];

(g) make provision applying, modifying or excluding an enactment, in such circumstances as may be specified and subject to any conditions which may be specified, in relation to a person entitled to take leave under [section 80A or 80B];

(h) make different provision for different cases or circumstances.

[(2) . . .]

NOTES

Inserted as noted to s 80A at **[1.979]**.

Sub-s (1) numbered as such, and sub-s (2) added, by the Work and Families Act 2006, s 11(1), Sch 1, para 38.

Words in square brackets in sub-s (1) substituted, and sub-s (2) repealed, by the Children and Families Act 2014, s 126, Sch 7, paras 29, 36, as from 5 April 2015 (note that these amendments do not have effect in relation to (a) children whose expected week of birth ends on or before 4 April 2015, and (b) children placed for adoption on or before that date: see the Children and Families Act 2014 (Commencement No 3, Transitional Provisions and Savings) Order 2014, SI 2014/1640, art 16).

[CHAPTER 4 PARENTAL BEREAVEMENT LEAVE

[1.984]

80EA Parental bereavement leave

(1) The Secretary of State must make regulations entitling an employee who is a bereaved parent to be absent from work on leave under this section.

(2) For the purposes of subsection (1) an employee is a "bereaved parent" if the employee satisfies conditions specified in the regulations as to relationship with a child who has died.
(3) The conditions specified under subsection (2) may be framed, in whole or in part, by reference to the employee's care of the child before the child's death.
(4) The regulations must include provision for determining—
- (a) the extent of an employee's entitlement to leave under this section in respect of a child;
- (b) when leave under this section may be taken.

(5) Provision under subsection (4)(a) must secure that where an employee is entitled to leave under this section in respect of a child the employee is entitled to at least two weeks' leave.
(6) Provision under subsection (4)(b) must secure that leave under this section must be taken before the end of a period of at least 56 days beginning with the date of the child's death.
(7) The regulations must secure that where a person is eligible under subsection (1) as the result of the death of more than one child, the person is entitled to leave in respect of each child.
(8) The regulations may make provision about how leave under this section is to be taken.
(9) In this section—
"child" means a person under the age of 18 (see also section 80EE for the application of this Chapter in relation to stillbirths);
"week" means any period of seven days.]

NOTES
Commencement: to be appointed.
Chapter 4 (ss 80EA–80EE) inserted by the Parental Bereavement (Leave and Pay) Act 2018, s 1(a), Schedule, Pt 1, paras 1, 2, as from a day to be appointed.
Regulations: as of 15 May 2019, no Regulations had been made under this section.

[1.985]
[80EB Rights during and after bereavement leave
(1) Regulations under section 80EA must provide—
- (a) that an employee who is absent on leave under that section is entitled, for such purposes and to such extent as the regulations may prescribe, to the benefit of the terms and conditions of employment which would have applied but for the absence,
- (b) that an employee who is absent on leave under that section is bound, for such purposes and to such extent as the regulations may prescribe, by obligations arising under those terms and conditions (except in so far as they are inconsistent with subsection (1) of that section), and
- (c) that an employee who is absent on leave under that section is entitled to return from leave to a job of a kind prescribed by regulations, subject to section 80EC(1).

(2) The reference in subsection (1)(c) to absence on leave under section 80EA includes, where appropriate, a reference to a continuous period of absence attributable partly to leave under that section and partly to any one or more of the following—
- (a) maternity leave,
- (b) paternity leave,
- (c) adoption leave,
- (d) shared parental leave, and
- (e) parental leave.

(3) In subsection (1)(a), "terms and conditions of employment"—
- (a) includes matters connected with an employee's employment whether or not they arise under the contract of employment, but
- (b) does not include terms and conditions about remuneration.

(4) Regulations under section 80EA may specify matters which are, or are not, to be treated as remuneration for the purposes of this section.
(5) Regulations under section 80EA may make provision, in relation to the right to return mentioned in subsection (1)(c), about—
- (a) seniority, pension rights and similar rights;
- (b) terms and conditions of employment on return.]

NOTES
Commencement: to be appointed.
Inserted as noted to s 80EA at **[1.984]**.
Regulations: as of 15 May 2019, no Regulations had been made under this section.

[1.986]
[80EC Special cases
(1) Regulations under section 80EA may make provision about—
- (a) redundancy, or
- (b) dismissal (other than by reason of redundancy),

during a period of leave under that section.
(2) Provision by virtue of subsection (1) may include—
- (a) provision requiring an employer to offer alternative employment;
- (b) provision for the consequences of failure to comply with the regulations (which may include provision for a dismissal to be treated as unfair for the purposes of Part 10).]

NOTES

Commencement: to be appointed.
Inserted as noted to s 80EA at **[1.984]**.
Regulations: as of 15 May 2019, no Regulations had been made under this section.

[1.987]
[80ED Chapter 4: supplemental
Regulations under section 80EA may—
- (a) make provision about notices to be given, evidence to be produced and other procedures to be followed by employees and employers;
- (b) make provision requiring employers or employees to keep records;
- (c) make provision for the consequences of failure to give notices, to produce evidence, to keep records or to comply with other procedural requirements;
- (d) make provision for the consequences of failure to act in accordance with a notice given by virtue of paragraph (a);
- (e) make special provision for cases where an employee has a right which corresponds to a right under section 80EA and which arises under the person's contract of employment or otherwise;
- (f) make provision modifying the effect of Chapter 2 of Part 14 (calculation of a week's pay) in relation to an employee who is or has been absent from work on leave under section 80EA;
- (g) make provision applying, modifying or excluding an enactment, in such circumstances as may be specified and subject to any conditions which may be specified, in relation to a person entitled to take leave under section 80EA;
- (h) make different provision for different cases or circumstances;
- (i) make consequential provision.]

NOTES

Commencement: to be appointed.
Inserted as noted to s 80EA at **[1.984]**.
Regulations: as of 15 May 2019, no Regulations had been made under this section.

[1.988]
[80EE Application in relation to stillbirths
In this Chapter—
- (a) references to a child include a child stillborn after twenty-four weeks of pregnancy, and
- (b) references to the death of a child are to be read, in relation to a stillborn child, as references to the birth of the child.]

NOTES

Commencement: to be appointed.
Inserted as noted to s 80EA at **[1.984]**.

[PART VIIIA
FLEXIBLE WORKING

[1.989]
80F Statutory right to request contract variation
(1) A qualifying employee may apply to his employer for a change in his terms and conditions of employment if—
- (a) the change relates to—
  - (i) the hours he is required to work,
  - (ii) the times when he is required to work,
  - (iii) where, as between his home and a place of business of his employer, he is required to work, or
  - (iv) such other aspect of his terms and conditions of employment as the Secretary of State may specify by regulations, . . .
- [(b) . . .]

(2) An application under this section must—
- (a) state that it is such an application,
- (b) specify the change applied for and the date on which it is proposed the change should become effective, [and]
- (c) explain what effect, if any, the employee thinks making the change applied for would have on his employer and how, in his opinion, any such effect might be dealt with, . . .
- (d) . . .

(3) . . .
(4) If an employee has made an application under this section, he may not make a further application under this section to the same employer before the end of the period of twelve months beginning with the date on which the previous application was made.
(5) The Secretary of State may by regulations make provision about—
- (a) the form of applications under this section, and
- (b) when such an application is to be taken as made.

(6), (7) . . .
(8) For the purposes of this section, an employee is—

(a) a qualifying employee if he—
(i) satisfies such conditions as to duration of employment as the Secretary of State may specify by regulations, and
(ii) is not an agency worker [(other than an agency worker who is returning to work from a period of parental leave under regulations under section 76)];
(b) an agency worker if he is supplied by a person ("the agent") to do work for another ("the principal") under a contract or other arrangement made between the agent and the principal.]

[(9) Regulations under this section may make different provision for different cases.

(10) . . .]

NOTES

Part VIIIA (ss 80F–80I) inserted by the Employment Act 2002, s 47(1), (2).

Sub-s (1): para (b) originally substituted by the Work and Families Act 2006, s 12(1), (2), and repealed (together with the preceding word) by the Children and Families Act 2014, s 131(1), (2)(a), as from 30 June 2014, except in relation to any application for a change in terms and conditions which is made on or before 29 June 2014 (see the Children and Families Act 2014 (Commencement No 3, Transitional Provisions and Savings) Order 2014, SI 2014/1640, art 10).

Sub-s (2): word in square brackets in para (b) inserted, and para (d) (together with the preceding word) repealed, by the Children and Families Act 2014, s 131(2)(b), (c), as from 30 June 2014, except in relation to any application for a change in terms and conditions which is made on or before 29 June 2014 (see SI 2014/1640, art 10).

Sub-ss (3), (6), (7): repealed by the Work and Families Act 2006, ss 12(1), (4), 15, Sch 2.

Sub-s (8): words in square brackets inserted by the Parental Leave (EU Directive) Regulations 2013, SI 2013/283, reg 2.

Sub-ss (9), (10): added by the Work and Families Act 2006, s 12(1), (5); sub-s (10) subsequently repealed by the Children and Families Act 2014, s 131(2)(d), as from 30 June 2014, except in relation to any application for a change in terms and conditions which is made on or before 29 June 2014 (see SI 2014/1640, art 10).

Regulations: the Flexible Working (Eligibility, Complaints and Remedies) (Amendment) (Revocation) Regulations 2011, SI 2011/989; the Flexible Working Regulations 2014, SI 2014/1398 at **[2.1481]**. Other Regulations made under this section that amended the Flexible Working (Eligibility, Complaints and Remedies) Regulations 2002, SI 2002/3236 (which was originally made under this section but has been revoked) are regarded as spent even though they have not been revoked.

[1.990]

[80G Employer's duties in relation to application under section 80F

(1) An employer to whom an application under section 80F is made—
[(a) shall deal with the application in a reasonable manner,
(aa) shall notify the employee of the decision on the application within the decision period, and]
(b) shall only refuse the application because he considers that one or more of the following grounds applies—
(i) the burden of additional costs,
(ii) detrimental effect on ability to meet customer demand,
(iii) inability to re-organise work among existing staff,
(iv) inability to recruit additional staff,
(v) detrimental impact on quality,
(vi) detrimental impact on performance,
(vii) insufficiency of work during the periods the employee proposes to work,
(viii) planned structural changes, and
(ix) such other grounds as the Secretary of State may specify by regulations.

[(1A) If an employer allows an employee to appeal a decision to reject an application, the reference in subsection (1)(aa) to the decision on the application is a reference to—
(a) the decision on the appeal, or
(b) if more than one appeal is allowed, the decision on the final appeal.

(1B) For the purposes of subsection (1)(aa) the decision period applicable to an employee's application under section 80F is—
(a) the period of three months beginning with the date on which the application is made, or
(b) such longer period as may be agreed by the employer and the employee.

(1C) An agreement to extend the decision period in a particular case may be made—
(a) before it ends, or
(b) with retrospective effect, before the end of a period of three months beginning with the day after that on which the decision period that is being extended came to an end.]

[(1D) An application under section 80F is to be treated as having been withdrawn by the employee if—
(a) the employee without good reason has failed to attend both the first meeting arranged by the employer to discuss the application and the next meeting arranged for that purpose, or
(b) where the employer allows the employee to appeal a decision to reject an application or to make a further appeal, the employee without good reason has failed to attend both the first meeting arranged by the employer to discuss the appeal and the next meeting arranged for that purpose,

and the employer has notified the employee that the employer has decided to treat that conduct of the employee as a withdrawal of the application.]

(2)–(4) . . .]

NOTES

Inserted as noted to s 80F at **[1.989]**.

Sub-s (1)(a), (aa) substituted (for the original (sub-s (1)(a)), sub-ss (1A)–(1D) inserted, and sub-ss (2)–(4) repealed, by the Children and Families Act 2014, s 132(1)–(4), (5)(b), as from 30 June 2014, except in relation to any application for a change in terms and conditions which is made on or before 29 June 2014 (see the Children and Families Act 2014 (Commencement No 3, Transitional Provisions and Savings) Order 2014, SI 2014/1640, art 10).

Regulations: the Flexible Working Regulations 2014, SI 2014/1398 at **[2.1481]** (note that the 2014 Regulations were made under sub-ss (2), (3) and have therefore lapsed in so far as made under those subsections, subject to the transitional provisions noted above).

[1.991]

[80H Complaints to employment tribunals

(1) An employee who makes an application under section 80F may present a complaint to an employment tribunal—

(a) that his employer has failed in relation to the application to comply with section 80G(1), . . .

(b) that a decision by his employer to reject the application was based on incorrect facts[, or

(c) that the employer's notification under section 80G(1D) was given in circumstances that did not satisfy one of the requirements in section 80G(1D)(a) and (b)].

(2) No complaint [under subsection (1)(a) or (b)] may be made in respect of an application which has been disposed of by agreement or withdrawn.

[(3) In the case of an application which has not been disposed of by agreement or withdrawn, no complaint under subsection (1)(a) or (b) may be made until—

(a) the employer notifies the employee of the employer's decision on the application, or

(b) if the decision period applicable to the application (see section 80G(1B)) comes to an end without the employer notifying the employee of the employer's decision on the application, the end of the decision period.

(3A) If an employer allows an employee to appeal a decision to reject an application, a reference in other subsections of this section to the decision on the application is a reference to the decision on the appeal or, if more than one appeal is allowed, the decision on the final appeal.

(3B) If an agreement to extend the decision period is made as described in section 80G(1C)(b), subsection (3)(b) is to be treated as not allowing a complaint until the end of the extended period.]

[(3C) A complaint under subsection (1)(c) may be made as soon as the notification under section 80G(1D) complained of is given to the employee.]

(4) . . .

(5) An employment tribunal shall not consider a complaint under this section unless it is presented—

(a) before the end of the period of three months beginning with the relevant date, or

(b) within such further period as the tribunal considers reasonable in a case where it is satisfied that it was not reasonably practicable for the complaint to be presented before the end of that period of three months.

(6) In subsection (5)(a), the reference to the [relevant date is a reference to the first date on which the employee may make a complaint under subsection (1)(a), (b) or (c), as the case may be].

[(7) Section 207A(3) (extension because of mediation in certain European cross-border disputes) [and section 207B (extension of time limits to facilitate conciliation before institution of proceedings) apply] for the purposes of subsection (5)(a).]]

NOTES

Inserted as noted to s 80F at **[1.989]**.

Sub-s (1): word omitted from para (a) repealed, and para (c) (and the preceding word) inserted, by the Children and Families Act 2014, s 133(1), (2), as from 30 June 2014, except in relation to any application for a change in terms and conditions which is made on or before 29 June 2014 (see the Children and Families Act 2014 (Commencement No 3, Transitional Provisions and Savings) Order 2014, SI 2014/1640, art 10).

Sub-ss (2), (6): words in square brackets substituted by the Children and Families Act 2014, s 133(1), (3), (6), as from 30 June 2014, except in relation to any application for a change in terms and conditions which is made on or before 29 June 2014 (see SI 2014/1640, art 10).

Sub-ss (3), (3A), (3B): substituted (for the original sub-s (3)) by the Children and Families Act 2014, s 133(1), (4), as from 30 June 2014, except in relation to any application for a change in terms and conditions which is made on or before 29 June 2014 (see SI 2014/1640, art 10).

Sub-s (3C): inserted by the Children and Families Act 2014, s 133(1), (5), as from 30 June 2014, except in relation to any application for a change in terms and conditions which is made on or before 29 June 2014 (see SI 2014/1640, art 10).

Sub-s (4): repealed by the Children and Families Act 2014, s 132(5)(c), as from 30 June 2014, except in relation to any application for a change in terms and conditions which is made on or before 29 June 2014 (see SI 2014/1640, art 10).

Sub-s (7): added by the Cross-Border Mediation (EU Directive) Regulations 2011, SI 2011/1133, regs 30, 45; words in square brackets substituted by the Enterprise and Regulatory Reform Act 2013, s 8, Sch 2, paras 15, 32; substituted by the Cross-Border Mediation (EU Directive) (EU Exit) Regulations 2019, SI 2019/469, reg 4, Sch 1, Pt 1, para 12(1), (22), as from exit day (as defined in the European Union (Withdrawal) Act 2018, s 20), as follows—

> "(7) Section 207B (extension of time limits to facilitate conciliation before institution of proceedings) applies for the purposes of subsection (5)(a).".

Conciliation: employment tribunal proceedings under this section are "relevant proceedings" for the purposes of the conciliation provisions contained in the Employment Tribunals Act 1996, ss 18–18C; see s 18(1)(b) of the 1996 Act at **[1.757]**.

Regulations: the Flexible Working Regulations 2014, SI 2014/1398 at **[2.1481]** (note that the 2014 Regulations were made under the original sub-s (3)(b) and have therefore lapsed in so far as made under that subsection, subject to the transitional provisions noted above).

[1.992]

[80I Remedies

(1) Where an employment tribunal finds a complaint under section 80H well-founded it shall make a declaration to that effect and may—

(a) make an order for reconsideration of the application, and

(b) make an award of compensation to be paid by the employer to the employee.

(2) The amount of compensation shall be such amount, not exceeding the permitted maximum, as the tribunal considers just and equitable in all the circumstances.

(3) For the purposes of subsection (2), the permitted maximum is such number of weeks' pay as the Secretary of State may specify by regulations.

(4) Where an employment tribunal makes an order under subsection (1)(a), section 80G . . . shall apply as if the application had been made on the date of the order.]

NOTES

Inserted as noted to s 80F at **[1.989]**.

Sub-s (4): words omitted repealed by the Children and Families Act 2014, s 132(5)(d), as from 30 June 2014, except in relation to any application for a change in terms and conditions which is made on or before 29 June 2014 (see the Children and Families Act 2014 (Commencement No 3, Transitional Provisions and Savings) Order 2014, SI 2014/1640, art 10).

Regulations: the Flexible Working Regulations 2014, SI 2014/1398 at **[2.1481]**.

PART IX
TERMINATION OF EMPLOYMENT

Minimum period of notice

[1.993]

86 Rights of employer and employee to minimum notice

(1) The notice required to be given by an employer to terminate the contract of employment of a person who has been continuously employed for one month or more—

(a) is not less than one week's notice if his period of continuous employment is less than two years,

(b) is not less than one week's notice for each year of continuous employment if his period of continuous employment is two years or more but less than twelve years, and

(c) is not less than twelve weeks' notice if his period of continuous employment is twelve years or more.

(2) The notice required to be given by an employee who has been continuously employed for one month or more to terminate his contract of employment is not less than one week.

(3) Any provision for shorter notice in any contract of employment with a person who has been continuously employed for one month or more has effect subject to subsections (1) and (2); but this section does not prevent either party from waiving his right to notice on any occasion or from accepting a payment in lieu of notice.

(4) Any contract of employment of a person who has been continuously employed for three months or more which is a contract for a term certain of one month or less shall have effect as if it were for an indefinite period; and, accordingly, subsections (1) and (2) apply to the contract.

(5) . . .

(6) This section does not affect any right of either party to a contract of employment to treat the contract as terminable without notice by reason of the conduct of the other party.

NOTES

Sub-s (5): repealed by the Fixed-term Employees (Prevention of Less Favourable Treatment) Regulations 2002, SI 2002/2034, reg 11, Sch 2, Pt 1, para 3(1), (4) (except in relation to Government training schemes, agency workers and apprentices; see regs 18–20 of the 2002 Regulations at **[2.571]** et seq).

General Note: the provisions of this Part of this Act relating to a minimum period of notice suggest that the intention of the Act is to incorporate into the contract of employment the statutory terms laid down and that an employee who wishes to enforce those terms should sue on his contract of employment as statutorily amended, and not on the statute; see *Secretary of State for Employment v Wilson* [1978] 3 All ER 137, [1978] 1 ICR 200, EAT (approved in *Westwood v Secretary of State for Employment* [1985] ICR 209, [1984] 1 All ER 874, HL), both cases being in relation to the statutory predecessors of this Part.

[1.994]

87 Rights of employee in period of notice

(1) If an employer gives notice to terminate the contract of employment of a person who has been continuously employed for one month or more, the provisions of sections 88 to 91 have effect as respects the liability of the employer for the period of notice required by section 86(1).

(2) If an employee who has been continuously employed for one month or more gives notice to terminate his contract of employment, the provisions of sections 88 to 91 have effect as respects the liability of the employer for the period of notice required by section 86(2).

(3) In sections 88 to 91 "period of notice" means—

(a) where notice is given by an employer, the period of notice required by section 86(1), and

(b) where notice is given by an employee, the period of notice required by section 86(2).

(4) This section does not apply in relation to a notice given by the employer or the employee if the notice to be given by the employer to terminate the contract must be at least one week more than the notice required by section 86(1).

[1.995]

88 Employments with normal working hours

(1) If an employee has normal working hours under the contract of employment in force during the period of notice and during any part of those normal working hours—

(a) the employee is ready and willing to work but no work is provided for him by his employer,

(b) the employee is incapable of work because of sickness or injury,

(c) the employee is absent from work wholly or partly because of pregnancy or childbirth [or on [adoption leave, [shared parental leave,] [parental bereavement leave,] parental leave or [paternity leave]]], or

(d) the employee is absent from work in accordance with the terms of his employment relating to holidays,

the employer is liable to pay the employee for the part of normal working hours covered by any of paragraphs (a), (b), (c) and (d) a sum not less than the amount of remuneration for that part of normal working hours calculated at the average hourly rate of remuneration produced by dividing a week's pay by the number of normal working hours.

(2) Any payments made to the employee by his employer in respect of the relevant part of the period of notice (whether by way of sick pay, statutory sick pay, maternity pay, statutory maternity pay, [paternity pay, [statutory paternity pay], adoption pay, statutory adoption pay,] [shared parental pay, statutory shared parental pay,] [parental bereavement pay, statutory parental bereavement pay,] holiday pay or otherwise) go towards meeting the employer's liability under this section.

(3) Where notice was given by the employee, the employer's liability under this section does not arise unless and until the employee leaves the service of the employer in pursuance of the notice.

NOTES

Sub-s (1) is amended as follows:

Words in first (outer) pair of square brackets in para (c) (ie, beginning with the words "or on") inserted by the Employment Relations Act 1999, s 9, Sch 4, Pt III, paras 1, 5, 10.

Words in second (inner) pair of square brackets in para (c) (ie, beginning with the words "adoption leave") substituted by the Employment Act 2002, s 53, Sch 7, paras 24, 29(1), (2).

Words in third (inner) pair of square brackets in para (c) (ie, the words "shared parental leave,") inserted by the Children and Families Act 2014, s 126, Sch 7, paras 29, 37(1), (2)(a), as from 1 December 2014.

Words "paternity leave" in square brackets in para (c) substituted by the Children and Families Act 2014, s 126, Sch 7, paras 29, 37(1), (2)(b), as from 5 April 2015 (note that this amendment does not have effect in relation to (a) children whose expected week of birth ends on or before 4 April 2015, and (b) children placed for adoption on or before that date: see the Children and Families Act 2014 (Commencement No 3, Transitional Provisions and Savings) Order 2014, SI 2014/1640, art 16).

Words "parental bereavement leave," in square brackets in para (c) inserted by the Parental Bereavement (Leave and Pay) Act 2018, s 1(c), Schedule, Pt 3, paras 20, 25(1), (2), as from a day to be appointed.

Sub-s (2) is amended as follows:

Words in first (outer) pair of square brackets inserted by the Employment Act 2002, s 53, Sch 7, paras 24, 29(1), (3).

Words in second (inner) pair of square brackets substituted by the Children and Families Act 2014, s 126(1), Sch 7, paras 29, 37(1), (3)(a), as from 5 April 2015 (note that this amendment does not have effect in relation to (a) children whose expected week of birth ends on or before 4 April 2015, and (b) children placed for adoption on or before that date: see SI 2014/1640, art 16).

Words in third pair of square brackets inserted by the Children and Families Act 2014, s 126(1), Sch 7, paras 29, 37(1), (3)(b), as from 1 December 2014.

Words in final pair of square brackets inserted by the Parental Bereavement (Leave and Pay) Act 2018, s 1(c), Schedule, Pt 3, paras 20, 25(1), (3), as from a day to be appointed.

Statutory paternity pay: as to the meaning of this, see the Children and Families Act 2014, s 126 at **[1.1894]**

[1.996]

89 Employments without normal working hours

(1) If an employee does not have normal working hours under the contract of employment in force in the period of notice, the employer is liable to pay the employee for each week of the period of notice a sum not less than a week's pay.

(2) The employer's liability under this section is conditional on the employee being ready and willing to do work of a reasonable nature and amount to earn a week's pay.

(3) Subsection (2) does not apply—

(a) in respect of any period during which the employee is incapable of work because of sickness or injury,

(b) in respect of any period during which the employee is absent from work wholly or partly because of pregnancy or childbirth [or on [adoption leave, [shared parental leave,] [parental bereavement leave,] parental leave or [paternity leave]]], or

(c) in respect of any period during which the employee is absent from work in accordance with the terms of his employment relating to holidays.

(4) Any payment made to an employee by his employer in respect of a period within subsection (3) (whether by way of sick pay, statutory sick pay, maternity pay, statutory maternity pay, [paternity pay, [statutory paternity pay], adoption pay, statutory adoption pay,] [shared parental pay, statutory shared parental pay,] [parental bereavement pay, statutory parental bereavement pay,] holiday pay or otherwise) shall be taken into account for the purposes of this section as if it were remuneration paid by the employer in respect of that period.

(5) Where notice was given by the employee, the employer's liability under this section does not arise unless and until the employee leaves the service of the employer in pursuance of the notice.

NOTES

Sub-s (3) is amended as follows:

Words in first (outer) pair of square brackets in para (b) (ie, beginning with the words "or on") inserted by the Employment Relations Act 1999, s 9, Sch 4, Pt III, paras 1, 5, 11.

Words in second (inner) pair of square brackets in para (b) (ie, beginning with the words "adoption leave,") substituted by the Employment Act 2002, s 53, Sch 7, paras 24, 30(1), (2)

Words "shared parental leave," in square brackets in para (b) inserted by the Children and Families Act 2014, s 126, Sch 7, paras 29, 38(1), (2)(a), as from 1 December 2014.

Words "paternity leave" in square brackets in para (b) substituted by the Children and Families Act 2014, s 126, Sch 7, paras 29, 38(1), (2)(b), as from 5 April 2015 (note that this amendment does not have effect in relation to (a) children whose expected week of birth ends on or before 4 April 2015, and (b) children placed for adoption on or before that date: see the Children and Families Act 2014 (Commencement No 3, Transitional Provisions and Savings) Order 2014, SI 2014/1640, art 16).

Words "parental bereavement leave," inserted by the Parental Bereavement (Leave and Pay) Act 2018, s 1(c), Schedule, Pt 3, paras 20, 26(1), (2), as from a day to be appointed.

Sub-s (4) is amended as follows:

Words in first (outer) pair of square brackets inserted by the Employment Act 2002, s 53, Sch 7, paras 24, 30(1), (3).

Words in second (inner) pair of square brackets substituted by the Children and Families Act 2014, s 126(1), Sch 7, paras 29, 38(1), (3)(a), as from 5 April 2015 (note that this amendment does not have effect in relation to (a) children whose expected week of birth ends on or before 4 April 2015, and (b) children placed for adoption on or before that date: see SI 2014/1640, art 16).

Words in third pair of square brackets inserted by the Children and Families Act 2014, s 126, Sch 7, paras 29, 38(1), (3)(b), as from 1 December 2014.

Words in fourth pair of square brackets inserted by the Parental Bereavement (Leave and Pay) Act 2018, s 1(c), Schedule, Pt 3, paras 20, 26(1), (3), as from a day to be appointed.

Statutory paternity pay: as to the meaning of this, see the Children and Families Act 2014, s 126 at **[1.1894]**

[1.997]

90 Short-term incapacity benefit[, contributory employment and support allowance] and industrial injury benefit

(1) This section has effect where the arrangements in force relating to the employment are such that—

(a) payments by way of sick pay are made by the employer to employees to whom the arrangements apply, in cases where any such employees are incapable of work because of sickness or injury, and

(b) in calculating any payment so made to any such employee an amount representing, or treated as representing, short-term incapacity benefit[, contributory employment and support allowance] or industrial injury benefit is taken into account, whether by way of deduction or by way of calculating the payment as a supplement to that amount.

(2) If—

(a) during any part of the period of notice the employee is incapable of work because of sickness or injury,

(b) one or more payments by way of sick pay are made to him by the employer in respect of that part of the period of notice, and

(c) in calculating any such payment such an amount as is referred to in paragraph (b) of subsection (1) is taken into account as mentioned in that paragraph,

for the purposes of section 88 or 89 the amount so taken into account shall be treated as having been paid by the employer to the employee by way of sick pay in respect of that part of that period, and shall go towards meeting the liability of the employer under that section accordingly.

NOTES

Section heading, sub-s (1): words in square brackets inserted by the Employment and Support Allowance (Consequential Provisions) (No 3) Regulations 2008, SI 2008/1879, reg 2.

[1.998]

91 Supplementary

(1) An employer is not liable under section 88 or 89 to make any payment in respect of a period during which an employee is absent from work with the leave of the employer granted at the request of the employee, including any period of time off taken in accordance with—

(a) Part VI of this Act, or

(b) section 168 or 170 of the Trade Union and Labour Relations (Consolidation) Act 1992 (trade union duties and activities).

(2) No payment is due under section 88 or 89 in consequence of a notice to terminate a contract given by an employee if, after the notice is given and on or before the termination of the contract, the employee takes part in a strike of employees of the employer.

(3) If, during the period of notice, the employer breaks the contract of employment, payments received under section 88 or 89 in respect of the part of the period after the breach go towards mitigating the damages recoverable by the employee for loss of earnings in that part of the period of notice.

(4) If, during the period of notice, the employee breaks the contract and the employer rightfully treats the breach as terminating the contract, no payment is due to the employee under section 88 or 89 in respect of the part of the period falling after the termination of the contract.

(5) If an employer fails to give the notice required by section 86, the rights conferred by sections 87 to 90 and this section shall be taken into account in assessing his liability for breach of the contract.

(6) Sections 86 to 90 and this section apply in relation to a contract all or any of the terms of which are terms which take effect by virtue of any provision contained in or having effect under an Act (whether public or local) as in relation to any other contract; and the reference in this subsection to an Act includes, subject to any express provision to the contrary, an Act passed after this Act.

Written statement of reasons for dismissal

[1.999]

92 Right to written statement of reasons for dismissal

(1) An employee is entitled to be provided by his employer with a written statement giving particulars of the reasons for the employee's dismissal—

(a) if the employee is given by the employer notice of termination of his contract of employment,

(b) if the employee's contract of employment is terminated by the employer without notice, or

[(c) if the employee is employed under a limited-term contract and the contract terminates by virtue of the limiting event without being renewed under the same contract].

(2) Subject to [subsections (4) and (4A)], an employee is entitled to a written statement under this section only if he makes a request for one; and a statement shall be provided within fourteen days of such a request.

(3) Subject to [subsections (4) and (4A)], an employee is not entitled to a written statement under this section unless on the effective date of termination he has been, or will have been, continuously employed for a period of not less than [two years] ending with that date.

(4) An employee is entitled to a written statement under this section without having to request it and irrespective of whether she has been continuously employed for any period if she is dismissed—

(a) at any time while she is pregnant, or

(b) after childbirth in circumstances in which her [ordinary or additional maternity leave period] ends by reason of the dismissal.

[(4A) An employee who is dismissed while absent from work during an ordinary or additional adoption leave period is entitled to a written statement under this section without having to request it and irrespective of whether he has been continuously employed for any period if he is dismissed in circumstances in which that period ends by reason of the dismissal.]

(5) A written statement under this section is admissible in evidence in any proceedings.

(6) Subject to subsection (7), in this section "the effective date of termination"—

(a) in relation to an employee whose contract of employment is terminated by notice, means the date on which the notice expires,

(b) in relation to an employee whose contract of employment is terminated without notice, means the date on which the termination takes effect, and

[(c) in relation to an employee who is employed under a limited-term contract which terminates by virtue of the limiting event without being renewed under the same contract, means the date on which the termination takes effect].

(7) Where—

(a) the contract of employment is terminated by the employer, and

(b) the notice required by section 86 to be given by an employer would, if duly given on the material date, expire on a date later than the effective date of termination (as defined by subsection (6)),

the later date is the effective date of termination.

(8) In subsection (7)(b) "the material date" means—

(a) the date when notice of termination was given by the employer, or

(b) where no notice was given, the date when the contract of employment was terminated by the employer.

NOTES

Sub-s (1): para (c) substituted by the Fixed-term Employees (Prevention of Less Favourable Treatment) Regulations 2002, SI 2002/2034, reg 11, Sch 2, Pt 1, para 3(1), (5) (except in relation to Government training schemes, agency workers and apprentices; see regs 18–20 of the 2002 Regulations at **[2.571]** et seq).

Sub-s (2): words in square brackets substituted by the Employment Act 2002, s 53, Sch 7, paras 24, 31.

Sub-s (3): words in first pair of square brackets substituted by the Employment Act 2002, s 53, Sch 7, paras 24, 31; words in second pair of square brackets substituted by the Unfair Dismissal and Statement of Reasons for Dismissal (Variation of Qualifying Period) Order 2012, SI 2012/989, art 2. Note that by virtue of art 4 of the 2012 Order, this amendment does not have effect in any case where the period of continuous employment began before 6 April 2012 (in such cases the previous period of one year continues to apply).

Sub-s (4): words in square brackets substituted by the Employment Relations Act 1999, s 9, Sch 4, Pt III, paras 1, 5, 12.

Sub-s (4A): inserted by the Employment Act 2002, s 53, Sch 7, paras 24, 31.

Sub-s (6): para (c) substituted by the Employment Relations Act 2004, s 57(1), Sch 1, para 28.

Modified as noted to s 66 at **[1.947]**.

[1.1000]

93 Complaints to [employment tribunal]

(1) A complaint may be presented to an [employment tribunal] by an employee on the ground that—

(a) the employer unreasonably failed to provide a written statement under section 92, or

(b) the particulars of reasons given in purported compliance with that section are inadequate or untrue.

(2) Where an [employment tribunal] finds a complaint under this section well-founded, the tribunal—

(a) may make a declaration as to what it finds the employer's reasons were for dismissing the employee, and

(b) shall make an award that the employer pay to the employee a sum equal to the amount of two weeks' pay.

(3) An [employment tribunal] shall not consider a complaint under this section relating to the reasons for a dismissal unless it is presented to the tribunal at such a time that the tribunal would, in accordance with section 111, consider a complaint of unfair dismissal in respect of that dismissal presented at the same time.

NOTES

Words in square brackets substituted by the Employment Rights (Dispute Resolution) Act 1998, s 1(2)(a).

Modified as noted to s 66 at **[1.947]**.

Conciliation: employment tribunal proceedings under this section are "relevant proceedings" for the purposes of the conciliation provisions contained in the Employment Tribunals Act 1996, ss 18–18C; see s 18(1)(b) of the 1996 Act at **[1.757]**.

PART X
UNFAIR DISMISSAL

NOTES

This Part (ss 94–134A) is applied, with modifications, in relation to governing bodies with delegated budgets, by the Education (Modification of Enactments Relating to Employment) (England) Order 2003, SI 2003/1964, art 3, Schedule at **[2.685]**, **[2.689]** and the Education (Modification of Enactments Relating to Employment) (Wales) Order 2006, SI 2006/1073, art 3, Schedule at **[2.915]**, **[2.918]**.

This Part is modified, in relation to an office holder who is dismissed in the circumstances described in reg 33(1) of the Ecclesiastical Offices (Terms of Service) Regulations 2009, SI 2009/2108 at **[2.985]**; see as to the modifications, reg 33(2) of the 2009 Regulations.

This Part is applied, in respect of a person who is to be treated as unfairly dismissed for the purposes of the Employee Study and Training (Procedural Requirements) Regulations 2010: see the Employee Study and Training (Procedural Requirements) Regulations 2010, SI 2010/155, reg 18 at **[2.1128]**.

This Part is applied, in respect of a person who is a worker who works under a zero hours contract: see the Exclusivity Terms in Zero Hours Contracts (Redress) Regulations 2015, SI 2015/2021, reg 2 at **[2.1926]**.

Recoupment of social security benefits: as to the power to provide for recoupment of social security benefits in relation to payments by employers to employees under this Part, that are the subject of proceedings before employment tribunals, see the Employment Tribunals Act 1996, s 16 at **[1.755]**.

CHAPTER I RIGHT NOT TO BE UNFAIRLY DISMISSED

The right

[1.1001]
94 The right

(1) An employee has the right not to be unfairly dismissed by his employer.

(2) Subsection (1) has effect subject to the following provisions of this Part (in particular sections 108 to 110) and to the provisions of the Trade Union and Labour Relations (Consolidation) Act 1992 (in particular sections 237 to 239).

NOTES

Modification and application of this section: see the notes following the Part heading *ante*.

Dismissal

[1.1002]
95 Circumstances in which an employee is dismissed

(1) For the purposes of this Part an employee is dismissed by his employer if (and, subject to subsection (2) . . . , only if)—

(a) the contract under which he is employed is terminated by the employer (whether with or without notice),

[(b) he is employed under a limited-term contract and that contract terminates by virtue of the limiting event without being renewed under the same contract, or]

(c) the employee terminates the contract under which he is employed (with or without notice) in circumstances in which he is entitled to terminate it without notice by reason of the employer's conduct.

(2) An employee shall be taken to be dismissed by his employer for the purposes of this Part if—

(a) the employer gives notice to the employee to terminate his contract of employment, and

(b) at a time within the period of that notice the employee gives notice to the employer to terminate the contract of employment on a date earlier than the date on which the employer's notice is due to expire;

and the reason for the dismissal is to be taken to be the reason for which the employer's notice is given.

NOTES

Sub-s (1): words omitted repealed by the Employment Relations Act 2004, s 57, Sch 1, para 29, Sch 2. Para (b) substituted by the Fixed-term Employees (Prevention of Less Favourable Treatment) Regulations 2002, SI 2002/2034, reg 11, Sch 2, para 3(1), (7) (except in relation to Government training schemes, agency workers and apprentices; see regs 18–20 of the 2002 Regulations at **[2.571]** et seq).

Modification and application of this section: see the notes following the Part heading *ante*.

96 *(Repealed by the Employment Relations Act 1999, ss 9, 44, Sch 4, Pt III, paras 1, 5, 13, Sch 9(2).)*

[1.1003]
97 Effective date of termination

(1) Subject to the following provisions of this section, in this Part "the effective date of termination"—

(a) in relation to an employee whose contract of employment is terminated by notice, whether given by his employer or by the employee, means the date on which the notice expires,

(b) in relation to an employee whose contract of employment is terminated without notice, means the date on which the termination takes effect, and

[(c) in relation to an employee who is employed under a limited-term contract which terminates by virtue of the limiting event without being renewed under the same contract, means the date on which the termination takes effect].

(2) Where—
(a) the contract of employment is terminated by the employer, and
(b) the notice required by section 86 to be given by an employer would, if duly given on the material date, expire on a date later than the effective date of termination (as defined by subsection (1)),

for the purposes of sections 108(1), 119(1) and 227(3) the later date is the effective date of termination.

(3) In subsection (2)(b) "the material date" means—
(a) the date when notice of termination was given by the employer, or
(b) where no notice was given, the date when the contract of employment was terminated by the employer.

(4) Where—
(a) the contract of employment is terminated by the employee,
(b) the material date does not fall during a period of notice given by the employer to terminate that contract, and
(c) had the contract been terminated not by the employee but by notice given on the material date by the employer, that notice would have been required by section 86 to expire on a date later than the effective date of termination (as defined by subsection (1)),

for the purposes of sections 108(1), 119(1) and 227(3) the later date is the effective date of termination.

(5) In subsection (4) "the material date" means—
(a) the date when notice of termination was given by the employee, or
(b) where no notice was given, the date when the contract of employment was terminated by the employee.

(6) . . .

NOTES

Sub-s (1): para (c) substituted by the Fixed-term Employees (Prevention of Less Favourable Treatment) Regulations 2002, SI 2002/2034, reg 11, Sch 2, para 3(1), (8) (except in relation to Government training schemes, agency workers and apprentices; see regs 18–20 of the 2002 Regulations at **[2.571]** et seq).

Sub-s (6): repealed by the Employment Relations Act 1999, ss 9, 44, Sch 4, Pt III, paras 1, 5, 14, Sch 9(2).

Modification and application of this section: see the notes following the Part heading *ante*.

Fairness

[1.1004]

98 General

(1) In determining for the purposes of this Part whether the dismissal of an employee is fair or unfair, it is for the employer to show—
(a) the reason (or, if more than one, the principal reason) for the dismissal, and
(b) that it is either a reason falling within subsection (2) or some other substantial reason of a kind such as to justify the dismissal of an employee holding the position which the employee held.

(2) A reason falls within this subsection if it—
(a) relates to the capability or qualifications of the employee for performing work of the kind which he was employed by the employer to do,
(b) relates to the conduct of the employee,
[(ba) . . .]
(c) is that the employee was redundant, or
(d) is that the employee could not continue to work in the position which he held without contravention (either on his part or on that of his employer) of a duty or restriction imposed by or under an enactment.

[(2A) . . .]

(3) In subsection (2)(a)—
(a) "capability", in relation to an employee, means his capability assessed by reference to skill, aptitude, health or any other physical or mental quality, and
(b) "qualifications", in relation to an employee, means any degree, diploma or other academic, technical or professional qualification relevant to the position which he held.

[(3A) . . .]

(4) [Where] the employer has fulfilled the requirements of subsection (1), the determination of the question whether the dismissal is fair or unfair (having regard to the reason shown by the employer)—
(a) depends on whether in the circumstances (including the size and administrative resources of the employer's undertaking) the employer acted reasonably or unreasonably in treating it as a sufficient reason for dismissing the employee, and
(b) shall be determined in accordance with equity and the substantial merits of the case.

(5) . . .

(6) [Subsection (4)] [is] subject to—
(a) sections [98A] to 107 of this Act, and
(b) sections 152, 153[, 238 and 238A] of the Trade Union and Labour Relations (Consolidation) Act 1992 (dismissal on ground of trade union membership or activities or in connection with industrial action).

NOTES

Sub-ss (2)(ba), (2A), (3A): inserted by the Employment Equality (Age) Regulations 2006, SI 2006/1031, reg 49(1), Sch 8, Pt 1, paras 21, 22(1)–(4), and repealed by the Employment Equality (Repeal of Retirement Age Provisions) Regulations 2011, SI 2011/1069, reg 3(1), (2)(a).

Sub-s (4): words in square brackets substituted by SI 2011/1069, reg 3(1), (2)(b).

Sub-s (5): repealed by the Employment Relations Act 1999, ss 9, Sch 4, Pt III, paras 1, 5, 15(a), Sch 9(2).

Sub-s (6): words in first pair of square brackets substituted by the Employment Relations Act 1999, s 9, Sch 4, Pt III, paras 1, 5, 15(b); word in second pair of square brackets and figure in third pair of square brackets substituted by the Employment Act 2002, s 53, Sch 7, paras 24, 32; words in fourth pair of square brackets substituted by the Employment Relations Act 2004, s 57(1), Sch 1, para 30. Note that the reference to s 98A has not been amended despite the repeal of that section by the Employment Act 2008.

Modification and application of this section: see the notes following the Part heading *ante*.

98ZA–98ZH *(Sections 98ZA–98ZH (Retirement) were inserted by the Employment Equality (Age) Regulations 2006, SI 2006/1031, reg 49(1), Sch 8, Pt 1, paras 21, 23, and repealed by the Employment Equality (Repeal of Retirement Age Provisions) Regulations 2011, SI 2011/1069, reg 3(1), (3).)*

[Other dismissals]

98A *(Inserted by the Employment Act 2002, s 34(1), (2), and repealed by the Employment Act 2008, ss 2, 20, Schedule, Pt 1.)*

[1.1005]

[98B Jury Service

(1) An employee who is dismissed shall be regarded for the purposes of this Part as unfairly dismissed if the reason (or, if more than one, the principal reason) for the dismissal is that the employee—

(a) has been summoned under the Juries Act 1974, [Part 1 of the Coroners and Justice Act 2009], the Court of Session Act 1988 or the Criminal Procedure (Scotland) Act 1995 to attend for service as a juror, or

(b) has been absent from work because he attended at any place in pursuance of being so summoned.

(2) Subsection (1) does not apply in relation to an employee who is dismissed if the employer shows—

(a) that the circumstances were such that the employee's absence in pursuance of being so summoned was likely to cause substantial injury to the employer's undertaking,

(b) that the employer brought those circumstances to the attention of the employee,

(c) that the employee refused or failed to apply to the appropriate officer for excusal from or a deferral of the obligation to attend in pursuance of being so summoned, and

(d) that the refusal or failure was not reasonable.

(3) In paragraph (c) of subsection (2) "the appropriate officer" means—

(a) in the case of a person who has been summoned under the Juries Act 1974, the officer designated for the purposes of section 8, 9 or, as the case may be, 9A of that Act;

(b) in the case of a person who has been summoned under the Coroners Act 1988, a person who is the appropriate officer for the purposes of any rules made under subsection (1) of section 32 of that Act by virtue of subsection (2) of that section;

(c) in the case of a person who has been summoned under the Court of Session Act 1988, either—

(i) the clerk of court issuing the citation to attend for jury service; or

(ii) the clerk of the court before which the person is cited to attend for jury service;

(d) in the case of a person who has been summoned under the Criminal Procedure (Scotland) Act 1995, either—

(i) the clerk of court issuing the citation to attend for jury service; or

(ii) the clerk of the court before which the person has been cited to attend for jury service;

and references in that paragraph to a refusal or failure to apply include references to a refusal or failure to give a notice under section 1(2)(b) of the Law Reform (Miscellaneous Provisions) (Scotland) Act 1980.]

NOTES

Inserted by the Employment Relations Act 2004, s 40(3).

Sub-s (1): words in square brackets substituted by the Coroners and Justice Act 2009, s 177(1), Sch 21, Pt 1, para 36(1), (3).

Modification and application of this section: see the notes following the Part heading *ante*.

[1.1006]

[99 Leave for family reasons

(1) An employee who is dismissed shall be regarded for the purposes of this Part as unfairly dismissed if—

(a) the reason or principal reason for the dismissal is of a prescribed kind, or

(b) the dismissal takes place in prescribed circumstances.

(2) In this section "prescribed" means prescribed by regulations made by the Secretary of State.

(3) A reason or set of circumstances prescribed under this section must relate to—

(a) pregnancy, childbirth or maternity,

[(aa) time off under section 57ZE,]

[(ab) time off under section 57ZJ or 57ZL,]

(b) ordinary, compulsory or additional maternity leave,

[(ba) ordinary or additional adoption leave,]

[(bb) shared parental leave,]

(c) parental leave,

[(ca) [paternity leave]],

[(cb) parental bereavement leave,] [or]

(d) time off under section 57A;

and it may also relate to redundancy or other factors.

(4) A reason or set of circumstances prescribed under subsection (1) satisfies subsection (3)(c) or (d) if it relates to action which an employee—

(a) takes,
(b) agrees to take, or
(c) refuses to take,

under or in respect of a collective or workforce agreement which deals with parental leave.

(5) Regulations under this section may—

(a) make different provision for different cases or circumstances
(b) apply any enactment, in such circumstances as may be specified and subject to any conditions specified, in relation to persons regarded as unfairly dismissed by reason of this section.]

NOTES

Substituted by the Employment Relations Act 1999, s 9, Sch 4, Pt III, paras 1, 5, 16.

Sub-s (3) is amended as follows:

Paras (aa), (ab) inserted by the Children and Families Act 2014, ss 127(2)(b), 128(2)(c), as from 30 June 2014.

Para (ba) inserted, and para (ca) substituted for the original word "or" at the end of para (c), by the Employment Act 2002, s 53, Sch 7, paras 24, 33.

Para (bb) inserted by the Children and Families Act 2014, s 126, Sch 7, paras 29, 39(a), as from 30 June 2014.

Para (ca) further substituted (together with word following para (cb)) by the Work and Families Act 2006, s 11(1), Sch 1, para 41.

Words in square brackets in para (ca) substituted by the Children and Families Act 2014, s 126, Sch 7, paras 29, 39(b), as from 5 April 2015 (note that this amendment does not have effect in relation to (a) children whose expected week of birth ends on or before 4 April 2015, and (b) children placed for adoption on or before that date: see the Children and Families Act 2014 (Commencement No 3, Transitional Provisions and Savings) Order 2014, SI 2014/1640, art 16).

Para (cb) inserted by the Parental Bereavement (Leave and Pay) Act 2018, s 1(c), Schedule, Pt 3, paras 20, 27, as from a day to be appointed.

Modification and application of this section: see the notes following the Part heading *ante*.

Regulations: the Maternity and Parental Leave etc Regulations 1999, SI 1999/3312 at **[2.447]**; the Paternity and Adoption Leave Regulations 2002, SI 2002/2788 at **[2.576]**; the Maternity and Parental Leave (Amendment) Regulations 2002, SI 2002/2789; the Paternity and Adoption Leave (Adoptions from Overseas) Regulations 2003, SI 2003/921; the Maternity and Parental Leave etc and the Paternity and Adoption Leave (Amendment) Regulations 2006, SI 2006/2014; the Maternity and Parental Leave etc and the Paternity and Adoption Leave (Amendment) Regulations 2008, SI 2008/1966; the Additional Paternity Leave Regulations 2010, SI 2010/1055; the Additional Paternity Leave (Adoptions from Overseas) Regulations 2010, SI 2010/1059; the Paternity and Adoption Leave (Amendment) Regulations 2014, SI 2014/2112 at **[2.1512]**; the Shared Parental Leave Regulations 2014, SI 2014/3050 at **[2.1577]**; the Shared Parental Leave and Paternity and Adoption Leave (Adoptions from Overseas) Regulations 2014, SI 2014/3092 at **[2.1704]**; the Paternity, Adoption and Shared Parental Leave (Parental Order Cases) Regulations 2014, SI 2014/3096 at **[2.1747]**.

[1.1007]

100 Health and safety cases

(1) An employee who is dismissed shall be regarded for the purposes of this Part as unfairly dismissed if the reason (or, if more than one, the principal reason) for the dismissal is that—

(a) having been designated by the employer to carry out activities in connection with preventing or reducing risks to health and safety at work, the employee carried out (or proposed to carry out) any such activities,

(b) being a representative of workers on matters of health and safety at work or member of a safety committee—

(i) in accordance with arrangements established under or by virtue of any enactment, or
(ii) by reason of being acknowledged as such by the employer,

the employee performed (or proposed to perform) any functions as such a representative or a member of such a committee,

[(ba) the employee took part (or proposed to take part) in consultation with the employer pursuant to the Health and Safety (Consultation with Employees) Regulations 1996 or in the election of representatives of employee safety within the meaning of those Regulations (whether as a candidate or otherwise),]

(c) being an employee at a place where—

(i) there was no such representative or safety committee, or
(ii) there was such a representative or safety committee but it was not reasonably practicable for the employee to raise the matter by those means,

he brought to his employer's attention, by reasonable means, circumstances connected with his work which he reasonably believed were harmful or potentially harmful to health or safety,

(d) in circumstances of danger which the employee reasonably believed to be serious and imminent and which he could not reasonably have been expected to avert, he left (or proposed to leave) or (while the danger persisted) refused to return to his place of work or any dangerous part of his place of work, or

(e) in circumstances of danger which the employee reasonably believed to be serious and imminent, he took (or proposed to take) appropriate steps to protect himself or other persons from the danger.

(2) For the purposes of subsection (1)(e) whether steps which an employee took (or proposed to take) were appropriate is to be judged by reference to all the circumstances including, in particular, his knowledge and the facilities and advice available to him at the time.

(3) Where the reason (or, if more than one, the principal reason) for the dismissal of an employee is that specified in subsection (1)(e), he shall not be regarded as unfairly dismissed if the employer shows that it was (or would have been) so negligent for the employee to take the steps which he took (or proposed to take) that a reasonable employer might have dismissed him for taking (or proposing to take) them.

NOTES

Sub-s (1): para (ba) inserted by the Health and Safety (Consultation with Employees) Regulations 1996, SI 1996/1513, reg 8.

Modification and application of this section: see the notes following the Part heading *ante*.

[1.1008]

101 Shop workers and betting workers who refuse Sunday work

(1) Where an employee who is—

(a) a protected shop worker or an opted-out shop worker, or

(b) a protected betting worker or an opted-out betting worker,

is dismissed, he shall be regarded for the purposes of this Part as unfairly dismissed if the reason (or, if more than one, the principal reason) for the dismissal is that he refused (or proposed to refuse) to do shop work, or betting work, on Sunday or on a particular Sunday.

(2) Subsection (1) does not apply in relation to an opted-out shop worker or an opted-out betting worker where the reason (or principal reason) for the dismissal is that he refused (or proposed to refuse) to do shop work, or betting work, on any Sunday or Sundays falling before the end of the notice period.

(3) A shop worker or betting worker who is dismissed shall be regarded for the purposes of this Part as unfairly dismissed if the reason (or, if more than one, the principal reason) for the dismissal is that the shop worker or betting worker gave (or proposed to give) an opting-out notice to the employer.

(4) For the purposes of section 36(2)(b) or 41(1)(b), the appropriate date in relation to this section is the effective date of termination.

[1.1009]

[101ZA Shop workers who refuse to work additional hours on Sunday

(1) Subsection (2) applies where a shop worker has given an objection notice that has not been withdrawn and he or she is dismissed.

(2) The shop worker is to be regarded for the purposes of this Part as unfairly dismissed if the reason (or the principal reason) for the dismissal is that he or she refused, or proposed to refuse, to do shop work for additional hours on Sunday or on a particular Sunday.

(3) Subsection (2) does not apply where the reason (or principal reason) for the dismissal is that the shop worker refused (or proposed to refuse) to do shop work for additional hours on any Sunday or Sundays falling before the end of the relevant period.

(4) A shop worker who is dismissed is to be regarded for the purposes of this Part as unfairly dismissed if the reason (or principal reason) for the dismissal is that the worker gave (or proposed to give) an objection notice to the employer.

(5) In this section—

"additional hours" and "objection notice" have the meanings given by section 41A(2);

"relevant period" means the period determined by section 43ZA(2) (but subject to section 41D(3)).]

NOTES

Commencement: to be appointed .

Inserted by the Enterprise Act 2016, s 33, Sch 5, paras 1, 9, as from a day to be appointed.

Modification and application of this section: see the notes following the Part heading *ante*.

[1.1010]

[101A Working time cases

[(1)] An employee who is dismissed shall be regarded for the purposes of this Part as unfairly dismissed if the reason (or, if more than one, the principal reason) for the dismissal is that the employee—

(a) refused (or proposed to refuse) to comply with a requirement which the employer imposed (or proposed to impose) in contravention of the Working Time Regulations 1998,

(b) refused (or proposed to refuse) to forgo a right conferred on him by those Regulations,

(c) failed to sign a workforce agreement for the purposes of those Regulations, or to enter into, or agree to vary or extend, any other agreement with his employer which is provided for in those Regulations, or

(d) being—

(i) a representative of members of the workforce for the purposes of Schedule 1 to those Regulations, or

(ii) a candidate in an election in which any person elected will, on being elected, be such a representative,

performed (or proposed to perform) any functions or activities as such a representative or candidate.]

[(2) A reference in this section to the Working Time Regulations 1998 includes a reference to—

[(a)] the Merchant Shipping (Working Time: Inland Waterways) Regulations 2003;]

[(b) the Fishing Vessels (Working Time: Sea-fishermen) Regulations 2004];

[(c) the Cross-border Railway Services (Working Time) Regulations 2008];

[(d) the Merchant Shipping (Maritime Labour Convention) (Hours of Work) Regulations 2018 (SI 2018/58)]].]

NOTES

Inserted by the Working Time Regulations 1998, SI 1998/1833, regs 2(1), 32(1).

Sub-s (1): numbered as such by the Merchant Shipping (Working Time: Inland Waterways) Regulations 2003, SI 2003/3049, reg 20, Sch 2, para 3(1), (3).

Sub-s (2): added by SI 2003/3049, reg 20, Sch 2, para 3(1), (3); letter "(a)" in square brackets, and para (b), added by the Fishing Vessels (Working Time: Sea-fishermen) Regulations 2004, SI 2004/1713, reg 21, Sch 2, para 2(1), (3)(a); para (c) added by the Cross-border Railway Services (Working Time) Regulations 2008, SI 2008/1660, reg 19, Sch 3, para 2(1), (3); para (d) originally added by the Merchant Shipping (Maritime Labour Convention) (Hours of Work) (Amendment) Regulations 2014, SI 2014/308, reg 3, Schedule, para 2(1), (3), and subsequently substituted by the Merchant Shipping (Maritime Labour Convention) (Hours of Work) Regulations 2018, SI 2018/58, reg 31, Sch 2, para 2(b), as from 6 April 2018.

Modification and application of this section: see the notes following the Part heading *ante*.

[1.1011]
[101B Participation in education or training

An employee who is dismissed shall be regarded for the purposes of this Part as unfairly dismissed if the reason (or, if more than one, the principal reason) for the dismissal is that, being a person entitled to be permitted to participate in education or training by section 27 or 28 of the Education and Skills Act 2008, the employee exercised, or proposed to exercise, that right.]

NOTES

Commencement: to be appointed.

Inserted by the Education and Skills Act 2008, s 38, as from a day to be appointed.

Corresponding provision for Wales: see the note to s 47AA at **[1.887]**.

Modification and application of this section: see the notes following the Part heading *ante*.

[1.1012]
102 Trustees of occupational pension schemes

(1) An employee who is dismissed shall be regarded for the purposes of this Part as unfairly dismissed if the reason (or, if more than one, the principal reason) for the dismissal is that, being a trustee of a relevant occupational pension scheme which relates to his employment, the employee performed (or proposed to perform) any functions as such a trustee.

[(1A) This section applies to an employee who is a director of a company which is a trustee of a relevant occupational pension scheme as it applies to an employee who is a trustee of such a scheme (references to such a trustee being read for this purpose as references to such a director).]

(2) In this section "relevant occupational pension scheme" means an occupational pension scheme (as defined in section 1 of the Pension Schemes Act 1993) established under a trust.

NOTES

Sub-s (1A): inserted by the Welfare Reform and Pensions Act 1999, s 18, Sch 2, para 19(1), (4).

Modification and application of this section: see the notes following the Part heading *ante*.

[1.1013]
103 Employee representatives

[(1)] An employee who is dismissed shall be regarded for the purposes of this Part as unfairly dismissed if the reason (or, if more than one, the principal reason) for the dismissal is that the employee, being—

- (a) an employee representative for the purposes of Chapter II of Part IV of the Trade Union and Labour Relations (Consolidation) Act 1992 (redundancies) or [regulations 9, 13 and 15 of the Transfer of Undertakings (Protection of Employment) Regulations 2006], or
- (b) a candidate in an election in which any person elected will, on being elected, be such an employee representative,

performed (or proposed to perform) any functions or activities as such an employee representative or candidate.

[(2) An employee who is dismissed shall be regarded for the purposes of this Part as unfairly dismissed if the reason (or, if more than one, the principal reason) for the dismissal is that the employee took part in an election of employee representatives for the purposes of Chapter II of Part IV of the Trade Union and Labour Relations (Consolidation) Act 1992 (redundancies) or [regulations 9, 13 and 15 of the Transfer of Undertakings (Protection of Employment) Regulations 2006].]

NOTES

Sub-s (1): numbered as such by the Collective Redundancies and Transfer of Undertakings (Protection of Employment) (Amendment) Regulations 1999, SI 1999/1925, reg 13; words in square brackets in para (a) substituted by the Transfer of Undertakings (Protection of Employment) Regulations 2006, SI 2006/246, reg 20, Sch 2, para 10.

Sub-s (2): added by SI 1999/1925, reg 13; words in square brackets substituted by SI 2006/246, reg 20, Sch 2, para 10.

Modification and application of this section: see the notes following the Part heading *ante*.

[1.1014]
[103A Protected disclosure

An employee who is dismissed shall be regarded for the purposes of this Part as unfairly dismissed if the reason (or, if more than one, the principal reason) for the dismissal is that the employee made a protected disclosure.]

NOTES

Inserted by the Public Interest Disclosure Act 1998, ss 5, 18(2).

Modification and application of this section: see the notes following the Part heading *ante*.

[1.1015]
104 Assertion of statutory right

(1) An employee who is dismissed shall be regarded for the purposes of this Part as unfairly dismissed if the reason (or, if more than one, the principal reason) for the dismissal is that the employee—

(a) brought proceedings against the employer to enforce a right of his which is a relevant statutory right, or

(b) alleged that the employer had infringed a right of his which is a relevant statutory right.

(2) It is immaterial for the purposes of subsection (1)—

(a) whether or not the employee has the right, or

(b) whether or not the right has been infringed;

but, for that subsection to apply, the claim to the right and that it has been infringed must be made in good faith.

(3) It is sufficient for subsection (1) to apply that the employee, without specifying the right, made it reasonably clear to the employer what the right claimed to have been infringed was.

(4) The following are relevant statutory rights for the purposes of this section—

(a) any right conferred by this Act for which the remedy for its infringement is by way of a complaint or reference to an [employment tribunal],

(b) the right conferred by section 86 of this Act, . . .

(c) the rights conferred by sections 68, 86, [145A, 145B,] 146, 168, [168A,] 169 and 170 of the Trade Union and Labour Relations (Consolidation) Act 1992 (deductions from pay, union activities and time off) [. . .

[(d) the rights conferred by the Working Time Regulations 1998, [the Merchant Shipping (Maritime Labour Convention) (Hours of Work) Regulations 2018 (SI 2018/58)], the Merchant Shipping (Working Time: Inland Waterway) Regulations 2003][, the Fishing Vessels (Working Time: Sea-fisherman) Regulations 2004 or the Cross-border Railway Services (Working Time) Regulations 2008]][, and

(e) the rights conferred by the Transfer of Undertakings (Protection of Employment) Regulations 2006].

[(5) In this section any reference to an employer includes, where the right in question is conferred by section 63A, the principal (within the meaning of section 63A(3)).]

NOTES

Sub-s (4) is amended as follows:

Words in square brackets in para (a) substituted by the Employment Rights (Dispute Resolution) Act 1998, s 1(2)(a).

Word omitted from para (b) repealed, and para (d) and the word immediately preceding it added, by the Working Time Regulations 1998, SI 1998/1833, regs 2(1), 32(2).

First figures in square brackets in para (c) inserted by the Employment Relations Act 2004, s 57(1), Sch 1, para 31.

Second figure in square brackets in para (c) inserted by the Employment Act 2002, s 53, Sch 7, paras 24, 34.

Word omitted from para (c) repealed, and para (e) and the word immediately preceding it added, by the Transfer of Undertakings (Protection of Employment) Regulations 2006, SI 2006/246, reg 19.

Para (d) substituted by the Fishing Vessels (Working Time: Sea-fishermen) Regulations 2004, SI 2004/1713, reg 21, Sch 2, para 2(1), (4).

Words in first pair of square brackets in para (d) substituted by the Merchant Shipping (Maritime Labour Convention) (Hours of Work) Regulations 2018, SI 2018/58, reg 31, Sch 2, para 2(c), as from 6 April 2018.

Words in second pair of square brackets in para (d) substituted by the Cross-border Railway Services (Working Time) Regulations 2008, SI 2008/1660, reg 19, Sch 3, para 2(1), (4).

Sub-s (5): added by the Teaching and Higher Education Act 1998, s 44(1), Sch 3, para 13.

Modification and application of this section: see the notes following the Part heading *ante*.

[1.1016]
[104A The national minimum wage

(1) An employee who is dismissed shall be regarded for the purposes of this Part as unfairly dismissed if the reason (or, if more than one, the principal reason) for the dismissal is that—

(a) any action was taken, or was proposed to be taken, by or on behalf of the employee with a view to enforcing, or otherwise securing the benefit of, a right of the employee's to which this section applies; or

(b) the employer was prosecuted for an offence under section 31 of the National Minimum Wage Act 1998 as a result of action taken by or on behalf of the employee for the purpose of enforcing, or otherwise securing the benefit of, a right of the employee's to which this section applies; or

(c) the employee qualifies, or will or might qualify, for the national minimum wage or for a particular rate of national minimum wage.

(2) It is immaterial for the purposes of paragraph (a) or (b) of subsection (1) above—

(a) whether or not the employee has the right, or

(b) whether or not the right has been infringed,

but, for that subsection to apply, the claim to the right and, if applicable, the claim that it has been infringed must be made in good faith.

(3) The following are the rights to which this section applies—

(a) any right conferred by, or by virtue of, any provision of the National Minimum Wage Act 1998 for which the remedy for its infringement is by way of a complaint to an employment tribunal; and

(b) any right conferred by section 17 of the National Minimum Wage Act 1998 (worker receiving less than national minimum wage entitled to additional remuneration).]

NOTES

Inserted by the National Minimum Wage Act 1998, s 25(1).

Agricultural workers: as to the application of this section to agricultural workers, see the Agricultural Wages Act 1948, s 3A, the Agricultural Wages (Scotland) Act 1949, s 3A, and the Agricultural Sector (Wales) Act 2014, s 5(8).

Modification and application of this section: see the notes following the Part heading *ante*.

[1.1017]

[104B Tax credits

(1) An employee who is dismissed shall be regarded for the purposes of this Part as unfairly dismissed if the reason (or, if more than one, the principal reason) for the dismissal is that—

(a) any action was taken, or was proposed to be taken, by or on behalf of the employee with a view to enforcing, or otherwise securing the benefit of, a right conferred on the employee by regulations under section 25 of the Tax Credits Act 2002,

(b) a penalty was imposed on the employer, or proceedings for a penalty were brought against him, under that Act, as a result of action taken by or on behalf of the employee for the purpose of enforcing, or otherwise securing the benefit of, such a right, or

(c) the employee is entitled, or will or may be entitled, to working tax credit.

(2) It is immaterial for the purposes of subsection (1)(a) or (b)—

(a) whether or not the employee has the right, or

(b) whether or not the right has been infringed,

but, for those provisions to apply, the claim to the right and (if applicable) the claim that it has been infringed must be made in good faith.]

NOTES

Inserted by the Tax Credits Act 1999, s 7, Sch 3, para 3(1); substituted by the Tax Credits Act 2002, s 27, Sch 1, para 3(1), (2).

Modification and application of this section: see the notes following the Part heading *ante*.

[1.1018]

[104C Flexible working

An employee who is dismissed shall be regarded for the purposes of this Part as unfairly dismissed if the reason (or, if more than one, the principal reason) for the dismissal is that the employee—

(a) made (or proposed to make) an application under section 80F,

(b) . . .

(c) brought proceedings against the employer under section 80H, or

(d) alleged the existence of any circumstance which would constitute a ground for bringing such proceedings.]

NOTES

Inserted by the Employment Act 2002, s 47(1), (4).

Para (b) repealed by the Children and Families Act 2014, s 132(5)(e), as from 30 June 2014, except in relation to any application for a change in terms and conditions which is made on or before 29 June 2014 (see the Children and Families Act 2014 (Commencement No 3, Transitional Provisions and Savings) Order 2014, SI 2014/1640, art 10).

Modification and application of this section: see the notes following the Part heading *ante*.

[1.1019]

[104D Pension enrolment

(1) An employee who is dismissed shall be regarded for the purposes of this Part as unfairly dismissed if the reason (or, if more than one, the principal reason) for the dismissal is that—

(a) any action was taken, or was proposed to be taken, with a view to enforcing in favour of the employee a requirement to which this section applies;

(b) the employer was prosecuted for an offence under section 45 of the Pensions Act 2008 as a result of action taken for the purpose of enforcing in favour of the employee a requirement to which this section applies; or

(c) any provision of Chapter 1 of that Part of that Act applies to the employee, or will or might apply.

(2) It is immaterial for the purposes of paragraph (a) or (b) of subsection (1) above—

(a) whether or not the requirement applies in favour of the employee, or

(b) whether or not the requirement has been contravened,

but, for that subsection to apply, the claim that the requirement applies and, if applicable, the claim that it has been contravened must be made in good faith.

(3) This section applies to any requirement imposed on the employer by or under any provision of Chapter 1 of Part 1 of the Pensions Act 2008.

(4) In this section references to enforcing a requirement include references to securing its benefit in any way.]

NOTES

Inserted by the Pensions Act 2008, s 57(1), (2).

Modification and application of this section: see the notes following the Part heading *ante*.

[1.1020]
[104E Study and training
An employee who is dismissed is to be regarded for the purposes of this Part as unfairly dismissed if the reason (or, if more than one, the principal reason) for the dismissal is that the employee—
(a) made (or proposed to make) a section 63D application,
(b) exercised (or proposed to exercise) a right conferred on the employee under section 63F,
(c) brought proceedings against the employer under section 63I, or
(d) alleged the existence of any circumstance which would constitute a ground for bringing such proceedings.]

NOTES
Commencement: 6 April 2010 (except in relation to small employers and their employees); to be appointed (otherwise).
Inserted by the Apprenticeships, Skills, Children and Learning Act 2009, s 40(1), (4), as from 6 April 2010 (except in relation to small employers and their employees), and as from a day to be appointed (otherwise) (as to the meaning of "small employers" etc, see further the notes at **[1.937]**).
Modification and application of this section: see the notes following the Part heading *ante*.

[1.1021]
[104F Blacklists
(1) An employee who is dismissed shall be regarded for the purposes of this Part as unfairly dismissed if the reason (or, if more than one, the principal reason) for the dismissal relates to a prohibited list, and either—
(a) the employer contravenes regulation 3 of the 2010 Regulations in relation to that prohibited list, or
(b) the employer—
(i) relies on information supplied by a person who contravenes that regulation in relation to that list, and
(ii) knows or ought reasonably to know that the information relied on is supplied in contravention of that regulation.
(2) If there are facts from which the tribunal could conclude, in the absence of any other explanation, that the employer—
(a) contravened regulation 3 of the 2010 Regulations, or
(b) relied on information supplied in contravention of that regulation,
the tribunal must find that such a contravention or reliance on information occurred, unless the employer shows that it did not.
(3) In this section—
"the 2010 Regulations" means the Employment Relations Act 1999 (Blacklists) Regulations 2010, and
"prohibited list" has the meaning given in those Regulations (see regulation 3(2)).]

NOTES
Inserted by the Employment Relations Act 1999 (Blacklists) Regulations 2010, SI 2010/493, reg 12(1), (2).
Modification and application of this section: see the notes following the Part heading *ante*.

[1.1022]
[104G Employee shareholder status
An employee who is dismissed is to be regarded for the purposes of this Part as unfairly dismissed if the reason (or, if more than one, the principal reason) for the dismissal is that the employee refused to accept an offer by the employer for the employee to become an employee shareholder (within the meaning of section 205A).]

NOTES
Inserted by the Growth and Infrastructure Act 2013, s 31(4).
Modification and application of this section: see the notes following the Part heading *ante*.

[1.1023]
105 Redundancy
(1) An employee who is dismissed shall be regarded for the purposes of this Part as unfairly dismissed if—
(a) the reason (or, if more than one, the principal reason) for the dismissal is that the employee was redundant,
(b) it is shown that the circumstances constituting the redundancy applied equally to one or more other employees in the same undertaking who held positions similar to that held by the employee and who have not been dismissed by the employer, and
[(c) it is shown that any of subsections [(2A) to [(7N)]] applies].
(2) . . .
[(2A) This subsection applies if the reason (or, if more than one, the principal reason) for which the employee was selected for dismissal was one of those specified in subsection (1) of section 98B (unless the case is one to which subsection (2) of that section applies).]
(3) This subsection applies if the reason (or, if more than one, the principal reason) for which the employee was selected for dismissal was one of those specified in subsection (1) of section 100 (read with subsections (2) and (3) of that section).
(4) This subsection applies if either—

(a) the employee was a protected shop worker or an opted-out shop worker, or a protected betting worker or an opted-out betting worker, and the reason (or, if more than one, the principal reason) for which the employee was selected for dismissal was that specified in subsection (1) of section 101 (read with subsection (2) of that section), or

(b) the employee was a shop worker or a betting worker and the reason (or, if more than one, the principal reason) for which the employee was selected for dismissal was that specified in subsection (3) of that section.

[(4A) This subsection applies if the reason (or, if more than one, the principal reason) for which the employee was selected for dismissal was one of those specified in section 101A.]

[(4B) This subsection applies if the reason (or, if more than one, the principal reason) for which the employee was selected for dismissal was that specified in section 101B.]

(5) This subsection applies if the reason (or, if more than one, the principal reason) for which the employee was selected for dismissal was that specified in section 102(1).

(6) This subsection applies if the reason (or, if more than one, the principal reason) for which the employee was selected for dismissal was that specified in section 103.

[(6A) This subsection applies if the reason (or, if more than one, the principal reason) for which the employee was selected for dismissal was that specified in section 103A.]

(7) This subsection applies if the reason (or, if more than one, the principal reason) for which the employee was selected for dismissal was one of those specified in subsection (1) of section 104 (read with subsections (2) and (3) of that section).

[(7A) This subsection applies if the reason (or, if more than one, the principal reason) for which the employee was selected for dismissal was one of those specified in subsection (1) of section 104A (read with subsection (2) of that section).]

[(7B) This subsection applies if the reason (or, if more than one, the principal reason) for which the employee was selected for dismissal was one of those specified in subsection (1) of section 104B (read with subsection (2) of that section).]

[(7BA) This subsection applies if the reason (or, if more than one, the principal reason) for which the employee was selected for dismissal was one of those specified in section 104C.]

[(7BB) This subsection applies if the reason (or, if more than one, the principal reason) for which the employee was selected for dismissal was one of those specified in section 104E.]

[(7C) This subsection applies if—

(a) the reason (or, if more than one, the principal reason) for which the employee was selected for dismissal was the reason mentioned in section 238A(2) of the Trade Union and Labour Relations (Consolidation) Act 1992 (participation in official industrial action), and

(b) subsection (3), (4) or (5) of that section applies to the dismissal.]

[(7D) This subsection applies if the reason (or, if more than one, the principal reason) for which the employee was selected for dismissal was one specified in paragraph (3) or (6) of regulation 28 of the Transnational Information and Consultation of Employees Regulations 1999 (read with paragraphs (4) and (7) of that regulation).]

[(7E) This subsection applies if the reason (or, if more than one, the principal reason) for which the employee was selected for dismissal was one specified in paragraph (3) of regulation 7 of the Part-time Workers (Prevention of Less Favourable Treatment) Regulations 2000 (unless the case is one to which paragraph (4) of that regulation applies).]

[(7F) This subsection applies if the reason (or, if more than one, the principal reason) for which the employee was selected for dismissal was one specified in paragraph (3) of regulation 6 of the Fixed-term Employees (Prevention of Less Favourable Treatment) Regulations 2002 (unless the case is one to which paragraph (4) of that regulation applies).]

[(7G) This subsection applies if the reason (or, if more than one, the principal reason) for which the employee was selected for dismissal was one specified in paragraph (3) or (6) of regulation 42 of the European Public Limited-Liability Company Regulations 2004 (read with paragraphs (4) and (7) of that regulation).]

[(7H) This subsection applies if the reason (or, if more than one, the principal reason) for which the employee was selected for dismissal was one specified in paragraph (3) or (6) of regulation 30 of the Information and Consultation of Employees Regulations 2004 (read with paragraphs (4) and (7) of that regulation).]

[(7I) This subsection applies if the reason (or, if more than one, the principal reason) for which the employee was selected for dismissal was one specified in paragraph 5(3) or (5) of the Schedule to the Occupational and Personal Pension Schemes (Consultation by Employers and Miscellaneous Amendment) Regulations 2006 (read with paragraph 5(6) of that Schedule).]

[(7IA) . . .]

[(7J) This subsection applies if the reason (or, if more than one, the principal reason) for which the employee was selected for dismissal was one specified in paragraph (3) or (6) of regulation 31 of the European Cooperative Society (Involvement of Employees) Regulations 2006 (read with paragraphs (4) and (7) of that regulation).]

[(7JA) This subsection applies if the reason (or, if more than one, the principal reason) for which the employee was selected for dismissal was one of those specified in subsection (1) of section 104D (read with subsection (2) of that section).]

[(7K) This subsection applies if the reason (or, if more than one, the principal reason) for which the employee was selected for dismissal was one specified in—

(a) paragraph (2) of regulation 46 of the Companies (Cross-Border Mergers) Regulations 2007 (read with paragraphs (3) and (4) of that regulation); or

(b) paragraph (2) of regulation 47 of the Companies (Cross-Border Mergers) Regulations 2007 (read with paragraph (3) of that regulation).]

[(7L) This subsection applies if the reason (or, if more than one, the principal reason) for which the employee was selected for dismissal was one specified in paragraph (3) or (6) of regulation 29 of the European Public Limited-Liability Company (Employee Involvement) (Great Britain) Regulations 2009 (SI 2009/2401) (read with paragraphs (4) and (7) of that regulation).]

[(7M) This subsection applies if—

(a) the reason (or, if more than one, the principal reason) for which the employee was selected for dismissal was the one specified in the opening words of section 104F(1), and

(b) the condition in paragraph (a) or (b) of that subsection was met.]

[(7N) This subsection applies if the reason (or, if more than one, the principal reason) for which the employee was selected for dismissal was one specified in paragraph (3) of regulation 17 of the Agency Workers Regulations 2010 (unless the case is one to which paragraph (4) of that regulation applies).]

(8) For the purposes of section 36(2)(b) or 41(1)(b), the appropriate date in relation to this section is the effective date of termination.

(9) In this Part "redundancy case" means a case where paragraphs (a) and (b) of subsection (1) of this section are satisfied.

NOTES

Sub-s (1): para (c) substituted by the European Cooperative Society (Involvement of Employees) Regulations 2006, SI 2006/2059, reg 32(1)(a); words in first (outer) pair of square brackets in para (c) substituted by the Companies (Cross-Border Mergers) Regulations 2007, SI 2007/2974, reg 48(1)(a); figure "(7N)" in second (inner) pair of square brackets substituted by the Agency Workers Regulations 2010, SI 2010/93, reg 25, Sch 2, Pt 1, paras 9, 15.

Sub-s (2): repealed by the Employment Relations Act 1999, ss 9, Sch 4, Pt III, paras 1, 5, 17, Sch 9(2).

Sub-s (2A): inserted by the Employment Relations Act 2004, s 40(5).

Sub-s (4A): inserted by the Working Time Regulations 1998, SI 1998/1833, regs 2(1), 32(3).

Sub-s (4B): inserted by the Education and Skills Act 2008, s 39(1), (3), as from a day to be appointed.

Sub-s (6A): inserted by the Public Interest Disclosure Act 1998, ss 6, 18(2).

Sub-s (7A): inserted by the National Minimum Wage Act 1998, s 25(2).

Sub-s (7B): inserted by the Tax Credits Act 1999, s 7, Sch 3, para 3(2).

Sub-s (7BA): inserted by the Employment Relations Act 2004, s 41(4).

Sub-s (7BB): inserted by the Apprenticeships, Skills, Children and Learning Act 2009, s 40(5), Sch 1, paras 1, 3, as from 6 April 2010 (except in relation to small employers and their employees), and as from a day to be appointed (otherwise) (as to the meaning of "small employers" etc, see further the notes at **[1.937]**).

Sub-s (7C): inserted by the Employment Relations Act 1999, s 16, Sch 5, para 5(1), (3).

Sub-s (7D): inserted by the Transnational Information and Consultation of Employees Regulations 1999, SI 1999/3323, reg 29(1).

Sub-s (7E): inserted by the Part-time Workers (Prevention of Less Favourable Treatment) Regulations 2000, SI 2000/1551, reg 10, Schedule, para 2(1).

Sub-s (7F): inserted by the Fixed-term Employees (Prevention of Less Favourable Treatment) Regulations 2002, SI 2002/2034, reg 11, Sch 2, Pt 1, para 3(1), (10) (except in relation to Government training schemes, agency workers and apprentices; see regs 18–20 of the 2002 Regulations at **[2.571]** et seq).

Sub-s (7G): inserted by the European Public Limited-Liability Company Regulations 2004, SI 2004/2326, reg 43(1)(b).

Sub-s (7H): inserted by the Information and Consultation of Employees Regulations 2004, SI 2004/3426, reg 31(1)(b).

Sub-s (7I): inserted by the Occupational and Personal Pension Schemes (Consultation by Employers and Miscellaneous Amendment) Regulations 2006, SI 2006/349, reg 17, Schedule, para 6(1)(b).

Sub-s (7IA): inserted by the Employment Equality (Age) (Consequential Amendments) Regulations 2007, SI 2007/825, reg 3, and repealed by the Employment Equality (Repeal of Retirement Age Provisions) Regulations 2011, SI 2011/1069, reg 3(1), (4).

Sub-s (7J): inserted by SI 2006/2059, reg 32(1)(b).

Sub-s (7JA): inserted by the Pensions Act 2008, s 57(1), (4).

Sub-s (7K): inserted by SI 2007/2974, reg 48(1)(b) and repealed by the Companies, Limited Liability Partnerships and Partnerships (Amendment etc) (EU Exit) Regulations 2019, SI 2019/348, reg 8, Sch 3, paras 5, 6, as from exit day (as defined in the European Union (Withdrawal) Act 2018, s 20).

Sub-s (7L): inserted by the European Public Limited-Liability Company (Employee Involvement) (Great Britain) Regulations 2009, SI 2009/2401, reg 30(1), (2).

Sub-s (7M): inserted by the Employment Relations Act 1999 (Blacklists) Regulations 2010, SI 2010/493, reg 12(1), (3)(b).

Sub-s (7N): inserted by SI 2010/93, reg 25, Sch 2, Pt 1, paras 9, 15 and substituted by the Agency Workers (Amendment) Regulations 2019, SI 2019/724, reg 8(1), (2), as from 6 April 2020, as follows—

> "(7N) This subsection applies if the reason (or, if more than one, the principal reason) for which the employee was selected for dismissal was one specified in—
>
> (a) paragraph (3) of regulation 17 of the Agency Workers Regulations 2010 (unless the case is one to which paragraph (4) of that regulation applies); or
>
> (b) paragraph (3) of regulation 5 of the Agency Workers (Amendment) Regulations 2019 (unless the case is one to which paragraph (4) of that regulation applies).".

Corresponding provision for Wales: see the note to s 47AA at **[1.887]**.

Modification and application of this section: see the notes following the Part heading *ante*.

[1.1024]

106 Replacements

(1) Where this section applies to an employee he shall be regarded for the purposes of section 98(1)(b) as having been dismissed for a substantial reason of a kind such as to justify the dismissal of an employee holding the position which the employee held.

(2) This section applies to an employee where—

(a) on engaging him the employer informs him in writing that his employment will be terminated on the resumption of work by another employee who is, or will be, absent wholly or partly because of pregnancy or childbirth, [or on adoption leave] [or [shared parental leave]] and
(b) the employer dismisses him in order to make it possible to give work to the other employee.

(3) This section also applies to an employee where—
(a) on engaging him the employer informs him in writing that his employment will be terminated on the end of a suspension of another employee from work on medical grounds or maternity grounds (within the meaning of Part VII), and
(b) the employer dismisses him in order to make it possible to allow the resumption of work by the other employee.

(4) Subsection (1) does not affect the operation of section 98(4) in a case to which this section applies.

NOTES

Sub-s (2): words in first pair of square brackets in para (a) inserted by the Employment Act 2002, s 53, Sch 7, paras 24, 35; word in second (inner) pair of square brackets in that paragraph (ie, now only the word "or") inserted by the Work and Families Act 2006, s 11(1), Sch 1, para 42; words "shared parental leave" in square brackets in that paragraph substituted by the Children and Families Act 2014, s 126, Sch 7, paras 29, 40, as from 1 December 2014, except in relation to (a) children whose expected week of birth ends on or before 4 April 2015; (b) children placed for adoption on or before 4 April 2015 (see the Children and Families Act 2014 (Commencement No 3, Transitional Provisions and Savings) Order 2014, SI 2014/1640, art 12).

Modification and application of this section: see the notes following the Part heading *ante*.

[1.1025]
107 Pressure on employer to dismiss unfairly

(1) This section applies where there falls to be determined for the purposes of this Part a question—
(a) as to the reason, or principal reason, for which an employee was dismissed,
(b) whether the reason or principal reason for which an employee was dismissed was a reason fulfilling the requirement of section 98(1)(b), or
(c) whether an employer acted reasonably in treating the reason or principal reason for which an employee was dismissed as a sufficient reason for dismissing him.

(2) In determining the question no account shall be taken of any pressure which by calling, organising, procuring or financing a strike or other industrial action, or threatening to do so, was exercised on the employer to dismiss the employee; and the question shall be determined as if no such pressure had been exercised.

NOTES

Modification and application of this section: see the notes following the Part heading *ante*.

Exclusion of right

[1.1026]
108 Qualifying period of employment

(1) Section 94 does not apply to the dismissal of an employee unless he has been continuously employed for a period of not less than [two years] ending with the effective date of termination.

(2) If an employee is dismissed by reason of any such requirement or recommendation as is referred to in section 64(2), subsection (1) has effect in relation to that dismissal as if for the words [two years] there were substituted the words "one month".

(3) Subsection (1) does not apply if—
(a) . . .
[(aa) subsection (1) of section 98B (read with subsection (2) of that section) applies,]
[(b) subsection (1) of section 99 (read with any regulations made under that section) applies,]
(c) subsection (1) of section 100 (read with subsections (2) and (3) of that section) applies,
(d) subsection (1) of section 101 (read with subsection (2) of that section) or subsection (3) of that section applies,
[(da) subsection (2) of section 101ZA applies (read with subsection (3) of that section) or subsection (4) of that section applies,]
[(dd) section 101A applies,]
[(de) section 101B applies,]
(e) section 102 applies,
(f) section 103 applies,
[(ff) section 103A applies,]
(g) subsection (1) of section 104 (read with subsections (2) and (3) of that section) applies, . . .
[(gg) subsection (1) of section 104A (read with subsection (2) of that section) applies, . . .]
[(gh) subsection (1) of section 104B (read with subsection (2) of that section) applies, . . .]
[(gi) section 104C applies,]
[(gj) subsection (1) of section 104D (read with subsection (2) of that section) applies,]
[(gk) subsection (1) of section 104F (read with subsection (2) of that section) applies,]
[(gk) section 104E applies,]
[(gl) subsection (1) of section 104F (read with subsection (2) of that section) applies,]
[(gm) section 104G applies,]
(h) section 105 applies, [. . .
(hh) paragraph (3) or (6) of regulation 28 of the Transnational Information and Consultation of Employees Regulations 1999 (read with paragraphs (4) and (7) of that regulation) applies], [. . .

(i) paragraph (1) of regulation 7 of the Part-time Workers (Prevention of Less Favourable Treatment) Regulations 2000 applies], [. . .

(j) paragraph (1) of regulation 6 of the Fixed-term Employees (Prevention of Less Favourable Treatment) Regulations 2002 applies], [. . .

(k) paragraph (3) or (6) of regulation 42 of the European Public Limited-Liability Company Regulations 2004 applies]; [. . .

(l) paragraph (3) or (6) of regulation 30 of the Information and Consultation of Employees Regulations 2004 (read with paragraphs (4) and (7) of that regulation) applies] [, . . .

(m) paragraph 5(3) or (5) of the Schedule to the Occupational and Personal Pension Schemes (Consultation by Employers and Miscellaneous Amendment) Regulations 2006 (read with paragraph 5(6) of that Schedule) applies] [, . . .

(n) . . .][, . . .

(o) paragraph (3) or (6) of regulation 31 of the European Cooperative Society (Involvement of Employees) Regulations 2006 (read with paragraphs (4) and (7) of that regulation) applies], [. . .

(p) regulation 46 or 47 of the Companies (Cross-Border Mergers) Regulations 2007 applies][, . . .

(q) paragraph (1)(a) or (b) of regulation 29 of the European Public Limited-Liability Company (Employee Involvement) (Great Britain) Regulations 2009 (SI 2009/2401) applies,] [or

(r) paragraph (1) of regulation 17 of the Agency Workers Regulations 2010 applies].

[(4) Subsection (1) does not apply if the reason (or, if more than one, the principal reason) for the dismissal is, or relates to, the employee's political opinions or affiliation.]

[(5) Subsection (1) does not apply if the reason (or, if more than one, the principal reason) for the dismissal is, or is connected with, the employee's membership of a reserve force (as defined in section 374 of the Armed Forces Act 2006).]

NOTES

Sub-ss (1), (2): words in square brackets substituted by the Unfair Dismissal and Statement of Reasons for Dismissal (Variation of Qualifying Period) Order 2012, SI 2012/989, art 3. Note that by virtue of art 4 of the 2012 Order, this amendment does not have effect in any case where the period of continuous employment began before 6 April 2012 (in such cases the previous period of one year continues to apply).

Sub-s (3) is amended as follows:

Para (a) repealed by the Employment Relations Act 1999, ss 9, 44, Sch 4, Pt III, paras 1, 5, 18, Sch 9(2).

Para (aa) inserted by the Employment Relations Act 2004, s 40(6).

Para (b) substituted by the Employment Relations Act 2004, s 57(1), Sch 1, para 32.

Para (da) inserted by the Enterprise Act 2016, s 33, Sch 5, paras 1, 10, as from a day to be appointed.

Para (dd) inserted by the Working Time Regulations 1998, SI 1998/1833, regs 2(1), 32(4).

Para (de) inserted by the Education and Skills Act 2008, s 39(1), (4), as from a day to be appointed.

Para (ff) inserted by the Public Interest Disclosure Act 1998, ss 7(1), 18(2).

Word omitted from para (g) repealed, and para (gg) inserted, by the National Minimum Wage Act 1998, ss 25(3), 53, Sch 3.

Word omitted from para (gg) repealed, and para (gh) inserted, by the Tax Credits Act 1999, ss 7, 19(4), Sch 3, para 3(3), Sch 6.

Word omitted from para (gh) repealed, and para (hh) and the word immediately preceding it inserted, by the Transnational Information and Consultation of Employees Regulations 1999, SI 1999/3323, reg 29(2).

Para (gi) inserted by the Employment Relations Act 2004, s 41(5).

Para (gj) inserted by the Pensions Act 2008, s 57(1), (5).

First para (gk) inserted by the Employment Relations Act 1999 (Blacklists) Regulations 2010, SI 2010/493, reg 12(1), (4).

Second para (gk) inserted by the Apprenticeships, Skills, Children and Learning Act 2009, s 40(5), Sch 1, paras 1, 4, as from 6 April 2010 (except in relation to small employers and their employees), and as from a day to be appointed (otherwise) (as to the meaning of "small employers" etc, see further the notes at **[1.937]**).

Para (gl): inserted by the Employment Relations Act 1999 (Blacklists) Regulations 2010, SI 2010/493, reg 12(1), (4).

Para (gm): inserted by the Growth and Infrastructure Act 2013, s 31(5).

Word omitted from para (h) repealed, and para (i) and the word immediately preceding it added, by the Part-time Workers (Prevention of Less Favourable Treatment) Regulations 2000, SI 2000/1551, reg 10, Schedule, para 2(2).

Word omitted from para (hh) repealed, and para (j) and the word immediately preceding it added, by the Fixed-term Employees (Prevention of Less Favourable Treatment) Regulations 2002, SI 2002/2034, reg 11, Sch 2, Pt 1, para 3(1), (11) (except in relation to Government training schemes, agency workers and apprentices; see regs 18–20 of the 2002 Regulations at **[2.571]** et seq).

Word omitted from para (i) repealed, and para (k) and the word immediately preceding it added, by the European Public Limited-Liability Company Regulations 2004, SI 2004/2326, reg 43(2).

Word omitted from para (j) repealed, and para (l) and the word immediately preceding it added, by the Information and Consultation of Employees Regulations 2004, SI 2004/3426, reg 31(2).

Word omitted from para (k) repealed, and para (m) and the word immediately preceding it added, by the Occupational and Personal Pension Schemes (Consultation by Employers and Miscellaneous Amendment) Regulations 2006, SI 2006/349, reg 17, Schedule, para 6(2).

Word omitted following para (l) repealed, and para (n) and the word immediately preceding it added, by the Employment Equality (Age) Regulations 2006, SI 2006/1031, reg 49(1), Sch 8, Pt 1, paras 21, 24.

Para (n) repealed by the Employment Equality (Repeal of Retirement Age Provisions) Regulations 2011, SI 2011/1069, reg 3(1), (5).

Word omitted following para (m) repealed, and para (o) and the word immediately preceding it added, by the European Cooperative Society (Involvement of Employees) Regulations 2006, SI 2006/2059, reg 32(2).

Word omitted following para (n) repealed, and para (p) and the word immediately preceding it added, by the Companies (Cross-Border Mergers) Regulations 2007, SI 2007/2974, reg 48(2).

Para (p) repealed by the Companies, Limited Liability Partnerships and Partnerships (Amendment etc) (EU Exit) Regulations 2019, SI 2019/348, reg 8, Sch 3, paras 5, 7, as from exit day (as defined in the European Union (Withdrawal) Act 2018, s 20).

Word omitted following para (o) repealed, and para (q) and the word immediately preceding it added, by the European Public Limited-Liability Company (Employee Involvement) (Great Britain) Regulations 2009, SI 2009/2401, reg 30(3).

Word omitted following para (p) repealed, and para (r) and the word immediately preceding it added, by the Agency Workers Regulations 2010, SI 2010/93, reg 25, Sch 2, Pt 1, paras 9, 16 (note that Sch 2, Pt 1, para 16 of the 2010 Regulations was amended by the Agency Workers (Amendment) Regulations 2011, SI 2011/1941, reg 2(1), (5) to correct a drafting error in the original Regulations which provided that the inserted paragraph should be paragraph (q) instead of paragraph (r)).

Sub-s (4): added by the Enterprise and Regulatory Reform Act 2013, s 13.

Sub-s (5): added by the Defence Reform Act 2014, s 48(1), (2), as from 1 October 2014, except where the effective date of termination is earlier than the day on which s 48 comes into force. (see s 48(4) of the 2014 Act).

Modification and application of this section: see the notes following the Part heading *ante*.

Exclusion: this section is excluded in relation to dismissal on grounds related to union membership or activities; see the Trade Union and Labour Relations (Consolidation) Act 1992, s 154 at **[1.466]**.

Corresponding provision for Wales: see the note to s 47AA at **[1.887]**.

109 *(Repealed by the Employment Equality (Age) Regulations 2006, SI 2006/1031, reg 49(1), Sch 8, Pt 1, paras 21, 25.)*

[1.1027]

110 Dismissal procedures agreements

(1) Where a dismissal procedures agreement is designated by an order under subsection (3) which is for the time being in force—

(a) the provisions of that agreement relating to dismissal shall have effect in substitution for any rights under section 94, and

(b) accordingly, section 94 does not apply to the dismissal of an employee from any employment if it is employment to which, and he is an employee to whom, those provisions of the agreement apply.

[(2) But if the agreement includes provision that it does not apply to dismissals of particular descriptions, subsection (1) does not apply in relation to a dismissal of any such description.]

(3) An order designating a dismissal procedures agreement may be made by the Secretary of State, on an application being made to him jointly by all the parties to the agreement, if he is satisfied that—

(a) every trade union which is a party to the agreement is an independent trade union,

(b) the agreement provides for procedures to be followed in cases where an employee claims that he has been, or is in the course of being, unfairly dismissed,

(c) those procedures are available without discrimination to all employees falling within any description to which the agreement applies,

(d) the remedies provided by the agreement in respect of unfair dismissal are on the whole as beneficial as (but not necessarily identical with) those provided in respect of unfair dismissal by this Part,

[(e) the agreement includes provision either for arbitration in every case or for—

(i) arbitration where (by reason of equality of votes or for any other reason) a decision under the agreement cannot otherwise be reached, and

(ii) a right to submit to arbitration any question of law arising out of such a decision, and]

(f) the provisions of the agreement are such that it can be determined with reasonable certainty whether or not a particular employee is one to whom the agreement applies.

[(3A) The Secretary of State may by order amend subsection (3) so as to add to the conditions specified in that subsection such conditions as he may specify in the order.]

(4) If at any time when an order under subsection (3) is in force in relation to a dismissal procedures agreement the Secretary of State is satisfied, whether on an application made to him by any of the parties to the agreement or otherwise, either—

(a) that it is the desire of all the parties to the agreement that the order should be revoked, or

(b) that the agreement no longer satisfies all the conditions specified in subsection (3),

the Secretary of State shall revoke the order by an order under this subsection.

(5) The transitional provisions which may be made in an order under subsection (4) include, in particular, provisions directing—

(a) that an employee—

(i) shall not be excluded from his right under section 94 where the effective date of termination falls within a transitional period which ends with the date on which the order takes effect and which is specified in the order, and

(ii) shall have an extended time for presenting a complaint under section 111 in respect of a dismissal where the effective date of termination falls within that period, and

(b) that, where the effective date of termination falls within such a transitional period, an [employment tribunal] shall, in determining any complaint of unfair dismissal presented by an employee to whom the dismissal procedures agreement applies, have regard to such considerations as are specified in the order (in addition to those specified in this Part and section 10(4) and (5) of [the Employment Tribunals Act 1996]).

[(6) Where an award is made under a designated dismissal procedures agreement—

(a) in England and Wales it may be enforced, by leave of [the county court], in the same manner as a judgment of the court to the same effect and, where leave is given, judgment may be entered in terms of the award, and

(b) in Scotland it may be recorded for execution in the Books of Council and Session and shall be enforceable accordingly.

NOTES

Sub-s (2): substituted by the Employment Rights (Dispute Resolution) Act 1998, s 12(1), (5).

Sub-s (3): words in square brackets substituted by the Employment Rights (Dispute Resolution) Act 1998, s 12(2), (5).

Sub-s (3A): inserted by the Employment Act 2002, s 44, as from a day to be appointed.

Sub-s (5): words in square brackets substituted by the Employment Rights (Dispute Resolution) Act 1998, s 1(2)(a), (b).

Sub-s (6): added by the Employment Rights (Dispute Resolution) Act 1998, s 12(3), (5); words in square brackets substituted by the Crime and Courts Act 2013, s 17(5), Sch 9, Pt 3.

Modification and application of this section: see the notes following the Part heading *ante*.

The only Order under the provisions re-enacted in this section (not made as a statutory instrument) is in relation to the electrical contracting industry. This order was revoked with effect from 1 June 2001 by the Dismissal Procedures Agreement Designation (Electrical Contracting Industry) Order 1991 Revocation Order 2001 (SI 2001/1752), subject to transitional provisions.

CHAPTER II REMEDIES FOR UNFAIR DISMISSAL

Introductory

[1.1028]

111 Complaints to [employment tribunal]

(1) A complaint may be presented to an [employment tribunal] against an employer by any person that he was unfairly dismissed by the employer.

(2) [Subject to the following provisions of this section], an [employment tribunal] shall not consider a complaint under this section unless it is presented to the tribunal—

(a) before the end of the period of three months beginning with the effective date of termination, or

(b) within such further period as the tribunal considers reasonable in a case where it is satisfied that it was not reasonably practicable for the complaint to be presented before the end of that period of three months.

[(2A) Section 207A(3) (extension because of mediation in certain European cross-border disputes) [and section 207B (extension of time limits to facilitate conciliation before institution of proceedings) apply] for the purposes of subsection (2)(a).]

(3) Where a dismissal is with notice, an [employment tribunal] shall consider a complaint under this section if it is presented after the notice is given but before the effective date of termination.

(4) In relation to a complaint which is presented as mentioned in subsection (3), the provisions of this Act, so far as they relate to unfair dismissal, have effect as if—

(a) references to a complaint by a person that he was unfairly dismissed by his employer included references to a complaint by a person that his employer has given him notice in such circumstances that he will be unfairly dismissed when the notice expires,

(b) references to reinstatement included references to the withdrawal of the notice by the employer,

(c) references to the effective date of termination included references to the date which would be the effective date of termination on the expiry of the notice, and

(d) references to an employee ceasing to be employed included references to an employee having been given notice of dismissal.

[(5) Where the dismissal is alleged to be unfair by virtue of section 104F (blacklists),

(a) subsection (2)(b) does not apply, and

(b) an employment tribunal may consider a complaint that is otherwise out of time if, in all the circumstances of the case, it considers that it is just and equitable to do so.]

NOTES

Words in first pair of square brackets in sub-s (2) substituted, and sub-s (5) added, by the Employment Relations Act 1999 (Blacklists) Regulations 2010, SI 2010/493, reg 12(1), (5).

Sub-s (2A) was inserted by the Cross-Border Mediation (EU Directive) Regulations 2011, SI 2011/1133, regs 30, 46; words in square brackets substituted by the Enterprise and Regulatory Reform Act 2013, s 8, Sch 2, paras 15, 33 and substituted by the Cross-Border Mediation (EU Directive) (EU Exit) Regulations 2019, SI 2019/469, reg 4, Sch 1, Pt 1, para 12(1), (23), as from exit day (as defined in the European Union (Withdrawal) Act 2018, s 20), as follows—

"(2A) Section 207B (extension of time limits to facilitate conciliation before institution of proceedings) applies for the purposes of subsection (2)(a).".

All other words in square brackets this section (including in the section heading) were substituted by the Employment Rights (Dispute Resolution) Act 1998, s 1(2)(a).

Conciliation: employment tribunal proceedings under this section are "relevant proceedings" for the purposes of the conciliation provisions contained in the Employment Tribunals Act 1996, ss 18–18C; see s 18(1)(b) of the 1996 Act at **[1.757]**.

Modification and application of this section: see the notes following the Part heading *ante*.

Tribunal jurisdiction: the Employment Act 2002, s 38 applies to proceedings before the employment tribunal relating to a claim under this section; see s 38(1) of, and Sch 5 to, the 2002 Act at **[1.1279]**, **[1.1287]**. See also the Trade Union and Labour Relations (Consolidation) Act 1992, s 207A at **[1.524]** (as inserted by the Employment Act 2008). That section provides that in proceedings before an employment tribunal relating to a claim by an employee under any of the jurisdictions listed in Sch A2 to the 1992 Act at **[1.704]** (which includes this section) the tribunal may adjust any award given if the employer or the employee has unreasonably failed to comply with a relevant Code of Practice as defined by s 207A(4). See also the revised Acas Code of Practice 1 – Disciplinary and Grievance Procedures (2015) at **[4.1]** and Acas Code of Practice 4 – Settlement Agreements at **[4.54]**.

National security: for the effect of national security considerations on a complaint under this section, see the Employment Tribunals Act 1996, s 10(1) at **[1.745]**.

[1.1029]
[111A Confidentiality of negotiations before termination of employment

(1) Evidence of pre-termination negotiations is inadmissible in any proceedings on a complaint under section 111.
This is subject to subsections (3) to (5).
(2) In subsection (1) "pre-termination negotiations" means any offer made or discussions held, before the termination of the employment in question, with a view to it being terminated on terms agreed between the employer and the employee.
(3) Subsection (1) does not apply where, according to the complainant's case, the circumstances are such that a provision (whenever made) contained in, or made under, this or any other Act requires the complainant to be regarded for the purposes of this Part as unfairly dismissed.
(4) In relation to anything said or done which in the tribunal's opinion was improper, or was connected with improper behaviour, subsection (1) applies only to the extent that the tribunal considers just.
(5) Subsection (1) does not affect the admissibility, on any question as to costs or expenses, of evidence relating to an offer made on the basis that the right to refer to it on any such question is reserved.]

NOTES

Inserted by the Enterprise and Regulatory Reform Act 2013, s 14.

Modification and application of this section: see the notes following the Part heading *ante*.

See further as to the application of sub-s (4) above, Acas Code of Practice 4 – Settlement Agreements at **[4.54]**.

[1.1030]
112 The remedies: orders and compensation

(1) This section applies where, on a complaint under section 111, an [employment tribunal] finds that the grounds of the complaint are well-founded.
(2) The tribunal shall—
(a) explain to the complainant what orders may be made under section 113 and in what circumstances they may be made, and
(b) ask him whether he wishes the tribunal to make such an order.
(3) If the complainant expresses such a wish, the tribunal may make an order under section 113.
(4) If no order is made under section 113, the tribunal shall make an award of compensation for unfair dismissal (calculated in accordance with sections 118 to [126] [. . .]) to be paid by the employer to the employee.
[(5), (6) . . .]

NOTES

Sub-s (1): words in square brackets substituted by the Employment Rights (Dispute Resolution) Act 1998, s 1(2)(a).

Sub-s (4): figure in square brackets substituted by the Employment Act 2002, s 53, Sch 7, paras 24, 36; the words omitted were originally inserted by the Public Interest Disclosure Act 1998, s 8(1), and repealed by the Employment Relations Act 1999, s 44, Sch 9(11).

Sub-ss (5), (6): added by the Employment Act 2002, s 34(1), (3); repealed by the Employment Equality (Repeal of Retirement Age Provisions) Regulations 2011, SI 2011/1069, reg 3(1), (6).

Modification and application of this section: see the notes following the Part heading *ante*.

Orders for Reinstatement or Re-engagement

[1.1031]
113 The orders

An order under this section may be—
(a) an order for reinstatement (in accordance with section 114), or
(b) an order for re-engagement (in accordance with section 115),
as the tribunal may decide.

NOTES

Modification and application of this section: see the notes following the Part heading *ante*.

[1.1032]
114 Order for reinstatement

(1) An order for reinstatement is an order that the employer shall treat the complainant in all respects as if he had not been dismissed.
(2) On making an order for reinstatement the tribunal shall specify—
(a) any amount payable by the employer in respect of any benefit which the complainant might reasonably be expected to have had but for the dismissal (including arrears of pay) for the period between the date of termination of employment and the date of reinstatement,
(b) any rights and privileges (including seniority and pension rights) which must be restored to the employee, and
(c) the date by which the order must be complied with.
(3) If the complainant would have benefited from an improvement in his terms and conditions of employment had he not been dismissed, an order for reinstatement shall require him to be treated as if he had benefited from that improvement from the date on which he would have done so but for being dismissed.

(4) In calculating for the purposes of subsection (2)(a) any amount payable by the employer, the tribunal shall take into account, so as to reduce the employer's liability, any sums received by the complainant in respect of the period between the date of termination of employment and the date of reinstatement by way of—

(a) wages in lieu of notice or ex gratia payments paid by the employer, or
(b) remuneration paid in respect of employment with another employer,

and such other benefits as the tribunal thinks appropriate in the circumstances.

(5) . . .

NOTES

Sub-s (5): repealed by the Employment Relations Act 1999, ss 9, 44, Sch 4, Pt III, paras 1, 5, 20, Sch 9(2).

Modification and application of this section: see the notes following the Part heading *ante*.

[1.1033]

115 Order for re-engagement

(1) An order for re-engagement is an order, on such terms as the tribunal may decide, that the complainant be engaged by the employer, or by a successor of the employer or by an associated employer, in employment comparable to that from which he was dismissed or other suitable employment.

(2) On making an order for re-engagement the tribunal shall specify the terms on which re-engagement is to take place, including—

(a) the identity of the employer,
(b) the nature of the employment,
(c) the remuneration for the employment,
(d) any amount payable by the employer in respect of any benefit which the complainant might reasonably be expected to have had but for the dismissal (including arrears of pay) for the period between the date of termination of employment and the date of re-engagement,
(e) any rights and privileges (including seniority and pension rights) which must be restored to the employee, and
(f) the date by which the order must be complied with.

(3) In calculating for the purposes of subsection (2)(d) any amount payable by the employer, the tribunal shall take into account, so as to reduce the employer's liability, any sums received by the complainant in respect of the period between the date of termination of employment and the date of re-engagement by way of—

(a) wages in lieu of notice or ex gratia payments paid by the employer, or
(b) remuneration paid in respect of employment with another employer,

and such other benefits as the tribunal thinks appropriate in the circumstances.

(4) . . .

NOTES

Sub-s (4): repealed by the Employment Relations Act 1999, ss 9, 44, Sch 4, Pt III, paras 1, 5, 21, Sch 9(2).

Modification and application of this section: see the notes following the Part heading *ante*.

[1.1034]

116 Choice of order and its terms

(1) In exercising its discretion under section 113 the tribunal shall first consider whether to make an order for reinstatement and in so doing shall take into account—

(a) whether the complainant wishes to be reinstated,
(b) whether it is practicable for the employer to comply with an order for reinstatement, and
(c) where the complainant caused or contributed to some extent to the dismissal, whether it would be just to order his reinstatement.

(2) If the tribunal decides not to make an order for reinstatement it shall then consider whether to make an order for re-engagement and, if so, on what terms.

(3) In so doing the tribunal shall take into account—

(a) any wish expressed by the complainant as to the nature of the order to be made,
(b) whether it is practicable for the employer (or a successor or an associated employer) to comply with an order for re-engagement, and
(c) where the complainant caused or contributed to some extent to the dismissal, whether it would be just to order his re-engagement and (if so) on what terms.

(4) Except in a case where the tribunal takes into account contributory fault under subsection (3)(c) it shall, if it orders re-engagement, do so on terms which are, so far as is reasonably practicable, as favourable as an order for reinstatement.

(5) Where in any case an employer has engaged a permanent replacement for a dismissed employee, the tribunal shall not take that fact into account in determining, for the purposes of subsection (1)(b) or (3)(b), whether it is practicable to comply with an order for reinstatement or re-engagement.

(6) Subsection (5) does not apply where the employer shows—

(a) that it was not practicable for him to arrange for the dismissed employee's work to be done without engaging a permanent replacement, or
(b) that—
  (i) he engaged the replacement after the lapse of a reasonable period, without having heard from the dismissed employee that he wished to be reinstated or re-engaged, and
  (ii) when the employer engaged the replacement it was no longer reasonable for him to arrange for the dismissed employee's work to be done except by a permanent replacement.

NOTES

Modification and application of this section: see the notes following the Part heading *ante*.

[1.1035]

117 Enforcement of order and compensation

(1) An [employment tribunal] shall make an award of compensation, to be paid by the employer to the employee, if—

(a) an order under section 113 is made and the complainant is reinstated or re-engaged, but

(b) the terms of the order are not fully complied with.

(2) Subject to section 124 [. . .], the amount of the compensation shall be such as the tribunal thinks fit having regard to the loss sustained by the complainant in consequence of the failure to comply fully with the terms of the order.

[(2A) There shall be deducted from any award under subsection (1) the amount of any award made under section 112(5) at the time of the order under section 113.]

(3) Subject to subsections (1) and (2) [. . .], if an order under section 113 is made but the complainant is not reinstated or re-engaged in accordance with the order, the tribunal shall make—

(a) an award of compensation for unfair dismissal (calculated in accordance with sections 118 to [126]), and

(b) except where this paragraph does not apply, an additional award of compensation of [an amount not less than twenty-six nor more than fifty-two weeks' pay],

to be paid by the employer to the employee.

(4) Subsection (3)(b) does not apply where—

(a) the employer satisfies the tribunal that it was not practicable to comply with the order, . . .

(b) . . .

(5), (6) . . .

(7) Where in any case an employer has engaged a permanent replacement for a dismissed employee, the tribunal shall not take that fact into account in determining for the purposes of subsection (4)(a) whether it was practicable to comply with the order for reinstatement or re-engagement unless the employer shows that it was not practicable for him to arrange for the dismissed employee's work to be done without engaging a permanent replacement.

(8) Where in any case an [employment tribunal] finds that the complainant has unreasonably prevented an order under section 113 from being complied with, in making an award of compensation for unfair dismissal . . . it shall take that conduct into account as a failure on the part of the complainant to mitigate his loss.

NOTES

Sub-s (1): words in square brackets substituted by the Employment Rights (Dispute Resolution) Act 1998, s 1(2)(a).

Sub-s (2): words omitted originally inserted by the Public Interest Disclosure Act 1998, s 8(2)(a), and repealed by the Employment Relations Act 1999, s 44, Sch 9(11).

Sub-s (2A): inserted by the Employment Act 2002, s 34(1), (4).

Sub-s (3): words omitted originally inserted by the Public Interest Disclosure Act 1998, s 8(2)(b), and repealed by the Employment Relations Act 1999, s 44, Sch 9(11); figure in square brackets in para (a) substituted by the Employment Act 2002, s 53, Sch 7, paras 24, 37; words in square brackets in para (b) substituted by the Employment Relations Act 1999, s 33(2).

Sub-s (4): para (b) and word immediately preceding it repealed by the Employment Relations Act 1999, ss 33(1)(a), 44, Sch 9(10).

Sub-ss (5), (6): repealed by the Employment Relations Act 1999, ss 33(2), 44, Sch 9(10).

Sub-s (8): words in square brackets substituted, and words omitted repealed, by the Employment Rights (Dispute Resolution) Act 1998, ss 1(2)(a), 15, Sch 2.

Modification and application of this section: see the notes following the Part heading *ante*.

Modifications: for modifications in relation to arbitration schemes for unfair dismissal cases, see the ACAS Arbitration Scheme (Great Britain) Order 2004, SI 2004/753 at **[2.717]**.

Compensation

[1.1036]

118 General

(1) [. . .] where a tribunal makes an award of compensation for unfair dismissal under section 112(4) or 117(3)(a) the award shall consist of—

(a) a basic award (calculated in accordance with sections 119 to 122 and 126), and

(b) a compensatory award (calculated in accordance with sections 123, 124, [124A and 126]).

(2), (3), [(4)] . . .

NOTES

Sub-s (1): words omitted originally inserted by the Public Interest Disclosure Act 1998, s 8(3), and repealed by the Employment Relations Act 1999, s 44, Sch 9(11); words in square brackets in para (b) substituted by the Employment Act 2002, s 53, Sch 7, paras 24, 38.

Sub-ss (2), (3): repealed by the Employment Relations Act 1999, ss 33(1)(a), 44, Sch 9(10).

Sub-s (4): added by the Employment Rights (Dispute Resolution) Act 1998, s 15, Sch 1, para 21(1), (3); repealed by the Employment Act 2002, s 54, Sch 8(1).

Modification and application of this section: see the notes following the Part heading *ante*.

[1.1037]

119 Basic award

(1) Subject to the provisions of this section, sections 120 to 122 and section 126, the amount of the basic award shall be calculated by—

(a) determining the period, ending with the effective date of termination, during which the employee has been continuously employed,

(b) reckoning backwards from the end of that period the number of years of employment falling within that period, and

(c) allowing the appropriate amount for each of those years of employment.

(2) In subsection (1)(c) "the appropriate amount" means—

(a) one and a half weeks' pay for a year of employment in which the employee was not below the age of forty-one,

(b) one week's pay for a year of employment (not within paragraph (a)) in which he was not below the age of twenty-two, and

(c) half a week's pay for a year of employment not within paragraph (a) or (b).

(3) Where twenty years of employment have been reckoned under subsection (1), no account shall be taken under that subsection of any year of employment earlier than those twenty years.

(4)–(6) . . .

NOTES

Sub-ss (4), (5): repealed by the Employment Equality (Age) Regulations 2006, SI 2006/1031, reg 49(1), Sch 8, Pt 1, paras 21, 27.

Sub-s (6): repealed by the Employment Relations Act 1999, ss 9, 44, Sch 4, Pt III, paras 1, 5, 23, Sch 9(2).

Modification and application of this section: see the notes following the Part heading *ante*.

[1.1038]

120 Basic award: minimum in certain cases

(1) The amount of the basic award (before any reduction under section 122) shall not be less than [£6,408] where the reason (or, if more than one, the principal reason)—

(a) in a redundancy case, for selecting the employee for dismissal, or

(b) otherwise, for the dismissal,

is one of those specified in section 100(1)(a) and (b), [101A(d),] 102(1) or 103.

[(1A), (1B) . . .]

[(1C) Where an employee is regarded as unfairly dismissed by virtue of section 104F (blacklists) (whether or not the dismissal is unfair or regarded as unfair for any other reason), the amount of the basic award of compensation (before any reduction is made under section 122) shall not be less than £5,000.]

(2) . . .

NOTES

Sub-s (1): sum in first pair of square brackets substituted by the Employment Rights (Increase of Limits) Order 2019, SI 2019/324, art 3, Schedule, as from 6 April 2019, in relation to any case where the appropriate date (as defined in the order) falls on or after that date (see SI 2019/324, art 4 at **[2.2117]**). The previous sum was £6,203 (see SI 2018/194). This sum may be varied by the Secretary of State (see the Employment Relations Act 1999, s 34(1)(a), (3)(b) at **[1.1258]**). Figure in second pair of square brackets inserted by the Working Time Regulations 1998, SI 1998/1833, regs 2(1), 32(5).

Sub-ss (1A), (1B): inserted by the Employment Act 2002, s 34(1), (6); repealed by the Employment Equality (Repeal of Retirement Age Provisions) Regulations 2011, SI 2011/1069, reg 3(1), (7).

Sub-s (1C): inserted by the Employment Relations Act 1999 (Blacklists) Regulations 2010, SI 2010/493, reg 12(1), (6).

Sub-s (2): repealed by the Employment Relations Act 1999, ss 36(1)(a), 44, Sch 9(10).

Modification and application of this section: see the notes following the Part heading *ante*.

[1.1039]

121 Basic award of two weeks' pay in certain cases

The amount of the basic award shall be two weeks' pay where the tribunal finds that the reason (or, where there is more than one, the principal reason) for the dismissal of the employee is that he was redundant and the employee—

(a) by virtue of section 138 is not regarded as dismissed for the purposes of Part XI, or

(b) by virtue of section 141 is not, or (if he were otherwise entitled) would not be, entitled to a redundancy payment.

NOTES

Modification and application of this section: see the notes following the Part heading *ante*.

[1.1040]

122 Basic award: reductions

(1) Where the tribunal finds that the complainant has unreasonably refused an offer by the employer which (if accepted) would have the effect of reinstating the complainant in his employment in all respects as if he had not been dismissed, the tribunal shall reduce or further reduce the amount of the basic award to such extent as it considers just and equitable having regard to that finding.

(2) Where the tribunal considers that any conduct of the complainant before the dismissal (or, where the dismissal was with notice, before the notice was given) was such that it would be just and equitable to reduce or further reduce the amount of the basic award to any extent, the tribunal shall reduce or further reduce that amount accordingly.

(3) Subsection (2) does not apply in a redundancy case unless the reason for selecting the employee for dismissal was one of those specified in section 100(1)(a) and (b), [101A(d),] 102(1) or 103; and in such a case subsection (2) applies only to so much of the basic award as is payable because of section 120.

[(3A) Where the complainant has been awarded any amount in respect of the dismissal under a designated dismissal procedures agreement, the tribunal shall reduce or further reduce the amount of the basic award to such extent as it considers just and equitable having regard to that award.]

(4) The amount of the basic award shall be reduced or further reduced by the amount of—

(a) any redundancy payment awarded by the tribunal under Part XI in respect of the same dismissal, or

(b) any payment made by the employer to the employee on the ground that the dismissal was by reason of redundancy (whether in pursuance of Part XI or otherwise).

[(5) Where a dismissal is regarded as unfair by virtue of section 104F (blacklists), the amount of the basic award shall be reduced or further reduced by the amount of any basic award in respect of the same dismissal under section 156 of the Trade Union and Labour Relations (Consolidation) Act 1992 (minimum basic award in case of dismissal on grounds related to trade union membership or activities).]

NOTES

Sub-s (3): figure in square brackets inserted by the Working Time Regulations 1998, SI 1998/1833, regs 2(1), 32(5).

Sub-s (3A): inserted by the Employment Rights (Dispute Resolution) Act 1998, s 15, Sch 1, para 22.

Sub-s (5): added by the Employment Relations Act 1999 (Blacklists) Regulations 2010, SI 2010/493, reg 12(1), (7).

Modification and application of this section: see the notes following the Part heading *ante*.

[1.1041]

123 Compensatory award

(1) Subject to the provisions of this section and sections 124[, 124A and 126], the amount of the compensatory award shall be such amount as the tribunal considers just and equitable in all the circumstances having regard to the loss sustained by the complainant in consequence of the dismissal in so far as that loss is attributable to action taken by the employer.

(2) The loss referred to in subsection (1) shall be taken to include—

(a) any expenses reasonably incurred by the complainant in consequence of the dismissal, and

(b) subject to subsection (3), loss of any benefit which he might reasonably be expected to have had but for the dismissal.

(3) The loss referred to in subsection (1) shall be taken to include in respect of any loss of—

(a) any entitlement or potential entitlement to a payment on account of dismissal by reason of redundancy (whether in pursuance of Part XI or otherwise), or

(b) any expectation of such a payment,

only the loss referable to the amount (if any) by which the amount of that payment would have exceeded the amount of a basic award (apart from any reduction under section 122) in respect of the same dismissal.

(4) In ascertaining the loss referred to in subsection (1) the tribunal shall apply the same rule concerning the duty of a person to mitigate his loss as applies to damages recoverable under the common law of England and Wales or (as the case may be) Scotland.

(5) In determining, for the purposes of subsection (1), how far any loss sustained by the complainant was attributable to action taken by the employer, no account shall be taken of any pressure which by—

(a) calling, organising, procuring or financing a strike or other industrial action, or

(b) threatening to do so,

was exercised on the employer to dismiss the employee; and that question shall be determined as if no such pressure had been exercised.

(6) Where the tribunal finds that the dismissal was to any extent caused or contributed to by any action of the complainant, it shall reduce the amount of the compensatory award by such proportion as it considers just and equitable having regard to that finding.

[(6A) Where—

(a) the reason (or principal reason) for the dismissal is that the complainant made a protected disclosure, and

(b) it appears to the tribunal that the disclosure was not made in good faith,

the tribunal may, if it considers it just and equitable in all the circumstances to do so, reduce any award it makes to the complainant by no more than 25%.]

(7) If the amount of any payment made by the employer to the employee on the ground that the dismissal was by reason of redundancy (whether in pursuance of Part XI or otherwise) exceeds the amount of the basic award which would be payable but for section 122(4), that excess goes to reduce the amount of the compensatory award.

[(8) Where the amount of the compensatory award falls to be calculated for the purposes of an award under section 117(3)(a), there shall be deducted from the compensatory award any award made under section 112(5) at the time of the order under section 113.]

NOTES

Sub-s (1): words in square brackets substituted by the Employment Act 2002, s 53, Sch 7, paras 24, 39.

Sub-s (6A): inserted by the Enterprise and Regulatory Reform Act 2013, s 18(5).

Sub-s (8): added by the Employment Act 2002, s 34(1), (5).

Modification and application of this section: see the notes following the Part heading *ante*.

[1.1042]

124 Limit of compensatory award etc

(1) The amount of—

(a) any compensation awarded to a person under section 117(1) and (2), or

(b) a compensatory award to a person calculated in accordance with section 123,

shall not exceed [the amount specified in subsection (1ZA)].

[(1ZA) The amount specified in this subsection is the lower of—

(a) [£86,444], and

(b) 52 multiplied by a week's pay of the person concerned.]

[(1A) Subsection (1) shall not apply to compensation awarded, or a compensatory award made, to a person in a case where he is regarded as unfairly dismissed by virtue of section 100, 103A, 105(3) or 105(6A).]

(2) . . .

(3) In the case of compensation awarded to a person under section 117(1) and (2), the limit imposed by this section may be exceeded to the extent necessary to enable the award fully to reflect the amount specified as payable under section 114(2)(a) or section 115(2)(d).

(4) Where—

(a) a compensatory award is an award under paragraph (a) of subsection (3) of section 117, and

(b) an additional award falls to be made under paragraph (b) of that subsection,

the limit imposed by this section on the compensatory award may be exceeded to the extent necessary to enable the aggregate of the compensatory and additional awards fully to reflect the amount specified as payable under section 114(2)(a) or section 115(2)(d).

(5) The limit imposed by this section applies to the amount which the [employment tribunal] would, apart from this section, award in respect of the subject matter of the complaint after taking into account—

(a) any payment made by the respondent to the complainant in respect of that matter, and

(b) any reduction in the amount of the award required by any enactment or rule of law.

NOTES

Sub-s (1): words in square brackets substituted by the Unfair Dismissal (Variation of the Limit of Compensatory Award) Order 2013, SI 2013/1949, art 2(1), (2).

Sub-s (1ZA): inserted by SI 2013/1949, art 2(1), (3). Sum in square brackets substituted by the Employment Rights (Increase of Limits) Order 2019, SI 2019/324, art 3, Schedule, as from 6 April 2019, in relation to any case where the appropriate date (as defined in the order) falls on or after that date (see SI 2019/324, art 4 at **[2.2117]**). The previous sum was £83,682, as from 6 April 2018 (see SI 2018/194).

Sub-s (1A): inserted by the Employment Relations Act 1999, s 37(1).

Sub-s (2): repealed by the Employment Relations Act 1999, ss 36(1)(a), 44, Sch 9(10).

Sub-s (5): words in square brackets substituted by the Employment Rights (Dispute Resolution) Act 1998, s 1(2)(a).

Modification and application of this section: see the notes following the Part heading *ante*.

The previous sums (specified for sub-s (1) prior to its amendment as noted above, and subsequently specified in sub-s (1ZA)) were: £80,541 as from 6 April 2017 (see SI 2017/175); £78,962 as from 6 April 2016 (see SI 2016/288); £78,335 as from 6 April 2015 (see SI 2015/226); £76,574 as from 6 April 2014 (see SI 2014/382); £74,200 as from 1 February 2013 (see SI 2012/3007); £72,300 as from 1 February 2012 (see SI 2011/3006); £68,400 as from 1 February 2011 (see SI 2010/2926); and £65,300 as from 1 February 2010 (see SI 2009/3274) in each case where the appropriate date fell after the commencement date. This sum may be varied by the Secretary of State, see the Employment Relations Act 1999, s 34(1)(a), (3)(c) at **[1.1258]**.

[1.1043]

[124A Adjustments under the Employment Act 2002

Where an award of compensation for unfair dismissal falls to be—

(a) reduced or increased under [section 207A of the Trade Union and Labour Relations (Consolidation) Act 1992 (effect of failure to comply with Code: adjustment of awards)], or

(b) increased under section 38 of that Act (failure to give statement of employment particulars),

the adjustment shall be in the amount awarded under section 118(1)(b) and shall be applied immediately before any reduction under section 123(6) or (7).]

NOTES

Inserted by the Employment Act 2002, s 39.

Words in square brackets in para (a) substituted by the Employment Act 2008, s 3(4).

Modification and application of this section: see the notes following the Part heading *ante*.

Despite the amendment to para (a) of this section, there has been no corresponding amendment to the section heading nor the text in (b) (where the text "section 38 *of that Act*" should presumably now be read as "section 38 *of the Employment Act 2002*").

125 *(Repealed by the Employment Relations Act 1999, ss 33(1)(a), 44, Sch 9(10).)*

[1.1044]

126 Acts which are both unfair dismissal and discrimination

(1) This section applies where compensation falls to be awarded in respect of any act both under—

(a) the provisions of this Act relating to unfair dismissal, and

[(b) the Equality Act 2010].

(2) An [employment tribunal] shall not award compensation under [either of those Acts] in respect of any loss or other matter which is or has been taken into account under [the other] by the tribunal (or another [employment tribunal]) in awarding compensation on the same or another complaint in respect of that act.

NOTES

Sub-s (1): para (b) substituted by the Equality Act 2010, s 211(1), Sch 26, Pt 1, para 33(1), (2).

Sub-s (2): words "employment tribunal" in square brackets in both places they occur substituted by the Employment Rights (Dispute Resolution) Act 1998, s 1(2)(a); other words in square brackets substituted by the Equality Act 2010, s 211(1), Sch 26, Pt 1, para 33(1), (3).
Modification and application of this section: see the notes following the Part heading *ante*.

127, 127A, 127B *(s 127 repealed by the Employment Relations Act 1999, ss 9, 44, Sch 4, Pt III, paras 1, 5, 24, Sch 9(2); s 127A originally inserted by the Employment Rights (Dispute Resolution) Act 1998, s 13, and repealed by the Employment Act 2002, ss 53, 54, Sch 7, paras 24, 40, Sch 8(1); s 127B originally inserted by the Public Interest Disclosure Act 1998, ss 8(4), 18(2), and repealed by the Employment Relations Act 1999, ss 37(2), 44, Sch 9(11).)*

Interim relief

[1.1045]

128 Interim relief pending determination of complaint

[(1) An employee who presents a complaint to an employment tribunal that he has been unfairly dismissed and—
- (a) that the reason (or if more than one the principal reason) for the dismissal is one of those specified in—
  - (i) section 100(1)(a) and (b), 101A(d), 102(1), 103 or 103A, or
  - (ii) paragraph 161(2) of Schedule A1 to the Trade Union and Labour Relations (Consolidation) Act 1992, or
- (b) that the reason (or, if more than one, the principal reason) for which the employee was selected for dismissal was the one specified in the opening words of section 104F(1) and the condition in paragraph (a) or (b) of that subsection was met,

may apply to the tribunal for interim relief.]

(2) The tribunal shall not entertain an application for interim relief unless it is presented to the tribunal before the end of the period of seven days immediately following the effective date of termination (whether before, on or after that date).

(3) The tribunal shall determine the application for interim relief as soon as practicable after receiving the application.

(4) The tribunal shall give to the employer not later than seven days before the date of the hearing a copy of the application together with notice of the date, time and place of the hearing.

(5) The tribunal shall not exercise any power it has of postponing the hearing of an application for interim relief except where it is satisfied that special circumstances exist which justify it in doing so.

NOTES

Sub-s (1): substituted by the Employment Relations Act 1999 (Blacklists) Regulations 2010, SI 2010/493, reg 12(1), (8).
Modification and application of this section: see the notes following the Part heading *ante*.

[1.1046]

129 Procedure on hearing of application and making of order

[(1) This section applies where, on hearing an employee's application for interim relief, it appears to the tribunal that it is likely that on determining the complaint to which the application relates the tribunal will find—
- (a) that the reason (or if more than one the principal reason) for the dismissal is one of those specified in—
  - (i) section 100(1)(a) and (b), 101A(d), 102(1), 103 or 103A, or
  - (ii) paragraph 161(2) of Schedule A1 to the Trade Union and Labour Relations (Consolidation) Act 1992, or
- (b) that the reason (or, if more than one, the principal reason) for which the employee was selected for dismissal was the one specified in the opening words of section 104F(1) and the condition in paragraph (a) or (b) of that subsection was met.]

(2) The tribunal shall announce its findings and explain to both parties (if present)—
- (a) what powers the tribunal may exercise on the application, and
- (b) in what circumstances it will exercise them.

(3) The tribunal shall ask the employer (if present) whether he is willing, pending the determination or settlement of the complaint—
- (a) to reinstate the employee (that is, to treat him in all respects as if he had not been dismissed), or
- (b) if not, to re-engage him in another job on terms and conditions not less favourable than those which would have been applicable to him if he had not been dismissed.

(4) For the purposes of subsection (3)(b) "terms and conditions not less favourable than those which would have been applicable to him if he had not been dismissed" means, as regards seniority, pension rights and other similar rights, that the period prior to the dismissal should be regarded as continuous with his employment following the dismissal.

(5) If the employer states that he is willing to reinstate the employee, the tribunal shall make an order to that effect.

(6) If the employer—
- (a) states that he is willing to re-engage the employee in another job, and
- (b) specifies the terms and conditions on which he is willing to do so,

the tribunal shall ask the employee whether he is willing to accept the job on those terms and conditions.

(7) If the employee is willing to accept the job on those terms and conditions, the tribunal shall make an order to that effect.

(8) If the employee is not willing to accept the job on those terms and conditions—
- (a) where the tribunal is of the opinion that the refusal is reasonable, the tribunal shall make an order for the continuation of his contract of employment, and
- (b) otherwise, the tribunal shall make no order.

(9) If on the hearing of an application for interim relief the employer—
- (a) fails to attend before the tribunal, or
- (b) states that he is unwilling either to reinstate or re-engage the employee as mentioned in subsection (3),

the tribunal shall make an order for the continuation of the employee's contract of employment.

NOTES

Sub-s (1): substituted by the Employment Relations Act 1999 (Blacklists) Regulations 2010, SI 2010/493, reg 12(1), (9).
Modification and application of this section: see the notes following the Part heading *ante*.

[1.1047]

130 Order for continuation of contract of employment

(1) An order under section 129 for the continuation of a contract of employment is an order that the contract of employment continue in force—
- (a) for the purposes of pay or any other benefit derived from the employment, seniority, pension rights and other similar matters, and
- (b) for the purposes of determining for any purpose the period for which the employee has been continuously employed,

from the date of its termination (whether before or after the making of the order) until the determination or settlement of the complaint.

(2) Where the tribunal makes such an order it shall specify in the order the amount which is to be paid by the employer to the employee by way of pay in respect of each normal pay period, or part of any such period, falling between the date of dismissal and the determination or settlement of the complaint.

(3) Subject to the following provisions, the amount so specified shall be that which the employee could reasonably have been expected to earn during that period, or part, and shall be paid—
- (a) in the case of a payment for any such period falling wholly or partly after the making of the order, on the normal pay day for that period, and
- (b) in the case of a payment for any past period, within such time as may be specified in the order.

(4) If an amount is payable in respect only of part of a normal pay period, the amount shall be calculated by reference to the whole period and reduced proportionately.

(5) Any payment made to an employee by an employer under his contract of employment, or by way of damages for breach of that contract, in respect of a normal pay period, or part of any such period, goes towards discharging the employer's liability in respect of that period under subsection (2); and, conversely, any payment under that subsection in respect of a period goes towards discharging any liability of the employer under, or in respect of breach of, the contract of employment in respect of that period.

(6) If an employee, on or after being dismissed by his employer, receives a lump sum which, or part of which, is in lieu of wages but is not referable to any normal pay period, the tribunal shall take the payment into account in determining the amount of pay to be payable in pursuance of any such order.

(7) For the purposes of this section, the amount which an employee could reasonably have been expected to earn, his normal pay period and the normal pay day for each such period shall be determined as if he had not been dismissed.

NOTES

Modification and application of this section: see the notes following the Part heading *ante*.

[1.1048]

131 Application for variation or revocation of order

(1) At any time between—
- (a) the making of an order under section 129, and
- (b) the determination or settlement of the complaint,

the employer or the employee may apply to an [employment tribunal] for the revocation or variation of the order on the ground of a relevant change of circumstances since the making of the order.

(2) Sections 128 and 129 apply in relation to such an application as in relation to an original application for interim relief except that, in the case of an application by the employer, section 128(4) has effect with the substitution of a reference to the employee for the reference to the employer.

NOTES

Sub-s (1): words in square brackets substituted by the Employment Rights (Dispute Resolution) Act 1998, s 1(2)(a).
Modification and application of this section: see the notes following the Part heading *ante*.

[1.1049]

132 Consequence of failure to comply with order

(1) If, on the application of an employee, an [employment tribunal] is satisfied that the employer has not complied with the terms of an order for the reinstatement or re-engagement of the employee under section 129(5) or (7), the tribunal shall—
- (a) make an order for the continuation of the employee's contract of employment, and
- (b) order the employer to pay compensation to the employee.

(2) Compensation under subsection (1)(b) shall be of such amount as the tribunal considers just and equitable in all the circumstances having regard—

(a) to the infringement of the employee's right to be reinstated or re-engaged in pursuance of the order, and

(b) to any loss suffered by the employee in consequence of the non-compliance.

(3) Section 130 applies to an order under subsection (1)(a) as in relation to an order under section 129.

(4) If on the application of an employee an [employment tribunal] is satisfied that the employer has not complied with the terms of an order for the continuation of a contract of employment subsection (5) or (6) applies.

(5) Where the non-compliance consists of a failure to pay an amount by way of pay specified in the order—

(a) the tribunal shall determine the amount owed by the employer on the date of the determination, and

(b) if on that date the tribunal also determines the employee's complaint that he has been unfairly dismissed, it shall specify that amount separately from any other sum awarded to the employee.

(6) In any other case, the tribunal shall order the employer to pay the employee such compensation as the tribunal considers just and equitable in all the circumstances having regard to any loss suffered by the employee in consequence of the non-compliance.

NOTES

Sub-ss (1), (4): words in square brackets substituted by the Employment Rights (Dispute Resolution) Act 1998, s 1(2)(a).

Modification and application of this section: see the notes following the Part heading *ante*.

CHAPTER III SUPPLEMENTARY

[1.1050]

133 Death of employer or employee

(1) Where—

(a) an employer has given notice to an employee to terminate his contract of employment, and

(b) before that termination the employee or the employer dies,

this Part applies as if the contract had been duly terminated by the employer by notice expiring on the date of the death.

(2) Where—

(a) an employee's contract of employment has been terminated,

(b) by virtue of subsection (2) or (4) of section 97 a date later than the effective date of termination as defined in subsection (1) of that section is to be treated for certain purposes as the effective date of termination, and

(c) the employer or the employee dies before that date,

subsection (2) or (4) of section 97 applies as if the notice referred to in that subsection as required by section 86 expired on the date of the death.

(3) Where an employee has died, sections 113 to 116 do not apply; and, accordingly, if the [employment tribunal] finds that the grounds of the complaint are well-founded, the case shall be treated as falling within section 112(4) as a case in which no order is made under section 113.

(4) Subsection (3) does not prejudice an order for reinstatement or re-engagement made before the employee's death.

(5) Where an order for reinstatement or re-engagement has been made and the employee dies before the order is complied with—

(a) if the employer has before the death refused to reinstate or re-engage the employee in accordance with the order, subsections (3) to (6) of section 117 apply, and an award shall be made under subsection (3)(b) of that section, unless the employer satisfies the tribunal that it was not practicable at the time of the refusal to comply with the order, and

(b) if there has been no such refusal, subsections (1) and (2) of that section apply if the employer fails to comply with any ancillary terms of the order which remain capable of fulfilment after the employee's death as they would apply to such a failure to comply fully with the terms of an order where the employee had been reinstated or re-engaged.

NOTES

Sub-s (3): words in square brackets substituted by the Employment Rights (Dispute Resolution) Act 1998, s 1(2)(a).

Modification and application of this section: see the notes following the Part heading *ante*.

[1.1051]

134 Teachers in aided schools

(1) Where a teacher in [a foundation, voluntary aided or foundation special school is dismissed by the governing body of the school in pursuance of a requirement of the [local authority] under [paragraph 7 of Schedule 2 to the Education Act 2002]], this Part has effect in relation to the dismissal as if—

(a) the [local authority] had at all material times been the teacher's employer,

(b) the [local authority] had dismissed him, and

(c) the reason or principal reason for which they did so had been the reason or principal reason for which they required his dismissal.

(2) For the purposes of a complaint under section 111 as it has effect by virtue of subsection (1)—

(a) section 117(4)(a) applies as if for the words "not practicable to comply" there were substituted the words "not practicable for the [local authority] to permit compliance", and

(b) section 123(5) applies as if the references in it to the employer were to the [local authority].

[(3) In this section "local authority" has the meaning given by section 579(1) of the Education Act 1996.]

NOTES

Sub-s (1): words in first (outer) pair of square brackets substituted by the School Standards and Framework Act 1998, s 140(1), Sch 30, para 55; words in third (inner) pair of square brackets substituted by the Education Act 2002, s 215(1), Sch 21, para 30; words "local authority" (in each place) substituted by the Local Education Authorities and Children's Services Authorities (Integration of Functions) Order 2010, SI 2010/1158, art 5, Sch 2, Pt 2, para 41(1), (3)(a).

Sub-s (2): words in square brackets substituted by SI 2010/1158, art 5(1), Sch 2, Pt 2, para 41(1), (3)(a).

Sub-s (3): added by SI 2010/1158, art 5, Sch 2, Pt 2, para 41(1), (3)(b).

Modification and application of this section: see the notes following the Part heading *ante*.

[1.1052]

[134A Application to police

(1) For the purposes of section 100, and of the other provisions of this Part so far as relating to the right not to be unfairly dismissed in a case where the dismissal is unfair by virtue of section 100, the holding, otherwise than under a contract of employment, of the office of constable or an appointment as police cadet shall be treated as employment by the relevant officer under a contract of employment.

[(2) In this section "the relevant officer", in relation to—

(a) a person holding the office of constable, or

(b) a person holding an appointment as a police cadet,

means the person who under section 51A of the Health and Safety at Work etc Act 1974 is to be treated as his employer for the purposes of Part 1 of that Act.]

[(3) Subsection (1) does not apply to the holding of the office of constable by a member of a police force on secondment to the [National Crime Agency].]]

NOTES

Inserted by the Police (Health and Safety) Act 1997, s 4.

Sub-s (2): substituted by the Serious Organised Crime and Police Act 2005, s 158(1), (2)(b), (3), (5).

Sub-s (3): added by the Serious Organised Crime and Police Act 2005, s 59, Sch 4, paras 84, 87; words in square brackets substituted by the Crime and Courts Act 2013, s 15(3), Sch 8, Pt 2, paras 49, 51.

PART XI
REDUNDANCY PAYMENTS ETC

CHAPTER I RIGHT TO REDUNDANCY PAYMENT

[1.1053]

135 The right

(1) An employer shall pay a redundancy payment to any employee of his if the employee—

(a) is dismissed by the employer by reason of redundancy, or

(b) is eligible for a redundancy payment by reason of being laid off or kept on short-time.

(2) Subsection (1) has effect subject to the following provisions of this Part (including, in particular, sections 140 to 144, 149 to 152, 155 to 161 and 164).

CHAPTER II RIGHT ON DISMISSAL BY REASON OF REDUNDANCY

Dismissal by reason of redundancy

[1.1054]

136 Circumstances in which an employee is dismissed

(1) Subject to the provisions of this section and sections 137 and 138, for the purposes of this Part an employee is dismissed by his employer if (and only if)—

(a) the contract under which he is employed by the employer is terminated by the employer (whether with or without notice),

[(b) he is employed under a limited term contract and that contract terminates by virtue of the limiting event without being renewed under the same contract, or]

(c) the employee terminates the contract under which he is employed (with or without notice) in circumstances in which he is entitled to terminate it without notice by reason of the employer's conduct.

(2) Subsection (1)(c) does not apply if the employee terminates the contract without notice in circumstances in which he is entitled to do so by reason of a lock-out by the employer.

(3) An employee shall be taken to be dismissed by his employer for the purposes of this Part if—

(a) the employer gives notice to the employee to terminate his contract of employment, and

(b) at a time within the obligatory period of notice the employee gives notice in writing to the employer to terminate the contract of employment on a date earlier than the date on which the employer's notice is due to expire.

(4) In this Part the "obligatory period of notice", in relation to notice given by an employer to terminate an employee's contract of employment, means—

(a) the actual period of the notice in a case where the period beginning at the time when the notice is given and ending at the time when it expires is equal to the minimum period which (by virtue of any enactment or otherwise) is required to be given by the employer to terminate the contract of employment, and

(b) the period which—

(i) is equal to the minimum period referred to in paragraph (a), and
(ii) ends at the time when the notice expires,
in any other case.

(5) Where in accordance with any enactment or rule of law—
(a) an act on the part of an employer, or
(b) an event affecting an employer (including, in the case of an individual, his death),
operates to terminate a contract under which an employee is employed by him, the act or event shall be taken for the purposes of this Part to be a termination of the contract by the employer.

NOTES

Sub-s (1): para (b) substituted by the Fixed-term Employees (Prevention of Less Favourable Treatment) Regulations 2002, SI 2002/2034, reg 11, Sch 2, Pt 1, para 3(1), (13) (except in relation to Government training schemes, agency workers and apprentices; see regs 18–20 of the 2002 Regulations at **[2.571]** et seq).

137 *(Repealed by the Employment Relations Act 1999, ss 9, 44, Sch 4, Pt III, paras 1, 5, 25, Sch 9(2).)*

[1.1055]
138 No dismissal in cases of renewal of contract or re-engagement

(1) Where—
(a) an employee's contract of employment is renewed, or he is re-engaged under a new contract of employment in pursuance of an offer (whether in writing or not) made before the end of his employment under the previous contract, and
(b) the renewal or re-engagement takes effect either immediately on, or after an interval of not more than four weeks after, the end of that employment,
the employee shall not be regarded for the purposes of this Part as dismissed by his employer by reason of the ending of his employment under the previous contract.

(2) Subsection (1) does not apply if—
(a) the provisions of the contract as renewed, or of the new contract, as to—
(i) the capacity and place in which the employee is employed, and
(ii) the other terms and conditions of his employment,
differ (wholly or in part) from the corresponding provisions of the previous contract, and
(b) during the period specified in subsection (3)—
(i) the employee (for whatever reason) terminates the renewed or new contract, or gives notice to terminate it and it is in consequence terminated, or
(ii) the employer, for a reason connected with or arising out of any difference between the renewed or new contract and the previous contract, terminates the renewed or new contract, or gives notice to terminate it and it is in consequence terminated.

(3) The period referred to in subsection (2)(b) is the period—
(a) beginning at the end of the employee's employment under the previous contract, and
(b) ending with—
(i) the period of four weeks beginning with the date on which the employee starts work under the renewed or new contract, or
(ii) such longer period as may be agreed in accordance with subsection (6) for the purpose of retraining the employee for employment under that contract;
and is in this Part referred to as the "trial period".

(4) Where subsection (2) applies, for the purposes of this Part—
(a) the employee shall be regarded as dismissed on the date on which his employment under the previous contract (or, if there has been more than one trial period, the original contract) ended, and
(b) the reason for the dismissal shall be taken to be the reason for which the employee was then dismissed, or would have been dismissed had the offer (or original offer) of renewed or new employment not been made, or the reason which resulted in that offer being made.

(5) Subsection (2) does not apply if the employee's contract of employment is again renewed, or he is again re-engaged under a new contract of employment, in circumstances such that subsection (1) again applies.

(6) For the purposes of subsection (3)(b)(ii) a period of retraining is agreed in accordance with this subsection only if the agreement—
(a) is made between the employer and the employee or his representative before the employee starts work under the contract as renewed, or the new contract,
(b) is in writing,
(c) specifies the date on which the period of retraining ends, and
(d) specifies the terms and conditions of employment which will apply in the employee's case after the end of that period.

[1.1056]
139 Redundancy

(1) For the purposes of this Act an employee who is dismissed shall be taken to be dismissed by reason of redundancy if the dismissal is wholly or mainly attributable to—
(a) the fact that his employer has ceased or intends to cease—
(i) to carry on the business for the purposes of which the employee was employed by him, or
(ii) to carry on that business in the place where the employee was so employed, or
(b) the fact that the requirements of that business—
(i) for employees to carry out work of a particular kind, or

(ii) for employees to carry out work of a particular kind in the place where the employee was employed by the employer,

have ceased or diminished or are expected to cease or diminish.

(2) For the purposes of subsection (1) the business of the employer together with the business or businesses of his associated employers shall be treated as one (unless either of the conditions specified in paragraphs (a) and (b) of that subsection would be satisfied without so treating them).

(3) For the purposes of subsection (1) the activities carried on by a [local authority] with respect to the schools maintained by it, and the activities carried on by the [governing bodies] of those schools, shall be treated as one business (unless either of the conditions specified in paragraphs (a) and (b) of that subsection would be satisfied without so treating them).

(4) Where—

(a) the contract under which a person is employed is treated by section 136(5) as terminated by his employer by reason of an act or event, and

(b) the employee's contract is not renewed and he is not re-engaged under a new contract of employment,

he shall be taken for the purposes of this Act to be dismissed by reason of redundancy if the circumstances in which his contract is not renewed, and he is not re-engaged, are wholly or mainly attributable to either of the facts stated in paragraphs (a) and (b) of subsection (1).

(5) In its application to a case within subsection (4), paragraph (a)(i) of subsection (1) has effect as if the reference in that subsection to the employer included a reference to any person to whom, in consequence of the act or event, power to dispose of the business has passed.

(6) In subsection (1) "cease" and "diminish" mean cease and diminish either permanently or temporarily and for whatever reason.

[(7) In subsection (3) "local authority" has the meaning given by section 579(1) of the Education Act 1996.]

NOTES

Sub-s (3): words in first pair of square brackets substituted by the Local Education Authorities and Children's Services Authorities (Integration of Functions) Order 2010, SI 2010/1158, art 5, Sch 2, Pt 2, para 41(1), (4)(a); words in second pair of square brackets substituted by the Education Act 2002, s 215(1), Sch 21, para 31.

Sub-s (7): added by SI 2010/1158, art 5, Sch 2, Pt 2, para 41(1), (4)(b).

Exclusions

[1.1057]

140 Summary dismissal

(1) Subject to subsections (2) and (3), an employee is not entitled to a redundancy payment by reason of dismissal where his employer, being entitled to terminate his contract of employment without notice by reason of the employee's conduct, terminates it either—

(a) without notice,

(b) by giving shorter notice than that which, in the absence of conduct entitling the employer to terminate the contract without notice, the employer would be required to give to terminate the contract, or

(c) by giving notice which includes, or is accompanied by, a statement in writing that the employer would, by reason of the employee's conduct, be entitled to terminate the contract without notice.

(2) Where an employee who—

(a) has been given notice by his employer to terminate his contract of employment, or

(b) has given notice to his employer under section 148(1) indicating his intention to claim a redundancy payment in respect of lay-off or short-time,

takes part in a strike at any relevant time in circumstances which entitle the employer to treat the contract of employment as terminable without notice, subsection (1) does not apply if the employer terminates the contract by reason of his taking part in the strike.

(3) Where the contract of employment of an employee who—

(a) has been given notice by his employer to terminate his contract of employment, or

(b) has given notice to his employer under section 148(1) indicating his intention to claim a redundancy payment in respect of lay-off or short-time,

is terminated as mentioned in subsection (1) at any relevant time otherwise than by reason of his taking part in a strike, an [employment tribunal] may determine that the employer is liable to make an appropriate payment to the employee if on a reference to the tribunal it appears to the tribunal, in the circumstances of the case, to be just and equitable that the employee should receive it.

(4) In subsection (3) "appropriate payment" means—

(a) the whole of the redundancy payment to which the employee would have been entitled apart from subsection (1), or

(b) such part of that redundancy payment as the tribunal thinks fit.

(5) In this section "relevant time"—

(a) in the case of an employee who has been given notice by his employer to terminate his contract of employment, means any time within the obligatory period of notice, and

(b) in the case of an employee who has given notice to his employer under section 148(1), means any time after the service of the notice.

NOTES

Sub-s (3): words in square brackets substituted by the Employment Rights (Dispute Resolution) Act 1998, s 1(2)(a).

[1.1058]
141 Renewal of contract or re-engagement

(1) This section applies where an offer (whether in writing or not) is made to an employee before the end of his employment—

(a) to renew his contract of employment, or

(b) to re-engage him under a new contract of employment,

with renewal or re-engagement to take effect either immediately on, or after an interval of not more than four weeks after, the end of his employment.

(2) Where subsection (3) is satisfied, the employee is not entitled to a redundancy payment if he unreasonably refuses the offer.

(3) This subsection is satisfied where—

(a) the provisions of the contract as renewed, or of the new contract, as to—

(i) the capacity and place in which the employee would be employed, and

(ii) the other terms and conditions of his employment,

would not differ from the corresponding provisions of the previous contract, or

(b) those provisions of the contract as renewed, or of the new contract, would differ from the corresponding provisions of the previous contract but the offer constitutes an offer of suitable employment in relation to the employee.

(4) The employee is not entitled to a redundancy payment if—

(a) his contract of employment is renewed, or he is re-engaged under a new contract of employment, in pursuance of the offer,

(b) the provisions of the contract as renewed or new contract as to the capacity or place in which he is employed or the other terms and conditions of his employment differ (wholly or in part) from the corresponding provisions of the previous contract,

(c) the employment is suitable in relation to him, and

(d) during the trial period he unreasonably terminates the contract, or unreasonably gives notice to terminate it and it is in consequence terminated.

[1.1059]
142 Employee anticipating expiry of employer's notice

(1) Subject to subsection (3), an employee is not entitled to a redundancy payment where—

(a) he is taken to be dismissed by virtue of section 136(3) by reason of giving to his employer notice terminating his contract of employment on a date earlier than the date on which notice by the employer terminating the contract is due to expire,

(b) before the employee's notice is due to expire, the employer gives him a notice such as is specified in subsection (2), and

(c) the employee does not comply with the requirements of that notice.

(2) The employer's notice referred to in subsection (1)(b) is a notice in writing—

(a) requiring the employee to withdraw his notice terminating the contract of employment and to continue in employment until the date on which the employer's notice terminating the contract expires, and

(b) stating that, unless he does so, the employer will contest any liability to pay to him a redundancy payment in respect of the termination of his contract of employment.

(3) An [employment tribunal] may determine that the employer is liable to make an appropriate payment to the employee if on a reference to the tribunal it appears to the tribunal, having regard to—

(a) the reasons for which the employee seeks to leave the employment, and

(b) the reasons for which the employer requires him to continue in it,

to be just and equitable that the employee should receive the payment.

(4) In subsection (3) "appropriate payment" means—

(a) the whole of the redundancy payment to which the employee would have been entitled apart from subsection (1), or

(b) such part of that redundancy payment as the tribunal thinks fit.

NOTES

Sub-s (3): words in square brackets substituted by the Employment Rights (Dispute Resolution) Act 1998, s 1(2)(a).

[1.1060]
143 Strike during currency of employer's notice

(1) This section applies where—

(a) an employer has given notice to an employee to terminate his contract of employment ("notice of termination"),

(b) after the notice is given the employee begins to take part in a strike of employees of the employer, and

(c) the employer serves on the employee a notice of extension.

(2) A notice of extension is a notice in writing which—

(a) requests the employee to agree to extend the contract of employment beyond the time of expiry by a period comprising as many available days as the number of working days lost by striking ("the proposed period of extension"),

(b) indicates the reasons for which the employer makes that request, and

(c) states that the employer will contest any liability to pay the employee a redundancy payment in respect of the dismissal effected by the notice of termination unless either—

(i) the employee complies with the request, or

(ii) the employer is satisfied that, in consequence of sickness or injury or otherwise, the employee is unable to comply with it or that (even though he is able to comply with it) it is reasonable in the circumstances for him not to do so.

(3) Subject to subsections (4) and (5), if the employee does not comply with the request contained in the notice of extension, he is not entitled to a redundancy payment by reason of the dismissal effected by the notice of termination.

(4) Subsection (3) does not apply if the employer agrees to pay a redundancy payment to the employee in respect of the dismissal effected by the notice of termination even though he has not complied with the request contained in the notice of extension.

(5) An [employment tribunal] may determine that the employer is liable to make an appropriate payment to the employee if on a reference to the tribunal it appears to the tribunal that—

(a) the employee has not complied with the request contained in the notice of extension and the employer has not agreed to pay a redundancy payment in respect of the dismissal effected by the notice of termination, but

(b) either the employee was unable to comply with the request or it was reasonable in the circumstances for him not to comply with it.

(6) In subsection (5) "appropriate payment" means—

(a) the whole of the redundancy payment to which the employee would have been entitled apart from subsection (3), or

(b) such part of that redundancy payment as the tribunal thinks fit.

(7) If the employee—

(a) complies with the request contained in the notice of extension, or

(b) does not comply with it but attends at his proper or usual place of work and is ready and willing to work on one or more (but not all) of the available days within the proposed period of extension,

the notice of termination has effect, and shall be deemed at all material times to have had effect, as if the period specified in it had been appropriately extended; and sections 87 to 91 accordingly apply as if the period of notice required by section 86 were extended to a corresponding extent.

(8) In subsection (7) "appropriately extended" means—

(a) in a case within paragraph (a) of that subsection, extended beyond the time of expiry by an additional period equal to the proposed period of extension, and

(b) in a case within paragraph (b) of that subsection, extended beyond the time of expiry up to the end of the day (or last of the days) on which he attends at his proper or usual place of work and is ready and willing to work.

NOTES

Sub-s (5): words in square brackets substituted by the Employment Rights (Dispute Resolution) Act 1998, s 1(2)(a).

[1.1061]

144 Provisions supplementary to section 143

(1) For the purposes of section 143 an employee complies with the request contained in a notice of extension if, but only if, on each available day within the proposed period of extension, he—

(a) attends at his proper or usual place of work, and

(b) is ready and willing to work,

whether or not he has signified his agreement to the request in any other way.

(2) The reference in section 143(2) to the number of working days lost by striking is a reference to the number of working days in the period—

(a) beginning with the date of service of the notice of termination, and

(b) ending with the time of expiry,

which are days on which the employee in question takes part in a strike of employees of his employer.

(3) In section 143 and this section—

"available day", in relation to an employee, means a working day beginning at or after the time of expiry which is a day on which he is not taking part in a strike of employees of the employer,

"available day within the proposed period of extension" means an available day which begins before the end of the proposed period of extension,

"time of expiry", in relation to a notice of termination, means the time at which the notice would expire apart from section 143, and

"working day", in relation to an employee, means a day on which, in accordance with his contract of employment, he is normally required to work.

(4) Neither the service of a notice of extension nor any extension by virtue of section 143(7) of the period specified in a notice of termination affects—

(a) any right either of the employer or of the employee to terminate the contract of employment (whether before, at or after the time of expiry) by a further notice or without notice, or

(b) the operation of this Part in relation to any such termination of the contract of employment.

Supplementary

[1.1062]

145 The relevant date

(1) For the purposes of the provisions of this Act relating to redundancy payments "the relevant date" in relation to the dismissal of an employee has the meaning given by this section.

(2) Subject to the following provisions of this section, "the relevant date"—

(a) in relation to an employee whose contract of employment is terminated by notice, whether given by his employer or by the employee, means the date on which the notice expires,

(b) in relation to an employee whose contract of employment is terminated without notice, means the date on which the termination takes effect, and

[(c) in relation to an employee who is employed under a limited-term contract which terminates by virtue of the limiting event without being renewed under the same contract, means the date on which the termination takes effect].

(3) Where the employee is taken to be dismissed by virtue of section 136(3) the "relevant date" means the date on which the employee's notice to terminate his contract of employment expires.

(4) Where the employee is regarded by virtue of section 138(4) as having been dismissed on the date on which his employment under an earlier contract ended, "the relevant date" means—

(a) for the purposes of section 164(1), the date which is the relevant date as defined by subsection (2) in relation to the renewed or new contract or, where there has been more than one trial period, the last such contract, and

(b) for the purposes of any other provision, the date which is the relevant date as defined by subsection (2) in relation to the previous contract or, where there has been more than one such trial period, the original contract.

(5) Where—

(a) the contract of employment is terminated by the employer, and

(b) the notice required by section 86 to be given by an employer would, if duly given on the material date, expire on a date later than the relevant date (as defined by the previous provisions of this section),

for the purposes of sections 155, 162(1) and 227(3) the later date is the relevant date.

(6) In subsection (5)(b) "the material date" means—

(a) the date when notice of termination was given by the employer, or

(b) where no notice was given, the date when the contract of employment was terminated by the employer.

(7) . . .

NOTES

Sub-s (2): para (c) substituted by the Fixed-term Employees (Prevention of Less Favourable Treatment) Regulations 2002, SI 2002/2034, reg 11, Sch 2, Pt 1, para 3(1), (14) (except in relation to Government training schemes, agency workers and apprentices; see regs 18–20 of the 2002 Regulations at **[2.571]** et seq).

Sub-s (7): repealed by the Employment Relations Act 1999, ss 9, 44, Sch 4, Pt III, paras 1, 5, 26, Sch 9(2).

[1.1063]

146 Provisions supplementing sections 138 and 141

(1) In sections 138 and 141—

(a) references to re-engagement are to re-engagement by the employer or an associated employer, and

(b) references to an offer are to an offer made by the employer or an associated employer.

(2) For the purposes of the application of section 138(1) or 141(1) to a contract under which the employment ends on a Friday, Saturday or Sunday—

(a) the renewal or re-engagement shall be treated as taking effect immediately on the ending of the employment under the previous contract if it takes effect on or before the next Monday after that Friday, Saturday or Sunday, and

(b) the interval of four weeks to which those provisions refer shall be calculated as if the employment had ended on that next Monday.

(3) . . .

NOTES

Sub-s (3): repealed by the Employment Relations Act 1999, ss 9, 44, Sch 4, Pt III, paras 1, 5, 27, Sch 9(2).

Modification: this section, and ss 155 and 162, are modified in relation to any person to whom the Redundancy Payments (Continuity of Employment in Local Government, etc) (Modification) Order 1999, SI 1999/2277 applies for the purposes of determining that person's entitlement to a redundancy payment under the this Act and the amount of such payment; see arts 2, 3 of, and Sch 2, Pt I to, the 1999 Order at **[2.410]**, **[2.411]**, **[2.415]**.

CHAPTER III RIGHT BY REASON OF LAY-OFF OR SHORT-TIME

Lay-off and short-time

[1.1064]

147 Meaning of "lay-off" and "short-time"

(1) For the purposes of this Part an employee shall be taken to be laid off for a week if—

(a) he is employed under a contract on terms and conditions such that his remuneration under the contract depends on his being provided by the employer with work of the kind which he is employed to do, but

(b) he is not entitled to any remuneration under the contract in respect of the week because the employer does not provide such work for him.

(2) For the purposes of this Part an employee shall be taken to be kept on short-time for a week if by reason of a diminution in the work provided for the employee by his employer (being work of a kind which under his contract the employee is employed to do) the employee's remuneration for the week is less than half a week's pay.

[1.1065]
148 Eligibility by reason of lay-off or short-time

(1) Subject to the following provisions of this Part, for the purposes of this Part an employee is eligible for a redundancy payment by reason of being laid off or kept on short-time if—

(a) he gives notice in writing to his employer indicating (in whatever terms) his intention to claim a redundancy payment in respect of lay-off or short-time (referred to in this Part as "notice of intention to claim"), and

(b) before the service of the notice he has been laid off or kept on short-time in circumstances in which subsection (2) applies.

(2) This subsection applies if the employee has been laid off or kept on short-time—

(a) for four or more consecutive weeks of which the last before the service of the notice ended on, or not more than four weeks before, the date of service of the notice, or

(b) for a series of six or more weeks (of which not more than three were consecutive) within a period of thirteen weeks, where the last week of the series before the service of the notice ended on, or not more than four weeks before, the date of service of the notice.

Exclusions

[1.1066]
149 Counter-notices

Where an employee gives to his employer notice of intention to claim but—

(a) the employer gives to the employee, within seven days after the service of that notice, notice in writing (referred to in this Part as a "counter-notice") that he will contest any liability to pay to the employee a redundancy payment in pursuance of the employee's notice, and

(b) the employer does not withdraw the counter-notice by a subsequent notice in writing,

the employee is not entitled to a redundancy payment in pursuance of his notice of intention to claim except in accordance with a decision of an [employment tribunal].

NOTES

Words in square brackets substituted by the Employment Rights (Dispute Resolution) Act 1998, s 1(2)(a).

[1.1067]
150 Resignation

(1) An employee is not entitled to a redundancy payment by reason of being laid off or kept on short-time unless he terminates his contract of employment by giving such period of notice as is required for the purposes of this section before the end of the relevant period.

(2) The period of notice required for the purposes of this section—

(a) where the employee is required by his contract of employment to give more than one week's notice to terminate the contract, is the minimum period which he is required to give, and

(b) otherwise, is one week.

(3) In subsection (1) "the relevant period"—

(a) if the employer does not give a counter-notice within seven days after the service of the notice of intention to claim, is three weeks after the end of those seven days,

(b) if the employer gives a counter-notice within that period of seven days but withdraws it by a subsequent notice in writing, is three weeks after the service of the notice of withdrawal, and

(c) if—

(i) the employer gives a counter-notice within that period of seven days, and does not so withdraw it, and

(ii) a question as to the right of the employee to a redundancy payment in pursuance of the notice of intention to claim is referred to an [employment tribunal],

is three weeks after the tribunal has notified to the employee its decision on that reference.

(4) For the purposes of subsection (3)(c) no account shall be taken of—

(a) any appeal against the decision of the tribunal, or

(b) any proceedings or decision in consequence of any such appeal.

NOTES

Sub-s (3): words in square brackets substituted by the Employment Rights (Dispute Resolution) Act 1998, s 1(2)(a).

[1.1068]
151 Dismissal

(1) An employee is not entitled to a redundancy payment by reason of being laid off or kept on short-time if he is dismissed by his employer.

(2) Subsection (1) does not prejudice any right of the employee to a redundancy payment in respect of the dismissal.

[1.1069]
152 Likelihood of full employment

(1) An employee is not entitled to a redundancy payment in pursuance of a notice of intention to claim if—

(a) on the date of service of the notice it was reasonably to be expected that the employee (if he continued to be employed by the same employer) would, not later than four weeks after that date, enter on a period of employment of not less than thirteen weeks during which he would not be laid off or kept on short-time for any week, and

(b) the employer gives a counter-notice to the employee within seven days after the service of the notice of intention to claim.

(2) Subsection (1) does not apply where the employee—

(a) continues or has continued, during the next four weeks after the date of service of the notice of intention to claim, to be employed by the same employer, and

(b) is or has been laid off or kept on short-time for each of those weeks.

Supplementary

[1.1070]

153 The relevant date

For the purposes of the provisions of this Act relating to redundancy payments "the relevant date" in relation to a notice of intention to claim or a right to a redundancy payment in pursuance of such a notice—

(a) in a case falling within paragraph (a) of subsection (2) of section 148, means the date on which of the last of the four or more consecutive weeks before the service of the notice came to an end, and

(b) in a case falling within paragraph (b) of that subsection, means the date on which the last of the series of six or more weeks before the service of the notice came to an end.

[1.1071]

154 Provisions supplementing sections 148 and 152

For the purposes of sections 148(2) and 152(2)—

(a) it is immaterial whether a series of weeks consists wholly of weeks for which the employee is laid off or wholly of weeks for which he is kept on short-time or partly of the one and partly of the other, and

(b) no account shall be taken of any week for which an employee is laid off or kept on short-time where the lay-off or short-time is wholly or mainly attributable to a strike or a lock-out (whether or not in the trade or industry in which the employee is employed and whether in Great Britain or elsewhere).

CHAPTER IV GENERAL EXCLUSIONS FROM RIGHT

[1.1072]

155 Qualifying period of employment

An employee does not have any right to a redundancy payment unless he has been continuously employed for a period of not less than two years ending with the relevant date.

NOTES

Modified as noted to s 146 at **[1.1063]**.

156 *(Repealed by the Employment Equality (Age) Regulations 2006, SI 2006/1031, reg 49(1), Sch 8, Pt 1, paras 21, 30, 33.)*

[1.1073]

157 Exemption orders

(1) Where an order under this section is in force in respect of an agreement covered by this section, an employee who, immediately before the relevant date, is an employee to whom the agreement applies does not have any right to a redundancy payment.

(2) An agreement is covered by this section if it is an agreement between—

(a) one or more employers or organisations of employers, and

(b) one or more trade unions representing employees,

under which employees to whom the agreement applies have a right in certain circumstances to payments on the termination of their contracts of employment.

(3) Where, on the application of all the parties to an agreement covered by this section, the Secretary of State is satisfied, having regard to the provisions of the agreement, that the employees to whom the agreement applies should not have any right to a redundancy payment, he may make an order under this section in respect of the agreement.

(4) The Secretary of State shall not make an order under this section in respect of an agreement unless the agreement indicates (in whatever terms) the willingness of the parties to it to submit to an [employment tribunal] any question arising under the agreement as to—

(a) the right of an employee to a payment on the termination of his employment, or

(b) the amount of such a payment.

(5) An order revoking an earlier order under this section may be made in pursuance of an application by all or any of the parties to the agreement in question or in the absence of such an application.

(6) . . .

NOTES

Sub-s (4): words in square brackets substituted by the Employment Rights (Dispute Resolution) Act 1998, s 1(2)(a).

Sub-s (6): repealed by the Employment Relations Act 1999, ss 9, 44, Sch 4, Pt III, paras 1, 5, 29, Sch 9(2).

Orders: as of 15 May 2019, no Orders had been made under this section but, by virtue of s 241 of, and Sch 2, Pt I, paras 1–4 to, this Act, the Redundancy Payments (Exemption) (No 1) Order 1969, SI 1969/207, the Redundancy Payments (Exemption) (No 1) Order 1970, SI 1970/354, and the Redundancy Payments (Exemption) Order 1980, SI 1980/1052, have effect as if made under this section.

158 *(Repealed by the Employment Equality (Age) Regulations 2006, SI 2006/1031, reg 49(1), Sch 8, Pt 1, paras 21, 31, 33.)*

[1.1074]
159 Public offices etc
A person does not have any right to a redundancy payment in respect of any employment which—
(a) is employment in a public office within the meaning of section 39 of the Superannuation Act 1965, or
(b) is for the purposes of pensions and other superannuation benefits treated (whether by virtue of that Act or otherwise) as service in the civil service of the State.

[1.1075]
160 Overseas government employment
(1) A person does not have any right to a redundancy payment in respect of employment in any capacity under the Government of an overseas territory.
(2) The reference in subsection (1) to the Government of an overseas territory includes a reference to—
(a) a Government constituted for two or more overseas territories, and
(b) any authority established for the purpose of providing or administering services which are common to, or relate to matters of common interest to, two or more overseas territories.
(3) In this section references to an overseas territory are to any territory or country outside the United Kingdom.

[1.1076]
161 Domestic servants
(1) A person does not have any right to a redundancy payment in respect of employment as a domestic servant in a private household where the employer is the parent (or step-parent), grandparent, child (or step-child), grandchild or brother or sister (or half-brother or half-sister) of the employee.
(2) Subject to that, the provisions of this Part apply to an employee who is employed as a domestic servant in a private household as if—
(a) the household were a business, and
(b) the maintenance of the household were the carrying on of that business by the employer.

NOTES
Step-parent; step-child: references to a step-parent or step-child include relationships arising through civil partnership; see the Civil Partnership Act 2004, ss 246, 247, Sch 21, para 42.

CHAPTER V OTHER PROVISIONS ABOUT REDUNDANCY PAYMENTS

[1.1077]
162 Amount of a redundancy payment
(1) The amount of a redundancy payment shall be calculated by—
(a) determining the period, ending with the relevant date, during which the employee has been continuously employed,
(b) reckoning backwards from the end of that period the number of years of employment falling within that period, and
(c) allowing the appropriate amount for each of those years of employment.
(2) In subsection (1)(c) "the appropriate amount" means—
(a) one and a half weeks' pay for a year of employment in which the employee was not below the age of forty-one,
(b) one week's pay for a year of employment (not within paragraph (a)) in which he was not below the age of twenty-two, and
(c) half a week's pay for each year of employment not within paragraph (a) or (b).
(3) Where twenty years of employment have been reckoned under subsection (1), no account shall be taken under that subsection of any year of employment earlier than those twenty years.
(4), (5) . . .
(6) [Subsections (1) to (3)] apply for the purposes of any provision of this Part by virtue of which an [employment tribunal] may determine that an employer is liable to pay to an employee—
(a) the whole of the redundancy payment to which the employee would have had a right apart from some other provision, or
(b) such part of the redundancy payment to which the employee would have had a right apart from some other provision as the tribunal thinks fit,
as if any reference to the amount of a redundancy payment were to the amount of the redundancy payment to which the employee would have been entitled apart from that other provision.
(7), (8) . . .

NOTES
Sub-ss (4), (5), (8): repealed by the Employment Equality (Age) Regulations 2006, SI 2006/1031, reg 49(1), Sch 8, Pt 1, paras 21, 32(1), (2), 33.
Sub-s (6): words in first pair of square brackets substituted by SI 2006/1031, reg 49(1), Sch 8, Pt 1, paras 21, 32(1), (3); words in second pair of square brackets substituted by the Employment Rights (Dispute Resolution) Act 1998, s 1(2)(a).
Sub-s (7): repealed by the Employment Relations Act 1999, ss 9, 44, Sch 4, Pt III, paras 1, 5, 30, Sch 9(2).
Modified as noted to s 146 at **[1.1063]**.

[1.1078]

163 References to [employment tribunals]

(1) Any question arising under this Part as to—

(a) the right of an employee to a redundancy payment, or

(b) the amount of a redundancy payment,

shall be referred to and determined by an [employment tribunal].

(2) For the purposes of any such reference, an employee who has been dismissed by his employer shall, unless the contrary is proved, be presumed to have been so dismissed by reason of redundancy.

(3) Any question whether an employee will become entitled to a redundancy payment if he is not dismissed by his employer and he terminates his contract of employment as mentioned in section 150(1) shall for the purposes of this Part be taken to be a question as to the right of the employee to a redundancy payment.

(4) Where an order under section 157 is in force in respect of an agreement, this section has effect in relation to any question arising under the agreement as to the right of an employee to a payment on the termination of his employment, or as to the amount of such a payment, as if the payment were a redundancy payment and the question arose under this Part.

[(5) Where a tribunal determines under subsection (1) that an employee has a right to a redundancy payment it may order the employer to pay to the worker such amount as the tribunal considers appropriate in all the circumstances to compensate the worker for any financial loss sustained by him which is attributable to the non-payment of the redundancy payment.]

NOTES

Section heading, sub-s (1): words in square brackets substituted by the Employment Rights (Dispute Resolution) Act 1998, s 1(2)(a), (b).

Sub-s (5): added by the Employment Act 2008, s 7(2).

Conciliation: employment tribunal proceedings under this section are "relevant proceedings" for the purposes of the conciliation provisions contained in the Employment Tribunals Act 1996, ss 18–18C; see s 18(1)(b) of the 1996 Act at **[1.757]**.

Tribunal jurisdiction: the Employment Act 2002, s 38 applies to proceedings before the employment tribunal relating to a claim under this section; see s 38(1) of, and Sch 5 to, the 2002 Act at **[1.1279]**, **[1.1287]**. See also the Trade Union and Labour Relations (Consolidation) Act 1992, s 207A at **[1.524]** (as inserted by the Employment Act 2008). That section provides that in proceedings before an employment tribunal relating to a claim by an employee under any of the jurisdictions listed in Sch A2 to the 1992 Act at **[1.704]** (which includes this section) the tribunal may adjust any award given if the employer or the employee has unreasonably failed to comply with a relevant Code of Practice as defined by s 207A(4). See also the revised Acas Code of Practice 1 – Disciplinary and Grievance Procedures (2015) at **[4.1]**, and the Acas Code of Practice 4 – Settlement Agreements (2013) at **[4.54]**.

[1.1079]

164 Claims for redundancy payment

(1) An employee does not have any right to a redundancy payment unless, before the end of the period of six months beginning with the relevant date—

(a) the payment has been agreed and paid,

(b) the employee has made a claim for the payment by notice in writing given to the employer,

(c) a question as to the employee's right to, or the amount of, the payment has been referred to an [employment tribunal], or

(d) a complaint relating to his dismissal has been presented by the employee under section 111.

(2) An employee is not deprived of his right to a redundancy payment by subsection (1) if, during the period of six months immediately following the period mentioned in that subsection, the employee—

(a) makes a claim for the payment by notice in writing given to the employer,

(b) refers to an [employment tribunal] a question as to his right to, or the amount of, the payment, or

(c) presents a complaint relating to his dismissal under section 111,

and it appears to the tribunal to be just and equitable that the employee should receive a redundancy payment.

(3) In determining under subsection (2) whether it is just and equitable that an employee should receive a redundancy payment an [employment tribunal] shall have regard to—

(a) the reason shown by the employee for his failure to take any such step as is referred to in subsection (2) within the period mentioned in subsection (1), and

(b) all the other relevant circumstances.

[(4) Subsections (1)(c) and (2) are subject to section 207A (extension because of mediation in certain European cross-border disputes).]

[(5) Section 207B (extension of time limits to facilitate conciliation before institution of proceedings) applies for the purposes of subsections (1)(c) and (2).]

NOTES

Sub-ss (1)–(3): words in square brackets substituted by the Employment Rights (Dispute Resolution) Act 1998, s 1(2)(a).

Sub-s (4): added by the Cross-Border Mediation (EU Directive) Regulations 2011, SI 2011/1133, regs 30, 47 and repealed by the Cross-Border Mediation (EU Directive) (EU Exit) Regulations 2019, SI 2019/469, reg 4, Sch 1, Pt 1, para 12(1), (24), as from exit day (as defined in the European Union (Withdrawal) Act 2018, s 20).

Sub-s (5): added by the Enterprise and Regulatory Reform Act 2013, s 8, Sch 2, paras 15, 34.

[1.1080]

165 Written particulars of redundancy payment

(1) On making any redundancy payment, otherwise than in pursuance of a decision of a tribunal which specifies the amount of the payment to be made, the employer shall give to the employee a written statement indicating how the amount of the payment has been calculated.

(2) An employer who without reasonable excuse fails to comply with subsection (1) is guilty of an offence and liable on summary conviction to a fine not exceeding level 1 on the standard scale.

(3) If an employer fails to comply with the requirements of subsection (1), the employee may by notice in writing to the employer require him to give to the employee a written statement complying with those requirements within such period (not being less than one week beginning with the day on which the notice is given) as may be specified in the notice.

(4) An employer who without reasonable excuse fails to comply with a notice under subsection (3) is guilty of an offence and liable on summary conviction to a fine not exceeding level 3 on the standard scale.

CHAPTER VI PAYMENTS BY SECRETARY OF STATE

[1.1081]

166 Applications for payments

(1) Where an employee claims that his employer is liable to pay to him an employer's payment and either—

(a) that the employee has taken all reasonable steps, other than legal proceedings, to recover the payment from the employer and the employer has refused or failed to pay it, or has paid part of it and has refused or failed to pay the balance, or

(b) that the employer is insolvent and the whole or part of the payment remains unpaid,

the employee may apply to the Secretary of State for a payment under this section.

(2) In this Part "employer's payment", in relation to an employee, means—

(a) a redundancy payment which his employer is liable to pay to him under this Part, . . .

[(aa) a payment which his employer is liable to make to him under an agreement to refrain from instituting or continuing proceedings for a contravention or alleged contravention of section 135 which has effect by virtue of section 203(2)(e) or (f), or]

(b) a payment which his employer is, under an agreement in respect of which an order is in force under section 157, liable to make to him on the termination of his contract of employment.

(3) In relation to any case where (in accordance with any provision of this Part) an [employment tribunal] determines that an employer is liable to pay part (but not the whole) of a redundancy payment the reference in subsection (2)(a) to a redundancy payment is to the part of the redundancy payment.

(4) In subsection (1)(a) "legal proceedings"—

(a) does not include any proceedings before an [employment tribunal], but

(b) includes any proceedings to enforce a decision or award of an [employment tribunal].

(5) An employer is insolvent for the purposes of subsection (1)(b)—

(a) where the employer is an individual, if (but only if) subsection *(6) [or (8A)]* is satisfied, . . .

(b) where the employer is a company, if (but only if) subsection *(7) [or (8A)]* is satisfied[, . . .

(c) where the employer is a limited liability partnership, if (but only if) subsection *(8) [or (8A)]* is satisfied][; and

(d) where the employer is not any of the above, if (but only if) subsection *(8A)* is satisfied.]

(6) This subsection is satisfied in the case of an employer who is an individual—

(a) in England and Wales if—

(i) he has been [made] bankrupt or has made a composition or arrangement with his creditors, or

(ii) he has died and his estate falls to be administered in accordance with an order under section 421 of the Insolvency Act 1986, and

(b) in Scotland if—

(i) sequestration of his estate has been awarded or he has executed a trust deed for his creditors or has entered into a composition contract, or

(ii) he has died and a judicial factor appointed under section 11A of the Judicial Factors (Scotland) Act 1889 is required by that section to divide his insolvent estate among his creditors.

(7) This subsection is satisfied in the case of an employer which is a company—

(a) if a winding up order . . . has been made, or a resolution for voluntary winding up has been passed, with respect to the company,

[(aa) if the company is in administration for the purposes of the Insolvency Act 1986,]

(b) if a receiver or (in England and Wales only) a manager of the company's undertaking has been duly appointed, or (in England and Wales only) possession has been taken, by or on behalf of the holders of any debentures secured by a floating charge, of any property of the company comprised in or subject to the charge, or

(c) if a voluntary arrangement proposed in the case of the company for the purposes of Part I of the Insolvency Act 1986 has been approved under that Part of that Act.

[(8) This subsection is satisfied in the case of an employer which is a limited liability partnership—

(a) if a winding-up order, an administration order or a determination for a voluntary winding-up has been made with respect to the limited liability partnership,

(b) if a receiver or (in England and Wales only) a manager of the undertaking of the limited liability partnership has been duly appointed, or (in England and Wales only) possession has been taken, by or on behalf of the holders of any debentures secured by a floating charge, of any property of the limited liability partnership comprised in or subject to the charge, or

(c) if a voluntary arrangement proposed in the case of the limited liability partnership for the purpose of Part I of the Insolvency Act 1986 has been approved under that Part of that Act.]

[(8ZA) This subsection is satisfied in the case of an employer if—

(a) the employer is a legal person,

(b) a request has been made for the first opening of collective proceedings—

(i) based on the insolvency of the employer, as provided for under the law of any part of the United Kingdom, and

(ii) involving the partial or total divestment of the employer's assets and the appointment of a liquidator or a person performing a similar task, and

(c) any of the following has decided to open the proceedings—

(i) a court,

(ii) a meeting of creditors, or

(iii) the creditors by a decision procedure.]

[(8A) This subsection is satisfied in the case of an employer if—

(a) a request has been made for the first opening of collective proceedings—

(i) based on the insolvency of the employer, as provided for under the laws, regulations and administrative provisions of a member State, and

(ii) involving the partial or total divestment of the employer's assets and the appointment of a liquidator or a person performing a similar task, and

(b) the competent authority has—

(i) decided to open the proceedings, or

(ii) established that the employer's undertaking or business has been definitively closed down and the available assets of the employer are insufficient to warrant the opening of the proceedings.

(8B) For the purposes of *subsection (8A)*—

(a) "liquidator or person performing a similar task" includes the official receiver or an administrator, trustee in bankruptcy, judicial factor, supervisor of a voluntary arrangement, or person performing a similar task,

(b) "competent authority" includes—

(i) a court,

(ii) a meeting of creditors,

(iii) a creditors' committee,

(iv) the creditors by a decision procedure, and

(v) an authority of a member State empowered to open insolvency proceedings, to confirm the opening of such proceedings or to take decisions in the course of such proceedings.

(8C) An employee may apply under this section only if he or she worked or habitually worked in Great Britain in that employment to which the application relates.]

[(9) In this section—

(a) references to a company are to be read as including references to a charitable incorporated organisation, and

(b) any reference to the Insolvency Act 1986 in relation to a company is to be read as including a reference to that Act as it applies to charitable incorporated organisations.]

NOTES

Sub-s (2): word omitted from para (a) repealed, and para (aa) inserted, by the Employment Rights (Dispute Resolution) Act 1998, ss 11(2), 15, Sch 2.

Sub-ss (3), (4): words in square brackets substituted by the Employment Rights (Dispute Resolution) Act 1998, s 1(2)(a).

Sub-s (5): the words "or (8A)" (in each place they occur) were inserted, the word omitted from para (b) was repealed, and para (d) (and the preceding word) was inserted, by the Employment Rights Act 1996 and Pension Schemes Act 1993 (Amendment) Regulations 2017, SI 2017/1205, reg 2(1), (2)(a), as from 26 December 2017. Word omitted from para (a) repealed, and para (c) and word immediately preceding it added, by the Limited Liability Partnerships Regulations 2001, SI 2001/1090, reg 9, Sch 5, para 18(1), (2). For the words in italics in paras (a), (b), (c), (d) there are substituted the words "(6), (8ZA) or (8A)", "(7), (8ZA) or (8A)", "(8), (8ZA) or (8A)", and "(8ZA) or (8A)" respectively, by the Insolvency (Amendment) (EU Exit) Regulations 2019, SI 2019/146, reg 2, Schedule, Pt 11, para 253(1), (2)(a), as from exit day (as defined in the European Union (Withdrawal) Act 2018, s 20) and subject to savings in regs 4, 5 thereof.

Sub-s (6): word in square brackets substituted by the Enterprise and Regulatory Reform Act 2013 (Consequential Amendments) (Bankruptcy) and the Small Business, Enterprise and Employment Act 2015 (Consequential Amendments) Regulations 2016, SI 2016/481, reg 2(1), Sch 1, Pt 2, para 18, as from 6 April 2016.

Sub-s (7): words omitted from para (a) repealed, and para (aa) inserted, by the Enterprise Act 2002, ss 248(3), 278(2), Sch 17, para 49(1), (2), Sch 26, subject to savings in relation to special administration regimes (within the meaning of s 249 of the 2002 Act).

Sub-s (8): added by SI 2001/1090, reg 9, Sch 5, para 18(1), (3).

Sub-s (8ZA): inserted by SI 2019/146, reg 2, Schedule, Pt 11, para 253(1), (2)(b), as from exit day (as defined in the European Union (Withdrawal) Act 2018, s 20) and subject to savings in regs 4, 5 thereof.

Sub-ss (8A)–(8C): inserted by SI 2017/1205, reg 2(1), (2)(b), as from 26 December 2017; for the words in italics in sub-s (8B) there are substituted the words "this section", by SI 2019/146, reg 2, Schedule, Pt 11, para 253(1), (2)(c), as from exit day (as defined in the European Union (Withdrawal) Act 2018, s 20) and subject to savings in regs 4, 5 thereof.

Sub-s (9): added by the Charitable Incorporated Organisations (Consequential Amendments) Order 2012, SI 2012/3014, art 3.

[1.1082]
167 Making of payments
(1) Where, on an application under section 166 by an employee in relation to an employer's payment, the Secretary of State is satisfied that the requirements specified in subsection (2) are met, he shall pay to the employee out of the National Insurance Fund a sum calculated in accordance with section 168 but reduced by so much (if any) of the employer's payment as has already been paid.
(2) The requirements referred to in subsection (1) are—
(a) that the employee is entitled to the employer's payment, and
(b) that one of the conditions specified in paragraphs (a) and (b) of subsection (1) of section 166 is fulfilled,
and, in a case where the employer's payment is a payment such as is mentioned in subsection (2)(b) of that section, that the employee's right to the payment arises by virtue of a period of continuous employment (computed in accordance with the provisions of the agreement in question) which is not less than two years.
(3) Where under this section the Secretary of State pays a sum to an employee in respect of an employer's payment—
(a) all rights and remedies of the employee with respect to the employer's payment, or (if the Secretary of State has paid only part of it) all the rights and remedies of the employee with respect to that part of the employer's payment, are transferred to and vest in the Secretary of State, and
(b) any decision of an [employment tribunal] requiring the employer's payment to be paid to the employee has effect as if it required that payment, or that part of it which the Secretary of State has paid, to be paid to the Secretary of State.
(4) Any money recovered by the Secretary of State by virtue of subsection (3) shall be paid into the National Insurance Fund.

NOTES
Sub-s (3): words in square brackets substituted by the Employment Rights (Dispute Resolution) Act 1998, s 1(2)(a).

[1.1083]
168 Amount of payments
(1) The sum payable to an employee by the Secretary of State under section 167—
(a) where the employer's payment to which the employee's application under section 166 relates is a redundancy payment or a part of a redundancy payment, is a sum equal to the amount of the redundancy payment or part, . . .
[(aa) where the employer's payment to which the employee's application under section 166 relates is a payment which his employer is liable to make to him under an agreement having effect by virtue of section 203(2)(e) or (f), is a sum equal to the amount of the employer's payment or of any redundancy payment which the employer would have been liable to pay to the employee but for the agreement, whichever is less, and]
(b) where the employer's payment to which the employee's application under section 166 relates is a payment which the employer is liable to make under an agreement in respect of which an order is in force under section 157, is a sum equal to the amount of the employer's payment or of the relevant redundancy payment, whichever is less.
(2) The reference in subsection (1)(b) to the amount of the relevant redundancy payment is to the amount of the redundancy payment which the employer would have been liable to pay to the employee on the assumptions specified in subsection (3).
(3) The assumptions referred to in subsection (2) are that—
(a) the order in force in respect of the agreement had not been made,
(b) the circumstances in which the employer's payment is payable had been such that the employer was liable to pay a redundancy payment to the employee in those circumstances,
(c) the relevant date, in relation to any such redundancy payment, had been the date on which the termination of the employee's contract of employment is treated as having taken effect for the purposes of the agreement, and
(d) in so far as the provisions of the agreement relating to the circumstances in which the continuity of an employee's period of employment is to be treated as broken, and the weeks which are to count in computing a period of employment, are inconsistent with the provisions of Chapter I of Part XIV, the provisions of the agreement were substituted for those provisions.

NOTES
Sub-s (1): word omitted from para (a) repealed, and para (aa) inserted, by the Employment Rights (Dispute Resolution) Act 1998, ss 11(3), 15, Sch 2.

[1.1084]
169 Information relating to applications for payments
(1) Where an employee makes an application to the Secretary of State under section 166, the Secretary of State may, by notice in writing given to the employer, require the employer—
(a) to provide the Secretary of State with such information, and
(b) to produce for examination on behalf of the Secretary of State documents in his custody or under his control of such description,
as the Secretary of State may reasonably require for the purpose of determining whether the application is well-founded.

(2) Where a person on whom a notice is served under subsection (1) fails without reasonable excuse to comply with a requirement imposed by the notice, he is guilty of an offence and liable on summary conviction to a fine not exceeding level 3 on the standard scale.

(3) A person is guilty of an offence if—

(a) in providing any information required by a notice under subsection (1), he makes a statement which he knows to be false in a material particular or recklessly makes a statement which is false in a material particular, or

(b) he produces for examination in accordance with a notice under subsection (1) a document which to his knowledge has been wilfully falsified.

(4) A person guilty of an offence under subsection (3) is liable—

(a) on summary conviction, to a fine not exceeding the statutory maximum or to imprisonment for a term not exceeding three months, or to both, or

(b) on conviction on indictment, to a fine or to imprisonment for a term not exceeding two years, or to both.

[1.1085]

170 References to [employment tribunals]

(1) Where on an application made to the Secretary of State for a payment under section 166 it is claimed that an employer is liable to pay an employer's payment, there shall be referred to an [employment tribunal]—

(a) any question as to the liability of the employer to pay the employer's payment, and

(b) any question as to the amount of the sum payable in accordance with section 168.

(2) For the purposes of any reference under this section an employee who has been dismissed by his employer shall, unless the contrary is proved, be presumed to have been so dismissed by reason of redundancy.

NOTES

Section heading, sub-s (1): words in square brackets substituted by the Employment Rights (Dispute Resolution) Act 1998, s 1(2)(a), (b).

CHAPTER VII SUPPLEMENTARY

Application of Part to particular cases

[1.1086]

171 Employment not under contract of employment

(1) The Secretary of State may by regulations provide that, subject to such exceptions and modifications as may be prescribed by the regulations, this Part and the provisions of this Act supplementary to this part have effect in relation to any employment of a description to which this section applies as may be so prescribed as if—

(a) it were employment under a contract of employment,

(b) any person engaged in employment of that description were an employee, and

(c) such person as may be determined by or under the regulations were his employer.

(2) This section applies to employment of any description which—

(a) is employment in the case of which secondary Class 1 contributions are payable under Part I of the Social Security Contributions and Benefits Act 1992 in respect of persons engaged in it, but

(b) is not employment under a contract of service or of apprenticeship or employment of any description falling within subsection (3).

(3) The following descriptions of employment fall within this subsection—

(a) any employment such as is mentioned in section 159 (whether as originally enacted or as modified by an order under section 209(1)),

(b) any employment remunerated out of the revenue of the Duchy of Lancaster or the Duchy of Cornwall,

(c) any employment remunerated out of [the Sovereign Grant], and

(d) any employment remunerated out of Her Majesty's Privy Purse.

NOTES

Sub-s (3): words in square brackets in para (c) substituted by the Sovereign Grant Act 2011, s 14, Sch 1, para 31.

Regulations: as of 15 May 2019, no Regulations had been made under this section but, by virtue of s 241 of, and Sch 2, Pt I, paras 1–4 to, this Act, the Redundancy Payments Office Holders Regulations 1965, SI 1965/2007 have effect as if made under this section.

[1.1087]

172 Termination of employment by statute

(1) The Secretary of State may by regulations provide that, subject to such exceptions and modifications as may be prescribed by the regulations, this Part has effect in relation to any person who by virtue of any statutory provisions—

(a) is transferred to, and becomes a member of, a body specified in those provisions, but

(b) at a time so specified ceases to be a member of that body unless before that time certain conditions so specified have been fulfilled,

as if the cessation of his membership of that body by virtue of those provisions were dismissal by his employer by reason of redundancy.

(2) The power conferred by subsection (1) is exercisable whether or not membership of the body in question constitutes employment within the meaning of section 230(5); and, where that membership does not constitute such employment, that power may be exercised in addition to any power exercisable under section 171.

NOTES

Regulations: as of 15 May 2019, no Regulations had been made under this section but, by virtue of s 241 of, and Sch 2, Pt I, paras 1–4 to, this Act, the Redundancy Payments Termination of Employment Regulations 1965, SI 1965/2022 (concerning chief constables and chief or assistant chief fire officers), have effect as if made under this section.

[1.1088]

173 Employees paid by person other than employer

(1) For the purposes of the operation of the provisions of this Part (and Chapter I of Part XIV) in relation to any employee whose remuneration is, by virtue of any statutory provision, payable to him by a person other than his employer, each of the references to the employer specified in subsection (2) shall be construed as a reference to the person by whom the remuneration is payable.

(2) The references referred to in subsection (1) are the first reference in section 135(1), the third reference in section 140(3), the first reference in section 142(3) and the first reference in section 143(2)(c) and the references in sections 142(2)(b), 143(4) and (5), 149(a) and (b), 150(3), 152(1)(b), 158(4), 162(6), 164 to 169, 170(1) and 214(5).

Death of employer or employee

[1.1089]

174 Death of employer: dismissal

(1) Where the contract of employment of an employee is taken for the purposes of this Part to be terminated by his employer by reason of the employer's death, this Part has effect in accordance with the following provisions of this section.

(2) Section 138 applies as if—

(a) in subsection (1)(a), for the words "in pursuance" onwards there were substituted "by a personal representative of the deceased employer",

(b) in subsection (1)(b), for the words "either immediately" onwards there were substituted "not later than eight weeks after the death of the deceased employer", and

(c) in subsections (2)(b) and (6)(a), for the word "employer" there were substituted "personal representative of the deceased employer".

(3) Section 141(1) applies as if—

(a) for the words "before the end of his employment" there were substituted "by a personal representative of the deceased employer", and

(b) for the words "either immediately" onwards there were substituted "not later than eight weeks after the death of the deceased employer."

(4) For the purposes of section 141—

(a) provisions of the contract as renewed, or of the new contract, do not differ from the corresponding provisions of the contract in force immediately before the death of the deceased employer by reason only that the personal representative would be substituted for the deceased employer as the employer, and

(b) no account shall be taken of that substitution in determining whether refusal of the offer was unreasonable or whether the employee acted reasonably in terminating or giving notice to terminate the new or renewed employment.

(5) Section 146 has effect as if—

(a) subsection (1) were omitted, and

(b) in subsection (2), paragraph (a) were omitted and, in paragraph (b), for the word "four" there were substituted "eight".

(6) For the purposes of the application of this Part (in accordance with section 161(2)) in relation to an employee who was employed as a domestic servant in a private household, references in this section and sections 175 and 218(4) and (5) to a personal representative include a person to whom the management of the household has passed, otherwise than in pursuance of a sale or other disposition for valuable consideration, in consequence of the death of the employer.

[1.1090]

175 Death of employer: lay-off and short-time

(1) Where an employee is laid off or kept on short-time and his employer dies, this Part has effect in accordance with the following provisions of this section.

(2) Where the employee—

(a) has been laid off or kept on short-time for one or more weeks before the death of the employer,

(b) has not given the deceased employer notice of intention to claim before the employer's death,

(c) after the employer's death has his contract of employment renewed, or is re-engaged under a new contract, by a personal representative of the deceased employer, and

(d) after renewal or re-engagement is laid off or kept on short-time for one or more weeks by the personal representative,

the week in which the employer died and the first week of the employee's employment by the personal representative shall be treated for the purposes of Chapter III as consecutive weeks (and references to four weeks or thirteen weeks shall be construed accordingly).

(3) The following provisions of this section apply where—

(a) the employee has given the deceased employer notice of intention to claim before the employer's death,
(b) the employer's death occurred before the end of the period of four weeks after the service of the notice, and
(c) the employee has not terminated his contract of employment by notice expiring before the employer's death.

(4) If the contract of employment is not renewed, and the employee is not re-engaged under a new contract, by a personal representative of the deceased employer before the end of the period of four weeks after the service of the notice of intention to claim—
(a) sections 149 and 152 do not apply, but
(b) (subject to that) Chapter III applies as if the employer had not died and the employee had terminated the contract of employment by a week's notice, or by the minimum notice which he is required to give to terminate the contract (if longer than a week), expiring at the end of that period.

(5) If—
(a) the contract of employment is renewed, or the employee is re-engaged under a new contract, by a personal representative of the deceased employer before the end of the period of four weeks after the service of the notice of intention to claim, and
(b) the employee was laid off or kept on short-time by the deceased employer for one or more of those weeks and is laid off or kept on short-time by the personal representative for the week, or for the next two or more weeks, following the renewal or re-engagement,

subsection (6) has effect.

(6) Where this subsection has effect Chapter III applies as if—
(a) all the weeks mentioned in subsection (5) were consecutive weeks during which the employee was employed (but laid off or kept on short-time) by the same employer, and
(b) the periods specified by section 150(3)(a) and (b) as the relevant period were extended by any week or weeks any part of which was after the death of the employer and before the date on which the renewal or re-engagement took effect.

[1.1091]
176 Death of employee

(1) Where an employee whose employer has given him notice to terminate his contract of employment dies before the notice expires, this part applies as if the contract had been duly terminated by the employer by notice expiring on the date of the employee's death.

(2) Where—
(a) an employee's contract of employment has been terminated by the employer,
(b) (by virtue of subsection (5) of section 145) a date later than the relevant date as defined by the previous provisions of that section is the relevant date for the purposes of certain provisions of this Act, and
(c) the employee dies before that date,

that subsection applies as if the notice to which it refers would have expired on the employee's death.

(3) Where—
(a) an employer has given notice to an employee to terminate his contract of employment and has offered to renew his contract of employment or to re-engage him under a new contract, and
(b) the employee dies without having accepted or refused the offer and without the offer having been withdrawn,

section 141(2) applies as if for the words "he unreasonably refuses" there were substituted "it would have been unreasonable on his part to refuse".

(4) Where an employee's contract of employment has been renewed or he has been re-engaged under a new contract—
(a) if he dies during the trial period without having terminated, or given notice to terminate, the contract, section 141(4) applies as if for paragraph (d) there were substituted—

"(d) it would have been unreasonable for the employee during the trial period to terminate or give notice to terminate the contract.", and

(b) if during that trial period he gives notice to terminate the contract but dies before the notice expires, sections 138(2) and 141(4) apply as if the notice had expired (and the contract had been terminated by its expiry) on the date of the employee's death.

(5) Where in the circumstances specified in paragraphs (a) and (b) of subsection (3) of section 136 the employee dies before the notice given by him under paragraph (b) of that subsection expires—
(a) if he dies before his employer has given him a notice such as is specified in subsection (2) of section 142, subsections (3) and (4) of that section apply as if the employer had given him such a notice and he had not complied with it, and
(b) if he dies after his employer has given him such a notice, that section applies as if the employee had not died but did not comply with the notice.

(6) Where an employee has given notice of intention to claim—
(a) if he dies before he has given notice to terminate his contract of employment and before the relevant period (as defined in subsection (3) of section 150) has expired, that section does not apply, and
(b) if he dies within the period of seven days after the service of the notice of intention to claim, and before the employer has given a counter-notice, Chapter III applies as if the employer had given a counter-notice within that period of seven days.

(7) Where a claim for a redundancy payment is made by a personal representative of a deceased employee—

(a) if the employee died before the end of the period of six months beginning with the relevant date, subsection (1) of section 164, and

(b) if the employee died after the end of the period of six months beginning with the relevant date but before the end of the following period of six months, subsection (2) of that section,

applies as if for the words "six months" there were substituted "one year".

Equivalent payments

[1.1092]

177 References to [employment tribunals]

(1) Where the terms and conditions (whether or not they constitute a contract of employment) on which a person is employed in employment of any description mentioned in section 171(3) include provision—

(a) for the making of a payment to which this section applies, and

(b) for referring to an [employment tribunal] any question as to the right of any person to such a payment in respect of that employment or as to the amount of such a payment,

the question shall be referred to and determined by an [employment tribunal].

(2) This section applies to any payment by way of compensation for loss of employment of any description mentioned in section 171(3) which is payable in accordance with arrangements falling within subsection (3).

(3) The arrangements which fall within this subsection are arrangements made with the approval of the Treasury (or, in the case of persons whose service is for the purposes of pensions and other superannuation benefits treated as service in the civil service of the State, of the Minister for the Civil Service) for securing that a payment will be made—

(a) in circumstances which in the opinion of the Treasury (or Minister) correspond (subject to the appropriate modifications) to those in which a right to a redundancy payment would have accrued if the provisions of this Part (apart from section 159 and this section) applied, and

(b) on a scale which in the opinion of the Treasury (or Minister), taking into account any sums payable in accordance with—

(i) a scheme made under section 1 of the Superannuation Act 1972, or

(ii) the Superannuation Act 1965 as it continues to have effect by virtue of section 23(1) of the Superannuation Act 1972,

to or in respect of the person losing the employment in question, corresponds (subject to the appropriate modifications) to that on which a redundancy payment would have been payable if those provisions applied.

NOTES

Section heading, sub-s (1): words in square brackets substituted by the Employment Rights (Dispute Resolution) Act 1998, s 1(2)(a), (b).

Conciliation: employment tribunal proceedings under this section are "relevant proceedings" for the purposes of the conciliation provisions contained in the Employment Tribunals Act 1996, ss 18–18C; see s 18(1)(b) of the 1996 Act at **[1.757]**.

Other supplementary provisions

[1.1093]

178 Old statutory compensation schemes

(1) The Secretary of State may make provision by regulations for securing that where—

(a) (apart from this section) a person is entitled to compensation under a statutory provision to which this section applies, and

(b) the circumstances are such that he is also entitled to a redundancy payment,

the amount of the redundancy payment shall be set off against the compensation to which he would be entitled apart from this section; and any statutory provision to which any such regulations apply shall have effect subject to the regulations.

(2) This section applies to any statutory provision—

(a) which was in force immediately before 6th December 1965, and

(b) under which the holders of such situations, places or employments as are specified in that provision are, or may become, entitled to compensation for loss of employment, or for loss or diminution of emoluments or of pension rights, in consequence of the operation of any other statutory provision referred to in that provision.

NOTES

Regulations: as of 15 May 2019, no Regulations had been made under this section but, by virtue of s 241 of, and Sch 2, Pt I, paras 1–4 to, this Act, the Redundancy Payments Statutory Compensation Regulations 1965, SI 1965/1988, have effect as if made under this section.

[1.1094]

179 Notices

(1) Any notice which under this Part is required or authorised to be given by an employer to an employee may be given by being delivered to the employee, or left for him at his usual or last-known place of residence, or sent by post addressed to him at that place.

(2) Any notice which under this Part is required or authorised to be given by an employee to an employer may be given either by the employee himself or by a person authorised by him to act on his behalf, and (whether given by or on behalf of the employee)—

(a) may be given by being delivered to the employer, or sent by post addressed to him at the pl[ace] where the employee is or was employed by him, or

(b) if arrangements have been made by the employer, may be given by being delivered to a perso[n] designated by the employer in pursuance of the arrangements, left for such a person at a place so designated or sent by post to such a person at an address so designated.

(3) In this section any reference to the delivery of a notice includes, in relation to a notice which is not required by this Part to be in writing, a reference to the oral communication of the notice.

(4) Any notice which, in accordance with any provision of this section, is left for a person at a place referred to in that provision shall, unless the contrary is proved, be presumed to have been received by him on the day on which it was left there.

(5) Nothing in subsection (1) or (2) affects the capacity of an employer to act by a servant or agent for the purposes of any provision of this Part (including either of those subsections).

(6) In relation to an employee to whom section 173 applies, this section has effect as if—

(a) any reference in subsection (1) or (2) to a notice required or authorised to be given by or to an employer included a reference to a notice which, by virtue of that section, is required or authorised to be given by or to the person by whom the remuneration is payable,

(b) in relation to a notice required or authorised to be given to that person, any reference to the employer in paragraph (a) or (b) of subsection (2) were a reference to that person, and

(c) the reference to an employer in subsection (5) included a reference to that person.

[1.1095]
180 Offences

(1) Where an offence under this Part committed by a body corporate is proved—

(a) to have been committed with the consent or connivance of, or

(b) to be attributable to any neglect on the part of,

any director, manager, secretary or other similar officer of the body corporate, or any person who was purporting to act in any such capacity, he (as well as the body corporate) is guilty of the offence and liable to be proceeded against and punished accordingly.

(2) In this section "director", in relation to a body corporate established by or under any enactment for the purpose of carrying on under national ownership any industry or part of an industry or undertaking, being a body corporate whose affairs are managed by its members, means a member of that body corporate.

[1.1096]
181 Interpretation

(1) In this Part—

"counter-notice" shall be construed in accordance with section 149(a),

"dismissal" and "dismissed" shall be construed in accordance with sections 136 to 138,

"employer's payment" has the meaning given by section 166,

"notice of intention to claim" shall be construed in accordance with section 148(1),

"obligatory period of notice" has the meaning given by section 136(4), and

"trial period" shall be construed in accordance with section 138(3).

(2) In this Part—

(a) references to an employee being laid off or being eligible for a redundancy payment by reason of being laid off, and

(b) references to an employee being kept on short-time or being eligible for a redundancy payment by reason of being kept on short-time,

shall be construed in accordance with sections 147 and 148.

PART XII
INSOLVENCY OF EMPLOYERS

NOTES

Bank insolvency or administration: in so far as any provision of this Act applies to liquidation or administration, it applies with specified modifications in the case of a bank insolvency or administration; see the Banking Act 2009 (Parts 2 and 3 Consequential Amendments) Order 2009, SI 2009/317.

[1.1097]
182 Employee's rights on insolvency of employer

If, on an application made to him in writing by an employee, the Secretary of State is satisfied that—

(a) the employee's employer has become insolvent,

(b) the employee's employment has been terminated, and

(c) on the appropriate date the employee was entitled to be paid the whole or part of any debt to which this Part applies,

the Secretary of State shall, subject to section 186, pay the employee out of the National Insurance Fund the amount to which, in the opinion of the Secretary of State, the employee is entitled in respect of the debt.

[1.1098]
183 Insolvency

(1) An employer has become insolvent for the purposes of this Part—

(a) where the employer is an individual, if (but only if) subsection *(2) [or (4A)]* is satisfied, . . .

(b) where the employer is a company, if (but only if) subsection *(3) [or (4A)]* is satisfied[, . . .

(c) where the employer is a limited liability partnership, if (but only if) subsection *(4) [or (4A)]* is satisfied][; and

(d) where the employer is not any of the above, if (but only if) subsection *(4A)* is satisfied.]

(2) This subsection is satisfied in the case of an employer who is an individual—

(a) in England and Wales if—

[(ai) a moratorium period under a debt relief order applies in relation to him,]

(i) he has been [made] bankrupt or has made a composition or arrangement with his creditors, or

(ii) he has died and his estate falls to be administered in accordance with an order under section 421 of the Insolvency Act 1986, and

(b) in Scotland if—

(i) sequestration of his estate has been awarded or he has executed a trust deed for his creditors or has entered into a composition contract, or

(ii) he has died and a judicial factor appointed under section 11A of the Judicial Factors (Scotland) Act 1889 is required by that section to divide his insolvent estate among his creditors.

(3) This subsection is satisfied in the case of an employer which is a company—

(a) if a winding up order . . . has been made, or a resolution for voluntary winding up has been passed, with respect to the company,

[(aa) if the company is in administration for the purposes of the Insolvency Act 1986,]

(b) if a receiver or (in England and Wales only) a manager of the company's undertaking has been duly appointed, or (in England and Wales only) possession has been taken, by or on behalf of the holders of any debentures secured by a floating charge, of any property of the company comprised in or subject to the charge, or

(c) if a voluntary arrangement proposed in the case of the company for the purposes of Part I of the Insolvency Act 1986 has been approved under that Part of that Act.

[(4) This subsection is satisfied in the case of an employer which is a limited liability partnership—

(a) if a winding-up order, an administration order or a determination for a voluntary winding-up has been made with respect to the limited liability partnership,

(b) if a receiver or (in England and Wales only) a manager of the undertaking of the limited liability partnership has been duly appointed, or (in England and Wales only) possession has been taken, by or on behalf of the holders of any debentures secured by a floating charge, of any property of the limited liability partnership comprised in or subject to the charge, or

(c) if a voluntary arrangement proposed in the case of the limited liability partnership for the purposes of Part I of the Insolvency Act 1986 has been approved under that Part of that Act.]

[(4ZA) This subsection is satisfied in the case of an employer if—

(a) the employer is a legal person,

(b) a request has been made for the first opening of collective proceedings—

(i) based on the insolvency of the employer, as provided for under the law of any part of the United Kingdom, and

(ii) involving the partial or total divestment of the employer's assets and the appointment of a liquidator or a person performing a similar task, and

(c) any of the following has decided to open the proceedings—

(i) a court,

(ii) a meeting of creditors, or

(iii) the creditors by a decision procedure.]

[(4A) This subsection is satisfied in the case of an employer if—

(a) a request has been made for the first opening of collective proceedings—

(i) based on the insolvency of the employer, as provided for under the laws, regulations and administrative provisions of a member State, and

(ii) involving the partial or total divestment of the employer's assets and the appointment of a liquidator or a person performing a similar task, and

(b) the competent authority has—

(i) decided to open the proceedings, or

(ii) established that the employer's undertaking or business has been definitively closed down and the available assets of the employer are insufficient to warrant the opening of the proceedings.

(4B) For the purposes of *subsection (4A)*—

(a) "liquidator or person performing a similar task" includes the official receiver or an administrator, trustee in bankruptcy, judicial factor, supervisor of a voluntary arrangement, or person performing a similar task,

(b) "competent authority" includes—

(i) a court,

(ii) a meeting of creditors,

(iii) a creditors' committee,

(iv) the creditors by a decision procedure, and

(v) an authority of a member State empowered to open insolvency proceedings, to confirm the opening of such proceedings or to take decisions in the course of such proceedings.

(4C) An employee may apply under section 182 (employee's rights on insolvency of employer) only if he or she worked or habitually worked in England, Wales or Scotland in that employment to which the application relates.]

[(5) In this section—

(a) references to a company are to be read as including references to a charitable incorporated organisation, and
(b) any reference to the Insolvency Act 1986 in relation to a company is to be read as including a reference to that Act as it applies to charitable incorporated organisations.]

NOTES

Sub-s (1): the words "or (4A)" (in each place they occur) were inserted, the word omitted from para (b) was repealed, and para (d) (and the preceding word) was inserted, by the Employment Rights Act 1996 and Pension Schemes Act 1993 (Amendment) Regulations 2017, SI 2017/1205, reg 2(1), (3)(a), as from 26 December 2017. Word omitted from para (a) repealed, and para (c) and word immediately preceding it added, by the Limited Liability Partnership Regulations, SI 2001/1090, reg 9, Sch 5, para 19(1), (2). For the words in italics in paras (a), (b), (c), (d) there are substituted the words "(2), (4ZA) or (4A)", "(3), (4ZA) or (4A)", "(4), (4ZA) or (4A)", "(4ZA) or (4A)" respectively, by the Insolvency (Amendment) (EU Exit) Regulations 2019, SI 2019/146, reg 2, Schedule, Pt 11, para 253(1), (3)(a), as from exit day (as defined in the European Union (Withdrawal) Act 2018, s 20) and subject to savings in regs 4, 5 thereof.

Sub-s (2): sub-para (a)(ai) inserted by the Tribunals, Courts and Enforcement Act 2007, s 108(3), Sch 20, Pt 2, para 17; word in square brackets in sub-para (a)(i) substituted by the Enterprise and Regulatory Reform Act 2013 (Consequential Amendments) (Bankruptcy) and the Small Business, Enterprise and Employment Act 2015 (Consequential Amendments) Regulations 2016, SI 2016/481, reg 2(1), Sch 1, Pt 2, para 18, as from 6 April 2016.

Sub-s (3): words omitted from para (a) repealed, and para (aa) inserted, by the Enterprise Act 2002, ss 248(3), 278(2), Sch 17, para 49(1), (3), Sch 26, subject to savings in relation to special administration regimes (within the meaning of s 249 of the 2002 Act).

Sub-s (4): added by SI 2001/1090, reg 9, Sch 5, para 19(1), (3).

Sub-s (4ZA): inserted by SI 2019/146, reg 2, Schedule, Pt 11, para 253(1), (3)(b), as from exit day (as defined in the European Union (Withdrawal) Act 2018, s 20) and subject to savings in regs 4, 5 thereof.

Sub-ss (4A)–(4C): inserted by SI 2017/1205, reg 2(1), (3)(b), as from 26 December 2017; for the words in italics in sub-s (4B) there are substituted the words "this section", by SI 2019/146, reg 2, Schedule, Pt 11, para 253(1), (3)(c), as from exit day (as defined in the European Union (Withdrawal) Act 2018, s 20) and subject to savings in regs 4, 5 thereof.

Sub-s (5): added by the Charitable Incorporated Organisations (Consequential Amendments) Order 2012, SI 2012/3014, art 4.

[1.1099]

184 Debts to which Part applies

(1) This Part applies to the following debts—
(a) any arrears of pay in respect of one or more (but not more than eight) weeks,
(b) any amount which the employer is liable to pay the employee for the period of notice required by section 86(1) or (2) or for any failure of the employer to give the period of notice required by section 86(1),
(c) any holiday pay—
(i) in respect of a period or periods of holiday not exceeding six weeks in all, and
(ii) to which the employee became entitled during the twelve months ending with the appropriate date,
(d) any basic award of compensation for unfair dismissal [or so much of an award under a designated dismissal procedures agreement as does not exceed any basic award of compensation for unfair dismissal to which the employee would be entitled but for the agreement], and
(e) any reasonable sum by way of reimbursement of the whole or part of any fee or premium paid by an apprentice or articled clerk.

(2) For the purposes of subsection (1)(a) the following amounts shall be treated as arrears of pay—
(a) a guarantee payment,
(b) any payment for time off under Part VI of this Act or section 169 of the Trade Union and Labour Relations (Consolidation) Act 1992 (payment for time off for carrying out trade union duties etc),
(c) remuneration on suspension on medical grounds under section 64 of this Act and remuneration on suspension on maternity grounds under section 68 of this Act, and
(d) remuneration under a protective award under section 189 of the Trade Union and Labour Relations (Consolidation) Act 1992.

(3) In subsection (1)(c) "holiday pay", in relation to an employee, means—
(a) pay in respect of a holiday actually taken by the employee, or
(b) any accrued holiday pay which, under the employee's contract of employment, would in the ordinary course have become payable to him in respect of the period of a holiday if his employment with the employer had continued until he became entitled to a holiday.

(4) A sum shall be taken to be reasonable for the purposes of subsection (1)(e) in a case where a trustee in bankruptcy, or (in Scotland) a [trustee or interim trustee in the sequestration of an estate under the Bankruptcy (Scotland) Act 2016], or liquidator has been or is required to be appointed—
(a) as respects England and Wales, if it is admitted to be reasonable by the trustee in bankruptcy or liquidator under section 348 of the Insolvency Act 1986 (effect of bankruptcy on apprenticeships etc), whether as originally enacted or as applied to the winding up of a company by rules under section 411 of that Act, and
(b) as respects Scotland, if it is accepted by the [trustee] or interim trustee or liquidator for the purposes of the sequestration or winding up.

NOTES

Sub-s (1): words in square brackets in para (d) inserted by the Employment Rights (Dispute Resolution) Act 1998, s 12(4).

Sub-s (4): words in square brackets substituted by the Bankruptcy (Scotland) Act 2016 (Consequential Provisions and Modifications) Order 2016, SI 2016/1034, art 7(1), Sch 1, Pt 1, para 16(1), (2)(a), as from 30 November 2016.

[1.1100]

185 The appropriate date

In this Part "the appropriate date"—

(a) in relation to arrears of pay (not being remuneration under a protective award made under section 189 of the Trade Union and Labour Relations (Consolidation) Act 1992) and to holiday pay, means the date on which the employer became insolvent,

(b) in relation to a basic award of compensation for unfair dismissal and to remuneration under a protective award so made, means whichever is the latest of—

(i) the date on which the employer became insolvent,

(ii) the date of the termination of the employee's employment, and

(iii) the date on which the award was made, and

(c) in relation to any other debt to which this Part applies, means whichever is the later of—

(i) the date on which the employer became insolvent, and

(ii) the date of the termination of the employee's employment.

[1.1101]

186 Limit on amount payable under section 182

(1) The total amount payable to an employee in respect of any debt to which this Part applies, where the amount of the debt is referable to a period of time, shall not exceed—

(a) [£525] in respect of any one week, or

(b) in respect of a shorter period, an amount bearing the same proportion to [£525] as that shorter period bears to a week.

(2) . . .

NOTES

Sub-s (1): sums in square brackets substituted by the Employment Rights (Increase of Limits) Order 2019, SI 2019/324, art 3, Schedule, as from 6 April 2019, in relation to any case where the appropriate date (as defined in the order) falls on or after that date (see SI 2019/324, art 4 at **[2.2117]**). Previous sums were as follows: £508 as from 6 April 2018 (see SI 2018/194); £489 as from 6 April 2017 (see SI 2017/175); £479 as from 6 April 2016 (see SI 2016/288); £475 as from 6 April 2015 (see SI 2015/226); £464 as from 6 April 2014 (see SI 2014/382); £450 as from 1 February 2013 (see SI 2012/3007); £430 as from 1 February 2012 (see SI 2011/3006); £400 as from 1 February 2011 (see SI 2010/2926); and £380 as from 1 October 2009 (see SI 2009/1903), in each case where the appropriate date fell after the commencement date. This sum may be varied by the Secretary of State (see the Employment Relations Act 1999, s 34(1)(a), (3)(a) at **[1.1258]**).

Sub-s (2): repealed by the Employment Relations Act 1999, ss 36(1)(a), 44, Sch 9(10).

[1.1102]

187 Role of relevant officer

(1) Where a relevant officer has been, or is required to be, appointed in connection with an employer's insolvency, the Secretary of State shall not make a payment under section 182 in respect of a debt until he has received a statement from the relevant officer of the amount of that debt which appears to have been owed to the employee on the appropriate date and to remain unpaid.

(2) If the Secretary of State is satisfied that he does not require a statement under subsection (1) in order to determine the amount of a debt which was owed to the employee on the appropriate date and remains unpaid, he may make a payment under section 182 in respect of the debt without having received such a statement.

(3) A relevant officer shall, on request by the Secretary of State, provide him with a statement for the purposes of subsection (1) as soon as is reasonably practicable.

(4) The following are relevant officers for the purposes of this section—

(a) a trustee in bankruptcy or a [trustee] or interim trustee (within the meaning of the Bankruptcy (Scotland) Act [2016]),

(b) a liquidator,

(c) an administrator,

(d) a receiver or manager,

(e) a trustee under a composition or arrangement between the employer and his creditors, and

(f) a trustee under a trust deed for his creditors executed by the employer.

(5) In subsection (4)(e) "trustee" includes the supervisor of a voluntary arrangement proposed for the purposes of, and approved under, Part I or VIII of the Insolvency Act 1986.

NOTES

Sub-s (4): word and year "2016" in square brackets in para (a) substituted by the Bankruptcy (Scotland) Act 2016 (Consequential Provisions and Modifications) Order 2016, SI 2016/1034, art 7(1), Sch 1, Pt 1, para 16(1), (3), as from 30 November 2016.

[1.1103]

188 Complaints to [employment tribunals]

(1) A person who has applied for a payment under section 182 may present a complaint to an [employment tribunal]—

(a) that the Secretary of State has failed to make any such payment, or

(b) that any such payment made by him is less than the amount which should have been paid.

(2) An [employment tribunal] shall not consider a complaint under subsection (1) unless it is presented—

(a) before the end of the period of three months beginning with the date on which the decision of the Secretary of State on the application was communicated to the applicant, or

(b) within such further period as the tribunal considers reasonable in a case where it is not reasonably practicable for the complaint to be presented before the end of that period of three months.

(3) Where an [employment tribunal] finds that the Secretary of State ought to make a payment under section 182, the tribunal shall—

(a) make a declaration to that effect, and

(b) declare the amount of any such payment which it finds the Secretary of State ought to make.

NOTES

Words in square brackets substituted by the Employment Rights (Dispute Resolution) Act 1998, s 1(2)(a), (b).

[1.1104]

189 Transfer to Secretary of State of rights and remedies

(1) Where, in pursuance of section 182, the Secretary of State makes a payment to an employee in respect of a debt to which this Part applies—

(a) on the making of the payment any rights and remedies of the employee in respect of the debt (or, if the Secretary of State has paid only part of it, in respect of that part) become rights and remedies of the Secretary of State, and

(b) any decision of an [employment tribunal] requiring an employer to pay that debt to the employee has the effect that the debt (or the part of it which the Secretary of State has paid) is to be paid to the Secretary of State.

(2) Where a debt (or any part of a debt) in respect of which the Secretary of State has made a payment in pursuance of section 182 constitutes—

(a) a preferential debt within the meaning of the Insolvency Act 1986 for the purposes of any provision of that Act (including any such provision as applied by any order made under that Act) or any provision of [the Companies Act 2006], or

(b) a preferred debt within the meaning of the Bankruptcy (Scotland) Act [2016] for the purposes of any provision of that Act (including any such provision as applied by section 11A of the Judicial Factors (Scotland) Act 1889),

the rights which become rights of the Secretary of State in accordance with subsection (1) include any right arising under any such provision by reason of the status of the debt (or that part of it) as a preferential or preferred debt.

(3) In computing for the purposes of any provision mentioned in subsection (2)(a) or (b) the aggregate amount payable in priority to other creditors of the employer in respect of—

(a) any claim of the Secretary of State to be paid in priority to other creditors of the employer by virtue of subsection (2), and

(b) any claim by the employee to be so paid made in his own right,

any claim of the Secretary of State to be so paid by virtue of subsection (2) shall be treated as if it were a claim of the employee.

(4) . . .

(5) Any sum recovered by the Secretary of State in exercising any right, or pursuing any remedy, which is his by virtue of this section shall be paid into the National Insurance Fund.

NOTES

Sub-s (1): words in square brackets substituted by the Employment Rights (Dispute Resolution) Act 1998, s 1(2)(a).

Sub-s (2): words in square brackets in para (a) substituted by the Companies Act 2006 (Consequential Amendments etc) Order 2008, SI 2008/948, arts 3(1)(b), 6, Sch 1, Pt 2, para 201; year "2016" in square brackets in para (b) substituted by the Bankruptcy (Scotland) Act 2016 (Consequential Provisions and Modifications) Order 2016, SI 2016/1034, art 7(1), Sch 1, Pt 1, para 16(1), (4), as from 30 November 2016.

Sub-s (4): repealed by the Enterprise Act 2002, ss 248(3), 278(2), Sch 17, para 49(1), (4), Sch 26, subject to savings in relation to special administration regimes (within the meaning of s 249 of the 2002 Act).

[1.1105]

190 Power to obtain information

(1) Where an application is made to the Secretary of State under section 182 in respect of a debt owed by an employer, the Secretary of State may require—

(a) the employer to provide him with such information as he may reasonably require for the purpose of determining whether the application is well-founded, and

(b) any person having the custody or control of any relevant records or other documents to produce for examination on behalf of the Secretary of State any such document in that person's custody or under his control which is of such a description as the Secretary of State may require.

(2) Any such requirement—

(a) shall be made by notice in writing given to the person on whom the requirement is imposed, and

(b) may be varied or revoked by a subsequent notice so given.

(3) If a person refuses or wilfully neglects to furnish any information or produce any document which he has been required to furnish or produce by a notice under this section he is guilty of an offence and liable on summary conviction to a fine not exceeding level 3 on the standard scale.

(4) If a person, in purporting to comply with a requirement of a notice under this section, knowingly or recklessly makes any false statement he is guilty of an offence and liable on summary conviction to a fine not exceeding level 5 on the standard scale.

(5) Where an offence under this section committed by a body corporate is proved—

(a) to have been committed with the consent or connivance of, or

(b) to be attributable to any neglect on the part of,

any director, manager, secretary or other similar officer of the body corporate, or any person who was purporting to act in any such capacity, he (as well as the body corporate) is guilty of the offence and liable to be proceeded against and punished accordingly.

(6) Where the affairs of a body corporate are managed by its members, subsection (5) applies in relation to the acts and defaults of a member in connection with his functions of management as if he were a director of the body corporate.

PART XIII MISCELLANEOUS

CHAPTER I PARTICULAR TYPES OF EMPLOYMENT

Crown employment etc

[1.1106]

191 Crown employment

(1) Subject to sections 192 and 193, the provisions of this Act to which this section applies have effect in relation to Crown employment and persons in Crown employment as they have effect in relation to other employment and other employees or workers.

(2) This section applies to—

(a) Parts I to III,

[(aa) Part IVA,]

(b) Part V, apart from section 45,

[(c) Parts 6 to 8A,]

(d) in Part IX, sections 92 and 93,

(e) Part X, apart from section 101, and

(f) this Part and Parts XIV and XV.

(3) In this Act "Crown employment" means employment under or for the purposes of a government department or any officer or body exercising on behalf of the Crown functions conferred by a statutory provision.

(4) For the purposes of the application of provisions of this Act in relation to Crown employment in accordance with subsection (1)—

(a) references to an employee or a worker shall be construed as references to a person in Crown employment,

(b) references to a contract of employment, or a worker's contract, shall be construed as references to the terms of employment of a person in Crown employment,

(c) references to dismissal, or to the termination of a worker's contract, shall be construed as references to the termination of Crown employment,

(d) references to redundancy shall be construed as references to the existence of such circumstances as are treated, in accordance with any arrangements falling within section 177(3) for the time being in force, as equivalent to redundancy in relation to Crown employment, . . .

[(da) the reference in section 98B(2)(a) to the employer's undertaking shall be construed as a reference to the national interest, and]

(e) [any other reference] to an undertaking shall be construed—

(i) in relation to a Minister of the Crown, as references to his functions or (as the context may require) to the department of which he is in charge, and

(ii) in relation to a government department, officer or body, as references to the functions of the department, officer or body or (as the context may require) to the department, officer or body.

(5) Where the terms of employment of a person in Crown employment restrict his right to take part in—

(a) certain political activities, or

(b) activities which may conflict with his official functions,

nothing in section 50 requires him to be allowed time off work for public duties connected with any such activities.

(6) Sections 159 and 160 are without prejudice to any exemption or immunity of the Crown.

NOTES

Sub-s (2): para (aa) inserted by the Public Interest Disclosure Act 1998, ss 10, 18(2); para (c) substituted by the Employment Act 2002, s 53, Sch 7, paras 24, 41.

Sub-s (4): word omitted from para (d) repealed, para (da) inserted, and words in square brackets in para (e) substituted, by the Employment Relations Act 2004, s 57, Sch 1, para 34, Sch 2.

[1.1107]

192 Armed forces

(1) Section 191—

(a) applies to service as a member of the naval, military or air forces of the Crown but subject to the following provisions of this section, and

(b) applies to employment by an association established for the purposes of Part XI of the Reserve Forces Act 1996.

(2) The provisions of this Act which have effect by virtue of section 191 in relation to service as a member of the naval, military or air forces of the Crown are—

(a) Part I,

[(aa) in Part V, [sections [43M,] 45A, 47C and 47D] and sections 48 and 49 so far as relating to [those sections],

[(ab) section 47C,]

(b) in Part VI, sections [55 to 57B],

(c) Parts VII and VIII,

(d) in Part IX, sections 92 and 93,

(e) Part X, apart from sections [98B(2) and (3),] 100 to 103[, 104C][, 108(5)] and 134, and

(f) this Part and Parts XIV and XV.

(3) Her Majesty may by Order in Council—

(a) amend subsection (2) by making additions to, or omissions from, the provisions for the time being specified in that subsection, and

(b) make any provision for the time being so specified apply to service as a member of the naval, military or air forces of the Crown subject to such exceptions and modifications as may be specified in the Order in Council,

but no provision contained in Part II may be added to the provisions for the time being specified in subsection (2).

(4) Modifications made by an Order in Council under subsection (3) may include provision precluding the making of a complaint or reference to any [employment tribunal] unless[—

(a) the person aggrieved has made [a service complaint]; and

(b) the Defence Council have made a determination with respect to the [service complaint]].

[(5) Where modifications made by an Order in Council under subsection (3) include provision such as is mentioned in subsection (4), the Order in Council shall also include provision—

(a) enabling a complaint or reference to be made to an [employment tribunal] in such circumstances as may be specified in the Order, notwithstanding that provision such as is mentioned in subsection (4) would otherwise preclude the making of the complaint or reference; and

(b) where a complaint or reference is made to an [employment tribunal] by virtue of provision such as is mentioned in paragraph (a), enabling [the service complaint procedures] to continue after the complaint or reference is made.]

[(6A) In subsections (4) and (5)—

"service complaint" means a complaint under section 334 of the Armed Forces Act 2006;

"the service complaint procedures" means the procedures prescribed by regulations under that section.]

(7) No provision shall be made by virtue of subsection (4) which has the effect of substituting a period longer than six months for any period specified as the normal period for a complaint or reference.

(8) In subsection (7) "the normal period for a complaint or reference", in relation to any matter within the jurisdiction of an [employment tribunal], means the period specified in the relevant enactment as the period within which the complaint or reference must be made (disregarding any provision permitting an extension of that period at the discretion of the tribunal).

NOTES

Commencement: to be appointed (see the note below).

By Sch 2, para 16 to this Act (at **[1.1158]**), until a day to be appointed by Order under sub-para (2)(b) of para 16, s 192 has effect as set out in para 16(1) of that Schedule, and the section set out above is not in force. This section, although not in force, has been amended as follows—

Sub-s (2): para (aa) inserted by the Working Time Regulations 1998, SI 1998/1833, regs 2(1), 31(4); words in first (outer) and final pairs of square brackets in para (aa) substituted by the Tax Credits Act 2002, s 27, Sch 1, para 1(1), (5); figure in second (inner) pair of square paragraphs in para (aa) inserted by the Employment Relations Act 2004, s 57(1), Sch 1, para 35(a); para (ab) inserted, and words in square brackets in para (b) substituted, by the Employment Relations Act 1999, s 9, Sch 4, Pt III, paras 1, 5, 31; para (ab) repealed by the Tax Credits Act 2002, s 60, Sch 6, as from a day to be appointed; words in first pair of square brackets in para (e) inserted by the Employment Relations Act 2004, s 57(1), Sch 1, para 35(b); figure in second pair of square brackets in para (e) inserted by the Employment Act 2002, s 53, Sch 7, paras 24, 42; figure in third pair of square brackets in para (e) inserted by the Defence Reform Act 2014, s 48(1), (3), as from 1 October 2014.

Sub-s (4): words in first pair of square brackets substituted by the Employment Rights (Dispute Resolution) Act 1998, s 1(2)(a); words in second (outer) pair of square brackets substituted by the Armed Forces Act 1996, s 26(1), (2); words in square brackets in paras (a), (b) substituted by the Armed Forces Act 2006, s 378(1), Sch 16, para 136(a).

Sub-s (5): substituted by the Armed Forces Act 1996, s 26(1), (3); words "employment tribunal" in square brackets substituted by the Employment Rights (Dispute Resolution) Act 1998, s 1(2)(a); other words in square brackets substituted by the Armed Forces Act 2006, s 378(1), Sch 16, para 136(b).

Sub-s (6A): substituted, for original sub-s (6), by the Armed Forces Act 2006, s 378(1), Sch 16, para 136(c).

Sub-s (8): words in square brackets substituted by the Employment Rights (Dispute Resolution) Act 1998, s 1(2)(a).

References to a service complaint, etc: see the Armed Forces Act 2006 (Transitional Provisions etc) Order 2009, SI 2009/1059, art 196, which provides: (i) references to a service complaint include a complaint made under the service redress procedures in sub-s (4) above, and (ii) references to the service complaint procedures include the service redress procedures in sub-s (5) above.

[1.1108]

[193 National security

Part IVA and section 47B of this Act do not apply in relation to employment for the purposes of—

(a) the Security Service,
(b) the Secret Intelligence Service, or
(c) the Government Communications Headquarters.]

NOTES

Substituted by the Employment Relations Act 1999, s 41, Sch 8, para 1.

Parliamentary staff

[1.1109]

194 House of Lords staff

(1) The provisions of this Act to which this section applies have effect in relation to employment as a relevant member of the House of Lords staff as they have effect in relation to other employment.

(2) This section applies to—

(a) Part I,
(b) Part III,
(c) in Part V, [sections [43M,] 44, 45A[, 47[, [47AA,] 47C[, 47D and 47E]]]], and sections 48 and 49 so far as relating to those sections,
(d) Part VI, apart from sections 58 to 60,
[(e) Parts [6A,] VII, VIII and VIIIA,]
(f) in Part IX, sections 92 and 93,
(g) Part X, apart from sections 101 and 102, and
(h) this Part and Parts XIV and XV.

[(2A) For the purposes of the application of section 98B(2) in relation to a relevant member of the House of Lords staff, the reference to the employer's undertaking shall be construed as a reference to the national interest or, if the case so requires, the interests of the House of Lords.]

(3) For the purposes of the application of [the other provisions] of this Act to which this section applies in relation to a relevant member of the House of Lords staff references to an undertaking shall be construed as references to the House of Lords.

(4) Nothing in any rule of law or the law or practice of Parliament prevents a relevant member of the House of Lords staff from bringing before the High Court or [the county court]—

(a) a claim arising out of or relating to a contract of employment or any other contract connected with employment, or
(b) a claim in tort arising in connection with employment.

(5) Where the terms of the contract of employment of a relevant member of the House of Lords staff restrict his right to take part in—

(a) certain political activities, or
(b) activities which may conflict with his official functions,

nothing in section 50 requires him to be allowed time off work for public duties connected with any such activities.

(6) In this section "relevant member of the House of Lords staff" means any person who is employed under a contract of employment with the Corporate Officer of the House of Lords.

(7) For the purposes of the application of—

(a) the provisions of this Act to which this section applies, or
(b) a claim within subsection (4),

in relation to a person continuously employed in or for the purposes of the House of Lords up to the time when he became so employed under a contract of employment with the Corporate Officer of the House of Lords, his employment shall not be treated as having been terminated by reason only of a change in his employer before or at that time.

NOTES

Sub-s (2) is amended as follows:

Words in first (outer) pair of square brackets in para (c) substituted by the Working Time Regulations 1998, SI 1998/1833, regs 2(1), 31(5).

Figure "43M," in para (c) inserted by the Employment Relations Act 2004, s 57(1), Sch 1, para 36(1), (2).

Figure ", 47" in para (c) substituted by the Employment Relations Act 1999, s 9, Sch 4, Pt II, paras 1, 5, 32.

Figure "47AA," in para (c) inserted by the Education and Skills Act 2008, s 39(1), (5), as from a day to be appointed.

Figure ", 47C" in para (c) substituted by both the Tax Credits Act 2002, s 27, Sch 1, para 1(1), (6)(a), and the Employment Act 2002, s 53, Sch 7, paras 24, 43(a).

Words ", 47D and 47E" in para (c) substituted by the Employment Relations Act 2004, s 41(7).

Para (e) substituted by the Employment Act 2002, s 53, Sch 7, paras 24, 43(b).

Figure "6A" in square brackets in para (e) inserted by the Apprenticeships, Skills, Children and Learning Act 2009, s 40(1), (5), Sch 1, paras 1, 5, as from 6 April 2010 (except in relation to small employers and their employees), and as from a day to be appointed (otherwise) (as to the meaning of "small employers" etc, see further the notes at **[1.937]**).

Sub-s (2A): inserted by the Employment Relations Act 2004, s 57(1), Sch 1, para 36(1), (3).

Sub-s (3): words in square brackets substituted by the Employment Relations Act 2004, s 57(1), Sch 1, para 36(1), (4).

Sub-s (4): words in square brackets substituted by the Crime and Courts Act 2013, s 17(5), Sch 9, Pt 3, para 52.

[1.1110]

195 House of Commons staff

(1) The provisions of this Act to which this section applies have in effect in relation to employment as a relevant member of the House of Commons staff as they have effect in relation to other employment.

(2) This section applies to—

(a) Part I,
(b) Part III,

(c) in Part V, [sections [43M,] 44, 45A[, 47[, [47AA,] 47C[, 47D and 47E]]]], and sections 48 and 49 so far as relating to those sections,
(d) Part VI, apart from sections 58 to 60,
[(e) Parts [6A,] VII, VIII and VIIIA,]
(f) in Part IX, sections 92 and 93,
(g) Part X, apart from sections 101 and 102, and
(h) this Part and Parts XIV and XV.

[(2A) For the purposes of the application of section 98B(2) in relation to a relevant member of the House of Commons staff, the reference to the employer's undertaking shall be construed as a reference to the national interest or, if the case so requires, the interests of the House of Commons.]

(3) For the purposes of the application of the provisions of this Act to which this section applies in relation to a relevant member of the House of Commons staff—
(a) references to an employee shall be construed as references to a relevant member of the House of Commons staff,
(b) references to a contract of employment shall be construed as including references to the terms of employment of a relevant member of the House of Commons staff,
(c) references to dismissal shall be construed as including references to the termination of the employment of a relevant member of the House of Commons staff, and
(d) references to an undertaking [(other than in section 98B)] shall be construed as references to the House of Commons.

(4) Nothing in any rule of law or the law or practice of Parliament prevents a relevant member of the House of Commons staff from bringing before the High Court or [the county court]—
(a) a claim arising out of or relating to a contract of employment or any other contract connected with employment, or
(b) a claim in tort arising in connection with employment.

(5) In this section "relevant member of the House of Commons staff" means any person—
(a) who was appointed by the House of Commons Commission or is employed in the refreshment department, or
(b) who is a member of the Speaker's personal staff.

(6) Subject to subsection (7), for the purposes of—
(a) the provisions of this Act to which this section applies,
(b) Part XI (where applicable to relevant members of the House of Commons staff), and
(c) a claim within subsection (4),

the House of Commons Commission is the employer of staff appointed by the Commission and the Speaker is the employer of his personal staff and of any person employed in the refreshment department and not appointed by the Commission.

(7) Where the House of Commons Commission or the Speaker designates a person to be treated for all or any of the purposes mentioned in subsection (6) as the employer of any description of staff (other than the Speaker's personal staff), the person so designated shall be treated for those purposes as their employer.

(8) Where any proceedings are brought by virtue of this section against—
(a) the House of Commons Commission,
(b) the Speaker, or
(c) any person designated under subsection (7),

the person against whom the proceedings are brought may apply to the court or [employment tribunal] concerned to have some other person against whom the proceedings could at the time of the application be properly brought substituted for him as a party to the proceedings.

(9) For the purposes mentioned in subsection (6)—
(a) a person's employment in or for the purposes of the House of Commons shall not (provided he continues to be employed in such employment) be treated as terminated by reason only of a change in his employer, and
(b) (provided he so continues) his first appointment to such employment shall be deemed after the change to have been made by his employer for the time being.

(10) In accordance with subsection (9)—
(a) an employee shall be treated for the purposes mentioned in subsection (6) as being continuously employed by his employer for the time being from the commencement of his employment until its termination, and
(b) anything done by or in relation to his employer for the time being in respect of his employment before the change shall be so treated as having been done by or in relation to the person who is his employer for the time being after the change.

(11) In subsections (9) and (10) "employer for the time being", in relation to a person who has ceased to be employed in or for the purposes of the House of Commons, means the person who was his employer immediately before he ceased to be so employed, except that where some other person would have been his employer for the time being if he had not ceased to be so employed it means that other person.

(12) If the House of Commons resolves at any time that any provision of subsections (5) to (8) should be amended in its application to any member of the staff of that House, Her Majesty may by Order in Council amend that provision accordingly.

NOTES

Sub-s (2) is amended as follows:

Words in first (outer) pair of square brackets in para (c) substituted by the Working Time Regulations 1998, SI 1998/1833, regs 2(1), 31(5).

Figure "43M," in para (c) inserted by the Employment Relations Act 2004, s 57(1), Sch 1, para 36(1), (2).

Figure ", 47" in para (c) substituted by the Employment Relations Act 1999, s 9, Sch 4, Pt II, paras 1, 5, 33.
Figure "47AA," in para (c) inserted by the Education and Skills Act 2008, s 39(1), (6), as from a day to be appointed.
Figure ", 47C" in para (c) substituted by both the Tax Credits Act 2002, s 27, Sch 1, para 1(1), (6)(a), and the Employment Act 2002, s 53, Sch 7, paras 24, 43(a).
Words ", 47D and 47E" in para (c) substituted by the Employment Relations Act 2004, s 41(7).
Para (e) substituted by the Employment Act 2002, s 53, Sch 7, paras 24, 43(b).
Figure "6A" in square brackets in para (e) inserted by the Apprenticeships, Skills, Children and Learning Act 2009, s 40(1), (5), Sch 1, paras 1, 6, as from 6 April 2010 (except in relation to small employers and their employees), and as from a day to be appointed (otherwise) (as to the meaning of "small employers" etc, see further the notes at **[1.937]**).
Sub-s (2A): inserted by the Employment Relations Act 2004, s 57(1), Sch 1, para 37(1), (3).
Sub-s (3): words in square brackets in para (d) inserted by the Employment Relations Act 2004, s 57(1), Sch 1, para 37(1), (4).
Sub-s (4): words in square brackets substituted by the Crime and Courts Act 2013, s 17(5), Sch 9, Pt 3, para 52.
Sub-s (8): words in square brackets substituted by the Employment Rights (Dispute Resolution) Act 1998, s 1(2)(a).

Excluded classes of employment

196, 197 *(S 196 repealed by the Employment Relations Act 1999, ss 32(3), 44, Sch 9(9). S 197 repealed by the Fixed-term Employees (Prevention of Less Favourable Treatment) Regulations 2002, SI 2002/2034, reg 11, Sch 2, Pt 1, para 3(1), (15) (except in relation to Government training schemes, agency workers and apprentices; see regs 18–20 of the 2002 Regulations at* **[2.571]** *et seq, and subject to transitional provisions in Sch 2, Pt 2, para 5 thereto at* **[2.575]***).)*

[1.1111]
198 Short-term employment
Sections 1 to 7 do not apply to an employee if his employment continues for less than one month.

NOTES
Repealed by the Employment Rights (Employment Particulars and Paid Annual Leave) (Amendment) Regulations 2018, SI 2018/1378, regs 2, 7, as from 6 April 2020.

[1.1112]
199 Mariners
(1) Sections 1 to 7, Part II and sections 86 to 91 do not apply to a person employed as a seaman in a ship registered in the United Kingdom under a crew agreement the provisions and form of which are of a kind approved by the Secretary of State [or an agreement specified in regulations under section 32(a) of the Merchant Shipping Act 1995].
(2) Sections 8 to 10, Part III, sections 44, 45, 47, [47C, [47E,] [47F,] 50 to 57B] and 61 to 63, [Parts [6A,] VII, VIII and VIIIA], sections 92 and 93 and . . . [Part X] do not apply to employment as master, or as a member of the crew, of a fishing vessel where the employee is remunerated only by a share in the profits or gross earnings of the vessel.
(3) . . .
(4) Sections 8 to 10 and 50 to 54 and *Part XII* do not apply to employment as a merchant seaman.
(5) In subsection (4) "employment as a merchant seaman"—
  (a) does not include employment in the fishing industry or employment on board a ship otherwise than by the owner, manager or charterer of that ship except employment as a radio officer, but
  (b) subject to that, includes—
    (i) employment as a master or a member of the crew of any ship,
    (ii) employment as a trainee undergoing training for the sea service, and
    (iii) employment in or about a ship in port by the owner, manager or charterer of the ship to do work of the kind ordinarily done by a merchant seaman on a ship while it is in port.
(6) . . .
[(7) The provisions mentioned in subsection (8) apply to employment on board a ship registered in the register maintained under section 8 of the Merchant Shipping Act 1995 if and only if—
  (a) the ship's entry in the register specifies a port in Great Britain as the port to which the vessel is to be treated as belonging,
  (b) under his contract of employment the person employed does not work wholly outside Great Britain, and
  (c) the person employed is ordinarily resident in Great Britain.
(8) The provisions are—
  (a) sections 8 to 10,
  (b) Parts II, III and V,
  (c) Part VI, apart from sections 58 to 60,
  [(d) Parts [6A,] VII, VIII and VIIIA,]
  (e) sections 92 and 93, and
  (f) Part X.]

NOTES
Sub-s (1): words in square brackets inserted by the Merchant Shipping (Maritime Labour Convention) (Consequential and Minor Amendments) Regulations 2014, SI 2014/1614, reg 3, as from 7 August 2014.
Sub-s (2) is amended as follows:
Words in first (outer) pair of square brackets (ie, the words from "47C" to "57B") substituted, and words omitted repealed, by the Employment Relations Act 1999, ss 9, 44, Sch 4, Pt III, paras 1, 5, 34(a), (b), Sch 9(2).
Figure "47E," in square brackets originally inserted by the Employment Act 2002, s 53, Sch 7, paras 24, 44(1), (2)(a), and substituted by the Employment Relations Act 2004, s 41(8).

Figures "47F," and "6A," in square brackets inserted by the Apprenticeships, Skills, Children and Learning Act 2009, s 40(5), Sch 1, paras 1, 7(a), (b), as from 6 April 2010 (except in relation to small employers and their employees), and as from a day to be appointed (otherwise) (as to the meaning of "small employers" etc, see further the notes at **[1.937]**).

Words in fourth pair of square brackets (ie, the words from "Parts" to "VIIIA") substituted by the Employment Act 2002, s 53, Sch 7, paras 24, 44(1), (2)(b).

The words "Part X" in square brackets were substituted (for the original words "Parts X to XII") by the Seafarers (Insolvency, Collective Redundancies and Information and Consultation Miscellaneous Amendments) Regulations 2018, SI 2018/407, reg 2(1), (2), as from 13 April 2018 (for transitional provisions see the final note below).

Sub-s (3): repealed by the Employment Relations Act 1999, ss 9, 44, Sch 4, Pt III, paras 1, 5, 34(c), Sch 9(2).

Sub-s (4): words in italics repealed by SI 2018/407, reg 2(1), (3), as from 13 April 2018 (for transitional provisions see the final note below).

Sub-s (6): repealed by the Fixed-term Employees (Prevention of Less Favourable Treatment) Regulations 2002, SI 2002/2034, reg 11, Sch 2, Pt 1, para 3(1), (16) (except in relation to Government training schemes, agency workers and apprentices; see regs 18–20 of the 2002 Regulations at **[2.571]** et seq, and subject to transitional provisions in Sch 2, Pt 2, para 5 thereto at **[2.575]**).

Sub-s (7): added by the Employment Relations Act 1999, s 32(4).

Sub-s (8): added by the Employment Relations Act 1999, s 32(4); para (d) substituted by the Employment Act 2002, s 53, Sch 7, paras 24, 44(1), (3); figure "6A," in square brackets inserted by the Apprenticeships, Skills, Children and Learning Act 2009, s 40(5), Sch 1, paras 1, 7(c), as from 6 April 2010 (except in relation to small employers and their employees), and as from a day to be appointed (otherwise) (as to the meaning of "small employers" etc, see further the notes at **[1.937]**).

Transitional provisions: the Seafarers (Insolvency, Collective Redundancies and Information and Consultation Miscellaneous Amendments) Regulations 2018, SI 2018/407, reg 2(4), (5) at **[2.2051]** provide as follows (note that the Regulations came into force on 13 April 2018):

> "(4) The amendment made by paragraph (2), insofar as it relates to Part XI of the Employment Rights Act 1996, only has effect in relation to employees who on or after the date on which these Regulations come into force—
>
> (a) are dismissed by reason of redundancy, or
>
> (b) become eligible for a redundancy payment by reason of being laid off or kept on short-time.
>
> (5) The amendment made by paragraph (2), insofar as it relates to Part XII of the Employment Rights Act 1996, and the amendment made by paragraph (3) only have effect in relation to employees whose employer has become insolvent on or after the date on which these Regulations come into force.".

[1.1113]

200 Police officers

(1) Sections 8 to 10, Part III[. . .], sections . . . , [43M,] 45, [45A,] 47[. . .], [47C,] 50 [to 57B] and 61 to 63, Parts VII and VIII, sections 92 and 93 [and], Part X [(except sections 100[, 103A] and 134A and the other provisions of that Part so far as relating to the right not to be unfairly dismissed in a case where the dismissal is unfair by virtue of section 100 [or 103A])] . . . do not apply to employment under a contract of employment in police service or to persons engaged in such employment.

(2) In subsection (1) "police service" means—

(a) service as a member of a constabulary maintained by virtue of an enactment, or

(b) subject to section 126 of the Criminal Justice and Public Order Act 1994 (prison staff not to be regarded as in police service), service in any other capacity by virtue of which a person has the powers or privileges of a constable.

NOTES

Sub-s (1) is amended as follows:

First and third words omitted originally inserted by the Public Interest Disclosure Act 1998, ss 13, 18(2), and repealed by the Police Reform Act 2002, ss 37(2)(a), 107, Sch 8.

Second word omitted repealed by the Police (Health and Safety) Act 1997, s 6(2)(a).

Figure "43M," in square brackets inserted by the Employment Relations Act 2004, s 57(1), Sch 1, para 38.

Figure "45A," in square brackets inserted by the Working Time Regulations 1998, SI 1998/1833, reg 31(6).

Figure "47C," in square brackets and the word "and" in square brackets inserted by the Employment Relations Act 1999, s 9, Sch 4, Pt III, paras 5, 35(a), (c).

Words "to 57B" in square brackets substituted by the Employment Relations Act 1999, s 9, Sch 4, Pt III, paras 5, 35(b).

Words in square brackets beginning with the words "(except sections 100" inserted by the Police (Health and Safety) Act 1997, s 6(2)(b).

Figure ", 103A" in square brackets and words "or 103A" in square brackets inserted by the Police Reform Act 2002, s 37(2)(b), (c).

Final words omitted repealed by the Employment Relations Act 1999, ss 9, 44, Sch 4, Pt III, paras 5, 35(d), Sch 9, Table 2.

Police service: a member of the staff of the Independent Office for Police Conduct, who is not a constable, is not treated as being in police service for the purposes of this Act; see the Police Reform Act 2002, s 13, Sch 3, Pt 3, para 19(5). A National Crime Agency (NCA) officer who is designated as having the powers and privileges of a constable is not to be regarded, by virtue of having those powers and privileges, as in police service for the purposes of any provision of this Act; see the Crime and Courts Act 2013, Sch 5, Pt 4, para 15.

Offshore employment

[1.1114]

201 Power to extend employment legislation to offshore employment

(1) In this section "offshore employment" means employment for the purposes of activities—

(a) in the territorial waters of the United Kingdom,

(b) connected with the exploration of the sea-bed or subsoil, or the exploitation of their natural resources, in the United Kingdom sector of the continental shelf, or

(c) connected with the exploration or exploitation, in a foreign sector of the continental shelf, of a cross-boundary petroleum field.

(2) Her Majesty may by Order in Council provide that—
(a) the provisions of this Act, and
(b) any Northern Ireland legislation making provision for purposes corresponding to any of the purposes of this Act,

apply, to such extent and for such purposes as may be specified in the Order (with or without modification), to or in relation to a person in offshore employment.

(3) An Order in Council under this section—
(a) may make different provision for different cases,
(b) may provide that all or any of the provisions referred to in subsection (2), as applied by such an Order in Council, apply—
(i) to individuals whether or not they are British subjects, and
(ii) to bodies corporate whether or not they are incorporated under the law of a part of the United Kingdom,

and apply even where the application may affect their activities outside the United Kingdom,
(c) may make provision for conferring jurisdiction on any court or class of court specified in the Order in Council, or on [employment tribunals], in respect of offences, causes of action or other matters arising in connection with offshore employment,
(d) may (without prejudice to subsection (2) and paragraph (a)) provide that the provisions referred to in subsection (2), as applied by the Order in Council, apply in relation to any person in employment in a part of the areas referred to in subsection (1)(a) and (b),
(e) may exclude from the operation of section 3 of the Territorial Waters Jurisdiction Act 1878 (consents required for prosecutions) proceedings for offences under the provisions referred to in subsection (2) in connection with offshore employment,
(f) may provide that such proceedings shall not be brought without such consent as may be required by the Order in Council,
(g) may (without prejudice to subsection (2)) modify or exclude the operation of any or all of sections . . . 199 and 215(2) to (6) or of any corresponding Northern Ireland legislation.

[(3A) Where an Order in Council under this section confers jurisdiction on an employment tribunal, the jurisdiction conferred includes power to make an order under section 12A of the Employment Tribunals Act 1996 (financial penalties), and that section applies accordingly.]

(4) Any jurisdiction conferred on a court or tribunal under this section is without prejudice to jurisdiction exercisable apart from this section by that or any other court or tribunal.

(5) In this section—

"cross-boundary petroleum field" means a petroleum field that extends across the boundary between the United Kingdom sector of the continental shelf and a foreign sector of the continental shelf,

"foreign sector of the continental shelf" means an area outside the territorial waters of any state, within which rights with respect to the sea-bed and subsoil and their natural resources are exercisable by a state other than the United Kingdom,

"petroleum field" means a geological structure identified as an oil or gas field by the Order in Council concerned, and

"United Kingdom sector of the continental shelf" means the area designated under section 1(7) of the Continental Shelf Act 1964.

NOTES

Sub-s (1): substituted by the Petroleum Act 1998, s 50, Sch 4, para 40(1), (2), as from a day to be appointed, as follows—

"(1) In this section "offshore employment" means employment for the purposes of—
(a) any activities in the territorial sea adjacent to the United Kingdom, or
(b) any such activities as are mentioned in section 11(2) of the Petroleum Act 1998 in waters within subsection (8)(b) or (c) of that section.".

Sub-s (3): words in square brackets in para (c) substituted by the Employment Rights (Dispute Resolution) Act 1998, s 1(2)(b); figure omitted from para (g) repealed by the Employment Relations Act 1999, s 44, Sch 9(9).

Sub-s (3A): inserted by the Enterprise and Regulatory Reform Act 2013, s 16(2), Sch 3, para 5.

Sub-s (5): repealed by the Petroleum Act 1998, ss 50, 51(1), Sch 4, para 40(1), (3), Sch 5, Pt I, as from a day to be appointed.

Orders: the Employment Relations (Offshore Employment) Order 2000, SI 2000/1828. Also, by virtue of s 241 of, and Sch 2, Pt I, paras 1–4 to, this Act, the Employment Protection (Offshore Employment) Order 1976, SI 1976/766, has effect as if made under this section.

CHAPTER II OTHER MISCELLANEOUS MATTERS

Restrictions on disclosure of information

[1.1115]

202 National security

(1) Where in the opinion of any Minister of the Crown the disclosure of any information would be contrary to the interests of national security—
(a) nothing in any of the provisions to which this section applies requires any person to disclose the information, and
(b) no person shall disclose the information in any proceedings in any court or tribunal relating to any of those provisions.

(2) This section applies to—
(a) Part I, so far as it relates to employment particulars,
(b) in Part V, [sections [43M,] 44, 45A[, 47 and 47C]], and sections 48 and 49 so far as relating to those sections,

(c) in Part VI, sections [55 to 57B] and 61 to 63,
(d) in Part VII, sections 66 to 68, and sections 69 and 70 so far as relating to those sections,
(e) Part VIII,
(f) in Part IX, sections 92 and 93 where they apply by virtue of section 92(4),
(g) Part X so far as relating to a dismissal which is treated as unfair—
[(i) by section [98B,] 99, 100, 101A(d) or 103, or by section 104 in its application in relation to time off under section 57A.]
(ii) by subsection (1) of section 105 by reason of the application of subsection [(2A)], (3) or (6) of that section [or by reason of the application of subsection (4A) in so far as it applies where the reason (or, if more than one, the principal reason) for which an employee was selected for dismissal was that specified in section 101A(d)], and
(h) this Part and Parts XIV and XV (so far as relating to any of the provisions in paragraphs (a) to (g)).

NOTES

Sub-s (2) is amended as follows:

Words in first (outer) pair of square brackets in para (b) substituted by the Working Time Regulations 1998, SI 1998/1833, reg 31(5).

Figure "43M," in square brackets in para (b) inserted by the Employment Relations Act 2004, s 57(1), Sch 1, para 39(1), (2).

Words ", 47 and 47C" in square brackets in para (b) substituted by the Employment Relations Act 1999, s 9, Sch 4, Pt III, paras 5, 36(a).

Words in square brackets in para (c) substituted by the Employment Relations Act 1999, s 9, Sch 4, Pt III, paras 5, 36(b).

Sub-para (g)(i) substituted by the Employment Relations Act 1999, s 9, Sch 4, Pt III, paras 5, 36(c).

Figure "98B," in square brackets in sub-para (g)(i) inserted by the Employment Relations Act 2004, s 57(1), Sch 1, para 39(1), (3)(a).

Figure "(2A)" in square brackets in sub-para (g)(ii) substituted by the Employment Relations Act 2004, s 57(1), Sch 1, para 39(1), (3)(b).

Words in second pair of square brackets in sub-para (g)(ii) inserted by SI 1998/1833, reg 32(6).

Contracting out etc and remedies

[1.1116]

203 Restrictions on contracting out

(1) Any provision in an agreement (whether a contract of employment or not) is void in so far as it purports—
(a) to exclude or limit the operation of any provision of this Act, or
(b) to preclude a person from bringing any proceedings under this Act before an [employment tribunal].

(2) Subsection (1)—
(a) does not apply to any provision in a collective agreement excluding rights under section 28 if an order under section 35 is for the time being in force in respect of it,
(b) does not apply to any provision in a dismissal procedures agreement excluding the right under section 94 if that provision is not to have effect unless an order under section 110 is for the time being in force in respect of it,
(c) does not apply to any provision in an agreement if an order under section 157 is for the time being in force in respect of it,
(d) . . .
(e) does not apply to any agreement to refrain from instituting or continuing proceedings where a conciliation officer has taken action under [any of sections 18A to 18C] of [the Employment Tribunals Act 1996], and
(f) does not apply to any agreement to refrain from instituting or continuing . . . any proceedings within [the following provisions of section 18(1) of the Employment Tribunals Act 1996 (cases where conciliation available)—
(i) [paragraph (b)] (proceedings under this Act),
(ii) [paragraph (l)] (proceedings arising out of the Part-time Workers (Prevention of Less Favourable Treatment) Regulations 2000,)]
[(iii) [paragraph (m)] (proceedings arising out of the Fixed-term Employees (Prevention of Less Favourable Treatment) Regulations 2002),
(iv) . . .]

if the conditions regulating [settlement] agreements under this Act are satisfied in relation to the agreement.

(3) For the purposes of subsection (2)(f) the conditions regulating [settlement] agreements under this Act are that—
(a) the agreement must be in writing,
(b) the agreement must relate to the particular [proceedings],
(c) the employee or worker must have received [advice from a relevant independent adviser] as to the terms and effect of the proposed agreement and, in particular, its effect on his ability to pursue his rights before an [employment tribunal],
(d) there must be in force, when the adviser gives the advice, a [contract of insurance, or an indemnity provided for members of a professional body,] covering the risk of a claim by the employee or worker in respect of loss arising in consequence of the advice,
(e) the agreement must identify the adviser, and
(f) the agreement must state that the conditions regulating [settlement] agreements under this Act are satisfied.

[(3A) A person is a relevant independent adviser for the purposes of subsection (3)(c)—
(a) if he is a qualified lawyer,
(b) if he is an officer, official, employee or member of an independent trade union who has been certified in writing by the trade union as competent to give advice and as authorised to do so on behalf of the trade union,
(c) if he works at an advice centre (whether as an employee or a volunteer) and has been certified in writing by the centre as competent to give advice and as authorised to do so on behalf of the centre, or
(d) if he is a person of a description specified in an order made by the Secretary of State.

(3B) But a person is not a relevant independent adviser for the purposes of subsection (3)(c) in relation to the employee or worker—
(a) if he is, is employed by or is acting in the matter for the employer or an associated employer,
(b) in the case of a person within subsection (3A)(b) or (c), if the trade union or advice centre is the employer or an associated employer,
(c) in the case of a person within subsection (3A)(c), if the employee or worker makes a payment for the advice received from him, or
(d) in the case of a person of a description specified in an order under subsection (3A)(d), if any condition specified in the order in relation to the giving of advice by persons of that description is not satisfied.

(4) In subsection (3A)(a) "qualified lawyer" means—
(a) as respects England and Wales, [a person who, for the purposes of the Legal Services Act 2007, is an authorised person in relation to an activity which constitutes the exercise of a right of audience or the conduct of litigation (within the meaning of that Act), and]
(b) as respects Scotland, an advocate (whether in practice as such or employed to give legal advice), or a solicitor who holds a practising certificate.]

[(5) An agreement under which the parties agree to submit a dispute to arbitration—
(a) shall be regarded for the purposes of subsection (2)(e) and (f) as being an agreement to refrain from instituting or continuing proceedings if—
(i) the dispute is covered by a scheme having effect by virtue of an order under section 212A of the Trade Union and Labour Relations (Consolidation) Act 1992, and
(ii) the agreement is to submit it to arbitration in accordance with the scheme, but
(b) shall be regarded as neither being nor including such an agreement in any other case.]

NOTES

Sub-s (1): words in square brackets substituted by the Employment Rights (Dispute Resolution) Act 1998, s 1(2)(a).

Sub-s (2) is amended as follows:

Para (d) repealed, and sub-paras (f)(iii), (iv) inserted, by the Fixed-term Employees (Prevention of Less Favourable Treatment) Regulations 2002, SI 2002/2034, reg 11, Sch 2, Pt 1, para 3(1), (17) (except in relation to Government training schemes, agency workers and apprentices; see regs 18–20 of the 2002 Regulations at **[2.571]** et seq, and subject to transitional provisions in Sch 2, Pt 2, para 5 thereto at **[2.575]**).

The words "any of sections 18A to 18C" in square brackets in para (e) were substituted by the Enterprise and Regulatory Reform Act 2013, s 7(2), Sch 1, para 10.

Words in second pair of square brackets in para (e) substituted, and first words omitted from para (f) repealed, by the Employment Rights (Dispute Resolution) Act 1998, ss 1(2)(c), 15, 44, Schs 2, 9(3).

Words in first (outer) pair of square brackets in para (f) substituted by the Part-time Workers (Prevention of Less Favourable Treatment) Regulations 2001, SI 2001/1107, reg 3.

Words "paragraph (b)", "paragraph (l)" and "paragraph (m)" in square brackets in sub-paras (f)(i), (ii) and (iii) respectively substituted, and sub-para (f)(iv) repealed, by the Employment Tribunals Act 1996 (Application of Conciliation Provisions) Order 2014, SI 2014/431, art 3, Schedule, paras 2, 4.

Final word in square brackets in para (f) substituted by the Enterprise and Regulatory Reform Act 2013, s 23(1)(b).

Sub-s (3): word "settlement" in square brackets in para (f) substituted by the Enterprise and Regulatory Reform Act 2013, s 23(1)(b); other words in square brackets substituted by the Employment Rights (Dispute Resolution) Act 1998, ss 1(2)(a), 9(1), (2)(e), 10(1), (2)(e), 15, Sch 1, para 24(1), (2).

Sub-ss (3A), (3B): substituted (together with sub-s (4)), for the original sub-s (4), by the Employment Rights (Dispute Resolution) Act 1998, s 15, Sch 1, para 24(1), (3).

Sub-s (4): substituted as noted above: words in square brackets in para (a) substituted by the Legal Services Act 2007, s 208(1), Sch 21, para 120.

Sub-s (5): added by the Employment Rights (Dispute Resolution) Act 1998, s 8(5).

The Employment Relations Act 1999, ss 10–13, are to be treated as provisions of Pt V of this Act for the purposes of sub-ss (1), (2)(e), (f), (3), (4) above; see s 14 of that Act at **[1.1251]**.

Orders: the Settlement Agreements (Description of Person) Order 2004, SI 2004/754 at **[2.725]**; the Compromise Agreements (Description of Person) Order 2004 (Amendment) Order 2004, SI 2004/2515. Note that the title of the first Order was amended by the Enterprise and Regulatory Reform Act 2013 (Consequential Amendments) (Employment) Order 2013, SI 2013/1956 (it was previously the Compromise Agreements (Description of Person) Order 2004); no amendment was made to the second Order though.

[1.1117]

204 Law governing employment

(1) For the purposes of this Act it is immaterial whether the law which (apart from this Act) governs any person's employment is the law of the United Kingdom, or of a part of the United Kingdom, or not.

(2) . . .

NOTES

Sub-s (2): repealed by the Employment Relations Act 1999, s 44, Sch 9(9).

[1.1118]
205 Remedy for infringement of certain rights
(1) The remedy of an employee for infringement of any of the rights conferred by section 8, Part III, Parts V to VIII, section 92, Part X and Part XII is, where provision is made for a complaint or the reference of a question to an [employment tribunal], by way of such a complaint or reference and not otherwise.
[(1ZA) In relation to the right conferred by section 45A, the reference in subsection (1) to an employee has effect as a reference to a worker.]
[(1A) In relation to the right conferred by section 47B, the reference in subsection (1) to an employee has effect as a reference to a worker.]
(2) The remedy of a worker in respect of any contravention of section 13, 15, 18(1) or 21(1) is by way of a complaint under section 23 and not otherwise.

NOTES
Sub-s (1): words in square brackets substituted by the Employment Rights (Dispute Resolution) Act 1998, s 1(2)(a).
Sub-s (1ZA): inserted by the Working Time Regulations 1998, SI 1998/1833, regs 2(1), 31(7).
Sub-s (1A): inserted by the Public Interest Disclosure Act 1998, ss 14, 18(2).

[Employee shareholder status

[1.1119]
205A Employee shareholders
(1) An individual who is or becomes an employee of a company is an "employee shareholder" if—
(a) the company and the individual agree that the individual is to be an employee shareholder,
(b) in consideration of that agreement, the company issues or allots to the individual fully paid up shares in the company, or procures the issue or allotment to the individual of fully paid up shares in its parent undertaking, which have a value, on the day of issue or allotment, of no less than £2,000,
(c) the company gives the individual a written statement of the particulars of the status of employee shareholder and of the rights which attach to the shares referred to in paragraph (b) ("the employee shares") (see subsection (5)), and
(d) the individual gives no consideration other than by entering into the agreement.
(2) An employee who is an employee shareholder does not have—
(a) the right to make an application under section 63D (request to undertake study or training),
(b) the right to make an application under section 80F (request for flexible working),
(c) the right under section 94 not to be unfairly dismissed, or
(d) the right under section 135 to a redundancy payment.
(3) The following provisions are to be read in the case of an employee who is an employee shareholder as if for "8 weeks' notice", in each place it appears, there were substituted "16 weeks' notice"—
(a) regulation 11 of the Maternity and Parental Leave etc Regulations 1999 (SI 1999/3312) (requirement for employee to notify employer of intention to return to work during maternity leave period), and
(b) regulation 25 of the Paternity and Adoption Leave Regulations 2002 (SI 2002/2788) (corresponding provision for adoption leave).
(4) Regulation 30 of the Additional Paternity Leave Regulations 2010 (SI 2010/1055) (requirement for employee to notify employer of intention to return to work during additional paternity leave period) is to be read in the case of an employee who is an employee shareholder as if for "six weeks' notice", in each place it appears, there were substituted "16 weeks' notice".
(5) The statement referred to in subsection (1)(c) must—
(a) state that, as an employee shareholder, the individual would not have the rights specified in subsection (2),
(b) specify the notice periods that would apply in the individual's case as a result of subsections (3) and (4),
(c) state whether any voting rights attach to the employee shares,
(d) state whether the employee shares carry any rights to dividends,
(e) state whether the employee shares would, if the company were wound up, confer any rights to participate in the distribution of any surplus assets,
(f) if the company has more than one class of shares and any of the rights referred to in paragraphs (c) to (e) attach to the employee shares, explain how those rights differ from the equivalent rights that attach to the shares in the largest class (or next largest class if the class which includes the employee shares is the largest),
(g) state whether the employee shares are redeemable and, if they are, at whose option,
(h) state whether there are any restrictions on the transferability of the employee shares and, if there are, what those restrictions are,
(i) state whether any of the requirements of sections 561 and 562 of the Companies Act 2006 are excluded in the case of the employee shares (existing shareholders' right of pre-emption), and
(j) state whether the employee shares are subject to drag-along rights or tag-along rights and, if they are, explain the effect of the shares being so subject.
(6) Agreement between a company and an individual that the individual is to become an employee shareholder is of no effect unless, before the agreement is made—
(a) the individual, having been given the statement referred to in subsection (1)(c), receives advice from a relevant independent adviser as to the terms and effect of the proposed agreement, and
(b) seven days have passed since the day on which the individual receives the advice.

(7) Any reasonable costs incurred by the individual in obtaining the advice (whether or not the individual becomes an employee shareholder) which would, but for this subsection, have to be met by the individual are instead to be met by the company.
(8) The reference in subsection (2)(b) to making an application under section 80F does not include a reference to making an application within the period of 14 days beginning with the day on which the employee shareholder returns to work from a period of parental leave under regulations under section 76.
(9) The reference in subsection (2)(c) to unfair dismissal does not include a reference to a dismissal—
(a) which is required to be regarded as unfair for the purposes of Part 10 by a provision (whenever made) contained in or made under this or any other Act, or
(b) which amounts to a contravention of the Equality Act 2010.
(10) The reference in subsection (2)(c) to the right not to be unfairly dismissed does not include a reference to that right in a case where section 108(2) (health and safety cases) applies.
(11) The Secretary of State may by order amend subsection (1) so as to increase the sum for the time being specified there.
(12) The Secretary of State may by regulations provide that any agreement for a company to buy back from an individual the shares referred to in subsection (1)(b) in the event that the individual ceases to be an employee shareholder or ceases to be an employee must be on terms which meet the specified requirements.
(13) In this section—
"company" means—
(a) a company or overseas company (within the meaning, in each case, of the Companies Act 2006) which has a share capital, or
(b) a European Public Limited-Liability Company (or Societas Europaea) within the meaning of Council Regulation 2157/2001/EC of 8 October 2001 on the Statute for a European company;
"drag-along rights", in relation to shares in a company, means the right of the holders of a majority of the shares, where they are selling their shares, to require the holders of the minority to sell theirs;
"parent undertaking" has the same meaning as in the Companies Act 2006;
"relevant independent adviser" has the meaning that it has for the purposes of section 203(3)(c);
"tag-along rights", in relation to shares in a company, means the right of the holders of a minority of the shares to sell their shares, where the holders of the majority are selling theirs, on the same terms as those on which the holders of the majority are doing so.
(14) The reference in this section to the value of shares in a company is a reference to their market value within the meaning of the Taxation of Chargeable Gains Act 1992 (see sections 272 and 273 of that Act).]

NOTES

Inserted, together with preceding heading, by the Growth and Infrastructure Act 2013, s 31(1).

Sub-s (13): in the definition "company", para (b) is substituted by the International Accounting Standards and European Public Limited-Liability Company (Amendment etc) (EU Exit) Regulations 2019, SI 2019/685, reg 21, Sch 3, Pt 3, para 18, as from exit day (as defined in the European Union (Withdrawal) Act 2018, s 20), as follows—

"(b) a United Kingdom Societas (or UK Societas) within the meaning of Council Regulation 2157/2001/EC of 8 October 2001 on the Statute for a European company;".

General provisions about death of employer or employee

[1.1120]

206 Institution or continuance of tribunal proceedings

(1) Where an employer has died, any tribunal proceedings arising under any of the provisions of this Act to which this section applies may be defended by a personal representative of the deceased employer.
(2) This section and section 207 apply to—
(a) Part I, so far as it relates to itemised pay statements,
(b) Part III,
(c) Part V,
(d) Part VI, apart from sections 58 to 60,
(e) Parts VII and VIII,
(f) in Part IX, sections 92 and 93, and
(g) Parts X to XII.
(3) Where an employee has died, any tribunal proceedings arising under any of the provisions of this Act to which this section applies may be instituted or continued by a personal representative of the deceased employee.
(4) If there is no personal representative of a deceased employee, any tribunal proceedings arising under any of the provisions of this Act to which this section applies may be instituted or continued on behalf of the estate of the deceased employee by any appropriate person appointed by the [employment tribunal].
(5) In subsection (4) "appropriate person" means a person who is—
(a) authorised by the employee before his death to act in connection with the proceedings, or
(b) the widow or widower, [surviving civil partner,] child, parent or brother or sister of the deceased employee;
and in Part XI and the following provisions of this section and section 207 references to a personal representative include a person appointed under subsection (4).
(6) In a case where proceedings are instituted or continued by virtue of subsection (4), any award mad by the [employment tribunal] shall be—

(a) made in such terms, and
(b) enforceable in such manner,

as the Secretary of State may by regulations provide.

(7) Any reference in the provisions of this Act to which this section applies to the doing of anything by or in relation to an employer or employee includes a reference to the doing of the thing by or in relation to a personal representative of the deceased employer or employee.

(8) Any reference in the provisions of this Act to which this section applies to a thing required or authorised to be done by or in relation to an employer or employee includes a reference to a thing required or authorised to be done by or in relation to a personal representative of the deceased employer or employee.

(9) Subsections (7) and (8) do not prevent a reference to a successor of an employer including a personal representative of a deceased employer.

NOTES

Sub-ss (4), (6): words in square brackets substituted by the Employment Rights (Dispute Resolution) Act 1998, s 1(2)(a).

Sub-s (5): words in square brackets in para (b) inserted by the Civil Partnership Act 2004 (Overseas Relationships and Consequential, etc Amendments) Order 2005, SI 2005/3129, art 4(4), Sch 4, para 11.

Regulations: as of 15 May 2019, no Regulations had been made under this section but, by virtue of s 241 of, and Sch 2, Pt I, paras 1–4 to, this Act, the Employment Tribunal Awards (Enforcement in case of Death) Regulations 1976, SI 1976/663, have effect as if made under this section.

[1.1121]

207 Rights and liabilities accruing after death

(1) Any right arising under any of the provisions of this Act to which this section applies which accrues after the death of an employee devolves as if it had accrued before his death.

(2) Where an [employment tribunal] determines under any provision of Part XI that an employer is liable to pay to a personal representative of a deceased employee—

(a) the whole of a redundancy payment to which he would have been entitled but for some provision of Part XI or section 206, or
(b) such part of such a redundancy payment as the tribunal thinks fit,

the reference in subsection (1) to a right includes any right to receive it.

(3) Where—

(a) by virtue of any of the provisions to which this section applies a personal representative is liable to pay any amount, and
(b) the liability has not accrued before the death of the employer,

it shall be treated as a liability of the deceased employer which had accrued immediately before his death.

NOTES

Sub-s (2): words in square brackets substituted by the Employment Rights (Dispute Resolution) Act 1998, s 1(2)(a).

[Mediation in certain cross-border disputes

[1.1122]

207A Extension of time limits because of mediation in certain cross-border disputes

(1) In this section—

(a) "Mediation Directive" means Directive 2008/52/EC of the European Parliament and of the Council of 21 May 2008 on certain aspects of mediation in civil and commercial matters,
(b) "mediation" has the meaning given by article 3(a) of the Mediation Directive,
(c) "mediator" has the meaning given by article 3(b) of the Mediation Directive, and
(d) "relevant dispute" means a dispute to which article 8(1) of the Mediation Directive applies (certain cross-border disputes).

(2) Subsection (3) applies where—

(a) this Act provides for that subsection to apply for the purposes of a provision of this Act,
(b) a time limit is set by that provision in relation to the whole or part of a relevant dispute,
(c) a mediation in relation to the relevant dispute starts before the time limit expires, and
(d) if not extended by this section, the time limit would expire before the mediation ends or less than four weeks after it ends.

(3) The time limit expires instead at the end of four weeks after the mediation ends (subject to subsection (4)).

(4) If a time limit mentioned in subsection (2)(b) has been extended by this section, subsections (2) and (3) apply to the extended time limit as they apply to a time limit mentioned in subsection (2)(b).

(5) Subsection (6) applies where—

(a) a time limit is set by section 164(1)(c) or (2) in relation to the whole or part of a relevant dispute,
(b) a mediation in relation to the relevant dispute starts before the time limit expires, and
(c) if not extended by this section, the time limit would expire before the mediation ends or less than eight weeks after it ends.

(6) The time limit expires instead at the end of eight weeks after the mediation ends (subject to subsection (7)).

(7) If a time limit mentioned in subsection (5)(a) has been extended by this section, subsections (5) and (6) apply to the extended time limit as they apply to a time limit mentioned in subsection (5)(a).

(8) Where more than one time limit applies in relation to a relevant dispute, the extension by subsection (3) or (6) of one of those time limits does not affect the others.

(9) For the purposes of this section, a mediation starts on the date of the agreement to mediate that is entered into by the parties and the mediator.

(10) For the purposes of this section, a mediation ends on the date of the first of these to occur—

- *(a) the parties reach an agreement in resolution of the relevant dispute,*
- *(b) a party completes the notification of the other parties that it has withdrawn from the mediation,*
- *(c) a party to whom a qualifying request is made fails to give a response reaching the other parties within 14 days of the request,*
- *(d) the parties, after being notified that the mediator's appointment has ended (by death, resignation or otherwise), fail to agree within 14 days to seek to appoint a replacement mediator,*
- *(e) the mediation otherwise comes to an end pursuant to the terms of the agreement to mediate.*

(11) For the purpose of subsection (10), a qualifying request is a request by a party that another (A) confirm to all parties that A is continuing with the mediation.

(12) In the case of any relevant dispute, references in this section to a mediation are references to the mediation so far as it relates to that dispute, and references to a party are to be read accordingly.

(13) Where an employment tribunal has power under this Act to extend a time limit to which subsection (3) applies, the power is exercisable in relation to the time limit as extended by this section.]

NOTES

Inserted, together with the preceding heading, by the Cross-Border Mediation (EU Directive) Regulations 2011, SI 2011/1133, regs 30, 48.

Repealed by the Cross-Border Mediation (EU Directive) (EU Exit) Regulations 2019, SI 2019/469, reg 4, Sch 1, Pt 1, para 12(1), (25), as from exit day (as defined in the European Union (Withdrawal) Act 2018, s 20) and subject to the modifications specified in Sch 2 to the 2019 Regulations for any mediation to which this section applies, issued before exit day (see reg 5, Sch 2, Pt 1, para 13 at **[2.2131]**, **[2.2132]**).

[1.1123]

[207B Extension of time limits to facilitate conciliation before institution of proceedings

(1) This section applies where this Act provides for it to apply for the purposes of a provision of this Act (a "relevant provision").

But it does not apply to a dispute that is (or so much of a dispute as is) a relevant dispute for the purposes of section 207A.

(2) In this section—

- (a) Day A is the day on which the complainant or applicant concerned complies with the requirement in subsection (1) of section 18A of the Employment Tribunals Act 1996 (requirement to contact ACAS before instituting proceedings) in relation to the matter in respect of which the proceedings are brought, and
- (b) Day B is the day on which the complainant or applicant concerned receives or, if earlier, is treated as receiving (by virtue of regulations made under subsection (11) of that section) the certificate issued under subsection (4) of that section.

(3) In working out when a time limit set by a relevant provision expires the period beginning with the day after Day A and ending with Day B is not to be counted.

(4) If a time limit set by a relevant provision would (if not extended by this subsection) expire during the period beginning with Day A and ending one month after Day B, the time limit expires instead at the end of that period.

(5) Where an employment tribunal has power under this Act to extend a time limit set by a relevant provision, the power is exercisable in relation to the time limit as extended by this section.]

NOTES

Inserted by the Enterprise and Regulatory Reform Act 2013, s 8, Sch 2, paras 15, 35.

Words in italics repealed by the Cross-Border Mediation (EU Directive) (EU Exit) Regulations 2019, SI 2019/469, reg 4, Sch 1, Pt 1, para 12(1), (26), as from exit day (as defined in the European Union (Withdrawal) Act 2018, s 20).

Modifications of Act

208 *(Repealed by the Employment Relations Act 1999, ss 36(2), 44, Sch 9(10).)*

[1.1124]

209 Powers to amend Act

(1) The Secretary of State may by order—

- (a) provide that any provision of this Act, other than any to which this paragraph does not apply, which is specified in the order shall not apply to persons, or to employments, of such classes as may be prescribed in the order,
- (b) provide that any provision of this Act, other than any to which this paragraph does not apply, shall apply to persons or employments of such classes as may be prescribed in the order subject to such exceptions and modifications as may be so prescribed, or
- (c) vary, or exclude the operation of, any of the provisions to which this paragraph applies.

(2) Subsection (1)(a) does not apply to—

- (a) Parts II and IV,
- (b) in Part V, sections 45 and 46, and sections 48 and 49 so far as relating to those sections,
- (c) in Part VI, sections 58 to 60,
- (d) in Part IX, sections 87(3), 88 to 90, 91(1) to (4) and (6) and 92(6) to (8),
- (e) in Part X, sections 95, 97(1) to (5), 98(1) to (4) and (6), 100, 101, [101A,] 102, 103, 105, 107, 110, 111, 120(2), 124(1), (2) and (5), 125(7) and 134,

(f) in Part XI, sections 143, 144, 160(2) and (3), 166 to 173 and 177 to 180,
(g) in Part XIII, sections . . . ,
(h) Chapter I of Part XIV, or
(j) in Part XV, section 236(3) so far as relating to sections 120(2), 124(2) and 125(7).

(3) Subsection (1)(b) does not apply to—
(a) any of the provisions to which subsection (1)(a) does not apply,
(b) sections 1 to 7, or
(c) the provisions of sections 86 to 91 not specified in subsection (2).

(4) The provision which may be made by virtue of paragraph (b) of subsection (1) in relation to section 94 does not include provision for application subject to exceptions or modifications; but this subsection does not prejudice paragraph (a) of that subsection.

(5) Subsection (1)(c) applies to sections 29(2), 65(2), 86(5), 92(3), 108(1), . . . 159, 160(1) . . . and 199(1), (2), (4) and (5).

(6), (7) . . .

(8) The provisions of this section are without prejudice to any other power of the Secretary of State to amend, vary or repeal any provision of this Act or to extend or restrict its operation in relation to any person or employment.

NOTES

Sub-s (2): figure in square brackets in para (e) inserted by the Working Time Regulations 1998, SI 1998/1833, regs 2(1), 32(7); words omitted from para (g) repealed by the Employment Relations Act 1999, s 44, Sch 9(3), (9) (it is unclear why the whole of para (g) was not repealed).

Sub-s (5): first words omitted repealed by the Employment Equality (Age) Regulations 2006, SI 2006/1031, reg 49(1), Sch 8, Pt 1, paras 21, 34; second words omitted repealed by the Employment Relations Act 1999, s 44, Sch 9(9).

Sub-s (6): repealed by the Employment Relations Act 1999, ss 9, 44, Sch 4, Pt III, paras 1, 5, 37, Sch 9(2).

Sub-s (7): repealed by the Employment Relations Act 1999, ss 23(6), 44, Sch 9(4).

Orders: the Redundancy Payments (Continuity of Employment in Local Government, etc) (Modification) Order 1999, SI 1999/2277 at **[2.409]**; the Redundancy Payments (Continuity of Employment in Local Government, etc) (Modification) (Amendment) Order 2001, SI 2001/866; the Redundancy Payments (Continuity of Employment in Local Government, etc) (Modification) (Amendment) Order 2002, SI 2002/532; the Redundancy Payments (Continuity of Employment in Local Government, etc) (Modification) (Amendment) Order 2004, SI 2004/1682; the Redundancy Payments (Continuity of Employment in Local Government, etc) (Modification) Order (Amendment) Order 2010, SI 2010/903; the Unfair Dismissal and Statement of Reasons for Dismissal (Variation of Qualifying Period) Order 2012, SI 2012/989; the Local Policing Bodies (Consequential Amendments and Transitional Provision) Order 2012, SI 2012/2733; the Redundancy Payments (Continuity of Employment in Local Government, etc) (Modification) (Amendment) Order 2013, SI 2013/1784; the Redundancy Payments (Continuity of Employment in Local Government, etc) (Modification) (Amendment) Order 2015, SI 2015/916; the Exclusivity Terms in Zero Hours Contracts (Redress) Regulations 2015, SI 2015/2021 at **[2.1925]**; the Seafarers (Insolvency, Collective Redundancies and Information and Consultation Miscellaneous Amendments) Regulations 2018, SI 2018/407 at **[2.2050]**. Also, by virtue of s 241 of, and Sch 2, Pt I, paras 1–4 to, this Act, the following Orders have effect as if made under this section: the Redundancy Payments (National Health Service) (Modification) Order 1993, SI 1993/3167 at **[2.208]**; the Employment Protection (Continuity of Employment of National Health Service Employees) (Modification) Order 1996, SI 1996/1023.

PART XIV
INTERPRETATION

CHAPTER I CONTINUOUS EMPLOYMENT

[1.1125]
210 Introductory

(1) References in any provision of this Act to a period of continuous employment are (unless provision is expressly made to the contrary) to a period computed in accordance with this Chapter.

(2) In any provision of this Act which refers to a period of continuous employment expressed in months or years—
(a) a month means a calendar month, and
(b) a year means a year of twelve calendar months.

(3) In computing an employee's period of continuous employment for the purposes of any provision of this Act, any question—
(a) whether the employee's employment is of a kind counting towards a period of continuous employment, or
(b) whether periods (consecutive or otherwise) are to be treated as forming a single period of continuous employment,

shall be determined week by week; but where it is necessary to compute the length of an employee's period of employment it shall be computed in months and years of twelve months in accordance with section 211.

(4) Subject to sections 215 to 217, a week which does not count in computing the length of a period of continuous employment breaks continuity of employment.

(5) A person's employment during any period shall, unless the contrary is shown, be presumed to have been continuous.

[1.1126]
211 Period of continuous employment

(1) An employee's period of continuous employment for the purposes of any provision of this Act—
(a) (subject to [subsection] (3)) begins with the day on which the employee starts work, and

(b) ends with the day by reference to which the length of the employee's period of continuous employment is to be ascertained for the purposes of the provision.

(2) . . .

(3) If an employee's period of continuous employment includes one or more periods which (by virtue of section 215, 216 or 217) while not counting in computing the length of the period do not break continuity of employment, the beginning of the period shall be treated as postponed by the number of days falling within that intervening period, or the aggregate number of days falling within those periods, calculated in accordance with the section in question.

NOTES

The word in square brackets in sub-s (1) was substituted, and sub-s (2) was repealed, by the Employment Equality (Age) Regulations 2006, SI 2006/1031, reg 49(1), Sch 8, Pt 1, paras 21, 35.

[1.1127]
212 Weeks counting in computing period

(1) Any week during the whole or part of which an employee's relations with his employer are governed by a contract of employment counts in computing the employee's period of employment.

(2) . . .

(3) Subject to subsection (4), any week (not within subsection (1)) during the whole or part of which an employee is—

(a) incapable of work in consequence of sickness or injury,

(b) absent from work on account of a temporary cessation of work, [or]

(c) absent from work in circumstances such that, by arrangement or custom, he is regarded as continuing in the employment of his employer for any purpose, . . .

(d) . . .

counts in computing the employee's period of employment.

(4) Not more than twenty-six weeks count under subsection (3)(a) . . . between any periods falling under subsection (1).

NOTES

Sub-s (2) was repealed, the word in square brackets in para (b) of sub-s (3) was inserted, and the words omitted from sub-s (3), (4) were repealed, by the Employment Relations Act 1999, ss 9, 44, Sch 4, Pt III, paras 1, 5, 38, Sch 9(2).

[1.1128]
213 Intervals in employment

(1) Where in the case of an employee a date later than the date which would be the effective date of termination by virtue of subsection (1) of section 97 is treated for certain purposes as the effective date of termination by virtue of subsection (2) or (4) of that section, the period of the interval between the two dates counts as a period of employment in ascertaining for the purposes of section 108(1) or 119(1) the period for which the employee has been continuously employed.

(2) Where an employee is by virtue of section 138(1) regarded for the purposes of Part XI as not having been dismissed by reason of a renewal or re-engagement taking effect after an interval, the period of the interval counts as a period of employment in ascertaining for the purposes of section 155 or 162(1) the period for which the employee has been continuously employed (except so far as it is to be disregarded under section 214 or 215).

(3) Where in the case of an employee a date later than the date which would be the relevant date by virtue of subsections (2) to (4) of section 145 is treated for certain purposes as the relevant date by virtue of subsection (5) of that section, the period of the interval between the two dates counts as a period of employment in ascertaining for the purposes of section 155 or 162(1) the period for which the employee has been continuously employed (except so far as it is to be disregarded under section 214 or 215).

[1.1129]
214 Special provisions for redundancy payments

(1) This section applies where a period of continuous employment has to be determined in relation to an employee for the purposes of the application of section 155 or 162(1).

(2) The continuity of a period of employment is broken where—

(a) a redundancy payment has previously been paid to the employee (whether in respect of dismissal or in respect of lay-off or short-time), and

(b) the contract of employment under which the employee was employed was renewed (whether by the same or another employer) or the employee was re-engaged under a new contract of employment (whether by the same or another employer).

(3) The continuity of a period of employment is also broken where—

(a) a payment has been made to the employee (whether in respect of the termination of his employment or lay-off or short-time) in accordance with a scheme under section 1 of the Superannuation Act 1972 or arrangements falling within section 177(3), and

(b) he commenced new, or renewed, employment.

(4) The date on which the person's continuity of employment is broken by virtue of this section—

(a) if the employment was under a contract of employment, is the date which was the relevant date in relation to the payment mentioned in subsection (2)(a) or (3)(a), and

(b) if the employment was otherwise than under a contract of employment, is the date which would have been the relevant date in relation to the payment mentioned in subsection (2)(a) or (3)(a) had the employment been under a contract of employment.

(5) For the purposes of this section a redundancy payment shall be treated as having been paid if—

(a) the whole of the payment has been paid to the employee by the employer,
(b) a tribunal has determined liability and found that the employer must pay part (but not all) of the redundancy payment and the employer has paid that part, or
(c) the Secretary of State has paid a sum to the employee in respect of the redundancy payment under section 167.

[1.1130]
215 Employment abroad etc

(1) This Chapter applies to a period of employment—
(a) (subject to the following provisions of this section) even where during the period the employee was engaged in work wholly or mainly outside Great Britain, and
(b) even where the employee was excluded by or under this Act from any right conferred by this Act.

(2) For the purposes of sections 155 and 162(1) a week of employment does not count in computing a period of employment if the employee—
(a) was employed outside Great Britain during the whole or part of the week, and
(b) was not during that week an employed earner for the purposes of the Social Security Contributions and Benefits Act 1992 in respect of whom a secondary Class 1 contribution was payable under that Act (whether or not the contribution was in fact paid).

(3) Where by virtue of subsection (2) a week of employment does not count in computing a period of employment, the continuity of the period is not broken by reason only that the week does not count in computing the period; and the number of days which, for the purposes of section 211(3), fall within the intervening period is seven for each week within this subsection.

(4) Any question arising under subsection (2) whether—
(a) a person was an employed earner for the purposes of the Social Security Contributions and Benefits Act 1992, or
(b) if so, whether a secondary Class 1 contribution was payable in respect of him under that Act,
shall be determined by [an officer of the Commissioners of Inland Revenue].

[(5) Part II of the Social Security Contributions (Transfer of Functions, etc) Act 1999 (decisions and appeals) shall apply in relation to the determination of any issue by the Inland Revenue under subsection (4) as if it were a decision falling within section 8(1) of that Act.]

(6) Subsection (2) does not apply in relation to a person who is—
(a) employed as a master or seaman in a British ship, and
(b) ordinarily resident in Great Britain.

NOTES

The words in square brackets in sub-s (4), and all of sub-s (5), were substituted by the Social Security Contributions (Transfer of Functions, etc) Act 1999, s 18, Sch 7, para 21.

Commissioners of Inland Revenue: a reference to the Commissioners of Inland Revenue is now to be taken as a reference to the Commissioners for Her Majesty's Revenue and Customs; see the Commissioners for Revenue and Customs Act 2005, s 50(1), (7).

[1.1131]
216 Industrial disputes

(1) A week does not count under section 212 if during the week, or any part of the week, the employee takes part in a strike.

(2) The continuity of an employee's period of employment is not broken by a week which does not count under this Chapter (whether or not by virtue only of subsection (1)) if during the week, or any part of the week, the employee takes part in a strike; and the number of days which, for the purposes of section 211(3), fall within the intervening period is the number of days between the last working day before the strike and the day on which work was resumed.

(3) The continuity of an employee's period of employment is not broken by a week if during the week, or any part of the week, the employee is absent from work because of a lock-out by the employer; and the number of days which, for the purposes of section 211(3), fall within the intervening period is the number of days between the last working day before the lock-out and the day on which work was resumed.

[1.1132]
217 Reinstatement after military service

(1) If a person who is entitled to apply to his former employer under the Reserve Forces (Safeguard of Employment) Act 1985 enters the employment of the employer not later than the end of the six month period mentioned in section 1(4)(b) of that Act, his period of service in the armed forces of the Crown in the circumstances specified in section 1(1) of that Act does not break his continuity of employment.

(2) In the case of such a person the number of days which, for the purposes of section 211(3), fall within the intervening period is the number of days between the last day of his previous period of employment with the employer (or, if there was more than one such period, the last of them) and the first day of the period of employment beginning in the six month period.

[1.1133]
218 Change of employer

(1) Subject to the provisions of this section, this Chapter relates only to employment by the one employer.

(2) If a trade or business, or an undertaking (whether or not established by or under an Act), is transferred from one person to another—

(a) the period of employment of an employee in the trade or business or undertaking at the time of the transfer counts as a period of employment with the transferee, and
(b) the transfer does not break the continuity of the period of employment.

(3) If by or under an Act (whether public or local and whether passed before or after this Act) a contract of employment between any body corporate and an employee is modified and some other body corporate is substituted as the employer—
(a) the employee's period of employment at the time when the modification takes effect counts as a period of employment with the second body corporate, and
(b) the change of employer does not break the continuity of the period of employment.

(4) If on the death of an employer the employee is taken into the employment of the personal representatives or trustees of the deceased—
(a) the employee's period of employment at the time of the death counts as a period of employment with the employer's personal representatives or trustees, and
(b) the death does not break the continuity of the period of employment.

(5) If there is a change in the partners, personal representatives or trustees who employ any person—
(a) the employee's period of employment at the time of the change counts as a period of employment with the partners, personal representatives or trustees after the change, and
(b) the change does not break the continuity of the period of employment.

(6) If an employee of an employer is taken into the employment of another employer who, at the time when the employee enters the second employer's employment, is an associated employer of the first employer—
(a) the employee's period of employment at that time counts as a period of employment with the second employer, and
(b) the change of employer does not break the continuity of the period of employment.

(7) If an employee of the [governing body] of a school maintained by a [local authority] is taken into the employment of the authority or an employee of a [local authority] is taken into the employment of the [governing body] of a school maintained by the authority—
(a) his period of employment at the time of the change of employer counts as a period of employment with the second employer, and
(b) the change does not break the continuity of the period of employment.

(8) If a person employed in relevant employment by a health service employer is taken into relevant employment by another such employer, his period of employment at the time of the change of employer counts as a period of employment with the second employer and the change does not break the continuity of the period of employment.

(9) For the purposes of subsection (8) employment is relevant employment if it is employment of a description—
(a) in which persons are engaged while undergoing professional training which involves their being employed successively by a number of different health service employers, and
(b) which is specified in an order made by the Secretary of State.

(10) The following are health service employers for the purposes of subsections (8) and (9)—
[(za) the National Health Service Commissioning Board,
(zb) a clinical commissioning group established under section 14D of the National Health Service Act 2006,]
(a) . . .
(b) Special Health Authorities established under [section 28 of [the National Health Service Act 2006] or section 22 of the National Health Service (Wales) Act 2006],
[(bb) . . .]
(c) National Health Service trusts established under *[[the National Health Service Act 2006] or* the National Health Service (Wales) Act 2006],
[(ca) NHS foundation trusts,]
[(cb) Local Health Boards established under section 11 of the National Health Service (Wales) Act 2006,]
[(cc) the National Institute for Health and Care Excellence,]
[(cd) the Health and Social Care Information Centre,]
(d), [(dd)], (e) . . .

[(11) In subsection (7) "local authority" has the meaning given by section 579(1) of the Education Act 1996.]

NOTES

Sub-s (7): words "governing body" in square brackets substituted by the Education Act 2002, s 215(1), Sch 21, para 32; words "local authority" in square brackets substituted by the Local Education Authorities and Children's Services Authorities (Integration of Functions) Order 2010, SI 2010/1158, art 5, Sch 2, Pt 2, para 41(1), (5)(a).

Sub-s (10) is amended as follows:

Paras (za), (zb) inserted by the Health and Social Care Act 2012, s 55(2), Sch 5, para 75(a).

Para (a) repealed by the Health and Social Care Act 2012, s 55(2), Sch 5, para 75(b).

In para (b), words in first (outer) pair of square brackets substituted by the National Health Service (Consequential Provisions) Act 2006, s 2, Sch 1, paras 177, 180(b), and words in second (inner) pair of square brackets substituted by the Health and Social Care Act 2012, s 55(2), Sch 5, para 75(c).

Para (bb) inserted by the Health Act 1999 (Supplementary, Consequential etc Provisions) Order 2000, SI 2000/90, art 3(1), Sch 1, para 30(1), (3), and repealed by the Health and Social Care Act 2012, s 55(2), Sch 5, para 75(d).

In para (c), words in first (outer) pair of square brackets substituted by the National Health Service (Consequential Provisions) Act 2006, s 2, Sch 1, paras 177, 180(d), words in second (inner) pair of square brackets substituted by the Health and Social Care Act 2012, s 55(2), Sch 5, para 75(e), and words in italics repealed by the Health and Social Care Act 2012, s 179(6), Sch 14, Pt 2, paras 68, 70, as from a day to be appointed.

Para (ca) inserted by the Health and Social Care (Community Health and Standards) Act 2003, s 34, Sch 4, paras 99, 1
Para (cb) inserted by SI 2007/961, art 3, Schedule, para 27(1), (4).
Para (cc) inserted by the Health and Social Care Act 2012, s 249, Sch 17, para 6(1), (3).
Para (cd) inserted by the Health and Social Care Act 2012, s 277, Sch 19, para 6(1), (3).
Paras (d), (e) (and the word immediately preceding para (e)) repealed by the Health and Social Care (Community Health and Standards) Act 2003, ss 190(2), 196, Sch 13, para 8, Sch 14, Pts 4, 7.
Para (dd) inserted by the Health Protection Agency Act 2004, s 11(1), Sch 3, para 13, and repealed by the Health and Social Care Act 2012, s 56(4), Sch 7, para 9.
Sub-s (11): added by SI 2010/1158, art 5(1), Sch 2, Pt 2, para 41(1), (5)(b).
Orders: as of 15 May 2019, no Orders had been made under this section but, by virtue of s 241 of, and Sch 2, Pt I, paras 1–4 to, this Act, the Employment Protection (National Health Service) Order 1996, SI 1996/638, has effect as if made under this section.

[1.1134]
219 Reinstatement or re-engagement of dismissed employee
(1) Regulations made by the Secretary of State may make provision—
(a) for preserving the continuity of a person's period of employment for the purposes of this Chapter or for the purposes of this Chapter as applied by or under any other enactment specified in the regulations, or
(b) for modifying or excluding the operation of section 214 subject to the recovery of any such payment as is mentioned in that section,

in cases where . . . a dismissed employee is reinstated [re-engaged or otherwise re-employed] by his employer or by a successor or associated employer of that employer [in any circumstances prescribed by the regulations].
(2)–(4) . . .

NOTES
Sub-s (1): words omitted repealed, words in first pair of square brackets substituted, and words in second pair of square brackets inserted, by the Employment Rights (Dispute Resolution) Act 1998, s 15, Sch 1, para 25(1), (2), Sch 2.
Sub-ss (2)–(4): repealed by the Employment Rights (Dispute Resolution) Act 1998, s 15, Sch 1, para 25(1), (3), Sch 2.
Regulations: the Employment Protection (Continuity of Employment) Regulations 1996, SI 1996/3147 at **[2.270]**; the Employment Protection (Continuity of Employment) (Amendment) Regulations 2001, SI 2001/1188.

CHAPTER II A WEEK'S PAY

Introductory

[1.1135]
220 Introductory
The amount of a week's pay of an employee shall be calculated for the purposes of this Act in accordance with this Chapter.

Employments with normal working hours

[1.1136]
221 General
(1) This section and sections 222 and 223 apply where there are normal working hours for the employee when employed under the contract of employment in force on the calculation date.
(2) Subject to section 222, if the employee's remuneration for employment in normal working hours (whether by the hour or week or other period) does not vary with the amount of work done in the period, the amount of a week's pay is the amount which is payable by the employer under the contract of employment in force on the calculation date if the employee works throughout his normal working hours in a week.
(3) Subject to section 222, if the employee's remuneration for employment in normal working hours (whether by the hour or week or other period) does vary with the amount of work done in the period, the amount of a week's pay is the amount of remuneration for the number of normal working hours in a week calculated at the average hourly rate of remuneration payable by the employer to the employee in respect of the period of twelve weeks ending—
(a) where the calculation date is the last day of a week, with that week, and
(b) otherwise, with the last complete week before the calculation date.

(4) In this section references to remuneration varying with the amount of work done includes remuneration which may include any commission or similar payment which varies in amount.
(5) This section is subject to sections 227 and 228.

[1.1137]
222 Remuneration varying according to time of work
(1) This section applies if the employee is required under the contract of employment in force on the calculation date to work during normal working hours on days of the week, or at times of the day, which differ from week to week or over a longer period so that the remuneration payable for, or apportionable to, any week varies according to the incidence of those days or times.
(2) The amount of a week's pay is the amount of remuneration for the average number of weekly normal working hours at the average hourly rate of remuneration.
(3) For the purposes of subsection (2)—
(a) the average number of weekly hours is calculated by dividing by twelve the total number of the employee's normal working hours during the relevant period of twelve weeks, and

(b) the average hourly rate of remuneration is the average hourly rate of remuneration payable by the employer to the employee in respect of the relevant period of twelve weeks.

(4) In subsection (3) "the relevant period of twelve weeks" means the period of twelve weeks ending—

(a) where the calculation date is the last day of a week, with that week, and

(b) otherwise, with the last complete week before the calculation date.

(5) This section is subject to sections 227 and 228.

[1.1138]
223 Supplementary

(1) For the purposes of sections 221 and 222, in arriving at the average hourly rate of remuneration, only—

(a) the hours when the employee was working, and

(b) the remuneration payable for, or apportionable to, those hours,

shall be brought in.

(2) If for any of the twelve weeks mentioned in sections 221 and 222 no remuneration within subsection (1)(b) was payable by the employer to the employee, account shall be taken of remuneration in earlier weeks so as to bring up to twelve the number of weeks of which account is taken.

(3) Where—

(a) in arriving at the average hourly rate of remuneration, account has to be taken of remuneration payable for, or apportionable to, work done in hours other than normal working hours, and

(b) the amount of that remuneration was greater than it would have been if the work had been done in normal working hours (or, in a case within section 234(3), in normal working hours falling within the number of hours without overtime),

account shall be taken of that remuneration as if the work had been done in such hours and the amount of that remuneration had been reduced accordingly.

Employments with no normal working hours

[1.1139]
224 Employments with no normal working hours

(1) This section applies where there are no normal working hours for the employee when employed under the contract of employment in force on the calculation date.

(2) The amount of a week's pay is the amount of the employee's average weekly remuneration in the period of twelve weeks ending—

(a) where the calculation date is the last day of a week, with that week, and

(b) otherwise, with the last complete week before the calculation date.

(3) In arriving at the average weekly remuneration no account shall be taken of a week in which no remuneration was payable by the employer to the employee and remuneration in earlier weeks shall be brought in so as to bring up to twelve the number of weeks of which account is taken.

(4) This section is subject to sections 227 and 228.

The calculation date

[1.1140]
225 Rights during employment

(1) Where the calculation is for the purposes of section 30, the calculation date is—

(a) where the employee's contract has been varied, or a new contract entered into, in connection with a period of short-time working, the last day on which the original contract was in force, and

(b) otherwise, the day in respect of which the guarantee payment is payable.

(2) Where the calculation is for the purposes of section 53 or 54, the calculation date is the day on which the employer's notice was given.

(3) Where the calculation is for the purposes of section 56, the calculation date is the day of the appointment.

[(3A) Where the calculation is for the purposes of section 57ZF, the calculation date is the day of the appointment.]

[(3B) Where the calculation is for the purposes of section 57ZK or 57ZM, the calculation date is the day of the appointment.]

(4) Where the calculation is for the purposes of section 62, the calculation date is the day on which the time off was taken or on which it is alleged the time off should have been permitted.

[(4A) Where the calculation is for the purposes of section 63B, the calculation date is the day on which the time off was taken or on which it is alleged the time off should have been permitted.]

[(4B) Where the calculation is for the purposes of section 63J, the calculation date is the day on which the section 63D application was made.]

(5) Where the calculation is for the purposes of section 69—

(a) in the case of an employee suspended on medical grounds, the calculation date is the day before that on which the suspension begins, and

(b) in the case of an employee suspended on maternity grounds, the calculation date is—

[(i) where the day before that on which the suspension begins falls during a period of ordinary or additional maternity leave, the day before the beginning of that period,]

(ii) otherwise, the day before that on which the suspension begins.

[(6) Where the calculation is for the purposes of section 80I, the calculation date is the day on which the application under section 80F was made.]

NOTES

Sub-ss (3A), (3B): inserted by the Children and Families Act 2014, ss 127(2)(c), 128(2)(d), as from 1 October 2014 (in relation to sub-s (3A)), and as from 5 April 2015 (in relation to sub-s (3B)).

Sub-s (4A): inserted by the Teaching and Higher Education Act 1998, s 44(1), Sch 3, paras 10, 14.

Sub-s (4B): inserted by the Apprenticeships, Skills, Children and Learning Act 2009, s 40(5), Sch 1, paras 1, 8, as from 6 April 2010 (except in relation to small employers and their employees), and as from a day to be appointed (otherwise) (as to the meaning of "small employers" etc, see further the notes at **[1.937]**).

Sub-s (5): sub-para (b)(i) substituted by the Employment Relations Act 1999, s 9, Sch 4, Pt III, paras 1, 5, 39.

Sub-s (6): added by the Employment Act 2002, s 53, Sch 7, paras 24, 45.

[1.1141]

226 Rights on termination

(1) Where the calculation is for the purposes of section 88 or 89, the calculation date is the day immediately preceding the first day of the period of notice required by section 86(1) or (2).

(2) Where the calculation is for the purposes of section 93, 117 or 125, the calculation date is—

(a) if the dismissal was with notice, the date on which the employer's notice was given, and

(b) otherwise, the effective date of termination.

(3) Where the calculation is for the purposes of section [112, 119, 120[, 121 or 124]], the calculation date is—

(a) . . .

(b) if by virtue of subsection (2) or (4) of section 97 a date later than the effective date of termination as defined in subsection (1) of that section is to be treated for certain purposes as the effective date of termination, the effective date of termination as so defined, and

(c) otherwise, the date specified in subsection (6).

(4) Where the calculation is for the purposes of section 147(2), the calculation date is the day immediately preceding the first of the four, or six, weeks referred to in section 148(2).

(5) Where the calculation is for the purposes of section 162, the calculation date is—

(a) . . .

(b) if by virtue of subsection (5) of section 145 a date is to be treated for certain purposes as the relevant date which is later than the relevant date as defined by the previous provisions of that section, the relevant date as so defined, and

(c) otherwise, the date specified in subsection (6).

(6) The date referred to in subsections (3)(c) and (5)(c) is the date on which notice would have been given had—

(a) the contract been terminable by notice and been terminated by the employer giving such notice as is required by section 86 to terminate the contract, and

(b) the notice expired on the effective date of termination, or the relevant date,

(whether or not those conditions were in fact fulfilled).

NOTES

Sub-s (3): words in first (outer) pair of square brackets substituted by the Employment Act 2002, s 53, Sch 7, paras 24, 46; words in second (inner) pair of square brackets substituted by the Unfair Dismissal (Variation of the Limit of Compensatory Award) Order 2013, SI 2013/1949, art 3; para (a) repealed by the Employment Relations Act 1999, ss 9, 44, Sch 4, Pt III, paras 1, 5, 40, Sch 9(2).

Sub-s (5): para (a) repealed by the Employment Relations Act 1999, ss 9, 44, Sch 4, Pt III, paras 1, 5, 40, Sch 9(2).

Maximum amount of week's pay

[1.1142]

227 Maximum amount

(1) For the purpose of calculating—

[(zza) an award of compensation under section 63J(1)(b),]

[(za) an award of compensation under section 80I(1)(b),]

(a) a basic award of compensation for unfair dismissal,

(b) an additional award of compensation for unfair dismissal,

[(ba) an award under section 112(5), or]

(c) a redundancy payment,

the amount of a week's pay shall not exceed [£525].

(2)–(4) . . .

NOTES

Sub-s (1) is amended as follows:

Para (zza) inserted by the Apprenticeships, Skills, Children and Learning Act 2009, s 40(5), Sch 1, paras 1, 9, as from 6 April 2010 (except in relation to small employers and their employees), and as from a day to be appointed (otherwise) (as to the meaning of "small employers" etc, see further the notes at **[1.937]**).

Para (za) inserted by the Employment Act 2002, s 53, Sch 7, paras 24, 47(1), (2).

Para (ba) substituted (for the original word "or" at the end of para (b)) by s 53 of, and Sch 7, paras 24, 47(1), (3) to, the 2002 Act.

Sum in square brackets substituted by the Employment Rights (Increase of Limits) Order 2019, SI 2019/324, art 3, Schedule, as from 6 April 2019, in relation to any case where the appropriate date (as defined in the order) falls on or after that date (see SI 2019/324, art 4 at **[2.2117]**). Previous sums were as follows: £508 as from 6 April 2018 (see SI 2018/194); £489 as from 6 April 2017 (see SI 2017/175); £479 as from 6 April 2016 (see SI 2016/288); £475 as from 6 April 2015 (see SI 2015/226); £464 as from 6 April 2014 (see SI 2014/382); £450 as from 1 February 2013 (see SI 2012/3007); £430 as from 1 February 2012 (see SI 2011/3006); £400 as from 1 February 2011 (see SI 2010/2926); and £380 as from 1 October 2009 (see SI 2009/1903).

in each case where the appropriate date fell after the commencement date). This sum may be varied by the Secretary of State (see the Employment Relations Act 1999, s 34(1)(a), (3)(a) at **[1.1258]**).
Sub-ss (2)–(4): repealed by the Employment Relations Act 1999, ss 36(1)(a), 44, Sch 9(10).

Miscellaneous

[1.1143]
228 New employments and other special cases

(1) In any case in which the employee has not been employed for a sufficient period to enable a calculation to be made under the preceding provisions of this Chapter, the amount of a week's pay is the amount which fairly represents a week's pay.

(2) In determining that amount the [employment tribunal]—
- (a) shall apply as nearly as may be such of the preceding provisions of this Chapter as it considers appropriate, and
- (b) may have regard to such of the considerations specified in subsection (3) as it thinks fit.

(3) The considerations referred to in subsection (2)(b) are—
- (a) any remuneration received by the employee in respect of the employment in question,
- (b) the amount offered to the employee as remuneration in respect of the employment in question,
- (c) the remuneration received by other persons engaged in relevant comparable employment with the same employer, and
- (d) the remuneration received by other persons engaged in relevant comparable employment with other employers.

(4) The Secretary of State may by regulations provide that in cases prescribed by the regulations the amount of a week's pay shall be calculated in such manner as may be so prescribed.

NOTES

Sub-s (2): words in square brackets substituted by the Employment Rights (Dispute Resolution) Act 1998, s 1(2)(a).
Regulations: as of 15 May 2019, no Regulations had been made under this section.

[1.1144]
229 Supplementary

(1) In arriving at—
- (a) an average hourly rate of remuneration, or
- (b) average weekly remuneration,

under this Chapter, account shall be taken of work for a former employer within the period for which the average is to be taken if, by virtue of Chapter I of this Part, a period of employment with the former employer counts as part of the employee's continuous period of employment.

(2) Where under this Chapter account is to be taken of remuneration or other payments for a period which does not coincide with the periods for which the remuneration or other payments are calculated, the remuneration or other payments shall be apportioned in such manner as may be just.

CHAPTER III OTHER INTERPRETATION PROVISIONS

[1.1145]
230 Employees, workers etc

(1) In this Act "employee" means an individual who has entered into or works under (or, where the employment has ceased, worked under) a contract of employment.

(2) In this Act "contract of employment" means a contract of service or apprenticeship, whether express or implied, and (if it is express) whether oral or in writing.

(3) In this Act "worker" (except in the phrases "shop worker" and "betting worker") means an individual who has entered into or works under (or, where the employment has ceased, worked under)—
- (a) a contract of employment, or
- (b) any other contract, whether express or implied and (if it is express) whether oral or in writing, whereby the individual undertakes to do or perform personally any work or services for another party to the contract whose status is not by virtue of the contract that of a client or customer of any profession or business undertaking carried on by the individual;

and any reference to a worker's contract shall be construed accordingly.

(4) In this Act "employer", in relation to an employee or a worker, means the person by whom the employee or worker is (or, where the employment has ceased, was) employed.

(5) In this Act "employment"—
- (a) in relation to an employee, means (except for the purposes of section 171) employment under a contract of employment, and
- (b) in relation to a worker, means employment under his contract;

and "employed" shall be construed accordingly.

[(6) This section has effect subject to sections 43K[, 47B(3) *and 49B(10)*]; and for the purposes of Part XIII so far as relating to Part IVA or section 47B, "worker", "worker's contract" and, in relation to a worker, "employer", "employment" and "employed" have the extended meaning given by section 43K.]

[(7) This section has effect subject to section 75K(3) and (5).]

NOTES

Sub-s (6): added by the Public Interest Disclosure Act 1998, ss 15(1), 18(2); words in square brackets substituted by the Small Business, Enterprise and Employment Act 2015, s 149(1), (3), as from 26 May 2015; for the words in italics there are substituted the words ", 49B(10) and 49C(12)" by the Children and Social Work Act 2017, s 32(1), (5), as from a day to be appointed.

Sub-s (7): added by the Children and Families Act 2014, s 126, Sch 7, paras 29, 41, as from 30 June 2014.

[1.1146]
231 Associated employers

For the purposes of this Act any two employers shall be treated as associated if—

(a) one is a company of which the other (directly or indirectly) has control, or

(b) both are companies of which a third person (directly or indirectly) has control;

and "associated employer" shall be construed accordingly.

[1.1147]
232 Shop workers

(1) In this Act "shop worker" means an employee who, under his contract of employment, is or may be required to do shop work.

(2) In this Act "shop work" means work in or about a shop . . . on a day on which the shop is open for the serving of customers.

(3) Subject to subsection (4), in this Act "shop" includes any premises where any retail trade or business is carried on.

(4) Where premises are used mainly for purposes other than those of retail trade or business and would not (apart from subsection (3)) be regarded as a shop, only such part of the premises as—

(a) is used wholly or mainly for the purposes of retail trade or business, or

(b) is used both for the purposes of retail trade or business and for the purposes of wholesale trade and is used wholly or mainly for those two purposes considered together,

is to be regarded as a shop for the purposes of this Act.

(5) In subsection (4)(b) "wholesale trade" means the sale of goods for use or resale in the course of a business or the hire of goods for use in the course of a business.

(6) In this section "retail trade or business" includes—

(a) the business of a barber or hairdresser,

(b) the business of hiring goods otherwise than for use in the course of a trade or business, and

(c) retail sales by auction,

but does not include catering business or the sale at theatres and places of amusement of programmes, catalogues and similar items.

(7) In subsection (6) "catering business" means—

(a) the sale of meals, refreshments or [alcohol] [. . .] for consumption on the premises on which they are sold, or

(b) the sale of meals or refreshments prepared to order for immediate consumption off the premises;

and in paragraph (a) ["alcohol" has the same meaning as in the Licensing Act 2003] [except that in Scotland "alcohol" has the meaning given in section 2 of the Licensing (Scotland) Act 2005].

(8) In this Act—

"notice period", in relation to an opted-out shop worker, has the meaning given by section 41(3),

"opted-out", in relation to a shop worker, shall be construed in accordance with section 41(1) and (2),

"opting-in notice", in relation to a shop worker, has the meaning given by section 36(6),

"opting-out notice", in relation to a shop worker, has the meaning given by section 40(2), and

"protected", in relation to a shop worker, shall be construed in accordance with section 36(1) to (5).

NOTES

Sub-s (2): words omitted repealed by the Sunday Working (Scotland) Act 2003, s 1(1), (3)(a).

Sub-s (7): word in first pair of square brackets in para (a) substituted by the Licensing Act 2003, s 198(1), Sch 6, para 114(a); words omitted from para (a) originally inserted by the Sunday Working (Scotland) Act 2003, s 1(1), (3)(b)(i), and repealed by the Licensing (Scotland) Act 2005 (Consequential Provisions) Order 2009, SSI 2009/248, art 2(1), Sch 1, Pt 1, para 7(a); penultimate words in square brackets substituted by the Licensing Act 2003, s 198(1), Sch 6, para 114(b); final words in square brackets substituted by SSI 2009/248, art 2(1), Sch 1, Pt 1, para 7(b).

[1.1148]
[233 Betting workers

(1) In this Act "betting worker" means an employee who under his contract of employment is or may be required to do betting work.

(2) In this Act "betting work" means—

(a) work which consists of or includes dealing with betting transactions at a track in England or Wales and which is carried out for a person who holds a general betting operating licence, a pool betting operating licence or a horse-race pool betting operating licence, and

(b) work on premises in respect of which a betting premises licence has effect at a time when the premises are used for betting transactions.

(3) In subsection (2) "betting transactions" includes the collection or payment of winnings.

(4) Expressions used in this section and in the Gambling Act 2005 have the same meaning in this section as in that Act.

(5) In this Act—

"notice period", in relation to an opted-out betting worker, has the meaning given by section 41(3),

"opted-out", in relation to a betting worker, shall be construed in accordance with section 41(1) and (2),

"opting-in notice", in relation to a betting worker, has the meaning given by section 36(6),

"opting-out notice", in relation to a betting worker, has the meaning given by section 40(2), and

"protected", in relation to a betting worker, shall be construed in accordance with section 36(1) to (5).]

NOTES

Substituted by the Gambling Act 2005, s 356(1), Sch 16, Pt 2, para 11.

[1.1149]

234 Normal working hours

(1) Where an employee is entitled to overtime pay when employed for more than a fixed number of hours in a week or other period, there are for the purposes of this Act normal working hours in his case.

(2) Subject to subsection (3), the normal working hours in such a case are the fixed number of hours.

(3) Where in such a case—

(a) the contract of employment fixes the number, or minimum number, of hours of employment in a week or other period (whether or not it also provides for the reduction of that number or minimum in certain circumstances), and

(b) that number or minimum number of hours exceeds the number of hours without overtime,

the normal working hours are that number or minimum number of hours (and not the number of hours without overtime).

[1.1150]

235 Other definitions

(1) In this Act, except in so far as the context otherwise requires—

"act" and "action" each includes omission and references to doing an act or taking action shall be construed accordingly,

"basic award of compensation for unfair dismissal" shall be construed in accordance with section 118,

"business" includes a trade or profession and includes any activity carried on by a body of persons (whether corporate or unincorporated),

"childbirth" means the birth of a living child or the birth of a child whether living or dead after twenty-four weeks of pregnancy,

"collective agreement" has the meaning given by section 178(1) and (2) of the Trade Union and Labour Relations (Consolidation) Act 1992,

"conciliation officer" means an officer designated by the Advisory, Conciliation and Arbitration Service under section 211 of that Act,

"dismissal procedures agreement" means an agreement in writing with respect to procedures relating to dismissal made by or on behalf of one or more independent trade unions and one or more employers or employers' associations,

"employers' association" has the same meaning as in the Trade Union and Labour Relations (Consolidation) Act 1992,

"expected week of childbirth" means the week, beginning with midnight between Saturday and Sunday, in which it is expected that childbirth will occur,

"guarantee payment" has the meaning given by section 28,

"independent trade union" means a trade union which—

(a) is not under the domination or control of an employer or a group of employers or of one or more employers' associations, and

(b) is not liable to interference by an employer or any such group or association (arising out of the provision of financial or material support or by any other means whatever) tending towards such control,

"job", in relation to an employee, means the nature of the work which he is employed to do in accordance with his contract and the capacity and place in which he is so employed,

. . .

["local authority", in relation to the placement of children under section 22C of the Children Act 1989, has the same meaning as in that Act (see section 105(1) of that Act);

"local authority foster parent" has the same meaning as in the Children Act 1989 (see [section 105(1)] of that Act);

["parental bereavement leave" means leave under section 80EA;]

["paternity leave" means leave under section 80A or 80B,]

"position", in relation to an employee, means the following matters taken as a whole—

(a) his status as an employee,

(b) the nature of his work, and

(c) his terms and conditions of employment,

["protected disclosure" has the meaning given by section 43A,]

"redundancy payment" has the meaning given by Part XI,

"relevant date" has the meaning given by sections 145 and 153,

"renewal" includes extension, and any reference to renewing a contract or a fixed term shall be construed accordingly,

["section 63D application" has the meaning given by section 63D(2);]

["shared parental leave" means leave under section 75E or 75G,]

"statutory provision" means a provision, whether of a general or a special nature, contained in, or in any document made or issued under, any Act, whether of a general or special nature,

"successor", in relation to the employer of an employee, means (subject to subsection (2)) a person who in consequence of a change occurring (whether by virtue of a sale or other disposition or by operation of law) in the ownership of the undertaking, or of the part of the undertaking, for the purposes of which the employee was employed, has become the owner of the undertaking or part, "trade union" has the meaning given by section 1 of the Trade Union and Labour Relatior (Consolidation) Act 1992,

"week"—

(a) in Chapter I of this Part means a week ending with Saturday, and

(b) otherwise, except in [sections [75F, 75H,] 80A, 80B[, 80EA] and 86], means, in relation to an employee whose remuneration is calculated weekly by a week ending with a day other than Saturday, a week ending with that other day and, in relation to any other employee, a week ending with Saturday.

(2) The definition of "successor" in subsection (1) has effect (subject to the necessary modifications) in relation to a case where—

(a) the person by whom an undertaking or part of an undertaking is owned immediately before a change is one of the persons by whom (whether as partners, trustees or otherwise) it is owned immediately after the change, or

(b) the persons by whom an undertaking or part of an undertaking is owned immediately before a change (whether as partners, trustees or otherwise) include the persons by whom, or include one or more of the persons by whom, it is owned immediately after the change,

as it has effect where the previous owner and the new owner are wholly different persons.

[(2A) For the purposes of this Act a contract of employment is a "limited-term contract" if—

(a) the employment under the contract is not intended to be permanent, and

(b) provision is accordingly made in the contract for it to terminate by virtue of a limiting event.

(2B) In this Act, "limiting event", in relation to a contract of employment means—

(a) in the case of a contract for a fixed-term, the expiry of the term,

(b) in the case of a contract made in contemplation of the performance of a specific task, the performance of the task, and

(c) in the case of a contract which provides for its termination on the occurrence of an event (or the failure of an event to occur), the occurrence of the event (or the failure of the event to occur).]

(3) References in this Act to redundancy, dismissal by reason of redundancy and similar expressions shall be construed in accordance with section 139.

(4) In sections 136(2), 154 and 216(3) and paragraph 14 of Schedule 2 "lock-out" means—

(a) the closing of a place of employment,

(b) the suspension of work, or

(c) the refusal by an employer to continue to employ any number of persons employed by him in consequence of a dispute,

done with a view to compelling persons employed by the employer, or to aid another employer in compelling persons employed by him, to accept terms or conditions of or affecting employment.

(5) In sections 91(2), 140(2) and (3), 143(1), 144(2) and (3), 154 and 216(1) and (2) and paragraph 14 of Schedule 2 "strike" means—

(a) the cessation of work by a body of employed persons acting in combination, or

(b) a concerted refusal, or a refusal under a common understanding, of any number of employed persons to continue to work for an employer in consequence of a dispute,

done as a means of compelling their employer or any employed person or body of employed persons, or to aid other employees in compelling their employer or any employed person or body of employed persons, to accept or not to accept terms or conditions of or affecting employment.

NOTES

Sub-s (1) is amended as follows:

Definitions omitted repealed by the Employment Relations Act 1999, ss 9, 44, Sch 4, Pt III, paras 1, 5, 41, Sch 9(2).

Definitions "local authority" and "local authority foster parent" inserted by the Children and Families Act 2014, s 128(2)(e), as from 5 April 2015; words in square brackets in definition "local authority foster parent" substituted by the Social Services and Well-being (Wales) Act 2014 (Consequential Amendments) Regulations 2016, SI 2016/413, regs 143, 148, as from 6 April 2016.

Definition "parental bereavement leave" inserted, and figure ", 80EA" in definition "week" inserted by the Parental Bereavement (Leave and Pay) Act 2018, s 1(c), Schedule, Pt 3, paras 20, 28, as from a day to be appointed.

Definition "paternity leave" substituted (for the previous definition "ordinary or additional paternity leave") by the Children and Families Act 2014, s 126, Sch 7, paras 29, 42(a), as from 5 April 2015 (note that this amendment does not have effect in relation to (a) children whose expected week of birth ends on or before 4 April 2015, and (b) children placed for adoption on or before that date: see the Children and Families Act 2014 (Commencement No 3, Transitional Provisions and Savings) Order 2014, SI 2014/1640, art 16).

Definition "protected disclosure" inserted by the Public Interest Disclosure Act 1998, ss 15(2), 18(2).

Definition "section 63D application" inserted by the Apprenticeships, Skills, Children and Learning Act 2009, s 40(5), Sch 1, paras 1, 10, as from 6 April 2010 (except in relation to small employers and their employees), and as from a day to be appointed (otherwise) (as to the meaning of "small employers" etc, see further the notes at **[1.937]**).

Definition "shared parental leave" inserted, and words in square brackets in definition "week" inserted, by the Children and Families Act 2014, s 126, Sch 7, paras 29, 42(b), (c), as from 30 June 2014.

Sub-ss (2A), (2B): inserted by the Fixed-term Employees (Prevention of Less Favourable Treatment) Regulations 2002, SI 2002/2034, reg 11, Sch 2, Pt 1, para 3(1), (18) (except in relation to Government training schemes, agency workers and apprentices; see regs 18–20 of the 2002 Regulations at **[2.571]** et seq).

PART XV
GENERAL AND SUPPLEMENTARY

General

[1.1151]

236 Orders and regulations

(1) Any power conferred by any provision of this Act to make any order (other than an Order in Council) or regulations is exercisable by statutory instrument.

(2) A statutory instrument made under any power conferred by this Act to make an Order in Council or other order or regulations, except—

(a) an Order in Council or other order [or regulations] to which subsection (3) applies,

(b) an order under section 35 or Part II of Schedule 2, or

(c) an order made in accordance with section 208,

is subject to annulment in pursuance of a resolution of either House of Parliament.

(3) No recommendation shall be made to Her Majesty to make an Order in Council under section 192(3), and no order [or regulations] shall be made under section [27B,] [41A that include provision under subsection (4)(c) of that section,] [43FA (but see subsection (3A)),] [43K(4)], [47C, [49B,] [49C,] [63D, 63F(7),], 71, 72, 73, [75A, 75B,] [75E, 75F(16), 75G, 75H(16), (17) or (18), 76, [80A, . . . 80B[, 80EA], . . . 80G], 99,] *120(2), 124(2)*[, 125(7) or 205A(11) or (12)] or (subject to subsection (4)) section 209, unless a draft of the Order in Council[, order or regulations] has been laid before Parliament and approved by a resolution of each House of Parliament.

[(3A) Subsection (3) does not apply to regulations under section 43FA that contain only the provision mentioned in section 43FA(2), (3) or (4).]

(4) Subsection (3) does not apply to an order under section 209(1)(b) which specifies only provisions contained in Part XI.

(5) Any power conferred by this Act which is exercisable by statutory instrument includes power to make such incidental, supplementary or transitional provisions as appear to the authority exercising the power to be necessary or expedient.

NOTES

Sub-s (2): words in square brackets in para (a) inserted by the Employment Relations Act 1999, s 9, Sch 4, Pt III, paras 1, 5, 42(1), (2); para (c) repealed by the Employment Relations Act 1999, s 44, Sch 9(10), as from a day to be appointed.

Sub-s (3) is amended as follows:

Words "or regulations" in square brackets inserted by the Employment Relations Act 1999, s 9, Sch 4, Pt III, paras 5, 42(1), (3)(a).

Figure "27B," in square brackets inserted by the Small Business, Enterprise and Employment Act 2015, s 153(1), (3), as from 26 May 2015.

Words "41A that include provision under subsection (4)(c) of that section," in square brackets inserted by the Enterprise Act 2016, s 33, Sch 5, paras 1, 11, as from 4 May 2016.

Words "43FA (but see subsection (3A))," in square brackets inserted by the Small Business, Enterprise and Employment Act 2015, s 148(1), (3)(a), as from 1 January 2016.

Figure "43K(4)" in square brackets inserted by the Enterprise and Regulatory Reform Act 2013, s 20(8).

Figures from "47C," to "99," in square brackets originally substituted by the Employment Relations Act 1999, s 9, Sch 4, Pt III, paras 5, 42(1), (3)(b).

Figure "49B," in square brackets inserted by the Small Business, Enterprise and Employment Act 2015, s 149(1), (4), as from 26 May 2015.

Figure "49C," in square brackets inserted by the Children and Social Work Act 2017, s 32(1), (6), as from a day to be appointed.

Figures "63D, 63F(7)," in square brackets inserted by the Apprenticeships, Skills, Children and Learning Act 2009, s 40(5), Sch 1, paras 1, 11, as from 6 April 2010 (except in relation to small employers and their employees), and as from a day to be appointed (otherwise) (as to the meaning of "small employers" etc, see further the notes at **[1.937]**).

Figures "75A, 75B" in square brackets inserted by the Employment Act 2002, s 53, Sch 7, paras 24, 49.

Figures "75E, 75F(16), 75G, 75H(16), (17) or (18)," in square brackets inserted by the Children and Families Act 2014, s 117(2), as from 30 June 2014.

Figures in square brackets beginning with the figure "80A" and ending with the figure "80G" substituted (for the original figures "80A, 80B, 80G") by the Work and Families Act 2006, s 11(1), Sch 1, para 44.

Figure ", 80EA" inserted by the Parental Bereavement (Leave and Pay) Act 2018, s 1(a), Schedule, Pt 1, paras 1, 3, as from a day to be appointed.

Figures omitted repealed by the Children and Families Act 2014, s 126, Sch 7, paras 29, 43, as from 5 April 2015 (note that this amendment does not have effect in relation to (a) children whose expected week of birth ends on or before 4 April 2015, and (b) children placed for adoption on or before that date: see the Children and Families Act 2014 (Commencement No 3, Transitional Provisions and Savings) Order 2014, SI 2014/1640, art 16).

Figures "120(2), 124(2)" in italics repealed by the Employment Relations Act 1999, s 44, Sch 9(10), as from a day to be appointed.

Words ", 125(7) or 205A(11) or (12)" in square brackets substituted by the Growth and Infrastructure Act 2013, s 31(6).

Words ", order or regulations" in square brackets substituted by the Employment Relations Act 1999, s 9, Sch 4, Pt III, paras 5, 42(1), (3)(c).

Sub-s (3A): inserted by the Small Business, Enterprise and Employment Act 2015, s 148(1), (3)(b), as from 1 January 2016.

An order made in accordance with section 208: note that s 208 was repealed by the Employment Relations Act 1999, ss 36(2), 44, Sch 9(10).

[1.1152]

237 Financial provisions

There shall be paid out of the National Insurance Fund into the Consolidated Fund sums equal to the amount of—

(a) any expenses incurred by the Secretary of State in consequence of Part XI, and
(b) any expenses incurred by the Secretary of State (or by persons acting on his behalf) in exercising his functions under Part XII.

238, 239 *(Provision for arrangements for co-ordinating provisions of Northern Ireland and Isle of Man legislation corresponding to this Act (previously contained in ss 157, 158 of the 1978 Act) outside the scope of this work.)*

Final provisions

240 *(Introduces Sch 1 (consequential amendments).)*

[1.1153]
241 Transitionals, savings and transitory provisions
Schedule 2 (transitional provisions, savings and transitory provisions) shall have effect.

242 *(Introduces Sch 3 (repeals and revocations).)*

[1.1154]
243 Commencement
This Act shall come into force at the end of the period of three months beginning with the day on which it is passed.

[1.1155]
244 Extent
(1) Subject to the following provisions, this Act extends to England and Wales and Scotland but not to Northern Ireland.
(2) [Sections 36(2) and (4), 37(1) and (5), 38 and 39] extend to England and Wales only.
(3) Sections 201 and 238 (and sections 236 and 243, this section and section 245) extend to Northern Ireland (as well as to England and Wales and Scotland).
(4) Sections 240 and 242 and Schedules 1 and 3 have the same extent as the provisions amended or repealed by this Act.

NOTES
Sub-s (2): words in square brackets substituted by the Sunday Working (Scotland) Act 2003, s 1(1), (5).

[1.1156]
245 Short title
This Act may be cited as the Employment Rights Act 1996.

SCHEDULES

SCHEDULE 1

(Consequential Amendments – in so far as these are relevant, they have been incorporated at the appropriate place.)

SCHEDULE 2
TRANSITIONAL PROVISIONS, SAVINGS AND TRANSITORY PROVISIONS

Section 241

PART I
TRANSITIONAL PROVISIONS AND SAVINGS

General transitionals and savings

[1.1157]
1. The substitution of this Act for the provisions repealed or revoked by this Act does not affect the continuity of the law.

2. (1) Anything done, or having effect as done, (including the making of subordinate legislation) under or for the purposes of any provision repealed or revoked by this Act has effect as if done under or for the purposes of any corresponding provision of this Act.
(2) Sub-paragraph (1) does not apply to the making of any subordinate legislation to the extent that it is reproduced in this Act.

3. Any reference (express or implied) in this Act or any other enactment, or in any instrument or document, to a provision of this Act is (so far as the context permits) to be read as (according to the context) being or including in relation to times, circumstances and purposes before the commencement of this Act a reference to the corresponding provision repealed or revoked by this Act.

4. (1) Any reference (express or implied) in any enactment, or in any instrument or document, to a provision repealed or revoked by this Act is (so far as the context permits) to be read as (according to the context) being or including in relation to times, circumstances and purposes after the commencement of this Act a reference to the corresponding provision of this Act.

(2) In particular, where a power conferred by an Act is expressed to be exercisable in relation to enactments contained in Acts passed before or in the same Session as the Act conferring the power, the power is also exercisable in relation to provisions of this Act which reproduce such enactments.

5. Paragraphs 1 to 4 have effect in place of section 17(2) of the Interpretation Act 1978 (but are without prejudice to any other provision of that Act).

Preservation of old transitionals and savings

6. (1) The repeal by this Act of an enactment previously repealed subject to savings (whether or not in the repealing enactment) does not affect the continued operation of those savings.

(2) The repeal by this Act of a saving made on the previous repeal of an enactment does not affect the operation of the saving in so far as it remains capable of having effect.

(3) Where the purpose of an enactment repealed by this Act was to secure that the substitution of the provisions of the Act containing that enactment for provisions repealed by that Act did not affect the continuity of the law, the enactment repealed by this Act continues to have effect in so far as it is capable of doing so.

Employment particulars [for pre-TURERA employees]

7. (1) In this paragraph "pre-TURERA employee" means an employee whose employment with his employer began before 30th November 1993 (the day on which section 26 of the Trade Union Reform and Employment Rights Act 1993 came into force), whether or not the provisions of sections 1 to 6 of the Employment Protection (Consolidation) Act 1978, as they had effect before the substitution made by that section, applied to him before that date.

(2) Subject to the following provisions of this paragraph [and paragraph 7B], sections 1 to 7 of this Act do not apply to a pre-TURERA employee (but the provisions of sections 1 to 6 of the Employment Protection (Consolidation) Act 1978, as they had effect before the substitution made by section 26 of the Trade Union Reform and Employment Rights Act 1993, continue in force in his case).

(3) Where a pre-TURERA employee, at any time [before 6 April 2020]—

- (a) on or after the day on which this Act comes into force, and
- (b) either before the end of his employment or within the period of three months beginning with the day on which his employment ends,

requests from his employer a statement under section 1 of this Act, the employer shall (subject to section 5 and any other provision disapplying or having the effect of disapplying sections 1 to 4) be treated as being required by section 1 to give him a written statement under that section not later than two months after the request is made; and section 4 of this Act shall (subject to that) apply in relation to the employee after he makes the request.

(4) An employer is not required to give an employee a statement under section 1 pursuant to sub-paragraph (3)—

- (a) on more than one occasion, or
- (b) if he has already given him a statement pursuant to paragraph 3(3) of Schedule 9 to the Trade Union Reform and Employment Rights Act 1993.

(5) Where—

- (a) on or after the day on which this Act comes into force there is in the case of a pre-TURERA employee a change in any of the matters particulars of which would, had he been given a statement of particulars on 30th November 1993 under section 1 of the Employment Protection (Consolidation) Act 1978 (as substituted by section 26 of the Trade Union Reform and Employment Rights Act 1993), have been included or referred to in the statement, and
- (b) he has not previously requested a statement under sub-paragraph (3) or paragraph 3(3) of Schedule 9 to the Trade Union Reform and Employment Rights Act 1993,

subsections (1) and (6) of section 4 of this Act shall be treated (subject to section 5 and any other provision disapplying or having the effect of disapplying section 4) as requiring his employer to give him a written statement containing particulars of the change at the time specified in subsection (3) of section 4; and the other provisions of section 4 apply accordingly.

[Employment particulars for pre-6 April 2020 employees

7A. (1) In this paragraph an "existing employee" means an employee whose employment with his employer began on or after 30th November 1993 and before 6th April 2020.

(2) Subject to paragraph 7B, sections 1 to 7 of this Act apply to an existing employee without the amendments made by regulations 2 to 6 of the Employment Rights (Employment Particulars and Paid Annual Leave) (Amendment) Regulations 2018.

Request for employment particulars by pre-6 April 2020 employee or pre-TURERA employee

7B. (1) Where an existing employee (as defined in paragraph 7A(1)) or a pre-TURERA employee (as defined in paragraph 7(1)) at any time—

- (a) on or after 6 April 2020, and
- (b) either before the end of the employee's employment or within the period of three months beginning with the day on which the employee's employment ends,

requests from the employer a statement under section 1 of this Act, the employer shall (subject to section 5 and any other provisions disapplying or having the effect of disapplying sections 1 to 4) be treated as being required by section 1 to give him a written statement under that section not later than

1 month after the request is made and section 4 of this Act shall (subject to that) apply in relation to th employee after he makes the request.

(4) An employer is not required to give an existing employee or a pre-TURERA employee a statement under section 1 pursuant to sub-paragraph (1) on more than one occasion.

(5) Where—

(a) on or after 6 April 2020 there is in the case of an existing employee or a pre-TURERA employee a change in any of the matters particulars of which would, had they have been given a statement of particulars on or after 6 April 2020 under section 1 of this Act (as amended), have been included or referred to in the statement, and

(b) he has not previously requested a statement under sub-paragraph (1),

subsection (1) of section 4 of this Act shall be treated (subject to section 5 and any other provision disapplying or having the effect of disapplying section 4) as requiring his employer to give him a written statement containing particulars of the change at the time specified in subsection (3) of section 4; and the other provisions of section 4 apply accordingly.

(6) A reference in this paragraph to section 1 or section 4 is a reference to that section as amended by the Employment Rights (Employment Particulars and Paid Annual Leave) (Amendment) Regulations 2018.]

Monetary limits in old cases

8. In relation to any case in which (but for this Act) a limit lower than that set by Article 3 of the Employment Protection (Increase of Limits) Order 1995 would have applied in accordance with Article 4 of that Order, this Act has effect as if it reproduced that lower limit.

Shop workers and betting workers to whom old maternity provisions applied

9. (1) This paragraph applies where an employee exercised a right to return to work under Part III of the Employment Protection (Consolidation) Act 1978 at a time when the amendments of that Part made by the Trade Union Reform and Employment Rights Act 1993 did not have effect in her case (so that her right was a right to return to work in the job in which she was employed under the original contract of employment).

(2) Section 36(4) shall have effect as if for paragraph (b) there were substituted—

"(b) under her original contract of employment, she was a shop worker, or a betting worker, but was not employed to work only on Sunday."

(3) If the employee was employed as a shop worker under her original contract of employment, she shall not be regarded as failing to satisfy the condition in section 36(2)(a) or (c) or 41(1)(c) merely because during her pregnancy she was employed under a different contract of employment by virtue of section 60(2) of the Employment Protection (Consolidation) Act 1978 (as it had effect before the commencement of section 24 of the Trade Union Reform and Employment Rights Act 1993) or otherwise by reason of her pregnancy.

(4) In this paragraph, and in section 36(4)(b) as substituted by sub-paragraph (2), "original contract of employment" has the meaning given by section 153(1) of the Employment Protection (Consolidation) Act 1978 as originally enacted.

Validity of provisions deriving from certain regulations

10. Any question as to the validity of any of sections 47, 61, 62, 63 and 103, which derive from the Collective Redundancies and Transfer of Undertakings (Protection of Employment) (Amendment) Regulations 1995 made under subsection (2) of section 2 of the European Communities Act 1972, shall be determined as if those provisions were contained in regulations made under that subsection [before the repeal of that subsection by section 1 of the European Union (Withdrawal) Act 2018].

Unfair dismissal

11. Part X does not apply to a dismissal from employment under a contract for a fixed term of two years or more (not being a contract of apprenticeship) if—

(a) the contract was made before 28th February 1972, and

(b) the dismissal consists only of the expiry of that term without its being renewed.

Redundancy payments

12. (1) Section 135 does not apply to an employee who immediately before the relevant date is employed under a contract for a fixed term of two years or more (not being a contract of apprenticeship) if the contract was made before 6th December 1965.

(2) Section 197(3) does not apply if the contract was made before 6th December 1965.

Periods of employment

13. (1) The reference in section 215(2)(b) to a person being an employed earner for the purposes of the Social Security Contributions and Benefits Act 1992 in respect of whom a secondary Class 1 contribution was payable under that Act (whether or not it was in fact paid) shall be construed—

(a) as respects a week of employment after 1st June 1976 and before 1st July 1992, as a reference to a person being an employed earner for the purposes of the Social Security Act 1975 in respect of whom a secondary Class 1 contribution was payable under that Act (whether or not it was in fact paid),

(b) as respects a week of employment after 6th April 1975 and before 1st June 1976, as a reference to a person being an employed earner for the purposes of the Social Security Act 1975, and

(c) as respects a week of employment before 6th April 1975, as a reference to a person being an employee in respect of whom an employer's contribution was payable in respect of the corresponding contribution week (whether or not it was in fact paid).

(2) For the purposes of the application of sub-paragraph (1) to a week of employment where the corresponding contribution week began before 5th July 1948, an employer's contribution shall be treated as payable as mentioned in that sub-paragraph if such a contribution would have been so payable had the statutory provisions relating to national insurance in force on 5th July 1948 been in force in that contribution week.

(3) The references in subsection (4) of section 215 to the Social Security Contributions and Benefits Act 1992 include the Social Security Act 1975; and that subsection applies to any question arising whether an employer's contribution was or would have been payable as mentioned in sub-paragraph (1) or (2).

(4) In this paragraph—

"employer's contribution" has the same meaning as in the National Insurance Act 1965, and

"corresponding contribution week", in relation to a week of employment, means a contribution week (within the meaning of that Act) of which so much as falls within the period beginning with midnight between Sunday and Monday and ending with Saturday also falls within that week of employment.

14. (1) Subject to paragraph 13 and sub-paragraphs (2) and (3) of this paragraph, Chapter I of Part XIV applies to periods before this Act comes into force as it applies to later periods.

(2) If, during the whole or any part of a week beginning before 6th July 1964, an employee was absent from work—

(a) because he was taking part in a strike, or

(b) because of a lock-out by his employer,

the week counts as a period of employment.

(3) Any week which counted as a period of employment in the computation of a period of employment for the purposes of the Employment Protection (Consolidation) Act 1978 counts as a period of employment for the purposes of this Act; and any week which did not break the continuity of a person's employment for the purposes of that Act shall not break the continuity of a period of employment for the purposes of this Act.

NOTES

Para 7: words in square brackets inserted by the Employment Rights (Employment Particulars and Paid Annual Leave) (Amendment) Regulations 2018, SI 2018/1378, reg 9(1), (2), as from 6 April 2020.

Paras 7A, 7B: inserted by SI 2018/1378, reg 9(1), (3), as from 6 April 2020.

Para 10: words in square brackets inserted by the Employment Rights (Amendment) (EU Exit) Regulations 2019, SI 2019/535, reg 2(1), Sch 1, Pt 1, paras 1, 3, as from exit day (as defined in the European Union (Withdrawal) Act 2018, s 20).

PART II
TRANSITORY PROVISIONS

[1.1158]

15. . . .

Armed forces

16. (1) If section 31 of the Trade Union Reform and Employment Rights Act 1993 has not come into force before the commencement of this Act, this Act shall have effect until the relevant commencement date as if for section 192 there were substituted—

"192 Armed forces

(1) Section 191—

(a) does not apply to service as a member of the naval, military or air forces of the Crown, but

(b) does apply to employment by an association established for the purposes of Part XI of the Reserve Forces Act 1996."

(2) The reference in sub-paragraph (1) to the relevant commencement date is a reference—

(a) if an order has been made before the commencement of this Act appointing a day after that commencement as the day on which section 31 of the Trade Union Reform and Employment Rights Act 1993 is to come into force, to the day so appointed, and

(b) otherwise, to such day as the Secretary of State may by order appoint.

17. (1) If Part XI of the Reserve Forces Act 1996 has not come into force before the commencement of this Act, section 192 of this Act shall have effect until the relevant commencement date as if for "Part XI of the Reserve Forces Act 1996" there were substituted "Part VI of the Reserve Forces Act 1980".

(2) The reference in sub-paragraph (1) to the relevant commencement date is a reference—

(a) if an order has been made before the commencement of this Act appointing a day after that commencement as the day on which Part XI of the Reserve Forces Act 1996 is to come into force, to the day so appointed, and

(b) otherwise, to such day as the Secretary of State may by order appoint.

Disability discrimination

18. . . .

NOTES

Para 15: repealed by the Statute Law (Repeals) Act 2004 (it was previously spent).

Para 16: section 31 of the Trade Union Reform and Employment Rights Act 1993 was not brought into force prior to its repeal by Sch 3 to this Act, and as of 15 May 2019, no Orders had been made under para 16(2)(b). Accordingly, s 192 of this Act (at **[1.1107]**) has effect as stated in para 16(1) until a date to be appointed by Order under para 16(2)(b).

Para 17: the Reserve Forces Act 1996, Pt XI was brought into force on 1 April 1997 by the Reserve Forces Act 1996 (Commencement No 1) Order 1997, SI 1997/305. That Order was made on 19 February 1997 (ie, after the commencement of this Act on 22 August 1996). As of 15 May 2019, no Orders had been made under para 17(2)(b). This paragraph can be regarded as spent.

Para 18: repealed by the Employment Rights (Dispute Resolution) Act 1998, s 15, Sch 2.

SCHEDULE 3

(Repeals and revocations – in so far as these are relevant, they have been incorporated.)

PROTECTION FROM HARASSMENT ACT 1997

(1997 c 40)

ARRANGEMENT OF SECTIONS

England and Wales

Scotland

General

An Act to make provision for protecting persons from harassment and similar conduct

[21 March 1997]

NOTES

Regulatory functions: the regulatory functions conferred by, or under, this Act are subject to the Legislative and Regulatory Reform Act 2006, ss 21, 22; see the Legislative and Regulatory Reform (Regulatory Functions) Order 2007, SI 2007/3544 (made under s 24(2) of the 2006 Act) for details.

Sections 1–7 of this Act apply only to England and Wales; ss 8–11 apply only to Scotland: see s 14 *post*.

See *Harvey* L(3)(C)(1).

England and Wales

[1.1159]

1 Prohibition of harassment

(1) A person must not pursue a course of conduct—

(a) which amounts to harassment of another, and

(b) which he knows or ought to know amounts to harassment of the other.

[(1A) A person must not pursue a course of conduct—

(a) which involves harassment of two or more persons, and

(b) which he knows or ought to know involves harassment of those persons, and

(c) by which he intends to persuade any person (whether or not one of those mentioned above)—

(i) not to do something that he is entitled or required to do, or

(ii) to do something that he is not under any obligation to do.]

(2) For the purposes of this section [or section 2A(2)(c)], the person whose course of conduct is in question ought to know that it amounts to [or involves] harassment of another if a reasonable person in possession of the same information would think the course of conduct amounted to [or involved] harassment of the other.

(3) Subsection (1) [or (1A)] does not apply to a course of conduct if the person who pursued it shows—

(a) that it was pursued for the purpose of preventing or detecting crime,

(b) that it was pursued under any enactment or rule of law or to comply with any condition or requirement imposed by any person under any enactment, or

(c) that in the particular circumstances the pursuit of the course of conduct was reasonable.

NOTES

Sub-s (1A): inserted by the Serious Organised Crime and Police Act 2005, s 125(1), (2)(a).

Sub-s (2): words in first pair of square brackets inserted by the Protection of Freedoms Act 2012, s 115(1), Sch 9, Pt 11, para 143(1), (2); words in second and third pairs of square brackets inserted by the Serious Organised Crime and Police Act 2005, s 125(1), (2)(b).

Sub-s (3): words in square brackets inserted by the Serious Organised Crime and Police Act 2005, s 125(1), (2)(c).

2, 2A, 2B (*Ss 2 (Offence of harassment), 2A (Offence of stalking) and 2B (Power of entry in relation to offence of stalking) (as inserted by the Protection of Freedoms Act 2012, ss 111, 112) are outside the scope of this work.*)

[1.1160]

3 Civil remedy

(1) An actual or apprehended breach of [section 1(1)] may be the subject of a claim in civil proceedings by the person who is or may be the victim of the course of conduct in question.

(2) On such a claim, damages may be awarded for (among other things) any anxiety caused by the harassment and any financial loss resulting from the harassment.

(3) Where—

(a) in such proceedings the High Court or [the county] court grants an injunction for the purpose of restraining the defendant from pursuing any conduct which amounts to harassment, and
(b) the plaintiff considers that the defendant has done anything which he is prohibited from doing by the injunction,

the plaintiff may apply for the issue of a warrant for the arrest of the defendant.
(4) An application under subsection (3) may be made—
(a) where the injunction was granted by the High Court, to a judge of that court, and
(b) where the injunction was granted by [the county] court, to a judge [of that] court.
(5) The judge . . . to whom an application under subsection (3) is made may only issue a warrant if—
(a) the application is substantiated on oath, and
(b) the judge . . . has reasonable grounds for believing that the defendant has done anything which he is prohibited from doing by the injunction.
(6) Where—
(a) the High Court or [the county] court grants an injunction for the purpose mentioned in subsection (3)(a), and
(b) without reasonable excuse the defendant does anything which he is prohibited from doing by the injunction,

he is guilty of an offence.
(7) Where a person is convicted of an offence under subsection (6) in respect of any conduct, that conduct is not punishable as a contempt of court.
(8) A person cannot be convicted of an offence under subsection (6) in respect of any conduct which has been punished as a contempt of court.
(9) A person guilty of an offence under subsection (6) is liable—
(a) on conviction on indictment, to imprisonment for a term not exceeding five years, or a fine, or both, or
(b) on summary conviction, to imprisonment for a term not exceeding six months, or a fine not exceeding the statutory maximum, or both.

NOTES

Sub-s (1): words in square brackets substituted by the Serious Organised Crime and Police Act 2005, s 125(1), (4).

Sub-ss (3), (4), (6): words in square brackets substituted by the Crime and Courts Act 2013, s 17(5), Sch 9, Pt 2, para 39(a), (b).

Sub-s (5): words omitted repealed by the Crime and Courts Act 2013, s 17(5), Sch 9, Pt 2, para 39(c).

3A *(S 3A (Injunctions to protect persons from harassment within section 1(1A)) is outside the scope of this work.)*

[1.1161]

4 Putting people in fear of violence

(1) A person whose course of conduct causes another to fear, on at least two occasions, that violence will be used against him is guilty of an offence if he knows or ought to know that his course of conduct will cause the other so to fear on each of those occasions.
(2) For the purposes of this section, the person whose course of conduct is in question ought to know that it will cause another to fear that violence will be used against him on any occasion if a reasonable person in possession of the same information would think the course of conduct would cause the other so to fear on that occasion.
(3) It is a defence for a person charged with an offence under this section to show that—
(a) his course of conduct was pursued for the purpose of preventing or detecting crime,
(b) his course of conduct was pursued under any enactment or rule of law or to comply with any condition or requirement imposed by any person under any enactment, or
(c) the pursuit of his course of conduct was reasonable for the protection of himself or another or for the protection of his or another's property.
(4) A person guilty of an offence under this section is liable—
(a) on conviction on indictment, to imprisonment for a term not exceeding [ten years], or a fine, or both, or
(b) on summary conviction, to imprisonment for a term not exceeding six months, or a fine not exceeding the statutory maximum, or both.
(5) If on the trial on indictment of a person charged with an offence under this section the jury find him not guilty of the offence charged, they may find him guilty of an offence under section 2 [or 2A].
(6) The Crown Court has the same powers and duties in relation to a person who is by virtue of subsection (5) convicted before it of an offence under section 2 [or 2A] as a magistrates' court would have on convicting him of the offence.

NOTES

Sub-s (4): words in square brackets substituted (for the original words "five years") by the Policing and Crime Act 2017, s 175(1)(a), as from 3 April 2017. Note that s 175(3), (4) of the 2017 Act provide that this amendment applies only in relation to an offence committed on or after that date, and where the course of conduct constituting an offence is found to have occurred over a period of 2 or more days, or at some time during a period of 2 or more days, the offence must be taken to have been committed on the last of those days.

Sub-ss (5), (6): words in square brackets inserted by the Protection of Freedoms Act 2012, s 115(1), Sch 9, Pt 11, para 143(1), (3).

4A–6 (*Ss 4A (Stalking involving fear of violence or serious alarm or distress), 5 (Restraining orders on conviction) and 5A (Restraining orders on acquittal) are outside the scope of this work. S 6 amends the Limitation Act 1980, s 11 at* **[1.125]**.)

[1.1162]
7 Interpretation of this group of sections

(1) This section applies for the interpretation of [sections 1 to 5A].

(2) References to harassing a person include alarming the person or causing the person distress.

[(3) A "course of conduct" must involve—

(a) in the case of conduct in relation to a single person (see section 1(1)), conduct on at least two occasions in relation to that person, or

(b) in the case of conduct in relation to two or more persons (see section 1(1A)), conduct on at least one occasion in relation to each of those persons.]

[(3A) A person's conduct on any occasion shall be taken, if aided, abetted, counselled or procured by another—

(a) to be conduct on that occasion of the other (as well as conduct of the person whose conduct it is); and

(b) to be conduct in relation to which the other's knowledge and purpose, and what he ought to have known, are the same as they were in relation to what was contemplated or reasonably foreseeable at the time of the aiding, abetting, counselling or procuring.]

(4) "Conduct" includes speech.

[(5) References to a person, in the context of the harassment of a person, are references to a person who is an individual.]

NOTES

Sub-s (1): words in square brackets substituted by the Domestic Violence, Crime and Victims Act 2004, s 58(1), Sch 10, para 44.

Sub-s (3): substituted by the Serious Organised Crime and Police Act 2005, s 125(1), (7)(a).

Sub-s (3A): inserted by the Criminal Justice and Police Act 2001, s 44(1).

Sub-s (5): added by the Serious Organised Crime and Police Act 2005, s 125(1), (7)(b).

Scotland

[1.1163]
8 Harassment

(1) Every individual has a right to be free from harassment and, accordingly, a person must not pursue a course of conduct which amounts to harassment of another and—

(a) is intended to amount to harassment of that person; or

(b) occurs in circumstances where it would appear to a reasonable person that it would amount to harassment of that person.

[(1A) Subsection (1) is subject to section 8A.]

(2) An actual or apprehended breach of subsection (1) may be the subject of a claim in civil proceedings by the person who is or may be the victim of the course of conduct in question; and any such claim shall be known as an action of harassment.

(3) For the purposes of this section—

"conduct" includes speech;

"harassment" of a person includes causing the person alarm or distress; and

a course of conduct must involve conduct on at least two occasions.

(4) It shall be a defence to any action of harassment to show that the course of conduct complained of—

(a) was authorised by, under or by virtue of any enactment or rule of law;

(b) was pursued for the purpose of preventing or detecting crime; or

(c) was, in the particular circumstances, reasonable.

(5) In an action of harassment the court may, without prejudice to any other remedies which it may grant—

(a) award damages;

(b) grant—

(i) interdict or interim interdict;

(ii) if it is satisfied that it is appropriate for it to do so in order to protect the person from further harassment, an order, to be known as a "non-harassment order", requiring the defender to refrain from such conduct in relation to the pursuer as may be specified in the order for such period (which includes an indeterminate period) as may be so specified,

but a person may not be subjected to the same prohibitions in an interdict or interim interdict and a non-harassment order at the same time.

(6) The damages which may be awarded in an action of harassment include damages for any anxiety caused by the harassment and any financial loss resulting from it.

(7) Without prejudice to any right to seek review of any interlocutor, a person against whom a non-harassment order has been made, or the person for whose protection the order was made, may apply to the court by which the order was made for revocation of or a variation of the order and, on any such application, the court may revoke the order or vary it in such manner as it considers appropriate.

(8) . . .

NOTES

Sub-s (1A): inserted by the Domestic Abuse (Scotland) Act 2011, s 1(1).

Sub-s (8): repealed by the Damages (Scotland) Act 2011, s 16, Sch 2.

8A–11 *(Ss 8A (Harassment amounting to domestic abuse), 9 (Breach of non-harassment order), 10 (Limitation), and 11 (Non-harassment order following criminal offence) are outside the scope of this work.)*

General

12, 13 *(Ss 12 (National security, etc) and 13 (Corresponding provision for Northern Ireland) are outside the scope of this work.)*

[1.1164]
14 Extent
(1) Sections 1 to 7 extend to England and Wales only.
(2) Sections 8 to 11 extend to Scotland only.
(3) This Act (except section 13) does not extend to Northern Ireland.

[1.1165]
15 Commencement
(1) Sections 1, 2, 4, 5 and 7 to 12 are to come into force on such day as the Secretary of State may by order made by statutory instrument appoint.
(2) Sections 3 and 6 are to come into force on such day as the Lord Chancellor may by order made by statutory instrument appoint.
(3) Different days may be appointed under this section for different purposes.

NOTES

Orders: the Protection from Harassment Act 1997 (Commencement) (No 1) Order 1997, SI 1997/1418; the Protection from Harassment Act 1997 (Commencement) (No 2) Order 1997, SI 1997/1498; the Protection from Harassment Act 1997 (Commencement) (No 3) Order 1998, SI 1998/1902.

[1.1166]
16 Short title
This Act may be cited as the Protection from Harassment Act 1997.

EMPLOYMENT RIGHTS (DISPUTE RESOLUTION) ACT 1998

(1998 c 8)

An Act to rename industrial tribunals and amend the law relating to those tribunals; to amend the law relating to dismissal procedures agreements and other alternative methods of resolving disputes about employment rights; to provide for the adjustment of awards of compensation for unfair dismissal in cases where no use is made of internal procedures for appealing against dismissal; to make provision about cases involving both unfair dismissal and disability discrimination; and for connected purposes

[8 April 1998]

NOTES

Most of this Act comprises amendments to the Employment Tribunals Act 1996 and related legislation. The relevant amendments are incorporated in the text and noted below. Where these are enabling provisions any Orders are noted to the text of the provisions as inserted or amended.

See *Harvey* PI.

PART I
EMPLOYMENT TRIBUNALS

Renaming of tribunals

[1.1167]
1 Industrial tribunals to be known as employment tribunals
(1) Industrial tribunals are renamed employment tribunals.
(2) Accordingly, the Industrial Tribunals Act 1996 may be cited as the Employment Tribunals Act 1996; and (wherever they occur in any enactment)—
- (a) for the words "industrial tribunal" substitute "employment tribunal",
- (b) for the words "industrial tribunals" substitute "employment tribunals",
- (c) for the words "the Industrial Tribunals Act 1996" substitute "the Employment Tribunals Act 1996",
- (d) for the words "President of the Industrial Tribunals (England and Wales)" substitute "President of the Employment Tribunals (England and Wales)", and
- (e) for the words "President of the Industrial Tribunals (Scotland)" substitute "President of the Employment Tribunals (Scotland)".

2–6 *(S 2 amends the Employment Tribunals Act 1996, s 7 at* **[1.740]***; ss 3–5 amend s 4 of the 1996 Act at* **[1.733]***; s 6 substitutes the Trade Union and Labour Relations (Consolidation) Act 1992, s 87 at* **[1.390]***.)*

PART II
OTHER METHODS OF DISPUTE RESOLUTION

7–12 *(S 7 inserts the Trade Union and Labour Relations (Consolidation) Act 1992, s 212A at* **[1.531]***; ss 8–10 amend s 288 of the 1992 Act at* **[1.622]***, the Employment Rights Act 1996, s 203 at* **[1.1116]***, and amended the Sex Discrimination Act 1975, s 77, the Race Relations Act 1976, s 72, and the Disability Discrimination Act 1995, s 9 (all repealed); s 11 amends the Employment Rights Act 1996, ss 166(2) and 168(1) at* **[1.1081]**, **[1.1083]** *and is spent in so far as it amended the Employment Tribunals Act 1996, s 18(1) as it has been superseded by a subsequent amendment; s 12 amends ss 110 and 184 of the Employment Rights Act 1996 at* **[1.1027]** *and* **[1.1099]**.*)*

PART III
AWARDS OF COMPENSATION

13, 14 *(S 13 inserted the Employment Rights Act 1996, s 127A (repealed), and was itself repealed by the Employment Act 2002, s 54, Sch 8; s 14(1) (repealed) originally amended s 117 of the 1996 Act; s 14(2) amends s 126 of the 1996 Act, at* **[1.1044]**.*)*

PART IV
SUPPLEMENTARY AND GENERAL

15, 16 *(S 15 introduces Sch 1 (minor and consequential amendments) and Sch 2 (repeals); s 16 relates to Northern Ireland.)*

[1.1168]
17 Commencement, transitional provisions and savings

(1) The provisions of this Act (apart from section 16, this section and section 18 and paragraph 17(2) of Schedule 1) shall not come into force until such day as the Secretary of State may by order made by statutory instrument appoint; and different days may be appointed for different purposes.
(2) An order under subsection (1) may contain such transitional provisions and savings as appear to the Secretary of State to be appropriate.
(3) The amendment made by paragraph 17(2) of Schedule 1 shall be deemed always to have had effect.
(4) . . .

NOTES

Sub-s (4): repealed by the Statute Law (Repeals) Act 2004.

Orders: the Employment Rights (Dispute Resolution) Act 1998 (Commencement No 1 and Transitional and Saving Provisions) Order 1998, SI 1998/1658.

[1.1169]
18 Short title

This Act may be cited as the Employment Rights (Dispute Resolution) Act 1998.

SCHEDULES 1 & 2

(Schs 1 and 2 contain minor and consequential amendments and repeals which, in so far as relevant to this work, have been incorporated at the appropriate place.)

PUBLIC INTEREST DISCLOSURE ACT 1998

(1998 c 23)

An Act to protect individuals who make certain disclosures of information in the public interest; to allow such individuals to bring action in respect of victimisation; and for connected purposes

[2 July 1998]

NOTES

This Act consists almost entirely of provisions adding to or amending existing legislation, principally the Employment Rights Act 1996. The provisions so added or amended are incorporated at the relevant point in the text and are noted below. The provisions of the Act not brought into force at Royal Assent (see s 18(4) below) were brought into force on 2 July 1999 (see SI 1999/1547). See also the Public Interest Disclosure (Prescribed Persons) Order 2014, SI 2014/2418 at **[2.1513]** (made under the Employment Rights Act 1996, s 43F, as inserted by s 1 of this Act).

See *Harvey* CIII, DII(H).

1–17 *(S 1 inserts the Employment Rights Act 1996, Pt IVA (ss 43A–43L) at* **[1.866]–[1.878]***, s 2 inserts 47B of the 1996 Act at* **[1.888]***; s 3 amends s 48 of the 1996 Act at* **[1.894]***; s 4 amends s 49 of the 1996 Act at* **[1.895]***; s 5 inserts s 103A of the 1996 Act at* **[1.1014]***; s 6 amends s 105 of the 1996 Act at* **[1.1023]**· *s 7 amends s 108 of the 1996 Act at* **[1.1026]** *and amended s 109 of that Act (repealed); s 8 repealed b the Employment Relations Act 1999, s 44, Sch 9(11); s 9 amends ss 128 and 129 of the 1996 Act* **[1.1045]** *and* **[1.1046]***; s 10 amends s 191 of the 1996 Act at* **[1.1106]***; s 11 repealed by the Employm Relations Act 1999, s 44, Sch 9(12); s 12 (which amended the repealed s 196 of the 1996 Act) is sp* *s 13 repealed by the Police Reform Act 2002, ss 37(3), 107(2), Sch 8; s 14 amends s 205 of the 1996 Act at* **[1.1118]**; *s 15 amends ss 230, 235 of the 1996 Act at* **[1.1145]**, **[1.1150]**; *s 16 amends the Trade Union and Labour Relations (Consolidation) Act 1992, s 237 at* **[1.568]**; *s 17 (Northern Ireland) outside the scope of this work.)*

[1.1170]
18 Short title, interpretation, commencement and extent
(1) This Act may be cited as the Public Interest Disclosure Act 1998.
(2) In this Act "the 1996 Act" means the Employment Rights Act 1996.
(3) Subject to subsection (4), this Act shall come into force on such day or days as the Secretary of State may by order made by statutory instrument appoint, and different days may be appointed for different purposes.
(4) The following provisions shall come into force on the passing of this Act—
  (a) section 1 so far as relating to the power to make an order under section 43F of the 1996 Act,
  (b) . . .
  (c) section 17, and
  (d) this section.
(5) This Act, except section 17, does not extend to Northern Ireland.

NOTES
Sub-s (4): para (b) repealed by the Employment Relations Act 1999, s 44, Sch 9(11).
Orders: the Public Interest Disclosure Act 1998 (Commencement) Order 1999, SI 1999/1547.

NATIONAL MINIMUM WAGE ACT 1998

(1998 c 39)

ARRANGEMENT OF SECTIONS

An Act to make provision for and in connection with a national minimum wage; to provide for the amendment of certain enactments relating to the remuneration of persons employed in agriculture; and for connected purposes

[31 July 1998]

NOTES

This Act is reproduced in full apart from ss 5–8 (which relate to the Low Pay Commission), 25–27, 29 and 30 (amendments to other Acts, incorporated therein), 46 and 47 (which relate to agricultural wages), 50 (publicity for the National Minimum Wage) and 53 (repeals and revocations) and Schs 1–3 (the Low Pay Commission, agricultural wages and repeals and revocations). The principal Regulations under this Act are now the National Minimum Wage Regulations 2015, SI 2015/621 at **[2.1860]** which revoked and replaced the National Minimum Wage Regulations 1999, SI 1999/584, as from 6 April 2015.

Employment Appeal Tribunal: an appeal lies to the Employment Appeal Tribunal on any question of law arising from any decision of, or in any proceedings before, an employment tribunal under or by virtue of this Act; see the Employment Tribunals Act 1996, s 21(1)(ga) at **[1.764]**.

An employee who is dismissed is to be regarded as unfairly dismissed if the reason (or, if more than one, the principal reason) for the dismissal is that any action was taken, or was proposed to be taken, by or on behalf of the employee with a view to enforcing, or otherwise securing the benefit of, any right conferred by, or by virtue of, this Act for which the remedy for its infringement is by way of complaint to an employment tribunal; see the Employment Rights Act 1996, s 104A at **[1.1016]**.

Note: the enforcement provisions of this Act are applied with modifications for the purposes of the Agricultural Sector (Wales) Act 2014; see s 5 of the 2014 Act at **[1.1911]**.

See *Harvey* BI(4).

Entitlement to the national minimum wage

[1.1171]

1 Workers to be paid at least the minimum wage

(1) A person who qualifies for the national minimum wage shall be remunerated by his employer in respect of his work in any pay reference period at a rate which is not less than the national minimum wage.

(2) A person qualifies for the national minimum wage if he is an individual who—

(a) is a worker;

(b) is working, or ordinarily works, in the United Kingdom under his contract; and

(c) has ceased to be of compulsory school age.

(3) The national minimum wage shall be such single hourly rate as the Secretary of State may from time to time prescribe.

(4) For the purposes of this Act a "pay reference period" is such period as the Secretary of State may prescribe for the purpose.

(5) Subsections (1) to (4) above are subject to the following provisions of this Act.

NOTES

Regulations: the National Minimum Wage Regulations 2015, SI 2015/621 at **[2.1860]**; reg 4 of which (the national living wage) prescribes £8.21 an hour as the single hourly rate of the national minimum wage for a worker who is aged 25 years or over (from 1 April 2019). See reg 4 of the 2015 Regulations at **[2.1863]** (as amended by the National Minimum Wage (Amendment) Regulations 2019, SI 2019/603, reg 2(1), (2)). The other rates of the national minimum wage as of 1 April 2019, are £7.70 an hour for those aged 21 or over, £6.15 an hour for those aged 18–20, £4.35 an hour for those aged 16 or 17, and £3.90 an hour for apprentices (see reg 4A of the 2015 Regulations). The National Minimum Wage (Amendment) Regulations 2015, SI 2015/1724, the National Minimum Wage (Amendment) Regulations 2016, SI 2016/68, the National Minimum Wage (Amendment) Regulations 2017, SI 2017/465, the National Minimum Wage (Amendment) Regulations 2018, SI 2018/455, and the National Minimum Wage (Amendment) Regulations 2019, SI 2019/603 were also made under this section.

The previous rates under the 2015 Regulations were: £7.83 (from 1 April 2018), £7.50 (from 1 April 2017); £7.20 (from 1 April 2016); £6.50 (as from the commencement of the 2015 Regulations on 6 April 2015 (note that this was the same rate that had effect as from 1 October 2014 – see below)). The previous rates (by virtue of the National Minimum Wage Regulations 1999, SI 1999/584) were: £3.60 (from 1 April 1999); £3.70 (from 1 October 2000); £4.10 (from 1 October 2001); £4.20 (from 1 October 2002); £4.50 (from 1 October 2003); £4.85 (from 1 October 2004); £5.05 (from 1 October 2005); £5.35 (from 1 October 2006); £5.52 (from 1 October 2007); £5.73 (from 1 October 2008); £5.80 (from 1 October 2009); £5.93 (from 1 October 2010); £6.08 (from 1 October 2011); £6.19 (from 1 October 2012); £6.31 (as from 1 October 2013); £6.50 (as from 1 October 2014). For provisions regarding those who do not qualify for the national minimum wage, see Part 6 of the 2015 Regulations (Exclusions) at **[2.1912]** et seq. For provisions relating to those who qualify at different rates, see regs 4A, 4B, 5 (at **[2.1864]** et seq).

Regulations relating to the national minimum wage

[1.1172]

2 Determination of hourly rate of remuneration

(1) The Secretary of State may by regulations make provision for determining what is the hourly rate at which a person is to be regarded for the purposes of this Act as remunerated by his employer in respect of his work in any pay reference period.

(2) The regulations may make provision for determining the hourly rate in cases where—

(a) the remuneration, to the extent that it is at a periodic rate, is at a single rate;

(b) the remuneration is, in whole or in part, at different rates applicable at different times or in different circumstances;

(c) the remuneration is, in whole or in part, otherwise than at a periodic rate or rates;

(d) the remuneration consists, in whole or in part, of benefits in kind.

(3) The regulations may make provision with respect to—

(a) circumstances in which, times at which, or the time for which, a person is to be treated as, or as not, working, and the extent to which a person is to be so treated;

(b) the treatment of periods of paid or unpaid absence from, or lack of, work and of remuneration in respect of such periods.

(4) The provision that may be made by virtue of paragraph (a) of subsection (3) above includes provision for or in connection with—

(a) treating a person as, or as not, working for a maximum or minimum time, or for a proportion of the time, in any period;

(b) determining any matter to which that paragraph relates by reference to the terms of an agreement.

(5) The regulations may make provision with respect to—

(a) what is to be treated as, or as not, forming part of a person's remuneration, and the extent to which it is to be so treated;

(b) the valuation of benefits in kind;

(c) the treatment of deductions from earnings;

(d) the treatment of any charges or expenses which a person is required to bear.

(6) The regulations may make provision with respect to—

(a) the attribution to a period, or the apportionment between two or more periods, of the whole or any part of any remuneration or work, whether or not the remuneration is received or the work is done within the period or periods in question;

(b) the aggregation of the whole or any part of the remuneration for different periods;

(c) the time at which remuneration is to be treated as received or accruing.

(7) Subsections (2) to (6) above are without prejudice to the generality of subsection (1) above.

(8) No provision shall be made under this section which treats the same circumstances differently in relation to—

(a) different areas;

(b) different sectors of employment;

(c) undertakings of different sizes;

(d) persons of different ages; or

(e) persons of different occupations.

NOTES

Regulations: the National Minimum Wage Regulations 2015, SI 2015/621 at **[2.1860]**; the National Minimum Wage (Amendment) Regulations 2015, SI 2015/1724; the National Minimum Wage (Amendment) (No 2) Regulations 2016, SI 2016/953; the National Minimum Wage (Amendment) Regulations 2017, SI 2017/465; the National Minimum Wage (Amendment) Regulations 2018, SI 2018/455; the National Minimum Wage (Amendment) Regulations 2019, SI 2019/603.

[1.1173]

3 Exclusion of, and modifications for, certain classes of person

(1) This section applies to persons who have not attained the age of 26.

[(1A) This section also applies to persons who have attained the age of 26 who are—

(a) within the first six months after the commencement of their employment with an employer by whom they have not previously been employed;

(b) participating in a scheme under which shelter is provided in return for work;

(c) participating in a scheme designed to provide training, work experience or temporary work;

(d) participating in a scheme to assist in the seeking or obtaining of work; . . .

(e) [undertaking] a course of higher education requiring attendance for a period of work experience; [or

(f) undertaking a course of further education requiring attendance for a period of work experience].]

(2) The Secretary of State may by regulations make provision in relation to any of the persons to whom this section applies—

(a) preventing them being persons who qualify for the national minimum wage; or

(b) prescribing an hourly rate for the national minimum wage other than the single hourly rate for the time being prescribed under section 1(3) above.

(3) No provision shall be made under subsection (2) above which treats persons differently in relation to—

(a) different areas;

(b) different sectors of employment;

(c) undertakings of different sizes; or

(d) different occupations.

(4) If any description of persons who have attained the age of 26 is added by regulations under section 4 below to the descriptions of person to whom this section applies, no provision shall be made under subsection (2) above which treats persons of that description differently in relation to different ages over 26.

NOTES

Sub-s (1A): inserted by the National Minimum Wage Act 1998 (Amendment) Regulations 1999, SI 1999/583, reg 2; word omitted from para (d) repealed, word in square brackets in para (e) substituted, and para (f) (and the word immediately preceding it) inserted, by the National Minimum Wage Act 1998 (Amendment) Regulations 2007, SI 2007/2042, reg 2.

Regulations: the National Minimum Wage Regulations 2015, SI 2015/621 at **[2.1860]**; the National Minimum Wage (Amendment) Regulations 2015, SI 2015/1724; the National Minimum Wage (Amendment) Regulations 2016, SI 2016/68; the National Minimum Wage (Amendment) (No 2) Regulations 2016, SI 2016/953; the National Minimum Wage (Amendment) Regulations 2017, SI 2017/465; the National Minimum Wage (Amendment) Regulations 2018, SI 2018/455; the National Minimum Wage (Amendment) Regulations 2019, SI 2019/603.

[1.1174]

4 Power to add to the persons to whom section 3 applies

(1) The Secretary of State may by regulations amend section 3 above by adding descriptions of persons who have attained the age of 26 to the descriptions of person to whom that section applies.

(2) No amendment shall be made under subsection (1) above which treats persons differently in relation to—

(a) different areas;

(b) different sectors of employment;

(c) undertakings of different sizes;

(d) different ages over 26; or

(e) different occupations.

NOTES

Regulations: National Minimum Wage Act 1998 (Amendment) Regulations 1999, SI 1999/583; the National Minimum Wage Act 1998 (Amendment) Regulations 2007, SI 2007/2042.

5–8 *((Establishment of, and references to, the Low Pay Commission) outside the scope of this work.)*

Records

[1.1175]

9 Duty of employers to keep records

For the purposes of this Act, the Secretary of State may by regulations make provision requiring employers—

(a) to keep, in such form and manner as may be prescribed, such records as may be prescribed; and

(b) to preserve those records for such period as may be prescribed.

NOTES

Regulations: the National Minimum Wage Regulations 2015, SI 2015/621 at [2.1860].

[1.1176]

10 Worker's right of access to records

(1) A worker may, in accordance with the following provisions of this section,—

(a) require his employer to produce any relevant records; and

(b) inspect and examine those records and copy any part of them.

(2) The rights conferred by subsection (1) above are exercisable only if the worker believes on reasonable grounds that he is or may be being, or has or may have been, remunerated for any pay reference period by his employer at a rate which is less than the national minimum wage.

(3) The rights conferred by subsection (1) above are exercisable only for the purpose of establishing whether or not the worker is being, or has been, remunerated for any pay reference period by his employer at a rate which is less than the national minimum wage.

(4) The rights conferred by subsection (1) above are exercisable—

(a) by the worker alone; or

(b) by the worker accompanied by such other person as the worker may think fit.

(5) The rights conferred by subsection (1) above are exercisable only if the worker gives notice (a "production notice") to his employer requesting the production of any relevant records relating to such period as may be described in the notice.

(6) If the worker intends to exercise the right conferred by subsection (4)(b) above, the production notice must contain a statement of that intention.

(7) Where a production notice is given, the employer shall give the worker reasonable notice of the place and time at which the relevant records will be produced.

(8) The place at which the relevant records are produced must be—

(a) the worker's place of work; or

(b) any other place at which it is reasonable, in all the circumstances, for the worker to attend to inspect the relevant records; or

(c) such other place as may be agreed between the worker and the employer.

(9) The relevant records must be produced—

(a) before the end of the period of fourteen days following the date of receipt of the production notice; or

(b) at such later time as may be agreed during that period between the worker and the employer.

(10) In this section—

"records" means records which the worker's employer is required to keep and, at the time of receipt of the production notice, preserve in accordance with section 9 above;

"relevant records" means such parts of, or such extracts from, any records as are relevant to establishing whether or not the worker has, for any pay reference period to which the records relate, been remunerated by the employer at a rate which is at least equal to the national minimum wage.

[1.1177]

11 Failure of employer to allow access to records

(1) A complaint may be presented to an employment tribunal by a worker on the ground that the employer—

(a) failed to produce some or all of the relevant records in accordance with subsections (8) and (9) of section 10 above; or

(b) failed to allow the worker to exercise some or all of the rights conferred by subsection (1)(b) or (4)(b) of that section.

(2) Where an employment tribunal finds a complaint under this section well-founded, the tribunal shall—

(a) make a declaration to that effect; and

(b) make an award that the employer pay to the worker a sum equal to 80 times the hourly amount of the national minimum wage (as in force when the award is made).

(3) An employment tribunal shall not consider a complaint under this section unless it is presented to the tribunal before the expiry of the period of three months following—

(a) the end of the period of fourteen days mentioned in paragraph (a) of subsection (9) of section 10 above; or

(b) in a case where a later day was agreed under paragraph (b) of that subsection, that later day.

(4) Where the employment tribunal is satisfied that it was not reasonably practicable for a complaint under this section to be presented before the expiry of the period of three months mentioned in subsection (3) above, the tribunal may consider the complaint if it is presented within such further period as the tribunal considers reasonable.

[(4A) Where the complaint is presented to an employment tribunal in England and Wales or Scotland, section 11A applies for the purposes of subsection (3).]

(5) Expressions used in this section and in section 10 above have the same meaning in this section as they have in that section.

NOTES

Sub-s (4A): inserted by the Enterprise and Regulatory Reform Act 2013, s 8, Sch 2, paras 36, 37.

Conciliation: employment tribunal proceedings under this section are "relevant proceedings" for the purposes of the conciliation provisions contained in the Employment Tribunals Act 1996, ss 18–18C; see s 18(1)(c) of the 1996 Act at **[1.757]**.

[1.1178]

[11A Extension of time limit to facilitate conciliation before institution of proceedings

(1) In this section—

(a) Day A is the day on which the worker concerned complies with the requirement in subsection (1) of section 18A of the Employment Tribunals Act 1996 (requirement to contact ACAS before instituting proceedings) in relation to the matter in respect of which the proceedings are brought, and

(b) Day B is the day on which the worker concerned receives or, if earlier, is treated as receiving (by virtue of regulations made under subsection (11) of that section) the certificate issued under subsection (4) of that section.

(2) In working out when the time limit set by section 11(3) expires the period beginning with the day after Day A and ending with Day B is not to be counted.

(3) If the time limit set by section 11(3) would (if not extended by this subsection) expire during the period beginning with Day A and ending one month after Day B, the time limit expires instead at the end of that period.

(4) The power conferred on the employment tribunal by subsection (4) of section 11 to extend the time limit set by subsection (3) of that section is exercisable in relation to that time limit as extended by this section.]

NOTES

Inserted by the Enterprise and Regulatory Reform Act 2013, s 8, Sch 2, paras 36, 38.

[1.1179]

12 Employer to provide worker with national minimum wage statement

(1) Regulations may make provision for the purpose of conferring on a worker the right to be given by his employer, at or before the time at which any payment of remuneration is made to the worker, a written statement.

(2) The regulations may make provision with respect to the contents of any such statement and may, in particular, require it to contain—

(a) prescribed information relating to this Act or any regulations under it; or

(b) prescribed information for the purpose of assisting the worker to determine whether he has been remunerated at a rate at least equal to the national minimum wage during the period to which the payment of remuneration relates.

(3) Any statement required to be given under this section to a worker by his employer may, if the worker is an employee, be included in the written itemised pay statement required to be given to him by his employer under section 8 of the Employment Rights Act 1996 or Article 40 of the Employment Rights (Northern Ireland) Order 1996, as the case may be.

(4) The regulations may make provision for the purpose of applying—

(a) sections 11 and 12 of the Employment Rights Act 1996 (references to employment tribunals and determination of references), or

(b) in relation to Northern Ireland, Articles 43 and 44 of the Employment Rights (Northern Ireland) Order 1996 (references to industrial tribunals and determination of references),

in relation to a worker and any such statement as is mentioned in subsection (1) above as they apply in relation to an employee and a statement required to be given to him by his employer under section 8 of that Act or Article 40 of that Order, as the case may be.

NOTES

Regulations: as of 15 May 2019, no Regulations had been made under this section.

Officers

[1.1180]

13 Appointment of officers

(1) The Secretary of State—

(a) may appoint officers to act for the purposes of this Act; and

(b) may, instead of or in addition to appointing any officers under this section, arrange with any [relevant authority for officers of that authority to] act for those purposes.

[(1A) The following are relevant authorities—

(a) any Minister of the Crown or government department;

(b) any body performing functions on behalf of the Crown;

(c) the Gangmasters and Labour Abuse Authority.]

(2) When acting for the purposes of this Act, an officer shall, if so required, produce some duly authenticated document showing his authority so to act.

(3) If it appears to an officer that any person with whom he is dealing while acting for the purposes of this Act does not know that he is an officer so acting, the officer shall identify himself as such to that person.

NOTES

Words in square brackets in sub-s (1) substituted, and sub-s (1A) inserted, by the Immigration Act 2016, s 11(1), Sch 2 paras 4, 5, as from 12 July 2016.

[1.1181]

14 Powers of officers

[(A1) This section does not apply to an officer acting for the purposes of this Act in relation to England and Wales if the officer is a labour abuse prevention officer within the meaning of section 114B of the Police and Criminal Evidence Act 1984 (PACE powers for labour abuse prevention officers).]

(1) An officer acting for the purposes of this Act shall have power for the performance of his duties—

(a) to require the production by a relevant person of any records required to be kept and preserved in accordance with regulations under section 9 above and to inspect and examine those records and to copy . . . them;

(b) to require a relevant person to furnish to him (either alone or in the presence of any other person, as the officer thinks fit) an explanation of any such records;

(c) to require a relevant person to furnish to him (either alone or in the presence of any other person, as the officer thinks fit) any additional information known to the relevant person which might reasonably be needed in order to establish whether this Act, or any enforcement notice under section 19 below, is being or has been complied with;

(d) at all reasonable times to enter any relevant premises in order to exercise any power conferred on the officer by paragraphs (a) to (c) above.

(2) No person shall be required under paragraph (b) or (c) of subsection (above to answer any question or furnish any information which might incriminate the person or, if [married or a civil partner, the person's spouse or civil partner].

(3) The powers conferred by subsection (1) above include power, on reasonable written notice, to require a relevant person—

(a) to produce any such records as are mentioned in paragraph (a) of that subsection to an officer at such time and place as may be specified in the notice; or

(b) to attend before an officer at such time and place as may be specified in the notice to furnish any such explanation or additional information as is mentioned in paragraph (b) or (c) of that subsection.

[(3A) The power of an officer to copy records under subsection (1)(a) includes a power to remove such records from the place where they are produced to him in order to copy them; but such records must be returned as soon as reasonably practicable to the relevant person by whom they are produced.]

(4) In this section "relevant person" means any person whom an officer acting for the purposes of this Act has reasonable cause to believe to be—

(a) the employer of a worker;

(b) a person who for the purposes of section 34 below is the agent or the principal;

(c) a person who supplies work to an individual who qualifies for the national minimum wage;

(d) a worker, servant or agent of a person falling within paragraph (a), (b) or (c) above; or

(e) a person who qualifies for the national minimum wage.

(5) In this section "relevant premises" means any premises which an officer acting for the purposes of this Act has reasonable cause to believe to be—

(a) premises at which an employer carries on business;

(b) premises which an employer uses in connection with his business (including any place used, in connection with that business, for giving out work to home workers, within the meaning of section 35 below); or

(c) premises of a person who for the purposes of section 34 below is the agent or the principal.

NOTES

Sub-s (A1): inserted by the Immigration Act 2016, s 11(1), Sch 2, paras 4, 6, as from 12 July 2016.

Sub-s (1): words omitted from para (a) repealed by the Employment Act 2008, s 10(1), (2), 20, Schedule, Pt 3.

Sub-s (2): words in square brackets substituted by the Civil Partnership Act 2004, s 261(1), Sch 27, para 155.

Sub-s (3A): inserted by the Employment Act 2008, s 10(1), (3).

Note that the Employment Act 2008, s 10(4) provides that nothing in this section (or Part 3 of the Schedule) affects this section as it has effect for the purposes of the Agricultural Wages (Scotland) Act 1949, or the Agricultural Wages (Regulation) (Northern Ireland) Order 1977 (SI 1977/2151).

Information

[1.1182]

15 Information obtained by officers

(1) This section applies to[—

(a)] any information obtained by an officer acting for the purposes of this Act, whether by virtue of paragraph (a) or paragraph (b) of section 13(1) above[, and

(b) any information obtained by an officer acting by virtue of section 26(2) of the Immigration Act 2016 (investigative functions in connection with labour market enforcement undertakings and orders)].

(2) Information to which this section applies vests in the Secretary of State.

(3) Information to which this section applies may be used for any purpose relating to this Act by—

(a) the Secretary of State; or

(b) any [eligible] relevant authority whose officer obtained the information.

(4) Information to which this section applies—

(a) may be supplied by, or with the authorisation of, the Secretary of State to any [eligible] relevant authority for any purpose relating to this Act; and

(b) may be used by the recipient for any purpose relating to this Act.

(5) Information supplied under subsection (4) above—

(a) shall not be supplied by the recipient to any other person or body unless it is supplied for the purposes of any civil or criminal proceedings relating to this Act; and

(b) shall not be supplied in those circumstances without the authorisation of the Secretary of State.

[(5A) Information to which this section applies—

(a) may be supplied by, or with the authorisation of, the Secretary of State to an officer acting for the purposes of the Employment Agencies Act 1973 for any purpose relating to that Act; and

(b) may be used by an officer acting for the purposes of that Act for any purpose relating to that Act.]

(5B) *(Inserted by the Employment Act (Northern Ireland) 2010 and applies to Northern Ireland only.)*

[(5C) Information to which this section applies—

(a) Secretary of State to an officer acting by virtue of section 26 of the Immigration Act 2016 (investigative functions in connection with labour market enforcement undertakings and orders); and

(b) may be used by an officer so acting for any purpose for which the officer is so acting.]

[(6) This section—

(a) does not limit the circumstances in which information may be supplied or used apart from this section; and

(b) is subject to section 148 of the Finance Act 2000 (use of minimum wage information).]

[(6A) Nothing in this section prevents a disclosure in accordance with section 16A below.]

(7) Subsection (2) above does not affect the title or rights of—

(a) any person whose property the information was immediately before it was obtained as mentioned in subsection (1) above; or

(b) any person claiming title or rights through or under such a person otherwise than by virtue of any power conferred by or under this Act.

(8) In this section ["eligible relevant authority" means any relevant authority within the meaning given by section 13(1A) which] is party to arrangements made with the Secretary of State which are in force under section 13(1)(b) above.

NOTES

Sub-s (1): para (a) designated as such, and para (b) (and the preceding word) added, by the Immigration Act 2016, s 31, Sch 3, para 7(1), (2), as from 12 July 2016.

Sub-ss (3), (4): word in square brackets inserted by the Immigration Act 2016, s 11(1), Sch 2, paras 4, 7(a), (b), as from 12 July 2016.

Sub-s (5A): inserted by the Employment Act 2008, s 18(1).

Sub-s (5C): inserted by the Immigration Act 2016, s 31, Sch 3, para 7(1), (3), as from 12 July 2016.

Sub-s (6): substituted by the Finance Act 2000, s 148(4).

Sub-s (6A): inserted by the Employment Relations Act 2004, s 57(1), Sch 1, para 40.

Sub-s (8): words in square brackets substituted by the Immigration Act 2016, s 11(1), Sch 2, paras 4, 7(c), as from 12 July 2016.

See further, as to the information to which this section applies, the Employment Relations Act 1999, s 39 at **[1.1261]**.

[1.1183]

16 Information obtained by agricultural wages officers

(1) This section applies to information which has been obtained by an officer acting for the purposes of any of the agricultural wages legislation.

(2) Information to which this section applies may, with the authorisation of the relevant authority, be supplied to the Secretary of State for use for any purpose relating to this Act.

(3) Information supplied under subsection (2) above may be supplied by the recipient to any Minister of the Crown, government department or other body if—

(a) arrangements made between the recipient and that Minister, department or body under section 13(1)(b) above are in force; and

(b) the information is supplied for any purpose relating to this Act.

(4) Except as provided by subsection (3) above, information supplied under subsection (2) or (3) above—

(a) shall not be supplied by the recipient to any other person or body unless it is supplied for the purposes of any civil or criminal proceedings relating to this Act; and

(b) shall not be supplied in those circumstances without the authorisation of the relevant authority.

(5) This section does not limit the circumstances in which information may be supplied or used apart from this section.

[(5A) Nothing in this section prevents a disclosure in accordance with section 16A below.]

(6) In this section—

"the agricultural wages legislation" means—

(a) the Agricultural Wages Act 1948;

(b) the Agricultural Wages (Scotland) Act 1949; and

(c) the Agricultural Wages (Regulation) (Northern Ireland) Order 1977;

"relevant authority" means—

(a) in relation to information obtained by an officer acting in England, the Minister of Agriculture, Fisheries and Food;

(b) in relation to information obtained by an officer acting in Wales, the Minister of the Crown with the function of appointing officers under section 12 of the Agricultural Wages Act 1948 in relation to Wales;

(c) *in relation to information obtained by an officer acting in an area which is partly in England and partly in Wales, the Ministers mentioned in paragraphs (a) and (b) above acting jointly;*

(d) in relation to information obtained by an officer acting in Scotland, the Minister of the Crown with the function of appointing officers under section 12 of the Agricultural Wages (Scotland) Act 1949; and

(e) in relation to information obtained by an officer acting in Northern Ireland, the Department of Agriculture for Northern Ireland.

NOTES

Sub-s (5A): inserted by the Employment Relations Act 2004, s 57(1), Sch 1, para 41.

Sub-s (6): words in italics repealed by the Enterprise and Regulatory Reform Act 2013, s 72(4), Sch 20, para 2, as from 1 October 2013 (in relation to England) and as from a day to be appointed (in relation to Wales).

Transfer of functions in relation to Wales: as to the transfer of functions under this section from Ministers of the Crown to the National Assembly for Wales, see the National Assembly for Wales (Transfer of Functions) Order 1999, SI 1999/672.

Minister of Agriculture, Fisheries and Food: the Ministry of Agriculture, Fisheries and Food was dissolved and the functions of the Minister were transferred to the Secretary of State by the Ministry of Agriculture, Fisheries and Food (Dissolution) Order 2002, SI 2002/794.

See further the Employment Relations Act 1999, s 39 at **[1.1261]**.

[1.1184]

[16A Disclosure of information by officers

(1) Subsection (2) applies to information obtained for the purposes of the relevant legislation by an enforcement officer so far as that information relates to an identifiable worker or agency worker.

(2) In order to enable or assist him to act for the purposes of the relevant legislation, the enforcement officer may disclose all or any of the information to the worker or, as the case may be, agency worker concerned.

(3) Subsection (4) applies to information obtained for the purposes of the relevant legislation by an enforcement officer so far as that information relates to an identifiable employer or person who is the agent or the principal for the purposes of section 34 below.

(4) In order to enable or assist him to act for the purposes of the relevant legislation, the officer may disclose all or any of the information to the employer, the agent or, as the case may be, the principal concerned.

(5) In this section—

"agency worker" shall be construed in accordance with section 34 below;

"enforcement officer" means—

(a) an officer acting for the purposes of this Act, whether by virtue of paragraph (a) or (b) of section 13(1) above;

(b) *an officer acting for the purposes of the Agricultural Wages Act 1948; or*

(c) an officer acting for the purposes of the Agricultural Wages (Regulation) (Northern Ireland) Order 1977;

"the relevant legislation" means—

(a) in relation to an enforcement officer acting for the purposes of this Act, this Act;

(b) *in relation to an enforcement officer acting for the purposes of the Agricultural Wages Act 1948, that Act; and*

(c) in relation to an enforcement officer acting for the purposes of the Agricultural Wages (Regulation) (Northern Ireland) Order 1977, that Order.]

NOTES

Inserted by the Employment Relations Act 2004, s 44.

Sub-s (5): words in italics repealed by the Enterprise and Regulatory Reform Act 2013, s 72(4), Sch 20, as from 1 October 2013 (in relation to England) and as from a day to be appointed (in relation to Wales).

Enforcement

[1.1185]

17 Non-compliance: worker entitled to additional remuneration

(1) If a worker who qualifies for the national minimum wage is remunerated for any pay reference period by his employer at a rate which is less than the national minimum wage, the worker shall [at any time ("the time of determination")] be taken to be entitled under his contract to be paid, as additional remuneration in respect of that period, [whichever is the higher of—

(a) the amount described in subsection (2) below, and

(b) the amount described in subsection (4) below].

(2) [The amount referred to in subsection (1)(a) above] is the difference between—

(a) the relevant remuneration received by the worker for the pay reference period; and

(b) the relevant remuneration which the worker would have received for that period had he been remunerated by the employer at a rate equal to the national minimum wage.

(3) In subsection (2) above, "relevant remuneration" means remuneration which falls to be brought into account for the purposes of regulations under section 2 above.

[(4) The amount referred to in subsection (1)(b) above is the amount determined by the formula—

$$(A / R1) \times R2$$

where—

A is the amount described in subsection (2) above,

R1 is the rate of national minimum wage which was payable in respect of the worker during the pay reference period, and

R2 is the rate of national minimum wage which would have been payable in respect of the worker during that period had the rate payable in respect of him during that period been determined by reference to regulations under section 1 and 3 above in force at the time of determination.

(5) Subsection (1) above ceases to apply to a worker in relation to any pay reference period when he is at any time paid the additional remuneration for that period to which he is at that time entitled under that subsection.

(6) Where any additional remuneration is paid to the worker under this section in relation to the pay reference period but subsection (1) above has not ceased to apply in relation to him, the amounts described in subsections (2) and (4) above shall be regarded as reduced by the amount of that remuneration.]

NOTES

Sub-s (1): words in first pair of square brackets inserted, and words in second pair of square brackets substituted, by the Employment Act 2008, s 8(1), (2).

Sub-s (2): words in square brackets substituted by the Employment Act 2008, s 8(1), (4).

Sub-ss (4)–(6): added by the Employment Act 2008, s 8(1), (5).

Note that the Employment Act 2008, s 8(7) provides that the amendments to this section do not affect the section as it has effect for the purposes of the Agricultural Wages (Scotland) Act 1949, or the Agricultural Wages (Regulation) (Northern Ireland) Order 1977 (SI 1977/2151).

[1.1186]

18 Enforcement in the case of special classes of worker

(1) If the persons who are the worker and the employer for the purposes of section 17 above would not (apart from this section) fall to be regarded as the worker and the employer for the purposes of—

(a) Part II of the Employment Rights Act 1996 (protection of wages), or

(b) in relation to Northern Ireland, Part IV of the Employment Rights (Northern Ireland) Order 1996,

they shall be so regarded for the purposes of the application of that Part in relation to the entitlement conferred by that section.

(2) In the application by virtue of subsection (1) above of—

(a) Part II of the Employment Rights Act 1996, or

(b) Part IV of the Employment Rights (Northern Ireland) Order 1996,

in a case where there is or was, for the purposes of that Part, no worker's contract between the persons who are the worker and the employer for the purposes of section 17 above, it shall be assumed that there is or, as the case may be, was such a contract.

(3) For the purpose of enabling the amount described as additional remuneration in subsection (1) of section 17 above to be recovered in civil proceedings on a claim in contract in a case where in fact there is or was no worker's contract between the persons who are the worker and the employer for the purposes of that section, it shall be assumed for the purpose of any civil proceedings, so far as relating to that amount, that there is or, as the case may be, was such a contract.

[1.1187]

[19 Notices of underpayment: arrears

(1) Subsection (2) below applies where an officer acting for the purposes of this Act is of the opinion that, on any day ("the relevant day"), a sum was due under section 17 above for any one or more pay reference periods ending before the relevant day to a worker who at any time qualified for the national minimum wage.

(2) Where this subsection applies, the officer may, subject to this section, serve a notice requiring the employer to pay to the worker, within the 28-day period, the sum due to the worker under section 17 above for any one or more of the pay reference periods referred to in subsection (1) above.

(3) In this Act, "notice of underpayment" means a notice under this section.

(4) A notice of underpayment must specify, for each worker to whom it relates—

(a) the relevant day in relation to that worker;

(b) the pay reference period or periods in respect of which the employer is required to pay a sum to the worker as specified in subsection (2) above;

(c) the amount described in section 17(2) above in relation to the worker in respect of each such period;

(d) the amount described in section 17(4) above in relation to the worker in respect of each of such period;

(e) the sum due under section 17 above to the worker for each such period.

(5) Where a notice of underpayment relates to more than one worker, the notice may identify the workers by name or by description.

(6) The reference in subsection (1) above to a pay reference period includes (subject to subsection (7) below) a pay reference period ending before the coming into force of this section.

(7) A notice of underpayment may not relate to a pay reference period ending more than six years before the date of service of the notice.

(8) In this section and sections 19A to 19C below "the 28-day period" means the period of 28 days beginning with the date of service of the notice of underpayment.]

NOTES

Sections 19, 19A–19H were substituted for the original ss 19–22, and ss 22A–22F (as inserted by the Employment Relations Act 2004, s 46(1)), by the Employment Act 2008, s 9(1).

Note that the Employment Act 2008, s 9(7) provides that nothing in this section (or Part 2 of the Schedule) affects any provision of the National Minimum Wage Act 1998 as that provision has effect for the purposes of the Agricultural Wages (Scotland) Act 1949, or the Agricultural Wages (Regulation) (Northern Ireland) Order 1977 (SI 1977/2151).

[1.1188]

[19A Notices of underpayment: financial penalty

(1) A notice of underpayment must, subject to this section, require the employer to pay a financial penalty specified in the notice to the Secretary of State within the 28-day period.

(2) The Secretary of State may by directions specify circumstances in which a notice of underpayment is not to impose a requirement to pay a financial penalty.

(3) Directions under subsection (2) may be amended or revoked by further such directions.

(4) The amount of any financial penalty is, subject as follows, to be [the total of the amounts for all workers to whom the notice relates calculated in accordance with subsections (5) to (5B)].

[(5) The amount for each worker to whom the notice relates is the relevant percentage of the amount specified under section 19(4)(c) in respect of each pay reference period specified under section 19(4)(b).

(5A) In subsection (5), "the relevant percentage", in relation to any pay reference period, means [200%].

(5B) If the amount as calculated under subsection (5) for any worker would be more than £20,000, the amount for the worker taken into account in calculating the financial penalty is to be £20,000.]

(6) If a financial penalty as calculated under subsection (4) above would be less than £100, the financial penalty specified in the notice shall be that amount.

(7) . . .

(8) The Secretary of State may by regulations—

(a) amend subsection [(5A)] above so as to substitute a different percentage for the percentage at any time specified there;

(b) amend subsection [(5B) or (6)] above so as to substitute a different amount for the amount at any time specified there.

(9) A notice of underpayment must, in addition to specifying the amount of any financial penalty, state how that amount was calculated.

(10) In a case where a notice of underpayment imposes a requirement to pay a financial penalty, if the employer on whom the notice is served, within the period of 14 days beginning with the day on which the notice was served—

(a) pays the amount required under section 19(2) above, and

(b) pays at least half the financial penalty,

he shall be regarded as having paid the financial penalty.

(11) A financial penalty paid to the Secretary of State pursuant to this section shall be paid by the Secretary of State into the Consolidated Fund.]

NOTES

Substituted as noted to s 19 at **[1.1187]**. See further the final note to s 19 at **[1.1187]**.

Sub-s (4): words in square brackets substituted by the Small Business, Enterprise and Employment Act 2015, s 152(1), (2), (6), as from 26 May 2015, in relation to notices of underpayment which relate only to pay reference periods commencing on or after that date.

Sub-ss (5)–(5A): substituted (for the original sub-s (5)) by the Small Business, Enterprise and Employment Act 2015, s 152(1), (3), (6), as from 26 May 2015, in relation to notices of underpayment which relate only to pay reference periods commencing on or after that date. Figure "200%" in square brackets in sub-s (5A) substituted (for the original figure "100%") by the National Minimum Wage (Amendment) Regulations 2016, SI 2016/68, regs 2, 4, as from 1 April 2016, except in respect of a pay reference period which began before that date.

Sub-s (7): repealed by the Small Business, Enterprise and Employment Act 2015, s 152(1), (4), (6), as from 26 May 2015, in relation to notices of underpayment which relate only to pay reference periods commencing on or after that date.

Sub-s (8): figure and words in square brackets substituted by the Small Business, Enterprise and Employment Act 2015, s 152(1), (5), (6), as from 26 May 2015, in relation to notices of underpayment which relate only to pay reference periods commencing on or after that date.

Regulations: the National Minimum Wage (Variation of Financial Penalty) Regulations 2014, SI 2014/547; the National Minimum Wage (Amendment) Regulations 2016, SI 2016/68.

[1.1189]

[19B Suspension of financial penalty

(1) This section applies in any case where it appears to the officer serving a notice of underpayment which imposes a requirement to pay a financial penalty that—

(a) relevant proceedings have been instituted; or

(b) relevant proceedings may be instituted.

(2) In this section "relevant proceedings" means proceedings against the employer for an offence under section 31(1) below in relation to a failure to remunerate any worker to whom the notice relates for any pay reference period specified under section 19(4)(b) above in relation to that worker.

(3) The notice of underpayment may contain provision suspending the requirement to pay the financial penalty payable under the notice until a notice terminating the suspension is served on the employer.

(4) An officer acting for the purposes of this Act may serve on the employer a notice terminating the suspension ("a penalty activation notice") if it appears to the officer—

(a) in a case referred to in subsection (1)(a) above, that relevant proceedings have concluded without the employer having been convicted of an offence under section 31(1) below, or
(b) in a case referred to in subsection (1)(b) above—
(i) that relevant proceedings will not be instituted; or
(ii) that relevant proceedings have been concluded without the employer having been convicted of an offence under section 31(1) below.

(5) Where a penalty activation notice is served, the requirement to pay the financial penalty has effect as if the notice of underpayment had been served on the day on which the penalty activation notice was served.

(6) An officer acting for the purposes of this Act must serve on the employer a notice withdrawing the requirement to pay the financial penalty if it appears to the officer that, pursuant to relevant proceedings, the employer has been convicted of an offence under section 31(1) below.]

NOTES

Substituted as noted to s 19 at **[1.1187]**. See further the final note to s 19 at **[1.1187]**.

[1.1190]

[19C Notices of underpayment: appeals

(1) A person on whom a notice of underpayment is served may in accordance with this section appeal against any one or more of the following—
(a) the decision to serve the notice;
(b) any requirement imposed by the notice to pay a sum to a worker;
(c) any requirement imposed by the notice to pay a financial penalty.

(2) An appeal under this section lies to an employment tribunal.

(3) An appeal under this section must be made before the end of the 28-day period.

(4) An appeal under subsection (1)(a) above must be made on the ground that no sum was due under section 17 above to any worker to whom the notice relates on the day specified under section 19(4)(a) above in relation to him in respect of any pay reference period specified under section 19(4)(b) above in relation to him.

(5) An appeal under subsection (1)(b) above in relation to a worker must be made on either or both of the following grounds—
(a) that, on the day specified under section 19(4)(a) above in relation to the worker, no sum was due to the worker under section 17 above in respect of any pay reference period specified under section 19(4)(b) above in relation to him;
(b) that the amount specified in the notice as the sum due to the worker is incorrect.

(6) An appeal under subsection (1)(c) above must be made on either or both of the following grounds—
(a) that the notice was served in circumstances specified in a direction under section 19A(2) above, or
(b) that the amount of the financial penalty specified in the notice of underpayment has been incorrectly calculated (whether because the notice is incorrect in some of the particulars which affect that calculation or for some other reason).

(7) Where the employment tribunal allows an appeal under subsection (1)(a) above, it must rescind the notice.

(8) Where, in a case where subsection (7) above does not apply, the employment tribunal allows an appeal under subsection (1)(b) or (c) above—
(a) the employment tribunal must rectify the notice, and
(b) the notice of underpayment shall have effect as rectified from the date of the employment tribunal's determination.]

NOTES

Substituted as noted to s 19 at **[1.1187]**. See further the final note to s 19 at **[1.1187]**.

[1.1191]

[19D Non-compliance with notice of underpayment: recovery of arrears

(1) If a requirement to pay a sum to a worker contained in a notice of underpayment is not complied with in whole or in part, an officer acting for the purposes of this Act may, on behalf of any worker to whom the requirement relates—
(a) present a complaint under section 23(1)(a) of the Employment Rights Act 1996 (deductions from worker's wages in contravention of section 13 of that Act) to an employment tribunal in respect of any sums due to the worker by virtue of section 17 above; or
(b) in relation to Northern Ireland, present a complaint under Article 55(1)(a) of the Employment Rights (Northern Ireland) Order 1996 (deductions from worker's wages in contravention of Article 45 of that Order) to an industrial tribunal in respect of any sums due to the worker by virtue of section 17 above; or
(c) commence other civil proceedings for the recovery, on a claim in contract, of any sums due to the worker by virtue of section 17 above.

(2) The powers conferred by subsection (1) above for the recovery of sums due from an employer to a worker shall not be in derogation of any right which the worker may have to recover such sums by civil proceedings.]

NOTES

Substituted as noted to s 19 at **[1.1187]**. See further the final note to s 19 at **[1.1187]**.

Conciliation: employment tribunal proceedings under this section are "relevant proceedings" for the purposes of the conciliation provisions contained in the Employment Tribunals Act 1996, ss 18–18C; see s 18(1)(c) of the 1996 Act at **[1.757]**.

[1.1192]
[19E Non-compliance with notice of underpayment: recovery of penalty
A financial penalty payable under a notice of underpayment—
(a) in England and Wales, is recoverable, if [the county court] so orders, under section 85 of the County Courts Act 1984 or otherwise as if it were payable under an order of that court;
(b) in Scotland, may be enforced in the same manner as an extract registered decree arbitral bearing a warrant for execution issued by the sheriff court of any sheriffdom in Scotland;
(c) in Northern Ireland, is recoverable, if the county court so orders, as if it were payable under an order of that court.]

NOTES
Substituted as noted to s 19 at **[1.1187]**. See further the final note to s 19 at **[1.1187]**.
Words in square brackets in para (a) substituted by the Crime and Courts Act 2013, s 17(5), Sch 9, Pt 3, para 52.

[1.1193]
[19F Withdrawal of notice of underpayment
(1) Where a notice of underpayment has been served (and not already withdrawn or rescinded) and it appears to an officer acting for the purposes of this Act that the notice incorrectly includes or omits any requirement or is incorrect in any particular, the officer may withdraw it by serving notice of the withdrawal on the employer.
(2) Where a notice of underpayment is withdrawn and no replacement notice of underpayment is served in accordance with section 19G below—
(a) any sum paid by or recovered from the employer by way of financial penalty payable under the notice must be repaid to him with interest at the appropriate rate running from the date when the sum was paid or recovered;
(b) any appeal against the notice must be dismissed;
(c) after the withdrawal no complaint may be presented or other civil proceedings commenced by virtue of section 19D above in reliance on any non-compliance with the notice before it was withdrawn;
(d) any complaint or proceedings so commenced before the withdrawal may be proceeded with despite the withdrawal.
(3) In a case where subsection (2) above applies, the notice of withdrawal must indicate the effect of that subsection (but a failure to do so does not make the withdrawal ineffective).
(4) In subsection (2)(a) above, "the appropriate rate" means the rate that, on the date the sum was paid or recovered, was specified in section 17 of the Judgments Act 1838.]

NOTES
Substituted as noted to s 19 at **[1.1187]**. See further the final note to s 19 at **[1.1187]**.

[1.1194]
[19G Replacement notice of underpayment
(1) Where an officer acting for the purposes of this Act serves a notice of withdrawal under section 19F above and is of the opinion referred to in section 19(1) above in relation to any worker specified in the notice which is being withdrawn ("the original notice"), he may at the same time serve another notice under section 19 above ("the replacement notice").
(2) The replacement notice may not relate to any worker to whom the original notice did not relate.
(3) If the replacement notice contravenes subsection (2) above, that fact shall be an additional ground of appeal for the purposes of section 19C above.
(4) The replacement notice may relate to a pay reference period ending after the date of service of the original notice.
(5) Section 19(7) above applies in relation to the replacement notice as if the reference to six years before the date of service of the notice were a reference to six years before the date of service of the original notice.
(6) The replacement notice must—
(a) indicate the differences between it and the original notice that it is reasonable for the officer to consider are material; and
(b) indicate the effect of section 19H below.
(7) Failure to comply with subsection (6) above does not make the replacement notice ineffective.
(8) Where a replacement notice is withdrawn under section 19F above, no further replacement notice may be served under subsection (1) above pursuant to the withdrawal.
(9) Nothing in this section affects any power that arises apart from this section to serve a notice of underpayment in relation to any worker.]

NOTES
Substituted as noted to s 19 at **[1.1187]**. See further the final note to s 19 at **[1.1187]**.

[1.1195]
[19H Effect of replacement notice of underpayment
(1) This section applies where a notice of underpayment is withdrawn under section 19F above and a replacement notice is served in accordance with section 19G above.

(2) If an appeal has been made under section 19C above against the original notice and the appeal has not been withdrawn or finally determined before the time when that notice is withdrawn—

(a) that appeal ("the earlier appeal") shall have effect after that time as if it were against the replacement notice; and

(b) the employer may exercise his right of appeal under section 19C above against the replacement notice only if he withdraws the earlier appeal.

(3) After the withdrawal no complaint may be presented or other civil proceedings commenced by virtue of section 19D above in reliance on any non-compliance with the notice before it was withdrawn; but any complaint or proceedings so commenced before the withdrawal may be proceeded with despite the withdrawal.

(4) If a sum was paid by or recovered from the employer by way of financial penalty under the original notice—

(a) an amount equal to that sum (or, if more than one, the total of those sums) shall be treated as having been paid in respect of the replacement notice; and

(b) any amount by which that sum (or total) exceeds the amount payable under the replacement notice must be repaid to the employer with interest at the appropriate rate running from the date when the sum (or, if more than one, the first of them) was paid or recovered.

(5) In subsection (4)(b) above "the appropriate rate" means the rate that, on the date mentioned in that provision, was specified in section 17 of the Judgments Act 1838.]

NOTES

Substituted as noted to s 19 at **[1.1187]**. See further the final note to s 19 at **[1.1187]**.

20–22, 22A–22H *(Substituted by new ss 19, 19A–19H, as noted to s 19 at* **[1.1187]**.*)*

Rights not to suffer unfair dismissal or other detriment

[1.1196]

23 The right not to suffer detriment

(1) A worker has the right not to be subjected to any detriment by any act, or any deliberate failure to act, by his employer, done on the ground that—

(a) any action was taken, or was proposed to be taken, by or on behalf of the worker with a view to enforcing, or otherwise securing the benefit of, a right of the worker's to which this section applies; or

(b) the employer was prosecuted for an offence under section 31 below as a result of action taken by or on behalf of the worker for the purpose of enforcing, or otherwise securing the benefit of, a right of the worker's to which this section applies; or

(c) the worker qualifies, or will or might qualify, for the national minimum wage or for a particular rate of national minimum wage.

(2) It is immaterial for the purposes of paragraph (a) or (b) of subsection (1) above—

(a) whether or not the worker has the right, or

(b) whether or not the right has been infringed,

but, for that subsection to apply, the claim to the right and, if applicable, the claim that it has been infringed must be made in good faith.

(3) The following are the rights to which this section applies—

(a) any right conferred by, or by virtue of, any provision of this Act for which the remedy for its infringement is by way of a complaint to an employment tribunal; and

(b) any right conferred by section 17 above.

[(4) This section does not apply where the detriment in question amounts to dismissal within the meaning of—

(a) Part X of the Employment Rights Act 1996 (unfair dismissal), or

(b) Part XI of the Employment Rights (Northern Ireland) Order 1996 (corresponding provision for Northern Ireland),

. . .]

NOTES

Sub-s (4): substituted by the Employment Relations Act 1999, s 18(4); words omitted repealed by the Employment Relations (Northern Ireland) Order 1999, SI 1999/2790, arts 20(5)(a), 40, Sch 9(3).

[1.1197]

24 Enforcement of the right

(1) A worker may present a complaint to an employment tribunal that he has been subjected to a detriment in contravention of section 23 above.

(2) Subject to the following provisions of this section, the provisions of—

(a) [sections 48(2) to (4A)] and 49 of the Employment Rights Act 1996 (complaints to employment tribunals and remedies), or

(b) in relation to Northern Ireland, Articles 71(2) to (4) and 72 of the Employment Rights (Northern Ireland) Order 1996 (complaints to industrial tribunals and remedies),

shall apply in relation to a complaint under this section as they apply in relation to a complaint under section 48 of that Act or Article 71 of that Order (as the case may be), but taking references in those provisions to the employer as references to the employer within the meaning of section 23(1) above.

(3) Where—

(a) the detriment to which the worker is subjected is the termination of his worker's contract, but

(b) that contract is not a contract of employment,

any compensation awarded under section 49 of the Employment Rights Act 1996 or Article 72 of the Employment Rights (Northern Ireland) Order 1996 by virtue of subsection (2) above must not exceed the limit specified in subsection (4) below.

(4) The limit mentioned in subsection (3) above is the total of—

(a) the sum which would be the basic award for unfair dismissal, calculated in accordance with section 119 of the Employment Rights Act 1996 or Article 153 of the Employment Rights (Northern Ireland) Order 1996 (as the case may be), if the worker had been an employee and the contract terminated had been a contract of employment; and

(b) the sum for the time being specified in section 124(1) of that Act or Article 158(1) of that Order (as the case may be) which is the limit for a compensatory award to a person calculated in accordance with section 123 of that Act or Article 157 of that Order (as the case may be).

(5) Where the worker has been working under arrangements which do not fall to be regarded as a worker's contract for the purposes of—

(a) the Employment Rights Act 1996, or

(b) in relation to Northern Ireland, the Employment Rights (Northern Ireland) Order 1996,

he shall be treated for the purposes of subsections (3) and (4) above as if any arrangements under which he has been working constituted a worker's contract falling within section 230(3)(b) of that Act or Article 3(3)(b) of that Order (as the case may be).

NOTES

Sub-s (2): words in square brackets substituted by the Enterprise and Regulatory Reform Act 2013, s 8, Sch 2, paras 36, 39.

Conciliation: employment tribunal proceedings under this section are "relevant proceedings" for the purposes of the conciliation provisions contained in the Employment Tribunals Act 1996, ss 18–18C; see s 18(1)(c) of the 1996 Act at **[1.757]**.

Tribunal jurisdiction: the Employment Act 2002, s 38 applies to proceedings before the employment tribunal relating to a claim under this section; see s 38(1) of, and Sch 5 to, the 2002 Act at **[1.1279]**, **[1.1287]**. See also the Trade Union and Labour Relations (Consolidation) Act 1992, s 207A at **[1.524]** (as inserted by the Employment Act 2008). That section provides that in proceedings before an employment tribunal relating to a claim by an employee under any of the jurisdictions listed in Sch A2 to the 1992 Act at **[1.704]** (which includes this section) the tribunal may adjust any award given if the employer or the employee has unreasonably failed to comply with a relevant Code of Practice as defined by s 207A(4). See also the revised Acas Code of Practice 1 – Disciplinary and Grievance Procedures (2015) at **[4.1]**, and the Acas Code of Practice 4 – Settlement Agreements (2013) at **[4.54]**.

25, 26 *(S 25 inserts the Employment Rights Act 1996, s 104A at* **[1.1016]***, amends ss 105, 108 of that Act at* **[1.1023]**, **[1.1026]***, and amended s 109 (repealed); s 26 applies to Northern Ireland (outside the scope of this work).)*

Civil procedure, evidence and appeals

27 *(Sub-s (1) amends the Employment Tribunals Act 1996, s 4(3) at* **[1.733]***; sub-s (2) applies to Northern Ireland (outside the scope of this work).)*

[1.1198]

28 Reversal of burden of proof

(1) Where in any civil proceedings any question arises as to whether an individual qualifies or qualified at any time for the national minimum wage, it shall be presumed that the individual qualifies or, as the case may be, qualified at that time for the national minimum wage unless the contrary is established.

(2) Where—

(a) a complaint is made—

(i) to an employment tribunal under section 23(1)(a) of the Employment Rights Act 1996 (unauthorised deductions from wages), or

(ii) to an industrial tribunal under Article 55(1)(a) of the Employment Rights (Northern Ireland) Order 1996, and

(b) the complaint relates in whole or in part to the deduction of the amount described as additional remuneration in section 17(1) above,

it shall be presumed for the purposes of the complaint, so far as relating to the deduction of that amount, that the worker in question was remunerated at a rate less than the national minimum wage unless the contrary is established.

(3) Where in any civil proceedings a person seeks to recover on a claim in contract the amount described as additional remuneration in section 17(1) above, it shall be presumed for the purposes of the proceedings, so far as relating to that amount, that the worker in question was remunerated at a rate less than the national minimum wage unless the contrary is established.

29 *(Amends the Employment Tribunals Act 1996, s 21(1) at* **[1.764]***.)*

Conciliation

30 *(Sub-s (1) is spent (it amended the Employment Tribunals Act 1996, s 18(1) and the amendment has been superseded by a subsequent amendment); sub-s (2) applies to Northern Ireland (outside the scope of this work).)*

Offences

[1.1199]

31 Offences

(1) If the employer of a worker who qualifies for the national minimum wage refuses or wilfully neglects to remunerate the worker for any pay reference period at a rate which is at least equal to the national minimum wage, that employer is guilty of an offence.

(2) If a person who is required to keep or preserve any record in accordance with regulations under section 9 above fails to do so, that person is guilty of an offence.
(3) If a person makes, or knowingly causes or allows to be made, in a record required to be kept in accordance with regulations under section 9 above any entry which he knows to be false in a material particular, that person is guilty of an offence.
(4) If a person, for purposes connected with the provisions of this Act, produces or furnishes, or knowingly causes or allows to be produced or furnished, any record or information which he knows to be false in a material particular, that person is guilty of an offence.
(5) If a person—
(a) intentionally delays or obstructs an officer acting for the purposes of this Act in the exercise of any power conferred by this Act, or
(b) refuses or neglects to answer any question, furnish any information or produce any document when required to do so under section 14(1) above,
that person is guilty of an offence.
(6) Where the commission by any person of an offence under subsection (1) or (2) above is due to the act or default of some other person, that other person is also guilty of the offence.
(7) A person may be charged with and convicted of an offence by virtue of subsection (6) above whether or not proceedings are taken against any other person.
(8) In any proceedings for an offence under subsection (1) or (2) above it shall be a defence for the person charged to prove that he exercised all due diligence and took all reasonable precautions to secure that the provisions of this Act, and of any relevant regulations made under it, were complied with by himself and by any person under his control.
(9) A person guilty of an offence under this section shall be liable—
[(a) on conviction on indictment, to a fine, or
(b) on summary conviction, to a fine not exceeding the statutory maximum].

NOTES

Sub-s (9): words in square brackets substituted by the Employment Act 2008, s 11(1).

Note that the Employment Act 2008, s 11(3) provides that nothing in this section (or Part 4 of the Schedule) affects this section as it has effect for the purposes of the Agricultural Wages (Scotland) Act 1949, or the Agricultural Wages (Regulation) (Northern Ireland) Order 1977 (SI 1977/2151).

[1.1200]
32 Offences by bodies corporate etc

(1) This section applies to any offence under this Act.
(2) If an offence committed by a body corporate is proved—
(a) to have been committed with the consent or connivance of an officer of the body, or
(b) to be attributable to any neglect on the part of such an officer,
the officer as well as the body corporate is guilty of the offence and liable to be proceeded against and punished accordingly.
(3) In subsection (2) above "officer", in relation to a body corporate, means a director, manager, secretary or other similar officer of the body, or a person purporting to act in any such capacity.
(4) If the affairs of a body corporate are managed by its members, subsection (2) above applies in relation to the acts and defaults of a member in connection with his functions of management as if he were a director of the body corporate.
(5) If an offence committed by a partnership in Scotland is proved—
(a) to have been committed with the consent or connivance of a partner, or
(b) to be attributable to any neglect on the part of a partner,
the partner as well as the partnership is guilty of the offence and liable to be proceeded against and punished accordingly.
(6) In subsection (5) above, "partner" includes a person purporting to act as a partner.

[1.1201]
33 Proceedings for offences

(1) The persons who may conduct proceedings for an offence under this Act—
(a) . . .
(b) in Northern Ireland, before a court of summary jurisdiction,
shall include any person authorised for the purpose by the Secretary of State even if that person is not a barrister or solicitor.
[(1A) The persons who may conduct proceedings for an offence under this Act in England and Wales, before a magistrates' court, shall include any person authorised for the purpose by the Secretary of State.]
(2)–(5) . . .

NOTES

Sub-s (1): para (a) repealed by the Legal Services Act 2007, ss 208(1), 210, Sch 21, paras 124, 125(a), Sch 23.
Sub-s (1A): inserted by the Legal Services Act 2007, s 208(1), Sch 21, paras 124, 125(b).
Sub-ss (2)–(5): repealed by the Employment Act 2008, ss 11(2), 20, Schedule, Pt 4.
Note that the Employment Act 2008, s 11(3) provides that nothing in this section (or Part 4 of the Schedule) affects this section as it has effect for the purposes of the Agricultural Wages (Scotland) Act 1949, or the Agricultural Wages (Regulation) (Northern Ireland) Order 1977 (SI 1977/2151).

Special classes of person

[1.1202]

34 Agency workers who are not otherwise "workers"

(1) This section applies in any case where an individual ("the agency worker")—

(a) is supplied by a person ("the agent") to do work for another ("the principal") under a contract or other arrangements made between the agent and the principal; but

(b) is not, as respects that work, a worker, because of the absence of a worker's contract between the individual and the agent or the principal; and

(c) is not a party to a contract under which he undertakes to do the work for another party to the contract whose status is, by virtue of the contract, that of a client or customer of any profession or business undertaking carried on by the individual.

(2) In a case where this section applies, the other provisions of this Act shall have effect as if there were a worker's contract for the doing of the work by the agency worker made between the agency worker and—

(a) whichever of the agent and the principal is responsible for paying the agency worker in respect of the work; or

(b) if neither the agent nor the principal is so responsible, whichever of them pays the agency worker in respect of the work.

[1.1203]

35 Home workers who are not otherwise "workers"

(1) In determining for the purposes of this Act whether a home worker is or is not a worker, section 54(3)(b) below shall have effect as if for the word "personally" there were substituted "(whether personally or otherwise)".

(2) In this section "home worker" means an individual who contracts with a person, for the purposes of that person's business, for the execution of work to be done in a place not under the control or management of that person.

[1.1204]

36 Crown employment

(1) Subject to section 37 below, the provisions of this Act have effect in relation to Crown employment and persons in Crown employment as they have effect in relation to other employment and other workers.

(2) In this Act, subject to section 37 below, "Crown employment" means employment under or for the purposes of a government department or any officer or body exercising on behalf of the Crown functions conferred by statutory provision.

(3) For the purposes of the application of the other provisions of this Act in relation to Crown employment in accordance with subsection (1) above—

(a) references to an employee or a worker shall be construed as references to a person in Crown employment;

(b) references to a contract of employment or a worker's contract shall be construed as references to the terms of employment of a person in Crown employment; and

(c) references to dismissal, or to the termination of a worker's contract, shall be construed as references to the termination of Crown employment.

[1.1205]

37 Armed forces

(1) A person serving as a member of the naval, military or air forces of the Crown does not qualify for the national minimum wage in respect of that service.

(2) Section 36 above applies to employment by an association established for the purposes of Part XI of the Reserve Forces Act 1996, notwithstanding anything in subsection (1) above.

[1.1206]

[37A Cadet Force Adult Volunteers

(1) A person (not being a person to whom section 37(1) above applies) who—

(a) is a member of any of the forces specified in subsection (2) below, and

(b) assists the activities of those forces otherwise than in the course of Crown employment,

does not qualify for the national minimum wage in respect of anything done by him in so assisting those activities.

(2) The forces referred to in subsection (1) above are—

(a) the Combined Cadet Force;

(b) the Sea Cadet Corps;

(c) the Army Cadet Force;

(d) the Air Training Corps.]

NOTES

Inserted by the Employment Act 2008, s 13.

[1.1207]

38 House of Lords staff

(1) Apart from section 21 above, the provisions of this Act have effect in relation to employment as a relevant member of the House of Lords staff as they have effect in relation to other employment.

(2) Nothing in any rule of law or the law or practice of Parliament prevents a relevant member of the House of Lords staff from bringing before the High Court or [the county court] any claim under this Act.

(3) In this section "relevant member of the House of Lords staff" means any person who is employed under a worker's contract with the Corporate Officer of the House of Lords.

NOTES

Sub-s (2): words in square brackets substituted by the Crime and Courts Act 2013, s 17(5), Sch 9, Pt 3, para 52.

[1.1208]

39 House of Commons staff

(1) Apart from section 21 above, the provisions of this Act have effect in relation to employment as a relevant member of the House of Commons staff as they have effect in relation to other employment.

(2) Nothing in any rule of law or the law or practice of Parliament prevents a relevant member of the House of Commons staff from bringing before the High Court or [the county court] any claim under this Act.

(3) In this section "relevant member of the House of Commons staff" means any person—

- (a) who was appointed by the House of Commons Commission; or
- (b) who is a member of the Speaker's personal staff.

NOTES

Sub-s (2): words in square brackets substituted by the Crime and Courts Act 2013, s 17(5), Sch 9, Pt 3, para 52.

[1.1209]

40 Mariners

For the purposes of this Act, an individual employed to work on board a ship registered in the United Kingdom under Part II of the Merchant Shipping Act 1995 shall be treated as an individual who under his contract ordinarily works in the United Kingdom unless—

- (a) the employment is wholly outside the United Kingdom; or
- (b) the person is not ordinarily resident in the United Kingdom;

and related expressions shall be construed accordingly.

Extensions

[1.1210]

41 Power to apply Act to individuals who are not otherwise "workers"

The Secretary of State may by regulations make provision for this Act to apply, with or without modifications, as if—

- (a) any individual of a prescribed description who would not otherwise be a worker for the purposes of this Act were a worker for those purposes;
- (b) there were in the case of any such individual a worker's contract of a prescribed description under which the individual works; and
- (c) a person of a prescribed description were the employer under that contract.

NOTES

Regulations: as of 15 May 2019, no Regulations had been made under this section.

[1.1211]

42 Power to apply Act to offshore employment

(1) In this section "offshore employment" means employment for the purposes of activities—

- (a) in the territorial waters of the United Kingdom, or
- (b) connected with the exploration of the sea-bed or subsoil, or the exploitation of their natural resources, in the United Kingdom sector of the continental shelf, or
- (c) connected with the exploration or exploitation, in a foreign sector of the continental shelf, of a cross-boundary petroleum field.

(2) Her Majesty may by Order in Council provide that the provisions of this Act apply, to such extent and for such purposes as may be specified in the Order (with or without modification), to or in relation to a person in offshore employment.

(3) An Order in Council under this section—

- (a) may provide that all or any of the provisions of this Act, as applied by such an Order in Council, apply—
  - (i) to individuals whether or not they are British subjects, and
  - (ii) to bodies corporate whether or not they are incorporated under the law of a part of the United Kingdom,

  and apply even where the application may affect their activities outside the United Kingdom,
- (b) may make provision for conferring jurisdiction on any court or class of court specified in the Order in Council, or on employment tribunals, in respect of offences, causes of action or other matters arising in connection with offshore employment,
- (c) may (without prejudice to subsection (2) above) provide that the provisions of this Act, as applied by the Order in Council, apply in relation to any person in employment in a part of the areas referred to in subsection (1)(a) and (b) above,
- (d) may exclude from the operation of section 3 of the Territorial Waters Jurisdiction Act 1878 (consents required for prosecutions) proceedings for offences under this Act in connection with offshore employment,
- (e) may provide that such proceedings shall not be brought without such consent as may be required by the Order in Council,

(f) may (without prejudice to subsection (2) above) modify or exclude the operation of sections 1(2)(b) and 40 above.

(4) Any jurisdiction conferred on a court or tribunal under this section is without prejudice to jurisdiction exercisable apart from this section by that or any other court or tribunal.

(5) In this section—

"cross-boundary petroleum field" means a petroleum field that extends across the boundary between the United Kingdom sector of the continental shelf and a foreign sector of the continental shelf,

"foreign sector of the continental shelf" means an area outside the territorial waters of any state, within which rights with respect to the sea-bed and subsoil and their natural resources are exercisable by a state other than the United Kingdom,

"petroleum field" means a geological structure identified as an oil or gas field by the Order in Council concerned, and

"United Kingdom sector of the continental shelf" means the area designated under section 1(7) of the Continental Shelf Act 1964.

NOTES

Orders: the National Minimum Wage (Offshore Employment) Order 1999, SI 1999/1128. This Order in Council has the effect of extending the provisions of this Act to workers who work, or ordinarily work, in the territorial waters of the UK. It also extends the operation of this Act to workers who work, or ordinarily work, in the UK sector of the continental shelf where the employment is: (a) connected with the exploration of the sea-bed or its subsoil, or the exploitation of their natural resources in the UK sector of the continental shelf; or (b) connected with the exploration or exploitation, in a foreign sector of the continental shelf, of a cross-boundary petroleum field. Note that the 1999 Order has no application in respect of ships in navigation, or engaged in fishing or dredging. As to the application of this Act to mariners, see s 40 *ante*.

Exclusions

[1.1212]

43 Share fishermen

A person—

(a) employed as master, or as a member of the crew, of a fishing vessel, and

(b) remunerated, in respect of that employment, only by a share in the profits or gross earnings of the vessel,

does not qualify for the national minimum wage in respect of that employment.

[1.1213]

44 Voluntary workers

(1) A worker employed by a charity, a voluntary organisation, an associated fund-raising body or a statutory body does not qualify for the national minimum wage in respect of that employment if he receives, and under the terms of his employment (apart from this Act) is entitled to,—

(a) no monetary payments of any description, or no monetary payments except in respect of expenses—

(i) actually incurred in the performance of his duties; or

(ii) reasonably estimated as likely to be or to have been so incurred; and

(b) no benefits in kind of any description, or no benefits in kind other than the provision of some or all of his subsistence or of such accommodation as is reasonable in the circumstances of the employment.

[(1A) For the purposes of subsection (1)(a) above, expenses which—

(a) are incurred in order to enable the worker to perform his duties,

(b) are reasonably so incurred, and

(c) are not accommodation expenses,

are to be regarded as actually incurred in the performance of his duties.]

(2) A person who would satisfy the conditions in subsection (1) above but for receiving monetary payments made solely for the purpose of providing him with means of subsistence shall be taken to satisfy those conditions if—

(a) he is employed to do the work in question as a result of arrangements made between a charity acting in pursuance of its charitable purposes and the body for which the work is done; and

(b) the work is done for a charity, a voluntary organisation, an associated fund-raising body or a statutory body.

(3) For the purposes of subsection (1)(b) above—

(a) any training (other than that which a person necessarily acquires in the course of doing his work) shall be taken to be a benefit in kind; but

(b) there shall be left out of account any training provided for the sole or main purpose of improving the worker's ability to perform the work which he has agreed to do.

(4) In this section—

"associated fund-raising body" means a body of persons the profits of which are applied wholly for the purposes of a charity or voluntary organisation;

"charity" means a body of persons, or the trustees of a trust, established for charitable purposes only;

"receive", in relation to a monetary payment or a benefit in kind, means receive in respect of, or otherwise in connection with, the employment in question (whether or not under the terms of the employment);

"statutory body" means a body established by or under an enactment (including an enactment comprised in Northern Ireland legislation) [and includes the Children's Panel];

"subsistence" means such subsistence as is reasonable in the circumstances of the employment in question, and does not include accommodation;

"voluntary organisation" means a body of persons, or the trustees of a trust, which is established only for charitable purposes (whether or not those purposes are charitable within the meaning of any rule of law), benevolent purposes or philanthropic purposes, but which is not a charity.

NOTES

Sub-s (1A): inserted by the Employment Act 2008, s 14.

Sub-s (4): words in square brackets in definition "statutory body" inserted by the Children's Hearings (Scotland) Act 2011 (Consequential and Transitional Provisions and Savings) Order 2013, SI 2013/1465, art 17(1), Sch 1, Pt 1, para 6.

[1.1214]

[44A Religious and other communities: resident workers

(1) A residential member of a community to which this section applies does not qualify for the national minimum wage in respect of employment by the community.

(2) Subject to subsection (3), this section applies to a community if—

(a) it is a charity or is established by a charity,

(b) a purpose of the community is to practise or advance a belief of a religious or similar nature, and

(c) all or some of its members live together for that purpose.

(3) This section does not apply to a community which—

(a) is an independent school [or an alternative provision Academy that is not an independent school], or

(b) provides a course of further or higher education.

(4) The residential members of a community are those who live together as mentioned in subsection (2)(c).

(5) In this section—

(a) "charity" has the same meaning as in section 44, and

(b) "independent school" has the same meaning as in section 463 of the Education Act 1996 (in England and Wales), section 135 of the Education (Scotland) Act 1980 (in Scotland) and Article 2 of the Education and Libraries (Northern Ireland) Order 1986 (in Northern Ireland).

(6) In this section "course of further or higher education" means—

(a) in England and Wales, a course of a description referred to in Schedule 6 to the Education Reform Act 1988 or Schedule 2 to the Further and Higher Education Act 1992;

(b) in Scotland, a course or programme of a description mentioned in or falling within section 6(1) or 38 of the Further and Higher Education (Scotland) Act 1992;

(c) in Northern Ireland, a course of a description referred to in Schedule 1 to the Further Education (Northern Ireland) Order 1997 or a course providing further education within the meaning of Article 3 of that Order.]

NOTES

Inserted by the Employment Relations Act 1999, s 22.

Sub-s (3): words in square brackets inserted by the Alternative Provision Academies (Consequential Amendments to Acts) (England) Order 2012, SI 2012/976, art 2, Schedule, para 10.

Further and Higher Education Act 1992: Sch 2 to that Act was repealed by the Learning and Skills Act 2000, s 153, Sch 11.

[1.1215]

45 Prisoners

(1) A prisoner does not qualify for the national minimum wage in respect of any work which he does in pursuance of prison rules.

(2) In this section—

"prisoner" means a person detained in, or on temporary release from, a prison;

"prison" includes any other institution to which prison rules apply;

"prison rules" means—

(a) in relation to England and Wales, rules made under section 47 [or 47A] of the Prison Act 1952;

(b) in relation to Scotland, rules made under section 39 of the Prisons (Scotland) Act 1989; and

(c) in relation to Northern Ireland, rules made under section 13 of the Prison Act (Northern Ireland) 1953.

NOTES

Sub-s (2): words in square brackets in the definition "prison rules" inserted by the Legal Aid, Sentencing and Punishment of Offenders Act 2012, s 129(9), as from a day to be appointed.

[1.1216]

[45A Persons discharging fines by unpaid work

A person does not qualify for the national minimum wage in respect of any work that he does in pursuance of a work order under Schedule 6 to the Courts Act 2003 (discharge of fines by unpaid work).]

NOTES

Inserted by the Courts Act 2003, s 109(1), Sch 8, para 382.

[1.1217]
[45B Immigration: detained persons
Section 153A of the Immigration and Asylum Act 1999 (c 33) (persons detained in removal centres) disqualifies certain persons for the national minimum wage.]

NOTES
Inserted by the Immigration, Asylum and Nationality Act 2006, s 59(2).

46, 47 (*Agricultural workers: outside the scope of this work.*)

Miscellaneous

[1.1218]
48 Application of Act to superior employers
Where—
(a) the immediate employer of a worker is himself in the employment of some other person, and
(b) the worker is employed on the premises of that other person,
that other person shall be deemed for the purposes of this Act to be the employer of the worker jointly with the immediate employer.

[1.1219]
49 Restrictions on contracting out
(1) Any provision in any agreement (whether a worker's contract or not) is void in so far as it purports—
(a) to exclude or limit the operation of any provision of this Act; or
(b) to preclude a person from bringing proceedings under this Act before an employment tribunal.
(2) Subsection (1) above does not apply to any agreement to refrain from instituting or continuing proceedings where a conciliation officer has taken action under—
(a) [any of sections 18A to 18C] of the Employment Tribunals Act 1996 (conciliation), or
(b) in relation to Northern Ireland, Article 20 of the Industrial Tribunals (Northern Ireland) Order 1996.
(3) Subsection (1) above does not apply to any agreement to refrain from instituting or continuing before an employment tribunal any proceedings within—
(a) [section 18(1)(c)] of the Employment Tribunals Act 1996 (proceedings under or by virtue of this Act where conciliation is available), or
(b) in relation to Northern Ireland, Article 20(1)(cc) of the Industrial Tribunals (Northern Ireland) Order 1996,
if the conditions regulating [settlement] agreements under this Act are satisfied in relation to the agreement.
(4) For the purposes of subsection (3) above the conditions regulating [settlement] agreements under this Act are that—
(a) the agreement must be in writing,
(b) the agreement must relate to the particular proceedings,
(c) the employee or worker must have received advice from a relevant independent adviser as to the terms and effect of the proposed agreement and, in particular, its effect on his ability to pursue his rights before an employment tribunal,
(d) there must be in force, when the adviser gives the advice, a contract of insurance, or an indemnity provided for members of a profession or a professional body, covering the risk of a claim by the employee or worker in respect of loss arising in consequence of the advice,
(e) the agreement must identify the adviser, and
(f) the agreement must state that the conditions regulating [settlement] agreements under this Act are satisfied.
(5) A person is a relevant independent adviser for the purposes of subsection (4)(c) above—
(a) if he is a qualified lawyer,
(b) if he is an officer, official, employee or member of an independent trade union who has been certified in writing by the trade union as competent to give advice and as authorised to do so on behalf of the trade union,
(c) if he works at an advice centre (whether as an employee or a volunteer) and has been certified in writing by the centre as competent to give advice and as authorised to do so on behalf of the centre, or
(d) if he is a person of a description specified in an order made by the Secretary of State.
(6) But a person is not a relevant independent adviser for the purposes of subsection (4)(c) above in relation to the employee or worker—
(a) if he is employed by, or is acting in the matter for, the employer or an associated employer,
(b) in the case of a person within subsection (5)(b) or (c) above, if the trade union or advice centre is the employer or an associated employer,
(c) in the case of a person within subsection (5)(c) above, if the employee or worker makes a payment for the advice received from him, or
(d) in the case of a person of a description specified in an order under subsection (5)(d) above, if any condition specified in the order in relation to the giving of advice by persons of that description is not satisfied.
(7) In this section "qualified lawyer" means—

[(a) as regards England and Wales, a person who, for the purposes of the Legal Services Act 2007, is an authorised person in relation to an activity which constitutes the exercise of a right of audience or the conduct of litigation (within the meaning of that Act);]

(b) as respects Scotland—

(i) an advocate (whether in practice as such or employed to give legal advice); or

(ii) a solicitor who holds a practising certificate; and

(c) as respects Northern Ireland—

(i) a barrister (whether in practice as such or employed to give legal advice); or

(ii) a solicitor who holds a practising certificate.

(8) For the purposes of this section any two employers shall be treated as associated if—

(a) one is a company of which the other (directly or indirectly) has control; or

(b) both are companies of which a third person (directly or indirectly) has control;

and "associated employer" shall be construed accordingly.

(8A)–(11) (*Apply to Northern Ireland: outside the scope of this work.*)

NOTES

Sub-s (2): words in square brackets in para (a) substituted by the Enterprise and Regulatory Reform Act 2013, s 7(2), Sch 1, para 11.

Sub-s (3): words in square brackets in para (a) substituted by the Employment Tribunals Act 1996 (Application of Conciliation Provisions) Order 2014, SI 2014/431, art 3, Schedule, para 5; word in second pair of square brackets substituted by the Enterprise and Regulatory Reform Act 2013, s 23(3)(a).

Sub-s (4): words in square brackets substituted by the Enterprise and Regulatory Reform Act 2013, s 23(3)(a).

Sub-s (7): para (a) substituted by the Legal Services Act 2007, s 208(1), Sch 21, paras 124, 126.

Orders: the Compromise Agreements (Description of Person) Order 2004, SI 2004/754 at **[2.725]**; the Compromise Agreements (Description of Person) Order 2004 (Amendment) Order 2004, SI 2004/2515.

50 (*(Publicity for the Act and Regulations) outside the scope of this work.*)

Supplementary

[1.1220]

51 Regulations and orders

(1) Except to the extent that this Act makes provision to the contrary, any power conferred by this Act to make an Order in Council, regulations or an order includes power—

(a) to make different provision for different cases or for different descriptions of person; and

(b) to make incidental, consequential, supplemental or transitional provision and savings.

(2) Paragraph (a) of subsection (1) above does not have effect in relation to regulations under section 1(3) above or an order under section 49 above.

(3) No recommendation shall be made to Her Majesty to make an Order in Council under any provision of this Act unless a draft of the Order in Council has been laid before Parliament and approved by a resolution of each House of Parliament.

(4) Any power of a Minister of the Crown to make regulations or an order under this Act shall be exercisable by statutory instrument.

(5) A statutory instrument containing (whether alone or with other provisions) regulations under this Act shall not be made unless a draft of the instrument has been laid before, and approved by a resolution of, each House of Parliament.

(6) Subsection (5) above shall not have effect in relation to a statutory instrument if the only regulations under this Act which the instrument contains are regulations under section . . . 47(2) or (4) above.

(7) A statutory instrument—

(a) which contains (whether alone or with other provisions) any regulations under section . . . 47(2) or (4) above or an order under section 49 above, and

(b) which is not subject to any requirement that a draft of the instrument be laid before, and approved by a resolution of, each House of Parliament,

shall be subject to annulment in pursuance of a resolution of either House of Parliament.

(8) The power—

(a) of the Department of Economic Development to make an order under section 26(6) above, or

(b) of the Department of Agriculture for Northern Ireland to make regulations under section 47 above,

shall be exercisable by statutory rule for the purposes of the Statutory Rules (Northern Ireland) Order 1979; and any such order or regulations shall be subject to negative resolution within the meaning of section 41(6) of the Interpretation Act (Northern Ireland) 1954.

NOTES

Sub-ss (6), (7): words omitted repealed by the Employment Act 2008, ss 9(3), 20, Schedule, Pt 2.

[1.1221]

52 Expenses

There shall be paid out of money provided by Parliament—

(a) any expenditure incurred under this Act by a Minister of the Crown or government department or by a body performing functions on behalf of the Crown; and

(b) any increase attributable to the provisions of this Act in the sums payable out of such money under any other Act.

53 (*Introduces Sch 3 (repeals and revocations).*)

[1.1222]
54 Meaning of "worker", "employee" etc

(1) In this Act "employee" means an individual who has entered into or works under (or, where the employment has ceased, worked under) a contract of employment.

(2) In this Act "contract of employment" means a contract of service or apprenticeship, whether express or implied, and (if it is express) whether oral or in writing.

(3) In this Act "worker" (except in the phrases "agency worker" and "home worker") means an individual who has entered into or works under (or, where the employment has ceased, worked under)—

- (a) a contract of employment; or
- (b) any other contract, whether express or implied and (if it is express) whether oral or in writing, whereby the individual undertakes to do or perform personally any work or services for another party to the contract whose status is not by virtue of the contract that of a client or customer of any profession or business undertaking carried on by the individual;

and any reference to a worker's contract shall be construed accordingly.

(4) In this Act "employer", in relation to an employee or a worker, means the person by whom the employee or worker is (or, where the employment has ceased, was) employed.

(5) In this Act "employment"—

- (a) in relation to an employee, means employment under a contract of employment; and
- (b) in relation to a worker, means employment under his contract;

and "employed" shall be construed accordingly.

[1.1223]
55 Interpretation

(1) In this Act, unless the context otherwise requires,—

"civil proceedings" means proceedings before an employment tribunal or civil proceedings before any other court;

"enforcement notice" shall be construed in accordance with section 19 above;

"government department" includes a Northern Ireland department, except in section 52(a) above;

"industrial tribunal" means a tribunal established under Article 3 of the Industrial Tribunals (Northern Ireland) Order 1996;

"notice" means notice in writing;

"pay reference period" shall be construed in accordance with section 1(4) above;

"penalty notice" shall be construed in accordance with section 21 above;

"person who qualifies for the national minimum wage" shall be construed in accordance with section 1(2) above; and related expressions shall be construed accordingly;

"prescribe" means prescribe by regulations;

"regulations" means regulations made by the Secretary of State, except in the case of regulations under section 47(2) or (4) above made *by the Secretary of State and the Minister of Agriculture, Fisheries and Food acting jointly or* by the Department of Agriculture for Northern Ireland.

(2) Any reference in this Act to a person being remunerated for a pay reference period is a reference to the person being remunerated by his employer in respect of his work in that pay reference period.

(3) Any reference in this Act to doing work includes a reference to performing services; and "work" and other related expressions shall be construed accordingly.

(4) For the purposes of this Act, a person ceases to be of compulsory school age in Scotland when he ceases to be of school age in accordance with sections 31 and 33 of the Education (Scotland) Act 1980.

(5) Any reference in this Act to a person ceasing to be of compulsory school age shall, in relation to Northern Ireland, be construed in accordance with Article 46 of the Education and Libraries (Northern Ireland) Order 1986.

(6) Any reference in this Act to an employment tribunal shall, in relation to Northern Ireland, be construed as a reference to an industrial tribunal.

NOTES

Sub-s (1): words in italics in the definition "regulations" repealed by the Enterprise and Regulatory Reform Act 2013, s 72(4), Sch 20, as from 1 October 2013 (in relation to England) and as from a day to be appointed (in relation to Wales and Scotland).

Note: with regard to the definitions "enforcement notice" and "penalty notice", note that ss 19 and 21 of this Act have been substituted as noted *ante* and no longer make reference to these terms.

Minister of Agriculture, Fisheries and Food: the Ministry of Agriculture, Fisheries and Food was dissolved and the functions of the Minister were transferred to the Secretary of State by the Ministry of Agriculture, Fisheries and Food (Dissolution) Order 2002, SI 2002/794.

[1.1224]
56 Short title, commencement and extent

(1) This Act may be cited as the National Minimum Wage Act 1998.

(2) Apart from this section and any powers to make an Order in Council or regulations or an order (which accordingly come into force on the day on which this Act is passed) the provisions of this Act shall come into force on such day or days as the Secretary of State may by order appoint; and different days may be appointed for different purposes.

(3) This Act extends to Northern Ireland.

NOTES

Orders: the National Minimum Wage Act 1998 (Commencement No 1 and Transitional Provisions) Order 1998, SI 1998/2574; the National Minimum Wage Act 1998 (Commencement No 2 and Transitional Provisions) Order 1999, SI 1999/685.

SCHEDULES 1–3

Sch 1 (provisions as to the Low Pay Commission), and Sch 2 (amendments to agricultural wages legislation) outside the scope of this work; Sch 3 contains repeals and revocations only and, in so far as relevant to this work, these have been incorporated at the appropriate place.)

HUMAN RIGHTS ACT 1998

(1998 c 42)

ARRANGEMENT OF SECTIONS

Introduction

An Act to give further effect to rights and freedoms guaranteed under the European Convention on Human Rights; to make provision with respect to holders of certain judicial offices who become judges of the European Court of Human Rights; and for connected purposes

[9 November 1998]

NOTES

Only certain provisions of this Act are included: those omitted are outside the scope of this work for reasons given in notes thereto.

Introduction

[1.1225]

1 The Convention Rights

(1) In this Act "the Convention rights" means the rights and fundamental freedoms set out in—

(a) Articles 2 to 12 and 14 of the Convention,

(b) Articles 1 to 3 of the First Protocol, and

(c) [Article 1 of the Thirteenth Protocol],

as read with Articles 16 to 18 of the Convention.

(2) Those Articles are to have effect for the purposes of this Act subject to any designated derogation or reservation (as to which see sections 14 and 15).

(3) The Articles are set out in Schedule 1.

(4) The [Secretary of State] may by order make such amendments to this Act as he considers appropriate to reflect the effect, in relation to the United Kingdom, of a protocol.

(5) In subsection (4) "protocol" means a protocol to the Convention—

(a) which the United Kingdom has ratified; or

(b) which the United Kingdom has signed with a view to ratification.

(6) No amendment may be made by an order under subsection (4) so as to come into force before the protocol concerned is in force in relation to the United Kingdom.

NOTES

Sub-s (1): words in square brackets in para (c) substituted by the Human Rights Act 1998 (Amendment) Order 2004, SI 2004/1574, art 2(1).

Sub-s (4): words in square brackets substituted by the Secretary of State for Constitutional Affairs Order 2003, SI 2003/1887, art 9, Sch 2, para 10(1).

Orders: the Human Rights Act 1998 (Amendment) Order 2004, SI 2004/1574.

[1.1226]

2 Interpretation of Convention rights

(1) A court or tribunal determining a question which has arisen in connection with a Convention right must take into account any—

(a) judgment, decision, declaration or advisory opinion of the European Court of Human Rights,

(b) opinion of the Commission given in a report adopted under Article 31 of the Convention,

(c) decision of the Commission in connection with Article 26 or 27(2) of the Convention, or

(d) decision of the Committee of Ministers taken under Article 46 of the Convention,

whenever made or given, so far as, in the opinion of the court or tribunal, it is relevant to the proceedings in which that question has arisen.

(2) Evidence of any judgment, decision, declaration or opinion of which account may have to be taken under this section is to be given in proceedings before any court or tribunal in such manner as may be provided by rules.

(3) In this section "rules" means rules of court or, in the case of proceedings before a tribunal, rules made for the purposes of this section—

(a) by . . . [the Lord Chancellor or] the Secretary of State, in relation to any proceedings outside Scotland;

(b) by the Secretary of State, in relation to proceedings in Scotland; or

(c) by a Northern Ireland department, in relation to proceedings before a tribunal in Northern Ireland—

(i) which deals with transferred matters; and

(ii) for which no rules made under paragraph (a) are in force.

NOTES

Sub-s (3): words omitted from para (a) repealed by the Secretary of State for Constitutional Affairs Order 2003, SI 2003/1887, art 9, Sch 2, para 10(2); words in square brackets in para (a) inserted by the Transfer of Functions (Lord Chancellor and Secretary of State) Order 2005, SI 2005/3429, art 8, Schedule, para 3.

Rules: the Act of Adjournal (Criminal Procedure Rules Amendment No 2) (Human Rights Act 1998) 2000, SSI 2000/315; the Act of Sederunt (Rules of the Court of Session Amendment No 6) (Human Rights Act 1998) 2000, SSI 2000/316.

Legislation

[1.1227]

3 Interpretation of legislation

(1) So far as it is possible to do so, primary legislation and subordinate legislation must be read and given effect in a way which is compatible with the Convention rights.

(2) This section—

(a) applies to primary legislation and subordinate legislation whenever enacted;

(b) does not affect the validity, continuing operation or enforcement of any incompatible primary legislation; and

(c) does not affect the validity, continuing operation or enforcement of any incompatible subordinate legislation if (disregarding any possibility of revocation) primary legislation prevents removal of the incompatibility.

[1.1228]

4 Declaration of incompatibility

(1) Subsection (2) applies in any proceedings in which a court determines whether a provision of primary legislation is compatible with a Convention right.

(2) If the court is satisfied that the provision is incompatible with a Convention right, it may make a declaration of that incompatibility.

(3) Subsection (4) applies in any proceedings in which a court determines whether a provision of subordinate legislation, made in the exercise of a power conferred by primary legislation, is compatible with a Convention right.

(4) If the court is satisfied—

(a) that the provision is incompatible with a Convention right, and

(b) that (disregarding any possibility of revocation) the primary legislation concerned prevents removal of the incompatibility,

it may make a declaration of that incompatibility.

(5) In this section "court" means—

[(a) the Supreme Court;]

(b) the Judicial Committee of the Privy Council;

(c) the [Court Martial Appeal Court];

(d) in Scotland, the High Court of Justiciary sitting otherwise than as a trial court or the Court of Session;

(e) in England and Wales or Northern Ireland, the High Court or the Court of Appeal;

[(f) the Court of Protection, in any matter being dealt with by the President of the Family Division, the [Chancellor of the High Court] or a puisne judge of the High Court].

(6) A declaration under this section ("a declaration of incompatibility")—

(a) does not affect the validity, continuing operation or enforcement of the provision in respect of which it is given; and

(b) is not binding on the parties to the proceedings in which it is made.

NOTES

Sub-s (5): para (a) substituted by the Constitutional Reform Act 2005, s 40, Sch 9, Pt 1, para 66(1), (2); words in square brackets in para (c) substituted by the Armed Forces Act 2006, s 378(1), Sch 16, para 156; para (f) added by the Mental Capacity Act 2005, s 67(1), Sch 6, para 43; words in square brackets in para (f) substituted by the Crime and Courts Act 2013, s 21(4), Sch 14, Pt 3, para 5(5).

5 (*Right of Crown to intervene in certain proceedings (outside the scope of this work).*)

Public authorities

[1.1229]

6 Acts of public authorities

(1) It is unlawful for a public authority to act in a way which is incompatible with a Convention right.

(2) Subsection (1) does not apply to an act if—

(a) as the result of one or more provisions of primary legislation, the authority could not have acted differently; or

(b) in the case of one or more provisions of, or made under, primary legislation which cannot be read or given effect in a way which is compatible with the Convention rights, the authority was acting so as to give effect to or enforce those provisions.

(3) In this section "public authority" includes—

(a) a court or tribunal, and

(b) any person certain of whose functions are functions of a public nature,

but does not include either House of Parliament or a person exercising functions in connection with proceedings in Parliament.

(4) . . .

(5) In relation to a particular act, a person is not a public authority by virtue only of subsection (3)(b) if the nature of the act is private.

(6) "An act" includes a failure to act but does not include a failure to—

(a) introduce in, or lay before, Parliament a proposal for legislation; or

(b) make any primary legislation or remedial order.

NOTES

Sub-s (4): repealed by the Constitutional Reform Act 2005, ss 40, 146, Sch 9, Pt 1, para 66(1), (4), Sch 18, Pt 5.

[1.1230]

7 Proceedings

(1) A person who claims that a public authority has acted (or proposes to act) in a way which is made unlawful by section 6(1) may—

(a) bring proceedings against the authority under this Act in the appropriate court or tribunal, or

(b) rely on the Convention right or rights concerned in any legal proceedings,

but only if he is (or would be) a victim of the unlawful act.

(2) In subsection (1)(a) "appropriate court or tribunal" means such court or tribunal as may be determined in accordance with rules; and proceedings against an authority include a counterclaim or similar proceeding.

(3) If the proceedings are brought on an application for judicial review, the applicant is to be taken to have a sufficient interest in relation to the unlawful act only if he is, or would be, a victim of that act.

(4) If the proceedings are made by way of a petition for judicial review in Scotland, the applicant shall be taken to have title and interest to sue in relation to the unlawful act only if he is, or would be, a victim of that act.

(5) Proceedings under subsection (1)(a) must be brought before the end of—

(a) the period of one year beginning with the date on which the act complained of took place; or

(b) such longer period as the court or tribunal considers equitable having regard to all the circumstances,

but that is subject to any rule imposing a stricter time limit in relation to the procedure in question.

(6) In subsection (1)(b) "legal proceedings" includes—

(a) proceedings brought by or at the instigation of a public authority; and

(b) an appeal against the decision of a court or tribunal.

(7) For the purposes of this section, a person is a victim of an unlawful act only if he would be a victim for the purposes of Article 34 of the Convention if proceedings were brought in the European Court of Human Rights in respect of that act.

(8) Nothing in this Act creates a criminal offence.

(9) In this section "rules" means—

(a) in relation to proceedings before a court or tribunal outside Scotland, rules made by . . . [the Lord Chancellor or] the Secretary of State for the purposes of this section or rules of court,

(b) in relation to proceedings before a court or tribunal in Scotland, rules made by the Secretary of State for those purposes,

(c) in relation to proceedings before a tribunal in Northern Ireland—

(i) which deals with transferred matters; and

(ii) for which no rules made under paragraph (a) are in force,

rules made by a Northern Ireland department for those purposes,

and includes provision made by order under section 1 of the Courts and Legal Services Act 1990.

(10) In making rules, regard must be had to section 9.

(11) The Minister who has power to make rules in relation to a particular tribunal may, to the extent he considers it necessary to ensure that the tribunal can provide an appropriate remedy in relation to an act (or proposed act) of a public authority which is (or would be) unlawful as a result of section 6(1), by order add to—

(a) the relief or remedies which the tribunal may grant; or

(b) the grounds on which it may grant any of them.

(12) An order made under subsection (11) may contain such incidental, supplemental, consequential or transitional provision as the Minister making it considers appropriate.

(13) "The Minister" includes the Northern Ireland department concerned.

NOTES

Sub-s (9): words omitted from para (a) repealed by the Secretary of State for Constitutional Affairs Order 2003, SI 2003/1887, art 9, Sch 2, para 10(2); words in square brackets in para (a) inserted by the Transfer of Functions (Lord Chancellor and Secretary of State) Order 2005, SI 2005/3429, art 8, Schedule, para 3.

Rules: the Human Rights Act 1998 (Jurisdiction) (Scotland) Rules 2000, SSI 2000/301; the Proscribed Organisations Appeal Commission (Human Rights Act 1998 Proceedings) Rules 2006, SI 2006/2290.

Orders: as of 15 May 2019, no Orders had been made under sub-s (11).

[1.1231]

8 Judicial remedies

(1) In relation to any act (or proposed act) of a public authority which the court finds is (or would be) unlawful, it may grant such relief or remedy, or make such order, within its powers as it considers just and appropriate.

(2) But damages may be awarded only by a court which has power to award damages, or to order the payment of compensation, in civil proceedings.

(3) No award of damages is to be made unless, taking account of all the circumstances of the case, including—

(a) any other relief or remedy granted, or order made, in relation to the act in question (by that or any other court), and

(b) the consequences of any decision (of that or any other court) in respect of that act,

the court is satisfied that the award is necessary to afford just satisfaction to the person in whose favour it is made.

(4) In determining—

(a) whether to award damages, or

(b) the amount of an award,

the court must take into account the principles applied by the European Court of Human Rights in relation to the award of compensation under Article 41 of the Convention.

(5) A public authority against which damages are awarded is to be treated—

(a) in Scotland, for the purposes of section 3 of the Law Reform (Miscellaneous Provisions) (Scotland) Act 1940 as if the award were made in an action of damages in which the authority has been found liable in respect of loss or damage to the person to whom the award is made;

(b) for the purposes of the Civil Liability (Contribution) Act 1978 as liable in respect of damage suffered by the person to whom the award is made.

(6) In this section—

"court" includes a tribunal;

"damages" means damages for an unlawful act of a public authority; and

"unlawful" means unlawful under section 6(1).

[1.1232]

9 Judicial acts

(1) Proceedings under section 7(1)(a) in respect of a judicial act may be brought only—

(a) by exercising a right of appeal;

(b) on an application (in Scotland a petition) for judicial review; or

(c) in such other forum as may be prescribed by rules.

(2) That does not affect any rule of law which prevents a court from being the subject of judicial review.

(3) In proceedings under this Act in respect of a judicial act done in good faith, damages may not be awarded otherwise than to compensate a person to the extent required by Article 5(5) of the Convention.

(4) An award of damages permitted by subsection (3) is to be made against the Crown; but no award may be made unless the appropriate person, if not a party to the proceedings, is joined.

(5) In this section—

"appropriate person" means the Minister responsible for the court concerned, or a person or government department nominated by him;

"court" includes a tribunal;

"judge" includes a member of a tribunal, a justice of the peace [(or, in Northern Ireland, a lay magistrate)] and a clerk or other officer entitled to exercise the jurisdiction of a court;

"judicial act" means a judicial act of a court and includes an act done on the instructions, or on behalf, of a judge; and

"rules" has the same meaning as in section 7(9).

NOTES

Sub-s (5): words in square brackets in the definition "judge" inserted by the Justice (Northern Ireland) Act 2002, s 10(6), Sch 4, para 39.

Rules: the Human Rights Act 1998 (Jurisdiction) (Scotland) Rules 2000, SSI 2000/301.

Remedial action

[1.1233]

10 Power to take remedial action

(1) This section applies if—

(a) a provision of legislation has been declared under section 4 to be incompatible with a Convention right and, if an appeal lies—

(i) all persons who may appeal have stated in writing that they do not intend to do so;

(ii) the time for bringing an appeal has expired and no appeal has been brought within that time; or

(iii) an appeal brought within that time has been determined or abandoned; or

(b) it appears to a Minister of the Crown or Her Majesty in Council that, having regard to a finding of the European Court of Human Rights made after the coming into force of this section in proceedings against the United Kingdom, a provision of legislation is incompatible with an obligation of the United Kingdom arising from the Convention.

(2) If a Minister of the Crown considers that there are compelling reasons for proceeding under this section, he may by order make such amendments to the legislation as he considers necessary to remove the incompatibility.

(3) If, in the case of subordinate legislation, a Minister of the Crown considers—

(a) that it is necessary to amend the primary legislation under which the subordinate legislation in question was made, in order to enable the incompatibility to be removed, and

(b) that there are compelling reasons for proceeding under this section,

he may by order make such amendments to the primary legislation as he considers necessary.

(4) This section also applies where the provision in question is in subordinate legislation and has been quashed, or declared invalid, by reason of incompatibility with a Convention right and the Minister proposes to proceed under paragraph 2(b) of Schedule 2.

(5) If the legislation is an Order in Council, the power conferred by subsection (2) or (3) is exercisable by Her Majesty in Council.

(6) In this section "legislation" does not include a Measure of the Church Assembly or of the General Synod of the Church of England.

(7) Schedule 2 makes further provision about remedial orders.

NOTES

Orders: the Marriage Act 1949 (Remedial) Order 2007, SI 2007/438; the Asylum and Immigration (Treatment of Claimants, etc) Act 2004 (Remedial) Order 2011, SI 2011/1158; the Sexual Offences Act 2003 (Remedial) Order 2012, SI 2012/1883.

Other rights and proceedings

[1.1234]

11 Safeguard for existing human rights

A person's reliance on a Convention right does not restrict—

(a) any other right or freedom conferred on him by or under any law having effect in any part of the United Kingdom; or

(b) his right to make any claim or bring any proceedings which he could make or bring apart from sections 7 to 9.

[1.1235]

12 Freedom of expression

(1) This section applies if a court is considering whether to grant any relief which, if granted, might affect the exercise of the Convention right to freedom of expression.

(2) If the person against whom the application for relief is made ("the respondent") is neither present nor represented, no such relief is to be granted unless the court is satisfied—

(a) that the applicant has taken all practicable steps to notify the respondent; or

(b) that there are compelling reasons why the respondent should not be notified.

(3) No such relief is to be granted so as to restrain publication before trial unless the court is satisfied that the applicant is likely to establish that publication should not be allowed.

(4) The court must have particular regard to the importance of the Convention right to freedom of expression and, where the proceedings relate to material which the respondent claims, or which appears to the court, to be journalistic, literary or artistic material (or to conduct connected with such material), to—

(a) the extent to which—

(i) the material has, or is about to, become available to the public; or

(ii) it is, or would be, in the public interest for the material to be published;

(b) any relevant privacy code.

(5) In this section—

"court" includes a tribunal; and

"relief" includes any remedy or order (other than in criminal proceedings).

[1.1236]

13 Freedom of thought, conscience and religion

(1) If a court's determination of any question arising under this Act might affect the exercise by a religious organisation (itself or its members collectively) of the Convention right to freedom of thought, conscience and religion, it must have particular regard to the importance of that right.

(2) In this section "court" includes a tribunal.

14–18 *(Ss 14–17 (derogations and reservations), s 18 (appointment of judges of the European Court of Human Rights) outside the scope of this work.)*

Parliamentary procedure

[1.1237]

19 Statements of compatibility

(1) A Minister of the Crown in charge of a Bill in either House of Parliament must, before Second Reading of the Bill—

(a) make a statement to the effect that in his view the provisions of the Bill are compatible with the Convention rights ("a statement of compatibility"); or

(b) make a statement to the effect that although he is unable to make a statement of compatibility the government nevertheless wishes the House to proceed with the Bill.

(2) The statement must be in writing and be published in such manner as the Minister making it considers appropriate.

Supplemental

[1.1238]

20 Orders etc under this Act

(1) Any power of a Minister of the Crown to make an order under this Act is exercisable by statutory instrument.

(2) The power of . . . [the Lord Chancellor or] the Secretary of State to make rules (other than rules of court) under section 2(3) or 7(9) is exercisable by statutory instrument.

(3) Any statutory instrument made under section 14, 15 or 16(7) must be laid before Parliament.

(4) No order may be made by . . . [the Lord Chancellor or] the Secretary of State under section 1(4), 7(11) or 16(2) unless a draft of the order has been laid before, and approved by, each House of Parliament.

(5) Any statutory instrument made under section 18(7) or Schedule 4, or to which subsection (2) applies, shall be subject to annulment in pursuance of a resolution of either House of Parliament.

(6) The power of a Northern Ireland department to make—

(a) rules under section 2(3)(c) or 7(9)(c), or

(b) an order under section 7(11),

is exercisable by statutory rule for the purposes of the Statutory Rules (Northern Ireland) Order 1979.

(7) Any rules made under section 2(3)(c) or 7(9)(c) shall be subject to negative resolution; and section 41(6) of the Interpretation Act (Northern Ireland) 1954 (meaning of "subject to negative resolution") shall apply as if the power to make the rules were conferred by an Act of the Northern Ireland Assembly.

(8) No order may be made by a Northern Ireland department under section 7(11) unless a draft of the order has been laid before, and approved by, the Northern Ireland Assembly.

NOTES

Sub-ss (2), (4): words omitted repealed by the Secretary of State for Constitutional Affairs Order 2003, SI 2003/1887, art 9, Sch 2, para 10(2); words in square brackets inserted by the Transfer of Functions (Lord Chancellor and Secretary of State) Order 2005, SI 2005/3429, art 8, Schedule, para 3.

[1.1239]

21 Interpretation, etc

(1) In this Act—

"amend" includes repeal and apply (with or without modifications);

"the appropriate Minister" means the Minister of the Crown having charge of the appropriate authorised government department (within the meaning of the Crown Proceedings Act 1947);

"the Commission" means the European Commission of Human Rights;

"the Convention" means the Convention for the Protection of Human Rights and Fundamental Freedoms, agreed by the Council of Europe at Rome on 4th November 1950 as it has effect for the time being in relation to the United Kingdom;

"declaration of incompatibility" means a declaration under section 4;

"Minister of the Crown" has the same meaning as in the Ministers of the Crown Act 1975;

"Northern Ireland Minister" includes the First Minister and the deputy First Minister in Northern Ireland;

"primary legislation" means any—

(a) public general Act;

(b) local and personal Act;

(c) private Act;

(d) Measure of the Church Assembly;

(e) Measure of the General Synod of the Church of England;

(f) Order in Council—

(i) made in exercise of Her Majesty's Royal Prerogative;

(ii) made under section 38(1)(a) of the Northern Ireland Constitution Act 1973 or the corresponding provision of the Northern Ireland Act 1998; or

(iii) amending an Act of a kind mentioned in paragraph (a), (b) or (c);

and includes an order or other instrument made under primary legislation (otherwise than by the [Welsh Ministers, the First Minister for Wales, the Counsel General to the Welsh Assembly Government], a member of the Scottish Executive, a Northern Ireland Minister or a Northern Ireland department) to the extent to which it operates to bring one or more provisions of that legislation into force or amends any primary legislation;

"the First Protocol" means the protocol to the Convention agreed at Paris on 20th March 1952;

. . .

"the Eleventh Protocol" means the protocol to the Convention (restructuring the control machinery established by the Convention) agreed at Strasbourg on 11th May 1994;

["the Thirteenth Protocol" means the protocol to the Convention (concerning the abolition of the death penalty in all circumstances) agreed at Vilnius on 3rd May 2002;]

"remedial order" means an order under section 10;

"subordinate legislation" means any—

(a) Order in Council other than one—

(i) made in exercise of Her Majesty's Royal Prerogative;

(ii) made under section 38(1)(a) of the Northern Ireland Constitution Act 1973 or the corresponding provision of the Northern Ireland Act 1998; or

(iii) amending an Act of a kind mentioned in the definition of primary legislation;

(b) Act of the Scottish Parliament;

[(ba) Measure of the National Assembly for Wales;

(bb) Act of the National Assembly for Wales;]

(c) Act of the Parliament of Northern Ireland;

(d) Measure of the Assembly established under section 1 of the Northern Ireland Assembly Act 1973;

(e) Act of the Northern Ireland Assembly;

(f) order, rules, regulations, scheme, warrant, byelaw or other instrument made under primary legislation (except to the extent to which it operates to bring one or more provisions of that legislation into force or amends any primary legislation);

(g) order, rules, regulations, scheme, warrant, byelaw or other instrument made under legislation mentioned in paragraph (b), (c), (d) or (e) or made under an Order in Council applying only to Northern Ireland;

(h) order, rules, regulations, scheme, warrant, byelaw or other instrument made by a member of the Scottish Executive[, Welsh Ministers, the First Minister for Wales, the Counsel General to the Welsh Assembly Government], a Northern Ireland Minister or a Northern Ireland department in exercise of prerogative or other executive functions of Her Majesty which are exercisable by such a person on behalf of Her Majesty;

"transferred matters" has the same meaning as in the Northern Ireland Act 1998; and

"tribunal" means any tribunal in which legal proceedings may be brought.

(2) The references in paragraphs (b) and (c) of section 2(1) to Articles are to Articles of the Convention as they had effect immediately before the coming into force of the Eleventh Protocol.

(3) The reference in paragraph (d) of section 2(1) to Article 46 includes a reference to Articles 32 and 54 of the Convention as they had effect immediately before the coming into force of the Eleventh Protocol.

(4) The references in section 2(1) to a report or decision of the Commission or a decision of the Committee of Ministers include references to a report or decision made as provided by paragraphs 3, 4 and 6 of Article 5 of the Eleventh Protocol (transitional provisions).

(5) . . .

NOTES

Sub-s (1) is amended as follows:

Words in square brackets in the definition "primary legislation" substituted by the Government of Wales Act 2006, s 160(1), Sch 10, para 56(1), (2).

Definition "the Sixth Protocol" (omitted) repealed, and definition "the Thirteenth Protocol" inserted, by the Human Rights Act 1998 (Amendment) Order 2004, SI 2004/1574, art 2(2).

In definition "subordinate legislation" paras (ba), (bb) inserted, and words in square brackets in para (h) inserted, by the Government of Wales Act 2006, s 160(1), Sch 10, para 56(1), (3), (4).

Sub-s (5): repealed by the Armed Forces Act 2006, s 378(2), Sch 17.

Welsh Assembly Government: see the Wales Act 2014, s 4 which provides that, unless the context requires otherwise, any reference to the Welsh Assembly Government is to be read as, or as including, a reference to the Welsh Government.

[1.1240]

22 Short title, commencement, application and extent

(1) This Act may be cited as the Human Rights Act 1998.

(2) Sections 18, 20 and 21(5) and this section come into force on the passing of this Act.

(3) The other provisions of this Act come into force on such day as the Secretary of State may by order appoint; and different days may be appointed for different purposes.

(4) Paragraph (b) of subsection (1) of section 7 applies to proceedings brought by or at the instigation of a public authority whenever the act in question took place; but otherwise that subsection does not apply to an act taking place before the coming into force of that section.

(5) This Act binds the Crown.

(6) This Act extends to Northern Ireland.

(7) . . .

NOTES

Sub-s (7): repealed by the Armed Forces Act 2006, s 378(2), Sch 17.

Orders: the Human Rights Act 1998 (Commencement) Order 1998, SI 1998/2882; the Human Rights Act 1998 (Commencement No 2) Order 2000, SI 2000/1851.

SCHEDULES

SCHEDULE 1
THE ARTICLES

Section 1(3)

PART I
THE CONVENTION

RIGHTS AND FREEDOMS

Article 2
Right to life

[1.1241]

1. Everyone's right to life shall be protected by law. No one shall be deprived of his life intentionally save in the execution of a sentence of a court following his conviction of a crime for which this penalty is provided by law.

2. Deprivation of life shall not be regarded as inflicted in contravention of this Article when it results from the use of force which is no more than absolutely necessary:

(a) in defence of any person from unlawful violence;

(b) in order to effect a lawful arrest or to prevent the escape of a person lawfully detained;

(c) in action lawfully taken for the purpose of quelling a riot or insurrection.

Article 3
Prohibition of torture

No one shall be subjected to torture or to inhuman or degrading treatment or punishment.

Article 4
Prohibition of slavery and forced labour

1. No one shall be held in slavery or servitude.

2. No one shall be required to perform forced or compulsory labour.

3. For the purpose of this Article the term "forced or compulsory labour" shall not include:

(a) any work required to be done in the ordinary course of detention imposed according to the provisions of Article 5 of this Convention or during conditional release from such detention;

(b) any service of a military character or, in case of conscientious objectors in countries where they are recognised, service exacted instead of compulsory military service;

(c) any service exacted in case of an emergency or calamity threatening the life or well-being of the community;

(d) any work or service which forms part of normal civic obligations.

Article 5
Right to liberty and security

1. Everyone has the right to liberty and security of person. No one shall be deprived of his liberty save in the following cases and in accordance with a procedure prescribed by law:

(a) the lawful detention of a person after conviction by a competent court;
(b) the lawful arrest or detention of a person for non-compliance with the lawful order of a court or in order to secure the fulfilment of any obligation prescribed by law;
(c) the lawful arrest or detention of a person effected for the purpose of bringing him before the competent legal authority on reasonable suspicion of having committed an offence or when it is reasonably considered necessary to prevent his committing an offence or fleeing after having done so;
(d) the detention of a minor by lawful order for the purpose of educational supervision or his lawful detention for the purpose of bringing him before the competent legal authority;
(e) the lawful detention of persons for the prevention of the spreading of infectious diseases, of persons of unsound mind, alcoholics or drug addicts or vagrants;
(f) the lawful arrest or detention of a person to prevent his effecting an unauthorised entry into the country or of a person against whom action is being taken with a view to deportation or extradition.

2. Everyone who is arrested shall be informed promptly, in a language which he understands, of the reasons for his arrest and of any charge against him.

3. Everyone arrested or detained in accordance with the provisions of paragraph 1(c) of this Article shall be brought promptly before a judge or other officer authorised by law to exercise judicial power and shall be entitled to trial within a reasonable time or to release pending trial. Release may be conditioned by guarantees to appear for trial.

4. Everyone who is deprived of his liberty by arrest or detention shall be entitled to take proceedings by which the lawfulness of his detention shall be decided speedily by a court and his release ordered if the detention is not lawful.

5. Everyone who has been the victim of arrest or detention in contravention of the provisions of this Article shall have an enforceable right to compensation.

Article 6
Right to a fair trial

1. In the determination of his civil rights and obligations or of any criminal charge against him, everyone is entitled to a fair and public hearing within a reasonable time by an independent and impartial tribunal established by law. Judgment shall be pronounced publicly but the press and public may be excluded from all or part of the trial in the interest of morals, public order or national security in a democratic society, where the interests of juveniles or the protection of the private life of the parties so require, or to the extent strictly necessary in the opinion of the court in special circumstances where publicity would prejudice the interests of justice.

2. Everyone charged with a criminal offence shall be presumed innocent until proved guilty according to law.

3. Everyone charged with a criminal offence has the following minimum rights:
(a) to be informed promptly, in a language which he understands and in detail, of the nature and cause of the accusation against him;
(b) to have adequate time and facilities for the preparation of his defence;
(c) to defend himself in person or through legal assistance of his own choosing or, if he has not sufficient means to pay for legal assistance, to be given it free when the interests of justice so require;
(d) to examine or have examined witnesses against him and to obtain the attendance and examination of witnesses on his behalf under the same conditions as witnesses against him;
(e) to have the free assistance of an interpreter if he cannot understand or speak the language used in court.

Article 7
No punishment without law

1. No one shall be held guilty of any criminal offence on account of any act or omission which did not constitute a criminal offence under national or international law at the time when it was committed. Nor shall a heavier penalty be imposed than the one that was applicable at the time the criminal offence was committed.

2. This Article shall not prejudice the trial and punishment of any person for any act or omission which, at the time when it was committed, was criminal according to the general principles of law recognised by civilised nations.

Article 8
Right to respect for private and family life

1. Everyone has the right to respect for his private and family life, his home and his correspondence.

2. There shall be no interference by a public authority with the exercise of this right except such as is in accordance with the law and is necessary in a democratic society in the interests of national security, public safety or the economic well-being of the country, for the prevention of disorder or crime, for the protection of health or morals, or for the protection of the rights and freedoms of others.

Article 9

Freedom of thought, conscience and religion

1. Everyone has the right to freedom of thought, conscience and religion; this right includes freedom to change his religion or belief and freedom, either alone or in community with others and in public or private, to manifest his religion or belief, in worship, teaching, practice and observance.

2. Freedom to manifest one's religion or beliefs shall be subject only to such limitations as are prescribed by law and are necessary in a democratic society in the interests of public safety, for the protection of public order, health or morals, or for the protection of the rights and freedoms of others.

Article 10

Freedom of expression

1. Everyone has the right to freedom of expression. This right shall include freedom to hold opinions and to receive and impart information and ideas without interference by public authority and regardless of frontiers. This Article shall not prevent States from requiring the licensing of broadcasting, television or cinema enterprises.

2. The exercise of these freedoms, since it carries with it duties and responsibilities, may be subject to such formalities, conditions, restrictions or penalties as are prescribed by law and are necessary in a democratic society, in the interests of national security, territorial integrity or public safety, for the prevention of disorder or crime, for the protection of health or morals, for the protection of the reputation or rights of others, for preventing the disclosure of information received in confidence, or for maintaining the authority and impartiality of the judiciary.

Article 11

Freedom of assembly and association

1. Everyone has the right to freedom of peaceful assembly and to freedom of association with others, including the right to form and to join trade unions for the protection of his interests.

2. No restrictions shall be placed on the exercise of these rights other than such as are prescribed by law and are necessary in a democratic society in the interests of national security or public safety, for the prevention of disorder or crime, for the protection of health or morals or for the protection of the rights and freedoms of others. This Article shall not prevent the imposition of lawful restrictions on the exercise of these rights by members of the armed forces, of the police or of the administration of the State.

Article 12

Right to marry

Men and women of marriageable age have the right to marry and to found a family, according to the national laws governing the exercise of this right.

Article 14

Prohibition of discrimination

The enjoyment of the rights and freedoms set forth in this Convention shall be secured without discrimination on any ground such as sex, race, colour, language, religion, political or other opinion, national or social origin, association with a national minority, property, birth or other status.

Article 16

Restrictions on political activity of aliens

Nothing in Articles 10, 11 and 14 shall be regarded as preventing the High Contracting Parties from imposing restrictions on the political activity of aliens.

Article 17

Prohibition of abuse of rights

Nothing in this Convention may be interpreted as implying for any State, group or person any right to engage in any activity or perform any act aimed at the destruction of any of the rights and freedoms set forth herein or at their limitation to a greater extent than is provided for in the Convention.

Article 18

Limitation on use of restrictions on rights

The restrictions permitted under this Convention to the said rights and freedoms shall not be applied for any purpose other than those for which they have been prescribed.

PART II
THE FIRST PROTOCOL

Article 1

Protection of property

[1.1242]
Every natural or legal person is entitled to the peaceful enjoyment of his possessions. No one shall be deprived of his possessions except in the public interest and subject to the conditions provided for by law and by the general principles of international law.

The preceding provisions shall not, however, in any way impair the right of a State to enforce such laws as it deems necessary to control the use of property in accordance with the general interest or to secure the payment of taxes or other contributions or penalties.

Article 2

Right to education

No person shall be denied the right to education. In the exercise of any functions which it assumes in relation to education and to teaching, the State shall respect the right of parents to ensure such education and teaching in conformity with their own religious and philosophical convictions.

Article 3

Right to free elections

The High Contracting Parties undertake to hold free elections at reasonable intervals by secret ballot, under conditions which will ensure the free expression of the opinion of the people in the choice of the legislature.

[PART III
ARTICLE 1 OF THE THIRTEENTH PROTOCOL

Abolition of the Death Penalty

[1.1243]
The death penalty shall be abolished. No one shall be condemned to such penalty or executed.]

NOTES

Substituted by the Human Rights Act 1998 (Amendment) Order 2004, SI 2004/1574, art 2(3).

SCHEDULE 2
REMEDIAL ORDERS

Section 10

Orders

[1.1244]
1. (1) A remedial order may—
- (a) contain such incidental, supplemental, consequential or transitional provision as the person making it considers appropriate;
- (b) be made so as to have effect from a date earlier than that on which it is made;
- (c) make provision for the delegation of specific functions;
- (d) make different provision for different cases.

(2) The power conferred by sub-paragraph (1)(a) includes—
- (a) power to amend primary legislation (including primary legislation other than that which contains the incompatible provision); and
- (b) power to amend or revoke subordinate legislation (including subordinate legislation other than that which contains the incompatible provision).

(3) A remedial order may be made so as to have the same extent as the legislation which it affects.

(4) No person is to be guilty of an offence solely as a result of the retrospective effect of a remedial order.

Procedure

2. No remedial order may be made unless—
- (a) a draft of the order has been approved by a resolution of each House of Parliament made after the end of the period of 60 days beginning with the day on which the draft was laid; or

(b) it is declared in the order that it appears to the person making it that, because of the urgency of the matter, it is necessary to make the order without a draft being so approved.

Orders laid in draft

3. (1) No draft may be laid under paragraph 2(a) unless—

(a) the person proposing to make the order has laid before Parliament a document which contains a draft of the proposed order and the required information; and

(b) the period of 60 days, beginning with the day on which the document required by this sub-paragraph was laid, has ended.

(2) If representations have been made during that period, the draft laid under paragraph 2(a) must be accompanied by a statement containing—

(a) a summary of the representations; and

(b) if, as a result of the representations, the proposed order has been changed, details of the changes.

Urgent cases

4. (1) If a remedial order ("the original order") is made without being approved in draft, the person making it must lay it before Parliament, accompanied by the required information, after it is made.

(2) If representations have been made during the period of 60 days beginning with the day on which the original order was made, the person making it must (after the end of that period) lay before Parliament a statement containing—

(a) a summary of the representations; and

(b) if, as a result of the representations, he considers it appropriate to make changes to the original order, details of the changes.

(3) If sub-paragraph (2)(b) applies, the person making the statement must—

(a) make a further remedial order replacing the original order; and

(b) lay the replacement order before Parliament.

(4) If, at the end of the period of 120 days beginning with the day on which the original order was made, a resolution has not been passed by each House approving the original or replacement order, the order ceases to have effect (but without that affecting anything previously done under either order or the power to make a fresh remedial order).

Definitions

5. In this Schedule—

"representations" means representations about a remedial order (or proposed remedial order) made to the person making (or proposing to make) it and includes any relevant Parliamentary report or resolution; and

"required information" means—

(a) an explanation of the incompatibility which the order (or proposed order) seeks to remove, including particulars of the relevant declaration, finding or order; and

(b) a statement of the reasons for proceeding under section 10 and for making an order in those terms.

Calculating periods

6. In calculating any period for the purposes of this Schedule, no account is to be taken of any time during which—

(a) Parliament is dissolved or prorogued; or

(b) both Houses are adjourned for more than four days.

[**7.** (1) This paragraph applies in relation to—

(a) any remedial order made, and any draft of such an order proposed to be made,—

(i) by the Scottish Ministers; or

(ii) within devolved competence (within the meaning of the Scotland Act 1998) by Her Majesty in Council; and

(b) any document or statement to be laid in connection with such an order (or proposed order).

(2) This Schedule has effect in relation to any such order (or proposed order), document or statement subject to the following modifications.

(3) Any reference to Parliament, each House of Parliament or both Houses of Parliament shall be construed as a reference to the Scottish Parliament.

(4) Paragraph 6 does not apply and instead, in calculating any period for the purposes of this Schedule, no account is to be taken of any time during which the Scottish Parliament is dissolved or is in recess for more than four days.]

NOTES

Para 7: added by the Scotland Act 1998 (Consequential Modifications) Order 2000, SI 2000/2040, art 2(1), Schedule, Pt I, para 21.

Orders: the Marriage Act 1949 (Remedial) Order 2007, SI 2007/438; the Asylum and Immigration (Treatment of Claimants, etc) Act 2004 (Remedial) Order 2011, SI 2011/1158; the Sexual Offences Act 2003 (Remedial) Order 2012, SI 2012/1883.

SCHEDULE 3
DEROGATION AND RESERVATION

Sections 14 and 15

PART I

(*Repealed by the Human Rights Act (Amendment) Order 2001, SI 2001/1216, art 4.*)

PART II
RESERVATION

[1.1245]
At the time of signing the present (First) Protocol, I declare that, in view of certain provisions of the Education Acts in the United Kingdom, the principle affirmed in the second sentence of Article 2 is accepted by the United Kingdom only so far as it is compatible with the provision of efficient instruction and training, and the avoidance of unreasonable public expenditure.

Dated 20 March 1952. Made by the United Kingdom Permanent Representative to the Council of Europe.

SCHEDULE 4

(Sch 4 (judicial pensions) outside the scope of this work.)

EMPLOYMENT RELATIONS ACT 1999

(1999 c 26)

ARRANGEMENT OF SECTIONS

An Act to amend the law relating to employment, to trade unions and to employment agencies and businesses

[27 July 1999]

NOTES

Much of this Act amends other legislation; the amendments are incorporated therein so far as within the scope of this work, and noted below. The Act is otherwise printed in full except where (and for the reasons) noted.

Employment Appeal Tribunal: an appeal lies to the Employment Appeal Tribunal on any question of law arising from any decision of, or in any proceedings before, an employment tribunal under or by virtue of this Act; see the Employment Tribunals Act 1996, s 21(1)(gb) at **[1.764]**.

See *Harvey* AI(2), AII(7), NI(7).

Trade unions

1, 2 *(S 1 adds the Trade Union and Labour Relations (Consolidation) Act 1992, Pt I, Ch VA (s 70A) and Sch A1, at* **[1.368]**, **[1.638]**; *s 2 introduces Sch 2 (Detriment related to trade union membership).)*

[1.1246]

3 Blacklists

(1) The Secretary of State may make regulations prohibiting the compilation of lists which—

(a) contain details of members of trade unions or persons who have taken part in the activities of trade unions, and

(b) are compiled with a view to being used by employers or employment agencies for the purposes of discrimination in relation to recruitment or in relation to the treatment of workers.

(2) The Secretary of State may make regulations prohibiting—

(a) the use of lists to which subsection (1) applies;

(b) the sale or supply of lists to which subsection (1) applies.

(3) Regulations under this section may, in particular—

(a) confer jurisdiction (including exclusive jurisdiction) on employment tribunals and on the Employment Appeal Tribunal;

(b) include provision for or about the grant and enforcement of specified remedies by courts and tribunals;

(c) include provision for the making of awards of compensation calculated in accordance with the regulations;

(d) include provision permitting proceedings to be brought by trade unions on behalf of members in specified circumstances;

(e) include provision about cases where an employee is dismissed by his employer and the reason or principal reason for the dismissal, or why the employee was selected for dismissal, relates to a list to which subsection (1) applies;

(f) create criminal offences;

(g) in specified cases or circumstances, extend liability for a criminal offence created under paragraph (f) to a person who aids the commission of the offence or to a person who is an agent, principal, employee, employer or officer of a person who commits the offence;

(h) provide for specified obligations or offences not to apply in specified circumstances;

(i) include supplemental, incidental, consequential and transitional provision, including provision amending an enactment;

(j) make different provision for different cases or circumstances.

(4) Regulations under this section creating an offence may not provide for it to be punishable—

(a) by imprisonment,

(b) by a fine in excess of level 5 on the standard scale in the case of an offence triable only summarily, or

(c) by a fine in excess of the statutory maximum in the case of summary conviction for an offence triable either way.

(5) In this section—

"list" includes any index or other set of items whether recorded electronically or by any other means, and

"worker" has the meaning given by section 13.

(6) Subject to subsection (5), expressions used in this section and in the Trade Union and Labour Relations (Consolidation) Act 1992 have the same meaning in this section as in that Act.

NOTES

Regulations: the Employment Relations Act 1999 (Blacklists) Regulations 2010, SI 2010/493 at **[2.1137]**.

4–9 *(S 4 introduces Sch 3 (Ballots and notices); s 5 inserts the Trade Union and Labour Relations (Consolidation) Act 1992, ss 70B, 70C at* **[1.369]**, **[1.370]**; *s 6 amends the Employment Rights Act 1996, ss 128, 129 at* **[1.1045]**, **[1.1046]**; *s 7 substitutes Pt VIII of the 1996 Act at* **[1.958]** *et seq; s 8 inserts ss 57A, 57B in the 1996 Act at* **[1.926]**, **[1.927]**; *s 9 introduces Sch 4, Pt III to this Act (amendments consequential on ss 7, 8).)*

Disciplinary and grievance hearings

[1.1247]

10 Right to be accompanied

(1) This section applies where a worker—

(a) is required or invited by his employer to attend a disciplinary or grievance hearing, and

(b) reasonably requests to be accompanied at the hearing.

[(2A) Where this section applies, the employer must permit the worker to be accompanied at the hearing by one companion who—

(a) is chosen by the worker; and

(b) is within subsection (3).

(2B) The employer must permit the worker's companion to—

(a) address the hearing in order to do any or all of the following—
(i) put the worker's case;
(ii) sum up that case;
(iii) respond on the worker's behalf to any view expressed at the hearing;
(b) confer with the worker during the hearing.

(2C) Subsection (2B) does not require the employer to permit the worker's companion to—
(a) answer questions on behalf of the worker;
(b) address the hearing if the worker indicates at it that he does not wish his companion to do so; or
(c) use the powers conferred by that subsection in a way that prevents the employer from explaining his case or prevents any other person at the hearing from making his contribution to it.]

(3) A person is within this subsection if he is—
(a) employed by a trade union of which he is an official within the meaning of sections 1 and 119 of the Trade Union and Labour Relations (Consolidation) Act 1992,
(b) an official of a trade union (within that meaning) whom the union has reasonably certified in writing as having experience of, or as having received training in, acting as a worker's companion at disciplinary or grievance hearings, or
(c) another of the employer's workers.

(4) If—
(a) a worker has a right under this section to be accompanied at a hearing,
(b) his chosen companion will not be available at the time proposed for the hearing by the employer, and
(c) the worker proposes an alternative time which satisfies subsection (5),
the employer must postpone the hearing to the time proposed by the worker.

(5) An alternative time must—
(a) be reasonable, and
(b) fall before the end of the period of five working days beginning with the first working day after the day proposed by the employer.

(6) An employer shall permit a worker to take time off during working hours for the purpose of accompanying another of the employer's workers in accordance with a request under subsection (1)(b).

(7) Sections 168(3) and (4), 169 and 171 to 173 of the Trade Union and Labour Relations (Consolidation) Act 1992 (time off for carrying out trade union duties) shall apply in relation to subsection (6) above as they apply in relation to section 168(1) of that Act.

NOTES

Sub-ss (2A)–(2C): substituted (for the original sub-s (2)) by the Employment Relations Act 2004, s 37(1).

See also the ACAS Code of Practice 1: Disciplinary and Grievance Procedures (2015) at **[4.1]**, and the accompanying Guide at **[4.6]**.

[1.1248]

11 Complaint to employment tribunal

(1) A worker may present a complaint to an employment tribunal that his employer has failed, or threatened to fail, to comply with section [10(2A), (2B)] or (4).

(2) A tribunal shall not consider a complaint under this section in relation to a failure or threat unless the complaint is presented—
(a) before the end of the period of three months beginning with the date of the failure or threat, or
(b) within such further period as the tribunal considers reasonable in a case where it is satisfied that it was not reasonably practicable for the complaint to be presented before the end of that period of three months.

[(2A) Section 207A(3) (extension because of mediation in certain European cross-border disputes) and section 207B (extension of time limits to facilitate conciliation before institution of proceedings) of the Employment Rights Act 1996 apply for the purposes of subsection (2)(a).

(2B) Subsections (2) and (2A) are to be treated as provisions of the Employment Rights Act 1996 for the purposes of *sections 207A and* 207B of that Act.]

(3) Where a tribunal finds that a complaint under this section is well-founded it shall order the employer to pay compensation to the worker of an amount not exceeding two weeks' pay.

(4) Chapter II of Part XIV of the Employment Rights Act 1996 (calculation of a week's pay) shall apply for the purposes of subsection (3); and in applying that Chapter the calculation date shall be taken to be—
(a) in the case of a claim which is made in the course of a claim for unfair dismissal, the date on which the employer's notice of dismissal was given or, if there was no notice, the effective date of termination, and
(b) in any other case, the date on which the relevant hearing took place (or was to have taken place).

(5) The limit in section 227(1) of the Employment Rights Act 1996 (maximum amount of week's pay) shall apply for the purposes of subsection (3) above.

(6) . . .

NOTES

Sub-s (1): figures in square brackets substituted by the Employment Relations Act 2004, s 37(2).

Sub-ss (2A), (2B): inserted by the Enterprise and Regulatory Reform Act 2013, s 8, Sch 2, para 40; sub-s (2A) substituted as set out below, and for the words in italics in sub-s (2B) there is substituted the word "section", by the Cross-Border Mediation (EU Directive) (EU Exit) Regulations 2019, SI 2019/469, reg 4, Sch 1, Pt 1, para 15, as from exit day (as defined in the

European Union (Withdrawal) Act 2018, s 20)—

"(2A) Section 207B (extension of time limits to facilitate conciliation before institution of proceedings) of the Employment Rights Act 1996 applies for the purposes of subsection (2)(a).".

Sub-s (6): repealed by the Employment Act 2002, s 54, Sch 8.

[1.1249]

12 Detriment and dismissal

(1) A worker has the right not to be subjected to any detriment by any act, or any deliberate failure to act, by his employer done on the ground that he—

(a) exercised or sought to exercise the right under section [10(2A), (2B)] or (4), or

(b) accompanied or sought to accompany another worker (whether of the same employer or not) pursuant to a request under that section.

(2) Section 48 of the Employment Rights Act 1996 shall apply in relation to contraventions of subsection (1) above as it applies in relation to contraventions of certain sections of that Act.

(3) A worker who is dismissed shall be regarded for the purposes of Part X of the Employment Rights Act 1996 as unfairly dismissed if the reason (or, if more than one, the principal reason) for the dismissal is that he—

(a) exercised or sought to exercise the right under section [10(2A), (2B)] or (4), or

(b) accompanied or sought to accompany another worker (whether of the same employer or not) pursuant to a request under that section.

(4) Sections 108 and 109 of that Act (qualifying period of employment and upper age limit) shall not apply in relation to subsection (3) above.

(5) Sections 128 to 132 of that Act (interim relief) shall apply in relation to dismissal for the reason specified in subsection (3)(a) or (b) above as they apply in relation to dismissal for a reason specified in section 128(1)(b) of that Act.

(6) In the application of Chapter II of Part X of that Act in relation to subsection (3) above, a reference to an employee shall be taken as a reference to a worker.

[(7) References in this section to a worker having accompanied or sought to accompany another worker include references to his having exercised or sought to exercise any of the powers conferred by section 10(2A) or (2B).]

NOTES

Sub-ss (1), (3): figures in square brackets substituted by the Employment Relations Act 2004, s 37(3)(a).

Sub-s (7): added by the Employment Relations Act 2004, s 37(3)(b).

[1.1250]

13 Interpretation

(1) In sections 10 to 12 and this section "worker" means an individual who is—

(a) a worker within the meaning of section 230(3) of the Employment Rights Act 1996,

(b) an agency worker,

(c) a home worker,

(d) a person in Crown employment within the meaning of section 191 of that Act, other than a member of the naval, military, air or reserve forces of the Crown, or

(e) employed as a relevant member of the House of Lords staff or the House of Commons staff within the meaning of section 194(6) or 195(5) of that Act.

(2) In subsection (1) "agency worker" means an individual who—

(a) is supplied by a person ("the agent") to do work for another ("the principal") by arrangement between the agent and the principal,

(b) is not a party to a worker's contract, within the meaning of section 230(3) of that Act, relating to that work, and

(c) is not a party to a contract relating to that work under which he undertakes to do the work for another party to the contract whose status is, by virtue of the contract, that of a client or customer of any professional or business undertaking carried on by the individual;

and, for the purposes of sections 10 to 12, both the agent and the principal are employers of an agency worker.

(3) In subsection (1) "home worker" means an individual who—

(a) contracts with a person, for the purposes of the person's business, for the execution of work to be done in a place not under the person's control or management, and

(b) is not a party to a contract relating to that work under which the work is to be executed for another party to the contract whose status is, by virtue of the contract, that of a client or customer of any professional or business undertaking carried on by the individual;

and, for the purposes of sections 10 to 12, the person mentioned in paragraph (a) is the home worker's employer.

(4) For the purposes of section 10 a disciplinary hearing is a hearing which could result in—

(a) the administration of a formal warning to a worker by his employer,

(b) the taking of some other action in respect of a worker by his employer, or

(c) the confirmation of a warning issued or some other action taken.

(5) For the purposes of section 10 a grievance hearing is a hearing which concerns the performance of a duty by an employer in relation to a worker.

(6) For the purposes of section 10(5)(b) in its application to a part of Great Britain a working day is a day other than—

(a) a Saturday or a Sunday,

(b) Christmas Day or Good Friday, or
(c) a day which is a bank holiday under the Banking and Financial Dealings Act 1971 in that part of Great Britain.

[1.1251]
14 Contracting out and conciliation
Sections 10 to 13 of this Act shall be treated as provisions of Part V of the Employment Rights Act 1996 for the purposes of—
(a) section 203(1), (2)(e) and (f), (3) and (4) of that Act (restrictions on contracting out), and
(b) [section 18(1)(b)] of the Employment Tribunals Act 1996 (conciliation).

NOTES
Words in square brackets in para (b) substituted by the Employment Tribunals Act 1996 (Application of Conciliation Provisions) Order 2014, SI 2014/431, art 3, Schedule, para 6.

[1.1252]
15 National security employees
Sections 10 to 13 of this Act shall not apply in relation to a person employed for the purposes of—
(a) the Security Service,
(b) the Secret Intelligence Service, or
(c) the Government Communications Headquarters.

Other rights of individuals

16–18 *(S 16 introduces Sch 5 (Unfair dismissal of striking workers); s 17 repealed by the Employment Relations Act 2004, ss 31(8), 57(2), Sch 2; s 18(1)–(4) amend the Employment Rights Act 1996, ss 44, 45A, 46, 47, 47A, 47B, at* **[1.880]**, **[1.883]**, **[1.884]**, **[1.885]**, **[1.886]**, **[1.888]**, *amended s 197 (repealed), and substitute the National Minimum Wage Act 1998, s 23(4) at* **[1.1196]**; *s 18(5) repealed by the Tax Credits Act 2002, s 60, Sch 6; s 18(6) repealed by Sch 9 to this Act.)*

[1.1253]
19 Part-time work: discrimination
(1) The Secretary of State shall make regulations for the purpose of securing that persons in part-time employment are treated, for such purposes and to such extent as the regulations may specify, no less favourably than persons in full-time employment.
(2) The regulations may—
(a) specify classes of person who are to be taken to be, or not to be, in part-time employment;
(b) specify classes of person who are to be taken to be, or not to be, in full-time employment;
(c) specify circumstances in which persons in part-time employment are to be taken to be, or not to be, treated less favourably than persons in full-time employment;
(d) make provision which has effect in relation to persons in part-time employment generally or provision which has effect only in relation to specified classes of persons in part-time employment.
(3) The regulations may—
(a) confer jurisdiction (including exclusive jurisdiction) on employment tribunals and on the Employment Appeal Tribunal;
(b) create criminal offences in relation to specified acts or omissions by an employer, by an organisation of employers, by an organisation of workers or by an organisation existing for the purposes of a profession or trade carried on by the organisation's members;
(c) in specified cases or circumstances, extend liability for a criminal offence created under paragraph (b) to a person who aids the commission of the offence or to a person who is an agent, principal, employee, employer or officer of a person who commits the offence;
(d) provide for specified obligations or offences not to apply in specified circumstances;
(e) make provision about notices or information to be given, evidence to be produced and other procedures to be followed;
(f) amend, apply with or without modifications, or make provision similar to any provision of the Employment Rights Act 1996 (including, in particular, Parts V, X and XIII) or the Trade Union and Labour Relations (Consolidation) Act 1992;
(g) provide for the provisions of specified agreements to have effect in place of provisions of the regulations to such extent and in such circumstances as may be specified;
(h) include supplemental, incidental, consequential and transitional provision, including provision amending an enactment;
(i) make different provision for different cases or circumstances.

(4) Without prejudice to the generality of this section the regulations may make any provision which appears to the Secretary of State to be necessary or expedient—
(a) for the purpose of implementing Council Directive 97/81/EC on the framework agreement on part-time work in its application to terms and conditions of employment;
(b) for the purpose of dealing with any matter arising out of or related to the United Kingdom's obligations under that Directive;
(c) for the purpose of any matter dealt with by the framework agreement or for the purpose of applying the provisions of the framework agreement to any matter relating to part-time workers.

(5) Regulations under this section which create an offence—
(a) shall provide for it to be triable summarily only, and
(b) may not provide for it to be punishable by imprisonment or by a fine in excess of level 5 on the standard scale.

NOTES

Sub-s (4): repealed by the Employment Rights (Amendment) (EU Exit) Regulations 2019, SI 2019/535, reg 2(1), Sch 1, Pt 1, para 4, as from exit day (as defined in the European Union (Withdrawal) Act 2018, s 20) and subject to savings in Sch 1, Pt 3, para 22 thereto, which provides that the repeal does not affect the validity of any regulations made under this section that came into force before exit day.

Regulations: the Part-time Workers (Prevention of Less Favourable Treatment) Regulations 2000, SI 2000/1551 at **[2.535]**; the Part-time Workers (Prevention of Less Favourable Treatment) Regulations 2001, SI 2001/1107.

[1.1254]

20 Part-time work: code of practice

(1) The Secretary of State may issue codes of practice containing guidance for the purpose of—

(a) eliminating discrimination in the field of employment against part-time workers;

(b) facilitating the development of opportunities for part-time work;

(c) facilitating the flexible organisation of working time taking into account the needs of workers and employers;

(d) any matter dealt with in the framework agreement on part-time work annexed to Council Directive 97/81/EC.

(2) The Secretary of State may revise a code and issue the whole or part of the revised code.

(3) A person's failure to observe a provision of a code does not make him liable to any proceedings.

(4) A code—

(a) is admissible in evidence in proceedings before an employment tribunal, and

(b) shall be taken into account by an employment tribunal in any case in which it appears to the tribunal to be relevant.

NOTES

Codes of Practice: as of 15 May 2019, no codes had been issued under this section.

[1.1255]

21 Code of practice: supplemental

(1) Before issuing or revising a code of practice under section 20 the Secretary of State shall consult such persons as he considers appropriate.

(2) Before issuing a code the Secretary of State shall—

(a) publish a draft code,

(b) consider any representations made to him about the draft,

(c) if he thinks it appropriate, modify the draft in the light of any representations made to him.

(3) If, having followed the procedure under subsection (2), the Secretary of State decides to issue a code, he shall lay a draft code before each House of Parliament.

(4) If the draft code is approved by resolution of each House of Parliament, the Secretary of State shall issue the code in the form of the draft.

(5) In this section and section 20(3) and (4)—

(a) a reference to a code includes a reference to a revised code,

(b) a reference to a draft code includes a reference to a draft revision, and

(c) a reference to issuing a code includes a reference to issuing part of a revised code.

22 *(Inserts the National Minimum Wage Act 1998, s 44A at* **[1.1214]**.*)*

[1.1256]

23 Power to confer rights on individuals

(1) This section applies to any right conferred on an individual against an employer (however defined) under or by virtue of any of the following—

(a) the Trade Union and Labour Relations (Consolidation) Act 1992;

(b) the Employment Rights Act 1996;

[(ba) the Employment Act 2002;]

(c) this Act;

(d) any instrument made under section 2(2) of the European Communities Act 1972.

(2) The Secretary of State may by order make provision which has the effect of conferring any such right on individuals who are of a specified description.

(3) The reference in subsection (2) to individuals includes a reference to individuals expressly excluded from exercising the right.

(4) An order under this section may—

(a) provide that individuals are to be treated as parties to workers' contracts or contracts of employment;

(b) make provision as to who are to be regarded as the employers of individuals;

(c) make provision which has the effect of modifying the operation of any right as conferred on individuals by the order;

(d) include such consequential, incidental or supplementary provisions as the Secretary of State thinks fit.

(5) An order under this section may make provision in such way as the Secretary of State thinks fit . . .

[(5A) The ways in which an order under this section may make provision include, in particular—

(a) amending any enactment;

(b) excluding or applying (whether with or without amendment) any enactment.

(5B) In subsection (5A) "enactment" includes an enactment comprised in subordinate legislation made under an Act.]

(6) Section 209(7) of the Employment Rights Act 1996 (which is superseded by this section) shall be omitted.

(7) Any order made or having effect as if made under section 209(7), so far as effective immediately before the commencement of this section, shall have effect as if made under this section.

NOTES

Sub-s (1): para (ba) inserted by the Employment Act 2002, s 53, Sch 7, para 54.

Sub-s (5): words omitted repealed by a combination of the Employment Act 2002, s 41, and the Employment Relations Act 2004, ss 39(1), (2), 57(2), Sch 2.

Sub-ss (5A), (5B): inserted by the Employment Relations Act 2004, s 39(1), (3).

Orders: the Employment Rights Act 1996 (Itemised Pay Statement) (Amendment) (No 2) Order 2018, SI 2018/529 at **[2.2054]**. As to Orders made or having effect as if made under the Employment Rights Act 1996, s 209(7) (and therefore having effect as if made under this section by virtue of sub-s (7) above) see the note to s 209 of the 1996 Act at **[1.1124]**.

CAC, ACAS, Commissioners and Certification Officer

24–29 *(Ss 24–27 contain various amendments to the Trade Union and Labour Relations (Consolidation) Act 1992 at* **[1.268]** et seq; *s 28(1), (2) abolished the office of Commissioner for the Rights of Trade Union Members and the office of Commissioner for Protection Against Unlawful Industrial Action and repealed the Trade Union and Labour Relations (Consolidation) Act 1992, Pt I, Ch VIII, ss 235B, 235C and 266–271, and were themselves repealed by the Statute Law (Repeals) Act 2004; s 28(3) amends s 32A of the 1992 Act; s 29 introduces Sch 6 (the Certification Officer).)*

Miscellaneous

[1.1257]

30 Partnerships at work

(1) The Secretary of State may spend money or provide money to other persons for the purpose of encouraging and helping employers (or their representatives) and employees (or their representatives) to improve the way they work together.

(2) Money may be provided in such way as the Secretary of State thinks fit (whether as grants or otherwise) and on such terms as he thinks fit (whether as to repayment or otherwise).

31–33 *(S 31 introduces Sch 7 (employment agencies); s 32 amends the Trade Union and Labour Relations (Consolidation) Act 1992, s 285 at* **[1.619]**, *inserts s 287(3A) of the 1992 Act at* **[1.621]**, *repeals the Employment Rights Act 1996, s 196 and amends s 199 of the 1996 Act at* **[1.1112]**; *s 33(1) repealed the Employment Rights Act 1996, ss 117(4)(b), 118(2), (3), 125 and the Trade Union and Labour Relations (Consolidation) Act 1992, ss 157, 158, and was repealed by the Statute Law (Repeals) Act 2004; s 33(2), (3) amend s 117 of the 1996 Act at* **[1.1035]**, *and the Employment Rights (Dispute Resolution) Act 1998, s 14, and were repealed in part by the Statute Law (Repeals) Act 2004.)*

[1.1258]

34 Indexation of amounts, &c

(1) This section applies to the sums specified in the following provisions—

(a) section 31(1) of the Employment Rights Act 1996 (guarantee payments: limits);

(b) section 120(1) of that Act (unfair dismissal: minimum amount of basic award);

(c) section 124(1) of that Act (unfair dismissal: limit of compensatory award);

(d) section 186(1)(a) and (b) of that Act (employee's rights on insolvency of employer: maximum amount payable);

(e) section 227(1) of that Act (maximum amount of a week's pay for purposes of certain calculations);

[(ea) section 145E(3) of the Trade Union and Labour Relations (Consolidation) Act 1992 (unlawful inducements: amount of award);

(f) section 156(1) of that Act (unfair dismissal: minimum basic award);]

(g) section [176(6A)] of that Act (right to membership of trade union: remedies).

(2) If the retail prices index for September of a year is higher or lower than the index for the previous September, the Secretary of State shall . . . make an order in relation to each sum mentioned in subsection (1)—

(a) increasing each sum, if the new index is higher, or

(b) decreasing each sum, if the new index is lower,

by the same percentage as the amount of the increase or decrease of the index[, with effect from the following 6th April].

(3) In making the calculation required by subsection (2) the Secretary of State shall [round the result to the nearest whole pound, taking 50p as nearest to the next whole pound above].

(4) For the sum specified in section 124(1) of the Employment Rights Act 1996 (unfair dismissal: limit of compensatory award) there shall be substituted the sum of £50,000 (subject to subsection (2) above).

[(4A) A reference in this section to a sum specified in section 124(1) of the Employment Rights Act 1996 does not include anything specified by virtue of section 15(2)(b)(ii) of the Enterprise and Regulatory Reform Act 2013 (specified number multiplied by a week's pay of the individual concerned).

(4B) As regards a sum specified in section 124(1) of the Employment Rights Act 1996, the duty under subsection (2) to make an order with effect from 6 April in a particular year does not arise where an order varying such a sum with effect from a day within 12 months before that date has been made under section 15(1) of the Enterprise and Regulatory Reform Act 2013.]

(5) In this section "the retail prices index" means—
- (a) the general index of retail prices (for all items) published by the [Statistics Board], or
- (b) where that index is not published for a month, any substituted index or figures published by [the Board].

(6) An order under this section—
- (a) shall be made by statutory instrument,
- (b) may include transitional provision, and
- (c) shall be laid before Parliament after being made.

NOTES

Sub-s (1): paras (ea), (f) substituted, for the original para (f), by the Employment Relations Act 2004, s 57(1), Sch 1, para 42(1), (2); figure in square brackets in para (g) substituted by s 57(1) of, and Sch 1, para 42(1), (3) to, the 2004 Act.

Sub-s (2): words omitted repealed, and words in square brackets added, by the Enterprise and Regulatory Reform Act 2013, s 22(1), (2).

Sub-s (3): words in square brackets substituted by the Enterprise and Regulatory Reform Act 2013, s 22(1), (3).

Sub-ss (4A), (4B): inserted by the Enterprise and Regulatory Reform Act 2013, s 15(10).

Sub-s (5): words in square brackets substituted by the Statistics and Registration Service Act 2007, s 60(1), Sch 3, para 11.

Orders: the current Order is the Employment Rights (Increase of Limits) Order 2018, SI 2019/324 at **[2.2114]**.

35 *(Amends the Employment Rights Act 1996, s 31 at* **[1.847]***.)*

[1.1259]

36 Sections 33 to 35: consequential

(1), (2) . . .

(3) An increase effected, before section 34 comes into force, by virtue of a provision repealed by this section shall continue to have effect notwithstanding this section (but subject to section 34(2) and (4)).

NOTES

Sub-ss (1), (2): repeal the Employment Rights Act 1996, ss 120(2), 124(2), 186(2), 208, 227(2)–(4), and the Trade Union and Labour Relations (Consolidation) Act 1992, ss 159, 176(7), (8).

37 *(S 37(1) amends the Employment Rights Act 1996, s 124 at* **[1.1042]**; *s 37(2) repealed s 127B of that Act, and was repealed by the Statute Law (Repeals) Act 2004.)*

[1.1260]

38 Transfer of undertakings

(1) This section applies where regulations under section 2(2) of the European Communities Act 1972 (general implementation of Treaties) make provision for the purpose of implementing, or for a purpose concerning, [an] [EU] obligation of the United Kingdom which relates to the treatment of employees on the transfer of an undertaking or business or part of an undertaking or business.

(2) The Secretary of State may by regulations make the same or similar provision in relation to the treatment of employees in circumstances other than those to which the [EU] obligation applies (including circumstances in which there is no transfer, or no transfer to which the [EU] obligation applies).

(3) Regulations under this section shall be subject to annulment in pursuance of a resolution of either House of Parliament.

NOTES

Sub-ss (1), (2): words in square brackets substituted by the Treaty of Lisbon (Changes in Terminology) Order 2011, SI 2011/1043, art 6(1)(e), (3).

Sub-ss (1), (2): substituted by new sub-ss (1), (2), (2A) set out below, by the Employment Rights (Amendment) (EU Exit) (No 2) Regulations 2019, SI 2019/536, reg 2, Schedule, Pt 1, para 1, as from exit day (as defined in the European Union (Withdrawal) Act 2018, s 20) and subject to Pt 3 of the Schedule to the 2019 Regulations at **[2.2185]**—

"(1) The Secretary of State may by regulations make TUPE-like provision in relation to the treatment of employees in circumstances other than those to which the main part of the TUPE regulations applies.

(2) In this section—
- (a) the "main part of the TUPE regulations" means so much of the Transfer of Undertakings (Protection of Employment) Regulations 2006 (SI 2006/246) as relates to the treatment of employees on the transfer of an undertaking, business or part of an undertaking or business;
- (b) "TUPE-like provision" means provision which is the same or similar to that made by the main part of the TUPE regulations.

(2A) The circumstances mentioned in subsection (1) include circumstances in which there is no transfer, or no transfer to which the main part of the TUPE regulations applies.".

Regulations: the Transfer of Undertakings (Protection of Employment) (Rent Officer Service) Regulations 1999, SI 1999/2511; the Transfer of Undertakings (Protection of Employment) (Transfer to OFCOM) Regulations 2003, SI 2003/2715; the Transfer of Undertakings (Protection of Employment) Regulations 2006, SI 2006/246 at **[2.867]**; the Transfer of Undertakings (Protection of Employment) (Consequential Amendments) Regulations 2006, SI 2006/2405; the Transfer of Undertakings (Protection of Employment) (RCUK Shared Services Centre Limited) Regulations 2012, SI 2012/2413; the Transfer of Undertakings (Protection of Employment) (Transfers of Public Health Staff) Regulations 2013, SI 2013/278; the Collective Redundancies and Transfer of Undertakings (Protection of Employment) (Amendment) Regulations 2014, SI 2014/16; the Transfer of Undertakings (Protection of Employment) (Transfer of Staff to the Department for Work and Pensions) Regulations 2014, SI 2014/1139.

[1.1261]

39 Minimum wage: information

(1) Information obtained by a revenue official in the course of carrying out a function of the Commissioners of Inland Revenue may be—

(a) supplied by the Commissioners of Inland Revenue to the Secretary of State for any purpose relating to the National Minimum Wage Act 1998;

(b) supplied by the Secretary of State with the authority of the Commissioners of Inland Revenue to any person acting under section 13(1)(b) of that Act;

(c) supplied by the Secretary of State with the authority of the Commissioners of Inland Revenue to an officer acting for the purposes of any of the agricultural wages legislation.

(2) In this section—

"revenue official" means an officer of the Commissioners of Inland Revenue appointed under section 4 of the Inland Revenue Regulation Act 1890 (appointment of collectors, officers and other persons), and

"the agricultural wages legislation" has the same meaning as in section 16 of the National Minimum Wage Act 1998 (agricultural wages officers).

NOTES

Commissioners of Inland Revenue: a reference to the Commissioners of Inland Revenue is now to be taken as a reference to the Commissioners for Her Majesty's Revenue and Customs; see the Commissioners for Revenue and Customs Act 2005, s 50(1), (7).

Inland Revenue Regulation Act 1890, s 4: repealed by the Commissioners for Revenue and Customs Act 2005, ss 50(6), 52(2), Sch 4, para 5, Sch 5.

40, 41 *(S 40 repealed by the Education Act 2002, s 215(2), Sch 22, Pt 3; s 41 introduces Sch 8 (national security).)*

General

[1.1262]

42 Orders and regulations

(1) Any power to make an order or regulations under this Act shall be exercised by statutory instrument.

(2) No order or regulations shall be made under section 3, 17, 19 or 23 unless a draft has been laid before, and approved by resolution of, each House of Parliament.

[1.1263]

43 Finance

There shall be paid out of money provided by Parliament—

(a) any increase attributable to this Act in the sums so payable under any other enactment;

(b) any other expenditure of the Secretary of State under this Act.

44 *(Introduces Sch 9 (repeals).)*

[1.1264]

45 Commencement

(1) The preceding provisions of this Act shall come into force in accordance with provision made by the Secretary of State by order made by statutory instrument.

(2) An order under this section—

(a) may make different provision for different purposes;

(b) may include supplementary, incidental, saving or transitional provisions.

NOTES

Orders: the Employment Relations Act 1999 (Commencement No 1 and Transitional Provisions) Order 1999, SI 1999/2509; the Employment Relations Act 1999 (Commencement No 2 and Transitional and Saving Provisions) Order 1999, SI 1999/2830; the Employment Relations Act 1999 (Commencement No 3 and Transitional Provision) Order 1999, SI 1999/3374; the Employment Relations Act 1999 (Commencement No 4 and Transitional Provision) Order 2000, SI 2000/420; the Employment Relations Act 1999 (Commencement No 5 and Transitional Provision) Order 2000, SI 2000/875; the Employment Relations Act 1999 (Commencement No 6 and Transitional Provisions) Order 2000, SI 2000/1338; the Employment Relations Act 1999 (Commencement No 7 and Transitional Provisions) Order 2000, SI 2000/2242; the Employment Relations Act 1999 (Commencement No 8) Order 2001, SI 2001/1187; the Employment Relations Act 1999 (Commencement No 8) (Amendment) Order 2001, SI 2001/1461; the Employment Relations Act 1999 (Commencement No 9) Order 2003, SI 2003/3357.

[1.1265]

46 Extent

(1) Any amendment or repeal in this Act has the same extent as the provision amended or repealed.

(2) An Order in Council under paragraph 1(1)(b) of Schedule 1 to the Northern Ireland Act 1974 (legislation for Northern Ireland in the interim period) which contains a statement that it is made only for purposes corresponding to any of the purposes of this Act—

(a) shall not be subject to paragraph 1(4) and (5) of that Schedule (affirmative resolution of both Houses of Parliament), but

(b) shall be subject to annulment in pursuance of a resolution of either House of Parliament.

(3) Apart from sections 39 and 45 and subject to subsection (1), the preceding sections of this Act shall not extend to Northern Ireland.

NOTES

Northern Ireland Act 1974: repealed by the Northern Ireland Act 1998, s 100(2), Sch 15.

[1.1266]
47 Citation

This Act may be cited as the Employment Relations Act 1999.

SCHEDULES 1–9

(In so far as still in force, Schedules 1–9 to this Act make a variety of amendments and repeals to (inter alia) the following: the Trade Union and Labour Relations (Consolidation) Act 1992, the Employment Rights Act 1996, the Employment Tribunals Act 1996, and the Employment Agencies Act 1973; they also amended the Race Relations Act 1976 and the Disability Discrimination Act 1995 (both now repealed). All such amendments and repeals are noted at the appropriate place where they are within the scope of this work.)

CONTRACTS (RIGHTS OF THIRD PARTIES) ACT 1999

(1999 c 31)

ARRANGEMENT OF SECTIONS

An Act to make provision for the enforcement of contractual terms by third parties

[11 November 1999]

NOTES

As to the commencement and application of this Act, see s 10(2), (3) at **[1.1275]**.
This Act does not apply to Scotland (see s 10(4), *post*).

[1.1267]
1 Right of third party to enforce contractual term

(1) Subject to the provisions of this Act, a person who is not a party to a contract (a "third party") may in his own right enforce a term of the contract if—

(a) the contract expressly provides that he may, or
(b) subject to subsection (2), the term purports to confer a benefit on him.

(2) subsection (1)(b) does not apply if on a proper construction of the contract it appears that the parties did not intend the term to be enforceable by the third party.

(3) The third party must be expressly identified in the contract by name, as a member of a class or as answering a particular description but need not be in existence when the contract is entered into.

(4) This section does not confer a right on a third party to enforce a term of a contract otherwise than subject to and in accordance with any other relevant terms of the contract.

(5) For the purpose of exercising his right to enforce a term of the contract, there shall be available to the third party any remedy that would have been available to him in an action for breach of contract if he had been a party to the contract (and the rules relating to damages, injunctions, specific performance and other relief shall apply accordingly).

(6) Where a term of a contract excludes or limits liability in relation to any matter references in this Act to the third party enforcing the term shall be construed as references to his availing himself of the exclusion or limitation.

(7) In this Act, in relation to a term of a contract which is enforceable by a third party—

"the promisor" means the party to the contract against whom the term is enforceable by the third party, and

"the promisee" means the party to the contract by whom the term is enforceable against the promisor.

[1.1268]

2 Variation and rescission of contract

(1) Subject to the provisions of this section, where a third party has a right under section 1 to enforce a term of the contract, the parties to the contract may not, by agreement, rescind the contract, or vary it in such a way as to extinguish or alter his entitlement under that right, without his consent if—

(a) the third party has communicated his assent to the term to the promisor,

(b) the promisor is aware that the third party has relied on the term, or

(c) the promisor can reasonably be expected to have foreseen that the third party would rely on the term and the third party has in fact relied on it.

(2) The assent referred to in subsection (1)(a)—

(a) may be by words or conduct, and

(b) if sent to the promisor by post or other means, shall not be regarded as communicated to the promisor until received by him.

(3) subsection (1) is subject to any express term of the contract under which—

(a) the parties to the contract may by agreement rescind or vary the contract without the consent of the third party, or

(b) the consent of the third party is required in circumstances specified in the contract instead of those set out in subsection (1)(a) to (c).

(4) Where the consent of a third party is required under subsection (1) or (3), the court or arbitral tribunal may, on the application of the parties to the contract, dispense with his consent if satisfied—

(a) that his consent cannot be obtained because his whereabouts cannot reasonably be ascertained, or

(b) that he is mentally incapable of giving his consent.

(5) The court or arbitral tribunal may, on the application of the parties to a contract, dispense with any consent that may be required under subsection (1)(c) if satisfied that it cannot reasonably be ascertained whether or not the third party has in fact relied on the term.

(6) If the court or arbitral tribunal dispenses with a third party's consent, it may impose such conditions as it thinks fit, including a condition requiring the payment of compensation to the third party.

(7) The jurisdiction conferred on the court by subsections (4) to (6) is exercisable [in England and Wales by both the High Court and the county court and in Northern Ireland] by both the High Court and a county court.

NOTES

Sub-s (7): words in square brackets inserted by the Crime and Courts Act 2013, s 17(5), Sch 9, Pt 3, para 71.

[1.1269]

3 Defences etc available to promisor

(1) Subsections (2) to (5) apply where, in reliance on section 1, proceedings for the enforcement of a term of a contract are brought by a third party.

(2) The promisor shall have available to him by way of defence or set-off any matter that—

(a) arises from or in connection with the contract and is relevant to the term, and

(b) would have been available to him by way of defence or set-off if the proceedings had been brought by the promisee.

(3) The promisor shall also have available to him by way of defence or set-off any matter if—

(a) an express term of the contract provides for it to be available to him in proceedings brought by the third party, and

(b) it would have been available to him by way of defence or set-off if the proceedings had been brought by the promisee.

(4) The promisor shall also have available to him—

(a) by way of defence or set-off any matter, and

(b) by way of counterclaim any matter not arising from the contract,

that would have been available to him by way of defence or set-off or, as the case may be, by way of counterclaim against the third party if the third party had been a party to the contract.

(5) Subsections (2) and (4) are subject to any express term of the contract as to the matters that are not to be available to the promisor by way of defence, set-off or counterclaim.

(6) Where in any proceedings brought against him a third party seeks in reliance on section 1 to enforce a term of a contract (including, in particular, a term purporting to exclude or limit liability), he may not do so if he could not have done so (whether by reason of any particular circumstances relating to him or otherwise) had he been a party to the contract.

[1.1270]

4 Enforcement of contract by promisee

Section 1 does not affect any right of the promisee to enforce any term of the contract.

[1.1271]

5 Protection of party promisor from double liability

Where under section 1 a term of a contract is enforceable by a third party, and the promisee has recovered from the promisor a sum in respect of—

(a) the third party's loss in respect of the term, or

(b) the expense to the promisee of making good to the third party the default of the promisor,

then, in any proceedings brought in reliance on that section by the third party, the court or arbitral tribunal shall reduce any award to the third party to such extent as it thinks appropriate to take account of the sum recovered by the promisee.

[1.1272]
6 Exceptions
(1) Section 1 confers no rights on a third party in the case of a contract on a bill of exchange, promissory note or other negotiable instrument.
(2) Section 1 confers no rights on a third party in the case of any contract binding on a company and its members under [section 33 of the Companies Act 2006 (effect of company's constitution)].
[(2A) Section 1 confers no rights on a third party in the case of any incorporation document of a limited liability partnership [or any agreement (express or implied) between the members of a limited liability partnership, or between a limited liability partnership and its members, that determines the mutual rights and duties of the members and their rights and duties in relation to the limited liability partnership].]
(3) Section 1 confers no right on a third party to enforce—
(a) any term of a contract of employment against an employee,
(b) any term of a worker's contract against a worker (including a home worker), or
(c) any term of a relevant contract against an agency worker.
(4) In subsection (3)—
(a) "contract of employment", "employee", "worker's contract", and "worker" have the meaning given by section 54 of the National Minimum Wage Act 1998,
(b) "home worker" has the meaning given by section 35(2) of that Act,
(c) "agency worker" has the same meaning as in section 34(1) of that Act, and
(d) "relevant contract" means a contract entered into, in a case where section 34 of that Act applies, by the agency worker as respects work falling within subsection (1)(a) of that section.
(5)–(8) *((Carriage of goods and cargo) outside the scope of this work.)*

NOTES
Sub-s (2): words in square brackets substituted by the Companies Act 2006 (Consequential Amendments, Transitional Provisions and Savings) Order 2009, SI 2009/1941, art 2(1), Sch 1, para 179(1), (2)(a).
Sub-s (2A): inserted by the Limited Liability Partnerships Regulations 2001, SI 2001/1090, reg 9(1), Sch 5, para 20; words in square brackets substituted by SI 2009/1941, art 2(1), Sch 1, para 179(1), (2)(b).

[1.1273]
7 Supplementary provisions relating to third party
(1) Section 1 does not affect any right or remedy of a third party that exists or is available apart from this Act.
(2) Section 2(2) of the Unfair Contract Terms Act 1977 (restriction on exclusion etc of liability for negligence) shall not apply where the negligence consists of the breach of an obligation arising from a term of a contract and the person seeking to enforce it is a third party acting in reliance on section 1.
(3) In sections 5 and 8 of the Limitation Act 1980 the references to an action founded on a simple contract and an action upon a specialty shall respectively include references to an action brought in reliance on section 1 relating to a simple contract and an action brought in reliance on that section relating to specialty.
(4) A third party shall not, by virtue of section 1(5) or 3(4) or (6), be treated as a party to the contract for the purposes of any other Act (or any instrument made under any other Act).

[1.1274]
8 Arbitration provisions
(1) Where—
(a) a right under section 1 to enforce a term ("the substantive term") is subject to a term providing for the submission of disputes to arbitration ("the arbitration agreement"), and
(b) the arbitration agreement is an agreement in writing for the purposes of Part I of the Arbitration Act 1996,

the third party shall be treated for the purposes of that Act as a party to the arbitration agreement as regards disputes between himself and the promisor relating to the enforcement of the substantive term by the third party.
(2) Where—
(a) a third party has a right under section 1 to enforce a term providing for one or more descriptions of dispute between the third party and the promisor to be submitted to arbitration ("the arbitration agreement"),
(b) the arbitration agreement is an agreement in writing for the purposes of Part I of the Arbitration Act 1996, and
(c) the third party does not fall to be treated under subsection (1) as a party to the arbitration agreement,

the third party shall, if he exercises the right, be treated for the purposes of that Act as a party to the arbitration agreement in relation to the matter with respect to which the right is exercised, and be treated as having been so immediately before the exercise of the right.

9 *(Applies to Northern Ireland (outside the scope of this work).)*

[1.1275]
10 Short title, commencement and extent
(1) This Act may be cited as the Contracts (Rights of Third Parties) Act 1999.
(2) This Act comes into force on the day on which it is passed but, subject to subsection (3), does not apply in relation to a contract entered into before the end of the period of six months beginning with that day.
(3) The restriction in subsection (2) does not apply in relation to a contract which—

(a) is entered into on or after the day on which this Act is passed, and
(b) expressly provides for the application of this Act.

(4) This Act extends as follows—
(a) section 9 extends to Northern Ireland only;
(b) the remaining provisions extend to England and Wales and Northern Ireland only.

NOTES

"On or after the day on which this Act is passed" in sub-s (3): this was 11 November 1999.

EMPLOYMENT ACT 2002

(2002 c 22)

ARRANGEMENT OF SECTIONS

PART 1
STATUTORY LEAVE AND PAY

CHAPTER 1
PATERNITY AND ADOPTION

Administration and enforcement: pay

PART 3
DISPUTE RESOLUTION ETC

Employment particulars

General

PART 4
MISCELLANEOUS AND GENERAL

Miscellaneous

General

SCHEDULES

An Act to make provision for statutory rights to paternity and adoption leave and pay; to amend the law relating to statutory maternity leave and pay; to amend the Employment Tribunals Act 1996; to make provision for the use of statutory procedures in relation to employment disputes; to amend the law relating to particulars of employment; to make provision about compromise agreements; to make provision for questionnaires in relation to equal pay; to make provision in connection with trade union learning representatives; to amend section 110 of the Employment Rights Act 1996; to make provision about fixed-term work; to make provision about flexible working; to amend the law relating to maternity allowance; to make provision for work-focused interviews for partners of benefit claimants; to make provision about the use of information for, or relating to, employment and training; and for connected purposes

[8 July 2002]

NOTES

Most of this major Act consists of amendments and additions to other legislation, principally the Employment Rights Act 1996 and the Social Security Contributions and Benefits Act 1992. These are cross referenced. The Act is otherwise printed in full save for those provisions that either have been repealed or are outside the scope of this work. In particular, ss 29–33 and Schs 2–4 were repealed by the Employment Act 2008, s 20, Schedule, Pt 1.

PART 1
STATUTORY LEAVE AND PAY

CHAPTER 1 PATERNITY AND ADOPTION

1–4 *(S 1 inserts the Employment Rights Act 1996, ss 80A, 80B, 80C–80E at* **[1.979]** *et seq; s 2 inserts the Social Security Contributions and Benefits Act 1992, ss 171ZA–171ZE, 171ZF–171ZK at* **[1.220]** *et seq; s 3 inserts the Employment Rights Act 1996, ss 75A–75D at* **[1.963]** *et seq; s 4 inserts the Social Security Contributions and Benefits Act 1992, ss 171ZL–171ZT at* **[1.231]** *et seq.)*

Administration and enforcement: pay

5, 6 *(S 5 repealed by the Commissioners for Revenue and Customs Act 2005, ss 50(6), 52(2), Sch 4, para 93, Sch 5; s 6 (financial arrangements) outside the scope of this work.)*

[1.1276]

7 Funding of employers' liabilities

(1) The Secretary of State shall by regulations make provision for the payment by employers of [statutory paternity pay,] statutory adoption pay *[and statutory shared parental pay]* to be funded by the Board to such extent as the regulations may specify.

(2) Regulations under subsection (1) shall—

(a) make provision for a person who has made a payment of [statutory paternity pay,] statutory adoption pay *[or statutory shared parental pay]* to be entitled, except in such circumstances as the regulations may provide, to recover an amount equal to the sum of

(i) the aggregate of such of those payments as qualify for small employers' relief; and

(ii) an amount equal to 92 per cent of the aggregate of such of those payments as do not so qualify; and

(b) include provision for a person who has made a payment of [statutory paternity pay,] statutory adoption pay *[or statutory shared parental pay]* qualifying for small employers' relief to be entitled, except in such circumstances as the regulations may provide, to recover an additional amount equal to the amount to which the person would have been entitled under section 167(2)(b) of the Social Security Contributions and Benefits Act 1992 (corresponding provision for statutory maternity pay) had the payment been a payment of statutory maternity pay.

(3) For the purposes of subsection (2), [a payment of] [statutory paternity pay,] statutory adoption pay *[or statutory shared parental pay]* qualifies for small employers' relief if it would have so qualified were it a payment of statutory maternity pay, [treating—

(a) the period for which the payment of statutory paternity pay is made,

(b) the payee's adoption pay period, *or*

(c) the period for which the payment of statutory shared parental pay is made, [or

(d) the period for which the payment of statutory parental bereavement pay is made,]

as the maternity pay period].

(4) Regulations under subsection (1) may, in particular—

(a) make provision for funding in advance as well as in arrear;

(b) make provision for funding, or the recovery of amounts due under provision made by virtue of subsection (2)(b), by means of deductions from such amounts for which employers are accountable to the Board as the regulations may provide, or otherwise;

(c) make provision for the recovery by the Board of any sums overpaid to employers under the regulations.

(5) Where in accordance with any provision of regulations under subsection (1) an amount has been deducted from an employer's contributions payments, the amount so deducted shall (except in such cases as the Secretary of State may by regulations provide) be treated for the purposes of any provision made by or under any enactment in relation to primary or secondary Class 1 contributions—

(a) as having been paid (on such date as may be determined in accordance with the regulations), and

(b) as having been received by the Board,

towards discharging the employer's liability in respect of such contributions.

(6) Regulations under this section must be made with the concurrence of the Board.

(7) In this section, "contributions payments", in relation to an employer, means any payments which the employer is required, by or under any enactment, to make in discharge of any liability in respect of primary or secondary Class 1 contributions.

NOTES

Sub-s (1): words in first pair of square brackets substituted by the Children and Families Act 2014, s 126(1), Sch 7, paras 50, 51(1), (2)(a), as from 5 April 2015 (note that this amendment does not have effect in relation to (a) children whose expected week of birth ends on or before 4 April 2015, and (b) children placed for adoption on or before that date: see the Children and Families Act 2014 (Commencement No 3, Transitional Provisions and Savings) Order 2014, SI 2014/1640, art 16); words in second pair of square brackets inserted by s 126(1) of, and Sch 7, paras 50, 51(1), (2)(b) to, the 2014 Act, as from 30 June 2014; for the words in italics there are substituted the words ", statutory shared parental pay and statutory parental bereavement pay", by the Parental Bereavement (Leave and Pay) Act 2018, s 1(c), Schedule, Pt 3, paras 35, 36(1), (2), as from a day to be appointed.

Sub-s (2): words "statutory paternity pay," in square brackets (in both places that they occur) substituted by the Children and Families Act 2014, s 126(1), Sch 7, paras 50, 51(1), (3)(a)(i), (b)(i), as from 5 April 2015 (for effect see the sub-s (1) note above); words "or statutory shared parental pay" in square brackets (in both places that they occur) inserted by s 126(1) of, and Sch 7, paras 50, 51(1), (3)(a)(ii), (b)(ii) to, the 2014 Act, as from 30 June 2014; for the words in italics in paras (a), (b) there are substituted the words ", statutory shared parental pay or statutory parental bereavement pay", by the Parental Bereavement (Leave and Pay) Act 2018, s 1(c), Schedule, Pt 3, paras 35, 36(1), (3), as from a day to be appointed.

Sub-s (3): words in first pair of square brackets substituted by the Work and Families Act 2006, s 11(1), Sch 1, para 50(1), (4); words in second pair of square brackets substituted by the Children and Families Act 2014, s 126(1), Sch 7, paras 50, 51(1), (4)(a), as from 5 April 2015 (for effect see the sub-s (1) note above); words in third pair of square brackets inserted by s 126(1) of, and Sch 7, paras 50, 51(1), (4)(b) to, the 2014 Act, as from 30 June 2014; words in final pair of square brackets substituted by s 126(1) of, and Sch 7, paras 50, 51(1), (4)(c) to, the 2014 Act, as from 30 June 2014 (except in relation to (a) children whose expected week of birth ends on or before 4 April 2015; (b) children placed for adoption on or before that date: see SI 2014/1640, art 9); for the first words in italics there are substituted the words ", statutory shared parental pay or statutory parental bereavement pay", the word in italics in para (b) is repealed, and para (d) is inserted, together with word preceding it, by the Parental Bereavement (Leave and Pay) Act 2018, s 1(c), Schedule, Pt 3, paras 35, 36(1), (4), as from a day to be appointed.

Statutory paternity pay: as to the meaning of this, see the Children and Families Act 2014, s 126 at **[1.1894]**.

Regulations: the Statutory Paternity Pay and Statutory Adoption Pay (Administration) Regulations 2002, SI 2002/2820 at **[2.611]**; the Statutory Paternity Pay (Adoption) and Statutory Adoption Pay (Adoptions from Overseas) (Administration) Regulations 2003, SI 2003/1192; the Additional Statutory Paternity Pay (Birth, Adoption and Adoptions from Overseas) (Administration) Regulations 2010, SI 2010/154; the Statutory Shared Parental Pay (Administration) Regulations 2014, SI 2014/2929 at **[2.1537]**.

[1.1277]

8 Regulations about payment

(1) The Secretary of State may make regulations with respect to the payment by employers of [statutory paternity pay,] statutory adoption pay *[and statutory shared parental pay]*.

(2) Regulations under subsection (1) may, in particular, include provision—

(a) about the records to be kept by employers in relation to payments of [statutory paternity pay,] statutory adoption pay *[and statutory shared parental pay]*, including the length of time for which they are to be retained;

(b) for the production of wages sheets and other documents and records to officers of the Board for the purpose of enabling them to satisfy themselves that [statutory paternity pay,] statutory adoption pay *[and statutory shared parental pay]* have been paid and are being paid, in accordance with the regulations, to employees who are entitled to them;

(c) for requiring employers to provide information to employees (in their itemised pay statements or otherwise);

(d) for requiring employers to make returns to the Board containing such particulars with respect to payments of [statutory paternity pay,] statutory adoption pay *[and statutory shared parental pay]* as the regulations may provide.

(3) Regulations under subsection (1) must be made with the concurrence of the Board.

NOTES

Sub-s (1): words in first pair of square brackets substituted by the Children and Families Act 2014, s 126(1), Sch 7, paras 50, 52(1), (2)(a), as from 5 April 2015 (note that this amendment does not have effect in relation to (a) children whose expected week of birth ends on or before 4 April 2015, and (b) children placed for adoption on or before that date: see the Children and Families Act 2014 (Commencement No 3, Transitional Provisions and Savings) Order 2014, SI 2014/1640, art 16); words in second pair of square brackets inserted by s 126(1) of, and Sch 7, paras 50, 52(1), (2)(b) to, the 2014 Act, as from 30 June 2014; for the words in italics there are substituted the words ", statutory shared parental pay and statutory parental bereavement pay", by the Parental Bereavement (Leave and Pay) Act 2018, s 1(c), Schedule, Pt 3, paras 35, 37, as from a day to be appointed.

Sub-s (2): words in first pair of square brackets in paras (a), (b), (d) substituted by the Children and Families Act 2014, s 126(1), Sch 7, paras 50, 52(1), (3)(a)(i), (b)(i), (c)(i), as from 5 April 2015 (for effect see the sub-s (1) note above); words in second pair of square brackets in those paragraphs inserted by s 126(1) of, and Sch 7, paras 50, 52(1), (3)(a)(ii), (b)(ii), (c)(ii) to, the 2014 Act, as from 30 June 2014; for the words in italics in paras (a), (b), (d) there are substituted the words ", statutory shared parental pay and statutory parental bereavement pay", by the Parental Bereavement (Leave and Pay) Act 2018, s 1(c), Schedule, Pt 3, paras 35, 37, as from a day to be appointed.

Statutory paternity pay: as to the meaning of this, see the Children and Families Act 2014, s 126 at **[1.1894]**

Regulations: the Statutory Paternity Pay and Statutory Adoption Pay (Administration) Regulations 2002, SI 2002/2820 at **[2.611]**; the Statutory Paternity Pay (Adoption) and Statutory Adoption Pay (Adoptions from Overseas) (Administration) Regulations 2003, SI 2003/1192; the Additional Statutory Paternity Pay (Birth, Adoption and Adoptions from Overseas) (Administration) Regulations 2010, SI 2010/154; the Statutory Paternity Pay and Statutory Adoption Pay (Parental Orders and Prospective Adopters) Regulations 2014, SI 2014/2934 at **[2.1551]**.

9–15 *(S 9 amends the Social Security Contributions (Transfer of Functions, etc) Act 1999; ss 10–15 (powers to require information, penalties and supply and use of information) outside the scope of this work.)*

[1.1278]

16 Interpretation

In sections 5 to 15—

"the Board" means the Commissioners of Inland Revenue;

"the Department" means the Department for Social Development or the Department for Employment and Learning;

"employer" and "employee" have the same meanings as in Parts 12ZA and 12ZB of the Social Security Contributions and Benefits Act 1992.

NOTES

Commissioners of Inland Revenue: a reference to the Commissioners of Inland Revenue is now to be taken as a reference to the Commissioners for Her Majesty's Revenue and Customs; see the Commissioners for Revenue and Customs Act 2005, s 50(1), (7).

17–28 *(In so far as these sections are still in force and not outside the scope of this work, they contain various amendments to the Employment Rights Act 1996 and the Social Security Contributions and Benefits Act 1992 which have been incorporated where appropriate.)*

PART 3
DISPUTE RESOLUTION ETC

Statutory procedures

29–34 *(Ss 29–33, 34(2) repealed by the Employment Act 2008, s 20, Schedule, Pt 1 (note that s 30 was never brought into effect); s 34(1) introduces the amendments that follow; s 34(3)–(6) amend ss 112, 117, 120, 123 of the 1996 Act at* **[1.1030]**, **[1.1035]**, **[1.1038]**, **[1.1041]**.*)*

Employment particulars

35–37 *(Ss 35, 36 amend the Employment Rights Act 1996, s 3 at* **[1.815]**; *s 37 inserts ss 7A, 7B of the 1996 Act at* **[1.820]**, **[1.821]**.*)*

[1.1279]

38 Failure to give statement of employment particulars etc

(1) This section applies to proceedings before an employment tribunal relating to a claim by *an employee* under any of the jurisdictions listed in Schedule 5.

(2) If in the case of proceedings to which this section applies—

- (a) the employment tribunal finds in favour of the *employee*, but makes no award to him in respect of the claim to which the proceedings relate, and
- (b) when the proceedings were begun the employer was in breach of his duty to the *employee* under section 1(1) or 4(1) of the Employment Rights Act 1996 (c 18) (duty to give a written statement of initial employment particulars or of particulars of change) [or [(in the case of a claim by an employee)] under section 41B or 41C of that Act (duty to give a written statement in relation to rights not to work on Sunday)],

the tribunal must, subject to subsection (5), make an award of the minimum amount to be paid by the employer to the *employee* and may, if it considers it just and equitable in all the circumstances, award the higher amount instead.

(3) If in the case of proceedings to which this section applies—

- (a) the employment tribunal makes an award to the *employee* in respect of the claim to which the proceedings relate, and
- (b) when the proceedings were begun the employer was in breach of his duty to the *employee* under section 1(1) or 4(1) of the Employment Rights Act 1996 [or [(in the case of a claim by an employee)] under section 41B or 41C of that Act],

the tribunal must, subject to subsection (5), increase the award by the minimum amount and may, if it considers it just and equitable in all the circumstances, increase the award by the higher amount instead.

(4) In subsections (2) and (3)—

- (a) references to the minimum amount are to an amount equal to two weeks' pay, and
- (b) references to the higher amount are to an amount equal to four weeks' pay.

(5) The duty under subsection (2) or (3) does not apply if there are exceptional circumstances which would make an award or increase under that subsection unjust or inequitable.

(6) The amount of a week's pay of *an employee* shall—

- (a) be calculated for the purposes of this section in accordance with Chapter 2 of Part 14 of the Employment Rights Act 1996 (c 18), and
- (b) not exceed the amount for the time being specified in section 227 of that Act (maximum amount of week's pay).

[(6A) The provisions referred to in subsection (6) shall apply for the purposes of that subsection—

- (a) as if a reference to an employee were a reference to a worker; and
- (b) as if a reference to an employee's contract of employment were a reference to a worker's contract of employment or other worker's contract.]

(7) For the purposes of Chapter 2 of Part 14 of the Employment Rights Act 1996 as applied by subsection (6), the calculation date shall be taken to be—

- (a) if the *employee* was employed by the employer on the date the proceedings were begun, that date, and
- *(b) if he was not, the effective date of termination as defined by section 97 of that Act.*

(8) The Secretary of State may by order—

- (a) amend Schedule 5 for the purpose of—
  - (i) adding a jurisdiction to the list in that Schedule, or
  - (ii) removing a jurisdiction from that list;
- (b) make provision, in relation to a jurisdiction listed in Schedule 5, for this section not to apply to proceedings relating to claims of a description specified in the order;
- (c) make provision for this section to apply, with or without modifications, as if—
  - (i) any individual of a description specified in the order who would not otherwise be an employee for the purposes of this section were an employee for those purposes, and
  - (ii) a person of a description specified in the order were, in the case of any such individual, the individual's employer for those purposes.

NOTES

Sub-s (1): for the words in italics there are substituted the words "a worker", by the Employment Rights (Miscellaneous Amendments) Regulations 2019, SI 2019/731, reg 17(1), (2), as from 6 April 2020.

Sub-s (2): for the word "employee" in each place it appears in italics, there is substituted the word "worker", and words in second (inner) pair of square brackets inserted, by SI 2019/731, reg 17(1), (3), as from 6 April 2020; words in first (outer) pair of square brackets in para (b) inserted by the Enterprise Act 2016, s 33, Sch 5, para 12, as from a day to be appointed.

Sub-s (3): for the word "employee" in each place it appears in italics, there is substituted the word "worker", and words in second (inner) pair of square brackets inserted, by SI 2019/731, reg 17(1), (4), as from 6 April 2020; words in first (outer) pair of square brackets in para (b) inserted by the Enterprise Act 2016, s 33, Sch 5, para 12, as from a day to be appointed.

Sub-s (6): for the words in italics there are substituted the words "a worker", by SI 2019/731, reg 17(1), (5), as from 6 April 2020.

Sub-s (6A): inserted by SI 2019/731, reg 17(1), (6), as from 6 April 2020.

Sub-s (7): for the word in italics in para (a) there is substituted the word "worker", and para (b) is substituted as follows, by SI 2019/731, reg 17(1), (7), as from 6 April 2020—

"(b) if he was not, in the case of an employee, the effective date of termination as defined by section 97 of that Act or in the case of all other workers the date on which the termination takes effect.".

The tribunal must . . . make an award, etc (sub-s (2)): where an award of compensation for unfair dismissal falls to be increased under this section, the adjustment is to be in the amount awarded under the Employment Rights Act 1996, s 118(1)(b), and is to be applied immediately before any reduction under s 123(6), (7) of that Act; see s 124A of the 1996 Act at **[1.1043]**.

Orders: the Employment Act 2002 (Amendment of Schedules 3, 4 and 5) Order 2007, SI 2007/30 (note that Schs 3 and 4 have been repealed as noted *post*).

General

39 *(Inserts the Employment Rights Act 1996, s 124A at* **[1.1043]**.*)*

[1.1280]
40 Interpretation of Part 3

In this Part—

"employer" and "employee" have the same meanings as in the Employment Rights Act 1996 (c 18);

. . .

["worker" has the same meaning as in the Employment Rights Act 1996.]

NOTES

Definition "statutory procedure" (omitted) repealed by the Employment Act 2008, s 20, Schedule, Pt 1; definition "worker" inserted by the Employment Rights (Miscellaneous Amendments) Regulations 2019, SI 2019/731, reg 18, as from 6 April 2020.

PART 4
MISCELLANEOUS AND GENERAL

Miscellaneous

41–44 *(S 41 repealed by the Employment Relations Act 2004, s 57(2); s 42 repealed by the Equality Act 2010, s 211(2), Sch 27, Pt 1; s 43 inserts the Trade Union and Labour Relations (Consolidation) Act 1992, s 168A at* **[1.478]**, *and amends ss 169, 170, 173, 199, 200, 203 of that Act; s 44 amends the Employment Rights Act 1996, s 110 at* **[1.1027]**.*)*

[1.1281]
45 Fixed-term work

(1) The Secretary of State shall make regulations—

(a) for the purpose of securing that employees in fixed-term employment are treated, for such purposes and to such extent as the regulations may specify, no less favourably than employees in permanent employment, and

(b) for the purpose of preventing abuse arising from the use of successive periods of fixed-term employment.

(2) The regulations may—

(a) specify classes of employee who are to be taken to be, or not to be, in fixed-term employment;

(b) specify classes of employee who are to be taken to be, or not to be, in permanent employment;

(c) specify circumstances in which employees in fixed-term employment are to be taken to be, or not to be, treated less favourably than employees in permanent employment;

(d) specify circumstances in which periods of fixed-term employment are to be taken to be, or not to be, successive;

(e) specify circumstances in which fixed-term employment is to have effect as permanent employment;

(f) make provision which has effect in relation to employees in fixed-term employment generally or provision which has effect only in relation to specified classes of employee in fixed-term employment.

(3) The regulations may—

(a) confer jurisdiction (including exclusive jurisdiction) on employment tribunals;

(b) provide for specified obligations not to apply in specified circumstances;

(c) make provision about notices or information to be given, evidence to be produced and other procedures to be followed;

(d) amend, apply with or without modifications, or make provision similar to any provision of—

(i) the Employment Rights Act 1996 (c 18) (including, in particular, Parts 5, 10 and 13),

(ii) the Trade Union and Labour Relations (Consolidation) Act 1992 (c 52), or

(iii) the Social Security Contributions and Benefits Act 1992 (c 4);

(e) provide for the provisions of specified agreements to have effect in place of provisions of the regulations to such extent and in such circumstances as may be specified.

(4) Without prejudice to the generality of this section, the regulations may make any provision in relation to employees which appears to the Secretary of State to be necessary or expedient—

(a) for the purpose of implementing Council Directive 99/70/EC on the framework agreement on fixed-term work in its application to terms and conditions of employment;

(b) for the purpose of dealing with any matter arising out of or related to the United Kingdom's obligations under that Directive;

(c) for the purpose of any matter dealt with by the framework agreement or for the purpose of applying the provisions of the framework agreement to any matter relating to fixed term workers.

(5) In its application to this section, section 51(1)(b) includes power to amend an enactment.

(6) In this section—

(a) "employee" means an individual who has entered into or works under (or, where the employment has ceased, worked under) a contract of employment, and

(b) "contract of employment" means a contract of service or apprenticeship, whether express or implied, and (if it is express) whether oral or in writing.

NOTES

Sub-s (4): repealed by the Employment Rights (Amendment) (EU Exit) Regulations 2019, SI 2019/535, reg 2(1), Sch 1, Pt 1, para 5, as from exit day (as defined in the European Union (Withdrawal) Act 2018, s 20) and subject to savings in Sch 1, Pt 3, para 22 thereto, which provides that the repeal does not affect the validity of any regulations made under this section that came into force before exit day.

Regulations: the Fixed-term Employees (Prevention of Less Favourable Treatment) Regulations 2002, SI 2002/2034 at **[2.553]**; the Fixed-term Employees (Prevention of Less Favourable Treatment) (Amendment) Regulations 2008, SI 2008/2776.

46–50 *(S 46 applies to Northern Ireland only; s 47 inserts the Employment Rights Act 1996, ss 47E, 80F–80I, 104C at* **[1.891]**, **[1.989]–[1.992]**, **[1.1018]**; *s 48 (Rate of maternity allowance), s 49 (Work-focused interviews for partners), s 50 (introduces Sch 6 (Use of information for, or relating to, employment and training)) outside the scope of this work. Note also that s 49 is repealed by the Welfare Reform Act 2012, s 147, Sch 14, Pt 1, as from a day to be appointed.)*

General

[1.1282]

51 Orders and regulations

(1) Any power of the Secretary of State to make orders or regulations under this Act includes power—

(a) to make different provision for different cases or circumstances;

(b) to make such incidental, supplementary, consequential or transitional provision as the Secretary of State thinks fit.

(2) Any power of the Secretary of State to make orders or regulations under this Act is exercisable by statutory instrument.

(3) No order may be made under this Act unless a draft of the order has been laid before and approved by resolution of each House of Parliament.

(4) No regulations may be made under section . . . 45 unless a draft of the regulations has been laid before and approved by resolution of each House of Parliament.

(5) A statutory instrument containing regulations under any other provision of this Act shall be subject to annulment in pursuance of a resolution of either House of Parliament.

(6) This section does not apply to orders under section 55(2).

NOTES

Sub-s (4): words omitted repealed by the Employment Act 2008, s 20, Schedule, Pt 1.

[1.1283]

52 Financial provisions

(1) There shall be paid out of money provided by Parliament—

(a) any expenses incurred by a Minister of the Crown or government department in consequence of this Act, and

(b) any increase attributable to this Act in the sums so provided under any other Act.

(2) There shall be paid into the Consolidated Fund any increase attributable to this Act in the sums payable into that Fund under any other Act.

[1.1284]

53 Minor and consequential amendments

Schedule 7 (which makes minor and consequential amendments) has effect.

[1.1285]

54 Repeals and revocations

The enactments and instruments specified in Schedule 8 are hereby repealed or revoked to the extent specified there.

[1.1286]

55 Short title etc

(1) This Act may be cited as the Employment Act 2002.

(2) This Act, except sections 45, 46, 51 and 52 and this section, shall come into force on such day as the Secretary of State may by order made by statutory instrument appoint, and different days may be so appointed for different purposes.

(3) An order under subsection (2) may contain such transitional provisions and savings as the Secretary of State considers necessary or expedient in connection with the coming into force of any of the provisions of this Act.

(4) The Secretary of State may by regulations make such transitional provisions and savings as he considers necessary or expedient for the purposes of or in connection with—

(a) the coming into force of section 19 or 48, or Schedule 7 so far as relating to any amendment made in consequence of either of those sections; or

(b) the operation of any enactment amended by any of those provisions during any period when the amendment is not wholly in force.

(5) Subject to subsections (6) and (7), this Act extends to England and Wales and Scotland only.

(6)–(8) (*Apply to Northern Ireland only.*)

NOTES

Orders: the Employment Act 2002 (Commencement No 1) Order 2002, SI 2002/1989; the Employment Act 2002 (Commencement No 2) Order 2002, SI 2002/2256; the Employment Act 2002 (Commencement No 3 and Transitional and Saving Provisions) Order 2002, SI 2002/2866; the Employment Act 2002 (Commencement No 4 and Transitional Provisions) Order 2003, SI 2003/1190; the Employment Act 2002 (Commencement No 5) Order 2003, SI 2003/1666; the Employment Act 2002 (Commencement No 6 and Transitional Provision) Order 2004, SI 2004/1717; the Employment Act 2002 (Commencement No 7) Order 2004, SI 2004/2185; the Employment Act 2002 (Commencement No 8) Order 2004, SI 2004/2822.

SCHEDULES

SCHEDULES 1–4

(Sch 1 (Penalties: procedure and appeals) outside the scope of this work; Schs 2–4 repealed by the Employment Act 2008, s 20, Schedule, Pt 1.)

SCHEDULE 5
TRIBUNAL JURISDICTIONS TO WHICH SECTION 38 APPLIES

Section 38

[1.1287]

. . .

. . .

[Section 145A of the Trade Union and Labour Relations (Consolidation) Act 1992 (inducements relating to union membership or activities)

Section 145B of that Act (inducements relating to collective bargaining)

Section 146 of that Act (detriment in relation to union membership and activities)]

Paragraph 156 of Schedule A1 to that Act (detriment in relation to union recognition rights)

. . .

Section 23 of the Employment Rights Act 1996 (c 18) (unauthorised deductions and payments)

Section 48 of that Act (detriment in employment)

Section 111 of that Act (unfair dismissal)

Section 163 of that Act (redundancy payments)

Section 24 of the National Minimum Wage Act 1998 (c 39) (detriment in relation to national minimum wage)

. . .

[Sections 120 and 127 of the Equality Act 2010 (discrimination etc in work cases)]

The Employment Tribunal Extension of Jurisdiction (England and Wales) Order 1994 (SI 1994/1623) (breach of employment contract and termination)

The Employment Tribunal Extension of Jurisdiction (Scotland) Order 1994 (SI 1994/1624) (corresponding provision for Scotland)

Regulation 30 of the Working Time Regulations 1998 (SI 1998/1833) (breach of regulations)

Regulation 32 of the Transnational Information and Consultation of Employees Regulations 1999 (SI 1999/3323) (detriment relating to European Works Councils)

[. . .]

[. . .]

[Regulation 45 of the European Public Limited-Liability Company Regulations 2004 (SI 2004/2326) (detriment in employment)

Regulation 33 of the Information and Consultation of Employees Regulations 2004 (SI 2004/3426) (detriment in employment)

Paragraph 8 of the Schedule to the Occupational and Personal Pension Schemes (Consultation by Employers and Miscellaneous Amendment) Regulations 2006 (SI 2006/349) (detriment in employment)]

[. . .]

[Regulation 34 of the European Cooperative Society (Involvement of Employees) Regulations 2006 (detriment in relation to involvement in a European Cooperative Society)]

[Regulation 51 of the Companies (Cross-Border Mergers) Regulations 2007 (detriment in relation to special negotiating body or employee participation)]

[Regulation 17 of the Cross-border Railways Services (Working Time) Regulations 2008 (breach of regulations)].

NOTES

Entries relating to the Equal Pay Act 1970, the Sex Discrimination Act 1975, the Race Relations Act 1976, and the Disability Discrimination Act 1995 (all omitted) repealed by the Equality Act 2010, s 211, Sch 26, Pt 1, para 49(1), (2)(a)–(d), Sch 27, Pt 1.

Entries relating to the Trade Union and Labour Relations (Consolidation) Act 1992 substituted by the Employment Relations Act 2004, s 57(1), Sch 1, para 43.

Entry relating to the Tax Credits Act 1999 (omitted) repealed by the Tax Credits Act 2002, s 60, Sch 6.

Entry relating to the Equality Act 2010 inserted by the Equality Act 2010, s 211(1), Sch 26, Pt 1, para 49(1), (3).

Entry relating to the Employment Equality (Sexual Orientation) Regulations 2003 (omitted) originally inserted by the Employment Equality (Sexual Orientation) Regulations 2003, SI 2003/1661, reg 39, Sch 5, para 4(c), and repealed by the Equality Act 2010, s 211, Sch 26, Pt 1, para 49(1), (2)(e), Sch 27, Pt 1.

Entry relating to the Employment Equality (Religion or Belief) Regulations 2003 (omitted) originally inserted by the Employment Equality (Religion or Belief) Regulations 2003, SI 2003/1660, reg 39(2), Sch 5, para 4(c), and repealed by the Equality Act 2010, s 211, Sch 26, Pt 1, para 49(1), (2)(f), Sch 27, Pt 1.

Entries relating to the European Public Limited-Liability Company Regulations 2004, the Information and Consultation of Employees Regulations 2004, and the Occupational and Personal Pension Schemes (Consultation by Employers and Miscellaneous Amendment) Regulations 2006 inserted by the Employment Act 2002 (Amendment of Schedules 3, 4 and 5) Order 2007, SI 2007/30, art 2.

Entry relating to the Employment Equality (Age) Regulations 2006 (omitted) originally inserted by the Employment Equality (Age) Regulations 2006, SI 2006/1031, reg 49(1), Sch 8, Pt 1, para 36(1), (2), and repealed by the Equality Act 2010, s 211, Sch 26, Pt 1, para 49(1), (2)(g), Sch 27, Pt 1.

Entry relating to the European Cooperative Society (Involvement of Employees) Regulations 2006 inserted by the European Cooperative Society (Involvement of Employees) Regulations 2006, SI 2006/2059, reg 34(4).

Entry relating to the Companies (Cross-Border Mergers) Regulations 2007 inserted by the Companies (Cross-Border Mergers) Regulations 2007, SI 2007/2974, reg 63(c) and repealed by the Companies, Limited Liability Partnerships and Partnerships (Amendment etc) (EU Exit) Regulations 2019, SI 2019/348, reg 8, Sch 3, para 8, as from exit day (as defined in the European Union (Withdrawal) Act 2018, s 20).

Entry relating to the Cross-border Railways Services (Working Time) Regulations 2008 inserted by the Cross-border Railways Services (Working Time) Regulations 2008, SI 2008/1660, reg 19, Sch 3, para 3(c).

Note that the entries relating to SI 1994/1623 and SI 1994/1624 are printed as in the Queen's Printers' copy of this Act; the correct titles of the said orders are the "Employment Tribunals Extension of Jurisdiction (England and Wales) Order 1994" and the "Employment Tribunals Extension of Jurisdiction (Scotland) Order 1994" respectively.

SCHEDULE 6

(Sch 6 (Miscellaneous amendments concerning the use of information for, or relating to, employment and training) outside the scope of this work; Schs 7 and 8 contain minor and consequential amendments and repeals respectively and, where relevant to this work, have been incorporated at the appropriate place.)

EDUCATION ACT 2002

(2002 c 32)

An Act to make provision about education, training and childcare

[24 July 2002]

NOTES

Most of this Act covers matters outside the scope of this work, and only those provisions most directly relevant to employment law are printed. For reasons of space, the subject matter of sections not printed is not annotated. The provisions printed here apply only to England and Wales.

ARRANGEMENT OF SECTIONS

PART 3
MAINTAINED SCHOOLS

CHAPTER 1
PATERNITY AND ADOPTION

PART 8
TEACHERS

Teacher misconduct etc: England

PART 11
MISCELLANEOUS AND GENERAL

General

SCHEDULES

PART 3
MAINTAINED SCHOOLS

CHAPTER 1 GOVERNMENT OF MAINTAINED SCHOOLS

[1.1288]
35 Staffing of community, voluntary controlled, community special and maintained nursery schools

(1) This section applies to—
- (a) community schools,
- (b) voluntary controlled schools,
- (c) community special schools, and
- (d) maintained nursery schools.

(2) Any teacher or other member of staff who is appointed to work under a contract of employment at a school to which this section applies is to be employed by the [local authority].

(3) The teaching staff of any school to which this section applies shall include—
- (a) a person appointed as head teacher, or
- (b) a person appointed to carry out the functions of the head teacher of the school—
  - (i) pending the appointment of a head teacher, or
  - (ii) in the absence of the head teacher.

(4) Regulations may make further provision with respect to the staffing of schools to which this section applies.

(5) Regulations under subsection (4) may, in particular—
- (a) make provision with respect to the appointment, discipline, suspension and dismissal of teachers and other staff,
- (b) make provision with respect to the appointment of teachers and other staff to work at a school otherwise than under a contract of employment,
- (c) make provision with respect to staff employed, or engaged otherwise than under a contract of employment, wholly or partly for the purposes of—
  - (i) the provision of facilities and services under section 27, or
  - (ii) any other activities which are not school activities but are carried on on the school premises under the management or control of the governing body, and
- (d) confer functions on [local authorities], governing bodies and head teachers.

(6) In relation to teachers at a voluntary controlled school who are reserved teachers within the meaning of section 58 of the School Standards and Framework Act 1998 (c 31) (appointment and dismissal of certain teachers at schools with a religious character), regulations under subsection (4) shall have effect subject to the provisions of that section.

(7) If at any time a school to which this section applies does not have a delegated budget by virtue of any suspension under . . . Schedule 15 to, the School Standards and Framework Act 1998[, or section 66 of the Education and Inspections Act 2006][, or section 8 of the School Standards and Organisation (Wales) Act 2013]—

(a) regulations under subsection (4) shall not apply, and

(b) the provisions of Part 1 of Schedule 2 shall apply instead.

(8) In discharging any function conferred by regulations under subsection (4), a [local authority] [in Wales] or the governing body or head teacher of a maintained school [in Wales] shall have regard to any guidance given from time to time—

(a) . . .

(b) . . . by the National Assembly for Wales.

NOTES

Sub-ss (2), (5): words in square brackets substituted by the Local Education Authorities and Children's Services Authorities (Integration of Functions) Order 2010, SI 2010/1158, art 5(1), Sch 2, Pt 1, para 11(1)–(3).

Sub-s (7): words omitted repealed, and words in second pair of square brackets inserted, by the School Standards and Organisation (Wales) Act 2013, s 99, Sch 5, Pt 1, para 6(1), (3); words in first pair of square brackets inserted by the Education Act 2011, s 19(1).

Sub-s (8): words in first pair of square brackets substituted by SI 2010/1158, art 5(1), Sch 2, Pt 1, para 11(1), (2); other words in square brackets inserted, and words omitted repealed, by the Deregulation Act 2015, s 66(5), Sch 16, para 4, as from 1 January 2016 (Sch 16, para 4 to the 2015 Act also repeals sub-s (8) in so far as it applies to England).

Regulations: the Staffing of Maintained Schools (Wales) Regulations 2006, SI 2006/873; the Staffing of Maintained Schools (Miscellaneous Amendments) (Wales) Regulations 2007, SI 2007/944; the Education (Miscellaneous Amendments relating to Safeguarding Children) (England) Regulations 2009, SI 2009/1924; the Education (Miscellaneous Amendments relating to Safeguarding Children) (Wales) Regulations 2009, SI 2009/2544; the School Staffing (England) Regulations 2009, SI 2009/2680 at **[2.1027]**; the Staffing of Maintained Schools (Wales) (Amendment) Regulations 2009, SI 2009/2708; the Staffing of Maintained Schools (Wales) (Amendment No 2) Regulations 2009, SI 2009/3161; the Federation of Maintained Schools and Miscellaneous Amendments (Wales) Regulations 2010, SI 2010/638; the School Governance (Federations) (England) Regulations 2012, SI 2012/1035; the School Staffing (England) (Amendment) Regulations 2012, SI 2012/1740; the School Staffing (England) (Amendment) Regulations 2013, SI 2013/1940; the School Staffing (England) (Amendment) Regulations 2014, SI 2014/798; the Federation of Maintained Schools (Wales) Regulations 2014, SI 2014/1132; the School Governance (Constitution and Federations) (England) (Amendment) Regulations 2014, SI 2014/1257; the Staffing of Maintained Schools (Wales) (Amendment) Regulations 2014, SI 2014/1609; the School Governance (Constitution and Federations) (England) (Amendment) (No 2) Regulations 2014, SI 2014/1959; the School Staffing (England) (Amendment) Regulations 2015, SI 2015/887.

[1.1289]

36 Staffing of foundation, voluntary aided and foundation special schools

(1) This section applies to—

(a) foundation schools,

(b) voluntary aided schools, and

(c) foundation special schools.

(2) Except as provided by regulations under subsection (4), any teacher or other member of staff who is appointed to work under a contract of employment at a school to which this section applies is to be employed by the governing body of the school.

(3) The teaching staff of any school to which this section applies shall include—

(a) a person appointed as head teacher, or

(b) a person appointed to carry out the functions of the head teacher of the school—

(i) pending the appointment of a head teacher, or

(ii) in the absence of the head teacher.

(4) Regulations may make further provision with respect to the staffing of schools to which this section applies.

(5) Regulations under subsection (4) may, in particular—

(a) make provision with respect to the appointment, discipline, suspension and dismissal of teachers and other staff,

(b) make provision with respect to the appointment of teachers and other staff to work at a school otherwise than under a contract of employment,

(c) make provision with respect to staff employed, or engaged otherwise than under a contract of employment, wholly or partly for the purposes of—

(i) the provision of facilities and services under section 27, or

(ii) any other activities which are not school activities but are carried on the school premises under the management or control of the governing body,

(d) enable teachers and other staff to be employed by the [local authority] in prescribed cases, and

(e) confer functions on [local authorities], governing bodies and head teachers.

(6) Regulations under subsection (4) shall have effect subject to section 58 of the School Standards and Framework Act 1998 (c 31) (appointment and dismissal of certain teachers at schools with a religious character).

(7) If at any time a school to which this section applies does not have a delegated budget by virtue of any suspension under . . . Schedule 15 to, the School Standards and Framework Act 1998[, or section 66 of the Education and Inspections Act 2006][, or section 8 of the School Standards and Organisation (Wales) Act 2013], regulations under subsection (4) shall have effect subject to the provisions of Part 2 of Schedule 2.

(8) In discharging any function conferred by regulations under subsection (4), a [local authority] [in Wales] or the governing body or head teacher of a maintained school [in Wales] shall have regard to any guidance given from time to time

(a) . . .

(b) . . . by the National Assembly for Wales.

NOTES

Sub-s (5): words in square brackets substituted by the Local Education Authorities and Children's Services Authorities (Integration of Functions) Order 2010, SI 2010/1158, art 5(1), Sch 2, Pt 1, para 11(1)–(3).

Sub-s (7): words omitted repealed and words in second pair of square brackets inserted by the School Standards and Organisation (Wales) Act 2013, s 99, Sch 5, Pt 1, para 6(1), (4); words in first pair of square brackets inserted by the Education Act 2011, s 19(2).

Sub-s (8): words in first pair of square brackets substituted by SI 2010/1158, art 5(1), Sch 2, Pt 1, para 11(1), (2); other words in square brackets inserted, and words omitted repealed, by the Deregulation Act 2015, s 66(5), Sch 16, para 5, as from 1 January 2016 (Sch 16, para 5 to the 2015 Act also repeals sub-s (8) in so far as it applies to England).

Regulations: see the note to s 35 *ante*.

[1.1290]

37 Payments in respect of dismissal, etc

(1) It shall be for the governing body of a maintained school to determine—

(a) whether any payment should be made by the [local authority] in respect of the dismissal, or for the purpose of securing the resignation, of any member of the staff of the school, and

(b) the amount of any such payment.

(2) Subsection (1) does not, however, apply in relation to a payment which the [local authority] are required to make—

(a) by virtue of any contract other than one made in contemplation of the impending dismissal or resignation of the member of staff concerned, or

(b) under any statutory provision.

(3) The [local authority]—

(a) shall take such steps as may be required for giving effect to any determination of the governing body under subsection (1), and

(b) shall not make, or agree to make, a payment in relation to which that subsection applies except in accordance with such a determination.

(4) Subject to subsection (7), costs incurred by the [local authority] in respect of any premature retirement of a member of the staff of a maintained school shall be met from the school's budget share for one or more [funding periods] except in so far as the authority agree with the governing body in writing (whether before or after the retirement occurs) that they shall not be so met.

(5) Subject to subsection (7), costs incurred by the [local authority] in respect of the dismissal, or for the purpose of securing the resignation, of any member of the staff of a maintained school shall not be met from the school's budget share for any [funding period] except in so far as the authority have good reason for deducting those costs, or any part of those costs, from that share.

(6) The fact that the authority have a policy precluding dismissal of their employees by reason of redundancy is not to be regarded as a good reason for the purposes of subsection (5); and in this subsection the reference to dismissal by reason of redundancy shall be read in accordance with section 139 of the Employment Rights Act 1996 (c 18).

(7) Where a [local authority] incur costs

(a) in respect of any premature retirement of any member of the staff of a maintained school who is employed for community purposes, or

(b) in respect of the dismissal, or for the purpose of securing the resignation, of any member of the staff of a maintained school who is employed for those purposes,

they shall recover those costs from the governing body except in so far as the authority agree with the governing body in writing (whether before or after the retirement, dismissal or resignation occurs) that they shall not be so recoverable.

[(7A) Any amount payable by virtue of subsection (7) by the governing body of a maintained school in England to the local authority may be met by the governing body out of the school's budget share for any funding period if and to the extent that the condition in subsection (7B) is met.

(7B) The condition is that the governing body are satisfied that meeting the amount out of the school's budget share will not to a significant extent interfere with the performance of any duty imposed on them by section 21(2) or by any other provision of the Education Acts.]

(8) Any amount payable by virtue of subsection (7) by the governing body of a maintained school [in Wales] to the [local authority] shall not be met by the governing body out of the school's budget share for any [funding period].

(9) Where a person is employed partly for community purposes and partly for other purposes, any payment or costs in respect of that person is to be apportioned between the two purposes; and the preceding provisions of this section shall apply separately to each part of the payment or costs.

(10) Regulations may make provision with respect to the recovery from governing bodies of amounts payable by virtue of subsection (7).

(11) Subsections (1) to (6) do not apply to a maintained school at any time when the school does not have a delegated budget by virtue of any suspension under . . . Schedule 15 to, the School Standards and Framework Act 1998 (c 31) [or section 8 of the School Standards and Organisation (Wales) Act 2013].

[(12) In this section—

"community purposes" means the purposes of the provision of facilities or services under section 27;

"funding period" has the meaning given by section 45(1B) of the School Standards and Framework Act 1998.]

NOTES

The words "funding periods" in sub-s (4), "funding period" in sub-ss (5), (8), and the whole of sub-s (12) were substituted by the Education Act 2005, s 117, Sch 18, para 14(1), (3), (4).

Sub-ss (7A), (7B) were inserted, and the words "in Wales" in square brackets in sub-s (8) were inserted, by the Education Act 2011, s 47(1).

In sub-s (11), words omitted repealed and words in square brackets inserted by the School Standards and Organisation (Wales) Act 2013, s 99, Sch 5, Pt 1, para 6(1), (5).

All other words in square brackets were substituted by the Local Education Authorities and Children's Services Authorities (Integration of Functions) Order 2010, SI 2010/1158, art 5(1), Sch 2, Pt 1, para 11(1), (2).

Regulations: as at 15 May 2019, no Regulations had been made under sub-s (10).

PART 8
TEACHERS

[Teacher misconduct etc: England

[1.1291]

141A Teachers to whom sections 141B to 141E apply

(1) Sections 141B to 141E apply to a person who is employed or engaged to carry out teaching work at—

(a) a school in England,

(b) a sixth form college in England,

[(ba) a 16 to 19 Academy,]

(c) relevant youth accommodation in England, or

(d) a children's home in England.

(2) In subsection (1)—

"children's home" has the same meaning as in the Care Standards Act 2000;

"teaching work" means work of a kind specified in regulations under this section (and such regulations may make provision by reference to specified activities or by reference to the circumstances in which activities are carried out).]

NOTES

Inserted, together with the preceding heading and ss 141B–141E, by the Education Act 2011, s 8(1).

Sub-s (1): para (ba) inserted by the Education Act 2011, s 54(1), Sch 13, para 13(1), (3).

Regulations: the Teachers' Disciplinary (England) Regulations 2012, SI 2012/560 at **[2.1252]**.

[1.1292]

[141B Investigation of disciplinary cases by Secretary of State

(1) The Secretary of State may investigate a case where an allegation is referred to the Secretary of State that a person to whom this section applies—

(a) may be guilty of unacceptable professional conduct or conduct that may bring the teaching profession into disrepute, or

(b) has been convicted (at any time) of a relevant offence.

(2) Where the Secretary of State finds on an investigation of a case under subsection (1) that there is a case to answer, the Secretary of State must decide whether to make a prohibition order in respect of the person.

(3) Schedule 11A (regulations about decisions under subsection (2)) has effect.

(4) In this section—

a "prohibition order" means an order prohibiting the person to whom it relates from carrying out teaching work;

(a) in the case of a conviction in England and Wales, a criminal offence other than one having no material relevance to the person's fitness to be a teacher, and

(b) in the case of a conviction elsewhere, an offence which, if committed in England and Wales, would be within paragraph (a).]

"relevant offence", in relation to a person, means—

"teaching work" has the same meaning as in section 141A(1);

NOTES

Inserted as noted to s 141A at **[1.1291]**.

[1.1293]

[141C List of persons prohibited from teaching etc

(1) The Secretary of State must keep a list containing—

(a) the names of persons in relation to whom a prohibition order has effect, and

(b) the names of persons who have begun, but have failed satisfactorily to complete, an induction period under section 135A in such circumstances as may be prescribed.

(2) The Secretary of State may include on the list the name of any person who has been prohibited from teaching in Wales, Scotland or Northern Ireland that the Secretary of State thinks appropriate to include on the list.

(3) The Secretary of State must secure that, where the name of a person is included on the list because an interim prohibition order has effect in respect of the person, there is an indication on the list to that effect.

(4) The Secretary of State must secure that, where the name of a person is included on the list because the person has failed satisfactorily to complete an induction period under section 135A, there is an indication on the list to that effect.

(5) The list may contain such other information in relation to the persons whose names are included on it as the Secretary of State considers appropriate.

(6) The list must be available for inspection by members of the public.

(7) In this section—

"prohibition order" has the same meaning as in section 141B;

"interim prohibition order" means an order made by virtue of paragraph 3 of Schedule 11A.]

NOTES

Inserted as noted to s 141A at **[1.1291]**.

Regulations: the Education (Induction Arrangements for School Teachers) (England) Regulations 2012, SI 2012/1115.

[1.1294]

[141D Supply of information following dismissal, resignation etc

(1) This section applies where a relevant employer has ceased to use the services of a teacher because the teacher has been guilty of serious misconduct.

(2) This section also applies where a relevant employer might have ceased to use the services of a teacher as mentioned in subsection (1) had the teacher not ceased to provide those services.

(3) The employer must consider whether it would be appropriate to provide prescribed information about the teacher to the Secretary of State.

(4) In this section—

"relevant employer" means—

(a) a local authority;

(b) a person exercising a function relating to the provision of education on behalf of a local authority;

(c) the proprietor of a school [or 16 to 19 Academy];

(d) a sixth form college corporation;

(e) a person who employs a person to teach in a children's home or in relevant youth accommodation;

"education" includes vocational, social, physical and recreational training;

"children's home" has the same meaning as in the Care Standards Act 2000;

"services" includes professional and voluntary services;

"teacher" means a person within section 141A(1).]

NOTES

Inserted as noted to s 141A at **[1.1291]**.

Sub-s (4): words in square brackets in para (c) of the definition "relevant employer" inserted by the Education Act 2011, s 54(1), Sch 13, para 13(1), (4).

Regulations: the Teachers' Disciplinary (England) Regulations 2012, SI 2012/560 at **[2.1252]**.

[1.1295]

[141E Supply of information by contractor, agency etc

(1) This section applies where arrangements have been made by a person (the "agent") for a teacher to carry out work at the request of or with the consent of a relevant employer (whether or not under a contract) and the agent has terminated the arrangements because the teacher has been guilty of serious misconduct.

(2) This section also applies where the agent—

(a) might have terminated the arrangements as mentioned in subsection (1) had the teacher not terminated them, or

(b) might have refrained from making new arrangements because of the teacher's serious misconduct had the teacher not ceased to be available for work.

(3) The agent must consider whether it would be appropriate to provide prescribed information about the teacher to the Secretary of State.

(4) In this section "relevant employer" and "teacher" have the same meanings as in section 141D.]

NOTES

Inserted as noted to s 141A at **[1.1291]**.

Regulations: the Teachers' Disciplinary (England) Regulations 2012, SI 2012/560 at **[2.1252]**.

PART 11
MISCELLANEOUS AND GENERAL

General

[1.1296]

216 Commencement

(1) The following provisions shall come into force on the day on which this Act is passed—

(*outside the scope of this work*),

this section and section 217.

(2), (3) *(Outside the scope of this work.)*
(4) Subject to subsections (1) to (3), this Act shall come into force—
(a) except in relation to Wales, in accordance with provision made by the Secretary of State by order, and
(b) in relation to Wales, in accordance with provision made by the National Assembly for Wales by order.
(5) An order under this section may—
(a) make provision generally or for specified purposes only,
(b) make different provision for different purposes, and
(c) contain such transitional provisions and savings as the person making the order thinks fit.

NOTES

Orders: commencement orders made under this section are outside the scope of this work.

[1.1297]

217 Short title and extent

(1) This Act may be cited as the Education Act 2002.
(2) This Act shall be included in the list of Education Acts set out in section 578 of the Education Act 1996 (c 56).
(3) Any amendment or repeal in this Act has the same extent as the provision amended or repealed.
(4) Except as provided by subsection (3), this Act extends to England and Wales only.

SCHEDULES

[SCHEDULE 11A
REGULATIONS ABOUT DECISIONS UNDER SECTION 141B

[Section 141B]

Regulations: general

[1.1298]

1. The Secretary of State must make regulations in accordance with the following provisions of this Schedule.

Procedure for decisions under section 141B(2)

2. (1) Regulations under paragraph 1 must make provision about the procedure to be followed by the Secretary of State in reaching a decision under section 141B(2).

(2) The regulations must not require a person to give evidence or produce any document or other material evidence which the person could not be compelled to give or produce in civil proceedings in any court in England and Wales.

(3) The regulations may make provision for any functions of the Secretary of State under section 141B to be excluded or restricted in such circumstances as may be specified in or determined under the regulations.

(4) The circumstances include, in particular, where the Secretary of State considers this to be appropriate taking into account the powers of the [Disclosure and Barring Service] under the Safeguarding Vulnerable Groups Act 2006.

Interim prohibition orders

3. (1) Regulations under paragraph 1 may make provision for the Secretary of State to make an interim prohibition order, pending the Secretary of State's final decision under section 141B(2).

(2) Regulations about interim prohibition orders must provide that an interim prohibition order may be made only if the Secretary of State considers that it is necessary in the public interest to do so.

(3) Regulations about interim prohibition orders must provide that the Secretary of State must review an interim prohibition order—
(a) within six months of the order being made, and
(b) within each subsequent six month period,
if the person to whom the order relates makes an application to the Secretary of State for such a review.

Prohibition orders

4. (1) Regulations under paragraph 1 may make provision—
(a) about the service on a person to whom a prohibition order relates of notice of the order and of the right to appeal against the order under paragraph 5;
(b) about the publication of information relating to the case of a person to whom a prohibition order relates;
(c) prescribing circumstances in which a person to whom a prohibition order relates may nevertheless carry out teaching work (within the meaning of section 141A).

(2) Regulations under paragraph 1 may also make provision—
(a) as to the time when a prohibition order takes effect;
(b) allowing a person to whom a prohibition order relates to apply to the Secretary of State for the order to be set aside;
(c) as to the minimum period for which a prohibition order must be in effect before such an application may be made;

(d) as to the procedure relating to such an application.

Appeals against prohibition orders

5. (1) Regulations under paragraph 1 must make provision conferring on a person to whom a prohibition order relates a right to appeal against the order to the High Court.

(2) The regulations must provide that an appeal must be brought within 28 days of the person being served with notice of the prohibition order.

(3) No appeal is to lie from any decision of the Court on such an appeal.

(4) In this paragraph, "prohibition order" does not include an interim prohibition order made by virtue of paragraph 3.

Supplementary provisions

6. (1) Regulations under paragraph 1 may make incidental and supplementary provision, including provision—

(a) where a prohibition order has effect in relation to a person, for the Secretary of State to serve notice of the order on the person's employer;

(b) requiring the employer of such a person to take such steps in consequence of the order (which may include dismissing the person) as may be prescribed;

(c) authorising the delegation of functions conferred by virtue of this Schedule and the determination of matters by any person or persons specified in the regulations.

(2) Regulations under paragraph 1 may also make provision—

(a) for the Secretary of State to make a decision in a particular case about the effect in England of an order prohibiting a person from teaching in schools in Wales, Scotland or Northern Ireland;

(b) about the effect in general in England of orders prohibiting a person from teaching in schools in Wales, Scotland or Northern Ireland.]

NOTES

Inserted by the Education Act 2011, s 8(2).

Para 2: words in square brackets in sub-para (4) substituted by the Protection of Freedoms Act 2012 (Disclosure and Barring Service Transfer of Functions) Order 2012, SI 2012/3006, art 13(1), (2)(e).

Regulations: the Teachers' Disciplinary (England) Regulations 2012, SI 2012/560 at **[2.1252]**.

INCOME TAX (EARNINGS AND PENSIONS) ACT 2003

(2003 c 1)

ARRANGEMENT OF SECTIONS

PART 1
OVERVIEW

PART 2
EMPLOYMENT INCOME: CHARGE TO TAX

CHAPTER 1
INTRODUCTION

CHAPTER 8
APPLICATION OF PROVISIONS TO WORKERS UNDER ARRANGEMENTS MADE BY INTERMEDIARIES

Application of this Chapter

The deemed employment payment

Supplementary provisions

An Act to restate, with minor changes, certain enactments relating to income tax on employment income, pension income and social security income; and for connected purposes

[6 March 2003]

NOTES

This substantial Act is essentially a re-enactment of the provisions of the Income and Corporation Taxes Act 1988 (referred to in this Act as ICTA) and later legislation, so far as relating to the taxation of earnings and pensions. Most of this Act covers matters outside the scope of this work, and only those provisions most directly relevant to employment law are printed. For reasons of space, the subject matter of sections not printed is not annotated.

PART 1
OVERVIEW

[1.1299]

1 Overview of contents of this Act

(1) This Act imposes charges to income tax on—
 (a) employment income (see Parts 2 to [7A]),
 (b) pension income (see Part 9), and
 (c) social security income (see [Chapters 1 to 7 of] Part 10).

(2) . . .

(3) This Act also—
 (a) confers certain reliefs in respect of liabilities of former employees (see Part 8),
 [(aa) makes provision for the high income child benefit charge (see Chapter 8 of Part 10),]
 (b) provides for the assessment, collection and recovery of income tax in respect of employment, pension or social security income that is PAYE income (see Part 11),
 [(ba) allows deductions to be made from such income in respect of certain debts payable to the Commissioners for Her Majesty's Revenue and Customs (see Part 11), and]
 (c) allows deductions to be made from such income in respect of payroll giving (see Part 12).

NOTES

Sub-s (1): figure "7A" in square brackets in para (a) substituted by the Finance Act 2011, s 26, Sch 2, paras 2, 3; words in square brackets in para (c) inserted by the Finance Act 2012, s 8, Sch 1, paras 5(1), (2)(a), 7(1), with effect for the tax year 2012–13 and subsequent tax years.

Sub-s (2): repealed by the Income Tax Act 2007, ss 1027, 1031, Sch 1, Pt 2, paras 425, 426, Sch 3, Pt 1 (for effect and transitional provisions see the introductory note to this Act).

Sub-s (3): para (aa) inserted by the Finance Act 2012, s 8, Sch 1, paras 5(1), (2)(b), 7(1); word omitted from para (b) repealed, and para (ba) inserted, by the Finance Act 2009 (Consequential Amendments) Order 2011, SI 2011/1583, art 2(1), (2).

PART 2
EMPLOYMENT INCOME: CHARGE TO TAX

CHAPTER 1 INTRODUCTION

[1.1300]
3 Structure of employment income Parts

(1) The structure of the employment income Parts is as follows—

this Part imposes the charge to tax on employment income, and sets out—

(a) how the amount charged to tax for a tax year is to be calculated, and

(b) who is liable for the tax charged;

Part 3 sets out what are earnings and provides for amounts to be treated as earnings;

Part 4 deals with exemptions from the charge to tax under this Part (and, in some cases, from other charges to tax);

Part 5 deals with deductions from taxable earnings;

Part 6 deals with employment income other than earnings or share-related income; and

Part 7 deals with [income and exemptions relating to securities and securities options acquired in connection with an employment].

(2) In this Act "the employment income Parts" means this Part and Parts 3 to [7A].

NOTES

Sub-s (1): words in square brackets in the entry relating to Part 7 substituted by the Finance Act 2003, s 140, Sch 22, paras 1, 16(1); entry relating to Part 7A inserted by the Finance Act 2011, s 26, Sch 2, paras 2, 4(1), (3)).

Sub-s (2): figure "7A" in square brackets substituted by the Finance Act 2011, s 26, Sch 2, paras 2, 4(1), (3).

[1.1301]
4 "Employment" for the purposes of the employment income Parts

(1) In the employment income Parts "employment" includes in particular—

(a) any employment under a contract of service,

(b) any employment under a contract of apprenticeship, and

(c) any employment in the service of the Crown.

(2) In those Parts "employed", "employee" and "employer" have corresponding meanings.

[1.1302]
5 Application to offices and office-holders

(1) The provisions of the employment income Parts that are expressed to apply to employments apply equally to offices, unless otherwise indicated.

(2) In those provisions as they apply to an office—

(a) references to being employed are to being the holder of the office;

(b) "employee" means the office-holder;

(c) "employer" means the person under whom the office-holder holds office.

(3) In the employment income Parts "office" includes in particular any position which has an existence independent of the person who holds it and may be filled by successive holders.

CHAPTER 8 APPLICATION OF PROVISIONS TO WORKERS UNDER ARRANGEMENTS MADE BY INTERMEDIARIES

Application of this Chapter

[1.1303]
49 Engagements to which this Chapter applies

(1) This Chapter applies where—

(a) an individual ("the worker") personally performs, or is under an obligation personally to perform, services [for another person] ("the client"),

[(aa) the client is not a public authority,]

(b) the services are provided not under a contract directly between the client and the worker but under arrangements involving a third party ("the intermediary"), and

[(c) the circumstances are such that—

(i) if the services were provided under a contract directly between the client and the worker, the worker would be regarded for income tax purposes as an employee of the client or the holder of an office under the client, or

(ii) the worker is an office-holder who holds that office under the client and the services relate to the office].

(2) . . .

(3) The reference in subsection (1)(b) to a "third party" includes a partnership or unincorporated body of which the worker is a member.

(4) The circumstances referred to in subsection (1)(c) include the terms on which the services are provided, having regard to the terms of the contracts forming part of the arrangements under which the services are provided.

[(4A) Holding office as statutory auditor of the client does not count as holding office under the client for the purposes of subsection (1)(c), and here "statutory auditor" means a statutory auditor within the meaning of Part 42 of the Companies Act 2006 (see section 1210 of that Act).]

(5) In this Chapter "engagement to which this Chapter applies" means any such provision of services as is mentioned in subsection (1).

NOTES

Sub-s (1): words in square brackets in para (a) substituted by the Finance Act 2003, s 136(1), (2); para (aa) inserted by the Finance Act 2017, s 6, Sch 1, Pt 1, paras 1, 3, with effect for the tax year 2017–18 and subsequent tax years; para (c) substituted by the Finance Act 2013, s 22.

Sub-s (2): repealed by the Finance Act 2003, ss 216, 136(1), (3)(a), Sch 43, Pt 3(1).

Sub-s (4A): inserted by the Finance Act 2017, s 6, Sch 1, Pt 3, para 11, with effect for the tax year 2017–18 and subsequent tax years.

[1.1304]

50 Worker treated as receiving earnings from employment

(1) If, in the case of an engagement to which this Chapter applies, in any tax year—

(a) the conditions specified in section 51, 52 or 53 are met in relation to the intermediary, and

(b) the worker, or an associate of the worker—

(i) receives from the intermediary, directly or indirectly, a payment or benefit that is not employment income, or

(ii) has rights which entitle, or which in any circumstances would entitle, the worker or associate to receive from the intermediary, directly or indirectly, any such payment or benefit,

the intermediary is treated as making to the worker, and the worker is treated as receiving, in that year a payment which is to be treated as earnings from an employment ("the deemed employment payment").

(2) A single payment is treated as made in respect of all engagements in relation to which the intermediary is treated as making a payment to the worker in the tax year.

(3) The deemed employment payment is treated as made at the end of the tax year, unless section 57 applies (earlier date of deemed payment in certain cases).

(4) In this Chapter "the relevant engagements", in relation to a deemed employment payment, means the engagements mentioned in subsection (2).

[1.1305]

51 Conditions of liability where intermediary is a company

(1) Where the intermediary is a company the conditions are that the intermediary is not an associated company of the client that falls within subsection (2) and either—

(a) the worker has a material interest in the intermediary, or

(b) the payment or benefit mentioned in section 50(1)(b)—

(i) is received or receivable by the worker directly from the intermediary, and

(ii) can reasonably be taken to represent remuneration for services provided by the worker to the client.

(2) An associated company of the client falls within this subsection if it is such a company by reason of the intermediary and the client being under the control—

(a) of the worker, or

(b) of the worker and other persons.

(3) A worker is treated as having a material interest in a company if—

(a) the worker, alone or with one or more associates of the worker, or

(b) an associate of the worker, with or without other such associates,

has a material interest in the company.

(4) For this purpose a material interest means—

(a) beneficial ownership of, or the ability to control, directly or through the medium of other companies or by any other indirect means, more than 5% of the ordinary share capital of the company; or

(b) possession of, or entitlement to acquire, rights entitling the holder to receive more than 5% of any distributions that may be made by the company; or

(c) where the company is a close company, possession of, or entitlement to acquire, rights that would in the event of the winding up of the company, or in any other circumstances, entitle the holder to receive more than 5% of the assets that would then be available for distribution among the participators.

(5) In subsection (4)(c) "participator" has the meaning given by [section 454 of CTA 2010].

NOTES

Sub-s (5): words in square brackets substituted by the Corporation Tax Act 2010, s 1177, Sch 1, Pt 2, paras 378, 380.

[1.1306]

52 Conditions of liability where intermediary is a partnership

(1) Where the intermediary is a partnership the conditions are as follows.

(2) In relation to any payment or benefit received or receivable by the worker as a member of the partnership the conditions are—

(a) that the worker, alone or with one or more relatives, is entitled to 60% or more of the profits of the partnership; or

(b) that most of the profits of the partnership concerned derive from the provision of services under engagements to which [one or other of this Chapter and Chapter 10] applies—

(i) to a single client, or

(ii) to a single client together with associates of that client; or

(c) that under the profit sharing arrangements the income of any of the partners is based on the amount of income generated by that partner by the provision of services under engagements to which [one or other of this Chapter and Chapter 10] applies.

In paragraph (a) "relative" means [spouse or civil partner], parent or child or remoter relation in the direct line, or brother or sister.

(3) In relation to any payment or benefit received or receivable by the worker otherwise than as a member of the partnership, the conditions are that the payment or benefit—

(a) is received or receivable by the worker directly from the intermediary, and

(b) can reasonably be taken to represent remuneration for services provided by the worker to the client.

NOTES

Sub-s (2): words in square brackets in paras (b), (c) substituted by the Finance Act 2017, s 6, Sch 1, Pt 1, paras 1, 4, with effect for the tax year 2017–18 and subsequent tax years; final words in square brackets substituted by the Tax and Civil Partnership Regulations 2005, SI 2005/3229, regs 137, 138.

[1.1307]

53 Conditions of liability where intermediary is an individual

Where the intermediary is an individual the conditions are that the payment or benefit—

(a) is received or receivable by the worker directly from the intermediary, and

(b) can reasonably be taken to represent remuneration for services provided by the worker to the client.

The deemed employment payment

[1.1308]

54 Calculation of deemed employment payment

(1) The amount of the deemed employment payment for a tax year ("the year") is the amount resulting from the following steps—

Step 1

Find (applying section 55) the total amount of all payments and benefits received by the intermediary in the year in respect of the relevant engagements, and reduce that amount by 5%.

Step 2

Add (applying that section) the amount of any payments and benefits received by the worker in the year in respect of the relevant engagements, otherwise than from the intermediary, that—

(a) are not chargeable to income tax as employment income, and

(b) would be so chargeable if the worker were employed by the client.

Step 3

Deduct (applying Chapters 1 to 5 of Part 5) the amount of any expenses met in the year by the intermediary that would have been deductible from the taxable earnings from the employment if—

(a) the worker had been employed by the client, and

(b) the expenses had been met by the worker out of those earnings.

If the result at this or any later point is nil or a negative amount, there is no deemed employment payment.

Step 4

Deduct the amount of any capital allowances in respect of expenditure incurred by the intermediary that could have been deducted from employment income under section 262 of CAA 2001 (employments and offices) if the worker had been employed by the client and had incurred the expenditure.

Step 5

Deduct any contributions made in the year for the benefit of the worker by the intermediary to a [registered pension scheme] that if made by an employer for the benefit of an employee would not be chargeable to income tax as income of the employee.

This does not apply to excess contributions made and later repaid.

Step 6

Deduct the amount of any employer's national insurance contributions paid by the intermediary for the year in respect of the worker.

Step 7

Deduct the amount of any payments and benefits received in the year by the worker from the intermediary—

(a) in respect of which the worker is chargeable to income tax as employment income, and

(b) which do not represent items in respect of which a deduction was made under step 3.

Step 8

Assume that the result of step 7 represents an amount together with employer's national insurance contributions on it, and deduct what (on that assumption) would be the amount of those contributions.

The result is the deemed employment payment.

[(1A) For the purposes of step 1 of subsection (1), any payment or benefit which is employment income of the worker by virtue of section 863G(4) of ITTOIA 2005 (salaried members of limited liability partnerships: anti-avoidance) is to be ignored.]

(2) If [section 61 of the Finance Act 2004] applies (sub-contractors in the construction industry: payments to be made under deduction), the intermediary is treated for the purposes of step 1 of subsection (1) as receiving the amount that would have been received had no deduction been made under that section.

(3) In step 3 of subsection (1), the reference to expenses met by the intermediary includes—

(a) expenses met by the worker and reimbursed by the intermediary, and

(b) where the intermediary is a partnership and the worker is a member of the partnership, expenses met by the worker for and on behalf of the partnership.

(4) In step 3 of subsection (1), the expenses deductible include the amount of any mileage allowance relief for the year which the worker would have been entitled to in respect of the use of a vehicle falling within subsection (5) if—

(a) the worker had been employed by the client, and

(b) the vehicle had not been a company vehicle (within the meaning of Chapter 2 of Part 4).

(5) A vehicle falls within this subsection if—

(a) it is provided by the intermediary for the worker, or

(b) where the intermediary is a partnership and the worker is a member of the partnership, it is provided by the worker for the purposes of the business of the partnership.

(6) Where, on the assumptions mentioned in paragraphs (a) and (b) of step 3 of subsection (1), the deductibility of the expenses is determined under sections 337 to 342 (travel expenses), the duties performed under the relevant engagements are treated as duties of a continuous employment with the intermediary.

(7) In step 7 of subsection (1), the amounts deductible include any payments received in the year from the intermediary that—

(a) are exempt from income tax by virtue of section 229 or 233 (mileage allowance payments and passenger payments), and

(b) do not represent items in respect of which a deduction was made under step 3.

(8) For the purposes of subsection (1) any necessary apportionment is to be made on a just and reasonable basis of amounts received by the intermediary that are referable—

(a) to the services of more than one worker, or

(b) partly to the services of the worker and partly to other matters.

NOTES

Sub-s (1): words in square brackets in step 5 substituted by the Finance Act 2004, s 281(1), Sch 35, paras 54, 56.

Sub-s (1A): inserted by the Finance Act 2014, s 74, Sch 17, Pt 1, para 5.

Sub-s (2): words in square brackets substituted by the Finance Act 2004, s 76, Sch 12, para 17.

See further, the Pension Protection Fund (Tax) Regulations 2006, SI 2006/575, reg 39, which provides as follows—

"39. Step 5 of section 54(1) of ITEPA 2003 (calculation of deemed employment payment under arrangements made by intermediaries) applies in relation to a payment, by the intermediary, of any sum in respect of any of the Pensions Act levies in the same way as it applies in relation to any contributions that may be deducted under that step.".

CAA 2001: Capital Allowances Act 2001.

[1.1309]

55 Application of rules relating to earnings from employment

(1) The following provisions apply in relation to the calculation of the deemed employment payment.

(2) A "payment or benefit" means anything that, if received by an employee for performing the duties of an employment, would be earnings from the employment.

(3) The amount of a payment or benefit is taken to be—

(a) in the case of a payment or cash benefit, the amount received, and

(b) in the case of a non-cash benefit, the cash equivalent of the benefit.

(4) The cash equivalent of a non-cash benefit is taken to be—

(a) the amount that would be earnings if the benefit were earnings from an employment, or

(b) in the case of living accommodation, whichever is the greater of that amount and the cash equivalent determined in accordance with section 398(2).

(5) A payment or benefit is treated as received—

(a) in the case of a payment or cash benefit, when payment is made of or on account of the payment or benefit;

(b) in the case of a non-cash benefit that is calculated by reference to a period within the tax year, at the end of that period;

(c) in the case of a non-cash benefit that is not so calculated, when it would have been treated as received for the purposes of Chapter 4 or 5 of this Part (see section 19 or 32) if—

(i) the worker had been an employee, and

(ii) the benefit had been provided by reason of the employment.

[1.1310]

56 Application of Income Tax Acts in relation to deemed employment

(1) The Income Tax Acts (in particular, the PAYE provisions) apply in relation to the deemed employment payment as follows.

(2) They apply as if—

(a) the worker were employed by the intermediary, and

(b) the relevant engagements were undertaken by the worker in the course of performing the duties of that employment.

(3) The deemed employment payment is treated in particular—

(a) as taxable earnings from the employment for the purpose of securing that any deductions under Chapters 2 to 6 of Part 5 do not exceed the deemed employment payment; and

(b) as taxable earnings from the employment for the purposes of section 232.

(4) The worker is not chargeable to tax in respect of the deemed employment payment if, or to the extent that, by reason of any combination of the factors mentioned in subsection (5), the worker would not be chargeable to tax if—

(a) the client employed the worker,
(b) the worker performed the services in the course of that employment, and
(c) the deemed employment payment were a payment by the client of earnings from that employment.

(5) The factors are—
[(a) the worker being resident or domiciled outside the United Kingdom or meeting the requirement of section 26A,]
(b) the client being resident . . . outside the United Kingdom, and
(c) the services in question being provided outside the United Kingdom.

(6) Where the intermediary is a partnership or unincorporated association, the deemed employment payment is treated as received by the worker in the worker's personal capacity and not as income of the partnership or association.

(7) Where—
(a) the worker is resident in the United Kingdom, [and]
(b) the services in question are provided in the United Kingdom, . . .
(c) . . .

the intermediary is treated as having a place of business in the United Kingdom, whether or not it in fact does so.

(8) . . .

NOTES

Sub-s (5): para (a) substituted, and words omitted from para (b) repealed, by the Finance Act 2013, s 219, Sch 46, Pt 2, paras 29, 30, 72.

Sub-s (7): word in square brackets in para (a) inserted, and para (c) and the word immediately preceding it repealed, by the Finance Act 2003, ss 136(1), (3)(b)(ii), 216, Sch 43, Pt 3(1).

Sub-s (8): repealed by the Finance Act 2004, s 326, Sch 42, Pt 3.

Supplementary provisions

[1.1311]

57 Earlier date of deemed employment payment in certain cases

(1) If in any tax year—
(a) a deemed employment payment is treated as made, and
(b) before the date on which the payment would be treated as made under section 50(2) any relevant event (as defined below) occurs in relation to the intermediary,

the deemed employment payment for that year is treated as having been made immediately before that event or, if there is more than one, immediately before the first of them.

(2) Where the intermediary is a company the following are relevant events—
(a) the company ceasing to trade;
(b) where the worker is a member of the company, the worker ceasing to be such a member;
(c) where the worker holds an office with the company, the worker ceasing to hold such an office;
(d) where the worker is employed by the company, the worker ceasing to be so employed.

(3) Where the intermediary is a partnership the following are relevant events—
(a) the dissolution of the partnership or the partnership ceasing to trade or a partner ceasing to act as such;
(b) where the worker is employed by the partnership, the worker ceasing to be so employed.

(4) Where the intermediary is an individual and the worker is employed by the intermediary, it is a relevant event if the worker ceases to be so employed.

(5) The fact that the deemed employment payment is treated as made before the end of the tax year does not affect what receipts and other matters are taken into account in calculating its amount.

[1.1312]

58 Relief in case of distributions by intermediary

(1) A claim for relief may be made under this section where the intermediary—
(a) is a company,
(b) is treated as making a deemed employment payment in any tax year, and
(c) either in that tax year (whether before or after that payment is treated as made), or in a subsequent tax year, makes a distribution (a "relevant distribution").

(2) A claim for relief under this section must be made—
(a) by the intermediary by notice to [an officer of Revenue and Customs], and
(b) within 5 years after the 31st January following the tax year in which the distribution is made.

(3) If on a claim being made [an officer of Revenue and Customs] [is] satisfied that relief should be given in order to avoid a double charge to tax, [the officer] must direct the giving of such relief by way of amending any assessment, by discharge or repayment of tax, or otherwise, as appears to [the officer] appropriate.

(4) Relief under this section is given by setting the amount of the deemed employment payment against the relevant distribution so as to reduce the distribution.

(5) In the case of more than one relevant distribution, [an officer of Revenue and Customs] must exercise the power conferred by this section so as to secure that so far as practicable relief is given by setting the amount of a deemed employment payment—
(a) against relevant distributions of the same tax year before those of other years,
(b) against relevant distributions received by the worker before those received by another person, and
(c) against relevant distributions of earlier years before those of later years.

(6) . . .

NOTES

Sub-ss (2), (3), (5): words in square brackets substituted by the Commissioners for Revenue and Customs Act 2005, s 50(6), Sch 4, paras 101, 102(1), 103(1)(a), 105.

Sub-s (6): repealed by the Finance Act 2016, s 5(11), Sch 1, para 61(1), (2), in relation to dividends paid or arising (or treated as paid), and other distributions made (or treated as made), in the tax year 2016–17 or at any later time.

[1.1313]

59 Provisions applicable to multiple intermediaries

(1) The provisions of this section apply where in the case of an engagement to which this Chapter applies the arrangements involve more than one relevant intermediary.

(2) All relevant intermediaries in relation to the engagement are jointly and severally liable, subject to subsection (3), to account for any amount required under the PAYE provisions to be deducted from a deemed employment payment treated as made by any of them—

(a) in respect of that engagement, or

(b) in respect of that engagement together with other engagements.

(3) An intermediary is not so liable if it has not received any payment or benefit in respect of that engagement or any such other engagement as is mentioned in subsection (2)(b).

(4) Subsection (5) applies where a payment or benefit has been made or provided, directly or indirectly, from one relevant intermediary to another in respect of the engagement.

(5) In that case, the amount taken into account in relation to any intermediary in step 1 or step 2 of section 54(1) is reduced to such extent as is necessary to avoid double-counting having regard to the amount so taken into account in relation to any other intermediary.

(6) Except as provided by subsections (2) to (5), the provisions of this Chapter apply separately in relation to each relevant intermediary.

(7) In this section "relevant intermediary" means an intermediary in relation to which the conditions specified in section 51, 52 or 53 are met.

[1.1314]

60 Meaning of "associate"

(1) In this Chapter "associate"—

(a) in relation to an individual, has the meaning given by [section 448 of CTA 2010], subject to the following provisions of this section;

(b) in relation to a company, means a person connected with the company; and

(c) in relation to a partnership, means any associate of a member of the partnership.

(2) Where an individual has an interest in shares or obligations of the company as a beneficiary of an employee benefit trust, the trustees are not regarded as associates of the individual by reason only of that interest except in the following circumstances.

(3) The exception is where—

(a) the individual, either alone or with any one or more associates of the individual, or

(b) any associate of the individual, with or without other such associates,

has at any time on or after 14th March 1989 been the beneficial owner of, or able (directly or through the medium of other companies or by any other indirect means) to control more than 5% of the ordinary share capital of the company.

(4) In subsection (3) "associate" does not include the trustees of an employee benefit trust as a result only of the individual's having an interest in shares or obligations of the trust.

(5) Sections 549 to 554 (attribution of interests in companies to beneficiaries of employee benefit trusts) apply for the purposes of subsection (3) as they apply for the purposes of the provisions listed in section 549(2).

(6) In this section "employee benefit trust" has the meaning given by sections 550 and 551.

NOTES

Sub-s (1): words in square brackets substituted by the Corporation Tax Act 2010, s 1177, Sch 1, Pt 2, paras 378, 381 (for general transitional provisions and savings see s 1180(1), Sch 2, Pts 1, 2).

[1.1315]

61 Interpretation

(1) In this Chapter—

"associate" has the meaning given by section 60;

"associated company" has the meaning given by [section 449 of CTA 2010];

"business" means any trade, profession or vocation and includes a [UK property business [within the meaning of Chapter 2 of Part 3 of ITTOIA 2005 or Chapter 2 of Part 4 of CTA 2009]];

"company" means a body corporate or unincorporated association, and does not include a partnership;

"employer's national insurance contributions" means secondary Class 1 or Class 1A national insurance contributions;

["engagement to which Chapter 10 applies" has the meaning given by section 61M(5);]

"engagement to which this Chapter applies" has the meaning given by section 49(5);

"national insurance contributions" means contributions under Part 1 of SSCBA 1992 or Part 1 of SSCB(NI)A 1992;

"PAYE provisions" means the provisions of Part 11 or PAYE regulations;

"the relevant engagements" has the meaning given by section 50(4).

(2) References in this Chapter to payments or benefits received or receivable from a partnership or unincorporated association include payments or benefits to which a person is or may be entitled in the person's capacity as a member of the partnership or association.

(3) For the purposes of this Chapter—

(a) anything done by or in relation to an associate of an intermediary is treated as done by or in relation to the intermediary, and

(b) a payment or other benefit provided to a member of an individual's family or household is treated as provided to the individual.

(4) For the purposes of this Chapter a man and a woman living together as husband and wife are treated as if they were married to each other.

[(5) For the purposes of this Chapter two people of the same sex living together as if they were civil partners of each other are treated as if they were civil partners of each other.

For the purposes of this Chapter, two people of the same sex are to be regarded as living together as if they were civil partners if, but only if, they would be regarded as living together as husband and wife were they instead two people of the opposite sex.]

NOTES

Sub-s (1): in the definition "associated company" words in square brackets substituted by the Corporation Tax Act 2010, s 1177, Sch 1, Pt 2, paras 378, 382; in the definition "business" words in first (outer) pair of square brackets inserted by the Income Tax (Trading and Other Income) Act 2005, s 882, Sch 1, Pt 2, paras 584, 586; words in second (inner) pair of square brackets in that definition substituted by the Corporation Tax Act 2009, s 1322, Sch 1, Pt 2, paras 548, 549; definition "engagement to which Chapter 10 applies" inserted by the Finance Act 2017, s 6, Sch 1, Pt 1, paras 1, 5, with effect for the tax year 2017–18 and subsequent tax years.

Sub-s (5): added by the Tax and Civil Partnership Regulations 2005, SI 2005/3229, regs 137, 139.

ICTA: Income and Corporation Taxes Act 1988.

ITTOIA 2005: the Income Tax (Trading and Other Income) Act 2005.

CTA 2009: the Corporation Tax Act 2009.

SSCBA 1992 and SSCB(NI)A 1992: the Social Security Contributions and Benefits Act 1992 and the Social Security Contributions and Benefits (Northern Ireland) Act 1992, respectively.

[CHAPTER 10 WORKERS' SERVICES PROVIDED TO PUBLIC SECTOR THROUGH INTERMEDIARIES

[1.1316]

61K Scope of this Chapter

(1) This Chapter has effect with respect to the provision of services to a public authority through an intermediary.

(2) Nothing in this Chapter—

(a) affects the operation of Chapter 7 of this Part (agency workers), or

(b) applies to payments or transfers to which section 966(3) or (4) of ITA 2007 applies (visiting performers: duty to deduct and account for sums representing income tax).]

NOTES

Commencement: see the note below.

Chapter 10 (ss 61K–61X) inserted by the Finance Act 2017, s 6, Sch 1, Pt 2, para 9. This amendment has effect in relation to deemed direct payments treated as made on or after 6 April 2017, and does so even if relating to services provided before that date: see the Finance Act 2017, s 6, Sch 1, Pt 4, para 16.

[1.1317]

[61L Meaning of "public authority"

(1) In this Chapter "public authority" means—

(a) a public authority as defined by the Freedom of Information Act 2000,

(b) a Scottish public authority as defined by the Freedom of Information (Scotland) Act 2002 (asp 13),

(c) the Corporate Officer of the House of Commons,

(d) the Corporate Officer of the House of Lords,

(e) the National Assembly for Wales Commission, or

(f) the Northern Ireland Assembly Commission.

(2) An authority within paragraph (a) or (b) of subsection (1) is a public authority for the purposes of this Chapter in relation to all its activities even if provisions of the Act mentioned in that paragraph do not apply to all information held by the authority.

(3) Subsection (1) is subject to subsection (4).

(4) primary-healthcare provider is a public authority for the purposes of this Chapter only if the primary-healthcare provider—

(a) has a registered patient list for the purposes of relevant medical-services regulations,

(b) is within paragraph 43A in Part 3 of Schedule 1 to the Freedom of Information Act 2000 (providers of primary healthcare services in England and Wales) by reason of being a person providing primary dental services,

(c) is within paragraph 51 in that Part of that Schedule (providers of healthcare services in Northern Ireland) by reason of being a person providing general dental services, or

(d) is within paragraph 33 in Part 4 of Schedule 1 to the Freedom of Information (Scotland) Act 2002 (providers of healthcare services in Scotland) by reason of being a person providing general dental services.

(5) In this section—

"primary-healthcare provider" means an authority that is within subsection (1)(a) or (b) only because it is within a relevant paragraph,

"relevant paragraph" means—

(a) any of paragraphs 43A to 45A and 51 in Part 3 of Schedule 1 to the Freedom of Information Act 2000, or

(b) any of paragraphs 33 to 35 in Part 4 of Schedule 1 to the Freedom of Information (Scotland) Act 2002, and

"relevant medical-services regulations" means any of the following—

(a) the Primary Medical Services (Sale of Goodwill and Restrictions on Sub-contracting) Regulations 2004 (SI 2004/906),

(b) the Primary Medical Services (Sale of Goodwill and Restrictions on Sub-contracting) (Wales) Regulations 2004 (SI 2004/1017),

(c) the Primary Medical Services (Sale of Goodwill and Restrictions on Sub-contracting) (Scotland) Regulations 2004 (SSI 2004/162), and

(d) the Primary Medical Services (Sale of Goodwill and Restrictions on Sub-contracting) Regulations (Northern Ireland) 2004 (SR (NI) 2004 No 477).

(6) The Commissioners for Her Majesty's Revenue and Customs may by regulations amend this section in consequence of—

(a) any amendment or revocation of any regulations for the time being referred to in this section,

(b) any amendment in Part 3 of Schedule 1 to the Freedom of Information Act 2000, or

(c) any amendment in Part 4 of Schedule 1 to the Freedom of Information (Scotland) Act 2002.]

NOTES

Commencement: see the note to s 61K at **[1.1316]**.

Inserted as noted to s 61K at **[1.1316]**.

[1.1318]

[61M Engagements to which Chapter applies

(1) Sections 61N to 61R apply where—

(a) an individual ("the worker") personally performs, or is under an obligation personally to perform, services for another person ("the client"),

(b) the client is a public authority,

(c) the services are provided not under a contract directly between the client and the worker but under arrangements involving a third party ("the intermediary"), and

(d) the circumstances are such that—

(i) if the services were provided under a contract directly between the client and the worker, the worker would be regarded for income tax purposes as an employee of the client or the holder of an office under the client, or

(ii) the worker is an office-holder who holds that office under the client and the services relate to the office.

(2) The reference in subsection (1)(c) to a "third party" includes a partnership or unincorporated association of which the worker is a member.

(3) The circumstances referred to in subsection (1)(d) include the terms on which the services are provided, having regard to the terms of the contracts forming part of the arrangements under which the services are provided.

(4) Holding office as statutory auditor of the client does not count as holding office under the client for the purposes of subsection (1)(d), and here "statutory auditor" means a statutory auditor within the meaning of Part 42 of the Companies Act 2006 (see section 1210 of that Act).

(5) In this Chapter "engagement to which this Chapter applies" means any such provision of services as is mentioned in subsection (1).]

NOTES

Commencement: see the note to s 61K at **[1.1316]**.

Inserted as noted to s 61K at **[1.1316]**.

[1.1319]

[61N Worker treated as receiving earnings from employment

(1) If one of Conditions A to C is met, identify the chain of two or more persons where—

(a) the highest person in the chain is the client,

(b) the lowest person in the chain is the intermediary, and

(c) each person in the chain above the lowest makes a chain payment to the person immediately below them in the chain.

(See section 61U for cases where one of Conditions A to C is treated as being met.)

(2) In this section and sections 61O to 61S—

"chain payment" means a payment, or money's worth or any other benefit, that can reasonably be taken to be for the worker's services to the client,

"make"—

(a) in relation to a chain payment that is money's worth, means transfer, and

(b) in relation to a chain payment that is a benefit other than a payment or money's worth, means provide, and

"the fee-payer" means the person in the chain immediately above the lowest.

(3) The fee-payer is treated as making to the worker, and the worker is treated as receiving, a payment which is to be treated as earnings from an employment ("the deemed direct payment"), but this is subject to subsections (5) to (7) and sections 61T and 61V.

(4) The deemed direct payment is treated as made at the same time as the chain payment made by the fee-payer.

(5) Subsections (6) and (7) apply, subject to sections 61T and 61V, if the fee-payer—

- (a) is not the client, and
- (b) is not a qualifying person.

(6) If there is no person in the chain below the highest and above the lowest who is a qualifying person, subsections (3) and (4) have effect as if for any reference to the fee-payer there were substituted a reference to the client.

(7) Otherwise, subsections (3) and (4) have effect as if for any reference to the fee-payer there were substituted a reference to the person in the chain who—

- (a) is above the lowest,
- (b) is a qualifying person, and
- (c) is lower in the chain than any other person in the chain who—
  - (i) is above the lowest, and
  - (ii) is a qualifying person.

(8) In subsections (5) to (7) a "qualifying person" is a person who—

- (a) is resident in the United Kingdom or has a place of business in the United Kingdom,
- (b) is not a person who is controlled by—
  - (i) the worker, alone or with one or more associates of the worker, or
  - (ii) an associate of the worker, with or without other associates of the worker, and
- (c) if a company, is not one in which—
  - (i) the worker, alone or with one or more associates of the worker, or
  - (ii) an associate of the worker, with or without other associates of the worker,

  has a material interest (within the meaning given by section 51(4) and (5)).

(9) Condition A is that—

- (a) the intermediary is a company, and
- (b) the conditions in section 61O are met in relation to the intermediary.

(10) Condition B is that—

- (a) the intermediary is a partnership,
- (b) the worker is a member of the partnership,
- (c) the provision of the services is by the worker as a member of the partnership, and
- (d) the condition in section 61P is met in relation to the intermediary.

(11) Condition C is that the intermediary is an individual.

(12) Where a payment, money's worth or any other benefit can reasonably be taken to be for both—

- (a) the worker's services to the client, and
- (b) anything else,

then, for the purposes of this Chapter, so much of it as can, on a just and reasonable apportionment, be taken to be for the worker's services is to be treated as (and the rest is to be treated as not being) a payment, or money's worth or another benefit, that can reasonably be taken to be for the worker's services.]

NOTES

Commencement: see the note to s 61K at **[1.1316]**.

Inserted as noted to s 61K at **[1.1316]**.

[1.1320]

[61O Conditions where intermediary is a company

(1) The conditions mentioned in section 61N(9)(b) are that—

- (a) the intermediary is not an associated company of the client that falls within subsection (2), and
- (b) the worker has a material interest in the intermediary.

(2) An associated company of the client falls within this subsection if it is such a company by reason of the intermediary and the client being under the control—

- (a) of the worker, or
- (b) of the worker and other persons.

(3) The worker is treated as having a material interest in the intermediary if—

- (a) the worker, alone or with one or more associates of the worker, or
- (b) an associate of the worker, with or without other associates of the worker,

has a material interest in the intermediary.

(4) For this purpose "material interest" has the meaning given by section 51(4) and (5).

(5) In this section "associated company" has the meaning given by section 449 of CTA 2010.]

NOTES

Commencement: see the note to s 61K at **[1.1316]**.

Inserted as noted to s 61K at **[1.1316]**.

CTA 2010: Corporation Tax Act 2010.

[1.1321]

[61P Conditions where intermediary is a partnership

(1) The condition mentioned in section 61N(10)(d) is—

(a) that the worker, alone or with one or more relatives, is entitled to 60% or more of the profits of the partnership, or
(b) that most of the profits of the partnership derive from the provision of services under engagements to which one or other of this Chapter and Chapter 8 applies—
(i) to a single client, or
(ii) to a single client together with associates of that client, or
(c) that under the profit sharing arrangements the income of any of the partners is based on the amount of income generated by that partner by the provision of services under engagements to which one or other of this Chapter and Chapter 8 applies.

(2) In subsection (1)(a) "relative" means spouse or civil partner, parent or child or remoter relation in the direct line, or brother or sister.

(3) Section 61(4) and (5) apply for the purposes of this section as they apply for the purposes of Chapter 8.]

NOTES

Commencement: see the note to s 61K at **[1.1316]**.
Inserted as noted to s 61K at **[1.1316]**.

[1.1322]
[61Q Calculation of deemed direct payment

(1) The amount of the deemed direct payment is the amount resulting from the following steps—

Step 1

Identify the amount or value of the chain payment made by the person who is treated as making the deemed direct payment, and deduct from that amount so much of it (if any) as is in respect of value added tax.

Step 2

Deduct, from the amount resulting from Step 1, so much of that amount as represents the direct cost to the intermediary of materials used, or to be used, in the performance of the services.

Step 3

Deduct, at the option of the person treated as making the deemed direct payment, from the amount resulting from Step 2, so much of that amount as represents expenses met by the intermediary that would have been deductible from the taxable earnings from the employment if—
(a) the worker had been employed by the client, and
(b) the expenses had been met by the worker out of those earnings.

Step 4

If the amount resulting from the preceding Steps is nil or negative, there is no deemed direct payment. Otherwise, that amount is the amount of the deemed direct payment.

(2) For the purposes of Step 1 of subsection (1), any part of the amount or value of the chain payment which is employment income of the worker by virtue of section 863G(4) of ITTOIA 2005 (salaried members of limited liability partnerships: anti-avoidance) is to be ignored.

(3) In subsection (1), the reference to the amount or value of the chain payment means the amount or value of that payment before the deduction (if any) permitted under section 61S.

(4) If the actual amount or value of the chain payment mentioned in Step 1 of subsection (1) is such that its recipient bears the cost of amounts due under PAYE regulations or contributions regulations in respect of the deemed direct payment, that Step applies as if the amount or value of that chain payment were what it would be if the burden of that cost were not being passed on through the setting of the level of the payment.

(5) In Step 3 of subsection (1), the reference to expenses met by the intermediary includes—
(a) expenses met by the worker and reimbursed by the intermediary, and
(b) where the intermediary is a partnership and the worker is a member of the partnership, expenses met by the worker for and on behalf of the partnership.

(6) In subsection (4) "contributions regulations" means regulations under the Contributions and Benefits Act providing for primary Class 1 contributions to be paid in a similar manner to income tax in relation to which PAYE regulations have effect (see, in particular, paragraph 6(1) of Schedule 1 to the Act); and here "primary Class 1 contribution" means a primary Class 1 contribution within the meaning of Part 1 of the Contributions and Benefits Act.]

NOTES

Commencement: see the note to s 61K at **[1.1316]**.
Inserted as noted to s 61K at **[1.1316]**.
ITTOIA 2005: the Income Tax (Trading and Other Income) Act 2005.

[1.1323]
[61R Application of Income Tax Acts in relation to deemed employment

(1) The Income Tax Acts (in particular, Part 11 and PAYE regulations) apply in relation to the deemed direct payment as follows.

(2) They apply as if—
(a) the worker were employed by the person treated as making the deemed direct payment, and
(b) the services were performed, or to be performed, by the worker in the course of performing the duties of that employment.

(3) The deemed direct payment is treated in particular—
(a) as taxable earnings from the employment for the purpose of securing that any deductions under Chapters 2 to 6 of Part 5 do not exceed the deemed direct payment, and

(b) as taxable earnings from the employment for the purposes of section 232.

(4) The worker is not chargeable to tax in respect of the deemed direct payment if, or to the extent that, by reason of any combination of the factors mentioned in subsection (5), the worker would not be chargeable to tax if—

(a) the client employed the worker,

(b) the worker performed the services in the course of that employment, and

(c) the deemed direct payment were a payment by the client of earnings from that employment.

(5) The factors are—

(a) the worker being resident or domiciled outside the United Kingdom or meeting the requirement of section 26A,

(b) the client being resident outside, or not resident in, the United Kingdom, and

(c) the services being provided outside the United Kingdom.

(6) Where the intermediary is a partnership or unincorporated association, the deemed direct payment is treated as received by the worker in the worker's personal capacity and not as income of the partnership or association.

(7) Where—

(a) the client is the person treated as making the deemed direct payment,

(b) the worker is resident in the United Kingdom,

(c) the services are provided in the United Kingdom,

(d) the client is not resident in the United Kingdom, and

(e) the client does not have a place of business in the United Kingdom,

the client is treated as resident in the United Kingdom.]

NOTES

Commencement: see the note to s 61K at **[1.1316]**.

Inserted as noted to s 61K at **[1.1316]**.

[1.1324]

[61S Deductions from chain payments

(1) This section applies if, as a result of section 61R, a person who is treated as making a deemed direct payment is required under PAYE Regulations to pay an amount to the Commissioners for Her Majesty's Revenue and Customs (the Commissioners) in respect of the payment.

(But see subsection (4)).

(2) The person may deduct from the underlying chain payment an amount which is equal to the amount payable to the Commissioners, but where the amount or value of the underlying chain payment is treated by section 61Q(4) as increased by the cost of any amount due under PAYE Regulations, the amount that may be deducted is limited to the difference (if any) between the amount payable to the Commissioners and the amount of that increase.

(3) Where a person in the chain other than the intermediary receives a chain payment from which an amount has been deducted in reliance on subsection (2) or this subsection, that person may deduct the same amount from the chain payment made by them.

(4) This section does not apply in a case to which 61V(2) applies (services-provider treated as making deemed direct payment).

(5) In subsection (2) "the underlying chain payment" means the chain payment whose amount is used at Step 1 of section 61Q(1) as the starting point for calculating the amount of the deemed direct payment.]

NOTES

Commencement: see the note to s 61K at **[1.1316]**.

Inserted as noted to s 61K at **[1.1316]**.

[1.1325]

[61T Information to be provided by clients and consequences of failure

(1) If the conditions in section 61M(1)(a) to (c) are met in any case, and a person as part of the arrangements mentioned in section 61M(1)(c) enters into a contract with the client, the client must inform that person (in the contract or otherwise) of which one of the following is applicable—

(a) the client has concluded that the condition in section 61M(1)(d) is met in the case;

(b) the client has concluded that the condition in section 61M(1)(d) is not met in the case.

(2) If the contract is entered into on or after 6 April 2017, the duty under subsection (1) must be complied with—

(a) on or before the time of entry into the contract, or

(b) if the services begin to be performed at a later time, before that later time.

(3) If the contract is entered into before 6 April 2017, the duty under subsection (1) must be complied with on or before the date of the first payment made under the contract on or after 6 April 2017.

(4) If the information which subsection (1) requires the client to give to a person has been given (whether in the contract, as required by subsection (2) or (3) or otherwise), the client must, on a written request by the person, provide the person with a written response to any questions raised by the person about the client's reasons for reaching the conclusion identified in the information.

(5) A response required by subsection (4) must be provided before the end of 31 days beginning with the day the request for it is received by the client.

(6) If—

(a) the client fails to comply with the duty under subsection (1) within the time allowed by subsection (2) or (3),

(b) the client fails to provide a response required by subsection (4) within the time allowed by subsection (5), or
(c) the client complies with the duty under subsection (1) but fails to take reasonable care in coming to its conclusion as to whether the condition in section 61M(1)(d) is met in the case,

section 61N(3) and (4) have effect in the case as if for any reference to the fee-payer there were substituted a reference to the client, but this is subject to section 61V.]

NOTES

Commencement: see the note to s 61K at **[1.1316]**.
Inserted as noted to s 61K at **[1.1316]**.

[1.1326]
[61U Information to be provided by worker and consequences of failure

(1) In the case of an engagement to which this Chapter applies, the worker must inform the potential deemed employer of which one of the following is applicable—
(a) that one of conditions A to C in section 61N is met in the case;
(b) that none of conditions A to C in section 61N is met in the case.

(2) If the worker has not complied with subsection (1), then for the purposes of section 61N(1), one of conditions A to C in section 61N is to be treated as met.

(3) In this section, "the potential deemed employer" is the person who, if one of conditions A to C in section 61N were met, would be treated as making a deemed direct payment to the worker under section 61N(3).]

NOTES

Commencement: see the note to s 61K at **[1.1316]**.
Inserted as noted to s 61K at **[1.1316]**.

[1.1327]
[61V Consequences of providing fraudulent information

(1) Subsection (2) applies if in any case—
(a) a person ("the deemed employer") would, but for this section, be treated by section 61N(3) as making a payment to another person ("the services-provider"), and
(b) the fraudulent documentation condition is met.

(2) Section 61N(3) has effect in the case as if the reference to the fee-payer were a reference to the services-provider, but—
(a) section 61N(4) continues to have effect as if the reference to the fee-payer were a reference to the deemed employer, and
(b) Step 1 of section 61Q(1) continues to have effect as referring to the chain payment made by the deemed employer.

(3) Subsection (2) has effect even though that involves the services-provider being treated as both employer and employee in relation to the deemed employment under section 61N(3).

(4) "The fraudulent documentation condition" is that a relevant person provided any person with a fraudulent document intended to constitute evidence—
(a) that the case is not an engagement to which this Chapter applies, or
(b) that none of conditions A to C in section 61N is met in the case.

(5) A "relevant person" is—
(a) the services-provider;
(b) a person connected with the services-provider;
(c) if the intermediary in the case is a company, an office-holder in that company.]

NOTES

Commencement: see the note to s 61K at **[1.1316]**.
Inserted as noted to s 61K at **[1.1316]**.

[1.1328]
[61W Prevention of double charge to tax and allowance of certain deductions

(1) Subsection (2) applies where—
(a) a person ("the payee") receives a payment or benefit ("the end-of-line remuneration") from another person ("the paying intermediary"),
(b) the end-of-line remuneration can reasonably be taken to represent remuneration for services of the payee to a public authority,
(c) a payment ("the deemed payment") has been treated by section 61N(3) as made to the payee,
(d) the underlying chain payment can reasonably be taken to be for the same services of the payee to that public authority, and
(e) the recipient of the underlying chain payment has (whether by deduction from that payment or otherwise) borne the cost of any amounts due, under PAYE regulations and contributions regulations in respect of the deemed payment, from the person treated by section 61N(3) as making the deemed payment.

(2) For income tax purposes, the paying intermediary and the payee may treat the amount of the end-of-line remuneration as reduced (but not below nil) by any one or more of the following—
(a) the amount (see section 61Q) of the deemed payment;

(b) the amount of any capital allowances in respect of expenditure incurred by the paying intermediary that could have been deducted from employment income under section 262 of CAA 2001 if the payee had been employed by the public authority and had incurred the expenditure;

(c) the amount of any contributions made, in the same tax year as the end-of-line remuneration, for the benefit of the payee by the paying intermediary to a registered pension scheme that if made by an employer for the benefit of an employee would not be chargeable to income tax as income of the employee.

(3) Subsection (2)(c)does not apply to—

(a) excess contributions paid and later repaid,

(b) contributions set under subsection (2) against another payment by the paying intermediary, or

(c) contributions deductible at Step 5 of section 54(1) in calculating the amount of the payment (if any) treated by section 50 as made in the tax year concerned by the paying intermediary to the payee.

(4) For the purposes of subsection (3)(c), the contributions to which Step 5 of section 54(1) applies in the case of the particular calculation are "deductible" at that Step so far as their amount does not exceed the result after Step 4 in that calculation.

(5) In subsection (1)(d) "the underlying chain payment" means the chain payment whose amount is used at Step 1 of section 61Q(1) as the starting point for calculating the amount of the deemed payment.

(6) Subsection (2) applies whether the end-of-line remuneration—

(a) is earnings of the payee,

(b) is a distribution of the paying intermediary, or

(c) takes some other form.]

NOTES

Commencement: see the note to s 61K at **[1.1316]**.

Inserted as noted to s 61K at **[1.1316]**.

CAA 2001: Capital Allowances Act 2001.

[1.1329]

[61X Interpretation

In this Chapter—

"associate" has the meaning given by section 60;

"company" means a body corporate or unincorporated association, and does not include a partnership;

"engagement to which Chapter 8 applies" has the meaning given by section 49(5).]

NOTES

Commencement: see the note to s 61K at **[1.1316]**.

Inserted as noted to s 61K at **[1.1316]**.

PART 3
EMPLOYMENT INCOME: EARNINGS AND BENEFITS ETC TREATED AS EARNINGS

CHAPTER 1 EARNINGS

[1.1330]

62 Earnings

(1) This section explains what is meant by "earnings" in the employment income Parts.

(2) In those Parts "earnings", in relation to an employment, means—

(a) any salary, wages or fee,

(b) any gratuity or other profit or incidental benefit of any kind obtained by the employee if it is money or money's worth, or

(c) anything else that constitutes an emolument of the employment.

(3) For the purposes of subsection (2) "money's worth" means something that is—

(a) of direct monetary value to the employee, or

(b) capable of being converted into money or something of direct monetary value to the employee.

(4) Subsection (1) does not affect the operation of statutory provisions that provide for amounts to be treated as earnings (and see section 721(7)).

CHAPTER 2 TAXABLE BENEFITS: THE BENEFITS CODE

The benefits code

[1.1331]

63 The benefits code

(1) In the employment income Parts "the benefits code" means—

this Chapter,

Chapter 3 (expenses payments),

Chapter 4 (vouchers and credit-tokens),

Chapter 5 (living accommodation),

Chapter 6 (cars, vans and related benefits),

Chapter 7 (loans), [and]

. . .

. . .

Chapter 10 (residual liability to charge), ...
. . .
(2)–(4) . . .
[(5) The benefits code has effect subject to section 554Z2(2).]

NOTES

Sub-s (1): word in square brackets in the entry relating to Chapter 7 inserted, and entry relating to Chapter 11 (and the preceding word) repealed, by the Finance Act 2015, s 13(3), Sch 1, Pt 1, paras 1, 5(1), (2), with effect for the tax year 2016–17 and subsequent tax years; entries relating to Chapters 8 and 9 repealed by the Finance Act 2003, ss 140, 216, Sch 22, paras 1, 20(1), Sch 43, Pt 3(4).

Sub-ss (2)–(4): repealed by the Finance Act 2015, s 13(3), Sch 1, Pt 1, paras 1, 5(1), (3), with effect for the tax year 2016–17 and subsequent tax years.

Sub-s (5): added by the Finance Act 2011, s 26, Sch 2, paras 2, 8.

CHAPTER 3 TAXABLE BENEFITS: EXPENSES PAYMENTS

[1.1332]
70 Sums in respect of expenses

(1) This Chapter applies to a sum paid to an employee in a tax year if the sum—
 (a) is paid to the employee in respect of expenses, and
 (b) is so paid by reason of the employment.
(2) This Chapter applies to a sum paid away by an employee in a tax year if the sum—
 (a) was put at the employee's disposal in respect of expenses,
 (b) was so put by reason of the employment, and
 (c) is paid away by the employee in respect of expenses.
(3) For the purposes of this Chapter it does not matter whether the employment is held at the time when the sum is paid or paid away so long as it is held at some point in the tax year in which the sum is paid or paid away.
(4) References in this Chapter to an employee accordingly include a prospective or former employee.
(5) This Chapter does not apply to the extent that the sum constitutes earnings from the employment by virtue of any other provision.

[1.1333]
71 Meaning of paid or put at disposal by reason of the employment

(1) If an employer pays a sum in respect of expenses to an employee it is to be treated as paid by reason of the employment unless—
 (a) the employer is an individual, and
 (b) the payment is made in the normal course of the employer's domestic, family or personal relationships.
(2) If an employer puts a sum at an employee's disposal in respect of expenses it is to be treated as put at the employee's disposal by reason of the employment unless—
 (a) the employer is an individual, and
 (b) the sum is put at the employee's disposal in the normal course of the employer's domestic, family or personal relationships.

[1.1334]
72 Sums in respect of expenses treated as earnings

(1) If this Chapter applies to a sum, the sum is to be treated as earnings from the employment for the tax year in which it is paid or paid away.
(2) Subsection (1) does not prevent the making of a deduction allowed under any of the provisions listed in subsection (3).
(3) The provisions are—
 section 336 (deductions for expenses: the general rule);
 section 337 (travel in performance of duties);
 section 338 (travel for necessary attendance);
 section 340 (travel between group employments);
 [section 340A (travel between linked employments);]
 section 341 (travel at start or finish of overseas employment);
 section 342 (travel between employments where duties performed abroad);
 section 343 (deduction for professional membership fees);
 section 344 (deduction for annual subscriptions);
 section 346 (deduction for employee liabilities);
 section 351 (expenses of ministers of religion);
 section 353 (deductions from earnings charged on remittance).

NOTES

Sub-s (3): entry relating to s 340A inserted by the Enactment of Extra-Statutory Concessions Order 2014, SI 2014/211, arts 3, 4.

CHAPTER 5 TAXABLE BENEFITS: LIVING ACCOMMODATION

Living accommodation

[1.1335]

97 Living accommodation to which this Chapter applies

(1) This Chapter applies to living accommodation provided for—

(a) an employee, or

(b) a member of an employee's family or household,

by reason of the employment.

[(1A) Where this Chapter applies to any living accommodation—

(a) the living accommodation is a benefit for the purposes of this Chapter (and accordingly it is immaterial whether the terms on which it is provided to any of those persons constitute a fair bargain), and

(b) sections 102 to 108 provide for [an amount in respect of] the benefit of the living accommodation to be treated as earnings.]

(2) Living accommodation provided for any of those persons by the employer is to be regarded as provided by reason of the employment unless—

(a) the employer is an individual, and

(b) the provision is made in the normal course of the employer's domestic, family or personal relationships.

NOTES

Sub-s (1A): inserted by the Finance Act 2016, s 7(1), (2), with effect for the tax year 2016–17 and subsequent tax years; words in square brackets in para (b) substituted by the Finance Act 2017, s 7, Sch 2, paras 2, 7, with effect for the tax year 2017–18 and subsequent tax years.

Exceptions

[1.1336]

98 Accommodation provided by local authority

[In section 102 (benefit of accommodation treated as earnings) subsection (1A) (accommodation provided otherwise than pursuant to optional remuneration arrangements)] does not apply to living accommodation provided for an employee if—

(a) the employer is a local authority,

(b) it is provided for the employee by the authority, and

(c) the terms on which it is provided are no more favourable than those on which similar accommodation is provided by the authority for persons who are not their employees but whose circumstances are otherwise similar to those of the employee.

NOTES

Words in square brackets substituted by the Finance Act 2017, s 7, Sch 2, paras 2, 8, with effect for the tax year 2017–18 and subsequent tax years.

[1.1337]

99 Accommodation provided for performance of duties

(1) [In section 102 (benefit of accommodation treated as earnings) subsection (1A) (accommodation provided otherwise than pursuant to optional remuneration arrangements)] does not apply to living accommodation provided for an employee if it is necessary for the proper performance of the employee's duties that the employee should reside in it.

(2) [In section 102 (benefit of accommodation treated as earnings) subsection (1A)] does not apply to living accommodation provided for an employee if—

(a) it is provided for the better performance of the duties of the employment, and

(b) the employment is one of the kinds of employment in the case of which it is customary for employers to provide living accommodation for employees.

(3) But if the accommodation is provided by a company and the employee ("E") is a director of the company or of an associated company, the exception in subsection (1) or (2) only applies if, in the case of each company of which E is a director—

(a) E has no material interest in the company, and

(b) either—

(i) E's employment is as a full-time working director, or

(ii) the company is non-profit-making or is [a charitable company].

(4) "Non-profit-making" means that the company does not carry on a trade and its functions do not consist wholly or mainly in the holding of investments or other property.

(5) A company is "associated" with another if—

(a) one has control of the other, or

(b) both are under the control of the same person.

NOTES

Sub-ss (1), (2): words in square brackets substituted by the Finance Act 2017, s 7, Sch 2, paras 2, 9, with effect for the tax year 2017–18 and subsequent tax years.

Sub-s (3): words in square brackets in para (b) substituted by the Finance Act 2010, s 30, Sch 6, Pt 2, para 17(1), (2).

CHAPTER 6 TAXABLE BENEFITS: CARS, VANS AND RELATED BENEFITS

General

[1.1338]

114 Cars, vans and related benefits

(1) This Chapter applies to a car or a van in relation to a particular tax year if in that year the car or van—

(a) is made available (without any transfer of the property in it) to an employee or a member of the employee's family or household,

(b) is so made available by reason of the employment (see section 117), and

(c) is available for the employee's or member's private use (see section 118).

[(1A) Where this Chapter applies to a car or van, the car or van is a benefit for the purposes of this Chapter (and accordingly it is immaterial whether the terms on which it is made available to the employee or member constitute a fair bargain).]

(2) Where this Chapter applies to a car or van—

(a) sections 120 to 148 provide for [an amount in respect of] the benefit of the car to be treated as earnings,

(b) sections 149 to 153 provide for [an amount in respect of] the benefit of any fuel provided for the car to be treated as earnings, . . .

(c) sections 154 to [159] provide for [an amount in respect of] the benefit of the van to be treated as earnings[; and

(d) sections 160 to 164 provide for [an amount in respect of] the benefit of any fuel provided for the van to be treated as earnings in certain circumstances].

(3) . . .

[(3A) This Chapter does not apply to a van in relation to a tax year if the private use of the van during the tax year by the employee or member of the employee's family or household is insignificant.]

(4) The following provisions of this Chapter provide for further exceptions—

section 167 (pooled cars);

section 168 (pooled vans);

section 169 (car available to more than one member of family or household employed by same employer);

[section 169A (van available to more than one member of family or household employed by same employer)].

NOTES

Sub-s (1A): inserted by the Finance Act 2016, s 7(1), (4), with effect for the tax year 2016–17 and subsequent tax years.

Sub-s (2): word omitted from para (b) repealed, figure in square brackets in para (c) substituted, and para (d) and the word immediately preceding it added, by the Finance Act 2004, ss 80(1), 326, Sch 14, paras 1, 2(1)–(3), Sch 42, Pt 2(9); all other words in square brackets substituted by the Finance Act 2017, s 7, Sch 2, paras 2, 19, with effect for the tax year 2017–18 and subsequent tax years.

Sub-s (3A): inserted by the Finance Act 2004, s 80(1), Sch 14, paras 1, 2(1), (4).

Sub-s (4): words in square brackets added by the Finance Act 2004, s 80(1), Sch 14, paras 1, 2(1), (4).

[1.1339]

115 Meaning of "car" and "van"

(1) In this Chapter—

"car" means a mechanically propelled road vehicle which is not—

(a) a goods vehicle,

(b) a motor cycle,

(c) an invalid carriage, or

(d) a vehicle of a type not commonly used as a private vehicle and unsuitable to be so used;

"van" means a mechanically propelled road vehicle which—

(a) is a goods vehicle, and

(b) has a design weight not exceeding 3,500 kilograms,

and which is not a motor cycle.

(2) For the purposes of subsection (1)—

"design weight" means the weight which a vehicle is designed or adapted not to exceed when in normal use and travelling on a road laden;

"goods vehicle" means a vehicle of a construction primarily suited for the conveyance of goods or burden of any description;

"invalid carriage" has the meaning given by section 185(1) of the Road Traffic Act 1988 (c 52);

"motor cycle" has the meaning given by section 185(1) of the Road Traffic Act 1988.

[1.1340]

116 Meaning of when car or van is available to employee

(1) For the purposes of this Chapter a car or van is available to an employee at a particular time if it is then made available, by reason of the employment and without any transfer of the property in it, to the employee or a member of the employee's family or household.

(2) References in this Chapter to—

(a) the time when a car [or van] is first made available to an employee are to the earliest time when the car [or van] is made available as mentioned in subsection (1), and

(b) the last day in a year on which a car [or van] is available to an employee are to the last day in the year on which the car [or van] is made available as mentioned in subsection (1).

(3) This section does not apply to section [124A or] 138 (automatic car for a disabled employee).

NOTES

Sub-s (2): words in square brackets inserted by the Finance Act 2004, s 80(1), Sch 14, paras 1, 3.

Sub-s (3): words in square brackets inserted by the Finance Act 2009, s 54(1), (2).

[1.1341]

[117 Meaning of car or van made available by reason of employment

(1) For the purposes of this Chapter a car or van made available by an employer to an employee or member of an employee's family or household is to be regarded as made available by reason of the employment unless subsection (2) or (3) excludes the application of this subsection.

(2) Subsection (1) does not apply where—

(a) the employer is an individual, and

(b) the car or van in question is made available in the normal course of the employer's domestic, family or personal relationships.

(3) Subsection (1) does not apply where—

(a) the employer carries on a vehicle hire business under which cars or vans of the same kind are made available to members of the public for hire,

(b) the car or van in question is hired to the employee or member in the normal course of that business, and

(c) in hiring that car or van the employee or member is acting as an ordinary member of the public.]

NOTES

Commencement: see the note below.

Substituted by the Finance Act 2016, s 7(1), (5), with effect for the tax year 2016–17 and subsequent tax years.

[1.1342]

118 Availability for private use

(1) For the purposes of this Chapter a car or van made available in a tax year to an employee or a member of the employee's family or household is to be treated as available for the employee's or member's private use unless in that year—

(a) the terms on which it is made available prohibit such use, and

(b) it is not so used.

(2) In this Chapter "private use", in relation to a car or van made available to an employee or a member of the employee's family or household, means any use other than for the employee's business travel (see section 171(1)).

CHAPTER 10 TAXABLE BENEFITS: RESIDUAL LIABILITY TO CHARGE

Introduction

[1.1343]

201 Employment-related benefits

(1) This Chapter applies to employment-related benefits.

(2) In this Chapter—

"benefit" means a benefit or facility of any kind;

"employment-related benefit" means a benefit, other than an excluded benefit, which is provided in a tax year—

(a) for an employee, or

(b) for a member of an employee's family or household,

by reason of the employment.

For the definition of "excluded benefit" see section 202.

(3) A benefit provided by an employer is to be regarded as provided by reason of the employment unless—

(a) the employer is an individual, and

(b) the provision is made in the normal course of the employer's domestic, family or personal relationships.

(4) For the purposes of this Chapter it does not matter whether the employment is held at the time when the benefit is provided so long as it is held at some point in the tax year in which the benefit is provided.

(5) References in this Chapter to an employee accordingly include a prospective or former employee.

[1.1344]

202 Excluded benefits

(1) A benefit is an "excluded benefit" for the purposes of this Chapter if—

(a) any of Chapters 3 to 9 of the benefits code applies to the benefit,

(b) any of those Chapters would apply to the benefit but for an exception, or

(c) the benefit consists in the right to receive, or the prospect of receiving, sums treated as earnings under section 221 (payments where employee absent because of sickness or disability).

[(1A) But a benefit provided to an employee or member of an employee's family or household is to be taken not to be an excluded benefit by virtue of subsection (1)(c) so far as it is provided under optional remuneration arrangements.]

(2) In this section "exception", in relation to the application of a Chapter of the benefits code to a benefit, means any enactment in the Chapter which provides that the Chapter does not apply to the benefit.

But for this purpose section 86 (transport vouchers under pre-26th March 1982 arrangements) is not an exception.

NOTES

Sub-s (1A): inserted by the Finance Act 2017, 7, Sch 2, paras 2, 47, with effect for the tax year 2017–18 and subsequent tax years.

Cash equivalent of benefit treated as earnings

[1.1345]

203 Cash equivalent of benefit treated as earnings

(1) The cash equivalent of an employment-related benefit is to be treated as earnings from the employment for the tax year in which it is provided.

(2) The cash equivalent of an employment-related benefit is the cost of the benefit less any part of that cost made good by the employee[, to the persons providing the benefit, on or before 6 July following the tax year in which it is provided].

(3) The cost of an employment-related benefit is determined in accordance with section 204 unless—

(a) section 205 provides that the cost is to be determined in accordance with that section, or

(b) section 206 provides that the cost is to be determined in accordance with that section.

NOTES

Sub-s (2): words in square brackets substituted by the Finance (No 2) Act 2017, s 1(1), (13), with effect for the tax year 2017–18 and subsequent tax years.

[1.1346]

[203A Employment-related benefit provided under optional remuneration arrangements

(1) Where an employment-related benefit is provided pursuant to optional remuneration arrangements—

(a) the relevant amount is to be treated as earnings from the employment for the tax year in which the benefit is provided, and

(b) section 203(1) does not apply.

(2) To find the relevant amount, first determine which (if any) is the greater of—

(a) the cost of the employment-related benefit, and

(b) the amount foregone with respect to the benefit (see section 69B).

(3) If the cost of the employment-related benefit is greater than or equal to the amount foregone, the "relevant amount" is the cash equivalent (see section 203(2)).

(4) Otherwise, the "relevant amount" is—

(a) the amount foregone with respect to the employment-related benefit, less

(b) any part of the cost of the benefit made good by the employee, to the persons providing the benefit, on or before 6 July following the tax year in which it is provided.

(5) For the purposes of subsections (2) and (3), assume that the cost of the employment-related benefit is zero if the condition in subsection (6) is met.

(6) The condition is that the employment-related benefit would be exempt from income tax but for section 228A (exclusion of certain exemptions).

(7) Where it is necessary for the purposes of subsections (2)(b) and (4) to apportion an amount of earnings to the benefit provided in the tax year, the apportionment is to be made on a just and reasonable basis.

In this subsection "earnings" is to be interpreted in accordance with section 69B(5).]

NOTES

Commencement: see the note below.

Inserted by the Finance Act 2017, 7, Sch 2, paras 2, 48, with effect for the tax year 2017–18 and subsequent tax years. For transitional provisions see Sch 7, para 62(5)–(9), (11)–(15).

Determination of the cost of the benefit

[1.1347]

204 Cost of the benefit: basic rule

The cost of an employment-related benefit is the expense incurred in or in connection with provision of the benefit (including a proper proportion of any expense relating partly to provision of the benefit and partly to other matters).

Supplementary provisions

[1.1348]

210 Power to exempt minor benefits

(1) The Treasury may make provision by regulations for exempting from the application of this Chapter such minor benefits as may be specified in the regulations.

(2) An exemption conferred by such regulations is conditional on the benefit being made available to the employer's employees generally on similar terms.

NOTES

Regulations: the Income Tax (Exemption of Minor Benefits) (Amendment) Regulations 2003, SI 2003/1434; the Income Tax (Exemption of Minor Benefits) (Amendment) Regulations 2004, SI 2004/3087; the Income Tax (Exemption of Minor Benefits) (Revocation) Regulations 2009, SI 2009/695; the Income Tax (Exemption of Minor Benefits) (Amendment) Regulations 2012, SI 2012/1808. Note also that the Income Tax (Benefits in Kind) (Exemption for Welfare Counselling) Regulations 2000, SI 2000/2080, the Income Tax (Exemption of Minor Benefits) Regulations 2002, SI 2002/205, and the Income Tax (Benefits in Kind) (Exemption for Employment Costs resulting from Disability) Regulations 2002, SI 2002/1596, all have effect as if made under this section by virtue of s 723(2) of, and Sch 7, para 3 to, this Act.

PART 4
EMPLOYMENT INCOME: EXEMPTIONS

CHAPTER 6 EXEMPTIONS: NON-CASH VOUCHERS AND CREDIT TOKENS

Exemptions for particular non-cash vouchers and credit tokens

[1.1349]

[270A Limited exemption for qualifying childcare vouchers

(1) If qualifying childcare vouchers are provided for an [eligible] [employee—
(a) no liability to income tax arises by virtue of section 62 (general definition of earnings), and
(b) liability] to income tax by virtue of Chapter 4 of Part 3 (taxable benefits: vouchers and credit tokens) arises only in respect of so much of the cash equivalent of the benefit as exceeds the exempt amount.

[For the meaning of "eligible employee", see section 270AA.]

(2) A "qualifying childcare voucher" means a non-cash voucher in relation to which Conditions A to [D] are met.

(3) Condition A is that the voucher is provided to enable an employee to obtain care for a child who—
(a) is a child or stepchild of the employee and is maintained (wholly or partly) at the employee's expense, or
(b) is resident with the employee and is a person in respect of whom the employee has parental responsibility.

(4) Condition B is that the voucher can only be used to obtain qualifying child care.

(5) Condition C is that the vouchers are provided under a scheme that is open—
(a) to the employer's [eligible] employees generally, or
(b) generally to those at a particular location.

[(5A) Where the scheme under which the vouchers are provided involves—
(a) relevant salary sacrifice arrangements, or
(b) relevant flexible remuneration arrangements,

Condition C is not prevented from being met by reason only that the scheme is not open to relevant low-paid employees.

(5B) In subsection (5A)—

"relevant salary sacrifice arrangements" means arrangements (whenever made) under which the employees for whom the vouchers are provided give up the right to receive an amount of general earnings or specific employment income in return for the provision of the vouchers;

"relevant flexible remuneration arrangements" means arrangements (whenever made) under which the employees for whom the vouchers are provided agree with the employer that they are to be provided with the vouchers rather than receive some other description of employment income;

"relevant low-paid employees" means any of the employer's employees who are remunerated by the employer at a rate such that, if the relevant salary sacrifice arrangements or relevant flexible remuneration arrangements applied to them, the rate at which they would then be so remunerated would be likely to be lower than the national minimum wage.]

[(5C) Condition D is that the employer has, at the required time, made an estimate of the employee's relevant earnings amount for the tax year in respect of which the voucher is provided (see section 270B).]

(6) For the purposes of this section the "exempt amount", in any tax year, is [the sum of—
(a) [the appropriate amount] for each qualifying week in that year, and
(b) the voucher administration costs for that year].

[(6ZA) In subsection (6)(a) "the appropriate amount", in the case of an employee, means—
(a) if the relevant earnings amount in the case of the employee for the tax year, as estimated in accordance with subsection (5C), exceeds the higher rate limit for the tax year, [£25],
(b) if the relevant earnings amount in the case of the employee for the tax year, as so estimated, exceeds the basic rate limit for the tax year but does not exceed the higher rate limit for the tax year, £28, and
(c) otherwise, £55.]

[(6A) The "voucher administration costs" for any tax year in respect of which qualifying childcare vouchers are provided for an employee means the difference between the cost of provision of the vouchers and their face value.

The face value of a voucher is the amount stated on or recorded in the voucher as the value of the provision of care for a child that may be obtained by using it.]

(7) A "qualifying week" means a tax week in respect of which a qualifying childcare voucher is received.

A "tax week" means one of the successive periods in a tax year beginning with the first day of that year and every seventh day after that (so that the last day of a tax year or, in the case of a tax year ending in a leap year, the last two days is treated as a separate week).

(8) An employee is only entitled to one exempt amount even if care is provided for more than one child.

But it does not matter that another person may also be entitled to an exempt amount in respect of the same child.

(9) An employee is not entitled to an exempt amount under this section and under section 318A (limited exemption for employer-contracted childcare) in respect of the same tax week.

(10) In this section "care", "child", "parental responsibility" and "qualifying child care" have the same meaning as in section 318A (see sections 318B and 318C).

[(10A) In this section "cost of provision", in relation to a childcare voucher, has the meaning given in section 87(3) and (3A).]

(11) The powers conferred by section 318D (childcare: power to vary [amounts] and qualifying conditions) are exercisable—

- (a) in relation to the [amounts] specified in subsection [(6ZA) above] as in relation to the [amounts] specified in section [318A(6A)], and
- (b) in relation to the qualifying conditions for the exemption conferred by this section as in relation to the qualifying conditions for the exemption conferred by section 318A.]

NOTES

Inserted by the Finance Act 2004, s 78(1), Sch 13, para 3.

Sub-s (1): words in first and final pairs of square brackets inserted by the Childcare Payments Act 2014, s 63(1), (2), as from 21 April 2017; words in second pair of square brackets substituted by the Finance Act 2005, s 16(1), (4).

Sub-s (2): reference to "D" in square brackets substituted by the Finance Act 2011, s 35, Sch 8, paras 1, 2(1), (2).

Sub-s (5): word in square brackets inserted by the Childcare Payments Act 2014, s 63(1), (3), as from 21 April 2017.

Sub-ss (5A), (5B): inserted by the Finance Act 2011, s 36(1).

Sub-s (5C): inserted by the Finance Act 2011, s 35, Sch 8, paras 1, 2(1), (3).

Sub-s (6): words in first (outer) pair of square brackets substituted by the Finance Act 2005, s 15(1), (2); words in square brackets in para (a) substituted by the Finance Act 2011, s 35, Sch 8, paras 1, 2(1), (4).

Sub-s (6ZA): inserted by the Finance Act 2011, s 35, Sch 8, paras 1, 2(1), (5); sum in square brackets substituted by the Income Tax (Exempt Amount for Childcare Vouchers and for Employer Contracted Childcare) Order 2013, SI 2013/513, art 2(1), (2).

Sub-ss (6A), (10A): inserted by the Finance Act 2005, s 15(1), (3), (4).

Sub-s (11): word "amounts" in square brackets in each place they occur substituted by the Finance Act 2011, s 35, Sch 8, paras 1, 2(1), (6)(a); other words in square brackets substituted by the Finance Act 2011, s 35, Sch 8, paras 1, 2(1), (6)(b), (c).

Orders: the Income Tax (Exempt Amounts for Childcare Vouchers and for Employer Contracted Childcare) Order 2006, SI 2006/882; the Income Tax (Exempt Amount for Childcare Vouchers and for Employer Contracted Childcare) Order 2013, SI 2013/513.

CHAPTER 10 EXEMPTIONS: TERMINATION OF EMPLOYMENT

Redundancy payments

[1.1350]

309 Limited exemptions for statutory redundancy payments

(1) No liability to income tax in respect of earnings arises by virtue of a redundancy payment or an approved contractual payment, except where subsection (2) applies.

(2) Where an approved contractual payment exceeds the amount which would have been due if a redundancy payment had been payable, the excess is liable to income tax.

(3) No liability to income tax in respect of employment income other than earnings arises by virtue of a redundancy payment or an approved contractual payment, except where it does so by virtue of Chapter 3 of Part 6 (payments and benefits on termination of employment etc).

(4) For the purposes of this section—

- (a) a statutory payment in respect of a redundancy payment is to be treated as paid on account of the redundancy payment, and
- (b) a statutory payment in respect of an approved contractual payment is to be treated as paid on account of the approved contractual payment.

(5) In this section—

"approved contractual payment" means a payment to a person on the termination of the person's employment under an agreement in respect of which an order is in force under section 157 of ERA 1996 or Article 192 of ER(NI)O 1996,

"redundancy payment" means a redundancy payment under Part 11 of ERA 1996 or Part 12 of ER(NI)O 1996, and

"statutory payment" means a payment under section 167(1) of ERA 1996 or Article 202(1) of ER(NI)O 1996.

(6) In subsection (5) "employment", in relation to a person, has the meaning given in section 230(5) of ERA 1996 or Article 3(5) of ER(NI)O 1996.

NOTES

ERA 1996 and ER(NI)O 1996: the Employment Rights Act 1996 and the Employment Rights (Northern Ireland) Order 1996, respectively.

Outplacement benefits

[1.1351]

310 Counselling and other outplacement services

(1) No liability to income tax arises in respect of—

(a) the provision of services to a person in connection with the cessation of the person's employment, or

(b) the payment or reimbursement of—

(i) fees for such provision, or

(ii) travelling expenses incurred in connection with such provision,

if conditions A to D and, in the case of travel expenses, condition E are met.

(2) Condition A is that the only or main purpose of the provision of the services is to enable the person to do either or both of the following—

(a) to adjust to the cessation of the employment, or

(b) to find other gainful employment (including self-employment).

(3) Condition B is that the services consist wholly of any or all of the following—

(a) giving advice and guidance,

(b) imparting or improving skills,

(c) providing or making available the use of office equipment or similar facilities.

(4) Condition C is that the person has been employed . . . in the employment which is ceasing throughout the period of 2 years ending—

(a) at the time when the services begin to be provided, or

(b) if earlier, at the time when the employment ceases.

(5) Condition D is that the opportunity to receive the services, on similar terms as to payment or reimbursement of any expenses incurred in connection with their provision, is available—

(a) generally to employees or former employees of the person's employer in that employment, or

(b) to a particular class or classes of them.

(6) Condition E is that the travel expenses are expenses—

(a) in respect of which, on the assumptions in subsection (7), mileage allowance relief under Chapter 2 of this Part would be available if no mileage allowance payments had been made, or

(b) which, on those assumptions, would be deductible under Part 5.

(7) The assumptions are—

(a) that receiving the services is one of the duties of the employee's employment,

(b) that the employee incurs and pays the expenses, and

(c) if the employment has in fact ceased, that it continues.

(8) In this section "mileage allowance payments" has the meaning given by section 229(2).

NOTES

Sub-s (4): words omitted repealed by the Finance Act 2005, ss 18(1), (2), 104, Sch 11, Pt 2(1).

PART 5
EMPLOYMENT INCOME: DEDUCTIONS ALLOWED FROM EARNINGS

CHAPTER 1 DEDUCTIONS ALLOWED FROM EARNINGS: GENERAL RULES

Introduction

[1.1352]

327 Deductions from earnings: general

(1) This Part provides for deductions that are allowed from the taxable earnings from an employment in a tax year in calculating the net taxable earnings from the employment in the tax year for the purposes of Part 2 (see section 11(1)).

(2) In this Part, unless otherwise indicated by the context—

(a) references to the earnings from which deductions are allowed are references to the taxable earnings mentioned in subsection (1), and

(b) references to the tax year are references to the tax year mentioned there.

(3) The deductions for which this Part provides are those allowed under—

Chapter 2 (deductions for employee's expenses),

Chapter 3 (deductions from benefits code earnings),

Chapter 4 (fixed allowances for employee's expenses),

Chapter 5 (deductions for earnings representing benefits or reimbursed expenses), and

Chapter 6 (deductions from seafarers' earnings).

(4) Further provision about deductions from earnings is made in—

section 232 (giving effect to mileage allowance relief),

. . .

section 262 of CAA 2001 (capital allowances to be given effect by treating them as deductions from earnings).

(5) Further provision about deductions from income including earnings is made in—

Part 12 (payroll giving),

[and sections 188 to 194 of FA 2004 (contributions to registered pension schemes)]

NOTES

Sub-s (4): words omitted repealed by the Finance Act 2004, ss 281, 326, Sch 35, paras 54, 60(1), (2), Sch 42, Pt 3.

Sub-s (5): words in square brackets substituted by the Finance Act 2004, s 281(1), Sch 35, paras 54, 60(1), (3).

CAA 2001: Capital Allowances Act 2001.

CHAPTER 2 DEDUCTIONS FOR EMPLOYEE'S EXPENSES

Introduction

[1.1353]
333 Scope of this Chapter: expenses paid by the employee

(1) A deduction from a person's earnings for an amount is allowed under the following provisions of this Chapter only if the amount—
(a) is paid by the person, or
(b) is paid on the person's behalf by someone else and is included in the earnings.

(2) In the following provisions of this Chapter, in relation to a deduction from a person's earnings, references to the person paying an amount include references to the amount being paid on the person's behalf by someone else if or to the extent that the amount is included in the earnings.

(3) Subsection (1)(b) does not apply to the deductions under—
(a) section 351(2) and (3) (expenses of ministers of religion), and
(b) section 355 (deductions for corresponding payments by non-domiciled employees with foreign employers),

and subsection (2) does not apply in the case of those deductions.

(4) Chapter 3 of this Part provides for deductions where—
(a) a person's earnings include an amount treated as earnings under Chapter 4, 5 or 10 of Part 3 (taxable benefits: vouchers etc, living accommodation and residual liability to charge), and
(b) an amount in respect of the benefit in question would be deductible under this Chapter if the person had incurred and paid it.

[1.1354]
334 Effect of reimbursement etc

(1) For the purposes of this Chapter, a person may be regarded as paying an amount despite—
(a) its reimbursement, or
(b) any other payment from another person in respect of the amount.

(2) But where a reimbursement or such other payment is made in respect of an amount, a deduction for the amount is allowed under the following provisions of this Chapter only if or to the extent that—
(a) the reimbursement, or
(b) so much of the other payment as relates to the amount,

is included in the person's earnings.

(3) This section does not apply to a deduction allowed under section 351 (expenses of ministers of religion).

(4) This section is to be disregarded for the purposes of the deductibility provisions.

General rule for deduction of employee's expenses

[1.1355]
336 Deductions for expenses: the general rule

(1) The general rule is that a deduction from earnings is allowed for an amount if—
(a) the employee is obliged to incur and pay it as holder of the employment, and
(b) the amount is incurred wholly, exclusively and necessarily in the performance of the duties of the employment.

(2) The following provisions of this Chapter contain additional rules allowing deductions for particular kinds of expenses and rules preventing particular kinds of deductions.

(3) No deduction is allowed under this section for an amount that is deductible under sections 337 to 342 (travel expenses).

Travel expenses

[1.1356]
337 Travel in performance of duties

(1) A deduction from earnings is allowed for travel expenses if—
(a) the employee is obliged to incur and pay them as holder of the employment, and
(b) the expenses are necessarily incurred on travelling in the performance of the duties of the employment.

(2) This section needs to be read with section 359 (disallowance of travel expenses: mileage allowances and reliefs).

[1.1357]
338 Travel for necessary attendance

(1) A deduction from earnings is allowed for travel expenses if—
(a) the employee is obliged to incur and pay them as holder of the employment, and
(b) the expenses are attributable to the employee's necessary attendance at any place in the performance of the duties of the employment.

(2) Subsection (1) does not apply to the expenses of ordinary commuting or travel between any two places that is for practical purposes substantially ordinary commuting.

(3) In this section "ordinary commuting" means travel between—
(a) the employee's home and a permanent workplace, or
(b) a place that is not a workplace and a permanent workplace.

(4) Subsection (1) does not apply to the expenses of private travel or travel between any two places that is for practical purposes substantially private travel.
(5) In subsection (4) "private travel" means travel between—
(a) the employee's home and a place that is not a workplace, or
(b) two places neither of which is a workplace.
(6) This section needs to be read with section 359 (disallowance of travel expenses: mileage allowances and reliefs).

[1.1358]
339 Meaning of "workplace" and "permanent workplace"
(1) In this Part "workplace", in relation to an employment, means a place at which the employee's attendance is necessary in the performance of the duties of the employment.
(2) In this Part "permanent workplace", in relation to an employment, means a place which—
(a) the employee regularly attends in the performance of the duties of the employment, and
(b) is not a temporary workplace.
This is subject to subsections (4) and (8).
(3) In subsection (2) "temporary workplace", in relation to an employment, means a place which the employee attends in the performance of the duties of the employment—
(a) for the purpose of performing a task of limited duration, or
(b) for some other temporary purpose.
This is subject to subsections (4) and (5).
(4) A place which the employee regularly attends in the performance of the duties of the employment is treated as a permanent workplace and not a temporary workplace if—
(a) it forms the base from which those duties are performed, or
(b) the tasks to be carried out in the performance of those duties are allocated there.
(5) A place is not regarded as a temporary workplace if the employee's attendance is—
(a) in the course of a period of continuous work at that place—
(i) lasting more than 24 months, or
(ii) comprising all or almost all of the period for which the employee is likely to hold the employment, or
(b) at a time when it is reasonable to assume that it will be in the course of such a period.
(6) For the purposes of subsection (5), a period is a period of continuous work at a place if over the period the duties of the employment are performed to a significant extent at the place.
(7) An actual or contemplated modification of the place at which duties are performed is to be disregarded for the purposes of subsections (5) and (6) if it does not, or would not, have any substantial effect on the employee's journey, or expenses of travelling, to and from the place where they are performed.
(8) An employee is treated as having a permanent workplace consisting of an area if—
(a) the duties of the employment are defined by reference to an area (whether or not they also require attendance at places outside it),
(b) in the performance of those duties the employee attends different places within the area,
(c) none of the places the employee attends in the performance of those duties is a permanent workplace, and
(d) the area would be a permanent workplace if subsections (2), (3), (5), (6) and (7) referred to the area where they refer to a place.

[1.1359]
[339A Travel for necessary attendance: employment intermediaries
(1) This section applies where an individual ("the worker")—
(a) personally provides services (which are not excluded services) to another person ("the client"), and
(b) the services are provided not under a contract directly between the client or a person connected with the client and the worker but under arrangements involving an employment intermediary.
This is subject to the following provisions of this section.
(2) Where this section applies, each engagement is for the purposes of sections 338 and 339 to be regarded as a separate employment.
(3) This section does not apply if it is shown that the manner in which the worker provides the services is not subject to (or to the right of) supervision, direction or control by any person.
(4) Subsection (3) does not apply in relation to an engagement if—
(a) Chapter 8 of Part 2 applies in relation to the engagement,
(b) the conditions in section 51, 52 or 53 are met in relation to the employment intermediary, and
(c) the employment intermediary is not a managed service company.
(5) This section does not apply in relation to an engagement if—
(a) Chapter 8 of Part 2 does not apply in relation to the engagement merely because the circumstances in section 49(1)(c) are not met,
(b) assuming those circumstances were met, the conditions in section 51, 52 or 53 would be met in relation to the employment intermediary, and
(c) the employment intermediary is not a managed service company.
(6) In determining for the purposes of subsection (4) or (5) whether the conditions in section 51, 52 or 53 are or would be met in relation to the employment intermediary—
(a) in section 51(1)—
(i) disregard "either" in the opening words, and
(ii) disregard paragraph (b) (and the preceding or), and

(b) read references to the intermediary as references to the employment intermediary.

[(6A) Subsection (3) does not apply in relation to an engagement if—

(a) sections 61N to 61R in Chapter 10 of Part 2 apply in relation to the engagement,

(b) one of Conditions A to C in section 61N is met in relation to the employment intermediary, and

(c) the employment intermediary is not a managed service company.

(6B) This section does not apply in relation to an engagement if—

(a) sections 61N to 61R in Chapter 10 of Part 2 do not apply in relation to the engagement because the circumstances in section 61M(1)(d) are not met,

(b) assuming those circumstances were met, one of Conditions A to C in section 61N would be met in relation to the employment intermediary, and

(c) the employment intermediary is not a managed service company.

(6C) In determining for the purposes of subsection (6A) or (6B) whether one of Conditions A to C in section 61N is or would be met in relation to the employment intermediary, read references to the intermediary as references to the employment intermediary.]

(7) Subsection (8) applies if—

(a) the client or a relevant person provides the employment intermediary (whether before or after the worker begins to provide the services) with a fraudulent document which is intended to constitute evidence that, by virtue of subsection (3), this section does not or will not apply in relation to the services,

(b) that section is taken not to apply in relation to the services, and

(c) in consequence, the employment intermediary does not under PAYE regulations deduct and account for an amount that would have been deducted and accounted for under those regulations if this section had been taken to apply in relation to the services.

(8) For the purpose of recovering the amount referred to in subsection (7)(c) ("the unpaid tax")—

(a) the worker is to be treated as having an employment with the client or relevant person who provided the document, the duties of which consist of the services, and

(b) the client or relevant person is under PAYE regulations to account for the unpaid tax as if it arose in respect of earnings from that employment.

(9) In subsections (7) and (8) "relevant person" means a person, other than the client, the worker or a person connected with the employment intermediary, who—

(a) is resident, or has a place of business, in the United Kingdom, and

(b) is party to a contract with the employment intermediary or a person connected with the employment intermediary under or in consequence of which—

(i) the services are provided, or

(ii) the employment intermediary, or a person connected with the employment intermediary, makes payments in respect of the services.

(10) In determining whether this section applies, no regard is to be had to any arrangements the main purpose, or one of the main purposes, of which is to secure that this section does not to any extent apply.

(11) In this section—

"arrangements" includes any scheme, transaction or series of transactions, agreement or understanding, whether or not enforceable, and any associated operations;

"employment intermediary" means a person, other than the worker or the client, who carries on a business (whether or not with a view to profit and whether or not in conjunction with any other business) of supplying labour;

"engagement" means any such provision of service as is mentioned in subsection (1)(a);

"excluded services" means services provided wholly in the client's home;

"managed service company" means a company which—

(a) is a managed service company within the meaning given by section 61B, or

(b) would be such a company disregarding subsection (1)(c) of that section.]

NOTES

Commencement: see the note below.

Inserted by the Finance Act 2016, s 14(1), with effect for the tax year 2016–17 and subsequent tax years.

Sub-ss (6A)–(6C): inserted by the Finance Act 2017, s 6, Sch 1, Pt 3, para 12, with effect for the tax year 2017–18 and subsequent tax years.

PART 6
EMPLOYMENT INCOME: INCOME WHICH IS NOT EARNINGS OR SHARE-RELATED

CHAPTER 3 PAYMENTS AND BENEFITS ON TERMINATION OF EMPLOYMENT ETC

Preliminary

[1.1360]

401 Application of this Chapter

(1) This Chapter applies to payments and other benefits which are received directly or indirectly in consideration or in consequence of, or otherwise in connection with—

(a) the termination of a person's employment,

(b) a change in the duties of a person's employment, or

(c) a change in the earnings from a person's employment,

by the person, or the person's spouse [or civil partner], blood relative, dependant or personal representatives.

(2) Subsection (1) is subject to subsection (3) and sections 405 to [414A] (exceptions for certain payments and benefits).
(3) This Chapter does not apply to any payment or other benefit chargeable to income tax apart from this Chapter.
(4) For the purposes of this Chapter—
- (a) a payment or other benefit which is provided on behalf of, or to the order of, the employee or former employee is treated as received by the employee or former employee, and
- (b) in relation to a payment or other benefit—
  - (i) any reference to the employee or former employee is to the person mentioned in subsection (1), and
  - (ii) any reference to the employer or former employer is to be read accordingly.

NOTES

Sub-s (1): words in square brackets inserted by the Tax and Civil Partnership Regulations 2005, SI 2005/3229, regs 137, 152.

Sub-s (2): figure in square brackets substituted by the Enactment of Extra-Statutory Concessions Order 2014, SI 2014/211, arts 5(1), (3)(a), 6.

[1.1361]
402 Meaning of "benefit"

(1) In this Chapter "benefit" includes anything in respect of which, were it received for performance of the duties of the employment, an amount—
- (a) would be taxable earnings from the employment, or
- (b) would be such earnings apart from an earnings-only exemption.

This is subject to subsections (2) to (4).
(2) In this Chapter "benefit" does not include a benefit received in connection with the termination of a person's employment that is a benefit which, were it received for performance of the duties of the employment, would fall within—
- (a) section 239(4) (exemption of benefits connected with taxable cars and vans and exempt heavy goods vehicles), so far as that section applies to a benefit connected with a car or van,
- (b) section 269 (exemption where benefits or money obtained in connection with taxable car or van or exempt heavy goods vehicle),
- (c) section 319 (mobile telephones), or
- (d) section 320 (limited exemption for computer equipment).

(3) In this Chapter "benefit" does not include a benefit received in connection with any change in the duties of, or earnings from, a person's employment to the extent that it is a benefit which, were it received for performance of the duties of the employment, would fall within section 271(1) (limited exemption of removal benefits and expenses).
(4) The right to receive a payment or benefit is not itself a benefit for the purposes of this Chapter.

Payments and benefits treated as employment income

[1.1362]
[402A Split of payments and other benefits between sections 402B and 403

(1) In this Chapter "termination award" means a payment or other benefit to which this Chapter applies because of section 401(1)(a).
(2) Section 402B (termination awards not benefiting from threshold treated as earnings) applies to termination awards to the extent determined under section 402C.
(3) Section 403 (charge on payment or benefit where threshold applies) applies to termination awards so far as they are not ones to which section 402B applies.
(4) Section 403 also applies to payments and other benefits to which this Chapter applies because of section 401(1)(b) or (c) (change in duties or earnings).]

NOTES

Commencement: see the note below.

Inserted by the Finance (No 2) Act 2017, s 5(1), (3), (10), with effect for the tax year 2018–19 and subsequent tax years.

[1.1363]
[402B Termination awards not benefiting from threshold to be treated as earnings

(1) The amount of a termination award to which this section applies is treated as an amount of earnings of the employee, or former employee, from the employment.
(2) See also section 7(3)(b) and (5)(ca) (which cause amounts treated as earnings under this section to be included in general earnings).
(3) Section 403(3) (when benefits are received) does not apply in relation to payments or other benefits to which this section applies.]

NOTES

Commencement: see the note below.

Inserted by the Finance (No 2) Act 2017, s 5(1), (3), (10), with effect for the tax year 2018–19 and subsequent tax years.

[1.1364]
[402C The termination awards to which section 402B applies

(1) This section has effect for the purpose of identifying the extent to which section 402B applies to termination awards in respect of the termination of the employment of the employee.
(2) In this section "relevant termination award" means a termination award that is neither—

(a) a redundancy payment, nor
(b) so much of an approved contractual payment as is equal to or less than the amount which would have been due if a redundancy payment had been payable.

(3) If the post-employment notice pay (see section 402D) in respect of the termination is greater than, or equal to, the total amount of the relevant termination awards in respect of the termination, section 402B applies to all of those relevant termination awards.

(4) If the post-employment notice pay in respect of the termination is less than the total amount of the relevant termination awards in respect of the termination but is not nil—
(a) section 402B applies to a part of those relevant termination awards, and
(b) the amount of that part is equal to the post-employment notice pay.

(5) Section 309(4) to (6) (meaning of "redundancy payment" and "approved contractual payment" etc) apply for the purposes of subsection (2) as they apply for the purposes of section 309.]

NOTES

Commencement: see the note below.

Inserted by the Finance (No 2) Act 2017, s 5(1), (3), (10), with effect for the tax year 2018–19 and subsequent tax years.

[1.1365]

[402D "Post-employment notice pay"

(1) "The post-employment notice pay" in respect of a termination is (subject to subsection (11)) given by—

((BP x D) / P) – T

where—

BP, D and P are given by subsections (3) to (7), and

T is the total of the amounts of any payment or benefit received in connection with the termination which—
(a) would fall within section 401(1)(a) but for section 401(3),
(b) is taxable as earnings under Chapter 1 of Part 3,
(c) is not pay in respect of holiday entitlement for a period before the employment ends, and
(d) is not a bonus payable for termination of the employment.

(2) If the amount given by the formula in subsection (1) is a negative amount, the post-employment notice pay is nil.

(3) Subject to subsections (5) and (6)—

BP is the employee's basic pay (see subsection (7)) from the employment in respect of the last pay period of the employee to end before the trigger date,

P is the number of days in that pay period, and

D is the number of days in the post-employment notice period.

(4) See section 402E for the meaning of "trigger date" and "post-employment notice period".

(5) If there is no pay period of the employee which ends before the trigger date then—

BP is the employee's basic pay from the employment in respect of the period starting with the first day of the employment and ending with the trigger date,

P is the number of days in that period, and

D is the number of days in the post-employment notice period.

(6) If the last pay period of the employee to end before the trigger date is a month, the minimum notice (see section 402E) is given by contractual terms and is expressed to be a whole number of months, and the post-employment notice period is equal in length to the minimum notice or is otherwise a whole number of months, then—

BP is the employee's basic pay from the employment in respect of the last pay period of the employee to end before the trigger date,

P is 1, and

D is the length of the post-employment notice period expressed in months.

(7) In this section "basic pay" means—
(a) employment income of the employee from the employment but disregarding—
 (i) any amount received by way of overtime, bonus, commission, gratuity or allowance,
 (ii) any amount received in connection with the termination of the employment,
 (iii) any amount treated as earnings under Chapters 2 to 10 of Part 3 (the benefits code) or which would be so treated apart from section 64,
 (iv) any amount which is treated as earnings under Chapter 12 of Part 3 (amounts treated as earnings),
 (v) any amount which counts as employment income by virtue of Part 7 (income relating to securities and securities options), and
 (vi) any employment-related securities that constitute earnings under Chapter 1 of Part 3 (earnings), and
(b) any amount which the employee has given up the right to receive but which would have fallen within paragraph (a) had the employee not done so.

(8) In subsection (7) "employment-related securities" has the same meaning as it has in Chapter 1 of Part 7 (see section 421B).

(9) The Treasury may by regulations amend this section for the purpose of altering the meaning of "basic pay".

(10) A statutory instrument containing regulations under subsection (9) may not be made unless a draft of it has been laid before, and approved by a resolution of, the House of Commons.

(11) Where the purpose, or one of the purposes, of any arrangements is the avoidance of tax by causing the post-employment notice pay calculated under subsection (1) to be less than it would otherwise be, the post-employment notice pay is to be treated as the amount which the post-employment notice pay would have been but for the arrangements.

(12) In subsection (11) "arrangements" includes any scheme, arrangement or understanding of any kind, whether or not legally enforceable, involving a single transaction or two or more transactions.]

NOTES

Commencement: see the note below.

Inserted by the Finance (No 2) Act 2017, s 5(1), (3), (10), with effect for the tax year 2018–19 and subsequent tax years.

Regulations: as of 15 May 2019, no Regulations had been made under this section.

[1.1366]

[402E Meaning of "trigger date" and "post-employment notice period" in section 402D

(1) Subsections (2) and (4) to (6) have effect for the purposes of section 402D (and subsection (4) has effect also for the purposes of this section).

(2) The "trigger date" is—

(a) if the termination is not a notice case, the last day of the employment, and

(b) if the termination is a notice case, the day the notice is given.

(3) For the purposes of this section, the termination is a "notice case" if the employer or employee gives notice to the other to terminate the employment, and here it does not matter—

(a) whether the notice is more or less than, or the same as, the minimum notice, or

(b) if the employment ends before the notice expires.

(4) The "minimum notice" is the minimum notice required to be given by the employer to terminate the employee's employment by notice in accordance with the law and contractual terms effective—

(a) where the termination is not a notice case—

(i) immediately before the employment ends, or

(ii) where the employment ends by agreement entered into after the start of the employment, immediately before the agreement is entered into, and

(b) where the termination is a notice case, immediately before the notice is given.

(5) The "post-employment notice period" is the period—

(a) beginning at the end of the last day of the employment, and

(b) ending with the earliest lawful termination date.

(But see subsection (8) for provision about limited-term contracts.)

(6) If the earliest lawful termination date is, or precedes, the last day of the employment, the number of days in the post-employment notice period is nil.

(7) "The earliest lawful termination date" is the last day of the period which—

(a) is equal in length to the minimum notice, and

(b) begins at the end of the trigger date.

(8) In the case of a contract of employment which is a limited-term contract and which does not include provision for termination by notice by the employer, the post-employment notice period is the period—

(a) beginning at the end of the last day of the employment, and

(b) ending with the day of the occurrence of the limiting event.

(9) If, in a case to which subsection (8) applies, on the last day of the employment the day of the occurrence of the limiting event is not ascertained or ascertainable (because, for example, the limiting event is the performance of a task), then subsection (8) has effect as if for paragraph (b) there were substituted—

"(b) ending with the day on which notice would have expired if the employer had, on the last day of the employment, given to the employee the minimum notice required to terminate the contract under section 86 of the Employment Rights Act 1996 (assuming that that section applies to the employment)."

(10) In this section "limited-term contract" and "limiting event" have the same meaning as in the Employment Rights Act 1996 (see section 235(2A) and (2B)).]

NOTES

Commencement: see the note below.

Inserted by the Finance (No 2) Act 2017, s 5(1), (3), (10), with effect for the tax year 2018–19 and subsequent tax years.

[1.1367]

403 Charge on payment or other benefit [where threshold applies]

(1) The amount of a payment or benefit to which this [section] applies counts as employment income of the employee or former employee for the relevant tax year if and to the extent that it exceeds the £30,000 threshold.

(2) In this section "the relevant tax year" means the tax year in which the payment or other benefit is received.

(3) For the purposes of this Chapter [(but see section 402B(3))]—

(a) a cash benefit is treated as received—

(i) when it is paid or a payment is made on account of it, or

(ii) when the recipient becomes entitled to require payment of or on account of it, and

(b) a non-cash benefit is treated as received when it is used or enjoyed.

(4) For the purposes of this Chapter the amount of a payment or benefit in respect of an employee or former employee exceeds the £30,000 threshold if and to the extent that, [when aggregated with—

(a) other payments or benefits in respect of the employee or former employee that are payments or benefits to which this section applies, and

(b) other payments or benefits in respect of the employee or former employee that are payments or benefits—

(i) received in the tax year 2017-18 or an earlier tax year, and

(ii) to which this Chapter applied in the tax year of receipt,

it exceeds] £30,000 according to the rules in section 404 (how the £30,000 threshold applies).

(5) If it is received after the death of the employee or former employee—

(a) the amount of a payment or benefit to which this [section] applies counts as the employment income of the personal representatives for the relevant year if or to the extent that it exceeds £30,000 according to the rules in section 404, and

(b) the tax is accordingly to be assessed and charged on them and is a debt due from and payable out of the estate.

(6) In this Chapter references to the taxable person are to the person in relation to whom subsection (1) or (5) provides for an amount to count as employment income [or, as the case may be, in relation to whom section 402B(1) provides for an amount to be treated as an amount of earnings].

NOTES

All words in square brackets in this section were substituted or inserted by the Finance (No 2) Act 2017, s 5(1), (4), (10), with effect for the tax year 2018–19 and subsequent tax years.

[1.1368]

404 How the £30,000 threshold applies

(1) For the purpose of the £30,000 threshold in section 403(4) and (5), the payments and other benefits provided in respect of an employee or former employee which are to be aggregated are those provided—

(a) in respect of the same employment,

(b) in respect of different employments with the same employer, and

(c) in respect of employments with employers who are associated.

(2) For this purpose employers are "associated" if on a termination or change date—

(a) one of them is under the control of the other, or

(b) one of them is under the control of a third person who on that termination or change date or another such date controls or is under the control of the other.

(3) In subsection (2)—

(a) references to an employer, or to a person controlling or controlled by an employer, include the successors of the employer or person, and

(b) "termination or change date" means a date on which a termination or change occurs in connection with which a payment or other benefit to which this [section 403] applies is received in respect of the employee or former employee.

(4) If payments and other benefits are received in different tax years, the £30,000 is set against the amount of payments and other benefits received in earlier years before those received in later years.

(5) If more than one payment or other benefit is received in a tax year in which the threshold is exceeded—

(a) the £30,000 (or the balance of it) is set against the amounts of cash benefits as they are received, and

(b) any balance at the end of the year is set against the aggregate amount of non-cash benefits received in the year.

[(6) In subsection (3)(b), the reference to a payment or other benefit to which section 403 applies includes a reference to a payment or other benefit—

(a) received in the tax year 2017–18 or an earlier tax year, and

(b) to which this Chapter applied in the tax year of receipt.]

NOTES

Words in square brackets in sub-s (4) substituted, and sub-s (6) added, by the Finance (No 2) Act 2017, s 5(1), (5), (10), with effect for the tax year 2018–19 and subsequent tax years.

[1.1369]

[404A Amounts charged to be treated as highest part of total income

(1) A payment or other benefit which counts as a person's employment income as a result of section 403 is treated as the highest part of the person's total income.

(2) Subsection (1) has effect for all income tax purposes except the purposes of sections 535 to 537 of ITTOIA 2005 (gains from contracts for life insurance etc: top slicing relief).

(3) See section 1012 of ITA 2007 (relationship between highest part rules) for the relationship between—

(a) the rule in subsection (1), and

(b) other rules requiring particular income to be treated as the highest part of a person's total income]

NOTES

Inserted by the Income Tax Act 2007, s 1027, Sch 1, Pt 2, paras 425, 437 (for effect and transitional provisions see the introductory note to this Act).

ITTOIA 2005: the Income Tax (Trading and Other Income) Act 2005.

ITA 2007: the Income Tax Act 2007.

[1.1370]

[404B Power to vary threshold

(1) The Treasury may by regulations amend the listed provisions by substituting, for the amount for the time being mentioned in those provisions, a different amount.

(2) The listed provisions are—

subsections (1), (4) and (5) of section 403, and

subsections (1), (4) and (5) of section 404 and its heading.

(3) Regulations under this section may include transitional provision.

(4) A statutory instrument containing regulations under this section which reduce the mentioned amount may not be made unless a draft of it has been laid before, and approved by a resolution of, the House of Commons.]

NOTES

Commencement: see the note below.

Inserted by the Finance (No 2) Act 2017, s 5(1), (6), (10), with effect for the tax year 2018–19 and subsequent tax years.

Regulations: as of 15 May 2019, no Regulations had been made under this section.

Exceptions and reductions

[1.1371]

405 Exception for certain payments exempted when received as earnings

(1) This Chapter does not apply to any payment received in connection with the termination of a person's employment which, were it received for the performance of the duties of the employment, would fall within section 308 (exemption of contributions to approved personal pension arrangements).

(2) This Chapter does not apply to any payment received in connection with any change in the duties of, or earnings from, a person's employment to the extent that, were it received for the performance of the duties of the employment, it would fall within section 271(1) (limited exemption of removal benefits and expenses).

[1.1372]

406 Exception for death or disability payments and benefits

[(1)] This Chapter does not apply to a payment or other benefit provided—

(a) in connection with the termination of employment by the death of an employee, or

(b) on account of injury to, or disability of, an employee.

[(2) Although "injury" in subsection (1) includes psychiatric injury, it does not include injured feelings.]

NOTES

Sub-s (1) numbered as such, and sub-s (2) added, by the Finance (No 2) Act 2017, s 5(1), (7), (10), with effect for the tax year 2018–19 and subsequent tax years.

[1.1373]

407 Exception for payments and benefits under tax-exempt pension schemes

(1) This Chapter does not apply to a payment or other benefit provided under a tax-exempt pension scheme if—

(a) the payment or other benefit is by way of compensation—

(i) for loss of employment, or

(ii) for loss or diminution of earnings, and

the loss or diminution is due to ill-health, or

(b) the payment or other benefit is properly regarded as earned by past service.

(2) For this purpose "tax-exempt pension scheme" means—

[(a) a registered pension scheme,

(aa) a scheme set up by a government outside the United Kingdom for the benefit of employees or primarily for their benefit, or]

(b) any such scheme or fund as was described in section 221(1) and (2) of ICTA 1970 (schemes to which payments could be made without charge to tax under section 220 of ICTA 1970).

(3) . . .

NOTES

Sub-s (2): paras (a), (aa) substituted, for the original para (a), by the Finance Act 2004, s 281(1), Sch 35, paras 54, 62(1), (2).

Sub-s (3): repealed by the Finance Act 2004, ss 281(1), 326, Sch 35, paras 54, 62(1), (3), Sch 42, Pt 3.

ICTA 1970: the Income and Corporation Taxes Act 1970 (repealed).

[1.1374]

408 Exception for contributions to [registered pension schemes]

(1) This Chapter does not apply to a contribution to a [registered pension scheme] [or an employer-financed retirement benefit scheme] if the contribution is made—

(a) as part of an arrangement relating to the termination of a person's employment, and

(b) in order to provide benefits for the person in accordance with the terms of the scheme or approved personal pension arrangements.

(2) . . .

NOTES

The words in square brackets in the section heading and the words in the first pair of square brackets in sub-s (1) were substituted, and sub-s (2) was repealed, by the Finance Act 2004, ss 281(1), 326, Sch 35, paras 54, 63, Sch 42, Pt 3.

The words in the second pair of square brackets in sub-s (1) were inserted by the Taxation of Pension Schemes (Consequential Amendments) (No 2) Order 2006, SI 2006/1963, art 2.

[1.1375]
409 Exception for payments and benefits in respect of [certain legal expenses etc] and indemnity insurance

(1) This Chapter does not apply to a payment or other benefit received by an individual if or to the extent that—

(a) in the case of a cash benefit, it is provided for meeting the cost of a deductible amount, or
(b) in the case of a non-cash benefit, it is or represents a benefit equivalent to the cost of paying a deductible amount.

(2) For the purposes of this section "deductible amount" means an amount which meets conditions A to C.

(3) Condition A is that the amount is paid by the individual [or by the employer or former employer on behalf of the individual].

(4) Condition B is that a deduction for the amount would have been allowed under section 346 from earnings from the relevant employment, if the individual still held the employment when the amount was paid.

(5) Condition C is that the amount is paid at a time which falls within the run-off period.

(6) In this section and section 410—

"relevant employment" means the employment mentioned in section 401(1);
"run-off period" means the period which—

(a) starts with the day on which the relevant employment terminated, and
(b) ends with the last day of the sixth tax year following the tax year in which the period started.

NOTES

The words in square brackets in the section heading were substituted, and the words in square brackets in sub-s (3) were inserted, by the Finance (No 2) Act 2017, s 4(1), (4), (8), with effect for the tax year 2017–18 and subsequent tax years.

[1.1376]
410 Exception for payments and benefits in respect of [certain legal expenses etc] and indemnity insurance: individual deceased

(1) This Chapter does not apply to a payment or other benefit received by an individual's personal representatives if or to the extent that—

(a) in the case of a cash benefit, it is provided for meeting the cost of a deductible amount, or
(b) in the case of a non-cash benefit, it is or represents a benefit equivalent to the cost of paying a deductible amount.

(2) For the purposes of this section "deductible amount" means an amount which meets conditions A to C.

(3) Condition A is that the amount is paid by the individual's personal representatives [or by the former employer on behalf of the individual's personal representatives].

(4) Condition B is that a deduction for the amount would have been allowed under section 346 from earnings from the relevant employment, if—

(a) the individual had not died,
(b) the amount had been paid by the individual, and
(c) the individual still held the employment when the amount was paid.

(5) Condition C is that the amount is paid at a time which falls within the run-off period.

NOTES

The words in square brackets in the section heading were substituted, and the words in square brackets in sub-s (3) were inserted, by the Finance (No 2) Act 2017, s 4(1), (5), (8), with effect for the tax year 2017–18 and subsequent tax years.

[1.1377]
411 Exception for payments and benefits for forces

[(1)] This Chapter does not apply to a payment or other benefit provided—

(a) under a Royal Warrant, Queen's Order or Order in Council relating to members of Her Majesty's forces, or
(b) by way of payment in commutation of annual or other periodical payments authorised by any such Warrant or Order.

[(2) This Chapter does not apply to a payment or other benefit provided under a scheme established by an order under section 1(1) of the Armed Forces (Pensions and Compensation) Act 2004.]

NOTES

Sub-s (1) numbered as such, and sub-s (2) added, by the Finance Act 2007, s 63.

[1.1378]
412 Exception for payments and benefits provided by foreign governments etc

(1) This Chapter does not apply to—

(a) a benefit provided under a pension scheme administered by the government of an overseas territory within the Commonwealth, or
(b) a payment of compensation for loss of career, interruption of service or disturbance made—
 (i) in connection with any change in the constitution of any such overseas territory, and

(ii) to a person who was employed in the public service of the territory before the change.

(2) References in subsection (1) to—

(a) an overseas territory,

(b) the government of such a territory, and

(c) employment in the public service of such a territory,

have the meanings given in section 615 of ICTA.

[1.1379]

413 Exception in certain cases of foreign service

[(A1) This section applies to a payment or other benefit if—

(a) the payment or other benefit is within section 401(1)(a), and the employee or former employee is non-UK resident for the tax year in which the employment terminates, or

(b) the payment or other benefit is within section 401(1)(b) or (c).]

(1) This Chapter does not apply if the service of the employee or former employee in the employment in respect of which the payment or other benefit is received included foreign service comprising—

(a) three-quarters or more of the whole period of service ending with the date of the termination or change in question, or

(b) if the period of service ending with that date exceeded 10 years, the whole of the last 10 years, or

(c) if the period of service ending with that date exceeded 20 years, one-half or more of that period, including any 10 of the last 20 years.

(2) In subsection (1) "foreign service" means service to which subsection [(2A),] (3), (4) or (6) applies.

[(2A) This subsection applies to service in or after the tax year 2013–14—

(a) to the extent that it consists of duties performed outside the United Kingdom in respect of which earnings would not be relevant earnings, or

(b) if a deduction equal to the whole amount of the earnings from the employment was or would have been allowable under Chapter 6 of Part 5 (deductions from seafarers' earnings).]

(3) This subsection applies to service in or after the tax year 2003–04 [but before the tax year 2013–14] such that—

[(a) any earnings from the employment would not be relevant earnings, or]

(b) a deduction equal to the whole amount of the earnings from the employment was or would have been allowable under Chapter 6 of Part 5 (deductions from seafarers' earnings).

[(3ZA) In subsection (2A)(a) "relevant earnings" means earnings for a tax year that are earnings to which section 15 applies and to which that section would apply even if the employee made a claim under section 809B of ITA 2007 (claim for remittance basis) for that year.]

[(3A) In subsection (3)(a) "relevant earnings" means—

(a) for service in or after the tax year 2008–09, earnings—

(i) which are for a tax year in which the employee is ordinarily UK resident,

(ii) to which section 15 applies, and

(iii) to which that section would apply, even if the employee made a claim under section 809B of ITA 2007 (claim for remittance basis) for that year, and

(b) for service before the tax year 2008–09, general earnings to which section 15 or 21 as originally enacted applies.]

(4) This subsection applies to service before the tax year 2003–04 and after the tax year 1973–74 such that—

(a) the emoluments from the employment were not chargeable under Case I of Schedule E, or would not have been so chargeable had there been any, or

(b) a deduction equal to the whole amount of the emoluments from the employment was or would have been allowable under a foreign earnings deduction provision.

(5) In subsection (4) "foreign earnings deduction provision" means—

(a) paragraph 1 of Schedule 2 to FA 1974,

(b) paragraph 1 of Schedule 7 to FA 1977, or

(c) section 192A or 193(1) of ICTA.

(6) This subsection applies to service before the tax year 1974–75 such that tax was not chargeable in respect of the emoluments of the employment—

(a) in the tax year 1956–57 or later, under Case I of Schedule E, or

(b) in earlier tax years, under Schedule E,

or it would not have been so chargeable had there been any such emoluments.

NOTES

Sub-s (A1): inserted by the Finance Act 2018, s 10(1), (2), (5). This amendment has effect where the payment or other benefit is received after 13 September 2017 and the date of the termination or change in question is, or is after, 6 April 2018.

Sub-s (2): figure in square brackets inserted by the Finance Act 2013, s 219, Sch 46, Pt 2, paras 29, 38(1), (2), 72.

Sub-s (2A): inserted by the Finance Act 2013, s 219, Sch 46, Pt 2, paras 29, 38(1), (3), 72.

Sub-s (3): words in first pair of square brackets inserted by the Finance Act 2013, s 219, Sch 46, Pt 2, paras 29, 38(1), (4), 72; para (a) substituted by the Finance Act 2008, s 25, Sch 7, Pt 1, paras 2, 30(1), (2).

Sub-s (3ZA): inserted by the Finance Act 2013, s 219, Sch 46, Pt 2, paras 29, 38(1), (5), 72.

Sub-s (3A): inserted by the Finance Act 2008, s 25, Sch 7, Pt 1, paras 2, 30(1), (3).

[1.1380]

[413A Exception for payment of certain legal costs

(1) This Chapter does not apply to a payment which meets conditions A and B.

(2) Condition A is that the payment meets the whole or part of legal costs incurred by the employee exclusively in connection with the termination of the employee's employment.
(3) Condition B is that either—
(a) the payment is made pursuant to an order of a court or tribunal, or
(b) the termination of the employee's employment results in a [settlement] agreement between the employer and the employee and—
(i) the [settlement] agreement provides for the payment to be made by the employer, and
(ii) the payment is made directly to the employee's lawyer.
(4) In this section—
. . .
"lawyer" has the same meaning as "qualified lawyer" in section 203(4) of the Employment Rights Act 1996 or article 245(4) of the Employment Rights (Northern Ireland) Order 1996;
"legal costs" means fees payable for the services and disbursements of a lawyer.]

NOTES
Inserted by the Enactment of Extra-Statutory Concessions Order 2011, SI 2011/1037, art 10(1), (3), (4).
Sub-s (3): words in square brackets substituted by the Enactment of Extra-Statutory Concessions Order 2013, SI 2013/234, art 3(1)(a), (2).
Sub-s (4): definition "compromise agreement" (omitted) repealed by SI 2013/234, art 3(1)(b), (2).

[1.1381]
414 Reduction in other cases of foreign service
(1) This section applies if—
[(za) either—
(i) the payment or other benefit is within section 401(1)(a), and the employee or former employee is non-UK resident for the tax year in which the employment terminates, or
(ii) the payment or other benefit is within section 401(1)(b) or (c),]
(a) the service of the employee or former employee in the employment in respect of which the payment or other benefit is received includes foreign service, and
[(b) section 413(1) does not except the payment or other benefit from the application of this Chapter].
(2) The taxable person may claim relief in the form of a proportionate reduction of the amount that would [otherwise—
(a) be treated as earnings by section 402B(1), or
(b) count as employment income as a result of section 403].
(3) The proportion is that which the length of the foreign service bears to the whole length of service in the employment before the date of the termination or change in question.
(4) A person's entitlement to relief under this section is limited as mentioned in subsection (5) if the person is entitled—
(a) to deduct, retain or satisfy income tax out of a payment which the person is liable to make, or
(b) to charge any income tax against another person.
(5) The relief must not reduce the amount of income tax for which the person is liable below the amount the person is entitled so to deduct, retain, satisfy or charge.
(6) In this section "foreign service" has the same meaning as in section 413(2).

NOTES
Sub-s (1): para (za) inserted, and para (b) substituted, by the Finance Act 2018, s 10(1), (3), (5). These amendments have effect where the payment or other benefit is received after 13 September 2017 and the date of the termination or change in question is, or is after, 6 April 2018.
Sub-s (2): words in square brackets substituted by the Finance (No 2) Act 2017, s 5(1), (8), (10), with effect for the tax year 2018–19 and subsequent tax years.

[1.1382]
[414A Exception for payments and benefits under section 615(3) schemes
(1) This Chapter does not apply to a payment or other benefit provided in the form of a lump sum under a section 615(3) scheme.
(2) In this section, "section 615(3) scheme" means a superannuation fund to which section 615(3) of ICTA applies.]

NOTES
Inserted by the Enactment of Extra-Statutory Concessions Order 2014, SI 2014/211, arts 5(1), (3)(b), 6.

[1.1383]
[414B Exception in certain cases of foreign service as seafarer
(1) This section applies to a payment or other benefit if—
(a) the payment or other benefit is within section 401(1)(a), and
(b) the employee or former employee is UK resident for the tax year in which the employment terminates.
(2) This Chapter does not apply if the service of the employee or former employee in the employment in respect of which the payment or other benefit is received included foreign seafaring service comprising—
(a) three-quarters or more of the whole period of service ending with the date of the termination in question, or

(b) if the period of service ending with that date exceeded 10 years, the whole of the last 10 years, or

(c) if the period of service ending with that date exceeded 20 years, one-half or more of that period, including any 10 of the last 20 years.

(3) In subsection (2) "foreign seafaring service" means service to which subsection (4), (5) or (7) applies.

(4) This subsection applies to service in or after the tax year 2003–04 such that a deduction equal to the whole amount of the earnings from the employment was or would have been allowable under Chapter 6 of Part 5 (deductions from seafarers' earnings).

(5) This subsection applies to service before the tax year 2003–04 and after the tax year 1973–74 such that a deduction equal to the whole amount of the emoluments from the employment was or would have been allowable under a seafarers' earnings deduction provision.

(6) In subsection (5) "seafarers' earnings deduction provision" means—

(a) paragraph 1 of Schedule 2 to FA 1974 so far as relating to employment as a seafarer,

(b) paragraph 1 of Schedule 7 to FA 1977 so far as relating to employment as a seafarer,

(c) section 192A of ICTA, or

(d) section 193(1) of ICTA so far as relating to employment as a seafarer.

(7) This subsection applies to service before the tax year 1974–75 in an employment as a seafarer such that tax was not chargeable in respect of the emoluments of the employment—

(a) in the tax year 1956–57 or later, under Case I of Schedule E, or

(b) in earlier tax years, under Schedule E,

or it would not have been so chargeable had there been any such emoluments.

(8) In this section "employment as a seafarer" is to be read in accordance with section 384.]

NOTES

Commencement: see the note below.

Inserted by the Finance Act 2018, s 10(1), (4), (5).This amendment has effect where the payment or other benefit is received after 13 September 2017 and the date of the termination or change in question is, or is after, 6 April 2018.

FA 1974: Finance Act 1974.

FA 1977: Finance Act 1977.

ICTA: Income and Corporation Taxes Act 1988.

[1.1384]

[414C Reduction in other cases of foreign service as seafarer

(1) This section applies if—

(a) the payment or other benefit is within section 401(1)(a),

(b) the employee or former employee is UK resident for the tax year in which the employment terminates,

(c) the service of the employee or former employee in the employment in respect of which the payment or other benefit is received includes foreign service, and

(d) section 414B(2) does not except the payment or other benefit from the application of this Chapter.

(2) The taxable person may claim relief in the form of a proportionate reduction of the amount that would otherwise—

(a) be treated as earnings by section 402B(1), or

(b) count as employment income as a result of section 403.

(3) The proportion is that which the length of the foreign seafaring service bears to the whole length of service in the employment before the date of the termination in question.

(4) A person's entitlement to relief under this section is limited as mentioned in subsection (5) if the person is entitled—

(a) to deduct, retain or satisfy income tax out of a payment which the person is liable to make, or

(b) to charge any income tax against another person.

(5) The relief must not reduce the amount of income tax for which the person is liable below the amount the person is entitled so to deduct, retain, satisfy or charge.

(6) In this section "foreign seafaring service" has the same meaning as in section 414B(2).]

NOTES

Commencement: see the note below.

Inserted by the Finance Act 2018, s 10(1), (4), (5).This amendment has effect where the payment or other benefit is received after 13 September 2017 and the date of the termination or change in question is, or is after, 6 April 2018.

General and supplementary provisions

[1.1385]

415 Valuation of benefits

(1) In the case of a cash benefit, for the purposes of this Chapter the amount of a payment or other benefit is taken to be the amount received.

(2) In the case of a non-cash benefit, for the purposes of this Chapter the amount of a payment or other benefit is taken to be the greater of—

(a) the amount of earnings (as defined in Chapter 1 of Part 3) that the benefit would give rise to if it were received by an employee within section 15 for performance of the duties of an employment (money's worth), and

(b) the cash equivalent of the benefit under the benefits code if it were so received and the code applied to it.

(3) For the purposes of subsection (2), the benefits code has effect with the modifications in subsections (4), (6) and (7).
(4) References in the benefits code to the employee are to be taken as references to the taxable person and any other person by whom the benefit is received.
(5) For the purposes of subsection (4), section 401(4)(a) is to be disregarded.
(6) References in the benefits code to the employer are to be taken as including references to the former employer.
(7) Where—

(a) section 106 (cash equivalent: cost of accommodation over £75,000) applies, and
(b) the sum referred to in section 105(2)(b) (the sum made good) exceeds the amount referred to in section 105(2)(a) (the rental value),

the amount to be subtracted under paragraph (b) of step 4 of the calculation in section 106(2) is that excess (and not only the excess rent referred to there).

[1.1386]
416 Notional interest treated as paid if amount charged for beneficial loan
(1) This section applies if an amount ("the taxable amount") consisting of, or including, an amount representing the benefit of a loan counts as a person's employment income in a tax year under section 403.
(2) That person is to be treated for the purposes of the Tax Acts (other than this Chapter) as having paid interest on the loan in the tax year equal to the lesser of—

(a) the amount representing the cash equivalent of the loan, and
(b) the taxable amount.

(3) The interest is to be treated—

(a) as accruing during the period in the tax year during which the loan is outstanding, and
(b) as paid at the end of the period.

(4) The interest is not to be treated—

(a) as income of the person making the loan, or
(b) as relevant loan interest to which section 369 of ICTA applies (mortgage interest payable under deduction of tax).

PART 13
SUPPLEMENTARY PROVISIONS

Amendments, repeals, citation etc

[1.1387]
723 Commencement and transitional provisions and savings
(1) This Act comes into force on 6th April 2003 and has effect—

(a) for the purposes of income tax, for the tax year 2003–04 and subsequent tax years, and
(b) for the purposes of corporation tax, for accounting periods ending after 5th April 2003.

(2) Subsection (1) is subject to Schedule 7, which contains transitional provisions and savings.

[1.1388]
725 Citation
This Act may be cited as the Income Tax (Earnings and Pensions) Act 2003.

LOCAL GOVERNMENT ACT 2003

(2003 c 26)

An Act to make provision about finance, and other provision, in connection with local and certain other authorities; to provide for changing the dates of local elections in 2004; to amend the Audit Commission Act 1998; and for connected purposes

[18 September 2003]

NOTES

Most of this Act covers matters outside the scope of this work, and only those provisions most directly relevant to employment law are printed. For reasons of space, the subject matter of sections not printed is not annotated. All provisions of the Act printed here apply to England and Wales. Sections 101 and 102 also apply to Scotland subject to the making of a commencement order by the Scottish Ministers (see s 128(5)) but, as at 15 May 2019, no such order had been made.

The Code of Practice on Workforce Matters in Local Authority Service Contracts, which was given legislative status by ss 101, 102 of this Act, was revoked on 23 March 2011 with immediate effect. However, the Best Value Authorities Staff Transfers (Pensions) Direction 2007, made under ss 101 and 102, remains in place.

PART 8
MISCELLANEOUS AND GENERAL

CHAPTER 1 MISCELLANEOUS

Contracting-out

[1.1389]
101 Staff transfer matters: general

(1) In exercising a power to contract with a person for the provision of services, [a relevant authority] must—

(a) deal with matters affecting—
(i) who will be the employer of existing staff if a contract is entered into and carried out, or
(ii) what will be the terms and conditions of employment of existing staff, or the arrangements for their pensions, if their employer changes as a result of a contract being entered into and carried out,
in accordance with directions given to it by the appropriate person;
(b) have regard to guidance issued to it by the appropriate person on matters relating to the employment or pensions of existing staff.

(2) In subsection (1), references to existing staff, in relation to a contract for the provision of services, are to staff who before the contract is carried out are engaged in the provision of any of the services.

(3) Where the provision of any services under a contract with [a relevant authority] for their provision is to cease in circumstances where they are to be provided instead by members of the authority's staff, the authority shall comply with directions given to it by the appropriate person for the purpose of requiring it to offer employment to staff who, before the services cease to be provided under the contract, are engaged in the provision of any of the services.

(4) The duties under Part 1 of the Local Government Act 1999 (c 27) (best value) of a best value authority have effect subject to subsections (1) and (3).

(5) The duties under sections 1 and 2 of the Local Government in Scotland Act 2003 (asp 1) (best value) of a relevant authority have effect subject to subsections (1) and (3).

[(5A) The duties under Part 1 of the Local Government (Wales) Measure 2009 (local government improvement) have effect subject to subsections (1) and (3).]

(6) Directions given, or guidance issued, for the purposes of subsection (1) or (3)—
(a) may be addressed to—
(i) [all relevant authorities], or
(ii) authorities of a particular description;
(b) may be different for different cases or authorities.

[(7) . . .]

[(7A) In this section, in relation to England and Wales, "relevant authority" means—
(a) a best value authority;
[(aa) a Welsh improvement authority;]
(b) a parish council;
(c) a parish meeting of a parish which does not have a separate parish council; or
(d) a community council.]

(8) In this section[, in relation to Scotland]—
"appropriate person" . . . means the Scottish Ministers; and
"relevant authority" means—
(a) a council constituted under section 2 of the Local Government etc (Scotland) Act 1994 (c 39),
(b) the Strathclyde Passenger Transport Authority, or
(c) any other body to which Part 1 of the Local Government in Scotland Act 2003 (asp 1) (best value and accountability) applies.

NOTES

Commencement: 18 November 2003 (so far as relating to England and to a best value authority in Wales mentioned in sub-s (7)); 27 November 2003 (so far as relating to a best value authority in Wales, other than one mentioned in sub-s (7)); to be appointed (so far as relating to Scotland). Note that sub-s (7) has been repealed, see further the note below.

Sub-ss (1), (3), (6): words in square brackets substituted by the Local Government and Public Involvement in Health Act 2007, s 136(3), Sch 7, para 3(1), (9)(a), (b).

Sub-s (5A): inserted by the Local Government (Wales) Measure 2009, s 51(1), Sch 1, paras 23, 30(a).

Sub-s (7): substituted by the Local Government and Public Involvement in Health Act 2007, s 144(2), Sch 8, Pt 2, para 25(1), (4); repealed by the Police Reform and Social Responsibility Act 2011, s 99, Sch 16, Pt 3, paras 316, 321.

Sub-s (7A): inserted by the Local Government and Public Involvement in Health Act 2007, s 136(3), Sch 7, para 3(1), (9)(c); para (aa) inserted by the Local Government (Wales) Measure 2009, s 51(1), Sch 1, paras 23, 30(b).

Sub-s (8): words in square brackets inserted, and words omitted repealed, by the Local Government and Public Involvement in Health Act 2007, s 136(3), Sch 7, para 3(1), (9)(d).

See further, the final note at the beginning of this Act.

[1.1390]
102 Staff transfer matters: pensions

(1) The appropriate person shall exercise his power to give directions under section 101(1) so as to secure that where a local authority is contracting with a person ("the contractor") for the provision of services that are to be provided under a contract instead of by employees of the authority, it does so on terms—

(a) that require the contractor, in the event of there being any transferring employees, to secure pension protection for each of them, and
(b) that, so far as relating to the securing of pension protection for a transferring employee, are enforceable by the employee.

(2) For the purposes of subsection (1)—
(a) "transferring employee" means an employee of the authority whose contract of employment becomes, by virtue of the application of the TUPE regulations in relation to what is done for the purposes of carrying out the contract between the authority and the contractor, a contract of employment with someone other than the authority, and
(b) "pension protection" is secured for a transferring employee if after that change in his employer he has, as an employee of his new employer, rights to acquire pension benefits and those rights—
(i) are the same as, or
(ii) under the directions count as being broadly comparable to or better than,
those that he had as an employee of the authority.

(3) The appropriate person shall exercise his power to give directions under section 101(1) so as to secure that where—
(a) a local authority has contracted with a person ("the first contractor") for the provision of services,
(b) the application of the TUPE regulations in relation to what was done for the purposes of carrying out the contract between the authority and the first contractor resulted in employees of the authority ("the original employees") becoming employees of someone other than the authority, and
(c) the authority is contracting with a person ("the subsequent contractor") for the provision of any of the services,
the authority contracts with the subsequent contractor on terms satisfying the requirements of subsection (4).

(4) Those requirements are that the terms—
(a) require the subsequent contractor, in the event of there being any transferring original employees, to secure pension protection for each of them, and
(b) so far as relating to the securing of pension protection for an original employee, are enforceable by the employee.

(5) For the purposes of subsection (4)—
(a) "transferring original employee" means an original employee—
(i) whose contract of employment becomes, by virtue of the application of the TUPE regulations in relation to what is done for the purposes of carrying out the contract between the authority and the subsequent contractor, a contract of employment with someone other than his existing employer, and
(ii) whose contract of employment on each occasion when an intervening contract was carried out became, by virtue of the application of the TUPE regulations in relation to what was done for the purposes of carrying out the intervening contract, a contract of employment with someone other than his existing employer;
(b) "pension protection" is secured for a transferring original employee if after the change in his employer mentioned in paragraph (a)(i) he has, as an employee of his new employer, rights to acquire pension benefits and those rights—
(i) are the same as, or
(ii) under the directions count as being broadly comparable to or better than,
those that he had before that change.

(6) In subsection (5)(a)(ii), "intervening contract" means a contract with the authority for the provision, at times after they are provided under the contract with the first contractor and before they are to be provided under a contract with the subsequent contractor, of the services to be provided under the contract with the subsequent contractor.

(7) Any expression used in this section, and in the TUPE regulations, has in this section the meaning that it has in the TUPE regulations.

[(7A) In this section, in relation to England, "local authority" means—
(a) a county council in England, a district council, a London borough council, a parish council or a parish meeting of a parish which does not have a separate parish council;
(b) the Council of the Isles of Scilly;
(c) the Common Council of the City of London in its capacity as a local authority; and
(d) the Greater London Authority so far as it exercises its functions through the Mayor.

(7B) In this section, in relation to Wales, "local authority" means a county council, county borough council or community council in Wales.]

(8) In this section[, in relation to Scotland]—
"appropriate person" . . . means the Scottish Ministers;
"local authority"—
(a) . . .
(b) . . . means a council constituted under section 2 of the Local Government etc (Scotland) Act 1994 (c 39);

[(9) In this section,]
"the TUPE regulations" means the [Transfer of Undertakings (Protection of Employment) Regulations 2006], or any regulations replacing those regulations, as from time to time amended.

NOTES

Commencement: 27 November 2003 (in relation to Wales); 1 April 2004 (in relation to England); to be appointed (in relation to Scotland).

Sub-ss (7A), (7B): inserted by the Local Government and Public Involvement in Health Act 2007, s 136(3), Sch 7, para 3(1), (10).

Sub-s (8): words in square brackets inserted, and words omitted repealed, by the Local Government and Public Involvement in Health Act 2007, s 136(3), Sch 7, para 3(1), (11)(a)–(c).

Sub-s (9): numbered as such, and words "In this section," in square brackets inserted, by the Local Government and Public Involvement in Health Act 2007, s 136(3), Sch 7, para 3(1), (11)(d); words in square brackets in definition "the TUPE regulations" substituted by the Transfer of Undertakings (Protection of Employment) Regulations 2006, SI 2006/246, Sch 2, para 1(i).

See further, the final note at the beginning of this Act.

CHAPTER 2 GENERAL

[1.1391]

124 General interpretation

In this Act—

"appropriate person" means—

(a) in relation to England, the Secretary of State, and

(b) in relation to Wales, the National Assembly for Wales;

"best value authority" means an authority or body which is a best value authority for the purposes of Part 1 of the Local Government Act 1999 (c 27);

"financial year" means a period of 12 months beginning with 1st April;

. . .

["Welsh improvement authority" means an authority which is a Welsh improvement authority within the meaning of section 1 of the Local Government (Wales) Measure 2009].

NOTES

Definition "valuation tribunal" (omitted) repealed by the Local Government and Public Involvement in Health Act 2007, ss 220(1), 241, Sch 16, paras 10, 12, Sch 18, Pt 17.

Definition "Welsh improvement authority" inserted by the Local Government (Wales) Measure 2009, s 51(1), Sch 1, paras 23, 31.

[1.1392]

128 Commencement

(1) The following provisions shall come into force on the day on which this Act is passed—

(a) this section and sections 30, 34, 35, 72, 73, 103, 104, 110, 114, 121, 123, 124 and 129;

(b), (c) (*outside the scope of this work.*)

(2) (*Outside the scope of this work.*)

(3) The following provisions shall come into force on such day as the Secretary of State may by order appoint—

(a) (*outside the scope of this work*);

(b) section 101, so far as relating to England and so far as relating to a best value authority in Wales mentioned in subsection (7) of that section;

(c)–(f) (*outside the scope of this work.*)

(4) The following provisions shall come into force on such day as the National Assembly for Wales may by order appoint—

(a), (b) (*outside the scope of this work*);

(c) section 101, so far as relating to a best value authority in Wales, other than one mentioned in subsection (7) of that section;

(d)–(g) (*outside the scope of this work.*)

(5) So far as relating to Scotland, sections 101 and 102 shall come into force on such day as the Scottish Ministers may by order appoint.

(6) The remaining provisions of this Act—

(a) so far as relating to England, shall come into force on such day as the Secretary of State may by order appoint, and

(b) so far as relating to Wales, shall come into force on such day as the National Assembly for Wales may by order appoint.

(7) Power to make orders under this section is exercisable by statutory instrument.

(8) Orders under this section may make different provision for different purposes.

(9) A person who has power under this section to appoint a day for the coming into force of a provision may by order make in connection with the coming into force of that provision such transitional provision or saving as the person considers necessary or expedient.

NOTES

Orders: the commencement orders relevant to the sections reproduced here are the Local Government Act 2003 (Commencement No 1 and Transitional Provisions and Savings) Order 2003, SI 2003/2938, and the Local Government Act 2003 (Commencement) (Wales) Order 2003, SI 2003/3034.

[1.1393]
129 Short title and extent
(1) This Act may be cited as the Local Government Act 2003.
(2) Subject to the following provisions, this Act extends to England and Wales only.
(3) Sections 83(2), 101 and 102 extend also to Scotland.
(4) The following provisions extend also to Scotland, Northern Ireland and Gibraltar—
  (a) sections 103, 104 and 128,
  (b) this section, and
  (c) *(outside the scope of this work.)*
(5)–(8) *(Outside the scope of this work.)*

GENDER RECOGNITION ACT 2004

(2004 c 7)

An Act to make provision for and in connection with change of gender

[1 July 2004]

NOTES
Most of this Act covers matters outside the scope of this work, and only those provisions most directly relevant to employment law are printed. For reasons of space, the subject matter of sections not printed is not annotated. The provisions reproduced here apply to the whole of the United Kingdom (s 28). All provisions which did not come into force on Royal assent came into force on 4 April 2005 (see SI 2005/54).

Consequences of issue of gender recognition certificate etc

[1.1394]
9 General
(1) Where a full gender recognition certificate is issued to a person, the person's gender becomes for all purposes the acquired gender (so that, if the acquired gender is the male gender, the person's sex becomes that of a man and, if it is the female gender, the person's sex becomes that of a woman).
(2) Subsection (1) does not affect things done, or events occurring, before the certificate is issued; but it does operate for the interpretation of enactments passed, and instruments and other documents made, before the certificate is issued (as well as those passed or made afterwards).
(3) Subsection (1) is subject to provision made by this Act or any other enactment or any subordinate legislation.

[1.1395]
13 Social security benefits and pensions
Schedule 5 (entitlement to benefits and pensions) has effect.

SCHEDULES

SCHEDULE 5
BENEFITS AND PENSIONS

Section 13

PART 1
INTRODUCTORY

[1.1396]
1. This Schedule applies where a full gender recognition certificate is issued to a person.

PART 3
OCCUPATIONAL PENSION SCHEMES

[1.1397]
14 Guaranteed minimum pensions etc: Great Britain
(1) In this paragraph "the 1993 Act" means the Pension Schemes Act 1993 (c 48); and expressions used in this paragraph and in that Act have the same meaning in this paragraph as in that Act.
(2) The fact that the person's gender has become the acquired gender does not affect the operation of section 14 of the 1993 Act (guaranteed minimum) in relation to the person, except to the extent that its operation depends on section 16 of the 1993 Act (revaluation); and sub-paragraphs (3) and (5) have effect subject to that.
(3) If (immediately before the certificate is issued) the person is a woman who is entitled to a guaranteed minimum pension but has not attained the age of 65—
  (a) the person is for the purposes of section 13 of the 1993 Act and the guaranteed minimum pension provisions to be treated after it is issued as not having attained pensionable age (so that the entitlement ceases) but as attaining pensionable age on subsequently attaining the age of 65, and

(b) in a case where the person's guaranteed minimum pension has commenced before the certificate is issued, it is to be treated for the purposes of Chapter 3 of Part 4 of the 1993 Act (anti-franking) as if it had not.

(4) But sub-paragraph (3)(a) does not—

(a) affect any pension previously paid to the person, or

(b) prevent section 15 of the 1993 Act (increase of guaranteed minimum where commencement of guaranteed minimum pension postponed) operating to increase the person's guaranteed minimum by reason of a postponement of the commencement of the person's guaranteed minimum pension for a period ending before the certificate is issued.

(5) If (immediately before the certificate is issued) the person is a man who—

(a) has attained the age of 60, but

(b) has not attained the age of 65,

the person is to be treated for the purposes of section 13 of the 1993 Act and the guaranteed minimum pension provisions as attaining pensionable age when it is issued.

(6) If at that time the person has attained the age of 65, the fact that the person's gender has become the acquired gender does not affect the person's pensionable age for those purposes.

(7) The fact that the person's gender has become the acquired gender does not affect any guaranteed minimum pension to which the person is entitled as a widow or widower immediately before the certificate is issued (except in consequence of the operation of the previous provisions of this Schedule).

(8) If a transaction to which section 19 of the 1993 Act applies which is carried out before the certificate is issued discharges a liability to provide a guaranteed minimum pension for or in respect of the person, it continues to do so afterwards.

(9) "The guaranteed minimum pension provision" means so much of the 1993 Act (apart from section 13) and of any other enactment as relates to guaranteed minimum pensions.

15. *(Applies to Northern Ireland only.)*

16 Equivalent pension benefits: Great Britain

(1) The provision that may be made by regulations under paragraph 15 of Schedule 3 to the Social Security (Consequential Provisions) Act 1992 (c 6) (power to retain provisions repealed by Social Security Act 1973 (c 38), with or without modification, for transitional purposes) includes provision modifying the preserved equivalent pension benefits provisions in consequence of this Act.

(2) "The preserved equivalent pension benefits provisions" are the provisions of the National Insurance Act 1965 (c 51) relating to equivalent pension benefits continued in force, with or without modification, by regulations having effect as if made under that paragraph.

17. *(Applies to Northern Ireland only.)*

HIGHER EDUCATION ACT 2004

(2004 c 8)

An Act to make provision about research in the arts and humanities and about complaints by students against institutions providing higher education; to make provision about fees payable by students in higher education; to provide for the appointment of a Director of Fair Access to Higher Education; to make provision about grants and loans to students in higher or further education; to limit the jurisdiction of visitors of institutions providing higher education; and for connected purposes

[1 July 2004]

NOTES

Most of this Act covers matters outside the scope of this work, and only s 46 is reproduced here. For reasons of space, the subject matter of sections not printed is not annotated. Section 46 came into force on 1 January 2005 in relation to both England and Wales (see SI 2004/2781 and SI 2004/3144) and applies to England and Wales only (see s 53 (Extent)).

PART 5
MISCELLANEOUS AND GENERAL

Staff disputes: jurisdiction of visitor

[1.1398]

46 Exclusion of visitor's jurisdiction in relation to staff disputes

(1) The visitor of a qualifying institution has no jurisdiction in respect of—

(a) any dispute relating to a member of staff which concerns his appointment or employment or the termination of his appointment or employment,

(b) any other dispute between a member of staff and the qualifying institution in respect of which proceedings could be brought before any court or tribunal, or

(c) any dispute as to the application of the statutes or other internal laws of the institution in relation to a matter falling within paragraph (a) or (b).

(2) In subsection (1) "qualifying institution" has the meaning given by section 11.

(3) In determining whether a dispute falls within subsection (1)(b) it is to be assumed that the visitor does not have jurisdiction to determine the dispute.
(4) Section 206 of the Education Reform Act 1988 (c 40) (which is superseded by subsection (1)) shall cease to have effect.

NOTES

Note for the purposes of this section that s 11 of this Act in Pt 2 provides as follows; note also that paras (e), (f) were inserted by the Consumer Rights Act 2015, s 89(1), (2), as from 1 September 2015—

"11 Qualifying institutions

In this Part "qualifying institution" means any of the following institutions in England or Wales—

(a) a university (whether or not receiving financial support under section 65 of the 1992 Act) whose entitlement to grant awards is conferred or confirmed by—
  (i) an Act of Parliament,
  (ii) a Royal Charter, or
  (iii) an order under section 76 of the 1992 Act;
(b) a constituent college, school or hall or other institution of a university falling within paragraph (a);
(c) an institution conducted by a higher education corporation;
(d) a designated institution, as defined by section 72(3) of the 1992 Act;
[(e) an institution (other than one within another paragraph of this section) which provides higher education courses which are designated for the purposes of section 22 of the 1998 Act by or under regulations under that section;
(f) an institution (other than one within another paragraph of this section) whose entitlement to grant awards is conferred by an order under section 76(1) of the 1992 Act]."

Note also that s 11 is amended by the Higher Education and Research Act 2017, s 89(2), as from 1 April 2018 (in so far as relating to the amendments set out in sub-para (h)(ii) below and only in so far as relating to England), and as from a day to be appointed (otherwise), as follows—

"(a) in the words before paragraph (a), omit "in England or Wales",
(b) in the opening words of paragraph (a)—
  (i) after "university" insert "in England or Wales", and
  (ii) after "the 1992 Act" insert "or section 39 or 93 of the Higher Education and Research Act 2017 ("the 2017 Act")",
(c) in paragraph (a)(iii), after "the 1992 Act" insert "or section 42 or 45 of the 2017 Act",
(d) in paragraph (b), after "institution" insert "in England or Wales",
(e) in paragraph (c), after "institution" insert "in England or Wales",
(f) in paragraph (d), at beginning insert "an institution in Wales which is",
(g) after paragraph (d), insert—

"(da) an institution in England which is a registered higher education provider as defined by section 85 of the 2017 Act (other than one within paragraph (a), (b), (c) or (d) of this section);",

(h) in paragraph (e)—
  (i) after "institution" insert "in England or Wales", and
  (ii) for "another paragraph" substitute "any of the preceding paragraphs",
(i) after paragraph (e), insert—

"(ea) an institution in England (other than one within any of the preceding paragraphs of this section) which provides higher education courses leading to the grant of an award by or on behalf of—
  (i) another institution in England within another paragraph of this section, or
  (ii) the Office for Students where the grant is authorised by regulations under section 51(1) of the 2017 Act;", and

(j) in paragraph (f)—
  (i) after "institution" insert "in England or Wales", and
  (ii) after "the 1992 Act" insert "or section 42 or 45 of the 2017 Act".".

"The 1992 Act": the Further and Higher Education Act 1992 (see s 48 of this Act).
"The 1998 Act": the Teaching and Higher Education Act 1998 (see *ibid*).

GANGMASTERS (LICENSING) ACT 2004

(2004 c 11)

ARRANGEMENT OF SECTIONS

Scope of Act

Part 1 Statutes

An Act to make provision for the licensing of activities involving the supply or use of workers in connection with agricultural work, the gathering of wild creatures and wild plants, the harvesting of fish from fish farms, and certain processing and packaging; and for connected purposes

[8 July 2004]

1, 2 ((*The Gangmasters Licensing Authority) outside the scope of this work. See also the Immigration Act 2016, s 10 which renames the Gangmasters Licensing Authority as the Gangmasters and Labour Abuse Authority as from 12 July 2016.*)

Scope of Act

[1.1399]

3 Work to which this Act applies

(1) The work to which this Act applies is—

(a) agricultural work,
(b) gathering shellfish, and
(c) processing or packaging—
  (i) any produce derived from agricultural work, or
  (ii) shellfish, fish or products derived from shellfish or fish.

This is subject to any provision made by regulations under subsection (5) below and to section 5 (territorial scope of application).

(2) In subsection (1)(a) "agricultural work" means work in agriculture.

(3) In this Act "agriculture" includes—

(a) dairy-farming,
(b) the production for the purposes of any trade, business or other undertaking (whether carried on for profit or not) of consumable produce,
(c) the use of land as grazing, meadow or pasture land,
(d) the use of land as an orchard or as osier land or woodland, and
(e) the use of land for market gardens or nursery grounds.

In paragraph (b) "consumable produce" means produce grown for sale, consumption or other use after severance from the land on which it is grown.

(4) In this Act "shellfish" means crustaceans and molluscs of any kind, and includes any part of a shellfish and any (or any part of any) brood, ware, halfware or spat of shellfish, and any spawn of shellfish, and the shell, or any part of the shell, of a shellfish.

(5) The Secretary of State may by regulations make provision—

(a) excluding work of a prescribed description from being work to which this Act applies;
(b) including work of [a prescribed description as being work to which this Act applies]

[(6) The Secretary of State must consult the Authority and the Director of Labour Market Enforcement before making regulations under subsection (5).]

NOTES

Sub-s (5): words in square brackets substituted by the Immigration Act 2016, s 31, Sch 3, paras 13, 17(a), as from 12 July 2016.

Sub-s (6): added by the Immigration Act 2016, s 31, Sch 3, paras 13, 17(b), as from 12 July 2016.

Regulations: as of 15 May 2019, no Regulations had been made under this section.

[1.1400]

4 Acting as a gangmaster

(1) This section defines what is meant in this Act by a person acting as a gangmaster.

(2) A person ("A") acts as a gangmaster if he supplies a worker to do work to which this Act applies for another person ("B").

(3) For the purposes of subsection (2) it does not matter—

(a) whether the worker works under a contract with A or is supplied to him by another person,
(b) whether the worker is supplied directly under arrangements between A and B or indirectly under arrangements involving one or more intermediaries,
(c) whether A supplies the worker himself or procures that the worker is supplied,
(d) whether the work is done under the control of A, B or an intermediary,
(e) whether the work done for B is for the purposes of a business carried on by him or in connection with services provided by him to another person.

(4) A person ("A") acts as a gangmaster if he uses a worker to do work to which this Act applies in connection with services provided by him to another person.

(5) A person ("A") acts as a gangmaster if he uses a worker to do any of the following work to which this Act applies for the purposes of a business carried on by him—

(a) harvesting or otherwise gathering agricultural produce following—

(i) a sale, assignment or lease of produce to A, or

(ii) the making of any other agreement with A,

where the sale, assignment, lease or other agreement was entered into for the purpose of enabling the harvesting or gathering to take place;

(b) gathering shellfish;

(c) processing or packaging agricultural produce harvested or gathered as mentioned in paragraph (a).

In this subsection "agricultural produce" means any produce derived from agriculture.

(6) For the purposes of subsection (4) or (5) A shall be treated as using a worker to do work to which this Act applies if he makes arrangements under which the worker does the work—

(a) whether the worker works for A (or for another) or on his own account, and

(b) whether or not he works under a contract (with A or another).

(7) Regulations under section 3(5)(b) may provide for the application of subsections (5) and (6) above in relation to work that is work to which this Act applies by virtue of the regulations.

[1.1401]

5 Territorial scope of application

(1) The work to which this Act applies is work—

(a) in the United Kingdom,

(b) on any portion of the shore or bed of the sea, or of an estuary or tidal river, adjacent to the United Kingdom, whether above or below (or partly above and partly below) the low water mark, or

(c) in UK coastal waters.

(2) In subsection (1)(c) "UK coastal waters" means waters adjacent to the United Kingdom to a distance of six miles measured from the baselines from which the breadth of the territorial sea is measured.

In this subsection "miles" means international nautical miles of 1,852 metres.

(3) The provisions of this Act apply where a person acts as a gangmaster, whether in the United Kingdom or elsewhere, in relation to work to which this Act applies.

Licensing

[1.1402]

6 Prohibition of unlicensed activities

(1) A person shall not act as a gangmaster except under the authority of a licence.

(2) Regulations made by the Secretary of State may specify circumstances in which a licence is not required.

NOTES

Regulations: the Gangmasters Licensing (Exclusions) Regulations 2013, SI 2013/2216.

[1.1403]

7 Grant of licence

(1) The Authority may grant a licence if it thinks fit.

(2) A licence shall describe the activities authorised by it and shall be granted for such period as the Authority thinks fit.

(3) A licence authorises activities—

(a) by the holder of the licence, and

(b) by persons employed or engaged by the holder of the licence who are named or otherwise specified in the licence.

(4) In the case of a licence held otherwise than by an individual, the reference in subsection (3)(a) to activities by the holder of the licence shall be read as a reference only to such activities as are mentioned in whichever of the following provisions applies—

section 20(2) (body corporate);

section 21(2) (unincorporated association);

section 22(4) (partnership that is regarded as a legal person under the law of the country or territory under which it is formed).

(5) A licence shall be granted subject to such conditions as the Authority considers appropriate.

[1.1404]

8 General power of Authority to make rules

(1) The Authority may [with the approval of the Secretary of State] make such rules as it thinks fit in connection with the licensing of persons acting as gangmasters.

(2) The rules may, in particular—

(a) prescribe the form and contents of applications for licences and other documents to be filed in connection with applications;

(b) regulate the procedure to be followed in connection with applications and authorise the rectification of procedural irregularities;

(c) prescribe time limits for doing anything required to be done in connection with an application and provide for the extension of any period so prescribed;
(d) prescribe the requirements which must be met before a licence is granted;
(e) provide for the manner in which the meeting of those requirements is to be verified;
(f) allow for the grant of licences on a provisional basis before it is determined whether the requirements for the grant of a licence are met and for the withdrawal of such licences (if appropriate) if it appears that those requirements are not met;
(g) prescribe the form of licences and the information to be contained in them;
(h) require the payment of such fees as may be prescribed or determined in accordance with the rules;
(i) provide that licences are to be granted subject to conditions requiring the licence holder—
(i) to produce, in prescribed circumstances, evidence in a prescribed form of his being licensed, and
(ii) to comply with any prescribed requirements relating to the recruitment, use and supply of workers.

(3) . . .

(4) In subsection (2) "prescribed" means prescribed by the rules.

NOTES

The words in square brackets in sub-s (1) were inserted, and sub-s (3) was repealed, by the Immigration Act 2016, s 31, Sch 3, paras 13, 18, as from 12 July 2016.

Rules: the Gangmasters (Licensing Conditions) Rules 2009, SI 2009/307 at **[2.948]**.

[1.1405]

9 Modification, revocation or transfer of licence

(1) The Authority may by notice in writing to the licensee modify or revoke any licence granted to him (including any of the conditions of that licence)—
(a) with the consent of the licensee, or
(b) where it appears to him that a condition of the licence or any requirement of this Act has not been complied with.

(2) The modifications that may be made include one suspending the effect of the licence for such period as the Authority may determine.

(3) A licence may be transferred with the written consent of the Authority and in such other cases as may be determined by the Authority.

[1.1406]

10 Appeals

(1) The Secretary of State shall by regulations make provision for an appeal against any decision of the Authority—
(a) to refuse an application for a licence,
(b) as to the conditions to which the grant of the licence is subject,
(c) to refuse consent to the transfer of a licence, or
(d) to modify or revoke a licence.

(2) The regulations shall make provision—
(a) for and in connection with the appointment of a person to hear and determine such appeals (including provision for the payment of remuneration and allowances to such a person), and
(b) as to the procedure to be followed in connection with an appeal.

NOTES

Regulations: the Gangmasters (Appeals) Regulations 2006, SI 2006/662.

[1.1407]

11 Register of licences

(1) The Authority shall establish and maintain a register of persons licensed under this Act.

(2) The register shall contain such particulars as the Authority may determine of every person who for the time being holds a licence or whose activities are authorised by a licence (whether or not they are named in the licence).

(3) The Authority shall ensure that appropriate arrangements are in force for allowing members of the public to inspect the contents of the register.

Offences

[1.1408]

12 Offences: acting as a gangmaster, being in possession of false documents etc

(1) A person commits an offence if he acts as a gangmaster in contravention of section 6 (prohibition of unlicensed activities).

For this purpose a person acting as a gangmaster does not contravene section 6 by reason only of the fact that he breaches a condition of the licence which authorises him to so act.

(2) A person commits an offence if he has in his possession or under his control—
(a) a relevant document that is false and that he knows or believes to be false,
(b) a relevant document that was improperly obtained and that he knows or believes to have been improperly obtained, or
(c) a relevant document that relates to someone else,

with the intention of inducing another person to believe that he or another person acting as a gangmaster in contravention of section 6 is acting under the authority of a licence.

(3) A person guilty of an offence under subsection (1) or (2) is liable on summary conviction—

(a) in England and Wales, to imprisonment for a term not exceeding twelve months, or to a fine not exceeding the statutory maximum, or to both;

(b) in Scotland or Northern Ireland, to imprisonment for a term not exceeding six months, or to a fine not exceeding the statutory maximum, or to both.

In relation to an offence committed before the commencement of section 154(1) of the Criminal Justice Act 2003 (c 44), for "twelve months" in paragraph (a) substitute "six months".

(4) A person guilty of an offence under subsection (1) or (2) is liable on conviction on indictment to imprisonment for a term not exceeding ten years, or to a fine, or to both.

(5) For the purposes of this section—

(a) except in Scotland, a document is false only if it is false within the meaning of Part 1 of the Forgery and Counterfeiting Act 1981 (c 45) (see section 9(1) of that Act), and

(b) a document was improperly obtained if false information was provided, in or in connection with the application for its issue or an application for its modification, to the person who issued it or (as the case may be) to a person entitled to modify it,

and references to the making of a false document include references to the modification of a document so that it becomes false.

(6) In this section "relevant document" means—

(a) a licence, or

(b) any document issued by the Authority in connection with a licence.

[1.1409]
13 Offences: entering into arrangements with gangmasters

(1) A person commits an offence if—

(a) he enters into arrangements under which a person ("the gangmaster") supplies him with workers or services, and

(b) the gangmaster in supplying the workers or services contravenes section 6 (prohibition of unlicensed activities).

(2) In proceedings against a person for an offence under subsection (1) it is a defence for him to prove that he—

(a) took all reasonable steps to satisfy himself that the gangmaster was acting under the authority of a valid licence, and

(b) did not know, and had no reasonable grounds for suspecting that the gangmaster was not the holder of a valid licence.

(3) The Secretary of State may by regulations make provision as to what constitutes "reasonable steps" for the purposes of subsection (2)(a).

(4) A person guilty of an offence under subsection (1) is liable—

(a) on summary conviction in England and Wales, to imprisonment for a term not exceeding 51 weeks, or to a fine not exceeding the statutory maximum, or to both,

(b) on summary conviction in Scotland or Northern Ireland, to imprisonment for a term not exceeding six months, or to a fine not exceeding the statutory maximum, or to both.

In relation to an offence committed before the commencement of section 281(5) of the Criminal Justice Act 2003 (c 44), for "51 weeks" in paragraph (a) substitute "six months".

NOTES

Regulations: as of 15 May 2019, no Regulations had been made under sub-s (3).

[1.1410]
14 Offences: supplementary provisions

(1) An enforcement officer (see section 15) has the powers of arrest mentioned in subsection (2) (in addition to powers under [section 24A] of the Police and Criminal Evidence Act 1984 (c 60)) in relation to any of the following offences—

(a) an offence under section 12(1) or (2),

(b) conspiring to commit any such offence,

(c) attempting to commit any such offence,

(d) inciting, aiding, abetting, counselling or procuring the commission of any such offence.

(2) Those powers are as follows—

(a) if he has reasonable grounds for suspecting that such an offence has been committed, he may arrest without warrant anyone whom he has reasonable grounds for suspecting to be guilty of the offence;

(b) he may arrest without warrant—

(i) anyone who is about to commit such an offence;

(ii) anyone whom he has reasonable grounds for suspecting to be about to commit such an offence.

[(2A) Subsections (1) and (2) do not apply to an enforcement officer who is acting for the purposes of this Act in relation to England and Wales if the officer is a labour abuse prevention officer within the meaning of section 114B of the Police and Criminal Evidence Act 1984 (PACE powers for labour abuse prevention officers).]

(3) Subsections (1) and (2) do not apply in Scotland.

(4) (*Amends the Proceeds of Crime Act 2002, Schs 2, 4, 5.*)

NOTES

Sub-s (1): words in square brackets substituted by the Serious Organised Crime and Police Act 2005, s 111, Sch 7, Pt 4, para 62(a).

Sub-s (2A): inserted by the Immigration Act 2016, s 31, Sch 3, paras 13, 19, as from 12 July 2016.

Attempt, conspiracy or incitement to commit an offence: see the Serious Crime Act 2007, s 63(1), (2), Sch 6, Pt 1, para 50 which provides that any reference however expressed to (or to conduct amounting to) the offence abolished by s 59 of the 2007 Act (abolition of common law offence of inciting the commission of another offence) has effect as a reference to (or to conduct amounting to) the offences of encouraging or assisting the commission of an offence.

15–22 *(Ss 15–19 (Enforcement), ss 20–22 (supplementary) outside the scope of this work.)*

Miscellaneous and general

22A–25 *(S 22A (Relationship with other agencies, etc), s 23 (Annual report), s 24 (financial provision), s 25 (general provisions about the making of Regulations, etc) outside the scope of this work.)*

[1.1411]
26 Meaning of "worker"

(1) In this Act "worker" means an individual who does work to which this Act applies.

(2) A person is not prevented from being a worker for the purposes of this Act by reason of the fact that he has no right to be, or to work, in the United Kingdom.

[1.1412]
27 Exclusion of provisions relating to employment agencies and businesses

(1) The Employment Agencies Act 1973 (c 35) does not apply to an employment agency or an employment business in so far as it consists of activities for which a licence is required under this Act.

(2) In subsection (1) "employment agency" and "employment business" have the same meaning as in that Act.

28 (*(Application to Northern Ireland) Outside the scope of this work.*)

[1.1413]
29 Commencement and transitional provision

(1) The provisions of this Act come into force on such day as the Secretary of State may by order appoint.

(2) Different days may be appointed for different purposes and for different areas.

(3) The Secretary of State may by order make such transitional provision as he considers appropriate in connection with the coming into force of any provision of this Act.

NOTES

Commencement: to be appointed.

Orders: the Gangmasters (Licensing) Act 2004 (Commencement No 1) Order 2004, SI 2004/2857; the Gangmasters (Licensing) Act 2004 (Commencement No 2) Order 2005, SI 2005/447; the Gangmasters (Licensing) Act 2004 (Commencement No 3) Order 2006, SI 2006/2406; the Gangmasters (Licensing) Act 2004 (Commencement No 4) Order 2006, SI 2006/2906; the Gangmasters (Licensing) Act 2004 (Commencement No 5) Order 2007, SI 2007/695.

Note that this section has never technically been brought into force; for the statutory basis of orders made under a section not yet in force, see the Interpretation Act 1978, s 13 (anticipatory exercise of powers).

[1.1414]
30 Short title and extent

(1) This Act may be cited as the Gangmasters (Licensing) Act 2004.

(2) This Act extends to England and Wales, Scotland and Northern Ireland.

SCHEDULES 1 AND 2

(Sch 1 (Consequential amendments), Sch 2 (Application to Northern Ireland) outside the scope of this work.)

EMPLOYMENT RELATIONS ACT 2004

(2004 c 24)

An Act to amend the law relating to the recognition of trade unions and the taking of industrial action; to make provision about means of voting in ballots under the Trade Union and Labour Relations (Consolidation) Act 1992; to amend provisions of that Act relating to rights of members and non-members of trade unions and to make other provision about rights of trade union members, employees and workers; to make further provision concerning the enforcement of legislation relating to minimum wages; to make further provision about proceedings before and appeals from the Certification Officer; to make further provision about the amalgamation of trade unions; to make provision facilitating the administration of trade unions and the carrying out by them of their functions; and for connected purposes

[16 September 2004]

NOTES

Most of this Act consists of amendments to other Acts and, where relevant, they have been incorporated at the appropriate place. The rest of the Act is printed in full save for provisions that have been repealed and ss 43, 47, and 58 which are outside the scope of this work.

1–28 *(Pt 1 (ss 1–21: Union Recognition) inserts the Trade Union and Labour Relations (Consolidation) Act 1992, s 210A at* **[1.528]**, *and amends Sch A1 to the 1992 Act at* **[1.638]** *et seq; Pt 2 (ss 22–28: Law Relating to Industrial Action) contains various amendments to the 1992 Act (these amendments have been incorporated at the appropriate place.))*

PART 3
RIGHTS OF TRADE UNION MEMBERS, WORKERS AND EMPLOYEES

29–34 *(S 29 inserts the Trade Union and Labour Relations (Consolidation) Act 1992, s 145A–145F at* **[1.452]** *et seq; ss 30–34 contain various amendments to the 1992 Act (these amendments have been incorporated at the appropriate place) and repeal the Employment Relations Act 1999, s 17.)*

Other rights of workers and employees

35–41 *(Substitute the Trade Union and Labour Relations (Consolidation) Act 1992, s 154 at* **[1.466]**, *and amend ss 237, 238 of that Act at* **[1.568]**, **[1.569]**, *amend the Employment Tribunals Act 1996, ss 10, 21 at* **[1.745]**, **[1.764]**, *amend the Employment Relations Act 1999, ss 10–12, 23 at* **[1.1247]–[1.1249]**, **[1.1256]**, *insert the Employment Rights Act 1996, ss 43M, 98B at* **[1.879]**, **[1.1005]**, *amend ss 48, 105, 108, 194, 195, 199 of that Act at* **[1.894]**, **[1.1023]**, **[1.1026]**, **[1.1109]**, **[1.1110]**, **[1.1112]**, *and amended s 109 (repealed).)*

[1.1415]
42 Information and consultation: Great Britain

(1) The Secretary of State may make regulations for the purpose of conferring on employees of an employer to whom the regulations apply, or on representatives of those employees, rights—
- (a) to be informed by the employer about prescribed matters;
- (b) to be consulted by the employer about prescribed matters.

(2) Regulations made under subsection (1) must make provision as to the employers to whom the regulations apply which may include provision—
- (a) applying the regulations by reference to factors including the number of employees in the United Kingdom in the employer's undertaking;
- (b) as to the method by which the number of employees in an employer's undertaking is to be calculated; and
- (c) applying the regulations to different descriptions of employer with effect from different dates.

(3) Regulations made under subsection (1) may make provision—
- (a) as to the circumstances in which the rights mentioned in subsection (1) arise and the extent of those rights;
- (b) for and about the initiation and conduct of negotiations between employers to whom the regulations apply and their employees for the purposes of reaching an agreement satisfying prescribed conditions about the provision of information to the employees, and consultation of them (whether that provision or consultation is to be direct or through representatives);
- (c) about the representatives the employees may have for the purposes of the regulations and the method by which those representatives are to be selected;
- (d) as to the resolution of disputes and the enforcement of obligations imposed by the regulations or by an agreement of the kind mentioned in paragraph (b).

(4) Regulations made under subsection (1) may—
- (a) confer jurisdiction (including exclusive jurisdiction) on employment tribunals and on the Employment Appeal Tribunal;
- (b) confer functions on the Central Arbitration Committee;
- (c) require or authorise the holding of ballots;
- (d) amend, apply with or without modifications, or make provision similar to any provision of the Employment Rights Act 1996 (c 18) (including, in particular, Parts 5, 10 and 13), the Employment Tribunals Act 1996 (c 17) or the 1992 Act;
- (e) include supplemental, incidental, consequential and transitional provision, including provision amending any enactment;
- (f) make different provision for different cases or circumstances.

(5) Regulations made under subsection (1) may make any provision which appears to the Secretary of State to be necessary or expedient—
- *(a) for the purpose of implementing Directive 2002/14/EC of the European Parliament and of the Council of 11 March 2002 establishing a general framework for informing and consulting employees in the European Community;*
- *(b) for the purpose of dealing with any matter arising out of or related to the United Kingdom's obligations under that Directive.*

(6) Nothing in subsections *(2) to (5)* prejudices the generality of this section.

(7) Regulations under this section shall be made by statutory instrument.
(8) No such regulations may be made unless a draft of the regulations has been laid before Parliament and approved by a resolution of each House of Parliament.
(9) In this section "prescribed" means prescribed by regulations under this section.

NOTES

Sub-s (5): repealed by the Employment Rights (Amendment) (EU Exit) Regulations 2019, SI 2019/535, reg 2(1), Sch 1, Pt 1, para 6(a), as from exit day (as defined in the European Union (Withdrawal) Act 2018, s 20) and subject to savings in Sch 1, Pt 3, para 22 thereto, which provides that the repeal does not affect the validity of any regulations made under this section that came into force before exit day.

Sub-s (6): for the words in italics there are substituted the words "(2) to (4)" by SI 2019/535, reg 2(1), Sch 1, Pt 1, para 6(b), as from exit day (as defined in the European Union (Withdrawal) Act 2018, s 20) and subject to savings as noted above.

Regulations: the Information and Consultation of Employees Regulations 2004, SI 2004/3426 at **[2.768]**; the Information and Consultation of Employees (Amendment) Regulations 2006, SI 2006/514; the Seafarers (Insolvency, Collective Redundancies and Information and Consultation Miscellaneous Amendments) Regulations 2018, SI 2018/407 at **[2.2050]**.

43–51 *(S 43 (Information and consultation: Northern Ireland) outside the scope of this work; ss 44–47 (Pt 4 Enforcement of Minimum Wage Legislation) are as follows: s 44 inserts the National Minimum Wage Act 1998,s 16A at* **[1.1184]**; *ss 45, 46 repealed by the Employment Act 2008, s 20, Schedule, Pt 2; s 47 contains miscellaneous amendments to agricultural wages legislation that are outside the scope of this work; ss 48–51 (Pt 5 The Certification Officer) insert the Trade Union and Labour Relations (Consolidation) Act 1992, ss 101A, 101B, 256ZA at* **[1.409]**, **[1.410]**, **[1.592]**, *contain various other amendments to the 1992 Act (incorporated as appropriate), and amend the Employment Tribunals Act 1996, ss 33, 42 at* **[1.778]**, **[1.807]**.)

PART 6
MISCELLANEOUS

52, 53 *(Amend the Trade Union and Labour Relations (Consolidation) Act 1992, ss 34, 36, 37, 46 at* **[1.319]**, **[1.321]**, **[1.322]**, **[1.340]**.)

[1.1416]

54 Means of voting in ballots and elections

(1) The Secretary of State may by order provide, in relation to any description of ballot or election authorised or required by the 1992 Act, that any ballot or election of that description is to be conducted by such one or more permissible means as the responsible person determines.
(2) A "permissible means" is a means of voting that the order provides is permissible for that description of ballot or election.
(3) "The responsible person" is a person specified, or of a description specified, by the order.
(4) An order under this section may—
- (a) include provision about the determinations that may be made by the responsible person, including provision requiring specified factors to be taken into account, or specified criteria to be applied, in making a determination;
- (b) allow the determination of different means of voting for voters in different circumstances;
- (c) allow a determination to be such that voters have a choice of means of voting.

(5) The means that an order specifies as permissible means must, in the case of any description of ballot or election, include (or consist of) postal voting.
(6) An order under this section may—
- (a) include supplemental, incidental and consequential provisions;
- (b) make different provision for different cases or circumstances.

(7) An order under this section may—
- (a) modify the provisions of the 1992 Act;
- (b) exclude or apply (with or without modifications) any provision of that Act;
- (c) make provision as respects any ballot or election conducted by specified means which is similar to any provision of that Act relating to ballots or elections.

(8) The power to make an order under this section is exercisable by statutory instrument.
(9) No order may be made under this section unless a draft of the order has been laid before Parliament and approved by a resolution of each House.
(10) The Secretary of State shall not make an order under this section which provides that a means of voting is permissible for a description of ballot or election unless he considers—
- (a) that a ballot or election of that description conducted by that means could, if particular conditions were satisfied, meet the required standard; and
- (b) that, in relation to any ballot or election of that description held after the order comes into force, the responsible person will not be permitted to determine that that means must or may be used by any voters unless he has taken specified factors into account or applied specified criteria.

(11) In specifying in an order under this section factors to be taken into account or criteria to be applied by the responsible person, the Secretary of State must have regard to the need for ballots and elections to meet the required standard.
(12) For the purposes of subsections (10) and (11) a ballot or election meets "the required standard" if it is such that—
- (a) those entitled to vote have an opportunity to do so;
- (b) votes cast are secret;
- (c) the risk of any unfairness or malpractice is minimised.

(13) In this section "specified" means specified in an order under this section.

NOTES

Orders: as of 15 May 2019, no Orders had been made under this section.

55 (*Inserts the Trade Union and Labour Relations (Consolidation) Act 1992, ss 116A, 118(8) at* **[1.421]**, **[1.424]**.)

PART 7
SUPPLEMENTARY PROVISIONS

[1.1417]

56 Meaning of "the 1992 Act"

In this Act "the 1992 Act" means the Trade Union and Labour Relations (Consolidation) Act 1992 (c 52).

57, 58 (*S 57 introduces Schs 1, 2 (Minor and consequential amendments and repeals); s 58 (Corresponding provision for Northern Ireland) outside the scope of this work.*)

[1.1418]

59 Citation, commencement and extent

(1) This Act may be cited as the Employment Relations Act 2004.

(2) This section and sections 42, 43, 56 and 58 shall come into force on the day on which this Act is passed.

(3) The other provisions of this Act shall not come into force until such day as the Secretary of State may by order made by statutory instrument appoint, and different days may be appointed for different purposes.

(4) An order under subsection (3) may contain such transitional provisions and savings as the Secretary of State considers necessary or expedient in connection with the coming into force of any of the provisions of this Act.

(5) Subject to subsections (6) and (7), this Act extends to England and Wales and to Scotland.

(6) Any amendment by this Act of an enactment (including an enactment contained in Northern Ireland legislation) has the same extent as the enactment amended.

(7) Sections 43 and 58 extend to Northern Ireland only.

NOTES

Orders: the Employment Relations Act 2004 (Commencement No 1 and Transitional Provisions) Order 2004, SI 2004/2566; the Employment Relations Act 2004 (Commencement No 2 and Transitional Provisions) Order 2004, SI 2004/3342; the Employment Relations Act 2004 (Commencement No 3 and Transitional Provisions) Order 2005, SI 2005/872; the Employment Relations Act 2004 (Commencement No 4 and Transitional Provisions) Order 2005, SI 2005/2419.

SCHEDULES 1, 2

(*Schs 1, 2 contain minor and consequential amendments and repeals; in so far as these are relevant to this work, they have been taken in at the appropriate place.*)

PENSIONS ACT 2004

(2004 c 35)

ARRANGEMENT OF SECTIONS

PART 5
OCCUPATIONAL AND PERSONAL PENSION SCHEMES: MISCELLANEOUS PROVISIONS

Requirements for member-nominated trustees and directors

Pension protection on transfer of employment

Consultation by employers

PART 9
MISCELLANEOUS AND SUPPLEMENTARY

Miscellaneous and Supplementary

An Act to make provision relating to pensions and financial planning for retirement and provision relating to entitlement to bereavement payments, and for connected purposes

[18 November 2004]

NOTES

Most of this Act covers matters outside the scope of this work, and only those provisions most directly relevant to employment law are printed. For reasons of space, the subject matter of sections not printed is not annotated. The substantive provisions reproduced here apply to Great Britain only (s 323), and came into force in accordance with provision made by the Secretary of State by order (s 322(1)).

See *Harvey* BI(9), F2(F).

PART 5
OCCUPATIONAL AND PERSONAL PENSION SCHEMES: MISCELLANEOUS PROVISIONS

Requirements for member-nominated trustees and directors

[1.1419]

241 Requirement for member-nominated trustees

(1) The trustees of an occupational trust scheme must secure—

(a) that, within a reasonable period of the commencement date, arrangements are in place which provide for at least one-third of the total number of trustees to be member-nominated trustees, and

(b) that those arrangements are implemented.

(2) "Member-nominated trustees" are trustees of an occupational trust scheme who—

(a) are nominated as the result of a process in which at least the following are eligible to participate—

(i) all the active members of the scheme or an organisation which adequately represents the active members, and

(ii) all the pensioner members of the scheme or an organisation which adequately represents the pensioner members, and

(b) are selected as a result of a process which involves some or all of the members of the scheme.

(3) The "commencement date", in relation to a scheme, is—

(a) the date upon which this section first applies in relation to the scheme, or

(b) in the case of a scheme to which this section has ceased to apply and then reapplies, the date on which the section reapplies to it.

(4) The arrangements may provide for a greater number of member-nominated trustees than that required to satisfy the one-third minimum mentioned in subsection (1)(a) only if the employer has approved the greater number.

(5) The arrangements—

(a) must provide for the nomination and selection process to take place within a reasonable period of any requirement arising under the arrangements to appoint a member-nominated trustee,

(b) must provide, where a vacancy is not filled because insufficient nominations are received, for the nomination and selection process to be repeated at reasonable intervals until the vacancy is filled,

(c) must provide that where the employer so requires, a person who is not a member of the scheme must have the employer's approval to qualify for selection as a member-nominated trustee, and

(d) subject to paragraph (c), may provide that, where the number of nominations received is equal to or less than the number of appointments required, the nominees are deemed to be selected.

(6) The arrangements must provide that the removal of a member-nominated trustee requires the agreement of all the other trustees.

(7) Nothing in the arrangements or in the provisions of the scheme may exclude member-nominated trustees from the exercise of functions exercisable by other trustees by reason only of the fact that they are member-nominated trustees.

(8) This section does not apply in relation to an occupational trust scheme if—

(a) every member of the scheme is a trustee of the scheme and no other person is such a trustee,

(b) every trustee of the scheme is a company, or

(c) the scheme is of a prescribed description.

(9) If, in the case of an occupational trust scheme, the arrangements required by subsection (1)—

(a) are not in place as required by subsection (1)(a), or

(b) are not being implemented,

section 10 of the Pensions Act 1995 (c 26) (civil penalties) applies to any trustee who has failed to take all reasonable steps to secure compliance.

NOTES

Regulations: the Occupational Pension Schemes (Member-nominated Trustees and Directors) Regulations 2006, SI 2006/714 (reg 5 of which modifies this section and s 242 in respect of schemes whose existing scheme rules require a higher proportion of trustees or directors to be member-nominated; it also provides for transitional provisions for schemes that were exempted under the Occupational Pension Schemes (Member-nominated Trustees and Directors) Regulations 1996 (SI 1996/1216)); the Occupational and Personal Pension Schemes (Miscellaneous Amendments) Regulations 2007, SI 2007/814; the Occupational Pension Schemes (Scottish Parliamentary Pensions Act 2009) Regulations 2009, SI 2009/1906.

[1.1420]
242 Requirement for member-nominated directors of corporate trustees

(1) Where a company is a trustee of an occupational trust scheme and every trustee of the scheme is a company, the company must secure—

(a) that, within a reasonable period of the commencement date, arrangements are in place which provide for at least one-third of the total number of directors of the company to be member-nominated directors, and

(b) that those arrangements are implemented.

(2) "Member-nominated directors" are directors of the company in question who—

(a) are nominated as the result of a process in which at least the following are eligible to participate—

(i) all the active members of the occupational trust scheme or an organisation which adequately represents the active members, and

(ii) all the pensioner members of the occupational trust scheme or an organisation which adequately represents the pensioner members, and

(b) are selected as a result of a process which involves some or all of the members of that scheme.

(3) The "commencement date", in relation to a company, is—

(a) the date upon which this section first applies in relation to the company, or

(b) in the case of a company to which this section has ceased to apply and then reapplies, the date on which the section reapplies to it.

(4) The arrangements may provide for a greater number of member-nominated directors than that required to satisfy the one-third minimum mentioned in subsection (1)(a) only if the employer has approved the greater number.

(5) The arrangements—

(a) must provide for the nomination and selection process to take place within a reasonable period of any requirement arising under the arrangements to appoint a member-nominated director,

(b) must provide, where a vacancy is not filled because insufficient nominations are received, for the nomination and selection process to be repeated at reasonable intervals until the vacancy is filled,

(c) must provide that where the employer so requires, a person who is not a member of the scheme must have the employer's approval to qualify for selection as a member-nominated director, and

(d) subject to paragraph (c), may provide that, where the number of nominations received is equal to or less than the number of appointments required, the nominees are deemed to be selected.

(6) The arrangements must provide that the removal of a member-nominated director requires the agreement of all the other directors.

(7) Nothing in the arrangements may exclude member-nominated directors from the exercise of functions exercisable by other directors by reason only of the fact that they are member-nominated directors.

(8) Where the same company is a trustee of two or more occupational trust schemes by reference to each of which this section applies to the company, then, subject to subsection (9), the preceding provisions of this section have effect as if—

(a) the schemes were a single scheme,

(b) the members of each of the schemes were members of that single scheme, and

(c) the references to "the employer" were references to all the employers in relation to the schemes.

(9) Where, apart from this subsection, subsection (8) would apply in relation to a company, the company may elect that subsection (8)—

(a) is not to apply as mentioned in that subsection, or

(b) is to apply but only in relation to some of the schemes to which it would otherwise apply.

(10) This section does not apply in relation to an occupational trust scheme if the scheme is of a prescribed description.

(11) If, in the case of a company which is a trustee of an occupational trust scheme, the arrangements required by subsection (1)—

(a) are not in place as required by subsection (1)(a), or

(b) are not being implemented,

section 10 of the Pensions Act 1995 (c 26) (civil penalties) applies to the company.

NOTES

Regulations: the Occupational Pension Schemes (Member-nominated Trustees and Directors) Regulations 2006, SI 2006/714 (see the note to s 241 *ante*); the Occupational and Personal Pension Schemes (Miscellaneous Amendments) Regulations 2007, SI 2007/814; the Occupational, Personal and Stakeholder Pensions (Miscellaneous Amendments) Regulations 2009, SI 2009/615.

[1.1421]
243 Member-nominated trustees and directors: supplementary

(1) The Secretary of State may, by order, amend sections 241(1)(a) and (4) and 242(1)(a) and (4) by substituting, in each of those provisions, "one-half" for "one-third".

(2) Regulations may modify sections 241 and 242 (including any of the provisions mentioned in subsection (1)) in their application to prescribed cases.

(3) In sections 241 and 242—

"company" means a company [as defined in section 1(1) of the Companies Act 2006] or a company which may be wound up under Part 5 of the Insolvency Act 1986 (c 45) (unregistered companies);

"occupational trust scheme" means an occupational pension scheme established under a trust.

NOTES

Sub-s (3): words in square brackets in the definition "company" substituted by the Companies Act 2006 (Consequential Amendments, Transitional Provisions and Savings) Order 2009, SI 2009/1941, art 2(1), Sch 1, para 243(1), (9).

Regulations: the Occupational Pension Schemes (Member-nominated Trustees and Directors) Regulations 2006, SI 2006/714 (see the note to s 241 *ante*); the Occupational, Personal and Stakeholder Pensions (Miscellaneous Amendments) Regulations 2009, SI 2009/615.

Pension protection on transfer of employment

[1.1422]

257 Conditions for pension protection

(1) This section applies in relation to a person ("the employee") where—

[(a) there is a relevant transfer within the meaning of the TUPE regulations,]

(b) by virtue of the transfer the employee ceases to be employed by the transferor and becomes employed by the transferee, and

(c) at the time immediately before the employee becomes employed by the transferee—

(i) there is an occupational pension scheme ("the scheme") in relation to which the transferor is the employer, and

(ii) one of subsections (2), (3) and (4) applies.

(2) This subsection applies where—

(a) the employee is an active member of the scheme, and

(b) if any of the benefits that may be provided under the scheme are money purchase benefits—

(i) the transferor is required to make contributions to the scheme in respect of the employee, or

(ii) the transferor is not so required but has made one or more such contributions.

(3) This subsection applies where—

(a) the employee is not an active member of the scheme but is eligible to be such a member, and

(b) if any of the benefits that may be provided under the scheme are money purchase benefits, the transferor would have been required to make contributions to the scheme in respect of the employee if the employee had been an active member of it.

(4) This subsection applies where—

(a) the employee is not an active member of the scheme, nor eligible to be such a member, but would have been an active member of the scheme or eligible to be such a member if, after the date on which he became employed by the transferor, he had been employed by the transferor for a longer period, and

(b) if any of the benefits that may be provided under the scheme are money purchase benefits, the transferor would have been required to make contributions to the scheme in respect of the employee if the employee had been an active member of it.

(5) For the purposes of this section, the condition in subsection (1)(c) is to be regarded as satisfied in any case where it would have been satisfied but for any action taken by the transferor by reason of the transfer.

(6), (7) . . .

(8) In this section—

the "TUPE Regulations" means the [Transfer of Undertakings (Protection of Employment) Regulations 2006];

references to the transferor include any associate of the transferor, and section 435 of the Insolvency Act 1986 (c 45) applies for the purposes of this section as it applies for the purposes of that Act.

NOTES

Sub-s (1): para (a) substituted by the Transfer of Undertakings (Protection of Employment) Regulations 2006, SI 2006/246, reg 20(3), Sch 2, paras 13(1), (2).

Sub-s (6): repealed by SI 2006/246, reg 20(3), Sch 2, paras 13(1), (3).

Sub-s (7): repealed by the Pensions Act 2007, ss 15(3)(a), 27(2), Sch 4, Pt 1, para 41, Sch 7, Pt 6.

Sub-s (8): words in square brackets in the definition "TUPE Regulations" substituted by SI 2006/246, reg 20(3), Sch 2, paras 13(1), (4).

Note: as to the application of this section to certain specified banks, see the Banking (Special Provisions) Act 2008, the Banking Act 2009, and Orders made under those Acts.

[1.1423]

258 Form of protection

(1) In a case where section 257 applies, it is a condition of the employee's contract of employment with the transferee that the requirements in subsection (2) or the requirement in subsection (3) are complied with.

(2) The requirements in this subsection are that—

(a) the transferee secures that, as from the relevant time, the employee is, or is eligible to be, an active member of an occupational pension scheme in relation to which the transferee is the employer, and

(b) in a case where the scheme is a *money purchase scheme*, as from the relevant time—

(i) the transferee makes relevant contributions to the scheme in respect of the employee, or
(ii) if the employee is not an active member of the scheme but is eligible to be such a member, the transferee would be required to make such contributions if the employee were an active member, and

(c) in a case where the scheme is not a *money purchase scheme*, as from the relevant time the scheme [complies with prescribed requirements]

(3) The requirement in this subsection is that, as from the relevant time, the transferee makes relevant contributions to a stakeholder pension scheme of which the employee is a member.

(4) The requirement in subsection (3) is for the purposes of this section to be regarded as complied with by the transferee during any period in relation to which the condition in subsection (5) is satisfied.

(5) The condition in this subsection is that the transferee has offered to make relevant contributions to a stakeholder pension scheme of which the employee is eligible to be a member (and the transferee has not withdrawn the offer).

(6) Subsection (1) does not apply in relation to a contract if or to the extent that the employee and the transferee so agree at any time after the time when the employee becomes employed by the transferee.

(7) In this section—

"the relevant time" means—

(a) in a case where section 257 applies by virtue of the application of subsection (2) or (3) of that section, the time when the employee becomes employed by the transferee;
(b) in a case where that section applies by virtue of the application of subsection (4) of that section, the time at which the employee would have been a member of the scheme referred to in subsection (1)(c)(i) of that section or (if earlier) would have been eligible to be such a member;

"relevant contributions" means such contributions in respect of such period or periods as may be prescribed;

"stakeholder pension scheme" means a pension scheme which is registered under section 2 of the Welfare Reform and Pensions Act 1999 (c 30).

NOTES

Sub-s (2) is amended as follows:

For the words "money purchase scheme" in italics in paras (b) and (c) there are substituted the words "scheme under which all the benefits that may be provided are money purchase benefits" by the Pension Schemes Act 2015, s 46, Sch 2, paras 23, 34, as from a day to be appointed.

Words "complies with prescribed requirements" in square brackets in para (c) substituted by the Pensions Act 2014, s 24(1), Sch 13, Pt 2, para 73, as from 6 April 2016.

Note: as to the application of this section to certain specified banks, see the Banking (Special Provisions) Act 2008, the Banking Act 2009, and Orders made under those Acts.

Regulations: the Transfer of Employment (Pension Protection) Regulations 2005, SI 2005/649 at **[2.838]**; the Occupational Pension Schemes (Miscellaneous Amendments) Regulations 2014, SI 2014/540.

Consultation by employers

[1.1424]

259 Consultation by employers: occupational pension schemes

(1) Regulations may require any prescribed person who is the employer in relation to an occupational pension scheme and who—

(a) proposes to make a prescribed decision in relation to the scheme, or
(b) has been notified by the trustees or managers of the scheme that they propose to make a prescribed decision in relation to the scheme,

to consult prescribed persons in the prescribed manner before the decision is made.

(2) Regulations may require the trustees or managers of an occupational pension scheme not to make a prescribed decision in relation to the scheme unless—

(a) they have notified the employer of the proposed decision, and
(b) they are satisfied that the employer has undertaken any consultation required by virtue of subsection (1).

(3) The validity of any decision made in relation to an occupational pension scheme is not affected by any failure to comply with regulations under this section.

(4) Section 261 contains further provisions about regulations under this section.

NOTES

Multi-employer Schemes: this section and s 261 are modified, in relation to multi-employer schemes, by the Occupational Pension Schemes (Consultation by Employers) (Modification for Multi-employer Schemes) Regulations 2006, SI 2006/16, reg 2, so that any reference in those sections to the trustees or managers of an occupational pension scheme is to be treated as if it included a reference to any other person who under the rules of a multi-employer scheme has power to make a decision in relation to the scheme.

Regulations: the Occupational and Personal Pension Schemes (Consultation by Employers and Miscellaneous Amendment) Regulations 2006, SI 2006/349 at **[2.890]**; the Occupational and Personal Pension Schemes (Miscellaneous Amendments) Regulations 2006, SI 2006/778; the Occupational and Personal Pension Schemes (Miscellaneous Amendments) Regulations 2007, SI 2007/814; the Occupational and Personal Pension Schemes (Miscellaneous Amendments) Regulations 2010, SI 2010/499; the Occupational and Personal Pension Schemes (Miscellaneous Amendments) Regulations 2011, SI 2011/672; the Pensions (Institute and Faculty of Actuaries and Consultation by Employers—Amendment) Regulations 2012, SI 2012/692; the Occupational Pension Schemes (Charges and Governance) Regulations 2015, SI 2015/879; the Occupational and Personal Pension Schemes (Modification of Schemes—Miscellaneous Amendments) Regulations 2016, SI 2016/231.

[1.1425]

260 Consultation by employers: personal pension schemes

(1) Regulations may require any prescribed person who—

- (a) is the employer in relation to a personal pension scheme where direct payment arrangements exist in respect of one or more members of the scheme who are his employees, and
- (b) proposes to make a prescribed decision affecting the application of the direct payment arrangements in relation to those employees,

to consult prescribed persons in the prescribed manner before he makes the decision.

(2) The validity of any decision prescribed for the purposes of subsection (1)(b) is not affected by any failure to comply with regulations under this section.

(3) Section 261 contains further provisions about regulations under this section.

NOTES

Regulations: the Occupational and Personal Pension Schemes (Consultation by Employers and Miscellaneous Amendment) Regulations 2006, SI 2006/349 at **[2.890]**; the Occupational and Personal Pension Schemes (Miscellaneous Amendments) Regulations 2006, SI 2006/778; the Occupational and Personal Pension Schemes (Miscellaneous Amendments) Regulations 2011, SI 2011/672; the Pensions (Institute and Faculty of Actuaries and Consultation by Employers—Amendment) Regulations 2012, SI 2012/692.

[1.1426]

261 Further provisions about regulations relating to consultation

(1) In this section "consultation regulations" means regulations under section 259 or 260.

(2) Consultation regulations may—

- (a) make provision about the time to be allowed for consultation;
- (b) prescribe the information which must be provided to the persons who are required to be consulted;
- (c) confer a discretion on the employer in prescribed cases as to the persons who are to be consulted;
- (d) make provision about the representatives the employees may have for the purposes of the regulations and the methods by which those representatives are to be selected;
- (e) require or authorise the holding of ballots;
- (f) amend, apply with or without modifications, or make provision similar to, any provision of the Employment Rights Act 1996 (c 18) (including, in particular, Parts 5, 10 and 13), the Employment Tribunals Act 1996 (c 17) or the Trade Union and Labour Relations (Consolidation) Act 1992 (c 52);
- (g) enable any requirement for consultation imposed by the regulations to be waived or relaxed by order of the Regulator;
- (h) require the employer to communicate to the trustees and managers of the scheme any representations received by the employer in response to any consultation required by the regulations.

(3) Persons on whom obligations are imposed by consultation regulations, either as employers or as the trustees or managers of occupational pension schemes, must, if so required by the Regulator, provide information to the Regulator about the action taken by them for the purpose of complying with the regulations.

(4) Consultation regulations may make provision as to—

- (a) the information to be provided under subsection (3);
- (b) the form and manner in which the information is to be provided;
- (c) the period within which the information is to be provided.

(5) Nothing in consultation regulations is to be regarded as affecting any duty to consult arising otherwise than under the regulations.

NOTES

Multi-employer Schemes: see the note to s 259 at **[1.1424]**.

Regulations under ss 259 or 260: see those sections *ante*.

PART 9
MISCELLANEOUS AND SUPPLEMENTARY

Miscellaneous and Supplementary

[1.1427]

325 Short title

This Act may be cited as the Pensions Act 2004.

EQUALITY ACT 2006

(2006 c 3)

ARRANGEMENT OF SECTIONS

PART 1
THE COMMISSION FOR EQUALITY AND HUMAN RIGHTS

The Commission

SCHEDULES

An Act to make provision for the establishment of the Commission for Equality and Human Rights; to dissolve the Equal Opportunities Commission, the Commission for Racial Equality and the Disability Rights Commission; to make provision about discrimination on grounds of religion or belief; to enable provision to be made about discrimination on grounds of sexual orientation; to impose duties relating to sex discrimination on persons performing public functions; to amend the Disability Discrimination Act 1995; and for connected purposes

[16 February 2006]

NOTES

This Act, in so far as still in force, is reproduced in full save for provisions omitted for reasons noted at the appropriate points below. In particular, as noted below, ss 25, 26, 33, and 43–81 were repealed by the Equality Act 2010.

Regulatory functions: the regulatory functions conferred by, or under, this Act are subject to the Legislative and Regulatory Reform Act 2006, ss 21, 22; see the Legislative and Regulatory Reform (Regulatory Functions) Order 2007, SI 2007/3544 (made under s 24(2) of the 2006 Act) for details.

Transfer of functions: (i) as to the transfer of the functions of the Secretary of State for Trade and Industry under Part 1 of this Act to the Secretary of State for Communities and Local Government, see the Secretary of State for Communities and Local Government Order 2006, SI 2006/1926, arts 7(1), (2), (3)(c), 8; (ii) see also the Transfer of Functions (Equality) Order 2007, SI 2007/2914, art 3(1), (2)(f), regarding the transfer of the functions of the Secretary of State under this Act (except s 66(2) and Sch 2, para 14(4)) to the Lord Privy Seal; (iii) see also the Transfer of Functions (Equality) Order 2010, SI 2010/1839, which makes provision in connection with the transfer of certain statutory functions relating to equality from the Lord Privy Seal to the Secretary of State (the Government Equalities Office, previously the department of the Lord Privy Seal, is now headed by the Secretary of State entrusted with responsibility for equality. As of 15 May 2019, this is the Secretary of State for Women and Equalities.

See *Harvey* L

PART 1
THE COMMISSION FOR EQUALITY AND HUMAN RIGHTS

The Commission

[1.1428]
1 Establishment

There shall be a body corporate known as the Commission for Equality and Human Rights.

[1.1429]
2 Constitution, &c

Schedule 1 (constitution of the Commission, proceedings, money, &c) shall have effect.

[1.1430]
3 General duty

The Commission shall exercise its functions under this Part with a view to encouraging and supporting the development of a society in which—

(a) people's ability to achieve their potential is not limited by prejudice or discrimination,
(b) there is respect for and protection of each individual's human rights,
(c) there is respect for the dignity and worth of each individual,
(d) each individual has an equal opportunity to participate in society, and
(e) there is mutual respect between groups based on understanding and valuing of diversity and on shared respect for equality and human rights.

[1.1431]
4 Strategic plan

(1) The Commission shall prepare a plan showing—

(a) activities or classes of activity to be undertaken by the Commission in pursuance of its functions under this Act,
(b) an expected timetable for each activity or class, and
(c) priorities for different activities or classes, or principles to be applied in determining priorities.

(2) The Commission shall review the plan—

(a) at least once during the period of three years beginning with its completion,
(b) at least once during each period of three years beginning with the completion of a review, and
(c) at such other times as the Commission thinks appropriate.

(3) If the Commission thinks it appropriate as a result of a review, the Commission shall revise the plan.

(4) The Commission shall send the plan and each revision to the [Secretary of State], who shall lay a copy before Parliament.

(5) The Commission shall publish the plan and each revision.

NOTES

Sub-s (4): words in square brackets substituted by the Transfer of Functions (Equality) Order 2010, SI 2010/1839, arts 3(1)(f), 7, Schedule, para 14(1), (2)(a).

[1.1432]

5 Strategic plan: consultation

Before preparing or reviewing a plan in accordance with section 4 the Commission shall—

(a) consult such persons having knowledge or experience relevant to the Commission's functions as the Commission thinks appropriate,

(b) consult such other persons as the Commission thinks appropriate,

(c) issue a general invitation to make representations, in a manner likely in the Commission's opinion to bring the invitation to the attention of as large a class of persons who may wish to make representations as is reasonably practicable, and

(d) take account of any representations made.

[1.1433]

6 Disclosure

(1) A person who is or was a Commissioner, an Investigating Commissioner, an employee of the Commission or a member of a committee established by the Commission commits an offence if he discloses information to which this section applies unless subsection (3) authorises the disclosure.

(2) This section applies to information acquired by the Commission—

(a) by way of representations made in relation to, or otherwise in the course of, an inquiry under section 16,

(b) by way of representations made in relation to, or otherwise in the course of, an investigation under section 20,

(c) by way of representations made in relation to, or otherwise in the course of, an assessment under section 31,

(d) by way of representations made in relation to, or otherwise in connection with, a notice under section 32, or

(e) from a person with whom the Commission enters into, or considers entering into, an agreement under section 23.

(3) This subsection authorises a disclosure made—

(a) for the purpose of the exercise of a function of the Commission under any of sections 16, 20, 21, 24, 25, 31 and 32,

(b) in a report of an inquiry, investigation or assessment published by the Commission,

(c) in pursuance of an order of a court or tribunal,

(d) with the consent of each person to whom the disclosed information relates,

(e) in a manner that ensures that no person to whom the disclosed information relates can be identified,

(f) for the purpose of civil or criminal proceedings to which the Commission is party, or

(g) if the information was acquired by the Commission more than 70 years before the date of the disclosure.

(4) But subsection (3) does not authorise, nor may the Commission make, a disclosure of information provided by or relating to an intelligence service unless the service has authorised the disclosure.

(5) In subsection (4) "intelligence service" means—

(a) the Security Service,

(b) the Secret Intelligence Service, and

(c) the Government Communications Headquarters.

(6) A person guilty of an offence under subsection (1) shall be liable on summary conviction to a fine not exceeding level 5 on the standard scale.

NOTES

Discloses information: in so far as it authorises the disclosure of information, this section is subject to the Anti-terrorism, Crime and Security Act 2001, s 17 (extension of existing disclosure powers); see Sch 4, Pt 1, para 53B to that Act.

[1.1434]

7 Scotland: human rights

(1) The Commission shall not take human rights action in relation to a matter if the Scottish Parliament has legislative competence to enable a person to take action of that kind in relation to that matter.

(2) In subsection (1) "human rights action" means action taken—

(a) in accordance with section 9(1), and

(b) under, by virtue of or in pursuance of—

(i) section 11(1) in so far as it relates to the Human Rights Act 1998 (c 42),

(ii) section 11(2)(c) or (d),

(iii) section 12,

(iv) section 13,

(v) section 16,

(vi) section 17, or

(vii) section 30.

(3) Despite section 9(4), the Commission shall not, in the course of fulfilling a duty under section 8 . . . , consider the question whether a person's human rights have been contravened if the Scottish Parliament has legislative competence to enable a person to consider that question.

(4) Subsections (1) and (3) shall not prevent the Commission from taking action with the consent (whether general or specific) of a person if—
- (a) the person is established by Act of the Scottish Parliament, and
- (b) the person's principal duties relate to human rights and are similar to any of the Commission's duties under section 9.

(5) Subsections (1) and (3) shall not prevent the Commission from relying on section 13(1)(f) so as to act jointly or cooperate (but not assist) for a purpose relating to human rights and connected with Scotland.

NOTES

Sub-s (3): words omitted repealed by the Enterprise and Regulatory Reform Act 2013, s 64(3), (4).

Duties

[1.1435]

8 Equality and diversity

(1) The Commission shall, by exercising the powers conferred by this Part—
- (a) promote understanding of the importance of equality and diversity,
- (b) encourage good practice in relation to equality and diversity,
- (c) promote equality of opportunity,
- (d) promote awareness and understanding of rights under the [Equality Act 2010],
- (e) enforce [that Act],
- (f) work towards the elimination of unlawful discrimination, and
- (g) work towards the elimination of unlawful harassment.

(2) In subsection (1)—

"diversity" means the fact that individuals are different,

"equality" means equality between individuals, and

"unlawful" is to be construed in accordance with section 34.

(3) In promoting equality of opportunity between disabled persons and others, the Commission may, in particular, promote the favourable treatment of disabled persons.

(4) In this Part "disabled person" means a person who—
- (a) is a disabled person within the meaning of the [Equality Act 2010], or
- (b) has been a disabled person within that meaning (whether or not at a time when that Act had effect).

NOTES

Sub-ss (1), (4): words in square brackets substituted by the Equality Act 2010, s 211(1), Sch 26, paras 61, 62.

[1.1436]

9 Human rights

(1) The Commission shall, by exercising the powers conferred by this Part—
- (a) promote understanding of the importance of human rights,
- (b) encourage good practice in relation to human rights,
- (c) promote awareness, understanding and protection of human rights, and
- (d) encourage public authorities to comply with section 6 of the Human Rights Act 1998 (c 42) (compliance with Convention rights).

(2) In this Part "human rights" means—
- (a) the Convention rights within the meaning given by section 1 of the Human Rights Act 1998, and
- (b) other human rights.

(3) In determining what action to take in pursuance of this section the Commission shall have particular regard to the importance of exercising the powers conferred by this Part in relation to the Convention rights.

(4) In fulfilling a duty under section 8 . . . the Commission shall take account of any relevant human rights.

(5) A reference in this Part (including this section) to human rights does not exclude any matter by reason only of its being a matter to which section 8 . . . relates.

NOTES

Sub-ss (4), (5): words omitted repealed by the Enterprise and Regulatory Reform Act 2013, s 64(3), (5).

[1.1437]

10 Groups

(1) . . .

(2) In this Part "group" means a group or class of persons who share a common attribute in respect of any of the following matters—
- (a) age,
- (b) disability,
- (c) gender,
- [(d) gender reassignment (within the meaning of section 7 of the Equality Act 2010),]
- (e) race,
- (f) religion or belief, and
- (g) sexual orientation.

(3) For the purposes of this Part a reference to a group (as defined in subsection (2)) includes a reference to a smaller group or smaller class, within a group, of persons who share a common attribute (in addition to the attribute by reference to which the group is defined) in respect of any of the matters specified in subsection (2)(a) to (g).

(4)–(7) . . .

NOTES

Sub-ss (1), (4)–(7): repealed by the Enterprise and Regulatory Reform Act 2013, s 64(1)(a).

Sub-s (2): para (d) substituted by the Equality Act 2010, s 211(1), Sch 26, paras 61, 63.

Orders: as of 15 May 2019, no Orders had been made under this section.

Note: the Enterprise and Regulatory Reform Act 2013, s 64(1)(a), states that sub-s (8) of this section is repealed, but sub-s (8) does not exist.

[1.1438]

11 Monitoring the law

(1) The Commission shall monitor the effectiveness of the equality and human rights enactments.

(2) The Commission may—

(a) advise central government about the effectiveness of any of the equality and human rights enactments;

(b) recommend to central government the amendment, repeal, consolidation (with or without amendments) or replication (with or without amendments) of any of the equality and human rights enactments;

(c) advise central or devolved government about the effect of an enactment (including an enactment in or under an Act of the Scottish Parliament);

(d) advise central or devolved government about the likely effect of a proposed change of law.

(3) In this section—

(a) "central government" means Her Majesty's Government,

(b) "devolved government" means—

(i) the Scottish Ministers, and

(ii) the [Welsh Ministers, the First Minister for Wales and the Counsel General to the Welsh Assembly Government], and

[(c) a reference to the equality and human rights enactments is a reference to the Human Rights Act 1998, this Act and the Equality Act 2010].

NOTES

Sub-s (3): words in square brackets in sub-para (b)(ii) substituted by the Government of Wales Act 2006 (Consequential Modifications and Transitional Provisions) Order 2007, SI 2007/1388, art 3, Sch 1, paras 112, 113; para (c) substituted by the Equality Act 2010, s 211(1), Sch 26, paras 61, 64.

Welsh Assembly Government: see the Wales Act 2014, s 4 which provides that, unless the context requires otherwise, any reference to the Welsh Assembly Government is to be read as, or as including, a reference to the Welsh Government.

[1.1439]

12 Monitoring progress

(1) The Commission shall from time to time identify—

(a) changes in society that have occurred or are expected to occur and are relevant to [the duties specified in sections 8 and 9],

(b) results at which to aim for the purpose of encouraging and supporting [changes in society that are consistent with those duties] ("outcomes"), and

(c) factors by reference to which progress towards those results may be measured ("indicators").

(2) In identifying outcomes and indicators the Commission shall—

(a) consult such persons having knowledge or experience relevant to the Commission's functions as the Commission thinks appropriate,

(b) consult such other persons as the Commission thinks appropriate,

(c) issue a general invitation to make representations, in a manner likely in the Commission's opinion to bring the invitation to the attention of as large a class of persons who may wish to make representations as is reasonably practicable, and

(d) take account of any representations made.

(3) The Commission shall from time to time monitor progress towards each identified outcome by reference to any relevant identified indicator.

(4) The Commission shall publish a report on progress towards the identified outcomes by reference to the identified indicators—

(a) within the period of three years beginning with the date on which this section comes into force, and

(b) within each period of [five] years beginning with the date on which a report is published under this subsection.

(5) The Commission shall send each report to the [Secretary of State], who shall lay a copy before Parliament.

NOTES

Sub-ss (1), (4): words in square brackets in paras (a), (b) substituted by the Enterprise and Regulatory Reform Act 2013, s 64(2), (3), (6).

Sub-s (5): words in square brackets substituted by the Transfer of Functions (Equality) Order 2010, SI 2010/1839, arts 3(1)(f), 7, Schedule, para 14(1), (2)(c).

General powers

[1.1440]

13 Information, advice, &c

(1) In pursuance of its duties under sections 8 [and 9] the Commission may—

(a) publish or otherwise disseminate ideas or information;
(b) undertake research;
(c) provide education or training;
(d) give advice or guidance (whether about the effect or operation of an enactment or otherwise);
(e) arrange for a person to do anything within paragraphs (a) to (d);
(f) act jointly with, co-operate with or assist a person doing anything within paragraphs (a) to (d).

(2) The reference to giving advice in subsection (1)(d) does not include a reference to preparing, or assisting in the preparation of, a document to be used for the purpose of legal proceedings.

NOTES

Sub-s (1): words in square brackets substituted by the Enterprise and Regulatory Reform Act 2013, s 64(3), (7).

[1.1441]

14 Codes of practice

[(1) The Commission may issue a code of practice in connection with any matter addressed by the Equality Act 2010.]

(2) A code of practice under subsection (1) shall contain provision designed—

(a) to ensure or facilitate compliance with [the Equality Act 2010 or an enactment made under that Act], or
(b) to promote equality of opportunity.

(3) The Commission may issue a code of practice giving practical guidance to landlords and tenants in England or Wales about—

(a) circumstances in which a tenant requires the consent of his landlord to make a relevant improvement, within the meaning of [section 190(7) of the Equality Act 2010] (improvements), to a dwelling house,
(b) reasonableness in relation to that consent, and
(c) the application in relation to relevant improvements (within that meaning) to dwelling houses of—
 (i) section 19(2) of the Landlord and Tenant Act 1927 (c 36) (consent to improvements),
 (ii) sections 81 to 85 of the Housing Act 1980 (c 51) (tenant's improvements),
 (iii) sections 97 to 99 of the Housing Act 1985 (c 68) (tenant's improvements), and
 [(iv) section 190 of the Equality Act 2010].

(4) The Commission may issue a code of practice giving practical guidance to landlords and tenants of houses (within the meaning of the Housing (Scotland) Act 2006 (asp 01)) in Scotland about—

(a) circumstances in which the tenant requires the consent of the landlord to carry out work in relation to the house for the purpose of making the house suitable for the accommodation, welfare or employment of any disabled person who occupies, or intends to occupy, the house as a sole or main residence,
(b) circumstances in which it is unreasonable to withhold that consent,
(c) circumstances in which any condition imposed on the granting of that consent is unreasonable, and
(d) the application in relation to such work of—
 (i) sections 28 to 31 and 34(6) of the Housing (Scotland) Act 2001 (asp 10), and
 (ii) sections 52, 53 and 64(6) of the Housing (Scotland) Act 2006 (asp 01).

(5) The Commission shall comply with a direction of the [Secretary of State] to issue a code under this section in connection with a specified matter if—

(a) the matter is not [a matter addressed by the Equality Act 2010], but
(b) the [Secretary of State] expects to add it by order under section 15(6).

(6) Before issuing a code under this section the Commission shall—

(a) publish proposals, and
(b) consult such persons as it thinks appropriate.

(7) Before issuing a code under this section the Commission shall submit a draft to the [Secretary of State], who shall—

(a) if he approves the draft—
 (i) notify the Commission, and
 (ii) lay a copy before Parliament, or
(b) otherwise, give the Commission written reasons why he does not approve the draft.

(8) Where a draft is laid before Parliament under subsection (7)(a)(ii), if neither House passes a resolution disapproving the draft within 40 days—

(a) the Commission may issue the code in the form of the draft, and
(b) it shall come into force in accordance with provision made by the [Secretary of State] by order.

(9) If, or in so far as, a code relates to a duty imposed by or under [section 149, 153 or 154 of the Equality Act 2010 (public sector equality duty)] the [Secretary of State] shall consult the Scottish Ministers and the [Welsh Ministers] before—

(a) approving a draft under subsection (7)(a) above, or
(b) making an order under subsection (8)(b) above.

(10) In relation to a code of practice under subsection (4), the [Secretary of State] shall consult the Scottish Ministers before—

(a) approving a draft under subsection (7)(a) above, or
(b) making an order under subsection (8)(b) above.

NOTES

Words "Secretary of State" in square brackets in every place they occur substituted by the Transfer of Functions (Equality) Order 2010, SI 2010/1839, arts 3(1)(f), 7, Schedule, para 14(1), (2)(d).

Other amendments to this section are as follows:

Sub-s (1): substituted by the Equality Act 2010, s 211(1), Sch 26, paras 61, 65(1), (2).

Sub-ss (2), (3): words in square brackets substituted by the Equality Act 2010, s 211(1), Sch 26, paras 61, 65(1), (3), (4).

Sub-s (5): words "a matter addressed by the Equality Act 2010" in square brackets substituted by the Equality Act 2010, s 211(1), Sch 26, paras 61, 65(1), (5).

Sub-s (9): words "Welsh Ministers" in square brackets substituted by the Government of Wales Act 2006 (Consequential Modifications and Transitional Provisions) Order 2007, SI 2007/1388, art 3, Sch 1, paras 112, 114; words "section 149, 153 or 154 of the Equality Act 2010 (public sector equality duty)" substituted by the Equality Act 2010, s 211(1), Sch 26, paras 61, 65(1), (6).

Orders: (i) the Disability Discrimination Code of Practice (Trade Organisations, Qualifications Bodies and General Qualifications Bodies) (Commencement) Order 2008, SI 2008/1335. This Order brings the revised Disability Discrimination Act 1995 Code of Practice for Trade Organisations, Qualifications Bodies and General Qualifications Bodies into force on 23 June 2008 (see **[4.112]**). (ii) the Equality Act 2010 Codes of Practice (Services, Public Functions and Associations, Employment, and Equal Pay) Order 2011, SI 2011/857. This Order brings into force (on 6 April 2011) the Equality Act 2010 Code of Practice on Services, Public Functions and Associations, the Equality Act 2010 Code of Practice on Employment at **[4.127]** and the Equality Act 2010 Code of Practice on Equal Pay at **[4.123]**.

[1.1442]

15 Codes of practice: supplemental

(1) The Commission may revise a code issued under section 14; and a reference in this section or in that section to the issue of a code shall be treated as including a reference to the revision of a code.

(2) The 40 day period specified in section 14(8)—
  (a) shall begin with the date on which the draft is laid before both Houses (or, if laid before each House on a different date, with the later date), and
  (b) shall be taken not to include a period during which—
    (i) Parliament is prorogued or dissolved, or
    (ii) both Houses are adjourned for more than four days.

(3) A code issued under section 14 may be revoked by the [Secretary of State], at the request of the Commission, by order.

(4) A failure to comply with a provision of a code shall not of itself make a person liable to criminal or civil proceedings; but a code—
  (a) shall be admissible in evidence in criminal or civil proceedings, and
  (b) shall be taken into account by a court or tribunal in any case in which it appears to the court or tribunal to be relevant.

(5) Subsection (4)(b) does not apply in relation to a code issued under section 14(4).

(6) The [Secretary of State] may by order amend section 14 so as to vary the range of matters that codes of practice under that section may address.

NOTES

Sub-ss (3), (6): words in square brackets substituted by the Transfer of Functions (Equality) Order 2010, SI 2010/1839, arts 3(1)(f), 7, Schedule, para 14(1), (2)(e).

Orders: as of 15 May 2019, no Orders had been made under this section.

[1.1443]

16 Inquiries

(1) The Commission may conduct an inquiry into a matter relating to any of the Commission's duties under sections 8 [and 9].

(2) If in the course of an inquiry the Commission begins to suspect that a person may have committed an unlawful act—
  (a) in continuing the inquiry the Commission shall, so far as possible, avoid further consideration of whether or not the person has committed an unlawful act,
  (b) the Commission may commence an investigation into that question under section 20,
  (c) the Commission may use information or evidence acquired in the course of the inquiry for the purpose of the investigation, and
  (d) the Commission shall so far as possible ensure (whether by aborting or suspending the inquiry or otherwise) that any aspects of the inquiry which concern the person investigated, or may require his involvement, are not pursued while the investigation is in progress.

(3) The report of an inquiry—
  (a) may not state (whether expressly or by necessary implication) that a specified or identifiable person has committed an unlawful act, and
  (b) shall not otherwise refer to the activities of a specified or identifiable person unless the Commission thinks that the reference—
    (i) will not harm the person, or
    (ii) is necessary in order for the report adequately to reflect the results of the inquiry.

(4) Subsections (2) and (3) shall not prevent an inquiry from considering or reporting a matter relating to human rights (whether or not a necessary implication arises in relation to the [Equality Act 2010]).

(5) Before settling a report of an inquiry which records findings which in the Commission's opinion are of an adverse nature and relate (whether expressly or by necessary implication) to a specified or identifiable person the Commission shall—

(a) send a draft of the report to the person,
(b) specify a period of at least 28 days during which he may make written representations about the draft, and
(c) consider any representations made.

(6) Schedule 2 makes supplemental provision about inquiries.

NOTES

Sub-s (1): words in square brackets substituted by the Enterprise and Regulatory Reform Act 2013, s 64(3), (8).
Sub-s (4): words in square brackets substituted by the Equality Act 2010, s 211(1), Sch 26, paras 61, 66.

[1.1444]
17 Grants

(1) In pursuance of any of its duties under sections 8 [and 9] the Commission may make grants to another person.

(2) A grant under subsection (1) may be made subject to conditions (which may, in particular, include conditions as to repayment).

(3) A power under this Part to co-operate with or assist a person may not be exercised by the provision of financial assistance otherwise than in accordance with this section.

NOTES

Sub-s (1): words in square brackets substituted by the Enterprise and Regulatory Reform Act 2013, s 64(3), (9).

[1.1445]
18 Human rights

In pursuance of its duties under section 9 the Commission may (without prejudice to the generality of section 13) co-operate with persons interested in human rights within the United Kingdom or elsewhere.

19 (*Repealed by the Enterprise and Regulatory Reform Act 2013, s 64(1)(a).*)

Enforcement powers

[1.1446]
20 Investigations

(1) The Commission may investigate whether or not a person—

(a) has committed an unlawful act,
(b) has complied with a requirement imposed by an unlawful act notice under section 21, or
(c) has complied with an undertaking given under section 23.

(2) The Commission may conduct an investigation under subsection (1)(a) only if it suspects that the person concerned may have committed an unlawful act.

(3) A suspicion for the purposes of subsection (2) may (but need not) be based on the results of, or a matter arising during the course of, an inquiry under section 16.

(4) Before settling a report of an investigation recording a finding that a person has committed an unlawful act or has failed to comply with a requirement or undertaking the Commission shall—

(a) send a draft of the report to the person,
(b) specify a period of at least 28 days during which he may make written representations about the draft, and
(c) consider any representations made.

(5) Schedule 2 makes supplemental provision about investigations.

[1.1447]
21 Unlawful act notice

(1) The Commission may give a person a notice under this section (an "unlawful act notice") if—

(a) he is or has been the subject of an investigation under section 20(1)(a), and
(b) the Commission is satisfied that he has committed an unlawful act.

(2) A notice must specify—

(a) the unlawful act, and
(b) the provision of the [Equality Act 2010] by virtue of which the act is unlawful.

(3) A notice must inform the recipient of the effect of—

(a) subsections (5) to (7),
(b) section 20(1)(b), and
(c) section 24(1).

(4) A notice may—

(a) require the person to whom the notice is given to prepare an action plan for the purpose of avoiding repetition or continuation of the unlawful act;
(b) recommend action to be taken by the person for that purpose.

(5) A person who is given a notice may, within the period of six weeks beginning with the day on which the notice is given, appeal to the appropriate court or tribunal on the grounds—

(a) that he has not committed the unlawful act specified in the notice, or
(b) that a requirement for the preparation of an action plan imposed under subsection (4)(a) is unreasonable.

(6) On an appeal under subsection (5) the court or tribunal may—

(a) affirm a notice;
(b) annul a notice;
(c) vary a notice;
(d) affirm a requirement;
(e) annul a requirement;
(f) vary a requirement;
(g) make an order for costs or expenses.

(7) In subsection (5) "the appropriate court or tribunal" means—
(a) an employment tribunal, if a claim in respect of the alleged unlawful act could be made to it, or
(b) [the county court] (in England and Wales) or the sheriff (in Scotland), if a claim in respect of the alleged unlawful act could be made to it or to him.

NOTES

Sub-s (2): words in square brackets substituted by the Equality Act 2010, s 211(1), Sch 26, paras 61, 67; for transitory provisions relating to ships and hovercraft, see the Equality Act 2010 (Commencement No 4, Savings, Consequential, Transitional, Transitory and Incidental Provisions and Revocation) Order 2010, SI 2010/2317, arts 10(4), 11(2).

Sub-s (7): words in square brackets in para (b) substituted by the Crime and Courts Act 2013, s 17(5), Sch 9, Pt 3, para 52.

[1.1448]
22 Action plans

(1) This section applies where a person has been given a notice under section 21 which requires him (under section 21(4)(a)) to prepare an action plan.
(2) The notice must specify a time by which the person must give the Commission a first draft plan.
(3) After receiving a first draft plan from a person the Commission shall—
(a) approve it, or
(b) give the person a notice which—
(i) states that the draft is not adequate,
(ii) requires the person to give the Commission a revised draft by a specified time, and
(iii) may make recommendations about the content of the revised draft.
(4) Subsection (3) shall apply in relation to a revised draft plan as it applies in relation to a first draft plan.
(5) An action plan comes into force—
(a) if the period of six weeks beginning with the date on which a first draft or revised draft is given to the Commission expires without the Commission—
(i) giving a notice under subsection (3)(b), or
(ii) applying for an order under subsection (6)(b), or
(b) upon a court's declining to make an order under subsection (6)(b) in relation to a revised draft of the plan.
(6) The Commission may apply to [the county court] (in England and Wales) or to the sheriff (in Scotland)—
(a) for an order requiring a person to give the Commission a first draft plan by a time specified in the order,
(b) for an order requiring a person who has given the Commission a revised draft plan to prepare and give to the Commission a further revised draft plan—
(i) by a time specified in the order, and
(ii) in accordance with any directions about the plan's content specified in the order, or
(c) during the period of five years beginning with the date on which an action plan prepared by a person comes into force, for an order requiring the person—
(i) to act in accordance with the action plan, or
(ii) to take specified action for a similar purpose.
(7) An action plan may be varied by agreement between the Commission and the person who prepared it.
(8) Paragraphs 10 to 14 of Schedule 2 apply (but omitting references to oral evidence) in relation to consideration by the Commission of the adequacy of a draft action plan as they apply in relation to the conduct of an inquiry.
(9) A person commits an offence if without reasonable excuse he fails to comply with an order under subsection (6); and a person guilty of an offence under this subsection shall be liable on summary conviction to a fine not exceeding level 5 on the standard scale.

NOTES

Sub-s (6): words in square brackets substituted by the Crime and Courts Act 2013, s 17(5), Sch 9, Pt 3, para 52.

[1.1449]
23 Agreements

(1) The Commission may enter into an agreement with a person under which—
(a) the person undertakes—
(i) not to commit an unlawful act of a specified kind, and
(ii) to take, or refrain from taking, other specified action (which may include the preparation of a plan for the purpose of avoiding an unlawful act), and
(b) the Commission undertakes not to proceed against the person under section 20 or 21 in respect of any unlawful act of the kind specified under paragraph (a)(i).
(2) The Commission may enter into an agreement with a person under this section only if it thinks that the person has committed an unlawful act.

(3) But a person shall not be taken to admit to the commission of an unlawful act by reason only of entering into an agreement under this section.

(4) An agreement under this section—

(a) may be entered into whether or not the person is or has been the subject of an investigation under section 20,

(b) may include incidental or supplemental provision (which may include provision for termination in specified circumstances), and

(c) may be varied or terminated by agreement of the parties.

(5) This section shall apply in relation to the breach of a duty specified in section 34(2) as it applies in relation to the commission of an unlawful act; and for that purpose the reference in subsection (1)(b) above to section 20 or 21 shall be taken as a reference to section 32.

[1.1450]
24 Applications to court

(1) If the Commission thinks that a person is likely to commit an unlawful act, it may apply—

(a) in England and Wales, to [the county court] for an injunction restraining the person from committing the act, or

(b) in Scotland, to the sheriff for an interdict prohibiting the person from committing the act.

(2) Subsection (3) applies if the Commission thinks that a party to an agreement under section 23 has failed to comply, or is likely not to comply, with an undertaking under the agreement.

(3) The Commission may apply to [the county court] (in England and Wales) or to the sheriff (in Scotland) for an order requiring the person—

(a) to comply with his undertaking, and

(b) to take such other action as the court or the sheriff may specify.

NOTES

Sub-ss (1), (3): words in square brackets substituted by the Crime and Courts Act 2013, s 17(5), Sch 9, Pt 3, para 52.

[1.1451]
[24A Enforcement powers: supplemental

(1) This section has effect in relation to—

(a) an act which is unlawful because, by virtue of any of sections 13 to 18 of the Equality Act 2010, it amounts to a contravention of any of Parts 3, 4, 5, 6 or 7 of that Act,

(b) an act which is unlawful because it amounts to a contravention of section 60(1) of that Act (or to a contravention of section 111 or 112 of that Act that relates to a contravention of section 60(1) of that Act) (enquiries about disability and health),

(c) an act which is unlawful because it amounts to a contravention of section 106 of that Act (information about diversity in range of election candidates etc),

(d) an act which is unlawful because, by virtue of section 108(1) of that Act, it amounts to a contravention of any of Parts 3, 4, 5, 6 or 7 of that Act, or

(e) the application of a provision, criterion or practice which, by virtue of section 19 of that Act, amounts to a contravention of that Act.

(2) For the purposes of sections 20 to 24 of this Act, it is immaterial whether the Commission knows or suspects that a person has been or may be affected by the unlawful act or application.

(3) For those purposes, an unlawful act includes making arrangements to act in a particular way which would, if applied to an individual, amount to a contravention mentioned in subsection (1)(a).

(4) Nothing in this Act affects the entitlement of a person to bring proceedings under the Equality Act 2010 in respect of a contravention mentioned in subsection (1).]

NOTES

Inserted by the Equality Act 2010, s 211(1), Sch 26, paras 61, 68.

25–27 *(Ss 25, 26 repealed by the Equality Act 2010, s 211, Sch 26, paras 61, 69, 70, Sch 27, Pt 1; for transitory provisions relating to ships and hovercraft, see the Equality Act 2010 (Commencement No 4, Savings, Consequential, Transitional, Transitory and Incidental Provisions and Revocation) Order 2010, SI 2010/2317, arts 10(4), 11(2). S 27 repealed by the Enterprise and Regulatory Reform Act 2013, s 64(1)(b).)*

[1.1452]
28 Legal assistance

(1) The Commission may assist an individual who is or may become party to legal proceedings if—

(a) the proceedings relate or may relate (wholly or partly) to a provision of the [Equality Act 2010], and

(b) the individual alleges that he has been the victim of behaviour contrary to a provision of [that Act].

(2) The Commission may assist an individual who is or may become party to legal proceedings in England and Wales if and in so far as the proceedings concern or may concern the question of a landlord's reasonableness in relation to consent to the making of an improvement to a dwelling where the improvement would be likely to facilitate the enjoyment of the premises by the tenant or another lawful occupier having regard to a disability.

(3) The Commission may assist an individual who is or may become a party to legal proceedings in Scotland if and in so far as the proceedings concern or may concern the question whether—

(a) it is unreasonable for a landlord to withhold consent to the carrying out of work in relation to a house (within the meaning of the Housing (Scotland) Act 2006 (asp 01)) for the purpose of making the house suitable for the accommodation, welfare or employment of any disabled person who occupies, or intends to occupy, the house as a sole or main residence, or
(b) any condition imposed by a landlord on consenting to the carrying out of such work is unreasonable.

(4) In giving assistance under this section the Commission may provide or arrange for the provision of—
(a) legal advice;
(b) legal representation;
(c) facilities for the settlement of a dispute;
(d) any other form of assistance.

(5) Assistance may not be given under subsection (1) in relation to alleged behaviour contrary to a provision of [Part 12 of the Equality Act 2010 (disabled persons:] transport).

(6) Where proceedings relate or may relate partly to a provision of [the Equality Act 2010] and partly to other matters—
(a) assistance may be given under subsection (1) in respect of any aspect of the proceedings while they relate to a provision of [that Act], but
(b) if the proceedings cease to relate to a provision of [that Act], assistance may not be continued under subsection (1) in respect of the proceedings (except in so far as it is permitted by virtue of subsection (7) or (8)).

(7) The Lord Chancellor may by order disapply subsection (6)(b), and enable the Commission to give assistance under subsection (1), in respect of legal proceedings which—
(a) when instituted, related (wholly or partly) to a provision of the [Equality Act 2010],
(b) have ceased to relate to the provision of [that Act], and
(c) relate (wholly or partly) to any of the Convention rights within the meaning given by section 1 of the Human Rights Act 1998 (c 42).

(8) The [Secretary of State] may by order enable the Commission to give assistance under this section in respect of legal proceedings in the course of which an individual who is or has been a disabled person relies or proposes to rely on a matter relating to his disability; but an order under this subsection may not permit assistance in relation to alleged behaviour contrary to a provision of [Part 12 of the Equality Act 2010].

(9) An order under subsection (7) or (8) may make provision generally or only in relation to proceedings of a specified kind or description (which in the case of an order under subsection (7) may, in particular, refer to specified provisions of the [Equality Act 2010]) or in relation to specified circumstances.

(10) This section is without prejudice to the effect of any restriction imposed, in respect of representation—
(a) by virtue of an enactment (including an enactment in or under an Act of the Scottish Parliament), or
(b) in accordance with the practice of a court.

(11) A legislative provision which requires insurance or an indemnity in respect of advice given in connection with a [settlement agreement] shall not apply to advice provided by the Commission under this section.

(12) [This section applies] to *a provision of* [EU] law which—
(a) relates to discrimination on grounds of sex (including reassignment of gender), racial origin, ethnic origin, religion, belief, disability, age or sexual orientation, and
(b) confers rights on individuals

[as it applies to [a provision of] the Equality Act 2010].

(13) In its application by virtue of subsection (12), subsection (1)(b) shall have effect as if it referred to an allegation by an individual that he is disadvantaged by—
(a) an enactment (including an enactment in or under an Act of the Scottish Parliament) which is contrary to *a provision of* [EU] law, or
(b) a failure by the United Kingdom to implement a right as required by [EU] law [(as it had effect before exit day)].

NOTES

Sub-ss (1), (5)–(7), (9): words in square brackets substituted by the Equality Act 2010, s 211(1), Sch 26, paras 61, 72(1)–(5), (7).

Sub-s (8): words in first pair of square brackets substituted by the Transfer of Functions (Equality) Order 2010, SI 2010/1839, arts 3(1)(f), 7, Schedule, para 14(1), (2)(g); words in second pair of square brackets substituted by the Equality Act 2010, s 211(1), Sch 26, paras 61, 72(1), (6).

Sub-s (11): words in square brackets substituted by the Enterprise and Regulatory Reform Act 2013, s 23(4).

Sub-s (12): words in first pair of square brackets substituted, and words in third (outer) pair of square brackets added, by the Equality Act 2010, s 211(1), Sch 26, paras 61, 72(1), (8); reference in second pair of square brackets substituted by the Treaty of Lisbon (Changes in Terminology) Order 2011, SI 2011/1043, art 6(2)(a); for the words in italics there are substituted the words "anything in retained" and words in fourth (inner) pair of square brackets inserted, by the Equality (Amendment and Revocation) (EU Exit) Regulations 2019, SI 2019/305, reg 4(1), (2)(a), as from exit day (as defined in the European Union (Withdrawal) Act 2018, s 20).

Sub-s (13): references to "EU" in square brackets substituted by SI 2011/1043, art 6(2)(a); for the words in italics in para (a) there are substituted the words "anything in retained" and words in square brackets in para (b) inserted, by SI 2019/305, reg 4(1), (2)(b), as from exit day (as defined in the European Union (Withdrawal) Act 2018, s 20).

[1.1453]

29 Legal assistance: costs

(1) This section applies where—

(a) the Commission has assisted an individual under section 28 in relation to proceedings, and

(b) the individual becomes entitled to some or all of his costs in the proceedings (whether by virtue of an award or by virtue of an agreement).

(2) The Commission's expenses in providing the assistance—

(a) shall be charged on sums paid to the individual by way of costs, and

(b) may be enforced as a debt due to the Commission.

(3) A requirement to pay money to the Commission under subsection (2) ranks, in England and Wales, after a requirement imposed by virtue of [section 25 of the Legal Aid, Sentencing and Punishment of Offenders Act 2012 (statutory charge in connection with civil legal aid)].

(4) Subsection (2), in its application to Scotland, shall not affect the operation of section 17(2A) of the Legal Aid (Scotland) Act 1986 (c 47) (requirement in certain cases to pay to the Scottish Legal Aid Board sums recovered under awards of, or agreements as to, expenses).

(5) For the purposes of subsection (2) the Commission's expenses shall be calculated in accordance with such provision (if any) as the [Secretary of State] makes for the purpose by regulations; and regulations may, in particular, provide for the apportionment of expenditure incurred by the Commission—

(a) partly for one purpose and partly for another, or

(b) for general purposes.

(6) In the application of this section to Scotland a reference to costs shall be taken as a reference to expenses.

NOTES

Sub-s (3): words in square brackets substituted by the Legal Aid, Sentencing and Punishment of Offenders Act 2012, s 39, Sch 5, Pt 1, para 67.

Sub-s (5): words in square brackets substituted by the Transfer of Functions (Equality) Order 2010, SI 2010/1839, arts 3(1)(f), 7, Schedule, para 14(1), (2)(h).

Regulations: as of 15 May 2019, no Regulations had been made under this section.

[1.1454]

30 Judicial review and other legal proceedings

(1) The Commission shall have capacity to institute or intervene in legal proceedings, whether for judicial review or otherwise, if it appears to the Commission that the proceedings are relevant to a matter in connection with which the Commission has a function.

(2) The Commission shall be taken to have title and interest in relation to the subject matter of any legal proceedings in Scotland which it has capacity to institute, or in which it has capacity to intervene, by virtue of subsection (1).

(3) The Commission may, in the course of legal proceedings for judicial review which it institutes (or in which it intervenes), rely on section 7(1)(b) of the Human Rights Act 1998 (c 42) (breach of Convention rights); and for that purpose—

(a) the Commission need not be a victim or potential victim of the unlawful act to which the proceedings relate,

(b) the Commission may act only if there is or would be one or more victims of the unlawful act,

(c) section 7(3) and (4) of that Act shall not apply, and

(d) no award of damages may be made to the Commission (whether or not the exception in section 8(3) of that Act applies);

and an expression used in this subsection and in section 7 of the Human Rights Act 1998 has the same meaning in this subsection as in that section.

(4) Subsections (1) and (2)—

(a) do not create a cause of action, and

(b) are, except as provided by subsection (3), subject to any limitation or restriction imposed by virtue of an enactment (including an enactment in or under an Act of the Scottish Parliament) or in accordance with the practice of a court.

[1.1455]

31 Public sector duties: assessment

[(1) The Commission may assess the extent to which or the manner in which a person has complied with a duty under or by virtue of section 149, 153 or 154 of the Equality Act 2010 (public sector equality duty).]

(2) Schedule 2 makes supplemental provision about assessments.

(3) This section is without prejudice to the generality of sections 16 and 20.

NOTES

Sub-s (1): substituted by the Equality Act 2010, s 211(1), Sch 26, paras 61, 73.

[1.1456]

32 Public sector duties: compliance notice

[(1) This section applies where the Commission thinks that a person has failed to comply with a duty under or by virtue of section 149, 153 or 154 of the Equality Act 2010 (public sector equality duty).]

(2) The Commission may give the person a notice requiring him—

(a) to comply with the duty, and

(b) to give the Commission, within the period of 28 days beginning with the date on which he receives the notice, written information of steps taken or proposed for the purpose of complying with the duty.

(3) A notice under this section may require a person to give the Commission information required by the Commission for the purposes of assessing compliance with the duty; in which case the notice shall specify—

(a) the period within which the information is to be given (which shall begin with the date on which the notice is received and shall not exceed three months), and

(b) the manner and form in which the information is to be given.

(4) The Commission may not give a notice under this section in respect of a duty under [section 149 of the Equality Act 2010] unless—

(a) the Commission has carried out an assessment under section 31 above, and

(b) the notice relates to the results of the assessment.

(5) A person who receives a notice under this section shall comply with it.

(6) But a notice under this section shall not oblige a person to give information—

(a) that he is prohibited from disclosing by virtue of an enactment, or

(b) that he could not be compelled to give in proceedings before the High Court or the Court of Session.

(7) Paragraphs 11 and 14 of Schedule 2 shall have effect (with any necessary modifications) in relation to a requirement imposed by a notice under this section as they have effect in relation to a requirement imposed by a notice under paragraph 9 of that Schedule.

(8) If the Commission thinks that a person, to whom a notice under this section has been given, has failed to comply with a requirement of the notice, the Commission may apply to the court for an order requiring the person to comply.

(9) In subsection (8) "the court" means—

(a) where the notice related to a duty under [section 149 of the Equality Act 2010], the High Court (in England and Wales) or (in Scotland) the Court of Session, and

(b) [where the notice related to a duty by virtue of section 153 or 154 of that Act], [the county court] (in England and Wales) or the sheriff (in Scotland).

(10) A notice under this section shall specify a time before which the Commission may not make an application under subsection (8) in respect of the notice.

(11) Legal proceedings in relation to a duty by virtue of [section 153 or 154 of the Equality Act 2010]—

(a) may be brought by the Commission in accordance with subsection (8) above, and

(b) may not be brought in any other way.

NOTES

Sub-s (1): substituted by the Equality Act 2010, s 211(1), Sch 26, paras 61, 74(1), (2).

Sub-s (4): words in square brackets substituted by the Equality Act 2010, s 211(1), Sch 26, paras 61, 74(1), (3).

Sub-s (9): words in first and second pairs of square brackets substituted by the Equality Act 2010, s 211(1), Sch 26, paras 61, 74(1), (4), (5); words in third pair of square brackets substituted by the Crime and Courts Act 2013, s 17(5), Sch 9, Pt 3, para 52.

Sub-s (11): words in square brackets substituted by the Equality Act 2010, s 211(1), Sch 26, paras 61, 74(1), (6).

Interpretation

33 (*Repealed by the Equality Act 2010, s 211, Sch 26, paras 61, 75, Sch 27, Pt 1; for transitory provisions relating to the public sector equality duty, see the Equality Act 2010 (Commencement No 4, Savings, Consequential, Transitional, Transitory and Incidental Provisions and Revocation) Order 2010, SI 2010/2317, art 9.*)

[1.1457]

34 Unlawful

(1) In this Part (except section 30(3)) "unlawful" means contrary to a provision of the [Equality Act 2010].

(2) But action is not unlawful for the purposes of this Part by reason only of the fact that it contravenes a duty under or by virtue of [any of the following provisions of the Equality Act 2010]—

[(a) section 1 (public sector duty regarding socio-economic inequalities),

(b) section 149, 153 or 154 (public sector equality duty),

(c) Part 12 (disabled persons: transport), or

(d) section 190 (disability: improvements to let dwelling houses).]

NOTES

Sub-s (1): words in square brackets substituted by the Equality Act 2010, s 211(1), Sch 26, paras 61, 76(1), (2).

Sub-s (2): words in first pair of square brackets inserted, and paras (a)–(d) substituted (for the original paras (a)–(c)), by the Equality Act 2010, s 211(1), Sch 26, paras 61, 76(1), (3). Note that these amendments came into force on 1 October 2010, except in so far as relating to the substituted paras (a), (b). Note also that in so far as it relates to para (b), this amendment was further commenced on 5 April 2011. It is still to be appointed in so far as relating to para (a). See the Equality Act 2010 (Commencement No 4, Savings, Consequential, Transitional, Transitory and Incidental Provisions and Revocation) Order 2010, SI 2010/2317, art 2(15)(e)(vii) and the Equality Act 2010 (Commencement No 6) Order, SI 2011/1066, art 2. For transitory provisions relating to the public sector equality duty, see art 9 of the 2010 Order.

[1.1458]

35 General

In this Part—

"act" includes deliberate omission,

"groups" has the meaning given by section 10,
"the Commission" means the Commission for Equality and Human Rights,
"disabled person" has the meaning given by section 8,
"human rights" has the meaning given by section 9,
[. . .]
"race" includes colour, nationality, ethnic origin and national origin,
"religion or belief" has the same meaning as in [section 10 of the Equality Act 2010], and
["sexual orientation" has the same meaning as in section 12 of the Equality Act 2010].

NOTES

Definition "the Minister" (omitted) originally inserted by the Transfer of Functions (Equality) Order 2007, SI 2007/2914, art 8, Schedule, para 15(1), and repealed by the Transfer of Functions (Equality) Order 2010, SI 2010/1839, arts 3(1)(f), 7, Schedule, para 14(1), (3).

Words in square brackets in definition "religion or belief" substituted, and definition "sexual orientation" substituted, by the Equality Act 2010, s 211(1), Sch 26, paras 61, 77.

Dissolution of Existing Commissions

[1.1459]

36 Dissolution

(1) The Secretary of State may by order provide for—
 (a) any of the former Commissions to cease to exist, or
 (b) the removal from any of the former Commissions of a specified function.

(2) In this Part "the former Commissions" means—
 (a) the Equal Opportunities Commission,
 (b) the Commission for Racial Equality, and
 (c) the Disability Rights Commission.

(3) The Secretary of State shall by exercising the power under subsection (1) ensure that each of the former Commissions ceases to exist not later than the end of 31st March 2009.

NOTES

"The Secretary of State": see the note on transfer of functions immediately before Part 1 of this Act.

Orders: the Equality Act 2006 (Dissolution of Commissions and Consequential and Transitional Provisions) Order 2007, SI 2007/2602; the Equality Act 2006 (Dissolution of Commissions and Consequential and Transitional Provisions) (Amendment) Order 2007, SI 2007/3555.

[1.1460]

37 Transfer of property, &c

(1) An order under section 36(1) in respect of any of the former Commissions may provide for the transfer to the Commission for Equality and Human Rights of specified property, rights and liabilities of the former Commission.

(2) The Secretary of State may give a former Commission any direction that the Secretary of State thinks appropriate in connection with the dissolution of the former Commission or the establishment of the Commission for Equality and Human Rights; and a direction may, in particular, require the former Commission—
 (a) to provide information in connection with property, rights or liabilities;
 (b) to provide information in connection with the exercise of functions;
 (c) to transfer specified property, rights and liabilities to a specified person;
 (d) to make property, staff or facilities available, on such terms or conditions as may be specified in the direction, to the Commission for Equality and Human Rights;
 (e) not to take action of a specified kind or in specified circumstances.

(3) The Secretary of State may direct a former Commission to prepare a scheme for the transfer of specified property, rights and liabilities to—
 (a) the Commission for Equality and Human Rights, or
 (b) another person specified in the direction.

(4) If the Secretary of State gives a direction under subsection (3)—
 (a) the former Commission shall prepare a scheme in accordance with the direction, having consulted either the Commission for Equality and Human Rights or the person specified under subsection (3)(b), and
 (b) the scheme shall have effect—
  (i) when approved by the Secretary of State, and
  (ii) subject to any modifications made by him, having consulted the former Commission and either the Commission for Equality and Human Rights or the person specified under subsection (3)(b).

(5) Where a former Commission ceases to exist by virtue of section 36(1)(a), its property, rights and liabilities shall by virtue of this subsection vest in the Commission for Equality and Human Rights (and this subsection operates in addition to any transfer provided for by virtue of subsection (1) above).

(6) An order, direction or scheme under or by virtue of this section may, in particular—
 (a) specify property, rights or liabilities;
 (b) specify a class or description of property, rights or liabilities;
 (c) specify property, rights or liabilities to a specified extent.

NOTES

"The Secretary of State": see the note on transfer of functions immediately before Part 1 of this Act.

[1.1461]
38 Transfer of property: supplemental

(1) A direction under section 37—
- (a) shall be in writing,
- (b) may be given only following consultation with the former Commission to which the direction relates and, where the Secretary of State thinks it appropriate, the Commission for Equality and Human Rights, and
- (c) may be varied or revoked by a further direction.

(2) In so far as is appropriate as a consequence of a transfer effected by or by virtue of section 37—
- (a) anything done by or in relation to any of the former Commissions which has effect immediately before the transfer shall continue to have effect as if done by or in relation to the Commission for Equality and Human Rights, and
- (b) anything (including any legal proceedings) which immediately before the transfer is in the process of being done by or in relation to any of the former Commissions may be continued by or in relation to the Commission for Equality and Human Rights.

(3) In so far as is appropriate in consequence of a transfer effected by or by virtue of section 37 a reference to any of the former Commissions in an agreement, instrument or other document shall be treated as a reference to the Commission for Equality and Human Rights.

(4) Section 37, and a direction, scheme or order under or by virtue of that section, shall operate in relation to property, rights or liabilities—
- (a) whether or not they would otherwise be capable of being transferred,
- (b) without any instrument or other formality being required, and
- (c) irrespective of any requirement for consent that would otherwise apply.

(5) A scheme or order under or by virtue of section 37 which relates to rights or liabilities under a contract of employment—
- (a) must provide for the application of the [Transfer of Undertakings (Protection of Employment) Regulations 2006], and
- (b) must provide that for any purpose relating to an employee of a former commission who becomes an employee of the Commission for Equality and Human Rights by virtue of the scheme or order—
  - (i) a period of employment with the former commission shall be treated as a period of employment with the Commission for Equality and Human Rights, and
  - (ii) the transfer to that Commission shall not be treated as a break in service.

NOTES

Sub-s (5): the Transfer of Undertakings (Protection of Employment) Regulations 2006, SI 2006/246, reg 20, Sch 2, para 1(l) provides that the words "Transfer of Undertakings (Protection of Employment) Regulations 2006" should be substituted for the words "Transfer of Undertakings (Protection of Employment) Regulations 1981 (SI 1981/1794)" in s 39(5) of this Act. It appears that this is a drafting error as the words in question occur in sub-s (5) of this section and not in s 39(5). The amendment has been taken in above.

"The Secretary of State": see the note on transfer of functions immediately before Part 1 of this Act.

Miscellaneous

[1.1462]
39 Orders and regulations

(1) An order of a Minister of the Crown under this Part and regulations under this Part shall be made by statutory instrument.

(2) An order of a Minister of the Crown under this Part and regulations under this Part—
- (a) may make provision generally or only for specified purposes,
- (b) may make different provision for different purposes, and
- (c) may include transitional, incidental or consequential provision.

(3) An order or regulations under any of the following provisions shall be subject to annulment in pursuance of a resolution of either House of Parliament—
- (a) section 15(3),
- (b) section 28,
- (c) section 29,
- (d) section 36, and
- (e) Part 5 of Schedule 1.

(4) An order under section [15(6)]—
- (a) may, in particular, make consequential amendment of an enactment (including this Act and including an enactment in or under an Act of the Scottish Parliament), and
- (b) may not be made unless a draft has been laid before and approved by resolution of each House of Parliament.

(5) An incidental provision included in an order or regulations by virtue of subsection (2)(c) may, in particular, impose a requirement for consent to action under or by virtue of the order or regulations.

NOTES

Sub-s (4): figure in square brackets substituted by the Enterprise and Regulatory Reform Act 2013, s 64(3), (10).

40 *(Introduces Sch 3 (consequential amendments).)*

[1.1463]
41 Transitional: the Commission

(1) If an order under section 93 provides for any of sections 1 to 3 and Schedule 1 to come into force (to any extent) at a time before any of sections 8 to 32 come into force (to any extent)—

(a) the period between that time and the commencement of any of sections 8 to 32 (to any extent) is the "transitional period" for the purposes of this section, and

(b) the following provisions of this section shall have effect.

(2) During the transitional period the minimum number of Commissioners shall be five (and not as provided by paragraph 1 of Schedule 1).

(3) The Secretary of State shall, as soon as is reasonably practicable after making the first appointments under that paragraph, appoint as additional members of the Commission (to be known as Transition Commissioners)—

(a) a commissioner of the Equal Opportunities Commission nominated by its chairman,

(b) a commissioner of the Commission for Racial Equality nominated by its chairman, and

(c) a commissioner of the Disability Rights Commission nominated by its chairman.

(4) A person may nominate himself as a Transition Commissioner.

(5) If a Transition Commissioner ceases to be a commissioner of the Commission whose chairman nominated him—

(a) he shall cease to be a Transition Commissioner,

(b) the chairman of that Commission shall nominate a replacement, and

(c) the Secretary of State shall appoint the nominated replacement.

(6) A person shall hold appointment as a Transition Commissioner until a time specified by order of the Secretary of State (subject to subsection (5)); and the Secretary of State shall specify a time which in his opinion is not more than two years after the time when, by virtue of section 36, the Commission whose chairman nominated the Transition Commissioner—

(a) ceases to exist, or

(b) loses its principal functions.

(7) In all other respects the provisions of this Part apply in relation to a Transition Commissioner as in relation to another Commissioner.

NOTES

"The Secretary of State": see the note on transfer of functions immediately before Part 1 of this Act.

Orders: the Equality Act 2006 (Termination of Appointments) Order 2007, SI 2007/2604.

[1.1464]
42 Transitional: functions of the dissolved Commissions

(1) An order under section 36(1)(a) or (b) may—

(a) provide for a former Commission to continue to exercise a function in respect of a transitional case of a kind specified;

(b) provide for the Commission for Equality and Human Rights to exercise a function of a former Commission in respect of a transitional case of a kind specified.

(2) An order under section 93 commencing a provision of Schedule 3 or 4 may include a saving or a consequential or incidental provision for the purpose of the operation of provision made by virtue of subsection (1) above; and the saving, consequential or incidental provision may, in particular, include provision applying, disapplying or modifying the application of a provision of this Act or of another enactment (including an enactment in or under an Act of the Scottish Parliament).

(3) A code of practice issued by a Commission dissolved by virtue of section 36, or which relates to a function of a Commission removed by virtue of section 36(1)(b)—

(a) shall continue to have effect until revoked by the Secretary of State, at the request of the Commission for Equality and Human Rights, by order made by statutory instrument, and

(b) may be revised by the Commission for Equality and Human Rights as if it had been issued under section 14.

(4) Consultation undertaken by a former Commission in relation to the issue or revision of a code of practice may be relied upon by the Commission for Equality and Human Rights for a purpose of section 14.

(5) An order under subsection (3)(a) shall be subject to annulment in pursuance of a resolution of either House of Parliament.

NOTES

"The Secretary of State": see the note on transfer of functions immediately before Part 1 of this Act.

Orders: the Equality Act 2006 (Dissolution of Commissions and Consequential and Transitional Provisions) Order 2007, SI 2007/2602; the Disability Discrimination Code of Practice (Trade Organisations and Qualifications Bodies) (Revocation) Order 2008, SI 2008/1336; the Former Equality Commissions' Codes of Practice (Employment, Equal Pay, and Rights of Access for Disabled Persons) (Revocation) Order 2011, SI 2011/776.

43–80 *(S 43 repealed by the Equality Act 2010, s 211, Sch 26, paras 61, 79, Sch 27, Pt 1; ss 44–80 (Pt 2: Discrimination on grounds of religion or belief in relation to goods, facilities and services) repealed by the Equality Act 2010, s 211, Sch 26, paras 61, 80, Sch 27, Pt 1.)*

PART 3
DISCRIMINATION ON GROUNDS OF SEXUAL ORIENTATION

81 (*Repealed by the Equality Act 2010, s 211, Sch 26, paras 61, 81, Sch 27, Pt 1; for transitory provisions relating to ships and hovercraft, see the Equality Act 2010 (Commencement No 4, Savings, Consequential, Transitional, Transitory and Incidental Provisions and Revocation) Order 2010, SI 2010/2317, art 10(2), Sch 1.*)

82–90 (*S 82 (Regulations for Northern Ireland) outside the scope of this work; ss 83–90 (Pt 4) contain various amendments to the Sex Discrimination Act 1975, the Race Relations Act 1976, and the Disability Discrimination Act 1995 (all repealed).*)

PART 5
GENERAL

91 (*Introduces Schedule 4 (Repeals).*)

[1.1465]
92 Crown application

This Act applies (except as is otherwise expressly provided) to—

(a) Ministers of the Crown,
(b) government departments,
(c) office-holders in the Scottish Administration (within the meaning of section 126(7) of the Scotland Act 1998 (c 46)),
[(ca) the Welsh Ministers, the First Minister for Wales and the Counsel General to the Welsh Assembly Government,] and
(d) other agents of the Crown.

NOTES

Para (ca) inserted by the Government of Wales Act 2006 (Consequential Modifications and Transitional Provisions) Order 2007, SI 2007/1388, art 3, Sch 1, paras 112, 119.

Construction of references to an office-holder in the Scottish Administration: unless the context otherwise requires, references to an office-holder in the Scottish Administration are to be taken to include a reference to the Scottish Courts and Tribunals Service: see the Judiciary and Courts (Scotland) Act 2008 (Consequential Provisions and Modifications) Order 2009, SI 2009/2231, art 3.

Welsh Assembly Government: see the Wales Act 2014, s 4 which provides that, unless the context requires otherwise, any reference to the Welsh Assembly Government is to be read as, or as including, a reference to the Welsh Government.

[1.1466]
93 Commencement

(1) The preceding provisions of this Act, except for sections 41, 42 and 86, shall come into force in accordance with provision made by the Secretary of State by order.
(2) An order under subsection (1)—

(a) shall be made by statutory instrument,
(b) may make provision generally or only for a specified purpose,
(c) may make different provision for different purposes, and
(d) may include transitional provisions and savings.

NOTES

"The Secretary of State": see the note on transfer of functions immediately before Part 1 of this Act.

Orders: the Equality Act 2006 (Commencement No 1) Order 2006, SI 2006/1082; the Equality Act 2006 (Commencement No 2) Order 2007, SI 2007/1092; the Equality Act 2006 (Commencement No 3 and Savings) Order 2007, SI 2007/2603.

[1.1467]
94 Extent

(1) This Act extends only to—

(a) England and Wales, and
(b) Scotland.

(2) But—

(a) section 82 extends only to Northern Ireland, and
(b) except as provided by subsection (3), an amendment of an enactment by this Act shall have the same extent as the enactment amended (or as the relevant part of the enactment amended).

(3) Paragraphs 36 to 38 . . . of Schedule 3 (which amend the Estate Agents Act 1979 (c 38) . . .), together with corresponding entries in Schedule 4, shall not extend to Northern Ireland.

NOTES

Sub-s (3): words omitted repealed by the Equality Act 2010, s 211, Sch 26, paras 61, 83, Sch 27, Pt 1.

[1.1468]
95 Short title

This Act may be cited as the Equality Act 2006.

SCHEDULES

SCHEDULE 1
THE COMMISSION: CONSTITUTION, &C

Section 2

PART 1
CONSTITUTION

Membership

[1.1469]

1. (1) The [Secretary of State] shall appoint not less than 10 or more than 15 individuals as members of the Commission (to be known as Commissioners).

(2) The chief executive of the Commission (appointed under paragraph 7 below) shall be a Commissioner *ex officio*.

2. (1) In appointing Commissioners the [Secretary of State] shall—

(a) appoint an individual only if the [Secretary of State] thinks that the individual—

(i) has experience or knowledge relating to a relevant matter, or

(ii) is suitable for appointment for some other special reason, and

(b) have regard to the desirability of the Commissioners together having experience and knowledge relating to the relevant matters.

(2) For the purposes of sub-paragraph (1) the relevant matters are those matters in respect of which the Commission has functions including, in particular—

(a) discrimination (whether on grounds of age, disability, gender, gender reassignment, race, religion or belief, sexual orientation or otherwise), and

(b) human rights.

(3) The [Secretary of State] shall ensure that the Commission includes—

(a) a Commissioner appointed under paragraph 1(1) who is (or has been) a disabled person,

(b) a Commissioner appointed under paragraph 1(1), with the consent of the Scottish Ministers, who knows about conditions in Scotland, and

(c) a Commissioner appointed under paragraph 1(1), with the consent of the [Welsh Ministers], who knows about conditions in Wales.

(4) A person may not be appointed for the purpose of satisfying more than one paragraph of sub-paragraph (3).

Tenure

3. (1) A Commissioner shall hold and vacate office in accordance with the terms of his appointment (subject to this Schedule).

(2) The appointment of a Commissioner must be expressed to be for a specified period of not less than two years or more than five years.

(3) A Commissioner whose period of membership has expired may be re-appointed.

(4) A Commissioner may resign by notice in writing to the [Secretary of State].

(5) The [Secretary of State] may dismiss a Commissioner who is, in the opinion of the [Secretary of State], unable, unfit or unwilling to perform his functions.

(6) This paragraph does not apply to the chief executive.

Chairman

4. (1) The [Secretary of State] shall appoint—

(a) a Commissioner as Chairman, and

(b) one or more Commissioners as deputy Chairman.

(2) The Chairman shall—

(a) preside over meetings of the Commission,

(b) perform such functions as may be specified in the terms of his appointment, and

(c) perform such other functions as may be assigned to him by the Commission.

(3) A deputy Chairman—

(a) may act for the Chairman when he is unavailable, and

(b) shall perform—

(i) such functions as may be specified in the terms of his appointment, and

(ii) such other functions as the Chairman may delegate or assign to him.

(4) The Chairman or a deputy Chairman—

(a) shall vacate office if he ceases to be a Commissioner,

(b) may resign by notice in writing to the [Secretary of State], and

(c) otherwise, shall hold and vacate office in accordance with the terms of his appointment (and may be reappointed).

(5) If the Chairman resigns he shall cease to be a Commissioner (but he may be reappointed as a Commissioner).

(6) The chief executive may not be appointed Chairman or deputy Chairman.

NOTES

The words "Secretary of State" in square brackets in every place they occur were substituted by the Transfer of Functions (Equality) Order 2010, SI 2010/1839, arts 3(1)(f), 7, Schedule, para 14(1), (2)(o).

The words in the second pair of square brackets in para 2(3) were substituted by the Government of Wales Act 2006 (Consequential Modifications and Transitional Provisions) Order 2007, SI 2007/1388, art 3, Sch 1, paras 112, 120.

PART 2
PROCEEDINGS

Procedure

[1.1470]

5. The Commission may regulate its own proceedings (subject to this Schedule).

6. (1) The Commission shall determine a quorum for its meetings.

(2) At least five Commissioners must participate in the process by which a determination under sub-paragraph (1) is made.

Staff

7. (1) The Commission—
- (a) shall appoint a chief executive, and
- (b) may appoint other staff.

(2) A person may be appointed under sub-paragraph (1)(a) only with the consent of the [Secretary of State].

(3) An appointment may be made under sub-paragraph (1)(b) only if consistent with arrangements determined by the Commission and approved by the [Secretary of State] as to—
- (a) numbers, and
- (b) terms and conditions of appointment.

8. (*Amends the Employers' Liability (Compulsory Insurance) Act 1969, s 3.*)

Investigating Commissioners

9. (1) The Commission may appoint one or more Investigating Commissioners.

(2) An Investigating Commissioner may be appointed only—
- (a) for the purpose of having delegated to him by the Commission the function of taking action of a kind listed in sub-paragraph (3), and
- (b) with the consent of the [Secretary of State].

(3) The kinds of action referred to in sub-paragraph (2)(a) are—
- (a) carrying out an inquiry under section 16,
- (b) carrying out an investigation under section 20,
- (c) giving an unlawful act notice under section 21, and
- (d) entering into an agreement under section 23.

(4) An Investigating Commissioner is not a Commissioner; but paragraphs 3(1), (4) and (5) and 33 apply to him as if he were (and with the substitution of references to the Commission for references to the [Secretary of State]).

Delegation

10. (1) The Commission may delegate a function—
- (a) to a Commissioner,
- (b) to staff, or
- (c) in accordance with paragraph 9, to an Investigating Commissioner.

(2) Paragraphs 15, 21, 22, 29, 30 and 52 make provision about delegation to committees.

Committees

11. (1) The Commission may establish one or more committees (to be known as advisory committees) to advise—
- (a) the Commission, or
- (b) an Investigating Commissioner.

(2) An advisory committee may include any of the following—
- (a) Commissioners;
- (b) staff;
- (c) other non-Commissioners.

12. (1) The Commission may establish one or more committees to whom the Commission may delegate functions (to be known as decision-making committees).

(2) A decision-making committee may include any of the following—
- (a) Commissioners;
- (b) staff;
- (c) other non-Commissioners.

(3) The Commission shall ensure that the Chairman of each decision-making committee is a Commissioner.

(4) In allocating its resources the Commission shall ensure that each decision-making committee receives a share sufficient to enable it to exercise its functions.

13. A member of a committee shall hold and vacate office in accordance with the terms of his appointment by the Commission (which may include provision for dismissal).

14. The Commission—

(a) may, to any extent, regulate the proceedings of a committee (and may, in particular, determine a quorum for meetings),

(b) may, to any extent, permit a committee to regulate its own proceedings (and may, in particular, enable a committee to determine a quorum for meetings), and

(c) may dissolve a committee.

15. (1) The Commission may delegate a function to a decision-making committee.

(2) This paragraph is subject to paragraphs 21, 22, 29, 30 and 52.

Scotland Committee

16. (1) The Commission shall establish a decision-making committee to be known as the Scotland Committee.

(2) The Commission shall ensure that the Scotland Committee is established before any of sections 8 to 12 comes into force (to any extent).

17. The Commission shall appoint as the Chairman of the Scotland Committee a Commissioner appointed for the purpose of satisfying paragraph 2(3)(b).

18. The Commission shall appoint each member of the Scotland Committee for a period of not less than two years or more than 5 years, subject to the possibilities of—

(a) reappointment, and

(b) dismissal in accordance with the terms of appointment.

19. The Scotland Committee shall advise the Commission about the exercise of the Commission's functions in so far as they affect Scotland.

20. Before exercising a function in a manner which in the opinion of the Commission is likely to affect persons in Scotland, the Commission shall consult the Scotland Committee.

21. (1) The power under section 13—

(a) shall be treated by virtue of this paragraph as having been delegated by the Commission to the Scotland Committee in so far as its exercise, in the opinion of the Commission, affects Scotland, and

(b) to that extent shall not be exercisable by the Commission.

(2) . . .

(3) Sub-paragraph (1) shall not prevent the Commission from making arrangements under section 13(1)(d) or (e) for the provision of advice or guidance to persons anywhere in Great Britain.

22. (1) The power under section 11(2)(c)—

(a) shall be treated by virtue of this paragraph as having been delegated by the Commission to the Scotland Committee in so far as it concerns the giving of advice to devolved government about enactments which, in the opinion of the Commission, affect only Scotland, and

(b) to that extent shall not be exercisable by the Commission.

(2) The power under section 11(2)(d)—

(a) shall be treated by virtue of this paragraph as having been delegated by the Commission to the Scotland Committee in so far as it concerns the giving of advice to devolved government about proposed changes in the law which, in the opinion of the Commission, would affect only Scotland, and

(b) to that extent shall not be exercisable by the Commission.

(3) . . .

23. In allocating its resources the Commission shall ensure that the Scotland Committee receives a share sufficient to enable it to exercise its functions.

Wales Committee

24. (1) The Commission shall establish a decision-making committee to be known as the Wales Committee.

(2) The Commission shall ensure that the Wales Committee is established before any of sections 8 to 12 comes into force (to any extent).

25. The Commission shall appoint as the Chairman of the Wales Committee a Commissioner appointed for the purpose of satisfying paragraph 2(3)(c).

26. The Commission shall appoint each member of the Wales Committee for a period of not less than two years or more than 5 years, subject to the possibilities of—

(a) reappointment, and
(b) dismissal in accordance with the terms of appointment.

27. The Wales Committee shall advise the Commission about the exercise of its functions in so far as they affect Wales.

28. Before exercising a function in a manner which in the opinion of the Commission is likely to affect persons in Wales, the Commission shall consult the Wales Committee.

29. (1) The power under section 13—
(a) shall be treated by virtue of this paragraph as having been delegated by the Commission to the Wales Committee in so far as its exercise, in the opinion of the Commission, affects Wales, and
(b) to that extent shall not be exercisable by the Commission.

(2) . . .

(3) Sub-paragraph (1) shall not prevent the Commission from making arrangements under section 13(1)(d) or (e) for the provision of advice or guidance to persons anywhere in Great Britain.

30. (1) The power under section 11(2)(c)—
(a) shall be treated by virtue of this paragraph as having been delegated by the Commission to the Wales Committee in so far as it concerns the giving of advice to devolved government about enactments which, in the opinion of the Commission, affect only Wales, and
(b) to that extent shall not be exercisable by the Commission.

(2) The power under section 11(2)(d)—
(a) shall be treated by virtue of this paragraph as having been delegated by the Commission to the Wales Committee in so far as it concerns the giving of advice to devolved government about proposed changes in the law which, in the opinion of the Commission, would affect only Wales, and
(b) to that extent shall not be exercisable by the Commission.

(3) . . .

31. In allocating its resources the Commission shall ensure that the Wales Committee receives a share sufficient to enable it to exercise its functions.

Annual report

32. (1) The Commission shall for each financial year prepare a report on the performance of its functions in that year (to be known as its annual report).

(2) An annual report shall, in particular, indicate in what manner and to what extent the Commission's performance of its functions has accorded to the plan under section 4.

(3) The matters addressed by an annual report shall, in particular, include the Commission's activities in relation to—
(a) Scotland, and
(b) Wales.

(4) The Commission shall send each annual report to the [Secretary of State] within such period, beginning with the end of the financial year to which the report relates, as he may specify.

(5) The [Secretary of State] shall lay before Parliament a copy of each annual report received under sub-paragraph (4).

(6) The Commission shall send a copy of each annual report to—
(a) the Scottish Parliament, and
(b) the National Assembly for Wales.

Savings

33. The validity of proceedings of the Commission shall not be affected by—
(a) a vacancy (whether for Commissioner, Chairman, deputy Chairman or chief executive), or
(b) a defect in relation to an appointment.

34. The validity of proceedings of a committee of the Commission shall not be affected by—
(a) a vacancy (including a vacancy in the office of Chairman), or
(b) a defect in relation to an appointment (including a defect in relation to the office of Chairman).

NOTES

The words "Secretary of State" in square brackets in every place they occur were substituted by the Transfer of Functions (Equality) Order 2010, SI 2010/1839, arts 3(1)(f), 7, Schedule, para 14(1), (2)(o).

Paras 21(2), 22(3), 29(2), 30(3) were repealed by the Equality Act 2006 (Dissolution of the Disability Committee) Order 2014, SI 2014/406, art 3(2), as from 31 March 2017.

PART 3
MONEY

Remuneration, &c

[1.1471]

35. (1) The Commission may pay to the Chairman, a deputy Chairman or another Commissioner—
(a) such remuneration as the [Secretary of State] may determine, and

(b) such travelling and other allowances as the [Secretary of State] may determine.

(2) The Commission may pay to or in respect of the Chairman, a deputy Chairman or another Commissioner such sums as the [Secretary of State] may determine by way of, or in respect of, pensions, allowances or gratuities.

(3) If the [Secretary of State] thinks that there are special circumstances that make it right for a person ceasing to hold office as Chairman, deputy Chairman or Commissioner to receive compensation, the Commission may pay to him such compensation as the [Secretary of State] may determine.

(4) This paragraph does not apply to the Chief Executive.

36. (1) The Commission may pay sums to or in respect of a member or former member of staff by way of or in respect of—

(a) remuneration,
(b) allowances,
(c) pensions,
(d) gratuities, or
(e) compensation for loss of employment.

(2) (*Amends the Superannuation Act 1972, Sch 1.*)

(3) The Commission shall pay to the Minister for the Civil Service such sums as he may determine in respect of any increase attributable to sub-paragraph (2) in the sums payable out of money provided by Parliament under the Superannuation Act 1972 (c 11).

37. (1) The Commission may, with the approval of the [Secretary of State], pay sums to or in respect of a member or former member of an advisory or decision-making committee by way of or in respect of —

(a) remuneration,
(b) allowances, or
(c) gratuities.

(2) This paragraph does not apply in relation to a person who is a member of staff of the Commission.

(3) Approval for the purposes of sub-paragraph (1) may be general or specific.

Funding by [Secretary of State]

38. The [Secretary of State] shall pay to the Commission such sums as appear to the [Secretary of State] reasonably sufficient for the purpose of enabling the Commission to perform its functions.

Charging

39. The Commission may make a charge for a service provided under section 13 . . .

Accounts

40. (1) The Commission shall—

(a) keep proper accounting records, and
(b) prepare a statement of accounts in respect of each financial year in such form as the [Secretary of State] may direct.

(2) The Commission shall send a copy of a statement under sub-paragraph (1)(b) to—

(a) the [Secretary of State], and
(b) the Comptroller and Auditor General.

(3) A copy of a statement must be sent under sub-paragraph (2) within such period, beginning with the end of the financial year to which the statement relates, as the [Secretary of State] may direct.

(4) The Comptroller and Auditor General shall—

(a) examine, certify and report on a statement received under this paragraph, and
(b) lay a copy of the statement and his report before Parliament.

(5) The [Secretary of State] may make a direction under sub-paragraph (1)(b) only with the consent of the Treasury.

Financial year

41. (1) The financial year of the Commission shall be the period of 12 months ending with 31st March.

(2) But the first financial year of the Commission shall be the period—

(a) beginning with the coming into force of section 1, and
(b) ending with—
  (i) the following 31st March, if that section comes into force on 1st April, and
  (ii) the second following 31st March, in any other case.

NOTES

The words "Secretary of State" in square brackets in every place they occur were substituted by the Transfer of Functions (Equality) Order 2010, SI 2010/1839, arts 3(1)(f), 7, Schedule, para 14(1), (2)(o).

Para 39: words omitted repealed by the Enterprise and Regulatory Reform Act 2013, s 64(3), (11)(a).

PART 4
STATUS, &C

Status

[1.1472]

42. (1) The Commission shall not—

(a) be regarded as the servant or agent of the Crown, or
(b) enjoy any status, immunity or privilege of the Crown.

(2) Service as Commissioner, Investigating Commissioner or employee of the Commission is not employment in the civil service of the State.

(3) The [Secretary of State] shall have regard to the desirability of ensuring that the Commission is under as few constraints as reasonably possible in determining—

(a) its activities,
(b) its timetables, and
(c) its priorities.

Supervision

43. (*Amends the Parliamentary Commissioner Act 1967, Sch 2.*)

Disqualifications

44, 45. (*Amend the House of Commons Disqualification Act 1975, Sch 1 and the Northern Ireland Assembly Disqualification Act 1975, Sch 1.*)

46. A Commissioner or Investigating Commissioner, and a member of a decision-making committee of the Commission, shall be disqualified from being a member of the National Assembly for Wales.

Records

47, 48. (*Amend the Public Records Act 1958, Sch 1, and the Freedom of Information Act 2000, Sch 1.*)

NOTES

Para 42: words in square brackets substituted by the Transfer of Functions (Equality) Order 2010, SI 2010/1839, arts 3(1)(f), 7, Schedule, para 14(1), (2)(o).

PART 5

(*Repealed by the Equality Act 2006 (Dissolution of the Disability Committee) Order 2014, SI 2014/406, art 3(1), as from 31 March 2017.*)

SCHEDULE 2
INQUIRIES, INVESTIGATIONS AND ASSESSMENTS

Sections 16, 20 and 31

Introduction

[1.1473]

1. This Schedule applies to—

(a) inquiries under section 16,
(b) investigations under section 20, and
(c) assessments under section 31.

Terms of reference

2. Before conducting an inquiry the Commission shall—

(a) publish the terms of reference of the inquiry in a manner that the Commission thinks is likely to bring the inquiry to the attention of persons whom it concerns or who are likely to be interested in it, and
(b) in particular, give notice of the terms of reference to any persons specified in them.

3. Before conducting an investigation the Commission shall—

(a) prepare terms of reference specifying the person to be investigated and the nature of the unlawful act which the Commission suspects,
(b) give the person to be investigated notice of the proposed terms of reference,
(c) give the person to be investigated an opportunity to make representations about the proposed terms of reference,
(d) consider any representations made, and
(e) publish the terms of reference once settled.

4. Before conducting an assessment of a person's compliance with a duty the Commission shall—

(a) prepare terms of reference,
(b) give the person notice of the proposed terms of reference,
(c) give the person an opportunity to make representations about the proposed terms of reference,
(d) consider any representations made, and
(e) publish the terms of reference once settled.

5. Paragraphs 2 to 4 shall apply in relation to revised terms of reference as they apply in relation to original terms of reference.

Representations

6. (1) The Commission shall make arrangements for giving persons an opportunity to make representations in relation to inquiries, investigations and assessments.

(2) In particular, in the course of an investigation, inquiry or assessment the Commission must give any person specified in the terms of reference an opportunity to make representations.

7. Arrangements under paragraph 6 may (but need not) include arrangements for oral representations.

8. (1) The Commission shall consider representations made in relation to an inquiry, investigation or assessment.

(2) But the Commission may, where they think it appropriate, refuse to consider representations—
  (a) made neither by nor on behalf of a person specified in the terms of reference, or
  (b) made on behalf of a person specified in the terms of reference by a person who is not [a relevant lawyer].

[(2A) "Relevant lawyer" means—
  (a) an advocate or solicitor in Scotland, or
  (b) a person who, for the purposes of the Legal Services Act 2007, is an authorised person in relation to an activity which constitutes the exercise of a right of audience or the conduct of litigation (within the meaning of that Act).]

(3) If the Commission refuse to consider representations in reliance on sub-paragraph (2) they shall give the person who makes them written notice of the Commission's decision and the reasons for it.

Evidence

9. In the course of an inquiry, investigation or assessment the Commission may give a notice under this paragraph to any person.

10. (1) A notice given to a person under paragraph 9 may require him—
  (a) to provide information in his possession,
  (b) to produce documents in his possession, or
  (c) to give oral evidence.

(2) A notice under paragraph 9 may include provision about—
  (a) the form of information, documents or evidence;
  (b) timing.

(3) A notice under paragraph 9—
  (a) may not require a person to provide information that he is prohibited from disclosing by virtue of an enactment,
  (b) may not require a person to do anything that he could not be compelled to do in proceedings before the High Court or the Court of Session, and
  (c) may not require a person to attend at a place unless the Commission undertakes to pay the expenses of his journey.

11. The recipient of a notice under paragraph 9 may apply to [the county court] (in England and Wales) or to the sheriff (in Scotland) to have the notice cancelled on the grounds that the requirement imposed by the notice is—
  (a) unnecessary having regard to the purpose of the inquiry, investigation or assessment to which the notice relates, or
  (b) otherwise unreasonable.

12. (1) Sub-paragraph (2) applies where the Commission thinks that a person—
  (a) has failed without reasonable excuse to comply with a notice under paragraph 9, or
  (b) is likely to fail without reasonable excuse to comply with a notice under paragraph 9.

(2) The Commission may apply to [the county court] (in England and Wales) or to the sheriff (in Scotland) for an order requiring a person to take such steps as may be specified in the order to comply with the notice.

13. (1) A person commits an offence if without reasonable excuse he—
  (a) fails to comply with a notice under paragraph 9 or an order under paragraph 12(2),
  (b) falsifies anything provided or produced in accordance with a notice under paragraph 9 or an order under paragraph 12(2), or
  (c) makes a false statement in giving oral evidence in accordance with a notice under paragraph 9.

(2) A person who is guilty of an offence under this paragraph shall be liable on summary conviction to a fine not exceeding level 5 on the standard scale.

14. (1) Where a person is given a notice under paragraph 9 he shall disregard it, and notify the Commission that he is disregarding it, in so far as he thinks it would require him—
  (a) to disclose sensitive information within the meaning of [paragraph 5 of Schedule 1 to the Justice and Security Act 2013] (Intelligence and Security Committee [of Parliament]),
  (b) to disclose information which might lead to the identification of an employee or agent of an intelligence service (other than one whose identity is already known to the Commission),

(c) to disclose information which might provide details of processes used in recruiting, selecting or training employees or agents of an intelligence service,

(d) to disclose information which might provide details of, or cannot practicably be separated from, information falling within any of paragraphs (a) to (c), or

(e) to make a disclosure of information relating to an intelligence service which would prejudice the interests of national security.

(2) In sub-paragraph (1) "intelligence service" means—

(a) the Security Service,

(b) the Secret Intelligence Service, and

(c) the Government Communications Headquarters.

(3) Where in response to a notice under paragraph 9 a person gives a notice to the Commission under sub-paragraph (1) above—

(a) paragraphs 12 and 13 shall not apply in relation to that part of the notice under paragraph 9 to which the notice under sub-paragraph (1) above relates,

(b) the Commission may apply to the tribunal established by section 65 of the Regulation of Investigatory Powers Act 2000 (c 23) for an order requiring the person to take such steps as may be specified in the order to comply with the notice,

(c) the following provisions of that Act shall apply in relation to proceedings under this paragraph as they apply in relation to proceedings under that Act (with any necessary modifications)—

(i) section 67(7), (8) and (10) to (12) (determination),

(ii) section 68 (procedure), and

(iii) section 69 (rules), and

(d) the tribunal shall determine proceedings under this paragraph by considering the opinion of the person who gave the notice under sub-paragraph (1) above in accordance with the principles that would be applied by a court on an application for judicial review of the giving of the notice.

(4) Where the Commission receives information or documents from or relating to an intelligence service in response to a notice under paragraph 9, the Commission shall store and use the information or documents in accordance with any arrangements specified by the Secretary of State.

(5) The recipient of a notice under paragraph 9 may apply to the High Court (in England and Wales) or the Court of Session (in Scotland) to have the notice cancelled on the grounds that the requirement imposed by the notice is undesirable for reasons of national security, other than for the reason that it would require a disclosure of a kind to which sub-paragraph (1) above applies.

Reports

15. The Commission shall publish a report of its findings on an inquiry, investigation or assessment.

Recommendations

16. (1) The Commission may make recommendations—

(a) as part of a report of an inquiry, investigation or assessment under paragraph 15, or

(b) in respect of a matter arising in the course of an inquiry, investigation or assessment.

(2) A recommendation may be addressed to any class of person.

Effect of report

17. (1) A court or tribunal—

(a) may have regard to a finding of the report of an inquiry, investigation or assessment, but

(b) shall not treat it as conclusive.

18. A person to whom a recommendation in the report of an inquiry, investigation or assessment is addressed shall have regard to it.

Courts and tribunals

19. An inquiry, investigation or assessment may not question (whether expressly or by necessary implication) the findings of a court or tribunal.

Intelligence services

20. (1) An inquiry may not consider—

(a) whether an intelligence service has acted (or is acting) in a way which is incompatible with a person's human rights, or

(b) other matters concerning human rights in relation to an intelligence service.

(2) In this paragraph "intelligence service" has the same meaning as in paragraph 14.

NOTES

Para 8: words in square brackets in sub-para (2)(b) substituted, and sub-para (2A) added, by the Legal Services Act 2007, s 208(1), Sch 21, para 152.

Paras 11, 12: words in square brackets substituted by the Crime and Courts Act 2013, s 17(5), Sch 9, Pt 3, para 52.

Para 14: in sub-para (1) words in first pair of square brackets substituted, and words in second pair of square brackets inserted, by the Justice and Security Act 2013, s 19(1), Sch 2, Pt 1, para 6.

SCHEDULES 3, 4

(Sch 3 (Amendments Consequential on Part 1) and Sch 4 (Repeals) contains various amendments and repeals; in so far as these are still in force and relevant to this Handbook, they have been incorporated at the appropriate place.)

IMMIGRATION, ASYLUM AND NATIONALITY ACT 2006

(2006 c 13)

ARRANGEMENT OF SECTIONS

Employment

An Act to make provision about immigration, asylum and nationality; and for connected purposes

[30 March 2006]

NOTES

Only those provisions of this Act relevant to employment law are reproduced. Provisions not reproduced are not annotated. The provisions reproduced here extend to the whole of the United Kingdom (see s 63 (Extent)).

See *Harvey* AI(5).

Employment

[1.1474]

15 Penalty

(1) It is contrary to this section to employ an adult subject to immigration control if—

(a) he has not been granted leave to enter or remain in the United Kingdom, or

(b) his leave to enter or remain in the United Kingdom—

(i) is invalid,

(ii) has ceased to have effect (whether by reason of curtailment, revocation, cancellation, passage of time or otherwise), or

(iii) is subject to a condition preventing him from accepting the employment.

(2) The Secretary of State may give an employer who acts contrary to this section a notice requiring him to pay a penalty of a specified amount not exceeding the prescribed maximum.

(3) An employer is excused from paying a penalty if he shows that he complied with any prescribed requirements in relation to the employment.

(4) But the excuse in subsection (3) shall not apply to an employer who knew, at any time during the period of the employment, that it was contrary to this section.

(5) The Secretary of State may give a penalty notice without having established whether subsection (3) applies.

(6) A penalty notice must—

(a) state why the Secretary of State thinks the employer is liable to the penalty,

(b) state the amount of the penalty,

(c) specify a date, at least 28 days after the date specified in the notice as the date on which it is given, before which the penalty must be paid,

(d) specify how the penalty must be paid,

(e) explain how the employer may object to the penalty [or make an appeal against it], and

(f) explain how the Secretary of State may enforce the penalty.

(7) An order prescribing requirements for the purposes of subsection (3) may, in particular—

(a) require the production to an employer of a document of a specified description;

(b) require the production to an employer of one document of each of a number of specified descriptions;

(c) require an employer to take specified steps to verify, retain, copy or record the content of a document produced to him in accordance with the order;

(d) require action to be taken before employment begins;

(e) require action to be taken at specified intervals or on specified occasions during the course of employment.

NOTES

Sub-s (6): words in square brackets in para (e) inserted by the Immigration Act 2014, s 73, Sch 9, Pt 5, para 61, as from 28 July 2014.

Orders: the Immigration (Restrictions on Employment) Order 2007, SI 2007/3290 at **[2.931]**; the Immigration (Employment of Adults Subject to Immigration Control) (Maximum Penalty) Order 2008, SI 2008/132 at **[2.946]**; the Immigration (Restrictions on Employment) (Amendment) Order 2009, SI 2009/2908; the Immigration (Restrictions on Employment) (Codes of Practice and Amendment) Order 2014, SI 2014/1183; the Immigration (Employment of Adults Subject to Immigration Control) (Maximum Penalty) (Amendment) Order 2014, SI 2014/1262.

[1.1475]
16 Objection

(1) This section applies where an employer to whom a penalty notice is given objects on the ground that—

(a) he is not liable to the imposition of a penalty,
(b) he is excused payment by virtue of section 15(3), or
(c) the amount of the penalty is too high.

(2) The employer may give a notice of objection to the Secretary of State.

(3) A notice of objection must—

(a) be in writing,
(b) give the objector's reasons,
(c) be given in the prescribed manner, and
(d) be given before the end of the prescribed period.

(4) Where the Secretary of State receives a notice of objection to a penalty he shall consider it and—

(a) cancel the penalty,
(b) reduce the penalty,
(c) increase the penalty, or
(d) determine to take no action.

(5) Where the Secretary of State considers a notice of objection he shall—

(a) have regard to the code of practice under section 19 (in so far as the objection relates to the amount of the penalty),
(b) inform the objector of his decision before the end of the prescribed period or such longer period as he may agree with the objector,
(c) if he increases the penalty, issue a new penalty notice under section 15, and
(d) if he reduces the penalty, notify the objector of the reduced amount.

NOTES

Orders: the Immigration (Restrictions on Employment) Order 2007, SI 2007/3290 at **[2.931]**.

[1.1476]
17 Appeal

(1) An employer to whom a penalty notice is given may appeal to the court on the ground that—

(a) he is not liable to the imposition of a penalty,
(b) he is excused payment by virtue of section 15(3), or
(c) the amount of the penalty is too high.

(2) The court may—

(a) allow the appeal and cancel the penalty,
(b) allow the appeal and reduce the penalty, or
(c) dismiss the appeal.

(3) An appeal shall be a re-hearing of the Secretary of State's decision to impose a penalty and shall be determined having regard to—

(a) the code of practice under section 19 that has effect at the time of the appeal (in so far as the appeal relates to the amount of the penalty), and
(b) any other matters which the court thinks relevant (which may include matters of which the Secretary of State was unaware);

and this subsection has effect despite any provision of rules of court.

[(4A) An appeal may be brought only if the employer has given a notice of objection under section 16 and the Secretary of State—

(a) has determined the objection by issuing to the employer the penalty notice (as a result of increasing the penalty under section 16(4)(c)),
(b) has determined the objection by—
    (i) reducing the penalty under section 16(4)(b), or
    (ii) taking no action under section 16(4)(d), or
(c) has not informed the employer of a decision before the end of the period that applies for the purposes of section 16(5)(b).

(4B) An appeal must be brought within the period of 28 days beginning with the relevant date.

(4C) Where the appeal is brought under subsection (4A)(a), the relevant date is the date specified in the penalty notice issued in accordance with section 16(5)(c) as the date on which it is given.

(4D) Where the appeal is brought under subsection (4A)(b), the relevant date is the date specified in the notice informing the employer of the decision for the purposes of section 16(5)(b) as the date on which it is given.

(4E) Where the appeal is brought under subsection (4A)(c), the relevant date is the date on which the period that applies for the purposes of section 16(5)(b) ends.]

(6) In this section "the court" means—

(a) where the employer has his principal place of business in England and Wales, [the county court],

(b) where the employer has his principal place of business in Scotland, the sheriff, and

(c) where the employer has his principal place of business in Northern Ireland, a county court.

NOTES

Sub-ss (4A)–(4E): substituted (for the original sub-ss (4), (5)) by the Immigration Act 2014, s 44, as from 28 July 2014, except in relation to an appeal in respect of a penalty notice issued before that date (including a penalty notice issued before that date but withdrawn and, after that date, re-issued) (see SI 2014/1820, art 5).

Sub-s (6): words in square brackets in para (a) substituted by the Crime and Courts Act 2013, s 17(5), Sch 9, Pt 3, para 52.

[1.1477]

18 Enforcement

[(1) This section applies where a sum is payable to the Secretary of State as a penalty under section 15.

(1A) In England and Wales the penalty is recoverable as if it were payable under an order of the county court.

(1B) In Scotland, the penalty may be enforced in the same manner as an extract registered decree arbitral bearing a warrant for execution issued by the sheriff court of any sheriffdom in Scotland.

(1C) In Northern Ireland the penalty is recoverable as if it were payable under an order of a county court in Northern Ireland.

(1D) Where action is taken under this section for the recovery of a sum payable as a penalty under section 15, the penalty is—

(a) in relation to England and Wales, to be treated for the purposes of section 98 of the Courts Act 2003 (register of judgments and orders etc) as if it were a judgment entered in the county court;

(b) in relation to Northern Ireland, to be treated for the purposes of Article 116 of the Judgments Enforcement (Northern Ireland) Order 1981 (SI 1981/226 (NI 6)) (register of judgments) as if it were a judgment in respect of which an application has been accepted under Article 22 or 23(1) of that Order.]

(3) Money paid to the Secretary of State by way of penalty shall be paid into the Consolidated Fund.

NOTES

Sub-ss (1)–(1D): substituted (for the original sub-ss (1), (2)) by the Immigration Act 2014, s 45, as from 28 July 2014, except in relation to a sum payable to the Secretary of State as a penalty under s 15 of the Immigration, Asylum and Nationality Act 2006 if proceedings for the enforcement of the penalty were commenced before that date (see SI 2014/1820, art 6).

[1.1478]

19 Code of practice

(1) The Secretary of State shall issue a code of practice specifying factors to be considered by him in determining the amount of a penalty imposed under section 15.

(2) The code—

(a) shall not be issued unless a draft has been laid before Parliament, and

(b) shall come into force in accordance with provision made by order of the Secretary of State.

(3) The Secretary of State shall from time to time review the code and may revise and re-issue it following a review; and a reference in this section to the code includes a reference to the code as revised.

NOTES

Orders: the Immigration (Restrictions on Employment) Order 2007, SI 2007/3290 at **[2.931]**; the Immigration (Restrictions on Employment) (Codes of Practice and Amendment) Order 2014, SI 2014/1183 at **[2.1480]**; the Immigration (Restrictions on Employment) (Code of Practice and Miscellaneous Amendments) Order 2018, SI 2018/1340 at **[2.2110]**.

Code of Practice: see the Home Office Code of Practice on preventing illegal working – Civil penalty scheme for employers (2019) at **[4.107]**.

[1.1479]

20 Orders

(1) An order of the Secretary of State under section 15, 16 or 19—

(a) may make provision which applies generally or only in specified circumstances,

(b) may make different provision for different circumstances,

(c) may include transitional or incidental provision, and

(d) shall be made by statutory instrument.

(2) An order under section 15(2) may not be made unless a draft has been laid before and approved by resolution of each House of Parliament.

(3) Any other order shall be subject to annulment in pursuance of a resolution of either House of Parliament.

[1.1480]

21 Offence

(1) A person commits an offence if he employs another ("the employee") knowing that the employee is [disqualified from employment by reason of the employee's immigration status].

[(1A) A person commits an offence if the person—

(a) employs another person ("the employee") who is disqualified from employment by reason of the employee's immigration status, and

(b) has reasonable cause to believe that the employee is disqualified from employment by reason of the employee's immigration status.

(1B) For the purposes of subsections (1) and (1A) a person is disqualified from employment by reason of the person's immigration status if the person is an adult subject to immigration control and—

(a) the person has not been granted leave to enter or remain in the United Kingdom, or

(b) the person's leave to enter or remain in the United Kingdom—

(i) is invalid,

(ii) has ceased to have effect (whether by reason of curtailment, revocation, cancellation, passage of time or otherwise), or

(iii) is subject to a condition preventing the person from accepting the employment.]

(2) A person guilty of an offence under this section shall be liable—

(a) on conviction on indictment—

(i) to imprisonment for a term not exceeding [five] years,

(ii) to a fine, or

(iii) to both, or

(b) on summary conviction—

(i) to imprisonment for a term not exceeding 12 months in England and Wales or 6 months in Scotland or Northern Ireland,

(ii) to a fine not exceeding the statutory maximum, or

(iii) to both.

(3) An offence under this section shall be treated as—

(a) a relevant offence for the purpose of sections 28B and 28D of the Immigration Act 1971 (c 77) (search, entry and arrest), and

(b) an offence under Part III of that Act (criminal proceedings) for the purposes of sections 28E, 28G and 28H (search after arrest).

(4) In relation to a conviction occurring before the commencement of section 154(1) of the Criminal Justice Act 2003 (c 44) (general limit on magistrates' powers to imprison) the reference to 12 months in subsection (2)(b)(i) shall be taken as a reference to 6 months.

NOTES

Sub-s (1): words in square brackets substituted by the Immigration Act 2016, s 35(1), (2), as from 12 July 2016.

Sub-ss (1A), (1B): inserted by the Immigration Act 2016, s 35(1), (3), as from 12 July 2016.

Sub-s (2): word in square brackets substituted by the Immigration Act 2016, s 35(1), (4), as from 12 July 2016.

[1.1481]

22 Offence: bodies corporate, &c

(1) For the purposes of section 21(1) a body (whether corporate or not) shall be treated as knowing a fact about an employee if a person who has responsibility within the body for an aspect of the employment knows the fact.

[(1A) For the purposes of section 21(1A) a body (whether corporate or not) shall be treated as having reasonable cause to believe a fact about an employee if a person who has responsibility within the body for an aspect of the employment has reasonable cause to believe that fact.]

(2) If an offence under section 21(1) [or (1A)] is committed by a body corporate with the consent or connivance of an officer of the body, the officer, as well as the body, shall be treated as having committed the offence.

(3) In subsection (2) a reference to an officer of a body includes a reference to—

(a) a director, manager or secretary,

(b) a person purporting to act as a director, manager or secretary, and

(c) if the affairs of the body are managed by its members, a member.

(4) Where an offence under section 21(1) [or (1A)] is committed by a partnership (whether or not a limited partnership) subsection (2) above shall have effect, but as if a reference to an officer of the body were a reference to—

(a) a partner, and

(b) a person purporting to act as a partner.

NOTES

Sub-s (1A) inserted, and words in square brackets in sub-ss (2), (4) inserted, by the Immigration Act 2016, s 35(5)–(7), as from 12 July 2016.

[1.1482]

23 Discrimination: code of practice

(1) The Secretary of State shall issue a code of practice specifying what an employer should or should not do in order to ensure that, while avoiding liability to a penalty under section 15 and while avoiding the commission of an offence under section 21, he also avoids contravening—

(a) [the Equality Act 2010, so far as relating to race], or

(b) the Race Relations (Northern Ireland) Order 1997 (SI 869 (NI 6)).

(2) Before issuing the code the Secretary of State shall—

(a) consult—

(i) the Commission for Equality and Human Rights,

(ii) the Equality Commission for Northern Ireland,

(iii) such bodies representing employers as he thinks appropriate, and

(iv) such bodies representing workers as he thinks appropriate,

(b) publish a draft code (after that consultation),

(c) consider any representations made about the published draft, and
(d) lay a draft code before Parliament (after considering representations under paragraph (c) and with or without modifications to reflect the representations).

(3) The code shall come into force in accordance with provision made by order of the Secretary of State; and an order—
(a) may include transitional provision,
(b) shall be made by statutory instrument, and
(c) shall be subject to annulment in pursuance of a resolution of either House of Parliament.

(4) A breach of the code—
(a) shall not make a person liable to civil or criminal proceedings, but
(b) may be taken into account by a court or tribunal.

(5) The Secretary of State shall from time to time review the code and may revise and re-issue it following a review; and a reference in this section to the code includes a reference to the code as revised.

(6) Until the dissolution of the Commission for Racial Equality, the reference in subsection (2)(a)(i) to the Commission for Equality and Human Rights shall be treated as a reference to the Commission for Racial Equality.

NOTES

Sub-s (1): words in square brackets in para (a) substituted by the Equality Act 2010, s 211(1), Sch 26, Pt 1, para 86.

Orders: the Immigration (Restrictions on Employment) (Codes of Practice and Amendment) Order 2014, SI 2014/1183.

Code of Practice: see the Home Office Code of Practice: Avoiding unlawful discrimination while preventing illegal working (2014) at **[4.79]**.

[1.1483]
24 [Immigration bail]

Where a person is at large in the United Kingdom by virtue of [a grant of immigration bail to the person under Schedule 10 to the Immigration Act 2016]—
(a) he shall be treated for the purposes of sections 15(1) and [21(1B)] as if he had been granted leave to enter the United Kingdom, and
(b) any restriction as to employment imposed under [that Schedule as a condition of that person's immigration bail] shall be treated for those purposes as a condition of leave.

NOTES

Figure "21(1B)" in square brackets in para (a) substituted by the Immigration Act 2016, s 35(5), (8), as from 12 July 2016.

Other words in square brackets (including in the section heading) substituted by the Immigration Act 2016, s 61(1), (2)(b), Sch 10, Pt 2, para 39, as from 15 January 2018 (for transitional provisions relating to persons at large at that date, and the treatment of existing recognizances and bail bonds, see the Immigration Act 2016 (Commencement No 7 and Transitional Provisions) Regulations 2017, SI 2017/1241, Schedule).

[1.1484]
25 Interpretation

In sections 15 to 24—
(a) "adult" means a person who has attained the age of 16,
(b) a reference to employment is to employment under a contract of service or apprenticeship, whether express or implied and whether oral or written,
(c) a person is subject to immigration control if under the Immigration Act 1971 he requires leave to enter or remain in the United Kingdom, and
(d) "prescribed" means prescribed by order of the Secretary of State.

[1.1485]
26 Repeal

Sections 8 and 8A of the Asylum and Immigration Act 1996 (c 49) (restrictions on employment) shall cease to have effect.

WORK AND FAMILIES ACT 2006

(2006 c 18)

An Act to make provision about statutory rights to leave and pay in connection with the birth or adoption of children; to amend section 80F of the Employment Rights Act 1996; to make provision about workers' entitlement to annual leave; to provide for the increase in the sums specified in section 186(1) and 227(1) of that Act; and for connected purposes

[21 June 2006]

NOTES

See *Harvey* CI(1), H(2), J(8).

1–11 (*S 1 amends the Social Security Contributions and Benefits Act 1992, s 165 at* **[1.213]**; *s 2 amends s 171ZN of the 1992 Act at* **[1.233]**; *ss 3–10 repealed by the Children and Families Act 2014, s 126(1), Sch 7, paras 65, 66, as from 5 April 2015 (note that this repeal does not have effect in relation to (a) children whose expected week of birth ends on or before 4 April 2015, and (b) children placed for* *adoption on or before that date: see the Children and Families Act 2014 (Commencement No 3, Transitional Provisions and Savings) Order 2014, SI 2014/1640, art 16); s 11 introduces Sch 1 to this Act.)*

Miscellaneous provisions about employment rights

12 *(Amends the Employment Rights Act 1996, s 80F at* **[1.989]**.*)*

[1.1486]

13 Annual leave

(1) The Secretary of State may by regulations make provision conferring on workers the right, except in prescribed cases, to a prescribed amount of annual leave in each leave year, as defined for the purposes of the regulations.

(2) The regulations may in particular—

(a) make provision for determining the amount of annual leave to which workers are to be entitled;

(b) make provision for determining the amount of pay in respect of any period of leave which is required by the regulations to be paid leave;

(c) make provision enabling a worker to elect when to take leave to which he is entitled by virtue of the regulations, subject to any provision of the regulations enabling his employer to require him to take, or not to take, that leave at a particular time;

(d) make provision for the payment of compensation in prescribed cases to a worker who has not taken leave to which he is entitled;

(e) make provision as to the relationship between the rights conferred by the regulations and a worker's rights to leave, pay or compensation under any contract or under any Act or subordinate legislation;

(f) enable a worker to present a complaint to an employment tribunal that his employer has refused to permit him to exercise any right he has under the regulations, or has failed to pay him any amount due to him under the regulations;

(g) make, in connection with any right conferred by the regulations (including any right to payment), any other provision which is the same as or similar to any provision made, in connection with any right relating to annual leave conferred in pursuance of any [EU] obligation, by any regulations under section 2(2) of the 1972 Act made at any time before the day on which the first regulations under this section are made.

(3) Regulations under this section may make provision as to—

(a) who is to be treated as a worker for the purposes of the regulations, and

(b) who is to be treated as the worker's employer.

(4) Regulations under this section may in particular—

(a) make provision applying to—

(i) Crown employment and persons in Crown employment;

(ii) service as a member of the armed forces;

(b) make provision conferring rights to and in connection with annual leave on persons falling within any other categories of persons on whom any [EU] obligation of the United Kingdom requires a right to annual leave to be conferred.

(5) Regulations under this section may not make provision in relation to the subject-matter of the Agricultural Wages (Scotland) Act 1949 (c 30) (as that Act had effect on 1st July 1999).

(6) Regulations under this section—

(a) are to be made by statutory instrument;

(b) may make different provision for different cases;

(c) may contain incidental, supplemental, consequential, transitional or saving provision, including provision amending any Act or subordinate legislation.

(7) No statutory instrument containing regulations under this section may be made unless a draft of the instrument has been laid before, and approved by a resolution of, each House of Parliament.

(8) In this section—

"the 1972 Act" means the European Communities Act 1972 (c 68);

"the armed forces" means any of the naval, military or air forces of the Crown;

"Crown employment" has the meaning given by section 191(3) of ERA 1996;

"subordinate legislation" has the same meaning as in the Interpretation Act 1978 (c 30).

NOTES

The references in square brackets in sub-ss (2)(g), (4)(b) were substituted by the Treaty of Lisbon (Changes in Terminology) Order 2011, SI 2011/1043, art 6(1)(e).

Sub-ss (2)(g), (4)(b) and the definition "the 1972 Act" in sub-s (8) are repealed by the Employment Rights (Amendment) (EU Exit) (No 2) Regulations 2019, SI 2019/536, reg 2, Schedule, Pt 1, para 2, as from exit day (as defined in the European Union (Withdrawal) Act 2018, s 20) and subject to Pt 3 of the Schedule to the 2019 Regulations at **[2.2185]**.

Regulations: the Working Time (Amendment) Regulations 2007, SI 2007/2079 (amending the Working Time Regulations 1998, SI 1998/1833 at **[2.274]**).

Supplementary

14, 15 *(S 14 (Increase of maximum amount of a week's pay for certain purposes) provided for a one off increase to sums in ERA 1996, ss 186(1), 227(1) and is considered spent; s 15 introduces Sch 2 (repeals).)*

[1.1487]

16 Interpretation

In this Act—

"ERA 1996" means the Employment Rights Act 1996 (c 18);

"SSCBA 1992" means the Social Security Contributions and Benefits Act 1992 (c 4).

17–19 *(S 17 (Corresponding provision for Northern Ireland), s 18 (Financial provisions), s 19 (Commencement) outside the scope of this work.)*

[1.1488]

20 Short title and extent

(1) This Act may be cited as the Work and Families Act 2006.

(2) Subject to subsection (3), this Act extends to England and Wales and Scotland only.

(3) The following provisions extend also to Northern Ireland—

(a) this section and sections 17 to 19;

(b) paragraphs 2, 45, 49, and 55 to 61 of Schedule 1, and section 11 so far as relating to those paragraphs;

(c) the entry in Schedule 2 relating to the Income Tax (Earnings and Pensions) Act 2003 (c 1), and section 15 so far as relating to that entry.

SCHEDULES 1 AND 2

(Sch 1 (Leave and pay related to birth or adoptions: further amendments) contains various consequential amendments to the Social Security Act 1989, the Finance Act 1989, the Social Security Contributions and Benefits Act 1992, the Social Security Administration Act 1992, the Employment Rights Act 1996, the Finance Act 1997, the Social Security Contributions (Transfer of Functions, etc) Act 1999, the Finance Act 1999, the Employment Act 2002, the Proceeds of Crime Act 2002, the Income Tax (Earnings and Pensions) Act 2003, and the Commissioners for Revenue and Customs Act 2005; in so far as relevant to this work, these have been incorporated at the appropriate place. Sch 2 repeals certain provisions in the Social Security Contributions and Benefits Act 1992, the Employment Rights Act 1996, the Employment Act 2002, and the Income Tax (Earnings and Pensions) Act 2003 (incorporated as appropriate).)

COMPANIES ACT 2006

(2006 c 46)

ARRANGEMENT OF SECTIONS

PART 10
A COMPANY'S DIRECTORS

CHAPTER 1
APPOINTMENT AND REMOVAL OF DIRECTORS

Requirement to have directors

Appointment

Removal

CHAPTER 2
GENERAL DUTIES OF DIRECTORS

Introductory

The general duties

Supplementary provisions

An Act to reform company law and restate the greater part of the enactments relating to companies; to make other provision relating to companies and other forms of business organisation; to make provision about directors' disqualification, business names, auditors and actuaries; to amend Part 9 of the Enterprise Act 2002; and for connected purposes

[8 November 2006]

NOTES

Only certain sections of this Act are directly relevant to employment law, and accordingly, only those sections of most relevance have been included in this work. The subject matter of the sections and Schedules omitted is not annotated.

Application to other bodies, etc: various provisions of this Act are applied with modifications to specified types of other bodies, etc; these include the following: (i) the Limited Liability Partnerships (Accounts and Audit) (Application of Companies Act 2006) Regulations 2008, SI 2008/1911 (application to LLPs); (ii) the Unregistered Companies Regulations 2009, SI 2009/2436 (application to unregistered companies); (iii) the Insurance Accounts Directive (Miscellaneous Insurance Undertakings) Regulations 2008, SI 2008/565 and the Insurance Accounts Directive (Lloyd's Syndicate and Aggregate Accounts) Regulations 2008, SI 2008/1950 (application to insurance undertakings); (iv) the Bank Accounts Directive (Miscellaneous Banks) Regulations 2008, SI 2008/567 (application to banks; as to the application of certain provisions of this Act to particular banks, see also the Banking (Special Provisions) Act 2008 and the Banking Act 2009, and the Orders made under those Acts); (v) the Partnerships (Accounts) Regulations 2008, SI 2008/569 (application to partnerships); (vi) the Overseas Companies Regulations 2009, SI 2009/1801 (application to overseas companies).

Civil Procedure Rules: the Civil Procedure Rules 1998, SI 1998/3132, rule 49 (as amended), states that those Rules apply to proceedings under this Act subject to the provisions of the relevant practice direction which applies to those proceedings.

PART 10
A COMPANY'S DIRECTORS

CHAPTER 1 APPOINTMENT AND REMOVAL OF DIRECTORS

Requirement to have directors

[1.1490]
154 Companies required to have directors

(1) A private company must have at least one director.
(2) A public company must have at least two directors.

[1.1491]
155 Companies required to have at least one director who is a natural person

(1) A company must have at least one director who is a natural person.
(2) This requirement is met if the office of director is held by a natural person as a corporation sole or otherwise by virtue of an office.

NOTES

Repealed by the Small Business, Enterprise and Employment Act 2015, s 87(1), (2), as from a day to be appointed.

As to the duty of the Secretary of State to carry out a review of the Small Business, Enterprise and Employment Act 2015, s 87, see s 88 of that Act at **[1.1923]**.

Appointment

[1.1492]

[156A Each director to be a natural person

(1) A person may not be appointed a director of a company unless the person is a natural person.

(2) Subsection (1) does not prohibit the holding of the office of director by a natural person as a corporation sole or otherwise by virtue of an office.

(3) An appointment made in contravention of this section is void.

(4) Nothing in this section affects any liability of a person under any provision of the Companies Acts or any other enactment if the person—

(a) purports to act as director, or

(b) acts as shadow director,

although the person could not, by virtue of this section, be validly appointed as a director.

(5) This section has effect subject to section 156B (power to provide for exceptions from requirement that each director be a natural person).

(6) If a purported appointment is made in contravention of this section, an offence is committed by—

(a) the company purporting to make the appointment,

(b) where the purported appointment is of a body corporate or a firm that is a legal person under the law by which it is governed, that body corporate or firm, and

(c) every officer of a person falling within paragraph (a) or (b) who is in default.

For this purpose a shadow director is treated as an officer of a company.

(7) A person guilty of an offence under this section is liable on summary conviction—

(a) in England and Wales, to a fine;

(b) in Scotland or Northern Ireland, to a fine not exceeding level 5 on the standard scale.]

NOTES

Commencement: to be appointed.

Inserted, together with ss 156B, 156C, by the Small Business, Enterprise and Employment Act 2015, s 87(1), (4), as from a day to be appointed.

As to the duty of the Secretary of State to carry out a review of the Small Business, Enterprise and Employment Act 2015, s 87, see s 88 of that Act at **[1.1923]**.

[1.1493]

[156B Power to provide for exceptions from requirement that each director be a natural person

(1) The Secretary of State may make provision by regulations for cases in which a person who is not a natural person may be appointed a director of a company.

(2) The regulations must specify the circumstances in which, and any conditions subject to which, the appointment may be made.

(3) Provision made by virtue of subsection (2) may in particular include provision that an appointment may be made only with the approval of a regulatory body specified in the regulations.

(4) The regulations must include provision that a company must have at least one director who is a natural person (and for this purpose the requirement is met if the office of director is held by a natural person as a corporation sole or otherwise by virtue of an office).

(5) Regulations under this section may amend section 164 so as to require particulars relating to exceptions to be contained in a company's register of directors.

(6) The regulations may make different provision for different parts of the United Kingdom.

This is without prejudice to the general power to make different provision for different cases.

(7) Regulations under this section are subject to affirmative resolution procedure.]

NOTES

Commencement: to be appointed.

Inserted as noted to s 156A at **[1.1492]**.

[1.1494]

[156C Existing director who is not a natural person

(1) In this section "the relevant day" is the day after the end of the period of 12 months beginning with the day on which section 156A comes into force.

(2) Where—

(a) a person appointed a director of a company before section 156A comes into force is not a natural person, and

(b) the case is not one excepted from that section by regulations under section 156B,

that person ceases to be a director on the relevant day.

(3) The company must—

(a) make the necessary consequential alteration in its register of directors, and

(b) give notice to the registrar of the change in accordance with section 167.

(4) If an election is in force under section 167A in respect of the company, the company must, in place of doing the things required by subsection (3), deliver to the registrar in accordance with section 167D the information of which the company would otherwise have been obliged to give notice under subsection (3).

(5) If it appears to the registrar that—

(a) a notice should have, but has not, been given in accordance with subsection (3)(b), or

(b) information should have, but has not, been delivered in accordance with subsection (4),

the registrar must place a note in the register recording the fact.]

NOTES

Commencement: to be appointed.

Inserted as noted to s 156A at **[1.1492]**.

[1.1495]

160 Appointment of directors of public company to be voted on individually

(1) At a general meeting of a public company a motion for the appointment of two or more persons as directors of the company by a single resolution must not be made unless a resolution that it should be so made has first been agreed to by the meeting without any vote being given against it.

(2) A resolution moved in contravention of this section is void, whether or not its being so moved was objected to at the time.

But where a resolution so moved is passed, no provision for the automatic reappointment of retiring directors in default of another appointment applies.

(3) For the purposes of this section a motion for approving a person's appointment, or for nominating a person for appointment, is treated as a motion for his appointment.

(4) Nothing in this section applies to a resolution amending the company's articles.

[1.1496]

161 Validity of acts of directors

(1) The acts of a person acting as a director are valid notwithstanding that it is afterwards discovered—

(a) that there was a defect in his appointment;

(b) that he was disqualified from holding office;

(c) that he had ceased to hold office;

(d) that he was not entitled to vote on the matter in question.

(2) This applies even if the resolution for his appointment is void under section 160 (appointment of directors of public company to be voted on individually).

Removal

[1.1497]

168 Resolution to remove director

(1) A company may by ordinary resolution at a meeting remove a director before the expiration of his period of office, notwithstanding anything in any agreement between it and him.

(2) Special notice is required of a resolution to remove a director under this section or to appoint somebody instead of a director so removed at the meeting at which he is removed.

(3) A vacancy created by the removal of a director under this section, if not filled at the meeting at which he is removed, may be filled as a casual vacancy.

(4) A person appointed director in place of a person removed under this section is treated, for the purpose of determining the time at which he or any other director is to retire, as if he had become director on the day on which the person in whose place he is appointed was last appointed a director.

(5) This section is not to be taken—

(a) as depriving a person removed under it of compensation or damages payable to him in respect of the termination of his appointment as director or of any appointment terminating with that as director, or

(b) as derogating from any power to remove a director that may exist apart from this section.

[1.1498]

169 Director's right to protest against removal

(1) On receipt of notice of an intended resolution to remove a director under section 168, the company must forthwith send a copy of the notice to the director concerned.

(2) The director (whether or not a member of the company) is entitled to be heard on the resolution at the meeting.

(3) Where notice is given of an intended resolution to remove a director under that section, and the director concerned makes with respect to it representations in writing to the company (not exceeding a reasonable length) and requests their notification to members of the company, the company shall, unless the representations are received by it too late for it to do so—

(a) in any notice of the resolution given to members of the company state the fact of the representations having been made; and

(b) send a copy of the representations to every member of the company to whom notice of the meeting is sent (whether before or after receipt of the representations by the company).

(4) If a copy of the representations is not sent as required by subsection (3) because received too late or because of the company's default, the director may (without prejudice to his right to be heard orally) require that the representations shall be read out at the meeting.

(5) Copies of the representations need not be sent out and the representations need not be read out at the meeting if, on the application either of the company or of any other person who claims to be aggrieved, the court is satisfied that the rights conferred by this section are being abused.

(6) The court may order the company's costs (in Scotland, expenses) on an application under subsection (5) to be paid in whole or in part by the director, notwithstanding that he is not a party to the application.

CHAPTER 2 GENERAL DUTIES OF DIRECTORS

Introductory

[1.1499]

170 Scope and nature of general duties

(1) The general duties specified in sections 171 to 177 are owed by a director of a company to the company.

(2) A person who ceases to be a director continues to be subject—

(a) to the duty in section 175 (duty to avoid conflicts of interest) as regards the exploitation of any property, information or opportunity of which he became aware at a time when he was a director, and

(b) to the duty in section 176 (duty not to accept benefits from third parties) as regards things done or omitted by him before he ceased to be a director.

To that extent those duties apply to a former director as to a director, subject to any necessary adaptations.

(3) The general duties are based on certain common law rules and equitable principles as they apply in relation to directors and have effect in place of those rules and principles as regards the duties owed to a company by a director.

(4) The general duties shall be interpreted and applied in the same way as common law rules or equitable principles, and regard shall be had to the corresponding common law rules and equitable principles in interpreting and applying the general duties.

[(5) The general duties apply to a shadow director of a company where and to the extent that they are capable of so applying.]

NOTES

Sub-s (5): substituted by the Small Business, Enterprise and Employment Act 2015, s 89(1), as from 26 May 2015 (see further s 89(2) of the 2015 Act at **[1.1924]**).

The general duties

[1.1500]

171 Duty to act within powers

A director of a company must—

(a) act in accordance with the company's constitution, and

(b) only exercise powers for the purposes for which they are conferred.

[1.1501]

172 Duty to promote the success of the company

(1) A director of a company must act in the way he considers, in good faith, would be most likely to promote the success of the company for the benefit of its members as a whole, and in doing so have regard (amongst other matters) to—

(a) the likely consequences of any decision in the long term,

(b) the interests of the company's employees,

(c) the need to foster the company's business relationships with suppliers, customers and others,

(d) the impact of the company's operations on the community and the environment,

(e) the desirability of the company maintaining a reputation for high standards of business conduct, and

(f) the need to act fairly as between members of the company.

(2) Where or to the extent that the purposes of the company consist of or include purposes other than the benefit of its members, subsection (1) has effect as if the reference to promoting the success of the company for the benefit of its members were to achieving those purposes.

(3) The duty imposed by this section has effect subject to any enactment or rule of law requiring directors, in certain circumstances, to consider or act in the interests of creditors of the company.

[1.1502]

173 Duty to exercise independent judgment

(1) A director of a company must exercise independent judgment.

(2) This duty is not infringed by his acting—

(a) in accordance with an agreement duly entered into by the company that restricts the future exercise of discretion by its directors, or

(b) in a way authorised by the company's constitution.

[1.1503]

174 Duty to exercise reasonable care, skill and diligence

(1) A director of a company must exercise reasonable care, skill and diligence.

(2) This means the care, skill and diligence that would be exercised by a reasonably diligent person with—

(a) the general knowledge, skill and experience that may reasonably be expected of a person carrying out the functions carried out by the director in relation to the company, and

(b) the general knowledge, skill and experience that the director has.

[1.1504]

175 Duty to avoid conflicts of interest

(1) A director of a company must avoid a situation in which he has, or can have, a direct or indirect interest that conflicts, or possibly may conflict, with the interests of the company.

(2) This applies in particular to the exploitation of any property, information or opportunity (and it is immaterial whether the company could take advantage of the property, information or opportunity).

(3) This duty does not apply to a conflict of interest arising in relation to a transaction or arrangement with the company.

(4) This duty is not infringed—

(a) if the situation cannot reasonably be regarded as likely to give rise to a conflict of interest; or

(b) if the matter has been authorised by the directors.

(5) Authorisation may be given by the directors—

(a) where the company is a private company and nothing in the company's constitution invalidates such authorisation, by the matter being proposed to and authorised by the directors; or

(b) where the company is a public company and its constitution includes provision enabling the directors to authorise the matter, by the matter being proposed to and authorised by them in accordance with the constitution.

(6) The authorisation is effective only if—

(a) any requirement as to the quorum at the meeting at which the matter is considered is met without counting the director in question or any other interested director, and

(b) the matter was agreed to without their voting or would have been agreed to if their votes had not been counted.

(7) Any reference in this section to a conflict of interest includes a conflict of interest and duty and a conflict of duties.

[1.1505]

176 Duty not to accept benefits from third parties

(1) A director of a company must not accept a benefit from a third party conferred by reason of—

(a) his being a director, or

(b) his doing (or not doing) anything as director.

(2) A "third party" means a person other than the company, an associated body corporate or a person acting on behalf of the company or an associated body corporate.

(3) Benefits received by a director from a person by whom his services (as a director or otherwise) are provided to the company are not regarded as conferred by a third party.

(4) This duty is not infringed if the acceptance of the benefit cannot reasonably be regarded as likely to give rise to a conflict of interest.

(5) Any reference in this section to a conflict of interest includes a conflict of interest and duty and a conflict of duties.

[1.1506]

177 Duty to declare interest in proposed transaction or arrangement

(1) If a director of a company is in any way, directly or indirectly, interested in a proposed transaction or arrangement with the company, he must declare the nature and extent of that interest to the other directors.

(2) The declaration may (but need not) be made—

(a) at a meeting of the directors, or

(b) by notice to the directors in accordance with—

(i) section 184 (notice in writing), or

(ii) section 185 (general notice).

(3) If a declaration of interest under this section proves to be, or becomes, inaccurate or incomplete, a further declaration must be made.

(4) Any declaration required by this section must be made before the company enters into the transaction or arrangement.

(5) This section does not require a declaration of an interest of which the director is not aware or where the director is not aware of the transaction or arrangement in question.

For this purpose a director is treated as being aware of matters of which he ought reasonably to be aware.

(6) A director need not declare an interest—

(a) if it cannot reasonably be regarded as likely to give rise to a conflict of interest;

(b) if, or to the extent that, the other directors are already aware of it (and for this purpose the other directors are treated as aware of anything of which they ought reasonably to be aware); or

(c) if, or to the extent that, it concerns terms of his service contract that have been or are to be considered—

(i) by a meeting of the directors, or

(ii) by a committee of the directors appointed for the purpose under the company's constitution.

Supplementary provisions

[1.1507]

178 Civil consequences of breach of general duties

(1) The consequences of breach (or threatened breach) of sections 171 to 177 are the same as would apply if the corresponding common law rule or equitable principle applied.

(2) The duties in those sections (with the exception of section 174 (duty to exercise reasonable care, skill and diligence)) are, accordingly, enforceable in the same way as any other fiduciary duty owed to a company by its directors.

[1.1508]
179 Cases within more than one of the general duties
Except as otherwise provided, more than one of the general duties may apply in any given case.

[1.1509]
180 Consent, approval or authorisation by members
(1) In a case where—
(a) section 175 (duty to avoid conflicts of interest) is complied with by authorisation by the directors, or
(b) section 177 (duty to declare interest in proposed transaction or arrangement) is complied with,
the transaction or arrangement is not liable to be set aside by virtue of any common law rule or equitable principle requiring the consent or approval of the members of the company.
This is without prejudice to any enactment, or provision of the company's constitution, requiring such consent or approval.
(2) The application of the general duties is not affected by the fact that the case also falls within Chapter 4 (transactions requiring approval of members) [or 4A], except that where [either of those Chapters] applies and—
(a) approval is given under [the Chapter concerned], or
(b) the matter is one as to which it is provided that approval is not needed,
it is not necessary also to comply with section 175 (duty to avoid conflicts of interest) or section 176 (duty not to accept benefits from third parties).
(3) Compliance with the general duties does not remove the need for approval under any applicable provision of Chapter 4 (transactions requiring approval of members) [or 4A].
(4) The general duties—
(a) have effect subject to any rule of law enabling the company to give authority, specifically or generally, for anything to be done (or omitted) by the directors, or any of them, that would otherwise be a breach of duty, and
(b) where the company's articles contain provisions for dealing with conflicts of interest, are not infringed by anything done (or omitted) by the directors, or any of them, in accordance with those provisions.
(5) Otherwise, the general duties have effect (except as otherwise provided or the context otherwise requires) notwithstanding any enactment or rule of law.

NOTES
Sub-s (2): words in first pair of square brackets inserted, and words in second and third pairs of square brackets substituted, by the Enterprise and Regulatory Reform Act 2013, s 81(1), (2)(a), (b).
Sub-s (3): words in square brackets added by the Enterprise and Regulatory Reform Act 2013, s 81(1), (2)(c).

[1.1510]
181 Modification of provisions in relation to charitable companies
(1) In their application to a company that is a charity, the provisions of this Chapter have effect subject to this section.
(2) Section 175 (duty to avoid conflicts of interest) has effect as if—
(a) for subsection (3) (which disapplies the duty to avoid conflicts of interest in the case of a transaction or arrangement with the company) there were substituted—

"(3) This duty does not apply to a conflict of interest arising in relation to a transaction or arrangement with the company if or to the extent that the company's articles allow that duty to be so disapplied, which they may do only in relation to descriptions of transaction or arrangement specified in the company's articles.";

(b) for subsection (5) (which specifies how directors of a company may give authority under that section for a transaction or arrangement) there were substituted—

"(5) Authorisation may be given by the directors where the company's constitution includes provision enabling them to authorise the matter, by the matter being proposed to and authorised by them in accordance with the constitution.".

(3) Section 180(2)(b) (which disapplies certain duties under this Chapter in relation to cases excepted from requirement to obtain approval by members under Chapter 4) applies only if or to the extent that the company's articles allow those duties to be so disapplied, which they may do only in relation to descriptions of transaction or arrangement specified in the company's articles.
(4) *(Inserted the Charities Act 1993, s 26(5A) and was repealed by the Charities Act 2011, s 354, Sch 10.)*
(5) This section does not extend to Scotland.

CHAPTER 3 DECLARATION OF INTEREST IN EXISTING TRANSACTION OR ARRANGEMENT

[1.1511]
182 Declaration of interest in existing transaction or arrangement
(1) Where a director of a company is in any way, directly or indirectly, interested in a transaction or arrangement that has been entered into by the company, he must declare the nature and extent of the interest to the other directors in accordance with this section.

This section does not apply if or to the extent that the interest has been declared under section 177 (duty to declare interest in proposed transaction or arrangement).

(2) The declaration must be made—

(a) at a meeting of the directors, or

(b) by notice in writing (see section 184), or

(c) by general notice (see section 185).

(3) If a declaration of interest under this section proves to be, or becomes, inaccurate or incomplete, a further declaration must be made.

(4) Any declaration required by this section must be made as soon as is reasonably practicable.

Failure to comply with this requirement does not affect the underlying duty to make the declaration.

(5) This section does not require a declaration of an interest of which the director is not aware or where the director is not aware of the transaction or arrangement in question.

For this purpose a director is treated as being aware of matters of which he ought reasonably to be aware.

(6) A director need not declare an interest under this section—

(a) if it cannot reasonably be regarded as likely to give rise to a conflict of interest;

(b) if, or to the extent that, the other directors are already aware of it (and for this purpose the other directors are treated as aware of anything of which they ought reasonably to be aware); or

(c) if, or to the extent that, it concerns terms of his service contract that have been or are to be considered—

(i) by a meeting of the directors, or

(ii) by a committee of the directors appointed for the purpose under the company's constitution.

[1.1512]

183 Offence of failure to declare interest

(1) A director who fails to comply with the requirements of section 182 (declaration of interest in existing transaction or arrangement) commits an offence.

(2) A person guilty of an offence under this section is liable—

(a) on conviction on indictment, to a fine;

(b) on summary conviction, to a fine not exceeding the statutory maximum.

[1.1513]

184 Declaration made by notice in writing

(1) This section applies to a declaration of interest made by notice in writing.

(2) The director must send the notice to the other directors.

(3) The notice may be sent in hard copy form or, if the recipient has agreed to receive it in electronic form, in an agreed electronic form.

(4) The notice may be sent—

(a) by hand or by post, or

(b) if the recipient has agreed to receive it by electronic means, by agreed electronic means.

(5) Where a director declares an interest by notice in writing in accordance with this section—

(a) the making of the declaration is deemed to form part of the proceedings at the next meeting of the directors after the notice is given, and

(b) the provisions of section 248 (minutes of meetings of directors) apply as if the declaration had been made at that meeting.

[1.1514]

185 General notice treated as sufficient declaration

(1) General notice in accordance with this section is a sufficient declaration of interest in relation to the matters to which it relates.

(2) General notice is notice given to the directors of a company to the effect that the director—

(a) has an interest (as member, officer, employee or otherwise) in a specified body corporate or firm and is to be regarded as interested in any transaction or arrangement that may, after the date of the notice, be made with that body corporate or firm, or

(b) is connected with a specified person (other than a body corporate or firm) and is to be regarded as interested in any transaction or arrangement that may, after the date of the notice, be made with that person.

(3) The notice must state the nature and extent of the director's interest in the body corporate or firm or, as the case may be, the nature of his connection with the person.

(4) General notice is not effective unless—

(a) it is given at a meeting of the directors, or

(b) the director takes reasonable steps to secure that it is brought up and read at the next meeting of the directors after it is given.

CHAPTER 4 TRANSACTIONS WITH DIRECTORS REQUIRING APPROVAL OF MEMBERS

Service contracts

[1.1515]

188 Directors' long-term service contracts: requirement of members' approval

(1) This section applies to provision under which the guaranteed term of a director's employment—

(a) with the company of which he is a director, or

(b) where he is the director of a holding company, within the group consisting of that company and its subsidiaries,

is, or may be, longer than two years.

(2) A company may not agree to such provision unless it has been approved—

(a) by resolution of the members of the company, and

(b) in the case of a director of a holding company, by resolution of the members of that company.

(3) The guaranteed term of a director's employment is—

(a) the period (if any) during which the director's employment—

(i) is to continue, or may be continued otherwise than at the instance of the company (whether under the original agreement or under a new agreement entered into in pursuance of it), and

(ii) cannot be terminated by the company by notice, or can be so terminated only in specified circumstances, or

(b) in the case of employment terminable by the company by notice, the period of notice required to be given,

or, in the case of employment having a period within paragraph (a) and a period within paragraph (b), the aggregate of those periods.

(4) If more than six months before the end of the guaranteed term of a director's employment the company enters into a further service contract (otherwise than in pursuance of a right conferred, by or under the original contract, on the other party to it), this section applies as if there were added to the guaranteed term of the new contract the unexpired period of the guaranteed term of the original contract.

(5) A resolution approving provision to which this section applies must not be passed unless a memorandum setting out the proposed contract incorporating the provision is made available to members—

(a) in the case of a written resolution, by being sent or submitted to every eligible member at or before the time at which the proposed resolution is sent or submitted to him;

(b) in the case of a resolution at a meeting, by being made available for inspection by members of the company both—

(i) at the company's registered office for not less than 15 days ending with the date of the meeting, and

(ii) at the meeting itself.

(6) No approval is required under this section on the part of the members of a body corporate that—

(a) is not a UK-registered company, or

(b) is a wholly-owned subsidiary of another body corporate.

(7) In this section "employment" means any employment under a director's service contract.

[1.1516]
189 Directors' long-term service contracts: civil consequences of contravention

If a company agrees to provision in contravention of section 188 (directors' long-term service contracts: requirement of members' approval)—

(a) the provision is void, to the extent of the contravention, and

(b) the contract is deemed to contain a term entitling the company to terminate it at any time by the giving of reasonable notice.

Payments for loss of office

[1.1517]
215 Payments for loss of office

(1) In this Chapter a "payment for loss of office" means a payment made to a director or past director of a company—

(a) by way of compensation for loss of office as director of the company,

(b) by way of compensation for loss, while director of the company or in connection with his ceasing to be a director of it, of—

(i) any other office or employment in connection with the management of the affairs of the company, or

(ii) any office (as director or otherwise) or employment in connection with the management of the affairs of any subsidiary undertaking of the company,

(c) as consideration for or in connection with his retirement from his office as director of the company, or

(d) as consideration for or in connection with his retirement, while director of the company or in connection with his ceasing to be a director of it, from—

(i) any other office or employment in connection with the management of the affairs of the company, or

(ii) any office (as director or otherwise) or employment in connection with the management of the affairs of any subsidiary undertaking of the company.

(2) The references to compensation and consideration include benefits otherwise than in cash and references in this Chapter to payment have a corresponding meaning.

(3) For the purposes of sections 217 to 221 (payments requiring members' approval)—

(a) payment to a person connected with a director, or

(b) payment to any person at the direction of, or for the benefit of, a director or a person connected with him,

is treated as payment to the director.

(4) References in those sections to payment by a person include payment by another person at the direction of, or on behalf of, the person referred to.

[(5) Nothing in this section or sections 216 to 222 applies in relation to a payment for loss of office to a director of a quoted company [or unquoted traded company] other than a payment to which section 226C does not apply by virtue of section 226D(6).]

[(6) "Unquoted traded company" means a traded company (as defined by section 360C) that is not a quoted company.]

NOTES

Sub-s (5): added by the Enterprise and Regulatory Reform Act 2013, s 81(1), (4), subject to transitional provisions in s 82(5) thereof at **[1.1828]**. Words in square brackets inserted by the Companies (Directors' Remuneration Policy and Directors' Remuneration Report) Regulations 2019, SI 2019/970, regs 3, 4(a), as from 10 June 2019 (for transitional provisions, etc, see reg 2 of the 2019 Regulations at **[2.2199]**).

Sub-s (6): added by SI 2019/970, regs 3, 4(b), as from 10 June 2019 (for transitional provisions, etc, see reg 2 of the 2019 Regulations at **[2.2199]**).

[1.1518]

216 Amounts taken to be payments for loss of office

(1) This section applies where in connection with any such transfer as is mentioned in section 218 or 219 (payment in connection with transfer of undertaking, property or shares) a director of the company—

(a) is to cease to hold office, or

(b) is to cease to be the holder of—

(i) any other office or employment in connection with the management of the affairs of the company, or

(ii) any office (as director or otherwise) or employment in connection with the management of the affairs of any subsidiary undertaking of the company.

(2) If in connection with any such transfer—

(a) the price to be paid to the director for any shares in the company held by him is in excess of the price which could at the time have been obtained by other holders of like shares, or

(b) any valuable consideration is given to the director by a person other than the company,

the excess or, as the case may be, the money value of the consideration is taken for the purposes of those sections to have been a payment for loss of office.

[1.1519]

217 Payment by company: requirement of members' approval

(1) A company may not make a payment for loss of office to a director of the company unless the payment has been approved by a resolution of the members of the company.

(2) A company may not make a payment for loss of office to a director of its holding company unless the payment has been approved by a resolution of the members of each of those companies.

(3) A resolution approving a payment to which this section applies must not be passed unless a memorandum setting out particulars of the proposed payment (including its amount) is made available to the members of the company whose approval is sought—

(a) in the case of a written resolution, by being sent or submitted to every eligible member at or before the time at which the proposed resolution is sent or submitted to him;

(b) in the case of a resolution at a meeting, by being made available for inspection by the members both—

(i) at the company's registered office for not less than 15 days ending with the date of the meeting, and

(ii) at the meeting itself.

(4) No approval is required under this section on the part of the members of a body corporate that—

(a) is not a UK-registered company, or

(b) is a wholly-owned subsidiary of another body corporate.

[1.1520]

218 Payment in connection with transfer of undertaking etc: requirement of members' approval

(1) No payment for loss of office may be made by any person to a director of a company in connection with the transfer of the whole or any part of the undertaking or property of the company unless the payment has been approved by a resolution of the members of the company.

(2) No payment for loss of office may be made by any person to a director of a company in connection with the transfer of the whole or any part of the undertaking or property of a subsidiary of the company unless the payment has been approved by a resolution of the members of each of the companies.

(3) A resolution approving a payment to which this section applies must not be passed unless a memorandum setting out particulars of the proposed payment (including its amount) is made available to the members of the company whose approval is sought—

(a) in the case of a written resolution, by being sent or submitted to every eligible member at or before the time at which the proposed resolution is sent or submitted to him;

(b) in the case of a resolution at a meeting, by being made available for inspection by the members both—

(i) at the company's registered office for not less than 15 days ending with the date of the meeting, and

(ii) at the meeting itself.

(4) No approval is required under this section on the part of the members of a body corporate that—

(a) is not a UK-registered company, or

(b) is a wholly-owned subsidiary of another body corporate.

(5) A payment made in pursuance of an arrangement—

(a) entered into as part of the agreement for the transfer in question, or within one year before or two years after that agreement, and
(b) to which the company whose undertaking or property is transferred, or any person to whom the transfer is made, is privy,

is presumed, except in so far as the contrary is shown, to be a payment to which this section applies.

[1.1521]
219 Payment in connection with share transfer: requirement of members' approval
(1) No payment for loss of office may be made by any person to a director of a company in connection with a transfer of shares in the company, or in a subsidiary of the company, resulting from a takeover bid unless the payment has been approved by a resolution of the relevant shareholders.
(2) The relevant shareholders are the holders of the shares to which the bid relates and any holders of shares of the same class as any of those shares.
(3) A resolution approving a payment to which this section applies must not be passed unless a memorandum setting out particulars of the proposed payment (including its amount) is made available to the members of the company whose approval is sought—
(a) in the case of a written resolution, by being sent or submitted to every eligible member at or before the time at which the proposed resolution is sent or submitted to him;
(b) in the case of a resolution at a meeting, by being made available for inspection by the members both—
(i) at the company's registered office for not less than 15 days ending with the date of the meeting, and
(ii) at the meeting itself.
(4) Neither the person making the offer, nor any associate of his (as defined in section 988), is entitled to vote on the resolution, but—
(a) where the resolution is proposed as a written resolution, they are entitled (if they would otherwise be so entitled) to be sent a copy of it, and
(b) at any meeting to consider the resolution they are entitled (if they would otherwise be so entitled) to be given notice of the meeting, to attend and speak and if present (in person or by proxy) to count towards the quorum.
(5) If at a meeting to consider the resolution a quorum is not present, and after the meeting has been adjourned to a later date a quorum is again not present, the payment is (for the purposes of this section) deemed to have been approved.
(6) No approval is required under this section on the part of shareholders in a body corporate that—
(a) is not a UK-registered company, or
(b) is a wholly-owned subsidiary of another body corporate.
(7) A payment made in pursuance of an arrangement—
(a) entered into as part of the agreement for the transfer in question, or within one year before or two years after that agreement, and
(b) to which the company whose shares are the subject of the bid, or any person to whom the transfer is made, is privy,

is presumed, except in so far as the contrary is shown, to be a payment to which this section applies.

[1.1522]
220 Exception for payments in discharge of legal obligations etc
(1) Approval is not required under section 217, 218 or 219 (payments requiring members' approval) for a payment made in good faith—
(a) in discharge of an existing legal obligation (as defined below),
(b) by way of damages for breach of such an obligation,
(c) by way of settlement or compromise of any claim arising in connection with the termination of a person's office or employment, or
(d) by way of pension in respect of past services.
(2) In relation to a payment within section 217 (payment by company) an existing legal obligation means an obligation of the company, or any body corporate associated with it, that was not entered into in connection with, or in consequence of, the event giving rise to the payment for loss of office.
(3) In relation to a payment within section 218 or 219 (payment in connection with transfer of undertaking, property or shares) an existing legal obligation means an obligation of the person making the payment that was not entered into for the purposes of, in connection with or in consequence of, the transfer in question.
(4) In the case of a payment within both section 217 and section 218, or within both section 217 and section 219, subsection (2) above applies and not subsection (3).
(5) A payment part of which falls within subsection (1) above and part of which does not is treated as if the parts were separate payments.

[1.1523]
221 Exception for small payments
(1) Approval is not required under section 217, 218 or 219 (payments requiring members' approval) if—
(a) the payment in question is made by the company or any of its subsidiaries, and
(b) the amount or value of the payment, together with the amount or value of any other relevant payments, does not exceed £200.
(2) For this purpose "other relevant payments" are payments for loss of office in relation to which the following conditions are met.

(3) Where the payment in question is one to which section 217 (payment by company) applies, the conditions are that the other payment was or is paid—
- (a) by the company making the payment in question or any of its subsidiaries,
- (b) to the director to whom that payment is made, and
- (c) in connection with the same event.

(4) Where the payment in question is one to which section 218 or 219 applies (payment in connection with transfer of undertaking, property or shares), the conditions are that the other payment was (or is) paid in connection with the same transfer—
- (a) to the director to whom the payment in question was made, and
- (b) by the company making the payment or any of its subsidiaries.

[1.1524]
222 Payments made without approval: civil consequences

(1) If a payment is made in contravention of section 217 (payment by company)—
- (a) it is held by the recipient on trust for the company making the payment, and
- (b) any director who authorised the payment is jointly and severally liable to indemnify the company that made the payment for any loss resulting from it.

(2) If a payment is made in contravention of section 218 (payment in connection with transfer of undertaking etc), it is held by the recipient on trust for the company whose undertaking or property is or is proposed to be transferred.

(3) If a payment is made in contravention of section 219 (payment in connection with share transfer)—
- (a) it is held by the recipient on trust for persons who have sold their shares as a result of the offer made, and
- (b) the expenses incurred by the recipient in distributing that sum amongst those persons shall be borne by him and not retained out of that sum.

(4) If a payment is in contravention of section 217 and section 218, subsection (2) of this section applies rather than subsection (1).

(5) If a payment is in contravention of section 217 and section 219, subsection (3) of this section applies rather than subsection (1), unless the court directs otherwise.

Supplementary

[1.1525]
223 Transactions requiring members' approval: application of provisions to shadow directors

(1) For the purposes of—
- (a) sections 188 and 189 (directors' service contracts),
- (b) sections 190 to 196 (property transactions),
- (c) sections 197 to 214 (loans etc), and
- (d) sections 215 to 222 (payments for loss of office),

a shadow director is treated as a director.

(2) Any reference in those provisions to loss of office as a director does not apply in relation to loss of a person's status as a shadow director.

[CHAPTER 4A DIRECTORS OF QUOTED COMPANIES [AND TRADED COMPANIES]: SPECIAL PROVISION

NOTES

Words in square brackets in the Chapter heading inserted by the Companies (Directors' Remuneration Policy and Directors' Remuneration Report) Regulations 2019, SI 2019/970, regs 3, 5, as from 10 June 2019 (for transitional provisions, etc, see reg 2 of the 2019 Regulations at **[2.2199]**).

Interpretation

[1.1526]
226A Key definitions

(1) In this Chapter—

"directors' remuneration policy" means the policy of a quoted company[, or of an unquoted traded company,] with respect to the making of remuneration payments and payments for loss of office;

"quoted company" has the same meaning as in Part 15 of this Act;

"remuneration payment" means any form of payment or other benefit made to or otherwise conferred on a person as consideration for the person—
- (a) holding, agreeing to hold or having held office as director of a company, or
- (b) holding, agreeing to hold or having held, during a period when the person is or was such a director—
  - (i) any other office or employment in connection with the management of the affairs of the company, or
  - (ii) any office (as director or otherwise) or employment in connection with the management of the affairs of any subsidiary undertaking of the company,

other than a payment for loss of office;

"payment for loss of office" has the same meaning as in Chapter 4 of this Part;

["unquoted traded company" means a traded company (as defined by section 360C) that is not a quoted company].

(2) Subsection (3) applies where, in connection with a relevant transfer, a director of a quoted company is—
- (a) to cease to hold office as director, or

(b) to cease to be the holder of—
  (i) any other office or employment in connection with the management of the affairs of the company, or
  (ii) any office (as director or otherwise) or employment in connection with the management of the affairs of any subsidiary undertaking of the company.

(3) If in connection with the transfer—
  (a) the price to be paid to the director for any shares in the company held by the director is in excess of the price which could at the time have been obtained by other holders of like shares, or
  (b) any valuable consideration is given to the director by a person other than the company,

the excess or, as the case may be, the money value of the consideration is taken for the purposes of section 226C to have been a payment for loss of office.

(4) In subsection (2), "relevant transfer" means—
  (a) a transfer of the whole or any part of the undertaking or property of the company or a subsidiary of the company;
  (b) a transfer of shares in the company, or in a subsidiary of the company, resulting from a takeover bid.

(5) References in this Chapter to the making of a remuneration payment or to the making of a payment for loss of office are to be read in accordance with this section.

(6) References in this Chapter to a payment by a company include a payment by another person at the direction of, or on behalf of, the company.

(7) References in this Chapter to a payment to a person ("B") who is, has been or is to be a director of a company include—
  (a) a payment to a person connected with B, or
  (b) a payment to a person at the direction of, or for the benefit of, B or a person connected with B.

(8) Section 252 applies for the purposes of determining whether a person is connected with a person who has been, or is to be, a director of a company as it applies for the purposes of determining whether a person is connected with a director.

(9) References in this Chapter to a director include a shadow director but references to loss of office as a director do not include loss of a person's status as a shadow director.

[(10) References in this Chapter (other than sections 226E(2)(b) and (5)) to a director of a company include a person who is not a director of the company but who is—
  (a) its chief executive officer (however described), or
  (b) where such a function exists in the company, its deputy chief executive officer (however described).]]

NOTES

This section and ss 226B–226F (Chapter 4A) were inserted by the Enterprise and Regulatory Reform Act 2013, s 80.

The definition "unquoted traded company" and the words in square brackets in the definition "directors' remuneration policy" in sub-s (1) were inserted, and sub-s (10) was added, by the Companies (Directors' Remuneration Policy and Directors' Remuneration Report) Regulations 2019, SI 2019/970, regs 3, 6 (this amendment applies to a quoted company from the first date on or after 10 June 2019 on which a relevant directors' remuneration policy for the company approved under s 439A of this Act takes effect – see reg 2 of the 2019 Regulations at **[2.2199]**).

Transitional provisions: see the Enterprise and Regulatory Reform Act 2013, s 82 at **[1.1828]**.

[Restrictions relating to remuneration or loss of office payments

[1.1527]

226B Remuneration payments

(1) A quoted company [or unquoted traded company] may not make a remuneration payment to a person who is, or is to be or has been, a director of the company unless—
  (a) the payment is consistent with the approved directors' remuneration policy, or
  [(b) an amendment to that policy authorising the company to make the payment has been approved by resolution of the members of the company.]

(2) The approved directors' remuneration policy is the most recent remuneration policy to have been approved by a resolution passed by the members of the company in general meeting.]

NOTES

Inserted as noted to s 226A at **[1.1526]**.

Sub-s (1): the words in the first pair of square brackets were inserted, and para (b) was substituted, by the Companies (Directors' Remuneration Policy and Directors' Remuneration Report) Regulations 2019, SI 2019/970, regs 3, 7 (this amendment applies to a quoted company from the first date on or after 10 June 2019 on which a relevant directors' remuneration policy for the company approved under s 439A of this Act takes effect – see reg 2 of the 2019 Regulations at **[2.2199]**). The original text read as follows—

"(b) the payment is approved by resolution of the members of the company.".

Transitional provisions: see the Enterprise and Regulatory Reform Act 2013, s 82 at **[1.1828]**.

[1.1528]

[226C Loss of office payments

(1) No payment for loss of office may be made by any person to a person who is, or has been, a director of a quoted company [or of an unquoted traded company] unless—
  (a) the payment is consistent with the approved directors' remuneration policy, or

[(b) an amendment to that policy authorising the company to make the payment has been approved by resolution of the members of the company.]

(2) The approved directors' remuneration policy is the most recent remuneration policy to have been approved by a resolution passed by the members of the company in general meeting.]

NOTES

Inserted as noted to s 226A at **[1.1526]**.

Sub-s (1): the words in the first pair of square brackets were inserted, and para (b) was substituted, by the Companies (Directors' Remuneration Policy and Directors' Remuneration Report) Regulations 2019, SI 2019/970, regs 3, 8 (this amendment applies to a quoted company from the first date on or after 10 June 2019 on which a relevant directors' remuneration policy for the company approved under s 439A of this Act takes effect – see reg 2 of the 2019 Regulations at **[2.2199]**). The original text read as follows—

"(b) the payment is approved by resolution of the members of the company.".

Transitional provisions: see the Enterprise and Regulatory Reform Act 2013, s 82 at **[1.1828]**.

[1.1529]

[226D Sections 226B and 226C: supplementary

(1) A resolution approving [an amendment] for the purposes of section 226B(1)(b) or 226C(1)(b) must not be passed unless a memorandum setting out particulars of the proposed payment [to which the amendment relates] (including its amount) is made available for inspection by the members of the company—

(a) at the company's registered office for not less than 15 days ending with the date of the meeting at which the resolution is to be considered, and

(b) at that meeting itself.

[(2) The memorandum must explain the ways in which the payment would be inconsistent with the approved directors' remuneration policy (within the meaning of the section in question) but for the amendment.]

(3) The company must ensure that the memorandum is made available on the company's website from the first day on which the memorandum is made available for inspection under subsection (1) until its next accounts meeting.

(4) Failure to comply with subsection (3) does not affect the validity of the meeting at which a resolution is passed approving [the amendment] to which the memorandum relates or the validity of anything done at the meeting.

(5) Nothing in section 226B or 226C authorises the making of a remuneration payment or (as the case may be) a payment for loss of office in contravention of the articles of the company concerned.

(6) Nothing in section 226B or 226C applies in relation to a remuneration payment or (as the case may be) a payment for loss of office made to a person who is, or is to be or has been, a director of a quoted company [or of an unquoted traded company] before the earlier of—

(a) the end of the first financial year of the company to begin on or after the day on which it becomes a quoted company [or (as the case may be) an unquoted traded company], and

(b) the date from which the company's first directors' remuneration policy to be approved under section 439A takes effect.

(7) In this section the "company's website" is the website on which the company makes material available under section 430.]

NOTES

Inserted as noted to s 226A at **[1.1526]**.

Sub-s (1): words in first pair of square brackets substituted (for the original words "an amendment"), and words in second pair of square brackets inserted, by the Companies (Directors' Remuneration Policy and Directors' Remuneration Report) Regulations 2019, SI 2019/970, regs 3, 9(a) (this amendment applies to a quoted company from the first date on or after 10 June 2019 on which a relevant directors' remuneration policy for the company approved under s 439A of this Act takes effect – see reg 2 of the 2019 Regulations at **[2.2199]**).

Sub-s (2) substituted by SI 2019/970, regs 3, 9(b) (this amendment applies to a quoted company from the first date on or after 10 June 2019 on which a relevant directors' remuneration policy for the company approved under s 439A of this Act takes effect – see reg 2 of the 2019 Regulations at **[2.2199]**). The original text read as follows—

"(2) The memorandum must explain the ways in which the payment is inconsistent with the approved directors' remuneration policy (within the meaning of the section in question).".

Sub-s (4): words in square brackets substituted (for the original words "the amendment") by SI 2019/970, regs 3, 9(c) (this amendment applies to a quoted company from the first date on or after 10 June 2019 on which a relevant directors' remuneration policy for the company approved under s 439A of this Act takes effect – see reg 2 of the 2019 Regulations at **[2.2199]**).

Sub-s (6): words in square brackets inserted by SI 2019/970, regs 3, 9(d) (this amendment applies to a quoted company from the first date on or after 10 June 2019 on which a relevant directors' remuneration policy for the company approved under s 439A of this Act takes effect – see reg 2 of the 2019 Regulations at **[2.2199]**).

Transitional provisions: see the Enterprise and Regulatory Reform Act 2013, s 82 at **[1.1828]**.

[Supplementary

[1.1530]

226E Payments made without approval: civil consequences

(1) An obligation (however arising) to make a payment which would be in contravention of section 226B or 226C has no effect.

(2) If a payment is made in contravention of section 226B or 226C—

(a) it is held by the recipient on trust for the company or other person making the payment, and

(b) in the case of a payment by a company, any director who authorised the payment is jointly and severally liable to indemnify the company that made the payment for any loss resulting from it.

(3) If a payment for loss of office is made in contravention of section 226C to a director of a quoted company [or of an unquoted traded company] in connection with the transfer of the whole or any part of the undertaking or property of the company or a subsidiary of the company—

(a) subsection (2) does not apply, and

(b) the payment is held by the recipient on trust for the company whose undertaking or property is or is proposed to be transferred.

(4) If a payment for loss of office is made in contravention of section 226C to a director of a quoted company [or of an unquoted traded company] in connection with a transfer of shares in the company, or in a subsidiary of the company, resulting from a takeover bid—

(a) subsection (2) does not apply,

(b) the payment is held by the recipient on trust for persons who have sold their shares as a result of the offer made, and

(c) the expenses incurred by the recipient in distributing that sum amongst those persons shall be borne by the recipient and not retained out of that sum.

(5) If in proceedings against a director for the enforcement of a liability under subsection (2)(b)—

(a) the director shows that he or she has acted honestly and reasonably, and

(b) the court considers that, having regard to all the circumstances of the case, the director ought to be relieved of liability,

the court may relieve the director, either wholly or in part, from liability on such terms as the court thinks fit.]

NOTES

Inserted as noted to s 226A at **[1.1526]**.

Sub-ss (3), (4): words in square brackets inserted by the Companies (Directors' Remuneration Policy and Directors' Remuneration Report) Regulations 2019, SI 2019/970, regs 3, 10 (this amendment applies to a quoted company from the first date on or after 10 June 2019 on which a relevant directors' remuneration policy for the company approved under s 439A of this Act takes effect – see reg 2 of the 2019 Regulations at **[2.2199]**).

Transitional provisions: see the Enterprise and Regulatory Reform Act 2013, s 82 at **[1.1828]**.

[1.1531]
[226F Relationship with requirements under Chapter 4

(1) This Chapter does not affect any requirement for approval by a resolution of the members of a company which applies in relation to the company under Chapter 4.

(2) Where the making of a payment to which section 226B or 226C applies requires approval by a resolution of the members of the company concerned under Chapter 4, approval obtained for the purposes of that Chapter is to be treated as satisfying the requirements of section 226B(1)(b) or (as the case may be) 226C(1)(b).]

NOTES

Inserted as noted to s 226A at **[1.1526]**.

Transitional provisions: see the Enterprise and Regulatory Reform Act 2013, s 82 at **[1.1828]**.

CHAPTER 5 DIRECTORS' SERVICE CONTRACTS

[1.1532]
227 Directors' service contracts

(1) For the purposes of this Part a director's "service contract", in relation to a company, means a contract under which—

(a) a director of the company undertakes personally to perform services (as director or otherwise) for the company, or for a subsidiary of the company, or

(b) services (as director or otherwise) that a director of the company undertakes personally to perform are made available by a third party to the company, or to a subsidiary of the company.

(2) The provisions of this Part relating to directors' service contracts apply to the terms of a person's appointment as a director of a company.

They are not restricted to contracts for the performance of services outside the scope of the ordinary duties of a director.

[1.1533]
228 Copy of contract or memorandum of terms to be available for inspection

(1) A company must keep available for inspection—

(a) a copy of every director's service contract with the company or with a subsidiary of the company, or

(b) if the contract is not in writing, a written memorandum setting out the terms of the contract.

(2) All the copies and memoranda must be kept available for inspection at—

(a) the company's registered office, or

(b) a place specified in regulations under section 1136.

(3) The copies and memoranda must be retained by the company for at least one year from the date of termination or expiry of the contract and must be kept available for inspection during that time.

(4) The company must give notice to the registrar—

(a) of the place at which the copies and memoranda are kept available for inspection, and

(b) of any change in that place,

unless they have at all times been kept at the company's registered office.
(5) If default is made in complying with subsection (1), (2) or (3), or default is made for 14 days in complying with subsection (4), an offence is committed by every officer of the company who is in default.
(6) A person guilty of an offence under this section is liable on summary conviction to a fine not exceeding level 3 on the standard scale and, for continued contravention, a daily default fine not exceeding one-tenth of level 3 on the standard scale.
(7) The provisions of this section apply to a variation of a director's service contract as they apply to the original contract.

[1.1534]
229 Right of member to inspect and request copy
(1) Every copy or memorandum required to be kept under section 228 must be open to inspection by any member of the company without charge.
(2) Any member of the company is entitled, on request and on payment of such fee as may be prescribed, to be provided with a copy of any such copy or memorandum.
The copy must be provided within seven days after the request is received by the company.
(3) If an inspection required under subsection (1) is refused, or default is made in complying with subsection (2), an offence is committed by every officer of the company who is in default.
(4) A person guilty of an offence under this section is liable on summary conviction to a fine not exceeding level 3 on the standard scale and, for continued contravention, a daily default fine not exceeding one-tenth of level 3 on the standard scale.
(5) In the case of any such refusal or default the court may by order compel an immediate inspection or, as the case may be, direct that the copy required be sent to the person requiring it.

NOTES
Regulations: the Companies (Fees for Inspection and Copying of Company Records) Regulations 2007, SI 2007/2612.

[1.1535]
230 Directors' service contracts: application of provisions to shadow directors
A shadow director is treated as a director for the purposes of the provisions of this Chapter.

CHAPTER 7 DIRECTORS' LIABILITIES

Provision protecting directors from liability

[1.1536]
232 Provisions protecting directors from liability
(1) Any provision that purports to exempt a director of a company (to any extent) from any liability that would otherwise attach to him in connection with any negligence, default, breach of duty or breach of trust in relation to the company is void.
(2) Any provision by which a company directly or indirectly provides an indemnity (to any extent) for a director of the company, or of an associated company, against any liability attaching to him in connection with any negligence, default, breach of duty or breach of trust in relation to the company of which he is a director is void, except as permitted by—
(a) section 233 (provision of insurance),
(b) section 234 (qualifying third party indemnity provision), or
(c) section 235 (qualifying pension scheme indemnity provision).
(3) This section applies to any provision, whether contained in a company's articles or in any contract with the company or otherwise.
(4) Nothing in this section prevents a company's articles from making such provision as has previously been lawful for dealing with conflicts of interest.

[1.1537]
233 Provision of insurance
Section 232(2) (voidness of provisions for indemnifying directors) does not prevent a company from purchasing and maintaining for a director of the company, or of an associated company, insurance against any such liability as is mentioned in that subsection.

[1.1538]
234 Qualifying third party indemnity provision
(1) Section 232(2) (voidness of provisions for indemnifying directors) does not apply to qualifying third party indemnity provision.
(2) Third party indemnity provision means provision for indemnity against liability incurred by the director to a person other than the company or an associated company.
Such provision is qualifying third party indemnity provision if the following requirements are met.
(3) The provision must not provide any indemnity against—
(a) any liability of the director to pay—
(i) a fine imposed in criminal proceedings, or
(ii) a sum payable to a regulatory authority by way of a penalty in respect of non-compliance with any requirement of a regulatory nature (however arising); or
(b) any liability incurred by the director—
(i) in defending criminal proceedings in which he is convicted, or

(ii) in defending civil proceedings brought by the company, or an associated company, in which judgment is given against him, or
(iii) in connection with an application for relief (see subsection (6)) in which the court refuses to grant him relief.

(4) The references in subsection (3)(b) to a conviction, judgment or refusal of relief are to the final decision in the proceedings.

(5) For this purpose—
(a) a conviction, judgment or refusal of relief becomes final—
(i) if not appealed against, at the end of the period for bringing an appeal, or
(ii) if appealed against, at the time when the appeal (or any further appeal) is disposed of; and
(b) an appeal is disposed of—
(i) if it is determined and the period for bringing any further appeal has ended, or
(ii) if it is abandoned or otherwise ceases to have effect.

(6) The reference in subsection (3)(b)(iii) to an application for relief is to an application for relief under—

section 661(3) or (4) (power of court to grant relief in case of acquisition of shares by innocent nominee), or

section 1157 (general power of court to grant relief in case of honest and reasonable conduct).

[1.1539]
235 Qualifying pension scheme indemnity provision

(1) Section 232(2) (voidness of provisions for indemnifying directors) does not apply to qualifying pension scheme indemnity provision.

(2) Pension scheme indemnity provision means provision indemnifying a director of a company that is a trustee of an occupational pension scheme against liability incurred in connection with the company's activities as trustee of the scheme.

Such provision is qualifying pension scheme indemnity provision if the following requirements are met.

(3) The provision must not provide any indemnity against—
(a) any liability of the director to pay—
(i) a fine imposed in criminal proceedings, or
(ii) a sum payable to a regulatory authority by way of a penalty in respect of non-compliance with any requirement of a regulatory nature (however arising); or
(b) any liability incurred by the director in defending criminal proceedings in which he is convicted.

(4) The reference in subsection (3)(b) to a conviction is to the final decision in the proceedings.

(5) For this purpose—
(a) a conviction becomes final—
(i) if not appealed against, at the end of the period for bringing an appeal, or
(ii) if appealed against, at the time when the appeal (or any further appeal) is disposed of; and
(b) an appeal is disposed of—
(i) if it is determined and the period for bringing any further appeal has ended, or
(ii) if it is abandoned or otherwise ceases to have effect.

(6) In this section "occupational pension scheme" means an occupational pension scheme as defined in section 150(5) of the Finance Act 2004 (c 12) that is established under a trust.

[1.1540]
236 Qualifying indemnity provision to be disclosed in directors' report

(1) This section requires disclosure in the directors' report of—
(a) qualifying third party indemnity provision, and
(b) qualifying pension scheme indemnity provision.

Such provision is referred to in this section as "qualifying indemnity provision".

(2) If when a directors' report is approved any qualifying indemnity provision (whether made by the company or otherwise) is in force for the benefit of one or more directors of the company, the report must state that such provision is in force.

(3) If at any time during the financial year to which a directors' report relates any such provision was in force for the benefit of one or more persons who were then directors of the company, the report must state that such provision was in force.

(4) If when a directors' report is approved qualifying indemnity provision made by the company is in force for the benefit of one or more directors of an associated company, the report must state that such provision is in force.

(5) If at any time during the financial year to which a directors' report relates any such provision was in force for the benefit of one or more persons who were then directors of an associated company, the report must state that such provision was in force.

CHAPTER 9 SUPPLEMENTARY PROVISIONS

Provision for employees on cessation or transfer of business

[1.1541]
247 Power to make provision for employees on cessation or transfer of business
(1) The powers of the directors of a company include (if they would not otherwise do so) power to make provision for the benefit of persons employed or formerly employed by the company, or any of its subsidiaries, in connection with the cessation or the transfer to any person of the whole or part of the undertaking of the company or that subsidiary.
(2) This power is exercisable notwithstanding the general duty imposed by section 172 (duty to promote the success of the company).
(3) In the case of a company that is a charity it is exercisable notwithstanding any restrictions on the directors' powers (or the company's capacity) flowing from the objects of the company.
(4) The power may only be exercised if sanctioned—
(a) by a resolution of the company, or
(b) by a resolution of the directors,
in accordance with the following provisions.
(5) A resolution of the directors—
(a) must be authorised by the company's articles, and
(b) is not sufficient sanction for payments to or for the benefit of directors, former directors or shadow directors.
(6) Any other requirements of the company's articles as to the exercise of the power conferred by this section must be complied with.
(7) Any payment under this section must be made—
(a) before the commencement of any winding up of the company, and
(b) out of profits of the company that are available for dividend.

Meaning of "director" and "shadow director"

[1.1542]
251 "Shadow director"
(1) In the Companies Acts "shadow director", in relation to a company, means a person in accordance with whose directions or instructions the directors of the company are accustomed to act.
(2) A person is not to be regarded as a shadow director by reason only that the directors act[—
(a) on advice given by that person in a professional capacity;
(b) in accordance with instructions, a direction, guidance or advice given by that person in the exercise of a function conferred by or under an enactment;
(c) in accordance with guidance or advice given by that person in that person's capacity as a Minister of the Crown (within the meaning of the Ministers of the Crown Act 1975)].
(3) A body corporate is not to be regarded as a shadow director of any of its subsidiary companies for the purposes of—
Chapter 2 (general duties of directors),
Chapter 4 (transactions requiring members' approval), or
Chapter 6 (contract with sole member who is also a director),
by reason only that the directors of the subsidiary are accustomed to act in accordance with its directions or instructions.

NOTES
Sub-s (2): words in square brackets substituted by the Small Business, Enterprise and Employment Act 2015, s 90(3), as from 26 May 2015.

PART 15
ACCOUNTS AND REPORTS

CHAPTER 6 QUOTED COMPANIES [AND TRADED COMPANIES]: DIRECTORS' REMUNERATION REPORT

NOTES
Words in square brackets in the Chapter heading inserted by the Companies (Directors' Remuneration Policy and Directors' Remuneration Report) Regulations 2019, SI 2019/970, regs 3, 11, as from 10 June 2019 (for transitional provisions, etc, see reg 2 of the 2019 Regulations at **[2.2199]**).

[1.1543]
420 Duty to prepare directors' remuneration report
(1) The directors of a quoted company[, or of a traded company (as defined by section 360C) that is not a quoted company,] must prepare a directors' remuneration report for each financial year of the company.
(2) In the case of failure to comply with the requirement to prepare a directors' remuneration report, every person who—
(a) was a director of the company immediately before the end of the period for filing accounts and reports for the financial year in question, and
(b) failed to take all reasonable steps for securing compliance with that requirement,
commits an offence.
(3) A person guilty of an offence under this section is liable—
(a) on conviction on indictment, to a fine;

(b) on summary conviction, to a fine not exceeding the statutory maximum.

NOTES

Sub-s (1): words in square brackets inserted by the Companies (Directors' Remuneration Policy and Directors' Remuneration Report) Regulations 2019, SI 2019/970, regs 3, 12, as from 10 June 2019 (for transitional provisions, etc, see reg 2 of the 2019 Regulations at **[2.2199]**).

Executives' remuneration reports: the Financial Services Act 2010, s 4 provides that the Treasury may make provision by Regulations about the preparation, approval and disclosure of executives' remuneration reports. Section 5(4) of the 2010 Act provides that Regulations under s 4 may apply any provision made by or under this Act relating to directors' remuneration reports, subject to such exceptions, adaptations and modifications as the Treasury consider appropriate.

[1.1544]
421 Contents of directors' remuneration report

(1) The Secretary of State may make provision by regulations as to—
(a) the information that must be contained in a directors' remuneration report,
(b) how information is to be set out in the report, and
(c) what is to be the auditable part of the report.

(2) Without prejudice to the generality of this power, the regulations may make any such provision as was made, immediately before the commencement of this Part, by Schedule 7A to the Companies Act 1985 (c 6).

[(2A) The regulations must provide that any information required to be included in the report as to the policy of the company with respect to the making of remuneration payments and payments for loss of office (within the meaning of Chapter 4A of Part 10) is to be set out in a separate part of the report.]

(3) It is the duty of—
(a) any director of a company, and
(b) any person who is or has at any time in the preceding five years been a director of the company,
to give notice to the company of such matters relating to himself as may be necessary for the purposes of regulations under this section.

(4) A person who makes default in complying with subsection (3) commits an offence and is liable on summary conviction to a fine not exceeding level 3 on the standard scale.

NOTES

Sub-s (2A): inserted by the Enterprise and Regulatory Reform Act 2013, s 79(1).

Executives' remuneration reports: see the note to s 420 at **[1.1543]**.

Regulations: the Large and Medium-sized Companies and Groups (Accounts and Reports) Regulations 2008, SI 2008/410; the Large and Medium-sized Companies and Groups (Accounts and Reports) (Amendment) Regulations 2013, SI 2013/1981; the Companies (Miscellaneous Reporting) Regulations 2018, SI 2018/860; the Companies (Directors' Remuneration Policy and Directors' Remuneration Report) Regulations 2019, SI 2019/970 at **[2.2198]**.

[1.1545]
422 Approval and signing of directors' remuneration report

(1) The directors' remuneration report must be approved by the board of directors and signed on behalf of the board by a director or the secretary of the company.

(2) If a directors' remuneration report is approved that does not comply with the requirements of this Act, every director of the company who—
(a) knew that it did not comply, or was reckless as to whether it complied, and
(b) failed to take reasonable steps to secure compliance with those requirements or, as the case may be, to prevent the report from being approved,
commits an offence.

(3) A person guilty of an offence under this section is liable—
(a) on conviction on indictment, to a fine;
(b) on summary conviction, to a fine not exceeding the statutory maximum.

NOTES

Executives' remuneration reports: see the note to s 420 at **[1.1543]**.

[1.1546]
[422A Revisions to directors' remuneration policy

(1) The directors' remuneration policy contained in a company's directors' remuneration report may be revised.

(2) Any such revision must be approved by the board of directors.

(3) The policy as so revised must be set out in a document signed on behalf of the board by a director or the secretary of the company.

(4) Regulations under section 421(1) may make provision as to—
(a) the information that must be contained in a document setting out a revised directors' remuneration policy, and
(b) how information is to be set out in the document.

(5) Sections 422(2) and (3), 454, 456 and 463 apply in relation to such a document as they apply in relation to a directors' remuneration report.

(6) In this section, "directors' remuneration policy" means the policy of a company with respect to the matters mentioned in section 421(2A).]

NOTES

Inserted by the Enterprise and Regulatory Reform Act 2013, s 79(2).

Regulations: the Large and Medium-sized Companies and Groups (Accounts and Reports) (Amendment) Regulations 2013, SI 2013/1981.

CHAPTER 9 QUOTED COMPANIES [AND TRADED COMPANIES]: MEMBERS' APPROVAL OF DIRECTORS' REMUNERATION REPORT

NOTES

Words in square brackets in the Chapter heading inserted by the Companies (Directors' Remuneration Policy and Directors' Remuneration Report) Regulations 2019, SI 2019/970, regs 3, 18, as from 10 June 2019 (for transitional provisions, etc, see reg 2 of the 2019 Regulations at **[2.2199]**).

[1.1547]

439 Quoted Companies [and traded companies]: members' approval of directors' remuneration report

(1) A [company to which this section applies] must, prior to the accounts meeting, give to the members of the company entitled to be sent notice of the meeting notice of the intention to move at the meeting, as an ordinary resolution, a resolution approving the directors' remuneration report for the financial year [other than the part containing the directors' remuneration policy (as to which see section 439A)].

[(1A) This section applies to—

(a) a quoted company, and

(b) a traded company (as defined by section 360C) that is not a quoted company.]

(2) The notice may be given in any manner permitted for the service on the member of notice of the meeting.

(3) The business that may be dealt with at the accounts meeting includes the resolution.

This is so notwithstanding any default in complying with subsection (1) or (2).

(4) The existing directors must ensure that the resolution is put to the vote of the meeting.

(5) No entitlement of a person to remuneration is made conditional on the resolution being passed by reason only of the provision made by this section.

(6) In this section—

"the accounts meeting" means the general meeting of the company before which the company's annual accounts for the financial year are to be laid; and

"existing director" means a person who is a director of the company immediately before that meeting.

NOTES

The words in square brackets in the section heading, and sub-s (1A), were inserted, and the words in the first pair of square brackets in subs (1) were substituted (for the original words "quoted company"), by the Companies (Directors' Remuneration Policy and Directors' Remuneration Report) Regulations 2019, SI 2019/970, regs 3, 19, as from 10 June 2019 (for transitional provisions, etc, see reg 2 of the 2019 Regulations at **[2.2199]**).

The words in the second pair of square brackets in sub-s (1) were inserted by the Enterprise and Regulatory Reform Act 2013, s 79(3).

[1.1548]

[439A Quoted Companies [and traded companies]: members' approval of directors' remuneration policy

(1) A quoted company [or unquoted traded company] must give notice of the intention to move, as an ordinary resolution, a resolution approving the relevant directors' remuneration policy—

(a) at the accounts meeting held in the first financial year which begins on or after the day on which the company becomes a quoted company [or (as the case may be) an unquoted traded company], and

(b) at an accounts or other general meeting held no later than the end of the period of three financial years beginning with the first financial year after the last accounts or other general meeting in relation to which notice is given under this subsection.

(2) A quoted company [or unquoted traded company] must give notice of the intention to move at an accounts meeting, as an ordinary resolution, a resolution approving the relevant directors' remuneration policy if—

(a) a resolution required to be put to the vote under section 439 was not passed at the last accounts meeting of the company, and

(b) no notice under this section was given in relation to that meeting or any other general meeting held before the next accounts meeting.

[(2A) A quoted company or unquoted traded company must give notice of the intention to move at an accounts or other general meeting, as an ordinary resolution, a resolution approving the relevant directors' remuneration policy if—

(a) a resolution required to be put to the vote under subsection (1) or (2) or this subsection was not passed at the last accounts or other general meeting of the company, and

(b) no notice under this section was given in relation to any other general meeting held before the next accounts meeting.]

(3) Subsection (2) does not apply in relation to a quoted company [or unquoted traded company] before the first meeting in relation to which it gives notice under subsection (1).

(4) A notice given under subsection (2) [or (2A)] is to be treated as given under subsection (1) for the purpose of determining the period within which the next notice under subsection (1) must be given.

(5) Notice of the intention to move a resolution to which this section applies must be given, prior to the meeting in question, to the members of the company entitled to be sent notice of the meeting.

(6) Subsections (2) to (4) of section 439 apply for the purposes of a resolution to which this section applies as they apply for the purposes of a resolution to which section 439 applies, with the modification that, for the purposes of a resolution relating to a general meeting other than an accounts meeting, subsection (3) applies as if for "accounts meeting" there were substituted "general meeting".

(7) For the purposes of this section, the relevant directors' remuneration policy is—

(a) in a case where notice is given in relation to an accounts meeting, the remuneration policy contained in the directors' remuneration report in respect of which a resolution under section 439 is required to be put to the vote at that accounts meeting;

(b) in a case where notice is given in relation to a general meeting other than an accounts meeting—

(i) the remuneration policy contained in the directors' remuneration report in respect of which such a resolution was required to be put to the vote at the last accounts meeting to be held before that other general meeting, or

(ii) where that policy has been revised in accordance with section 422A, the policy as so revised.

(8) In this section—

(a) "accounts meeting" means a general meeting of the company before which the company's annual accounts for a financial year are to be laid;

(b) "directors' remuneration policy" means the policy of the company with respect to the matters mentioned in section 421(2A);

[(c) "unquoted traded company" means a traded company (as defined by section 360C) that is not a quoted company.]]

NOTES

Inserted by the Enterprise and Regulatory Reform Act 2013, s 79(4).

All words in square brackets in this section (including sub-s (2A) and the words in square brackets in the section heading) were inserted by the Companies (Directors' Remuneration Policy and Directors' Remuneration Report) Regulations 2019, SI 2019/970, regs 3, 20, as from 10 June 2019 (for transitional provisions, etc, see reg 2 of the 2019 Regulations at **[2.2199]**).

Transitional provisions: see the Enterprise and Regulatory Reform Act 2013, s 82 at **[1.1828]**.

PART 47
FINAL PROVISIONS

[1.1549]
1298 Short title

The short title of this Act is the Companies Act 2006.

[1.1550]
1299 Extent

Except as otherwise provided (or the context otherwise requires), the provisions of this Act extend to the whole of the United Kingdom.

[1.1551]
1300 Commencement

(1) The following provisions come into force on the day this Act is passed—

(a) Part 43 (transparency obligations and related matters), except the amendment in paragraph 11(2) of Schedule 15 of the definition of "regulated market" in Part 6 of the Financial Services and Markets Act 2000 (c 8),

(b) in Part 44 (miscellaneous provisions)—
section 1274 (grants to bodies concerned with actuarial standards etc), and
section 1276 (application of provisions to Scotland and Northern Ireland),

(c) Part 46 (general supplementary provisions), except section 1295 and Schedule 16 (repeals), and

(d) this Part.

(2) The other provisions of this Act come into force on such day as may be appointed by order of the Secretary of State or the Treasury.

NOTES

Orders: the Companies Act 2006 (Commencement No 1, Transitional Provisions and Savings) Order 2006, SI 2006/3428; the Companies Act 2006 (Commencement No 2, Consequential Amendments, Transitional Provisions and Savings) Order 2007, SI 2007/1093; the Companies Act 2006 (Commencement No 3, Consequential Amendments, Transitional Provisions and Savings) Order 2007, SI 2007/2194; the Companies Act 2006 (Commencement No 4 and Commencement No 3 (Amendment)) Order 2007, SI 2007/2607; the Companies Act 2006 (Commencement No 5, Transitional Provisions and Savings) Order 2007, SI 2007/3495; the Companies Act 2006 (Commencement No 6, Saving and Commencement Nos 3 and 5 (Amendment)) Order 2008, SI 2008/674; the Companies Act 2006 (Commencement No 7, Transitional Provisions and Savings) Order 2008, SI 2008/1886; the Companies Act 2006 (Commencement No 8, Transitional Provisions and Savings) Order 2008, SI 2008/2860; the Companies Act 2006 (Consequential Amendments, Transitional Provisions and Savings) Order 2009, SI 2009/1941; the Companies Act 2006 and Limited Liability Partnerships (Transitional Provisions and Savings) (Amendment) Regulations 2009, SI 2009/2476; the Companies and Limited Liability Partnerships (Forms, etc) Amendment Regulations 2013, SI 2013/1947.

TRIBUNALS, COURTS AND ENFORCEMENT ACT 2007

(2007 c 15)

ARRANGEMENT OF SECTIONS

An Act to make provision about tribunals and inquiries; to establish an Administrative Justice and Tribunals Council; to amend the law relating to judicial appointments and appointments to the Law Commission; to amend the law relating to the enforcement of judgments and debts; to make further provision about the management and relief of debt; to make provision protecting cultural objects from seizure or forfeiture in certain circumstances; to amend the law relating to the taking of possession of land affected by compulsory purchase; to alter the powers of the High Court in judicial review applications; and for connected purposes

[19 July 2007]

NOTES

Only those provisions of this Act relevant to employment law are reproduced. Provisions not reproduced are not annotated. The provisions reproduced here extend to the whole of the United Kingdom (see s 147).

See *Harvey* PI.

PART 1
TRIBUNALS AND INQUIRIES

CHAPTER 1 TRIBUNAL JUDICIARY: INDEPENDENCE AND SENIOR PRESIDENT

[1.1552]

1 Independence of tribunal judiciary

In section 3 of the Constitutional Reform Act 2005 (c 4) (guarantee of continued judicial independence), after subsection (7) insert—

"(7A) In this section "the judiciary" also includes every person who—
(a) holds an office listed in Schedule 14 or holds an office listed in subsection (7B), and
(b) but for this subsection would not be a member of the judiciary for the purposes of this section.

(7B) The offices are those of—
(a) Senior President of Tribunals;
(b) President of Employment Tribunals (Scotland);
(c) Vice President of Employment Tribunals (Scotland);
(d) member of a panel of chairmen of Employment Tribunals (Scotland);
(e) member of a panel of members of employment tribunals that is not a panel of chairmen;

(f) adjudicator appointed under section 5 of the Criminal Injuries Compensation Act 1995."

[1.1553]

2 Senior President of Tribunals

(1) Her Majesty may, on the recommendation of the Lord Chancellor, appoint a person to the office of Senior President of Tribunals.

(2) Schedule 1 makes further provision about the Senior President of Tribunals and about recommendations for appointment under subsection (1).

(3) A holder of the office of Senior President of Tribunals must, in carrying out the functions of that office, have regard to—

- (a) the need for tribunals to be accessible,
- (b) the need for proceedings before tribunals—
  - (i) to be fair, and
  - (ii) to be handled quickly and efficiently,
- (c) the need for members of tribunals to be experts in the subject-matter of, or the law to be applied in, cases in which they decide matters, and
- (d) the need to develop innovative methods of resolving disputes that are of a type that may be brought before tribunals.

(4) In subsection (3) "tribunals" means—

- (a) the First-tier Tribunal,
- (b) the Upper Tribunal,
- (c) employment tribunals, [and]
- (d) the Employment Appeal Tribunal, . . .
- (e) . . .

NOTES

Sub-s (4): word "and" in square brackets at the end of para (c) inserted, and para (e) (and the word immediately preceding it) repealed, by the Transfer of Functions of the Asylum and Immigration Tribunal Order 2010, SI 2010/21, art 5(1), Sch 1, paras 36, 37.

CHAPTER 2 FIRST-TIER TRIBUNAL AND UPPER TRIBUNAL

Establishment

[1.1554]

3 The First-tier Tribunal and the Upper Tribunal

(1) There is to be a tribunal, known as the First-tier Tribunal, for the purpose of exercising the functions conferred on it under or by virtue of this Act or any other Act.

(2) There is to be a tribunal, known as the Upper Tribunal, for the purpose of exercising the functions conferred on it under or by virtue of this Act or any other Act.

(3) Each of the First-tier Tribunal, and the Upper Tribunal, is to consist of its judges and other members.

(4) The Senior President of Tribunals is to preside over both of the First-tier Tribunal and the Upper Tribunal.

(5) The Upper Tribunal is to be a superior court of record.

Members and composition of tribunals

[1.1555]

6 Certain judges who are also judges of First-tier Tribunal and Upper Tribunal

(1) A person is within this subsection (and so, by virtue of sections 4(1)(c) and 5(1)(g), is a judge of the First-tier Tribunal and of the Upper Tribunal) if the person—

- [(za) is the Lord Chief Justice of England and Wales,
- (zb) is the Master of the Rolls,
- (zc) is the President of the Queen's Bench Division of the High Court in England and Wales,
- (zd) is the President of the Family Division of the High Court in England and Wales,
- (ze) is the Chancellor of the High Court in England and Wales,]
- (a) is an ordinary judge of the Court of Appeal in England and Wales (including the vice-president, if any, of either division of that Court),
- (b) is a Lord Justice of Appeal in Northern Ireland,
- (c) is a judge of the Court of Session,
- (d) is a puisne judge of the High Court in England and Wales or Northern Ireland,
- [(da) is a deputy judge of the High Court in England and Wales,
- (db) is the Judge Advocate General,]
- (e) is a circuit judge,
- [(ea) is a Recorder,]
- (f) is a sheriff in Scotland,
- (g) is a county court judge in Northern Ireland,
- (h) is a district judge in England and Wales or Northern Ireland, . . .
- (i) is a District Judge (Magistrates' Courts),
- [(j) is the President of Employment Tribunals (England and Wales),
- (k) is the President of Employment Tribunals (Scotland),
- (l) is the Vice President of Employment Tribunals (Scotland), or
- (m) is a Regional Employment Judge].

(2) References in subsection (1)(c) to (i) to office-holders do not include deputies or temporary office-holders.

NOTES

Sub-s (1): paras (za)–(ze), (da), (db) inserted by the Crime and Courts Act 2013, s 21(4), Sch 14, Pt 4, paras 6, 8; para (ea) inserted, word omitted from para (h) repealed and paras (j)–(m) added, by the Courts and Tribunals (Judiciary and Functions of Staff) Act 2018, s 1(2), as from 20 February 2019.

CHAPTER 4 ADMINISTRATIVE MATTERS IN RESPECT OF CERTAIN TRIBUNALS

[1.1556]

39 The general duty

(1) The Lord Chancellor is under a duty to ensure that there is an efficient and effective system to support the carrying on of the business of—

(a) the First-tier Tribunal,

(b) the Upper Tribunal,

(c) employment tribunals, [and]

(d) the Employment Appeal Tribunal, . . .

(e) . . .

and that appropriate services are provided for those tribunals (referred to in this section and in sections 40 and 41 as "the tribunals").

(2) Any reference in this section, or in section 40 or 41, to the Lord Chancellor's general duty in relation to the tribunals is to his duty under subsection (1).

(3) The Lord Chancellor must annually prepare and lay before each House of Parliament a report as to the way in which he has discharged his general duty in relation to the tribunals.

NOTES

Sub-s (1): word "and" in square brackets at the end of para (c) inserted, and para (e) (and the word immediately preceding it) repealed, by the Transfer of Functions of the Asylum and Immigration Tribunal Order 2010, SI 2010/21, art 5(1), Sch 1, paras 36, 40.

[1.1557]

40 Tribunal staff and services

(1) The Lord Chancellor may appoint such staff as appear to him appropriate for the purpose of discharging his general duty in relation to the tribunals.

(2) Subject to subsections (3) and (4), the Lord Chancellor may enter into such contracts with other persons for the provision, by them or their sub-contractors, of staff or services as appear to him appropriate for the purpose of discharging his general duty in relation to the tribunals.

(3) The Lord Chancellor may not enter into contracts for the provision of staff to discharge functions which involve making judicial decisions or exercising any judicial discretion.

(4) The Lord Chancellor may not enter into contracts for the provision of staff to carry out the administrative work of the tribunals unless an order made by the Lord Chancellor authorises him to do so.

(5) Before making an order under subsection (4) the Lord Chancellor must consult the Senior President of Tribunals as to what effect (if any) the order might have on the proper and efficient administration of justice.

(6) An order under subsection (4) may authorise the Lord Chancellor to enter into contracts for the provision of staff to discharge functions—

(a) wholly or to the extent specified in the order,

(b) generally or in cases or areas specified in the order, and

(c) unconditionally or subject to the fulfilment of conditions specified in the order.

NOTES

Orders: the Contracting Out (Administrative Work of Tribunals) Order 2009, SI 2009/121. This Order (as amended) enables the Lord Chancellor to enter into contracts with other persons for the provision of staff for carrying out the administrative work of the tribunals listed in art 2 of the Order. These tribunals are: (a) the First-tier Tribunal, (b) the Upper Tribunal, (c) employment tribunals, and (d) the Employment Appeal Tribunal.

[1.1558]

41 Provision of accommodation

(1) The Lord Chancellor may provide, equip, maintain and manage such tribunal buildings, offices and other accommodation as appear to him appropriate for the purpose of discharging his general duty in relation to the tribunals.

(2) The Lord Chancellor may enter into such arrangements for the provision, equipment, maintenance or management of tribunal buildings, offices or other accommodation as appear to him appropriate for the purpose of discharging his general duty in relation to the tribunals.

(3) The powers under—

(a) section 2 of the Commissioners of Works Act 1852 (c 28) (acquisition by agreement), and

(b) section 228(1) of the Town and Country Planning Act 1990 (c 8) (compulsory acquisition),

to acquire land necessary for the public service are to be treated as including power to acquire land for the purpose of its provision under arrangements entered into under subsection (2).

(4) In this section "tribunal building" means any place where any of the tribunals sits, including the precincts of any building in which it sits.

[1.1559]

42 Fees

(1) The Lord Chancellor may by order prescribe fees payable in respect of—

(a) anything dealt with by the First-tier Tribunal,
(b) anything dealt with by the Upper Tribunal,
(c) . . .
(d) anything dealt with by an added tribunal, and
(e) mediation conducted by staff appointed under section 40(1).

(2) An order under subsection (1) may, in particular, contain provision as to—

(a) scales or rates of fees;
(b) exemptions from or reductions in fees;
(c) remission of fees in whole or in part.

(3) In subsection (1)(d) "added tribunal" means a tribunal specified in an order made by the Lord Chancellor.

(4) A tribunal may be specified in an order under subsection (3) only if—

(a) it is established by or under an enactment, whenever passed or made, and
(b) is not an ordinary court of law.

(5) Before making an order under this section, the Lord Chancellor must consult—

(a) the Senior President of Tribunals . . .
(b) . . .

(6) The making of an order under subsection (1) requires the consent of the Treasury except where the order contains provision only for the purpose of altering amounts payable by way of fees already prescribed under that subsection.

(7) The Lord Chancellor must take such steps as are reasonably practicable to bring information about fees under subsection (1) to the attention of persons likely to have to pay them.

(8) Fees payable under subsection (1) are recoverable summarily as a civil debt.

(9) Subsection (8) does not apply to the recovery in Scotland of fees payable under this section.

(10) . . .

NOTES

Sub-s (1): para (c) repealed by the Transfer of Functions of the Asylum and Immigration Tribunal Order 2010, SI 2010/21, art 5(1), Sch 1, paras 36, 41.

Sub-s (5): para (b) and the word omitted immediately preceding it repealed by the Public Bodies (Abolition of Administrative Justice and Tribunals Council) Order 2013, SI 2013/2042, art 2(2), Schedule, paras 31, 32(a).

Sub-s (10): repealed by SI 2013/2042, art 2(2), Schedule, paras 31, 32(b).

Orders: many Orders have been made under this section, the vast majority of which are outside the scope of this work. The ones relevant to employment law are: the Added Tribunals (Employment Tribunals and Employment Appeal Tribunal) Order 2013, SI 2013/1892 at **[2.1453]**; the Employment Tribunals and the Employment Appeal Tribunal Fees Order 2013, SI 2013/1893; the Courts and Tribunals Fee Remissions Order 2013, SI 2013/2302; the Employment Tribunals and the Employment Appeal Tribunal Fees (Amendment) Order 2015, SI 2015/414. Note that SI 2013/1893 was quashed by the Supreme Court in *R (UNISON) v Lord Chancellor* [2017] UKSC 51, [2017] ICR 1037.

[1.1560]

43 Report by Senior President of Tribunals

(1) Each year the Senior President of Tribunals must give the Lord Chancellor a report covering, in relation to relevant tribunal cases—

(a) matters that the Senior President of Tribunals wishes to bring to the attention of the Lord Chancellor, and
(b) matters that the Lord Chancellor has asked the Senior President of Tribunals to cover in the report.

(2) The Lord Chancellor must publish each report given to him under subsection (1).

(3) In this section "relevant tribunal cases" means—

(a) cases coming before the First-tier Tribunal,
(b) cases coming before the Upper Tribunal,
(c) cases coming before the Employment Appeal Tribunal, . . . [and]
(d) cases coming before employment tribunals[, . . .
(e) . . .].

NOTES

Sub-s (3) is amended as follows:

The original word "and" omitted from para (c) was repealed, and para (e) (and the word immediately preceding it) was originally inserted, by the UK Borders Act 2007, ss 56(1), 58, Schedule.

The word "and" in square brackets at the end of para (c) was reinserted, and para (e) (and the word immediately preceding it) was repealed, by the Transfer of Functions of the Asylum and Immigration Tribunal Order 2010, SI 2010/21, art 5(1), Sch 1, paras 36, 42.

CHAPTER 6 SUPPLEMENTARY

[1.1561]

49 Orders and regulations under Part 1: supplemental and procedural provisions

(1) Power—

(a) of the Lord Chancellor to make an order, or regulations, under this Part,
(b) of the Senior President of Tribunals to make an order under section 7(9), or

(c) of the Scottish Ministers, or the Welsh Ministers, to make an order under paragraph 25(2) of Schedule 7,

is exercisable by statutory instrument.

(2) The Statutory Instruments Act 1946 (c 36) shall apply in relation to the power to make orders conferred on the Senior President of Tribunals by section 7(9) as if the Senior President of Tribunals were a Minister of the Crown.

(3) Any power mentioned in subsection (1) includes power to make different provision for different purposes.

(4) Without prejudice to the generality of subsection (3), power to make an order under section 30 or 31 includes power to make different provision in relation to England, Scotland, Wales and Northern Ireland respectively.

(5) *No order mentioned in subsection (6) is to be made unless a draft of the statutory instrument containing it* (whether alone or with other provision) has been laid before, and approved by a resolution of, each House of Parliament.

(6) *Those orders* are—

(a) an order under section 11(8), 13(6) or (14), 30, 31(1), 32, 33, 34, 35, 36, 37 or 42(3);

[(aa) regulations under section 29D(4);]

(b) an order under paragraph 15 of Schedule 4;

(c) an order under section 42(1)(a) to (d) that provides for fees to be payable in respect of things for which fees have never been payable;

(d) an order under section 31(2), (7) or (9), or paragraph 30(1) of Schedule 5, that contains provision taking the form of an amendment or repeal of an enactment comprised in an Act.

(7) A statutory instrument that—

(a) contains—

(i) an order mentioned in subsection (8), or

(ii) regulations under Part 3 of Schedule 9, and

(b) is not subject to any requirement that a draft of the instrument be laid before, and approved by a resolution of, each House of Parliament,

is subject to annulment in pursuance of a resolution of either House of Parliament.

(8) Those orders are—

(a) an order made by the Lord Chancellor under this Part;

(b) an order made by the Senior President of Tribunals under section 7(9).

(9) A statutory instrument that contains an order made by the Scottish Ministers under paragraph 25(2) of Schedule 7 is subject to annulment in pursuance of a resolution of the Scottish Parliament.

(10) A statutory instrument that contains an order made by the Welsh Ministers under paragraph 25(2) of Schedule 7 is subject to annulment in pursuance of a resolution of the National Assembly for Wales.

NOTES

Sub-s (5): for the words in italics there are substituted the words "None of the orders or regulations mentioned in subsection (6) may be made unless a draft of the statutory instrument containing the order or regulations", by the Courts and Tribunals (Judiciary and Functions of Staff) Act 2018, s 3, Schedule, Pt 2, paras 39, 42(1), (2), as from a day to be appointed.

Sub-s (6): for the words in italics there are substituted the words "The orders and regulations", and para (aa) is inserted, by the Courts and Tribunals (Judiciary and Functions of Staff) Act 2018, s 3, Schedule, Pt 2, paras 39, 42(1), (3), as from a day to be appointed.

EMPLOYMENT ACT 2008

(2008 c 24)

An Act to make provision about the procedure for the resolution of employment disputes; to provide for compensation for financial loss in cases of unlawful underpayment or non-payment; to make provision about the enforcement of minimum wages legislation and the application of the national minimum wage to Cadet Force Adult Volunteers and voluntary workers; to make provision about the enforcement of offences under the Employment Agencies Act 1973; to make provision about the right of trade unions to expel or exclude members on the grounds of membership of a political party; and for connected purposes

[13 November 2008]

[1.1562]

NOTES

This Act is, to a large extent, amending only. A brief summary of the effect of each section and Schedule is given below (with the exception of ss 22, 23 which are reproduced in full). As to the commencement of this Act, see s 22 below, the Employment Act 2008 (Commencement No 1, Transitional Provisions and Savings) Order 2008, SI 2008/3232, and the Employment Act 2008 (Commencement No 2, Transitional Provisions and Savings) Order 2009, SI 2009/603. All amendments made by this Act have been incorporated at the appropriate place. Amendments to the Employment Act 2002 are at **[1.1276]** et seq; amendments to the Employment Rights Act 1996 are at **[1.813]** et seq; amendments to the Trade Union and Labour Relations (Consolidation) Act 1992 are at **[1.268]** et seq; amendments to the Employment Tribunals Act 1996 are at **[1.771]** et seq; amendments to the National Minimum Wage Act 1998 are at **[1.1171]** et seq; and amendments to the Employment Agencies Act 1973 are at **[1.20]** et seq. Transitional provisions and savings have also been noted where relevant.

See *Harvey* AII(7), BI(4).

Dispute resolution

1 Statutory dispute resolution procedures
(Repeals the Employment Act 2002, ss 29–33 and Schs 2–4.)

2 Procedural fairness
(Repeals the Employment Rights Act 1996, s 98A.)

3 Non-compliance with statutory Codes of Practice
(Inserts the Trade Union and Labour Relations (Consolidation) Act 1992, s 207A, Sch A2, and amends the Employment Rights Act 1996, s 124A.)

4 Determination of proceedings without hearing
(Amends the Employment Tribunals Act 1996, s 7.)

5 Conciliation before bringing of proceedings
(Amended the Employment Tribunals Act 1996, s 18 and was repealed by the Enterprise and Regulatory Reform Act 2013, s 7(2), Sch 1, para 12.)

6 Conciliation after bringing of proceedings
(Repeals the Employment Tribunals Act 1996, ss 18(2A), 19(2).)

7 Compensation for financial loss
(Amends the Employment Rights Act 1996, ss 24, 163.)

National minimum wage etc

8 Arrears payable in cases of non-compliance
(Amends the National Minimum Wage Act 1998, s 17 and the Agricultural Wages Act 1948, s 3A. Repealed in part by the Enterprise and Regulatory Reform Act 2013, s 72(4), Sch 20, as from 1 October 2013 (in relation to England) and as from a day to be appointed (in relation to Wales).)

9 Notices of underpayment
(Section 9(1) substitutes the National Minimum Wage Act 1998, ss 19, 19A–19H for the existing ss 19–22F. Section 9(3)–(6) amend the National Minimum Wage Act 1998, s 51, the Employment Tribunals Act 1996, s 4, the Commissioners for Revenue and Customs Act 2005, s 44, and the Agricultural Wages Act 1948, s 3A. Repealed in part by the Enterprise and Regulatory Reform Act 2013, s 72(4), Sch 20, as from a day to be appointed.)

10 Powers of officers to take copies of records
(Section 10(1)–(3) amend the National Minimum Wage Act 1998, s 14.)

11 Offences: mode of trial and penalties
(Amends the National Minimum Wage Act 1998, ss 31, 33.)

12 Powers to investigate criminal offences
(Amends the Finance Act 2007, s 84 and the Criminal Law (Consolidation) (Scotland) Act 1995, s 23A.)

13 Cadet Force Adult Volunteers
(Inserts the National Minimum Wage Act 1998, s 37A.)

14 Voluntary workers
(Inserts the National Minimum Wage Act 1998, s 44(1A).)

Employment agencies

15 Offences: mode of trial and penalties
(Amends the Employment Agencies Act 1973, ss 3B, 5, 6.)

16 Enforcement powers
(Amends the Employment Agencies Act 1973, s 9.)

17 Offences by partnerships in Scotland
(Amends the Employment Agencies Act 1973, s 11.)

Miscellaneous

18 Employment agencies and national minimum wage legislation: information
(Inserts the National Minimum Wage Act 1998, s 15(5A) and amends the Employment Agencies Act 1973, s 9.)

19 Exclusion or expulsion from trade union for membership of political party
(Inserts the Trade Union and Labour Relations (Consolidation) Act 1992, s 174(4C)–(4H) and amends s 176 of that Act.)

General

20 Repeals
(Introduces the Schedule to this Act (repeals).)

21 Extent
(Provides only that an amendment or repeal effected by this Act has the same extent as the enactment (or the relevant part of the enactment) to which it relates.)

[1.1563]
22 Commencement
(1) The provisions of this Act come into force as follows—
(a) sections 1 to 9 and Parts 1 and 2 of the Schedule come into force on such day as the Secretary of State may by order appoint;

(b) section 10 and Part 3 of the Schedule come into force at the end of the period of two months beginning with the day on which this Act is passed;
(c) sections 11 and 12 and Part 4 of the Schedule come into force on such day as the Secretary of State may by order appoint;
(d) sections 13 and 14 come into force at the end of the period of two months beginning with the day on which this Act is passed;
(e) sections 15 to 17 and Part 5 of the Schedule come into force on 6 April 2009;
(f) sections 18 and 19 come into force on such day as the Secretary of State may by order appoint;
(g) the remaining provisions of this Act come into force on the day on which this Act is passed.

(2) An order under subsection (1) is to be made by statutory instrument.

(3) An order under subsection (1) may—
(a) appoint different days for different purposes;
(b) contain transitional provision, or savings.

NOTES

Orders: the Employment Act 2008 (Commencement No 1, Transitional Provisions and Savings) Order 2008, SI 2008/3232; the Employment Act 2008 (Commencement No 2, Transitional Provisions and Savings) Order 2009, SI 2009/603.

[1.1564]

23 Short title

This Act may be cited as the Employment Act 2008.

SCHEDULE

(Contains various repeals which are noted at the appropriate place where they are within the scope of this work.)

PENSIONS ACT 2008

(2008 c 30)

ARRANGEMENT OF SECTIONS

PART 1
PENSION SCHEME MEMBERSHIP FOR JOBHOLDERS

CHAPTER 1
EMPLOYERS' DUTIES

Jobholders

Employers' duties

Duty in relation to workers without qualifying earnings

Supplementary provision about the duties

Qualifying earnings and earnings trigger

Qualifying schemes and automatic enrolment schemes

An Act to make provision relating to pensions; and for connected purposes

[26 November 2008]

NOTES

Only certain parts of this Act most relevant to employment law are reproduced. Provisions omitted are not annotated. Duties of employers to enrol employees are being brought into effect in stages from 1 October 2012 (see the Employers' Duties (Implementation) Regulations 2010, SI 2010/4, reg 4 at **[2.1079]**, as amended).

Employment Appeal Tribunal: an appeal lies to the Employment Appeal Tribunal on any question of law arising from any decision of, or in any proceedings before, an employment tribunal under or by virtue of this Act; see the Employment Tribunals Act 1996, s 21(1)(gd) at **[1.764]**.

See *Harvey* BI(8).

PART 1
PENSION SCHEME MEMBERSHIP FOR JOBHOLDERS

CHAPTER 1 EMPLOYERS' DUTIES

Jobholders

[1.1565]

1 Jobholders

(1) For the purposes of this Part a jobholder is a worker—
- (a) who is working or ordinarily works in Great Britain under the worker's contract,
- (b) who is aged at least 16 and under 75, and
- (c) to whom qualifying earnings are payable by the employer in the relevant pay reference period (see sections 13 and 15).

(2) Where a jobholder has more than one employer, or a succession of employers, this Chapter applies separately in relation to each employment.

(3) Accordingly—
- (a) references to the employer are references to the employer concerned;
- (b) references to membership of a pension scheme are references to membership in relation to the employment concerned.

Employers' duties

[1.1566]

2 Continuity of scheme membership

(1) If a jobholder is an active member of a qualifying scheme, the employer must not take any action, or make any omission, by which (without the jobholder ceasing to be employed by the employer)—
- (a) the jobholder ceases to be an active member of the scheme, or
- (b) the scheme ceases to be a qualifying scheme.

(2) Subsection (1) is not contravened if the jobholder remains an active member of another qualifying scheme.

[(3) Subsection (1) is not contravened if by virtue of section 5 the jobholder becomes an active member of an automatic enrolment scheme with effect from—
- (a) the day after the cessation referred to in paragraph (a) or (b) of subsection (1), or
- (b) a day within the prescribed period (if a period is prescribed).]

(4) Subsection (1) is not contravened if the action or omission is at the jobholder's request.

(5) In this Part as it applies in the case of any jobholder, references to a qualifying scheme are references to a pension scheme which is a qualifying scheme in relation to that jobholder (see section 16).

NOTES

Sub-s (3): substituted by the Pensions Act 2011, s 4(1).

Regulations: the Occupational and Personal Pension Schemes (Automatic Enrolment) Regulations 2010, SI 2010/772 at **[2.1153]**; the Automatic Enrolment (Miscellaneous Amendments) Regulations 2012, SI 2012/215; the Occupational and Personal Pension Schemes (Automatic Enrolment) (Amendment) Regulations 2012, SI 2012/1257.

[1.1567]

3 Automatic enrolment

[(1) This section applies to a jobholder—
- (a) who is aged at least 22,
- (b) who has not reached pensionable age, and
- (c) to whom earnings of more than [£10,000] are payable by the employer in the relevant pay reference period (see section 15).]

(2) The employer must make prescribed arrangements by which the jobholder becomes an active member of an automatic enrolment scheme with effect from the automatic enrolment date.

(3) Subsection (2) does not apply if the jobholder was an active member of a qualifying scheme on the automatic enrolment date.

(4) Subsection (2) does not apply if, within the prescribed period before the automatic enrolment date, the jobholder ceased to be an active member of a qualifying scheme because of any action or omission by the jobholder.

(5) For the purposes of arrangements under subsection (2) regulations may require information to be provided to any person by the employer or—

(a) where the arrangements relate to an occupational pension scheme, the trustees or managers of the scheme;
(b) where the arrangements relate to a personal pension scheme, the provider of the scheme.

(6) For the purposes of arrangements made under subsection (2) in relation to a personal pension scheme, regulations may deem an agreement to exist (subject to section 8) between the jobholder and the provider of the scheme for the jobholder to be an active member of the scheme on terms and conditions determined in accordance with the regulations.

[(6A) In this section "earnings" has the meaning given in section 13(3).

(6B) In the case of a pay reference period of less or more than 12 months, subsection (1) applies as if the amount in paragraph (c) were proportionately less or more.]

(7) The automatic enrolment date, in relation to any person, is the first day on which this section applies to the person as a jobholder of the employer. [This is subject to section 4.]

(8) In this Part as it applies in the case of any jobholder, references to an automatic enrolment scheme are references to a pension scheme which is an automatic enrolment scheme in relation to that jobholder (see section 17).

NOTES

Sub-s (1): substituted by the Pensions Act 2011, s 5(1); sum in square brackets in para (c) substituted by the Automatic Enrolment (Earnings Trigger and Qualifying Earnings Band) Order 2014, SI 2014/623, art 2(1), as from 6 April 2014. (Note the previous sum was £9,440, as substituted for the sum of £8,105 by SI 2013/667.)

Sub-ss (6A), (6B): inserted by the Pensions Act 2011, s 5(2).

Sub-s (7): words in square brackets inserted by the Pensions Act 2011, s 6(1).

Regulations: the Occupational and Personal Pension Schemes (Automatic Enrolment) Regulations 2010, SI 2010/772 at **[2.1153]**; the Automatic Enrolment (Miscellaneous Amendments) Regulations 2012, SI 2012/215; the Occupational and Personal Pension Schemes (Automatic Enrolment) (Amendment) Regulations 2012, SI 2012/1257; the Automatic Enrolment (Miscellaneous Amendments) Regulations 2013, SI 2013/2556; the Occupational and Personal Pension Schemes (Automatic Enrolment) (Amendment) Regulations 2015, SI 2015/501; the Employers' Duties (Implementation) (Amendment) Regulations 2017, SI 2017/347.

See further: for rounded figures for the purposes of sub-s (6B) above in respect of specified pay reference periods, the Automatic Enrolment (Earnings Trigger and Qualifying Earnings Band) Order 2019, SI 2019/374 at **[2.2119]**.

[1.1568]

[4 Postponement or disapplication of automatic enrolment

(1) Where—
(a) an employer (E) gives to a person employed by E on E's staging date ("the worker") notice that E intends to defer automatic enrolment for the worker until a date specified in the notice ("the deferral date"), and
(b) any prescribed requirements in relation to the notice are met,

the worker's automatic enrolment date is the deferral date if on that date section 3 applies to the worker as a jobholder of E; if not, subsection (4) applies.

(2) Where—
(a) a person ("the worker") begins to be employed by an employer (E) after E's staging date,
(b) E gives the worker notice that E intends to defer automatic enrolment until a date specified in the notice ("the deferral date"), and
(c) any prescribed requirements in relation to the notice are met,

the worker's automatic enrolment date is the deferral date if on that date section 3 applies to the worker as a jobholder of E; if not, subsection (4) applies.

(3) Where—
(a) a person ("the worker") employed by an employer (E) becomes, after E's staging date, a jobholder to whom section 3 applies,
(b) E gives the worker notice that E intends to defer automatic enrolment until a date specified in the notice ("the deferral date"), and
(c) any prescribed requirements in relation to the notice are met,

the worker's automatic enrolment date is the deferral date if on that date section 3 applies to the worker as a jobholder of E; if not, subsection (4) applies.

(4) Where this subsection applies, section 3(2) does not apply in relation to any employment of the worker by E in the period beginning with the starting day and ending with the deferral date.

(5) A notice under this section may be given on or before the starting day or within a prescribed period after that day.

(6) The deferral date may be any date in the period of three months after the starting day.

(7) An employer who gives a worker a notice under subsection (1) or (2) may not give the worker a notice under subsection (3) in relation to any occasion on or before the deferral date specified in the notice on which the worker becomes a jobholder to whom section 3 applies.

(8) In this section—

"staging date", in relation to an employer of a particular description, means the date prescribed under section 12 in relation to employers of that description;

"starting day" means—
(a) E's staging date, in the case of a notice under subsection (1);
(b) the day on which the worker begins to be employed by E, in the case of a notice under subsection (2);
(c) the day on which the worker becomes a jobholder to whom section 3 applies, in the case of a notice under subsection (3).]

NOTES

Substituted by the Pensions Act 2011, s 6(2).

Regulations: the Automatic Enrolment (Miscellaneous Amendments) Regulations 2012, SI 2012/215; the Automatic Enrolment (Miscellaneous Amendments) Regulations 2013, SI 2013/2556; the Occupational and Personal Pension Schemes (Automatic Enrolment) (Amendment) Regulations 2015, SI 2015/501.

[1.1569]

5 Automatic re-enrolment

[(1) This section applies to a jobholder—

(a) who is aged at least 22,

(b) who has not reached pensionable age, and

(c) to whom earnings of more than [£10,000] are payable by the employer in the relevant pay reference period (see section 15).]

[(1A) This section also applies to a jobholder who—

(a) is aged at least 22,

(b) has not reached pensionable age, and

(c) is not an active member of a qualifying scheme because there has been a period beginning at any time after the jobholder's automatic enrolment date during which the requirements of section 1(1)(a) or (c) were not met (so that the person was not a jobholder for that period).

(1B) This section also applies to a jobholder who has ceased to be an active member of a qualifying scheme because of something other than an action or omission by the jobholder.]

(2) The employer must make prescribed arrangements by which the jobholder becomes an active member of an automatic enrolment scheme with effect from the automatic re-enrolment date.

(3) Subsection (2) does not apply if the jobholder was an active member of a qualifying scheme on the automatic re-enrolment date.

[(3A) Subsection (2) does not apply if the jobholder's automatic enrolment date is deferred under section 4 from a date before the automatic re-enrolment date to a date after the automatic re-enrolment date.]

[(4) . . .]

(5) . . .

(6) For the purposes of arrangements under subsection (2) regulations may require information to be provided to any person by the employer or—

(a) where the arrangements relate to an occupational pension scheme, the trustees or managers of the scheme;

(b) where the arrangements relate to a personal pension scheme, the provider of the scheme.

(7) For the purposes of arrangements made under subsection (2) in relation to a personal pension scheme, regulations may deem an agreement to exist (subject to section 8) between the jobholder and the provider of the scheme for the jobholder to be an active member of the scheme on terms and conditions determined in accordance with the regulations.

[(7A) In this section "earnings" has the meaning given in section 13(3).

(7B) In the case of a pay reference period of less or more than 12 months, subsection (1) applies as if the amount in paragraph (c) were proportionately less or more.]

(8) Automatic re-enrolment dates are dates . . . that are to be determined in accordance with regulations.

NOTES

Sub-s (1): substituted by the Pensions Act 2011, s 5(3); sum in square brackets in para (c) substituted by the Automatic Enrolment (Earnings Trigger and Qualifying Earnings Band) Order 2014, SI 2014/623, art 2(1), as from 6 April 2014. (Note the previous sum was £9,440, as substituted for the sum of £8,105 by SI 2013/667.)

Sub-ss (1A), (1B): inserted by the Pensions Act 2011, s 4(2).

Sub-s (3A): inserted by the Pensions Act 2014, s 37(1), (2), as from 11 September 2014.

Sub-s (4): substituted by the Pensions Act 2011, s 4(3); and repealed by the Pensions Act 2014, s 38(3), as from 11 September 2014.

Sub-s (5): repealed by the Pensions Act 2011, s 6(3).

Sub-ss (7A), (7B): inserted by the Pensions Act 2011, s 5(4).

Sub-s (8): words omitted repealed by the Pensions Act 2011, s 4(4).

Regulations: the Occupational and Personal Pension Schemes (Automatic Enrolment) Regulations 2010, SI 2010/772 at **[2.1153]**; the Automatic Enrolment (Miscellaneous Amendments) Regulations 2012, SI 2012/215; the Occupational and Personal Pension Schemes (Automatic Enrolment) (Amendment) Regulations 2012, SI 2012/1257; the Automatic Enrolment (Miscellaneous Amendments) Regulations 2013, SI 2013/2556; the Occupational and Personal Pension Schemes (Automatic Enrolment) (Amendment) Regulations 2015, SI 2015/501.

See further: for rounded figures for the purposes of sub-s (7B) above in respect of specified pay reference periods, the Automatic Enrolment (Earnings Trigger and Qualifying Earnings Band) Order 2019, SI 2019/374 at **[2.2119]**.

[1.1570]

6 Timing of automatic re-enrolment

(1) Regulations under section 5(8) must either—

(a) secure that for any jobholder there is no automatic re-enrolment date less than three years after the jobholder's automatic enrolment date, and that there is not more than one automatic re-enrolment date in any period of three years, or

(b) secure that for any employer there is not more than one automatic re-enrolment date in any period of [2 years and 9 months].

(2) Subsection (1) does not restrict the provision that regulations may make about the timing of a jobholder's automatic re-enrolment date ("the relevant date") in the following cases.

(3) . . .

(4) The [first case] is where—

(a) . . . the jobholder ceases to be an active member of a qualifying scheme . . . ,

(b) that event is not the effect of any action or omission by the jobholder . . . , and

(c) the relevant date is the jobholder's first automatic re-enrolment date after that [event].

(5) The [second case] is where—

(a) there is a period beginning at any time after the jobholder's automatic enrolment date during which the requirements of section 1(1)(a) or (c) are not met (so that the person is not a jobholder for that period), and

(b) the relevant date is the jobholder's first automatic re-enrolment date after that period.

(6) . . .

NOTES

Sub-s (1): words in square brackets substituted by the Pensions Act 2011, s 7, as from 3 November 2011 (in so far as relating to the making of regulations), and as from 1 April 2015 (otherwise).

Sub-ss (3), (6): repealed by the Pensions Act 2011, s 6(4)(a).

Sub-s (4): words in square brackets substituted, and words omitted repealed, by the Pensions Act 2011, ss 4(5), 6(4)(b).

Sub-s (5): words in square brackets substituted by the Pensions Act 2011, s 6(4)(c).

[1.1571]

7 Jobholder's right to opt in

(1) This section applies to a jobholder who is not an active member of a qualifying scheme.

(2) But it does not apply at a time when—

(a) arrangements are required to be made under section 3 or 5 in respect of the jobholder, . . .

(b) . . .

(3) The jobholder may by notice require the employer to arrange for the jobholder to become an active member of an automatic enrolment scheme.

(4) The Secretary of State may by regulations make provision—

(a) about the form and content of the notice;

(b) about the arrangements that the employer is required to make;

(c) for determining the date with effect from which the jobholder is to become an active member under the arrangements.

(5) For the purposes of arrangements under subsection (3) regulations may require information to be provided to any person by the employer or—

(a) where the arrangements relate to an occupational pension scheme, the trustees or managers of the scheme;

(b) where the arrangements relate to a personal pension scheme, the provider of the scheme.

(6) For the purposes of arrangements made under subsection (3) in relation to a personal pension scheme, regulations may deem an agreement to exist (subject to section 8) between the jobholder and the provider of the scheme for the jobholder to be an active member of the scheme on terms and conditions determined in accordance with the regulations.

(7) Subsections (8) and (9) apply where a jobholder becomes an active member of an automatic enrolment scheme in pursuance of a notice under this section and, within the period of 12 months beginning with the day on which that notice was given—

(a) ceases to be an active member of that scheme, and

(b) gives the employer a further notice under this section.

(8) The further notice does not have effect to require the employer to arrange for the jobholder to become an active member of an automatic enrolment scheme.

(9) But any arrangements the employer makes for the jobholder to become, within that period, an active member of such a scheme must be made in accordance with regulations under this section.

NOTES

Sub-s (2): para (b) and word immediately preceding it repealed by the Pensions Act 2011, s 6(5).

Regulations: the Occupational and Personal Pension Schemes (Automatic Enrolment) Regulations 2010, SI 2010/772 at **[2.1153]**; the Automatic Enrolment (Miscellaneous Amendments) Regulations 2012, SI 2012/215; the Occupational and Personal Pension Schemes (Automatic Enrolment) (Amendment) Regulations 2012, SI 2012/1257; the Employers' Duties (Implementation) (Amendment) Regulations 2017, SI 2017/347.

[1.1572]

8 Jobholder's right to opt out

(1) This section applies on any occasion when arrangements under section 3(2), 5(2) or 7(3) apply to a jobholder (arrangements for the jobholder to become an active member of an automatic enrolment scheme).

(2) If the jobholder gives notice under this section—

(a) the jobholder is to be treated for all purposes as not having become an active member of the scheme on that occasion;

(b) any contributions paid by the jobholder, or by the employer on behalf or in respect of the jobholder, on the basis that the jobholder has become an active member of the scheme on that occasion must be refunded in accordance with prescribed requirements.

(3) Regulations under subsection (2)(b) may, in particular, make provision about—

(a) the time within which contributions must be refunded;

(b) how the amount to be refunded is calculated;
(c) the procedure for refunding contributions.

(4) The Secretary of State may by regulations make further provision in relation to notices under this section.

(5) The regulations may in particular make provision—
(a) as to the form and content of a notice;
(b) as to the period within which a notice must be given;
(c) as to the person to whom a notice must be given;
(d) requiring any person to make prescribed arrangements for enabling notices to be given;
(e) requiring any person to take prescribed action in consequence of a notice (in addition to any action prescribed under subsection (2)(b)).

(6) The regulations must provide for the notice—
(a) to include information about the effect in relation to jobholders of giving notice under this section, and
(b) to be signed or otherwise authorised by the jobholder.

NOTES

Regulations: the Occupational and Personal Pension Schemes (Automatic Enrolment) Regulations 2010, SI 2010/772 at **[2.1153]**; the Occupational and Personal Pension Schemes (Automatic Enrolment) (Amendment) Regulations 2012, SI 2012/1257; the Automatic Enrolment (Miscellaneous Amendments) Regulations 2013, SI 2013/2556.

Duty in relation to workers without qualifying earnings

[1.1573]

9 Workers without qualifying earnings

(1) This section applies to a worker—
(a) to whom paragraphs (a) and (b) of section 1(1) apply (working in Great Britain and aged between 16 and 75),
(b) to whom paragraph (c) of section 1(1) does not apply (qualifying earnings), and
(c) who is not an active member of a pension scheme that satisfies the requirements of this section.

(2) The worker may by notice require the employer to arrange for the worker to become an active member of a pension scheme that satisfies the requirements of this section.

(3) The Secretary of State may by regulations make provision—
(a) about the form and content of the notice;
(b) about the arrangements that the employer is required to make;
(c) for determining the date with effect from which the worker is (subject to compliance with any requirements of the scheme) to become an active member under the arrangements.

(4) Subsections (5) and (6) apply where a worker becomes an active member of a pension scheme in pursuance of a notice under this section and, within the period of 12 months beginning with the day on which that notice was given—
(a) ceases to be an active member of that scheme because of any action or omission by the worker, and
(b) gives the employer a further notice under this section.

(5) The further notice does not have effect to require the employer to arrange for the worker to become an active member of a pension scheme.

(6) But any arrangements the employer makes for the worker to become, within that period, an active member of a pension scheme that satisfies the requirements of this section must be made in accordance with regulations under this section.

(7) A pension scheme satisfies the requirements of this section if—
(a) it is registered under Chapter 2 of Part 4 of the Finance Act 2004 (c 12), and
(b) in the case of a personal pension scheme, there are, in relation to the worker concerned, direct payment arrangements (within the meaning of section 111A of the Pension Schemes Act 1993 (c 48)) between the worker and the employer.

NOTES

Regulations: the Occupational and Personal Pension Schemes (Automatic Enrolment) Regulations 2010, SI 2010/772 at **[2.1153]**; the Occupational and Personal Pension Schemes (Automatic Enrolment) (Amendment) Regulations 2012, SI 2012/1257; the Occupational and Personal Pension Schemes (Automatic Enrolment) (Amendment) Regulations 2015, SI 2015/501.

Supplementary provision about the duties

[1.1574]

10 Information to be given to workers

(1) The Secretary of State [may] make provision by regulations—
(a) for . . . jobholders to be given information about the effect of sections 2 to 8 in relation to them;
(b) for . . . workers to whom section 9 applies to be given information about the effect of that section in relation to them;
(c) for a prescribed person to be required to provide the information.

(2) Regulations under this section [may in particular make provision about]—
(a) what information must be given;
(b) in what circumstances it must be given;
(c) how and when it must be given.

NOTES

Words in square brackets substituted, and words omitted repealed, by the Pensions Act 2014, s 38(1), as from 11 September 2014.

Regulations: the Occupational and Personal Pension Schemes (Automatic Enrolment) Regulations 2010, SI 2010/772 at **[2.1153]**; the Automatic Enrolment (Miscellaneous Amendments) Regulations 2012, SI 2012/215; the Occupational and Personal Pension Schemes (Automatic Enrolment) (Amendment) Regulations 2012, SI 2012/1257; the Automatic Enrolment (Miscellaneous Amendments) Regulations 2013, SI 2013/2556; the Occupational and Personal Pension Schemes (Automatic Enrolment) (Amendment) Regulations 2015, SI 2015/501; the Employers' Duties (Implementation) (Amendment) Regulations 2017, SI 2017/347.

[1.1575]

11 Information to be given to the Pensions Regulator

(1) The Secretary of State may make regulations requiring employers to provide the Pensions Regulator ("the Regulator") with information about action they have taken or intend to take for the purposes of any provision of, or of regulations under, sections 2 to 10.

(2) The regulations may in particular—

(a) require an employer to provide information about pension schemes to which any action relates;

(b) require an employer to identify which of any prescribed descriptions a scheme falls within;

(c) require an employer to provide information that appears to the Secretary of State to be required for the performance by the Regulator of its functions under Chapter 2 of this Part;

(d) make provision about how and in what form any information is to be provided.

NOTES

Regulations: the Employers' Duties (Registration and Compliance) Regulations 2010, SI 2010/5; the Automatic Enrolment (Miscellaneous Amendments) Regulations 2012, SI 2012/215; the Automatic Enrolment (Miscellaneous Amendments) Regulations 2013, SI 2013/2556; the Occupational and Personal Pension Schemes (Automatic Enrolment) (Miscellaneous Amendments) Regulations 2016, SI 2016/311; the Employers' Duties (Miscellaneous Amendments) Regulations 2017, SI 2017/868.

[1.1576]

12 Introduction of employers' duties

The Secretary of State may by regulations provide that sections 2 to 9 do not apply in the case of an employer of any description until such date after the commencement of those sections as is prescribed in relation to employers of that description.

NOTES

Regulations: the Employers' Duties (Implementation) Regulations 2010, SI 2010/4 at **[2.1076]**; the Automatic Enrolment (Miscellaneous Amendments) Regulations 2012, SI 2012/215; Employers' Duties (Implementation) (Amendment) Regulations 2012, SI 2012/1813; the Occupational and Personal Pension Schemes (Automatic Enrolment) (Miscellaneous Amendments) Regulations 2016, SI 2016/311; the Employers' Duties (Implementation) (Amendment) Regulations 2017, SI 2017/347; the Employers' Duties (Miscellaneous Amendments) Regulations 2017, SI 2017/868.

[Qualifying earnings and earnings trigger]

[1.1577]

13 Qualifying earnings

(1) A person's qualifying earnings in a pay reference period of 12 months are the part (if any) of the gross earnings payable to that person in that period that is—

(a) more than [£6,136], and

(b) not more than [£50,000].

(2) In the case of a pay reference period of less or more than 12 months, subsection (1) applies as if the amounts in paragraphs (a) and (b) were proportionately less or more.

(3) In this section, "earnings", in relation to a person, means sums of any of the following descriptions that are payable to the person in connection with the person's employment—

(a) salary, wages, commission, bonuses and overtime;

(b) statutory sick pay under Part 11 of the Social Security Contributions and Benefits Act 1992 (c 4);

(c) statutory maternity pay under Part 12 of that Act;

(d) [statutory paternity pay] under Part 12ZA of that Act;

(e) statutory adoption pay under Part 12ZB of that Act;

[(ea) statutory shared parental pay under Part 12ZC of that Act;]

[(eb) statutory parental bereavement pay under Part 12ZD of that Act;]

(f) sums prescribed for the purposes of this section.

NOTES

Words in square brackets in the cross-heading preceding this section substituted by the Pensions Act 2011, s 8(2).

Sub-s (1): sums in square brackets in paras (a) and (b) substituted by the Automatic Enrolment (Earnings Trigger and Qualifying Earnings Band) Order 2019, SI 2019/374, art 2, as from 6 April 2019. See further the notes below.

Note that the previous sums in para (a) were: £6,032 (as from 6 April 2018, see SI 2018/367); £5,876 (as from 6 April 2017, see SI 2017/394); £5,824 (as from 6 April 2015, see SI 2015/428); £5,772 (as from 6 April 2014, see SI 2014/623); £5,668 (as from 6 April 2013, see SI 2013/667); £5,564 (as from 15 June 2012, see SI 2012/1506).

Note that the previous sums in para (b) were: £46,350 (as from 6 April 2018, see SI 2018/367); £45,000 (as from 6 April 2017, see SI 2017/394); £43,000 (as from 6 April 2016, see SI 2016/435); £42,385 (as from 6 April 2015, see SI 2015/468); £41,865 (as from 6 April 2014, see SI 2014/623); £41,450 (as from 6 April 2013, see SI 2013/667); £42,475 (as from 15 June 2012, see SI 2012/1506).

Sub-s (3) is amended as follows:

Words in square brackets in para (d) substituted by the Children and Families Act 2014, s 126(1), Sch 7, para 74(a), as from 5 April 2015 (note that this amendment does not have effect in relation to (a) children whose expected week of birth ends on or before 4 April 2015, and (b) children placed for adoption on or before that date: see the Children and Families Act 2014 (Commencement No 3, Transitional Provisions and Savings) Order 2014, SI 2014/1640, art 16).

Para (ea) inserted by the Children and Families Act 2014, s 126(1), Sch 7, para 74(b), as from 1 December 2014.

Para (eb) inserted by the Parental Bereavement (Leave and Pay) Act 2018, s 1(c), Schedule, Pt 3, para 55, as from a day to be appointed.

Statutory paternity pay: as to the meaning of this, see the Children and Families Act 2014, s 126 at **[1.1894]**.

Regulations: as of 15 May 2019, no Regulations had been made under this section.

See further: for rounded figures for the purposes of sub-s (2) above in respect of specified pay reference periods, the Automatic Enrolment (Earnings Trigger and Qualifying Earnings Band) Order 2019, SI 2019/374 at **[2.2119]**.

[1.1578]

[14 Review of earnings trigger and qualifying earnings band

(1) The Secretary of State must in each tax year consider whether any of the amounts in sections 3(1)(c), 5(1)(c) and 13(1)(a) and (b) should be increased or decreased.

(2) If the Secretary of State considers that any of those amounts should be increased or decreased, the Secretary of State may make an order substituting in the provisions in question the amounts that the Secretary of State thinks appropriate.

(3) For the purposes of subsection (1) the Secretary of State may take into account any of the factors specified in subsection (4) (as well as any others that the Secretary of State thinks relevant).

(4) The factors are—

(a) the amounts for the time being specified in Chapter 2 of Part 3 (personal allowances) of the Income Tax Act 2007;

(b) the amounts for the time being specified in regulations under section 5 of the Social Security Contributions and Benefits Act 1992 (earnings limits and thresholds for Class 1 national insurance contributions);

[(c) the amounts for the time being specified in section 44(4) of that Act (rate of basic state pension) and in regulations under section 3(1) of the Pensions Act 2014 (full rate of state pension);] (d) the general 1

(d) the general level of prices in Great Britain, and the general level of earnings there, estimated in such manner as the Secretary of State thinks fit.]

NOTES

Substituted by the Pensions Act 2011, s 8(1).

Sub-s (4): para (c) substituted by the Pensions Act 2014 (Consequential and Supplementary Amendments) Order 2016, SI 2016/224, art 7, as from 6 April 2016.

Orders: the Automatic Enrolment (Earnings Trigger and Qualifying Earnings Band) Order 2012, SI 2012/1506; the Automatic Enrolment (Earnings Trigger and Qualifying Earnings Band) Order 2013, SI 2013/667; the Automatic Enrolment (Earnings Trigger and Qualifying Earnings Band) Order 2014, SI 2014/623; the Automatic Enrolment (Earnings Trigger and Qualifying Earnings Band) Order 2019, SI 2019/374 at **[2.2119]**.

[1.1579]

15 Pay reference period

(1) In relation to any person a pay reference period is the period prescribed.

(2) The Secretary of State may by regulations—

(a) make provision for determining a person's earnings in any pay reference period;

(b) make provision for determining the first date of each pay reference period in relation to a person.

(3) A reference in any provision to the relevant pay reference period is a reference to the period determined in accordance with regulations under this section, as they apply for the purposes of that provision in the case concerned.

NOTES

Regulations: the Occupational and Personal Pension Schemes (Automatic Enrolment) Regulations 2010, SI 2010/772 at **[2.1153]**; the Automatic Enrolment (Miscellaneous Amendments) Regulations 2012, SI 2012/215; the Occupational and Personal Pension Schemes (Automatic Enrolment) (Amendment) Regulations 2012, SI 2012/1257; the Automatic Enrolment (Miscellaneous Amendments) Regulations 2013, SI 2013/2556.

[1.1580]

[15A Power to specify rounded figures

[(1) The Secretary of State may by order specify rounded figures for the purposes of section 3(6B), 5(7B) or 13(2) in the case of pay reference periods of any length specified in the order.

(2) A rounded figure so specified applies in place of the amount that would otherwise apply ("the exact amount").

(3) The Secretary of State must decide in relation to any particular amount whether to specify—

(a) a figure that is a whole number of pounds, or

(b) a figure that is divisible by 10 pence, or

(c) a figure that includes a whole number of pennies.

(4) It is for the Secretary of State to decide whether to round any particular amount up or down. Accordingly, a figure specified under this section may be the figure within paragraph (a) or (b) or (c) of subsection (3) that is closest to the exact amount or the one that is next closest to it (or, if two figures are joint closest, it may be either of those).]

NOTES

Inserted by the Pensions Act 2011, s 9.

Orders: the Automatic Enrolment (Earnings Trigger and Qualifying Earnings Band) Order 2012, SI 2012/1506; the Automatic Enrolment (Earnings Trigger and Qualifying Earnings Band) Order 2013, SI 2013/667; the Automatic Enrolment (Earnings Trigger and Qualifying Earnings Band) Order 2014, SI 2014/623; the Automatic Enrolment (Earnings Trigger and Qualifying Earnings Band) Order 2019, SI 2019/374 at **[2.2119]**.

Qualifying schemes and automatic enrolment schemes

[1.1581]

16 Qualifying schemes

(1) A pension scheme is a qualifying scheme in relation to a jobholder (J) if—

(a) the scheme is an occupational pension scheme or a personal pension scheme,

(b) the scheme is registered under Chapter 2 of Part 4 of the Finance Act 2004 (c 12), and

(c) while J is an active member, the scheme satisfies the quality requirement in relation to J.

(2) The Secretary of State may by regulations provide that subsection (1)(b) does not apply in relation to a scheme to which section 25 or 27 applies, if prescribed requirements are satisfied.

(3) The Secretary of State may by regulations provide that a scheme is not a qualifying scheme in relation to J if—

(a)–(ab) . . .

(b) while J is an active member, the contributions that must be paid to the scheme by, or on behalf or in respect of, J exceed a prescribed amount, or

(c) the scheme provides for average salary benefits to be provided to or in respect of J and contains prescribed features.

[(3A) See also paragraphs 1(4) and 2(4) of Schedule 18 to the Pensions Act 2014, which confer power to make regulations providing for a scheme not to be a qualifying scheme in relation to a jobholder in certain circumstances.]

[(4), (5) . . .]

NOTES

Sub-s (3): paras (a), (aa), (ab) substituted (for the original para (a)) by the Pensions Act 2011, s 10(1), (2), and subsequently repealed by the Pensions Act 2014, s 43, Sch 18, para 11(1), (2), as from 11 September 2014.

Sub-s (3A): inserted by the Pensions Act 2014, s 43, Sch 18, para 11(1), (3), as from 11 September 2014.

Sub-ss (4), (5): inserted by the Pensions Act 2011, s 10(1), (3); and repealed by the Pensions Act 2014, s 43, Sch 18, para 11(1), (4), as from 11 September 2014.

Regulations: the Occupational and Personal Pension Schemes (Automatic Enrolment) Regulations 2010, SI 2010/772 at **[2.1153]**; the Automatic Enrolment (Miscellaneous Amendments) Regulations 2012, SI 2012/215; the Occupational and Personal Pension Schemes (Automatic Enrolment) (Amendment) Regulations 2012, SI 2012/1257; the Occupational and Personal Pension Schemes (Automatic Enrolment) (Amendment) (No 3) Regulations 2012, SI 2012/2691; the Occupational and Personal Pension Schemes (Automatic Enrolment) (Amendment) Regulations 2014, SI 2014/715.

[1.1582]

17 Automatic enrolment schemes

(1) A pension scheme is an automatic enrolment scheme in relation to a jobholder (J) if—

(a) it is a qualifying scheme in relation to J,

(b) it satisfies the conditions in subsection (2), and

(c) it satisfies any further conditions prescribed.

(2) The conditions mentioned in subsection (1)(b) are that—

(a) no provision of the scheme prevents the employer from making arrangements prescribed by regulations under section 3(2), 5(2) or 7(4) for J to become an active member of the scheme;

(b) no provision of the scheme requires J to express a choice in relation to any matter, or to provide any information, in order to remain an active member.

NOTES

Regulations: the Occupational and Personal Pension Schemes (Automatic Enrolment) (Amendment) Regulations 2012, SI 2012/1257; the Occupational and Personal Pension Schemes (Automatic Enrolment) (Amendment) Regulations 2013, SI 2013/2328.

[1.1583]

18 Occupational pension schemes

For the purposes of this Part, each of these is an occupational pension scheme—

(a) an occupational pension scheme within the meaning of section 1(1) of the Pension Schemes Act 1993 (c 48) that has its main administration in the United Kingdom;

(b) an institution for occupational retirement provision within the meaning of Article 6(a) of the IORP Directive, that has its main administration in an EEA State other than the United Kingdom;

(c) a pension scheme that is prescribed or is of a prescribed description and that has its main administration elsewhere than in *an EEA State*.

NOTES

Para (b) is repealed and for the words in italics in para (c) there are substituted the words "the United Kingdom", by the Occupational and Personal Pension Schemes (Amendment etc) (EU Exit) Regulations 2019, SI 2019/192, reg 6(1), (2), as from exit day (as defined in the European Union (Withdrawal) Act 2018, s 20).

Regulations: the Occupational and Personal Pension Schemes (Automatic Enrolment) Regulations 2010, SI 2010/772 at **[2.1153]**; the Occupational and Personal Pension Schemes (Automatic Enrolment) (Amendment) Regulations 2012, SI 2012/1257.

[1.1584]

19 Personal pension schemes

For the purposes of this Part, a personal pension scheme is a pension scheme that is not an occupational pension scheme.

Miscellaneous

[1.1585]

33 Deduction of contributions

(1) An employer who arranges for a person to become a member of a scheme in accordance with section 3(2), 5(2) or 7(3), or of an occupational pension scheme in accordance with section 9(2), may deduct the person's contributions to the scheme from the person's remuneration and pay them to the trustees or managers of the scheme (in the case of an occupational pension scheme) or the provider of the scheme (in the case of a personal pension scheme).

(2) Regulations prescribing arrangements for the purposes of section 3(2), 5(2), 7(3) or 9(2), may require the employer to make such a deduction or payment at any time on or after the date with effect from which the jobholder is to become an active member of a scheme under the arrangements.

NOTES

Regulations: the Occupational and Personal Pension Schemes (Automatic Enrolment) Regulations 2010, SI 2010/772 at **[2.1153]**; the Occupational and Personal Pension Schemes (Automatic Enrolment) (Amendment) Regulations 2012, SI 2012/1257; the Automatic Enrolment (Miscellaneous Amendments) Regulations 2013, SI 2013/2556.

CHAPTER 2 COMPLIANCE

Effect of failure to comply

[1.1586]

34 Effect of failure to comply

(1) Contravention of any of the employer duty provisions does not give rise to a right of action for breach of statutory duty.

(2) But nothing in the employer duty provisions or this Chapter affects any right of action arising apart from those provisions.

(3) In this Chapter, references to the employer duty provisions are references to any provision of sections 2 to 11 or of regulations under those sections.

Compliance notices and unpaid contributions notices

[1.1587]

35 Compliance notices

(1) The Regulator may issue a compliance notice to a person if the Regulator is of the opinion that the person has contravened one or more of the employer duty provisions.

(2) A compliance notice is a notice directing the person to whom it is issued to take, or refrain from taking, the steps specified in the notice in order to remedy the contravention.

(3) A compliance notice may, in particular—

(a) state the period within which any step must be taken or must cease to be taken;

(b) require the person to whom it is issued to provide within a specified period specified information relating to the contravention;

(c) require the person to inform the Regulator, within a specified period, how the person has complied or is complying with the notice;

(d) state that, if the person fails to comply with the requirements of the notice, the Regulator may issue a fixed penalty notice under section 40.

(4) The steps specified in the notice may, in particular, include such steps as the Regulator thinks appropriate for placing the worker in the same position (as nearly as possible) as if the contravention had not occurred.

(5) If the compliance notice is issued in respect of a failure to comply with an enrolment duty and the specified steps relate to membership of *a defined benefits scheme or a hybrid scheme*, the notice may, in particular, require the employer to ensure that the worker is entitled to the same benefits under the scheme as if the employer had complied with that duty.

NOTES

Sub-s (5): for the words in italics there are substituted the words "an occupational defined benefits scheme or a shared risk scheme" by the Pension Schemes Act 2015, s 46, Sch 2, paras 39, 48, as from a day to be appointed.

[1.1588]

36 Third party compliance notices

(1) The Regulator may issue a third party compliance notice if it is of the opinion that—

(a) a person has contravened one or more of the employer duty provisions,
(b) the contravention is or was, wholly or partly, a result of a failure of another person (the "third party") to do any thing, and
(c) that failure is not itself a contravention of any of the employer duty provisions.

(2) A third party compliance notice is a notice directing the third party to take, or refrain from taking, the steps specified in the notice in order to remedy or prevent a recurrence of the failure.

(3) A third party notice may, in particular—
(a) state the period within which any step must be taken or must cease to be taken;
(b) require the third party to inform the Regulator, within a specified period, how the third party has complied or is complying with the notice;
(c) state that, if the third party fails to comply with the requirements of the notice, the Regulator may issue a fixed penalty notice under section 40.

(4) A third party notice may give the third party a choice between different ways of remedying or preventing the recurrence of the third party's failure.

[1.1589]
37 Unpaid contributions notices
(1) The Regulator may issue an unpaid contributions notice to an employer if it is of the opinion that relevant contributions have not been paid on or before the due date.
(2) An unpaid contributions notice is a notice requiring an employer to pay into a pension scheme by a specified date an amount in respect of relevant contributions that have not been paid.
(3) "Due date" has the meaning prescribed.
(4) An unpaid contributions notice may, in particular—
(a) specify the scheme to which the contributions are due;
(b) specify the workers, or category of workers, in respect of whom the contributions are due;
(c) state the period in respect of which the contributions are due;
(d) state the due date in respect of the contributions;
(e) require the employer to take such other steps in relation to remedying the failure to pay the contributions as the Regulator considers appropriate;
(f) state that if the employer fails to comply with the notice, the Regulator may issue a fixed penalty notice under section 40.

(5) In this section, "employer" in relation to a worker means the person by whom the worker is or, if the employment has ceased, was employed.

NOTES

Regulations: the Occupational and Personal Pension Schemes (Automatic Enrolment) Regulations 2010, SI 2010/772 at **[2.1153]**; the Automatic Enrolment (Miscellaneous Amendments) Regulations 2012, SI 2012/215; the Occupational and Personal Pension Schemes (Automatic Enrolment) (Amendment) Regulations 2012, SI 2012/1257; the Automatic Enrolment (Miscellaneous Amendments) Regulations 2013, SI 2013/2556.

Penalty notices

[1.1590]
40 Fixed penalty notices
(1) The Regulator may issue a fixed penalty notice to a person if it is of the opinion that the person has failed to comply with—
(a) a compliance notice under section 35,
(b) a third party compliance notice under section 36,
(c) an unpaid contributions notice under section 37, or
(d) a notice issued under section 72 of the Pensions Act 2004 (c 35) (provision of information)[, so far as relevant to the exercise of any of its functions under or by virtue of this Part].

(2) The Regulator may issue a fixed penalty notice to a person if it is of the opinion that the person has contravened—
(a) any provision of regulations under section 3(2) or 5(2) (prescribed arrangements for automatic enrolment or re-enrolment),
(b) any provision of regulations under section 7(4) (prescribed arrangements: jobholder's right to opt in),
(c) section 8(2)(b) (refund of contributions if jobholder opts out of scheme membership), and any provision of regulations under that provision,
(d) section 10 (requirement to give information to workers), and any provision of regulations under that section, or
(e) any provision of regulations under section 60 (requirement to keep records).

(3) A fixed penalty notice is a notice requiring the person to whom it is issued to pay a penalty within the period specified in the notice.
(4) The penalty—
(a) is to be determined in accordance with regulations, and
(b) must not exceed £50,000.
(5) A fixed penalty notice must—
(a) state the amount of the penalty;
(b) state the date, which must be at least 4 weeks after the date on which the notice is issued, by which the penalty must be paid;
(c) state the period to which the penalty relates;
(d) if the notice is issued under subsection (1), specify the failure to which the notice relates;

(e) if the notice is issued under subsection (2), specify the provision or provisions that have been contravened;
(f) if the notice is issued under subsection (1), state that, if the failure to comply continues, the Regulator may issue an escalating penalty notice under section 41;
(g) notify the person to whom the notice is issued of the review process under section 43 and the right of referral to the [a tribunal] under section 44.

NOTES

Commencement: 26 November 2008 (in so far as it confers any power to make Regulations); 30 June 2012 (sub-ss (1)(a)–(c), (2)–(5) (for remaining purposes) and sub-s (1)(d) (for the purposes of the exercise of the Regulator's functions under or by virtue of Part 1 of this Act)); to be appointed (sub-s (1)(d) for remaining purposes).

Sub-s (1): words in square brackets inserted by the Pensions Act 2014, s 41(1), as from 14 July 2014.

Sub-s (5): words in square brackets in para (g) substituted by the Transfer of Tribunal Functions Order 2010, SI 2010/22, art 5(1), Sch 2, paras 146, 147.

Regulations: the Employers' Duties (Registration and Compliance) Regulations 2010, SI 2010/5; the Automatic Enrolment (Miscellaneous Amendments) Regulations 2012, SI 2012/215.

[1.1591]

41 Escalating penalty notices

(1) The Regulator may issue an escalating penalty notice to a person if it is of the opinion that the person has failed to comply with—
(a) a compliance notice under section 35,
(b) a third party compliance notice under section 36,
(c) an unpaid contributions notice under section 37, or
(d) a notice under section 72 of the Pensions Act 2004 (c 35) (provision of information)[, so far as relevant to the exercise of any of its functions under or by virtue of this Part].

(2) But the Regulator may not issue an escalating penalty notice if—
(a) it relates to failure to comply with a notice within subsection (1)(a), (b) or (c), the person to whom that notice was issued has applied for a review of it under section 43, and any review has not been completed;
(b) it relates to failure to comply with any notice within subsection (1), the person has exercised the right of referral to [a tribunal] under section 44 in respect of a fixed penalty notice issued in relation to that notice, and the reference has not been determined.

(3) An escalating penalty notice is a notice requiring a person to pay an escalating penalty if the person fails to comply with a notice referred to in subsection (1) before a specified date.

(4) An escalating penalty is a penalty which is calculated by reference to a prescribed daily rate.

(5) The prescribed daily rate—
(a) is to be determined in accordance with regulations, and
(b) must not exceed £10,000.

(6) An escalating penalty notice must—
(a) specify the failure to which the notice relates;
(b) state that, if the person fails to comply with the notice referred to in subsection (1) before a specified date, the person will be liable to pay an escalating penalty;
(c) state the daily rate of the escalating penalty and the way in which the penalty is calculated;
(d) state the date from which the escalating penalty will be payable, which must not be earlier than the date specified in the fixed penalty notice under section 40(5)(b);
(e) state that the escalating penalty will continue to be payable at the daily rate until the date on which the person complies with the notice referred to in subsection (1) or such earlier date as the Regulator may determine;
(f) notify the person of the review process under section 43 and the right of referral to [a tribunal] under section 44.

NOTES

Commencement: 26 November 2008 (in so far as it confers any power to make Regulations); 30 June 2012 (sub-ss (1)(a)–(c), (2)–(6) (for remaining purposes) and sub-s (1)(d) (for the purposes of the exercise of the Regulator's functions under or by virtue of Part 1 of this Act)); to be appointed (sub-s (1)(d) for remaining purposes).

Sub-s (1): words in square brackets inserted by the Pensions Act 2014, s 41(1), as from 14 July 2014.

Sub-ss (2), (6): words in square brackets substituted by the Transfer of Tribunal Functions Order 2010, SI 2010/22, art 5(1), Sch 2, paras 146, 148.

Regulations: the Employers' Duties (Registration and Compliance) Regulations 2010, SI 2010/5; the Automatic Enrolment (Miscellaneous Amendments) Regulations 2012, SI 2012/215.

[1.1592]
42 Penalty notices: recovery

(1) Any penalty payable under section 40 or section 41 is recoverable by the Regulator.

(2) In England and Wales, any such penalty is, if [the county court] so orders, recoverable under section 85 of the County Courts Act 1984 (c 28) or otherwise as if it were payable under an order of that court.

(3) In Scotland, a fixed penalty notice or escalating penalty notice is enforceable as if it were an extract registered decree arbitral bearing a warrant for execution issued by the sheriff court of any sheriffdom in Scotland.

(4) The Regulator must pay into the Consolidated Fund any penalty recovered under this section.

NOTES

Sub-s (2): words in square brackets substituted by the Crime and Courts Act 2013, s 17(5), Sch 9, Pt 3, para 52.

Reviews and references

[1.1593]
43 Review of notices

(1) The Regulator may review a notice to which this section applies—
 (a) on the written application of the person to whom the notice was issued, or
 (b) if the Regulator otherwise considers it appropriate.

(2) This section applies to—
 (a) a compliance notice issued under section 35;
 (b) a third party compliance notice issued under section 36;
 (c) an unpaid contributions notice issued under section 37;
 (d) a fixed penalty notice issued under section 40;
 (e) an escalating penalty notice issued under section 41.

(3) Regulations may prescribe the period within which—
 (a) an application to review a notice may be made under subsection (1)(a);
 (b) a notice may be reviewed under subsection (1)(b).

(4) On a review of a notice, the effect of the notice is suspended for the period beginning when the Regulator determines to carry out the review and ending when the review is completed.

(5) In carrying out a review, the Regulator must consider any representations made by the person to whom the notice was issued.

(6) The Regulator's powers on a review include power to—
 (a) confirm, vary or revoke the notice;
 (b) substitute a different notice.

NOTES

Regulations: the Employers' Duties (Registration and Compliance) Regulations 2010, SI 2010/5; the Automatic Enrolment (Miscellaneous Amendments) Regulations 2012, SI 2012/215.

[1.1594]
44 References to [First-tier Tribunal or upper Tribunal]

(1) A person to whom a notice is issued under section 40 or 41 may, if one of the conditions in subsection (2) is satisfied, make a reference to [the Tribunal] in respect of—
 (a) the issue of the notice;
 (b) the amount of the penalty payable under the notice.

(2) The conditions are—
 (a) that the Regulator has completed a review of the notice under section 43;
 (b) that the person to whom the notice was issued has made an application for the review of the notice under section 43(1)(a) and the Regulator has determined not to carry out such a review.

(3) On a reference to [the Tribunal] in respect of a notice, the effect of the notice is suspended for the period beginning when the Tribunal receives notice of the reference and ending—
 (a) when the reference is withdrawn or completed, or
 (b) if the reference is made out of time, on the Tribunal determining not to allow the reference to proceed.

(4) For the purposes of subsection (3), a reference is completed when—
 (a) the reference has been determined,
 (b) the Tribunal has remitted the matter to the Regulator, and
 (c) any directions of the Tribunal for giving effect to its determination have been complied with.

[(4A) In this section "the Tribunal", in relation to a reference under this section, means—
 (a) the Upper Tribunal, in any case where it is determined by or under Tribunal Procedure Rules that the Upper Tribunal is to hear the reference;
 (b) the First-tier Tribunal, in any other case.]

(5)–(9) . . .

NOTES

Sub-s (4A) was inserted, and the words in square brackets in the section heading and in sub-ss (1), (3) were substituted, by the Transfer of Tribunal Functions Order 2010, SI 2010/22, art 5(1), Sch 2, paras 146, 149.

Sub-ss (5)–(9): repealed by SI 2010/22, art 5(3), Sch 4.

Offences and monitoring

[1.1595]

45 Offences of failing to comply

(1) An offence is committed by an employer who wilfully fails to comply with—

(a) the duty under section 3(2) (automatic enrolment),

(b) the duty under section 5(2) (automatic re-enrolment), or

(c) the duty under section 7(3) (jobholder's right to opt in).

(2) A person guilty of an offence under this section is liable—

(a) on conviction on indictment, to imprisonment for a term not exceeding two years, or to a fine, or both;

(b) on summary conviction to a fine not exceeding the statutory maximum.

[1.1596]

46 Offences by bodies corporate

(1) Subsection (2) applies where an offence under section 45 committed by a body corporate is proved—

(a) to have been committed with the consent or connivance of an officer of the body corporate, or

(b) to be attributable to any neglect on the part of an officer of the body corporate.

(2) The officer, as well as the body corporate, is guilty of the offence and is liable to be proceeded against and punished accordingly.

(3) "Officer" in this section means—

(a) a director, manager, secretary or other similar officer, or

(b) a person purporting to act in such a capacity.

(4) Where the affairs of a body corporate are managed by its members, this section applies in relation to the acts and defaults of a member in connection with the member's functions of management as if the member were an officer of the body corporate.

[1.1597]

47 Offences by partnerships and unincorporated associations

(1) Proceedings for an offence under section 45 alleged to have been committed by a partnership or an unincorporated association may be brought in the name of the partnership or association.

(2) For the purposes of such proceedings—

(a) rules of court relating to the service of documents are to have effect as if the partnership or association were a body corporate;

(b) the following provisions apply in relation to the partnership or association as they apply in relation to a body corporate—

(i) section 33 of the Criminal Justice Act 1925 (c 86) and Schedule 3 to the Magistrates' Courts Act 1980 (c 43);

(ii) section 70 of the Criminal Procedure (Scotland) Act 1995 (c 46).

(3) A fine imposed on a partnership or association on its conviction of an offence under section 45 is to be paid out of the funds of the partnership or association.

(4) Subsection (5) applies where an offence under section 45 committed by a partnership is proved—

(a) to have been committed with the consent or connivance of a partner, or

(b) to be attributable to any neglect on the part of a partner.

(5) The partner, as well as the partnership, is guilty of the offence and is liable to be proceeded against and punished accordingly.

(6) Subsection (7) applies where an offence under section 45 committed by an unincorporated association is proved—

(a) to have been committed with the consent or connivance of an officer of the association, or

(b) to be attributable to any neglect on the part of an officer of the association.

(7) The officer, as well as the association, is guilty of the offence and is liable to be proceeded against and punished accordingly.

(8) "Officer" in this section means—

(a) an officer of the association or a member of its governing body, or

(b) a person purporting to act in such capacity.

(9) "Partner" in this section includes a person purporting to act as a partner.

CHAPTER 3 SAFEGUARDS: EMPLOYMENT AND PRE-EMPLOYMENT

Prohibited recruitment conduct

[1.1598]

50 Prohibited recruitment conduct

(1) An employer contravenes this section if any statement made or question asked by or on behalf of the employer for the purposes of recruitment indicates (expressly or impliedly) that an application for employment with the employer may be determined by reference to whether or not an applicant might opt out of automatic enrolment.

(2) The reference in subsection (1) to a statement made or a question asked for the purposes of recruitment is a reference to one made or asked in the course of any of the following—

(a) inviting applications for employment;

(b) requesting information from an applicant, referee or other person in connection with an application for employment;

(c) providing information about employment;

(d) proposing terms or conditions of employment.

(3) The reference in subsection (1) to an applicant opting out of automatic enrolment is a reference to the applicant, if becoming at any time in the course of the employment a jobholder to whom section 3 or 5 applies, giving notice in accordance with section 8 in relation to arrangements made by the employer under the relevant section.
(4) In this section and sections 51 and 52, "employer" means the prospective employer in relation to any employment.

[1.1599]
51 Compliance notices
(1) The Regulator may issue a compliance notice to an employer if the Regulator is of the opinion that the employer has contravened section 50.
(2) A compliance notice is a notice directing the employer to take, or refrain from taking, the steps specified in the notice in order to—
(a) remedy the contravention, or
(b) prevent the contravention being repeated.
(3) A compliance notice may, in particular—
(a) state the period within which any step must be taken or must cease to be taken;
(b) require the employer to provide within a specified period specified information relating to the contravention;
(c) require the employer to inform the Regulator, within a specified period, how the employer has complied or is complying with the notice;
(d) state that, if the employer fails to comply with the requirements of the notice, the Regulator may issue a penalty notice under section 52.
(4) A compliance notice must specify the contravention to which the notice relates.

[1.1600]
52 Penalty notices
(1) The Regulator may issue a penalty notice to an employer if the Regulator is of the opinion that the employer—
(a) has contravened section 50, or
(b) has failed to comply with a compliance notice under section 51.
(2) A penalty notice is a notice requiring the person to whom it is issued to pay a penalty within the period specified in the notice.
(3) The penalty—
(a) is to be determined in accordance with regulations, and
(b) must not exceed £50,000.
(4) A penalty notice must—
(a) state the amount of the penalty;
(b) state the date, which must be at least 4 weeks after the date on which the notice is issued, by which the penalty must be paid;
(c) specify the contravention or failure to which the notice relates;
(d) notify the employer of the review process under section 43 and the right to make a reference under section 44 (as applied by section 53).
(5) Section 42 (penalty notices: recovery) applies to a penalty payable under this section, and to a notice under this section, as it applies to a penalty payable under section 40, and to a notice under that section.

NOTES
Regulations: the Employers' Duties (Registration and Compliance) Regulations 2010, SI 2010/5; the Automatic Enrolment (Miscellaneous Amendments) Regulations 2012, SI 2012/215.

[1.1601]
53 Review of notices and references to Pensions Regulator Tribunal
(1) Section 43 (review of notices) also applies to a compliance notice issued under section 51 and to a penalty notice issued under section 52.
(2) Section 44 (references to the [First-tier Tribunal or Upper Tribunal]) applies in relation to a penalty notice issued under section 52 as it applies in relation to a notice issued under section 40 or 41.

NOTES
Sub-s (2): words in square brackets substituted by the Transfer of Tribunal Functions Order 2010, SI 2010/22, art 5(1), Sch 2, paras 146, 150.

Inducements

[1.1602]
54 Inducements
(1) An employer contravenes this section if the employer takes any action for the sole or main purpose of—
(a) inducing a worker to give up membership of a relevant scheme without becoming an active member of another relevant scheme [with effect from—
(i) the day after the membership is given up, or
(ii) a day within the prescribed period (if a period is prescribed)], or
(b) inducing a jobholder to give a notice under section 8 without becoming an active member of a qualifying scheme [with effect from—

(i) the day on which the jobholder became an active member of the scheme to which the notice relates, or

(ii) a day within the prescribed period (if a period is prescribed)].

(2) Section 35 applies in relation to a contravention of this section as it applies in relation to a contravention of section 2(1), and sections 38 to 44 apply accordingly.

(3) But the Regulator may not issue a compliance notice in respect of a contravention of this section unless the contravention occurred within the prescribed period before—

(a) the time when a complaint was made to the Regulator about the contravention, or

(b) the time when the Regulator informed the employer of an investigation of the contravention, if no complaint was made before that time.

(4) A compliance notice in respect of a contravention of this section may direct the employer to take or refrain from taking specified steps in order to prevent the contravention being repeated.

(5) For the purposes of this section a worker gives up membership of a relevant scheme if the worker—

(a) takes action or makes an omission by which the worker, without ceasing to be employed by the employer, ceases to be an active member of the scheme, or

(b) requests or authorises the employer to take such action or to make such an omission.

(6) In this section, "relevant scheme" means—

(a) in relation to a jobholder, a qualifying scheme;

(b) in relation to a worker to whom section 9 applies, a scheme which satisfies the requirements of that section.

NOTES

Sub-s (1): words in square brackets substituted by the Pensions Act 2011, s 4(6).

Regulations: the Employers' Duties (Registration and Compliance) Regulations 2010, SI 2010/5; the Automatic Enrolment (Miscellaneous Amendments) Regulations 2012, SI 2012/215.

Protection of employment rights

[1.1603]

55 The right not to suffer detriment

(1) A worker has the right not to be subjected to any detriment by an act, or a deliberate failure to act, by the worker's employer, done on the ground that—

(a) any action was taken, or was proposed to be taken, with a view to enforcing in favour of the worker a requirement to which this section applies,

(b) the employer was prosecuted for an offence under section 45 as a result of action taken for the purpose of enforcing in favour of the worker a requirement to which this section applies, or

(c) any provision of Chapter 1 of this Part applies to the worker, or will or might apply.

(2) It is immaterial for the purposes of paragraph (a) or (b) of subsection (1)—

(a) whether or not the requirement applies in favour of the worker, or

(b) whether or not the requirement has been contravened,

but, for that subsection to apply, the claim that the requirement applies and, if applicable, the claim that it has been contravened must be made in good faith.

(3) This section applies to any requirement imposed on the employer by or under any provision of Chapter 1 of this Part.

(4) This section does not apply where the detriment in question amounts to dismissal within the meaning of Part 10 of the Employment Rights Act 1996 (c 18) (unfair dismissal).

(5) In this section references to enforcing a requirement include references to securing its benefit in any way.

[1.1604]

56 Enforcement of the right

(1) A worker may present a complaint to an employment tribunal that the worker has been subjected to a detriment in contravention of section 55.

(2) Subject to the following provisions of this section, the provisions of [sections 48(2) to (4A)] and 49 of the Employment Rights Act 1996 (complaints to employment tribunals and remedies), apply in relation to a complaint under this section as they apply in relation to a complaint under section 48 of that Act, but taking references in those provisions to the employer as references to the employer within the meaning of section 55(1).

(3) Where—

(a) the detriment to which the worker is subjected is the termination of the worker's contract, but

(b) that contract is not a contract of employment,

any compensation awarded under section 49 of the Employment Rights Act 1996 by virtue of subsection (2) must not exceed the limit specified in subsection (4).

(4) The limit is the total of—

(a) the sum which would be the basic award for unfair dismissal, calculated in accordance with section 119 of the Employment Rights Act 1996, if the worker had been an employee within the meaning of that Act and the contract terminated had been a contract of employment, and

(b) the sum for the time being specified in section 124(1) of that Act which is the limit for a compensatory award to a person calculated in accordance with section 123 of that Act.

(5) Where the worker has been working under arrangements which do not fall to be regarded as a worker's contract for the purposes of the Employment Rights Act 1996, the worker is to be treated for the purposes of subsections (3) and (4) as if any arrangements under which the worker has been working constituted a worker's contract falling within section 230(3)(b) of that Act.

(6) *(Spent (amended the Employment Tribunals Act 1996, s 18(1) and the amendment has been superseded by a subsequent amendment).)*

NOTES

Sub-s (2): words in square brackets substituted by the Enterprise and Regulatory Reform Act 2013, s 8, Sch 2, para 41.

Conciliation: employment tribunal proceedings under this section are "relevant proceedings" for the purposes of the conciliation provisions contained in the Employment Tribunals Act 1996, ss 18–18C; see s 18(1)(d) of the 1996 Act at **[1.757]**.

57 *(Inserts the Employment Rights Act 1996, s 104D at* **[1.1019]**, *and amends ss 105, 108 of the 1996 Act at* **[1.1023]**, **[1.1026]**, *and the Trade Union and Labour Relations (Consolidation) Act 1992, ss 237, 238 at* **[1.568]**, **[1.569]**.*)*

[1.1605]

58 Restrictions on agreements to limit operation of this Part

(1) Any provision in any agreement (whether a worker's contract or not) is void in so far as it purports—

(a) to exclude or limit the operation of any provision of this Part, or

(b) to preclude a person from bringing proceedings under section 56 before an employment tribunal.

(2) The fact that an agreement is to any extent void under subsection (1) does not entitle the employer to recover any property transferred, or the value of any benefit conferred, as an inducement to enter into, or otherwise in connection with, the agreement.

(3) Subsection (1) does not apply to any agreement to refrain from instituting or continuing proceedings where a conciliation officer has taken action under [any of sections 18A to 18C] of the Employment Tribunals Act 1996 (c 17) (conciliation).

(4) Subsection (1) does not apply to any agreement to refrain from instituting or continuing before an employment tribunal any proceedings within section 18(1)(v) of the Employment Tribunals Act 1996 (proceedings under this Act where conciliation is available) if the conditions regulating [settlement] agreements under this Act are satisfied in relation to the agreement.

(5) For the purposes of subsection (4) the conditions regulating [settlement] agreements under this Act are that—

(a) the agreement must be in writing,

(b) the agreement must relate to the particular proceedings,

(c) the worker must have received advice from a relevant independent adviser as to the terms and effect of the proposed agreement and, in particular, its effect on his ability to pursue his rights before an employment tribunal,

(d) there must be in force, when the adviser gives the advice, a contract of insurance, or an indemnity provided for members of a profession or a professional body, covering the risk of a claim by the worker in respect of loss arising in consequence of the advice,

(e) the agreement must identify the adviser, and

(f) the agreement must state that the conditions regulating [settlement] agreements under this Act are satisfied.

(6) A person is a relevant independent adviser for the purposes of subsection (5)(c) if that person—

(a) is a qualified lawyer,

(b) is an officer, official, employee or member of an independent trade union who has been certified in writing by the trade union as competent to give advice and as authorised to do so on behalf of the trade union,

(c) works at an advice centre (whether as an employee or a volunteer) and has been certified in writing by the centre as competent to give advice and as authorised to do so on behalf of the centre, or

(d) is a person of a description specified in an order made by the Secretary of State.

(7) But a person is not a relevant independent adviser for the purposes of subsection (5)(c) in relation to the worker—

(a) if the person is employed by, or is acting in the matter for, the employer or an associated employer,

(b) in the case of a person within subsection (6)(b) or (c), if the trade union or advice centre is the employer or an associated employer,

(c) in the case of a person within subsection (6)(c), if the worker makes a payment for the advice received from the person, or

(d) in the case of a person of a description specified in an order under subsection (6)(d), if any condition specified in the order in relation to the giving of advice by persons of that description is not satisfied.

(8) In this section "qualified lawyer" means—

(a) as respects England and Wales—

(i) a barrister (whether in practice as such or employed to give legal advice),

(ii) a solicitor who holds a practising certificate, or

(iii) a person other than a barrister or solicitor who is an authorised advocate or authorised litigator (within the meaning of the Courts and Legal Services Act 1990);

(b) as respects Scotland—

(i) an advocate (whether in practice as such or employed to give legal advice), or

(ii) a solicitor who holds a practising certificate.

(9) For the purposes of this section any two employers are associated if—

(a) one is a company of which the other (directly or indirectly) has control, or

(b) both are companies of which a third person (directly or indirectly) has control;
and "associated employer" is to be read accordingly.

NOTES

Sub-s (3): words in square brackets substituted by the Enterprise and Regulatory Reform Act 2013, s 7(2), Sch 1, para 13.

Sub-ss (4), (5): words in square brackets substituted by the Enterprise and Regulatory Reform Act 2013, s 23(1)(c).

Orders: the Compromise Agreements (Automatic Enrolment) (Description of Person) Order 2012, SI 2012/212. This Order specifies that, for the purposes of sub-s (5)(c) above, a legal executive authorised by the Institute of Legal Executives who is practising subject to the regulatory arrangements of the Institute is a "relevant independent adviser" for the purposes of being able to give advice in relation to compromise agreements (now renamed "settlement agreements" by the amendments to sub-ss (4), (5) noted above) under this Act.

59 *(Amends the Employment Tribunals Act 1996, s 21 at* **[1.764]***.)*

CHAPTER 8 APPLICATION AND INTERPRETATION

Workers

[1.1606]

88 "Employer", "worker" and related expressions

(1) This section applies for the purposes of this Part.

(2) "Contract of employment" means a contract of service or apprenticeship, whether express or implied, and (if it is express) whether oral or in writing.

(3) "Worker" means an individual who has entered into or works under—

(a) a contract of employment, or

(b) any other contract by which the individual undertakes to do work or perform services personally for another party to the contract.

(4) But a contract is not within subsection (3)(b) if the status of the other party is by virtue of the contract that of a client or customer of a profession or business undertaking carried on by the individual concerned.

(5) For the purposes of subsection (3)(b), it does not matter whether the contract is express or implied or (if it is express) whether it is oral or in writing.

(6) Any reference to a worker's contract is to be read in accordance with subsections (3) to (5).

(7) "Employer", in relation to a worker, means the person by whom the worker is employed (subject to sections 37(5) and 38(6)).

(8) "Employment" in relation to a worker, means employment under the worker's contract, and related expressions are to be read accordingly.

[1.1607]

89 Agency workers

(1) This section applies to an individual ("the agency worker")—

(a) who is supplied by a person ("the agent") to do work for another person ("the principal") under a contract or other arrangements made between the agent and the principal,

(b) who is not, as respects that work, a worker, because of the absence of a worker's contract between the individual and the agent or the principal, and

(c) who is not a party to a contract under which the agency worker undertakes to do the work for another party to the contract whose status is, by virtue of the contract, that of a client or customer of a profession or business undertaking carried on by the individual.

(2) Where this section applies, the other provisions of this Part have effect—

(a) as if there were a worker's contract for the doing of the work by the agency worker, made between the agency worker and the relevant person under subsection (3), and

(b) as if that person were the agency worker's employer.

(3) The relevant person is—

(a) whichever of the agent and the principal is responsible for paying the agency worker in respect of the work, or

(b) if neither the agent nor the principal is responsible for doing so, whichever of them pays the agency worker in respect of the work.

[1.1608]

90 Directors

(1) A person who holds office as a director of a company is not, by virtue of that office or of any employment by the company, a worker for the purposes of this Part, unless—

(a) the person is employed by the company under a contract of employment, and

(b) there is at least one other person who is employed by the company under a contract of employment.

(2) In this section, "company" includes any body corporate.

[1.1609]
91 Crown employment

(1) This Part has effect in relation to employment by or under the Crown as it has effect in relation to other employment.

(2) For the purposes of the application of the provisions of this Part in accordance with subsection (1)—

(a) references to a worker are to be construed as references to a person employed by or under the Crown;

(b) references to a worker's contract are to be construed as references to the terms of employment of a person employed by or under the Crown.

(3) This section does not impose criminal liability on the Crown.

(4) But on the application of the Regulator the High Court or the Court of Session may declare unlawful a failure by the Crown to comply with any of the duties mentioned in section 45(1).

[1.1610]
92 Armed forces

(1) A person serving as a member of the naval, military or air forces of the Crown is not, by virtue of that service, a worker for the purposes of this Part.

(2) A member of any of the forces specified in subsection (3) who assists the activities of any of those forces is not, by virtue of anything done in assisting those activities, a worker for the purposes of this Part.

(3) The forces are—

(a) the Combined Cadet Force;

(b) the Sea Cadet Corps;

(c) the Army Cadet Force;

(d) the Air Training Corps.

[1.1611]
93 House of Lords staff

(1) This Part has effect in relation to employment as a relevant member of the House of Lords staff as it has effect in relation to other employment.

(2) In this section, "relevant member of the House of Lords staff" means any person who is employed under a worker's contract with the Corporate Officer of the House of Lords.

[1.1612]
94 House of Commons staff

(1) This Part has effect in relation to employment as a relevant member of the House of Commons staff as it has effect in relation to other employment.

(2) In this section, "relevant member of the House of Commons staff" means any person—

(a) who was appointed by the House of Commons Commission, or

(b) who is a member of the Speaker's personal staff.

(3) For the purposes of the application of the provisions of this Part in relation to a relevant member of the House of Commons staff—

(a) references to a worker are to be read as references to a relevant member of the House of Commons staff, and

(b) references to a worker's contract are to be read as references to the terms of employment of a relevant member of the House of Commons staff.

[1.1613]
95 Police

(1) This Part has effect in relation to a person who—

(a) holds the office of constable or an appointment as a police cadet, and

(b) does not hold that office or appointment under a contract of employment,

as if the person were employed by the [relevant local policing body or] relevant police authority under a worker's contract.

(2) A [local policing body, or a] police authority that maintains a police force is the relevant [local policing body, or relevant] police authority—

(a) in relation to a constable, if the constable is a member of that police force;

(b) in relation to a police cadet, if the cadet is undergoing training with a view to becoming a member of that police force.

NOTES

Words in square brackets inserted by the Police Reform and Social Responsibility Act 2011, s 99, Sch 16, Pt 3, para 371.

[1.1614]

96 Persons working on vessels

(1) Subject to regulations under this section, a person employed or engaged in any capacity on board a ship is not, by virtue of that employment or engagement, a worker for the purposes of this Part.

(2) The Secretary of State may by regulations provide that, to the extent and for the purposes specified in the regulations, the relevant provisions apply, with or without modification, in relation to a person employed or engaged in any capacity on board a ship (whether or not that person is working or ordinarily works in any part of the United Kingdom).

(3) For the purposes of this section, the relevant provisions are—

(a) this Part (and any enactment as amended by this Part), and

(b) any provision in force in Northern Ireland corresponding to any provision of this Part (and any enactment as amended by such a provision).

(4) Regulations under this section—

(a) may provide for a provision to apply in relation to individuals whether or not they are British subjects;

(b) may provide for a provision to apply in relation to bodies corporate whether or not they are incorporated under the law of a part of the United Kingdom;

(c) may do so even where the application may affect the individual's or body's activities outside the United Kingdom.

(5) Regulations under this section—

(a) may provide for a court or tribunal on which jurisdiction is conferred by the relevant provisions to have jurisdiction, in respect of offences or other matters, for the purposes of any provision as it applies by virtue of the regulations;

(b) may exclude from the operation of section 3 of the Territorial Waters Jurisdiction Act 1878 (c 73) (consents required for prosecutions) proceedings for offences under any provision as it applies by virtue of the regulations;

(c) may provide that such proceedings may not be brought without such consent as may be required by the regulations.

(6) Any jurisdiction conferred on a court or tribunal under this section is without prejudice to jurisdiction exercisable apart from this section by that or any other court or tribunal.

(7) In this section, "ship" includes—

(a) a hovercraft within the meaning of the Hovercraft Act 1968 (c 59), and

(b) every description of vessel used in navigation.

NOTES

Regulations: the Occupational and Personal Pension Schemes (Automatic Enrolment) (Amendment) Regulations 2012, SI 2012/1257.

[1.1615]
97 Persons in offshore employment

(1) Her Majesty may by Order in Council provide that, to the extent and for the purposes specified in the Order, the relevant provisions apply, with or without modification, in relation to a person in offshore employment.

(2) For the purposes of this section, the relevant provisions are—
- (a) this Part (and any enactment as amended by this Part), and
- (b) any provision in force in Northern Ireland corresponding to any provision of this Part (and any enactment as amended by such a provision).

(3) In this section, "offshore employment" has the same meaning as in section 201(1) of the Employment Rights Act 1996 (c 18).

(4) An Order in Council under this section—
- (a) may provide for a provision to apply in relation to individuals whether or not they are British subjects;
- (b) may provide for a provision to apply in relation to bodies corporate whether or not they are incorporated under the law of a part of the United Kingdom;
- (c) may do so even where the application may affect the individual's or body's activities outside the United Kingdom.

(5) An Order in Council under this section—
- (a) may make different provision for different cases;
- (b) may provide for a court or tribunal on which jurisdiction is conferred by the relevant provisions to have jurisdiction, in respect of offences or other matters, for the purposes of any provision as it applies by virtue of the Order;
- (c) may (without prejudice to subsection (1) and paragraph (a)) provide for a provision to apply in relation to any person in employment in a part of the areas referred to in section 201(1)(a) and (b) of the Employment Rights Act 1996 (c 18);
- (d) may exclude from the operation of section 3 of the Territorial Waters Jurisdiction Act 1878 (c 73) (consents required for prosecutions) proceedings for offences under any provision as it applies by virtue of the Order;
- (e) may provide that such proceedings may not be brought without such consent as may be required by the Order.

(6) Any jurisdiction conferred on a court or tribunal under this section is without prejudice to jurisdiction exercisable apart from this section by that or any other court or tribunal.

(7) No Order in Council may be made under this section unless a draft of the Order has been laid before and approved by a resolution of each House of Parliament.

NOTES

Orders: as of 15 May 2019, no Orders had been made under this section.

[1.1616]
98 Extension of definition of worker

The Secretary of State may by regulations make provision for this Part to apply with or without modifications—
- (a) as if any individual of a prescribed description (who would not otherwise be a worker) were a worker,
- (b) as if there were in the case of any such individual a worker's contract of a prescribed description under which the individual works, and
- (c) as if a person of a prescribed description were the employer under that contract.

NOTES

Commencement: 26 November 2008 (in so far as it confers any power to make Regulations); to be appointed (otherwise).

Regulations: the Occupational and Personal Pension Schemes (Automatic Enrolment) (Amendment) Regulations 2012, SI 2012/1257.

General

[1.1617]
99 Interpretation of Part

In this Part—

"active member"—
- (a) in relation to an occupational pension scheme, means a person who is in pensionable service under the scheme;
- (b) in relation to a personal pension scheme, means a jobholder in relation to whom there is an agreement within section 26(4) between the provider of the scheme and the employer or (where section 9 applies) a worker in relation to whom there are direct payment arrangements (within the meaning of section 111A of the Pension Schemes Act 1993 (c 48)) between the worker and the employer;

"automatic enrolment scheme" is to be read in accordance with section 3(8);

"average salary benefits" means benefits the rate or amount of which is calculated by reference to the average salary of a member over the period of service on which the benefits are based;

["collective benefit" has the meaning given by section 8 of the Pension Schemes Act 2015;]

"contract of employment" has the meaning given by section 88;

"defined benefits", in relation to a member of an occupational pension scheme, means benefits which are not money purchase benefits (but the rate or amount of which is calculated by reference to earnings or service of the member or any other factor other than an amount available for their provision);

"defined benefits scheme" means an occupational pension scheme under which all the benefits that may be provided are defined benefits;

["defined contributions scheme" has the meaning given by section 4 of the Pension Schemes Act 2015;]

"employer", "employment" and related expressions have the meaning given by section 88;

"enrolment duty" means a duty under section 3(2), 5(2), 7(3) or 9(2);

"hybrid scheme" means an occupational pension scheme which is neither a defined benefits scheme nor a money purchase scheme;

the "IORP Directive" means Directive 2003/41/EC of the European Parliament and of the Council on the activities and supervision of institutions for occupational retirement provision;

"jobholder" has the meaning given by section 1(1);

"money purchase benefits", in relation to a member of a pension scheme, means benefits the rate or amount of which is calculated by reference to a payment or payments made by the member or by any other person in respect of the member and [which fall within section 99A];

"money purchase scheme" means an occupational pension scheme under which all the benefits that may be provided are money purchase benefits;

["occupational", in relation to a defined benefits scheme, shared risk scheme or defined contributions scheme, means an occupational pension scheme of that description;]

"occupational pension scheme" has the meaning given by section 18;

"pension scheme" has the meaning given by section 1(5) of the Pension Schemes Act 1993 (c 48);

"pensionable age" has the meaning given by the rules in paragraph 1 of Schedule 4 to the Pensions Act 1995 (c 26);

"pensionable service", in relation to a member of an occupational pension scheme, means service in any description of employment to which the scheme relates which qualifies the member (on the assumption that it continues for the appropriate period) for pension or other benefits under the scheme;

"personal pension scheme" has the meaning given by section 19;

"prescribed" means prescribed by regulations;

"provider"—

(a) in relation to a personal pension scheme to which section 26 applies, means the person referred to in subsection (1)(b) of that section;

(b) in relation to any other personal pension scheme, has the meaning prescribed;

"qualifying earnings" has the meaning given by section 13;

"qualifying scheme" is to be read in accordance with section 2(5);

"regulations" means regulations made by the Secretary of State;

"the Regulator" means the Pensions Regulator;

["shared risk scheme" has the meaning given by section 3 of the Pension Schemes Act 2015;]

"tax year" means the 12 months beginning with 6th April in any year;

"trustee or manager"—

(a) in relation to England and Wales or Scotland, is to be construed in accordance with section 178 of the Pension Schemes Act 1993 (c 48) (trustees and managers of schemes: interpretation);

(b) in relation to Northern Ireland, is to be construed in accordance with section 173 of the Pension Schemes (Northern Ireland) Act 1993 (c 49) (trustees or managers of schemes);

"worker" has the meaning given by section 88.

NOTES

Definitions "collective benefit", "defined contributions scheme", "occupational", and "shared risk scheme" inserted, definitions "defined benefits", "hybrid scheme", and "money purchase scheme" repealed, and definition "defined benefits scheme" substituted (as follows), by the Pension Schemes Act 2015, s 46, Sch 2, paras 39, 50, as from a day to be appointed—

""defined benefits scheme" has the meaning given by section 2 of the Pension Schemes Act 2015;".

Definition "IORP Directive" repealed by the Occupational and Personal Pension Schemes (Amendment etc) (EU Exit) Regulations 2019, SI 2019/192, reg 6(1), (3), as from exit day (as defined in the European Union (Withdrawal) Act 2018, s 20).

Words in square brackets in the definition "money purchase benefits" substituted by the Pensions Act 2011, s 29(3), with retrospective effect.

PART 6
GENERAL

[1.1618]

150 Extent

(1) Subject to the following provisions, this Act extends to England and Wales and Scotland.

(2) The following provisions extend also to Northern Ireland—

- (a) Chapters 5 and 6 of Part 1 and section 99 so far as it relates to those Chapters;
- (b) section 96(2) to (7);
- (c) section 97;
- (d), (e) (*outside the scope of this work*);
- (f) sections [143, 144, 145 and 146];
- (g) section 149, this section and section 151.

(3) An amendment or repeal by this Act has the same extent as the enactment amended or repealed (subject to the provision made by section 63(3), section 64(2) and paragraph 9 of Schedule 10).

NOTES

Sub-s (2): words in brackets in para (f) substituted by the Pensions Act 2011, s 36(3).

[1.1619]

151 Short title

This Act may be cited as the Pensions Act 2008.

EQUALITY ACT 2010

(2010 c 15)

ARRANGEMENT OF SECTIONS

PART 1
SOCIO-ECONOMIC INEQUALITIES

PART 2
EQUALITY: KEY CONCEPTS

CHAPTER 1
PROTECTED CHARACTERISTICS

CHAPTER 2
PROHIBITED CONDUCT

Discrimination

Adjustments for disabled persons

Discrimination: supplementary

Other prohibited conduct

PART 5
WORK

CHAPTER 1
EMPLOYMENT, ETC

Employees

Police officers

Partners

PART 6
EDUCATION

CHAPTER 3
GENERAL QUALIFICATIONS BODIES

PART 8
PROHIBITED CONDUCT: ANCILLARY

PART 9
ENFORCEMENT

CHAPTER 1
INTRODUCTORY

CHAPTER 2
CIVIL COURTS

CHAPTER 3
EMPLOYMENT TRIBUNALS

CHAPTER 4
EQUALITY OF TERMS

CHAPTER 5
MISCELLANEOUS

PART 10
CONTRACTS, ETC

Contracts and other agreements

SCHEDULES

An Act to make provision to require Ministers of the Crown and others when making strategic decisions about the exercise of their functions to have regard to the desirability of reducing socio-economic inequalities; to reform and harmonise equality law and restate the greater part of the enactments relating to discrimination and harassment related to certain personal characteristics; to enable certain employers to be required to publish information about the differences in pay between male and female employees; to prohibit victimisation in certain circumstances; to require the exercise of certain functions to be with regard to the need to eliminate discrimination and other prohibited conduct; to enable duties to be imposed in relation to the exercise of public procurement functions; to increase equality of opportunity; to amend the law relating to rights and responsibilities in family relationships; and for connected purposes

[8 April 2010]

NOTES

This Act covers unlawful discrimination both in the employment and related fields and in relation to goods, facilities, services, transport and certain public services. Only those Parts of the Act which deal with employment and related areas, and the provisions of general application, such as definitions and provisions relating to enforcement and remedies, are reproduced. Other provisions are omitted for reasons of space and/or as outside the scope of this work.

The Act is largely a re-enactment in a more accessible and coherent form of the many and disparate provisions of previous legislation on unlawful discrimination, but also effects significant changes in the law. Details may be found in commentaries on the Act; see in particular the Explanatory Notes to the Act, available alongside the Act itself on the official government legislation website (www.legislation.gov.uk).

As of 15 May 2019, a total of thirteen commencement orders have been made under s 216 bringing various provisions into force on various dates (see **[1.1767]** for details). The main one for the purposes of the provisions reproduced here is the Equality Act 2010 (Commencement No 4, Savings, Consequential, Transitional, Transitory and Incidental Provisions and Revocation) Order 2010, SI 2010/2317 which also contains a variety of transitional provisions affecting the commencement of this Act, and savings with regard to the repeal and revocation of the previous discrimination legislation. These transitional provisions etc are now considered spent, and the Order is not reproduced in this edition.

Note also that this Act was amended by the Equality Act 2010 (Consequential Amendments, Saving and Supplementary Provisions) Order 2010, SI 2010/2279 (as noted below where relevant). In particular, note that the original Schs 26 and 27 (Amendments and Repeals & revocations) were heavily renumbered and amended. The new paragraph number is given for all amendments to other material elsewhere in this Handbook.

Employment Appeal Tribunal: an appeal lies to the Employment Appeal Tribunal on any question of law arising from any decision of, or in any proceedings before, an employment tribunal under or by virtue of this Act; see the Employment Tribunals Act 1996, s 21(1)(ge) at **[1.764]**.

PART 1
SOCIO-ECONOMIC INEQUALITIES

[1.1620]

1 Public sector duty regarding socio-economic inequalities

(1) An authority to which this section applies must, when making decisions of a strategic nature about how to exercise its functions, have due regard to the desirability of exercising them in a way that is designed to reduce the inequalities of outcome which result from socio-economic disadvantage.

(2) In deciding how to fulfil a duty to which it is subject under subsection (1), an authority must take into account any guidance issued [in accordance with subsection (2A)].

[(2A) The guidance to be taken into account under subsection (2) is—

(a) in the case of a duty imposed on an authority in relation to devolved Scottish functions, guidance issued by the Scottish Ministers;

[(aa) in the case of a duty imposed on an authority in relation to devolved Welsh functions, guidance issued by the Welsh Ministers;]

(b) in any other case, guidance issued by a Minister of the Crown.]

(3) The authorities to which this section applies are—

(a) a Minister of the Crown;

(b) a government department other than the Security Service, the Secret Intelligence Service or the Government Communications Head-quarters;

(c) a county council or district council in England;

(d) the Greater London Authority;

(e) a London borough council;

(f) the Common Council of the City of London in its capacity as a local authority;

(g) the Council of the Isles of Scilly;

(h)–(j) . . .

(k) a [police and crime commissioner] established for an area in England.

(4), (5) . . .

(6) The reference to inequalities in subsection (1) does not include any inequalities experienced by a person as a result of being a person subject to immigration control within the meaning given by section 115(9) of the Immigration and Asylum Act 1999.

NOTES

Commencement: 1 April 2018 (sub-ss (1)–(3), (6) in relation to Scotland); to be appointed (otherwise). See further the final note below.

Sub-s (2): words in square brackets substituted by the Scotland Act 2016, s 38(1)–(3), as from 23 May 2016.

Sub-s (2A): inserted by the Scotland Act 2016, s 38(1), (4), as from 23 May 2016. Para (aa) inserted by the Wales Act 2017, s 45(1), (2), as from 1 April 2018.

Sub-s (3) is amended as follows:

Substituted in relation to Scotland only as noted below.

Paras (h), (i) repealed by the Health and Social Care Act 2012, s 55(2), Sch 5, paras 180, 181.

Para (j) repealed by the Public Bodies Act 2011, s 30(3), Sch 6.

Words in square brackets in para (k) substituted by the Police Reform and Social Responsibility Act 2011, s 99, Sch 16, Pt 3, paras 380, 381.

Sub-ss (4), (5): repealed by the Deregulation Act 2015, s 100(2)(g), as from 26 May 2015.

Note: the Equality Act 2010 (Commencement No 13) (Scotland) Order 2017, SSI 2017/403, art 1 (which commences sub-ss (1)–(3), (6) in relation to Scotland as noted above) also provides that, for the avoidance of doubt, sub-s (3) above is commenced as originally enacted. Sub-s (3) has been subsequently substituted in relation to Scotland only, by the Equality Act 2010 (Authorities subject to the Socio-economic Inequality Duty) (Scotland) Regulations 2018, SSI 2018/101, reg 2, as from 1 April 2018, as follows—

"(3) The authorities to which this section applies are—

(a) the Scottish Ministers;

(b) Food Standards Scotland;

(c) Keeper of the Registers of Scotland;

(d) National Records of Scotland;

(e) Revenue Scotland;

(f) Scottish Courts and Tribunals Service;

(g) a council constituted under section 2 of the Local Government etc (Scotland) Act 1994;

(h) an integration joint board established under section 9(2) of the Public Bodies (Joint Working) (Scotland) Act 2014;

(i) a Health Board constituted under section 2(1)(a) of the National Health Service (Scotland) Act 1978;

(j) a Special Health Board constituted under section 2(1)(b) of that Act;

(k) Scottish Police Authority;

(l) Highlands and Islands Enterprise;

(m) Scottish Enterprise.".

[1.1621]

2 Power to amend section 1

(1) A Minister of the Crown may by regulations amend section 1 so as to—

(a) add a public authority to the authorities that are subject to the duty under subsection (1) of that section;

(b) remove an authority from those that are subject to the duty;

(c) make the duty apply, in the case of a particular authority, only in relation to certain functions that it has;

(d) in the case of an authority to which the application of the duty is already restricted to certain functions, remove or alter the restriction.

(2) In subsection (1) "public authority" means an authority that has functions of a public nature.

(3) Provision made under subsection (1) may not impose a duty on an authority in relation to any devolved Scottish functions or devolved Welsh functions.

(4) The Scottish Ministers or the Welsh Ministers may by regulations amend section 1 so as to—

(a) add a relevant authority to the authorities that are subject to the duty under subsection (1) of that section;

(b) remove a relevant authority from those that are subject to the duty;
(c) make the duty apply, in the case of a particular relevant authority, only in relation to certain functions that it has;
(d) in the case of a relevant authority to which the application of the duty is already restricted to certain functions, remove or alter the restriction.

(5) For the purposes of the power conferred by subsection (4) on the Scottish Ministers, "relevant authority" means an authority whose functions—
(a) are exercisable only in or as regards Scotland,
(b) are wholly or mainly devolved Scottish functions, and
(c) correspond or are similar to those of an authority for the time being specified in section 1(3).

(6) For the purposes of the power conferred by subsection (4) on the Welsh Ministers, "relevant authority" means [a devolved Welsh authority (within the meaning given by section 157A of the Government of Wales Act 2006) whose functions correspond] or are similar to those of an authority for the time being specified in subsection (3) of section 1 or referred to in subsection (4) of that section.

(7) . . .

(8) Regulations under this section may make any amendments of section 1 that appear to the Minister or Ministers to be necessary or expedient in consequence of provision made under subsection (1) or (as the case may be) subsection (4).

(9), (10) . . .

(11) For the purposes of this [Part]—
(a) a function is a devolved Scottish function if it is exercisable in or as regards Scotland and it does not relate to reserved matters (within the meaning of the Scotland Act 1998);
(b) . . .

NOTES

Commencement: 1 April 2018 (in so far as it confers a power on the Scottish Ministers); to be appointed (otherwise).

Sub-s (6): words in square brackets substituted by the Wales Act 2017, s 69(1), Sch 6, Pt 3, para 83(1), (2), as from 1 April 2018.

Sub-ss (7), (9), (10): repealed by the Wales Act 2017, s 45(1), (3), as from 1 April 2018.

Sub-s (11): word in square brackets substituted by the Scotland Act 2016, s 38(1), (5), (8), as from 23 May 2016. Para (b) repealed by the Wales Act 2017, s 69(1), Sch 6, Pt 3, para 83(1), (3), as from 1 April 2018.

Regulations: as of 15 May 2019, no Regulations had been made under this section.

[1.1622]
3 Enforcement

A failure in respect of a performance of a duty under section 1 does not confer a cause of action at private law.

NOTES

Commencement: 1 April 2018 (in relation to Scotland); to be appointed (otherwise).

PART 2
EQUALITY: KEY CONCEPTS

CHAPTER 1 PROTECTED CHARACTERISTICS

[1.1623]
4 The protected characteristics

The following characteristics are protected characteristics—
age;
disability;
gender reassignment;
marriage and civil partnership;
pregnancy and maternity;
race;
religion or belief;
sex;
sexual orientation.

[1.1624]
5 Age

(1) In relation to the protected characteristic of age—
(a) a reference to a person who has a particular protected characteristic is a reference to a person of a particular age group;
(b) a reference to persons who share a protected characteristic is a reference to persons of the same age group.

(2) A reference to an age group is a reference to a group of persons defined by reference to age, whether by reference to a particular age or to a range of ages.

[1.1625]
6 Disability

(1) A person (P) has a disability if—
(a) P has a physical or mental impairment, and

(b) the impairment has a substantial and long-term adverse effect on P's ability to carry out normal day-to-day activities.

(2) A reference to a disabled person is a reference to a person who has a disability.

(3) In relation to the protected characteristic of disability—

(a) a reference to a person who has a particular protected characteristic is a reference to a person who has a particular disability;

(b) a reference to persons who share a protected characteristic is a reference to persons who have the same disability.

(4) This Act (except Part 12 and section 190) applies in relation to a person who has had a disability as it applies in relation to a person who has the disability; accordingly (except in that Part and that section)—

(a) a reference (however expressed) to a person who has a disability includes a reference to a person who has had the disability, and

(b) a reference (however expressed) to a person who does not have a disability includes a reference to a person who has not had the disability.

(5) A Minister of the Crown may issue guidance about matters to be taken into account in deciding any question for the purposes of subsection (1).

(6) Schedule 1 (disability: supplementary provision) has effect.

NOTES

Guidance under sub-s (5): see the Guidance on matters to be taken into account in determining questions relating to the definition of disability (April 2011) at **[4.274]**. See also the Equality Act 2010 (Guidance on the Definition of Disability) Appointed Day Order 2011, SI 2011/1159 which was made under this section and which commences the Guidance from 1 May 2011 and, in art 3, provides for transitional provisions with regard to the continued operation of the 1996 Guidance.

[1.1626]

7 Gender reassignment

(1) A person has the protected characteristic of gender reassignment if the person is proposing to undergo, is undergoing or has undergone a process (or part of a process) for the purpose of reassigning the person's sex by changing physiological or other attributes of sex.

(2) A reference to a transsexual person is a reference to a person who has the protected characteristic of gender reassignment.

(3) In relation to the protected characteristic of gender reassignment—

(a) a reference to a person who has a particular protected characteristic is a reference to a transsexual person;

(b) a reference to persons who share a protected characteristic is a reference to transsexual persons.

[1.1627]

8 Marriage and civil partnership

(1) A person has the protected characteristic of marriage and civil partnership if the person is married or is a civil partner.

(2) In relation to the protected characteristic of marriage and civil partnership—

(a) a reference to a person who has a particular protected characteristic is a reference to a person who is married or is a civil partner;

(b) a reference to persons who share a protected characteristic is a reference to persons who are married or are civil partners.

[1.1628]

9 Race

(1) Race includes—

(a) colour;

(b) nationality;

(c) ethnic or national origins.

(2) In relation to the protected characteristic of race—

(a) a reference to a person who has a particular protected characteristic is a reference to a person of a particular racial group;

(b) a reference to persons who share a protected characteristic is a reference to persons of the same racial group.

(3) A racial group is a group of persons defined by reference to race; and a reference to a person's racial group is a reference to a racial group into which the person falls.

(4) The fact that a racial group comprises two or more distinct racial groups does not prevent it from constituting a particular racial group.

(5) A Minister of the Crown . . . —

(a) [must by order] amend this section so as to provide for caste to be an aspect of race;

(b) [may by order] amend this Act so as to provide for an exception to a provision of this Act to apply, or not to apply, to caste or to apply, or not to apply, to caste in specified circumstances.

(6) The power under section 207(4)(b), in its application to subsection (5), includes power to amend this Act.

NOTES

Sub-s (5): words omitted repealed, and words in square brackets in paras (a), (b) inserted, by the Enterprise and Regulatory Reform Act 2013, s 97(1)–(4).

Review: as to the review of the effect of sub-s (5) of this section (and orders made under it) and whether it remains appropriate, see the Enterprise and Regulatory Reform Act 2013, s 97(5)–(10) at **[1.1829]**.

Orders: as of 15 May 2019, no Orders had been made under this section.

[1.1629]
10 Religion or belief
(1) Religion means any religion and a reference to religion includes a reference to a lack of religion.
(2) Belief means any religious or philosophical belief and a reference to belief includes a reference to a lack of belief.
(3) In relation to the protected characteristic of religion or belief—
- (a) a reference to a person who has a particular protected characteristic is a reference to a person of a particular religion or belief;
- (b) a reference to persons who share a protected characteristic is a reference to persons who are of the same religion or belief.

[1.1630]
11 Sex
In relation to the protected characteristic of sex—
- (a) a reference to a person who has a particular protected characteristic is a reference to a man or to a woman;
- (b) a reference to persons who share a protected characteristic is a reference to persons of the same sex.

[1.1631]
12 Sexual orientation
(1) Sexual orientation means a person's sexual orientation towards—
- (a) persons of the same sex,
- (b) persons of the opposite sex, or
- (c) persons of either sex.

(2) In relation to the protected characteristic of sexual orientation—
- (a) a reference to a person who has a particular protected characteristic is a reference to a person who is of a particular sexual orientation;
- (b) a reference to persons who share a protected characteristic is a reference to persons who are of the same sexual orientation.

CHAPTER 2 PROHIBITED CONDUCT

Discrimination

[1.1632]
13 Direct discrimination
(1) A person (A) discriminates against another (B) if, because of a protected characteristic, A treats B less favourably than A treats or would treat others.
(2) If the protected characteristic is age, A does not discriminate against B if A can show A's treatment of B to be a proportionate means of achieving a legitimate aim.
(3) If the protected characteristic is disability, and B is not a disabled person, A does not discriminate against B only because A treats or would treat disabled persons more favourably than A treats B.
(4) If the protected characteristic is marriage and civil partnership, this section applies to a contravention of Part 5 (work) only if the treatment is because it is B who is married or a civil partner.
(5) If the protected characteristic is race, less favourable treatment includes segregating B from others.
(6) If the protected characteristic is sex—
- (a) less favourable treatment of a woman includes less favourable treatment of her because she is breast-feeding;
- (b) in a case where B is a man, no account is to be taken of special treatment afforded to a woman in connection with pregnancy or childbirth.

(7) Subsection (6)(a) does not apply for the purposes of Part 5 (work).
(8) This section is subject to sections 17(6) and 18(7).

[1.1633]
14 Combined discrimination: dual characteristics
(1) A person (A) discriminates against another (B) if, because of a combination of two relevant protected characteristics, A treats B less favourably than A treats or would treat a person who does not share either of those characteristics.
(2) The relevant protected characteristics are—
- (a) age;
- (b) disability;
- (c) gender reassignment;
- (d) race
- (e) religion or belief;
- (f) sex;
- (g) sexual orientation.

(3) For the purposes of establishing a contravention of this Act by virtue of subsection (1), B need not show that A's treatment of B is direct discrimination because of each of the characteristics in the combination (taken separately).

(4) But B cannot establish a contravention of this Act by virtue of subsection (1) if, in reliance on another provision of this Act or any other enactment, A shows that A's treatment of B is not direct discrimination because of either or both of the characteristics in the combination.

(5) Subsection (1) does not apply to a combination of characteristics that includes disability in circumstances where, if a claim of direct discrimination because of disability were to be brought, it would come within section 116 (special educational needs).

(6) A Minister of the Crown may by order amend this section so as to—

(a) make further provision about circumstances in which B can, or in which B cannot, establish a contravention of this Act by virtue of subsection (1);

(b) specify other circumstances in which subsection (1) does not apply.

(7) The references to direct discrimination are to a contravention of this Act by virtue of section 13.

NOTES

Commencement: to be appointed.

Orders: as of 15 May 2019, no Orders had been made under this section.

[1.1634]

15 Discrimination arising from disability

(1) A person (A) discriminates against a disabled person (B) if—

(a) A treats B unfavourably because of something arising in consequence of B's disability, and

(b) A cannot show that the treatment is a proportionate means of achieving a legitimate aim.

(2) Subsection (1) does not apply if A shows that A did not know, and could not reasonably have been expected to know, that B had the disability.

[1.1635]

16 Gender reassignment discrimination: cases of absence from work

(1) This section has effect for the purposes of the application of Part 5 (work) to the protected characteristic of gender reassignment.

(2) A person (A) discriminates against a transsexual person (B) if, in relation to an absence of B's that is because of gender reassignment, A treats B less favourably than A would treat B if—

(a) B's absence was because of sickness or injury, or

(b) B's absence was for some other reason and it is not reasonable for B to be treated less favourably.

(3) A person's absence is because of gender reassignment if it is because the person is proposing to undergo, is undergoing or has undergone the process (or part of the process) mentioned in section 7(1).

[1.1636]

17 Pregnancy and maternity discrimination: non-work cases

(1) This section has effect for the purposes of the application to the protected characteristic of pregnancy and maternity of—

(a) Part 3 (services and public functions);

(b) Part 4 (premises);

(c) Part 6 (education);

(d) Part 7 (associations).

(2) A person (A) discriminates against a woman if A treats her unfavourably because of a pregnancy of hers.

(3) A person (A) discriminates against a woman if, in the period of 26 weeks beginning with the day on which she gives birth, A treats her unfavourably because she has given birth.

(4) The reference in subsection (3) to treating a woman unfavourably because she has given birth includes, in particular, a reference to treating her unfavourably because she is breast-feeding.

(5) For the purposes of this section, the day on which a woman gives birth is the day on which—

(a) she gives birth to a living child, or

(b) she gives birth to a dead child (more than 24 weeks of the pregnancy having passed).

(6) Section 13, so far as relating to sex discrimination, does not apply to anything done in relation to a woman in so far as—

(a) it is for the reason mentioned in subsection (2), or

(b) it is in the period, and for the reason, mentioned in subsection (3).

[1.1637]

18 Pregnancy and maternity discrimination: work cases

(1) This section has effect for the purposes of the application of Part 5 (work) to the protected characteristic of pregnancy and maternity.

(2) A person (A) discriminates against a woman if, in the protected period in relation to a pregnancy of hers, A treats her unfavourably—

(a) because of the pregnancy, or

(b) because of illness suffered by her as a result of it.

(3) A person (A) discriminates against a woman if A treats her unfavourably because she is on compulsory maternity leave.

(4) A person (A) discriminates against a woman if A treats her unfavourably because she is exercising or seeking to exercise, or has exercised or sought to exercise, the right to ordinary or additional maternity leave.

(5) For the purposes of subsection (2), if the treatment of a woman is in implementation of a decision taken in the protected period, the treatment is to be regarded as occurring in that period (even if the implementation is not until after the end of that period).

(6) The protected period, in relation to a woman's pregnancy, begins when the pregnancy begins, and ends—

- (a) if she has the right to ordinary and additional maternity leave, at the end of the additional maternity leave period or (if earlier) when she returns to work after the pregnancy;
- (b) if she does not have that right, at the end of the period of 2 weeks beginning with the end of the pregnancy.

(7) Section 13, so far as relating to sex discrimination, does not apply to treatment of a woman in so far as—

- (a) it is in the protected period in relation to her and is for a reason mentioned in paragraph (a) or (b) of subsection (2), or
- (b) it is for a reason mentioned in subsection (3) or (4).

[1.1638]

19 Indirect discrimination

(1) A person (A) discriminates against another (B) if A applies to B a provision, criterion or practice which is discriminatory in relation to a relevant protected characteristic of B's.

(2) For the purposes of subsection (1), a provision, criterion or practice is discriminatory in relation to a relevant protected characteristic of B's if—

- (a) A applies, or would apply, it to persons with whom B does not share the characteristic,
- (b) it puts, or would put, persons with whom B shares the characteristic at a particular disadvantage when compared with persons with whom B does not share it,
- (c) it puts, or would put, B at that disadvantage, and
- (d) A cannot show it to be a proportionate means of achieving a legitimate aim.

(3) The relevant protected characteristics are—

age;
disability;
gender reassignment;
marriage and civil partnership;
race;
religion or belief;
sex;
sexual orientation.

Adjustments for disabled persons

[1.1639]

20 Duty to make adjustments

(1) Where this Act imposes a duty to make reasonable adjustments on a person, this section, sections 21 and 22 and the applicable Schedule apply; and for those purposes, a person on whom the duty is imposed is referred to as A.

(2) The duty comprises the following three requirements.

(3) The first requirement is a requirement, where a provision, criterion or practice of A's puts a disabled person at a substantial disadvantage in relation to a relevant matter in comparison with persons who are not disabled, to take such steps as it is reasonable to have to take to avoid the disadvantage.

(4) The second requirement is a requirement, where a physical feature puts a disabled person at a substantial disadvantage in relation to a relevant matter in comparison with persons who are not disabled, to take such steps as it is reasonable to have to take to avoid the disadvantage.

(5) The third requirement is a requirement, where a disabled person would, but for the provision of an auxiliary aid, be put at a substantial disadvantage in relation to a relevant matter in comparison with persons who are not disabled, to take such steps as it is reasonable to have to take to provide the auxiliary aid.

(6) Where the first or third requirement relates to the provision of information, the steps which it is reasonable for A to have to take include steps for ensuring that in the circumstances concerned the information is provided in an accessible format.

(7) A person (A) who is subject to a duty to make reasonable adjustments is not (subject to express provision to the contrary) entitled to require a disabled person, in relation to whom A is required to comply with the duty, to pay to any extent A's costs of complying with the duty.

(8) A reference in section 21 or 22 or an applicable Schedule to the first, second or third requirement is to be construed in accordance with this section.

(9) In relation to the second requirement, a reference in this section or an applicable Schedule to avoiding a substantial disadvantage includes a reference to—

- (a) removing the physical feature in question,
- (b) altering it, or
- (c) providing a reasonable means of avoiding it.

(10) A reference in this section, section 21 or 22 or an applicable Schedule (apart from paragraphs 2 to 4 of Schedule 4) to a physical feature is a reference to—

- (a) a feature arising from the design or construction of a building,
- (b) a feature of an approach to, exit from or access to a building,
- (c) a fixture or fitting, or furniture, furnishings, materials, equipment or other chattels, in or on premises, or
- (d) any other physical element or quality.

(11) A reference in this section, section 21 or 22 or an applicable Schedule to an auxiliary aid includes a reference to an auxiliary service.
(12) A reference in this section or an applicable Schedule to chattels is to be read, in relation to Scotland, as a reference to moveable property.
(13) The applicable Schedule is, in relation to the Part of this Act specified in the first column of the Table, the Schedule specified in the second column.

Part of this Act	Applicable Schedule
Part 3 (services and public functions)	Schedule 2
Part 4 (premises)	Schedule 4
Part 5 (work)	Schedule 8
Part 6 (education)	Schedule 13
Part 7 (associations)	Schedule 15
Each of the Parts mentioned above	Schedule 21

[1.1640]
21 Failure to comply with duty
(1) A failure to comply with the first, second or third requirement is a failure to comply with a duty to make reasonable adjustments.
(2) A discriminates against a disabled person if A fails to comply with that duty in relation to that person.
(3) A provision of an applicable Schedule which imposes a duty to comply with the first, second or third requirement applies only for the purpose of establishing whether A has contravened this Act by virtue of subsection (2); a failure to comply is, accordingly, not actionable by virtue of another provision of this Act or otherwise.

[1.1641]
22 Regulations
(1) Regulations may prescribe—
- (a) matters to be taken into account in deciding whether it is reasonable for A to take a step for the purposes of a prescribed provision of an applicable Schedule;
- (b) descriptions of persons to whom the first, second or third requirement does not apply.

(2) Regulations may make provision as to—
- (a) circumstances in which it is, or in which it is not, reasonable for a person of a prescribed description to have to take steps of a prescribed description;
- (b) what is, or what is not, a provision, criterion or practice;
- (c) things which are, or which are not, to be treated as physical features;
- (d) things which are, or which are not, to be treated as alterations of physical features;
- (e) things which are, or which are not, to be treated as auxiliary aids.

(3) Provision made by virtue of this section may amend an applicable Schedule.

NOTES
Regulations: the Equality Act 2010 (Disability) Regulations 2010, SI 2010/2128 at **[2.1184]**.

Discrimination: supplementary

[1.1642]
23 Comparison by reference to circumstances
(1) On a comparison of cases for the purposes of section 13, 14, or 19 there must be no material difference between the circumstances relating to each case.
(2) The circumstances relating to a case include a person's abilities if—
- (a) on a comparison for the purposes of section 13, the protected characteristic is disability;
- (b) on a comparison for the purposes of section 14, one of the protected characteristics in the combination is disability.

(3) If the protected characteristic is sexual orientation, the fact that one person (whether or not the person referred to as B) is a civil partner while another is married [to a person of the opposite sex] is not a material difference between the circumstances relating to each case.
[(4) If the protected characteristic is sexual orientation, the fact that one person (whether or not the person referred to as B) is married to a person of the same sex while another is married to a person of the opposite sex is not a material difference between the circumstances relating to each case.]

NOTES
Words in square brackets in sub-s (3) inserted, and sub-s (4) added, by the Marriage (Same Sex Couples) Act 2013, s 17(4), Sch 7, Pt 2, paras 42, 43.

[1.1643]
24 Irrelevance of alleged discriminator's characteristics
(1) For the purpose of establishing a contravention of this Act by virtue of section 13(1), it does not matter whether A has the protected characteristic.
(2) For the purpose of establishing a contravention of this Act by virtue of section 14(1), it does not matter—

(a) whether A has one of the protected characteristics in the combination;
(b) whether A has both.

[1.1644]
25 References to particular strands of discrimination
(1) Age discrimination is—
(a) discrimination within section 13 because of age;
(b) discrimination within section 19 where the relevant protected characteristic is age.
(2) Disability discrimination is—
(a) discrimination within section 13 because of disability;
(b) discrimination within section 15;
(c) discrimination within section 19 where the relevant protected characteristic is disability;
(d) discrimination within section 21.
(3) Gender reassignment discrimination is—
(a) discrimination within section 13 because of gender reassignment;
(b) discrimination within section 16;
(c) discrimination within section 19 where the relevant protected characteristic is gender reassignment.
(4) Marriage and civil partnership discrimination is—
(a) discrimination within section 13 because of marriage and civil partnership;
(b) discrimination within section 19 where the relevant protected characteristic is marriage and civil partnership.
(5) Pregnancy and maternity discrimination is discrimination within section 17 or 18.
(6) Race discrimination is—
(a) discrimination within section 13 because of race;
(b) discrimination within section 19 where the relevant protected characteristic is race.
(7) Religious or belief-related discrimination is—
(a) discrimination within section 13 because of religion or belief;
(b) discrimination within section 19 where the relevant protected characteristic is religion or belief.
(8) Sex discrimination is—
(a) discrimination within section 13 because of sex;
(b) discrimination within section 19 where the relevant protected characteristic is sex.
(9) Sexual orientation discrimination is—
(a) discrimination within section 13 because of sexual orientation;
(b) discrimination within section 19 where the relevant protected characteristic is sexual orientation.

Other prohibited conduct

[1.1645]
26 Harassment
(1) A person (A) harasses another (B) if—
(a) A engages in unwanted conduct related to a relevant protected characteristic, and
(b) the conduct has the purpose or effect of—
(i) violating B's dignity, or
(ii) creating an intimidating, hostile, degrading, humiliating or offensive environment for B.
(2) A also harasses B if—
(a) A engages in unwanted conduct of a sexual nature, and
(b) the conduct has the purpose or effect referred to in subsection (1)(b).
(3) A also harasses B if—
(a) A or another person engages in unwanted conduct of a sexual nature or that is related to gender reassignment or sex,
(b) the conduct has the purpose or effect referred to in subsection (1)(b), and
(c) because of B's rejection of or submission to the conduct, A treats B less favourably than A would treat B if B had not rejected or submitted to the conduct.
(4) In deciding whether conduct has the effect referred to in subsection (1)(b), each of the following must be taken into account—
(a) the perception of B;
(b) the other circumstances of the case;
(c) whether it is reasonable for the conduct to have that effect.
(5) The relevant protected characteristics are—
age;
disability;
gender reassignment;
race;
religion or belief;
sex;
sexual orientation.

[1.1646]
27 Victimisation
(1) A person (A) victimises another person (B) if A subjects B to a detriment because—
(a) B does a protected act, or
(b) A believes that B has done, or may do, a protected act.

(2) Each of the following is a protected act—
(a) bringing proceedings under this Act;
(b) giving evidence or information in connection with proceedings under this Act;
(c) doing any other thing for the purposes of or in connection with this Act;
(d) making an allegation (whether or not express) that A or another person has contravened this Act.
(3) Giving false evidence or information, or making a false allegation, is not a protected act if the evidence or information is given, or the allegation is made, in bad faith.
(4) This section applies only where the person subjected to a detriment is an individual.
(5) The reference to contravening this Act includes a reference to committing a breach of an equality clause or rule.

28–38 *(Ss 28–31 (Part 3: Services and Public Functions) and ss 32–38 (Part 4: Premises) are outside the scope of this work.)*

PART 5
WORK

NOTES

Offshore work: as to the application of this Part to offshore work, see the Equality Act 2010 (Offshore Work) Order 2010, SI 2010/1835 at **[2.1180]**.

Work on ships and hovercraft: as to the application of this Part to seafarers working on UK ships and hovercraft, or on ships and hovercraft from other EEA States, see the Equality Act 2010 (Work on Ships and Hovercraft) Regulations 2011, SI 2011/1771 at **[2.1246]**.

CHAPTER 1 EMPLOYMENT, ETC

Employees

[1.1647]
39 Employees and applicants
(1) An employer (A) must not discriminate against a person (B)—
(a) in the arrangements A makes for deciding to whom to offer employment;
(b) as to the terms on which A offers B employment;
(c) by not offering B employment.
(2) An employer (A) must not discriminate against an employee of A's (B)—
(a) as to B's terms of employment;
(b) in the way A affords B access, or by not affording B access, to opportunities for promotion, transfer or training or for receiving any other benefit, facility or service;
(c) by dismissing B;
(d) by subjecting B to any other detriment.
(3) An employer (A) must not victimise a person (B)—
(a) in the arrangements A makes for deciding to whom to offer employment;
(b) as to the terms on which A offers B employment;
(c) by not offering B employment.
(4) An employer (A) must not victimise an employee of A's (B)—
(a) as to B's terms of employment;
(b) in the way A affords B access, or by not affording B access, to opportunities for promotion, transfer or training or for any other benefit, facility or service;
(c) by dismissing B;
(d) by subjecting B to any other detriment.
(5) A duty to make reasonable adjustments applies to an employer.
(6) Subsection (1)(b), so far as relating to sex or pregnancy and maternity, does not apply to a term that relates to pay—
(a) unless, were B to accept the offer, an equality clause or rule would have effect in relation to the term, or
(b) if paragraph (a) does not apply, except in so far as making an offer on terms including that term amounts to a contravention of subsection (1)(b) by virtue of section 13, 14 or 18.
(7) In subsections (2)(c) and (4)(c), the reference to dismissing B includes a reference to the termination of B's employment—
(a) by the expiry of a period (including a period expiring by reference to an event or circumstance);
(b) by an act of B's (including giving notice) in circumstances such that B is entitled, because of A's conduct, to terminate the employment without notice.
(8) Subsection (7)(a) does not apply if, immediately after the termination, the employment is renewed on the same terms.

[1.1648]
40 Employees and applicants: harassment
(1) An employer (A) must not, in relation to employment by A, harass a person (B)—
(a) who is an employee of A's;
(b) who has applied to A for employment.
(2)–(4) . . .

NOTES

Sub-ss (2)–(4): repealed by the Enterprise and Regulatory Reform Act 2013, s 65.

[1.1649]
41 Contract workers

(1) A principal must not discriminate against a contract worker—
  (a) as to the terms on which the principal allows the worker to do the work;
  (b) by not allowing the worker to do, or to continue to do, the work;
  (c) in the way the principal affords the worker access, or by not affording the worker access, to opportunities for receiving a benefit, facility or service;
  (d) by subjecting the worker to any other detriment.

(2) A principal must not, in relation to contract work, harass a contract worker.

(3) A principal must not victimise a contract worker—
  (a) as to the terms on which the principal allows the worker to do the work;
  (b) by not allowing the worker to do, or to continue to do, the work;
  (c) in the way the principal affords the worker access, or by not affording the worker access, to opportunities for receiving a benefit, facility or service;
  (d) by subjecting the worker to any other detriment.

(4) A duty to make reasonable adjustments applies to a principal (as well as to the employer of a contract worker).

(5) A "principal" is a person who makes work available for an individual who is—
  (a) employed by another person, and
  (b) supplied by that other person in furtherance of a contract to which the principal is a party (whether or not that other person is a party to it).

(6) "Contract work" is work such as is mentioned in subsection (5).

(7) A "contract worker" is an individual supplied to a principal in furtherance of a contract such as is mentioned in subsection (5)(b).

Police officers

[1.1650]
42 Identity of employer

(1) For the purposes of this Part, holding the office of constable is to be treated as employment—
  (a) by the chief officer, in respect of any act done by the chief officer in relation to a constable or appointment to the office of constable;
  (b) by the responsible authority, in respect of any act done by the authority in relation to a constable or appointment to the office of constable.

(2) For the purposes of this Part, holding an appointment as a police cadet is to be treated as employment—
  (a) by the chief officer, in respect of any act done by the chief officer in relation to a police cadet or appointment as one;
  (b) by the responsible authority, in respect of any act done by the authority in relation to a police cadet or appointment as one.

(3) Subsection (1) does not apply to service with the Civil Nuclear Constabulary (as to which, see section 55(2) of the Energy Act 2004).

(4) Subsection (1) does not apply to a constable at [NCA] [or SPA].

(5) A constable at [NCA] or [SPA] is to be treated as employed by it, in respect of any act done by it in relation to the constable.

(6) . . .

NOTES

The references to the "NCA" in square brackets in sub-ss (4), (5) were substituted by the Crime and Courts Act 2013, s 15(3), Sch 8, Pt 2, paras 180, 181.

The references to the "SPA" in square brackets in sub-ss (4), (5) were substituted, and sub-s (6) was repealed, by the Police and Fire Reform (Scotland) Act 2012 (Consequential Provisions and Modifications) Order 2013, SI 2013/602, art 26, Sch 2, Pt 1, para 63(1), (2).

For the meaning of "NCA" and "SPA" see respectively s 43(5) and s 43(5A) of this Act at **[1.1651]**.

[1.1651]
43 Interpretation

(1) This section applies for the purposes of section 42.

(2) "Chief officer" means—
  (a) in relation to an appointment under a relevant Act, the chief officer of police for the police force to which the appointment relates;
  (b) in relation to any other appointment, the person under whose direction and control the body of constables or other persons to which the appointment relates is;
  (c) in relation to a constable or other person under the direction and control of a chief officer of police, that chief officer of police;
  (d) in relation to any other constable or any other person, the person under whose direction and control the constable or other person is.

(3) "Responsible authority" means—
  (a) in relation to an appointment under a relevant Act, the [local policing body or police authority] that maintains the police force to which the appointment relates;
  (b) in relation to any other appointment, the person by whom a person would (if appointed) be paid;
  (c) in relation to a constable or other person under the direction and control of a chief officer of police, the [local policing body or police authority] that maintains the police force for which that chief officer is the chief officer of police;

(d) in relation to any other constable or any other person, the person by whom the constable or other person is paid.

(4) "Police cadet" means a person appointed to undergo training with a view to becoming a constable.

[(5) "NCA" means the National Crime Agency; and a reference to a constable at NCA is a reference to a constable seconded to it to serve as an NCA officer.]

[(5A) "SPA" means the Scottish Police Authority; and a reference to a constable at SPA is a reference to a constable serving as a member of its staff by virtue of paragraph 7(1) of schedule 1 to the Police and Fire Reform (Scotland) Act 2012.]

(7) . . .

(8) For the purposes of this section, the relevant Acts are—

(a) the Metropolitan Police Act 1829;
(b) the City of London Police Act 1839;
(c) the [Police and Fire Reform (Scotland) Act 2012];
[(d) the Police Reform and Social Responsibility Act 2011]

[(9) Subsections (2) and (3) apply in relation to Scotland as follows—

(a) a reference to a police authority includes a reference to the Scottish Police Authority;
(b) a reference to a police force includes a reference to the Police Service of Scotland; and9;
(c) a reference to a chief officer of police includes a reference to the chief constable of the Police Service of Scotland.]

NOTES

The words in square brackets in sub-s (3) were substituted, and sub-s (8)(d) was substituted, by the Police Reform and Social Responsibility Act 2011, s 99, Sch 16, Pt 3, paras 380, 382.

Sub-s (5) was substituted by the Crime and Courts Act 2013, s 15(3), Sch 8, Pt 2, paras 180, 182.

Sub-s (5A) was substituted (for the original sub-s (6)), sub-s (7) was repealed, the words in square brackets in sub-s (8)(c) were substituted, and sub-s (9) was substituted, by the Police and Fire Reform (Scotland) Act 2012 (Consequential Provisions and Modifications) Order 2013, SI 2013/602, art 26, Sch 2, Pt 1, para 63(1), (3).

Partners

[1.1652]

44 Partnerships

(1) A firm or proposed firm must not discriminate against a person—

(a) in the arrangements it makes for deciding to whom to offer a position as a partner;
(b) as to the terms on which it offers the person a position as a partner;
(c) by not offering the person a position as a partner.

(2) A firm (A) must not discriminate against a partner (B)—

(a) as to the terms on which B is a partner;
(b) in the way A affords B access, or by not affording B access, to opportunities for promotion, transfer or training or for receiving any other benefit, facility or service;
(c) by expelling B;
(d) by subjecting B to any other detriment.

(3) A firm must not, in relation to a position as a partner, harass—

(a) a partner;
(b) a person who has applied for the position.

(4) A proposed firm must not, in relation to a position as a partner, harass a person who has applied for the position.

(5) A firm or proposed firm must not victimise a person—

(a) in the arrangements it makes for deciding to whom to offer a position as a partner;
(b) as to the terms on which it offers the person a position as a partner;
(c) by not offering the person a position as a partner.

(6) A firm (A) must not victimise a partner (B)—

(a) as to the terms on which B is a partner;
(b) in the way A affords B access, or by not affording B access, to opportunities for promotion, transfer or training or for receiving any other benefit, facility or service;
(c) by expelling B;
(d) by subjecting B to any other detriment.

(7) A duty to make reasonable adjustments applies to—

(a) a firm;
(b) a proposed firm.

(8) In the application of this section to a limited partnership within the meaning of the Limited Partnerships Act 1907, "partner" means a general partner within the meaning of that Act.

[1.1653]

45 Limited liability partnerships

(1) An LLP or proposed LLP must not discriminate against a person—

(a) in the arrangements it makes for deciding to whom to offer a position as a member;
(b) as to the terms on which it offers the person a position as a member;
(c) by not offering the person a position as a member.

(2) An LLP (A) must not discriminate against a member (B)—

(a) as to the terms on which B is a member;
(b) in the way A affords B access, or by not affording B access, to opportunities for promotion, transfer or training or for receiving any other benefit, facility or service;
(c) by expelling B;

(d) by subjecting B to any other detriment.

(3) An LLP must not, in relation to a position as a member, harass—

(a) a member;

(b) a person who has applied for the position.

(4) A proposed LLP must not, in relation to a position as a member, harass a person who has applied for the position.

(5) An LLP or proposed LLP must not victimise a person—

(a) in the arrangements it makes for deciding to whom to offer a position as a member;

(b) as to the terms on which it offers the person a position as a member;

(c) by not offering the person a position as a member.

(6) An LLP (A) must not victimise a member (B)—

(a) as to the terms on which B is a member;

(b) in the way A affords B access, or by not affording B access, to opportunities for promotion, transfer or training or for receiving any other benefit, facility or service;

(c) by expelling B;

(d) by subjecting B to any other detriment.

(7) A duty to make reasonable adjustments applies to—

(a) an LLP;

(b) a proposed LLP.

[1.1654]

46 Interpretation

(1) This section applies for the purposes of sections 44 and 45.

(2) "Partnership" and "firm" have the same meaning as in the Partnership Act 1890.

(3) "Proposed firm" means persons proposing to form themselves into a partnership.

(4) "LLP" means a limited liability partnership (within the meaning of the Limited Liability Partnerships Act 2000).

(5) "Proposed LLP" means persons proposing to incorporate an LLP with themselves as members.

(6) A reference to expelling a partner of a firm or a member of an LLP includes a reference to the termination of the person's position as such—

(a) by the expiry of a period (including a period expiring by reference to an event or circumstance);

(b) by an act of the person (including giving notice) in circumstances such that the person is entitled, because of the conduct of other partners or members, to terminate the position without notice;

(c) (in the case of a partner of a firm) as a result of the dissolution of the partnership.

(7) Subsection (6)(a) and (c) does not apply if, immediately after the termination, the position is renewed on the same terms.

The Bar

[1.1655]

47 Barristers

(1) A barrister (A) must not discriminate against a person (B)—

(a) in the arrangements A makes for deciding to whom to offer a pupillage or tenancy;

(b) as to the terms on which A offers B a pupillage or tenancy;

(c) by not offering B a pupillage or tenancy.

(2) A barrister (A) must not discriminate against a person (B) who is a pupil or tenant—

(a) as to the terms on which B is a pupil or tenant;

(b) in the way A affords B access, or by not affording B access, to opportunities for training or gaining experience or for receiving any other benefit, facility or service;

(c) by terminating the pupillage;

(d) by subjecting B to pressure to leave chambers;

(e) by subjecting B to any other detriment.

(3) A barrister must not, in relation to a pupillage or tenancy, harass—

(a) the pupil or tenant;

(b) a person who has applied for the pupillage or tenancy.

(4) A barrister (A) must not victimise a person (B)—

(a) in the arrangements A makes for deciding to whom to offer a pupillage or tenancy;

(b) as to the terms on which A offers B a pupillage or tenancy;

(c) by not offering B a pupillage or tenancy.

(5) A barrister (A) must not victimise a person (B) who is a pupil or tenant—

(a) as to the terms on which B is a pupil or tenant;

(b) in the way A affords B access, or by not affording B access, to opportunities for training or gaining experience or for receiving any other benefit, facility or service;

(c) by terminating the pupillage;

(d) by subjecting B to pressure to leave chambers;

(e) by subjecting B to any other detriment.

(6) A person must not, in relation to instructing a barrister—

(a) discriminate against a barrister by subjecting the barrister to a detriment;

(b) harass the barrister;

(c) victimise the barrister.

(7) A duty to make reasonable adjustments applies to a barrister.

(8) The preceding provisions of this section (apart from subsection (6)) apply in relation to a barrister's clerk as they apply in relation to a barrister; and for that purpose the reference to a barrister's clerk includes a reference to a person who carries out the functions of a barrister's clerk.
(9) A reference to a tenant includes a reference to a barrister who is permitted to work in chambers (including as a squatter or door tenant); and a reference to a tenancy is to be construed accordingly.

[1.1656]
48 Advocates
(1) An advocate (A) must not discriminate against a person (B)—
(a) in the arrangements A makes for deciding who to take as A's devil or to whom to offer membership of a stable;
(b) as to the terms on which A offers to take B as A's devil or offers B membership of a stable;
(c) by not offering to take B as A's devil or not offering B membership of a stable.
(2) An advocate (A) must not discriminate against a person (B) who is a devil or a member of a stable—
(a) as to the terms on which B is a devil or a member of the stable;
(b) in the way A affords B access, or by not affording B access, to opportunities for training or gaining experience or for receiving any other benefit, facility or service;
(c) by terminating A's relationship with B (where B is a devil);
(d) by subjecting B to pressure to leave the stable;
(e) by subjecting B to any other detriment.
(3) An advocate must not, in relation to a relationship with a devil or membership of a stable, harass—
(a) a devil or member;
(b) a person who has applied to be taken as the advocate's devil or to become a member of the stable.
(4) An advocate (A) must not victimise a person (B)—
(a) in the arrangements A makes for deciding who to take as A's devil or to whom to offer membership of a stable;
(b) as to the terms on which A offers to take B as A's devil or offers B membership of a stable;
(c) by not offering to take B as A's devil or not offering B membership of a stable.
(5) An advocate (A) must not victimise a person (B) who is a devil or a member of a stable—
(a) as to the terms on which B is a devil or a member of the stable;
(b) in the way A affords B access, or by not affording B access, to opportunities for training or gaining experience or for receiving any other benefit, facility or service;
(c) by terminating A's relationship with B (where B is a devil);
(d) by subjecting B to pressure to leave the stable;
(e) by subjecting B to any other detriment.
(6) A person must not, in relation to instructing an advocate—
(a) discriminate against the advocate by subjecting the advocate to a detriment;
(b) harass the advocate;
(c) victimise the advocate.
(7) A duty to make reasonable adjustments applies to an advocate.
(8) This section (apart from subsection (6)) applies in relation to an advocate's clerk as it applies in relation to an advocate; and for that purpose the reference to an advocate's clerk includes a reference to a person who carries out the functions of an advocate's clerk.
(9) "Advocate" means a practising member of the Faculty of Advocates.

Office-holders

[1.1657]
49 Personal offices: appointments, etc
(1) This section applies in relation to personal offices.
(2) A personal office is an office or post—
(a) to which a person is appointed to discharge a function personally under the direction of another person, and
(b) in respect of which an appointed person is entitled to remuneration.
(3) A person (A) who has the power to make an appointment to a personal office must not discriminate against a person (B)—
(a) in the arrangements A makes for deciding to whom to offer the appointment;
(b) as to the terms on which A offers B the appointment;
(c) by not offering B the appointment.
(4) A person who has the power to make an appointment to a personal office must not, in relation to the office, harass a person seeking, or being considered for, the appointment.
(5) A person (A) who has the power to make an appointment to a personal office must not victimise a person (B)—
(a) in the arrangements A makes for deciding to whom to offer the appointment;
(b) as to the terms on which A offers B the appointment;
(c) by not offering B the appointment.
(6) A person (A) who is a relevant person in relation to a personal office must not discriminate against a person (B) appointed to the office—
(a) as to the terms of B's appointment;
(b) in the way A affords B access, or by not affording B access, to opportunities for promotion, transfer or training or for receiving any other benefit, facility or service;
(c) by terminating B's appointment;

(d) by subjecting B to any other detriment.

(7) A relevant person in relation to a personal office must not, in relation to that office, harass a person appointed to it.

(8) A person (A) who is a relevant person in relation to a personal office must not victimise a person (B) appointed to the office—

(a) as to the terms of B's appointment;

(b) in the way A affords B access, or by not affording B access, to opportunities for promotion, transfer or training or for receiving any other benefit, facility or service;

(c) by terminating B's appointment;

(d) by subjecting B to any other detriment.

(9) A duty to make reasonable adjustments applies to—

(a) a person who has the power to make an appointment to a personal office;

(b) a relevant person in relation to a personal office.

(10) For the purposes of subsection (2)(a), a person is to be regarded as discharging functions personally under the direction of another person if that other person is entitled to direct the person as to when and where to discharge the functions.

(11) For the purposes of subsection (2)(b), a person is not to be regarded as entitled to remuneration merely because the person is entitled to payments—

(a) in respect of expenses incurred by the person in discharging the functions of the office or post, or

(b) by way of compensation for the loss of income or benefits the person would or might have received had the person not been discharging the functions of the office or post.

(12) Subsection (3)(b), so far as relating to sex or pregnancy and maternity, does not apply to a term that relates to pay—

(a) unless, were B to accept the offer, an equality clause or rule would have effect in relation to the term, or

(b) if paragraph (a) does not apply, except in so far as making an offer on terms including that term amounts to a contravention of subsection (3)(b) by virtue of section 13, 14 or 18.

[1.1658]

50 Public offices: appointments, etc

(1) This section and section 51 apply in relation to public offices.

(2) A public office is—

(a) an office or post, appointment to which is made by a member of the executive;

(b) an office or post, appointment to which is made on the recommendation of, or subject to the approval of, a member of the executive;

(c) an office or post, appointment to which is made on the recommendation of, or subject to the approval of, the House of Commons, the House of Lords, the National Assembly for Wales or the Scottish Parliament[

[(d) an office or post, appointment to which is made by the Lord Chief Justice or the Senior President of Tribunals.]

(3) A person (A) who has the power to make an appointment to a public office within subsection (2)(a)[, (b) or (d)] must not discriminate against a person (B)—

(a) in the arrangements A makes for deciding to whom to offer the appointment;

(b) as to the terms on which A offers B the appointment;

(c) by not offering B the appointment.

(4) A person who has the power to make an appointment to a public office within subsection (2)(a)[, (b) or (d)] must not, in relation to the office, harass a person seeking, or being considered for, the appointment.

(5) A person (A) who has the power to make an appointment to a public office within subsection (2)(a)[, (b) or (d)] must not victimise a person (B)—

(a) in the arrangements A makes for deciding to whom to offer the appointment;

(b) as to the terms on which A offers B the appointment;

(c) by not offering B the appointment.

(6) A person (A) who is a relevant person in relation to a public office within subsection (2)(a)[, (b) or (d)] must not discriminate against a person (B) appointed to the office—

(a) as to B's terms of appointment;

(b) in the way A affords B access, or by not affording B access, to opportunities for promotion, transfer or training or for receiving any other benefit, facility or service;

(c) by terminating the appointment;

(d) by subjecting B to any other detriment.

(7) A person (A) who is a relevant person in relation to a public office within subsection (2)(c) must not discriminate against a person (B) appointed to the office—

(a) as to B's terms of appointment;

(b) in the way A affords B access, or by not affording B access, to opportunities for promotion, transfer or training or for receiving any other benefit, facility or service;

(c) by subjecting B to any other detriment (other than by terminating the appointment).

(8) A relevant person in relation to a public office must not, in relation to that office, harass a person appointed to it.

(9) A person (A) who is a relevant person in relation to a public office within subsection (2)(a) *or (b)* must not victimise a person (B) appointed to the office—

(a) as to B's terms of appointment;

(b) in the way A affords B access, or by not affording B access, to opportunities for promotion, transfer or training or for receiving any other benefit, facility or service;
(c) by terminating the appointment;
(d) by subjecting B to any other detriment.

(10) A person (A) who is a relevant person in relation to a public office within subsection (2)(c) must not victimise a person (B) appointed to the office—
(a) as to B's terms of appointment;
(b) in the way A affords B access, or by not affording B access, to opportunities for promotion, transfer or training or for receiving any other benefit, facility or service;
(c) by subjecting B to any other detriment (other than by terminating the appointment).

(11) A duty to make reasonable adjustments applies to—
(a) a relevant person in relation to a public office;
(b) a person who has the power to make an appointment to a public office within subsection (2)(a)[, (b) or (d)].

(12) Subsection (3)(b), so far as relating to sex or pregnancy and maternity, does not apply to a term that relates to pay—
(a) unless, were B to accept the offer, an equality clause or rule would have effect in relation to the term, or
(b) if paragraph (a) does not apply, except in so far as making an offer on terms including that term amounts to a contravention of subsection (3)(b) by virtue of section 13, 14 or 18.

NOTES

Sub-s (2)(d) inserted, and words in square brackets in sub-ss (3)–(6), (9), (11) substituted, by the Crime and Courts Act 2013, s 20, Sch 13, Pt 4, para 50.

[1.1659]

51 Public offices: recommendations for appointments, etc

(1) A person (A) who has the power to make a recommendation for or give approval to an appointment to a public office within section 50(2)(a)[, (b) or (d)], must not discriminate against a person (B)—
(a) in the arrangements A makes for deciding who to recommend for appointment or to whose appointment to give approval;
(b) by not recommending B for appointment to the office;
(c) by making a negative recommendation of B for appointment to the office;
(d) by not giving approval to the appointment of B to the office.

(2) A person who has the power to make a recommendation for or give approval to an appointment to a public office within section 50(2)(a)[, (b) or (d)] must not, in relation to the office, harass a person seeking or being considered for the recommendation or approval.

(3) A person (A) who has the power to make a recommendation for or give approval to an appointment to a public office within section 50(2)(a)[, (b) or (d)], must not victimise a person (B)—
(a) in the arrangements A makes for deciding who to recommend for appointment or to whose appointment to give approval;
(b) by not recommending B for appointment to the office;
(c) by making a negative recommendation of B for appointment to the office;
(d) by not giving approval to the appointment of B to the office.

(4) A duty to make reasonable adjustments applies to a person who has the power to make a recommendation for or give approval to an appointment to a public office within section 50(2)(a)[, (b) or (d)].

(5) A reference in this section to a person who has the power to make a recommendation for or give approval to an appointment to a public office within section 50(2)(a) [or (d)] is a reference only to a relevant body which has that power; and for that purpose "relevant body" means a body established—
(a) by or in pursuance of an enactment, or
(b) by a member of the executive.

NOTES

Words in square brackets in sub-ss (1)–(4) substituted, and words in square brackets in sub-s (5) inserted, by the Crime and Courts Act 2013, s 20, Sch 13, Pt 4, para 51.

[1.1660]

52 Interpretation and exceptions

(1) This section applies for the purposes of sections 49 to 51.
(2) "Personal office" has the meaning given in section 49.
(3) "Public office" has the meaning given in section 50.
(4) An office or post which is both a personal office and a public office is to be treated as being a public office only.
(5) Appointment to an office or post does not include election to it.
(6) "Relevant person", in relation to an office, means the person who, in relation to a matter specified in the first column of the table, is specified in the second column (but a reference to a relevant person does not in any case include the House of Commons, the House of Lords, the National Assembly for Wales or the Scottish Parliament).

Matter	Relevant person
A term of appointment	The person who has the power to set the term.

Matter	Relevant person
Access to an opportunity	The person who has the power to afford access to the opportunity (or, if there is no such person, the person who has the power to make the appointment).
Terminating an appointment	The person who has the power to terminate the appointment.
Subjecting an appointee to any other detriment	The person who has the power in relation to the matter to which the conduct in question relates (or, if there is no such person, the person who has the power to make the appointment).
Harassing an appointee	The person who has the power in relation to the matter to which the conduct in question relates.

(7) A reference to terminating a person's appointment includes a reference to termination of the appointment—

(a) by the expiry of a period (including a period expiring by reference to an event or circumstance);

(b) by an act of the person (including giving notice) in circumstances such that the person is entitled, because of the relevant person's conduct, to terminate the appointment without notice.

(8) Subsection (7)(a) does not apply if, immediately after the termination, the appointment is renewed on the same terms.

(9) Schedule 6 (excluded offices) has effect.

Qualifications

[1.1661]
53 Qualifications bodies

(1) A qualifications body (A) must not discriminate against a person (B)—

(a) in the arrangements A makes for deciding upon whom to confer a relevant qualification;

(b) as to the terms on which it is prepared to confer a relevant qualification on B;

(c) by not conferring a relevant qualification on B.

(2) A qualifications body (A) must not discriminate against a person (B) upon whom A has conferred a relevant qualification—

(a) by withdrawing the qualification from B;

(b) by varying the terms on which B holds the qualification;

(c) by subjecting B to any other detriment.

(3) A qualifications body must not, in relation to conferment by it of a relevant qualification, harass—

(a) a person who holds the qualification, or

(b) a person who applies for it.

(4) A qualifications body (A) must not victimise a person (B)—

(a) in the arrangements A makes for deciding upon whom to confer a relevant qualification;

(b) as to the terms on which it is prepared to confer a relevant qualification on B;

(c) by not conferring a relevant qualification on B.

(5) A qualifications body (A) must not victimise a person (B) upon whom A has conferred a relevant qualification—

(a) by withdrawing the qualification from B;

(b) by varying the terms on which B holds the qualification;

(c) by subjecting B to any other detriment.

(6) A duty to make reasonable adjustments applies to a qualifications body.

(7) The application by a qualifications body of a competence standard to a disabled person is not disability discrimination unless it is discrimination by virtue of section 19.

[1.1662]
54 Interpretation

(1) This section applies for the purposes of section 53.

(2) A qualifications body is an authority or body which can confer a relevant qualification.

(3) A relevant qualification is an authorisation, qualification, recognition, registration, enrolment, approval or certification which is needed for, or facilitates engagement in, a particular trade or profession.

(4) An authority or body is not a qualifications body in so far as—

(a) it can confer a qualification to which section 96 applies,

(b) it is the responsible body of a school to which section 85 applies,

(c) it is the governing body of an institution to which section 91 applies,

(d) it exercises functions under the Education Acts, or

(e) it exercises functions under the Education (Scotland) Act 1980.

(5) A reference to conferring a relevant qualification includes a reference to renewing or extending the conferment of a relevant qualification.

(6) A competence standard is an academic, medical or other standard applied for the purpose of determining whether or not a person has a particular level of competence or ability.

Employment services

[1.1663]

55 Employment service-providers

(1) A person (an "employment service-provider") concerned with the provision of an employment service must not discriminate against a person—

(a) in the arrangements the service-provider makes for selecting persons to whom to provide, or to whom to offer to provide, the service;

(b) as to the terms on which the service-provider offers to provide the service to the person;

(c) by not offering to provide the service to the person.

(2) An employment service-provider (A) must not, in relation to the provision of an employment service, discriminate against a person (B)—

(a) as to the terms on which A provides the service to B;

(b) by not providing the service to B;

(c) by terminating the provision of the service to B;

(d) by subjecting B to any other detriment.

(3) An employment service-provider must not, in relation to the provision of an employment service, harass—

(a) a person who asks the service-provider to provide the service;

(b) a person for whom the service-provider provides the service.

(4) An employment service-provider (A) must not victimise a person (B)—

(a) in the arrangements A makes for selecting persons to whom to provide, or to whom to offer to provide, the service;

(b) as to the terms on which A offers to provide the service to B;

(c) by not offering to provide the service to B.

(5) An employment service-provider (A) must not, in relation to the provision of an employment service, victimise a person (B)—

(a) as to the terms on which A provides the service to B;

(b) by not providing the service to B;

(c) by terminating the provision of the service to B;

(d) by subjecting B to any other detriment.

(6) A duty to make reasonable adjustments applies to an employment service-provider, except in relation to the provision of a vocational service.

(7) The duty imposed by section 29(7)(a) applies to a person concerned with the provision of a vocational service; but a failure to comply with that duty in relation to the provision of a vocational service is a contravention of this Part for the purposes of Part 9 (enforcement).

[1.1664]

56 Interpretation

(1) This section applies for the purposes of section 55.

(2) The provision of an employment service includes—

(a) the provision of vocational training;

(b) the provision of vocational guidance;

(c) making arrangements for the provision of vocational training or vocational guidance;

(d) the provision of a service for finding employment for persons;

(e) the provision of a service for supplying employers with persons to do work;

(f) the provision of a service in pursuance of arrangements made under section 2 of the Employment and Training Act 1973 (functions of the Secretary of State relating to employment);

(g) the provision of a service in pursuance of arrangements made or a direction given under section 10 of that Act (careers services);

(h) the exercise of a function in pursuance of arrangements made under section 2(3) of the Enterprise and New Towns (Scotland) Act 1990 (functions of Scottish Enterprise, etc relating to employment);

(i) an assessment related to the conferment of a relevant qualification within the meaning of section 53 above (except in so far as the assessment is by the qualifications body which confers the qualification).

(3) This section does not apply in relation to training or guidance in so far as it is training or guidance in relation to which another provision of this Part applies.

(4) This section does not apply in relation to training or guidance for pupils of a school to which section 85 applies in so far as it is training or guidance to which the responsible body of the school has power to afford access (whether as the responsible body of that school or as the responsible body of any other school at which the training or guidance is provided).

(5) This section does not apply in relation to training or guidance for students of an institution to which section 91 applies in so far as it is training or guidance to which the governing body of the institution has power to afford access.

(6) "Vocational training" means—

(a) training for employment, or

(b) work experience (including work experience the duration of which is not agreed until after it begins).

(7) A reference to the provision of a vocational service is a reference to the provision of an employment service within subsection (2)(a) to (d) (or an employment service within subsection (2)(f) or (g) in so far as it is also an employment service within subsection (2)(a) to (d)); and for that purpose—

(a) the references to an employment service within subsection (2)(a) do not include a reference to vocational training within the meaning given by subsection (6)(b), and
(b) the references to an employment service within subsection (2)(d) also include a reference to a service for assisting persons to retain employment.
(8) A reference to training includes a reference to facilities for training.

Trade organisations

[1.1665]
57 Trade organisations
(1) A trade organisation (A) must not discriminate against a person (B)—
(a) in the arrangements A makes for deciding to whom to offer membership of the organisation;
(b) as to the terms on which it is prepared to admit B as a member;
(c) by not accepting B's application for membership.
(2) A trade organisation (A) must not discriminate against a member (B)—
(a) in the way it affords B access, or by not affording B access, to opportunities for receiving a benefit, facility or service;
(b) by depriving B of membership;
(c) by varying the terms on which B is a member;
(d) by subjecting B to any other detriment.
(3) A trade organisation must not, in relation to membership of it, harass—
(a) a member, or
(b) an applicant for membership.
(4) A trade organisation (A) must not victimise a person (B)—
(a) in the arrangements A makes for deciding to whom to offer membership of the organisation;
(b) as to the terms on which it is prepared to admit B as a member;
(c) by not accepting B's application for membership.
(5) A trade organisation (A) must not victimise a member (B)—
(a) in the way it affords B access, or by not affording B access, to opportunities for receiving a benefit, facility or service;
(b) by depriving B of membership;
(c) by varying the terms on which B is a member;
(d) by subjecting B to any other detriment.
(6) A duty to make reasonable adjustments applies to a trade organisation.
(7) A trade organisation is—
(a) an organisation of workers,
(b) an organisation of employers, or
(c) any other organisation whose members carry on a particular trade or profession for the purposes of which the organisation exists.

Local authority members

[1.1666]
58 Official business of members
(1) A local authority must not discriminate against a member of the authority in relation to the member's carrying out of official business—
(a) in the way the authority affords the member access, or by not affording the member access, to opportunities for training or for receiving any other facility;
(b) by subjecting the member to any other detriment.
(2) A local authority must not, in relation to a member's carrying out of official business, harass the member.
(3) A local authority must not victimise a member of the authority in relation to the member's carrying out of official business—
(a) in the way the authority affords the member access, or by not affording the member access, to opportunities for training or for receiving any other facility;
(b) by subjecting the member to any other detriment.
(4) A member of a local authority is not subjected to a detriment for the purposes of subsection (1)(b) or (3)(b) only because the member is—
(a) not appointed or elected to an office of the authority,
(b) not appointed or elected to, or to an office of, a committee or sub-committee of the authority, or
(c) not appointed or nominated in exercise of an appointment power of the authority.
(5) In subsection (4)(c), an appointment power of a local authority is a power of the authority, or of a group of bodies including the authority, to make—
(a) appointments to a body;
(b) nominations for appointment to a body.
(6) A duty to make reasonable adjustments applies to a local authority.

[1.1667]
59 Interpretation
(1) This section applies for the purposes of section 58.
(2) "Local authority" means—
(a) a county council in England;
(b) a district council in England;
(c) the Greater London Authority;
(d) a London borough council;

(e) the Common Council of the City of London;
(f) the Council of the Isles of Scilly;
(g) a parish council in England;
(h) a county council in Wales;
(i) a community council in Wales;
(j) a county borough council in Wales;
(k) a council constituted under section 2 of the Local Government etc (Scotland) Act 1994;
(l) a community council in Scotland.

(3) A Minister of the Crown may by order amend subsection (2) so as to add, vary or omit a reference to a body which exercises functions that have been conferred on a local authority within paragraph (a) to (l).

(4) A reference to the carrying-out of official business by a person who is a member of a local authority is a reference to the doing of anything by the person—
(a) as a member of the authority,
(b) as a member of a body to which the person is appointed by, or appointed following nomination by, the authority or a group of bodies including the authority, or
(c) as a member of any other public body.

(5) "Member", in relation to the Greater London Authority, means—
(a) the Mayor of London;
(b) a member of the London Assembly.

NOTES

Orders: as of 15 May 2019, no Orders had been made under this section.

Recruitment

[1.1668]

60 Enquiries about disability and health

(1) A person (A) to whom an application for work is made must not ask about the health of the applicant (B)—
(a) before offering work to B, or
(b) where A is not in a position to offer work to B, before including B in a pool of applicants from whom A intends (when in a position to do so) to select a person to whom to offer work.

(2) A contravention of subsection (1) (or a contravention of section 111 or 112 that relates to a contravention of subsection (1)) is enforceable as an unlawful act under Part 1 of the Equality Act 2006 (and, by virtue of section 120(8), is enforceable only by the Commission under that Part).

(3) A does not contravene a relevant disability provision merely by asking about B's health; but A's conduct in reliance on information given in response may be a contravention of a relevant disability provision.

(4) Subsection (5) applies if B brings proceedings before an employment tribunal on a complaint that A's conduct in reliance on information given in response to a question about B's health is a contravention of a relevant disability provision.

(5) In the application of section 136 to the proceedings, the particulars of the complaint are to be treated for the purposes of subsection (2) of that section as facts from which the tribunal could decide that A contravened the provision.

(6) This section does not apply to a question that A asks in so far as asking the question is necessary for the purpose of—
(a) establishing whether B will be able to comply with a requirement to undergo an assessment or establishing whether a duty to make reasonable adjustments is or will be imposed on A in relation to B in connection with a requirement to undergo an assessment,
(b) establishing whether B will be able to carry out a function that is intrinsic to the work concerned,
(c) monitoring diversity in the range of persons applying to A for work,
(d) taking action to which section 158 would apply if references in that section to persons who share (or do not share) a protected characteristic were references to disabled persons (or persons who are not disabled) and the reference to the characteristic were a reference to disability, or
(e) if A applies in relation to the work a requirement to have a particular disability, establishing whether B has that disability.

(7) In subsection (6)(b), where A reasonably believes that a duty to make reasonable adjustments would be imposed on A in relation to B in connection with the work, the reference to a function that is intrinsic to the work is to be read as a reference to a function that would be intrinsic to the work once A complied with the duty.

(8) Subsection (6)(e) applies only if A shows that, having regard to the nature or context of the work—
(a) the requirement is an occupational requirement, and
(b) the application of the requirement is a proportionate means of achieving a legitimate aim.

(9) "Work" means employment, contract work, a position as a partner, a position as a member of an LLP, a pupillage or tenancy, being taken as a devil, membership of a stable, an appointment to a personal or public office, or the provision of an employment service; and the references in subsection (1) to offering a person work are, in relation to contract work, to be read as references to allowing a person to do the work.

(10) A reference to offering work is a reference to making a conditional or unconditional offer of work (and, in relation to contract work, is a reference to allowing a person to do the work subject to fulfilment of one or more conditions).

(11) The following, so far as relating to discrimination within section 13 because of disability, are relevant disability provisions—
- (a) section 39(1)(a) or (c);
- (b) section 41(1)(b);
- (c) section 44(1)(a) or (c);
- (d) section 45(1)(a) or (c);
- (e) section 47(1)(a) or (c);
- (f) section 48(1)(a) or (c);
- (g) section 49(3)(a) or (c);
- (h) section 50(3)(a) or (c);
- (i) section 51(1);
- (j) section 55(1)(a) or (c).

(12) An assessment is an interview or other process designed to give an indication of a person's suitability for the work concerned.
(13) For the purposes of this section, whether or not a person has a disability is to be regarded as an aspect of that person's health.
(14) This section does not apply to anything done for the purpose of vetting applicants for work for reasons of national security.

CHAPTER 2 OCCUPATIONAL PENSION SCHEMES

[1.1669]
61 Non-discrimination rule

(1) An occupational pension scheme must be taken to include a non-discrimination rule.
(2) A non-discrimination rule is a provision by virtue of which a responsible person (A)—
- (a) must not discriminate against another person (B) in carrying out any of A's functions in relation to the scheme;
- (b) must not, in relation to the scheme, harass B;
- (c) must not, in relation to the scheme, victimise B.

(3) The provisions of an occupational pension scheme have effect subject to the non-discrimination rule.
(4) The following are responsible persons—
- (a) the trustees or managers of the scheme;
- (b) an employer whose employees are, or may be, members of the scheme;
- (c) a person exercising an appointing function in relation to an office the holder of which is, or may be, a member of the scheme.

(5) A non-discrimination rule does not apply in relation to a person who is a pension credit member of a scheme.
(6) An appointing function is any of the following—
- (a) the function of appointing a person;
- (b) the function of terminating a person's appointment;
- (c) the function of recommending a person for appointment;
- (d) the function of approving an appointment.

(7) A breach of a non-discrimination rule is a contravention of this Part for the purposes of Part 9 (enforcement).
(8) It is not a breach of a non-discrimination rule for the employer or the trustees or managers of a scheme to maintain or use in relation to the scheme rules, practices, actions or decisions relating to age which are of a description specified by order by a Minister of the Crown.
(9) An order authorising the use of rules, practices, actions or decisions which are not in use before the order comes into force must not be made unless the Minister consults such persons as the Minister thinks appropriate.
(10) A non-discrimination rule does not have effect in relation to an occupational pension scheme in so far as an equality rule has effect in relation to it (or would have effect in relation to it but for Part 2 of Schedule 7).
(11) A duty to make reasonable adjustments applies to a responsible person.

NOTES

Orders: the Equality Act (Age Exceptions for Pension Schemes) Order 2010, SI 2010/2133 at **[2.1204]**; the Equality Act (Age Exceptions for Pension Schemes) (Amendment) Order 2010, SI 2010/2285.

[1.1670]
62 Non-discrimination alterations

(1) This section applies if the trustees or managers of an occupational pension scheme do not have power to make non-discrimination alterations to the scheme.
(2) This section also applies if the trustees or managers of an occupational pension scheme have power to make non-discrimination alterations to the scheme but the procedure for doing so—
- (a) is liable to be unduly complex or protracted, or
- (b) involves obtaining consents which cannot be obtained or which can be obtained only with undue delay or difficulty.

(3) The trustees or managers may by resolution make non-discrimination alterations to the scheme.
(4) Non-discrimination alterations may have effect in relation to a period before the date on which they are made.

(5) Non-discrimination alterations to an occupational pension scheme are such alterations to the scheme as may be required for the provisions of the scheme to have the effect that they have in consequence of section 61(3).

[1.1671]

63 Communications

(1) In their application to communications the following provisions apply in relation to a disabled person who is a pension credit member of an occupational pension scheme as they apply in relation to a disabled person who is a deferred member or pensioner member of the scheme—

(a) section 61;

(b) section 120;

(c) section 126;

(d) paragraph 19 of Schedule 8 (and such other provisions of that Schedule as apply for the purposes of that paragraph).

(2) Communications include—

(a) the provision of information;

(b) the operation of a dispute resolution procedure.

CHAPTER 3 EQUALITY OF TERMS

Sex equality

[1.1672]

64 Relevant types of work

(1) Sections 66 to 70 apply where—

(a) a person (A) is employed on work that is equal to the work that a comparator of the opposite sex (B) does;

(b) a person (A) holding a personal or public office does work that is equal to the work that a comparator of the opposite sex (B) does.

(2) The references in subsection (1) to the work that B does are not restricted to work done contemporaneously with the work done by A.

[1.1673]

65 Equal work

(1) For the purposes of this Chapter, A's work is equal to that of B if it is—

(a) like B's work,

(b) rated as equivalent to B's work, or

(c) of equal value to B's work.

(2) A's work is like B's work if—

(a) A's work and B's work are the same or broadly similar, and

(b) such differences as there are between their work are not of practical importance in relation to the terms of their work.

(3) So on a comparison of one person's work with another's for the purposes of subsection (2), it is necessary to have regard to—

(a) the frequency with which differences between their work occur in practice, and

(b) the nature and extent of the differences.

(4) A's work is rated as equivalent to B's work if a job evaluation study—

(a) gives an equal value to A's job and B's job in terms of the demands made on a worker, or

(b) would give an equal value to A's job and B's job in those terms were the evaluation not made on a sex-specific system.

(5) A system is sex-specific if, for the purposes of one or more of the demands made on a worker, it sets values for men different from those it sets for women.

(6) A's work is of equal value to B's work if it is—

(a) neither like B's work nor rated as equivalent to B's work, but

(b) nevertheless equal to B's work in terms of the demands made on A by reference to factors such as effort, skill and decision-making.

[1.1674]

66 Sex equality clause

(1) If the terms of A's work do not (by whatever means) include a sex equality clause, they are to be treated as including one.

(2) A sex equality clause is a provision that has the following effect—

(a) if a term of A's is less favourable to A than a corresponding term of B's is to B, A's term is modified so as not to be less favourable;

(b) if A does not have a term which corresponds to a term of B's that benefits B, A's terms are modified so as to include such a term.

(3) Subsection (2)(a) applies to a term of A's relating to membership of or rights under an occupational pension scheme only in so far as a sex equality rule would have effect in relation to the term.

(4) In the case of work within section 65(1)(b), a reference in subsection (2) above to a term includes a reference to such terms (if any) as have not been determined by the rating of the work (as well as those that have).

[1.1675]

67 Sex equality rule

(1) If an occupational pension scheme does not include a sex equality rule, it is to be treated as including one.

(2) A sex equality rule is a provision that has the following effect—

(a) if a relevant term is less favourable to A than it is to B, the term is modified so as not to be less favourable;

(b) if a term confers a relevant discretion capable of being exercised in a way that would be less favourable to A than to B, the term is modified so as to prevent the exercise of the discretion in that way.

(3) A term is relevant if it is—

(a) a term on which persons become members of the scheme, or

(b) a term on which members of the scheme are treated.

(4) A discretion is relevant if its exercise in relation to the scheme is capable of affecting—

(a) the way in which persons become members of the scheme, or

(b) the way in which members of the scheme are treated.

(5) The reference in subsection (3)(b) to a term on which members of a scheme are treated includes a reference to the term as it has effect for the benefit of dependants of members.

(6) The reference in subsection (4)(b) to the way in which members of a scheme are treated includes a reference to the way in which they are treated as the scheme has effect for the benefit of dependants of members.

[(7) If the effect of a relevant matter on a person (A) differs according to the effect it has on a person of the same sex as A, according to whether A is married, in a civil partnership, or for some other reason due to A's family status, a comparison for the purposes of this section of the effect of that matter on persons of the opposite sex must be with a person of the opposite sex to A who is in the same position as A and in particular—

(a) where A is married to someone of the opposite sex, A is to be compared to a person of the opposite sex to A ("B") where B is married to someone of the opposite sex to B;

(b) where A is married to someone of the same sex as A or is in a civil partnership, A is to be compared to B where B is married to someone of the same sex as B or is in a civil partnership.]

(8) A relevant matter is—

(a) a relevant term;

(b) a term conferring a relevant discretion;

(c) the exercise of a relevant discretion in relation to an occupational pension scheme.

(9) This section, so far as relating to the terms on which persons become members of an occupational pension scheme, does not have effect in relation to pensionable service before 8 April 1976.

(10) This section, so far as relating to the terms on which members of an occupational pension scheme are treated, does not have effect in relation to pensionable service before 17 May 1990.

NOTES

Sub-s (7): substituted, in relation to England and Wales, by the Marriage (Same Sex Couples) Act 2013 (Consequential and Contrary Provisions and Scotland) Order 2014, SI 2014/560, art 2, Sch 1, para 35(1), (2). Note that an identical substitution was also made by the Marriage and Civil Partnership (Scotland) Act 2014 and Civil Partnership Act 2004 (Consequential Provisions and Modifications) Order 2014, SI 2014/3229, art 29, Sch 5, para 19(1), (2), as from 16 December 2014. The relevant provision of SI 2014/3229 extends to England, Wales and Scotland.

[1.1676]

68 Sex equality rule: consequential alteration of schemes

(1) This section applies if the trustees or managers of an occupational pension scheme do not have power to make sex equality alterations to the scheme.

(2) This section also applies if the trustees or managers of an occupational pension scheme have power to make sex equality alterations to the scheme but the procedure for doing so—

(a) is liable to be unduly complex or protracted, or

(b) involves obtaining consents which cannot be obtained or which can be obtained only with undue delay or difficulty.

(3) The trustees or managers may by resolution make sex equality alterations to the scheme.

(4) Sex equality alterations may have effect in relation to a period before the date on which they are made.

(5) Sex equality alterations to an occupational pension scheme are such alterations to the scheme as may be required to secure conformity with a sex equality rule.

[1.1677]

69 Defence of material factor

(1) The sex equality clause in A's terms has no effect in relation to a difference between A's terms and B's terms if the responsible person shows that the difference is because of a material factor reliance on which—

(a) does not involve treating A less favourably because of A's sex than the responsible person treats B, and

(b) if the factor is within subsection (2), is a proportionate means of achieving a legitimate aim.

(2) A factor is within this subsection if A shows that, as a result of the factor, A and persons of the same sex doing work equal to A's are put at a particular disadvantage when compared with persons of the opposite sex doing work equal to A's.

(3) For the purposes of subsection (1), the long-term objective of reducing inequality between men's and women's terms of work is always to be regarded as a legitimate aim.
(4) A sex equality rule has no effect in relation to a difference between A and B in the effect of a relevant matter if the trustees or managers of the scheme in question show that the difference is because of a material factor which is not the difference of sex.
(5) "Relevant matter" has the meaning given in section 67.
(6) For the purposes of this section, a factor is not material unless it is a material difference between A's case and B's.

[1.1678]
70 Exclusion of sex discrimination provisions
(1) The relevant sex discrimination provision has no effect in relation to a term of A's that—
(a) is modified by, or included by virtue of, a sex equality clause or rule, or
(b) would be so modified or included but for section 69 or Part 2 of Schedule 7.
(2) Neither of the following is sex discrimination for the purposes of the relevant sex discrimination provision—
(a) the inclusion in A's terms of a term that is less favourable as referred to in section 66(2)(a);
(b) the failure to include in A's terms a corresponding term as referred to in section 66(2)(b).
(3) The relevant sex discrimination provision is, in relation to work of a description given in the first column of the table, the provision referred to in the second column so far as relating to sex.

Description of work	Provision
Employment	Section 39(2)
Appointment to a personal office	Section 49(6)
Appointment to a public office	Section 50(6)

[1.1679]
71 Sex discrimination in relation to contractual pay
(1) This section applies in relation to a term of a person's work—
(a) that relates to pay, but
(b) in relation to which a sex equality clause or rule has no effect.
(2) The relevant sex discrimination provision (as defined by section 70) has no effect in relation to the term except in so far as treatment of the person amounts to a contravention of the provision by virtue of section 13 or 14.

Pregnancy and maternity equality

[1.1680]
72 Relevant types of work
Sections 73 to 76 apply where a woman—
(a) is employed, or
(b) holds a personal or public office.

[1.1681]
73 Maternity equality clause
(1) If the terms of the woman's work do not (by whatever means) include a maternity equality clause, they are to be treated as including one.
(2) A maternity equality clause is a provision that, in relation to the terms of the woman's work, has the effect referred to in section 74(1), (6) and (8).
(3) In the case of a term relating to membership of or rights under an occupational pension scheme, a maternity equality clause has only such effect as a maternity equality rule would have.

[1.1682]
74 Maternity equality clause: pay
(1) A term of the woman's work that provides for maternity-related pay to be calculated by reference to her pay at a particular time is, if each of the following three conditions is satisfied, modified as mentioned in subsection (5).
(2) The first condition is that, after the time referred to in subsection (1) but before the end of the protected period—
(a) her pay increases, or
(b) it would have increased had she not been on maternity leave.
(3) The second condition is that the maternity-related pay is not—
(a) what her pay would have been had she not been on maternity leave, or
(b) the difference between the amount of statutory maternity pay to which she is entitled and what her pay would have been had she not been on maternity leave.
(4) The third condition is that the terms of her work do not provide for the maternity-related pay to be subject to—
(a) an increase as mentioned in subsection (2)(a), or
(b) an increase that would have occurred as mentioned in subsection (2)(b).
(5) The modification referred to in subsection (1) is a modification to provide for the maternity-related pay to be subject to—
(a) any increase as mentioned in subsection (2)(a), or
(b) any increase that would have occurred as mentioned in subsection (2)(b).

(6) A term of her work that—
(a) provides for pay within subsection (7), but
(b) does not provide for her to be given the pay in circumstances in which she would have been given it had she not been on maternity leave,

is modified so as to provide for her to be given it in circumstances in which it would normally be given.

(7) Pay is within this subsection if it is—
(a) pay (including pay by way of bonus) in respect of times before the woman is on maternity leave,
(b) pay by way of bonus in respect of times when she is on compulsory maternity leave, or
(c) pay by way of bonus in respect of times after the end of the protected period.

(8) A term of the woman's work that—
(a) provides for pay after the end of the protected period, but
(b) does not provide for it to be subject to an increase to which it would have been subject had she not been on maternity leave,

is modified so as to provide for it to be subject to the increase.

(9) Maternity-related pay is pay (other than statutory maternity pay) to which a woman is entitled—
(a) as a result of being pregnant, or
(b) in respect of times when she is on maternity leave.

(10) A reference to the protected period is to be construed in accordance with section 18.

[1.1683]
75 Maternity equality rule

(1) If an occupational pension scheme does not include a maternity equality rule, it is to be treated as including one.

(2) A maternity equality rule is a provision that has the effect set out in subsections (3) and (4).

(3) If a relevant term does not treat time when the woman is on maternity leave as it treats time when she is not, the term is modified so as to treat time when she is on maternity leave as time when she is not.

(4) If a term confers a relevant discretion capable of being exercised so that time when she is on maternity leave is treated differently from time when she is not, the term is modified so as not to allow the discretion to be exercised in that way.

(5) A term is relevant if it is—
(a) a term relating to membership of the scheme,
(b) a term relating to the accrual of rights under the scheme, or
(c) a term providing for the determination of the amount of a benefit payable under the scheme.

(6) A discretion is relevant if its exercise is capable of affecting—
(a) membership of the scheme,
(b) the accrual of rights under the scheme, or
(c) the determination of the amount of a benefit payable under the scheme.

(7) This section does not require the woman's contributions to the scheme in respect of time when she is on maternity leave to be determined otherwise than by reference to the amount she is paid in respect of that time.

(8) This section, so far as relating to time when she is on ordinary maternity leave but is not being paid by her employer, applies only in a case where the expected week of childbirth began on or after 6 April 2003.

(9) This section, so far as relating to time when she is on additional maternity leave but is not being paid by her employer—
(a) does not apply to the accrual of rights under the scheme in any case;
(b) applies for other purposes only in a case where the expected week of childbirth began on or after 5 October 2008.

(10) In this section—
(a) a reference to being on maternity leave includes a reference to having been on maternity leave, and
(b) a reference to being paid by the employer includes a reference to receiving statutory maternity pay from the employer.

[1.1684]
76 Exclusion of pregnancy and maternity discrimination provisions

(1) The relevant pregnancy and maternity discrimination provision has no effect in relation to a term of the woman's work that is modified by a maternity equality clause or rule.

[(1A) The relevant pregnancy and maternity discrimination provision has no effect in relation to a term of the woman's work—
(a) that relates to pay, but
(b) in relation to which a maternity equality clause or rule has no effect.]

(2) The inclusion in the woman's terms of a term that requires modification by virtue of section 73(2) or (3) is not pregnancy and maternity discrimination for the purposes of the relevant pregnancy and maternity discrimination provision.

(3) The relevant pregnancy and maternity discrimination provision is, in relation to a description of work given in the first column of the table, the provision referred to in the second column so far as relating to pregnancy and maternity.

Description of work	***Provision***
Employment	Section 39(2)

Description of work	Provision
Appointment to a personal office	Section 49(6)
Appointment to a public office	Section 50(6)

NOTES

Sub-s (1A): inserted by the Equality Act 2010 (Amendment) Order 2010, SI 2010/2622, art 2.

Disclosure of information

[1.1685]

77 Discussions about pay

(1) A term of a person's work that purports to prevent or restrict the person (P) from disclosing or seeking to disclose information about the terms of P's work is unenforceable against P in so far as P makes or seeks to make a relevant pay disclosure.

(2) A term of a person's work that purports to prevent or restrict the person (P) from seeking disclosure of information from a colleague about the terms of the colleague's work is unenforceable against P in so far as P seeks a relevant pay disclosure from the colleague; and "colleague" includes a former colleague in relation to the work in question.

(3) A disclosure is a relevant pay disclosure if made for the purpose of enabling the person who makes it, or the person to whom it is made, to find out whether or to what extent there is, in relation to the work in question, a connection between pay and having (or not having) a particular protected characteristic.

(4) The following are to be treated as protected acts for the purposes of the relevant victimisation provision—

(a) seeking a disclosure that would be a relevant pay disclosure;
(b) making or seeking to make a relevant pay disclosure;
(c) receiving information disclosed in a relevant pay disclosure.

(5) The relevant victimisation provision is, in relation to a description of work specified in the first column of the table, section 27 so far as it applies for the purposes of a provision mentioned in the second column.

Description of work	Provision by virtue of which section 27 has effect
Employment	Section 39(3) or (4)
Appointment to a personal office	Section 49(5) or (8)
Appointment to a public office	Section 50(5) or (9)

[1.1686]

78 Gender pay gap information

(1) Regulations may require employers to publish information relating to the pay of employees for the purpose of showing whether, by reference to factors of such description as is prescribed, there are differences in the pay of male and female employees.

(2) This section does not apply to—

(a) an employer who has fewer than 250 employees;
(b) a person specified in Schedule 19;
(c) a government department or part of the armed forces not specified in that Schedule.

(3) The regulations may prescribe—

(a) descriptions of employer;
(b) descriptions of employee;
(c) how to calculate the number of employees that an employer has;
(d) descriptions of information;
(e) the time at which information is to be published;
(f) the form and manner in which it is to be published.

(4) Regulations under subsection (3)(e) may not require an employer, after the first publication of information, to publish information more frequently than at intervals of 12 months.

(5) The regulations may make provision for a failure to comply with the regulations—

(a) to be an offence punishable on summary conviction by a fine not exceeding level 5 on the standard scale;
(b) to be enforced, otherwise than as an offence, by such means as are prescribed.

(6) The reference to a failure to comply with the regulations includes a reference to a failure by a person acting on behalf of an employer.

NOTES

Commencement: 22 August 2016.

Regulations: the Equality Act 2010 (Gender Pay Gap Information) Regulations 2017, SI 2017/172 at **[2.1978]**.

Supplementary

[1.1687]

79 Comparators

(1) This section applies for the purposes of this Chapter.

(2) If A is employed, B is a comparator if subsection (3) or (4) applies.

(3) This subsection applies if—

(a) B is employed by A's employer or by an associate of A's employer, and
(b) A and B work at the same establishment.

(4) This subsection applies if—
(a) B is employed by A's employer or an associate of A's employer,
(b) B works at an establishment other than the one at which A works, and
(c) common terms apply at the establishments (either generally or as between A and B).

(5) If A holds a personal or public office, B is a comparator if—
(a) B holds a personal or public office, and
(b) the person responsible for paying A is also responsible for paying B.

(6) If A is a relevant member of the House of Commons staff, B is a comparator if—
(a) B is employed by the person who is A's employer under subsection (6) of section 195 of the Employment Rights Act 1996, or
(b) if subsection (7) of that section applies in A's case, B is employed by the person who is A's employer under that subsection.

(7) If A is a relevant member of the House of Lords staff, B is a comparator if B is also a relevant member of the House of Lords staff.

(8) Section 42 does not apply to this Chapter; accordingly, for the purposes of this Chapter only, holding the office of constable is to be treated as holding a personal office.

(9) For the purposes of this section, employers are associated if—
(a) one is a company of which the other (directly or indirectly) has control, or
(b) both are companies of which a third person (directly or indirectly) has control.

[1.1688]

80 Interpretation and exceptions

(1) This section applies for the purposes of this Chapter.

(2) The terms of a person's work are—
(a) if the person is employed, the terms of the person's employment that are in the person's contract of employment, contract of apprenticeship or contract to do work personally;
(b) if the person holds a personal or public office, the terms of the person's appointment to the office.

(3) If work is not done at an establishment, it is to be treated as done at the establishment with which it has the closest connection.

(4) A person (P) is the responsible person in relation to another person if—
(a) P is the other's employer;
(b) P is responsible for paying remuneration in respect of a personal or public office that the other holds.

(5) A job evaluation study is a study undertaken with a view to evaluating, in terms of the demands made on a person by reference to factors such as effort, skill and decision-making, the jobs to be done—
(a) by some or all of the workers in an undertaking or group of undertakings, or
(b) in the case of the armed forces, by some or all of the members of the armed forces.

(6) In the case of Crown employment, the reference in subsection (5)(a) to an undertaking is to be construed in accordance with section 191(4) of the Employment Rights Act 1996.

(7) . . .

(8) Schedule 7 (exceptions) has effect.

NOTES

Sub-s (7): repealed, in relation to England and Wales, by the Marriage (Same Sex Couples) Act 2013 (Consequential and Contrary Provisions and Scotland) Order 2014, SI 2014/560, art 2, Sch 1, para 35(1), (3). Note that the same repeal was also made by the Marriage and Civil Partnership (Scotland) Act 2014 and Civil Partnership Act 2004 (Consequential Provisions and Modifications) Order 2014, SI 2014/3229, art 29, Sch 5, para 19(1), (3), as from 16 December 2014. The relevant provision of SI 2014/3229 extends to England, Wales and Scotland.

CHAPTER 4 SUPPLEMENTARY

[1.1689]

81 Ships and hovercraft

(1) This Part applies in relation to—
(a) work on ships,
(b) work on hovercraft, and
(c) seafarers,

only in such circumstances as are prescribed.

(2) For the purposes of this section, it does not matter whether employment arises or work is carried out within or outside the United Kingdom.

(3) "Ship" has the same meaning as in the Merchant Shipping Act 1995.

(4) "Hovercraft" has the same meaning as in the Hovercraft Act 1968.

(5) "Seafarer" means a person employed or engaged in any capacity on board a ship or hovercraft.

(6) Nothing in this section affects the application of any other provision of this Act to conduct outside England and Wales or Scotland.

NOTES

Regulations: the Equality Act 2010 (Work on Ships and Hovercraft) Regulations 2011, SI 2011/1771 at **[2.1246]**.

[1.1690]
82 Offshore work

(1) Her Majesty may by Order in Council provide that in the case of persons in offshore work—
(a) specified provisions of this Part apply (with or without modification);
(b) Northern Ireland legislation making provision for purposes corresponding to any of the purposes of this Part applies (with or without modification).

(2) The Order may—
(a) provide for these provisions, as applied by the Order, to apply to individuals (whether or not British citizens) and bodies corporate (whether or not incorporated under the law of a part of the United Kingdom), whether or not such application affects activities outside the United Kingdom;
(b) make provision for conferring jurisdiction on a specified court or class of court or on employment tribunals in respect of offences, causes of action or other matters arising in connection with offshore work;
(c) exclude from the operation of section 3 of the Territorial Waters Jurisdiction Act 1878 (consents required for prosecutions) proceedings for offences under the provisions mentioned in subsection (1) in connection with offshore work;
(d) provide that such proceedings must not be brought without such consent as may be required by the Order.

(3) "Offshore work" is work for the purposes of—
(a) activities in the territorial sea adjacent to the United Kingdom,
(b) activities such as are mentioned in subsection (2) of section 11 of the Petroleum Act 1998 in waters within subsection (8)(b) or (c) of that section, or
(c) activities mentioned in paragraphs (a) and (b) of section 87(1) of the Energy Act 2004 in waters to which that section applies.

(4) Work includes employment, contract work, a position as a partner or as a member of an LLP, or an appointment to a personal or public office.

(5) Northern Ireland legislation includes an enactment contained in, or in an instrument under, an Act that forms part of the law of Northern Ireland.

(6) In the application to Northern Ireland of subsection (2)(b), the reference to employment tribunals is to be read as a reference to industrial tribunals.

(7) Nothing in this section affects the application of any other provision of this Act to conduct outside England and Wales or Scotland.

NOTES

Orders: the Equality Act 2010 (Offshore Work) Order 2010, SI 2010/1835 at **[2.1180]**.

[1.1691]
83 Interpretation and exceptions

(1) This section applies for the purposes of this Part.

(2) "Employment" means—
(a) employment under a contract of employment, a contract of apprenticeship or a contract personally to do work;
(b) Crown employment;
(c) employment as a relevant member of the House of Commons staff;
(d) employment as a relevant member of the House of Lords staff.

(3) This Part applies to service in the armed forces as it applies to employment by a private person; and for that purpose—
(a) references to terms of employment, or to a contract of employment, are to be read as including references to terms of service;
(b) references to associated employers are to be ignored.

(4) A reference to an employer or an employee, or to employing or being employed, is (subject to section 212(11)) to be read with subsections (2) and (3); and a reference to an employer also includes a reference to a person who has no employees but is seeking to employ one or more other persons.

(5) "Relevant member of the House of Commons staff" has the meaning given in section 195 of the Employment Rights Act 1996; and such a member of staff is an employee of—
(a) the person who is the employer of that member under subsection (6) of that section, or
(b) if subsection (7) of that section applies in the case of that member, the person who is the employer of that member under that subsection.

(6) "Relevant member of the House of Lords staff" has the meaning given in section 194 of that Act (which provides that such a member of staff is an employee of the Corporate Officer of the House of Lords).

(7) In the case of a person in Crown employment, or in employment as a relevant member of the House of Commons staff, a reference to the person's dismissal is a reference to the termination of the person's employment.

(8) A reference to a personal or public office, or to an appointment to a personal or public office, is to be construed in accordance with section 52.

(9) "Crown employment" has the meaning given in section 191 of the Employment Rights Act 1996.

(10) Schedule 8 (reasonable adjustments) has effect.

(11) Schedule 9 (exceptions) has effect.

PART 6
EDUCATION

84–94 *(Ss 84–89 (Chapter 1: Schools) and ss 90–94 (Chapter 2: Further and Higher Education) are outside the scope of this work.)*

CHAPTER 3 GENERAL QUALIFICATIONS BODIES

[1.1692]
95 Application of this Chapter
This Chapter does not apply to the protected characteristic of marriage and civil partnership.

[1.1693]
96 Qualifications bodies
(1) A qualifications body (A) must not discriminate against a person (B)—
(a) in the arrangements A makes for deciding upon whom to confer a relevant qualification;
(b) as to the terms on which it is prepared to confer a relevant qualification on B;
(c) by not conferring a relevant qualification on B.
(2) A qualifications body (A) must not discriminate against a person (B) upon whom A has conferred a relevant qualification—
(a) by withdrawing the qualification from B;
(b) by varying the terms on which B holds the qualification;
(c) by subjecting B to any other detriment.
(3) A qualifications body must not, in relation to conferment by it of a relevant qualification, harass—
(a) a person who holds the qualification, or
(b) a person who applies for it.
(4) A qualifications body (A) must not victimise a person (B)—
(a) in the arrangements A makes for deciding upon whom to confer a relevant qualification;
(b) as to the terms on which it is prepared to confer a relevant qualification on B;
(c) by not conferring a relevant qualification on B.
(5) A qualifications body (A) must not victimise a person (B) upon whom A has conferred a relevant qualification—
(a) by withdrawing the qualification from B;
(b) by varying the terms on which B holds the qualification;
(c) by subjecting B to any other detriment.
(6) A duty to make reasonable adjustments applies to a qualifications body.
(7) Subsection (6) does not apply to the body in so far as the appropriate regulator specifies provisions, criteria or practices in relation to which the body—
(a) is not subject to a duty to make reasonable adjustments;
(b) is subject to a duty to make reasonable adjustments, but in relation to which such adjustments as the regulator specifies should not be made.
(8) For the purposes of subsection (7) the appropriate regulator must have regard to—
(a) the need to minimise the extent to which disabled persons are disadvantaged in attaining the qualification because of their disabilities;
(b) the need to secure that the qualification gives a reliable indication of the knowledge, skills and understanding of a person upon whom it is conferred;
(c) the need to maintain public confidence in the qualification.
(9) The appropriate regulator—
(a) must not specify any matter for the purposes of subsection (7) unless it has consulted such persons as it thinks appropriate;
(b) must publish matters so specified (including the date from which they are to have effect) in such manner as is prescribed.
(10) The appropriate regulator is—
(a) in relation to a qualifications body that confers qualifications in England, a person prescribed by a Minister of the Crown;
(b) in relation to a qualifications body that confers qualifications in Wales, a person prescribed by the Welsh Ministers;
(c) in relation to a qualifications body that confers qualifications in Scotland, a person prescribed by the Scottish Ministers.
(11) For the purposes of subsection (10), a qualification is conferred in a part of Great Britain if there are, or may reasonably be expected to be, persons seeking to obtain the qualification who are or will be assessed for those purposes wholly or mainly in that part.

NOTES
Regulations: the Equality Act 2010 (General Qualifications Bodies Regulator and Relevant Qualifications) (Wales) Regulations 2010, SI 2010/2217 at **[2.1214]**; the Equality Act 2010 (General Qualifications Bodies) (Appropriate Regulator and Relevant Qualifications) Regulations 2010, SI 2010/2245 at **[2.1221]**; the Equality Act 2010 (Qualifications Body Regulator and Relevant Qualifications) (Scotland) Regulations 2010, SSI 2010/315 at **[2.1218]**.

[1.1694]
97 Interpretation
(1) This section applies for the purposes of section 96.
(2) A qualifications body is an authority or body which can confer a relevant qualification.

(3) A relevant qualification is an authorisation, qualification, approval or certification of such description as may be prescribed—

(a) in relation to conferments in England, by a Minister of the Crown;
(b) in relation to conferments in Wales, by the Welsh Ministers;
(c) in relation to conferments in Scotland, by the Scottish Ministers.

(4) An authority or body is not a qualifications body in so far as—

(a) it is the responsible body of a school to which section 85 applies,
(b) it is the governing body of an institution to which section 91 applies,
(c) it exercises functions under the Education Acts, or
(d) it exercises functions under the Education (Scotland) Act 1980.

(5) A qualifications body does not include an authority or body of such description, or in such circumstances, as may be prescribed.

(6) A reference to conferring a relevant qualification includes a reference—

(a) to renewing or extending the conferment of a relevant qualification;
(b) to authenticating a relevant qualification conferred by another person.

(7) A reference in section 96(8), (10) or (11) to a qualification is a reference to a relevant qualification.

(8) Subsection (11) of section 96 applies for the purposes of subsection (3) of this section as it applies for the purposes of subsection (10) of that section.

NOTES

Regulations: the Equality Act 2010 (General Qualifications Bodies) (Appropriate Regulator and Relevant Qualifications) (Amendment) (England) Regulations 2017, SI 2017/705.

98–107 *(Ss 98, 99 (Chapter 4: Miscellaneous) and ss 100–107 (Part 7: Associations) are outside the scope of this work.)*

PART 8
PROHIBITED CONDUCT: ANCILLARY

[1.1695]
108 Relationships that have ended

(1) A person (A) must not discriminate against another (B) if—

(a) the discrimination arises out of and is closely connected to a relationship which used to exist between them, and
(b) conduct of a description constituting the discrimination would, if it occurred during the relationship, contravene this Act.

(2) A person (A) must not harass another (B) if—

(a) the harassment arises out of and is closely connected to a relationship which used to exist between them, and
(b) conduct of a description constituting the harassment would, if it occurred during the relationship, contravene this Act.

(3) It does not matter whether the relationship ends before or after the commencement of this section.

(4) A duty to make reasonable adjustments applies to A [if B is] placed at a substantial disadvantage as mentioned in section 20.

(5) For the purposes of subsection (4), sections 20, 21 and 22 and the applicable Schedules are to be construed as if the relationship had not ended.

(6) For the purposes of Part 9 (enforcement), a contravention of this section relates to the Part of this Act that would have been contravened if the relationship had not ended.

(7) But conduct is not a contravention of this section in so far as it also amounts to victimisation of B by A.

NOTES

Sub-s (4): words in square brackets substituted by the Equality Act 2010 (Consequential Amendments, Saving and Supplementary Provisions) Order 2010, SI 2010/2279, arts 2, 5.

Note that in *Rowstock Ltd v Jessemey* [2014] EWCA Civ 185, [2014] IRLR 368, [2014] ICR 550, the Court of Appeal (per Underhill LJ at para 48) held that sub-s (1) should be interpreted as if there were added at the end the words "In this section 'discrimination' includes 'victimisation'".

[1.1696]
109 Liability of employers and principals

(1) Anything done by a person (A) in the course of A's employment must be treated as also done by the employer.

(2) Anything done by an agent for a principal, with the authority of the principal, must be treated as also done by the principal.

(3) It does not matter whether that thing is done with the employer's or principal's knowledge or approval.

(4) In proceedings against A's employer (B) in respect of anything alleged to have been done by A in the course of A's employment it is a defence for B to show that B took all reasonable steps to prevent A—

(a) from doing that thing, or
(b) from doing anything of that description.

(5) This section does not apply to offences under this Act (other than offences under Part 12 (disabled persons: transport)).

[1.1697]

110 Liability of employees and agents

(1) A person (A) contravenes this section if—

(a) A is an employee or agent,

(b) A does something which, by virtue of section 109(1) or (2), is treated as having been done by A's employer or principal (as the case may be), and

(c) the doing of that thing by A amounts to a contravention of this Act by the employer or principal (as the case may be).

(2) It does not matter whether, in any proceedings, the employer is found not to have contravened this Act by virtue of section 109(4).

(3) A does not contravene this section if—

(a) A relies on a statement by the employer or principal that doing that thing is not a contravention of this Act, and

(b) it is reasonable for A to do so.

(4) A person (B) commits an offence if B knowingly or recklessly makes a statement mentioned in subsection (3)(a) which is false or misleading in a material respect.

(5) A person guilty of an offence under subsection (4) is liable on summary conviction to a fine not exceeding level 5 on the standard scale.

[(5A) A does not contravene this section if A—

(a) does not conduct a relevant marriage,

(b) is not present at, does not carry out, or does not otherwise participate in, a relevant marriage, or

(c) does not consent to a relevant marriage being conducted,

for the reason that the marriage is the marriage of a same sex couple.

(5B) Subsection (5A) applies to A only if A is within the meaning of "person" for the purposes of section 2 of the Marriage (Same Sex Couples) Act 2013; and other expressions used in subsection (5A) and section 2 of that Act have the same meanings in that subsection as in that section.]

[(5C) A does not contravene this section by refusing to solemnise a relevant Scottish marriage for the reason that the marriage is the marriage of two persons of the same sex.

(5D) A does not contravene this section by refusing to register a relevant Scottish civil partnership for the reason that the civil partnership is between two persons of the same sex.

(5E) Subsections (5C) and (5D) apply only if A is an approved celebrant.

(5F) Expressions used in subsections (5C) to (5E) have the same meaning as in paragraph 25B of Schedule 3.

(5G) A chaplain does not contravene this section by refusing to solemnise a relevant Scottish forces marriage for the reason that the marriage is the marriage of two persons of the same sex.

(5H) Expressions used in subsection (5G) have the same meaning as in paragraph 25C of Schedule 3.]

(6) Part 9 (enforcement) applies to a contravention of this section by A as if it were the contravention mentioned in subsection (1)(c).

(7) The reference in subsection (1)(c) to a contravention of this Act does not include a reference to disability discrimination in contravention of Chapter 1 of Part 6 (schools).

NOTES

Sub-ss (5A), (5B): inserted by the Marriage (Same Sex Couples) Act 2013, s 2(5).

Sub-ss (5C)–(5H): inserted by the Marriage and Civil Partnership (Scotland) Act 2014 and Civil Partnership Act 2004 (Consequential Provisions and Modifications) Order 2014, SI 2014/3229, art 29, Sch 5, para 19(1), (4), as from 16 December 2014.

[1.1698]

111 Instructing, causing or inducing contraventions

(1) A person (A) must not instruct another (B) to do in relation to a third person (C) anything which contravenes Part 3, 4, 5, 6 or 7 or section 108(1) or (2) or 112(1) (a basic contravention).

(2) A person (A) must not cause another (B) to do in relation to a third person (C) anything which is a basic contravention.

(3) A person (A) must not induce another (B) to do in relation to a third person (C) anything which is a basic contravention.

(4) For the purposes of subsection (3), inducement may be direct or indirect.

(5) Proceedings for a contravention of this section may be brought—

(a) by B, if B is subjected to a detriment as a result of A's conduct;

(b) by C, if C is subjected to a detriment as a result of A's conduct;

(c) by the Commission.

(6) For the purposes of subsection (5), it does not matter whether—

(a) the basic contravention occurs;

(b) any other proceedings are, or may be, brought in relation to A's conduct.

(7) This section does not apply unless the relationship between A and B is such that A is in a position to commit a basic contravention in relation to B.

(8) A reference in this section to causing or inducing a person to do something includes a reference to attempting to cause or induce the person to do it.

(9) For the purposes of Part 9 (enforcement), a contravention of this section is to be treated as relating—

(a) in a case within subsection (5)(a), to the Part of this Act which, because of the relationship between A and B, A is in a position to contravene in relation to B;

(b) in a case within subsection (5)(b), to the Part of this Act which, because of the relationship between B and C, B is in a position to contravene in relation to C.

[1.1699]
112 Aiding contraventions

(1) A person (A) must not knowingly help another (B) to do anything which contravenes Part 3, 4, 5, 6 or 7 or section 108(1) or (2) or 111 (a basic contravention).

(2) It is not a contravention of subsection (1) if—

(a) A relies on a statement by B that the act for which the help is given does not contravene this Act, and

(b) it is reasonable for A to do so.

(3) B commits an offence if B knowingly or recklessly makes a statement mentioned in subsection (2)(a) which is false or misleading in a material respect.

(4) A person guilty of an offence under subsection (3) is liable on summary conviction to a fine not exceeding level 5 on the standard scale.

(5) For the purposes of Part 9 (enforcement), a contravention of this section is to be treated as relating to the provision of this Act to which the basic contravention relates.

(6) The reference in subsection (1) to a basic contravention does not include a reference to disability discrimination in contravention of Chapter 1 of Part 6 (schools).

PART 9
ENFORCEMENT

CHAPTER 1 INTRODUCTORY

[1.1700]
113 Proceedings

(1) Proceedings relating to a contravention of this Act must be brought in accordance with this Part.

(2) Subsection (1) does not apply to proceedings under Part 1 of the Equality Act 2006.

(3) Subsection (1) does not prevent—

(a) a claim for judicial review;

(b) proceedings under the Immigration Acts;

(c) proceedings under the Special Immigration Appeals Commission Act 1997;

(d) in Scotland, an application to the supervisory jurisdiction of the Court of Session.

(4) This section is subject to any express provision of this Act conferring jurisdiction on a court or tribunal.

(5) The reference to a contravention of this Act includes a reference to a breach of an equality clause or rule.

(6) Chapters 2 and 3 do not apply to proceedings relating to an equality clause or rule except in so far as Chapter 4 provides for that.

(7) This section does not apply to—

(a) proceedings for an offence under this Act;

(b) proceedings relating to a penalty under Part 12 (disabled persons: transport).

CHAPTER 2 CIVIL COURTS

[1.1701]
114 Jurisdiction

(1) [The county court] or, in Scotland, the sheriff has jurisdiction to determine a claim relating to—

(a) a contravention of Part 3 (services and public functions);

(b) a contravention of Part 4 (premises);

(c) a contravention of Part 6 (education);

(d) a contravention of Part 7 (associations);

(e) a contravention of section 108, 111 or 112 that relates to Part 3, 4, 6 or 7.

(2) Subsection (1)(a) does not apply to a claim within section 115.

(3) Subsection (1)(c) does not apply to a claim within section 116.

(4) Subsection (1)(d) does not apply to a contravention of section 106.

(5) For the purposes of proceedings on a claim within subsection (1)(a)—

(a) a decision in proceedings on a claim mentioned in section 115(1) that an act is a contravention of Part 3 is binding;

(b) it does not matter whether the act occurs outside the United Kingdom.

(6) The county court or sheriff—

(a) must not grant an interim injunction or interdict unless satisfied that no criminal matter would be prejudiced by doing so;

(b) must grant an application to stay or sist proceedings under subsection (1) on grounds of prejudice to a criminal matter unless satisfied the matter will not be prejudiced.

(7) In proceedings in England and Wales on a claim within subsection (1), the power under section 63(1) of the County Courts Act 1984 (appointment of assessors) must be exercised unless the judge is satisfied that there are good reasons for not doing so.

(8) In proceedings in Scotland on a claim within subsection (1), the power under rule 44.3 of Schedule 1 to the Sheriff Court (Scotland) Act 1907 (appointment of assessors) must be exercised unless the sheriff is satisfied that there are good reasons for not doing so.

(9) The remuneration of an assessor appointed by virtue of subsection (8) is to be at a rate determined by the Lord President of the Court of Session.

NOTES

Sub-s (1): words in square brackets substituted by the Crime and Courts Act 2013, s 17(5), Sch 9, Pt 3, para 52.

115, 116 *(S 115 (Immigration cases) and s 116 (Education cases) are outside the scope of this work.)*

[1.1702]

117 National security

(1) Rules of court may, in relation to proceedings on a claim within section 114, confer power as mentioned in subsections (2) to (4); but a power so conferred is exercisable only if the court thinks it expedient to do so in the interests of national security.

(2) The rules may confer power to exclude from all or part of the proceedings—

(a) the claimant or pursuer;

(b) a representative of the claimant or pursuer;

(c) an assessor.

(3) The rules may confer power to permit a claimant, pursuer or representative who has been excluded to make a statement to the court before the commencement of the proceedings, or part of the proceedings, to which the exclusion relates.

(4) The rules may confer power to take steps to keep secret all or part of the reasons for the court's decision.

(5) The Attorney General or, in Scotland, the Advocate General for Scotland may appoint a person to represent the interests of a claimant or pursuer in, or in any part of, proceedings to which an exclusion by virtue of subsection (2)(a) or (b) relates.

(6) A person (P) may be appointed under subsection (5) only if—

(a) in relation to proceedings in England and Wales, P is a person who, for the purposes of the Legal Services Act 2007, is an authorised person in relation to an activity which constitutes the exercise of a right of audience or the conduct of litigation;

(b) in relation to proceedings in Scotland, P is an advocate or qualified to practice as a solicitor in Scotland.

(7) P is not responsible to the person whose interests P is appointed to represent.

NOTES

Subordinate Legislation: the Act of Sederunt (Sheriff Court Rules) (Equality Act 2010) 2010, SSI 2010/340.

[1.1703]

118 Time limits

(1) [Subject to [*sections 140A and* 140AA]] Proceedings on a claim within section 114 may not be brought after the end of—

(a) the period of 6 months starting with the date of the act to which the claim relates, or

(b) such other period as the county court or sheriff thinks just and equitable.

(2) If subsection (3) . . . applies, subsection (1)(a) has effect as if for "6 months" there were substituted "9 months".

(3) This subsection applies if—

(a) the claim relates to the act of a qualifying institution, and

(b) a complaint relating to the act is referred under the student complaints scheme before the end of the period of 6 months starting with the date of the act.

(4) . . .

(5) If it has been decided under the immigration provisions that the act of an immigration authority in taking a relevant decision is a contravention of Part 3 (services and public functions), subsection (1) has effect as if for paragraph (a) there were substituted—

"(a) the period of 6 months starting with the day after the expiry of the period during which, as a result of section 114(2), proceedings could not be brought in reliance on section 114(1)(a);".

(6) For the purposes of this section—

(a) conduct extending over a period is to be treated as done at the end of the period;

(b) failure to do something is to be treated as occurring when the person in question decided on it.

(7) In the absence of evidence to the contrary, a person (P) is to be taken to decide on failure to do something—

(a) when P does an act inconsistent with doing it, or

(b) if P does no inconsistent act, on the expiry of the period in which P might reasonably have been expected to do it.

(8) In this section—

"immigration authority", "immigration provisions" and "relevant decision" each have the meaning given in section 115;

"qualifying institution" has the meaning given in section 11 of the Higher Education Act 2004[, and includes an institution which is treated as continuing to be a qualifying institution for the purposes of Part 2 of that Act (see section 20A(2) of that Act)];

"the student complaints scheme" means a scheme for the review of qualifying complaints (within the meaning of section 12 of that Act) that is provided by the designated operator (within the meaning of section 13(5)(b) of that Act).

NOTES

Sub-s (1): words in first (outer) pair of square brackets inserted by the Cross-Border Mediation (EU Directive) Regulations 2011, SI 2011/1133, regs 54, 55; words in second (inner) pair of square brackets substituted by the Alternative Dispute Resolution for Consumer Disputes (Amendment) Regulations 2015, SI 2015/1392, reg 7(1), (2), as from 9 July 2015, in relation to cases where the contract to which the dispute relates was entered into on or after that date; for the words in italics there is substituted the word "section", by the Cross-Border Mediation (EU Directive) (EU Exit) Regulations 2019, SI 2019/469, reg 4, Sch 1, Pt 1, para 17(1), (2), as from exit day (as defined in the European Union (Withdrawal) Act 2018, s 20).

Sub-s (2): words omitted repealed by the Enterprise and Regulatory Reform Act 2013, s 64(12), (13)(a).

Sub-s (4): repealed by the Enterprise and Regulatory Reform Act 2013, s 64(12), (13)(b).

Sub-s (8): words in square brackets in the definition "qualifying institution" inserted by the Higher Education and Research Act 2017, s 89(6), as from 1 April 2018.

[1.1704]
119 Remedies

(1) This section applies if [the county court] or the sheriff finds that there has been a contravention of a provision referred to in section 114(1).

(2) The county court has power to grant any remedy which could be granted by the High Court—
   (a) in proceedings in tort;
   (b) on a claim for judicial review.

(3) The sheriff has power to make any order which could be made by the Court of Session—
   (a) in proceedings for reparation;
   (b) on a petition for judicial review.

(4) An award of damages may include compensation for injured feelings (whether or not it includes compensation on any other basis).

(5) Subsection (6) applies if the county court or sheriff—
   (a) finds that a contravention of a provision referred to in section 114(1) is established by virtue of section 19, but
   (b) is satisfied that the provision, criterion or practice was not applied with the intention of discriminating against the claimant or pursuer.

(6) The county court or sheriff must not make an award of damages unless it first considers whether to make any other disposal.

(7) The county court or sheriff must not grant a remedy other than an award of damages or the making of a declaration unless satisfied that no criminal matter would be prejudiced by doing so.

NOTES

Sub-s (1): words in square brackets substituted by the Crime and Courts Act 2013, s 17(5), Sch 9, Pt 3, para 52.

CHAPTER 3 EMPLOYMENT TRIBUNALS

[1.1705]
120 Jurisdiction

(1) An employment tribunal has, subject to section 121, jurisdiction to determine a complaint relating to—
   (a) a contravention of Part 5 (work);
   (b) a contravention of section 108, 111 or 112 that relates to Part 5.

(2) An employment tribunal has jurisdiction to determine an application by a responsible person (as defined by section 61) for a declaration as to the rights of that person and a worker in relation to a dispute about the effect of a non-discrimination rule.

(3) An employment tribunal also has jurisdiction to determine an application by the trustees or managers of an occupational pension scheme for a declaration as to their rights and those of a member in relation to a dispute about the effect of a non-discrimination rule.

(4) An employment tribunal also has jurisdiction to determine a question that—
   (a) relates to a non-discrimination rule, and
   (b) is referred to the tribunal by virtue of section 122.

(5) In proceedings before an employment tribunal on a complaint relating to a breach of a non-discrimination rule, the employer—
   (a) is to be treated as a party, and
   (b) is accordingly entitled to appear and be heard.

(6) Nothing in this section affects such jurisdiction as the High Court, [the county court], the Court of Session or the sheriff has in relation to a non-discrimination rule.

(7) Subsection (1)(a) does not apply to a contravention of section 53 in so far as the act complained of may, by virtue of an enactment, be subject to an appeal or proceedings in the nature of an appeal.

(8) In subsection (1), the references to Part 5 do not include a reference to section 60(1).

NOTES

Sub-s (6): words in square brackets substituted by the Crime and Courts Act 2013, s 17(5), Sch 9, Pt 3, para 52.

Tribunal jurisdiction: the Employment Act 2002, s 38 applies to proceedings before the employment tribunal relating to a claim under this section; see s 38(1) of, and Sch 5 to, the 2002 Act at **[1.1279]**, **[1.1287]**. See also the Trade Union and Labour Relations (Consolidation) Act 1992, s 207A at **[1.524]** (as inserted by the Employment Act 2008). That section provides that in proceedings before an employment tribunal relating to a claim by an employee under any of the jurisdictions listed in Sch A2 to the 1992 Act at **[1.704]** (which includes this section) the tribunal may adjust any award given if the employer or the employee has unreasonably failed to comply with a relevant Code of Practice as defined by s 207A(4). See also the revised Acas Code of Practice 1 – Disciplinary and Grievance Procedures (2015) at **[4.1]**, and the Acas Code of Practice 4 – Settlement Agreements (2013) at **[4.54]**.

Conciliation: employment tribunal proceedings under this section are "relevant proceedings" for the purposes of the conciliation provisions contained in the Employment Tribunals Act 1996, ss 18–18C; see s 18(1)(e) of the 1996 Act at **[1.757]**.

[1.1706]

121 Armed forces cases

(1) Section 120(1) does not apply to a complaint relating to an act done when the complainant was serving as a member of the armed forces unless—

(a) the complainant has made a service complaint about the matter, and

(b) the complaint has not been withdrawn.

[(2) Where the complaint is dealt with by a person or panel appointed by the Defence Council by virtue of section 340C(1)(a) of the 2006 Act, it is to be treated for the purposes of subsection (1)(b) as withdrawn if—

(a) the period allowed in accordance with service complaints regulations for bringing an appeal against the person's or panel's decision expires, and

(b) either—

(i) the complainant does not apply to the Service Complaints Ombudsman for a review by virtue of section 340D(6) of the 2006 Act (review of decision that appeal brought out of time cannot proceed), or

(ii) the complainant does apply for such a review and the Ombudsman decides that an appeal against the person's or panel's decision cannot be proceeded with.]

(3), (4) . . .

(5) The making of a complaint to an employment tribunal in reliance on subsection (1) does not affect the continuation of [the procedures set out in service complaints regulations].

[(6) In this section—

"the 2006 Act" means the Armed Forces Act 2006;

"service complaints regulations" means regulations made under section 340B(1) of the 2006 Act.6

NOTES

Sub-s (2): substituted by the Armed Forces (Service Complaints and Financial Assistance) Act 2015, s 3, Schedule, paras 12, 13(1), (2), as from 1 January 2016 (subject to transitional provisions as noted below).

Sub-ss (3), (4): repealed by the Armed Forces (Service Complaints and Financial Assistance) Act 2015, s 3, Schedule, paras 12, 13(1), (3), as from 1 January 2016 (subject to transitional provisions as noted below).

Sub-s (5): words in square brackets substituted by the Armed Forces (Service Complaints and Financial Assistance) Act 2015, s 3, Schedule, paras 12, 13(1), (4), as from 1 January 2016 (subject to transitional provisions as noted below).

Sub-s (6): added by the Armed Forces (Service Complaints and Financial Assistance) Act 2015, s 3, Schedule, paras 12, 13(1), (5), as from 1 January 2016 (subject to transitional provisions as noted below).

Transitional provisions: the Armed Forces (Service Complaints and Financial Assistance) Act 2015 (Transitional and Savings Provisions) Regulations 2015, SI 2015/1969, reg 18 provides that the amendments and revocations made by s 3 of, and the Schedule to, the Armed Forces (Service Complaints and Financial Assistance) Act 2015 are of no effect in relation to a pre-commencement complaint (except a "Part 3 complaint"). See further reg 2 of the 2015 Regulations (interpretation).

[1.1707]

122 References by court to tribunal, etc

(1) If it appears to a court in which proceedings are pending that a claim or counter-claim relating to a non-discrimination rule could more conveniently be determined by an employment tribunal, the court may strike out the claim or counter-claim.

(2) If in proceedings before a court a question arises about a non-discrimination rule, the court may (whether or not on an application by a party to the proceedings)—

(a) refer the question, or direct that it be referred by a party to the proceedings, to an employment tribunal for determination, and

(b) stay or sist the proceedings in the meantime.

[1.1708]

123 Time limits

(1) [Subject to [*sections 140A and* 140B],] Proceedings on a complaint within section 120 may not be brought after the end of—

(a) the period of 3 months starting with the date of the act to which the complaint relates, or

(b) such other period as the employment tribunal thinks just and equitable.

(2) Proceedings may not be brought in reliance on section 121(1) after the end of—

(a) the period of 6 months starting with the date of the act to which the proceedings relate, or

(b) such other period as the employment tribunal thinks just and equitable.

(3) For the purposes of this section—

(a) conduct extending over a period is to be treated as done at the end of the period;

(b) failure to do something is to be treated as occurring when the person in question decided on it.

(4) In the absence of evidence to the contrary, a person (P) is to be taken to decide on failure to do something—

(a) when P does an act inconsistent with doing it, or

(b) if P does no inconsistent act, on the expiry of the period in which P might reasonably have been expected to do it.

NOTES

Sub-s (1): words in first (outer) pair of square brackets inserted by the Cross-Border Mediation (EU Directive) Regulations 2011, SI 2011/1133, regs 54, 56; words in second (inner) pair of square brackets substituted by the Enterprise and Regulatory Reform Act 2013, s 8, Sch 2, paras 42, 43; for the words in italics there is substituted the word "section", by the Cross-Border Mediation (EU Directive) (EU Exit) Regulations 2019, SI 2019/469, reg 4, Sch 1, Pt 1, para 17(1), (3), as from exit day (as defined in the European Union (Withdrawal) Act 2018, s 20).

[1.1709]

124 Remedies: general

(1) This section applies if an employment tribunal finds that there has been a contravention of a provision referred to in section 120(1).

(2) The tribunal may—

(a) make a declaration as to the rights of the complainant and the respondent in relation to the matters to which the proceedings relate;

(b) order the respondent to pay compensation to the complainant;

(c) make an appropriate recommendation.

(3) An appropriate recommendation is a recommendation that within a specified period the respondent takes specified steps for the purpose of obviating or reducing the adverse effect [on the complainant] of any matter to which the proceedings relate—

(a), (b) . . .

(4) Subsection (5) applies if the tribunal—

(a) finds that a contravention is established by virtue of section 19, but

(b) is satisfied that the provision, criterion or practice was not applied with the intention of discriminating against the complainant.

(5) It must not make an order under subsection (2)(b) unless it first considers whether to act under subsection (2)(a) or (c).

(6) The amount of compensation which may be awarded under subsection (2)(b) corresponds to the amount which could be awarded by [the county court] or the sheriff under section 119.

(7) If a respondent fails, without reasonable excuse, to comply with an appropriate recommendation . . . , the tribunal may—

(a) if an order was made under subsection (2)(b), increase the amount of compensation to be paid;

(b) if no such order was made, make one.

NOTES

Sub-s (3): words in square brackets inserted, and paras (a), (b) repealed, by the Deregulation Act 2015, s 2(1), as from 1 October 2015, subject to transitional provisions in the Deregulation Act 2015 (Commencement No 1 and Transitional and Saving Provisions) Order 2015, SI 2015/994, Schedule, which provide that the amendments made by s 2 of the 2015 Act do not affect ss 124 and 125 of this Act as they apply to proceedings that are commenced before 1 October 2015.

Sub-s (6): words in square brackets substituted by the Crime and Courts Act 2013, s 17(5), Sch 9, Pt 3, para 52.

Sub-s (7): words omitted repealed by the Deregulation Act 2015, s 2(2)(a), as from 1 October 2015 (subject to transitional provisions as noted above).

125 *(Repealed by the Deregulation Act 2015, s 2(2)(b), as from 1 October 2015, subject to transitional provisions in the Deregulation Act 2015 (Commencement No 1 and Transitional and Saving Provisions) Order 2015, SI 2015/994, Schedule, which provide that the amendments made by s 2 of the 2015 Act do not affect ss 124 and 125 of this Act as they apply to proceedings that are commenced before 1 October 2015.)*

[1.1710]

126 Remedies: occupational pension schemes

(1) This section applies if an employment tribunal finds that there has been a contravention of a provision referred to in section 120(1) in relation to—

(a) the terms on which persons become members of an occupational pension scheme, or

(b) the terms on which members of an occupational pension scheme are treated.

(2) In addition to anything which may be done by the tribunal under section 124 the tribunal may also by order declare—

(a) if the complaint relates to the terms on which persons become members of a scheme, that the complainant has a right to be admitted to the scheme;

(b) if the complaint relates to the terms on which members of the scheme are treated, that the complainant has a right to membership of the scheme without discrimination.

(3) The tribunal may not make an order under subsection (2)(b) of section 124 unless—

(a) the compensation is for injured feelings, or

(b) the order is made by virtue of subsection (7) of that section.

(4) An order under subsection (2)—

(a) may make provision as to the terms on which or the capacity in which the claimant is to enjoy the admission or membership;

(b) may have effect in relation to a period before the order is made.

CHAPTER 4 EQUALITY OF TERMS

[1.1711]

127 Jurisdiction

(1) An employment tribunal has, subject to subsection (6), jurisdiction to determine a complaint relating to a breach of an equality clause or rule.

(2) The jurisdiction conferred by subsection (1) includes jurisdiction to determine a complaint arising out of a breach of an equality clause or rule; and a reference in this Chapter to a complaint relating to such a breach is to be read accordingly.

(3) An employment tribunal also has jurisdiction to determine an application by a responsible person for a declaration as to the rights of that person and a worker in relation to a dispute about the effect of an equality clause or rule.

(4) An employment tribunal also has jurisdiction to determine an application by the trustees or managers of an occupational pension scheme for a declaration as to their rights and those of a member in relation to a dispute about the effect of an equality rule.

(5) An employment tribunal also has jurisdiction to determine a question that—

(a) relates to an equality clause or rule, and

(b) is referred to the tribunal by virtue of section 128(2).

(6) This section does not apply to a complaint relating to an act done when the complainant was serving as a member of the armed forces unless—

(a) the complainant has made a service complaint about the matter, and

(b) the complaint has not been withdrawn.

(7) [Subsections (2) to (6)] of section 121 apply for the purposes of subsection (6) of this section as they apply for the purposes of subsection (1) of that section.

(8) In proceedings before an employment tribunal on a complaint relating to a breach of an equality rule, the employer—

(a) is to be treated as a party, and

(b) is accordingly entitled to appear and be heard.

(9) Nothing in this section affects such jurisdiction as the High Court, [the county court], the Court of Session or the sheriff has in relation to an equality clause or rule.

NOTES

Sub-s (7): words in square brackets substituted by the Armed Forces (Service Complaints and Financial Assistance) Act 2015, s 3, Schedule, paras 12, 14, as from 1 January 2016 (for transitional provisions see the note to s 121 at **[1.1706]**).

Sub-s (9): words in square brackets substituted by the Crime and Courts Act 2013, s 17(5), Sch 9, Pt 3, para 52.

Tribunal jurisdiction: the Employment Act 2002, s 38 applies to proceedings before the employment tribunal relating to a claim under this section; see s 38(1) of, and Sch 5 to, the 2002 Act at **[1.1279]**, **[1.1287]**. See also the Trade Union and Labour Relations (Consolidation) Act 1992, s 207A at **[1.524]** (as inserted by the Employment Act 2008). That section provides that in proceedings before an employment tribunal relating to a claim by an employee under any of the jurisdictions listed in Sch A2 to the 1992 Act at **[1.704]** (which includes this section) the tribunal may adjust any award given if the employer or the employee has unreasonably failed to comply with a relevant Code of Practice as defined by s 207A(4). See also the revised Acas Code of Practice 1 – Disciplinary and Grievance Procedures (2015) at **[4.1]**, and the Acas Code of Practice 4 – Settlement Agreements (2013) at **[4.54]**.

Conciliation: employment tribunal proceedings under this section are "relevant proceedings" for the purposes of the conciliation provisions contained in the Employment Tribunals Act 1996, ss 18–18C; see s 18(1)(e) of the 1996 Act at **[1.757]**.

[1.1712]

128 References by court to tribunal, etc

(1) If it appears to a court in which proceedings are pending that a claim or counter-claim relating to an equality clause or rule could more conveniently be determined by an employment tribunal, the court may strike out the claim or counter-claim.

(2) If in proceedings before a court a question arises about an equality clause or rule, the court may (whether or not on an application by a party to the proceedings)—

(a) refer the question, or direct that it be referred by a party to the proceedings, to an employment tribunal for determination, and

(b) stay or sist the proceedings in the meantime.

[1.1713]

129 Time limits

(1) This section applies to—

(a) a complaint relating to a breach of an equality clause or rule;

(b) an application for a declaration referred to in section 127(3) or (4).

(2) Proceedings on the complaint or application may not be brought in an employment tribunal after the end of the qualifying period.

(3) If the complaint or application relates to terms of work other than terms of service in the armed forces, the qualifying period is, in a case mentioned in the first column of the table, the period mentioned in the second column[, subject to [*sections 140A and* 140B]].

Case	Qualifying period
A standard case	The period of 6 months beginning with the last day of the employment or appointment.

Case	Qualifying period
A stable work case (but not if it is also a concealment or incapacity case (or both))	The period of 6 months beginning with the day on which the stable working relationship ended.
A concealment case (but not if it is also an incapacity case)	The period of 6 months beginning with the day on which the worker discovered (or could with reasonable diligence have discovered) the qualifying fact.
An incapacity case (but not if it is also a concealment case)	The period of 6 months beginning with the day on which the worker ceased to have the incapacity.
A case which is a concealment case and an incapacity case.	The period of 6 months beginning with the later of the days on which the period would begin if the case were merely a concealment or incapacity case.

(4) If the complaint or application relates to terms of service in the armed forces, the qualifying period is, in a case mentioned in the first column of the table, the period mentioned in the second column[, subject to section 140B].

Case	Qualifying period
A standard case	The period of 9 months beginning with the last day of the period of service during which the complaint arose.
A concealment case (but not if it is also an incapacity case)	The period of 9 months beginning with the day on which the worker discovered (or could with reasonable diligence have discovered) the qualifying fact.
An incapacity case (but not if it is also a concealment case)	The period of 9 months beginning with the day on which the worker ceased to have the incapacity.
A case which is a concealment case and an incapacity case.	The period of 9 months beginning with the later of the days on which the period would begin if the case were merely a concealment or incapacity case.

NOTES

Sub-s (3): words in first (outer) pair of square brackets inserted by the Cross-Border Mediation (EU Directive) Regulations 2011, SI 2011/1133, regs 54, 57; words in second (inner) pair of square brackets substituted by the Enterprise and Regulatory Reform Act 2013, s 8, Sch 2, paras 42, 44(a); for the words in italics there is substituted the word "section", by the Cross-Border Mediation (EU Directive) (EU Exit) Regulations 2019, SI 2019/469, reg 4, Sch 1, Pt 1, para 17(1), (4), as from exit day (as defined in the European Union (Withdrawal) Act 2018, s 20).

Sub-s (4): words in square brackets inserted by the Enterprise and Regulatory Reform Act 2013, s 8, Sch 2, paras 42, 44(b).

[1.1714]
130 Section 129: supplementary

(1) This section applies for the purposes of section 129.

(2) A standard case is a case which is not—
- (a) a stable work case,
- (b) a concealment case,
- (c) an incapacity case, or
- (d) a concealment case and an incapacity case.

(3) A stable work case is a case where the proceedings relate to a period during which there was a stable working relationship between the worker and the responsible person (including any time after the terms of work had expired).

(4) A concealment case in proceedings relating to an equality clause is a case where—
- (a) the responsible person deliberately concealed a qualifying fact from the worker, and
- (b) the worker did not discover (or could not with reasonable diligence have discovered) the qualifying fact until after the relevant day.

(5) A concealment case in proceedings relating to an equality rule is a case where—
- (a) the employer or the trustees or managers of the occupational pension scheme in question deliberately concealed a qualifying fact from the member, and
- (b) the member did not discover (or could not with reasonable diligence have discovered) the qualifying fact until after the relevant day.

(6) A qualifying fact for the purposes of subsection (4) or (5) is a fact—
- (a) which is relevant to the complaint, and
- (b) without knowledge of which the worker or member could not reasonably have been expected to bring the proceedings.

(7) An incapacity case in proceedings relating to an equality clause with respect to terms of work other than terms of service in the armed forces is a case where the worker had an incapacity during the period of 6 months beginning with the later of—

(a) the relevant day, or

(b) the day on which the worker discovered (or could with reasonable diligence have discovered) the qualifying fact deliberately concealed from the worker by the responsible person.

(8) An incapacity case in proceedings relating to an equality clause with respect to terms of service in the armed forces is a case where the worker had an incapacity during the period of 9 months beginning with the later of—

(a) the last day of the period of service during which the complaint arose, or

(b) the day on which the worker discovered (or could with reasonable diligence have discovered) the qualifying fact deliberately concealed from the worker by the responsible person.

(9) An incapacity case in proceedings relating to an equality rule is a case where the member of the occupational pension scheme in question had an incapacity during the period of 6 months beginning with the later of—

(a) the relevant day, or

(b) the day on which the member discovered (or could with reasonable diligence have discovered) the qualifying fact deliberately concealed from the member by the employer or the trustees or managers of the scheme.

(10) The relevant day for the purposes of this section is—

(a) the last day of the employment or appointment, or

(b) the day on which the stable working relationship between the worker and the responsible person ended.

[1.1715]

131 Assessment of whether work is of equal value

(1) This section applies to proceedings before an employment tribunal on—

(a) a complaint relating to a breach of an equality clause or rule, or

(b) a question referred to the tribunal by virtue of section 128(2).

(2) Where a question arises in the proceedings as to whether one person's work is of equal value to another's, the tribunal may, before determining the question, require a member of the panel of independent experts to prepare a report on the question.

(3) The tribunal may withdraw a requirement that it makes under subsection (2); and, if it does so, it may—

(a) request the panel member to provide it with specified documentation;

(b) make such other requests to that member as are connected with the withdrawal of the requirement.

(4) If the tribunal requires the preparation of a report under subsection (2) (and does not withdraw the requirement), it must not determine the question unless it has received the report.

(5) Subsection (6) applies where—

(a) a question arises in the proceedings as to whether the work of one person (A) is of equal value to the work of another (B), and

(b) A's work and B's work have been given different values by a job evaluation study.

(6) The tribunal must determine that A's work is not of equal value to B's work unless it has reasonable grounds for suspecting that the evaluation contained in the study—

(a) was based on a system that discriminates because of sex, or

(b) is otherwise unreliable.

(7) For the purposes of subsection (6)(a), a system discriminates because of sex if a difference (or coincidence) between values that the system sets on different demands is not justifiable regardless of the sex of the person on whom the demands are made.

(8) A reference to a member of the panel of independent experts is a reference to a person—

(a) who is for the time being designated as such by the Advisory, Conciliation and Arbitration Service (ACAS) for the purposes of this section, and

(b) who is neither a member of the Council of ACAS nor one of its officers or members of staff.

(9) "Job evaluation study" has the meaning given in section 80(5).

[1.1716]

132 Remedies in non-pensions cases

(1) This section applies to proceedings before a court or employment tribunal on a complaint relating to a breach of an equality clause, other than a breach with respect to membership of or rights under an occupational pension scheme.

(2) If the court or tribunal finds that there has been a breach of the equality clause, it may—

(a) make a declaration as to the rights of the parties in relation to the matters to which the proceedings relate;

(b) order an award by way of arrears of pay or damages in relation to the complainant.

(3) The court or tribunal may not order a payment under subsection (2)(b) in respect of a time before the arrears day.

(4) In relation to proceedings in England and Wales, the arrears day is, in a case mentioned in the first column of the table, the day mentioned in the second column.

Case	Arrears day
A standard case	The day falling 6 years before the day on which the proceedings were instituted.

Case	Arrears day
A concealment case or an incapacity case (or a case which is both).	The day on which the breach first occurred.

(5) In relation to proceedings in Scotland, the arrears day is the first day of—
(a) the period of 5 years ending with the day on which the proceedings were commenced, or
(b) if the case involves a relevant incapacity, or a relevant fraud or error, [the period determined in accordance with section 135(6) and (7)].

NOTES

Sub-s (5): words in square brackets in para (b) substituted by the Equality Act 2010 (Consequential Amendments, Saving and Supplementary Provisions) Order 2010, SI 2010/2279, arts 2, 6.

[1.1717]
133 Remedies in pensions cases

(1) This section applies to proceedings before a court or employment tribunal on a complaint relating to—
(a) a breach of an equality rule, or
(b) a breach of an equality clause with respect to membership of, or rights under, an occupational pension scheme.
(2) If the court or tribunal finds that there has been a breach as referred to in subsection (1)—
(a) it may make a declaration as to the rights of the parties in relation to the matters to which the proceedings relate;
(b) it must not order arrears of benefits or damages or any other amount to be paid to the complainant.
(3) Subsection (2)(b) does not apply if the proceedings are proceedings to which section 134 applies.
(4) If the breach relates to a term on which persons become members of the scheme, the court or tribunal may declare that the complainant is entitled to be admitted to the scheme with effect from a specified date.
(5) A date specified for the purposes of subsection (4) must not be before 8 April 1976.
(6) If the breach relates to a term on which members of the scheme are treated, the court or tribunal may declare that the complainant is, in respect of a specified period, entitled to secure the rights that would have accrued if the breach had not occurred.
(7) A period specified for the purposes of subsection (6) must not begin before 17 May 1990.
(8) If the court or tribunal makes a declaration under subsection (6), the employer must provide such resources to the scheme as are necessary to secure for the complainant (without contribution or further contribution by the complainant or other members) the rights referred to in that subsection.

[1.1718]
134 Remedies in claims for arrears brought by pensioner members

(1) This section applies to proceedings before a court or employment tribunal on a complaint by a pensioner member of an occupational pension scheme relating to a breach of an equality clause or rule with respect to a term on which the member is treated.
(2) If the court or tribunal finds that there has been a breach referred to in subsection (1), it may—
(a) make a declaration as to the rights of the complainant and the respondent in relation to the matters to which the proceedings relate;
(b) order an award by way of arrears of benefits or damages or of any other amount in relation to the complainant.
(3) The court or tribunal must not order an award under subsection (2)(b) in respect of a time before the arrears day.
(4) If the court or tribunal orders an award under subsection (2)(b), the employer must provide such resources to the scheme as are necessary to secure for the complainant (without contribution or further contribution by the complainant or other members) the amount of the award.
(5) In relation to proceedings in England and Wales, the arrears day is, in a case mentioned in the first column of the table, the day mentioned in the second column.

Case	Arrears day
A standard case	The day falling 6 years before the day on which the proceedings were commenced.
A concealment case or an incapacity case (or a case which is both).	The day on which the breach first occurred.

(6) In relation to proceedings in Scotland, the arrears day is the first day of—
(a) the period of 5 years ending with the day on which the proceedings were commenced, or
(b) if the case involves a relevant incapacity, or a relevant fraud or error, [the period determined in accordance with section 135(6) and (7)].

NOTES

Sub-s (6): words in square brackets in para (b) substituted by the Equality Act 2010 (Consequential Amendments, Saving and Supplementary Provisions) Order 2010, SI 2010/2279, arts 2, 6.

[1.1719]
135 Supplementary
(1) This section applies for the purposes of sections 132 to 134.
(2) A standard case is a case which is not—
(a) a concealment case,
(b) an incapacity case, or
(c) a concealment case and an incapacity case.
(3) A concealment case in relation to an equality clause is a case where—
(a) the responsible person deliberately concealed a qualifying fact (as defined by section 130) from the worker, and
(b) the worker commenced the proceedings before the end of the period of 6 years beginning with the day on which the worker discovered (or could with reasonable diligence have discovered) the qualifying fact.
(4) A concealment case in relation to an equality rule is a case where—
(a) the employer or the trustees or managers of the occupational pension scheme in question deliberately concealed a qualifying fact (as defined by section 130) from the member, and
(b) the member commenced the proceedings before the end of the period of 6 years beginning with the day on which the member discovered (or could with reasonable diligence have discovered) the qualifying fact.
(5) An incapacity case is a case where the worker or member—
(a) had an incapacity when the breach first occurred, and
(b) commenced the proceedings before the end of the period of 6 years beginning with the day on which the worker or member ceased to have the incapacity.
(6) A case involves a relevant incapacity or a relevant fraud or error if the period of 5 years referred to in section 132(5)(a) [or 134(6)(a)] is, as a result of subsection (7) below, reckoned as a period of more than [5 years; and—
(a) if, as a result of subsection (7), that period is reckoned as a period of more than 5 years but no more than 20 years, the period for the purposes of section 132(5)(b) or (as the case may be) section 134(6)(b) is that extended period;
(b) if, as a result of subsection (7), that period is reckoned as a period of more than 20 years, the period for the purposes of section 132(5)(b) or (as the case may be) section 134(6)(b) is a period of 20 years].
(7) For the purposes of the reckoning referred to in subsection (6), no account is to be taken of time when the worker or member—
(a) had an incapacity, or
(b) was induced by a relevant fraud or error to refrain from commencing proceedings (not being a time after the worker or member could with reasonable diligence have discovered the fraud or error).
(8) For the purposes of subsection (7)—
(a) a fraud is relevant in relation to an equality clause if it is a fraud on the part of the responsible person;
(b) an error is relevant in relation to an equality clause if it is induced by the words or conduct of the responsible person;
(c) a fraud is relevant in relation to an equality rule if it is a fraud on the part of the employer or the trustees or managers of the scheme;
(d) an error is relevant in relation to an equality rule if it is induced by the words or conduct of the employer or the trustees or managers of the scheme.
(9) A reference in subsection (8) to the responsible person, the employer or the trustees or managers includes a reference to a person acting on behalf of the person or persons concerned.
(10) In relation to terms of service, a reference in section 132(5) or subsection (3) or (5)(b) of this section to commencing proceedings is to be read as a reference to making a service complaint.
(11) A reference to a pensioner member of a scheme includes a reference to a person who is entitled to the present payment of pension or other benefits derived through a member.
(12) In relation to proceedings before a court—
(a) a reference to a complaint is to be read as a reference to a claim, and
(b) a reference to a complainant is to be read as a reference to a claimant.

NOTES
Sub-s (6): words in first pair of square brackets inserted, and words in second pair of square brackets substituted, by the Equality Act 2010 (Consequential Amendments, Saving and Supplementary Provisions) Order 2010, SI 2010/2279, arts 2, 7.

CHAPTER 5 MISCELLANEOUS

[1.1720]
136 Burden of proof
(1) This section applies to any proceedings relating to a contravention of this Act.
(2) If there are facts from which the court could decide, in the absence of any other explanation, that a person (A) contravened the provision concerned, the court must hold that the contravention occurred.
(3) But subsection (2) does not apply if A shows that A did not contravene the provision.
(4) The reference to a contravention of this Act includes a reference to a breach of an equality clause or rule.
(5) This section does not apply to proceedings for an offence under this Act.
(6) A reference to the court includes a reference to—

(a) an employment tribunal;
(b) the Asylum and Immigration Tribunal;
(c) the Special Immigration Appeals Commission;
(d) the First-tier Tribunal;
(e) the *Special Educational Needs Tribunal for Wales*;
(f) [the First-tier Tribunal for Scotland Health and Education Chamber].

NOTES

Sub-s (6): for the words in italics in para (e) there are substituted the words "Education Tribunal for Wales" by the Additional Learning Needs and Education Tribunal (Wales) Act 2018, s 96, Sch 1, para 19(1), (3), as from a day to be appointed; words in square brackets in para (f) substituted by the First-tier Tribunal for Scotland (Transfer of Functions of the Additional Support Needs Tribunals for Scotland) Regulations 2018, SSI 2018/4, reg 5, Sch 2, Pt 1, para 4(1), (3), as from 12 January 2018.

[1.1721]

137 Previous findings

(1) A finding in relevant proceedings in respect of an act which has become final is to be treated as conclusive in proceedings under this Act.

(2) Relevant proceedings are proceedings before a court or employment tribunal under any of the following—
(a) section 19 or 20 of the Race Relations Act 1968;
(b) the Equal Pay Act 1970;
(c) the Sex Discrimination Act 1975;
(d) the Race Relations Act 1976;
(e) section 6(4A) of the Sex Discrimination Act 1986;
(f) the Disability Discrimination Act 1995;
(g) Part 2 of the Equality Act 2006;
(h) the Employment Equality (Religion and Belief) Regulations 2003 (SI 2003/1660);
(i) the Employment Equality (Sexual Orientation) Regulations 2003 (SI 2003/1661);
(j) the Employment Equality (Age) Regulations 2006 (SI 2006/1031);
(k) the Equality Act (Sexual Orientation) Regulations 2007 (SI 2007/1263).

(3) A finding becomes final—
(a) when an appeal against the finding is dismissed, withdrawn or abandoned, or
(b) when the time for appealing expires without an appeal having been brought.

138 (*Repealed by the Enterprise and Regulatory Reform Act 2013, s 66(1).*)

[1.1722]

139 Interest

(1) Regulations may make provision—
(a) for enabling an employment tribunal to include interest on an amount awarded by it in proceedings under this Act;
(b) specifying the manner in which, and the periods and rate by reference to which, the interest is to be determined.

(2) Regulations may modify the operation of an order made under section 14 of the Employment Tribunals Act 1996 (power to make provision as to interest on awards) in so far as it relates to an award in proceedings under this Act.

NOTES

Regulations: the Employment Tribunals (Interest on Awards in Discrimination Cases) (Amendment) Regulations 2013, SI 2013/1669. Also, the Employment Tribunals (Interest on Awards in Discrimination Cases) Regulations 1996, SI 1996/2803 at **[2.263]** have effect as if made under this section by virtue of the Equality Act 2010 (Commencement No 4, Savings, Consequential, Transitional, Transitory and Incidental Provisions and Revocation) Order 2010, SI 2010/2317, art 21, Sch 7.

Orders: the Employment Tribunals (Interest) Order (Amendment) Order 2013, SI 2013/1671. This Order was made under sub-ss (1)(b), (2) but note that this section confers a power to make Regulations rather than Orders.

The rate of interest prescribed by the 1996 Regulations (as amended) for claims presented after 28 July 2013 is 8%; for the rates applicable to claims presented on or before that date, see the notes to the 1996 Regulations at **[2.263]** et seq.

[1.1723]

[139A Equal pay audits

(1) Regulations may make provision requiring an employment tribunal to order the respondent to carry out an equal pay audit in any case where the tribunal finds that there has been an equal pay breach.

(2) An equal pay breach is—
(a) a breach of an equality clause, or
(b) a contravention in relation to pay of section 39(2), 49(6) or 50(6), so far as relating to sex discrimination.

(3) An equal pay audit is an audit designed to identify action to be taken to avoid equal pay breaches occurring or continuing.

(4) The regulations may make further provision about equal pay audits, including provision about—
(a) the content of an audit;
(b) the powers and duties of a tribunal for deciding whether its order has been complied with;
(c) any circumstances in which an audit may be required to be published or may be disclosed to any person.

(5) The regulations must provide for an equal pay audit not to be ordered where the tribunal considers that—

(a) an audit completed by the respondent in the previous 3 years meets requirements prescribed for this purpose,
(b) it is clear without an audit whether any action is required to avoid equal pay breaches occurring or continuing,
(c) the breach the tribunal has found gives no reason to think that there may be other breaches, or
(d) the disadvantages of an equal pay audit would outweigh its benefits.

(6) The regulations may provide for an employment tribunal to have power, where a person fails to comply with an order to carry out an equal pay audit, to order that person to pay a penalty to the Secretary of State of not more than an amount specified in the regulations.

(7) The regulations may provide for that power—
(a) to be exercisable in prescribed circumstances;
(b) to be exercisable more than once, if the failure to comply continues.

(8) The first regulations made by virtue of subsection (6) must not specify an amount of more than £5,000.

(9) Sums received by the Secretary of State under the regulations must be paid into the Consolidated Fund.

(10) The first regulations under this section must specify an exemption period during which the requirement to order an equal pay audit does not apply in the case of a business that—
(a) had fewer than 10 employees immediately before a specified time, or
(b) was begun as a new business in a specified period.

(11) For the purposes of subsection (10)—
(a) "specified" means specified in the regulations, and
(b) the number of employees a business had or the time when a business was begun as a new business is to be determined in accordance with the regulations.

(12) Before making regulations under this section, a Minister of the Crown must consult any other Minister of the Crown with responsibility for employment tribunals.]

NOTES

Inserted by the Enterprise and Regulatory Reform Act 2013, s 98(1), (2).

Regulations: the Equality Act 2010 (Equal Pay Audits) Regulations 2014, SI 2014/2559 at **[2.1517]**.

[1.1724]

140 Conduct giving rise to separate proceedings

(1) This section applies in relation to conduct which has given rise to two or more separate proceedings under this Act, with at least one being for a contravention of section 111 (instructing, causing or inducing contraventions).

(2) A court may transfer proceedings to an employment tribunal.

(3) An employment tribunal may transfer proceedings to a court.

(4) A court or employment tribunal is to be taken for the purposes of this Part to have jurisdiction to determine a claim or complaint transferred to it under this section; accordingly—
(a) a reference to a claim within section 114(1) includes a reference to a claim transferred to a court under this section, and
(b) a reference to a complaint within section 120(1) includes a reference to a complaint transferred to an employment tribunal under this section.

(5) A court or employment tribunal may not make a decision that is inconsistent with an earlier decision in proceedings arising out of the conduct.

(6) "Court" means—
(a) in relation to proceedings in England and Wales, [the county court];
(b) in relation to proceedings in Scotland, the sheriff.

NOTES

Sub-s (6): words in square brackets substituted by the Crime and Courts Act 2013, s 17(5), Sch 9, Pt 3, para 52.

[1.1725]

[140A Extension of time limits because of mediation in certain cross-border disputes

(1) In this section—
(a) "Mediation Directive" means Directive 2008/52/EC of the European Parliament and of the Council of 21 May 2008 on certain aspects of mediation in civil and commercial matters,
(b) "mediation" has the meaning given by article 3(a) of the Mediation Directive,
(c) "mediator" has the meaning given by article 3(b) of the Mediation Directive, and
(d) "relevant dispute" means a dispute to which article 8(1) of the Mediation Directive applies (certain cross-border disputes).

(2) Subsection (3) applies where—
(a) a time limit is set by section 118(1)(a), 118(2) or 129(3) in relation to the whole or part of a relevant dispute,
(b) a mediation in relation to the relevant dispute starts before the time limit expires, and
(c) if not extended by this section, the time limit would expire before the mediation ends or less than eight weeks after it ends.

(3) The time limit expires instead at the end of eight weeks after the mediation ends (subject to subsection (4)).

(4) If a time limit mentioned in subsection (2)(a) has been extended by this section, subsections (2) and (3) apply to the extended time limit as they apply to a time limit mentioned in subsection (2)(a).

(5) Subsection (6) applies where—

(a) a time limit is set by section 123(1)(a) in relation to the whole or part of a relevant dispute,
(b) a mediation in relation to the relevant dispute starts before the time limit expires, and
(c) if not extended by this section the time limit would expire before the mediation ends or less than four weeks after it ends.

(6) The time limit expires instead at the end of four weeks after the mediation ends (subject to subsection (7)).

(7) If a time limit mentioned in subsection (5)(a) has been extended by this section, subsections (5) and (6) apply to the extended time limit as they apply to a time limit mentioned in subsection (5)(a).

(8) Where more than one time limit applies in relation to a relevant dispute, the extension by subsection (3) or (6) of one of those time limits does not affect the others.

(9) For the purposes of this section, a mediation starts on the date of the agreement to mediate that is entered into by the parties and the mediator.

(10) For the purposes of this section, a mediation ends on the date of the first of these to occur—
(a) the parties reach an agreement in resolution of the relevant dispute,
(b) a party completes the notification of the other parties that it has withdrawn from the mediation,
(c) a party to whom a qualifying request is made fails to give a response reaching the other parties within 14 days of the request,
(d) the parties, after being notified that the mediator's appointment has ended (by death, resignation or otherwise), fail to agree within 14 days to seek to appoint a replacement mediator,
(e) the mediation otherwise comes to an end pursuant to the terms of the agreement to mediate.

(11) For the purpose of subsection (10), a qualifying request is a request by a party that another (A) confirm to all parties that A is continuing with the mediation.

(12) In the case of any relevant dispute, references in this section to a mediation are references to the mediation so far as it relates to that dispute, and references to a party are to be read accordingly.

(13) Where a court or tribunal has power under section 118(1)(b) or 123(1)(b) to extend a period of limitation, the power is exercisable in relation to the period of limitation as extended by this section.]

NOTES

Inserted by the Cross-Border Mediation (EU Directive) Regulations 2011, SI 2011/1133, regs 54, 58.

Repealed by the Cross-Border Mediation (EU Directive) (EU Exit) Regulations 2019, SI 2019/469, reg 4, Sch 1, Pt 1, para 17(1), (5), as from exit day (as defined in the European Union (Withdrawal) Act 2018, s 20) and subject to the modifications specified in Sch 2 to the 2019 Regulations for any mediation to which this section applies, issued before exit day (see reg 5, Sch 2, Pt 1, para 17 at **[2.2131]**, **[2.2132]**).

[1.1726]

[140AA Extension of time limits because of alternative dispute resolution in certain cross border or domestic contractual disputes

(1) In this section—
(a) "ADR Directive" means Directive 2013/11/EU of the European Parliament and of the Council of 21 May 2013 on alternative dispute resolution for consumer disputes and amending Regulation (EC) No 2006/2004 and Directive 2009/22/EC;
(b) "ADR entity" has the meaning given by *article 4(1)(h) of the ADR Directive*;
(c) . . .
(d) "ADR procedure" has the meaning given by article 4(1)(g) of the ADR Directive;
(e) "non-binding ADR procedure" means an ADR procedure the outcome of which is not binding on the parties;
(f) "relevant dispute" means a dispute to which Article 12(1) of the ADR Directive applies (certain cross-border or domestic contractual disputes brought by a consumer against a trader).

(2) Subsection (3) applies where—
(a) a time limit is set by section 118(1)(a) and (2) in relation to the whole or part of a relevant dispute;
(b) a non-binding ADR procedure in relation to the relevant dispute starts before the time limit expires; and
(c) if not extended by this section, the time limit would expire before the non-binding ADR procedure ends or less than eight weeks after it ends.

(3) For the purposes of initiating judicial proceedings, the time limit expires instead at the end of eight weeks after the non-binding ADR procedure ends (subject to subsection (4)).

(4) If a time limit has been extended by this section, subsections (2) and (3) apply to the extended time limit as they apply to a time limit mentioned in subsection (2)(a).

(5) Where more than one time limit applies in relation to a relevant dispute, the extension by subsection (3) of one of those time limits does not affect the others.

(6) For the purposes of this section, a non-binding ADR procedure starts in relation to a relevant dispute on the date when the dispute is first sent or otherwise communicated to the ADR entity in accordance with the entity's rules regarding the submission of complaints.

(7) For the purposes of this section, the non-binding ADR procedure ends on the date of the first of these to occur—
(a) the parties reach an agreement in resolution of the relevant dispute;
(b) a party completes the notification of the other parties that it has withdrawn from the non-binding ADR procedure;
(c) a party to whom a qualifying request is made fails to give a response reaching the other parties within 14 days of the request;

(d) that the ADR entity notifies the party that submitted the relevant dispute to the ADR entity that, in accordance with its policy, the ADR entity refuses to deal with the relevant dispute;
(e) after the parties are notified that the ADR entity can no longer act in relation to the relevant dispute (for whatever reason), the parties fail to agree within 14 days to submit the dispute to an alternative ADR entity;
(f) the non-binding ADR procedure otherwise comes to an end pursuant to the rules of the ADR entity.

(8) For the purpose of subsection (6), a qualifying request is a request by a party that another (A) confirm to all parties that A is continuing with the non-binding ADR procedure.
(9) In the case of any relevant dispute, references in this section to a non-binding ADR procedure are references to the non-binding ADR procedure so far as it relates to that dispute, and references to a party are to be read accordingly.
(10) Where a court or tribunal has power under section 118(1)(b) to extend a period of limitation, the power is exercisable in relation to the period of limitation as extended by this section.]

NOTES

Commencement: 9 July 2015.

Inserted by the Alternative Dispute Resolution for Consumer Disputes (Amendment) Regulations 2015, SI 2015/1392, reg 7(1), (3), as from 9 July 2015, in relation to cases where the contract to which the dispute relates was entered into on or after that date.

Sub-s (1): para (c) is repealed by the Alternative Dispute Resolution for Consumer Disputes (Amendment) (No 2) Regulations 2015, SI 2015/1972, reg 5, as from 9 January 2016. Para (a) is repealed, for the words in italics in para (b) there are substituted the words "regulation 4 of the Alternative Dispute Resolution for Consumer Disputes (Competent Authorities and Information) Regulations 2015 (SI 2015/542)", and paras (d), (f) are substituted as follows, by the Equality (Amendment and Revocation) (EU Exit) Regulations 2019, SI 2019/305, reg 5(1), (2), as from exit day (as defined in the European Union (Withdrawal) Act 2018, s 20)—

"(d) "ADR procedure" means a procedure for the out-of-court resolution of disputes through the intervention of an ADR entity which proposes or imposes a solution or brings the parties together with the aim of facilitating an amicable solution;";
(f) "relevant dispute" means a dispute that—
(a) concerns obligations under a contract of sale or for services, and
(b) is between a trader established in the United Kingdom or the European Union and a consumer resident in the United Kingdom, which the parties attempt to settle by recourse to a non-binding ADR procedure.".

[1.1727]

[140B Extension of time limits to facilitate conciliation before institution of proceedings

(1) This section applies where a time limit is set by section 123(1)(a) or 129(3) or (4).
But it does not apply to a dispute that is (or so much of a dispute as is) a relevant dispute for the purposes of section 140A.
(2) In this section—
(a) Day A is the day on which the complainant or applicant concerned complies with the requirement in subsection (1) of section 18A of the Employment Tribunals Act 1996 (requirement to contact ACAS before instituting proceedings) in relation to the matter in respect of which the proceedings are brought, and
(b) Day B is the day on which the complainant or applicant concerned receives or, if earlier, is treated as receiving (by virtue of regulations made under subsection (11) of that section) the certificate issued under subsection (4) of that section.

(3) In working out when the time limit set by section 123(1)(a) or 129(3) or (4) expires the period beginning with the day after Day A and ending with Day B is not to be counted.
(4) If the time limit set by section 123(1)(a) or 129(3) or (4) would (if not extended by this subsection) expire during the period beginning with Day A and ending one month after Day B, the time limit expires instead at the end of that period.
(5) The power conferred on the employment tribunal by subsection (1)(b) of section 123 to extend the time limit set by subsection (1)(a) of that section is exercisable in relation to that time limit as extended by this section.]

NOTES

Inserted by the Enterprise and Regulatory Reform Act 2013, s 8, Sch 2, paras 42, 45.

Sub-s (1): words in italics repealed by the Cross-Border Mediation (EU Directive) (EU Exit) Regulations 2019, SI 2019/469, reg 4, Sch 1, Pt 1, para 17(1), (6), as from exit day (as defined in the European Union (Withdrawal) Act 2018, s 20).

[1.1728]

141 Interpretation, etc

(1) This section applies for the purposes of this Part.
(2) A reference to the responsible person, in relation to an equality clause or rule, is to be construed in accordance with Chapter 3 of Part 5.
(3) A reference to a worker is a reference to the person to the terms of whose work the proceedings in question relate; and, for the purposes of proceedings relating to an equality rule or a non-discrimination rule, a reference to a worker includes a reference to a member of the occupational pension scheme in question.
(4) A reference to the terms of a person's work is to be construed in accordance with Chapter 3 of Part 5.

(5) A reference to a member of an occupational pension scheme includes a reference to a prospective member.
(6) In relation to proceedings in England and Wales, a person has an incapacity if the person—
(a) has not attained the age of 18, or
(b) lacks capacity (within the meaning of the Mental Capacity Act 2005).
(7) In relation to proceedings in Scotland, a person has an incapacity if the person—
(a) has not attained the age of 16, or
(b) is incapable (within the meaning of the Adults with Incapacity (Scotland) Act 2000 (asp 4)).
[(8) Service complaint" means a complaint made under section 340A(1) or (2) of the Armed Forces Act 2006.]
(9) "Criminal matter" means—
(a) an investigation into the commission of an alleged offence;
(b) a decision whether to commence criminal proceedings;
(c) criminal proceedings.

NOTES

Sub-s (8): substituted by the Armed Forces (Service Complaints and Financial Assistance) Act 2015, s 3, Schedule, paras 12, 15, as from 1 January 2016 (for transitional provisions see the note to s 121 at **[1.1706]**).

PART 10
CONTRACTS, ETC

Contracts and other agreements

[1.1729]
142 Unenforceable terms

(1) A term of a contract is unenforceable against a person in so far as it constitutes, promotes or provides for treatment of that or another person that is of a description prohibited by this Act.
(2) A relevant non-contractual term is unenforceable against a person in so far as it constitutes, promotes or provides for treatment of that or another person that is of a description prohibited by this Act, in so far as this Act relates to disability.
(3) A relevant non-contractual term is a term which—
(a) is a term of an agreement that is not a contract, and
(b) relates to the provision of an employment service within section 56(2)(a) to (e) or to the provision under a group insurance arrangement of facilities by way of insurance.
(4) A reference in subsection (1) or (2) to treatment of a description prohibited by this Act does not include—
(a) a reference to the inclusion of a term in a contract referred to in section 70(2)(a) or 76(2), or
(b) a reference to the failure to include a term in a contract as referred to in section 70(2)(b).
(5) Subsection (4) does not affect the application of section 148(2) to this section.

[1.1730]
143 Removal or modification of unenforceable terms

(1) [The county court] or the sheriff may, on an application by a person who has an interest in a contract or other agreement which includes a term that is unenforceable as a result of section 142, make an order for the term to be removed or modified.
(2) An order under this section must not be made unless every person who would be affected by it—
(a) has been given notice of the application (except where notice is dispensed with in accordance with rules of court), and
(b) has been afforded an opportunity to make representations to the county court or sheriff.
(3) An order under this section may include provision in respect of a period before the making of the order.

NOTES

Sub-s (1): words in square brackets substituted by the Crime and Courts Act 2013, s 17(5), Sch 9, Pt 3, para 52.

[1.1731]
144 Contracting out

(1) A term of a contract is unenforceable by a person in whose favour it would operate in so far as it purports to exclude or limit a provision of or made under this Act.
(2) A relevant non-contractual term (as defined by section 142) is unenforceable by a person in whose favour it would operate in so far as it purports to exclude or limit a provision of or made under this Act, in so far as the provision relates to disability.
(3) This section does not apply to a contract which settles a claim within section 114.
(4) This section does not apply to a contract which settles a complaint within section 120 if the contract—
(a) is made with the assistance of a conciliation officer, or
(b) is a qualifying [settlement agreement].
(5) A contract within subsection (4) includes a contract which settles a complaint relating to a breach of an equality clause or rule or of a non-discrimination rule.
(6) A contract within subsection (4) includes an agreement by the parties to a dispute to submit the dispute to arbitration if—
(a) the dispute is covered by a scheme having effect by virtue of an order under section 212A of the Trade Union and Labour Relations (Consolidation) Act 1992, and

(b) the agreement is to submit the dispute to arbitration in accordance with the scheme.

NOTES

Sub-s (4): words in square brackets substituted by the Enterprise and Regulatory Reform Act 2013, s 23(5).

Collective agreements and rules of undertakings

[1.1732]

145 Void and unenforceable terms

(1) A term of a collective agreement is void in so far as it constitutes, promotes or provides for treatment of a description prohibited by this Act.

(2) A rule of an undertaking is unenforceable against a person in so far as it constitutes, promotes or provides for treatment of the person that is of a description prohibited by this Act.

[1.1733]

146 Declaration in respect of void term, etc

(1) A qualifying person (P) may make a complaint to an employment tribunal that a term is void, or that a rule is unenforceable, as a result of section 145.

(2) But subsection (1) applies only if—

(a) the term or rule may in the future have effect in relation to P, and

(b) where the complaint alleges that the term or rule provides for treatment of a description prohibited by this Act, P may in the future be subjected to treatment that would (if P were subjected to it in present circumstances) be of that description.

(3) If the tribunal finds that the complaint is well-founded, it must make an order declaring that the term is void or the rule is unenforceable.

(4) An order under this section may include provision in respect of a period before the making of the order.

(5) In the case of a complaint about a term of a collective agreement, where the term is one made by or on behalf of a person of a description specified in the first column of the table, a qualifying person is a person of a description specified in the second column.

Description of person who made collective agreement	**Qualifying person**
Employer	A person who is, or is seeking to be, an employee of that employer
Organisation of employers	A person who is, or is seeking to be, an employee of an employer who is a member of that organisation
Association of organisations of employers	A person who is, or is seeking to be, an employee of an employer who is a member of an organisation in that association

(6) In the case of a complaint about a rule of an undertaking, where the rule is one made by or on behalf of a person of a description specified in the first column of the table, a qualifying person is a person of a description specified in the second column.

Description of person who made rule of undertaking	**Qualifying person**
Employer	A person who is, or is seeking to be, an employee of that employer
Trade organisation or qualifications body	A person who is, or is seeking to be, a member of the organisation or body
	A person upon whom the body has conferred a relevant qualification
	A person seeking conferment by the body of a relevant qualification

Supplementary

[1.1734]

147 Meaning of "qualifying [settlement agreement]"

(1) This section applies for the purposes of this Part.

(2) A qualifying [settlement agreement] is a contract in relation to which each of the conditions in subsection (3) is met.

(3) Those conditions are that—

(a) the contract is in writing,

(b) the contract relates to the particular complaint,

(c) the complainant has, before entering into the contract, received advice from an independent adviser about its terms and effect (including, in particular, its effect on the complainant's ability to pursue the complaint before an employment tribunal),

(d) on the date of the giving of the advice, there is in force a contract of insurance, or an indemnity provided for members of a profession or professional body, covering the risk of a claim by the complainant in respect of loss arising from the advice,
(e) the contract identifies the adviser, and
(f) the contract states that the conditions in paragraphs (c) and (d) are met.

(4) Each of the following is an independent adviser—
(a) a qualified lawyer;
(b) an officer, official, employee or member of an independent trade union certified in writing by the trade union as competent to give advice and as authorised to do so on its behalf;
(c) a worker at an advice centre (whether as an employee or a volunteer) certified in writing by the centre as competent to give advice and as authorised to do so on its behalf;
(d) a person of such description as may be specified by order.

(5) Despite subsection (4), none of the following is an independent adviser [to the complainant] in relation to a qualifying [settlement agreement]—
(a) a person [(other than the complainant)] who is a party to the contract or the complaint;
(b) a person who is connected to a person within paragraph (a);
(c) a person who is employed by a person within paragraph (a) or (b);
(d) a person who is acting for a person within paragraph (a) or (b) in relation to the contract or the complaint;
(e) a person within subsection (4)(b) or (c), if the trade union or advice centre is a person within paragraph (a) or (b);
(f) a person within subsection (4)(c) to whom the complainant makes a payment for the advice.

(6) A "qualified lawyer", for the purposes of subsection (4)(a), is—
(a) in relation to England and Wales, a person who, for the purposes of the Legal Services Act 2007, is an authorised person in relation to an activity which constitutes the exercise of a right of audience or the conduct of litigation;
(b) in relation to Scotland, an advocate (whether in practice as such or employed to give legal advice) or a solicitor who holds a practising certificate.

(7) "Independent trade union" has the meaning given in section 5 of the Trade Union and Labour Relations (Consolidation) Act 1992.

(8) Two persons are connected for the purposes of subsection (5) if—
(a) one is a company of which the other (directly or indirectly) has control, or
(b) both are companies of which a third person (directly or indirectly) has control.

(9) Two persons are also connected for the purposes of subsection (5) in so far as a connection between them gives rise to a conflict of interest in relation to the contract or the complaint.

NOTES

Words "settlement agreement" (in each place that they occur) substituted by the Enterprise and Regulatory Reform Act 2013, s 23(6).

Other words in square brackets in sub-s (5) inserted by the Equality Act 2010 (Amendment) Order 2012, SI 2012/334, art 2.

Orders: the Equality Act 2010 (Qualifying Settlement Contract Specified Person) Order 2010, SI 2010/2192 at **[2.1212]**.

[1.1735]
148 Interpretation

(1) This section applies for the purposes of this Part.

(2) A reference to treatment of a description prohibited by this Act does not include treatment in so far as it is treatment that would contravene—
(a) Part 1 (public sector duty regarding socio-economic inequalities), or
(b) Chapter 1 of Part 11 (public sector equality duty).

(3) "Group insurance arrangement" means an arrangement between an employer and another person for the provision by that other person of facilities by way of insurance to the employer's employees (or a class of those employees).

(4) "Collective agreement" has the meaning given in section 178 of the Trade Union and Labour Relations (Consolidation) Act 1992.

(5) A rule of an undertaking is a rule within subsection (6) or (7).

(6) A rule within this subsection is a rule made by a trade organisation or a qualifications body for application to—
(a) its members or prospective members,
(b) persons on whom it has conferred a relevant qualification, or
(c) persons seeking conferment by it of a relevant qualification.

(7) A rule within this subsection is a rule made by an employer for application to—
(a) employees,
(b) persons who apply for employment, or
(c) persons the employer considers for employment.

(8) "Trade organisation", "qualifications body" and "relevant qualification" each have the meaning given in Part 5 (work).

PART 11
ADVANCEMENT OF EQUALITY

CHAPTER 1 PUBLIC SECTOR EQUALITY DUTY

[1.1736]
149 Public sector equality duty
(1) A public authority must, in the exercise of its functions, have due regard to the need to—
(a) eliminate discrimination, harassment, victimisation and any other conduct that is prohibited by or under this Act;
(b) advance equality of opportunity between persons who share a relevant protected characteristic and persons who do not share it;
(c) foster good relations between persons who share a relevant protected characteristic and persons who do not share it.

(2) A person who is not a public authority but who exercises public functions must, in the exercise of those functions, have due regard to the matters mentioned in subsection (1).
(3) Having due regard to the need to advance equality of opportunity between persons who share a relevant protected characteristic and persons who do not share it involves having due regard, in particular, to the need to—
(a) remove or minimise disadvantages suffered by persons who share a relevant protected characteristic that are connected to that characteristic;
(b) take steps to meet the needs of persons who share a relevant protected characteristic that are different from the needs of persons who do not share it;
(c) encourage persons who share a relevant protected characteristic to participate in public life or in any other activity in which participation by such persons is disproportionately low.

(4) The steps involved in meeting the needs of disabled persons that are different from the needs of persons who are not disabled include, in particular, steps to take account of disabled persons' disabilities.
(5) Having due regard to the need to foster good relations between persons who share a relevant protected characteristic and persons who do not share it involves having due regard, in particular, to the need to—
(a) tackle prejudice, and
(b) promote understanding.

(6) Compliance with the duties in this section may involve treating some persons more favourably than others; but that is not to be taken as permitting conduct that would otherwise be prohibited by or under this Act.
(7) The relevant protected characteristics are—
age;
disability;
gender reassignment;
pregnancy and maternity;
race;
religion or belief;
sex;
sexual orientation.
(8) A reference to conduct that is prohibited by or under this Act includes a reference to—
(a) a breach of an equality clause or rule;
(b) a breach of a non-discrimination rule.

(9) Schedule 18 (exceptions) has effect.

[1.1737]
150 Public authorities and public functions
(1) A public authority is a person who is specified in Schedule 19.
(2) In that Schedule—
Part 1 specifies public authorities generally;
Part 2 specifies relevant Welsh authorities;
Part 3 specifies relevant Scottish authorities.
(3) A public authority specified in Schedule 19 is subject to the duty imposed by section 149(1) in relation to the exercise of all of its functions unless subsection (4) applies.
(4) A public authority specified in that Schedule in respect of certain specified functions is subject to that duty only in respect of the exercise of those functions.
(5) A public function is a function that is a function of a public nature for the purposes of the Human Rights Act 1998.

[1.1738]
151 Power to specify public authorities
(1) A Minister of the Crown may by order amend Part 1, 2 or 3 of Schedule 19.
(2) The Welsh Ministers may by order amend Part 2 of Schedule 19.
(3) The Scottish Ministers may by order amend Part 3 of Schedule 19.
(4) The power under subsection (1), (2) or (3) may not be exercised so as to—
(a) add an entry to Part 1 relating to a relevant Welsh or Scottish authority or a cross-border Welsh or Scottish authority;
(b) add an entry to Part 2 relating to a person who is not a relevant Welsh authority;
(c) add an entry to Part 3 relating to a person who is not a relevant Scottish authority.

(5) A Minister of the Crown may by order amend Schedule 19 so as to make provision relating to a cross-border Welsh or Scottish authority.

(6) On the first exercise of the power under subsection (5) to add an entry relating to a cross-border Welsh or Scottish authority to Schedule 19, a Minister of the Crown must—

(a) add a Part 4 to the Schedule for cross-border authorities, and

(b) add the cross-border Welsh or Scottish authority to that Part.

(7) Any subsequent exercise of the power under subsection (5) to add an entry relating to a cross-border Welsh or Scottish authority to Schedule 19 must add that entry to Part 4 of the Schedule.

(8) An order may not be made under this section so as to extend the application of section 149 unless the person making it considers that the extension relates to a person by whom a public function is exercisable.

(9) An order may not be made under this section so as to extend the application of section 149 to—

(a) the exercise of a function referred to in paragraph 3 of Schedule 18 (judicial functions, etc);

(b) a person listed in paragraph 4(2)(a) to (e) of that Schedule (Parliament, devolved legislatures and General Synod);

(c) the exercise of a function listed in paragraph 4(3) of that Schedule (proceedings in Parliament or devolved legislatures).

NOTES

Orders: the Equality Act 2010 (Specification of Public Authorities) (Scotland) Order 2011, SSI 2011/233; the Equality Act 2010 (Public Authorities and Consequential and Supplementary Amendments) Order 2011, SI 2011/1060; the Equality Act 2010 (Specification of Relevant Welsh Authorities) Order 2011, SI 2011/1063; the Equality Act 2010 (Specification of Public Authorities) (Scotland) Order 2012, SSI 2012/55; the Equality Act 2010 (Specification of Public Authorities) (Scotland) Order 2013, SSI 2013/170; the Equality Act 2010 (Specification of Public Authorities) (Scotland) Order 2015, SSI 2015/83; the Equality Act 2010 (Specific Duties and Public Authorities) Regulations 2017, SI 2017/353 at **[2.2008]**.

[1.1739]

152 Power to specify public authorities: consultation . . .

(1) Before making an order under a provision specified in the first column of the Table, a Minister of the Crown must consult the person or persons specified in the second column.

Provision	Consultees
Section 151(1)	The Commission
Section 151(1), so far as relating to a relevant Welsh authority	The Welsh Ministers
Section 151(1), so far as relating to a relevant Scottish authority	The Scottish Ministers
Section 151(5)	The Commission
Section 151(5), so far as relating to a cross-border Welsh authority	The Welsh Ministers
Section 151(5), so far as relating to a cross-border Scottish authority	The Scottish Ministers

(2) Before making an order under section 151(2), the Welsh Ministers must [consult the Commission, and after making such an order they must inform a Minister of the Crown]

(3) Before making an order under section 151(3), the Scottish Ministers must [consult the Commission, and after making such an order they must inform a Minister of the Crown].

NOTES

Section heading: words omitted repealed by the Wales Act 2017, s 44(1), (2)(b), as from 1 April 2018.

Sub-s (2): words in square brackets substituted by the Wales Act 2017, s 44(1), (2)(a), as from 1 April 2018.

Sub-s (3): words in square brackets substituted by the Scotland Act 2016, s 37(6), (7), as from 23 May 2016.

[1.1740]

153 Power to impose specific duties

(1) A Minister of the Crown may by regulations impose duties on a public authority specified in Part 1 of Schedule 19 for the purpose of enabling the better performance by the authority of the duty imposed by section 149(1).

(2) The Welsh Ministers may by regulations impose duties on a public authority specified in Part 2 of Schedule 19 for that purpose.

(3) The Scottish Ministers may by regulations impose duties on a public authority specified in Part 3 of Schedule 19 for that purpose.

(4) Before making regulations under this section, the person making them must consult the Commission.

NOTES

Regulations: the Equality Act 2010 (Statutory Duties) (Wales) Regulations 2011, SI 2011/1064 at **[2.1226]**; the Equality Act 2010 (Specific Duties) Regulations 2011, SI 2011/2260; the Equality Act 2010 (Specific Duties) (Scotland) Regulations 2012, SSI 2012/162 at **[2.1277]**; the Equality Act 2010 (Specific Duties) (Scotland) Amendment Regulations 2015, SSI 2015/254; the Equality Act 2010 (Specific Duties) (Scotland) Amendment Regulations 2016, SSI 2016/159; the Equality Act 2010 (Specific Duties and Public Authorities) Regulations 2017, SI 2017/353 at **[2.2008]**.

[1.1741]

154 Power to impose specific duties: cross-border authorities

(1) If a Minister of the Crown exercises the power in section 151(5) to add an entry for a public authority to Part 4 of Schedule 19, the Minister must include after the entry a letter specified in the first column of the Table in subsection (3).

(2) Where a letter specified in the first column of the Table in subsection (3) is included after an entry for a public authority in Part 4 of Schedule 19, the person specified in the second column of the Table—

(a) may by regulations impose duties on the authority for the purpose of enabling the better performance by the authority of the duty imposed by section 149(1), subject to such limitations as are specified in that column;

(b) must in making the regulations comply with the procedural requirement specified in that column.

(3) This is the Table—

Letter	Person by whom regulations may be made and procedural requirements
A	Regulations may be made by a Minister of the Crown in relation to the authority's functions that are not devolved Welsh functions.
	The Minister of the Crown must consult the Welsh Ministers before making the regulations.
	Regulations may be made by the Welsh Ministers in relation to the authority's devolved Welsh functions.
	[The Welsh Ministers must inform a Minister of the Crown after] making the regulations.
B	Regulations may be made by a Minister of the Crown in relation to the authority's functions that are not devolved Scottish functions.
	The Minister of the Crown must consult the Scottish Ministers before making the regulations.
	Regulations may be made by the Scottish Ministers in relation to the authority's devolved Scottish functions.
	[The Scottish Ministers must inform a Minister of the Crown after] making the regulations.
C	Regulations may be made by a Minister of the Crown in relation to the authority's functions that are neither devolved Welsh functions nor devolved Scottish functions.
	The Minister of the Crown must consult the Welsh Ministers and the Scottish Ministers before making the regulations.
	Regulations may be made by the Welsh Ministers in relation to the authority's devolved Welsh functions.
	[The Welsh Ministers must inform a Minister of the Crown after] making the regulations.
	Regulations may be made by the Scottish Ministers in relation to the authority's devolved Scottish functions.
	[The Scottish Ministers must inform a Minister of the Crown after] making the regulations.
D	The regulations may be made by a Minister of the Crown.
	The Minister of the Crown must consult the Welsh Ministers before making the regulations.

(4) Before making regulations under subsection (2), the person making them must consult the Commission.

NOTES

The table in sub-s (3) has been amended as follows:

Words "The Welsh Ministers must inform a Minister of the Crown after" in square brackets (in both places they occur) substituted by the Wales Act 2017, s 44(1), (3), as from 1 April 2018.

Words "The Scottish Ministers must inform a Minister of the Crown after" in square brackets (in both places they occur) substituted by the Scotland Act 2016, s 37(6), (8), as from 23 May 2016.

Regulations: the Equality Act 2010 (Specific Duties and Public Authorities) Regulations 2017, SI 2017/353 at **[2.2008]**.

[1.1742]

155 Power to impose specific duties: supplementary

(1) Regulations under section 153 or 154 may require a public authority to consider such matters as may be specified from time to time by—

(a) a Minister of the Crown, where the regulations are made by a Minister of the Crown;

(b) the Welsh Ministers, where the regulations are made by the Welsh Ministers;

(c) the Scottish Ministers, where the regulations are made by the Scottish Ministers.

(2) Regulations under section 153 or 154 may impose duties on a public authority that is a contracting authority within the meaning of the *Public Sector Directive* in connection with its public procurement functions.

(3) In subsection (2)—

"public procurement functions" means functions the exercise of which is regulated by the Public Sector Directive;

[“the Public Sector Directive” means Directive 2014/24/EU of the European Parliament and of the Council of 26 February 2014 on public procurement and repealing Directive 2004/18/EC, as amended from time to time].

(4) Subsections (1) and (2) do not affect the generality of section 153 or 154(2)(a).

(5) A duty imposed on a public authority under section 153 or 154 may be modified or removed by regulations made by—

- (a) a Minister of the Crown, where the original duty was imposed by regulations made by a Minister of the Crown;
- (b) the Welsh Ministers, where the original duty was imposed by regulations made by the Welsh Ministers;
- (c) the Scottish Ministers, where the original duty was imposed by regulations made by the Scottish Ministers.

NOTES

Sub-s (2): for the words in italics there are substituted the words “Public Contracts Regulations”, by the Public Procurement (Amendment etc) (EU Exit) Regulations 2019, SI 2019/560, reg 3(1), (2)(a), as from exit day (as defined in the European Union (Withdrawal) Act 2018, s 20).

Sub-s (3): definition “the Public Sector Directive” substituted by the Public Procurement (Amendments, Repeals and Revocations) Regulations 2016, SI 2016/275, reg 2, Sch 1, para 7, as from 18 April 2016 (subject to various transitional provisions in reg 5 of the 2016 Regulations); definitions in italics substituted by SI 2019/560, reg 3(1), (2)(b), as from exit day (as defined in the European Union (Withdrawal) Act 2018, s 20), as follows—

> "“Public Contracts Regulations” means the Public Contracts Regulations 2015 (SI 2015/102) or, in Scotland, the Public Contracts (Scotland) Regulations 2015 (SSI 2015/446), as amended from time to time;
>
> “public procurement functions” means functions the exercise of which is regulated by Part 2 of the Public Contracts Regulations 2015 (SI 2015/102) or by the Public Contracts (Scotland) Regulations 2015 (SSI 2015/446), as amended from time to time.”.

Regulations: the Equality Act 2010 (Specific Duties) (Scotland) Regulations 2012, SSI 2012/162 at **[2.1277]**; the Equality Act 2010 (Specific Duties) (Scotland) Amendment Regulations 2015, SSI 2015/254.

[1.1743]

156 Enforcement

A failure in respect of a performance of a duty imposed by or under this Chapter does not confer a cause of action at private law.

[1.1744]

157 Interpretation

(1) This section applies for the purposes of this Chapter.

[(2) A relevant Welsh authority is a devolved Welsh authority (within the meaning given by section 157A of the Government of Wales Act 2006) other than the Assembly Commission.]

(3) A cross-border Welsh authority is a person other than a relevant Welsh authority (or the Assembly Commission) who has any function that—

- (a) is exercisable in or as regards Wales, and
- (b) is a devolved Welsh function.

(4) The Assembly Commission has the same meaning as in the Government of Wales Act 2006.

[(5) A function is a devolved Welsh function if—

- (a) it relates to a matter in respect of which functions are exercisable by the Welsh Ministers, the First Minister for Wales or the Counsel General to the Welsh Government, or
- (b) provision conferring the function would be within the legislative competence of the National Assembly for Wales.]

(6) A relevant Scottish authority is a public body, public office or holder of a public office—

- (a) which is not a cross-border Scottish authority or the Scottish Parliamentary Corporate Body,
- (b) whose functions are exercisable only in or as regards Scotland, and
- (c) at least some of whose functions do not relate to reserved matters.

(7) A cross-border Scottish authority is a cross-border public authority within the meaning given by section 88(5) of the Scotland Act 1998.

(8) A function is a devolved Scottish function if it—

- (a) is exercisable in or as regards Scotland, and
- (b) does not relate to reserved matters.

(9) Reserved matters has the same meaning as in the Scotland Act 1998.

NOTES

Sub-ss (2), (5): substituted by the Wales Act 2017, s 69(1), Sch 6, Pt 3, para 84, as from 1 April 2018.

CHAPTER 2 POSITIVE ACTION

[1.1745]
158 Positive action: general

(1) This section applies if a person (P) reasonably thinks that—
- (a) persons who share a protected characteristic suffer a disadvantage connected to the characteristic,
- (b) persons who share a protected characteristic have needs that are different from the needs of persons who do not share it, or
- (c) participation in an activity by persons who share a protected characteristic is disproportionately low.

(2) This Act does not prohibit P from taking any action which is a proportionate means of achieving the aim of—
- (a) enabling or encouraging persons who share the protected characteristic to overcome or minimise that disadvantage,
- (b) meeting those needs, or
- (c) enabling or encouraging persons who share the protected characteristic to participate in that activity.

(3) Regulations may specify action, or descriptions of action, to which subsection (2) does not apply.

(4) This section does not apply to—
- (a) action within section 159(3), or
- (b) anything that is permitted by virtue of section 104.

(5) If section 104(7) is repealed by virtue of section 105, this section will not apply to anything that would have been so permitted but for the repeal.

(6) This section does not enable P to do anything that is prohibited by or under an enactment other than this Act.

NOTES

Regulations: as of 15 May 2019, no Regulations had been made under this section.

[1.1746]
159 Positive action: recruitment and promotion

(1) This section applies if a person (P) reasonably thinks that—
- (a) persons who share a protected characteristic suffer a disadvantage connected to the characteristic, or
- (b) participation in an activity by persons who share a protected characteristic is disproportionately low.

(2) Part 5 (work) does not prohibit P from taking action within subsection (3) with the aim of enabling or encouraging persons who share the protected characteristic to—
- (a) overcome or minimise that disadvantage, or
- (b) participate in that activity.

(3) That action is treating a person (A) more favourably in connection with recruitment or promotion than another person (B) because A has the protected characteristic but B does not.

(4) But subsection (2) applies only if—
- (a) A is as qualified as B to be recruited or promoted,
- (b) P does not have a policy of treating persons who share the protected characteristic more favourably in connection with recruitment or promotion than persons who do not share it, and
- (c) taking the action in question is a proportionate means of achieving the aim referred to in subsection (2).

(5) "Recruitment" means a process for deciding whether to—
- (a) offer employment to a person,
- (b) make contract work available to a contract worker,
- (c) offer a person a position as a partner in a firm or proposed firm,
- (d) offer a person a position as a member of an LLP or proposed LLP,
- (e) offer a person a pupillage or tenancy in barristers' chambers,
- (f) take a person as an advocate's devil or offer a person membership of an advocate's stable,
- (g) offer a person an appointment to a personal office,
- (h) offer a person an appointment to a public office, recommend a person for such an appointment or approve a person's appointment to a public office, or
- (i) offer a person a service for finding employment.

(6) This section does not enable P to do anything that is prohibited by or under an enactment other than this Act.

160–188 *(Ss 160–188 (Part 12—Disabled Persons: Transport) outside the scope of this work.)*

PART 13
DISABILITY: MISCELLANEOUS

[1.1747]
189 Reasonable adjustments

Schedule 21 (reasonable adjustments: supplementary) has effect.

190 *(S 190 (Improvements to let dwelling houses) outside the scope of this work.)*

PART 14
GENERAL EXCEPTIONS

[1.1748]
191 Statutory provisions
Schedule 22 (statutory provisions) has effect.

[1.1749]
192 National security
A person does not contravene this Act only by doing, for the purpose of safeguarding national security, anything it is proportionate to do for that purpose.

[1.1750]
193 Charities
(1) A person does not contravene this Act only by restricting the provision of benefits to persons who share a protected characteristic if—
- (a) the person acts in pursuance of a charitable instrument, and
- (b) the provision of the benefits is within subsection (2).

(2) The provision of benefits is within this subsection if it is—
- (a) a proportionate means of achieving a legitimate aim, or
- (b) for the purpose of preventing or compensating for a disadvantage linked to the protected characteristic.

(3) It is not a contravention of this Act for—
- (a) a person who provides supported employment to treat persons who have the same disability or a disability of a prescribed description more favourably than those who do not have that disability or a disability of such a description in providing such employment;
- (b) a Minister of the Crown to agree to arrangements for the provision of supported employment which will, or may, have that effect.

(4) If a charitable instrument enables the provision of benefits to persons of a class defined by reference to colour, it has effect for all purposes as if it enabled the provision of such benefits—
- (a) to persons of the class which results if the reference to colour is ignored, or
- (b) if the original class is defined by reference only to colour, to persons generally.

(5) It is not a contravention of this Act for a charity to require members, or persons wishing to become members, to make a statement which asserts or implies membership or acceptance of a religion or belief; and for this purpose restricting the access by members to a benefit, facility or service to those who make such a statement is to be treated as imposing such a requirement.
(6) Subsection (5) applies only if—
- (a) the charity, or an organisation of which it is part, first imposed such a requirement before 18 May 2005, and
- (b) the charity or organisation has not ceased since that date to impose such a requirement.

(7) It is not a contravention of section 29 for a person, in relation to an activity which is carried on for the purpose of promoting or supporting a charity, to restrict participation in the activity to persons of one sex.
(8) A charity regulator does not contravene this Act only by exercising a function in relation to a charity in a manner which the regulator thinks is expedient in the interests of the charity, having regard to the charitable instrument.
(9) Subsection (1) does not apply to a contravention of—
- (a) section 39;
- (b) section 40;
- (c) section 41;
- (d) section 55, so far as relating to the provision of vocational training.

(10) Subsection (9) does not apply in relation to disability.

NOTES
Regulations: as of 15 May 2019, no Regulations had been made under this section.

[1.1751]
194 Charities: supplementary
(1) This section applies for the purposes of section 193.
(2) That section does not apply to race, so far as relating to colour.
(3) "Charity"—
- (a) in relation to England and Wales, has the meaning given by [section 1(1) of the Charities Act 2011];
- (b) in relation to Scotland, means a body entered in the Scottish Charity Register.

(4) "Charitable instrument" means an instrument establishing or governing a charity (including an instrument made or having effect before the commencement of this section).
(5) The charity regulators are—
- (a) the Charity Commission for England and Wales;
- (b) the Scottish Charity Regulator.

(6) Section 107(5) applies to references in subsection (5) of section 193 to members, or persons wishing to become members, of a charity.
(7) "Supported employment" means facilities provided, or in respect of which payments are made, under section 15 of the Disabled Persons (Employment) Act 1944.

NOTES

Sub-s (3): words in square brackets in para (a) substituted by the Charities Act 2011, s 354(1), Sch 7, Pt 2, para 144.

[1.1752]
195 Sport

(1) A person does not contravene this Act, so far as relating to sex, only by doing anything in relation to the participation of another as a competitor in a gender-affected activity.
(2) A person does not contravene section 29, 33, 34 or 35, so far as relating to gender reassignment, only by doing anything in relation to the participation of a transsexual person as a competitor in a gender-affected activity if it is necessary to do so to secure in relation to the activity—
- (a) fair competition, or
- (b) the safety of competitors.

(3) A gender-affected activity is a sport, game or other activity of a competitive nature in circumstances in which the physical strength, stamina or physique of average persons of one sex would put them at a disadvantage compared to average persons of the other sex as competitors in events involving the activity.
(4) In considering whether a sport, game or other activity is gender-affected in relation to children, it is appropriate to take account of the age and stage of development of children who are likely to be competitors.
(5) A person who does anything to which subsection (6) applies does not contravene this Act only because of the nationality or place of birth of another or because of the length of time the other has been resident in a particular area or place.
(6) This subsection applies to—
- (a) selecting one or more persons to represent a country, place or area or a related association, in a sport or game or other activity of a competitive nature;
- (b) doing anything in pursuance of the rules of a competition so far as relating to eligibility to compete in a sport or game or other such activity.

[(7) A person does not contravene this Act, so far as relating to age discrimination, only by doing anything in relation to the participation of another as a competitor in an age-banded activity if it is necessary to do so—
- (a) to secure in relation to the activity fair competition or the safety of competitors,
- (b) to comply with the rules of a national or international competition, or
- (c) to increase participation in that activity.

(8) For the purposes of subsection (7), an age-banded activity is a sport, game or other activity of a competitive nature in circumstances in which the physical or mental strength, agility, stamina, physique, mobility, maturity or manual dexterity of average persons of a particular age group would put them at a disadvantage compared to average persons of another age group as competitors in events involving the activity.]

NOTES

Sub-ss (7), (8): added by the Equality Act 2010 (Age Exceptions) Order 2012, SI 2012/2466, art 9.

[1.1753]
196 General

Schedule 23 (general exceptions) has effect.

[1.1754]
197 Age

(1) A Minister of the Crown may by order amend this Act to provide that any of the following does not contravene this Act so far as relating to age—
- (a) specified conduct;
- (b) anything done for a specified purpose;
- (c) anything done in pursuance of arrangements of a specified description.

(2) Specified conduct is conduct—
- (a) of a specified description,
- (b) carried out in specified circumstances, or
- (c) by or in relation to a person of a specified description.

(3) An order under this section may—
- (a) confer on a Minister of the Crown or the Treasury a power to issue guidance about the operation of the order (including, in particular, guidance about the steps that may be taken by persons wishing to rely on an exception provided for by the order);
- (b) require the Minister or the Treasury to carry out consultation before issuing guidance under a power conferred by virtue of paragraph (a);
- (c) make provision (including provision to impose a requirement) that refers to guidance issued under a power conferred by virtue of paragraph (a).

(4) Guidance given by a Minister of the Crown or the Treasury in anticipation of the making of an order under this section is, on the making of the order, to be treated as if it has been issued in accordance with the order.
(5) For the purposes of satisfying a requirement imposed by virtue of subsection (3)(b), the Minister or the Treasury may rely on consultation carried out before the making of the order that imposes the requirement (including consultation carried out before the commencement of this section).
(6) Provision by virtue of subsection (3)(c) may, in particular, refer to provisions of the guidance that themselves refer to a document specified in the guidance.

(7) Guidance issued (or treated as issued) under a power conferred by virtue of subsection (3)(a) comes into force on such day as the person who issues the guidance may by order appoint; and an order under this subsection may include the text of the guidance or of extracts from it.
(8) This section is not affected by any provision of this Act which makes special provision in relation to age.
(9) The references to this Act in subsection (1) do not include references to—
(a) Part 5 (work);
(b) Chapter 2 of Part 6 (further and higher education).

NOTES

Orders: the Equality Act 2010 (Age Exceptions) Order 2012, SI 2012/2466.

198–201 *(Ss 198–201 (Part 15: Family Property) outside the scope of this work.)*

PART 16
GENERAL AND MISCELLANEOUS

202 *(S 202 (Civil partnerships on religious premises) outside the scope of this work.)*

EU obligations

[1.1755]
203 Harmonisation

(1) This section applies if—
(a) there is [an EU] obligation of the United Kingdom which a Minister of the Crown thinks relates to the subject matter of the Equality Acts,
(b) the obligation is to be implemented by the exercise of the power under section 2(2) of the European Communities Act 1972 (the implementing power), and
(c) the Minister thinks that it is appropriate to make harmonising provision in the Equality Acts.
(2) The Minister may by order make the harmonising provision.
(3) If the Minister proposes to make an order under this section, the Minister must consult persons and organisations the Minister thinks are likely to be affected by the harmonising provision.
(4) If, as a result of the consultation under subsection (3), the Minister thinks it appropriate to change the whole or part of the proposal, the Minister must carry out such further consultation with respect to the changes as the Minister thinks appropriate.
(5) The Equality Acts are the Equality Act 2006 and this Act.
(6) Harmonising provision is provision made in relation to relevant subject matter of the Equality Acts—
(a) which corresponds to the implementing provision, or
(b) which the Minister thinks is necessary or expedient in consequence of or related to provision made in pursuance of paragraph (a) or the implementing provision.
(7) The implementing provision is provision made or to be made in exercise of the implementing power in relation to so much of the subject matter of the Equality Acts as implements [an EU] obligation.
(8) Relevant subject matter of the Equality Acts is so much of the subject matter of those Acts as does not implement [an EU] obligation.
(9) A harmonising provision may amend a provision of the Equality Acts.
(10) The reference to this Act does not include a reference to this section or Schedule 24 or to a provision specified in that Schedule.
(11) A Minister of the Crown must report to Parliament on the exercise of the power under subsection (2)—
(a) at the end of the period of 2 years starting on the day this section comes into force;
(b) at the end of each succeeding period of 2 years.

NOTES

Repealed by the Equality (Amendment and Revocation) (EU Exit) Regulations 2019, SI 2019/305, reg 5(1), (4), as from exit day (as defined in the European Union (Withdrawal) Act 2018, s 20).

Sub-ss (1), (7), (8): words in square brackets substituted by the Treaty of Lisbon (Changes in Terminology) Order 2011, SI 2011/1043, art 6(1)(e), (3).

Orders: as of 15 May 2019, no Orders had been made under this section.

[1.1756]
204 Harmonisation: procedure

(1) If, after the conclusion of the consultation required under section 203, the Minister thinks it appropriate to proceed with the making of an order under that section, the Minister must lay before Parliament—
(a) a draft of a statutory instrument containing the order, together with
(b) an explanatory document.
(2) The explanatory document must—
(a) introduce and give reasons for the harmonising provision;
(b) explain why the Minister thinks that the conditions in subsection (1) of section 203 are satisfied;
(c) give details of the consultation carried out under that section;
(d) give details of the representations received as a result of the consultation;
(e) give details of such changes as were made as a result of the representations.

(3) Where a person making representations in response to the consultation has requested the Minister not to disclose them, the Minister must not disclose them under subsection (2)(d) if, or to the extent that, to do so would (disregarding any connection with proceedings in Parliament) constitute an actionable breach of confidence.

(4) If information in representations made by a person in response to consultation under section 203 relates to another person, the Minister need not disclose the information under subsection (2)(d) if or to the extent that—

- *(a) the Minister thinks that the disclosure of information could adversely affect the interests of that other person, and*
- *(b) the Minister has been unable to obtain the consent of that other person to the disclosure.*

(5) The Minister may not act under subsection (1) before the end of the period of 12 weeks beginning with the day on which the consultation under section 203(3) begins.

(6) Laying a draft of a statutory instrument in accordance with subsection (1) satisfies the condition as to laying imposed by subsection (8) of section 208, in so far as that subsection applies in relation to orders under section 203.

NOTES

Repealed by the Equality (Amendment and Revocation) (EU Exit) Regulations 2019, SI 2019/305, reg 5(1), (5), as from exit day (as defined in the European Union (Withdrawal) Act 2018, s 20).

Application

[1.1757]

205 Crown application

(1) The following provisions of this Act bind the Crown—

- (a) Part 1 (public sector duty regarding socio-economic inequalities);
- (b) Part 3 (services and public functions), so far as relating to the exercise of public functions;
- (c) Chapter 1 of Part 11 (public sector equality duty).

(2) Part 5 (work) binds the Crown as provided for by that Part.

(3) The remainder of this Act applies to Crown acts as it applies to acts done by a private person.

(4) For the purposes of subsection (3), an act is a Crown act if (and only if) it is done—

- (a) by or on behalf of a member of the executive,
- (b) by a statutory body acting on behalf of the Crown, or
- (c) by or on behalf of the holder of a statutory office acting on behalf of the Crown.

(5) A statutory body or office is a body or office established by an enactment.

(6) The provisions of Parts 2 to 4 of the Crown Proceedings Act 1947 apply to proceedings against the Crown under this Act as they apply to proceedings in England and Wales which, as a result of section 23 of that Act, are treated for the purposes of Part 2 of that Act as civil proceedings by or against the Crown.

(7) The provisions of Part 5 of that Act apply to proceedings against the Crown under this Act as they apply to proceedings in Scotland which, as a result of that Part, are treated as civil proceedings by or against the Crown.

(8) But the proviso to section 44 of that Act (removal of proceedings from the sheriff to the Court of Session) does not apply to proceedings under this Act.

[1.1758]

206 Information society services

Schedule 25 (information society services) has effect.

Subordinate legislation

[1.1759]

207 Exercise of power

(1) A power to make an order or regulations under this Act is exercisable by a Minister of the Crown, unless there is express provision to the contrary.

(2) Orders, regulations or rules under this Act must be made by statutory instrument.

(3) Subsection (2) does not apply to—

- (a) a transitional exemption order under Part 1 of Schedule 11,
- (b) a transitional exemption order under Part 1 of Schedule 12, or
- (c) an order under paragraph 1(3) of Schedule 14 that does not modify an enactment.

(4) Orders or regulations under this Act—

- (a) may make different provision for different purposes;
- (b) may include consequential, incidental, supplementary, transitional, transitory or saving provision.

(5) Nothing in section 163(4), 174(4)[, 181A(5), 181B(6)] or 182(3) affects the generality of the power under subsection (4)(a).

(6) The power under subsection (4)(b), in its application to section 37, [139A,] 153, 154(2), 155(5), 197 or 216 or to paragraph 7(1) of Schedule 11 or paragraph 1(3) or 2(3) of Schedule 14, includes power to amend an enactment (including, in the case of section [139A,] 197 or 216, this Act).

(7) In the case of section 216 (commencement), provision by virtue of subsection (4)(b) may be included in a separate order from the order that provides for the commencement to which the provision relates; and, for that purpose, it does not matter—

- (a) whether the order providing for the commencement includes provision by virtue of subsection (4)(b);
- (b) whether the commencement has taken place.

(8) A statutory instrument containing an Order in Council under section 82 (offshore work) is subject to annulment in pursuance of a resolution of either House of Parliament.

NOTES

Sub-s (5): figures in square brackets inserted by the Bus Services Act 2017, s 17(2), as from 26 June 2018.

Sub-s (6): figures in square brackets inserted by the Enterprise and Regulatory Reform Act 2013, s 98(1), (3).

[1.1760]

208 Ministers of the Crown, etc

(1) This section applies where the power to make an order or regulations under this Act is exercisable by a Minister of the Crown or the Treasury.

(2) A statutory instrument containing (whether alone or with other provision) an order or regulations that amend this Act or another Act of Parliament, or an Act of the Scottish Parliament or an Act or Measure of the National Assembly for Wales, is subject to the affirmative procedure.

(3) But a statutory instrument is not subject to the affirmative procedure by virtue of subsection (2) merely because it contains—

(a) an order under section 59 (local authority functions);
(b) an order under section 151 (power to amend list of public authorities for the purposes of the public sector equality duty) that provides for the omission of an entry where the authority concerned has ceased to exist or the variation of an entry where the authority concerned has changed its name;
(c) an order under paragraph 1(3) of Schedule 14 (educational charities and endowments) that modifies an enactment.

(4) A statutory instrument containing (whether alone or with other provision) an order or regulations mentioned in subsection (5) is subject to the affirmative procedure.

(5) The orders and regulations referred to in subsection (4) are—

(a) regulations under section 30 (services: ships and hovercraft);
(b) regulations under section 78 (gender pay gap information);
(c) regulations under section 81 (work: ships and hovercraft);
(d) an order under section 105 (election candidates: expiry of provision);
(e) regulations under section 106 (election candidates: diversity information);
[(ea) regulations under section 139A (equal pay audits);]
(f) regulations under section 153 or 154(2) (public sector equality duty: powers to impose specific duties);
[(fa) regulations under section 181A or 181B (information for bus passengers);]
(g) . . .
(h) an order under section 203 (EU obligations: harmonisation);
(i) regulations under paragraph 9(3) of Schedule 20 (rail vehicle accessibility: determination of turnover for purposes of penalties).

(6) A statutory instrument that is not subject to the affirmative procedure by virtue of subsection (2) or (4) is subject to the negative procedure.

(7) But a statutory instrument is not subject to the negative procedure by virtue of subsection (6) merely because it contains—

(a) . . . ;
(b) an order under section 216 (commencement) that—
    (i) does not amend an Act of Parliament, an Act of the Scottish Parliament or an Act or Measure of the National Assembly for Wales, and
    (ii) is not made in reliance on section 207(7).

(8) If a statutory instrument is subject to the affirmative procedure, the order or regulations contained in it must not be made unless a draft of the instrument is laid before and approved by a resolution of each House of Parliament.

(9) If a statutory instrument is subject to the negative procedure, it is subject to annulment in pursuance of a resolution of either House of Parliament.

(10) If a draft of a statutory instrument containing an order or regulations under section 2, 151, 153, 154(2) or 155(5) would, apart from this subsection, be treated for the purposes of the Standing Orders of either House of Parliament as a hybrid instrument, it is to proceed in that House as if it were not a hybrid instrument.

NOTES

Sub-s (5): para (ea) inserted by the Enterprise and Regulatory Reform Act 2013, s 98(1), (4). Para (fa) inserted by the Bus Services Act 2017, s 17(3), as from 26 June 2018. Para (g) repealed by the Deregulation Act 2015, s 51, Sch 10, Pt 7, para 30(c)(i), as from 1 October 2015. Para (h) repealed by the Equality (Amendment and Revocation) (EU Exit) Regulations 2019, SI 2019/305, reg 5(1), (6), as from exit day (as defined in the European Union (Withdrawal) Act 2018, s 20).

Sub-s (7): para (a) repealed by the Deregulation Act 2015, s 51, Sch 10, Pt 7, para 30(c)(ii), as from 1 October 2015.

[1.1761]

209 The Welsh Ministers

(1) This section applies where the power to make an order or regulations under this Act is exercisable by the Welsh Ministers.

(2) A statutory instrument containing (whether alone or with other provision) an order or regulations mentioned in subsection (3) is subject to the affirmative procedure.

(3) The orders and regulations referred to in subsection (2) are—

(a) regulations under section 2 (socio-economic inequalities);

(b) an order under section 151 (power to amend list of public authorities for the purposes of the public sector equality duty);
(c) regulations under section 153 or 154(2) (public sector equality duty: powers to impose specific duties);
(d) regulations under section 155(5) that amend an Act of Parliament or an Act or Measure of the National Assembly for Wales (public sector equality duty: power to modify or remove specific duties);
[(e) regulations under paragraph 6, 6A or 6F of Schedule 17 (tribunal procedure, case friends and capacity of parents and persons over compulsory school age)].

(4) But a statutory instrument is not subject to the affirmative procedure by virtue of subsection (2) merely because it contains an order under section 151 that provides for—
(a) the omission of an entry where the authority concerned has ceased to exist, or
(b) the variation of an entry where the authority concerned has changed its name.

(5) A statutory instrument that is not subject to the affirmative procedure by virtue of subsection (2) is subject to the negative procedure.

(6) If a statutory instrument is subject to the affirmative procedure, the order or regulations contained in it must not be made unless a draft of the instrument is laid before and approved by a resolution of the National Assembly for Wales.

(7) If a statutory instrument is subject to the negative procedure, it is subject to annulment in pursuance of a resolution of the National Assembly for Wales.

NOTES

Sub-s (3): para (e) inserted by the Additional Learning Needs and Education Tribunal (Wales) Act 2018, s 96, Sch 1, para 19(1), (4), as from a day to be appointed.

[1.1762]

210 The Scottish Ministers

(1) This section applies where the power to make an order, regulations or rules under this Act is exercisable by the Scottish Ministers.

(2) A statutory instrument containing (whether alone or with other provision) an order or regulations mentioned in subsection (3) is subject to the affirmative procedure.

(3) The orders and regulations referred to in subsection (2) are—
(a) regulations under section 2 (socio-economic inequalities);
(b) regulations under section 37 (power to make provision about adjustments to common parts in Scotland);
(c) an order under section 151 (power to amend list of public authorities for the purposes of the public sector equality duty);
(d) regulations under section 153 or 154(2) (public sector equality duty: powers to impose specific duties);
(e) regulations under section 155(5) that amend an Act of Parliament or an Act of the Scottish Parliament (public sector equality duty: power to modify or remove specific duties).

(4) But a statutory instrument is not subject to the affirmative procedure by virtue of subsection (2) merely because it contains an order under section 151 that provides for—
(a) the omission of an entry where the authority concerned has ceased to exist, or
(b) the variation of an entry where the authority concerned has changed its name.

(5) A statutory instrument that is not subject to the affirmative procedure by virtue of subsection (2) is subject to the negative procedure.

(6) If a statutory instrument is subject to the affirmative procedure, the order or regulations contained in it must not be made unless a draft of the instrument is laid before and approved by a resolution of the Scottish Parliament.

(7) If a statutory instrument is subject to the negative procedure, it is subject to annulment in pursuance of a resolution of the Scottish Parliament.

Amendments, etc

211 *(Introduces Sch 26 (Amendments) and Sch 27 (Repeals and Revocations.)*

Interpretation

[1.1763]

212 General interpretation

(1) In this Act—

"armed forces" means any of the naval, military or air forces of the Crown;
"the Commission" means the Commission for Equality and Human Rights;
"detriment" does not, subject to subsection (5), include conduct which amounts to harassment;
"the Education Acts" has the meaning given in section 578 of the Education Act 1996;
"employment" and related expressions are (subject to subsection (11)) to be read with section 83;
"enactment" means an enactment contained in—
(a) an Act of Parliament,
(b) an Act of the Scottish Parliament,
(c) an Act or Measure of the National Assembly for Wales, or
(d) subordinate legislation;
"equality clause" means a sex equality clause or maternity equality clause;
"equality rule" means a sex equality rule or maternity equality rule;

"man" means a male of any age;
"maternity equality clause" has the meaning given in section 73;
"maternity equality rule" has the meaning given in section 75;
"non-discrimination rule" has the meaning given in section 61;
"occupational pension scheme" has the meaning given in section 1 of the Pension Schemes Act 1993;
"parent" has the same meaning as in—
(a) the Education Act 1996 (in relation to England and Wales);
(b) the Education (Scotland) Act 1980 (in relation to Scotland);
"prescribed" means prescribed by regulations;
"profession" includes a vocation or occupation;
"sex equality clause" has the meaning given in section 66;
"sex equality rule" has the meaning given in section 67;
"subordinate legislation" means—
(a) subordinate legislation within the meaning of the Interpretation Act 1978, or
(b) an instrument made under an Act of the Scottish Parliament or an Act or Measure of the National Assembly for Wales;
"substantial" means more than minor or trivial;
"trade" includes any business;
"woman" means a female of any age.

(2) A reference (however expressed) to an act includes a reference to an omission.

(3) A reference (however expressed) to an omission includes (unless there is express provision to the contrary) a reference to—
(a) a deliberate omission to do something;
(b) a refusal to do it;
(c) a failure to do it.

(4) A reference (however expressed) to providing or affording access to a benefit, facility or service includes a reference to facilitating access to the benefit, facility or service.

(5) Where this Act disapplies a prohibition on harassment in relation to a specified protected characteristic, the disapplication does not prevent conduct relating to that characteristic from amounting to a detriment for the purposes of discrimination within section 13 because of that characteristic.

(6) A reference to occupation, in relation to premises, is a reference to lawful occupation.

(7) The following are members of the executive—
(a) a Minister of the Crown;
(b) a government department;
(c) the Welsh Ministers, the First Minister for Wales or the Counsel General to the Welsh Assembly Government;
(d) any part of the Scottish Administration.

(8) A reference to a breach of an equality clause or rule is a reference to a breach of a term modified by, or included by virtue of, an equality clause or rule.

(9) A reference to a contravention of this Act does not include a reference to a breach of an equality clause or rule, unless there is express provision to the contrary.

(10) "Member", in relation to an occupational pension scheme, means an active member, a deferred member or a pensioner member (within the meaning, in each case, given by section 124 of the Pensions Act 1995).

(11) "Employer", "deferred member", "pension credit member", "pensionable service", "pensioner member" and "trustees or managers" each have, in relation to an occupational pension scheme, the meaning given by section 124 of the Pensions Act 1995.

(12) A reference to the accrual of rights under an occupational pension scheme is to be construed in accordance with that section.

(13) Nothing in section 28, 32, 84, 90, 95 or 100 is to be regarded as an express exception.

NOTES

Welsh Assembly Government: see the Wales Act 2014, s 4 which provides that, unless the context requires otherwise, any reference to the Welsh Assembly Government is to be read as, or as including, a reference to the Welsh Government.

[1.1764]

213 References to maternity leave, etc

(1) This section applies for the purposes of this Act.

(2) A reference to a woman on maternity leave is a reference to a woman on—
(a) compulsory maternity leave,
(b) ordinary maternity leave, or
(c) additional maternity leave.

(3) A reference to a woman on compulsory maternity leave is a reference to a woman absent from work because she satisfies the conditions prescribed for the purposes of section 72(1) of the Employment Rights Act 1996.

(4) A reference to a woman on ordinary maternity leave is a reference to a woman absent from work because she is exercising the right to ordinary maternity leave.

(5) A reference to the right to ordinary maternity leave is a reference to the right conferred by section 71(1) of the Employment Rights Act 1996.

(6) A reference to a woman on additional maternity leave is a reference to a woman absent from work because she is exercising the right to additional maternity leave.

(7) A reference to the right to additional maternity leave is a reference to the right conferred by section 73(1) of the Employment Rights Act 1996.

(8) "Additional maternity leave period" has the meaning given in section 73(2) of that Act.

[1.1765]

214 Index of defined expressions

Schedule 28 lists the places where expressions used in this Act are defined or otherwise explained.

Final provisions

[1.1766]

215 Money

There is to be paid out of money provided by Parliament any increase attributable to this Act in the expenses of a Minister of the Crown.

[1.1767]

216 Commencement

(1) The following provisions come into force on the day on which this Act is passed—

(a) section 186(2) (rail vehicle accessibility: compliance);

(b) this Part (except sections 202 (civil partnerships on religious premises), 206 (information society services) and 211 (amendments, etc)).

(2) Part 15 (family property) comes into force on such day as the Lord Chancellor may by order appoint.

(3) [Subject to [subsections (4) and (6)],] the other provisions of this Act come into force on such day as a Minister of the Crown may by order appoint.

[(4) The following provisions of Part 1 (socio-economic inequalities) come into force on such day as the Scottish Ministers may by order appoint—

(a) section 1, so far as it applies to a relevant authority as defined by section 2(5);

(b) section 2, so far as it confers a power on the Scottish Ministers;

(c) section 3, for the purposes of section 1 to the extent mentioned in paragraph (a).

(5) The following do not apply to an order under subsection (4)—

(a) section 207(2) (see instead section 27 of the Interpretation and Legislative Reform (Scotland) Act 2010: powers exercisable by Scottish statutory instrument), and

(b) section 210.]

[(6) The following provisions of Part 1 come into force on such day as the Welsh Ministers may by order appoint—

(a) section 1, so far as it applies to a relevant authority as defined by section 2(6);

(b) section 2, so far as it confers a power on the Welsh Ministers;

(c) section 3, for the purposes of section 1 to the extent mentioned in paragraph (a).

(7) Section 209 does not apply to an order under subsection (6).]

NOTES

Words in first (outer) pair of square brackets in sub-s (3) inserted, and sub-ss (4), (5) added, by the Scotland Act 2016, s 38(9), as from 23 May 2016.

Words in second (inner) pair of square brackets in sub-s (3) substituted, and sub-ss (6), (7) added, by the Wales Act 2017, s 45(1), (4)–(6), as from 1 April 2018.

Orders: the Equality Act 2010 (Commencement No 1) Order 2010, SI 2010/1736; the Equality Act 2010 (Commencement No 2) Order 2010, SI 2010/1966; the Equality Act 2010 (Commencement No 3) Order 2010, SI 2010/2191; the Equality Act 2010 (Consequential Amendments, Saving and Supplementary Provisions) Order 2010, SI 2010/2279; the Equality Act 2010 (Commencement No 4, Savings, Consequential, Transitional, Transitory and Incidental Provisions and Revocation) Order 2010, SI 2010/2317; the Equality Act 2010 (Commencement No 4, Savings, Consequential, Transitional, Transitory and Incidental Provisions and Revocation) Order 2010 (Amendment) Order 2010, SI 2010/2337; the Equality Act 2010 (Commencement No 5) Order 2011, SI 2011/96; the Equality Act 2010 (Commencement No 6) Order 2011, SI 2011/1066; the Equality Act 2010 (Commencement No 7) Order 2011, SI 2011/1636; the Equality Act 2010 (Commencement No 8) Order 2011, SI 2011/2646; the Equality Act 2010 (Commencement No 9) Order 2012, SI 2012/1569; the Equality Act 2010 (Commencement No 10) Order 2012, SI 2012/2184; the Equality Act 2010 (Commencement No 11) Order 2016, SI 2016/839; the Equality Act 2010 (Commencement No 12) Order 2017, SI 2017/107; the Equality Act 2010 (Commencement No 13) (Scotland) Order 2017, SSI 2017/403.

[1.1768]

217 Extent

(1) This Act forms part of the law of England and Wales.

(2) This Act, apart from section 190 (improvements to let dwelling houses) and Part 15 (family property), forms part of the law of Scotland.

(3) Each of the following also forms part of the law of Northern Ireland—

(a) section 82 (offshore work);

(b) section 105(3) and (4) (expiry of Sex Discrimination (Election Candidates) Act 2002);

(c) section 199 (abolition of presumption of advancement).

[1.1769]

218 Short title

This Act may be cited as the Equality Act 2010.

SCHEDULES

SCHEDULE 1
DISABILITY: SUPPLEMENTARY PROVISION

Section 6

PART 1
DETERMINATION OF DISABILITY

[1.1770]
1. Impairment

Regulations may make provision for a condition of a prescribed description to be, or not to be, an impairment.

2. Long-term effects

(1) The effect of an impairment is long-term if—
(a) it has lasted for at least 12 months,
(b) it is likely to last for at least 12 months, or
(c) it is likely to last for the rest of the life of the person affected.

(2) If an impairment ceases to have a substantial adverse effect on a person's ability to carry out normal day-to-day activities, it is to be treated as continuing to have that effect if that effect is likely to recur.

(3) For the purposes of sub-paragraph (2), the likelihood of an effect recurring is to be disregarded in such circumstances as may be prescribed.

(4) Regulations may prescribe circumstances in which, despite sub-paragraph (1), an effect is to be treated as being, or as not being, long-term.

3. Severe disfigurement

(1) An impairment which consists of a severe disfigurement is to be treated as having a substantial adverse effect on the ability of the person concerned to carry out normal day-to-day activities.

(2) Regulations may provide that in prescribed circumstances a severe disfigurement is not to be treated as having that effect.

(3) The regulations may, in particular, make provision in relation to deliberately acquired disfigurement.

4. Substantial adverse effects

Regulations may make provision for an effect of a prescribed description on the ability of a person to carry out normal day-to-day activities to be treated as being, or as not being, a substantial adverse effect.

5. Effect of medical treatment

(1) An impairment is to be treated as having a substantial adverse effect on the ability of the person concerned to carry out normal day-to-day activities if—
(a) measures are being taken to treat or correct it, and
(b) but for that, it would be likely to have that effect.

(2) "Measures" includes, in particular, medical treatment and the use of a prosthesis or other aid.

(3) Sub-paragraph (1) does not apply—
(a) in relation to the impairment of a person's sight, to the extent that the impairment is, in the person's case, correctable by spectacles or contact lenses or in such other ways as may be prescribed;
(b) in relation to such other impairments as may be prescribed, in such circumstances as are prescribed.

6. Certain medical conditions

(1) Cancer, HIV infection and multiple sclerosis are each a disability.

(2) HIV infection is infection by a virus capable of causing the Acquired Immune Deficiency Syndrome.

7. Deemed disability

(1) Regulations may provide for persons of prescribed descriptions to be treated as having disabilities.

(2) The regulations may prescribe circumstances in which a person who has a disability is to be treated as no longer having the disability.

(3) This paragraph does not affect the other provisions of this Schedule.

8. Progressive conditions

(1) This paragraph applies to a person (P) if—
(a) P has a progressive condition,
(b) as a result of that condition P has an impairment which has (or had) an effect on P's ability to carry out normal day-to-day activities, but
(c) the effect is not (or was not) a substantial adverse effect.

(2) P is to be taken to have an impairment which has a substantial adverse effect if the condition is likely to result in P having such an impairment.

(3) Regulations may make provision for a condition of a prescribed description to be treated as being, or as not being, progressive.

9. Past disabilities

(1) A question as to whether a person had a disability at a particular time ("the relevant time") is to be determined, for the purposes of section 6, as if the provisions of, or made under, this Act were in force when the act complained of was done had been in force at the relevant time.

(2) The relevant time may be a time before the coming into force of the provision of this Act to which the question relates.

NOTES

Regulations: the Equality Act 2010 (Disability) Regulations 2010, SI 2010/2128 at **[2.1184]**.

PART 2
GUIDANCE

[1.1771]

10. Preliminary

This Part of this Schedule applies in relation to guidance referred to in section 6(5).

11. Examples

The guidance may give examples of—

(a) effects which it would, or would not, be reasonable, in relation to particular activities, to regard as substantial adverse effects;

(b) substantial adverse effects which it would, or would not, be reasonable to regard as long-term.

12. Adjudicating bodies

(1) In determining whether a person is a disabled person, an adjudicating body must take account of such guidance as it thinks is relevant.

(2) An adjudicating body is—

(a) a court;

(b) a tribunal;

(c) a person (other than a court or tribunal) who may decide a claim relating to a contravention of Part 6 (education).

13. Representations

Before issuing the guidance, the Minister must—

(a) publish a draft of it;

(b) consider any representations made to the Minister about the draft;

(c) make such modifications as the Minister thinks appropriate in the light of the representations.

14. Parliamentary procedure

(1) If the Minister decides to proceed with proposed guidance, a draft of it must be laid before Parliament.

(2) If, before the end of the 40-day period, either House resolves not to approve the draft, the Minister must take no further steps in relation to the proposed guidance.

(3) If no such resolution is made before the end of that period, the Minister must issue the guidance in the form of the draft.

(4) Sub-paragraph (2) does not prevent a new draft of proposed guidance being laid before Parliament.

(5) The 40-day period—

(a) begins on the date on which the draft is laid before both Houses (or, if laid before each House on a different date, on the later date);

(b) does not include a period during which Parliament is prorogued or dissolved;

(c) does not include a period during which both Houses are adjourned for more than 4 days.

15. Commencement

The guidance comes into force on the day appointed by order by the Minister.

16. Revision and revocation

(1) The Minister may—

(a) revise the whole or part of guidance and re-issue it;

(b) by order revoke guidance.

(2) A reference to guidance includes a reference to guidance which has been revised and re-issued.

NOTES

Guidance issued under this Part: see the Guidance on matters to be taken into account in determining questions relating to the definition of disability (2011) at **[4.274]**.

Orders: the Equality Act 2010 (Guidance on the Definition of Disability) Appointed Day Order 2011, SI 2011/1159.

SCHEDULES 2–5

(Sch 2 (Services and Public Functions: Reasonable Adjustments), Sch 3 (Services and Public Functions: Exceptions), Sch 4 (Premises: Reasonable Adjustments), Sch 5 (Premises: Exceptions) outside the scope of this work.)

SCHEDULE 6
OFFICE-HOLDERS: EXCLUDED OFFICES

Section 52

[1.1772]

1. Work to which other provisions apply

(1) An office or post is not a personal or public office in so far as one or more of the provisions mentioned in sub-paragraph (2)—
- (a) applies in relation to the office or post, or
- (b) would apply in relation to the office or post but for the operation of some other provision of this Act.

(2) Those provisions are—
- (a) section 39 (employment);
- (b) section 41 (contract work);
- (c) section 44 (partnerships).
- (d) section 45 (LLPs);
- (e) section 47 (barristers);
- (f) section 48 (advocates);
- (g) section 55 (employment services) so far as applying to the provision of work experience within section 56(2)(a) or arrangements within section 56(2)(c) for such provision.

2. Political offices

(1) An office or post is not a personal or public office if it is a political office.

(2) A political office is an office or post set out in the second column of the following Table—

Political setting	Office or post
Houses of Parliament	An office of the House of Commons held by a member of that House
	An office of the House of Lords held by a member of that House
	A Ministerial office within the meaning of section 2 of the House of Commons Disqualification Act 1975
	The office of the Leader of the Opposition within the meaning of the Ministerial and other Salaries Act 1975
	The office of the Chief Opposition Whip, or of an Assistant Opposition Whip, within the meaning of that Act
Scottish Parliament	An office of the Scottish Parliament held by a member of the Parliament
	The office of a member of the Scottish Executive
	The office of a junior Scottish Minister
National Assembly for Wales	An office of the National Assembly for Wales held by a member of the Assembly
	The office of a member of the Welsh Assembly Government
Local government in England (outside London)	An office of a county council, district council or parish council in England held by a member of the council
	An office of the Council of the Isles of Scilly held by a member of the Council
Local government in London	An office of the Greater London Authority held by the Mayor of London or a member of the London Assembly
	An office of a London borough council held by a member of the council
	An office of the Common Council of the City of London held by a member of the Council
Local government in Wales	An office of a county council, county borough council or community council in Wales held by a member of the council
Local government in Scotland	An office of a council constituted under section 2 of the Local Government etc (Scotland) Act 1994 held by a member of the council
	An office of a council established under section 51 of the Local Government (Scotland) Act 1973 held by a member of the council
Political parties	An office of a registered political party

(3) The reference to a registered political party is a reference to a party registered in the Great Britain register under Part 2 of the Political Parties, Elections and Referendums Act 2000.

3. Honours etc

A life peerage (within the meaning of the Life Peerages Act 1958), or any other dignity or honour conferred by the Crown, is not a personal or public office.

[4. Bishops

The office of diocesan or suffragan bishop is not a public office.]

NOTES

Para 4: added by the Bishops and Priests (Consecration and Ordination of Women) Measure 2014, s 2, as from 17 November 2014.

Welsh Assembly Government: see the Wales Act 2014, s 4 which provides that, unless the context requires otherwise, any reference to the Welsh Assembly Government is to be read as, or as including, a reference to the Welsh Government.

SCHEDULE 7
EQUALITY OF TERMS: EXCEPTIONS

Section 80

PART 1
TERMS OF WORK

[1.1773]

1. Compliance with laws regulating employment of women, etc

Neither a sex equality clause nor a maternity equality clause has effect in relation to terms of work affected by compliance with laws regulating—

(a) the employment of women;

(b) the appointment of women to personal or public offices.

2. Pregnancy, etc

A sex equality clause does not have effect in relation to terms of work affording special treatment to women in connection with pregnancy or childbirth.

PART 2
OCCUPATIONAL PENSION SCHEMES

Preliminary

[1.1774]

3. (1) A sex equality rule does not have effect in relation to a difference as between men and women in the effect of a relevant matter if the difference is permitted by or by virtue of this Part of this Schedule.

(2) "Relevant matter" has the meaning given in section 67.

4. State retirement pensions

(1) This paragraph applies where a man and a woman are eligible, in such circumstances as may be prescribed, to receive different amounts by way of pension.

(2) The difference is permitted if, in prescribed circumstances, it is attributable only to differences between men and women in the retirement benefits to which, in prescribed circumstances, the man and woman are or would be entitled.

(3) "Retirement benefits" are benefits under sections 43 to 55 of the Social Security Contributions and Benefits Act 1992 (state retirement pensions) [or sections 2 to 12 of the Pensions Act 2014 (state pension)].

5. Actuarial factors

(1) A difference as between men and women is permitted if it consists of applying to the calculation of the employer's contributions to an occupational pension scheme actuarial factors which—

(a) differ for men and women, and

(b) are of such description as may be prescribed.

(2) A difference as between men and women is permitted if it consists of applying to the determination of benefits of such description as may be prescribed actuarial factors which differ for men and women.

6. Power to amend

(1) Regulations may amend this Part of this Schedule so as to add, vary or omit provision about cases where a difference as between men and women in the effect of a relevant matter is permitted.

(2) The regulations may make provision about pensionable service before the date on which they come into force (but not about pensionable service before 17 May 1990).

NOTES

Para 4: words in square brackets in sub-para (3) inserted by the Pensions Act 2014 (Consequential and Supplementary Amendments) Order 2016, SI 2016/224, art 8, as from 6 April 2016.

Regulations: the Equality Act 2010 (Sex Equality Rule) (Exceptions) Regulations 2010, SI 2010/2132 at **[2.1200]**; the Pensions Act 2011 (Transitional, Consequential and Supplementary Provisions) Regulations 2014, SI 2014/1711.

SCHEDULE 8
WORK: REASONABLE ADJUSTMENTS

Section 83

PART 1
INTRODUCTORY

[1.1775]

1. Preliminary

This Schedule applies where a duty to make reasonable adjustments is imposed on A by this Part of this Act.

2. The duty

(1) A must comply with the first, second and third requirements.

(2) For the purposes of this paragraph—

(a) the reference in section 20(3) to a provision, criterion or practice is a reference to a provision, criterion or practice applied by or on behalf of A;

(b) the reference in section 20(4) to a physical feature is a reference to a physical feature of premises occupied by A;

(c) the reference in section 20(3), (4) or (5) to a disabled person is to an interested disabled person.

(3) In relation to the first and third requirements, a relevant matter is any matter specified in the first column of the applicable table in Part 2 of this Schedule.

(4) In relation to the second requirement, a relevant matter is—

(a) a matter specified in the second entry of the first column of the applicable table in Part 2 of this Schedule, or

(b) where there is only one entry in a column, a matter specified there.

(5) If two or more persons are subject to a duty to make reasonable adjustments in relation to the same interested disabled person, each of them must comply with the duty so far as it is reasonable for each of them to do so.

3. (1) This paragraph applies if a duty to make reasonable adjustments is imposed on A by section 55 (except where the employment service which A provides is the provision of vocational training within the meaning given by section 56(6)(b)).

(2) The reference in section 20(3), (4) and (5) to a disabled person is a reference to an interested disabled person.

(3) In relation to each requirement, the relevant matter is the employment service which A provides.

(4) Sub-paragraph (5) of paragraph 2 applies for the purposes of this paragraph as it applies for the purposes of that paragraph.

PART 2
INTERESTED DISABLED PERSON

[1.1776]

4. Preliminary

An interested disabled person is a disabled person who, in relation to a relevant matter, is of a description specified in the second column of the applicable table in this Part of this Schedule.

5. Employers (see section 39)

(1) This paragraph applies where A is an employer.

Relevant matter	Description of disabled person
Deciding to whom to offer employment.	A person who is, or has notified A that the person may be, an applicant for the employment.
Employment by A.	An applicant for employment by A.
	An employee of A's.

(2) Where A is the employer of a disabled contract worker (B), A must comply with the first, second and third requirements on each occasion when B is supplied to a principal to do contract work.

(3) In relation to the first requirement (as it applies for the purposes of sub-paragraph (2))—

(a) the reference in section 20(3) to a provision, criterion or practice is a reference to a provision, criterion or practice applied by or on behalf of all or most of the principals to whom B is or might be supplied,

(b) the reference to being put at a substantial disadvantage is a reference to being likely to be put at a substantial disadvantage that is the same or similar in the case of each of the principals referred to in paragraph (a), and

(c) the requirement imposed on A is a requirement to take such steps as it would be reasonable for A to have to take if the provision, criterion or practice were applied by or on behalf of A.

(4) In relation to the second requirement (as it applies for the purposes of sub-paragraph (2))—

(a) the reference in section 20(4) to a physical feature is a reference to a physical feature of premises occupied by each of the principals referred to in sub-paragraph (3)(a),

(b) the reference to being put at a substantial disadvantage is a reference to being likely to be put at a substantial disadvantage that is the same or similar in the case of each of those principals, and

(c) the requirement imposed on A is a requirement to take such steps as it would be reasonable for A to have to take if the premises were occupied by A.

(5) In relation to the third requirement (as it applies for the purposes of sub-paragraph (2))—

(a) the reference in section 20(5) to being put at a substantial disadvantage is a reference to being likely to be put at a substantial disadvantage that is the same or similar in the case of each of the principals referred to in sub-paragraph (3)(a), and

(b) the requirement imposed on A is a requirement to take such steps as it would be reasonable for A to have to take if A were the person to whom B was supplied.

6. Principals in contract work (see section 41)

(1) This paragraph applies where A is a principal.

Relevant matter	Description of disabled person
Contract work that A may make available.	A person who is, or has notified A that the person may be, an applicant to do the work.
Contract work that A makes available.	A person who is supplied to do the work.

(2) A is not required to do anything that a disabled person's employer is required to do by virtue of paragraph 5.

7. Partnerships (see section 44)

(1) This paragraph applies where A is a firm or a proposed firm.

Relevant matter	Description of disabled person
Deciding to whom to offer a position as a partner.	A person who is, or has notified A that the person may be, a candidate for the position.
A position as a partner.	A candidate for the position.
	The partner who holds the position.

(2) Where a firm or proposed firm (A) is required by this Schedule to take a step in relation to an interested disabled person (B)—

(a) the cost of taking the step is to be treated as an expense of A;

(b) the extent to which B should (if B is or becomes a partner) bear the cost is not to exceed such amount as is reasonable (having regard in particular to B's entitlement to share in A's profits).

8. LLPs (see section 45)

(1) This paragraph applies where A is an LLP or a proposed LLP.

Relevant matter	Description of disabled person
Deciding to whom to offer a position as a member.	A person who is, or has notified A that the person may be, a candidate for the position.
A position as a member.	A candidate for the position.
	The member who holds the position.

(2) Where an LLP or proposed LLP (A) is required by this Schedule to take a step in relation to an interested disabled person (B)—

(a) the cost of taking the step is to be treated as an expense of A;

(b) the extent to which B should (if B is or becomes a member) bear the cost is not to exceed such amount as is reasonable (having regard in particular to B's entitlement to share in A's profits).

9. Barristers and their clerks (see section 47)

This paragraph applies where A is a barrister or barrister's clerk.

Relevant matter	Description of disabled person
Deciding to whom to offer a pupillage or tenancy.	A person who is, or has notified A that the person may be, an applicant for the pupillage or tenancy.
A pupillage or tenancy.	An applicant for the pupillage or tenancy.
	The pupil or tenant.

10. Advocates and their clerks (see section 48)

This paragraph applies where A is an advocate or advocate's clerk.

Relevant matter	Description of disabled person
Deciding who to offer to take as a devil or to whom to offer membership of a stable.	A person who applies, or has notified A that the person may apply, to be taken as a devil or to become a member of the stable.
The relationship with a devil or membership of a stable.	An applicant to be taken as a devil or to become a member of the stable.
	The devil or member.

11. Persons making appointments to offices etc (see sections 49 to 51)

This paragraph applies where A is a person who has the power to make an appointment to a personal or public office.

Relevant matter	Description of disabled person
Deciding to whom to offer the appointment.	A person who is, or has notified A that the person may be, seeking the appointment.
	A person who is being considered for the appointment.
Appointment to the office.	A person who is seeking, or being considered for, appointment to the office.

12. This paragraph applies where A is a relevant person in relation to a personal or public office.

Relevant matter	Description of disabled person
Appointment to the office.	A person appointed to the office.

13. This paragraph applies where A is a person who has the power to make a recommendation for, or give approval to, an appointment to a public office.

Relevant matter	Description of disabled person
Deciding who to recommend or approve for appointment to the office.	A person who is, or has notified A that the person may be, seeking recommendation or approval for appointment to the office.
	A person who is being considered for recommendation or approval for appointment to the office.
An appointment to the office.	A person who is seeking, or being considered for, appointment to the office in question.

14. In relation to the second requirement in a case within paragraph 11, 12 or 13, the reference in paragraph 2(2)(b) to premises occupied by A is to be read as a reference to premises—

(a) under the control of A, and

(b) at or from which the functions of the office concerned are performed.

15. Qualifications bodies (see section 53)

(1) This paragraph applies where A is a qualifications body.

Relevant matter	Description of disabled person
Deciding upon whom to confer a relevant qualification.	A person who is, or has notified A that the person may be, an applicant for the conferment of the qualification.
Conferment by the body of a relevant qualification.	An applicant for the conferment of the qualification.
	A person who holds the qualification.

(2) A provision, criterion or practice does not include the application of a competence standard.

16. Employment service-providers (see section 55)

This paragraph applies where—

(a) A is an employment service-provider, and

(b) the employment service which A provides is vocational training within the meaning given by section 56(6)(b).

Relevant matter	Description of disabled person
Deciding to whom to offer to provide the service.	A person who is, or has notified A that the person may be, an applicant for the provision of the service.
Provision by A of the service.	A person who applies to A for the provision of the service.
	A person to whom A provides the service.

17. Trade organisations (see section 57)

This paragraph applies where A is a trade organisation.

Relevant matter	Description of disabled person
Deciding to whom to offer membership of the organisation.	A person who is, or has notified A that the person may be, an applicant for membership.
Membership of the organisation.	An applicant for membership.
	A member.

18. Local authorities (see section 58)

(1) This paragraph applies where A is a local authority.

Relevant matter	Description of disabled person
A member's carrying-out of official business.	The member.

(2) Regulations may, for the purposes of a case within this paragraph, make provision—

- (a) as to circumstances in which a provision, criterion or practice is, or is not, to be taken to put a disabled person at the disadvantage referred to in the first requirement;
- (b) as to circumstances in which a physical feature is, or is not, to be taken to put a disabled person at the disadvantage referred to in the second requirement;
- (c) as to circumstances in which it is, or in which it is not, reasonable for a local authority to be required to take steps of a prescribed description;
- (d) as to steps which it is always, or which it is never, reasonable for a local authority to take.

19. Occupational pensions (see section 61)

This paragraph applies where A is, in relation to an occupational pension scheme, a responsible person within the meaning of section 61.

Relevant matter	Description of disabled person
Carrying out A's functions in relation to the scheme.	A person who is or may be a member of the scheme.

NOTES

Regulations: as of 15 May 2019, no Regulations had been made under this Part.

PART 3
LIMITATIONS ON THE DUTY

[1.1777]

20. Lack of knowledge of disability, etc

(1) A is not subject to a duty to make reasonable adjustments if A does not know, and could not reasonably be expected to know—

- (a) in the case of an applicant or potential applicant, that an interested disabled person is or may be an applicant for the work in question;
- (b) [in any case referred to in Part 2 of this Schedule], that an interested disabled person has a disability and is likely to be placed at the disadvantage referred to in the first, second or third requirement.

(2) An applicant is, in relation to the description of A specified in the first column of the table, a person of a description specified in the second column (and the reference to a potential applicant is to be construed accordingly).

Description of A	Applicant
An employer	An applicant for employment
A firm or proposed firm	A candidate for a position as a partner
An LLP or proposed LLP	A candidate for a position as a member
A barrister or barrister's clerk	An applicant for a pupillage or tenancy

Description of A	Applicant
An advocate or advocate's clerk	An applicant for being taken as an advocate's devil or for becoming a member of a stable
A relevant person in relation to a personal or public office	A person who is seeking appointment to, or recommendation or approval for appointment to, the office
A qualifications body	An applicant for the conferment of a relevant qualification
An employment service-provider	An applicant for the provision of an employment service
A trade organisation	An applicant for membership

(3) If the duty to make reasonable adjustments is imposed on A by section 55, this paragraph applies only in so far as the employment service which A provides is vocational training within the meaning given by section 56(6)(b).

NOTES

Para 20: words in square brackets in sub-para (1)(b) substituted by Equality Act 2010 (Public Authorities and Consequential and Supplementary Amendments) Order, SI 2011/1060, art 6(1), (2).

SCHEDULE 9
WORK: EXCEPTIONS

Section 83

PART 1
OCCUPATIONAL REQUIREMENTS

[1.1778]

1. General

(1) A person (A) does not contravene a provision mentioned in sub-paragraph (2) by applying in relation to work a requirement to have a particular protected characteristic, if A shows that, having regard to the nature or context of the work—

(a) it is an occupational requirement,
(b) the application of the requirement is a proportionate means of achieving a legitimate aim, and
(c) the person to whom A applies the requirement does not meet it (or A has reasonable grounds for not being satisfied that the person meets it).

(2) The provisions are—

(a) section 39(1)(a) or (c) or (2)(b) or (c);
(b) section 41(1)(b);
(c) section 44(1)(a) or (c) or (2)(b) or (c);
(d) section 45(1)(a) or (c) or (2)(b) or (c);
(e) section 49(3)(a) or (c) or (6)(b) or (c);
(f) section 50(3)(a) or (c) or (6)(b) or (c);
(g) section 51(1).

(3) The references in sub-paragraph (1) to a requirement to have a protected characteristic are to be read—

(a) in the case of gender reassignment, as references to a requirement not to be a transsexual person (and section 7(3) is accordingly to be ignored);
(b) in the case of marriage and civil partnership, as references to a requirement not to be married or a civil partner (and section 8(2) is accordingly to be ignored).

(4) In the case of a requirement to be of a particular sex, sub-paragraph (1) has effect as if in paragraph (c), the words from "(or" to the end were omitted.

2. Religious requirements relating to sex, marriage etc, sexual orientation

(1) A person (A) does not contravene a provision mentioned in sub-paragraph (2) by applying in relation to employment a requirement to which sub-paragraph (4) applies if A shows that—

(a) the employment is for the purposes of an organised religion,
(b) the application of the requirement engages the compliance or non-conflict principle, and
(c) the person to whom A applies the requirement does not meet it (or A has reasonable grounds for not being satisfied that the person meets it).

(2) The provisions are—

(a) section 39(1)(a) or (c) or (2)(b) or (c);
(b) section 49(3)(a) or (c) or (6)(b) or (c);
(c) section 50(3)(a) or (c) or (6)(b) or (c);
(d) section 51(1).

(3) A person does not contravene section 53(1) or (2)(a) or (b) by applying in relation to a relevant qualification (within the meaning of that section) a requirement to which sub-paragraph (4) applies if the person shows that—

(a) the qualification is for the purposes of employment mentioned in sub-paragraph (1)(a), and
(b) the application of the requirement engages the compliance or non-conflict principle.

(4) This sub-paragraph applies to—
(a) a requirement to be of a particular sex;
(b) a requirement not to be a transsexual person;
(c) a requirement not to be married or a civil partner;
[(ca) a requirement not to be married to a person of the same sex;]
(d) a requirement not to be married to, or the civil partner of, a person who has a living former spouse or civil partner;
(e) a requirement relating to circumstances in which a marriage or civil partnership came to an end;
(f) a requirement related to sexual orientation.

(5) The application of a requirement engages the compliance principle if the requirement is applied so as to comply with the doctrines of the religion.

(6) The application of a requirement engages the non-conflict principle if, because of the nature or context of the employment, the requirement is applied so as to avoid conflicting with the strongly held religious convictions of a significant number of the religion's followers.

(7) A reference to employment includes a reference to an appointment to a personal or public office.

(8) In the case of a requirement within sub-paragraph (4)(a), sub-paragraph (1) has effect as if in paragraph (c) the words from "(or" to the end were omitted.

3. Other requirements relating to religion or belief

A person (A) with an ethos based on religion or belief does not contravene a provision mentioned in paragraph 1(2) by applying in relation to work a requirement to be of a particular religion or belief if A shows that, having regard to that ethos and to the nature or context of the work—
(a) it is an occupational requirement,
(b) the application of the requirement is a proportionate means of achieving a legitimate aim, and
(c) the person to whom A applies the requirement does not meet it (or A has reasonable grounds for not being satisfied that the person meets it).

4. Armed forces

(1) A person does not contravene section 39(1)(a) or (c) or (2)(b) by applying in relation to service in the armed forces a relevant requirement if the person shows that the application is a proportionate means of ensuring the combat effectiveness of the armed forces.

(2) A relevant requirement is—
(a) a requirement to be a man;
(b) a requirement not to be a transsexual person.

(3) This Part of this Act, so far as relating to age or disability, does not apply to service in the armed forces; and section 55, so far as relating to disability, does not apply to work experience in the armed forces.

5. Employment services

(1) A person (A) does not contravene section 55(1) or (2) if A shows that A's treatment of another person relates only to work the offer of which could be refused to that other person in reliance on paragraph 1, 2, 3 or 4.

(2) A person (A) does not contravene section 55(1) or (2) if A shows that A's treatment of another person relates only to training for work of a description mentioned in sub-paragraph (1).

(3) A person (A) does not contravene section 55(1) or (2) if A shows that—
(a) A acted in reliance on a statement made to A by a person with the power to offer the work in question to the effect that, by virtue of sub-paragraph (1) or (2), A's action would be lawful, and
(b) it was reasonable for A to rely on the statement.

(4) A person commits an offence by knowingly or recklessly making a statement such as is mentioned in sub-paragraph (3)(a) which in a material respect is false or misleading.

(5) A person guilty of an offence under sub-paragraph (4) is liable on summary conviction to a fine not exceeding level 5 on the standard scale.

6. Interpretation

(1) This paragraph applies for the purposes of this Part of this Schedule.

(2) A reference to contravening a provision of this Act is a reference to contravening that provision by virtue of section 13.

(3) A reference to work is a reference to employment, contract work, a position as a partner or as a member of an LLP, or an appointment to a personal or public office.

(4) A reference to a person includes a reference to an organisation.

(5) A reference to section 39(2)(b), 44(2)(b), 45(2)(b), 49(6)(b) or 50(6)(b) is to be read as a reference to that provision with the omission of the words "or for receiving any other benefit, facility or service".

(6) A reference to section 39(2)(c), 44(2)(c), 45(2)(c), 49(6)(c), 50(6)(c), 53(2)(a) or 55(2)(c) (dismissal, etc) does not include a reference to that provision so far as relating to sex.

(7) The reference to paragraph (b) of section 41(1), so far as relating to sex, is to be read as if that paragraph read—

"(b) by not allowing the worker to do the work."

NOTES

Para 2: sub-para (4)(ca) inserted by the Marriage (Same Sex Couples) Act 2013, s 17(4), Sch 7, Pt 2, paras 42, 45.

PART 2
EXCEPTIONS RELATING TO AGE

[1.1779]

7. Preliminary

For the purposes of this Part of this Schedule, a reference to an age contravention is a reference to a contravention of this Part of this Act, so far as relating to age.

8, 9. . . .

10. Benefits based on length of service

(1) It is not an age contravention for a person (A) to put a person (B) at a disadvantage when compared with another (C), in relation to the provision of a benefit, facility or service in so far as the disadvantage is because B has a shorter period of service than C.

(2) If B's period of service exceeds 5 years, A may rely on sub-paragraph (1) only if A reasonably believes that doing so fulfils a business need.

(3) A person's period of service is whichever of the following A chooses—

(a) the period for which the person has been working for A at or above a level (assessed by reference to the demands made on the person) that A reasonably regards as appropriate for the purposes of this paragraph, or

(b) the period for which the person has been working for A at any level.

(4) The period for which a person has been working for A must be based on the number of weeks during the whole or part of which the person has worked for A.

(5) But for that purpose A may, so far as is reasonable, discount—

(a) periods of absence;

(b) periods that A reasonably regards as related to periods of absence.

(6) For the purposes of sub-paragraph (3)(b), a person is to be treated as having worked for A during any period in which the person worked for a person other than A if—

(a) that period counts as a period of employment with A as a result of section 218 of the Employment Rights Act 1996, or

(b) if sub-paragraph (a) does not apply, that period is treated as a period of employment by an enactment pursuant to which the person's employment was transferred to A.

(7) For the purposes of this paragraph, the reference to a benefit, facility or service does not include a reference to a benefit, facility or service which may be provided only by virtue of a person's ceasing to work.

11. The national minimum wage: young workers

(1) It is not an age contravention for a person to pay a young worker (A) at a lower rate than that at which the person pays an older worker (B) if—

(a) the hourly rate for the national minimum wage for a person of A's age is lower than that for a person of B's age, and

(b) the rate at which A is paid is below the single hourly rate.

(2) A young worker is a person who qualifies for the national minimum wage at a lower rate than the single hourly rate; and an older worker is a person who qualifies for the national minimum wage at a higher rate than that at which the young worker qualifies for it.

(3) The single hourly rate is the rate prescribed under section 1(3) of the National Minimum Wage Act 1998.

12. The national minimum wage: apprentices

(1) It is not an age contravention for a person to pay an apprentice who does not qualify for the national minimum wage at a lower rate than the person pays an apprentice who does.

(2) An apprentice is a person who—

(a) is employed under a contract of apprenticeship, or

(b) as a result of provision made by virtue of section 3(2)(a) of the National Minimum Wage Act 1998 (persons not qualifying), is treated as employed under a contract of apprenticeship.

13. Redundancy

(1) It is not an age contravention for a person to give a qualifying employee an enhanced redundancy payment of an amount less than that of an enhanced redundancy payment which the person gives to another qualifying employee, if each amount is calculated on the same basis.

(2) It is not an age contravention to give enhanced redundancy payments only to those who are qualifying employees by virtue of sub-paragraph (3)(a) or (b).

(3) A person is a qualifying employee if the person—

(a) is entitled to a redundancy payment as a result of section 135 of the Employment Rights Act 1996,

(b) agrees to the termination of the employment in circumstances where the person would, if dismissed, have been so entitled,

(c) would have been so entitled but for section 155 of that Act (requirement for two years' continuous employment), or

(d) agrees to the termination of the employment in circumstances where the person would, if dismissed, have been so entitled but for that section.

(4) An enhanced redundancy payment is a payment the amount of which is, subject to sub-paragraphs (5) and (6), calculated in accordance with section 162(1) to (3) of the Employment Rights Act 1996.

(5) A person making a calculation for the purposes of sub-paragraph (4)—

(a) may treat a week's pay as not being subject to a maximum amount;

(b) may treat a week's pay as being subject to a maximum amount above that for the time being specified in section 227(1) of the Employment Rights Act 1996;

(c) may multiply the appropriate amount for each year of employment by a figure of more than one.

(6) Having made a calculation for the purposes of sub-paragraph (4) (whether or not in reliance on sub-paragraph (5)), a person may multiply the amount calculated by a figure of more than one.

(7) In sub-paragraph (5), "the appropriate amount" has the meaning given in section 162 of the Employment Rights Act 1996, and "a week's pay" is to be read with Chapter 2 of Part 14 of that Act.

(8) For the purposes of sub-paragraphs (4) to (6), the reference to "the relevant date" in subsection (1)(a) of section 162 of that Act is, in the case of a person who is a qualifying employee by virtue of sub-paragraph (3)(b) or (d), to be read as reference to the date of the termination of the employment.

[14. Insurance etc

(1) It is not an age contravention for an employer to make arrangements for, or afford access to, the provision of insurance or a related financial service to or in respect of an employee for a period ending when the employee attains whichever is the greater of—

(a) the age of 65, and

(b) the state pensionable age.

(2) It is not an age contravention for an employer to make arrangements for, or afford access to, the provision of insurance or a related financial service to or in respect of only such employees as have not attained whichever is the greater of—

(a) the age of 65, and

(b) the state pensionable age.

(3) Sub-paragraphs (1) and (2) apply only where the insurance or related financial service is, or is to be, provided to the employer's employees or a class of those employees—

(a) in pursuance of an arrangement between the employer and another person, or

(b) where the employer's business includes the provision of insurance or financial services of the description in question, by the employer.

(4) The state pensionable age is the pensionable age determined in accordance with the rules in paragraph 1 of Schedule 4 to the Pensions Act 1995.]

15. Child care

(1) A person does not contravene a relevant provision, so far as relating to age, only by providing, or making arrangements for or facilitating the provision of, care for children of a particular age group.

(2) The relevant provisions are—

(a) section 39(2)(b);
(b) section 41(1)(c);
(c) section 44(2)(b);
(d) section 45(2)(b);
(e) section 47(2)(b);
(f) section 48(2)(b);
(g) section 49(6)(b);
(h) section 50(6)(b);
(i) section 57(2)(a);
(j) section 58(3)(a).

(3) Facilitating the provision of care for a child includes—

(a) paying for some or all of the cost of the provision;

(b) helping a parent of the child to find a suitable person to provide care for the child;

(c) enabling a parent of the child to spend more time providing care for the child or otherwise assisting the parent with respect to the care that the parent provides for the child.

(4) A child is a person who has not attained the age of 17.

(5) A reference to care includes a reference to supervision.

16. Contributions to personal pension schemes

(1) A Minister of the Crown may by order provide that it is not an age contravention for an employer to maintain or use, with respect to contributions to personal pension schemes, practices, actions or decisions relating to age which are of a specified description.

(2) An order authorising the use of practices, actions or decisions which are not in use before the order comes into force must not be made unless the Minister consults such persons as the Minister thinks appropriate.

(3) "Personal pension scheme" has the meaning given in section 1 of the Pension Schemes Act 1993; and "employer", in relation to a personal pension scheme, has the meaning given in section 318(1) of the Pensions Act 2004.

NOTES

Paras 8, 9 repealed, and para 14 substituted, by the Employment Equality (Repeal of Retirement Age Provisions) Regulations 2011, SI 2011/1069, reg 2; for savings in relation to para 8, see reg 5 thereof.

Orders: the Equality Act (Age Exceptions for Pension Schemes) Order 2010, SI 2010/2133 at **[2.1204]**; the Equality Act (Age Exceptions for Pension Schemes) (Amendment) Order 2010, SI 2010/2285.

PART 3
OTHER EXCEPTIONS

[1.1780]

17. Non-contractual payments to women on maternity leave

(1) A person does not contravene section 39(1)(b) or (2), so far as relating to pregnancy and maternity, by depriving a woman who is on maternity leave of any benefit from the terms of her employment relating to pay.

(2) The reference in sub-paragraph (1) to benefit from the terms of a woman's employment relating to pay does not include a reference to—
- (a) maternity-related pay (including maternity-related pay that is increase-related),
- (b) pay (including increase-related pay) in respect of times when she is not on maternity leave, or
- (c) pay by way of bonus in respect of times when she is on compulsory maternity leave.

(3) For the purposes of sub-paragraph (2), pay is increase-related in so far as it is to be calculated by reference to increases in pay that the woman would have received had she not been on maternity leave.

(4) A reference to terms of her employment is a reference to terms of her employment that are not in her contract of employment, her contract of apprenticeship or her contract to do work personally.

(5) "Pay" means benefits—
- (a) that consist of the payment of money to an employee by way of wages or salary, and
- (b) that are not benefits whose provision is regulated by the contract referred to in sub-paragraph (4).

(6) "Maternity-related pay" means pay to which a woman is entitled—
- (a) as a result of being pregnant, or
- (b) in respect of times when she is on maternity leave.

18. Benefits dependent on marital status, etc

(1) A person does not contravene this Part of this Act, so far as relating to sexual orientation, by doing anything which prevents or restricts a person who is not [within sub-paragraph (1A)] from having access to a benefit, facility or service—
- (a) the right to which accrued before 5 December 2005 (the day on which section 1 of the Civil Partnership Act 2004 came into force), or
- (b) which is payable in respect of periods of service before that date.

[(1A) A person is within this sub-paragraph if the person is—
- (a) a man who is married to a woman, or
- (b) a woman who is married to a man, or
- (c) married to a person of the same sex in a relevant gender change case.

(1B) The reference in sub-paragraph (1A)(c) to a relevant gender change case is a reference to a case where—
- (a) the married couple were of the opposite sex at the time of their marriage, and
- (b) a full gender recognition certificate has been issued to one of the couple under the Gender Recognition Act 2004.]

(2) A person does not contravene this Part of this Act, so far as relating to sexual orientation, by providing married persons and civil partners (to the exclusion of all other persons) with access to a benefit, facility or service.

19. Provision of services etc to the public

(1) A does not contravene a provision mentioned in sub-paragraph (2) in relation to the provision of a benefit, facility or service to B if A is concerned with the provision (for payment or not) of a benefit, facility or service of the same description to the public.

(2) The provisions are—
- (a) section 39(2) and (4);
- (b) section 41(1) and (3);
- (c) sections 44(2) and (6) and 45(2) and (6);
- (d) sections 49(6) and (8) and 50(6), (7), (9) and (10).

(3) Sub-paragraph (1) does not apply if—
- (a) the provision by A to the public differs in a material respect from the provision by A to comparable persons,

(b) the provision to B is regulated by B's terms, or
(c) the benefit, facility or service relates to training.

(4) "Comparable persons" means—
(a) in relation to section 39(2) or (4), the other employees;
(b) in relation to section 41(1) or (3), the other contract workers supplied to the principal;
(c) in relation to section 44(2) or (6), the other partners of the firm;
(d) in relation to section 45(2) or (6), the other members of the LLP;
(e) in relation to section 49(6) or (8) or 50(6), (7), (9) or (10), persons holding offices or posts not materially different from that held by B.

(5) "B's terms" means—
(a) the terms of B's employment,
(b) the terms on which the principal allows B to do the contract work,
(c) the terms on which B has the position as a partner or member, or
(d) the terms of B's appointment to the office.

(6) A reference to the public includes a reference to a section of the public which includes B.

20. Insurance contracts, etc

(1) It is not a contravention of this Part of this Act, so far as relating to relevant discrimination, to do anything in relation to an annuity, life insurance policy, accident insurance policy or similar matter involving the assessment of risk if—
(a) that thing is done by reference to actuarial or other data from a source on which it is reasonable to rely, and
(b) it is reasonable to do it.

(2) "Relevant discrimination" is—
(a) gender reassignment discrimination;
(b) marriage and civil partnership discrimination;
(c) pregnancy and maternity discrimination;
(d) sex discrimination.

NOTES

Para 18: the word in square brackets in sub-para (1) was substituted (for the original word "married"), and sub-paras (1A), (1B) were inserted, by the Marriage (Same Sex Couples) Act 2013, s 11(4), Sch 4, Pt 6, para 17, as from 13 March 2014 (except in so far as it relating to a relevant gender change case for the purposes of this Act), and as from a day to be appointed (otherwise).

SCHEDULES 10–17

(Sch 10 (Accessibility for Disabled Pupils), Sch 11 (Schools: Exceptions), Sch 12 (Further and Higher Education Exceptions), Sch 13 (Education: Reasonable Adjustments), Sch 14 (Educational Charities and Endowments), Sch 15 (Associations: Reasonable Adjustments), Sch 16 (Associations: Exceptions), Sch 17 (Disabled Pupils: Enforcement) are outside the scope of this work.)

SCHEDULE 18
PUBLIC SECTOR EQUALITY DUTY: EXCEPTIONS

Section 149

[1.1781]

1. Children

(1) Section 149, so far as relating to age, does not apply to the exercise of a function relating to—
(a) the provision of education to pupils in schools;
(b) the provision of benefits, facilities or services to pupils in schools;
(c) the provision of accommodation, benefits, facilities or services in community homes pursuant to section 53(1) of the Children Act 1989;
(d) the provision of accommodation, benefits, facilities or services pursuant to arrangements under section 82(5) of that Act (arrangements by the Secretary of State relating to the accommodation of children);
(e) the provision of accommodation, benefits, facilities or services in residential establishments pursuant to section 26(1)(b) of the Children (Scotland) Act 1995.

(2) "Pupil" and "school" each have the same meaning as in Chapter 1 of Part 6.

2. Immigration

(1) In relation to the exercise of immigration and nationality functions, section 149 has effect as if subsection (1)(b) did not apply to the protected characteristics of age, race or religion or belief; but for that purpose "race" means race so far as relating to—
(a) nationality, or
(b) ethnic or national origins.

(2) "Immigration and nationality functions" means functions exercisable by virtue of—
(a) the Immigration Acts (excluding sections 28A to 28K of the Immigration Act 1971 so far as they relate to criminal offences),
(b) the British Nationality Act 1981,
(c) the British Nationality (Falkland Islands) Act 1983,

(d) the British Nationality (Hong Kong) Act 1990,
(e) the Hong Kong (War Wives and Widows) Act 1996,
(f) the British Nationality (Hong Kong) Act 1997,
(g) the Special Immigration Appeals Commission Act 1997, or
(h) *a provision made under section 2(2) of the European Communities Act 1972, or of [EU law], which* relates to the subject matter of an enactment within paragraphs (a) to (g).

3. Judicial functions, etc

(1) Section 149 does not apply to the exercise of—
(a) a judicial function;
(b) a function exercised on behalf of, or on the instructions of, a person exercising a judicial function.

(2) The references to a judicial function include a reference to a judicial function conferred on a person other than a court or tribunal.

4. Exceptions that are specific to section 149(2)

(1) Section 149(2) (application of section 149(1) to persons who are not public authorities but by whom public functions are exercisable) does not apply to—
(a) a person listed in sub-paragraph (2);
(b) the exercise of a function listed in sub-paragraph (3).

(2) Those persons are—
(a) the House of Commons;
(b) the House of Lords;
(c) the Scottish Parliament;
(d) the National Assembly for Wales;
(e) the General Synod of the Church of England;
(f) the Security Service;
(g) the Secret Intelligence Service;
(h) the Government Communications Headquarters;
(i) a part of the armed forces which is, in accordance with a requirement of the Secretary of State, assisting the Government Communications Headquarters.

(3) Those functions are—
(a) a function in connection with proceedings in the House of Commons or the House of Lords;
(b) a function in connection with proceedings in the Scottish Parliament (other than a function of the Scottish Parliamentary Corporate Body);
(c) a function in connection with proceedings in the National Assembly for Wales (other than a function of the Assembly Commission).

5. Power to amend Schedule

(1) A Minister of the Crown may by order amend this Schedule so as to add, vary or omit an exception to section 149.

(2) But provision by virtue of sub-paragraph (1) may not amend this Schedule—
(a) so as to omit an exception in paragraph 3;
(b) so as to omit an exception in paragraph 4(1) so far as applying for the purposes of paragraph 4(2)(a) to (e) or (3);
(c) so as to reduce the extent to which an exception referred to in paragraph (a) or (b) applies.

NOTES

Para 2: words in square brackets in sub-para (2)(h) substituted by the Equality Act 2010 (Consequential Amendments, Saving and Supplementary Provisions) Order 2010, SI 2010/2279, arts 2, 11; for the words in italics there are substituted the words "anything which forms part of retained EU law by virtue of section 2(2)(a), 3 or 4 of the European Union (Withdrawal) Act 2018 and", by the Equality (Amendment and Revocation) (EU Exit) Regulations 2019, SI 2019/305, reg 5(1), (8), as from exit day (as defined in the European Union (Withdrawal) Act 2018, s 20).

Orders: as of 15 May 2019, no Orders had been made under this Schedule.

SCHEDULE 19
PUBLIC AUTHORITIES

Section 150

PART 1
PUBLIC AUTHORITIES: GENERAL

Ministers of the Crown and government departments

[1.1782]

A Minister of the Crown.

A government department other than the Security Service, the Secret Intelligence Service or the Government Communications Headquarters.

[Broadcasting

The British Broadcasting Corporation ("BBC"), except in respect of functions relating to the provision of a content service (within the meaning given by section 32(7) of the Communications Act 2003); and the reference to the BBC includes a reference to a body corporate which—

(a) is a wholly owned subsidiary of the BBC,
(b) is not operated with a view to generating a profit, and
(c) undertakes activities primarily in order to promote the BBC's public purposes.

The Channel Four Television Corporation, except in respect of—

(a) functions relating to the provision of a content service (within the meaning given by section 32(7) of the Communications Act 2003), and
(b) the function of carrying on the activities referred to in section 199 of that Act.

The Welsh Authority (as defined by section 56(1) of the Broadcasting Act 1990), except in respect of functions relating to the provision of a content service (within the meaning given by section 32(7) of the Communications Act 2003).]

[Civil liberties

The Commission for Equality and Human Rights.

The Information Commissioner.]

[Court services and legal services

The Children and Family Court Advisory and Support Service.

The Judicial Appointments Commission.

The Legal Services Board.

. . .]

[Criminal justice

Her Majesty's Chief Inspector of Constabulary.

Her Majesty's Chief Inspector of the Crown Prosecution Service.

Her Majesty's Chief Inspector of Prisons.

Her Majesty's Chief Inspector of Probation for England and Wales.

The Parole Board for England and Wales.

[A recall adjudicator (as defined in section 239A of the Criminal Justice Act 2003).]

A probation trust established by an order made under section 5(1) of the Offender Management Act 2007.

The Youth Justice Board for England and Wales.]

[Environment, housing and development

The Homes and Communities Agency.

Natural England.

. . . .

. . .]

Armed forces

Any of the armed forces other than any part of the armed forces which is, in accordance with a requirement of the Secretary of State, assisting the Government Communications Headquarters.

[Health, social care and social security

[The National Health Service Commissioning Board.

A clinical commissioning group established under section 14D of the National Health Service Act 2006.]

The Care Quality Commission.

. . .

[Health Education England.]

[The Health Research Authority.]

The Health Service Commissioner for England, in respect of—

(a) the Commissioner's functions set out in paragraph 11 of Schedule 1 to the Health Service Commissioners Act 1993; and

(b) the Commissioner's public procurement functions (as defined in section 155(3) of this Act).

[Monitor].

An NHS foundation trust within the meaning given by section 30 of the National Health Service Act 2006.

An NHS trust established under section 25 of [the National Health Service Act 2006].

. . .

A Special Health Authority established under section 28 of that Act other than NHS Blood and Transplant and the NHS Business Services Authority.

. . .

[The National Institute for Health and Care Excellence.]
[The Health and Social Care Information Centre.]

[The National Data Guardian for Health and Social Care.]]

[Industry, business, finance etc

The Advisory, Conciliation and Arbitration Service.

The Bank of England [(including the Bank in its capacity as the Prudential Regulation Authority)], in respect of its public functions.

[The Board of the Pension Protection Fund.]

The Civil Aviation Authority.

[The Coal Authority.]

. . .

[. . .]

[The Comptroller and Auditor General.]

[The Construction Industry Training Board.]

[The Engineering Construction Industry Training Board.]

[The Financial Conduct Authority.]

[The Money and Pensions Service.]

The National Audit Office.

[The Nuclear Decommissioning Authority.]

The Office of Communications.

[The Office of Tax Simplification.]

[The Oil and Gas Authority.]

[The Office for Budget Responsibility.]

[The Payment Systems Regulator established under section 40 of the Financial Services (Banking Reform) Act 2013.]

[. . .]

[. . .]

[United Kingdom Research and Innovation.]]

Local government

A county council, district council or parish council in England.

A parish meeting constituted under section 13 of the Local Government Act 1972.

Charter trustees constituted under section 246 of that Act for an area in England.

The Greater London Authority.

A London borough council.

The Common Council of the City of London in its capacity as a local authority or port health authority.

The Sub-Treasurer of the Inner Temple or the Under-Treasurer of the Middle Temple, in that person's capacity as a local authority.

. . .

[The London Fire Commissioner.]

Transport for London.

[A Mayoral development corporation.]

The Council of the Isles of Scilly.

The Broads Authority established by section 1 of the Norfolk and Suffolk Broads Act 1988.

. . .

A fire and rescue authority constituted by a scheme under section 2 of the Fire and Rescue Services Act 2004, or a scheme to which section 4 of that Act applies, for an area in England.

[A fire and rescue authority created by an order under section 4A of that Act.]

An internal drainage board which is continued in being by virtue of section 1 of the Land Drainage Act 1991 for an area in England.

A National Park authority established by an order under section 63 of the Environment Act 1995 for an area in England.

A Passenger Transport Executive for an integrated transport area in England (within the meaning of Part 2 of the Transport Act 1968).

A port health authority constituted by an order under section 2 of the Public Health (Control of Disease) Act 1984 for an area in England.

A waste disposal authority established by virtue of an order under section 10(1) of the Local Government Act 1985.

A joint authority established under Part 4 of that Act for an area in England (including, by virtue of section 77(9) of the Local Transport Act 2008, an Integrated Transport Authority established under Part 5 of that Act of 2008).

[A sub-national transport body established under section 102E of the Local Transport Act 2008.]

A body corporate established pursuant to an order under section 67 of the Local Government Act 1985.

A joint committee constituted in accordance with section 102(1)(b) of the Local Government Act 1972 for an area in England.

A joint board which is continued in being by virtue of section 263(1) of that Act for an area in England.

[. . .

A Local Commissioner in England as defined by section 23(3) of the Local Government Act 1974, in respect of—

(a) the Commissioner's functions under sections 29(6A) and 34G(6) of that Act, and section 210(5) of the Apprenticeships, Skills, Children and Learning Act 2009; and
(b) the Commissioner's public procurement functions (as defined in section 155(3) of this Act).

. . .]

[A combined authority established by an order made under section 103(1) of the Local Democracy, Economic Development and Construction Act 2009.]

[An economic prosperity board established by an order made under section 88(1) of the Local Democracy, Economic Development and Construction Act 2009.]

Other educational bodies

The governing body of an educational establishment maintained by an English local authority (within the meaning of section 162 of the Education and Inspections Act 2006).

The governing body of an institution in England within the further education sector (within the meaning of section 91(3) of the Further and Higher Education Act 1992).

The governing body of an institution in England within the higher education sector (within the meaning of section 91(5) of that Act).

[. . .

A local authority with respect to the pupil referral units it establishes and maintains by virtue of section 19 of the Education Act 1996.

[The National Citizen Service Trust.]

[The Office for Students.]

[The proprietor of a City Technology College, a City College for Technology of the Arts, or an Academy.]]

[Parliamentary and devolved bodies

The National Assembly for Wales Commission (Comisiwn Cynulliad Cenedlaethol Cymru).

The Parliamentary Commissioner for Administration, in respect of—

(a) the Commissioner's functions set out in section 3(1) and (1A) of the Parliamentary Commissioner Act 1967; and

(b) the Commissioner's public procurement functions (as defined in section 155(3) of this Act).

The Scottish Parliamentary Corporate Body.]

[Police

The British Transport Police Force.

A chief constable of a police force maintained under section 2 of the Police Act 1996.

The Chief Inspector of the UK Border Agency.

The Civil Nuclear Police Authority.

[The College of Policing.]

The Commissioner of Police for the City of London.

The Commissioner of Police of the Metropolis.

The Common Council of the City of London in its capacity as a police authority.

[The Director General of the Independent Office for Police Conduct.]

[The Independent Office for Police Conduct.]

. . .

[A police and crime commissioner established under section 1 of the Police Reform and Social Responsibility Act 2011.]

[The Mayor's Office for Policing and Crime established under section 3 of that Act.]

A Port Police Force established under an order made under section 14 of the Harbours Act 1964.

The Port Police Force established under Part 10 of the Port of London Act 1968.

A Port Police Force established under section 79 of the Harbours, Docks and Piers Clauses Act 1847.

. . .]

[Regulators

. . .

[The Association of Chartered Certified Accountants, in respect of its public functions.]

. . .

The Chartered Institute of Patent Attorneys, in respect of its public functions.

The Council for Licensed Conveyancers, in respect of its public functions.

[The Disclosure and Barring Service.]

[The Gambling Commission.]

[The Gangmasters and Labour Abuse Authority.]

The General Chiropractic Council, in respect of its public functions.

The General Council of the Bar, in respect of its public functions.

The General Dental Council, in respect of its public functions.

The General Medical Council, in respect of its public functions.

[The General Optical Council, in respect of its public functions.]

[The General Osteopathic Council, in respect of its public functions.]

[The General Pharmaceutical Council, in respect of its public functions.]

[The Health and Care Professions Council, in respect of its public functions.]

The Health and Safety Executive.

[The Independent Monitor appointed under section 119B of the Police Act 1997.]

[The Office for Nuclear Regulation.]

The Insolvency Practitioners Association, in respect of its public functions.

The Institute of Chartered Accountants in England and Wales, in respect of its public functions.

The Institute of Legal Executives, in respect of its public functions.

The Institute of Trade Mark Attorneys, in respect of its public functions.

The Law Society of England and Wales, in respect of its public functions.

The Nursing and Midwifery Council, in respect of its public functions.

The Office of the Immigration Services Commissioner.]

[The Pensions Regulator.]

[The Regulator of Social Housing.]

[The Security Industry Authority.]

[Social Work England.]

[Transport

High Speed Two (HS2) Limited.

Highways England Company Limited.

Network Rail Limited.]

NOTES

Heading "Broadcasting" and related entries inserted by the Equality Act 2010 (Public Authorities and Consequential and Supplementary Amendments) Order 2011, SI 2011/1060, art 2(1), (2), Sch 1, paras 1, 2.

Heading "Civil liberties" and related entries inserted by SI 2011/1060, art 2(1), (2), Sch 1, paras 1, 2.

Heading "Court services and legal services" and related entries inserted by SI 2011/1060, art 2(1), (2), Sch 1, paras 1, 2. The entries under this heading are subsequently amended as follows:

Entry "The Legal Services Commission" (omitted) repealed by the Legal Aid, Sentencing and Punishment of Offenders Act 2012, s 39, Sch 5, Pt 1, para 70.

Heading "Criminal justice" and related entries inserted by SI 2011/1060, art 2(1), (2), Sch 1, paras 1, 2. The entries under this heading are subsequently amended as follows:

Entry "A recall adjudicator (as defined in section 239A of the Criminal Justice Act 2003)" inserted by the Criminal Justice and Courts Act 2015, s 8(3), Sch 3, para 17, as from a day to be appointed.

Heading "Environment, housing and development" and related entries inserted by SI 2011/1060, art 2(1), (2), Sch 1, paras 1, 2. The entries under this heading are subsequently amended as follows:

Entry "The Office for Tenants and Social Landlords" (omitted) repealed by the Localism Act 2011, ss 178, 237, Sch 16, Pt 2, para 62, Sch 25, Pt 26.

Entry "The Olympic Delivery Authority" (omitted) repealed by the Olympic Delivery Authority (Dissolution) Order 2014, SI 2014/3184, art 2(2), Schedule, para 14, as from 2 December 2014.

Heading "Health, social care and social security" and related entries substituted, for heading "National Health Service" and related entries as originally enacted, by SI 2011/1060, art 2(1), (2), Sch 1, paras 1, 3. The entries under this heading are subsequently amended as follows:

Entries "The National Health Service Commissioning Board" and "A clinical commissioning group" inserted by the Health and Social Care Act 2012, s 55(2), Sch 5, para 182(a).

Entry "The Child Maintenance and Enforcement Commission" (omitted) repealed by the Public Bodies (Child Maintenance and Enforcement Commission: Abolition and Transfer of Functions) Order 2012, SI 2012/2007, art 3(2), Schedule, Pt 1, para 109(e).

Entry "Health Education England" inserted by the Care Act 2014, s 96(2), Sch 5, Pt 4, para 35, as from 1 April 2015.

Entry "The Health Research Authority" inserted by the Care Act 2014, s 109(2), Sch 7, Pt 4, para 27, as from 1 January 2015.

Entry "Monitor" substituted, for entry "The Independent Regulator of NHS Foundation Trusts" as originally enacted, by the Health and Social Care Act 2012, s 150(5), Sch 13, para 19.

In entry relating to "An NHS trust" words in square brackets substituted by the Health and Social Care Act 2012, s 55(2), Sch 5, para 182(b), and the entry is repealed by the Health and Social Care Act 2012, s 179(6), Sch 14, Pt 2, para 116, as from a day to be appointed.

Entries relating to "A Primary Care Trust" and "A Strategic Health Authority" (omitted) repealed by the Health and Social Care Act 2012, s 55(2), Sch 5, para 182(c), (d).

Entries "The Health and Social Care Information Centre" and "The National Institute for Health and Care Excellence" inserted by the Health and Social Care Act 2012, ss 249(1), 277, Sch 17, para 14, Sch 19, para 13.

Entry "The National Data Guardian for Health and Social Care" inserted by the Health and Social Care (National Data Guardian) Act 2018, s 3, Sch 2, para 5, as from 1 April 2019 (in relation to England) and as from a day to be appointed (in relation to Wales).

Heading "Industry, business, finance etc" and related entries inserted by SI 2011/1060, art 2(1), (2), Sch 1, paras 1, 4. The entries under this heading are subsequently amended as follows:

Words in square brackets in entry "Bank of England" inserted by the Bank of England and Financial Services (Consequential Amendments) Regulations 2017, SI 2017/80, reg 2, Schedule, Pt 1, para 19(a), as from 1 March 2017.

Entries "The Board of the Pension Protection Fund", "The Coal Authority", "The Construction Industry Training Board", "The Engineering Construction Industry Training Board", "The Nuclear Decommissioning Authority", and "The Oil and Gas Authority" inserted by the Equality Act 2010 (Specific Duties and Public Authorities) Regulations 2017, SI 2017/353, reg 8, Sch 3, paras 1, 2(b), as from 31 March 2017.

Entry "The Competition Commission" (omitted) repealed by the Enterprise and Regulatory Reform Act 2013 (Competition) (Consequential, Transitional and Saving Provisions) Order 2014, SI 2014/892, art 2, Sch 1, Pt 2, para 182.

Entries "The Comptroller and Auditor General" and "The Office for Budget Responsibility" inserted by the Budget Responsibility and National Audit Act 2011, ss 3, 26, Sch 1, para 28, Sch 5, Pt 2, para 34.

Entry "The Competition and Markets Authority" (omitted) originally inserted by the Enterprise and Regulatory Reform Act 2013, s 25(4), Sch 4, Pt 1, para 26; subsequently repealed by SI 2017/353, reg 8, Sch 3, paras 1, 2(a), as from 31 March 2017.

Entry "The Financial Conduct Authority" substituted (for original entry "The Financial Services Authority"), and entry "The Prudential Regulation Authority" inserted, by the Financial Services Act 2012, s 114(1), Sch 18, Pt 2, para 131; entry "The Prudential Regulation Authority" (omitted) subsequently repealed by SI 2017/80, reg 2, Schedule, Pt 1, para 19(b), as from 1 March 2017.

Entry "The Money and Pensions Service." inserted by the Financial Guidance and Claims Act 2018 (Naming and Consequential Amendments) Regulations 2019, SI 2019/383, reg 3, Schedule, Pt 1, para 9(b), as from 6 April 2019.

Entry "The Office of Tax Simplification." inserted by the Finance Act 2016, s 184(2), Sch 25, para 15, as from 28 November 2016.

Entry relating to "The Payment Systems Regulator" inserted by the Financial Services (Banking Reform) Act 2013, s 40(5), Sch 4, para 16.

Entry "The single financial guidance body" inserted by Financial Guidance and Claims Act 2018, s 25, Sch 3, para 24, as from 1 October 2018 and repealed by SI 2019/383, reg 3, Schedule, Pt 1, para 9(a), as from 6 April 2019.

Entry "United Kingdom Research and Innovation" inserted by the Higher Education and Research Act 2017, s 91, Sch 9, para 23, as from 30 March 2018.

Under the heading "Local government", entry "The London Development Agency" (omitted) repealed by the Localism Act 2011, s 237, Sch 25, Pt 32.

Under the heading "Local government", entry "The London Fire Commissioner" substituted (for the original entry "The London Fire and Emergency Planning Authority") by the Policing and Crime Act 2017, s 9(3)(c), Sch 2, Pt 2, para 116, as from 1 April 2018.

Under the heading "Local government", entry "A Mayoral development corporation" inserted by the Localism Act 2011, s 222, Sch 22, para 62.

Under the heading "Local government", entry "A regional development agency" (omitted) repealed by the Public Bodies Act 2011, s 30(3), Sch 6.

Under heading "Local government", entry "A fire and rescue authority created by an order under section 4A of that Act" inserted by the Policing and Crime Act 2017, s 6, Sch 1, Pt 2, para 85, as from 3 April 2017.

Under heading "Local government", entry "A sub-national transport body established under section 102E of the Local Transport Act 2008" inserted, in relation to England and Wales, by the Cities and Local Government Devolution Act 2016, s 23(1), Sch 5, para 31, as from 28 March 2016.

Under the heading "Local government", entry "The Audit Commission for Local Authorities and the National Health Service in England" (omitted) originally inserted by SI 2011/1060, art 2(1), (2), Sch 1, paras 1, 5; subsequently repealed by the Local Audit and Accountability Act 2014, s 45, Sch 12, para 114, as from 1 April 2015.

Under the heading "Local government", entry beginning "A Local Commissioner in England as defined by section 23(3) of the Local Government Act 1974" inserted by SI 2011/1060, art 2(1), (2), Sch 1, paras 1, 5.

Under the heading "Local government", entry "The Standards Board for England" (omitted) originally inserted by SI 2011/1060, art 2(1), (2), Sch 1, paras 1, 5; subsequently repealed by SI 2017/353, reg 8, Sch 3, paras 1, 3(a), as from 31 March 2017.

Under the heading "Local government", the final three entries in square brackets were added by SI 2017/353, reg 8, Sch 3, paras 1, 3(b), as from 31 March 2017.

Under the heading "Other educational bodies", entries "The Higher Education Funding Council for England" (omitted), "A local authority with respect to the pupil referral units it establishes and maintains by virtue of section 19 of the Education Act 1996", and entry beginning "The proprietor of a City Technology College" inserted by SI 2011/1060, art 2(1), (2), Sch 1, paras 1, 6. Entry "The Higher Education Funding Council for England" subsequently repealed by the Higher Education and Research Act 2017, s 122, Sch 11, para 32, as from 1 April 2018. Entry "The Office for Students" inserted by the Higher Education and Research Act 2017, s 1, Sch 1, para 21, as from 1 January 2018. Entry "The National Citizen Service Trust" inserted by the National Citizen Service Act 2017, s 11, Sch 2, para 4, as from 1 December 2018. Entry beginning "The proprietor of a City Technology College" subsequently substituted by SI 2017/353, reg 8, Sch 3, paras 1, 4, as from 31 March 2017.

Heading "Parliamentary and devolved bodies" and related entries inserted by SI 2011/1060, art 2(1), (2), Sch 1, paras 1, 7.

Heading "Police" and related entries substituted by SI 2011/1060, art 2(1), (2), Sch 1, paras 1, 8. The entries under this heading are subsequently amended as follows:

Entry "The College of Policing" inserted by the Anti-social Behaviour, Crime and Policing Act 2014, s 181(1), Sch 11, Pt 3, para 96.

Entries "The Director General of the Independent Office for Police Conduct" and "The Independent Office for Police Conduct" inserted, and entry "The Independent Police Complaints Commission" (omitted) repealed, by the Policing and Crime Act 2017, s 33(9), Sch 9, Pt 3, para 72, as from 8 January 2018.

Entries "A police and crime commissioner established under section 1 of the Police Reform and Social Responsibility Act 2011" and "The Mayor's Office for Policing and Crime established under section 3 of that Act" substituted by the Police Reform and Social Responsibility Act 2011, s 99, Sch 16, Pt 3, paras 380, 383.

Entry "The Serious Organised Crime Agency" (omitted) repealed by the Crime and Courts Act 2013, s 15(3), Sch 8, Pt 2, paras 180, 183.

Heading "Regulators" and related entries inserted by SI 2011/1060, art 2(1), (2), Sch 1, paras 1, 9. The entries under this heading are subsequently amended as follows:

Entries "The Association of Authorised Public Accountants, in respect of its public functions" and "The Association of International Accountants, in respect of its public functions" (omitted) repealed by SI 2017/353, reg 8, Sch 3, paras 1, 5(a), as from 31 March 2017.

Entry "The Association of Chartered Certified Accountants, in respect of its public functions" substituted by SI 2017/353, reg 8, Sch 3, paras 1, 5(b), as from 31 March 2017.

Entry "The Office for Nuclear Regulation" inserted by the Energy Act 2013, s 116(1), Sch 12, Pt 5, para 102.

Entry "The Regulator of Social Housing." inserted, in relation to England, by the Legislative Reform (Regulator of Social Housing) (England) Order 2018, SI 2018/1040, art 2, Schedule, Pt 2, para 42, as from 1 October 2018.

Entry "Social Work England." inserted by the Social Workers Regulations 2018, SI 2018/893, reg 40, as from 23 July 2018.

All other entries in square brackets under this heading were inserted by SI 2017/353, reg 8, Sch 3, paras 1, 5(c), as from 31 March 2017.

Heading "Transport" and related entries inserted by inserted by SI 2017/353, reg 8, Sch 3, paras 1, 6, as from 31 March 2017.

PART 2
PUBLIC AUTHORITIES: RELEVANT WELSH AUTHORITIES

Welsh Assembly Government, etc

[1.1783]
The Welsh Ministers.

The First Minister for Wales.

The Counsel General to the Welsh Assembly Government.

A subsidiary of the Welsh Ministers (within the meaning given by section 134(4) of the Government of Wales Act 2006).

National Health Service

A Local Health Board established under section 11 of the National Health Service (Wales) Act 2006.

An NHS trust established under section 18 of that Act.

. . .

A Community Health Council in Wales.

[The Board of Community Health Councils in Wales or Bwrdd Cynghorau Iechyd Cymuned Cymru.]

Local government

[A county council or county borough council in Wales.]

. . .

A fire and rescue authority constituted by a scheme under section 2 of the Fire and Rescue Services Act 2004, or a scheme to which section 4 of that Act applies, for an area in Wales.

. . .

A National Park authority established by an order under section 63 of the Environment Act 1995 for an area in Wales.

. . .

. . .

. . .

. . .

Other educational bodies

The governing body of an educational establishment maintained by a Welsh local authority (within the meaning of section 162 of the Education and Inspections Act 2006).

The governing body of an institution in Wales within the further education sector (within the meaning of section 91(3) of the Further and Higher Education Act 1992).

The governing body of an institution in Wales within the higher education sector (within the meaning of section 91(5) of that Act).

[The Higher Education Funding Council for Wales or Cyngor Cyllido Addysg Uwch Cymru.

The General Teaching Council for Wales or Cyngor Addysgu Cyffredinol Cymru.

Her Majesty's Chief Inspector of Education and Training in Wales or Prif Arolygydd Ei Mawrhydi dros Addysg a Hyfforddiant yng Nghymru.

[Qualifications Wales]

Other public authorities

The Auditor General for Wales or Archwilydd Cyffredinol Cymru.

[The Welsh Revenue Authority or Awdurdod Cyllid Cymru.]

The Public Services Ombudsman for Wales or Ombwdsmon Gwasanaethau Cyhoeddus Cymru.

[Social Care Wales or Gofal Cymdeithasol Cymru.]

The Arts Council for Wales or Cyngor Celfyddydau Cymru.

The National Museum of Wales or Amgueddfa Genedlaethol Cymru.

The National Library of Wales or Llyfrgell Genedlaethol Cymru.

The Sports Council for Wales or Cyngor Chwaraeon Cymru.

[Comisiynydd y Gymraeg (The Welsh Language Commissioner).]

. . .

The Commissioner for Older People in Wales or Comisiynydd Pobl Hyn Cymru.

The Children's Commissioner for Wales or Comisiynydd Plant Cymru.

[the Wales Audit Office or Swyddfa Archwilio Cymru.]]

NOTES

Entry "Comisiynydd y Gymraeg (The Welsh Language Commissioner)" substituted (for the original entry "The Welsh Language Board or Bwrdd yr Iaith Gymraeg") by the Welsh Language (Wales) Measure 2011 (Transfer of functions, Transitional and Consequential Provisions) Order 2012, SI 2012/990, art 11.

Entry "The Countryside Council for Wales or Cyngor Cefn Gwlad Cymru" (omitted) repealed by the Natural Resources Body for Wales (Functions) Order 2013, SI 2013/755, art 4(1), Sch 2, para 450(1), (2).

Entry "Qualifications Wales" inserted by the Qualifications Wales Act 2015, s 2(2), Sch 1, Pt 2, para 40, as from 21 September 2015.

Entry "the Wales Audit Office or Swyddfa Archwilio Cymru." inserted by the Public Audit (Wales) Act 2013, s 34, Sch 4, para 92.

Entry "Social Care Wales or Gofal Cymdeithasol Cymru" substituted (for the original entry "The Care Council for Wales or Cyngor Gofal Cymru") by SI 2017/353, reg 8, Sch 3, paras 7, 8, as from 31 March 2017.

Entry "The Welsh Revenue Authority or Awdurdod Cyllid Cymru" inserted by the Tax Collection and Management (Wales) Act 2016 (Consequential and Supplemental Provisions) Regulations 2018, SI 2018/285, reg 3, as from 1 April 2018.

All other amendments to this Part were made by the Equality Act 2010 (Specification of Relevant Welsh Authorities) Order 2011, SI 2011/1063, art 2.

Welsh Assembly Government: see the Wales Act 2014, s 4 which provides that, unless the context requires otherwise, any reference to the Welsh Assembly Government is to be read as, or as including, a reference to the Welsh Government.

PART 3
PUBLIC AUTHORITIES: RELEVANT SCOTTISH AUTHORITIES

Scottish Administration

[1.1784]
An office-holder in the Scottish Administration (within the meaning given by section 126(7)(a) of the Scotland Act 1998).

National Health Service

A Health Board constituted under section 2 of the National Health Service (Scotland) Act 1978.

A Special Health Board constituted under that section.

Local government

A council constituted under section 2 of the Local Government etc (Scotland) Act 1994.

A community council established under section 51 of the Local Government (Scotland) Act 1973.

A joint board within the meaning of section 235(1) of that Act.

. . .

A licensing board established under section 5 of the Licensing (Scotland) Act 2005, or continued in being by virtue of that section.

A National Park authority established by a designation order made under section 6 of the National Parks (Scotland) Act 2000.

Scottish Enterprise and Highlands and Islands Enterprise, established under the Enterprise and New Towns (Scotland) Act 1990.

Other educational bodies

An education authority in Scotland (within the meaning of section 135(1) of the Education (Scotland) Act 1980).

The managers of a grant-aided school (within the meaning of that section).

The board of management of a college of further education (within the meaning of section 36(1) of the Further and Higher Education (Scotland) Act 1992).

In the case of such a college of further education not under the management of a board of management, the board of governors of the college or any person responsible for the management of the college, whether or not formally constituted as a governing body or board of governors.

The governing body of an institution within the higher education sector (within the meaning of Part 2 of the Further and Higher Education (Scotland) Act 1992).

[Police and Fire]

[The Scottish Police Authority.]

[The chief constable of the Police Service of Scotland.]

[The Scottish Fire and Rescue Service.]

[The Chief Officer of the Scottish Fire and Rescue Service.]

[Other bodies and offices added on 6th April 2011

Accounts Commission for Scotland.

Audit Scotland.

Board of Trustees of the National Galleries of Scotland.

Board of Trustees of the National Museums of Scotland.

Board of Trustees of the Royal Botanic Garden, Edinburgh.

Bòrd na Gàidhlig.

. . .

A chief officer of a community justice authority.

. . .

Commissioner for Children and Young People in Scotland.

Commission for Ethical Standards in Public Life in Scotland.

The Common Services Agency for the Scottish Health Service.

A community justice authority.

Creative Scotland.

The Crofters Commission.

The General Teaching Council for Scotland.

Healthcare Improvement Scotland

Learning and Teaching Scotland.

The Mental Welfare Commission for Scotland.

[The Police Investigations and Review Commissioner.]

Quality Meat Scotland.

A regional Transport Partnership created by an order under section 1(1) of the Transport (Scotland) Act 2005.

Risk Management Authority.

Royal Commission on the Ancient and Historical Monuments of Scotland.

Scottish Children's Reporter Administration.

Scottish Commission for Human Rights.

The Scottish Criminal Cases Review Commission.

Scottish Environment Protection Agency.

Scottish Further and Higher Education Funding Council.

Scottish Futures Trust Ltd.

Scottish Information Commissioner.

The Scottish Legal Aid Board.

The Scottish Legal Complaints Commission.

Scottish Natural Heritage.

. . .

Scottish Public Services Ombudsman.

Scottish Qualifications Authority.

The Scottish Road Works Commissioner.

The Scottish Social Services Council.

The Scottish Sports Council.

Scottish Water.

Skills Development Scotland.

Social Care and Social Work Improvement Scotland.

The Standards Commission for Scotland.

[The National Library of Scotland.]

VisitScotland.

A Water Customer Consultation Panel.

The Water Industry Commission for Scotland.]

[Other bodies and offices added on 5th March 2012

Children's Hearings Scotland.

The National Convener of Children's Hearings Scotland.]

[Other bodies added on 1st April 2015

Historic Environment Scotland.

An integration joint board established by order under section 9(2) of the Public Bodies (Joint Working) (Scotland) Act 2014.

A regional board (within the meaning of section 35(1) of the Further and Higher Education (Scotland) Act 2005).]

[Other body added on 28th June 2018

ILF Scotland.]

NOTES

Entries "A joint fire and rescue board constituted by a scheme under section 2(1) of the Fire (Scotland) Act 2005", "A Chief Constable of a police force maintained under section 1 of the Police (Scotland) Act 1967", "A Chief Officer of a relevant authority appointed under section 7 of the Fire (Scotland) Act 2005" and "The Scottish Police Services Authority" (all omitted) were repealed, the heading "Police and Fire" was substituted (for the original heading "Police"), the entry "The Scottish Police Authority" was substituted (for the original entry "A police authority established under section 2 of the Police (Scotland) Act 1967"), and the entries "The chief constable of the Police Service of Scotland", "The Scottish Fire and Rescue Service" and "The Chief Officer of the Scottish Fire and Rescue Service" were inserted, by the Police and Fire Reform (Scotland) Act 2012 (Consequential Provisions and Modifications) Order 2013, SI 2013/602, art 26, Sch 2, Pt 1, para 63.

The heading "Other bodies and offices added on 6th April 2011" and associated entries were added by the Equality Act 2010 (Specification of Public Authorities) (Scotland) Order 2011, SSI 2011/233. The entry "The Police Investigations and Review Commissioner" in square brackets was substituted (for the original entry "The Police Complaints Commissioner for Scotland") by the Police and Fire Reform (Scotland) Act 2012, s 61(3); entry "The National Library of Scotland" substituted (for the original entry "The Trustees of the National Library of Scotland") by the Equality Act 2010 (Specification of Public Authorities) (Scotland) Order 2013, SSI 2013/170, art 2.

The heading "Other bodies and offices added on 5th March 2012" and associated entries were added by the Equality Act 2010 (Specification of Public Authorities) (Scotland) Order 2012, SSI 2012/55.

The heading "Other bodies added on 1st April 2015" and associated entries were added by the Equality Act 2010 (Specification of Public Authorities) (Scotland) Order 2015, SSI 2015/83, art 2, as from 1 April 2015.

The heading "Other body added on 28th June 2018" and the associated entry was added by the ILF Scotland (Miscellaneous Listings) Order 2018, SSI 2018/214, art 4, as from 28 June 2018.

[PART 4
PUBLIC AUTHORITIES: CROSS-BORDER AUTHORITIES

Cross-border Welsh authorities

[1.1785]

The Environment Agency—D

[The Natural Resources Body for Wales—A]

NHS Blood and Transplant—D

The NHS Business Services Authority—D

The Student Loans Company Limited—D]

NOTES

Inserted by the Equality Act 2010 (Public Authorities and Consequential and Supplementary Amendments) Order 2011, SI 2011/1060, art 2(1), (3), Sch 2.

Entry in square brackets inserted by the Natural Resources Body for Wales (Functions) Order 2013, SI 2013/755, art 4(1), Sch 2, para 450(1), (3).

SCHEDULE 20

(Sch 20 (Rail Vehicle Accessibility: Compliance) was outside the scope of this work and has now been repealed.)

SCHEDULE 21
REASONABLE ADJUSTMENTS: SUPPLEMENTARY

Section 189

[1.1786]

1. Preliminary

This Schedule applies for the purposes of Schedules 2, 4, 8, 13 and 15.

2. Binding obligations, etc

(1) This paragraph applies if—

(a) a binding obligation requires A to obtain the consent of another person to an alteration of premises which A occupies,

(b) where A is a controller of let premises, a binding obligation requires A to obtain the consent of another person to a variation of a term of the tenancy, or

(c) where A is a responsible person in relation to common parts, a binding obligation requires A to obtain the consent of another person to an alteration of the common parts.

(2) For the purpose of discharging a duty to make reasonable adjustments—

(a) it is always reasonable for A to have to take steps to obtain the consent, but

(b) it is never reasonable for A to have to make the alteration before the consent is obtained.

(3) In this Schedule, a binding obligation is a legally binding obligation in relation to premises, however arising; but the reference to a binding obligation in sub-paragraph (1)(a) or (c) does not include a reference to an obligation imposed by a tenancy.

(4) The steps referred to in sub-paragraph (2)(a) do not include applying to a court or tribunal.

3. Landlord's consent

(1) This paragraph applies if—

(a) A occupies premises under a tenancy,

(b) A is proposing to make an alteration to the premises so as to comply with a duty to make reasonable adjustments, and

(c) but for this paragraph, A would not be entitled to make the alteration.

(2) This paragraph also applies if—

(a) A is a responsible person in relation to common parts,

(b) A is proposing to make an alteration to the common parts so as to comply with a duty to make reasonable adjustments,

(c) A is the tenant of property which includes the common parts, and

(d) but for this paragraph, A would not be entitled to make the alteration.

(3) The tenancy has effect as if it provided—

(a) for A to be entitled to make the alteration with the written consent of the landlord,

(b) for A to have to make a written application for that consent,

(c) for the landlord not to withhold the consent unreasonably, and

(d) for the landlord to be able to give the consent subject to reasonable conditions.

(4) If a question arises as to whether A has made the alteration (and, accordingly, complied with a duty to make reasonable adjustments), any constraint attributable to the tenancy must be ignored unless A has applied to the landlord in writing for consent to the alteration.

(5) For the purposes of sub-paragraph (1) or (2), A must be treated as not entitled to make the alteration if the tenancy—

(a) imposes conditions which are to apply if A makes an alteration, or

(b) entitles the landlord to attach conditions to a consent to the alteration.

4. Proceedings before county court or sheriff

(1) This paragraph applies if, in a case within Part 3, 4, 6 or 7 of this Act—

(a) A has applied in writing to the landlord for consent to the alteration, and

(b) the landlord has refused to give consent or has given consent subject to a condition.

(2) A (or a disabled person with an interest in the alteration being made) may refer the matter to [the county court] or, in Scotland, the sheriff.

(3) The county court or sheriff must determine whether the refusal or condition is unreasonable.

(4) If the county court or sheriff finds that the refusal or condition is unreasonable, the county court or sheriff—

(a) may make such declaration as it thinks appropriate;

(b) may make an order authorising A to make the alteration specified in the order (and requiring A to comply with such conditions as are so specified).

5. Joining landlord as party to proceedings

(1) This paragraph applies to proceedings relating to a contravention of this Act by virtue of section 20.

(2) A party to the proceedings may request the employment tribunal, county court or sheriff ("the judicial authority") to direct that the landlord is joined or sisted as a party to the proceedings.

(3) The judicial authority—

(a) must grant the request if it is made before the hearing of the complaint or claim begins;

(b) may refuse the request if it is made after the hearing begins;

(c) must refuse the request if it is made after the complaint or claim has been determined.

(4) If the landlord is joined or sisted as a party to the proceedings, the judicial authority may determine whether—

(a) the landlord has refused to consent to the alteration;

(b) the landlord has consented subject to a condition;

(c) the refusal or condition was unreasonable.

(5) If the judicial authority finds that the refusal or condition was unreasonable, it—

(a) may make such declaration as it thinks appropriate;

(b) may make an order authorising A to make the alteration specified in the order (and requiring A to comply with such conditions as are so specified);

(c) may order the landlord to pay compensation to the complainant or claimant.

(6) An employment tribunal may act in reliance on sub-paragraph (5)(c) instead of, or in addition to, acting in reliance on section 124(2); but if it orders the landlord to pay compensation it must not do so in reliance on section 124(2).

(7) If [the county court] or the sheriff orders the landlord to pay compensation, it may not order A to do so.

6. Regulations

(1) Regulations may make provision as to circumstances in which a landlord is taken for the purposes of this Schedule to have—

(a) withheld consent;

(b) withheld consent reasonably;

(c) withheld consent unreasonably.

(2) Regulations may make provision as to circumstances in which a condition subject to which a landlord gives consent is taken—

(a) to be reasonable;

(b) to be unreasonable.

(3) Regulations may make provision supplementing or modifying the preceding paragraphs of this Schedule, or provision made under this paragraph, in relation to a case where A's tenancy is a sub-tenancy.

(4) Provision made by virtue of this paragraph may amend the preceding paragraphs of this Schedule.

7. Interpretation

An expression used in this Schedule and in Schedule 2, 4, 8, 13 or 15 has the same meaning in this Schedule as in that Schedule.

NOTES

Paras 4, 5: words in square brackets substituted by the Crime and Courts Act 2013, s 17(5), Sch 9, Pt 3, para 52.

Regulations : the Equality Act 2010 (Disability) Regulations 2010, SI 2010/2128 at **[2.1184]**. See further reg 14 of those Regulations at **[2.1197]** (modification of this Schedule in relation to any case where the occupier occupies premises under a sub-tenancy).

SCHEDULE 22
STATUTORY PROVISIONS

Section 191

[1.1787]

1. Statutory authority

(1) A person (P) does not contravene a provision specified in the first column of the table, so far as relating to the protected characteristic specified in the second column in respect of that provision, if P does anything P must do pursuant to a requirement specified in the third column.

Specified provision	Protected characteristic	Requirement
Parts 3 to 7	Age	A requirement of an enactment
Parts 3 to 7 and 12	Disability	A requirement of an enactment A relevant requirement or condition imposed by virtue of an enactment
Parts 3 to 7	Religion or belief	A requirement of an enactment A relevant requirement or condition imposed by virtue of an enactment
Section 29(6) and Parts 6 and 7	Sex	A requirement of an enactment
Parts 3, 4, 6 and 7	Sexual orientation	A requirement of an enactment A relevant requirement or condition imposed by virtue of an enactment

(2) A reference in the table to Part 6 does not include a reference to that Part so far as relating to vocational training.

(3) In this paragraph a reference to an enactment includes a reference to—
- (a) a Measure of the General Synod of the Church of England;
- (b) an enactment passed or made on or after the date on which this Act is passed.

(4) In the table, a relevant requirement or condition is a requirement or condition imposed (whether before or after the passing of this Act) by—
- (a) a Minister of the Crown;
- (b) a member of the Scottish Executive;
- (c) the National Assembly for Wales (constituted by the Government of Wales Act 1998);
- (d) the Welsh Ministers, the First Minister for Wales or the Counsel General to the Welsh Assembly Government.

2. Protection of women

(1) A person (P) does not contravene a specified provision only by doing in relation to a woman (W) anything P is required to do to comply with—
- (a) a pre-1975 Act enactment concerning the protection of women;
- (b) a relevant statutory provision (within the meaning of Part 1 of the Health and Safety at Work etc Act 1974) if it is done for the purpose of the protection of W (or a description of women which includes W);
- (c) a requirement of a provision specified in Schedule 1 to the Employment Act 1989 (provisions concerned with protection of women at work).

(2) The references to the protection of women are references to protecting women in relation to—
- (a) pregnancy or maternity, or
- (b) any other circumstances giving rise to risks specifically affecting women.

(3) It does not matter whether the protection is restricted to women.

(4) These are the specified provisions—
- (a) Part 5 (work);
- (b) Part 6 (education), so far as relating to vocational training.

(5) A pre-1975 Act enactment is an enactment contained in—
- (a) an Act passed before the Sex Discrimination Act 1975;
- (b) an instrument approved or made by or under such an Act (including one approved or made after the passing of the 1975 Act).

(6) If an Act repeals and re-enacts (with or without modification) a pre-1975 enactment then the provision re-enacted must be treated as being in a pre-1975 enactment.

(7) For the purposes of sub-paragraph (1)(c), a reference to a provision in Schedule 1 to the Employment Act 1989 includes a reference to a provision for the time being having effect in place of it.

(8) This paragraph applies only to the following protected characteristics—
- (a) pregnancy and maternity;
- (b) sex.

3. Educational appointments, etc: religious belief

(1) A person does not contravene Part 5 (work) only by doing a relevant act in connection with the employment of another in a relevant position.

(2) A relevant position is—

(a) the head teacher or principal of an educational establishment;

(b) the head, a fellow or other member of the academic staff of a college, or institution in the nature of a college, in a university;

(c) a professorship of a university which is a canon professorship or one to which a canonry is annexed.

(3) A relevant act is anything it is necessary to do to comply with—

(a) a requirement of an instrument relating to the establishment that the head teacher or principal must be a member of a particular religious order;

(b) a requirement of an instrument relating to the college or institution that the holder of the position must be a woman;

(c) an Act or instrument in accordance with which the professorship is a canon professorship or one to which a canonry is annexed.

(4) Sub-paragraph (3)(b) does not apply to an instrument taking effect on or after 16 January 1990 (the day on which section 5(3) of the Employment Act 1989 came into force).

(5) A Minister of the Crown may by order provide that anything in sub-paragraphs (1) to (3) does not have effect in relation to—

(a) a specified educational establishment or university;

(b) a specified description of educational establishments.

(6) An educational establishment is—

(a) a school within the meaning of the Education Act 1996 or the Education (Scotland) Act 1980;

(b) a college, or institution in the nature of a college, in a university;

(c) an institution designated by order made, or having effect as if made, under section 129 of the Education Reform Act 1988;

(d) a college of further education within the meaning of section 36 of the Further and Higher Education (Scotland) Act 1992;

(e) a university in Scotland;

(f) an institution designated by order under section 28 of the Further and Higher Education Act 1992 or section 44 of the Further and Higher Education (Scotland) Act 1992.

(7) This paragraph does not affect paragraph 2 of Schedule 9.

4. A person does not contravene this Act only by doing anything which is permitted for the purposes of—

(a) section 58(6) or (7) of the School Standards and Framework Act 1998 (dismissal of teachers because of failure to give religious education efficiently);

(b) section 60(4) and (5) of that Act (religious considerations relating to certain appointments);

(c) section 124A of that Act (preference for certain teachers at independent schools of a religious character);

[(d) section 124AA(5) to (7) of that Act (religious considerations relating to certain teachers at Academies with religious character)].

5. Crown employment, etc

(1) A person does not contravene this Act—

(a) by making or continuing in force rules mentioned in sub-paragraph (2);

(b) by publishing, displaying or implementing such rules;

(c) by publishing the gist of such rules.

(2) The rules are rules restricting to persons of particular birth, nationality, descent or residence—

(a) employment in the service of the Crown;

(b) employment by a prescribed public body;

(c) holding a public office (within the meaning of section 50).

(3) The power to make regulations for the purpose of sub-paragraph (2)(b) is exercisable by the Minister for the Civil Service.

(4) In this paragraph "public body" means a body (whether corporate or unincorporated) exercising public functions (within the meaning given by section 31(4)).

NOTES

Para 4: sub-para (d) inserted by the Education Act 2011, s 62(1), (4)(c).

Welsh Assembly Government: see the Wales Act 2014, s 4 which provides that, unless the context requires otherwise, any reference to the Welsh Assembly Government is to be read as, or as including, a reference to the Welsh Government.

Orders: as of 15 May 2019, no Orders had been made under this Schedule.

Regulations: as of 15 May 2019, no Regulations had been made under this Schedule, but by virtue of the Equality Act 2010 (Commencement No 4, Savings, Consequential, Transitional, Transitory and Incidental Provisions and Revocation) Order 2010, SI 2010/2317, art 21(1), Sch 7, the Race Relations (Prescribed Public Bodies) (No 2) Regulations 1994, SI 1994/1986 have effect as if made under para 5(2)(b).

SCHEDULE 23
GENERAL EXCEPTIONS

Section 196

[1.1788]

1. Acts authorised by statute or the executive

(1) This paragraph applies to anything done—
- (a) in pursuance of an enactment;
- (b) in pursuance of an instrument made by a member of the executive under an enactment;
- (c) to comply with a requirement imposed (whether before or after the passing of this Act) by a member of the executive by virtue of an enactment;
- (d) in pursuance of arrangements made (whether before or after the passing of this Act) by or with the approval of, or for the time being approved by, a Minister of the Crown;
- (e) to comply with a condition imposed (whether before or after the passing of this Act) by a Minister of the Crown.

(2) A person does not contravene Part 3, 4, 5 or 6 by doing anything to which this paragraph applies which discriminates against another because of the other's nationality.

(3) A person (A) does not contravene Part 3, 4, 5 or 6 if, by doing anything to which this paragraph applies, A discriminates against another (B) by applying to B a provision, criterion or practice which relates to—
- (a) B's place of ordinary residence;
- (b) the length of time B has been present or resident in or outside the United Kingdom or an area within it.

2. Organisations relating to religion or belief

(1) This paragraph applies to an organisation the purpose of which is—
- (a) to practise a religion or belief,
- (b) to advance a religion or belief,
- (c) to teach the practice or principles of a religion or belief,
- (d) to enable persons of a religion or belief to receive any benefit, or to engage in any activity, within the framework of that religion or belief, or
- (e) to foster or maintain good relations between persons of different religions or beliefs.

(2) This paragraph does not apply to an organisation whose sole or main purpose is commercial.

(3) The organisation does not contravene Part 3, 4 or 7, so far as relating to religion or belief or sexual orientation, only by restricting—
- (a) membership of the organisation;
- (b) participation in activities undertaken by the organisation or on its behalf or under its auspices;
- (c) the provision of goods, facilities or services in the course of activities undertaken by the organisation or on its behalf or under its auspices;
- (d) the use or disposal of premises owned or controlled by the organisation.

(4) A person does not contravene Part 3, 4 or 7, so far as relating to religion or belief or sexual orientation, only by doing anything mentioned in sub-paragraph (3) on behalf of or under the auspices of the organisation.

(5) A minister does not contravene Part 3, 4 or 7, so far as relating to religion or belief or sexual orientation, only by restricting—
- (a) participation in activities carried on in the performance of the minister's functions in connection with or in respect of the organisation;
- (b) the provision of goods, facilities or services in the course of activities carried on in the performance of the minister's functions in connection with or in respect of the organisation.

(6) Sub-paragraphs (3) to (5) permit a restriction relating to religion or belief only if it is imposed—
- (a) because of the purpose of the organisation, or
- (b) to avoid causing offence, on grounds of the religion or belief to which the organisation relates, to persons of that religion or belief.

(7) Sub-paragraphs (3) to (5) permit a restriction relating to sexual orientation only if it is imposed—
- (a) because it is necessary to comply with the doctrine of the organisation, or
- (b) to avoid conflict with strongly held convictions within sub-paragraph (9).

(8) In sub-paragraph (5), the reference to a minister is a reference to a minister of religion, or other person, who—
- (a) performs functions in connection with a religion or belief to which the organisation relates, and
- (b) holds an office or appointment in, or is accredited, approved or recognised for the purposes of the organisation.

(9) The strongly held convictions are—
- (a) in the case of a religion, the strongly held religious convictions of a significant number of the religion's followers;
- (b) in the case of a belief, the strongly held convictions relating to the belief of a significant number of the belief's followers.

[(9A) An organisation does not contravene Part 3, 4 or 7 only by refusing to allow premises owned or controlled by the organisation to be used—
- (a) to solemnise a relevant Scottish marriage for the reason that the marriage is the marriage of two persons of the same sex;

(b) to register a relevant Scottish civil partnership for the reason that the civil partnership is between two persons of the same sex.

(9B) A person (or a group of persons) does not contravene Part 3, 4 or 7 only by refusing to allow premises owned or controlled by the person (or the group) on behalf of an organisation to be used—

(a) to solemnise a relevant Scottish marriage for the reason that the marriage is the marriage of two persons of the same sex;

(b) to register a relevant Scottish civil partnership for the reason that the civil partnership is between two persons of the same sex.

(9C) An organisation does not contravene section 29 only by allowing an approved celebrant of the organisation to act as set out in sub-paragraph (1) or (2) of paragraph 25B of Schedule 3.

(9D) In sub-paragraphs (9A) to (9C), "approved celebrant", "relevant Scottish marriage" and "relevant Scottish civil partnership" have the same meaning as in paragraph 25B of Schedule 3.]

(10) This paragraph does not permit anything which is prohibited by section 29, so far as relating to sexual orientation, if it is done—

(a) on behalf of a public authority, and

(b) under the terms of a contract between the organisation and the public authority.

(11) In the application of this paragraph in relation to sexual orientation, sub-paragraph (1)(e) must be ignored.

(12) In the application of this paragraph in relation to sexual orientation, in sub-paragraph (3)(d), "disposal" does not include disposal of an interest in premises by way of sale if the interest being disposed of is—

(a) the entirety of the organisation's interest in the premises, or

(b) the entirety of the interest in respect of which the organisation has power of disposal.

(13) In this paragraph—

(a) "disposal" is to be construed in accordance with section 38;

(b) "public authority" has the meaning given in section 150(1).

3. Communal accommodation

(1) A person does not contravene this Act, so far as relating to sex discrimination or gender reassignment discrimination, only because of anything done in relation to—

(a) the admission of persons to communal accommodation;

(b) the provision of a benefit, facility or service linked to the accommodation.

(2) Sub-paragraph (1)(a) does not apply unless the accommodation is managed in a way which is as fair as possible to both men and women.

(3) In applying sub-paragraph (1)(a), account must be taken of—

(a) whether and how far it is reasonable to expect that the accommodation should be altered or extended or that further accommodation should be provided, and

(b) the frequency of the demand or need for use of the accommodation by persons of one sex as compared with those of the other.

(4) In applying sub-paragraph (1)(a) in relation to gender reassignment, account must also be taken of whether and how far the conduct in question is a proportionate means of achieving a legitimate aim.

(5) Communal accommodation is residential accommodation which includes dormitories or other shared sleeping accommodation which for reasons of privacy should be used only by persons of the same sex.

(6) Communal accommodation may include—

(a) shared sleeping accommodation for men and for women;

(b) ordinary sleeping accommodation;

(c) residential accommodation all or part of which should be used only by persons of the same sex because of the nature of the sanitary facilities serving the accommodation.

(7) A benefit, facility or service is linked to communal accommodation if—

(a) it cannot properly and effectively be provided except for those using the accommodation, and

(b) a person could be refused use of the accommodation in reliance on sub-paragraph (1)(a).

(8) This paragraph does not apply for the purposes of Part 5 (work) unless such arrangements as are reasonably practicable are made to compensate for—

(a) in a case where sub-paragraph (1)(a) applies, the refusal of use of the accommodation;

(b) in a case where sub-paragraph (1)(b) applies, the refusal of provision of the benefit, facility or service.

4. Training provided to non-*EEA* residents, etc

(1) A person (A) does not contravene this Act, so far as relating to nationality, only by providing a non-resident (B) with training, if A thinks that B does not intend to exercise in Great Britain skills B obtains as a result.

(2) A non-resident is a person who is not ordinarily resident in *an EEA state*.

(3) The reference to providing B with training is—

(a) if A employs B in relevant employment, a reference to doing anything in or in connection with the employment;

(b) if A as a principal allows B to do relevant contract work, a reference to doing anything in or in connection with allowing B to do the work;

(c) in a case within paragraph (a) or (b) or any other case, a reference to affording B access to facilities for education or training or ancillary benefits.

(4) Employment or contract work is relevant if its sole or main purpose is the provision of training in skills.

(5) In the case of training provided by the armed forces or Secretary of State for purposes relating to defence, sub-paragraph (1) has effect as if—

(a) the reference in sub-paragraph (2) to an EEA state were a reference to Great Britain, and
(b) in sub-paragraph (4), for "its sole or main purpose is" there were substituted "it is for purposes including".

(6) "Contract work" and "principal" each have the meaning given in section 41.

NOTES

Para 2: sub-paras (9A)–(9D) inserted by the Marriage and Civil Partnership (Scotland) Act 2014 and Civil Partnership Act 2004 (Consequential Provisions and Modifications) Order 2014, SI 2014/3229, art 29, Sch 5, para 19(1), (6), as from 16 December 2014.

Para 4: reference to "EEA" in the heading repealed, for the words in italics in sub-para (2) there are substituted the words "Great Britain" and sub-para (5)(a) is repealed, by the Equality (Amendment and Revocation) (EU Exit) Regulations 2019, SI 2019/305, reg 5(1), (9), as from exit day (as defined in the European Union (Withdrawal) Act 2018, s 20).

SCHEDULE 24
HARMONISATION: EXCEPTIONS

Section 203

[1.1789]
Part 1 (public sector duty regarding socio-economic inequalities)

Chapter 2 of Part 5 (occupational pensions)

Section 78 (gender pay gap)

Section 106 (election candidates: diversity information)

Chapters 1 to 3 and 5 of Part 9 (enforcement), except section 136

Sections 142 and 146 (unenforceable terms, declaration in respect of void terms)

Chapter 1 of Part 11 (public sector equality duty)

Part 12 (disabled persons: transport)

Part 13 (disability: miscellaneous)

Section 197 (power to specify age exceptions)

Part 15 (family property)

Part 16 (general and miscellaneous)

Schedule 1 (disability: supplementary provision)

In Schedule 3 (services and public functions: exceptions)—

(a) in Part 3 (health and care), paragraphs 13 and 14;
(b) Part 4 (immigration);
(c) Part 5 (insurance);
(d) Part 6 (marriage);
(e) Part 7 (separate and single services), except paragraph 30;
(f) Part 8 (television, radio and on-line broadcasting and distribution);
(g) Part 9 (transport);
(h) Part 10 (supplementary)

Schedule 4 (premises: reasonable adjustments)

Schedule 5 (premises: exceptions), except paragraph 1

Schedule 6 (office-holders: excluded offices), except so far as relating to colour or nationality or marriage and civil partnership

Schedule 8 (work: reasonable adjustments)

In Schedule 9 (work: exceptions)—

(a) Part 1 (general), except so far as relating to colour or nationality;
(b) Part 2 (exceptions relating to age);
(c) Part 3 (other exceptions), except paragraph 19 so far as relating to colour or nationality

Schedule 10 (education: accessibility for disabled pupils)

Schedule 13 (education: reasonable adjustments), except paragraphs 2, 5, 6 and 9

Schedule 17 (education: disabled pupils: enforcement)

Schedule 18 (public sector equality duty: exceptions)

Schedule 19 (list of public authorities)

Schedule 20 (rail vehicle accessibility: compliance)

Schedule 21 (reasonable adjustments: supplementary)

In Schedule 22 (exceptions: statutory provisions), paragraphs 2 and 5

Schedule 23 (general exceptions), except paragraph 2

Schedule 25 (information society services)

NOTES

Repealed by the Equality (Amendment and Revocation) (EU Exit) Regulations 2019, SI 2019/305, reg 5(1), (4), as from exit day (as defined in the European Union (Withdrawal) Act 2018, s 20).

SCHEDULE 25
INFORMATION SOCIETY SERVICES

Section 206

[1.1790]

1. Service providers

(1) This paragraph applies where a person concerned with the provision of an information society service (an "information society service provider") is established in Great Britain.

(2) This Act applies to anything done by the person in an EEA state (other than the United Kingdom) in providing the service as this Act would apply if the act in question were done by the person in Great Britain.

2. (1) This paragraph applies where an information society service provider is established in an EEA state (other than the United Kingdom).

(2) This Act does not apply to anything done by the person in providing the service.

3. Exceptions for mere conduits

(1) An information society service provider does not contravene this Act only by providing so much of an information society service as consists in—

- (a) the provision of access to a communication network, or
- (b) the transmission in a communication network of information provided by the recipient of the service.

(2) But sub-paragraph (1) applies only if the service provider does not—

- (a) initiate the transmission,
- (b) select the recipient of the transmission, or
- (c) select or modify the information contained in the transmission.

(3) For the purposes of sub-paragraph (1), the provision of access to a communication network, and the transmission of information in a communication network, includes the automatic, intermediate and transient storage of the information transmitted so far as the storage is solely for the purpose of carrying out the transmission in the network.

(4) Sub-paragraph (3) does not apply if the information is stored for longer than is reasonably necessary for the transmission.

4. Exception for caching

(1) This paragraph applies where an information society service consists in the transmission in a communication network of information provided by a recipient of the service.

(2) The information society service provider does not contravene this Act only by doing anything in connection with the automatic, intermediate and temporary storage of information so provided if—

- (a) the storage of the information is solely for the purpose of making more efficient the onward transmission of the information to other recipients of the service at their request, and
- (b) the condition in sub-paragraph (3) is satisfied.

(3) The condition is that the service-provider—

- (a) does not modify the information,
- (b) complies with such conditions as are attached to having access to the information, and
- (c) (where sub-paragraph (4) applies) expeditiously removes the information or disables access to it.

(4) This sub-paragraph applies if the service-provider obtains actual knowledge that—

- (a) the information at the initial source of the transmission has been removed from the network,
- (b) access to it has been disabled, or
- (c) a court or administrative authority has required the removal from the network of, or the disablement of access to, the information.

5. Exception for hosting

(1) An information society service provider does not contravene this Act only by doing anything in providing so much of an information society service as consists in the storage of information provided by a recipient of the service, if—

(a) the service provider had no actual knowledge when the information was provided that its provision amounted to a contravention of this Act, or

(b) on obtaining actual knowledge that the provision of the information amounted to a contravention of that section, the service provider expeditiously removed the information or disabled access to it.

(2) Sub-paragraph (1) does not apply if the recipient of the service is acting under the authority of the control of the service provider.

6. Monitoring obligations

An injunction or interdict under Part 1 of the Equality Act 2006 may not impose on a person concerned with the provision of a service of a description given in paragraph 3(1), 4(1) or 5(1)—

(a) a liability the imposition of which would contravene Article 12, 13 or 14 of the E-Commerce Directive;

(b) a general obligation of the description given in Article 15 of that Directive.

7. Interpretation

(1) This paragraph applies for the purposes of this Schedule.

(2) "Information society service"—

(a) has the meaning given in Article 2(a) of the E-Commerce Directive (which refers to Article 1(2) of Directive 98/34/EC of the European Parliament and of the Council of 22 June 1998 laying down a procedure for the provision of information in the field of technical standards and regulations), and

(b) is summarised in recital 17 of the E-Commerce Directive as covering "any service normally provided for remuneration, at a distance, by means of electronic equipment for the processing (including digital compression) and storage of data, and at the individual request of a recipient of a service".

(3) "The E-Commerce Directive" means Directive 2000/31/EC of the European Parliament and of the Council of 8 June 2000 on certain legal aspects of information society services, in particular electronic commerce, in the Internal Market (Directive on electronic commerce).

(4) "Recipient" means a person who (whether for professional purposes or not) uses an information society service, in particular for seeking information or making it accessible.

(5) An information society service-provider is "established" in a country or territory if the service-provider—

(a) effectively pursues an economic activity using a fixed establishment in that country or territory for an indefinite period, and

(b) is a national of an EEA state or a body mentioned in [Article 54 of the Treaty on the Functioning of the European Union].

(6) The presence or use in a particular place of equipment or other technical means of providing an information society service is not itself sufficient to constitute the establishment of a service-provider.

(7) Where it cannot be decided from which of a number of establishments an information society service is provided, the service is to be regarded as provided from the establishment at the centre of the information society service provider's activities relating to that service.

(8) Section 212(4) does not apply to references to providing a service.

NOTES

Para 7: words in square brackets in sub-para (5)(b) substituted by the Treaty of Lisbon (Changes in Terminology or Numbering) Order 2012, SI 2012/1809, art 3(1), Schedule, Pt 1.

SCHEDULES 26 AND 27

(Sch 26 (Amendments) contains various amendments which, in so far as relevant to this work, are incorporated in the appropriate place (see further the introductory notes to this Act); Sch 27 (Repeals and Revocations) contains various repeals and revocations, including the following: the Equal Pay Act 1970, the Sex Discrimination Act 1975, the Race Relations Act 1976, the Sex Discrimination Act 1986, the Employment Act 1989, ss 1–7, 9, the Social Security Act 1989, Sch 5, para 5, the Disability Discrimination Act 1995, the Pensions Act 1995, ss 62–65, the Equality Act 2006, ss 25, 26, 33, 43–81, 83–90, 94 (in part), Sch 3, paras 6–35, 41–56, the Occupational Pension Schemes (Equal Treatment) Regulations 1995 (SI 1995/3183), the Employment Equality (Religion or Belief) Regulations 2003 (SI 2003/1660), the Employment Equality (Sexual Orientation) Regulations 2003 (SI 2003/1661), the Disability Discrimination Act 1995 (Pensions) Regulations 2003 (SI 2003/2770), the Occupational Pension Schemes (Equal Treatment) (Amendment) Regulations 2005 (SI 2005/1923), the Employment Equality (Age) Regulations 2006 (SI 2006/1031) (the whole Regulations other than Schs 6 and 8), the Equality Act (Sexual Orientation) Regulations 2007 (SI 2007/1263), and the Sex Discrimination (Amendment of Legislation) Regulations 2008 (SI 2008/963).)

SCHEDULE 28
INDEX OF DEFINED EXPRESSIONS

Section 214

[1.1791]

Expression	Provision
Accrual of rights, in relation to an occupational pension scheme	Section 212(12)
Additional maternity leave	Section 213(6) and (7)
Additional maternity leave period	Section 213(8)
Age discrimination	Section 25(1)
Age group	Section 5(2)
Armed forces	Section 212(1)
Association	Section 107(2)
Auxiliary aid	Section 20(11)
Belief	Section 10(2)
Breach of an equality clause or rule	Section 212(8)
The Commission	Section 212(1)
Commonhold	Section 38(7)
Compulsory maternity leave	Section 213(3)
Contract work	Section 41(6)
Contract worker	Section 41(7)
Contravention of this Act	Section 212(9)
Crown employment	Section 83(9)
Detriment	Section 212(1) and (5)
Disability	Section 6(1)
Disability discrimination	Section 25(2)
Disabled person	Section 6(2) and (4)
Discrimination	Sections 13 to 19, 21 and 108
Disposal, in relation to premises	Section 38(3) to (5)
Education Acts	Section 212(1)
Employer, in relation to an occupational pension scheme	Section 212(11)
Employment	Section 212(1)
Enactment	Section 212(1)
Equality clause	Section 212(1)
Equality rule	Section 212(1)
Firm	Section 46(2)
Gender reassignment	Section 7(1)
Gender reassignment discrimination	Section 25(3)
Harassment	Section 26(1)
Independent educational institution	Section 89(7)
LLP	Section 46(4)
Man	Section 212(1)
Marriage and civil partnership	Section 8
Marriage and civil partnership discrimination	Section 25(4)

Expression	Provision
Maternity equality clause	Section 212(1)
Maternity equality rule	Section 212(1)
Maternity leave	Section 213(2)
Member, in relation to an occupational pension scheme	Section 212(10)
Member of the executive	Section 212(7)
Non-discrimination rule	Section 212(1)
Occupation, in relation to premises	Section 212(6)
Occupational pension scheme	Section 212(1)
Offshore work	Section 82(3)
Ordinary maternity leave	Section 213(4) and (5)
Parent	Section 212(1)
Pension credit member	Section 212(11)
Pensionable service	Section 212(11)
Pensioner member	Section 212(11)
Personal office	Section 49(2)
Physical feature	Section 20(10)
Pregnancy and maternity discrimination	Section 25(5)
Premises	Section 38(2)
Prescribed	Section 212(1)
Profession	Section 212(1)
Proposed firm	Section 46(3)
Proposed LLP	Section 46(5)
Proprietor, in relation to a school	Section 89(4)
Protected characteristics	Section 4
Protected period, in relation to pregnancy	Section 18(6)
Provision of a service	Sections 31 and 212(4)
Public function	Sections 31(4) and 150(5)
Public office	Sections 50(2) and 52(4)
Pupil	Section 89(3)
Race	Section 9(1)
Race discrimination	Section 25(6)
Reasonable adjustments, duty to make	Section 20
Relevant member of the House of Commons staff	Section 83(5)
Relevant member of the House of Lords staff	Section 83(6)
Relevant person, in relation to a personal or public office	Section 52(6)
Religion	Section 10(1)
Religious or belief-related discrimination	Section 25(7)
Requirement, the first, second or third	Section 20
Responsible body, in relation to a further or higher education institution	Section 91(12)
Responsible body, in relation to a school	Section 85(9)
School	Section 89(5) and (6)
Service-provider	Section 29(1)
Sex	Section 11
Sex discrimination	Section 25(8)
Sex equality clause	Section 212(1)
Sex equality rule	Section 212(1)
Sexual orientation	Section 12(1)
Sexual orientation discrimination	Section 25(9)
Student	Section 94(3)
Subordinate legislation	Section 212(1)
Substantial	Section 212(1)
Taxi, for the purposes of Part 3 (services and public functions)	Schedule 2, paragraph 4
Taxi, for the purposes of Chapter 1 of Part 12 (disabled persons: transport)	Section 173(1)

Expression	Provision
Tenancy	Section 38(6)
Trade	Section 212(1)
Transsexual person	Section 7(2)
Trustees or managers, in relation to an occupational pension scheme	Section 212(11)
University	Section 94(4)
Victimisation	Section 27(1)
Vocational training	Section 56(6)
Woman	Section 212(1)

BRIBERY ACT 2010

(2010 c 23)

ARRANGEMENT OF SECTIONS

An Act to make provision about offences relating to bribery; and for connected purposes

[8 April 2010]

General bribery offences

[1.1792]

1 Offences of bribing another person

(1) A person ("P") is guilty of an offence if either of the following cases applies.

(2) Case 1 is where—

(a) P offers, promises or gives a financial or other advantage to another person, and

(b) P intends the advantage—

(i) to induce a person to perform improperly a relevant function or activity, or

(ii) to reward a person for the improper performance of such a function or activity.

(3) Case 2 is where—

(a) P offers, promises or gives a financial or other advantage to another person, and

(b) P knows or believes that the acceptance of the advantage would itself constitute the improper performance of a relevant function or activity.

(4) In case 1 it does not matter whether the person to whom the advantage is offered, promised or given is the same person as the person who is to perform, or has performed, the function or activity concerned.

(5) In cases 1 and 2 it does not matter whether the advantage is offered, promised or given by P directly or through a third party.

[1.1793]

2 Offences relating to being bribed

(1) A person ("R") is guilty of an offence if any of the following cases applies.

(2) Case 3 is where R requests, agrees to receive or accepts a financial or other advantage intending that, in consequence, a relevant function or activity should be performed improperly (whether by R or another person).

(3) Case 4 is where—

(a) R requests, agrees to receive or accepts a financial or other advantage, and

(b) the request, agreement or acceptance itself constitutes the improper performance by R of a relevant function or activity.

(4) Case 5 is where R requests, agrees to receive or accepts a financial or other advantage as a reward for the improper performance (whether by R or another person) of a relevant function or activity.
(5) Case 6 is where, in anticipation of or in consequence of R requesting, agreeing to receive or accepting a financial or other advantage, a relevant function or activity is performed improperly—
(a) by R, or
(b) by another person at R's request or with R's assent or acquiescence.
(6) In cases 3 to 6 it does not matter—
(a) whether R requests, agrees to receive or accepts (or is to request, agree to receive or accept) the advantage directly or through a third party,
(b) whether the advantage is (or is to be) for the benefit of R or another person.
(7) In cases 4 to 6 it does not matter whether R knows or believes that the performance of the function or activity is improper.
(8) In case 6, where a person other than R is performing the function or activity, it also does not matter whether that person knows or believes that the performance of the function or activity is improper.

[1.1794]
3 Function or activity to which bribe relates
(1) For the purposes of this Act a function or activity is a relevant function or activity if—
(a) it falls within subsection (2), and
(b) meets one or more of conditions A to C.
(2) The following functions and activities fall within this subsection—
(a) any function of a public nature,
(b) any activity connected with a business,
(c) any activity performed in the course of a person's employment,
(d) any activity performed by or on behalf of a body of persons (whether corporate or unincorporate).
(3) Condition A is that a person performing the function or activity is expected to perform it in good faith.
(4) Condition B is that a person performing the function or activity is expected to perform it impartially.
(5) Condition C is that a person performing the function or activity is in a position of trust by virtue of performing it.
(6) A function or activity is a relevant function or activity even if it—
(a) has no connection with the United Kingdom, and
(b) is performed in a country or territory outside the United Kingdom.
(7) In this section "business" includes trade or profession.

[1.1795]
4 Improper performance to which bribe relates
(1) For the purposes of this Act a relevant function or activity—
(a) is performed improperly if it is performed in breach of a relevant expectation, and
(b) is to be treated as being performed improperly if there is a failure to perform the function or activity and that failure is itself a breach of a relevant expectation.
(2) In subsection (1) "relevant expectation"—
(a) in relation to a function or activity which meets condition A or B, means the expectation mentioned in the condition concerned, and
(b) in relation to a function or activity which meets condition C, means any expectation as to the manner in which, or the reasons for which, the function or activity will be performed that arises from the position of trust mentioned in that condition.
(3) Anything that a person does (or omits to do) arising from or in connection with that person's past performance of a relevant function or activity is to be treated for the purposes of this Act as being done (or omitted) by that person in the performance of that function or activity.

[1.1796]
5 Expectation test
(1) For the purposes of sections 3 and 4, the test of what is expected is a test of what a reasonable person in the United Kingdom would expect in relation to the performance of the type of function or activity concerned.
(2) In deciding what such a person would expect in relation to the performance of a function or activity where the performance is not subject to the law of any part of the United Kingdom, any local custom or practice is to be disregarded unless it is permitted or required by the written law applicable to the country or territory concerned.
(3) In subsection (2) "written law" means law contained in—
(a) any written constitution, or provision made by or under legislation, applicable to the country or territory concerned, or
(b) any judicial decision which is so applicable and is evidenced in published written sources.

Bribery of foreign public officials

[1.1797]
6 Bribery of foreign public officials
(1) A person ("P") who bribes a foreign public official ("F") is guilty of an offence if P's intention is to influence F in F's capacity as a foreign public official.
(2) P must also intend to obtain or retain—
(a) business, or

(b) an advantage in the conduct of business.

(3) P bribes F if, and only if—

(a) directly or through a third party, P offers, promises or gives any financial or other advantage—

(i) to F, or

(ii) to another person at F's request or with F's assent or acquiescence, and

(b) F is neither permitted nor required by the written law applicable to F to be influenced in F's capacity as a foreign public official by the offer, promise or gift.

(4) References in this section to influencing F in F's capacity as a foreign public official mean influencing F in the performance of F's functions as such an official, which includes—

(a) any omission to exercise those functions, and

(b) any use of F's position as such an official, even if not within F's authority.

(5) "Foreign public official" means an individual who—

(a) holds a legislative, administrative or judicial position of any kind, whether appointed or elected, of a country or territory outside the United Kingdom (or any subdivision of such a country or territory),

(b) exercises a public function—

(i) for or on behalf of a country or territory outside the United Kingdom (or any subdivision of such a country or territory), or

(ii) for any public agency or public enterprise of that country or territory (or subdivision), or

(c) is an official or agent of a public international organisation.

(6) "Public international organisation" means an organisation whose members are any of the following—

(a) countries or territories,

(b) governments of countries or territories,

(c) other public international organisations,

(d) a mixture of any of the above.

(7) For the purposes of subsection (3)(b), the written law applicable to F is—

(a) where the performance of the functions of F which P intends to influence would be subject to the law of any part of the United Kingdom, the law of that part of the United Kingdom,

(b) where paragraph (a) does not apply and F is an official or agent of a public international organisation, the applicable written rules of that organisation,

(c) where paragraphs (a) and (b) do not apply, the law of the country or territory in relation to which F is a foreign public official so far as that law is contained in—

(i) any written constitution, or provision made by or under legislation, applicable to the country or territory concerned, or

(ii) any judicial decision which is so applicable and is evidenced in published written sources.

(8) For the purposes of this section, a trade or profession is a business.

Failure of commercial organisations to prevent bribery

[1.1798]

7 Failure of commercial organisations to prevent bribery

(1) A relevant commercial organisation ("C") is guilty of an offence under this section if a person ("A") associated with C bribes another person intending—

(a) to obtain or retain business for C, or

(b) to obtain or retain an advantage in the conduct of business for C.

(2) But it is a defence for C to prove that C had in place adequate procedures designed to prevent persons associated with C from undertaking such conduct.

(3) For the purposes of this section, A bribes another person if, and only if, A—

(a) is, or would be, guilty of an offence under section 1 or 6 (whether or not A has been prosecuted for such an offence), or

(b) would be guilty of such an offence if section 12(2)(c) and (4) were omitted.

(4) See section 8 for the meaning of a person associated with C and see section 9 for a duty on the Secretary of State to publish guidance.

(5) In this section—

"partnership" means—

(a) a partnership within the Partnership Act 1890, or

(b) a limited partnership registered under the Limited Partnerships Act 1907,

or a firm or entity of a similar character formed under the law of a country or territory outside the United Kingdom,

"relevant commercial organisation" means—

(a) a body which is incorporated under the law of any part of the United Kingdom and which carries on a business (whether there or elsewhere),

(b) any other body corporate (wherever incorporated) which carries on a business, or part of a business, in any part of the United Kingdom,

(c) a partnership which is formed under the law of any part of the United Kingdom and which carries on a business (whether there or elsewhere), or

(d) any other partnership (wherever formed) which carries on a business, or part of a business, in any part of the United Kingdom,

and, for the purposes of this section, a trade or profession is a business.

[1.1799]

8 Meaning of associated person

(1) For the purposes of section 7, a person ("A") is associated with C if (disregarding any bribe under consideration) A is a person who performs services for or on behalf of C.

(2) The capacity in which A performs services for or on behalf of C does not matter.

(3) Accordingly A may (for example) be C's employee, agent or subsidiary.

(4) Whether or not A is a person who performs services for or on behalf of C is to be determined by reference to all the relevant circumstances and not merely by reference to the nature of the relationship between A and C.

(5) But if A is an employee of C, it is to be presumed unless the contrary is shown that A is a person who performs services for or on behalf of C.

[1.1800]

9 Guidance about commercial organisations preventing bribery

(1) The Secretary of State must publish guidance about procedures that relevant commercial organisations can put in place to prevent persons associated with them from bribing as mentioned in section 7(1).

(2) The Secretary of State may, from time to time, publish revisions to guidance under this section or revised guidance.

(3) The Secretary of State must consult the Scottish Ministers [and the Department of Justice in Northern Ireland] before publishing anything under this section.

(4) Publication under this section is to be in such manner as the Secretary of State considers appropriate.

(5) Expressions used in this section have the same meaning as in section 7.

NOTES

Sub-s (3): words in square brackets inserted by the Northern Ireland Act 1998 (Devolution of Policing and Justice Functions) Order 2012, SI 2012/2595, art 19(1), (2).

Prosecution and penalties

[1.1801]

10 Consent to prosecution

(1) No proceedings for an offence under this Act may be instituted in England and Wales except by or with the consent of—

(a) the Director of Public Prosecutions, [or]
(b) the Director of the Serious Fraud Office, . . .
(c) . . .

(2) No proceedings for an offence under this Act may be instituted in Northern Ireland except by or with the consent of—

(a) the Director of Public Prosecutions for Northern Ireland, or
(b) the Director of the Serious Fraud Office.

(3) No proceedings for an offence under this Act may be instituted in England and Wales or Northern Ireland by a person—

(a) who is acting—
  (i) under the direction or instruction of the Director of Public Prosecutions [or the Director of the Serious Fraud Office], or
  (ii) on behalf of such a Director, or
(b) to whom such a function has been assigned by such a Director,

except with the consent of the Director concerned to the institution of the proceedings.

(4) The Director of Public Prosecutions [and the Director of the Serious Fraud Office] must exercise personally any function under subsection (1), (2) or (3) of giving consent.

(5) The only exception is if—

(a) the Director concerned is unavailable, and
(b) there is another person who is designated in writing by the Director acting personally as the person who is authorised to exercise any such function when the Director is unavailable.

(6) In that case, the other person may exercise the function but must do so personally.

(7) Subsections (4) to (6) apply instead of any other provisions which would otherwise have enabled any function of the Director of Public Prosecutions [or the Director of the Serious Fraud Office] under subsection (1), (2) or (3) of giving consent to be exercised by a person other than the Director concerned.

(8) No proceedings for an offence under this Act may be instituted in Northern Ireland by virtue of section 36 of the Justice (Northern Ireland) Act 2002 (delegation of the functions of the Director of Public Prosecutions for Northern Ireland to persons other than the Deputy Director) except with the consent of the Director of Public Prosecutions for Northern Ireland to the institution of the proceedings.

(9) The Director of Public Prosecutions for Northern Ireland must exercise personally any function under subsection (2) or (8) of giving consent unless the function is exercised personally by the Deputy Director of Public Prosecutions for Northern Ireland by virtue of section 30(4) or (7) of the Act of 2002 (powers of Deputy Director to exercise functions of Director).

(10) Subsection (9) applies instead of section 36 of the Act of 2002 in relation to the functions of the Director of Public Prosecutions for Northern Ireland and the Deputy Director of Public Prosecutions for Northern Ireland under, or (as the case may be) by virtue of, subsections (2) and (8) above of giving consent.

NOTES

The word "or" in square brackets in sub-s (1)(a) was inserted, sub-s (1)(c) and the preceding word were repealed, and the words in square brackets in sub-ss (3), (4), (7) were substituted, by the Public Bodies (Merger of the Director of Public Prosecutions and the Director of Revenue and Customs Prosecutions) Order 2014, SI 2014/834, art 3(3)(b), Sch 2, para 74.

[1.1802]

11 Penalties

(1) An individual guilty of an offence under section 1, 2 or 6 is liable—

(a) on summary conviction, to imprisonment for a term not exceeding 12 months, or to a fine not exceeding the statutory maximum, or to both,

(b) on conviction on indictment, to imprisonment for a term not exceeding 10 years, or to a fine, or to both.

(2) Any other person guilty of an offence under section 1, 2 or 6 is liable—

(a) on summary conviction, to a fine not exceeding the statutory maximum,

(b) on conviction on indictment, to a fine.

(3) A person guilty of an offence under section 7 is liable on conviction on indictment to a fine.

(4) The reference in subsection (1)(a) to 12 months is to be read—

(a) in its application to England and Wales in relation to an offence committed before the commencement of section 154(1) of the Criminal Justice Act 2003, and

(b) in its application to Northern Ireland,

as a reference to 6 months.

Other provisions about offences

[1.1803]

12 Offences under this Act: territorial application

(1) An offence is committed under section 1, 2 or 6 in England and Wales, Scotland or Northern Ireland if any act or omission which forms part of the offence takes place in that part of the United Kingdom.

(2) Subsection (3) applies if—

(a) no act or omission which forms part of an offence under section 1, 2 or 6 takes place in the United Kingdom,

(b) a person's acts or omissions done or made outside the United Kingdom would form part of such an offence if done or made in the United Kingdom, and

(c) that person has a close connection with the United Kingdom.

(3) In such a case—

(a) the acts or omissions form part of the offence referred to in subsection (2)(a), and

(b) proceedings for the offence may be taken at any place in the United Kingdom.

(4) For the purposes of subsection (2)(c) a person has a close connection with the United Kingdom if, and only if, the person was one of the following at the time the acts or omissions concerned were done or made—

(a) a British citizen,

(b) a British overseas territories citizen,

(c) a British National (Overseas),

(d) a British Overseas citizen,

(e) a person who under the British Nationality Act 1981 was a British subject,

(f) a British protected person within the meaning of that Act,

(g) an individual ordinarily resident in the United Kingdom,

(h) a body incorporated under the law of any part of the United Kingdom,

(i) a Scottish partnership.

(5) An offence is committed under section 7 irrespective of whether the acts or omissions which form part of the offence take place in the United Kingdom or elsewhere.

(6) Where no act or omission which forms part of an offence under section 7 takes place in the United Kingdom, proceedings for the offence may be taken at any place in the United Kingdom.

(7) Subsection (8) applies if, by virtue of this section, proceedings for an offence are to be taken in Scotland against a person.

(8) Such proceedings may be taken—

(a) in any sheriff court district in which the person is apprehended or in custody, or

(b) in such sheriff court district as the Lord Advocate may determine.

(9) In subsection (8) "sheriff court district" is to be read in accordance with section 307(1) of the Criminal Procedure (Scotland) Act 1995.

[1.1804]

13 Defence for certain bribery offences etc

(1) It is a defence for a person charged with a relevant bribery offence to prove that the person's conduct was necessary for—

(a) the proper exercise of any function of an intelligence service, or

(b) the proper exercise of any function of the armed forces when engaged on active service.

(2) The head of each intelligence service must ensure that the service has in place arrangements designed to ensure that any conduct of a member of the service which would otherwise be a relevant bribery offence is necessary for a purpose falling within subsection (1)(a).

(3) The Defence Council must ensure that the armed forces have in place arrangements designed to ensure that any conduct of—

(a) a member of the armed forces who is engaged on active service, or

(b) a civilian subject to service discipline when working in support of any person falling within paragraph (a),

which would otherwise be a relevant bribery offence is necessary for a purpose falling within subsection (1)(b).

(4) The arrangements which are in place by virtue of subsection (2) or (3) must be arrangements which the Secretary of State considers to be satisfactory.

(5) For the purposes of this section, the circumstances in which a person's conduct is necessary for a purpose falling within subsection (1)(a) or (b) are to be treated as including any circumstances in which the person's conduct—

(a) would otherwise be an offence under section 2, and

(b) involves conduct by another person which, but for subsection (1)(a) or (b), would be an offence under section 1.

(6) In this section—

"active service" means service in—

(a) an action or operation against an enemy,

(b) an operation outside the British Islands for the protection of life or property, or

(c) the military occupation of a foreign country or territory,

"armed forces" means Her Majesty's forces (within the meaning of the Armed Forces Act 2006),

"civilian subject to service discipline" and "enemy" have the same meaning as in the Act of 2006,

"GCHQ" has the meaning given by section 3(3) of the Intelligence Services Act 1994,

"head" means—

(a) in relation to the Security Service, the Director General of the Security Service,

(b) in relation to the Secret Intelligence Service, the Chief of the Secret Intelligence Service, and

(c) in relation to GCHQ, the Director of GCHQ,

"intelligence service" means the Security Service, the Secret Intelligence Service or GCHQ,

"relevant bribery offence" means—

(a) an offence under section 1 which would not also be an offence under section 6,

(b) an offence under section 2,

(c) an offence committed by aiding, abetting, counselling or procuring the commission of an offence falling within paragraph (a) or (b),

(d) an offence of attempting or conspiring to commit, or of inciting the commission of, an offence falling within paragraph (a) or (b), or

(e) an offence under Part 2 of the Serious Crime Act 2007 (encouraging or assisting crime) in relation to an offence falling within paragraph (a) or (b).

[1.1805]

14 Offences under sections 1, 2 and 6 by bodies corporate etc

(1) This section applies if an offence under section 1, 2 or 6 is committed by a body corporate or a Scottish partnership.

(2) If the offence is proved to have been committed with the consent or connivance of—

(a) a senior officer of the body corporate or Scottish partnership, or

(b) a person purporting to act in such a capacity,

the senior officer or person (as well as the body corporate or partnership) is guilty of the offence and liable to be proceeded against and punished accordingly.

(3) But subsection (2) does not apply, in the case of an offence which is committed under section 1, 2 or 6 by virtue of section 12(2) to (4), to a senior officer or person purporting to act in such a capacity unless the senior officer or person has a close connection with the United Kingdom (within the meaning given by section 12(4)).

(4) In this section—

"director", in relation to a body corporate whose affairs are managed by its members, means a member of the body corporate,

"senior officer" means—

(a) in relation to a body corporate, a director, manager, secretary or other similar officer of the body corporate, and

(b) in relation to a Scottish partnership, a partner in the partnership.

[1.1806]

15 Offences under section 7 by partnerships

(1) Proceedings for an offence under section 7 alleged to have been committed by a partnership must be brought in the name of the partnership (and not in that of any of the partners).

(2) For the purposes of such proceedings—

(a) rules of court relating to the service of documents have effect as if the partnership were a body corporate, and

(b) the following provisions apply as they apply in relation to a body corporate—

(i) section 33 of the Criminal Justice Act 1925 and Schedule 3 to the Magistrates' Courts Act 1980,

(ii) section 18 of the Criminal Justice Act (Northern Ireland) 1945 (c 15 (NI)) and Schedule 4 to the Magistrates' Courts (Northern Ireland) Order 1981 (SI 1981/1675 (NI 26)),

(iii) section 70 of the Criminal Procedure (Scotland) Act 1995.

(3) A fine imposed on the partnership on its conviction for an offence under section 7 is to be paid out of the partnership assets.

(4) In this section "partnership" has the same meaning as in section 7.

Supplementary and final provisions

[1.1807]

16 Application to Crown

This Act applies to individuals in the public service of the Crown as it applies to other individuals.

[1.1808]

17 Consequential provision

(1) The following common law offences are abolished—

(a) the offences under the law of England and Wales and Northern Ireland of bribery and embracery,

(b) the offences under the law of Scotland of bribery and accepting a bribe.

(2) Schedule 1 (which contains consequential amendments) has effect.

(3) Schedule 2 (which contains repeals and revocations) has effect.

(4) The relevant national authority may by order make such supplementary, incidental or consequential provision as the relevant national authority considers appropriate for the purposes of this Act or in consequence of this Act.

(5) The power to make an order under this section—

(a) is exercisable by statutory instrument [(subject to subsection (9A))],

(b) includes power to make transitional, transitory or saving provision,

(c) may, in particular, be exercised by amending, repealing, revoking or otherwise modifying any provision made by or under an enactment (including any Act passed in the same Session as this Act).

(6) Subject to subsection (7), a statutory instrument containing an order of the Secretary of State under this section may not be made unless a draft of the instrument has been laid before, and approved by a resolution of, each House of Parliament.

(7) A statutory instrument containing an order of the Secretary of State under this section which does not amend or repeal a provision of a public general Act or of devolved legislation is subject to annulment in pursuance of a resolution of either House of Parliament.

(8) Subject to subsection (9), a statutory instrument containing an order of the Scottish Ministers under this section may not be made unless a draft of the instrument has been laid before, and approved by a resolution of, the Scottish Parliament.

(9) A statutory instrument containing an order of the Scottish Ministers under this section which does not amend or repeal a provision of an Act of the Scottish Parliament or of a public general Act is subject to annulment in pursuance of a resolution of the Scottish Parliament.

[(9A) The power of the Department of Justice in Northern Ireland to make an order under this section is exercisable by statutory rule for the purposes of the Statutory Rules (Northern Ireland) Order 1979 (and not by statutory instrument).

(9B) Subject to subsection (9C), an order of the Department of Justice in Northern Ireland made under this section is subject to affirmative resolution (within the meaning of section 41(4) of the Interpretation Act (Northern Ireland) 1954).

(9C) An order of the Department of Justice in Northern Ireland made under this section which does not amend or repeal a provision of an Act of the Northern Ireland Assembly or of a public general Act is subject to negative resolution (within the meaning of section 41(6) of the Interpretation Act (Northern Ireland) 1954).]

(10) In this section—

"devolved legislation" means an Act of the Scottish Parliament, a Measure of the National Assembly for Wales or an Act of the Northern Ireland Assembly,

"enactment" includes an Act of the Scottish Parliament and Northern Ireland legislation,

"relevant national authority" means—

(a) in the case of provision which would be within the legislative competence of the Scottish Parliament if it were contained in an Act of that Parliament, the Scottish Ministers, . . .

[(aa) in the case of provision which could be made by an Act of the Northern Ireland Assembly without the consent of the Secretary of State (see sections 6 to 8 of the Northern Ireland Act 1998), the Department of Justice in Northern Ireland, and]

(b) in any other case, the Secretary of State.

NOTES

Sub-s (5): words in square brackets inserted by the Northern Ireland Act 1998 (Devolution of Policing and Justice Functions) Order 2012, SI 2012/2595, art 19(1), (3)(a).

Sub-ss (9A)–(9C): inserted by SI 2012/2595, art 19(1), (3)(b).

Sub-s (10): in definition "relevant national authority", word omitted repealed, and para (aa) inserted, by SI 2012/2595, art 19(1), (3)(c).

Orders: the Bribery Act 2010 (Consequential Amendments) Order 2011, SI 2011/1441.

[1.1809]

18 Extent

(1) Subject as follows, this Act extends to England and Wales, Scotland and Northern Ireland.

(2) Subject to subsections (3) to (5), any amendment, repeal or revocation made by Schedule 1 or 2 has the same extent as the provision amended, repealed or revoked.

(3) The amendment of, and repeals in, the Armed Forces Act 2006 do not extend to the Channel Islands.

(4) The amendments of the International Criminal Court Act 2001 extend to England and Wales and Northern Ireland only.

(5) Subsection (2) does not apply to the repeal in the Civil Aviation Act 1982.

[1.1810]
19 Commencement and transitional provision etc
(1) Subject to subsection (2), this Act comes into force on such day as the Secretary of State may by order made by statutory instrument appoint.
(2) Sections 16, 17(4) to (10) and 18, this section (other than subsections (5) to (7)) and section 20 come into force on the day on which this Act is passed.
(3) An order under subsection (1) may—
  (a) appoint different days for different purposes,
  (b) make such transitional, transitory or saving provision as the Secretary of State considers appropriate in connection with the coming into force of any provision of this Act.
(4) The Secretary of State must consult the Scottish Ministers before making an order under this section in connection with any provision of this Act which would be within the legislative competence of the Scottish Parliament if it were contained in an Act of that Parliament.
(5) This Act does not affect any liability, investigation, legal proceeding or penalty for or in respect of—
  (a) a common law offence mentioned in subsection (1) of section 17 which is committed wholly or partly before the coming into force of that subsection in relation to such an offence, or
  (b) an offence under the Public Bodies Corrupt Practices Act 1889 or the Prevention of Corruption Act 1906 committed wholly or partly before the coming into force of the repeal of the Act by Schedule 2 to this Act.
(6) For the purposes of subsection (5) an offence is partly committed before a particular time if any act or omission which forms part of the offence takes place before that time.
(7) Subsections (5) and (6) are without prejudice to section 16 of the Interpretation Act 1978 (general savings on repeal).

NOTES
Orders: the Bribery Act 2010 (Commencement) Order 2011, SI 2011/1418.

[1.1811]
20 Short title
This Act may be cited as the Bribery Act 2010.

SCHEDULES 1 AND 2

(Sch 1 (Consequential Amendments) and Sch 2 (Repeals and Revocations) contain various amendments, repeals and revocations of enactments that are outside the scope of this work.)

EUROPEAN UNION ACT 2011

(2011 c 12)

An Act to make provision about treaties relating to the European Union and decisions made under them, including provision implementing the Protocol signed at Brussels on 23 June 2010 amending the Protocol (No 36) on transitional provisions annexed to the Treaty on European Union, to the Treaty on the Functioning of the European Union and to the Treaty establishing the European Atomic Energy Community; and to make provision about the means by which directly applicable or directly effective European Union law has effect in the United Kingdom

[19 July 2011]

NOTES
The whole of this Act is repealed by the European Union (Withdrawal) Act 2018, s 23(8), Sch 9, as from exit day (as defined in s 20 of that Act).
Most of this Act covers matters outside the scope of this work. Section 15 amends the European Communities Act 1972, s 1 at **[1.14]**. Only s 18 below is directly relevant to employment law. For reasons of space, the subject matter of sections not printed is not annotated. This Act applies to the whole of the United Kingdom (see s 20). Sections 15 and 18 came into force on 19 July 2011 (ie, the date of Royal assent) by virtue of s 21 of this Act.

PART 3
GENERAL

Status of EU law

[1.1812]
18 Status of EU law dependent on continuing statutory basis
Directly applicable or directly effective EU law (that is, the rights, powers, liabilities, obligations, restrictions, remedies and procedures referred to in section 2(1) of the European Communities Act 1972) falls to be recognised and available in law in the United Kingdom only by virtue of that Act or where it is required to be recognised and available in law by virtue of any other Act.

LOCALISM ACT 2011

(2011 c 20)

ARRANGEMENT OF SECTIONS

PART I
LOCAL GOVERNMENT

CHAPTER 8
PAY ACCOUNTABILITY

An Act to make provision about the functions and procedures of local and certain other authorities; to make provision about the functions of the Commission for Local Administration in England; to enable the recovery of financial sanctions imposed by the Court of Justice of the European Union on the United Kingdom from local and public authorities; to make provision about local government finance; to make provision about town and country planning, the Community Infrastructure Levy and the authorisation of nationally significant infrastructure projects; to make provision about social and other housing; to make provision about regeneration in London; and for connected purposes

[15 November 2011]

NOTES

Most of this Act covers matters outside the scope of this work and, for reasons of space, the subject matter of sections not printed is not annotated. Sections 38–43 came into force on 15 January 2012 in relation to England (by virtue of s 240(1)(b) of this Act), and on 31 January 2012 in relation to Wales (by virtue of the Localism Act 2011 (Commencement No 1) (Wales) Order 2012, SI 2012/193 which was made under s 240(3)). The provisions of the Act reproduced here apply to England and Wales only (see s 239).

PART 1
LOCAL GOVERNMENT

CHAPTER 8 PAY ACCOUNTABILITY

[1.1813]
38 Pay policy statements

(1) A relevant authority must prepare a pay policy statement for the financial year 2012-2013 and each subsequent financial year.

(2) A pay policy statement for a financial year must set out the authority's policies for the financial year relating to—

(a) the remuneration of its chief officers,
(b) the remuneration of its lowest-paid employees, and
(c) the relationship between—
  (i) the remuneration of its chief officers, and
  (ii) the remuneration of its employees who are not chief officers.

(3) The statement must state—

(a) the definition of "lowest-paid employees" adopted by the authority for the purposes of the statement, and
(b) the authority's reasons for adopting that definition.

(4) The statement must include the authority's policies relating to—

(a) the level and elements of remuneration for each chief officer,
(b) remuneration of chief officers on recruitment,
(c) increases and additions to remuneration for each chief officer,
(d) the use of performance-related pay for chief officers,
(e) the use of bonuses for chief officers,
(f) the approach to the payment of chief officers on their ceasing to hold office under or to be employed by the authority, and
(g) the publication of and access to information relating to remuneration of chief officers.

(5) A pay policy statement for a financial year may also set out the authority's policies for the financial year relating to the other terms and conditions applying to the authority's chief officers.

[1.1814]
39 Supplementary provisions relating to statements

(1) A relevant authority's pay policy statement must be approved by a resolution of the authority before it comes into force.

(2) The first statement must be prepared and approved before the end of 31 March 2012.
(3) Each subsequent statement must be prepared and approved before the end of the 31 March immediately preceding the financial year to which it relates.
(4) A relevant authority may by resolution amend its pay policy statement (including after the beginning of the financial year to which it relates).
(5) As soon as is reasonably practicable after approving or amending a pay policy statement, the authority must publish the statement or the amended statement in such manner as it thinks fit (which must include publication on the authority's website).

[1.1815]
40 Guidance
(1) A relevant authority in England must, in performing its functions under section 38 or 39, have regard to any guidance issued or approved by the Secretary of State.
(2) A relevant authority in Wales must, in performing its functions under section 38 or 39, have regard to any guidance issued or approved by the Welsh Ministers.

[1.1816]
41 Determinations relating to remuneration etc
(1) This section applies to a determination that—
(a) is made by a relevant authority in a financial year beginning on or after 1 April 2012 and
(b) relates to the remuneration of or other terms and conditions applying to a chief officer of the authority.
(2) The relevant authority must comply with its pay policy statement for the financial year in making the determination.
(3) Any power of a fire and rescue authority within section 43(1)(i) [or (j)] to appoint officers and employees is subject to the requirement in subsection (2).
(4) *(Amends the Local Government Act 1972, s 112.)*

NOTES
Sub-s (3): words in square brackets inserted by the Policing and Crime Act 2017, s 6, Sch 1, Pt 2, para 94(1), (2), as from 3 April 2017.

[1.1817]
42 Exercise of functions
(1) The functions conferred on a relevant authority by this Chapter are not to be the responsibility of an executive of the authority under executive arrangements.
(2) Section 101 of the Local Government Act 1972 (arrangements for discharge of functions by local authorities) does not apply to the function of passing a resolution under this Chapter.
(3) The function of a fire and rescue authority within section 43(1)(i) of passing a resolution under this Chapter may not be delegated by the authority.

[1.1818]
43 Interpretation
(1) In this Chapter "relevant authority" means—
(a) a county council,
(b) a county borough council,
(c) a district council,
(d) a London borough council,
(e) the Common Council of the City of London in its capacity as a local authority,
(f) the Council of the Isles of Scilly,
[(g) in relation only to sections 38, 40 and 41 and this section, the London Fire Commissioner,]
(h) a metropolitan county fire and rescue authority,
(i) a fire and rescue authority constituted by a scheme under section 2 of the Fire and Rescue Services Act 2004 or a scheme to which section 4 of that Act applies, [or
(j) in relation only to sections 38, 40 and 41 and this section, a fire and rescue authority created by an order under section 4A of that Act].
(2) In this Chapter "chief officer", in relation to a relevant authority, means each of the following—
(a) the head of its paid service designated under section 4(1) of the Local Government and Housing Act 1989;
(b) its monitoring officer designated under section 5(1) of that Act;
(c) a statutory chief officer mentioned in section 2(6) of that Act;
(d) a non-statutory chief officer mentioned in section 2(7) of that Act;
(e) a deputy chief officer mentioned in section 2(8) of that Act.
(3) In this Chapter "remuneration", in relation to a chief officer and a relevant authority, means—
(a) the chief officer's salary or, in the case of a chief officer engaged by the authority under a contract for services, payments made by the authority to the chief officer for those services,
(b) any bonuses payable by the authority to the chief officer,
(c) any charges, fees or allowances payable by the authority to the chief officer,
(d) any benefits in kind to which the chief officer is entitled as a result of the chief officer's office or employment,
(e) any increase in or enhancement of the chief officer's pension entitlement where the increase or enhancement is as a result of a resolution of the authority, and

(f) any amounts payable by the authority to the chief officer on the chief officer ceasing to hold office under or be employed by the authority, other than amounts that may be payable by virtue of any enactment.

(4) In this Chapter "terms and conditions", in relation to a chief officer and a relevant authority, means the terms and conditions on which the chief officer holds office under or is employed by the authority.

(5) References in this Chapter to the remuneration of, or the other terms and conditions applying to, a chief officer include—

(a) the remuneration that may be provided to, or the terms and conditions that may apply to, that chief officer in the future, and

(b) the remuneration that is to be provided to, or the terms and conditions that are to apply to, chief officers of that kind that the authority may appoint in the future.

(6) In this Chapter "remuneration", in relation to a relevant authority and an employee of its who is not a chief officer, means—

(a) the employee's salary,

(b) any bonuses payable by the authority to the employee,

(c) any allowances payable by the authority to the employee,

(d) any benefits in kind to which the employee is entitled as a result of the employee's employment,

(e) any increase in or enhancement of the employee's pension entitlement where the increase or enhancement is as a result of a resolution of the authority, and

(f) any amounts payable by the authority to the employee on the employee ceasing to be employed by the authority, other than any amounts that may be payable by virtue of any enactment.

(7) References in this Chapter to the remuneration of an employee who is not a chief officer include—

(a) the remuneration that may be provided to that employee in the future, and

(b) the remuneration that is to be provided to employees of the same kind that the authority may employ in the future.

(8) In this Chapter—

"enactment" includes an enactment comprised in subordinate legislation (within the meaning of the Interpretation Act 1978);

"financial year" means the period of 12 months ending with 31 March in any year.

NOTES

Sub-s (1) is amended as follows:

Para (g) substituted by the Policing and Crime Act 2017, s 9(3)(c), Sch 2, Pt 2, paras 118, 120, as from 1 April 2018.

Word omitted from para (h) repealed, and para (j) and the preceding word inserted by the Policing and Crime Act 2017, s 6, Sch 1, Pt 2, para 94(1), (3), as from 3 April 2017.

HEALTH AND SOCIAL CARE ACT 2012

(2012 c 7)

An Act to establish and make provision about a National Health Service Commissioning Board and clinical commissioning groups and to make other provision about the National Health Service in England; to make provision about public health in the United Kingdom; to make provision about regulating health and adult social care services; to make provision about public involvement in health and social care matters, scrutiny of health matters by local authorities and co-operation between local authorities and commissioners of health care services; to make provision about regulating health and social care workers; to establish and make provision about a National Institute for Health and Care Excellence; to establish and make provision about a Health and Social Care Information Centre and to make other provision about information relating to health or social care matters; to abolish certain public bodies involved in health or social care; to make other provision about health care; and for connected purposes

[27 March 2012]

NOTES

Only the three provisions of this Act most relevant to employment law are reproduced. Provisions omitted are not annotated. Sections 300, 301 and Sch 23 apply to England and Wales, and also apply to Scotland and Northern Ireland insofar as they confer powers in connection with the abolition of the Health Protection Agency (see s 308(1), (3)(i)). Certain specified provisions of this Act (which are outside the scope of this work) came into force on the date of Royal assent (27 March 2012). This Act also came into force on 27 March 2012 so far as necessary for enabling the exercise on or after that day of any power to make an Order or Regulations or to give directions. For all other purposes, this Act comes into force in accordance with Orders made under s 306. The provisions reproduced here came into force on 1 July 2012 (except insofar as relating to (a) the National Health Service Commissioning Board, (b) a clinical commissioning group, (c) any person with whom the Secretary of State has made, or has decided to make, an agreement under section 12ZA(1) of the Mental Health Act 1983, (d) the National Institute for Health and Care Excellence and (e) the Health and Social Care Information Centre); on 1 October 2012 (insofar as relating to the Board and a clinical commissioning group); and on 1 April 2013 (otherwise).

PART 11
MISCELLANEOUS

Transfer schemes

[1.1819]
300 Transfer schemes

(1) The Secretary of State may make a property transfer scheme or a staff transfer scheme in connection with—
(a) the establishment or abolition of a body by this Act, or
(b) the modification of the functions of a body or other person by or under this Act.

(2) A property transfer scheme is a scheme for the transfer from a body or other person mentioned in the first column of the Table in Schedule 22 of any property, rights or liabilities, other than rights or liabilities under or in connection with a contract of employment, to a body or other person mentioned in the corresponding entry in the second column.

(3) A staff transfer scheme is a scheme for the transfer from a body or other person mentioned in the first column of the Table in Schedule 23 of any rights or liabilities under or in connection with a contract of employment to a body or other person mentioned in the corresponding entry in the second column.

(4) The Secretary of State may direct the Board or a qualifying company to exercise the functions of the Secretary of State in relation to the making of a property transfer scheme or a staff transfer scheme in connection with the abolition of—
(a) one or more Primary Care Trusts specified in the direction, or
(b) one or more Strategic Health Authorities so specified.

(5) Where the Secretary of State gives a direction under subsection (4), the Secretary of State may give directions to the Board or (as the case may be) the company about its exercise of the functions.

(6) For the purposes of this section and section 301—
(a) an individual who holds employment in the civil service is to be treated as employed by virtue of a contract of employment, and
(b) the terms of the individual's employment in the civil service are to be regarded as constituting the terms of the contract of employment.

(7) In this section and sections 301 and 302 references to the transfer of property include references to the grant of a lease.

(8) In this section and Schedules 22 and 23, "qualifying company" means—
(a) a company which is formed under section 223 of the National Health Service Act 2006 and wholly or partly owned by the Secretary of State or the Board, or
(b) a subsidiary of a company which is formed under that section and wholly owned by the Secretary of State.

(9) In section 301 and Schedules 22 and 23—
"local authority" means—
(a) a county council in England;
(b) a district council in England, other than a council for a district in a county for which there is a county council;
(c) a London borough council;
(d) the Council of the Isles of Scilly;
(e) the Common Council of the City of London;
"public authority" means any body or other person which has functions conferred by or under an Act or by royal charter.

NOTES

Regulations: the National Health Service and Public Health (Functions and Miscellaneous Provisions) Regulations 2013, SI 2013/261.

[1.1820]
301 Transfer schemes: supplemental

(1) The things that may be transferred under a property transfer scheme or a staff transfer scheme include—
(a) property, rights and liabilities that could not otherwise be transferred;
(b) property acquired, and rights and liabilities arising, after the making of the scheme;
(c) criminal liabilities but only where the transfer is to a person mentioned in subsection (2).

(2) Those persons are—
(a) the National Health Service Commissioning Board;
(b) a clinical commissioning group;
(c) a local authority;
(d) the Care Quality Commission;
(e) Monitor;
(f) the National Institute for Health and Care Excellence;
(g) the Health and Social Care Information Centre;
(h) the Health and Care Professions Council;
(i) a public authority other than a Minister of the Crown.

(3) A property transfer scheme or a staff transfer scheme may make supplementary, incidental, transitional and consequential provision and may in particular—
(a) create rights, or impose liabilities, in relation to property or rights transferred;
(b) make provision about the continuing effect of things done by the transferor in respect of anything transferred;

(c) make provision about the continuation of things (including legal proceedings) in the process of being done by, on behalf of or in relation to the transferor in respect of anything transferred;

(d) make provision for references to the transferor in an instrument or other document in respect of anything transferred to be treated as references to the transferee.

(4) A property transfer scheme may make provision for the shared ownership or use of property.

(5) A staff transfer scheme may make provision which is the same or similar to the TUPE regulations.

(6) A property transfer scheme or a staff transfer scheme may provide—

(a) for the scheme to be modified by agreement after it comes into effect, and

(b) for any such modifications to have effect from the date when the original scheme comes into effect.

(7) Where a Primary Care Trust, a Strategic Health Authority or a Special Health Authority is abolished by this Act, the Secretary of State must exercise the powers conferred by section 300 and this section so as to secure that all the body's liabilities (other than criminal liabilities) are dealt with.

(8) In this section, "TUPE regulations" means the Transfer of Undertakings (Protection of Employment) Regulations 2006 (SI 2006/246).

SCHEDULES

SCHEDULE 23
STAFF TRANSFER SCHEMES

Section 300(3)

[1.1821]

Transferor	**Permitted transferees**
Any Primary Care Trust	The Secretary of State
	The National Health Service Commissioning Board
	A clinical commissioning group
	A local authority
	The Care Quality Commission
	A Special Health Authority
	Any public authority which exercises functions in relation to health and is prescribed in regulations
	A qualifying company
	Any person with whom the Secretary of State has made, or has decided to make, an agreement under section 12ZA(1) of the Mental Health Act 1983
Any Strategic Health Authority	The Secretary of State
	The National Health Service Commissioning Board
	A clinical commissioning group
	The Care Quality Commission
	Monitor
	A Special Health Authority
	Any public authority which exercises functions in relation to health and is prescribed in regulations
	A qualifying company
	Any person with whom the Secretary of State has made, or has decided to make, an agreement under section 12ZA(1) of the Mental Health Act 1983
The Special Health Authority known as National Institute for Health and Clinical Excellence	The National Institute for Health and Care Excellence (established under section 232)
The Special Health Authority known as the Health and Social Care Information Centre	The Health and Social Care Information Centre (established under section 252)
The Special Health Authority known as the NHS Institute for Innovation and Improvement	The National Health Service Commissioning Board
The Special Health Authority known as the National Patient Safety Agency	The National Health Service Commissioning Board
	The Health and Social Care Information Centre
The Special Health Authority known as the NHS Business Services Authority	The Health and Social Care Information Centre
The Appointments Commission	A Minister of the Crown

Transferor	Permitted transferees
	A Special Health Authority
The General Social Care Council	The Secretary of State
	The Health and Care Professions Council
	A person authorised by the Secretary of State under subsection (5)(b) of section 67 of the Care Standards Act 2000 to exercise functions of the Secretary of State under that section
	Any other person who carries on activities in connection with social work or social care work
The Health Protection Agency	The Secretary of State
The Secretary of State	The National Health Service Commissioning Board
	The Care Quality Commission
	Monitor
	The Health and Social Care Information Centre

NOTES

Regulations: the National Health Service and Public Health (Functions and Miscellaneous Provisions) Regulations 2013, SI 2013/261.

ENTERPRISE AND REGULATORY REFORM ACT 2013

(2013 c 24)

ARRANGEMENT OF SECTIONS

An Act to make provision about the UK Green Investment Bank; to make provision about employment law; to establish and make provision about the Competition and Markets Authority and to abolish the Competition Commission and the Office of Fair Trading; to amend the Competition Act 1998 and the Enterprise Act 2002; to make provision for the reduction of legislative burdens; to make provision about copyright and rights in performances; to make provision about payments to company directors; to make provision about redress schemes relating to lettings agency work and property management work; to make provision about the supply of customer data; to make provision for the protection of essential supplies in cases of insolvency; to make provision about certain bodies established by Royal Charter; to amend section 9(5) of the Equality Act 2010; and for connected purposes.

[25 April 2013]

1–6A *((Pt 1) Outside the scope of this work.)*

PART 2
EMPLOYMENT

7–12 *(S 7 inserts the Employment Tribunals Act 1996, ss 18A, 18B at* **[1.758]**, **[1.759]** *and introduces Sch 1 (conciliation: minor and consequential amendments) to the Act; s 8 introduces Sch 2 (extension of limitation periods to allow for conciliation) to the Act; ss 9, 11, 12 amend various provisions in the Employment Tribunals Act 1996 at* **[1.729]** *et seq; s 10 inserts the Trade Union and Labour Relations (Consolidation) Act 1992, 251B at* **[1.586]**.*)*

Unfair dismissal

13, 14 *(S 13 amends the Employment Rights Act 1996, s 108 at* **[1.1026]**; *s 14 inserts s 111A thereof at* **[1.1029]**.*)*

[1.1822]

15 Power by order to increase or decrease limit of compensatory award

(1) The Secretary of State may by order made by statutory instrument amend section 124 of the Employment Rights Act 1996 (limit of compensatory award etc) so as to vary the limit imposed for the time being by subsection (1) of that section.

(2) The limit as so varied may be—
- (a) a specified amount, or
- (b) the lower of—
  - (i) a specified amount, and
  - (ii) a specified number multiplied by a week's pay of the individual concerned.

(3) Different amounts may be specified by virtue of subsection (2)(a) or (b)(i) in relation to employers of different descriptions.

(4) An amount specified by virtue of subsection (2)(a) or (b)(i)—
- (a) may not be less than median annual earnings;
- (b) may not be more than three times median annual earnings.

(5) A number specified by virtue of subsection (2)(b)(ii) may not be less than 52.

(6) An order under this section may make consequential, supplemental, transitional, transitory or saving provision.

(7) The consequential provision that may be made under subsection (6) includes provision inserting a reference to section 124 of the Employment Rights Act 1996 in section 226(3) of that Act (week's pay: calculation date in unfair dismissal cases).

(8) A statutory instrument containing an order under this section is not to be made unless a draft of the instrument has been laid before each House of Parliament and approved by a resolution of each House.

(9) In this section "median annual earnings" means—
- (a) the latest figure for median gross annual earnings of full-time employees in the United Kingdom published by the Statistics Board (disregarding any provisional figures), or
- (b) if that figure was published by the Statistics Board more than two years before the laying of the draft of the statutory instrument in question, an estimate of the current amount of such earnings worked out in whatever way the Secretary of State thinks fit.

(10) . . .

NOTES

Commencement: 25 April 2013 (so far as is necessary for enabling the exercise of any power to make orders); 25 June 2013 (otherwise).

Sub-s (10): amends the Employment Relations Act 1999, s 34 at **[1.1258]**.

Orders: the Unfair Dismissal (Variation of the Limit of Compensatory Award) Order 2013, SI 2013/1949.

16 *(Inserts the Employment Tribunals Act 1996, s 12A at* **[1.750]** *and introduces Sch 3 (financial penalties: minor and consequential amendments) to this Act.)*

Protected disclosures

17–19 *(Amend various provisions of the Employment Rights Act 1996 at* **[1.813]** *et seq.)*

[1.1823]

20 Extension of meaning of "worker"

(1)–(9) . . .

(10) Until the coming into force of the repeal (made by Schedule 3 to the Smoking, Health and Social Care (Scotland) Act 2005 (asp 13)) of sections 27 to 28 of the National Health Service (Scotland) Act 1978 ("the 1978 Act"), section 43K(1)(c)(ii) of the Employment Rights Act 1996 has effect as if it included a reference to section 27A of the 1978 Act.

NOTES

Sub-ss (1)–(8): amend the Employment Rights Act 1996, ss 43K, 236 at **[1.876]**, **[1.1151]**.

Sub-s (9): amends the Smoking, Health and Social Care (Scotland) Act 2005 (Consequential Modifications) (England, Wales and Northern Ireland) Order 2006, SI 2006/1056.

Note: as of 15 May 2019, Schedule 3 to the Smoking, Health and Social Care (Scotland) Act 2005 had not been brought into force in so far as relating to the repeal of ss 27 and 28 of the National Health Service (Scotland) Act 1978.

21–23 (*Make various amendments which, in so far as relevant to this work, have been incorporated at the appropriate place.*)

General

[1.1824]

24 Transitional provision

(1) Section 10 does not apply in relation to a disclosure, or a request for information, made before that section comes into force.

(2) Section 12 does not apply in relation to proceedings that are in the process of being heard by the Employment Appeal Tribunal when that section comes into force.

(3) Section 13 does not apply where the effective date of termination of the contract of employment in question is earlier than the date on which that section comes into force.

"Effective date of termination" here has the meaning given by section 97(1) of the Employment Rights Act 1996.

(4) Section 14 does not apply to any offer made or discussions held before the commencement of that section.

(5) Section 16 does not apply in relation to any claim presented before the end of the sixth month after the day on which this Act is passed (or before the commencement of that section).

(6) Section 17, 18, 19 or 20 does not apply to a qualifying disclosure made before the section comes into force.

"Qualifying disclosure" here has the meaning given by section 43B of the Employment Rights Act 1996.

25–58 (*Pt 3 (ss 25–28: The Competition and Markets Authority) and Pt 4 (ss 29–58: Competition Reform) outside the scope of this work.*)

PART 5
REDUCTION OF LEGISLATIVE BURDENS

59–63 (*Outside the scope of this work.*)

Equality Acts

64, 65 (*Amend various provisions in the Equality Act 2006 at* **[1.1428]** *et seq and the Equality Act 2010 at* **[1.1620]** *et seq.*)

[1.1825]

66 Equality Act 2010: obtaining information for proceedings

(1) . . .

(2) That does not affect section 138 for the purposes of proceedings that relate to a contravention occurring before this section comes into force.

NOTES

Sub-s (1): repeals the Equality Act 2010, s 138.

Note that this section came into force on 6 April 2014.

67, 68 (*Outside the scope of this work.*)

Miscellaneous

[1.1826]

69 Civil liability for breach of health and safety duties

(1)–(7) . . .

(8) Where, on the commencement of this section, there is in force an Order in Council made under section 84(3) of the Health and Safety at Work etc Act 1974 that applies to matters outside Great Britain any of the provisions of that Act that are amended by this section, that Order is to be taken as applying those provisions as so amended.

(9) The amendments made by this section do not apply in relation to breach of a duty which it would be within the legislative competence of the Scottish Parliament to impose by an Act of that Parliament.

(10) The amendments made by this section do not apply in relation to breach of a duty where that breach occurs before the commencement of this section.

NOTES

Sub-ss (1)–(7): amend the Health and Safety at Work etc Act 1974, s 47 at **[1.71]**.

70, 71 (*Outside the scope of this work.*)

[1.1827]

72 Abolition of Agricultural Wages Board and related English bodies

(1) The Agricultural Wages Board for England and Wales is abolished.

(2) Every agricultural wages committee for an area in England is abolished.

(3) Every agricultural dwelling-house advisory committee for an area in England is abolished.

(4) Schedule 20 (abolition of Agricultural Wages Board and related English bodies: consequential provision) has effect.

NOTES

Commencement: 25 June 2013 (sub-s (1)); 16 December 2013 (sub-s (2), (3)); as to the commencement of sub-s (4), see the note below.

Schedule 20 contains various amendments and repeals consequential on the abolition of the Agricultural Wages Board and related English bodies by sub-ss (1)–(3) above. That Schedule came into force on various dates between 25 June 2013 and 31 December 2014; and is not in force for other purposes.

Transitional provisions and savings: for transitional provisions and savings in relation to the operation of the Agricultural Wages Act 1948 and the Agricultural Wages (England and Wales) Order 2012, see the Enterprise and Regulatory Reform Act 2013 (Commencement No 1, Transitional Provisions and Savings) Order 2013, SI 2013/1455, art 4, Sch 3, the Agricultural Sector (Wales) Act 2014, s 12, and the Agricultural Wages (Wales) Order 2016, SI 2016/107. Note that the regulation of agricultural wages in Wales is now governed by the 2014 Act; see, in particular, the Agricultural Wages (Wales) Order 2019, SI 2019/511 at **[2.2142]**. Relevant provisions of the 2014 Act are at **[1.1909]**.

73 (*Outside the scope of this work.*)

PART 6
MISCELLANEOUS AND GENERAL

74–78 (*Outside the scope of this work.*)

Payments to directors of quoted companies

79–81 (*Amend the Companies Act 2006 at* **[1.1490]** *et seq.*)

[1.1828]

82 Payments to directors: transitional provision

(1) In relation to a company that is a quoted company immediately before the day on which section 79 of this Act comes into force, section 439A(1)(a) of the Companies Act 2006 (as inserted by section 79(4) of this Act) applies as if—

- (a) the reference to the day on which the company becomes a quoted company were a reference to the day on which section 79 of this Act comes into force, and
- (b) at the end of the paragraph (but before the ", and") there were inserted "or at an earlier general meeting".

(2) In relation to a company that is a quoted company immediately before the day on which section 79 of this Act comes into force, section 226D(6)(a) of the Companies Act 2006 (as inserted by section 80 of this Act) applies as if the reference to the day on which the company becomes a quoted company were a reference to the day on which section 79 of this Act comes into force.

(3) Chapter 4A of Part 10 of the Companies Act 2006 does not apply in relation to remuneration payments or payments for loss of office that are required to be made under an agreement entered into before 27 June 2012 or in consequence of any other obligation arising before that date.

(4) An agreement entered into, or any other obligation arising, before 27 June 2012 that is modified or renewed on or after that date is to be treated for the purposes of subsection (3) as having been entered into or (as the case may be) as having arisen on the date on which it was modified or renewed.

(5) The amendment made by section 81(4) does not apply in relation to a payment for loss of office to which subsection (3) of this section applies.

83–96 (*Outside the scope of this work.*)

Caste as an aspect of race

[1.1829]

97 Equality Act 2010: caste as an aspect of race

(1)–(4) . . .

(5) A Minister of the Crown—

- (a) may carry out a review of the effect of section 9(5) of the Equality Act 2010 (and orders made under it) and whether it remains appropriate, and
- (b) must publish a report on the outcome of any such review.

(6) The power under subsection (5)(a) may not be exercised before the end of the period of 5 years beginning with the day on which this Act is passed (but may be exercised on more than one occasion after that).

(7) If a Minister of the Crown considers it appropriate in the light of the outcome of a review under subsection (5), the Minister may by order repeal or otherwise amend section 9(5) of the Equality Act 2010.

(8) The power to make an order under subsection (7) includes power to make incidental, supplementary, consequential, transitional or saving provision, including doing so by amending an Act or subordinate legislation (within the meaning of the Interpretation Act 1978).

(9) An order under subsection (7) must be made by statutory instrument.

(10) A statutory instrument containing an order under subsection (7) may not be made unless a draft of the instrument has been laid before, and approved by a resolution of, each House of Parliament.

NOTES

Commencement: 25 April 2013 (for enabling the exercise on or after that date of any power to make provision by Order made by statutory instrument); 25 June 2013 (otherwise).

Sub-ss (1)–(4): amend the Equality Act 2010, s 9 at **[1.1628]**.

Orders: as of 15 May 2019, no Orders had been made under sub-s (7).

98 *(Inserts the Equality Act 2010, s 139A at* **[1.1723]** *and amends ss 207, 208 thereof at* **[1.1759]**, **[1.1760]**.*)*

General

[1.1830]

99 Consequential amendments, repeals and revocations

(1) The Secretary of State may by order made by statutory instrument make such provision as the Secretary of State considers appropriate in consequence of this Act.

(2) The power conferred by subsection (1) includes power—

(a) to make transitional, transitory or saving provision;

(b) to amend, repeal, revoke or otherwise modify any provision made by or under an enactment (including any enactment passed or made in the same Session as this Act).

(3) An order under subsection (1) which makes provision for the transfer of a function from the Competition Commission or the Office of Fair Trading to the Competition and Markets Authority in consequence of Part 3 of this Act may make such modifications to the function as the Secretary of State considers appropriate in consequence of the transfer.

(4) The modifications mentioned in subsection (3) may, in particular, alter the circumstances in which, or the conditions under which, the function is exercisable.

(5) A statutory instrument containing (whether alone or with other provision) an order under this section which amends, repeals or revokes any provision of primary legislation is not to be made unless a draft of the instrument has been laid before, and approved by a resolution of, each House of Parliament.

(6) A statutory instrument containing an order under this section which does not amend, repeal or revoke any provision of primary legislation is subject to annulment in pursuance of a resolution of either House of Parliament.

(7) In this section—

"enactment" includes an Act of the Scottish Parliament, a Measure or Act of the National Assembly for Wales and Northern Ireland legislation;

"primary legislation" means—

(a) an Act of Parliament,

(b) an Act of the Scottish Parliament,

(c) a Measure or Act of the National Assembly for Wales, and

(d) Northern Ireland legislation.

NOTES

Orders: the Enterprise and Regulatory Reform Act 2013 (Health and Safety) (Consequential Amendments) Order 2013, SI 2013/1666; the Enterprise and Regulatory Reform Act 2013 (Consequential Amendments) (Employment) Order 2013, SI 2013/1956; the Enterprise and Regulatory Reform Act 2013 (Consequential Amendments) (Employment) Order 2014, SI 2014/386; the Enterprise and Regulatory Reform Act 2013 (Consequential Amendments) (Employment) (No 2) Order 2014, SI 2014/853; other Orders made under this section (eg relating to competition and planning law) are outside the scope of this work.

[1.1831]

100 Transitional, transitory or saving provision

The Secretary of State may by order made by statutory instrument make such transitional, transitory or saving provision as the Secretary of State considers appropriate in connection with the coming into force of any provision of this Act.

NOTES

Orders: as of 15 May 2019, the only Orders made under this section are commencement orders and the Enterprise and Regulatory Reform Act 2013 (Abolition of Conservation Area Consent) (Consequential and Saving Provisions) (England) Order 2013, SI 2013/2146.

[1.1832]

101 Financial provision

There is to be paid out of money provided by Parliament—

(a) any expenditure incurred under or by virtue of this Act by the Secretary of State or the Competition and Markets Authority, and

(b) any increase attributable to this Act in the sums payable under any other Act out of money so provided.

[1.1833]

102 Extent

(1) Part 1 extends to England and Wales, Scotland and Northern Ireland.

(2) Part 2 extends only to England and Wales and Scotland, except that the following provisions of that Part extend also to Northern Ireland—

(a) section 23(3);
(b) paragraph 11 of Schedule 1;
(c) paragraphs 36 to 39 of Schedule 2.

(3), (4) *(Outside the scope of this work.)*

(5) Part 5 extends as follows—

(a) sections 59, 62, 67, 68 and 70 and Part 1 of Schedule 21 extend to England and Wales, Scotland and Northern Ireland,
(b) section 69 extends only to England and Wales and Scotland except that it also extends to Northern Ireland so far as Parts 1 and 4 of the Health and Safety at Work etc Act 1974 extend there,
(c) sections 64, 65 and 66 and paragraphs 1, 56 to 58, 60 and 66 of Schedule 19 (and section 71(3) so far as it relates to those paragraphs) extend only to England and Wales and Scotland,
(d) sections 60, 61, 63, 71(1) and (2) and 72(1) to (3), Schedules 16, 17 and 18, paragraphs 2 to 55, 59, 61 to 65 of Schedule 19 (and section 71(3) so far as it relates to those paragraphs) and Parts 2 and 3 of Schedule 21 extend only to England and Wales, and
(e) an amendment, repeal or revocation made by Schedule 20 has the same extent as the provision amended, repealed or revoked, subject to subsection (6).

(6), (7) *(Outside the scope of this work.)*

(8) This Part extends to England and Wales, Scotland and Northern Ireland except that—

(a) sections 92, 93, 95, 97 and 98 extend only to England and Wales and Scotland;
(b) sections 83 to 88, 94 and 96 extend only to England and Wales.

[1.1834]

103 Commencement

(1) The following provisions come into force on the day on which this Act is passed—

(a) section 10;
(b) section 24;
(c)–(g) *(outside the scope of this work)*;
(h) sections 98 to 104;
(i) any other provision so far as is necessary for enabling the exercise on or after the day on which this Act is passed of any power (arising under or by virtue of that provision) to make provision by regulations, rules or order made by statutory instrument.

(2) The following provisions (so far as not already in force by virtue of subsection (1)(i)) come into force at the end of the period of 2 months beginning with the day on which this Act is passed—

(a) Part 1;
(b) sections 12, 13, 15, 17, 18, 20, 21 and 22;
(c) *(outside the scope of this work)*;
(d) section 64;
(e) section 97;
(f), (g) *(outside the scope of this work)*.

(3) Except as provided by subsections (1) and (2), the provisions of this Act come into force on such day as the Secretary of State may by order made by statutory instrument appoint.

(4) An order under subsection (3) may appoint different days for different purposes.

NOTES

Orders: the Enterprise and Regulatory Reform Act 2013 (Commencement No 1, Transitional Provisions and Savings) Order 2013, SI 2013/1455; the Enterprise and Regulatory Reform Act 2013 (Commencement No 2) Order 2013, SI 2013/1648; the Enterprise and Regulatory Reform Act 2013 (Commencement No 3, Transitional Provisions and Savings) Order 2013, SI 2013/2227; the Enterprise and Regulatory Reform Act 2013 (Commencement No 1, Transitional Provisions and Savings) (Amendment) Order 2013, SI 2013/2271; the Enterprise and Regulatory Reform Act 2013 (Commencement No 4 and Saving Provision) Order 2013, SI 2013/2979; the Enterprise and Regulatory Reform Act 2013 (Commencement No 5, Transitional Provisions and Savings) Order 2014, SI 2014/253; the Enterprise and Regulatory Reform Act 2013 (Commencement No 6, Transitional Provisions and Savings) Order 2014, SI 2014/416; the Enterprise and Regulatory Reform Act 2013 (Commencement No 4 and Saving Provision) (Amendment) Order 2014, SI 2014/824; the Enterprise and Regulatory Reform Act 2013 (Commencement No 7 and Amendment) Order 2014, SI 2014/2481; the Enterprise and Regulatory Reform Act 2013 (Commencement No 8 and Saving Provisions) Order 2015, SI 2015/641; the Enterprise and Regulatory Reform Act 2013 (Commencement No 9 and Saving Provisions) Order 2016, SI 2016/191; the Enterprise and Regulatory Reform Act 2013 (Commencement No 10 and Saving Provisions) Order 2016, SI 2016/593.

[1.1835]

104 Short title

This Act may be cited as the Enterprise and Regulatory Reform Act 2013.

SCHEDULES 1–21

(Schs 1–3, 20 contain amendments, repeals and revocations which, in so far as relevant to this work, have been incorporated at the appropriate place; Schs 4–18, 21 are outside the scope of this work; Sch 19 amends the Insolvency Act 1986, s 285 at **[1.158]** *and other provisions of that Act which are outside the scope of this work.)*

PUBLIC SERVICE PENSIONS ACT 2013

(2013 c 25)

ARRANGEMENT OF SECTIONS

Establishment of new schemes

Governance

Design

Cost control

Administration

Transitional

Procedure for scheme regulations

New schemes: supplementary

Existing schemes: supplementary

Public body pension schemes

Parliamentary and other pension schemes

General

Final

SCHEDULES

An Act to make provision for public service pension schemes; and for connected purposes.

[25 April 2013]

Establishment of new schemes

[1.1836]

1 Schemes for persons in public service

(1) Regulations may establish schemes for the payment of pensions and other benefits to or in respect of persons specified in subsection (2).

(2) Those persons are—

(a) civil servants;
(b) the judiciary;
(c) local government workers for England, Wales and Scotland;
(d) teachers for England, Wales and Scotland;
(e) health service workers for England, Wales and Scotland;
(f) fire and rescue workers for England, Wales and Scotland;
(g) members of police forces for England, Wales and Scotland;
(h) the armed forces.

(3) These terms are defined in Schedule 1.

(4) In this Act, regulations under this section are called "scheme regulations".

NOTES

Regulations: The Regulations made under this section and ss 2 and 3 are too numerous to list individually. The principal sets of Regulations are: the Teachers' Pension Scheme Regulations 2014, SI 2014/512; the Public Service (Civil Servants and Others) Pensions Regulations 2014, SI 2014/1964; the Armed Forces Early Departure Payments Scheme Regulations 2014, SI 2014/2328; the Armed Forces Pension Regulations 2014, SI 2014/2336; the Firefighters' Pension Scheme (England) Regulations 2014, SI 2014/2848; the National Health Service Pension Scheme Regulations 2015, SI 2015/94; the Judicial Pensions Regulations 2015, SI 2015/182; the Police Pensions Regulations 2015, SI 2015/445; the Teachers (Compensation for Redundancy and Premature Retirement) Regulations 2015, SI 2015/601; the Firefighters' Pension Scheme (Wales) Regulations 2015, SI 2015/622; the Civil Service (Other Crown Servants) Pension Scheme Regulations 2016, SI 2016/326; the Teachers' Pension Scheme (Scotland) (No 2) Regulations 2014, SSI 2014/292; the Firefighters' Pension Scheme (Scotland) Regulations 2015, SSI 2015/19; the National Health Service Pension Scheme (Scotland) Regulations 2015, SSI 2015/94; the Police Pension Scheme (Scotland) Regulations 2015, SSI 2015/142; the Local Government Pension Scheme (Scotland) Regulations 2018, SSI 2018/141.

[1.1837]

2 Responsible authority for schemes

(1) The persons who may make scheme regulations are set out in Schedule 2.

(2) In this Act, the person who may make scheme regulations for any description of persons specified in section 1(2) is called the "responsible authority" for the scheme for those persons.

NOTES

Regulations: see the note to s 1 at **[1.1836]**.

[1.1838]

3 Scheme regulations

(1) Scheme regulations may, subject to this Act, make such provision in relation to a scheme under section 1 as the responsible authority considers appropriate.

(2) That includes in particular—

(a) provision as to any of the matters specified in Schedule 3;
(b) consequential, supplementary, incidental or transitional provision in relation to the scheme or any provision of this Act.

(3) Scheme regulations may—

(a) make different provision for different purposes or cases (including different provision for different descriptions of persons);
(b) make retrospective provision (but see section 23);
(c) allow any person to exercise a discretion.

(4) The consequential provision referred to in subsection (2)(b) includes consequential provision amending any primary legislation passed before or in the same session as this Act (as well as consequential provision amending any secondary legislation).

(5) Scheme regulations require the consent of the Treasury before being made, unless one of the following exceptions applies.

(6) The exceptions are—

(a) scheme regulations of the Scottish Ministers relating to local government workers, fire and rescue workers and members of a police force;
(b) scheme regulations of the Welsh Ministers relating to fire and rescue workers.

NOTES

Regulations: see the note to s 1 at **[1.1836]**.

Governance

[1.1839]

4 Scheme manager

(1) Scheme regulations for a scheme under section 1 must provide for a person to be responsible for managing or administering—
(a) the scheme, and
(b) any statutory pension scheme that is connected with it.

(2) In this Act, that person is called the "scheme manager" for the scheme (or schemes).

(3) The scheme manager may in particular be the responsible authority.

(4) Subsection (1) does not apply to a scheme under section 1 which is an injury or compensation scheme.

(5) Scheme regulations may comply with the requirement in subsection (1)(a) or (b) by providing for different persons to be responsible for managing or administering different parts of a scheme (and references in this Act to the "scheme manager", in such a case, are to be construed accordingly).

(6) For the purposes of this Act, a scheme under section 1 and another statutory pension scheme are connected if and to the extent that the schemes make provision in relation to persons of the same description.

(7) Scheme regulations may specify exceptions to subsection (6).

NOTES

Commencement: 28 February 2014 (for the purpose of making scheme regulations to establish schemes for the payment of pensions and other benefits to or in respect of teachers); 1 April 2014 (all remaining purposes except for the purpose of making scheme regulations to establish schemes for the payment of pensions and other benefits to or in respect of (i) local government workers in England and Wales and (ii) fire and rescue workers); 1 April 2015 (otherwise).

Regulations: the Teachers' Pension Scheme Regulations 2014, SI 2014/512; the Public Service (Civil Servants and Others) Pensions Regulations 2014, SI 2014/1964; the Armed Forces Pension Regulations 2014, SI 2014/2336; the Teachers' Pension Scheme (Amendment) Regulations 2014, SI 2014/2652; the Firefighters' Pension Scheme (England) Regulations 2014, SI 2014/2848; the National Health Service Pension Scheme Regulations 2015, SI 2015/94; the Judicial Pensions Regulations 2015, SI 2015/182; the Police Pensions Regulations 2015, SI 2015/445; the Civil Service (Other Crown Servants) Pension Scheme Regulations 2016, SI 2016/326; the Judicial Pensions (Additional Voluntary Contributions) Regulations 2017, SI 2017/512.

[1.1840]

5 Pension board

(1) Scheme regulations for a scheme under section 1 must provide for the establishment of a board with responsibility for assisting the scheme manager (or each scheme manager) in relation to the following matters.

(2) Those matters are—
(a) securing compliance with the scheme regulations and other legislation relating to the governance and administration of the scheme and any statutory pension scheme that is connected with it;
(b) securing compliance with requirements imposed in relation to the scheme and any connected scheme by the Pensions Regulator;
(c) such other matters as the scheme regulations may specify.

(3) In making the regulations the responsible authority must have regard to the desirability of securing the effective and efficient governance and administration of the scheme and any connected scheme.

(4) The regulations must include provision—
(a) requiring the scheme manager—
  (i) to be satisfied that a person to be appointed as a member of the board does not have a conflict of interest, and
  (ii) to be satisfied from time to time that none of the members of the board has a conflict of interest;
(b) requiring a member of the board, or a person proposed to be appointed as a member of the board, to provide the scheme manager with such information as the scheme manager reasonably requires for the purposes of provision under paragraph (a);
(c) requiring the board to include employer representatives and member representatives in equal numbers.

(5) In subsection (4)(a) "conflict of interest", in relation to a person, means a financial or other interest which is likely to prejudice the person's exercise of functions as a member of the board (but does not include a financial or other interest arising merely by virtue of membership of the scheme or any connected scheme).

(6) In subsection (4)(c)—
(a) "employer representatives" means persons appointed to the board for the purpose of representing employers for the scheme and any connected scheme;
(b) "member representatives" means persons appointed to the board for the purpose of representing members of the scheme and any connected scheme.

(7) Where the scheme manager of a scheme under section 1 is a committee of a local authority, the scheme regulations may provide for that committee also to be the board for the purposes of this section.
(8) In this Act, a board established under this section is called a "pension board".
(9) This section does not apply to a scheme under section 1 which is an injury or compensation scheme.

NOTES

Commencement: 28 February 2014 (for the purpose of making scheme regulations to establish schemes for the payment of pensions and other benefits to or in respect of teachers); 1 April 2014 (all remaining purposes except for the purpose of making scheme regulations to establish schemes for the payment of pensions and other benefits to or in respect of (i) local government workers in England and Wales and (ii) fire and rescue workers); 1 April 2015 (otherwise).

Regulations: the Teachers' Pension Scheme Regulations 2014, SI 2014/512; the Public Service (Civil Servants and Others) Pensions Regulations 2014, SI 2014/1964; the Armed Forces Pension Regulations 2014, SI 2014/2336; the Teachers' Pension Scheme (Amendment) Regulations 2014, SI 2014/2652; the Local Government Pension Scheme (Amendment) (Governance) Regulations 2015, SI 2015/57; the National Health Service Pension Scheme Regulations 2015, SI 2015/94; the Judicial Pensions Regulations 2015, SI 2015/182; the Police Pensions Regulations 2015, SI 2015/445; the Local Government Pension Scheme (Governance) (Scotland) Regulations 2015, SSI 2015/60; the Civil Service (Other Crown Servants) Pension Scheme Regulations 2016, SI 2016/326; the Judicial Pensions (Additional Voluntary Contributions) Regulations 2017, SI 2017/512.

[1.1841]

6 Pension board: information

(1) The scheme manager for a scheme under section 1 and any statutory pension scheme that is connected with it must publish information about the pension board for the scheme or schemes (and keep that information up-to-date).
(2) That information must include information about—
- (a) who the members of the board are,
- (b) representation on the board of members of the scheme or schemes, and
- (c) the matters falling within the board's responsibility.

(3) This section does not apply to a scheme under section 1 which is an injury or compensation scheme.

NOTES

Commencement: 28 February 2014 (for the purpose of making scheme regulations to establish schemes for the payment of pensions and other benefits to or in respect of teachers); 1 April 2014 (all remaining purposes except for the purpose of making scheme regulations to establish schemes for the payment of pensions and other benefits to or in respect of (i) local government workers in England and Wales and (ii) fire and rescue workers); 1 April 2015 (otherwise).

[1.1842]

7 Scheme advisory board

(1) Scheme regulations for a scheme under section 1 which is a defined benefits scheme must provide for the establishment of a board with responsibility for providing advice to the responsible authority, at the authority's request, on the desirability of changes to the scheme.
(2) Where, by virtue of section 4(5), there is more than one scheme manager for a scheme mentioned in subsection (1) (and accordingly there is more than one pension board for the scheme), the regulations may also provide for the board to provide advice (on request or otherwise) to the scheme managers or the scheme's pension boards in relation to the effective and efficient administration and management of—
- (a) the scheme and any statutory pension scheme that is connected with it, or
- (b) any pension fund of the scheme and any connected scheme.

(3) A person to whom advice is given by virtue of subsection (1) or (2) must have regard to the advice.
(4) The regulations must include provision—
- (a) requiring the responsible authority—
  - (i) to be satisfied that a person to be appointed as a member of the board does not have a conflict of interest, and
  - (ii) to be satisfied from time to time that none of the members of the board has a conflict of interest;
- (b) requiring a member of the board, or a person proposed to be appointed as a member of the board, to provide the responsible authority with such information as the authority reasonably requires for the purposes of provision under paragraph (a).

(5) In subsection (4)(a) "conflict of interest", in relation to a person, means a financial or other interest which is likely to prejudice the person's exercise of functions as a member of the board (but does not include a financial or other interest arising merely by virtue of membership of the scheme or any connected scheme).
(6) In this Act, a board established under this section is called a "scheme advisory board".

NOTES

Commencement: 28 February 2014 (for the purpose of making scheme regulations to establish schemes for the payment of pensions and other benefits to or in respect of teachers); 1 April 2014 (all remaining purposes except for the purpose of making scheme regulations to establish schemes for the payment of pensions and other benefits to or in respect of (i) local government workers in England and Wales and (ii) fire and rescue workers); 1 April 2015 (otherwise).

Regulations: the Teachers' Pension Scheme Regulations 2014, SI 2014/512; the Armed Forces Pension Regulations 2014, SI 2014/2336; the Teachers' Pension Scheme (Amendment) Regulations 2014, SI 2014/2652; the Local Government Pension Scheme (Amendment) (Governance) Regulations 2015, SI 2015/57; the National Health Service Pension Scheme Regulations 2015, SI 2015/94; the Police Pensions Regulations 2015, SI 2015/445; the Firefighters' Pension Scheme (Amendment) (Governance) Regulations 2015, SI 2015/465; the Local Government Pension Scheme (Governance) (Scotland) Regulations 2015, SSI 2015/60.

Design

[1.1843]

8 Types of scheme

(1) Scheme regulations may establish a scheme under section 1 as—

(a) a defined benefits scheme,

(b) a defined contributions scheme, or

(c) a scheme of any other description.

(2) A scheme under section 1 which is a defined benefits scheme must be—

(a) a career average revalued earnings scheme, or

(b) a defined benefits scheme of such other description as Treasury regulations may specify.

(3) Treasury regulations may not specify a final salary scheme under subsection (2)(b).

(4) A scheme under section 1 is a "career average revalued earnings scheme" if—

(a) the pension payable to or in respect of a person, so far as it is based on the person's pensionable service, is determined by reference to the person's pensionable earnings in each year of pensionable service, and

(b) those earnings, or a proportion of those earnings accrued as a pension, are under the scheme revalued each year until the person leaves pensionable service.

(5) Treasury regulations under this section are subject to the negative Commons procedure.

NOTES

Regulations: the Teachers' Pension Scheme Regulations 2014, SI 2014/512; the Public Service (Civil Servants and Others) Pensions Regulations 2014, SI 2014/1964; the Armed Forces Pension Regulations 2014, SI 2014/2336; the Teachers' Pension Scheme (Amendment) Regulations 2014, SI 2014/2652; the National Health Service Pension Scheme Regulations 2015, SI 2015/94; the Judicial Pensions Regulations 2015, SI 2015/182; the Police Pensions Regulations 2015, SI 2015/445; the Civil Service (Other Crown Servants) Pension Scheme Regulations 2016, SI 2016/326; the Teachers' Pensions Schemes (Miscellaneous Amendments) Regulations 2017, SI 2017/1084; the Teachers' Pensions Schemes (Amendment) Regulations 2018, SI 2018/218.

[1.1844]

9 Revaluation

(1) This section applies in relation to a scheme under section 1 which—

(a) requires a revaluation of pensionable earnings of a person, or a proportion of those earnings accrued as a pension, until the person leaves pensionable service, and

(b) requires such a revaluation to be by reference to a change in prices or earnings (or both) in a given period.

(2) The change in prices or earnings to be applied for the purposes of such a revaluation is to be such percentage increase or decrease as a Treasury order may specify in relation to the period.

(3) For the purposes of making such an order the Treasury may determine the change in prices or earnings in any period by reference to the general level of prices or earnings estimated in such manner as the Treasury consider appropriate.

(4) A Treasury order under this section—

(a) must be made in each year;

(b) may make different provision for different purposes.

(5) A Treasury order under this section is subject to—

(a) the affirmative Commons procedure, if the order specifies a percentage decrease for the purposes of subsection (2), and

(b) the negative Commons procedure, in any other case.

(6) For the purposes of subsection (1) any gap in the person's pensionable service which does not exceed five years is to be disregarded.

NOTES

Commencement: 28 February 2014 (sub-ss (1)–(3), (4)(b), (5), (6)); 1 April 2015 (sub-s (4)(a) for the purposes of an order in respect of scheme regulations to establish schemes for the payment of pensions and other benefits to or in respect of local government workers in England and Wales); 1 April 2016 (otherwise).

Orders: the Public Service Pensions Revaluation Order 2015, SI 2015/769 (providing that for the purposes of sub-s (2) above, the change in prices to be applied in relation to the scheme year ending with 31 March 2015 is an increase of 1.2 per cent); the Public Service Pensions Revaluation (Earnings) Order 2016, SI 2016/95 (providing that for the purposes of sub-s (2) above, the change in earnings specified in relation to the period beginning on 1 April 2015 and ending on 31 March 2016 is an increase of 2 per cent); the Public Service Pensions Revaluation (Prices) Order 2016, SI 2016/438 (providing that for the purposes of sub-s (2) above, the change in prices specified in relation to the period beginning on 1 April 2015 and ending on 31 March 2016 is a decrease of 0.1 per cent); the Public Service Pensions Revaluation Order 2017, SI 2017/242 (providing that for the purposes of sub-s (2) above, the change in prices specified in relation to the period beginning on 1 April 2016 and ending on 31 March 2017 is an increase of 1 per cent, and the change in earnings is an increase of 2.6 per cent); the Public Service Pensions Revaluation Order 2018, SI 2018/338 (providing that for the purposes of sub-s (2) above, the change in prices specified in relation to the period beginning on 1 April 2017 and ending on 31 March 2018 is an increase of 3 per cent, and the change in earnings is an increase of 3 per cent); the Public Service Pensions Revaluation Order 2019, SI 2019/455 providing that for the purposes of sub-s (2) above, the change in prices specified in relation to the period beginning on 1 April 2018 and ending on 31 March 2019 is an increase of 2.4 per cent, and the change in earnings is an increase of 2.8 per cent).

[1.1845]

10 Pension age

(1) The normal pension age of a person under a scheme under section 1 must be—

(a) the same as the person's state pension age, or

(b) 65, if that is higher.

(2) Subsection (1) does not apply in relation to—
- (a) fire and rescue workers who are firefighters,
- (b) members of a police force, and
- (c) members of the armed forces.

The normal pension age of such persons under a scheme under section 1 must be 60.

(3) The deferred pension age of a person under a scheme under section 1 must be—
- (a) the same as the person's state pension age, or
- (b) 65, if that is higher.

(4) Where—
- (a) a person's state pension age changes, and
- (b) the person's normal or deferred pension age under a scheme under section 1 changes as a result of subsection (1) or (3),

the change to the person's normal or deferred pension age must under the scheme apply in relation to all the benefits (including benefits already accrued under the scheme) which may be paid to or in respect of the person under the scheme and to which the normal or deferred pension age is relevant.

(5) In this Act—
- (a) "normal pension age", in relation to a person and a scheme, means the earliest age at which the person is entitled to receive benefits under the scheme (without actuarial adjustment) on leaving the service to which the scheme relates (and disregarding any special provision as to early payment of benefits on the grounds of ill-health or otherwise);
- (b) "deferred pension age", in relation to a person and a scheme, means the earliest age at which the person is entitled to receive benefits under the scheme (without actuarial adjustment) after leaving the service to which the scheme relates at a time before normal pension age (and disregarding any special provision as to early payment of benefits on the grounds of ill-health or otherwise);
- (c) "state pension age", in relation to a person, means the pensionable age of the person as specified from time to time in Part 1 of Schedule 4 to the Pensions Act 1995.

NOTES

Commencement: 25 June 2013 (for the purposes of the report under s 36 of this Act); 28 February 2014 (for the purpose of making scheme regulations to establish schemes for the payment of pensions and other benefits to or in respect of teachers); 1 April 2014 (all remaining purposes except for the purposes of any requirements relating to transitional councillor members in connection with their membership of schemes for the payment of pensions and other benefits to or in respect of local government workers in England and Wales); to be appointed (otherwise).

Cost control

[1.1846]

11 Valuations

(1) Scheme regulations for a scheme under section 1 which is a defined benefits scheme must provide for actuarial valuations to be made of—
- (a) the scheme, and
- (b) any statutory pension scheme that is connected with it.

(2) Such a valuation is to be carried out in accordance with Treasury directions.

(3) Treasury directions under subsection (2) may in particular specify—
- (a) how and when a valuation is to be carried out;
- (b) the time in relation to which a valuation is to be carried out;
- (c) the data, methodology and assumptions to be used in a valuation;
- (d) the matters to be covered by a valuation;
- (e) where a scheme under section 1 and another statutory pension scheme are connected, whether the schemes are to be valued separately or together (and if together, how);
- (f) the period within which any changes to the employer contribution rate under a scheme under section 1 must take effect following a valuation.

(4) Treasury directions under subsection (2), and variations and revocations of such directions, may only be made after the Treasury has consulted the Government Actuary.

(5) Scheme regulations for a scheme under section 1 which is not a defined benefits scheme may provide for actuarial valuations to be made of the scheme and any statutory pension scheme that is connected with it; and if they do, subsections (2) to (4) apply.

NOTES

Commencement: 1 December 2013 (sub-ss (2)–(4) for the purposes of making Treasury directions under sub-s (2)); 1 April 2015 (otherwise)

Regulations: the Armed Forces Pension Regulations 2014, SI 2014/2336; the Teachers' Pension Scheme (Amendment) Regulations 2014, SI 2014/2652; the National Health Service Pension Scheme Regulations 2015, SI 2015/94.

[1.1847]

12 Employer cost cap

(1) Scheme regulations for a scheme under section 1 which is a defined benefits scheme must set a rate, expressed as a percentage of pensionable earnings of members of the scheme, to be used for the purpose of measuring changes in the cost of the scheme.

(2) In this section, the rate set under subsection (1) is called the "employer cost cap".

(3) The employer cost cap is to be set in accordance with Treasury directions.

(4) Treasury directions may in particular specify—

(a) how the first valuation under section 11 of a scheme under section 1 is to be taken into account in setting the cap;

(b) the costs, or changes in costs, that are to be taken into account on subsequent valuations of a scheme under section 1 for the purposes of measuring changes in the cost of the scheme against the cap;

(c) the extent to which costs or changes in the costs of any statutory pension scheme which is connected with a scheme under section 1 are to be taken into account for the purposes of this section.

(5) Treasury regulations must make—

(a) provision requiring the cost of a scheme (and any connected scheme) to remain within specified margins either side of the employer cost cap, and

(b) for cases where the cost of a scheme would otherwise go beyond either of those margins, provision specifying a target cost within the margins.

(6) For cases where the cost of the scheme would otherwise go beyond the margins, scheme regulations may provide for—

(a) a procedure for the responsible authority, the scheme manager (if different), employers and members (or representatives of employers and members) to reach agreement on the steps required to achieve the target cost for the scheme, and

(b) the steps to be taken for that purpose if agreement is not reached under that procedure.

(7) The steps referred to in subsection (6) may include the increase or decrease of members' benefits or contributions.

(8) Treasury regulations under this section may—

(a) include consequential or supplementary provision;

(b) make different provision for different schemes.

(9) Treasury regulations under this section are subject to the negative Commons procedure.

NOTES

Commencement: 1 December 2013 (sub-ss (2)–(5), (8), (9) for the purposes of making Treasury directions or regulations under sub-ss (3) and (5)); 28 February 2014 (sub-ss (2)–(5), (8), (9) for the purpose of making Treasury directions under sub-s (3) and Treasury regulations under sub-s (5)); 1 April 2015 (except for the purpose of making scheme regulations to establish schemes for the payment of pensions and other benefits to or in respect of local government workers in Scotland and Northern Ireland); 1 April 2016 (otherwise).

Regulations: the Public Service Pensions (Employer Cost Cap) Regulations 2014, SI 2014/575; the Public Service (Civil Servants and Others) Pensions Regulations 2014, SI 2014/1964; the Armed Forces Pension Regulations 2014, SI 2014/2336; the Teachers' Pension Scheme (Amendment) Regulations 2014, SI 2014/2652; the Local Government Pension Scheme (Amendment) (Governance) Regulations 2015, SI 2015/57; the National Health Service Pension Scheme Regulations 2015, SI 2015/94; the Judicial Pensions Regulations 2015, SI 2015/182; the Police Pensions Regulations 2015, SI 2015/445; the Firefighters' Pension Scheme (Amendment) (Governance) Regulations 2015, SI 2015/465; the Civil Service (Other Crown Servants) Pension Scheme Regulations 2016, SI 2016/326; the Local Government Pension Scheme (Scotland) Amendment Regulations 2016, SSI 2016/32.

[1.1848]

13 Employer contributions in funded schemes

(1) This section applies in relation to a scheme under section 1 which is a defined benefits scheme with a pension fund.

(2) Scheme regulations must provide for the rate of employer contributions to be set at an appropriate level to ensure—

(a) the solvency of the pension fund, and

(b) the long-term cost-efficiency of the scheme, so far as relating to the pension fund.

(3) For that purpose, scheme regulations must require actuarial valuations of the pension fund.

(4) Where an actuarial valuation under subsection (3) has taken place, a person appointed by the responsible authority is to report on whether the following aims are achieved—

(a) the valuation is in accordance with the scheme regulations;

(b) the valuation has been carried out in a way which is not inconsistent with other valuations under subsection (3);

(c) the rate of employer contributions is set as specified in subsection (2).

(5) A report under subsection (4) must be published; and a copy must be sent to the scheme manager and (if different) the responsible authority.

(6) If a report under subsection (4) states that, in the view of the person making the report, any of the aims in that subsection has not been achieved—

(a) the report may recommend remedial steps;

(b) the scheme manager must—

(i) take such remedial steps as the scheme manager considers appropriate, and

(ii) publish details of those steps and the reasons for taking them;

(c) the responsible authority may—

(i) require the scheme manager to report on progress in taking remedial steps;

(ii) direct the scheme manager to take such remedial steps as the responsible authority considers appropriate.

(7) The person appointed under subsection (4) must, in the view of the responsible authority, be appropriately qualified.

NOTES

Regulations: the Armed Forces Pension Regulations 2014, SI 2014/2336.

Administration

[1.1849]

14 Information about benefits

(1) Scheme regulations must require the scheme manager for a scheme under section 1 which is a defined benefits scheme to provide benefit information statements to each person in pensionable service under the scheme in accordance with this section.

(2) A benefit information statement must include—

(a) a description of the benefits earned by the person in respect of his or her pensionable service, and

(b) such other information as Treasury directions may specify.

(3) The information included in a benefit information statement must comply with such requirements as Treasury directions may specify.

(4) A benefit information statement must be provided—

(a) no later than the relevant date, and

(b) at least once in each year ending with the anniversary of that date.

(5) The relevant date is the last day of the period of 17 months beginning with the day on which scheme regulations establishing the scheme come into force.

(6) A benefit information statement must be provided in such manner as Treasury directions may specify.

NOTES

Regulations: the Teachers' Pension Scheme Regulations 2014, SI 2014/512; Armed Forces Pension Regulations 2014, SI 2014/2336; the National Health Service Pension Scheme Regulations 2015, SI 2015/94.

[1.1850]

15 Information about schemes

(1) Treasury directions may require the scheme manager or responsible authority of a scheme under section 1 to—

(a) publish scheme information, or

(b) provide scheme information to the Treasury.

(2) In subsection (1), "scheme information" means information about the scheme and any statutory pension scheme that is connected with it.

(3) The information to which Treasury directions under this section may relate includes in particular—

(a) scheme accounts;

(b) information about any scheme funding, assets and liabilities;

(c) information about scheme membership;

(d) information about employer and member contributions;

(e) information about scheme administration and governance.

(4) Treasury directions under this section may specify how and when information is to be published or provided.

(5) Treasury directions under this section may not require publication or provision of anything that the scheme manager or responsible authority could not otherwise lawfully publish or provide.

NOTES

Commencement: 1 April 2015.

[1.1851]

16 Records

(1) The scheme manager for a scheme under section 1 and any statutory pension scheme that is connected with it must keep such records as may be specified in regulations made by the Secretary of State.

(2) Regulations under this section are subject to the negative procedure.

NOTES

Commencement: 1 November 2013 (for the purposes of making Regulations); 1 April 2015 (otherwise).

Regulations: the Public Service Pensions (Record Keeping and Miscellaneous Amendments) Regulations 2014, SI 2014/3138.

17 (*Outside the scope of this work.*)

Transitional

[1.1852]

18 Restriction of existing pension schemes

(1) No benefits are to be provided under an existing scheme to or in respect of a person in relation to the person's service after the closing date.

(2) In this Act "existing scheme" means a scheme listed in Schedule 5 (whether made before or after this section comes into force).

(3) Subsection (1) does not apply—

(a) in relation to an existing scheme which is a defined contributions scheme;

(b) to benefits excepted by Schedule 5.

(4) The closing date is—

(a) 31 March 2014 for an existing scheme which is a relevant local government scheme, and

(b) 31 March 2015 in any other case.

This is subject to subsection (7).

(5) Scheme regulations may provide for exceptions to subsection (1) in the case of—

(a) persons who were members of an existing scheme, or who were eligible to be members of such a scheme, immediately before 1 April 2012, and

(b) such other persons as the regulations may specify, being persons who before that date had ceased to be members of an existing scheme or to be eligible for membership of such a scheme.

[(5A) Scheme regulations may also provide for exceptions to subsection (1) in the case of—

(a) persons who were members of a public body pension scheme specified in the regulations, or who were eligible to be members of such a scheme, immediately before 1 April 2012, and

(b) such other persons as the regulations may specify, being persons who before that date had ceased to be members of a scheme referred to in paragraph (a) or to be eligible for membership of such a scheme.]

(6) Exceptions under subsection (5) [or (5A)] may, in particular, be framed by reference to the satisfaction of a specified condition (for example, the attainment of normal pension age under the existing scheme or another specified age) before a specified date.

(7) Where an exception to subsection (1) is framed by reference to the satisfaction of a specified condition before a specified date, scheme regulations may also provide for a different closing date for persons in whose case the condition—

(a) is not satisfied before the specified date, but

(b) is satisfied no more than 4 years after that date.

(8) Provision made under subsection (5) [or (5A)] or (7) may in particular be made by amending the relevant existing scheme.

(9) In subsection (1), the reference to benefits in relation to a person's service includes benefits relating to the person's death in service.

(10) In subsection (4), "relevant local government scheme" means regulations under section 7 of the Superannuation Act 1972 which relate to persons in England and Wales.

NOTES

Commencement: 28 February 2014 (for the purpose of making scheme regulations to establish schemes for the payment of pensions and other benefits to or in respect of teachers); 1 April 2014 (except for the purposes of any requirements relating to transitional councillor members in connection with their membership of schemes for the payment of pensions and other benefits to or in respect of local government workers in England and Wales); to be appointed (otherwise).

Sub-s (5A) inserted, and words in square brackets in sub-ss (6), (8) inserted, by the Pensions Act 2014, s 52, as from 23 July 2014.

Regulations: the Teachers' Pension Scheme Regulations 2014, SI 2014/512; the Public Service (Civil Servants and Others) Pensions Regulations 2014, SI 2014/1964; the Armed Forces Pension Regulations 2014, SI 2014/2336; the Teachers' Pension Scheme (Amendment) Regulations 2014, SI 2014/2652; the National Health Service Pension Scheme Regulations 2015, SI 2015/94; the National Health Service Pension Scheme (Transitional and Consequential Provisions) Regulations 2015, SI 2015/95; the Judicial Pensions Regulations 2015, SI 2015/182; the Police Pensions Regulations 2015, SI 2015/445; the Armed Forces (Transitional Provisions) Pensions Regulations 2015, SI 2015/568; the Teachers' Pension Scheme (Amendment) Regulations 2015, SI 2015/592; the Firefighters' Pension Scheme (England) (Transitional and Consequential Provisions) Regulations 2015, SI 2015/589; the Firefighters' Pension Scheme (Wales) (Transitional and Consequential Provisions) Regulations 2015, SI 2015/1016; the National Health Service Pension Scheme (Transitional and Consequential Provisions) (Scotland) Regulations 2015, SSI 2015/95; the Civil Service (Other Crown Servants) Pension Scheme Regulations 2016, SI 2016/326; the Judicial Pensions (Amendment) Regulations 2017, SI 2017/508; the Firefighters' Pension Scheme (England) (Amendment) Regulations 2017, SI 2017/888; the Firefighters' Pension Scheme (Wales) (Amendment) Regulations 2018, SI 2018/576; the National Health Service Pension Schemes, Additional Voluntary Contributions and Injury Benefits (Amendment) Regulations 2019, SI 2019/418.

[1.1853]

19 Closure of existing injury and compensation schemes

(1) Scheme regulations for a scheme under section 1 may secure that no benefits are to be provided under a scheme listed in Schedule 6 that is connected with it.

(2) Where Schedule 6 specifies particular benefits in relation to a scheme, the power under subsection (1) is exercisable only in relation to those benefits.

(3) Scheme regulations may provide for exceptions to subsection (1).

(4) Provision made under this section may in particular be made by amending the connected scheme.

[1.1854]

20 Final salary link

Schedule 7 contains provision for a "final salary link" in relation to schemes to which section 18(1) applies (and see section 31(14)).

Procedure for scheme regulations

[1.1855]

21 Consultation

(1) Before making scheme regulations the responsible authority must consult such persons (or representatives of such persons) as appear to the authority likely to be affected by them.

(2) The responsible authority must publish a statement indicating the persons that the authority would normally expect to consult under subsection (1) (and keep the statement up-to-date).

(3) Subsection (1) may be satisfied by consultation before, as well as by consultation after, the coming into force of this section.

[1.1856]

22 Procedure for protected elements

(1) This section applies where, after the coming into force of scheme regulations establishing a scheme under section 1, the responsible authority proposes to make further scheme regulations containing provision changing the protected elements of the scheme within the protected period.

(2) The responsible authority must—

(a) consult the persons specified in subsection (3) with a view to reaching agreement with them, and

(b) lay a report before the appropriate legislature.

(3) The persons referred to in subsection (2)(a) are the persons (or representatives of the persons) who appear to the responsible authority to be likely to be affected by the regulations if they were made.

(4) The report under subsection (2)(b) must set out why the responsible authority proposes to make the regulations, having regard to the desirability of not making a change to the protected elements of a scheme under section 1 within the protected period.

(5) In this section—

"the appropriate legislature" means—

(a) Parliament, where the responsible authority is the Secretary of State, the Minister for the Civil Service or the Lord Chancellor;

(b) the Scottish Parliament, where the responsible authority is the Scottish Ministers;

(c) the National Assembly for Wales, where the responsible authority is the Welsh Ministers;

"protected period" means the period beginning with the coming into force of this section and ending with 31 March 2040;

"protected elements", in relation to a scheme under section 1, means—

(a) the extent to which the scheme is a career average revalued earnings scheme;

(b) members' contribution rates under the scheme;

(c) benefit accrual rates under the scheme.

(6) In this section, references to a change to the protected elements do not include a change appearing to the responsible authority to be required by or consequential upon section 12 (employer cost cap).

(7) In a case where this section applies, there is no requirement to consult under section 21(1).

[1.1857]

23 Procedure for retrospective provision

(1) Where the responsible authority proposes to make scheme regulations containing retrospective provision which appears to the authority to have significant adverse effects in relation to the pension payable to or in respect of members of the scheme, the authority must first obtain the consent of the persons referred to in subsection (3).

(2) Where the responsible authority proposes to make scheme regulations containing retrospective provision which appears to the authority—

(a) not to have significant adverse effects as specified in subsection (1), but

(b) to have significant adverse effects in any other way in relation to members of the scheme (for example, in relation to injury or compensation benefits),

the authority must first consult the persons specified in subsection (3) with a view to reaching agreement with them.

(3) The persons referred to in subsections (1) and (2) are the persons (or representatives of the persons) who appear to the responsible authority to be likely to be affected by the provision if it were made.

(4) The responsible authority must, in a case falling within subsection (1) or (2), lay a report before the appropriate legislature (as defined in section 22).

(5) In a case falling within subsection (1) or (2) there is no requirement to consult under section 21(1).

[1.1858]

24 Other procedure

(1) Scheme regulations are subject to the affirmative procedure if—

(a) they amend primary legislation,

(b) section 23(1) or (2) (procedure for retrospective provision having significant adverse effects) applies, or

(c) they are scheme regulations for a scheme relating to the judiciary, unless the pension board for that scheme has stated that it considers the regulations to be minor or wholly beneficial.

(2) Scheme regulations are subject to the negative procedure in any other case.

(3) If scheme regulations otherwise subject to the negative procedure are combined with scheme regulations subject to the affirmative procedure, the combined regulations are subject to the affirmative procedure.

New schemes: supplementary

[1.1859]

25 Extension of schemes

(1) Scheme regulations for a scheme under section 1 may make provision for the payment of pensions and other benefits to or in respect of—

(a) persons who are specified in section 1(2), but

(b) in relation to whom the responsible authority could not otherwise make a scheme under section 1.

(2) Scheme regulations for a scheme under section 1 may make provision to deem persons of any description to fall within a given description of persons specified in section 1(2).

(3) Scheme regulations for a scheme under section 1 may specify persons, not being persons specified in section 1(2), as persons to whom the scheme may potentially relate.
(4) The persons specified under subsection (3) may be any persons (other than persons specified in section 1(2)) that the responsible authority considers appropriate.
(5) The responsible authority may then at any time determine that the scheme is to relate to some or all of those persons.
(6) By virtue of a determination under subsection (5) the scheme regulations then apply to the persons to whom the determination relates as they apply to other persons to or in respect of whom pensions and other benefits are provided under the scheme (or such class of other persons as may be specified in the determination).
(7) Subsection (6) is subject to—
(a) any special provision made in the scheme regulations, and
(b) a direction under subsection (8).
(8) Scheme regulations made under subsection (2) or (3) in relation to any persons may include provision authorising the responsible authority by direction to modify provisions of the regulations in their application to those persons for the purpose of—
(a) securing appropriate protection against additional costs to the scheme that might result from the application of the scheme regulations to those persons,
(b) obtaining information about those persons, their employers and other relevant persons, or
(c) taking appropriate account of—
(i) the arrangements under which those persons are employed, and
(ii) the organisational structures of their employers.
(9) The responsible authority for a scheme under section 1 must publish a list of the persons to whom the scheme relates by virtue of determinations under subsection (5) (and keep the published list up-to-date).
(10) A determination under subsection (5) may have retrospective effect.
(11) Where, by virtue of section 4(5), there is more than one scheme manager for a scheme under section 1, the responsible authority may delegate its functions under subsection (5) or (9) to the scheme managers, subject to such conditions as the responsible authority considers appropriate.

NOTES

Regulations: the Public Service (Civil Servants and Others) Pensions Regulations 2014, SI 2014/1964; the Armed Forces Pension Regulations 2014, SI 2014/2336; the National Health Service Pension Scheme Regulations 2015, SI 2015/94; the Police Pensions Regulations 2015, SI 2015/445; the National Health Service Pension Scheme (Amendment) Regulations 2015, SI 2015/581; the Civil Service (Other Crown Servants) Pension Scheme Regulations 2016, SI 2016/326; the National Health Service Pension Scheme and Additional Voluntary Contributions (Amendment) Regulations 2017, SI 2017/275; the Judicial Pensions (Amendment) Regulations 2017, SI 2017/508; the London Government (London Fire Commissioner and Policing) (Amendment) Regulations 2018, SI 2018/269; the Local Government Pension Scheme (Amendment) Regulations 2018, SI 2018/493.

[1.1860]
26 Non-scheme benefits
(1) The scheme manager or employer for a scheme under section 1 may make such payments as the scheme manager or employer considers appropriate towards the provision, otherwise than by virtue of the scheme, of pensions and other benefits to or in respect of—
(a) persons within the description of persons specified in section 1(2) for which the responsible authority may make the scheme, and
(b) any other persons to whom the scheme relates by virtue of section 25.
(2) Subsection (1) is subject to any provision made in the scheme regulations for the scheme that restricts or otherwise affects the power to make payments under that subsection.

27 *(Introduces Sch 8 to the Act (consequential and minor amendments).)*

Existing schemes: supplementary

[1.1861]
28 Existing local government schemes
(1) This section applies in relation to regulations under section 7 of the Superannuation Act 1972 which relate to persons in England and Wales which are in force immediately before the coming into force of this section.
(2) To the extent that—
(a) such regulations make provision for the payment of pensions and other benefits to or in respect of a person in relation to the person's service on or after 1 April 2014, and
(b) that provision could be made under scheme regulations,
the regulations are to have effect as if they were scheme regulations relating to local government workers in England and Wales.
(3) Accordingly, to that extent a scheme under such regulations is to have effect as a scheme under section 1.

29 *(Introduces Sch 9 to the Act (amendments to the Superannuation Act 1972).)*

Public body pension schemes

[1.1862]

30 New public body pension schemes

(1) The following provisions of this Act apply in relation to a new public body pension scheme (and any statutory pension scheme that is connected with it) as to a scheme under section 1 (and any connected scheme)—

(a) section 3(1) and (2) and Schedule 3 (scheme regulations);

(b) section 4 (scheme manager);

(c) sections 5 and 6 (pension board), if the scheme has more than one member;

(d) sections 8 to 10 (scheme design);

(e) sections 11 and 12 (cost control);

(f) sections 14 to 16 (information and records).

(2) For the purposes of subsection (1), the provisions referred to in that subsection are to be read with the following modifications—

(a) references to scheme regulations are to be read as references to the rules of the scheme;

(b) references to the responsible authority are to be read as references to the public authority which established the scheme.

(3) A new public body pension scheme, and any variation to the rules of the scheme, requires the consent of the Treasury.

(4) This section does not apply to a new public body pension scheme which relates to a devolved body or office.

(5) In this Act—

"public body pension scheme" means a scheme (other than an existing scheme) [or a scheme established under section 18A of the Judicial Pensions and Retirement Act 1993] established by a public authority for the payment of pensions and other benefits to or in respect of members or staff of a statutory body or the holder of a statutory office;

"new public body pension scheme" means a public body pension scheme established after the coming into force of this section.

NOTES

Commencement: 1 April 2015.

Sub-s (5): words in square brackets in the definition "public body pension scheme" inserted by the Pension Schemes Act 2015 (Judicial Pensions) (Consequential Provision) Regulations 2017, SI 2017/393, reg 2, as from 14 March 2017.

[1.1863]

31 Restriction of certain existing public body pension schemes

(1) This section applies to a public body pension scheme which relates to members or staff of a body, or the holder of an office, listed in Schedule 10.

(2) The public authority responsible for the scheme must make provision to secure that no benefits are provided under the scheme to or in respect of a person in relation to the person's service after a date determined by the authority.

(3) Subsection (2) does not apply—

(a) in relation to a public body pension scheme which is a defined contributions scheme, or

(b) to injury or compensation benefits.

(4) The public authority responsible for a scheme to which subsection (2) applies may provide for exceptions to the provision made under subsection (2), and section 18(6) and (7) apply in relation to any such exceptions (reading references to scheme regulations as references to rules of the scheme).

(5) Provision made under subsection (2) or (4) may in particular be made by amending the public body pension scheme.

(6) In subsection (2), the reference to benefits in relation to a person's service includes benefits relating to the person's death in service.

(7) If any of the persons to whom a scheme to which subsection (2) applies relates are not eligible for membership of a scheme under section 1, the public authority responsible for the scheme may establish a new scheme for the payment of pensions or other benefits to or in respect of those persons (and see section 30).

(8) Where a scheme to which subsection (2) applies was established in exercise of a statutory function or other power, the function or power may not be exercised again so as to establish a new defined benefits scheme in relation to the body or office.

(9) In the case of a scheme established by deed of trust, subsections (2) and (4) apply irrespective of the provisions of the deed or the law relating to trusts.

(10) A Treasury order may amend Schedule 10 so as to—

(a) remove any body or office specified there;

(b) add any body or office to it (by name or description),

but may not add a devolved body or office.

(11) A Treasury order under subsection (10) may make consequential or supplementary provision, including in particular provision made by amending any legislation.

(12) A Treasury order under subsection (10) is subject to the negative procedure.

(13) It is immaterial for the purposes of subsection (1) whether a scheme is made before or after the coming into force of this section.

(14) Schedule 7 contains provision for a "final salary link" in relation to schemes to which subsection (2) applies.

NOTES

Commencement: 1 April 2015.

Orders: as of 15 May 2019, no Orders had been made under this section.

[1.1864]

32 Existing public body pension schemes: pension age

(1) A public body pension scheme established before the coming into force of this section may include—

- (a) provision securing that the normal and deferred pension age of a person under the scheme is—
  - (i) the same as the person's state pension age, or
  - (ii) 65, if that is higher, and
- (b) provision securing that changes in the person's normal or deferred pension age occurring in consequence of provision under paragraph (a) apply in relation to relevant accrued benefits (as well as other benefits).

(2) In subsection (1)(b) "relevant accrued benefits", in relation to a person and a scheme, means benefits accrued after the coming into force of the provision under subsection (1) which may be paid to or in respect of the person under the scheme and to which the normal or deferred pension age is relevant.

(3) This section does not apply to a public body pension scheme which relates to a devolved body or office.

NOTES

Commencement: 1 April 2015.

Parliamentary and other pension schemes

[1.1865]

33 Great offices of state

Schedule 11 makes provision about pension arrangements for the offices of—

- (a) Prime Minister and First Lord of the Treasury,
- (b) Lord Chancellor, and
- (c) Speaker of the House of Commons.

34–36 *(Outside the scope of this work.)*

General

[1.1866]

37 General interpretation

In this Act—

"the affirmative procedure" and "the affirmative Commons procedure" have the meanings given in section 38;

"armed forces" has the meaning given in Schedule 1;

"body" includes an unincorporated body or organisation of persons (for example, a committee or board of trustees);

"career average revalued earnings scheme" has the meaning given in section 8(4);

"civil servants" has the meaning given in Schedule 1;

"compensation benefits" means benefits by way of compensation for loss of office or employment;

"connected", in relation to a scheme under section 1 and another statutory pension scheme, or a new public body pension scheme and another statutory pension scheme, has the meaning given by section 4(6);

"defined benefits scheme": a pension scheme is a "defined benefits scheme" if or to the extent that the benefits that may be provided under the scheme are not money purchase benefits (within the meaning of the Pension Schemes Act 1993) or injury and compensation benefits;

"defined contributions scheme": a pension scheme is a "defined contributions scheme" if or to the extent that the benefits that may be provided under the scheme are money purchase benefits (within the meaning of the Pension Schemes Act 1993);

"deferred pension age" has the meaning given in section 10(5);

"devolved": a body or office is "devolved" if or to the extent that provision about pensions payable to or in respect of members or staff of the body, or a holder of the office—

- (a) would be within the legislative competence of the Northern Ireland Assembly were that provision contained in an Act of the Assembly, or
- (b) is not a reserved matter within the meaning of the Scotland Act 1998;

"earnings" includes any remuneration or profit derived from an employment;

"employer", in relation to a pension scheme, means—

- (a) any employer of persons to whom the scheme relates,
- (b) the person responsible for the remuneration of an office-holder to whom the scheme relates, or
- (c) such other persons (in addition to, or instead of, any person falling within paragraph (a) or (b)) as scheme regulations or (in the case of a public body pension scheme) the rules of the scheme may provide;

"existing scheme" has the meaning given in section 18(2);

"final salary", in relation to a person to or in respect of whom a pension under a pension scheme is payable, means the person's pensionable earnings, or highest, average or representative pensionable earnings, in a specified period ending at, or defined by reference to, the time when the person's pensionable service in relation to that scheme terminates;

"final salary scheme": a pension scheme is a "final salary scheme" if entitlement to the pension payable to or in respect of a person which is based on the pensionable service of that person is or may be determined to any extent by reference to the person's final salary;

"fire and rescue workers" has the meaning given in Schedule 1;

"injury benefits" means benefits by way of compensation for incapacity or death as a result of injury or illness;

"injury or compensation scheme": a pension scheme is an "injury or compensation scheme" if it provides only for injury or compensation benefits (or both);

"judiciary" has the meaning given in Schedule 1;

"health service workers" has the meaning given in Schedule 1;

"legislation" means primary or secondary legislation;

"local authority" means—

(a) a local authority in England and Wales within the meaning of Part 1 of the Local Government and Housing Act 1989, or

(b) a council constituted under section 2 of the Local Government etc (Scotland) Act 1994;

"local government workers" has the meaning given in Schedule 1;

"members of a police force" has the meaning given in Schedule 1;

"the negative procedure" and "the negative Commons procedure" have the meanings given in section 38;

"normal pension age" has the meaning given in section 10(5);

"pension board" has the meaning given by section 5(8);

"pension scheme" means a scheme for the payment of pensions or other benefits to or in respect of persons with service of a particular description;

"pensionable earnings", in relation to a pension scheme and a member of it, means earnings by reference to which a pension or other benefits under the scheme are calculated;

"pensionable service", in relation to a pension scheme, means service which qualifies a person to a pension or other benefits under that scheme;

"primary legislation" means an Act, Act of the Scottish Parliament, Act or Measure of the National Assembly for Wales or Northern Ireland legislation;

"public authority" means—

(a) a Minister of the Crown (as defined by section 8 of the Ministers of the Crown Act 1975),

(b) a statutory body or the holder of a statutory office, or

(c) a person exercising a statutory function;

"public body pension scheme" and "new public body pension scheme" have the meanings given in section 30(5);

"responsible authority", in relation to a scheme under section 1, has the meaning given by section 2(2);

"scheme" includes arrangements of any description;

"scheme advisory board" has the meaning given by section 7(6);

"scheme manager", in relation to a scheme under section 1, has the meaning given in section 4(2);

"scheme regulations" has the meaning given in section 1(4);

"secondary legislation" means an instrument made under primary legislation;

"staff", in relation to a body, includes any employee or officer of the body;

"state pension age" has the meaning given in section 10(5);

"statutory body" and "statutory office" mean a body or office established under any legislation;

"statutory function" means a function conferred by any legislation;

"statutory pension scheme" means—

(a) a pension scheme which is established by or under any legislation, and

(b) a public body pension scheme which is not so established;

"teachers" has the meaning given in Schedule 1;

"Treasury directions" means directions given by the Treasury;

"Treasury order" means an order made by the Treasury;

"Treasury regulations" means regulations made by the Treasury.

NOTES

Regulations: the Teachers' Pension Scheme (Amendment) Regulations 2014, SI 2014/2652 (made under para (c) of the definition "employer").

[1.1867]

38 Regulations, orders and directions

(1) For the purposes of this Act any power of the Secretary of State, the Minister for the Civil Service, the Treasury, the Lord Chancellor or the Welsh Ministers to make regulations or an order is exercisable by statutory instrument.

(2) In this Act, the "affirmative procedure" means—

(a) in the case of regulations or an order of the Secretary of State, the Minister for the Civil Service or the Lord Chancellor, that the regulations or order may not be made unless a draft of the instrument containing them or it has been laid before, and approved by resolution of, each House of Parliament;

(b) in the case of regulations of the Welsh Ministers, that the regulations may not be made unless a draft of the instrument containing them has been laid before, and approved by resolution of, the National Assembly for Wales.

(3) In this Act, the "negative procedure" means—

(a) in the case of regulations or an order of the Secretary of State, the Minister for the Civil Service, the Lord Chancellor or the Treasury, that the instrument containing them or it is subject to annulment in pursuance of a resolution of either House of Parliament;

(b) in the case of regulations or an order of the Welsh Ministers, that the instrument containing them or it is subject to annulment in pursuance of a resolution of the National Assembly for Wales.

(4) In this Act, the "affirmative Commons procedure", in relation to a Treasury order, means that the order may not be made unless a draft of the instrument containing it has been laid before, and approved by resolution of, the House of Commons.

(5) In this Act, the "negative Commons procedure", in relation to Treasury regulations or a Treasury order, means that the instrument containing them or it is subject to annulment in pursuance of a resolution of the House of Commons.

(6) For regulations and orders of the Scottish Ministers, see Part 2 of the Interpretation and Legislative Reform (Scotland) Act 2010 (asp 10).

(7) Treasury directions under this Act may be varied or revoked.

Final

[1.1868]
39 Financial provision

(1) Scheme regulations may provide for any pension or other sum payable under the regulations to or in respect of a person who has held an office specified in Part 1 of Schedule 1 to the Judicial Pensions and Retirement Act 1993 to be charged on, and paid out of, the Consolidated Fund.

(2) There shall be paid out of money provided by Parliament—

(a) any expenditure incurred under or by virtue of this Act by a Minister of the Crown, and

(b) any increase attributable to this Act in the sums payable under or by virtue of any other Act out of money so provided.

[1.1869]
40 Extent

(1) An amendment or repeal in this Act has the same extent as the provision amended or repealed.

(2) That aside, this Act extends to England and Wales, Scotland and Northern Ireland.

[1.1870]
41 Commencement

(1) The following provisions of this Act come into force on the day on which this Act is passed—

(a) section 29 and Schedule 9 (existing schemes for civil servants: extension of access);

(b) section 33 and Schedule 11 (great offices of state);

(c) sections 37 to 40, this section and section 42.

(2) The other provisions of this Act come into force on such day or days as may be appointed by Treasury order.

(3) An order under subsection (2) may—

(a) appoint different days for different purposes;

(b) make transitional, transitory or saving provision.

NOTES

Orders: the Public Service Pensions Act 2013 (Commencement No 1) Order 2013, SI 2013/1518; the Public Service Pensions Act 2013 (Commencement No 2 and Transitional Provisions) Order 2013, SI 2013/2818; the Public Service Pensions Act 2013 (Commencement No 3) Order 2014, SI 2014/433; the Public Service Pensions Act 2013 (Commencement No 4) Order 2014, SI 2014/839; the Public Service Pensions Act 2013 (Commencement No 5) Order 2014, SI 2014/1912; the Public Service Pensions Act 2013 (Commencement No 6, Saving Provision and Amendment) Order 2015, SI 2015/4.

[1.1871]
42 Short title

This Act may be cited as the Public Service Pensions Act 2013.

SCHEDULES

SCHEDULE 1
PERSONS IN PUBLIC SERVICE: DEFINITIONS

Section 1(3)

Civil servants

[1.1872]
1 In this Act, "civil servants" means persons employed in the civil service of the State (not including the civil service of Northern Ireland).

Judiciary

2 (1) In this Act, "the judiciary" means holders of an office specified in an order made by—

(a) the Secretary of State, in relation to an office with a jurisdiction exercised exclusively in relation to Scotland, or
(b) the Lord Chancellor, in any other case.

(2) An order under sub-paragraph (1) may only specify an office in or as regards Scotland or Northern Ireland if the office is not a devolved office.

(3) An order under this paragraph is subject to the negative procedure.

Local government workers

3 (1) In this Act, "local government workers" means persons employed in local government service and specified in scheme regulations.

(2) In this paragraph, "local government service" means service specified in scheme regulations.

Teachers

4 In this Act, "teachers" includes persons who are employed otherwise than as teachers—
(a) in a capacity connected with education which to a substantial extent involves the control or supervision of teachers, or
(b) in employment which involves the performance of duties in connection with the provision of education or services ancillary to education, and

who are specified in scheme regulations.

Health service workers

5 (1) In this Act, "health service workers" means persons engaged in health services and specified in scheme regulations.

(2) In this paragraph, "health services" means services specified in scheme regulations.

Fire and rescue workers

6 In this Act, "fire and rescue workers" means persons employed by—
(a) a fire and rescue authority in England or Wales,
[(aa) the chief constable of the police force for a police area having been—
(i) transferred to the chief constable under a scheme made under section 4I(1) of the Fire and Rescue Services Act 2004, . . .
(ii) appointed by the chief constable under section 4I(4) of that Act,
[(iii) transferred to the chief constable under a scheme made by virtue of section 107EC(1) of the Local Democracy, Economic Development and Construction Act 2009, or
(iv) appointed by the chief constable under section 107EC(2) of that Act, or]
(b) the Scottish Fire and Rescue Service.

Police forces

7 In this Act "members of a police force"—
(a) in relation to England and Wales, includes special constables and police cadets;
(b) in relation to Scotland, means members of the Police Service of Scotland and police cadets.

Armed forces

8 In this Act, "the armed forces" means the naval, military and air forces of the Crown.

Transitional provision

9 In relation to a time before the coming into force of section 101 of the Police and Fire Reform (Scotland) Act 2012 (asp 8), the reference in paragraph 6(b) to the Scottish Fire and Rescue Service is to be read as a reference to a relevant authority (as defined in section 6 of the Fire (Scotland) Act 2005 (asp 5)).

10 In relation to a time before the coming into force of section 6 of the Police and Fire Reform (Scotland) Act 2012, the reference in paragraph 7(b) to the Police Service of Scotland is to be read as a reference to a police force within the meaning of the Police (Scotland) Act 1967.

NOTES

Para 6 is amended as follows:

Sub-para (aa) was substituted for the word "or" at the end of para (a) by the Policing and Crime Act 2017, s 6, Sch 1, Pt 2, para 95, as from 3 April 2017.

The word omitted from sub-para (aa)(i) was repealed, and sub-paras (aa)(iii), (iv) were substituted for the word "or" at the end of sub-para (aa)(ii), by the Policing and Crime Act 2017, s 8(11), as from 17 July 2017.

Regulations: the Teachers' Pension Scheme Regulations 2014, SI 2014/512; the Armed Forces Pension Regulations 2014, SI 2014/2336; the Teachers' Pension Scheme (Amendment) Regulations 2014, SI 2014/2652; the Public Service Pensions Act 2013 (Judicial Offices) Order 2015, SI 2015/580; the Public Service Pensions Act 2013 (Judicial Offices) (Amendment) Order 2015, SI 2015/1483; the Local Government Pension Scheme (Wandsworth and Richmond Fund Merger) Regulations 2016, SI 2016/1241; the Teachers' Pensions Schemes (Miscellaneous Amendments) Regulations 2017, SI 2017/1084; the Public Service Pensions Act 2013 (Judicial Offices) (Amendment) Order 2018, SI 2018/186; the Teachers' Pensions Schemes (Amendment) Regulations 2018, SI 2018/218.

SCHEDULE 2
RESPONSIBLE AUTHORITIES

Section 2(1)

Civil servants and judiciary

[1.1873]

1 Scheme regulations for civil servants may be made by the Minister for the Civil Service.

2 (1) Scheme regulations for the judiciary may be made by the Lord Chancellor.

(2) Before making scheme regulations in relation to an office with a jurisdiction exercised exclusively in relation to Scotland, the Lord Chancellor must consult the Secretary of State.

Local government workers

3 Scheme regulations for local government workers may be made by—

(a) the Secretary of State, in or as regards England and Wales;
(b) the Scottish Ministers, in or as regards Scotland.

Teachers

4 Scheme regulations for teachers may be made by—

(a) the Secretary of State, in or as regards England and Wales;
(b) the Scottish Ministers, in or as regards Scotland.

Health service workers

5 Scheme regulations for health service workers may be made by—

(a) the Secretary of State, in or as regards England and Wales;
(b) the Scottish Ministers, in or as regards Scotland.

Fire and rescue workers

6 Scheme regulations for fire and rescue workers may be made by—

(a) the Secretary of State, in or as regards England;
(b) the Welsh Ministers, in or as regards Wales;
(c) the Scottish Ministers, in or as regards Scotland.

Police forces

7 Scheme regulations for members of a police force may be made by—

(a) the Secretary of State, in or as regards England and Wales;
(b) the Scottish Ministers, in or as regards Scotland.

Armed forces

8 Scheme regulations for the armed forces may be made by the Secretary of State.

NOTES

Commencement: 28 February 2014.

Regulations: the Regulations made under this Schedule are too numerous to list individually. The principal Regulations include: the Teachers' Pension Scheme Regulations 2014, SI 2014/512; the Public Service (Civil Servants and Others) Pensions Regulations 2014, SI 2014/1964; the Armed Forces Pension Regulations 2014, SI 2014/2336; the National Health Service Pension Scheme Regulations 2015, SI 2015/94; the Judicial Pensions Regulations 2015, SI 2015/182; the Police Pensions Regulations 2015, SI 2015/445; the Firefighters' Pension Scheme (Scotland) Regulations 2015, SSI 2015/19; the National Health Service Pension Scheme (Scotland) Regulations 2015, SSI 2015/94; the Police Pension Scheme (Scotland) Regulations 2015, SSI 2015/142; and the Civil Service (Other Crown Servants) Pension Scheme Regulations 2016, SI 2016/326; the Local Government Pension Scheme (Scotland) Regulations 2018, SSI 2018/141.

SCHEDULE 3
SCOPE OF SCHEME REGULATIONS: SUPPLEMENTARY MATTERS

Section 3(2)(a)

[1.1874]

1 Eligibility and admission to membership.

This includes—

(a) specifying who, of the persons in relation to whom the scheme regulations may be made, is eligible for membership;
(b) conditions of eligibility.

2 The benefits which must or may be paid under the scheme.

Those benefits may include—

(a) pensions and other benefits on leaving service to which the scheme relates (whether before, at or after normal pension age);
(b) benefits payable on death (in service or otherwise);
(c) compensation payments (including for death, injury or redundancy);
(d) discretionary payments and concessions.

3 The persons to whom benefits under the scheme are payable.

Those persons may include—

(a) active, deferred and pensioner members of the scheme;
(b) pension credit members of the scheme;
(c) widows, widowers, surviving civil partners and surviving dependants.

4 The conditions subject to which benefits are payable.

5 The assignment of benefits, including restrictions on assignment.

6 The forfeiture or suspension of benefits.

7 The recovery of overpaid benefits.

8 The exclusion of double recovery of compensation or damages.

This includes—

(a) exclusion or modification of rights to compensation or damages in respect of any matter in a case where benefits are paid under the scheme in respect of the same matter;
(b) exclusion or modification of rights to benefits under the scheme where compensation or damages are received in respect of the same matter from another source.

9 Contributions, including—

(a) the making of contributions by employers and members;
(b) contribution rates;
(c) interest on late payment of contributions;
(d) the return of contributions (with or without interest).

10 The payment or receipt of transfer values or other lump sum payments for the purpose of creating or restoring rights to benefits (under the scheme or otherwise).

11 Pension funds (for schemes which have them).

This includes the administration, management and winding-up of any pension funds.

12 The administration and management of the scheme, including—

(a) the giving of guidance or directions by the responsible authority to the scheme manager (where those persons are different);
(b) the person by whom benefits under the scheme are to be provided;
(c) the provision or publication of information about the scheme.

13 The delegation of functions under scheme regulations, including—

(a) delegation of functions by the scheme manager or responsible authority;
(b) further delegation of functions by any delegatee.

14 The payment by an employer of—

(a) any costs relating to the administration of the scheme;
(b) any costs incurred because of a failure by the employer to comply with the employer's obligations under the scheme;
(c) interest relating to payments to be made by virtue of this paragraph.

15 The resolution of disputes and appeals (including the referral to a court of law of questions of law which under the scheme fall to be determined by the responsible authority).

NOTES

Regulations: the Regulations made under this Schedule are too numerous to list individually. The principal Regulations include: the Teachers' Pension Scheme Regulations 2014, SI 2014/512; the Public Service (Civil Servants and Others) Pensions Regulations 2014, SI 2014/1964; the Armed Forces Pension Regulations 2014, SI 2014/2336; the National Health Service Pension Scheme Regulations 2015, SI 2015/94; the Judicial Pensions Regulations 2015, SI 2015/182; the Police Pensions Regulations 2015, SI 2015/445; the Teachers (Compensation for Redundancy and Premature Retirement) Regulations 2015, SI 2015/601; and the Civil Service (Other Crown Servants) Pension Scheme Regulations 2016, SI 2016/326.

SCHEDULE 4

(*Sch 4 amends provisions of the Pensions Act 2004 that are outside the scope of this work.*)

SCHEDULE 5
EXISTING PENSION SCHEMES

Section 18

Civil servants

[1.1875]

1 A scheme under section 1 of the Superannuation Act 1972 [other than a scheme which relates to staff of the Secret Intelligence Service or Security Service].

Exception: injury benefits and compensation benefits

Judiciary

2 A scheme constituted by section 20 of the Sheriff Courts (Scotland) Act 1907.

3 A scheme constituted by paragraph 23 of Schedule 9 to the Agriculture Act 1947, so far as relating to payment of pension benefits.

4 A scheme constituted by or made under any provision of Part XIII of the County Courts Act (Northern Ireland) 1959 (c 25 (NI)).

5 A scheme constituted by or made under any provision of the District Judges (Magistrates' Courts) Pensions Act (Northern Ireland) 1960 (c 2 (NI)).

6 A scheme constituted by or made under any provision of the Sheriffs' Pensions (Scotland) Act 1961.

7 A scheme under paragraph 7A of Schedule 10 to the Rent Act 1977.
Exception: injury benefits and compensation benefits

8 A scheme constituted by or made under any provision of the Judicial Pensions Act 1981.
Exception: injury benefits under a scheme constituted by or made under Part 3 of Schedule 1 to that Act

9 A scheme constituted by paragraph 9 of Schedule 4 to the Rent (Scotland) Act 1984.

10 A scheme constituted by or made under any provision of Part 1 or section 19 of the Judicial Pensions and Retirement Act 1993.
Except i on: benefits payable to or in respect of a holder of a devolved office

11 A scheme constituted by paragraph 4(1) of Schedule 1 to the Scottish Land Court Act 1993.

12 A scheme constituted by or made under paragraph 6 of Schedule 2 to the Mental Health (Care and Treatment) (Scotland) Act 2003 (asp 13).

13 A scheme constituted by or made under paragraph 9 of Schedule 1 to the Education (Additional Support for Learning) (Scotland) Act 2004 (asp 4).

14 A scheme constituted by paragraph 2(1)(b) of Schedule 2 to the Charities and Trustee Investment (Scotland) Act 2005 (asp 10), so far as relating to payment of pension benefits.

15 A scheme constituted by paragraph 6(3) of Schedule 11 to the Welsh Language (Wales) Measure 2011 (nawm 1).

Local government workers

16 A scheme constituted by paragraph 2 of Schedule 1 to the Coroners Act 1988.

17 Regulations under section 7 of the Superannuation Act 1972.
Exception: injury benefits

Teachers

18 Regulations under section 9 of the Superannuation Act 1972.
Exception: injury benefits

Health service workers

19 Regulations under section 10 of the Superannuation Act 1972.
Exception: injury benefits

Fire and rescue workers

20 A scheme under section 26 of the Fire Services Act 1947.

21 A scheme under section 34 of the Fire and Rescue Services Act 2004.
Exception: injury benefits and compensation benefits

Members of police forces

22 Regulations under section 1 of the Police Pensions Act 1976.
Exception: injury benefits

23 A scheme under section 48 of the Police and Fire Reform (Scotland) Act 2012 (asp 8).
Exception: injury benefits and compensation benefits

Armed forces

24 The scheme constituted by the Royal Warrant of 19 December 1949 (see Army Order 151 of 1949).
Exception: injury benefits

25 An Order in Council under section 3 of the Naval and Marine Pay and Pensions Act 1865.
Exception: injury benefits

26 An order under section 2 of the Pensions and Yeomanry Pay Act 1884.
Exception: injury benefits

27 An order under section 2 of the Air Force (Constitution) Act 1917.
Exception: injury benefits

28 Orders or regulations under section 4 of the Reserve Forces Act 1996 containing provision made under section 8 of that Act.
Exception: injury benefits and compensation benefits

29 (1) A scheme under section 1(1) of the Armed Forces (Pensions and Compensation) Act 2004.
Exception: injury benefits and compensation benefits

(2) For the purposes of sub-paragraph (1), "compensation benefits" includes benefits by way of payments for resettlement or retraining.

NOTES

Commencement: 28 February 2014 (for the purpose of making scheme regulations to establish schemes for the payment of pensions and other benefits to or in respect of teachers); to be appointed (otherwise).

Para 1: words in square brackets inserted by the Pension Schemes Act 2015, s 80, as from 3 March 2015.

Regulations: the Teachers' Pension Scheme Regulations 2014, SI 2014/512; the Armed Forces Pension Regulations 2014, SI 2014/2336; the Teachers' Pension Scheme (Amendment) Regulations 2014, SI 2014/2652; the Teachers' Pension Scheme (Amendment) Regulations 2015, SI 2015/592. Note that despite this Schedule being in force only for the purpose of making scheme regulations to establish schemes for the payment of pensions and other benefits to or in respect of teachers, the power to make regulations relating to the armed forces is derived from s 13 of the Interpretation Act 1978 (Anticipatory exercise of powers).

SCHEDULE 6
EXISTING INJURY AND COMPENSATION SCHEMES

Section 19

Civil servants

[1.1876]

1 A scheme under section 1 of the Superannuation Act 1972.
Specified benefits: injury benefits and compensation benefits

Judiciary

2 A scheme under paragraph 7A of Schedule 10 to the Rent Act 1977.
Specified benefits: injury benefits and compensation benefits

3 A scheme constituted by or made under Part 3 of Schedule 1 to the Judicial Pensions Act 1981.

4 A scheme constituted by section 11(b) of the Judicial Pensions Act 1981.

Local government workers

5 Regulations under section 7 of the Superannuation Act 1972.
Specified benefits: injury benefits

Teachers

6 Regulations under section 9 of the Superannuation Act 1972.
Specified benefits: injury benefits

Health service workers

7 Regulations under section 10 of the Superannuation Act 1972.
Specified benefits: injury benefits

Fire and rescue workers

8 A scheme under section 34 of the Fire and Rescue Services Act 2004.
Specified benefits: injury benefits and compensation benefits

Members of police forces

9 Regulations under section 1 of the Police Pensions Act 1976.
Specified benefits: injury benefits

10 A scheme under section 48 of the Police and Fire Reform (Scotland) Act 2012 (asp 8).
Specified benefits: injury benefits and compensation benefits

Armed forces

11 The scheme constituted by the Royal Warrant of 19 December 1949 (see Army Order 151 of 1949).
Specified benefits: injury benefits

12 An Order in Council under section 3 of the Naval and Marine Pay and Pensions Act 1865.
Specified benefits: injury benefits

13 An order under section 2 of the Pensions and Yeomanry Pay Act 1884.
Specified benefits: injury benefits

14 An order under section 2 of the Air Force (Constitution) Act 1917.
Specified benefits: injury benefits

15 An order or regulations under section 4 of the Reserve Forces Act 1996 containing provision made under section 8 of that Act.
Specified benefits: injury benefits and compensation benefits

16 (1) A scheme under section 1(1) of the Armed Forces (Pensions and Compensation) Act 2004.
Specified benefits: injury benefits and compensation benefits

(2) For the purposes of sub-paragraph (1), "compensation benefits" includes benefits by way of payments for resettlement or retraining.

17 A scheme under section 1(2) of the Armed Forces (Pensions and Compensation) Act 2004.

Compensation schemes for loss of office etc

18 Regulations under section 24 of the Superannuation Act 1972.

NOTES

Regulations: the Teachers' Pension Scheme Regulations 2014, SI 2014/512; the Armed Forces Pension Regulations 2014, SI 2014/2336.

SCHEDULE 7
FINAL SALARY LINK

Sections 20 and 31

Persons who remain in an old scheme for past service

[1.1877]

1 (1) This paragraph applies in a case where—
(a) a person is a member of an existing scheme to which section 18(1) applies or a scheme to which section 31(2) applies ("the old scheme") by virtue of his or her pensionable service for that scheme ("the old scheme service"), and
(b) the person is also a member of a scheme under section 1 or a new public body pension scheme ("the new scheme") by virtue of his or her pensionable service for that scheme ("the new scheme service").

(2) If, in a case where this paragraph applies—
(a) the old scheme service and the new scheme service are continuous, and
(b) the person's employer in relation to the old scheme service is the person's employer in relation to the new scheme service (or any other employer in relation to the new scheme),

then, in determining the person's final salary for any purpose of the old scheme—
(i) the old scheme service is to be regarded as having ended when the new scheme service ended, and
(ii) such earnings as scheme regulations for the new scheme may specify, being earnings derived by the person from the new scheme service, are to be regarded as derived from the old scheme service (subject to sub-paragraph (3)).

(3) The amount of the earnings that are to be regarded as derived from the old scheme service must not be materially less than the amount of the earnings that would have been the person's pensionable earnings derived from that service had the new scheme service been old scheme service.

Persons whose benefits under an old scheme are transferred to another closed scheme

2 (1) This paragraph applies in a case where—
(a) a person has been a member of an existing scheme to which section 18(1) applies or a scheme to which section 31(2) applies ("the old scheme") by virtue of his or her pensionable service for that scheme ("the old scheme service"),
(b) the person is also a member of a scheme under section 1 or a new public body pension scheme ("the new scheme") by virtue of his or her pensionable service for that scheme ("the new scheme service"),
(c) the person's rights to benefit under the old scheme have been transferred after the date referred to in section 18(1) or 31(2) to an existing scheme to which section 18(1) applies or a scheme to which section 31(2) applies ("the transfer scheme"), and
(d) the old scheme service is treated, by virtue of that transfer, as pensionable service of the person for the transfer scheme ("the deemed transfer scheme service").

(2) If, in a case where this paragraph applies—
(a) the deemed transfer scheme service and the new scheme service are continuous, and
(b) the person's employer in relation to the new scheme service is an employer in relation to the transfer scheme,

then, in determining the person's final salary for any purpose of the transfer scheme—

(i) the deemed transfer scheme service is to be regarded as having ended when the new scheme service ended, and
(ii) such earnings as scheme regulations for the new scheme may specify, being earnings derived by the person from the new scheme service, are to be regarded as derived from the deemed transfer scheme service (subject to sub-paragraph (3)).

(3) The amount of the earnings that are to be regarded as derived from the deemed transfer scheme service must not be materially less than the amount of the earnings that would have been the person's pensionable earnings derived from that service had the new scheme service been deemed transfer scheme service.

(4) In sub-paragraph (1)(c), the reference to a transfer of rights to benefit includes the making of a transfer payment in respect of such rights.

Continuity of employment

3 (1) For the purposes of paragraphs 1(2)(a) and 2(2)(a), there are to be disregarded—
(a) any gap in service where the person was in pensionable public service;
(b) a single gap of service where the person was not in pensionable public service, if that gap does not exceed five years;
(c) two or more gaps in service where the person was not in pensionable public service, if none of the gaps exceeds five years.

(2) In this paragraph, "pensionable public service" means service which is pensionable service in relation to—
(a) a scheme under section 1, or
(b) a new public body pension scheme.

Movement between new schemes

4 Where the condition in sub-paragraph (1)(b) of paragraph 1 or 2 applies by virtue of periods of pensionable service for two or more different schemes—
(a) identify the last period of pensionable service by virtue of which that paragraph applies and the scheme to which that service relates, and
(b) disregard, for the purposes of that sub-paragraph, periods of pensionable service relating to other schemes.

Final salary link not to apply again to a pension in payment

5 (1) Scheme regulations may provide that where a pension in payment under a scheme to which section 18(1) or 31(2) applies has been calculated by reference to this Schedule, the pension cannot be recalculated by reference to this Schedule where there is a subsequent period of pensionable public service (within the meaning of paragraph 3).

(2) Provision made under sub-paragraph (1) may in particular be made by amending the scheme under which the pension is in payment.

NOTES

Regulations: the Teachers' Pension Scheme Regulations 2014, SI 2014/512; the Public Service (Civil Servants and Others) Pensions Regulations 2014, SI 2014/1964; the Armed Forces Pension Regulations 2014, SI 2014/2336; the Teachers' Pension Scheme (Amendment) Regulations 2014, SI 2014/2652; the Judicial Pensions Regulations 2015, SI 2015/182; the Police Pensions Regulations 2015, SI 2015/445; the Firefighters' Pension Scheme (England) (Transitional and Consequential Provisions) Regulations 2015, SI 2015/589; the Firefighters' Pension Scheme (Wales) (Transitional and Consequential Provisions) Regulations 2015, SI 2015/1016; the Civil Service (Other Crown Servants) Pension Scheme Regulations 2016, SI 2016/326.

SCHEDULES 8, 9

(Sch 8 contains consequential and minor amendments which, in so far as relevant to this work, have been incorporated at the appropriate place; Sch 9 amends the Superannuation Act 1972, s 1 at **[1.6]** *and inserts s 1A thereof at* **[1.7]**.)

SCHEDULE 10
PUBLIC BODIES WHOSE PENSION SCHEMES MUST BE RESTRICTED

Section 31(1)

[1.1878]

1 Arts and Humanities Research Council.

2 Biotechnology and Biological Sciences Research Council.

3 Civil Nuclear Police Authority.

4 Commissioners of Irish Lights.

5 Economic and Social Research Council.

6 Engineering and Physical Sciences Research Council.

7 Natural Environment Research Council.

8 Commissioners of Northern Lighthouses.

9 Science and Technology Facilities Council.

10 Secret Intelligence Service.

11 Security Service.

12 Technology Strategy Board.

13 Trinity House Lighthouse Service.

14 United Kingdom Atomic Energy Authority.

[15 United Kingdom Research and Innovation.]

NOTES

Commencement: 1 April 2015.

Para 15: added by the Higher Education and Research Act 2017, s 122, Sch 12, para 28, as from 1 April 2018.

SCHEDULE 11

(*Sch 11 amends legislation outside the scope of this work.*)

GROWTH AND INFRASTRUCTURE ACT 2013

(2013 c 27)

An Act to make provision in connection with facilitating or controlling the following, namely, the provision or use of infrastructure, the carrying-out of development, and the compulsory acquisition of land; to make provision about when rating lists are to be compiled; to make provision about the rights of employees of companies who agree to be employee shareholders; and for connected purposes.

[25 April 2013]

NOTES

Most of this Act covers matters outside the scope of this work and the subject matter of provisions not printed is not annotated. The Act comes into force in accordance with s 35 *post* and Orders made thereunder.

Economic measures

31 (*Inserts the Employment Rights Act 1996, ss 47G, 104G, 205A at* **[1.893]**, **[1.1022]**, **[1.1119]** *and amends ss 48, 108, 236 thereof at* **[1.894]**, **[1.1026]**, **[1.1151]**.)

General provisions

[1.1879]

32 Orders

(1) Any power of the Secretary of State to make an order under this Act—

(a) is exercisable by statutory instrument, and

(b) includes—

(i) power to make different provision for different purposes, and

(ii) power to make incidental, supplementary, consequential, transitional or transitory provision or savings.

(2) The Secretary of State may not make an order to which subsection (3) applies unless a draft of the statutory instrument containing the order (whether alone or with other provisions) has been laid before, and approved by a resolution of, each House of Parliament.

(3) This subsection applies to—

(a) an order under section 7(5);

(b) an order under section 33 which amends or repeals any provision of an Act of Parliament, an Act of the Scottish Parliament or an Act or Measure of the National Assembly for Wales.

(4) A statutory instrument that—

(a) contains an order made by the Secretary of State under this Act, and

(b) is not subject to any requirement that a draft of the instrument be laid before, and approved by a resolution of, each House of Parliament,

is subject to annulment in pursuance of a resolution of either House of Parliament.

(5) Subsection (4) does not apply to an order under section 7(6).

(6) Subsections (1)(b) and (4) do not apply to an order under section 35.

[1.1880]

33 Consequential amendments

(1) The Secretary of State may by order make such provision as the Secretary of State considers appropriate in consequence of this Act.

(2) The power to make an order under this section may, in particular, be exercised by amending, repealing, revoking or otherwise modifying any provision made by or under an enactment.

(3) In this section "enactment" means an enactment whenever passed or made, and includes an Act of the Scottish Parliament or an Act or Measure of the National Assembly for Wales.

NOTES

Orders: as of 15 May 2019, the Orders made under this section are all outside the scope of this work.

[1.1881]
34 Financial provisions
There is to be paid out of money provided by Parliament any increase attributable to this Act in the sums payable under any other Act out of money so provided.

NOTES

Commencement: to be appointed; the omission of any reference to this section in s 35(2) below appears to be a drafting error.

[1.1882]
35 Commencement
(1) Subject as follows, this Act comes into force on such day as the Secretary of State may by order appoint; and different days may be appointed for different purposes.
(2) Section 1(1) so far as it inserts the new section 62B, sections 4, 7, 9, 16, 19, 26, 32 and 33, this section and section 36, and Schedules 2 and 4, come into force on the day on which this Act is passed.
(3), (4) *(Outside the scope of this work.)*
(5) The Scottish Ministers may by order make such transitional, transitory or saving provision as the Scottish Ministers consider appropriate in connection with the coming into force of section 21(4) to (6).
(6) The Secretary of State may by order make such transitional, transitory or saving provision as the Secretary of State considers appropriate in connection with the coming into force of any other provision of this Act.
(7) Power to make an order under subsection (5) or (6) includes power to make different provision for different purposes.

NOTES

Orders: various commencement orders have been made under this section; the only one relevant to the provisions reproduced here is the Growth and Infrastructure Act 2013 (Commencement No 3 and Savings) Order 2013, SI 2013/1766.

[1.1883]
36 Short title and extent
(1) This Act may be cited as the Growth and Infrastructure Act 2013.
(2) Subject as follows, this Act extends to England and Wales only.
(3) Sections 9(4) and 32 to 35, and this section, extend also to Scotland and Northern Ireland.
(4) Any amendment or repeal made by this Act has the same extent as the provision to which it relates, subject to subsection (5).
(5), (6) *(Outside the scope of this work.)*

TRANSPARENCY OF LOBBYING, NON-PARTY CAMPAIGNING AND TRADE UNION ADMINISTRATION ACT 2014 (NOTE)

(2014 c 4)

[1.1884]

NOTES

Only Part 3 (ss 40–43) of this Act (Trade Unions' Registers of Members) and certain provisions in Part 4 (Supplementary) are relevant to employment law.

Section 40 (Duty to provide membership audit certificate) inserts the Trade Union and Labour Relations (Consolidation) Act 1992, s 24ZA at **[1.292]**, and makes consequential amendments to s 44 at **[1.334]** and s 118 at **[1.424]**.

Section 41 (Duty to appoint an assurer etc) inserts ss 24ZB–24ZG of the 1992 Act at **[1.293]** et seq, and amends s 24A at **[1.303]**, s 44 at **[1.334]**, and s 299 at **[1.633]**.

Section 42 (Investigatory powers) inserts ss 24ZH–24ZK of the 1992 Act at **[1.299]** et seq, and amends s 24 at **[1.291]**.

Section 43 (Enforcement) inserts ss 24B, 24C of the 1992 Act at **[1.304]** et seq, and amends ss 24–26 at **[1.291]** et seq, and ss 45D and 256 at **[1.339]** and **[1.591]**.

Section 44 (Financial provision) provides that there is to be paid out of money provided by Parliament (a) any expenditure incurred by a Minister of the Crown under or by virtue of this Act, and (b) any increase attributable to this Act in the sums payable under any other Act out of money so provided.

Section 45 (Commencement) provides: (i) s 41 of this Act comes into force on 30 January 2014 (only for the purposes of the exercise of the power to make subordinate legislation conferred by s 24ZB(3) of the 1992 Act (which is inserted by that section)); (ii) Part 4 (ss 44–49) of this Act also comes into force on 30 January 2014; and (iii) the other provisions of Part 3 come into force on such day as the Minister may appoint by order made by statutory instrument. The Transparency of Lobbying, Non-Party Campaigning and Trade Union Administration Act 2014 (Commencement No 2 and Transitional Provision) Order 2015, SI 2015/717 (made under s 45(1)(c), (2)) provides for the following commencement dates for the provisions of Part 3:

— section 40: 6 April 2015;
— section 41: 6 April 2015 (in so far as not already in force);
— sections 42, 43: 1 June 2016;

Section 48 (Extent) provides, inter alia, that any amendment or repeal made by Part 3 of this Act has the same extent as the enactment amended or repealed.

CHILDREN AND FAMILIES ACT 2014

(2014 c 6)

ARRANGEMENT OF SECTIONS

PART 7
STATUTORY RIGHTS TO LEAVE AND PAY

Shared parental leave

An Act to make provision about children, families, and people with special educational needs or disabilities; to make provision about the right to request flexible working; and for connected purposes

13 March 2014

NOTES

Most of this Act covers matters outside the scope of this work, and only Parts 7–9 are directly relevant to employment law. For reasons of space, the subject matter of sections not printed is not annotated.

PART 7
STATUTORY RIGHTS TO LEAVE AND PAY

Shared parental leave

[1.1885]

117 Shared parental leave

(*This section inserts ss 75E–75K of the Employment Rights Act 1996, at* **[1.967]** *et seq, and amends s 236 of that Act, at* **[1.1151]**.)

NOTES

Commencement: 30 June 2014.

[1.1886]

118 Exclusion or curtailment of other statutory rights to leave

(*This section amends the Employment Rights Act 1996, ss 71, 73, 75A, 75B, 80A, 80B (see* **[1.958]** *et seq).*)

NOTES

Commencement: 30 June 2014.

Statutory shared parental pay

[1.1887]

119 Statutory shared parental pay

(*This section inserts the Social Security Contributions and Benefits Act 1992, ss 171ZU–171ZZ5 (Part 12ZC Statutory Shared Parental Pay), (see* **[1.240]** *et seq), and amends s 176.*)

NOTES

Commencement: 30 June 2014.

[1.1888]

120 Exclusion or curtailment of other statutory rights to pay

(*This section amends the Social Security Contributions and Benefits Act 1992, ss 35, 165, 171ZE, 171ZN at* **[1.213]**, **[1.224]**, **[1.233]**.)

NOTES

Commencement: 30 June 2014.

Other statutory rights

[1.1889]

121 Statutory rights to leave and pay of prospective adopters with whom looked after children are placed

(*This section amends the Employment Rights Act 1996, ss 75A, 80B at* **[1.963]**, **[1.980]**, *and the Social Security Contributions and Benefits Act 1992, ss 171ZB, 171ZE, 171ZJ, 171ZL, 171ZN (see* **[1.221]** *et seq).*)

NOTES

Commencement: 30 June 2014.

[1.1890]

122 Statutory rights to leave and pay of applicants for parental orders

(*This section amends the Employment Rights Act 1996, ss 75A, 75B, 75D, 80B (see* **[1.963]** *et seq), and the Social Security Contributions and Benefits Act 1992, ss 171ZK, 171ZT at* **[1.230]**, **[1.239]**.)

NOTES

Commencement: 30 June 2014.

[1.1891]

123 Statutory paternity pay: notice requirement and period of payment

(*This section amends the Social Security Contributions and Benefits Act 1992, ss 171ZC, 171ZE at* **[1.222]**, **[1.224]**, *and s 176.*)

NOTES

Commencement: 30 June 2014 (in so far as relating to the amendments to s 171ZC); to be appointed (otherwise).

Transitional provisions: the Children and Families Act 2014 (Commencement No 3, Transitional Provisions and Savings) Order 2014, SI 2014/1640, art 9 provides that the amendment to s 171ZC does not have effect in relation to (a) children whose expected week of birth ends on or before 4 April 2015; (b) children placed for adoption on or before that date.

[1.1892]

124 Rate of statutory adoption pay

(*This section amends the Social Security Contributions and Benefits Act 1992, s 171ZN at* **[1.233]**, *and s 176.*)

NOTES

Commencement: 5 April 2015.

Transitional provisions: the Children and Families Act 2014 (Commencement No 3, Transitional Provisions and Savings) Order 2014, SI 2014/1640, art 13 provides that the amendments to s 171ZN have effect only in relation to any adoption pay period which begins on or after 5 April 2015 (and for this purpose, "adoption pay period" has the meaning given in s 171ZN(2) of the 1992 Act).

[1.1893]
125 Abolition of additional paternity leave and additional statutory paternity pay
(1) In Part 8 of the Employment Rights Act 1996, sections 80AA and 80BB (entitlement to additional paternity leave: birth and adoption) are repealed.
(2) In Part 12ZA of the Social Security Contributions and Benefits Act 1992, sections 171ZEA to 171ZEE (additional statutory paternity pay: birth and adoption) are repealed.

NOTES
Commencement: 5 April 2015.
Transitional provisions: the Children and Families Act 2014 (Commencement No 3, Transitional Provisions and Savings) Order 2014, SI 2014/1640, art 14 provides that the repeals made by this section do not have effect in relation to (a) children whose expected week of birth ends on or before 4 April 2015; (b) children placed for adoption on or before that date.

Further amendments

[1.1894]
126 Further amendments
(1) Schedule 7 (which contains further amendments relating to statutory rights to leave and pay) has effect.
(2) A reference to ordinary statutory paternity pay in an instrument or document made before the commencement of paragraphs 12 and 13 of Schedule 7 is to be read, in relation to any time after that commencement, as a reference to statutory paternity pay.
(3) A reference to statutory paternity pay in an enactment (including an enactment amended by this Act) or in an instrument or document is to be read, in relation to any time that falls—
(a) after the commencement of paragraphs 12 and 13 of Schedule 1 to the Work and Families Act 2006, and
(b) before the commencement of paragraphs 12 and 13 of Schedule 7,
as a reference to ordinary statutory paternity pay.
(4) Subsection (3) does not apply to the extent that a reference to statutory paternity pay is a reference to additional statutory paternity pay.

NOTES
Commencement: sub-s (1) (which introduces the amendments made by Sch 7) came into force on various dates between 30 June 2014 and 5 April 2015 and is not yet in force for certain (minor) purposes. Sub-ss (2)–(4) came into force on 5 April 2015.
Transitional provisions: the Children and Families Act 2014 (Commencement No 3, Transitional Provisions and Savings) Order 2014, SI 2014/1640, art 15 provides that sub-ss (2)–(4) do not have effect in relation to (a) children whose expected week of birth ends on or before 4 April 2015; (b) children placed for adoption on or before that date.

PART 8
TIME OFF WORK: ANTE-NATAL CARE ETC

[1.1895]
127 Time off work to accompany to ante-natal appointments
(*This section inserts the Employment Rights Act 1996, ss 57ZE–57ZI (see* **[1.911]** *et seq), and amends ss 47C, 99, 225 of that Act at* **[1.889]**, **[1.997]**, **[1.1140]**.)

NOTES
Commencement: 30 June 2014 (in so far as amending ss 47C, 99 of the 1996 Act); 1 October 2014 (otherwise).

[1.1896]
128 Time off work to attend adoption appointments
(*This section inserts the Employment Rights Act 1996, ss 57ZJ–57ZS (see* **[1.916]** *et seq), and amends ss 47C, 80B, 99, 225, 235 at* **[1.889]**, **[1.980]**, **[1.997]**, **[1.1140]**.)

NOTES
Commencement: 30 June 2014 (in so far as amending ss 47C, 80B, 99 of the 1996 Act); 5 April 2015 (otherwise).

[1.1897]
129 Right not to be subjected to detriment: agency workers
(*This section amends the Employment Rights Act 1996, ss 47C, 48, 49 at* **[1.889]**, **[1.894]**, **[1.895]**.)

NOTES
Commencement: 1 October 2014 (in so far as inserting s 47C(5)(a), (b), (6) and (7) of the 1996 Act, and in so far as amending ss 48, 49 of that Act); 5 April 2015 (otherwise).

[1.1898]
130 Time off work for ante-natal care: increased amount of award
(*This section amends the Employment Rights Act 1996, ss 57, 57ZC at* **[1.906]**, **[1.909]**.)

NOTES
Commencement: 1 October 2014.

Transitional provisions: the Children and Families Act 2014 (Commencement No 3, Transitional Provisions and Savings) Order 2014, SI 2014/1640, art 11 provides that the amendments made by this section have effect only in relation to any refusal to permit time off which is made on or after 1 October 2014.

PART 9
RIGHT TO REQUEST FLEXIBLE WORKING

[1.1899]
131 Removal of requirement to be a carer
(*This section amends the Employment Rights Act 1996, s 80F at* **[1.989]**.)

NOTES
Commencement: 30 June 2014.
Transitional provisions: the Children and Families Act 2014 (Commencement No 3, Transitional Provisions and Savings) Order 2014, SI 2014/1640, art 10 provides that the amendments made by this section do not have effect in relation to any application for a change in terms and conditions which is made on or before 29 June 2014.

[1.1900]
132 Dealing with applications
(*This section amends the Employment Rights Act 1996, ss 80G, 80I at* **[1.990]**, **[1.992]** *and repeals ss 47E(1)(b), 80H(4), 104C(1)(b) at* **[1.891]**, **[1.991]**, **[1.1018]**.)

NOTES
Commencement: 30 June 2014.
Transitional provisions: the Children and Families Act 2014 (Commencement No 3, Transitional Provisions and Savings) Order 2014, SI 2014/1640, art 10 provides that the amendments made by this section do not have effect in relation to any application for a change in terms and conditions which is made on or before 29 June 2014.

[1.1901]
133 Complaints to employment tribunals
(*This section amends the Employment Rights Act 1996, s 80H at* **[1.991]**.)

NOTES
Commencement: 30 June 2014.
Transitional provisions: the Children and Families Act 2014 (Commencement No 3, Transitional Provisions and Savings) Order 2014, SI 2014/1640, art 10 provides that the amendments made by this section do not have effect in relation to any application for a change in terms and conditions which is made on or before 29 June 2014.

[1.1902]
134 Review of sections 131 to 133
(1) The Secretary of State must from time to time—
(a) carry out a review of sections 131 to 133,
(b) set out the conclusions of the review in a report, and
(c) publish the report.
(2) The report must in particular—
(a) set out the objectives intended to be achieved by the amendments of the Employment Rights Act 1996 made by sections 131 to 133,
(b) assess the extent to which those objectives are achieved, and
(c) assess whether those objectives remain appropriate and, if so, the extent to which they could be achieved in a way that imposes less regulation.
(3) The first report to be published under this section must be published before the end of the period of seven years beginning with the day on which sections 131 to 133 come into force.
(4) Reports under this section are afterwards to be published at intervals not exceeding seven years.

NOTES
Commencement: 30 June 2014.

PART 10
GENERAL PROVISIONS

[1.1903]
135 Orders and regulations
(1) A power to make an order or regulations under this Act is exercisable by statutory instrument.
(2) A power to make an order or regulations under this Act includes power—
(a) to make different provision for different purposes (including different areas);
(b) to make provision generally or in relation to specific cases.
(3) A power to make an order or regulations under this Act (except a power conferred by section 78(6), 137 or 139) includes power to make incidental, supplementary, consequential, transitional or transitory provision or savings.
(4) Subject to subsection (5), a statutory instrument that contains an order or regulations made under this Act by the Secretary of State or the Lord Chancellor is subject to annulment in pursuance of a resolution of either House of Parliament.
(5) Subsection (4) does not apply to—

(a) a statutory instrument containing an order under section 78(6), 137 or 139, or
(b) a statutory instrument to which subsection (6) applies.

(6) A statutory instrument containing (whether alone or with other provision)—
(a) the first regulations to be made under section 49,
(b) an order under section 58(1) or 59(1),
(c) regulations under section 70(3),
(d) regulations under section 92 or 93,
(e) regulations under subsection (6), (8), (9) or (10) of section 94,
(f) regulations under subsection (11) of that section which amend, repeal or revoke any provision of an enactment within the meaning of that section, or
(g) an order under section 136 which amends or repeals any provision of primary legislation,

is not to be made unless a draft of the instrument has been laid before, and approved by a resolution of, each House of Parliament.

(7) "Primary legislation" means—
(a) an Act of Parliament;
(b) a Measure or Act of the National Assembly for Wales.

[1.1904]
136 Consequential amendments, repeals and revocations

(1) The Secretary of State or the Lord Chancellor may by order make provision in consequence of any provision of this Act.

(2) The power conferred by subsection (1) includes power to amend, repeal, revoke or otherwise modify any provision made by or under an enactment (including any enactment passed or made in the same Session as this Act).

(3) "Enactment" includes a Measure or Act of the National Assembly for Wales.

NOTES

Orders: the Child Arrangements Order (Consequential Amendments to Subordinate Legislation) Order 2014, SI 2014/852; the Special Educational Needs (Consequential Amendments to Subordinate Legislation) Order 2014, SI 2014/2103; the Shared Parental Leave and Statutory Shared Parental Pay (Consequential Amendments to Subordinate Legislation) Order 2014, SI 2014/3255; the Care Act 2014 and Children and Families Act 2014 (Consequential Amendments) Order 2015, SI 2015/914.

[1.1905]
137 Transitional, transitory or saving provision

(1) The Secretary of State or the Lord Chancellor may by order make transitional, transitory or saving provision in connection with the coming into force of any provision of this Act.

(2)–(5) (*Outside the scope of this work.*)

NOTES

Orders: the Children and Families Act 2014 (Transitional Provisions) Order 2014, SI 2014/1042; the Children and Families Act 2014 (Commencement No 3, Transitional Provisions and Savings) Order 2014, SI 2014 1640; the Children and Families Act 2014 (Transitional and Saving Provisions) (No 2) Order 2014, SI 2014/2270; the Children and Families Act 2014 (Commencement No 5 and Transitional Provision) Order 2014, SI 2014/2749; the Children and Families Act 2014 (Transitional and Saving Provisions) (Amendment) Order 2015, SI 2015/505; the Children and Families Act 2014 (Transitional and Saving Provisions) (Amendment) (No 2) Order 2015, SI 2015/1619.

[1.1906]
138 Financial provision

(1) There is to be paid out of money provided by Parliament—
(a) any expenses incurred by a Minister of the Crown or a government department under this Act, and
(b) any increase attributable to this Act in the sums payable under any other Act out of money so provided.

(2) There is to be paid into the Consolidated Fund any increase attributable to this Act in the sums payable into that Fund under any other Act.

[1.1907]
139 Commencement

(1) This Part comes into force on the day on which this Act is passed.

(2)–(5) (*Outside the scope of this work.*)

(6) The remaining provisions of this Act come into force on such day as the Secretary of State appoints by order.

(7) An order under subsection (2), (3) or (6) may appoint different days for different purposes.

NOTES

Orders: the Children and Families Act 2014 (Commencement No 1) Order 2014, SI 2014/793; the Children and Families Act 2014 (Commencement No 2) Order 2014, SI 2014/889; the Children and Families Act 2014 (Commencement No 2) (Amendment) Order 2014, SI 2014/1134; the Children and Families Act 2014 (Commencement No 3, Transitional Provisions and Savings) Order 2014, SI 2014 1640; the Children and Families Act 2014 (Commencement No 4) Order 2014, SI 2014/2609; the Children and Families Act 2014 (Commencement No 5 and Transitional Provision) Order 2014, SI 2014/2749; the Children and Families Act 2014 (Commencement No 6) Order 2015, SI 2015/375; the Children and Families Act 2014 (Commencement) (Wales) Order 2015, SI 2015/1808.

[1.1908]

140 Short title and extent

(1) This Act may be cited as the Children and Families Act 2014.

(2) (*Outside the scope of this work.*)

(3) This Act extends to England and Wales only, subject to the following subsections.

(4) (*Outside the scope of this work.*)

(5) Sections 126(2) to (4) and 134 extend to England and Wales and Scotland.

(6) Section 126(3) and (4), so far as relating to paragraphs 5, 56 to 62 and 64 of Schedule 7, extends to Northern Ireland.

(7) This Part extends to the whole of the United Kingdom.

(8) An amendment or repeal made by this Act has the same extent as the provision to which it relates (ignoring extent by virtue of an Order in Council), subject to subsection (9).

(9) (*Outside the scope of this work.*)

SCHEDULE 7

(Sch 7 (Statutory Rights to Leave and pay: Further Amendments) makes amendments consequential on Part 7 of this Act. It amends, inter alia, the Social Security Act 1989, the Social Security Contributions and Benefits Act 1992, the Employment Rights Act 1996, and the Employment Act 2002. All amendments have been incorporated at the appropriate place ante.)

AGRICULTURAL SECTOR (WALES) ACT 2014

(2014 anaw 6)

ARRANGEMENT OF SECTIONS

An Act of the National Assembly for Wales to make provision in relation to the agricultural sector in Wales; and for connected purposes.

30 July 2014

Introduction

[1.1909]

1 Overview

This Act makes provision for—

(a) the establishment of the Agricultural Advisory Panel for Wales,

(b) the making of orders which set the terms and conditions for persons employed in agriculture in Wales ("agricultural workers"), and

(c) the enforcement of such terms and conditions.

NOTES

Commencement: 30 July 2014.

Agricultural Advisory Panel for Wales

2 (*S 2 (Agricultural Advisory Panel for Wales) outside the scope of this work.*)

Agricultural Wages Orders

[1.1910]

3 Agricultural wages orders

(1) An agricultural wages order is an order making provision about the minimum rates of remuneration and other terms and conditions of employment for agricultural workers.

(2) An agricultural wages order may, in particular, include provision—

(a) specifying the minimum rates of remuneration to be paid to agricultural workers (including rates for periods when such workers are absent in consequence of sickness or injury);

(b) about any benefits or advantages which, for the purposes of a minimum rate of remuneration, may be reckoned as remuneration in lieu of payment in cash;

(c) requiring employers of agricultural workers to allow such workers to take such holidays and other leave as may be specified in the order.

(3) An agricultural wages order may specify different rates and make different provision for different descriptions of agricultural workers.

(4) An agricultural wages order may not include any provision about the pensions of agricultural workers.

(5) No minimum rate of remuneration may be specified in an order under this section which is less than the national minimum wage.

NOTES

Commencement: 30 July 2014.

Orders: the Agricultural Wages (Wales) Order 2019, SI 2019/511 at **[2.2142]** (revoking and replacing the Agricultural Wages (Wales) Order 2018, SI 2018/433, also made under this section).

4 (*S 4 (Agricultural wages orders: powers of the Welsh Ministers) outside the scope of this work.*)

Enforcement

[1.1911]

5 Enforcement of minimum rates

(1) The enforcement provisions of the 1998 Act listed in subsection (2) are to have effect for the purposes of this Act as they have effect for the purposes of that Act (except so far as they relate to Northern Ireland or Scotland), but with the modifications specified in subsections (3) to (7) of this section.

(2) The enforcement provisions are—

(a) sections 10 and 11 (records);

(b) section 14 (powers of officers);

(c) section 17 (entitlement of worker to additional remuneration), except for subsection (3);

(d) section 19 (notices of underpayment: arrears);

(e) section 19C (notices of underpayment: appeals), except for subsections (1)(c) and (6) and, so far as relating to appeals under subsection (1)(c), subsection (8);

(f) section 19D (non-compliance with notice of underpayment: recovery of arrears);

(g) section 19F (withdrawal of notice of underpayment), except for subsections (2)(a) and (4);

(h) section 19G (replacement notice of underpayment);

(i) section 19H (effect of replacement notice of underpayment), except for subsections (4) and (5);

(j) sections 23 and 24 (right not to suffer detriment);

(k) section 28 (evidence: reversal of burden of proof in civil proceedings);

(l) sections 31 and 33 (offences);

(m) section 48 (superior employers);

(n) section 49 (restriction on contracting out).

(3) In the application of any of those enforcement provisions—

(a) any reference to the 1998 Act, other than a reference to a specific provision of it, includes a reference to this Act;

(b) any reference to a worker (within the meaning of the 1998 Act) is to be construed as a reference to an agricultural worker (within the meaning of this Act);

(c) any reference to a person (however described) who qualifies for the national minimum wage is to be construed as a reference to an agricultural worker;

(d) any reference to a record includes a reference to any record which the employer of an agricultural worker is required to keep and preserve in accordance with regulations made under section 7 of this Act;

(e) any reference to an officer acting for the purposes of the 1998 Act is to be construed as a reference to an officer acting for the purposes of this Act;

(f) subject to paragraph (c), any reference to the national minimum wage, other than a reference to the hourly amount of the national minimum wage, is to be construed as a reference to the minimum rate applicable by virtue of this Act;

(g) subject to paragraph (c), any reference to qualifying for the national minimum wage is to be construed as being entitled to the minimum rate applicable by virtue of this Act.

(4) In the application of sections 10(10), 14(1)(a) and 31 of the 1998 Act, the references to a record required to be kept in accordance with regulations made under section 9 of the 1998 Act includes references to a record required to be kept in accordance with regulations made under section 7 of this Act.

(5) In the application of section 14 of the 1998 Act, after subsection (2) insert—

"(2A) Where an officer wishes to exercise the power under paragraph (d) of subsection (1) in relation to a dwelling house, the officer must first give reasonable notice."

(6) In the application of section 17 of the 1998 Act—

(a) for subsection (2) substitute—

"(2) The amount referred to in subsection (1)(a) is the difference between—

(a) the remuneration received by the worker as an agricultural worker for the pay reference period from the worker's employer, and

(b) the amount which the worker would have received as an agricultural worker for that period had the worker been remunerated by the employer at the minimum rate applicable by virtue of the Agricultural Sector (Wales) Act 2014;",

(b) for subsection (4) substitute—

"(4) the amount referred to in subsection (1)(b) is the amount determined by the formula—

(A / R1) x R2

where—

A is the amount described in subsection (2),

R1 is the minimum rate applicable by virtue of the Agricultural Sector (Wales) Act 2014 in respect of the worker during the pay reference period, and

R2 is the minimum rate which would have been applicable by virtue of that Act in respect of the worker during the pay reference period had the minimum rate applicable by virtue of that Act in respect of the worker during that period been determined by reference to any order under section 3 of that Act in force at the time of determination."

(7) In the application of section 33(1A) of the 1998 Act (authorisation for conducting proceedings) for "Secretary of State" substitute "Welsh Ministers".

(8) In section 104A of the Employment Rights Act 1996 (unfair dismissal: national minimum wage), in subsection (1)(c)—

(a) any reference to a person qualifying for the national minimum wage includes a reference to a person being or becoming entitled to a minimum rate applicable by virtue of this Act, and

(b) any reference to a person qualifying for a particular rate of national minimum wage includes a reference to a person being or becoming entitled to a particular minimum rate applicable by virtue of this Act.

NOTES

Commencement: 30 July 2014.

[1.1912]

6 Enforcement of holiday entitlement

(1) It is an offence for an employer of an agricultural worker to fail to allow the worker to take the holidays specified in an agricultural wages order.

(2) A person guilty of an offence under this section is liable on summary conviction to a fine not exceeding level 3 on the standard scale.

(3) In any proceedings against a person under this section it is for the person to prove that the agricultural worker was allowed to take the holidays to which the worker was entitled.

NOTES

Commencement: 30 July 2014.

Records

[1.1913]

7 Duty of employers to keep records

(1) For the purposes of this Act, the Welsh Ministers may, by regulations, make provision requiring employers of agricultural workers—

(a) to keep, in such form and manner as may be specified, such records as may be specified, and

(b) to preserve those records for such period as may be specified.

(2) In this section, "specified" means specified in the regulations made under subsection (1).

NOTES

Commencement: 30 July 2014.

Agricultural Enforcement Officers

8, 9 (*Ss 8 and 9 concern Agricultural Enforcement Officers and are outside the scope of this work.*)

Miscellaneous

[1.1914]

10 Meaning of "the national minimum wage"

(1) Subject to subsections (2) to (5), "the national minimum wage" means the single hourly rate for the time being in force by virtue of regulations under section 1(3) of the 1998 Act.

(2) Subsection (3) applies if, in the case of persons of any description, regulations under section 3(2) of the 1998 Act prevent them from being persons who (within the meaning of that Act) qualify for the national minimum wage.

(3) This Act is to have effect in relation to persons of that description as if the national minimum wage were nil.

(4) Subsection (5) applies if, in the case of persons of any description, regulations under section 3(2) of the 1998 Act prescribe a rate ("the reduced rate") for the national minimum wage other than the single hourly rate for the time being prescribed under section 1(3) of that Act.

(5) This Act is to have effect in relation to persons of that description as if the national minimum wage were the reduced rate.

NOTES

Commencement: 30 July 2014.

11–13 (*S 11 amends the Working Time Regulations 1998,SI 1998/1833 at* **[2.274]** *et seq. S 12 contains transitional provisions in relation to the Agricultural Wages (England and Wales) Order 2012. S 13 provides for the review of this Act by the Welsh Ministers.*)

[1.1915]

14 Duration of this Act

(1) This Act (other than subsection (3) and, for the purposes of that subsection, sections 17(1), 17(2) and 18) ceases to have effect at the end of the expiration period, unless an order is made under subsection (2).

(2) The Welsh Ministers may, by order, after the end of the review period but before the end of the expiration period, provide that this Act is to continue in effect despite subsection (1).

(3) The Welsh Ministers may, by order, make such provision (including provision modifying any enactment) as may be necessary or expedient in consequence of this Act ceasing to have effect.

(4) In this section—

"the expiration period" ("*y cyfnod dod i ben*") means the period of 4 years beginning with the day on which this Act comes into force;

"the review period" ("*y cyfnod adolygu*") has the same meaning as in section 13.

NOTES

Commencement: 30 July 2014.

Orders: the Agricultural Sector (Wales) Act 2014 (Continuation of Effect) Order 2018, SI 2018/515, which provides that this Act continues to have effect despite sub-s (1) above.

General

[1.1916]

15 Offences by bodies corporate

(1) This section applies where an offence under this Act is committed by a body corporate.

(2) If the offence is proved to have been committed with the consent or connivance of, or to be attributable to any neglect on the part of—

(a) any director, manager or secretary of the body corporate, or

(b) any person who was purporting to act in any such capacity,

that director, manager, secretary or person purporting to act as such (as well as the body corporate) is guilty of the offence and liable to be proceeded against and punished accordingly.

(3) The reference to the director, manager or secretary of the body corporate includes a reference—

(a) to any similar officer of the body;

(b) where the body is a body corporate whose affairs are managed by its members, to any officer or member of the body.

NOTES

Commencement: 30 July 2014.

[1.1917]

16 Ancillary provision

(1) The Welsh Ministers may, by order, make such incidental, consequential, supplemental, transitional, transitory or saving provision as they consider appropriate for the purposes of, or in connection with, giving full effect to any provision made by or under this Act.

(2) An order under this section may modify this or any other enactment.

NOTES

Commencement: 30 July 2014.

Orders: the Agricultural Sector (Wales) Act 2014 (Consequential Modification) Order 2015, SI 2015/2001; the Agricultural Advisory Panel for Wales (Establishment) Order 2016, SI 2016/255.

[1.1918]

17 Orders and regulations

(1) Any power of the Welsh Ministers to make an order or regulations under this Act is exercisable by statutory instrument and includes power to—

(a) make such incidental, consequential, supplemental, transitional, transitory or saving provision as the Welsh Ministers consider necessary or expedient for the purposes of, or in connection with, this Act, and

(b) make different provision for different purposes.

(2) A statutory instrument which contains (whether alone or with other provisions)—

(a) an order under section 2,

(b) regulations under section 7,

(c) an order under section 14, or

(d) an order under section 16 which includes provision which adds to, amends or omits the text of an Act of Parliament or a Measure or Act of the National Assembly for Wales,

is not to be made until a draft of the instrument has been laid before, and approved by resolution of, the National Assembly for Wales.

(3) Any other statutory instrument containing an order or regulations under this Act is to be subject to annulment in pursuance of a resolution of the National Assembly for Wales.

NOTES

Commencement: 30 July 2014.

[1.1919]
18 Interpretation

In this Act, unless the context requires otherwise—

"1998 Act" ("*Deddf 1998*") means the National Minimum Wage Act 1998 (c 39);

"agricultural wages order" ("*gorchymyn cyflogau amaethyddol*") is to be construed in accordance with section 3 (but see also section 12(3));

"agricultural worker" ("*gweithiwr amaethyddol*") means a person employed in agriculture in Wales, whether or not the whole of the work undertaken by virtue of that employment is undertaken in Wales;

"agriculture" ("*amaethyddiaeth*") includes—

(a) dairy farming;

(b) the production of any consumable produce for the purposes of a trade or business or any other undertaking (whether carried on for profit or not);

(c) the use of land as grazing, meadow or pasture land;

(d) the use of land for orchards, osier land or woodland;

(e) the use of land for market gardens or nursery grounds;

"consumable produce" ("*cynnyrch defnyddiadwy*") means produce grown for consumption or for other use after severance from the land on which it is grown;

"employment" ("*cyflogaeth*") means employed under a contract of service or apprenticeship and "employed" ("*a gyflogir*") and "employer" ("*cyflogwr*") are to be construed accordingly;

"modify" ("*addasu*"), in relation to an enactment, includes amend or repeal;

"the national minimum wage" ("*isafswm cyflog cenedlaethol*") has the meaning given by section 10.

NOTES

Commencement: 30 July 2014.

[1.1920]
19 Commencement

The provisions of this Act come into force on the day on which this Act receives Royal Assent.

NOTES

Commencement: 30 July 2014.

[1.1921]
20 Short title

The short title of this Act is the Agricultural Sector (Wales) Act 2014.

NOTES

Commencement: 30 July 2014.

DEREGULATION ACT 2015 (NOTE)

(2015 c 20)

[1.1922]

NOTES

Only a few provisions of this Act are relevant to Employment law; provisions not reproduced are not annotated.

Section 1 (Health and safety at work: general duty of self-employed persons) amends the Health and Safety at Work etc Act 1974, ss 3, 11, 82 at **[1.32]**, **[1.39]**, **[1.81]**. It further provides that where this section comes into force at a time when there is in force an Order in Council made under the Health and Safety at Work etc Act 1974, s 84(3) that applies ss 3 or 11 of the 1974 Act to matters outside Great Britain, that Order is to be taken as applying that section as amended by this section. Section 115 (Commencement) provides that s 1 comes into force on 26 March 2015 (but only so far as is necessary for enabling the exercise on or after that day of any power to make provision by an order or regulations made by statutory instrument). Section

1 was brought into force for remaining purposes on 1 October 2015 (see the Deregulation Act 2015 (Commencement No 3 and Transitional and Saving Provisions) Order 2015, SI 2015/1732).

Section 2 (Removal of employment tribunals' power to make wider recommendations) amends the Equality Act 2010, s 124 at **[1.1709]** and repeals s 125 of that Act. Section 2 came into force on 1 October 2015 (see the Deregulation Act 2015 (Commencement No 1 and Transitional and Saving Provisions) Order 2015, SI 2015/994). The Schedule to the 2015 Order (Transitional Provisions) provides that the amendments made by s 2 do not affect ss 124 and 125 of the Equality Act 2010 as they apply to proceedings that are commenced before 1 October 2015.

Section 6 (Requirements to wear safety helmets: exemption for Sikhs) amends the Employment Act 1989, ss 11, 12 at **[1.187]**, **[1.188]**. Section 6 came into force on 1 October 2015 (see SI 2015/994). Article 12 of the 2015 Order provides for various transitional provisions and savings in connection with the commencement of this section; these are set out in ss 11 and 12 of the 1989 Act itself at **[1.187]**, **[1.188]**.

Section 92 (Gangmasters (Licensing) Act 2004: enforcement) amends the Gangmasters (Licensing) Act 2004, s 15. As of 15 May 2019, this section had not been brought into force.

Section 114 (Extent) provides that a repeal, revocation or other amendment or modification made by this Act has the same extent as the provision repealed, revoked or otherwise amended or modified.

SMALL BUSINESS, ENTERPRISE AND EMPLOYMENT ACT 2015

(2015 c 26)

ARRANGEMENT OF SECTIONS

PART 7
COMPANIES: TRANSPARENCY

Corporate Directors

Shadow Directors

PART 11
EMPLOYMENT

Equal Pay

Employment Tribunals

National Minimum Wage

Public Sector Exit Payments

PART 12
GENERAL

An Act to make provision about improved access to finance for businesses and individuals; to make provision about regulatory provisions relating to business and certain voluntary and community bodies; to make provision about the exercise of procurement functions by certain public authorities; to make provision for the creation of a Pubs Code and Adjudicator for the regulation of dealings by pub-owning businesses with their tied pub tenants; to make provision about the regulation of the provision of childcare; to make provision about information relating to the evaluation of education; to make provision about the regulation of companies; to make provision about company filing requirements; to make provision about the disqualification from appointments relating to companies; to make provision about insolvency; to make provision about the law relating to employment; and for connected purposes.

[26 March 2015]

NOTES

Most of this Act covers matters outside the scope of this work, and only those provisions relevant to employment law are reproduced. For reasons of space, the subject matter of sections not printed is not annotated.

PART 7
COMPANIES: TRANSPARENCY

Corporate Directors

87 (*Amends the Companies Act 2006, s 156, repeals s 155 at* **[1.1491]**, *and inserts s 156A–156C at* **[1.1492]–[1.1494]**.)

[1.1923]

88 Review of section 87

(1) The Secretary of State must, before the end of each review period—
- (a) carry out a review of section 87, and
- (b) prepare and publish a report setting out the conclusions of the review.

(2) The report must in particular—
- (a) set out the objectives intended to be achieved by the section,
- (b) assess the extent to which those objectives have been achieved, and
- (c) assess whether those objectives remain appropriate and, if so, the extent to which they could be achieved in another way which imposed less regulation.

(3) The Secretary of State must lay the report before Parliament.

(4) Each of the following is a review period for the purposes of this section—
- (a) the period of 5 years beginning with the day on which section 87 comes into force (whether wholly or partly), and
- (b) each successive period of 5 years.

NOTES

Commencement: to be appointed.

Shadow Directors

[1.1924]

89 Application of directors' general duties to shadow directors

(1) (*Amends the Companies Act 2006, s 170 at* **[1.1499]**.)

(2) The Secretary of State may by regulations make provision about the application of the general duties of directors to shadow directors.

(3) The regulations may, in particular, make provision—
- (a) for prescribed general duties of directors to apply to shadow directors with such adaptations as may be prescribed;
- (b) for prescribed general duties of directors not to apply to shadow directors.

(4) In this section—

"director" and "shadow director" have the same meanings as in the Companies Act 2006;
"general duties of directors" means the duties specified in sections 171 to 177 of that Act;
"prescribed" means prescribed in regulations.

(5) Regulations under this section are subject to affirmative resolution procedure.

NOTES

Commencement: 26 May 2015.

PART 11
EMPLOYMENT

Equal Pay

[1.1925]

147 Equal pay: transparency

(1) The Secretary of State must, as soon as possible and no later than 12 months after the passing of this Act, make regulations under section 78 of the Equality Act 2010 (gender pay gap information) for the purpose of requiring the publication of information showing whether there are differences in the pay of males and females.

(2) The Secretary of State must consult such persons as the Secretary of State thinks appropriate on the details of such regulations prior to publication.

NOTES

Commencement: to be appointed.

Whistleblowing

148, 149 *(S 148 inserts the Employment Rights Act 1996, s 43FA at* **[1.872]** *and amends s 236 of that Act at* **[1.1151]**; *s 149 inserts s 49B at* **[1.897]**, *and amends ss 230(6), 236(3) of the 1996 Act at* **[1.1145]**, **[1.1151]**.)

Employment Tribunals

[1.1926]
150 Financial penalty for failure to pay sums ordered by employment tribunal etc
(1)–(7) *(Inserts the Employment Tribunals Act 1996 ss 37A–37Q, (Pt 2A) at* **[1.783]** *et seq, amends ss 12A, 19A, 41, 42(1) of the 1996 Act at* **[1.750]**, **[1.762]**, **[1.806]**, **[1.807]** *and amends the Trade Union and Labour Relations (Consolidation) Act 1992, s 251B at* **[1.586]**.)
(8) The amendments made by this section have effect only in relation to relevant sums where—
(a) in the case of a financial award, the decision of the employment tribunal on the claim to which the financial award relates is made on or after the day on which this section comes into force;
(b) in the case of a settlement sum, the certificate under section 19A(1) of the Employment Tribunals Act 1996 in respect of the settlement under whose terms it is payable is issued on or after that day.

NOTES
Commencement: 6 April 2016.

151 *(Amends the Employment Tribunals Act 1996, ss 7, 13, 13A at* **[1.740]**, **[1.751]**, **[1.752]**.)

National Minimum Wage

[1.1927]
152 Amount of financial penalty for underpayment of national minimum wage
(1)–(5) *(Amends the National Minimum Wage Act 1998, s 19A at* **[1.1188]**.)
(6) The amendments made by this section have effect in relation to notices of underpayment which relate only to pay reference periods commencing on or after the day on which this section comes into force.

NOTES
Commencement: 26 May 2015.

Exclusivity in Zero Hours Contracts

153 *(Inserts the Employment Rights Act 1996, ss 27A, 27B (Pt 2A), at* **[1.842]** *et seq, and amends s 236(3) of that Act at* **[1.1151]**.)

Public Sector Exit Payments

[1.1928]
[153A Regulations to restrict public sector exit payments
(1) Regulations may make provision to secure that the total amount of exit payments made to a person in respect of a relevant public sector exit does not exceed £95,000.
(2) Where provision is made under subsection (1) it must also secure that if, in any period of 28 consecutive days, two or more relevant public sector exits occur in respect of the same person, the total amount of exit payments made to the person in respect of those exits does not exceed the amount provided for in subsection (1).
(3) An exit payment is in respect of a relevant public sector exit if it is made—
(a) to an employee of a prescribed public sector authority in consequence of the employee leaving employment, or
(b) to a holder of a prescribed public sector office in consequence of the office-holder leaving office.
(4) An exit payment is a payment of a prescribed description.
(5) The descriptions of payment which may be prescribed include—
(a) any payment on account of dismissal by reason of redundancy (read in accordance with section 139 of the Employment Rights Act 1996);
(b) any payment on voluntary exit;
(c) any payment to reduce or eliminate an actuarial reduction to a pension on early retirement or in respect of the cost to a pension scheme of such a reduction not being made;
(d) any severance payment or other ex gratia payment;
(e) any payment in respect of an outstanding entitlement;
(f) any payment of compensation under the terms of a contract;
(g) any payment in lieu of notice;
(h) any payment in the form of shares or share options.
(6) In this section a reference to a payment made to a person includes a reference to a payment made in respect of that person to another person.
(7) For the purposes of subsection (2), a public sector exit occurs when the person leaves the employment or office in question (regardless of when any exit payment is made).
(8) Regulations may include—
(a) provision which exempts from any provision made under subsection (1) exit payments, or exit payments of a prescribed description, made in prescribed circumstances;

(b) provision which, in consequence of provision made under subsection (1), amends a relevant public sector scheme so as to make any duty or power under the scheme to make exit payments subject to any restriction imposed by regulations under subsection (1) (taking account of any relaxation of such a restriction which may be made under section 153C);

(c) provision which makes an amendment of any provision made by or under an enactment (whenever passed or made) which is necessary or expedient in consequence of any provision made by or under this section.

(9) Regulations may substitute a different amount for the amount for the time being specified in subsection (1).

(10) Nothing in this section applies in relation to payments made by authorities who wholly or mainly exercise functions which could be conferred by provision included in an Act of the Northern Ireland Assembly made without the consent of the Secretary of State (see sections 6 to 8 of the Northern Ireland Act 1998).

(11) In this section—

"enactment" includes an Act of the Scottish Parliament, a Measure or Act of the National Assembly for Wales and Northern Ireland legislation;

"prescribed" means prescribed by regulations under this section;

"relevant public sector scheme" means—

(a) a scheme under section 1 of the Superannuation Act 1972 (civil servants);

(b) a scheme under section 7 of that Act (local government workers);

(c) a scheme under section 9 of that Act (teachers);

(d) a scheme under section 10 of that Act (health service workers);

(e) a scheme under section 1 of the Public Service Pensions Act 2013 (schemes for persons in public service);

(f) a scheme under section 26 of the Fire Services Act 1947 or section 34 of the Fire and Rescue Services Act 2004 (fire and rescue workers);

(g) a scheme under section 1 of the Police Pensions Act 1976 or section 48 of the Police and Fire Reform (Scotland) Act 2012 (members of police forces);

(h) any other prescribed scheme (whether established by or under an enactment or otherwise).]

NOTES

Commencement: 1 February 2017.

Inserted by the Enterprise Act 2016, s 41(1), as from 1 February 2017.

Regulations: as of 15 May 2019, no regulations had been made under this section.

[1.1929]

[153B Supplementary provision about regulations under section 153A

(1) Subject to subsection (2), the power to make regulations under section 153A is exercisable—

(a) by the Scottish Ministers, in relation to payments made by a relevant Scottish authority;

(b) by the Welsh Ministers, in relation to relevant Welsh exit payments;

(c) by the Treasury, in relation to any other payments.

(2) Where the relevant Scottish authority is the Scottish Administration (or a part of it) the power to make regulations under section 153A is exercisable by the Treasury (instead of the Scottish Ministers)—

(a) in relation to payments made to the holders of offices in the Scottish Administration which are not ministerial offices (read in accordance with section 126(8) of the Scotland Act 1998), and

(b) in relation to payments made to members of the staff of the Scottish Administration (read in accordance with section 126(7)(b) of that Act).

(3) The power to make provision of the kind mentioned in section 153A(8)(b) (power to amend public sector schemes), so far as exercisable by the Treasury, is also exercisable concurrently by any other Minister of the Crown (within the meaning of the Ministers of the Crown Act 1975) with the consent of the Treasury.

(4) Regulations under section 153A—

(a) if made by the Treasury, are subject to the affirmative resolution procedure;

(b) if made by the Scottish Ministers, are subject to the affirmative procedure;

(c) if made by the Welsh Ministers, may not be made unless a draft of the statutory instrument containing them has been laid before, and approved by a resolution of, the National Assembly for Wales.

(5) In this section "relevant Scottish authority" means—

(a) the Scottish Parliamentary Corporate Body, or

(b) any authority which wholly or mainly exercises functions within devolved competence (within the meaning of section 54 of the Scotland Act 1998).

(6) In this section "relevant Welsh exit payments" means exit payments made to holders of the following offices—

(a) member of the National Assembly for Wales;

(b) the First Minister for Wales;

(c) Welsh Minister appointed under section 48 of the Government of Wales Act 2006;

(d) Counsel General to the Welsh Government;

(e) Deputy Welsh Minister;

(f) member of a county council or a county borough council in Wales;

(g) member of a National Park Authority in Wales;

(h) member of a Fire and Rescue Authority in Wales.]

NOTES

Commencement: 1 February 2017.

Inserted by the Enterprise Act 2016, s 41(1), as from 1 February 2017.

[1.1930]

[153C Power to relax restriction on public sector exit payments

(1) A Minister of the Crown may relax any restriction imposed by regulations made by the Treasury under section 153A.

(2) The Scottish Ministers may relax any restriction imposed by regulations made by the Scottish Ministers under section 153A.

(3) The Welsh Ministers may relax any restriction imposed by regulations made by the Welsh Ministers under section 153A.

(4) A requirement may be relaxed—

(a) in respect of a particular employee or office-holder or a description of employees or office-holders;

(b) in relation to the whole or any part of an exit payment, or a description of exit payments.

(5) Regulations under section 153A made by the Treasury may—

(a) make provision for the power under subsection (1) to be exercisable on behalf of a Minister of the Crown by a person specified in the regulations;

(b) except in relation to exit payments made by a [devolved Welsh authority], make provision for a requirement to be relaxed only—

(i) with the consent of the Treasury, or

(ii) following compliance with any directions given by the Treasury;

(c) make provision as to the publication of information about any relaxation of a requirement granted.

(6) Regulations under section 153A made by the Scottish Ministers may—

(a) make provision for the power under subsection (2) to be exercisable on behalf of the Scottish Ministers by a person specified in the regulations;

(b) where provision is made by virtue of paragraph (a), make provision for a requirement to be relaxed only—

(i) with the consent of the Scottish Ministers, or

(ii) following compliance with any directions given by the Scottish Ministers;

(c) make provision as to the publication of information about any relaxation of a requirement granted.

(7) Regulations under section 153A made by the Welsh Ministers may—

(a) make provision for the power under subsection (3) to be exercisable on behalf of the Welsh Ministers by a person specified in the regulations;

(b) where provision is made by virtue of paragraph (a), make provision for a requirement to be relaxed only—

(i) with the consent of the Welsh Ministers, or

(ii) following compliance with any directions given by the Welsh Ministers;

(c) make provision as to the publication of information about any relaxation of a requirement granted.

(8) Regulations made by the Treasury under section 153A(1)—

(a) must, if they make provision in relation to exit payments made by a [devolved Welsh authority], provide for the power conferred on a Minister of the Crown by subsection (1) to be exercised instead by the Welsh Ministers in relation to those exit payments;

(b) may provide for the power conferred on a Minister of the Crown by subsection (1) to be exercised instead by the Welsh Ministers in relation to exit payments made by any other authority who is not a [devolved Welsh authority] but who wholly or mainly exercises functions in relation to Wales (but this does not limit the provision that may be made under subsection (5)(a)).

(9) In this section—

"Minister of the Crown" has the same meaning as in the Ministers of the Crown Act 1975;

["devolved Welsh authority" has the same meaning as in the Government of Wales Act 2006 (see section 157A of that Act)].]

NOTES

Commencement: 1 February 2017.

Inserted by the Enterprise Act 2016, s 41(1), as from 1 February 2017.

Words in square brackets in sub-ss (5), (8) substituted, and definition "devolved Welsh authority" substituted (for the original definition "relevant Welsh authority"), by the Wales Act 2017, s 69(1), Sch 6, Pt 3, para 109, as from 1 April 2018.

[1.1931]

154 Regulations in connection with [repayment of] public sector exit payments

(1) Regulations may make provision requiring the repayment of some or all of any qualifying exit payment in qualifying circumstances (see section 155).

(2) The regulations may make such other provision in connection with the repayment mentioned in subsection (1) as the person making the regulations thinks fit.

(3) A qualifying exit payment is a payment of a prescribed description—

(a) made to an employee of a prescribed public sector authority in consequence of the employee leaving employment, or

(b) made to a holder of a prescribed public sector office in consequence of the office holder leaving office.

(4) The descriptions of payment which may be prescribed by virtue of subsection (3) include—

(a) any payment on account of dismissal by reason of redundancy (read in accordance with section 139 of the Employment Rights Act 1996),
(b) any payment on voluntary exit,
(c) any payment to reduce or eliminate an actuarial reduction to a pension on early retirement [or in respect of the cost to a pension scheme of such a reduction not being made],
(d) any severance payment or other ex gratia payment,
(e) any payment in respect of an outstanding entitlement (such as to annual leave or an allowance),
(f) any payment of compensation under the terms of a contract,
(g) any payment in lieu of notice, and
(h) any payment in the form of shares or share options.

(5) If more than one qualifying exit payment is payable to an employee or office holder the provision made in the exit payments regulations is to apply in relation to the aggregated payments.

(6) For the purposes of this section and sections 155 and 157—

an "exit payee" is an employee or office holder to whom any qualifying exit payment is payable,
the "exit payments regulations" are regulations under subsection (1),
a "responsible authority" means an authority by which any qualifying exit payments are payable, and
"prescribed" means prescribed by the exit payments regulations.

[(7) In this section a reference to a payment made to a person includes a reference to a payment made in respect of that person to another person.]

NOTES

Commencement: 1 January 2016.

The words in square brackets in the section heading and in sub-s (4)(c) were inserted, and sub-s (7) was added, by the Enterprise Act 2016, s 41(2), Sch 6, para 1, as from 1 February 2017.

Regulations: as of 15 May 2019, no regulations had been made under this section.

[1.1932]

155 Section 154(1): further provision

(1) For the purposes of section 154(1) circumstances are qualifying circumstances if—

(a) an exit payee becomes—
  (i) an employee or a contractor of a prescribed public sector authority, or
  (ii) a holder of a prescribed public sector office,
(b) less than one year has elapsed between the exit payee leaving the employment or office in respect of which a qualifying exit payment is payable and the event mentioned in paragraph (a), and
(c) any other prescribed conditions are met.

(2) The exit payment regulations may, in particular, make provision—

(a) exempting an exit payee from the requirement to repay in the prescribed circumstances;
(b) exempting some or all of a qualifying exit payment from that requirement in the prescribed circumstances;
(c) for the amount required to be repaid to be tapered according to the time which has elapsed between an exit payee leaving employment or office and the event mentioned in subsection (1)(a);
(d) imposing duties, in connection with a qualifying exit payment, on—
  (i) an exit payee,
  (ii) a responsible authority, and
  (iii) a subsequent authority;
(e) as to the arrangements required to be made by an exit payee to repay to a responsible authority the amount of a qualifying exit payment required to be repaid;
(f) for preventing an exit payee from becoming an employee or a contractor, or a holder of a public sector office, as mentioned in subsection (1)(a) until the arrangements required by virtue of paragraph (e) have been made;
(g) as to the consequences of an exit payee failing to repay the amount required to be repaid (including the dismissal of the exit payee).

(3) In subsection (2)(d)(iii) a "subsequent authority" means—

(a) in relation to an exit payee who becomes an employee or a contractor, a public sector authority of which the exit payee becomes an employee or a contractor, or
(b) in relation to an exit payee who becomes a holder of a public sector office, an authority which is responsible for the appointment.

(4) For the purposes of this section an exit payee becomes a contractor of a public sector authority if the exit payee provides services to the authority under a contract for services.

NOTES

Commencement: 1 January 2016.

[1.1933]

156 Power to make regulations [under section 154(1)] to be exercisable by the Treasury or Scottish Ministers

(1) The power to make regulations under section 154(1) is exercisable—

(a) by the Scottish Ministers in relation to payments made by a relevant Scottish authority;
(b) by the Treasury in relation to any other payments,
(but this subsection is subject to subsection (2)).

(2) Where the relevant Scottish authority is the Scottish Administration the power to make regulations under section 154(1) is exercisable by the Treasury (instead of the Scottish Ministers) in relation to payments made to—
(a) the holders of offices in the Scottish Administration which are not ministerial offices (read in accordance with section 126(8) of the Scotland Act 1998), and
(b) the members of the staff of the Scottish Administration (read in accordance with section 126(7)(b) of that Act).

(3) In this section "relevant Scottish authority" means—
(a) the Scottish Parliamentary Corporate Body, or
(b) any authority which wholly or mainly exercises functions which would be within devolved competence (within the meaning of section 54 of the Scotland Act 1998).

[(4) The first regulations made by the Treasury under section 154(1) are subject to the affirmative resolution procedure.

(4A) The first regulations made by the Scottish Ministers under section 154(1) are subject to the affirmative procedure.]

(5) Any other regulations under section 154(1)—
(a) if made by the Treasury, are subject to negative resolution procedure;
(b) if made by the Scottish Ministers, are subject to the negative procedure.

NOTES

Commencement: 1 January 2016.

The words in square brackets in the section heading were inserted, and sub-ss (4), (4A) were substituted (for the original sub-s (4)), by the Enterprise Act 2016, s 41(2), Sch 6, paras 1, 2, as from 1 February 2017.

[1.1934]

157 Power of Secretary of State to waive repayment requirement

(1) The Secretary of State may waive the whole or any part of any repayment required by regulations made by the Treasury under section 154(1).

(2) The Scottish Ministers may waive the whole or any part of any repayment required by regulations made by the Scottish Ministers under section 154(1).

(3) A waiver may be given in respect of—
(a) a particular exit payee, or
(b) a description of exit payees.

(4) The exit payments regulations made by the Treasury may—
(a) make provision for the power under subsection (1) to be exercisable on behalf of the Secretary of State by a prescribed person,
(b) make provision for a waiver to be given only—
(i) with the consent of the Treasury, or
(ii) following compliance with any directions given by the Treasury, and
(c) make provision as to the publication of information about any waivers given.

(5) The exit payments regulations made by the Scottish Ministers may—
(a) make provision for the power under subsection (2) to be exercisable on behalf of the Scottish Ministers by a prescribed person,
(b) make provision for a waiver to be given only—
(i) with the consent of the Scottish Ministers, or
(ii) following compliance with any directions given by the Scottish Ministers,
(where provision is made by virtue of paragraph (a)), and
(c) make provision as to the publication of information about any waivers given.

(6) The exit payments regulations made by the Treasury may make provision for the power conferred on the Secretary of State by subsection (1) to be exercised instead—
(a) by the Department of Finance and Personnel in Northern Ireland, in relation to qualifying exit payments made by responsible authorities who wholly or mainly exercise functions which could be conferred by provision included in an Act of the Northern Ireland Assembly made without the consent of the Secretary of State (see sections 6 to 8 of the Northern Ireland Act 1998);
(b) by the Welsh Ministers, in relation to qualifying exit payments made by responsible authorities who [are devolved Welsh authorities within the meaning given by section 157A of the Government of Wales Act 2006].

NOTES

Commencement: 1 January 2016.

Sub-s (6): words in square brackets substituted by the Wales Act 2017, s 69(1), Sch 6, Pt 3, para 110, as from 1 April 2018.

PART 12
GENERAL

[1.1935]

159 Consequential amendments, repeals and revocations

(1) A Minister of the Crown may by regulations make such provision as the Minister considers appropriate in consequence of this Act (other than sections 35 and 36 as they apply in Wales).

(2) The power conferred by subsection (1) includes power—

(a) to make transitional, transitory or saving provision;
(b) to amend, repeal, revoke or otherwise modify any provision made by or under an enactment (including an enactment contained in this Act and any enactment passed or made in the same Session as this Act).

(3) Subject to subsection (4)(b), regulations under subsection (1) which amend, repeal or revoke any provision of primary legislation are subject to affirmative resolution procedure.

(4) Regulations under subsection (1) which—
(a) do not amend, repeal or revoke any provision of primary legislation, or
(b) amend, repeal or revoke any provision of primary legislation only in connection with there ceasing to be any share warrants (see section 84),

are subject to negative resolution procedure.

(5) The Welsh Ministers may by regulations make such provision as they consider appropriate in consequence of section 35 or 36 as it applies in Wales.

(6) The power conferred by subsection (5) includes power—
(a) to make transitional, transitory or saving provision;
(b) to amend, repeal, revoke or otherwise modify any provision made by or under any Act (including this Act and any Act passed in the same Session as this Act) or any Measure or Act of the National Assembly for Wales.

(7) A statutory instrument containing regulations under subsection (5) which amend or repeal an Act or a Measure or Act of the National Assembly for Wales may not be made unless a draft of the instrument has been laid before, and approved by a resolution of, the National Assembly for Wales.

(8) A statutory instrument containing regulations under subsection (5), other than a statutory instrument within subsection (7), is subject to annulment in pursuance of a resolution of the National Assembly for Wales.

(9) In this Part—

"enactment" includes an Act of the Scottish Parliament, a Measure or Act of the National Assembly for Wales and Northern Ireland legislation;

"Minister of the Crown" has the same meaning as in the Ministers of the Crown Act 1975;

"primary legislation" means—
(a) an Act of Parliament,
(b) an Act of the Scottish Parliament,
(c) a Measure or Act of the National Assembly for Wales, and
(d) Northern Ireland legislation.

NOTES

Commencement: 26 March 2015.

Regulations: the Small Business, Enterprise and Employment Act 2015 (Consequential Amendments) (Insolvency and Company Directors Disqualification) Regulations 2015, SI 2015/1651. Other Regulations made under this section concern such areas as childcare and education and are, therefore, outside the scope of this work.

[1.1936]

160 Transitional, transitory or saving provision

(1) A Minister of the Crown may by regulations make such transitional, transitory or saving provision as the Minister considers appropriate in connection with the coming into force of this Act (other than sections 35 and 36 as they apply in Wales).

(2) The Welsh Ministers may by regulations make such transitional, transitory or saving provision as they consider appropriate in connection with the coming into force of section 35 or 36 as it applies in Wales.

NOTES

Commencement: 26 March 2015.

Regulations: as of 15 May 2019, the only regulations made under this section are commencement regulations (as to which, see s 164 *post*).

[1.1937]

161 Supplementary provision about regulations

(1) Regulations under this Act, other than regulations made by the Scottish Ministers under section 1[, 153A] or 154(1), are to be made by statutory instrument.

(2) Regulations under this Act may make—
(a) different provision for different purposes or cases;
(b) different provision for different areas;
(c) provision generally or for specific cases;
(d) provision subject to exceptions;
(e) incidental, supplementary, consequential, transitional or transitory provision or savings.

(3) Where regulations under this Act are subject to "negative resolution procedure" the statutory instrument containing the regulations is subject to annulment in pursuance of a resolution of either House of Parliament.

(4) Where regulations under this Act are subject to "affirmative resolution procedure" the regulations may not be made unless a draft of the statutory instrument containing them has been laid before Parliament and approved by a resolution of each House of Parliament.

(5) Any provision that may be included in an instrument under this Act for which no Parliamentary procedure is prescribed may be made by regulations subject to negative or affirmative resolution procedure.

(6) Any provision that may be included in an instrument under this Act subject to negative resolution procedure may be made by regulations subject to affirmative resolution procedure.

NOTES

Commencement: 26 March 2015.

Sub-s (1): figure in square brackets inserted by the Enterprise Act 2016, s 41(2), Sch 6, paras 1, 3, as from 1 February 2017.

[1.1938]

162 Financial provisions

There is to be paid out of money provided by Parliament—

(a) any expenditure incurred under or by virtue of this Act by a Minister of the Crown, and

(b) any increase attributable to this Act in the sums payable under any other Act out of money so provided.

NOTES

Commencement: 26 March 2015.

[1.1939]

163 Extent

(1) Subject to subsections (2) to (4), this Act extends to England and Wales, Scotland and Northern Ireland.

(2) Any amendment, repeal or revocation made by this Act has the same extent as the enactment amended, repealed or revoked, except the amendments made by sections 113 and 114, which extend as mentioned in subsection (1).

(3) Part 4 extends to England and Wales only.

(4) In Part 10, sections 144 to 146 and Schedule 11 extend to England and Wales and Scotland only.

NOTES

Commencement: 26 March 2015.

[1.1940]

164 Commencement

(1) The provisions of this Act come into force on such day as a Minister of the Crown may by regulations appoint, subject to subsections (2) to (5).

(2) The following provisions of this Act come into force on the day this Act is passed—

(a) in Part 1, sections 4 to 7 (regulations about financial information on small and medium sized businesses);

(b) in Part 3, section 39 (regulations about procurement);

(c) in Part 5, section 74 (funding for free of charge early years provision);

(d) in Part 11, section 151 (employment tribunal procedure regulations: postponements);

(e) this Part.

(3)–(6) (*Outside the scope of this work.*)

NOTES

Commencement: 26 March 2015.

Regulations: the Small Business, Enterprise and Employment Act 2015 (Commencement No 1) Regulations 2015, SI 2015/1329; the Small Business, Enterprise and Employment Act 2015 (Commencement No 2 and Transitional Provisions) Regulations 2015, SI 2015/1689; the Small Business, Enterprise and Employment Act 2015 (Commencement No 1) (Wales) Regulations 2015, SI 2015/1710; the Small Business, Enterprise and Employment Act 2015 (Commencement No 3) Regulations 2015, SI 2015/2029; the Small Business, Enterprise and Employment Act 2015 (Commencement No 4, Transitional and Savings Provisions) Regulations 2016, SI 2016/321; the Small Business, Enterprise and Employment Act 2015 (Commencement No 5 and Saving Provision) Regulations 2016, SI 2016/532; the Small Business, Enterprise and Employment Act 2015 (Commencement No 6 and Transitional and Savings Provisions) Regulations 2016, SI 2016/1020; the Small Business, Enterprise and Employment Act 2015 (Commencement No 7, Consequential, Transitional and Savings Provisions) Regulations 2019, SI 2019/816.

[1.1941]

165 Short title

This Act may be cited as the Small Business, Enterprise and Employment Act 2015.

NOTES

Commencement: 26 March 2015.

MODERN SLAVERY ACT 2015

(2015 c 30)

ARRANGEMENT OF SECTIONS

PART 1
OFFENCES

Offences

SCHEDULES

An Act to make provision about slavery, servitude and forced or compulsory labour and about human trafficking, including provision for the protection of victims; to make provision for an Independent Anti-slavery Commissioner; and for connected purposes.

26th March 2015

NOTES

Much of this Act covers matters outside the scope of this work, and only those provisions relevant to employment law are reproduced. For reasons of space, the subject matter of sections not printed is not annotated.

PART 1
OFFENCES

Offences

[1.1942]

1 Slavery, servitude and forced or compulsory labour

(1) A person commits an offence if—

(a) the person holds another person in slavery or servitude and the circumstances are such that the person knows or ought to know that the other person is held in slavery or servitude, or

(b) the person requires another person to perform forced or compulsory labour and the circumstances are such that the person knows or ought to know that the other person is being required to perform forced or compulsory labour.

(2) In subsection (1) the references to holding a person in slavery or servitude or requiring a person to perform forced or compulsory labour are to be construed in accordance with Article 4 of the Human Rights Convention.

(3) In determining whether a person is being held in slavery or servitude or required to perform forced or compulsory labour, regard may be had to all the circumstances.

(4) For example, regard may be had—

(a) to any of the person's personal circumstances (such as the person being a child, the person's family relationships, and any mental or physical illness) which may make the person more vulnerable than other persons;

(b) to any work or services provided by the person, including work or services provided in circumstances which constitute exploitation within section 3(3) to (6).

(5) The consent of a person (whether an adult or a child) to any of the acts alleged to constitute holding the person in slavery or servitude, or requiring the person to perform forced or compulsory labour, does not preclude a determination that the person is being held in slavery or servitude, or required to perform forced or compulsory labour.

NOTES

Commencement: 31 July 2015.

Transitional provisions: the Modern Slavery Act 2015 (Commencement No 1, Saving and Transitional Provisions) Regulations 2015, SI 2015/1476, regs 5–8 provide as follows—

"**5.**

(1) This regulation applies where in any proceedings—

(a) a person ("D") is charged in respect of the same conduct with—

(i) an offence under section 71 of the Coroners and Justice Act 2009; and

(ii) an offence under section 1 of the 2015 Act;

(b) the only thing preventing D from being found guilty of an offence under section 1 of the 2015 Act is the fact that it has not been proved beyond reasonable doubt that the offence was committed wholly on or after 31st July 2015;

(c) the only thing preventing D from being found guilty of an offence under section 71 of the Coroners and Justice Act 2009 is the fact that it has not been proved beyond reasonable doubt that the offence was committed wholly or partly before 31st July 2015.

(2) For the purpose of determining D's guilt it shall be conclusively presumed that the offence was committed wholly or partly before 31st July 2015.

6. (1) This regulation applies where in any proceedings—

(a) a person ("D") is charged in respect of the same conduct with—

(i) an offence under section 4 of the Asylum and Immigration (Treatment of Claimants, etc) Act 2004 or section 59A of the Sexual Offences Act 2003; and

(ii) an offence under section 2 of the 2015 Act;

(b) the only thing preventing D from being found guilty of an offence under section 2 of the 2015 Act is the fact that it has not been proved beyond reasonable doubt that the offence was committed wholly on or after 31st July 2015;

(c) the only thing preventing D from being found guilty of an offence under section 4 of the Asylum and Immigration (Treatment of Claimants, etc) Act 2004 or section 59A of the Sexual Offences Act 2003 is the fact that it has not been proved beyond reasonable doubt that the offence was committed wholly or partly before 31st July 2015.

(2) For the purpose of determining D's guilt it shall be conclusively presumed that the offence was committed wholly or partly before 31st July 2015.

7. A reference in regulations 5 and 6 to an offence includes a reference to—

(a) aiding, abetting, counselling or procuring the commission of the offence;

(b) conspiracy to commit the offence;

(c) an attempt to commit the offence; and
(d) an offence under Part 2 of the Serious Crime Act 2007 (encouraging or assisting crime) in relation to the offence.

8.
For the purposes of regulations 3 to 6 an offence is partly committed before 31st July 2015 if any act or omission which forms part of the offence takes place before that day.".

[1.1943]
2 Human trafficking

(1) A person commits an offence if the person arranges or facilitates the travel of another person ("V") with a view to V being exploited.
(2) It is irrelevant whether V consents to the travel (whether V is an adult or a child).
(3) A person may in particular arrange or facilitate V's travel by recruiting V, transporting or transferring V, harbouring or receiving V, or transferring or exchanging control over V.
(4) A person arranges or facilitates V's travel with a view to V being exploited only if—
(a) the person intends to exploit V (in any part of the world) during or after the travel, or
(b) the person knows or ought to know that another person is likely to exploit V (in any part of the world) during or after the travel.
(5) "Travel" means—
(a) arriving in, or entering, any country,
(b) departing from any country,
(c) travelling within any country.
(6) A person who is a UK national commits an offence under this section regardless of—
(a) where the arranging or facilitating takes place, or
(b) where the travel takes place.
(7) A person who is not a UK national commits an offence under this section if—
(a) any part of the arranging or facilitating takes place in the United Kingdom, or
(b) the travel consists of arrival in or entry into, departure from, or travel within, the United Kingdom.

NOTES
Commencement: 31 July 2015
Transitional provisions: see the note to s 1 at **[1.1942]**.

[1.1944]
3 Meaning of exploitation

(1) For the purposes of section 2 a person is exploited only if one or more of the following subsections apply in relation to the person.

Slavery, servitude and forced or compulsory labour

(2) The person is the victim of behaviour—
(a) which involves the commission of an offence under section 1, or
(b) which would involve the commission of an offence under that section if it took place in England and Wales.
(3)–(6) (*Outside the scope of this work.*)

NOTES
Commencement: 31 July 2015.

[1.1945]
4 Committing offence with intent to commit offence under section 2

A person commits an offence under this section if the person commits any offence with the intention of committing an offence under section 2 (including an offence committed by aiding, abetting, counselling or procuring an offence under that section).

NOTES
Commencement: 31 July 2015.

Penalties and Sentencing

[1.1946]
5 Penalties

(1) A person guilty of an offence under section 1 or 2 is liable—
(a) on conviction on indictment, to imprisonment for life;
(b) on summary conviction, to imprisonment for a term not exceeding 12 months or a fine or both.
(2) A person guilty of an offence under section 4 is liable (unless subsection (3) applies)—
(a) on conviction on indictment, to imprisonment for a term not exceeding 10 years;
(b) on summary conviction, to imprisonment for a term not exceeding 12 months or a fine or both.
(3) Where the offence under section 4 is committed by kidnapping or false imprisonment, a person guilty of that offence is liable, on conviction on indictment, to imprisonment for life.
(4) In relation to an offence committed before section 154(1) of the Criminal Justice Act 2003 comes into force, the references in subsections (1)(b) and (2)(b) to 12 months are to be read as references to 6 months.

NOTES
Commencement: 31 July 2015.

[1.1947]
6 Sentencing
(This section amends the Criminal Justice Act 2003, Sch 15, Pts 1, 2 and Sch 15B, Pt 1.)

[1.1948]
7 Confiscation of assets
(This section amends the Proceeds of Crime Act 2002, Sch 2.)

[1.1949]
8 Power to make slavery and trafficking reparation orders
(1) The court may make a slavery and trafficking reparation order against a person if—
(a) the person has been convicted of an offence under section 1, 2 or 4, and
(b) a confiscation order is made against the person in respect of the offence.
(2) The court may also make a slavery and trafficking reparation order against a person if—
(a) by virtue of section 28 of the Proceeds of Crime Act 2002 (defendants who abscond during proceedings) a confiscation order has been made against a person in respect of an offence under section 1, 2 or 4, and
(b) the person is later convicted of the offence.
(3) The court may make a slavery and trafficking reparation order against the person in addition to dealing with the person in any other way (subject to section 10(1)).
(4) In a case within subsection (1) the court may make a slavery and trafficking reparation order against the person even if the person has been sentenced for the offence before the confiscation order is made.
(5) In determining whether to make a slavery and trafficking reparation order against the person the court must have regard to the person's means.
(6) If the court considers that—
(a) it would be appropriate both to impose a fine and to make a slavery and trafficking reparation order, but
(b) the person has insufficient means to pay both an appropriate fine and appropriate compensation under such an order,
the court must give preference to compensation (although it may impose a fine as well).
(7) In any case in which the court has power to make a slavery and trafficking reparation order it must—
(a) consider whether to make such an order (whether or not an application for such an order is made), and
(b) if it does not make an order, give reasons.
(8) In this section—
(a) "the court" means—
(i) the Crown Court, or
(ii) any magistrates' court that has power to make a confiscation order by virtue of an order under section 97 of the Serious Organised Crime and Police Act 2005 (confiscation orders by magistrates' courts);
(b) "confiscation order" means a confiscation order under section 6 of the Proceeds of Crime Act 2002;
(c) a confiscation order is made in respect of an offence if the offence is the offence (or one of the offences) concerned for the purposes of Part 2 of that Act.

NOTES
Commencement: 31 July 2015.

[1.1950]
9 Effect of slavery and trafficking reparation orders
(1) A slavery and trafficking reparation order is an order requiring the person against whom it is made to pay compensation to the victim of a relevant offence for any harm resulting from that offence.
(2) "Relevant offence" means—
(a) the offence under section 1, 2 or 4 of which the person is convicted;
(b) any other offence under section 1, 2 or 4 which is taken into consideration in determining the person's sentence.
(3) The amount of the compensation is to be such amount as the court considers appropriate having regard to any evidence and to any representations made by or on behalf of the person or the prosecutor, but subject to subsection (4).
(4) The amount of the compensation payable under the slavery and trafficking reparation order (or if more than one order is made in the same proceedings, the total amount of the compensation payable under those orders) must not exceed the amount the person is required to pay under the confiscation order.
(5) In determining the amount to be paid by the person under a slavery and trafficking reparation order the court must have regard to the person's means.
(6) In subsection (4) "the confiscation order" means the confiscation order within section 8(1)(b) or (2)(a) (as the case may be).

NOTES
Commencement: 31 July 2015.

[1.1951]

10 Slavery and trafficking reparation orders: supplementary provision

(1) A slavery and trafficking reparation order and a compensation order under section 130 of the Powers of Criminal Courts (Sentencing) Act 2000 may not both be made in respect of the same offence.

(2) Where the court makes a slavery and trafficking reparation order as mentioned in section 8(4), for the purposes of the following provisions the person's sentence is to be regarded as imposed or made on the day on which the order is made—

(a) section 18(2) of the Criminal Appeal Act 1968 (time limit for notice of appeal or application for leave to appeal);

(b) paragraph 1 of Schedule 3 to the Criminal Justice Act 1988 (time limit for notice of application for leave to refer a case under section 36 of that Act).

(3) Sections 132 to 134 of the Powers of Criminal Courts (Sentencing) Act 2000 (appeals, review etc of compensation orders) apply to slavery and trafficking reparation orders as if—

(a) references to a compensation order were references to a slavery and trafficking reparation order;

(b) references to the court of trial were references to the court (within the meaning of section 8 above);

(c) references to injury, loss or damage were references to harm;

(d) the reference in section 133(3)(c)(iii) to a slavery and trafficking reparation order under section 8 above were to a compensation order under section 130 of that Act;

(e) in section 134 the references to service compensation orders were omitted.

(4) If under section 21 or 22 of the Proceeds of Crime Act 2002 the court varies a confiscation order so as to increase the amount required to be paid under that order, it may also vary any slavery and trafficking reparation order made by virtue of the confiscation order so as to increase the amount required to be paid under the slavery and trafficking reparation order.

(5) If under section 23 or 29 of that Act the court varies a confiscation order so as to reduce the amount required to be paid under that order, it may also—

(a) vary any relevant slavery and trafficking reparation order so as to reduce the amount which remains to be paid under that order;

(b) discharge any relevant slavery and trafficking reparation order.

(6) If under section 24 [or 25A] of that Act the court discharges a confiscation order, it may also discharge any relevant slavery and trafficking reparation order.

(7) For the purposes of subsections (5) and (6) a slavery and trafficking reparation order is relevant if it is made by virtue of the confiscation order and some or all of the amount required to be paid under it has not been paid.

(8) If on an appeal under section 31 of the Proceeds of Crime Act 2002 the Court of Appeal—

(a) quashes a confiscation order, it must also quash any slavery and trafficking reparation order made by virtue of the confiscation order;

(b) varies a confiscation order, it may also vary any slavery and trafficking reparation order made by virtue of the confiscation order;

(c) makes a confiscation order, it may make any slavery and trafficking reparation order that could have been made under section 8 above by virtue of the confiscation order.

(9) If on an appeal under section 33 of that Act the Supreme Court—

(a) quashes a confiscation order, it must also quash any slavery and trafficking reparation order made by virtue of the confiscation order;

(b) varies a confiscation order, it may also vary any slavery and trafficking reparation order made by virtue of the confiscation order.

(10) For the purposes of this section—

(a) a slavery and trafficking reparation order made under section 8(1) is made by virtue of the confiscation order within section 8(1)(b);

(b) a slavery and trafficking reparation order made under section 8(2) is made by virtue of the confiscation order within section 8(2)(a).

NOTES

Commencement: 31 July 2015.

Sub-s (6): words in square brackets inserted by the Modern Slavery Act 2015 (Consequential Amendments) Regulations 2016, SI 2016/244, reg 28, as from 17 March 2016.

[1.1952]

11 Forfeiture of land vehicle, ship or aircraft

(1) This section applies if a person is convicted on indictment of an offence under section 2.

(2) The court may order the forfeiture of a land vehicle used or intended to be used in connection with the offence if the convicted person—

(a) owned the vehicle at the time the offence was committed,

(b) was at that time a director, secretary or manager of a company which owned the vehicle,

(c) was at that time in possession of the vehicle under a hire-purchase agreement,

(d) was at that time a director, secretary or manager of a company which was in possession of the vehicle under a hire-purchase agreement, or

(e) was driving the vehicle in the course of the commission of the offence.

(3) The court may order the forfeiture of a ship or aircraft used or intended to be used in connection with the offence if the convicted person—

(a) owned the ship or aircraft at the time the offence was committed,

(b) was at that time a director, secretary or manager of a company which owned the ship or aircraft,

(c) was at that time in possession of the ship or aircraft under a hire-purchase agreement,

(d) was at that time a director, secretary or manager of a company which was in possession of the ship or aircraft under a hire-purchase agreement,
(e) was at that time a charterer of the ship or aircraft, or
(f) committed the offence while acting as captain of the ship or aircraft.

(4) But where subsection (3)(a) or (b) does not apply to the convicted person, forfeiture of a ship or aircraft may be ordered only if subsection (5) applies or—
(a) in the case of a ship other than a hovercraft, its gross tonnage is less than 500 tons;
(b) in the case of an aircraft, the maximum weight at which it may take off in accordance with its certificate of airworthiness is less than 5,700 kilogrammes.

(5) This subsection applies where a person who, at the time the offence was committed—
(a) owned the ship or aircraft, or
(b) was a director, secretary or manager of a company which owned it,

knew or ought to have known of the intention to use it in the course of the commission of an offence under section 2.

(6) Where a person who claims to have an interest in a land vehicle, ship or aircraft applies to a court to make representations about its forfeiture, the court may not order its forfeiture without giving the person an opportunity to make representations.

NOTES

Commencement: 31 July 2015.

[1.1953]

[11A Enforcement by Gangmasters and Labour Abuse Authority

(1) The Secretary of State may make arrangements with the Gangmasters and Labour Abuse Authority for officers of the Authority to act for the purposes of this Part in taking action in circumstances in which it appears that an offence under this Part which is a labour market offence (within the meaning of section 3 of the Immigration Act 2016) has been, is being or may be committed.

(2) For provision about the powers of such an officer who is acting for the purposes of this Part, see section 114B of the Police and Criminal Evidence Act 1984 (PACE powers for labour abuse prevention officers).]

NOTES

Commencement: 12 July 2016.
Inserted by the Immigration Act 2016, s 11, Sch 2, paras 8, 9, as from 12 July 2016.

Supplementary

[1.1954]

12 Detention of land vehicle, ship or aircraft

(1) If a person ("P") has been arrested for an offence under section 2, a constable or senior immigration officer may detain a relevant land vehicle, ship or aircraft.

(2) A land vehicle, ship or aircraft is relevant if the constable or officer has reasonable grounds to believe that an order for its forfeiture could be made under section 11 if P were convicted of the offence.

(3) The land vehicle, ship or aircraft may be detained—
(a) until a decision is taken as to whether or not to charge P with the offence,
(b) if P has been charged, until P is acquitted, the charge against P is dismissed or the proceedings are discontinued, or
(c) if P has been charged and convicted, until the court decides whether or not to order forfeiture of the vehicle, ship or aircraft.

(4) A person (other than P) may apply to the court for the release of the land vehicle, ship or aircraft on the grounds that the person—
(a) owns the vehicle, ship or aircraft,
(b) was, immediately before the detention of the vehicle, ship or aircraft, in possession of it under a hire-purchase agreement, or
(c) is a charterer of the ship or aircraft.

(5) The court to which an application is made under subsection (4) may, if satisfactory security or surety is tendered, release the land vehicle, ship or aircraft on condition that it is made available to the court if—
(a) P is convicted, and
(b) an order for its forfeiture is made under section 11.

(6) In this section, "the court" means—
(a) if P has not been charged, or P has been charged but proceedings for the offence have not begun to be heard, a magistrates' court;
(b) if P has been charged and proceedings for the offence have begun to be heard, the court hearing the proceedings.

(7) In this section, "senior immigration officer" means an immigration officer not below the rank of chief immigration officer.

NOTES

Commencement: 31 July 2015.

[1.1955]
13 Interpretation of Part 1

(1) In this Part—

"captain" means master (of a ship) or commander (of an aircraft);

"confiscation order" has the meaning given by section 8(8);

"the Human Rights Convention" means the Convention for the Protection of Human Rights and Fundamental Freedoms agreed by the Council of Europe at Rome on 4th November 1950;

"land vehicle" means any vehicle other than a ship or aircraft;

"ship" includes every description of vessel (including a hovercraft) used in navigation;

"slavery and trafficking reparation order" means an order made under section 8;

"UK national" means—

(a) a British citizen,

(b) a person who is a British subject by virtue of Part 4 of the British Nationality Act 1981 and who has a right of abode in the United Kingdom, or

(c) a person who is a British overseas territories citizen by virtue of a connection with Gibraltar.

(2) In sections 8 and 10, references to provisions of the Proceeds of Crime Act 2002 include references to those provisions as amended or otherwise modified by virtue of an order (whenever made) under section 97 of the Serious Organised Crime and Police Act 2005 (confiscation orders by magistrates' courts).

(3) In sections 11 and 12, a reference to being an owner of a vehicle, ship or aircraft includes a reference to being any of a number of persons who jointly own it.

NOTES

Commencement: 31 July 2015.

PART 2
PREVENTION ORDERS

Slavery and Trafficking Prevention Orders

[1.1956]
14 Slavery and trafficking prevention orders on sentencing

(1) A court may make a slavery and trafficking prevention order against a person ("the defendant") where it deals with the defendant in respect of—

(a) a conviction for a slavery or human trafficking offence,

(b) a finding that the defendant is not guilty of a slavery or human trafficking offence by reason of insanity, or

(c) a finding that the defendant is under a disability and has done the act charged against the defendant in respect of a slavery or human trafficking offence.

(2) The court may make the order only if it is satisfied that—

(a) there is a risk that the defendant may commit a slavery or human trafficking offence, and

(b) it is necessary to make the order for the purpose of protecting persons generally, or particular persons, from the physical or psychological harm which would be likely to occur if the defendant committed such an offence.

(3) A "slavery or human trafficking offence" means an offence listed in Schedule 1.

(4) The Secretary of State may by regulations amend Schedule 1.

(5) For the purposes of this section, convictions and findings include those taking place before this section comes into force.

NOTES

Commencement: 31 July 2015.

Regulations: as of 15 May 2019, no regulations had been made under this section.

[1.1957]
15 Slavery and trafficking prevention orders on application

(1) A magistrates' court may make a slavery and trafficking prevention order against a person ("the defendant") on an application by—

(a) a chief officer of police,

(b) an immigration officer, . . .

(c) the Director General of the National Crime Agency ("the Director General")[, or

(d) the Gangmasters and Labour Abuse Authority].

(2) The court may make the order only if it is satisfied that—

(a) the defendant is a relevant offender (see section 16), and

(b) since the defendant first became a relevant offender, the defendant has acted in a way which means that the condition in subsection (3) is met.

(3) The condition is that—

(a) there is a risk that the defendant may commit a slavery or human trafficking offence, and

(b) it is necessary to make the order for the purpose of protecting persons generally, or particular persons, from the physical or psychological harm which would be likely to occur if the defendant committed such an offence.

(4) A chief officer of police may make an application under this section only in respect of a person—

(a) who lives in the chief officer's police area, or

(b) who the chief officer believes is in that area or is intending to come to it.

(5) An application under this section is to be made by complaint, and may be made to any magistrates' court acting for a local justice area that includes—

(a) any part of a relevant police area, or

(b) any place where it is alleged that the defendant acted in a way mentioned in subsection (2)(b).

(6) Where the defendant is under 18, a reference in this section to a magistrates' court is to be taken as referring to a youth court (subject to any rules of court made under section 32).

(7) Where an immigration officer[, the Director General or the Gangmasters and Labour Abuse Authority] makes an application under this section, the officer[, the Director General or the Authority] must give notice of the application to the chief officer of police for a relevant police area.

(8) In this section "relevant police area" means—

(a) where the applicant is a chief officer of police, the officer's police area;

(b) where the applicant is an immigration officer[, the Director General or the Gangmasters and Labour Abuse Authority], the police area where the defendant lives or a police area which the officer[, the Director General or the Authority] believes the defendant is in or is intending to come to.

(9) The acts of the defendant which may be relied on for the purposes of subsection (2)(b) include acts taking place before this section comes into force.

NOTES

Commencement: 31 July 2015.

Sub-s (1): word omitted from para (b) repealed, and para (d) and the preceding word added, by the Immigration Act 2016, s 11(1), Sch 2, paras 8, 10(1), (2), as from 12 July 2016.

Sub-ss (7), (8): words in square brackets substituted by the Immigration Act 2016, s 11(1), Sch 2, paras 8, 10(1), (3), (4), as from 12 July 2016.

[1.1958]

16 Meaning of "relevant offender"

(1) A person is a "relevant offender" for the purposes of section 15 if subsection (2) or (3) applies to the person.

(2) This subsection applies to a person if—

(a) the person has been convicted of a slavery or human trafficking offence,

(b) a court has made a finding that the person is not guilty of a slavery or human trafficking offence by reason of insanity,

(c) a court has made a finding that the person is under a disability and has done the act charged against the person in respect of a slavery or human trafficking offence, or

(d) the person has been cautioned in respect of a slavery or human trafficking offence.

(3) This subsection applies to a person if, under the law of a country outside the United Kingdom—

(a) the person has been convicted of an equivalent offence (whether or not the person has been punished for it),

(b) a court has made, in relation to an equivalent offence, a finding equivalent to a finding that the person is not guilty by reason of insanity,

(c) a court has made, in relation to an equivalent offence, a finding equivalent to a finding that the person is under a disability and has done the act charged against the person, or

(d) the person has been cautioned in respect of an equivalent offence.

(4) An "equivalent offence" means an act which—

(a) constituted an offence under the law of the country concerned, and

(b) would have constituted a slavery or human trafficking offence under the law of England and Wales if it had been done in England and Wales, or by a UK national, or as regards the United Kingdom.

(5) For the purposes of subsection (4) an act punishable under the law of a country outside the United Kingdom constitutes an offence under that law, however it is described in that law.

(6) On an application under section 15 where subsection (3) is alleged to apply to the defendant, the condition in subsection (4)(b) is to be taken as met unless—

(a) not later than provided by rules of court, the defendant serves on the applicant a notice which states that in the defendant's opinion the condition is not met, shows the grounds for that opinion, and requires the applicant to prove that the condition is met, or

(b) the court permits the defendant to require the applicant to prove that the condition is met without service of such a notice.

(7) References in this section to convictions, findings and cautions include those taking place before this section comes into force.

NOTES

Commencement: 31 July 2015.

Rules: the Magistrates' Courts (Modern Slavery Act 2015) Rules 2015, SI 2015/1478.

[1.1959]

17 Effect of slavery and trafficking prevention orders

(1) A slavery and trafficking prevention order is an order prohibiting the defendant from doing anything described in the order.

(2) The only prohibitions that may be included in the order are those which the court is satisfied are necessary for the purpose of protecting persons generally, or particular persons, from the physical or psychological harm which would be likely to occur if the defendant committed a slavery or human trafficking offence.

(3) The order may prohibit the defendant from doing things in any part of the United Kingdom, and anywhere outside the United Kingdom.

(4) Subject to section 18(1), a prohibition contained in a slavery and trafficking prevention order has effect—

(a) for a fixed period, specified in the order, of at least 5 years, or

(b) until further order.

(5) A slavery and trafficking prevention order—

(a) may specify that some of its prohibitions have effect until further order and some for a fixed period;

(b) may specify different periods for different prohibitions.

(6) If a court makes a slavery and trafficking prevention order in relation to a person who is already subject to such an order (whether made by that court or another), the earlier order ceases to have effect.

NOTES

Commencement: 31 July 2015.

[1.1960]

18 Prohibitions on foreign travel

(1) A prohibition on foreign travel contained in a slavery and trafficking prevention order must be for a fixed period of not more than 5 years.

(2) A "prohibition on foreign travel" means—

(a) a prohibition on travelling to any country outside the United Kingdom named or described in the order,

(b) a prohibition on travelling to any country outside the United Kingdom other than a country named or described in the order, or

(c) a prohibition on travelling to any country outside the United Kingdom.

(3) Subsection (1) does not prevent a prohibition on foreign travel from being extended for a further period (of no more than 5 years each time) under section 20.

(4) A slavery and trafficking prevention order that contains a prohibition within subsection (2)(c) must require the defendant to surrender all of the defendant's passports at a police station specified in the order—

(a) on or before the date when the prohibition takes effect, or

(b) within a period specified in the order.

(5) Any passports surrendered must be returned as soon as reasonably practicable after the person ceases to be subject to a slavery and trafficking prevention order containing a prohibition within subsection (2)(c).

(6) Subsection (5) does not apply in relation to—

(a) a passport issued by or on behalf of the authorities of a country outside the United Kingdom if the passport has been returned to those authorities;

(b) a passport issued by or on behalf of an international organisation if the passport has been returned to that organisation.

NOTES

Commencement: 31 July 2015.

[1.1961]

19 Requirement to provide name and address

(1) A slavery and trafficking prevention order may (as well as imposing prohibitions on the defendant) require the defendant to comply with subsections (3) to (6).

(2) It may do so only if the court is satisfied that the requirement is necessary for the purpose of protecting persons generally, or particular persons, from the physical or psychological harm which would be likely to occur if the defendant committed a slavery or human trafficking offence.

(3) Before the end of the period of 3 days beginning with the day on which a slavery and trafficking prevention order requiring the defendant to comply with subsections (3) to (6) is first served the defendant must, in the way specified in the order, notify the person specified in the order of the relevant matters.

(4) The relevant matters are—

(a) the defendant's name and, where the defendant uses one or more other names, each of those names, and

(b) the defendant's home address.

(5) If while the defendant is subject to the order the defendant—

(a) uses a name which has not been notified under the order, or

(b) changes home address,

the defendant must, in the way specified in the order, notify the person specified in the order of the new name or the new home address.

(6) The notification must be given before the end of the period of 3 days beginning with the day on which the defendant uses the name or changes home address.

(7) Where the order requires the defendant to notify the Director General of the National Crime Agency[, an immigration officer or the Gangmasters and Labour Abuse Authority], the Director General[, the officer or the Authority] must give details of any notification to the chief officer of police for each relevant police area.

(8) "Relevant police area" means—

(a) where the defendant notifies a new name, the police area where the defendant lives;

(b) where the defendant notifies a change of home address, the police area where the defendant lives and (if different) the police area where the defendant lived before the change of home address.

NOTES

Commencement: 31 July 2015.

Sub-s (7): words in square brackets substituted by the Immigration Act 2016, s 11(1), Sch 2, paras 8, 11, as from 12 July 2016.

[1.1962]

20 Variation, renewal and discharge

(1) A person within subsection (2) may apply to the appropriate court for an order varying, renewing or discharging a slavery and trafficking prevention order.

(2) The persons are—

(a) the defendant;

(b) the chief officer of police for the area in which the defendant lives;

(c) a chief officer of police who believes that the defendant is in, or is intending to come to, that officer's police area;

(d) where the order was made on an application under section 15 by a chief officer of police, that officer;

(e) where the order was made on an application under section 15 by an immigration officer, an immigration officer;

(f) where the order was made on an application under section 15 by the Director General of the National Crime Agency ("the Director General"), the Director General;

[(g) where the order was made on an application under section 15 by the Gangmasters and Labour Abuse Authority, the Authority].

(3) On the application the court, after hearing—

(a) the person making the application, and

(b) the other persons mentioned in subsection (2) (if they wish to be heard),

may make any order varying, renewing or discharging the slavery and trafficking prevention order that the court considers appropriate.

(4) An order may be renewed, or varied so as to impose additional prohibitions on the defendant or require the defendant to comply with section 19(3) to (6), only if the court is satisfied that—

(a) there is a risk that the defendant may commit a slavery or human trafficking offence, and

(b) it is necessary to renew or vary the order for the purpose of protecting persons generally, or particular persons, from the physical or psychological harm which would be likely to occur if the defendant committed such an offence.

(5) Any renewed or varied order—

(a) may contain only those prohibitions which the court is satisfied are necessary for that purpose,

(b) may require the defendant to comply with section 19(3) to (6) only if the court is satisfied that the requirement is necessary for that purpose.

(6) The court must not discharge an order before the end of 5 years beginning with the day on which the order was made, without the consent of—

(a) the defendant and the chief officer of police for the area in which the defendant lives, or

(b) where the application is made by a chief officer of police, the defendant and that chief officer.

(7) Subsection (6) does not apply to an order containing a prohibition on foreign travel and no other prohibitions.

(8) An application under this section may be made—

(a) where the appropriate court is the Crown Court, in accordance with rules of court;

(b) in any other case, by complaint.

(9) Where an immigration officer[, the Director General or the Gangmasters and Labour Abuse Authority] makes an application under this section, the officer[, the Director General or the Authority] must give notice of the application to the chief officer of police for—

(a) the police area where the defendant lives, or

(b) a police area which the immigration officer[, the Director General or the Authority] believes the defendant is in or is intending to come to.

(10) In this section "the appropriate court" means—

(a) where the Crown Court or the Court of Appeal made the slavery and trafficking prevention order, the Crown Court;

(b) where an adult magistrates' court made the order—

(i) that court,

(ii) an adult magistrates' court for the area in which the defendant lives, or

(iii) where the application is made by a chief officer of police, any adult magistrates' court acting for a local justice area that includes any part of the chief officer's police area;

(c) where a youth court made the order and the defendant is under 18—

(i) that court,

(ii) a youth court for the area in which the defendant lives, or

(iii) where the application is made by a chief officer of police, any youth court acting for a local justice area that includes any part of the chief officer's police area;

(d) where a youth court made the order and the defendant is 18 or over—

(i) an adult magistrates' court for the area in which the defendant lives, or

(ii) where the application is made by a chief officer of police, any adult magistrates' court acting for a local justice area that includes any part of the chief officer's police area.

NOTES

Commencement: 31 July 2015.

Sub-s (2): para (g) inserted by the Immigration Act 2016, s 11(1), Sch 2, paras 8, 12(1), (2), as from 12 July 2016.

Sub-s (9): words in square brackets substituted by the Immigration Act 2016, s 11(1), Sch 2, paras 8, 12(1), (3), as from 12 July 2016.

[1.1963]

21 Interim slavery and trafficking prevention orders

(1) This section applies where an application under section 15 ("the main application") has not been determined.

(2) An application for an interim slavery and trafficking prevention order—

(a) may be made by the complaint by which the main application is made, or

(b) if the main application has been made, may be made by the person who has made that application, by complaint to the court to which that application has been made.

(3) The court may, if it considers it just to do so, make an interim slavery and trafficking prevention order.

(4) An interim slavery and trafficking prevention order is an order which prohibits the defendant from doing anything described in the order.

(5) The order may prohibit the defendant from doing things in any part of the United Kingdom, and anywhere outside the United Kingdom.

(6) The order may (as well as imposing prohibitions on the defendant) require the defendant to comply with subsections (3) to (6) of section 19.

If it does, those subsections apply as if references to a slavery and trafficking prevention order were to an interim slavery and trafficking prevention order.

(7) The order—

(a) has effect only for a fixed period, specified in the order;

(b) ceases to have effect, if it has not already done so, on the determination of the main application.

(8) The applicant or the defendant may by complaint apply to the court that made the interim slavery and trafficking prevention order for the order to be varied, renewed or discharged.

NOTES

Commencement: 31 July 2015.

Offences and Supplementary Provision

[1.1964]

30 Offences

(1) A person who, without reasonable excuse, does anything that the person is prohibited from doing by—

(a) a slavery and trafficking prevention order,

(b) an interim slavery and trafficking prevention order,

(c) a slavery and trafficking risk order,

(d) an interim slavery and trafficking risk order,

(e) a slavery and trafficking prevention order under Schedule 3 to the Human Trafficking and Exploitation (Criminal Justice and Support for Victims) Act (Northern Ireland) 2015 (c 2 (NI)), . . .

(f) an interim slavery and trafficking prevention order under that Schedule to that Act,

[(g) a trafficking and exploitation prevention order under section 17 or 18 of the Human Trafficking and Exploitation (Scotland) Act 2015 (asp 12),

(h) an interim trafficking and exploitation prevention order under section 24 of that Act,

(i) a trafficking and exploitation risk order under section 26 of that Act, or

(j) an interim trafficking and exploitation risk order under section 30 of that Act,]

commits an offence.

(2) A person commits an offence if, without reasonable excuse, the person fails to comply with a requirement imposed under—

(a) section 18(4) or 25(4) (requirement to surrender passports), or

(b) section 19(1), 21(6), 26(1) or 28(6) (requirement to provide name and address).

(3) A person guilty of an offence under this section is liable—

(a) on conviction on indictment, to imprisonment for a term not exceeding 5 years;

(b) on summary conviction, to imprisonment for a term not exceeding 6 months or a fine or both.

(4) Where a person is convicted of an offence under this section, it is not open to the court by or before which the person is convicted to make an order for conditional discharge in respect of the offence.

NOTES

Commencement: 31 July 2015.

Sub-s (1): word omitted from para (e) repealed, and paras (g)–(j) inserted, by the Human Trafficking and Exploitation (Scotland) Act 2015 (Consequential Provisions and Modifications) Order 2016, SI 2016/1031, art 3, Schedule, para 3(1), (2), as from 17 December 2016.

[1.1965]
[30A Enforcement by Gangmasters and Labour Abuse Authority
(1) The Secretary of State may make arrangements with the Gangmasters and Labour Abuse Authority for officers of the Authority to act for the purposes of this Part in taking action in circumstances in which it appears that an offence under this Part which is a labour market offence (within the meaning of section 3 of the Immigration Act 2016) has been, is being or may be committed.
(2) For provision about the powers of such an officer who is acting for the purposes of this Part, see section 114B of the Police and Criminal Evidence Act 1984 (PACE powers for labour abuse prevention officers).]

NOTES
Commencement: 12 July 2016.
Inserted by the Immigration Act 2016, s 11(1), Sch 2, paras 8, 16, as from 12 July 2016.

PART 5
PROTECTION OF VICTIMS

[1.1966]
45 Defence for slavery or trafficking victims who commit an offence
(1) A person is not guilty of an offence if—
(a) the person is aged 18 or over when the person does the act which constitutes the offence,
(b) the person does that act because the person is compelled to do it,
(c) the compulsion is attributable to slavery or to relevant exploitation, and
(d) a reasonable person in the same situation as the person and having the person's relevant characteristics would have no realistic alternative to doing that act.
(2) A person may be compelled to do something by another person or by the person's circumstances.
(3) Compulsion is attributable to slavery or to relevant exploitation only if—
(a) it is, or is part of, conduct which constitutes an offence under section 1 or conduct which constitutes relevant exploitation, or
(b) it is a direct consequence of a person being, or having been, a victim of slavery or a victim of relevant exploitation.
(4) A person is not guilty of an offence if—
(a) the person is under the age of 18 when the person does the act which constitutes the offence,
(b) the person does that act as a direct consequence of the person being, or having been, a victim of slavery or a victim of relevant exploitation, and
(c) a reasonable person in the same situation as the person and having the person's relevant characteristics would do that act.
(5) For the purposes of this section—
"relevant characteristics" means age, sex and any physical or mental illness or disability;
"relevant exploitation" is exploitation (within the meaning of section 3) that is attributable to the exploited person being, or having been, a victim of human trafficking.
(6) In this section references to an act include an omission.
(7) Subsections (1) and (4) do not apply to an offence listed in Schedule 4.
(8) The Secretary of State may by regulations amend Schedule 4.

NOTES
Commencement: 31 July 2015.

[1.1967]
53 Overseas domestic workers
(1) Immigration rules must make provision for leave to remain in the United Kingdom to be granted to an overseas domestic worker—
(a) who has been determined to be a victim of slavery or human trafficking, and
(b) in relation to whom such other requirements are met as may be provided for by the rules.
(2) Immigration rules must make provision as to the conditions on which such leave is to be granted, and must in particular provide—
(a) that the leave is to be for the purpose of working as a domestic worker in a private household;
(b) for a person who has such leave to be able to change employer (subject to paragraph (a)).
(3) Immigration rules may specify a maximum period for which a person may have leave to remain in the United Kingdom by virtue of subsection (1).
If they do so, the specified maximum period must not be less than 6 months.
(4) For the purposes of this section an overseas domestic worker has been determined to be a victim of slavery or human trafficking if a public authority has determined that he or she is such a victim—
(a) under regulations made under section 50(2)(b), or
(b) where no such regulations apply, under arrangements identified in the immigration rules.
(5) The Secretary of State must issue guidance to persons having functions under the Immigration Acts about the exercise of those functions in relation to an overseas domestic worker who may be a victim of slavery or human trafficking.
(6) The guidance must provide for a period during which no enforcement action should be taken against such an overseas domestic worker in respect of his or her—
(a) remaining in the United Kingdom beyond the time limited by his or her leave to enter or remain, or
(b) breaching a condition of that leave relating to his or her employment,

if he or she did so because of the matters relied on as slavery or human trafficking.

(7) In this section—

"enforcement action" has the meaning given by section 24A of the Immigration Act 1971;

"immigration rules" has the same meaning as in that Act;

"overseas domestic worker" means a person who, under the immigration rules, has (or last had) leave to enter or remain in the United Kingdom as—

(a) a domestic worker in a private household, or

(b) a private servant in a diplomatic household.

NOTES

Commencement: 15 October 2015.

PART 6
TRANSPARENCY IN SUPPLY CHAINS ETC

[1.1968]

54 Transparency in supply chains etc

(1) A commercial organisation within subsection (2) must prepare a slavery and human trafficking statement for each financial year of the organisation.

(2) A commercial organisation is within this subsection if it—

(a) supplies goods or services, and

(b) has a total turnover of not less than an amount prescribed by regulations made by the Secretary of State.

(3) For the purposes of subsection (2)(b), an organisation's total turnover is to be determined in accordance with regulations made by the Secretary of State.

(4) A slavery and human trafficking statement for a financial year is—

(a) a statement of the steps the organisation has taken during the financial year to ensure that slavery and human trafficking is not taking place—

(i) in any of its supply chains, and

(ii) in any part of its own business, or

(b) a statement that the organisation has taken no such steps.

(5) An organisation's slavery and human trafficking statement may include information about—

(a) the organisation's structure, its business and its supply chains;

(b) its policies in relation to slavery and human trafficking;

(c) its due diligence processes in relation to slavery and human trafficking in its business and supply chains;

(d) the parts of its business and supply chains where there is a risk of slavery and human trafficking taking place, and the steps it has taken to assess and manage that risk;

(e) its effectiveness in ensuring that slavery and human trafficking is not taking place in its business or supply chains, measured against such performance indicators as it considers appropriate;

(f) the training about slavery and human trafficking available to its staff.

(6) A slavery and human trafficking statement—

(a) if the organisation is a body corporate other than a limited liability partnership, must be approved by the board of directors (or equivalent management body) and signed by a director (or equivalent);

(b) if the organisation is a limited liability partnership, must be approved by the members and signed by a designated member;

(c) if the organisation is a limited partnership registered under the Limited Partnerships Act 1907, must be signed by a general partner;

(d) if the organisation is any other kind of partnership, must be signed by a partner.

(7) If the organisation has a website, it must—

(a) publish the slavery and human trafficking statement on that website, and

(b) include a link to the slavery and human trafficking statement in a prominent place on that website's homepage.

(8) If the organisation does not have a website, it must provide a copy of the slavery and human trafficking statement to anyone who makes a written request for one, and must do so before the end of the period of 30 days beginning with the day on which the request is received.

(9) The Secretary of State—

(a) may issue guidance about the duties imposed on commercial organisations by this section;

(b) must publish any such guidance in a way the Secretary of State considers appropriate.

(10) The guidance may in particular include further provision about the kind of information which may be included in a slavery and human trafficking statement.

(11) The duties imposed on commercial organisations by this section are enforceable by the Secretary of State bringing civil proceedings in the High Court for an injunction or, in Scotland, for specific performance of a statutory duty under section 45 of the Court of Session Act 1988.

(12) For the purposes of this section—

"commercial organisation" means—

(a) a body corporate (wherever incorporated) which carries on a business, or part of a business, in any part of the United Kingdom, or

(b) a partnership (wherever formed) which carries on a business, or part of a business, in any part of the United Kingdom,

and for this purpose "business" includes a trade or profession;

"partnership" means—

(a) a partnership within the Partnership Act 1890,

(b) a limited partnership registered under the Limited Partnerships Act 1907, or

(c) a firm, or an entity of a similar character, formed under the law of a country outside the United Kingdom;

"slavery and human trafficking" means—

(a) conduct which constitutes an offence under any of the following—

(i) section 1, 2 or 4 of this Act,

(ii) section 1, 2 or 4 of the Human Trafficking and Exploitation (Criminal Justice and Support for Victims) Act (Northern Ireland) 2015 (c 2 (NI)) (equivalent offences in Northern Ireland),

[(iii) section 1 or 4 of the Human Trafficking and Exploitation (Scotland) Act 2015 (asp 12) (equivalent offences in Scotland), or]

(b) conduct which would constitute an offence in a part of the United Kingdom under any of those provisions if the conduct took place in that part of the United Kingdom.

NOTES

Commencement: 29 October 2015.

Sub-s (12): in the definition "slavery and human trafficking" sub-para (a)(iii) was substituted (for the original sub-paras (a)(iii)–(v)) by the Human Trafficking and Exploitation (Scotland) Act 2015 (Consequential Provisions and Modifications) Order 2016, SI 2016/1031, art 3, Schedule, para 3(1), (5), as from 17 December 2016.

Transitional provision: the Modern Slavery Act 2015 (Commencement No 3 and Transitional Provision) Regulations 2015, SI 2015/1816, reg 3 provides that this section does not have effect in respect of a financial year ending before 31 March 2016.

Guidance issued under sub-s (9) above: see Transparency in Supply Chains etc – A practical guide (2015) at **[4.91]**.

Regulations: the Modern Slavery Act 2015 (Transparency in Supply Chains) Regulations 2015, SI 2015/1833 (prescribing a total turnover of £36 million for the purposes of sub-s (2)(b)).

PART 7
MISCELLANEOUS AND GENERAL

Miscellaneous

[1.1969]

[54A Gangmasters and Labour Abuse Authority: information gateways

(1) A specified person may disclose information to the Gangmasters and Labour Abuse Authority (the "Authority") or a relevant officer if the disclosure is made for the purposes of the exercise of any function of the Authority or the officer under this Act.

(2) Information obtained by the Authority or a relevant officer in connection with the exercise of any function of the Authority or the officer under this Act may be used by the Authority or the officer in connection with the exercise of any other such function of the Authority or the officer.

(3) The Authority or a relevant officer may disclose to a specified person information obtained in connection with the exercise of any function of the Authority or the officer under this Act if the disclosure is made for the purposes of the exercise of any function of the specified person.

(4) A disclosure of information which is authorised by this section does not breach—

(a) an obligation of confidence owed by the person making the disclosure, or

(b) any other restriction on the disclosure of information (however imposed).

(5) But nothing in this section authorises the making of a disclosure which—

(a) contravenes [the data protection legislation], or

(b) is prohibited by Part 1 of the Regulation of Investigatory Powers Act 2000.

(6) This section does not limit the circumstances in which information may be disclosed apart from this section.

(7) "Specified person" means a person specified in Schedule 4A (information gateways: specified persons).

(8) The Secretary of State may by regulations amend Schedule 4A.

(9) In this section[–

"the data protection legislation" has the same meaning as in the Data Protection Act 2018 (see section 3 of that Act);]

"relevant officer" means an officer of the Authority who is acting for the purposes of Part 1 or 2 of this Act (see sections 11A and 30A).]

NOTES

Commencement: 12 July 2016.

Inserted by the Immigration Act 2016, s 31, Sch 3, paras 28, 30, as from 12 July 2016.

Sub-s (5): words in square brackets substituted by the Data Protection Act 2018, s 211, Sch 19, Pt 1, para 191(1), (2), as from 25 May 2018 (for transitional provisions and savings relating to the repeal of the Data Protection Act 1998, see Sch 20 to the 2018 Act at **[1.2232]**)

Sub-s (9): definition "the data protection legislation" (and the preceding dash) inserted by the Data Protection Act 2018, s 211, Sch 19, Pt 1, para 191(1), (3), as from 25 May 2018 (for transitional provisions and savings relating to the repeal of the Data Protection Act 1998, see Sch 20 to the 2018 Act at **[1.2232]**)

Regulations: as of 15 May 2019, no Regulations had been made under this section.

General

[1.1970]

56 Interpretation

(1) For the purposes of this Act a person is a victim of slavery if he or she is a victim of—

(a) conduct which constitutes an offence under section 1, or

(b) conduct which would have constituted an offence under that section if that section had been in force when the conduct occurred.

(2) For the purposes of this Act a person is a victim of human trafficking if he or she is the victim of—

(a) conduct which constitutes an offence under section 2, or would constitute an offence under that section if the person responsible for the conduct were a UK national, or

(b) conduct which would have been within paragraph (a) if section 2 had been in force when the conduct occurred.

(3) In this Act—

"child" means a person under the age of 18;

"country" includes territory or other part of the world;

"immigration officer" means a person appointed as an immigration officer under paragraph 1 of Schedule 2 to the Immigration Act 1971;

"public authority" means any public authority within the meaning of section 6 of the Human Rights Act 1998, other than a court or tribunal;

"UK national" has the meaning given by section 13.

NOTES

Commencement: 26 March 2015.

[1.1971]

57 Consequential provision

(1) Schedule 5 contains minor and consequential amendments.

(2) The Secretary of State may by regulations make whatever provision the Secretary of State thinks appropriate in consequence of this Act.

(3) The provision which may be made by regulations under subsection (2) includes provision amending, repealing or revoking any provision of an Act or subordinate legislation (including an Act passed or subordinate legislation made in the same session as this Act).

NOTES

Commencement: 26 March 2015 (sub-ss (2), (3)); 31 July 2015 (sub-s (1) certain purposes); 17 March 2016 (otherwise).

Regulations: the Modern Slavery Act 2015 (Consequential Amendments) Regulations 2015, SI 2015/1472; the Modern Slavery Act 2015 (Consequential Amendments) Regulations 2016, SI 2016/244

[1.1972]

58 Regulations

(1) Any power of the Secretary of State to make regulations under this Act is exercisable by statutory instrument.

(2) A statutory instrument containing regulations made by the Secretary of State under this Act is subject to annulment in pursuance of a resolution of either House of Parliament, unless—

(a) it contains only regulations under section 61 (commencement), or

(b) it contains regulations to which subsection (4) applies.

(3) A statutory instrument containing regulations to which subsection (4) applies may not be made unless a draft of the instrument has been laid before, and approved by a resolution of, each House of Parliament.

(4) This section applies to—

(a) regulations under section 14(4) (power to amend Schedule 1);

(b) regulations under section 31(1) (power to amend section 30);

(c) regulations under section 43(9) which remove a public authority from Schedule 3, other than in consequence of the authority having ceased to exist;

(d) regulations under section 43(9) which contain the provision mentioned in section 43(10) (power to modify section 43);

(e) regulations under section 45(8) (power to amend Schedule 4);

(f) regulations under section 48(6) (independent child trafficking advocates);

(g) regulations under section 50 (identifying and supporting victims);

(h) regulations under section 52(6) which remove a public authority from section 52(5), other than in consequence of the authority having ceased to exist;

(i) regulations under section 54(2) (minimum turnover for application of section 54);

(j) the first regulations under section 54(3) (definition of turnover for purposes of section 54);

[(ja) regulations under section 54A(8) (power to amend Schedule 4A);]

(k) regulations under section 57(2) (consequential provision) which amend, or repeal any provision of, an Act.

(5) Regulations made by the Scottish Ministers under section 43(7)—

(a) are subject to the affirmative procedure if they contain—

(i) provision removing a public authority from Schedule 3, other than in consequence of the authority having ceased to exist, or

(ii) the provision mentioned in section 43(10) (power to modify section 43);

(b) otherwise, are subject to the negative procedure.

(6) The power of the Department of Justice in Northern Ireland to make regulations under section 43(8) is exercisable by statutory rule for the purposes of the Statutory Rules (Northern Ireland) Order 1979 (SI 1979/1573 (NI 12)).

(7) Regulations made by the Department of Justice in Northern Ireland under section 43(8) are subject to negative resolution (within the meaning of section 41(6) of the Interpretation (Northern Ireland) Act 1954 (c 33 (NI))), unless they are regulations to which subsection (9) applies.

(8) The Department of Justice in Northern Ireland may not make regulations to which subsection (9) applies unless a draft of the regulations has been laid before, and approved by a resolution of, the Northern Ireland Assembly.

(9) This subsection applies to regulations under section 43(8) which contain—

- (a) provision removing a public authority from Schedule 3, other than in consequence of the authority having ceased to exist, or
- (b) the provision mentioned in section 43(10) (power to modify section 43).

(10) Regulations made under this Act may—

- (a) make different provision for different purposes;
- (b) include saving, transitional, transitory, supplementary or consequential provision.

(11) This section (apart from subsection (10)) does not apply to regulations under paragraph 5 of Schedule 2.

NOTES

Commencement: 26 March 2015.

Sub-s (4): para (ja) inserted by the Immigration Act 2016, s 31, Sch 3, paras 28, 32, as from 12 July 2016.

[1.1973]

59 Financial provisions

There is to be paid out of money provided by Parliament—

- (a) any expenditure incurred under or by virtue of this Act by the Secretary of State;
- (b) any increase attributable to this Act in the sums payable under any other Act out of money so provided.

NOTES

Commencement: 26 March 2015.

[1.1974]

60 Extent

(1) Parts 1, 2 and 5 (except for section 53) [and section 54A, and Schedule 4A, in Part 7] extend to England and Wales only, subject to subsection (4).

(2) *(Relates to the extent of Part 3 and is outside the scope of this work.)*

(3) Part 4, section 53 in Part 5 and Parts 6 and 7 [(except for section 54A and Schedule 4A)] extend to England and Wales, Scotland and Northern Ireland, subject to subsections (4) and (5).

(4) An amendment or repeal made by this Act has the same extent as the provision amended or repealed.

(5) *(Relates to the extent of Sch 5 and is outside the scope of this work.)*

(6) Her Majesty may by Order in Council provide for any of the provisions of this Act to extend, with or without modifications, to any of the Channel Islands or to the Isle of Man.

NOTES

Commencement: 26 March 2015.

Sub-ss (1), (3): words in square brackets inserted by the Immigration Act 2016, s 31, Sch 3, paras 28, 33, as from 12 July 2016.

[1.1975]

61 Commencement

(1) This Act comes into force on whatever day or days the Secretary of State appoints by regulations, subject to subsections (2) and (3).

(2) Section 48(7) comes into force at the end of the period of 2 months beginning with the day on which this Act is passed.

(3) This Part, other than section 57(1) and Schedule 5, comes into force on the day on which this Act is passed.

(4) Before making regulations bringing into force any of the provisions of Part 3, the Secretary of State must consult—

- (a) the Scottish Ministers, so far as the provisions extend to Scotland;
- (b) the Department of Justice in Northern Ireland, so far as the provisions extend to Northern Ireland.

(5) The Secretary of State may not make regulations under subsection (1) bringing into force section 48(1) to (6) (or any part of it) before the end of the period of 9 months beginning with the day on which this Act is passed.

(6) After the end of that period—

- (a) if a resolution is passed by each House of Parliament that section 48(1) to (6) (or any part of it) should come into force, the Secretary of State must make regulations under subsection (1) bringing into force that section (or that part of it);
- (b) the Secretary of State may not make regulations under subsection (1) bringing into force section 48(1) to (6) (or any part of it) unless required to do so by paragraph (a).

(7) Regulations made by virtue of subsection (6)(a) must bring into force section 48(1) to (6) (or the part of it specified in the resolutions) before the end of the period of one month beginning with the day on which the resolutions are passed (or, if they are passed on different days, the day on which the later of them is passed).

(8) The Secretary of State may by regulations make whatever saving, transitory or transitional provision the Secretary of State thinks appropriate in connection with the coming into force of any provision of this Act.

NOTES

Commencement: 26 March 2015.

Regulations: the Modern Slavery Act 2015 (Commencement No 1, Saving and Transitional Provisions) Regulations 2015, SI 2015/1476; the Modern Slavery Act 2015 (Commencement No 2) Regulations 2015, SI 2015/1690; the Modern Slavery Act 2015 (Commencement No 3 and Transitional Provision) Regulations 2015, SI 2015/1816; the Modern Slavery Act 2015 (Commencement No 4) Regulations 2016, SI 2016/243; the Modern Slavery Act 2015 (Commencement No 5) Regulations 2016, SI 2016/740.

[1.1976]

62 Short title

This Act may be cited as the Modern Slavery Act 2015.

NOTES

Commencement: 26 March 2015.

SCHEDULES

SCHEDULE 1
SLAVERY AND HUMAN TRAFFICKING OFFENCES

Section 14

Nationality, Immigration and Asylum Act 2002 (c 41)

[1.1977]

1. An offence under section 145 of the Nationality, Immigration and Asylum Act 2002 (trafficking for prostitution).

Sexual Offences Act 2003 (c 42)

2. (1) An offence under section 57, 58, 58A, 59 or 59A of the Sexual Offences Act 2003 (trafficking for sexual exploitation).

(2) An offence under section 62 of that Act (committing offence with intent to commit relevant sexual offence), where the relevant sexual offence the person in question intended to commit was an offence under section 57, 58, 58A, 59 or 59A of that Act.

Criminal Justice (Scotland) Act 2003 (asp 7)

3. An offence under section 22 of the Criminal Justice (Scotland) Act 2003 (traffic in prostitution etc).

Asylum and Immigration (Treatment of Claimants, etc) Act 2004 (c 19)

4. An offence under section 4 of the Asylum and Immigration (Treatment of Claimants, etc) Act 2004 (trafficking for exploitation).

Coroners and Justice Act 2009 (c 25)

5. An offence under section 71 of the Coroners and Justice Act 2009 (slavery, servitude and forced or compulsory labour).

Criminal Justice and Licensing (Scotland) Act 2010 (asp 13)

6. An offence under section 47 of the Criminal Justice and Licensing (Scotland) Act 2010 (slavery, servitude and forced or compulsory labour).

Modern Slavery Act 2015 (c 30)

7. An offence under section 1, 2 or 4 of this Act.

Human Trafficking and Exploitation (Criminal Justice and Support for Victims) Act (Northern Ireland) 2015 (c 2 (NI))

8. An offence under section 1, 2 or 4 of the Human Trafficking and Exploitation (Criminal Justice and Support for Victims) Act (Northern Ireland) 2015 (slavery, servitude and forced or compulsory labour; human trafficking).

[Human Trafficking and Exploitation (Scotland) Act 2015 (asp 12)

8A. (1) An offence under section 1 or 4 of the Human Trafficking and Exploitation (Scotland) Act 2015 (human trafficking; slavery, servitude and forced or compulsory labour).

(2) An offence aggravated by a connection with human trafficking activity in accordance with section 5 of that Act (general aggravation of offence).]

Ancillary offences

9. (1) An offence of attempting or conspiring to commit an offence listed in this Schedule.

(2) An offence committed by aiding, abetting, counselling, procuring or inciting the commission of an offence listed in this Schedule.

(3) An offence under Part 2 of the Serious Crime Act 2007 (encouraging or assisting) where the offence (or one of the offences) which the person in question intends or believes would be committed is an offence listed in this Schedule.

NOTES

Commencement: 31 July 2015.

Para 8A: inserted by the Human Trafficking and Exploitation (Scotland) Act 2015 (Consequential Provisions and Modifications) Order 2016, SI 2016/1031, art 3, Schedule, para 3(1), (6), as from 17 December 2016.

[SCHEDULE 4A
INFORMATION GATEWAYS: SPECIFIED PERSONS]

[Section 54A]

[1.1978]

[Authorities with functions in connection with the labour market etc

The Secretary of State.

A person by whom, or by whose officers, labour market enforcement functions (within the meaning given by section 3 of the Immigration Act 2016) are exercisable.

Law enforcement and border security

A chief officer of police for a police area in England and Wales.

The chief constable of the British Transport Police Force.

An immigration officer.

Local government

A county council in England or Wales.

A county borough council in Wales.

A district council in England.

A London borough council.

The Greater London Authority.

The Common Council of the City of London.

The Council of the Isles of Scilly.

Health bodies

A National Health Service trust established under section 25 of the National Health Service Act 2006 or section 18 of the National Health Service (Wales) Act 2006.

An NHS foundation trust within the meaning given by section 30 of the National Health Service Act 2006.

A Local Health Board established under section 11 of the National Health Service (Wales) Act 2006.

Other

The Independent Anti-slavery Commissioner.]

NOTES

Commencement: 12 July 2016.

Inserted by the Immigration Act 2016, s 31, Sch 3, paras 28, 35, as from 12 July 2016.

HUMAN TRAFFICKING AND EXPLOITATION (SCOTLAND) ACT 2015

(2015 asp 12)

ARRANGEMENT OF SECTIONS

PART 1
OFFENCES

Human Trafficking

An Act of the Scottish Parliament to make provision about human trafficking and slavery, servitude and forced or compulsory labour, including provision about offences and sentencing, provision for victim support and provision to reduce activity related to offences.

4 November 2015

NOTES

Most of this Act covers matters outside the scope of this work and only a few sections are reproduced here. For reasons of space, the subject matter of sections not printed is not annotated.

PART 1
OFFENCES

Human Trafficking

[1.1979]

1 Offence of human trafficking

(1) A person commits an offence if the person—
- (a) takes a relevant action, and
- (b) does so with a view to another person being exploited.

(2) In this Part, "relevant action" means an action which is any of the following—
- (a) the recruitment of another person,
- (b) the transportation or transfer of another person,
- (c) the harbouring or receiving of another person,
- (d) the exchange or transfer of control over another person, or
- (e) the arrangement or facilitation of any of the actions mentioned in paragraphs (a) to (d).

(3) It is irrelevant whether the other person consents to any part of the relevant action.

(4) For the purposes of subsection (1), a person takes a relevant action with a view to another person being exploited only if—
- (a) the person intends to exploit the other person (in any part of the world) during or after the relevant action, or
- (b) the person knows or ought to know the other person is likely to be exploited (in any part of the world) during or after the relevant action.

(5) An offence under this section is to be known as the offence of human trafficking.

(6) A person who commits an offence of human trafficking is liable
(a) on summary conviction, to imprisonment for a term not exceeding 12 months or a fine not exceeding the statutory maximum (or both),
(b) on conviction on indictment, to imprisonment for life or a fine (or both).

NOTES
Commencement: 31 May 2016.

[1.1980]
2 Application of offence to conduct in United Kingdom and elsewhere
(1) A person mentioned in subsection (2) commits an offence of human trafficking regardless of where the relevant action takes place.
(2) The persons are—
(a) a person who is a UK national,
(b) a person who at the time of the offence was habitually resident in Scotland,
(c) a body incorporated under the law of a part of the United Kingdom.
(3) A person not mentioned in subsection (2) commits an offence of human trafficking if—
(a) any part of the relevant action takes place in the United Kingdom, or
(b) the relevant action is taken with a view to a person arriving in or entering into, departing from, or travelling within, the United Kingdom.

NOTES
Commencement: 31 May 2016.

[1.1981]
3 Exploitation for purposes of offence of human trafficking
(1) For the purposes of section 1, a person is exploited only if one or more of the following subsections apply in relation to that person.
Slavery, servitude and forced or compulsory labour
(2) The person is the victim of conduct which—
(a) involves the commission of an offence under section 4, or
(b) would constitute such an offence were it done in Scotland.
(3)–(8) (*Outside the scope of this work.*)

NOTES
Commencement: 31 May 2016.

Slavery, Servitude and Forced or Compulsory Labour

[1.1982]
4 Slavery, servitude and forced or compulsory labour
(1) A person commits an offence if—
(a) the person holds another person in slavery or servitude and the circumstances are such that the person knows or ought to know that the other person is so held, or
(b) the person requires another person to perform forced or compulsory labour and the circumstances are such that the person knows or ought to know that the other person is being required to perform such labour.
(2) In subsection (1) the references to holding a person in slavery or servitude or requiring a person to perform forced or compulsory labour are to be construed in accordance with Article 4 of the Human Rights Convention (which prohibits a person from being held in slavery or servitude or being required to perform forced or compulsory labour).
(3) In determining whether a person is being held in slavery or servitude or required to perform forced or compulsory labour, regard is to be had in particular to any personal circumstances of the person (for example the person being a child, or the person's age, or the person's family relationships or health) that may make the person more vulnerable than other persons.
(4) The consent of a person to any of the acts alleged to constitute holding the person in slavery or servitude or requiring the person to perform forced or compulsory labour, does not preclude a determination that the person is being held in slavery or servitude or required to perform forced or compulsory labour.
(5) A person who commits an offence under this section is liable—
(a) on summary conviction, to imprisonment for a term not exceeding 12 months or a fine not exceeding the statutory maximum (or both),
(b) on conviction on indictment, to imprisonment for life or a fine (or both).
(6) In this section "the Human Rights Convention" means the Convention for the Protection of Human Rights and Fundamental Freedoms agreed by the Council of Europe at Rome on 4 November 1950.

NOTES
Commencement: 31 May 2016.

Aggravation as to Human Trafficking

[1.1983]
5 General aggravation of offence
(1) This subsection applies where it is—

(a) libelled in an indictment or specified in a complaint that an offence is aggravated by a connection with human trafficking activity, and
(b) proved that the offence is so aggravated.

(2) An offence is aggravated by a connection with human trafficking activity if the offender is motivated (wholly or partly) by the objective of committing or conspiring to commit the offence of human trafficking.

(3) It is immaterial whether or not in committing an offence the offender in fact enables the offender or another person to commit the offence of human trafficking.

(4) Evidence from a single source is sufficient to prove that an offence is aggravated by a connection with human trafficking activity.

(5) Where subsection (1) applies, the court must—
(a) state on conviction that the offence is aggravated by a connection with human trafficking activity,
(b) record the conviction in a way that shows that the offence is so aggravated,
(c) take the aggravation into account in determining the appropriate sentence, and
(d) state—
(i) where the sentence in respect of the offence is different from that which the court would have imposed if the offence were not so aggravated, the extent of and the reasons for that difference, or
(ii) otherwise, the reasons for there being no such difference.

NOTES

Commencement: 31 May 2016.

[1.1984]

7 Aggravation involving public official

(1) This subsection applies where it is—
(a) libelled in an indictment or specified in a complaint that the offence of human trafficking is aggravated by an abuse of a public position, and
(b) proved that the offence is so aggravated.

(2) The offence of human trafficking is aggravated by an abuse of a public position if the offender is, at the time of committing the offence—
(a) a public official, and
(b) acting or purporting to act in the course of official duties.

(3) Evidence from a single source is sufficient to prove that the offence is aggravated by an abuse of a public position.

(4) Where subsection (1) applies, the court must—
(a) state on conviction that the offence is aggravated by an abuse of a public position,
(b) record the conviction in a way that shows that the offence is so aggravated,
(c) take the aggravation into account in determining the appropriate sentence, and
(d) state—
(i) where the sentence in respect of the offence is different from that which the court would have imposed if the offence were not so aggravated, the extent of and the reasons for that difference, or
(ii) otherwise, the reasons for there being no such difference.

(5) In this section "a public official" means an individual who (whether in Scotland or elsewhere)—
(a) holds a legislative or judicial position of any kind,
(b) exercises a public function in an administrative or other capacity, or
(c) is an official or agent of an international organisation.

(6) For the purpose of subsection (5)(c), "an international organisation" means an organisation whose members are—
(a) countries or territories,
(b) governments of countries or territories,
(c) other international organisations, or
(d) a mixture of any of the above.

(7) The Scottish Ministers may by regulations modify subsections (5) and (6).

NOTES

Commencement: 31 May 2016.
Regulations: as of 15 May 2019, no regulations had been made under this section.

PART 2
PROTECTION OF VICTIMS

Prosecution of Victims

[1.1985]

8 Lord Advocate's instructions on prosecution of victims of offences

(1) The Lord Advocate must issue and publish instructions about the prosecution of a person who is, or appears to be, the victim of an offence—
(a) of human trafficking,
(b) under section 4.

(2) The instructions must in particular include factors to be taken into account or steps to be taken by the prosecutor when deciding whether to prosecute a person in the circumstances mentioned in subsections (3) and (4).

(3) The circumstances are where—

(a) an adult does an act which constitutes an offence because the adult has been compelled to do so, and

(b) the compulsion appears to be directly attributable to the adult being a victim of an offence mentioned in subsection (1).

(4) The circumstances are where—

(a) a child does an act which constitutes an offence, and

(b) the act appears to be done as a consequence of the child being a victim of an offence mentioned in subsection (1).

(5) The Lord Advocate may from time to time revise the instructions.

(6) In this section "prosecutor" means Lord Advocate, Crown Counsel or procurator fiscal (and any person duly authorised to represent or act for them).

NOTES

Commencement: 31 May 2016.

PART 6
FINAL PROVISIONS

[1.1986]

39 Offences by bodies corporate etc

(1) Where—

(a) an offence under this Act has been committed by a body corporate or a Scottish partnership or other unincorporated association, and

(b) it is proved that the offence was committed with the consent or connivance of, or was attributable to any neglect on the part of—

(i) a relevant individual, or

(ii) an individual purporting to act in the capacity of a relevant individual,

the individual (as well as the body corporate, partnership or, as the case may be, other unincorporated association) commits the offence and is liable to be proceeded against and punished accordingly.

(2) In subsection (1), "relevant individual" means—

(a) in relation to a body corporate—

(i) a director, manager, secretary or other similar officer of the body,

(ii) where the affairs of the body are managed by its members, the members,

(b) in relation to a Scottish partnership, a partner,

(c) in relation to an unincorporated association other than a Scottish partnership, a person who is concerned in the management or control of the association.

NOTES

Commencement: 31 May 2016.

[1.1987]

40 Interpretation

In this Act—

"adult" means an individual aged 18 or over,

"captain" means master of a ship or commander of an aircraft,

"child" means a person under 18 years of age,

"ship" includes every description of vessel (including a hovercraft) used in navigation,

"UK national" means—

(a) a British citizen,

(b) a person who is a British subject by virtue of Part 4 of the British Nationality Act 1981 and who has a right of abode in the United Kingdom, or

(c) a person who is a British overseas territories citizen by virtue of a connection with Gibraltar,

"vehicle" means any vehicle other than a ship or an aircraft.

NOTES

Commencement: 5 November 2015.

[1.1988]

41 Regulations

(1) Any power of the Scottish Ministers to make regulations under this Act includes power to make—

(a) different provision for different purposes,

(b) incidental, supplementary, consequential, transitional, transitory or saving provision.

(2) Regulations under—

(a) section 7(7),

(b) section 9(2)(b)(i),

(c) section 9(8),

(d) section 10,

(e) section 12(5),

(f) section 16(2),
(g) section 33(1),
(h) section 42(1) which contain provisions that add to, replace or omit any part of the text of an Act, are subject to the affirmative procedure.

(3) All other regulations under this Act are subject to the negative procedure.

(4) This section does not apply to regulations under section 45.

NOTES

Commencement: 5 November 2015.

[1.1989]

42 Ancillary provision

(1) The Scottish Ministers may by regulations make such incidental, supplementary, consequential, transitional, transitory or saving provision as they consider necessary or expedient for the purposes of, or in connection with, any provision made by or under this Act.

(2) Regulations under subsection (1) may modify any enactment (including this Act).

NOTES

Commencement: 5 November 2015.

Regulations: as of 15 May 2019, no regulations had been made under this section.

[1.1990]

44 Crown application

(1) No contravention by the Crown of any provision made by or under this Act makes the Crown criminally liable.

(2) But the Court of Session may, on the application of the Scottish Ministers or any public body or office-holder having responsibility for enforcing the provision, declare unlawful any act or omission of the Crown which constitutes such a contravention.

(3) Despite subsection (1), any provision made by or under the provisions of this Act applies to persons in the public service of the Crown as it applies to other persons.

NOTES

Commencement: 5 November 2015.

[1.1991]

45 Commencement

(1) This section and sections 40, 41, 42, 44 and 46 come into force on the day after Royal Assent.

(2) The other provisions of this Act come into force on such day as the Scottish Ministers may by regulations appoint.

(3) Different days may be appointed for different purposes.

(4) Regulations under subsection (2) may contain transitional, transitory or saving provision.

NOTES

Commencement: 5 November 2015.

Regulations: the Human Trafficking and Exploitation (Scotland) Act 2015 (Commencement No 1 and Transitory Provisions) Regulations 2016, SSI 2016/128; the Human Trafficking and Exploitation (Scotland) Act 2015 (Commencement No 2 and Transitional Provisions) Regulations 2016, SSI 2016/385; the Human Trafficking and Exploitation (Scotland) Act 2015 (Commencement No 3 and Transitional Provisions) Regulations 2017, SSI 2017/140; the Human Trafficking and Exploitation (Scotland) Act 2015 (Commencement No 4) Regulations 2018, SSI 2018/9.

[1.1992]

46 Short title

The short title of this Act is the Human Trafficking and Exploitation (Scotland) Act 2015.

NOTES

Commencement: 5 November 2015.

SCOTLAND ACT 2016

(2016 c 11)

An Act to amend the Scotland Act 1998 and make provision about the functions of the Scottish Ministers; and for connected purposes.

[23rd March 2016]

NOTES

Most of this Act covers matters outside the scope of this work and only a few sections are reproduced here. For reasons of space, the subject matter of sections not printed is not annotated. By virtue of s 72 (not reproduced) ss 37–39 came into force on 23 May 2016, and ss 70, 71, 73 came into force on 23 March 2016.

PART 4
OTHER LEGISLATIVE COMPETENCE

[1.1993]
37 Equal opportunities

(1) Section L2 in Part 2 of Schedule 5 to the Scotland Act 1998 (equal opportunities) is amended as follows.
(2) Omit the words from ", including the subject-matter of" to "1995".
(3) Under the heading "Exceptions", at the end insert—

"Equal opportunities so far as relating to the inclusion of persons with protected characteristics in non-executive posts on boards of Scottish public authorities with mixed functions or no reserved functions.
Equal opportunities in relation to the Scottish functions of any Scottish public authority or cross-border public authority, other than any function that relates to the inclusion of persons in non-executive posts on boards of Scottish public authorities with mixed functions or no reserved functions. The provision falling within this exception does not include any modification of the Equality Act 2010, or of any subordinate legislation made under that Act, but does include—
(a) provision that supplements or is otherwise additional to provision made by that Act;
(b) in particular, provision imposing a requirement to take action that that Act does not prohibit;
(c) provision that reproduces or applies an enactment contained in that Act, with or without modification, without affecting the enactment as it applies for the purposes of that Act."

(4) Under the heading "Interpretation", at the appropriate places insert—

""Board" includes any other equivalent management body."
""Non-executive post" in relation to an authority means any position the holder of which is not an employee of the authority."
""Protected characteristic" has the same meaning as in the Equality Act 2010."

(5) Under that heading, at the end insert—

"The references to the Equality Act 2010 and any subordinate legislation made under that Act are to be read as references to those enactments, as at the day on which section 37 of the Scotland Act 2016 comes into force, but treating any provision of them that is not yet in force on that day as if it were in force."

(6)–(8) (*Amend the Equality Act 2010, ss 152, 154 at* **[1.1739]** *and* **[1.1741]**).

NOTES
Commencement: 23 May 2016.

38 (*Amends the Equality Act 2010, ss 1, 2, 216 at* **[1.1620]** *et seq, and amends the Interpretation and Legislative Reform (Scotland) Act 2010 (outside the scope of this work).*)

[1.1994]
39 Tribunals
(1) In Part 3 of Schedule 5 to the Scotland Act 1998 (reserved matters: general provisions) after paragraph 2 insert—

"Tribunals

2A.
(1) This Schedule does not reserve the transfer to a Scottish tribunal of functions of a tribunal that relate to reserved matters, so far as those functions are exercisable in relation to Scottish cases.
(2) "Scottish cases" has the meaning given by an Order in Council made by Her Majesty under this sub-paragraph.
(3) Sub-paragraph (1) does not apply where a function is excluded from transfer.
(4) Where a function is not excluded from transfer but is subject to qualified transfer, sub-paragraph (1) applies only if the transfer of the function is in accordance with provision made by Her Majesty by Order in Council.
(5) An Order in Council under sub-paragraph (4)—
(a) must specify the function to which it relates,
(b) must specify the Scottish tribunal to which the function may be transferred, and
(c) may make any other provision which Her Majesty considers necessary or expedient for the purposes of or in consequence of the transfer of the function and its exercise by the Scottish tribunal.
(6) The functions that are subject to qualified transfer are the functions of the following tribunals—
(a) the First-tier Tribunal or the Upper Tribunal that are established under section 3 of the Tribunals, Courts and Enforcement Act 2007;
(b) an employment tribunal or the Employment Appeal Tribunal;
(c) a tribunal listed in Schedule 1 to the Tribunals and Inquiries Act 1992;

(d) a tribunal listed in Schedule 6 to the Tribunals, Courts and Enforcement Act 2007.

(7) Sub-paragraph (6)(c) and (d) include a tribunal added to the Schedule concerned after this paragraph comes into force.

(8) Provision made by virtue of sub-paragraph (5)(c) may—

(a) include provision that—

(i) modifies the function;

(ii) imposes conditions or restrictions (including conditions or restrictions relating to the composition or rules of procedure of the Scottish tribunal, or to its staff or accommodation);

(b) be made with a view to purposes including—

(i) securing consistency in any respect in practice or procedure or otherwise between the Scottish tribunal and other tribunals;

(ii) promoting judicial co-operation in the interests of consistency.

(9) Sub-paragraph (8) does not limit the provision that may be made by virtue of sub-paragraph (5)(c).

(10) The following functions are excluded from transfer—

(a) functions of a national security tribunal;

(b) functions of a regulator, or of a person or body that exercises functions on behalf of a regulator;

(c) functions of the Comptroller-General of Patents, Designs and Trade Marks.

(11) In this paragraph—

a "national security tribunal" means—

(a) the Pathogens Access Appeal Commission;

(b) the Proscribed Organisations Appeal Commission;

(c) the Special Immigration Appeals Commission;

(d) the tribunal established by section 65(1) of the Regulation of Investigatory Powers Act 2000 (investigatory powers tribunal);

(e) any other tribunal that has functions relating to matters falling within Section B8 of Part 2 of this Schedule, except a tribunal mentioned in sub-paragraph (6);

a "regulator" means a person or body that has regulatory functions (within the meaning given by section 32 of the Legislative and Regulatory Reform Act 2006);

a "Scottish tribunal" means a tribunal in Scotland—

(a) that does not have functions in or as regards any other country or territory, except for purposes ancillary to its functions in or as regards Scotland, and

(b) that is not, and does not have as a member, a member of the Scottish Government.

(12) The powers conferred by this paragraph do not affect the powers conferred by section 30 or section 113."

(2) In paragraph 1(2) of Schedule 7 to that Act (procedure for subordinate legislation) at the appropriate place insert—

"Schedule 5, Part 3, paragraph 2A Type A"

(3)–(7) (*Contain various amendments to the Tribunals and Inquiries Act 1992 (outside the scope of this work).*)

NOTES

Commencement: 23 May 2016.

Orders in Council: as of 15 May 2019, no Orders in Council had been made under the inserted paragraph 2A.

PART 7
GENERAL

[1.1995]

70 Transitional provision

(1) Nothing in a provision of this Act affects the validity of anything done by or in relation to a Minister of the Crown before the provision comes into force.

(2) Anything (including legal proceedings) which is in the process of being done by or in relation to a Minister of the Crown at the time when a provision of this Act comes into force may, so far as it relates to a function transferred to the Scottish Ministers by virtue of that provision, be continued by or in relation to the Scottish Ministers.

(3) Anything done (or which has effect as if done) by or in relation to a Minister of the Crown—

(a) which is in force when a provision of this Act comes into force, and

(b) which was done for the purposes of or in connection with a function transferred by virtue of that provision,

has effect as if done by or in relation to the Scottish Ministers, so far as that is required for continuing its effect.

(4) This section applies subject to any provision made by regulations under section 71.

(5) In this section "Minister of the Crown" has the same meaning as in the Ministers of the Crown Act 1975.

NOTES

Commencement: 23 March 2016.

[1.1996]
71 Power to make consequential, transitional and saving provision
(1) The Secretary of State may by regulations make—
(a) such consequential provision in connection with any provision of Part 1, 3, 4, 5 or 6, or
(b) such transitional or saving provision in connection with the coming into force of any provision of Part 1, 3, 4, 5 or 6,

as the Secretary of State considers appropriate.
(2) Regulations under this section may amend, repeal, revoke or otherwise modify any of the following—
(a) an enactment or an instrument made under an enactment;
(b) a prerogative instrument;
(c) any other instrument or document.

(3) For the purposes of making provision in connection with, or with the coming into force of, a provision of Part 3, subsection (2) applies to an enactment, instrument or document whenever passed or made.
(4) Otherwise, subsection (2) applies to—
(a) an Act of Parliament passed before or in the same session as this Act;
(b) an Act of the Scottish Parliament passed, or an instrument or document made, before the end of the session in which this Act is passed.

(5) Regulations under this section may make—
(a) different provision for different purposes or cases;
(b) provision generally or for specific cases;
(c) provision subject to exceptions;
(d) provision for the delegation of functions;
(e) transitional or saving provision.

(6) Regulations under this section must be made by statutory instrument.
(7) A statutory instrument containing regulations under this section which includes provision amending or repealing any provision of primary legislation may not be made unless a draft of the instrument has been laid before and approved by a resolution of each House of Parliament.
(8) Any other statutory instrument containing regulations under this section, if made without a draft having been approved by a resolution of each House of Parliament, is subject to annulment in pursuance of a resolution of either House of Parliament.
(9) In this section—
"enactment"—
(a) includes an Act of the Scottish Parliament, and
(b) for the purposes of making provision in connection with, or with the coming into force of, a provision of Part 3, also includes a Measure or Act of the National Assembly for Wales and Northern Ireland legislation;

"prerogative instrument" means an Order in Council, warrant, charter or other instrument made under the prerogative;
"primary legislation" means—
(a) an Act of Parliament,
(b) an Act of the Scottish Parliament,
(c) a Measure or Act of the National Assembly for Wales, and
(d) Northern Ireland legislation.

(10) (*Amends the Scotland Act 1998 (outside the scope of this work).*)

NOTES
Commencement: 23 March 2016.
Regulations: the Scotland Act 2016 (Saving) Regulations 2016, SI 2016/761; the Scotland Act 2016 (Commencement No 4, Transitional and Savings) Regulations 2017, SI 2017/300; the Scotland Act 2016 (Transitional) Regulations 2017, SI 2017/444. Other Regulations made under this section are outside the scope of this work.

[1.1997]
73 Short title
This Act may be cited as the Scotland Act 2016.

NOTES
Commencement: 23 March 2016.

ENTERPRISE ACT 2016 (NOTE)

(2016 c 12)

[1.1998]

NOTES
Only a few provisions of this Act are relevant to Employment law; provisions not reproduced are not annotated.
Section 33 (Sunday working) introduces Schedule 5 to this Act, which contains amendments to employment legislation relating to the rights of shop workers to opt out of working on Sunday.

Section 41 (Restriction on public sector exit payments) inserts the Small Business, Enterprise and Employment Act 2015, s 153A (Regulations to restrict public sector exit payments), s 153B (Supplementary provision about regulations under section 153A), and s 153C (Power to relax restriction on public sector exit payments) at **[1.1928]** et seq. This section also introduces Sch 6 to this Act.

Section 44 (Commencement) provides that s 33 and Sch 5 come into force on 4 May 2016 (for the purpose of enabling the exercise of any power to make Regulations under any provision of the Employment Rights Act 1996 inserted by that Schedule). Section 41 came into force on 1 February 2017 (see SI 2017/70). As of 15 May 2019, s 33 and Sch 5 had not been brought into force for remaining purposes.

Section 45 (Extent) provides that any amendment, repeal or revocation made by this Act has the same extent as the enactment amended, repealed or revoked.

Schedule 5 (Sunday working) amends the Employment Rights Act 1996, ss 41, 42, 43, 48, 108, 236, and inserts ss 41A–41D, 43ZA, 43ZB, 45ZA, 101ZA (see the 1996 Act at **[1.813]** et seq). It also amends the Employment Act 2002, s 38 at **[1.1279]**.

In Schedule 6 (Restriction on Public Sector Exit Payments: Consequential and Related Provision), paras 1–3 amend the Small Business, Enterprise and Employment Act 2015, s 155, 156, 161 at **[1.1932]** et seq. Paragraph 5 amends the Local Government Pension Scheme Regulations 2013, SI 2013/2356 (outside the scope of this work). Paragraph 4 provides as follows—

"Power to amend public sector schemes

4. (1) Regulations may amend any relevant public sector scheme to ensure that if any exit payment restriction would have effect to prevent retirement benefits becoming immediately payable under the scheme without reduction—

(a) the retirement benefits may become immediately payable under the scheme subject to the appropriate early payment deduction, and

(b) the member may opt to buy out all or part of that deduction.

(2) Regulations may also amend any relevant public sector scheme to ensure that if any exit payment restriction has effect to prevent a payment being made by the employer under the scheme in respect of the whole or any part of an extra charge arising to the scheme as a result of retirement benefits becoming immediately payable to a member without reduction—

(a) the retirement benefits become payable immediately subject to the appropriate early payment deduction except to the extent that the extra charge arising to the scheme as a result of not making that deduction has been met by a payment made by the employer under the scheme, but

(b) the member may opt to buy out all or part of that early payment deduction.

(3) Regulations under this paragraph may be made—

(a) in relation to exit payments made by a relevant Scottish authority (other than exit payments to which section 153B(2) of the Small Business, Enterprise and Employment Act 2015 applies), by the Scottish Ministers, and

(b) in any other case, by—

(i) the Treasury, or

(ii) another Minister of the Crown with the consent of the Treasury.

(4) Regulations under this paragraph may make—

(a) consequential, incidental or supplemental provision;

(b) transitional or transitory provision, or savings;

(c) different provision for different purposes.

(5) Regulations under this paragraph (other than regulations made by the Scottish Ministers) are to be made by statutory instrument.

(6) A statutory instrument containing regulations under this paragraph is subject to annulment in pursuance of a resolution of either House of Parliament.

(7) Regulations under this paragraph made by the Scottish Ministers are subject to the negative procedure.

(8) In this paragraph—

"the appropriate early payment deduction" means such adjustment as is shown as appropriate in actuarial guidance issued by the Secretary of State;

"exit payment restriction" means a restriction imposed by regulations under section 153A of the Small Business, Enterprise and Employment Act 2015;

"Minister of the Crown" has the same meaning as in the Ministers of the Crown Act 1975;

"relevant public sector scheme" has the same meaning as in section 153A of the Small Business, Enterprise and Employment Act 2015;

"relevant Scottish authority" has the meaning given by section 153B of that Act.".

Paras 1–4 of Sch 6 came into force on 1 February 2017 (see SI 2017/70) but, as of 15 May 2019, no Regulations had been made under this paragraph.

TRADE UNION ACT 2016

(2016 c 15)

ARRANGEMENT OF SECTIONS

Introduction

Ballot thresholds for industrial action

Electronic balloting

An Act to make provision about industrial action, trade unions, employers' associations and the functions of the Certification Officer.

[4 May 2016]

Introduction

[1.1999]

1 Meaning of "the 1992 Act"

In this Act "the 1992 Act" means the Trade Union and Labour Relations (Consolidation) Act 1992.

NOTES

Commencement: 3 November 2016.

Note that the 1992 Act is at **[1.268]** et seq.

Ballot thresholds for industrial action

[1.2000]

2 Ballots: 50% turnout requirement

(1) (*Amends the Trade Union and Labour Relations (Consolidation) Act 1992, s 226(2) at* **[1.547]**.)

(2) Subsection (1) does not apply to any ballot opened before the day on which this section comes into force.

For this purpose a ballot is "opened" on the first day when a voting paper is sent to any person entitled to vote in the ballot.

NOTES

Commencement: 1 March 2017.

[1.2001]

3 Ballots: 40% support requirement in important public services

(1), (2) (*Amend the Trade Union and Labour Relations (Consolidation) Act 1992, s 226 at* **[1.547]**.)

(3) This section does not apply to any ballot opened before the day on which this section comes into force.

For this purpose a ballot is "opened" on the first day when a voting paper is sent to any person entitled to vote in the ballot.

NOTES

Commencement: 5 December 2016 (for the purpose of enabling the exercise of the power to make regulations under s 226(2D) of the 1992 Act as inserted by sub-s (1) above); 1 March 2017 (otherwise).

Electronic balloting

[1.2002]

4 Provision for electronic balloting: review and piloting scheme

(1) The Secretary of State shall commission an independent review, the report of which shall be laid before each House of Parliament, on the delivery of secure methods of electronic balloting for the purpose of ballots held under section 226 of the 1992 Act (requirement of ballot before action by trade union).

(2) The use of pilot schemes shall be permitted to inform the design and implementation of electronic balloting before it is rolled out across union strike ballots.

(3) The Secretary of State must consider the report and publish and lay before each House of Parliament his or her response to it.

(4) For the purpose of preparing the response under subsection (3), the Secretary of State must consult relevant organisations including professionals from expert associations to seek their advice and recommendations.

(5) The review under subsection (1) shall be commissioned within six months of the passing of this Act.

NOTES

Commencement: 3 November 2016.

Information requirements relating to industrial action

[1.2003]

5 Information to be included on voting paper

(1) (*Amends the Trade Union and Labour Relations (Consolidation) Act 1992, s 229 at* **[1.554]**.)

(2) Subsection (1) does not apply to any ballot opened before the day on which this section comes into force.

For this purpose a ballot is "opened" on the first day when a voting paper is sent to any person entitled to vote in the ballot.

NOTES

Commencement: 1 March 2017.

[1.2004]

6 Information to members etc about result of ballot

(1) (*Amends the Trade Union and Labour Relations (Consolidation) Act 1992, s 231 at* **[1.556]**.)

(2) Subsection (1) does not apply to any ballot opened before the day on which this section comes into force.

For this purpose a ballot is "opened" on the first day when a voting paper is sent to any person entitled to vote in the ballot.

NOTES

Commencement: 1 March 2017.

[1.2005]

7 Information to Certification Officer about industrial action etc

(1) (*Inserts the Trade Union and Labour Relations (Consolidation) Act 1992, s 32ZA at* **[1.314]**.)

(2) Subsection (1) applies only to returns for periods that begin after the day on which this section comes into force.

NOTES

Commencement: 1 March 2017.

Timing and duration of industrial action

[1.2006]

8 Two weeks' notice to be given to employers of industrial action

(1) (*Amends the Trade Union and Labour Relations (Consolidation) Act 1992, s 234A at* **[1.564]**.)

(2) Subsection (1) does not apply to any industrial action in relation to which the employer receives a relevant notice before the day on which this section comes into force.

"Relevant notice" here has the same meaning as in section 234A of the 1992 Act (see subsection (3) of that section).

NOTES

Commencement: 1 March 2017.

[1.2007]

9 Expiry of mandate for industrial action

(1) (*Amends the Trade Union and Labour Relations (Consolidation) Act 1992, s 234 at* **[1.563]**.)

(2) Subsection (1) and paragraphs 13 and 14 of Schedule 4 do not apply to any industrial action the ballot for which opened before the day on which this section comes into force.

For this purpose a ballot is "opened" on the first day when a voting paper is sent to any person entitled to vote in the ballot.

NOTES

Commencement: 1 March 2017.

Picketing

[1.2008]

10 Union supervision of picketing

(*Amends the Trade Union and Labour Relations (Consolidation) Act 1992, s 219 at* **[1.539]** *and inserts s 220A at* **[1.541]**.)

NOTES

Commencement: 1 March 2017.

Transitional provisions: the Trade Union Act 2016 (Commencement No 3 and Transitional) Regulations 2017, SI 2017/139, reg 3 provides that the amendments made by this section apply in relation to a trade union organising or encouraging members after 1 March 2017 to take part in picketing (in accordance with s 220A(1) of the Trade Union and Labour Relations (Consolidation) Act 1992).

Application of funds for political objects

[1.2009]

11 Opting in by union members to contribute to political funds

(1)–(4) (*Amend the Trade Union and Labour Relations (Consolidation) Act 1992, s 82 at* **[1.384]**, *substitute ss 84, 85 of that Act at* **[1.386]**, **[1.388]**, *and insert s 84A at* **[1.387]**.)

(5) The amendments made by subsections (1) to (4) apply only after the end of the transition period, and only to a person—

(a) who after the end of that period joins a trade union that has a political fund, or

(b) who is a member of a trade union that has a political fund but did not have one immediately before the end of that period.

(6) In subsection (5) "the transition period" means a period of not less than 12 months, starting on the day on which this section comes into force, specified by the Secretary of State in regulations made by statutory instrument.

(7) Before making regulations under subsection (6) the Secretary of State must consult—

(a) the Certification Officer, and

(b) all trade unions that have a political fund.

(8) A statutory instrument containing regulations under subsection (6) may not be made unless a draft of the instrument has been laid before, and approved by a resolution of, each House of Parliament.

NOTES

Commencement: 5 December 2016 (for the purpose of enabling the exercise of the power to make regulations under sub-ss (6)–(8)); 1 March 2017 (otherwise).

Regulations: the Trade Union Act 2016 (Political Funds) (Transition Period) Regulations 2017, SI 2017/130 at **[2.1962]** (reg 2 of which provides that the transition period referred to in sub-s (5) above is the period of 12 months beginning on 1 March 2017).

[1.2010]

12 Union's annual return to include details of political expenditure

(1)–(3) (*Insert the Trade Union and Labour Relations (Consolidation) Act 1992, s 32ZB at* **[1.315]**, *and amend ss 131, 132 of that Act at* **[1.437]**, **[1.438]**.)

(4) Subsections (1) to (3) apply only to returns for periods that begin after the day on which this section comes into force.

NOTES

Commencement: 1 March 2017.

Facility time and check-off

[1.2011]

13 Publication requirements

(*Inserts the Trade Union and Labour Relations (Consolidation) Act 1992, s 172A at* **[1.483]**.)

NOTES

Commencement: 1 March 2017.

[1.2012]
14 Reserve powers
(*Inserts the Trade Union and Labour Relations (Consolidation) Act 1992, s 172B at* **[1.484]**.)

NOTES
Commencement: to be appointed.

[1.2013]
15 Restriction on deduction of union subscriptions from wages in public sector
(*Inserts the Trade Union and Labour Relations (Consolidation) Act 1992, s 116B at* **[1.422]**, *and amends s 296 of that Act at* **[1.628]**.)

NOTES
Commencement: 1 March 2017 (for the purpose of making regulations under s 116B of the 1992 Act as inserted by this section); to be appointed (otherwise).

Certification Officer

[1.2014]
16 Certification Officer not subject to ministerial direction
(*Amends the Trade Union and Labour Relations (Consolidation) Act 1992, s 254 at* **[1.589]**.)

NOTES
Commencement: to be appointed.

[1.2015]
17 Investigatory powers etc
(1) (*Inserts the Trade Union and Labour Relations (Consolidation) Act 1992, s 256C at* **[1.595]**.)
(2) After Schedule A2 to the 1992 Act insert, as Schedule A3, the Schedule set out in Schedule 1 to this Act.
(3) Schedule 2, which makes amendments to the 1992 Act to enable the Certification Officer to exercise certain powers without an application or complaint being made to the Officer, has effect.

NOTES
Commencement: to be appointed.

[1.2016]
18 Enforcement by Certification Officer of new annual return requirements
(1) (*Inserts the Trade Union and Labour Relations (Consolidation) Act 1992, s 32ZC at* **[1.316]**.)
(2) Subsection (1) applies only to returns for periods that begin after the day on which this section comes into force.
(3), (4) (*Amend the Trade Union and Labour Relations (Consolidation) Act 1992, ss 45, 45D at* **[1.335]**, **[1.339]**.)

NOTES
Commencement: 1 March 2017.

[1.2017]
19 Further powers of Certification Officer where enforcement order made
(1) (*Inserts the Trade Union and Labour Relations (Consolidation) Act 1992, s 256D at* **[1.596]**.)
(2) After Schedule A3 to the 1992 Act (inserted by section 17 above) insert, as Schedule A4, the Schedule set out in Schedule 3 to this Act.
(3) Subsections (1) and (2) do not apply in relation to any acts or omissions of a trade union or other person occurring before this section comes into force.
(4) (*Amends the Trade Union and Labour Relations (Consolidation) Act 1992, ss 24B, 25, 31, 45C, 55, 72A, 80, 82 and 108B at* **[1.304]**, **[1.306]**, **[1.312]**, **[1.338]**, **[1.350]**, **[1.373]**, **[1.382]**, **[1.384]**, **[1.419]** *respectively*.)

NOTES
Commencement: to be appointed.

[1.2018]
20 Power to impose levy
(*Inserts the Trade Union and Labour Relations (Consolidation) Act 1992, s 257A at* **[1.598]** *and amends s 258 of that Act at* **[1.599]**.)

NOTES
Commencement: to be appointed.

[1.2019]
21 Rights of appeal not limited to questions of law
(*Amends the Trade Union and Labour Relations (Consolidation) Act 1992, ss 45D, 56A, 95, 104 and 108C at* **[1.339]**, **[1.352]**, **[1.397]**, **[1.413]**, **[1.420]**.)

NOTES

Commencement: to be appointed.

General

[1.2020]

22 Minor and consequential amendments

Schedule 4 (minor and consequential amendments) has effect.

NOTES

Commencement: 1 March 2017 (in so far as it relates to specified paragraphs of Sch 4) to be appointed (otherwise).

[1.2021]

23 Financial provision

There is to be paid out of money provided by Parliament any increase attributable to this Act in the sums payable under any other Act out of money so provided.

NOTES

Commencement: 4 May 2016.

[1.2022]

24 Extent

An amendment or repeal made by this Act has the same extent as the enactment to which it relates.

NOTES

Commencement: 4 May 2016.

[1.2023]

25 Commencement

(1) This Act, apart from sections 23 to 26 (which come into force on the day on which this Act is passed), comes into force on whatever day or days the Secretary of State appoints by regulations made by statutory instrument.

(2) Regulations under this section may include saving, transitional or transitory provision.

NOTES

Commencement: 4 May 2016.

Regulations: Trade Union Act 2016 (Commencement No 1) Regulations 2016, SI 2016/1051; the Trade Union Act 2016 (Commencement No 2) Regulations 2016, SI 2016/1170; the Trade Union Act 2016 (Commencement No 3 and Transitional) Regulations 2017, SI 2017/139 at **[2.1974]**.

[1.2024]

26 Short title

This Act may be cited as the Trade Union Act 2016.

NOTES

Commencement: 4 May 2016.

SCHEDULES

SCHEDULE 1
CERTIFICATION OFFICER: INVESTIGATORY POWERS: SCHEDULE TO BE INSERTED INTO THE 1992 ACT

[1.2025]

(*Inserts the Trade Union and Labour Relations (Consolidation) Act 1992, Sch A3 (Certification Officer: Investigatory Powers) at* **[1.705]**.)

SCHEDULE 2
CERTIFICATION OFFICER: EXERCISE OF POWERS WITHOUT APPLICATION ETC

[1.2026]

(*Amends the Trade Union and Labour Relations (Consolidation) Act 1992, ss 45C, 54, 55, 72A, 79, 80, 82, and 103 at* **[1.338]**, **[1.349]**, **[1.350]**, **[1.373]**, **[1.381]**, **[1.382]**, **[1.412]**, **[1.384]**.)

SCHEDULE 3
CERTIFICATION OFFICER: POWER TO IMPOSE FINANCIAL PENALTIES: SCHEDULE TO BE INSERTED INTO THE 1992 ACT

[1.2027]

(*Inserts the Trade Union and Labour Relations (Consolidation) Act 1992, Sch A4 (Certification Officer: Power to Impose Financial Penalties) at* **[1.706]**.)

SCHEDULE 4
MINOR AND CONSEQUENTIAL AMENDMENTS

[1.2028]

(Paras 1–19 contain minor amendments to the Trade Union and Labour Relations (Consolidation) Act 1992 at **[1.268]** *et seq (which have been incorporated ante). Para 20 amends Northern Ireland legislation (outside the scope of this work). Para 21 repeals the Trade Union Reform and Employment Rights Act 1993, Sch 8, para 47(b), the Employment Relations Act 1999, Sch 3, para 10, Sch 6, paras 17(2), 18(2), and the Employment Relations Act 2004, s 24(2), Sch 1, para 14.)*

IMMIGRATION ACT 2016

(2016 c 19)

ARRANGEMENT OF SECTIONS

PART 1
LABOUR MARKET AND ILLEGAL WORKING

CHAPTER 1
LABOUR MARKET

Director of Labour Market Enforcement

Gangmasters and Labour Abuse Authority

Labour market enforcement undertakings

Labour market enforcement orders

LME undertakings and orders: supplementary

Supplementary provision

CHAPTER 2
ILLEGAL WORKING

Offences

NOTES

Only some provisions of this Act are relevant to employment law; provisions not reproduced are not annotated.

An Act to make provision about the law on immigration and asylum; to make provision about access to services, facilities, licences and work by reference to immigration status; to make provision about the enforcement of certain legislation relating to the labour market; to make provision about language requirements for public sector workers; to make provision about fees for passports and civil registration; and for connected purposes.

[12 May 2016]

PART 1
LABOUR MARKET AND ILLEGAL WORKING

CHAPTER 1 LABOUR MARKET

Director of Labour Market Enforcement

[1.2029]

1 Director of Labour Market Enforcement

(1) The Secretary of State must appoint a person as the Director of Labour Market Enforcement (referred to in this Chapter as "the Director").

(2) The Director is to hold office in accordance with the terms of his or her appointment.

(3) The functions of the Director are exercisable on behalf of the Crown.

(4) The Secretary of State must provide the Director with such staff, goods, services, accommodation and other resources as the Secretary of State considers the Director needs for the exercise of his or her functions.

(5) The Secretary of State must—

(a) pay the Director such expenses, remuneration and allowances, and

(b) pay or make provision for the payment of such pension to or in respect of the Director,

as may be provided for by or under the terms of the Director's appointment.

NOTES

Commencement: 12 July 2016.

[1.2030]

2 Labour market enforcement strategy

(1) The Director must before the beginning of each financial year prepare a labour market enforcement strategy for that year and submit it to the Secretary of State for approval.

(2) A labour market enforcement strategy (referred to in this Chapter as a "strategy") is a document which—

(a) sets out the Director's assessment of—

(i) the scale and nature of non-compliance in the labour market during the year before the one to which the strategy relates, and
(ii) the likely scale and nature of such non-compliance during the year to which the strategy relates and the following two years,

(b) contains a proposal for the year to which the strategy relates setting out—
(i) how labour market enforcement functions should be exercised,
(ii) the education, training and research activities the Secretary of State, and any other person by whom, or by whose officers, labour market enforcement functions are exercisable, should undertake or facilitate in connection with those functions,
(iii) the information, or descriptions of information, that should be provided to the Director for the purposes of his or her functions by any person by whom, or by whose officers, labour market enforcement functions are exercisable, and
(iv) the form and manner in which, and frequency with which, that information should be provided,

(c) sets out the activities the Director proposes to undertake during the year to which the strategy relates in the exercise of his or her functions under section 8, and
(d) deals with such other matters as the Director considers appropriate.

(3) The proposal mentioned in paragraph (b) of subsection (2) must, in particular, set out how the funding available for the purposes of the functions and activities mentioned in sub-paragraphs (i) and (ii) of that paragraph should be allocated.

(4) The Director may at any time prepare a revised strategy and submit it to the Secretary of State for approval.

(5) The Secretary of State may approve a strategy either with or without modifications (but a modification may not relate to the assessment described in paragraph (a) of subsection (2)).

(6) Any person by whom labour market enforcement functions are exercisable during a year to which a strategy approved under this section relates must, in exercising those functions, have regard to the strategy.

NOTES

Commencement: 12 July 2016.

[1.2031]

3 Non-compliance in the labour market etc: interpretation

(1) For the purposes of this Chapter each of the following constitutes "non-compliance in the labour market"—
(a) the commission of a labour market offence;
(b) failure to comply with the requirement under section 1 of the National Minimum Wage Act 1998 (workers to be paid at least national minimum wage);
(c) failure to pay any financial penalty required to be paid by a notice of underpayment served under section 19 of that Act (see section 19A of that Act);
(d) breach of a condition of a licence granted under section 7 of the Gangmasters (Licensing) Act 2004;
(e) failure to comply with any other requirement imposed by or under any enactment and which is prescribed by regulations made by the Secretary of State.

(2) In this Chapter "labour market enforcement functions" means—
(a) any function of the Secretary of State in connection with prohibition orders made under section 3A of the Employment Agencies Act 1973,
(b) any function of an officer acting for the purposes of that Act (see section 8A of that Act),
(c) any function of an officer acting for the purposes of the National Minimum Wage Act 1998 (see section 13 of that Act),
(d) any function of the Gangmasters and Labour Abuse Authority conferred by section 1(2)(a) to (c) of the Gangmasters (Licensing) Act 2004,
(e) any function of an enforcement officer or a compliance officer acting for the purposes of that Act (see section 15 of that Act),
(f) any function of the Gangmasters and Labour Abuse Authority under Part 2 of the Modern Slavery Act 2015 (slavery and trafficking prevention orders etc),
(g) any function of an officer of that Authority acting for the purposes of Part 1 or 2 of that Act (see sections 11A and 30A of that Act),
(h) any function of an enforcing authority under this Chapter,
(i) any function an officer has by virtue of section 26, and
(j) any other function prescribed by regulations made by the Secretary of State.

(3) In this section "labour market offence" means—
(a) an offence under the Employment Agencies Act 1973 other than one under section 9(4)(b) of that Act;
(b) an offence under the National Minimum Wage Act 1998;
(c) an offence under the Gangmasters (Licensing) Act 2004;
(d) an offence under section 1 of the Modern Slavery Act 2015;
(e) an offence under section 2 or 4 of that Act—
(i) which is committed in relation to a worker or a person seeking work, or
(ii) which is otherwise committed in circumstances where subsection (2) of section 3 of that Act applies;
(f) an offence under section 30(1) or (2) of that Act which is committed in relation to—

(i) an order which was made on the application of the Gangmasters and Labour Abuse Authority, or
(ii) an order which was made under section 14 of that Act and which falls within subsection (4) below;
(g) an offence under section 27;
(h) any other offence prescribed by regulations made by the Secretary of State;
(i) an offence of attempting or conspiring to commit an offence mentioned in paragraphs (a) to (h);
(j) an offence under Part 2 of the Serious Crime Act 2007 in relation to an offence so mentioned;
(k) an offence of inciting a person to commit an offence so mentioned;
(l) an offence of aiding, abetting, counselling or procuring the commission of an offence so mentioned.

(4) An order made under section 14 of the Modern Slavery Act 2015 falls within this subsection if—
(a) the order was made following—
(i) the conviction of the defendant of an offence mentioned in subsection (3)(d), (e) or (i) to (l), or
(ii) a finding of a kind mentioned in section 14(1)(b) or (c) of that Act in connection with any such offence, and
(b) the prosecution resulted from an investigation conducted by a labour abuse prevention officer (within the meaning of section 114B of the Police and Criminal Evidence Act 1984).

(5) In this section "worker" has the same meaning as in the Employment Rights Act 1996 (see section 230 of that Act) and the reference to a person seeking work is to be read accordingly.

(6) In this section references to the Gangmasters (Licensing) Act 2004 are references to that Act only so far as it applies in relation to England and Wales and Scotland.

NOTES

Commencement: 12 July 2016.

Regulations: as of 15 May 2019, no regulations had been made under this section.

[1.2032]

4 Annual and other reports

(1) As soon as reasonably practicable after the end of each financial year in respect of which the Secretary of State has approved a strategy under section 2, the Director must submit to the Secretary of State an annual report for that year.

(2) An annual report must include—
(a) an assessment of the extent to which labour market enforcement functions were exercised, and activities of the kind mentioned in section 2(2)(b)(ii) were carried out, in accordance with the strategy during the year to which the report relates,
(b) an assessment of the extent to which the strategy had an effect on the scale and nature of non-compliance in the labour market during that year, and
(c) a statement of the activities the Director undertook during that year in the exercise of his or her functions under section 8.

(3) The Director must submit to the Secretary of State a report dealing with any matter—
(a) which the Secretary of State has requested the Director to report on, or
(b) which a strategy approved by the Secretary of State under section 2 states is a matter the Director proposes to report on,
and must do so as soon as reasonably practicable after the request is made or the strategy is approved.

NOTES

Commencement: 12 July 2016.

[1.2033]

5 Publication of strategy and reports

(1) The Secretary of State must lay before Parliament—
(a) any strategy the Secretary of State approves under section 2, and
(b) any annual or other report the Secretary of State receives under section 4,
and must do so as soon as reasonably practicable after approving the strategy or receiving the report.

(2) A document laid under subsection (1) must not contain material removed under subsection (3).

(3) The Secretary of State may remove from a document to be laid under subsection (1) any material the publication of which the Secretary of State considers—
(a) would be against the interests of national security,
(b) might jeopardise the safety of any person in the United Kingdom, or
(c) might prejudice the investigation or prosecution of an offence under the law of England and Wales, Scotland or Northern Ireland.

NOTES

Commencement: 12 July 2016.

[1.2034]

6 Information gateways

(1) A person may disclose information to the Director or a relevant staff member if the disclosure is made for the purposes of the exercise of any function of the Director.

(2) Information obtained by the Director or a relevant staff member in connection with the exercise of any function of the Director may be used by the Director or a relevant staff member in connection with the exercise of any other function of the Director.

(3) The Director or a relevant staff member may disclose information obtained in connection with the exercise of any function of the Director to a specified person if the disclosure is made for the purposes of the exercise of any function of the specified person.

(4) "Specified person" means a person specified in Schedule 1 (persons to whom Director etc may disclose information).

(5) The Secretary of State may by regulations amend Schedule 1.

(6) In this section, "relevant staff member" means a member of staff provided to the Director under section 1(4).

NOTES

Commencement: 12 July 2016.

Regulations: as of 15 May 2019, no regulations had been made under this section.

[1.2035]

7 Information gateways: supplementary

(1) A disclosure of information which is authorised by section 6 does not breach—

(a) an obligation of confidence owed by the person making the disclosure, or

(b) any other restriction on the disclosure of information (however imposed).

(2) But nothing in section 6 authorises the making of a disclosure which—

(a) contravenes [the data protection legislation], or

(b) is prohibited by [any of Parts 1 to 7 or Chapter 1 of Part 9 of the Investigatory Powers Act 2016].

(3) Section 6 does not limit the circumstances in which information may be disclosed apart from that section.

(4) Section 6(1) does not authorise a person serving in an intelligence service to disclose information to the Director or a relevant staff member.

But this does not affect the disclosures which such a person may make in accordance with intelligence service disclosure arrangements.

(5) Intelligence service information may not be disclosed by the Director or a relevant staff member without authorisation from the appropriate service chief.

(6) If the Director or a relevant staff member has disclosed intelligence service information to a person, that person may not further disclose that information without authorisation from the appropriate service chief.

(7) HMRC information may not be disclosed by the Director or a relevant staff member without authorisation from HMRC Commissioners.

(8) If the Director or a relevant staff member has disclosed HMRC information to a person, that person may not further disclose that information without authorisation from HMRC Commissioners.

(9) Subsections (7) and (8) do not apply to national minimum wage information.

(10) If a person contravenes subsection (7) or (8) by disclosing revenue and customs information relating to a person whose identity—

(a) is specified in the disclosure, or

(b) can be deduced from it,

section 19 of the Commissioners for Revenue and Customs Act 2005 (wrongful disclosure) applies in relation to that disclosure as it applies in relation to a disclosure of such information in contravention of section 20(9) of that Act.

(11) In this section—

"appropriate service chief" means—

(a) the Director-General of the Security Service (in the case of information obtained by the Director or a relevant staff member from that Service or a person acting on its behalf);

(b) the Chief of the Secret Intelligence Service (in the case of information so obtained from that Service or a person acting on its behalf);

(c) the Director of GCHQ (in the case of information so obtained from GCHQ or a person acting on its behalf);

["the data protection legislation" has the same meaning as in the Data Protection Act 2018 (see section 3 of that Act);]

"GCHQ" has the same meaning as in the Intelligence Services Act 1994;

"HMRC information" means information disclosed to the Director or a relevant staff member under section 6 by HMRC Commissioners or a person acting on behalf of HMRC Commissioners;

"intelligence service" means—

(a) the Security Service;

(b) the Secret Intelligence Service;

(c) GCHQ;

"intelligence service disclosure arrangements" means—

(a) arrangements made by the Director-General of the Security Service under section 2(2)(a) of the Security Service Act 1989 about the disclosure of information by that Service,

(b) arrangements made by the Chief of the Intelligence Service under section 2(2)(a) of the Intelligence Services Act 1994 about the disclosure of information by that Service, and

(c) arrangements made by the Director of GCHQ under section 4(2)(a) of that Act about the disclosure of information by GCHQ;

"intelligence service information" means information obtained from an intelligence service or a person acting on behalf of an intelligence service;

"national minimum wage information" means information obtained by an officer in the course of acting—

(a) for the purposes of the National Minimum Wage Act 1998 (see section 13 of that Act), or

(b) by virtue of section 26(2);

"relevant staff member" has the same meaning as in section 6;

"revenue and customs information relating to a person" has the meaning given in section 19(2) of the Commissioners for Revenue and Customs Act 2005.

NOTES

Commencement: 12 July 2016.

Sub-s (2): words in square brackets in para (a) substituted by the Data Protection Act 2018, s 211, Sch 19, Pt 1, para 197(1), (2), as from 25 May 2018 (for transitional provisions and savings relating to the repeal of the Data Protection Act 1998, see Sch 20 to the 2018 Act at **[1.2232]**). Words in square brackets in para (b) substituted by the Investigatory Powers Act 2016, s 271(1), Sch 10, Pt 1, para 35, as from 27 June 2018.

Sub-s (11): definition "the data protection legislation" inserted by the Data Protection Act 2018, s 211, Sch 19, Pt 1, para 197(1), (3), as from 25 May 2018 (for transitional provisions and savings relating to the repeal of the Data Protection Act 1998, see Sch 20 to the 2018 Act at **[1.2232]**).

[1.2036]

8 Information hub

(1) The Director must gather, store, process, analyse and disseminate information relating to non-compliance in the labour market.

(2) The Director may request any person by whom, or by whose officers, labour market enforcement functions are exercisable to provide the Director with any non-compliance information specified or of a description specified in the request.

(3) "Non-compliance information" means information relating to non-compliance in the labour market which the Director considers would facilitate the exercise of any of his or her functions.

(4) A person by whom, or by whose officers, labour market enforcement functions are exercisable may request the Director to provide the person, or an officer of the person, with any enforcement information specified or of a description specified in the request.

(5) "Enforcement information" means information which the person making the request considers would facilitate the exercise of any labour market enforcement function of the person or of an officer of the person.

(6) A person who receives a request under this section must respond to it in writing within a reasonable period.

NOTES

Commencement: 12 July 2016.

[1.2037]

9 Restriction on exercising functions in relation to individual cases

(1) The Director must not in exercising any function make any recommendation in relation to an individual case.

(2) Subsection (1) does not prevent the Director considering individual cases and drawing conclusions about them for the purpose of, or in the context of, considering a general issue.

NOTES

Commencement: 12 July 2016.

Gangmasters and Labour Abuse Authority

[1.2038]

10 Renaming of Gangmasters Licensing Authority

(1) The Gangmasters Licensing Authority is renamed the Gangmasters and Labour Abuse Authority.

(2) In any enactment passed before the day on which this section comes into force, and in any instrument or other document made before that day, references to the Gangmasters Licensing Authority are to be read, in relation to any time on or after that day, as references to the Gangmasters and Labour Abuse Authority.

NOTES

Commencement: 12 July 2016.

[1.2039]

11 Functions in relation to labour market

(1) Schedule 2 (functions in relation to labour market) has effect.

(2) The Secretary of State may by regulations confer other functions on the Gangmasters and Labour Abuse Authority or its officers.

NOTES

Commencement: 12 July 2016.

Regulations: as of 15 May 2019, no regulations had been made under sub-s (2).

Labour market enforcement undertakings

[1.2040]

14 Power to request LME undertaking

(1) This section applies where an enforcing authority believes that a person has committed, or is committing, a trigger offence.

(2) An enforcing authority may give a notice to the person—

(a) identifying the trigger offence which the authority believes has been or is being committed;

(b) giving the authority's reasons for the belief;

(c) inviting the person to give the authority a labour market enforcement undertaking in the form attached to the notice.

(3) A labour market enforcement undertaking (an "LME undertaking") is an undertaking by the person giving it (the "subject") to comply with any prohibitions, restrictions and requirements set out in the undertaking (as to which see section 15).

(4) "Trigger offence" means—

(a) an offence under the Employment Agencies Act 1973 other than one under section 9(4)(b) of that Act;

(b) an offence under the National Minimum Wage Act 1998;

(c) an offence under the Gangmasters (Licensing) Act 2004;

(d) any other offence prescribed by regulations made by the Secretary of State;

(e) an offence of attempting or conspiring to commit an offence mentioned in paragraphs (a) to (d);

(f) an offence under Part 2 of the Serious Crime Act 2007 in relation to an offence so mentioned;

(g) an offence of inciting a person to commit an offence so mentioned;

(h) an offence of aiding, abetting, counselling or procuring the commission of an offence so mentioned.

(5) "Enforcing authority"—

(a) in relation to a trigger offence under the Employment Agencies Act 1973, means the Secretary of State or any authority whose officers are acting for the purposes of that Act (see section 8A of that Act);

(b) in relation to a trigger offence under the National Minimum Wage Act 1998, means the Secretary of State or any authority whose officers are acting for the purposes of that Act (see section 13 of that Act);

(c) in relation to a trigger offence under the Gangmasters (Licensing) Act 2004, means the Secretary of State or any authority whose officers are acting as enforcement officers for the purposes of that Act (see section 15 of that Act);

(d) in relation to an offence which is a trigger offence by virtue of subsection (4)(d) (including an offence mentioned in subsection (4)(e) to (h) in connection with such an offence), has the meaning prescribed in regulations made by the Secretary of State.

(6) In subsection (5), a reference to an offence under an Act includes a reference to an offence mentioned in subsection (4)(e) to (h) in connection with such an offence.

(7) In this section references to the Gangmasters (Licensing) Act 2004 are references to that Act only so far as it applies in relation to England and Wales and Scotland.

NOTES

Commencement: 25 November 2016.

Regulations: as of 15 May 2019, no regulations had been made under this section.

[1.2041]

15 Measures in LME undertakings

(1) An LME undertaking may include a prohibition, restriction or requirement (each a "measure") if, and only if—

(a) the measure falls within subsection (2) or (3) (or both), and

(b) the enforcing authority considers that the measure is just and reasonable.

(2) A measure falls within this subsection if it is for the purpose of—

(a) preventing or reducing the risk of the subject not complying with any requirement imposed by or under the relevant enactment, or

(b) bringing to the attention of persons likely to be interested in the matter—

(i) the existence of the LME undertaking,

(ii) the circumstances in which it was given, and

(iii) any action taken (or not taken) by the subject in order to comply with the undertaking.

(3) A measure falls within this subsection if it is prescribed, or is of a description prescribed, in regulations made by the Secretary of State.

(4) The enforcing authority must not—

(a) invite the subject to give an LME undertaking, or

(b) agree to the form of an undertaking,

unless the authority believes that at least one measure in the undertaking is necessary for the purpose mentioned in subsection (5).

(5) That purpose is preventing or reducing the risk of the subject—

(a) committing a further trigger offence under the relevant enactment, or

(b) continuing to commit the trigger offence.

(6) An LME undertaking must set out how each measure included for the purpose mentioned in subsection (2)(a) is expected to achieve that purpose.

(7) In this section, the "relevant enactment" means the enactment under which the enforcing authority believes the trigger offence concerned has been or is being committed.

NOTES

Commencement: 25 November 2016.

Regulations: as of 15 May 2019, no regulations had been made under this section.

[1.2042]

16 Duration

(1) An LME undertaking has effect from when it is accepted by the enforcing authority or from the later time specified in it for this purpose.

(2) An LME undertaking has effect for the period specified in it but the maximum period for which an undertaking may have effect is 2 years.

(3) The enforcing authority may release the subject from an LME undertaking.

(4) The enforcing authority must release the subject from an LME undertaking if at any time during the period for which it has effect the authority believes that no measure in it is necessary for the purpose mentioned in section 15(5).

(5) If the enforcing authority releases the subject from an LME undertaking it must take such steps as it considers appropriate to bring that fact to the attention of—

(a) the subject;

(b) any other persons likely to be interested in the matter.

NOTES

Commencement: 25 November 2016.

[1.2043]

17 Further provision about giving notice under section 14

(1) A notice may be given under section 14 to a person by—

(a) delivering it to the person,

(b) leaving it at the person's proper address,

(c) sending it by post to the person at that address, or

(d) subject to subsection (6), sending it to the person by electronic means.

(2) A notice to a body corporate may be given to any officer of that body.

(3) A notice to a partnership may be given to any partner.

(4) A notice to an unincorporated association (other than a partnership) may be given to any member of the governing body of the association.

(5) For the purposes of this section and of section 7 of the Interpretation Act 1978 (service of documents by post) in its application to this section, the proper address of a person is the person's last known address (whether of the person's residence or of a place where the person carries on business or is employed) and also—

(a) in the case of a body corporate or an officer of the body, the address of the body's registered or principal office in the United Kingdom;

(b) in the case of a partnership or a partner, the address of the principal office of the partnership in the United Kingdom;

(c) in the case of an unincorporated association (other than a partnership) or a member of its governing body, the principal office of the association in the United Kingdom.

(6) A notice may be sent to a person by electronic means only if—

(a) the person has indicated that notices under section 14 may be given to the person by being sent to an electronic address and in an electronic form specified for that purpose, and

(b) the notice is sent to that address in that form.

(7) A notice sent to a person by electronic means is, unless the contrary is proved, to be treated as having been given on the working day immediately following the day on which it was sent.

(8) In this section—

"electronic address" means any number or address used for the purposes of sending or receiving documents or information by electronic means;

"officer", in relation to a body corporate, means a director, manager, secretary or other similar officer of the body;

"working day" means a day other than a Saturday, a Sunday, Christmas Day, Good Friday or a bank holiday under the Banking and Financial Dealings Act 1971 in any part of the United Kingdom.

NOTES

Commencement: 25 November 2016.

Labour market enforcement orders

[1.2044]

18 Power to make LME order on application

(1) The appropriate court may, on an application by an enforcing authority under section 19, make a labour market enforcement order against a person if the court—

(a) is satisfied, on the balance of probabilities, that the person has committed, or is committing, a trigger offence, and

(b) considers that it is just and reasonable to make the order.

(2) A labour market enforcement order (an "LME order") is an order which—

(a) prohibits or restricts the person against whom it is made ("the respondent") from doing anything set out in the order;
(b) requires the respondent to do anything set out in the order.

See section 21.

(3) In this section "the appropriate court"—
(a) where the conduct constituting the trigger offence took or is taking place primarily in England and Wales, means a magistrates' court;
(b) where that conduct took or is taking place primarily in Scotland, means the sheriff;
(c) where that conduct took or is taking place primarily in Northern Ireland, means a court of summary jurisdiction.

(4) An application for an LME order under this section is—
(a) in England and Wales, to be made by complaint;
(b) in Northern Ireland, to be made by complaint under Part 8 of the Magistrates' Courts (Northern Ireland) Order 1981 (SI 1981/1675 (NI 26)).

NOTES

Commencement: 25 November 2016.

[1.2045]

19 Applications

(1) An enforcing authority may apply for an LME order to be made under section 18 against a person (the "proposed respondent") if—
(a) the authority has served a notice on the proposed respondent under section 14, and
(b) the proposed respondent—
(i) refuses to give an LME undertaking, or
(ii) otherwise fails, before the end of the negotiation period, to give an LME undertaking in the form attached to the notice or in such other form as may be agreed with the enforcing authority.

(2) An enforcing authority may also apply for an LME order if the proposed respondent—
(a) has given an LME undertaking to the enforcing authority, and
(b) has failed to comply with the undertaking.

(3) In subsection (1) "the negotiation period" means—
(a) the period of 14 days beginning with the day after that on which the notice mentioned in paragraph (a) of that subsection was given, or
(b) such longer period as may be agreed between the enforcing authority and the proposed respondent.

NOTES

Commencement: 25 November 2016.

[1.2046]

20 Power to make LME order on conviction

(1) This section applies where a court deals with a person in respect of a conviction for a trigger offence.

(2) The court may make an LME order against the person if the court considers it is just and reasonable to do so.

(3) An LME order must not be made under this section except—
(a) in addition to a sentence imposed in respect of the offence concerned, or
(b) in addition to an order discharging the person conditionally or, in Scotland, discharging the person absolutely.

NOTES

Commencement: 25 November 2016.

[1.2047]

21 Measures in LME orders

(1) An LME order may include a prohibition, restriction or requirement (each a "measure") if, and only if, the measure falls within subsection (2) or (3) (or both).

(2) A measure falls within this subsection if it is for the purpose of—
(a) preventing or reducing the risk of the respondent not complying with any requirement imposed by or under the relevant enactment, or
(b) bringing to the attention of persons likely to be interested in the matter—
(i) the existence of the LME order,
(ii) the circumstances in which it was made, and
(iii) any action taken (or not taken) by the respondent in order to comply with the order.

(3) A measure falls within this subsection if it is prescribed, or is of a description prescribed, in regulations made by the Secretary of State.

(4) Where an LME order includes a measure for the purpose mentioned in subsection (2)(a), the order must set out how the measure is expected to achieve that purpose.

(5) In this section the "relevant enactment" means the enactment under which the trigger offence concerned has been or is being committed.

NOTES

Commencement: 25 November 2016.

Regulations: as of 15 May 2019, no regulations had been made under this section.

[1.2048]

22 Further provision about LME orders

(1) An LME order has effect for the period specified in it but the maximum period for which an order may have effect is 2 years.

(2) An LME order may not be made against an individual who is under 18.

(3) If a court makes an LME order, the court may also—

(a) release the respondent from any LME undertaking given in relation to the trigger offence concerned;

(b) discharge any other LME order which is in force against the respondent and which was made by the court or any other court in the same part of the United Kingdom as the court.

NOTES

Commencement: 25 November 2016.

[1.2049]

23 Variation and discharge

(1) The appropriate court may by order vary or discharge an LME order—

(a) on the application of the respondent;

(b) if the order was made under section 18, on the application of the enforcing authority who applied for the order;

(c) if the order was made under section 20, on the application of the enforcing authority whose officer conducted the investigation which resulted in the prosecution of the respondent for the trigger offence.

(2) In this section "the appropriate court"—

(a) in relation to an LME order made in England and Wales (whether made under section 18 or 20), means a magistrates' court;

(b) in relation to such an order made in Scotland, means the sheriff;

(c) in relation to such an order made in Northern Ireland, means a court of summary jurisdiction.

(3) An application for an order under this section is—

(a) if made to a magistrates' court in England and Wales, to be made by complaint;

(b) if made to a court of summary jurisdiction in Northern Ireland, to be made by complaint under Part 8 of the Magistrates' Courts (Northern Ireland) Order 1981 (SI 1981/1675 (NI 26)).

NOTES

Commencement: 25 November 2016.

[1.2050]

24 Appeals

(1) A respondent may appeal against—

(a) the making of an LME order under section 18;

(b) the making of, or refusal to make, an order under section 23.

(2) An appeal under subsection (1) is to be made—

(a) where the order was made or refused by a magistrates' court in England and Wales, to the Crown Court;

(b) where the order was made or refused by the sheriff, to the Sheriff Appeal Court;

(c) where the order was made or refused by a court of summary jurisdiction in Northern Ireland, to a county court.

(3) On an appeal under subsection (1) the court hearing the appeal may make such orders as may be necessary to give effect to its determination of the appeal, and may also make such incidental or consequential orders as appear to it to be just and reasonable.

(4) An LME order that has been varied by virtue of subsection (3) remains an order of the court that first made it for the purposes of section 23.

(5) A respondent may appeal against the making of an LME order under section 20 as if the order were a sentence passed on the respondent for the trigger offence.

NOTES

Commencement: 25 November 2016.

LME undertakings and orders: supplementary

[1.2051]

25 Code of practice

(1) The Secretary of State must issue a code of practice giving guidance to enforcing authorities about the exercise of their functions under sections 14 to 23.

(2) The Secretary of State may revise the code from time to time.

(3) The code and any revised code—

(a) must not be issued unless a draft has been laid before Parliament, and

(b) comes into force on such day as the Secretary of State appoints by regulations.

(4) The Secretary of State must publish the code and any revised code.

(5) An enforcing authority must have regard to the current version of the code in exercising its functions under sections 14 to 23.

NOTES

Commencement: 25 November 2016.

Code of Practice: see the Code of Practice on Labour Market Enforcement Undertakings and Orders at **[4.84]**.

Regulations: the Labour Market Enforcement (Code of Practice on Labour Market Enforcement Undertakings and Orders: Appointed Day) Regulations 2016, SI 2016/1044 (which brings the above-mentioned Code of Practice into force on 25 November 2016).

[1.2052]

26 Investigative functions

(1) An officer acting for the purposes of the Employment Agencies Act 1973—

- (a) may also act for the purposes of taking action where it appears that a person has failed to comply with an LME undertaking or an LME order where the trigger offence to which the undertaking or order relates is an offence under that Act, and
- (b) in doing so, has the same powers and duties as he or she has when acting for the purposes of that Act.

(2) An officer acting for the purposes of the National Minimum Wage Act 1998—

- (a) may also act for the purposes of taking action where it appears that a person has failed to comply with an LME undertaking or an LME order where the trigger offence to which the undertaking or order relates is an offence under that Act, and
- (b) in doing so, has the same powers and duties as he or she has when acting for the purposes of that Act.

(3) An officer acting as an enforcement officer for the purposes of the Gangmasters (Licensing) Act 2004—

- (a) may also act for the purposes of taking action where it appears that a person has failed to comply with an LME undertaking or an LME order where the trigger offence to which the undertaking or order relates is an offence under that Act, and
- (b) in doing so, has the same powers and duties as he or she has when acting as an enforcement officer for the purposes of that Act.

(4) In this section references to the Gangmasters (Licensing) Act 2004 are references to that Act only so far as it applies in relation to England and Wales and Scotland.

NOTES

Commencement: 25 November 2016.

[1.2053]

27 Offence

(1) A person against whom an LME order is made commits an offence if the person, without reasonable excuse, fails to comply with the order.

(2) A person guilty of an offence under this section is liable—

- (a) on conviction on indictment, to imprisonment for a term not exceeding 2 years, to a fine or to both;
- (b) on summary conviction in England and Wales, to imprisonment for a term not exceeding 12 months, to a fine or to both;
- (c) on summary conviction in Scotland, to imprisonment for a term not exceeding 12 months, to a fine not exceeding the statutory maximum or to both;
- (d) on summary conviction in Northern Ireland, to imprisonment for a term not exceeding 6 months, to a fine not exceeding the statutory maximum or to both.

(3) In relation to an offence committed before the commencement of section 154(1) of the Criminal Justice Act 2003, the reference in subsection (2)(b) to 12 months is to be read as a reference to 6 months.

NOTES

Commencement: 25 November 2016.

[1.2054]

28 Offences by bodies corporate

(1) If an offence under section 27 committed by a body corporate is proved—

- (a) to have been committed with the consent or connivance of an officer of the body, or
- (b) to be attributable to any neglect on the part of such an officer,

the officer, as well as the body corporate, is guilty of the offence and liable to be proceeded against and punished accordingly.

(2) In subsection (1) "officer", in relation to a body corporate, means—

- (a) a director, manager, secretary or other similar officer of the body;
- (b) a person purporting to act in any such capacity.

(3) If the affairs of a body corporate are managed by its members, subsection (1) applies in relation to the acts and defaults of a member in connection with the member's functions of management as if the member were a director of the body corporate.

NOTES

Commencement: 25 November 2016.

[1.2055]
29 Application to unincorporated associations

(1) In a case falling within subsection (2), an unincorporated association is to be treated as a legal person for the purposes of sections 14 to 27.

(2) A case falls within this subsection if it relates to a trigger offence for which it is possible to bring proceedings against an unincorporated association in the name of the association.

(3) Proceedings for an offence under section 27 alleged to have been committed by an unincorporated association may be brought against the association in the name of the association.

(4) For the purposes of such proceedings—

(a) rules of court relating to the service of documents have effect as if the association were a body corporate, and

(b) the following provisions apply as they apply in relation to a body corporate—

(i) section 33 of the Criminal Justice Act 1925 and Schedule 3 to the Magistrates' Courts Act 1980;

(ii) sections 70 and 143 of the Criminal Procedure (Scotland) Act 1995;

(iii) section 18 of the Criminal Justice Act (Northern Ireland) 1945 (c 15 (NI)) and Schedule 4 to the Magistrates' Courts (Northern Ireland) Order 1981 (SI 1981/1675 (NI 26)).

(5) A fine imposed on the association on its conviction of an offence is to be paid out of the funds of the association.

(6) If an offence under section 27 committed by an unincorporated association is proved—

(a) to have been committed with the consent or connivance of an officer of the association, or

(b) to be attributable to any neglect on the part of such an officer,

the officer, as well as the association, is guilty of the offence and liable to be proceeded against and punished accordingly.

(7) In subsection (6) "officer", in relation to any association, means—

(a) an officer of the association or a member of its governing body;

(b) a person purporting to act in such a capacity.

NOTES

Commencement: 25 November 2016.

[1.2056]
30 Application to partnerships

(1) If an offence under section 27 committed by a partner of a partnership which is not regarded as a legal person is shown—

(a) to have been committed with the consent or connivance of another partner, or

(b) to be attributable to any neglect on the part of another partner,

that other partner, as well as the first-mentioned partner, is guilty of the offence and liable to be proceeded against and punished accordingly.

(2) Proceedings for an offence under section 27 alleged to have been committed by a partnership which is regarded as a legal person may be brought against the partnership in the firm name.

(3) For the purposes of such proceedings—

(a) rules of court relating to the service of documents have effect as if the partnership were a body corporate, and

(b) the following provisions apply as they apply in relation to a body corporate—

(i) section 33 of the Criminal Justice Act 1925 and Schedule 3 to the Magistrates' Courts Act 1980;

(ii) sections 70 and 143 of the Criminal Procedure (Scotland) Act 1995;

(iii) section 18 of the Criminal Justice Act (Northern Ireland) 1945 (c 15 (NI)) and Schedule 4 to the Magistrates' Courts (Northern Ireland) Order 1981 (SI 1981/1675 (NI 26)).

(4) A fine imposed on a partnership on its conviction of an offence is to be paid out of the funds of the partnership.

(5) If an offence under section 27 committed by a partnership is proved—

(a) to have been committed with the consent or connivance of a partner, or

(b) to be attributable to any neglect on the part of a partner,

the partner, as well as the partnership, is guilty of the offence and liable to be proceeded against and punished accordingly.

(6) In subsections (1) and (5) "partner" includes a person purporting to act as a partner.

(7) For the purposes of this section a partnership is, or is not, "regarded as a legal person" if it is, or is not, so regarded under the law of the country or territory under which it was formed.

NOTES

Commencement: 25 November 2016.

Supplementary provision

31 (*Introduces Schedule 3 (Consequential and Related Amendments).*)

[1.2057]
32 Regulations under Chapter 1

(1) Regulations under section 3 or 14 must not prescribe a requirement, function or offence if provision imposing the requirement, conferring the function or creating the offence falls within subsection (3).

(2) Regulations under section 11 must not confer a function if provision doing so falls within subsection (3).

(3) Provision falls within this subsection if—

(a) it would be within the legislative competence of the Scottish Parliament if contained in an Act of that Parliament,

(b) it would be within the legislative competence of the National Assembly for Wales if contained in an Act of that Assembly, or

(c) it would be within the legislative competence of the Northern Ireland Assembly if contained in an Act of that Assembly made without the consent of the Secretary of State.

(4) Regulations under section 3, 11 or 14 may make such provision amending, repealing or revoking any provision of any enactment, including this Chapter, as the Secretary of State considers appropriate in consequence of the regulations.

NOTES

Commencement: 12 July 2016.

[1.2058]

33 Interpretation of Chapter 1

In this Chapter—

"the Director" has the meaning given by section 1;

"enactment" includes—

(a) an enactment contained in subordinate legislation within the meaning of the Interpretation Act 1978;

(b) an enactment contained in, or in an instrument made under, an Act of the Scottish Parliament;

(c) an enactment contained in, or in an instrument made under, a Measure or Act of the National Assembly for Wales;

(d) an enactment contained in, or in an instrument made under, Northern Ireland legislation;

"enforcing authority" has the meaning given by section 14;

"financial year" means a period of 12 months ending with 31 March;

"HMRC Commissioners" means the Commissioners for Her Majesty's Revenue and Customs;

"labour market enforcement functions" has the meaning given by section 3;

"LME order" has the meaning given by section 18;

"LME undertaking" has the meaning given by section 14;

"non-compliance in the labour market" has the meaning given by section 3;

"the respondent" has the meaning given by section 18;

"strategy" has the meaning given by section 2;

"subject" has the meaning given by section 14;

"trigger offence" has the meaning given by section 14.

NOTES

Commencement: 12 July 2016.

CHAPTER 2 ILLEGAL WORKING

Offences

[1.2059]

34 Offence of illegal working

(1) The Immigration Act 1971 is amended as follows.

(2) In section 3(1)(c)(i) (power to grant limited leave to enter or remain in the United Kingdom subject to condition restricting employment or occupation) for "employment" substitute "work".

(3) After section 24A insert—

"24B Illegal working

(1) A person ("P") who is subject to immigration control commits an offence if—

(a) P works at a time when P is disqualified from working by reason of P's immigration status, and

(b) at that time P knows or has reasonable cause to believe that P is disqualified from working by reason of P's immigration status.

(2) For the purposes of subsection (1) a person is disqualified from working by reason of the person's immigration status if—

(a) the person has not been granted leave to enter or remain in the United Kingdom, or

(b) the person's leave to enter or remain in the United Kingdom—

(i) is invalid,

(ii) has ceased to have effect (whether by reason of curtailment, revocation, cancellation, passage of time or otherwise), or

(iii) is subject to a condition preventing the person from doing work of that kind.

(3) A person who is guilty of an offence under subsection (1) is liable on summary conviction—

(a) in England and Wales, to imprisonment for a term not exceeding 51 weeks or a fine, or both,

(b) in Scotland or Northern Ireland, to imprisonment for a term not exceeding 6 months or a fine not exceeding level 5 on the standard scale, or both.

(4) In relation to an offence committed before section 281(5) of the Criminal Justice Act 2003 comes into force, the reference in subsection (3)(a) to 51 weeks is to be read as a reference to 6 months.

(5) If a person is convicted of an offence under subsection (1) in England and Wales, the prosecutor must consider whether to ask the court to commit the person to the Crown Court under section 70 of the Proceeds of Crime Act 2002 (committal with view to confiscation order being considered).

(6) If a person is convicted of an offence under subsection (1) in Scotland, the prosecutor must consider whether to ask the court to act under section 92 of the Proceeds of Crime Act 2002 (making of confiscation order).

(7) If a person is convicted of an offence under subsection (1) in Northern Ireland, the prosecutor must consider whether to ask the court to commit the person to the Crown Court under section 218 of the Proceeds of Crime Act 2002 (committal with view to confiscation order being considered).

(8) The reference in subsection (1) to a person who is subject to immigration control is to a person who under this Act requires leave to enter or remain in the United Kingdom.

(9) Where a person is on immigration bail within the meaning of Part 1 of Schedule 10 to the Immigration Act 2016—

(a) the person is to be treated for the purposes of subsection (2) as if the person had been granted leave to enter the United Kingdom, but

(b) any condition as to the person's work in the United Kingdom to which the person's immigration bail is subject is to be treated for those purposes as a condition of leave.

(10) The reference in subsection (1) to a person working is to that person working—

(a) under a contract of employment,

(b) under a contract of apprenticeship,

(c) under a contract personally to do work,

(d) under or for the purposes of a contract for services,

(e) for a purpose related to a contract to sell goods,

(f) as a constable,

(g) in the course of Crown employment,

(h) as a relevant member of the House of Commons staff, or

(i) as a relevant member of the House of Lords staff.

(11) In subsection (10)—

"contract to sell goods" means a contract by which a person acting in the course of a trade, business, craft or profession transfers or agrees to transfer the property in goods to another person (and for this purpose "goods" means any tangible moveable items);

"Crown employment"—

(a) in relation to England and Wales and Scotland, has the meaning given by section 191(3) of the Employment Rights Act 1996;

(b) in relation to Northern Ireland, has the meaning given by Article 236(3) of the Employment Rights (Northern Ireland) Order 1996 (SI 1996/1919 (NI 16));

"relevant member of the House of Commons staff" has the meaning given by section 195(5) of the Employment Rights Act 1996;

"relevant member of the House of Lords staff" has the meaning given by section 194(6) of the Employment Rights Act 1996.

(12) Subsection (1) does not apply to—

(a) service as a member of the naval, military or air forces of the Crown, or

(b) employment by an association established for the purposes of Part 11 of the Reserve Forces Act 1996.

(13) In this section "contract" means a contract whether express or implied and, if express, whether oral or in writing."

(4)–(8) (*Contain other amendments to the Immigration Act 1971.*)

NOTES

Commencement: 12 July 2016.

[1.2060]

35 Offence of employing illegal worker

(1) Section 21 of the Immigration, Asylum and Nationality Act 2006 (offence of knowingly employing illegal worker) is amended in accordance with subsections (2) to (4).

(2) In subsection (1) for the words from "an adult" to the end of the subsection substitute "disqualified from employment by reason of the employee's immigration status."

(3) After subsection (1) insert—

"(1A) A person commits an offence if the person—

(a) employs another person ("the employee") who is disqualified from employment by reason of the employee's immigration status, and

(b) has reasonable cause to believe that the employee is disqualified from employment by reason of the employee's immigration status.

(1B) For the purposes of subsections (1) and (1A) a person is disqualified from employment by reason of the person's immigration status if the person is an adult subject to immigration control and—

(a) the person has not been granted leave to enter or remain in the United Kingdom, or

(b) the person's leave to enter or remain in the United Kingdom—

(i) is invalid,

(ii) has ceased to have effect (whether by reason of curtailment, revocation, cancellation, passage of time or otherwise), or

(iii) is subject to a condition preventing the person from accepting the employment."

(4) In subsection (2)(a)(i) (maximum term of imprisonment for conviction of offence on indictment) for "two" substitute "five".

(5) Section 22 of the Immigration, Asylum and Nationality Act 2006 (offences by bodies corporate etc) is amended in accordance with subsections (6) and (7).

(6) After subsection (1) insert—

"(1A) For the purposes of section 21(1A) a body (whether corporate or not) shall be treated as having reasonable cause to believe a fact about an employee if a person who has responsibility within the body for an aspect of the employment has reasonable cause to believe that fact."

(7)–(10) *(Contain other amendments to the Immigration, Asylum and Nationality Act 2006 and the Immigration Act 1971.)*

NOTES

Commencement: 12 July 2016.

Illegal working notices and orders

[1.2061]

38 Illegal working closure notices and illegal working compliance orders

Schedule 6 (illegal working closure notices and illegal working compliance orders) has effect.

NOTES

Commencement: 1 December 2016.

PART 7
LANGUAGE REQUIREMENTS FOR PUBLIC SECTOR WORKERS

NOTES

Transfer of functions: the functions of the Secretary of State under this Part which were exercisable concurrently with the Chancellor of the Duchy of Lancaster ceased to be exercisable concurrently with the Chancellor of the Duchy of Lancaster and are instead exercisable concurrently with the Minister for the Cabinet Office; see the Transfer of Functions (Elections, Referendums, Third Sector and Information) Order 2016, SI 2016/997, art 3, Sch 1. See also the amendments made to ss 83 and 93 by that Order *post*.

[1.2062]

77 English language requirements for public sector workers

(1) A public authority must ensure that each person who works for the public authority in a customer-facing role speaks fluent English.

(2) In determining how to comply with subsection (1), a public authority must have regard to the code of practice under section 80 that is for the time being applicable to that authority.

(3) A public authority must operate an adequate procedure for enabling complaints to be made to the authority about breaches by the authority of subsection (1) and for the consideration of such complaints.

(4) In determining whether a procedure is adequate for the purposes of subsection (3), a public authority must have regard to the code of practice under section 80 that is for the time being applicable to that authority.

(5) For the purposes of this Part a person works for a public authority if the person works—

(a) under a contract of employment with the public authority,

(b) under a contract of apprenticeship with the public authority,

(c) under a contract to do work personally with the public authority,

(d) in England and Wales or Scotland, as an agency worker within the meaning of the Agency Workers Regulations 2010 (SI 2010/93) in respect of whom the public authority is the hirer within the meaning of those regulations,

(e) in Northern Ireland, as an agency worker within the meaning of the Agency Workers Regulations (Northern Ireland) 2011 (SR 2011/350) in respect of whom the public authority is the hirer within the meaning of those regulations,

(f) for the public authority as a constable, or

(g) for the public authority in the course of Crown employment.

(6) In subsection (5) "Crown employment"—

(a) in relation to England and Wales and Scotland, has the meaning given by section 191(3) of the Employment Rights Act 1996,

(b) in relation to Northern Ireland, has the meaning given by Article 236(3) of the Employment Rights (Northern Ireland) Order 1996 (SI 1996/1919 (NI 16)), and

(c) includes service as a member of the armed forces of the Crown and employment by an association established for the purposes of Part 11 of the Reserve Forces Act 1996.

(7) References in this Part to a person who works in a customer-facing role are to a person who, as a regular and intrinsic part of the person's role, is required to speak to members of the public in English.

(8) For the purposes of this Part a person speaks fluent English if the person has a command of spoken English which is sufficient to enable the effective performance of the person's role.

(9) This section applies in relation to a person who is working in a customer-facing role for a public authority when this section comes into force as well as to a person who begins to work in such a role after that time.

(10) This section does not apply in relation to a person whose work is carried out wholly or mainly outside the United Kingdom.

NOTES

Commencement: 21 November 2016.

Code of Practice issued under s 80: see the Code of Practice on the English language requirements for public sector workers (November 2016) at **[4.317]**.

[1.2063]

78 Meaning of "public authority"

(1) Subject as follows, in this Part "public authority" means a person with functions of a public nature.

(2) A person is not a public authority for the purposes of this Part if, apart from this subsection, the person would be a public authority for those purposes merely because the person exercises functions on behalf of another public authority.

(3) A person who exercises functions in relation to Scotland is a public authority for the purposes of this Part in relation to those functions only if and to the extent that those functions relate to a reserved matter.

(4) In subsection (3) "Scotland" and "reserved matter" have the same meanings as in the Scotland Act 1998.

(5) A person who exercises functions in relation to Wales is a public authority for the purposes of this Part in relation to those functions only if and to the extent that those [functions are functions that could not be conferred by provision falling within] the legislative competence of the National Assembly for Wales.

(6) A person who exercises functions in relation to Northern Ireland is a public authority for the purposes of this Part in relation to those functions only if and to the extent that those functions relate to an excepted matter.

(7) In subsection (6) "Northern Ireland" and "excepted matter" have the same meanings as in the Northern Ireland Act 1998.

(8) The following are not public authorities for the purposes of this Part—

(a) the Security Service;

(b) the Secret Intelligence Service;

(c) the Government Communications Headquarters.

(9) The relevant Minister may by regulations amend subsection (8) so as to add, modify or remove a reference to a person or description of person with functions of a public nature.

NOTES

Commencement: 21 November 2016.

Sub-s (5): words in square brackets substituted by the Wales Act 2017, s 69(1), Sch 6, Pt 3, para 113, as from 1 April 2018.

Regulations: as of 15 May 2019, no regulations had been made under this section.

[1.2064]

79 Power to expand meaning of person working for public authority

(1) The relevant Minister may by regulations amend section 77 with the effect that a person who works for a contractor of a public authority is a person who works for the authority for the purposes of this Part.

(2) In subsection (1) "contractor", in relation to a public authority, means a person who—

(a) provides a service to members of the public as a result of an arrangement made with a public authority (whether or not by that person), but

(b) is not a public authority.

(3) For the purposes of subsection (1) a person works for a contractor if the person works—

(a) under a contract of employment with the contractor,

(b) under a contract of apprenticeship with the contractor,

(c) under a contract to do work personally with the contractor,

(d) in England and Wales or Scotland, as an agency worker within the meaning of the Agency Workers Regulations 2010 (SI 2010/93) in respect of whom the contractor is the hirer within the meaning of those regulations, or

(e) in Northern Ireland, as an agency worker within the meaning of the Agency Workers Regulations (Northern Ireland) 2011 (SR 2011/350) in respect of whom the contractor is the hirer within the meaning of those regulations.

NOTES

Commencement: 21 November 2016.

Regulations: as of 15 May 2019, no regulations had been made under this section.

[1.2065]

80 Duty to issue codes of practice

(1) The relevant Minister must issue a code or codes of practice for the purposes of section 77.

(2) A code of practice must include provision about the following matters—

(a) the standard of spoken English to be met by a person working for a public authority to which the code applies in a customer-facing role;

(b) the action available to such a public authority where such a person does not meet that standard;

(c) the procedure to be operated by such a public authority for enabling complaints to be made to the authority about breaches by the authority of section 77(1) and for the consideration of such complaints;
(d) how the public authority is to comply with its other legal obligations as well as complying with the duty in section 77(1).

(3) A code of practice may make such other provision as the relevant Minister considers appropriate for securing that a person who works for a public authority to which the code applies in a customer-facing role speaks fluent English.

(4) A code of practice may make provision in relation to—
(a) all public authorities,
(b) particular descriptions of public authority, or
(c) particular public authorities.

(5) But the relevant Minister must ensure that there is at all times a code of practice in force which applies to each public authority.

(6) A code of practice may make different provision for different purposes, including different provision for different public authorities or descriptions of public authority.

NOTES

Commencement: 21 November 2016.

Code of Practice: see the Code of Practice on the English language requirements for public sector workers (November 2016) at **[4.317]**.

[1.2066]
81 Procedure for codes of practice

(1) In preparing a code of practice the relevant Minister must consult such persons as the relevant Minister thinks appropriate.

(2) Before issuing a code of practice the relevant Minister must lay a draft of the code before Parliament.

(3) A code of practice comes into force in accordance with provision made by regulations made by the relevant Minister.

(4) After a code of practice has come into force the relevant Minister must publish it in such manner as the relevant Minister thinks appropriate.

(5) The relevant Minister may from time to time review a code of practice and may revise and re-issue it following a review.

(6) References in subsections (1) to (4) to a code of practice include a revised code.

NOTES

Commencement: 21 November 2016.

Regulations: the Code of Practice (English Language Requirements for Public Sector Workers) Regulations 2016, SI 2016/1157 (which brings into force the Code of Practice issued under s 80 on 22 December 2016).

[1.2067]
82 Application of Part to Wales

(1) Subsection (2) makes provision about the application of this Part in relation to—
(a) a public authority that exercises functions only in Wales, and
(b) a public authority that exercises functions outside Wales and in Wales, to the extent that it exercises functions in Wales.

(2) In the provisions of this Part listed in subsection (3) references to English are to be read as references to English or Welsh.

(3) Those provisions are—
(a) section 77(1), (7) and (8), and
(b) section 80(2)(a) and (3).

NOTES

Commencement: 21 November 2016.

[1.2068]
83 Interpretation of Part

In this Part—

"contract" means a contract whether express or implied and, if express, whether oral or in writing;
"public authority" has the meaning given by section 78;
"relevant Minister" means the Secretary of State or the [Minister for the Cabinet Office];
"Wales" has the same meaning as in the Government of Wales Act 2006.

NOTES

Commencement: 21 November 2016.

In the definition "relevant Minister" words in square brackets substituted by the Transfer of Functions (Elections, Referendums, Third Sector and Information) Order 2016, SI 2016/997, art 13, Sch 2, Pt 1, para 32(a), as from 9 November 2016.

[1.2069]
84 Crown application

This Part binds the Crown.

NOTES
Commencement: 21 November 2016.

PART 9
MISCELLANEOUS AND GENERAL

Final provisions

[1.2070]
91 Financial provisions
The following are to be paid out of money provided by Parliament—
(a) any expenditure incurred under or by virtue of this Act by a Minister of the Crown, a person holding office under Her Majesty or a government department, and
(b) any increase attributable to the Act in the sums payable under any other Act out of money so provided.

NOTES
Commencement: 12 May 2016.

[1.2071]
92 Transitional and consequential provision
(1) The Secretary of State may by regulations make such transitional, transitory or saving provision as the Secretary of State considers appropriate in connection with the coming into force of any provision of this Act.
(2) The Secretary of State may by regulations make such provision as the Secretary of State considers appropriate in consequence of this Act.
(3) The provision that may be made by regulations under subsection (2) includes provision amending, repealing or revoking any enactment.
(4) "Enactment" includes—
(a) an enactment contained in subordinate legislation within the meaning of the Interpretation Act 1978;
(b) an enactment contained in, or in an instrument made under, an Act of the Scottish Parliament;
(c) an enactment contained in, or in an instrument made under, a Measure or Act of the National Assembly for Wales;
(d) an enactment contained in, or in an instrument made under, Northern Ireland legislation.
(5) (*Amends the UK Borders Act 2007.*)

NOTES
Commencement: 12 May 2016.
Regulations: the Immigration Act 2016 (Consequential Amendments) Regulations 2016, SI 2016/655; the Immigration Act 2016 (Transitional Provision) Regulations 2016, SI 2016/712; the Immigration Act 2016 (Consequential Amendments) (Biometrics and Legal Aid) Regulations 2017, SI 2017/617; the Immigration Act 2016 (Consequential Amendments) Regulations 2017, SI 2017/931; the Immigration Act 2016 (Commencement No 7 and Transitional Provisions) Regulations 2017, SI 2017/1241; the Immigration Act 2016 (Consequential Amendments) (Immigration Bail) Regulations 2017, SI 2017/1242; the Immigration Act 2016 (Consequential Amendments) (Licensing of Booking Offices: Scotland) Regulations 2017, SI 2017/1317; the Immigration Act 2016 (Commencement No 7 and Transitional Provisions) (Amendment) Regulations 2018, SI 2018/31.

[1.2072]
93 Regulations
(1) Regulations made by the Secretary of State or the [Minister for the Cabinet Office] under this Act are to be made by statutory instrument.
(2) A statutory instrument containing (whether alone or with other provision) any of the following regulations may not be made unless a draft of the instrument has been laid before, and approved by a resolution of, each House of Parliament—
(a), (b) (*outside the scope of this work*),
(c) regulations under section 11 which amend or repeal primary legislation,
(d)–(g) (*outside the scope of this work*),
(h) regulations under section 78(9),
(i) regulations under section 79(1),
(j)–(m) (*outside the scope of this work*),
(3) Primary legislation means any of the following—
(a) an Act of Parliament;
(b) an Act of the Scottish Parliament;
(c) a Measure or Act of the National Assembly for Wales;
(d) Northern Ireland legislation.
(4) A statutory instrument—
(a) containing any other regulations made by the Secretary of State or the [Minister for the Cabinet Office] under this Act, and
(b) to which subsection (2) does not apply,
is subject to annulment in pursuance of a resolution of either House of Parliament.
(5) Subsection (4) does not apply to regulations under section 92(1) or 94(1).
(6) Regulations made by the Secretary of State or the [Minister for the Cabinet Office] under this Act—

(a) may make different provision for different purposes or areas,
(b) may make provision which applies generally or for particular purposes or areas,
(c) may make transitional, transitory or saving provision, or
(d) may make incidental, supplementary or consequential provision.

NOTES

Commencement: 12 May 2016.

Sub-ss (1), (4), (6): words "Minister for the Cabinet Office" in square brackets substituted by the Transfer of Functions (Elections, Referendums, Third Sector and Information) Order 2016, SI 2016/997, art 13, Sch 2, Pt 1, para 32(b), as from 9 November 2016.

[1.2073]

94 Commencement

(1) Subject to subsections (3) to (5) this Act comes into force on such day as the Secretary of State appoints by regulations.

(2) Regulations under subsection (1) may appoint different days for different purposes or areas.

(3) Subsections (3) to (5) of section 61 come into force on the day on which this Act is passed.

(4) (*Outside the scope of this work.*)

(5) This Part comes into force on the day on which this Act is passed.

NOTES

Commencement: 12 May 2016.

Regulations: the Immigration Act 2016 (Commencement No 1) Regulations 2016, SI 2016/603; the Immigration Act 2016 (Commencement No 2 and Transitional Provisions) Regulations 2016, SI 2016/1037; the Immigration Act 2016 (Commencement No 3 and Transitional Provision) Regulations 2017, SI 2017/380; the Immigration Act 2016 (Commencement No 4) Regulations 2017, SI 2017/799; the Immigration Act 2016 (Commencement No 5) Regulations 2017, SI 2017/929; the Immigration Act 2016 (Commencement No 6) Regulations 2017, SI 2017/1210; the Immigration Act 2016 (Commencement No 7 and Transitional Provisions) Regulations 2017, SI 2017/1241.

[1.2074]

95 Extent

(1) This Act extends to England and Wales, Scotland and Northern Ireland, subject as follows.

(2) (*Outside the scope of this work.*)

(3) Any amendment, repeal or revocation made by this Act has the same extent within the United Kingdom as the provision to which it relates.

(4) But subsection (3) does not apply to the amendments made to the Modern Slavery Act 2015 by paragraphs 30 and 35 of Schedule 3 (for the extent of which, see the amendments to section 60 of that Act made by paragraph 33 of that Schedule).

(5)–(7) (*Outside the scope of this work.*)

NOTES

Commencement: 12 May 2016.

[1.2075]

96 Short title

This Act may be cited as the Immigration Act 2016.

NOTES

Commencement: 12 May 2016.

SCHEDULES

SCHEDULE 1
PERSONS TO WHOM DIRECTOR ETC MAY DISCLOSE INFORMATION

Section 6

[1.2076]

Authorities with functions in connection with the labour market or the work place etc

The Secretary of State.
HMRC Commissioners.
A person by whom, or by whose officers, labour market enforcement functions are exercisable.
The Health and Safety Executive.
An enforcing authority within the meaning of Part 1 of the Health and Safety at Work etc Act 1974 (see section 18(7) of that Act).
An inspector appointed by such an enforcing authority (see section 19 of that Act).
An enforcement authority within the meaning of regulation 28 of the Working Time Regulations 1998 (SI 1998/1833).
An inspector appointed by such an enforcement authority (see Schedule 3 to those Regulations).
The Low Pay Commission.
The Pensions Regulator.

Law enforcement and border security

A chief officer of police for a police area in England and Wales.
A local policing body within the meaning given by section 101(1) of the Police Act 1996.

The chief constable of the British Transport Police Force.
The chief constable of the Police Service of Scotland.
The Chief Constable of the Police Service of Northern Ireland.
A person appointed as an immigration officer under paragraph 1 of Schedule 2 to the Immigration Act 1971.

Local government
A county or district council in England.
A London borough council.
The Greater London Authority.
The Common Council of the City of London.
The Council of the Isles of Scilly.
A county or county borough council in Wales.
A council constituted under section 2 of the Local Government etc (Scotland) Act 1994.
A district council in Northern Ireland.

Health bodies
The Care Quality Commission.
A National Health Service trust established under section 25 of the National Health Service Act 2006 or section 18 of the National Health Service (Wales) Act 2006.
An NHS foundation trust within the meaning given by section 30 of the National Health Service Act 2006.
A Local Health Board established under section 11 of the National Health Service (Wales) Act 2006.

Other
The Independent Anti-slavery Commissioner.
A Northern Ireland department.

NOTES
Commencement: 12 July 2016.

SCHEDULES 2, 3

(*Schedule 2 (Functions in relation to labour market) contains a variety of amendments including amendments to the Employment Agencies Act 1973 and the National Minimum Wage Act 1998 which, in so far as relevant, have been incorporated ante. Schedule 3 (Consequential and related amendments) contains a variety of amendments including amendments to the National Minimum Wage Act 1998, the Gangmasters (Licensing) Act 2004, and the Modern Slavery Act 2015 which, in so far as relevant, have been incorporated ante. Other amendments made by Schedules 2 and 3 are outside the scope of this work.*)

SCHEDULE 6
ILLEGAL WORKING CLOSURE NOTICES AND ILLEGAL WORKING COMPLIANCE ORDERS

Section 38

Illegal working closure notices

[1.2077]
1. (1) An immigration officer of at least the rank of chief immigration officer may issue an illegal working closure notice in respect of premises if satisfied on reasonable grounds that the conditions in sub-paragraphs (3) and (6) are met.

(2) An illegal working closure notice is a notice which prohibits, for a period specified in the notice—
- (a) access to the premises other than by a person who habitually lives on the premises, except where authorised in writing by an immigration officer;
- (b) paid or voluntary work being performed on the premises, except where so authorised.

(3) The condition in this sub-paragraph is that an employer operating at the premises is employing a person over the age of 16 and subject to immigration control—
- (a) who has not been granted leave to enter or remain in the United Kingdom, or
- (b) whose leave to enter or remain in the United Kingdom—
  - (i) is invalid,
  - (ii) has ceased to have effect (whether by reason of curtailment, revocation, cancellation, passage of time or otherwise), or
  - (iii) is subject to a condition preventing the person from accepting the employment.

(4) Where a person is on immigration bail within the meaning of Part 1 of Schedule 10—
- (a) the person is to be treated for the purposes of sub-paragraph (3) as if the person had been granted leave to enter the United Kingdom, but
- (b) any condition as to the person's work in the United Kingdom to which the person's immigration bail is subject is to be treated for those purposes as a condition of leave.

(5) A person falling within sub-paragraph (3) is referred to in this Schedule as an "illegal worker".

(6) The condition in this sub-paragraph is that the employer, or a connected person in relation to the employer—
- (a) has been convicted of an offence under section 21 of the Immigration, Asylum and Nationality Act 2006 ("the 2006 Act"),

(b) has, during the period of three years ending with the date on which the illegal working closure notice is issued, been required to pay a penalty under section 15 of the 2006 Act, or

(c) has at any time been required to pay such a penalty and failed to pay it.

(7) Sub-paragraph (6)(a) does not apply in relation to a conviction which is a spent conviction for the purposes of the Rehabilitation of Offenders Act 1974 or the Rehabilitation of Offenders (Northern Ireland) Order 1978 (SI 1978/1908 (NI 27)).

(8) For the purposes of sub-paragraph (6)(b) and (c)—

(a) a person to whom a penalty notice under section 15 of the 2006 Act has been given is not to be treated as having been required to pay the penalty if—

(i) the person is excused payment by virtue of section 15(3) of that Act, or

(ii) the penalty is cancelled by virtue of section 16 or 17 of that Act;

(b) a person to whom such a notice has been given is not to be treated as having been required to pay the penalty until such time as—

(i) the period for giving a notice of objection under section 16 of the 2006 Act has expired and the Secretary of State has considered any notice given within that period, and

(ii) if a notice of objection was given within that period, the period for appealing under section 17 of that Act has expired and any appeal brought within that period has been finally determined, abandoned or withdrawn.

(9) For the purposes of sub-paragraph (6), a person is a connected person in relation to an employer if—

(a) where the employer is a body corporate, the person is—

(i) a director, manager or secretary of the body corporate,

(ii) purporting to act as a director, manager or secretary of the body corporate, or

(iii) if the affairs of the body corporate are managed by its members, a member of the body corporate;

(b) where the employer is a partnership (whether or not a limited partnership), the person is a partner or purporting to act as a partner;

(c) where the employer is an individual, the person is—

(i) a body corporate of which the individual has at any time been a director, manager or secretary,

(ii) a body corporate in relation to which the individual has at any time purported to act as a director, manager or secretary,

(iii) a body corporate whose affairs are managed by its members and the individual has at any time been a member of the body corporate,

(iv) a partnership (whether or not a limited partnership) in which the individual has at any time been a partner or in relation to which the individual has at any time purported to act as a partner.

(10) An illegal working closure notice may not be issued if the employer shows in relation to the employment of each illegal worker that if a penalty notice were given under section 15 of the 2006 Act the employer would be excused under subsection (3) of that section from paying the penalty.

(11) An illegal working closure notice may be issued only if reasonable efforts have been made to inform—

(a) people who live on the premises (whether habitually or not), and

(b) any person who has an interest in the premises,

that the notice is going to be issued.

(12) Before issuing an illegal working closure notice the immigration officer must ensure that any person the officer thinks appropriate has been consulted.

(13) The Secretary of State may by regulations amend sub-paragraph (1) to change the rank specified in that sub-paragraph.

2. (1) An illegal working closure notice must—

(a) identify the premises;

(b) explain the effect of the notice;

(c) state that failure to comply with the notice is an offence;

(d) state that an application will be made under paragraph 5 for an illegal working compliance order;

(e) specify when and where the application will be heard;

(f) explain the effect of an illegal working compliance order.

(2) The maximum period that may be specified in an illegal working closure notice is 24 hours unless sub-paragraph (3) applies.

(3) The maximum period is 48 hours if the notice is issued by an immigration officer of at least the rank of immigration inspector.

(4) In calculating when the period of 48 hours ends, Christmas Day is to be disregarded.

(5) The period specified in an illegal working closure notice to which sub-paragraph (3) does not apply may be extended by up to 24 hours if an extension notice is issued by an officer of at least the rank of immigration inspector.

(6) An extension notice is a notice which—

(a) identifies the illegal working closure notice to which it relates, and

(b) specifies the period of the extension.

(7) The Secretary of State may by regulations amend sub-paragraph (3) or sub-paragraph (5) to change the rank specified in that sub-paragraph.

Cancellation of illegal working closure notices

3. (1) An immigration officer may by the issue of a cancellation notice cancel an illegal working closure notice if—

(a) the immigration officer considers that the condition in paragraph 1(3) or (6) is not met, or
(b) the employer shows in relation to the employment of each illegal worker that if a penalty notice were given under section 15 of the 2006 Act the employer would be excused under subsection (3) of that section from paying the penalty.

(2) A cancellation notice may be issued only—

(a) by an immigration officer of at least the rank of the immigration officer who issued the illegal working closure notice, or
(b) where the illegal working closure notice has been extended by an extension notice, by an immigration officer of at least the rank of the immigration officer who issued the extension notice.

Service of notices

4. (1) A notice under paragraph 1, 2 or 3 must be served by an immigration officer.

(2) The immigration officer must if possible—

(a) fix a copy of the notice to at least one prominent place on the premises,
(b) fix a copy of the notice to each normal means of access to the premises,
(c) fix a copy of the notice to any outbuildings that appear to the immigration officer to be used with or as part of the premises,
(d) give a copy of the notice to at least one person who appears to the immigration officer to have control of or responsibility for the premises,
(e) give a copy of the notice to the people who live on the premises and to any person who does not live there but was informed (under paragraph 1(11)) that the notice was going to be issued.

(3) If the immigration officer reasonably believes, at the time of serving the notice, that there are persons occupying another part of the building or other structure in which the premises are situated whose access to that part will be impeded if an illegal working compliance order is made under paragraph 5, the immigration officer must also if possible serve the notice on those persons.

(4) The immigration officer may enter any premises, using reasonable force if necessary, for the purposes of complying with sub-paragraph (2)(a).

Illegal working compliance orders

5. (1) Whenever an illegal working closure notice is issued an application must be made to the court for an illegal working compliance order (unless the notice has been cancelled under paragraph 3).

(2) An application for an illegal working compliance order must be made by an immigration officer.

(3) The application must be heard by the court not later than 48 hours after service of the illegal working closure notice.

(4) In calculating when the period of 48 hours ends, Christmas Day is to be disregarded.

(5) The court may make an illegal working compliance order in respect of premises if it is satisfied, on the balance of probabilities—

(a) that the conditions in paragraph 1(3) and (6) are met, and
(b) that it is necessary to make the illegal working compliance order to prevent an employer operating at the premises from employing an illegal worker.

(6) An illegal working compliance order may—

(a) prohibit or restrict access to the premises;
(b) require a person specified in the order to carry out, at such times as may be so specified, such checks relating to the right to work as may be prescribed by the Secretary of State in regulations;
(c) require a person specified in the order to produce to an immigration officer, at such times and such places as may be so specified, such documents relating to the right to work as may be prescribed by the Secretary of State in regulations;
(d) specify the times at which and the circumstances in which an immigration officer may enter the premises to carry out such investigations or inspections as may be specified in the order;
(e) make such other provision as the court considers appropriate.

(7) Different provisions in an illegal working compliance order may have effect for different periods.

(8) The maximum period for which an illegal working compliance order or any provision in it may have effect is 12 months.

(9) Provision included in an illegal working compliance order which prohibits or restricts access may make such provision—

(a) in relation to all persons, all persons except those specified, or all persons except those of a specified description;
(b) having effect at all times, or at all times except those specified;
(c) having effect in all circumstances, or in all circumstances except those specified.

(10) An illegal working compliance order, or any provision of it, may—

(a) be made in respect of the whole or any part of the premises;

(b) include provision about access to a part of the building or structure of which the premises form part.

(11) The court must notify the relevant licensing authority if it makes an illegal working compliance order in relation to premises in England and Wales in respect of which a premises licence is in force.

Illegal working compliance orders: adjournment of hearing

6. (1) This paragraph applies where an application has been made under paragraph 5 for an illegal working compliance order.

(2) The court may adjourn the hearing of the application for a period of not more than 14 days to enable any person who has an interest in the premises to show why an illegal working compliance order should not be made.

(3) If the court adjourns the hearing it may order that the illegal working closure notice continues in force until the end of the period of adjournment.

Extension of illegal working compliance orders

7. (1) An immigration officer may apply to the court for an extension (or further extension) of the period for which any provision of an illegal working compliance order is in force.

(2) The court may grant an application under this paragraph only if it is satisfied, on the balance of probabilities, that it is necessary to grant it to prevent an employer operating at the premises from employing an illegal worker.

(3) Where an application is made under this section, the court may issue a summons directed to—

- (a) any person on whom the illegal working closure notice was served under paragraph 4, or
- (b) any other person who appears to the court to have an interest in the premises,

requiring the person to appear before the court to respond to the application.

(4) If a summons is issued, a notice stating the date, time and place of the hearing of the application must be served on the persons to whom the summons is directed.

(5) No application may be granted under this paragraph such that an illegal working compliance order, or any provision in it—

- (a) is extended for a period exceeding 6 months, or
- (b) is in force for a period exceeding 24 months in total.

Variation or discharge of illegal working compliance orders

8. (1) An application may be made to the court under this paragraph—

- (a) by an immigration officer for an illegal working compliance order to be varied or discharged,
- (b) by a person on whom the illegal working closure notice was served under paragraph 4, or by any other person who has an interest in the premises, for an illegal working compliance order to be varied or discharged.

(2) Where an application is made under this paragraph, the court may issue a summons directed to—

- (a) an immigration officer,
- (b) any person on whom the illegal working closure notice was served under paragraph 4, or
- (c) any other person who appears to the court to have an interest in the premises,

requiring the person to appear before the court to respond to the application.

(3) If a summons is issued, a notice stating the date, time and place of the hearing of the application must be served on the persons to whom the summons is directed.

(4) The court may not discharge an illegal working compliance order unless it is satisfied, on the balance of probabilities, that it is no longer necessary to prevent an employer operating at the premises from employing an illegal worker.

Notice and orders: appeals

9. (1) An appeal against a decision—

- (a) to make, extend or vary an illegal working compliance order;
- (b) not to discharge an illegal working compliance order;
- (c) to order that an illegal working closure notice continues in force,

may be made by a person on whom the illegal working closure notice was served under paragraph 4, or any other person who has an interest in the premises.

(2) An appeal against a decision—

- (a) not to make an illegal working compliance order;
- (b) not to extend a provision of an illegal working compliance order, or not to vary such an order, made on the application of an immigration officer;
- (c) to vary or discharge an illegal working compliance order;
- (d) not to order that an illegal working closure notice continues in force,

may be made by an immigration officer.

(3) An appeal under this paragraph—

- (a) if it is in relation to premises in England and Wales or Northern Ireland, is to the Crown Court,
- (b) if it is in relation to premises in Scotland, is to the sheriff appeal court.

(4) An appeal under this paragraph must be made within the period of 21 days beginning with the date of the decision to which it relates.

(5) On an appeal under this paragraph the court may make whatever order it thinks appropriate.

(6) The court must notify the relevant licensing authority if it makes an illegal working compliance order in relation to premises in England and Wales in respect of which a premises licence is in force.

Notices and orders: enforcement

10. (1) Where access to premises is prohibited or restricted by virtue of an illegal working closure notice or an illegal working compliance order an immigration officer or a constable may enter the premises and do anything necessary to secure the premises against entry.

(2) A person acting under sub-paragraph (1) may use reasonable force.

(3) An immigration officer or a constable, together with any person acting under that person's supervision, may also enter such premises to carry out essential maintenance or repairs.

Notices and orders: offences

11. (1) A person who without reasonable excuse remains on or enters premises in contravention of an illegal working closure notice commits an offence.

(2) A person who without reasonable excuse contravenes an illegal working compliance order commits an offence.

(3) A person who without reasonable excuse obstructs a person acting under paragraph 4 or paragraph 10 commits an offence.

(4) A person guilty of an offence under this paragraph is liable on summary conviction—
- (a) in England and Wales, to imprisonment for a term not exceeding 51 weeks, to a fine or to both;
- (b) in Scotland, to imprisonment for a term not exceeding 12 months, to a fine not exceeding level 5 on the standard scale or to both;
- (c) in Northern Ireland, to imprisonment for a term not exceeding 6 months, to a fine not exceeding level 5 on the standard scale or to both.

(5) In relation to an offence committed before section 281(5) of the Criminal Justice Act 2003 comes into force, the reference in sub-paragraph (4)(a) to 51 weeks is to be read as a reference to 6 months.

Access to other premises

12. (1) Where—
- (a) access to premises is prohibited or restricted by a provision of an illegal working compliance order,
- (b) those premises are part of a building or structure, and
- (c) there is another part of that building or structure that is not subject to the prohibition or restriction,

an occupier or owner of that other part may apply to the court for an order under this paragraph.

(2) Notice of an application under this paragraph must be given to—
- (a) whatever immigration officer the court thinks appropriate;
- (b) each person on whom the illegal working closure notice was served under paragraph 4,
- (c) any other person who has an interest in the premises.

(3) On an application under this paragraph the court may make whatever order it thinks appropriate in relation to access to any part of the building or structure mentioned in sub-paragraph (1).

(4) For the purposes of sub-paragraph (3), it does not matter whether provision has been made under paragraph 5(10)(b).

Reimbursement of costs

13. (1) Where the Secretary of State incurs expenditure for the purpose of clearing, securing or maintaining premises in respect of which an illegal working compliance order is in force, the Secretary of State may apply to the court for an order under this paragraph.

(2) On an application under this paragraph the court may make whatever order it thinks appropriate for the reimbursement (in full or in part) by the owner or occupier of the premises of the expenditure mentioned in sub-paragraph (1).

(3) An application for an order under this paragraph may not be heard unless it is made before the end of the period of 3 months starting with the day on which the illegal working compliance order ceases to have effect.

(4) An order under this paragraph may be made only against a person who has been served with the application for the order.

Exemption from liability

14. (1) Each of the following—
- (a) the Secretary of State,
- (b) an immigration officer,
- (c) a police officer,
- (d) the chief officer of police under whose direction or control a police officer acts,

is not liable for damages in proceedings for judicial review or the tort of negligence or misfeasance in public office, arising out of anything done or omitted to be done by the person in the exercise or purposed exercise of a power under this Schedule.

(2) Sub-paragraph (1) does not apply to an act or omission shown to have been in bad faith.

(3) Sub-paragraph (1) does not apply so as to prevent an award of damages made in respect of an act or omission on the ground that the act or omission was unlawful by virtue of section 6(1) of the Human Rights Act 1998.

(4) This paragraph does not affect any other exemption from liability (whether at common law or otherwise).

Compensation

15. (1) A person who claims to have incurred financial loss in consequence of an illegal working closure notice, other than one cancelled under paragraph 3(1)(b), may apply to the court for compensation.

(2) An application under this paragraph may not be heard unless it is made before the end of the period of 3 months starting with the day on which the notice ceases to have effect.

(3) On an application under this paragraph the court may order the payment of compensation out of money provided by Parliament if it is satisfied—

(a) that at the time the notice was issued, the condition in paragraph 1(3) or (6) was not met;

(b) that the applicant has incurred financial loss in consequence of the notice; and

(c) that having regard to all the circumstances it is appropriate to order payment of compensation in respect of that loss.

Guidance

16. (1) The Secretary of State may issue guidance about the exercise of functions under this Schedule.

(2) The Secretary of State may revise any guidance issued under this paragraph.

(3) Before issuing or revising guidance under this paragraph the Secretary of State must consult—

(a) persons whom the Secretary of State considers to represent the views of immigration officers and of chief officers of police, and

(b) such other persons as the Secretary of State considers appropriate.

(4) The Secretary of State must arrange for any guidance issued or revised under this paragraph to be published.

Interpretation

17. (1) In this Schedule—

"court", except where the context otherwise requires, means—

(a) in relation to premises in England and Wales or Northern Ireland, the magistrates' court;

(b) in relation to premises in Scotland, the sheriff court;

"owner" in relation to premises, means—

(a) a person (other than a mortgagee not in possession) entitled to dispose of the fee simple of the premises, whether in possession or in reversion;

(b) a person who holds or is entitled to the rents and profits of the premises under a lease that (when granted) was for a term of not less than 3 years;

"person who has an interest", in relation to premises, includes—

(a) the owner;

(b) any person with control of or responsibility for the premises;

(c) any person who otherwise occupies the premises;

"premises" includes—

(a) any land, vehicle, vessel or other place (whether enclosed or not);

(b) any outbuildings that are, or are used as, part of premises;

"premises licence" has the meaning given by section 11 of the Licensing Act 2003;

"relevant licensing authority" has the meaning given by section 12 of that Act.

(2) In this Schedule—

(a) a reference to employment is to employment under a contract of service or apprenticeship, whether express or implied and whether oral or written;

(b) a person is subject to immigration control if under the Immigration Act 1971 the person requires leave to enter or remain in the United Kingdom.

Amendment of Licensing Act 2003

18. (*Amends the Licensing Act 2003 (outside the scope of this work).*)

NOTES

Commencement: 1 December 2016.

Transitional provisions: see the Immigration Act 2016 (Commencement No 2 and Transitional Provisions) Regulations 2016, SI 2016/1037, reg 7 which provides that where a person is at large in the UK by virtue of the Immigration Act 1971, Sch 2, para 21(1): (a) the person is to be treated for the purposes of para 1(3) above as if the person had been granted leave to enter the UK, but (b) any restriction as to employment imposed under paragraph 21(2) of Schedule 2 to the 1971 Act is to be treated as a condition of leave.

Regulations: the Illegal Working Compliance Orders Regulations 2016, SI 2016/1058 at **[2.1948]**.

TRADE UNION (WALES) ACT 2017

(2017 anaw 4)

An Act of the National Assembly for Wales to make provision about industrial action and trade union activity in relation to the operations of, and services provided by, devolved public authorities.

[7 September 2017]

1 (*Amends the Trade Union and Labour Relations (Consolidation) Act 1992, ss 116B, 172A, 226, 299 at* **[1.422]**, **[1.483]**, **[1.547]**, **[1.633]**, *and inserts s 297B at* **[1.631]**.)

[1.2078]
2 Prohibition on using temporary workers to cover industrial action

(1) A devolved Welsh authority may not hire a worker supplied by a person carrying on an employment business to perform—

(a) duties normally performed by a member of its staff ("S") while S is taking part in a strike or other industrial action, or

(b) the duties of any other member of its staff assigned to perform the duties normally performed by S.

(2) But subsection (1) does not apply if either the strike or other industrial action is unofficial.

(3) For the purposes of this section a strike or other industrial action is unofficial if it would be regarded as unofficial for the purposes of section 237 of the Trade Union and Labour Relations (Consolidation) Act 1992 (c 52).

(4) In this section—

"devolved Welsh authority" ("*awdurdod datganoledig Cymreig*") has the same meaning as in section 157A of the Government of Wales Act 2006 (c 32);

"employment business" ("*busnes cyflogaeth*") has the same meaning as in section 13(3) of the Employment Agencies Act 1973 (c 35).

NOTES

Commencement: 13 September 2017.

[1.2079]
3 Coming into force

The provisions in section 1 and section 2 come into force on whatever day or days the Welsh Ministers appoint by order made by statutory instrument (and this section and section 4 come into force on the day after this Act receives Royal Assent).

NOTES

Commencement: 8 September 2017.

Orders: Trade Union (Wales) Act 2017 (Commencement) Order 2017, SI 2017/903.

[1.2080]
4 Short title

The short title of this Act is the Trade Union (Wales) Act 2017.

NOTES

Commencement: 8 September 2017.

CONTRACT (THIRD PARTY RIGHTS) (SCOTLAND) ACT 2017

(2017 asp 5)

ARRANGEMENT OF SECTIONS

An Act of the Scottish Parliament to make provision about the enforcement of contractual terms by third parties.

[30 October 2017]

[1.2081]

1 Creation of a third-party right

(1) A person who is not a party to a contract acquires a third-party right under it where—

(a) the contract contains an undertaking that one or more of the contracting parties will do, or not do, something for the person's benefit, and

(b) at the relevant time it was the intention of the contracting parties that the person should be legally entitled to enforce or otherwise invoke the undertaking.

(2) The third-party right is the right to enforce or otherwise invoke the undertaking.

(3) The person who is to acquire a third-party right under a contract must be identifiable from the contract by being either named or described in it.

(4) A third-party right may be acquired by a person despite the fact that at the relevant time the person—

(a) was not in existence, or

(b) did not fall within the description of persons (if any) whom the contracting parties intended should benefit from, and be legally entitled to enforce or otherwise invoke, the undertaking.

(5) In subsections (1)(b) and (4), "the relevant time" means—

(a) the time when the contract was constituted, or

(b) if the undertaking was added to the contract by a modification of its terms, the time when the modification was made.

NOTES

Commencement: 26 February 2018.

[1.2082]

2 Creation: further provision

(1) This section makes provision elaborating on section 1.

(2) The undertaking referred to in section 1(1)(a) may be one which depends on something happening or not happening (whether or not it is certain that that thing will or will not happen).

(3) The intention of the contracting parties referred to in section 1(1)(b) may be express or implied.

(4) A person may acquire a third-party right to enforce or otherwise invoke an undertaking despite the fact that—

(a) the undertaking may be cancelled or modified,

(b) there has been no delivery, intimation or communication of the undertaking to the person.

(5) The reference in section 1(1)(a) to an undertaking to do something includes an undertaking to indemnify a person.

(6) The reference in section 1(1)(a) to an undertaking not to do something includes an undertaking—

(a) not to hold a person liable in a matter,

(b) not to enforce, or not to enforce in full, a person's liability in a matter.

(7) This Act is without prejudice to any other enactment, or rule of law, that imposes requirements which must be fulfilled if an enforceable obligation is to be created.

NOTES

Commencement: 26 February 2018.

[1.2083]

3 Contracting parties' freedom to alter third party's entitlement

(1) An undertaking contained in a contract which has given rise to a third-party right may be cancelled or modified by the contracting parties.

(2) Nothing in this Act precludes a contract from providing that an undertaking, which is contained in the contract and in relation to which a third-party right has arisen, will not be cancelled or modified by the contracting parties.

(3) Subsection (1) is subject to sections 4 to 6.

NOTES

Commencement: 26 February 2018.

[1.2084]

4 Protection of third party's entitlement from retroactive change

(1) No account is to be taken of the cancellation or modification of an undertaking contained in a contract where and in so far as the undertaking is being enforced or otherwise invoked—

(a) by virtue of a person's third-party right to do so, and

(b) in consequence of something happening or not happening prior to the undertaking being cancelled or (as the case may be) the modification being made.

(2) Subsection (1) does not apply in relation to a cancellation or modification if the contract provided that it may be made with retroactive effect.

NOTES

Commencement: 26 February 2018.

[1.2085]
5 Protection of third party's entitlement after notice given

(1) Subsection (2) applies (subject to subsections (3) and (4)) where—

(a) a person who has a third-party right arising from an undertaking contained in a contract is given notice of the undertaking by a contracting party, and

(b) the undertaking is subsequently cancelled or modified.

(2) No account is to be taken of the cancellation or (as the case may be) modification of the undertaking when it is being enforced or otherwise invoked by virtue of the third-party right.

(3) Subsection (2) does not apply if—

(a) the undertaking is one which depends on something happening or not happening, and

(b) it remained uncertain whether that thing would happen or not at the time when the notice mentioned in subsection (1)(a) was given.

(4) Subsection (2) does not apply in relation to the cancellation or modification of the undertaking if—

(a) at the time when the notice mentioned in subsection (1)(a) was given, the person given the notice was told by the contracting party that the undertaking may be cancelled or (as the case may be) that the modification may be made, or

(b) the person who has the third-party right has given assent to the cancellation or (as the case may be) modification of the undertaking.

NOTES

Commencement: 26 February 2018.

[1.2086]
6 Protection of third party's entitlement after undertaking relied on

(1) Subsection (2) applies (subject to subsections (3) and (4)) where—

(a) a person has a third-party right to enforce or otherwise invoke an undertaking contained in a contract,

(b) the person has done something, or refrained from doing something, in reliance on the undertaking,

(c) doing or (as the case may be) refraining from doing the thing has affected the person's position to a material extent,

(d) either—

(i) the contracting parties acquiesced in the person doing or (as the case may be) refraining from doing the thing, or

(ii) the person's doing or (as the case may be) refraining from doing the thing in reliance on the undertaking could reasonably have been foreseen by the contracting parties, and

(e) subsequent to the person doing or (as the case may be) refraining from doing the thing mentioned in paragraph (b), the undertaking has been cancelled or modified.

(2) Where the person is enforcing or otherwise invoking the undertaking by virtue of having the third-party right, no account is to be taken of the cancellation or modification of the undertaking if the person's position would be adversely affected to a material extent were the undertaking treated as having been cancelled or (as the case may be) modified.

(3) Subsection (2) does not apply in relation to the cancellation or modification of the undertaking if—

(a) the contract provides—

(i) that the contracting parties are entitled to cancel or (as the case may be) modify the undertaking, and

(ii) that their entitlement to do so will not be affected by the person doing, or refraining from doing, something in reliance on the undertaking, and

(b) the person knew or ought to have known about that provision of the contract before the person did, or refrained from doing, the thing mentioned in subsection (1)(b).

(4) Subsection (2) does not apply in relation to the cancellation or modification of the undertaking if the person has given assent to it.

(5) In legal proceedings, a person seeking to enforce or otherwise invoke an undertaking by virtue of having a third-party right to do so may not plead that a contracting party—

(a) is personally barred from cancelling or modifying the undertaking, or

(b) has waived any right to cancel or modify the undertaking.

NOTES

Commencement: 26 February 2018.

[1.2087]
7 Remedies available to third party

(1) This section applies where a person has a third-party right to enforce or otherwise invoke an undertaking contained in a contract.

(2) The person has available, as a remedy for breach of the undertaking, any remedy for breach which a contracting party would be entitled to were the undertaking one in favour of the contracting party.

(3) Subsection (2) is subject to any contrary provision made in the contract.

NOTES

Commencement: 26 February 2018.

[1.2088]

8 Defences available against third party

(1) This section applies where a person has a third-party right to enforce or otherwise invoke an undertaking contained in a contract.

(2) A contracting party has available, as a defence against a claim by the person that the undertaking has been breached, any defence which is both—

(a) a defence that a contracting party would have against any other contracting party, and

(b) relevant to the undertaking.

(3) Subsection (2) is subject to any contrary provision made in the contract.

NOTES

Commencement: 26 February 2018.

[1.2089]

9 Arbitration

(1) In relation to a dispute to which subsection (2) or (3) applies, the person who has the third-party right mentioned in subsection (2) or (as the case may be) (3) is to be regarded as a party to the arbitration agreement mentioned in that subsection.

(2) This subsection applies to a dispute if—

(a) the dispute concerns an undertaking being enforced or otherwise invoked by virtue of a person's third-party right to do so, and

(b) an arbitration agreement provides for a dispute on the matter under dispute to be resolved by arbitration.

(3) This subsection applies to a dispute if—

(a) subsection (2) does not apply to the dispute,

(b) an arbitration agreement provides for a dispute on the matter under dispute to be resolved by arbitration,

(c) a person has a third-party right to enforce or otherwise invoke an undertaking to resolve a dispute on the matter by arbitration under the agreement, and

(d) the person who has the third-party right has—

(i) submitted the dispute to arbitration, or

(ii) sought a sist of legal proceedings concerning the matter under dispute on the basis that an arbitration agreement provides for a dispute on the matter to be resolved by arbitration.

(4) For the purpose of subsection (3)(d)(i), the person who has the third-party right is to be regarded as having submitted the dispute to arbitration if the person has done whatever a party to the agreement would need to do in order to submit the dispute to arbitration.

(5) A person is not to be regarded as having renounced a third-party right to enforce or otherwise invoke an undertaking to resolve a dispute by arbitration by bringing legal proceedings in relation to the dispute.

(6) In this section—

"arbitration agreement" has the meaning given by section 4 of the Arbitration (Scotland) Act 2010, and
"dispute" is to be construed in accordance with section 2(1) of that Act.

NOTES

Commencement: 26 February 2018.

[1.2090]

10 Prescription

(1) An undertaking contained in a contract which is capable of being enforced or otherwise invoked by virtue of a third-party right is an obligation arising from the contract for the purposes of the Prescription and Limitation (Scotland) Act 1973.

(2) In subsection (1), "third-party right" means a right which has arisen by virtue of either—

(a) section 1, or

(b) the rule of law mentioned in section 11.

NOTES

Commencement: 26 February 2018.

[1.2091]

11 Abolition of common-law rule: jus quaesitum tertio

(1) The rule of law by which a person who is not a party to a contract may acquire a right to enforce or otherwise invoke the contract's terms does not apply in relation to contracts constituted on or after the day this section comes into force.

(2) If a contract constituted before this section comes into force is modified so that an undertaking it contains gives rise to a third-party right under section 1, a person who may enforce or otherwise invoke the undertaking by virtue of that right may not do so by virtue of any right acquired by operation of the rule of law mentioned in subsection (1).

(3) A right rendered unenforceable by subsection (2) remains incapable of being enforced or invoked notwithstanding—

(a) its transfer to another person, or

(b) the third-party right under section 1 referred to in that subsection being relinquished (whether by transfer, waiver or otherwise).

NOTES

Commencement: 26 February 2018.

[1.2092]

12 Application

Nothing in sections 1 to 9 applies in relation to an undertaking constituted before the day on which section 1 comes into force, unless the contract containing the undertaking provides otherwise.

NOTES

Commencement: 31 October 2017.

[1.2093]

13 Commencement

(1) This section and sections 12 and 14 come into force on the day after Royal Assent.

(2) The other provisions of this Act come into force on such day as the Scottish Ministers may by regulations appoint.

NOTES

Commencement: 31 October 2017.

Regulations: Contract (Third Party Rights) (Scotland) Act 2017 (Commencement) Regulations 2018, SSI 2018/8.

[1.2094]

14 Short title

The short title of this Act is the Contract (Third Party Rights) (Scotland) Act 2017.

NOTES

Commencement: 31 October 2017.

GENDER REPRESENTATION ON PUBLIC BOARDS (SCOTLAND) ACT 2018

(2018 asp 4)

ARRANGEMENT OF SECTIONS

SCHEDULES

An Act of the Scottish Parliament to make provision about gender representation on boards of Scottish public authorities.

[1.2095]

1 Gender representation objective

(1) The "gender representation objective" for a public board is that it has 50% of non-executive members who are women.

(2) Where a public board has an odd number of non-executive members, the percentage mentioned in subsection (1) applies as if the board had one fewer non-executive member.

NOTES

Commencement: to be appointed.

[1.2096]

2 Key definitions

In this Act—

"appointing person" means, in relation to the function of appointing a non-executive member of a public board, a person who has that function,

"excluded position", in relation to a public authority, means a position mentioned in the second column of the table in schedule 1 which corresponds with the public authority mentioned in the first column,

"non-executive member", in relation to a public authority, means a position on its public board—

(a) that is not an excluded position,

(b) that is not held by an employee of the authority,

"public authority" means an authority listed, or within a description listed, in the first column of the table in schedule 1,

"public board" means—

(a) if the public authority is a company, the directors,

(b) if the public authority has a statutory board or other equivalent statutory management body, that board or body,

(c) in relation to any other public authority, the membership of the authority,

"woman" includes a person who has the protected characteristic of gender reassignment (within the meaning of section 7 of the Equality Act 2010) if, and only if, the person is living as a woman and is proposing to undergo, is undergoing or has undergone a process (or part of a process) for the purpose of becoming female.

NOTES

Commencement: 1 December 2018.

[1.2097]

3 Duty when appointing non-executive members

(1) Subsection (2) applies where there is—

(a) a vacancy in a position of non-executive member of a public board,

(b) more than one candidate for the position,

(c) at least one candidate who is a woman, and

(d) at least one candidate who is not a woman.

(2) The appointing person must, in making the appointment to fill the vacancy, act in accordance with section 4 with a view to achieving (or making progress towards achieving) the gender representation objective immediately after the appointment takes effect.

(3) When an appointing person is making more than one appointment—

(a) both or all of those appointments must be taken into account in identifying the number of non-executive members, and

(b) the appointing person must act with a view to achieving (or making progress towards achieving) the gender representation objective immediately after all of those appointments have taken effect.

NOTES

Commencement: to be appointed.

[1.2098]

4 Consideration of candidates

(1) The appointing person must determine whether any particular candidate is best qualified for the appointment.

(2) If no particular candidate is best qualified for the appointment, the appointing person must identify candidates it considers are equally qualified.

(3) Subject to subsection (4), the appointing person must give preference to a candidate identified under subsection (2) who is a woman if appointing that candidate will result in the board achieving (or making progress towards achieving) the gender representation objective.

(4) The appointing person—

(a) must consider whether the appointment of a candidate identified under subsection (2) who is not a woman is justified on the basis of a characteristic or situation particular to that candidate, and

(b) if so, may give preference to that candidate.

(5) In subsection (4), "characteristic" includes a protected characteristic (within the meaning of section 4 of the Equality Act 2010).

NOTES

Commencement: to be appointed.

[1.2099]

5 Encouragement of applications by women

(1) An appointing person for a public board must take such steps as it considers appropriate to encourage women to apply to become non-executive members of the public board.

(2) A public authority to which a public board relates must take such steps as it considers appropriate to encourage women to apply to become non-executive members of the public board.

(3) For the avoidance of doubt, nothing in subsections (1) and (2) prevents an appointing person or a public authority from taking such steps as it considers appropriate to encourage persons with other protected characteristics (within the meaning of section 4 of the Equality Act 2010) to apply to become non-executive members of the public board.

NOTES

Commencement: to be appointed.

[1.2100]

6 Duty to take steps towards achieving objective

(1) This section applies whenever the gender representation objective is not achieved in relation to a public board.

(2) An appointing person for the public board must, in addition to anything done under sections 3 to 5, take such other steps as it considers appropriate with a view to achieving the gender representation objective by 31 December 2022.

(3) The public authority to which the public board relates must, in addition to anything done under section 5(2), take such other steps as it considers appropriate with a view to achieving the gender representation objective by 31 December 2022.

NOTES

Commencement: to be appointed.

[1.2101]

7 Guidance on operation of Act

(1) The Scottish Ministers must publish guidance on the operation of this Act.

(2) The guidance must in particular cover—

(a) an appointing person's functions in—

(i) appointing non-executive members under sections 3 and 4,

(ii) encouraging applications by women under section 5(1),

(iii) taking any steps under section 6(2),

(iv) reporting under section 8(4),

(b) a public authority's functions in—

(i) encouraging applications by women under section 5(2),

(ii) taking any steps under section 6(3),

(iii) reporting under section 8(5).

(3) An appointing person must have regard to the guidance in carrying out its functions under this Act.

(4) A public authority must have regard to the guidance in carrying out its functions under this Act.

NOTES

Commencement: 1 December 2018.

[1.2102]

8 Reports on operation of Act

(1) The Scottish Ministers must lay before the Scottish Parliament reports on the operation of this Act in accordance with provision made in regulations under subsection (6).

(2) Regulations under subsection (6) must ensure that reports under subsection (1) are laid before the Scottish Parliament at intervals of no more than two years.

(3) The Scottish Ministers must publish reports on the carrying out of their functions under sections 3 to 6 in accordance with provision made in regulations under subsection (6).

(4) An appointing person (other than the Scottish Ministers) specified in regulations under subsection (6) must publish reports on the carrying out of its functions under sections 3 to 6 in accordance with provision made in regulations under subsection (6).

(5) A public authority specified in regulations under subsection (6) must publish reports on the carrying out of its functions under sections 5 and 6 in accordance with provision made in regulations under subsection (6).

(6) The Scottish Ministers may by regulations—

(a) specify appointing persons for the purposes of subsection (4),

(b) specify public authorities for the purposes of subsection (5),

(c) make further provision about reports mentioned in subsections (1) to (5).

NOTES

Commencement: 1 December 2018.

Regulations: as of 15 May 2019, no regulations had been made under this section.

[1.2103]

9 Power to modify schedule 1

The Scottish Ministers may by regulations modify schedule 1 so as to add an entry, vary the description of an entry or remove an entry.

NOTES

Commencement: to be appointed.

Regulations: as of 15 May 2019, no regulations had been made under this section.

[1.2104]

10 Application of Act to certain public authorities

Schedule 2 makes provision about the application of this Act in relation to certain public authorities.

NOTES

Commencement: to be appointed.

[1.2105]

11 Equality Act 2010

(1) Sections 158 and 159 of the Equality Act 2010 (positive action) do not apply to any action taken under this Act.

(2) Part 5 of the Equality Act 2010 (work) does not prohibit any action taken under this Act.

NOTES

Commencement: to be appointed.

[1.2106]

12 Regulations

(1) Regulations under sections 8 and 9 may—

(a) include incidental, supplementary, consequential, transitional, transitory or saving provision,

(b) make different provision for different purposes.

(2) Regulations under section 9 may modify this Act.

(3) Regulations under section 8 are subject to the negative procedure.

(4) Regulations under section 9 are subject to the affirmative procedure.

NOTES

Commencement: 1 December 2018.

[1.2107]

13 Commencement

(1) This section and section 14 come into force on the day after Royal Assent.

(2) The other provisions of this Act come into force on such day as the Scottish Ministers may by regulations appoint.

(3) Regulations under this section may—

(a) include transitional, transitory or saving provision,

(b) make different provision for different purposes.

NOTES

Commencement: 10 March 2018.

Regulations: the Gender Representation on Public Boards (Scotland) Act 2018 (Commencement No 1) Regulations 2018, SSI 2018/340.

[1.2108]

14 Short title

The short title of this Act is the Gender Representation on Public Boards (Scotland) Act 2018.

NOTES

Commencement: 10 March 2018.

SCHEDULES

SCHEDULE 1
PUBLIC AUTHORITIES

(introduced by section 2)

[1.2109]

Authority	*Excluded position*
Accounts Commission for Scotland	
Architecture and Design Scotland (company number SC267870)	
Board of Trustees for the National Galleries of Scotland	
Board of Trustees of the National Museums of Scotland	
Board of Trustees of the Royal Botanic Garden, Edinburgh	
Bòrd na Gàidhlig	
British Waterways Board	

Authority	*Excluded position*
Cairngorms National Park Authority	Members elected under article 5(2) of the Cairngorms National Park Designation, Transitional and Consequential Provisions (Scotland) Order 2003 (SSI 2003/1) Members nominated under article 5(4) of that Order
Caledonian Maritime Assets Limited (company number SC001854)	
Children's Hearings Scotland	
A college of further education other than a regional college (within the meanings given to those terms by the Further and Higher Education (Scotland) Act 1992)	All members other than those appointed under paragraph 3A(2)(a) and (f) of schedule 2 of that Act
A regional college (within the meaning given by the Further and Higher Education (Scotland) Act 1992)	All members other than those appointed under paragraph 3(2)(a) and (f) of schedule 2 of that Act
Common Services Agency for the Scottish Health Service	
Community Justice Scotland	
Creative Scotland	
Crofting Commission	Members elected by virtue of paragraph 7 of schedule 1 of the Crofting Reform (Scotland) Act 2010
Crown Estate Scotland (Interim Management)	
David MacBrayne Limited (company number SC015304)	
Food Standards Scotland	
A Health Board constituted under section 2(1)(a) of the National Health Service (Scotland) Act 1978	Councillors appointed under paragraph 2(1)(b) of schedule 1 of that Act Members of Health Boards mentioned in regulation 3 of the Health Boards (Membership and Procedure) (Scotland) Regulations 2001 (SSI 2001/302) who hold a post in a university with a medical or dental school Members appointed only by virtue of being nominated for membership
Healthcare Improvement Scotland	The member mentioned in paragraph 2(1)(b) of schedule 5A of the National Health Service (Scotland) Act 1978 (the person appointed to chair Social Care and Social Work Improvement Scotland)
A higher education institution (within the meaning given by the Higher Education Governance (Scotland) Act 2016)	All members other than those appointed by the governing body (which has the same meaning as in Part II of the Further and Higher Education (Scotland) Act 1992) (for this purpose a member is not appointed by the governing body if that member is appointed only by virtue of being the winning candidate in an election for membership or by virtue of being nominated for membership by another person)
Highlands and Islands Airports Limited (company number SC097647)	
Highlands and Islands Enterprise	
Historic Environment Scotland	
ILF Scotland (company number SC500075)	
Judicial Appointments Board for Scotland	
Local Government Boundary Commission for Scotland	
Loch Lomond and the Trossachs National Park Authority	Members elected under article 5(2) of the Loch Lomond and The Trossachs National Park Designation, Transitional and Consequential Provisions (Scotland) Order 2002 (SSI 2002/201) Members nominated under article 5(4) of that Order
Mental Welfare Commission for Scotland	

Authority	***Excluded position***
Mobility and Access Committee for Scotland	
National Confidential Forum	
National Library of Scotland	The member mentioned in paragraph 2(2) of schedule 1 of the National Library of Scotland Act 2012 (the member who is selected from persons nominated by the Dean of the Faculty of Advocates)
Newbattle Abbey College (company number SC262968)	A director nominated by the University of Aberdeen, the University of Edinburgh, the University of Glasgow or the University of St. Andrews A director who is also a member of the college
Quality Meat Scotland	
Regional Board for Glasgow Colleges	All members other than those appointed under paragraph 3(2)(a) and (f) of schedule 2B of the Further and Higher Education (Scotland) Act 2005
A regional Transport Partnership created under section 1(1) of the Transport (Scotland) Act 2005	Councillor members (mentioned in section 1(2)(b) of that Act) Members appointed only by virtue of being nominated for membership by a Health Board mentioned in section 6(1)(a)(ii) of that Act A member appointed only by virtue of being nominated for membership by Highlands and Islands Enterprise A member appointed only by virtue of being nominated for membership by Scottish Enterprise
Revenue Scotland	
Risk Management Authority	
Sabhal Mòr Ostaig (company number SC361752)	A director who is also a student of Sabhal Mòr Ostaig
Scottish Advisory Committee on Distinction Awards	All members other than the Chair, the Medical Director and the lay representatives
Scottish Agricultural Wages Board	Persons nominated or elected under paragraph 1(a) of schedule 1 of the Agricultural Wages (Scotland) Act 1949 (persons representing employers and workers)
Scottish Charity Regulator	
Scottish Children's Reporter Administration	
Scottish Commission for Human Rights	The member appointed to chair the commission under paragraph 1(1)(a) of the Scottish Commission for Human Rights Act 2006
Scottish Courts and Tribunals Service	The Lord President The Lord Justice Clerk The President of the Scottish Tribunals
Scottish Criminal Cases Review Commission	
Scottish Enterprise	
Scottish Environment Protection Agency	
Scottish Fire and Rescue Service	
Scottish Fiscal Commission	
Scottish Further and Higher Education Funding Council	
Scottish Futures Trust Limited (company number SC348382)	
Scottish Housing Regulator	
Scottish Land Commission	
Scottish Legal Aid Board	
Scottish Legal Complaints Commission	
Scottish Natural Heritage	
Scottish Police Authority	
Scottish Qualifications Authority	

Authority	Excluded position
Scottish Social Services Council	The member mentioned in regulation 2(3) of the Scottish Social Services Council (Appointments, Procedure and Access to the Register) Regulations 2001 (SSI 2001/303) (the person who is the chair or a member of Social Care and Social Work Improvement Scotland)
Scottish Sports Council	
Scottish Water	
Skills Development Scotland Co. Limited (company number SC202659)	
Social Care and Social Work Improvement Scotland	The member mentioned in paragraph 2(1)(b) of schedule 11 of the Public Services Reform (Scotland) Act 2010 (the person appointed to chair Healthcare Improvement Scotland) The member mentioned in paragraph 2(1)(c) of that schedule (the person appointed as convener of the Scottish Social Services Council)
A Special Health Board constituted under section 2(1)(b) of the National Health Service (Scotland) Act 1978	Councillors appointed under paragraph 2(1)(b) of schedule 1 of that Act Members appointed only by virtue of being nominated for membership
Standards Commission for Scotland	
VisitScotland	
Water Industry Commission for Scotland	
West Highland College UHI (company number SC153921)	A director who is also a student of the college

NOTES

Commencement: 1 December 2018.

For the words "*Crown Estate Scotland (Interim Management)*" in italics there are substituted the words "Crown Estate Scotland", by the Scottish Crown Estate Act 2019, s 1(3), Sch 1, para 8, as from a day to be appointed.

SCHEDULE 2
APPLICATION OF ACT TO CERTAIN PUBLIC AUTHORITIES

(introduced by section 10)

[1.2110]

Judicial Appointments Board for Scotland

1. When the Lord President is making an appointment of a judicial member under paragraph 2(a) of schedule 1 of the Judiciary and Courts (Scotland) Act 2008, the Lord President must act with a view to achieving the gender representation objective in relation to the judicial members only.

2. When the Scottish Ministers are making an appointment of a legal member or a lay member under paragraph 2(b) or (c) of that schedule, they must act with a view to achieving the gender representation objective in relation to the legal members and lay members only (taken together).

Regional Board for Glasgow Colleges

3. When the Scottish Ministers are making an appointment under paragraph 3(2)(a) of schedule 2B of the Further and Higher Education (Scotland) Act 2005 ("schedule 2B") they may, for the purpose of identifying the number of non-executive members, disregard a vacancy in a position mentioned in paragraph 3(2)(f) of schedule 2B.

4. When the board mentioned in paragraph 3(2)(f) of schedule 2B is making an appointment under that paragraph, the board may, for the purpose of identifying the number of non-executive members, disregard a vacancy in a position mentioned in paragraph 3(2)(a) of schedule 2B.

Regional colleges

5. When the Scottish Ministers are making an appointment under paragraph 3(2)(a) of schedule 2 of the Further and Higher Education (Scotland) Act 1992 ("schedule 2") they may, for the purpose of identifying the number of non-executive members, disregard a vacancy in a position mentioned in paragraph 3(2)(f) of schedule 2.

6. When the board mentioned in paragraph 3(2)(f) of schedule 2 is making an appointment under that paragraph, the board may, for the purpose of identifying the number of non-executive members, disregard a vacancy in a position mentioned in paragraph 3(2)(a) of schedule 2.

Scottish Criminal Cases Review Commission

7. For the purposes of the application of this Act in relation to appointments to the Scottish Criminal Cases Review Commission—

(a) the Scottish Ministers, in making a recommendation under section 194A(4) of the Criminal Procedure (Scotland) Act 1995, are to be treated as the appointing person (instead of Her Majesty), and

(b) references in this Act to the making of an appointment are to be construed as references to the making of a recommendation under that section.

NOTES

Commencement: to be appointed.

DATA PROTECTION ACT 2018

(2018 c 12)

An Act to make provision for the regulation of the processing of information relating to individuals; to make provision in connection with the Information Commissioner's functions under certain regulations relating to information; to make provision for a direct marketing code of practice; and for connected purposes.

[23 May 2018]

NOTES

Only certain provisions of this Act are relevant to this work. The subject matter of provisions not included is not annotated.

Commencement: the commencement of this Act is provided for by s 212 at **[1.2211]**. Subsection (2)(a)–(e) of that section provide that certain provisions of this Act come into force on the day on which this Act is passed (23 May 2018). Subsection (3) provides that certain specified provisions come into force on 23 July 2018. Note that sub-(2)(f) provides that "any other provision of this Act so far as it confers power to make regulations or Tribunal Procedure Rules or is otherwise necessary for enabling the exercise of such a power on or after the day on which this Act is passed" shall also come into force on 23 May 2018. Except as noted *ante*, s 212 provides that this Act shall come into force on such day as the Secretary of State may by regulations appoint (see sub-s (1) of that section). See also the Data Protection Act 2018 (Commencement No 1 and Transitional and Saving Provisions) Regulations 2018, SI 2018/625. Those Regulations provide that most of the remaining provisions of this Act come into force on 25 May 2018 (see reg 2) and 23 July 2018 (see reg 3).

This Act is extensively amended by the Data Protection, Privacy and Electronic Communications (Amendments etc) (EU Exit) Regulations 2019, SI 2019/419, as from exit day (as defined in the European Union (Withdrawal) Act 2018, s 20) and subject to transitional provisions; for these, see the 2019 Regulations at **[2.2122]** et seq.

ARRANGEMENT OF SECTIONS

PART 1
PRELIMINARY

PART 2
GENERAL PROCESSING

CHAPTER 1
SCOPE AND DEFINITIONS

CHAPTER 2
THE GDPR

Meaning of certain terms used in the GDPR

Lawfulness of processing

Special categories of personal data

Rights of the data subject

Restrictions on data subject's rights

Assessment notices

Information notices and assessment notices: destruction of documents etc

Enforcement notices

Powers of entry and inspection

Penalties

Guidance

Appeals etc

Complaints

Remedies in the court

Offences relating to personal data

Jurisdiction of courts

Definitions

PART 7
SUPPLEMENTARY AND FINAL PROVISION

Regulations under this Act

Rights of the data subject

Representation of data subjects

Offences

PART 1
PRELIMINARY

[1.2111]

1 Overview

(1) This Act makes provision about the processing of personal data.

(2) Most processing of personal data is subject to the *GDPR*.

(3) Part 2 supplements the *GDPR (see Chapter 2) and applies a broadly equivalent regime to certain types of processing to which the GDPR does not apply (see Chapter 3).*

(4) Part 3 makes provision about the processing of personal data by competent authorities for law enforcement purposes *and implements the Law Enforcement Directive*.

(5) Part 4 makes provision about the processing of personal data by the intelligence services.

(6) Part 5 makes provision about the Information Commissioner.

(7) Part 6 makes provision about the enforcement of the data protection legislation.

(8) Part 7 makes supplementary provision, including provision about the application of this Act to the Crown and to Parliament.

NOTES

Commencement: 23 May 2018 (see also the introductory notes to this Act preceding s 1 at **[1.2111]**).

For "GDPR" in italics in sub-s (1) and for the words in italics in sub-s (2) there is substituted "UK GDPR", and the words in italics in sub-s (4) are repealed, by the Data Protection, Privacy and Electronic Communications (Amendments etc) (EU Exit) Regulations 2019, SI 2019/419, reg 4, Sch 2, paras 1, 2, as from exit day (as defined in the European Union (Withdrawal) Act 2018, s 20), for transitional provisions etc, see the 2019 Regulations at **[2.2122]** et seq.

[1.2112]

2 Protection of personal data

(1) The *GDPR, the applied GDPR* and this Act protect individuals with regard to the processing of personal data, in particular by—

(a) requiring personal data to be processed lawfully and fairly, on the basis of the data subject's consent or another specified basis,

(b) conferring rights on the data subject to obtain information about the processing of personal data and to require inaccurate personal data to be rectified, and

(c) conferring functions on the Commissioner, giving the holder of that office responsibility for monitoring and enforcing their provisions.

(2) When carrying out functions under the *GDPR, the applied GDPR* and this Act, the Commissioner must have regard to the importance of securing an appropriate level of protection for personal data, taking account of the interests of data subjects, controllers and others and matters of general public interest.

NOTES

Commencement: 25 May 2018 (see also the introductory notes to this Act preceding s 1 at **[1.2111]**).

Sub-ss (1), (2): for the words in italics there are substituted the words "UK GDPR" by the Data Protection, Privacy and Electronic Communications (Amendments etc) (EU Exit) Regulations 2019, SI 2019/419, reg 4, Sch 2, paras 1, 3, as from exit day (as defined in the European Union (Withdrawal) Act 2018, s 20), for transitional provisions etc, see the 2019 Regulations at **[2.2122]** et seq.

[1.2113]

3 Terms relating to the processing of personal data

(1) This section defines some terms used in this Act.

(2) "Personal data" means any information relating to an identified or identifiable living individual (subject to subsection (14)(c)).

(3) "Identifiable living individual" means a living individual who can be identified, directly or indirectly, in particular by reference to—

(a) an identifier such as a name, an identification number, location data or an online identifier, or

(b) one or more factors specific to the physical, physiological, genetic, mental, economic, cultural or social identity of the individual.

(4) "Processing", in relation to information, means an operation or set of operations which is performed on information, or on sets of information, such as—

(a) collection, recording, organisation, structuring or storage,

(b) adaptation or alteration,

(c) retrieval, consultation or use,

(d) disclosure by transmission, dissemination or otherwise making available,

(e) alignment or combination, or

(f) restriction, erasure or destruction,

(subject to subsection (14)(c) and sections 5(7), 29(2) and 82(3), which make provision about references to processing in the different Parts of this Act).

(5) "Data subject" means the identified or identifiable living individual to whom personal data relates.

(6) "Controller" and "processor", in relation to the processing of personal data to which *Chapter 2 or 3 of* Part 2, Part 3 or Part 4 applies, have the same meaning as in that Chapter or Part (see sections 5, 6, 32 and 83 and see also subsection (14)(d)).

(7) "Filing system" means any structured set of personal data which is accessible according to specific criteria, whether held by automated means or manually and whether centralised, decentralised or dispersed on a functional or geographical basis.

(8) "The Commissioner" means the Information Commissioner (see section 114).

(9) "The data protection legislation" means—

(*a*) *the GDPR,*

(*b*) *the applied GDPR,*

(c) this Act,

(d) regulations made under this Act, and

(e) regulations made under section 2(2) of the European Communities Act 1972 which relate to *the GDPR* or the Law Enforcement Directive.

(10) "*The GDPR*" means Regulation (EU) 2016/679 of the European Parliament and of the Council of 27 April 2016 on the protection of natural persons with regard to the processing of personal data and on the free movement of such data *(General Data Protection Regulation)*.

[(10A) "The EU GDPR" means Regulation (EU) 2016/679 of the European Parliament and of the Council of 27th April 2016 on the protection of natural persons with regard to the processing of personal data and on the free movement of such data (General Data Protection Regulation) as it has effect in EU law.]

(11) "The applied GDPR" means the GDPR as applied by Chapter 3 of Part 2.

(12) "The Law Enforcement Directive" means Directive (EU) 2016/680 of the European Parliament and of the Council of 27 April 2016 on the protection of natural persons with regard to the processing of personal data by competent authorities for the purposes of the prevention, investigation, detection or prosecution of criminal offences or the execution of criminal penalties, and on the free movement of such data, and repealing Council Framework Decision 2008/977/JHA.

(13) "The Data Protection Convention" means the Convention for the Protection of Individuals with regard to Automatic Processing of Personal Data which was opened for signature on 28 January 1981, as amended up to the day on which this Act is passed.

(14) In Parts 5 to 7, except where otherwise provided—

(*a*) *references to the GDPR are to the GDPR read with Chapter 2 of Part 2 and include the applied GDPR read with Chapter 3 of Part 2 ;*

(*b*) *references to Chapter 2 of Part 2, or to a provision of that Chapter, include that Chapter or that provision as applied by Chapter 3 of Part 2;*

(c) references to personal data, and the processing of personal data, are to personal data and processing to which *Chapter 2 or 3 of* Part 2, Part 3 or Part 4 applies;

(d) references to a controller or processor are to a controller or processor in relation to the processing of personal data to which *Chapter 2 or 3 of* Part 2, Part 3 or Part 4 applies.

(15) There is an index of defined expressions in section 206.

NOTES

Commencement: 23 May 2018 (see also the introductory notes to this Act preceding s 1 at **[1.2111]**).

Sub-s (6): words in italics repealed by the Data Protection, Privacy and Electronic Communications (Amendments etc) (EU Exit) Regulations 2019, SI 2019/419, reg 4, Sch 2, paras 1, 4(1), (2), as from exit day (as defined in the European Union (Withdrawal) Act 2018, s 20), for transitional provisions etc, see the 2019 Regulations at **[2.2122]** et seq.

Sub-s (9): para (a) is substituted (as set out below), para (b) is repealed, and for the words in italics in para (e) there are substituted the words "the EU GDPR", by SI 2019/419, reg 4, Sch 2, paras 1, 4(1), (3), as from exit day (as defined in the European Union (Withdrawal) Act 2018, s 20), for transitional provisions etc, see the 2019 Regulations at **[2.2122]** et seq—

"(a) the UK GDPR,".

Sub-s (10): for the first words in italics there are substituted the words "The UK GDPR", and for the second words in italics there are substituted the words "(United Kingdom General Data Protection Regulation), as it forms part of the law of England and Wales, Scotland and Northern Ireland by virtue of section 3 of the European Union (Withdrawal) Act 2018 (and see section 205(4))", SI 2019/419, reg 4, Sch 2, paras 1, 4(1), (4), as from exit day (as defined in the European Union (Withdrawal) Act 2018, s 20), for transitional provisions etc, see the 2019 Regulations at **[2.2122]** et seq.

Sub-s (10A): inserted by SI 2019/419, reg 4, Sch 2, paras 1, 4(1), (5), as from exit day (as defined in the European Union (Withdrawal) Act 2018, s 20), for transitional provisions etc, see the 2019 Regulations at **[2.2122]** et seq.

Sub-s (11): repealed by SI 2019/419, reg 4, Sch 2, paras 1, 4(1), (6), as from exit day (as defined in the European Union (Withdrawal) Act 2018, s 20), for transitional provisions etc, see the 2019 Regulations at **[2.2122]** et seq.

Sub-s (14): para (a) is substituted (as set out below), and para (b) and the words in italics in paras (c), (d) are repealed, by SI 2019/419, reg 4, Sch 2, paras 1, 4(1), (7), as from exit day (as defined in the European Union (Withdrawal) Act 2018, s 20), for transitional provisions etc, see the 2019 Regulations at **[2.2122]** et seq—

"(a) references to the UK GDPR are to the UK GDPR read with Part 2;".

PART 2
GENERAL PROCESSING

CHAPTER 1 SCOPE AND DEFINITIONS

[1.2114]

4 Processing to which this Part applies

(1) This Part is relevant to most processing of personal data.

(2) *Chapter 2 of this Part*—

(a) applies to the types of processing of personal data to which the *GDPR* applies by virtue of Article 2 of the *GDPR*, and

(b) supplements, and must be read with, the *GDPR*.

(3) Chapter 3 of this Part—

(*a*) *applies to certain types of processing of personal data to which the GDPR does not apply (see section 21), and*

(b) *makes provision for a regime broadly equivalent to the GDPR to apply to such processing.*

NOTES

Commencement: 25 May 2018 (see also the introductory notes to this Act preceding s 1 at **[1.2111]**).

For the first words in italics in sub-s (2) there are substituted the words "This Part", for "GDPR" in italics in each place that it occurs in that subsection there is substituted "UK GDPR", and sub-s (3) is repealed, by the Data Protection, Privacy and Electronic Communications (Amendments etc) (EU Exit) Regulations 2019, SI 2019/419, reg 4, Sch 2, paras 1, 5, as from exit day (as defined in the European Union (Withdrawal) Act 2018, s 20), for transitional provisions etc, see the 2019 Regulations at **[2.2122]** et seq.

[1.2115]

5 Definitions

(1) Terms used in *Chapter 2 of* this Part and in the *GDPR* have the same meaning in *Chapter 2 as* they have in the *GDPR.*

(2) In subsection (1), the reference to a term's meaning in the *GDPR* is to its meaning in the *GDPR* read with any provision of *Chapter 2* which modifies the term's meaning for the purposes of the *GDPR.*

(3) Subsection (1) is subject to any provision in *Chapter 2* which provides expressly for the term to have a different meaning and to section 204.

(4) Terms used in Chapter 3 of this Part and in the applied GDPR have the same meaning in Chapter 3 as they have in the applied GDPR.

(5) In subsection (4), the reference to a term's meaning in the applied GDPR is to its meaning in the GDPR read with any provision of Chapter 2 (as applied by Chapter 3) or Chapter 3 which modifies the term's meaning for the purposes of the applied GDPR.

(6) Subsection (4) is subject to any provision in Chapter 2 (as applied by Chapter 3) or Chapter 3 which provides expressly for the term to have a different meaning.

(7) A reference in *Chapter 2 or Chapter 3 o*f this Part to the processing of personal data is to processing to which *the Chapter* applies.

(8) Sections 3 and 205 include definitions of other expressions used in this Part.

NOTES

Commencement: 25 May 2018 (see also the introductory notes to this Act preceding s 1 at **[1.2111]**).

Sub-s (1): the first words in italics are repealed, for "GDPR" in italics in each place that it occurs there is substituted "UK GDPR", and for the words "Chapter 2 as" in italics there are substituted the words "this Part as", by the Data Protection, Privacy and Electronic Communications (Amendments etc) (EU Exit) Regulations 2019, SI 2019/419, reg 4, Sch 2, paras 1, 6(1), (2), as from exit day (as defined in the European Union (Withdrawal) Act 2018, s 20), for transitional provisions etc, see the 2019 Regulations at **[2.2122]** et seq.

Sub-s (2): for "GDPR" in italics in each place that it occurs there is substituted "UK GDPR", and for the words "Chapter 2" in italics there are substituted the words "this Part", by SI 2019/419, reg 4, Sch 2, paras 1, 6(1), (3), as from exit day (as defined in the European Union (Withdrawal) Act 2018, s 20), for transitional provisions etc, see the 2019 Regulations at **[2.2122]** et seq.

Sub-s (3): for the words in italics there are substituted the words "this Part" by SI 2019/419, reg 4, Sch 2, paras 1, 6(1), (4), as from exit day (as defined in the European Union (Withdrawal) Act 2018, s 20), for transitional provisions etc, see the 2019 Regulations at **[2.2122]** et seq.

Sub-ss (4)–(6): repealed by SI 2019/419, reg 4, Sch 2, paras 1, 6(1), (5), as from exit day (as defined in the European Union (Withdrawal) Act 2018, s 20), for transitional provisions etc, see the 2019 Regulations at **[2.2122]** et seq.

Sub-s (7): the first words in italics are repealed, and for the second words in italics there are substituted the words "this Part", by SI 2019/419, reg 4, Sch 2, paras 1, 6(1), (6), as from exit day (as defined in the European Union (Withdrawal) Act 2018, s 20), for transitional provisions etc, see the 2019 Regulations at **[2.2122]** et seq.

CHAPTER 2 *THE GDPR*

NOTES

The Chapter heading is substituted (by the new heading "The UK GDPR") by the Data Protection, Privacy and Electronic Communications (Amendments etc) (EU Exit) Regulations 2019, SI 2019/419, reg 4, Sch 2, paras 1, 7, as from exit day (as defined in the European Union (Withdrawal) Act 2018, s 20), for transitional provisions etc, see the 2019 Regulations at **[2.2122]** et seq.

Meaning of certain terms used in the GDPR

NOTES

For "GDPR" in the above heading there is substituted "UK GDPR" by the Data Protection, Privacy and Electronic Communications (Amendments etc) (EU Exit) Regulations 2019, SI 2019/419, reg 4, Sch 2, paras 1, 8, as from exit day (as defined in the European Union (Withdrawal) Act 2018, s 20), for transitional provisions etc, see the 2019 Regulations at **[2.2122]** et seq.

[1.2116]

6 Meaning of "controller"

(1) The definition of "controller" in Article 4(7) of the *GDPR* has effect subject to—

- (a) subsection (2),
- (b) section 209, and
- (c) section 210.

(2) For the purposes of the *GDPR*, where personal data is processed only—

- (a) for purposes for which it is required by an enactment to be processed, and
- (b) by means by which it is required by an enactment to be processed,

the person on whom the obligation to process the data is imposed by the enactment (or, if different, one of the enactments) is the controller.

NOTES

Commencement: 25 May 2018 (see also the introductory notes to this Act preceding s 1 at **[1.2111]**).

Sub-ss (1), (2): for "GDPR" in italics there is substituted "UK GDPR" by the Data Protection, Privacy and Electronic Communications (Amendments etc) (EU Exit) Regulations 2019, SI 2019/419, reg 4, Sch 2, paras 1, 9, as from exit day (as defined in the European Union (Withdrawal) Act 2018, s 20), for transitional provisions etc, see the 2019 Regulations at **[2.2122]** et seq.

[1.2117]

7 Meaning of "public authority" and "public body"

(1) For the purposes of the *GDPR*, the following (and only the following) are "public authorities" and "public bodies" *under the law of the United Kingdom*—

(a) a public authority as defined by the Freedom of Information Act 2000,

(b) a Scottish public authority as defined by the Freedom of Information (Scotland) Act 2002 (asp 13), and

(c) an authority or body specified or described by the Secretary of State in regulations,

subject to subsections (2), (3) and (4).

(2) An authority or body that falls within subsection (1) is only a "public authority" or "public body" for the purposes of the *GDPR* when performing a task carried out in the public interest or in the exercise of official authority vested in it.

(3) The references in subsection (1)(a) and (b) to public authorities and Scottish public authorities as defined by the Freedom of Information Act 2000 and the Freedom of Information (Scotland) Act 2002 (asp 13) do not include any of the following that fall within those definitions—

(a) a parish council in England;

(b) a community council in Wales;

(c) a community council in Scotland;

(d) a parish meeting constituted under section 13 of the Local Government Act 1972;

(e) a community meeting constituted under section 27 of that Act;

(f) charter trustees constituted—

(i) under section 246 of that Act,

(ii) under Part 1 of the Local Government and Public Involvement in Health Act 2007, or

(iii) by the Charter Trustees Regulations 1996 (SI 1996/263).

(4) The Secretary of State may by regulations provide that a person specified or described in the regulations that is a public authority described in subsection (1)(a) or (b) is not a "public authority" or "public body" for the purposes of the *GDPR*.

(5) Regulations under this section are subject to the affirmative resolution procedure.

NOTES

Commencement: 25 May 2018 (see also the introductory notes to this Act preceding s 1 at **[1.2111]**).

For "GDPR" in italics in each place that it occurs there is substituted "UK GDPR", and the words "under the law of the United Kingdom" in italics in sub-s (1) are repealed, by the Data Protection, Privacy and Electronic Communications (Amendments etc) (EU Exit) Regulations 2019, SI 2019/419, reg 4, Sch 2, paras 1, 10, as from exit day (as defined in the European Union (Withdrawal) Act 2018, s 20), for transitional provisions etc, see the 2019 Regulations at **[2.2122]** et seq.

Lawfulness of processing

[1.2118]

8 Lawfulness of processing: public interest etc

In Article 6(1) of the *GDPR* (lawfulness of processing), the reference in point (e) to processing of personal data that is necessary for the performance of a task carried out in the public interest or in the exercise of the controller's official authority includes processing of personal data that is necessary for—

(a) the administration of justice,

(b) the exercise of a function of either House of Parliament,

(c) the exercise of a function conferred on a person by an enactment or rule of law,

(d) the exercise of a function of the Crown, a Minister of the Crown or a government department, or

(e) an activity that supports or promotes democratic engagement.

NOTES

Commencement: 25 May 2018 (see also the introductory notes to this Act preceding s 1 at **[1.2111]**).

For "GDPR" in italics there is substituted "UK GDPR" by the Data Protection, Privacy and Electronic Communications (Amendments etc) (EU Exit) Regulations 2019, SI 2019/419, reg 4, Sch 2, paras 1, 11, as from exit day (as defined in the European Union (Withdrawal) Act 2018, s 20), for transitional provisions etc, see the 2019 Regulations at **[2.2122]** et seq.

Special categories of personal data

[1.2119]

10 Special categories of personal data and criminal convictions etc data

(1) Subsections (2) and (3) make provision about the processing of personal data described in Article 9(1) of the *GDPR* (prohibition on processing of special categories of personal data) in reliance on an exception in one of the following points of Article 9(2)—

(a) point (b) (employment, social security and social protection);

(b) point (g) (substantial public interest);

(c) point (h) (health and social care);
(d) point (i) (public health);
(e) point (j) (archiving, research and statistics).

(2) The processing meets the requirement in point (b), (h), (i) or (j) of Article 9(2) of the *GDPR* for authorisation by, or a basis in, the law of the United Kingdom or a part of the United Kingdom only if it meets a condition in Part 1 of Schedule 1.

(3) The processing meets the requirement in point (g) of Article 9(2) of the *GDPR* for a basis in the law of the United Kingdom or a part of the United Kingdom only if it meets a condition in Part 2 of Schedule 1.

(4) Subsection (5) makes provision about the processing of personal data relating to criminal convictions and offences or related security measures that is not carried out under the control of official authority.

(5) The processing meets the requirement in Article *10 of the GDPR* for authorisation by the law of the United Kingdom or a part of the United Kingdom only if it meets a condition in Part 1, 2 or 3 of Schedule 1.

(6) The Secretary of State may by regulations—
(a) amend Schedule 1—
(i) by adding or varying conditions or safeguards, and
(ii) by omitting conditions or safeguards added by regulations under this section, and
(b) consequentially amend this section.

(7) Regulations under this section are subject to the affirmative resolution procedure.

NOTES

Commencement: 25 May 2018 (see also the introductory notes to this Act preceding s 1 at **[1.2111]**).

For "GDPR" in italics in each place that it occurs in sub-ss (1)–(3) there is substituted "UK GDPR", and for the words "10 of the GDPR" in italics in sub-s (5) there are substituted the words "10(1) of the UK GDPR", by the Data Protection, Privacy and Electronic Communications (Amendments etc) (EU Exit) Regulations 2019, SI 2019/419, reg 4, Sch 2, paras 1, 13, as from exit day (as defined in the European Union (Withdrawal) Act 2018, s 20), for transitional provisions etc, see the 2019 Regulations at **[2.2122]** et seq.

[1.2120]

11 Special categories of personal data etc: supplementary

(1) For the purposes of Article 9(2)(h) of the *GDPR* (processing for health or social care purposes etc), the circumstances in which the processing of personal data is carried out subject to the conditions and safeguards referred to in Article 9(3) of the *GDPR* (obligation of secrecy) include circumstances in which it is carried out—
(a) by or under the responsibility of a health professional or a social work professional, or
(b) by another person who in the circumstances owes a duty of confidentiality under an enactment or rule of law.

(2) In Article 10 of the *GDPR* and section 10, references to personal data relating to criminal convictions and offences or related security measures include personal data relating to—
(a) the alleged commission of offences by the data subject, or
(b) proceedings for an offence committed or alleged to have been committed by the data subject or the disposal of such proceedings, including sentencing.

NOTES

Commencement: 25 May 2018 (see also the introductory notes to this Act preceding s 1 at **[1.2111]**).

For "GDPR" in italics in each place that it occurs there is substituted "UK GDPR" by the Data Protection, Privacy and Electronic Communications (Amendments etc) (EU Exit) Regulations 2019, SI 2019/419, reg 4, Sch 2, paras 1, 14, as from exit day (as defined in the European Union (Withdrawal) Act 2018, s 20), for transitional provisions etc, see the 2019 Regulations at **[2.2122]** et seq.

Rights of the data subject

[1.2121]

12 Limits on fees that may be charged by controllers

(1) The Secretary of State may by regulations specify limits on the fees that a controller may charge in reliance on—
(a) Article 12(5) of the *GDPR* (reasonable fees when responding to manifestly unfounded or excessive requests), or
(b) Article 15(3) of the *GDPR* (reasonable fees for provision of further copies).

(2) The Secretary of State may by regulations—
(a) require controllers of a description specified in the regulations to produce and publish guidance about the fees that they charge in reliance on those provisions, and
(b) specify what the guidance must include.

(3) Regulations under this section are subject to the negative resolution procedure.

NOTES

Commencement: 25 May 2018 (see also the introductory notes to this Act preceding s 1 at **[1.2111]**).

Sub-s (1): for "GDPR" in italics in each place that it occurs there is substituted "UK GDPR" by the Data Protection, Privacy and Electronic Communications (Amendments etc) (EU Exit) Regulations 2019, SI 2019/419, reg 4, Sch 2, paras 1, 15, as from exit day (as defined in the European Union (Withdrawal) Act 2018, s 20), for transitional provisions etc, see the 2019 Regulations at **[2.2122]** et seq.

[1.2122]

14 Automated decision-making authorised by law: safeguards

(1) This section makes provision for the purposes of Article 22(2)(b) of the *GDPR* (exception from Article 22(1) of the *GDPR* for significant decisions based solely on automated processing that are *authorised by law* and subject to safeguards for the data subject's rights, freedoms and legitimate interests).

(2) A decision is a "significant decision" for the purposes of this section if, in relation to a data subject, it—

(a) produces legal effects concerning the data subject, or

(b) similarly significantly affects the data subject.

(3) A decision is a "qualifying significant decision" for the purposes of this section if—

(a) it is a significant decision in relation to a data subject,

(b) it is required or authorised by law, and

(c) it does not fall within Article 22(2)(a) or (c) of the *GDPR* (decisions necessary to a contract or made with the data subject's consent).

(4) Where a controller takes a qualifying significant decision in relation to a data subject based solely on automated processing—

(a) the controller must, as soon as reasonably practicable, notify the data subject in writing that a decision has been taken based solely on automated processing, and

(b) the data subject may, before the end of the period of 1 month beginning with receipt of the notification, request the controller to—

(i) reconsider the decision, or

(ii) take a new decision that is not based solely on automated processing.

(5) If a request is made to a controller under subsection (4), the controller must, within the period described in Article 12(3) of the *GDPR*—

(a) consider the request, including any information provided by the data subject that is relevant to it,

(b) comply with the request, and

(c) by notice in writing inform the data subject of—

(i) the steps taken to comply with the request, and

(ii) the outcome of complying with the request.

(6) In connection with this section, a controller has the powers and obligations under Article 12 of the *GDPR* (transparency, procedure for extending time for acting on request, fees, manifestly unfounded or excessive requests etc) that apply in connection with Article 22 of the *GDPR*.

(7) The Secretary of State may by regulations make such further provision as the Secretary of State considers appropriate to provide suitable measures to safeguard a data subject's rights, freedoms and legitimate interests in connection with the taking of qualifying significant decisions based solely on automated processing.

(8) Regulations under subsection (7)—

(a) may amend this section, and

(b) are subject to the affirmative resolution procedure.

NOTES

Commencement: 25 May 2018 (see also the introductory notes to this Act preceding s 1 at **[1.2111]**).

For "GDPR" in italics in each place that it occurs there is substituted "UK GDPR", and for the words "authorised by law" in italics in sub-s (1) there are substituted the words "required or authorised under the law of the United Kingdom or a part of the United Kingdom", by the Data Protection, Privacy and Electronic Communications (Amendments etc) (EU Exit) Regulations 2019, SI 2019/419, reg 4, Sch 2, paras 1, 17, as from exit day (as defined in the European Union (Withdrawal) Act 2018, s 20), for transitional provisions etc, see the 2019 Regulations at **[2.2122]** et seq.

Restrictions on data subject's rights

NOTES

The above heading is substituted (by the new heading "Exemptions etc") by the Data Protection, Privacy and Electronic Communications (Amendments etc) (EU Exit) Regulations 2019, SI 2019/419, reg 4, Sch 2, paras 1, 18, as from exit day (as defined in the European Union (Withdrawal) Act 2018, s 20), for transitional provisions etc, see the 2019 Regulations at **[2.2122]** et seq.

[1.2123]

15 Exemptions etc

(1) Schedules 2, 3 and 4 make provision for exemptions from, and restrictions and adaptations of the application of, rules of the *GDPR*.

(2) In Schedule 2—

(a) Part 1 makes provision adapting or restricting the application of rules contained in Articles 13 to 21 and 34 of the *GDPR* in specified circumstances, *as allowed for by* Article 6(3) and Article 23(1) of the *GDPR*;

(b) Part 2 makes provision restricting the application of rules contained in Articles 13 to 21 and 34 of the *GDPR* in specified circumstances, *as allowed for by* Article 23(1) of the *GDPR*;

(c) Part 3 makes provision restricting the application of Article 15 of the *GDPR* where this is necessary to protect the rights of others, *as allowed for by* Article 23(1) of the *GDPR*;

(d) Part 4 makes provision restricting the application of rules contained in Articles 13 to 15 of the *GDPR* in specified circumstances, *as allowed for by* Article 23(1) of the *GDPR*;

(e) Part 5 makes provision containing exemptions or derogations from Chapters II, III, IV, *V and VII of the GDPR* for reasons relating to freedom of expression, *as allowed for by Article 85(2) of the GDPR*;

(f) Part 6 makes provision containing derogations from rights contained in Articles 15, 16, 18, 19, 20 and 21 of the *GDPR* for scientific or historical research purposes, statistical purposes and archiving purposes, *as allowed for by Article 89(2) and (3) of the GDPR*.

(3) Schedule 3 makes provision restricting the application of rules contained in Articles 13 to 21 of the *GDPR* to health, social work, education and child abuse data, *as allowed for by* Article 23(1) of the *GDPR*.

(4) Schedule 4 makes provision restricting the application of rules contained in Articles 13 to 21 of the *GDPR* to information the disclosure of which is prohibited or restricted by an enactment, *as allowed for by* Article 23(1) of the *GDPR*.

[(4A) In connection with the manual unstructured processing of personal data held by an FOI public authority, see Chapter 3 of this Part (sections 21, 24 and 25).]

(5) In connection with the safeguarding of national security and with defence, see Chapter 3 of this Part *and the exemption in section 26*.

NOTES

Commencement: 25 May 2018 (see also the introductory notes to this Act preceding s 1 at **[1.2111]**).

For "GDPR" in italics in sub-s (1) there is substituted "UK GDPR" by the Data Protection, Privacy and Electronic Communications (Amendments etc) (EU Exit) Regulations 2019, SI 2019/419, reg 4, Sch 2, paras 1, 19(1), (2), as from exit day (as defined in the European Union (Withdrawal) Act 2018, s 20), for transitional provisions etc, see the 2019 Regulations at **[2.2122]** et seq.

In sub-ss (2)(a)–(d), (3) and (4), for "GDPR" in italics (in the first place it occurs) there is substituted "UK GDPR", for ", as allowed for by" in italics there is substituted "(of a kind described in", and for "GDPR" in italics (in the second place it occurs) there is substituted "UK GDPR)", by SI 2019/419, reg 4, Sch 2, paras 1, 19(1), (3)–(6), (9), (10), as from exit day (as defined in the European Union (Withdrawal) Act 2018, s 20), for transitional provisions etc, see the 2019 Regulations at **[2.2122]** et seq.

For the first words in italics in sub-s (2)(e) there are substituted the words "and V of the UK GDPR", and for the second words in italics in sub-s (2)(e) there are substituted the words "(of a kind described in Article 85(2) of the UK GDPR)", by SI 2019/419, reg 4, Sch 2, paras 1, 19(1), (7), as from exit day (as defined in the European Union (Withdrawal) Act 2018, s 20), for transitional provisions etc, see the 2019 Regulations at **[2.2122]** et seq.

For "GDPR" in italics in sub-s (2)(f) there is substituted "UK GDPR", and the second words in italics are repealed, by SI 2019/419, reg 4, Sch 2, paras 1, 19(1), (8), as from exit day (as defined in the European Union (Withdrawal) Act 2018, s 20), for transitional provisions etc, see the 2019 Regulations at **[2.2122]** et seq.

Sub-s (4A) is inserted by SI 2019/419, reg 4, Sch 2, paras 1, 19(1), (11), as from exit day (as defined in the European Union (Withdrawal) Act 2018, s 20), for transitional provisions etc, see the 2019 Regulations at **[2.2122]** et seq.

For the words in italics in sub-s (5) there are substituted the words "(sections 26 to 28)" by SI 2019/419, reg 4, Sch 2, paras 1, 19(1), (12), as from exit day (as defined in the European Union (Withdrawal) Act 2018, s 20), for transitional provisions etc, see the 2019 Regulations at **[2.2122]** et seq.

[1.2124]

16 Power to make further exemptions etc by regulations

(1) The following powers to make provision altering the application of the *GDPR* may be exercised by way of regulations made by the Secretary of State under this section—

(a) the power in Article 6(3) *for Member State law* to lay down a legal basis containing specific provisions to adapt the application of rules of the *GDPR* where processing is necessary for compliance with a legal obligation, for the performance of a task in the public interest or in the exercise of official authority;

(b) the power in Article 23(1) to make *a legislative measure* restricting the scope of the obligations and rights mentioned in that Article where necessary and proportionate to safeguard certain objectives of general public interest;

(c) the power in Article 85(2) to provide for exemptions or derogations from certain Chapters of the *GDPR* where necessary to reconcile the protection of personal data with the freedom of expression and information.

(2) Regulations under this section may—

(a) amend Schedules 2 to 4—

(i) by adding or varying provisions, and

(ii) by omitting provisions added by regulations under this section, *and*

(b) consequentially amend section 15[, and

(c) consequentially amend the UK GDPR by adding, varying or omitting a reference to section 15, Schedule 2, 3 or 4, this section or regulations under this section].

(3) Regulations under this section are subject to the affirmative resolution procedure.

NOTES

Commencement: 25 May 2018 (see also the introductory notes to this Act preceding s 1 at **[1.2111]**).

For "GDPR" in italics in each place that it occurs there is substituted "UK GDPR", the words "for Member State law" in italics in sub-s (1)(a) are repealed, for the words "a legislative measure" in italics in sub-s (1)(b) there is substituted "provision", the word "and" in italics in sub-s (2)(a)(ii) is repealed, and sub-s (2)(c) and the preceding word are inserted, by the Data Protection, Privacy and Electronic Communications (Amendments etc) (EU Exit) Regulations 2019, SI 2019/419, reg 4, Sch 2, paras 1, 20, as from exit day (as defined in the European Union (Withdrawal) Act 2018, s 20), for transitional provisions etc, see the 2019 Regulations at **[2.2122]** et seq.

Minor definition

[1.2125]

20 Meaning of "court"

Section 5(1) (terms used in *this Chapter* to have the same meaning as in the *GDPR*) does not apply to references in *this Chapter* to a court and, accordingly, such references do not include a tribunal.

NOTES

Commencement: 25 May 2018 (see also the introductory notes to this Act preceding s 1 at **[1.2111]**).

For "this Chapter" in italics in both places it occurs there is substituted "this Part", and for "GDPR" in italics there is substituted "UK GDPR", by the Data Protection, Privacy and Electronic Communications (Amendments etc) (EU Exit) Regulations 2019, SI 2019/419, reg 4, Sch 2, paras 1, 26, as from exit day (as defined in the European Union (Withdrawal) Act 2018, s 20), for transitional provisions etc, see the 2019 Regulations at **[2.2122]** et seq.

CHAPTER 3 OTHER GENERAL PROCESSING

NOTES

The above heading is substituted (by the new heading "Exemptions for manual unstructured processing and for national security and defence purposes") by the Data Protection, Privacy and Electronic Communications (Amendments etc) (EU Exit) Regulations 2019, SI 2019/419, reg 4, Sch 2, paras 1, 27, as from exit day (as defined in the European Union (Withdrawal) Act 2018, s 20), for transitional provisions etc, see the 2019 Regulations at **[2.2122]** et seq.

Scope

NOTES

The above heading is substituted (by the new heading "Definitions") by the Data Protection, Privacy and Electronic Communications (Amendments etc) (EU Exit) Regulations 2019, SI 2019/419, reg 4, Sch 2, paras 1, 28, as from exit day (as defined in the European Union (Withdrawal) Act 2018, s 20), for transitional provisions etc, see the 2019 Regulations at **[2.2122]** et seq.

[1.2126]

21 Processing to which this Chapter applies

(1) This Chapter applies to the automated or structured processing of personal data in the course of—

(a) an activity which is outside the scope of European Union law, or

(b) an activity which falls within the scope of Article 2(2)(b) of the GDPR (common foreign and security policy activities),

provided that the processing is not processing by a competent authority for any of the law enforcement purposes (as defined in Part 3) or processing to which Part 4 (intelligence services processing) applies.

(2) This Chapter also applies to the manual unstructured processing of personal data held by an FOI public authority.

(3) This Chapter does not apply to the processing of personal data by an individual in the course of a purely personal or household activity.

(4) In this section—

"the automated or structured processing of personal data" means—

(a) the processing of personal data wholly or partly by automated means, and

(b) the processing otherwise than by automated means of personal data which forms part of a filing system or is intended to form part of a filing system;

"the manual unstructured processing of personal data" means the processing of personal data which is not the automated or structured processing of personal data.

(5) In this Chapter, "FOI public authority" means—

(a) a public authority as defined in the Freedom of Information Act 2000, or

(b) a Scottish public authority as defined in the Freedom of Information (Scotland) Act 2002 (asp 13).

(6) References in this Chapter to personal data "held" by an FOI public authority are to be interpreted—

(a) in relation to England and Wales and Northern Ireland, in accordance with section 3(2) of the Freedom of Information Act 2000, and

(b) in relation to Scotland, in accordance with section 3(2), (4) and (5) of the Freedom of Information (Scotland) Act 2002 (asp 13),

but such references do not include information held by an intelligence service (as defined in section 82) on behalf of an FOI public authority.

(7) But personal data is not to be treated as "held" by an FOI public authority for the purposes of this Chapter, where—

(a) section 7 of the Freedom of Information Act 2000 prevents Parts 1 to 5 of that Act from applying to the personal data, or

(b) section 7(1) of the Freedom of Information (Scotland) Act 2002 (asp 13) prevents that Act from applying to the personal data.

NOTES

Commencement: 25 May 2018 (see also the introductory notes to this Act preceding s 1 at **[1.2111]**).

The section heading is substituted (by the new heading "Definitions"), and sub-ss (1)–(4) are repealed, by the Data Protection, Privacy and Electronic Communications (Amendments etc) (EU Exit) Regulations 2019, SI 2019/419, reg 4, Sch 2, paras 1, 29, as from exit day (as defined in the European Union (Withdrawal) Act 2018, s 20), for transitional provisions etc, see the 2019 Regulations at **[2.2122]** et seq.

Application of the GDPR

[1.2127]

22 Application of the GDPR to processing to which this Chapter applies

(1) The GDPR applies to the processing of personal data to which this Chapter applies but as if its Articles were part of an Act extending to England and Wales, Scotland and Northern Ireland.

(2) Chapter 2 of this Part applies for the purposes of the applied GDPR as it applies for the purposes of the GDPR.

(3) In this Chapter, "the applied Chapter 2 " means Chapter 2 of this Part as applied by this Chapter.

(4) Schedule 6 contains provision modifying—

(a) the GDPR as it applies by virtue of subsection (1) (see Part 1);

(b) Chapter 2 of this Part as it applies by virtue of subsection (2) (see Part 2).

(5) A question as to the meaning or effect of a provision of the applied GDPR, or the applied Chapter 2 , is to be determined consistently with the interpretation of the equivalent provision of the GDPR, or Chapter 2 of this Part, as it applies otherwise than by virtue of this Chapter, except so far as Schedule 6 requires a different interpretation.

NOTES

Commencement: 25 May 2018 (see also the introductory notes to this Act preceding s 1 at **[1.2111]**).

This section (and the preceding heading) is repealed by the Data Protection, Privacy and Electronic Communications (Amendments etc) (EU Exit) Regulations 2019, SI 2019/419, reg 4, Sch 2, paras 1, 30, as from exit day (as defined in the European Union (Withdrawal) Act 2018, s 20), for transitional provisions etc, see the 2019 Regulations at **[2.2122]** et seq.

[1.2128]

23 Power to make provision in consequence of regulations related to the GDPR

(1) The Secretary of State may by regulations make provision in connection with the processing of personal data to which this Chapter applies which is equivalent to that made by GDPR regulations, subject to such modifications as the Secretary of State considers appropriate.

(2) In this section, "GDPR regulations" means regulations made under section 2(2) of the European Communities Act 1972 which make provision relating to the GDPR.

(3) Regulations under subsection (1) may apply a provision of GDPR regulations, with or without modification.

(4) Regulations under subsection (1) may amend or repeal a provision of—

(a) the applied GDPR;

(b) this Chapter;

(c) Parts 5 to 7, in so far as they apply in relation to the applied GDPR.

(5) Regulations under this section are subject to the affirmative resolution procedure.

NOTES

Commencement: 25 May 2018 (see also the introductory notes to this Act preceding s 1 at **[1.2111]**).

This section is repealed by the Data Protection, Privacy and Electronic Communications (Amendments etc) (EU Exit) Regulations 2019, SI 2019/419, reg 4, Sch 2, paras 1, 31, as from exit day (as defined in the European Union (Withdrawal) Act 2018, s 20), for transitional provisions etc, see the 2019 Regulations at **[2.2122]** et seq.

PART 5
THE INFORMATION COMMISSIONER

The Commissioner

[1.2129]

114 The Information Commissioner

(1) There is to continue to be an Information Commissioner.

(2) Schedule 12 makes provision about the Commissioner.

NOTES

Commencement: 25 May 2018 (see also the introductory notes to this Act preceding s 1 at **[1.2111]**).

General functions

[1.2130]

115 General functions under the *GDPR* and safeguards

(1) The Commissioner is to be the supervisory authority in the United Kingdom for the purposes of Article 51 of the GDPR.

(2) General functions are conferred on the Commissioner by—

(a) Article 57 of the *GDPR* (tasks), and

(b) Article 58 of the GDPR (powers),

(and see also the Commissioner's duty under section 2 [and section 28(5)]).

(3) The Commissioner's functions in relation to the processing of personal data to which the *GDPR* applies include—

(a) a duty to advise Parliament, the government and other institutions and bodies on legislative and administrative measures relating to the protection of individuals' rights and freedoms with regard to the processing of personal data, and

(b) a power to issue, on the Commissioner's own initiative or on request, opinions to Parliament, the government or other institutions and bodies as well as to the public on any issue related to the protection of personal data.

(4) The Commissioner's functions under Article 58 of the *GDPR* are subject to the safeguards in subsections (5) to (9).

(5) The Commissioner's power under Article 58(1)(a) of the *GDPR* (power to require a controller or processor to provide information that the Commissioner requires for the performance of the Commissioner's tasks under the *GDPR*) is exercisable only by giving an information notice under section 142.

(6) The Commissioner's power under Article 58(1)(b) of the *GDPR* (power to carry out data protection audits) is exercisable only in accordance with section 146.

(7) The Commissioner's powers under Article 58(1)(e) and (f) of the *GDPR* (power to obtain information from controllers and processors and access to their premises) are exercisable only—

(a) in accordance with Schedule 15 (see section 154), or

(b) to the extent that they are exercised in conjunction with the power under Article 58(1)(b) of the *GDPR*, in accordance with section 146.

(8) The following powers are exercisable only by giving an enforcement notice under section 149—

(a) the Commissioner's powers under Article 58(2)(c) to (g) and (j) of the *GDPR* (certain corrective powers);

(b) the Commissioner's powers under Article 58(2)(h) to order a certification body to withdraw, or not to issue, a certification under Articles 42 and 43 of the *GDPR*.

(9) The Commissioner's powers under Articles 58(2)(i) and 83 of the *GDPR* (administrative fines) are exercisable only by giving a penalty notice under section 155.

(10) This section is without prejudice to other functions conferred on the Commissioner, whether by the *GDPR*, this Act or otherwise.

NOTES

Commencement: 25 May 2018 (see also the introductory notes to this Act preceding s 1 at **[1.2111]**).

Sub-s (1) is repealed, for "GDPR" in italics in each place that it occurs (including in the section heading) there is substituted "UK GDPR", and the words in square brackets in sub-s (2) are inserted, by the Data Protection, Privacy and Electronic Communications (Amendments etc) (EU Exit) Regulations 2019, SI 2019/419, reg 4, Sch 2, paras 1, 47, as from exit day (as defined in the European Union (Withdrawal) Act 2018, s 20), for transitional provisions etc, see the 2019 Regulations at **[2.2122]** et seq.

[1.2131]

116 Other general functions

[(A1) The Commissioner is responsible for monitoring the application of Part 3 of this Act, in order to protect the fundamental rights and freedoms of individuals in relation to processing by a competent authority for any of the law enforcement purposes (as defined in Part 3) and to facilitate the free flow of personal data.]

(1) The Commissioner—

(a) is to be the supervisory authority in the United Kingdom for the purposes of Article 41 of the Law Enforcement Directive, and

(b) is to continue to be the designated authority in the United Kingdom for the purposes of Article 13 of the Data Protection Convention.

(2) Schedule 13 confers general functions on the Commissioner in connection with processing to which the *GDPR* does not apply (and see also the Commissioner's duty under section 2).

(3) This section and Schedule 13 are without prejudice to other functions conferred on the Commissioner, whether by this Act or otherwise.

NOTES

Commencement: 25 May 2018 (see also the introductory notes to this Act preceding s 1 at **[1.2111]**).

Sub-s (A1): is inserted, para (a) of sub-s (1) is repealed, and for "GDPR" in italics in sub-s (2) there is substituted "UK GDPR", by the Data Protection, Privacy and Electronic Communications (Amendments etc) (EU Exit) Regulations 2019, SI 2019/419, reg 4, Sch 2, paras 1, 48, as from exit day (as defined in the European Union (Withdrawal) Act 2018, s 20), for transitional provisions etc, see the 2019 Regulations at **[2.2122]** et seq.

[1.2132]

117 Competence in relation to courts etc

Nothing in this Act [or the UK GDPR] permits or requires the Commissioner to exercise functions in relation to the processing of personal data by—

(a) an individual acting in a judicial capacity, or

(b) a court or tribunal acting in its judicial capacity,

(and see also Article 55(3) of the GDPR).

NOTES

Commencement: 25 May 2018 (see also the introductory notes to this Act preceding s 1 at **[1.2111]**).

Words in square brackets inserted, and words in italics repealed, by the Data Protection, Privacy and Electronic Communications (Amendments etc) (EU Exit) Regulations 2019, SI 2019/419, reg 4, Sch 2, paras 1, 49, as from exit day (as defined in the European Union (Withdrawal) Act 2018, s 20), for transitional provisions etc, see the 2019 Regulations at **[2.2122]** et seq.

International role

[1.2133]

118 *Co-operation and mutual assistance*

(1) Articles 60 to 62 of the GDPR confer functions on the Commissioner in relation to co-operation and mutual assistance between, and joint operations of, supervisory authorities under the GDPR.

(2) References to the GDPR in subsection (1) do not include the applied GDPR.

(3) Article 61 of the applied GDPR confers functions on the Commissioner in relation to co-operation with other supervisory authorities (as defined in Article 4(21) of the applied GDPR).

(4) Part 1 of Schedule 14 makes provision as to the functions to be carried out by the Commissioner for the purposes of Article 50 of the Law Enforcement Directive (mutual assistance).

(5) Part 2 of Schedule 14 makes provision as to the functions to be carried out by the Commissioner for the purposes of Article 13 of the Data Protection Convention (co-operation between parties).

NOTES

Commencement: 25 May 2018 (see also the introductory notes to this Act preceding s 1 at **[1.2111]**).

The section heading is substituted (by the new heading "Co-operation between parties to the Data Protection Convention"), and sub-ss (1)–(4) are repealed, by the Data Protection, Privacy and Electronic Communications (Amendments etc) (EU Exit) Regulations 2019, SI 2019/419, reg 4, Sch 2, paras 1, 50, as from exit day (as defined in the European Union (Withdrawal) Act 2018, s 20), for transitional provisions etc, see the 2019 Regulations at **[2.2122]** et seq.

[1.2134]

119 Inspection of personal data in accordance with international obligations

(1) The Commissioner may inspect personal data where the inspection is necessary in order to discharge an international obligation of the United Kingdom, subject to the restriction in subsection (2).

(2) The power under subsection (1) is exercisable only if the personal data—

(a) is processed wholly or partly by automated means, or

(b) is processed otherwise than by automated means and forms part of a filing system or is intended to form part of a filing system.

(3) The power under subsection (1) includes power to inspect, operate and test equipment which is used for the processing of personal data.

(4) Before exercising the power under subsection (1), the Commissioner must by written notice inform the controller and any processor that the Commissioner intends to do so.

(5) Subsection (4) does not apply if the Commissioner considers that the case is urgent.

(6) It is an offence—

(a) intentionally to obstruct a person exercising the power under subsection (1), or

(b) to fail without reasonable excuse to give a person exercising that power any assistance the person may reasonably require.

(7) Paragraphs (c) and (d) of section 3(14) do not apply to references in this section to personal data, the processing of personal data, a controller or a processor.

NOTES

Commencement: 25 May 2018 (see also the introductory notes to this Act preceding s 1 at **[1.2111]**).

[1.2135]

[119A Standard clauses for transfers to third countries etc

(1) The Commissioner may issue a document specifying standard data protection clauses which the Commissioner considers provide appropriate safeguards for the purposes of transfers of personal data to a third country or an international organisation in reliance on Article 46 of the UK GDPR (and see also section 17C).

(2) The Commissioner may issue a document that amends or withdraws a document issued under subsection (1).

(3) A document issued under this section—

(a) must specify when it comes into force,

(b) may make different provision for different purposes, and

(c) may include transitional provision or savings.

(4) Before issuing a document under this section, the Commissioner must consult the Secretary of State and such of the following as the Commissioner considers appropriate—

(a) trade associations;

(b) data subjects;

(c) persons who appear to the Commissioner to represent the interests of data subjects.

(5) After a document is issued under this section—

(a) the Commissioner must send a copy to the Secretary of State, and

(b) the Secretary of State must lay it before Parliament.

(6) If, within the 40-day period, either House of Parliament resolves not to approve the document then, with effect from the end of the day on which the resolution is passed, the document is to be treated as not having been issued under this section (so that the document, and any amendment or withdrawal made by the document, is to be disregarded for the purposes of Article 46(2)(d) of the UK GDPR).

(7) Nothing in subsection (6)—

(a) affects any transfer of personal data previously made in reliance on the document, or

(b) prevents a further document being laid before Parliament.

(8) The Commissioner must publish—

(a) a document issued under this section, and

(b) a notice identifying any document which, under subsection (6), is treated as not having been issued under this section.

(9) The Commissioner must keep under review the clauses specified in a document issued under this section for the time being in force.

(10) In this section, "the 40-day period" means—

(a) if the document is laid before both Houses of Parliament on the same day, the period of 40 days beginning with that day, or

(b) if the document is laid before the Houses of Parliament on different days, the period of 40 days beginning with the later of those days.

(11) In calculating the 40-day period, no account is to be taken of any period during which Parliament is dissolved or prorogued or during which both Houses of Parliament are adjourned for more than 4 days.

(12) In this section, "trade association" includes a body representing controllers or processors.]

NOTES

Commencement: exit day (as defined in the European Union (Withdrawal) Act 2018, s 20).

Inserted by the Data Protection, Privacy and Electronic Communications (Amendments etc) (EU Exit) Regulations 2019, SI 2019/419, reg 4, Sch 2, paras 1, 51, as from exit day (as defined in the European Union (Withdrawal) Act 2018, s 20), for transitional provisions etc, see the 2019 Regulations at **[2.2122]** et seq.

[1.2136]

120 Further international role

(1) The Commissioner must, in relation to third countries and international organisations, take appropriate steps to—

(a) develop international co-operation mechanisms to facilitate the effective enforcement of legislation for the protection of personal data;

(b) provide international mutual assistance in the enforcement of legislation for the protection of personal data, subject to appropriate safeguards for the protection of personal data and other fundamental rights and freedoms;

(c) engage relevant stakeholders in discussion and activities aimed at furthering international co-operation in the enforcement of legislation for the protection of personal data;

(d) promote the exchange and documentation of legislation and practice for the protection of personal data, including legislation and practice relating to jurisdictional conflicts with third countries.

(2) Subsection (1) applies only in connection with the processing of personal data to which the *GDPR* does not apply; for the equivalent duty in connection with the processing of personal data to which the *GDPR* applies, see Article 50 of the *GDPR* (international co-operation for the protection of personal data).

[(2A) The Commissioner may contribute to the activities of international organisations with data protection functions.]

(3) The Commissioner must carry out data protection functions which the Secretary of State directs the Commissioner to carry out for the purpose of enabling Her Majesty's Government in the United Kingdom to give effect to an international obligation of the United Kingdom.

(4) The Commissioner may provide an authority carrying out data protection functions under the law of a British overseas territory with assistance in carrying out those functions.

(5) The Secretary of State may direct that assistance under subsection (4) is to be provided on terms, including terms as to payment, specified or approved by the Secretary of State.

(6) In this section—

"data protection functions" means functions relating to the protection of individuals with respect to the processing of personal data;

"mutual assistance in the enforcement of legislation for the protection of personal data" includes assistance in the form of notification, complaint referral, investigative assistance and information exchange;

"third country" means a country or territory *that is not a member State*.

(7) Section 3(14)(c) does not apply to references to personal data and the processing of personal data in this section.

NOTES

Commencement: 25 May 2018 (see also the introductory notes to this Act preceding s 1 at **[1.2111]**).

For "GDPR" in italics in each place that it occurs in sub-s (2) there is substituted "UK GDPR", sub-s (2A) is inserted, and for the words in italics in the definition "third country" in sub-s (6) there are substituted the words "outside the United Kingdom", by the Data Protection, Privacy and Electronic Communications (Amendments etc) (EU Exit) Regulations 2019, SI 2019/419, reg 4, Sch 2, paras 1, 52, as from exit day (as defined in the European Union (Withdrawal) Act 2018, s 20), for transitional provisions etc, see the 2019 Regulations at **[2.2122]** et seq.

Codes of practice

[1.2137]

121 Data-sharing code

(1) The Commissioner must prepare a code of practice which contains—

(a) practical guidance in relation to the sharing of personal data in accordance with the requirements of the data protection legislation, and

(b) such other guidance as the Commissioner considers appropriate to promote good practice in the sharing of personal data.

(2) Where a code under this section is in force, the Commissioner may prepare amendments of the code or a replacement code.

(3) Before preparing a code or amendments under this section, the Commissioner must consult the Secretary of State and such of the following as the Commissioner considers appropriate—

(a) trade associations;

(b) data subjects;

(c) persons who appear to the Commissioner to represent the interests of data subjects.

(4) A code under this section may include transitional provision or savings.

(5) In this section—

"good practice in the sharing of personal data" means such practice in the sharing of personal data as appears to the Commissioner to be desirable having regard to the interests of data subjects and others, including compliance with the requirements of the data protection legislation;

"the sharing of personal data" means the disclosure of personal data by transmission, dissemination or otherwise making it available;

"trade association" includes a body representing controllers or processors.

NOTES

Commencement: 25 May 2018 (see also the introductory notes to this Act preceding s 1 at **[1.2111]**).

[1.2138]

125 Approval of codes prepared under sections 121 to 124

(1) When a code is prepared under section 121, 122, 123 or 124—

(a) the Commissioner must submit the final version to the Secretary of State, and

(b) the Secretary of State must lay the code before Parliament.

(2) In relation to the first code under section 123—

(a) the Commissioner must prepare the code as soon as reasonably practicable and must submit it to the Secretary of State before the end of the period of 18 months beginning when this Act is passed, and

(b) the Secretary of State must lay it before Parliament as soon as reasonably practicable.

(3) If, within the 40-day period, either House of Parliament resolves not to approve a code prepared under section 121, 122, 123 or 124, the Commissioner must not issue the code.

(4) If no such resolution is made within that period—

(a) the Commissioner must issue the code, and

(b) the code comes into force at the end of the period of 21 days beginning with the day on which it is issued.

(5) If, as a result of subsection (3), there is no code in force under section 121, 122, 123 or 124, the Commissioner must prepare another version of the code.

(6) Nothing in subsection (3) prevents another version of the code being laid before Parliament.

(7) In this section, "the 40-day period" means—

(a) if the code is laid before both Houses of Parliament on the same day, the period of 40 days beginning with that day, or

(b) if the code is laid before the Houses of Parliament on different days, the period of 40 days beginning with the later of those days.

(8) In calculating the 40-day period, no account is to be taken of any period during which Parliament is dissolved or prorogued or during which both Houses of Parliament are adjourned for more than 4 days.

(9) This section, other than subsections (2) and (5), applies in relation to amendments prepared under section 121, 122, 123 or 124 as it applies in relation to codes prepared under those sections.

NOTES

Commencement: 23 July 2018 (see also the introductory notes to this Act preceding s 1 at **[1.2111]**).

[1.2139]

126 Publication and review of codes issued under section 125(4)

(1) The Commissioner must publish a code issued under section 125(4).

(2) Where an amendment of a code is issued under section 125(4), the Commissioner must publish—

(a) the amendment, or

(b) the code as amended by it.

(3) The Commissioner must keep under review each code issued under section 125(4) for the time being in force.

(4) Where the Commissioner becomes aware that the terms of such a code could result in a breach of an international obligation of the United Kingdom, the Commissioner must exercise the power under section 121(2), 122(2), 123(2) or 124(2) with a view to remedying the situation.

NOTES

Commencement: 23 July 2018 (see also the introductory notes to this Act preceding s 1 at **[1.2111]**).

[1.2140]

127 Effect of codes issued under section 125(4)

(1) A failure by a person to act in accordance with a provision of a code issued under section 125(4) does not of itself make that person liable to legal proceedings in a court or tribunal.

(2) A code issued under section 125(4), including an amendment or replacement code, is admissible in evidence in legal proceedings.

(3) In any proceedings before a court or tribunal, the court or tribunal must take into account a provision of a code issued under section 125(4) in determining a question arising in the proceedings if—

(a) the question relates to a time when the provision was in force, and

(b) the provision appears to the court or tribunal to be relevant to the question.

(4) Where the Commissioner is carrying out a function described in subsection (5), the Commissioner must take into account a provision of a code issued under section 125(4) in determining a question arising in connection with the carrying out of the function if—

(a) the question relates to a time when the provision was in force, and

(b) the provision appears to the Commissioner to be relevant to the question.

(5) Those functions are functions under—

(a) the data protection legislation, or

(b) the Privacy and Electronic Communications (EC Directive) Regulations 2003 (SI 2003/2426).

NOTES

Commencement: 23 July 2018 (see also the introductory notes to this Act preceding s 1 at **[1.2111]**).

[1.2141]

128 Other codes of practice

(1) The Secretary of State may by regulations require the Commissioner—

(a) to prepare appropriate codes of practice giving guidance as to good practice in the processing of personal data, and

(b) to make them available to such persons as the Commissioner considers appropriate.

(2) Before preparing such codes, the Commissioner must consult such of the following as the Commissioner considers appropriate—

(a) trade associations;

(b) data subjects;

(c) persons who appear to the Commissioner to represent the interests of data subjects.

(3) Regulations under this section—

(a) must describe the personal data or processing to which the code of practice is to relate, and

(b) may describe the persons or classes of person to whom it is to relate.

(4) Regulations under this section are subject to the negative resolution procedure.

(5) In this section—

"good practice in the processing of personal data" means such practice in the processing of personal data as appears to the Commissioner to be desirable having regard to the interests of data subjects and others, including compliance with the requirements of the data protection legislation;

"trade association" includes a body representing controllers or processors.

NOTES

Commencement: 25 May 2018 (see also the introductory notes to this Act preceding s 1 at **[1.2111]**).

Consensual audits

[1.2142]

129 Consensual audits

(1) The Commissioner's functions under Article 58(1) of the *GDPR* and paragraph 1 of Schedule 13 include power, with the consent of a controller or processor, to carry out an assessment of whether the controller or processor is complying with good practice in the processing of personal data.

(2) The Commissioner must inform the controller or processor of the results of such an assessment.

(3) In this section, "good practice in the processing of personal data" has the same meaning as in section 128.

NOTES

Commencement: 25 May 2018 (see also the introductory notes to this Act preceding s 1 at **[1.2111]**).

Sub-s (1): for "GDPR" in italics there is substituted "UK GDPR" by the Data Protection, Privacy and Electronic Communications (Amendments etc) (EU Exit) Regulations 2019, SI 2019/419, reg 4, Sch 2, paras 1, 54, as from exit day (as defined in the European Union (Withdrawal) Act 2018, s 20), for transitional provisions etc, see the 2019 Regulations at **[2.2122]** et seq.

Information provided to the Commissioner

[1.2143]

131 Disclosure of information to the Commissioner

(1) No enactment or rule of law prohibiting or restricting the disclosure of information precludes a person from providing the Commissioner with information necessary for the discharge of the Commissioner's functions.

(2) But this section does not authorise the making of a disclosure which is prohibited by any of Parts 1 to 7 or Chapter 1 of Part 9 of the Investigatory Powers Act 2016.

(3) Until the repeal of Part 1 of the Regulation of Investigatory Powers Act 2000 by paragraphs 45 and 54 of Schedule 10 to the Investigatory Powers Act 2016 is fully in force, subsection (2) has effect as if it included a reference to that Part.

NOTES

Commencement: 25 May 2018 (see also the introductory notes to this Act preceding s 1 at **[1.2111]**).

[1.2144]

132 Confidentiality of information

(1) A person who is or has been the Commissioner, or a member of the Commissioner's staff or an agent of the Commissioner, must not disclose information which—

(a) has been obtained by, or provided to, the Commissioner in the course of, or for the purposes of, the discharging of the Commissioner's functions,

(b) relates to an identified or identifiable individual or business, and

(c) is not available to the public from other sources at the time of the disclosure and has not previously been available to the public from other sources,

unless the disclosure is made with lawful authority.

(2) For the purposes of subsection (1), a disclosure is made with lawful authority only if and to the extent that—

(a) the disclosure was made with the consent of the individual or of the person for the time being carrying on the business,

(b) the information was obtained or provided as described in subsection (1)(a) for the purpose of its being made available to the public (in whatever manner),

(c) the disclosure was made for the purposes of, and is necessary for, the discharge of one or more of the Commissioner's functions,

(d) the disclosure was made for the purposes of, and is necessary for, the discharge of an EU obligation,

(e) the disclosure was made for the purposes of criminal or civil proceedings, however arising, or

(f) having regard to the rights, freedoms and legitimate interests of any person, the disclosure was necessary in the public interest.

(3) It is an offence for a person knowingly or recklessly to disclose information in contravention of subsection (1).

NOTES

Commencement: 25 May 2018 (see also the introductory notes to this Act preceding s 1 at **[1.2111]**).

Sub-s (2): para (d) is repealed by the Data Protection, Privacy and Electronic Communications (Amendments etc) (EU Exit) Regulations 2019, SI 2019/419, reg 4, Sch 2, paras 1, 55, as from exit day (as defined in the European Union (Withdrawal) Act 2018, s 20), for transitional provisions etc, see the 2019 Regulations at **[2.2122]** et seq.

[1.2145]

133 Guidance about privileged communications

(1) The Commissioner must produce and publish guidance about—

(a) how the Commissioner proposes to secure that privileged communications which the Commissioner obtains or has access to in the course of carrying out the Commissioner's functions are used or disclosed only so far as necessary for carrying out those functions, and

(b) how the Commissioner proposes to comply with restrictions and prohibitions on obtaining or having access to privileged communications which are imposed by an enactment.

(2) The Commissioner—

(a) may alter or replace the guidance, and

(b) must publish any altered or replacement guidance.

(3) The Commissioner must consult the Secretary of State before publishing guidance under this section (including altered or replacement guidance).

(4) The Commissioner must arrange for guidance under this section (including altered or replacement guidance) to be laid before Parliament.

(5) In this section, "privileged communications" means—

(a) communications made—

(i) between a professional legal adviser and the adviser's client, and

(ii) in connection with the giving of legal advice to the client with respect to legal obligations, liabilities or rights, and

(b) communications made—

(i) between a professional legal adviser and the adviser's client or between such an adviser or client and another person,

(ii) in connection with or in contemplation of legal proceedings, and

(iii) for the purposes of such proceedings.

(6) In subsection (5)—

(a) references to the client of a professional legal adviser include references to a person acting on behalf of the client, and

(b) references to a communication include—

(i) a copy or other record of the communication, and

(ii) anything enclosed with or referred to in the communication if made as described in subsection (5)(a)(ii) or in subsection (5)(b)(ii) and (iii).

NOTES

Commencement: 25 May 2018 (see also the introductory notes to this Act preceding s 1 at **[1.2111]**).

Fees

[1.2146]

134 Fees for services

The Commissioner may require a person other than a data subject or a data protection officer to pay a reasonable fee for a service provided to the person, or at the person's request, which the Commissioner is required or authorised to provide under the data protection legislation.

NOTES

Commencement: 25 May 2018 (see also the introductory notes to this Act preceding s 1 at **[1.2111]**).

[1.2147]

135 Manifestly unfounded or excessive requests by data subjects etc

(1) Where a request to the Commissioner from a data subject or a data protection officer is manifestly unfounded or excessive, the Commissioner may—

(a) charge a reasonable fee for dealing with the request, or

(b) refuse to act on the request.

(2) An example of a request that may be excessive is one that merely repeats the substance of previous requests.

(3) In any proceedings where there is an issue as to whether a request described in subsection (1) is manifestly unfounded or excessive, it is for the Commissioner to show that it is.

(4) Subsections (1) and (3) apply only in cases in which the Commissioner does not already have such powers and obligations under Article 57(4) of the *GDPR*.

NOTES

Commencement: 25 May 2018 (see also the introductory notes to this Act preceding s 1 at **[1.2111]**).

Sub-s (4): for "GDPR" in italics there is substituted "UK GDPR" by the Data Protection, Privacy and Electronic Communications (Amendments etc) (EU Exit) Regulations 2019, SI 2019/419, reg 4, Sch 2, paras 1, 56, as from exit day (as defined in the European Union (Withdrawal) Act 2018, s 20), for transitional provisions etc, see the 2019 Regulations at **[2.2122]** et seq.

[1.2148]

136 Guidance about fees

(1) The Commissioner must produce and publish guidance about the fees the Commissioner proposes to charge in accordance with—

(a) section 134 or 135, or

(b) Article 57(4) of the *GDPR*.

(2) Before publishing the guidance, the Commissioner must consult the Secretary of State.

NOTES

Commencement: 25 May 2018 (see also the introductory notes to this Act preceding s 1 at **[1.2111]**).

Sub-s (1): for "GDPR" in italics there is substituted "UK GDPR" by the Data Protection, Privacy and Electronic Communications (Amendments etc) (EU Exit) Regulations 2019, SI 2019/419, reg 4, Sch 2, paras 1, 57, as from exit day (as defined in the European Union (Withdrawal) Act 2018, s 20), for transitional provisions etc, see the 2019 Regulations at **[2.2122]** et seq.

Charges

[1.2149]

137 Charges payable to the Commissioner by controllers

(1) The Secretary of State may by regulations require controllers to pay charges of an amount specified in the regulations to the Commissioner.

(2) Regulations under subsection (1) may require a controller to pay a charge regardless of whether the Commissioner has provided, or proposes to provide, a service to the controller.

(3) Regulations under subsection (1) may—

(a) make provision about the time or times at which, or period or periods within which, a charge must be paid;

(b) make provision for cases in which a discounted charge is payable;

(c) make provision for cases in which no charge is payable;

(d) make provision for cases in which a charge which has been paid is to be refunded.

(4) In making regulations under subsection (1), the Secretary of State must have regard to the desirability of securing that the charges payable to the Commissioner under such regulations are sufficient to offset—

(a) expenses incurred by the Commissioner in discharging the Commissioner's functions—

(i) under the data protection legislation,

(ii) under the Data Protection Act 1998,

(iii) under or by virtue of sections 108 and 109 of the Digital Economy Act 2017, and

(iv) under or by virtue of the Privacy and Electronic Communications (EC Directive) Regulations 2003 (SI 2003/2426),

(b) any expenses of the Secretary of State in respect of the Commissioner so far as attributable to those functions,

(c) to the extent that the Secretary of State considers appropriate, any deficit previously incurred (whether before or after the passing of this Act) in respect of the expenses mentioned in paragraph (a), and

(d) to the extent that the Secretary of State considers appropriate, expenses incurred by the Secretary of State in respect of the inclusion of any officers or staff of the Commissioner in any scheme under section 1 of the Superannuation Act 1972 or section 1 of the Public Service Pensions Act 2013.

(5) The Secretary of State may from time to time require the Commissioner to provide information about the expenses referred to in subsection (4)(a).

(6) The Secretary of State may by regulations make provision—

(a) requiring a controller to provide information to the Commissioner, or

(b) enabling the Commissioner to require a controller to provide information to the Commissioner,

for either or both of the purposes mentioned in subsection (7).

(7) Those purposes are—

(a) determining whether a charge is payable by the controller under regulations under subsection (1);

(b) determining the amount of a charge payable by the controller.

(8) The provision that may be made under subsection (6)(a) includes provision requiring a controller to notify the Commissioner of a change in the controller's circumstances of a kind specified in the regulations.

NOTES

Commencement: 25 May 2018 (see also the introductory notes to this Act preceding s 1 at **[1.2111]**).

[1.2150]

138 Regulations under section 137: supplementary

(1) Before making regulations under section 137(1) or (6), the Secretary of State must consult such representatives of persons likely to be affected by the regulations as the Secretary of State thinks appropriate (and see also section 182).

(2) The Commissioner—

(a) must keep under review the working of regulations under section 137(1) or (6), and

(b) may from time to time submit proposals to the Secretary of State for amendments to be made to the regulations.

(3) The Secretary of State must review the working of regulations under section 137(1) or (6)—

(a) at the end of the period of 5 years beginning with the making of the first set of regulations under section 108 of the Digital Economy Act 2017, and

(b) at the end of each subsequent 5 year period.

(4) Regulations under section 137(1) are subject to the negative resolution procedure if—

(a) they only make provision increasing a charge for which provision is made by previous regulations under section 137(1) or section 108(1) of the Digital Economy Act 2017, and

(b) they do so to take account of an increase in the retail prices index since the previous regulations were made.

(5) Subject to subsection (4), regulations under section 137(1) or (6) are subject to the affirmative resolution procedure.

(6) In subsection (4), "the retail prices index" means—

(a) the general index of retail prices (for all items) published by the Statistics Board, or

(b) where that index is not published for a month, any substitute index or figures published by the Board.

(7) Regulations under section 137(1) or (6) may not apply to—

(a) Her Majesty in her private capacity,

(b) Her Majesty in right of the Duchy of Lancaster, or

(c) the Duke of Cornwall.

NOTES

Commencement: 25 May 2018 (see also the introductory notes to this Act preceding s 1 at **[1.2111]**).

Reports etc

[1.2151]

139 Reporting to Parliament

(1) The Commissioner must—

(a) produce a general report on the carrying out of the Commissioner's functions annually,

(b) arrange for it to be laid before Parliament, and

(c) publish it.

(2) The report must include the annual report required under Article 59 of the *GDPR*.

(3) The Commissioner may produce other reports relating to the carrying out of the Commissioner's functions and arrange for them to be laid before Parliament.

NOTES

Commencement: 25 May 2018 (see also the introductory notes to this Act preceding s 1 at **[1.2111]**).

Sub-s (2): for "GDPR" in italics there is substituted "UK GDPR" by the Data Protection, Privacy and Electronic Communications (Amendments etc) (EU Exit) Regulations 2019, SI 2019/419, reg 4, Sch 2, paras 1, 58, as from exit day (as defined in the European Union (Withdrawal) Act 2018, s 20), for transitional provisions etc, see the 2019 Regulations at **[2.2122]** et seq.

[1.2152]
140 Publication by the Commissioner
A duty under this Act for the Commissioner to publish a document is a duty for the Commissioner to publish it, or to arrange for it to be published, in such form and manner as the Commissioner considers appropriate.

NOTES
Commencement: 25 May 2018 (see also the introductory notes to this Act preceding s 1 at **[1.2111]**).

[1.2153]
141 Notices from the Commissioner
(1) This section applies in relation to a notice authorised or required by this Act to be given to a person by the Commissioner.
(2) The notice may be given to an individual—
(a) by delivering it to the individual,
(b) by sending it to the individual by post addressed to the individual at his or her usual or last-known place of residence or business, or
(c) by leaving it for the individual at that place.
(3) The notice may be given to a body corporate or unincorporate—
(a) by sending it by post to the proper officer of the body at its principal office, or
(b) by addressing it to the proper officer of the body and leaving it at that office.
(4) The notice may be given to a partnership in Scotland—
(a) by sending it by post to the principal office of the partnership, or
(b) by addressing it to that partnership and leaving it at that office.
(5) The notice may be given to the person by other means, including by electronic means, with the person's consent.
(6) In this section—
"principal office", in relation to a registered company, means its registered office;
"proper officer", in relation to any body, means the secretary or other executive officer charged with the conduct of its general affairs;
"registered company" means a company registered under the enactments relating to companies for the time being in force in the United Kingdom.
(7) This section is without prejudice to any other lawful method of giving a notice.

NOTES
Commencement: 25 May 2018 (see also the introductory notes to this Act preceding s 1 at **[1.2111]**).

PART 6
ENFORCEMENT

Information notices

[1.2154]
142 Information notices
(1) The Commissioner may, by written notice (an "information notice")—
(a) require a controller or processor to provide the Commissioner with information that the Commissioner reasonably requires for the purposes of carrying out the Commissioner's functions under the data protection legislation, or
(b) require any person to provide the Commissioner with information that the Commissioner reasonably requires for the purposes of—
(i) investigating a suspected failure of a type described in section 149(2) or a suspected offence under this Act, or
(ii) determining whether the processing of personal data is carried out by an individual in the course of a purely personal or household activity.
(2) An information notice must state—
(a) whether it is given under subsection (1)(a), (b)(i) or (b)(ii), and
(b) why the Commissioner requires the information.
(3) An information notice—
(a) may specify or describe particular information or a category of information;
(b) may specify the form in which the information must be provided;
(c) may specify the time at which, or the period within which, the information must be provided;
(d) may specify the place where the information must be provided;
(but see the restrictions in subsections (5) to (7)).
(4) An information notice must provide information about—
(a) the consequences of failure to comply with it, and
(b) the rights under sections 162 and 164 (appeals etc).
(5) An information notice may not require a person to provide information before the end of the period within which an appeal can be brought against the notice.
(6) If an appeal is brought against an information notice, the information need not be provided pending the determination or withdrawal of the appeal.
(7) If an information notice—
(a) states that, in the Commissioner's opinion, the information is required urgently, and
(b) gives the Commissioner's reasons for reaching that opinion,

subsections (5) and (6) do not apply but the notice must not require the information to be provided before the end of the period of 24 hours beginning when the notice is given.

(8) The Commissioner may cancel an information notice by written notice to the person to whom it was given.

(9) In subsection (1), in relation to a person who is a controller or processor for the purposes of the *GDPR*, the reference to a controller or processor includes a representative of a controller or processor designated under Article 27 of the *GDPR* (representatives of controllers or processors not established in *the European Union*).

(10) Section 3(14)(c) does not apply to the reference to the processing of personal data in subsection (1)(b).

NOTES

Commencement: 25 May 2018 (see also the introductory notes to this Act preceding s 1 at **[1.2111]**).

Sub-s (9): for "GDPR" in italics in both places it occurs there is substituted "UK GDPR", and for the words "the European Union" in italics there are substituted the words "the United Kingdom", by the Data Protection, Privacy and Electronic Communications (Amendments etc) (EU Exit) Regulations 2019, SI 2019/419, reg 4, Sch 2, paras 1, 59, as from exit day (as defined in the European Union (Withdrawal) Act 2018, s 20), for transitional provisions etc, see the 2019 Regulations at **[2.2122]** et seq.

[1.2155]

143 Information notices: restrictions

(1) The Commissioner may not give an information notice with respect to the processing of personal data for the special purposes unless—

- (a) a determination under section 174 with respect to the data or the processing has taken effect, or
- (b) the Commissioner—
  - (i) has reasonable grounds for suspecting that such a determination could be made, and
  - (ii) the information is required for the purposes of making such a determination.

(2) An information notice does not require a person to give the Commissioner information to the extent that requiring the person to do so would involve an infringement of the privileges of either House of Parliament.

(3) An information notice does not require a person to give the Commissioner information in respect of a communication which is made—

- (a) between a professional legal adviser and the adviser's client, and
- (b) in connection with the giving of legal advice to the client with respect to obligations, liabilities or rights under the data protection legislation.

(4) An information notice does not require a person to give the Commissioner information in respect of a communication which is made—

- (a) between a professional legal adviser and the adviser's client or between such an adviser or client and another person,
- (b) in connection with or in contemplation of proceedings under or arising out of the data protection legislation, and
- (c) for the purposes of such proceedings.

(5) In subsections (3) and (4), references to the client of a professional legal adviser include references to a person acting on behalf of the client.

(6) An information notice does not require a person to provide the Commissioner with information if doing so would, by revealing evidence of the commission of an offence expose the person to proceedings for that offence.

(7) The reference to an offence in subsection (6) does not include an offence under—

- (a) this Act;
- (b) section 5 of the Perjury Act 1911 (false statements made otherwise than on oath);
- (c) section 44(2) of the Criminal Law (Consolidation) (Scotland) Act 1995 (false statements made otherwise than on oath);
- (d) Article 10 of the Perjury (Northern Ireland) Order 1979 (SI 1979/1714 (NI 19)) (false statutory declarations and other false unsworn statements).

(8) An oral or written statement provided by a person in response to an information notice may not be used in evidence against that person on a prosecution for an offence under this Act (other than an offence under section 144) unless in the proceedings—

- (a) in giving evidence the person provides information inconsistent with the statement, and
- (b) evidence relating to the statement is adduced, or a question relating to it is asked, by that person or on that person's behalf.

(9) In subsection (6), in relation to an information notice given to a representative of a controller or processor designated under Article 27 of the *GDPR*, the reference to the person providing the information being exposed to proceedings for an offence includes a reference to the controller or processor being exposed to such proceedings.

NOTES

Commencement: 25 May 2018 (see also the introductory notes to this Act preceding s 1 at **[1.2111]**).

Sub-s (9): for "GDPR" in italics there is substituted "UK GDPR" by the Data Protection, Privacy and Electronic Communications (Amendments etc) (EU Exit) Regulations 2019, SI 2019/419, reg 4, Sch 2, paras 1, 60, as from exit day (as defined in the European Union (Withdrawal) Act 2018, s 20), for transitional provisions etc, see the 2019 Regulations at **[2.2122]** et seq.

[1.2156]

144 False statements made in response to information notices

It is an offence for a person, in response to an information notice—

- (a) to make a statement which the person knows to be false in a material respect, or
- (b) recklessly to make a statement which is false in a material respect.

NOTES

Commencement: 25 May 2018 (see also the introductory notes to this Act preceding s 1 at **[1.2111]**).

[1.2157]

145 Information orders

(1) This section applies if, on an application by the Commissioner, a court is satisfied that a person has failed to comply with a requirement of an information notice.

(2) The court may make an order requiring the person to provide to the Commissioner some or all of the following—

- (a) information referred to in the information notice;
- (b) other information which the court is satisfied the Commissioner requires, having regard to the statement included in the notice in accordance with section 142(2)(b).

(3) The order—

- (a) may specify the form in which the information must be provided,
- (b) must specify the time at which, or the period within which, the information must be provided, and
- (c) may specify the place where the information must be provided.

NOTES

Commencement: 25 May 2018 (see also the introductory notes to this Act preceding s 1 at **[1.2111]**).

Assessment notices

[1.2158]

146 Assessment notices

(1) The Commissioner may by written notice (an "assessment notice") require a controller or processor to permit the Commissioner to carry out an assessment of whether the controller or processor has complied or is complying with the data protection legislation.

(2) An assessment notice may require the controller or processor to do any of the following—

- (a) permit the Commissioner to enter specified premises;
- (b) direct the Commissioner to documents on the premises that are of a specified description;
- (c) assist the Commissioner to view information of a specified description that is capable of being viewed using equipment on the premises;
- (d) comply with a request from the Commissioner for a copy (in such form as may be requested) of—
  - (i) the documents to which the Commissioner is directed;
  - (ii) the information which the Commissioner is assisted to view;
- (e) direct the Commissioner to equipment or other material on the premises which is of a specified description;
- (f) permit the Commissioner to inspect or examine the documents, information, equipment or material to which the Commissioner is directed or which the Commissioner is assisted to view;
- (g) provide the Commissioner with an explanation of such documents, information, equipment or material;
- (h) permit the Commissioner to observe the processing of personal data that takes place on the premises;
- (i) make available for interview by the Commissioner a specified number of people of a specified description who process personal data on behalf of the controller, not exceeding the number who are willing to be interviewed.

(3) In subsection (2), references to the Commissioner include references to the Commissioner's officers and staff.

(4) An assessment notice must, in relation to each requirement imposed by the notice, specify the time or times at which, or period or periods within which, the requirement must be complied with (but see the restrictions in subsections (6) to (9)).

(5) An assessment notice must provide information about—

- (a) the consequences of failure to comply with it, and
- (b) the rights under sections 162 and 164 (appeals etc).

(6) An assessment notice may not require a person to do anything before the end of the period within which an appeal can be brought against the notice.

(7) If an appeal is brought against an assessment notice, the controller or processor need not comply with a requirement in the notice pending the determination or withdrawal of the appeal.

(8) If an assessment notice—

- (a) states that, in the Commissioner's opinion, it is necessary for the controller or processor to comply with a requirement in the notice urgently,
- (b) gives the Commissioner's reasons for reaching that opinion, and
- (c) does not meet the conditions in subsection (9)(a) to (d),

subsections (6) and (7) do not apply but the notice must not require the controller or processor to comply with the requirement before the end of the period of 7 days beginning when the notice is given.

(9) If an assessment notice—

(a) states that, in the Commissioner's opinion, there are reasonable grounds for suspecting that a controller or processor has failed or is failing as described in section 149(2) or that an offence under this Act has been or is being committed,
(b) indicates the nature of the suspected failure or offence,
(c) does not specify domestic premises,
(d) states that, in the Commissioner's opinion, it is necessary for the controller or processor to comply with a requirement in the notice in less than 7 days, and
(e) gives the Commissioner's reasons for reaching that opinion,

subsections (6) and (7) do not apply.

(10) The Commissioner may cancel an assessment notice by written notice to the controller or processor to whom it was given.

(11) Where the Commissioner gives an assessment notice to a processor, the Commissioner must, so far as reasonably practicable, give a copy of the notice to each controller for whom the processor processes personal data.

(12) In this section—

"domestic premises" means premises, or a part of premises, used as a dwelling;

"specified" means specified in an assessment notice.

NOTES

Commencement: 25 May 2018 (see also the introductory notes to this Act preceding s 1 at **[1.2111]**).

[1.2159]

147 Assessment notices: restrictions

(1) An assessment notice does not require a person to do something to the extent that requiring the person to do it would involve an infringement of the privileges of either House of Parliament.

(2) An assessment notice does not have effect so far as compliance would result in the disclosure of a communication which is made—
(a) between a professional legal adviser and the adviser's client, and
(b) in connection with the giving of legal advice to the client with respect to obligations, liabilities or rights under the data protection legislation.

(3) An assessment notice does not have effect so far as compliance would result in the disclosure of a communication which is made—
(a) between a professional legal adviser and the adviser's client or between such an adviser or client and another person,
(b) in connection with or in contemplation of proceedings under or arising out of the data protection legislation, and
(c) for the purposes of such proceedings.

(4) In subsections (2) and (3)—
(a) references to the client of a professional legal adviser include references to a person acting on behalf of such a client, and
(b) references to a communication include—
(i) a copy or other record of the communication, and
(ii) anything enclosed with or referred to in the communication if made as described in subsection (2)(b) or in subsection (3)(b) and (c).

(5) The Commissioner may not give a controller or processor an assessment notice with respect to the processing of personal data for the special purposes.

(6) The Commissioner may not give an assessment notice to—
(a) a body specified in section 23(3) of the Freedom of Information Act 2000 (bodies dealing with security matters), or
(b) the Office for Standards in Education, Children's Services and Skills in so far as it is a controller or processor in respect of information processed for the purposes of functions exercisable by Her Majesty's Chief Inspector of Education, Children's Services and Skills by virtue of section 5(1)(a) of the Care Standards Act 2000.

NOTES

Commencement: 25 May 2018 (see also the introductory notes to this Act preceding s 1 at **[1.2111]**).

Information notices and assessment notices: destruction of documents etc

[1.2160]

148 Destroying or falsifying information and documents etc

(1) This section applies where a person—
(a) has been given an information notice requiring the person to provide the Commissioner with information, or
(b) has been given an assessment notice requiring the person to direct the Commissioner to a document, equipment or other material or to assist the Commissioner to view information.

(2) It is an offence for the person—
(a) to destroy or otherwise dispose of, conceal, block or (where relevant) falsify all or part of the information, document, equipment or material, or
(b) to cause or permit the destruction, disposal, concealment, blocking or (where relevant) falsification of all or part of the information, document, equipment or material,

with the intention of preventing the Commissioner from viewing, or being provided with or directed to, all or part of the information, document, equipment or material.

(3) It is a defence for a person charged with an offence under subsection (2) to prove that the destruction, disposal, concealment, blocking or falsification would have occurred in the absence of the person being given the notice.

NOTES

Commencement: 25 May 2018 (see also the introductory notes to this Act preceding s 1 at **[1.2111]**).

Enforcement notices

[1.2161]

149 Enforcement notices

(1) Where the Commissioner is satisfied that a person has failed, or is failing, as described in subsection (2), (3), (4) or (5), the Commissioner may give the person a written notice (an "enforcement notice") which requires the person—

(a) to take steps specified in the notice, or

(b) to refrain from taking steps specified in the notice,

or both (and see also sections 150 and 151).

(2) The first type of failure is where a controller or processor has failed, or is failing, to comply with any of the following—

(a) a provision of Chapter II of the *GDPR* or Chapter 2 of Part 3 or Chapter 2 of Part 4 of this Act (principles of processing);

(b) a provision of Articles 12 to 22 of the *GDPR* or Part 3 or 4 of this Act conferring rights on a data subject;

(c) a provision of Articles 25 to 39 of the *GDPR* or section 64 or 65 of this Act (obligations of controllers and processors);

(d) a requirement to communicate a personal data breach to the Commissioner or a data subject under section 67, 68 or 108 of this Act;

(e) the principles for transfers of personal data to third countries, non-Convention countries and international organisations in Articles 44 to 49 of the *GDPR* or in sections 73 to 78 or 109 of this Act.

(3) The second type of failure is where a monitoring body has failed, or is failing, to comply with an obligation under Article 41 of the *GDPR* (monitoring of approved codes of conduct).

(4) The third type of failure is where a person who is a certification provider—

(a) does not meet the requirements for accreditation,

(b) has failed, or is failing, to comply with an obligation under Article 42 or 43 of the *GDPR* (certification of controllers and processors), or

(c) has failed, or is failing, to comply with any other provision of the *GDPR* (whether in the person's capacity as a certification provider or otherwise).

(5) The fourth type of failure is where a controller has failed, or is failing, to comply with regulations under section 137.

(6) An enforcement notice given in reliance on subsection (2), (3) or (5) may only impose requirements which the Commissioner considers appropriate for the purpose of remedying the failure.

(7) An enforcement notice given in reliance on subsection (4) may only impose requirements which the Commissioner considers appropriate having regard to the failure (whether or not for the purpose of remedying the failure).

(8) The Secretary of State may by regulations confer power on the Commissioner to give an enforcement notice in respect of other failures to comply with the data protection legislation.

(9) Regulations under this section—

(a) may make provision about the giving of an enforcement notice in respect of the failure, including by amending this section and sections 150 to 152,

(b) may make provision about the giving of an information notice, an assessment notice or a penalty notice, or about powers of entry and inspection, in connection with the failure, including by amending sections 142, 143, 146, 147 and 155 to 157 and Schedules 15 and 16, and

(c) are subject to the affirmative resolution procedure.

NOTES

Commencement: 25 May 2018 (see also the introductory notes to this Act preceding s 1 at **[1.2111]**).

For "GDPR" in italics in each place that it occurs there is substituted "UK GDPR" by the Data Protection, Privacy and Electronic Communications (Amendments etc) (EU Exit) Regulations 2019, SI 2019/419, reg 4, Sch 2, paras 1, 61, as from exit day (as defined in the European Union (Withdrawal) Act 2018, s 20), for transitional provisions etc, see the 2019 Regulations at **[2.2122]** et seq.

[1.2162]

150 Enforcement notices: supplementary

(1) An enforcement notice must—

(a) state what the person has failed or is failing to do, and

(b) give the Commissioner's reasons for reaching that opinion.

(2) In deciding whether to give an enforcement notice in reliance on section 149(2), the Commissioner must consider whether the failure has caused or is likely to cause any person damage or distress.

(3) In relation to an enforcement notice given in reliance on section 149(2), the Commissioner's power under section 149(1)(b) to require a person to refrain from taking specified steps includes power—

(a) to impose a ban relating to all processing of personal data, or

(b) to impose a ban relating only to a specified description of processing of personal data, including by specifying one or more of the following—
(i) a description of personal data;
(ii) the purpose or manner of the processing;
(iii) the time when the processing takes place.

(4) An enforcement notice may specify the time or times at which, or period or periods within which, a requirement imposed by the notice must be complied with (but see the restrictions in subsections (6) to (8)).

(5) An enforcement notice must provide information about—
(a) the consequences of failure to comply with it, and
(b) the rights under sections 162 and 164 (appeals etc).

(6) An enforcement notice must not specify a time for compliance with a requirement in the notice which falls before the end of the period within which an appeal can be brought against the notice.

(7) If an appeal is brought against an enforcement notice, a requirement in the notice need not be complied with pending the determination or withdrawal of the appeal.

(8) If an enforcement notice—
(a) states that, in the Commissioner's opinion, it is necessary for a requirement to be complied with urgently, and
(b) gives the Commissioner's reasons for reaching that opinion,

subsections (6) and (7) do not apply but the notice must not require the requirement to be complied with before the end of the period of 24 hours beginning when the notice is given.

(9) In this section, "specified" means specified in an enforcement notice.

NOTES

Commencement: 25 May 2018 (see also the introductory notes to this Act preceding s 1 at **[1.2111]**).

[1.2163]

151 Enforcement notices: rectification and erasure of personal data etc

(1) Subsections (2) and (3) apply where an enforcement notice is given in respect of a failure by a controller or processor—
(a) to comply with a data protection principle relating to accuracy, or
(b) to comply with a data subject's request to exercise rights under Article 16, 17 or 18 of the *GDPR* (right to rectification, erasure or restriction on processing) or section 46, 47 or 100 of this Act.

(2) If the enforcement notice requires the controller or processor to rectify or erase inaccurate personal data, it may also require the controller or processor to rectify or erase any other data which—
(a) is held by the controller or processor, and
(b) contains an expression of opinion which appears to the Commissioner to be based on the inaccurate personal data.

(3) Where a controller or processor has accurately recorded personal data provided by the data subject or a third party but the data is inaccurate, the enforcement notice may require the controller or processor—
(a) to take steps specified in the notice to ensure the accuracy of the data,
(b) if relevant, to secure that the data indicates the data subject's view that the data is inaccurate, and
(c) to supplement the data with a statement of the true facts relating to the matters dealt with by the data that is approved by the Commissioner,

(as well as imposing requirements under subsection (2)).

(4) When deciding what steps it is reasonable to specify under subsection (3)(a), the Commissioner must have regard to the purpose for which the data was obtained and further processed.

(5) Subsections (6) and (7) apply where—
(a) an enforcement notice requires a controller or processor to rectify or erase personal data, or
(b) the Commissioner is satisfied that the processing of personal data which has been rectified or erased by the controller or processor involved a failure described in subsection (1).

(6) An enforcement notice may, if reasonably practicable, require the controller or processor to notify third parties to whom the data has been disclosed of the rectification or erasure.

(7) In determining whether it is reasonably practicable to require such notification, the Commissioner must have regard, in particular, to the number of people who would have to be notified.

(8) In this section, "data protection principle relating to accuracy" means the principle in—
(a) Article 5(1)(d) of the *GDPR*,
(b) section 38(1) of this Act, or
(c) section 89 of this Act.

NOTES

Commencement: 25 May 2018 (see also the introductory notes to this Act preceding s 1 at **[1.2111]**).

Sub-ss (1), (8): for "GDPR" in italics there is substituted "UK GDPR" by the Data Protection, Privacy and Electronic Communications (Amendments etc) (EU Exit) Regulations 2019, SI 2019/419, reg 4, Sch 2, paras 1, 62, as from exit day (as defined in the European Union (Withdrawal) Act 2018, s 20), for transitional provisions etc, see the 2019 Regulations at **[2.2122]** et seq.

[1.2164]
152 Enforcement notices: restrictions
(1) The Commissioner may not give a controller or processor an enforcement notice in reliance on section 149(2) with respect to the processing of personal data for the special purposes unless—
(a) a determination under section 174 with respect to the data or the processing has taken effect, and
(b) a court has granted leave for the notice to be given.
(2) A court must not grant leave for the purposes of subsection (1)(b) unless it is satisfied that—
(a) the Commissioner has reason to suspect a failure described in section 149(2) which is of substantial public importance, and
(b) the controller or processor has been given notice of the application for leave in accordance with rules of court or the case is urgent.
(3) An enforcement notice does not require a person to do something to the extent that requiring the person to do it would involve an infringement of the privileges of either House of Parliament.
(4) In the case of a joint controller in respect of the processing of personal data to which Part 3 or 4 applies whose responsibilities for compliance with that Part are determined in an arrangement under section 58 or 104, the Commissioner may only give the controller an enforcement notice in reliance on section 149(2) if the controller is responsible for compliance with the provision, requirement or principle in question.

NOTES
Commencement: 25 May 2018 (see also the introductory notes to this Act preceding s 1 at **[1.2111]**).

[1.2165]
153 Enforcement notices: cancellation and variation
(1) The Commissioner may cancel or vary an enforcement notice by giving written notice to the person to whom it was given.
(2) A person to whom an enforcement notice is given may apply in writing to the Commissioner for the cancellation or variation of the notice.
(3) An application under subsection (2) may be made only—
(a) after the end of the period within which an appeal can be brought against the notice, and
(b) on the ground that, by reason of a change of circumstances, one or more of the provisions of that notice need not be complied with in order to remedy the failure identified in the notice.

NOTES
Commencement: 25 May 2018 (see also the introductory notes to this Act preceding s 1 at **[1.2111]**).

Powers of entry and inspection

[1.2166]
154 Powers of entry and inspection
Schedule 15 makes provision about powers of entry and inspection.

NOTES
Commencement: 25 May 2018 (see also the introductory notes to this Act preceding s 1 at **[1.2111]**).

Penalties

[1.2167]
155 Penalty notices
(1) If the Commissioner is satisfied that a person—
(a) has failed or is failing as described in section 149(2), (3), (4) or (5), or
(b) has failed to comply with an information notice, an assessment notice or an enforcement notice,
the Commissioner may, by written notice (a "penalty notice"), require the person to pay to the Commissioner an amount in sterling specified in the notice.
(2) Subject to subsection (4), when deciding whether to give a penalty notice to a person and determining the amount of the penalty, the Commissioner must have regard to the following, so far as relevant—
(a) to the extent that the notice concerns a matter to which the *GDPR* applies, the matters listed in Article 83(1) and (2) of the *GDPR*;
(b) to the extent that the notice concerns another matter, the matters listed in subsection (3).
(3) Those matters are—
(a) the nature, gravity and duration of the failure;
(b) the intentional or negligent character of the failure;
(c) any action taken by the controller or processor to mitigate the damage or distress suffered by data subjects;
(d) the degree of responsibility of the controller or processor, taking into account technical and organisational measures implemented by the controller or processor in accordance with section 57, 66, 103 or 107;
(e) any relevant previous failures by the controller or processor;
(f) the degree of co-operation with the Commissioner, in order to remedy the failure and mitigate the possible adverse effects of the failure;
(g) the categories of personal data affected by the failure;
(h) the manner in which the infringement became known to the Commissioner, including whether, and if so to what extent, the controller or processor notified the Commissioner of the failure;

(i) the extent to which the controller or processor has complied with previous enforcement notices or penalty notices;
(j) adherence to approved codes of conduct or certification mechanisms;
(k) any other aggravating or mitigating factor applicable to the case, including financial benefits gained, or losses avoided, as a result of the failure (whether directly or indirectly);
(l) whether the penalty would be effective, proportionate and dissuasive.

(4) Subsections (2) and (3) do not apply in the case of a decision or determination relating to a failure described in section 149(5).

(5) Schedule 16 makes further provision about penalty notices, including provision requiring the Commissioner to give a notice of intent to impose a penalty and provision about payment, variation, cancellation and enforcement.

(6) The Secretary of State may by regulations—
(a) confer power on the Commissioner to give a penalty notice in respect of other failures to comply with the data protection legislation, and
(b) provide for the maximum penalty that may be imposed in relation to such failures to be either the standard maximum amount or the higher maximum amount.

(7) Regulations under this section—
(a) may make provision about the giving of penalty notices in respect of the failure,
(b) may amend this section and sections 156 to 158, and
(c) are subject to the affirmative resolution procedure.

(8) In this section, "higher maximum amount" and "standard maximum amount" have the same meaning as in section 157.

NOTES

Commencement: 25 May 2018 (see also the introductory notes to this Act preceding s 1 at **[1.2111]**).

Sub-s (2): for "GDPR" in italics in both places it occurs there is substituted "UK GDPR" by the Data Protection, Privacy and Electronic Communications (Amendments etc) (EU Exit) Regulations 2019, SI 2019/419, reg 4, Sch 2, paras 1, 63, as from exit day (as defined in the European Union (Withdrawal) Act 2018, s 20), for transitional provisions etc, see the 2019 Regulations at **[2.2122]** et seq.

[1.2168]

156 Penalty notices: restrictions

(1) The Commissioner may not give a controller or processor a penalty notice in reliance on section 149(2) with respect to the processing of personal data for the special purposes unless—
(a) a determination under section 174 with respect to the data or the processing has taken effect, and
(b) a court has granted leave for the notice to be given.

(2) A court must not grant leave for the purposes of subsection (1)(b) unless it is satisfied that—
(a) the Commissioner has reason to suspect a failure described in section 149(2) which is of substantial public importance, and
(b) the controller or processor has been given notice of the application for leave in accordance with rules of court or the case is urgent.

(3) The Commissioner may not give a controller or processor a penalty notice with respect to the processing of personal data where the purposes and manner of the processing are determined by or on behalf of either House of Parliament.

(4) The Commissioner may not give a penalty notice to—
(a) the Crown Estate Commissioners, or
(b) a person who is a controller by virtue of section 209(4) (controller for the Royal Household etc).

(5) In the case of a joint controller in respect of the processing of personal data to which Part 3 or 4 applies whose responsibilities for compliance with that Part are determined in an arrangement under section 58 or 104, the Commissioner may only give the controller a penalty notice in reliance on section 149(2) if the controller is responsible for compliance with the provision, requirement or principle in question.

NOTES

Commencement: 25 May 2018 (see also the introductory notes to this Act preceding s 1 at **[1.2111]**).

[1.2169]

157 Maximum amount of penalty

(1) In relation to an infringement of a provision of the *GDPR*, the maximum amount of the penalty that may be imposed by a penalty notice is—
(a) the amount specified in Article 83 of the *GDPR*, or
(b) if an amount is not specified there, the standard maximum amount.

(2) In relation to an infringement of a provision of Part 3 of this Act, the maximum amount of the penalty that may be imposed by a penalty notice is—
(a) in relation to a failure to comply with section 35, 36, 37, 38(1), 39(1), 40, 44, 45, 46, 47, 48, 49, 52, 53, 73, *74,* 75, 76, 77 or 78, the higher maximum amount, and
(b) otherwise, the standard maximum amount.

(3) In relation to an infringement of a provision of Part 4 of this Act, the maximum amount of the penalty that may be imposed by a penalty notice is—
(a) in relation to a failure to comply with section 86, 87, 88, 89, 90, 91, 93, 94, 100 or 109, the higher maximum amount, and

(b) otherwise, the standard maximum amount.

(4) In relation to a failure to comply with an information notice, an assessment notice or an enforcement notice, the maximum amount of the penalty that may be imposed by a penalty notice is the higher maximum amount.

(5) The "higher maximum amount" is—

(a) in the case of an undertaking, *20 million Euros* or 4% of the undertaking's total annual worldwide turnover in the preceding financial year, whichever is higher, or

(b) in any other case, *20 million Euros*.

(6) The "standard maximum amount" is—

(a) in the case of an undertaking, *10 million Euros* or 2% of the undertaking's total annual worldwide turnover in the preceding financial year, whichever is higher, or

(b) in any other case, *10 million Euros*.

(7) The maximum amount of a penalty in sterling must be determined by applying the spot rate of exchange set by the Bank of England on the day on which the penalty notice is given.

NOTES

Commencement: 25 May 2018 (see also the introductory notes to this Act preceding s 1 at **[1.2111]**).

Sub-s (1): for "GDPR" in italics in both places that it occurs there is substituted "UK GDPR" by the Data Protection, Privacy and Electronic Communications (Amendments etc) (EU Exit) Regulations 2019, SI 2019/419, reg 4, Sch 2, paras 1, 64(1), (2), as from exit day (as defined in the European Union (Withdrawal) Act 2018, s 20), for transitional provisions etc, see the 2019 Regulations at **[2.2122]** et seq.

Sub-s (2): figure in italics repealed by SI 2019/419, reg 4, Sch 2, paras 1, 64(1), (3), as from exit day (as defined in the European Union (Withdrawal) Act 2018, s 20), for transitional provisions etc, see the 2019 Regulations at **[2.2122]** et seq.

Sub-s (5): for "20 million Euros" in italics in both places that it occurs there is substituted "£17,500,000" by SI 2019/419, reg 4, Sch 2, paras 1, 64(1), (4), as from exit day (as defined in the European Union (Withdrawal) Act 2018, s 20), for transitional provisions etc, see the 2019 Regulations at **[2.2122]** et seq.

Sub-s (6): for "10 million Euros" in italics in both places that it occurs there is substituted "£8,700,000" by SI 2019/419, reg 4, Sch 2, paras 1, 64(1), (5), as from exit day (as defined in the European Union (Withdrawal) Act 2018, s 20), for transitional provisions etc, see the 2019 Regulations at **[2.2122]** et seq.

Sub-s (7): repealed by SI 2019/419, reg 4, Sch 2, paras 1, 64(1), (6), as from exit day (as defined in the European Union (Withdrawal) Act 2018, s 20), for transitional provisions etc, see the 2019 Regulations at **[2.2122]** et seq.

[1.2170]

158 Fixed penalties for non-compliance with charges regulations

(1) The Commissioner must produce and publish a document specifying the amount of the penalty for a failure to comply with regulations made under section 137.

(2) The Commissioner may specify different amounts for different types of failure.

(3) The maximum amount that may be specified is 150% of the highest charge payable by a controller in respect of a financial year in accordance with the regulations, disregarding any discount available under the regulations.

(4) The Commissioner—

(a) may alter or replace the document, and

(b) must publish any altered or replacement document.

(5) Before publishing a document under this section (including any altered or replacement document), the Commissioner must consult—

(a) the Secretary of State, and

(b) such other persons as the Commissioner considers appropriate.

(6) The Commissioner must arrange for a document published under this section (including any altered or replacement document) to be laid before Parliament.

NOTES

Commencement: 25 May 2018 (see also the introductory notes to this Act preceding s 1 at **[1.2111]**).

[1.2171]

159 Amount of penalties: supplementary

(1) For the purposes of Article 83 of the *GDPR* and section 157, the Secretary of State may by regulations—

(a) provide that a person of a description specified in the regulations is or is not an undertaking, and

(b) make provision about how an undertaking's turnover is to be determined.

(2) For the purposes of Article 83 of the *GDPR*, section 157 and section 158, the Secretary of State may by regulations provide that a period is or is not a financial year.

(3) Regulations under this section are subject to the affirmative resolution procedure.

NOTES

Commencement: 25 May 2018 (see also the introductory notes to this Act preceding s 1 at **[1.2111]**).

Sub-ss (1), (2): for "GDPR" in italics there is substituted "UK GDPR" by the Data Protection, Privacy and Electronic Communications (Amendments etc) (EU Exit) Regulations 2019, SI 2019/419, reg 4, Sch 2, paras 1, 65, as from exit day (as defined in the European Union (Withdrawal) Act 2018, s 20), for transitional provisions etc, see the 2019 Regulations at **[2.2122]** et seq.

Guidance

[1.2172]
160 Guidance about regulatory action

(1) The Commissioner must produce and publish guidance about how the Commissioner proposes to exercise the Commissioner's functions in connection with—

(a) information notices,
(b) assessment notices,
(c) enforcement notices, and
(d) penalty notices.

(2) The Commissioner may produce and publish guidance about how the Commissioner proposes to exercise the Commissioner's other functions under this Part.

(3) In relation to information notices, the guidance must include—

(a) provision specifying factors to be considered in determining the time at which, or the period within which, information is to be required to be provided;
(b) provision about the circumstances in which the Commissioner would consider it appropriate to give an information notice to a person in reliance on section 142(7) (urgent cases);
(c) provision about how the Commissioner will determine how to proceed if a person does not comply with an information notice.

(4) In relation to assessment notices, the guidance must include—

(a) provision specifying factors to be considered in determining whether to give an assessment notice to a person;
(b) provision about the circumstances in which the Commissioner would consider it appropriate to give an assessment notice in reliance on section 146(8) or (9) (urgent cases);
(c) provision specifying descriptions of documents or information that—
  (i) are not to be examined or inspected in accordance with an assessment notice, or
  (ii) are to be so examined or inspected only by a person of a description specified in the guidance;
(d) provision about the nature of inspections and examinations carried out in accordance with an assessment notice;
(e) provision about the nature of interviews carried out in accordance with an assessment notice;
(f) provision about the preparation, issuing and publication by the Commissioner of assessment reports in respect of controllers and processors that have been given assessment notices;
(g) provision about how the Commissioner will determine how to proceed if a person does not comply with an assessment notice.

(5) The guidance produced in accordance with subsection (4)(c) must include provisions that relate to—

(a) documents and information concerning an individual's physical or mental health;
(b) documents and information concerning the provision of social care for an individual.

(6) In relation to enforcement notices, the guidance must include—

(a) provision specifying factors to be considered in determining whether to give an enforcement notice to a person;
(b) provision about the circumstances in which the Commissioner would consider it appropriate to give an enforcement notice to a person in reliance on section 150(8) (urgent cases);
(c) provision about how the Commissioner will determine how to proceed if a person does not comply with an enforcement notice.

(7) In relation to penalty notices, the guidance must include—

(a) provision about the circumstances in which the Commissioner would consider it appropriate to issue a penalty notice;
(b) provision about the circumstances in which the Commissioner would consider it appropriate to allow a person to make oral representations about the Commissioner's intention to give the person a penalty notice;
(c) provision explaining how the Commissioner will determine the amount of penalties;
(d) provision about how the Commissioner will determine how to proceed if a person does not comply with a penalty notice.

(8) The Commissioner—

(a) may alter or replace guidance produced under this section, and
(b) must publish any altered or replacement guidance.

(9) Before producing guidance under this section (including any altered or replacement guidance), the Commissioner must consult—

(a) the Secretary of State, and
(b) such other persons as the Commissioner considers appropriate.

(10) Section 161 applies in relation to the first guidance under subsection (1).

(11) The Commissioner must arrange for other guidance under this section (including any altered or replacement guidance) to be laid before Parliament.

(12) In this section, "social care" has the same meaning as in Part 1 of the Health and Social Care Act 2008 (see section 9(3) of that Act).

NOTES

Commencement: 25 May 2018 (see also the introductory notes to this Act preceding s 1 at **[1.2111]**).

[1.2173]

161 Approval of first guidance about regulatory action

(1) When the first guidance is produced under section 160(1)—

(a) the Commissioner must submit the final version to the Secretary of State, and

(b) the Secretary of State must lay the guidance before Parliament.

(2) If, within the 40-day period, either House of Parliament resolves not to approve the guidance—

(a) the Commissioner must not issue the guidance, and

(b) the Commissioner must produce another version of the guidance (and this section applies to that version).

(3) If, within the 40-day period, no such resolution is made—

(a) the Commissioner must issue the guidance, and

(b) the guidance comes into force at the end of the period of 21 days beginning with the day on which it is issued.

(4) Nothing in subsection (2)(a) prevents another version of the guidance being laid before Parliament.

(5) In this section, "the 40-day period" means—

(a) if the guidance is laid before both Houses of Parliament on the same day, the period of 40 days beginning with that day, or

(b) if the guidance is laid before the Houses of Parliament on different days, the period of 40 days beginning with the later of those days.

(6) In calculating the 40-day period, no account is to be taken of any period during which Parliament is dissolved or prorogued or during which both Houses of Parliament are adjourned for more than 4 days.

NOTES

Commencement: 25 May 2018 (see also the introductory notes to this Act preceding s 1 at **[1.2111]**).

Appeals etc

[1.2174]

162 Rights of appeal

(1) A person who is given any of the following notices may appeal to the Tribunal—

(a) an information notice;

(b) an assessment notice;

(c) an enforcement notice;

(d) a penalty notice;

(e) a penalty variation notice.

(2) A person who is given an enforcement notice may appeal to the Tribunal against the refusal of an application under section 153 for the cancellation or variation of the notice.

(3) A person who is given a penalty notice or a penalty variation notice may appeal to the Tribunal against the amount of the penalty specified in the notice, whether or not the person appeals against the notice.

(4) Where a determination is made under section 174 in respect of the processing of personal data, the controller or processor may appeal to the Tribunal against the determination.

NOTES

Commencement: 25 May 2018 (see also the introductory notes to this Act preceding s 1 at **[1.2111]**).

[1.2175]

163 Determination of appeals

(1) Subsections (2) to (4) apply where a person appeals to the Tribunal under section 162(1) or (3).

(2) The Tribunal may review any determination of fact on which the notice or decision against which the appeal is brought was based.

(3) If the Tribunal considers—

(a) that the notice or decision against which the appeal is brought is not in accordance with the law, or

(b) to the extent that the notice or decision involved an exercise of discretion by the Commissioner, that the Commissioner ought to have exercised the discretion differently,

the Tribunal must allow the appeal or substitute another notice or decision which the Commissioner could have given or made.

(4) Otherwise, the Tribunal must dismiss the appeal.

(5) On an appeal under section 162(2), if the Tribunal considers that the enforcement notice ought to be cancelled or varied by reason of a change in circumstances, the Tribunal must cancel or vary the notice.

(6) On an appeal under section 162(4), the Tribunal may cancel the Commissioner's determination.

NOTES

Commencement: 25 May 2018 (see also the introductory notes to this Act preceding s 1 at **[1.2111]**).

[1.2176]

164 Applications in respect of urgent notices

(1) This section applies where an information notice, an assessment notice or an enforcement notice given to a person contains an urgency statement.

(2) The person may apply to the court for either or both of the following—

(a) the disapplication of the urgency statement in relation to some or all of the requirements of the notice;

(b) a change to the time at which, or the period within which, a requirement of the notice must be complied with.

(3) On an application under subsection (2), the court may do any of the following—

(a) direct that the notice is to have effect as if it did not contain the urgency statement;

(b) direct that the inclusion of the urgency statement is not to have effect in relation to a requirement of the notice;

(c) vary the notice by changing the time at which, or the period within which, a requirement of the notice must be complied with;

(d) vary the notice by making other changes required to give effect to a direction under paragraph (a) or (b) or in consequence of a variation under paragraph (c).

(4) The decision of the court on an application under this section is final.

(5) In this section, "urgency statement" means—

(a) in relation to an information notice, a statement under section 142(7)(a),

(b) in relation to an assessment notice, a statement under section 146(8)(a) or (9)(d), and

(c) in relation to an enforcement notice, a statement under section 150(8)(a).

NOTES

Commencement: 25 May 2018 (see also the introductory notes to this Act preceding s 1 at **[1.2111]**).

Complaints

[1.2177]

165 Complaints by data subjects

(1) Articles 57(1)(f) and (2) and 77 of the *GDPR* (data subject's right to lodge a complaint) confer rights on data subjects to complain to the Commissioner if the data subject considers that, in connection with personal data relating to him or her, there is an infringement of the *GDPR*.

(2) A data subject may make a complaint to the Commissioner if the data subject considers that, in connection with personal data relating to him or her, there is an infringement of Part 3 or 4 of this Act.

(3) The Commissioner must facilitate the making of complaints under subsection (2) by taking steps such as providing a complaint form which can be completed electronically and by other means.

(4) If the Commissioner receives a complaint under subsection (2), the Commissioner must—

(a) take appropriate steps to respond to the complaint,

(b) inform the complainant of the outcome of the complaint,

(c) inform the complainant of the rights under section 166, and

(d) if asked to do so by the complainant, provide the complainant with further information about how to pursue the complaint.

(5) The reference in subsection (4)(a) to taking appropriate steps in response to a complaint includes—

(a) investigating the subject matter of the complaint, to the extent appropriate, and

(b) informing the complainant about progress on the complaint, including about whether further investigation or co-ordination with *another supervisory authority or* foreign designated authority is necessary.

(6) If the Commissioner receives a complaint relating to the infringement of a data subject's rights under provisions adopted by a member State other than the United Kingdom pursuant to the Law Enforcement Directive, the Commissioner must—

(a) send the complaint to the relevant supervisory authority for the purposes of that Directive,

(b) inform the complainant that the Commissioner has done so, and

(c) if asked to do so by the complainant, provide the complainant with further information about how to pursue the complaint.

(7) In this section—

"foreign designated authority" means an authority designated for the purposes of Article 13 of the Data Protection Convention by a party, other than the United Kingdom, which is bound by that Convention;

"supervisory authority" means a supervisory authority for the purposes of Article 51 of the GDPR or Article 41 of the Law Enforcement Directive in a member State other than the United Kingdom.

NOTES

Commencement: 25 May 2018 (see also the introductory notes to this Act preceding s 1 at **[1.2111]**).

Sub-s (1): for "GDPR" in italics in both places that it occurs there is substituted "UK GDPR", for the words in italics in sub-s (5) there is substituted "a", and sub-s (6) and the definition "supervisory authority" in sub-s (7) are repealed, by the Data Protection, Privacy and Electronic Communications (Amendments etc) (EU Exit) Regulations 2019, SI 2019/419, reg 4, Sch 2, paras 1, 66, as from exit day (as defined in the European Union (Withdrawal) Act 2018, s 20), for transitional provisions etc, see the 2019 Regulations at **[2.2122]** et seq.

[1.2178]

166 Orders to progress complaints

(1) This section applies where, after a data subject makes a complaint under section 165 or Article 77 of the *GDPR*, the Commissioner—

(a) fails to take appropriate steps to respond to the complaint,

(b) fails to provide the complainant with information about progress on the complaint, or of the outcome of the complaint, before the end of the period of 3 months beginning when the Commissioner received the complaint, or

(c) if the Commissioner's consideration of the complaint is not concluded during that period, fails to provide the complainant with such information during a subsequent period of 3 months.

(2) The Tribunal may, on an application by the data subject, make an order requiring the Commissioner—

(a) to take appropriate steps to respond to the complaint, or

(b) to inform the complainant of progress on the complaint, or of the outcome of the complaint, within a period specified in the order.

(3) An order under subsection (2)(a) may require the Commissioner—

(a) to take steps specified in the order;

(b) to conclude an investigation, or take a specified step, within a period specified in the order.

(4) Section 165(5) applies for the purposes of subsections (1)(a) and (2)(a) as it applies for the purposes of section 165(4)(a).

NOTES

Commencement: 25 May 2018 (see also the introductory notes to this Act preceding s 1 at **[1.2111]**).

Sub-s (1): for "GDPR" in italics there is substituted "UK GDPR" by the Data Protection, Privacy and Electronic Communications (Amendments etc) (EU Exit) Regulations 2019, SI 2019/419, reg 4, Sch 2, paras 1, 67, as from exit day (as defined in the European Union (Withdrawal) Act 2018, s 20), for transitional provisions etc, see the 2019 Regulations at **[2.2122]** et seq.

Remedies in the court

[1.2179]

167 Compliance orders

(1) This section applies if, on an application by a data subject, a court is satisfied that there has been an infringement of the data subject's rights under the data protection legislation in contravention of that legislation.

(2) A court may make an order for the purposes of securing compliance with the data protection legislation which requires the controller in respect of the processing, or a processor acting on behalf of that controller—

(a) to take steps specified in the order, or

(b) to refrain from taking steps specified in the order.

(3) The order may, in relation to each step, specify the time at which, or the period within which, it must be taken.

(4) In subsection (1)—

(a) the reference to an application by a data subject includes an application made in exercise of the right under Article 79(1) of the *GDPR* (right to an effective remedy against a controller or processor);

(b) the reference to the data protection legislation does not include Part 4 of this Act or regulations made under that Part.

(5) In relation to a joint controller in respect of the processing of personal data to which Part 3 applies whose responsibilities are determined in an arrangement under section 58, a court may only make an order under this section if the controller is responsible for compliance with the provision of the data protection legislation that is contravened.

NOTES

Commencement: 25 May 2018 (see also the introductory notes to this Act preceding s 1 at **[1.2111]**).

Sub-s (4): for "GDPR" in italics there is substituted "UK GDPR" by the Data Protection, Privacy and Electronic Communications (Amendments etc) (EU Exit) Regulations 2019, SI 2019/419, reg 4, Sch 2, paras 1, 68, as from exit day (as defined in the European Union (Withdrawal) Act 2018, s 20), for transitional provisions etc, see the 2019 Regulations at **[2.2122]** et seq.

[1.2180]

168 Compensation for contravention of the *GDPR*

(1) In Article 82 of the *GDPR* (right to compensation for material or non-material damage), "non-material damage" includes distress.

(2) Subsection (3) applies where—

(a) in accordance with rules of court, proceedings under Article 82 of the *GDPR* are brought by a representative body on behalf of a person, and

(b) a court orders the payment of compensation.

(3) The court may make an order providing for the compensation to be paid on behalf of the person to—

(a) the representative body, or

(b) such other person as the court thinks fit.

NOTES

Commencement: 25 May 2018 (see also the introductory notes to this Act preceding s 1 at **[1.2111]**).

For "GDPR" in italics in each place that it occurs (including in the section heading) there is substituted "UK GDPR" by the Data Protection, Privacy and Electronic Communications (Amendments etc) (EU Exit) Regulations 2019, SI 2019/419, reg 4, Sch 2, paras 1, 69, as from exit day (as defined in the European Union (Withdrawal) Act 2018, s 20), for transitional provisions etc, see the 2019 Regulations at **[2.2122]** et seq.

[1.2181]

169 Compensation for contravention of other data protection legislation

(1) A person who suffers damage by reason of a contravention of a requirement of the data protection legislation, other than the *GDPR*, is entitled to compensation for that damage from the controller or the processor, subject to subsections (2) and (3).

(2) Under subsection (1)—

- (a) a controller involved in processing of personal data is liable for any damage caused by the processing, and
- (b) a processor involved in processing of personal data is liable for damage caused by the processing only if the processor—
  - (i) has not complied with an obligation under the data protection legislation specifically directed at processors, or
  - (ii) has acted outside, or contrary to, the controller's lawful instructions.

(3) A controller or processor is not liable as described in subsection (2) if the controller or processor proves that the controller or processor is not in any way responsible for the event giving rise to the damage.

(4) A joint controller in respect of the processing of personal data to which Part 3 or 4 applies whose responsibilities are determined in an arrangement under section 58 or 104 is only liable as described in subsection (2) if the controller is responsible for compliance with the provision of the data protection legislation that is contravened.

(5) In this section, "damage" includes financial loss and damage not involving financial loss, such as distress.

NOTES

Commencement: 25 May 2018 (see also the introductory notes to this Act preceding s 1 at **[1.2111]**).

Sub-s (1): for "GDPR" in italics there is substituted "UK GDPR" by the Data Protection, Privacy and Electronic Communications (Amendments etc) (EU Exit) Regulations 2019, SI 2019/419, reg 4, Sch 2, paras 1, 70, as from exit day (as defined in the European Union (Withdrawal) Act 2018, s 20), for transitional provisions etc, see the 2019 Regulations at **[2.2122]** et seq.

Offences relating to personal data

[1.2182]

170 Unlawful obtaining etc of personal data

(1) It is an offence for a person knowingly or recklessly—

- (a) to obtain or disclose personal data without the consent of the controller,
- (b) to procure the disclosure of personal data to another person without the consent of the controller, or
- (c) after obtaining personal data, to retain it without the consent of the person who was the controller in relation to the personal data when it was obtained.

(2) It is a defence for a person charged with an offence under subsection (1) to prove that the obtaining, disclosing, procuring or retaining—

- (a) was necessary for the purposes of preventing or detecting crime,
- (b) was required or authorised by an enactment, by a rule of law or by the order of a court or tribunal, or
- (c) in the particular circumstances, was justified as being in the public interest.

(3) It is also a defence for a person charged with an offence under subsection (1) to prove that—

- (a) the person acted in the reasonable belief that the person had a legal right to do the obtaining, disclosing, procuring or retaining,
- (b) the person acted in the reasonable belief that the person would have had the consent of the controller if the controller had known about the obtaining, disclosing, procuring or retaining and the circumstances of it, or
- (c) the person acted—
  - (i) for the special purposes,
  - (ii) with a view to the publication by a person of any journalistic, academic, artistic or literary material, and
  - (iii) in the reasonable belief that in the particular circumstances the obtaining, disclosing, procuring or retaining was justified as being in the public interest.

(4) It is an offence for a person to sell personal data if the person obtained the data in circumstances in which an offence under subsection (1) was committed.

(5) It is an offence for a person to offer to sell personal data if the person—

- (a) has obtained the data in circumstances in which an offence under subsection (1) was committed, or
- (b) subsequently obtains the data in such circumstances.

(6) For the purposes of subsection (5), an advertisement indicating that personal data is or may be for sale is an offer to sell the data.

(7) In this section—

- (a) references to the consent of a controller do not include the consent of a person who is a controller by virtue of Article 28(10) of the *GDPR* or section 59(8) or 105(3) of this Act (processor to be treated as controller in certain circumstances);
- (b) where there is more than one controller, such references are references to the consent of one or more of them.

NOTES

Commencement: 25 May 2018 (see also the introductory notes to this Act preceding s 1 at **[1.2111]**).

Sub-s (7): for "GDPR" in italics there is substituted "UK GDPR" by the Data Protection, Privacy and Electronic Communications (Amendments etc) (EU Exit) Regulations 2019, SI 2019/419, reg 4, Sch 2, paras 1, 71, as from exit day (as defined in the European Union (Withdrawal) Act 2018, s 20), for transitional provisions etc, see the 2019 Regulations at **[2.2122]** et seq.

[1.2183]

171 Re-identification of de-identified personal data

(1) It is an offence for a person knowingly or recklessly to re-identify information that is de-identified personal data without the consent of the controller responsible for de-identifying the personal data.

(2) For the purposes of this section and section 172—

(a) personal data is "de-identified" if it has been processed in such a manner that it can no longer be attributed, without more, to a specific data subject;

(b) a person "re-identifies" information if the person takes steps which result in the information no longer being de-identified within the meaning of paragraph (a).

(3) It is a defence for a person charged with an offence under subsection (1) to prove that the re-identification—

(a) was necessary for the purposes of preventing or detecting crime,

(b) was required or authorised by an enactment, by a rule of law or by the order of a court or tribunal, or

(c) in the particular circumstances, was justified as being in the public interest.

(4) It is also a defence for a person charged with an offence under subsection (1) to prove that—

(a) the person acted in the reasonable belief that the person—

(i) is the data subject to whom the information relates,

(ii) had the consent of that data subject, or

(iii) would have had such consent if the data subject had known about the re-identification and the circumstances of it,

(b) the person acted in the reasonable belief that the person—

(i) is the controller responsible for de-identifying the personal data,

(ii) had the consent of that controller, or

(iii) would have had such consent if that controller had known about the re-identification and the circumstances of it,

(c) the person acted—

(i) for the special purposes,

(ii) with a view to the publication by a person of any journalistic, academic, artistic or literary material, and

(iii) in the reasonable belief that in the particular circumstances the re-identification was justified as being in the public interest, or

(d) the effectiveness testing conditions were met (see section 172).

(5) It is an offence for a person knowingly or recklessly to process personal data that is information that has been re-identified where the person does so—

(a) without the consent of the controller responsible for de-identifying the personal data, and

(b) in circumstances in which the re-identification was an offence under subsection (1).

(6) It is a defence for a person charged with an offence under subsection (5) to prove that the processing—

(a) was necessary for the purposes of preventing or detecting crime,

(b) was required or authorised by an enactment, by a rule of law or by the order of a court or tribunal, or

(c) in the particular circumstances, was justified as being in the public interest.

(7) It is also a defence for a person charged with an offence under subsection (5) to prove that—

(a) the person acted in the reasonable belief that the processing was lawful,

(b) the person acted in the reasonable belief that the person—

(i) had the consent of the controller responsible for de-identifying the personal data, or

(ii) would have had such consent if that controller had known about the processing and the circumstances of it, or

(c) the person acted—

(i) for the special purposes,

(ii) with a view to the publication by a person of any journalistic, academic, artistic or literary material, and

(iii) in the reasonable belief that in the particular circumstances the processing was justified as being in the public interest.

(8) In this section—

(a) references to the consent of a controller do not include the consent of a person who is a controller by virtue of Article 28(10) of the *GDPR* or section 59(8) or 105(3) of this Act (processor to be treated as controller in certain circumstances);

(b) where there is more than one controller, such references are references to the consent of one or more of them.

NOTES

Commencement: 25 May 2018 (see also the introductory notes to this Act preceding s 1 at **[1.2111]**).

Sub-s (8): for "GDPR" in italics there is substituted "UK GDPR" by the Data Protection, Privacy and Electronic Communications (Amendments etc) (EU Exit) Regulations 2019, SI 2019/419, reg 4, Sch 2, paras 1, 72, as from exit day (as defined in the European Union (Withdrawal) Act 2018, s 20), for transitional provisions etc, see the 2019 Regulations at **[2.2122]** et seq.

[1.2184]
172 Re-identification: effectiveness testing conditions

(1) For the purposes of section 171, in relation to a person who re-identifies information that is de-identified personal data, "the effectiveness testing conditions" means the conditions in subsections (2) and (3).

(2) The first condition is that the person acted—

(a) with a view to testing the effectiveness of the de-identification of personal data,

(b) without intending to cause, or threaten to cause, damage or distress to a person, and

(c) in the reasonable belief that, in the particular circumstances, re-identifying the information was justified as being in the public interest.

(3) The second condition is that the person notified the Commissioner or the controller responsible for de-identifying the personal data about the re-identification—

(a) without undue delay, and

(b) where feasible, not later than 72 hours after becoming aware of it.

(4) Where there is more than one controller responsible for de-identifying personal data, the requirement in subsection (3) is satisfied if one or more of them is notified.

NOTES

Commencement: 25 May 2018 (see also the introductory notes to this Act preceding s 1 at **[1.2111]**).

[1.2185]
173 Alteration etc of personal data to prevent disclosure to data subject

(1) Subsection (3) applies where—

(a) a request has been made in exercise of a data subject access right, and

(b) the person making the request would have been entitled to receive information in response to that request.

(2) In this section, "data subject access right" means a right under—

(a) Article 15 of the *GDPR* (right of access by the data subject);

(b) Article 20 of the *GDPR* (right to data portability);

(c) section 45 of this Act (law enforcement processing: right of access by the data subject);

(d) section 94 of this Act (intelligence services processing: right of access by the data subject).

(3) It is an offence for a person listed in subsection (4) to alter, deface, block, erase, destroy or conceal information with the intention of preventing disclosure of all or part of the information that the person making the request would have been entitled to receive.

(4) Those persons are—

(a) the controller, and

(b) a person who is employed by the controller, an officer of the controller or subject to the direction of the controller.

(5) It is a defence for a person charged with an offence under subsection (3) to prove that—

(a) the alteration, defacing, blocking, erasure, destruction or concealment of the information would have occurred in the absence of a request made in exercise of a data subject access right, or

(b) the person acted in the reasonable belief that the person making the request was not entitled to receive the information in response to the request.

NOTES

Commencement: 25 May 2018 (see also the introductory notes to this Act preceding s 1 at **[1.2111]**).

Sub-s (2): for "GDPR" in italics in both places that it occurs there is substituted "UK GDPR" by the Data Protection, Privacy and Electronic Communications (Amendments etc) (EU Exit) Regulations 2019, SI 2019/419, reg 4, Sch 2, paras 1, 73, as from exit day (as defined in the European Union (Withdrawal) Act 2018, s 20), for transitional provisions etc, see the 2019 Regulations at **[2.2122]** et seq.

Jurisdiction of courts

[1.2186]
180 Jurisdiction

(1) The jurisdiction conferred on a court by the provisions listed in subsection (2) is exercisable—

(a) in England and Wales, by the High Court or the county court,

(b) in Northern Ireland, by the High Court or a county court, and

(c) in Scotland, by the Court of Session or the sheriff,

subject to subsections (3) and (4).

(2) Those provisions are—

(a) section 145 (information orders);

(b) section 152 (enforcement notices and processing for the special purposes);

(c) section 156 (penalty notices and processing for the special purposes);

(d) section 167 and Article 79 of the *GDPR* (compliance orders);

(e) sections 168 and 169 and Article 82 of the *GDPR* (compensation).

(3) In relation to the processing of personal data to which Part 4 applies, the jurisdiction conferred by the provisions listed in subsection (2) is exercisable only by the High Court or, in Scotland, the Court of Session.

(4) In relation to an information notice which contains a statement under section 142(7), the jurisdiction conferred on a court by section 145 is exercisable only by the High Court or, in Scotland, the Court of Session.

(5) The jurisdiction conferred on a court by section 164 (applications in respect of urgent notices) is exercisable only by the High Court or, in Scotland, the Court of Session.

NOTES

Commencement: 25 May 2018 (see also the introductory notes to this Act preceding s 1 at **[1.2111]**).

Sub-s (2): for "GDPR" in italics in both places that it occurs there is substituted "UK GDPR" by the Data Protection, Privacy and Electronic Communications (Amendments etc) (EU Exit) Regulations 2019, SI 2019/419, reg 4, Sch 2, paras 1, 75, as from exit day (as defined in the European Union (Withdrawal) Act 2018, s 20), for transitional provisions etc, see the 2019 Regulations at **[2.2122]** et seq.

Definitions

[1.2187]

181 Interpretation of Part 6

In this Part—

"assessment notice" has the meaning given in section 146;

"certification provider" has the meaning given in section 17;

"enforcement notice" has the meaning given in section 149;

"information notice" has the meaning given in section 142;

"penalty notice" has the meaning given in section 155;

"penalty variation notice" has the meaning given in Schedule 16;

"representative", in relation to a controller or processor, means a person designated by the controller or processor under Article 27 of the *GDPR* to represent the controller or processor with regard to the controller's or processor's obligations under the *GDPR*.

NOTES

Commencement: 25 May 2018 (see also the introductory notes to this Act preceding s 1 at **[1.2111]**).

For "GDPR" in italics in both places that it occurs in the definition "representative" there is substituted "UK GDPR" by the Data Protection, Privacy and Electronic Communications (Amendments etc) (EU Exit) Regulations 2019, SI 2019/419, reg 4, Sch 2, paras 1, 76, as from exit day (as defined in the European Union (Withdrawal) Act 2018, s 20), for transitional provisions etc, see the 2019 Regulations at **[2.2122]** et seq.

PART 7
SUPPLEMENTARY AND FINAL PROVISION

Regulations under this Act

[1.2188]

182 Regulations and consultation

(1) Regulations under this Act are to be made by statutory instrument.

(2) Before making regulations under this Act, the Secretary of State must consult—

(a) the Commissioner, and

(b) such other persons as the Secretary of State considers appropriate.

(3) Subsection (2) does not apply to regulations made under—

(a) section 23;

(b) section 30;

(c) section 211;

(d) section 212;

(e) section 213;

(f) paragraph 15 of Schedule 2.

(4) Subsection (2) does not apply to regulations made under section 18 where the Secretary of State has made an urgency statement in respect of them.

(5) Regulations under this Act may—

(a) make different provision for different purposes;

(b) include consequential, supplementary, incidental, transitional, transitory or saving provision.

(6) Where regulations under this Act are subject to "the negative resolution procedure" the statutory instrument containing the regulations is subject to annulment in pursuance of a resolution of either House of Parliament.

(7) Where regulations under this Act are subject to "the affirmative resolution procedure" the regulations may not be made unless a draft of the statutory instrument containing them has been laid before Parliament and approved by a resolution of each House of Parliament.

(8) Where regulations under this Act are subject to "the made affirmative resolution procedure"—

(a) the statutory instrument containing the regulations must be laid before Parliament after being made, together with the urgency statement in respect of them, and

(b) the regulations cease to have effect at the end of the period of 120 days beginning with the day on which the instrument is made, unless within that period the instrument is approved by a resolution of each House of Parliament.

(9) In calculating the period of 120 days, no account is to be taken of any time during which—

(a) Parliament is dissolved or prorogued, or

(b) both Houses of Parliament are adjourned for more than 4 days.

(10) Where regulations cease to have effect as a result of subsection (8), that does not—

(a) affect anything previously done under the regulations, or

(b) prevent the making of new regulations.

(11) Any provision that may be included in regulations under this Act subject to the negative resolution procedure may be made by regulations subject to the affirmative resolution procedure or the made affirmative resolution procedure.

(12) If a draft of a statutory instrument containing regulations under section 7 would, apart from this subsection, be treated for the purposes of the standing orders of either House of Parliament as a hybrid instrument, it is to proceed in that House as if it were not such an instrument.

(13) A requirement under a provision of this Act to consult may be satisfied by consultation before, as well as by consultation after, the provision comes into force.

(14) In this section, "urgency statement" has the meaning given in section 18(4).

NOTES

Commencement: 23 May 2018 (see also the introductory notes to this Act preceding s 1 at **[1.2111]**).

Sub-s (3): para (a) repealed by the Data Protection, Privacy and Electronic Communications (Amendments etc) (EU Exit) Regulations 2019, SI 2019/419, reg 4, Sch 2, paras 1, 77, as from exit day (as defined in the European Union (Withdrawal) Act 2018, s 20), for transitional provisions etc, see the 2019 Regulations at **[2.2122]** et seq.

Rights of the data subject

[1.2189]

184 Prohibition of requirement to produce relevant records

(1) It is an offence for a person ("P1") to require another person to provide P1 with, or give P1 access to, a relevant record in connection with—

(a) the recruitment of an employee by P1,

(b) the continued employment of a person by P1, or

(c) a contract for the provision of services to P1.

(2) It is an offence for a person ("P2") to require another person to provide P2 with, or give P2 access to, a relevant record if—

(a) P2 is involved in the provision of goods, facilities or services to the public or a section of the public, and

(b) the requirement is a condition of providing or offering to provide goods, facilities or services to the other person or to a third party.

(3) It is a defence for a person charged with an offence under subsection (1) or (2) to prove that imposing the requirement—

(a) was required or authorised by an enactment, by a rule of law or by the order of a court or tribunal, or

(b) in the particular circumstances, was justified as being in the public interest.

(4) The imposition of the requirement referred to in subsection (1) or (2) is not to be regarded as justified as being in the public interest on the ground that it would assist in the prevention or detection of crime, given Part 5 of the Police Act 1997 (certificates of criminal records etc).

(5) In subsections (1) and (2), the references to a person who requires another person to provide or give access to a relevant record include a person who asks another person to do so—

(a) knowing that, in the circumstances, it would be reasonable for the other person to feel obliged to comply with the request, or

(b) being reckless as to whether, in the circumstances, it would be reasonable for the other person to feel obliged to comply with the request,

and the references to a "requirement" in subsections (3) and (4) are to be interpreted accordingly.

(6) In this section—

"employment" means any employment, including—

(a) work under a contract for services or as an office-holder,

(b) work under an apprenticeship,

(c) work experience as part of a training course or in the course of training for employment, and

(d) voluntary work,

and "employee" is to be interpreted accordingly;

"relevant record" has the meaning given in Schedule 18 and references to a relevant record include—

(a) a part of such a record, and

(b) a copy of, or of part of, such a record.

NOTES

Commencement: 25 May 2018 (see also the introductory notes to this Act preceding s 1 at **[1.2111]**).

[1.2190]

185 Avoidance of certain contractual terms relating to health records

(1) A term or condition of a contract is void in so far as it purports to require an individual to supply another person with a record which—

(a) consists of the information contained in a health record, and

(b) has been or is to be obtained by a data subject in the exercise of a data subject access right.

(2) A term or condition of a contract is also void in so far as it purports to require an individual to produce such a record to another person.

(3) The references in subsections (1) and (2) to a record include a part of a record and a copy of all or part of a record.

(4) In this section, "data subject access right" means a right under—

(a) Article 15 of the *GDPR* (right of access by the data subject);

(b) Article 20 of the *GDPR* (right to data portability);
(c) section 45 of this Act (law enforcement processing: right of access by the data subject);
(d) section 94 of this Act (intelligence services processing: right of access by the data subject).

NOTES

Commencement: 25 May 2018 (see also the introductory notes to this Act preceding s 1 at **[1.2111]**).

Sub-s (4): for "GDPR" in italics in both places that it occurs there is substituted "UK GDPR" by the Data Protection, Privacy and Electronic Communications (Amendments etc) (EU Exit) Regulations 2019, SI 2019/419, reg 4, Sch 2, paras 1, 79, as from exit day (as defined in the European Union (Withdrawal) Act 2018, s 20), for transitional provisions etc, see the 2019 Regulations at **[2.2122]** et seq.

[1.2191]

186 Data subject's rights and other prohibitions and restrictions

(1) An enactment or rule of law prohibiting or restricting the disclosure of information, or authorising the withholding of information, does not remove or restrict the obligations and rights provided for in the provisions listed in subsection (2), except as provided by or under the provisions listed in subsection (3).

(2) The provisions providing obligations and rights are—
(a) Chapter III of the *GDPR* (rights of the data subject),
(b) Chapter 3 of Part 3 of this Act (law enforcement processing: rights of the data subject), and
(c) Chapter 3 of Part 4 of this Act (intelligence services processing: rights of the data subject).

(3) The provisions providing exceptions are—
(a) in Chapter 2 of Part 2 of this Act, sections 15 and 16 and Schedules 2, 3 and 4,
(b) in Chapter 3 of Part 2 of this Act, sections *23,* 24, 25 and 26,
(c) in Part 3 of this Act, sections 44(4), 45(4) and 48(3), and
(d) in Part 4 of this Act, Chapter 6.

NOTES

Commencement: 25 May 2018 (see also the introductory notes to this Act preceding s 1 at **[1.2111]**).

For "GDPR" in italics in sub-s (2) there is substituted "UK GDPR", and the figure in italics in sub-s (3) is repealed, by the Data Protection, Privacy and Electronic Communications (Amendments etc) (EU Exit) Regulations 2019, SI 2019/419, reg 4, Sch 2, paras 1, 80, as from exit day (as defined in the European Union (Withdrawal) Act 2018, s 20), for transitional provisions etc, see the 2019 Regulations at **[2.2122]** et seq.

Representation of data subjects

[1.2192]

187 Representation of data subjects with their authority

(1) In relation to the processing of personal data to which the *GDPR applies*—
(a) *Article 80(1) of the GDPR (representation of data subjects)* enables a data subject to authorise a body or other organisation which meets the conditions set out in *that Article* to exercise the data subject's rights under Articles 77, 78 and 79 of the *GDPR* (rights to lodge complaints and to an effective judicial remedy) on the data subject's behalf, and
(b) *a data subject may also authorise* such a body or organisation to exercise the data subject's rights under Article 82 of the *GDPR* (right to compensation).

(2) In relation to the processing of personal data to which the *GDPR* does not apply, a body or other organisation which meets the conditions in subsections (3) and (4), if authorised to do so by a data subject, may exercise some or all of the following rights of a data subject on the data subject's behalf—
(a) rights under section 165(2)*, (4)(d) and (6)(c)* (complaints to the Commissioner);
(b) rights under section 166(2) (orders for the Commissioner to progress complaints);
(c) rights under section 167(1) (compliance orders);
(d) the right to bring judicial review proceedings against the Commissioner.

(3) The first condition is that the body or organisation, by virtue of its constitution or an enactment—
(a) is required (after payment of outgoings) to apply the whole of its income and any capital it expends for charitable or public purposes,
(b) is prohibited from directly or indirectly distributing amongst its members any part of its assets (otherwise than for charitable or public purposes), and
(c) has objectives which are in the public interest.

(4) The second condition is that the body or organisation is active in the field of protection of data subjects' rights and freedoms with regard to the protection of their personal data.

(5) In this Act, references to a "representative body", in relation to a right of a data subject, are to a body or other organisation authorised to exercise the right on the data subject's behalf under Article 80 of the *GDPR* or this section.

NOTES

Commencement: 25 May 2018 (see also the introductory notes to this Act preceding s 1 at **[1.2111]**).

Sub-s (1): for the first words in italics there are substituted the words "UK GDPR applies, Article 80(1) of the UK GDPR (representation of data subjects)", the first words in italics in para (a) are repealed, for the second words in italics in para (a) there are substituted the words "subsections (3) and (4)", for "GDPR" in italics in para (a) there is substituted "UK GDPR", for the first words in italics in para (b) there are substituted the words "also authorises", and for "GDPR" in italics in para (b) there is substituted "UK GDPR", by the Data Protection, Privacy and Electronic Communications (Amendments etc) (EU Exit) Regulations 2019, SI 2019/419, reg 4, Sch 2, paras 1, 81(1)–(4), as from exit day (as defined in the European Union (Withdrawal) Act 2018, s 20), for transitional provisions etc, see the 2019 Regulations at **[2.2122]** et seq.

Sub-s (2): for "GDPR" in italics there is substituted "UK GDPR", and for the second words in italics there are substituted the words "and (4)(d)", by SI 2019/419, reg 4, Sch 2, paras 1, 81(1), (5), as from exit day (as defined in the European Union (Withdrawal) Act 2018, s 20), for transitional provisions etc, see the 2019 Regulations at **[2.2122]** et seq.

Sub-s (5): for "GDPR" in italics there is substituted "UK GDPR" by SI 2019/419, reg 4, Sch 2, paras 1, 81(1), (6), as from exit day (as defined in the European Union (Withdrawal) Act 2018, s 20), for transitional provisions etc, see the 2019 Regulations at **[2.2122]** et seq.

[1.2193]

188 Representation of data subjects with their authority: collective proceedings

(1) The Secretary of State may by regulations make provision for representative bodies to bring proceedings before a court or tribunal in England and Wales or Northern Ireland combining two or more relevant claims.

(2) In this section, "relevant claim", in relation to a representative body, means a claim in respect of a right of a data subject which the representative body is authorised to exercise on the data subject's behalf under Article 80(1) of the *GDPR* or section 187.

(3) The power under subsection (1) includes power—

- (a) to make provision about the proceedings;
- (b) to confer functions on a person, including functions involving the exercise of a discretion;
- (c) to make different provision in relation to England and Wales and in relation to Northern Ireland.

(4) The provision mentioned in subsection (3)(a) includes provision about—

- (a) the effect of judgments and orders;
- (b) agreements to settle claims;
- (c) the assessment of the amount of compensation;
- (d) the persons to whom compensation may or must be paid, including compensation not claimed by the data subject;
- (e) costs.

(5) Regulations under this section are subject to the negative resolution procedure.

NOTES

Commencement: 23 July 2018 (see also the introductory notes to this Act preceding s 1 at **[1.2111]**).

Sub-s (2): for "GDPR" in italics there is substituted "UK GDPR" by the Data Protection, Privacy and Electronic Communications (Amendments etc) (EU Exit) Regulations 2019, SI 2019/419, reg 4, Sch 2, paras 1, 82, as from exit day (as defined in the European Union (Withdrawal) Act 2018, s 20), for transitional provisions etc, see the 2019 Regulations at **[2.2122]** et seq.

[1.2194]

189 Duty to review provision for representation of data subjects

(1) Before the end of the review period, the Secretary of State must—

- (a) review the matters listed in subsection (2) in relation to England and Wales and Northern Ireland,
- (b) prepare a report of the review, and
- (c) lay a copy of the report before Parliament.

(2) Those matters are—

- (a) the operation of Article 80(1) of the *GDPR*,
- (b) the operation of section 187,
- (c) the merits of exercising the power under Article 80(2) of the *GDPR* (power to enable a body or other organisation which meets the conditions in Article 80(1) of the *GDPR* to exercise some or all of a data subject's rights under Articles 77, 78 and 79 of the *GDPR* without being authorised to do so by the data subject),
- (d) the merits of making equivalent provision in relation to data subjects' rights under Article 82 of the *GDPR* (right to compensation), and
- (e) the merits of making provision for a children's rights organisation to exercise some or all of a data subject's rights under Articles 77, 78, 79 and 82 of the *GDPR* on behalf of a data subject who is a child, with or without being authorised to do so by the data subject.

(3) "The review period" is the period of 30 months beginning when section 187 comes into force.

(4) In carrying out the review, the Secretary of State must—

- (a) consider the particular needs of children separately from the needs of adults,
- (b) have regard to the fact that children have different needs at different stages of development,
- (c) carry out an analysis of the particular challenges that children face in authorising, and deciding whether to authorise, other persons to act on their behalf under Article 80(1) of the *GDPR* or section 187,
- (d) consider the support and advice available to children in connection with the exercise of their rights under Articles 77, 78, 79 and 82 of the *GDPR* by another person on their behalf and the merits of making available other support or advice, and
- (e) have regard to the United Kingdom's obligations under the United Nations Convention on the Rights of the Child.

(5) Before preparing the report under subsection (1), the Secretary of State must consult the Commissioner and such other persons as the Secretary of State considers appropriate, including—

- (a) persons active in the field of protection of data subjects' rights and freedoms with regard to the protection of their personal data,
- (b) children and parents,
- (c) children's rights organisations and other persons who appear to the Secretary of State to represent the interests of children,
- (d) child development experts, and
- (e) trade associations.

(6) In this section—

"children's rights organisation" means a body or other organisation which—

(a) is active in representing the interests of children, and

(b) has objectives which are in the public interest;

"trade association" includes a body representing controllers or processors;

"the United Nations Convention on the Rights of the Child" means the Convention on the Rights of the Child adopted by the General Assembly of the United Nations on 20 November 1989 (including any Protocols to that Convention which are in force in relation to the United Kingdom), subject to any reservations, objections or interpretative declarations by the United Kingdom for the time being in force.

NOTES

Commencement: 23 July 2018 (see also the introductory notes to this Act preceding s 1 at **[1.2111]**).

Sub-ss (2), (4): for "GDPR" in italics in each place that it occurs there is substituted "UK GDPR" by the Data Protection, Privacy and Electronic Communications (Amendments etc) (EU Exit) Regulations 2019, SI 2019/419, reg 4, Sch 2, paras 1, 83, as from exit day (as defined in the European Union (Withdrawal) Act 2018, s 20), for transitional provisions etc, see the 2019 Regulations at **[2.2122]** et seq.

[1.2195]

190 Post-review powers to make provision about representation of data subjects

(1) After the report under section 189(1) is laid before Parliament, the Secretary of State may by regulations—

(a) exercise the powers under Article 80(2) of the *GDPR* in relation to England and Wales and Northern Ireland,

(b) make provision enabling a body or other organisation which meets the conditions in Article 80(1) of the *GDPR* to exercise a data subject's rights under Article 82 of the *GDPR* in England and Wales and Northern Ireland without being authorised to do so by the data subject, and

(c) make provision described in section 189(2)(e) in relation to the exercise in England and Wales and Northern Ireland of the rights of a data subject who is a child.

(2) The powers under subsection (1) include power—

(a) to make provision enabling a data subject to prevent a body or other organisation from exercising, or continuing to exercise, the data subject's rights;

(b) to make provision about proceedings before a court or tribunal where a body or organisation exercises a data subject's rights;

(c) to make provision for bodies or other organisations to bring proceedings before a court or tribunal combining two or more claims in respect of a right of a data subject;

(d) to confer functions on a person, including functions involving the exercise of a discretion;

(e) to amend sections 166 to 168, 180, 187, 203, 205 and 206;

(f) to insert new sections and Schedules into Part 6 or 7 ;

(g) to make different provision in relation to England and Wales and in relation to Northern Ireland.

(3) The powers under subsection (1)(a) and (b) include power to make provision in relation to data subjects who are children or data subjects who are not children or both.

(4) The provision mentioned in subsection (2)(b) and (c) includes provision about—

(a) the effect of judgments and orders;

(b) agreements to settle claims;

(c) the assessment of the amount of compensation;

(d) the persons to whom compensation may or must be paid, including compensation not claimed by the data subject;

(e) costs.

(5) Regulations under this section are subject to the affirmative resolution procedure.

NOTES

Commencement: 23 July 2018 (see also the introductory notes to this Act preceding s 1 at **[1.2111]**).

Sub-s (1): for "GDPR" in italics in each place that it occurs there is substituted "UK GDPR" by the Data Protection, Privacy and Electronic Communications (Amendments etc) (EU Exit) Regulations 2019, SI 2019/419, reg 4, Sch 2, paras 1, 84, as from exit day (as defined in the European Union (Withdrawal) Act 2018, s 20), for transitional provisions etc, see the 2019 Regulations at **[2.2122]** et seq.

Offences

[1.2196]

196 Penalties for offences

(1) A person who commits an offence under section 119 or 173 or paragraph 15 of Schedule 15 is liable—

(a) on summary conviction in England and Wales, to a fine;

(b) on summary conviction in Scotland or Northern Ireland, to a fine not exceeding level 5 on the standard scale.

(2) A person who commits an offence under section 132, 144, 148, 170, 171 or 184 is liable—

(a) on summary conviction in England and Wales, to a fine;

(b) on summary conviction in Scotland or Northern Ireland, to a fine not exceeding the statutory maximum;

(c) on conviction on indictment, to a fine.

(3) Subsections (4) and (5) apply where a person is convicted of an offence under section 170 or 184.

(4) The court by or before which the person is convicted may order a document or other material to be forfeited, destroyed or erased if—

(a) it has been used in connection with the processing of personal data, and
(b) it appears to the court to be connected with the commission of the offence,

subject to subsection (5).

(5) If a person, other than the offender, who claims to be the owner of the material, or to be otherwise interested in the material, applies to be heard by the court, the court must not make an order under subsection (4) without giving the person an opportunity to show why the order should not be made.

NOTES

Commencement: 25 May 2018 (see also the introductory notes to this Act preceding s 1 at **[1.2111]**).

[1.2197]

197 Prosecution

(1) In England and Wales, proceedings for an offence under this Act may be instituted only—
(a) by the Commissioner, or
(b) by or with the consent of the Director of Public Prosecutions.

(2) In Northern Ireland, proceedings for an offence under this Act may be instituted only—
(a) by the Commissioner, or
(b) by or with the consent of the Director of Public Prosecutions for Northern Ireland.

(3) Subject to subsection (4), summary proceedings for an offence under section 173 (alteration etc of personal data to prevent disclosure) may be brought within the period of 6 months beginning with the day on which the prosecutor first knew of evidence that, in the prosecutor's opinion, was sufficient to bring the proceedings.

(4) Such proceedings may not be brought after the end of the period of 3 years beginning with the day on which the offence was committed.

(5) A certificate signed by or on behalf of the prosecutor and stating the day on which the 6 month period described in subsection (3) began is conclusive evidence of that fact.

(6) A certificate purporting to be signed as described in subsection (5) is to be treated as so signed unless the contrary is proved.

(7) In relation to proceedings in Scotland, section 136(3) of the Criminal Procedure (Scotland) Act 1995 (deemed date of commencement of proceedings) applies for the purposes of this section as it applies for the purposes of that section.

NOTES

Commencement: 25 May 2018 (see also the introductory notes to this Act preceding s 1 at **[1.2111]**).

[1.2198]

198 Liability of directors etc

(1) Subsection (2) applies where—
(a) an offence under this Act has been committed by a body corporate, and
(b) it is proved to have been committed with the consent or connivance of or to be attributable to neglect on the part of—
 (i) a director, manager, secretary or similar officer of the body corporate, or
 (ii) a person who was purporting to act in such a capacity.

(2) The director, manager, secretary, officer or person, as well as the body corporate, is guilty of the offence and liable to be proceeded against and punished accordingly.

(3) Where the affairs of a body corporate are managed by its members, subsections (1) and (2) apply in relation to the acts and omissions of a member in connection with the member's management functions in relation to the body as if the member were a director of the body corporate.

(4) Subsection (5) applies where—
(a) an offence under this Act has been committed by a Scottish partnership, and
(b) the contravention in question is proved to have occurred with the consent or connivance of, or to be attributable to any neglect on the part of, a partner.

(5) The partner, as well as the partnership, is guilty of the offence and liable to be proceeded against and punished accordingly.

NOTES

Commencement: 25 May 2018 (see also the introductory notes to this Act preceding s 1 at **[1.2111]**).

[1.2199]

199 Recordable offences

(1) The National Police Records (Recordable Offences) Regulations 2000 (SI 2000/1139) have effect as if the offences under the following provisions were listed in the Schedule to the Regulations—
(a) section 119;
(b) section 132;
(c) section 144;
(d) section 148;
(e) section 170;
(f) section 171;
(g) section 173;
(h) section 184;
(i) paragraph 15 of Schedule 15.

(2) Regulations under section 27(4) of the Police and Criminal Evidence Act 1984 (recordable offences) may repeal subsection (1).

NOTES

Commencement: 25 May 2018 (see also the introductory notes to this Act preceding s 1 at **[1.2111]**).

[1.2200]

200 Guidance about PACE codes of practice

(1) The Commissioner must produce and publish guidance about how the Commissioner proposes to perform the duty under section 67(9) of the Police and Criminal Evidence Act 1984 (duty to have regard to codes of practice under that Act when investigating offences and charging offenders) in connection with offences under this Act.

(2) The Commissioner—

(a) may alter or replace the guidance, and

(b) must publish any altered or replacement guidance.

(3) The Commissioner must consult the Secretary of State before publishing guidance under this section (including any altered or replacement guidance).

(4) The Commissioner must arrange for guidance under this section (including any altered or replacement guidance) to be laid before Parliament.

NOTES

Commencement: 25 May 2018 (see also the introductory notes to this Act preceding s 1 at **[1.2111]**).

The Tribunal

[1.2201]

201 Disclosure of information to the Tribunal

(1) No enactment or rule of law prohibiting or restricting the disclosure of information precludes a person from providing the First-tier Tribunal or the Upper Tribunal with information necessary for the discharge of—

(a) its functions under the data protection legislation, or

(b) its other functions relating to the Commissioner's acts and omissions.

(2) But this section does not authorise the making of a disclosure which is prohibited by any of Parts 1 to 7 or Chapter 1 of Part 9 of the Investigatory Powers Act 2016.

(3) Until the repeal of Part 1 of the Regulation of Investigatory Powers Act 2000 by paragraphs 45 and 54 of Schedule 10 to the Investigatory Powers Act 2016 is fully in force, subsection (2) has effect as if it included a reference to that Part.

NOTES

Commencement: 25 May 2018 (see also the introductory notes to this Act preceding s 1 at **[1.2111]**).

[1.2202]

202 Proceedings in the First-tier Tribunal: contempt

(1) This section applies where—

(a) a person does something, or fails to do something, in relation to proceedings before the First-tier Tribunal—

(i) on an appeal under section 27, 79, 111 or 162, or

(ii) for an order under section 166, and

(b) if those proceedings were proceedings before a court having power to commit for contempt, the act or omission would constitute contempt of court.

(2) The First-tier Tribunal may certify the offence to the Upper Tribunal.

(3) Where an offence is certified under subsection (2), the Upper Tribunal may—

(a) inquire into the matter, and

(b) deal with the person charged with the offence in any manner in which it could deal with the person if the offence had been committed in relation to the Upper Tribunal.

(4) Before exercising the power under subsection (3)(b), the Upper Tribunal must—

(a) hear any witness who may be produced against or on behalf of the person charged with the offence, and

(b) hear any statement that may be offered in defence.

NOTES

Commencement: 25 May 2018 (see also the introductory notes to this Act preceding s 1 at **[1.2111]**).

[1.2203]

203 Tribunal Procedure Rules

(1) Tribunal Procedure Rules may make provision for regulating—

(a) the exercise of the rights of appeal conferred by section 27, 79, 111 or 162, and

(b) the exercise of the rights of data subjects under section 166, including their exercise by a representative body.

(2) In relation to proceedings involving the exercise of those rights, Tribunal Procedure Rules may make provision about—

(a) securing the production of material used for the processing of personal data, and

(b) the inspection, examination, operation and testing of equipment or material used in connection with the processing of personal data.

NOTES

Commencement: 25 May 2018 (see also the introductory notes to this Act preceding s 1 at **[1.2111]**).

Interpretation

[1.2204]

205 General interpretation

(1) In this Act—

"biometric data" means personal data resulting from specific technical processing relating to the physical, physiological or behavioural characteristics of an individual, which allows or confirms the unique identification of that individual, such as facial images or dactyloscopic data;

"data concerning health" means personal data relating to the physical or mental health of an individual, including the provision of health care services, which reveals information about his or her health status;

"enactment" includes—

(a) an enactment passed or made after this Act,

(b) an enactment comprised in subordinate legislation,

(c) an enactment comprised in, or in an instrument made under, a Measure or Act of the National Assembly for Wales,

(d) an enactment comprised in, or in an instrument made under, an Act of the Scottish Parliament, *and*

(e) an enactment comprised in, or in an instrument made under, Northern Ireland legislation[, and

(f) any retained direct EU legislation;]

"genetic data" means personal data relating to the inherited or acquired genetic characteristics of an individual which gives unique information about the physiology or the health of that individual and which results, in particular, from an analysis of a biological sample from the individual in question;

"government department" includes the following (except in the expression "United Kingdom government department")—

(a) a part of the Scottish Administration;

(b) a Northern Ireland department;

(c) the Welsh Government;

(d) a body or authority exercising statutory functions on behalf of the Crown;

"health record" means a record which—

(a) consists of data concerning health, and

(b) has been made by or on behalf of a health professional in connection with the diagnosis, care or treatment of the individual to whom the data relates;

"inaccurate", in relation to personal data, means incorrect or misleading as to any matter of fact;

"international obligation of the United Kingdom" includes—

(a) an EU obligation, and

(b) an obligation that arises under an international agreement or arrangement to which the United Kingdom is a party;

"international organisation" means an organisation and its subordinate bodies governed by international law, or any other body which is set up by, or on the basis of, an agreement between two or more countries;

"Minister of the Crown" has the same meaning as in the Ministers of the Crown Act 1975;

"publish" means make available to the public or a section of the public (and related expressions are to be read accordingly);

"subordinate legislation" has the meaning given in the Interpretation Act 1978;

"tribunal" means any tribunal in which legal proceedings may be brought;

"the Tribunal", in relation to an application or appeal under this Act, means—

(a) the Upper Tribunal, in any case where it is determined by or under Tribunal Procedure Rules that the Upper Tribunal is to hear the application or appeal, or

(b) the First-tier Tribunal, in any other case.

[(1A) In this Act, references to a fundamental right or fundamental freedom (however expressed) are to a fundamental right or fundamental freedom which continues to form part of domestic law on and after exit day by virtue of section 4 of the European Union (Withdrawal) Act 2018, as the right or freedom is amended or otherwise modified by the law of the United Kingdom, or of a part of the United Kingdom, from time to time on or after exit day.]

(2) References in this Act to a period expressed in hours, days, weeks, months or years are to be interpreted in accordance with Article 3 of Regulation (EEC, Euratom) No 1182/71 of the Council of 3 June 1971 determining the rules applicable to periods, dates and time limits, except in—

[(za) section 119A(10) and (11);]

(a) section 125(4), (7) and (8);

(b) section 161(3), (5) and (6);

(c) section 176(2);

(d) section 178(2);

(e) section 182(8) and (9);

(f) section 183(4);

(g) section 192(3), (5) and (6);

(h) section 197(3) and (4);

(i) paragraph 23(4) and (5) of Schedule 1;
(j) paragraphs 5(4) and 6(4) of Schedule 3;
(k) Schedule 5;
(l) paragraph 11(5) of Schedule 12;
(m) Schedule 15;

(and the references in section 5 to terms used in *Chapter 2 or 3 of* Part 2 do not include references to a period expressed in hours, days, weeks, months or years).

(3) Section 3(14)(b) (interpretation of references to Chapter 2 of Part 2 in Parts 5 to 7) and the amendments in Schedule 19 which make equivalent provision are not to be treated as implying a contrary intention for the purposes of section 20(2) of the Interpretation Act 1978, or any similar provision in another enactment, as it applies to other references to, or to a provision of, Chapter 2 of Part 2 of this Act.

[(4) In the definition of "the UK GDPR" in section 3(10)—
(a) the reference to Regulation (EU) 2016/679 as it forms part of the law of England and Wales, Scotland and Northern Ireland by virtue of section 3 of the European Union (Withdrawal) Act 2018 is to be treated as a reference to that Regulation as modified by Schedule 1 to the Data Protection, Privacy and Electronic Communications (Amendments etc) (EU Exit) Regulations 2019 ("the 2019 Regulations"), but
(b) nothing in the definition or in paragraph (a) determines whether, where Regulation (EU) 2016/679 is modified on or after exit day by the law of England and Wales, Scotland or Northern Ireland (other than by Schedule 1 to the 2019 Regulations), the reference to Regulation (EU) 2016/679 is then to be read as a reference to that Regulation as modified.

(5) Subsection (4) is not to be read as implying anything about how other references to Regulation (EU) 2016/679 or references to other retained EU law are to be interpreted.]

NOTES

Commencement: 23 May 2018 (see also the introductory notes to this Act preceding s 1 at **[1.2111]**).

Sub-s (1): the word "and" in italics in para (d) of the definition "enactment" is repealed, para (e) of that definition (and the preceding word) is added, and para (a) of the definition "international obligation of the United Kingdom" is repealed, by the Data Protection, Privacy and Electronic Communications (Amendments etc) (EU Exit) Regulations 2019, SI 2019/419, reg 4, Sch 2, paras 1, 85(1)–(3), as from exit day (as defined in the European Union (Withdrawal) Act 2018, s 20), for transitional provisions etc, see the 2019 Regulations at **[2.2122]** et seq.

Sub-s (1A): inserted by SI 2019/419, reg 4, Sch 2, paras 1, 85(1), (4), as from exit day (as defined in the European Union (Withdrawal) Act 2018, s 20), for transitional provisions etc, see the 2019 Regulations at **[2.2122]** et seq.

Sub-s (2): para (za) is inserted, and the words in italics are repealed, by SI 2019/419, reg 4, Sch 2, paras 1, 85(1), (5), as from exit day (as defined in the European Union (Withdrawal) Act 2018, s 20), for transitional provisions etc, see the 2019 Regulations at **[2.2122]** et seq.

Sub-s (3): repealed by SI 2019/419, reg 4, Sch 2, paras 1, 85(1), (6), as from exit day (as defined in the European Union (Withdrawal) Act 2018, s 20), for transitional provisions etc, see the 2019 Regulations at **[2.2122]** et seq.

Sub-ss (4), (5): added by SI 2019/419, reg 4, Sch 2, paras 1, 85(1), (7), as from exit day (as defined in the European Union (Withdrawal) Act 2018, s 20), for transitional provisions etc, see the 2019 Regulations at **[2.2122]** et seq.

[1.2205]

206 Index of defined expressions

The Table below lists provisions which define or otherwise explain terms defined for this Act, for a Part of this Act or for Chapter 2 or 3 of Part 2 of this Act.

the affirmative resolution procedure	section 182
the applied Chapter 2 (in Chapter 3 of Part 2)	*section 22*
the applied GDPR	*section 3*
assessment notice (in Part 6)	section 181
biometric data	section 205
certification provider (in Part 6)	section 181
the Commissioner	section 3
competent authority (in Part 3)	section 30
consent (in Part 4)	section 84
controller	section 3
data concerning health	section 205
the Data Protection Convention	section 3
the data protection legislation	section 3
data subject	section 3
employee (in Parts 3 and 4)	sections 33 and 84
enactment	section 205
enforcement notice (in Part 6)	section 181
[the EU GDPR	section 3
filing system	section 3

FOI public authority (in Chapter 3 of Part 2)	section 21
the GDPR	*section 3*
genetic data	section 205
government department	section 205
health professional	section 204
health record	section 205
identifiable living individual	section 3
inaccurate	section 205
information notice (in Part 6)	section 181
intelligence service (in Part 4)	section 82
international obligation of the United Kingdom	section 205
international organisation	section 205
the Law Enforcement Directive	section 3
the law enforcement purposes (in Part 3)	section 31
the made affirmative resolution procedure	section 182
Minister of the Crown	section 205
the negative resolution procedure	section 182
penalty notice (in Part 6)	section 181
penalty variation notice (in Part 6)	section 181
personal data	section 3
personal data breach (in Parts 3 and 4)	sections 33 and 84
processing	section 3
processor	section 3
profiling (in Part 3)	section 33
public authority (in the *GDPR* and Part 2)	section 7
public body (in the *GDPR* and Part 2)	section 7
publish	section 205
recipient (in Parts 3 and 4)	sections 33 and 84
representative (in Part 6)	section 181
representative body (in relation to a right of a data subject)	section 187
restriction of processing (in Parts 3 and 4)	sections 33 and 84
social work professional	section 204
the special purposes (in Part 6)	section 174
special purposes proceedings (in Part 6)	section 174
subordinate legislation	section 205
third country (in Part 3)	section 33
tribunal	section 205
the Tribunal	section 205
[the UK GDPR	section 3]

NOTES

Commencement: 23 May 2018 (see also the introductory notes to this Act preceding s 1 at **[1.2111]**).

The entries "the applied Chapter 2", "the applied GDPR" and "the GDPR" are repealed, the entries "the EU GDPR" and "the UK GDPR" are inserted, and for "GDPR" in italics in the entries "public authority" and "public body" there is substituted "UK GDPR", by the Data Protection, Privacy and Electronic Communications (Amendments etc) (EU Exit) Regulations 2019, SI 2019/419, reg 4, Sch 2, paras 1, 86, as from exit day (as defined in the European Union (Withdrawal) Act 2018, s 20), for transitional provisions etc, see the 2019 Regulations at **[2.2122]** et seq.

Territorial application

[1.2206]

207 Territorial application of this Act

(1) This Act applies only to processing of personal data described in subsections *(2) and (3)*.

[(1A) In the case of the processing of personal data to which Part 2 (the UK GDPR) applies, it applies to the types of such processing to which the UK GDPR applies by virtue of Article 3 of the UK GDPR.]

(2) *It applies to the processing of personal data* in the context of the activities of an establishment of a controller or processor in the United Kingdom, whether or not the processing takes place in the United Kingdom.

(3) It also applies to the processing of personal data to which Chapter 2 of Part 2 (the GDPR) applies where—

(a) the processing is carried out in the context of the activities of an establishment of a controller or processor in a country or territory that is not a member State, whether or not the processing takes place in such a country or territory,

(b) the personal data relates to a data subject who is in the United Kingdom when the processing takes place, and

(c) the processing activities are related to—

(i) the offering of goods or services to data subjects in the United Kingdom, whether or not for payment, or

(ii) the monitoring of data subjects' behaviour in the United Kingdom.

(4) *Subsections (1) to (3)* have effect subject to any provision in or made under section 120 providing for the Commissioner to carry out functions in relation to other processing of personal data.

(5) Section 3(14)(c) does not apply to the reference to the processing of personal data in subsection (2).

(6) The reference in subsection (3) to Chapter 2 of Part 2 (the GDPR) does not include that Chapter as applied by Chapter 3 of Part 2 (the applied GDPR).

(7) In this section, references to a person who has an establishment in the United Kingdom include the following—

(a) an individual who is ordinarily resident in the United Kingdom,

(b) a body incorporated under the law of the United Kingdom or a part of the United Kingdom,

(c) a partnership or other unincorporated association formed under the law of the United Kingdom or a part of the United Kingdom, and

(d) a person not within paragraph (a), (b) or (c) who maintains, and carries on activities through, an office, branch or agency or other stable arrangements in the United Kingdom,

and references to a person who has an establishment in another country or territory have a corresponding meaning.

NOTES

Commencement: 25 May 2018 (see also the introductory notes to this Act preceding s 1 at **[1.2111]**).

Sub-s (1): for the words in italics there are substituted the words "(1A) and (2)" by the Data Protection, Privacy and Electronic Communications (Amendments etc) (EU Exit) Regulations 2019, SI 2019/419, reg 4, Sch 2, paras 1, 87(1), (2), as from exit day (as defined in the European Union (Withdrawal) Act 2018, s 20), for transitional provisions etc, see the 2019 Regulations at **[2.2122]** et seq.

Sub-s (1A): inserted by SI 2019/419, reg 4, Sch 2, paras 1, 87(1), (3), as from exit day (as defined in the European Union (Withdrawal) Act 2018, s 20), for transitional provisions etc, see the 2019 Regulations at **[2.2122]** et seq.

Sub-s (2): for the words in italics there are substituted the words "In the case of the processing of personal data to which Part 2 does not apply, it applies where such processing is carried out" by SI 2019/419, reg 4, Sch 2, paras 1, 87(1), (4), as from exit day (as defined in the European Union (Withdrawal) Act 2018, s 20), for transitional provisions etc, see the 2019 Regulations at **[2.2122]** et seq.

Sub-ss (3), (6): repealed by SI 2019/419, reg 4, Sch 2, paras 1, 87(1), (5), (7), as from exit day (as defined in the European Union (Withdrawal) Act 2018, s 20), for transitional provisions etc, see the 2019 Regulations at **[2.2122]** et seq.

Sub-s (4): for the words in italics there are substituted the words "Subsections (1), (1A) and (2)" by SI 2019/419, reg 4, Sch 2, paras 1, 87(1), (6), as from exit day (as defined in the European Union (Withdrawal) Act 2018, s 20), for transitional provisions etc, see the 2019 Regulations at **[2.2122]** et seq.

Sub-s (7): words in italics repealed by SI 2019/419, reg 4, Sch 2, paras 1, 87(1), (8), as from exit day (as defined in the European Union (Withdrawal) Act 2018, s 20), for transitional provisions etc, see the 2019 Regulations at **[2.2122]** et seq.

General

[1.2207]

208 Children in Scotland

(1) Subsections (2) and (3) apply where a question falls to be determined in Scotland as to the legal capacity of a person aged under 16 to—

(a) exercise a right conferred by the data protection legislation, or

(b) give consent for the purposes of the data protection legislation.

(2) The person is to be taken to have that capacity where the person has a general understanding of what it means to exercise the right or give such consent.

(3) A person aged 12 or over is to be presumed to be of sufficient age and maturity to have such understanding, unless the contrary is shown.

NOTES

Commencement: 25 May 2018 (see also the introductory notes to this Act preceding s 1 at **[1.2111]**).

[1.2208]

209 Application to the Crown

(1) This Act binds the Crown.

(2) For the purposes of the *GDPR* and this Act, each government department is to be treated as a person separate from the other government departments (to the extent that is not already the case).

(3) Where government departments are not able to enter into contracts with each other, a provision of the *GDPR* or this Act that would require relations between them to be governed by a contract (or other binding legal act) in writing is to be treated as satisfied if the relations are the subject of a memorandum of understanding between them.

(4) Where the purposes for which and the manner in which personal data is, or is to be, processed are determined by a person acting on behalf of the Royal Household, the Duchy of Lancaster or the Duchy of Cornwall, the controller in respect of that data for the purposes of the *GDPR* and this Act is—

(a) in relation to the Royal Household, the Keeper of the Privy Purse,
(b) in relation to the Duchy of Lancaster, such person as the Chancellor of the Duchy appoints, and
(c) in relation to the Duchy of Cornwall, such person as the Duke of Cornwall, or the possessor for the time being of the Duchy of Cornwall, appoints.

(5) Different persons may be appointed under subsection (4)(b) or (c) for different purposes.

(6) As regards criminal liability—
(a) a government department is not liable to prosecution under this Act;
(b) nothing in subsection (4) makes a person who is a controller by virtue of that subsection liable to prosecution under this Act;
(c) a person in the service of the Crown is liable to prosecution under the provisions of this Act listed in subsection (7).

(7) Those provisions are—
(a) section 119;
(b) section 170;
(c) section 171;
(d) section 173;
(e) paragraph 15 of Schedule 15.

NOTES

Commencement: 23 May 2018 (see also the introductory notes to this Act preceding s 1 at **[1.2111]**).

Sub-ss (2)–(4): for "GDPR" in italics there is substituted "UK GDPR" by the Data Protection, Privacy and Electronic Communications (Amendments etc) (EU Exit) Regulations 2019, SI 2019/419, reg 4, Sch 2, paras 1, 88, as from exit day (as defined in the European Union (Withdrawal) Act 2018, s 20), for transitional provisions etc, see the 2019 Regulations at **[2.2122]** et seq.

[1.2209]

210 Application to Parliament

(1) Parts 1, 2 and 5 to 7 of this Act apply to the processing of personal data by or on behalf of either House of Parliament.

(2) Where the purposes for which and the manner in which personal data is, or is to be, processed are determined by or on behalf of the House of Commons, the controller in respect of that data for the purposes of the *GDPR* and this Act is the Corporate Officer of that House.

(3) Where the purposes for which and the manner in which personal data is, or is to be, processed are determined by or on behalf of the House of Lords, the controller in respect of that data for the purposes of the *GDPR* and this Act is the Corporate Officer of that House.

(4) Subsections (2) and (3) do not apply where the purposes for which and the manner in which the personal data is, or is to be, processed are determined by or on behalf of the Intelligence and Security Committee of Parliament.

(5) As regards criminal liability—
(a) nothing in subsection (2) or (3) makes the Corporate Officer of the House of Commons or the Corporate Officer of the House of Lords liable to prosecution under this Act;
(b) a person acting on behalf of either House of Parliament is liable to prosecution under the provisions of this Act listed in subsection (6).

(6) Those provisions are—
(a) section 170;
(b) section 171;
(c) section 173;
(d) paragraph 15 of Schedule 15.

NOTES

Commencement: 23 May 2018 (see also the introductory notes to this Act preceding s 1 at **[1.2111]**).

Sub-ss (2), (3): for "GDPR" in italics there is substituted "UK GDPR" by the Data Protection, Privacy and Electronic Communications (Amendments etc) (EU Exit) Regulations 2019, SI 2019/419, reg 4, Sch 2, paras 1, 89, as from exit day (as defined in the European Union (Withdrawal) Act 2018, s 20), for transitional provisions etc, see the 2019 Regulations at **[2.2122]** et seq.

[1.2210]

211 Minor and consequential provision

(1) In Schedule 19—
(a) Part 1 contains minor and consequential amendments of primary legislation;
(b) Part 2 contains minor and consequential amendments of other legislation;
(c) Part 3 contains consequential modifications of legislation;
(d) Part 4 contains supplementary provision.

(2) The Secretary of State may by regulations make provision that is consequential on any provision made by this Act.

(3) Regulations under subsection (2)—
(a) may include transitional, transitory or saving provision;
(b) may amend, repeal or revoke an enactment.

(4) The reference to an enactment in subsection (3)(b) does not include an enactment passed or made after the end of the Session in which this Act is passed.

(5) Regulations under this section that amend, repeal or revoke primary legislation are subject to the affirmative resolution procedure.

(6) Any other regulations under this section are subject to the negative resolution procedure.

(7) In this section, "primary legislation" means—
(a) an Act;
(b) an Act of the Scottish Parliament;
(c) a Measure or Act of the National Assembly for Wales;
(d) Northern Ireland legislation.

NOTES

Commencement: 25 May 2018 (see also the introductory notes to this Act preceding s 1 at **[1.2111]**).

Final

[1.2211]

212 Commencement

(1) Except as provided by subsections (2) and (3), this Act comes into force on such day as the Secretary of State may by regulations appoint.

(2) This section and the following provisions come into force on the day on which this Act is passed—
(a) sections 1 and 3;
(b) section 182;
(c) sections 204, 205 and 206;
(d) sections 209 and 210;
(e) sections 213(2), 214 and 215;
(f) any other provision of this Act so far as it confers power to make regulations or Tribunal Procedure Rules or is otherwise necessary for enabling the exercise of such a power on or after the day on which this Act is passed.

(3) The following provisions come into force at the end of the period of 2 months beginning when this Act is passed—
(a) section 124;
(b) sections 125, 126 and 127, so far as they relate to a code prepared under section 124;
(c) section 177;
(d) section 178 and Schedule 17;
(e) section 179.

(4) Regulations under this section may make different provision for different areas.

NOTES

Commencement: 23 May 2018 (see also the introductory notes to this Act preceding s 1 at **[1.2111]**).

Regulations: the Data Protection Act 2018 (Commencement No 1 and Transitional and Saving Provisions) Regulations 2018, SI 2018/625.

[1.2212]

213 Transitional provision

(1) Schedule 20 contains transitional, transitory and saving provision.

(2) The Secretary of State may by regulations make transitional, transitory or saving provision in connection with the coming into force of any provision of this Act or with the *GDPR* beginning to apply, including provision amending or repealing a provision of Schedule 20.

(3) Regulations under this section that amend or repeal a provision of Schedule 20 are subject to the negative resolution procedure.

[(4) Schedule 21 contains further transitional, transitory and saving provision made in connection with the amendment of this Act and the UK GDPR by regulations under section 8 of the European Union (Withdrawal) Act 2018.]

NOTES

Commencement: 23 May 2018 (sub-s (2)); 25 May 2018 (otherwise) (see also the introductory notes to this Act preceding s 1 at **[1.2111]**).

For "GDPR" in italics in sub-s (2) there is substituted "EU GDPR", and sub-s (4) is added, by the Data Protection, Privacy and Electronic Communications (Amendments etc) (EU Exit) Regulations 2019, SI 2019/419, reg 4, Sch 2, paras 1, 90, as from exit day (as defined in the European Union (Withdrawal) Act 2018, s 20), for transitional provisions etc, see the 2019 Regulations at **[2.2122]** et seq.

Regulations: the Data Protection Act 2018 (Commencement No 1 and Transitional and Saving Provisions) Regulations 2018, SI 2018/625.

[1.2213]

214 Extent

(1) This Act extends to England and Wales, Scotland and Northern Ireland, subject to—
(a) subsections (2) to (5), and
(b) paragraph 12 of Schedule 12.

(2) Section 199 extends to England and Wales only.

(3) Sections 188, 189 and 190 extend to England and Wales and Northern Ireland only.

(4) An amendment, repeal or revocation made by this Act has the same extent in the United Kingdom as the enactment amended, repealed or revoked.

(5) This subsection and the following provisions also extend to the Isle of Man—
(a) paragraphs 332 and 434 of Schedule 19;
(b) sections 211(1), 212(1) and 213(2), so far as relating to those paragraphs.

(6) Where there is a power to extend a part of an Act by Order in Council to any of the Channel Islands, the Isle of Man or any of the British overseas territories, the power may be exercised in relation to an amendment or repeal of that part which is made by or under this Act.

NOTES

Commencement: 23 May 2018 (see also the introductory notes to this Act preceding s 1 at **[1.2111]**).

[1.2214]

215 Short title

This Act may be cited as the Data Protection Act 2018.

NOTES

Commencement: 23 May 2018 (see also the introductory notes to this Act preceding s 1 at **[1.2111]**).

SCHEDULES

SCHEDULE 1
SPECIAL CATEGORIES OF PERSONAL DATA AND CRIMINAL CONVICTIONS ETC DATA

Section 10

PART 1
CONDITIONS RELATING TO EMPLOYMENT, HEALTH AND RESEARCH ETC

Employment, social security and social protection

[1.2215]

1. (1) This condition is met if—

(a) the processing is necessary for the purposes of performing or exercising obligations or rights which are imposed or conferred by law on the controller or the data subject in connection with employment, social security or social protection, and

(b) when the processing is carried out, the controller has an appropriate policy document in place (see paragraph 39 in Part 4 of this Schedule).

(2) See also the additional safeguards in Part 4 of this Schedule.

(3) In this paragraph—

"social security" includes any of the branches of social security listed in Article 3(1) of Regulation (EC) No 883/2004 of the European Parliament and of the Council on the co-ordination of social security systems (as amended from time to time);

"social protection" includes an intervention described in Article 2(b) of Regulation (EC) 458/2007 of the European Parliament and of the Council of 25 April 2007 on the European system of integrated social protection statistics (ESSPROS) *(as amended from time to time)*.

NOTES

Commencement: 25 May 2018 (see also the introductory notes to this Act preceding s 1 at **[1.2111]**).

Para 1: in the definition "social protection" in sub-para (3), for the words in italics there are substituted the words "as it had effect in EU law immediately before exit day", by the UK Statistics (Amendment etc) (EU Exit) Regulations 2019, SI 2019/489, reg 3, as from exit day (as defined in the European Union (Withdrawal) Act 2018, s 20).

PART 2
SUBSTANTIAL PUBLIC INTEREST CONDITIONS

Equality of opportunity or treatment

[1.2216]

8. (1) This condition is met if the processing—

(a) is of a specified category of personal data, and

(b) is necessary for the purposes of identifying or keeping under review the existence or absence of equality of opportunity or treatment between groups of people specified in relation to that category with a view to enabling such equality to be promoted or maintained,

subject to the exceptions in sub-paragraphs (3) to (5).

(2) In sub-paragraph (1), "specified" means specified in the following table—

Category of personal data	*Groups of people (in relation to a category of personal data)*
Personal data revealing racial or ethnic origin	People of different racial or ethnic origins
Personal data revealing religious or philosophical beliefs	People holding different religious or philosophical beliefs
Data concerning health	People with different states of physical or mental health
Personal data concerning an individual's sexual orientation	People of different sexual orientation

(3) Processing does not meet the condition in sub-paragraph (1) if it is carried out for the purposes of measures or decisions with respect to a particular data subject.

(4) Processing does not meet the condition in sub-paragraph (1) if it is likely to cause substantial damage or substantial distress to an individual.

(5) Processing does not meet the condition in sub-paragraph (1) if—

(a) an individual who is the data subject (or one of the data subjects) has given notice in writing to the controller requiring the controller not to process personal data in respect of which the individual is the data subject (and has not given notice in writing withdrawing that requirement),

(b) the notice gave the controller a reasonable period in which to stop processing such data, and

(c) that period has ended.

Racial and ethnic diversity at senior levels of organisations

9. (1) This condition is met if the processing—

(a) is of personal data revealing racial or ethnic origin,

(b) is carried out as part of a process of identifying suitable individuals to hold senior positions in a particular organisation, a type of organisation or organisations generally,

(c) is necessary for the purposes of promoting or maintaining diversity in the racial and ethnic origins of individuals who hold senior positions in the organisation or organisations, and

(d) can reasonably be carried out without the consent of the data subject,

subject to the exception in sub-paragraph (3).

(2) For the purposes of sub-paragraph (1)(d), processing can reasonably be carried out without the consent of the data subject only where—

(a) the controller cannot reasonably be expected to obtain the consent of the data subject, and

(b) the controller is not aware of the data subject withholding consent.

(3) Processing does not meet the condition in sub-paragraph (1) if it is likely to cause substantial damage or substantial distress to an individual.

(4) For the purposes of this paragraph, an individual holds a senior position in an organisation if the individual—

(a) holds a position listed in sub-paragraph (5), or

(b) does not hold such a position but is a senior manager of the organisation.

(5) Those positions are—

(a) a director, secretary or other similar officer of a body corporate;

(b) a member of a limited liability partnership;

(c) a partner in a partnership within the Partnership Act 1890, a limited partnership registered under the Limited Partnerships Act 1907 or an entity of a similar character formed under the law of a country or territory outside the United Kingdom.

(6) In this paragraph, "senior manager", in relation to an organisation, means a person who plays a significant role in—

(a) the making of decisions about how the whole or a substantial part of the organisation's activities are to be managed or organised, or

(b) the actual managing or organising of the whole or a substantial part of those activities.

(7) The reference in sub-paragraph (2)(b) to a data subject withholding consent does not include a data subject merely failing to respond to a request for consent.

Preventing or detecting unlawful acts

10. (1) This condition is met if the processing—

(a) is necessary for the purposes of the prevention or detection of an unlawful act,

(b) must be carried out without the consent of the data subject so as not to prejudice those purposes, and

(c) is necessary for reasons of substantial public interest.

(2) If the processing consists of the disclosure of personal data to a competent authority, or is carried out in preparation for such disclosure, the condition in sub-paragraph (1) is met even if, when the processing is carried out, the controller does not have an appropriate policy document in place (see paragraph 5 of this Schedule).

(3) In this paragraph—

"act" includes a failure to act;

"competent authority" has the same meaning as in Part 3 of this Act (see section 30).

Support for individuals with a particular disability or medical condition

16. (1) This condition is met if the processing—

(a) is carried out by a not-for-profit body which provides support to individuals with a particular disability or medical condition,

(b) is of a type of personal data falling within sub-paragraph (2) which relates to an individual falling within sub-paragraph (3),

(c) is necessary for the purposes of—

(i) raising awareness of the disability or medical condition, or

(ii) providing support to individuals falling within sub-paragraph (3) or enabling such individuals to provide support to each other,

(d) can reasonably be carried out without the consent of the data subject, and

(e) is necessary for reasons of substantial public interest.

(2) The following types of personal data fall within this sub-paragraph—

(a) personal data revealing racial or ethnic origin;

(b) genetic data or biometric data;

(c) data concerning health;

(d) personal data concerning an individual's sex life or sexual orientation.

(3) An individual falls within this sub-paragraph if the individual is or has been a member of the body mentioned in sub-paragraph (1)(a) and—

(a) has the disability or condition mentioned there, has had that disability or condition or has a significant risk of developing that disability or condition, or

(b) is a relative or carer of an individual who satisfies paragraph (a) of this sub-paragraph.

(4) For the purposes of sub-paragraph (1)(d), processing can reasonably be carried out without the consent of the data subject only where—

(a) the controller cannot reasonably be expected to obtain the consent of the data subject, and

(b) the controller is not aware of the data subject withholding consent.

(5) In this paragraph—

"carer" means an individual who provides or intends to provide care for another individual other than—

(a) under or by virtue of a contract, or

(b) as voluntary work;

"disability" has the same meaning as in the Equality Act 2010 (see section 6 of, and Schedule 1 to, that Act).

(6) The reference in sub-paragraph (4)(b) to a data subject withholding consent does not include a data subject merely failing to respond to a request for consent.

Counselling etc

17. (1) This condition is met if the processing—

(a) is necessary for the provision of confidential counselling, advice or support or of another similar service provided confidentially,

(b) is carried out without the consent of the data subject for one of the reasons listed in sub-paragraph (2), and

(c) is necessary for reasons of substantial public interest.

(2) The reasons mentioned in sub-paragraph (1)(b) are—

(a) in the circumstances, consent to the processing cannot be given by the data subject;

(b) in the circumstances, the controller cannot reasonably be expected to obtain the consent of the data subject to the processing;

(c) the processing must be carried out without the consent of the data subject because obtaining the consent of the data subject would prejudice the provision of the service mentioned in sub-paragraph (1)(a).

Safeguarding of economic well-being of certain individuals

19. (1) This condition is met if the processing—

(a) is necessary for the purposes of protecting the economic well-being of an individual at economic risk who is aged 18 or over,

(b) is of data concerning health,

(c) is carried out without the consent of the data subject for one of the reasons listed in sub-paragraph (2), and

(d) is necessary for reasons of substantial public interest.

(2) The reasons mentioned in sub-paragraph (1)(c) are—

(a) in the circumstances, consent to the processing cannot be given by the data subject;

(b) in the circumstances, the controller cannot reasonably be expected to obtain the consent of the data subject to the processing;

(c) the processing must be carried out without the consent of the data subject because obtaining the consent of the data subject would prejudice the provision of the protection mentioned in sub-paragraph (1)(a).

(3) In this paragraph, "individual at economic risk" means an individual who is less able to protect his or her economic well-being by reason of physical or mental injury, illness or disability.

Occupational pensions

21. (1) This condition is met if the processing—

(a) is necessary for the purpose of making a determination in connection with eligibility for, or benefits payable under, an occupational pension scheme,

(b) is of data concerning health which relates to a data subject who is the parent, grandparent, great-grandparent or sibling of a member of the scheme,

(c) is not carried out for the purposes of measures or decisions with respect to the data subject, and

(d) can reasonably be carried out without the consent of the data subject.

(2) For the purposes of sub-paragraph (1)(d), processing can reasonably be carried out without the consent of the data subject only where—

(a) the controller cannot reasonably be expected to obtain the consent of the data subject, and

(b) the controller is not aware of the data subject withholding consent.

(3) In this paragraph—

"occupational pension scheme" has the meaning given in section 1 of the Pension Schemes Act 1993;

"member", in relation to a scheme, includes an individual who is seeking to become a member of the scheme.

(4) The reference in sub-paragraph (2)(b) to a data subject withholding consent does not include a data subject merely failing to respond to a request for consent.

Publication of legal judgments

26. This condition is met if the processing—

(a) consists of the publication of a judgment or other decision of a court or tribunal, or

(b) is necessary for the purposes of publishing such a judgment or decision.

NOTES

Commencement: 25 May 2018 (see also the introductory notes to this Act preceding s 1 at **[1.2111]**).

PART 3
ADDITIONAL CONDITIONS RELATING TO CRIMINAL CONVICTIONS ETC

Consent

[1.2217]

29. This condition is met if the data subject has given consent to the processing.

Protecting individual's vital interests

30. This condition is met if—

(a) the processing is necessary to protect the vital interests of an individual, and

(b) the data subject is physically or legally incapable of giving consent.

Processing by not-for-profit bodies

31. This condition is met if the processing is carried out—

(a) in the course of its legitimate activities with appropriate safeguards by a foundation, association or other not-for-profit body with a political, philosophical, religious or trade union aim, and

(b) on condition that—

(i) the processing relates solely to the members or to former members of the body or to persons who have regular contact with it in connection with its purposes, and

(ii) the personal data is not disclosed outside that body without the consent of the data subjects.

Personal data in the public domain

32. This condition is met if the processing relates to personal data which is manifestly made public by the data subject.

Legal claims

33. This condition is met if the processing—

(a) is necessary for the purpose of, or in connection with, any legal proceedings (including prospective legal proceedings),

(b) is necessary for the purpose of obtaining legal advice, or

(c) is otherwise necessary for the purposes of establishing, exercising or defending legal rights.

Judicial acts

34. This condition is met if the processing is necessary when a court or tribunal is acting in its judicial capacity.

NOTES

Commencement: 25 May 2018 (see also the introductory notes to this Act preceding s 1 at **[1.2111]**).

PART 4
APPROPRIATE POLICY DOCUMENT AND ADDITIONAL SAFEGUARDS

Application of this Part of this Schedule

[1.2218]

38. This Part of this Schedule makes provision about the processing of personal data carried out in reliance on a condition in Part 1, 2 or 3 of this Schedule which requires the controller to have an appropriate policy document in place when the processing is carried out.

Requirement to have an appropriate policy document in place

39. The controller has an appropriate policy document in place in relation to the processing of personal data in reliance on a condition described in paragraph 38 if the controller has produced a document which—

(a) explains the controller's procedures for securing compliance with the principles in Article 5 of the *GDPR* (principles relating to processing of personal data) in connection with the processing of personal data in reliance on the condition in question, and

(b) explains the controller's policies as regards the retention and erasure of personal data processed in reliance on the condition, giving an indication of how long such personal data is likely to be retained.

Additional safeguard: retention of appropriate policy document

40. (1) Where personal data is processed in reliance on a condition described in paragraph 38, the controller must during the relevant period—

(a) retain the appropriate policy document,

(b) review and (if appropriate) update it from time to time, and

(c) make it available to the Commissioner, on request, without charge.

(2) "Relevant period", in relation to the processing of personal data in reliance on a condition described in paragraph 38, means a period which—

(a) begins when the controller starts to carry out processing of personal data in reliance on that condition, and

(b) ends at the end of the period of 6 months beginning when the controller ceases to carry out such processing.

Additional safeguard: record of processing

41. A record maintained by the controller, or the controller's representative, under Article 30 of the *GDPR* in respect of the processing of personal data in reliance on a condition described in paragraph 38 must include the following information—

(a) which condition is relied on,

(b) how the processing satisfies Article 6 of the *GDPR* (lawfulness of processing), and

(c) whether the personal data is retained and erased in accordance with the policies described in paragraph 39(b) and, if it is not, the reasons for not following those policies.

NOTES

Commencement: 25 May 2018 (see also the introductory notes to this Act preceding s 1 at **[1.2111]**).

Paras 39, 41: for "GDPR" in italics there is substituted "UK GDPR" by the Data Protection, Privacy and Electronic Communications (Amendments etc) (EU Exit) Regulations 2019, SI 2019/419, reg 4, Sch 2, paras 1, 91, as from exit day (as defined in the European Union (Withdrawal) Act 2018, s 20), for transitional provisions etc, see the 2019 Regulations at **[2.2122]** et seq.

SCHEDULE 2
EXEMPTIONS ETC FROM THE *GDPR*

NOTES

For "GDPR" in italics in the Schedule heading there is substituted "UK GDPR" by the Data Protection, Privacy and Electronic Communications (Amendments etc) (EU Exit) Regulations 2019, SI 2019/419, reg 4, Sch 2, paras 1, 93(1), (2), as from exit day (as defined in the European Union (Withdrawal) Act 2018, s 20), for transitional provisions etc, see the 2019 Regulations at **[2.2122]** et seq.

Section 15

PART 1
ADAPTATIONS AND RESTRICTIONS *BASED ON* ARTICLES 6(3) AND 23(1)

GDPR provisions to be adapted or restricted: "the listed GDPR provisions"

[1.2219]

1. In this Part of this Schedule, "the listed GDPR provisions" means—

(a) the following provisions of the *GDPR* (the rights and obligations in which may be restricted by virtue of Article 23(1) of the *GDPR*)—

(i) Article 13(1) to (3) (personal data collected from data subject: information to be provided);

(ii) Article 14(1) to (4) (personal data collected other than from data subject: information to be provided);

(iii) Article 15(1) to (3) (confirmation of processing, access to data and safeguards for third country transfers);

(iv) Article 16 (right to rectification);

(v) Article 17(1) and (2) (right to erasure);

(vi) Article 18(1) (restriction of processing);

(vii) Article 19 (notification obligation regarding rectification or erasure of personal data or restriction of processing);

(viii) Article 20(1) and (2) (right to data portability);

(ix) Article 21(1) (objections to processing);

(x) Article 5 (general principles) so far as its provisions correspond to the rights and obligations provided for in the provisions mentioned in sub-paragraphs (i) to (ix); and

(b) the following provisions of the *GDPR* (the application of which may be adapted by virtue of Article 6(3) of the *GDPR*)—

(i) Article 5(1)(a) (lawful, fair and transparent processing), other than the lawfulness requirements set out in Article 6;
(ii) Article 5(1)(b) (purpose limitation).

Information required to be disclosed by law etc or in connection with legal proceedings

5. (1) The listed GDPR provisions do not apply to personal data consisting of information that the controller is obliged by an enactment to make available to the public, to the extent that the application of those provisions would prevent the controller from complying with that obligation.

(2) The listed GDPR provisions do not apply to personal data where disclosure of the data is required by an enactment, a rule of law or an order of a court or tribunal, to the extent that the application of those provisions would prevent the controller from making the disclosure.

(3) The listed GDPR provisions do not apply to personal data where disclosure of the data—
(a) is necessary for the purpose of, or in connection with, legal proceedings (including prospective legal proceedings),
(b) is necessary for the purpose of obtaining legal advice, or
(c) is otherwise necessary for the purposes of establishing, exercising or defending legal rights,
to the extent that the application of those provisions would prevent the controller from making the disclosure.

NOTES

Commencement: 25 May 2018 (see also the introductory notes to this Act preceding s 1 at **[1.2111]**).

For the words "based on" in italics in the Part heading there are substituted the words "as described in", and for "GDPR" in italics in each place that it occurs in para 1 (including in the first place that it occurs in the heading preceding that paragraph) there is substituted "UK GDPR", by the Data Protection, Privacy and Electronic Communications (Amendments etc) (EU Exit) Regulations 2019, SI 2019/419, reg 4, Sch 2, paras 1, 92(1), (3)–(5), as from exit day (as defined in the European Union (Withdrawal) Act 2018, s 20), for transitional provisions etc, see the 2019 Regulations at **[2.2122]** et seq.

PART 2
RESTRICTIONS *BASED ON* ARTICLE 23(1): RESTRICTIONS OF RULES IN ARTICLES 13 TO 21 AND 34

GDPR provisions to be restricted: "the listed GDPR provisions"

[1.2220]

6. In this Part of this Schedule, "the listed GDPR provisions" means the following provisions of the *GDPR* (the rights and obligations in which may be restricted by virtue of Article 23(1) of the *GDPR*)—
(a) Article 13(1) to (3) (personal data collected from data subject: information to be provided);
(b) Article 14(1) to (4) (personal data collected other than from data subject: information to be provided);
(c) Article 15(1) to (3) (confirmation of processing, access to data and safeguards for third country transfers);
(d) Article 16 (right to rectification);
(e) Article 17(1) and (2) (right to erasure);
(f) Article 18(1) (restriction of processing);
(g) Article 19 (notification obligation regarding rectification or erasure of personal data or restriction of processing);
(h) Article 20(1) and (2) (right to data portability);
(i) Article 21(1) (objections to processing);
(j) Article 5 (general principles) so far as its provisions correspond to the rights and obligations provided for in the provisions mentioned in sub-paragraphs (a) to (i).

Functions designed to protect the public etc

7. The listed GDPR provisions do not apply to personal data processed for the purposes of discharging a function that—
(a) is designed as described in column 1 of the Table, and
(b) meets the condition relating to the function specified in column 2 of the Table,
to the extent that the application of those provisions would be likely to prejudice the proper discharge of the function.

Table

Description of function design	*Condition*
1 The function is designed to protect members of the public against— (a) financial loss due to dishonesty, malpractice or other seriously improper conduct by, or the unfitness or incompetence of, persons concerned in the provision of banking, insurance, investment or other financial services or in the management of bodies corporate, or (b) financial loss due to the conduct of discharged or undischarged bankrupts.	The function is— (a) conferred on a person by an enactment, (b) a function of the Crown, a Minister of the Crown or a government department, or (c) of a public nature, and is exercised in the public interest.

Description of function design	*Condition*
2 The function is designed to protect members of the public against— (a) dishonesty, malpractice or other seriously improper conduct, or (b) unfitness or incompetence.	The function is— (a) conferred on a person by an enactment, (b) a function of the Crown, a Minister of the Crown or a government department, or (c) of a public nature, and is exercised in the public interest.
3 The function is designed— (a) to protect charities or community interest companies against misconduct or mismanagement (whether by trustees, directors or other persons) in their administration, (b) to protect the property of charities or community interest companies from loss or misapplication, or (c) to recover the property of charities or community interest companies.	The function is— (a) conferred on a person by an enactment, (b) a function of the Crown, a Minister of the Crown or a government department, or (c) of a public nature, and is exercised in the public interest.
4 The function is designed— (a) to secure the health, safety and welfare of persons at work, or (b) to protect persons other than those at work against risk to health or safety arising out of or in connection with the action of persons at work.	The function is— (a) conferred on a person by an enactment, (b) a function of the Crown, a Minister of the Crown or a government department, or (c) of a public nature, and is exercised in the public interest.
5 The function is designed to protect members of the public against— (a) maladministration by public bodies, (b) failures in services provided by public bodies, or (c) a failure of a public body to provide a service which it is a function of the body to provide.	The function is conferred by any enactment on— (a) the Parliamentary Commissioner for Administration, (b) the Commissioner for Local Administration in England, (c) the Health Service Commissioner for England, (d) the Public Services Ombudsman for Wales, (e) the Northern Ireland Public Services Ombudsman, (f) the Prison Ombudsman for Northern Ireland, or (g) the Scottish Public Services Ombudsman.
6 The function is designed— (a) to protect members of the public against conduct which may adversely affect their interests by persons carrying on a business, (b) to regulate agreements or conduct which have as their object or effect the prevention, restriction or distortion of competition in connection with any commercial activity, or (c) to regulate conduct on the part of one or more undertakings which amounts to the abuse of a dominant position in a market.	The function is conferred on the Competition and Markets Authority by an enactment.

Judicial appointments, judicial independence and judicial proceedings

14. (1) The listed GDPR provisions do not apply to personal data processed for the purposes of assessing a person's suitability for judicial office or the office of Queen's Counsel.

(2) The listed GDPR provisions do not apply to personal data processed by—

(a) an individual acting in a judicial capacity, or

(b) a court or tribunal acting in its judicial capacity.

(3) As regards personal data not falling within sub-paragraph (1) or (2), the listed GDPR provisions do not apply to the extent that the application of those provisions would be likely to prejudice judicial independence or judicial proceedings.

NOTES

Commencement: 25 May 2018 (see also the introductory notes to this Act preceding s 1 at **[1.2111]**).

For the words "based on" in italics in the Part heading there are substituted the words "as described in", and for "GDPR" in italics in each place that it occurs in para 6 (including in the first place that it occurs in the heading preceding that paragraph) there is substituted "UK GDPR", by the Data Protection, Privacy and Electronic Communications (Amendments etc) (EU Exit) Regulations 2019, SI 2019/419, reg 4, Sch 2, paras 1, 92(1), (9)–(11), as from exit day (as defined in the European Union (Withdrawal) Act 2018, s 20), for transitional provisions etc, see the 2019 Regulations at **[2.2122]** et seq.

PART 3
RESTRICTION *BASED ON ARTICLE 23(1):* PROTECTION OF RIGHTS OF OTHERS

Protection of the rights of others: general

[1.2221]

16. (1) Article 15(1) to (3) of the *GDPR* (confirmation of processing, access to data and safeguards for third country transfers), and Article 5 of the *GDPR* so far as its provisions correspond to the rights and obligations provided for in Article 15(1) to (3), do not oblige a controller to disclose information to the data subject to the extent that doing so would involve disclosing information relating to another individual who can be identified from the information.

(2) Sub-paragraph (1) does not remove the controller's obligation where—

(a) the other individual has consented to the disclosure of the information to the data subject, or

(b) it is reasonable to disclose the information to the data subject without the consent of the other individual.

(3) In determining whether it is reasonable to disclose the information without consent, the controller must have regard to all the relevant circumstances, including—

(a) the type of information that would be disclosed,

(b) any duty of confidentiality owed to the other individual,

(c) any steps taken by the controller with a view to seeking the consent of the other individual,

(d) whether the other individual is capable of giving consent, and

(e) any express refusal of consent by the other individual.

(4) For the purposes of this paragraph—

(a) "information relating to another individual" includes information identifying the other individual as the source of information;

(b) an individual can be identified from information to be provided to a data subject by a controller if the individual can be identified from—

(i) that information, or

(ii) that information and any other information that the controller reasonably believes the data subject is likely to possess or obtain.

NOTES

Commencement: 25 May 2018 (see also the introductory notes to this Act preceding s 1 at **[1.2111]**).

For the words "based on Article 23(1):" in italics in the Part heading there are substituted the words "for the", and for "GDPR" in italics in both places that it occurs in para 16 there is substituted "UK GDPR", by the Data Protection, Privacy and Electronic Communications (Amendments etc) (EU Exit) Regulations 2019, SI 2019/419, reg 4, Sch 2, paras 1, 92(1), (13), (14), as from exit day (as defined in the European Union (Withdrawal) Act 2018, s 20), for transitional provisions etc, see the 2019 Regulations at **[2.2122]** et seq.

PART 4
RESTRICTIONS *BASED ON* ARTICLE 23(1): RESTRICTIONS OF RULES IN ARTICLES 13 TO 15

GDPR provisions to be restricted: "the listed GDPR provisions"

[1.2222]

18. In this Part of this Schedule, "the listed GDPR provisions" means the following provisions of the *GDPR* (the rights and obligations in which may be restricted by virtue of Article 23(1) of the *GDPR*)—

(a) Article 13(1) to (3) (personal data collected from data subject: information to be provided);

(b) Article 14(1) to (4) (personal data collected other than from data subject: information to be provided);

(c) Article 15(1) to (3) (confirmation of processing, access to data and safeguards for third country transfers);

(d) Article 5 (general principles) so far as its provisions correspond to the rights and obligations provided for in the provisions mentioned in sub-paragraphs (a) to (c).

Legal professional privilege

19. The listed GDPR provisions do not apply to personal data that consists of—

(a) information in respect of which a claim to legal professional privilege or, in Scotland, confidentiality of communications, could be maintained in legal proceedings, or

(b) information in respect of which a duty of confidentiality is owed by a professional legal adviser to a client of the adviser.

Negotiations

23. The listed GDPR provisions do not apply to personal data that consists of records of the intentions of the controller in relation to any negotiations with the data subject to the extent that the application of those provisions would be likely to prejudice those negotiations.

Confidential references

24. The listed GDPR provisions do not apply to personal data consisting of a reference given (or to be given) in confidence for the purposes of—

(a) the education, training or employment (or prospective education, training or employment) of the data subject,

(b) the placement (or prospective placement) of the data subject as a volunteer,
(c) the appointment (or prospective appointment) of the data subject to any office, or
(d) the provision (or prospective provision) by the data subject of any service.

NOTES

Commencement: 25 May 2018 (see also the introductory notes to this Act preceding s 1 at **[1.2111]**).

For the words "based on" in italics in the Part heading there are substituted the words "as described in", and for "GDPR" in italics in each place that it occurs in para 18 (including in the first place that it occurs in the heading preceding that paragraph) there is substituted "UK GDPR", by the Data Protection, Privacy and Electronic Communications (Amendments etc) (EU Exit) Regulations 2019, SI 2019/419, reg 4, Sch 2, paras 1, 92(1), (15)–(17), as from exit day (as defined in the European Union (Withdrawal) Act 2018, s 20), for transitional provisions etc, see the 2019 Regulations at **[2.2122]** et seq.

SCHEDULE 6
THE APPLIED GDPR AND THE APPLIED CHAPTER 2

Section 22

PART 1
MODIFICATIONS TO THE GDPR

Introductory

[1.2223]

1. *In its application by virtue of section 22(1), the GDPR has effect as if it were modified as follows.*

References to the GDPR and its provisions

2. *(1) References to "this Regulation" and to provisions of the GDPR have effect as references to the applied GDPR and to the provisions of the applied GDPR.*

(2) But sub-paragraph (1) does not have effect—

(a) in the case of the references which are modified or inserted by paragraphs 9(f)(ii), 15(b), 16(a)(ii), 35, 36(a) and (e)(ii) and 38(a)(i);

(b) in relation to the references in points (a) and (b) of paragraph 2 of Article 61, as inserted by paragraph 49.

References to Union law and Member State law

3. *(1) References to "Union law", "Member State law", "the law of a Member State" and "Union or Member State law" have effect as references to domestic law.*

(2) Sub-paragraph (1) is subject to the specific modifications made in this Part of this Schedule.

(3) In this paragraph, "domestic law" means the law of the United Kingdom, or of a part of the United Kingdom, and includes law in the form of an enactment, an instrument made under Her Majesty's prerogative or a rule of law.

References to the Union and to Member States

4. *(1) References to "the Union", "a Member State" and "Member States" have effect as references to the United Kingdom.*

(2) Sub-paragraph (1) is subject to the specific modifications made in this Part of this Schedule (including paragraph 3(1)).

References to supervisory authorities

5. *(1) References to a "supervisory authority", a "competent supervisory authority" or "supervisory authorities", however expressed, have effect as references to the Commissioner.*

(2) Sub-paragraph (1) does not apply to the references in—

(a) Article 4(21) as modified by paragraph 9(f);

(b) Article 57(1)(h);

(c) Article 61(1) inserted by paragraph 49.

(3) Sub-paragraph (1) is also subject to the specific modifications made in this Part of this Schedule.

References to the national parliament

6. *References to "the national parliament" have effect as references to both Houses of Parliament.*

Chapter I of the GDPR (general provisions)

7. *For Article 2 (material scope) substitute—*

> **"2.** *This Regulation applies to the processing of personal data to which Chapter 3 of Part 2 of the 2018 Act applies (see section 21 of that Act)."*

8. *For Article 3 substitute—*

"Article 3

Territorial application

Subsections (1), (2) and (7) of section 207 of the 2018 Act have effect for the purposes of this Regulation as they have effect for the purposes of that Act but as if the following were omitted—

(a) in subsection (1), the reference to subsection (3), and
(b) in subsection (7), the words following paragraph (d)."

9. *In Article 4 (definitions)—*

(a) in paragraph (7) (meaning of "controller"), for "; where the purposes and means of such processing are determined by Union or Member State law, the controller or the specific criteria for its nomination may be provided for by Union or Member State law" substitute ", subject to section 6 of the 2018 Act (meaning of "controller")";
(b) after paragraph (7) insert—

"(7A) "the 2018 Act" means the Data Protection Act 2018 as applied by section 22 of that Act and further modified by section 3 of that Act.";

(c) omit paragraph (16) (meaning of "main establishment");
(d) omit paragraph (17) (meaning of "representative");
(e) in paragraph (20) (meaning of "binding corporate rules"), for "on the territory of a Member State" substitute "in the United Kingdom";
(f) in paragraph (21) (meaning of "supervisory authority")—
 (i) after "a Member State" insert "(other than the United Kingdom)";
 (ii) for "Article 51" substitute "Article 51 of the GDPR";
(g) after paragraph (21) insert—

"(21A) "the Commissioner" means the Information Commissioner (see section 114 of the 2018 Act);";

(h) omit paragraph (22) (meaning of "supervisory authority concerned");
(i) omit paragraph (23) (meaning of "cross-border processing");
(j) omit paragraph (24) (meaning of "relevant and reasoned objection");
(k) after paragraph (26) insert—

"(27) "the GDPR" has the meaning given in section 3(10) of the 2018 Act.
(28) "domestic law" has the meaning given in paragraph 3(3) of Schedule 6 to the 2018 Act."

Chapter II of the GDPR (principles)

10. *In Article 6 (lawfulness of processing)—*

(a) omit paragraph 2;
(b) in paragraph 3, for the first subparagraph substitute—

"In addition to the provision made in section 15 of and Part 1 of Schedule 2 to the 2018 Act, a legal basis for the processing referred to in point (c) and (e) of paragraph 1 may be laid down by the Secretary of State in regulations (see section 16 of the 2018 Act).";

(c) in paragraph 3, in the second subparagraph, for "The Union or the Member State law shall" substitute "The regulations must".

12. *In Article 9 (processing of special categories of personal data)—*

(a) in paragraph 2(a), omit ", except where Union or Member State law provide that the prohibition referred to in paragraph 1 may not be lifted by the data subject";
(b) in paragraph 2(b), for "Union or Member State law" substitute "domestic law (see section 10 of the 2018 Act)";
(c) in paragraph 2, for point (g) substitute—

"(g) processing is necessary for reasons of substantial public interest and is authorised by domestic law (see section 10 of the 2018 Act);";

(d) in paragraph 2(h), for "Union or Member State law" substitute "domestic law (see section 10 of the 2018 Act)";
(e) in paragraph 2(i), for "Union or Member State law" insert "domestic law (see section 10 of the 2018 Act);";
(f) in paragraph 2, for point (j) substitute—

"(j) processing is necessary for archiving purposes in the public interest, scientific or historical research purposes or statistical purposes in accordance with Article 89(1) (as supplemented by section 19 of the 2018 Act) and is authorised by domestic law (see section 10 of that Act).";

(g) in paragraph 3, for "national competent bodies", in both places, substitute "a national competent body of the United Kingdom";
(h) omit paragraph 4.

13. *In Article 10 (processing of personal data relating to criminal convictions and offences), in the first sentence, for "Union or Member State law providing for appropriate safeguards for the rights and freedoms of data subjects" substitute "domestic law (see section 10 of the 2018 Act)".*

Section 1 of Chapter III of the GDPR (rights of the data subject: transparency and modalities)

14. *In Article 12 (transparent information etc for the exercise of the rights of the data subject), omit paragraph 8.*

Section 2 of Chapter III of the GDPR (rights of the data subject: information and access to personal data)

15. *In Article 13 (personal data collected from data subject: information to be provided), in paragraph 1—*

(a) *in point (a), omit "and, where applicable, of the controller's representative";*

(b) *in point (f), after "the Commission" insert "pursuant to Article 45(3) of the GDPR".*

16. *In Article 14 (personal data collected other than from data subject: information to be provided)—*

(a) *in paragraph 1—*

(i) *in point (a), omit "and, where applicable, of the controller's representative";*

(ii) *in point (f), after "the Commission" insert "pursuant to Article 45(3) of the GDPR";*

(b) *in paragraph 5(c), for "Union or Member State law to which the controller is subject" substitute "a rule of domestic law".*

Section 3 of Chapter III of the GDPR (rights of the data subject: rectification and erasure)

17. *In Article 17 (right to erasure ('right to be forgotten'))—*

(a) *in paragraph 1(e), for "in Union or Member State law to which the controller is subject" substitute "under domestic law";*

(b) *in paragraph 3(b), for "by Union or Member State law to which the controller is subject" substitute "under domestic law".*

18. *In Article 18 (right to restriction of processing), in paragraph 2, for "of the Union or of a Member State" substitute "of the United Kingdom".*

Section 4 of Chapter III of the GDPR (rights of the data subject: right to object and automated individual decision-making)

19. *In Article 21 (right to object), in paragraph 5, omit ", and notwithstanding Directive 2002/58/EC,".*

20. *In Article 22 (automated individual decision-making, including profiling), for paragraph 2(b) substitute—*

"(b) is a qualifying significant decision for the purposes of section 14 of the 2018 Act; or".

Section 5 of Chapter III of the GDPR (rights of the data subject: restrictions)

21. *In Article 23 (restrictions), in paragraph 1—*

(a) *for "Union or Member State law to which the data controller or processor is subject" substitute "In addition to the provision made by section 15 of and Schedules 2, 3 and 4 to the 2018 Act, the Secretary of State";*

(b) *in point (e), for "of the Union or of a Member State", in both places, substitute "of the United Kingdom";*

(c) *after point (j) insert—*

"See section 16 of the 2018 Act."

Section 1 of Chapter IV of the GDPR (controller and processor: general obligations)

22. *In Article 26 (joint controllers), in paragraph 1, for "Union or Member State law to which the controllers are subject" substitute "domestic law".*

25. *In Article 30 (records of processing activities)—*

(a) *in paragraph 1, in the first sentence, omit "and, where applicable, the controller's representative,";*

(b) *in paragraph 1, in point (a), omit ", the controller's representative";*

(c) *in paragraph 1, in point (g), after "32(1)" insert "or section 28(3) of the 2018 Act";*

(d) *in paragraph 2, in the first sentence, omit "and, where applicable, the processor's representative";*

(e) *in paragraph 2, in point (a), omit "the controller's or the processor's representative, and";*

(f) *in paragraph 2, in point (d), after "32(1)" insert "or section 28(3) of the 2018 Act";*

(g) *in paragraph 4, omit "and, where applicable, the controller's or the processor's representative,".*

26. *In Article 31 (co-operation with the supervisory authority), omit "and, where applicable, their representatives,".*

Section 3 of Chapter IV of the GDPR (controller and processor: data protection impact assessment and prior consultation)

27. *In Article 35 (data protection impact assessment), omit paragraphs 4, 5, 6 and 10.*

28. *In Article 36 (prior consultation)—*

(a) *for paragraph 4 substitute—*

"4. *The Secretary of State must consult the Commissioner during the preparation of any proposal for a legislative measure which relates to processing.";*

(b) *omit paragraph 5.*

Section 4 of Chapter IV of the GDPR (controller and processor: data protection officer)

29. *In Article 37 (designation of data protection officers), omit paragraph 4.*

30. *In Article 39 (tasks of the data protection officer), in paragraph 1(a) and (b), for "other Union or Member State data protection provisions" substitute "other rules of domestic law relating to data protection".*

Section 5 of Chapter IV of the GDPR (controller and processor: codes of conduct and certification)

31. *In Article 40 (codes of conduct)—*
(a) in paragraph 1, for "The Member States, the supervisory authorities, the Board and the Commission shall" substitute "The Commissioner must";
(b) omit paragraph 3;
(c) in paragraph 6, omit ", and where the code of conduct concerned does not relate to processing activities in several Member States";
(d) omit paragraphs 7 to 11.

32. *In Article 41 (monitoring of approved codes of conduct), omit paragraph 3.*

Section 1 of Chapter VI of the GDPR (independent supervisory authorities: independent status)

40. *In Article 51 (supervisory authority)—*
(a) in paragraph 1—
(i) for "Each Member State shall provide for one or more independent public authorities to be" substitute "The Commissioner is";
(ii) omit "and to facilitate the free flow of personal data within the Union ('supervisory authority')";
(b) omit paragraphs 2 to 4.

41. *In Article 52 (independence)—*
(a) in paragraph 2—
(i) for "The member or members of each supervisory authority" substitute "The Commissioner";
(ii) for "their", in both places, substitute "the Commissioner's";
(b) in paragraph 3—
(i) for "Member or members of each supervisory authority" substitute "The Commissioner";
(ii) for "their", in both places, substitute "the Commissioner's";
(c) omit paragraphs 4 to 6.

42. *Omit Article 53 (general conditions for the members of the supervisory authority).*

43. *Omit Article 54 (rules on the establishment of the supervisory authority).*

Section 2 of Chapter VI of the GDPR (independent supervisory authorities: competence, tasks and powers)

44. *In Article 55 (competence)—*
(a) in paragraph 1, omit "on the territory of its own Member State";
(b) omit paragraph 2.

45. *Omit Article 56 (competence of the lead supervisory authority).*

46. *In Article 57 (tasks)—*
(a) in paragraph 1, in the first sentence, for "each supervisory authority shall on its territory" substitute "the Commissioner is to";
(b) in paragraph 1, in point (e), omit "and, if appropriate, cooperate with the supervisory authorities in other Member States to that end";
(c) in paragraph 1, in point (f), omit "or coordination with another supervisory authority";
(d) in paragraph 1, omit points (g), (k) and (t);
(e) after paragraph 1 insert—

"1A *In this Article and Article 58, references to "this Regulation" have effect as references to this Regulation and section 28(3) of the 2018 Act."*

47. *In Article 58 (powers)—*
(a) in paragraph 1, in point (a), omit ", and, where applicable, the controller's or the processor's representative";
(b) in paragraph 1, in point (f), for "Union or Member State procedural law" substitute "domestic law";
(c) in paragraph 3, in point (b), for "the Member State government" substitute "the Secretary of State";
(d) in paragraph 3, omit point (c);
(e) omit paragraphs 4 to 6.

48. *In Article 59 (activity reports)—*
(a) for ", the government and other authorities as designated by Member State law" substitute "and the Secretary of State";

(b) *omit ", to the Commission and to the Board".*

Chapter VII of the GDPR (co-operation and consistency)

49. *For Articles 60 to 76 substitute—*

"Article 61

Co-operation with other supervisory authorities etc

1. *The Commissioner may, in connection with carrying out the Commissioner's functions under this Regulation—*

(a) *co-operate with, provide assistance to and seek assistance from other supervisory authorities;*

(b) *conduct joint operations with other supervisory authorities, including joint investigations and joint enforcement measures.*

2. *The Commissioner must, in carrying out the Commissioner's functions under this Regulation, have regard to—*

(a) *decisions, advice, guidelines, recommendations and best practices issued by the European Data Protection Board established under Article 68 of the GDPR;*

(b) *any implementing acts adopted by the Commission under Article 67 of the GDPR (exchange of information)."*

Chapter VIII of the GDPR (remedies, liability and penalties)

50. *In Article 77 (right to lodge a complaint with a supervisory authority)—*

(a) *in paragraph 1, omit "in particular in the Member State of his or her habitual residence, place of work or place of the alleged infringement";*

(b) *in paragraph 2, for "The supervisory authority with which the complaint has been lodged" substitute "The Commissioner".*

51. *In Article 78 (right to an effective judicial remedy against a supervisory authority)—*

(a) *omit paragraph 2;*

(b) *for paragraph 3 substitute—*

"3. *Proceedings against the Commissioner are to be brought before a court in the United Kingdom.";*

(c) *omit paragraph 4.*

52. *In Article 79 (right to an effective judicial remedy against a controller or processor), for paragraph 2 substitute—*

"2. *Proceedings against a controller or a processor are to be brought before a court (see section 180 of the 2018 Act)."*

53. *In Article 80 (representation of data subjects)—*

(a) *in paragraph 1, omit "where provided for by Member State law";*

(b) *in paragraph 2, for "Member States" substitute "The Secretary of State";*

(c) *after that paragraph insert—*

"3. *The power under paragraph 2 may only be exercised by making regulations under section 190 of the 2018 Act."*

54. *Omit Article 81 (suspension of proceedings).*

55. *In Article 82 (right to compensation and liability), for paragraph 6 substitute—*

"6. *Proceedings for exercising the right to receive compensation are to be brought before a court (see section 180 of the 2018 Act)."*

56. *In Article 83 (general conditions for imposing administrative fines)—*

(a) *in paragraph 5, in point (d), for "pursuant to Member State law adopted under Chapter IX" substitute "under Part 5 or 6 of Schedule 2 to the 2018 Act or under regulations made under section 16 of that Act";*

(b) *in paragraph 7—*

(i) *for "each Member State" substitute "the Secretary of State";*

(ii) *for "that Member State" substitute "the United Kingdom";*

(c) *for paragraph 8 substitute—*

"8. *Section 115(9) of the 2018 Act makes provision about the exercise of the Commissioner's powers under this Article.";*

(d) *omit paragraph 9.*

57. *In Article 84 (penalties)—*

(a) *for paragraph 1 substitute—*

"1. The rules on other penalties applicable to infringements of this Regulation are set out in the 2018 Act (see in particular Part 6 (enforcement)).";

(b) omit paragraph 2.

Chapter IX of the GDPR (provisions relating to specific processing situations)

58. *In Article 85 (processing and freedom of expression and information)—*

(a) omit paragraph 1;

(b) in paragraph 2, for "Member States shall" substitute "the Secretary of State, in addition to the relevant provisions, may by way of regulations (see section 16 of the 2018 Act),";

(c) in paragraph 2, at the end insert—

"In this paragraph, "the relevant provisions" means section 15 of and Part 5 of Schedule 2 to the 2018 Act.";

(d) omit paragraph 3.

59. *In Article 86 (processing and public access to official documents), for "Union or Member State law to which the public authority or body is subject" substitute "domestic law".*

60. *Omit Article 87 (processing of national identification number).*

61. *Omit Article 88 (processing in the context of employment).*

63. *Omit Article 90 (obligations of secrecy).*

64. *Omit Article 91 (existing data protection rules of churches and religious associations).*

Chapter X of the GDPR (delegated acts and implementing acts)

65. *Omit Article 92 (exercise of the delegation).*

66. *Omit Article 93 (committee procedure).*

Chapter XI of the GDPR (final provisions)

67. *Omit Article 94 (repeal of Directive 95/46/EC).*

68. *Omit Article 95 (relationship with Directive 2002/58/EC).*

69. *In Article 96 (relationship with previously concluded Agreements), for "by Member States" substitute "by the United Kingdom or the Commissioner".*

70. *Omit Article 97 (Commission reports).*

71. *Omit Article 98 (Commission reviews).*

72. *Omit Article 99 (entry into force and application).*

NOTES

Commencement: 25 May 2018 (except para 62); to be appointed (para 62) (see also the introductory notes to this Act preceding s 1 at **[1.2111]**).

Repealed by the Data Protection, Privacy and Electronic Communications (Amendments etc) (EU Exit) Regulations 2019, SI 2019/419, reg 4, Sch 2, paras 1, 96, as from exit day (as defined in the European Union (Withdrawal) Act 2018, s 20), for transitional provisions etc, see the 2019 Regulations at **[2.2122]** et seq.

PART 2

MODIFICATIONS TO CHAPTER 2 OF PART 2

Introductory

[1.2224]

73. *In its application by virtue of section 22(2), Chapter 2 of Part 2 has effect as if it were modified as follows.*

General modifications

74. *(1) References to Chapter 2 of Part 2 and the provisions of that Chapter have effect as references to the applied Chapter 2 and the provisions of the applied Chapter 2 .*

(2) References to the GDPR and to the provisions of the GDPR have effect as references to the applied GDPR and to the provisions of the applied GDPR, except in section 18(2)(a).

(3) References to the processing of personal data to which Chapter 2 applies have effect as references to the processing of personal data to which Chapter 3 applies.

Exemptions

75. *In section 16 (power to make further exemptions etc by regulations), in subsection (1)(a), for "Member State law" substitute "the Secretary of State".*

NOTES

Commencement: 25 May 2018 (see also the introductory notes to this Act preceding s 1 at **[1.2111]**).

Repealed by the Data Protection, Privacy and Electronic Communications (Amendments etc) (EU Exit) Regulations 2019, SI 2019/419, reg 4, Sch 2, paras 1, 96, as from exit day (as defined in the European Union (Withdrawal) Act 2018, s 20), for transitional provisions etc, see the 2019 Regulations at **[2.2122]** et seq.

SCHEDULE 12
THE INFORMATION COMMISSIONER

Section 114

Status and capacity

[1.2225]

1. (1) The Commissioner is to continue to be a corporation sole.

(2) The Commissioner and the Commissioner's officers and staff are not to be regarded as servants or agents of the Crown.

Appointment

2. (1) The Commissioner is to be appointed by Her Majesty by Letters Patent.

(2) No recommendation may be made to Her Majesty for the appointment of a person as the Commissioner unless the person concerned has been selected on merit on the basis of fair and open competition.

(3) The Commissioner is to hold office for such term not exceeding 7 years as may be determined at the time of the Commissioner's appointment, subject to paragraph 3.

(4) A person cannot be appointed as the Commissioner more than once.

Resignation and removal

3. (1) The Commissioner may be relieved of office by Her Majesty at the Commissioner's own request.

(2) The Commissioner may be removed from office by Her Majesty on an Address from both Houses of Parliament.

(3) No motion is to be made in either House of Parliament for such an Address unless a Minister of the Crown has presented a report to that House stating that the Minister is satisfied that one or both of the following grounds is made out—

(a) the Commissioner is guilty of serious misconduct;

(b) the Commissioner no longer fulfils the conditions required for the performance of the Commissioner's functions.

Salary etc

4. (1) The Commissioner is to be paid such salary as may be specified by a resolution of the House of Commons.

(2) There is to be paid in respect of the Commissioner such pension as may be specified by a resolution of the House of Commons.

(3) A resolution for the purposes of this paragraph may—

(a) specify the salary or pension,

(b) specify the salary or pension and provide for it to be increased by reference to such variables as may be specified in the resolution, or

(c) provide that the salary or pension is to be the same as, or calculated on the same basis as, that payable to, or in respect of, a person employed in a specified office under, or in a specified capacity in the service of, the Crown.

(4) A resolution for the purposes of this paragraph may take effect from—

(a) the date on which it is passed, or

(b) from an earlier date or later date specified in the resolution.

(5) A resolution for the purposes of this paragraph may make different provision in relation to the pension payable to, or in respect of, different holders of the office of Commissioner.

(6) A salary or pension payable under this paragraph is to be charged on and issued out of the Consolidated Fund.

(7) In this paragraph, "pension" includes an allowance or gratuity and a reference to the payment of a pension includes a reference to the making of payments towards the provision of a pension.

Officers and staff

5. (1) The Commissioner—

(a) must appoint one or more deputy commissioners, and

(b) may appoint other officers and staff.

(2) The Commissioner is to determine the remuneration and other conditions of service of people appointed under this paragraph.

(3) The Commissioner may pay pensions, allowances or gratuities to, or in respect of, people appointed under this paragraph, including pensions, allowances or gratuities paid by way of compensation in respect of loss of office or employment.

(4) The references in sub-paragraph (3) to paying pensions, allowances or gratuities includes making payments towards the provision of pensions, allowances or gratuities.

(5) In making appointments under this paragraph, the Commissioner must have regard to the principle of selection on merit on the basis of fair and open competition.

(6) The Employers' Liability (Compulsory Insurance) Act 1969 does not require insurance to be effected by the Commissioner.

Carrying out of the Commissioner's functions by officers and staff

6. (1) The functions of the Commissioner are to be carried out by the deputy commissioner or deputy commissioners if—

(a) there is a vacancy in the office of the Commissioner, or

(b) the Commissioner is for any reason unable to act.

(2) When the Commissioner appoints a second or subsequent deputy commissioner, the Commissioner must specify which deputy commissioner is to carry out which of the Commissioner's functions in the circumstances referred to in sub-paragraph (1).

(3) A function of the Commissioner may, to the extent authorised by the Commissioner, be carried out by any of the Commissioner's officers or staff.

Authentication of the seal of the Commissioner

7. The application of the seal of the Commissioner is to be authenticated by—

(a) the Commissioner's signature, or

(b) the signature of another person authorised for the purpose.

Presumption of authenticity of documents issued by the Commissioner

8. A document purporting to be an instrument issued by the Commissioner and to be—

(a) duly executed under the Commissioner's seal, or

(b) signed by or on behalf of the Commissioner,

is to be received in evidence and is to be deemed to be such an instrument unless the contrary is shown.

Money

9. The Secretary of State may make payments to the Commissioner out of money provided by Parliament.

Fees etc and other sums

10. (1) All fees, charges, penalties and other sums received by the Commissioner in carrying out the Commissioner's functions are to be paid by the Commissioner to the Secretary of State.

(2) Sub-paragraph (1) does not apply where the Secretary of State, with the consent of the Treasury, otherwise directs.

(3) Any sums received by the Secretary of State under sub-paragraph (1) are to be paid into the Consolidated Fund.

Accounts

11. (1) The Commissioner must—

(a) keep proper accounts and other records in relation to the accounts, and

(b) prepare in respect of each financial year a statement of account in such form as the Secretary of State may direct.

(2) The Commissioner must send a copy of the statement to the Comptroller and Auditor General—

(a) on or before 31 August next following the end of the year to which the statement relates, or

(b) on or before such earlier date after the end of that year as the Treasury may direct.

(3) The Comptroller and Auditor General must examine, certify and report on the statement.

(4) The Commissioner must arrange for copies of the statement and the Comptroller and Auditor General's report to be laid before Parliament.

(5) In this paragraph, "financial year" means a period of 12 months beginning with 1 April.

Scotland

12. Paragraphs 1(1), 7 and 8 do not extend to Scotland.

NOTES

Commencement: 25 May 2018 (see also the introductory notes to this Act preceding s 1 at **[1.2111]**).

SCHEDULE 13
OTHER GENERAL FUNCTIONS OF THE COMMISSIONER

Section 116

General tasks

[1.2226]

1. (1) The Commissioner must—

(a) monitor and enforce Parts 3 and 4 of this Act;

(b) promote public awareness and understanding of the risks, rules, safeguards and rights in relation to processing of personal data to which those Parts apply;

(c) advise Parliament, the government and other institutions and bodies on legislative and administrative measures relating to the protection of individuals' rights and freedoms with regard to processing of personal data to which those Parts apply;

(d) promote the awareness of controllers and processors of their obligations under Parts 3 and 4 of this Act;

(e) on request, provide information to a data subject concerning the exercise of the data subject's rights under Parts 3 and 4 of this Act and, if appropriate, co-operate with *LED supervisory authorities and* foreign designated authorities to provide such information;

(f) co-operate with *LED supervisory authorities and* foreign designated authorities with a view to ensuring the consistency of application and enforcement of *the Law Enforcement Directive and* the Data Protection Convention, including by sharing information and providing mutual assistance;

(g) conduct investigations on the application of Parts 3 and 4 of this Act, including on the basis of information received from *an LED supervisory authority,* a foreign designated authority or another public authority;

(h) monitor relevant developments to the extent that they have an impact on the protection of personal data, including the development of information and communication technologies;

(i) contribute to the activities of the European Data Protection Board established by the GDPR in connection with the processing of personal data to which the Law Enforcement Directive applies.

(2) Section 3(14)(c) does not apply to the reference to personal data in sub-paragraph (1)(h).

General powers

2. The Commissioner has the following investigative, corrective, authorisation and advisory powers in relation to processing of personal data to which Part 3 or 4 of this Act applies—

(a) to notify the controller or the processor of an alleged infringement of Part 3 or 4 of this Act;

(b) to issue warnings to a controller or processor that intended processing operations are likely to infringe provisions of Part 3 or 4 of this Act;

(c) to issue reprimands to a controller or processor where processing operations have infringed provisions of Part 3 or 4 of this Act;

(d) to issue, on the Commissioner's own initiative or on request, opinions to Parliament, the government or other institutions and bodies as well as to the public on any issue related to the protection of personal data.

Definitions

3. In this Schedule—

"foreign designated authority" means an authority designated for the purposes of Article 13 of the Data Protection Convention by a party, other than the United Kingdom, which is bound by that Convention;

"LED supervisory authority" means a supervisory authority for the purposes of Article 41 of the Law Enforcement Directive in a member State other than the United Kingdom.

NOTES

Commencement: 25 May 2018 (see also the introductory notes to this Act preceding s 1 at **[1.2111]**).

All words in italics are repealed by the Data Protection, Privacy and Electronic Communications (Amendments etc) (EU Exit) Regulations 2019, SI 2019/419, reg 4, Sch 2, paras 1, 97, as from exit day (as defined in the European Union (Withdrawal) Act 2018, s 20), for transitional provisions etc, see the 2019 Regulations at **[2.2122]** et seq.

SCHEDULE 15
POWERS OF ENTRY AND INSPECTION

Section 154

Issue of warrants in connection with non-compliance and offences

[1.2227]

1. (1) This paragraph applies if a judge of the High Court, a circuit judge or a District Judge (Magistrates' Courts) is satisfied by information on oath supplied by the Commissioner that—

(a) there are reasonable grounds for suspecting that—

  (i) a controller or processor has failed or is failing as described in section 149(2), or

  (ii) an offence under this Act has been or is being committed, and

(b) there are reasonable grounds for suspecting that evidence of the failure or of the commission of the offence is to be found on premises specified in the information or is capable of being viewed using equipment on such premises.

(2) The judge may grant a warrant to the Commissioner.

Issue of warrants in connection with assessment notices

2. (1) This paragraph applies if a judge of the High Court, a circuit judge or a District Judge (Magistrates' Courts) is satisfied by information on oath supplied by the Commissioner that a controller or processor has failed to comply with a requirement imposed by an assessment notice.

(2) The judge may, for the purpose of enabling the Commissioner to determine whether the controller or processor has complied or is complying with the data protection legislation, grant a warrant to the Commissioner in relation to premises that were specified in the assessment notice.

Restrictions on issuing warrants: processing for the special purposes

3. A judge must not issue a warrant under this Schedule in respect of personal data processed for the special purposes unless a determination under section 174 with respect to the data or the processing has taken effect.

Restrictions on issuing warrants: procedural requirements

4. (1) A judge must not issue a warrant under this Schedule unless satisfied that—

(a) the conditions in sub-paragraphs (2) to (4) are met,

(b) compliance with those conditions would defeat the object of entry to the premises in question, or

(c) the Commissioner requires access to the premises in question urgently.

(2) The first condition is that the Commissioner has given 7 days' notice in writing to the occupier of the premises in question demanding access to the premises.

(3) The second condition is that—

(a) access to the premises was demanded at a reasonable hour and was unreasonably refused, or

(b) entry to the premises was granted but the occupier unreasonably refused to comply with a request by the Commissioner or the Commissioner's officers or staff to be allowed to do any of the things referred to in paragraph 5.

(4) The third condition is that, since the refusal, the occupier of the premises—

(a) has been notified by the Commissioner of the application for the warrant, and

(b) has had an opportunity to be heard by the judge on the question of whether or not the warrant should be issued.

(5) In determining whether the first condition is met, an assessment notice given to the occupier is to be disregarded.

Content of warrants

5. (1) A warrant issued under this Schedule must authorise the Commissioner or any of the Commissioner's officers or staff—

(a) to enter the premises,

(b) to search the premises, and

(c) to inspect, examine, operate and test any equipment found on the premises which is used or intended to be used for the processing of personal data.

(2) A warrant issued under paragraph 1 must authorise the Commissioner or any of the Commissioner's officers or staff—

(a) to inspect and seize any documents or other material found on the premises which may be evidence of the failure or offence mentioned in that paragraph,

(b) to require any person on the premises to provide, in an appropriate form, a copy of information capable of being viewed using equipment on the premises which may be evidence of that failure or offence,

(c) to require any person on the premises to provide an explanation of any document or other material found on the premises and of any information capable of being viewed using equipment on the premises, and

(d) to require any person on the premises to provide such other information as may reasonably be required for the purpose of determining whether the controller or processor has failed or is failing as described in section 149(2).

(3) A warrant issued under paragraph 2 must authorise the Commissioner or any of the Commissioner's officers or staff—

(a) to inspect and seize any documents or other material found on the premises which may enable the Commissioner to determine whether the controller or processor has complied or is complying with the data protection legislation,

(b) to require any person on the premises to provide, in an appropriate form, a copy of information capable of being viewed using equipment on the premises which may enable the Commissioner to make such a determination,

(c) to require any person on the premises to provide an explanation of any document or other material found on the premises and of any information capable of being viewed using equipment on the premises, and

(d) to require any person on the premises to provide such other information as may reasonably be required for the purpose of determining whether the controller or processor has complied or is complying with the data protection legislation.

(4) A warrant issued under this Schedule must authorise the Commissioner or any of the Commissioner's officers or staff to do the things described in sub-paragraphs (1) to (3) at any time in the period of 7 days beginning with the day on which the warrant is issued.

(5) For the purposes of this paragraph, a copy of information is in an "appropriate form" if—

(a) it can be taken away, and

(b) it is visible and legible or it can readily be made visible and legible.

Copies of warrants

6. A judge who issues a warrant under this Schedule must—

(a) issue two copies of it, and

(b) certify them clearly as copies.

Execution of warrants: reasonable force

7. A person executing a warrant issued under this Schedule may use such reasonable force as may be necessary.

Execution of warrants: time when executed

8. A warrant issued under this Schedule may be executed only at a reasonable hour, unless it appears to the person executing it that there are grounds for suspecting that exercising it at a reasonable hour would defeat the object of the warrant.

Execution of warrants: occupier of premises

9. (1) If an occupier of the premises in respect of which a warrant is issued under this Schedule is present when the warrant is executed, the person executing the warrant must—

(a) show the occupier the warrant, and
(b) give the occupier a copy of it.

(2) Otherwise, a copy of the warrant must be left in a prominent place on the premises.

Execution of warrants: seizure of documents etc

10. (1) This paragraph applies where a person executing a warrant under this Schedule seizes something.

(2) The person must, on request—

(a) give a receipt for it, and
(b) give an occupier of the premises a copy of it.

(3) Sub-paragraph (2)(b) does not apply if the person executing the warrant considers that providing a copy would result in undue delay.

(4) Anything seized may be retained for so long as is necessary in all the circumstances.

Matters exempt from inspection and seizure: privileged communications

11. (1) The powers of inspection and seizure conferred by a warrant issued under this Schedule are not exercisable in respect of a communication which is made—

(a) between a professional legal adviser and the adviser's client, and
(b) in connection with the giving of legal advice to the client with respect to obligations, liabilities or rights under the data protection legislation.

(2) The powers of inspection and seizure conferred by a warrant issued under this Schedule are not exercisable in respect of a communication which is made—

(a) between a professional legal adviser and the adviser's client or between such an adviser or client and another person,
(b) in connection with or in contemplation of proceedings under or arising out of the data protection legislation, and
(c) for the purposes of such proceedings.

(3) Sub-paragraphs (1) and (2) do not prevent the exercise of powers conferred by a warrant issued under this Schedule in respect of—

(a) anything in the possession of a person other than the professional legal adviser or the adviser's client, or
(b) anything held with the intention of furthering a criminal purpose.

(4) The references to a communication in sub-paragraphs (1) and (2) include—

(a) a copy or other record of the communication, and
(b) anything enclosed with or referred to in the communication if made as described in sub-paragraph (1)(b) or in sub-paragraph (2)(b) and (c).

(5) In sub-paragraphs (1) to (3), the references to the client of a professional legal adviser include a person acting on behalf of such a client.

Matters exempt from inspection and seizure: Parliamentary privilege

12. The powers of inspection and seizure conferred by a warrant issued under this Schedule are not exercisable where their exercise would involve an infringement of the privileges of either House of Parliament.

Partially exempt material

13. (1) This paragraph applies if a person in occupation of premises in respect of which a warrant is issued under this Schedule objects to the inspection or seizure of any material under the warrant on the grounds that it consists partly of matters in respect of which those powers are not exercisable.

(2) The person must, if the person executing the warrant so requests, provide that person with a copy of so much of the material as is not exempt from those powers.

Return of warrants

14. (1) Where a warrant issued under this Schedule is executed—

(a) it must be returned to the court from which it was issued after being executed, and

(b) the person by whom it is executed must write on the warrant a statement of the powers that have been exercised under the warrant.

(2) Where a warrant issued under this Schedule is not executed, it must be returned to the court from which it was issued within the time authorised for its execution.

Offences

15. (1) It is an offence for a person—

(a) intentionally to obstruct a person in the execution of a warrant issued under this Schedule, or

(b) to fail without reasonable excuse to give a person executing such a warrant such assistance as the person may reasonably require for the execution of the warrant.

(2) It is an offence for a person—

(a) to make a statement in response to a requirement under paragraph 5(2)(c) or (d) or (3)(c) or (d) which the person knows to be false in a material respect, or

(b) recklessly to make a statement in response to such a requirement which is false in a material respect.

Self-incrimination

16. (1) An explanation given, or information provided, by a person in response to a requirement under paragraph 5(2)(c) or (d) or (3)(c) or (d) may only be used in evidence against that person—

(a) on a prosecution for an offence under a provision listed in sub-paragraph (2), or

(b) on a prosecution for any other offence where—

(i) in giving evidence that person makes a statement inconsistent with that explanation or information, and

(ii) evidence relating to that explanation or information is adduced, or a question relating to it is asked, by that person or on that person's behalf.

(2) Those provisions are—

(a) paragraph 15,

(b) section 5 of the Perjury Act 1911 (false statements made otherwise than on oath),

(c) section 44(2) of the Criminal Law (Consolidation) (Scotland) Act 1995 (false statements made otherwise than on oath), or

(d) Article 10 of the Perjury (Northern Ireland) Order 1979 (SI 1979/1714 (NI 19)) (false statutory declarations and other false unsworn statements).

Vessels, vehicles etc

17. In this Schedule—

(a) "premises" includes a vehicle, vessel or other means of transport, and

(b) references to the occupier of premises include the person in charge of a vehicle, vessel or other means of transport.

Scotland

18. In the application of this Schedule to Scotland—

(a) references to a judge of the High Court have effect as if they were references to a judge of the Court of Session,

(b) references to a circuit judge have effect as if they were references to the sheriff or the summary sheriff,

(c) references to information on oath have effect as if they were references to evidence on oath, and

(d) references to the court from which the warrant was issued have effect as if they were references to the sheriff clerk.

Northern Ireland

19. In the application of this Schedule to Northern Ireland—

(a) references to a circuit judge have effect as if they were references to a county court judge, and

(b) references to information on oath have effect as if they were references to a complaint on oath.

NOTES

Commencement: 25 May 2018 (see also the introductory notes to this Act preceding s 1 at **[1.2111]**).

SCHEDULE 16
PENALTIES

Section 155

Meaning of "penalty"

[1.2228]

1. In this Schedule, "penalty" means a penalty imposed by a penalty notice.

Notice of intent to impose penalty

2. (1) Before giving a person a penalty notice, the Commissioner must, by written notice (a "notice of intent") inform the person that the Commissioner intends to give a penalty notice.

(2) The Commissioner may not give a penalty notice to a person in reliance on a notice of intent after the end of the period of 6 months beginning when the notice of intent is given, subject to sub-paragraph (3).

(3) The period for giving a penalty notice to a person may be extended by agreement between the Commissioner and the person.

Contents of notice of intent

3. (1) A notice of intent must contain the following information—
- (a) the name and address of the person to whom the Commissioner proposes to give a penalty notice;
- (b) the reasons why the Commissioner proposes to give a penalty notice (see sub-paragraph (2));
- (c) an indication of the amount of the penalty the Commissioner proposes to impose, including any aggravating or mitigating factors that the Commissioner proposes to take into account.

(2) The information required under sub-paragraph (1)(b) includes—
- (a) a description of the circumstances of the failure, and
- (b) where the notice is given in respect of a failure described in section 149(2), the nature of the personal data involved in the failure.

(3) A notice of intent must also—
- (a) state that the person may make written representations about the Commissioner's intention to give a penalty notice, and
- (b) specify the period within which such representations may be made.

(4) The period specified for making written representations must be a period of not less than 21 days beginning when the notice of intent is given.

(5) If the Commissioner considers that it is appropriate for the person to have an opportunity to make oral representations about the Commissioner's intention to give a penalty notice, the notice of intent must also—
- (a) state that the person may make such representations, and
- (b) specify the arrangements for making such representations and the time at which, or the period within which, they may be made.

Giving a penalty notice

4. (1) The Commissioner may not give a penalty notice before a time, or before the end of a period, specified in the notice of intent for making oral or written representations.

(2) When deciding whether to give a penalty notice to a person and determining the amount of the penalty, the Commissioner must consider any oral or written representations made by the person in accordance with the notice of intent.

Contents of penalty notice

5. (1) A penalty notice must contain the following information—
- (a) the name and address of the person to whom it is addressed;
- (b) details of the notice of intent given to the person;
- (c) whether the Commissioner received oral or written representations in accordance with the notice of intent;
- (d) the reasons why the Commissioner proposes to impose the penalty (see sub-paragraph (2));
- (e) the reasons for the amount of the penalty, including any aggravating or mitigating factors that the Commissioner has taken into account;
- (f) details of how the penalty is to be paid;
- (g) details of the rights of appeal under section 162;
- (h) details of the Commissioner's enforcement powers under this Schedule.

(2) The information required under sub-paragraph (1)(d) includes—
- (a) a description of the circumstances of the failure, and
- (b) where the notice is given in respect of a failure described in section 149(2), the nature of the personal data involved in the failure.

Period for payment of penalty

6. (1) A penalty must be paid to the Commissioner within the period specified in the penalty notice.

(2) The period specified must be a period of not less than 28 days beginning when the penalty notice is given.

Variation of penalty

7. (1) The Commissioner may vary a penalty notice by giving written notice (a "penalty variation notice") to the person to whom it was given.

(2) A penalty variation notice must specify—
- (a) the penalty notice concerned, and
- (b) how it is varied.

(3) A penalty variation notice may not—
- (a) reduce the period for payment of the penalty;
- (b) increase the amount of the penalty;
- (c) otherwise vary the penalty notice to the detriment of the person to whom it was given.

(4) If—

(a) a penalty variation notice reduces the amount of the penalty, and

(b) when that notice is given, an amount has already been paid that exceeds the amount of the reduced penalty,

the Commissioner must repay the excess.

Cancellation of penalty

8. (1) The Commissioner may cancel a penalty notice by giving written notice to the person to whom it was given.

(2) If a penalty notice is cancelled, the Commissioner—

(a) may not take any further action under section 155 or this Schedule in relation to the failure to which that notice relates, and

(b) must repay any amount that has been paid in accordance with that notice.

Enforcement of payment

9. (1) The Commissioner must not take action to recover a penalty unless—

(a) the period specified in accordance with paragraph 6 has ended,

(b) any appeals against the penalty notice have been decided or otherwise ended,

(c) if the penalty notice has been varied, any appeals against the penalty variation notice have been decided or otherwise ended, and

(d) the period for the person to whom the penalty notice was given to appeal against the penalty, and any variation of it, has ended.

(2) In England and Wales, a penalty is recoverable—

(a) if the county court so orders, as if it were payable under an order of that court;

(b) if the High Court so orders, as if it were payable under an order of that court.

(3) In Scotland, a penalty may be enforced in the same manner as an extract registered decree arbitral bearing a warrant for execution issued by the sheriff court of any sheriffdom in Scotland.

(4) In Northern Ireland, a penalty is recoverable—

(a) if a county court so orders, as if it were payable under an order of that court;

(b) if the High Court so orders, as if it were payable under an order of that court.

NOTES

Commencement: 25 May 2018 (see also the introductory notes to this Act preceding s 1 at **[1.2111]**).

SCHEDULE 18
RELEVANT RECORDS

Section 184

Relevant records

[1.2229]

1. (1) In section 184, "relevant record" means—

(a) a relevant health record (see paragraph 2),

(b) a relevant record relating to a conviction or caution (see paragraph 3), or

(c) a relevant record relating to statutory functions (see paragraph 4).

(2) A record is not a "relevant record" to the extent that it relates, or is to relate, only to personal data which falls within *section 21(2)* (manual unstructured personal data held by FOI public authorities).

Relevant health records

2. "Relevant health record" means a health record which has been or is to be obtained by a data subject in the exercise of a data subject access right.

Relevant records relating to a conviction or caution

3. (1) "Relevant record relating to a conviction or caution" means a record which—

(a) has been or is to be obtained by a data subject in the exercise of a data subject access right from a person listed in sub-paragraph (2), and

(b) contains information relating to a conviction or caution.

(2) Those persons are—

(a) the chief constable of a police force maintained under section 2 of the Police Act 1996;

(b) the Commissioner of Police of the Metropolis;

(c) the Commissioner of Police for the City of London;

(d) the Chief Constable of the Police Service of Northern Ireland;

(e) the chief constable of the Police Service of Scotland;

(f) the Director General of the National Crime Agency;

(g) the Secretary of State.

(3) In this paragraph—

"caution" means a caution given to a person in England and Wales or Northern Ireland in respect of an offence which, at the time when the caution is given, is admitted;

"conviction" has the same meaning as in the Rehabilitation of Offenders Act 1974 or the Rehabilitation of Offenders (Northern Ireland) Order 1978 (SI 1978/1908 (NI 27)).

Relevant records relating to statutory functions

4. (1) "Relevant record relating to statutory functions" means a record which—

(a) has been or is to be obtained by a data subject in the exercise of a data subject access right from a person listed in sub-paragraph (2), and

(b) contains information relating to a relevant function in relation to that person.

(2) Those persons are—

(a) the Secretary of State;

(b) the Department for Communities in Northern Ireland;

(c) the Department of Justice in Northern Ireland;

(d) the Scottish Ministers;

(e) the Disclosure and Barring Service.

(3) In relation to the Secretary of State, the "relevant functions" are—

(a) the Secretary of State's functions in relation to a person sentenced to detention under—

(i) section 92 of the Powers of Criminal Courts (Sentencing) Act 2000,

(ii) section 205(2) or 208 of the Criminal Procedure (Scotland) Act 1995, or

(iii) Article 45 of the Criminal Justice (Children) (Northern Ireland) Order 1998 (SI 1998/1504 (NI 9));

(b) the Secretary of State's functions in relation to a person imprisoned or detained under—

(i) the Prison Act 1952,

(ii) the Prisons (Scotland) Act 1989, or

(iii) the Prison Act (Northern Ireland) 1953 (c 18 (NI));

(c) the Secretary of State's functions under—

(i) the Social Security Contributions and Benefits Act 1992,

(ii) the Social Security Administration Act 1992,

(iii) the Jobseekers Act 1995,

(iv) Part 5 of the Police Act 1997,

(v) Part 1 of the Welfare Reform Act 2007, or

(vi) Part 1 of the Welfare Reform Act 2012.

(4) In relation to the Department for Communities in Northern Ireland, the "relevant functions" are its functions under—

(a) the Social Security Contributions and Benefits (Northern Ireland) Act 1992,

(b) the Social Security Administration (Northern Ireland) Act 1992,

(c) the Jobseekers (Northern Ireland) Order 1995 (SI 1995/2705 (NI 15)), or

(d) Part 1 of the Welfare Reform Act (Northern Ireland) 2007 (c 2 (NI)).

(5) In relation to the Department of Justice in Northern Ireland, the "relevant functions" are its functions under Part 5 of the Police Act 1997.

(6) In relation to the Scottish Ministers, the "relevant functions" are their functions under

(a) Part 5 of the Police Act 1997, or

(b) Parts 1 and 2 of the Protection of Vulnerable Groups (Scotland) Act 2007 (asp 14).

(7) In relation to the Disclosure and Barring Service, the "relevant functions" are its functions under—

(a) Part 5 of the Police Act 1997,

(b) the Safeguarding Vulnerable Groups Act 2006, or

(c) the Safeguarding Vulnerable Groups (Northern Ireland) Order 2007 (SI 2007/1351 (NI 11)).

Data subject access right

5. In this Schedule, "data subject access right" means a right under—

(a) Article 15 of the *GDPR* (right of access by the data subject);

(b) Article 20 of the *GDPR* (right to data portability);

(c) section 45 of this Act (law enforcement processing: right of access by the data subject);

(d) section 94 of this Act (intelligence services processing: right of access by the data subject).

Records stating that personal data is not processed

6. For the purposes of this Schedule, a record which states that a controller is not processing personal data relating to a particular matter is to be taken to be a record containing information relating to that matter.

Power to amend

7. (1) The Secretary of State may by regulations amend this Schedule.

(2) Regulations under this paragraph are subject to the affirmative resolution procedure.

NOTES

Commencement: 25 May 2018 (see also the introductory notes to this Act preceding s 1 at **[1.2111]**).

For the words in italics in para 1 there are substituted the words "Article 2(1A) of the UK GDPR", and for "GDPR" in italics in both places that it occurs in para 5 there is substituted "UK GDPR", by the Data Protection, Privacy and Electronic Communications (Amendments etc) (EU Exit) Regulations 2019, SI 2019/419, reg 4, Sch 2, paras 1, 99, as from exit day (as defined in the European Union (Withdrawal) Act 2018, s 20), for transitional provisions etc, see the 2019 Regulations at **[2.2122]** et seq.

SCHEDULE 19
MINOR AND CONSEQUENTIAL AMENDMENTS

Section 211

PARTS 1 AND 2

(Part 1 of this Schedule contains amendments to primary legislation (including the repeal of the Data Protection Act 1998). Part 2 contains amendments to other legislation. In so far as relevant to this work, they have been incorporated at the appropriate place.)

PART 3
MODIFICATIONS

Introduction

[1.2230]

430. (1) Unless the context otherwise requires, legislation described in sub-paragraph (2) has effect on and after the day on which this Part of this Schedule comes into force as if it were modified in accordance with this Part of this Schedule.

(2) That legislation is—

(a) subordinate legislation made before the day on which this Part of this Schedule comes into force;

(b) primary legislation that is passed or made before the end of the Session in which this Act is passed.

(3) In this Part of this Schedule—

"primary legislation" has the meaning given in section 211(7);

"references" includes any references, however expressed.

General modifications

431. (1) References to a particular provision of, or made under, the Data Protection Act 1998 have effect as references to the equivalent provision or provisions of, or made under, the data protection legislation.

(2) Other references to the Data Protection Act 1998 have effect as references to the data protection legislation.

(3) References to disclosure, use or other processing of information that is prohibited or restricted by an enactment which include disclosure, use or other processing of information that is prohibited or restricted by the Data Protection Act 1998 have effect as if they included disclosure, use or other processing of information that is prohibited or restricted by *the GDPR or the applied GDPR*.

Specific modification of references to terms used in the Data Protection Act 1998

432. (1) References to personal data, and to the processing of such data, as defined in the Data Protection Act 1998, have effect as references to personal data, and to the processing of such data, as defined for the purposes of Parts 5 to 7 of this Act (see section 3(2), (4) and (14)).

(2) References to processing as defined in the Data Protection Act 1998, in relation to information, have effect as references to processing as defined in section 3(4).

(3) References to a data subject as defined in the Data Protection Act 1998 have effect as references to a data subject as defined in section 3(5).

(4) References to a data controller as defined in the Data Protection Act 1998 have effect as references to a controller as defined for the purposes of Parts 5 to 7 of this Act (see section 3(6) and (14)).

(5) References to the data protection principles set out in the Data Protection Act 1998 have effect as references to the principles set out in—

(a) Article 5(1) of *the GDPR and the applied GDPR*, and

(b) sections 34(1) and 85(1) of this Act.

(6) References to direct marketing as defined in section 11 of the Data Protection Act 1998 have effect as references to direct marketing as defined in section 122 of this Act.

(7) References to a health professional within the meaning of section 69(1) of the Data Protection Act 1998 have effect as references to a health professional within the meaning of section 204 of this Act.

(8) References to a health record within the meaning of section 68(2) of the Data Protection Act 1998 have effect as references to a health record within the meaning of section 205 of this Act.

NOTES

Commencement: 25 May 2018 (see also the introductory notes to this Act preceding s 1 at **[1.2111]**).

Paras 431, 432: for the words in italics in there are substituted the words "the UK GDPR" by the Data Protection, Privacy and Electronic Communications (Amendments etc) (EU Exit) Regulations 2019, SI 2019/419, reg 4, Sch 2, paras 1, 100, as from exit day (as defined in the European Union (Withdrawal) Act 2018, s 20), for transitional provisions etc, see the 2019 Regulations at **[2.2122]** et seq.

PART 4
SUPPLEMENTARY

Definitions

[1.2231]

433. Section 3(14) does not apply to this Schedule.

Provision inserted in subordinate legislation by this Schedule

434. Provision inserted into subordinate legislation by this Schedule may be amended or revoked as if it had been inserted using the power under which the subordinate legislation was originally made.

NOTES

Commencement: 25 May 2018 (see also the introductory notes to this Act preceding s 1 at **[1.2111]**).

SCHEDULE 20
TRANSITIONAL PROVISION ETC

Section 213

PART 1
GENERAL

Interpretation

[1.2232]

1. (1) In this Schedule—

"the 1984 Act" means the Data Protection Act 1984;

"the 1998 Act" means the Data Protection Act 1998;

"the 2014 Regulations" means the Criminal Justice and Data Protection (Protocol No 36) Regulations 2014 (SI 2014/3141);

"data controller" has the same meaning as in the 1998 Act (see section 1 of that Act);

"the old data protection principles" means the principles set out in—

(a) Part 1 of Schedule 1 to the 1998 Act, and

(b) regulation 30 of the 2014 Regulations.

(2) A provision of the 1998 Act that has effect by virtue of this Schedule is not, by virtue of that, part of the data protection legislation (as defined in section 3).

NOTES

Commencement: 25 May 2018 (see also the introductory notes to this Act preceding s 1 at **[1.2111]**).

PART 2
RIGHTS OF DATA SUBJECTS

Right of access to personal data under the 1998 Act

[1.2233]

2. (1) The repeal of sections 7 to 9A of the 1998 Act (right of access to personal data) does not affect the application of those sections after the relevant time in a case in which a data controller received a request under section 7 of that Act (right of access to personal data) before the relevant time.

(2) The repeal of sections 7 and 8 of the 1998 Act and the revocation of regulation 44 of the 2014 Regulations (which applies those sections with modifications) do not affect the application of those sections and that regulation after the relevant time in a case in which a UK competent authority received a request under section 7 of the 1998 Act (as applied by that regulation) before the relevant time.

Right to prevent processing likely to cause damage or distress under the 1998 Act

3. (1) The repeal of section 10 of the 1998 Act (right to prevent processing likely to cause damage or distress) does not affect the application of that section after the relevant time in a case in which an individual gave notice in writing to a data controller under that section before the relevant time.

(2) In this paragraph, "the relevant time" means the time when the repeal of section 10 of the 1998 Act comes into force.

Automated processing under the 1998 Act

5. (1) The repeal of section 12 of the 1998 Act (rights in relation to automated decision-taking) does not affect the application of that section after the relevant time in relation to a decision taken by a person before that time if—

(a) in taking the decision the person failed to comply with section 12(1) of the 1998 Act, or

(b) at the relevant time—

(i) the person had not taken all of the steps required under section 12(2) or (3) of the 1998 Act, or

(ii) the period specified in section 12(2)(b) of the 1998 Act (for an individual to require a person to reconsider a decision) had not expired.

(2) In this paragraph, "the relevant time" means the time when the repeal of section 12 of the 1998 Act comes into force.

Compensation for contravention of the 1998 Act or Part 4 of the 2014 Regulations

6. (1) The repeal of section 13 of the 1998 Act (compensation for failure to comply with certain requirements) does not affect the application of that section after the relevant time in relation to damage or distress suffered at any time by reason of an act or omission before the relevant time.

(2) The revocation of regulation 45 of the 2014 Regulations (right to compensation) does not affect the application of that regulation after the relevant time in relation to damage or distress suffered at any time by reason of an act or omission before the relevant time.

(3) "The relevant time" means—

(a) in sub-paragraph (1), the time when the repeal of section 13 of the 1998 Act comes into force;

(b) in sub-paragraph (2), the time when the revocation of regulation 45 of the 2014 Regulation comes into force.

Rectification, blocking, erasure and destruction under the 1998 Act

7. (1) The repeal of section 14(1) to (3) and (6) of the 1998 Act (rectification, blocking, erasure and destruction of inaccurate personal data) does not affect the application of those provisions after the relevant time in a case in which an application was made under subsection (1) of that section before the relevant time.

(2) The repeal of section 14(4) to (6) of the 1998 Act (rectification, blocking, erasure and destruction: risk of further contravention in circumstances entitling data subject to compensation under section 13 of the 1998 Act) does not affect the application of those provisions after the relevant time in a case in which an application was made under subsection (4) of that section before the relevant time.

(3) In this paragraph, "the relevant time" means the time when the repeal of section 14 of the 1998 Act comes into force.

Jurisdiction and procedure under the 1998 Act

8. The repeal of section 15 of the 1998 Act (jurisdiction and procedure) does not affect the application of that section in connection with sections 7 to 14 of the 1998 Act as they have effect by virtue of this Schedule.

Exemptions under the 1998 Act

9. (1) The repeal of Part 4 of the 1998 Act (exemptions) does not affect the application of that Part after the relevant time in connection with a provision of Part 2 of the 1998 Act as it has effect after that time by virtue of paragraphs 2 to 7 of this Schedule.

(2) The revocation of the relevant Orders, and the repeal mentioned in sub-paragraph (1), do not affect the application of the relevant Orders after the relevant time in connection with a provision of Part 2 of the 1998 Act as it has effect as described in sub-paragraph (1).

(3) In this paragraph—

"the relevant Orders" means—

(a) the Data Protection (Corporate Finance Exemption) Order 2000 (SI 2000/184);

(b) the Data Protection (Subject Access Modification) (Health) Order 2000 (SI 2000/413);

(c) the Data Protection (Subject Access Modification) (Education) Order 2000 (SI 2000/414);

(d) the Data Protection (Subject Access Modification) (Social Work) Order 2000 (SI 2000/415);

(e) the Data Protection (Crown Appointments) Order 2000 (SI 2000/416);

(f) Data Protection (Miscellaneous Subject Access Exemptions) Order 2000 (SI 2000/419);

(g) Data Protection (Designated Codes of Practice) (No 2) Order 2000 (SI 2000/1864);

"the relevant time" means the time when the repeal of the provision of Part 2 of the 1998 Act in question comes into force.

(4) As regards certificates issued under section 28(2) of the 1998 Act, see Part 5 of this Schedule.

NOTES

Commencement: 25 May 2018 (see also the introductory notes to this Act preceding s 1 at **[1.2111]**).

PART 5
NATIONAL SECURITY CERTIFICATES

National security certificates: processing of personal data under the 1998 Act

[1.2234]

17. (1) The repeal of section 28(2) to (12) of the 1998 Act does not affect the application of those provisions after the relevant time with respect to the processing of personal data to which the 1998 Act (including as it has effect by virtue of this Schedule) applies.

(2) A certificate issued under section 28(2) of the 1998 Act continues to have effect after the relevant time with respect to the processing of personal data to which the 1998 Act (including as it has effect by virtue of this Schedule) applies.

(3) Where a certificate continues to have effect under sub-paragraph (2) after the relevant time, it may be revoked or quashed in accordance with section 28 of the 1998 Act after the relevant time.

(4) In this paragraph, "the relevant time" means the time when the repeal of section 28 of the 1998 Act comes into force.

NOTES

Commencement: 25 May 2018 (see also the introductory notes to this Act preceding s 1 at **[1.2111]**).

PART 6
THE INFORMATION COMMISSIONER

Appointment etc

[1.2235]

19. (1) On and after the relevant day, the individual who was the Commissioner immediately before that day—

(a) continues to be the Commissioner,

(b) is to be treated as having been appointed under Schedule 12 to this Act, and

(c) holds office for the period—

(i) beginning with the relevant day, and

(ii) lasting for 7 years less a period equal to the individual's pre-commencement term.

(2) On and after the relevant day, a resolution passed by the House of Commons for the purposes of paragraph 3 of Schedule 5 to the 1998 Act (salary and pension of Commissioner), and not superseded before that day, is to be treated as having been passed for the purposes of paragraph 4 of Schedule 12 to this Act.

(3) In this paragraph—

"pre-commencement term", in relation to an individual, means the period during which the individual was the Commissioner before the relevant day;

"the relevant day" means the day on which Schedule 12 to this Act comes into force.

Requests for assessment

27. (1) The repeal of section 42 of the 1998 Act (requests for assessment) does not affect the application of that section after the relevant time in a case in which the Commissioner received a request under that section before the relevant time, subject to sub-paragraph (2).

(2) The Commissioner is only required to make an assessment of acts and omissions that took place before the relevant time.

(3) In this paragraph, "the relevant time" means the time when the repeal of section 42 of the 1998 Act comes into force.

NOTES

Commencement: 25 May 2018 (see also the introductory notes to this Act preceding s 1 at **[1.2111]**).

PART 7
ENFORCEMENT ETC UNDER THE 1998 ACT

Assessment notices

[1.2236]

32. (1) The repeal of sections 41A and 41B of the 1998 Act (assessment notices) does not affect the application of those sections after the relevant time in a case in which—

(a) the Commissioner served a notice under section 41A of the 1998 Act before the relevant time (and did not cancel it before that time), or

(b) the Commissioner considers it appropriate, after the relevant time, to investigate—

(i) whether a data controller complied with the old data protection principles before that time, or

(ii) whether a data controller complied with the sixth data protection principle sections after that time.

(2) The revocation of the Data Protection (Assessment Notices) (Designation of National Health Service Bodies) Order 2014 (SI 2014/3282), and the repeals mentioned in sub-paragraph (1), do not affect the application of that Order in a case described in sub-paragraph (1).

(3) Sub-paragraph (1) does not enable the Secretary of State, after the relevant time, to make an order under section 41A(2)(b) or (c) of the 1998 Act (data controllers on whom an assessment notice may be served) designating a public authority or person for the purposes of that section.

(4) Section 41A of the 1998 Act, as it has effect by virtue of sub-paragraph (1), has effect as if subsections (8) and (11) (duty to review designation orders) were omitted.

(5) The repeal of section 41C of the 1998 Act (code of practice about assessment notice) does not affect the application, after the relevant time, of the code issued under that section and in force immediately before the relevant time in relation to the exercise of the Commissioner's functions under and in connection with section 41A of the 1998 Act, as it has effect by virtue of sub-paragraph (1).

(6) In this paragraph, "the relevant time" means the time when the repeal of section 41A of the 1998 Act comes into force.

Enforcement notices

33. (1) The repeal of sections 40 and 41 of the 1998 Act (enforcement notices) does not affect the application of those sections after the relevant time in a case in which—

(a) the Commissioner served a notice under section 40 of the 1998 Act before the relevant time (and did not cancel it before that time), or

(b) the Commissioner is satisfied, after that time, that a data controller—

(i) contravened the old data protection principles before that time, or

(ii) contravened the sixth data protection principle sections after that time.

(2) In this paragraph, "the relevant time" means the time when the repeal of section 40 of the 1998 Act comes into force.

Offences

36. (1) The repeal of sections 47, 60 and 61 of the 1998 Act (offences of failing to comply with certain notices and of providing false information etc in response to a notice) does not affect the application of those sections after the relevant time in connection with an information notice, special information notice or enforcement notice served under Part 5 of the 1998 Act—

(a) before the relevant time, or

(b) after that time in reliance on this Schedule.

(2) In this paragraph, "the relevant time" means the time when the repeal of section 47 of the 1998 Act comes into force.

Monetary penalties

38. (1) The repeal of sections 55A, 55B, 55D and 55E of the 1998 Act (monetary penalties) does not affect the application of those provisions after the relevant time in a case in which—

(a) the Commissioner served a monetary penalty notice under section 55A of the 1998 Act before the relevant time,

(b) the Commissioner served a notice of intent under section 55B of the 1998 Act before the relevant time, or

(c) the Commissioner considers it appropriate, after the relevant time, to serve a notice mentioned in paragraph (a) or (b) in respect of—

(i) a contravention of section 4(4) of the 1998 Act before the relevant time, or

(ii) a contravention of the sixth data protection principle sections after the relevant time.

(2) The revocation of the relevant subordinate legislation, and the repeals mentioned in sub-paragraph (1), do not affect the application of the relevant subordinate legislation (or of provisions of the 1998 Act applied by them) after the relevant time in a case described in sub-paragraph (1).

(3) Guidance issued under section 55C of the 1998 Act (guidance about monetary penalty notices) which is in force immediately before the relevant time continues in force after that time for the purposes of the Commissioner's exercise of functions under sections 55A and 55B of the 1998 Act as they have effect by virtue of this paragraph.

(4) In this paragraph—

"the relevant subordinate legislation" means—

(a) the Data Protection (Monetary Penalties) (Maximum Penalty and Notices) Regulations 2010 (SI 2010/31);

(b) the Data Protection (Monetary Penalties) Order 2010 (SI 2010/910);

"the relevant time" means the time when the repeal of section 55A of the 1998 Act comes into force.

Appeals

39. (1) The repeal of sections 48 and 49 of the 1998 Act (appeals) does not affect the application of those sections after the relevant time in relation to a notice served under the 1998 Act or a determination made under section 45 of that Act—

(a) before the relevant time, or

(b) after that time in reliance on this Schedule.

(2) In this paragraph, "the relevant time" means the time when the repeal of section 48 of the 1998 Act comes into force.

NOTES

Commencement: 25 May 2018 (see also the introductory notes to this Act preceding s 1 at **[1.2111]**).

"SCHEDULE 21
FURTHER TRANSITIONAL PROVISION ETC

Section 213

PART 1
INTERPRETATION

The applied GPDR

[1.2237]

1. In this Schedule, "the applied GDPR" means the EU GDPR as applied by Chapter 3 of Part 2 before exit day.

NOTES

Commencement: exit day (as defined in the European Union (Withdrawal) Act 2018, s 20).

Inserted by the Data Protection, Privacy and Electronic Communications (Amendments etc) (EU Exit) Regulations 2019, SI 2019/419, reg 4, Sch 2, paras 1, 102, as from exit day (as defined in the European Union (Withdrawal) Act 2018, s 20), for transitional provisions etc, see the 2019 Regulations at **[2.2122]** et seq.

PART 2
CONTINUATION OF EXISTING ACTS ETC

Merger of the directly applicable GDPR and the applied GDPR

[1.2238]

2. (1) On and after exit day, references in an enactment to the UK GDPR (including the reference in the definition of "the data protection legislation" in section 3(9)) include—

(a) the EU GDPR as it was directly applicable to the United Kingdom before exit day, read with Chapter 2 of Part 2 of this Act as it had effect before exit day, and

(b) the applied GDPR, read with Chapter 3 of Part 2 of this Act as it had effect before exit day.

(2) On and after exit day, references in an enactment to, or to a provision of, Chapter 2 of Part 2 of this Act (including general references to this Act or to Part 2 of this Act) include that Chapter or that provision as applied by Chapter 3 of Part 2 of this Act as it had effect before exit day.

(3) Sub-paragraphs (1) and (2) have effect—

(a) in relation to references in this Act, except as otherwise provided;

(b) in relation to references in other enactments, unless the context otherwise requires.

3. (1) Anything done in connection with the EU GDPR as it was directly applicable to the United Kingdom before exit day, the applied GDPR or this Act—

(a) if in force or effective immediately before exit day, continues to be in force or effective on and after exit day, and

(b) if in the process of being done immediately before exit day, continues to be done on and after exit day.

(2) References in this paragraph to anything done include references to anything omitted to be done.

NOTES

Commencement: exit day (as defined in the European Union (Withdrawal) Act 2018, s 20).

Inserted by the Data Protection, Privacy and Electronic Communications (Amendments etc) (EU Exit) Regulations 2019, SI 2019/419, reg 4, Sch 2, paras 1, 102, as from exit day (as defined in the European Union (Withdrawal) Act 2018, s 20), for transitional provisions etc, see the 2019 Regulations at **[2.2122]** et seq.

EUROPEAN UNION (WITHDRAWAL) ACT 2018

(2018 c 16)

NOTES

Only the provisions of this Act most relevant to employment law are reproduced. Provisions not reproduced are not annotated.

This Act makes provision for the legal consequences of the withdrawal of the United Kingdom from the European Union, as from exit day (as defined in s 20 at **[1.2248]**). As at 15 May 2019, exit day is defined as 11pm on 31 October 2019; s 20(3) and (4) confer powers on a Minister of the Crown to amend the definition of exit day. As it is not known whether this power will be exercised, those provisions of this Act which will come into force on exit day are shown with the annotation "Commencement: to be appointed".

ARRANGEMENT OF SECTIONS

SCHEDULES

An Act to repeal the European Communities Act 1972 and make other provision in connection with the withdrawal of the United Kingdom from the EU.

[26 June 2018]

Repeal of the ECA

[1.2239]

1 Repeal of the European Communities Act 1972

The European Communities Act 1972 is repealed on exit day.

NOTES

Commencement: to be appointed.

Retention of existing EU law

[1.2240]

2 Saving for EU-derived domestic legislation

(1) EU-derived domestic legislation, as it has effect in domestic law immediately before exit day, continues to have effect in domestic law on and after exit day.

(2) In this section "EU-derived domestic legislation" means any enactment so far as—

(a) made under section 2(2) of, or paragraph 1A of Schedule 2 to, the European Communities Act 1972,

(b) passed or made, or operating, for a purpose mentioned in section 2(2)(a) or (b) of that Act,

(c) relating to anything—

(i) which falls within paragraph (a) or (b), or

(ii) to which section 3(1) or 4(1) applies, or

(d) relating otherwise to the EU or the EEA,

but does not include any enactment contained in the European Communities Act 1972.

(3) This section is subject to section 5 and Schedule 1 (exceptions to savings and incorporation).

NOTES

Commencement: to be appointed.

[1.2241]

3 Incorporation of direct EU legislation

(1) Direct EU legislation, so far as operative immediately before exit day, forms part of domestic law on and after exit day.

(2) In this Act "direct EU legislation" means—

(a) any EU regulation, EU decision or EU tertiary legislation, as it has effect in EU law immediately before exit day and so far as—

(i) it is not an exempt EU instrument (for which see section 20(1) and Schedule 6),

(ii) it is not an EU decision addressed only to a member State other than the United Kingdom, and

(iii) its effect is not reproduced in an enactment to which section 2(1) applies,

(b) any Annex to the EEA agreement, as it has effect in EU law immediately before exit day and so far as—

(i) it refers to, or contains adaptations of, anything falling within paragraph (a), and

(ii) its effect is not reproduced in an enactment to which section 2(1) applies, or

(c) Protocol 1 to the EEA agreement (which contains horizontal adaptations that apply in relation to EU instruments referred to in the Annexes to that agreement), as it has effect in EU law immediately before exit day.

(3) For the purposes of this Act, any direct EU legislation is operative immediately before exit day if—

(a) in the case of anything which comes into force at a particular time and is stated to apply from a later time, it is in force and applies immediately before exit day,

(b) in the case of a decision which specifies to whom it is addressed, it has been notified to that person before exit day, and

(c) in any other case, it is in force immediately before exit day.

(4) This section—

(a) brings into domestic law any direct EU legislation only in the form of the English language version of that legislation, and

(b) does not apply to any such legislation for which there is no such version,

but paragraph (a) does not affect the use of the other language versions of that legislation for the purposes of interpreting it.

(5) This section is subject to section 5 and Schedule 1 (exceptions to savings and incorporation).

NOTES

Commencement: to be appointed.

[1.2242]

4 Saving for rights etc under section 2(1) of the ECA

(1) Any rights, powers, liabilities, obligations, restrictions, remedies and procedures which, immediately before exit day—

(a) are recognised and available in domestic law by virtue of section 2(1) of the European Communities Act 1972, and

(b) are enforced, allowed and followed accordingly,

continue on and after exit day to be recognised and available in domestic law (and to be enforced, allowed and followed accordingly).

(2) Subsection (1) does not apply to any rights, powers, liabilities, obligations, restrictions, remedies or procedures so far as they—

(a) form part of domestic law by virtue of section 3, or

(b) arise under an EU directive (including as applied by the EEA agreement) and are not of a kind recognised by the European Court or any court or tribunal in the United Kingdom in a case decided before exit day (whether or not as an essential part of the decision in the case).

(3) This section is subject to section 5 and Schedule 1 (exceptions to savings and incorporation).

NOTES

Commencement: to be appointed.

[1.2243]

5 Exceptions to savings and incorporation

(1) The principle of the supremacy of EU law does not apply to any enactment or rule of law passed or made on or after exit day.

(2) Accordingly, the principle of the supremacy of EU law continues to apply on or after exit day so far as relevant to the interpretation, disapplication or quashing of any enactment or rule of law passed or made before exit day.

(3) Subsection (1) does not prevent the principle of the supremacy of EU law from applying to a modification made on or after exit day of any enactment or rule of law passed or made before exit day if the application of the principle is consistent with the intention of the modification.

(4) The Charter of Fundamental Rights is not part of domestic law on or after exit day.

(5) Subsection (4) does not affect the retention in domestic law on or after exit day in accordance with this Act of any fundamental rights or principles which exist irrespective of the Charter (and references to the Charter in any case law are, so far as necessary for this purpose, to be read as if they were references to any corresponding retained fundamental rights or principles).

(6) Schedule 1 (which makes further provision about exceptions to savings and incorporation) has effect.

NOTES

Commencement: 4 July 2018 (sub-s (6) certain purposes); to be appointed (otherwise).

[1.2244]

6 Interpretation of retained EU law

(1) A court or tribunal—

(a) is not bound by any principles laid down, or any decisions made, on or after exit day by the European Court, and

(b) cannot refer any matter to the European Court on or after exit day.

(2) Subject to this and subsections (3) to (6), a court or tribunal may have regard to anything done on or after exit day by the European Court, another EU entity or the EU so far as it is relevant to any matter before the court or tribunal.

(3) Any question as to the validity, meaning or effect of any retained EU law is to be decided, so far as that law is unmodified on or after exit day and so far as they are relevant to it—

(a) in accordance with any retained case law and any retained general principles of EU law, and

(b) having regard (among other things) to the limits, immediately before exit day, of EU competences.

(4) But—

(a) the Supreme Court is not bound by any retained EU case law,

(b) the High Court of Justiciary is not bound by any retained EU case law when—

(i) sitting as a court of appeal otherwise than in relation to a compatibility issue (within the meaning given by section 288ZA(2) of the Criminal Procedure (Scotland) Act 1995) or a devolution issue (within the meaning given by paragraph 1 of Schedule 6 to the Scotland Act 1998), or

(ii) sitting on a reference under section 123(1) of the Criminal Procedure (Scotland) Act 1995, and

(c) no court or tribunal is bound by any retained domestic case law that it would not otherwise be bound by.

(5) In deciding whether to depart from any retained EU case law, the Supreme Court or the High Court of Justiciary must apply the same test as it would apply in deciding whether to depart from its own case law.

(6) Subsection (3) does not prevent the validity, meaning or effect of any retained EU law which has been modified on or after exit day from being decided as provided for in that subsection if doing so is consistent with the intention of the modifications.

(7) In this Act—

"retained case law" means—

(a) retained domestic case law, and
(b) retained EU case law;

"retained domestic case law" means any principles laid down by, and any decisions of, a court or tribunal in the United Kingdom, as they have effect immediately before exit day and so far as they—

(a) relate to anything to which section 2, 3 or 4 applies, and
(b) are not excluded by section 5 or Schedule 1,

(as those principles and decisions are modified by or under this Act or by other domestic law from time to time);

"retained EU case law" means any principles laid down by, and any decisions of, the European Court, as they have effect in EU law immediately before exit day and so far as they—

(a) relate to anything to which section 2, 3 or 4 applies, and
(b) are not excluded by section 5 or Schedule 1,

(as those principles and decisions are modified by or under this Act or by other domestic law from time to time);

"retained EU law" means anything which, on or after exit day, continues to be, or forms part of, domestic law by virtue of section 2, 3 or 4 or subsection (3) or (6) above (as that body of law is added to or otherwise modified by or under this Act or by other domestic law from time to time);

"retained general principles of EU law" means the general principles of EU law, as they have effect in EU law immediately before exit day and so far as they—

(a) relate to anything to which section 2, 3 or 4 applies, and
(b) are not excluded by section 5 or Schedule 1,

(as those principles are modified by or under this Act or by other domestic law from time to time).

NOTES

Commencement: 4 July 2018 (sub-s (7)); to be appointed (otherwise).

[1.2245]

7 Status of retained EU law

(1) Anything which—

(a) was, immediately before exit day, primary legislation of a particular kind, subordinate legislation of a particular kind or another enactment of a particular kind, and
(b) continues to be domestic law on and after exit day by virtue of section 2,

continues to be domestic law as an enactment of the same kind.

(2) Retained direct principal EU legislation cannot be modified by any primary or subordinate legislation other than—

(a) an Act of Parliament,
(b) any other primary legislation (so far as it has the power to make such a modification), or
(c) any subordinate legislation so far as it is made under a power which permits such a modification by virtue of—
 (i) paragraph 3, 5(3)(a) or (4)(a), 8(3), 10(3)(a) or (4)(a), 11(2)(a) or 12(3) of Schedule 8,
 (ii) any other provision made by or under this Act,
 (iii) any provision made by or under an Act of Parliament passed before, and in the same Session as, this Act, or
 (iv) any provision made on or after the passing of this Act by or under primary legislation.

(3) Retained direct minor EU legislation cannot be modified by any primary or subordinate legislation other than—

(a) an Act of Parliament,
(b) any other primary legislation (so far as it has the power to make such a modification), or
(c) any subordinate legislation so far as it is made under a power which permits such a modification by virtue of—
 (i) paragraph 3, 5(2) or (4)(a), 8(3), 10(2) or (4)(a) or 12(3) of Schedule 8,
 (ii) any other provision made by or under this Act,
 (iii) any provision made by or under an Act of Parliament passed before, and in the same Session as, this Act, or
 (iv) any provision made on or after the passing of this Act by or under primary legislation.

(4) Anything which is retained EU law by virtue of section 4 cannot be modified by any primary or subordinate legislation other than—

(a) an Act of Parliament,
(b) any other primary legislation (so far as it has the power to make such a modification), or
(c) any subordinate legislation so far as it is made under a power which permits such a modification by virtue of—
 (i) paragraph 3, 5(3)(b) or (4)(b), 8(3), 10(3)(b) or (4)(b), 11(2)(b) or 12(3) of Schedule 8,
 (ii) any other provision made by or under this Act,

(iii) any provision made by or under an Act of Parliament passed before, and in the same Session as, this Act, or

(iv) any provision made on or after the passing of this Act by or under primary legislation.

(5) For other provisions about the status of retained EU law, see—

(a) section 5(1) to (3) (status of retained EU law in relation to other enactments or rules of law),

(b) section 6 (status of retained case law and retained general principles of EU law),

(c) section 15(2) and Part 2 of Schedule 5 (status of retained EU law for the purposes of the rules of evidence),

(d) paragraphs 13 to 16 of Schedule 8 (affirmative and enhanced scrutiny procedure for, and information about, instruments which amend or revoke subordinate legislation under section 2(2) of the European Communities Act 1972 including subordinate legislation implementing EU directives),

(e) paragraphs 19 and 20 of that Schedule (status of certain retained direct EU legislation for the purposes of the Interpretation Act 1978), and

(f) paragraph 30 of that Schedule (status of retained direct EU legislation for the purposes of the Human Rights Act 1998).

(6) In this Act—

"retained direct minor EU legislation" means any retained direct EU legislation which is not retained direct principal EU legislation;

"retained direct principal EU legislation" means—

(a) any EU regulation so far as it—

(i) forms part of domestic law on and after exit day by virtue of section 3, and

(ii) was not EU tertiary legislation immediately before exit day, or

(b) any Annex to the EEA agreement so far as it—

(as modified by or under this Act or by other domestic law from time to time).

(i) forms part of domestic law on and after exit day by virtue of section 3, and

(ii) refers to, or contains adaptations of, any EU regulation so far as it falls within paragraph (a),

NOTES

Commencement: to be appointed.

Main powers in connection with withdrawal

[1.2246]

8 Dealing with deficiencies arising from withdrawal

(1) A Minister of the Crown may by regulations make such provision as the Minister considers appropriate to prevent, remedy or mitigate—

(a) any failure of retained EU law to operate effectively, or

(b) any other deficiency in retained EU law,

arising from the withdrawal of the United Kingdom from the EU.

(2) Deficiencies in retained EU law are where the Minister considers that retained EU law—

(a) contains anything which has no practical application in relation to the United Kingdom or any part of it or is otherwise redundant or substantially redundant,

(b) confers functions on, or in relation to, EU entities which no longer have functions in that respect under EU law in relation to the United Kingdom or any part of it,

(c) makes provision for, or in connection with, reciprocal arrangements between—

(i) the United Kingdom or any part of it or a public authority in the United Kingdom, and

(ii) the EU, an EU entity, a member State or a public authority in a member State,

which no longer exist or are no longer appropriate,

(d) makes provision for, or in connection with, other arrangements which—

(i) involve the EU, an EU entity, a member State or a public authority in a member State, or

(ii) are otherwise dependent upon the United Kingdom's membership of the EU,

and which no longer exist or are no longer appropriate,

(e) makes provision for, or in connection with, any reciprocal or other arrangements not falling within paragraph (c) or (d) which no longer exist, or are no longer appropriate, as a result of the United Kingdom ceasing to be a party to any of the EU Treaties,

(f) does not contain any functions or restrictions which—

(i) were in an EU directive and in force immediately before exit day (including any power to make EU tertiary legislation), and

(ii) it is appropriate to retain, or

(g) contains EU references which are no longer appropriate.

(3) There is also a deficiency in retained EU law where the Minister considers that there is—

(a) anything in retained EU law which is of a similar kind to any deficiency which falls within subsection (2), or

(b) a deficiency in retained EU law of a kind described, or provided for, in regulations made by a Minister of the Crown.

(4) But retained EU law is not deficient merely because it does not contain any modification of EU law which is adopted or notified, comes into force or only applies on or after exit day.

(5) Regulations under subsection (1) may make any provision that could be made by an Act of Parliament.

(6) Regulations under subsection (1) may (among other things) provide for functions of EU entities or public authorities in member States (including making an instrument of a legislative character or providing funding) to be—

(a) exercisable instead by a public authority (whether or not established for the purpose) in the United Kingdom, or

(b) replaced, abolished or otherwise modified.

(7) But regulations under subsection (1) may not—

(a) impose or increase taxation or fees,

(b) make retrospective provision,

(c) create a relevant criminal offence,

(d) establish a public authority,

(e) be made to implement the withdrawal agreement,

(f) amend, repeal or revoke the Human Rights Act 1998 or any subordinate legislation made under it, or

(g) amend or repeal the Scotland Act 1998, the Government of Wales Act 2006 or the Northern Ireland Act 1998 (unless the regulations are made by virtue of paragraph 21(b) of Schedule 7 to this Act or are amending or repealing any provision of those Acts which modifies another enactment).

(8) No regulations may be made under this section after the end of the period of two years beginning with exit day.

(9) The reference in subsection (1) to a failure or other deficiency arising from the withdrawal of the United Kingdom from the EU includes a reference to any failure or other deficiency arising from that withdrawal taken together with the operation of any provision, or the interaction between any provisions, made by or under this Act.

NOTES

Commencement: 26 June 2018.

Regulations: the European Public Limited-Liability Company (Amendment etc) (EU Exit) Regulations 2018, SI 2018/1298 at **[2.2101]**; the Data Protection, Privacy and Electronic Communications (Amendments etc) (EU Exit) Regulations 2019, SI 2019/419 at **[2.2122]**; the Cross-Border Mediation (EU Directive) (EU Exit) Regulations 2019, SI 2019/469 at **[2.2130]**; the Civil Jurisdiction and Judgments (Amendment) (EU Exit) Regulations 2019, SI 2019/479 at **[2.2134]**; the Employment Rights (Amendment) (EU Exit) Regulations 2019, SI 2019/535 at **[2.2180]**; the Employment Rights (Amendment) (EU Exit) (No 2) Regulations 2019, SI 2019/536 at **[2.2183]**. Note that only Regulations reproduced in this Handbook are listed; the numerous other Regulations made under this section are considered outside the scope of this work.

Financial and other matters

[1.2247]

19 Future interaction with the law and agencies of the EU

Nothing in this Act shall prevent the United Kingdom from—

(a) replicating in domestic law any EU law made on or after exit day, or

(b) continuing to participate in, or have a formal relationship with, the agencies of the EU after exit day.

NOTES

Commencement: 4 July 2018.

General and final provision

[1.2248]

20 Interpretation

(1) In this Act—

"Charter of Fundamental Rights" means the Charter of Fundamental Rights of the European Union of 7 December 2000, as adapted at Strasbourg on 12 December 2007;

"devolved authority" means—

(a) the Scottish Ministers,

(b) the Welsh Ministers, or

(c) a Northern Ireland department;

"domestic law" means—

(a) in section 3, the law of England and Wales, Scotland and Northern Ireland, and

(b) in any other case, the law of England and Wales, Scotland or Northern Ireland;

"the EEA" means the European Economic Area;

"enactment" means an enactment whenever passed or made and includes—

(a) an enactment contained in any Order in Council, order, rules, regulations, scheme, warrant, byelaw or other instrument made under an Act,

(b) an enactment contained in any Order in Council made in exercise of Her Majesty's Prerogative,

(c) an enactment contained in, or in an instrument made under, an Act of the Scottish Parliament,

(d) an enactment contained in, or in an instrument made under, a Measure or Act of the National Assembly for Wales,

(e) an enactment contained in, or in an instrument made under, Northern Ireland legislation,

(f) an enactment contained in any instrument made by a member of the Scottish Government, the Welsh Ministers, the First Minister for Wales, the Counsel General to the Welsh Government, a Northern Ireland Minister, the First Minister in Northern

Ireland, the deputy First Minister in Northern Ireland or a Northern Ireland department in exercise of prerogative or other executive functions of Her Majesty which are exercisable by such a person on behalf of Her Majesty,

(g) an enactment contained in, or in an instrument made under, a Measure of the Church Assembly or of the General Synod of the Church of England, and

(h) except in sections 2 and 7 or where there is otherwise a contrary intention, any retained direct EU legislation;

"EU decision" means—

(a) a decision within the meaning of Article 288 of the Treaty on the Functioning of the European Union, or

(b) a decision under former Article 34(2)(c) of the Treaty on European Union;

"EU directive" means a directive within the meaning of Article 288 of the Treaty on the Functioning of the European Union;

"EU entity" means an EU institution or any office, body or agency of the EU;

"EU reference" means—

(a) any reference to the EU, an EU entity or a member State,

(b) any reference to an EU directive or any other EU law, or

(c) any other reference which relates to the EU;

"EU regulation" means a regulation within the meaning of Article 288 of the Treaty on the Functioning of the European Union;

"EU tertiary legislation" means—

(a) any provision made under—

(i) an EU regulation,

(ii) a decision within the meaning of Article 288 of the Treaty on the Functioning of the European Union, or

(iii) an EU directive,

by virtue of Article 290 or 291(2) of the Treaty on the Functioning of the European Union or former Article 202 of the Treaty establishing the European Community, or

(b) any measure adopted in accordance with former Article 34(2)(c) of the Treaty on European Union to implement decisions under former Article 34(2)(c),

but does not include any such provision or measure which is an EU directive;

"exempt EU instrument" means anything which is an exempt EU instrument by virtue of Schedule 6;

"exit day" [means 31 October 2019 at 11.00 p.m. (and] see subsections (2) to (5));

"member State" (except in the definitions of "direct EU legislation" and "EU reference") does not include the United Kingdom;

"Minister of the Crown" has the same meaning as in the Ministers of the Crown Act 1975 and also includes the Commissioners for Her Majesty's Revenue and Customs;

"modify" includes amend, repeal or revoke (and related expressions are to be read accordingly);

"Northern Ireland devolved authority" means the First Minister and deputy First Minister in Northern Ireland acting jointly, a Northern Ireland Minister or a Northern Ireland department;

"primary legislation" means—

(a) an Act of Parliament,

(b) an Act of the Scottish Parliament,

(c) a Measure or Act of the National Assembly for Wales, or

(d) Northern Ireland legislation;

"public authority" means a public authority within the meaning of section 6 of the Human Rights Act 1998;

"relevant criminal offence" means an offence for which an individual who has reached the age of 18 (or, in relation to Scotland or Northern Ireland, 21) is capable of being sentenced to imprisonment for a term of more than 2 years (ignoring any enactment prohibiting or restricting the imprisonment of individuals who have no previous convictions);

"retained direct EU legislation" means any direct EU legislation which forms part of domestic law by virtue of section 3 (as modified by or under this Act or by other domestic law from time to time, and including any instruments made under it on or after exit day);

"retrospective provision", in relation to provision made by regulations, means provision taking effect from a date earlier than the date on which the regulations are made;

"subordinate legislation" means—

(a) any Order in Council, order, rules, regulations, scheme, warrant, byelaw or other instrument made under any Act, or

(b) any instrument made under an Act of the Scottish Parliament, Northern Ireland legislation or a Measure or Act of the National Assembly for Wales,

and (except in section 7 or Schedule 2 or where there is a contrary intention) includes any Order in Council, order, rules, regulations, scheme, warrant, byelaw or other instrument made on or after exit day under any retained direct EU legislation;

"tribunal" means any tribunal in which legal proceedings may be brought;

"Wales" and "Welsh zone" have the same meaning as in the Government of Wales Act 2006 (see section 158 of that Act);

"withdrawal agreement" means an agreement (whether or not ratified) between the United Kingdom and the EU under Article 50(2) of the Treaty on European Union which sets out the arrangements for the United Kingdom's withdrawal from the EU.

(2) In this [Act references to before, after or on exit day, or to beginning with exit day, are to be read as references to before, after or at 11.00 p.m. on 31 October 2019 or (as the case may be) to beginning with 11.00 p.m. on that day].

(3) Subsection (4) applies if the day or time on or at which the Treaties are to cease to apply to the United Kingdom in accordance with Article 50(3) of the Treaty on European Union is different from that specified in the definition of "exit day" in subsection (1).

(4) A Minister of the Crown may by regulations—

(a) amend the definition of "exit day" in subsection (1) to ensure that the day and time specified in the definition are the day and time that the Treaties are to cease to apply to the United Kingdom, and

(b) amend subsection (2) in consequence of any such amendment.

(5) In subsections (3) and (4) "the Treaties" means the Treaty on European Union and the Treaty on the Functioning of the European Union.

(6) In this Act references to anything which continues to be domestic law by virtue of section 2 include references to anything to which subsection (1) of that section applies which continues to be domestic law on or after exit day (whether or not it would have done so irrespective of that section).

(7) In this Act references to anything which is retained EU law by virtue of section 4 include references to any modifications, made by or under this Act or by other domestic law from time to time, of the rights, powers, liabilities, obligations, restrictions, remedies or procedures concerned.

(8) References in this Act (however expressed) to a public authority in the United Kingdom include references to a public authority in any part of the United Kingdom.

(9) References in this Act to former Article 34(2)(c) of the Treaty on European Union are references to that Article as it had effect at any time before the coming into force of the Treaty of Lisbon.

(10) Any other reference in this Act to—

(a) an Article of the Treaty on European Union or the Treaty on the Functioning of the European Union, or

(b) Article 10 of Title VII of Protocol 36 to those treaties,

includes a reference to that Article as applied by Article 106a of the Euratom Treaty.

NOTES

Commencement: 26 June 2018.

Sub-s (1): words in square brackets in the definition "exit day" substituted by the European Union (Withdrawal) Act 2018 (Exit Day) (Amendment) (No 2) Regulations 2019, SI 2019/859, reg 2(1), (2), as from 11 April 2019.

Sub-s (2): words in square brackets substituted by SI 2019/859, reg 2(1), (3), as from 11 April 2019.

Regulations: the European Union (Withdrawal) Act 2018 (Exit Day) (Amendment) Regulations 2019, SI 2019/718; the European Union (Withdrawal) Act 2018 (Exit Day) (Amendment) (No 2) Regulations 2019, SI 2019/859. Note that the amendments made by the European Union (Withdrawal) Act 2018 (Exit Day) (Amendment) (No 2) Regulations 2019 supersede the amendments made by the earlier Regulations.

[1.2249]

21 Index of defined expressions

(1) In this Act, the expressions listed in the left-hand column have the meaning given by, or are to be interpreted in accordance with, the provisions listed in the right-hand column.

Expression	*Provision*
Anything which continues to be domestic law by virtue of section 2	Section 20(6)
Anything which is retained EU law by virtue of section 4	Section 20(7)
Article (in relation to the Treaty on European Union or the Treaty on the Functioning of the European Union)	Section 20(10)
Charter of Fundamental Rights	Section 20(1)
Devolved authority	Section 20(1)
Direct EU legislation	Section 3(2)
Domestic law	Section 20(1)
The EEA	Section 20(1)
EEA agreement	Schedule 1 to the Interpretation Act 1978
Enactment	Section 20(1)
The EU	Schedule 1 to the Interpretation Act 1978
EU decision	Section 20(1)
EU directive	Section 20(1)
EU entity	Section 20(1)
EU institution	Schedule 1 to the Interpretation Act 1978
EU instrument	Schedule 1 to the Interpretation Act 1978
Euratom Treaty	Schedule 1 to the Interpretation Act 1978
EU reference	Section 20(1)

Expression	*Provision*
EU regulation	Section 20(1)
European Court	Schedule 1 to the Interpretation Act 1978
EU tertiary legislation	Section 20(1)
EU Treaties	Schedule 1 to the Interpretation Act 1978
Exempt EU instrument	Section 20(1)
Exit day (and related expressions)	Section 20(1) to (5)
Former Article 34(2)(c) of Treaty on European Union	Section 20(9)
Member State	Section 20(1) and Schedule 1 to the Interpretation Act 1978
Minister of the Crown	Section 20(1)
Modify (and related expressions)	Section 20(1)
Northern Ireland devolved authority	Section 20(1)
Operative (in relation to direct EU legislation)	Section 3(3)
Primary legislation	Section 20(1)
Public authority	Section 20(1)
Public authority in the United Kingdom (however expressed)	Section 20(8)
Relevant criminal offence	Section 20(1) (and paragraph 44 of Schedule 8)
Retained case law	Section 6(7)
Retained direct EU legislation	Section 20(1)
Retained direct minor EU legislation	Section 7(6)
Retained direct principal EU legislation	Section 7(6)
Retained domestic case law	Section 6(7)
Retained EU case law	Section 6(7)
Retained EU law	Section 6(7)
Retained general principles of EU law	Section 6(7)
Retrospective provision	Section 20(1)
Subordinate legislation	Section 20(1)
Tribunal	Section 20(1)
Wales	Section 20(1)
Welsh zone	Section 20(1)
Withdrawal agreement	Section 20(1)

(2) See paragraph 22 of Schedule 8 for amendments made by this Act to Schedule 1 to the Interpretation Act 1978.

NOTES

Commencement: 26 June 2018.

[1.2250]

23 Consequential and transitional provision

(1) A Minister of the Crown may by regulations make such provision as the Minister considers appropriate in consequence of this Act.

(2) The power to make regulations under subsection (1) may (among other things) be exercised by modifying any provision made by or under an enactment.

(3) In subsection (2) "enactment" does not include primary legislation passed or made after the end of the Session in which this Act is passed.

(4) No regulations may be made under subsection (1) after the end of the period of 10 years beginning with exit day.

(5) Parts 1 and 2 of Schedule 8 (which contain consequential provision) have effect.

(6) A Minister of the Crown may by regulations make such transitional, transitory or saving provision as the Minister considers appropriate in connection with the coming into force of any provision of this Act (including its operation in connection with exit day).

(7) Parts 3 and 4 of Schedule 8 (which contain transitional, transitory and saving provision) have effect.

(8) The enactments mentioned in Schedule 9 (which contains repeals not made elsewhere in this Act) are repealed to the extent specified.

NOTES

Commencement: 26 June 2018 (sub-ss (1)–(4), (6), and sub-s (7) for certain purposes); 4 July 2018 (sub-ss (5), (7), (8) for certain purposes); 1 March 2019 (sub-s (7) for certain purposes); exit day (as defined in the European Union (Withdrawal) Act 2018, s 20) (sub-s (8) for certain purposes); to be appointed (otherwise).

Regulations: the European Union (Withdrawal) Act 2018 (Commencement and Transitional Provisions) Regulations 2018, SI 2018/808; the European Communities (Designation Orders) (Revocation) (EU Exit) Regulations 2018, SI 2018/1011; the European Union (Definition of Treaties Orders) (Revocation) (EU Exit) Regulations 2018, SI 2018/1012. Other Regulations made under this section are not listed as they are outside the scope of this work.

[1.2251]

24 Extent

(1) Subject to subsections (2) and (3), this Act extends to England and Wales, Scotland and Northern Ireland.

(2) Any provision of this Act which amends or repeals an enactment has the same extent as the enactment amended or repealed.

(3) Regulations under section 8(1) or 23 may make provision which extends to Gibraltar—

- (a) modifying any enactment which—
  - (i) extends to Gibraltar and relates to European Parliamentary elections, or
  - (ii) extends to Gibraltar for any purpose which is connected with Gibraltar forming part of an electoral region, under the European Parliamentary Elections Act 2002, for the purposes of such elections, or
- (b) which is supplementary, incidental, consequential, transitional, transitory or saving provision in connection with a modification within paragraph (a).

NOTES

Commencement: 26 June 2018.

[1.2252]

25 Commencement and short title

(1) The following provisions—

- (a) sections 8 to 11 (including Schedule 2),
- (b) paragraphs 4, 5, 21(2)(b), 48(b), 51(2)(c) and (d) and (4) of Schedule 3 (and section 12(8) and (12) so far as relating to those paragraphs),
- (c) sections 13 and 14 (including Schedule 4),
- (d) sections 16 to 18,
- (e) sections 20 to 22 (including Schedules 6 and 7),
- (f) section 23(1) to (4) and (6),
- (g) paragraph 41(10), 43 and 44 of Schedule 8 (and section 23(7) so far as relating to those paragraphs),
- (h) section 24, and
- (i) this section,

come into force on the day on which this Act is passed.

(2) In section 12—

- (a) subsection (2) comes into force on the day on which this Act is passed for the purposes of making regulations under section 30A of the Scotland Act 1998,
- (b) subsection (4) comes into force on that day for the purposes of making regulations under section 109A of the Government of Wales Act 2006, and
- (c) subsection (6) comes into force on that day for the purposes of making regulations under section 6A of the Northern Ireland Act 1998.

(3) In Schedule 3—

- (a) paragraph 1(b) comes into force on the day on which this Act is passed for the purposes of making regulations under section 57(4) of the Scotland Act 1998,
- (b) paragraph 2 comes into force on that day for the purposes of making regulations under section 80(8) of the Government of Wales Act 2006,
- (c) paragraph 3(b) comes into force on that day for the purposes of making regulations under section 24(3) of the Northern Ireland Act 1998,
- (d) paragraph 24(2) comes into force on that day for the purposes of making regulations under section 30A of the Scotland Act 1998,
- (e) paragraph 24(3) comes into force on that day for the purposes of making regulations under section 57(4) of the Scotland Act 1998,
- (f) paragraph 25 comes into force on that day for the purposes of making regulations under section 30A or 57(4) of the Scotland Act 1998,
- (g) paragraph 43 comes into force on that day for the purposes of making regulations under section 80(8) or 109A of the Government of Wales Act 2006, and
- (h) paragraphs 57 and 58 come into force on that day for the purposes of making regulations under section 6A or 24(3) of the Northern Ireland Act 1998;

and section 12(7) and (12), so far as relating to each of those paragraphs, comes into force on that day for the purposes of making the regulations mentioned above in relation to that paragraph.

(4) The provisions of this Act, so far as they are not brought into force by subsections (1) to (3), come into force on such day as a Minister of the Crown may by regulations appoint; and different days may be appointed for different purposes.

(5) This Act may be cited as the European Union (Withdrawal) Act 2018.

NOTES

Commencement: 26 June 2018.

Regulations: the European Union (Withdrawal) Act 2018 (Commencement and Transitional Provisions) Regulations 2018, SI 2018/808; the European Union (Withdrawal) Act 2018 (Commencement No 2) Regulations 2019, SI 2019/399.

SCHEDULES

SCHEDULE 1
FURTHER PROVISION ABOUT EXCEPTIONS TO SAVINGS AND INCORPORATION

Section 5(6)

Challenges to validity of retained EU law

[1.2253]

1. (1) There is no right in domestic law on or after exit day to challenge any retained EU law on the basis that, immediately before exit day, an EU instrument was invalid.

(2) Sub-paragraph (1) does not apply so far as—

(a) the European Court has decided before exit day that the instrument is invalid, or

(b) the challenge is of a kind described, or provided for, in regulations made by a Minister of the Crown.

(3) Regulations under sub-paragraph (2)(b) may (among other things) provide for a challenge which would otherwise have been against an EU institution to be against a public authority in the United Kingdom.

General principles of EU law

2. No general principle of EU law is part of domestic law on or after exit day if it was not recognised as a general principle of EU law by the European Court in a case decided before exit day (whether or not as an essential part of the decision in the case).

3. (1) There is no right of action in domestic law on or after exit day based on a failure to comply with any of the general principles of EU law.

(2) No court or tribunal or other public authority may, on or after exit day—

(a) disapply or quash any enactment or other rule of law, or

(b) quash any conduct or otherwise decide that it is unlawful,

because it is incompatible with any of the general principles of EU law.

Rule in Francovich

4. There is no right in domestic law on or after exit day to damages in accordance with the rule in *Francovich*.

Interpretation

5. (1) References in section 5 and this Schedule to the principle of the supremacy of EU law, the Charter of Fundamental Rights, any general principle of EU law or the rule in *Francovich* are to be read as references to that principle, Charter or rule so far as it would otherwise continue to be, or form part of, domestic law on or after exit day in accordance with this Act.

(2) Accordingly (among other things) the references to the principle of the supremacy of EU law in section 5(2) and (3) do not include anything which would bring into domestic law any modification of EU law which is adopted or notified, comes into force or only applies on or after exit day.

NOTES

Commencement: 4 July 2018 (para 1(2)(b) for the purpose of making regulations, and para 1(3)); to be appointed (otherwise).

Regulations: the Challenges to Validity of EU Instruments (EU Exit) Regulations 2019, SI 2019/673.

SCHEDULE 8
CONSEQUENTIAL, TRANSITIONAL, TRANSITORY AND SAVING PROVISION

Section 23(5) and (7)

PART 1
GENERAL CONSEQUENTIAL PROVISION

Existing ambulatory references to retained direct EU legislation

[1.2254]

1. (1) Any reference which, immediately before exit day—

(a) exists in—

(i) any enactment,

(ii) any EU regulation, EU decision, EU tertiary legislation or provision of the EEA agreement which is to form part of domestic law by virtue of section 3, or

(iii) any document relating to anything falling within sub-paragraph (i) or (ii), and

(b) is a reference to (as it has effect from time to time) any EU regulation, EU decision, EU tertiary legislation or provision of the EEA agreement which is to form part of domestic law by virtue of section 3,

is to be read, on or after exit day, as a reference to the EU regulation, EU decision, EU tertiary legislation or provision of the EEA agreement as it forms part of domestic law by virtue of section 3 and, unless the contrary intention appears, as modified by domestic law from time to time.

(2) Sub-paragraph (1) does not apply to any reference which forms part of a power to make, confirm or approve subordinate legislation so far as the power to make the subordinate legislation—

(a) continues to be part of domestic law by virtue of section 2, and

(b) is subject to a procedure before Parliament, the Scottish Parliament, the National Assembly for Wales or the Northern Ireland Assembly.

(3) Sub-paragraphs (1) and (2) are subject to any other provision made by or under this Act or any other enactment.

Other existing ambulatory references

2. (1) Any reference which—

(a) exists, immediately before exit day, in—

(i) any enactment,

(ii) any EU regulation, EU decision, EU tertiary legislation or provision of the EEA agreement which is to form part of domestic law by virtue of section 3, or

(iii) any document relating to anything falling within sub-paragraph (i) or (ii),

(b) is not a reference to which paragraph 1(1) applies, and

(c) is, immediately before exit day, a reference to (as it has effect from time to time) any of the EU Treaties, any EU instrument or any other document of an EU entity,

is to be read, on or after exit day, as a reference to the EU Treaty, instrument or document as it has effect immediately before exit day.

(2) Sub-paragraph (1) does not apply to any reference which forms part of a power to make, confirm or approve subordinate legislation so far as the power to make the subordinate legislation—

(a) continues to be part of domestic law by virtue of section 2, and

(b) is subject to a procedure before Parliament, the Scottish Parliament, the National Assembly for Wales or the Northern Ireland Assembly.

(3) Sub-paragraphs (1) and (2) are subject to any other provision made by or under this Act or any other enactment.

Existing powers to make subordinate legislation etc

3. (1) Any power to make, confirm or approve subordinate legislation which—

(a) was conferred before the day on which this Act is passed, and

(b) is capable of being exercised to amend or repeal (or, as the case may be, result in the amendment or repeal of) an enactment contained in primary legislation,

is to be read, so far as the context permits or requires, as being capable of being exercised to modify (or, as the case may be, result in the modification of) any retained direct EU legislation or anything which is retained EU law by virtue of section 4.

(2) But sub-paragraph (1) does not apply if the power to make, confirm or approve subordinate legislation is only capable of being exercised to amend or repeal (or, as the case may be, result in the amendment or repeal of) an enactment contained in Northern Ireland legislation which is an Order in Council.

4. (1) Any subordinate legislation which—

(a) is, or is to be, made, confirmed or approved by virtue of paragraph 3, and

(b) amends or revokes any retained direct principal EU legislation,

is to be subject to the same procedure (if any) before Parliament, the Scottish Parliament, the National Assembly for Wales or the Northern Ireland Assembly as would apply to that legislation if it were amending or repealing an enactment contained in primary legislation.

(2) Any subordinate legislation which—

(a) is, or is to be, made, confirmed or approved by virtue of paragraph 3, and

(b) either—

(i) modifies (otherwise than as a connected modification and otherwise than by way of amending or revoking it) any retained direct principal EU legislation, or

(ii) modifies (otherwise than as a connected modification) anything which is retained EU law by virtue of section 4,

is to be subject to the same procedure (if any) before Parliament, the Scottish Parliament, the National Assembly for Wales or the Northern Ireland Assembly as would apply to that legislation if it were amending or repealing an enactment contained in primary legislation.

(3) Any subordinate legislation which—

(a) is, or is to be, made, confirmed or approved by virtue of paragraph 3, and

(b) amends or revokes any retained direct minor EU legislation,

is to be subject to the same procedure (if any) before Parliament, the Scottish Parliament, the National Assembly for Wales or the Northern Ireland Assembly as would apply to that legislation if it were amending or revoking an enactment contained in subordinate legislation made under a different power.

(4) Any subordinate legislation which—

(a) is, or is to be, made, confirmed or approved by virtue of paragraph 3, and

(b) modifies (otherwise than as a connected modification and otherwise than by way of amending or revoking it) any retained direct minor EU legislation,

is to be subject to the same procedure (if any) before Parliament, the Scottish Parliament, the National Assembly for Wales or the Northern Ireland Assembly as would apply to that legislation if it were amending or revoking an enactment contained in subordinate legislation made under a different power.

(5) Any subordinate legislation which—

(a) is, or is to be, made, confirmed or approved by virtue of paragraph 3, and

(b) modifies as a connected modification any retained direct EU legislation or anything which is retained EU law by virtue of section 4,

is to be subject to the same procedure (if any) before Parliament, the Scottish Parliament, the National Assembly for Wales or the Northern Ireland Assembly as would apply to the modification to which it is connected.

(6) Any provision which may be made, confirmed or approved by virtue of paragraph 3 may be included in the same instrument as any other provision which may be so made, confirmed or approved.

(7) Where more than one procedure of a kind falling within sub-paragraph (8) would otherwise apply in the same legislature for an instrument falling within sub-paragraph (6), the higher procedure is to apply in the legislature concerned.

(8) The order of procedures is as follows (the highest first)—

(a) a procedure which requires a statement of urgency before the instrument is made and the approval of the instrument after it is made to enable it to remain in force,

(b) a procedure which requires the approval of the instrument in draft before it is made,

(c) a procedure not falling within paragraph (a) which requires the approval of the instrument after it is made to enable it to come into, or remain in, force,

(d) a procedure which provides for the annulment of the instrument after it is made,

(e) a procedure not falling within any of the above paragraphs which provides for the laying of the instrument after it is made,

(f) no procedure.

(9) The references in this paragraph to amending or repealing an enactment contained in primary legislation or amending or revoking an enactment contained in subordinate legislation do not include references to amending or repealing or (as the case may be) amending or revoking an enactment contained in any Northern Ireland legislation which is an Order in Council.

(10) In this paragraph "connected modification" means a modification which is supplementary, incidental, consequential, transitional or transitory, or a saving, in connection with—

(a) another modification under the power of retained direct EU legislation or anything which is retained EU law by virtue of section 4, or

(b) anything else done under the power.

5. (1) This paragraph applies to any power to make, confirm or approve subordinate legislation—

(a) which was conferred before the day on which this Act is passed, and

(b) is not capable of being exercised as mentioned in paragraph 3(1)(b) or is only capable of being so exercised in relation to Northern Ireland legislation which is an Order in Council.

(2) Any power to which this paragraph applies (other than a power to which sub-paragraph (4) applies) is to be read—

(a) so far as is consistent with any retained direct principal EU legislation or anything which is retained EU law by virtue of section 4, and

(b) so far as the context permits or requires,

as being capable of being exercised to modify (or, as the case may be, result in the modification of) any retained direct minor EU legislation.

(3) Any power to which this paragraph applies (other than a power to which sub-paragraph (4) applies) is to be read, so far as the context permits or requires, as being capable of being exercised to modify (or, as the case may be, result in the modification of)—

(a) any retained direct principal EU legislation, or

(b) anything which is retained EU law by virtue of section 4,

so far as the modification is supplementary, incidental or consequential in connection with any modification of any retained direct minor EU legislation by virtue of sub-paragraph (2).

(4) Any power to which this paragraph applies so far as it is a power to make, confirm or approve transitional, transitory or saving provision is to be read, so far as the context permits or requires, as being capable of being exercised to modify (or, as the case may be, result in the modification of)—

(a) any retained direct EU legislation, or

(b) anything which is retained EU law by virtue of section 4.

6. Any subordinate legislation which is, or is to be, made, confirmed or approved by virtue of paragraph 5(2), (3) or (4) is to be subject to the same procedure (if any) before Parliament, the Scottish Parliament, the National Assembly for Wales or the Northern Ireland Assembly as would apply to that legislation if it were doing anything else under the power.

7. Any power to make, confirm or approve subordinate legislation which, immediately before exit day, is subject to an implied restriction that it is exercisable only compatibly with EU law is to be read on or after exit day without that restriction or any corresponding restriction in relation to compatibility with retained EU law.

8. (1) Paragraphs 3 to 7 and this paragraph—

(a) do not prevent the conferral of wider powers,
(b) do not apply so far as section 57(4) of the Scotland Act 1998, section 80(8) of the Government of Wales Act 2006 or section 24(3) of the Northern Ireland Act 1998 applies (or would apply when in force on and after exit day), and
(c) are subject to any other provision made by or under this Act or any other enactment.

(2) For the purposes of paragraphs 3 and 5—
(a) a power is conferred whether or not it is in force, and
(b) a power in retained direct EU legislation is not conferred before the day on which this Act is passed.

(3) A power which, by virtue of paragraph 3 or 5 or any Act of Parliament passed before, and in the same Session as, this Act, is capable of being exercised to modify any retained EU law is capable of being so exercised before exit day so as to come into force on or after exit day.

Affirmative procedure for instruments which amend or revoke subordinate legislation made under section 2(2) of the ECA (including subordinate legislation implementing EU directives)

13. (1) A statutory instrument which—
(a) is to be made on or after exit day by a Minister of the Crown under a power conferred before the beginning of the Session in which this Act is passed,
(b) is not to be made jointly with any person who is not a Minister of the Crown,
(c) amends or revokes any subordinate legislation made under section 2(2) of the European Communities Act 1972, and
(d) would otherwise be subject to a lower procedure before each House of Parliament and no procedure before any other legislature,

may not be made unless a draft of the instrument has been laid before, and approved by a resolution of, each House of Parliament.

(2) Sub-paragraph (1) has effect instead of any other provision which would otherwise apply in relation to the procedure for such an instrument before each House of Parliament but does not affect any other requirements which apply in relation to making, confirming or approving the instrument.

(3) Any provision which—
(a) may be made under the power mentioned in sub-paragraph (1)(a),
(b) is not provision which falls within sub-paragraph (1)(c), and
(c) is subject to a lower procedure than the procedure provided for by sub-paragraph (1),

may be included in an instrument to which sub-paragraph (1) applies (and is accordingly subject to the procedure provided for by that sub-paragraph instead of the lower procedure).

(4) If a draft of a statutory instrument which—
(a) is to be made on or after exit day by a Minister of the Crown under a power conferred before the beginning of the Session in which this Act is passed,
(b) is not to be made jointly with any person who is not a Minister of the Crown,
(c) amends or revokes any provision, made otherwise than under section 2(2) of the European Communities Act 1972 (whether or not by way of amendment), of subordinate legislation made under that section, and
(d) would otherwise be subject to a lower procedure before each House of Parliament and no procedure before any other legislature,

is laid before, and approved by a resolution of, each House of Parliament, then the instrument is not subject to the lower procedure.

(5) This paragraph applies to an instrument which is subject to a procedure before the House of Commons only as it applies to an instrument which is subject to a procedure before each House of Parliament but as if the references to each House of Parliament were references to the House of Commons only.

(6) For the purposes of this paragraph, the order of procedures is as follows (the highest first)—
(a) a procedure which requires a statement of urgency before the instrument is made and the approval of the instrument after it is made to enable it to remain in force,
(b) a procedure which requires the approval of the instrument in draft before it is made,
(c) a procedure not falling within paragraph (a) which requires the approval of the instrument after it is made to enable it to come into, or remain in, force,
(d) a procedure which provides for the annulment of the instrument after it is made,
(e) a procedure not falling within any of the above paragraphs which provides for the laying of the instrument after it is made,
(f) no procedure.

(7) For the purposes of this paragraph a power is conferred whether or not it is in force.

(8) References in this paragraph, other than in sub-paragraph (4), to subordinate legislation made under section 2(2) of the European Communities Act 1972—
(a) do not include references to any provision of such legislation which is made (whether or not by way of amendment) otherwise than under section 2(2) of that Act, and
(b) do include references to subordinate legislation made otherwise than under section 2(2) of that Act so far as that legislation is amended by provision made under that section (but do not include references to any primary legislation so far as so amended).

(9) This paragraph is subject to any other provision made by or under this Act or any other enactment.

Enhanced scrutiny procedure for instruments which amend or revoke subordinate legislation under section 2(2) of the ECA (including subordinate legislation implementing EU directives)

14. (1) This paragraph applies where, on or after exit day—

(a) a statutory instrument which—

(i) amends or revokes subordinate legislation made under section 2(2) of the European Communities Act 1972, and

(ii) is made under a power conferred before the beginning of the Session in which this Act is passed, or

(b) a draft of such an instrument,

is to be laid before each House of Parliament and subject to no procedure before any other legislature.

(2) The relevant authority must publish, in such manner as the relevant authority considers appropriate, a draft of the instrument at least 28 days before the instrument or draft is laid.

(3) The relevant authority must make a scrutiny statement before the instrument or draft is laid.

(4) A scrutiny statement is a statement—

(a) setting out the steps which the relevant authority has taken to make the draft instrument published in accordance with sub-paragraph (2) available to each House of Parliament,

(b) containing information about the relevant authority's response to—

(i) any recommendations made by a committee of either House of Parliament about the published draft instrument, and

(ii) any other representations made to the relevant authority about the published draft instrument, and

(c) containing any other information that the relevant authority considers appropriate in relation to the scrutiny of the instrument or draft instrument which is to be laid.

(5) A scrutiny statement must be in writing and must be published in such manner as the relevant authority considers appropriate.

(6) Sub-paragraphs (2) to (5) do not apply if the relevant authority—

(a) makes a statement in writing to the effect that the relevant authority is of the opinion that, by reason of urgency, sub-paragraphs (2) to (5) should not apply, and

(b) publishes the statement in such manner as the relevant authority considers appropriate.

(7) This paragraph does not apply in relation to any laying before each House of Parliament of an instrument or draft instrument where an equivalent draft instrument (ignoring any differences relating to procedure) has previously been laid before both Houses.

(8) This paragraph applies to an instrument which is subject to a procedure before the House of Commons only as it applies to an instrument which is subject to a procedure before each House of Parliament but as if references to each or either House of Parliament, or both Houses, were references to the House of Commons only.

(9) For the purposes of this paragraph—

(a) a power is conferred whether or not it is in force,

(b) the draft instrument published under sub-paragraph (2) need not be identical to the final version of the instrument or draft instrument as laid,

(c) where an instrument or draft is laid before each House of Parliament on different days, the earlier day is to be taken as the day on which it is laid before both Houses, and

(d) in calculating the period of 28 days, no account is to be taken of any time during which—

(i) Parliament is dissolved or prorogued, or

(ii) either House of Parliament is adjourned for more than four days.

(10) Sub-paragraph (8) of paragraph 13 applies for the purposes of this paragraph as it applies for the purposes of sub-paragraph (1) of that paragraph.

(11) In this paragraph "the relevant authority" means—

(a) in the case of an Order in Council or Order of Council, the Minister of the Crown who has responsibility in relation to the instrument,

(b) in the case of any other statutory instrument which is not to be made by a Minister of the Crown, the person who is to make the instrument, and

(c) in any other case, the Minister of the Crown who is to make the instrument.

(12) This paragraph is subject to any other provision made by or under this Act or any other enactment.

Explanatory statements for instruments amending or revoking regulations etc under section 2(2) of the ECA

15. (1) This paragraph applies where, on or after exit day—

(a) a statutory instrument which amends or revokes any subordinate legislation made under section 2(2) of the European Communities Act 1972, or

(b) a draft of such an instrument,

is to be laid before each House of Parliament or before the House of Commons only.

(2) Before the instrument or draft is laid, the relevant authority must make a statement as to why, in the opinion of the relevant authority, there are good reasons for the amendment or revocation.

(3) Before the instrument or draft is laid, the relevant authority must make a statement otherwise explaining—

(a) the law which is relevant to the amendment or revocation, and

(b) the effect of the amendment or revocation on retained EU law.

(4) If the relevant authority fails to make a statement required by sub-paragraph (2) or (3) before the instrument or draft is laid—

(a) a Minister of the Crown, or

(b) where the relevant authority is not a Minister of the Crown, the relevant authority,

must make a statement explaining why the relevant authority has failed to make the statement as so required.

(5) A statement under sub-paragraph (2), (3) or (4) must be made in writing and be published in such manner as the person making it considers appropriate.

(6) For the purposes of this paragraph, where an instrument or draft is laid before each House of Parliament on different days, the earlier day is to be taken as the day on which it is laid before both Houses.

(7) This paragraph applies in relation to instruments whether the power to make them is conferred before, on or after exit day including where the power is conferred by regulations under this Act (but not where it is conferred by this Act).

(8) This paragraph does not apply in relation to any laying before each House of Parliament, or before the House of Commons only, of an instrument or draft instrument where an equivalent draft instrument (ignoring any differences relating to procedure) has previously been laid before both Houses or before the House of Commons only.

(9) Sub-paragraph (8) of paragraph 13 applies for the purposes of this paragraph as it applies for the purposes of sub-paragraph (1) of that paragraph.

(10) In this paragraph "the relevant authority" means—

(a) in the case of an Order in Council or Order of Council, the Minister of the Crown who has responsibility in relation to the instrument,

(b) in the case of any other statutory instrument which is not made by a Minister of the Crown, the person who makes, or is to make, the instrument, and

(c) in any other case, the Minister of the Crown who makes, or is to make, the instrument.

16. (1) This paragraph applies where, on or after exit day—

(a) a Scottish statutory instrument which amends or revokes any subordinate legislation made under section 2(2) of the European Communities Act 1972, or

(b) a draft of such an instrument,

is to be laid before the Scottish Parliament.

(2) Before the instrument or draft is laid, the relevant authority must make a statement as to why, in the opinion of the relevant authority, there are good reasons for the amendment or revocation.

(3) Before the instrument or draft is laid, the relevant authority must make a statement otherwise explaining—

(a) the law which is relevant to the amendment or revocation, and

(b) the effect of the amendment or revocation on retained EU law.

(4) If the relevant authority fails to make a statement required by sub-paragraph (2) or (3) before the instrument or draft is laid, the relevant authority must make a statement explaining why the relevant authority has failed to make the statement as so required.

(5) A statement under sub-paragraph (2), (3) or (4) must be made in writing and be published in such manner as the relevant authority considers appropriate.

(6) This paragraph applies in relation to instruments whether the power to make them is conferred before, on or after exit day including where the power is conferred by regulations under this Act (but not where it is conferred by this Act).

(7) Sub-paragraph (8) of paragraph 13 applies for the purposes of this paragraph as it applies for the purposes of sub-paragraph (1) of that paragraph.

(8) In this paragraph "the relevant authority" means—

(a) in the case of a Scottish statutory instrument which is not made by the Scottish Ministers, other than an Order in Council, the person who makes, or is to make, the instrument, and

(b) in any other case, the Scottish Ministers.

NOTES

Commencement: to be appointed.

PART 4
SPECIFIC TRANSITIONAL, TRANSITORY AND SAVING PROVISION

Retention of existing EU law

[1.2255]

38. Section 4(2)(b) does not apply in relation to any rights, powers, liabilities, obligations, restrictions, remedies or procedures so far as they are of a kind recognised by a court or tribunal in the United Kingdom in a case decided on or after exit day but begun before exit day (whether or not as an essential part of the decision in the case).

39. (1) Subject as follows and subject to any provision made by regulations under section 23(6), section 5(4) and paragraphs 1 to 4 of Schedule 1 apply in relation to anything occurring before exit day (as well as anything occurring on or after exit day).

(2) Section 5(4) and paragraphs 1 to 4 of Schedule 1 do not affect any decision of a court or tribunal made before exit day.

(3) Section 5(4) and paragraphs 3 and 4 of Schedule 1 do not apply in relation to any proceedings begun, but not finally decided, before a court or tribunal in the United Kingdom before exit day.

(4) Paragraphs 1 to 4 of Schedule 1 do not apply in relation to any conduct which occurred before exit day which gives rise to any criminal liability.

(5) Paragraph 3 of Schedule 1 does not apply in relation to any proceedings begun within the period of three years beginning with exit day so far as—

(a) the proceedings involve a challenge to anything which occurred before exit day, and

(b) the challenge is not for the disapplication or quashing of—

(i) an Act of Parliament or a rule of law which is not an enactment, or

(ii) any enactment, or anything else, not falling within sub-paragraph (i) which, as a result of anything falling within that sub-paragraph, could not have been different or which gives effect to, or enforces, anything falling within that sub-paragraph.

(6) Paragraph 3(2) of Schedule 1 does not apply in relation to any decision of a court or tribunal, or other public authority, on or after exit day which is a necessary consequence of any decision of a court or tribunal made before exit day or made on or after that day by virtue of this paragraph.

(7) Paragraph 4 of Schedule 1 does not apply in relation to any proceedings begun within the period of two years beginning with exit day so far as the proceedings relate to anything which occurred before exit day.

Main powers in connection with withdrawal

40. The prohibition on making regulations under section 8, 9 or 23(1) or Schedule 2 after a particular time does not affect the continuation in force of regulations made at or before that time (including the exercise after that time of any power conferred by regulations made at or before that time).

Devolution

41. (1) The amendments made by section 12 and Part 1 of Schedule 3 do not affect the validity of—

(a) any provision of an Act of the Scottish Parliament, Act of the National Assembly for Wales or Act of the Northern Ireland Assembly made before exit day,

(b) any subordinate legislation which is subject to confirmation or approval and is made and confirmed or approved before exit day, or

(c) any other subordinate legislation made before exit day.

(2) Accordingly and subject to sub-paragraphs (3) to (10), the validity of anything falling within sub-paragraph (1)(a), (b) or (c) is to be decided by reference to the law before exit day.

(3) Section 29(2)(d) of the Scotland Act 1998, so far as relating to EU law, does not apply to any provision of an Act of the Scottish Parliament made before exit day if the provision—

(a) comes into force on or after exit day or comes into force before that day and is a power to make, confirm or approve subordinate legislation, and

(b) is made when there are no regulations under section 30A of the Scotland Act 1998 by virtue of which the provision would be in breach of the restriction in subsection (1) of that section when the provision comes into force (or, in the case of a provision which comes into force before exit day, on or after exit day) if the provision were made and the regulations were in force at that time.

(4) Section 108A(2)(e) of the Government of Wales Act 2006, so far as relating to EU law, does not apply to any provision of an Act of the National Assembly for Wales made before exit day if the provision—

(a) comes into force on or after exit day or comes into force before that day and is a power to make, confirm or approve subordinate legislation, and

(b) is made when there are no regulations under section 109A of the Government of Wales Act 2006 by virtue of which the provision would be in breach of the restriction in subsection (1) of that section when the provision comes into force (or, in the case of a provision which comes into force before exit day, on or after exit day) if the provision were made and the regulations were in force at that time.

(5) Section 6(2)(d) of the Northern Ireland Act 1998, so far as relating to EU law, does not apply to any provision of an Act of the Northern Ireland Assembly made before exit day if the provision—

(a) comes into force on or after exit day or comes into force before that day and is a power to make, confirm or approve subordinate legislation, and

(b) is made when there are no regulations under section 6A of the Northern Ireland Act 1998 by virtue of which the provision would be in breach of the restriction in subsection (1) of that section when the provision comes into force (or, in the case of a provision which comes into force before exit day, on or after exit day) if the provision were made and the regulations were in force at that time.

(6) Section 57(2) of the Scotland Act 1998, so far as relating to EU law, does not apply to the making, confirming or approving before exit day of any subordinate legislation if the legislation—

(a) comes into force on or after exit day, and

(b) is made, confirmed or approved when there are no regulations under subsection (4) of section 57 of the Scotland Act 1998 by virtue of which the making, confirming or approving would be in breach of the restriction in that subsection when the legislation comes into force if—

(i) the making, confirming or approving had occurred at that time,
(ii) in the case of legislation confirmed or approved, the legislation was made at that time, and
(iii) the regulations were in force at that time.

(7) Section 80(8) of the Government of Wales Act 2006, so far as relating to EU law, does not apply to the making, confirming or approving before exit day of any subordinate legislation if the legislation—
(a) comes into force on or after exit day, and
(b) is made, confirmed or approved when there are no regulations under subsection (8) of section 80 of the Government of Wales Act 2006 by virtue of which the making, confirming or approving would be in breach of the restriction in that subsection, so far as relating to retained EU law, when the legislation comes into force if—
(i) the making, confirming or approving had occurred at that time,
(ii) in the case of legislation confirmed or approved, the legislation was made at that time, and
(iii) the regulations were in force at that time.

(8) Section 24(1)(b) of the Northern Ireland Act 1998, so far as relating to EU law, does not apply to the making, confirming or approving before exit day of any subordinate legislation if the legislation—
(a) comes into force on or after exit day, and
(b) is made, confirmed or approved when there are no regulations under subsection (3) of section 24 of the Northern Ireland Act 1998 by virtue of which the making, confirming or approving would be in breach of the restriction in that subsection when the legislation comes into force if—
(i) the making, confirming or approving had occurred at that time,
(ii) in the case of legislation confirmed or approved, the legislation was made at that time, and
(iii) the regulations were in force at that time.

(9) For the purposes of sub-paragraphs (3) to (8) assume that the restrictions relating to retained EU law in—
(a) sections 30A(1) and 57(4) of the Scotland Act 1998,
(b) sections 80(8) and 109A(1) of the Government of Wales Act 2006, and
(c) sections 6A(1) and 24(3) of the Northern Ireland Act 1998,
come into force on exit day.

(10) Section 57(2) of the Scotland Act 1998, section 80(8) of the Government of Wales Act 2006 and section 24(1)(b) of the Northern Ireland Act 1998, so far as relating to EU law, do not apply to the making of regulations under Schedule 2 or 4.

Other provision

44. (1) The definition of "relevant criminal offence" in section 20(1) is to be read, until the appointed day, as if for the words "the age of 18 (or, in relation to Scotland or Northern Ireland, 21)" there were substituted "the age of 21".

(2) In sub-paragraph (1), "the appointed day" means the day on which the amendment made to section 81(3)(a) of the Regulation of Investigatory Powers Act 2000 by paragraph 211 of Schedule 7 to the Criminal Justice and Court Services Act 2000 comes into force.

45. (1) The amendment made by paragraph 17 does not affect whether the payment of any fees or other charges may be required under section 56 of the Finance Act 1973 in connection with a service or facilities provided, or an authorisation, certificate or other document issued, before that amendment comes into force.

(2) Sub-paragraph (3) applies where—
(a) immediately before the amendment made by paragraph 17 comes into force, the payment of fees or other charges could be required, under section 56 of the Finance Act 1973, in connection with the provision of a service or facilities, or issuing an authorisation, certificate or other document, in pursuance of an EU obligation, and
(b) after the amendment made by paragraph 17 comes into force—
(i) regulations made under that section (whether or not modified under Part 2 of Schedule 4 or otherwise) prescribing the fees or charges, or under which the fees or charges are to be determined, form part of retained EU law, and
(ii) the service or facilities are provided, or the authorisation, certificate or other document is issued, under or in connection with retained EU law.

(3) Despite the amendment made by paragraph 17, the payment of fees or other charges may be required, under that section and in accordance with the regulations, in connection with the provision of the service or facilities, or the issuing of the authorisation, certificate or other document.

NOTES

Commencement: 26 June 2018 (paras 41(10), 43, 44); 4 July 2018 (para 40); 1 March 2019 para 41(3)–(9)); to be appointed (otherwise).

PARENTAL BEREAVEMENT (LEAVE AND PAY) ACT 2018

2018 c 24

An Act to make provision about leave and pay for employees whose children have died.

[13 September 2018]

[1.2256]

1 Parental bereavement leave and pay

In the Schedule—

(a) Part 1 creates a statutory entitlement to parental bereavement leave,

(b) Part 2 creates a statutory entitlement to parental bereavement pay, and

(c) Part 3 contains related amendments.

NOTES

Commencement: to be appointed.

[1.2257]

2 Extent, commencement and short title

(1) An amendment or repeal made by the Schedule has the same extent as the provision to which it relates.

(2) Section 1 and the Schedule come into force on such day as the Secretary of State may by regulations made by statutory instrument appoint; and different days may be appointed for different purposes.

(3) This section comes into force on the day on which this Act is passed.

(4) This Act may be cited as the Parental Bereavement (Leave and Pay) Act 2018.

NOTES

Commencement: 13 September 2018.

SCHEDULE

(*Pt 1 of the Schedule inserts the Employment Rights Act 1996, ss 80EA–80EE at* **[1.984]** *et seq and amends s 236 thereof at* **[1.1151]**. *Pt 2 inserts the Social Security Contributions and Benefits Act 1992, Pt 12ZD (ss 171ZZ6–171ZZ15) at* **[1.251]** *et seq. Pt 3 contains further amendments relating to parental bereavement leave and pay, which in so far as relevant to this work have been incorporated at the appropriate place.*)

PART 2
STATUTORY INSTRUMENTS

TRADE UNIONS AND EMPLOYERS' ASSOCIATIONS (AMALGAMATIONS, ETC) REGULATIONS 1975

(SI 1975/536)

NOTES

Made: 26 March 1975.

Authority: originally made under the Trade Union (Amalgamations, etc) Act 1964, s 7 (repealed); now have effect under the Trade Union and Labour Relations (Consolidation) Act 1992, s 108.

Commencement: 12 May 1975.

See *Harvey* M8.

ARRANGEMENT OF REGULATIONS

SCHEDULES

[2.1]

1 Citation, commencement and revocation

(1) These Regulations may be cited as the Trade Unions and Employers' Associations (Amalgamations, etc) Regulations 1975 and shall come into operation on 12th May 1975.

(2) . . .

NOTES

Para (2): revokes the Employers' and Workers' Organisations (Amalgamations, etc) Regulations 1971, SI 1971/1542.

[2.2]

2 Interpretation

(1) The Interpretation Act 1889 shall apply to these Regulations as it applies to an Act of Parliament.

(2) For the purposes of these Regulations, unless the context otherwise requires, the following expressions shall have the meanings hereby assigned to them respectively, that is to say—

"the 1964 Act" means the Trade Union (Amalgamations, etc) Act 1964;

"the 1974 Act" means the Trade Union and Labour Relations Act 1974;

["the Certification Officer" means the officer appointed under section 7(1) of the Employment Protection Act 1975 or any assistant certification officer appointed under section 7(4) of the said Act to whom, in accordance with section 7(5) of the said Act, functions have been delegated in relation to any matter authorised or required to be dealt with under these Regulations];

"duly authenticated" means bearing the signature of [the Certification Officer] and the date of the signature;

"organisation" means any trade union as defined in section 28(1) of the 1974 Act, or any employers' association as defined in section 28(2) of the 1974 Act which is not a corporate body;

"Northern Ireland union" has the meaning assigned to it by section 10(5) of the 1964 Act.

NOTES

Para (2): definition "the Certification Officer" substituted by the Trade Unions and Employers' Associations (Amalgamations, etc) (Amendment) Regulations 1978, SI 1978/1344, reg 2. As to the appointment of the Certification Officer, see now the Trade Union and Labour Relations (Consolidation) Act 1992, s 254.

Interpretation Act 1889: see now the Interpretation Act 1978.

Trade Union (Amalgamations, etc) Act 1964; Trade Union and Labour Relations Act 1974: repealed and replaced by the Trade Union and Labour Relations (Consolidation) Act 1992.

[2.3]

3 Approval of proposed instruments and notices

(1) An application pursuant to section 1(4) of the 1964 Act for approval of a proposed instrument of amalgamation or transfer shall be submitted to [the Certification Officer]—

(a) in the case of a proposed instrument of amalgamation, by one of the amalgamating organisations; and

(b) in the case of a proposed instrument of transfer, by the transferor organisation, and the application shall be accompanied by two copies of the proposed instrument both of which shall be signed as required by paragraph 6 of Schedule 1 or, as the case may be, paragraph 4 of Schedule 2 to these Regulations [by the fee prescribed by Regulation 11(1)], and by copies of the current rules of the organisations which are parties to the instrument.

(2) An application pursuant to section 1(4) of the 1964 Act for approval of a proposed notice to be supplied to members of an organisation in accordance with section 1(2)(d) of that Act shall be accompanied by two copies of the proposed notice.

(3) [The Certification Officer] shall signify his approval of such instrument or notice by returning to the applicant organisation one of the copies endorsed with the word "Approved" and duly authenticated.

NOTES

Para (1): words in first pair of square brackets substituted by the Trade Unions and Employers' Associations (Amalgamations, etc) (Amendment) Regulations 1978, SI 1978/1344, reg 3; words in second pair of square brackets substituted by the Certification Officer (Amendment of Fees) Regulations 1988, SI 1988/310, reg 2.

Para (3): words in square brackets substituted by SI 1978/1344, reg 3.

[2.4]

4 Contents of instrument of amalgamation or transfer

(1) Subject to Regulation 5 an instrument of amalgamation shall contain the particulars and information specified in Schedule 1 to these Regulations.

(2) Subject to Regulation 5 an instrument of transfer shall contain the particulars and information specified in Schedule 2 to these Regulations.

[2.5]

5

Regulation 4 shall not apply to any instrument of amalgamation or instrument of transfer which, before the coming into operation of these Regulations, has been approved by the Chief [Certification Officer] of Trade Unions and Employers' Associations or by any assistant registrar appointed by him for the purpose of section 8 of the 1964 Act.

NOTES

Words in square brackets substituted by the Trade Unions and Employers' Associations (Amalgamations, etc) (Amendment) Regulations 1978, SI 1978/1344, reg 3.

[2.6]

6 Application for registration of instruments

(1) An application pursuant to section 1(5) of the 1964 Act for registration of an instrument of amalgamation shall be signed by three members of the committee of management or other governing body and the secretary of each of the amalgamating organisations and shall be submitted to [the Certification Officer] in the form to be provided by him for that purpose. The application shall be accompanied by two copies of the instrument and two copies of the proposed rules of the amalgamated organisation and by a statutory declaration from each of the amalgamating organisations in the form to be provided by [the Certification Officer] for that purpose. Each copy of the proposed rules shall be signed by the secretary of each of the amalgamating organisations.

(2) An application pursuant to section 1(5) of the 1964 Act for registration of an instrument of transfer shall be signed by three members of the committee of management or other governing body and the secretary of each of the organisations concerned and shall be submitted to [the Certification Officer] by the transferee organisation in the form to be provided by him for that purpose. The application shall be accompanied by two copies of the instrument and by statutory declarations made by the secretary of the transferor organisation and the secretary of the transferee organisation in the forms to be provided by [the Certification Officer] for that purpose. The application shall also be accompanied by two copies of any amendments to the rules of the transferee organisation made since the date of the application for approval of the proposed instrument of transfer under Regulation 3(1).

(3) In any case where he considers it desirable with a view to ensuring that adequate publicity is given to the date by which complaints must be made to him, under section 4 of the 1964 Act, as to the validity of a resolution approving an instrument of amalgamation or transfer, [the Certification Officer] may, not later than seven days after the date on which he receives the application for registration of the instrument, require notice to be given or published in such manner, in such form, and on or before such date, as he may direct of the fact that the application for registration has been or is to be made to him.

NOTES

Words in square brackets substituted by the Trade Unions and Employers' Associations (Amalgamations, etc) (Amendment) Regulations 1978, SI 1978/1344, reg 3.

[2.7]

7 Registration of instruments

(1) Before registering an instrument of amalgamation, [the Certification Officer] shall satisfy himself that the proposed rules of the amalgamated organisation are in no way inconsistent with the terms of the said instrument.

(2) Upon registering the instrument [the Certification Officer] shall send to the address specified for that purpose on the form of application for registration one copy of the instrument endorsed with the word "Registered" and duly authenticated.

NOTES

Words in square brackets substituted by the Trade Unions and Employers' Associations (Amalgamations, etc) (Amendment) Regulations 1978, SI 1978/1344, reg 3.

[2.8]
8

(1) Before registering an instrument of transfer [the Certification Officer] shall satisfy himself that the rules of the transferee organisation are in no way inconsistent with the terms of the said instrument.

(2) Upon registering the instrument [the Certification Officer] shall send to the transferee organisation one copy of the instrument endorsed with the word "Registered" and duly authenticated.

NOTES

Words in square brackets substituted by the Trade Unions and Employers' Associations (Amalgamations, etc) (Amendment) Regulations 1978, SI 1978/1344, reg 3.

[2.9]
9 Approval of change of name

(1) An application by an organisation pursuant to section 6(2) of the 1964 Act for the approval of a change of name shall be signed by three members of the committee of management or other governing body and the secretary of the organisation and shall be submitted to [the Certification Officer] in duplicate in the form to be provided by him for that purpose.

(2) The application shall be accompanied by a statutory declaration as to the manner in which the change of name was effected by the secretary of the organisation in the form to be provided by [the Certification Officer] for the purpose.

(3) Upon approving the change of name [the Certification Officer] shall return to the organisation one copy of the application endorsed with the word "Approved" and duly authenticated.

NOTES

Words in square brackets substituted by the Trade Unions and Employers' Associations (Amalgamations, etc) (Amendment) Regulations 1978, SI 1978/1344, reg 3.

[2.10]
10 Amalgamations of transfers involving Northern Ireland Unions

Where a Northern Ireland union is a party to an amalgamation or transfer of engagements, these Regulations shall have effect subject to the following modifications, that is to say:—

(a) Regulations 3 and 6(3) shall not apply to a Northern Ireland union;

(b) Regulation 4(2) shall not apply to an instrument of transferor if the transfer organisation is a Northern Ireland union;

(c) Regulation 6 shall not require any statutory declaration from a Northern Ireland union;

(d) the application to the Certification Officer under Regulation 6(2) for the registration of an instrument of transfer shall be submitted by the transferor organisation of the transferee organisation is a Northern Ireland union.

[2.11]
[11 Fees

(1) The fee referred to in Regulation 3(1) (fee to accompany an application for approval of a proposed instrument of amalgamation or transfer) shall be [£1850].

(2) The following fees shall be payable in advance—

For approval of a change of name	[£96]
For every inspection on the same day of documents kept by the Certification Officer under the 1964 Act relating to one and the same organisation	[£19].]

NOTES

Substituted by the Certification Officer (Amendment of Fees) Regulations 1988, SI 1988/310, reg 2.

Sums in square brackets substituted by the Certification Officer (Amendment of Fees) Regulations 2005, SI 2005/713, regs 2, 3.

[2.12]
[12

A fee of [£41] shall be payable for the entry of an amalgamated organisation on the list of trade unions or employers' associations maintained by the Certification Officer under section 8 of the 1974 Act where each of the amalgamating organisations is already entered on the list.]

NOTES

Substituted by the Trade Unions and Employers' Associations (Amalgamations, etc) (Amendment) Regulations 1978, SI 1978/1344, reg 5.

Sum in square brackets substituted by the Certification Officer (Amendment of Fees) Regulations 2005, SI 2005/713, reg 4.

SCHEDULES

SCHEDULE 1
CONTENTS OF INSTRUMENT OF AMALGAMATION

Regulation 4(1)

[2.13]

1. The instrument shall state that it is an instrument of amalgamation between the organisations named therein as the amalgamating organisations, and that upon the coming into operation of the instrument the members of the amalgamating organisations will become members of the amalgamated organisation and be subject to that organisation's rules.

2. The instrument shall either set out the proposed rules of the amalgamated organisation or state who are the persons authorised to draw up those rules.

3. If the instrument does not set out the proposed rules it shall contain a summary of what those rules will provide with regard to the following matters:—

(i) the name and principal purposes of the amalgamated organisation;
(ii) the conditions of admission to membership;
(iii) the structure of the amalgamated organisation;
(iv) the method of appointing and removing its governing body and principal officials and of altering its rules;
(v) the contributions and benefits applicable to members of the amalgamating organisations.

4. The instrument shall specify property held for the benefit of any of the amalgamating organisations or for the benefit of a branch of any of those organisations which is not to be vested in the appropriate trustees as defined in section 5(3) of the 1964 Act, and shall state the proposed disposition of any such property.

5. Without prejudice to section 1(5) of the 1964 Act, the instrument shall state the date on which it is to take effect.

6. The instrument shall be signed by three members of the committee of management or other governing body and the secretary of each of the amalgamating organisations.

SCHEDULE 2
CONTENTS OF INSTRUMENT OF TRANSFER

Regulation 4(2)

[2.14]

1. The instrument shall state that it is an instrument of transfer of the engagements of the organisation named therein as the transferor organisation to the organisation named therein as the transferee organisation, and that upon the coming into operation of the instrument the members of the transferor organisation will become members of the transferee organisation and be subject to that organisation's rules.

2. The instrument shall:—

(i) state what contributions and benefits will be applicable to members of the transferor organisation under the transferee organisation's rules;
(ii) if members of the transferor organisation are to be allocated to a branch or section or to branches or sections of the transferee organisation, give particulars of such allocation or the method by which it is to be decided;
(iii) state whether before registration of the instrument the transferee organisation's rules are to be altered in their application to members of the transferor organisation and, if so, the effect of any alterations;
(iv) without prejudice to section 1(5) of the 1964 Act, state the date on which the instrument is to take effect.

3. The instrument shall specify any property held for the benefit of the transferor organisation or for the benefit of a branch of the transferor organisation which is not to be vested in the appropriate trustees as defined in section 5(3) of the 1964 Act, and shall state the proposed disposition of any such property.

4. The instrument shall be signed by three members of the committee of management or other governing body and the secretary of each of the organisations.

REHABILITATION OF OFFENDERS ACT 1974 (EXCEPTIONS) ORDER 1975

(SI 1975/1023)

NOTES

Made: 24 June 1975.

Authority: Rehabilitation of Offenders Act 1974, ss 4(4), 7(4).

Commencement: 1 July 1975.

Note: this Order was revoked in relation to Scotland by the Rehabilitation of Offenders Act 1974 (Exclusions and Exceptions) (Scotland) Order 2003, SSI 2003/231, art 6(a), as from 29 March 2003. This Order remains in force for England and Wales only. Amendments made to this Order before 29 March 2003 which applied to Scotland only have now been omitted from the Order as reproduced here. The current Order relating to Scotland is the Rehabilitation of Offenders Act 1974 (Exclusions and Exceptions) (Scotland) Order 2013, SSI 2013/50 at **[2.1310]**.

See *Harvey* DI(9), (13).

[2.15]
1

This Order may be cited as the Rehabilitation of Offenders Act 1974 (Exceptions) Order 1975 and shall come into operation on 1st July 1975.

NOTES

Revoked in relation to Scotland as noted at the beginning of this Order.

[2.16]
2

[(1) In this Order, except where the context otherwise requires—

["the 2000 Act" means the Financial Services and Markets Act 2000;]

["the 2006 Act" means the Safeguarding Vulnerable Groups Act 2006;]

["the 2016 Act" means the Regulation and Inspection of Social Care (Wales) Act 2016;]

"the Act" means the Rehabilitation of Offenders Act 1974;

["administration of justice offence" means—

(a) the offence of perverting the course of justice,

(b) any offence under section 51 of the Criminal Justice and Public Order Act 1994 (intimidation etc of witnesses, jurors and others),

(c) an offence under section 1, 2, 6 or 7 of the Perjury Act 1911 (perjury),

or any offence committed under the law of any part of the United Kingdom (other than England or Wales) or of any other country where the conduct which constitutes the offence would, if it all took place in England or Wales, constitute one or more of the offences specified by paragraph (a) to (c);]

["adoption agency" has the meaning given by section 2(1) of the Adoption and Children Act 2002;

["adoption service"—

(a) in relation to England, means the discharge by a local authority in England of relevant adoption functions within the meaning of section 43(3)(a) of the Care Standards Act 2000, and

(b) in relation to Wales, means the discharge by a local authority in Wales of functions under the Adoption and Children Act 2002 of making or participating in arrangements for the adoption of children or the provision of adoption support services as defined in section 2(6) of that Act;]

"adoption support agency" has the meaning given by section 8 of the Adoption and Children Act 2002;]

["associate", in relation to a person ("A"), means someone who is a controller, director or manager of A or, where A is a partnership, any partner of A;]

["authorised payment institution" has the meaning given by regulation 2(1) of the [Payment Services Regulations 2017];]

. . .

["childminder agency" has the meaning given in section 98(1) of the Childcare Act 2006;]

["child minding" means—

[(a) child minding within the meaning of section 79A of the Children Act 1989; and

(b) early years childminding within the meaning of section 96(4) of the Childcare Act 2006, or later years childminding within the meaning of section 96(8) of that Act;]]

["children's home"—

(a) in relation to England, has the meaning given by section 1 of the Care Standards Act 2000; and

[(b) in relation to Wales, means premises at which—

(i) a care home service is provided wholly or mainly to persons under the age of 18, or

(ii) a secure accommodation service is provided,

and in this paragraph "care home service" and "secure accommodation service" have the meaning given in Part 1 of the 2016 Act;]

["collective investment scheme" has the meaning given by section 235 of the 2000 Act;]

[. . .]

["contracting authority" has the meaning given by regulation 2(1) of the Public Contracts Regulations 2015, regulation 4(1) of the Utilities Contracts Regulations 2016 or regulation 4 of the Concession Contracts Regulations 2016, as appropriate;]

[. . .]

["controller" has the meaning given by section 422 of the 2000 Act;]

[. . .]

["Council of Lloyd's" means the council constituted by section 3 of Lloyd's Act 1982;]

["day care" means—

[(a) day care for which registration is required by section 79D(5) of the Children Act 1989; and

(b) early years provision within the meaning of section 96(2) of the Childcare Act 2006 (other than early years childminding), or later years provision within the meaning of section 96(6) of that Act (other than later years childminding), for which registration is required, or permitted, under Part 3 of that Act;]]

["day care premises" means any premises on which day care is provided, but does not include any part of the premises where children are not looked after;]

["depositary", in relation to an authorised contractual scheme, has the meaning given in section 237(2) of the 2000 Act;]

[. . .]

[. . .]

["director" has the meaning given by section 417 of the 2000 Act;]

["electronic money institution" has the meaning given by regulation 2(1) of the Electronic Money Regulations 2011;]

["the FCA" means the Financial Conduct Authority;]

["fostering agency"—

(a) in relation to England, has the meaning given by section 4(4) of the Care Standards Act 2000, and

(b) in relation to Wales, means a provider of a fostering service within the meaning of paragraph 5 of Schedule 1 to the 2016 Act;]

["fostering service"—

(a) in relation to England, the discharge by a local authority in England of relevant fostering functions within the meaning of section 43(3)(b)(i) of the Care Standards Act 2000, and

(b) in relation to Wales, the discharge by a local authority in Wales of functions under section 81 of the Social Services and Well-being (Wales) Act 2014 (in connection with placements with local authority foster parents) or regulations made under or by virtue of any of sections 87, 92(1)(a), (b), (d) or 93 of that Act;]

["key worker" means—

(a) any individual who is likely, in the course of exercising the duties of that individual's office or employment, to play a significant role in the decision making process of the FCA, the PRA or the Bank of England in relation to the exercise of its public functions (within the meaning of section 349(5) of the 2000 Act); or

(b) any individual who is likely, in the course of exercising the duties of that individual's office or employment, to support directly an individual mentioned in paragraph (a);]

["manager" has the meaning given by section 423 of the 2000 Act;]

["open-ended investment company" has the meaning given by section 236 of the 2000 Act;]

["operator", in relation to an authorised contractual scheme, has the meaning given in section 237(2) of the 2000 Act;]

["Part 4A permission" has the meaning given by section 55A(5) of the 2000 Act;]

["the PRA" means the Prudential Regulation Authority;]

["protected caution" means a caution of the kind described in article 2A(1);

"protected conviction" means a conviction of the kind described in article 2A(2);]

["payment services" has the meaning given by regulation 2(1) of the [Payment Services Regulations 2017];]

["recognised clearing house" means a recognised clearing house as defined in section 285 of the 2000 Act;]

["recognised CSD" has the meaning given by section 285(1)(e) of the 2000 Act;]

["registered account information service provider" has the meaning given by regulation 2(1) of the Payment Services Regulations 2017;]

["relevant collective investment scheme" means a collective investment scheme which is recognised under section *264 (schemes constituted in other EEA States)* . . . *or* 272 (individually recognised overseas schemes) of the 2000 Act;]

"residential family centre"—

(a) in relation to England, has the meaning given by section 4(2) of the Care Standards Act 2000; and

(b) in relation to Wales, means a place at which a residential family centre service, within the meaning of Part 1 of the Regulation and Inspection of Social Care (Wales) Act 2016, is provided;]

. . .

["small payment institution" has the meaning given by regulation 2(1) of the [Payment Services Regulations 2017];]

["taxi driver licence" means a licence granted under—
  [(i) section 46 of the Town Police Clauses Act 1847;]
  (ii) section 8 of the Metropolitan Public Carriage Act 1869;
  (iii) section 9 of the Plymouth City Council Act 1975;
  (iv) section 51 of the Local Government (Miscellaneous Provisions) Act 1976; or
  (v) section 13 of the Private Hire Vehicles (London) Act 1998;]

["trustee", in relation to a unit trust scheme, has the meaning given by section 237 of the 2000 Act;]

[. . .]

["UK recognised investment exchange" means an investment exchange in relation to which a recognition order under section 290 of the 2000 Act, otherwise than by virtue of section 292(2) of that Act (overseas investment exchanges), is in force;]

["voluntary adoption agency"—
  (a) in relation to England, has the meaning given by section 4(7) of the Care Standards Act 2000, and
  (b) in relation to Wales, means a provider of an adoption service within the meaning of paragraph 4(a) of Schedule 1 to the 2016 Act;]

["work" includes—
  (a) work of any kind, whether paid or unpaid, and whether under a contract of service or apprenticeship, under a contract for services, or otherwise than under a contract; and
  (b) an office established by or by virtue of an enactment;]

["work with children" means work of the kind described in paragraph 14[, 14A, 14B or 14C] of [Part 2 of] Schedule 1 to this Order;]

. . .

(2) . . .]

[(2ZA) In this Order references to the Bank of England do not include the Bank acting in its capacity as the Prudential Regulation Authority.]

[(2A) Nothing in this Order applies in relation to a conviction for a service offence which is not a recordable service offence; and for this purpose—
  (a) "service offence" means an offence which is a service offence within the meaning of the Armed Forces Act 2006 or an SDA offence within the meaning of the Armed Forces Act 2006 (Transitional Provisions etc) Order 2009;
  (b) "recordable service offence" means an offence which is a recordable service offence within the meaning of the Police and Criminal Evidence Act 1984 (Armed Forces) Order 2009.]

(3) Part IV of Schedule 1 to this Order shall have effect for the interpretation of expressions used in that Schedule.

(4) In this Order a reference to any enactment shall be construed as a reference to that enactment as amended, extended or applied by or under any other enactment.

[(4A) In this Order any reference to a conviction shall where relevant include a reference to a caution, and any reference to spent convictions shall be construed accordingly.]

(5) The Interpretation Act 1889 shall apply to the interpretation of this Order as it applies to the interpretation of an Act of Parliament.

NOTES

Revoked in relation to Scotland as noted at the beginning of this Order.

Para (1) is amended as follows:

Substituted, together with para (2), by the Rehabilitation of Offenders Act 1974 (Exceptions) (Amendment No 2) Order 1986, SI 1986/2268, art 2(1), Schedule, para 1.

Definitions "the 2000 Act", "administration of justice offence", "associate", "collective investment scheme", "the competent authority for listing", "controller", "Council of Lloyd's", "director", "key worker", "manager", "open-ended investment company", "trustee", "UK recognised clearing house", and "UK recognised investment exchange" inserted by the Rehabilitation of Offenders Act 1974 (Exceptions) (Amendment) (No 2) Order 2001, SI 2001/3816, arts 2, 3(1).

Definition "the 2006 Act" inserted by the Rehabilitation of Offenders Act 1974 (Exceptions) (Amendment) (England and Wales) Order 2009, SI 2009/1818, arts 2, 3.

Definition "the 2016 Act" inserted, definitions "adoption service", "fostering agency", "fostering service", "voluntary adoption agency" substituted, and in definition "children's home" para (b) substituted, by the Regulation and Inspection of Social Care (Wales) Act 2016 (Consequential Amendments to Secondary Legislation) Regulations 2019, SI 2019/237, reg 2, Sch 1, para 1(1), (2), as from 29 April 2019.

Definitions "adoption agency", "child minding", "day care", "day care premises", "work", and "work with children" inserted by the Rehabilitation of Offenders Act 1974 (Exceptions) (Amendment) Order 2001, SI 2001/1192, arts 2, 3.

Definitions "adoption agency", "adoption service" and "adoption support agency" substituted (for the original definition "adoption agency" as inserted as noted above), definitions "childminder agency", "children's home", "fostering agency", "fostering service", "residential family centre" and "voluntary adoption agency" inserted, and words in first pair of square brackets in definition "work with children" inserted, by the Rehabilitation of Offenders Act 1974 (Exceptions) Order 1975 (Amendment) (England and Wales) Order 2014, SI 2014/1707, arts 2, 3, as from 1 July 2014 (with the exception of the insertion of the definition "childminder agency"), and as from 1 September 2014 (otherwise). Definitions "children's home" and "residential family centre" subsequently substituted by the Regulation and Inspection of Social Care (Wales) Act 2016 (Consequential Amendments to Secondary Legislation) Regulations 2018, SI 2018/48, reg 2, Sch 1, para 1(1), (2), as from 2 April 2018.

Definitions "authorised payment institution", "payment services", and "small payment institution" inserted by the Rehabilitation of Offenders Act 1974 (Exceptions) (Amendment) (England and Wales) Order 2011, SI 2011/1800, art 2(1), (2). Words in square brackets in those definitions substituted by the Payment Services Regulations 2017, SI 2017/752, reg 156, Sch 8, Pt 3, para 6(a), as from 13 January 2018.

Definition "the Building Societies Commission" (omitted) revoked by SI 2001/3816, arts 2, 3(3).

Paras (a), (b) of definitions "child minding" and "day care" substituted, and words in second pair of square brackets in definition "work with children" inserted, by the Rehabilitation of Offenders Act 1974 (Exceptions) (Amendment) (England and Wales) Order 2008, SI 2008/3259, arts 2, 3(1).

Definition "child minding" further amended in relation to Wales by the Children and Families (Wales) Measure 2010 (Commencement No 2, Savings and Transitional Provisions) Order 2010, SI 2010/2582, art 5, Sch 4, para 1(1), (2)(a), as follows: in para (a) for "section 79A of the Children Act 1989" substitute "section 19 of the Children and Families (Wales) Measure 2010". Definition "day care" also amended in relation to Wales by SI 2010/2582, art 5, Sch 4, para 1(1), (2)(b), as follows: in para (a) for "section 79D(5) of the Children Act 1989" substitute "section 23(1) of the Children and Families (Wales) Measure 2010".

Definition "the competent authority for listing" (omitted) revoked, definitions "the FCA" and "the PRA" inserted, definition "key worker" substituted and definition "Part 4A permission" substituted for definition "Part IV permission" (as originally inserted by SI 2001/3816, arts 2, 3(1)), by the Financial Services Act 2012 (Consequential Amendments and Transitional Provisions) Order 2013, SI 2013/472, art 3, Sch 2, para 1(1), (2).

Definition "contracting authority" substituted, definitions "contracting entity", "Directive 2004/17/EC" and "Directive 2004/18/EC" (omitted) revoked, and definition "utility" inserted, by the Public Procurement (Amendments, Repeals and Revocations) Regulations 2016, SI 2016/275, reg 3, Sch 2, Pt 2, paras 25, 26, as from 18 April 2016. The definitions "contracting authority", "contracting entity", "Directive 2004/17/EC", and "Directive 2004/18/EC" were originally inserted by the Rehabilitation of Offenders Act 1974 (Exceptions) (Amendment) (England and Wales) Order 2006, SI 2006/2143, arts 2, 3(b).

Definition "Council" (omitted) originally inserted by the Rehabilitation of Offenders Act 1974 (Exceptions) (Amendment) (England and Wales) Order 2003, SI 2003/965, arts 2, 3(a), and revoked by SI 2012/1957, arts 2, 4.

Definitions "depositary" and "operator" inserted by the Collective Investment in Transferable Securities (Contractual Scheme) Regulations 2013, SI 2013/1388, reg 7(1), (2).

Definition "electronic money institution" inserted by the Electronic Money Regulations 2011, SI 2011/99, reg 79, Sch 4, Pt 2, para 7(a).

Definitions "protected caution" and "protected conviction" inserted by the Rehabilitation of Offenders Act 1974 (Exceptions) Order 1975 (Amendment) (England and Wales) Order 2013, SI 2013/1198, arts 2, 3(1), (2).

Definition "recognised clearing house" inserted by the Financial Services and Markets Act 2000 (Over the Counter Derivatives, Central Counterparties and Trade Repositories) Regulations 2013, SI 2013/504, reg 28(1), (2)(b).

Definition "recognised CSD" inserted by the Central Securities Depositories Regulations 2017, SI 2017/1064, reg 10, Schedule, Pt 2, para 18(1), (2), as from 28 November 2017.

Definition "registered account information service provider" inserted by SI 2017/752, reg 156, Sch 8, Pt 3, para 6(a)(ii), as from 13 January 2018.

Definition "relevant collective investment scheme" inserted by the Rehabilitation of Offenders Act 1974 (Exceptions) (Amendment) (No 2) Order 2001, SI 2001/3816, arts 2, 3(1); words omitted revoked by the Alternative Investment Fund Managers Regulations 2013, SI 2013/1773, reg 81, Sch 2, Part 2, para 2(1), (2); words in italics revoked by the Collective Investment Schemes (Amendment etc) (EU Exit) Regulations 2019, SI 2019/325, reg 48, as from exit day (as defined in the European Union (Withdrawal) Act 2018, s 20).

Definition "relevant offence" (omitted) revoked by the Rehabilitation of Offenders Act 1974 (Exceptions) (Amendment) (England and Wales) Order 2007, SI 2007/2149, arts 2, 3(1).

Definition "taxi driver licence" inserted by SI 2003/965, arts 2, 3(a); para (i) substituted by SI 2006/2143, arts 2, 3(a).

Definition "UK recognised clearing house" (omitted) originally inserted by SI 2001/3816, arts 2, 3(1); revoked by SI 2013/504, reg 28(1), (2)(a).

Final words omitted revoked by SI 2001/3816, arts 2, 3(3).

Para (2): substituted as noted above; revoked by SI 2013/1198, arts 2, 3(1), (3).

Para (2ZA): inserted by the Bank of England and Financial Services (Consequential Amendments) Regulations 2017, SI 2017/80, reg 2, Schedule, Pt 2, para 21, as from 1 March 2017.

Para (2A): inserted by SI 2013/1198, arts 2, 3(1), (4).

Para (4A): inserted by SI 2008/3259, arts 2, 3(2).

Adoption Act 1976, s 1: repealed by the Adoption and Children Act 2002, s 139(3), Sch 5. As to the meaning of "adoption agency", see now s 2(1) of the 2002 Act.

Children Act 1989, ss 79A, 79D(5): repealed in relation to Wales by the Children and Families (Wales) Measure 2010, s 73, Sch 2 (as to the meaning of "child minding" in the 2010 Measure, see s 19 thereof, and as to the registration of day care providers under the 2010 Measure, see s 23).

Interpretation Act 1889: repealed and replaced by the Interpretation Act 1978.

[2.17]
[2A

(1) For the purposes of this Order, a caution is a protected caution if it was given to a person for an offence other than a listed offence and—

(a) where the person was under 18 years at the time the caution was given, two years or more have passed since the date on which the caution was given; or

(b) where the person was 18 years or over at the time the caution was given, six years or more have passed since the date on which the caution was given.

(2) For the purposes of this Order, a person's conviction is a protected conviction if the conditions in paragraph (3) are satisfied and—

(a) where the person was under 18 years at the time of the conviction, five years and six months or more have passed since the date of the conviction; or

(b) where the person was 18 years or over at the time of the conviction, 11 years or more have passed since the date of the conviction.

(3) The conditions referred to in paragraph (2) are that—

(a) the offence of which the person was convicted was not a listed offence;

(b) no sentence mentioned in paragraph (4) was imposed in respect of the conviction; and

(c) the person has not been convicted of any other offence at any time.

(4) The sentences referred to in paragraph (3)(b) are—
(a) a custodial sentence, and
(b) a sentence of service detention,
within the meaning of section 5(8) of the Act, as to be substituted by section 139(1) and (4) of the Legal Aid, Sentencing and Punishment of Offenders Act 2012.

(5) In paragraphs (1) and (3)(a) "listed offence" means—
(a) an offence under section 67(1A) of the Medicines Act 1968;
(b) an offence under any of sections 126 to 129 of the Mental Health Act 1983;
(c) an offence specified in the Schedule to the Disqualification from Caring for Children (England) Regulations 2002;
(d) an offence specified in Schedule 15 to the Criminal Justice Act 2003;
(e) an offence under section 44 of, or under paragraph 4 of Schedule 1 or paragraph 4 of Schedule 4 to, the Mental Capacity Act 2005;
(f) an offence under section 7, 9 or 19 of the Safeguarding Vulnerable Groups Act 2006;
(g) an offence specified in section 17(3)(a), (b) or (c) of the Health and Social Care Act 2008, apart from an offence under section 76 of that Act;
(h) an offence specified in the Schedule to the Safeguarding Vulnerable Groups Act 2006 (Prescribed Criteria and Miscellaneous Provisions) Regulations 2009;
(i) an offence specified in Schedule 2 or 3 of the Childcare (Disqualification) Regulations 2009;
(j) an offence superseded (whether directly or indirectly) by any offence falling within paragraphs (a) to (i);
(k) an offence of—
(i) attempting or conspiring to commit any offence falling within paragraphs (a) to (j), or
(ii) inciting or aiding, abetting, counselling or procuring the commission of any such offence,
or an offence under Part 2 of the Serious Crime Act 2007 (encouraging or assisting crime) committed in relation to any such offence;
(l) an offence under the law of Scotland or Northern Ireland, or any country or territory outside the United Kingdom, which corresponds to any offence under the law of England and Wales falling within paragraphs (a) to (k);
(m) an offence under section 42 of the Armed Forces Act 2006 in relation to which the corresponding offence under the law of England and Wales (within the meaning of that section) is an offence falling within paragraphs (a) to (k); or
(n) an offence under section 70 of the Army Act 1955, section 70 of the Air Force Act 1955 or section 42 of the Naval Discipline Act 1957 of which the corresponding civil offence (within the meaning of that Act) is an offence falling within paragraphs (a) to k).]

NOTES

Inserted by the Rehabilitation of Offenders Act 1974 (Exceptions) Order 1975 (Amendment) (England and Wales) Order 2013, SI 2013/1198, arts 2, 4.

[2.18]
3

[(1)] [[Subject to paragraph (2), neither] section 4(2) of, nor paragraph 3(3) of Schedule 2 to,] the Act shall apply in relation to—
(a) any question asked by or on behalf of any person, in the course of the duties of his office or employment, in order to assess the suitability—
(i) of the person to whom the question relates for admission to any of the professions specified in Part I of Schedule 1 to this Order; or
[(ii) of the person to whom the question relates for any office or employment specified in Part II of the said Schedule 1 [apart from one specified in paragraph [1,] 6, 16, 17, 18, 18A, 31, 32, 35 or 36] or for any other work specified in paragraph [12A, 13, [13A,] 14, 14A, [14AA,] [14B, 14C,] [14D,] [14E,] 20, 21, ... [38, 40 or 43]] of Part II of the said Schedule 1; or]
(iii) of the person to whom the question relates or of any other person to pursue any occupation specified in Part III of the said Schedule 1 [apart from one specified in paragraph 1 or 8] or to pursue it subject to a particular condition or restriction; or
(iv) of the person to whom the question relates or of any other person to hold a licence, certificate or permit of a kind specified in Schedule 2 to this Order [apart from one specified in [paragraph 1, 3 or 6]] or to hold it subject to a particular condition or restriction,
where the person questioned is informed at the time the question is asked that, by virtue of this Order, spent convictions are to be disclosed;
[(aa) any question asked by or on behalf of any person, in the course of the duties of his work, in order to assess the suitability of a person to work with children, where—
(i) the question relates to the person whose suitability is being assessed;
(ii) the person whose suitability is being assessed lives on the premises where his work with children would normally take place and the question relates to a person living in the same household as him;
(iii) the person whose suitability is being assessed lives on the premises where his work with children would normally take place and the question relates to a person who regularly works on those premises at a time when the work with children usually takes place; or

(iv) the work for which the person's suitability is being assessed is child minding which would normally take place on premises other than premises where that person lives and the question relates to a person who lives on those other premises or to a person who regularly works on them at a time when the child minding takes place,

and where the person to whom the question relates is informed at the time the question is asked that, by virtue of this Order, spent convictions are to be disclosed;]

[(ab) . . .]

(b) . . .

[(bb) any question asked by or on behalf of

(i) the Civil Aviation Authority,

(ii) any other person authorised to provide air traffic services under section 4 or section 5 of the Transport Act 2000 (in any case where such person is a company, an "authorised company"),

(iii) any company which is a subsidiary (within the meaning given by section 736(1) of the Companies Act 1985) of an authorised company, or

(iv) any company of which an authorised company is a subsidiary,

where, in the case of sub-paragraphs (iii) and (iv) of this paragraph the question is put in relation to the provision of air traffic services, and in all cases, where the question is put in order to assess, for the purpose of safeguarding national security, the suitability of the person to whom the question relates or of any other person for any office or employment where the person questioned is informed at the time the question is asked that, by virtue of this Order, spent convictions are to be disclosed for the purpose of safeguarding national security;]

[(e) any question asked by or on behalf of any person in the course of his duties as a person employed by an adoption agency for the purpose of assessing the suitability of any person to adopt children in general or a child in particular where—

(i) the question relates to the person whose suitability is being assessed; or

(ii) the question relates to a person over the age of 18 living in the same household as the person whose suitability is being assessed,

and where the person to whom the question relates is informed at the time the question is asked that, by virtue of this Order, spent convictions are to be disclosed;

[(ea) any question asked by or on behalf of any person in the course of his duties as a person employed by a local authority in England or Wales for the purpose of preparing a report for the court under section 14A(8) of the Children Act 1989 regarding the suitability of any person to be a special guardian, where—

(i) the question relates to the person whose suitability is being assessed; or

(ii) the question relates to a person over the age of 18 living in the same household as the person whose suitability is being assessed;

and where the person to whom the question relates is informed at the time the question is asked that, by virtue of this Order, spent convictions are to be disclosed;]

(f) any question asked by or on behalf of any person, in the course of the duties of his work, in order to assess the suitability of a person to provide day care where—

(i) the question relates to the person whose suitability is being assessed; or

(ii) the question relates to a person who lives on the premises which are or are proposed to be day care premises,

and where the person to whom the question relates is informed at the time the question is asked that, by virtue of this Order, spent convictions are to be disclosed];

[(fa) any question asked by or on behalf of Her Majesty's Chief Inspector of Education, Children's Services and Skills in assessing a person's suitability for registration as a childminder agency under Part 3 of the Childcare Act 2006, where the person to whom the question relates is informed at the time the question is asked that, by virtue of this Order, spent convictions are to be disclosed;]

[(g) any question asked by, or on behalf of, the person listed in the second column of any entry in the table below to the extent that it relates to a conviction . . . (or any circumstances ancillary to . . . a conviction) of any individual, but only if—

(i) the person questioned is informed at the time the question is asked that, by virtue of this Order, spent convictions . . . are to be disclosed; and

(ii) the question is asked in order to assess the suitability of the individual to whom the question relates to have the status specified in the first column of that entry.

	[Status	*Questioner*
1	A person with Part 4A permission.	The FCA, the PRA or the Bank of England.

[Status		Questioner
2	(a) A person in relation to whom an approval is given under section 59 of the 2000 Act (approval for particular arrangements). An associate of the person (whether or not an individual) mentioned in sub-paragraph (a).	The FCA, the PRA or the authorised person (within the meaning of section 31(2) of the 2000 Act) or the applicant for Part 4A permission who made the application for the approval of the appropriate regulator (within the meaning of section 59(4) of the 2000 Act) under section 59 of the 2000 Act in relation to the person mentioned in sub-paragraph (a) of the first column.
3	(a) The manager or trustee of an authorised unit trust scheme (within the meaning of section 237 of the 2000 Act). An associate of the person (whether or not an individual) mentioned in sub-paragraph (a).	The FCA or the unit trust scheme mentioned in the first column.
[3A	(a) The operator or depositary of an authorised contractual scheme (within the meaning of section 237(3) of the 2000 Act). (b) An associate of the person (whether or not an individual) mentioned in sub-paragraph (a).	The FCA.]
4	(a) A director of an open-ended investment company. (b) An associate of that person (whether or not an individual) mentioned in sub-paragraph (a).	The FCA, the PRA or the open-ended investment company mentioned in the first column.
5	An associate of the operator or trustee of a relevant collective investment scheme.	The FCA, the PRA or the collective investment scheme mentioned in the first column.
[6	An associate of a UK recognised investment exchange or recognised clearing house.	The FCA, the PRA, or the Bank of England or the investment exchange or clearing house mentioned in the first column.]
7	A controller of a person with Part 4A permission.	The FCA, the PRA or the person with Part 4A permission mentioned in the first column.
8	(a) A person who carries on a regulated activity (within the meaning of section 22 of the 2000 Act) but to whom the general prohibition does not apply by virtue of section 327 of the 2000 Act (exemption from the general prohibition for members of a designated professional body). (b) An associate of the person (whether or not an individual) mentioned in sub-paragraph (a).	The FCA or the PRA. In the case of a person mentioned in sub-paragraph (b) of the first column, the person mentioned in sub-paragraph (a) of that column.
9	A key worker of the FCA, the PRA or the Bank of England.	The FCA, the PRA or the Bank of England.
10	An ombudsman (within the meaning of Schedule 17 to the 2000 Act) of the Financial Ombudsman Service.	The scheme operator (within the meaning of section 225 of the 2000 Act) of the Financial Ombudsman Service.
11	An associate of the issuer of securities which have been admitted to the official list maintained by the FCA for listing under section 74 of the 2000 Act.	The FCA.
12	A sponsor (within the meaning of section 88(2) of the 2000 Act).	The FCA.
13	(a) A Primary information provider (within the meaning of section 89P of the 2000 Act).	The FCA or the PRA.

Part 2 Statutory Instruments

[Status		Questioner
	(b) An associate of the person (whether or not an individual) mentioned in sub-paragraph (a).	In the case of a person mentioned in sub-paragraph (2) of the first column, the person mentioned in sub-paragraph (1) of that column.
14	An associate of a person who has a Part 4A permission and who is admitted to Lloyd's as an underwriting agent (within the meaning of section 2 of Lloyd's Act 1982).	(a) The Council of Lloyd's. (b) The person with Part 4A permission specified in the first column (or a person applying for such permission).
15	An associate of the Council of Lloyd's.	The Council of Lloyd's.
16	[(a) Any member of a UK recognised investment exchange or recognised clearing house.	The UK recognised investment exchange or recognised clearing house specified in the first column.]
	(b) An associate of the person (whether or not an individual) mentioned in sub-paragraph (a).	In the case of a person mentioned in sub-paragraph (b) of the first column, the person mentioned in sub-paragraph (a) of that column.
17	A director or person responsible for the management of the electronic money or payment services business of an electronic money institution.	The FCA.
18	A controller of an electronic money institution.	The FCA.
19	A director or a person responsible for the management of an authorised payment institution[, a registered account information service provider] or a small payment institution.	The FCA.
20	A person responsible for the management of payment services provided, or to be provided, by an authorised payment institution[, a registered account information service provider] or a small payment institution.	The FCA.
21	A controller of an authorised payment institution[, a registered account information service provider] or a small payment institution.	The FCA.]]

[(h) any question asked by or on behalf of the [Gambling Commission] for the purpose of determining whether to grant or revoke a licence under Part I of the National Lottery etc Act 1993 where the question relates to an individual—

(i) who manages the business or any part of the business carried on under the licence (or who is likely to do so if the licence is granted), or

(ii) for whose benefit that business is carried on (or is likely to be carried on if the licence is granted),

and where the person to whom the question relates is informed at the time that the question is asked that, by virtue of this Order, spent convictions are to be disclosed];

[(i) any question asked by or on behalf of [Social Care Wales] for the purpose of determining whether or not to grant an application for registration under [Part 4 of the Regulation and Inspection of Social Care (Wales) Act 2016], where the person questioned is informed at the time the question is asked that, by virtue of this Order, spent convictions are to be disclosed];

[(j) any question asked by or on behalf of a contracting authority or utility in relation to a conviction for an offence listed in regulation 57(1) of the Public Contracts Regulations 2015 or regulation 38(8) of the Concession Contracts Regulations 2016 which is a spent conviction (or any circumstances ancillary to such a conviction) for the purpose of determining whether or not a person is excluded—

(i) for the purposes of regulation 57 of the Public Contracts Regulations 2015,

(ii) from participation in a design contest for the purposes of regulation 80 of the Public Contracts Regulations 2015,

(iii) for the purposes of regulation 80 of the Utilities Contracts Regulations 2016,

(iv) from participation in a design contest for the purposes of regulation 96 of the Utilities Contracts Regulations 2016, or

(v) for the purposes of regulation 38 of the Concession Contracts Regulations 2016,

where the person questioned is informed at the time the question is asked that, by virtue of this Order, spent convictions for such offences are to be disclosed;]

(ja) . . .]

(k) any question asked, by or on behalf of the Football Association[, Football League] or Football Association Premier League in order to assess the suitability of the person to whom the question relates or of any other person to be approved as able to undertake, in the course of acting as a steward at a sports ground at which football matches are played or as a supervisor or manager of such a person, licensable conduct within the meaning of the Private Security Industry Act 2001 without a licence issued under that Act, in accordance with . . . section 4 of that Act];

[(l) any question asked by the [Disclosure and Barring Service] for the purpose of considering the suitability of an individual to have access to information released under sections 113A and 113B of the Police Act 1997];

[(m) any question asked by or on behalf of the Master Locksmiths Association for the purposes of assessing the suitability of any person who has applied to be granted membership of that Association;

(n) any question asked by or on behalf of the Secretary of State for the purpose of assessing the suitability of any person or body to obtain or retain a licence under regulation 5 of the Misuse of Drugs Regulations 2001 or under Article 3(2) of Regulation 2004/273/EC or under article 6(1) of Regulation 2005/111/EC where—

(i) the question relates to the holder of, or an applicant for, such a licence or any person who as a result of his role in the company or other body concerned is required to be named in the application for such a licence (or would have been so required if that person had had that role at the time the application was made), and

(ii) any person to whom the question relates is informed at the time the question is asked that by virtue of this Order, spent convictions are to be disclosed];

[(o) any question asked by or on behalf of any body which is a licensing authority within the meaning of section 73(1) of the Legal Services Act 2007 (licensing authorities and relevant licensing authorities) where—

(i) it is asked in order to assess whether, for the purposes of Schedule 13 to that Act (ownership of licensed bodies), the approval requirements are met in relation to a person's holding of a restricted interest in a licensed body; and

(ii) the person to whom the question relates is informed at the time that the question is asked that, by virtue of this Order, spent convictions are to be disclosed.]

[(2) Paragraph (1) does not apply in relation to a protected caution or a protected conviction.]

NOTES

Revoked in relation to Scotland as noted at the beginning of this Order.

Para (1) is amended as follows:

Numbered as such by the Rehabilitation of Offenders Act 1974 (Exceptions) Order 1975 (Amendment) (England and Wales) Order 2013, SI 2013/1198, arts 2, 5(a).

Words in square brackets ending with the words "section 4(2) of, nor paragraph 3(3) of Schedule 2 to," substituted by the Rehabilitation of Offenders Act 1974 (Exceptions) (Amendment) (England and Wales) Order 2008, SI 2008/3259, arts 2, 4.

Words "Subject to paragraph (2), neither" in square brackets substituted by SI 2013/1198, arts 2, 5(b).

Sub-para (a)(ii) substituted by the Rehabilitation of Offenders Act 1974 (Exceptions) (Amendment) Order 2001, SI 2001/1192, arts 2, 4(1).

Words "apart from one specified in paragraph 6, 16, 17, 18, 18A, 31, 32, 35 or 36" in square brackets in sub-para (a)(ii) inserted by SI 2013/1198, arts 2, 5(c)(i).

Figures "1", 14AA" and "14E" in square brackets in sub-para (a)(ii) inserted by the Rehabilitation of Offenders Act 1974 (Exceptions) Order 1975 (Amendment) (England and Wales) Order 2016, SI 2016/824, art 2(1)–(3), as from 4 August 2016.

Words in square brackets in sub-para (a)(ii) beginning with the words "12A, 13" substituted by the Rehabilitation of Offenders Act 1974 (Exceptions) (Amendment) (England and Wales) Order 2009, SI 2009/1818, arts 2, 4(1).

Figure "13A" in square brackets in sub-para (a)(ii) inserted by the Rehabilitation of Offenders Act 1974 (Exceptions) Order 1975 (Amendment) (England and Wales) Order 2015, SI 2015/317, art 2(1), (2), as from 10 March 2015.

Figures "14B, 14C," in square brackets in sub-para (a)(ii) inserted by the Rehabilitation of Offenders Act 1974 (Exceptions) Order 1975 (Amendment) (England and Wales) Order 2014, SI 2014/1707, arts 2, 4(a), as from 1 July 2014.

Figure "14D," in square brackets in sub-para (a)(ii) inserted by SI 2014/1707, arts 2, 4(b), as from 1 September 2014.

First figures omitted from sub-para (a)(ii) revoked by SI 2013/1198, arts 2, 5(c)(i).

Second figure omitted from sub-para (a)(ii) revoked by the Rehabilitation of Offenders Act 1974 (Exceptions) (Amendment) (England and Wales) Order 2012, SI 2012/1957, arts 2, 8.

Words "38, 40 or 43" in square brackets in sub-para (a)(ii) substituted by the Protection of Freedoms Act 2012 (Disclosure and Barring Service Transfer of Functions) Order 2012, SI 2012/3006, arts 18, 19.

Words "apart from one specified in paragraph 1 or 8" in square brackets in sub-para (a)(iii) inserted by SI 2013/1198, arts 2, 5(c)(ii).

Words in first (outer) pair of square brackets in sub-para (a)(iv) inserted by SI 2013/1198, arts 2, 5(c)(iii).

Words "paragraph 1, 3 or 6" in square brackets in sub-para (a)(iv) substituted by the Control of Explosives Precursors Regulations 2014, SI 2014/1942, reg 17(1), (2), as from 2 September 2014.

Sub-para (aa) originally inserted by the Rehabilitation of Offenders Act 1974 (Exceptions) (Amendment) Order 1986, SI 1986/1249, art 2, Schedule; subsequently substituted by SI 2001/1192, arts 2, 4(2).

Sub-para (ab) originally inserted by the Rehabilitation of Offenders Act 1974 (Exceptions) (Amendment No 2) Order 1986, SI 1986/2268, art 2(1), Schedule, para 2; subsequently revoked by the Rehabilitation of Offenders Act 1974 (Exceptions) (Amendment) (No 2) Order 2001, SI 2001/3816, arts 2, 4(1), (2).

Sub-para (b) revoked by SI 2013/1198, arts 2, 5(d).

Sub-para (bb) inserted by the Rehabilitation of Offenders Act 1974 (Exceptions) (Amendment) Order 2002, SI 2002/441, arts 2, 3(3), as from a day to be appointed (ie, the day on which the Police Act 1997, s 133(d) comes into force in England and Wales).

Sub-paras (e), (f) added by SI 2001/1192, arts 2, 4(3). Note that SI 2001/1192 purports to insert these paragraphs after sub-para (d) but it is believed that this is a drafting error as this article does not contain a sub-para (d).

Sub-paras (ea), (fa) inserted by SI 2014/1707, arts 2, 4(c), (d), as from 1 July 2014 (in so far as relating to sub-para (ea)), and as from 1 September 2014 (in so far as relating to sub-para (fa)).

Sub-para (g) inserted by SI 2001/3816, arts 2, 4(1), (4).

Words omitted from sub-para (g) revoked by the Rehabilitation of Offenders Act 1974 (Exceptions) (Amendment) (England and Wales) Order 2007, SI 2007/2149, arts 2, 4(2), (3).

The table in sub-para (g) was substituted by the Financial Services Act 2012 (Consequential Amendments and Transitional Provisions) Order 2013, SI 2013/472, art 3, Sch 2, para 1(1), (3)(b); and has subsequently been amended as follows—

Entry 3A was inserted by the Collective Investment in Transferable Securities (Contractual Scheme) Regulations 2013, SI 2013/1388, reg 7(1), (3).

Entries 6, 16(a) were substituted by the Financial Services and Markets Act 2000 (Over the Counter Derivatives, Central Counterparties and Trade Repositories) Regulations 2013, SI 2013/504, reg 28(1), (3).

The words in square brackets in entries 19, 20 and 21 were inserted by the Payment Systems and Services and Electronic Money (Miscellaneous Amendments) Regulations 2017, SI 2017/1173, reg 3, as from 22 December 2017.

Sub-para (h) added by SI 2002/441, arts 2, 3(4).

Words in square brackets in sub-para (h) substituted by the Public Bodies (Merger of the Gambling Commission and the National Lottery Commission) Order 2013, SI 2013/2329, art 4, Schedule, para 30.

Sub-para (i) added by SI 2003/965, arts 2, 5; words in square brackets in that sub-paragraph substituted by the Regulation and Inspection of Social Care (Wales) Act 2016 (Consequential Amendments to Secondary Legislation) Regulations 2017, SI 2017/52, reg 2, Sch 1, para 1(1), (2)(a), as from 3 April 2017.

Sub-para (j) originally added (together with sub-para (k)) by the Rehabilitation of Offenders Act 1974 (Exceptions) (Amendment) (England and Wales) Order 2006, SI 2006/2143, arts 2, 4; sub-para (j) was subsequently substituted (together with para (ja)), by the Public Contracts Regulations 2015, SI 2015/102, reg 116, Sch 6, Pt 2, as from 26 February 2015; sub-para (j) was further substituted, and sub-para (ja) was revoked, by the Public Procurement (Amendments, Repeals and Revocations) Regulations 2016, SI 2016/275, reg 3, Sch 2, Pt 2, paras 25, 27, as from 18 April 2016.

Sub-para (k) added as noted above; words in square brackets inserted, and words omitted revoked, by the Rehabilitation of Offenders Act 1974 (Exceptions) (Amendment No 2) (England and Wales) Order 2006, SI 2006/3290, art 2.

Sub-para (l) added by SI 2007/2149, arts 2, 4(4); words in square brackets substituted by SI 2012/3006, arts 69, 70.

Sub-paras (m), (n) added by SI 2009/1818, arts 2, 4(2).

Sub-para (o) added by the Rehabilitation of Offenders Act 1974 (Exceptions) (Amendment) (England and Wales) (No 2) Order 2011, SI 2011/2865, art 2.

Para (2): added by SI 2013/1198, arts 2, 5(e).

[2.19]
[3ZA

Neither section 4(2) of, nor paragraph 3(3) of Schedule 2 to, the Act applies in relation to—

(a) any question asked by or on behalf of any person, in the course of the duties of his office or employment, in order to assess the suitability—
   (i) of the person to whom the question relates for an office or employment specified in paragraph [1,] 6, 16, 17, 18, 18A, 31, 32, 35 or 36 of Part II of that Schedule or for any other work specified in paragraph 35 or 36 of that Part of that Schedule; or
   (ii) of the person to whom the question relates or of any other person to pursue an occupation specified in paragraph 1 or 8 of Part III of that Schedule or to pursue it subject to a particular condition or restriction; or
   (iii) of the person to whom the question relates or of any other person to hold a licence, certificate or permit of a kind specified in [paragraph 1, 3 or 6] of Schedule 2 to this Order or to hold it subject to a particular condition or restriction,

   where the person questioned is informed at the time the question is asked that, by virtue of this Order, spent convictions are to be disclosed; or

(b) any question asked by or on behalf of any person, in the course of his duties as a person employed in the service of the Crown, the United Kingdom Atomic Energy Authority or the FCA or the PRA in order to assess, for the purpose of safeguarding national security, the suitability of the person to whom the question relates or of any other person for any office or employment where the person questioned is informed at the time the question is asked that, by virtue of this Order, spent convictions are to be disclosed for the purpose of safeguarding national security.]

NOTES

Inserted by the Rehabilitation of Offenders Act 1974 (Exceptions) Order 1975 (Amendment) (England and Wales) Order 2013, SI 2013/1198, arts 2, 6.

Figure "1" in square brackets in sub-para (a)(i) inserted by the Rehabilitation of Offenders Act 1974 (Exceptions) Order 1975 (Amendment) (England and Wales) Order 2016, SI 2016/824, art 2(1), (3), as from 4 August 2016.

Words in square brackets in sub-para (a)(iii) substituted by the Control of Explosives Precursors Regulations 2014, SI 2014/1942, reg 17(1), (3), as from 2 September 2014.

Note: references to the Crown in para (b) above are to be treated as including the National Assembly for Wales Commission; see the National Assembly for Wales Commission (Crown Status) Order 2016, SI 2016/159, art 2 (with effect from 10 March 2016).

[2.20]
[3A

(1) [Subject to paragraph (1A), neither] section 4(2) of, nor paragraph 3(3) of Schedule 2 to, the Act applies to a question to which paragraph (2) or (3) applies.

[(1A) Paragraph (1) does not apply in relation to a protected caution or a protected conviction.]

(2) This paragraph applies to any question asked by or on behalf of any person ("A"), in the course of the duties of A's office or employment, in order to assess the suitability of the person to whom the question relates ("B") for any work which is a controlled activity relating to children within the meaning of section 21 of the 2006 Act [as it had effect immediately before the coming into force of section 68 of the Protection of Freedoms Act 2012], where the person questioned is told at the time the question is asked, that by virtue of this Order, spent convictions are to be disclosed but only if that person knows that B—

(a) is a person barred from regulated activity relating to children within the meaning of section 3(2) of the 2006 Act;
(b) is included in the list kept under section 1 of the Protection of Children Act 1999; or
(c) is subject to a direction made under section 142 of the Education Act 2002.

(3) This paragraph applies to any question asked by or on behalf of any person ("A"), in the course of the duties of A's office or employment, in order to assess the suitability of the person to whom the question relates ("B") for any work which is a controlled activity relating to vulnerable adults within the meaning of section 22 of the 2006 Act [as it had effect immediately before the coming into force of section 68 of the Protection of Freedoms Act 2012], where the person questioned is told at the time the question is asked, that by virtue of this Order, spent convictions are to be disclosed but only if that person knows that B—

(a) is a person barred from regulated activity relating to vulnerable adults within the meaning of section 3(3) of the 2006 Act; or
(b) is included in the list kept under section 81 of the Care Standards Act 2000.]

NOTES

Inserted by the Rehabilitation of Offenders Act 1974 (Exceptions) (Amendment) (England and Wales) Order 2010, SI 2010/1153, arts 2, 3.

Para (1): words in square brackets substituted by the Rehabilitation of Offenders Act 1974 (Exceptions) Order 1975 (Amendment) (England and Wales) Order 2013, SI 2013/1198, arts 2, 7(a).

Para (1A): inserted by SI 2013/1198, arts 2, 7(b).

Paras (2), (3): words in square brackets inserted by the Rehabilitation of Offenders Act 1974 (Exceptions) (Amendment) (England and Wales) Order 2012, SI 2012/1957, arts 2, 9.

Protection of Children Act 1999, s 1; Care Standards Act 2000, s 81; Education Act 2002, s 142: repealed by the Safeguarding Vulnerable Groups Act 2006, s 63, Sch 9, Pt 1, paras 8(1), (2), 9, Sch 10, as from 12 October 2009, but partly as from a day to be appointed in the case of the repeal of s 142 of the 2002 Act (subject to transitional provisions and savings (see SI 2009/2611)).

[2.21]
4

[(1)] [[Subject to paragraph (2), neither] paragraph (b) of section 4(3) of, nor paragraph 3(5) of Schedule 2 to, the Act shall apply] in relation to—

(a) the dismissal or exclusion of any person from any profession specified in Part I of Schedule 1 to this Order;
[(b) any office, employment or occupation specified in Part II or [of that Schedule apart from one specified in paragraph [1,] 6, 16, 17, 18, 18A, 31, 32, 35 or 36 or in Part III of that Schedule apart from one specified in paragraph 1 or 8] or any other work specified in paragraph [12A, 13, [13A,] 14, 14A, [14AA,] [14B, 14C,] [14D,] [14E,] 20, 21, ... 40, 43 or 44] of Part II of the said Schedule 1;]
(c) . . .
[(d) [any decision by the FCA, the PRA or the Bank of England]—
(i) to refuse an application for [Part 4A permission] under the 2000 Act,
(ii) to vary or to cancel such permission (or to refuse to vary or cancel such permission) or to impose a requirement under [section 55L, 55M or 55O] of that Act or,
(iii) to make, or to refuse to vary or revoke, an order under section 56 of that Act (prohibition orders),
(iv) to refuse an application for . . . approval under section 59 of that Act or to withdraw such approval,
(v) to refuse to make, or to revoke, an order declaring a unit trust scheme to be an authorised unit trust scheme under section 243 of the 2000 Act or to refuse to give its approval under section 251 of the 2000 Act to a proposal to replace the manager or trustee of such a scheme,
(vi) to give a direction under section 257 of the 2000 Act (authorised unit trust schemes), or to vary (or to refuse to vary or revoke) such a direction,
[(via) to refuse to make, or to revoke, an order declaring a contractual scheme to be an authorised contractual scheme under section 261D of the 2000 Act or to refuse to give its approval under section 261Q of the 2000 Act to a proposal to replace the operator or depositary of such a scheme,
(vib) to give a direction under section 261X of the 2000 Act or to vary (or to refuse to vary or revoke) such a direction,]
(vii) to refuse to make, or to revoke, an authorisation order under regulation 14 of the Open-Ended Investment Companies Regulations 2001 or to refuse to give its approval under regulation 21 of those Regulations to a proposal to replace a director or to appoint an additional director of an open-ended investment company,
(viii) to give a direction to an open-ended investment company under regulation 25 of those Regulations or to vary (or refuse to vary or revoke) such a direction,

(ix) . . . to refuse to make, or to revoke, an order declaring a collective investment scheme to be a recognised scheme under section 272 of [the 2000 Act],

(x) to refuse to make, or to revoke, a recognition order under section 290 of the 2000 Act, otherwise than by virtue of section 292(2) of that Act [to refuse to vary a recognition order under section 290ZA(1) of the 2000 Act, to vary a recognition order under section 290ZA(2) of the 2000 Act], [to refuse to grant an authorisation of the sort referred to in section 290ZB(1)(a) of the 2000 Act, to withdraw an authorisation of the sort referred to in section 290ZB(1)(c) of the 2000 Act,] or to give a direction to a UK recognised investment exchange[, recognised clearing house or recognised CSD] under section 296 [or 296A] of the 2000 Act,

(xi) to make, or to refuse to vary or to revoke, an order under section 329 (orders in respect of members of a designated professional body in relation to the general prohibition), . . .

(xii) to dismiss, fail to promote or exclude a person from being a key worker of [the FCA or the PRA],

[(xiii) to refuse an application for registration as an authorised electronic money institution or a small electronic money institution under the Electronic Money Regulations 2011, . . .

(xiv) to vary or cancel such registration (or to refuse to vary or cancel such registration) or to impose a requirement under regulation 7 of those Regulations,]

[(xv) to refuse an application for registration as an authorised payment institution [, a registered account information service provider] or a small payment institution under the Payment Services Regulations [2017], . . .]

(xvi) to vary or cancel such registration (or to refuse to vary or cancel such registration) or to impose a requirement under regulation 7 of those Regulations,]

[(xvii) in a case requiring any decision referred to in paragraphs (i) to (xvi), where the FCA, the PRA or the Bank of England has the function of deciding whether to give consent or conditional consent in relation to the decision which is proposed in that case, to give or refuse to give consent or to give conditional consent, or

(xviii) in a case requiring any decision referred to in paragraphs (i) to (xvi), where the FCA, the PRA or the Bank of England has the power under the 2000 Act to direct another regulator as to the decision to be taken in that case, to decide whether to give a direction and, if a direction is to be given, what direction to give,]

by reason of, or partly by reason of, a spent conviction of an individual . . . , or of any circumstances ancillary to such a conviction or of a failure (whether or not by that individual) to disclose such a conviction or any such circumstances;

(e) any decision by the scheme operator (within the meaning of section 225 of the 2000 Act) of the Financial Ombudsman Service to dismiss, or not to appoint, an individual as, an ombudsman (within the meaning of Schedule 17 to the 2000 Act) of the Financial Ombudsman Service by reason of, or partly by reason of, his spent conviction . . . , or of any circumstances ancillary to such a conviction or of a failure (whether or not by that individual) to disclose such a conviction or any such circumstances;

(f) [any decision of the FCA]—

(i) to refuse an application for listing under Part VI of the 2000 Act or to discontinue or suspend the listing of any securities under section 77 of that Act,

(ii) to refuse to grant a person's application for approval as a sponsor under section 88 of the 2000 Act or to cancel such approval, . . .

(iii) to dismiss, fail to promote or exclude a person from being a key worker of [the FCA in relation to the exercise of its functions under Part 6 of the 2000 Act, or],

[(iv) to refuse to grant a person's application under information provider rules (within the meaning of section 89P(9) of the 2000 Act) for approval as a Primary information provider, to impose limitations or other restrictions on the giving of information to which such an approval relates or to cancel such an approval,]

by reason of, or partly by reason of, a spent conviction of an individual . . . , or of any circumstances ancillary to such a conviction or of a failure (whether or not by that individual) to disclose such a conviction or any such circumstances;

(g) any decision of anyone who is specified in any of sub-paragraphs 2 to 4 or 5 to 7 of the second column of the table in article 3(g), other than [the FCA or the PRA], to dismiss an individual who has, or to fail to promote or exclude an individual who is seeking to obtain, the status specified in the corresponding entry in the first column of that table (but not, where applicable, the status of being an associate of another person), by reason of, or partly by reason of, a spent conviction of that individual or of his associate . . . , or of any circumstances ancillary to such a conviction or of a failure (whether or not by that individual) to disclose such a conviction or any such circumstances;

(h) any decision of anyone who is specified in sub-paragraph 8(a), 14(a) or 16(a) of the second column of the table in article 3(g) to dismiss an individual who has, or to fail to promote or exclude an individual who is seeking to obtain, the status specified in the corresponding entry in sub-paragraph (b) of the first column of that table (associate), by reason of, or partly by reason of, a spent conviction of that individual . . . , or of any circumstances ancillary to such a conviction or of a failure (whether or not by that individual) to disclose such a conviction or any such circumstances;

(i) any decision of the Council of Lloyd's—

(i) to refuse to admit any person as, or to exclude, an underwriting agent (within the meaning of section 2 of Lloyd's Act 1982), where that person has, or who has applied for, [Part 4A permission], or

(ii) to dismiss, or to exclude a person from being, an associate of the Council of Lloyd's,

by reason of, or partly by reason of, a spent conviction of an individual . . . , or of any circumstances ancillary to such a conviction or of a failure (whether or not by that individual) to disclose such a conviction or any such circumstances;

(j) any decision of a UK recognised investment exchange[, recognised clearing house or recognised CSD] to refuse to admit any person as, or to exclude, a member by reason of, or partly by reason of, a spent conviction of an individual . . . , or of any circumstances ancillary to such a conviction or of a failure (whether or not by that individual) to disclose such a conviction or any such circumstances;]

[(ja) any decision by the relevant registration authority, as defined by section 5 of the Care Standards Act 2000, to refuse to grant an application for registration under Part 2 of that Act or to suspend or remove or refuse to restore a person's registration under that Part of that Act;]

[(jb) any decision by the Welsh Ministers—

(i) to refuse an application for registration under section 7 of the 2016 Act,

(ii) to refuse (under section 12 of the 2016 Act) an application made by a person under section 11(1)(a)(i) or (ii) of the 2016 Act to vary their registration,

(iii) to cancel a person's registration under section 15(1)(b) to (f) or 23(1) of the 2016 Act,

(iv) to vary a person's registration under section 13(3)(b) or (4)(b) or 23(1) of the 2016 Act;]

[(k) any decision by [Social Care Wales] to refuse to grant an application for registration under [Part 4 of the Regulation and Inspection of Social Care (Wales) Act 2016] or to suspend, remove or refuse to restore a person's registration under that Part;

[(ka) any decision of Her Majesty's Chief Inspector of Education, Children's Services and Skills to refuse to grant a person's application for registration as a childminder agency or to suspend, cancel or impose a condition on a person's registration as a childminder agency under Part 3 of the Childcare Act 2006;]

(l) any decision to refuse to grant a taxi driver licence, to grant such a licence subject to conditions or to suspend, revoke or refuse to renew such a licence;

(m) any decision by the Security Industry Authority to refuse to grant a licence under section 8 of the Private Security Industry Act 2001, to grant such a licence subject to conditions, to modify such a licence (including any of the conditions of that licence) or to revoke such a licence];

[(n) any decision by the Football Association[, Football League] or Football Association Premier League to refuse to approve a person as able to undertake, in the course of acting as a steward at a sports ground at which football matches are played or as a supervisor or manager of such a person, licensable conduct within the meaning of the Private Security Industry Act 2001 without a licence issued under that Act, in accordance with . . . section 4 of that Act].

[(2) Paragraph (1) does not apply in relation to a protected caution or a protected conviction.]

NOTES

Revoked in relation to Scotland as noted at the beginning of this Order.

Para (1) is amended as follows:

Numbered as such by the Rehabilitation of Offenders Act 1974 (Exceptions) Order 1975 (Amendment) (England and Wales) Order 2013, SI 2013/1198, arts 2, 8(a).

Words in square brackets ending with the words "nor paragraph 3(5) of Schedule 2 to, the Act shall apply" substituted by the Rehabilitation of Offenders Act 1974 (Exceptions) (Amendment) (England and Wales) Order 2008, SI 2008/3259, arts 2, 5.

Words "Subject to paragraph (2), neither" in square brackets substituted by SI 2013/1198, arts 2, 8(b).

Sub-para (b) substituted by the Rehabilitation of Offenders Act 1974 (Exceptions) (Amendment) Order 2001, SI 2001/1192, arts 2, 5.

Words in first pair of square brackets in sub-para (b) substituted by SI 2013/1198, arts 2, 8(c)(i).

Figures "1", 14AA" and "14E" in square brackets in sub-para (b) inserted by the Rehabilitation of Offenders Act 1974 (Exceptions) Order 1975 (Amendment) (England and Wales) Order 2016, SI 2016/824, art 2(1)–(3), as from 4 August 2016.

Words in square brackets in sub-para (b) beginning with the words "12A, 13" substituted by the Rehabilitation of Offenders Act 1974 (Exceptions) (Amendment) (England and Wales) Order 2009, SI 2009/1818, arts 2, 5.

Figure "13A," in square brackets in sub-para (b) inserted by the Rehabilitation of Offenders Act 1974 (Exceptions) Order 1975 (Amendment) (England and Wales) Order 2015, SI 2015/317, art 2(1), (3), as from 10 March 2015.

Figures "14B, 14C," in square brackets in sub-para (b) inserted by the Rehabilitation of Offenders Act 1974 (Exceptions) Order 1975 (Amendment) (England and Wales) Order 2014, SI 2014/1707, arts 2, 5(a), as from 1 July 2014.

Figure "14D," in square brackets in sub-para (b) inserted by SI 2014/1707, arts 2, 5(b), as from 1 September 2014.

First figures omitted from sub-para (b) revoked by SI 2013/1198, arts 2, 8(c)(ii).

Second figure omitted from sub-para (b) revoked by the Rehabilitation of Offenders Act 1974 (Exceptions) (Amendment) (England and Wales) Order 2012, SI 2012/1957, arts 2, 8.

Sub-para (c) revoked by SI 2013/1198, arts 2, 8(d).

Sub-para (d) originally inserted by the Rehabilitation of Offenders Act 1974 (Exceptions) (Amendment No 2) Order 1986, SI 1986/2268, art 2(1), Schedule, para 3.

Sub-paras (d)–(j) substituted (for the original sub-para (d)) by the Rehabilitation of Offenders Act 1974 (Exceptions) (Amendment) (No 2) Order 2001, SI 2001/3816, arts 2, 5.

Words in first, second and third pairs of square brackets in sub-para (d) substituted by the Financial Services Act 2012 (Consequential Amendments and Transitional Provisions) Order 2013, SI 2013/472, art 3, Sch 2, para 1(1), (4)(a)(i)–(iii).

Words omitted from sub-para (d)(iv) revoked by SI 2013/472, art 3, Sch 2, para 1(1), (4)(a)(iv).

Sub-paras (d)(via), (vib) inserted by the Collective Investment in Transferable Securities (Contractual Scheme) Regulations 2013, SI 2013/1388, reg 7(1), (4).

Words omitted from sub-para (d)(ix) revoked, and words in square brackets in that sub-paragraph substituted, by the Alternative Investment Fund Managers Regulations 2013, SI 2013/1773, reg 81, Sch 2, Part 2, para 2(1), (3).

Words in first pair of square brackets in sub-para (d)(x) inserted by the Financial Services and Markets Act 2000 (Over the Counter Derivatives, Central Counterparties and Trade Repositories) Regulations 2013, SI 2013/504, reg 28(1), (4)(a).

Words in second pair of square brackets in sub-para (d)(x) inserted, and words in third pair of square brackets substituted by the Central Securities Depositories Regulations 2017, SI 2017/1064, reg 10, Schedule, Pt 2, para 18(1), (4)(a), as from 28 November 2017.

Words "or 296A" in square brackets in sub-para (d)(x) inserted by SI 2013/472, art 3, Sch 2, para 1(1), (4)(a)(v).

Word omitted from sub-para (d)(xi) revoked, and sub-paras (d)(xiii), (xiv) added, by the Electronic Money Regulations 2011, SI 2011/99, reg 79, Sch 4, Pt 2, para 7(c).

Words in square brackets in sub-para (d)(xii) substituted by SI 2013/472, art 3, Sch 2, para 1(1), (4)(a)(vi).

Word omitted from sub-para (d)(xiii) revoked, and sub-paras (d)(xv), (xvi) added, by the Rehabilitation of Offenders Act 1974 (Exceptions) (Amendment) (England and Wales) Order 2011, SI 2011/1800, art 2(1), (4).

Words in first pair of square brackets in sub-para (d)(xv) inserted, and year "2017" in square brackets substituted, by the Payment Services Regulations 2017, SI 2017/752, reg 156, Sch 8, Pt 3, para 6(b), as from 13 January 2018.

Word omitted from sub-para (d)(xv) revoked, and sub-paras (d)(xvii), (xviii) added, by SI 2013/472, art 3, Sch 2, para 1(1), (4)(a)(viii).

All other words omitted from sub-para (d) revoked by SI 2007/2149, arts 2, 5(1).

Sub-para (e) substituted as noted above; words omitted revoked by SI 2007/2149, arts 2, 5(1).

Sub-para (f) substituted as noted above; words in first pair of square brackets and words in square brackets in sub-para (f)(iii) substituted, word omitted from sub-para (f)(ii) revoked, and sub-para (f)(iv) inserted, by SI 2013/472, art 3, Sch 2, para 1(1), (4)(b); final words omitted revoked by SI 2007/2149, arts 2, 5(1).

Sub-para (g) substituted as noted above; words in square brackets substituted by SI 2013/472, art 3, Sch 2, para 1(1), (4)(c); words omitted revoked by SI 2007/2149, arts 2, 5(1).

Sub-para (h) substituted as noted above; words omitted revoked by SI 2007/2149, arts 2, 5(1).

Sub-para (i): substituted as noted above; words in square brackets substituted by SI 2013/472, art 3, Sch 2, para 1(1), (4)(d); words omitted revoked by SI 2007/2149, arts 2, 5(1).

Sub-para (j) substituted as noted above; words in square brackets substituted by SI 2017/1064, reg 10, Schedule, Pt 2, para 18(1), (4)(b), as from 28 November 2017; words omitted revoked by SI 2007/2149, arts 2, 5(1).

Sub-paras (ja), (ka) inserted by SI 2014/1707, arts 2, 5(c), (d), as from 1 July 2014 (in so far as relating to sub-para (ja)), and as from 1 September 2014 (in so far as relating to sub-para (ka)).

Sub-para (jb) inserted by the Regulation and Inspection of Social Care (Wales) Act 2016 (Consequential Amendments to Secondary Legislation) Regulations 2019, SI 2019/237, reg 2, Sch 1, para 1(1), (3), as from 29 April 2019.

Sub-paras (k)–(m) added by SI 2003/965, arts 2, 7; words in square brackets in sub-para (k) substituted by the Regulation and Inspection of Social Care (Wales) Act 2016 (Consequential Amendments to Secondary Legislation) Regulations 2017, SI 2017/52, reg 2, Sch 1, para 1(1), (2)(a), as from 3 April 2017.

Sub-para (n) added by the Rehabilitation of Offenders Act 1974 (Exceptions) (Amendment) (England and Wales) Order 2006, SI 2006/2143, arts 2, 5; words in square brackets inserted, and words omitted revoked, by the Rehabilitation of Offenders Act 1974 (Exceptions) (Amendment No 2) (England and Wales) Order 2006, SI 2006/3290, art 2.

[2.22]
[4ZA

Neither paragraph (b) of section 4(3) of, nor paragraph 3(5) of Schedule 2 to, the Act applies in relation to—

(a) any office, employment or occupation specified in paragraph [1,] 6, 16, 17, 18, 18A, 31, 32, 35 or 36 of Part II of that Schedule or paragraph 1 or 8 of Part III of that Schedule or any other work specified in paragraph 35 or 36 of Part II of that Schedule;

(b) any action taken for the purpose of safeguarding national security.]

NOTES

Inserted by the Rehabilitation of Offenders Act 1974 (Exceptions) Order 1975 (Amendment) (England and Wales) Order 2013, SI 2013/1198, arts 2, 9.

Figure "1" in square brackets in sub-para (a) inserted by the Rehabilitation of Offenders Act 1974 (Exceptions) Order 1975 (Amendment) (England and Wales) Order 2016, SI 2016/824, art 2(1), (3), as from 4 August 2016.

[2.23]
[4A

(1) Section 4(2) of the Act shall not apply to a question asked by or on behalf of any person, in the course of the duties of the person's office or employment, in order to assess whether the person to whom the question relates is disqualified by reason of section 66(3)(c) of the 2011 Act from being elected as, or being, a police and crime commissioner.

(2) Section 4(3)(a) of the Act shall not apply in relation to any obligation to disclose any matter if the obligation is imposed in order to assess whether a person is disqualified by reason of section 66(3)(c) of the 2011 Act from being elected as, or being, a police and crime commissioner.

(3) Section 4(3)(b) of the Act shall not apply in relation to the disqualification of a person from being elected as, or being, a police and crime commissioner under section 66(3)(c) of the 2011 Act.

(4) In this article—

"the 2011 Act" means the Police Reform and Social Responsibility Act 2011; and

"police and crime commissioner" means a police and crime commissioner established under section 1 of the 2011 Act.]

NOTES

Inserted by the Rehabilitation of Offenders Act 1974 (Exceptions) (Amendment) (England and Wales) Order 2012, SI 2012/1957, arts 2, 3.

[2.24]
[5

(1) [Neither section 4(1) of, nor paragraph 3(1) of Schedule 2 to, the Act shall]—

(a) apply in relation to any proceedings specified in Schedule 3 to this Order;

(b) apply in relation to any proceedings specified in paragraph (2) below to the extent that there falls to be determined therein any issue relating to a person's spent conviction . . . or to circumstances ancillary thereto;

(c) prevent, in any proceedings specified in paragraph (2) below, the admission or requirement of any evidence relating to a person's spent conviction . . . or to circumstances ancillary thereto.

[(2) The proceedings referred to in paragraph (1) above are any proceedings with respect to a decision or proposed decision of the kind specified in article [4(1)(d) to (n)].]]

NOTES

Revoked in relation to Scotland as noted at the beginning of this Order.

Substituted by the Rehabilitation of Offenders Act 1974 (Exceptions) (Amendment No 2) Order 1986, SI 1986/2268, art 2(1), Schedule, para 4.

Para (1): words in square brackets substituted by the Rehabilitation of Offenders Act 1974 (Exceptions) (Amendment) (England and Wales) Order 2008, SI 2008/3259, arts 2, 6(1); words omitted revoked by the Rehabilitation of Offenders Act 1974 (Exceptions) (Amendment) (England and Wales) Order 2007, SI 2007/2149, arts 2, 6.

Para (2): substituted by the Rehabilitation of Offenders Act 1974 (Exceptions) (Amendment) (No 2) Order 2001, SI 2001/3816, arts 2, 6; words in square brackets substituted by the Rehabilitation of Offenders Act 1974 (Exceptions) Order 1975 (Amendment) (England and Wales) Order 2015, SI 2015/317, art 2(1), (4), as from 10 March 2015.

[2.25]
[6

(1) Neither section 4(2) of, nor paragraph 3(3) of Schedule 2 to, the Act applies to a question to which paragraph (2) applies.

(2) This paragraph applies to a question asked by or on behalf of any person in the course of that person's office or employment in the Channel Islands or the Isle of Man in order to assess the suitability of the person to whom the question relates for any purposes referred to in article 3[, 3ZA] or 3A, where—

(a) the person asking the question states that a corresponding question and purpose are also provided for in—

(i) the Rehabilitation of Offenders (Exceptions) (Jersey) Regulations 2002 ("the Jersey Regulations");

(ii) the Rehabilitation of Offenders (Bailiwick of Guernsey) Law 2002 (Commencement, Exclusions and Exceptions) Ordinance 2006 ("the Guernsey Ordinance"); or

(iii) the Rehabilitation of Offenders Act 2001 (Exceptions) Order 2001 ("the Isle of Man Exceptions Order"), and

(b) the person questioned is one to whom article 3 or 3A would apply [in relation to the caution or conviction in question, or paragraph 3ZA would apply,] and is informed at the time the question is asked that spent convictions are to be disclosed.

(3) Neither subsection (1) or (3) of section 4 of, nor paragraph 3(1) or (5) of Schedule 2 to, the Act apply to a question to which paragraph (4) applies.

(4) This paragraph applies to a question asked by or on behalf of any person in the course of that person's office or employment in the Channel Islands or the Isle of Man in respect of a case or class of case and conviction specified in article 4 [or 4ZA] or for a purpose mentioned in article 5, where the person asking the question states that the Jersey Regulations or the Guernsey Ordinance or the Isle of Man Exceptions Order provides for a corresponding case or class of case and conviction or a corresponding purpose, and the person questioned is a person to whom [article 4 or 4ZA would apply in relation to the caution or conviction in question, or article 5 would apply].]

NOTES

Inserted by the Rehabilitation of Offenders Act 1974 (Exceptions) (Amendment) (England and Wales) Order 2009, SI 2009/1818, arts 2, 6, and substituted by the Rehabilitation of Offenders Act 1974 (Exceptions) (Amendment) (England and Wales) Order 2010, SI 2010/1153, arts 2, 4.

Words in square brackets in paras (2), (4) inserted or substituted by the Rehabilitation of Offenders Act 1974 (Exceptions) Order 1975 (Amendment) (England and Wales) Order 2013, SI 2013/1198, arts 2, 10.

SCHEDULES
SCHEDULE 1
[EXCEPTED PROFESSIONS, OFFICES, EMPLOYMENTS, WORK AND OCCUPATIONS]

Article 2(3), 3, 4

PART I
PROFESSIONS

[2.26]
[**1.** Health care professional.]

Part 2 Statutory Instruments

2. Barrister (in England and Wales), . . . solicitor.

3. Chartered accountant, certified accountant.

4. . . .

5. Veterinary surgeon.

6–8A, 9, 10–13. . .

14. Actuary.

15. Registered foreign lawyer.

[**16.** Chartered legal executive or other CILEx authorised person.]

17. Receiver appointed by the Court of Protection.]

[**18.** Home inspector.]

NOTES

Revoked in relation to Scotland as noted at the beginning of this Order.

Schedule heading: substituted by the Rehabilitation of Offenders Act 1974 (Exceptions) (Amendment) Order 2001, SI 2001/1192, arts 2, 6(1).

Para 1: substituted the Rehabilitation of Offenders Act 1974 (Exceptions) (Amendment) (England and Wales) Order 2012, SI 2012/1957, arts 2, 6(1), (2).

Para 2: words omitted revoked by the Rehabilitation of Offenders Act 1974 (Exceptions) Order 1975 (Amendment) (England and Wales) Order 2013, SI 2013/1198, arts 2, 11(1), (2)(a).

Paras 4, 6, 7, 10: revoked by SI 2012/1957, arts 2, 6(1), (3).

Paras 8, 8A: substituted, for the original para 8, by the Pharmacists and Pharmacy Technicians Order 2007, SI 2007/289, art 67, Sch 1, Pt 2, para 12(a); revoked by SI 2012/1957, arts 2, 6(1), (3).

Para 9: revoked by SI 2013/1198, arts 2, 11(1), (2)(b).

Para 11: originally added by the Osteopaths Act 1993, s 39(2); revoked by SI 2012/1957, arts 2, 6(1), (3).

Para 12: originally added by the Chiropractors Act 1994, s 40(2); revoked by SI 2012/1957, arts 2, 6(1), (3).

Paras 13–17: added by the Rehabilitation of Offenders Act 1974 (Exceptions) (Amendment) Order 2002, SI 2002/441, arts 2, 5(1); para 13 revoked by SI 2009/1182, art 4(1), Sch 4, Pt 1, para 1(a); para 16 subsequently substituted by the Rehabilitation of Offenders Act 1974 (Exceptions) Order 1975 (Amendment) (England and Wales) Order 2014, SI 2014/1707, arts 2, 6(a), as from 1 July 2014.

Para 18: added by the Rehabilitation of Offenders Act 1974 (Exceptions) (Amendment) (England and Wales) Order 2006, SI 2006/2143, arts 2, 6.

Solicitor: the reference to a solicitor should now be read as including a reference to a registered European lawyer, see the European Communities (Lawyer's Practice) Regulations 2000, SI 2000/1119, reg 37(3), Sch 4, para 19 (note that SI 2000/1119 is revoked by the Services of Lawyers and Lawyer's Practice (Revocation etc) (EU Exit) Regulations 2019, SI 2019/375, reg 3, as from exit day (as defined in the European Union (Withdrawal) Act 2018, s 20)).

PART II
[OFFICES, EMPLOYMENTS AND WORK]

[2.27]

1. Judicial appointments.

[**2.** The Director of Public Prosecutions and any office or employment in the Crown Prosecution Service.]

3. . . .

[**4.** [Designated officers for magistrates' courts, for justices of the peace or for local justice areas], justices' clerks [and assistants to justices' clerks].]

5. . . .

[**6.** Constables and persons appointed as police cadets to undergo training with a view to becoming constables and naval, military and air force police.

6A. Persons employed for the purposes of, or to assist the constables of, a police force established under any enactment.]

7. Any employment which is concerned with the administration of, or is otherwise normally carried out wholly or partly within the precincts of, a prison, remand centre, [removal centre, short-term holding facility,] [young offender institution] or young offenders institution, and members of boards of visitors appointed under section 6 of the Prison Act 1952 . . .

8. Traffic wardens appointed under section 81 of the Road Traffic Regulation Act 1967 . . .

[**9.** Officers of providers of probation services as defined in section 9 of the Offender Management Act 2007.]

10, 11. . . .

[**12.** Any office or employment which is concerned with:

(a) the provision of care services to vulnerable adults; or

(b) the representation of, or advocacy services for, vulnerable adults by a service that has been approved by the Secretary of State or created under any enactment;

and which is of such a kind as to enable a person, in the course of his normal duties, to have access to vulnerable adults in receipt of such services.]

[12A. Any work which is regulated activity relating to vulnerable adults within the meaning of Part 2 of Schedule 4 to the 2006 Act [including that Part] [as it had effect immediately before the coming into force of section 66 of the Protection of Freedoms Act 2012].]

[13. Any employment or other work which is concerned with the provision of health services and which is of such a kind as to enable the holder of that employment or the person engaged in that work to have access to persons in receipt of such services in the course of his normal duties.]

[13A. Any employment or other work in England or Wales concerned with—

(a) the investigation of fraud, corruption or other unlawful activity affecting the national health service, or

(b) security management in the national health service,

where "the national health service" means, in respect of England, the health service continued under section 1(1) of the National Health Service Act 2006 and, in respect of Wales, that continued under section 1(1) of the National Health Service (Wales) Act 2006.]

[14. Any work which is—

(a) work in a regulated position; or

(b) work in a further education institution [or 16 to 19 Academy] where the normal duties of that work involve regular contact with persons aged under 18.]

[14A. Any work which is regulated activity relating to children within the meaning of Part 1 of Schedule 4 to the 2006 Act [including that Part] [as it had effect immediately before the coming into force of section 64 of the Protection of Freedoms Act 2012].]

[14AA. Any work done infrequently which, if done frequently, would be regulated activity relating to children within the meaning of Part 1 of Schedule 4 to the 2006 Act including that Part as it had effect immediately before the coming into force of section 64 of the Protection of Freedoms Act 2012.]

[14B. Any employment or other work that is carried out at a children's home or residential family centre.

14C. Any employment or other work which is carried out for the purposes of an adoption service, an adoption support agency, a voluntary adoption agency, a fostering service or a fostering agency and which is of such a kind as to enable a person, in the course of his normal duties, to have contact with children or access to sensitive or personal information about children.]

[14D. Any employment or office which is concerned with the management of a childminder agency or any work for a childminder agency which is of such a kind as to require the person engaged in that work to enter day care premises or premises on which child minding is provided and as to enable the person, in the course of his normal duties, to have contact with children for whom child minding or day care is provided or access to sensitive or personal information about children for whom childminding or day care is provided.]

[14E. [The Director General, or any member or member of staff, of the Independent Office for Police Conduct] who in the course of his normal duties—

(a) has contact with vulnerable adults; or

(b) has access to sensitive or personal information about children or vulnerable adults.]

[15. Any employment in the Royal Society for the Prevention of Cruelty to Animals where the person employed or working, as part of his duties, may carry out the [humane] killing of animals.

16. Any office or employment in the Serious Fraud Office.

17. Any office or employment in the [National Crime Agency].

[18. The Commissioners for Her Majesty's Revenue and Customs and any office or employment in their service.

18A. . . .]

19. Any employment which is concerned with the monitoring, for the purposes of child protection, of communications by means of the internet.]

[20. Any employment or other work which is normally carried out in premises approved under section 9 of the Criminal Justice and Court Services Act 2000.

21. Any employment or other work which is normally carried out in a hospital used only for the provision of high security psychiatric services.]

[22. An individual designated under section 2 of the Traffic Management Act 2004.

23. Judges' clerks, secretaries and legal secretaries within the meaning of section 98 of the [Senior Courts Act 1981].

Part 2 Statutory Instruments

24. Court officers and court contractors, who in the course of their work, have face to face contact with judges of the Supreme Court, or access to such judges' lodgings.

25. Persons who in the course of their work have regular access to personal information relating to an identified or identifiable member of the judiciary.

26. Court officers and court contractors, who, in the course of their work, attend either the Royal Courts of Justice or the Central Criminal Court.

27. Court security officers, and tribunal security officers.

28. Court contractors, who, in the course of their work, have unsupervised access to court-houses, offices and other accommodation used in relation to the courts.

29. Contractors, sub-contractors, and any person acting under the authority of such a contractor or sub-contractor, who, in the course of their work, have unsupervised access to tribunal buildings, offices and other accommodation used in relation to tribunals.

30. The following persons—

(a) Court officers who execute county court warrants;

(b) High Court enforcement officers;

(c) sheriffs and under-sheriffs;

(d) tipstaffs;

(e) any other persons who execute High Court writs or warrants who act under the authority of a person listed at (a) to (d);

(f) persons who execute writs of sequestration;

(g) civilian enforcement officers as defined in section 125A of the Magistrates' Courts Act 1980;

(h) persons who are authorised to execute warrants under section 125B(1) of the Magistrates' Courts Act 1980, and any other person, (other than a constable), who is authorised to execute a warrant under section 125(2) of the 1980 Act;

(i) persons who execute clamping orders, as defined in paragraph 38(2) of Schedule 5 to the Courts Act 2003.

31. The Official Solicitor and his deputy.

32. Persons appointed to the office of Public Trustee or deputy Public Trustee, and officers of the Public Trustee.

33. Court officers and court contractors who exercise functions in connection with the administration and management of funds in court including the deposit, payment, delivery and transfer in, into and out of any court of funds in court and regulating the evidence of such deposit, payment, delivery or transfer and court officers and court contractors, who receive payments in pursuance of a conviction or order of a magistrates' court.]

[**34.** People working in [the Department for Education], the Office for Standards in Education, Children's Services and Skills . . . with access to sensitive or personal information about children . . . .

35. Any office, employment or other work which is concerned with the establishment or operation of a database under section 12 of the Children Act 2004, and which is of such a kind as to enable the holder of that office or employment, or the person engaged in that work, to have access to information included in the database.

36. Any office, employment or other work which is of such a kind that the person is or may be permitted or required to be given access to a database under section 12 of the Children Act 2004.

37. . . .

38. The chairman, other members, and members of staff (including any person seconded to serve as a member of staff) of the [Disclosure and Barring Service][, and any other work in the Disclosure and Barring Service].

39. Staff working within the Public Guardianship Office, (to be known as the Office of the Public Guardian from October 2007), with access to data relating to children and vulnerable adults.

40. The Commissioner for Older People in Wales, and his deputy, and any person appointed by the Commissioner to assist him in the discharge of his functions or authorised to discharge his functions on his behalf.

41. The Commissioners for the Gambling Commission and any office or employment in their service.

42. Individuals seeking authorisation from the Secretary of State for the Home Department to become authorised search officers.

43. Any employment or other work where the normal duties

(a) involve caring for, training, supervising, or being solely in charge of, persons aged under 18 serving in the naval, military or air forces of the Crown; or

(b) include supervising or managing a person employed or working in a capacity referred to in paragraph (a).]

[44. . . .]

NOTES

Revoked in relation to Scotland as noted at the beginning of this Order.

Schedule heading: substituted as noted *ante*.

Part heading: substituted by the Rehabilitation of Offenders Act 1974 (Exceptions) (Amendment) Order 2001, SI 2001/1192, arts 2, 6(21).

Para 2: substituted by the Rehabilitation of Offenders Act 1974 (Exceptions) (Amendment) Order 2002, SI 2002/441, arts 2, 5(2)(a), (b).

Para 3: revoked by the Rehabilitation of Offenders Act 1974 (Exceptions) (Amendment) (England and Wales) Order 2006, SI 2006/2143, arts 2, 7(a).

Para 4: substituted by SI 2001/1192, arts 2, 6(3); words in first pair of square brackets substituted by the Courts Act 2003 (Consequential Provisions) (No 2) Order 2005, SI 2005/617, art 2, Schedule, para 55; words in second pair of square brackets substituted by SI 2006/2143, arts 2, 7(b)(i).

Para 5: revoked by the Rehabilitation of Offenders Act 1974 (Exceptions) Order 1975 (Amendment) (England and Wales) Order 2013, SI 2013/1198, arts 2, 11(1), (3)(a).

Paras 6, 6A: substituted (for the original para 6) by SI 2013/1198, arts 2, 11(1), (3)(b).

Para 7: words in first pair of square brackets inserted by SI 2006/2143, arts 2, 7(b)(ii); words in second pair of square brackets substituted by virtue of the Criminal Justice Act 1988, s 123(6), Sch 8, paras 1, 3; words omitted revoked by SI 2013/1198, arts 2, 11(1), (3)(c).

Para 8: words omitted revoked by SI 2013/1198, arts 2, 11(1), (3)(d).

Para 9: substituted by the Rehabilitation of Offenders Act 1974 (Exceptions) Order 1975 (Amendment) (England and Wales) Order 2014, SI 2014/1707, arts 2, 6(b)(i), as from 1 July 2014.

Paras 10, 11: revoked by the Rehabilitation of Offenders Act 1974 (Exceptions) (Amendment) Order 1986, SI 1986/1249, art 2, Schedule.

Para 12: substituted by SI 2006/2143, arts 2, 7(c).

Paras 12A, 14A: inserted by the Rehabilitation of Offenders Act 1974 (Exceptions) (Amendment) (England and Wales) Order 2009, SI 2009/1818, arts 2, 7(1); words in first pair of square brackets in those paragraphs inserted by the Rehabilitation of Offenders Act 1974 (Exceptions) Order 1975 (Amendment) (England and Wales) Order 2015, SI 2015/317, art 2(1), (5)(a)(i), (iii), as from 10 March 2015; words in second pair of square brackets in those paragraphs inserted by the Rehabilitation of Offenders Act 1974 (Exceptions) (Amendment) (England and Wales) Order 2012, SI 2012/1957, arts 2, 10(1)–(3).

Para 13: substituted by SI 2001/1192, arts 2, 6(4).

Para 13A: inserted by SI 2015/317, art 2(1), (5)(a)(i), (ii), as from 10 March 2015.

Para 14: substituted, for the original paras 14, 15, by SI 1986/1249, art 2, Schedule; further substituted by SI 2001/1192, arts 2, 6(5); words in square brackets in sub-para (b) inserted by the Alternative Provision Academies and 16 to 19 Academies (Consequential Amendments to Subordinate Legislation) (England) Order 2012, SI 2012/979, art 2, Schedule, para 2.

Para 14AA: inserted by the Rehabilitation of Offenders Act 1974 (Exceptions) Order 1975 (Amendment) (England and Wales) Order 2016, SI 2016/824, art 2(1), (4), as from 4 August 2016.

Paras 14B–14D: inserted by SI 2014/1707, arts 2, 6(b)(ii), (iii), as from 1 July 2014 (in so far as relating to paras 14B, 14C), and as from 1 September 2014 (in so far as relating to para 14D).

Para 14E: inserted by SI 2016/824, art 2(1), (4), as from 4 August 2016; words in square brackets substituted by the Independent Office for Police Conduct (Transitional and Consequential) Regulations 2017, SI 2017/1250, reg 3, as from 8 January 2018.

Para 15: added (together with paras 16, 17, 18, 19) by SI 2002/441, arts 2, 5(2)(c); word in square brackets inserted by SI 2006/2143, arts 2, 7(b)(iii).

Paras 16, 19: added as noted above.

Para 17: added as noted above; words in square brackets substituted by virtue of the Crime and Courts Act 2013, s 15(3), Sch 8, Pt 4, para 190 (for general transitional provisions and savings relating to the abolition of SOCA, see s 15(3), Sch 8, Pt 1 thereto).

Paras 18, 18A: para 18 originally added as noted above; subsequently substituted by new paras 18, 18A by SI 2006/2143, arts 2, 7(d); para 18A subsequently revoked by the Public Bodies (Merger of the Director of Public Prosecutions and the Director of Revenue and Customs Prosecutions) Order 2014, SI 2014/834, art 3(3), Sch 3, para 1 (for general transitional provisions, etc, relating to the abolition of the Revenue and Customs Prosecutions Office and the transfer of the functions of the Director of Revenue and Customs Prosecutions to the Director of Public Prosecutions, see arts 4–10 of the 2014 Order).

Paras 20, 21: added by the Rehabilitation of Offenders Act 1974 (Exceptions) (Amendment) (England and Wales) Order 2003, SI 2003/965, arts 2, 8.

Paras 22–33: added by SI 2006/2143, arts 2, 7(e); words in square brackets in para 23 substituted by the Constitutional Reform Act 2005, s 59(5), Sch 11, Pt 1, para 1(2).

Paras 34–43: added by the Rehabilitation of Offenders Act 1974 (Exceptions) (Amendment) (England and Wales) Order 2007, SI 2007/2149, arts 2, 7; words in square brackets in para 34 substituted by the Secretary of State for Education Order 2010, SI 2010/1836, art 6, Schedule, Pt 2, para 11(a); words omitted from para 34 revoked, and para 37 revoked, by SI 2012/1957, arts 2, 10(1), (4), (5); words in first pair of square brackets in para 38 substituted, and words in second pair of square brackets in that paragraph inserted, by the Protection of Freedoms Act 2012 (Disclosure and Barring Service Transfer of Functions) Order 2012, SI 2012/3006, arts 18, 20(1), (2).

Paras 44: originally added by SI 2009/1818, arts 2, 7(1), and revoked by SI 2012/3006, arts 18, 20(1), (3), 69, 71.

Criminal Justice and Court Services Act 2000, s 9: repealed by the Offender Management Act 2007, s 39, Sch 5, Pt 1; as to premises approved under the 2007 Act, see s 13 thereof.

Powers of Criminal Courts Act 1973, Sch 3: repealed. As to arrangements for the provision of probation services, see now the Offender Management Act 2007, Pt I (ss 1–15).

Prison Act 1952, s 6: Boards of visitors appointed under the Prison Act 1952, s 6 have been renamed as independent monitoring boards by the Offender Management Act 2007, s 26(1).

Road Traffic Regulation Act 1967, s 81: repealed by the Road Traffic Regulation Act 1984 and replaced by s 95 of that Act.

PART III
REGULATED OCCUPATIONS

[2.28]
1. Firearms dealer.

2. Any occupation in respect of which an application to the Gaming Board for Great Britain for a licence, certificate or registration is required by or under any enactment.

3. . . .

4. Dealer in securities.

5. Manager or trustee under a unit trust scheme.

6. Any occupation which is concerned with—
(a) the management of a place in respect of which the approval of the Secretary of State is required by section 1 of the Abortion Act 1967; or
(b) in England and Wales, carrying on [a regulated activity in respect of which a person is required to be registered under Part 1 of the Health and Social Care Act 2008];
(c) . . .

7. . . .

8. Any occupation in respect of which the holder, as occupier of premises on which explosives are kept, is required [pursuant to [regulations 4, 5 and 11 of the Explosives Regulations 2014] to obtain from the chief officer of police a valid explosives certificate certifying him to be a fit person to acquire or acquire and keep explosives].

[**9.** . . .]

[**10.** Approved legal services body manager.]

[**11.** A regulated immigration adviser.]

[**12.** A head of finance and administration of a licensed body.]

[**13.** A head of legal practice of a licensed body.]

[**14.** CILEx approved manager.]

NOTES

Revoked in relation to Scotland as noted at the beginning of this Order.

Schedule heading: substituted as noted *ante*.

Para 3: revoked by the Rehabilitation of Offenders Act 1974 (Exceptions) (Amendment) (No 2) Order 2001, SI 2001/3816, arts 2, 7(a).

Paras 4, 5: revoked by the Rehabilitation of Offenders Act 1974 (Exceptions) (Amendment No 2) Order 1986, SI 1986/2268, art 2(2)(a), as from the date on which the Financial Services Act 1986, s 189, Sch 14 are brought into force for the purposes of this revocation. Note, however, that the 1986 Act was repealed by the Financial Services and Markets Act 2000 (Consequential Amendments and Repeals) Order 2001, SI 2001/3649, art 3(1)(c), without ever having been brought into force for these purposes. Therefore, these revocations cannot, under the present drafting of SI 1986/2268, ever be brought into force.

Para 6: words in square brackets in sub-para (b) substituted, and sub-para (c) revoked, by the Rehabilitation of Offenders Act 1974 (Exceptions) Order 1975 (Amendment) (England and Wales) Order 2013, SI 2013/1198, arts 2, 11(1), (4)(a).

Para 7: revoked by SI 2013/1198, arts 2, 11(1), (4)(b).

Para 8: words in square brackets substituted by the Manufacture and Storage of Explosives Regulations 2005, SI 2005/1082, reg 28(1), Sch 5, Pt 2, para 27(1), (2); words in second (inner) pair of square brackets substituted by the Explosives Regulations 2014, SI 2014/1638, reg 48(1), Sch 13, Pt 2, para 11(a), as from 1 October 2014.

Para 9: originally added by the Rehabilitation of Offenders Act 1974 (Exceptions) (Amendment) Order 2002, SI 2002/441, arts 2, 5(3)(a), and revoked by the Rehabilitation of Offenders Act 1974 (Exceptions) (Amendment) (England and Wales) Order 2003, SI 2003/965, arts 2, 9.

Para 10: added by the Rehabilitation of Offenders Act 1974 (Exceptions) (Amendment) (England and Wales) Order 2008, SI 2008/3259, arts 2, 7(1).

Para 11: added by the Rehabilitation of Offenders Act 1974 (Exceptions) (Amendment) (England and Wales) Order 2009, SI 2009/1818, arts 2, 7(2).

Paras 12, 13: added by the Rehabilitation of Offenders Act 1974 (Exceptions) (Amendment) (England and Wales) Order 2011, SI 2011/1800, art 2(1), (5).

Para 14: added by the Rehabilitation of Offenders Act 1974 (Exceptions) Order 1975 (Amendment) (England and Wales) Order 2014, SI 2014/1707, arts 2, 6(c), as from 1 July 2014.

Gaming Board for Great Britain: functions, etc, transferred to the Gambling Commission by the Gambling Act 2005, s 21, Sch 5.

Public Health Act 1936, s 187; Mental Health Act 1959, s 14: repealed. In England the registration of health and adult social care is now under the Health and Social Care Act 2008, Pt 1, Chapter 2, and the registration of all children's services is under the Care Standards Act 2000, Pt II. In Wales the registration of health and all social care is under Pt II of the 2000 Act.

National Assistance Act 1948, s 37: repealed. That section made provision for the registration of disabled persons' and old persons' homes; see now the note above.

PART IV
INTERPRETATION

[2.29]
In this Schedule—

["actuary" means a member of [the Institute and Faculty of Actuaries];

["approved legal services body manager" means a person who must be approved by the Law Society under section 9A(2)(e) of the Administration of Justice Act 1985;]

["assistants to justices' clerks" has the meaning given by section 27(5) of the Courts Act 2003;]

["authorised search officer" means a person authorised to carry out searches in accordance with sections 40 and 41 of the Immigration, Asylum and Nationality Act 2006;]

"care services" means

(i) accommodation and nursing or personal care in a care home (where "care home" has the same meaning as in the Care Standards Act 2000);

(ii) personal care or nursing or support for a person to live independently in his own home;

(iii) social care services; or

(iv) any services provided in an establishment catering for a person with learning difficulties;]

"certified accountant" means a member of the Association of Certified Accountants;

"chartered accountant" means a member of the Institute of Chartered Accountants in England and Wales or of the Institute of Chartered Accountants of Scotland;

["chartered legal executive" means a fellow of the Chartered Institute of Legal Executives;]

[. . .]

["child" means a person under the age of eighteen (and "children" is to be construed accordingly);]

["CILEx approved manager" means a person authorised by the Chartered Institute of Legal Executives to be concerned in the management of a body which is a CILEx authorised person.

"CILEx authorised person" means a person authorised by the Chartered Institute of Legal Executives to provide a reserved legal activity in accordance with the Legal Services Act 2007;]

["court contractor" means a person who has entered into a contract with the Lord Chancellor under section 2(4) of the Courts Act 2003, such a person's sub-contractor, and persons acting under the authority of such a contractor or sub-contractor for the purpose of discharging the Lord Chancellor's general duty in relation to the courts;]

["court officer" means a person appointed by the Lord Chancellor under section 2(1) of the Courts Act 2003;]

["court security officers" has the meaning given by section 51 of the Courts Act 2003;]

"dealer in securities" means a person dealing in securities within the meaning of section 26(1) of the Prevention of Fraud (Investments) Act 1958;

"firearms dealer" has the meaning assigned to that expression by section 57(4) of the Firearms Act 1968;

["funds in court" has the meaning given by section 47 of the Administration of Justice Act 1982;]

"further education" has the meaning assigned to that expression by section 41 of the Education Act 1944 or, in Scotland, section 4 of the Education (Scotland) Act 1962;

["further education institution" has the meaning given to it by paragraph 3 of the Education (Restriction of Employment) Regulations 2000;]

["head of finance and administration of a licensed body" means an individual who is designated as head of finance and administration and whose designation is approved in accordance with licensing rules made under section 83 of, and paragraphs 13 and 14 of Schedule 11 to, the Legal Services Act 2007;

"head of legal practice of a licensed body" means an individual who is designated as head of legal practice and whose designation is approved in accordance with licensing rules made under section 83 of, and paragraphs 11 and 12 of Schedule 11 to, the Legal Services Act 2007;]

["health care professional" means a person who is a member of a profession regulated by a body mentioned in subsection (3) of section 25 of the National Health Service Reform and Health Care Professions Act 2002 (and for the purposes of this definition subsection (3A) of that section is to be ignored);]

"health services" means services provided under the National Health Service Acts 1946 to 1973 or the National Health Service (Scotland) Acts 1947 to 1973 and similar services provided otherwise than under the National Health Service;

["high security psychiatric services" has the meaning given by section 4 of the National Health Service Act 1977;]

["home inspector" means a person who is a member of a certification scheme approved by the Secretary of State in accordance with section 164(3) of the Housing Act 2004;]

. . .

["judges of the Supreme Court" means the Lord Chief Justice, the Master of the Rolls, the President of the Queen's Bench Division, the President of the Family Division, the Chancellor of the High Court, the Lords Justices of Appeal and the puisne judges of the High Court;]

"judicial appointment" means an appointment to any office by virtue of which the holder has power (whether alone or with others) under any enactment or rule of law to determine any question affecting the rights, privileges, obligations or liabilities of any person;

[. . .]

["members of the judiciary" means persons appointed to any office by virtue of which the holder has power (whether alone or with others) under any enactment or rule of law to determine any question affecting the rights, privileges, obligations or liabilities of any person;]

["personal information" means any information which is of a personal or confidential nature and is not in the public domain and it includes information in any form but excludes anything disclosed for the purposes of proceedings in a particular cause or matter;]

"proprietor" and "independent school" have the meanings assigned to those expressions by section 114(1) of the Education Act 1944 or, in Scotland, section 145 of the Education (Scotland) Act 1962;

[. . .]

[. . .]

["registered foreign lawyer" has the meaning given by section 89 of the Courts and Legal Services Act 1990;]

[. . .]

[. . .]

[. . .]

"registered teacher" means a teacher registered under the Teaching Council (Scotland) Act 1965 and includes a provisionally registered teacher;

["regulated immigration adviser" means any person who provides immigration advice or immigration services as defined in section 82(1) of the Immigration and Asylum Act 1999 and is—

(i) a registered person under Part 5 of that Act, or

(ii) a person who acts on behalf of and under the supervision of such a registered person, or

(iii) a person who falls within section 84(4)(a), (b) or (c) of that Act;]

["regulated position" means a position which is a regulated position for the purposes of Part II of the Criminal Justice and Court Services Act 2000 [other than a position which would not be a regulated position if in section 36(4) of that Act "employment" included unpaid employment];]

["removal centre" and "short-term holding facility" have the meaning given by section 147 of the Immigration and Asylum Act 1999;]

"school" has the meaning assigned to that expression by section 114(1) of the Education Act 1944 or, in Scotland, section 145 of the Education (Scotland) Act 1962;

["security management" means activity carried out pursuant to the Secretary of State's security management functions within the meaning given by section 195(3) of the National Health Service Act 2006 and in respect of Wales, the corresponding functions of Welsh Ministers;]

[. . .]

"teacher" includes a warden of a community centre, leader of a youth club or similar institution, youth worker and, in Scotland, youth and community worker;

["tribunal security officers" means persons who, in the course of their work, guard tribunal buildings, offices and other accommodation used in relation to tribunals against unauthorised access or occupation, against outbreaks of disorder or against damage;]

["tribunals" means any person exercising the judicial power of the State, that is not a court listed in section 1(1) of the Courts Act 2003;]

"unit trust scheme" has the meaning assigned to that expression by section 26(1) of the Prevention of Fraud (Investments) Act 1958 and, in relation thereto, "manager" and "trustee" shall be construed in accordance with section 26(3) of that Act

["vulnerable adult" has the meaning given by section 59 of the 2006 Act as it had effect immediately before the coming into force of section 65 of the Protection of Freedoms Act 2012].

NOTES

Revoked in relation to Scotland as noted at the beginning of this Order.

Schedule heading: substituted as noted *ante*.

Definitions "actuary", "care services", "chartered psychologist" (omitted), "legal executive" (omitted), "registered foreign lawyer", and "vulnerable adult" inserted by the Rehabilitation of Offenders Act 1974 (Exceptions) (Amendment) Order 2002, SI 2002/441, arts 2, 5(4); definition "chartered psychologist" revoked by the Health Care and Associated Professions (Miscellaneous Amendments and Practitioner Psychologists) Order 2009, SI 2009/1182, art 4(1), Sch 4, Pt 1, para 1(b); definition "legal executive" subsequently revoked by the Rehabilitation of Offenders Act 1974 (Exceptions) Order 1975 (Amendment) (England and Wales) Order 2014, SI 2014/1707, arts 2, 6(d)(iii), as from 1 July 2014; definition "vulnerable adult" subsequently substituted by the Rehabilitation of Offenders Act 1974 (Exceptions) (Amendment) (England and Wales) Order 2012, SI 2012/1957, arts 2, 11(1), (2).

Words in square brackets in the definition "actuary" substituted, and definitions "head of finance and administration of a licensed body" and "head of legal practice of a licensed body" inserted, by the Rehabilitation of Offenders Act 1974 (Exceptions) (Amendment) (England and Wales) Order 2011, SI 2011/1800, art 2(1), (6).

Definition "approved legal services body manager" inserted by the Rehabilitation of Offenders Act 1974 (Exceptions) (Amendment) (England and Wales) Order 2008, SI 2008/3259, arts 2, 7(2).

Definitions "assistants to justices' clerks", "court contractor", "court officer", "court security officers", "funds in court", "home inspector", "judges of the Supreme Court", "members of the judiciary", "personal information", "removal centre", "short-term holding facility", "tribunal security officers", and "tribunals" inserted by the Rehabilitation of Offenders Act 1974 (Exceptions) (Amendment) (England and Wales) Order 2006, SI 2006/2143, arts 2, 8.

Definitions "authorised search officer" and "child" inserted by the Rehabilitation of Offenders Act 1974 (Exceptions) (Amendment) (England and Wales) Order 2007, SI 2007/2149, arts 2, 8.

Definitions "chartered legal executive", "CILEx approved manager", and "CILEx authorised person" inserted by SI 2014/1707, arts 2, 6(d)(i), (ii), as from 1 July 2014.

Definitions "dealer in securities" and "unit trust scheme" revoked by the Rehabilitation of Offenders Act 1974 (Exceptions) (Amendment No 2) Order 1986, SI 1986/2268, art 2(2)(a), as from the date on which the Financial Services Act 1986, s 189, Sch 14 are brought into force for the purposes of this revocation. Note, however, that the 1986 Act was repealed by the Financial

Services and Markets Act 2000 (Consequential Amendments and Repeals) Order 2001, SI 2001/3649, art 3(1)(c), without ever having been brought into force for these purposes. Therefore, these revocations cannot, under the present drafting of SI 1986/2268, ever be brought into force.

Definitions "further education institution" and "regulated position" inserted by the Rehabilitation of Offenders Act 1974 (Exceptions) (Amendment) Order 2001, SI 2001/1192, arts 2, 6(6)(a), (b); words in square brackets in definition "regulated position" inserted by SI 2012/1957, arts 2, 11(1), (3).

Definition "health care professional" inserted by SI 2012/1957, arts 2, 6(1), (3)(a).

Definition "high security psychiatric services" inserted by the Rehabilitation of Offenders Act 1974 (Exceptions) (Amendment) (England and Wales) Order 2003, SI 2003/965, arts 2, 10(a).

Definition "insurance company" (omitted) revoked by the Rehabilitation of Offenders Act 1974 (Exceptions) (Amendment) (No 2) Order 2001, SI 2001/3816, arts 2, 7(b).

Definition "registered chiropractor" (omitted) originally inserted by the Chiropractors Act 1994, s 40(4), and revoked by SI 2012/1957, arts 2, 6(1), (3)(b).

Definition "registered dental care professional" (omitted) originally inserted by SI 2009/1182, art 4(1), Sch 4, Pt 6, para 37(b), and revoked by SI 2012/1957, arts 2, 6(1), (3)(b).

Definition "registered osteopath" (omitted) originally inserted by the Osteopaths Act 1993, s 39(4), and revoked by SI 2012/1957, arts 2, 6(1), (3)(b).

Definitions "registered pharmacist" and "registered pharmacy technician" (omitted) originally inserted by the Pharmacists and Pharmacy Technicians Order 2007, SI 2007/289, art 67, Sch 1, Pt 2, para 12(b), and revoked by SI 2012/1957, arts 2, 6(1), (3)(b).

Definition "regulated immigration adviser" inserted by the Rehabilitation of Offenders Act 1974 (Exceptions) (Amendment) (England and Wales) Order 2009, SI 2009/1818, arts 2, 7(3).

Definition "security management" inserted by the Rehabilitation of Offenders Act 1974 (Exceptions) Order 1975 (Amendment) (England and Wales) Order 2015, SI 2015/317, art 2(1), (5)(b), as from 10 March 2015.

Definition "social services" (omitted) revoked by SI 2002/441, arts 2, 5(4)(e).

Definition "taxi driver" (omitted) originally inserted by SI 2002/441, arts 2, 5(4), and revoked by SI 2003/965, arts 2, 10(b).

Criminal Justice and Court Services Act 2000, Pt II: largely repealed by the Safeguarding Vulnerable Groups Act 2006, s 63(2), Sch 10, partly as from a day to be appointed. "Regulated position" is defined for the purposes of Pt II (ss 26–42) of the 2000 Act by s 36 thereof; as to "regulated activity" under the 2006 Act, see s 5 thereof.

Education Act 1944, ss 41, 114(1): repealed by the Education Act 1996, s 582(2), Sch 38, Pt I, and replaced by ss 2(3), 4(1), 463, 579(1) of the 1996 Act.

National Health Service Acts 1946 to 1973: repealed and consolidated in the National Health Service Act 1977 (now itself repealed). See now, generally, the National Health Service Act 2006 and the National Health Service (Wales) Act 2006.

Prevention of Fraud (Investments) Act 1958: repealed by the Financial Services Act 1986, s 212, Sch 17 (now itself repealed).

Education (Restriction of Employment) Regulations 2000: revoked by the Education (Prohibition from Teaching or Working with Children) Regulations 2003, SI 2003/1184.

SCHEDULES 2 AND 3

(Sch 2 (Excepted Licences, Certificates and Permits) and Sch 3 (Excepted Proceedings) are outside the scope of this work.)

SAFETY REPRESENTATIVES AND SAFETY COMMITTEES REGULATIONS 1977

(SI 1977/500)

NOTES

Made: 16 March 1997.

Authority: Health and Safety at Work etc Act 1974, ss 2(4), (7), 15(1), (3)(b), (5)(b), 80(1), (4), 82(3)(a).

Commencement: 1 October 1978.

Conciliation: employment tribunal proceedings under reg 11 are "relevant proceedings" for the purposes of the conciliation provisions contained in the Employment Tribunals Act 1996, ss 18–18C; see s 18(1)(f) of the 1996 Act at **[1.757]**.

See also the Health and Safety Commission Codes of Practice 'Safety Representatives and Safety Committees' (1978) and 'Time off for the Training of Safety Representatives' (1978) at **[4.163]** and **[4.165]** respectively.

See *Harvey* NI(13), NIII(7)(D).

ARRANGEMENT OF REGULATIONS

SCHEDULES

[2.30]

1 Citation and commencement

These Regulations may be cited as the Safety Representatives and Safety Committees Regulations 1977 and shall come into operation on 1st October 1978.

[2.31]

2 Interpretation

(1) In these Regulations, unless the context otherwise requires—

"the 1974 Act" means the Health and Safety at Work etc Act 1974 as amended by the 1975 Act;

"the 1975 Act" means the Employment Protection Act 1975;

"employee" has the meaning assigned by section 53(1) of the 1974 Act and "employer" shall be construed accordingly;

"recognised trade union" [. . . .] means an independent trade union as defined in section 30(1) of the Trade Union and Labour Relations Act 1974 which the employer concerned recognises for the purpose of negotiations relating to or connected with one or more of the matters specified in section 29(1) of that Act in relation to persons employed by him or as to which the Advisory, Conciliation and Arbitration Service has made a recommendation for recognition under the 1975 Act which is operative within the meaning of section 15 of that Act;

["relevant nuclear provisions" means—

(a) sections 1, *3 to 6*, 22 and 24A of the Nuclear Installations Act 1965;

(b) to the extent they are treated as nuclear regulations, the provisions of the Carriage of Dangerous Goods and Transportable Pressure Equipment Regulations 2009;

(c) the provisions of the Nuclear Industries Security Regulations 2003;

(d) the provisions of nuclear regulations other than any provision of such regulations identified in accordance with section 74(9) of the Energy Act 2013 as made for the nuclear safeguards purposes;

"relevant nuclear site" means a site which is—

(a) a GB nuclear site (within the meaning given in section 68 of the Energy Act 2013);

(b) an authorised defence site (within the meaning given in regulation 2(1) of the Health and Safety (Enforcing Authority) Regulations 1998); or

(c) a new nuclear build site (within the meaning given in regulation 2A of those Regulations);]

"safety representative" means a person appointed under Regulation 3(1) of these Regulations to be a safety representative;

"welfare at work" means those aspects of welfare at work which are the subject of health and safety regulations or of any of the existing statutory provisions within the meaning of section 53(1) of the 1974 Act;

"workplace" in relation to a safety representative means any place or places where the group or groups of employees he is appointed to represent are likely to work or which they are likely to frequent in the course of their employment or incidentally to it.

(2) The Interpretation Act 1889 shall apply to the interpretation of these Regulations as it applies to the interpretation of an Act of Parliament.

(3) These Regulations shall not be construed as giving any person a right to inspect any place, article, substance or document which is the subject of restrictions on the grounds of national security unless he satisfies any test or requirement imposed on those grounds by or on behalf of the Crown.

NOTES

Para (1): in definition "recognised trade union" words omitted originally inserted by the Police (Health and Safety) Regulations 1999, SI 1999/860, reg 3(1), (2), and revoked by the Serious Organised Crime and Police Act 2005 (Consequential and Supplementary Amendments to Secondary Legislation) Order 2006, SI 2006/594, art 2, Schedule, para 3(1), (2)(a) (note that the Queen's Printer's copy of SI 2006/594 actually provides that the words be omitted from the definition "regional trade union"); definitions "relevant nuclear provisions" and "relevant nuclear site" inserted by the Energy Act 2013 (Office for Nuclear Regulation) (Consequential Amendments, Transitional Provisions and Savings) Order 2014, SI 2014/469, art 6(2), Sch 3, Pt 3, paras 30, 31; for the words in italics in the definition "relevant nuclear provisions" there are substituted the words "3 to 5, 6 (so far as it relates to sites in respect of which nuclear site licences have been granted)" by the Nuclear Installations (Liability for Damage) Order 2016, SI 2016/562, art 39, Sch 2, Pt 2, para 5, as from a day to be appointed.

Employment Protection Act 1975: largely repealed and consolidated in the Trade Union and Labour Relations (Consolidation) Act 1992.

Trade Union and Labour Relations Act 1974: see now the Trade Union and Labour Relations (Consolidation) Act 1992. As to s 29(1) of the 1974 Act, see s 218 of the 1992 Act, and as to s 30(1) of the 1974 Act, see s 5 of the 1992 Act.

The reference in the definition of "recognised trade union" to the 1975 Act is now otiose, the relevant provisions of the 1975 Act having been repealed by the Employment Act 1980.

Interpretation Act 1889: see now the Interpretation Act 1978.

2A *(Inserted by the Police (Health and Safety) Regulations 1999, SI 1999/860, reg 3(1), (3); revoked by the Serious Organised Crime and Police Act 2005 (Consequential and Supplementary Amendments to Secondary Legislation) Order 2006, SI 2006/594, art 2, Schedule, para 3(1), (2)(a).)*

[2.32]

3 Appointment of safety representatives

(1) For the purposes of section 2(4) of the 1974 Act, a recognised trade union may appoint safety representatives from amongst the employees in all cases where one or more employees are employed by an employer by whom it is recognised, . . .

(2) Where the employer has been notified in writing by or on behalf of a trade union of the names of the persons appointed as safety representatives under this Regulation and the group or groups of employees they represent, each such safety representative shall have the functions set out in Regulation 4 below.

(3) A person shall cease to be a safety representative for the purposes of these Regulations when—

- (a) the trade union which appointed him notifies the employer in writing that his appointment has been terminated; or
- (b) he ceases to be employed at the workplace but if he was appointed to represent employees at more than one workplace he shall not cease by virtue of this sub-paragraph to be a safety representative so long as he continues to be employed at any one of them; or
- (c) he resigns.

(4) A person appointed under paragraph (1) above as a safety representative shall so far as is reasonably practicable either have been employed by his employer throughout the preceding two years or have had at least two years experience in similar employment.

NOTES

Para (1): words omitted revoked by the Health and Safety (Consultation with Employees) Regulations 1996, SI 1996/1513, reg 13.

[2.33]

4 Functions of safety representatives

(1) In addition to his function under section 2(4) of the 1974 Act to represent the employees in consultations with the employer under section 2(6) of the 1974 Act (which requires every employer to consult safety representatives with a view to the making and maintenance of arrangements which will enable him and his employees to cooperate effectively in promoting and developing measures to ensure the health and safety at work of the employees and in checking the effectiveness of such measures), each safety representative shall have the following functions—

- (a) to investigate potential hazards and dangerous occurrences at the workplace (whether or not they are drawn to his attention by the employees he represents) and to examine the causes of accidents at the workplace;
- (b) to investigate complaints by any employee he represents relating to that employee's health, safety or welfare at work;
- (c) to make representations to the employer on matters arising out of sub-paragraphs (a) and (b) above;
- (d) to make representations to the employer on general matters affecting the health, safety or welfare at work of the employees at the workplace;
- (e) to carry out inspections in accordance with Regulations 5, 6 and 7 below;
- (f) to represent the employees he was appointed to represent in consultations at the workplace with inspectors of the Health and Safety Executive[, the Office for Nuclear Regulation] and of any other enforcing authority;
- [(g) to receive information—
    - (i) in relation to premises which are, or are on, a relevant nuclear site, from inspectors under paragraph 23 of Schedule 8 to the Energy Act 2013;
    - (ii) otherwise, from inspectors in accordance with section 28(8) of the 1974 Act;]
- (h) to attend meetings of safety committees where he attends in his capacity as a safety representative in connection with any of the above functions;

but, without prejudice to sections 7 and 8 of the 1974 Act [or sections 102 and 103 of the Energy Act 2013], no function given to a safety representative by this paragraph shall be construed as imposing any duty on him.

(2) An employer shall permit a safety representative to take such time off with pay during the employee's working hours as shall be necessary for the purposes of—

- (a) performing his functions under section 2(4) of the 1974 Act and paragraph (1)(a) to (h) above;
- (b) undergoing such training in aspects of those functions as may be reasonable in all the circumstances having regard to any relevant provisions of a code of practice relating to time off for training approved for the time being by the [the Health and Safety Executive] under section 16 of the 1974 Act.

In this paragraph "with pay" means with pay in accordance with [Schedule 2] to these Regulations.

NOTES

Para (1): words in square brackets in sub-para (f) and final words in square brackets inserted, and sub-para (g) substituted, by the Energy Act 2013 (Office for Nuclear Regulation) (Consequential Amendments, Transitional Provisions and Savings) Order 2014, SI 2014/469, art 6(2), Sch 3, Pt 3, paras 30, 32.

Para (2): words in first pair of square brackets substituted by the Legislative Reform (Health and Safety Executive) Order 2008, SI 2008/960, art 22, Sch 3; words in second pair of square brackets substituted by the Police (Health and Safety) Regulations 1999, SI 1999/860, reg 3(1), (4).

[2.34]
[4A Employer's duty to consult and provide facilities and assistance

(1) Without prejudice to the generality of section 2(6) of the Health and Safety at Work etc Act 1974, every employer shall consult safety representatives in good time with regard to—

(a) the introduction of any measure at the workplace which may substantially affect the health and safety of the employees the safety representatives concerned represent;

(b) his arrangements for appointing or, as the case may be, nominating persons in accordance with [regulations 7(1) and 8(1)(b) of the Management of Health and Safety at Work Regulations 1999] [or article 13(3)(b) of the Regulatory Reform (Fire Safety) Order 2005];

(c) any health and safety information he is required to provide to the employees the safety representatives concerned represent by or under the relevant statutory provisions [or the relevant nuclear provisions];

(d) the planning and organisation of any health and safety training he is required to provide to the employees the safety representatives concerned represent by or under the relevant statutory provisions [or the relevant nuclear provisions]; and

(e) the health and safety consequences for the employees the safety representatives concerned represent of the introduction (including the planning thereof) of new technologies into the workplace.

(2) Without prejudice to regulations 5 and 6 of these Regulations, every employer shall provide such facilities and assistance as safety representatives may reasonably require for the purpose of carrying out their functions under section 2(4) of the 1974 Act and under these Regulations.]

NOTES

Inserted by the Management of Health and Safety at Work Regulations 1992, SI 1992/2051, reg 17, Schedule.

Para (1): words in first pair of square brackets in sub-para (b) substituted by the Management of Health and Safety at Work Regulations 1999, SI 1999/3242, reg 29(2), Sch 2; words in second pair of square brackets in sub-para (b) originally inserted by the Fire Precautions (Workplace) Regulations 1997, SI 1997/1840, reg 21(1), and substituted by the Regulatory Reform (Fire Safety) Order 2005, SI 2005/1541, art 41(1), in relation to England and Wales only. A corresponding amendment has been made in relation to Scotland by the Fire (Scotland) Act 2005 (Consequential Modifications and Savings) (No 2) Order 2006, SSI 2006/457, which provides that the words should now read "or regulation 12(3)(b) of the Fire Safety (Scotland) Regulations 2006"; words in square brackets in sub-paras (c), (d) inserted by the Energy Act 2013 (Office for Nuclear Regulation) (Consequential Amendments, Transitional Provisions and Savings) Order 2014, SI 2014/469, art 6(2), Sch 3, Pt 3, paras 30, 33.

[2.35]
5 Inspections of the workplace

(1) Safety representatives shall be entitled to inspect the workplace or a part of it if they have given the employer or his representative reasonable notice in writing of their intention to do so and have not inspected it, or that part of it, as the case may be, in the previous three months; and may carry out more frequent inspections by agreement with the employer.

(2) Where there has been a substantial change in the conditions of work (whether because of the introduction of new machinery or otherwise) or new information has been published by . . . the [relevant authority] relevant to the hazards of the workplace since the last inspection under this Regulation, the safety representatives after consultation with the employer shall be entitled to carry out a further inspection of the part of the workplace concerned notwithstanding that three months have not elapsed since the last inspection.

[(2A) In paragraph (2), "relevant authority" means—

(a) in relation to a workplace which is, or is on, a relevant nuclear site, the Office for Nuclear Regulation;

(b) otherwise, the Health and Safety Executive.]

(3) The employer shall provide such facilities and assistance as the safety representatives may reasonably require (including facilities for independent investigation by them and private discussion with the employees) for the purpose of carrying out an inspection under this Regulation, but nothing in this paragraph shall preclude the employer or his representative from being present in the workplace during the inspection.

(4) An inspection carried out under . . . [. . . regulation 40 of the Quarries Regulations 1999] shall count as an inspection under this Regulation.

NOTES

Para (2): words omitted revoked by the Legislative Reform (Health and Safety Executive) Order 2008, SI 2008/960, art 22, Sch 3; words in square brackets substituted by the Energy Act 2013 (Office for Nuclear Regulation) (Consequential Amendments, Transitional Provisions and Savings) Order 2014, SI 2014/469, art 6(2), Sch 3, Pt 3, paras 30, 34(1), (2).

Para (2A): inserted by SI 2014/469, art 6(2), Sch 3, Pt 3, paras 30, 34(1), (3).

Para (4): words omitted revoked by the Mines Regulations 2014, SI 2014/3248, reg 75, Sch 5, para 4, as from 6 April 2015; words in square brackets inserted by the Quarries Regulations 1999, SI 1999/2024, reg 48(1), Sch 5, Pt II.

[2.36]

6 Inspections following notifiable accidents, occurrences and diseases

(1) Where there has been [an over three day injury,] notifiable accident or dangerous occurrence in a workplace or a notifiable disease has been contracted there and—

(a) it is safe for an inspection to be carried out; and

(b) the interests of employees in the group or groups which safety representatives are appointed to represent might be involved,

those safety representatives may carry out an inspection of the part of the workplace concerned and so far as is necessary for the purpose of determining the cause they may inspect any other part of the workplace; where it is reasonably practicable to do so they shall notify the employer or his representative of their intention to carry out the inspection.

(2) The employer shall provide such facilities and assistance as the safety representatives may reasonably require (including facilities for independent investigation by them and private discussion with the employees) for the purpose of carrying out an inspection under this Regulation; but nothing in this paragraph shall preclude the employer or his representative from being present in the workplace during the inspection.

[(3) In this regulation—

"notifiable accident or dangerous occurrence" and "notifiable disease" mean any accident, dangerous occurrence or disease, as the case may be, notice of which is required to be given by virtue of any of the relevant statutory provisions within the meaning of section 53(1) of the 1974 Act [or the relevant nuclear provisions]; and

"over three day injury" means an injury required to be recorded in accordance with regulation 12(1)(b) of the Reporting of Injuries, Diseases and Dangerous Occurrences Regulations 2013.]

NOTES

Para (1): words in square brackets substituted by the Reporting of Injuries, Diseases and Dangerous Occurrences (Amendment) Regulations 2012, SI 2012/199, reg 6(1), (2)(a); see further the final note below.

Para (3): substituted by the Reporting of Injuries, Diseases and Dangerous Occurrences Regulations 2013, SI 2013/1471, reg 18(2), Sch 4; words in square brackets inserted by the Energy Act 2013 (Office for Nuclear Regulation) (Consequential Amendments, Transitional Provisions and Savings) Order 2014, SI 2014/469, art 6(2), Sch 3, Pt 3, paras 30, 35.

Note that Sch 4 to the 2013 Regulations also provides that "For the first "a" in regulation 6(1) substitute "an over three day injury,"". It is assumed that this is a drafting error as it does not take account of the same amendment made by SI 2012/199, reg 6(1), (2)(a) as noted above.

[2.37]

7 Inspection of documents and provision of information

(1) Safety representatives shall for the performance of their functions under section 2(4) of the 1974 Act [or the relevant nuclear provisions] and under Regulations, if they have given the employer reasonable notice, be entitled to inspect and take copies of any document relevant to the workplace or to the employees the safety representatives represent which the employer is required to keep by virtue of any relevant statutory provision within the meaning of section 53(1) of the 1974 Act except a document consisting of or relating to any health record of an identifiable individual.

(2) An employer shall make available to safety representatives the information, within the employer's knowledge, necessary to enable them to fulfil their functions except—

(a) any information the disclosure of which would be against the interests of national security; or

(b) any information which he could not disclose without contravening a prohibition imposed by or under an enactment; or

(c) any information relating specifically to an individual, unless he has consented to its being disclosed; or

(d) any information the disclosure of which would, for reasons other than its effect on health, safety or welfare at work, cause substantial injury to the employer's undertaking or, where the information was supplied to him by some other person, to the undertaking of that other person; or

(e) any information obtained by the employer for the purpose of bringing, prosecuting or defending any legal proceedings.

(3) Paragraph (2) above does not require an employer to produce or allow inspection of any document or part of a document which is not related to health, safety or welfare.

NOTES

Para (1): words in square brackets inserted by the Energy Act 2013 (Office for Nuclear Regulation) (Consequential Amendments, Transitional Provisions and Savings) Order 2014, SI 2014/469, art 6(2), Sch 3, Pt 3, paras 30, 36.

[2.38]

8 Cases where safety representatives need not be employees

(1) In the cases mentioned in paragraph (2) below safety representatives appointed under Regulation 3(1) of these Regulations need not be employees of the employer concerned; and section 2(4) of the 1974 Act shall be modified accordingly.

(2) The said cases are those in which the employees in the group or groups the safety representatives are appointed to represent are members of the British Actors' Equity Association or of the Musicians' Union.

(3) Regulations 3(3)(b) and (4) and 4(2) of these Regulations shall not apply to safety representatives appointed by virtue of this Regulation and in the case of safety representatives to be so appointed Regulation 3(1) shall have effect as if the words "from amongst the employees" were omitted.

[2.39]
9 Safety committees

(1) For the purposes of section 2(7) of the 1974 Act (which requires an employer in prescribed cases to establish a safety committee if requested to do so by safety representatives) the prescribed cases shall be any cases in which at least two safety representatives request the employer in writing to establish a safety committee.

(2) Where an employer is requested to establish a safety committee in a case prescribed in paragraph (1) above, he shall establish it in accordance with the following provisions—

(a) he shall consult with the safety representatives who made the request and with the representatives of recognised trade unions whose members work in any workplace in respect of which he proposes that the committee should function;

(b) the employer shall post a notice stating the composition of the committee and the workplace or workplaces to be covered by it in a place where it may be easily read by the employees;

(c) the committee shall be established not later than three months after the request for it.

[2.40]
10 Power of [the Health and Safety Executive] to grant exemptions

The [the Health and Safety Executive] may grant exemptions from any requirement imposed by these Regulations and any such exemption may be unconditional or subject to such conditions as [the Executive] may impose and may be with or without a limit of time.

NOTES

Words in square brackets substituted by the Legislative Reform (Health and Safety Executive) Order 2008, SI 2008/960, art 22, Sch 3.

[2.41]
11 Provisions as to [employment tribunals]

(1) A safety representative may, in accordance with the jurisdiction conferred on [employment tribunals] by paragraph 16(2) of Schedule 1 to the Trade Union and Labour Relations Act 1974, present a complaint to an [employment tribunal] that—

(a) the employer has failed to permit him to take time off in accordance with Regulation 4(2) of these Regulations; or

(b) the employer has failed to pay him in accordance with Regulation 4(2) of and the Schedule to these Regulations.

(2) An [employment tribunal] shall not consider a complaint under paragraph (1) above unless it is presented within three months of the date when the failure occurred or within such further period as the tribunal considers reasonable in a case where it is satisfied that it was not reasonably practicable for the complaint to be presented within the period of three months.

[(2A) Regulation 12 (extension of time limits to facilitate conciliation before institution of proceedings) applies for the purposes of paragraph (2).]

(3) Where an [employment tribunal] finds a complaint under paragraph (1)(a) above well-founded the tribunal shall make a declaration to that effect and may make an award of compensation to be paid by the employer to the employee which shall be of such amount as the tribunal considers just and equitable in all the circumstances having regard to the employer's default in failing to permit time off to be taken by the employee and to any loss sustained by the employee which is attributable to the matters complained of.

(4) Where on a complaint under paragraph (1)(b) above an [employment tribunal] finds that the employer has failed to pay the employee the whole or part of the amount required to be paid under paragraph (1)(b), the tribunal shall order the employer to pay the employee the amount which it finds due to him.

(5) . . .

NOTES

Para (2A): inserted by the Employment Tribunals Act 1996 (Application of Conciliation Provisions) Order 2014, SI 2014/431, art 3, Schedule, paras 7, 8.

All other words in square brackets substituted by the Employment Rights (Dispute Resolution) Act 1998, s 1(2)(a), (b).

Para (5): amended the Trade Union and Labour Relations Act 1974, Sch 1, para 16 (and is now spent).

Conciliation: employment tribunal proceedings under this regulation are "relevant proceedings" for the purposes of the conciliation provisions contained in the Employment Tribunals Act 1996, ss 18–18C; see s 18(1)(a) of the 1996 Act at **[1.757]**.

1974 Act: the references to the 1974 Act in para (1) have been superseded; the jurisdiction of employment tribunals is now conferred by the Employment Tribunals Act 1996, s 2.

[2.42]
[12 Extension of time limit to facilitate conciliation before institution of proceedings

(1) In this regulation—

(a) Day A is the day on which the worker concerned complies with the requirement in subsection (1) of section 18A of the Employment Tribunals Act 1996 (requirement to contact ACAS before instituting proceedings) in relation to the matter in respect of which the proceedings are brought, and

(b) Day B is the day on which the worker concerned receives or, if earlier, is treated as receiving (by virtue of regulations made under subsection (11) of that section) the certificate issued under subsection (4) of that section.

(2) In working out when the three month time limit set by regulation 11(2) expires the period beginning with the day after Day A and ending with Day B is not to be counted.

(3) If the three month time limit set by regulation 11(2) would (if not extended by this paragraph) expire during the period beginning with Day A and ending one month after Day B, the time limit expires instead at the end of that period.

(4) The power conferred on the employment tribunal by paragraph (2) of regulation 11 to extend the three month time limit set by that paragraph is exercisable in relation to that time limit as extended by this regulation.]

NOTES

Added by the Employment Tribunals Act 1996 (Application of Conciliation Provisions) Order 2014, SI 2014/431, art 3, Schedule, paras 7, 9.

SCHEDULES

SCHEDULE 1

(Sch 1 inserted by the Police (Health and Safety) Regulations 1999, SI 1999/860, reg 3(1), (5), and revoked by the Serious Organised Crime and Police Act 2005 (Consequential and Supplementary Amendments to Secondary Legislation) Order 2006, SI 2006/594, art 2, Schedule, para 3(1), (2)(a).)

[SCHEDULE 2]
PAY FOR TIME OFF ALLOWED TO SAFETY REPRESENTATIVES

Regulation 4(2)

[2.43]

1. Subject to paragraph 3 below, where a safety representative is permitted to take time off in accordance with Regulation 4(2) of these Regulations, his employer shall pay him—

(a) where the safety representative's remuneration for the work he would ordinarily have been doing during that time does not vary with the amount of work done, as if he had worked at that work for the whole of that time;

(b) where the safety representative's remuneration for that work varies with the amount of work done, an amount calculated by reference to the average hourly earnings for that work (ascertained in accordance with paragraph 2 below).

2. The average hourly earnings referred to in paragraph 1(b) above are the average hourly earnings of the safety representative concerned or, if no fair estimate can be made of those earnings, the average hourly earnings for work of that description of persons in comparable employment with the same employer or, if there are no such persons, a figure of average hourly earnings which is reasonable in the circumstances.

3. Any payment to a safety representative by an employer in respect of a period of time off—

(a) if it is a payment which discharges any liability which the employer may have under section 57 of the 1975 Act in respect of that period, shall also discharge his liability in respect of the same period under Regulation 4(2) of these Regulations;

(b) if it is a payment under any contractual obligation, shall go towards discharging the employer's liability in respect of the same period under Regulation 4(2) of these Regulations;

(c) if it is a payment under Regulation 4(2) of these Regulations shall go towards discharging any liability of the employer to pay contractual remuneration in respect of the same period.

NOTES

Original Schedule renumbered as Schedule 2 by the Police (Health and Safety) Regulations 1999, SI 1999/860, reg 3(1), (6).
"Section 57": see now the Trade Union and Labour Relations (Consolidation) Act 1992, s 169.

STATUTORY SICK PAY (GENERAL) REGULATIONS 1982

(SI 1982/894)

NOTES

Made: 30 June 1982.

Authority: Social Security and Housing Benefits Act 1982, ss 1(3), (4), 3(5), (7), 4(2), 5(5), 6(1), 8(1)–(3), 17(4), 18(1), 20, 26(1), (3)–(5), Sch 1, para 1, Sch 2, paras 2(3), 3(2) (repealed). These Regulations now have effect as if made under the Social Security Contributions and Benefits Act 1992, ss 151(4)–(6), 153(5), (6), (10), 154(2), 155(5), 156(1), 163(1), (3)–(5), Sch 12, paras 2(3), 3(2), and the Social Security Administration Act 1992, ss 5, 130(1), (2), (3)(c)(i), (4), by virtue of the Social Security (Consequential Provisions) Act 1992, s 2(2).

Commencement: 6 April 1983.

Transfer of functions: the functions of the Secretary of State conferred by regs 9A–9C, 10, 14 were transferred to the Commissioners of Inland Revenue by the Social Security Contributions (Transfer of Functions, etc) Act 1999, s 1(2), Sch 2. Note also that a reference to the Commissioners of Inland Revenue is now to be taken as a reference to the Commissioners for Her Majesty's Revenue and Customs; see the Commissioners for Revenue and Customs Act 2005, s 50(1), (7).

See *Harvey* BI(2)(B).

ARRANGEMENT OF REGULATIONS

[2.44]

1 Citation, commencement and interpretation

(1) These regulations may be cited as the Statutory Sick Pay (General) Regulations 1982, and shall come into operation on 6th April 1983.

(2) In these regulations—

"the Act" means the Social Security and Housing Benefits Act 1982;

["the Contributions and Benefits Act" means the Social Security Contributions and Benefits Act 1992;]

["income tax month" means the period beginning on the 6th day of any calendar month and ending on the 5th day of the following calendar month;]

"Part I" means Part I of the Act;

and other expressions, unless the context otherwise requires, have the same meanings as in Part I.

(3) Unless the context otherwise requires, any reference—

(a) in these regulations to a numbered section or Schedule is a reference to the section or Schedule, as the case may be, of or to the Act bearing that number;

(b) in these regulations to a numbered regulation is a reference to the regulation bearing that number in these regulations; and

(c) in any of these regulations to a numbered paragraph is a reference to the paragraph bearing that number in that regulation.

NOTES

Para (2): definition "the Contributions and Benefits Act" inserted by the Social Security (Miscellaneous Provisions) Amendment Regulations 1992, SI 1992/2595, reg 14; definition "income tax month" inserted by the Social Security Contributions, Statutory Maternity Pay and Statutory Sick Pay (Miscellaneous Amendments) Regulations 1996, SI 1996/777, reg 2(1), (2).

Social Security and Housing Benefits Act 1982: largely repealed by the Social Security (Consequential Provisions) Act 1992; see now the Social Security Administration Act 1992 and the Social Security Contributions and Benefits Act 1992.

[2.45]

2 Persons deemed incapable of work

(1) A person who is not incapable of work of which he can reasonably be expected to do under a particular contract of service may be deemed to be incapable of work of such a kind by reason of some specific disease or bodily or mental disablement for any day on which either—

(a)

(i) he is under medical care in respect of a disease or disablement as aforesaid,
(ii) it is stated by a registered medical practitioner that for precautionary or convalescent reasons consequential on such disease or disablement he should abstain from work, or from work of such a kind, and
(iii) he does not work under that contract of service, or

[(b) he is—
(i) excluded or abstains from work, or from work of such a kind, pursuant to a request or notice in writing lawfully made under an enactment; or
(ii) otherwise prevented from working pursuant to an enactment,

[by reason of it being known or reasonably suspected that he is infected or contaminated by, or has been in contact with a case of, a relevant infection or contamination]].

(2) A person who at the commencement of any day is, or thereafter on that day becomes, incapable of work of such a kind by reason of some specific disease or bodily or mental disablement, and

(a) on that day, under that contract of service, does no work, or no work except during a shift which ends on that day having begun on the previous day; and
(b) does no work under that contract of service during a shift which begins on that day and ends on the next,

shall be deemed to be incapable of work of such a kind by reason of that disease or bodily or mental disablement throughout that day.

[(3) For the purposes of paragraph (1)(b)—

"enactment" includes an enactment comprised in, or in an instrument made under—

(a) an Act; or
(b) an Act of the Scottish Parliament; and

["relevant infection or contamination" means—

(a) in England and Wales—
(i) any incidence or spread of infection or contamination, within the meaning of section 45A(3) of the Public Health (Control of Disease) Act 1984 in respect of which regulations are made under Part 2A of that Act (public health protection) for the purpose of preventing, protecting against, controlling or providing a public health response to, such incidence or spread, or
(ii) any disease, food poisoning, infection, infectious disease or notifiable disease to which regulation 9 (powers in respect of persons leaving aircraft) of the Public Health (Aircraft) Regulations 1979 applies or to which regulation 10 (powers in respect of certain persons on ships) of the Public Health (Ships) Regulations 1979 applies; and

(b) in Scotland, any—
(i) infectious disease within the meaning of section 1(5) of the Public Health etc (Scotland) Act 2008, or exposure to an organism causing that disease, or
(ii) contamination within the meaning of section 1(5) of that Act, or exposure to a contaminant,

to which sections 56 to 58 of that Act (compensation) apply.]]

NOTES

Para (1): sub-para (b) substituted by the Statutory Sick Pay (General) Amendment Regulations 2006, SI 2006/799, reg 2(1), (2); words in square brackets in sub-para (b) substituted by the Social Security (Miscellaneous Amendments) (No 3) Regulations 2011, SI 2011/2425, reg 6(a).

Para (3): added by SI 2006/799, reg 2(1), (3); definition "relevant infection or contamination" substituted (for the original definition "relevant disease") by SI 2011/2425, reg 6(b).

2A *(Spent; this regulation was inserted by the Statutory Sick Pay (General) Amendment Regulations 1986, SI 1986/477, reg 2, and amended the Social Security and Housing Benefits Act 1982, s 2(3), which was repealed by the Social Security (Consequential Provisions) Act 1992, s 3(1), Sch 1.)*

[2.46]

3 Period of entitlement ending or not arising

(1) In a case where an employee is detained in legal custody or sentenced to a term of imprisonment (except where the sentence is suspended) on a day which in relation to him falls within a period of entitlement, that period shall end with that day.

(2) A period of entitlement shall not arise in relation to a period of incapacity for work where at any time on the first day of that period of incapacity for work the employee in question is in legal custody or sentenced to or undergoing a term of imprisonment (except where the sentence is suspended).

[(2A) A period of entitlement in respect of an employee who was entitled to incapacity benefit, maternity allowance or severe disablement allowance shall not arise in relation to any day within a period of incapacity for work beginning with the first day on which paragraph 2(d) of Schedule 11 to the Contributions and Benefits Act ceases to have effect where the employee in question is a person to whom regulation 13A of the Social Security (Incapacity for Work) (General) Regulations 1995 (welfare to work beneficiary) applies.]

[(2B) Paragraph (2A) shall not apply, in the case of an employee who was entitled to incapacity benefit, where paragraph 2(d)(i) of Schedule 11 to the Contributions and Benefits Act ceases to have effect by virtue of paragraph 5A of that Schedule.]

[(2C) A period of entitlement in respect of an employee who was entitled to employment and support allowance shall not arise in relation to any day within a period of limited capability for work beginning with the first day on which paragraph 2(dd) of Schedule 11 to the Contributions and Benefits Act ceases to have effect where the employee in question is a person to whom regulation 148 of the Employment and Support Allowance Regulations 2008 (work and training beneficiaries) applies.]

[(3) A period of entitlement as between an employee and his employer shall end after 3 years if it has not otherwise ended in accordance with [section 153(2) of the Contributions and Benefits Act] or with regulations (other than this paragraph) made under [section 153(6) of the Contributions and Benefits Act.]

[[(4) Where a period of entitlement is current as between an employee and her employer and the employee—

(a) is pregnant or has been confined; and
(b) is incapable of work wholly or partly because of pregnancy or confinement on any day which falls on or after the beginning of the [4th week] before the expected week of confinement; and
(c) is not by virtue of that pregnancy or confinement entitled to statutory maternity pay under Part XII of the Contributions and Benefits Act or to maternity allowance under section 35 of that Act;

the period of entitlement shall end on that day or, if earlier, on the day she was confined.

(5) Where an employee—

(a) is pregnant or has been confined; and
(b) is incapable of work wholly or partly because of pregnancy or confinement on any day which falls on or after the beginning of the [4th week] before the expected week of confinement; and
(c) is not by virtue of that pregnancy or confinement entitled to statutory maternity pay under Part XII of the Contributions and Benefits Act or to maternity allowance under section 35 of that Act;

a period of entitlement as between her and her employer shall not arise in relation to a period of incapacity for work where the first day in that period falls within 18 weeks of the beginning of the week containing the day referred to at (b) above or, if earlier, of the week in which she was confined.]

(6) In paragraphs (4) and (5) "confinement" and "confined" have the same meanings as in [section 171 of the Contributions and Benefits Act.]]

NOTES

Para (2A): inserted by the Social Security (Welfare to Work) Regulations 1998, SI 1998/2231, reg 6.

Para (2B): inserted by the Employment Equality (Age) (Consequential Amendments) Regulations 2007, SI 2007/825, reg 5(1), (2).

Para (2C): inserted by the Employment and Support Allowance (Consequential Provisions) (No 2) Regulations 2008, SI 2008/1554, reg 45.

Para (3): added by the Statutory Sick Pay (General) Amendment Regulations 1986, SI 1986/477, reg 3; words in square brackets substituted by the Social Security Maternity Benefits and Statutory Sick Pay (Amendment) Regulations 1994, SI 1994/1367, reg 9(1), (2).

Paras (4), (5): added by the Statutory Sick Pay (General) Amendment (No 2) Regulations 1987, SI 1987/868, reg 2, and substituted by SI 1994/1367, reg 9(1), (3), (4); words in square brackets substituted by the Social Security, Statutory Maternity Pay and Statutory Sick Pay (Miscellaneous Amendments) Regulations 2002, SI 2002/2690, reg 13.

Para (6): added by SI 1987/868, reg 2; words in square brackets substituted by SI 1994/1367, reg 9(1), (5).

3A *(Inserted by the Statutory Sick Pay (General) Amendment Regulations 1986, SI 1986/477, reg 4; revoked by the Statutory Sick Pay (General) (Amendment) Regulations 2008, SI 2008/1735, reg 3.)*

[2.47]

4 Contract of service ended for the purpose of avoiding liability for statutory sick pay

(1) The provisions of this regulation apply in any case where an employer's contract of service with an employee is brought to an end by the employer solely or mainly for the purpose of avoiding liability for statutory sick pay.

(2) Where a period of entitlement is current on the day on which the contract is brought to an end, the employer shall be liable to pay statutory sick pay to the employee until the occurrence of an event which, if the contract had still been current, would have caused the period of entitlement to come to an end under section 3(2)(a), (b) or (d) or regulation 3(1) [of these regulations or regulation 10(2) of the Statutory Sick Pay (Mariners, Airmen and Persons Abroad) Regulations 1982], or (if earlier) until the date on which the contract would have expired.

NOTES

Para (2): words in square brackets inserted by the Statutory Sick Pay (Mariners, Airmen and Persons Abroad) Regulations 1982, SI 1982/1349, reg 10(3).

[2.48]

5 Qualifying days

(1) In this regulation "week" means a period of 7 consecutive days beginning with Sunday.

(2) Where an employee and an employer of his have not agreed which day or days in any week are or were qualifying days [or where in any week the only day or days are or were such as are referred to in paragraph (3)], the qualifying day or days in that week shall be—

(a) the day or days on which it is agreed between the employer and the employee that the employee is or was required to work (if not incapable) for that employer or, if it is so agreed that there is or was no such day,

(b) the Wednesday, or, if there is no such agreement between the employer and employee as mentioned in sub-paragraph (a),

(c) every day, except that or those (if any) on which it is agreed between the employer and the employee that none of that employer's employees are or were required to work (any agreement that all days are or were such days being ignored).

[(3) No effect shall be given to any agreement between an employee and his employer to treat as qualifying days—

(a) any day where the day is identified, whether expressly or otherwise, by reference to that or another day being a day of incapacity for work in relation to the employee's contract of service with an employer;

(b) any day identified, whether expressly or otherwise, by reference to a period of entitlement or to a period of incapacity for work.]

NOTES

Para (2): words in square brackets inserted by the Statutory Sick Pay (General) Amendment Regulations 1985, SI 1985/126, reg 2.

Para (3): added by SI 1985/126, reg 2.

[2.49]

6 Calculation of entitlement limit

(1) Where an employee's entitlement to statutory sick pay is calculated by reference to different weekly rates in the same period of entitlement . . ., the entitlement limit shall be calculated in the manner described in paragraphs (2) and (3), or, as the case may be, (4) and (5); and where a number referred to in paragraph (2)(b) or (d) or (4)(a)(ii) or (d)(ii) is not a whole number [of thousandths, it shall be rounded up to the next thousandth].

(2) For the purpose of determining whether an employee has reached his maximum entitlement to statutory sick pay in respect of a period of entitlement, there shall be calculated—

(a) the amount of statutory sick pay to which the employee became entitled during the part of the period of entitlement before the change in the weekly rate;

(b) the number by which the weekly rate (before the change) must be multiplied in order to produce the amount mentioned in sub-paragraph (a);

(c) the amount of statutory sick pay to which the employee has so far become entitled during the part of the period of entitlement after the change in the weekly rate; and

(d) the number by which the weekly rate (after the change) must be multiplied in order to produce the amount mentioned in sub-paragraph (c);

(e) the sum of the amounts mentioned in sub-paragraphs (a) and (c); and

(f) the sum of the numbers mentioned in sub-paragraphs (b) and (d).

(3) When the sum mentioned in paragraph (2)(f) reaches [28], the sum mentioned in paragraph (2)(e) reaches the entitlement limit.

(4), (5) . . .

NOTES

Para (1): words omitted revoked by the Statutory Sick Pay (General) Amendment Regulations 1986, SI 1986/477, reg 9; words in square brackets substituted by the Statutory Sick Pay (General) Amendment Regulations 1984, SI 1984/385, reg 2.

Para (3): number in square brackets substituted by SI 1986/477, reg 9.

Paras (4), (5): revoked by SI 1986/477, reg 9.

[2.50]

7 Time and manner of notification of incapacity for work

(1) Subject to paragraph (2), notice of any day of incapacity for work shall be given by or on behalf of an employee to his employer—

(a) in a case where the employer has decided on a time limit (not being one which requires the notice to be given earlier than . . . the first qualifying day in the period of incapacity for work which includes that day of incapacity for work [or by a specified time during that qualifying day]) and taken reasonable steps to make it known to the employee, within that time limit; and

(b) in any other case, on or before the seventh day after that day of incapacity for work.

(2) Notice of any day of incapacity for work may be given [one month] later than as provided by paragraph (1) where there is good cause for giving it later [or if in the particular circumstances that is not practicable, as soon as it is reasonably practicable thereafter], so however that it shall in any event be given on or before the 91st day after that day.

(3) A notice contained in a letter which is properly addressed and sent by prepaid post shall be deemed to have been given on the day on which it was posted.

(4) Notice of any day of incapacity for work shall be given by or on behalf of an employee to his employer—

(a) in a case where the employer has decided on a manner in which it is to be given (not being a manner which imposes a requirement such as is specified in paragraph (5)) and taken reasonable steps to make it known to the employee, in that manner; and

(b) in any other case, in any manner, so however that unless otherwise agreed between the employer and employee it shall be given in writing.

(5) The requirements mentioned in paragraph (4)(a) are that notice shall be given—

(a) personally;
(b) in the form of medical evidence;
(c) more than one in every 7 days during a period of entitlement;
(d) on a document supplied by the employer; or
(e) on a printed form.

NOTES

Para (1): words omitted revoked, and words in square brackets inserted, by the Statutory Sick Pay (General) Amendment Regulations 1984, SI 1984/385, reg 2.

Para (2): words in square brackets inserted by the Social Security Contributions, Statutory Maternity Pay and Statutory Sick Pay (Miscellaneous Amendments) Regulations 1996, SI 1996/777, reg 2(1), (3).

[2.51]

8 Manner in which statutory sick pay may not be paid

Statutory sick pay may not be paid in kind or by way of the provision of board or lodging or of services or other facilities.

[2.52]

9 Time limits for paying statutory sick pay

(1) In this regulation, "pay day" means a day on which it has been agreed, or it is the normal practice, between an employer and an employee of his, that payments by way of remuneration are to be made, or, where there is no such agreement or normal practice, the last day of a calendar month.

(2) In any case where—

(a) a decision has been made by an [adjudication officer], [social security appeal tribunal] or Commissioner in proceedings under Part I that an employee is entitled to an amount of statutory sick pay; and
(b) the time for bringing an appeal against the decision has expired and either—
   (i) no such appeal has been brought; or
   (ii) such an appeal has been brought and has been finally disposed of,

that amount of statutory sick pay is to be paid within the time specified in paragraph (3).

(3) Subject to paragraphs (4) and (5), the employer is required to pay the amount not later than the first pay day after—

(a) where an appeal has been brought, the day on which the employer receives notification that it has been finally disposed of;
(b) where leave to appeal has been refused and there remains no further opportunity to apply for leave, the day on which the employer receives notification of the refusal; and
(c) in any other case, the day on which the time for bringing an appeal expires.

(4) Subject to paragraph (5), where it is impracticable, in view of the employer's methods of accounting for and paying remuneration, for the requirement of payment referred to in paragraph (3) to be met by the pay day referred to in that paragraph, it shall be met not later than the next following pay day.

(5) Where the employer would not have remunerated the employee for his work on the day of incapacity for work in question (if it had not been a day of incapacity for work) as early as the pay day specified in paragraph (3) or (if it applies) paragraph (4), the requirement of payment shall be met on the first day on which the employee would have been remunerated for his work on that day.

NOTES

Para (2): words in square brackets substituted by virtue of the Health and Social Services and Social Security Adjudications Act 1983, s 25, Sch 8, Pt I, para 1(1), (3)(a).

[2.53]

[9A Liability of the [Commissioners of Inland Revenue] for payments of statutory sick pay

(1) Notwithstanding the provisions of section 1 of the Act and subject to paragraph (4), where—

(a) an adjudicating authority has determined that an employer is liable to make payments of statutory sick pay to an employee, and
(b) the time for appealing against that determination has expired, and
(c) no appeal against the determination has been lodged or leave to appeal against the determination is required and has been refused,

then for any day of incapacity for work in respect of which it was determined the employer was liable to make those payments, and for any further days of incapacity for work which fall within the same spell of incapacity for work and in respect of which the employer was liable to make payments of statutory sick pay to that employee, the liability to make payments of statutory sick pay in respect of those days shall, to the extent that payment has not been made by the employer, be that of the [Commissioners of Inland Revenue] and not the employer.

(2) For the purposes of this regulation a spell of incapacity for work consists of consecutive days of incapacity for work with no day of the week disregarded.

(3) In paragraph (1) above "adjudicating authority" means, as the case may be, the Chief or other adjudication officer, [the First-tier Tribunal or the Upper Tribunal].

(4) This regulation shall not apply to any liability of an employer to make a payment of statutory sick pay where the day of incapacity for work in respect of which the liability arose falls within a period of entitlement which commenced before 6th April 1987.]

NOTES

Inserted by the Statutory Sick Pay (General) Amendment Regulations 1987, SI 1987/372, reg 2.

Regulation heading, para (1): words in square brackets substituted by virtue of the Social Security Contributions (Transfer of Functions, etc) Act 1999, s 1(2), Sch 2.

Para (3): words in square brackets substituted by the Tribunals, Courts and Enforcement Act 2007 (Transitional and Consequential Provisions) Order 2008, SI 2008/2683, art 6(1), Sch 1, para 18.

Commissioners of Inland Revenue: a reference to the Commissioners of Inland Revenue is now to be taken as a reference to the Commissioners for Her Majesty's Revenue and Customs; see the Commissioners for Revenue and Customs Act 2005, s 50(1), (7).

[2.54]
[9B Insolvency of employer

(1) Notwithstanding the provisions of section 1 of the Act and subject to paragraph (3), any liability arising under Part I of the Act to make a payment of statutory sick pay in respect of a day of incapacity for work in relation to an employee's contract of service with his employer shall be that of the [Commissioners of Inland Revenue] and not that of the employer where the employer is insolvent on that day.

(2) For the purposes of paragraph (1) an employer shall be taken to be insolvent if, and only if—

(a) in England and Wales—

(i) he has been adjudged bankrupt or has made a composition or arrangement with his creditors;

(ii) he has died and his estate falls to be administered in accordance with an order under section 421 of the Insolvency Act 1986; or

(iii) where an employer is a company, a winding-up order . . . is made or a resolution for voluntary winding-up is passed with respect to it [or it enters administration], or a receiver or manager of its undertaking is duly appointed, or possession is taken by or on behalf of the holders of any debentures secured by a floating charge, or any property of the company comprised in or subject to the charge or a voluntary arrangement proposed for the purposes of Part I of the Insolvency Act 1986 is approved under that Part;

(b) in Scotland—

(i) an award of sequestration is made on his estate or he executes a trust deed for his creditors or enters into a composition contract;

(ii) he has died and a judicial factor appointed under section 11A of the Judicial Factors (Scotland) Act 1889 is required by that section to divide his insolvent estate among his creditors; or

(iii) where the employer is a company, a winding-up order . . . is made or a resolution for voluntary winding-up is passed with respect to it [or it enters administration] or a receiver of its undertaking is duly appointed or a voluntary arrangement proposed for the purposes of Part I of the Insolvency Act 1986 is approved under that Part.

(3) This regulation shall not apply where the employer became insolvent before 6th April 1987].

NOTES

Inserted by the Statutory Sick Pay (General) Amendment Regulations 1987, SI 1987/372, reg 2.

Para (1): words in square brackets substituted by virtue of the Social Security Contributions (Transfer of Functions, etc) Act 1999, s 1(2), Sch 2.

Para (2): words omitted revoked, and words in square brackets inserted, by the Enterprise Act 2002 (Insolvency) Order 2003, SI 2003/2096, art 5, Schedule, Pt 2, para 42.

Commissioners of Inland Revenue: a reference to the Commissioners of Inland Revenue is now to be taken as a reference to the Commissioners for Her Majesty's Revenue and Customs; see the Commissioners for Revenue and Customs Act 2005, s 50(1), (7).

[2.55]
[9C Payments by the [Commissioners of Inland Revenue]

Where the [Commissioners of Inland Revenue became] liable in accordance with regulation 9A or 9B to make payments of statutory sick pay to a person, the first payment shall be made as soon as reasonably practicable after he becomes so liable, and payments thereafter shall be made at weekly intervals, by means of an instrument of payment[, instrument for benefit payment] or by such other means as appears to the [Commissioners of Inland Revenue] to be appropriate in the circumstances of the particular case.]

NOTES

Inserted by the Statutory Sick Pay (General) Amendment Regulations 1987, SI 1987/372, reg 2.

Words "Commissioners of Inland Revenue" and "Commissioners of Inland Revenue became" in square brackets substituted by virtue of the Social Security Contributions (Transfer of Functions, etc) Act 1999, s 1(2), Sch 2; other words in square brackets inserted by the Social Security (Claims and Payments Etc) Amendment Regulations 1996, SI 1996/672, reg 3.

Commissioners of Inland Revenue: a reference to the Commissioners of Inland Revenue is now to be taken as a reference to the Commissioners for Her Majesty's Revenue and Customs; see the Commissioners for Revenue and Customs Act 2005, s 50(1), (7).

[2.56]
10 Persons unable to act

(1) Where in the case of any employee—

(a) statutory sick pay is payable to him or he is alleged to be entitled to it;
(b) he is unable for the time being to act; and
(c) either—
(i) no receiver has been appointed by the Court of Protection with power to receive statutory sick pay on his behalf, or
(ii) in Scotland, his estate is not being administered by any tutor, curator or other guardian acting or appointed in terms of law,

the [Commissioners of Inland Revenue] may, upon written application to [them] by a person who, if a natural person, is over the age of 18, appoint that person to exercise, on behalf of the employee, any right to which he may be entitled under Part I and to deal on his behalf with any sums payable to him.

(2) Where the [Commissioners of Inland Revenue have] made an appointment under paragraph (1)—
(a) [they] may at any time in [their] absolute discretion revoke it;
(b) the person appointed may resign his office after having given one month's notice in writing to the [Commissioners of Inland Revenue] of his intention to do so; and
(c) the appointment shall terminate when the [Commissioners of Inland Revenue are] notified that a receiver or other person to whom paragraph (1)(c) applies has been appointed.

(3) Anything required by Part I to be done by or to any employee who is unable to act may be done by or to the person appointed under this regulation to act on his behalf, and the receipt of the person so appointed shall be a good discharge to the employee's employer for any sum paid.

NOTES

Words in square brackets substituted by virtue of the Social Security Contributions (Transfer of Functions, etc) Act 1999, s 1(2), Sch 2.

Commissioners of Inland Revenue: a reference to the Commissioners of Inland Revenue is now to be taken as a reference to the Commissioners for Her Majesty's Revenue and Customs; see the Commissioners for Revenue and Customs Act 2005, s 50(1), (7).

[2.57]

11 Rounding to avoid fractional amounts

Where any payment of statutory sick pay is made and the statutory sick pay due for the period for which the payment purports to be made includes a fraction of a penny, the payment shall be rounded up to the next whole number of pence.

[2.58]

12 Days not to be treated as, or as parts of, periods of interruption of employment

In a case to which paragraph 3 of Schedule 2 applies, the day of incapacity for work mentioned in sub-paragraph (1)(b) of that paragraph shall not be, or form part of, a period of interruption of employment where it is a day which, by virtue of section 17(1) or (2) of the Social Security Act 1975 or any regulations made thereunder, is not to be treated as a day of incapacity for work.

NOTES

Section 17(1) or (2) of the Social Security Act 1975: repealed.

13 (*Revoked by the Statutory Sick Pay (Maintenance of Records) (Revocation) Regulations 2014, SI 2014/55, reg 2.*)

[2.59]

[13A Production of employer's records

(1) An authorised officer of the Commissioners of Inland Revenue may by notice require an employer to produce to him at the place of keeping such records as are in the employer's possession or power and as (in the officer's reasonable opinion) contain, or may contain, information relevant to satisfy him that statutory sick pay has been paid and is being paid in accordance with these regulations to employees or former employees who are entitled to it.

(2) A notice referred to in paragraph (1) shall be in writing and the employer shall produce the records referred to in that paragraph within 30 days after the date of such a notice.

(3) The production of records in pursuance of this regulation shall be without prejudice to any lien which a third party may have in respect of those records.

(4) References in this regulation to "records" means—
(a) any wage sheet or deductions working sheet; or
(b) any other document which relates to the calculation or payment of statutory sick pay to his employees or former employees,

whether kept in written form, electronically, or otherwise.

(5) In paragraph (1), "place of keeping" means such place in Great Britain that an employer and an authorised officer may agree upon, or, in the absence of such agreement—
(a) any place in Great Britain where records referred to in paragraph (1) are normally kept; or
(b) if there is no such place, the employer's principal place of business in Great Britain.]

NOTES

Inserted by the Statutory Maternity Pay (General) and Statutory Sick Pay (General) (Amendment) Regulations 2005, SI 2005/989, reg 3(1), (2).

Commissioners of Inland Revenue: a reference to the Commissioners of Inland Revenue is now to be taken as a reference to the Commissioners for Her Majesty's Revenue and Customs; see the Commissioners for Revenue and Customs Act 2005, s 50(1), (7).

[2.60]

14 Provision of information in connection with determination of questions

Any person claiming to be entitled to statutory sick pay, or any other person who is a party to proceedings arising under Part I, shall, if he receives notification from the [Commissioners of Inland Revenue] that any information is required from him for the determination of any question arising in connection therewith, furnish that information to the [Commissioners of Inland Revenue] within 10 days of receiving that notification.

NOTES

Words in square brackets substituted by virtue of the Social Security Contributions (Transfer of Functions, etc) Act 1999, s 1(2), Sch 2.

Commissioners of Inland Revenue: a reference to the Commissioners of Inland Revenue is now to be taken as a reference to the Commissioners for Her Majesty's Revenue and Customs; see the Commissioners for Revenue and Customs Act 2005, s 50(1), (7).

[2.61]

15 Provision of information by employers to employees

(1) [Subject to paragraph (1A),] in a case which falls within paragraph (a), (b) or (c) of section 18(3) (provision of information by employers in connection with the making of claims for [short-term incapacity] and other benefits), the employer shall furnish to his employee, in writing on a form approved by the Secretary of State for the purpose [or in a form in which it can be processed by equipment operating automatically in response to instructions given for that purpose], the information specified in paragraph (2), (3) or (4) below respectively within the time specified in the appropriate one of those paragraphs.

[(1A) For the purposes of paragraph (1), where, in the particular circumstances of a case, it is not practicable for the employer to furnish the information within the specified time mentioned in paragraph (2), (3), (4)(b)(ii) or (5), he shall, not later than the first pay day within the meaning of regulation 9(1) immediately following the relevant specified time, furnish the information to his employee.]

(2) In a case which falls within paragraph (a) (no period of entitlement arising in relation to a period of incapacity for work) of section 18(3)—

(a) the information mentioned in paragraph (1) is a statement of all the reasons why, under the provisions of paragraph 1 of Schedule 1 and regulations made thereunder, a period of entitlement does not arise; and

(b) it shall be furnished not more than 7 days after the day on which the employer is notified by or on behalf of the employee of the employee's incapacity for work on the fourth day of the period of incapacity for work.

(3) In a case which falls within paragraph (b) (period of entitlement ending but period of incapacity for work continuing) of section 18(3)—

[[(a) the information mentioned in paragraph (1) above is a statement informing the employee of—

(i) the reason why the period of entitlement ended;

(ii) the date of the last day in respect of which the employer is or was liable to make a payment of statutory sick pay to him]; and

(b) the statement shall be furnished not more than 7 days after the day on which the period of entitlement ended, or if earlier, on the day on which it is already required to be furnished under paragraph (4).]

(4) In a case which falls within paragraph (c) (period of entitlement expected to end before period of incapacity for work ends, on certain assumptions) of section 18(3)—

[[(a) the information mentioned in paragraph (1) above is a statement informing the employee of—

(i) the reason why the period of entitlement is expected to end;

(ii) the date of the last day in respect of which the employer is or was expected to be liable to make a payment of statutory sick pay to him]; and

(b) the statement shall be furnished—

(i) in a case where the period of entitlement is expected to end in accordance with section 3(2)(b) of the Act (maximum entitled to statutory sick pay), on or before the 42nd day before the period of entitlement is expected to end, or

(ii) in any other case, on or before the seventh day before the period of entitlement is expected to end,

. . .]

(5) For the purposes of section 18(3)(c)(i) (period for which the period of incapacity for work is to be assumed to continue to run) the prescribed period shall be 14 days.

NOTES

Para (1): words in first and third pairs of square brackets inserted by the Social Security Contributions, Statutory Maternity Pay and Statutory Sick Pay (Miscellaneous Amendments) Regulations 1996, SI 1996/777, reg 2(1), (5)(a); words in second pair of square brackets substituted by the Social Security (Incapacity Benefit) (Consequential and Transitional Amendments and Savings) Regulations 1995, SI 1995/829, reg 15.

Para (1A): inserted by SI 1996/777, reg 2(1), (5)(b).

Para (3): sub-paras (a), (b) substituted by the Statutory Sick Pay (General) Amendment Regulations 1986, SI 1986/477, reg 6; sub-para (a) further substituted by the Statutory Sick Pay (General) (Amendment) Regulations 2008, SI 2008/1735, reg 2(1), (2)(a).

Para (4): sub-paras (a), (b) substituted by SI 1986/477, reg 6; sub-para (a) further substituted by SI 2008/1735, reg 2(1), (2)(b); words omitted from sub-para (b) revoked by SI 1996/777, reg 2(1), (5)(c).

Section 18(3): see now the Social Security Administration Act 1992, s 130(2), (3).

15A *(Inserted by the Statutory Sick Pay (General) Amendment Regulations 1986, SI 1986/477, reg 7; revoked by the Statutory Sick Pay (General) (Amendment) Regulations 2008, SI 2008/1735, reg 3.)*

[2.62]

16 Meaning of "employee"

(1) [Subject to paragraph (1ZA),] in a case where, and in so far as, a person . . . is treated as an employed earner by virtue of the Social Security (Categorisation of Earners) Regulations 1978, he shall be treated as an employee for the purposes of Part I and in a case where, and in so far as, such a person is treated otherwise than as an employed earner by virtue of those regulations, he shall not be treated as an employee for the purposes of Part I.

[(1ZA) Paragraph (1) shall have effect in relation to a person who—

(a) is under the age of 16; and

(b) would or, as the case may be, would not have been treated as an employed earner by virtue of the Social Security (Categorisation of Earners) Regulations 1978 had he been over that age,

as it has effect in relation to a person who is or, as the case may be, is not so treated.]

[(1A) Any person who is in employed earner's employment within the meaning of the Social Security Act 1975 under a contract of apprenticeship shall be treated as an employee for the purposes of Part I.]

(2) A person who is in employed earner's employment within the meaning of the Social Security Act 1975 but whose employer—

(a) does not fulfil the conditions prescribed in regulation 119(1)(b) of the Social Security (Contributions) Regulations 1979 as to residence or presence in Great Britain, or

(b) is a person who, by reason of any international treaty to which the United Kingdom is a party or of any international convention binding the United Kingdom—

(i) is exempt from the provisions of the Social Security Act 1975, or

(ii) is a person against whom the provisions of that Act are not enforceable,

shall not be treated as an employee for the purposes of Part I.

NOTES

Para (1): words in square brackets inserted, and words omitted revoked, by the Employment Equality (Age) Regulations 2006, SI 2006/1031, reg 49(1), Sch 8, Pt 2, paras 49, 50(1), (2).

Para (1ZA): inserted by SI 2006/1031, reg 49(1), Sch 8, Pt 2, paras 49, 50(1), (3); substituted by the Employment Equality (Age) (Consequential Amendments) Regulations 2007, SI 2007/825, reg 5(1), (3).

Para (1A): inserted by the Statutory Sick Pay (Compensation of Employers) and Miscellaneous Provisions Regulations 1983, SI 1983/376, reg 5(2).

Social Security Act 1975: see now the Social Security Contributions and Benefits Act 1992.

[2.63]

17 Meaning of "earnings"

(1) . . .

[(2) For the purposes of section 163(2) of the Contributions and Benefits Act, the expression "earnings" refers to gross earnings and includes any remuneration or profit derived from a person's employment except any payment or amount which is—

(a) excluded [or disregarded in the calculation of a person's earnings under regulation 25, 27 or 123 of, or Schedule 3 to, the Social Security (Contributions) Regulations 2001] [(or would have been so excluded had he not been under the age of 16)];

(b) a chargeable emolument under section 10A of the Social Security Contributions and Benefits Act 1992, except where, in consequence of such a chargeable emolument being excluded from earnings, a person would not be entitled to statutory sick pay [(or where such a payment or amount would have been so excluded and in consequence he would not have been entitled to statutory sick pay had he not been under the age of 16)].]

[(2A) . . .]

(3) For the purposes of [section 163(2) of the Contributions and Benefits Act] the expression "earnings" includes also—

[(za) any amount retrospectively treated as earnings by regulations made by virtue of section 4B(2) of the Contributions and Benefits Act;]

(a) any sum payable by way of maternity pay or payable by the Secretary of State in pursuance of section 40 of the Employment Protection (Consolidation) Act 1978 in respect of maternity pay;

(b) any sum which is payable by the Secretary of State by virtue of section 122(3)(a) of that Act in respect of arrears of pay and which by virtue of section 42(1) of that Act is to go towards discharging a liability to pay maternity pay;

(c) any sum payable in respect of arrears of pay in pursuance of an order for re-instatement or re-engagement under that Act;

(d) any sum payable by way of pay in pursuance of an order under the Act for the continuation of a contract of employment;

(e) any sum payable by way of remuneration in pursuance of a protective award under the Employment Protection Act 1975;

(f) any sum payable to any employee under the Temporary Short-time Working Compensation Scheme administered under powers conferred by the Employment Subsidies Act 1978;

(g) any sum paid in satisfaction of any entitlement to statutory sick pay;

[(h) any sum payable by way of statutory maternity pay under Part V of the Social Security Act 1986, including sums payable in accordance with regulations made under section 46(8)(b) of that Act];

[(i) any sum payable by way of statutory paternity pay, including any sums payable in accordance with regulations made under section 171ZD(3) of the Contributions and Benefits Act;

(j) any sum payable by way of statutory adoption pay, including any sums payable in accordance with regulations made under section 171ZM(3) of the Contributions and Benefits Act];

[(k) any sum payable by way of statutory shared parental pay, including any sums payable in accordance with regulations made under section 171ZX(3) of the Contributions and Benefits Act.]

(4), (5) . . .

NOTES

Paras (1), (4), (5): revoked by the Social Security (Miscellaneous Provisions) Amendment Regulations 1992, SI 1992/2595, reg 15.

Para (2): substituted by the Social Security Contributions, Statutory Maternity Pay and Statutory Sick Pay (Miscellaneous Amendments) Regulations 1999, SI 1999/567, reg 13; words in first pair of square brackets in sub-para (a) substituted by the Social Security, Occupational Pension Schemes and Statutory Payments (Consequential Provisions) Regulations 2007, SI 2007/1154, reg 5(1), (2); words in second pair of square brackets in sub-para (a) and words in square brackets in sub-para (b) inserted by the Employment Equality (Age) Regulations 2006, SI 2006/1031, reg 49(1), Sch 8, Pt 2, para 51.

Para (2A): inserted by the Statutory Sick Pay (Compensation of Employers) and Miscellaneous Provisions Regulations 1983, SI 1983/376, reg 5(3); revoked by SI 1992/2595, reg 15.

Para (3): words in first pair of square brackets substituted by the Social Security, Statutory Maternity Pay and Statutory Sick Pay (Miscellaneous Amendments) Regulations 2002, SI 2002/2690, reg 14(a); sub-para (za) inserted by SI 2007/1154, reg 5(1), (3); sub-para (h) added by the Statutory Sick Pay (General) Amendment (No 2) Regulations 1987, SI 1987/868, reg 4(b); sub-paras (i), (j) added by SI 2002/2690, reg 14(b); sub-para (k) added by the Shared Parental Leave and Statutory Shared Parental Pay (Consequential Amendments to Subordinate Legislation) Order 2014, SI 2014/3255, art 3, as from 31 December 2014.

Statutory paternity pay: as to the meaning of this, see the Children and Families Act 2014, s 126 at **[1.1894]**.

"Section 40 of the Employment Protection (Consolidation) Act 1978": s 40 as then in force was repealed by the Social Security Act 1986: see now the Social Security Contributions and Benefits Act 1992, Pt XII.

"Section 122(3)(a) of that Act": see now the Employment Rights Act 1996, s 184(1).

"Employment Protection Act 1975": relevant provisions are now contained in the Trade Union and Labour Relations (Consolidation) Act 1992, s 188 et seq.

"Part V of the Social Security Act 1986": see now the Social Security Contributions and Benefits Act 1992, Pt XII.

[2.64]

18 Payments to be treated or not to be treated as contractual remuneration

For the purposes of paragraph 2(1) and (2) of Schedule 2 to the Act, those things which are included within the expression "earnings" by regulation 17 (except paragraph (3)(g) thereof) shall be, and those things which are excluded from that expression by that regulation shall not be, treated as contractual remuneration.

[2.65]

19 Normal weekly earnings

(1) For the purposes of section 26(2) and (4), an employee's normal weekly earnings shall be determined in accordance with the provisions of this regulation.

(2) In this regulation—

"the critical date" means the first day of the period of entitlement in relation to which a person's normal weekly earnings fall to be determined, or, in a case to which paragraph 2(c) of Schedule 1 applies, the relevant date within the meaning of Schedule 1;

"normal pay day" means a day on which the terms of an employee's contract of service require him to be paid, or the practice in his employment is for him to be paid, if any payment is due to him; and

"day of payment" means a day on which the employee was paid.

(3) Subject to paragraph (4), the relevant period (referred to in section 26(2)) is the period between—

(a) the last normal pay day to fall before the critical date; and

(b) the last normal pay day to fall at least 8 weeks earlier than the normal pay day mentioned in sub-paragraph (a),

including the normal pay day mentioned in sub-paragraph (a) but excluding that first mentioned in sub-paragraph (b).

(4) In a case where an employee has no identifiable normal pay day, paragraph (3) shall have effect as if the words "day of payment" were substituted for the words "normal pay day" in each place where they occur.

(5) In a case where an employee has normal pay days at intervals of or approximating to one or more calendar months (including intervals of or approximating to a year) his normal weekly earnings shall be calculated by dividing his earnings in the relevant period by the number of calendar months in that period (or, if it is not a whole number, the nearest whole number), multiplying the result by 12 and dividing by 52.

(6) In a case to which paragraph (5) does not apply and the relevant period is not an exact number of weeks, the employee's normal weekly earnings shall be calculated by dividing his earnings in the relevant period by the number of days in the relevant period and multiplying the result by 7.

(7) In a case where the normal pay day mentioned in sub-paragraph (a) of paragraph (3) exists but that first mentioned in sub-paragraph (b) of that paragraph does not yet exist, the employee's normal weekly earnings shall be calculated as if the period for which all the earnings under his contract of service received by him before the critical date represented payment were the relevant period.

(8) In a case where neither of the normal pay days mentioned in paragraph (3) yet exists, the employee's normal weekly earnings shall be the remuneration to which he is entitled, in accordance with the terms of his contract of service, for, as the case may be—

(a) a week's work; or

(b) a number of calendar months' work, divided by that number of months, multiplied by 12 and divided by 52.

[2.66]

20 Treatment of one or more employers as one

(1) In a case where the earnings paid to an employee in respect of 2 or more employments are aggregated and treated as a single payment of earnings under regulation 12(1) of the Social Security (Contributions) Regulations 1979, the employers of the employee in respect of those employments shall be treated as one for all purposes of Part I.

(2) Where 2 or more employers are treated as one under the provisions of paragraph (1), liability for the statutory sick pay payable by them to the employee shall be apportioned between them in such proportions as they may agree or, in default of agreement, in the proportions which the employee's earnings from each employment bear to the amount of the aggregated earnings.

(3) [Subject to paragraphs (4) and (5)] where a contract of service ("the current contract") was preceded by a contract of service entered into between the same employer and employee ("the previous contract"), and the interval between the date on which the previous contract ceased to have effect and that on which the current contract came into force was not more than 8 weeks, then for the purposes of establishing the employee's maximum entitlement within the meaning of section 5 (limitation on entitlement to statutory sick pay in any one period of entitlement or tax year), the provisions of Part I shall not have effect as if the employer were a different employer in relation to each of those contracts of service.

[(4) Where a contract of service ("the current contract") was preceded by two or more contracts of service entered into between the same employer and employee ("the previous contracts") and the previous contracts—

(a) existed concurrently for at least part of their length, and

(b) the intervals between the dates on which each of the previous contracts ceased to have effect and that on which the current contract came into force was not more than 8 weeks,

then for the purposes of establishing the employee's maximum entitlement within the meaning of section 5 the provisions of Part I shall not have effect as if the employer were a different employer in relation to the current contract and whichever of the previous contracts was the contract by virtue of which the employer had become liable to pay the greatest proportion of statutory sick pay in respect of any tax year or period of entitlement.

(5) If, in any case to which paragraph (4) applies, the same proportion of the employer's liability for statutory sick pay becomes due under each of the previous contracts, then for the purpose of establishing the employee's maximum entitlement within the meaning of section 5, the provisions of Part I shall have effect in relation to only one of the previous contracts.]

NOTES

Words in square brackets in para (3) inserted, and paras (4), (5) added, by the Statutory Sick Pay (Compensation of Employers) and Miscellaneous Provisions Regulations 1983, SI 1983/376, reg 3(4).

[2.67]

21 Treatment of more than one contract of service as one

Where 2 or more contracts of service exist concurrently between one employer and one employee, they shall be treated as one for all purposes of Part I except where, by virtue of regulation 11 of the Social Security (Contributions) Regulations 1979, the earnings from those contracts of service are not aggregated for the purposes of earnings-related contributions.

[2.68]

[21A Election to be treated as different employers not to apply to recovery of statutory sick pay

(1) Paragraph (2) below applies for the purposes of section 159A of the Contributions and Benefits Act (power to provide for recovery by employers of sums paid by way of statutory sick pay) and of any order made under that section.

(2) Where an employer has made 2 or more elections under regulation 3 of the Income Tax (Employments) Regulations 1993 to be treated as a different employer in respect of each of the groups of employees specified in the election, the different employers covered by each of those elections shall be treated as one employer.]

NOTES

Inserted by the Statutory Sick Pay Percentage Threshold Order 1995, SI 1995/513, art 3.

22 *(Revoked by the Statutory Maternity Pay (General) and Statutory Sick Pay (General) (Amendment) Regulations 2005, SI 2005/989, reg 3(1), (3).)*

STATUTORY SICK PAY (MEDICAL EVIDENCE) REGULATIONS 1985

(SI 1985/1604)

NOTES

Made: 22 October 1985.

Authority: Social Security and Housing Benefits Act 1982, s 17(2A), as inserted by the Social Security Act 1985, s 20 (repealed). By virtue of the Social Security (Consequential Provisions) Act 1992, s 2(2), these Regulations now have effect as if made under the Social Security Administration Act 1992, s 14(2).

Commencement: 6 April 1986.

See *Harvey* BI(2)(B).

[2.69]

1 Citation, commencement and interpretation

(1) These regulations may be cited as the Statutory Sick Pay (Medical Evidence) Regulations 1985 and shall come into operation on 6th April 1986.

(2) In these regulations, unless the context otherwise requires—

["the 1992 Act" means the Social Security Administration Act 1992;

"signature" means, in relation to a statement given in accordance with these regulations, the name by which the person giving that statement is usually known (any name other than the surname being either in full or otherwise indicated) written by that person in his own handwriting; and "signed" shall be construed accordingly.

(3) . . .

NOTES

Para (2): definition "the 1992 Act" substituted (for the original definition "the 1982 Act") by the Social Security (Medical Evidence) and Statutory Sick Pay (Medical Evidence) (Amendment) Regulations 2010, SI 2010/137, reg 3(1), (2).

Para (3): revoked by the Social Security (Miscellaneous Provisions) Amendment Regulations 1992, SI 1992/247, reg 6(1), (2).

[2.70]

2 Medical information

[(1) Medical information required under section 14(1) of the 1992 Act relating to incapacity for work shall be provided either—

(a) in the form of a statement given by a doctor in accordance with the rules set out in Part 1 of Schedule 1 to these Regulations; or

(b) by such other means as may be sufficient in the circumstances of any particular case.]

(2) An employee shall not be required under [section 14(1) of the 1992 Act] to provide medical information in respect of the first 7 days in any spell of incapacity for work; and for this purpose "spell of incapacity" means a continuous period of incapacity for work which is immediately preceded by a day on which the claimant either worked or was not incapable of work.

NOTES

Para (1): substituted by the Social Security (Medical Evidence) and Statutory Sick Pay (Medical Evidence) (Amendment) Regulations 2010, SI 2010/137, reg 3(1), (3)(a).

Para (2): words in square brackets substituted by SI 2010/137, reg 3(1), (3)(b).

SCHEDULES

[SCHEDULE 1

Regulation 2(1)(a)

PART I
RULES

[2.71]

1. In these rules, unless the context otherwise requires—

"assessment" means either a consultation between a patient and a doctor which takes place in person or by telephone or a consideration by a doctor of a written report by another doctor or other health care professional;

"condition" means a specific disease or bodily or mental disability;

"doctor" means a registered medical practitioner not being the patient;

"other health care professional" means a person (other than a registered medical practitioner and not being the patient) who is a registered nurse, a registered midwife, an occupational therapist or physiotherapist registered with a regulatory body established by an Order in Council under section 60 of the Health Act 1999, or a member of any profession regulated by a body mentioned in section 25(3) of the National Health Service Reform and Health Care Professions Act 2002;

"patient" means the person in respect of whom a statement is given in accordance with these rules.

2. Where a doctor issues a statement to a patient in accordance with an obligation arising under a contract, agreement or arrangement under Part 4 of the National Health Service Act 2006 or Part 4 of the National Health Service (Wales) Act 2006 or Part 1 of the National Health Service (Scotland) Act 1978 the doctor's statement shall be in a form set out at Part 2 of this Schedule and shall be signed by that doctor.

3. Where a doctor issues a statement in any case other than in accordance with rule 2, the doctor's statement shall be in the form set out in Part 2 of this Schedule or in a form to like effect and shall be signed by the doctor attending the patient.

4. A doctor's statement must be based on an assessment made by that doctor.

5. A doctor's statement shall be completed in ink or other indelible substance and shall contain the following particulars—

(a) the patient's name;

(b) the date of the assessment (whether by consultation or consideration of a report as the case may be) on which the doctor's statement is based;

(c) the condition in respect of which the doctor advises the patient they are not fit for work;

(d) a statement, where the doctor considers it appropriate, that the patient may be fit for work;

(e) a statement that the doctor will or, as the case may be will not, need to assess the patient's fitness for work again;

(f) the date on which the doctor's statement is given;

(g) the address of the doctor,

and shall bear, opposite the words "Doctor's signature", the signature in ink of the doctor making the statement.

6. Subject to rule 8, the condition in respect of which the doctor is advising the patient is not fit for work or, as the case may be, which has caused the patient's absence from work shall be specified as precisely as the doctor's knowledge of the patient's condition at the time of the assessment permits.

7. Where a doctor considers that a patient may be fit for work the doctor shall state the reasons for that advice and where this is considered appropriate, the arrangements which the patient might make, with their employer's agreement, to return to work.

8. The condition may be specified less precisely where, in the doctor's opinion, disclosure of the precise condition would be prejudicial to the patient's well-being, or to the patient's position with their employer.

9. A doctor's statement may be given on a date after the date of the assessment on which it is based, however no further statement shall be furnished in respect of that assessment other than a doctor's statement by way of replacement of an original which has been lost, in which case it shall be clearly marked "duplicate".

10. Where, in the doctor's opinion, the patient will become fit for work on a day not later than 14 days after the date of the assessment on which the doctor's statement is based, the doctor's statement shall specify that day.

11. Subject to rules 12 and 13, the doctor's statement shall specify the minimum period for which, in the doctor's opinion, the patient will not be fit for work or, as the case may be, for which they may be fit for work.

12. The period specified shall begin on the date of the assessment on which the doctor's statement is based and shall not exceed 3 months unless the patient has, on the advice of a doctor, refrained from work for at least 6 months immediately preceding that date.

13. Where—

(a) the patient has been advised by a doctor that they are not fit for work and, in consequence, has refrained from work for at least 6 months immediately preceding the date of the assessment on which the doctor's statement is based; and

(b) in the doctor's opinion, the patient will not be fit for work for the foreseeable future,

instead of specifying a period, the doctor may, having regard to the circumstances of the particular case, enter, after the words "case for", the words "an indefinite period".]

NOTES

Original Schedule numbered as Sch 1 by the Social Security (Miscellaneous Provisions) Amendment Regulations 1992, SI 1992/247, reg 6(1), (4); Sch 1 subsequently substituted by the Social Security (Medical Evidence) and Statutory Sick Pay (Medical Evidence) (Amendment) Regulations 2010, SI 2010/137, reg 3(1), (4).

[PART II
FORM OF DOCTOR'S STATEMENT

STATEMENT OF FITNESS FOR WORK FOR SOCIAL SECURITY OR STATUTORY SICK PAY

[2.72]

Patient's name Mr, Mrs, Miss, Ms ....

I assessed your case on: ..../..../....

and, because of the following condition(s): ....

I advise you that:
☐ you are not fit for work.
☐ you may be fit for work taking account of the following advice:

If available, and with your employer's agreement, you may benefit from:

☐ a phased return to work
☐ altered hours
☐ amended duties
☐ workplace adaptations

Comments, including functional effects of your condition(s):
....
....

This will be the case for ....
or from ..../..../.... to ..../..../....

I will/will not need to assess your fitness for work again at the end of this period.
(Please delete as applicable)

Doctor's signature ....
Date of statement ..../..../....
Doctor's address ....]

NOTES

Substituted as noted to Pt I of this Schedule at **[2.71]**.

SCHEDULE 1A

(Sch 1A added by the Social Security (Miscellaneous Provisions) Amendment Regulations 1992, SI 1992/247, reg 6(1), (5), Sch 2; revoked by the Social Security (Medical Evidence) and Statutory Sick Pay (Medical Evidence) (Amendment) Regulations 2010, SI 2010/137, reg 3(1), (5).)

STATUTORY MATERNITY PAY (GENERAL) REGULATIONS 1986

(SI 1986/1960)

NOTES

Made: 17 November 1986.

Authority: Social Security Act 1986, ss 46(4), (7), (8), 47(1), (3), (6), (7), 48(3), (6), 50(1), (2), (4), (5), 51(1)(g), (k), (n), (r), (4), 54(1), 83(1), 84(1), Sch 4, paras 6, 8, 12(3) (repealed apart from ss 54(1), 83(1), 84(1)). By virtue of the Social Security (Consequential Provisions) Act 1992, s 2(2), these Regulations now have effect as if made under the Social Security Contributions and Benefits Act 1992, ss 164(4), (8), (9), 165(1), (3), (7), 166(3), 171(1), (2), (5), (6), Sch 13, and the Social Security Administration Act 1992, ss 5, 132.

Commencement: 6 April 1987.

Transfer of functions: the functions of the Secretary of State conferred by regs 7, 25, 30, 31 have been transferred to the Commissioners of Inland Revenue by the Social Security Contributions (Transfer of Functions, etc) Act 1999, s 1(2), Sch 2. Note also that a reference to the Commissioners of Inland Revenue is now to be taken as a reference to the Commissioners for Her Majesty's Revenue and Customs; see the Commissioners for Revenue and Customs Act 2005, s 50(1), (7).

See *Harvey* J(2).

ARRANGEMENT OF REGULATIONS

PART I
INTRODUCTION

PART II
ENTITLEMENT

PART II
CONTINUOUS EMPLOYMENT AND NORMAL WORKING HOURS

PART IV
GENERAL PROVISIONS

PART V
ADMINISTRATION

PART VI
PAYMENT

PART I
INTRODUCTION

[2.73]

1 Citation, commencement and interpretation

(1) These regulations may be cited as the Statutory Maternity Pay (General) Regulations 1986 and shall come into operation in the case of regulations 1, 22 and 23 on 15th March 1987, and in the case of the remainder of the regulations on 6th April 1987.

(2) In these regulations, unless the context otherwise requires—

"the 1975 Act" means the Social Security Act 1975;

"the 1978 Act" means the Employment Protection (Consolidation) Act 1978;

"the 1986 Act" means the Social Security Act 1986;

["the Contributions and Benefits Act" means the Social Security Contributions and Benefits Act 1992];

["statutory maternity leave" means ordinary maternity leave and any additional maternity leave under, respectively, sections 71 and 73 of the Employment Rights Act 1996].

(3) Unless the context otherwise requires, any references in these regulations to—

(a) a numbered regulation is a reference to the regulation bearing that number in these regulations and any reference in a regulation to a numbered paragraph is a reference to the paragraph of that regulation bearing that number;

(b) any provision made by or contained in an enactment or instrument shall be construed as a reference to that provision as amended or extended by any enactment or instrument and as including a reference to any provision which it re-enacts or replaces, or which may re-enact or replace it, with or without modifications.

NOTES

Para (2): definition "the Contributions and Benefits Act" added by the Social Security (Miscellaneous Provisions) Amendment (No 2) Regulations 1992, SI 1992/2595, reg 12; definition "statutory maternity leave" added by the Statutory Maternity Pay (General) (Amendment) Regulations 2005, SI 2005/729, reg 2.

Social Security Act 1975, Social Security Act 1986: largely repealed and consolidated in the Social Security Contributions and Benefits Act 1992 and the Social Security Administration Act 1992.

Employment Protection (Consolidation) Act 1978: repealed and largely consolidated in the Trade Union and Labour Relations (Consolidation) Act 1992, the Employment Rights Act 1996 and the Employment Tribunals Act 1996.

PART II
ENTITLEMENT

[2.74]

[2 The Maternity Pay Period

(1) Subject to paragraphs (3) to (5), where—

(a) a woman gives notice to her employer of the date from which she expects his liability to pay her statutory maternity pay to begin; and

(b) in conformity with that notice ceases to work for him in a week which is later than the 12th week before the expected week of confinement,

the first day of the maternity pay period shall be the day on which she expects his liability to pay her statutory maternity pay to begin in conformity with that notice provided that day is not later than the day immediately following the day on which she is confined.

(2) The maternity pay period shall be a period of 39 consecutive weeks.

(3) In a case where a woman is confined—

(a) before the 11th week before the expected week of confinement; or

(b) after the 12th week before the expected week of confinement and the confinement occurs on a day which precedes that mentioned in a notice given to her employer as being the day on which she expects his liability to pay her statutory maternity pay to begin,

section 165 of the Contributions and Benefits Act shall have effect so that the first day of the maternity pay period shall be the day following the day on which she is so confined.

(4) In a case where a woman is absent from work wholly or partly because of pregnancy or confinement on any day—

(a) which falls on or after the beginning of the 4th week before the expected week of confinement; but

(b) not later than the day immediately following the day on which she is confined,

the first day of the maternity pay period shall be the day following the day on which she is so absent.

(5) In a case where a woman leaves her employment—

(a) at any time falling after the beginning of the 11th week before the expected week of confinement and before the start of the maternity pay period, but

(b) not later than the day on which she is confined,

the first day of the maternity pay period shall be the day following the day on which she leaves her employment.]

NOTES

Substituted by the Statutory Maternity Pay, Social Security (Maternity Allowance) and Social Security (Overlapping Benefits) (Amendment) Regulations 2006, SI 2006/2379, reg 3(1), (2).

Part 2 Statutory Instruments

[2.75]

3 Contract of service ended for the purpose of avoiding liability for statutory maternity pay

(1) A former employer shall be liable to make payments of statutory maternity pay to any woman who was employed by him for a continuous period of at least 8 weeks and whose contract of service with him was brought to an end by the former employer solely or mainly for the purpose of avoiding liability for statutory maternity pay.

(2) In order to determine the amount payable by the former employer—

(a) the woman shall be deemed for the purposes of Part V of the 1986 Act to have been employed by him from the date her employment with him ended until the end of the week immediately preceding the 14th week before the expected week of confinement on the same terms and conditions of employment as those subsisting immediately before her employment ended, and

(b) her normal weekly earnings for the period of 8 weeks immediately preceding the 14th week before the expected week of confinement shall for those purposes be calculated by reference to her normal weekly earnings for the period of 8 weeks ending with the last day in respect of which she was paid under her former contract of service.

NOTES

"Part V of the 1986 Act": see now the Social Security Contributions and Benefits Act 1992, Pt XII.

[2.76]

4 Modification of entitlement provisions

(1) . . .

(2) In relation to a woman in employed earner's employment who was confined before the 14th week before the expected week of confinement [section 164(2)(a) and (b) of the Contributions and Benefits Act] shall have effect as if for the conditions there set out, there was substituted the conditions that—

(a) she would but for her confinement have been in employed earner's employment with an employer for a continuous period of at least 26 weeks ending with the week immediately preceding the 14th week before the expected week of confinement, and

(b) her normal weekly earnings for the period of 8 weeks ending with the week immediately preceding the week of her confinement are not less than the lower earnings limit in force under [section 5(1)(a) of the Contributions and Benefits Act] immediately before the commencement of the week of her confinement.

[(3) In relation to a woman to whom paragraph (2) applies, section 166 of the Contributions and Benefits Act shall be modified so that subsection (2) has effect as if the reference to the period of 8 weeks immediately preceding the 14th week before the expected week of confinement was a reference to the period of 8 weeks immediately preceding the week in which her confinement occurred.]

NOTES

Para (1): revoked by the Social Security Maternity Benefits and Statutory Sick Pay (Amendment) Regulations 1994, SI 1994/1367, reg 3(1), (2).

Para (2): words in square brackets substituted by SI 1994/1367, reg 3(1), (3).

Para (3): added by the Statutory Maternity Pay (General) Amendment Regulations 1988, SI 1988/532, reg 2; substituted by SI 1994/1367, reg 3(1), (4).

"Lower earnings limit": this is currently £118 per week, as from 6 April 2019: see the Social Security (Contributions) Regulations 2001, SI 2001/1004, reg 10(a) (as amended by SI 2019/262, regs 6, 7(b)). The previous sums were: £116 (as from 6 April 2018, see SI 2018/337, regs 6, 7(b)); £113 (as from 6 April 2017; see SI 2017/415, regs 6, 7(a)); £112 (as from 6 April 2015; see SI 2015/557, regs 2, 3(c)); £111 (as from 6 April 2014; see SI 2014/569, regs 2, 3(b)); £109 (as from 6 April 2013: see SI 2013/558, regs 2, 3(b)); £107 (as from 6 April 2012: see SI 2012/804, regs 2, 3(b)); £102 (as from 6 April 2011; see SI 2011/940, regs 2, 3(b)). Note that there was no increase for the financial year commencing 6 April 2016.

[2.77]

5 Treatment of more than one contract of service as one

Where 2 or more contracts of service exist concurrently between one employer and one employee, they shall be treated as one for the purposes of Part V of the 1986 Act, except where, by virtue of regulation 11 of the Social Security (Contributions) Regulations 1979 the earnings from those contracts of service are not aggregated for the purposes of earnings-related contributions.

NOTES

"Part V of the 1986 Act": see now the Social Security Contributions and Benefits Act 1992, Pt XII.

[2.78]

[6 Prescribed rate of statutory maternity pay

The rate of statutory maternity pay prescribed under section 166(1)(b) of the Contributions and Benefits Act is a weekly rate of [£148.68].]

NOTES

Substituted by the Social Security, Statutory Maternity Pay and Statutory Sick Pay (Miscellaneous Amendments) Regulations 2002, SI 2002/2690, reg 3.

Sum in square brackets substituted by the Social Security Benefits Up-rating Order 2019, SI 2019/480, art 10, as from 7 April 2019 (except for the purpose of determining the rate of maternity allowance in accordance with the Social Security Contributions and Benefits Act 1992, s 35A(1), for which purpose it came into force on 8 April 2019).

The previous amounts were: £145.18, as from 1 April 2018 (except for the purpose of determining the rate of maternity allowance in accordance with the Social Security Contributions and Benefits Act 1992, s 35A(1), for which purpose it came into force on 9 April 2018), see SI 2018/281, art 10; £140.98, as from 2 April 2017 (except for the purpose of determining the rate of maternity allowance in accordance with the Social Security Contributions and Benefits Act 1992, s 35A(1), for which purpose it came into force on 10 April 2017), see SI 2017/260, art 10; £139.58, (as from 5 April 2015 and 6 April 2015 respectively), see SI 2015/30, art 4. Note that there was no increase in April 2016. Prior to those dates the amounts were £138.18 (see SI 2014/147, art 4); £136.78 (see SI 2013/574, art 9); £135.45 (see SI 2012/780, art 10); £128.73 (see SI 2011/821, art 10), £124.88 (see SI 2010/793, art 10), £123.06 (see SI 2009/947, art 10), £117.18 (see SI 2008/632, art 10), £112.75 (see SI 2007/688, art 10) and £108.80 (see SI 2006/645, art 10).

[2.79]

7 Liability of [Commissioners of Inland Revenue] to pay statutory maternity pay

(1) Where—

(a) an adjudicating authority has determined that an employer is liable to make payments of statutory maternity pay to a woman, and

(b) the time for appealing against that determination has expired, and

(c) no appeal against the determination has been lodged or leave to appeal against the determination is required and has been refused,

then for any week in respect of which the employer was liable to make payments of statutory maternity pay but did not do so, and for any subsequent weeks in the maternity pay period the liability to make those payments shall, notwithstanding section 46(3) of the 1986 Act, be that of the [Commissioners of Inland Revenue] and not the employer.

(2) In paragraph (1) adjudicating authority means, as the case may be, the Chief or any other adjudication officer, [the First-tier Tribunal or the Upper Tribunal].

(3) Liability to make payments of statutory maternity pay shall, notwithstanding section 46(3) of the 1986 Act, be a liability of the [Commissioners of Inland Revenue] and not the employer as from the week in which the employer first becomes insolvent until the end of the maternity pay period.

(4) For the purposes of paragraph (3) an employer shall be taken to be insolvent if, and only if—

(a) in England and Wales—

(i) he has been adjudged bankrupt or has made a composition or arrangement with his creditors;

(ii) he has died and his estate falls to be administered in accordance with an order under section 421 of the Insolvency Act 1986; or

(iii) where an employer is a company, a winding-up order . . . is made or a resolution for voluntary winding-up is passed with respect to it [or it enters administration], or a receiver or manager of its undertaking is duly appointed, or possession is taken by or on behalf of the holders of any debentures secured by a floating charge, of any property of the company comprised in or subject to the charge or a voluntary arrangement proposed for the purposes of Part I of the Insolvency Act 1986 is approved under that Part;

(b) in Scotland—

(i) an award of sequestration is made on his estate or he executes a trust deed for his creditors or enters into a composition contract;

(ii) he has died and a judicial factor appointed under section 11A of the Judicial Factors (Scotland) Act 1889 is required by that section to divide his insolvent estate among his creditors; or

(iii) where the employer is a company, a winding-up order . . . is made or a resolution for voluntary winding-up is passed with respect to it [or it enters administration] or a receiver of its undertaking is duly appointed or a voluntary arrangement proposed for the purposes of Part I of the Insolvency Act 1986 is approved under that Part.

NOTES

Regulation heading, paras (1), (3): words in square brackets substituted by virtue of the Social Security Contributions (Transfer of Functions, etc) Act 1999, s 1(2), Sch 2.

Para (2): words in square brackets substituted by the Tribunals, Courts and Enforcement Act 2007 (Transitional and Consequential Provisions) Order 2008, SI 2008/2683, art 6(1), Sch 1, para 42.

Para (4): words omitted revoked, and words in square brackets inserted, by the Enterprise Act 2002 (Insolvency) Order 2003, SI 2003/2096, art 5, Schedule, Pt 2, para 44.

Commissioners of Inland Revenue: a reference to the Commissioners of Inland Revenue is now to be taken as a reference to the Commissioners for Her Majesty's Revenue and Customs; see the Commissioners for Revenue and Customs Act 2005, s 50(1), (7).

"Section 46(3) of the 1986 Act": see now the Social Security Contributions and Benefits Act 1992, s 164(3).

[2.80]

8 Work after confinement

(1) Where in the week immediately preceding the 14th week before the expected week of confinement a woman had 2 or more employers but one or more of them were not liable to make payments to her of statutory maternity pay ("non-liable employer"), section 47(6) of the 1986 Act shall not apply in respect of any week after the week of confinement but within the maternity pay period in which she works only for a non-liable employer.

(2) Where after her confinement a woman—

(a) works for an employer who is not liable to pay her statutory maternity pay and is not a non-liable employer, but

(b) before the end of her maternity pay period ceases to work for that employer, the person who before she commenced work was liable to make payments of statutory maternity pay to her shall, notwithstanding section 46 of the 1986 Act, not be liable to make such payments to her for any weeks in the maternity pay period after she ceases work.

NOTES

"Section 47(6) of the 1986 Act": see now the Social Security Contributions and Benefits Act 1992, s 165(6); as to s 46 of the 1986 Act, see now s 164 of the 1992 Act.

[2.81]

9 No liability to pay statutory maternity pay

Notwithstanding the provisions of section 46(1) of the 1986 Act, no liability to make payments of statutory maternity pay to a woman shall arise in respect of a week within the maternity pay period for any part of which she is detained in legal custody or sentenced to a term of imprisonment (except where the sentence is suspended), or of any subsequent week within that period.

NOTES

"Section 46(1) of the 1986 Act": see now the Social Security Contributions and Benefits Act 1992, s 164(1).

[2.82]

[9A Working for not more than 10 days in the Maternity Pay Period

In a case where a woman does any work under a contract of service with her employer on any day, but for not more than 10 days (whether consecutive or not), during her maternity pay period, statutory maternity pay shall continue to be payable to the employee by the employer.]

NOTES

Inserted by the Statutory Maternity Pay, Social Security (Maternity Allowance) and Social Security (Overlapping Benefits) (Amendment) Regulations 2006, SI 2006/2379, reg 3(1), (3).

[2.83]

10 Death of woman

An employer shall not be liable to make payments of statutory maternity pay in respect of a woman for any week within the maternity pay period which falls after the week in which she dies.

PART III
CONTINUOUS EMPLOYMENT AND NORMAL WORKING HOURS

[2.84]

11 Continuous employment

(1) Subject to the following provisions of this regulation, where in any week a woman is, for the whole or part of the week,—

(a) incapable of work in consequence of sickness or injury, or

(b) absent from work on account of a temporary cessation of work, or

(c) absent from work in circumstances such that, by arrangement or custom, she is regarded as continuing in the employment of her employer for all or any purpose, or

(d) absent from work wholly or partly because of pregnancy or confinement, [or]

[(e) absent from work in consequence of taking paternity leave, adoption leave[, shared parental leave] or parental leave under Part 8 of the Employment Rights Act 1996,]

and returns to work for her employer after the incapacity for or absence from work, that week shall be treated for the purposes of Part V of the 1986 Act as part of a continuous period of employment with that employer, notwithstanding that no contract of service exists with that employer in respect of that week.

(2) Incapacity for work which lasts for more than 26 consecutive weeks shall not count for the purposes of paragraph (1)(a).

(3) Paragraph (1)(d) shall only apply to a woman who—

(a) has a contract of service with the same employer both before and after the confinement but not during any period of absence from work due to her confinement and the period between those contracts does not exceed 26 weeks, or

(b) returns to work in accordance with section 45(1) of the 1978 Act or in pursuance of an offer made in circumstances described in section 56A(2) of that Act after a period of absence from work wholly or partly occasioned by pregnancy or confinement.

[(3A) Where a woman who is pregnant—

(a) is an employee in an employed earner's employment in which the custom is for the employer—

(i) to offer work for a fixed period of not more than 26 consecutive weeks;

(ii) to offer work for such period on 2 or more occasions in a year for periods which do not overlap; and

(iii) to offer the work available to those persons who had worked for him during the last or a recent such period, but

(b) is absent from work—

(i) wholly or partly because of the pregnancy or her confinement, or

(ii) because of incapacity arising from some specific disease or bodily or mental disablement,

then in her case paragraph (1) shall apply as if the words "and returns to work for an employer after the incapacity for or absence from work" were omitted and paragraph (4) shall not apply.]

(4) Where a woman is employed under a contract of service for part only of the week immediately preceding the 14th week before the expected week of confinement, the whole of that week shall count in computing any period of continuous employment for the purposes of Part V of the 1986 Act.

NOTES

Para (1): word in square brackets in sub-para (d) added, and sub-para (e) added by the Social Security, Statutory Maternity Pay and Statutory Sick Pay (Miscellaneous Amendments) Regulations 2002, SI 2002/2690, reg 4; words in square brackets in sub-para (e) inserted by the Shared Parental Leave and Statutory Shared Parental Pay (Consequential Amendments to Subordinate Legislation) Order 2014, SI 2014/3255, art 4(1), (2), as from 31 December 2014.

Para (3A): inserted by the Statutory Maternity Pay (General) Amendment Regulations 1990, SI 1990/622, reg 2.

"Part V of the 1986 Act": see now the Social Security Contributions and Benefits Act 1992, Pt XII.

"Section 45(1) of the 1978 Act": see now the Employment Rights Act 1996, s 66.

"Section 56A(2) of that Act": replaced by the Employment Rights Act 1996, s 96(3) (repealed).

[2.85]

12 Continuous employment and unfair dismissal

(1) This regulation applies to a woman in relation to whose dismissal an action is commenced which consists—

(a) of the presentation by her of a complaint under section 67(1) of the 1978 Act; or

(b) of her making a claim in accordance with a dismissals procedure agreement designated by an order under section 65 of that Act; or

(c) of any action taken by a conciliation officer under section 134(3) of that Act; [or

(d) of a decision arising out of the use of a statutory dispute resolution procedure contained in Schedule 2 to the Employment Act 2002 in a case where, in accordance with the Employment Act 2002 (Dispute Resolution) Regulations 2004, such a procedure applies].

(2) If in consequence of an action of the kind specified in paragraph (1) a woman is reinstated or re-engaged by her employer or by a successor or associated employer of that employer the continuity of her employment shall be preserved for the purposes of Part V of the 1986 Act and any week which falls within the interval beginning with the effective date of termination and ending with the date of reinstatement or re-engagement, as the case may be, shall count in the computation of her period of continuous employment.

(3) In this regulation—

"successor" and "dismissals procedure agreement" have the same meanings as in section 30(3) and (4) of the Trade Union and Labour Relations Act 1974, and

"associated employer" shall be construed in accordance with section 153(4) of the 1978 Act.

NOTES

Para (1): sub-para (d) and the word immediately preceding it inserted by the Statutory Maternity Pay (General) and Statutory Paternity Pay and Statutory Adoption Pay (General) (Amendment) Regulations 2005, SI 2005/358, reg 3. Note that Sch 2 to the 2002 Act was repealed by the Employment Act 2008, s 1 and the 2004 Regulations lapsed as from 6 April 2009, subject to transitional provisions, but there has been no amendment to sub-para (1)(d) to reflect this.

"Section 67(1) of the 1978 Act": see now the Employment Rights Act 1996, s 111(1).

"Section 65 of that Act": see now the Employment Rights Act 1996, s 110.

"Section 134(3) of that Act": replaced by the Employment Tribunals Act 1996, s 18(5) (repealed).

"Part V of the 1986 Act": see now the Social Security Contributions and Benefits Act 1992, Pt XII.

"Section 30(3) and (4) of the Trade Union and Labour Relations Act 1974": see now the Employment Rights Act 1996, s 235.

"Section 153(4) of the 1978 Act": see now the Employment Rights Act 1996, s 231 and the Employment Tribunals Act 1996, s 42(3).

[2.86]

13 Continuous employment and stoppages of work

(1) Where for any week or part of a week a woman does no work because there is, within the meaning of section 19 of the 1975 Act a stoppage of work due to a trade dispute at her place of employment the continuity of her employment shall, subject to paragraph (2), be treated as continuing throughout the stoppage but, subject to paragraph (3), no such week shall count in the computation of her period of employment.

(2) Subject to paragraph (3), where during the stoppage of work a woman is dismissed from her employment, the continuity of her employment shall not be treated in accordance with paragraph (1) as continuing beyond the commencement of the day she stopped work.

(3) The provisions of paragraph (1) to the extent that they provide that a week in which a stoppage of work occurred shall not count in the computation of a period of employment, and paragraph (2) shall not apply to a woman who proves that at no time did she have a direct interest in the trade dispute in question.

NOTES

"Section 19 of the 1975 Act": replaced by the Social Security Contributions and Benefits Act 1992, s 27 (repealed); see now the Jobseekers Act 1995, s 14.

[2.87]

14 Change of employer

A woman's employment shall, notwithstanding the change of employer, be treated as continuous employment with the second employer where—

(a) the employer's trade or business or an undertaking (whether or not it is an undertaking established by or under an Act of Parliament) is transferred from one person to another;

(b) by or under an Act of Parliament, whether public or local and whenever passed, a contract of employment between any body corporate and the woman is modified and some other body corporate is substituted as her employer;

(c) on the death of her employer, the woman is taken into the employment of the personal representatives or trustees of the deceased;

(d) the woman is employed by partners, personal representatives or trustees and there is a change in the partners, or, as the case may be, personal representatives or trustees;

(e) the woman is taken into the employment of an employer who is, at the time she entered his employment, an associated employer of her previous employer, and for this purpose "associated employer" shall be construed in accordance with section 153(4) of the 1978 Act;

(f) on the termination of her employment with an employer she is taken into the employment of another employer and [those employers are the governors of a school maintained by a [local authority (within the meaning of the Education Act 1996)] and that authority].

NOTES

Para (f): words in first (outer) pair of square brackets substituted by the Statutory Maternity Pay (General) Amendment Regulations 1990, SI 1990/622, reg 3; words in second (inner) pair of square brackets substituted by the Local Education Authorities and Children's Services Authorities (Integration of Functions) (Local and Subordinate Legislation) Order 2010, SI 2010/1172, art 5, Sch 3, para 11.

"Section 153(4) of the 1978 Act": see now the Employment Rights Act 1996, s 231 and the Employment Tribunals Act 1996, s 42(3).

[2.88]

15 Reinstatement after service with the armed forces etc

If a woman who is entitled to apply to her former employer under the Reserve Forces (Safeguard of Employment) Act 1985 enters the employment of that employer not later than the 6 month period mentioned in section 1(4)(b) of that Act, her previous period of employment with that employer (or if there was more than one such period, the last of those periods) and the period of employment beginning in the said period of 6 months shall be treated as continuous.

[2.89]

16 Normal working weeks

(1) For the purposes of section 48(5) of the 1986 Act, a woman's contract of service shall be treated as not normally involving or having involved employment for less than 16 hours weekly where she is normally employed for 16 hours or more weekly.

(2) Where a woman's relations with her employer were governed for a continuous period of at least 2 years by a contract of service which normally involved employment for not less than 16 hours weekly and this period was followed by a further period, ending with the week immediately preceding the 14th week before the expected week of confinement, in which her relations with that employer were governed by a contract of service which normally involved employment for less than 16 hours, but not less than 8 hours weekly, then her contract of service shall be treated for the purpose of section 48(5) of the 1986 Act as not normally involving or having involved employment for less than 16 hours weekly.

(3) Where a woman's relations with her employer are or were governed for a continuous period of at least 2 years by a contract of service which involved

(a) for not more than 26 weeks in that period, employment for 8 hours or more but less than 16 hours weekly, and

(b) for the whole of the remainder of that period employment for not less than 16 hours weekly,

the contract of service shall be treated for the purposes of section 48(5) of the 1986 Act as not normally involving or having involved employment for less than 16 hours weekly.

NOTES

"Section 48(5) of the 1986 Act": replaced by the Social Security Contributions and Benefits Act 1992, s 166(5) (repealed).

[2.90]

[16A Meaning of "week"

Where a woman has been in employed earner's employment with the same employer in each of 26 consecutive weeks (but no more than 26 weeks) ending with the week immediately preceding the 14th week before the expected week of confinement then for the purpose of determining whether that employment amounts to a continuous period of at least 26 weeks, the first of those 26 weeks shall be a period commencing on the first day of her employment with the employer and ending at midnight on the first Saturday thereafter or on that day where her first day is a Saturday.]

NOTES

Inserted by the Statutory Maternity Pay (General) Amendment Regulations 1990, SI 1990/622, reg 4.

PART IV
GENERAL PROVISIONS

[2.91]

17 Meaning of "employee"

(1) [Subject to paragraph (1A),] in a case where, and in so far as, a woman . . . is treated as an employed earner by virtue of the Social Security (Categorisation of Earners) Regulations 1978 she shall be treated as an employee for the purposes of Part V of the 1986 Act and in a case where, and in so far as, such a woman is treated otherwise than as an employed earner by virtue of those regulations, she shall not be treated as an employee for the purposes of Part V.

[(1A) Paragraph (1) shall have effect in relation to a woman who—
- (a) is under the age of 16; and
- (b) would or, as the case may be, would not have been treated as an employed earner by virtue of the Social Security (Categorisation of Earners) Regulations 1978 had she been over that age,

as it has effect in relation to a woman who is, or, as the case may be, is not so treated.]

(2) Any woman who is in employed earner's employment within the meaning of the 1975 Act under a contract of apprenticeship shall be treated as an employee for the purposes of Part V.

(3) A woman who is in employed earner's employment within the meaning of the 1975 Act but whose employer—
- (a) does not fulfil the conditions prescribed in regulation 119(1)(b) of the Social Security (Contributions) Regulations 1979 as to residence or presence in Great Britain, or
- (b) is a woman who, by reason of any international treaty to which the United Kingdom is a party or of any international convention binding the United Kingdom—
  - (i) is exempt from the provisions of the 1975 Act, or
  - (ii) is a woman against whom the provisions of that Act are not enforceable,

shall not be treated as an employee for the purposes of Part V of the 1986 Act.

NOTES

Para (1): words in square brackets inserted, and words omitted revoked, by the Employment Equality (Age) Regulations 2006, SI 2006/1031, reg 49(1), Sch 8, Pt 2, paras 52, 53(1), (2).

Para (1A): inserted by SI 2006/1031, reg 49(1), Sch 8, Pt 2, paras 52, 53(1), (3); substituted by the Employment Equality (Age) (Consequential Amendments) Regulations 2007, SI 2007/825, reg 6.

"Part V of the 1986 Act": see now the Social Security Contributions and Benefits Act 1992, Pt XII.

[2.92]

18 Treatment of two or more employers as one

(1) In a case where the earnings paid to a woman in respect of 2 or more employments are aggregated and treated as a single payment of earnings under regulation 12(1) of the Social Security (Contributions) Regulations 1979, the employers of the woman in respect of those employments shall be treated as one for all purposes of Part V of the 1986 Act.

(2) Where 2 or more employers are treated as one under the provisions of paragraph (1), liability for statutory maternity pay payable by them to a woman shall be apportioned between them in such proportions as they may agree or, in default of agreement, in the proportions which the woman's earnings from each employment bear to the amount of the aggregated earnings.

NOTES

"Part V of the 1986 Act": see now the Social Security Contributions and Benefits Act 1992, Pt XII.

[2.93]

19 Payments to be treated as contractual remuneration

For the purposes of paragraph 12(1) and (2) of Schedule 4 to the 1986 Act, the payments which are to be treated as contractual remuneration are sums payable under the contract of service—
- (a) by way of remuneration;
- (b) for incapacity for work due to sickness or injury, and
- (c) by reason of pregnancy or confinement.

NOTES

"1986 Act, Sch 4, para 12": see now the Social Security Contributions and Benefits Act 1992, Sch 13, para 3.

[2.94]

20 Meaning of "earnings"

(1) . . .

[(2) For the purposes of section 171(4) of the Contributions and Benefits Act, the expression "earnings" refers to gross earnings and includes any remuneration or profit derived from a woman's employment except any payment or amount which is—
- (a) excluded [or disregarded in the calculation of a person's earnings under regulation 25, 27 or 123 of, or Schedule 3 to, the Social Security (Contributions) Regulations 2001] (payments to be disregarded and payments to directors to be disregarded respectively) [(or would have been so excluded had she not been under the age of 16)];
- (b) a chargeable emolument under section 10A of the Social Security Contributions and Benefits Act 1992, except where, in consequence of such a chargeable emolument being excluded from

earnings, a woman would not be entitled to statutory maternity pay [(or where such a payment or amount would have been so excluded and in consequence she would not have been entitled to statutory maternity pay had she not been under the age of 16)].]

(3) . . .

(4) For the purposes of [section 171(4) of the Contributions and Benefits Act] the expression "earnings" includes also—

[(za) any amount retrospectively treated as earnings by regulations made by virtue of section 4B(2) of the Contributions and Benefits Act;]

(a) any sum payable in respect of arrears of pay in pursuance of an order for reinstatement or re-engagement under the 1978 Act;

(b) any sum payable by way of pay in pursuance of an order under the 1978 Act for the continuation of a contract of employment;

(c) any sum payable by way of remuneration in pursuance of a protective award under the Employment Protection Act 1975;

(d) any sum payable by way of statutory sick pay, including sums payable in accordance with regulations made under section 1(5) of the Social Security and Housing Benefits Act 1982;

[(e) any sum payable by way of statutory maternity pay, including sums payable in accordance with regulations made under section 164(9)(b) of the Contributions and Benefits Act;

(f) any sum payable by way of statutory paternity pay, including sums payable in accordance with regulations made under section 171ZD(3) of the Contributions and Benefits Act;

(g) any sum payable by way of statutory adoption pay, including sums payable in accordance with regulations made under section 171ZM(3) of the Contributions and Benefits Act];

[(h) any sum payable by way of statutory shared parental pay, including any sums payable in accordance with regulations made under section 171ZX(3) of the Contributions and Benefits Act.]

(5), (6) . . .

NOTES

Paras (1), (3), (5), (6): revoked by the Social Security (Miscellaneous Provisions) Amendment (No 2) Regulations 1992, SI 1992/2595, reg 13(1), (2), (4).

Para (2): substituted by the Social Security Contributions, Statutory Maternity Pay and Statutory Sick Pay (Miscellaneous Amendments) Regulations 1999, SI 1999/567, reg 12; words in first pair of square brackets in sub-para (a) substituted by the Social Security, Occupational Pension Schemes and Statutory Payments (Consequential Provisions) Regulations 2007, SI 2007/1154, reg 4(1), (2); words in second pair of square brackets in sub-para (a) and words in square brackets in sub-para (b) inserted by the Employment Equality (Age) Regulations 2006, SI 2006/1031, reg 49(1), Sch 8, Pt 2, paras 52, 54.

Para (4): words in first pair of square brackets substituted by the Social Security, Statutory Maternity Pay and Statutory Sick Pay (Miscellaneous Amendments) Regulations 2002, SI 2002/2690, reg 5(a); sub-para (za) inserted by SI 2007/1154, reg 4(1), (3); sub-paras (e)–(g) added by reg 5(b) of the 2002 Regulations; sub-para (h) added by the Shared Parental Leave and Statutory Shared Parental Pay (Consequential Amendments to Subordinate Legislation) Order 2014, SI 2014/3255, art 4(1), (3), as from 31 December 2014.

Statutory paternity pay: as to the meaning of this, see the Children and Families Act 2014, s 126 at **[1.1894]**.

"Protective award under the Employment Protection Act 1975": see now the Trade Union and Labour Relations (Consolidation) Act 1992, ss 189–191.

"Section 1(5) of the Social Security and Housing Benefits Act 1982": see now the Social Security Contributions and Benefits Act 1992, s 151(4)–(6).

[2.95]

21 Normal weekly earnings

(1) For the purposes of [Part XII of the Contributions and Benefits Act], a woman's normal weekly earnings shall be calculated in accordance with the following provisions of this regulation.

(2) In this regulation—

"the appropriate date" means the first day of the 14th week before the expected week of confinement, or the first day in the week in which the woman is confined, whichever is the earlier, . . .

"normal pay day" means a day on which the terms of a woman's contract of service require her to be paid, or the practice in her employment is for her to be paid, if any payment is due to her; and

"day of payment" means a day on which the woman was paid.

(3) Subject to paragraph (4), the relevant period for the purposes of [section 171(4) of the Contributions and Benefits Act] is the period between—

(a) the last normal pay day to fall before the appropriate date; and

(b) the last normal pay day to fall at least 8 weeks earlier than the normal pay day mentioned in sub-paragraph (a),

including the normal pay day mentioned in sub-paragraph (a) but excluding that first mentioned in sub-paragraph (b).

(4) In a case where a woman has no identifiable normal pay day, paragraph (3) shall have effect as if the words "day of payment" were substituted for the words "normal pay day" in each place where they occur.

(5) In a case where a woman has normal pay days at intervals of or approximating to one or more calendar months (including intervals of or approximating to a year) her normal weekly earnings shall be calculated by dividing her earnings in the relevant period by the number of calendar months in that period (or, if it is not a whole number, the nearest whole number), multiplying the result by 12 and dividing by 52.

(6) In a case to which paragraph (5) does not apply and the relevant period is not an exact number of weeks, the woman's normal weekly earnings shall be calculated by dividing her earnings in the relevant period by the number of days in the relevant period and multiplying the result by 7.

[(7) In any case where—

(a) a woman is awarded a pay increase (or would have been awarded such an increase had she not then been absent on statutory maternity leave); and

(b) that pay increase applies to the whole or any part of the period between the beginning of the relevant period and the end of her period of statutory maternity leave,

her normal weekly earnings shall be calculated as if such an increase applied in each week of the relevant period.]

NOTES

Paras (1), (3): words in square brackets substituted by the Social Security Maternity Benefits and Statutory Sick Pay (Amendment) Regulations 1994, SI 1994/1367, reg 5(1), (2), (4).

Para (2): words omitted revoked by SI 1994/1367, reg 5(1), (3).

Para (7): added by the Statutory Maternity Pay (General) Amendment Regulations 1996, SI 1996/1335, reg 2, and substituted by the Statutory Maternity Pay (General) (Amendment) Regulations 2005, SI 2005/729, reg 3.

21A *(Inserted by the Statutory Maternity Pay (General) Amendment Regulations 1988, SI 1988/532, reg 3; revoked by the Social Security, Statutory Maternity Pay and Statutory Sick Pay (Miscellaneous Amendments) Regulations 2002, SI 2002/2690, reg 6.)*

[2.96]

[21B Effect of maternity allowance on statutory maternity pay

Where a woman, in any week which falls within the maternity pay period, is—

(a) in receipt of maternity allowance pursuant to the provisions of sections 35 and 35A of the Contributions and Benefits Act; and

(b) entitled to receive statutory maternity pay in consequence of[—

(i) receiving a pay increase referred to in regulation 21(7), or

(ii) being treated as having been paid retrospective earnings under regulation 20(4)(za)],

the employer shall not be liable to make payments of statutory maternity pay in respect of such a week unless, and to the extent by which, the rate of statutory maternity pay exceeds the rate of maternity allowance received by her in that week.]

NOTES

Inserted by the Statutory Maternity Pay (General) Amendment Regulations 1996, SI 1996/1335, reg 3, and substituted by the Statutory Maternity Pay (General) (Amendment) Regulations 2005, SI 2005/729, reg 4.

Sub-paras (b)(i), (ii) substituted by the Social Security, Occupational Pension Schemes and Statutory Payments (Consequential Provisions) Regulations 2007, SI 2007/1154, reg 4(1), (4).

PART V
ADMINISTRATION

[2.97]

22 Evidence of expected week of confinement or of confinement

(1) A woman shall in accordance with the following provisions of this regulation, provide the person who is liable to pay her statutory maternity pay with evidence as to—

(a) the week in which the expected date of confinement occurs, and

(b) where her entitlement to statutory maternity pay depends upon the fact of her confinement, the week in which she was confined.

(2) For the purpose of paragraph (1)(b) a certificate of birth shall be sufficient evidence that the woman was confined in the week in which the birth occurred.

(3) The evidence shall be submitted to the person who will be liable to make payments of statutory maternity pay not later than the end of the third week of the maternity pay period so however that where the woman has good cause the evidence may be submitted later than that date but not later than the end of the 13th week of the maternity pay period.

(4) For the purposes of paragraph (3) evidence contained in an envelope which is properly addressed and sent by prepaid post shall be deemed to have been submitted on the day on which it was posted.

[2.98]

23 Notice of absence from work

(1) Where a woman is confined before the beginning of the 14th week before the expected week of confinement, she shall be entitled to payments of statutory maternity pay only if—

(a) she gives notice to the person who will be liable to pay it [of the date on which she was confined], and

(b) that notice is given within [28 days] of the date she was confined or if in the particular circumstances that is not practicable, as soon as is reasonably practicable thereafter; and

(c) where the person so requests, the notice is in writing.

(2) Where a woman is confined before the date stated in a notice provided in accordance with [section 164(4) of the Contributions and Benefits Act] as being the date her absence from work is due to begin, she shall be entitled to payments of statutory maternity pay only if—

Part 2 Statutory Instruments

(a) she gives a further notice to the person who will be liable to pay it specifying the date she was confined and the date her absence from work . . . began, and

(b) that further notice is given within [28 days] of the date she was confined or if in the particular circumstances that is not practicable, as soon as is reasonably practicable thereafter; and

(c) where the person so requests, the notice is in writing.

(3) For the purposes of this regulation, a notice contained in an envelope which is properly addressed and sent by prepaid post shall be deemed to be given on the date on which it is posted.

[(4) Subject to paragraph (5), section 164(4) of the Contributions and Benefits Act (statutory maternity pay-entitlement and liability to pay) shall not have effect in the case of a woman who leaves her employment with the person who will be liable to pay her statutory maternity pay after the beginning of the week immediately preceding the 14th week before the expected week of confinement.]

[(5) A woman who is exempted from section 164(4) of the Contributions and Benefits Act by paragraph (4) but who is confined before the 11th week before the expected week of confinement shall only be entitled to statutory maternity pay if she gives the person who will be liable to pay it notice specifying the date she was confined.]

NOTES

Para (1): words in square brackets substituted by the Social Security, Statutory Maternity Pay and Statutory Sick Pay (Miscellaneous Amendments) Regulations 2002, SI 2002/2690, reg 6(1), (2).

Para (2): words in first pair of square brackets substituted by the Social Security Maternity Benefits and Statutory Sick Pay (Amendment) Regulations 1994, SI 1994/1367, reg 6(1), (2); words omitted revoked, and words in second pair of square brackets substituted, by SI 2002/2690, reg 6(1), (3).

Para (4): substituted by SI 2002/2690, reg 6(1), (4).

Para (5): substituted by SI 1994/1367, reg 6(1), (3).

[2.99]

24 Notification of employment after confinement

A woman who after the date of confinement but within the maternity pay period commences work in employed earner's employment with a person who is not liable to make payments of statutory maternity pay to her and is not a non-liable employer for the purposes of regulation 8(1), shall within 7 days of the day she commenced work inform any person who is so liable of the date she commenced work.

[2.100]

25 Provision of information in connection with determination of questions

Any woman claiming to be entitled to statutory maternity pay, or any other person who is a party to proceedings arising under the 1986 Act relating to statutory maternity pay, shall, if she receives notification from the [Commissioners of Inland Revenue] that any information is required from her for the determination of any question arising in connection therewith, furnish that information to the [Commissioners of Inland Revenue] within 10 days of receiving that notification.

NOTES

Words in square brackets substituted by virtue of the Social Security Contributions (Transfer of Functions, etc) Act 1999, s 1(2), Sch 2.

Commissioners of Inland Revenue: see the note to reg 7 at **[2.79]**.

[2.101]

[25A Provision of information relating to claims for certain other benefits

(1) Where an employer who has been given notice in accordance with [section 164(4)(a) or (9)(ea) of the Contributions and Benefits Act] or regulation 23 by a woman who is or has been an employee—

(a) decides that he has no liability to make payments of statutory maternity pay to her, or

(b) has made one or more payments of statutory maternity pay to her but decides, before the end of the maternity pay period and for a reason specified in paragraph (3), that he has no liability to make further payments to her,

then, in connection with the making of a claim by the woman for a maternity allowance[, incapacity benefit or an employment and support allowance], he shall furnish her with the information specified in the following provisions of this regulation.

(2) Where the employer decides he has no liability to make payments of statutory maternity pay to the woman, he shall furnish her with details of the decision and the reasons for it.

(3) Where the employer decides he has no liability to make further payments of statutory maternity pay to the woman because . . . she has within the maternity pay period been detained in legal custody or sentenced to a term of imprisonment which was not suspended, . . . he shall furnish her with—

(a) details of his decision and the reasons for it; and

(b) details of the last week in respect of which a liability to pay statutory maternity pay arose and the total number of weeks within the maternity pay period in which such a liability arose.

(4) The employer shall—

(a) return to the woman any maternity certificate provided by her in support of the notice referred to in paragraph (1); and

(b) comply with any requirements imposed by the preceding provisions of this regulation—

(i) in a case to which paragraph (2) applies, within 7 days of the decision being made, or, if earlier, within [28 days] of the day the woman gave notice of her intended absence or of her confinement if that had occurred; or

(ii) in a case to which paragraph (3) refers, within 7 days of being notified of the woman's detention or sentence . . .

(5) In this regulation, "incapacity benefit" means [incapacity benefit] or a severe disablement allowance.]

NOTES

Inserted by the Statutory Maternity Pay (General) Amendment Regulations 1990, SI 1990/622, reg 7.

Para (1): words in first pair of square brackets substituted by the Social Security, Statutory Maternity Pay and Statutory Sick Pay (Miscellaneous Amendments) Regulations 2002, SI 2002/2690, reg 8(1), (2); words in second pair of square brackets substituted by the Employment and Support Allowance (Consequential Provisions) (No 2) Regulations 2008, SI 2008/1554, reg 46.

Para (3): words omitted revoked by SI 2002/2690, reg 8(1), (3).

Para (4): words in square brackets substituted, and words omitted revoked, by SI 2002/2690, reg 8(1), (4).

Para (5): words in square brackets substituted by the Social Security (Incapacity Benefit) (Consequential and Transitional Amendments and Savings) Regulations 1995, SI 1995/829, reg 18(1), (3).

[2.102]

26 Records to be maintained by employers

(1) Every employer shall maintain for 3 years after the end of the tax year in which the maternity pay period ends a record in relation to any woman who is or was an employee of his of—

(a) the date of the first day of absence from work wholly or partly because of pregnancy or confinement as notified by her and, if different, the date of the first day when such absence commenced;

(b) the weeks in that tax year in which statutory maternity pay was paid and the amount paid in each week; and

(c) any week in that tax year which was within her maternity pay period but for which no payment of statutory maternity pay was made to her and the reasons no payment was made.

(2) Except where he was not liable to make a payment of statutory maternity pay and subject to paragraphs (3) and (4), every employer shall retain for 3 years after the end of the tax year in which the maternity pay period ends any medical certificate or other evidence relating to the expected week of confinement, or as the case may be, the confinement which was provided to him by a woman who is or was an employee of his.

(3) Where an employer returns a medical certificate to an employee of his for the purpose of enabling her to make a claim for benefit under the 1975 Act, it shall be sufficient for the purposes of paragraph (2) if he retains a copy of that certificate.

(4) An employer shall not retain any certificate of birth provided to him as evidence of confinement by a woman who is or was an employee of his, but shall retain a record of the date of birth.

[2.103]

[26A Production of employer's records

(1) An authorised officer of the Commissioners of Inland Revenue may by notice require an employer to produce to him at the place of keeping such records as are in the employer's possession or power and as (in the officer's reasonable opinion) contain, or may contain, information relevant to satisfy him that statutory maternity pay has been paid and is being paid in accordance with these regulations to employees or former employees who are entitled to it.

(2) A notice referred to in paragraph (1) shall be in writing and the employer shall produce the records referred to in that paragraph within 30 days after the date of such a notice.

(3) The production of records in pursuance of this regulation shall be without prejudice to any lien which a third party may have in respect of those records.

(4) References in this regulation to "records" means—

(a) any wage sheet or deductions working sheet; or

(b) any other document which relates to the calculation or payment of statutory maternity pay to his employees or former employees,

whether kept in written form, electronically, or otherwise.

(5) In paragraph (1), "place of keeping" means such place in Great Britain that an employer and an authorised officer may agree upon, or, in the absence of such agreement—

(a) any place in Great Britain where records referred to in paragraph (1) are normally kept; or

(b) if there is no such place, the employer's principal place of business in Great Britain.]

NOTES

Inserted by the Statutory Maternity Pay (General) and Statutory Sick Pay (General) (Amendment) Regulations 2005, SI 2005/989, reg 2(1), (2).

Commissioners of Inland Revenue: see the note to reg 7 at **[2.79]**.

PART VI
PAYMENT

[2.104]

27 Payment of statutory maternity pay

Payment of statutory maternity pay may be made in a like manner to payments of remuneration but shall not include payments in kind or by way of the provision of board or lodgings or of services or other facilities.

[2.105]
[28 Rounding to avoid fractional amounts

Where any payment of statutory maternity pay is paid for any week or part of a week and the amount due includes a fraction of a penny, the payment shall be rounded up to the next whole number of pence.]

NOTES

Substituted by the Statutory Maternity Pay, Social Security (Maternity Allowance) and Social Security (Overlapping Benefits) (Amendment) Regulations 2006, SI 2006/2379, reg 3(1), (4).

[2.106]
29 Time when statutory maternity pay is to be paid

(1) In this regulation, "pay day" means a day on which it has been agreed, or it is the normal practice between an employer or former employer and a woman who is or was an employee of his, that payments by way of remuneration are to be made, or, where there is no such agreement or normal practice, the last day of a calendar month.

(2) In any case where—
- (a) a decision has been made by an adjudication officer, appeal tribunal or Commissioner in proceedings under Part III of the 1975 Act as a result of which a woman is entitled to an amount of statutory maternity pay; and
- (b) the time for bringing an appeal against the decision has expired and either—
  - (i) no such appeal has been brought; or
  - (ii) such an appeal has been brought and has been finally disposed of,

that amount of statutory maternity pay shall be paid within the time specified in paragraph (3).

(3) Subject to paragraphs (4) and (5), the employer or former employer shall pay the amount not later than the first pay day after—
- (a) where an appeal has been brought, the day on which the employer or former employer receives notification that it has been finally disposed of;
- (b) where leave to appeal has been refused and there remains no further opportunity to apply for leave, the day on which the employer or former employer receives notification of the refusal; and
- (c) in any other case, the day on which the time for bringing an appeal expires.

(4) Subject to paragraph (5), where it is impracticable, in view of the employer's or former employer's methods of accounting for and paying remuneration, for the requirement of payment referred to in paragraph (3) to be met by the pay day referred to in that paragraph, it shall be met not later than the next following pay day.

(5) Where the employer or former employer would not have remunerated the woman for her work in the week in question as early as the pay day specified in paragraph (3) or (if it applies) paragraph (4), the requirement of payment shall be met on the first day on which the woman would have been remunerated for her work in that week.

[2.107]
30 Payments by the [Commissioners of Inland Revenue]

Where the [Commissioners of Inland Revenue become] liable in accordance with regulation 7 to make payments of statutory maternity pay to a woman, the first payment shall be made as soon as reasonably practicable after he becomes so liable, and payments thereafter shall be made at weekly intervals, by means of an instrument of payment or by such other means as appears to the [Commissioners of Inland Revenue] to be appropriate in the circumstances of any particular case.

NOTES

Words in square brackets substituted by virtue of the Social Security Contributions (Transfer of Functions, etc) Act 1999, s 1(2), Sch 2.

Commissioners of Inland Revenue: see the note to reg 7 at **[2.79]**.

[2.108]
31 Persons unable to act

(1) Where in the case of any woman—
- (a) statutory maternity pay is payable to her or she is alleged to be entitled to it;
- (b) she is unable for the time being to act; and
- (c) either—
  - (i) no receiver has been appointed by the Court of Protection with power to receive statutory maternity pay on her behalf, or
  - (ii) in Scotland, her estate is not being administered by any tutor, curator or other guardian acting or appointed in terms of law,

the [Commissioners of Inland Revenue] may, upon written application to him by a person who, if a natural person, is over the age of 18, appoint that person to exercise, on behalf of the woman any right to which she may be entitled under Part V of the 1986 Act and to deal on her behalf with any sums payable to her.

(2) Where the [Commissioners of Inland Revenue have] made an appointment under paragraph (1)—
- (a) [they] may at any time in [their] absolute discretion revoke it;

(b) the person appointed may resign his office after having given one month's notice in writing to the [Commissioners of Inland Revenue] of his intention to do so; and

(c) the appointment shall terminate when the [Commissioners of Inland Revenue are] notified that a receiver or other person to whom paragraph (1)(c) applies has been appointed.

(3) Anything required by Part V of the 1986 Act to be done by or to any woman who is unable to act may be done by or to the person appointed under this regulation to act on her behalf, and the receipt of the person so appointed shall be a good discharge to the woman's employer or former employer for any sum paid.

NOTES

Paras (1), (2): words in square brackets substituted by virtue of the Social Security Contributions (Transfer of Functions, etc) Act 1999, s 1(2), Sch 2.

Commissioners of Inland Revenue: see the note to reg 7 at **[2.79]**.

"Part V of the 1986 Act": see now the Social Security Contributions and Benefits Act 1992, Pt XII.

32 *(Reg 32 (Pt V) revoked by the Statutory Maternity Pay (General) and Statutory Sick Pay (General) (Amendment) Regulations 2005, SI 2005/989, reg 2(1), (3).)*

STATUTORY MATERNITY PAY (MEDICAL EVIDENCE) REGULATIONS 1987

(SI 1987/235)

NOTES

Made: 19 February 1987.

Authority: Social Security Act 1986, ss 49 (repealed), 84(1), Sch 4, para 6 (repealed). These Regulations now have effect as if made under the Social Security Administration Act 1992, s 15(1), by virtue of the Social Security (Consequential Provisions) Act 1992, s 2(2).

Commencement: 15 March 1987.

See *Harvey* J(2).

[2.109]

1 Citation, commencement and interpretation

(1) These regulations may be cited as the Statutory Maternity Pay (Medical Evidence) Regulations 1987 and shall come into force on 15th March 1987.

(2) In these regulations, unless the context otherwise requires—

"the Act" means the Social Security Act 1986;

["registered midwife" means a midwife who is registered as a midwife with the Nursing and Midwifery Council under the Nursing and Midwifery Order 2001;]

"doctor" means a registered medical practitioner;

[. . .]

"signature" means, in relation to any statement or certificate given in accordance with these regulations, the name by which the person giving that statement or certificate, as the case may be, is usually known (any name other than the surname being either in full or otherwise indicated) written by that person in his own handwriting; and "signed" shall be construed accordingly.

NOTES

Para (2): definition "registered midwife" substituted by the Nursing and Midwifery Order 2001 (Consequential Amendments) Order 2002, SI 2002/881, art 2, Schedule, para 2; definition "Primary Care Trust" (omitted) originally inserted by the National Health Service Reform and Health Care Professions Act 2002 (Supplementary, Consequential etc Provisions) Regulations 2002, SI 2002/2469, reg 11, Sch 8, and revoked by the National Treatment Agency (Abolition) and the Health and Social Care Act 2012 (Consequential, Transitional and Saving Provisions) Order 2013, SI 2013/235, art 11, Sch 2, Pt 1, para 9(1), (2).

Social Security Act 1986: largely repealed and consolidated in the Social Security Contributions and Benefits Act 1992 and the Social Security Administration Act 1992.

[2.110]

2 Evidence of pregnancy and confinement

The evidence as to pregnancy and the expected date of confinement which a woman is required to provide to a person who is liable to pay her statutory maternity pay shall be furnished in the form of a maternity certificate given by a doctor or by a registered midwife, not earlier than the beginning of the [20th week] before the expected week of confinement, in accordance with the rules set out in Part I of the Schedule to these regulations—

(a) in the appropriate form as set out in Part II of that Schedule, or

(b) in a form substantially to the like effect with such variations as the circumstances may require.

NOTES

Words in square brackets substituted by the Social Security (Medical Evidence) and Statutory Maternity Pay (Medical Evidence) (Amendment) Regulations 2001, SI 2001/2931, reg 3(1), (2).

SCHEDULE

Regulation 2

PART I
RULES

[2.111]

1. In these rules any reference to a woman is a reference to the woman in respect of whom a maternity certificate is given in accordance with these rules.

2. A maternity certificate shall be given by a doctor or registered midwife attending the woman and shall not be given by the woman herself.

3. The maternity certificate shall be on a form provided by the Secretary of State for the purpose and the wording shall be that set out in the appropriate part of the form specified in Part II of this Schedule.

4. Every maternity certificate shall be completed in ink or other indelible substance and shall contain the following particulars—

(a) the woman's name;

(b) the week in which the woman is expected to be confined or, if the maternity certificate is given after confinement, the date of that confinement and the date the confinement was expected to take place . . . ;

(c) the date of the examination on which the maternity certificate is based;

(d) the date on which the maternity certificate is signed; and

[(e) the address of the doctor or where the maternity certificate is signed by a registered midwife the personal identification number given to her on her registration in . . . the register maintained by the Nursing and Midwifery Council [("NMC") under article 5 of] the Nursing and Midwifery Order 2001 and the expiry date of that registration,]

and shall bear opposite the word "Signature", the signature of the person giving the maternity certificate written after there has been entered on the maternity certificate the woman's name and the expected date or, as the case may be, the date of the confinement.

5. After a maternity certificate has been given, no further maternity certificate based on the same examination shall be furnished other than a maternity certificate by way of replacement of an original which has been lost or mislaid, in which case it shall be clearly marked "duplicate".

NOTES

Para 4: words omitted from sub-para (b) revoked by the Social Security (Miscellaneous Provisions) Amendment Regulations 1991, SI 1991/2284, reg 23; sub-para (e) substituted by the Nursing and Midwifery Order 2001 (Consequential Amendments) Order 2002, SI 2002/881, art 2, Schedule, para 3; words omitted from sub-para (e) revoked, and words in square brackets in that paragraph substituted, by the Health Act 1999 (Consequential Amendments) (Nursing and Midwifery) Order 2004, SI 2004/1771, art 3, Schedule, Pt 2, para 51(a).

[PART II
FORM OF CERTIFICATE

MATERNITY CERTIFICATE

[2.112]

Please fill in this form in ink

Name of patient . . . .

Fill in this part if you are giving the certificate before the confinement. *Do not fill this in more [than 20 weeks] before the week the baby is expected.*	*Fill in this part if you are giving the certificate after the confinement.*
I certify that I examined you on the date given below. In my opinion you can expect to have your baby in the week that includes . . . . /. . . . . / . . . . *Weeks means a period of 7 days starting on a Sunday and ending on a Saturday*	I certify that I attended you in connection with the birth which took place on . . . . /. . . . . / . . . . when you were delivered of a child [ ] children. In my opinion your baby was expected in the week that includes. . . . . / . . . . /. . . . .
Date of examination. . . . . / . . . . /.	Registered midwives
Date of signing. . . . . / . . . . /.	Please give your [NMC] Personal Identification Number and the expiry date of your registration with the [NMC].
Signature.	. . . . Doctors

Please stamp your name and address here [(unless the form has been stamped, in Wales, by the Local Health Board in whose medical performers list you are included or, in Scotland,] [by the Health Board in whose primary medical services performers list you are included)]

. . . .

NOTES

Substituted by the Social Security (Miscellaneous Provisions) Amendment Regulations 1991, SI 1991/2284, reg 24.

Words in square brackets in the left-hand column substituted by the Social Security (Medical Evidence) and Statutory Maternity Pay (Medical Evidence) (Amendment) Regulations 2001, SI 2001/2931, reg 3(1), (3); "NMC" in square brackets in both places it occurs in the right-hand column substituted by the Health Act 1999 (Consequential Amendments) (Nursing and Midwifery) Order 2004, SI 2004/1771, art 3, Schedule, Pt 2, para 51(b); words in penultimate pair of square brackets in the right-hand column substituted by the National Treatment Agency (Abolition) and the Health and Social Care Act 2012 (Consequential, Transitional and Saving Provisions) Order 2013, SI 2013/235, art 11, Sch 2, Pt 1, para 9(1), (3); final words in square brackets in the right-hand column substituted, in relation to England and Scotland, by the General Medical Services and Personal Medical Services Transitional and Consequential Provisions Order 2004, SI 2004/865, art 119, Sch 1, para 5, and in relation to Wales by the General Medical Services Transitional and Consequential Provisions (Wales) (No 2) Order 2004, SI 2004/1016, art 95, Sch 1, para 5.

HEALTH AND SAFETY INFORMATION FOR EMPLOYEES REGULATIONS 1989

(SI 1989/682)

NOTES

Made: 18 April 1989.

Authority: Health and Safety at Work etc Act 1974, s 15(1), (2), (3)(a), (4)(a), (5)(b), (6)(b), Sch 3, para 15(1).

Commencement: 18 October 1989.

See *Harvey* NI(13).

ARRANGEMENT OF REGULATIONS

[2.113]

1 Citation and commencement

These Regulations may be cited as the Health and Safety Information for Employees Regulations 1989 and shall come into force on 18th October 1989.

[2.114]

2 Interpretation and application

(1) In these Regulations, unless the context otherwise requires—

"the 1974" Act means the Health and Safety at Work etc Act 1974;

["the 1995 Order" means the Health and Safety at Work etc Act 1974 (Application outside Great Britain) Order 1995;]

"the approved poster" and "the approved leaflet" have the meanings assigned by regulation 3;

"employment medical advisory service" means the employment medical advisory service referred to in section 55 of the 1974 Act;

"ship" has the meaning assigned to it by section 742 of the Merchant Shipping Act 1894.

(2) Any reference in these Regulations to the enforcing authority for premises is a reference to the enforcing authority which has responsibility for the enforcement of section 2 of the 1974 Act in relation to the main activity carried on in those premises.

(3) Any reference in these Regulations to—

(a) a numbered regulation is a reference to the regulation so numbered in these Regulations;

(b) a numbered paragraph is a reference to the paragraph so numbered in the regulation in which the reference appears.

Part 2 Statutory Instruments

(4) These Regulations shall have effect for the purpose of providing information to employees relating to health, safety and welfare but they shall not apply in relation to the master and crew of a sea going ship [(except to the extent that the master and crew are engaging in activities falling within articles 4, 5 and 6 of the 1995 Order)].

[(5) These Regulations shall, subject to paragraph (4) apply to and in relation to the premises and activities outside Great Britain to which sections 1 to 59 and 80 and 82 of the Health and Safety at Work etc Act 1974 apply by virtue of the 1995 Order as they apply to premises and activities within Great Britain.]

NOTES

Para (1): definition "the 1995 Order" inserted by the Health and Safety Information for Employees (Modifications and Repeals) Regulations 1995, SI 1995/2923, reg 2(a)(i).

Para (4): words in square brackets added by SI 1995/2923, reg 2(a)(ii).

Para (5): added by SI 1995/2923, reg 2(a)(iii).

The Health and Safety at Work etc Act 1974 (Application outside Great Britain) Order 1995, SI 1995/263: revoked and replaced by the Health and Safety at Work etc Act 1974 (Application outside Great Britain) Order 2001, SI 2001/2127; see now the Health and Safety at Work etc Act 1974 (Application outside Great Britain) Order 2013, SI 2013/240.

[2.115]

3 Meaning of and revisions to the approved poster and leaflet

(1) In these Regulations "the approved poster" or "the approved leaflet" means, respectively, a poster or leaflet in the form approved and published for the purposes of these Regulations by the Health and Safety Executive, as revised from time to time in accordance with paragraph (2).

(2) The Health and Safety Executive may approve a revision (in whole or in part) to the form of poster or leaflet; and where it does so it shall publish the revised form of poster or leaflet and issue a notice in writing specifying the date the revision was approved.

(3) Such a revision shall not take effect until [five years] after the date of its approval, but during that time the employer may use the approved poster or the approved leaflet incorporating that revision for the purposes of regulation 4(1).

[(4) The Health and Safety Executive may approve a particular form of poster or leaflet for use in relation to a particular employment or class of employment and where any such form has been approved the Executive shall publish it and issue a notice in writing specifying the date that form was approved and the particular employment or class of employment in respect of which it is approved.

(5) Where a particular form of poster or leaflet has been approved under paragraph (4) then paragraphs (2) and (3) shall apply to the revision of that particular form as they apply to the revision of an approved poster or an approved leaflet save that the notice in writing issued under paragraph (2) in respect of the revised form shall also specify the employment or class of employment in respect of which the revised form is approved.

(6) An employer may, in respect of employment for which a particular poster or leaflet has been approved under paragraph (4), comply with the requirements of regulation 4(1) by displaying that particular form of poster or giving that particular form of leaflet and in connection with any such compliance regulation 4 shall be construed as if the references to the approved poster and the approved leaflet in that regulation were references to the particular form of poster and the particular form of leaflet approved under paragraph (4) and as if the reference in regulation 4(3) to revision pursuant to regulation 3(2) were a reference to a revision pursuant to regulation 3(5).]

NOTES

Para (3): words in square brackets substituted by the Health and Safety Information for Employees (Amendment) Regulations 2009, SI 2009/606, reg 2(1), (2).

Paras (4)–(6): added by the Health and Safety Information for Employees (Modifications and Repeals) Regulations 1995, SI 1995/2923, reg 2(b).

[2.116]

4 Provision of poster or leaflet

(1) An employer shall, in relation to each of his employees—

(a) ensure that the approved poster is kept displayed in a readable condition—

(i) at a place which is reasonably accessible to the employee while he is at work, and

(ii) in such a position in that place as to be easily seen and read by that employee; or

(b) give to the employee the approved leaflet.

(2) An employer shall be treated as having complied with paragraph (1)(b) from the date these Regulations come into force or the date the employee commences employment with him (if later) if he gives to the employee the approved leaflet as soon as is reasonably practicable after that date.

(3) Where the form of poster or leaflet is revised pursuant to regulation 3(2), then on or before the date the revision takes effect—

(a) an employer relying on compliance with paragraph (1)(a) shall ensure that the approved poster displayed is the one as revised;

(b) an employer relying on compliance with paragraph (1)(b) shall either give to the employees concerned fresh approved leaflets (as so revised) or bring the revision to their notice in writing.

[2.117]
5 Provision of further information

(1) An employer relying on compliance with regulation 4(1)(a) shall, subject to paragraph (2), ensure that the following information is clearly and indelibly written on the poster in the appropriate space—

(a) the name of the enforcing authority for the premises where the poster is displayed and the address of the office of that authority for the area in which those premises are situated; and

(b) the address of the office of the employment medical advisory service for the area in which those premises are situated[; or

(c) information as to how any of his employees may obtain the information referred to in (a) and (b) above].

(2) Where there is a change in any of the matters referred to in paragraph (1) it shall be sufficient compliance with that paragraph for the corresponding amendment to the poster to be made within six months from the date thereof.

(3) An employer who gives to his employee a leaflet pursuant to regulation 4(1)(b) shall give with the leaflet a written notice containing—

(a) the name of the enforcing authority for the premises where the employee works, and the address of the office of that authority for the area in which those premises are situated; and

(b) the address of the office of the employment medical advisory service for the area in which those premises are situated[; or

(c) information as to how any of his employees may obtain the information referred to in (a) and (b) above].

(4) Where the employee works in more than one location he shall, for the purposes of paragraph (3), be treated as working at the premises from which his work is administered, and if his work is administered from two or more premises, the employer may choose any one of them for the purpose of complying with that paragraph.

(5) Where an employer relies on compliance with regulation 4(1)(b) and there is a change in any of the matters referred to in paragraph (3) the employer shall within six months of the date thereof give to the employee a written notice specifying the change.

NOTES

Paras (1), (3): sub-para (c) and the word immediately preceding it inserted by the Health and Safety Information for Employees (Amendment) Regulations 2009, SI 2009/606, reg 2(1), (3), (4).

[2.118]
6 Exemption certificates

(1) Subject to paragraph (2) the Health and Safety Executive may, by a certificate in writing, exempt any person or class of persons from all or any of the requirements imposed by these Regulations and any such exemption may be granted subject to conditions and to a limit of time and may be revoked in writing at any time.

(2) The Executive shall not grant any such exemption unless, having regard to the circumstances of the case, and in particular to—

(a) the conditions if any, which it proposes to attach to the exemption; and

(b) any other requirements imposed by or under any enactment which apply to the case;

it is satisfied that the health, safety and welfare of persons who are likely to be affected by the exemption will not be prejudiced in consequence of it.

[2.119]
7 Defence

In any proceedings for an offence for a contravention of these Regulations it shall be a defence for the accused to prove that he took all reasonable precautions and exercised all due diligence to avoid the commission of that offence.

8 *(Introduces the repeals, revocations and modifications set out in the Schedule.)*

SCHEDULE

(Schedule (Repeals, revocations and modifications) outside the scope of this work.)

SEX DISCRIMINATION ACT 1975 (EXEMPTION OF SPECIAL TREATMENT FOR LONE PARENTS) ORDER 1989

(SI 1989/2140)

NOTES

Made: 17 November 1989.
Authority: Employment Act 1989, ss 8, 28.
Commencement: 19 December 1989.

Part 2 Statutory Instruments

[2.120]
1 Citation and commencement

This Order may be cited as the Sex Discrimination Act 1975 (Exemption of Special Treatment for Lone Parents) Order 1989 and shall come into force on 19th December 1989.

[2.121]
2 Interpretation

In this Order—

"child of that lone parent" means a person who for the purposes of any regulations made in pursuance of section 20(1)(a) of the Social Security Act 1986 is—
(a) a child or young person for whom that lone parent is responsible, and
(b) a member of the same household as that lone parent; and

"Employment Training" means the arrangements known by that name made under section 2 of the Employment and Training Act 1973 [or section 2 of the Enterprise and New Towns (Scotland) Act 1990].

NOTES

In definition "Employment Training" words in square brackets added by the Enterprise (Scotland) Consequential Amendments Order 1991, SI 1991/387, art 2, Schedule.

Social Security Act 1986: largely repealed and consolidated in the Social Security Contributions and Benefits Act 1992 and the Social Security Administration Act 1992. As to s 20(1)(a) of the 1986 Act, see now the Social Security Contributions and Benefits Act 1992, s 123(1).

[2.122]
3 Exemption of Special Treatment

With respect to Employment Training, section 8 of the Employment Act 1989 shall apply to any special treatment afforded—
(a) by the making of any payment, in connection with the participation of a lone parent in Employment Training, to a person having the care of a child of that lone parent, or
(b) by the fixing of any special condition for the participation of lone parents in Employment Training.

[EMPLOYMENT TRIBUNALS] (INTEREST) ORDER 1990

(SI 1990/479)

NOTES

Made: 6 March 1990.

Authority: Employment Protection (Consolidation) Act 1978, Sch 9, paras 1, 6A (repealed). These Regulations now have effect as if made under the Employment Tribunals Act 1996, s 14.

Commencement: 1 April 1990.

Title: words in square brackets substituted by the Employment Rights (Dispute Resolution) Act 1998, s 1(2)(b).

See *Harvey* PI(1), (2A).

ARRANGEMENT OF ARTICLES

[2.123]
1 Citation, commencement and transitional provisions

(1) This Order may be cited as the [Employment Tribunals] (Interest) Order 1990 and shall come into force on 1st April 1990.

(2) Where a relevant decision day or a day to be treated as if it were a relevant decision day would, but for this paragraph of this Article, fall on a day before 1st April 1990, the relevant decision day or day to be treated as if it were that day shall be 1st April 1990.

NOTES

Para (1): words in square brackets substituted by the Employment Rights (Dispute Resolution) Act 1998, s 1(2)(b).

[2.124]

2 Interpretation

(1) In this Order, except in so far as the context otherwise requires—

"appellate court" means the Employment Appeal Tribunal, the High Court, the Court of Appeal, the Court of Session or the House of Lords as the case may be;

["the calculation day" in relation to a relevant decision day means the day immediately following the relevant decision day;]

"interest" means simple interest which accrues from day to day;

"relevant decision" in relation to a tribunal means any award or other determination of the tribunal by virtue of which one party to proceedings before the tribunal is required to pay a sum of money, excluding a sum representing costs or expenses, to another party to those proceedings;

"Rules of Procedure" means rules having effect in relation to proceedings before a tribunal by virtue of any regulations or order made pursuant to an enactment;

"the stipulated rate of interest" has the meaning assigned to it in Article 4 below;

"tribunal" means in England and Wales an [employment tribunal] (England and Wales) established in pursuance of the Industrial Tribunals (England and Wales) Regulations 1965 and in Scotland an [employment tribunal] (Scotland) established in pursuance of the Industrial Tribunals (Scotland) Regulations 1965.

(2) For the purposes of this Order a sum of money is required to be paid by one party to proceedings to another such party if, and only if, an amount of money required to be so paid is—

(a) specified in an award or other determination of a tribunal or, as the case may be, in an order or decision of an appellate court; or

(b) otherwise ascertainable solely by reference to the terms of such an award or determination or, as the case may be, solely by reference to the terms of such an order or decision,

but where a tribunal or, as the case may be, appellate court has made a declaration as to entitlement under a contract nothing in this Order shall be taken to provide for interest to be payable on any payment under that contract in respect of which no obligation to make the payment has arisen under that contract before the declaration was made.

(3) In this Order, except in so far as the context otherwise requires, "decision day" means the day signified by the date recording the sending of the document which is sent to the parties recording an award or other determination of a tribunal and "relevant decision day", subject to Article 5, 6 and 7 below, means the day so signified in relation to a relevant decision.

(4) In this Order "party" includes the Secretary of State where he has elected to appear as if he were a party in accordance with a Rule of Procedure entitling him so to elect.

NOTES

Para (1) is amended as follows:

Definition "the calculation day" substituted by the Employment Tribunals (Interest) Order (Amendment) Order 2013, SI 2013/1671, arts 2, 4, except in relation to a claim which is presented to an Employment Tribunal Office on or before 28 July 2013.

In the definition "tribunal" words in square brackets substituted by the Employment Rights (Dispute Resolution) Act 1998, s 1(2)(a).

Industrial Tribunals (England and Wales) Regulations 1965, Industrial Tribunals (Scotland) Regulations 1965: see now Employment Tribunals (Constitution and Rules of Procedure) Regulations 2013, SI 2013/1237 at **[2.1323]**.

[2.125]

3 Computation of interest

(1) Subject to paragraphs (2) and (3) of this Article and to Article 11 below, where the whole or any part of a sum of money payable by virtue of a relevant decision of a tribunal remains unpaid on the calculation day the sum of money remaining unpaid on the calculation day shall carry interest at the stipulated rate of interest from the calculation day (including that day).

(2) Where, after the calculation day, a party pays to another party some but not all of such a sum of money remaining unpaid on the calculation day, then beginning with the day on which the payment is made interest shall continue to accrue only on that part of the sum of money which then remains unpaid.

(3) For the purposes of the computation of interest under this Order, there shall be disregarded—

(a) any part of a sum of money which pursuant to the Employment Protection (Recoupment of Unemployment Benefit and Supplementary Benefit) Regulations 1977 has been claimed by the Secretary of State in a recoupment notice; and

(b) any part of a sum of money which the party required to pay the sum of money is required, by virtue of any provision contained in or having effect under any enactment, to deduct and pay over to a public authority in respect of income tax or contributions under Part I of the Social Security Act 1975.

[(4) Notwithstanding paragraph (1), no interest shall be payable if payment of the full amount of the award (including any interest under regulation 2 of the Employment Tribunals (Interest on Awards in Discrimination Cases) Regulations 1996) is made within 14 days after the relevant decision day.]

NOTES

Para (4): added by the Employment Tribunals (Interest) Order (Amendment) Order 2013, SI 2013/1671, arts 3, 4, except in relation to a claim which is presented to an Employment Tribunal Office on or before 28 July 2013.

Employment Protection (Recoupment of Unemployment Benefit and Supplementary Benefit) Regulations 1977 (SI 1977/674): revoked and replaced by the Employment Protection (Recoupment of Jobseeker's Allowance and Income Support) Regulations 1996, SI 1996/2349 at **[2.252]**.

Social Security Act 1975, Pt I: repealed by the Social Security (Consequential Provisions) Act 1992, and replaced by the Social Security Contributions and Benefits Act 1992, Pt I.

[2.126]
4 Rate of interest

The stipulated rate of interest shall be the rate of interest specified in section 17 of the Judgments Act 1838 on the relevant decision day.

NOTES

The specified rate is (as of 15 May 2019) 8% per annum. This has been the rate since 1 April 1993 (see SI 1993/564 which amends the Judgments Act 1838, s 17).

[2.127]
5 Reviews

Where a tribunal reviews its decision pursuant to the Rules of Procedure and the effect of the review, or of any re-hearing which takes place as a result of the review, is that a sum of money payable by one party to another party is confirmed or varied the relevant decision day shall be the decision day of the decision which is the subject of the review.

[2.128]
6 Decisions on remission to a tribunal

Where an appellate court remits a matter to a tribunal for re-assessment of the sum of money which would have been payable by virtue of a previous relevant decision or by virtue of an order of another appellate court, the relevant decision day shall be the decision day of that previous relevant decision or the day on which the other appellate court promulgated its order, as the case may be.

[2.129]
7 Appeals from relevant decisions

Where, on an appeal from a relevant decision, or on a further appeal arising from a relevant decision an appellate court makes an order which confirms or varies the sum of money which would have been payable by virtue of that relevant decision if there had been no appeal, the relevant decision day shall be the decision day of that relevant decision.

[2.130]
8 Other appeals

(1) This Article applies in relation to any order made by an appellate court on an appeal from a determination of any issue by a tribunal which is not a relevant decision, or on any further appeal arising from such a determination, where the effect of the order is that for the first time in relation to that issue one party to the proceedings is required to pay a sum of money, other than a sum representing costs or expenses, to another party to the proceedings.

(2) Where this Article applies in relation to an order, Articles 3 and 4 above shall apply to the sum of money payable by virtue of the order as if it was a sum of money payable by virtue of a relevant decision and as if the day on which the appellate court promulgated the order was the relevant decision day.

[2.131]
9

Where, on an appeal from an order in relation to which Article 8 applies or on a further appeal arising from such an order, an appellate court makes an order which confirms or varies the sum of money which would have been payable by virtue of the order in relation to which Article 8 applies if there had been no appeal, the day to be treated as the relevant decision day shall be the day on which the order in relation to which Article 8 applies was promulgated.

[2.132]
10 Reviews by the Employment Appeal Tribunal

Where the Employment Appeal Tribunal reviews an order to which Article 8 above applies, the day to be treated as the relevant decision day shall be the day on which the order reviewed was promulgated.

[2.133]
11 Variations of the sum of money on appeal etc

Where a sum of money payable by virtue of a relevant decision is varied under one of the procedures referred to in Articles 5, 6 and 7 above, or a sum of money treated as being so payable by virtue of Article 8 above is varied under one of the procedures referred to in Articles 6, 9 and 10 above, the reference in paragraph (1) of Article 3 above, to a sum of money payable by virtue of a relevant decision shall be treated as if it were a reference to that sum as so varied.

[2.134]
12 Notices

(1) Where a decision of a tribunal is a relevant decision and a copy of a document recording that decision is sent to all parties entitled to receive that decision, it shall be the duty of the Secretary of the Central Office of the [Employment Tribunals] (England and Wales) or the Secretary of the Central Office of the [Employment Tribunals] (Scotland), as the case may be, to cause a notice containing the matters detailed in paragraph (2) below to accompany that document.

(2) The notice referred to in paragraph (1) above shall specify the decision day, the stipulated rate of interest and the calculation day in respect of the decision concerned.

(3) The failure to discharge the duty under paragraph (1) above correctly or at all shall have no effect on the liability of one party to pay to another party any sum of money which is payable by virtue of this Order.

NOTES

Para (1): words in square brackets substituted by virtue of the Employment Rights (Dispute Resolution) Act 1998, s 1.

SEX DISCRIMINATION ACT 1975 (EXEMPTION OF SPECIAL TREATMENT FOR LONE PARENTS) ORDER 1991

(SI 1991/2813)

NOTES

Made: 12 December 1991.
Authority: Employment Act 1989, ss 8, 28.
Commencement: 14 January 1992.

[2.135]
1 Citation and commencement

This Order may be cited as the Sex Discrimination Act 1975 (Exemption of Special Treatment for Lone Parents) Order 1991 and shall come into force on 14th January 1992.

[2.136]
2 Interpretation

In this Order—

"the Council" means the National Council for One Parent Families;

"the Return to Work Programme" means arrangements known by that name made under section 2 of the Employment and Training Act 1973 for the provision by or on behalf of the Council of training and other assistance to persons wishing to obtain employment.

[2.137]
3 Exemption of special treatment

With respect to the Return to Work Programme, section 8 of the Employment Act 1989 shall apply to any special treatment afforded to or in respect of lone parents—

(a) by the fixing of any special condition for participation in the Programme, or

(b) by the making of any payment in respect of the care of a child of a lone parent while that lone parent is participating in the Programme.

TRADE UNION BALLOTS AND ELECTIONS (INDEPENDENT SCRUTINEER QUALIFICATIONS) ORDER 1993

(SI 1993/1909)

NOTES

Made: 27 July 1993.
Authority: Trade Union and Labour Relations (Consolidation) Act 1992, ss 49(2), 75(2), 100A(2), 226B(2).
Commencement: 30 August 1993.
See *Harvey* M(5).

[2.138]
1 Citation, commencement and interpretation

(1) This Order may be cited as the Trade Union Ballots and Elections (Independent Scrutineer Qualifications) Order 1993 and shall come into force on 30 August 1993.

(2) In this Order, unless the context otherwise requires—

"an individual potentially qualified to be a scrutineer" means an individual who satisfies the requirement specified in either paragraph (a) of article 3 or paragraph (a) of article 4;

"the 1992 Act" means the Trade Union and Labour Relations (Consolidation) Act 1992;

"the relevant provisions" means the provisions of sections 49(2)(a), 75(2)(a), 100A(2)(a) and 226B(2)(a) of the 1992 Act.

[2.139]
2 Qualifications

An individual satisfies the condition specified for the purposes of the relevant provisions in relation to a ballot or election, (as the case may be), if he satisfies the condition specified in article 3 or 4.

[2.140]
3

An individual satisfies this condition if—

(a) he has in force a practising certificate issued by the Law Society of England and Wales or the Law Society of Scotland; and
(b) he is not disqualified from satisfying this condition by virtue of article 5.

[2.141]
4

An individual satisfies this condition if—

(a) he is qualified to be an auditor of a trade union by virtue of section 34(1) of the 1992 Act; and
(b) he is not disqualified from satisfying this condition by virtue of article 5.

[2.142]
5

(1) An individual potentially qualified to be a scrutineer does not satisfy the condition specified in article 3 or 4 if he or any existing partner of his has—

(a) during the preceding 12 months, been a member, an officer or an employee of the trade union proposing to hold the ballot or election; or
(b) in acting at any time as a scrutineer for any trade union, knowingly permitted any member, officer or employee of the trade union to assist him in carrying out any of the functions referred to in sections 49(3), 75(3), 100A(3) and 226B(1) of the 1992 Act.

(2) References in this article to an officer shall be construed as not including an auditor.

[2.143]
6

A partnership satisfies the condition specified for the purposes of the relevant provisions in relation to a ballot or election, (as the case may be), if—

(a) every member of the partnership is an individual potentially qualified to be a scrutineer; and
(b) no member of the partnership is disqualified from being a scrutineer by virtue of article 5.

[2.144]
[7

The following persons are specified for the purpose of the relevant provisions—

Electoral Reform Services Limited;
Involvement and Participation Association;
Popularis Limited;
Print Image Network Limited (trading as UK Engage);
Democracy Technology Limited (trading as Mi-Voice);
Kanto Elect Limited.]

NOTES

Commencement: 1 October 2017.

Substituted by the Trade Union Ballots and Elections (Independent Scrutineer Qualifications) (Amendment) Order 2017, SI 2017/877, art 2, as from 1 October 2017.

8 *(Revokes the Trade Union Ballots and Elections (Independent Scrutineer Qualifications) Order 1988, SI 1988/2117.)*

EMPLOYMENT APPEAL TRIBUNAL RULES 1993

(SI 1993/2854)

NOTES

Made: 23 November 1993.

Authority: Employment Protection (Consolidation) Act 1978, s 154(3), Sch 11, paras 17(1), 18, 18A(1), 19(1) (repealed). These rules have effect as if made under the Employment Tribunals Act 1996, ss 30(1), (2), 31, 34, 41(4).

Commencement: 16 December 1993.

See also the Employment Appeal Tribunal Practice Direction 2018 at **[5.28]**.

Transfer of the functions of the Lord Advocate: as to the transfer of certain functions of the Lord Advocate, see the Transfer of Functions (Lord Advocate and Secretary of State) Order 1999, SI 1999/678 and the Transfer of Functions (Lord Advocate and Advocate General for Scotland) Order 1999, SI 1999/679.

See *Harvey* PI(2), U3.

ARRANGEMENT OF RULES

[2.145]
1 Citation and commencement

(1) These Rules may be cited as the Employment Appeal Tribunal Rules 1993 and shall come into force on 16th December 1993.

(2) As from that date the Employment Appeal Tribunal Rules 1980, the Employment Appeal Tribunal (Amendment) Rules 1985 and the Employment Appeal Tribunal (Amendment) Rules 1988 shall be revoked.

[2.146]
[2 Interpretation

(1) In these rules—

"the 1992 Act" means the Trade Union and Labour Relations (Consolidation) Act 1992;

"the 1996 Act" means the Employment Tribunals Act 1996;

"the 1999 Regulations" means the Transnational Information and Consultation of Employees Regulations 1999;

Part 2 Statutory Instruments

["the 2004 Regulations" means the European and Public Limited-Liability Company Regulations 2004;]

["the Information and Consultation Regulations" means the Information and Consultation of Employees Regulations 2004;]

["the 2007 Regulations" means the Companies (Cross-Border Mergers) Regulations 2007;]

"the Appeal Tribunal" means the Employment Appeal Tribunal established under section 87 of the Employment Protection Act 1975 and continued in existence under section 20(1) of the 1996 Act and includes the President, a judge, a member or the Registrar acting on behalf of the Tribunal;

"the CAC" means the Central Arbitration Committee;

"the Certification Officer" means the person appointed to be the Certification Officer under section 254(2) of the 1992 Act;

"costs officer" means any officer of the Appeal Tribunal authorised by the President to assess costs or expenses;

"Crown employment proceedings" has the meaning given by section 10(8) of the 1996 Act;

["document" includes a document delivered by way of electronic communication;]

["electronic communication" shall have the meaning given to it by section 15(1) of the Electronic Communications Act 2000;]

"excluded person" means, in relation to any proceedings, a person who has been excluded from all or part of the proceedings by virtue of—

(a) a direction of a Minister of the Crown under rule 30A(1)(b) or (c); or

(b) an order of the Appeal Tribunal under rule 30A(2)(a) read with rule 30A(1)(b) or (c);

"judge" means a judge of the Appeal Tribunal nominated under section 22(1)(a) or (b) of the 1996 Act and includes a judge nominated under section 23(2) of, or a judge appointed under section 24(1) of, the 1996 Act to be a temporary additional judge of the Appeal Tribunal;

["legal representative" shall mean a person, including a person who is a party's employee, who—

(a) has a general qualification within the meaning of the Courts and Legal Services Act 1990;

(b) is an advocate or solicitor in Scotland; or

(c) is a member of the Bar of Northern Ireland or a [Solicitor of the Court of Judicature of Northern Ireland];]

"member" means a member of the Appeal Tribunal appointed under section 22(1)(c) of the 1996 Act and includes a member appointed under section 23(3) of the 1996 Act to act temporarily in the place of a member appointed under that section;

["national security proceedings" shall have the meaning given to it in [regulation 3 of the Employment Tribunals (Constitution and Rules of Procedure) Regulations 2013];]

"the President" means the judge appointed under section 22(3) of the 1996 Act to be President of the Appeal Tribunal and includes a judge nominated under section 23(1) of the 1996 Act to act temporarily in his place;

"the Registrar" means the person appointed to be Registrar of the Appeal Tribunal and includes any officer of the Tribunal authorised by the President to act on behalf of the Registrar;

"the Secretary of Employment Tribunals" means the person acting for the time being as the Secretary of the Central Office of the Employment Tribunals (England and Wales) or, as may be appropriate, of the Central Office of the Employment Tribunals (Scotland);

"special advocate" means a person appointed pursuant to rule 30A(4);

["writing" includes writing delivered by means of electronic communication].

(2) . . .

(3) Any reference in these Rules to a person who was the [claimant] or, as the case may be, the respondent in the proceedings before an employment tribunal includes, where those proceedings are still continuing, a reference to a person who is the [claimant] or, as the case may be, is the respondent in those proceedings.]

NOTES

Substituted by the Employment Appeal Tribunal (Amendment) Rules 2001, SI 2001/1128, r 2.

Para (1): definitions "the 2004 Regulations", "document", "electronic communication", "legal representative", "national security proceedings", and "writing" inserted by the Employment Appeal Tribunal (Amendment) Rules 2004, SI 2004/2526, r 2(1). Definition "the Information and Consultation Regulations" inserted by the Information and Consultation of Employees Regulations 2004, SI 2004/3426, reg 41(a). Definition "the 2007 Regulations" inserted by the Companies (Cross-Border Mergers) Regulations 2007, SI 2007/2974, reg 64(1) and revoked by the Companies, Limited Liability Partnerships and Partnerships (Amendment etc) (EU Exit) Regulations 2019, SI 2019/348, reg 8, Sch 3, paras 9, 10, as from exit day (as defined in the European Union (Withdrawal) Act 2018, s 20). In definition "legal representative" words in square brackets substituted by the Constitutional Reform Act 2005, s 59(5), Sch 11, Pt 3, para 5. In definition "national security proceedings" words in square brackets substituted by the Employment Appeal Tribunal (Amendment) Rules 2013, SI 2013/1693, r 2.

Para (2): revoked by SI 2004/2526, r 2(2).

Para (3): words in square brackets substituted by SI 2004/2526, r 2(3).

[2.147]
[2A

(1) The overriding objective of these Rules is to enable the Appeal Tribunal to deal with cases justly.

(2) Dealing with a case justly includes, so far as practicable —

(a) ensuring that the parties are on an equal footing;

(b) dealing with the case in ways which are proportionate to the importance and complexity of the issues;

(c) ensuring that it is dealt with expeditiously and fairly; and
(d) saving expense.

(3) The parties shall assist the Appeal Tribunal to further the overriding objective.]

NOTES

Inserted by the Employment Appeal Tribunal (Amendment) Rules 2004, SI 2004/2526, r 3.

[2.148]
[3 Institution of Appeal

(1) Every appeal to the Appeal Tribunal shall, subject to paragraphs (2) and (4), be instituted by serving on the Tribunal the following documents—

(a) a notice of appeal in, or substantially in, accordance with Form 1, 1A or 2 in the Schedule to these rules;
[(b) in the case of an appeal from a judgment of an employment tribunal a copy of any claim and response in the proceedings before the employment tribunal or an explanation as to why either is not included; and]
[(c) in the case of an appeal from a judgment of an employment tribunal a copy of the written record of the judgment of the employment tribunal which is subject to appeal and the written reasons for the judgment, or an explanation as to why written reasons are not included;] and
(d) in the case of an appeal made pursuant to regulation 38(8) of the 1999 Regulations [or regulation 47(6) of the 2004 Regulations] [or regulation 35(6) of the Information and Consultation Regulations] *[or regulation 57(6) of the 2007 Regulations]* from a declaration or order of the CAC, a copy of that declaration or order[; and]
[(e) in the case of an appeal from an order of an employment tribunal a copy of the written record of the order of the employment tribunal which is subject to appeal and (if available) the written reasons for the order;
(f) in the case of an appeal from a decision or order of the Certification Officer a copy of the decision or order of the Certification Officer which is subject to appeal and the written reasons for that decision or order.]

[(2) In an appeal from a judgment or order of the employment tribunal in relation to national security proceedings where the appellant was the claimant—

(i) the appellant shall not be required by virtue of paragraph (1)(b) to serve on the Appeal Tribunal a copy of the response if the response was not disclosed to the appellant; and
(ii) the appellant shall not be required by virtue of paragraph (1)(c) or (e) to serve on the Appeal Tribunal a copy of the written reasons for the judgment or order if the written reasons were not sent to the appellant but if a document containing edited reasons was sent to the appellant, he shall serve a copy of that document on the Appeal Tribunal.]

(3) The period within which an appeal to the Appeal Tribunal may be instituted is—

[(a) in the case of an appeal from a judgment of the employment tribunal—
 (i) where the written reasons for the judgment subject to appeal—
  (aa) were requested orally at the hearing before the employment tribunal or in writing within 14 days of the date on which the written record of the judgment was sent to the parties; or
  (bb) were reserved and given in writing by the employment tribunal
 42 days from the date on which the written reasons were sent to the parties;
 (ii) in an appeal from a judgment given in relation to national security proceedings, where there is a document containing edited reasons for the judgment subject to appeal, 42 days from the date on which that document was sent to the parties; or
 (iii) where the written reasons for the judgment subject to appeal—
  (aa) were not requested orally at the hearing before the employment tribunal or in writing within 14 days of the date on which the written record of the judgment was sent to the parties; and
  (bb) were not reserved and given in writing by the employment tribunal
 42 days from the date on which the written record of the judgment was sent to the parties;]
[(b) in the case of an appeal from an order of an employment tribunal, 42 days from the date of the order;]
(c) in the case of an appeal from a decision of the Certification Officer, 42 days from the date on which the written record of that decision was sent to the appellant;
(d) in the case of an appeal from a declaration or order of the CAC under regulation 38(8) of the 1999 Regulations [or regulation 47(6) of the 2004 Regulations] [or regulation 35(6) of the Information and Consultation Regulations] [or regulation 57(6) of the 2007 Regulations], 42 days from the date on which the written notification of that declaration or order was sent to the appellant.

(4) In the case of [an appeal from a judgment or order of the employment tribunal in relation to national security proceedings], the appellant shall not set out the grounds of appeal in his notice of appeal and shall not append to his notice of appeal the [written reasons for the judgment] of the tribunal.

(5) In [an appeal from the employment tribunal in relation to national security proceedings] in relation to which the appellant was the respondent in the proceedings before the employment tribunal, the appellant shall, within the period described in paragraph (3)(a), provide to the Appeal Tribunal a document setting out the grounds on which the appeal is brought.

(6) In [an appeal from the employment tribunal in relation to national security proceedings] in relation to which the appellant was the [claimant] in the proceedings before the employment tribunal—

(a) the appellant may, within the period described in [paragraph 3(a)(ii) or (iii) or paragraph 3(b), whichever is applicable,] provide to the Appeal Tribunal a document setting out the grounds on which the appeal is brought; and

(b) a special advocate appointed in respect of the appellant may, within the period described in [paragraph 3(a)(ii) or (iii) or paragraph 3(b), whichever is applicable,] or within 21 days of his appointment, whichever is later, provide to the Appeal Tribunal a document setting out the grounds on which the appeal is brought or providing supplementary grounds of appeal.

[(7) Where it appears to a judge or the Registrar that a notice of appeal or a document provided under paragraph (5) or (6)—

(a) discloses no reasonable grounds for bringing the appeal; or

(b) is an abuse of the Appeal Tribunal's process or is otherwise likely to obstruct the just disposal of proceedings,

he shall notify the Appellant or special advocate accordingly informing him of the reasons for his opinion and, subject to [paragraph (10)], no further action shall be taken on the notice of appeal or document provided under paragraph (5) or (6).]

[(7ZA) Where a judge or the Registrar has taken a decision under paragraph (7), and also considers that the notice of appeal or document provided under paragraph (5) or (6) is totally without merit, the judge or Registrar may order that the appellant or special advocate is not entitled to have the matter heard before a judge under paragraph (10), with such order to be included as part of the notice issued under paragraph (7).]

[(7A) In paragraphs (7)[, (7ZA)] and (10) reference to a notice of appeal or a document provided under paragraph (5) or (6) includes reference to part of a notice of appeal or document provided under paragraph (5) or (6).]

(8), (9) . . .

[(10) [Subject to paragraph (7ZA), where] notification has been given under paragraph (7) and within 28 days of the date the notification was sent, an appellant or special advocate expresses dissatisfaction in writing with the reasons given by the judge or Registrar for his opinion, he is entitled to have the matter heard before a judge who shall make a direction as to whether any further action should be taken on the notice of appeal or document under paragraph (5) or (6).]

NOTES

Substituted by the Employment Appeal Tribunal (Amendment) Rules 2001, SI 2001/1128, r 3.

Para (1): sub-paras (b), (c) substituted, words in first pair of square brackets in sub-para (d) inserted, word in final pair of square brackets in that paragraph substituted, and sub-paras (e), (f) inserted, by the Employment Appeal Tribunal (Amendment) Rules 2004, SI 2004/2526, r 4(1); words in second pair of square brackets in sub-para (d) inserted by the Information and Consultation of Employees Regulations 2004, SI 2004/3426, reg 41(b); words in third pair of square brackets in sub-para (d) inserted by the Companies (Cross-Border Mergers) Regulations 2007, SI 2007/2974, reg 64(2) and revoked by the Companies, Limited Liability Partnerships and Partnerships (Amendment etc) (EU Exit) Regulations 2019, SI 2019/348, reg 8, Sch 3, paras 9, 11, as from exit day (as defined in the European Union (Withdrawal) Act 2018, s 20).

Para (2): substituted by SI 2004/2526, r 4(2).

Para (3): sub-paras (a), (b) substituted, and words in first pair of square brackets in sub-para (d) inserted, by SI 2004/2526, r 4(3); words in second pair of square brackets in sub-para (d) inserted by SI 2004/3426, reg 41(b); words in third pair of square brackets in sub-para (d) inserted by SI 2007/2974, reg 64(2).

Paras (4)–(6): words in square brackets substituted by SI 2004/2526, r 4(4)–(6).

Para (7): substituted by SI 2004/2526, r 4(7); words in square brackets substituted by the Employment Appeal Tribunal (Amendment) Rules 2013, SI 2013/1693, r 3(a).

Para (7ZA): inserted by SI 2013/1693, r 3(b).

Para (7A): inserted by SI 2004/2526, r 4(8); reference to ", (7ZA)" in square brackets inserted by SI 2013/1693, r 3(c).

Paras (8), (9): revoked by SI 2013/1693, r 3(d).

Para (10): substituted by SI 2004/2526, r 4(11); words in square brackets substituted by SI 2013/1693, r 3(e).

[2.149]

4 Service of notice of appeal

[(1)] On receipt of notice under rule 3, the Registrar shall seal the notice with the Appeal Tribunal's seal and shall serve a sealed copy on the appellant and on—

(a) every person who, in accordance with rule 5, is a respondent to the appeal; and

(b) the Secretary of [Employment Tribunals] in the case of an appeal from an [employment tribunal]; or

(c) the Certification Officer in the case of an appeal from any of his decisions; or

(d) the Secretary of State in the case of an appeal under . . . Chapter II of Part IV of the 1992 Act [or Part XI of the Employment Rights Act 1996] to which he is not a respondent[; or

(e) the Chairman of the CAC in the case of an appeal from the CAC under regulation 38(8) of the 1999 Regulations [or regulation 47(6) of the 2004 Regulations] [or regulation 35(6) of the Information and Consultation Regulations] *[or regulation 57(6) of the 2007 Regulations]*].

[(2) On receipt of a document provided under rule 3(5)—

(a) the Registrar shall not send the document to a person in respect of whom a Minister of the Crown has informed the Registrar that he wishes to address the Appeal Tribunal in accordance with rule 30A(3) with a view to the Appeal Tribunal making an order applicable to this stage of the proceedings under rule 30A(2)(a) read with 30A(1)(b) or (c) (exclusion of a party or his representative), at any time before the Appeal Tribunal decides whether or not to make such an order; but if it decides not to make such an order, the Registrar shall, subject to sub-paragraph (b), send the document to such a person 14 days after the Appeal Tribunal's decision not to make the order; and

(b) the Registrar shall not send a copy of the document to an excluded person, but if a special advocate is appointed in respect of such a person, the Registrar shall send a copy of the document to the special advocate.

(3) On receipt of a document provided under rule 3(6)(a) or (b), the Registrar shall not send a copy of the document to an excluded person, but shall send a copy of the document to the respondent.]

NOTES

Para (1): numbered as such, words omitted from sub-para (d) revoked, words in square brackets in that paragraph inserted, and para (e) and the word immediately preceding it added, by the Employment Appeal Tribunal (Amendment) Rules 2001, SI 2001/1128, r 4(a)–(d); words in square brackets in sub-para (b) substituted by the Employment Rights (Dispute Resolution) Act 1998, s 1(2)(a), (b); words in first pair of square brackets in sub-para (e) inserted by the Employment Appeal Tribunal (Amendment) Rules 2004, SI 2004/2526, r 5; words in second pair of square brackets in sub-para (e) inserted by the Information and Consultation of Employees Regulations 2004, SI 2004/3426, reg 41(b); words in third pair of square brackets in sub-para (e) inserted by the Companies (Cross-Border Mergers) Regulations 2007, SI 2007/2974, reg 64(2) and revoked by the Companies, Limited Liability Partnerships and Partnerships (Amendment etc) (EU Exit) Regulations 2019, SI 2019/348, reg 8, Sch 3, paras 9, 12, as from exit day (as defined in the European Union (Withdrawal) Act 2018, s 20).

Paras (2), (3): added by SI 2001/1128, r 4(d).

[2.150]

5 Respondents to appeals

The respondents to an appeal shall be—

(a) in the case of an appeal from an [employment tribunal] or of an appeal made pursuant to [section 45D, 56A, 95, 104 or 108C] of the 1992 Act from a decision of the Certification Officer, the parties (other than the appellant) to the proceedings before the [employment tribunal] or the Certification Officer;

(b) in the case of an appeal made pursuant to [section 9 or 126] of the 1992 Act from a decision of the Certification Officer, that Officer;

[(c) in the case of an appeal made pursuant to regulation 38(8) of the 1999 Regulations [or regulation 47(6) of the 2004 Regulations] [or regulation 35(6) of the Information and Consultation Regulations] *[or regulation 57(6) of the 2007 Regulations]* from a declaration or order of the CAC, the parties (other than the appellant) to the proceedings before the CAC].

NOTES

Words in first and third pairs of square brackets substituted by the Employment Rights (Dispute Resolution) Act 1998, s 1(2)(a); words in second and fourth pairs of square brackets substituted, and para (c) added, by the Employment Appeal Tribunal (Amendment) Rules 2001, SI 2001/1128, r 5; words in first pair of square brackets in sub-para (c) inserted by the Employment Appeal Tribunal (Amendment) Rules 2004, SI 2004/2526, r 6; words in second pair of square brackets in sub-para (c) inserted by the Information and Consultation of Employees Regulations 2004, SI 2004/3426, reg 41(b); words in third pair of square brackets in sub-para (c) inserted by the Companies (Cross-Border Mergers) Regulations 2007, SI 2007/2974, reg 64(2) and revoked by the Companies, Limited Liability Partnerships and Partnerships (Amendment etc) (EU Exit) Regulations 2019, SI 2019/348, reg 8, Sch 3, paras 9, 13, as from exit day (as defined in the European Union (Withdrawal) Act 2018, s 20).

[2.151]

6 Respondent's answer and notice of cross-appeal

(1) The Registrar shall, as soon as practicable, notify every respondent of the date appointed by the Appeal Tribunal by which any answer under this rule must be delivered.

(2) A respondent who wishes to resist an appeal shall, [subject to paragraph (6), and] within the time appointed under paragraph (1) of this rule, deliver to the Appeal Tribunal an answer in writing in, or substantially in, accordance with Form 3 in the Schedule to these Rules, setting out the grounds on which he relies, so, however, that it shall be sufficient for a respondent to an appeal referred to in rule 5(a) [or 5(c)] who wishes to rely on any ground which is the same as a ground relied on by the [employment tribunal][, the Certification Officer or the CAC] for making the [judgment,] decision[, declaration] or order appealed from to state that fact in his answer.

(3) A respondent who wishes to cross-appeal may [subject to paragraph (6),] do so by including in his answer a statement of the grounds of his cross-appeal, and in that event an appellant who wishes to resist the cross-appeal shall, within a time to be appointed by the Appeal Tribunal, deliver to the Tribunal a reply in writing setting out the grounds on which he relies.

(4) The Registrar shall serve a copy of every answer and reply to a cross-appeal on every party other than the party by whom it was delivered.

(5) Where the respondent does not wish to resist an appeal, the parties may deliver to the Appeal Tribunal an agreed draft of an order allowing the appeal and the Tribunal may, if it thinks it right to do so, make an order allowing the appeal in the terms agreed.

[(6) In [an appeal from the employment tribunal in relation to national security proceedings], the respondent shall not set out the grounds on which he relies in his answer to an appeal, nor include in his answer a statement of the grounds of any cross-appeal.

(7) In [an appeal from the employment tribunal in relation to national security proceedings] in relation to which the respondent was not the [claimant] in the proceedings before the employment tribunal, the respondent shall, within the time appointed under paragraph (1), provide to the Registrar a document, setting out the grounds on which he intends to resist the appeal, and may include in that document a statement of the grounds of any cross-appeal.

(8) In [an appeal from the employment tribunal in relation to national security proceedings] in relation to which the respondent was the [claimant] in the proceedings before the employment tribunal—

(a) the respondent may, within the time appointed under paragraph (1) provide to the Registrar a document, setting out the grounds on which he intends to resist the appeal, and may include in that document a statement of the grounds of any cross-appeal; and

(b) a special advocate appointed in respect of the respondent may, within the time appointed under paragraph (1), or within 21 days of his appointment, whichever is the later, provide to the Registrar a document, setting out the grounds, or the supplementary grounds, on which the respondent intends to resist the appeal, and may include in that document a statement of the grounds, or the supplementary grounds, of any cross-appeal.

(9) In [an appeal from the employment tribunal in relation to national security proceedings], if the respondent, or any special advocate appointed in respect of a respondent, provides in the document containing grounds for resisting an appeal a statement of grounds of cross-appeal and the appellant wishes to resist the cross-appeal—

(a) where the appellant was not the [claimant] in the proceedings before the employment tribunal, the appellant shall within a time to be appointed by the Appeal Tribunal deliver to the Tribunal a reply in writing setting out the grounds on which he relies; and

(b) where the appellant was the [claimant] in the proceedings before the employment tribunal, the appellant, or any special advocate appointed in respect of him, may within a time to be appointed by the Appeal Tribunal deliver to the Tribunal a reply in writing setting out the grounds on which the appellant relies.

(10) Any document provided under paragraph (7) or (9)(a) shall be treated by the Registrar in accordance with rule 4(2), as though it were a document received under rule 3(5).

(11) Any document provided under paragraph (8) or (9)(b) shall be treated by the Registrar in accordance with rule 4(3), as though it were a document received under rule 3(6)(a) or (b).]

[(12) Where it appears to a judge or the Registrar that a statement of grounds of cross-appeal contained in [the] respondent's answer or document provided under paragraph (7) or (8)—

(a) discloses no reasonable grounds for bringing the cross-appeal; or

(b) is an abuse of the Appeal Tribunal's process or is otherwise likely to obstruct the just disposal of proceedings,

he shall notify the [respondent] or special advocate accordingly informing him of the reasons for his opinion and, subject to [paragraph (16)], no further action shall be taken on the statement of grounds of cross-appeal.

[(12A) Where a judge or the Registrar has taken a decision under paragraph (12), and also considers that the statement of grounds of cross-appeal contained in the respondent's answer or document provided under paragraph (7) or (8) is totally without merit, the judge or Registrar may order that the respondent is not entitled to have the matter heard before a judge under paragraph (16), with such order to be included as part of the notice issued under paragraph (12).]

(13) In paragraphs (12)[, (12A)] and (16) reference to a statement of grounds of cross-appeal includes reference to part of a statement of grounds of cross-appeal.

(14), (15) . . .

(16) [Subject to paragraph (12A), where] notification has been given under paragraph (12) and within 28 days of the date the notification was sent, a respondent or special advocate expresses dissatisfaction in writing with the reasons given by the judge or Registrar for his opinion, he is entitled to have the matter heard before a judge who shall make a direction as to whether any further action should be taken on the statement of grounds of cross-appeal.]

NOTES

Para (2): words in first, second and sixth pairs of square brackets inserted, and words in fourth pair of square brackets substituted, by the Employment Appeal Tribunal (Amendment) Rules 2001, SI 2001/1128, r 6(a), (b); words in third pair of square brackets substituted by the Employment Rights (Dispute Resolution) Act 1998, s 1(2)(a); word in fifth pair of square brackets inserted by the Employment Appeal Tribunal (Amendment) Rules 2004, SI 2004/2526, r 7(1)(a).

Para (3): words in square brackets substituted by SI 2001/1128, r 6(b).

Paras (6)–(11): added by SI 2001/1128, r 6(c); words in square brackets in paras (6)–(9) substituted by SI 2004/2526, r 7(1)(b), (c).

Paras (12), (13)–(16): added by SI 2004/2526, r 7(2); the words in square brackets in paras (12), (13), (16) were substituted or inserted, and paras (14), (15) were revoked, by the Employment Appeal Tribunal (Amendment) Rules 2013, SI 2013/1693, r 4(a), (c)–(e).

Para (12A): inserted by SI 2013/1693, r 4(b).

[2.152]

7 Disposal of appeal

(1) The Registrar shall, as soon as practicable, give notice of the arrangements made by the Appeal Tribunal for hearing the appeal to—

(a) every party to the proceedings; and

(b) the Secretary of [Employment Tribunals] in the case of an appeal from an [employment tribunal]; or

(c) the Certification Officer in the case of an appeal from one of his decisions; or

(d) the Secretary of State in the case of an appeal under [Part XI of the Employment Rights Act 1996] or Chapter II of Part IV of the 1992 Act to which he is not a respondent[; or

(e) the Chairman of the CAC in the case of an appeal from a declaration or order of, or arising in any proceedings before, the CAC under regulation 38(8) of the 1999 Regulations [or regulation 47(6) of the 2004 Regulations] [or regulation 35(6) of the Information and Consultation Regulations] *[or regulation 57(6) of the 2007 Regulations]*].

(2) Any such notice shall state the date appointed by the Appeal Tribunal by which any [interim] application must be made.

NOTES

Para (1): words in square brackets in sub-para (b) substituted by the Employment Rights (Dispute Resolution) Act 1998, s 1(2)(a), (b); words in square brackets in sub-para (d) substituted, and sub-para (e) and word immediately preceding it added, by the Employment Appeal Tribunal (Amendment) Rules 2001, SI 2001/1128, r 7; words in first pair of square brackets in sub-para (e) inserted by the Employment Appeal Tribunal (Amendment) Rules 2004, SI 2004/2526, r 8(1); words in second pair of square brackets in sub-para (e) inserted by the Information and Consultation of Employees Regulations 2004, SI 2004/3426, reg 41(b); words in third pair of square brackets in sub-para (e) inserted by the Companies (Cross-Border Mergers) Regulations 2007, SI 2007/2974, reg 64(2) and revoked by the Companies, Limited Liability Partnerships and Partnerships (Amendment etc) (EU Exit) Regulations 2019, SI 2019/348, reg 8, Sch 3, paras 9, 14, as from exit day (as defined in the European Union (Withdrawal) Act 2018, s 20).

Para (2): word in square brackets substituted by SI 2004/2526, r 8(2).

[2.153]

8 Application in respect of exclusion or expulsion from, or unjustifiable discipline by, a trade union

Every application under section 67 or 176 of the 1992 Act to the Appeal Tribunal for—

(a) an award of compensation for exclusion or expulsion from a trade union; or

(b) one or both of the following, that is to say—

(i) an award of compensation for unjustifiable discipline;

(ii) an order that the union pay to the applicant an amount equal to any sum which he has paid in pursuance of any such determination as is mentioned in section 64(2)(b) of the 1992 Act;

shall be made in writing in, or substantially in, accordance with Form 4 in the Schedule to these Rules and shall be served on the Appeal Tribunal together with a copy of the decision or order declaring that the applicant's complaint against the trade union was well-founded.

[2.154]

9

If on receipt of an application under rule 8(a) it becomes clear that at the time the application was made the applicant had been admitted or re-admitted to membership of the union against which the complaint was made, the Registrar shall forward the application to the Central Office of [Employment Tribunals].

NOTES

Words in square brackets substituted by the Employment Rights (Dispute Resolution) Act 1998, s 1(2)(b).

[2.155]

10 Service of application under rule 8

On receipt of an application under rule 8, the Registrar shall seal it with the Appeal Tribunal's seal and shall serve a sealed copy on the applicant and on the respondent trade union and the Secretary of [Employment Tribunals].

NOTES

Words in square brackets substituted by the Employment Rights (Dispute Resolution) Act 1998, s 1(2)(b).

[2.156]

11 Appearance by respondent trade union

(1) Subject to paragraph (2) of this rule, a respondent trade union wishing to resist an application under rule 8 shall within 14 days of receiving the sealed copy of the application enter an appearance in, or substantially in, accordance with Form 5 in the Schedule to these Rules and setting out the grounds on which the union relies.

(2) Paragraph (1) above shall not require a respondent trade union to enter an appearance where the application is before the Appeal Tribunal by virtue of having been transferred there by an [employment tribunal] and, prior to that transfer, the respondent had entered an appearance to the proceedings before the [employment tribunal].

NOTES

Para (2): words in square brackets substituted by the Employment Rights (Dispute Resolution) Act 1998, s 1(2)(a).

[2.157]
12

On receipt of the notice of appearance under rule 11 the Registrar shall serve a copy of it on the applicant.

[2.158]
13 Application for restriction of proceedings order

Every application to the Appeal Tribunal by the Attorney General or the Lord Advocate under [section 33 of the 1996 Act] for a restriction of proceedings order shall be made in writing in, or substantially in, accordance with Form 6 in the Schedule to these Rules, accompanied by an affidavit in support, and shall be served on the Tribunal.

NOTES

Words in square brackets substituted by the Employment Appeal Tribunal (Amendment) Rules 2001, SI 2001/1128, r 8.

[2.159]
14 Service of application under rule 13

On receipt of an application under rule 13, the Registrar shall seal it with the Appeal Tribunal's seal and shall serve a sealed copy on the Attorney General or the Lord Advocate, as the case may be, on the Secretary of [Employment Tribunals] and on the person named in the application.

NOTES

Words in square brackets substituted by the Employment Rights (Dispute Resolution) Act 1998, s 1(2)(b).

[2.160]
15 Appearance by person named in application under rule 13

A person named in an application under rule 13 who wishes to resist the application shall within 14 days of receiving the sealed copy of the application enter an appearance in, or substantially in, accordance with Form 7 in the Schedule to these Rules, accompanied by an affidavit in support.

[2.161]
16

On receipt of the notice of appearance under rule 15 the Registrar shall serve a copy of it on the Attorney General or the Lord Advocate, as the case may be.

16A *(This rule was originally inserted (together with rr 16B–16D) by the Employment Appeal Tribunal (Amendment) Rules 2001, SI 2001/1128, r 9; it was revoked by the Transnational Information and Consultation of Employees (Amendment) Regulations 2010, SI 2010/1088, reg 30(1), (2).)*

[2.162]
[16AA Applications under regulation 33(6) of the 2004 Regulations

Every application under regulation 33(6) of the 2004 Regulations [or regulation 22(6) of the Information and Consultation Regulations] *[or regulation 53(6) of the 2007 Regulations]* [or regulation 20(7), 21(6) or 21A(5) of the 1999 Regulations] shall be made by way of application in writing in, or substantially in, accordance with Form 4B in the Schedule to these Rules and shall be served on the Appeal Tribunal together with a copy of the declaration referred to in regulation 33(4) of [the 2004 Regulations or regulation 22(4) of the Information and Consultation Regulations] *[or regulation 53(4) of the 2007 Regulations]* [or the decision referred to in regulation 20(4), 21(4) or 21A(3) of the 1999 Regulations], or an explanation as to why none is included.]

NOTES

Inserted by the Employment Appeal Tribunal (Amendment) Rules 2004, SI 2004/2526, r 9.

Words in first pair of square brackets inserted, and words in fourth pair of square brackets substituted, by the Information and Consultation of Employees Regulations 2004, SI 2004/3426, reg 41(c); words in second and fifth pairs of square brackets inserted by the Companies (Cross-Border Mergers) Regulations 2007, SI 2007/2974, reg 64(3) and revoked by the Companies, Limited Liability Partnerships and Partnerships (Amendment etc) (EU Exit) Regulations 2019, SI 2019/348, reg 8, Sch 3, paras 9, 15, as from exit day (as defined in the European Union (Withdrawal) Act 2018, s 20); words in third and sixth pairs of square brackets inserted by the Transnational Information and Consultation of Employees (Amendment) Regulations 2010, SI 2010/1088, reg 30(1), (3).

[2.163]
[16B Service of application under rule 16AA

On receipt of an application under rule 16AA, the Registrar shall seal it with the Appeal Tribunal's seal and shall serve a sealed copy on the applicant and on the respondent.]

NOTES

Inserted (together with rr 16A (now revoked) and rr 16C, 16D) by the Employment Appeal Tribunal (Amendment) Rules 2001, SI 2001/1128, r 9

Substituted by the Transnational Information and Consultation of Employees (Amendment) Regulations 2010, SI 2010/1088, reg 30(1), (4).

[2.164]
[16C Appearance by respondent

A respondent wishing to resist an application under rule . . . [16AA] shall within 14 days of receiving the sealed copy of the application enter an appearance in, or substantially in, accordance with Form 5A in the Schedule to these Rules and setting out the grounds on which the respondent relies.]

NOTES

Inserted as noted to r 16B at **[2.163]**.

Words omitted revoked by the Transnational Information and Consultation of Employees (Amendment) Regulations 2010, SI 2010/1088, reg 30(1), (5); figure in square brackets inserted by the Employment Appeal Tribunal (Amendment) Rules 2004, SI 2004/2526, r 10.

[2.165]
[16D

On receipt of the notice of appearance under rule 16C the Registrar shall serve a copy of it on the applicant.]

NOTES

Inserted as noted to r 16B at **[2.163]**.

[2.166]
17 Disposal of application

(1) The Registrar shall, as soon as practicable, give notice to the parties to an application under rule 8[, 13[, . . . or 16AA]] of the arrangements made by the Appeal Tribunal for hearing the application.

(2) Any such notice shall state the date appointed by the Appeal Tribunal by which any [interim] application must be made.

NOTES

Para (1): words in first (outer) pair of square brackets substituted by the Employment Appeal Tribunal (Amendment) Rules 2001, SI 2001/1128, r 10; words in second (inner) pair of square brackets substituted by the Employment Appeal Tribunal (Amendment) Rules 2004, SI 2004/2526, r 11; figure omitted revoked by the Transnational Information and Consultation of Employees (Amendment) Regulations 2010, SI 2010/1088, reg 30(1), (6).

Para (2): word in square brackets substituted by SI 2004/2526, r 12.

[2.167]
[17A Non-payment of fee

(1) The Registrar must strike out an appeal, and must notify each party that the appeal has been struck out, where—

(a) upon receipt of a notice of appeal, or following a direction by the Appeal Tribunal that a matter proceed to an oral hearing, the Lord Chancellor has issued a notice to an appellant specifying that a fee is payable; and

(b) the appellant has not paid the fee or presented a remission application on or before the date specified in that notice.

(2) Where an appeal has been struck out under paragraph (1), the appeal may be reinstated by the Registrar if—

(a) the appellant applies to have the appeal reinstated; and

(b) the fee specified in the Lord Chancellor's notice has been paid or a remission application has been presented and accepted.

(3) The Registrar must strike out an appeal, and must notify each party that the appeal has been struck out, where—

(a) after consideration of a remission application the Lord Chancellor has issued a notice to an appellant specifying that a fee is payable; and

(b) the appellant has not paid the fee on or before the date specified in that notice.

(4) Where an appeal has been struck out under paragraph (3) the appeal may be reinstated by the Registrar if—

(a) the appellant applies to have the appeal reinstated; and

(b) the fee specified in the Lord Chancellor's notice has been paid.

(5) An application for reinstatement under paragraph (2) or (4) is deemed to be an interim application for the purposes of rule 20.]

NOTES

Inserted by the Employment Appeal Tribunal (Amendment) Rules 2013, SI 2013/1693, r 5.

This rule has not been revoked, as of 15 May 2019, despite the judgment of the Supreme Court in *R (UNISON) v Lord Chancellor* [2017] UKSC 51, [2017] ICR 1037 quashing the Employment Tribunals and the Employment Appeal Tribunal Fees Order 2013, SI 2013/1893, which imposed obligations to pay fees on those appealing to the Employment Appeal Tribunal.

[2.168]
18 Joinder of parties

The Appeal Tribunal may, on the application of any person or of its own motion, direct that any person not already a party to the proceedings be added as a party, or that any party to proceedings shall cease to be a party, and in either case may give such consequential directions as it considers necessary.

[2.169]
19 [Interim] applications

(1) An [interim] application may be made to the Appeal Tribunal by giving notice in writing specifying the direction or order sought.

(2) On receipt of a notice under paragraph (1) of this rule, the Registrar shall serve a copy on every other party to the proceedings who appears to him to be concerned in the matter to which the notice relates and shall notify the applicant and every such party of the arrangements made by the Appeal Tribunal for disposing of the application.

NOTES

Words in square brackets substituted by the Employment Appeal Tribunal (Amendment) Rules 2004, SI 2004/2526, r 12.

[2.170]
[20 Disposal of interim applications

(1) Every interim application made to the Appeal Tribunal shall be considered in the first place by the Registrar who shall have regard to rule 2A (the overriding objective) and, where applicable, to rule 23(5).

(2) Subject to sub-paragraphs (3) and (4), every interim application shall be disposed of by the Registrar except that any matter which he thinks should properly be decided by the President or a judge shall be referred by him to the President or judge who may dispose of it himself or refer it in whole or part to the Appeal Tribunal as required to be constituted by section 28 of the 1996 Act or refer it back to the Registrar with such directions as he thinks fit.

(3) Every interim application for a restricted reporting order shall be disposed of by the President or a judge or, if he so directs, the application shall be referred to the Appeal Tribunal as required to be constituted by section 28 of the 1996 Act who shall dispose of it.

(4) Every interim application for permission to institute or continue or to make a claim or application in any proceedings before an employment tribunal or the Appeal Tribunal, pursuant to section 33(4) of the 1996 Act, shall be disposed of by the President or a judge, or, if he so directs, the application shall be referred to the Appeal Tribunal as required to be constituted by section 28 of the 1996 Act who shall dispose of it.]

NOTES

Substituted by the Employment Appeal Tribunal (Amendment) Rules 2004, SI 2004/2526, r 13.

[2.171]
21 Appeals from Registrar

(1) Where an application is disposed of by the Registrar in pursuance of rule 20(2) any party aggrieved by his decision may appeal to a judge and in that case . . . the judge may determine the appeal himself or refer it in whole or in part to the Appeal Tribunal as required to be constituted by [section 28 of the 1996 Act].

(2) Notice of appeal under paragraph (1) of this rule may be given to the Appeal Tribunal, either orally or in writing, within five days of the decision appealed from and the Registrar shall notify every other party who appears to him to be concerned in the appeal and shall inform every such party and the appellant of the arrangements made by the Tribunal for disposing of the appeal.

NOTES

Para (1): words omitted revoked, and words in square brackets substituted, by the Employment Appeal Tribunal (Amendment) Rules 2001, SI 2001/1128, r 12.

[2.172]
22 Hearing of interlocutory applications

(1) The Appeal Tribunal may, subject to [any direction of a Minister of the Crown under rule 30A(1) or order of the Appeal Tribunal under rule 30A(2)(a) read with rule 30A(1),] and, where applicable, to rule 23(6), sit either in private or in public for the hearing of any [interim] application.

(2) . . .

NOTES

Para (1): words in first pair of square brackets substituted by the Employment Appeal Tribunal (Amendment) Rules 2001, SI 2001/1128, r 13(a); word in second pair of square brackets substituted by the Employment Appeal Tribunal (Amendment) Rules 2004, SI 2004/2526, r 14.

Para (2): revoked by SI 2001/1128, r 13(b).

[2.173]
23 Cases involving allegations of sexual misconduct or the commission of sexual offences

(1) This rule applies to any proceedings to which [section 31 of the 1996 Act] applies.

(2) In any such proceedings where the appeal appears to involve allegations of the commission of a sexual offence, the Registrar shall omit from any register kept by the Appeal Tribunal, which is available to the public, or delete from any order, judgment or other document, which is available to the public, any identifying matter which is likely to lead members of the public to identify any person affected by or making such an allegation.

(3) In any proceedings to which this rule applies where the appeal involves allegations of sexual misconduct the Appeal Tribunal may at any time before promulgation of its decision either on the application of a party or of its own motion make a restricted reporting order having effect, if not revoked earlier by the Appeal Tribunal, until the promulgation of its decision.

(4) A restricted reporting order shall specify the persons who may not be identified.

[(5) Subject to paragraph (5A) the Appeal Tribunal shall not make a full restricted reporting order unless it has given each party to the proceedings an opportunity to advance oral argument at a hearing, if they so wish.]

[(5A) The Appeal Tribunal may make a temporary restricted reporting order without a hearing.

(5B) Where a temporary restricted reporting order has been made the Registrar shall inform the parties to the proceedings in writing as soon as possible of:

(a) the fact that the order has been made; and

(b) their right to apply to have the temporary restricted reporting order revoked or converted into a full restricted reporting order within 14 days of the temporary order being made.

(5C) If no such application is made under subparagraph (5B)(b) within the 14 days, the temporary restricted reporting order shall lapse and cease to have any effect on the fifteenth day after it was made. When such an application is made the temporary restricted reporting order shall continue to have effect until the Hearing at which the application is considered.]

(6) Any . . . hearing shall, subject to [any direction of a Minister of the Crown under rule 30A(1) or order of the Appeal Tribunal under rule 30A(2)(a) read with rule 30A(1),] or unless the Appeal Tribunal decides for any of the reasons mentioned in rule 29(2) to sit in private to hear evidence, be held in public.

(7) The Appeal Tribunal may revoke a restricted reporting order at any time where it thinks fit.

(8) Where the Appeal Tribunal makes a restricted reporting order, the Registrar shall ensure that a notice of that fact is displayed on the notice board of the Appeal Tribunal at the office in which the proceedings in question are being dealt with, on the door of the room in which those proceedings are taking place and with any list of the proceedings taking place before the Appeal Tribunal.

(9) In this rule, "promulgation of its decision" means the date recorded as being the date on which the Appeal Tribunal's order finally disposing of the appeal is sent to the parties.

NOTES

Para (1): words in square brackets substituted by the Employment Appeal Tribunal (Amendment) Rules 2001, SI 2001/1128, r 14(a).

Para (5): substituted by the Employment Appeal Tribunal (Amendment) Rules 2004, SI 2004/2526, r 15(1).

Paras (5A)–(5C): inserted by SI 2004/2526, r 15(2).

Para (6): word omitted revoked by SI 2004/2526, r 15(3); words in square brackets substituted by SI 2001/1128, r 14(b).

[2.174]

[23A Restricted reporting orders in disability cases

(1) This rule applies to proceedings to which section 32(1) of [the [1996 Act]] applies.

(2) In proceedings to which this rule applies the Appeal Tribunal may, on the application of the complainant or of its own motion, make a restricted reporting order having effect, if not revoked earlier by the Appeal Tribunal, until the promulgation of its decision.

(3) Where the Appeal Tribunal makes a restricted reporting order under paragraph (2) of this rule in relation to an appeal which is being dealt with by the Appeal Tribunal together with any other proceedings, the Appeal Tribunal may direct that the order is to apply also in relation to those other proceedings or such part of them as it may direct.

(4) Paragraphs (5) to (9) of rule 23 apply in relation to the making of a restricted reporting order under this rule as they apply in relation to the making of a restricted reporting order under that rule.]

NOTES

Inserted by the Employment Appeal Tribunal (Amendment) Rules 1996, SI 1996/3216, r 2.

Para (1): word in first (outer) pair of square brackets substituted by the Employment Rights (Dispute Resolution) Act 1998, s 1(2)(c); words in second (inner) pair of square brackets substituted by the Employment Appeal Tribunal (Amendment) Rules 2001, SI 2001/1128, r 15.

[2.175]

24 Appointment for direction

(1) Where it appears to the Appeal Tribunal that the future conduct of any proceedings would thereby be facilitated, the Tribunal may (either of its own motion or on application) at any stage in the proceedings appoint a date for a meeting for directions as to their future conduct and thereupon the following provisions of this rule shall apply.

(2) The Registrar shall give to every party in the proceedings notice of the date appointed under paragraph (1) of this rule and any party applying for directions shall, if practicable, before that date give to the Appeal Tribunal particulars of any direction for which he asks.

(3) The Registrar shall take such steps as may be practicable to inform every party of any directions applied for by any other party.

(4) On the date appointed under paragraph (1) of this rule, the Appeal Tribunal shall consider every application for directions made by any party and any written representations relating to the application submitted to the Tribunal and shall give such directions as it thinks fit for the purpose of securing the just, expeditious and economical disposal of the proceedings, including, where appropriate, directions in pursuance of rule 36, for the purpose of ensuring that the parties are enabled to avail themselves of opportunities for conciliation.

(5) Without prejudice to the generality of paragraph (4) of this rule, the Appeal Tribunal may give such directions as it thinks fit as to—

(a) the amendment of any notice, answer or other document;
(b) the admission of any facts or documents;
(c) the admission in evidence of any documents;
(d) the mode in which evidence is to be given at the hearing;
(e) the consolidation of the proceedings with any other proceedings pending before the Tribunal;
(f) the place and date of the hearing.

(6) An application for further directions or for the variation of any directions already given may be made in accordance with rule 19.

[2.176]
25 Appeal Tribunal's power to give directions

The Appeal Tribunal may either of its own motion or on application, at any stage of the proceedings, give any party directions as to any steps to be taken by him in relation to the proceedings.

[2.177]
26 Default by parties

[(1)] If a respondent to any proceedings fails to deliver an answer or, in the case of an application made under section 67 or 176 of the 1992 Act[, section 33 of the 1996 Act[,] [regulation 20, 21 or 21A of the 1999 Regulations]], [. . . regulation 33 of the 2004 Regulations] [or] [. . . regulation 22 of the Information and Consultation Regulations] *[or regulation 53 the 2007 Regulations]*, a notice of appearance within the time appointed under these Rules, or if any party fails to comply with an order or direction of the Appeal Tribunal, the Tribunal may order that he be debarred from taking any further part in the proceedings, or may make such other order as it thinks just.

[(2) An order made by the Appeal Tribunal under paragraph (1) may include, but is not limited to, an order that all or part of an appeal or answer is to be struck out.

(3) An appeal or answer, or part of an appeal or answer, may not be struck out unless the party in question has been given a reasonable opportunity to make representations, either in writing, or if requested by the party, at a hearing.]

NOTES

Para (1) numbered as such, and paras (2), (3) added, by the Employment Appeal Tribunal (Amendment) Rules 2013, SI 2013/1693, r 6.

The text that now forms para (1) was previously amended as follows:

Words in first (outer) pair of square brackets substituted by the Employment Appeal Tribunal (Amendment) Rules 2001, SI 2001/1128, r 16.

The comma in second (inner) pair of square brackets was substituted (for the original word "or") by the Employment Appeal Tribunal (Amendment) Rules 2004, SI 2004/2526, r 17(1).

Words in third (inner) pair of square brackets substituted by the Transnational Information and Consultation of Employees (Amendment) Regulations 2010, SI 2010/1088, reg 30(1), (7).

Words in fourth pair of square brackets inserted by SI 2004/2526, r 17(2), and the words omitted therefrom were revoked by the Information and Consultation of Employees Regulations 2004, SI 2004/3426, reg 41(d)(i).

Word in fifth pair of square brackets inserted by the Companies, Limited Liability Partnerships and Partnerships (Amendment etc) (EU Exit) Regulations 2019, SI 2019/348, reg 8, Sch 3, paras 9, 16, as from exit day (as defined in the European Union (Withdrawal) Act 2018, s 20).

Words in penultimate pair of square brackets inserted by SI 2004/3426, reg 41(d)(ii), and the words omitted therefrom were revoked by the Companies (Cross-Border Mergers) Regulations 2007, SI 2007/2974, reg 64(4).

Words in final pair of square brackets inserted by SI 2007/2974, reg 64(4) and revoked by SI 2019/348, reg 8, Sch 3, paras 9, 16, as from exit day (as defined in the European Union (Withdrawal) Act 2018, s 20).

[2.178]
27 Attendance of witnesses and production of documents

(1) The Appeal Tribunal may, on the application of any party, order any person to attend before the Tribunal as a witness or to produce any document.

[(1A) Where—

(a) a Minister has at any stage issued a direction under rule 30A(1)(b) or (c) (exclusion of a party or his representative), or the Appeal Tribunal has at any stage made an order under rule 30A(2)(a) read with rule 30A(1)(b) or (c); and
(b) the Appeal Tribunal is considering whether to impose, or has imposed, a requirement under paragraph (1) on any person,

the Minister (whether or not he is a party to the proceedings) may make an application to the Appeal Tribunal objecting to the imposition of a requirement under paragraph (1) or, where a requirement has been imposed, an application to vary or set aside the requirement, as the case may be. The Appeal Tribunal shall hear and determine the Minister's application in private and the Minister shall be entitled to address the Appeal Tribunal thereon. The application shall be made by notice to the Registrar and the

Registrar shall give notice of the application to each party.]

(2) No person to whom an order is directed under paragraph (1) of this rule shall be treated as having failed to obey that order unless at the time at which the order was served on him there was tendered to him a sufficient sum of money to cover his costs of attending before the Appeal Tribunal.

NOTES

Para (1A): inserted by the Employment Appeal Tribunal (Amendment) Rules 2001, SI 2001/1128, r 17.

[2.179]

28 Oaths

The Appeal Tribunal may, either of its own motion or on application, require any evidence to be given on oath.

[2.180]

29 Oral hearings

(1) Subject to paragraph (2) of this rule and to [any direction of a Minister of the Crown under rule 30A(1)(a) or order of the Appeal Tribunal under rule 30A(2)(a) read with rule 30A(1)(a),] an oral hearing at which any proceedings before the Appeal Tribunal are finally disposed of shall take place in public before, where applicable, such members of the Tribunal as (subject to [section 28 of the 1996 Act]) the President may nominate for the purpose.

[(2) Notwithstanding paragraph (1), the Appeal Tribunal may sit in private for the purpose of hearing evidence from any person which in the opinion of the Tribunal is likely to consist of—

(a) information which he could not disclose without contravening a prohibition imposed by or by virtue of any enactment;

(b) information which has been communicated to him in confidence or which he has otherwise obtained in consequence of the confidence reposed in him by another person; or

(c) information the disclosure of which would, for reasons other than its effect on negotiations with respect to any of the matters mentioned in section 178(2) of the 1992 Act, cause substantial injury to any undertaking of his or in which he works.]

NOTES

Para (1): words in square brackets substituted by the Employment Appeal Tribunal (Amendment) Rules 2001, SI 2001/1128, r 18(a).

Para (2): substituted by SI 2001/1128, r 18(b).

[2.181]

[30 Duty of Appeal Tribunal concerning disclosure of information

When exercising its functions, the Appeal Tribunal shall ensure that information is not disclosed contrary to the interests of national security.]

NOTES

Substituted, together with r 30A, for the original r 30, by the Employment Appeal Tribunal (Amendment) Rules 2001, SI 2001/1128, r 19.

[2.182]

[30A Proceedings in cases concerning national security

(1) A Minister of the Crown (whether or not he is a party to the proceedings) may, if he considers it expedient in the interests of national security, direct the Appeal Tribunal by notice to the Registrar to—

(a) sit in private for all or part of particular Crown employment proceedings;

(b) exclude any party who was the [claimant] in the proceedings before the employment tribunal from all or part of particular Crown employment proceedings;

(c) exclude the representatives of any party who was the [claimant] in the proceedings before the employment tribunal from all or part of particular Crown employment proceedings;

(d) take steps to conceal the identity of a particular witness in particular Crown employment proceedings.

(2) The Appeal Tribunal may, if it considers it expedient in the interests of national security, by order—

(a) do [in relation to particular proceedings before it] anything of a kind which the Appeal Tribunal can be required to do [in relation to particular Crown employment proceedings] by direction under paragraph (1) of this rule;

(b) direct any person to whom any document (including any decision or record of the proceedings) has been provided for the purposes of the proceedings not to disclose any such document or the content thereof—

(i) to any excluded person;

(ii) in any case in which a direction has been given under paragraph (1)(a) or an order has been made under paragraph (2)(a) read with paragraph (1)(a), to any person excluded from all or part of the proceedings by virtue of such direction or order; or

(iii) in any case in which a Minister of the Crown has informed the Registrar in accordance with paragraph (3) that he wishes to address the Appeal Tribunal with a view to the Tribunal making an order under paragraph (2)(a) read with paragraph (1)(b) or (c), to any person who may be excluded from all or part of the proceedings by virtue of such an order, if an order is made, at any time before the Appeal Tribunal decides whether or not to make such an order;

Part 2 Statutory Instruments

(c) take steps to keep secret all or part of the reasons for any order it makes.

The Appeal Tribunal shall keep under review any order it makes under this paragraph.

(3) In any proceedings in which a Minister of the Crown considers that it would be appropriate for the Appeal Tribunal to make an order as referred to in paragraph (2), he shall (whether or not he is a party to the proceedings) be entitled to appear before and to address the Appeal Tribunal thereon. The Minister shall inform the Registrar by notice that he wishes to address the Appeal Tribunal and the Registrar shall copy the notice to the parties.

(4) In any proceedings in which there is an excluded person, the Appeal Tribunal shall inform the Attorney General or, in the case of an appeal from an employment tribunal in Scotland, the Advocate General for Scotland, of the proceedings before it with a view to the Attorney General (or, as the case may be, the Advocate General), if he thinks it fit to do so, appointing a special advocate to represent the interests of the person who was the [claimant] in the proceedings before the employment tribunal in respect of those parts of the proceedings from which—

(a) any representative of his is excluded;

(b) both he and his representative are excluded; or

(c) he is excluded, where he does not have a representative.

(5) A special advocate shall have a general qualification within the meaning of section 71 of the Courts and Legal Services Act 1990, or, in the case of an appeal from an employment tribunal in Scotland, shall be—

(a) an advocate; or

(b) a solicitor who has by virtue of section 25A of the Solicitors (Scotland) Act 1980 rights of audience in the Court of Session or the High Court of Justiciary.

(6) Where the excluded person is a party to the proceedings, he shall be permitted to make a statement to the Appeal Tribunal before the commencement of the proceedings, or the part of the proceedings, from which he is excluded.

(7) Except in accordance with paragraphs (8) to (10), the special advocate may not communicate directly or indirectly with any person (including an excluded person)—

(a) (except in the case of the Appeal Tribunal or the party who was the respondent in the proceedings before the employment tribunal) on any matter contained in the documents referred to in rule 3(5), 3(6), 6(7) or 6(8)(b); or

(b) (except in the case of a person who was present) on any matter discussed or referred to during any part of the proceedings in which the Appeal Tribunal sat in private pursuant to a direction of the Minister under paragraph (1)(a) or an order of the Appeal Tribunal under paragraph (2)(a) read with paragraph (1)(a).

(8) The special advocate may apply for directions from the Appeal Tribunal authorising him to seek instructions from, or otherwise to communicate with, an excluded person—

(a) on any matter contained in the documents referred to in rule 3(5), 3(6), 6(7) or 6(8)(b); or

(b) on any matter discussed or referred to during any part of the proceedings in which the Appeal Tribunal sat in private as referred to in paragraph (7)(b).

(9) An application under paragraph (8) shall be made by presenting to the Registrar a notice of application, which shall state the title of the proceedings and set out the grounds of the application.

(10) The Registrar shall notify the Minister of an application for directions under paragraph (8) and the Minister shall be entitled to address the Appeal Tribunal on the application.

(11) In these rules, in any case in which a special advocate has been appointed in respect of a party, any reference to a party shall (save in those references specified in paragraph (12)) include the special advocate.

(12) The references mentioned in paragraph (11) are those in rules 5 and 18, the first and second references in rule 27(1A), paragraphs (1) and (6) of this rule, the first reference in paragraph (3) of this rule, rule 34(1), the reference in item 4 of Form 1, and in item 4 of Form 1A, in the Schedule to these Rules.]

NOTES

Substituted as noted to r 30 at **[2.181]**.

Paras (1), (4): words in square brackets substituted by the Employment Appeal Tribunal (Amendment) Rules 2004, SI 2004/2526, r 16.

Para (2): words in square brackets in sub-para (a) inserted by the Employment Appeal Tribunal (Amendment) Rules 2005, SI 2005/1871, r 2.

[2.183]

31 Drawing up, reasons for, and enforcement of orders

(1) Every order of the Appeal Tribunal shall be drawn up by the Registrar and a copy, sealed with the seal of the Tribunal, shall be served by the Registrar on every party to the proceedings to which it relates and—

(a) in the case of an order disposing of an appeal from an [employment tribunal] or of an order under [section 33 of the 1996 Act] on the Secretary of the [Employment Tribunals]; . . .

(b) in the case of an order disposing of an appeal from the Certification Officer, on that Officer.

[(c) in the case of an order imposing a penalty notice [regulation 20, 21 or 21A of the 1999 Regulations], [. . . regulation 33 of the 2004 Regulations] [or] [regulation 22 of the Information and Consultation Regulations] *[. . . regulation 53 the 2007 Regulations]*, on the Secretary of State; or

(d) in the case of an order disposing of an appeal from the CAC made under regulation 38(8) of the 1999 Regulations, on the Chairman of the CAC.]

(2) [Subject to rule 31A,] the Appeal Tribunal shall, on the application of any party made within 14 days after the making of an order finally disposing of any proceedings, give its reasons in writing for the order unless it was made after the delivery of a reasoned judgment.

(3) Subject to any order made by the Court of Appeal or Court of Session and to any directions given by the Appeal Tribunal, an appeal from the Tribunal shall not suspend the enforcement of any order made by it.

NOTES

Para (1) is amended as follows:

Words in first and third pairs of square brackets in sub-para (a) substituted by the Employment Rights (Dispute Resolution) Act 1998, s 1(2)(a), (b).

Words in second pair of square brackets in sub-para (a) substituted, word omitted from the end of that paragraph revoked, and sub-paras (c), (d) added, by the Employment Appeal Tribunal (Amendment) Rules 2001, SI 2001/1128, r 20(a)–(c).

Words in first pair of square brackets in sub-para (c) substituted by the Transnational Information and Consultation of Employees (Amendment) Regulations 2010, SI 2010/1088, reg 30(1), (8).

Words in second pair of square brackets in sub-para (c) inserted by the Employment Appeal Tribunal (Amendment) Rules 2004, SI 2004/2526, r 18.

Word in third pair of square brackets inserted by the Companies, Limited Liability Partnerships and Partnerships (Amendment etc) (EU Exit) Regulations 2019, SI 2019/348, reg 8, Sch 3, paras 9, 17, as from exit day (as defined in the European Union (Withdrawal) Act 2018, s 20).

First word omitted from sub-para (c) revoked, and words in fourth pair of square brackets in that paragraph inserted, by the Information and Consultation of Employees Regulations 2004, SI 2004/3426, reg 41(d)(ii).

Second word omitted from sub-para (c) revoked, and words in final pair of square brackets in that paragraph inserted, by the Companies (Cross-Border Mergers) Regulations 2007, SI 2007/2974, reg 64(4) and revoked by SI 2019/348, reg 8, Sch 3, paras 9, 17, as from exit day (as defined in the European Union (Withdrawal) Act 2018, s 20).

Para (2): words in square brackets inserted by SI 2001/1128, r 20(d).

[2.184]

[31A Reasons for orders in cases concerning national security

(1) Paragraphs (1) to (5) of this rule apply to the document setting out the reasons for the Appeal Tribunal's order prepared under rule 31(2) or any reasoned judgment of the Appeal Tribunal as referred to in rule 31(2), in any particular Crown employment proceedings in which a direction of a Minister of the Crown has been given under rule 30A(1)(a), (b) or (c) or an order of the Appeal Tribunal has been made under rule 30A(2)(a) read with rule 30A(1)(a), (b) or (c).

(2) Before the Appeal Tribunal gives its reasons in writing for any order or delivers any reasoned judgment, the Registrar shall send a copy of the reasons or judgment to the Minister.

(3) If the Minister considers it expedient in the interests of national security, he may—

(a) direct the Appeal Tribunal that the document containing its reasons for any order or its reasoned judgment shall not be disclosed to any person who was excluded from all or part of the proceedings and to prepare a further document setting out the reasons for its order, or a further reasoned judgment, but with the omission of such reasons as are specified in the direction; or

(b) direct the Appeal Tribunal that the document containing its reasons for any order or its reasoned judgment shall not be disclosed to any person who was excluded from all or part of the proceedings, but that no further document setting out the Appeal Tribunal's reasons for its order or further reasoned judgment should be prepared.

(4) Where the Minister has directed the Appeal Tribunal in accordance with paragraph (3)(a), the document prepared pursuant to that direction shall be marked in each place where an omission has been made. The document may then be given by the Registrar to the parties.

(5) The Registrar shall send the document prepared pursuant to a direction of the Minister in accordance with paragraph (3)(a) and the full document without the omissions made pursuant to that direction—

(a) to whichever of the appellant and the respondent was not the [claimant] in the proceedings before the employment tribunal;

(b) if he was not an excluded person, to the person who was the [claimant] in the proceedings before the employment tribunal and, if he was not an excluded person, to his representative;

(c) if applicable, to the special advocate; and

(d) where there are proceedings before a superior court relating to the order in question, to that court.

(6) Where the Appeal Tribunal intends to take steps under rule 30A(2)(c) to keep secret all or part of the reasons for any order it makes, it shall send the full reasons for its order to the persons listed in sub-paragraphs (a) to (d) of paragraph (5), as appropriate.]

NOTES

Inserted by the Employment Appeal Tribunal (Amendment) Rules 2001, SI 2001/1128, r 21.

Para (5): words in square brackets in sub-paras (a), (b) substituted by the Employment Appeal Tribunal (Amendment) Rules 2004, SI 2004/2526, r 16.

[2.185]

32 Registration and proof of awards in respect of exclusion or expulsion from, or unjustifiable discipline by, a trade union

(1) This rule applies where an application has been made to the Appeal Tribunal under section 67 or 176 of the 1992 Act.

(2) Without prejudice to rule 31, where the Appeal Tribunal makes an order in respect of an application to which this rule applies, and that order—

(a) makes an award of compensation, or

(b) is or includes an order of the kind referred to in rule 8(b)(ii),

or both, the Registrar shall as soon as may be enter a copy of the order, sealed with the seal of the Tribunal, into a register kept by the Tribunal (in this rule referred to as "the Register").

(3) The production in any proceedings in any court of a document, purporting to be certified by the Registrar to be a true copy of an entry in the Register of an order to which this rule applies shall, unless the contrary is proved, be sufficient evidence of the document and of the facts stated therein.

[2.186]

33 Review of decisions and correction of errors

(1) The Appeal Tribunal may, either of its own motion or on application, review any order made by it and may, on such review, revoke or vary that order on the grounds that—

(a) the order was wrongly made as the result of an error on the part of the Tribunal or its staff;

(b) a party did not receive proper notice of the proceedings leading to the order; or

(c) the interests of justice require such review.

(2) An application under paragraph (1) above shall be made within 14 days of the date of the order.

(3) A clerical mistake in any order arising from an accidental slip or omission may at any time be corrected by, or on the authority of, a judge or member.

[(4) The decision to grant or refuse an application for review may be made by a judge.]

NOTES

Para (4): added by the Employment Appeal Tribunal (Amendment) Rules 2004, SI 2004/2526, r 19.

[2.187]

[34 General power to make costs or expenses orders

(1) In the circumstances listed in rule 34A the Appeal Tribunal may make an order ("a costs order") that a party or a special advocate, ("the paying party") make a payment in respect of the costs incurred by another party or a special advocate ("the receiving party").

(2) For the purposes of these Rules "costs" includes fees, charges, disbursements and expenses incurred by or on behalf of a party or special advocate in relation to the proceedings, including the reimbursement allowed to a litigant in person under rule 34D. In Scotland, all references to costs or costs orders (except in the expression "wasted costs") shall be read as references to expenses or orders for expenses.

(3) A costs order may be made against or in favour of a respondent who has not had an answer accepted in the proceedings in relation to the conduct of any part which he has taken in the proceedings.

(4) A party or special advocate may apply to the Appeal Tribunal for a costs order to be made at any time during the proceedings. An application may also be made at the end of a hearing, or in writing to the Registrar within 14 days of the date on which the order of the Appeal Tribunal finally disposing of the proceedings was sent to the parties.

(5) No costs order shall be made unless the Registrar has sent notice to the party or special advocate against whom the order may be made giving him the opportunity to give reasons why the order should not be made. This paragraph shall not be taken to require the Registrar to send notice to the party or special advocate if the party or special advocate has been given an opportunity to give reasons orally to the Appeal Tribunal as to why the order should not be made.

(6) Where the Appeal Tribunal makes a costs order it shall provide written reasons for doing so if a request for written reasons is made within 21 days of the date of the costs order. The Registrar shall send a copy of the written reasons to all the parties to the proceedings.]

NOTES

Substituted by the Employment Appeal Tribunal (Amendment) Rules 2004, SI 2004/2526, r 20.

[2.188]

[34A When a costs or expenses order may be made

(1) Where it appears to the Appeal Tribunal that any proceedings brought by the paying party were unnecessary, improper, vexatious or misconceived or that there has been unreasonable delay or other unreasonable conduct in the bringing or conducting of proceedings by the paying party, the Appeal Tribunal may make a costs order against the paying party.

(2) The Appeal Tribunal may in particular make a costs order against the paying party when—

(a) he has not complied with a direction of the Appeal Tribunal;

(b) he has amended its notice of appeal, document provided under rule 3 sub- paragraphs (5) or (6), Respondent's answer or statement of grounds of cross-appeal, or document provided under rule 6 sub-paragraphs (7) or (8); or

(c) he has caused an adjournment of proceedings.

[(2A) If the Appeal Tribunal allows an appeal, in full or in part, it may make a costs order against the respondent specifying the respondent pay to the appellant an amount no greater than any fee paid by the appellant under a notice issued by the Lord Chancellor.]

(3) Nothing in paragraph (2) [or (2A)] shall restrict the Appeal Tribunal's discretion to award costs under paragraph (1).]

NOTES

Inserted, together with rr 34B–34D, by the Employment Appeal Tribunal (Amendment) Rules 2004, SI 2004/2526, r 21.

Para (2A) inserted, and words in square brackets in para (3) inserted, by the Employment Appeal Tribunal (Amendment) Rules 2013, SI 2013/1693, r 7.

[2.189]

[34B The amount of a costs or expenses order

(1) Subject to sub-paragraphs (2) and (3) the amount of a costs order against the paying party can be determined in the following ways:

(a) the Appeal Tribunal may specify the sum which the paying party must pay to the receiving party;

(b) the parties may agree on a sum to be paid by the paying party to the receiving party and if they do so the costs order shall be for the sum agreed; or

(c) the Appeal Tribunal may order the paying party to pay the receiving party the whole or a specified part of the costs of the receiving party with the amount to be paid being determined by way of detailed assessment in the High Court in accordance with the Civil Procedure Rules 1998 or in Scotland the Appeal Tribunal may direct that it be taxed by the Auditor of the Court of Session, from whose decision an appeal shall lie to a judge.

(2) The Appeal Tribunal may have regard to the paying party's ability to pay when considering the amount of a costs order.

(3) The costs of an assisted person in England and Wales shall be determined by detailed assessment in accordance with the Civil Procedure Rules.]

NOTES

Inserted as noted to r 34A at **[2.188]**.

[2.190]

[34C Personal liability of representatives for costs

(1) The Appeal Tribunal may make a wasted costs order against a party's representative.

(2) In a wasted costs order the Appeal Tribunal may disallow or order the representative of a party to meet the whole or part of any wasted costs of any party, including an order that the representative repay to his client any costs which have already been paid.

(3) "Wasted costs" means any costs incurred by a party (including the representative's own client and any party who does not have a legal representative):

(a) as a result of any improper, unreasonable or negligent act or omission on the part of any representative; or

(b) which, in the light of any such act or omission occurring after they were incurred, the Appeal Tribunal considers it reasonable to expect that party to pay.

(4) In this rule "representative" means a party's legal or other representative or any employee of such representative . . .

(5) Before making a wasted costs order, the Appeal Tribunal shall give the representative a reasonable opportunity to make oral or written representations as to reasons why such an order should not be made. The Appeal Tribunal may also have regard to the representative's ability to pay when considering whether it shall make a wasted costs order or how much that order should be.

(6) When the Appeal Tribunal makes a wasted costs order, it must specify in the order the amount to be disallowed or paid.

(7) The Registrar shall inform the representative's client in writing—

(a) of any proceedings under this rule; or

(b) of any order made under this rule against the party's representative.

(8) Where the Appeal Tribunal makes a wasted costs order it shall provide written reasons for doing so if a request is made for written reasons within 21 days of the date of the wasted costs order. The Registrar shall send a copy of the written reasons to all parties to the proceedings.]

NOTES

Inserted as noted to r 34A at **[2.188]**.

Para (4): words omitted revoked by the Employment Appeal Tribunal (Amendment) Rules 2013, SI 2013/1693, r 8.

[2.191]

[34D Litigants in person and party litigants

(1) This rule applies where the Appeal Tribunal makes a costs order in favour of a party who is a litigant in person.

(2) The costs allowed under this rule must not exceed, except in the case of a disbursement, two-thirds of the amount which would have been allowed if the litigant in person had been represented by a legal representative.

(3) The litigant in person shall be allowed—
(a) costs for the same categories of—
(i) work; and
(ii) disbursements,
which would have been allowed if the work had been done or the disbursements had been made by a legal representative on the litigant in person's behalf;
(b) the payments reasonably made by him for legal services relating to the conduct of the proceedings;
(c) the costs of obtaining expert assistance in assessing the costs claim; and
(d) other expenses incurred by him in relation to the proceedings.

(4) The amount of costs to be allowed to the litigant in person for any item of work claimed shall be—
(a) where the litigant in person can prove financial loss, the amount that he can prove he had lost for the time reasonably spent on doing the work; or
(b) where the litigant in person cannot prove financial loss, an amount for the time which the Tribunal considers reasonably spent on doing the work at the rate of £25.00 per hour;

(5) For the year commencing 6th April 2006 the hourly rate of £25.00 shall be increased by the sum of £1.00 and for each subsequent year commencing on 6 April, the hourly rate for the previous year shall also be increased by the sum of £1.00.

(6) A litigant in person who is allowed costs for attending at court to conduct his case is not entitled to a witness allowance in respect of such attendance in addition to those costs.

(7) For the purpose of this rule, a litigant in person includes—
(a) a company or other corporation which is acting without a legal representative; and
(b) in England and Wales a barrister, solicitor, solicitor's employee or other authorised litigator (as defined in the Courts and Legal Services Act), who is acting for himself; and
(c) in Scotland, an advocate or solicitor (within the meaning of the Solicitors (Scotland) Act 1980) who is acting for himself.

(8) In the application of this rule to Scotland, references to a litigant in person shall be read as references to a party litigant.]

NOTES

Inserted as noted to r 34A at **[2.188]**.
The hourly rate, as of 15 May 2019, is £38.

[2.192]
35 Service of documents

(1) Any notice or other document required or authorised by these Rules to be served on, or delivered to, any person may be sent to him by post to his address for service or, where no address for service has been given, to his registered office, principal place of business, head or main office or last known address, as the case may be, and any notice or other document required or authorised to be served on, or delivered to, the Appeal Tribunal may be sent by post or delivered to the Registrar—
(a) in the case of a notice instituting proceedings, at the central office or any other office of the Tribunal; or
(b) in any other case, at the office of the Tribunal in which the proceedings in question are being dealt with in accordance with rule 38(2).

(2) Any notice or other document required or authorised to be served on, or delivered to, an unincorporated body may be sent to its secretary, manager or other similar officer.

(3) Every document served by post shall be assumed, in the absence of evidence to the contrary, to have been delivered in the normal course of post.

(4) The Appeal Tribunal may inform itself in such manner as it thinks fit of the posting of any document by an officer of the Tribunal.

(5) The Appeal Tribunal may direct that service of any document be dispensed with or be effected otherwise than in the manner prescribed by these Rules.

[2.193]
36 Conciliation

Where at any stage of any proceedings it appears to the Appeal Tribunal that there is a reasonable prospect of agreement being reached between the parties [or of disposal of the appeal or a part of it by consensual means], the Tribunal may take such steps as it thinks fit to enable the parties to avail themselves of any opportunities for conciliation, whether by adjourning any proceedings or otherwise.

NOTES

Words in square brackets inserted by the Employment Appeal Tribunal (Amendment) Rules 2004, SI 2004/2526, r 22.

[2.194]
37 Time

(1) The time prescribed by these Rules or by order of the Appeal Tribunal for doing any act may be extended (whether it has already expired or not) or abridged, and the date appointed for any purpose may be altered, by order of the Tribunal.

[(1A) Where an act is required to be done on or before a particular day it shall be done by 4 pm on that day.]

(2) Where the last day for the doing of any act falls on a day on which the appropriate office of the Tribunal is closed and by reason thereof the act cannot be done on that day, it may be done on the next day on which that office is open.

(3) An application for an extension of the time prescribed for the doing of an act, including the institution of an appeal under rule 3, shall be heard and determined as an [interim] application under rule 20.

[(4) An application for an extension of the time prescribed for the institution of an appeal under rule3 shall not be heard until the notice of the appeal has been served on the Appeal Tribunal.]

NOTES

Para (1A): inserted by the Employment Appeal Tribunal (Amendment) Rules 2004, SI 2004/2526, r 23(1).
Para (3): word in square brackets substituted by SI 2004/2526, r 23(2).
Para (4): added by the Employment Appeal Tribunal (Amendment) Rules 2001, SI 2001/1128, r 23.

[2.195]
38 Tribunal offices and allocation of business

(1) The central office and any other office of the Appeal Tribunal shall be open at such times as the President may direct.

(2) Any proceedings before the Tribunal may be dealt with at the central office or at such other office as the President may direct.

[2.196]
39 Non-compliance with, and waiver of, rules

(1) Failure to comply with any requirements of these Rules shall not invalidate any proceedings unless the Appeal Tribunal otherwise directs.

(2) The Tribunal may, if it considers that to do so would lead to the more expeditious or economical disposal of any proceedings or would otherwise be desirable in the interests of justice, dispense with the taking of any step required or authorised by these Rules, or may direct that any such steps be taken in some manner other than that prescribed by these Rules.

(3) The powers of the Tribunal under paragraph (2) extend to authorising the institution of an appeal notwithstanding that the period prescribed in rule 3(2) may not have commenced.

[2.197]
40 Transitional provisions

(1) Where, prior to 16th December 1993, an [employment tribunal] has given full written reasons for its decision or order, those reasons shall be treated as extended written reasons for the purposes of rule 3(1)(c) and rule 3(2) and for the purposes of Form 1 in the Schedule to these Rules.

(2) Anything validly done under or pursuant to the Employment Appeal Tribunal Rules 1980 shall be treated as having been done validly for the purposes of these Rules, whether or not what was done could have been done under or pursuant to these Rules.

NOTES

Para (1): words in square brackets substituted by the Employment Rights (Dispute Resolution) Act 1998, s 1(2)(a).
Employment Appeal Tribunal Rules 1980, SI 1980/2035: revoked by r 1(2) of these Rules.

SCHEDULE

[FORM 1

Rule 3

Notice of Appeal from Decision of Employment Tribunal

[2.198]

1. The appellant is (*name and address of appellant*).

2. Any communication relating to this appeal may be sent to the appellant at (*appellant's address for service, including telephone number if any*).

3. The appellant appeals from (*here give particulars of the judgment, decision or order of the employment tribunal from which the appeal is brought including the location of the employment tribunal and the date*).

4. The parties to the proceedings before the employment tribunal, other than the appellant, were (*name and addresses of other parties to the proceedings resulting in judgment, decision or order appealed from*).

5. Copies of—

(a) the written record of the employment tribunal's judgment, decision or order and the written reasons of the employment tribunal;
(b) the claim (ET1);
(c) the response (ET3); and/or (*where relevant*)
(d) an explanation as to why any of these documents are not included;

are attached to this notice.

6. If the appellant has made an application to the employment tribunal for a review of its judgment or decision, copies of—

(a) the review application;

(b) the judgment;

(c) the written reasons of the employment tribunal in respect of that review application; and /or;

(d) a statement by or on behalf of the appellant, if such be the case, that a judgment is awaited

are attached to this Notice. If any of these documents exist but cannot be included, then a written explanation must be given.

7. The grounds upon which this appeal is brought are that the employment tribunal erred in law in that (*here set out in paragraphs the various grounds of appeal*).

Date . . . .

Signed . . . .

[Once you have submitted an appeal you will be asked to pay a fee or you can apply for a fee remission. If you fail to do so on or before the date such fee is due, your appeal will be struck out.]

NB. The details entered on your Notice of Appeal must be legible and suitable for photocopying or electronic scanning. The use of black ink or typescript is recommended.]

NOTES

Substituted by the Employment Appeal Tribunal (Amendment) Rules 2005, SI 2005/1871, r 3(a).

Words in square brackets inserted by the Employment Appeal Tribunal (Amendment) Rules 2013, SI 2013/1693, r 9.

[FORM 1A

Rule 3

Notice of Appeal from the CAC Made Pursuant to Regulation 38(8) of the Transnational Information and Consultation of Employees Regulations 1999, [. . . regulation 47(6) of the European Public Limited-Liability Company Regulations 2004] [. . . regulation 35(6) of the Information and Consultation of Employees Regulations 2004] [or regulation 57(6) of the Companies (Cross-Border Mergers) Regulations 2007]

[2.199]

1. The appellant is *(name and address of appellant).*

2. Any communication relating to this appeal may be sent to the appellant at *(appellant's address for service, including telephone number if any).*

3. The appellant appeals from *(here give particulars of the decision, declaration or order of the CAC from which the appeal is brought including the date).*

4. The parties to the proceedings before the CAC, other than the appellant, were *(names and addresses of other parties to the proceedings resulting in decision appealed from).*

5. A copy of the CAC's decision, declaration or order appealed from is attached to this notice.

6. The grounds upon which this appeal is brought are that the CAC erred in law in that *(here set out in paragraphs the various grounds of appeal).*

Date. . . . .

Signed. . . . .]

NOTES

Inserted by the Employment Appeal Tribunal (Amendment) Rules 2001, SI 2001/1128, r 24.

Words in first pair of square brackets in the heading inserted by the Employment Appeal Tribunal (Amendment) Rules 2004, SI 2004/2526, r 25(1); first word omitted from the heading revoked, and words in second pair of square brackets inserted, by the Information and Consultation of Employees Regulations 2004, SI 2004/3426, reg 41(e); second word omitted from the heading revoked, and words in final pair of square brackets added, by the Companies (Cross-Border Mergers) Regulations 2007, SI 2007/2974, reg 64(5).

Note: all other references to the "Companies (Cross-Border Mergers) Regulations 2007" in these Rules are prospectively revoked by SI 2019/348, but the reference to the 2007 Regulations in the title to this Form has not been specifically revoked; it is assumed this is a drafting error.

FORM 2

Rule 3

Notice of Appeal from Decision of Certification Officer

[2.200]

1. The appellant is *(name and address of appellant).*

2. Any communication relating to this appeal may be sent to the appellant at *(appellant's address for service, including telephone number if any).*

3. The appellant appeals from

(here give particulars of the order or decision of the Certification Officer from which the appeal is brought).

4. The appellant's grounds of appeal are:
(here state the grounds of appeal).

5. A copy of the Certification Officer's decision is attached to this notice.
Date. . . . .
Signed. . . . .

FORM 3

Rule 6

Respondent's Answer

[2.201]
1. The respondent is *(name and address of respondent).*

2. Any communication relating to this appeal may be sent to the respondent at *(respondent's address for service, including telephone number if any).*

3. The respondent intends to resist the appeal of (here give the name of appellant). The grounds on which the respondent will rely are (the grounds relied upon by the [employment tribunal]/Certification Officer for making the [judgment,] decision or order appealed from) (and) (the following grounds):
(here set out any grounds which differ from those relied upon by the [employment tribunal] or Certification Officer, as the case may be).

4. The respondent cross-appeals from
(here give particulars of the decision appealed from).

5. The respondent's grounds of appeal are:
(here state the grounds of appeal).
Date. . . . .
Signed. . . . .

NOTES

Para 3: words in first and third pairs of square brackets substituted by the Employment Rights (Dispute Resolution) Act 1998, s 1(2)(a); word in second pair of square brackets inserted by the Employment Appeal Tribunal (Amendment) Rules 2005, SI 2005/1871, r 3(b)(ii).

FORM 4

Rule 8

Application to the Employment Appeal Tribunal for Compensation for Exclusion or Expulsion from a Trade Union or for Compensation or an Order in respect of Unjustifiable Discipline

[2.202]
1. My name is
My address is

2. Any communication relating to this application may be sent to me at
(state address for service, including telephone number, if any).

3. My complaint against *(state the name and address of the trade union)* was declared to be well-founded by *(state tribunal)* on *(give date of decision or order).*

4. *(Where the application relates to exclusion or expulsion from a trade union)* I have not been admitted/re-admitted* to membership of the above-named trade union and hereby apply for compensation on the following grounds.
(Where the application relates to unjustifiable discipline) The determination infringing my right not to be unjustifiably disciplined has not been revoked./ The trade union has failed to take all the steps necessary for securing the reversal of things done for the purpose of giving effect to the determination.*
(*Delete as appropriate)
Date. . . . .
Signed. . . . .
NB.—A copy of the decision or order declaring the complaint against the trade union to be well-founded must be enclosed with this application.

FORM 4A

. . .

NOTES

Inserted by the Employment Appeal Tribunal (Amendment) Rules 2001, SI 2001/1128, r 25.

Revoked by the Transnational Information and Consultation of Employees (Amendment) Regulations 2010, SI 2010/1088, reg 30(1), (9)(a).

[FORM 4B

Rule 16AA

Applications under Regulation 33 of the European Public Limited–Liability Company Regulations 2004 [or regulation 22 of the Information and Consultation of Employees Regulations 2004] [or regulation 53 of the Companies (Cross-Border Mergers) Regulations 2007] [or regulation 20, 21 or 21A of the 1999 Regulations]

[2.203]

1. The applicant's name is *(name and address of applicant)*

2. Any communication relating to this application may be sent to the applicant at *(applicant's address for service, including telephone number if any).*

3. The application is made against *(state identity of respondent)*

4. The address of the respondent is

5. The Central Arbitration Committee made a declaration [or decision *(delete which does not apply)*] in my favour on [] *(insert date)* and I request the Employment Tribunal to issue a penalty notice in accordance with regulation 33 of the European Public Limited-Liability Company Regulations 2004 [or regulation 22 of the Information and Consultation of Employees Regulations 2004 [or regulation 53 of the Companies (Cross-Border Mergers) Regulations 2007] [or regulation 20, 21 or 21A of the Transnational Information and Consultation of Employees Regulations 1999] *(delete which does not apply)*].

Date. . . . .

Signed. . . . .]

NOTES

Inserted by the Employment Appeal Tribunal (Amendment) Rules 2004, SI 2004/2526, r 25(2).

Words in first pair of square brackets in the heading, and second (outer) pair of square brackets in para 5, inserted by the Information and Consultation of Employees Regulations 2004, SI 2004/3426, reg 41(f); words in second pair of square brackets in the heading, and third (inner) pair of square brackets in para 5, inserted by the Companies (Cross-Border Mergers) Regulations 2007, SI 2007/2974, reg 64(6); words in third pair of square brackets in the heading, and words in first and fourth (inner) pairs of square brackets in para 5 inserted by the Transnational Information and Consultation of Employees (Amendment) Regulations 2010, SI 2010/1088, reg 30(1), (9)(b), (c).

Note: all other references to the "Companies (Cross-Border Mergers) Regulations 2007" in these Rules are prospectively revoked by SI 2019/348, but the reference to the 2007 Regulations in the title to this Form has not been specifically revoked; it is assumed this is a drafting error.

FORM 5

Rule 11

Notice of appearance to Application to Employment Appeal Tribunal for Compensation for Exclusion or Expulsion from a Trade Union or for Compensation or an Order in respect of Unjustifiable Discipline

[2.204]

1. The respondent trade union is *(name and address of union).*

2. Any communication relating to this application may be sent to the respondent at *(respondent's address for service, including telephone number, if any).*

3. The respondent intends to resist the application of *(here give name of the applicant).*
The grounds on which the respondent will rely are as follows:

4. *(Where the application relates to exclusion or expulsion from the trade union, state whether or not the applicant had been admitted or re-admitted to membership on or before the date of application.)*
(Where the application relates to unjustifiable discipline, state whether—

(a) *the determination infringing the applicant's right not to be unjustifiably disciplined has been revoked; and*

(b) *the trade union has taken all the steps necessary for securing the reversal of anything done for the purpose of giving effect to the determination.)*

Date. . . . .

Signed. . . . .

Position in union. . . . .

[FORM 5A

Rule 16C

Notice of Appearance to the Employment Appeal Tribunal under [Regulation 20, 21 or 21A of the Transnational Information and Consultation of Employees Regulations 1999 or Regulation 20(6) of the European Public Limited-Liability Company (Employee Involvement) (Great Britain) Regulations 2009 or Regulation 22(6) of the Information and Consultation of Employees Regulations 2004 or Regulation 53(6) of the Companies (Cross-Border Mergers) Regulations 2007]

[2.205]

1. The respondent is *(name and address of respondent).*

2. Any communication relating to this application may be sent to the respondent at *(respondent's address for service, including telephone number, if any).*

3. The respondent intends to resist the application of *(here give the name or description of the applicant).*

The grounds on which the respondent will rely are as follows: *(give particulars, set out in paragraphs and making reference to the specific provisions in the Transnational Information and Consultation of Employees Regulations 1999 [or European Public Limited-Liability Company (Employee Involvement) (Great Britain) Regulations 2009 or Information and Consultation of Employees Regulations 2004 or Companies (Cross-Border Mergers) Regulations 2007] alleged to have been breached).*

Date. . . . .

Signed. . . . .

Position in respondent company or undertaking:. . . . .

(Where appropriate give position in respondent central or local management or position held in relation to respondent Works Council).]

NOTES

Inserted by the Employment Appeal Tribunal (Amendment) Rules 2001, SI 2001/1128, r 26.

Words in square brackets in the heading substituted, and words in square brackets in para 3 inserted, by the Transnational Information and Consultation of Employees (Amendment) Regulations 2010, SI 2010/1088, reg 30(1), (9)(d), (e).

Note: all other references to the "Companies (Cross-Border Mergers) Regulations 2007" in these Rules are prospectively revoked by SI 2019/348, but the reference to the 2007 Regulations in the title to this Form has not been specifically revoked; it is assumed this is a drafting error.

FORM 6

Rule 13

Application to the Employment Appeal Tribunal Under [section 33 of the 1996 Act] for a Restriction of Proceedings Order

[2.206]

1. The applicant is *(the Attorney General/Lord Advocate).*

2. Any communication relating to this application may be sent to the applicant at *(state address for service, including telephone number).*

3. The application is for a restriction of proceedings order to be made against *(state the name and address of the person against whom the order is sought).*

4. An affidavit in support of the application is attached.

Date. . . . .

Signed. . . . .

NOTES

Words in square brackets substituted by the Employment Appeal Tribunal (Amendment) Rules 2001, SI 2001/1128, r 27.

FORM 7

Rule 15

Notice of appearance to Application to the Employment Appeal Tribunal under [section 33 of the 1996 Act] for a Restriction of Proceedings Order

[2.207]

1. The respondent is *(state name and address of respondent).*

2. Any communication relating to this application may be sent to the respondent at *(respondent's address for service, including telephone number, if any).*

3. The respondent intends to resist the application. An affidavit in support is attached to this notice.

Date. . . . .

Signed. . . . .

NOTES

Words in square brackets substituted by the Employment Appeal Tribunal (Amendment) Rules 2001, SI 2001/1128, r 27.

REDUNDANCY PAYMENTS (NATIONAL HEALTH SERVICE) (MODIFICATION) ORDER 1993

(SI 1993/3167)

NOTES

Made: 16 December 1993.

Authority: Employment Protection (Consolidation) Act 1978, ss 149(1)(b), 154(3) (repealed). This Order now has effect as if made under the Employment Rights Act 1996, ss 209(1)(b), 236(5).

Commencement: 13 January 1994.

See *Harvey* E(3)(H)

ARRANGEMENT OF ARTICLES

SCHEDULES

[2.208]

1 Citation, commencement and interpretation

(1) This Order may be cited as the Redundancy Payments (National Health Service) (Modification) Order 1993 and shall come into force on 13th January 1994.

(2) In this Order, unless the context otherwise requires—

(a) "relevant event" means any event occurring on or after the coming into force of this Order on the happening of which an employee may become entitled to a redundancy payment in accordance with the provisions of the 1978 Act;

(b) "the 1978 Act" means the Employment Protection (Consolidation) Act 1978.

NOTES

Employment Protection (Consolidation) Act 1978: repealed and largely consolidated in the Trade Union and Labour Relations (Consolidation) Act 1992, the Employment Rights Act 1996 and the Employment Tribunals Act 1996.

[2.209]

2 Application of order

This Order applies to any person who immediately before the occurrence of the relevant event is employed by an employer described in Schedule 1 to this Order, for the purposes of determining that person's entitlement to a redundancy payment under the 1978 Act and the amount of such payment.

NOTES

"The 1978 Act": as to redundancy payments, etc see now the Employment Rights Act 1996, Pt XI (ss 135–181).

[2.210]

3 Application of certain redundancy payments provisions with modifications

In relation to any person to whom this Order applies the provisions of the 1978 Act mentioned in Schedule 2 to this Order shall have effect subject to the modifications specified in that Schedule.

[2.211]

4 Transitional, supplementary and incidental provisions

(1) Any reference to the 1978 Act in any enactment shall have effect as a reference to that Act as modified by this Order in relation to persons to whom this Order applies.

(2) Any document which refers, whether specifically or by means of a general description, to an enactment which is modified by any provision of this Order shall, except so far as the context otherwise requires, be construed as referring, or as including a reference, to that provision.

(3) Where a period of employment of a person to whom this Order applies falls to be computed in accordance with the provisions of the 1978 Act as modified by this Order, the provisions of this Order shall have effect in relation to any period whether falling wholly or partly before or after the coming into force of this Order.

SCHEDULES

SCHEDULE 1
EMPLOYMENT TO WHICH THIS ORDER APPLIES: EMPLOYERS IMMEDIATELY BEFORE THE RELEVANT EVENT

Article 2

[2.212]
[**1.** a Strategic Health Authority or Health Authority established under section 8 of the National Health Service Act 1977 ("the 1977 Act");

1A. a Special Health Authority established under section 11 of the 1977 Act;]

2. a National Health Service trust established by an order made under section 5(1) of the National Health Service and Community Care Act 1990;

[**2ZA.** an NHS foundation trust within the meaning of section 1(1) of the Health and Social Care (Community Health and Standards) Act 2003;]

[**2A.** a Primary Care Trust established under section 16A of the 1977 Act;]

[**2B.** a clinical commissioning group established under section 14D of the National Health Service Act 2006;

2C. the National Health Service Commissioning Board;

2D. the National Institute for Health and Care Excellence;

2E. the Health and Social Care Information Centre;]

3. a Family Health Services Authority (formerly called a Family Practitioner Committee) established by an order made under section 10(1) of the 1977 Act;

4. the Dental Practice Board (formerly called the Dental Estimates Board) constituted by regulations made under section 37(1) of the 1977 Act;

5. . . .

6. a Health Board or a special Health Board constituted under section 2(1)(a) or section 2(1)(b) respectively of the National Health Service (Scotland) Act 1978 (hereinafter in this Schedule referred to as "the 1978 Act");

7. . . .

8. the Common Services Agency for the Scottish Health Service established under section 10 of the 1978 Act;

9. a National Health Service trust established under section 12A(1) of the 1978 Act;

10. the Scottish Dental Practice Board (formerly called the Scottish Dental Estimates Board) constituted by regulations made under section 4 of the 1978 Act.

NOTES

Paras 1, 1A: substituted, for the original para 1, by the National Health Service Reform and Health Care Professions Act 2002 (Supplementary, Consequential etc Provisions) Regulations 2002, SI 2002/2469, reg 4, Sch 1, Pt 2, para 61.

Para 2ZA: inserted by the Health and Social Care (Community Health and Standards) Act 2003 (Supplementary and Consequential Provision) (NHS Foundation Trusts) Order 2004, SI 2004/696, art 3(1), Sch 1, para 14.

Para 2A: inserted by the Health Act 1999 (Supplementary, Consequential etc Provisions) (No 2) Order 2000, SI 2000/694, art 3, Schedule, Pt II, para 6.

Paras 2B–2E: inserted by the National Treatment Agency (Abolition) and the Health and Social Care Act 2012 (Consequential, Transitional and Saving Provisions) Order 2013, SI 2013/235, art 11, Sch 2, Pt 1, para 24.

Para 5: revoked by the Health and Social Care (Community Health and Standards) Act 2003 (Public Health Laboratory Service Board) (Consequential Provisions) Order 2005, SI 2005/1622, art 3, Schedule.

Para 7: revoked by the Mental Health (Care and Treatment) (Scotland) Act 2003 (Consequential Provisions) Order 2005, SI 2005/2078, art 15, Sch 2, para 16 (in relation to England and Wales), and by the Mental Health (Care and Treatment) (Scotland) Act 2003 (Modification of Subordinate Legislation) Order 2005, SSI 2005/445, art 2, Schedule, para 20 (in relation to Scotland).

SCHEDULE 2
MODIFICATIONS TO CERTAIN REDUNDANCY PAYMENTS PROVISIONS OF THE 1978 ACT

Article 3

[2.213]
1. Section 81 of the 1978 Act shall have effect as if:—
(a) in subsection (1) for the words "has been continuously employed for the requisite period" there were substituted the words "has been employed in relevant health service for the requisite

period" and for the words "Schedules 4, 13 and 14" there were substituted the words "Schedule 4, as modified by the Redundancy Payments (National Health Service) (Modification) Order 1993, and Schedules 13 and 14";

(b) after subsection (4) there were inserted the following subsection:—

"(5) In this section and Schedule 4—

(a) "relevant health service" means—

(i) continuous employment by an employer referred to in the Appendix to Schedule 2 to the Redundancy Payments (National Health Service) (Modification) Order 1993, or

(ii) where immediately before the relevant event a person has been successively employed by two or more employers referred to in the Appendix to Schedule 2 to the said Order, such aggregate period of service with such employers as would be continuous employment if they were a single employer;

(b) "relevant event" means any event occurring on or after the coming into force of the Redundancy Payments (National Health Service) (Modification) Order 1993 on the happening of which an employee may become entitled to a redundancy payment in accordance with this Act.".

2. Section 82 of the 1978 Act shall have effect as if immediately after subsection (7) there were inserted—

"(7A) Any reference in this section to re-engagement by the employer shall be construed as including a reference to re-engagement by any employer referred to in the Appendix to Schedule 2 to the Redundancy Payments (National Health Service) (Modification) Order 1993 and any reference in this section to an offer by the employer shall be construed as including a reference to an offer made by any such employer."

3. Section 84 of the 1978 Act shall have effect as if immediately after subsection (7) thereof there were inserted the following subsection—

"(7A) Any reference in this section to re-engagement by the employer shall be construed as including a reference to re-engagement by any employer referred to in the Appendix to Schedule 2 to the Redundancy Payments (National Health Service) (Modification) Order 1993 and any reference in this section to an offer made by the employer shall be construed as including a reference to an offer made by any such employer."

4. Schedule 4 to the 1978 Act shall have effect as if for paragraph 1 there were substituted the following paragraph—

"1. The amount of a redundancy payment to which an employee is entitled in any case to which the Redundancy Payments (National Health Service) (Modification) Order 1993 applies shall, subject to the following provisions of this Schedule, be calculated by reference to the period ending with the relevant date during which he has been employed in relevant health service."

5. Schedule 6 to the 1978 Act shall have effect as if in paragraph 1 for the words "Schedule 4" there were substituted the words "Schedule 4 as modified by the Redundancy Payments (National Health Service) (Modification) Order 1993".

NOTES

"The 1978 Act": for provisions as to redundancy payments, etc see now the Employment Rights Act 1996, Pt XI (ss 135–181). In particular, ss 82(7) and 84(7) of the 1978 Act are now s 146(1) of the 1996 Act; Sch 4, para 1 to the 1978 Act is now s 162(1) of the 1996 Act.

APPENDIX
EMPLOYERS WITH WHICH EMPLOYMENT MAY CONSTITUTE RELEVANT HEALTH SERVICE

[2.214]

Any employer described in Schedule 1 whether or not in existence at the time of the relevant event.

[EMPLOYMENT TRIBUNALS] EXTENSION OF JURISDICTION (ENGLAND AND WALES) ORDER 1994

(SI 1994/1623)

NOTES

Made: 11 July 1994.

Authority: Employment Protection (Consolidation) Act 1978, ss 131(1), (4A), (5), (5A), 154(3) (repealed). This Order now has effect as if made under the Employment Tribunals Act 1996, ss 3(1), 8(2)–(4), 41(4).

Commencement: 12 July 1994.

Title: words in square brackets substituted by the Employment Rights (Dispute Resolution) Act 1998, s 1(2)(b).

This Order applies only to England and Wales. For the equivalent Scottish Order, see the Employment Tribunals Extension of Jurisdiction (Scotland) Order 1994, SI 1994/1624 at **[2.227]**.

Tribunal jurisdiction: the Employment Act 2002, s 38 applies to proceedings before the employment tribunal relating to a claim under this Order; see s 38(1) of, and Sch 5 to, the 2002 Act at **[1.1279]**, **[1.1287]**. See also the Trade Union and Labour

Relations (Consolidation) Act 1992, s 207A at **[1.524]** (as inserted by the Employment Act 2008). That section provides that in proceedings before an employment tribunal relating to a claim by an employee under any of the jurisdictions listed in Sch A2 to the 1992 Act at **[1.704]** (which includes this Order) the tribunal may adjust any award given if the employer or the employee has unreasonably failed to comply with a relevant Code of Practice as defined by s 207A(4). See also the revised Acas Code of Practice 1 – Disciplinary and Grievance Procedures (2015) at **[4.1]**, and the Acas Code of Practice 4 – Settlement Agreements (2013) at **[4.54]**.

Conciliation: employment tribunal proceedings under art 6 are "relevant proceedings" for the purposes of the conciliation provisions contained in the Employment Tribunals Act 1996, ss 18–18C; see s 18(1)(g) of the 1996 Act at **[1.757]**.

See *Harvey* PI(1), U2.

ARRANGEMENT OF ARTICLES

[2.215]

1 Citation, commencement and interpretation

(1) This Order may be cited as the [Employment Tribunals] Extension of Jurisdiction (England and Wales) Order 1994 and comes into force on the first day after it is made.

(2) In this Order—

"contract claim" means a claim in respect of which proceedings may be brought before an [employment tribunal] by virtue of article 3 or 4; and

"the 1978 Act" means the Employment Protection (Consolidation) Act 1978.

NOTES

Words in square brackets substituted by the Employment Rights (Dispute Resolution) Act 1998, s 1(2)(a), (b).

Employment Protection (Consolidation) Act 1978: repealed and largely consolidated in the Trade Union and Labour Relations (Consolidation) Act 1992, the Employment Rights Act 1996 and the Employment Tribunals Act 1996.

[2.216]

2 Transitional provision

This Order does not enable proceedings in respect of a contract claim to be brought before an [employment tribunal] unless—

(a) the effective date of termination (as defined in section 55(4) of the 1978 Act) in respect of the contract giving rise to the claim, or

(b) where there is no effective date of termination, the last day upon which the employee works in the employment which has terminated,

occurs on or after the day on which the Order comes into force.

NOTES

Words in square brackets substituted by the Employment Rights (Dispute Resolution) Act 1998, s 1(2)(a).

"Section 55(4) of the 1978 Act": see now the Employment Rights Act 1996, s 97(1).

[2.217]

3 Extension of jurisdiction

Proceedings may be brought before an [employment tribunal] in respect of a claim of an employee for the recovery of damages or any other sum (other than a claim for damages, or for a sum due, in respect of personal injuries) if—

(a) the claim is one to which section 131(2) of the 1978 Act applies and which a court in England and Wales would under the law for the time being in force have jurisdiction to hear and determine;

(b) the claim is not one to which article 5 applies; and

(c) the claim arises or is outstanding on the termination of the employee's employment.

NOTES

Words in square brackets substituted by the Employment Rights (Dispute Resolution) Act 1998, s 1(2)(a).

"Section 131(2) of the 1978 Act": see now the Employment Tribunals Act 1996, s 3(2).

[2.218]

4

Proceedings may be brought before an [employment tribunal] in respect of a claim of an employer for the recovery of damages or any other sum (other than a claim for damages, or for a sum due, in respect of personal injuries) if—

Part 2 Statutory Instruments

(a) the claim is one to which section 131(2) of the 1978 Act applies and which a court in England and Wales would under the law for the time being in force have jurisdiction to hear and determine;
(b) the claim is not one to which article 5 applies;
(c) the claim arises or is outstanding on the termination of the employment of the employee against whom it is made; and
(d) proceedings in respect of a claim of that employee have been brought before an [employment tribunal] by virtue of this Order.

NOTES

Words in square brackets substituted by the Employment Rights (Dispute Resolution) Act 1998, s 1(2)(a).
"Section 131(2) of the 1978 Act": see now the Employment Tribunals Act 1996, s 3(2).

[2.219]
5

This article applies to a claim for breach of a contractual term of any of the following descriptions—
(a) a term requiring the employer to provide living accommodation for the employee;
(b) a term imposing an obligation on the employer or the employee in connection with the provision of living accommodation;
(c) a term relating to intellectual property;
(d) a term imposing an obligation of confidence;
(e) a term which is a covenant in restraint of trade.

In this article, "intellectual property" includes copyright, rights in performances, moral rights, design right, registered designs, patents and trade marks.

[2.220]
6 Manner in which proceedings may be brought

Proceedings on a contract claim may be brought before an [employment tribunal] by presenting a complaint to an [employment tribunal].

NOTES

Words in square brackets substituted by the Employment Rights (Dispute Resolution) Act 1998, s 1(2)(a).
Conciliation: employment tribunal proceedings under this article are "relevant proceedings" for the purposes of the conciliation provisions contained in the Employment Tribunals Act 1996, ss 18–18C; see s 18(1)(g) of the 1996 Act at **[1.757]**.

[2.221]
7 Time within which proceedings may be brought

[Subject to [*articles 8A and* 8B], an employment tribunal] shall not entertain a complaint in respect of an employee's contract claim unless it is presented—
(a) within the period of three months beginning with the effective date of termination of the contract giving rise to the claim, or
(b) where there is no effective date of termination, within the period of three months beginning with the last day upon which the employee worked in the employment which has terminated, or
[(ba) where the period within which a complaint must be presented in accordance with paragraph (a) or (b) is extended by regulation 15 of the Employment Act 2002 (Dispute Resolution) Regulations 2004, the period within which the complaint must be presented shall be the extended period rather than the period in paragraph (a) or (b)],
(c) where the tribunal is satisfied that it was not reasonably practicable for the complaint to be presented within whichever of those periods is applicable, within such further period as the tribunal considers reasonable.

NOTES

Words in first (outer) pair of square brackets substituted by the Cross-Border Mediation (EU Directive) Regulations 2011, SI 2011/1133, regs 59, 60; words in second (inner) pair of square brackets substituted by the Employment Tribunals Act 1996 (Application of Conciliation Provisions) Order 2014, SI 2014/431, art 3, Schedule, paras 10, 11.
For the words in italics there is substituted the word "article", by the Cross-Border Mediation (EU Directive) (EU Exit) Regulations 2019, SI 2019/469, reg 4, Sch 1, Pt 2, para 18(1), (2), as from exit day (as defined in the European Union (Withdrawal) Act 2018, s 20).
Para (ba) inserted by the Employment Act 2002 (Dispute Resolution) Regulations 2004, SI 2004/752, reg 17(c).
Note that reg 17(c) (and reg 15 of the 2004 Regulations) lapsed on the repeal of the enabling provisions of the Employment Act 2002.

[2.222]
8

[Subject to [*articles 8A and* 8B], an employment tribunal] shall not entertain a complaint in respect of an employer's contract claim unless—
(a) it is presented at a time when there is before the tribunal a complaint in respect of a contract claim of a particular employee which has not been settled or withdrawn;
(b) it arises out of a contract with that employee; and
(c) it is presented—
(i) within the period of six weeks beginning with the day, or if more than one the last of the days, on which the employer (or other person who is the respondent party to the

employee's contract claim) received from the tribunal a copy of an originating application in respect of a contract claim of that employee; or

(ii) where the tribunal is satisfied that it was not reasonably practicable for the complaint to be presented within that period, within such further period as the tribunal considers reasonable.

NOTES

Words in first (outer) pair of square brackets substituted by the Cross-Border Mediation (EU Directive) Regulations 2011, SI 2011/1133, regs 59, 61; words in second (inner) pair of square brackets substituted by the Employment Tribunals Act 1996 (Application of Conciliation Provisions) Order 2014, SI 2014/431, art 3, Schedule, paras 10, 11.

For the words in italics there is substituted the word "article", by the Cross-Border Mediation (EU Directive) (EU Exit) Regulations 2019, SI 2019/469, reg 4, Sch 1, Pt 2, para 18(1), (3), as from exit day (as defined in the European Union (Withdrawal) Act 2018, s 20).

[2.223]

[8A Extension of time limits because of mediation in certain cross-border disputes

(1) In this article—

(a) "Mediation Directive" means Directive 2008/52/EC of the European Parliament and of the Council of 21 May 2008 on certain aspects of mediation in civil and commercial matters;

(b) "mediation" has the meaning given by article 3(a) of the Mediation Directive;

(c) "mediator" has the meaning given by article 3(b) of the Mediation Directive; and

(d) "relevant dispute" means a dispute to which article 8(1) of the Mediation Directive applies (certain cross-border disputes).

(2) Paragraph (3) applies where—

(a) a time limit is set by article 7(a) or (b) in relation to the whole or part of a relevant dispute;

(b) a mediation in relation to the relevant dispute starts before the period expires; and

(c) if not extended by this article, the time limit would expire before the mediation ends or less than four weeks after it ends.

(3) The time limit expires instead at the end of four weeks after the mediation ends (subject to paragraph (4)).

(4) If a time limit mentioned in paragraph (2)(a) has been extended by this article, paragraphs (2) and (3) apply to the extended time limit as they apply to a time limit mentioned in paragraph (2)(a).

(5) Paragraph (6) applies where—

(a) a time limit is set by article 8(c)(i) in relation to the whole or part of a relevant dispute;

(b) a mediation in relation to the relevant dispute starts before the time limit expires; and

(c) if not extended by this article the time limit would expire before the mediation ends or less than two weeks after it ends.

(6) The time limit expires instead at the end of two weeks after the mediation ends (subject to paragraph (7)).

(7) If a time limit mentioned in paragraph (5)(a) has been extended by this article, paragraphs (5) and (6) apply to the extended time limit as they apply to a time limit mentioned in paragraph (5)(a).

(8) Where more than one time limit applies in relation to a relevant dispute, the extension by paragraph (3) or (6) of one of those time limits does not affect the others.

(9) For the purposes of this article, a mediation starts on the date of the agreement to mediate that is entered into by the parties and the mediator.

(10) For the purposes of this article, a mediation ends on the date of the first of these to occur—

(a) the parties reach an agreement in resolution of the relevant dispute;

(b) a party completes the notification of the other parties that it has withdrawn from the mediation;

(c) a party to whom a qualifying request is made fails to give a response reaching the other parties within 14 days of the request;

(d) the parties, after being notified that the mediator's appointment has ended (by death, resignation or otherwise), fail to agree within 14 days to seek to appoint a replacement mediator; or

(e) the mediation otherwise comes to an end pursuant to the terms of the agreement to mediate.

(11) For the purpose of paragraph (10), a qualifying request is a request by a party that another (A) confirm to all parties that A is continuing with the mediation.

(12) In the case of any relevant dispute, references in this article to a mediation are references to the mediation so far as it relates to that dispute, and references to a party are to be read accordingly.

(13) Where the tribunal has the power under article 7(c) or 8(c)(ii) to extend a period of limitation, the power is exercisable in relation to the period of limitation as extended by this article.]

NOTES

Inserted by the Cross-Border Mediation (EU Directive) Regulations 2011, SI 2011/1133, regs 59, 62.

Revoked by the Cross-Border Mediation (EU Directive) (EU Exit) Regulations 2019, SI 2019/469, reg 4, Sch 1, Pt 2, para 18(1), (4), as from exit day (as defined in the European Union (Withdrawal) Act 2018, s 20) and subject to the modifications specified in Sch 2 to the 2019 Regulations for any mediation to which this article applies, issued before exit day (see reg 5, Sch 2, Pt 2, para 18 at **[2.2131]**, **[2.2133]**).

[2.224]
[8B Extension of time limit to facilitate conciliation before institution of proceedings

(1) This article applies where this Order provides for it to apply for the purposes of a provision of this Order ("a relevant provision").

(2) In this article—

(a) Day A is the day on which the worker concerned complies with the requirement in subsection (1) of section 18A of the Employment Tribunals Act 1996 (requirement to contact ACAS before instituting proceedings) in relation to the matter in respect of which the proceedings are brought, and

(b) Day B is the day on which the worker concerned receives or, if earlier, is treated as receiving (by virtue of regulations made under subsection (11) of that section) the certificate issued under subsection (4) of that section.

(3) In working out when the time limit set by a relevant provision expires the period beginning with the day after Day A and ending with Day B is not to be counted.

(4) If the time limit set by a relevant provision would (if not extended by this paragraph) expire during the period beginning with Day A and ending one month after Day B, the time limit expires instead at the end of that period.

(5) Where an employment tribunal has power under this Order to extend the time limit set by a relevant provision, the power is exercisable in relation to that time limit as extended by this regulation.]

NOTES

Inserted by the Employment Tribunals Act 1996 (Application of Conciliation Provisions) Order 2014, SI 2014/431, art 3, Schedule, paras 10, 12.

[2.225]
9 Death and bankruptcy

(1) Where proceedings in respect of a contract claim have been brought before an [employment tribunal] and an employee or employer party to them dies before their conclusion, the proceedings shall not abate by reason of the death and the tribunal may, if it thinks it necessary in order to ensure that all matters in dispute may be effectually and completely determined and adjudicated upon, order the personal representatives of the deceased party, or other persons whom the tribunal considers appropriate, to be made parties and the proceedings to be carried on as if they had been substituted for the deceased party.

(2) Where proceedings in respect of a contract claim have been brought before an [employment tribunal] and the employee or employer who is the applicant party to them becomes bankrupt before their conclusion, the proceedings shall not abate by reason of the bankruptcy and the tribunal may, if it thinks it necessary in order to ensure that all matters in dispute may be effectually and completely adjudicated upon, order the person in whom the interest of the bankrupt party has vested to be made a party and the proceedings to be carried on as if he had been substituted for the bankrupt party.

NOTES

Words in square brackets substituted by the Employment Rights (Dispute Resolution) Act 1998, s 1(2)(a).

[2.226]
10 Limit on payment to be ordered

An [employment tribunal] shall not in proceedings in respect of a contract claim, or in respect of a number of contract claims relating to the same contract, order the payment of an amount exceeding £25,000.

NOTES

Words in square brackets substituted by the Employment Rights (Dispute Resolution) Act 1998, s 1(2)(a).

[EMPLOYMENT TRIBUNALS] EXTENSION OF JURISDICTION (SCOTLAND) ORDER 1994

(SI 1994/1624)

NOTES

Made: 11 July 1994.

Authority: Employment Protection (Consolidation) Act 1978, ss 131(1), (4A), (5), (5A), 154(3) (repealed). This Order now has effect as if made under the Employment Tribunals Act 1996, ss 3(1), 8(2)–(4), 41(4).

Commencement: 12 July 1994.

Title: words in square brackets substituted by the Employment Rights (Dispute Resolution) Act 1998, s 1(2)(b).

This Order applies only to Scotland. For the equivalent Order applying to England and Wales, see the Employment Tribunals Extension of Jurisdiction (England and Wales) Order 1994, SI 1994/1623 at **[2.215]**.

Tribunal jurisdiction: the Employment Act 2002, s 38 applies to proceedings before the employment tribunal relating to a claim under this Order; see s 38(1) of, and Sch 5 to, the 2002 Act at **[1.1279]**, **[1.1287]**. See also the Trade Union and Labour Relations (Consolidation) Act 1992, s 207A at **[1.524]** (as inserted by the Employment Act 2008). That section provides that in proceedings before an employment tribunal relating to a claim by an employee under any of the jurisdictions listed in Sch A2 to the 1992 Act at **[1.704]** (which includes this Order) the tribunal may adjust any award given if the employer or the employee has unreasonably failed to comply with a relevant Code of Practice as defined by s 207A(4). See also the revised Acas Code of Practice 1 – Disciplinary and Grievance Procedures (2015) at **[4.1]**, and the Acas Code of Practice 4 – Settlement Agreements (2013) at **[4.54]**.

Conciliation: employment tribunal proceedings under art 6 are "relevant proceedings" for the purposes of the conciliation provisions contained in the Employment Tribunals Act 1996, ss 18–18C; see s 18(1)(h) of the 1996 Act at **[1.757]**.

See *Harvey* PI(1), U2.

ARRANGEMENT OF ARTICLES

[2.227]
1 Citation, commencement and interpretation

(1) This Order may be cited as the [Employment Tribunals] Extension of Jurisdiction (Scotland) Order 1994 and comes into force on the first day after it is made.

(2) In this Order—

"contract claim" means a claim in respect of which proceedings may be brought before an [employment tribunal] by virtue of article 3 or 4; and

"the 1978 Act" means the Employment Protection (Consolidation) Act 1978.

NOTES

Words in square brackets substituted by the Employment Rights (Dispute Resolution) Act 1998, s 1(2)(a), (b).

Employment Protection (Consolidation) Act 1978: repealed and largely consolidated in the Trade Union and Labour Relations (Consolidation) Act 1992, the Employment Rights Act 1996 and the Employment Tribunals Act 1996.

[2.228]
2 Transitional provision

This Order does not enable proceedings in respect of a contract claim to be brought before an [employment tribunal] unless—

(a) the effective date of termination (as defined in section 55(4) of the 1978 Act) in respect of the contract giving rise to the claim, or
(b) where there is no effective date of termination, the last day upon which the employee works in the employment which has terminated,

occurs on or after the day on which the Order comes into force.

NOTES

Words in square brackets substituted by the Employment Rights (Dispute Resolution) Act 1998, s 1(2)(a).

"Section 55(4) of the 1978 Act": see now the Employment Rights Act 1996, s 97(1).

[2.229]
3 Extension of jurisdiction

Proceedings may be brought before an [employment tribunal] in respect of a claim of an employee for the recovery of damages or any other sum (other than a claim for damages, or for a sum due, in respect of personal injuries) if—

(a) the claim is one to which section 131(2) of the 1978 Act applies and which a court in Scotland would under the law for the time being in force have jurisdiction to hear and determine;
(b) the claim is not one to which article 5 applies; and
(c) the claim arises or is outstanding on the termination of the employee's employment.

NOTES

Words in square brackets substituted by the Employment Rights (Dispute Resolution) Act 1998, s 1(2)(a).

"Section 131(2) of the 1978 Act": see now the Employment Tribunals Act 1996, s 3(2).

[2.230]
4

Proceedings may be brought before an [employment tribunal] in respect of a claim of an employer for the recovery of damages or any other sum (other than a claim for damages, or for a sum due, in respect of personal injuries) if—

(a) the claim is one to which section 131(2) of the 1978 Act applies and which a court in Scotland would under the law for the time being in force have jurisdiction to hear and determine;
(b) the claim is not one to which article 5 applies;

(c) the claim arises or is outstanding on the termination of the employment of the employee against whom it is made; and
(d) proceedings in respect of a claim of that employee have been brought before an [employment tribunal] by virtue of this Order.

NOTES

Words in square brackets substituted by the Employment Rights (Dispute Resolution) Act 1998, s 1(2)(a).

"Section 131(2) of the 1978 Act": see now the Employment Tribunals Act 1996, s 3(2).

[2.231]

5

This article applies to a claim for breach of a contractual term of any of the following descriptions—

(a) a term requiring the employer to provide living accommodation for the employee;
(b) a term imposing an obligation on the employer or the employee in connection with the provision of living accommodation;
(c) a term relating to intellectual property;
(d) a term imposing an obligation of confidence;
(e) a term which is a covenant in restraint of trade.

In this article, "intellectual property" includes copyright, rights in performances, moral rights, design right, registered designs, patents and trade marks.

[2.232]

6 Manner in which proceedings may be brought

Proceedings on a contract claim may be brought before an [employment tribunal] by presenting a complaint to an [employment tribunal].

NOTES

Words in square brackets substituted by the Employment Rights (Dispute Resolution) Act 1998, s 1(2)(a).

Conciliation: employment tribunal proceedings under this article are "relevant proceedings" for the purposes of the conciliation provisions contained in the Employment Tribunals Act 1996, ss 18–18C; see s 18(1)(h) of the 1996 Act at **[1.757]**.

[2.233]

7 Time within which proceedings may be brought

[Subject to [*articles 8A and* 8B], an employment tribunal] shall not entertain a complaint in respect of an employee's contract claim unless it is presented—

(a) within the period of three months beginning with the effective date of termination of the contract giving rise to the claim, or
(b) where there is no effective date of termination, within the period of three months beginning with the last day upon which the employee worked in the employment which has terminated, or
[(ba) where the period within which a complaint must be presented in accordance with paragraph (a) or (b) is extended by regulation 15 of the Employment Act 2002 (Dispute Resolution) Regulations 2004, the period within which the complaint must be presented shall be the extended period rather than the period in paragraph (a) or (b).]
(c) where the tribunal is satisfied that it was not reasonably practicable for the complaint to be presented within whichever of those periods is applicable, within such further period as the tribunal considers reasonable.

NOTES

Words in first (outer) pair of square brackets substituted by the Cross-Border Mediation (EU Directive) Regulations 2011, SI 2011/1133, regs 63, 64. Words in second (inner) pair of square brackets substituted by the Employment Tribunals Act 1996 (Application of Conciliation Provisions) Order 2014, SI 2014/431, art 3, Schedule, paras 13, 14. For the words in italics there is substituted the word "article", by the Cross-Border Mediation (EU Directive) (EU Exit) Regulations 2019, SI 2019/469, reg 4, Sch 1, Pt 2, para 19(1), (2), as from exit day (as defined in the European Union (Withdrawal) Act 2018, s 20).

Para (ba) inserted by the Employment Act 2002 (Dispute Resolution) Regulations 2004, SI 2004/752, reg 17(d).

Note that reg 17(d) (and reg 15 of the 2004 Regulations) lapsed on the repeal of the enabling provisions of the Employment Act 2002.

[2.234]

8

[Subject to [*articles 8A and* 8B], an employment tribunal] shall not entertain a complaint in respect of an employer's contract claim unless—

(a) it is presented at a time when there is before the tribunal a complaint in respect of a contract claim of a particular employee which has not been settled or withdrawn;
(b) it arises out of a contract with that employee; and
(c) it is presented—
    (i) within the period of six weeks beginning with the day, or if more than one the last of the days, on which the employer (or other person who is the respondent party to the employee's contract claim) received from the tribunal a copy of an originating application in respect of a contract claim of that employee; or
    (ii) where the tribunal is satisfied that it was not reasonably practicable for the complaint to be presented within that period, within such further period as the tribunal considers reasonable.

NOTES

Words in first (outer) pair of square brackets substituted by the Cross-Border Mediation (EU Directive) Regulations 2011, SI 2011/1133, regs 63, 65; words in second (inner) pair of square brackets substituted by the Employment Tribunals Act 1996 (Application of Conciliation Provisions) Order 2014, SI 2014/431, art 3, Schedule, paras 13, 14. For the words in italics there is substituted the word "article", by the Cross-Border Mediation (EU Directive) (EU Exit) Regulations 2019, SI 2019/469, reg 4, Sch 1, Pt 2, para 19(1), (3), as from exit day (as defined in the European Union (Withdrawal) Act 2018, s 20).

[2.235]

[8A Extension of time limits because of mediation in certain cross-border disputes

(1) In this article—

(a) "Mediation Directive" means Directive 2008/52/EC of the European Parliament and of the Council of 21 May 2008 on certain aspects of mediation in civil and commercial matters;

(b) "mediation" has the meaning given by article 3(a) of the Mediation Directive;

(c) "mediator" has the meaning given by article 3(b) of the Mediation Directive; and

(d) "relevant dispute" means a dispute to which article 8(1) of the Mediation Directive applies (certain cross-border disputes).

(2) Paragraph (3) applies where—

(a) a time limit is set by article 7(a) or (b) in relation to the whole or part of a relevant dispute;

(b) a mediation in relation to the relevant dispute starts before the period expires; and

(c) if not extended by this article, the time limit would expire before the mediation ends or less than four weeks after it ends.

(3) The time limit expires instead at the end of four weeks after the mediation ends (subject to paragraph (4)).

(4) If a time limit mentioned in paragraph (2)(a) has been extended by this article, paragraphs (2) and (3) apply to the extended time limit as they apply to a time limit mentioned in paragraph (2)(a).

(5) Paragraph (6) applies where—

(a) a time limit is set by article 8(c)(i) in relation to the whole or part of a relevant dispute;

(b) a mediation in relation to the relevant dispute starts before the time limit expires; and

(c) if not extended by this article the time limit would expire before the mediation ends or less than two weeks after it ends.

(6) The time limit expires instead at the end of two weeks after the mediation ends (subject to paragraph (7)).

(7) If a time limit mentioned in paragraph (5)(a) has been extended by this article, paragraphs (5) and (6) apply to the extended time limit as they apply to a time limit mentioned in paragraph (5)(a).

(8) Where more than one time limit applies in relation to a relevant dispute, the extension by paragraph (3) or (6) of one of those time limits does not affect the others.

(9) For the purposes of this article, a mediation starts on the date of the agreement to mediate that is entered into by the parties and the mediator.

(10) For the purposes of this article, a mediation ends on the date of the first of these to occur—

(a) the parties reach an agreement in resolution of the relevant dispute;

(b) a party completes the notification of the other parties that it has withdrawn from the mediation;

(c) a party to whom a qualifying request is made fails to give a response reaching the other parties within 14 days of the request;

(d) the parties, after being notified that the mediator's appointment has ended (by death, resignation or otherwise), fail to agree within 14 days to seek to appoint a replacement mediator; or

(e) the mediation otherwise comes to an end pursuant to the terms of the agreement to mediate.

(11) For the purpose of paragraph (10), a qualifying request is a request by a party that another (A) confirm to all parties that A is continuing with the mediation.

(12) In the case of any relevant dispute, references in this article to a mediation are references to the mediation so far as it relates to that dispute, and references to a party are to be read accordingly.

(13) Where the tribunal has the power under article 7(c) or 8(c)(ii) to extend a period of limitation, the power is exercisable in relation to the period of limitation as extended by this article.]

NOTES

Inserted by the Cross-Border Mediation (EU Directive) Regulations 2011, SI 2011/1133, regs 63, 66.

Revoked by the Cross-Border Mediation (EU Directive) (EU Exit) Regulations 2019, SI 2019/469, reg 4, Sch 1, Pt 2, para 19(1), (4), as from exit day (as defined in the European Union (Withdrawal) Act 2018, s 20) and subject to the modifications specified in Sch 2 to the 2019 Regulations for any mediation to which this regulation applies, issued before exit day (see reg 5, Sch 2, Pt 2, para 19 at **[2.2131]**, **[2.2133]**).

[2.236]

[8B Extension of time limit to facilitate conciliation before institution of proceedings

(1) This article applies where this Order provides for it to apply for the purposes of a provision of this Order ("a relevant provision").

(2) In this article—

(a) Day A is the day on which the worker concerned complies with the requirement in subsection (1) of section 18A of the Employment Tribunals Act 1996 (requirement to contact ACAS before instituting proceedings) in relation to the matter in respect of which the proceedings are brought, and

(b) Day B is the day on which the worker concerned receives or, if earlier, is treated as receiving (by virtue of regulations made under subsection (11) of that section) the certificate issued under subsection (4) of that section.

(3) In working out when the time limit set by a relevant provision expires the period beginning with the day after Day A and ending with Day B is not to be counted.

(4) If the time limit set by a relevant provision would (if not extended by this paragraph) expire during the period beginning with Day A and ending one month after Day B, the time limit expires instead at the end of that period.

(5) Where an employment tribunal has power under this Order to extend the time limit set by a relevant provision, the power is exercisable in relation to that time limit as extended by this regulation.]

NOTES

Inserted by the Employment Tribunals Act 1996 (Application of Conciliation Provisions) Order 2014, SI 2014/431, art 3, Schedule, paras 13, 15.

[2.237]
9 Death and legal incapacity

Where proceedings in respect of a contract claim have been brought before an [employment tribunal] and an employee or employer party to them dies or comes under legal incapacity before the conclusion of the proceedings, the tribunal may order any person who represents that party or his estate to be made a party to the proceedings in place of the party who has died or come under legal incapacity and the proceedings to be carried on accordingly.

NOTES

Words in square brackets substituted by the Employment Rights (Dispute Resolution) Act 1998, s 1(2)(a).

[2.238]
10 Limit on payment to be ordered

An [employment tribunal] shall not in proceedings in respect of a contract claim, or in respect of a number of contract claims relating to the same contract, order the payment of an amount exceeding £25,000.

NOTES

Words in square brackets substituted by the Employment Rights (Dispute Resolution) Act 1998, s 1(2)(a).

HEALTH AND SAFETY (CONSULTATION WITH EMPLOYEES) REGULATIONS 1996

(SI 1996/1513)

NOTES

Made: 10 June 1996.
Authority: European Communities Act 1972, s 2(2).
Commencement: 1 October 1996.
Note: with regard to the authority for these Regulations, note that the European Communities Act 1972 is repealed by the European Union (Withdrawal) Act 2018, s 1, as from exit day (as defined in s 20 of that Act); but note also that provision is made for the continuation in force of any subordinate legislation made under the authority of s 2(2) of the 1972 Act by s 2 of the 2018 Act at **[1.2240]**, subject to the provisions of s 5 of, and Sch 1 to, the 2018 Act at **[1.2243]**, **[1.2253]**.
Conciliation: employment tribunal proceedings under Sch 2, para 2 are "relevant proceedings" for the purposes of the conciliation provisions contained in the Employment Tribunals Act 1996, ss 18–18C; see s 18(1)(i) of the 1996 Act at **[1.757]**.
See *Harvey* NI(13), NIII(7).

ARRANGEMENT OF REGULATIONS

SCHEDULES

[2.239]
1 Citation, extent and commencement

These Regulations, which extend to Great Britain, may be cited as the Health and Safety (Consultation with Employees) Regulations 1996 and shall come into force on 1st October 1996.

[2.240]
2 Interpretation

(1) In these Regulations, unless the context otherwise requires—

"the 1974 Act" means the Health and Safety at Work etc Act 1974;

"the 1977 Regulations" means the Safety Representatives and Safety Committees Regulations 1977;

"employee" has the meaning assigned to it by section 53(1) of the 1974 Act but shall not include a person employed as a domestic servant in a private household; and "employer" shall be construed accordingly;

"the relevant statutory provisions" has the meaning assigned to it by section 53(1) of the 1974 Act;

"representatives of employee safety" shall be construed in accordance with regulation 4(1)(b);

"safety representative" has the meaning assigned to it by regulation 2(1) of the 1977 Regulations;

"workplace" means, in relation to an employee, any place or places where that employee is likely to work or which he is likely to frequent in the course of his employment or incidentally to it and, in relation to a representative of employee safety, any place or places where the employees he represents are likely so to work or frequent.

(2) Any reference in these Regulations to consulting employees directly or consulting representatives of employee safety is a reference to consulting them pursuant to regulation 3 and regulation 4(1)(a) or (b), as the case may be.

(3) Unless the context otherwise requires, any reference in these Regulations to—

(a) a numbered regulation or schedule is a reference to the regulation or schedule in these Regulations so numbered; and

(b) a numbered paragraph is a reference to the paragraph so numbered in the regulation or schedule in which the reference appears.

[2.241]
3 Duty of employer to consult

Where there are employees who are not represented by safety representatives under the 1977 Regulations, the employer shall consult those employees in good time on matters relating to their health and safety at work and, in particular, with regard to—

(a) the introduction of any measure at the workplace which may substantially affect the health and safety of those employees;

(b) his arrangements for appointing or, as the case may be, nominating persons in accordance with [regulations 7(1) and 8(1)(b) of the Management of Health and Safety at Work Regulations 1999] [or article 13(3)(b) of the Regulatory Reform (Fire Safety) Order 2005]];

(c) any health and safety information he is required to provide to those employees by or under the relevant statutory provisions;

(d) the planning and organisation of any health and safety training he is required to provide to those employees by or under the relevant statutory provisions; and

(e) the health and safety consequences for those employees of the introduction (including the planning thereof) of new technologies into the workplace.

NOTES

Para (b): words in first pair of square brackets substituted by the Management of Health and Safety at Work Regulations 1999, SI 1999/3242, reg 29(2), Sch 2; words in second pair of square brackets originally inserted by the Fire Precautions (Workplace) Regulations 1997, SI 1997/1840, reg 21(1), and substituted by the Regulatory Reform (Fire Safety) Order 2005, SI 2005/1541, art 41(2), in relation to England and Wales only. A corresponding amendment has been made in relation to Scotland by the Fire (Scotland) Act 2005 (Consequential Modifications and Savings) (No 2) Order 2006, SSI 2006/457, which provides that the words should now read "or regulation 12(3)(b) of the Fire Safety (Scotland) Regulations 2006".

[2.242]
4 Persons to be consulted

(1) The consultation required by regulation 3 is consultation with either—

(a) the employees directly; or

(b) in respect of any group of employees, one or more persons in that group who were elected, by the employees in that group at the time of the election, to represent that group for the purposes of such consultation (and any such persons are in these Regulations referred to as "representatives of employee safety").

(2) Where an employer consults representatives of employee safety he shall inform the employees represented by those representatives of—

(a) the names of those representatives; and

(b) the group of employees represented by those representatives.

(3) An employer shall not consult a person as a representative of employee safety if—

(a) that person has notified the employer that he does not intend to represent the group of employees for the purposes of such consultation;

(b) that person has ceased to be employed in the group of employees which he represents;

(c) the period for which that person was elected has expired without that person being re-elected; or

(d) that person has become incapacitated from carrying out his functions under these regulations;

and where pursuant to this paragraph an employer discontinues consultation with that person he shall inform the employees in the group concerned of that fact.

(4) Where an employer who has been consulting representatives of employee safety decides to consult employees directly he shall inform the employees and the representatives of that fact.

[2.243]

5 Duty of employer to provide information

(1) Where an employer consults employees directly he shall, subject to paragraph (3), make available to those employees such information, within the employer's knowledge, as is necessary to enable them to participate fully and effectively in the consultation.

(2) Where an employer consults representatives of employee safety he shall, subject to paragraph (3), make available to those representatives such information, within the employer's knowledge, as is—

(a) necessary to enable them to participate fully and effectively in the consultation and in the carrying out of their functions under these Regulations;

(b) contained in any record which he is required to keep by [regulation 12 of the Reporting of Injuries, Diseases and Dangerous Occurrences Regulations 2013] and which relates to the workplace or the group of employees represented by those representatives.

(3) Nothing in paragraph (1) or (2) shall require an employer to make available any information—

(a) the disclosure of which would be against the interests of national security;

(b) which he could not disclose without contravening a prohibition imposed by or under any enactment;

(c) relating specifically to an individual, unless he has consented to its being disclosed;

(d) the disclosure of which would, for reasons other than its effect on health or safety, cause substantial injury to the employer's undertaking or, where the information was supplied to him by some other person, to the undertaking of that other person; or

(e) obtained by the employer for the purpose of bringing, prosecuting or defending any legal proceedings;

or to provide or allow the inspection of any document or part of a document which is not related to health or safety.

NOTES

Para (2): words in square brackets in sub-para (b) substituted by the Reporting of Injuries, Diseases and Dangerous Occurrences Regulations 2013, SI 2013/1471, reg 18(2), Sch 4.

[2.244]

6 Functions of representatives of employee safety

Where an employer consults representatives of employee safety each of those representatives shall, for the period for which that representative is so consulted, have the following functions—

(a) to make representations to the employer on potential hazards and dangerous occurrences at the workplace which affect, or could affect, the group of employees he represents;

(b) to make representations to the employer on general matters affecting the health and safety at work of the group of employees he represents and, in particular, on such matters as he is consulted about by the employer under regulation 3; and

(c) to represent the group of employees he represents in consultations at the workplace with inspectors appointed under section 19(1) of the 1974 Act.

[2.245]

7 Training, time off and facilities for representatives of employee safety and time off for candidates

(1) Where an employer consults representatives of employee safety, he shall—

(a) ensure that each of those representatives is provided with such training in respect of that representative's functions under these Regulations as is reasonable in all the circumstances and the employer shall meet any reasonable costs associated with such training including travel and subsistence costs; and

(b) permit each of those representatives to take such time off with pay during that representative's working hours as shall be necessary for the purpose of that representative performing his functions under these Regulations or undergoing any training pursuant to paragraph (l)(a).

(2) An employer shall permit a candidate standing for election as a representative of employee safety reasonable time off with pay during that person's working hours in order to perform his functions as such a candidate.

(3) Schedule 1 (pay for time off) and Schedule 2 (provisions as to [employment tribunals]) shall have effect.

(4) An employer shall provide such other facilities and assistance as a representative of employee safety may reasonably require for the purpose of carrying out his functions under these Regulations.

NOTES

Para (3): words in square brackets substituted by the Employment Rights (Dispute Resolution) Act 1998, s 1(2)(b).

8 *(Amends the Employment Rights Act 1996, ss 44, 100 at* **[1.880]**, **[1.1007]**.*)*

[2.246]

9 Exclusion of civil liability

Breach of a duty imposed by these Regulations shall, subject to regulation 7(3) and Schedule 2, not confer any right of action in any civil proceedings.

[2.247]

10 Application of health and safety legislation

Sections 16 to 21, 23, 24, 26, 28, 33, 34, 36 to 39, 42(1) to (3) and 46 of the 1974 Act, the Health and Safety (Enforcing Authority) Regulations 1989 and the Health and Safety (Training for Employment) Regulations 1990 shall apply as if any references therein to health and safety regulations or to the relevant statutory provisions included references to these Regulations.

NOTES

Health and Safety (Enforcing Authority) Regulations 1989: revoked and replaced by the Health and Safety (Enforcing Authority) Regulations 1998, SI 1998/494.

[2.248]

11 Application to the Crown and armed forces

(1) Section 48 of the 1974 Act shall, subject to paragraph (2), apply in respect of these Regulations as it applies in respect of regulations made under Part I of that Act.

(2) These Regulations shall apply in respect of members of the armed forces of the Crown subject to the following—

(a) references to "representatives of employee safety" (in regulation 4(1)(b) and elsewhere) shall, in respect of any group of employees, be references to one or more persons in that group who were appointed by the employer to represent that group for the purposes of such consultation;

(b) references to "elected" and "re-elected" in regulation 4(3)(c) shall be, respectively, references to "appointed" and "re-appointed"; and

(c) regulation 7(1)(b), (2) and (3) shall not apply.

[2.249]

12 Disapplication to sea-going ships

These Regulations shall not apply to or in relation to the master or crew of a seagoing ship or to the employer of such persons in respect of the normal ship-board activities of a ship's crew under the direction of the master.

13 *(Amends the Safety Representatives and Safety Committees Regulations 1977, SI 1977/500, reg 3 at* **[2.32]**.*)*

SCHEDULES

SCHEDULE 1
PAY FOR TIME OFF

Regulation 7(3)

[2.250]

1. Subject to paragraph 3 below, where a person is permitted to take time off in accordance with regulation 7(1)(b) or 7(2), his employer shall pay him—

(a) where the person's remuneration for the work he would ordinarily have been doing during that time does not vary with the amount of work done, as if he had worked at that work for the whole of that time;

(b) where the person's remuneration for that work varies with the amount of work done, an amount calculated by reference to the average hourly earnings for that work (ascertained in accordance with paragraph 2).

2. The average hourly earnings referred to in paragraph 1(b) are the average hourly earnings of the person concerned or, if no fair estimate can be made of those earnings, the average hourly earnings for work of that description of persons in comparable employment with the same employer or, if there are no such persons, a figure of average hourly earnings which is reasonable in all the circumstances.

3. Any payment to a person by an employer in respect of a period of time off—

Part 2 Statutory Instruments

(a) if it is a payment which discharges any liability which the employer may have under sections 168 or 169 of the Trade Union and Labour Relations (Consolidation) Act 1992, in respect of that period, shall also discharge his liability in respect of the same period under regulation 7(l)(b) or 7(2);

(b) if it is a payment under any contractual obligation, shall go towards discharging the employer's liability in respect of the same period under regulation 7(l)(b) or 7(2);

(c) if it is a payment under regulation 7(l)(b) or 7(2), shall go towards discharging any liability of the employer to pay contractual remuneration in respect of the same period.

SCHEDULE 2
PROVISIONS AS TO [EMPLOYMENT TRIBUNALS]

Regulation 7(3)

[2.251]

1. An [employment tribunal] shall have jurisdiction to determine complaints in accordance with the following provisions of this Schedule.

2. A person (referred to in this Schedule as the "complainant") may present a complaint to an [employment tribunal] that—

(a) his employer has failed to permit him to take time off in accordance with regulation 7(1)(b) or 7(2); or

(b) his employer has failed to pay him in accordance with regulation 7(1)(b) or 7(2) and Schedule 1.

3. [Subject to paragraph 3A an employment tribunal] shall not consider a complaint under paragraph 2 unless it is presented within three months of the date when the failure occurred or within such further period as the tribunal considers reasonable in a case where it is satisfied that it was not reasonably practicable for the complaint to be presented within the period of three months.

[**3A.** (1) In this paragraph—

(a) Day A is the day on which the worker concerned complies with the requirement in subsection (1) of section 18A of the Employment Tribunals Act 1996 (requirement to contact ACAS before instituting proceedings) in relation to the matter in respect of which the proceedings are brought, and

(b) Day B is the day on which the worker concerned receives or, if earlier, is treated as receiving (by virtue of regulations made under subsection (11) of that section) the certificate issued under subsection (4) of that section.

(2) In working out when the three month time limit set by paragraph 3 expires the period beginning with the day after Day A and ending with Day B is not to be counted.

(3) If the three month time limit set by paragraph 3 would (if not extended by this sub-paragraph) expire during the period beginning with Day A and ending one month after Day B, the time limit expires instead at the end of that period.

(4) The power conferred on the employment tribunal by paragraph 3 to extend the three month time limit set by that paragraph is exercisable in relation to that time limit as extended by this paragraph.]

4. Where an [employment tribunal] finds a complaint under paragraph 2(a) well-founded the tribunal shall make a declaration to that effect and may make an award of compensation to be paid by the employer to the complainant which shall be of such amount as the tribunal considers just and equitable in all the circumstances having regard to the employer's default in failing to permit time off to be taken by the complainant and to any loss sustained by the complainant which is attributable to the matters complained of.

5. Where on a complaint under paragraph 2(b) an [employment tribunal] finds that the employer has failed to pay the complainant the whole or part of the amount required to be paid in accordance with regulation 7(1)(b) or 7(2) and Schedule 1, the tribunal shall order the employer to pay the complainant the amount which it finds due to him.

NOTES

Words in square brackets in para 3 substituted, and para 3A inserted, by the Employment Tribunals Act 1996 (Application of Conciliation Provisions) Order 2014, SI 2014/431, art 3, Schedule, paras 16–18.

All other words in square brackets substituted by the Employment Rights (Dispute Resolution) Act 1998, s 1(2)(a), (b).

Conciliation: employment tribunal proceedings under para 2 above are "relevant proceedings" for the purposes of the conciliation provisions contained in the Employment Tribunals Act 1996, ss 18–18C; see s 18(1)(i) of the 1996 Act at **[1.757]**.

EMPLOYMENT PROTECTION (RECOUPMENT OF [BENEFITS]) REGULATIONS 1996

(SI 1996/2349)

NOTES

Made: 10 September 1996.

Authority: Employment Tribunals Act 1996, ss 16, 41(4); Social Security Administration Act 1992, s 58(1) (repealed subject to certain exceptions). Now have effect wholly under the Employment Tribunals Act 1996, ss 16, 41(4) (as amended by the Social Security Act 1998, s 86, Sch 7, para 147, Sch 8).

Commencement: 7 October 1996.

Title: word in square brackets substituted by the Universal Credit (Consequential, Supplementary, Incidental and Miscellaneous Provisions) Regulations 2013, SI 2013/630, reg 50(1), (2).

See *Harvey* DI(19)(D5).

ARRANGEMENT OF REGULATIONS

PART I
INTRODUCTORY

PART II
EMPLOYMENT TRIBUNAL PROCEEDINGS

PART III
RECOUPMENT OF BENEFIT

PART IV
DETERMINATION OF BENEFIT RECOUPED

PART I
INTRODUCTORY

[2.252]

1 Citation and Commencement

These Regulations may be cited as the Employment Protection (Recoupment of [Benefits]) Regulations 1996 and shall come into force on 7th October 1996.

NOTES

Word in square brackets substituted by the Universal Credit (Consequential, Supplementary, Incidental and Miscellaneous Provisions) Regulations 2013, SI 2013/630, reg 50(1), (3).

[2.253]

2 Interpretation

(1) In these Regulations, unless the context otherwise requires, the following expressions have the meanings hereby assigned to them respectively, that is to say—

"the 1992 Act" means the Trade Union and Labour Relations (Consolidation) Act 1992;

"the 1996 Act" means the Employment Rights Act 1996;

"prescribed element" has the meaning assigned to it in Regulation 3 below and the Schedule to these Regulations;

"protected period" has the same meaning as in section 189(5) of the 1992 Act;

"protective award" has the same meaning as in section 189(3) of the 1992 Act;

"recoupable benefit" means any jobseeker's allowance[, income-related employment and support allowance][, universal credit] or income support as the case may be, which is recoupable under these Regulations;

"recoupment notice" means a notice under these Regulations;

"Secretary of the Tribunals" means the Secretary of the Central Office of the [Employment Tribunals] (England and Wales) or, as the case may require, the Secretary of the Central Office of the [Employment Tribunals] (Scotland) for the time being;

["universal credit" means universal credit under Part 1 of the Welfare Reform Act 2012].

(2) In the Schedule to these Regulations references to sections are references to sections of the 1996 Act unless otherwise indicated and references in column 3 of the table to the conclusion of the tribunal proceedings are references to the conclusion of the proceedings mentioned in the corresponding entry in column 2.

(3) For the purposes of these Regulations (and in particular for the purposes of any calculations to be made by an [employment tribunal] as respects the prescribed element) the conclusion of the tribunal proceedings shall be taken to occur—

(a) where the [employment tribunal] at the hearing announces the effect of its decision to the parties, on the date on which that announcement is made;

(b) in any other case, on the date on which the decision of the tribunal is sent to the parties.

(4) References to parties in relevant [employment tribunal] proceedings shall be taken to include references to persons appearing on behalf of parties in a representative capacity.

(5) References in these Regulations to anything done, or to be done, in, or in consequence of, any tribunal proceedings include references to anything done, or to be done, in, or in consequence of any such proceedings as are in the nature of a review, or re-hearing or a further hearing consequent on an appeal.

NOTES

Words in first pair of square brackets in the definition "recoupable benefit" inserted by the Social Security (Miscellaneous Amendments) (No 5) Regulations 2010, SI 2010/2429, reg 5(a); words in second pair of square brackets in the definition "recoupable benefit" inserted, and definition "universal credit" inserted, by the Universal Credit (Consequential, Supplementary, Incidental and Miscellaneous Provisions) Regulations 2013, SI 2013/630, reg 50(1), (4); all other words in square brackets substituted by the Employment Rights (Dispute Resolution) Act 1998, s 1(2)(a), (b).

Note that "protected period" is actually defined in s 189(4) of the 1992 Act, and not s 189(5) as stated in para (1) above.

PART II
[EMPLOYMENT TRIBUNAL] PROCEEDINGS

[2.254]

3 Application to payments and proceedings

(1) Subject to paragraph (2) below these Regulations apply—

(a) to the payments described in column 1 of the table contained in the Schedule to these Regulations, being, in each case, payments which are the subject of [employment tribunal] proceedings of the kind described in the corresponding entry in column 2 and the prescribed element in relation to each such payment is so much of the relevant monetary award as is attributable to the matter described in the corresponding entry in column 3; and

(b) to payments of remuneration in pursuance of a protective award.

(2) The payments to which these Regulations apply by virtue of paragraph (1)(a) above include payments in proceedings under section 192 of the 1992 Act and, accordingly, where an order is made on an employee's complaint under that section, the relevant protective award shall, as respects that employee and to the appropriate extent, be taken to be subsumed in the order made under section 192 so that the provisions of these Regulations relating to monetary awards shall apply to payments under that order to the exclusion of the provisions relating to protective awards, but without prejudice to anything done under the latter in connection with the relevant protective award before the making of the order under section 192.

NOTES

Words in square brackets in para (1) and in the heading preceding this regulation substituted by the Employment Rights (Dispute Resolution) Act 1998, s 1(2)(a).

[2.255]

4 Duties of the [employment tribunals] and of the Secretary of the Tribunals in respect of monetary awards

(1) Where these Regulations apply, no regard shall be had, in assessing the amount of a monetary award, to the amount of any jobseeker's allowance[, income-related employment and support allowance][, universal credit] or any income support which may have been paid to or claimed by the employee for a period which coincides with any part of a period to which the prescribed element is attributable.

(2) Where the [employment tribunal] in arriving at a monetary award makes a reduction on account of the employee's contributory fault or on account of any limit imposed by or under the 1992 Act or 1996 Act, a proportionate reduction shall be made in arriving at the amount of the prescribed element.

(3) Subject to the following provisions of this Regulation it shall be the duty of the [employment tribunal] to set out in any decision which includes a monetary award the following particulars—

(a) the monetary award;

(b) the amount of the prescribed element, if any;

(c) the dates of the period to which the prescribed element is attributable;

(d) the amount, if any, by which the monetary award exceeds the prescribed element.

(4) Where the [employment tribunal] at the hearing announces to the parties the effect of a decision which includes a monetary award it shall inform those parties at the same time of the amount of any prescribed element included in the monetary award and shall explain the effect of Regulations 7 and 8 below in relation to the prescribed element.

(5) Where the [employment tribunal] has made such an announcement as is described in paragraph (4) above the Secretary of the Tribunals shall forthwith notify the Secretary of State that the tribunal has decided to make a monetary award including a prescribed element and shall notify him of the particulars set out in paragraph (3) above.

(6) As soon as reasonably practicable after the Secretary of the Tribunals has sent a copy of a decision containing the particulars set out in paragraph (3) above to the parties he shall send a copy of that decision to the Secretary of State.

(7) In addition to containing the particulars required under paragraph (3) above, any such decision as is mentioned in that paragraph shall contain a statement explaining the effect of Regulations 7 and 8 below in relation to the prescribed element.

(8) The requirements of paragraphs (3) to (7) above do not apply where the tribunal is satisfied that in respect of each day falling within the period to which the prescribed element relates the employee has neither received nor claimed jobseeker's allowance[, income-related employment and support allowance][, universal credit] or income support.

NOTES

Words in first pair of square brackets in paras (1), (8) inserted by the Social Security (Miscellaneous Amendments) (No 5) Regulations 2010, SI 2010/2429, reg 5(b); words in second pair of square brackets in paras (1), (8) inserted by the Universal Credit (Consequential, Supplementary, Incidental and Miscellaneous Provisions) Regulations 2013, SI 2013/630, reg 50(1), (5); all other words in square brackets substituted by the Employment Rights (Dispute Resolution) Act 1998, s 1(2)(a), (b).

[2.256]

5 Duties of the [employment tribunals] and of the Secretary of the Tribunals in respect of protective awards

(1) Where, on a complaint under section 189 of the 1992 Act, an [employment tribunal]—

(a) at the hearing announces to the parties the effect of a decision to make a protective award; or

(b) (where it has made no such announcement) sends a decision to make such an award to the parties;

the Secretary of the Tribunals shall forthwith notify the Secretary of State of the following particulars relating to the award—

(i) where the [employment tribunal] has made such an announcement as is described in paragraph (1)(a) above, the date of the hearing or where it has made no such announcement, the date on which the decision was sent to the parties;

(ii) the location of the tribunal;

(iii) the name and address of the employer;

(iv) the description of the employees to whom the award relates; and

(v) the dates of the protected period.

(2)

(a) Where an [employment tribunal] makes such an announcement as is described in paragraph (1)(a) above in the presence of the employer or his representative it shall advise him of his duties under Regulation 6 below and shall explain the effect of Regulations 7 and 8 below in relation to remuneration under the protective award.

(b) Without prejudice to (a) above any decision of an [employment tribunal] to make a protective award under section 189 of the 1992 Act shall contain a statement advising the employer of his duties under Regulation 6 below and an explanation of the effect of Regulations 7 and 8 below in relation to remuneration under the protective award.

NOTES

Words in square brackets substituted by the Employment Rights (Dispute Resolution) Act 1998, s 1(2)(a), (b).

[2.257]

6 Duties of the employer to give information about protective awards

(1) Where an [employment tribunal] makes a protective award under section 189 of the 1992 Act against an employer, the employer shall give to the Secretary of State the following information in writing—

(a) the name, address and national insurance number of every employee to whom the award relates; and

(b) the date of termination (or proposed termination) of the employment of each such employee.

(2) Subject to paragraph (3) below the employer shall comply with paragraph (1) above within the period of ten days commencing on the day on which the [employment tribunal] at the hearing announces to the parties the effect of a decision to make a protective award or (in the case where no such announcement is made) on the day on which the relevant decision is sent to the parties.

(3) Where, in any case, it is not reasonably practicable for the employer to comply with paragraph (1) above within the period applicable under paragraph (2) above he shall comply as soon as reasonably practicable after the expiration of that period.

NOTES

Words in square brackets substituted by the Employment Rights (Dispute Resolution) Act 1998, s 1(2)(a).

PART III
RECOUPMENT OF BENEFIT

[2.258]
7 Postponement of Awards

(1) This Regulation shall have effect for the purpose of postponing relevant awards in order to enable the Secretary of State to initiate recoupment under Regulation 8 below.

(2) Accordingly—

(a) so much of the monetary award as consists of the prescribed element;

(b) payment of any remuneration to which an employee would otherwise be entitled under a protective award,

shall be treated as stayed (in Scotland, sisted) as respects the relevant employee until—

(i) the Secretary of State has served a recoupment notice on the employer; or

(ii) the Secretary of State has notified the employer in writing that he does not intend to serve a recoupment notice.

(3) The stay or sist under paragraph (2) above is without prejudice to the right of an employee under section 192 of the 1992 Act to present a complaint to an [employment tribunal] of his employer's failure to pay remuneration under a protective award and Regulation 3(2) above has effect as respects any such complaint and as respects any order made under section 192(3) of that Act.

NOTES

Para (3): words in square brackets substituted by the Employment Rights (Dispute Resolution) Act 1998, s 1(2)(a).

[2.259]
8 Recoupment of Benefit

(1) Recoupment shall be initiated by the Secretary of State serving on the employer a recoupment notice claiming by way of total or partial recoupment of jobseeker's allowance[, income-related employment and support allowance][, universal credit] or income support the appropriate amount, computed, as the case may require, under paragraph (2) or (3) below.

(2) In the case of monetary awards the appropriate amount shall be whichever is the less of the following two sums—

(a) the amount of the prescribed element (less any tax or social security contributions which fall to be deducted therefrom by the employer); or

(b)

[(i)] the amount paid by way of or paid as on account of jobseeker's allowance[, income-related employment and support allowance] or income support to the employee for any period which coincides with any part of the period to which the prescribed element is attributable[; or

(ii) in the case of an employee entitled to an award of universal credit for any period ("the UC period") which coincides with any part of the period to which the prescribed element is attributable, any amount paid by way of or on account of universal credit for the UC period that would not have been paid if the person's earned income for that period was the same as immediately before the period to which the prescribed element is attributable].

(3) In the case of remuneration under a protective award the appropriate amount shall be whichever is the less of the following two sums—

(a) the amount (less any tax or social security contributions which fall to be deducted therefrom by the employer) accrued due to the employee in respect of so much of the protected period as falls before the date on which the Secretary of State receives from the employer the information required under Regulation 6 above; or

(b)

[(i)] the amount paid by way of or paid as on account of jobseeker's allowance[, income-related employment and support allowance] or income support to the employee for any period which coincides with any part of the protected period falling before the date described in (a) above[; or

(ii) in the case of an employee entitled to an award of universal credit for any period ("the UC period") which coincides with any part of the protected period falling before the date described in (a) above, any amount paid by way of or on account of universal credit for the UC period that would not have been paid if the person's earned income for that period was the same as immediately before the protected period].

(4) A recoupment notice shall be served on the employer by post or otherwise and copies shall likewise be sent to the employee and, if requested, to the Secretary of the Tribunals.

(5) The Secretary of State shall serve a recoupment notice on the employer, or notify the employer that he does not intend to serve such a notice, within the period applicable, as the case may require, under paragraph (6) or (7) below, or as soon as practicable thereafter.

(6) In the case of a monetary award the period shall be—

(a) in any case in which the tribunal at the hearing announces to the parties the effect of its decision as described in Regulation 4(4) above, the period ending 21 days after the conclusion of the hearing or the period ending 9 days after the decision has been sent to the parties, whichever is the later; or

(b) in any other case, the period ending 21 days after the decision has been sent to the parties.

(7) In the case of a protective award the period shall be the period ending 21 days after the Secretary of State has received from the employer the information required under Regulation 6 above.

(8) A recoupment notice served on an employer shall operate as an instruction to the employer to pay, by way of deduction out of the sum due under the award, the recoupable amount to the Secretary of State and it shall be the duty of the employer to comply with the notice. The employer's duty under this paragraph shall not affect his obligation to pay any balance that may be due to the employee under the relevant award.

(9) The duty imposed on the employer by service of the recoupment notice shall not be discharged by payment of the recoupable amount to the employee during the postponement period or thereafter if a recoupment notice is served on the employer during the said period.

(10) Payment by the employer to the Secretary of State under this Regulation shall be a complete discharge in favour of the employer as against the employee in respect of any sum so paid but without prejudice to any rights of the employee under Regulation 10 below.

(11) The recoupable amount shall be recoverable by the Secretary of State from the employer as a debt.

[(12) For the purposes of paragraphs (2)(b)(ii) and (3)(b)(ii), "earned income" has the meaning given in regulation 52 of the Universal Credit Regulations 2013.]

NOTES

Para (1): words in first pair of square brackets inserted by the Social Security (Miscellaneous Amendments) (No 5) Regulations 2010, SI 2010/2429, reg 5(c); words in second pair of square brackets inserted by the Universal Credit (Consequential, Supplementary, Incidental and Miscellaneous Provisions) Regulations 2013, SI 2013/630, reg 50(1), (6)(a).

Para (2): sub-para (b)(i) numbered as such, and sub-para (b)(ii) (and the preceding word) inserted, by SI 2013/630, reg 50(1), (6)(b); words in square brackets in sub-para (b)(i) inserted by SI 2010/2429, reg 5(c).

Para (3): sub-para (b)(i) numbered as such and sub-para (b)(ii) (and the preceding word) inserted, by SI 2013/630, reg 50(1), (6)(c); words in square brackets in sub-para (b)(i) inserted by SI 2010/2429, reg 5(c).

Para (12): added by SI 2013/630, reg 50(1), (6)(d).

[2.260]

9 Order made in secondary proceedings

(1) In the application of any of the above provisions in the case of—

(a) proceedings for an award under section 192 of the 1992 Act; or

(b) proceedings in the nature of a review, a re-hearing or a further hearing consequent on an appeal,

it shall be the duty of the [employment tribunal] or, as the case may require, the Secretary of State, to take the appropriate account of anything done under or in consequence of these Regulations in relation to any award made in the original proceedings.

(2) For the purposes of this Regulation the original proceedings are—

(a) where paragraph (1)(a) above applies the proceedings under section 189 of the 1992 Act; or

(b) where paragraph (1)(b) above applies the proceedings in respect of which the re-hearing, the review or the further hearing consequent on an appeal takes place.

NOTES

Para (1): words in square brackets substituted by the Employment Rights (Dispute Resolution) Act 1998, s 1(2)(a).

PART IV
DETERMINATION . . . OF BENEFIT RECOUPED

[2.261]

10 Provisions relating to determination of amount paid by way of or paid as on account of benefit

(1) Without prejudice to the right of the Secretary of State to recover from an employer the recoupable benefit, an employee on whom a copy of a recoupment notice has been served in accordance with Regulation 8 above may, within 21 days of the date on which such notice was served on him or within such further time as the Secretary of State may for special reasons allow, give notice in writing to the Secretary of State that he does not accept that the amount specified in the recoupment notice in respect of jobseeker's allowance[, income-related employment and support allowance][, universal credit] or income support is correct.

[(2) Where an employee has given notice in writing to the Secretary of State under paragraph (1) above that he does not accept that an amount specified in the recoupment notice is correct, the Secretary of State shall make a decision as to the amount of jobseeker's allowance[, income-related employment and support allowance][, universal credit] or, as the case may be, income support paid in respect of the period to which the prescribed element is attributable or, as appropriate, in respect of so much of the protected period as falls before the date on which the employer complies with Regulation 6 above.

(2A) The Secretary of State may revise either upon application made for the purpose or on his own initiative a decision under paragraph (2) above.

(2B) The employee shall have a right of appeal to [the First-tier Tribunal] against a decision of the Secretary of State whether as originally made under paragraph (2) or as revised under paragraph (2A) above.

(2C) The Social Security and Child Support (Decisions and Appeals) Regulations 1999 shall apply for the purposes of paragraphs (2A) and (2B) above as though a decision of the Secretary of State under paragraph (2A) above were made under section 9 of the 1998 Act and any appeal from such a decision were made under section 12 of that Act.

(2D) In this Regulation "the 1998 Act" means the Social Security Act 1998.

(3) Where the Secretary of State recovers too much money from an employer under these Regulations the Secretary of State shall pay to the employee an amount equal to the excess.]

(4) In any case where, after the Secretary of State has recovered from an employer any amount by way of recoupment of benefit, the decision given by the [employment tribunal] in consequence of which such recoupment took place is set aside or varied on appeal or on a re-hearing by the [employment tribunal], the Secretary of State shall make such repayment to the employer or payment to the employee of the whole or part of the amount recovered as he is satisfied should properly be made having regard to the decision given on appeal or re-hearing.

NOTES

The words omitted from the heading preceding this regulation were revoked, and paras (2), (2A)–(2D), (3), were substituted (for the original paras (2), (3)), by the Social Security Act 1998 (Commencement No 12 and Consequential and Transitional Provisions) Order 1999, SI 1999/3178, art 3(1), (14), Sch 14.

The words in the first pair of square brackets in paras (1), (2) were inserted by the Social Security (Miscellaneous Amendments) (No 5) Regulations 2010, SI 2010/2429, reg 5(d), and the words in the second pair of square brackets in paras (1), (2) were inserted by the Universal Credit (Consequential, Supplementary, Incidental and Miscellaneous Provisions) Regulations 2013, SI 2013/630, reg 50(1), (7).

The words in square brackets in para (2B) were substituted by the Tribunals, Courts and Enforcement Act 2007 (Transitional and Consequential Provisions) Order 2008, SI 2008/2683, art 6(1), Sch 1, para 73.

The words in square brackets in para (4) were substituted by the Employment Rights (Dispute Resolution) Act 1998, s 1(2)(a).

11 *(Revokes the Employment Protection (Recoupment of Unemployment Benefit and Supplementary Benefit) Regulations 1977, SI 1977/674.)*

SCHEDULE
TABLE RELATING TO MONETARY AWARDS

Regulation 3

[2.262]

Column 1	*Column 2*	*Column 3*
Payment	*Proceedings*	*Matter to which prescribed element is attributable*
1. Guarantee payments under section 28.	1. Complaint under section 34.	1. Any amount found to be due to the employee and ordered to be paid under section 34(3) for a period before the conclusion of the tribunal proceedings.
2. Payments under any collective agreement having regard to which the appropriate Minister has made an exemption order under section 35.	2. Complaint under section 35(4).	2. Any amount found to be due to the employee and ordered to be paid under section 34(3), as applied by section 35(4), for a period before the conclusion of the tribunal proceedings.
3. Payments of remuneration in respect of a period of suspension on medical grounds under section 64 and section 108(2).	3. Complaint under section 70.	3. Any amount found to be due to the employee and ordered to be paid under section 70(3) for a period before the conclusion of the tribunal proceedings.
4. Payments of remuneration in respect of a period of suspension on maternity grounds under section 68.	4. Complaint under section 70.	4. Any amount found to be due to the employee and ordered to be paid under section 70(3) for a period before the conclusion of the tribunal proceedings.
5. Payments under an order for reinstatement under section 114(1).	5. Complaint of unfair dismissal under section 111(1).	5. Any amount ordered to be paid under section 114(2)(a) in respect of arrears of pay for a period before the conclusion of the tribunal proceedings.
6. Payments under an order for re-engagement under section 117(8).	6. Complaint of unfair dismissal under section 111(1).	6. Any amount ordered to be paid under section 115(2)(d) in respect of arrears of pay for a period before the conclusion of the tribunal proceedings.

Column 1	***Column 2***	***Column 3***
7. Payments under an award of compensation for unfair dismissal in cases falling under section 112(4) (cases where no order for reinstatement or re-engagement has been made).	7. Complaint of unfair dismissal under section 111(1).	7. Any amount ordered to be paid and calculated under section 123 in respect of compensation for loss of wages for a period before the conclusion of the tribunal proceedings.
8. Payments under an award of compensation for unfair dismissal under section 117(3) where reinstatement order not complied with.	8. Proceedings in respect of non-compliance with order.	8. Any amount ordered to be paid and calculated under section 123 in respect of compensation for loss of wages for a period before the conclusion of the tribunal proceedings.
9. Payments under an award of compensation for unfair dismissal under section 117(3) where re-engagement order not complied with.	9. Proceedings in respect of non-compliance with order.	9. Any amount ordered to be paid and calculated under section 123 in respect of compensation for loss of wages for a period before the conclusion of the tribunal proceedings.
10. Payments under an interim order for reinstatement under section 163(4) of the 1992 Act.	10. Proceedings on an application for an order for interim relief under section 161(1) of the 1992 Act.	10. Any amount found to be due to the complainant and ordered to be paid in respect of arrears of pay for the period between the date of termination of employment and the conclusion of the tribunal proceedings.
11. Payments under an interim order for re-engagement under section 163(5)(a) of the 1992 Act.	11. Proceedings on an application for an order for interim relief under section 161(1) of the 1992 Act.	11. Any amount found to be due to the complainant and ordered to be paid in respect of arrears of pay for the period between the date of termination of employment and the conclusion of the tribunal proceedings.
12. Payments under an order for the continuation of a contract of employment under section 163(5)(b) of the 1992 Act where employee reasonably refuses re-engagement.	12. Proceedings on an application for an order for interim relief under section 161(1) of the 1992 Act.	12. Any amount found to be due to the complainant and ordered to be paid in respect of arrears of pay for the period between the date of termination of employment and the conclusion of the tribunal proceedings.
13. Payments under an order for the continuation of a contract of employment under section 163(6) of the 1992 Act where employer fails to attend or is unwilling to reinstate or re-engage.	13. Proceedings on an application for an order for interim relief under section 161(1) of the 1992 Act.	13. Any amount found to be due to the complainant and ordered to be paid in respect of arrears of pay for the period between the date of termination of employment and the conclusion of the tribunal proceedings.
14. Payments under an order for the continuation of a contract of employment under sections 166(1) and (2) of the 1992 Act where reinstatement or re-engagement order not complied with.	14. Proceedings in respect of non-compliance with order.	14. Any amount ordered to be paid to the employee by way of compensation under section 166(1)(b) of the 1992 Act for loss of wages for the period between the date of termination of employment and the conclusion of the tribunal proceedings.
15. Payments under an order for compensation under sections 166(3)(5) of the 1992 Act where order for the continuation of contract of employment not complied with.	15. Proceedings in respect of non-compliance with order.	15. Any amount ordered to be paid to the employee by way of compensation under section 166(3)(4) of the 1992 Act for loss of wages for the period between the date of termination of employment and the conclusion of the tribunal proceedings.

Column 1	Column 2	Column 3
16. Payments under an order under section 192(3) of the 1992 Act on employer's default in respect of remuneration due to employee under protective award.	16. Complaint under section 192(1) of the 1992 Act.	16. Any amount ordered to be paid to the employee in respect of so much of the relevant protected period as falls before the date of the conclusion of the tribunal proceedings.

[EMPLOYMENT TRIBUNALS] (INTEREST ON AWARDS IN DISCRIMINATION CASES) REGULATIONS 1996

(SI 1996/2803)

NOTES

Made: 5 November 1996.

Authority: European Communities Act 1972, s 2(2); Race Relations Act 1976, s 56(5), (6); Disability Discrimination Act 1995, s 17A(6), (7). In so far as these Regulations were made under provisions of the 1976 and 1995 Acts (which were repealed by the Equality Act 2010, s 211(2), Sch 27, Pt 1, as from 1 October 2010), they now have effect under the Equality Act 2010, s 139 (see the Equality Act 2010 (Commencement No 4, Savings, Consequential, Transitional, Transitory and Incidental Provisions and Revocation) Order 2010, SI 2010/2317, art 21, Sch 7).

Commencement: 2 December 1996.

Note: with regard to the authority for these Regulations, note that the European Communities Act 1972 is repealed by the European Union (Withdrawal) Act 2018, s 1, as from exit day (as defined in s 20 of that Act); but note also that provision is made for the continuation in force of any subordinate legislation made under the authority of s 2(2) of the 1972 Act by s 2 of the 2018 Act at **[1.2240]**, subject to the provisions of s 5 of, and Sch 1 to, the 2018 Act at **[1.2243]**, **[1.2253]**.

Title: words in square brackets substituted by the Employment Rights (Dispute Resolution) Act 1998, s 1(2)(b).

See *Harvey* PI(1)(ZA).

ARRANGEMENT OF REGULATIONS

[2.263]
1 Citation, commencement, interpretation and revocation

(1) These Regulations may be cited as the [Employment Tribunals] (Interest on Awards in Discrimination Cases) Regulations 1996 and shall come into force on 2nd December 1996.

(2) In these Regulations—

"the 1970 Act" means the Equal Pay Act 1970;
"the 1975 Act" means the Sex Discrimination Act 1975;
"the 1976 Act" means the Race Relations Act 1976;
"the 1995 Act" means the Disability Discrimination Act 1995 and;
"an award under the relevant legislation" means—

(a) an award under the 1970 Act of arrears of remuneration or damages, or

(b) an order under section 65(1)(b) of the 1975 Act, section 56(1)(b) of the 1976 Act . . . section 8(2)(b) of the 1995 Act [. . . regulation 30(1)(b) of the Employment Equality (Sexual Orientation) Regulations 2003] [. . . regulation 30(1)(b) of the Employment Equality (Religion or Belief) Regulations 2003] [or regulation 38(1)(b) of the Employment Equality (Age) Regulations 2006] for payment of compensation,

but does not include an award of costs under rule 12 in Schedule 1 to the [Employment Tribunals] (Constitution and Rules of Procedure) Regulations 1993, or of expenses under rule 12 in Schedule 1 to the [Employment Tribunals] (Constitution and Rules of Procedure) (Scotland) Regulations 1993, even if the award of costs or expenses is made in the same proceedings as an award under the 1970 Act or such an order.

(3) (*Revokes the Sex Discrimination and Equal Pay (Remedies) Regulations 1993, SI 1993/2978, and the Race Relations (Interest on Awards) Regulations 1994, SI 1994/1748.*)

NOTES

Para (1): words in square brackets substituted by the Employment Rights (Dispute Resolution) Act 1998, s 1(2)(b).

Para (2): in definition "an award under the relevant legislation" first words omitted from para (b) revoked, and words in first pair of square brackets in that paragraph inserted, by the Employment Equality (Sexual Orientation) Regulations 2003, SI 2003/1661, reg 39, Sch 5, para 3; second words omitted from para (b) of that definition revoked, and words in second pair of square brackets in that paragraph inserted, by the Employment Equality (Religion or Belief) Regulations 2003, SI 2003/1660, reg 39(2), Sch 5, para 3; final words omitted from para (b) of that definition revoked, and words in final pair of square brackets in that paragraph inserted, by the Employment Equality (Age) Regulations 2006, SI 2006/1031, reg 49(1), Sch 8, Pt 2, para 56(1), (2)(a); other words in square brackets in that definition substituted by the Employment Rights (Dispute Resolution) Act 1998, s 1(2)(b).

Employment Tribunals (Constitution and Rules of Procedure) Regulations 1993, SI 1993/2867; Employment Tribunals (Constitution and Rules of Procedure) (Scotland) Regulations 1993, SI 1993/2688: revoked and replaced; see now, the Employment Tribunals (Constitution and Rules of Procedure) Regulations 2013, SI 2013/1237 at **[2.1323]**.

Note that the Equal Pay Act 1970, the Sex Discrimination Act 1975, the Race Relations Act 1976, the Disability Discrimination Act 1995, the Employment Equality (Sexual Orientation) Regulations 2003, reg 30, the Employment Equality (Religion or Belief) Regulations 2003, reg 30, and the Employment Equality (Age) Regulations 2006, reg 38 were all repealed or revoked by the Equality Act 2010, s 211(2), Sch 27. However, these Regulations have not been amended to insert a reference to awards made under the 2010 Act. See further as to this, the Interpretation Act 1978,s 17(2)(a). Note also that the Disability Discrimination Act 1995, s 8(2)(b) became s 17A(2)(b) following the amendments made to the 1995 Act by the Disability Discrimination Act 1995 (Amendment) Regulations 2003, SI 2003/1673.

[2.264]

2 Interest on awards

(1) Where, at any time after the commencement of these Regulations, an [employment tribunal] makes an award under the relevant legislation—

(a) it may, subject to the following provisions of these Regulations, include interest on the sums awarded; and

(b) it shall consider whether to do so, without the need for any application by a party in the proceedings.

(2) Nothing in paragraph (1) shall prevent the tribunal from making an award or decision, with regard to interest, in terms which have been agreed between the parties.

NOTES

Para (1): words in square brackets substituted by the Employment Rights (Dispute Resolution) Act 1998, s 1(2)(a).

[2.265]

3 Rate of interest

(1) Interest shall be calculated as simple interest which accrues from day to day.

[(2) Subject to paragraph (3), the rate of interest to be applied shall be, in England and Wales, the rate fixed, for the time being, by section 17 of the Judgments Act 1838 and, in Scotland, the rate fixed, for the time being, by section 9 of the Sheriff Courts (Scotland) Extracts Act 1892.]

(3) Where the rate of interest in paragraph (2) has varied during a period for which interest is to be calculated, the tribunal may, if it so desires in the interests of simplicity, apply such median or average of those rates as seems to it appropriate.

NOTES

Para (2): substituted by the Employment Tribunals (Interest on Awards in Discrimination Cases) (Amendment) Regulations 2013, SI 2013/1669, reg 2, except in relation to a claim which is presented to an Employment Tribunal Office on or before 28 July 2013.

Rate of interest: the rate of interest currently prescribed for England and Wales under the Judgments Act 1838, s 17 is (and has been since 1993) 8%. The rate of interest prescribed for Scotland under the 1892 Act is also 8%.

[2.266]

4 Calculation of interest

(1) In this regulation and regulations 5 and 6, "day of calculation" means the day on which the amount of interest is calculated by the tribunal.

(2) In regulation 6, "mid-point date" means the day which falls half-way through the period mentioned in paragraph (3) or, where the number of days in that period is even, the first day of the second half of the period.

(3) The period referred to in paragraph (2) is the period beginning on the date, in the case of an award under the 1970 Act, of the contravention and, in other cases, of the act of discrimination complained of, and ending on the day of calculation.

[2.267]

5

No interest shall be included in respect of any sum awarded for a loss or matter which will occur after the day of calculation or in respect of any time before the contravention or act of discrimination complained of.

[2.268]

6

(1) Subject to the following paragraphs of this regulation—

(a) in the case of any sum for injury to feelings, interest shall be for the period beginning on the date of the contravention or act of discrimination complained of and ending on the day of calculation;

(b) in the case of all other sums of damages or compensation (other than any sum referred to in regulation 5) and all arrears of remuneration, interest shall be for the period beginning on the mid-point date and ending on the day of calculation.

(2) Where any payment has been made before the day of calculation to the complainant by or on behalf of the respondent in respect of the subject matter of the award, interest in respect of that part of the award covered by the payment shall be calculated as if the references in paragraph (1), and in the definition of "mid-point date" in regulation 4, to the day of calculation were to the date on which the payment was made.

(3) Where the tribunal considers that in the circumstances, whether relating to the case as a whole or to a particular sum in an award, serious injustice would be caused if interest were to be awarded in respect of the period or periods in paragraphs (1) or (2), it may—

(a) calculate interest, or as the case may be interest on the particular sum, for such different period, or

(b) calculate interest for such different periods in respect of various sums in the award,

as it considers appropriate in the circumstances, having regard to the provisions of these Regulations.

[2.269]
7 Decision in writing

(1) The tribunal's written statement of reasons for its decision shall contain a statement of the total amount of any interest awarded under regulation 2 and, unless this amount has been agreed between the parties, either a table showing how it has been calculated or a description of the manner in which it has been calculated.

(2) The tribunal's written statement of reasons shall include reasons for any decision not to award interest under regulation 2.

8 (*Revoked by the Employment Tribunals (Interest on Awards in Discrimination Cases) (Amendment) Regulations 2013, SI 2013/1669, reg 3, except in relation to a claim which is presented to an Employment Tribunal Office on or before 28 July 2013.*)

EMPLOYMENT PROTECTION (CONTINUITY OF EMPLOYMENT) REGULATIONS 1996

(SI 1996/3147)

NOTES

Made: 16 December 1996.
Authority: Employment Rights Act 1996, s 219.
Commencement: 13 January 1997.
See *Harvey* H(1).

[2.270]
1 Citation, commencement and revocation

(1) These Regulations may be cited as the Employment Protection (Continuity of Employment) Regulations 1996 and shall come into force on 13th January 1997.

(2) The Employment Protection (Continuity of Employment) Regulations 1993 are revoked.

[2.271]
2 Application

These Regulations apply to any action taken in relation to the dismissal of an employee which consists of—

(a) his making a claim in accordance with a dismissal procedures agreement designated by an order under section 110 of the Employment Rights Act 1996,

(b) the presentation by him of a relevant complaint of dismissal,

(c) any action taken by a conciliation officer under [any of sections 18A to 18C] of [the Employment Tribunals Act 1996] . . .

(d) the making of a relevant [settlement agreement][, . . .

(e) the making of an agreement to submit a dispute to arbitration in accordance with a scheme having effect by virtue of an order under section 212A of the Trade Union and Labour Relations (Consolidation) Act 1992,][. . .

(f) a decision taken arising out of the use of a statutory dispute resolution procedure contained in Schedule 2 to the Employment Act 2002 in a case where, in accordance with the Employment Act 2002 (Dispute Resolution) Regulations 2004, such a procedure applies][, or

(g) a decision taken arising out of the use of the statutory duty to consider procedure contained in Schedule 6 to the Employment Equality (Age) Regulations 2006].

NOTES

Words in first pair of square brackets in para (c) substituted by the Enterprise and Regulatory Reform Act 2013 (Consequential Amendments) (Employment) Order 2014, SI 2014/386, art 2, Schedule, para 1.

Words in second pair of square brackets in para (c) substituted by the Employment Rights (Dispute Resolution) Act 1998, s 1(2)(c).

Word omitted from para (c) revoked, and para (e) and the word immediately preceding it added, by the Employment Protection (Continuity of Employment) (Amendment) Regulations 2001, SI 2001/1188, reg 2.

Words in square brackets in para (d) substituted by the Enterprise and Regulatory Reform Act 2013 (Consequential Amendments) (Employment) Order 2013, SI 2013/1956, art 2, Schedule, para 1.

Word omitted from para (d) revoked, and para (f) and the word immediately preceding it added, by the Employment Act 2002 (Dispute Resolution) Regulations 2004, SI 2004/752, reg 17(e).

Word omitted from para (e) revoked, and para (g) and the word immediately preceding it added, by the Employment Equality (Age) Regulations 2006, SI 2006/1031, reg 49(1), Sch 8, Pt 2, para 57.

Employment Act 2002 (Dispute Resolution) Regulations 2004; Employment Equality (Age) Regulations 2006: lapsed and revoked respectively (both subject to transitional provisions).

[2.272]

3 Continuity of employment where employee re-engaged

(1) The provisions of this regulation shall have effect to preserve the continuity of a person's period of employment for the purposes of—

(a) Chapter I of Part XIV of the Employment Rights Act 1996 (continuous employment), and

(b) that Chapter as applied by subsection (2) of section 282 of the Trade Union and Labour Relations (Consolidation) Act 1992 for the purposes of that section.

(2) If in consequence of any action to which these Regulations apply a dismissed employee is reinstated or re-employed by his employer or by a successor or associated employer of the employer—

(a) the continuity of that employee's period of employment shall be preserved, and

(b) the period beginning with the date on which the dismissal takes effect and ending with the date of reinstatement or re-engagement shall count in the computation of the employee's period of continuous employment.

[2.273]

4 Exclusion of operation of section 214 of the Employment Rights Act 1996 where redundancy or equivalent payment repaid

(1) Section 214 of the Employment Rights Act 1996 (continuity broken where employee re-employed after the making of a redundancy payment or equivalent payment) shall not apply where—

(a) in consequence of any action to which these Regulations apply a dismissed employee is reinstated or re-employed by his employer or by a successor or associated employer of the employer,

(b) the terms upon which he is so reinstated or re-engaged include provision for him to repay the amount of a redundancy payment or an equivalent payment paid in respect of the relevant dismissal, and

(c) that provision is complied with.

(2) For the purposes of this regulation the cases in which a redundancy payment shall be treated as having been paid are the cases mentioned in section 214(5) of the Employment Rights Act 1996.

WORKING TIME REGULATIONS 1998

(SI 1998/1833)

NOTES

Made: 30 July 1998.

Authority: European Communities Act 1972, s 2(2).

Commencement: 1 October 1998.

Note: with regard to the authority for these Regulations, note that the European Communities Act 1972 is repealed by the European Union (Withdrawal) Act 2018, s 1, as from exit day (as defined in s 20 of that Act); but note also that provision is made for the continuation in force of any subordinate legislation made under the authority of s 2(2) of the 1972 Act by s 2 of the 2018 Act at **[1.2240]**, subject to the provisions of s 5 of, and Sch 1 to, the 2018 Act at **[1.2243]**, **[1.2253]**.

These Regulations are the domestic implementation of Council Directive 93/104/EC on working time, and (in part) of Council Directive 94/33/EC on the protection of young people at work at **[3.155]**. The 1993 Directive was repealed by Council Directive 2003/88/EC concerning certain aspects of the organisation of working time at **[3.330]**, which consolidates the 1993 Directive and a subsequent amending Directive, as from 2 August 2004.

Conciliation: employment tribunal proceedings under reg 30 are "relevant proceedings" for the purposes of the conciliation provisions contained in the Employment Tribunals Act 1996, ss 18–18C; see s 18(1)(j) of the 1996 Act at **[1.757]**.

Employment Appeal Tribunal: an appeal lies to the Employment Appeal Tribunal on any question of law arising from any decision of, or in any proceedings before, an employment tribunal under or by virtue of these Regulations; see the Employment Tribunals Act 1996, s 21(1)(h) at **[1.764]**.

The rights conferred by these Regulations are "relevant statutory rights" for the purposes of the Employment Rights Act 1996, s 104 (dismissal on grounds of assertion of statutory right); see s 104(4)(d) of that Act at **[1.1015]**.

See *Harvey* CI(1).

ARRANGEMENT OF REGULATIONS

PART I
GENERAL

PART II
RIGHTS AND OBLIGATIONS CONCERNING WORKING TIME

PART III
EXCEPTIONS

PART IV
MISCELLANEOUS

PART V
SPECIAL CLASSES OF PERSON

SCHEDULES

PART I
GENERAL

[2.274]
1 Citation, commencement and extent

(1) These Regulations may be cited as the Working Time Regulations 1998 and shall come into force on 1st October 1998.

(2) These Regulations extend to Great Britain only.

[2.275]
2 Interpretation

(1) In these Regulations—

"the 1996 Act" means the Employment Rights Act 1996;

"adult worker" means a worker who has attained the age of 18;

"the armed forces" means any of the naval, military and air forces of the Crown;

"calendar year" means the period of twelve months beginning with 1st January in any year;

"the civil protection services" includes the police, fire brigades and ambulance services, the security and intelligence services, customs and immigration officers, the prison service, the coastguard, and lifeboat crew and other voluntary rescue services;

"collective agreement" means a collective agreement within the meaning of section 178 of the Trade Union and Labour Relations (Consolidation) Act 1992, the trade union parties to which are independent trade unions within the meaning of section 5 of that Act;

"day" means a period of 24 hours beginning at midnight;

"employer", in relation to a worker, means the person by whom the worker is (or, where the employment has ceased, was) employed;

"employment", in relation to a worker, means employment under his contract, and "employed" shall be construed accordingly;

["fishing vessel" has the same meaning as in section 313 of the Merchant Shipping Act 1995;

"mobile worker" means any worker employed as a member of travelling or flying personnel by an undertaking which operates transport services for passengers or goods by road or air;]

"night time", in relation to a worker, means a period—

(a) the duration of which is not less than seven hours, and

(b) which includes the period between midnight and 5 am,

which is determined for the purposes of these Regulations by a relevant agreement, or, in default of such a determination, the period between 11 pm and 6 am;

"night work" means work during night time;

"night worker" means a worker—

(a) who, as a normal course, works at least three hours of his daily working time during night time, or

(b) who is likely, during night time, to work at least such proportion of his annual working time as may be specified for the purposes of these Regulations in a collective agreement or a workforce agreement;

and, for the purpose of paragraph (a) of this definition, a person works hours as a normal course (without prejudice to the generality of that expression) if he works such hours on the majority of days on which he works;

["offshore work" means work performed mainly on or from offshore installations (including drilling rigs), directly or indirectly in connection with the exploration, extraction or exploitation of mineral resources, including hydrocarbons, and diving in connection with such activities, whether performed from an offshore installation or a vessel[, including any such work performed in the territorial waters of the United Kingdom adjacent to Great Britain or in any area (except one or part of one in which the law of Northern Ireland applies) designated under section 1(7) of the Continental Shelf Act 1964];]

"relevant agreement", in relation to a worker, means a workforce agreement which applies to him, any provision of a collective agreement which forms part of a contract between him and his employer, or any other agreement in writing which is legally enforceable as between the worker and his employer;

"relevant training" means work experience provided pursuant to a training course or programme, training for employment, or both, other than work experience or training—

(a) the immediate provider of which is an educational institution or a person whose main business is the provision of training, and

(b) which is provided on a course run by that institution or person;

"rest period", in relation to a worker, means a period which is not working time, other than a rest break or leave to which the worker is entitled under these Regulations;

Part 2 Statutory Instruments

["the restricted period", in relation to a worker, means the period between 10 pm and 6 am or, where the worker's contract provides for him to work after 10 pm, the period between 11 pm and 7 am;]

["ship" has the same meaning as in section 313 of the Merchant Shipping Act 1995;]

"worker" means an individual who has entered into or works under (or, where the employment has ceased, worked under)—

(a) a contract of employment; or

(b) any other contract, whether express or implied and (if it is express) whether oral or in writing, whereby the individual undertakes to do or perform personally any work or services for another party to the contract whose status is not by virtue of the contract that of a client or customer of any profession or business undertaking carried on by the individual;

and any reference to a worker's contract shall be construed accordingly;

"worker employed in agriculture" has the same meaning as in the Agricultural Wages Act 1948 or the Agricultural Wages (Scotland) Act 1949, and a reference to a worker partly employed in agriculture [means, in relation to Wales, an agricultural worker within the meaning of section 18 of the Agricultural Sector (Wales) Act 2014 and otherwise] is to a worker employed in agriculture whose employer also employs him for non-agricultural purposes;

"workforce agreement" means an agreement between an employer and workers employed by him or their representatives in respect of which the conditions set out in Schedule 1 to these Regulations are satisfied;

"working time", in relation to a worker, means—

(a) any period during which he is working, at his employer's disposal and carrying out his activity or duties,

(b) any period during which he is receiving relevant training, and

(c) any additional period which is to be treated as working time for the purpose of these Regulations under a relevant agreement;

and "work" shall be construed accordingly;

"Working Time Directive" means Council Directive 93/104/EC of 23rd November 1993 concerning certain aspects of the organization of working time;

"young worker" means a worker who has attained the age of 15 but not the age of 18 and who, as respects England and Wales, is over compulsory school age (construed in accordance with section 8 of the Education Act 1996) and, as respects Scotland, is over school age (construed in accordance with section 31 of the Education (Scotland) Act 1980), and

"Young Workers Directive" means Council Directive 94/33/EC of 22nd June 1994 on the protection of young people at work.

(2) In the absence of a definition in these Regulations, words and expressions used in particular provisions which are also used in corresponding provisions of the Working Time Directive or the Young Workers Directive have the same meaning as they have in those corresponding provisions.

(3) In these Regulations—

(a) a reference to a numbered regulation is to the regulation in these Regulations bearing that number;

(b) a reference in a regulation to a numbered paragraph is to the paragraph in that regulation bearing that number; and

(c) a reference in a paragraph to a lettered sub-paragraph is to the sub-paragraph in that paragraph bearing that letter.

NOTES

Para (1): definitions "fishing vessel", "mobile worker", "offshore work", and "ship" inserted by the Working Time (Amendment) Regulations 2003, SI 2003/1684, regs 2, 3; words in square brackets in definition "offshore work" inserted by the Working Time (Amendment) (No 2) Regulations 2006, SI 2006/2389, reg 2; definition "the restricted period" inserted by the Working Time (Amendment) Regulations 2002, SI 2002/3128, regs 2, 3; in definition "worker employed in agriculture", words in square brackets inserted, in relation to Wales, by the Agricultural Sector (Wales) Act 2014, s 11(1), (2), as from 30 July 2014.

PART II
RIGHTS AND OBLIGATIONS CONCERNING WORKING TIME

[2.276]
3 General

[(1)] The provisions of this Part have effect subject to the exceptions provided for in Part III of these Regulations.

[(2) Where, in this Part, separate provision is made as respects the same matter in relation to workers generally and to young workers, the provision relating to workers generally applies only to adult workers and those young workers to whom, by virtue of any exception in Part 3, the provision relating to young workers does not apply.]

NOTES

Para (1) numbered as such, and para (2) added, by the Working Time (Amendment) Regulations 2002, SI 2002/3128, regs 2, 4.

[2.277]

4 Maximum weekly working time

(1) [Unless his employer has first obtained the worker's agreement in writing to perform such work], a worker's working time, including overtime, in any reference period which is applicable in his case shall not exceed an average of 48 hours for each seven days.

(2) An employer shall take all reasonable steps, in keeping with the need to protect the health and safety of workers, to ensure that the limit specified in paragraph (1) is complied with in the case of each worker employed by him in relation to whom it applies [and shall keep up-to-date records of all workers who carry out work to which it does not apply by reason of the fact that the employer has obtained the worker's agreement as mentioned in paragraph (1)].

(3) Subject to paragraphs (4) and (5) and any agreement under regulation 23(b), the reference periods which apply in the case of a worker are—

(a) where a relevant agreement provides for the application of this regulation in relation to successive periods of 17 weeks, each such period, or

(b) in any other case, any period of 17 weeks in the course of his employment.

(4) Where a worker has worked for his employer for less than 17 weeks, the reference period applicable in his case is the period that has elapsed since he started work for his employer.

(5) Paragraphs (3) and (4) shall apply to a worker who is excluded from the scope of certain provisions of these Regulations by regulation 21 as if for each reference to 17 weeks there were substituted a reference to 26 weeks.

(6) For the purposes of this regulation, a worker's average working time for each seven days during a reference period shall be determined according to the formula—

$$A + B / C$$

where—

A is the aggregate number of hours comprised in the worker's working time during the course of the reference period;

B is the aggregate number of hours comprised in his working time during the course of the period beginning immediately after the end of the reference period and ending when the number of days in that subsequent period on which he has worked equals the number of excluded days during the reference period; and

C is the number of weeks in the reference period.

(7) In paragraph (6), "excluded days" means days comprised in—

(a) any period of annual leave taken by the worker in exercise of his entitlement under regulation 13;

(b) any period of sick leave taken by the worker;

(c) any period of maternity [paternity, adoption or parental] leave taken by the worker; and

(d) any period in respect of which the limit specified in paragraph (1) did not apply in relation to the worker [by reason of the fact that the employer has obtained the worker's agreement as mentioned in paragraph (1)].

NOTES

Para (1): words in square brackets substituted by the Working Time Regulations 1999, SI 1999/3372, regs 1(1), 3(1)(a).

Para (2): words in square brackets added by SI 1999/3372, regs 1(1), 3(1)(b).

Para (7): words in first pair of square brackets inserted by the Working Time (Amendment) Regulations 2002, SI 2002/3128, regs 2, 5; words in second pair of square brackets substituted by the Working Time Regulations 1999, SI 1999/3372, regs 1(1), 3(1)(a), (c).

[2.278]

5 Agreement to exclude the maximum

(1) . . .

(2) An agreement for the purposes of [regulation 4]—

(a) may either relate to a specified period or apply indefinitely; and

(b) subject to any provision in the agreement for a different period of notice, shall be terminable by the worker by giving not less than seven days' notice to his employer in writing.

(3) Where an agreement for the purposes of [regulation 4] makes provision for the termination of the agreement after a period of notice, the notice period provided for shall not exceed three months.

(4) . . .

NOTES

Paras (1), (4): revoked by the Working Time Regulations 1999, SI 1999/3372, regs 1(1), 3(2)(a).

Paras (2), (3): words in square brackets substituted by SI 1999/3372, regs 1(1), 3(2)(b).

[2.279]

[5A Maximum working time for young workers

(1) A young worker's working time shall not exceed—

(a) eight hours a day, or

(b) 40 hours a week.

(2) If, on any day, or, as the case may be, during any week, a young worker is employed by more than one employer, his working time shall be determined for the purpose of paragraph (1) by aggregating the number of hours worked by him for each employer.

(3) For the purposes of paragraphs (1) and (2), a week starts at midnight between Sunday and Monday.

(4) An employer shall take all reasonable steps, in keeping with the need to protect the health and safety of workers, to ensure that the limits specified in paragraph (1) are complied with in the case of each worker employed by him in relation to whom they apply.]

NOTES

Inserted by the Working Time (Amendment) Regulations 2002, SI 2002/3128, regs 2, 6.

[2.280]

6 Length of night work

(1) A night worker's normal hours of work in any reference period which is applicable in his case shall not exceed an average of eight hours for each 24 hours.

(2) An employer shall take all reasonable steps, in keeping with the need to protect the health and safety of workers, to ensure that the limit specified in paragraph (1) is complied with in the case of each night worker employed by him.

(3) The reference periods which apply in the case of a night worker are—

(a) where a relevant agreement provides for the application of this regulation in relation to successive periods of 17 weeks, each such period, or

(b) in any other case, any period of 17 weeks in the course of his employment.

(4) Where a worker has worked for his employer for less than 17 weeks, the reference period applicable in his case is the period that has elapsed since he started work for his employer.

(5) For the purposes of this regulation, a night worker's average normal hours of work for each 24 hours during a reference period shall be determined according to the formula—

$$A / B - C$$

where—

A is the number of hours during the reference period which are normal working hours for that worker;

B is the number of days during the reference period, and

C is the total number of hours during the reference period comprised in rest periods spent by the worker in pursuance of his entitlement under regulation 11, divided by 24.

(6) . . .

(7) An employer shall ensure that no night worker employed by him whose work involves special hazards or heavy physical or mental strain works for more than eight hours in any 24-hour period during which the night worker performs night work.

(8) For the purposes of paragraph (7), the work of a night worker shall be regarded as involving special hazards or heavy physical or mental strain if—

(a) it is identified as such in—

(i) a collective agreement, or

(ii) a workforce agreement,

which takes account of the specific effects and hazards of night work, or

(b) it is recognised in a risk assessment made by the employer under [regulation 3 of the Management of Health and Safety at Work Regulations 1999] as involving a significant risk to the health or safety of workers employed by him.

NOTES

Para (6): revoked by the Working Time (Amendment) Regulations 2002, SI 2002/3128, regs 2, 7.

Para (8): words in square brackets substituted by the Management of Health and Safety at Work Regulations 1999, SI 1999/3242, reg 29(2), Sch 2.

[2.281]

[6A Night work by young workers

An employer shall ensure that no young worker employed by him works during the restricted period.]

NOTES

Inserted by the Working Time (Amendment) Regulations 2002, SI 2002/3128, regs 2, 8.

[2.282]

7 Health assessment and transfer of night workers to day work

(1) An employer—

(a) shall not assign an adult worker to work which is to be undertaken during periods such that the worker will become a night worker unless—

(i) the employer has ensured that the worker will have the opportunity of a free health assessment before he takes up the assignment; or

(ii) the worker had a health assessment before being assigned to work to be undertaken during such periods on an earlier occasion, and the employer has no reason to believe that that assessment is no longer valid, and

(b) shall ensure that each night worker employed by him has the opportunity of a free health assessment at regular intervals of whatever duration may be appropriate in his case.

(2) Subject to paragraph (4), an employer—

(a) shall not assign a young worker to work during [the restricted period] unless—

(i) the employer has ensured that the young worker will have the opportunity of a free assessment of his health and capacities before he takes up the assignment; or

(ii) the young worker had an assessment of his health and capacities before being assigned to work during the restricted period on an earlier occasion, and the employer has no reason to believe that that assessment is no longer valid; and

(b) shall ensure that each young worker employed by him and assigned to work during the restricted period has the opportunity of a free assessment of his health and capacities at regular intervals of whatever duration may be appropriate in his case.

(3) For the purposes of paragraphs (1) and (2), an assessment is free if it is at no cost to the worker to whom it relates.

(4) The requirements in paragraph (2) do not apply in a case where the work a young worker is assigned to do is of an exceptional nature.

(5) No person shall disclose an assessment made for the purposes of this regulation to any person other than the worker to whom it relates, unless—

(a) the worker has given his consent in writing to the disclosure, or

(b) the disclosure is confined to a statement that the assessment shows the worker to be fit—

(i) in a case where paragraph (1)(a)(i) or (2)(a)(i) applies, to take up an assignment, or

(ii) in a case where paragraph (1)(b) or (2)(b) applies, to continue to undertake an assignment.

(6) Where—

(a) a registered medical practitioner has advised an employer that a worker employed by the employer is suffering from health problems which the practitioner considers to be connected with the fact that the worker performs night work, and

(b) it is possible for the employer to transfer the worker to work—

(i) to which the worker is suited, and

(ii) which is to be undertaken during periods such that the worker will cease to be a night worker,

the employer shall transfer the worker accordingly.

NOTES

Para (2): words in square brackets substituted by the Working Time (Amendment) Regulations 2002, SI 2002/3128, regs 2, 9.

[2.283]

8 Pattern of work

Where the pattern according to which an employer organizes work is such as to put the health and safety of a worker employed by him at risk, in particular because the work is monotonous or the work-rate is predetermined, the employer shall ensure that the worker is given adequate rest breaks.

[2.284]

9 Records

An employer shall—

(a) keep records which are adequate to show whether the limits specified in regulations 4(1)[, 5A(1)] and 6(1) and (7) and the requirements in regulations [6A and] 7(1) and (2) are being complied with in the case of each worker employed by him in relation to whom they apply; and

(b) retain such records for two years from the date on which they were made.

NOTES

Words in square brackets inserted by the Working Time (Amendment) Regulations 2002, SI 2002/3128, regs 2, 10.

[2.285]

10 Daily rest

(1) [A worker] is entitled to a rest period of not less than eleven consecutive hours in each 24-hour period during which he works for his employer.

(2) Subject to paragraph (3), a young worker is entitled to a rest period of not less than twelve consecutive hours in each 24-hour period during which he works for his employer.

(3) The minimum rest period provided for in paragraph (2) may be interrupted in the case of activities involving periods of work that are split up over the day or of short duration.

NOTES

Para (1): words in square brackets substituted by the Working Time (Amendment) Regulations 2002, SI 2002/3128, regs 2, 11.

[2.286]

11 Weekly rest period

(1) Subject to paragraph (2), [a worker] is entitled to an uninterrupted rest period of not less than 24 hours in each seven-day period during which he works for his employer.

(2) If his employer so determines, [a worker] shall be entitled to either—

(a) two uninterrupted rest periods each of not less than 24 hours in each 14-day period during which he works for his employer; or

(b) one uninterrupted rest period of not less than 48 hours in each such 14-day period, in place of the entitlement provided for in paragraph (1).

(3) Subject to paragraph (8), a young worker is entitled to a rest period of not less than 48 hours in each seven-day period during which he works for his employer.

(4) For the purpose of paragraphs (1) to (3), a seven-day period or (as the case may be) 14-day period shall be taken to begin—

(a) at such times on such days as may be provided for the purposes of this regulation in a relevant agreement; or

(b) where there are no provisions of a relevant agreement which apply, at the start of each week or (as the case may be) every other week.

(5) In a case where, in accordance with paragraph (4), 14-day periods are to be taken to begin at the start of every other week, the first such period applicable in the case of a particular worker shall be taken to begin—

(a) if the worker's employment began on or before the date on which these Regulations come into force, on 5th October 1998; or

(b) if the worker's employment begins after the date on which these Regulations come into force, at the start of the week in which that employment begins.

(6) For the purposes of paragraphs (4) and (5), a week starts at midnight between Sunday and Monday.

(7) The minimum rest period to which [a worker] is entitled under paragraph (1) or (2) shall not include any part of a rest period to which the worker is entitled under regulation 10(1), except where this is justified by objective or technical reasons or reasons concerning the organization of work.

(8) The minimum rest period to which a young worker is entitled under paragraph (3)—

(a) may be interrupted in the case of activities involving periods of work that are split up over the day or are of short duration; and

(b) may be reduced where this is justified by technical or organization reasons, but not to less than 36 consecutive hours.

NOTES

Paras (1), (2), (7): words in square brackets substituted by the Working Time (Amendment) Regulations 2002, SI 2002/3128, regs 2, 12.

[2.287]

12 Rest breaks

(1) Where [a worker's] daily working time is more than six hours, he is entitled to a rest break.

(2) The details of the rest break to which [a worker] is entitled under paragraph (1), including its duration and the terms on which it is granted, shall be in accordance with any provisions for the purposes of this regulation which are contained in a collective agreement or a workforce agreement.

(3) Subject to the provisions of any applicable collective agreement or workforce agreement, the rest break provided for in paragraph (1) is an uninterrupted period of not less than 20 minutes, and the worker is entitled to spend it away from his workstation if he has one.

(4) Where a young worker's daily working time is more than four and a half hours, he is entitled to a rest break of at least 30 minutes, which shall be consecutive if possible, and he is entitled to spend it away from his workstation if he has one.

(5) If, on any day, a young worker is employed by more than one employer, his daily working time shall be determined for the purpose of paragraph (4) by aggregating the number of hours worked by him for each employer.

NOTES

Paras (1), (2): words in square brackets substituted by the Working Time (Amendment) Regulations 2002, SI 2002/3128, regs 2, 13.

[2.288]

13 Entitlement to annual leave

[(1) Subject to paragraph (5), a worker is entitled to four weeks' annual leave in each leave year.]

(2) . . .

(3) A worker's leave year, for the purposes of this regulation, begins—

(a) on such date during the calendar year as may be provided for in a relevant agreement; or

(b) where there are no provisions of a relevant agreement which apply—

(i) if the worker's employment began on or before 1st October 1998, on that date and each subsequent anniversary of that date; or

(ii) if the worker's employment begins after 1st October 1998, on the date on which that employment begins and each subsequent anniversary of that date.

(4) Paragraph (3) does not apply to a worker to whom Schedule 2 applies (workers employed in agriculture [in Wales or Scotland]) except where, in the case of a worker partly employed in agriculture [in Wales or Scotland], a relevant agreement so provides.

(5) Where the date on which a worker's employment begins is later than the date on which (by virtue of a relevant agreement) his first leave year begins, the leave to which he is entitled in that leave year is a proportion of the period applicable under [paragraph (1)] equal to the proportion of that leave year remaining on the date on which his employment begins.

(6)–(8) . . .

(9) Leave to which a worker is entitled under this regulation may be taken in instalments, but—

- (a) it may only be taken in the leave year in respect of which it is due, and
- (b) it may not be replaced by a payment in lieu except where the worker's employment is terminated.

NOTES

Para (1): substituted by the Working Time (Amendment) Regulations 2001, SI 2001/3256, art 2(1), (2).

Paras (2), (7), (8): revoked by SI 2001/3256, art 2(1), (3), (6).

Para (4): words in square brackets inserted by the Working Time (Amendment) (England) Regulations 2013, SI 2013/2228, regs 2(1), (2), 3, except in relation to a worker employed in agriculture in England in relation to that employment if (a) that employment commenced before 1 October 2013, and (b) the worker remains so employed under that employment.

Para (5): words in square brackets substituted by SI 2001/3256, art 2(1), (4).

Para (6): revoked by the Working Time (Amendment) Regulations 2007, SI 2007/2079, reg 2(1), (4).

[2.289]

[13A Entitlement to additional annual leave

(1) Subject to regulation 26A and paragraphs (3) and (5), a worker is entitled in each leave year to a period of additional leave determined in accordance with paragraph (2).

(2) The period of additional leave to which a worker is entitled under paragraph (1) is—

- (a) in any leave year beginning on or after 1st October 2007 but before 1st April 2008, 0.8 weeks;
- (b) in any leave year beginning before 1st October 2007, a proportion of 0.8 weeks equivalent to the proportion of the year beginning on 1st October 2007 which would have elapsed at the end of that leave year;
- (c) in any leave year beginning on 1st April 2008, 0.8 weeks;
- (d) in any leave year beginning after 1st April 2008 but before 1st April 2009, 0.8 weeks and a proportion of another 0.8 weeks equivalent to the proportion of the year beginning on 1st April 2009 which would have elapsed at the end of that leave year;
- (e) in any leave year beginning on or after 1st April 2009, 1.6 weeks.

(3) The aggregate entitlement provided for in paragraph (2) and regulation 13(1) is subject to a maximum of 28 days.

(4) A worker's leave year begins for the purposes of this regulation on the same date as the worker's leave year begins for the purposes of regulation 13.

(5) Where the date on which a worker's employment begins is later than the date on which his first leave year begins, the additional leave to which he is entitled in that leave year is a proportion of the period applicable under paragraph (2) equal to the proportion of that leave year remaining on the date on which his employment begins.

(6) Leave to which a worker is entitled under this regulation may be taken in instalments, but it may not be replaced by a payment in lieu except where—

- (a) the worker's employment is terminated; or
- (b) the leave is an entitlement that arises under paragraph (2)(a), (b) or (c); or
- (c) the leave is an entitlement to 0.8 weeks that arises under paragraph (2)(d) in respect of that part of the leave year which would have elapsed before 1st April 2009.

(7) A relevant agreement may provide for any leave to which a worker is entitled under this regulation to be carried forward into the leave year immediately following the leave year in respect of which it is due.

(8) This regulation does not apply to workers to whom the Agricultural Wages (Scotland) Act 1949 applies (as that Act had effect on 1 July 1999).]

NOTES

Inserted by the Working Time (Amendment) Regulations 2007, SI 2007/2079, reg 2(1), (2).

[2.290]

14 Compensation related to entitlement to leave

(1) This regulation applies where—

- (a) a worker's employment is terminated during the course of his leave year, and
- (b) on the date on which the termination takes effect ("the termination date"), the proportion he has taken of the leave to which he is entitled in the leave year under [regulation 13] [and regulation 13A] differs from the proportion of the leave year which has expired.

(2) Where the proportion of leave taken by the worker is less than the proportion of the leave year which has expired, his employer shall make him a payment in lieu of leave in accordance with paragraph (3).

(3) The payment due under paragraph (2) shall be—

(a) such sum as may be provided for the purposes of this regulation in a relevant agreement, or

(b) where there are no provisions of a relevant agreement which apply, a sum equal to the amount that would be due to the worker under regulation 16 in respect of a period of leave determined according to the formula—

$$(A \times B) - C$$

where—

A is the period of leave to which the worker is entitled under [regulation 13] [and regulation 13A];

B is the proportion of the worker's leave year which expired before the termination date, and

C is the period of leave taken by the worker between the start of the leave year and the termination date.

(4) A relevant agreement may provide that, where the proportion of leave taken by the worker exceeds the proportion of the leave year which has expired, he shall compensate his employer, whether by a payment, by undertaking additional work or otherwise.

NOTES

Paras (1), (3): words in first pair of square brackets substituted by the Working Time (Amendment) Regulations 2001, SI 2001/3256, art 3; words in second pair of square brackets inserted by the Working Time (Amendment) Regulations 2007, SI 2007/2079, reg 2(1), (5).

[2.291]

15 Dates on which leave is taken

(1) A worker may take leave to which he is entitled under [regulation 13] [and regulation 13A] on such days as he may elect by giving notice to his employer in accordance with paragraph (3), subject to any requirement imposed on him by his employer under paragraph (2).

(2) A worker's employer may require the worker—

(a) to take leave to which the worker is entitled under [regulation 13] [or regulation 13A]; or

(b) not to take such leave,

on particular days, by giving notice to the worker in accordance with paragraph (3).

(3) A notice under paragraph (1) or (2)—

(a) may relate to all or part of the leave to which a worker is entitled in a leave year;

(b) shall specify the days on which leave is or (as the case may be) is not to be taken and, where the leave on a particular day is to be in respect of only part of the day, its duration; and

(c) shall be given to the employer or, as the case may be, the worker before the relevant date.

(4) The relevant date, for the purposes of paragraph (3), is the date—

(a) in the case of a notice under paragraph (1) or (2)(a), twice as many days in advance of the earliest day specified in the notice as the number of days or part-days to which the notice relates, and

(b) in the case of a notice under paragraph (2)(b), as many days in advance of the earliest day so specified as the number of days or part-days to which the notice relates.

(5) Any right or obligation under paragraphs (1) to (4) may be varied or excluded by a relevant agreement.

(6) This regulation does not apply to a worker to whom Schedule 2 applies (workers employed in agriculture [in Wales or Scotland]) except where, in the case of a worker partly employed in agriculture [in Wales or Scotland], a relevant agreement so provides.

NOTES

Paras (1), (2): words in first pair of square brackets substituted by the Working Time (Amendment) Regulations 2001, SI 2001/3256, art 3; words in second pair of square brackets inserted by the Working Time (Amendment) Regulations 2007, SI 2007/2079, reg 2(1), (5), (6).

Para (6): words in square brackets inserted by the Working Time (Amendment) (England) Regulations 2013, SI 2013/2228, regs 2(1), (3), 3, except in relation to a worker employed in agriculture in England in relation to that employment if (a) that employment commenced before 1 October 2013, and (b) the worker remains so employed under that employment.

[2.292]

[15A Leave during the first year of employment

(1) During the first year of his employment, the amount of leave a worker may take at any time in exercise of his entitlement under regulation 13 [or regulation 13A] is limited to the amount which is deemed to have accrued in his case at that time under paragraph (2) [or (2A)], as modified under paragraph (3) in a case where that paragraph applies, less the amount of leave (if any) that he has already taken during that year.

(2) For the purposes of paragraph (1), [in the case of workers to whom the Agricultural Wages (Scotland) Act 1949 applies,] leave is deemed to accrue over the course of the worker's first year of employment, at the rate of one-twelfth of the amount specified in regulation 13(1) on the first day of each month of that year.

[(2A) Except where paragraph (2) applies, for the purposes of paragraph (1), leave is deemed to accrue over the course of the worker's first year of employment, at the rate of one-twelfth of the amount specified in regulation 13(1) and regulation 13A(2), subject to the limit contained in regulation 13A(3), on the first day of each month of that year.]

(3) Where the amount of leave that has accrued in a particular case includes a fraction of a day other than a half-day, the fraction shall be treated as a half-day if it is less than a half-day and as a whole day if it is more than a half-day.

(4) This regulation does not apply to a worker whose employment began on or before 25th October 2001.]

NOTES

Inserted by the Working Time (Amendment) Regulations 2001, SI 2001/3256, art 4.

Paras (1), (2): words in square brackets inserted by the Working Time (Amendment) Regulations 2007, SI 2007/2079, reg 2(1), (6)–(8).

Para (2A): inserted by SI 2007/2079, reg 2(1), (9).

[2.293]

16 Payment in respect of periods of leave

(1) A worker is entitled to be paid in respect of any period of annual leave to which he is entitled under regulation 13 [and regulation 13A], at the rate of a week's pay in respect of each week of leave.

(2) Sections 221 to 224 of the 1996 Act shall apply for the purpose of determining the amount of a week's pay for the purposes of this regulation, subject to the modifications set out in paragraph (3) [and the exception in paragraph (3A)].

(3) The provisions referred to in paragraph (2) shall apply—

- (a) as if references to the employee were references to the worker;
- (b) as if references to the employee's contract of employment were references to the worker's contract;
- (c) as if the calculation date were the first day of the period of leave in question; *and*
- (d) as if the references to sections 227 and 228 did not apply.
- [(e) subject to the exception in sub-paragraph (f)(ii), as if in sections 221(3), 222(3) and (4), 223(2) and 224(2) and (3) references to twelve were references to—
  - (i) in the case of a worker who on the calculation date has been employed by their employer for less than 52 complete weeks, the number of complete weeks for which the worker has been employed, or
  - (ii) in any other case, 52; and
- (f) in any case where section 223(2) or 224(3) applies as if—
  - (i) account were not to be taken of remuneration in weeks preceding the period of 104 weeks ending—
    - (aa) where the calculation date is the last day of a week, with that week, and
    - (bb) otherwise, with the last complete week before the calculation date; and
  - (ii) the period of weeks required for the purposes of sections 221(3), 222(3) and (4) and 224(2) was the number of weeks of which account is taken.]

[(3A) In any case where applying sections 221 to 224 of the 1996 Act subject to the modifications set out in paragraph (3) gives no weeks of which account is taken, the amount of a week's pay is not to be determined by applying those sections, but is the amount which fairly represents a week's pay having regard to the considerations specified in section 228(3) as if references in that section to the employee were references to the worker.

(3B) For the purposes of paragraphs (3) and (3A) "week" means, in relation to a worker whose remuneration is calculated weekly by a week ending with a day other than Saturday, a week ending with that other day and, in relation to any other worker, a week ending with Saturday.]

(4) A right to payment under paragraph (1) does not affect any right of a worker to remuneration under his contract ("contractual remuneration") [(and paragraph (1) does not confer a right under that contract)].

(5) Any contractual remuneration paid to a worker in respect of a period of leave goes towards discharging any liability of the employer to make payments under this regulation in respect of that period; and, conversely, any payment of remuneration under this regulation in respect of a period goes towards discharging any liability of the employer to pay contractual remuneration in respect of that period.

NOTES

Para (1): words in square brackets inserted by the Working Time (Amendment) Regulations 2007, SI 2007/2079, reg 2(1), (5).

Para (2): words in square brackets added by the Employment Rights (Employment Particulars and Paid Annual Leave) (Amendment) Regulations 2018, SI 2018/1378, reg 10(1), (2), as from 6 April 2020.

Para (3): word "and" in italics in sub-para (c) revoked and sub-paras (e), (f) inserted, by SI 2018/1378, reg 10(1), (3), as from 6 April 2020.

Paras (3A), (3B): inserted by SI 2018/1378, reg 10(1), (4), as from 6 April 2020.

Para (4): words in square brackets added by the Deduction from Wages (Limitation) Regulations 2014, SI 2014/3322, reg 3, as from 8 January 2015.

Part 2 Statutory Instruments

[2.294]
17 Entitlements under other provisions

Where during any period a worker is entitled to a rest period, rest break or annual leave both under a provision of these Regulations and under a separate provision (including a provision of his contract), he may not exercise the two rights separately, but may, in taking a rest period, break or leave during that period, take advantage of whichever right is, in any particular respect, the more favourable.

PART III
EXCEPTIONS

[2.295]
[18 Excluded sectors

[(1) These Regulations do not apply—

[(a) to workers to whom [the Merchant Shipping (Maritime Labour Convention) (Hours of Work) Regulations 2018] apply;]

[(b) to workers to whom the Fishing Vessels (Working Time: Sea-fishermen) Regulations 2004 apply;] or

[(c) to workers to whom the Merchant Shipping (Working Time: Inland Waterways) Regulations 2003 apply].

(2) Regulations 4(1) and (2), 6(1), (2) and (7), 7(1) and (6), 8, 10(1), 11(1) and (2), 12(1), 13[, 13A] and 16 do not apply—

(a) where characteristics peculiar to certain specific services such as the armed forces or the police, or to certain specific activities in the civil protection services, inevitably conflict with the provisions of these Regulations;

[(aa) to workers to whom the Civil Aviation (Working Time) Regulations 2004 apply;]

(b) to workers to whom the European Agreement on the organisation of working time of mobile staff in civil aviation concluded on 22nd March 2000 and implemented by Council Directive 2000/79/EC of 27th November 2000 applies; or

(c) to the activities of workers who are doctors in training.

(3) Paragraph (2)(c) has effect only until 31st July 2004.

(4) Regulations 4(1) and (2), 6(1), (2) and (7), 8, 10(1), 11(1) and (2) and 12(1) do not apply to workers to whom *Directive 2002/15/EC of the European Parliament and of the Council on the organisation of the working time of persons performing mobile road transport activities, dated 11th March 2002 applies*.]

[(5) Regulation 24 does not apply to workers to whom the Cross-border Railways Services (Working Time) Regulations 2008 apply.]]

NOTES

Substituted by the Working Time (Amendment) Regulations 2003, SI 2003/1684, regs 2, 4.

Para (1): sub-para (a) substituted by the Merchant Shipping (Maritime Labour Convention) (Hours of Work) (Amendment) Regulations 2014, SI 2014/308, reg 3, Schedule, para 5; words in square brackets in sub-para (a) substituted by the Merchant Shipping (Maritime Labour Convention) (Hours of Work) Regulations 2018, SI 2018/58, reg 31, Sch 2, para 5, as from 6 April 2018; sub-para (b) substituted by the Fishing Vessels (Working Time: Sea-fishermen) Regulations 2004, SI 2004/1713, reg 21, Sch 2, para 5; sub-para (c) substituted by the Merchant Shipping (Working Time: Inland Waterways) Regulations 2003, SI 2003/3049, reg 20, Sch 2, para 6.

Para (2): figure in first pair of square brackets inserted by the Working Time (Amendment) Regulations 2007, SI 2007/2079, reg 2(1), (10). Sub-para (aa) inserted and sub-para (b) revoked, by the Employment Rights (Amendment) (EU Exit) Regulations 2019, SI 2019/535, reg 2(1), Sch 1, Pt 2, paras 7, 8(a), as from exit day (as defined in the European Union (Withdrawal) Act 2018, s 20).

Para (4): for the words in italics there are substituted the words "the Road Transport (Working Time) Regulations 2005 apply", by SI 2019/535, reg 2(1), Sch 1, Pt 2, paras 7, 8(b), as from exit day (as defined in the European Union (Withdrawal) Act 2018, s 20).

Para (5): added by the Cross-border Railway Services (Working Time) Regulations 2008, SI 2008/1660, reg 19, Sch 3, para 4.

[2.296]
19 Domestic service

Regulations 4(1) and (2), [5A(1) and (4),] 6(1), (2) and (7), [6A,] 7(1), (2) and (6) and 8 do not apply in relation to a worker employed as a domestic servant in a private household.

NOTES

Words in square brackets inserted by the Working Time (Amendment) Regulations 2002, SI 2002/3128, regs 2, 14.

[2.297]
20 Unmeasured working time

[(1)] Regulations 4(1) and (2), 6(1), (2) and (7), 10(1), 11(1) and (2) and 12(1) do not apply in relation to a worker where, on account of the specific characteristics of the activity in which he is engaged, the duration of his working time is not measured or predetermined or can be determined by the worker himself, as may be the case for—

(a) managing executives or other persons with autonomous decision-taking powers;

(b) family workers; or

(c) workers officiating at religious ceremonies in churches and religious communities.

[(2) . . .]

NOTES

Para (1): numbered as such by the Working Time Regulations 1999, SI 1999/3372, regs 1(1), 4.

Para (2): added by SI 1999/3372, regs 1(1), 4, and revoked by the Working Time (Amendment) Regulations 2006, SI 2006/99, reg 2.

[2.298]

21 Other special cases

Subject to regulation 24, regulations 6(1), (2) and (7), 10(1), 11(1) and (2) and 12(1) do not apply in relation to a worker—

(a) where the worker's activities are such that his place of work and place of residence are distant from one another[, including cases where the worker is employed in offshore work,] or his different places of work are distant from one another;

(b) where the worker is engaged in security and surveillance activities requiring a permanent presence in order to protect property and persons, as may be the case for security guards and caretakers or security firms;

(c) where the worker's activities involve the need for continuity of service or production, as may be the case in relation to—

(i) services relating to the reception, treatment or care provided by hospitals or similar establishments [(including the activities of doctors in training)], residential institutions and prisons;

(ii) work at docks or airports;

(iii) press, radio, television, cinematographic production, postal and telecommunications services and civil protection services;

(iv) gas, water and electricity production, transmission and distribution, household refuse collection and incineration;

(v) industries in which work cannot be interrupted on technical grounds;

(vi) research and development activities;

(vii) agriculture;

[(viii) the carriage of passengers on regular urban transport services;]

(d) where there is a foreseeable surge of activity, as may be the case in relation to—

(i) agriculture;

(ii) tourism; and

(iii) postal services;

(e) where the worker's activities are affected by—

(i) an occurrence due to unusual and unforeseeable circumstances, beyond the control of the worker's employer;

(ii) exceptional events, the consequences of which could not have been avoided despite the exercise of all due care by the employer; or

(iii) an accident or the imminent risk of an accident;

[(f) where the worker works in railway transport and—

(i) his activities are intermittent;

(ii) he spends his working time on board trains; or

(iii) his activities are linked to transport timetables and to ensuring the continuity and regularity of traffic].

NOTES

Words in square brackets in paras (a), (c)(i) inserted, and paras (c)(viii), (f) added, by the Working Time (Amendment) Regulations 2003, SI 2003/1684, regs 2, 5.

[2.299]

22 Shift workers

(1) Subject to regulation 24—

(a) regulation 10(1) does not apply in relation to a shift worker when he changes shift and cannot take a daily rest period between the end of one shift and the start of the next one;

(b) paragraphs (1) and (2) of regulation 11 do not apply in relation to a shift worker when he changes shift and cannot take a weekly rest period between the end of one shift and the start of the next one; and

(c) neither regulation 10(1) nor paragraphs (1) and (2) of regulation 11 apply to workers engaged in activities involving periods of work split up over the day, as may be the case for cleaning staff.

(2) For the purposes of this regulation—

"shift worker" means any worker whose work schedule is part of shift work; and

"shift work" means any method of organizing work in shifts whereby workers succeed each other at the same workstations according to a certain pattern, including a rotating pattern, and which may be continuous or discontinuous, entailing the need for workers to work at different times over a given period of days or weeks.

[2.300]

23 Collective and workforce agreements

A collective agreement or a workforce agreement may—

(a) modify or exclude the application of regulations 6(1) to (3) and (7), 10(1), 11(1) and (2) and 12(1), and

Part 2 Statutory Instruments

(b) for objective or technical reasons or reasons concerning the organization of work, modify the application of regulation 4(3) and (4) by the substitution, for each reference to 17 weeks, of a different period, being a period not exceeding 52 weeks,

in relation to particular workers or groups of workers.

[2.301]

24 Compensatory rest

Where the application of any provision of these Regulations is excluded by regulation 21 or 22, or is modified or excluded by means of a collective agreement or a workforce agreement under regulation 23(a), and a worker is accordingly required by his employer to work during a period which would otherwise be a rest period or rest break—

(a) his employer shall wherever possible allow him to take an equivalent period of compensatory rest, and

(b) in exceptional cases in which it is not possible, for objective reasons, to grant such a period of rest, his employer shall afford him such protection as may be appropriate in order to safeguard the worker's health and safety.

[2.302]

[24A Mobile workers

(1) Regulations 6(1), (2) and (7), 10(1), 11(1) and (2) and 12(1) do not apply to a mobile worker in relation to whom the application of those regulations is not excluded by any provision of regulation 18.

(2) A mobile worker, to whom paragraph (1) applies, is entitled to adequate rest, except where the worker's activities are affected by any of the matters referred to in regulation 21(e).

(3) For the purposes of this regulation, "adequate rest" means that a worker has regular rest periods, the duration of which are expressed in units of time and which are sufficiently long and continuous to ensure that, as a result of fatigue or other irregular working patterns, he does not cause injury to himself, to fellow workers or to others and that he does not damage his health, either in the short term or in the longer term.]

NOTES

Inserted by the Working Time (Amendment) Regulations 2003, SI 2003/1684, regs 2, 6.

[2.303]

25 Workers in the armed forces

(1) Regulation 9 does not apply in relation to a worker serving as a member of the armed forces.

(2) Regulations [5A, 6A,] 10(2) and 11(3) do not apply in relation to a young worker serving as a member of the armed forces.

(3) In a case where a young worker is accordingly required to work during [the restricted period, or is not permitted the minimum rest period provided for in regulation 10(2) or 11(3),] he shall be allowed an appropriate period of compensatory rest.

NOTES

Para (2): figures in square brackets inserted by the Working Time (Amendment) Regulations 2002, SI 2002/3128, regs 2, 15(a).

Para (3): words in square brackets substituted by SI 2002/3128, regs 2, 15(b).

[2.304]

[25A Doctors in training

[[(1) Paragraph (1) of regulation 4 is modified in its application to workers to whom this paragraph applies by substituting for the reference to 48 hours a reference to 52 hours—

(a) in the case of doctors in training who are employed in an employment falling within Table 1 of Schedule 2A, with effect from 1st August 2009 until 31st July 2011; and

(b) in the case of doctors in training who are employed in an employment falling within Table 2 of Schedule 2A, with effect from 2nd November 2009 until 31st July 2011.]

(1A) Paragraph (1) applies to workers who are doctors in training who are employed—

(a) by an employer who is listed in column 1 of [Table 1 or Table 2] contained in Schedule 2A,

(b) at a place listed in column 2 of [the applicable table] in respect of that employer,

(c) to provide at that place one of the specialist services listed in column 3 of [the applicable table] in respect of that place, and

(d) in one of the grades listed in column 4 of [the applicable table] in respect of that specialist service and, where applicable, working as part of a rota referred to in that column in respect of that grade, or those grades.]

(2) In the case of workers who are doctors in training, paragraphs (3)–(5) of regulation 4 shall not apply and paragraphs (3) and (4) of this regulation shall apply in their place.

(3) Subject to paragraph (4), the reference period which applies in the case of a worker who is a doctor in training is, with effect from 1st August 2004—

(a) where a relevant agreement provides for the application of this regulation in relation to successive periods of 26 weeks, each such period; and

(b) in any other case, any period of 26 weeks in the course of his employment.

(4) Where a doctor in training has worked for his employer for less than 26 weeks, the reference period applicable in his case is the period that has elapsed since he started work for his employer.]

NOTES

Inserted by the Working Time (Amendment) Regulations 2003, SI 2003/1684, regs 2, 7.

Para (1): substituted, together with para (1A) for original para (1), by the Working Time (Amendment) Regulations 2009, SI 2009/1567, reg 2; further substituted by the Working Time (Amendment) (No 2) Regulations 2009, SI 2009/2766, reg 2(a).

Para (1A): substituted as noted above; words in square brackets substituted by SI 2009/2766, reg 2(b).

Schedule 2A: this lists the hospitals, and categories of doctors, to whom para (1) applied (until 31 July 2011), and is now spent.

[2.305]

[25B Workers employed in offshore work

(1) In the case of workers employed in offshore work, paragraphs (3)–(5) of regulation 4 shall not apply and paragraphs (2) and (3) of this regulation shall apply in their place.

(2) Subject to paragraph (3), the reference period which applies in the case of workers employed in offshore work is—

(a) where a relevant agreement provides for the application of this regulation in relation to successive periods of 52 weeks, each such period; and

(b) in any other case, any period of 52 weeks in the course of his employment.

(3) Where a worker employed in offshore work has worked for his employer for less than 52 weeks, the reference period applicable in his case is the period that has elapsed since he started work for his employer.]

NOTES

Inserted by the Working Time (Amendment) Regulations 2003, SI 2003/1684, regs 2, 8.

26 (*Revoked by the Working Time (Amendment) Regulations 2003, SI 2003/1684, regs 2, 9.*)

[2.306]

[26A Entitlement to additional annual leave under a relevant agreement

(1) Regulation 13A does not apply in relation to a worker whose employer, as at 1st October 2007 and by virtue of a relevant agreement, provides each worker employed by him with an annual leave entitlement of 1.6 weeks or 8 days (whichever is the lesser) in addition to each worker's entitlement under regulation 13, provided that such additional annual leave—

(a) may not be replaced by a payment in lieu except in relation to a worker whose employment is terminated;

(b) may not be carried forward into a leave year other than that which immediately follows the leave year in respect of which the leave is due; and

(c) is leave for which the worker is entitled to be paid at not less than the rate of a week's pay in respect of each week of leave, calculated in accordance with sections 221 to 224 of the 1996 Act, modified such that—

(i) references to the employee are references to the worker;

(ii) references to the employee's contract of employment are references to the worker's contract;

(iii) the calculation date is the first day of the period of leave in question; and

(iv) the references to sections 227 and 228 do not apply.

(2) Notwithstanding paragraph (1), any additional annual leave in excess of 1.6 weeks or 8 days (whichever is the lesser) to which a worker is entitled, shall not be subject to the conditions of that paragraph.

(3) This regulation shall cease to apply to a worker from the day when an employer ceases to provide additional annual leave in accordance with the conditions in paragraph (1).

(4) This regulation does not apply to workers to whom the Agricultural Wages (Scotland) Act 1949 applies (as that Act had effect on 1 July 1999).]

NOTES

Inserted by the Working Time (Amendment) Regulations 2007, SI 2007/2079, reg 2(1), (3).

[2.307]

27 Young workers: force majeure

(1) Regulations [5A, 6A,] 10(2) and 12(4) do not apply in relation to a young worker where his employer requires him to undertake work which no adult worker is available to perform and which—

(a) is occasioned by either—

(i) an occurrence due to unusual and unforeseeable circumstances, beyond the employer's control, or

(ii) exceptional events, the consequences of which could not have been avoided despite the exercise of all due care by the employer;

(b) is of a temporary nature; and

(c) must be performed immediately.

(2) Where the application of regulation [5A, 6A,] 10(2) or 12(4) is excluded by paragraph (1), and a young worker is accordingly required to work during a period which would otherwise be a rest period or rest break, his employer shall allow him to take an equivalent period of compensatory rest within the following three weeks.

NOTES

Figures in square brackets inserted by the Working Time (Amendment) Regulations 2002, SI 2002/3128, regs 2, 18.

[2.308]

[27A Other exceptions relating to young workers

(1) Regulation 5A does not apply in relation to a young worker where—

(a) the young worker's employer requires him to undertake work which is necessary either to maintain continuity of service or production or to respond to a surge in demand for a service or product;

(b) no adult worker is available to perform the work, and

(c) performing the work would not adversely affect the young worker's education or training.

(2) Regulation 6A does not apply in relation to a young worker employed—

(a) in a hospital or similar establishment, or

(b) in connection with cultural, artistic, sporting or advertising activities,

in the circumstances referred to in paragraph (1).

(3) Regulation 6A does not apply, except in so far as it prohibits work between midnight and 4 am, in relation to a young worker employed in—

(a) agriculture;

(b) retail trading;

(c) postal or newspaper deliveries;

(d) a catering business;

(e) a hotel, public house, restaurant, bar or similar establishment, or

(f) a bakery,

in the circumstances referred to in paragraph (1).

(4) Where the application of regulation 6A is excluded by paragraph (2) or (3), and a young worker is accordingly required to work during a period which would otherwise be a rest period or rest break—

(a) he shall be supervised by an adult worker where such supervision is necessary for the young worker's protection, and

(b) he shall be allowed an equivalent period of compensatory rest.]

NOTES

Inserted by the Working Time (Amendment) Regulations 2002, SI 2002/3128, regs 2, 17.

PART IV
MISCELLANEOUS

[2.309]

[28 Enforcement

(1) In this regulation, regulations 29–29E and Schedule 3—

"the 1974 Act" means the Health and Safety at Work etc Act 1974;

["2013 Act" means the Energy Act 2013;]

"the Civil Aviation Authority" means the authority referred to in section 2(1) of the Civil Aviation Act 1982;

"code of practice" includes a standard, a specification and any other documentary form of practical guidance;

. . .

["DVSA" means the Driver and Vehicle Standards Agency;]

"enforcement authority" means the Executive, a local authority, the Civil Aviation Authority[, [DVSA][, the ONR] or [the Office of Rail and Road]];

"the Executive" means the Health and Safety Executive referred to in [section 10(1)] of the 1974 Act;

"local authority" means—

(a) in relation to England, a county council so far as they are the council for an area for which there are no district councils, a district council, a London borough council, the Common Council of the City of London, the Sub-Treasurer of the Inner Temple or the Under-Treasurer of the Middle Temple;

(b) in relation to Wales, a county council or a county borough council;

(c) in relation to Scotland, a council constituted under section 2 of the Local Government etc (Scotland) Act 1994;

["ONR" means the Office for Nuclear Regulation;]

"premises" includes any place and, in particular, includes—

(a) any vehicle, vessel, aircraft or hovercraft;

(b) any installation on land (including the foreshore and other land intermittently covered by water), any offshore installation, and any other installation (whether floating, or resting on the seabed or the subsoil thereof, or resting on other land covered with water or the subsoil thereof) and

(c) any tent or movable structure;

"relevant civil aviation worker" means a mobile worker who works mainly on board civil aircraft, excluding any worker to whom regulation 18(2)(b) applies;

"the relevant requirements" means the following provisions—

(a) regulations 4(2), 5A(4), 6(2) and (7), 6A, 7(1), (2) and (6), 8, 9 and 27A(4)(a);

(b) regulation 24, in so far as it applies where regulation 6(1), (2) or (7) is modified or excluded, and

(c) regulation 24A(2), in so far as it applies where regulations 6(1), (2) or (7) is excluded;

["relevant nuclear provisions" means—

(a) sections 1, 3 to 6, 22 and 24A of the Nuclear Installations Act 1965;

(b) the provisions of the 2013 Act;

(c) the provisions of nuclear regulations other than any provision of such regulations identified in accordance with section 74(9) of the 2013 Act as made for the nuclear safeguards purposes;]

["relevant nuclear site" means a site which is—

(a) a GB nuclear site (within the meaning given by section 68 of the 2013 Act);

(b) an authorised defence site (within the meaning given in regulation 2(1) of the Health and Safety (Enforcing Authority) Regulations 1998); or

(c) a new nuclear build site (within the meaning given in regulation 2A of those Regulations);]

"relevant road transport worker" means a mobile worker to whom one or more of the following applies—

(a) [Council Regulation (EC) No 561/2006],

(b) the European Agreement concerning the Work of Crews of Vehicles engaged in International Road Transport (AETR) of 1st July 1970, and

(c) the United Kingdom domestic driver's hours code, which is set out in Part VI of the Transport Act 1968;

"the relevant statutory provisions" means—

(a) the provisions of the 1974 Act and of any regulations made under powers contained in that Act; and

(b) while and to the extent that they remain in force, the provisions of the Acts mentioned in Schedule 1 to the 1974 Act and which are specified in the third column of that Schedule and the regulations, orders or other instruments of a legislative character made or having effect under a provision so specified; . . .

. . .

(2) It shall be the duty of the Executive to make adequate arrangements for the enforcement of the relevant requirements except to the extent that—

(a) a local authority is made responsible for their enforcement by paragraph (3);

(b) the Civil Aviation Authority is made responsible for their enforcement by paragraph (5); . . .

(c) [DVSA] is made responsible for their enforcement by paragraph (6);

[(d) [the Office of Rail and Road] is made responsible for their enforcement by paragraph (3A)];

[(e) the ONR is made responsible for their enforcement by paragraph (3AA).]

(3) Where the relevant requirements apply in relation to workers employed in premises in respect of which a local authority is responsible, under the Health and Safety (Enforcing Authority) Regulations 1998, for enforcing any of the relevant statutory provisions, it shall be the duty of that authority to enforce those requirements.

[(3A) Where the relevant requirements apply in relation to workers employed in the carrying out of any of the activities specified in regulation 3(2) of the Health and Safety (Enforcing Authority for Railways and Other Guided Transport Systems) Regulations 2006 it shall be the duty of [the Office of Rail and Road] to enforce those requirements.]

[(3AA) Where the relevant requirements apply in relation to workers employed in premises which are or are on a relevant nuclear site, it shall be the duty of the ONR to enforce those requirements.]

(4) The duty imposed on local authorities by paragraph (3) shall be performed in accordance with such guidance as may be given to them by [the Executive].

(5) It shall be the duty of the Civil Aviation Authority to enforce the relevant requirements in relation to relevant civil aviation workers.

(6) It shall be the duty of [DVSA] to enforce the relevant requirements in relation to relevant road transport workers.

(7) The provisions of Schedule 3 shall apply in relation to the enforcement of the relevant requirements.

(8) . . .]

NOTES

Substituted by the Working Time (Amendment) Regulations 2003, SI 2003/1684, regs 2, 10.

Para (1) is amended as follows:

Definitions "2013 Act", "ONR", "relevant nuclear provisions" and "relevant nuclear site" inserted, and words ", the ONR" in third (inner) pair of square brackets in definition "enforcement authority" inserted, by the Energy Act 2013 (Office for Nuclear Regulation) (Consequential Amendments, Transitional Provisions and Savings) Order 2014, SI 2014/469, art 6(2), Sch 3, Pt 3, paras 80, 81(1), (2).

Definition "the Commission" (omitted) revoked by the Legislative Reform (Health and Safety Executive) Order 2008, SI 2008/960, art 22, Sch 3.

Definition "DVSA" inserted, word in second (inner) pair of square brackets in definition "enforcement authority" substituted, word omitted from para (b) of the definition "the relevant statutory provisions" revoked, and definition "VOSA" (omitted) revoked, by the Driving Standards Agency and the Vehicle and Operator Services Agency (Merger) (Consequential Amendments) Regulations 2014, SI 2014/480, reg 9(1), (2).

Words in first (outer) pair of square brackets in definition "enforcement authority" substituted by the Health and Safety (Enforcing Authority for Railways and Other Guided Transport Systems) Regulations 2006, SI 2006/557, reg 6, Schedule, para 7(a).

Words "the Office of Rail and Road" in square brackets in definition "enforcement authority" substituted by the Office of Rail Regulation (Change of Name) Regulations 2015, SI 2015/1682, reg 2(2), Schedule, Pt 2, para 10(d), as from 16 October 2015.

Words in square brackets in definition "the Executive" substituted by SI 2008/960, art 22, Sch 3.

Words in square brackets in definition "relevant road transport worker" substituted by the Employment Rights (Amendment) (EU Exit) Regulations 2019, SI 2019/535, reg 2(1), Sch 1, Pt 2, paras 7, 9, as from 5 March 2019.

Para (2) is amended as follows:

Word omitted from sub-para (b) revoked, and sub-para (d) added, by SI 2006/557, reg 6, Schedule, para 7(b)(ii).

Word in square brackets in sub-para (c) substituted by SI 2014/480, reg 9(1), (3).

Words in square brackets in sub-para (d) substituted by SI 2015/1682, reg 2(2), Schedule, Pt 2, para 10(d), as from 16 October 2015.

Sub-para (e) added by SI 2014/469, art 6(2), Sch 3, Pt 3, paras 80, 81(1), (3).

Para (3A): inserted by SI 2006/557, reg 6, Schedule, para 7(c); words in square brackets substituted by SI 2015/1682, reg 2(2), Schedule, Pt 2, para 10(d), as from 16 October 2015.

Para (3AA): inserted by SI 2014/469, art 6(2), Sch 3, Pt 3, paras 80, 81(1), (4).

Para (4): words in square brackets substituted by SI 2008/960, art 22, Sch 3.

Para (6): word in square brackets substituted by SI 2014/480, reg 9(1), (4).

Para (8): revoked by SI 2008/960, art 22, Sch 3.

[2.310]
[29 Offences

[(1) An employer who fails to comply with any of the relevant requirements shall be guilty of an offence.

(2) The provisions of paragraph (3) shall apply where an inspector is exercising or has exercised any power conferred by Schedule 3.

(3) It is an offence for a person—

(a) to contravene any requirement imposed by the inspector under paragraph 2 of Schedule 3;

(b) to prevent or attempt to prevent any other person from appearing before the inspector or from answering any question to which the inspector may by virtue of paragraph 2(2)(e) of Schedule 3 require an answer;

(c) to contravene any requirement or prohibition imposed by an improvement notice or a prohibition notice (including any such notice as is modified on appeal);

(d) intentionally to obstruct the inspector in the exercise or performance of his powers or duties;

(e) to use or disclose any information in contravention of paragraph 8 of Schedule 3;

(f) to make a statement which he knows to be false or recklessly to make a statement which is false, where the statement is made in purported compliance with a requirement to furnish any information imposed by or under these Regulations.

(4) An employer guilty of an offence under paragraph (1) shall be liable—

(a) on summary conviction, to a fine not exceeding the statutory maximum;

(b) on conviction on indictment, to a fine.

(5) A person guilty of an offence under paragraph (3) shall be liable to the penalty prescribed in relation to that provision by paragraphs (6), (7) or (8) as the case may be.

(6) A person guilty of an offence under sub-paragraph (3)(a), (b) or (d) shall be liable on summary conviction to a fine not exceeding level 5 on the standard scale.

(7) A person guilty of an offence under sub-paragraph (3)(c) shall be liable—

(a) on summary conviction, to imprisonment for a term not exceeding three months, or a fine not exceeding the statutory maximum;

(b) on conviction on indictment, to imprisonment for a term not exceeding two years, or a fine, or both.

(8) A person guilty of an offence under any of the sub-paragraphs of paragraph (3) not falling within paragraphs (6) or (7) above, shall be liable—

(a) on summary conviction, to a fine not exceeding the statutory maximum;

(b) on conviction on indictment—

(i) if the offence is under sub-paragraph (3)(e), to imprisonment for a term not exceeding two years or a fine or both;

(ii) if the offence is not one to which the preceding sub-paragraph applies, to a fine.

(9) The provisions set out in regulations 29A–29E below shall apply in relation to the offences provided for in paragraphs (1) and (3).]

NOTES

Substituted, together with regs 29A–29E for the original reg 29, by the Working Time (Amendment) Regulations 2003, SI 2003/1684, regs 2, 10.

[2.311]
[29A Offences due to fault of other person

Where the commission by any person of an offence is due to the act or default of some other person, that other person shall be guilty of the offence, and a person may be charged with and convicted of the offence by virtue of this paragraph whether or not proceedings are taken against the first-mentioned person.]

NOTES

Substituted as noted to reg 29 at **[2.310]**.

[2.312]
[29B Offences by bodies corporate

(1) Where an offence committed by a body corporate is proved to have been committed with the consent or connivance of, or to have been attributable to any neglect on the part of, any director, manager, secretary or other similar officer of the body corporate or a person who was purporting to act in any such capacity, he as well as the body corporate shall be guilty of that offence and shall be liable to be proceeded against and punished accordingly.

(2) Where the affairs of a body corporate are managed by its members, the preceding paragraph shall apply in relation to the acts and defaults of a member in connection with his functions of management as if he were a director of the body corporate.]

NOTES

Substituted as noted to reg 29 at **[2.310]**.

[2.313]
[29C Restriction on institution of proceedings in England and Wales

Proceedings for an offence shall not, in England and Wales, be instituted except by an inspector or by or with the consent of the Director of Public Prosecutions.]

NOTES

Substituted as noted to reg 29 at **[2.310]**.

[2.314]
[29D Prosecutions by inspectors

(1) An inspector, if authorised in that behalf by an enforcement authority, may, although not of counsel or a solicitor, prosecute before a magistrate's court proceedings for an offence under these Regulations.

(2) This regulation shall not apply to Scotland.]

NOTES

Substituted as noted to reg 29 at **[2.310]**.

[2.315]
[29E Power of court to order cause of offence to be remedied

(1) Where a person is convicted of an offence in respect of any matters which appear to the court to be matters which it is in his power to remedy, the court may, in addition to or instead of imposing any punishment, order him, within such time as may be fixed by the order, to take such steps as may be specified in the order for remedying the said matters.

(2) The time fixed by an order under paragraph (1) may be extended or further extended by order of the court on an application made before the end of that time as originally fixed or as extended under this paragraph, as the case may be.

(3) Where a person is ordered under paragraph (1) to remedy any matters, that person shall not be liable under these Regulations in respect of those matters in so far as they continue during the time fixed by the order or any further time allowed under paragraph (2).]

NOTES

Substituted as noted to reg 29 at **[2.310]**.

[2.316]
30 Remedies

(1) A worker may present a complaint to an employment tribunal that his employer—

(a) has refused to permit him to exercise any right he has under—

[(i) regulation 10(1) or (2), 11(1), (2) or (3), 12(1) or (4), 13 or 13A;]

(ii) regulation 24, in so far as it applies where regulation 10(1), 11(1) or (2) or 12(1) is modified or excluded; . . .

[(iii) regulation 24A, in so far as it applies where regulation 10(1), 11(1) or (2) or 12(1) is excluded; or

(iv) regulation 25(3), 27A(4)(b) or 27(2); or]

(b) has failed to pay him the whole or any part of any amount due to him under regulation 14(2) or 16(1).

(2) [Subject to [*regulations 30A and* 30B], an employment tribunal] shall not consider a complaint under this regulation unless it is presented—

(a) before the end of the period of three months (or, in a case to which regulation 38(2) applies, six months) beginning with the date on which it is alleged that the exercise of the right should have been permitted (or in the case of a rest period or leave extending over more than one day, the date on which it should have been permitted to begin) or, as the case may be, the payment should have been made;

(b) within such further period as the tribunal considers reasonable in a case where it is satisfied that it was not reasonably practicable for the complaint to be presented before the end of that period of three or, as the case may be, six months.

[(2A) Where the period within which a complaint must be presented in accordance with paragraph (2) is extended by regulation 15 of the Employment Act 2002 (Dispute Resolution) Regulations 2004, the period within which the complaint must be presented shall be the extended period rather than the period in paragraph (2).]

(3) Where an employment tribunal finds a complaint under paragraph (1)(a) well-founded, the tribunal—

(a) shall make a declaration to that effect, and

(b) may make an award of compensation to be paid by the employer to the worker.

(4) The amount of the compensation shall be such as the tribunal considers just and equitable in all the circumstances having regard to—

(a) the employer's default in refusing to permit the worker to exercise his right, and

(b) any loss sustained by the worker which is attributable to the matters complained of.

(5) Where on a complaint under paragraph (1)(b) an employment tribunal finds that an employer has failed to pay a worker in accordance with regulation 14(2) or 16(1), it shall order the employer to pay to the worker the amount which it finds to be due to him.

NOTES

Para (1): sub-para (a)(i) substituted by the Working Time (Amendment) Regulations 2007, SI 2007/2079, reg 2(1), (11); word omitted from sub-para (a)(ii) revoked, and sub-paras (a)(iii), (iv) substituted (for the original sub-para (a)(iii)), by the Working Time (Amendment) Regulations 2003, SI 2003/1684, regs 2, 11.

Para (2): words in first (outer) pair of square brackets substituted by the Cross-Border Mediation (EU Directive) Regulations 2011, SI 2011/1133, regs 67, 68; words in second (inner) pair of square brackets substituted by the Enterprise and Regulatory Reform Act 2013 (Consequential Amendments) (Employment) Order 2014, SI 2014/386, art 2, Schedule, paras 2, 3. For the words in italics there is substituted the word "regulation", by the Cross-Border Mediation (EU Directive) (EU Exit) Regulations 2019, SI 2019/469, reg 4, Sch 1, Pt 2, para 20(1), (2), as from exit day (as defined in the European Union (Withdrawal) Act 2018, s 20).

Para (2A): inserted by the Employment Act 2002 (Dispute Resolution) Regulations 2004, SI 2004/752, reg 17(f). Note that this paragraph has not been revoked despite the 2004 Regulations lapsing on 6 April 2009.

Conciliation: employment tribunal proceedings under this regulation are "relevant proceedings" for the purposes of the conciliation provisions contained in the Employment Tribunals Act 1996, ss 18–18C; see s 18(1)(j) of the 1996 Act at **[1.757]**.

Tribunal jurisdiction: the Employment Act 2002, s 38 applies to proceedings before the employment tribunal relating to a claim under this regulation; see s 38(1) of, and Sch 5 to, the 2002 Act at **[1.1279]**, **[1.1287]**. See also the Trade Union and Labour Relations (Consolidation) Act 1992, s 207A at **[1.524]** (as inserted by the Employment Act 2008). That section provides that in proceedings before an employment tribunal relating to a claim by an employee under any of the jurisdictions listed in Sch A2 to the 1992 Act at **[1.704]** (which includes this regulation) the tribunal may adjust any award given if the employer or the employee has unreasonably failed to comply with a relevant Code of Practice as defined by s 207A(4). See also the revised Acas Code of Practice 1 – Disciplinary and Grievance Procedures (2015) at **[4.1]**, and the Acas Code of Practice 4 – Settlement Agreements (2013) at **[4.54]**.

[2.317]

[30A Extension of time limits because of mediation in certain cross-border disputes

(1) In this regulation—

(a) "Mediation Directive" means Directive 2008/52/EC of the European Parliament and of the Council of 21 May 2008 on certain aspects of mediation in civil and commercial matters;

(b) "mediation" has the meaning given by article 3(a) of the Mediation Directive;

(c) "mediator" has the meaning given by article 3(b) of the Mediation Directive; and

(d) "relevant dispute" means a dispute to which article 8(1) of the Mediation Directive applies (certain cross-border disputes).

(2) Paragraph (3) applies where—

(a) a three month time limit is set by regulation 30(2) in relation to the whole or part of a relevant dispute;

(b) a mediation in relation to the relevant dispute starts before the period expires; and

(c) if not extended by this regulation, the time limit would expire before the mediation ends or less than four weeks after it ends.

(3) The time limit expires instead at the end of four weeks after the mediation ends (subject to paragraph (4)).

(4) If a time limit mentioned in paragraph (2)(a) has been extended by this article, paragraphs (2) and (3) apply to the extended time limit as they apply to a time limit mentioned in paragraph (2)(a).

(5) Where more than one time limit applies in relation to a relevant dispute, the extension by paragraph (3) of one of those time limits does not affect the others.

(6) For the purposes of this regulation, a mediation starts on the date of the agreement to mediate that is entered into by the parties and the mediator.

(7) For the purposes of this regulation, a mediation ends on the date of the first of these to occur—

(a) the parties reach an agreement in resolution of the relevant dispute;

(b) a party completes the notification of the other parties that it has withdrawn from the mediation;

(c) a party to whom a qualifying request is made fails to give a response reaching the other parties within 14 days of the request;

(d) the parties, after being notified that the mediator's appointment has ended (by death, resignation or otherwise), fail to agree within 14 days to seek to appoint a replacement mediator; or

(e) the mediation otherwise comes to an end pursuant to the terms of the agreement to mediate.

(8) For the purpose of paragraph (7), a qualifying request is a request by a party that another (A) confirm to all parties that A is continuing with the mediation.

(9) In the case of any relevant dispute, references in this regulation to a mediation are references to the mediation so far as it relates to that dispute, and references to a party are to be read accordingly.

(10) Where the tribunal has the power under regulation 30(2)(b) to extend a period of limitation, the power is exercisable in relation to the period of limitation as extended by this regulation.]

NOTES

Inserted by the Cross-Border Mediation (EU Directive) Regulations 2011, SI 2011/1133, regs 67, 69.

Revoked by the Cross-Border Mediation (EU Directive) (EU Exit) Regulations 2019, SI 2019/469, reg 4, Sch 1, Pt 2, para 20(1), (3), as from exit day (as defined in the European Union (Withdrawal) Act 2018, s 20) and subject to the modifications specified in Sch 2 to the 2019 Regulations for any mediation to which this regulation applies, issued before exit day (see reg 5, Sch 2, Pt 2, para 20 at **[2.2131]**, **[2.2133]**).

[2.318]

[30B Extension of time limit to facilitate conciliation before institution of proceedings

(1) In this regulation—

(a) Day A is the day on which the worker concerned complies with the requirement in subsection (1) of section 18A of the Employment Tribunals Act 1996 (requirement to contact ACAS before instituting proceedings) in relation to the matter in respect of which the proceedings are brought, and

(b) Day B is the day on which the worker concerned receives or, if earlier, is treated as receiving (by virtue of regulations made under subsection (11) of that section) the certificate issued under subsection (4) of that section.

(2) In working out when the time limit set by regulation 30(2)(a) expires the period beginning with the day after Day A and ending with Day B is not to be counted.

(3) If the time limit set by regulation 30(2)(a) would (if not extended by this paragraph) expire during the period beginning with Day A and ending one month after Day B, the time limit expires instead at the end of that period.

(4) The power conferred on the employment tribunal by regulation 30(2)(b) to extend the time limit set by paragraph (2)(a) of that regulation is exercisable in relation to that time limit as extended by this regulation.]

NOTES

Inserted by the Enterprise and Regulatory Reform Act 2013 (Consequential Amendments) (Employment) Order 2014, SI 2014/386, art 2, Schedule, paras 2, 4.

31–34 *(Regs 31, 32 contain various amendments to the Employment Rights Act 1996 which have been incorporated at the appropriate place (see that Act at* **[1.813]** *et seq); reg 33 amended the Employment Tribunals Act 1996, s 18 (and is now spent following subsequent amendments to that section); reg 34 amends 21 of the 1996 Act at* **[1.764]**.)

[2.319]

35 Restrictions on contracting out

(1) Any provision in an agreement (whether a contract of employment or not) is void in so far as it purports—

(a) to exclude or limit the operation of any provision of these Regulations, save in so far as these Regulations provide for an agreement to have that effect, or

(b) to preclude a person from bringing proceedings under these Regulations before an employment tribunal.

(2) Paragraph (1) does not apply to—

(a) any agreement to refrain from instituting or continuing proceedings where a conciliation officer has taken action under [any of sections 18A to 18C] of the Employment Tribunals Act 1996 (conciliation); or

(b) any agreement to refrain from instituting or continuing proceedings within [section 18(1)(j)] of the Employment Tribunals Act 1996 (proceedings under these Regulations where conciliation is available), if the conditions regulating [settlement] agreements under these Regulations are satisfied in relation to the agreement.

(3) For the purposes of paragraph (2)(b) the conditions regulating [settlement] agreements under these Regulations are that—

(a) the agreement must be in writing,

(b) the agreement must relate to the particular complaint,

(c) the worker must have received advice from a relevant independent adviser as to the terms and effect of the proposed agreement and, in particular, its effect on his ability to pursue his rights before an employment tribunal,

(d) there must be in force, when the adviser gives the advice, a contract of insurance, or an indemnity provided for members of a profession or professional body, covering the risk of a claim by the worker in respect of loss arising in consequence of the advice,

(e) the agreement must identify the adviser, and

(f) the agreement must state that the conditions regulating [settlement] agreements under these Regulations are satisfied.

(4) A person is a relevant independent adviser for the purposes of paragraph (3)(c)—

(a) if he is a qualified lawyer,

(b) if he is an officer, official, employee or member of an independent trade union who has been certified in writing by the trade union as competent to give advice and as authorised to do so on behalf of the trade union, or

(c) if he works at an advice centre (whether as an employee or as a volunteer) and has been certified in writing by the centre as competent to give advice and as authorised to do so on behalf of the centre.

(5) But a person is not a relevant independent adviser for the purposes of paragraph (3)(c) in relation to the worker—

(a) if he, is employed by or is acting in the matter for the employer or an associated employer,

(b) in the case of a person within paragraph (4)(b) or (c), if the trade union or advice centre is the employer or an associated employer, or

(c) in the case of a person within paragraph (4)(c), if the worker makes a payment for the advice received from him.

(6) In paragraph (4)(a), "qualified lawyer" means—

(a) as respects England and Wales, [a person who, for the purposes of the Legal Services Act 2007), is an authorised person in relation to an activity which constitutes the exercise of a right of audience or the conduct of litigation (within the meaning of that Act)]; and

(b) as respects Scotland, an advocate (whether in practice as such or employed to give legal advice), or a solicitor who holds a practising certificate.

[(6A) A person shall be treated as being a qualified lawyer within paragraph (6)(a) if he is a Fellow of the Institute of Legal Executives [practising in a solicitor's practice (including a body recognised under section 9 of the Administration of Justice Act 1985)].]

(7) For the purposes of paragraph (5) any two employers shall be treated as associated if—

(a) one is a company of which the other (directly or indirectly) has control; or

(b) both are companies of which a third person (directly or indirectly) has control; and "associated employer" shall be construed accordingly.

NOTES

Para (2): words in square brackets in sub-para (a) substituted by the Enterprise and Regulatory Reform Act 2013 (Consequential Amendments) (Employment) Order 2014, SI 2014/386, art 2, Schedule, paras 2, 5; words in first pair of square brackets in sub-para (b) substituted by the Employment Tribunals Act 1996 (Application of Conciliation Provisions) Order 2014, SI 2014/431, art 3, Schedule, para 19; word in second pair of square brackets in sub-para (b) substituted by the Enterprise and Regulatory Reform Act 2013 (Consequential Amendments) (Employment) Order 2013, SI 2013/1956, art 2, Schedule, para 2.

Para (6): words in square brackets substituted by the Legal Services Act 2007 (Consequential Amendments) Order 2009, SI 2009/3348, art 23, Sch 2.

Para (6A): inserted by the Working Time Regulations 1998 (Amendment) Regulations 2004, SI 2004/2516, reg 2; words in square brackets substituted by SI 2009/3348, art 22, Sch 1.

[2.320]
[35A

(1) The Secretary of State shall, after consulting persons appearing to him to represent the two sides of industry, arrange for the publication, in such form and manner as he considers appropriate, of information and advice concerning the operation of these Regulations.

(2) The information and advice shall be such as appear to him best calculated to enable employers and workers affected by these Regulations to understand their respective rights and obligations under them.]

NOTES

Inserted by the Working Time Regulations 1999, SI 1999/3372, regs 1(1), 5.

PART V
SPECIAL CLASSES OF PERSON

[2.321]
36 Agency workers not otherwise "workers"

(1) This regulation applies in any case where an individual ("the agency worker")—

(a) is supplied by a person ("the agent") to do work for another ("the principal") under a contract or other arrangements made between the agent and the principal; but

(b) is not, as respects that work, a worker, because of the absence of a worker's contract between the individual and the agent or the principal; and

(c) is not a party to a contract under which he undertakes to do the work for another party to the contract whose status is, by virtue of the contract, that of a client or customer of any profession or business undertaking carried on by the individual.

(2) In a case where this regulation applies, the other provisions of these Regulations shall have effect as if there were a worker's contract for the doing of the work by the agency worker made between the agency worker and—

(a) whichever of the agent and the principal is responsible for paying the agency worker in respect of the work; or

(b) if neither the agent nor the principal is so responsible, whichever of them pays the agency worker in respect of the work,

and as if that person were the agency worker's employer.

[2.322]
37 Crown employment

(1) Subject to paragraph (4) and regulation 38, these Regulations have effect in relation to Crown employment and persons in Crown employment as they have effect in relation to other employment and other workers.

(2) In paragraph (1) "Crown employment" means employment under or for the purposes of a government department or any officer or body exercising on behalf of the Crown functions conferred by a statutory provision.

(3) For the purposes of the application of the provisions of these Regulations in relation to Crown employment in accordance with paragraph (1)—

(a) references to a worker shall be construed as references to a person in Crown employment; and

(b) references to a worker's contract shall be construed as references to the terms of employment of a person in Crown employment.

(4) No act or omission by the Crown which is an offence under regulation 29 shall make the Crown criminally liable, but the High Court or, in Scotland, the Court of Session may, on the application of a person appearing to the Court to have an interest, declare any such act or omission unlawful.

[2.323]
38 Armed forces

(1) Regulation 37 applies—

(a) subject to paragraph (2), to service as a member of the armed forces, and

(b) to employment by an association established for the purposes of Part XI of the Reserve Forces Act 1996.

(2) No complaint concerning the service of any person as a member of the armed forces may be presented to an employment tribunal under regulation 30 unless—

(a) that person has made a complaint in respect of the same matter to an officer under the service redress procedures, and

(b) that complaint has not been withdrawn.

[(3) For the purpose of paragraph (2)(b), a person shall be treated as having withdrawn his complaint if, having made a complaint to an officer under the service redress procedures—

(a) where the service redress procedures are those referred to in section 334 of the Armed Forces Act 2006, neither that officer nor a superior officer has decided to refer the complaint to the Defence Council, and the person who made the complaint fails to apply for such a reference to be made;

(b) in any other case, the person who made the complaint fails to submit the complaint to the Defence Council under the service redress procedures.]

(4) Where a complaint of the kind referred to in paragraph (2) is presented to an employment tribunal, the service redress procedures may continue after the complaint is presented.

(5) In this regulation, "the service redress procedures" means the procedures, excluding those which relate to the making of a report on a complaint to Her Majesty, referred to in section 180 of the Army Act 1955, section 180 of the Air Force Act 1955[, section 130 of the Naval Discipline Act 1957 or section 334 of the Armed Forces Act 2006].

NOTES

Para (3): substituted by the Armed Forces (Service Complaints) (Consequential Amendments) Order 2008, SI 2008/1696, art 2(1), (2).

Para (5): words in square brackets substituted by SI 2008/1696, art 2(1), (3).

[2.324]
39 House of Lords staff

(1) These Regulations have effect in relation to employment as a relevant member of the House of Lords staff as they have effect in relation to other employment.

(2) Nothing in any rule of law or the law or practice of Parliament prevents a relevant member of the House of Lords staff from presenting a complaint to an employment tribunal under regulation 30.

(3) In this regulation "relevant member of the House of Lords staff" means any person who is employed under a worker's contract with the Corporate Officer of the House of Lords.

[2.325]
40 House of Commons staff

(1) These Regulations have effect in relation to employment as a relevant member of the House of Commons staff as they have effect in relation to other employment.

(2) For the purposes of the application of the provisions of these Regulations in relation to a relevant member of the House of Commons staff—

(a) references to a worker shall be construed as references to a relevant member of the House of Commons staff; and

Part 2 Statutory Instruments

(b) references to a worker's contract shall be construed as references to the terms of employment of a relevant member of the House of Commons staff.

(3) Nothing in any rule of law or the law or practice of Parliament prevents a relevant member of the House of Commons staff from presenting a complaint to an employment tribunal under regulation 30.

(4) In this regulation "relevant member of the House of Commons staff" means any person—

(a) who was appointed by the House of Commons Commission; or

(b) who is a member of the Speaker's personal staff.

[2.326]

41 Police service

(1) [Subject to paragraph (1A),] for the purposes of these Regulations, the holding, otherwise than under a contract of employment, of the office of constable or an appointment as a police cadet shall be treated as employment, under a worker's contract, by the relevant officer.

[(1A) For the purposes of these Regulations, any constable who has been seconded to [the National Crime Agency] to serve as a member of its staff shall be treated as employed by [the National Crime Agency].]

(2) Any matter relating to the employment of a worker which may be provided for the purposes of these Regulations in a workforce agreement may be provided for the same purposes in relation to the service of a person holding the office of constable or an appointment as a police cadet by an agreement between the relevant officer and [a branch board or a joint branch board (as the case may be)].

(3) In this regulation—

["a branch board" means a branch board constituted in accordance with regulation 10 of the Police Federation (England and Wales) Regulations 2017,]

"a joint branch board" means a joint branch board constituted in accordance with . . . or regulation 7(3) of the Police Federation (Scotland) Regulations 1985, and

"the relevant officer" means—

(a) in relation to a member of a police force or a special constable or police cadet appointed for a police area, the chief officer of police (or, in Scotland, the chief constable);

(b) . . .

(c) in relation to any other person holding the office of constable or an appointment as a police cadet, the person who has the direction and control of the body of constables or cadets in question.

[(4) For the purposes of these Regulations the relevant officer, as defined by paragraph (3), shall be treated as a corporation sole.

(5) Where, in a case in which the relevant officer, as so defined, is guilty of an offence under these Regulations, it is proved—

(a) that the office-holder personally consented to the commission of the offence;

(b) that he personally connived in its commission; or

(c) that the commission of the offence was attributable to personal neglect on his part,

the office-holder (as well as the corporation sole) shall be guilty of an offence and shall be liable to be proceeded against and punished accordingly.

(6) In paragraph (5) above "the office-holder", in relation to the relevant officer, means an individual who, at the time of the consent, connivance or neglect—

(a) held the office or other position mentioned in paragraph (3) above as the office or position of that officer; or

(b) was for the time being responsible for exercising and performing the powers and duties of that office or position.

(7) In the application of this regulation to Scotland—

(a) paragraph (4) shall have effect as if for the words "corporation sole" there were substituted "distinct juristic person (that is to say, as a juristic person distinct from the individual who for the time being is the office-holder)";

(b) paragraph (5) shall have effect as if for the words "corporation sole" there were substituted "juristic person"; and

(c) paragraph (6) shall have effect as if for the words "paragraph (5)" there were substituted "paragraphs (4) and (5)".]

NOTES

Para (1): words in square brackets inserted by the Serious Organised Crime and Police Act 2005 (Consequential and Supplementary Amendments to Secondary Legislation) Order 2006, SI 2006/594, art 2, Schedule, para 16(1), (2).

Para (1A): inserted by SI 2006/594, art 2, Schedule, para 16(1), (3); words in square brackets substituted by virtue of the Crime and Courts Act 2013, s 15(3), Sch 8, Pt 4, para 190 (for general transitional provisions and savings relating to the abolition of the Serious Organised Crime Agency, see s 15(3), Sch 8, Pt 1 thereto).

Para (2): words in square brackets substituted, in relation to England and Wales only, by the Police Federation (England and Wales) Regulations 2017, SI 2017/1140, reg 23, Sch 1, para 2(1), (2)(a), as from 31 December 2017. The original words (which still apply in Scotland) were "a joint branch board".

Para (3): the definition "a branch board" was inserted, and the words "regulation 7(3) of the Police Federation Regulations 1969 or" omitted from the definition "a joint branch board" were revoked, in relation to England and Wales only, by SI 2017/1140, reg 23, Sch 1, para 2(1), (2)(b), as from 31 December 2017. Para (b) of definition "the relevant officer" revoked by SI 2006/594, art 2, Schedule, para 16(1), (4).

Paras (4)–(7): added by the Working Time Regulations 1998 (Amendment) Order 2005, SI 2005/2241, art 2.

[2.327]

42 Non-employed trainees

For the purposes of these Regulations, a person receiving relevant training, otherwise than under a contract of employment, shall be regarded as a worker, and the person whose undertaking is providing the training shall be regarded as his employer.

[2.328]

43 [Workers employed in agriculture in Wales or Scotland]

The provisions of Schedule 2 have effect in relation to workers employed in agriculture [in Wales or Scotland].

NOTES

The regulation heading was substituted and the words in square brackets were inserted, by the Working Time (Amendment) (England) Regulations 2013, SI 2013/2228, regs 2(1), (4), 3, except in relation to a worker employed in agriculture in England in relation to that employment if (a) that employment commenced before 1 October 2013, and (b) the worker remains so employed under that employment.

SCHEDULES

SCHEDULE 1
WORKFORCE AGREEMENTS

Regulation 2

[2.329]

1. An agreement is a workforce agreement for the purposes of these Regulations if the following conditions are satisfied—

(a) the agreement is in writing;
(b) it has effect for a specified period not exceeding five years;
(c) it applies either—
  (i) to all of the relevant members of the workforce, or
  (ii) to all of the relevant members of the workforce who belong to a particular group;
(d) the agreement is signed—
  (i) in the case of an agreement of the kind referred to in sub-paragraph (c)(i), by the representatives of the workforce, and in the case of an agreement of the kind referred to in sub-paragraph (c)(ii) by the representatives of the group to which the agreement applies (excluding, in either case, any representative not a relevant member of the workforce on the date on which the agreement was first made available for signature), or
  (ii) if the employer employed 20 or fewer workers on the date referred to in sub-paragraph (d)(i), either by the appropriate representatives in accordance with that sub-paragraph or by the majority of the workers employed by him;
(e) before the agreement was made available for signature, the employer provided all the workers to whom it was intended to apply on the date on which it came into effect with copies of the text of the agreement and such guidance as those workers might reasonably require in order to understand it fully.

2. For the purposes of this Schedule—

"a particular group" is a group of the relevant members of a workforce who undertake a particular function, work at a particular workplace or belong to a particular department or unit within their employer's business;

"relevant members of the workforce" are all of the workers employed by a particular employer, excluding any worker whose terms and conditions of employment are provided for, wholly or in part, in a collective agreement;

"representatives of the workforce" are workers duly elected to represent the relevant members of the workforce, "representatives of the group" are workers duly elected to represent the members of a particular group, and representatives are "duly elected" if the election at which they were elected satisfied the requirements of paragraph 3 of this Schedule.

3. The requirements concerning elections referred to in paragraph 2 are that—

(a) the number of representatives to be elected is determined by the employer;
(b) the candidates for election as representatives of the workforce are relevant members of the workforce, and the candidates for election as representatives of a group are members of the group;
(c) no worker who is eligible to be a candidate is unreasonably excluded from standing for election;
(d) all the relevant members of the workforce are entitled to vote for representatives of the workforce, and all the members of a particular group are entitled to vote for representatives of the group;
(e) the workers entitled to vote may vote for as many candidates as there are representatives to be elected;
(f) the election is conducted so as to secure that—
  (i) so far as is reasonably practicable, those voting do so in secret, and
  (ii) the votes given at the election are fairly and accurately counted.

SCHEDULE 2
WORKERS EMPLOYED IN AGRICULTURE [IN WALES OR SCOTLAND]

Regulations 13(4), 15(6) and 43

[2.330]

1. Except where, in the case of a worker partly employed in agriculture [in Wales or Scotland], different provision is made by a relevant agreement—

(a) for the purposes of regulation 13 [and regulation 13A], the leave year of a worker employed in agriculture [in Wales or Scotland] begins on 6th April each year or such other date as may be specified in an agricultural wages order which applies to him; and

(b) the dates on which leave is taken by a worker employed in agriculture [in Wales or Scotland] shall be determined in accordance with an agricultural wages order which applies to him.

2. Where, in the case referred to in paragraph 1 above, a relevant agreement makes provision different from sub-paragraph (a) or (b) of that paragraph—

(a) neither section 11 of the Agricultural Wages Act 1948 nor section 11 of the Agricultural Wages (Scotland) Act 1949 shall apply to that provision; and

(b) an employer giving effect to that provision shall not thereby be taken to have failed to comply with the requirements of an agricultural wages order.

3. In this Schedule, "an agricultural wages order" means an order under section 3 of the Agricultural Wages Act 1948[, section 3 of the Agricultural Sector (Wales) Act 2014] or section 3 of the Agricultural Wages (Scotland) Act 1949.

NOTES

The words "in Wales or Scotland" in square brackets (in each place that they occur) were inserted by the Working Time (Amendment) (England) Regulations 2013, SI 2013/2228, regs 2(1), (5), 3, except in relation to a worker employed in agriculture in England in relation to that employment if (a) that employment commenced before 1 October 2013, and (b) the worker remains so employed under that employment.

Other words in square brackets in para 1 inserted by the Working Time (Amendment) Regulations 2007, SI 2007/2079, reg 2(1), (5).

Words in square brackets in para 3 inserted by the Agricultural Sector (Wales) Act 2014, s 11(1), (3), as from 30 July 2014.

SCHEDULE 2A

(Sch 2A is now spent and is omitted for that reason.)

[SCHEDULE 3
ENFORCEMENT

Regulation 28(7)

[2.331]

1 Appointment of inspectors

(1) Each enforcement authority may appoint as inspectors (under whatever title it may from time to time determine) such persons having suitable qualifications as it thinks necessary for carrying into effect these Regulations within its field of responsibility, and may terminate any appointment made under this paragraph.

(2) Every appointment of a person as an inspector under this paragraph shall be made by an instrument in writing specifying which of the powers conferred on inspectors by these Regulations are to be exercisable by the person appointed; and an inspector shall in right of his appointment under this paragraph—

(a) be entitled to exercise only such of those powers as are so specified; and

(b) be entitled to exercise the powers so specified only within the field of responsibility of the authority which appointed him.

(3) So much of an inspector's instrument of appointment as specifies the powers which he is entitled to exercise may be varied by the enforcement authority which appointed him.

(4) An inspector shall, if so required when exercising or seeking to exercise any power conferred on him by these Regulations, produce his instrument of appointment or a duly authenticated copy thereof.

2 Powers of inspectors

(1) Subject to the provisions of paragraph 1 and this sub-paragraph, an inspector may, for the purpose of carrying into effect these Regulations within the field of responsibility of the enforcement authority which appointed him, exercise the powers set out in sub-paragraph (2) below.

(2) The powers of an inspector referred to in the preceding sub-paragraph are the following, namely—

(a) at any reasonable time (or, in a situation which in his opinion is or may be dangerous, at any time) to enter any premises which he has reason to believe it is necessary for him to enter for the purpose mentioned in sub-paragraph (1) above;

(b) to take with him a constable if he has reasonable cause to apprehend any serious obstruction in the execution of his duty;

(c) without prejudice to the preceding sub-paragraph, on entering any premises by virtue of paragraph (a) above to take with him—

(i) any other person duly authorised by the inspector's enforcement authority; and

(ii) any equipment or materials required for any purpose for which the power of entry is being exercised;

(d) to make such examination and investigation as may in any circumstances be necessary for the purpose mentioned in sub-paragraph (1) above;

(e) to require any person whom he has reasonable cause to believe to be able to give any information relevant to any examination or investigation under paragraph (d) above to answer (in the absence of persons other than a person nominated by him to be present and any persons whom the inspector may allow to be present) such questions as the inspector thinks fit to ask and to sign a declaration of the truth of his answers;

(f) to require the production of, inspect, and take copies of or of any entry in—

(i) any records which by virtue of these Regulations are required to be kept, and

(ii) any other books, records or documents which it is necessary for him to see for the purposes of any examination or investigation under paragraph (d) above;

(g) to require any person to afford him such facilities and assistance with respect to any matters or things within that person's control or in relation to which that person has responsibilities as are necessary to enable the inspector to exercise any of the powers conferred on him by this paragraph;

(h) any other power which is necessary for the purpose mentioned in sub-paragraph (1) above.

(3) No answer given by a person in pursuance of a requirement imposed under sub-paragraph (2)(e) above shall be admissible in evidence against that person or the [spouse or civil partner] of that person in any proceedings.

(4) Nothing in this paragraph shall be taken to compel the production by any person of a document of which he would on grounds of legal professional privilege be entitled to withhold production on an order for discovery in an action in the High Court or, as the case may be, on an order for the production of documents in an action in the Court of Session.

3 Improvement notices

If an inspector is of the opinion that a person—

(a) is contravening one or more of these Regulations; or

(b) has contravened one or more of these Regulations in circumstances that make it likely that the contravention will continue or be repeated,

he may serve on him a notice (in this Schedule referred to as "an improvement notice") stating that he is of that opinion, specifying the provision or provisions as to which he is of that opinion, giving particulars of the reasons why he is of that opinion, and requiring that person to remedy the contravention or, as the case may be, the matters occasioning it within such period (ending not earlier than the period within which an appeal against the notice can be brought under paragraph 6) as may be specified in the notice.

4 Prohibition notices

(1) This paragraph applies to any activities which are being or are likely to be carried on by or under the control of any person, being activities to or in relation to which any of these Regulations apply or will, if the activities are so carried on, apply.

(2) If as regards any activities to which this paragraph applies an inspector is of the opinion that, as carried on or likely to be carried on by or under the control of the person in question, the activities involve or, as the case may be, will involve a risk of serious personal injury, the inspector may serve on that person a notice (in this Schedule referred to as "a prohibition notice").

(3) A prohibition notice shall—

(a) state that the inspector is of the said opinion;

(b) specify the matters which in his opinion give or, as the case may be, will give rise to the said risk;

(c) where in his opinion any of those matters involves or, as the case may be, will involve a contravention of any of these Regulations, state that he is of that opinion, specify the regulation or regulations as to which he is of that opinion, and give particulars of the reasons why he is of that opinion; and

(d) direct that the activities to which the notice relates shall not be carried on by or under the control of the person on whom the notice is served unless the matters specified in the notice in pursuance of paragraph (b) above and any associated contraventions of provisions so specified in pursuance of paragraph (c) above have been remedied.

(4) A direction contained in a prohibition notice in pursuance of sub-paragraph (3)(d) above shall take effect—

(a) at the end of the period specified in the notice; or

(b) if the notice so declares, immediately.

5 Provisions supplementary to paragraphs 3 and 4

(1) In this paragraph "a notice" means an improvement notice or a prohibition notice.

(2) A notice may (but need not) include directions as to the measures to be taken to remedy any contravention or matter to which the notice relates; and any such directions—

(a) may be framed to any extent by reference to any approved code of practice; and

(b) may be framed so as to afford the person on whom the notice is served a choice between different ways of remedying the contravention or matter.

(3) Where an improvement notice or a prohibition notice which is not to take immediate effect has been served—

(a) the notice may be withdrawn by an inspector at any time before the end of the period specified therein in pursuance of paragraph 3 or paragraph 4(4) as the case may be; and

(b) the period so specified may be extended or further extended by an inspector at any time when an appeal against the notice is not pending.

6 Appeal against improvement or prohibition notice

(1) In this paragraph "a notice" means an improvement or a prohibition notice.

(2) A person on whom a notice is served may within 21 days from the date of its service appeal to an employment tribunal; and on such an appeal the tribunal may either cancel or affirm the notice and, if it affirms it, may do so either in its original form or with such modifications as the tribunal may in the circumstances think fit.

(3) Where an appeal under this paragraph is brought against a notice within the period allowed under the preceding sub-paragraph, then—

(a) in the case of an improvement notice, the bringing of the appeal shall have the effect of suspending the operation of the notice until the appeal is finally disposed of or, if the appeal is withdrawn, until the withdrawal of the appeal;

(b) in the case of a prohibition notice, the bringing of the appeal shall have the like effect if, but only if, on the application of the appellant the tribunal so directs (and then only from the giving of the direction).

(4) One or more assessors may be appointed for the purposes of any proceedings brought before an employment tribunal under this paragraph.

7 Power of enforcement authority to indemnify inspectors

Where an action has been brought against an inspector in respect of an act done in the execution or purported execution of these Regulations and the circumstances are such that he is not legally entitled to require the enforcement authority to indemnify him, that authority may, nevertheless, indemnify him against the whole or part of any damages and costs or expenses which he may have been ordered to pay or may have incurred, if the authority is satisfied that the inspector honestly believed that the act complained of was within his powers and that his duty as an inspector required or entitled him to do it.

8 Restrictions on disclosure of information

(1) In this and the two following sub-paragraphs—

(a) "relevant information" means information obtained by an inspector in pursuance of a requirement imposed under paragraph 2(2)(e) or (f); and

(b) "the recipient", in relation to any relevant information, means the person by whom that information was so obtained or to whom that information was so furnished, as the case may be.

(2) Subject to the following sub-paragraph, no relevant information shall be disclosed without the consent of the person by whom it was furnished.

(3) The preceding sub-paragraph shall not apply to—

(a) disclosure of information to the Commission[, the ONR], a government department or any enforcement authority;

(b) without prejudice to paragraph (a) above, disclosure by the recipient of information to any person for the purpose of any function conferred on the recipient by or under any of the relevant statutory provisions[, relevant nuclear provisions] or under these Regulations;

(c) without prejudice to paragraph (a) above, disclosure by the recipient of information to—

(i) an officer of a local authority who is authorised by that authority to receive it; or

(ii) a constable authorised by a chief officer of police to receive it; or

(d) disclosure by the recipient of information in a form calculated to prevent it from being identified as relating to a particular person or case.

(4) In the preceding sub-paragraph any reference to the Commission[, the ONR], a government department or an enforcement authority includes respectively a reference to an officer of that body or authority (including in the case of an enforcement authority, any inspector appointed by it), and also, in the case of a reference to the Commission, includes a reference to—

(a) a person performing any functions of the Commission or the Executive on its behalf by virtue of section 13(1)(a) of the 1974 Act;

(b) an officer of a body which is so performing any such functions; and

(c) an adviser appointed in pursuance of section 13(1)(d) of the 1974 Act.

[(4A) In sub-paragraph (3) a reference to the ONR also includes a reference to—

(a) a person performing functions of the ONR on its behalf by virtue of section 95 of the 2013 Act;

(b) an officer of a body which is so performing any such functions; and

(c) a person appointed to provide advice to the ONR.]

(5) A person to whom information is disclosed in pursuance of sub-paragraph (3) above shall not use the information for a purpose other than—

(a) in a case falling within sub-paragraph (3)(a), a purpose of the Commission[, or the ONR], of the government department, or of the enforcement authority in question in connection with these Regulations[, the relevant nuclear provisions] or with the relevant statutory provisions, as the case may be;

(b) in the case of information given to an officer of a body which is a local authority, the purposes of the body in connection with the relevant statutory provisions[, the relevant nuclear provisions] or any enactment whatsoever relating to working time, public health, public safety or the protection of the environment;

(c) in the case of information given to a constable, the purposes of the police in connection with these Regulations, the relevant statutory provisions[, the relevant nuclear provisions] or any enactment whatsoever relating to working time, public health, public safety or the safety of the State.

(6) A person shall not disclose any information obtained by him as a result of the exercise of any power conferred by paragraph 2 of this Schedule (including in particular any information with respect to any trade secret obtained by him in any premises entered by him by virtue of any such power) except—

(a) for the purposes of his functions;
(b) for the purposes of any legal proceedings; or
(c) with the relevant consent.

In this sub-paragraph "the relevant consent" means the consent of the person who furnished it, and, in any other case, the consent of a person having responsibilities in relation to the premises where the information was obtained.

(7) Notwithstanding anything in the preceding sub-paragraph an inspector shall, in circumstances in which it is necessary to do so for the purpose of assisting in keeping persons (or the representatives of persons) employed at any premises adequately informed about matters affecting their health, safety and welfare or working time, give to such persons or their representatives the following descriptions of information, that is to say—

(a) factual information obtained by him as mentioned in that sub-paragraph which relates to those premises or anything which was or is therein or was or is being done therein; and
(b) information with respect to any action which he has taken or proposes to take in or in connection with those premises in the performance of his functions;

and, where an inspector does as aforesaid, he shall give the like information to the employer of the first-mentioned persons.

(8) Notwithstanding anything in sub-paragraph (6) above, a person who has obtained such information as is referred to in that sub-paragraph may furnish to a person who appears to him to be likely to be a party to any civil proceedings arising out of any accident, occurrence, situation or other matter, a written statement of the relevant facts observed by him in the course of exercising any of the powers referred to in that sub-paragraph.]

NOTES

Added by the Working Time (Amendment) Regulations 2003, SI 2003/1684, regs 2, 12.

Para 2: words in square brackets in sub-para (3) substituted, in relation to England and Wales only, by the Marriage (Same Sex Couples) Act 2013 (Consequential Provisions) Order 2014, SI 2014/107, art 2, Sch 1, para 25. A corresponding amendment has been made in relation to Scotland by the Marriage and Civil Partnership (Scotland) Act 2014 and Civil Partnership Act 2004 (Consequential Provisions and Modifications) Order 2014, SI 2014/3229, art 29, Sch 6, para 17, as from 16 December 2014.

Para 8: words in square brackets in sub-paras (3), (4), (5) inserted, and sub-para (4A) inserted, by the Energy Act 2013 (Office for Nuclear Regulation) (Consequential Amendments, Transitional Provisions and Savings) Order 2014, SI 2014/469, art 6(2), Sch 3, Pt 3, paras 80, 82.

CIVIL PROCEDURE RULES 1998

(SI 1998/3132)

NOTES

Made: 10 December 1998.

Authority: Civil Procedure Act 1997, ss 1, 2.

Commencement: 26 April 1999.

These Rules apply to England and Wales only.

Most of these Rules cover matters outside the scope of this work, and only those provisions most directly relevant to employment law are printed. For reasons of space, the subject matter of rules not printed is not annotated.

ARRANGEMENT OF RULES

PART 1
OVERRIDING OBJECTIVE

PART 2
APPLICATION AND INTERPRETATION OF THE RULES

PART 3
THE COURT'S CASE AND COSTS MANAGEMENT POWERS
Section I—Case Management

PART 18
FURTHER INFORMATION

PART 24
SUMMARY JUDGMENT

PART 31
DISCLOSURE AND INSPECTION OF DOCUMENTS

PART 35
EXPERTS AND ASSESSORS

PART 36
OFFERS TO SETTLE

SECTION I
PART 36 OFFERS TO SETTLE

PART 1
OVERRIDING OBJECTIVE

[2.332]
1.1 The overriding objective

(1) These Rules are a new procedural code with the overriding objective of enabling the court to deal with cases justly [and at proportionate cost].

(2) Dealing with a case justly [and at proportionate cost] includes, so far as is practicable—
- (a) ensuring that the parties are on an equal footing;
- (b) saving expense;
- (c) dealing with the case in ways which are proportionate—
  - (i) to the amount of money involved;
  - (ii) to the importance of the case;
  - (iii) to the complexity of the issues; and
  - (iv) to the financial position of each party;
- (d) ensuring that it is dealt with expeditiously and fairly; . . .
- (e) allotting to it an appropriate share of the court's resources, while taking into account the need to allot resources to other cases[; and
- (f) enforcing compliance with rules, practice directions and orders.]

NOTES

Para (1): words in square brackets added by the Civil Procedure (Amendment) Rules 2013, SI 2013/262, r 4(a).
Para (2): words in square brackets inserted, and word omitted revoked, by SI 2013/262, r 4(b).

[2.333]
1.2 Application by the court of the overriding objective

The court must seek to give effect to the overriding objective when it—
- (a) exercises any power given to it by the Rules; or
- (b) interprets any rule[, subject to [rules 76.2, 79.2[, 80.2[, 82.2 and 88.2]]]].

NOTES

Words in first (outer) pair of square brackets in para (b) inserted by the Civil Procedure (Amendment No 2) Rules 2005, SI 2005/656, r 3; words in second (inner) pair of square brackets in that paragraph substituted by the Civil Procedure (Amendment No 3) Rules 2011, SI 2011/2970, r 3; words in third (inner) pair of square brackets in that paragraph substituted by the Civil Procedure (Amendment No 5) Rules 2013, SI 2013/1571, r 3; words in fourth (inner) pair of square brackets in that paragraph substituted by the Civil Procedure (Amendment) Rules 2015, SI 2015/406, r 3, as from 27 February 2015.

[2.334]
1.3 Duty of the parties

The parties are required to help the court to further the overriding objective.

Part 2 Statutory Instruments

[2.335]
1.4 Court's duty to manage cases

(1) The court must further the overriding objective by actively managing cases.

(2) Active case management includes—

(a) encouraging the parties to co-operate with each other in the conduct of the proceedings;
(b) identifying the issues at an early stage;
(c) deciding promptly which issues need full investigation and trial and accordingly disposing summarily of the others;
(d) deciding the order in which issues are to be resolved;
(e) encouraging the parties to use an alternative dispute resolution procedure if the court considers that appropriate and facilitating the use of such procedure;
(f) helping the parties to settle the whole or part of the case;
(g) fixing timetables or otherwise controlling the progress of the case;
(h) considering whether the likely benefits of taking a particular step justify the cost of taking it;
(i) dealing with as many aspects of the case as it can on the same occasion;
(j) dealing with the case without the parties needing to attend at court;
(k) making use of technology; and
(l) giving directions to ensure that the trial of a case proceeds quickly and efficiently.

PART 2
APPLICATION AND INTERPRETATION OF THE RULES

[2.336]
2.8 Time

(1) This rule shows how to calculate any period of time for doing any act which is specified—

(a) by these Rules;
(b) by a practice direction; or
(c) by a judgment or order of the court.

(2) A period of time expressed as a number of days shall be computed as clear days.

(3) In this rule "clear days" means that in computing the number of days—

(a) the day on which the period begins; and
(b) if the end of the period is defined by reference to an event, the day on which that event occurs,

are not included.

Examples

(i) Notice of an application must be served at least 3 days before the hearing.
An application is to be heard on Friday 20 October.
The last date for service is Monday 16 October.

(ii) The court is to fix a date for a hearing.
The hearing must be at least 28 days after the date of notice.
If the court gives notice of the date of the hearing on 1 October, the earliest date for the hearing is 30 October.

(iii) Particulars of claim must be served within 14 days of service of the claim form.
The claim form is served on 2 October.
The last day for service of the particulars of claim is 16 October.

(4) Where the specified period—

(a) is 5 days or less; and
(b) includes—
 (i) a Saturday or Sunday; or
 (ii) a Bank Holiday, Christmas Day or Good Friday,

that day does not count.

Example

Notice of an application must be served at least 3 days before the hearing.
An application is to be heard on Monday 20 October.
The last date for service is Tuesday 14 October.

(5) [Subject to the provisions of Practice Direction 5C, when the period specified—]

(a) by these Rules or a practice direction; or
(b) by any judgment or court order,

for doing any act at the court office ends on a day on which the office is closed, that act shall be in time if done on the next day on which the court office is open.

NOTES

Para (5): words in square brackets substituted by the Civil Procedure (Amendment No 2) Rules 2009, SI 2009/3390, r 3(b).

[2.337]
2.9 Dates for compliance to be calendar dates and to include time of day

(1) Where the court gives a judgment, order or direction which imposes a time limit for doing any act, the last date for compliance must, wherever practicable—

(a) be expressed as a calendar date; and
(b) include the time of day by which the act must be done.

(2) Where the date by which an act must be done is inserted in any document, the date must, wherever practicable, be expressed as a calendar date.

[2.338]

2.10 Meaning of "month" in judgments, etc

Where "month" occurs in any judgment, order, direction or other document, it means a calendar month.

[2.339]

2.11 Time limits may be varied by parties

Unless these Rules or a practice direction provide otherwise or the court orders otherwise, the time specified by a rule or by the court for a person to do any act may be varied by the written agreement of the parties.

(Rules 3.8 (sanctions have effect unless defaulting party obtains relief), 28.4 (variation of case management timetable—fast track) and 29.5 (variation of case management timetable—multi-track) provide for time limits that cannot be varied by agreement between the parties).

PART 3
THE COURT'S CASE [AND COSTS] MANAGEMENT POWERS

NOTES

Part heading: words in square brackets inserted by the Civil Procedure (Amendment) Rules 2013, SI 2013/262, r 5(a).

[SECTION I CASE MANAGEMENT]

NOTES

Section heading: inserted by the Civil Procedure (Amendment) Rules 2013, SI 2013/262, r 5(c).

[2.340]

3.1 The court's general powers of management

(1) The list of powers in this rule is in addition to any powers given to the court by any other rule or practice direction or by any other enactment or any powers it may otherwise have.

(2) Except where these Rules provide otherwise, the court may—

(a) extend or shorten the time for compliance with any rule, practice direction or court order (even if an application for extension is made after the time for compliance has expired);

(b) adjourn or bring forward a hearing;

[(bb) require that any proceedings in the High Court be heard by a Divisional Court of the High Court;]

(c) require a party or a party's legal representative to attend the court;

(d) hold a hearing and receive evidence by telephone or by using any other method of direct oral communication;

(e) direct that part of any proceedings (such as a counterclaim) be dealt with as separate proceedings;

(f) stay the whole or part of any proceedings or judgment either generally or until a specified date or event;

(g) consolidate proceedings;

(h) try two or more claims on the same occasion;

(i) direct a separate trial of any issue;

(j) decide the order in which issues are to be tried;

(k) exclude an issue from consideration;

(l) dismiss or give judgment on a claim after a decision on a preliminary issue;

[(ll) order any party to file and [exchange a costs budget];]

(m) take any other step or make any other order for the purpose of managing the case and furthering the overriding objective[, including hearing an Early Neutral Evaluation with the aim of helping the parties settle the case].

(3) When the court makes an order, it may—

(a) make it subject to conditions, including a condition to pay a sum of money into court; and

(b) specify the consequence of failure to comply with the order or a condition.

[(3A) Where the court has made a direction in accordance with paragraph (2)(bb) the proceedings shall be heard by a Divisional Court of the High Court and not by a single judge.]

(4) Where the court gives directions it [will] take into account whether or not a party has complied with [the Practice Direction (Pre-Action Conduct) and] any relevant pre-action protocol.

(5) The court may order a party to pay a sum of money into court if that party has, without good reason, failed to comply with a rule, practice direction or a relevant pre-action protocol.

(6) When exercising its power under paragraph (5) the court must have regard to—

(a) the amount in dispute; and

(b) the costs which the parties have incurred or which they may incur.

[(6A) Where a party pays money into court following an order under paragraph (3) or (5), the money shall be security for any sum payable by that party to any other party in the proceedings . . .].

(7) A power of the court under these Rules to make an order includes a power to vary or revoke the order.

[(8) The court may contact the parties from time to time in order to monitor compliance with directions. The parties must respond promptly to any such enquiries from the court.]

NOTES

Para (2): sub-para (bb) inserted by the Civil Procedure (Amendment No 2) Rules 2017, SI 2017/889, rr 2, 3(a), as from 1 October 2017; sub-para (ll) inserted by the Civil Procedure (Amendment No 3) Rules 2005, SI 2005/2292, r 3; words in square brackets in that sub-paragraph substituted by the Civil Procedure (Amendment No 7) Rules 2013, SI 2013/1974, r 4(a); words in square brackets in sub-para (m) inserted by the Civil Procedure (Amendment No 4) Rules 2015, SI 2015/1569, rr 2, 4, as from 1 October 2015.

Para (3A): inserted by SI 2017/889, rr 2, 3(b), as from 1 October 2017.

Para (4): word in first pair of square brackets substituted, and words in second pair of square brackets inserted, by the Civil Procedure (Amendment No 3) Rules 2008, SI 2008/3327, r 3.

Para (6A): inserted by the Civil Procedure (Amendment) Rules 1999, SI 1999/1008, r 4; words omitted revoked by the Civil Procedure (Amendment No 3) Rules 2006, SI 2006/3435, r 3.

Para (8): added by the Civil Procedure (Amendment) Rules 2013, SI 2013/262, r 5(d).

[2.341]
[3.1A Case management – unrepresented parties

(1) This rule applies in any proceedings where at least one party is unrepresented.

(2) When the court is exercising any powers of case management, it must have regard to the fact that at least one party is unrepresented.

(3) Both the parties and the court must, when drafting case management directions in the multi-track and fast track, take as their starting point any relevant standard directions which can be found online at www.justice.gov.uk/courts/procedure-rules/civil and adapt them as appropriate to the circumstances of the case.

(4) The court must adopt such procedure at any hearing as it considers appropriate to further the overriding objective.

(5) At any hearing where the court is taking evidence this may include—
- (a) ascertaining from an unrepresented party the matters about which the witness may be able to give evidence or on which the witness ought to be cross-examined; and
- (b) putting, or causing to be put, to the witness such questions as may appear to the court to be proper.]

NOTES

Commencement: 1 October 2015.

Inserted by the Civil Procedure (Amendment No 4) Rules 2015, SI 2015/1569, rr 2, 5, as from 1 October 2015.

[2.342]
3.2 Court officer's power to refer to a judge

Where a step is to be taken by a court officer—
- (a) the court officer may consult a judge before taking that step;
- (b) the step may be taken by a judge instead of the court officer.

[2.343]
3.3 Court's power to make order of its own initiative

(1) Except where a rule or some other enactment provides otherwise, the court may exercise its powers on an application or of its own initiative.

(Part 23 sets out the procedure for making an application).

(2) Where the court proposes to make an order of its own initiative—
- (a) it may give any person likely to be affected by the order an opportunity to make representations; and
- (b) where it does so it must specify the time by and the manner in which the representations must be made.

(3) Where the court proposes—
- (a) to make an order of its own initiative; and
- (b) to hold a hearing to decide whether to make the order,

it must give each party likely to be affected by the order at least 3 days' notice of the hearing.

(4) The court may make an order of its own initiative without hearing the parties or giving them an opportunity to make representations.

(5) Where the court has made an order under paragraph (4)—
- (a) a party affected by the order may apply to have it set aside, varied or stayed; and
- (b) the order must contain a statement of the right to make such an application.

(6) An application under paragraph (5)(a) must be made—
- (a) within such period as may be specified by the court; or
- (b) if the court does not specify a period, not more than 7 days after the date on which the order was served on the party making the application.

[(7) If the court of its own initiative strikes out a statement of case or dismisses an application [(including an application for permission to appeal or for permission to apply for judicial review)], and it considers that the claim or application is totally without merit—
- (a) the court's order must record that fact; and

(b) the court must at the same time consider whether it is appropriate to make a civil restraint order.]

NOTES

Para (7): added by the Civil Procedure (Amendment No 2) Rules 2004, SI 2004/2072, r 4; words in square brackets inserted by the Civil Procedure (Amendment No 3) Rules 2005, SI 2005/2292, r 4.

[2.344]

3.4 Power to strike out a statement of case

(1) In this rule and rule 3.5, reference to a statement of case includes reference to part of a statement of case.

(2) The court may strike out a statement of case if it appears to the court—

(a) that the statement of case discloses no reasonable grounds for bringing or defending the claim;

(b) that the statement of case is an abuse of the court's process or is otherwise likely to obstruct the just disposal of the proceedings; or

(c) that there has been a failure to comply with a rule, practice direction or court order.

(3) When the court strikes out a statement of case it may make any consequential order it considers appropriate.

(4) Where—

(a) the court has struck out a claimant's statement of case;

(b) the claimant has been ordered to pay costs to the defendant; and

(c) before the claimant pays those costs, [the claimant] starts another claim against the same defendant, arising out of facts which are the same or substantially the same as those relating to the claim in which the statement of case was struck out,

the court may, on the application of the defendant, stay that other claim until the costs of the first claim have been paid.

(5) Paragraph (2) does not limit any other power of the court to strike out a statement of case.

[(6) If the court strikes out a claimant's statement of case and it considers that the claim is totally without merit—

(a) the court's order must record that fact; and

(b) the court must at the same time consider whether it is appropriate to make a civil restraint order.]

NOTES

Para (4): words in square brackets in sub-para (c) substituted by the Civil Procedure (Amendment) Rules 2014, SI 2014/407, r 6(a).

Para (6): added by the Civil Procedure (Amendment No 2) Rules 2004, SI 2004/2072, r 5.

[2.345]

3.8 Sanctions have effect unless defaulting party obtains relief

(1) Where a party has failed to comply with a rule, practice direction or court order, any sanction for failure to comply imposed by the rule, practice direction or court order has effect unless the party in default applies for and obtains relief from the sanction.

(Rule 3.9 sets out the circumstances which the court [will] consider on an application to grant relief from a sanction).

(2) Where the sanction is the payment of costs, the party in default may only obtain relief by appealing against the order for costs.

(3) Where a rule, practice direction or court order—

(a) requires a party to do something within a specified time, and

(b) specifies the consequence of failure to comply,

the time for doing the act in question may not be extended by agreement between the parties [except as provided in paragraph (4)].

[(4) In the circumstances referred to in paragraph (3) and unless the court orders otherwise, the time for doing the act in question may be extended by prior written agreement of the parties for up to a maximum of 28 days, provided always that any such extension does not put at risk any hearing date.]

NOTES

Para (1): word in square brackets substituted by the Civil Procedure (Amendment) Rules 2013, SI 2013/262, r 5(f).

Words in square brackets in para (3) inserted, and para (4) added, by the Civil Procedure (Amendment No 5) Rules 2014, SI 2014/1233, r 3.

[2.346]

3.9 Relief from sanctions

[(1) On an application for relief from any sanction imposed for a failure to comply with any rule, practice direction or court order, the court will consider all the circumstances of the case, so as to enable it to deal justly with the application, including the need—

(a) for litigation to be conducted efficiently and at proportionate cost; and

(b) to enforce compliance with rules, practice directions and orders.]

(2) An application for relief must be supported by evidence.

NOTES

Para (1): substituted by the Civil Procedure (Amendment) Rules 2013, SI 2013/262, r 5(g).

PART 18
FURTHER INFORMATION

[2.347]

18.1 Obtaining further information

(1) The court may at any time order a party to—

(a) clarify any matter which is in dispute in the proceedings; or

(b) give additional information in relation to any such matter,

whether or not the matter is contained or referred to in a statement of case.

(2) Paragraph (1) is subject to any rule of law to the contrary.

(3) Where the court makes an order under paragraph (1), the party against whom it is made must—

(a) file his response; and

(b) serve it on the other parties,

within the time specified by the court.

(Part 22 requires a response to be verified by a statement of truth).

[(Part 53 (defamation) restricts requirements for providing further information about sources of information in defamation claims).]

NOTES

Words in square brackets inserted by the Civil Procedure (Amendment) Rules 2000, SI 2000/221, r 8.

[2.348]

18.2 Restriction on the use of further information

The court may direct that information provided by a party to another party (whether given voluntarily or following an order made under rule 18.1) must not be used for any purpose except for that of the proceedings in which it is given.

PART 24
SUMMARY JUDGMENT

[2.349]

24.1 Scope of this Part

This Part sets out a procedure by which the court may decide a claim or a particular issue without a trial.

[(Part 53 makes special provision about summary disposal of defamation claims in accordance with the Defamation Act 1996).]

NOTES

Words in square brackets inserted by the Civil Procedure (Amendment) Rules 2000, SI 2000/221, r 12(a).

[2.350]

24.2 Grounds for summary judgment

The court may give summary judgment against a claimant or defendant on the whole of a claim or on a particular issue if—

(a) it considers that—

(i) that claimant has no real prospect of succeeding on the claim or issue; or

(ii) that defendant has no real prospect of successfully defending the claim or issue; and

(b) there is no other [compelling] reason why the case or issue should be disposed of at a trial.

(Rule 3.4 makes provision for the court to strike out a statement of case or part of a statement of case if it appears that it discloses no reasonable grounds for bringing or defending a claim).

NOTES

Word in square brackets in para (b) inserted by the Civil Procedure (Amendment No 3) Rules 2000, SI 2000/1317, r 9.

[2.351]

24.5 Evidence for the purposes of a summary judgment hearing

(1) If the respondent to an application for summary judgment wishes to rely on written evidence at the hearing, he must—

(a) file the written evidence; and

(b) serve copies on every other party to the application, at least 7 days before the summary judgment hearing.

(2) If the applicant wishes to rely on written evidence in reply, he must—

(a) file the written evidence; and

(b) serve a copy on the respondent,

at least 3 days before the summary judgment hearing.

(3) Where a summary judgment hearing is fixed by the court of its own initiative—

(a) any party who wishes to rely on written evidence at the hearing must—

(i) file the written evidence; and
(ii) unless the court orders otherwise, serve copies on every other party to the proceedings, at least 7 days before the date of the hearing;

(b) any party who wishes to rely on written evidence at the hearing in reply to any other party's written evidence must—
(i) file the written evidence in reply; and
(ii) unless the court orders otherwise serve copies on every other party to the proceedings, at least 3 days before the date of the hearing.

(4) This rule does not require written evidence—
(a) to be filed if it has already been filed; or
(b) to be served on a party on whom it has already been served.

[2.352]
24.6 Court's powers when it determines a summary judgment application

When the court determines a summary judgment application it may—
(a) give directions as to the filing and service of a defence;
(b) give further directions about the management of the case.

(Rule 3.1(3) provides that the court may attach conditions when it makes an order).

PART 31
DISCLOSURE AND INSPECTION OF DOCUMENTS

[2.353]
31.1 Scope of this Part

(1) This Part sets out rules about the disclosure and inspection of documents.

(2) This Part applies to all claims except a claim on the small claims track.

[2.354]
31.2 Meaning of disclosure

A party discloses a document by stating that the document exists or has existed.

[2.355]
31.3 Right of inspection of a disclosed document

(1) A party to whom a document has been disclosed has a right to inspect that document except where—
(a) the document is no longer in the control of the party who disclosed it;
(b) the party disclosing the document has a right or a duty to withhold inspection of it; . . . [or]
(c) paragraph (2) applies*[; or*
(d) rule 78.26 applies].

(Rule 31.8 sets out when a document is in the control of a party).

(Rule 31.19 sets out the procedure for claiming a right or duty to withhold inspection).

[(Rule 78.26 contains rules in relation to the disclosure and inspection of evidence arising out of mediation of certain cross-border disputes.)]

(2) Where a party considers that it would be disproportionate to the issues in the case to permit inspection of documents within a category or class of document disclosed under rule 31.6(b)—
(a) he is not required to permit inspection of documents within that category or class; but
(b) he must state in his disclosure statement that inspection of those documents will not be permitted on the grounds that to do so would be disproportionate.

(Rule 31.6 provides for standard disclosure).

(Rule 31.10 makes provision for a disclosure statement).

(Rule 31.12 provides for a party to apply for an order for specific inspection of documents).

NOTES

Word omitted from para (b) revoked by the Civil Procedure (Amendment) Rules 2011, SI 2011/88, r 9(a)(i).

Word "or" in square brackets in para (b) inserted by the Civil Procedure Rules 1998 (Amendment) (EU Exit) Regulations 2019, SI 2019/521, reg 10(1), (2)(a)(i), as from exit day (as defined in the European Union (Withdrawal) Act 2018, s 20).

Words in square brackets and italics inserted by SI 2011/88, r 9(a)(ii), (iii), (b) and subsequently revoked by SI 2019/521, reg 10(1), (2)(a)(ii), (iii), (b), as from exit day (as defined in the European Union (Withdrawal) Act 2018, s 20).

[2.356]
31.4 Meaning of document

In this Part—
"document" means anything in which information of any description is recorded; and
"copy", in relation to a document, means anything onto which information recorded in the document has been copied, by whatever means and whether directly or indirectly.

[2.357]
[31.5 Disclosure . . .

(1) In all claims to which rule 31.5(2) does not apply—

(a) an order to give disclosure is an order to give standard disclosure unless the court directs otherwise;
(b) the court may dispense with or limit standard disclosure; and
(c) the parties may agree in writing to dispense with or to limit standard disclosure.

(2) Unless the court otherwise orders, paragraphs (3) to (8) apply to all multi-track claims, other than those which include a claim for personal injuries.

(3) Not less than 14 days before the first case management conference each party must file and serve a report verified by a statement of truth, which—
(a) describes briefly what documents exist or may exist that are or may be relevant to the matters in issue in the case;
(b) describes where and with whom those documents are or may be located;
(c) in the case of electronic documents, describes how those documents are stored;
(d) estimates the broad range of costs that could be involved in giving standard disclosure in the case, including the costs of searching for and disclosing any electronically stored documents; and
(e) states which of the directions under paragraphs (7) or (8) are to be sought.

(4) In cases where the Electronic Documents Questionnaire has been exchanged, the Questionnaire should be filed with the report required by paragraph (3).

(5) Not less than seven days before the first case management conference, and on any other occasion as the court may direct, the parties must, at a meeting or by telephone, discuss and seek to agree a proposal in relation to disclosure that meets the overriding objective.

(6) If—
(a) the parties agree proposals for the scope of disclosure; and
(b) the court considers that the proposals are appropriate in all the circumstances,
the court may approve them without a hearing and give directions in the terms proposed.

(7) At the first or any subsequent case management conference, the court will decide, having regard to the overriding objective and the need to limit disclosure to that which is necessary to deal with the case justly, which of the following orders to make in relation to disclosure—
(a) an order dispensing with disclosure;
(b) an order that a party disclose the documents on which it relies, and at the same time request any specific disclosure it requires from any other party;
(c) an order that directs, where practicable, the disclosure to be given by each party on an issue by issue basis;
(d) an order that each party disclose any documents which it is reasonable to suppose may contain information which enables that party to advance its own case or to damage that of any other party, or which leads to an enquiry which has either of those consequences;
(e) an order that a party give standard disclosure;
(f) any other order in relation to disclosure that the court considers appropriate.

(8) The court may at any point give directions as to how disclosure is to be given, and in particular—
(a) what searches are to be undertaken, of where, for what, in respect of which time periods and by whom and the extent of any search for electronically stored documents;
(b) whether lists of documents are required;
(c) how and when the disclosure statement is to be given;
(d) in what format documents are to be disclosed (and whether any identification is required);
(e) what is required in relation to documents that once existed but no longer exist; and
(f) whether disclosure shall take place in stages.

(9) To the extent that the documents to be disclosed are electronic, the provisions of Practice Direction 31B—Disclosure of Electronic Documents will apply in addition to paragraphs (3) to (8).]

NOTES

Substituted by the Civil Procedure (Amendment) Rules 2013, SI 2013/262, r 11.

Words omitted from the rule heading revoked by the Civil Procedure (Amendment No 7) Rules 2013, SI 2013/1974, r 13.

[2.358]

31.6 Standard disclosure—what documents are to be disclosed

Standard disclosure requires a party to disclose only—
(a) the documents on which he relies; and
(b) the documents which—
 (i) adversely affect his own case;
 (ii) adversely affect another party's case; or
 (iii) support another party's case; and
(c) the documents which he is required to disclose by a relevant practice direction.

[2.359]

31.7 Duty of search

(1) When giving standard disclosure, a party is required to make a reasonable search for documents falling within rule 31.6(b) or (c).

(2) The factors relevant in deciding the reasonableness of a search include the following—
(a) the number of documents involved;
(b) the nature and complexity of the proceedings;

(c) the ease and expense of retrieval of any particular document; and
(d) the significance of any document which is likely to be located during the search.

(3) Where a party has not searched for a category or class of document on the grounds that to do so would be unreasonable, he must state this in his disclosure statement and identify the category or class of document.

(Rule 31.10 makes provision for a disclosure statement).

[2.360]
31.8 Duty of disclosure limited to documents which are or have been in party's control

(1) A party's duty to disclose documents is limited to documents which are or have been in his control.

(2) For this purpose a party has or has had a document in his control if—
(a) it is or was in his physical possession;
(b) he has or has had a right to possession of it; or
(c) he has or has had a right to inspect or take copies of it.

[2.361]
31.9 Disclosure of copies

(1) A party need not disclose more than one copy of a document.

(2) A copy of a document that contains a modification, obliteration or other marking or feature—
(a) on which a party intends to rely; or
(b) which adversely affects his own case or another party's case or supports another party's case;
shall be treated as a separate document.

(Rule 31.4 sets out the meaning of a copy of a document).

[2.362]
31.10 Procedure for standard disclosure

(1) The procedure for standard disclosure is as follows.

(2) Each party must make and serve on every other party, a list of documents in the relevant practice form.

(3) The list must identify the documents in a convenient order and manner and as concisely as possible.

(4) The list must indicate—
(a) those documents in respect of which the party claims a right or duty to withhold inspection; and
(b)
(i) those documents which are no longer in the party's control; and
(ii) what has happened to those documents.

(Rule 31.19(3) and (4) require a statement in the list of documents relating to any documents inspection of which a person claims he has a right or duty to withhold).

(5) The list must include a disclosure statement.

(6) A disclosure statement is a statement made by the party disclosing the documents—
(a) setting out the extent of the search that has been made to locate documents which he is required to disclose;
(b) certifying that he understands the duty to disclose documents; and
(c) certifying that to the best of his knowledge he has carried out that duty.

(7) Where the party making the disclosure statement is a company, firm, association or other organisation, the statement must also—
(a) identify the person making the statement; and
(b) explain why he is considered an appropriate person to make the statement.

(8) The parties may agree in writing—
(a) to disclose documents without making a list; and
(b) to disclose documents without the disclosing party making a disclosure statement.

(9) A disclosure statement may be made by a person who is not a party where this is permitted by a relevant practice direction.

[2.363]
31.11 Duty of disclosure continues during proceedings

(1) Any duty of disclosure continues until the proceedings are concluded.

(2) If documents to which that duty extends come to a party's notice at any time during the proceedings, he must immediately notify every other party.

[2.364]
31.12 Specific disclosure or inspection

(1) The court may make an order for specific disclosure or specific inspection.

(2) An order for specific disclosure is an order that a party must do one or more of the following things—
(a) disclose documents or classes of documents specified in the order;
(b) carry out a search to the extent stated in the order;
(c) disclose any documents located as a result of that search.

(3) An order for specific inspection is an order that a party permit inspection of a document referred to in rule 31.3(2).

(Rule 31.3(2) allows a party to state in his disclosure statement that he will not permit inspection of a document on the grounds that it would be disproportionate to do so).

[(Rule 78.26 contains rules in relation to the disclosure and inspection of evidence arising out of mediation of certain cross-border disputes.)]

NOTES

Words in square brackets and italics inserted by the Civil Procedure (Amendment) Rules 2011, SI 2011/88, r 9(c) and subsequently revoked by the Civil Procedure Rules 1998 (Amendment) (EU Exit) Regulations 2019, SI 2019/521, reg 10(1), (3), as from exit day (as defined in the European Union (Withdrawal) Act 2018, s 20).

[2.365]
31.13 Disclosure in stages

The parties may agree in writing, or the court may direct, that disclosure or inspection or both shall take place in stages.

[2.366]
31.14 Documents referred to in statements of case etc

[(1)] A party may inspect a document mentioned in—
(a) a statement of case;
(b) a witness statement;
(c) a witness summary; [or]
(d) an affidavit[.]
(e) . . .

[(2) Subject to rule 35.10(4), a party may apply for an order for inspection of any document mentioned in an expert's report which has not already been disclosed in the proceedings.]

(Rule 35.10(4) makes provision in relation to instructions referred to in an expert's report).

NOTES

Para (1) was numbered as such, para (2) was added, and all amendments to para (1) were made, by the Civil Procedure (Amendment No 5) Rules 2001, SI 2001/4015, r 20.

[2.367]
31.15 Inspection and copying of documents

Where a party has a right to inspect a document—
(a) that party must give the party who disclosed the document written notice of his wish to inspect it;
(b) the party who disclosed the document must permit inspection not more than 7 days after the date on which he received the notice; and
(c) that party may request a copy of the document and, if he also undertakes to pay reasonable copying costs, the party who disclosed the document must supply him with a copy not more than 7 days after the date on which he received the request.

(Rule 31.3 and 31.14 deal with the right of a party to inspect a document).

[2.368]
31.16 Disclosure before proceedings start

(1) This rule applies where an application is made to the court under any Act for disclosure before proceedings have started.
(2) The application must be supported by evidence.
(3) The court may make an order under this rule only where—
(a) the respondent is likely to be a party to subsequent proceedings;
(b) the applicant is also likely to be a party to those proceedings;
(c) if proceedings had started, the respondent's duty by way of standard disclosure, set out in rule 31.6, would extend to the documents or classes of documents of which the applicant seeks disclosure; and
(d) disclosure before proceedings have started is desirable in order to—
(i) dispose fairly of the anticipated proceedings;
(ii) assist the dispute to be resolved without proceedings; or
(iii) save costs.
(4) An order under this rule must—
(a) specify the documents or the classes of documents which the respondent must disclose; and
(b) require him, when making disclosure, to specify any of those documents—
(i) which are no longer in his control; or
(ii) in respect of which he claims a right or duty to withhold inspection.
(5) Such an order may—
(a) require the respondent to indicate what has happened to any documents which are no longer in his control; and
(b) specify the time and place for disclosure and inspection.

[(Rule 78.26 contains rules in relation to the disclosure and inspection of evidence arising out of mediation of certain cross-border disputes.)]

NOTES

Words in square brackets and italics inserted by the Civil Procedure (Amendment) Rules 2011, SI 2011/88, r 9(d) and subsequently revoked by the Civil Procedure Rules 1998 (Amendment) (EU Exit) Regulations 2019, SI 2019/521, reg 10(1), (4), as from exit day (as defined in the European Union (Withdrawal) Act 2018, s 20).

[2.369]
31.17 Orders for disclosure against a person not a party

(1) This rule applies where an application is made to the court under any Act for disclosure by a person who is not a party to the proceedings.

(2) The application must be supported by evidence.

(3) The court may make an order under this rule only where—
- (a) the documents of which disclosure is sought are likely to support the case of the applicant or adversely affect the case of one of the other parties to the proceedings; and
- (b) disclosure is necessary in order to dispose fairly of the claim or to save costs.

(4) An order under this rule must—
- (a) specify the documents or the classes of documents which the respondent must disclose; and
- (b) require the respondent, when making disclosure, to specify any of those documents—
  - (i) which are no longer in his control; or
  - (ii) in respect of which he claims a right or duty to withhold inspection.

(5) Such an order may—
- (a) require the respondent to indicate what has happened to any documents which are no longer in his control; and
- (b) specify the time and place for disclosure and inspection.

[(Rule 78.26 contains rules in relation to the disclosure and inspection of evidence arising out of mediation of certain cross-border disputes.)]

NOTES

Words in square brackets and italics inserted by the Civil Procedure (Amendment) Rules 2011, SI 2011/88, r 9(e) and subsequently revoked by the Civil Procedure Rules 1998 (Amendment) (EU Exit) Regulations 2019, SI 2019/521, reg 10(1), (5), as from exit day (as defined in the European Union (Withdrawal) Act 2018, s 20).

[2.370]
31.18 Rules not to limit other powers of the court to order disclosure

Rules 31.16 and 31.17 do not limit any other power which the court may have to order—
- (a) disclosure before proceedings have started; and
- (b) disclosure against a person who is not a party to proceedings.

[2.371]
31.19 Claim to withhold inspection or disclosure of a document

(1) A person may apply, without notice, for an order permitting him to withhold disclosure of a document on the ground that disclosure would damage the public interest.

(2) Unless the court orders otherwise, an order of the court under paragraph (1)—
- (a) must not be served on any other person; and
- (b) must not be open to inspection by any person.

(3) A person who wishes to claim that he has a right or a duty to withhold inspection of a document, or part of a document, must state in writing—
- (a) that he has such a right or duty; and
- (b) the grounds on which he claims that right or duty.

(4) The statement referred to in paragraph (3) must be made—
- (a) in the list in which the document is disclosed; or
- (b) if there is no list, to the person wishing to inspect the document.

(5) A party may apply to the court to decide whether a claim made under paragraph (3) should be upheld.

(6) For the purpose of deciding an application under paragraph (1) (application to withhold disclosure) or paragraph (3) (claim to withhold inspection) the court may—
- (a) require the person seeking to withhold disclosure or inspection of a document to produce that document to the court; and
- (b) invite any person, whether or not a party, to make representations.

(7) An application under paragraph (1) or paragraph (5) must be supported by evidence.

(8) This Part does not affect any rule of law which permits or requires a document to be withheld from disclosure or inspection on the ground that its disclosure or inspection would damage the public interest.

[2.372]
31.20 Restriction on use of a privileged document inspection of which has been inadvertently allowed

Where a party inadvertently allows a privileged document to be inspected, the party who has inspected the document may use it or its contents only with the permission of the court.

[2.373]
31.21 Consequence of failure to disclose documents or permit inspection

A party may not rely on any document which he fails to disclose or in respect of which he fails to permit inspection unless the court gives permission.

[2.374]
31.22 Subsequent use of disclosed documents [and completed Electronic Document Questionnaires]

(1) A party to whom a document has been disclosed may use the document only for the purpose of the proceedings in which it is disclosed, except where—

(a) the document has been read to or by the court, or referred to, at a hearing which has been held in public;
(b) the court gives permission; or
(c) the party who disclosed the document and the person to whom the document belongs agree.

(2) The court may make an order restricting or prohibiting the use of a document which has been disclosed, even where the document has been read to or by the court, or referred to, at a hearing which has been held in public.

(3) An application for such an order may be made—

(a) by a party; or
(b) by any person to whom the document belongs.

[(4) For the purpose of this rule, an Electronic Documents Questionnaire which has been completed and served by another party pursuant to Practice Direction 31B is to be treated as if it is a document which has been disclosed.]

NOTES

Words in square brackets in the rule heading added, and para (4) added, by the Civil Procedure (Amendment No 2) Rules 2010, SI 2010/1953, r 4.

[2.375]
[31.23 False disclosure statements

(1) Proceedings for contempt of court may be brought against a person if he makes, or causes to be made, a false disclosure statement, without an honest belief in its truth.

[(Section 6 of Part 81 contains provisions in relation to committal for making a false disclosure statement.)]

(2) . . .]

NOTES

Added by the Civil Procedure (Amendment) Rules 2000, SI 2000/221, r 16.
Para (1): words in square brackets added by the Civil Procedure (Amendment No 2) Rules 2012, SI 2012/2208, r 5(a).
Para (2): revoked by SI 2012/2208, r 5(b).

PART 35
EXPERTS AND ASSESSORS

[2.376]
35.1 Duty to restrict expert evidence

Expert evidence shall be restricted to that which is reasonably required to resolve the proceedings.

[2.377]
[35.2 Interpretation and definitions

(1) A reference to an 'expert' in this Part is a reference to a person who has been instructed to give or prepare expert evidence for the purpose of proceedings.

(2) 'Single joint expert' means an expert instructed to prepare a report for the court on behalf of two or more of the parties (including the claimant) to the proceedings.]

NOTES

Substituted by the Civil Procedure (Amendment) Rules 2009, SI 2009/2092, r 5(b).

[2.378]
35.3 Experts—overriding duty to the court

(1) [It is the duty of experts to help the court on matters within their expertise].

(2) This duty overrides any obligation to the person from whom [experts have received instructions or by whom they are paid].

NOTES

Words in square brackets substituted by the Civil Procedure (Amendment) Rules 2009, SI 2009/2092, r 5(c), (d).

[2.379]
35.4 Court's power to restrict expert evidence—

(1) No party may call an expert or put in evidence an expert's report without the court's permission.

[(2) When parties apply for permission they must [provide an estimate of the costs of the proposed expert evidence and] identify—

(a) the field in which expert evidence is required [and the issues which the expert evidence will address]; and
(b) where practicable, the name of the proposed expert.]

(3) If permission is granted . . . it shall be in relation only to the expert named or the field identified under paragraph (2). [The order granting permission may specify the issues which the expert evidence should address.]

[(3A) Where a claim has been allocated to the small claims track or the fast track, if permission is given for expert evidence, it will normally be given for evidence from only one expert on a particular issue.

[(3B), (3C) (*Outside the scope of this work.*)]

[(4) The court may limit the amount of a party's expert's fees and expenses that may be recovered from any other party.]

NOTES

Para (2): substituted by the Civil Procedure (Amendment) Rules 2009, SI 2009/2092, r 5(e); words in square brackets inserted by the Civil Procedure (Amendment) Rules 2013, SI 2013/262, r 13(a), (b).

Para (3): words omitted revoked by SI 2009/2092, r 5(f); words in square brackets added by SI 2013/262, r 13(c).

Para (3A): inserted by SI 2009/2092, r 5(g); words in square brackets substituted by the Civil Procedure (Amendment No 2) Rules 2009, SI 2009/3390, r 18(a).

Para (4): substituted by SI 2009/2092, r 5(h).

[2.380]
35.5 General requirement for expert evidence to be given in a written report

(1) Expert evidence is to be given in a written report unless the court directs otherwise.

(2) If a claim is on the [small claims track or the] fast track, the court will not direct an expert to attend a hearing unless it is necessary to do so in the interests of justice.

NOTES

Para (2): words in square brackets inserted by the Civil Procedure (Amendment) Rules 2009, SI 2009/2092, r 5(i).

[2.381]
35.6 Written questions to experts

[(1) A party may put written questions about an expert's report (which must be proportionate) to—

(a) an expert instructed by another party; or
(b) a single joint expert appointed under rule 35.7.]

(2) Written questions under paragraph (1)—

(a) may be put once only;
(b) must be put within 28 days of service of the expert's report; and
(c) must be for the purpose only of clarification of the report,

unless in any case,

(i) the court gives permission; or
(ii) the other party agrees.

(3) An expert's answers to questions put in accordance with paragraph (1) shall be treated as part of the expert's report.

(4) Where—

(a) a party has put a written question to an expert instructed by another party . . . ; and
(b) the expert does not answer that question,

the court may make one or both of the following orders in relation to the party who instructed the expert—

(i) that the party may not rely on the evidence of that expert; or
(ii) that the party may not recover the fees and expenses of that expert from any other party.

NOTES

Para (1): substituted by the Civil Procedure (Amendment) Rules 2009, SI 2009/2092, r 5(j)(i).

Para (4): words omitted from sub-para (a) revoked by SI 2009/2092, r 5(j)(ii).

[2.382]
[35.7 Court's power to direct that evidence is to be given by a single joint expert

(1) Where two or more parties wish to submit expert evidence on a particular issue, the court may direct that the evidence on that issue is to be given by a single joint expert.

(2) Where the parties who wish to submit the evidence ("the relevant parties") cannot agree who should be the single joint expert, the court may—

(a) select the expert from a list prepared or identified by the relevant parties; or
(b) direct that the expert be selected in such other manner as the court may direct.]

NOTES

Substituted by the Civil Procedure (Amendment) Rules 2009, SI 2009/2092, r 5(k).

[2.383]

35.8 Instructions to a single joint expert

(1) Where the court gives a direction under rule 35.7 for a single joint expert to be used, [any relevant] party may give instructions to the expert.

[(2) When a party gives instructions to the expert that party must, at the same time, send a copy to the other relevant parties.]

(3) The court may give directions about—
- (a) the payment of the expert's fees and expenses; and
- (b) any inspection, examination or experiments which the expert wishes to carry out.

(4) The court may, before an expert is instructed—
- (a) limit the amount that can be paid by way of fees and expenses to the expert; and
- (b) direct that [some or all of the relevant] parties pay that amount into court.

(5) Unless the court otherwise directs, the [relevant] parties are jointly and severally liable for the payment of the expert's fees and expenses.

NOTES

Paras (1), (4), (5): words in square brackets substituted by the Civil Procedure (Amendment) Rules 2009, SI 2009/2092, r 5(l), (n), (o).

Para (2): substituted by SI 2009/2092, r 5(m).

[2.384]

35.9 Power of court to direct a party to provide information

Where a party has access to information which is not reasonably [available to another party], the court may direct the party who has access to the information to—
- (a) prepare and file a document recording the information; and
- (b) serve a copy of that document on the other party.

NOTES

Words in square brackets substituted by the Civil Procedure (Amendment) Rules 2009, SI 2009/2092, r 5(p).

[2.385]

35.10 Contents of report

(1) An expert's report must comply with the requirements set out in [[Practice Direction] 35].

[(2) At the end of an expert's report there must be a statement that the expert understands and has complied with their duty to the court.]

(3) The expert's report must state the substance of all material instructions, whether written or oral, on the basis of which the report was written.

(4) The instructions referred to in paragraph (3) shall not be privileged against disclosure but the court will not, in relation to those instructions—
- (a) order disclosure of any specific document; or
- (b) permit any questioning in court, other than by the party who instructed the expert,

unless it is satisfied that there are reasonable grounds to consider the statement of instructions given under paragraph (3) to be inaccurate or incomplete.

NOTES

Para (1): words in first (outer) pair of square brackets substituted by the Civil Procedure (Amendment) Rules 2009, SI 2009/2092, r 5(q)(i); words in second (inner) pair of square brackets substituted by the Civil Procedure (Amendment No 2) Rules 2009, SI 2009/3390, r 18(b).

Para (2): substituted by SI 2009/2092, r 5(q)(ii).

[2.386]

35.11 Use by one party of expert's report disclosed by another

Where a party has disclosed an expert's report, any party may use that expert's report as evidence at the trial.

[2.387]

35.12 Discussions between experts

(1) The court may, at any stage, direct a discussion between experts for the purpose of requiring the experts to—
- [(a) identify and discuss the expert issues in the proceedings; and
- (b) where possible, reach an agreed opinion on those issues].

(2) The court may specify the issues which the experts must discuss.

[(3) The court may direct that following a discussion between the experts they must prepare a statement for the court setting out those issues on which—
- (a) they agree; and
- (b) they disagree, with a summary of their reasons for disagreeing.]

(4) The content of the discussion between the experts shall not be referred to at the trial unless the parties agree.

(5) Where experts reach agreement on an issue during their discussions, the agreement shall not bind the parties unless the parties expressly agree to be bound by the agreement.

NOTES

Para (1): sub-paras (a), (b) substituted by the Civil Procedure (Amendment No 5) Rules 2001, SI 2001/4015, r 21.

Para (3): substituted by the Civil Procedure (Amendment) Rules 2009, SI 2009/2092, r 5(r).

[2.388]

35.13 Consequence of failure to disclose expert's report

A party who fails to disclose an expert's report may not use the report at the trial or call the expert to give evidence orally unless the court gives permission.

[PART 36
OFFERS TO SETTLE

[2.389]

36.1 Scope of this Part

(1) This Part contains a self-contained procedural code about offers to settle made pursuant to the procedure set out in this Part ("Part 36 offers").

(2) Section I of this Part contains general rules about Part 36 offers.

(3) Section II of this Part contains rules about offers to settle where the parties have followed the Pre-Action Protocol for Low Value Personal Injury Claims in Road Traffic Accidents ("the RTA Protocol") or the Pre-Action Protocol for Low Value Personal Injury (Employers' Liability and Public Liability) Claims ("the EL/PL Protocol") and have started proceedings under Part 8 in accordance with Practice Direction 8B.]

NOTES

Commencement: 6 April 2015.

Part 36 (rr 36.1–36.30) were substituted by the Civil Procedure (Amendment No 8) Rules 2014, SI 2014/3299, rr 4, 7, Sch 1, as from 6 April 2015, subject to transitional provisions in r 18(1), (2) thereof.

[SECTION 1 PART 36 OFFERS TO SETTLE

GENERAL

[2.390]

36.2 Scope of this Section

(1) This Section does not apply to an offer to settle to which Section II of this Part applies.

(2) Nothing in this Section prevents a party making an offer to settle in whatever way that party chooses, but if the offer is not made in accordance with rule 36.5, it will not have the consequences specified in this Section.

(Rule 44.2 requires the court to consider an offer to settle that does not have the costs consequences set out in this Section in deciding what order to make about costs.)

(3) A Part 36 offer may be made in respect of the whole, or part of, or any issue that arises in—
- (a) a claim, counterclaim or other additional claim; or
- (b) an appeal or cross-appeal from a decision made at a trial.

(Rules 20.2 and 20.3 provide that counterclaims and other additional claims are treated as claims and that references to a claimant or a defendant include a party bringing or defending an additional claim.)]

NOTES

Commencement: 6 April 2015.

Substituted as noted to r 36.1 at **[2.389]**.

Note: Section II of this Part (omitted) applies to road traffic accident cases and is outside the scope of this work.

[2.391]

[36.3 Definitions

In this Section—
- (a) the party who makes an offer is the "offeror";
- (b) the party to whom an offer is made is the "offeree";
- (c) a "trial" means any trial in a case whether it is a trial of all issues or a trial of liability, quantum or some other issue in the case;
- (d) a trial is "in progress" from the time when it starts until the time when judgment is given or handed down;
- (e) a case is "decided" when all issues in the case have been determined, whether at one or more trials;
- (f) "trial judge" includes the judge (if any) allocated in advance to conduct a trial; and
- (g) "the relevant period" means—
  - (i) in the case of an offer made not less than 21 days before a trial, the period specified under rule 36.5(1)(c) or such longer period as the parties agree;
  - (ii) otherwise, the period up to the end of such trial.]

Part 2 Statutory Instruments

NOTES

Commencement: 6 April 2015.
Substituted as noted to r 36.1 at **[2.389]**.

[2.392]
[36.4 Application of Part 36 to appeals

(1) Except where a Part 36 offer is made in appeal proceedings, it shall have the consequences set out in this Section only in relation to the costs of the proceedings in respect of which it is made, and not in relation to the costs of any appeal from a decision in those proceedings.

(2) Where a Part 36 offer is made in appeal proceedings, references in this Section to a term in the first column below shall be treated, unless the context requires otherwise, as references to the corresponding term in the second column—

Term	*Corresponding term*
Claim	Appeal
Counterclaim	Cross-appeal
Case	Appeal proceedings
Claimant	Appellant
Defendant	Respondent
Trial	Appeal hearing
Trial judge	Appeal judge]

NOTES

Commencement: 6 April 2015.
Substituted as noted to r 36.1 at **[2.389]**.

[MAKING OFFERS

[2.393]
36.5 Form and content of a Part 36 offer

(1) A Part 36 offer must—
- (a) be in writing;
- (b) make clear that it is made pursuant to Part 36;
- (c) specify a period of not less than 21 days within which the defendant will be liable for the claimant's costs in accordance with rule 36.13 or 36.20 if the offer is accepted;
- (d) state whether it relates to the whole of the claim or to part of it or to an issue that arises in it and if so to which part or issue; and
- (e) state whether it takes into account any counterclaim.

(Rule 36.7 makes provision for when a Part 36 offer is made.)

(2) Paragraph (1)(c) does not apply if the offer is made less than 21 days before the start of a trial.

(3) In appropriate cases, a Part 36 offer must contain such further information as is required by rule 36.18 (personal injury claims for future pecuniary loss), rule 36.19 (offer to settle a claim for provisional damages), and rule 36.22 (deduction of benefits).

(4) A Part 36 offer which offers to pay or offers to accept a sum of money will be treated as inclusive of all interest until—
- (a) the date on which the period specified under rule 36.5(1)(c) expires; or
- (b) if rule 36.5(2) applies, a date 21 days after the date the offer was made.]

NOTES

Commencement: 6 April 2015.
Substituted as noted to r 36.1 at **[2.389]**.

[2.394]
[36.6 Part 36 offers—defendant's offer

(1) Subject to rules 36.18(3) and 36.19(1), a Part 36 offer by a defendant to pay a sum of money in settlement of a claim must be an offer to pay a single sum of money.

(2) A defendant's offer that includes an offer to pay all or part of the sum at a date later than 14 days following the date of acceptance will not be treated as a Part 36 offer unless the offeree accepts the offer.]

NOTES

Commencement: 6 April 2015.
Substituted as noted to r 36.1 at **[2.389]**.

[2.395]
[36.7 Time when a Part 36 offer is made

(1) A Part 36 offer may be made at any time, including before the commencement of proceedings.

(2) A Part 36 offer is made when it is served on the offeree.

(Part 6 provides detailed rules about service of documents.)]

NOTES

Commencement: 6 April 2015.
Substituted as noted to r 36.1 at **[2.389]**.

[CLARIFYING, WITHDRAWING AND CHANGING THE TERMS OF OFFERS

[2.396]
36.8 Clarification of a Part 36 offer

(1) The offeree may, within 7 days of a Part 36 offer being made, request the offeror to clarify the offer.

(2) If the offeror does not give the clarification requested under paragraph (1) within 7 days of receiving the request, the offeree may, unless the trial has started, apply for an order that the offeror do so.

(Part 23 contains provisions about making an application to the court.)

(3) If the court makes an order under paragraph (2), it must specify the date when the Part 36 offer is to be treated as having been made.]

NOTES

Commencement: 6 April 2015.
Substituted as noted to r 36.1 at **[2.389]**.

[2.397]
[36.9 Withdrawing or changing the terms of a Part 36 offer generally

(1) A Part 36 offer can only be withdrawn, or its terms changed, if the offeree has not previously served notice of acceptance.

(2) The offeror withdraws the offer or changes its terms by serving written notice of the withdrawal or change of terms on the offeree.

(Rule 36.17(7) deals with the costs consequences following judgment of an offer which is withdrawn.)

(3) Subject to rule 36.10, such notice of withdrawal or change of terms takes effect when it is served on the offeree.

(Rule 36.10 makes provision about when permission is required to withdraw or change the terms of an offer before the expiry of the relevant period.)

(4) Subject to paragraph (1), after expiry of the relevant period—

- (a) the offeror may withdraw the offer or change its terms without the permission of the court; or
- (b) the offer may be automatically withdrawn in accordance with its terms.

(5) Where the offeror changes the terms of a Part 36 offer to make it more advantageous to the offeree—

- (a) such improved offer shall be treated, not as the withdrawal of the original offer; but as the making of a new Part 36 offer on the improved terms; and
- (b) subject to rule 36.5(2), the period specified under rule 36.5(1)(c) shall be 21 days or such longer period (if any) identified in the written notice referred to in paragraph (2).]

NOTES

Commencement: 6 April 2015.
Substituted as noted to r 36.1 at **[2.389]**.

[2.398]
[36.10 Withdrawing or changing the terms of a Part 36 offer before the expiry of the relevant period

(1) Subject to rule 36.9(1), this rule applies where the offeror serves notice before expiry of the relevant period of withdrawal of the offer or change of its terms to be less advantageous to the offeree.

(2) Where this rule applies—

- (a) if the offeree has not served notice of acceptance of the original offer by the expiry of the relevant period, the offeror's notice has effect on the expiry of that period; and
- (b) if the offeree serves notice of acceptance of the original offer before the expiry of the relevant period, that acceptance has effect unless the offeror applies to the court for permission to withdraw the offer or to change its terms—
  - (i) within 7 days of the offeree's notice of acceptance; or
  - (ii) if earlier, before the first day of trial.

(3) On an application under paragraph (2)(b), the court may give permission for the original offer to be withdrawn or its terms changed if satisfied that there has been a change of circumstances since the making of the original offer and that it is in the interests of justice to give permission.]

NOTES

Commencement: 6 April 2015.
Substituted as noted to r 36.1 at **[2.389]**.

[ACCEPTING OFFERS

[2.399]
36.11 Acceptance of a Part 36 offer

(1) A Part 36 offer is accepted by serving written notice of acceptance on the offeror.

Part 2 Statutory Instruments

(2) Subject to paragraphs (3) and (4) and to rule 36.12, a Part 36 offer may be accepted at any time (whether or not the offeree has subsequently made a different offer), unless it has already been withdrawn.
(Rule 21.10 deals with compromise, etc by or on behalf of a child or protected party.)
(Rules 36.9 and 36.10 deal with withdrawal of Part 36 offers.)

(3) The court's permission is required to accept a Part 36 offer where—

(a) rule 36.15(4) applies;
(b) rule 36.22(3)(b) applies, the relevant period has expired and further deductible amounts have been paid to the claimant since the date of the offer;
(c) an apportionment is required under rule 41.3A; or
(d) a trial is in progress.

(Rule 36.15 deals with offers by some but not all of multiple defendants.)
(Rule 36.22 defines "deductible amounts".)
(Rule 41.3A requires an apportionment in proceedings under the Fatal Accidents Act 1976 and Law Reform (Miscellaneous Provisions) Act 1934.)

(4) Where the court gives permission under paragraph (3), unless all the parties have agreed costs, the court must make an order dealing with costs, and may order that the costs consequences set out in rule 36.13 apply.]

NOTES

Commencement: 6 April 2015.
Substituted as noted to r 36.1 at **[2.389]**.

[2.400]
[36.12 Acceptance of a Part 36 offer in a split-trial case

(1) This rule applies in any case where there has been a trial but the case has not been decided within the meaning of rule 36.3.

(2) Any Part 36 offer which relates only to parts of the claim or issues that have already been decided can no longer be accepted.

(3) Subject to paragraph (2) and unless the parties agree, any other Part 36 offer cannot be accepted earlier than 7 clear days after judgment is given or handed down in such trial.]

NOTES

Commencement: 6 April 2015.
Substituted as noted to r 36.1 at **[2.389]**.

[2.401]
[36.13 Costs consequences of acceptance of a Part 36 offer

(1) Subject to paragraphs (2) and (4) and to rule 36.20, where a Part 36 offer is accepted within the relevant period the claimant will be entitled to the costs of the proceedings (including their recoverable pre-action costs) up to the date on which notice of acceptance was served on the offeror.
(Rule 36.20 makes provision for the costs consequences of accepting a Part 36 offer in certain personal injury claims where the claim no longer proceeds under the RTA or EL/PL Protocol.)

(2) Where—

(a) a defendant's Part 36 offer relates to part only of the claim; and
(b) at the time of serving notice of acceptance within the relevant period the claimant abandons the balance of the claim,

the claimant will only be entitled to the costs of such part of the claim unless the court orders otherwise.

(3) Except where the recoverable costs are fixed by these Rules, costs under paragraphs (1) and (2) are to be assessed on the standard basis if the amount of costs is not agreed.
(Rule 44.3(2) explains the standard basis for the assessment of costs.)
(Rule 44.9 contains provisions about when a costs order is deemed to have been made and applying for an order under section 194(3) of the Legal Services Act 2007.)
(Part 45 provides for fixed costs in certain classes of case.)

(4) Where—

(a) a Part 36 offer which was made less than 21 days before the start of a trial is accepted; or
(b) a Part 36 offer which relates to the whole of the claim is accepted after expiry of the relevant period; or
(c) subject to paragraph (2), a Part 36 offer which does not relate to the whole of the claim is accepted at any time,

the liability for costs must be determined by the court unless the parties have agreed the costs.

(5) Where paragraph (4)(b) applies but the parties cannot agree the liability for costs, the court must, unless it considers it unjust to do so, order that—

(a) the claimant be awarded costs up to the date on which the relevant period expired; and
(b) the offeree do pay the offeror's costs for the period from the date of expiry of the relevant period to the date of acceptance.

(6) In considering whether it would be unjust to make the orders specified in paragraph (5), the court must take into account all the circumstances of the case including the matters listed in rule 36.17(5).

(7) The claimant's costs include any costs incurred in dealing with the defendant's counterclaim if the Part 36 offer states that it takes it into account.]

NOTES

Commencement: 6 April 2015.
Substituted as noted to r 36.1 at **[2.389]**.

[2.402]
[36.14 Other effects of acceptance of a Part 36 offer

(1) If a Part 36 offer is accepted, the claim will be stayed.

(2) In the case of acceptance of a Part 36 offer which relates to the whole claim, the stay will be upon the terms of the offer.

(3) If a Part 36 offer which relates to part only of the claim is accepted, the claim will be stayed as to that part upon the terms of the offer.

(4) If the approval of the court is required before a settlement can be binding, any stay which would otherwise arise on the acceptance of a Part 36 offer will take effect only when that approval has been given.

(5) Any stay arising under this rule will not affect the power of the court—
- (a) to enforce the terms of a Part 36 offer; or
- (b) to deal with any question of costs (including interest on costs) relating to the proceedings.

(6) Unless the parties agree otherwise in writing, where a Part 36 offer that is or includes an offer to pay or accept a single sum of money is accepted, that sum must be paid to the claimant within 14 days of the date of—
- (a) acceptance; or
- (b) the order when the court makes an order under rule 41.2 (order for an award of provisional damages) or rule 41.8 (order for an award of periodical payments), unless the court orders otherwise.

(7) If such sum is not paid within 14 days of acceptance of the offer, or such other period as has been agreed, the claimant may enter judgment for the unpaid sum.

(8) Where—
- (a) a Part 36 offer (or part of a Part 36 offer) which is not an offer to which paragraph (6) applies is accepted; and
- (b) a party alleges that the other party has not honoured the terms of the offer,

that party may apply to enforce the terms of the offer without the need for a new claim.]

NOTES

Commencement: 6 April 2015.
Substituted as noted to r 36.1 at **[2.389]**.

[2.403]
[36.15 Acceptance of a Part 36 offer made by one or more, but not all, defendants

(1) This rule applies where the claimant wishes to accept a Part 36 offer made by one or more, but not all, of a number of defendants.

(2) If the defendants are sued jointly or in the alternative, the claimant may accept the offer if—
- (a) the claimant discontinues the claim against those defendants who have not made the offer; and
- (b) those defendants give written consent to the acceptance of the offer.

(3) If the claimant alleges that the defendants have a several liability[(GL)] to the claimant, the claimant may—
- (a) accept the offer; and
- (b) continue with the claims against the other defendants if entitled to do so.

(4) In all other cases the claimant must apply to the court for permission to accept the Part 36 offer.]

NOTES

Commencement: 6 April 2015.
Substituted as noted to r 36.1 at **[2.389]**.

[UNACCEPTED OFFERS

[2.404]
36.16 Restriction on disclosure of a Part 36 offer

(1) A Part 36 offer will be treated as "without prejudice except as to costs".

(2) The fact that a Part 36 offer has been made and the terms of such offer must not be communicated to the trial judge until the case has been decided.

(3) Paragraph (2) does not apply—
- (a) where the defence of tender before claim has been raised;
- (b) where the proceedings have been stayed under rule 36.14 following acceptance of a Part 36 offer;
- (c) where the offeror and the offeree agree in writing that it should not apply; or
- (d) where, although the case has not been decided—
  - (i) any part of, or issue in, the case has been decided; and
  - (ii) the Part 36 offer relates only to parts or issues that have been decided.

(4) In a case to which paragraph (3)(d)(i) applies, the trial judge—

(a) may be told whether or not there are Part 36 offers other than those referred to in paragraph (3)(d)(ii); but
(b) must not be told the terms of any such other offers unless any of paragraphs (3)(a) to (c) applies.]

NOTES

Commencement: 6 April 2015.
Substituted as noted to r 36.1 at **[2.389]**.

[2.405]
[36.17 Costs consequences following judgment

(1) Subject to rule 36.21, this rule applies where upon judgment being entered—
(a) a claimant fails to obtain a judgment more advantageous than a defendant's Part 36 offer; or
(b) judgment against the defendant is at least as advantageous to the claimant as the proposals contained in a claimant's Part 36 offer.

(Rule 36.21 makes provision for the costs consequences following judgment in certain personal injury claims where the claim no longer proceeds under the RTA or EL/PL Protocol.)

(2) For the purposes of paragraph (1), in relation to any money claim or money element of a claim, "more advantageous" means better in money terms by any amount, however small, and "at least as advantageous" shall be construed accordingly.

(3) Subject to paragraphs (7) and (8), where paragraph (1)(a) applies, the court must, unless it considers it unjust to do so, order that the defendant is entitled to—
(a) costs (including any recoverable pre-action costs) from the date on which the relevant period expired; and
(b) interest on those costs.

(4) Subject to paragraph (7), where paragraph (1)(b) applies, the court must, unless it considers it unjust to do so, order that the claimant is entitled to—
(a) interest on the whole or part of any sum of money (excluding interest) awarded, at a rate not exceeding 10% above base rate for some or all of the period starting with the date on which the relevant period expired;
(b) costs (including any recoverable pre-action costs) on the indemnity basis from the date on which the relevant period expired;
(c) interest on those costs at a rate not exceeding 10% above base rate; and
(d) provided that the case has been decided and there has not been a previous order under this sub-paragraph, an additional amount, which shall not exceed £75,000, calculated by applying the prescribed percentage set out below to an amount which is—
  (i) the sum awarded to the claimant by the court; or
  (ii) where there is no monetary award, the sum awarded to the claimant by the court in respect of costs—

Amount awarded by the court	Prescribed percentage
Up to £500,000	10% of the amount awarded
Above £500,000	10% of the first £500,000 and (subject to the limit of £75,000) 5% of any amount above that figure.

(5) In considering whether it would be unjust to make the orders referred to in paragraphs (3) and (4), the court must take into account all the circumstances of the case including—
(a) the terms of any Part 36 offer;
(b) the stage in the proceedings when any Part 36 offer was made, including in particular how long before the trial started the offer was made;
(c) the information available to the parties at the time when the Part 36 offer was made;
(d) the conduct of the parties with regard to the giving of or refusal to give information for the purposes of enabling the offer to be made or evaluated; and
(e) whether the offer was a genuine attempt to settle the proceedings.

(6) Where the court awards interest under this rule and also awards interest on the same sum and for the same period under any other power, the total rate of interest must not exceed 10% above base rate.

(7) Paragraphs (3) and (4) do not apply to a Part 36 offer—
(a) which has been withdrawn;
(b) which has been changed so that its terms are less advantageous to the offeree where the offeree has beaten the less advantageous offer;
(c) made less than 21 days before trial, unless the court has abridged the relevant period.

(8) Paragraph (3) does not apply to a soft tissue injury claim to which rule 36.21 applies.

(Rule 44.2 requires the court to consider an offer to settle that does not have the costs consequences set out in this Section in deciding what order to make about costs.)]

NOTES

Commencement: 6 April 2015.
Substituted as noted to r 36.1 at **[2.389]**.

[MISCELLANEOUS

[2.406]
36.23 Cases in which the offeror's costs have been limited to court fees

(1) This rule applies in any case where the offeror is treated as having filed a costs budget limited to applicable court fees, or is otherwise limited in their recovery of costs to such fees.
(Rule 3.14 provides that a litigant may be treated as having filed a budget limited to court fees for failure to file a budget.)

(2) "Costs" in rules 36.13(5)(b), 36.17(3)(a) and 36.17(4)(b) shall mean—

(a) in respect of those costs subject to any such limitation, 50% of the costs assessed without reference to the limitation; together with

(b) any other recoverable costs.]

NOTES
Commencement: 6 April 2015.
Substituted as noted to r 36.1 at **[2.389]**.

POLICE (HEALTH AND SAFETY) REGULATIONS 1999

(SI 1999/860)

NOTES
Made: 17 March 1999.
Authority: Health and Safety at Work etc Act 1974, ss 2(4), 15(1), (2), (8), 51A(4), 82(3)(a), Sch 3, paras 1(1)(a), (2), 11.
Commencement: 14 April 1999.

[2.407]
1 Citation and commencement

These Regulations may be cited as the Police (Health and Safety) Regulations 1999 and shall come into force on 14th April 1999.

[2.408]
2 Amendment to the meaning of "employee" and "at work" in regulations made under Part I of the Health and Safety at Work etc Act 1974

For the purposes of regulations made under Part I of the 1974 Act before the coming into force of the Police (Health and Safety) Act 1997—

(a) a person who, otherwise than under a contract of employment, holds the office of constable or an appointment as police cadet shall be treated as an employee of the relevant officer referred to in section 51A of the 1974 Act; and

(b) a person holding the office of constable shall be treated as at work throughout the time when he is on duty but not otherwise,

and any reference to an "employee" and "at work" in those regulations shall have effect accordingly.

3–5 *(Reg 3 amended the Safety Representatives and Safety Committees Regulations 1977, SI 1977/500, reg 2(1), and inserted reg 2A (revoked) and is now spent; regs 4, 5 amend the Personal Protective Equipment at Work Regulations 1992, SI 1992/2966, and the Provision and Use of Work Equipment Regulations 1998, SI 1998/2306.)*

SCHEDULE

(The Schedule set out the Safety Representatives and Safety Committees Regulations 1977, SI 1977/500, Sch 1 (revoked) and is now spent.)

REDUNDANCY PAYMENTS (CONTINUITY OF EMPLOYMENT IN LOCAL GOVERNMENT, ETC) (MODIFICATION) ORDER 1999

(SI 1999/2277)

NOTES
Made: 11 August 1999.
Authority: Employment Rights Act 1996, ss 209(1)(b), 236.
Commencement: 1 September 1999.

ARRANGEMENT OF ARTICLES

Part 2 Statutory Instruments

SCHEDULES

[2.409]

1 Citation, commencement and interpretation

(1) This Order may be cited as the Redundancy Payments (Continuity of Employment in Local Government, etc) (Modification) Order 1999 and shall come into force on 1st September 1999.

(2) In this Order—

- (a) "the 1983 Order" means the Redundancy Payments (Local Government) (Modification) Order 1983;
- (b) "the 1972 Act" means the Local Government Act 1972;
- (c) "the 1978 Act" means the Employment Protection (Consolidation) Act 1978;
- (d) "the 1980 Act" means the Education (Scotland) Act 1980;
- (e) "the 1985 Act" means the Local Government Act 1985;
- (f) "the 1988 Act" means the Education Reform Act 1988;
- (g) "the 1992 Act" means the Further and Higher Education Act 1992;
- (h) "the 1994 Act" means the Local Government etc (Scotland) Act 1994;
- (i) "the 1996 Act" means the Employment Rights Act 1996;
- (j) "the 1998 Act" means the School Standards and Framework Act 1998;
- (k) "the Education Act" means the Education Act 1996.

(3) Subject to paragraph (4) below, in this Order "relevant event" in relation to a person means any event occurring on or after the day on which this Order comes into force on the happening of which that person may become entitled to a redundancy payment in accordance with the 1996 Act.

(4) Where an event has occurred on or after 21st June 1998 but before the day on which this Order comes into force, on the happening of which a person employed immediately before that event by the English Sports Council may have become entitled to a redundancy payment in accordance with the 1996 Act, "relevant event" in this Order includes that event in relation to that person.

[2.410]

2 Application of this Order

(1) This Order applies to any person who immediately before the occurrence of a relevant event is employed by an employer specified in Schedule 1 to this Order.

(2) Where a person commenced employment with a Further Education Funding Council established by section 1 of the 1992 Act before 1st April 1996 and left that employment either—

- (a) before that date, or
- (b) by reason of a relevant event after the date on which this Order comes into force,

this Order applies to that person as if that Council were specified in Schedule 1 to this Order.

[2.411]

3 Modification of certain redundancy payments provisions

In relation to any person to whom this Order applies, the provisions of the 1996 Act mentioned in Part I of Schedule 2 to this Order shall, for the purposes of determining that person's entitlement to a redundancy payment under the 1996 Act and the amount of such payment, have effect subject to the modifications specified in that Part.

[2.412]

4 Revocation

The Orders specified in Schedule 3 to this Order are revoked.

[2.413]

5 Transitional, supplementary and incidental provisions

(1) In relation to a person to whom this Order applies—

- (a) any reference to the 1996 Act in any enactment shall have effect as a reference to that Act as modified by this Order; and
- (b) any document which refers, whether specifically or by means of a general description, to the 1996 Act shall, except so far as the context otherwise requires, be construed as referring to that Act as modified by this Order.

(2) Where a period of employment of a person to whom this Order applies falls to be calculated in accordance with the provisions of the 1996 Act as modified by this Order, the provisions of this Order shall have effect in relation to that calculation whether the period in question falls wholly or partly before or wholly after this Order comes into force.

(3) Notwithstanding the revocation by article 4 above of the Orders specified in Schedule 3 to this Order, in relation to determining any person's entitlement to a redundancy payment following an event which occurred before the date on which this Order comes into force (or, in the case of a person such as is referred to in paragraph (4) of article 1, before the date referred to in that paragraph), and which would have been a relevant event if it had occurred on or after that date, the 1983 Order shall continue to have effect as it had effect on the date of that event.

SCHEDULES

SCHEDULE 1
EMPLOYMENT TO WHICH THIS ORDER APPLIES: EMPLOYERS IMMEDIATELY BEFORE THE RELEVANT EVENT

Article 2

Section 1—Local Government

[2.414]

1. In relation to England, a county council, a district council, a London borough council, the Common Council of the City of London, the Council of the Isles of Scilly; in relation to Wales, a county council or a county borough council, established under section 20 of the 1972 Act.

2. A council constituted under section 2 of the 1994 Act.

3. In relation to England, a parish council, a common parish council, a parish meeting; in relation to Wales, a community council, a common community council.

4. Any authority established by an order under section 10 of the 1985 Act.

5. A joint board or joint body constituted by or under any enactment for the purposes of exercising the functions of two or more bodies described in any of paragraphs 1 to 4 above.

6. Any other authority or body, not specified in any of paragraphs 1 to 4 above, established by or under any enactment for the purpose of exercising the functions of, or advising, one or more of the bodies specified in paragraphs 1 to 4 above.

[6A. The Greater London Authority.

6B. Transport for London.]

[6C. A functional body as defined in section 424 of the Greater London Authority Act 1999 but excluding Transport for London.

6D. The London Transport Users' Committee established under section 247 of the 1999 Act.

6E. The Cultural Strategy Group for London established under section 375 of that Act.]

7. Any committee (including a joint committee) established by or under any enactment for the purpose of exercising the functions of, or advising, one or more of the bodies specified in any of paragraphs 1 to 6 above.

8. Any two or more bodies described in any of paragraphs 1 to 7 above acting jointly or as a combined authority.

9. Any association which is representative of any two or more authorities described in any of paragraphs 1 to 4 above.

10. Any committee established by one or more of the associations described in paragraph 9 above for the purpose of exercising the functions of, or advising, one or more of such associations.

11. An association which is representative of one or more of the associations described in paragraph 9 above and of another body or other bodies, and included in whose objects is the assembling and dissemination of information and advising with regard to conditions of service in local government service and generally.

12. An organisation which is representative of an association or associations described in paragraph 9 above and employees' organisations and among whose objects is the negotiation of pay and conditions of service in local government service.

13. A National Park authority established under section 63 of the Environment Act 1995.

[13A. A National Park Authority established under sections 6 to 8 of the National Parks (Scotland) Act 2000.]

14. A residuary body established by section 57(1)(b) of the 1985 Act.

15. The Residuary Body for Wales (Corff Gweddilliol Cymru).

[16. Audit Scotland.]

17. The Commission for Local Administration in England.

18. The Commission for Local Administration in Wales.

19. The Commission for Local Administration in Scotland.

20. The Local Government Management Board.

21. Employers Organisation for Local Government.

22. Improvement and Development Agency for Local Government.

[23. Improvement Service Company.]

Section 2—Planning and development

1. One North East.

2. Yorkshire Forward.

3. North West Development Agency (NWDA).

4. Advantage West Midlands.

[4A. Dewsbury Partnership Limited.]

5. East Midlands Development Agency (EMDA).

6. East of England Development Agency (EEDA).

7. South East of England Development Agency (SEEDA).

[7A. SEERA Limited.]

8. South West of England Development Agency (SWERDA).

9. A development corporation within the meaning of the New Towns Act 1981.

[9A. A Mayoral development corporation within the meaning of section 198 of the Localism Act 2011.]

10. An Urban Development Corporation established under section 135 of the Local Government Planning and Land Act 1980.

11. A housing action trust established under Part III of the Housing Act 1988.

12. The Broads Authority, established under the Norfolk and Suffolk Broads Act 1988.

[13. . . .]

14. The Countryside Commission for Scotland.

15. The Development Board for Rural Wales.

16. The Edinburgh New Town Conservation Committee.

[17. The Regulator of Social Housing.]

18. Huddersfield Pride Limited.

19. Scottish Enterprise, established under the Enterprise and New Towns (Scotland) Act 1990.

20. Scottish Homes, established under the Housing (Scotland) Act 1988.

21. Springfield Horseshoe Housing Management Co-operative Limited.

22. Housing for Wales (Tai Cymru).

23. . . .

24. Batley Action Limited.

25. Bethnal Green City Challenge Company Limited.

26. The Blackburn City Challenge Partnership Board.

27. Bolton City Challenge Partnership Limited.

28. Bradford City Challenge Limited.

29. Brixton Challenge Company Limited.

30. Community North (Sunderland) Limited.

31. Dalston City Partnership Limited.

32. Deptford City Challenge Limited.

33. Derby Pride Limited.

34. Douglas Valley Partnership Limited.

35. Harlesden City Challenge Limited.

36. Hulme Regeneration Limited.

37. Leicester City Challenge Limited.

[**37A.** Manchester Investment and Development Agency Service Limited (MIDAS).]

38. Newcastle West End Partnership Limited.

39. Newtown South Aston City Challenge Limited.

40. North Kensington City Challenge Company Limited.

41. North Tyneside City Challenge Partnership Limited.

[**41A.** . . .]

42. Stratford Development Partnership Limited.

43. Wolverhampton City Challenge Limited.

44. . . .

[**45.** Pennine Housing 2000 Limited.

46. Twin Valley Homes Limited.

47. Urban Futures London Limited.]

[**48.** Aire-Wharfe Community Housing Trust Limited.

49. Bradford Building Services Limited.

50. Bradford Community Housing Trust Limited.

51. Bradford West City Community Housing Trust Limited.

[**51A.** City Building (Glasgow) LLP.]

52. Coast & County Housing Limited.

53. Dumfries and Galloway Housing Partnership Limited.

54. East Bradford Community Housing Trust Limited.

55. Knowsley Housing Trust.

56. North Bradford Community Housing Trust Limited.

57. Northern Housing Consortium Limited.

58. Shipley Community Housing Trust Limited.

59. South Bradford Community Housing Trust Limited.

60. Sunderland Housing Group.]

Section 3—Education

1. The governing body of a further education establishment for the time being mainly dependent for its maintenance on assistance from [local authorities (within the meaning of the Education Act)], or grants under section 485 of the Education Act or on such assistance and grants taken together.

2. The governing body of an aided school within the meaning of the Education Act.

3. The governing body of a foundation school, voluntary aided school or foundation special school within the meaning of the 1998 Act.

4. The managers of a grant-aided school as defined in section 135(1) of the 1980 Act.

5. The governing body of a central institution as defined in section 135(1) of the 1980 Act other than a college of agriculture.

6. The governing body of a College of Education as defined in section 135(1) of the 1980 Act.

7. The managers, other than a local authority, of a school which before any direction made by the Secretary of State under paragraph 2(1) of Schedule 7 to the Social Work (Scotland) Act 1968 was a school which immediately before the commencement of Part III of that Act was approved under section 83 of the Children and Young Persons (Scotland) Act 1937 if the employee was employed by those managers at the date the direction became effective.

8. A person carrying on a city technology college[, a city college for the technology of the arts or [an Academy]] established under an agreement with the Secretary of State under section 482 of the Education Act.

9. A company formed to manage a college of further education by virtue of section 65(1) of the Self-Governing Schools etc (Scotland) Act 1989.

10. The board of management of a self-governing school as defined in section 80(1) of the Self-Governing Schools etc (Scotland) Act 1989.

11. A further education corporation established under section 15 or 16 of the 1992 Act or in respect of which an order has been made under section 47 of that Act.

12. The governing body of an institution which is a designated institution for the purposes of Part I of the 1992 Act or, in the case of such an institution conducted by a company, that company.

13. The board of management of a college of further education, established under Part I of the Further and Higher Education (Scotland) Act 1992.

14. The governing body of a designated institution within the meaning of section 44(2) of the Further and Higher Education (Scotland) Act 1992.

15. A higher education corporation established under section 121 or 122 of the 1988 Act or in respect of which an order has been made under section 122A of that Act.

16. The governing body of an institution designated under section 129 of the 1988 Act or, in the case of such an institution conducted by a company, that company.

17. An Education Action Forum established under sections 10 and 11 of the 1998 Act.

18. The governing body of a grant-maintained school.

19. The governing body of a grant-maintained special school.

20. The Central Council for Education and Training in Social Work.

21. The Centre for Information on Language Teaching and Research.

[**21A.** The Centre for Literacy in Primary Education.

21B. Connexions Lancashire Limited.]

22. Cwmni Cynnal.

23. The General Teaching Council for Scotland, established under the [Public Services Reform (General Teaching Council for Scotland) Order 2011].

24. The National Institute of Adult Continuing Education (England and Wales).

25. Newbattle Abbey College.

26. The Scottish Community Education Council.

27. Scottish Consultative Council on the Curriculum.

28. The Scottish Council for Educational Technology.

29. The Scottish Council for Research in Education.

30. The Scottish Examination Board.

31. The Scottish Vocational Education Council.

[[**32.** Shetland Arts Development Agency.]

33. VT Four S Limited.]

Section 4—Careers guidance

1. Argyll & Bute Careers Partnership Limited.

2. Calderdale and Kirklees Careers Service Partnership Limited.

3. Cambridgeshire Careers Guidance Limited.

4. Capital Careers Limited.

5. Career Connections Limited.

6. Career Decisions Limited.

7. Career Development Edinburgh and Lothians.

8. Career Path (Northamptonshire) Limited.

9. Careerpaths (Cardiff and Vale) Limited.

10. Careers and Education Business Partnership.

11. Careers Central Limited.

[**11A.** Careers Enterprise (Futures) Limited.]

12. Careers Partnership Limited.

13. Careers Service Lancashire Area West Limited.

14. Central Careers Limited.

15. Cornwall and Devon Careers Limited.

[**15A.** Coventry, Solihull and Warwickshire Partnership Limited.]

16. Derbyshire Careers Service Limited.

17. East Lancashire Careers Services Limited.

18. Education Business Partnership (Wigan) Limited.

19. Essex Careers and Business Partnership Limited.

20. Future Steps Limited.

21. Futures Careers Limited.

22. Grampian Careers.

23. Guidance Enterprises Group Limited.

24. GuideLine Career Services Limited.

25. Gwent Careers Service Partnership Limited.

26. Hereford and Worcester Careers Service Limited.

27. Hertfordshire Careers Services Limited.

28. Highland Careers Services Limited.

29. The Humberside Partnership.

30. Learning Partnership West.

31. Leeds Careers Guidance.

32. Leicestershire Careers and Guidance Services Limited.

33. Lifetime Careers Barnsley, Doncaster and Rotherham Limited.

34. Lifetime Careers Bolton, Bury and Rochdale Limited.

35. Lifetime Careers Brent and Harrow Limited.

36. Lifetime Careers Stockport and High Peak Limited.

37. Lifetime Careers Wiltshire Limited.

38. Lincolnshire Careers and Guidance Services Limited.

[**38A.** London South Bank Careers.]

39. Mid Glamorgan Careers Limited.

40. Norfolk Careers Services Limited.

41. North East Wales Careers Service Company Limited.

[**41A.** Oldham Education Business and Guidance Services.]

42. Orkney Opportunities Centre.

43. Prospects Careers Services Limited.

44. Quality Careers Services Limited.

45. St Helens Careers Service Limited.

46. Sheffield Careers Guidance Services.

47. Shropshire Careers Service Limited.

48. Suffolk Careers Limited.

49. Tayside Careers Limited.

50. West Glamorgan Careers and Education Business Company Limited.

Section 5—Public transport

1. A Passenger Transport Executive established under section 9(1) of the Transport Act 1968.

2. A metropolitan county passenger transport authority established by section 28 of the 1985 Act.

3. The Forth Road Bridge Joint Board.

4. The Tay Road Bridge Joint Board.

Section 6—Police, fire and civil defence

1. A fire authority constituted by a combination scheme made under the Fire Services Act 1947.

[**1A.** A fire and rescue authority constituted by a scheme under section 2 of the Fire and Rescue Services Act 2004 or a scheme to which section 4 of that Act applies.]

[**1B.** A combined authority established under section 103 of the Local Democracy, Economic Development and Construction Act 2009 which is a fire and rescue authority for the purposes of the Fire and Rescue Services Act 2004 in relation to persons deployed wholly or partly in relation to the combined authority's fire and rescue functions.]

[**1C.** A fire and rescue authority created by an order under section 4A of the Fire and Rescue Services Act 2004.]

[**2.** A police and crime commissioner established under section 1 of the Police Reform and Social Responsibility Act 2011.

2A. A chief constable established under section 2 of the Police Reform and Social Responsibility Act 2011.

2B. The Commissioner of Police of the Metropolis established under section 4 of the Police Reform and Social Responsibility Act 2011.]

3. A [metropolitan county fire and rescue authority] established by section 26 of the 1985 Act.

[**4.** A company the members of which comprise fire and rescue authorities in England and whose objects include the operation of a regional fire control centre.]

Section 7—Sports Councils

1. The English Sports Council.

2. The Scottish Sports Council.

3. The Sports Council for Wales.

4. The United Kingdom Sports Council.

Section 8—Social services

1. Coverage Care Limited.

[**1ZA.** Essex Cares Limited.

1ZB. Essex Community Support Limited.

1ZC. Essex Employment and Inclusion Limited.

1ZD. Essex Equipment Services Limited.]

[**1A.** Forfarshire Society for the Blind.

1B. Harlow Welfare Rights & Advice.]

2. The Humberside Independent Care Association.

[**2A.** New Charter Building Company Limited.

2B. New Charter Housing Trust Limited.]

3. Quantum Care Limited.

4. Sandwell Community Caring Trust Limited.

[[**4ZA.** Social Care and Social Work Improvement Scotland.]

4ZB. The Scottish Social Services Council.

4ZC. Shetland Council of Social Services.]

[**4A.** Shetland Welfare Trust.

4AA. Tynedale Housing Company Limited.]

5. Waltham Forest Specialist Housing Consortium Limited.

6. The Wrekin Housing Trust Limited.

Section 9—Museums

1. The Board of Governors of the Museum of London.

2. The Board of Trustees of The National Museums and Galleries on Merseyside.

3. Coventry Museum of British Road Transport.

4. The Geffrye Museum Trust.

5. The Horniman Public Museum and Public Park Trust.

6. National Coal Mining Museum for England Trust Limited.

7. The Scottish Museums Council.

[**8.** Woodhorn Charitable Trust.]

Section 10—Miscellaneous bodies

[**1.** A valuation tribunal in Wales established under the Local Government Finance Act 1988.]

2. . . .

3. An area tourist board established by virtue of an order made under section 172, 173 or 174 of the 1994 Act.

4. A probation committee within the meaning of the Probation Service Act 1993.

[**4A.** A local probation board within the meaning of the Criminal Justice and Court Services Act 2000.]

[**4B.** a probation trust.]

5. A magistrates' courts committee or the Committee of Magistrates for the Inner London Area, within the meaning of the Justices of the Peace Act 1979.

[**5A.** A body designated as a Care Trust under section 45 of the Health and Social Care Act 2001.]

[**5B.** A community justice authority under section 3 of the Management of Offenders (Scotland) Act 2005.

[**5BA.** A person who performs a function of a local authority pursuant to a direction under section 497A(4) or (4A) of the Education Act (which confers power on the Secretary of State to secure the proper performance of local authority education functions, and is applied to social services functions relating to children by section 50 of the Children Act 2004 and to functions relating to childcare by section 15 of the Childcare Act 2006).]

5C. Active Stirling Limited.

5D. Ardroy Outdoor Learning Trust.

5E. Arts and Theatres Trust Fife Limited.]

[**6.** Blyth Valley Arts and Leisure Limited.

6A. The Business Shop—Angus Limited.

6AA. The Care Quality Commission.]

6B. The Care Standards Inspectorate for Wales.

6C. The Children and Family Court Advisory and Support Service.]

[**6D.** City Markets (Glasgow) LLP.

6E. City Parking (Glasgow) LLP.

6F. City Property (Glasgow) LLP.]

7. CIP (Hounslow) Limited.

[**7A.** Clackmannanshire Leisure.]

8. Community Initiative Partnerships.

[8AA. Cordia (Services) LLP.]

[8A. Coventry Sports Trust Limited.]

[8B. CV One Limited.]

[8C. Culture and Sport Glasgow.

8D. Culture and Sport Glasgow (Trading) CIC.]

9. Derwentside Leisure Limited.

[9ZA. East End Partnership Limited.]

[9A. Edinburgh Leisure.

9AA. Enfield Leisure Centres Limited.]

[9B. Enjoy East Lothian Limited.]

10. The Environment Agency.

[10A. Fife Coast and Countryside Trust.

10B. Fife Sports and Leisure Trust Limited.

10C. Forth Valley GIS Limited.

10D. Glasgow Community and Safety Services Limited.]

11. Greenwich Leisure Limited.

[11A. Herefordshire Community Leisure Trust.]

12. Hounslow Cultural and Community Services.

13. Hounslow Sports and Recreation Services.

[13A. The Islesburgh Trust.

13B. Kirklees Active Leisure Trust.]

14. The Land Authority for Wales.

15. Leisure Tynedale.

16. The Lee Valley Regional Park Authority.

17. The London Pensions Fund Authority.

[17A. The National Care Standards Commission.]

[17B, 17C. . . .]

18. National Mobility Services Trust Limited.

19. New Park Village TMC Limited.

[19ZA. North Lanarkshire Leisure Limited.

19ZB. Nuneaton and Bedworth Leisure Trust.]

[19A. Oldham Community Leisure Limited.

[19AA. Pendle Leisure Limited.]

19B. Renfrewshire Leisure Limited.

19C. Salford Community Leisure Limited.

[19CA. Sandwell Arts Trust.]

19D. Sandwell Sport and Leisure Trust.]

20. The Scottish Children's Reporter Administration established under section 128 of the 1994 Act [and continued by section 15 (the Scottish Children's Reporter Administration) of the Children's Hearings (Scotland) Act 2011].

21. The Scottish Environment Protection Agency.

[22. Scottish Water.]

[22A. Shetland Recreational Trust.]

[22B. Somerset Leisure Limited.]

23. The South Yorkshire Pensions Authority.

[23A. Sport Aberdeen.]

24. Strathclyde European Partnerships Limited.

[24A. Tameside Sports Trust.

24B. Tees Active Limited.

24C. The Valuation Tribunal Service.

24D. The Water Industry Commissioner for Scotland.]

25. West Lothian Leisure Limited.

[26. Wigan Leisure and Culture Trust.]

NOTES

Section 1: paras 6A–6E inserted by the London Government (Continuity of Employment) Order 2000, SI 2000/1042, art 4(1)–(3); paras 13A, 23 inserted, and para 16 substituted, by the Redundancy Payments (Continuity of Employment in Local Government, etc) (Modification) Order (Amendment) Order 2010, SI 2010/903, arts 2, 3.

Section 2: paras 4A, 37A, 48–60 inserted and added respectively by the Redundancy Payments (Continuity of Employment in Local Government, etc) (Modification) (Amendment) Order 2004, SI 2004/1682, art 2(1), (2); para 7A inserted by the Redundancy Payments (Continuity of Employment in Local Government, etc) (Modification) (Amendment) Order 2001, SI 2001/866, art 2(1), (2); para 9A inserted by the Localism Act 2011 (Housing and Regeneration Functions in Greater London) (Consequential, Transitory, Transitional and Saving Provisions) Order 2012, SI 2012/666, art 8(1), Sch 1, para 2(1), (2)(a); paras 13, 17 substituted by the Housing and Regeneration Act 2008 (Consequential Provisions) (No 2) Order 2008, SI 2008/2831, arts 3, 4, Sch 1, para 10, Sch 2, para 3; para 13 subsequently revoked by the Localism Act 2011 (Regulation of Social Housing) (Consequential Provisions) Order 2012, SI 2012/641, art 2(4); para 23 revoked by the Welsh Development Agency (Transfer of Functions to the National Assembly for Wales and Abolition) Order 2005, SI 2005/3226, art 7(1)(b), Sch 2, Pt 1, para 4; paras 41A, 51A inserted by SI 2010/903, arts 2, 4; para 41A subsequently revoked by SI 2012/666, art 8(1), Sch 1, para 2(1), (2)(b); para 44 revoked by the Abolition of the Commission for the New Towns and the Urban Regeneration Agency (Appointed Day and Consequential Amendments) Order 2009, SI 2009/801, reg 3(1); paras 45–47 added by the Redundancy Payments (Continuity of Employment in Local Government, etc) (Modification) (Amendment) Order 2002, SI 2002/532, art 2(1), (2)(a).

Section 3: words in square brackets in para 1 substituted by the Local Education Authorities and Children's Services Authorities (Integration of Functions) (Local and Subordinate Legislation) Order 2010, SI 2010/1172, art 4, Sch 3, para 33(1), (2); words in first (outer) pair of square brackets in para 8 substituted by SI 2001/866, art 2(1), (3); words in second (inner) pair of square brackets in para 8 substituted, and paras 21A, 21B, 32, 33 inserted and added respectively, by SI 2004/1682, art 2(1), (3); words in square brackets in para 23 substituted by the Public Services Reform (General Teaching Council for Scotland) Order 2011, SSI 2011/215, art 33(1), Sch 6, para 4; para 32 substituted by SI 2010/903, arts 2, 5.

Section 4: para 11A inserted by SI 2001/866, art 2(1), (7); paras 15A, 41A inserted by SI 2004/1682, art 2(1), (4); para 38A inserted by SI 2002/532, art 2(1), (3).

Section 6: para 1A inserted, in relation to England, by the Fire and Rescue Services Act 2004 (Consequential Amendments) (England) Order 2004, SI 2004/3168, art 50, and, in relation to Wales, by the Fire and Rescue Services Act 2004 (Consequential Amendments) (Wales) Order 2005, SI 2005/2929, art 50; para 1B inserted by the Greater Manchester Combined Authority (Fire and Rescue Functions) Order 2017, SI 2017/469, art 13, as from 8 May 2017; para 1C inserted, in relation to England, by the Fire and Rescue Authority (Police and Crime Commissioner) (Application of Local Policing Provisions, Inspection, Powers to Trade and Consequential Amendments) Order 2017, SI 2017/863, art 29, Sch 2, para 3, as from 1 October 2017; paras 2, 2A, 2B substituted, for original para 2, by the Local Policing Bodies (Consequential Amendments and Transitional Provision) Order 2012, SI 2012/2733, art 2; words in square brackets in para 3 substituted by the Civil Contingencies Act 2004, s 32(1), Sch 2, Pt 1, para 10(1), (2); original para 4 revoked by SI 2000/1042, art 4(1), (4)(b) and new para 4 added by SI 2010/903, arts 2, 6.

Section 8: paras 1ZA–1ZD inserted by SI 2010/903, arts 2, 7; paras 1A, 1B, 4ZA–4ZC inserted by SI 2004/1682, art 2(1), (5); paras 2A, 2B inserted by SI 2001/866, art 2(1), (5); paras 4A, 4AA substituted, for para 4A (as inserted by SI 2001/866, art 2(1), (5)), by SI 2002/532, art 2(1), (4)(a); para 4ZA substituted by SI 2011/2581, art 2, Sch 2, Pt 2, para 27.

Section 9: para 8 added by SI 2010/903, arts 2, 8.

Section 10: paras 1, 22 substituted, para 2 revoked, paras 4A, 8B, 9ZA, 11A, 13A, 13B, 19A–19D, 22A, 24A–24D, 26 inserted, and paras 6, 6A, 6B, 6C substituted (for para 6 as originally enacted), para 6A (as inserted by SI 2001/866, art 2(1), (6)(a)), and original para 6AA (as inserted by SI 2002/532, art 2(1), (5)(b)), by SI 2004/1682, art 2(1), (6); para 4B inserted by the Offender Management Act 2007 (Consequential Amendments) Order 2008, SI 2008/912, art 3, Sch 2, para 1; paras 5A, 7A, 8A, 17A inserted, and paras 9A, 9AA substituted, for para 9A (as inserted by SI 2001/866, art 2(1), (6)(b)), by SI 2002/532, art 2(1), (5); paras 5B–5E, 6D–6F, 8AA, 8C, 8D, 9B, 10A–10D, 19ZA, 19ZB, 19AA, 19CA, 22B, 23A inserted by SI 2010/903, arts 2, 9; para 5BA inserted by the Redundancy Payments (Continuity of Employment in Local Government, etc) (Modification) (Amendment) Order 2015, SI 2015/916, art 2(1), as from 1 July 2015; new para 6AA inserted by the Health and Social Care Act 2008 (Consequential Amendments and Transitory Provisions) Order 2008, SI 2008/2250, art 2(1), (3); paras 17B, 17C (as inserted by SI 2004/664, art 2, Sch 1, para 2) (omitted) revoked by the Health and Social Care Act 2008 (Commencement No 9, Consequential Amendments and Transitory, Transitional and Saving Provisions) Order 2009, SI 2009/462, art 12, Sch 5, para 6; words in square brackets in para 20 inserted by the Children's Hearings (Scotland) Act 2011 (Consequential and Transitional Provisions and Savings) Order 2013, SI 2013/1465, art 17(1), Sch 1, Pt 2, para 15.

The Commission for Local Administration in Wales was abolished by the Public Services Ombudsman (Wales) Act 2005, s 36(1) on 1 April 2006.

The reference to a metropolitan county passenger transport authority in Section 5, para 2 above is to be read as a reference to an Integrated Transport Authority: see the Local Transport Act 2008, s 77(2), (4)(a).

SCHEDULE 2

PART I
MODIFICATIONS TO CERTAIN REDUNDANCY PAYMENTS PROVISIONS OF THE 1996 ACT

Article 3

[2.415]

1. Section 146 of the 1996 Act shall have effect as if immediately after subsection (1) there were inserted—

SI 1999/2277 "(1A) The reference in subsection (1) to re-engagement by the employer includes a reference to re-engagement by any employer specified in Part II of Schedule 2 to the Redundancy Payments (Continuity of Employment in Local Government, etc) (Modification) Order 1999 and the reference in subsection (1) to an offer made by the employer includes a reference to an offer made by any employer so specified."

2. Section 155 of the 1996 Act shall have effect as if—

for the words "continuously employed" there were substituted the words "employed in relevant service";

the provisions of that section modified as provided in sub-paragraph (a) were subsection (1) of that section; and

after that subsection there were inserted the following subsections—

SI 1999/2277 "(2) In subsection (1) "relevant service" means

(a) continuous employment by an employer specified in Part II of Schedule 2 to the Redundancy Payments (Continuity of Employment in Local Government, etc) (Modification) Order 1999 ("the 1999 Order"), or

(b) where immediately before the relevant event a person has been successively employed by two or more employers specified in Part II of that Schedule, such aggregate period of service with such employers as would be continuous employment if they were a single employer.

(3) In subsection (2)(b) "relevant event" has the same meaning as in the 1999 Order."

3. Section 162 of the 1996 Act shall have effect as if—

for the words "continuously employed" in subsection (1)(a) there were substituted the words "employed in relevant service"; and

after subsection (1) there were inserted the following subsections—

SI 1999/2277 "(1A) In subsection (1)(a) "relevant service" means—

(a) continuous employment by an employer specified in Part II of Schedule 2 to the Redundancy Payments (Continuity of Employment in Local Government, etc) (Modification) Order 1999 ("the 1999 Order"), or

(b) where immediately before the relevant event a person has been successively employed by two or more employers specified in Part II of that Schedule, such aggregate period of service with such employers as would be continuous employment if they were a single employer.

(1B) In subsection (1A)(b) "relevant event" has the same meaning as in the 1999 Order."

PART II
EMPLOYERS WITH WHOM EMPLOYMENT MAY CONSTITUTE RELEVANT SERVICE

Section 1

Any employer specified in Schedule 1 to this Order whether or not in existence at the time of the relevant event.

Section 2—Local government

[2.416]

1. The Greater London Council.

2. The London Residuary Body established by section 57(1)(a) of the 1985 Act.

3. The council of an administrative county, county borough (other than one established under section 20 of the 1972 Act), metropolitan borough or county district.

4. A regional council, islands council or district council established by or under the Local Government (Scotland) Act 1973.

5. The council of a county, county of a city, large burgh, small burgh or district ceasing to exist after 15th May 1975.

6. Any joint board or joint body constituted by or under any enactment for the purpose of exercising the functions of two or more of the bodies described in any of paragraphs 1 to 5 above, and any special planning board within the meaning of paragraph 3 of Schedule 17 to the 1972 Act.

7. Any other body, not specified in any of paragraphs 1 to 6 above, established by or under any enactment for the purpose of exercising the functions of, or advising, one or more of the bodies specified in any of paragraphs 1 to 6 above.

8. Any committee (including a joint committee) established by or under any enactment for the purpose of exercising the functions of, or advising, one or more of the bodies described in any of paragraphs 1 to 6 above.

9. Any two or more bodies described in any of paragraphs 1 to 8 above acting jointly or as a combined authority.

10. Any association which was representative of any two or more bodies described in any of paragraphs 1 to 5 above.

11. Any committee established by one or more of the associations described in paragraph 10 above for the purpose of exercising the functions of, or advising, one or more of such associations.

12. An organisation which was representative of an association or associations described in paragraph 10 above and employees' organisations and among whose objects was to negotiate pay and conditions of service in local government service.

13. The council of a county or district in Wales ceasing to exist after 31st March 1996.

14. The Local Government Training Board.

[**15.** The Accounts Commission for Scotland.]

Section 3—Planning and development

1. A development corporation within the meaning of the New Towns Act 1946 or the New Towns Act 1965.

2. A development corporation established under section 2 of the New Towns (Scotland) Act 1968.

[**2A.** Olympic Park Legacy Company Limited.]

3. The Scottish Development Agency.

4. The Scottish Special Housing Association.

5. The English Industrial Estates Corporation established by the Local Employment Act 1960.

Section 4—Education

1. The governing body of an aided school within the meaning of the Education Act.

2. The governing body of a grant-maintained school.

3. The governing body of a grant-maintained special school.

4. The proprietor (within the meaning of section 579(1) of the Education Act) of a school for the time being recognised as a grammar school for the purposes of regulation 4(1) of the Direct Grant Schools Regulations 1959, being a school in relation to which, before 1st January 1976, the Secretary of State was satisfied as mentioned in regulation 3(1) of the Direct Grant Grammar Schools (Cessation of Grant) Regulations 1975.

5. The proprietor (within the meaning of section 114(1) of the Education Act 1944) of a school not falling within paragraph 1 of this section which throughout the period of employment was recognised as a grammar school or, as the case may be, as a direct grant grammar school for the purposes of regulation 4(1) of the Direct Grant Schools Regulations 1959, of Part IV of the Schools Grant Regulations 1951 or of Part IV of the Primary and Secondary Schools (Grant Conditions) Regulations 1945.

6. The managers of a school which during the period of employment was approved under section 83 of the Children and Young Persons (Scotland) Act 1937.

7. The managers of a school which during the period of employment was a grant-aided school within the meaning of section 143(1) of the Education (Scotland) Act 1946, section 145(22) of the Education (Scotland) Act 1962 or section 135(1) of the 1980 Act.

8. The managers of a school which during the period of employment was a school which, immediately before the commencement of Part III of the Social Work (Scotland) Act 1968, was approved under section 83 of the Children and Young Persons (Scotland) Act 1937.

9. An institution within the PCFC funding sector, within the meaning of section 132(6) of the 1988 Act.

10. The Further Education Staff College.

11. The Inner London Education Authority, known as the Inner London Interim Education Authority for a period prior to the abolition date as defined in section 1(2) of the 1985 Act.

12. The National Advisory Body for Public Sector Higher Education.

13. The Polytechnics and College Funding Council as established by section 132 of the 1988 Act.

14. The Scottish Association for National Certificates and Diplomas.

15. The Scottish Business Education Council.

16. The Scottish Council for Commercial, Administrative and Professional Education.

17. The Scottish Technical Education Council.

18. The Secretary of State for Defence in relation only to employees in schools administered by the Service Children's Education Authority.

19. The Secretary of State for Education and Employment[, the Secretary of State for Education and Skills] [the Secretary of State for Children, Schools and Families or the Secretary of State for Education], in relation only to teachers employed under contract in the European School established under Article 1 of the Statute of the European School and in schools designated as European Schools under Article 1 of the Protocol to that Statute.

[19A. Shetland Arts Trust.]

[20. . . .]

Section 5—Careers guidance

1. Black Country Careers Services Limited.

2. Buckinghamshire Careers Service Limited.

3. Kent Careers and Guidance Service Limited.

Section 6—[Police, fire and civil defence]

[1.] A previous police authority in relation to which Schedule 11 to the Police Act 1964 had effect or which was the police authority for an area or district which was before 1st April 1947 or after 31st March 1946 a separate police area or, in Scotland, a previous police authority for an area which was before 16th May 1975 a separate or combined police area.

[1A. A police authority established under section 3 of the Police Act 1996.

1B. The Metropolitan Police Authority established under section 5B of the Police Act 1996.]

[**2.** The London Fire and Civil Defence Authority.]

Section 7—Sports Councils

The Sports Council.

Section 8—Social services

A person or body of persons responsible for the management of an assisted community home within the meaning of section 36 of the Children and Young Persons Act 1969 or of an approved institution within the meaning of section 46 of that Act.

Section 9—Miscellaneous

1. A regional water board established under section 5 of the Water (Scotland) Act 1967.

2. A river purification board established under section 2 of the Rivers (Prevention of Pollution) (Scotland) Act 1951.

3. A river purification board established under section 135 of the Local Government (Scotland) Act 1973.

4. A local valuation panel constituted under the Local Government Act 1948 or established under the General Rate Act 1967.

[**4A.** A valuation tribunal in England established under the Local Government Finance Act 1988.]

5. The Central Scotland Water Development Board.

6. The Scottish Industrial Estates Corporation (formerly the Industrial Estates Management Corporation for Scotland) established by section 8 of the Local Employment Act 1960.

7. The Small Industries Council for Rural Areas of Scotland, being a company which was dissolved by section 15(5) of the Scottish Development Agency Act 1975 and was until then registered under the Companies Acts from time to time in force.

[**7A.** The Traffic Director for London.]

8. The Welsh Industrial Estates Corporation (formerly the Industrial Estates Management Corporation for Wales) established by section 8 of the Local Employment Act 1960.

NOTES

Section 2: para 15 added by the Redundancy Payments (Continuity of Employment in Local Government, etc) (Modification) Order (Amendment) Order 2010, SI 2010/903, arts 10, 11.

Section 3: para 2A inserted by the Localism Act 2011 (Housing and Regeneration Functions in Greater London) (Consequential, Transitory, Transitional and Saving Provisions) Order 2012, SI 2012/666, art 8(1), Sch 1, para 2(1), (3).

Section 4: words in first pair of square brackets in para 19 substituted by the Secretaries of State for Children, Schools and Families, for Innovation, Universities and Skills and for Business, Enterprise and Regulatory Reform Order 2007, SI 2007/3224, art 15, Schedule, Pt 2, para 26; words in second pair of square brackets in para 19 substituted by the Secretary of State for Education Order 2010, SI 2010/1836, art 6, Schedule, Pt 2, para 5; para 19A inserted by SI 2010/903, arts 10, 12; para 20 originally added by the Redundancy Payments (Continuity of Employment in Local Government, etc) (Modification) (Amendment) Order 2001, SI 2001/866, art 2(1), (7), substituted by the Local Education Authorities and Children's Services Authorities (Integration of Functions) (Local and Subordinate Legislation) Order 2010, SI 2010/1172, art 4, Sch 3, para 33(1), (3), and revoked by the Redundancy Payments (Continuity of Employment in Local Government, etc) (Modification) (Amendment) Order 2015, SI 2015/916, art 2(1), as from 1 July 2015.

Section 6: words in square brackets in the heading substituted, para 1 numbered as such, and para 2 added, by the London Government (Continuity of Employment) Order 2000, SI 2000/1042, art 4(1), (5); paras 1A, 1B inserted by the Redundancy Payments (Continuity of Employment in Local Government, etc) (Modification) (Amendment) Order 2013, SI 2013/1784, art 2.

Section 9: para 4A inserted by the Redundancy Payments (Continuity of Employment in Local Government, etc) (Modification) (Amendment) Order 2004, SI 2004/1682, art 2(1), (7); para 7A inserted by SI 2010/903, arts 10, 13.

SCHEDULE 3

(Sch 3 revokes the Redundancy Payments (Local Government) (Modification) Order 1983, SI 1983/1160 (and the various Orders that amended the 1983 Order).)

MANAGEMENT OF HEALTH AND SAFETY AT WORK REGULATIONS 1999

(SI 1999/3242)

NOTES

Made: 3 December 1999.

Authority: European Communities Act 1972, s 2(2), Health and Safety at Work etc Act 1974, ss 15(1), (2), (3)(a), (5), (9), 47(2), 52(2), (3), 80(1), 82(3)(a), Sch 3, paras 6(1), 7, 8(1), 10, 14, 15, 16.

Commencement: 29 December 1999.

Note: with regard to the authority for these Regulations, note that the European Communities Act 1972 is repealed by the European Union (Withdrawal) Act 2018, s 1, as from exit day (as defined in s 20 of that Act); but note also that provision is made for the continuation in force of any subordinate legislation made under the authority of s 2(2) of the 1972 Act by s 2 of the 2018 Act at **[1.2240]**, subject to the provisions of s 5 of, and Sch 1 to, the 2018 Act at **[1.2243]**, **[1.2253]**.

These Regulations revoke and replace the Management of Health and Safety at Work Regulations 1992, SI 1992/2051, and are the continuing domestic implementation of Council Directive 89/391 at **[3.104]** and, in part, Council Directive 92/85 at **[3.137]**.

See also the Code of Practice "Management of Health and Safety at Work" (not printed in this work) issued in conjunction with the 1992 Regulations by the Health and Safety Commission under the Health and Safety at Work, etc Act 1974, s 16.

See *Harvey* J(6).

ARRANGEMENT OF REGULATIONS

[2.417]

1 Citation, commencement and interpretation

(1) These Regulations may be cited as the Management of Health and Safety at Work Regulations 1999 and shall come into force on 29th December 1999.

(2) In these Regulations—

"the 1996 Act" means the Employment Rights Act 1996;

"the assessment" means, in the case of an employer or self-employed person, the assessment made or changed by him in accordance with regulation 3;

"child"—

(a) as respects England and Wales, means a person who is not over compulsory school age, construed in accordance with section 8 of the Education Act 1996; and

(b) as respects Scotland, means a person who is not over school age, construed in accordance with section 31 of the Education (Scotland) Act 1980;

["Directive 2014/27/EU" means Directive 2014/27/EU of the European Parliament and of the Council of 26 February 2014 amending Council Directives 92/58/EEC, 92/85/EEC, 94/33/EC, 98/24/EC and Directive 2004/37/EC of the European Parliament and of the Council in order to align them to Regulation (EC) No 1272/2008 on classification, labelling and packaging of substances and mixtures;]

"employment business" means a business (whether or not carried on with a view to profit and whether or not carried on in conjunction with any other business) which supplies persons (other than seafarers) who are employed in it to work for and under the control of other persons in any capacity;

"fixed-term contract of employment" means a contract of employment for a specific term which is fixed in advance or which can be ascertained in advance by reference to some relevant circumstance;

"given birth" means delivered a living child or, after twenty-four weeks of pregnancy, a stillborn child;

"new or expectant mother" means an employee who is pregnant; who has given birth within the previous six months; or who is breastfeeding;

"the preventive and protective measures" means the measures which have been identified by the employer or by the self-employed person in consequence of the assessment as the measures he needs to take to comply with the requirements and prohibitions imposed upon him by or under the relevant statutory provisions . . . ;

"young person" means any person who has not attained the age of eighteen.

(3) Any reference in these Regulations to—

(a) a numbered regulation or Schedule is a reference to the regulation or Schedule in these Regulations so numbered; or

(b) a numbered paragraph is a reference to the paragraph so numbered in the regulation in which the reference appears.

NOTES

Para (2): definition "Directive 2014/27/EU" inserted by the Classification, Labelling and Packaging of Chemicals (Amendments to Secondary Legislation) Regulations 2015, SI 2015/21, reg 8(1), (2), as from 1 June 2015; words omitted from the definition "the preventive and protective measures" revoked by the Regulatory Reform (Fire Safety) Order 2005, SI 2005/1541, art 53(2), Sch 5 (in relation to England and Wales), and by the Fire (Scotland) Act 2005 (Consequential Modifications and Savings) (No 2) Order 2006, SSI 2006/457, art 2(2), Sch 2 (in relation to Scotland).

[2.418]
[2 Disapplication of these Regulations

(1) These Regulations shall not apply to or in relation to the master or crew of a ship, or to the employer of such persons, in respect of the normal ship-board activities of a ship's crew which are carried out solely by the crew under the direction of the master.

(2) Regulations 3(4), (5), 10(2) and 19 shall not apply to occasional work or short-term work involving work regarded as not being harmful, damaging or dangerous to young people in a family undertaking.

(3) In this regulation—

"normal ship-board activities" include—

(a) the construction, reconstruction or conversion of a ship outside, but not inside, Great Britain; and

(b) the repair of a ship save repair when carried out in dry dock;

"ship" includes every description of vessel used in navigation, other than a ship belonging to Her Majesty which forms part of Her Majesty's Navy.]

NOTES

Substituted by the Management of Health and Safety at Work and Fire Precautions (Workplace) (Amendment) Regulations 2003, SI 2003/2457, regs 2, 3.

[2.419]
3 Risk assessment

(1) Every employer shall make a suitable and sufficient assessment of—

(a) the risks to the health and safety of his employees to which they are exposed whilst they are at work; and

(b) the risks to the health and safety of persons not in his employment arising out of or in connection with the conduct by him of his undertaking,

for the purpose of identifying the measures he needs to take to comply with the requirements and prohibitions imposed upon him by or under the relevant statutory provisions . . .

(2) Every [relevant self-employed person] shall make a suitable and sufficient assessment of—

(a) the risks to his own health and safety to which he is exposed whilst he is at work; and

(b) the risks to the health and safety of persons not in his employment arising out of or in connection with the conduct by him of his undertaking,

for the purpose of identifying the measures he needs to take to comply with the requirements and prohibitions imposed upon him by or under the relevant statutory provisions.

(3) Any assessment such as is referred to in paragraph (1) or (2) shall be reviewed by the employer or [relevant self-employed person] who made it if—

(a) there is reason to suspect that it is no longer valid; or

(b) there has been a significant change in the matters to which it relates;

and where as a result of any such review changes to an assessment are required, the employer or [relevant self-employed person] concerned shall make them.

[(3A) In this regulation "relevant self-employed person" means a self-employed person who conducts an undertaking of a prescribed description for the purposes of section 3(2) of the Health and Safety at Work etc Act 1974.]

(4) An employer shall not employ a young person unless he has, in relation to risks to the health and safety of young persons, made or reviewed an assessment in accordance with paragraphs (1) and (5).

(5) In making or reviewing the assessment, an employer who employs or is to employ a young person shall take particular account of—

(a) the inexperience, lack of awareness of risks and immaturity of young persons;

(b) the fitting-out and layout of the workplace and the workstation;

(c) the nature, degree and duration of exposure to physical, biological and chemical agents;

(d) the form, range, and use of work equipment and the way in which it is handled;

(e) the organisation of processes and activities;

(f) the extent of the health and safety training provided or to be provided to young persons; and

[(g) risks from agents, processes and work listed in the Annex to Council Directive 94/33/EC on the protection of young people at work, as amended by Directive 2014/27/EU.]

(6) Where the employer employs five or more employees, he shall record—

(a) the significant findings of the assessment; and

(b) any group of his employees identified by it as being especially at risk.

NOTES

Para (1): words omitted revoked by the Regulatory Reform (Fire Safety) Order 2005, SI 2005/1541, art 53(2), Sch 5 (in relation to England and Wales), and by the Fire (Scotland) Act 2005 (Consequential Modifications and Savings) (No 2) Order 2006, SSI 2006/457, art 2(2), Sch 2 (in relation to Scotland).

Paras (2), (3): words in square brackets substituted by the Deregulation Act 2015 (Health and Safety at Work) (General Duties of Self-Employed Persons) (Consequential Amendments) Order 2015, SI 2015/1637, art 2, Schedule, para 6(a), (b), as from 1 October 2015.

Para (3A): inserted by SI 2015/1637, art 2, Schedule, para 6(c), as from 1 October 2015.

Para (5): sub-para (g) substituted by the Classification, Labelling and Packaging of Chemicals (Amendments to Secondary Legislation) Regulations 2015, SI 2015/21, reg 8(1), (3), as from 1 June 2015.

As to the layout of this regulation, see the Management of Health and Safety at Work and Fire Precautions (Workplace) (Amendment) Regulations 2003, SI 2003/2457, reg 4 which provides as follows—

"In regulation 3(3) the words "and where" to the end shall follow and not appear in sub-paragraph (b).".

[2.420]
4 Principles of prevention to be applied

Where an employer implements any preventive and protective measures he shall do so on the basis of the principles specified in Schedule 1 to these Regulations.

[2.421]
5 Health and safety arrangements

(1) Every employer shall make and give effect to such arrangements as are appropriate, having regard to the nature of his activities and the size of his undertaking, for the effective planning, organisation, control, monitoring and review of the preventive and protective measures.

(2) Where the employer employs five or more employees, he shall record the arrangements referred to in paragraph (1).

[2.422]
6 Health surveillance

Every employer shall ensure that his employees are provided with such health surveillance as is appropriate having regard to the risks to their health and safety which are identified by the assessment.

[2.423]
7 Health and safety assistance

(1) Every employer shall, subject to paragraphs (6) and (7), appoint one or more competent persons to assist him in undertaking the measures he needs to take to comply with the requirements and prohibitions imposed upon him by or under the relevant statutory provisions . . .

(2) Where an employer appoints persons in accordance with paragraph (1), he shall make arrangements for ensuring adequate co-operation between them.

(3) The employer shall ensure that the number of persons appointed under paragraph (1), the time available for them to fulfil their functions and the means at their disposal are adequate having regard to the size of his undertaking, the risks to which his employees are exposed and the distribution of those risks throughout the undertaking.

(4) The employer shall ensure that—

(a) any person appointed by him in accordance with paragraph (1) who is not in his employment—
  (i) is informed of the factors known by him to affect, or suspected by him of affecting, the health and safety of any other person who may be affected by the conduct of his undertaking, and
  (ii) has access to the information referred to in regulation 10; and

(b) any person appointed by him in accordance with paragraph (1) is given such information about any person working in his undertaking who is—
  (i) employed by him under a fixed-term contract of employment, or
  (ii) employed in an employment business,

as is necessary to enable that person properly to carry out the function specified in that paragraph.

(5) A person shall be regarded as competent for the purposes of paragraphs (1) and (8) where he has sufficient training and experience or knowledge and other qualities to enable him properly to assist in undertaking the measures referred to in paragraph (1).

(6) Paragraph (1) shall not apply to a self-employed employer who is not in partnership with any other person where he has sufficient training and experience or knowledge and other qualities properly to undertake the measures referred to in that paragraph himself.

(7) Paragraph (1) shall not apply to individuals who are employers and who are together carrying on business in partnership where at least one of the individuals concerned has sufficient training and experience or knowledge and other qualities—

(a) properly to undertake the measures he needs to take to comply with the requirements and prohibitions imposed upon him by or under the relevant statutory provisions; and

(b) properly to assist his fellow partners in undertaking the measures they need to take to comply with the requirements and prohibitions imposed upon them by or under the relevant statutory provisions.

(8) Where there is a competent person in the employer's employment, that person shall be appointed for the purposes of paragraph (1) in preference to a competent person not in his employment.

NOTES

Para (1): words omitted revoked by the Regulatory Reform (Fire Safety) Order 2005, SI 2005/1541, art 53(2), Sch 5 (in relation to England and Wales), and by the Fire (Scotland) Act 2005 (Consequential Modifications and Savings) (No 2) Order 2006, SSI 2006/457, art 2(2), Sch 2 (in relation to Scotland).

[2.424]
8 Procedures for serious and imminent danger and for danger areas

(1) Every employer shall—

(a) establish and where necessary give effect to appropriate procedures to be followed in the event of serious and imminent danger to persons at work in his undertaking;

(b) nominate a sufficient number of competent persons to implement those procedures in so far as they relate to the evacuation from premises of persons at work in his undertaking; and

(c) ensure that none of his employees has access to any area occupied by him to which it is necessary to restrict access on grounds of health and safety unless the employee concerned has received adequate health and safety instruction.

(2) Without prejudice to the generality of paragraph (1)(a), the procedures referred to in that sub-paragraph shall—

(a) so far as is practicable, require any persons at work who are exposed to serious and imminent danger to be informed of the nature of the hazard and of the steps taken or to be taken to protect them from it;

(b) enable the persons concerned (if necessary by taking appropriate steps in the absence of guidance or instruction and in the light of their knowledge and the technical means at their disposal) to stop work and immediately proceed to a place of safety in the event of their being exposed to serious, imminent and unavoidable danger; and

(c) save in exceptional cases for reasons duly substantiated (which cases and reasons shall be specified in those procedures), require the persons concerned to be prevented from resuming work in any situation where there is still a serious and imminent danger.

(3) A person shall be regarded as competent for the purposes of paragraph (1)(b) where he has sufficient training and experience or knowledge and other qualities to enable him properly to implement the evacuation procedures referred to in that sub-paragraph.

[2.425]

9 Contacts with external services

Every employer shall ensure that any necessary contacts with external services are arranged, particularly as regards first-aid, emergency medical care and rescue work.

[2.426]

10 Information for employees

(1) Every employer shall provide his employees with comprehensible and relevant information on—

(a) the risks to their health and safety identified by the assessment;

(b) the preventive and protective measures;

(c) the procedures referred to in regulation 8(1)(a) . . . ;

(d) the identity of those persons nominated by him in accordance with regulation 8(1)(b) . . . ; and

(e) the risks notified to him in accordance with regulation 11(1)(c).

(2) Every employer shall, before employing a child, provide a parent of the child with comprehensible and relevant information on—

(a) the risks to his health and safety identified by the assessment;

(b) the preventive and protective measures; and

(c) the risks notified to him in accordance with regulation 11(1)(c).

(3) The reference in paragraph (2) to a parent of the child includes—

(a) in England and Wales, a person who has parental responsibility, within the meaning of section 3 of the Children Act 1989, for him; and

(b) in Scotland, a person who has parental rights, within the meaning of section 8 of the Law Reform (Parent and Child) (Scotland) Act 1986 for him.

NOTES

Para (1): words omitted from sub-paras (c), (d) revoked by the Regulatory Reform (Fire Safety) Order 2005, SI 2005/1541, art 53(2), Sch 5 (in relation to England and Wales), and by the Fire (Scotland) Act 2005 (Consequential Modifications and Savings) (No 2) Order 2006, SSI 2006/457, art 2(2), Sch 2 (in relation to Scotland).

[2.427]

11 Co-operation and co-ordination

(1) Where two or more employers share a workplace (whether on a temporary or a permanent basis) each such employer shall—

(a) co-operate with the other employers concerned so far as is necessary to enable them to comply with the requirements and prohibitions imposed upon them by or under the relevant statutory provisions . . . ;

(b) (taking into account the nature of his activities) take all reasonable steps to co-ordinate the measures he takes to comply with the requirements and prohibitions imposed upon him by or under the relevant statutory provisions . . . with the measures the other employers concerned are taking to comply with the requirements and prohibitions imposed upon them by that legislation; and

(c) take all reasonable steps to inform the other employers concerned of the risks to their employees' health and safety arising out of or in connection with the conduct by him of his undertaking.

(2) Paragraph (1) . . . shall apply to employers sharing a workplace with self-employed persons and to self-employed persons sharing a workplace with other self-employed persons as it applies to employers sharing a workplace with other employers; and the references in that paragraph to employers and the reference in the said paragraph to their employees shall be construed accordingly.

NOTES

Paras (1), (2): words omitted revoked by the Regulatory Reform (Fire Safety) Order 2005, SI 2005/1541, art 53(2), Sch 5 (in relation to England and Wales), and by the Fire (Scotland) Act 2005 (Consequential Modifications and Savings) (No 2) Order 2006, SSI 2006/457, art 2(2), Sch 2 (in relation to Scotland).

[2.428]

12 Persons working in host employers' or self-employed persons' undertakings

(1) Every employer and every self-employed person shall ensure that the employer of any employees from an outside undertaking who are working in his undertaking is provided with comprehensible information on—

(a) the risks to those employees' health and safety arising out of or in connection with the conduct by that first-mentioned employer or by that self-employed person of his undertaking; and

(b) the measures taken by that first-mentioned employer or by that self-employed person in compliance with the requirements and prohibitions imposed upon him by or under the relevant statutory provisions . . . in so far as the said requirements and prohibitions relate to those employees.

(2) Paragraph (1) . . . shall apply to a self-employed person who is working in the undertaking of an employer or a self-employed person as it applies to employees from an outside undertaking who are working therein; and the reference in that paragraph to the employer of any employees from an outside undertaking who are working in the undertaking of an employer or a self-employed person and the references in the said paragraph to employees from an outside undertaking who are working in the undertaking of an employer or a self-employed person shall be construed accordingly.

(3) Every employer shall ensure that any person working in his undertaking who is not his employee and every self-employed person (not being an employer) shall ensure that any person working in his undertaking is provided with appropriate instructions and comprehensible information regarding any risks to that person's health and safety which arise out of the conduct by that employer or self-employed person of his undertaking.

(4) Every employer shall—

(a) ensure that the employer of any employees from an outside undertaking who are working in his undertaking is provided with sufficient information to enable that second-mentioned employer to identify any person nominated by that first mentioned employer in accordance with regulation 8(1)(b) to implement evacuation procedures as far as those employees are concerned; and

(b) take all reasonable steps to ensure that any employees from an outside undertaking who are working in his undertaking receive sufficient information to enable them to identify any person nominated by him in accordance with regulation 8(1)(b) to implement evacuation procedures as far as they are concerned.

(5) Paragraph (4) shall apply to a self-employed person who is working in an employer's undertaking as it applies to employees from an outside undertaking who are working therein; and the reference in that paragraph to the employer of any employees from an outside undertaking who are working in an employer's undertaking and the references in the said paragraph to employees from an outside undertaking who are working in an employer's undertaking shall be construed accordingly.

NOTES

Paras (1), (2): words omitted revoked by the Regulatory Reform (Fire Safety) Order 2005, SI 2005/1541, art 53(2), Sch 5 (in relation to England and Wales), and by the Fire (Scotland) Act 2005 (Consequential Modifications and Savings) (No 2) Order 2006, SSI 2006/457, art 2(2), Sch 2 (in relation to Scotland).

[2.429]

13 Capabilities and training

(1) Every employer shall, in entrusting tasks to his employees, take into account their capabilities as regards health and safety.

(2) Every employer shall ensure that his employees are provided with adequate health and safety training—

(a) on their being recruited into the employer's undertaking; and

(b) on their being exposed to new or increased risks because of—

(i) their being transferred or given a change of responsibilities within the employer's undertaking,

(ii) the introduction of new work equipment into or a change respecting work equipment already in use within the employer's undertaking,

(iii) the introduction of new technology into the employer's undertaking, or

(iv) the introduction of a new system of work into or a change respecting a system of work already in use within the employer's undertaking.

(3) The training referred to in paragraph (2) shall—

(a) be repeated periodically where appropriate;

(b) be adapted to take account of any new or changed risks to the health and safety of the employees concerned; and

(c) take place during working hours.

[2.430]
14 Employees' duties

(1) Every employee shall use any machinery, equipment, dangerous substance, transport equipment, means of production or safety device provided to him by his employer in accordance both with any training in the use of the equipment concerned which has been received by him and the instructions respecting that use which have been provided to him by the said employer in compliance with the requirements and prohibitions imposed upon that employer by or under the relevant statutory provisions.

(2) Every employee shall inform his employer or any other employee of that employer with specific responsibility for the health and safety of his fellow employees—

(a) of any work situation which a person with the first-mentioned employee's training and instruction would reasonably consider represented a serious and immediate danger to health and safety; and

(b) of any matter which a person with the first-mentioned employee's training and instruction would reasonably consider represented a shortcoming in the employer's protection arrangements for health and safety,

in so far as that situation or matter either affects the health and safety of that first mentioned employee or arises out of or in connection with his own activities at work, and has not previously been reported to his employer or to any other employee of that employer in accordance with this paragraph.

[2.431]
15 Temporary workers

(1) Every employer shall provide any person whom he has employed under a fixed-term contract of employment with comprehensible information on—

(a) any special occupational qualifications or skills required to be held by that employee if he is to carry out his work safely; and

(b) any health surveillance required to be provided to that employee by or under any of the relevant statutory provisions,

and shall provide the said information before the employee concerned commences his duties.

(2) Every employer and every self-employed person shall provide any person employed in an employment business who is to carry out work in his undertaking with comprehensible information on—

(a) any special occupational qualifications or skills required to be held by that employee if he is to carry out his work safely; and

(b) health surveillance required to be provided to that employee by or under any of the relevant statutory provisions.

(3) Every employer and every self-employed person shall ensure that every person carrying on an employment business whose employees are to carry out work in his undertaking is provided with comprehensible information on—

(a) any special occupational qualifications or skills required to be held by those employees if they are to carry out their work safely; and

(b) the specific features of the jobs to be filled by those employees (in so far as those features are likely to affect their health and safety);

and the person carrying on the employment business concerned shall ensure that the information so provided is given to the said employees.

[2.432]
16 Risk assessment in respect of new or expectant mothers

(1) Where—

(a) the persons working in an undertaking include women of child-bearing age; and

(b) the work is of a kind which could involve risk, by reason of her condition, to the health and safety of a new or expectant mother, or to that of her baby, from any processes or working conditions, or physical, biological or chemical agents, including those specified in Annexes I and II of Council Directive 92/85/EEC on the introduction of measures to encourage improvements in the safety and health at work of pregnant workers and workers who have recently given birth or are breastfeeding, [as amended by Directive 2014/27/EU,]

the assessment required by regulation 3(1) shall also include an assessment of such risk.

(2) Where, in the case of an individual employee, the taking of any other action the employer is required to take under the relevant statutory provisions would not avoid the risk referred to in paragraph (1) the employer shall, if it is reasonable to do so, and would avoid such risks, alter her working conditions or hours of work.

(3) If it is not reasonable to alter the working conditions or hours of work, or if it would not avoid such risk, the employer shall, subject to section 67 of the 1996 Act suspend the employee from work for so long as is necessary to avoid such risk.

(4) In paragraphs (1) to (3) references to risk, in relation to risk from any infectious or contagious disease, are references to a level of risk at work which is in addition to the level to which a new or expectant mother may be expected to be exposed outside the workplace.

NOTES

Para (1): words in square brackets in sub-para (b) inserted by the Classification, Labelling and Packaging of Chemicals (Amendments to Secondary Legislation) Regulations 2015, SI 2015/21, reg 8(1), (4), as from 1 June 2015.

[2.433]
[16A Alteration of working conditions in respect of new or expectant mothers (agency workers)

(1) Where, in the case of an individual agency worker, the taking of any other action the hirer is required to take under the relevant statutory provisions would not avoid the risk referred to in regulation 16(1) the hirer shall, if it is reasonable to do so, and would avoid such risks, alter her working conditions or hours of work.

(2) If it is not reasonable to alter the working conditions or hours of work, or if it would not avoid such risk, the hirer shall without delay inform the temporary work agency, who shall then end the supply of that agency worker to the hirer.

(3) In paragraphs (1) and (2) references to risk, in relation to risk from any infectious or contagious disease, are references to a level of risk at work which is in addition to the level to which a new or expectant mother may be expected to be exposed outside the workplace.]

NOTES

Inserted by the Agency Workers Regulations 2010, SI 2010/93, reg 25, Sch 2, Pt 2, para 17.

[2.434]
17 Certificate from registered medical practitioner in respect of new or expectant mothers

Where—

(a) a new or expectant mother works at night; and

(b) a certificate from a registered medical practitioner or a registered midwife shows that it is necessary for her health or safety that she should not be at work for any period of such work identified in the certificate,

the employer shall, subject to section 67 of the 1996 Act, suspend her from work for so long as is necessary for her health or safety.

[2.435]
[17A Certificate from registered medical practitioner in respect of new or expectant mothers (agency workers)

Where—

(a) a new or expectant mother works at night; and

(b) a certificate from a registered medical practitioner or a registered midwife shows that it is necessary for her health or safety that she should not be at work for any period of such work identified in the certificate,

the hirer shall without delay inform the temporary work agency, who shall then end the supply of that agency worker to the hirer.]

NOTES

Inserted by the Agency Workers Regulations 2010, SI 2010/93, reg 25, Sch 2, Pt 2, paras 17(1), 18.

[2.436]
18 Notification by new or expectant mothers

(1) Nothing in paragraph (2) or (3) of regulation 16 shall require the employer to take any action in relation to an employee until she has notified the employer in writing that she is pregnant, has given birth within the previous six months, or is breastfeeding.

(2) Nothing in paragraph (2) or (3) of regulation 16 or in regulation 17 shall require the employer to maintain action taken in relation to an employee—

(a) in a case—

(i) to which regulation 16(2) or (3) relates; and

(ii) where the employee has notified her employer that she is pregnant, where she has failed, within a reasonable time of being requested to do so in writing by her employer, to produce for the employer's inspection a certificate from a registered medical practitioner or a registered midwife showing that she is pregnant;

(b) once the employer knows that she is no longer a new or expectant mother; or

(c) if the employer cannot establish whether she remains a new or expectant mother.

[2.437]
[18A Notification by new or expectant mothers (agency workers)

(1) Nothing in regulation 16A(1) or (2) shall require the hirer to take any action in relation to an agency worker until she has notified the hirer in writing that she is pregnant, has given birth within the previous six months, or is breastfeeding.

(2) Nothing in regulation 16A(2) shall require the temporary work agency to end the supply of the agency worker until she has notified the temporary work agency in writing that she is pregnant, has given birth within the previous six months, or is breastfeeding.

(3) Nothing in regulation 16A(1) shall require the hirer to maintain action taken in relation to an agency worker—

(a) in a case—

(i) to which regulation 16A(1) relates; and

(ii) where the agency worker has notified the hirer, that she is pregnant, where she has failed, within a reasonable time of being requested to do so in writing by the hirer, to produce for the hirer's inspection a certificate from a registered medical practitioner or a registered midwife showing that she is pregnant; or

(b) once the hirer knows that she is no longer a new or expectant mother; or

(c) if the hirer cannot establish whether she remains a new or expectant mother.]

NOTES

Inserted, together with reg 18AB, by the Agency Workers Regulations 2010, SI 2010/93, reg 25, Sch 2, Pt 2, paras 17(1), 19.

[2.438]

[18AB Agency workers: general provisions

(1) Without prejudice to any other duties of the hirer or temporary work agency under any enactment or rule of law in relation to health and safety at work, regulation 16A, 17A and 18A shall not apply where the agency worker—

(a) has not completed the qualifying period, or

(b) is no longer entitled to the rights conferred by regulation 5 of the Agency Workers Regulations 2010 pursuant to regulation 8(a) or (b) of those Regulations.

(2) Nothing in regulations 16A or 17A imposes a duty on the hirer or temporary work agency beyond the original intended duration, or likely duration of the assignment, whichever is the longer.

(3) This regulation, and regulations 16A, 17A and 18A do not apply in circumstances where regulations 16, 17 and 18 apply.

(4) For the purposes of this regulation and regulations 16A, 17A or 18A the following have the same meaning as in the Agency Workers Regulations 2010—

"agency worker";
"assignment";
"hirer";
"qualifying period";
"temporary work agency".]

NOTES

Inserted as noted to reg 18A at **[2.437]**.

[2.439]

19 Protection of young persons

(1) Every employer shall ensure that young persons employed by him are protected at work from any risks to their health or safety which are a consequence of their lack of experience, or absence of awareness of existing or potential risks or the fact that young persons have not yet fully matured.

(2) Subject to paragraph (3), no employer shall employ a young person for work—

(a) which is beyond his physical or psychological capacity;

(b) involving harmful exposure to agents which are toxic or carcinogenic, cause heritable genetic damage or harm to the unborn child or which in any other way chronically affect human health;

(c) involving harmful exposure to radiation;

(d) involving the risk of accidents which it may reasonably be assumed cannot be recognised or avoided by young persons owing to their insufficient attention to safety or lack of experience or training; or

(e) in which there is a risk to health from—

(i) extreme cold or heat;

(ii) noise; or

(iii) vibration,

and in determining whether work will involve harm or risks for the purposes of this paragraph, regard shall be had to the results of the assessment.

(3) Nothing in paragraph (2) shall prevent the employment of a young person who is no longer a child for work—

(a) where it is necessary for his training;

(b) where the young person will be supervised by a competent person; and

(c) where any risk will be reduced to the lowest level that is reasonably practicable.

(4) . . .

NOTES

Para (4): revoked by the Management of Health and Safety at Work and Fire Precautions (Workplace) (Amendment) Regulations 2003, SI 2003/2457, regs 2, 5.

[2.440]

20 Exemption certificates

(1) The Secretary of State for Defence may, in the interests of national security, by a certificate in writing exempt—

(a) any of the home forces, any visiting force or any headquarters from those requirements of these Regulations which impose obligations other than those in [regulations 16–18AB] on employers; or

(b) any member of the home forces, any member of a visiting force or any member of a headquarters from the requirements imposed by regulation 14;

and any exemption such as is specified in sub-paragraph (a) or (b) of this paragraph may be granted subject to conditions and to a limit of time and may be revoked by the said Secretary of State by a further certificate in writing at any time.

(2) In this regulation—

(a) "the home forces" has the same meaning as in section 12(1) of the Visiting Forces Act 1952;
(b) "headquarters" means a headquarters for the time being specified in Schedule 2 to the Visiting Forces and International Headquarters (Application of Law) Order 1999;
(c) "member of a headquarters" has the same meaning as in paragraph 1(1) of the Schedule to the International Headquarters and Defence Organisations Act 1964; and
(d) "visiting force" has the same meaning as it does for the purposes of any provision of Part I of the Visiting Forces Act 1952.

NOTES

Para (1): words in square brackets substituted by the Agency Workers Regulations 2010, SI 2010/93, reg 25, Sch 2, Pt 2, paras 17(1), 20.

[2.441]
21 Provisions as to liability

Nothing in the relevant statutory provisions shall operate so as to afford an employer a defence in any criminal proceedings for a contravention of those provisions by reason of any act or default of—

(a) an employee of his, or
(b) a person appointed by him under regulation 7.

[2.442]
[22 Restriction of civil liability for breach of statutory duty

(1) Breach of a duty imposed by regulation 16, 16A, 17 or 17A shall, so far as it causes damage, be actionable by the new or expectant mother.

(2) Any term of an agreement which purports to exclude or restrict any liability for such a breach is void.]

NOTES

Substituted by the Health and Safety at Work etc Act 1974 (Civil Liability) (Exceptions) Regulations 2013, SI 2013/1667, reg 3.

[2.443]
23 Extension outside Great Britain

(1) These Regulations shall, subject to regulation 2, apply to and in relation to the premises and activities outside Great Britain to which sections 1 to 59 and 80 to 82 of the Health and Safety at Work etc Act 1974 apply by virtue of the Health and Safety at Work etc Act 1974 (Application Outside Great Britain) Order 1995 as they apply within Great Britain.

(2) For the purposes of Part I of the 1974 Act, the meaning of "at work" shall be extended so that an employee or a self-employed person shall be treated as being at work throughout the time that he is present at the premises to and in relation to which these Regulations apply by virtue of paragraph (1); and, in that connection, these Regulations shall have effect subject to the extension effected by this paragraph.

NOTES

The Health and Safety at Work etc Act 1974 (Application outside Great Britain) Order 1995, SI 1995/263 was revoked and replaced by the Health and Safety at Work etc Act 1974 (Application outside Great Britain) Order 2001, SI 2001/2127. See now the Health and Safety at Work etc Act 1974 (Application outside Great Britain) Order 2013, SI 2013/240 (which revokes and replaces the 2001 Order).

24–28 *Reg 24 revokes the Health and Safety (First-Aid) Regulations 1981, SI 1981/917, reg 6; reg 25 amends the Offshore Installations and Pipeline Works (First-Aid) Regulations 1989, SI 1989/1671, reg 7; reg 26 amends the Mines Miscellaneous Health and Safety Provisions Regulations 1995, SI 1995/2005, reg 4; reg 27 revoked by the Construction (Design and Management) Regulations 2007, SI 2007/320, reg 48(1), Sch 4; reg 28 revoked by the Regulatory Reform (Fire Safety) Order 2005, SI 2005/1541, art 53(2), Sch 5 (in relation to England and Wales), and by the Fire (Scotland) Act 2005 (Consequential Modifications and Savings) (No 2) Order 2006, SSI 2006/457, art 2(2), Sch 2 (in relation to Scotland).)*

[2.444]
29 Revocations and consequential amendments

(1) The Management of Health and Safety at Work Regulations 1992, the Management of Health and Safety at Work (Amendment) Regulations 1994, the Health and Safety (Young Persons) Regulations 1997 and Part III of the Fire Precautions (Workplace) Regulations 1997 are hereby revoked.

(2) The instruments specified in column 1 of Schedule 2 shall be amended in accordance with the corresponding provisions in column 3 of that Schedule.

[2.445]
30 Transitional provision
The substitution of provisions in these Regulations for provisions of the Management of Health and Safety at Work Regulations 1992 shall not affect the continuity of the law; and accordingly anything done under or for the purposes of such provision of the 1992 Regulations shall have effect as if done under or for the purposes of any corresponding provision of these Regulations.

SCHEDULES

SCHEDULE 1
GENERAL PRINCIPLES OF PREVENTION

Regulation 4

[2.446]
(This Schedule specifies the general principles of prevention set out in Article 6(2) of Council Directive 89/391/EEC)

(a) avoiding risks;
(b) evaluating the risks which cannot be avoided;
(c) combating the risks at source;
(d) adapting the work to the individual, especially as regards the design of workplaces, the choice of work equipment and the choice of working and production methods, with a view, in particular, to alleviating monotonous work and work at a predetermined work-rate and to reducing their effect on health;
(e) adapting to technical progress;
(f) replacing the dangerous by the non-dangerous or the less dangerous;
(g) developing a coherent overall prevention policy which covers technology, organisation of work, working conditions, social relationships and the influence of factors relating to the working environment;
(h) giving collective protective measures priority over individual protective measures; and
(i) giving appropriate instructions to employees.

SCHEDULE 2

(Sch 2 (consequential amendments) in so far as these are within the scope of this work, they have been incorporated at the appropriate place.)

MATERNITY AND PARENTAL LEAVE ETC REGULATIONS 1999

(SI 1999/3312)

NOTES

Made: 10 December 1999.

Authority: Employment Rights Act 1996, ss 47C(2), (3), 71(1)–(3), (6), 72(1), (2), 73(1), (2), (4), (7), 74(1), (3), (4), 75(1), 76(1), (2), (5), 77(1), (4), 78(1), (2), (7), 79(1), (2), 99(1).

Commencement: 15 December 1999.

These Regulations, so far as relating to parental leave, are the domestic implementation of Directive 96/34/EC, as extended to the UK by Directive 97/75/EC. Note that Directive 96/34/EC was repealed and replaced by Directive 2010/18/EU at **[3.515]** et seq).

See *Harvey* DII, J(3), (7), (8).

ARRANGEMENT OF REGULATIONS

PART I
GENERAL

PART I
GENERAL

[2.447]

1 Citation and commencement

These Regulations may be cited as the Maternity and Parental Leave etc Regulations 1999 and shall come into force on 15th December 1999.

[2.448]

2 Interpretation

(1) In these Regulations—

"the 1996 Act" means the Employment Rights Act 1996;

["additional adoption leave" means leave under section 75B of the 1996 Act;]

"additional maternity leave" means leave under section 73 of the 1996 Act;

["armed forces independence payment" means armed forces independence payment under the Armed Forces and Reserve Forces (Compensation Scheme) Order 2011;]

"business" includes a trade or profession and includes any activity carried on by a body of persons (whether corporate or unincorporated);

"child" means a person under the age of eighteen;

"childbirth" means the birth of a living child or the birth of a child whether living or dead after 24 weeks of pregnancy;

"collective agreement" means a collective agreement within the meaning of section 178 of the Trade Union and Labour Relations (Consolidation) Act 1992, the trade union parties to which are independent trade unions within the meaning of section 5 of that Act;

"contract of employment" means a contract of service or apprenticeship, whether express or implied, and (if it is express) whether oral or in writing;

"disability living allowance" means the disability living allowance provided for in Part III of the Social Security Contributions and Benefits Act 1992;

"employee" means an individual who has entered into or works under (or, where the employment has ceased, worked under) a contract of employment;

"employer" means the person by whom an employee is (or, where the employment has ceased, was) employed;

"expected week of childbirth" means the week, beginning with midnight between Saturday and Sunday, in which it is expected that childbirth will occur, and "week of childbirth" means the week, beginning with midnight between Saturday and Sunday, in which childbirth occurs;

"job", in relation to an employee returning after . . . maternity leave or parental leave, means the nature of the work which she is employed to do in accordance with her contract and the capacity and place in which she is so employed;

"ordinary maternity leave" means leave under section 71 of the 1996 Act;

"parental leave" means leave under regulation 13(1);

"parental responsibility" has the meaning given by section 3 of the Children Act 1989, and "parental responsibilities" has the meaning given by section 1(3) of the Children (Scotland) Act 1995;

["personal independence payment" means personal independence payment under Part 4 of the Welfare Reform Act 2012;]

["statutory leave" means leave provided for in Part 8 of the 1996 Act;]

["statutory maternity leave" means ordinary maternity leave and additional maternity leave;

"statutory maternity leave period" means the period during which the employee is on statutory maternity leave;]

"workforce agreement" means an agreement between an employer and his employees or their representatives in respect of which the conditions set out in Schedule 1 to these Regulations are satisfied.

(2) A reference in any provision of these Regulations to a period of continuous employment is to a period computed in accordance with Chapter I of Part XIV of the 1996 Act, as if that provision were a provision of that Act.

(3) For the purposes of these Regulations any two employers shall be treated as associated if—

(a) one is a company of which the other (directly or indirectly) has control; or

(b) both are companies of which a third person (directly or indirectly) has control;

and "associated employer" shall be construed accordingly.

(4) In these Regulations, unless the context otherwise requires,—

(a) a reference to a numbered regulation or schedule is to the regulation or schedule in these Regulations bearing that number;

(b) a reference in a regulation or schedule to a numbered paragraph is to the paragraph in that regulation or schedule bearing that number, and

(c) a reference in a paragraph to a lettered sub-paragraph is to the sub-paragraph in that paragraph bearing that letter.

NOTES

Para (1): definitions "additional adoption leave" and "statutory leave" inserted, and word omitted from definition "job" revoked, by the Maternity and Parental Leave (Amendment) Regulations 2002, SI 2002/2789, regs 3, 4; definition "armed forces independence payment" inserted by the Armed Forces and Reserve Forces Compensation Scheme (Consequential Provisions: Subordinate Legislation) Order 2013, SI 2013/591, art 7, Schedule, para 16(1), (2); definition "personal independence payment" inserted by the Personal Independence Payment (Supplementary Provisions and Consequential Amendments) Regulations 2013, SI 2013/388, reg 8, Schedule, Pt 2, para 22(1), (2); definitions "statutory maternity leave" and "statutory maternity leave period" inserted by the Maternity and Parental Leave etc and the Paternity and Adoption Leave (Amendment) Regulations 2006, SI 2006/2014, regs 3, 4.

[2.449]

3 Application

(1) The provisions of Part II of these Regulations have effect only in relation to employees whose expected week of childbirth begins on or after 30th April 2000.

(2) Regulation 19 (protection from detriment) has effect only in relation to an act or failure to act which takes place on or after 15th December 1999.

(3) For the purposes of paragraph (2)—

(a) where an act extends over a period, the reference to the date of the act is a reference to the last day of that period, and

(b) a failure to act is to be treated as done when it was decided on.

(4) For the purposes of paragraph (3), in the absence of evidence establishing the contrary an employer shall be taken to decide on a failure to act—

(a) when he does an act inconsistent with doing the failed act, or

(b) if he has done no such inconsistent act, when the period expires within which he might reasonably have been expected to do the failed act if it was to be done.

(5) Regulation 20 (unfair dismissal) has effect only in relation to dismissals where the effective date of termination (within the meaning of section 97 of the 1996 Act) falls on or after 15th December 1999.

PART II
MATERNITY LEAVE

[2.450]

4 Entitlement to ordinary maternity leave [and to additional maternity leave]

(1) An employee is entitled to ordinary maternity leave [and to additional maternity leave] provided that she satisfies the following conditions—

(a) [no later than the end of the fifteenth week before her expected week of childbirth], or, if that is not reasonably practicable, as soon as is reasonably practicable, she notifies her employer of—

(i) her pregnancy;

(ii) the expected week of childbirth, and

(iii) the date on which she intends her ordinary maternity leave period to start,

and

(b) if requested to do so by her employer, she produces for his inspection a certificate from—

(i) a registered medical practitioner, or

(ii) a registered midwife,

stating the expected week of childbirth.

[(1A) An employee who has notified her employer under paragraph (1)(a)(iii) of the date on which she intends her ordinary maternity leave period to start may subsequently vary that date, provided that she notifies her employer of the variation at least—

(a) 28 days before the date varied, or

(b) 28 days before the new date,

whichever is the earlier, or, if that is not reasonably practicable, as soon as is reasonably practicable.]

(2) [Notification under paragraph (1)(a)(iii) or (1A)]—

(a) shall be given in writing, if the employer so requests, and

(b) shall not specify a date earlier than the beginning of the eleventh week before the expected week of childbirth.

(3) Where, by virtue of regulation 6(1)(b), an employee's ordinary maternity leave period commences with [the day which follows] the first day after the beginning of [the fourth week] before the expected week of childbirth on which she is absent from work wholly or partly because of pregnancy—

(a) paragraph (1) does not require her to notify her employer of the date specified in that paragraph, but

(b) (whether or not she has notified him of that date) she is not entitled to ordinary maternity leave [or to additional maternity leave] unless she notifies him as soon as is reasonably practicable that she is absent from work wholly or partly because of pregnancy [and of the date on which her absence on that account began].

(4) Where, by virtue of regulation 6(2), an employee's ordinary maternity leave period commences [on the day which follows] the day on which childbirth occurs—

(a) paragraph (1) does not require her to notify her employer of the date specified in that paragraph, but

(b) (whether or not she has notified him of that date) she is not entitled to ordinary maternity leave [or to additional maternity leave] unless she notifies him as soon as is reasonably practicable after the birth that she has given birth [and of the date on which the birth occurred].

(5) The notification provided for in paragraphs (3)(b) and (4)(b) shall be given in writing, if the employer so requests.

NOTES

Regulation heading: words in square brackets added by the Maternity and Parental Leave etc and the Paternity and Adoption Leave (Amendment) Regulations 2006, SI 2006/2014, regs 3, 5(a).

Para (1): words in first pair of square brackets inserted by SI 2006/2014, regs 3, 5(a); words in second pair of square brackets substituted by the Maternity and Parental Leave (Amendment) Regulations 2002, SI 2002/2789, regs 3, 5(a).

Para (1A): inserted by SI 2002/2789, regs 3, 5(b).

Para (2): words in square brackets substituted by SI 2002/2789, regs 3, 5(c).

Para (3): words in first and final pairs of square brackets inserted, and words in second pair of square brackets substituted, by SI 2002/2789, regs 3, 5(d); words in third pair of square brackets inserted by SI 2006/2014, regs 3, 5(b).

Para (4): words in first pair of square brackets substituted, and words in third pair of square brackets inserted, by SI 2002/2789, regs 3, 5(e); words in second pair of square brackets inserted by SI 2006/2014, regs 3, 5(b).

5 (*Revoked by the Maternity and Parental Leave etc and the Paternity and Adoption Leave (Amendment) Regulations 2006, SI 2006/2014, regs 3, 6.*)

[2.451]

6 Commencement of maternity leave periods

(1) Subject to paragraph (2), an employee's ordinary maternity leave period commences with the earlier of—

(a) the date which . . . she notifies to her employer[, in accordance with regulation 4,] as the date on which she intends her ordinary maternity leave period to start, [or, if by virtue of the provision for variation in that regulation she has notified more than one such date, the last date she notifies,] and

(b) [the day which follows] the first day after the beginning of [the fourth week] before the expected week of childbirth on which she is absent from work wholly or partly because of pregnancy.

(2) Where the employee's ordinary maternity leave period has not commenced by virtue of paragraph (1) when childbirth occurs, her ordinary maternity leave period commences [on the day which follows] the day on which childbirth occurs.

(3) An employee's additional maternity leave period commences on the day after the last day of her ordinary maternity leave period.

NOTES

Para (1): words omitted revoked, words in first, second and third pairs of square brackets inserted, and words in fourth pair of square brackets substituted, by the Maternity and Parental Leave (Amendment) Regulations 2002, SI 2002/2789, regs 3, 7(a), (b).

Para (2): words in square brackets substituted by SI 2002/2789, regs 3, 7(c).

[2.452]

7 Duration of maternity leave periods

(1) Subject to paragraphs (2) and (5), an employee's ordinary maternity leave period continues for the period of [26 weeks] from its commencement, or until the end of the compulsory maternity leave period provided for in regulation 8 if later.

(2) Subject to paragraph (5), where any requirement imposed by or under any relevant statutory provision prohibits the employee from working for any period after the end of the period determined under paragraph (1) by reason of her having recently given birth, her ordinary maternity leave period continues until the end of that later period.

(3) In paragraph (2), "relevant statutory provision" means a provision of—

(a) an enactment, or

(b) an instrument under an enactment,

other than a provision for the time being specified in an order under section 66(2) of the 1996 Act.

(4) Subject to paragraph (5), where an employee is entitled to additional maternity leave her additional maternity leave period continues until the end of the period of [26 weeks from the day on which it commenced].

(5) Where the employee is dismissed after the commencement of an ordinary or additional maternity leave period but before the time when (apart from this paragraph) that period would end, the period ends at the time of the dismissal.

[(6) An employer who is notified under any provision of regulation 4 of the date on which, by virtue of any provision of regulation 6, an employee's ordinary maternity leave period will commence or has commenced shall notify the employee of the date on which [her additional maternity leave period shall end]—

(a), (b) . . .

(7) The notification provided for in paragraph (6) shall be given to the employee—

(a) where the employer is notified under regulation 4(1)(a)(iii), (3)(b) or (4)(b), within 28 days of the date on which he received the notification;

(b) where the employer is notified under regulation 4(1A), within 28 days of the date on which the employee's ordinary maternity leave period commenced.]

NOTES

Paras (1), (4): words in square brackets substituted by the Maternity and Parental Leave (Amendment) Regulations 2002, SI 2002/2789, regs 3, 8(a), (b).

Para (6): added, together with para (7), by SI 2002/2789, regs 3, 8(c); words in square brackets inserted, and paras (a), (b) revoked, by the Maternity and Parental Leave etc and the Paternity and Adoption Leave (Amendment) Regulations 2006, SI 2006/2014, regs 3, 7.

Para (7): added as noted above.

[2.453]

8 Compulsory maternity leave

The prohibition in section 72 of the 1996 Act, against permitting an employee who satisfies prescribed conditions to work during a particular period (referred to as a "compulsory maternity leave period"), applies—

(a) in relation to an employee who is entitled to ordinary maternity leave, and

(b) in respect of the period of two weeks which commences with the day on which childbirth occurs.

[2.454]

[9 Application of terms and conditions during ordinary maternity leave [and additional maternity leave]

(1) An employee who takes ordinary maternity leave [or additional maternity leave]—

(a) is entitled, during the period of leave, to the benefit of all of the terms and conditions of employment which would have applied if she had not been absent, and

(b) is bound, during that period, by any obligations arising under those terms and conditions, subject only to [the exceptions in sections 71(4)(b) and 73(4)(b)] of the 1996 Act.

(2) In paragraph (1)(a), "terms and conditions" has the meaning given by [sections 71(5) and 73(5)] of the 1996 Act, and accordingly does not include terms and conditions about remuneration.

(3) For the purposes of [sections 71 and 73] of the 1996 Act, only sums payable to an employee by way of wages or salary are to be treated as remuneration.

[(4) In the case of accrual of rights under an employment-related benefit scheme within the meaning given by Schedule 5 to the Social Security Act 1989, nothing in paragraph (1)(a) concerning the treatment of additional maternity leave shall be taken to impose a requirement which exceeds the requirements of paragraph 5 of that Schedule.]]

NOTES

Substituted by the Maternity and Parental Leave (Amendment) Regulations 2002, SI 2002/2789, regs 3, 9.

Regulation heading: words in square brackets inserted by the Maternity and Parental Leave etc and the Paternity and Adoption Leave (Amendment) Regulations 2008, SI 2008/1966, regs 2(1), 3, 4(1)(a).

Para (1): words in first pair of square brackets inserted, and words in second pair of square brackets substituted, by SI 2008/1966, regs 2(1), 3, 4(1)(b), (c)).

Paras (2), (3): words in square brackets substituted by SI 2008/1966, regs 2(1), 3, 4(1)(d), (e).

Para (4): added by SI 2008/1966, regs 2(1), 3, 4(1)(f).

[2.455]

10 Redundancy during maternity leave

(1) This regulation applies where, during an employee's ordinary or additional maternity leave period, it is not practicable by reason of redundancy for her employer to continue to employ her under her existing contract of employment.

(2) Where there is a suitable available vacancy, the employee is entitled to be offered (before the end of her employment under her existing contract) alternative employment with her employer or his successor, or an associated employer, under a new contract of employment which complies with paragraph (3) (and takes effect immediately on the ending of her employment under the previous contract).

(3) The new contract of employment must be such that—

(a) the work to be done under it is of a kind which is both suitable in relation to the employee and appropriate for her to do in the circumstances, and

(b) its provisions as to the capacity and place in which she is to be employed, and as to the other terms and conditions of her employment, are not substantially less favourable to her than if she had continued to be employed under the previous contract.

[2.456]

11 Requirement to notify intention to return during a maternity leave period

[(1) An employee who intends to return to work earlier than the end of her additional maternity leave period, shall give to her employer not less than 8 weeks' notice of the date on which she intends to return.]

(2) If an employee attempts to return to work earlier than the end of [her additional maternity leave period] without complying with paragraph (1), her employer is entitled to postpone her return to a date such as will secure, subject to paragraph (3), that he has [8 weeks'] notice of her return.

[(2A) An employee who complies with her obligations in paragraph (1) or whose employer has postponed her return in the circumstances described in paragraph (2), and who then decides to return to work—

(a) earlier than the original return date, must give her employer not less than 8 weeks' notice of the date on which she now intends to return;

(b) later than the original return date, must give her employer not less than 8 weeks' notice ending with the original return date.

(2B) In paragraph (2A) the "original return date" means the date which the employee notified to her employer as the date of her return to work under paragraph (1), or the date to which her return was postponed by her employer under paragraph (2).]

(3) An employer is not entitled under paragraph (2) to postpone an employee's return to work to a date after the end of the relevant maternity leave period.

(4) If an employee whose return to work has been postponed under paragraph (2) has been notified that she is not to return to work before the date to which her return was postponed, the employer is under no contractual obligation to pay her remuneration until the date to which her return was postponed if she returns to work before that date.

[(5) This regulation does not apply in a case where the employer did not notify the employee in accordance with regulation 7(6) and (7) of the date on which [her additional maternity leave period] would end.]

NOTES

Para (1): substituted by the Maternity and Parental Leave etc and the Paternity and Adoption Leave (Amendment) Regulations 2006, SI 2006/2014, regs 3, 8(a).

Para (2): words in square brackets substituted by SI 2006/2014, regs 3, 8(b).

Paras (2A), (2B): inserted by SI 2006/2014, regs 3, 8(c).

Para (5): added by the Maternity and Parental Leave (Amendment) Regulations 2002, SI 2002/2789, regs 3, 10(c); words in square brackets substituted by SI 2006/2014, regs 3, 8(d).

Modification: this regulation is modified in relation to an employee who is an 'employee shareholder', as if for "8 weeks' notice", in each place it occurs, there were substituted "16 weeks' notice"; see the Employment Rights Act 1996, s 205A(3) at **[1.1119]** (as inserted by the Growth and Infrastructure Act 2013, s 31(1)).

12 *(Revoked by the Maternity and Parental Leave (Amendment) Regulations 2002, SI 2002/2789, regs 3, 11.)*

[2.457]

[12A Work during maternity leave period

[(1) Subject to paragraph (5), an employee may carry out up to 10 days' work for her employer during her statutory maternity leave period without bringing her maternity leave to an end.

(2) For the purposes of this regulation, any work carried out on any day shall constitute a day's work.

(3) Subject to paragraph (4), for the purposes of this regulation, work means any work done under the contract of employment and may include training or any activity undertaken for the purposes of keeping in touch with the workplace.

(4) Reasonable contact from time to time between an employee and her employer which either party is entitled to make during a maternity leave period (for example to discuss an employee's return to work) shall not bring that period to an end.

(5) Paragraph (1) shall not apply in relation to any work carried out by the employee at any time from childbirth to the end of the period of two weeks which commences with the day on which childbirth occurs.

(6) This regulation does not confer any right on an employer to require that any work be carried out during the statutory maternity leave period, nor any right on an employee to work during the statutory maternity leave period.

(7) Any days' work carried out under this regulation shall not have the effect of extending the total duration of the statutory maternity leave period.]

NOTES

Inserted by the Maternity and Parental Leave etc and the Paternity and Adoption Leave (Amendment) Regulations 2006, SI 2006/2014, regs 3, 9.

PART III
PARENTAL LEAVE

[2.458]

13 Entitlement to parental leave

(1) An employee who—

(a) has been continuously employed for a period of not less than a year [or is to be treated as having been so employed by virtue of paragraph (1A)]; and

(b) has, or expects to have, responsibility for a child,

is entitled, in accordance with these Regulations, to be absent from work on parental leave for the purpose of caring for that child.

[(1A) . . .]

(2) An employee has responsibility for a child, for the purposes of paragraph (1), if—

(a) he has parental responsibility or, in Scotland, parental responsibilities for the child; or

(b) he has been registered as the child's father under any provision of section 10(1) or 10A(1) of the Births and Deaths Registration Act 1953 or of section 18(1) or (2) of the Registration of Births, Deaths and Marriages (Scotland) Act 1965.

(3) . . .

NOTES

Words in square brackets in sub-para (1)(a) inserted, para (1A) inserted, and para (3) revoked, by the Maternity and Parental Leave (Amendment) Regulations 2001, SI 2001/4010, regs 2, 3.

Para (1A) revoked by the Maternity and Parental Leave etc (Amendment) Regulations 2014, SI 2014/3221, regs 2, 3, as from 5 April 2015.

[2.459]

14 Extent of entitlement

[(1) An employee is entitled to eighteen weeks' leave in respect of any individual child.]

[(1A) . . .]

(2) Where the period for which an employee is normally required, under his contract of employment, to work in the course of a week does not vary, a week's leave for the employee is a period of absence from work which is equal in duration to the period for which he is normally required to work.

(3) Where the period for which an employee is normally required, under his contract of employment, to work in the course of a week varies from week to week or over a longer period, or where he is normally required under his contract to work in some weeks but not in others, a week's leave for the employee is a period of absence from work which is equal in duration to the period calculated by dividing the total of the periods for which he is normally required to work in a year by 52.

(4) Where an employee takes leave in periods shorter than the period which constitutes, for him, a week's leave under whichever of paragraphs (2) and (3) is applicable in his case, he completes a week's leave when the aggregate of the periods of leave he has taken equals the period constituting a week's leave for him under the applicable paragraph.

NOTES

Para (1): substituted by the Parental Leave (EU Directive) Regulations 2013, SI 2013/283, reg 3(1), (2)(a).

Para (1A): inserted by the Maternity and Parental Leave (Amendment) Regulations 2001, SI 2001/4010, regs 2, 4(b), and revoked by SI 2013/283, reg 3(1), (2)(b).

[2.460]

[15 When parental leave may be taken

An employee may not exercise any entitlement to parental leave in respect of a child after the date of the child's 18th birthday.]

NOTES

Commencement: 5 April 2015.

Substituted by the Maternity and Parental Leave etc (Amendment) Regulations 2014, SI 2014/3221, regs 2, 4, as from 5 April 2015.

[2.461]

16 Default provisions in respect of parental leave

The provisions set out in Schedule 2 apply in relation to parental leave in the case of an employee whose contract of employment does not include a provision which—

(a) confers an entitlement to absence from work for the purpose of caring for a child, and

(b) incorporates or operates by reference to all or part of a collective agreement or workforce agreement.

[2.462]
[16A Review

(1) The Secretary of State must from time to time—
- (a) carry out a review of regulations 13 to 16 and Schedule 2,
- (b) set out the conclusions of the review in a report, and
- (c) publish the report.

(2) In carrying out the review the Secretary of State must, so far as is reasonable, have regard to how Council Directive 2010/18/EU of 8 March 2010 implementing the revised framework agreement on parental leave (which is implemented by means of regulations 13 to 16 and Schedule 2) is implemented in other member States.

(3) The report must in particular—
- (a) set out the objectives intended to be achieved by the regulatory system established by those regulations,
- (b) assess the extent to which those objectives are achieved, and
- (c) assess whether those objectives remain appropriate and, if so, the extent to which they could be achieved with a system that imposes less regulation.

(4) The first report under this regulation must be published before the end of the period of five years beginning with the day on which this regulation comes into force.

(5) Reports under this regulation are afterwards to be published at intervals not exceeding five years.]

NOTES

Inserted by the Parental Leave (EU Directive) Regulations 2013, SI 2013/283, reg 3(1), (3).

PART IV
PROVISIONS APPLICABLE IN RELATION TO MORE THAN ONE KIND OF ABSENCE

[2.463]
17 Application of terms and conditions during periods of leave

An employee who takes . . . parental leave—
- (a) is entitled, during the period of leave, to the benefit of her employer's implied obligation to her of trust and confidence and any terms and conditions of her employment relating to—
  - (i) notice of the termination of the employment contract by her employer;
  - (ii) compensation in the event of redundancy, or
  - (iii) disciplinary or grievance procedures;
- (b) is bound, during that period, by her implied obligation to her employer of good faith and any terms and conditions of her employment relating to—
  - (i) notice of the termination of the employment contract by her;
  - (ii) the disclosure of confidential information;
  - (iii) the acceptance of gifts or other benefits, or
  - (iv) the employee's participation in any other business.

NOTES

Words omitted revoked by the Maternity and Parental Leave etc and the Paternity and Adoption Leave (Amendment) Regulations 2008, SI 2008/1966, regs 2(1), 3, 4(2).

[2.464]
[18 Right to return after maternity or parental leave

(1) An employee who returns to work after a period of ordinary maternity leave, or a period of parental leave of four weeks or less, which was—
- (a) an isolated period of leave, or
- [(b) the last of two or more consecutive periods of statutory leave which did not include—
  - (i) any period of parental leave of more than four weeks; or
  - (ii) any period of statutory leave which when added to any other period of statutory leave (excluding parental leave) taken in relation to the same child means that the total amount of statutory leave taken in relation to that child totals more than 26 weeks,]

is entitled to return to the job in which she was employed before her absence.

(2) An employee who returns to work after—
- (a) a period of additional maternity leave, or a period of parental leave of more than four weeks, whether or not preceded by another period of statutory leave, or
- (b) a period of ordinary maternity leave, or a period of parental leave of four weeks or less, not falling within the description in paragraph (1)(a) or (b) above,

is entitled to return from leave to the job in which she was employed before her absence or, if it is not reasonably practicable for the employer to permit her to return to that job, to another job which is both suitable for her and appropriate for her to do in the circumstances.

(3) The reference in paragraphs (1) and (2) to the job in which an employee was employed before her absence is a reference to the job in which she was employed—
- (a) if her return is from an isolated period of statutory leave, immediately before that period began;
- (b) if her return is from consecutive periods of statutory leave, immediately before the first such period.

(4) This regulation does not apply where regulation 10 applies.]

NOTES

Substituted, together with reg 18A, for the original reg 18, by the Maternity and Parental Leave (Amendment) Regulations 2002, SI 2002/2789, regs 3, 12.

Para (1): sub-para (b) substituted by the Maternity and Parental Leave etc (Amendment) Regulations 2014, SI 2014/3221, regs 2, 5, as from 1 December 2014.

[2.465]

[18A Incidents of the right to return

(1) An employee's right to return under regulation 18(1) or (2) is a right to return—

[(a) with her seniority, pension rights and similar rights as they would have been if she had not been absent, and]

(b) on terms and conditions not less favourable than those which would have applied if she had not been absent.

[(2) In the case of accrual of rights under an employment-related benefit scheme within the meaning given by Schedule 5 to the Social Security Act 1989, nothing in paragraph (1)(a) concerning the treatment of additional maternity leave shall be taken to impose a requirement which exceeds the requirements of paragraphs 5 and 6 of that Schedule.]

(3) The provisions [in paragraph (1)] for an employee to be treated as if she had not been absent refer to her absence—

(a) if her return is from an isolated period of statutory leave, since the beginning of that period;

(b) if her return is from consecutive periods of statutory leave, since the beginning of the first such period.]

NOTES

Substituted as noted to reg 18 at **[2.464]**.

Para (1): sub-para (a) substituted by the Maternity and Parental Leave etc and the Paternity and Adoption Leave (Amendment) Regulations 2008, SI 2008/1966, regs 2(1), 3, 5(a).

Para (2): substituted by SI 2008/1966, regs 2(1), 3, 5(b).

Para (3): words in square brackets substituted by SI 2008/1966, regs 2(1), 3, 5(c).

[2.466]

19 Protection from detriment

(1) An employee is entitled under section 47C of the 1996 Act not to be subjected to any detriment by any act, or any deliberate failure to act, by her employer done for any of the reasons specified in paragraph (2).

(2) The reasons referred to in paragraph (1) are that the employee—

(a) is pregnant;

(b) has given birth to a child;

(c) is the subject of a relevant requirement, or a relevant recommendation, as defined by section 66(2) of the 1996 Act;

(d) took, sought to take or availed herself of the benefits of, ordinary maternity leave [or additional maternity leave];

(e) took or sought to take—

(i) . . .

(ii) parental leave, or

(iii) time off under section 57A of the 1996 Act;

[(ee) failed to return after a period of ordinary or additional maternity leave in a case where—

(i) the employer did not notify her, in accordance with regulation 7(6) and (7) or otherwise, of the date on which the period in question would end, and she reasonably believed that that period had not ended, or

(ii) the employer gave her less than 28 days' notice of the date on which the period in question would end, and it was not reasonably practicable for her to return on that date;]

[(eee) undertook, considered undertaking or refused to undertake work in accordance with regulation 12A;]

(f) declined to sign a workforce agreement for the purpose of these Regulations, or

(g) being—

(i) a representative of members of the workforce for the purposes of Schedule 1, or

(ii) a candidate in an election in which any person elected will, on being elected, become such a representative,

performed (or proposed to perform) any functions or activities as such a representative or candidate.

(3) For the purposes of paragraph (2)(d), a woman avails herself of the benefits of ordinary maternity leave if, during her ordinary maternity leave period, she avails herself of the benefit of any of the terms and conditions of her employment preserved by section 71 of the 1996 Act [and regulation 9] during that period.

[(3A) For the purposes of paragraph (2)(d), a woman avails herself of the benefits of additional maternity leave if, during her additional maternity leave period, she avails herself of the benefit of any of the terms and conditions of her employment preserved by section 73 of the 1996 Act and regulation 9 during that period.]

Part 2 Statutory Instruments

(4) Paragraph (1) does not apply in a case where the detriment in question amounts to dismissal within the meaning of Part X of the 1996 Act.

(5) Paragraph (2)(b) only applies where the act or failure to act takes place during the employee's ordinary or additional maternity leave period.

(6) For the purposes of paragraph (5)—

(a) where an act extends over a period, the reference to the date of the act is a reference to the last day of that period, and

(b) a failure to act is to be treated as done when it was decided on.

(7) For the purposes of paragraph (6), in the absence of evidence establishing the contrary an employer shall be taken to decide on a failure to act—

(a) when he does an act inconsistent with doing the failed act, or

(b) if he has done no such inconsistent act, when the period expires within which he might reasonably have been expected to do the failed act if it were to be done.

NOTES

Para (2) is amended as follows:

Words in square brackets in sub-para (d) inserted, and sub-para (e)(i) revoked, by the Maternity and Parental Leave etc and the Paternity and Adoption Leave (Amendment) Regulations 2008, SI 2008/1966, regs 2(1), 3, 6(a), (b).

Sub-para (ee) inserted by the Maternity and Parental Leave (Amendment) Regulations 2002, SI 2002/2789, regs 3, 13(a).

Sub-para (eee) inserted by the Maternity and Parental Leave etc and the Paternity and Adoption Leave (Amendment) Regulations 2006, SI 2006/2014, regs 3, 10.

Para (3): words in square brackets inserted by SI 2002/2789, regs 3, 13(b).

Para (3A): inserted by SI 2008/1966, regs 2(1), 3, 6(c).

[2.467]

20 Unfair dismissal

(1) An employee who is dismissed is entitled under section 99 of the 1996 Act to be regarded for the purposes of Part X of that Act as unfairly dismissed if—

(a) the reason or principal reason for the dismissal is of a kind specified in paragraph (3), or

(b) the reason or principal reason for the dismissal is that the employee is redundant, and regulation 10 has not been complied with.

(2) An employee who is dismissed shall also be regarded for the purposes of Part X of the 1996 Act as unfairly dismissed if—

(a) the reason (or, if more than one, the principal reason) for the dismissal is that the employee was redundant;

(b) it is shown that the circumstances constituting the redundancy applied equally to one or more employees in the same undertaking who held positions similar to that held by the employee and who have not been dismissed by the employer, and

(c) it is shown that the reason (or, if more than one, the principal reason) for which the employee was selected for dismissal was a reason of a kind specified in paragraph (3).

(3) The kinds of reason referred to in paragraphs (1) and (2) are reasons connected with—

(a) the pregnancy of the employee;

(b) the fact that the employee has given birth to a child;

(c) the application of a relevant requirement, or a relevant recommendation, as defined by section 66(2) of the 1996 Act;

(d) the fact that she took, sought to take or availed herself of the benefits of, ordinary maternity leave [or additional maternity leave];

(e) the fact that she took or sought to take—

(i) . . .

(ii) parental leave, or

(iii) time off under section 57A of the 1996 Act;

[(ee) the fact that she failed to return after a period of ordinary or additional maternity leave in a case where—

(i) the employer did not notify her, in accordance with regulation 7(6) and (7) or otherwise, of the date on which the period in question would end, and she reasonably believed that that period had not ended, or

(ii) the employer gave her less than 28 days' notice of the date on which the period in question would end, and it was not reasonably practicable for her to return on that date;]

[(eee) the fact that she undertook, considered undertaking or refused to undertake work in accordance with regulation 12A;]

(f) the fact that she declined to sign a workforce agreement for the purposes of these Regulations, or

(g) the fact that the employee, being—

(i) a representative of members of the workforce for the purposes of Schedule 1, or

(ii) a candidate in an election in which any person elected will, on being elected, become such a representative,

performed (or proposed to perform) any functions or activities as such a representative or candidate.

(4) Paragraphs (1)(b) and (3)(b) only apply where the dismissal ends the employee's ordinary or additional maternity leave period.

[(5) Paragraphs (3) and (3A) of regulation 19 apply for the purposes of paragraph (3)(d) as they apply for the purposes of paragraph (2)(d) of that regulation.]

(6) . . .

(7) Paragraph (1) does not apply in relation to an employee if—

(a) it is not reasonably practicable for a reason other than redundancy for the employer (who may be the same employer or a successor of his) to permit her to return to a job which is both suitable for her and appropriate for her to do in the circumstances;

(b) an associated employer offers her a job of that kind, and

(c) she accepts or unreasonably refuses that offer.

(8) Where on a complaint of unfair dismissal any question arises as to whether the operation of paragraph (1) is excluded by the provisions of paragraph . . . (7), it is for the employer to show that the provisions in question were satisfied in relation to the complainant.

NOTES

Para (3) is amended as follows:

Words in square brackets in sub-para (d) inserted, and sub-para (e)(i) revoked, by the Maternity and Parental Leave etc and the Paternity and Adoption Leave (Amendment) Regulations 2008, SI 2008/1966, regs 2(1), 3, 7(a), (b).

Sub-para (ee) inserted by the Maternity and Parental Leave (Amendment) Regulations 2002, SI 2002/2789, regs 3, 14.

Sub-para (eee) inserted by the Maternity and Parental Leave etc and the Paternity and Adoption Leave (Amendment) Regulations 2006, SI 2006/2014, regs 3, 11(a).

Para (5): substituted by SI 2008/1966, regs 2(1), 3, 7(c).

Para (6): revoked by SI 2006/2014, regs 3, 11(b).

Para (8): words omitted revoked by SI 2006/2014, regs 3, 11(c).

[2.468]

21 Contractual rights to maternity or parental leave

(1) This regulation applies where an employee is entitled to—

(a) ordinary maternity leave;

(b) additional maternity leave, or

(c) parental leave,

(referred to in paragraph (2) as a "statutory right") and also to a right which corresponds to that right and which arises under the employee's contract of employment or otherwise.

(2) In a case where this regulation applies—

(a) the employee may not exercise the statutory right and the corresponding right separately but may, in taking the leave for which the two rights provide, take advantage of whichever right is, in any particular respect, the more favourable, and

(b) the provisions of the 1996 Act and of these Regulations relating to the statutory right apply, subject to any modifications necessary to give effect to any more favourable contractual terms, to the exercise of the composite right described in sub-paragraph (a) as they apply to the exercise of the statutory right.

[2.469]

22 Calculation of a week's pay

Where—

(a) under Chapter II of Part XIV of the 1996 Act, the amount of a week's pay of an employee falls to be calculated by reference to the average rate of remuneration, or the average amount of remuneration, payable to the employee in respect of a period of twelve weeks ending on a particular date (referred to as "the calculation date");

(b) during a week in that period, the employee was absent from work on ordinary or additional maternity leave or parental leave, and

(c) remuneration is payable to the employee in respect of that week under her contract of employment, but the amount payable is less than the amount that would be payable if she were working,

that week shall be disregarded for the purpose of the calculation and account shall be taken of remuneration in earlier weeks so as to bring up to twelve the number of weeks of which account is taken.

SCHEDULES

SCHEDULE 1
WORKFORCE AGREEMENTS

Regulation 2(1)

[2.470]

1. An agreement is a workforce agreement for the purposes of these Regulations if the following conditions are satisfied—

(a) the agreement is in writing;

(b) it has effect for a specified period not exceeding five years;

(c) it applies either—

(i) to all of the relevant members of the workforce, or

(ii) to all of the relevant members of the workforce who belong to a particular group;

(d) the agreement is signed—

(i) in the case of an agreement of the kind referred to in sub-paragraph (c)(i), by the representatives of the workforce, and in the case of an agreement of the kind referred to in sub-paragraph (c)(ii), by the representatives of the group to which the agreement applies (excluding, in either case, any representative not a relevant member of the workforce on the date on which the agreement was first made available for signature), or

(ii) if the employer employed 20 or fewer employees on the date referred to in sub-paragraph (d)(i), either by the appropriate representatives in accordance with that sub-paragraph or by the majority of the employees employed by him;

and

(e) before the agreement was made available for signature, the employer provided all the employees to whom it was intended to apply on the date on which it came into effect with copies of the text of the agreement and such guidance as those employees might reasonably require in order to understand it in full.

2. For the purposes of this Schedule—

"a particular group" is a group of the relevant members of a workforce who undertake a particular function, work at a particular workplace or belong to a particular department or unit within their employer's business;

"relevant members of the workforce" are all of the employees employed by a particular employer, excluding any employee whose terms and conditions of employment are provided for, wholly or in part, in a collective agreement;

"representatives of the workforce" are employees duly elected to represent the relevant members of the workforce, "representatives of the group" are employees duly elected to represent the members of a particular group, and representatives are "duly elected" if the election at which they were elected satisfied the requirements of paragraph 3 of this Schedule.

3. The requirements concerning elections referred to in paragraph 2 are that—

(a) the number of representatives to be elected is determined by the employer;

(b) the candidates for election as representatives of the workforce are relevant members of the workforce, and the candidates for election as representatives of a group are members of the group;

(c) no employee who is eligible to be a candidate is unreasonably excluded from standing for election;

(d) all the relevant members of the workforce are entitled to vote for representatives of the workforce, and all the members of a particular group are entitled to vote for representatives of the group;

(e) the employees entitled to vote may vote for as many candidates as there are representatives to be elected, and

(f) the election is conducted so as to secure that—

(i) so far as is reasonably practicable, those voting do so in secret, and

(ii) the votes given at the election are fairly and accurately counted.

SCHEDULE 2
DEFAULT PROVISIONS IN RESPECT OF PARENTAL LEAVE

Regulation 16

Conditions of entitlement

[2.471]

1. An employee may not exercise any entitlement to parental leave unless—

(a) he has complied with any request made by his employer to produce for the employer's inspection evidence of his entitlement, of the kind described in paragraph 2;

(b) he has given his employer notice, in accordance with whichever of paragraphs 3 to 5 is applicable, of the period of leave he proposes to take, and

(c) in a case where paragraph 6 applies, his employer has not postponed the period of leave in accordance with that paragraph.

2. The evidence to be produced for the purpose of paragraph 1(a) is such evidence as may reasonably be required of—

(a) the employee's responsibility or expected responsibility for the child in respect of whom the employee proposes to take parental leave;

(b) the child's date of birth or, in the case of a child who was placed with the employee for adoption, the date on which the placement began, . . .

(c) . . .

[**2A.** Where regulation 13(1A) applies, and the employee's entitlement to parental leave arises out of a period of employment by a person other than the person who was his employer on 9th January 2002, the employee may not exercise the entitlement unless he has given his employer notice of that period of employment, and provided him with such evidence of it as the employer may reasonably require.]

Notice to be given to employer

3. Except in a case where paragraph 4 or 5 applies, the notice required for the purpose of paragraph 1(b) is notice which—

(a) specifies the dates on which the period of leave is to begin and end, and

(b) is given to the employer at least 21 days before the date on which that period is to begin.

4. Where the employee is the father of the child in respect of whom the leave is to be taken, and the period of leave is to begin on the date on which the child is born, the notice required for the purpose of paragraph 1(b) is notice which—

(a) specifies the expected week of childbirth and the duration of the period of leave, and

(b) is given to the employer at least 21 days before the beginning of the expected week of childbirth.

5. Where the child in respect of whom the leave is to be taken is to be placed with the employee for adoption by him and the leave is to begin on the date of the placement, the notice required for the purpose of paragraph 1(b) is notice which—

(a) specifies the week in which the placement is expected to occur and the duration of the period of leave, and

(b) is given to the employer at least 21 days before the beginning of that week, or, if that is not reasonably practicable, as soon as is reasonably practicable.

Postponement of leave

6. An employer may postpone a period of parental leave where—

(a) neither paragraph 4 nor paragraph 5 applies, and the employee has accordingly given the employer notice in accordance with paragraph 3;

(b) the employer considers that the operation of his business would be unduly disrupted if the employee took leave during the period identified in his notice;

(c) the employer agrees to permit the employee to take a period of leave—

(i) of the same duration as the period identified in the employee's notice, . . .

(ii) beginning on a date determined by the employer after consulting the employee, which is no later than six months after the commencement of that period; [and

(iii) ending before the date of the child's eighteenth birthday.]

(d) the employer gives the employee notice in writing of the postponement which—

(i) states the reason for it, and

(ii) specifies the dates on which the period of leave the employer agrees to permit the employee to take will begin and end,

and

(e) that notice is given to the employee not more than seven days after the employee's notice was given to the employer.

Minimum periods of leave

7. An employee may not take parental leave in a period other than the period which constitutes a week's leave for him under regulation 14 or a multiple of that period, except in a case where the child in respect of whom leave is taken is entitled to a disability living allowance[, armed forces independence payment] [or personal independence payment].

Maximum annual leave allowance

8. An employee may not take more than four weeks' leave in respect of any individual child during a particular year.

9. For the purposes of paragraph 8, a year is the period of twelve months beginning—

(a) except where sub-paragraph (b) applies, on the date on which the employee first became entitled to take parental leave in respect of the child in question, or

(b) in a case where the employee's entitlement has been interrupted at the end of a period of continuous employment, on the date on which the employee most recently became entitled to take parental leave in respect of that child,

and each successive period of twelve months beginning on the anniversary of that date.

NOTES

Para 2: word omitted from sub-para (b), and sub-para (c), revoked by the Maternity and Parental Leave etc (Amendment) Regulations 2014, SI 2014/3221, regs 2, 6, as from 5 April 2015.

Para 2A: inserted by the Maternity and Parental Leave (Amendment) Regulations 2001, SI 2001/4010, regs 2, 6(a).

Para 6: word omitted from sub-para (c)(i) revoked, and sub-para (c)(ii) and word immediately preceding it added, by SI 2001/4010, regs 2, 6(b).

Para 7: words in first pair of square brackets inserted by the Armed Forces and Reserve Forces Compensation Scheme (Consequential Provisions: Subordinate Legislation) Order 2013, SI 2013/591, art 7, Schedule, para 16(1), (5)(b); words in second pair of square brackets inserted by the Personal Independence Payment (Supplementary Provisions and Consequential Amendments) Regulations 2013, SI 2013/388, reg 8, Schedule, Pt 2, para 22(1), (5)(b).

TRANSNATIONAL INFORMATION AND CONSULTATION OF EMPLOYEES REGULATIONS 1999

(SI 1999/3323)

NOTES

Made: 12 December 1999.

Authority: European Communities Act 1972, s 2(2).

Commencement: 15 January 2000.

Part 2 Statutory Instruments

Note: with regard to the authority for these Regulations, note that the European Communities Act 1972 is repealed by the European Union (Withdrawal) Act 2018, s 1, as from exit day (as defined in s 20 of that Act); but note also that provision is made for the continuation in force of any subordinate legislation made under the authority of s 2(2) of the 1972 Act by s 2 of the 2018 Act at **[1.2240]**, subject to the provisions of s 5 of, and Sch 1 to, the 2018 Act at **[1.2243]**, **[1.2253]**.

These Regulations are the domestic implementation for the UK of Directive 94/45/EC, as extended to the UK by Directive 97/74/EC. Note that Directive 94/45/EC was repealed and replaced by Directive 2009/38/EC at **[3.491]** et seq. Amendments to these Regulations to give effect to Directive 2009/38/EC were made by the Transnational Information and Consultation of Employees (Amendment) Regulations 2010, SI 2010/1088, as noted below.

Employment Appeal Tribunal: an appeal lies to the Employment Appeal Tribunal on any question of law arising from any decision of, or in any proceedings before, an employment tribunal under or by virtue of these Regulations; see the Employment Tribunals Act 1996, s 21(1)(i) at **[1.764]**.

Conciliation: employment tribunal proceedings under regs 27, 32 are "relevant proceedings" for the purposes of the conciliation provisions contained in the Employment Tribunals Act 1996, ss 18–18C; see s 18(1)(k) of the 1996 Act at **[1.757]**.

See *Harvey* NIII(3).

References to "Member State" and "Member States": for the words "Member State" and "Member States" in each place they appear in these Regulations, there are substituted the words "Relevant State" and "Relevant States" respectively, by the Employment Rights (Amendment) (EU Exit) Regulations 2019, SI 2019/535, reg 2(2), Sch 2, Pt 1, paras 1, 2, as from exit day (as defined in the European Union (Withdrawal) Act 2018, s 20) and subject to savings and transitional provisions in Sch 2, Pt 2 at **[2.2182]**.

ARRANGEMENT OF REGULATIONS

PART I
GENERAL

PART II
EMPLOYEE NUMBERS & REQUEST TO NEGOTIATE ESTABLISHMENT OF A EUROPEAN WORKS COUNCIL OR INFORMATION AND CONSULTATION PROCEDURE

PART III
SPECIAL NEGOTIATING BODY

PART IV
EUROPEAN WORKS COUNCIL AND INFORMATION AND CONSULTATION PROCEDURE

PART V
COMPLIANCE AND ENFORCEMENT

PART I
GENERAL

[2.472]

1 Citation, commencement and extent

(1) These Regulations may be cited as the Transnational Information and Consultation of Employees Regulations 1999 and shall come into force on 15th January 2000.

(2) These Regulations extend to Northern Ireland.

[2.473]

2 Interpretation

(1) In these Regulations—

"the 1996 Act" means the Employment Rights Act 1996;

"the 1996 Order" means the Employment Rights (Northern Ireland) Order 1996;

"ACAS" means the Advisory, Conciliation and Arbitration Service;

["agency worker" has the meaning provided for in regulation 3 of the Agency Workers Regulations 2010;]

"Appeal Tribunal" means the Employment Appeal Tribunal;

"CAC" means the Central Arbitration Committee;

"central management" means—

(a) the central management of a Community-scale undertaking, or
(b) in the case of a Community-scale group of undertakings, the central management of the controlling undertaking,

or, where appropriate, the central management of an undertaking or group of undertakings that could be or is claimed to be a Community-scale undertaking or Community-scale group of undertakings;

"Community-scale undertaking" means an undertaking with at least 1000 employees within the Member States and at least 150 employees in each of at least two Member States;

"Community-scale group of undertakings" means a group of undertakings which has—

(a) at least 1000 employees within the Member States,

(b) at least two group undertakings in different Member States, and

(c) at least one group undertaking with at least 150 employees in one Member State and at least one other group undertaking with at least 150 employees in another Member State;

"consultation" means the exchange of views and establishment of dialogue between members of a European Works Council in the context of a European Works Council, or information and consultation representatives in the context of an information and consultation procedure, and central management or any more appropriate level of management;

"contract of employment" means a contract of service or apprenticeship, whether express or implied, and (if it is express) whether oral or in writing;

"controlled undertaking" has the meaning assigned to it by regulation 3;

"controlling undertaking" has the meaning assigned to it by regulation 3;

"employee" means an individual who has entered into or works under a contract of employment and in Part VII and regulation 41 includes, where the employment has ceased, an individual who worked under a contract of employment;

"employees' representatives" means—

(a) if the employees are of a description in respect of which an independent trade union is recognised by their employer for the purpose of collective bargaining, representatives of the trade union who normally take part as negotiators in the collective bargaining process, and

(b) any other employee representatives elected or appointed by employees to positions in which they are expected to receive, on behalf of the employees, information—

(i) which is relevant to the terms and conditions of employment of the employees, or

(ii) about the activities of the undertaking which may significantly affect the interests of the employees,

but excluding representatives who are expected to receive information relevant only to a specific aspect of the terms and conditions or interests of the employees, such as health and safety or collective redundancies;

"European Works Council" means the council, established under and in accordance with—

(a) regulation 17, or regulation 18 and the provisions of the Schedule, or

(b) where appropriate, the provisions of the law or practice of a Member State other than the United Kingdom which are designed to give effect to Article 6 of, or Article 7 of and the Annex to, the Transnational Information and Consultation Directive,

with the purpose of informing and consulting employees;

"Extension Directive" means Council Directive 97/74/EC of 15 December 1997 extending, to the United Kingdom, the Transnational Information and Consultation Directive;

"group of undertakings" means a controlling undertaking and its controlled undertakings;

"group undertaking" means an undertaking which is part of a Community-scale group of undertakings;

["hirer" has the meaning provided for in regulation 2 of the Agency Workers Regulations 2010;]

"independent trade union" has the same meaning as in the Trade Union and Labour Relations (Consolidation) Act 1992, or in Northern Ireland the 1996 Order;

"information and consultation procedure" means one or more information and consultation procedures agreed under—

(a) regulation 17 [before exit day], or

(b) where appropriate, the provisions of the law or practice of a Member State other than the United Kingdom which are designed to give effect to Article 6(3) of the Transnational Information and Consultation Directive;

"information and consultation representative" means a person who represents employees in the context of an information and consultation procedure;

"local management" means the management of one or more establishments in a Community-scale undertaking or of one or more undertakings in a Community-scale group of undertakings which is not the central management;

"Member State" means a state which is a Contracting Party to the Agreement on the European Economic Area signed at Oporto on 2nd May 1992 as adjusted by the Protocol signed at Brussels on 17th March 1993;

["national employee representation body" means—

(a) where the employees are of a description in respect of which an independent trade union is recognised by their employer for the purpose of collective bargaining, that trade union, and

(b) a body which has not been established with information and consultation on transnational matters as its main purpose, to which any employee representatives are elected or appointed by employees, as a result of which they hold positions in which they are expected to receive, on behalf of the employees, information—

(i) which is relevant to the terms and conditions of employment of the employees, or

(ii) about the activities of the undertaking which may significantly affect the interests of the employees,

(including information relevant only to a specific aspect of the terms and conditions or interests of the employees, such as health and safety or collective redundancies);

"relevant date" has the meaning given to it in regulation 6(4);]

"special negotiating body" means the body established [before exit day] for the purposes of negotiating with central management an agreement for a European Works Council or an information and consultation procedure;

["suitable information relating to the use of agency workers" means—

(a) the number of agency workers working temporarily for and under the supervision and direction of the undertaking;

(b) the parts of the undertaking in which those agency workers are working; and

(c) the type of work those agency workers are carrying out;

"temporary work agency" has the meaning provided for in regulation 4 of the Agency Workers Regulations 2010;]

"Transnational Information and Consultation Directive" means Council Directive 94/45/EC of 22 September 1994 on the establishment of a European Works Council or a procedure in Community-scale undertakings and Community-scale groups of undertakings for the purposes of informing and consulting employees;

"UK management" means the management which *is, or would be,* subject to the obligation in regulation 13(2) or paragraph 4(1) of the Schedule, being either the central management in the United Kingdom or the local management in the United Kingdom;

"UK member of the special negotiating body" means a member of the special negotiating body who represents UK employees for the purposes of negotiating with central management an agreement for a European Works Council or an information and consultation procedure.

(2) To the extent that the Transnational Information and Consultation Directive and the Extension Directive permit the establishment of more than one European Works Council in a Community-scale undertaking or Community-scale group of undertakings, these Regulations shall be construed accordingly.

(3) In paragraphs (1) and (4) of this regulation and in *regulations 6, 13 to 15* and paragraphs 3 to 5 of the Schedule, references to "UK employees" are references to employees who are employed in the United Kingdom by a Community-scale undertaking or Community-scale group of undertakings.

(4) In *regulations 13 and 15 and* paragraphs 3 and 4 of the Schedule, references to "UK employees' representatives" are references to employees' representatives who represent UK employees.

[(4A) In paragraph (1) in the definition of "national employee representation body" and in regulation 18A, matters are transnational where they concern—

(a) the Community-scale undertaking or Community-scale group of undertakings as a whole, or

(b) at least two undertakings or establishments of the Community-scale undertaking or Community-scale group of undertakings situated in two different Member States.

(4B) The arrangements to link information and consultation of a European Works Council with information and consultation of the national employee representation bodies—

(a) in regulation 17(4)(c) may relate to any matters including, as the case may be—

(i) the content of the information, the time when, or manner in which it is given, or

(ii) the content of the consultation, the time when, or manner in which it takes place;

(b) in *regulations 17(4)(c) and* 19E are subject to the limitation in regulation 18A(7); and

(c) in *regulations 17(4)(c) and* 19E shall not affect the main purpose for which a national employee representation body was established.

(4C) An agency worker who has a contract within regulation 3(1)(b) of the Agency Workers Regulations 2010 (contract with the temporary work agency) with a temporary work agency which is a Community-scale undertaking or Community-scale group of undertakings at the relevant date, which is not a contract of employment, shall be treated as being employed by that agency for the duration of their assignment with a hirer for the purposes of—

(a) calculating the number of employees within the definitions of "Community-scale undertaking" and "Community-scale group of undertakings" in this regulation; and

(b) the means of calculating the number of employees in regulation 6.]

(5) In the absence of a definition in these Regulations, words and expressions used in particular regulations and particular paragraphs of the Schedule to these Regulations which are also used in the provisions of the Transnational Information and Consultation Directive or the Extension Directive to which they *are designed* to give effect have the same meaning as they have in those provisions.

NOTES

Para (1): all definitions in square brackets were inserted by the Transnational Information and Consultation of Employees (Amendment) Regulations 2010, SI 2010/1088, regs 2, 3(a).

Paras (4A)–(4C): inserted by SI 2010/1088, regs 2, 3(b).

This regulation is amended by the Employment Rights (Amendment) (EU Exit) Regulations 2019, SI 2019/535, reg 2(2), Sch 2, Pt 1, paras 1, 3, as from exit day (as defined in the European Union (Withdrawal) Act 2018, s 20) and subject to savings and transitional provisions in Sch 2, Pt 2 at **[2.2182]**, as follows—

Para (1): amended as follows—

The definition "European Works Council" is substituted as follows—

""European Works Council" means the council, established—

(a) before exit day under and in accordance with regulation 17, or regulation 18 and the provisions of the Schedule, or

(b) where appropriate, under and in accordance with the provisions of the law or practice of a Relevant State other than the United Kingdom which are designed to give effect to Article 6 of, or Article 7 of and the Annex to, the Transnational Information and Consultation Directive,

with the purpose of informing and consulting employees;".

In the definitions "information and consultation procedure" and "special negotiating body" the words in square brackets are inserted.

The definitions "Member State" and "UK member of the special negotiating body" are revoked.

The definition "Relevant State" is inserted as follows—

""Relevant State" means—

(a) a state which is a Contracting Party to the Agreement on the European Economic Area signed at Oporto on 2nd May 1992 as adjusted by the Protocol signed at Brussels on 17th March 1993; and

(b) the United Kingdom;".

In the definition of "UK management" for the words in italics there are substituted the words "before exit day was, or would have been,".

Para (3): for the words in italics there are substituted the words "regulation 6".

Para (4): the words in italics are revoked.

Para (4B): sub-para (a) is revoked and for the words in italics in sub-paras (b), (c) there is substituted the word "regulation".

Para (5): for the words in italics there are substituted the words "were designed".

[2.474]

3 Controlled and Controlling Undertaking

(1) In these Regulations "controlling undertaking" means an undertaking which can exercise a dominant influence over another undertaking by virtue, for example, of ownership, financial participation or the rules which govern it and "controlled undertaking" means an undertaking over which such a dominant influence can be exercised.

(2) The ability of an undertaking to exercise a dominant influence over another undertaking shall be presumed, unless the contrary is proved, when in relation to another undertaking it directly or indirectly—

(a) can appoint more than half of the members of that undertaking's administrative, management or supervisory body;

(b) controls a majority of the votes attached to that undertaking's issued share capital; or

(c) holds a majority of that undertaking's subscribed capital.

(3) In applying the criteria in paragraph (2), a controlling undertaking's rights as regards voting and appointment shall include—

(a) the rights of its other controlled undertakings; and

(b) the rights of any person or body acting in his or its own name but on behalf of the controlling undertaking or of any other of the controlling undertaking's controlled undertakings.

(4) Notwithstanding paragraphs (1) and (2) an undertaking shall not be a controlling undertaking of another undertaking in which it has holdings where the first undertaking is a company *referred to* in Article 3(5)(a) or (c) of Council Regulation [(EC) No 139/2004 of 20 January 2004] on the control of concentrations between undertakings [(whether or not the Regulation applies to that company)].

(5) A dominant influence shall not be presumed to be exercised solely by virtue of the fact that an office holder is exercising functions, according to the law of a Member State, relating to liquidation, winding-up, insolvency, cessation of payments, compositions of creditors or analogous proceedings.

(6) Where the law governing an undertaking is the law of a Member State, the law applicable in order to determine whether an undertaking is a controlling undertaking shall be the law of that Member State.

(7) Where the law governing an undertaking is not that of a Member State the law applicable shall be the law of the Member State within whose territory—

(a) the representative of the undertaking is situated; or

(b) in the absence of such a representative, the management of the group undertaking which employs the greatest number of employees is situated.

(8) If two or more undertakings (whether situated in the same or in different Member States) meet one or more of the criteria in paragraph (2) in relation to another undertaking, the criteria shall be applied in the order listed in relation to each of the first-mentioned undertakings and that which meets the criterion that is highest in the order listed shall be presumed, unless the contrary is proved, to exercise a dominant influence over the undertaking in question.

NOTES

Para (4): words in first pair of square brackets substituted by the EC Merger Control (Consequential Amendments) Regulations 2004, SI 2004/1079, reg 2, Schedule, para 4; for the words in italics there is substituted the word "described", and words in second pair of square brackets inserted, by the Employment Rights (Amendment) (EU Exit) Regulations 2019, SI 2019/535, reg 2(2), Sch 2, Pt 1, paras 1, 4, as from exit day (as defined in the European Union (Withdrawal) Act 2018, s 20) and subject to savings and transitional provisions in Sch 2, Pt 2 at **[2.2182]**.

[2.475]

4 Circumstances in which provisions of these Regulations apply

(1) Subject to paragraph (2) the provisions of regulations *7 to 41* and of regulation 46 shall apply in relation to a Community-scale undertaking or Community-scale group of undertakings only where, in accordance with regulation 5, the central management is situated in the United Kingdom.

(2) The following regulations shall apply in relation to a Community-scale undertaking or Community-scale group of undertakings whether or not the central management is situated in the United Kingdom—

(a) regulations 7 and 8(1), (2) and (4) (provision of information on employee numbers);

(b) regulations 13 to 15 (UK members of the special negotiating body);

(c) regulation 18 to the extent it applies paragraphs 3 to 5 of the Schedule (UK members of the European Works Council);

(d) regulations 23(1) to (5) (breach of statutory duty);

(e) regulations 25 to 33 (protections for members of a European Works Council, etc);

(f) regulations 34 to 39 (enforcement bodies) to the extent they relate to applications made or complaints presented under any of the other regulations referred to in this paragraph;

(g) regulations 40 and 41 (restrictions on contracting out).

NOTES

For the words in italics in para (1) there are substituted the words "17 to 41", and para (2)(a), (b) is revoked, by the Employment Rights (Amendment) (EU Exit) Regulations 2019, SI 2019/535, reg 2(2), Sch 2, Pt 1, paras 1, 5, as from exit day (as defined in the European Union (Withdrawal) Act 2018, s 20) and subject to savings and transitional provisions in Sch 2, Pt 2 at **[2.2182]**.

[2.476]

5 The central management

(1) *The central management shall be responsible for creating the conditions and means necessary for the setting up of a European Works Council or an information and consultation procedure in a Community-scale undertaking or Community-scale group of undertakings where—*

(a) the central management is situated in the United Kingdom;

(b) the central management is not situated in a Member State and the representative agent of the central management (to be designated if necessary) is situated in the United Kingdom; or

(c) neither the central management nor the representative agent (whether or not as a result of being designated) is situated in a Member State and—

(i) in the case of a Community-scale undertaking, there are employed in an establishment, which is situated in the United Kingdom, more employees than are employed in any other establishment which is situated in a Member State, or

(ii) in the case of a Community-scale group of undertakings, there are employed in a group undertaking, which is situated in the United Kingdom, more employees than are employed in any other group undertaking which is situated in a Member State,

and the central management initiates, or by virtue of regulation 9(1) is required to initiate, negotiations for a European Works Council or information and consultation procedure.

(2) Where *the circumstances described in paragraph (1)(b) or (1)(c) apply*, the central management shall be treated, for the purposes of these Regulations, as being situated in the United Kingdom and—

(a) the representative agent referred to in paragraph (1)(b); or

(b) the management of the establishment referred to in paragraph (1)(c)(i) or of the group undertaking, referred to in paragraph (1)(c)(ii),

shall be treated, respectively, as being the central management.

NOTES

Para (1): for the first words in italics there are substituted the words "This regulation applies where", and sub-para (a) and the final words in italics are revoked, by the Employment Rights (Amendment) (EU Exit) Regulations 2019, SI 2019/535, reg 2(2), Sch 2, Pt 1, paras 1, 6(a), as from exit day (as defined in the European Union (Withdrawal) Act 2018, s 20) and subject to savings and transitional provisions in Sch 2, Pt 2 at **[2.2182]**.

Para (2): for the words in italics there are substituted the words "this regulation applies", by SI 2019/535, reg 2(2), Sch 2, Pt 1, paras 1, 6(b), as from exit day (as defined in the European Union (Withdrawal) Act 2018, s 20) and subject to savings and transitional provisions in Sch 2, Pt 2 at **[2.2182]**.

PART II
EMPLOYEE NUMBERS & *REQUEST TO NEGOTIATE ESTABLISHMENT OF A EUROPEAN WORKS COUNCIL OR INFORMATION AND CONSULTATION PROCEDURE*

NOTES

Words in italics revoked by the Employment Rights (Amendment) (EU Exit) Regulations 2019, SI 2019/535, reg 2(2), Sch 2, Pt 1, paras 1, 7, as from exit day (as defined in the European Union (Withdrawal) Act 2018, s 20) and subject to savings and transitional provisions in Sch 2, Pt 2 at **[2.2182]**.

[2.477]

6 Calculation of numbers of employees

(1) For the purposes of determining whether an undertaking is a Community-scale undertaking or a group of undertakings is a Community-scale group of undertakings, the number of employees employed by the undertaking, or group of undertakings, shall be determined—

Part 2 Statutory Instruments

(a) in the case of UK employees, by ascertaining the average number of employees employed during a two year period, calculated in accordance with paragraph (2) below;

(b) in the case of employees in another Member State, by ascertaining the average number of employees employed during a two year period, calculated in accordance with the provisions of the law or practice of that Member State which is designed to give effect to the Transnational Information and Consultation Directive.

(2) Subject to paragraph (3), the average number of UK employees is to be ascertained by—

(a) determining the number of UK employees in each month in the two year period preceding the relevant date (whether they were employed throughout the month or not);

(b) adding together all of the monthly numbers, and

dividing the number so determined by 24.

(3) For the purposes of the calculation in paragraph 2(a) if for the whole of a month within the two year period an employee works under a contract by virtue of which he would have worked for 75 hours or less in that month—

(a) were the month to have contained 21 working days;

(b) were the employee to have had no absences from work; and

(c) were the employee to have worked no overtime,

the employee may be counted as half a person for the month in question, if the UK management so decides.

(4) For the purposes of this regulation, [regulations 2(4C), *7 to 10, 19F* and 20] "relevant date" means—

(a) where a request under regulation 7 is made and no valid request under regulation 9 has been made, the last day of the month preceding the month in which the request under regulation 7 is made; and

(b) where a valid request under regulation 9 is made (whether or not a request under regulation 7 has been made), the last day of the month preceding the month in which the request under regulation 9 is made.

(5) Where appropriate, the references in paragraph (4) to regulations 7 and 9 shall be read, instead, as references to the provisions of the law or practice of a Member State other than the United Kingdom which are designed to give effect to, respectively, Article 11(2) and Article 5(1) of the Transnational Information and Consultation Directive.

NOTES

Para (4): words in square brackets substituted by the Transnational Information and Consultation of Employees (Amendment) Regulations 2010, SI 2010/1088, regs 2, 4. First words in italics revoked and paras (a), (b) substituted as follows, by the Employment Rights (Amendment) (EU Exit) Regulations 2019, SI 2019/535, reg 2(2), Sch 2, Pt 1, paras 1, 8, as from exit day (as defined in the European Union (Withdrawal) Act 2018, s 20) and subject to savings and transitional provisions in Sch 2, Pt 2 at **[2.2182]**—

"(a) where a request under regulation 7 was made before exit day but no valid request under regulation 9 was made before that day, the last day of the month preceding the month in which the request under regulation 7 was made;

(b) where a valid request under regulation 9 was made before exit day (whether or not a request under regulation 7 was made), the last day of the month preceding the month in which the request under regulation 9 was made.".

[2.478]

7 Entitlement to information

(1) An employee or an employees' representative may request information from the management of an establishment, or of an undertaking, in the United Kingdom for the purpose of determining whether, in the case of an establishment, it is part of a Community-scale undertaking or Community-scale group of undertakings or, in the case of an undertaking, it is a Community-scale undertaking or is part of a Community-scale group of undertakings.

(2) In this regulation and regulation 8, the management of an establishment or undertaking to which a request under paragraph (1) is made is referred to as the "recipient".

[(3) The recipient must obtain and provide the employee or employees' representative who has made the request with information—

(a) on the average number of employees employed by the undertaking, or as the case may be the group of undertakings, in the United Kingdom and in each of the other Member States in the last two years; and

(b) relating to the structure of—

(i) the undertaking, or as the case may be the group of undertakings, and

(ii) its workforce,

in the United Kingdom and in each of the other Member States in the last two years.

(4) Where information disclosed under paragraph (3) includes information as to the employment situation in the undertaking, or as the case may be the group of undertakings, this shall include suitable information relating to the use of agency workers (if any).]

NOTES

Revoked by the Employment Rights (Amendment) (EU Exit) Regulations 2019, SI 2019/535, reg 2(2), Sch 2, Pt 1, paras 1, 9, as from exit day (as defined in the European Union (Withdrawal) Act 2018, s 20) and subject to savings and transitional provisions in Sch 2, Pt 2 at **[2.2182]**.

Paras (3), (4): substituted (for the original para (3)) by the Transnational Information and Consultation of Employees (Amendment) Regulations 2010, SI 2010/1088, regs 2, 5.

[2.479]
8 Complaint of failure to provide information

(1) An employee or employees' representative who has requested information under regulation 7 may present a complaint to the CAC that—

[(a) the recipient has failed to provide, or as the case may be obtain and provide, the information referred to in regulation 7(3); or]

(b) the information which has been provided by the recipient is false or incomplete in a material particular.

[(2) Where the CAC finds the complaint well-founded it shall make an order requiring the recipient to disclose information to the complainant which order shall specify—

(a) the information in respect of which the CAC finds that the complaint is well-founded and which is to be disclosed, or as the case may be obtained and disclosed, to the complainant;

(b) the date (or if more than one, the earliest date) on which the recipient refused or failed to disclose, or as the case may be obtain and disclose, information, or disclosed false or incomplete information; and

(c) a date (not less than one week from the date of the order) by which the recipient must disclose, or as the case may be obtain and disclose, the information specified in the order.]

(3) If the CAC considers that, from the information it has obtained in considering the complaint, it is beyond doubt that the undertaking is, or that the establishment is part of, a Community-scale undertaking or that the establishment or undertaking is part of a Community-scale group of undertakings, it may make a declaration to that effect.

(4) The CAC shall not consider a complaint presented under this regulation unless it is made after the expiry of a period of one month beginning on the date on which the complainant made his request for information under regulation 7.

NOTES

Revoked by the Employment Rights (Amendment) (EU Exit) Regulations 2019, SI 2019/535, reg 2(2), Sch 2, Pt 1, paras 1, 9, as from exit day (as defined in the European Union (Withdrawal) Act 2018, s 20) and subject to savings and transitional provisions in Sch 2, Pt 2 at **[2.2182]**.

Sub-para (1)(a) and para (2) substituted by the Transnational Information and Consultation of Employees (Amendment) Regulations 2010, SI 2010/1088, regs 2, 6.

[2.480]
9 Request to negotiate an agreement for a European Works Council or information and consultation procedure

(1) The central management shall initiate negotiations for the establishment of a European Works Council or an information and consultation procedure where—

(a) a valid request has been made by employees or employees' representatives; and

(b) on the relevant date the undertaking is a Community-scale undertaking or the group of undertakings is a Community-scale group of undertakings.

(2) A valid request may consist of—

(a) a single request made by at least 100 employees, or employees' representatives who represent at least that number, in at least two undertakings or establishments in at least two different Member States; or

(b) a number of separate requests made on the same or different days by employees, or by employees' representatives, which when taken together mean that at least 100 employees, or employees' representatives who represent at least that number, in at least two undertakings or establishments in at least two different Member States have made requests.

(3) To amount to a valid request the single request referred to in paragraph (2)(a) or each separate request referred to in paragraph (2)(b) must—

(a) be in writing;

(b) be sent to—

(i) the central management, or

(ii) the local management;

(c) specify the date on which it was sent; and

(d) where appropriate, be made after the expiry of a period of two years, commencing on the date of a decision under regulation 16(3) (unless the special negotiating body and central management have otherwise agreed).

(4) The date on which a valid request is made is—

(a) where it consists of a single request satisfying paragraph 2(a) or of separate requests made on the same day satisfying paragraph 2(b), the date on which the request is or requests are sent; and

(b) where it consists of separate requests made on different days satisfying paragraph 2(b), the date of the sending of the request which resulted in that paragraph being satisfied.

(5) The central management may initiate the negotiations referred to in paragraph (1) on its own initiative.

NOTES

Revoked by the Employment Rights (Amendment) (EU Exit) Regulations 2019, SI 2019/535, reg 2(2), Sch 2, Pt 1, paras 1, 9, as from exit day (as defined in the European Union (Withdrawal) Act 2018, s 20) and subject to savings and transitional provisions in Sch 2, Pt 2 at **[2.2182]**.

[2.481]

10 Dispute as to whether valid request made or whether obligation in regulation 9(1) applies

(1) If the central management considers that a request (or separate request) did not satisfy any requirement of regulation 9(2) or (3) it may apply to the CAC for a declaration as to whether the request satisfied the requirement.

(2) The CAC shall only consider an application for a declaration made under paragraph (1) if—

(a) the application is made within a three month period beginning on the date when a request, or if more than one the first request, was made for the purposes of regulation 9, whether or not that request satisfied the requirements of regulations 9(2) and (3);

(b) the application is made before the central management takes any step to initiate negotiations for the establishment of a European Works Council or an information and consultation procedure; and

(c) at the time when the application is made, there has been no application by the central management for a declaration under paragraph (3).

(3) If the central management considers for any reason that the obligation in regulation 9(1) did not apply to it on the relevant date, it may, within a period of three months commencing on the date on which the valid request was made, apply to the CAC for a declaration as to whether that obligation applied to it on the relevant date.

(4) Where the date on which the valid request was made is a date falling before the date of any declaration made pursuant to an application made under this regulation the operation of the periods of time specified in paragraphs (1)(b) and (1)(c) of regulation 18 shall be suspended for a period of time—

(a) commencing on the date of the application; and

(b) ending on the date of the declaration.

(5) If on an application for a declaration under this regulation the CAC does not make any declaration in favour of the central management and considers that the central management has, in making the application or conducting the proceedings, acted frivolously, vexatiously, or otherwise unreasonably, the CAC shall make a declaration to the effect that paragraph (4) does not apply.

NOTES

Revoked by the Employment Rights (Amendment) (EU Exit) Regulations 2019, SI 2019/535, reg 2(2), Sch 2, Pt 1, paras 1, 9, as from exit day (as defined in the European Union (Withdrawal) Act 2018, s 20) and subject to savings and transitional provisions in Sch 2, Pt 2 at **[2.2182]**.

PART III
SPECIAL NEGOTIATING BODY

[2.482]

11 Functions of the special negotiating body

The special negotiating body shall have the task of determining, with the central management, by written agreement, the scope, composition, functions, and term of office of a European Works Council or the arrangements for implementing an information and consultation procedure.

NOTES

Pt III (regs 11–15) revoked by the Employment Rights (Amendment) (EU Exit) Regulations 2019, SI 2019/535, reg 2(2), Sch 2, Pt 1, paras 1, 10, as from exit day (as defined in the European Union (Withdrawal) Act 2018, s 20) and subject to savings and transitional provisions in Sch 2, Pt 2 at **[2.2182]**.

[2.483]

[12 Composition of the special negotiating body

(1) Subject to paragraph (3), the special negotiating body shall be constituted in accordance with paragraph (2).

(2) In each Member State in which employees of a Community-scale undertaking or Community-scale group of undertakings are employed to work, those employees shall elect or appoint one member of the special negotiating body for each 10% (or fraction of 10%) which those employees represent of the total number of employees of the Community-scale undertaking or Community-scale group of undertakings employed in those Member States.

(3) Paragraph (1) does not apply to a special negotiating body constituted before 5th June 2011.

(4) The special negotiating body shall inform the central management, local managements and the European social partner organisations of the composition of the special negotiating body and of the date they propose to start the negotiations.]

NOTES

Substituted by the Transnational Information and Consultation of Employees (Amendment) Regulations 2010, SI 2010/1088, regs 2, 7.

Revoked as noted to reg 11 at **[2.482]**.

[2.484]

13 Ballot arrangements

(1) Subject to regulation 15, the UK members of the special negotiating body shall be elected by a ballot of the UK employees.

(2) The UK management must arrange for the holding of a ballot of employees referred to in paragraph (1), which satisfies the requirements specified in paragraph (3).

(3) The requirements referred to in paragraph (2) are that—

(a) the ballot of the UK employees must comprise a single ballot but may instead, if the UK management so decides, comprise separate ballots of employees in such constituencies as the UK management may determine where—

(i) the number of UK members of the special negotiating body to be elected is more than one, and

(ii) the UK management considers that if separate ballots were held for those constituencies, the UK members of the special negotiating body to be elected would better reflect the interests of the UK employees as a whole than if a single ballot were held;

(b) a UK employee who is an employee of the Community-scale undertaking or the Community-scale group of undertakings on the day on which votes may be cast in the ballot, or if the votes may be cast on more than one day, on the first day of those days, is entitled to vote in the ballot of the UK employees;

(c) any UK employee, or UK employees' representative, who is an employee of, or an employees' representative in, the Community-scale undertaking or Community scale group of undertakings immediately before the latest time at which a person may become a candidate in the ballot, is entitled to stand in the ballot of the UK employees as a candidate for election as a UK member of the special negotiating body;

(d) the UK management must, in accordance with paragraph (7), appoint an independent ballot supervisor to supervise the conduct of the ballot of the UK employees but may instead, where there are to be separate ballots, appoint more than one independent ballot supervisor in accordance with that paragraph, each of whom is to supervise such of the separate ballots as the UK management may determine, provided that each separate ballot is supervised by a supervisor;

(e) after the UK management has formulated proposals as to the arrangements for the ballot of the UK employees and before it has published the final arrangements under sub-paragraph (f) it must, so far as reasonably practicable, consult with the UK employees' representatives on the proposed arrangements for the ballot of the UK employees;

(f) the UK management must publish the final arrangements for the ballot of the UK employees in such manner as to bring them to the attention of, so far as reasonably practicable, the UK employees and the UK employees' representatives.

(4) Any UK employee or UK employees' representative who believes that the arrangements for the ballot of the UK employees are defective may, within a period of 21 days beginning on the date on which the UK management published the final arrangements under sub-paragraph (f), present a complaint to the CAC.

(5) Where the CAC finds the complaint well-founded it shall make a declaration to that effect and may make an order requiring the UK management to modify the arrangements it has made for the ballot of the UK employees or to satisfy the requirements in sub-paragraph (e) or (f) of paragraph (3).

(6) An order under paragraph (5) shall specify the modifications to the arrangements which the UK management is required to make and the requirements which it must satisfy.

(7) A person is an independent ballot supervisor for the purposes of paragraph (3)(d) if the UK management reasonably believes that he will carry out any functions conferred on him in relation to the ballot competently and has no reasonable grounds for believing that his independence in relation to the ballot might reasonably be called into question.

(8) For the purposes of paragraph (4) the arrangements for the ballot of the UK employees are defective if—

(a) any of the requirements specified in sub-paragraphs (b) to (f) of paragraph (3) is not satisfied; or

(b) in a case where the ballot is to comprise separate ballots, the constituencies determined by the UK management do not reflect adequately the interests of the UK employees as a whole.

NOTES

Revoked as noted to reg 11 at **[2.482]**.

[2.485]

14 Conduct of ballot

(1) The UK management must—

(a) ensure that a ballot supervisor appointed under regulation 13(3)(d) carries out his functions under this regulation and that there is no interference with his carrying out of those functions from the UK management, or the central management (where it is not also the UK management); and

(b) comply with all reasonable requests made by a ballot supervisor for the purposes of, or in connection with, the carrying out of those functions.

(2) A ballot supervisor's appointment shall require that he—

(a) supervises the conduct of the ballot, or the separate ballots he is being appointed to supervise, in accordance with the arrangements for the ballot of the UK employees published by the UK management under regulation 13(3)(f) or, where appropriate, in accordance with the arrangements as required to be modified by an order made as a result of a complaint presented under regulation 13(4);

Part 2 Statutory Instruments

(b) *does not conduct the ballot or any of the separate ballots before the UK management has satisfied the requirement specified in regulation 13(3)(e) and—*
(i) *where no complaint has been presented under regulation 13(4), before the expiry of a period of 21 days beginning on the date on which the UK management published its arrangements under regulation 13(3)(f); or*
(ii) *where a complaint has been presented under regulation 13(4), before the complaint has been determined and, where appropriate, the arrangements have been modified as required by an order made as a result of the complaint;*
(c) *conducts the ballot, or each separate ballot, so as to secure that—*
(i) *so far as reasonably practicable, those entitled to vote are given the opportunity to vote,*
(ii) *so far as reasonably practicable, those entitled to stand as candidates are given the opportunity to stand,*
(iii) *so far as is reasonably practicable, those voting are able to do so in secret, and*
(iv) *the votes given in the ballot are fairly and accurately counted.*

(3) As soon as reasonably practicable after the holding of the ballot, the ballot supervisor must publish the results of the ballot in such manner as to make them available to the UK management and, so far as reasonably practicable, the UK employees entitled to vote in the ballot and the persons who stood as candidates in the ballot.

(4) A ballot supervisor shall publish a report ("an ineffective ballot report") where he considers (whether or not on the basis of representations made to him by another person) that—
(a) *any of the requirements referred to in paragraph (2) was not satisfied with the result that the outcome of the ballot would have been different; or*
(b) *there was interference with the carrying out of his functions or a failure by management to comply with all reasonable requests made by him with the result that he was unable to form a proper judgment as to whether each of the requirements referred to in paragraph (2) was satisfied in relation to the ballot.*

(5) Where a ballot supervisor publishes an ineffective ballot report the report must be published within a period of one month commencing on the date on which the ballot supervisor publishes the results of the ballot under paragraph (3).

(6) A ballot supervisor shall publish an ineffective ballot report in such manner as to make it available to the UK management and, so far as reasonably practicable, the UK employees entitled to vote in the ballot and the persons who stood as candidates in the ballot.

(7) Where a ballot supervisor publishes an ineffective ballot report then—
(a) *if there has been a single ballot or an ineffective ballot report has been published in respect of every separate ballot, the outcome of the ballot or ballots shall have no effect and the UK management shall again be under the obligation in regulation 13(2);*
(b) *if there have been separate ballots and sub-paragraph (a) does not apply—*
(i) *the UK management shall arrange for the separate ballot or ballots in respect of which an ineffective ballot report was issued to be reheld in accordance with regulation 13 and this regulation, and*
(ii) *no such ballot shall have effect until it has been reheld and no ineffective ballot report has been published in respect of it.*

(8) All costs relating to the holding of a ballot, including payments made to a ballot supervisor for supervising the conduct of the ballot, shall be borne by the central management (whether or not an ineffective ballot report has been made).

NOTES

Revoked as noted to reg 11 at **[2.482]**.

[2.486]
15 Consultative Committee

(1) Where a consultative committee exists—
(a) *no UK member of the special negotiating body shall be elected by a ballot of the UK employees, except in the circumstances specified in paragraphs (2), (3) or (9) below; and*
(b) *the committee shall be entitled to nominate from its number the UK members of the special negotiating body.*

(2) Where the consultative committee fails to nominate any UK members of the special negotiating body, all of the UK members of the special negotiating body shall be elected by a ballot of the UK employees in accordance with regulations 13 and 14.

(3) Where the consultative committee nominates such number of persons to be a UK member, or UK members, of the special negotiating body, which number is less or more than the number of UK members of the special negotiating body required, the consultative committee shall be treated as having failed to have nominated any UK members of the special negotiating body.

(4) In this regulation, "a consultative committee" means a body of persons—
(a) *whose normal functions include or comprise the carrying out of an information and consultation function;*
(b) *which is able to carry out its information and consultation function without interference from the UK management, or from the central management (where it is not also the UK management);*

(c) *which, in carrying out its information and consultation function, represents all the UK employees; and*

(d) *which consists wholly of persons who were elected by a ballot (which may have consisted of a number of separate ballots) in which all the employees who, at the time, were UK employees were entitled to vote.*

(5) In paragraph (4) "information and consultation function" means the function of—

(a) *receiving, on behalf of all the UK employees, information which may significantly affect the interests of the UK employees, but excluding information which is relevant only to a specific aspect of the interests of the employees, such as health and safety or collective redundancies; and*

(b) *being consulted by the UK management or the central management (where it is not also the UK management) on the information referred to in sub-paragraph (a) above.*

(6) The consultative committee must publish the names of the persons whom it has nominated to be UK members of the special negotiating body in such manner as to bring them to the attention of the UK management and, so far as reasonably practicable, the UK employees and UK employees' representatives.

(7) Where the UK management, a UK employee or a UK employees' representative believes that—

(a) *the consultative committee does not satisfy the requirements in paragraph (4) above; or*

(b) *any of the persons nominated by the consultative committee is not entitled to be nominated,*

it, or as the case may be he, may, within a period of 21 days beginning on the date on which the consultative committee published under paragraph (6) the names of persons nominated, present a complaint to the CAC.

(8) Where the CAC finds the complaint well-founded it shall make a declaration to that effect.

(9) Where the CAC has made a declaration under paragraph (8)—

(a) *no nomination made by the consultative committee shall have effect; and*

(b) *all of the UK members of the special negotiating body shall be elected by a ballot of the UK employees in accordance with regulations 13 and 14.*

(10) Where the consultative committee nominates any person to be a UK member of the special negotiating body, that nomination shall have effect after—

(a) *where no complaint has been presented under paragraph (7), the expiry of a period of 21 days beginning on the date on which the consultative committee published under paragraph (6) the names of persons nominated; or*

(b) *where a complaint has been presented under paragraph (7), the complaint has been determined without a declaration under paragraph (8) having been made.*

NOTES

Revoked as noted to reg 11 at **[2.482]**.

PART IV
EUROPEAN WORKS COUNCIL AND INFORMATION AND CONSULTATION PROCEDURE

[2.487]

16 Negotiation procedure

(1) With a view to concluding an agreement referred to in regulation 17 the central management must convene a meeting with the special negotiating body and must inform local managements accordingly.

[(1A) Within a reasonable time both before and after any meeting with the central management, the members of the special negotiating body are entitled to meet without the central management or its representatives being present, using any means necessary for communication at those meetings.]

(2) Subject to paragraph (3), the special negotiating body shall take decisions by a majority of the votes cast by its members and each member of the special negotiating body is to have one vote.

(3) The special negotiating body may decide not to open negotiations with central management or to terminate negotiations. Any such decision must be taken by at least two thirds of the votes cast by its members.

(4) Any decision made under paragraph (3) shall have the following effects—

(a) *the procedure to negotiate and conclude the agreement referred to in regulation 17 shall cease from the date of the decision; and*

(b) *a purported request made under regulation 9 less than two years after the date of the decision shall not be treated as such a request, unless the special negotiating body and the central management otherwise agree.*

(5) For the purpose of the negotiations, the special negotiating body may be assisted by experts of its choice [(which may include representatives of European trade union organisations) who may, at the request of the special negotiating body, attend in an advisory capacity any meeting convened in accordance with paragraph (1)].

(6) The central management shall pay for any reasonable expenses relating to the negotiations that are necessary to enable the special negotiating body to carry out its functions in an appropriate manner; but where the special negotiating body is assisted by more than one expert the central management is not required to pay such expenses in respect of more than one of them.

NOTES

Revoked by the Employment Rights (Amendment) (EU Exit) Regulations 2019, SI 2019/535, reg 2(2), Sch 2, Pt 1, paras 1, 11, as from exit day (as defined in the European Union (Withdrawal) Act 2018, s 20) and subject to savings and transitional provisions in Sch 2, Pt 2 at **[2.2182]**.

Para (1A): inserted by the Transnational Information and Consultation of Employees (Amendment) Regulations 2010, SI 2010/1088, regs 2, 8(a).

Para (5): words in square brackets inserted by SI 2010/1088, regs 2, 8(b).

[2.488]

17 Content and scope of a European Works Council agreement and information and consultation procedure

(1) The central management and the special negotiating body are under a duty to negotiate in a spirit of cooperation with a view to reaching a written agreement on the detailed arrangements for the information and consultation of employees in a Community-scale undertaking or Community-scale group of undertakings.

(2) In this regulation and regulations 18 and 20, the central management and the special negotiating body are referred to as "the parties".

(3) The parties may decide in writing to establish an information and consultation procedure instead of a European Works Council.

(4) Without prejudice to the autonomy of the parties, where the parties decide to proceed with the establishment of a European Works Council, the agreement establishing it shall determine—

(a) the undertakings of the Community-scale group of undertakings or the establishments of the Community-scale undertaking which are covered by the agreement;

(b) the composition of the European Works Council, the number of members, the allocation of seats and the term of office of the members;

(c) the functions and the procedure for information and consultation of the European Works Council [and arrangements to link information and consultation of the European Works Council with information and consultation of national employee representation bodies];

(d) the venue, frequency and duration of meetings of the European Works Council;

[(dd) where the parties decide that it is necessary to establish a select committee, the composition of the select committee, the procedure for appointing its members, the functions and the procedural rules;]

(e) the financial and material resources to be allocated to the European Works Council; and

[(f) the date of entry into force of the agreement and its duration, the arrangements for amending or terminating the agreement, the circumstances in which the agreement is to be renegotiated including where the structure of the Community-scale undertaking or Community-scale group of undertakings changes and the procedure for renegotiation of the agreement.]

[(4A) In determining the allocation of seats under paragraph (4)(b), an agreement shall, so far as reasonably practicable, take into account the need for balanced representation of employees with regard to their role and gender and the sector in which they work.]

[(5) If the parties decide to establish an information and consultation procedure instead of a European Works Council, the agreement establishing the procedure must specify a method by which the information and consultation representatives are to enjoy the right to meet to discuss the information conveyed to them.]

(6) An agreement referred to in paragraph (4) or (5) is not to be subject to the provisions of the Schedule, except to the extent that the parties provide in the agreement that any of those requirements are to apply.

(7) Where a Community-scale group of undertakings comprises one or more undertakings or groups of undertakings which are themselves Community-scale undertakings or Community-scale groups of undertakings, the European Works Council shall be established at the level of the first-mentioned Community-scale group of undertakings, unless an agreement referred to in paragraph (4) provides otherwise.

(8) Unless a wider scope is provided for in an agreement referred to in paragraph (1), the powers and competence of a European Works Council and the scope of an information and consultation procedure shall, in the case of a Community-scale undertaking, cover all the establishments located within the Member States and, in the case of a Community-scale group of undertakings, all group undertakings located within the Member States.

[(9) Where information disclosed under a European Works Council agreement or an information and consultation procedure includes information as to the employment situation in the Community-scale undertaking or, as the case may be, the Community-scale group of undertakings, this shall include suitable information relating to the use of agency workers (if any).]

NOTES

Paras (1)–(8): revoked by the Employment Rights (Amendment) (EU Exit) Regulations 2019, SI 2019/535, reg 2(2), Sch 2, Pt 1, paras 1, 12, as from exit day (as defined in the European Union (Withdrawal) Act 2018, s 20) and subject to savings and transitional provisions in Sch 2, Pt 2 at **[2.2182]**.

Para (4): revoked as noted above; words in square brackets in sub-para (c) inserted, sub-para (dd) inserted, and sub-para (f) substituted, by the Transnational Information and Consultation of Employees (Amendment) Regulations 2010, SI 2010/1088, regs 2, 9(a)–(c).

Para (4A): inserted by SI 2010/1088, regs 2, 9(d); revoked as noted above.

Para (5): substituted by SI 2010/1088, regs 2, 9(e); revoked as noted above.
Para (9): added by SI 2010/1088, regs 2, 9(f).

[2.489]
18 Subsidiary requirements

(1) The provisions of the Schedule shall apply if—

(a) the parties so agree;

(b) within the period of six months beginning on the date on which a valid request referred to in regulation 9 was made, the central management refuses to commence negotiations; or

(c) after the expiry of a period of three years beginning on the date on which a valid request referred to in regulation 9 was made, the parties have failed to conclude an agreement under regulation 17 and the special negotiating body has not taken the decision under regulation 16(3).

NOTES

Substituted by the Employment Rights (Amendment) (EU Exit) Regulations 2019, SI 2019/535, reg 2(2), Sch 2, Pt 1, paras 1, 13, as from exit day (as defined in the European Union (Withdrawal) Act 2018, s 20) and subject to savings and transitional provisions in Sch 2, Pt 2 at **[2.2182]**, as follows—

"**18 Subsidiary requirements**
The provisions of the Schedule continue to apply on and after exit day in any case where they applied before exit day.".

[2.490]
[18A Information and consultation

(1) This regulation applies where—

(a) a European Works Council or information and consultation procedure has been established [before exit day] under regulation 17; or

(b) a European Works Council has been established [before exit day] by virtue of regulation 18.

(2) The central management, or any more appropriate level of management, shall give information to—

(a) members of a European Works Council; or

(b) information and consultation representatives,

as the case may be, in accordance with paragraph (3).

(3) The content of the information, the time when, and manner in which it is given, must be such as to enable the recipients to—

(a) acquaint themselves with and examine its subject matter;

(b) undertake a detailed assessment of its possible impact; and

(c) where appropriate, prepare for consultation.

(4) The central management, or any more appropriate level of management, shall consult with—

(a) members of a European Works Council; or

(b) information and consultation representatives,

as the case may be, in accordance with paragraph (5).

(5) The content of the consultation, the time when, and manner in which it takes place, must be such as to enable a European Works Council or information and consultation representatives to express an opinion on the basis of the information provided to them.

(6) The opinion referred to in paragraph (5) shall be provided within a reasonable time after the information is provided to the European Works Council or the information and consultation representatives and, having regard to the responsibilities of management to take decisions effectively, may be taken into account by the central management or any more appropriate level of management.

(7) The information provided to the members of a European Works Council or information and consultation representatives, and the consultation of the members of a European Works Council or information and consultation representatives shall be limited to transnational matters.

(8) Where information as to the employment situation in the Community-scale undertaking or, as the case may be, the Community-scale group of undertakings, is disclosed by the central management or any more appropriate level of management, this shall include suitable information relating to the use of agency workers (if any).]

NOTES

Inserted by the Transnational Information and Consultation of Employees (Amendment) Regulations 2010, SI 2010/1088, regs 2, 10.

Para (1): words in square brackets inserted by the Employment Rights (Amendment) (EU Exit) Regulations 2019, SI 2019/535, reg 2(2), Sch 2, Pt 1, paras 1, 14, as from exit day (as defined in the European Union (Withdrawal) Act 2018, s 20) and subject to savings and transitional provisions in Sch 2, Pt 2 at **[2.2182]**.

[2.491]
19 Cooperation

(1) The central management and the European Works Council are under a duty to work in a spirit of cooperation with due regard to their reciprocal rights and obligations.

(2) The duty in paragraph (1) shall apply also to the central management and information and consultation representatives.

[2.492]
[19A Means required

(1) Subject to paragraph (2), the central management shall provide the members of a European Works Council with the means required to fulfil their duty to represent collectively the interests of the employees of the Community-scale undertaking or Community-scale group of undertakings under these Regulations.

(2) The obligation on central management in paragraph (1) does not include an obligation to provide a member of a European Works Council with—

(a) time off during working hours to perform functions as such a member, or remuneration for such time off (as required by regulations 25 and 26);
(b) the means required to undertake training (as required by regulation 19B); or
(c) time off during working hours to undertake training, or remuneration for such time off (as required by regulations 25 and 26).]

NOTES

Inserted, together with regs 19B–19F by the Transnational Information and Consultation of Employees (Amendment) Regulations 2010, SI 2010/1088, regs 2, 11.

[2.493]
[19B Right to training for members of a European Works Council, etc

(1) Subject to paragraph (2), the central management shall provide an employee who is—

(a) a member of a special negotiating body; or
(b) a member of a European Works Council,

with the means required to undertaking training to the extent necessary for the exercise of the employee's representative duties.

(2) The obligation on central management referred to in paragraph (1) does not include an obligation to provide time off during working hours to undertaking training, or remuneration for such time off (as required by regulations 25 and 26).]

NOTES

Inserted as noted to reg 19A at **[2.492]**.

Para (1): sub-para (a) revoked by the Employment Rights (Amendment) (EU Exit) Regulations 2019, SI 2019/535, reg 2(2), Sch 2, Pt 1, paras 1, 15, as from exit day (as defined in the European Union (Withdrawal) Act 2018, s 20) and subject to savings and transitional provisions in Sch 2, Pt 2 at **[2.2182]**.

[2.494]
[19C European Works Council to inform, etc

Subject to regulation 23, a European Works Council shall inform—

(a) the employees' representatives in the establishments of a Community-scale undertaking or in the undertakings of a Community-scale group of undertakings; or
(b) to the extent that any employees are not represented by employees' representatives, the employees themselves,

of the content and outcome of the information and consultation procedure carried out in accordance with these Regulations.]

NOTES

Inserted as noted to reg 19A at **[2.492]**.

[2.495]
[19D Complaint of failure to inform

(1) An employee or employees' representative may present a complaint to the CAC that—

(a) the European Works Council has failed to inform them under regulation 19C of the content or outcome of the information and consultation procedure; or
(b) the information which has been provided by the European Works Council is false or incomplete in a material particular.

(2) Where the CAC finds the complaint well-founded it shall make an order requiring the European Works Council to disclose information to the complainant which order shall specify—

(a) the information in respect of which the CAC finds that the complaint is well-founded and which is to be disclosed to the complainant;
(b) the date (or if more than one, the earliest date) on which the European Works Council refused or failed to disclose information, or disclosed false or incomplete information; and
(c) a date (not less than one week from the date of the order) by which the European Works Council must disclose the information specified in the order.

(3) The CAC shall not find a complaint under this regulation well-founded where it considers that the failure to inform, or the provision of false or incomplete information, resulted from a failure by the central management to provide the members of the European Works Council with the means required to fulfil their duty to represent collectively the interests of the employees of the Community-scale undertaking or Community-scale group of undertakings (as required by regulation 19A).

(4) A complaint brought under paragraph (1) must be brought within a period of six months beginning with the date of the alleged failure to inform, or the provision of false or incomplete information.]

NOTES

Inserted as noted to reg 19A at **[2.492]**.

[2.496]

[19E Links between information and consultation of European Works Council and national employee representation bodies

(1) Paragraph (2) applies where—

(a) no arrangements to link information and consultation of a European Works Council with information and consultation of national employee representation bodies *have been made* under regulation 17(4)(c), and

(b) there are circumstances likely to lead to substantial changes in work organisation or contractual relations.

(2) Subject to regulation 2(4B), the—

(a) management of every undertaking belonging to the Community-scale group of undertakings;

(b) central management; or

(c) representative agent or the management treated as the central management of the Community-scale undertaking or Community-scale group of undertakings within the meaning of regulation 5(2),

as the case may be, shall ensure that the procedures for informing and consulting the European Works Council and the national employee representation bodies in relation to the substantial changes in work organisation or contractual relations referred to in sub-paragraph (b) of paragraph (1) are linked so as to begin within a reasonable time of each other.

(3) The national employee representation bodies referred to in paragraph (2) are those bodies which are entitled, whether by law, agreement or custom and practice, to be informed and consulted on the substantial changes in work organisation or contractual relations referred to in sub-paragraph (b) of paragraph (1).]

NOTES

Inserted as noted to reg 19A at **[2.492]**.

Para (1): for the words in italics there are substituted the words "were made before exit day", by the Employment Rights (Amendment) (EU Exit) Regulations 2019, SI 2019/535, reg 2(2), Sch 2, Pt 1, paras 1, 16, as from exit day (as defined in the European Union (Withdrawal) Act 2018, s 20) and subject to savings and transitional provisions in Sch 2, Pt 2 at **[2.2182]**.

[2.497]

[19F Adaptation

(1) The central management shall initiate negotiations for the establishment of a European Works Council or an information and consultation procedure where the structure of a Community-scale undertaking or Community-scale group of undertakings changes significantly and paragraphs (2) and (3) apply.

(2) This paragraph applies where there is—

(a) one European Works Council agreement, or one agreement for an information and consultation procedure;

(b) more than one European Works Council agreement;

(c) more than one agreement for an information and consultation procedure;

(d) at least one European Works Council agreement and at least one agreement for an information and consultation procedure,

in force and there are no provisions for the continuance of the European Works Council or information and consultation procedure, as the case may be, where there are significant changes in the structure of the Community-scale undertaking or Community-scale group of undertakings or there are such provisions, but there is a conflict between them.

(3) This paragraph applies where a valid request within the meaning of regulation 9(2) and (3) has been made by employees or employees' representatives and on the relevant date the undertaking is a Community-scale undertaking or the group of undertakings is a Community-scale group of undertakings.

(4) Notwithstanding paragraph (1), the central management may initiate the negotiations referred to in paragraph (1) on its own initiative.

(5) Where the central management has initiated negotiations under paragraph (1) or (4), there shall be on the special negotiating body at least three members of every existing European Works Council in addition to the members elected or appointed in accordance with regulation 12(2).

(6) Before the establishment of a European Works Council or an information and consultation procedure under paragraph (1) or (4), any agreement establishing an existing European Works Council or information and consultation procedure—

(a) shall continue to operate in accordance with its terms, and

(b) may be adapted by agreement between the members of the European Works Council and the central management, or the information and consultation representatives and the central management, as the case may be, as a result of the change in structured referred to in paragraph (1).

Part 2 Statutory Instruments

(7) Where information is to be disclosed under a European Works Council agreement or an information and consultation procedure which includes information as to the employment situation in the Community-scale undertaking or, as the case may be, the Community-scale group of undertakings, this shall include suitable information relating to the use of agency workers (if any).]

NOTES

Inserted as noted to reg 19A at **[2.492]**.

Revoked by the Employment Rights (Amendment) (EU Exit) Regulations 2019, SI 2019/535, reg 2(2), Sch 2, Pt 1, paras 1, 17, as from exit day (as defined in the European Union (Withdrawal) Act 2018, s 20) and subject to savings and transitional provisions in Sch 2, Pt 2 at **[2.2182]**.

PART V
COMPLIANCE AND ENFORCEMENT

[2.498]

20 Failure to establish European Works Council or information and consultation procedure

[(A1) In this regulation the central management and the special negotiating body are referred to as "the parties".]

(1) A complaint may be presented to the [CAC] by a relevant applicant who considers—

(a) that the parties have reached agreement [before exit day] on the establishment of a European Works Council or an information and consultation procedure, or that regulation 18 applies; and

(b) that, because of a failure of the central management, the European Works Council or information and consultation procedure has not been established at all, or has not been established fully in accordance with the terms of the agreement [made before exit day] under regulation 17 or, as the case may be, in accordance with the provisions of the Schedule.

(2) In this regulation "failure" means an act or omission and a failure by the local management shall be treated as a failure by the central management.

(3) In this regulation "relevant applicant" means—

(a) in a case where a special negotiating body exists, the special negotiating body; or

(b) in a case where a special negotiating body does not exist, an employee, employees' representative, or person who was a member of the special negotiating body (if that body existed previously).

(4) Where the [CAC] finds the complaint well-founded it shall make a decision to that effect and may make an order requiring the central management to take such steps as are necessary to establish the European Works Council or information and consultation procedure in accordance with the terms of the agreement [made before exit day] under regulation 17 or, as the case may be, to establish a European Works Council in accordance with the provisions of the Schedule.

(5) The [CAC] shall not find a complaint under this regulation to be well-founded where—

(a) the central management made no application [before exit day] in relation to the request under regulation 10(1), or where the request consisted of separate requests was unable by reason of the time limit in sub-paragraph (a) of that regulation to make an application [before exit day] under the regulation in relation to a particular request, and shows that the request was not a valid request because a requirement of regulation 9(2) or (3) [that applied before exit day] was not satisfied; or

(b) the central management made no application [before exit day] under regulation 10(3) but shows that the obligation in regulation 9(1) did not, for any reason, apply to it on the relevant date.

(6) An order under paragraph (4) shall specify—

(a) the steps which the central management is required to take;

(b) the date of the failure of the central management; and

(c) the period within which the order must be complied with.

[(7) If the Appeal Tribunal makes a decision under paragraph (4) the relevant applicant may, within the period of three months beginning with the date on which the decision is made, make an application to the Appeal Tribunal for a penalty notice to be issued.]

[(7A) Where such an application is made, the Appeal Tribunal shall issue a written penalty notice to the central management requiring it to pay a penalty to the Secretary of State in respect of the failure.]

(8) Paragraph [(7A)] shall not apply if the Appeal Tribunal is satisfied, on hearing the representations of the central management, that the failure resulted from a reason beyond the central management's control or that it has some other reasonable excuse for its failure.

(9) Regulation 22 shall apply in respect of a penalty notice issued under this regulation.

(10) No order of the [CAC] under this regulation shall have the effect of suspending or altering the effect of any act done or of any agreement made by the central management or the local management.

NOTES

Para (A1): inserted by the Employment Rights (Amendment) (EU Exit) Regulations 2019, SI 2019/535, reg 2(2), Sch 2, Pt 1, paras 1, 18(a), as from exit day (as defined in the European Union (Withdrawal) Act 2018, s 20) and subject to savings and transitional provisions in Sch 2, Pt 2 at **[2.2182]**.

Paras (1), (4), (5): word "CAC" in square brackets in each place it appears substituted by the Transnational Information and Consultation of Employees (Amendment) Regulations 2010, SI 2010/1088, regs 2, 12(a); all other words in square brackets inserted by SI 2019/535, reg 2(2), Sch 2, Pt 1, paras 1, 18(b)–(d), as from exit day (as defined in the European Union (Withdrawal) Act 2018, s 20) and subject to savings and transitional provisions in Sch 2, Pt 2 at **[2.2182]**.

Para (7): substituted by SI 2010/1088, regs 2, 12(b).

Para (7A): inserted by SI 2010/1088, regs 2, 12(c).

Para (8): figure in square brackets substituted by SI 2010/1088, regs 2, 12(d).

Para (10): word in square brackets substituted by SI 2010/1088, regs 2, 12(a).

Note: the amendments to paras (1), (4), (5) substituting the word "CAC" were not replicated in relation to the final reference to "the Appeal Tribunal" in para (7); this appears to be a drafting error in SI 2010/1088.

[2.499]

21 Disputes about operation of European Works Council or information and consultation procedure

[(1) Where—

(a) a European Works Council or information and consultation procedure has been established [before exit day] under regulation 17; or

(b) a European Works Council has been established [before exit day] by virtue of regulation 18,

a complaint may be presented to the CAC by a relevant applicant where paragraph (1A) applies.]

[(1A) This paragraph applies where a relevant applicant considers that, because of the failure of a defaulter—

(a) the terms of the agreement [made before exit day] under regulation 17 or, as the case may be, the provisions of the Schedule, have not been complied with; or

(b) regulation 18A has not been complied with, or the information which has been provided by the management under regulation 18A is false or incomplete in a material particular.

(1B) A complaint brought under paragraph (1) must be brought within a period of six months beginning with the date of the alleged failure or non-compliance.]

(2) In this regulation, "failure" means an act or omission and a failure by the local management shall be treated as a failure by the central management.

(3) In this regulation "relevant applicant" means—

(a) in the case of a failure concerning a European Works Council, either the central management or the European Works Council; or

(b) in the case of a failure concerning an information and consultation procedure, either the central management or any one or more of the information and consultation representatives,

and "defaulter" means the persons mentioned in sub-paragraph (a) or (b) against whom the complaint is presented.

(4) Where the [CAC] finds the complaint well-founded it shall make a decision to that effect and may make an order requiring the defaulter to take such steps as are necessary to comply with the terms of the agreement [made before exit day] under regulation 17 or, as the case may be, the provisions of the Schedule.

(5) An order made under paragraph (4) shall specify—

(a) the steps which the defaulter is required to take;

(b) the date of the failure; and

(c) the period within which the order must be complied with.

(6) If the [CAC] makes a decision under paragraph (4) and the defaulter in question is the central management [the relevant applicant may, within the period of three months beginning with the date on which the decision is made, make an application to the Appeal Tribunal for a penalty notice to be issued].

[(6A) Where such an application is made, the Appeal Tribunal shall issue a written penalty notice to the central management requiring it to pay a penalty to the Secretary of State in respect of the failure.]

(7) Paragraph [(6A)] shall not apply if the Appeal Tribunal is satisfied, on hearing the representations of the central management, that the failure resulted from a reason beyond the central management's control or that it has some other reasonable excuse for its failure.

(8) Regulation 22 shall apply in respect of a penalty notice issued under this regulation.

(9) No order of the [CAC] under this regulation shall have the effect of suspending or altering the effect of any act done or of any agreement made by the central management or the local management.

NOTES

Para (1): substituted by the Transnational Information and Consultation of Employees (Amendment) Regulations 2010, SI 2010/1088, regs 2, 13(a); words in square brackets inserted by the Employment Rights (Amendment) (EU Exit) Regulations 2019, SI 2019/535, reg 2(2), Sch 2, Pt 1, paras 1, 19(a), as from exit day (as defined in the European Union (Withdrawal) Act 2018, s 20) and subject to savings and transitional provisions in Sch 2, Pt 2 at **[2.2182]**.

Paras (1A), (1B), (6A): inserted by SI 2010/1088, regs 2, 13(b), (e); words in square brackets in para (1A) inserted by SI 2019/535, reg 2(2), Sch 2, Pt 1, paras 1, 19(b), as from exit day (as defined in the European Union (Withdrawal) Act 2018, s 20) and subject to savings and transitional provisions in Sch 2, Pt 2 at **[2.2182]**.

Para (4): word in first pair of square brackets substituted by SI 2010/1088, regs 2, 13(c); words in second pair of square brackets inserted by SI 2019/535, reg 2(2), Sch 2, Pt 1, paras 1, 19(b), as from exit day (as defined in the European Union (Withdrawal) Act 2018, s 20) and subject to savings and transitional provisions in Sch 2, Pt 2 at **[2.2182]**.

Para (6): words in square brackets substituted by SI 2010/1088, regs 2, 13(d).

Para (7): figure in square brackets substituted by SI 2010/1088, regs 2, 13(f).

Para (9): word in square brackets substituted by SI 2010/1088, regs 2, 13(c).

[2.500]

[21A Disputes about failures of management

(1) A complaint may be presented to the CAC by a relevant applicant who considers that—

(a) *because of the failure of a defaulter, the members of the special negotiating body have been unable to meet in accordance with regulation 16(1A);*

(b) because of the failure of a defaulter, the members of the European Works Council have not been provided with the means required to fulfil their duty to represent collectively the interests of the employees of the Community-scale undertaking or Community-scale group of undertakings in accordance with regulation 19A;

(c) because of the failure of a defaulter, *a member of a special negotiating body or* a member of the European Works Council has not been provided with the means required to undertake the training referred to in regulation 19B; or

(d) regulation 19E(2) applies and that, because of the failure of a defaulter, the European Works Council and the national employee representation bodies have not been informed and consulted in accordance with that regulation.

(2) A complaint brought under paragraph (1) must be brought within a period of six months beginning with the date of the alleged failure.

(3) Where the CAC finds the complaint well-founded it shall make a decision to that effect and may make an order requiring the defaulter to take such steps as are necessary to comply with regulation *16(1A),* 19A, 19B or 19E(2), as the case may be.

(4) An order made under paragraph (3) shall specify—

(a) the steps which the defaulter is required to take;

(b) the date of the failure; and

(c) the period within which the order must be complied with.

(5) If the CAC makes a decision under paragraph (3), the relevant applicant may, within the period of three months beginning with the date on which the decision is made, make an application to the Appeal Tribunal for a penalty notice to be issued.

(6) Where such an application is made, the Appeal Tribunal shall issue a written penalty notice to the defaulter requiring it to pay a penalty to the Secretary of State in respect of the failure.

(7) Paragraph (6) shall not apply if the Appeal Tribunal is satisfied, on hearing the representations of the defaulter, that the failure resulted from a reason beyond the defaulter's control or that it has some other reasonable excuse for its failure.

(8) Regulation 22 shall apply to a penalty notice issued under this regulation.

(9) No order of the CAC under this regulation shall have the effect of suspending or altering the effect of any act done or of any agreement made by the central management or the local management.

(10) In this regulation—

(a) "defaulter" means, as the case may be—

(i) the management of any undertaking belonging to the Community-scale group of undertakings;

(ii) the central management; or

(iii) the representative agent or the management treated as the central management of the Community-scale undertaking or Community-scale group of undertakings within the meaning of regulation 5(2);

(b) "failure" means an act or omission and a failure by the local management shall be treated as a failure by the central management;

(c) "relevant applicant" means—

(i) for a complaint in relation to regulation 16(1A), a member of the special negotiating body;

(ii) for a complaint in relation to regulation 19A, a member of the European Works Council;

(iii) for a complaint in relation to regulation 19B, *a member of the special negotiating body or* a member of the European Works Council;

(iv) for a complaint in relation to regulation 19E(2), a member of the European Works Council, a national employee representation body, an employee, or an employees' representative.]

NOTES

Inserted by the Transnational Information and Consultation of Employees (Amendment) Regulations 2010, SI 2010/1088, regs 2, 14.

Paras (1), (3), (10): all words in italics are revoked by the Employment Rights (Amendment) (EU Exit) Regulations 2019, SI 2019/535, reg 2(2), Sch 2, Pt 1, paras 1, 20, as from exit day (as defined in the European Union (Withdrawal) Act 2018, s 20) and subject to savings and transitional provisions in Sch 2, Pt 2 at **[2.2182]**.

[2.501]

22 Penalties

(1) A penalty notice issued under [regulation 20, 21 or 21A] shall specify—

(a) the amount of the penalty which is payable;

(b) the date before which the penalty must be paid; and

(c) the failure and period to which the penalty relates.

(2) No penalty set by the Appeal Tribunal under this regulation may exceed [£100,000].

(3) When setting the amount of the penalty, the Appeal Tribunal shall take into account—

(a) the gravity of the failure;

(b) the period of time over which the failure occurred;

(c) the reason for the failure;

(d) the number of employees affected by the failure; and
(e) the number of employees of the Community-scale undertaking or Community-scale group of undertakings in the Member States.

(4) The date specified under paragraph (1)(b) above must not be earlier than the end of the period within which an appeal against a decision or order made by the [CAC] under [regulation 20, 21 or 21A] may be made.

(5) If the specified date in a penalty notice has passed and—
(a) the period during which an appeal may be made has expired without an appeal having been made; or
(b) such an appeal has been made and determined,

the Secretary of State may recover from the central management, as a civil debt due to him, any amount payable under the penalty notice which remains outstanding.

(6) The making of an appeal suspends the effect of a penalty notice.

[(7) Any sums received by the Secretary of State, or in Northern Ireland the Department for Employment and Learning, under regulation 20, 21 or 21A or this regulation shall be paid into, respectively, the Consolidated Fund or the Consolidated Fund of Northern Ireland.]

NOTES

The words in square brackets in paras (1), (2), (4) were substituted, and para (7) was substituted, by the Transnational Information and Consultation of Employees (Amendment) Regulations 2010, SI 2010/1088, regs 2, 15.

PART VI
CONFIDENTIAL INFORMATION

[2.502]
23 Breach of statutory duty

(1) A person who is or at any time was—
(a) a member of a special negotiating body or a European Works Council;
(b) an information and consultation representative; or
(c) an expert assisting a special negotiating body, a European Works Council or its select committee, or information and consultation representatives,

shall not disclose any information or document which is or has been in his possession by virtue of his position as described in sub-paragraph (a), (b) or (c) of this paragraph, which the central management has entrusted to him on terms requiring it to be held in confidence.

(2) In this regulation and in regulation 24, a person specified in paragraph (1)(a), (b) or (c) of this regulation is referred to as a "recipient".

(3) The obligation to comply with paragraph (1) is a duty owed to the central management, and a breach of the duty is actionable accordingly (subject to the defences and other incidents applying to actions for breach of statutory duty).

(4) Paragraph (3) shall not affect the liability which any person may incur, nor affect any right which any person may have, apart from paragraph (3).

(5) No action shall lie under paragraph (3) where the recipient reasonably believed the disclosure to be a "protected disclosure" within the meaning given to that expression by section 43A of the 1996 Act or, as the case may be, Article 67A of the 1996 Order.

(6) A recipient whom the central management (which is situated in the United Kingdom) has entrusted with any information or document on terms requiring it to be held in confidence may apply to the CAC for a declaration as to whether it was reasonable for the central management to impose such a requirement.

(7) If the CAC considers that the disclosure of the information or document by the recipient would not, or would not be likely to, prejudice or cause serious harm to the undertaking, it shall make a declaration that it was not reasonable for the central management to require the recipient to hold the information or document in confidence.

(8) If a declaration is made under paragraph (7), the information or document shall not at any time thereafter be regarded as having been entrusted to the recipient who made the application under paragraph (6), or to any other recipient, on terms requiring it to be held in confidence.

[2.503]
24 Withholding of information by central management

(1) The central management is not required to disclose any information or document to a recipient when the nature of the information or document is such that, according to objective criteria, the disclosure of the information or document would seriously harm the functioning of, or would be prejudicial to, the undertaking or group of undertakings concerned.

(2) Where there is a dispute between the central management and a recipient as to whether the nature of the information or document which the central management has failed to provide is such as is described in paragraph (1), the central management or a recipient may apply to the CAC for a declaration as to whether the information or document is of such a nature.

(3) If the CAC makes a declaration that the disclosure of the information or document in question would not, according to objective criteria, seriously harm the functioning of, or be prejudicial to, the undertaking or group of undertakings concerned, the CAC shall order the central management to disclose the information or document.

(4) An order under paragraph (3) above shall specify—
(a) the information or document to be disclosed;
(b) the recipient or recipients to whom the information or document is to be disclosed;
(c) any terms on which the information or document is to be disclosed; and
(d) the date before which the information or document is to be disclosed.

PART VII
PROTECTIONS FOR MEMBERS OF A EUROPEAN WORKS COUNCIL, ETC

[2.504]
25 Right to time off for members of a European Works Council, etc

(1) An employee who is—
(a) a member of a special negotiating body;
(b) a member of a European Works Council;
(c) an information and consultation representative; or
(d) a candidate in an election in which any person elected will, on being elected, be such a member or representative,

is entitled to be permitted by his employer to take reasonable time off during the employee's working hours in order to perform his functions as such a member, representative or candidate.

[(1A) An employer shall permit an employee who is—
(a) a member of a special negotiating body; or
(b) a member of a European Works Council,

to take reasonable time off during the employee's working hours in order to undertake the training referred to in regulation 19B.]

(2) For the purposes of this regulation the working hours of an employee shall be taken to be any time when, in accordance with his contract of employment, the employee is required to be at work.

NOTES

Para (1): sub-para (a) revoked by the Employment Rights (Amendment) (EU Exit) Regulations 2019, SI 2019/535, reg 2(2), Sch 2, Pt 1, paras 1, 21(a), as from exit day (as defined in the European Union (Withdrawal) Act 2018, s 20) and subject to savings and transitional provisions in Sch 2, Pt 2 at **[2.2182]**.

Para (1A): inserted by the Transnational Information and Consultation of Employees (Amendment) Regulations 2010, SI 2010/1088, regs 2, 16; sub-para (a) revoked by SI 2019/535, reg 2(2), Sch 2, Pt 1, paras 1, 21(b), as from exit day (as defined in the European Union (Withdrawal) Act 2018, s 20) and subject to savings and transitional provisions in Sch 2, Pt 2 at **[2.2182]**.

[2.505]
26 Right to remuneration for time off under regulation 25

(1) An employee who is permitted to take time off under regulation 25 is entitled to be paid remuneration by his employer for the time taken off at the appropriate hourly rate.

(2) Chapter II of Part XIV of the 1996 Act (a week's pay) and, in relation to Northern Ireland, Chapter IV of Part I of the 1996 Order shall apply in relation to this regulation as they apply, respectively, in relation to section 62 of the 1996 Act and Article 90 of the 1996 Order.

(3) The appropriate hourly rate, in relation to an employee, is the amount of one week's pay divided by the number of normal working hours in a week for that employee when employed under the contract of employment in force on the day when the time is taken.

(4) But where the number of normal working hours differs from week to week or over a longer period, the amount of one week's pay shall be divided instead by—
(a) the average number of normal working hours calculated by dividing by twelve the total number of the employee's normal working hours during the period of twelve weeks ending with the last complete week before the day on which the time off is taken; or
(b) where the employee has not been employed for a sufficient period to enable the calculation to be made under sub-paragraph (a), a number which fairly represents the number of normal working hours in a week having regard to such of the considerations specified in paragraph (5) as are appropriate in the circumstances.

(5) The considerations referred to in paragraph (4)(b) are—
(a) the average number of normal working hours in a week which the employee could expect in accordance with the terms of his contract; and
(b) the average number of normal working hours of other employees engaged in relevant comparable employment with the same employer.

(6) A right to any amount under paragraph (1) does not affect any right of an employee in relation to remuneration under his contract of employment ("contractual remuneration").

(7) Any contractual remuneration paid to an employee in respect of a period of time off under regulation 25 goes towards discharging any liability of the employer to pay remuneration under paragraph (1) in respect of that period, and, conversely, any payment of remuneration under paragraph (1) in respect of a period goes towards discharging any liability of the employer to pay contractual remuneration in respect of that period.

[2.506]
27 Right to time off: complaints to tribunals

(1) An employee may present a complaint, in Great Britain to an employment tribunal and in Northern Ireland to an industrial tribunal, that his employer—

(a) has unreasonably refused to permit him to take time off as required by regulation 25; or

(b) has failed to pay the whole or any part of any amount to which the employee is entitled under regulation 26.

(2) A tribunal shall not consider a complaint under this regulation unless it is presented—

(a) before the end of the period of three months beginning with the day on which the time off was taken or on which it is alleged the time off should have been permitted; or

(b) within such further period as the tribunal considers reasonable in a case where it is satisfied that it was not reasonably practicable for the complaint to be presented before the end of that period of three months.

[(2A) Regulation 27A (extension of time limits to facilitate conciliation before institution of proceedings) applies for the purposes of paragraph (2).]

(3) Where a tribunal finds a complaint under this regulation well-founded, the tribunal shall make a declaration to that effect.

(4) If the complaint is that the employer has unreasonably refused to permit the employee to take time off, the tribunal shall also order the employer to pay to the employee an amount equal to the remuneration to which he would have been entitled under regulation 26 if the employer had not refused.

(5) If the complaint is that the employer has failed to pay the employee the whole or part of any amount to which he is entitled under regulation 26, the tribunal shall also order the employer to pay to the employee the amount which it finds due to him.

NOTES

Para (2A): inserted by the Enterprise and Regulatory Reform Act 2013 (Consequential Amendments) (Employment) Order 2014, SI 2014/386, art 2, Schedule, paras 6, 7.

Conciliation: employment tribunal proceedings under this regulation are "relevant proceedings" for the purposes of the conciliation provisions contained in the Employment Tribunals Act 1996, ss 18–18C; see s 18(1)(k) of the 1996 Act at **[1.757]**.

[2.507]
[27A Extension of time limit to facilitate conciliation before institution of proceedings

(1) In this regulation—

(a) Day A is the day on which the worker concerned complies with the requirement in subsection (1) of section 18A of the Employment Tribunals Act 1996 (requirement to contact ACAS before instituting proceedings) in relation to the matter in respect of which the proceedings are brought, and

(b) Day B is the day on which the worker concerned receives or, if earlier, is treated as receiving (by virtue of regulations made under subsection (11) of that section) the certificate issued under subsection (4) of that section.

(2) In working out when the time limit set by regulation 27(2)(a) expires the period beginning with the day after Day A and ending with Day B is not to be counted.

(3) If the time limit set by regulation 27(2)(a) would (if not extended by this paragraph) expire during the period beginning with Day A and ending one month after Day B, the time limit expires instead at the end of that period.

(4) The power conferred on the employment tribunal by regulation 27(2)(b) to extend the time limit set by paragraph (2)(a) of that regulation is exercisable in relation to that time limit as extended by this regulation.]

NOTES

Inserted by the Enterprise and Regulatory Reform Act 2013 (Consequential Amendments) (Employment) Order 2014, SI 2014/386, art 2, Schedule, paras 6, 8.

[2.508]
28 Unfair dismissal

(1) An employee who is dismissed and to whom paragraph (2) or (5) applies shall be regarded, if the reason (or, if more than one, the principal reason) for the dismissal is a reason specified in, respectively, paragraph (3) or (6), as unfairly dismissed for the purposes of Part X of the 1996 Act and of Part XI of the 1996 Order.

(2) This paragraph applies to an employee who is—

(a) a member of a special negotiating body;

(b) a member of a European Works Council;

(c) an information and consultation representative; or

(d) a candidate in an election in which any person elected will, on being elected, be such a member or representative.

(3) The reason is that—

(a) the employee performed any functions or activities as such a member, representative or candidate; or

(b) the employee or a person acting on his behalf made a request to exercise an entitlement conferred on the employee by regulation 25 or 26;

or proposed to do so.

(4) The reason in paragraph (3)(a) does not apply where the reason (or principal reason) for the dismissal is that in the performance, or purported performance, of the employee's functions or activities he has disclosed any information or document in breach of the duty in regulation 23(1), unless the employee reasonably believed the disclosure to be a "protected disclosure" within the meaning given to that expression by section 43A of the 1996 Act or, as the case may be, by Article 67A of the 1996 Order.

(5) This paragraph applies to any employee whether or not he is an employee to whom paragraph (2) applies.

(6) The reasons are that the employee—

(a) took, or proposed to take, any proceedings before an employment tribunal or industrial tribunal to enforce a right or secure an entitlement conferred on him by these Regulations;

(b) exercised, or proposed to exercise, any entitlement to apply or complain to the Appeal Tribunal or the CAC, or in Northern Ireland [the High Court or] the Industrial Court, conferred by these Regulations;

(c) requested, or proposed to request, information in accordance with regulation 7;

(d) acted with a view to securing that a special negotiating body, a European Works Council or an information and consultation procedure did or did not come into existence;

(e) indicated that he supported or did not support the coming into existence of a special negotiating body, a European Works Council or an information and consultation procedure;

(f) stood as a candidate in an election in which any person elected would, on being elected, be a member of a special negotiating body or of a European Works Council or an information and consultation representative;

(g) influenced or sought to influence the way in which votes were to be cast by other employees in a ballot arranged under these Regulations;

(h) voted in such a ballot;

(i) expressed doubts, whether to a ballot supervisor or otherwise, as to whether such a ballot had been properly conducted; or

(j) proposed to do, failed to do, or proposed to decline to do, any of the things mentioned in sub-paragraphs (d) to (i).

(7) It is immaterial for the purposes of paragraph (6)(a)—

(a) whether or not the employee has the right; or

(b) whether or not the right has been infringed;

but for that paragraph to apply, the claim to the right and, if applicable, the claim that it has been infringed must be made in good faith.

NOTES

Para (6): words in square brackets in sub-para (b) inserted by the Transnational Information and Consultation of Employees (Amendment) Regulations 2010, SI 2010/1088, regs 2, 17.

29, 30 *(Reg 29 amends the Employment Rights Act 1996, ss 105, 108, and amended s 109 (repealed); reg 30 applies to Northern Ireland and is outside the scope of this work.)*

[2.509]

31 Detriment

(1) An employee to whom paragraph (2) or (5) applies has the right not to be subjected to any detriment by any act, or deliberate failure to act, by his employer, done on a ground specified in, respectively, paragraph (3) or (6).

(2) This paragraph applies to an employee who is—

(a) a member of a special negotiating body;

(b) a member of a European Works Council;

(c) an information and consultation representative; or

(d) a candidate in an election in which any person elected will, on being elected, be such a member or representative.

(3) The ground is that—

(a) the employee performed any functions or activities as such a member, representative or candidate; or

(b) the employee or a person acting on his behalf made a request to exercise an entitlement conferred on the employee by regulation 25 or 26;

or proposed to do so.

(4) The ground in paragraph (3)(a) does not apply where the ground for the subjection to detriment is that in the performance, or purported performance, of the employee's functions or activities he has disclosed any information or document in breach of the duty in regulation 23(1), unless the employee reasonably believed the disclosure to be a "protected disclosure" within the meaning given to that expression by section 43A of the 1996 Act or, as the case may be, Article 67A of the 1996 Order.

(5) This paragraph applies to any employee, whether or not he is an employee to whom paragraph (2) applies.

(6) The grounds are that the employee—

(a) took, or proposed to take, any proceedings before an employment tribunal or industrial tribunal to enforce a right or secure an entitlement conferred on him by these Regulations;

(b) exercised, or proposed to exercise, any entitlement to apply or complain to the Appeal Tribunal, the CAC, or in Northern Ireland [the High Court or] the Industrial Court, conferred by these Regulations;
(c) requested, or proposed to request, information in accordance with regulation 7;
(d) acted with a view to securing that a special negotiating body, a European Works Council or an information and consultation procedure did or did not come into existence;
(e) indicated that he supported or did not support the coming into existence of a special negotiating body, a European Works Council or an information and consultation procedure;
(f) stood as a candidate in an election in which any person elected would, on being elected, be a member of a special negotiating body or of a European Works Council or an information and consultation representative;
(g) influenced or sought to influence the way in which votes were to be cast by other employees in a ballot arranged under these Regulations;
(h) voted in such a ballot;
(i) expressed doubts, whether to a ballot supervisor or otherwise, as to whether such a ballot had been properly conducted; or
(j) proposed to do, failed to do, or proposed to decline to do, any of the things mentioned in sub-paragraphs (d) to (i).

(7) It is immaterial for the purposes of paragraph (6)(a)—
(a) whether or not the employee has the right; or
(b) whether or not the right has been infringed;
but for that paragraph to apply, the claim to the right and, if applicable, the claim that it has been infringed must be made in good faith.

NOTES

Para (6): words in square brackets in sub-para (b) inserted by the Transnational Information and Consultation of Employees (Amendment) Regulations 2010, SI 2010/1088, regs 2, 18.

[2.510]
32 Detriment: enforcement and subsidiary provisions

(1) An employee may present a complaint, in Great Britain to an employment tribunal and in Northern Ireland to an industrial tribunal, that he has been subjected to a detriment in contravention of regulation 31.

(2) The provisions of—
(a) sections 48(2) to (4) and 49 of the 1996 Act (complaints to employment tribunals and remedies); or
(b) in relation to Northern Ireland, Articles 71(2) to (4) and 72 of the 1996 Order (complaints to industrial tribunals and remedies);
shall apply in relation to a complaint under this regulation as they apply in relation to a complaint under section 48 of that Act or Article 71 of that Order (as the case may be), but taking references in those provisions to the employer as references to the employer within the meaning of regulation 31(1) above.

(3) Regulation 31 does not apply where the detriment in question amounts to dismissal.

NOTES

Conciliation: employment tribunal proceedings under this regulation are "relevant proceedings" for the purposes of the conciliation provisions contained in the Employment Tribunals Act 1996, ss 18–18C; see s 18(1)(k) of the 1996 Act at **[1.757]**.

Tribunal jurisdiction: the Employment Act 2002, s 38 applies to proceedings before the employment tribunal relating to a claim under this regulation; see s 38(1) of, and Sch 5 to, the 2002 Act at **[1.1279]**, **[1.1287]**. See also the Trade Union and Labour Relations (Consolidation) Act 1992, s 207A at **[1.524]** (as inserted by the Employment Act 2008). That section provides that in proceedings before an employment tribunal relating to a claim by an employee under any of the jurisdictions listed in Sch A2 to the 1992 Act at **[1.704]** (which includes this regulation) the tribunal may adjust any award given if the employer or the employee has unreasonably failed to comply with a relevant Code of Practice as defined by s 207A(4). See also the revised Acas Code of Practice 1 – Disciplinary and Grievance Procedures (2015) at **[4.1]**, and the Acas Code of Practice 4 – Settlement Agreements (2013) at **[4.54]**.

33 *(Para (1) amended the Employment Tribunals Act 1996, s 18 at* **[1.757]**, *but is now effectively spent following the further amendment of s 18 by the Employment Tribunals Act 1996 (Application of Conciliation Provisions) Order 2014, SI 2014/431; para (2) applies to Northern Ireland and is outside the scope of this work.)*

PART VIII
MISCELLANEOUS

The Appeal Tribunal, Industrial Court, CAC, ACAS and the Labour Relations Agency

[2.511]
34 Appeal Tribunal: jurisdiction

(1) Any proceedings before the Appeal Tribunal arising under these Regulations, other than proceedings before the Appeal Tribunal under paragraph (i) of section 21(1) of the Employment Tribunals Act 1996, shall—
(a) where the central management is situated in England and Wales, be in England and Wales;
(b) where the central management is situated in Scotland, be in Scotland.

(2) Paragraph (1) shall apply to proceedings before the Appeal Tribunal arising under regulation 8 as if for the words "central management" there were substituted the words "recipient (within the meaning given to that term by regulation 7)".

(3) Paragraph (1) shall apply to proceedings before the Appeal Tribunal arising under *regulation 13 or 15 or* paragraph 4 of the Schedule as if for the words "central management" there were substituted the words "UK management".

NOTES

Para (2) and the words in italics in para (3) are revoked by the Employment Rights (Amendment) (EU Exit) Regulations 2019, SI 2019/535, reg 2(2), Sch 2, Pt 1, paras 1, 22, as from exit day (as defined in the European Union (Withdrawal) Act 2018, s 20) and subject to savings and transitional provisions in Sch 2, Pt 2 at **[2.2182]**.

35–37 (*Reg 35 amends the Employment Tribunals Act 1996, ss 20, 21, 30 at* **[1.763]**, **[1.764]**, **[1.775]**; *regs 36, 37 apply to Northern Ireland and are outside the scope of this work.*)

[2.512]

38 CAC: proceedings

(1) Where under these Regulations a person presents a complaint or makes an application to the CAC the complaint or application must be in writing and in such form as the CAC may require.

(2) In its consideration of an application or complaint under these Regulations, the CAC shall make such enquiries as it sees fit and give any person whom it considers has a proper interest in the application or complaint an opportunity to be heard.

(3) Where the central management is situated in England and Wales—

- (a) a declaration or order made by the CAC under these Regulations may be relied on as if it were a declaration or order made by the High Court in England and Wales; and
- (b) an order made by the CAC under these Regulations may be enforced in the same way as an order of the High Court in England and Wales.

(4) Where the central management is situated in Scotland—

- (a) a declaration or order made by the CAC under these Regulations may be relied on as if it were a declaration or order made by the Court of Session; and
- (b) an order made by the CAC under these Regulations may be enforced in the same way as an order of the Court of Session.

(5) Paragraphs (3) and (4) shall apply to an order made under regulation 8 as if for the words "central management" there were substituted the word "recipient".

(6) Paragraphs (3) and (4) shall apply, as appropriate, to a declaration or order made under *regulation 13 or 15 or* paragraph 4 of the Schedule as if for the words "central management" there were substituted the words "UK management".

(7) A declaration or order made by the CAC under these Regulations must be in writing and state the reasons for the CAC's findings.

(8) An appeal lies to the Appeal Tribunal on any question of law arising from any declaration or order of, or arising in any proceedings before, the CAC under these Regulations.

NOTES

Para (5) and the words in italics in para (6) are revoked by the Employment Rights (Amendment) (EU Exit) Regulations 2019, SI 2019/535, reg 2(2), Sch 2, Pt 1, paras 1, 24, as from exit day (as defined in the European Union (Withdrawal) Act 2018, s 20) and subject to savings and transitional provisions in Sch 2, Pt 2 at **[2.2182]**.

[2.513]

39 ACAS and the Labour Relations Agency

(1) If on receipt of an application or complaint under these Regulations the CAC, . . . or as the case may be the Industrial Court, is of the opinion that it is reasonably likely to be settled by conciliation, it shall refer the application or complaint to ACAS or to the Labour Relations Agency and shall notify the applicant or complainant and any persons whom it considers have a proper interest in the application or complaint accordingly, whereupon ACAS, or as the case may be the Labour Relations Agency, shall seek to promote a settlement of the matter.

(2) If an application or complaint so referred is not settled or withdrawn and ACAS, or as the case may be the Labour Relations Agency, is of the opinion that further attempts at conciliation are unlikely to result in a settlement, it shall inform the CAC, . . . or as the case may be the Industrial Court, of its opinion.

(3) If the application or complaint is not referred to ACAS or to the Labour Relations Agency, or if it is so referred, on ACAS, or as the case may be the Labour Relations Agency, informing the CAC, . . . or as the case may be the Industrial Court, of its opinion that further attempts at conciliation are unlikely to result in a settlement, the CAC, . . . or as the case may be the Industrial Court, shall proceed to hear and determine the application or complaint.

NOTES

Words omitted revoked by the Transnational Information and Consultation of Employees (Amendment) Regulations 2010, SI 2010/1088, regs 2, 21.

Restrictions on contracting out

[2.514]

40 Restrictions on contracting out: general

(1) Any provision in any agreement (whether an employee's contract or not) is void in so far as it purports—

(a) to exclude or limit the operation of any provision of these Regulations other than a provision of Part VII; or

(b) to preclude a person from bringing any proceedings before the Appeal Tribunal or the CAC, or in Northern Ireland [the High Court or] the Industrial Court, under any provision of these Regulations other than a provision of Part VII.

(2) Paragraph (1) does not apply to any agreement to refrain from continuing any proceedings referred to in sub-paragraph (b) of that paragraph made after the proceedings have been instituted.

NOTES

Para (1): words in square brackets in sub-para (b) inserted by the Transnational Information and Consultation of Employees (Amendment) Regulations 2010, SI 2010/1088, regs 2, 22.

[2.515]

41 Restrictions on contracting out: Part VII

(1) Any provision in any agreement (whether an employee's contract or not) is void in so far as it purports—

(a) to exclude or limit the operation of any provision of Part VII of these Regulations; or

(b) to preclude a person from bringing any proceedings before an employment tribunal, or in Northern Ireland an industrial tribunal, under that Part.

(2) Paragraph (1) does not apply to any agreement to refrain from instituting or continuing proceedings before an employment tribunal or, in Northern Ireland, an industrial tribunal where—

(a) a conciliation officer has taken action under [any of sections 18A to 18C] of the Employment Tribunals Act 1996 (conciliation); or

(b) in relation to Northern Ireland, the Labour Relations Agency has taken action under Article 20 of the Industrial Tribunals (Northern Ireland) Order 1996 (conciliation).

(3) Paragraph (1) does not apply to any agreement to refrain from instituting or continuing before an employment tribunal, or in Northern Ireland an industrial tribunal, proceedings within—

(a) [section 18(1)(k)] of the Employment Tribunals Act 1996 (proceedings under these Regulations where conciliation is available); or

(b) in relation to Northern Ireland, Article 20(1)(g) of the Industrial Tribunals (Northern Ireland) Order 1996,

if the conditions regulating [settlement] agreements under these Regulations are satisfied in relation to the agreement.

(4) For the purposes of paragraph (3) the conditions regulating [settlement] agreements are that—

(a) the agreement must be in writing;

(b) the agreement must relate to the particular proceedings;

(c) the employee must have received advice from a relevant independent adviser as to the terms and effect of the proposed agreement and, in particular, its effect on his ability to pursue his rights before an employment tribunal or, in Northern Ireland, an industrial tribunal;

(d) there must be in force, when the adviser gives the advice, a contract of insurance, or an indemnity provided for members of a profession or professional body, covering the risk of a claim by the employee in respect of loss arising in consequence of the advice;

(e) the agreement must identify the adviser; and

(f) the agreement must state that the conditions in sub-paragraphs (a) to (e) are satisfied.

(5) A person is a relevant independent adviser for the purposes of paragraph (4)(c)—

(a) if he is a qualified lawyer;

(b) if he is an officer, official, employee or member of an independent trade union who has been certified in writing by the trade union as competent to give advice and as authorised to do so on behalf of the trade union; or

(c) if he works at an advice centre (whether as an employee or as a volunteer) and has been certified in writing by the centre as competent to give advice and as authorised to do so on behalf of the centre.

(6) But a person is not a relevant independent adviser for the purposes of paragraph (4)(c) in relation to the employee—

(a) if he is, is employed by or is acting in the matter for the employer or an associated employer;

(b) in the case of a person within paragraph (5)(b) or (c), if the trade union or advice centre is the employer or an associated employer; or

(c) in the case of a person within paragraph (5)(c), if the employee makes a payment for the advice received from him.

(7) In paragraph (5)(a), "qualified lawyer" means—

(a) as respects England and Wales, [a person who, for the purposes of the Legal Services Act 2007), is an authorised person in relation to an activity which constitutes the exercise of a right of audience or the conduct of litigation (within the meaning of that Act)];

(b) as respects Scotland, an advocate (whether in practice as such or employed to give legal advice) or a solicitor who holds a practising certificate; and

(c) as respects Northern Ireland, a barrister (whether in practice as such or employed to give legal advice) or a solicitor who holds a practising certificate.

[(7A) A person shall be treated as being a qualified lawyer within paragraph (7)(a) if he is a Fellow of the Institute of Legal Executives [practising in a solicitor's practice (including a body recognised under section 9 of the Administration of Justice Act 1985)].]

(8) For the purposes of paragraph (6) any two employers shall be treated as associated if—

(a) one is a company of which the other (directly or indirectly) has control; or

(b) both are companies of which a third person (directly or indirectly) has control;

and "associated employer" shall be construed accordingly.

[(9) In the application of this regulation in relation to Northern Ireland, paragraphs (3) and (4) above shall have effect as if for "settlement agreements" there were substituted "compromise agreements.]

NOTES

Para (2): words in square brackets substituted by the Enterprise and Regulatory Reform Act 2013 (Consequential Amendments) (Employment) Order 2014, SI 2014/386, art 2, Schedule, paras 6, 9.

Para (3): words in square brackets in sub-para (a) substituted by the Employment Tribunals Act 1996 (Application of Conciliation Provisions) Order 2014, SI 2014/431, art 3, Schedule, para 20; word in second pair of square brackets substituted by the Enterprise and Regulatory Reform Act 2013 (Consequential Amendments) (Employment) Order 2013, SI 2013/1956, art 2, Schedule, para 3(a).

Para (4): word in square brackets substituted by SI 2013/1956, art 2, Schedule, para 3(a).

Para (7): words in square brackets substituted by the Legal Services Act 2007 (Consequential Amendments) Order 2009, SI 2009/3348, art 23, Sch 2.

Para (7A): inserted by the Transnational Information and Consultation of Employees Regulations 1999 (Amendment) Regulations 2004, SI 2004/2518, reg 2; words in square brackets substituted by SI 2009/3348, art 22, Sch 1.

Para (9): added by SI 2013/1956, art 2, Schedule, para 3(b).

PART IX
EXCEPTIONS

[2.516]

42 Article 6 agreements

(1) Where, in accordance with regulation 5, the central management is situated in the United Kingdom and, immediately before the date on which these Regulations come into force an Article 6 agreement is in force, those provisions referred to in regulation 4(1) which apply only where the central management is situated in the United Kingdom shall only apply if—

(a) the parties to the Article 6 agreement agree or have agreed (whether before or after these Regulations come into force) to the effect that the provisions of these Regulations which would have applied in respect of the agreement had it been made [before exit day] under regulation 17 should apply in respect of the Article 6 agreement; or

(b) the Article 6 agreement ceases to have effect.

(2) In paragraph (1) and regulation 47 "Article 6 agreement" means an agreement for the establishment of a European Works Council or information and consultation procedure made under the provisions of the law or practice of a Member State other than the United Kingdom which are designed to give effect to Article 6 of the Transnational Information and Consultation Directive.

(3) Where paragraph (1)(a) applies these Regulations shall apply as if the Article 6 agreement had been made [before exit day] under regulation 17.

NOTES

Paras (1), (3): words in square brackets inserted by the Employment Rights (Amendment) (EU Exit) Regulations 2019, SI 2019/535, reg 2(2), Sch 2, Pt 1, paras 1, 25, as from exit day (as defined in the European Union (Withdrawal) Act 2018, s 20) and subject to savings and transitional provisions in Sch 2, Pt 2 at **[2.2182]**.

[2.517]

43 Article 7 European Works Councils

(1) Where, in accordance with regulation 5, the central management is situated in the United Kingdom, and immediately before the date these Regulations come into force an Article 7 European Works Council exists, those provisions referred to in regulation 4(1) which apply only where the central management is situated in the United Kingdom shall only apply if—

(a) the central management and European Works Council agree or have agreed (whether before or after these Regulations come into force) to the effect that the provisions of these Regulations which would have applied in respect of the European Works Council had it been made [before exit day], by virtue of regulation 18, under these Regulations should apply in respect of the Article 7 European Works Council; or

(b) the European Works Council decides, under the provisions of the law or practice of a Member State other than the United Kingdom which are designed to give effect to paragraph 1(f) of the Annex to the Transnational Information and Consultation Directive, to negotiate an agreement for a European Works Council or an information and consultation procedure.

(2) In paragraph (1) and regulations 47 and 48 "Article 7 European Works Council" means a European Works Council established under the provisions of the law or practice of a Member State other than the United Kingdom which are designed to give effect to Article 7 of, and the Annex to, the Transnational Information and Consultation Directive.

(3) Where paragraph (1)(a) or (b) applies these Regulations shall apply, subject to the modifications referred to in paragraphs (4) to (6) of regulation 48, as if the Article 7 European Works Council had been established [before exit day], by virtue of regulation 18, under these Regulations and, in a case where paragraph (1)(b) applies, as if a decision had been taken under paragraph 10(2) of the Schedule.

NOTES

Paras (1), (3): words in square brackets inserted by the Employment Rights (Amendment) (EU Exit) Regulations 2019, SI 2019/535, reg 2(2), Sch 2, Pt 1, paras 1, 26, as from exit day (as defined in the European Union (Withdrawal) Act 2018, s 20) and subject to savings and transitional provisions in Sch 2, Pt 2 at **[2.2182]**.

[2.518]

[44 Article 3 agreements

(1) *Subject to paragraphs (4) and (5),* none of the obligations in these Regulations, *except those in regulation 19F,* applies to a Community-scale undertaking or Community-scale group of undertakings where the conditions specified in Article 3 of the Extension Directive are satisfied.

(2) The conditions referred to in paragraph (1) are that—

- (a) an agreement is in force which—
  - (i) was in force immediately before 16th December 1999;
  - (ii) covers the entire workforce in the Member States; and
  - (iii) provides for the transnational information and consultation of employees, and
- (b) the obligation (whether arising under these Regulations or under the national law or practice of any other Member State) to initiate negotiations for the establishment of a European Works Council or information and consultation procedure would, but for this paragraph, have applied to the Community-scale undertaking or Community-scale group of undertakings solely as a result of the Extension Directive.

(3) If an agreement when taken together with one or more other agreements satisfies the requirements specified in paragraph (2)(a), that agreement, when taken together with such other agreements, shall be treated as an agreement for the purposes of that paragraph.

(4) Regulations 9 to 18 apply where the structure of a Community-scale undertaking or Community-scale group of undertakings changes significantly and there is—

- *(a) one European Works Council agreement, or one agreement for an information and consultation procedure;*
- *(b) more than one European Works Council agreement;*
- *(c) more than one agreement for an information and consultation procedure; or*
- *(d) at least one European Works Council agreement and at least one agreement for an information and consultation procedure,*

in force and there are no provisions for the continuance of the European Works Council or information and consultation procedure, as the case may be, where there are significant changes in the structure of the Community-scale undertaking or Community-scale group of undertakings or there are such provisions, but there is a conflict between them.

(5) Regulations 25(1) and (2), 26 to 28, 31 and 32 apply to an employee who is a member of a special negotiating body or a candidate in an election in which any person elected will, on being elected, be such a member, where the structure of a Community-scale undertaking or Community-scale group of undertakings changes significantly and paragraphs (6) and (7) apply.

(6) This paragraph applies where there is—

- *(a) one European Works Council agreement, or one agreement for an information and consultation procedure;*
- *(b) more than one European Works Council agreement;*
- *(c) more than one agreement for an information and consultation procedure; or*
- *(d) at least one European Works Council agreement and at least one agreement for an information and consultation procedure,*

in force and there are no provisions for the continuance of the European Works Council or information and consultation procedure, as the case may be, where there are significant changes in the structure of the Community-scale undertaking or Community-scale group of undertakings or there are such provisions, but there is a conflict between them.

(7) This paragraph applies where the central management has initiated negotiations for the establishment of a European Works Council or an information and consultation procedure under regulation 19F(1) or (3).]

NOTES

Regulations 44, 45, 45A substituted (for the original regs 44, 45), by the Transnational Information and Consultation of Employees (Amendment) Regulations 2010, SI 2010/1088, regs 2, 23.

The words in italics in para (1), and the whole of paras (4)–(7), are revoked by the Employment Rights (Amendment) (EU Exit) Regulations 2019, SI 2019/535, reg 2(2), Sch 2, Pt 1, paras 1, 27, as from exit day (as defined in the European Union (Withdrawal) Act 2018, s 20) and subject to savings and transitional provisions in Sch 2, Pt 2 at **[2.2182]**.

[2.519]
[45 Article 13 agreements

(1) *Subject to paragraphs (4) and (5),* none of the obligations in these Regulations, *except those in regulation 19F,* applies to a Community-scale undertaking or Community-scale group of undertakings where the conditions specified in Article 13 of the Transnational Information and Consultation Directive are satisfied.

(2) The conditions referred to in paragraph (1) are that an agreement is in force which—
- (a) was in force immediately before whichever is the earlier of 23rd September 1996 and the day after the date on which the national law or practice giving effect to the Transnational Information and Consultation Directive came into force in the Member State (other than the United Kingdom) whose national law governs the agreement;
- (b) covers the entire workforce in the Member States; and
- (c) provides for the transnational information and consultation of employees.

(3) If an agreement when taken together with one or more other agreements satisfies the requirements specified in paragraph (2), that agreement, when taken together with such other agreements, shall be treated as an agreement for the purposes of that paragraph.

(4) Regulations 9 to 18 apply where the structure of a Community-scale undertaking or Community-scale group of undertakings changes significantly and there is—
- *(a) one European Works Council agreement or one agreement for an information and consultation procedure;*
- *(b) more than one European Works Council agreement;*
- *(c) more than one agreement for an information and consultation procedure; or*
- *(d) at least one European Works Council agreement and at least one agreement for an information and consultation procedure,*

in force and there are no provisions for the continuance of the European Works Council or information and consultation procedure, as the case may be, where there are significant changes in the structure of the Community-scale undertaking or Community-scale group of undertakings or there are such provisions, but there is a conflict between them.

(5) Regulations 25(1) and (2), 26 to 28, 31 and 32 apply to an employee who is a member of a special negotiating body or a candidate in an election in which any person elected will, on being elected, be such a member, where the structure of a Community-scale undertaking or Community-scale group of undertakings changes significantly and paragraphs (6) and (7) apply.

(6) This paragraph applies where there is—
- *(a) one European Works Council agreement, or one agreement for an information and consultation procedure;*
- *(b) more than one European Works Council agreement;*
- *(c) more than one agreement for an information and consultation procedure; or*
- *(d) at least one European Works Council agreement and at least one agreement for an information and consultation procedure,*

in force and there are no provisions for the continuance of the European Works Council or information and consultation procedure, as the case may be, where there are significant changes in the structure of the Community-scale undertaking or Community-scale group of undertakings or there are such provisions, but there is a conflict between them.

(7) This paragraph applies where the central management has initiated negotiations for the establishment of a European Works Council or an information and consultation procedure under regulation 19F(1) or (3).]

NOTES

Substituted as noted to reg 44 at **[2.518]**.

The words in italics in para (1), and the whole of paras (4)–(7), are revoked by the Employment Rights (Amendment) (EU Exit) Regulations 2019, SI 2019/535, reg 2(2), Sch 2, Pt 1, paras 1, 28, as from exit day (as defined in the European Union (Withdrawal) Act 2018, s 20) and subject to savings and transitional provisions in Sch 2, Pt 2 at **[2.2182]**.

[2.520]
[45A Agreements signed or revised on or after 5th June 2009 and before 5th June 2011

(1) Subject to paragraph (4), where the conditions specified in paragraph (2) are satisfied, these Regulations shall apply to a Community-scale undertaking or Community-scale group of undertakings as if the amendments listed in paragraph (3) had not been made.

(2) The conditions referred to in paragraph (1) are that an agreement is in force which—
- (a) establishes a European Works Council or information and consultation procedure [before exit day] under regulation 17 of these Regulations; and
- (b) is signed or revised on or after 5th June 2009 and before 5th June 2011.

(3) The amendments referred to in paragraph *(1)* are those made by the following provisions of the 2010 Regulations—
- (a) regulation 3, in so far as it inserts the definition of "national employee representation bodies" and paragraphs (4A) and (4B) into regulation 2 of these Regulations;
- (b) regulations 5 to 10;
- (c) regulation 11, in so far as it inserts regulations 19A, 19B, 19C, 19D and 19E into these Regulations;
- (d) regulation 13, in so far as it inserts paragraph (1A)(b) into regulation 21 of these Regulations;

(e) regulation 14, in so far as it inserts regulation 21A(1)(b), (c) and (d) into these Regulations and makes provision for the resolution of complaints in relation to regulations 19A, 19B and 19E(2);
(f) regulation 16;
(g) regulation 23, in so far as it amends regulations 44 and 45 of these Regulations; and
(h) regulations 24 to 29.

[(3A) The amendments referred to in paragraph (1)(b) are those made by paragraphs 14, 15, 20, 21(b), 27 and 28 of Schedule 2 to the 2019 Regulations.]

(4) Regulations 9 to 18 apply where the structure of a Community-scale undertaking or Community-scale group of undertakings changes significantly and there is—
(a) one European Works Council agreement, or one agreement for an information and consultation procedure;
(b) more than one European Works Council agreement;
(c) more than one agreement for an information and consultation procedure; or
(d) at least one European Works Council agreement and at least one agreement for an information and consultation procedure,

in force and there are no provisions for the continuance of the European Works Council or information and consultation procedure, as the case may be, where there are significant changes in the structure of the Community-scale undertaking or Community-scale group of undertakings or there are such provisions, but there is a conflict between them.

(5) In this regulation "the 2010 Regulations" means the Transnational Information and Consultation of Employees (Amendment) Regulations 2010.]

NOTES

Substituted as noted to reg 44 at **[2.518]**.

This regulation is amended by the Employment Rights (Amendment) (EU Exit) Regulations 2019, SI 2019/535, reg 2(2), Sch 2, Pt 1, paras 1, 29, as from exit day (as defined in the European Union (Withdrawal) Act 2018, s 20) and subject to savings and transitional provisions in Sch 2, Pt 2 at **[2.2182]**, as follows—

Para (1) is substituted as follows—

"(1) Where the conditions specified in paragraph (2) are satisfied, these Regulations shall apply to a Community-scale undertaking or Community-scale group of undertakings as if the amendments listed—
(a) in paragraph (3) in relation to the 2010 Regulations, and
(b) in paragraph (3A) in relation to the 2019 Regulations,

had not been made.".

Para (2): the words in square brackets in sub-para (a) are inserted.
Para (3): for the figure in italics there is substituted the figure "(1)(a)".
Para (3A) is inserted.
Para (4) is revoked.
Para (5) is substituted as follows—

"(5) In this regulation—
(a) "the 2010 Regulations" means the Transnational Information and Consultation of Employees (Amendment) Regulations 2010, and
(b) "the 2019 Regulations" means the Employment Rights (Amendment) (EU Exit) Regulations 2019.".

[2.521]
[46 Merchant Navy

(1) Subject to paragraph (2), a member *of a special negotiating body or* of a European Works Council or an information and consultation representative, or an alternate of such member or representative, who is a member of the crew of a seagoing vessel, is entitled to participate in a meeting *of the special negotiating body or* of the European Works Council, or in any other meeting under any procedures established [before exit day] pursuant to regulation 17(3).

(2) A member or representative or alternate referred to in paragraph (1) may only participate in a meeting where that member, representative or alternate is not at sea or in a port in a country other than that in which the shipping company is domiciled, when the meeting takes place.

(3) Paragraph (2) does not apply to—
(a) a ferry worker; or
(b) a person who normally works on voyages the duration of which is less than 48 hours.

(4) The meetings must, where practicable, be scheduled to facilitate the participation of a member, representative or alternate referred to in paragraph (1).

(5) In cases where a member or a representative or alternate referred to in paragraph (1) is unable to attend a meeting, the use of information and communication technology to enable that person's participation in the meeting must be considered.]

NOTES

Substituted by the Seafarers (Transnational Information and Consultation, Collective Redundancies and Insolvency Miscellaneous Amendments) Regulations 2018, SI 2018/26, reg 2, as from 6 February 2018. Note that the 2018 Regulations do not provide for a heading for the new regulation, and the original heading has been retained above.

Para (1): words in italics revoked, and words in square brackets inserted, by the Employment Rights (Amendment) (EU Exit) Regulations 2019, SI 2019/535, reg 2(2), Sch 2, Pt 1, paras 1, 30, as from exit day (as defined in the European Union (Withdrawal) Act 2018, s 20) and subject to savings and transitional provisions in Sch 2, Pt 2 at **[2.2182]**.

[2.522]
[46A

(1) These regulations do not apply to *an SE* that is—

(a) a Community-scale undertaking, or

(b) a controlling undertaking of a Community-scale group of undertakings,

except where the special negotiating body has taken the decision referred to in regulation 17 of the European Public Limited-Liability Company (Employee Involvement) (Great Britain) Regulations 2009 (decision not to open, or to terminate, negotiations) (SI 2009/2401) or, as the case may be, regulation 17 of the European Public Limited-Liability Company (Employee Involvement) (Northern Ireland) Regulations 2009 (SI 2009/2402).

(2) In this regulation an "SE" means a company established in accordance with the European Public Limited-Liability Company Regulations 2004 (SI 2004/2326).]

NOTES

Inserted by the European Public Limited-Liability Company Regulations 2004, SI 2004/2326, reg 53, and substituted by the European Public Limited-Liability Company (Employee Involvement) (Great Britain) Regulations 2009, SI 2009/2401, reg 40.

For the words in italics in para (1) there are substituted the words "a UK Societas" and para (2) is substituted as follows, by the International Accounting Standards and European Public Limited-Liability Company (Amendment etc) (EU Exit) Regulations 2019, SI 2019/685, reg 21, Sch 3, Pt 3, para 19, as from exit day (as defined in the European Union (Withdrawal) Act 2018, s 20)—

> "(2) In this regulation "UK Societas" means a United Kingdom Societas within the meaning of Council Regulation 2157/2001/EC of 8 October 2001 on the Statute for a European Company.".

[2.523]
[46B

[(1) These regulations do not apply to an SCE that is—

(a) a Community-scale undertaking, or

(b) a controlling undertaking of a Community-scale group of undertakings,

except where the special negotiating body has taken the decision referred to in regulation 19 of, or paragraph 13 of Schedule 1 to, the European Cooperative Society (Involvement of Employees) Regulations 2006 (decision not to open, or to terminate, negotiations).

(2) In this regulation an "SCE" means a European Cooperative Society established in accordance with the European Cooperative Society Regulations 2006.]

NOTES

Inserted by the European Cooperative Society (Involvement of Employees) Regulations 2006, SI 2006/2059, reg 42.

PART X
TRANSITIONALS

[2.524]
47 Transitionals: special negotiating body

(1) Where immediately before the date on which these Regulations come into force—

(a) a special negotiating body has been validly requested or established under the provisions of the law or practice of a Member State other than the United Kingdom which is designed to give effect to the Transnational Information and Consultation Directive;

(b) no Article 6 agreement is in force; and

(c) no Article 7 European Works Council has been established—

paragraphs (2) and (3) shall apply.

(2) Where the central management is situated in the United Kingdom these Regulations shall apply, with the modifications specified in paragraphs (4) to (6), as if a valid request had been made under regulation 9 and, where appropriate, as if the special negotiating body had been established under these Regulations.

(3) Where the central management is not situated in the United Kingdom the regulations referred to in regulation 4(2) shall apply with the modifications specified in paragraphs (5) and (6) of this regulation.

(4) Regulation 12 shall apply in respect of the composition of the special negotiating body only to the extent that it determines the number of UK members on the special negotiating body but shall not affect in any way the number of non-UK members on the special negotiating body.

(5) Where, as a result of the implementation of the Extension Directive by a Member State (including the United Kingdom) there are required to be UK members on the special negotiating body and immediately before the date on which these Regulations come into force—

(a) no person has been designated to attend meetings of the special negotiating body as a representative of employees in the United Kingdom; or

(b) one or more persons have been designated to attend meetings of the special negotiating body as a representative of employees in the United Kingdom,

then in the case mentioned in sub-paragraph (a), the UK members of the special negotiating body shall be elected or appointed in accordance with regulations 13 to 15, and in the case mentioned in sub-paragraph (b), the person or persons shall be treated as from the date on which these Regulations come into force as a UK member of the special negotiating body who has been elected or appointed in accordance with regulations 13 to 15.

(6) Where the number of persons referred to in paragraph (5)(b) is—

(a) in a case where regulation 12 applies, less than the number of UK members of the special negotiating body required by that regulation, or

(b) in a case where regulation 12 does not apply, less than the number of UK members of the special negotiating body required by the provisions of the law or practice of the Member State under which the special negotiating body was established,

the additional number of UK members of the special negotiating body needed to secure compliance with regulation 12 or, as the case may be, the law or practice of the Member State referred to in sub-paragraph (b) of this paragraph shall be elected or appointed in accordance with regulations 13 to 15.

NOTES

Revoked by the Employment Rights (Amendment) (EU Exit) Regulations 2019, SI 2019/535, reg 2(2), Sch 2, Pt 1, paras 1, 31, as from exit day (as defined in the European Union (Withdrawal) Act 2018, s 20) and subject to savings and transitional provisions in Sch 2, Pt 2 at **[2.2182]**.

[2.525]

48 Transitionals: Article 7 European Works Councils

(1) Where, immediately before the date on which these Regulations come into force, a European Works Council has been established under the provisions of the law or practice of a Member State other than the United Kingdom, which are designed to give effect to Article 7 of, and the Annex to, the Transnational Information and Consultation Directive, paragraphs (2) and (3) shall apply.

(2) Where the central management is situated in the United Kingdom and regulation 43(1) (a) or 43(1)(b) applies these Regulations shall apply with the modifications specified in paragraphs (4) to (6) as if the European Works Council had been established under these Regulations.

(3) Where the central management is not situated in the United Kingdom, or is situated in the United Kingdom but neither regulation 43(1)(a) nor 43(1)(b) applies, the regulations referred to in regulation 4(2) shall apply with the modifications specified in paragraphs (5) and (6) of this regulation.

(4) Paragraph 2 of the Schedule shall apply in respect of the composition of the European Works Council only to the extent that it determines the number of UK members on the European Works Council but shall not affect in any way the number of non-UK members on the European Works Council.

(5) Where, as a result of the implementation of the Extension Directive by a Member State (including the United Kingdom), there are required to be UK members on the European Works Council and immediately before the date on which these Regulations come into force—

(a) no person has been designated to attend meetings of the European Works Council as a representative of employees in the United Kingdom; or

(b) one or more persons have been designated to attend meetings of the European Works Council as a representative of employees in the United Kingdom,

then in the case mentioned in sub-paragraph (a), the UK members of the European Works Council shall be appointed or elected in accordance with paragraphs 3 to 5 of the Schedule, and in the case mentioned in sub-paragraph (b), the person or persons shall be treated as from the date on which these Regulations come into force as a UK member of the European Works Council who has been elected or appointed in accordance with paragraphs 3 to 5 of the Schedule.

(6) Where the number of persons referred to in paragraph (5)(b) is—

(a) in a case where paragraph 2 of the Schedule applies, less than the number of UK members of the European Works Council required by that paragraph; or

(b) in a case where paragraph 2 of the Schedule does not apply, less than the number of UK members of the European Works Council required by the law or practice of the Member State under which the European Works Council was established,

the additional number of UK members needed to secure compliance with paragraph 2 or, as the case may be, the law or practice of the Member State referred to in sub-paragraph (b) of this paragraph shall be elected or appointed in accordance with paragraphs 3 to 5 of the Schedule.

SCHEDULE
SUBSIDIARY REQUIREMENTS

Regulation 18

[2.526]

1 Establishment of European Works Council

A European Works Council shall be established in the Community-scale undertaking or Community-scale group of undertakings in accordance with the provisions in this Schedule.

[2 Composition of the European Works Council

(1) The European Works Council shall be constituted in accordance with sub-paragraph (2).

(2) In each Member State in which employees of a Community-scale undertaking or Community-scale group of undertakings are employed to work, those employees shall elect or appoint one member of the European Works Council for each 10% (or fraction of 10%) which those employees represent of the total number of employees of the Community-scale undertaking or Community-scale group of undertakings employed in those Member States.

(3) The European Works Council shall inform the central management and any more appropriate level of management of the composition of the European Works Council.

Part 2 Statutory Instruments

(4) To ensure that it can co-ordinate its activities, the European Works Council shall elect from among its members a select committee comprising no more than five members who are to act on behalf of the European Works Council.]

3 Appointment or election of UK members of the European Works Council

(1) The UK members of the European Works Council must be UK employees and—

(a) in a case where all of those employees are represented by UK employees' representatives, shall be elected or appointed by such employees' representatives;

(b) in a case where not all of those employees are represented by UK employees' representatives, shall be elected by ballot.

(2) For the purposes of this paragraph all of the UK employees are represented by UK employees' representatives if each of the employees referred to in sub-paragraph (1) is a UK employee—

(a) in respect of which an independent trade union is recognised by his employer for the purpose of collective bargaining; or

(b) who has elected or appointed an employees' representative for the purpose of receiving, on the employee's behalf, information—

(i) which is relevant to the employee's terms and conditions of employment; or

(ii) about the activities of the undertaking which may significantly affect the employee's interests

but excluding representatives who are expected to receive information relevant only to a specific aspect of the terms and conditions or interests of the employee, such as health and safety or collective redundancies.

(3) Where sub-paragraph (1)(a) above applies, the election or appointment of members of the European Works Council shall be carried out by whatever method the UK employees' representatives decide.

(4) Where sub-paragraph (1)(b) applies, the UK members of the European Works Council are to be elected by a ballot of the UK employees in accordance with paragraphs 4 and 5.

4 Ballot arrangements

(1) The UK management must arrange for the holding of a ballot of employees referred to in paragraph 3(4), which satisfies the requirements specified in sub-paragraph (2).

(2) The requirements referred to in sub-paragraph (1) are that—

(a) the ballot of the UK employees must comprise a single ballot, but may instead, if the UK management so decides, comprise separate ballots of employees in such constituencies as the UK management may determine where—

(i) the number of UK members of the European Works Council to be elected is more than one, and

(ii) the UK management considers that if separate ballots were held for those constituencies, the UK members of the European Works Council to be elected would better reflect the interests of the UK employees as a whole than if a single ballot were held;

(b) a UK employee who is an employee of the Community-scale undertaking or the Community-scale group of undertakings on the day on which votes may be cast in the ballot or, if the votes may be cast on more than one day, on the first day of those days is entitled to vote in a ballot of the UK employees;

(c) any UK employee who is an employee of the Community-scale undertaking or Community-scale group of undertakings immediately before the latest time at which a person may become a candidate in the ballot, is entitled to stand in the ballot of the UK employees as a candidate for election as a UK member of the European Works Council;

(d) the UK management must, in accordance with sub-paragraph (6), appoint an independent ballot supervisor to supervise the conduct of the ballot of the UK employees but may instead, where there are to be separate ballots, appoint more than one independent ballot supervisor in accordance with that sub-paragraph, each of whom is to supervise such of the separate ballots as the UK management may determine, provided that each separate ballot is supervised by a supervisor;

(e) after the UK management has formulated proposals as to the arrangements for the ballot of the UK employees and before it has published the final arrangements under paragraph (f) it must, so far as reasonably practicable, consult with the UK employees' representatives on the proposed arrangements for the ballot of the UK employees;

(f) the UK management must publish the final arrangements for the ballot of the UK employees in such manner as to bring them to the attention of, so far as reasonably practicable, the UK employees and the UK employees' representatives.

(3) Any UK employee or UK employees' representative who believes that the arrangements for the ballot of the UK employees are defective may, within a period of 21 days beginning on the date the UK management published the final arrangements under paragraph (f), present a complaint to the CAC.

(4) Where the CAC finds the complaint well-founded it shall make a declaration to that effect and may make an order requiring the UK management to modify the arrangements it has made for the ballot of the UK employees or to satisfy the requirements in paragraph (e) or (f) of sub-paragraph (2).

(5) An order under sub-paragraph (4) shall specify the modifications to the arrangements which the UK management is required to make and the requirements which it must satisfy.

(6) A person is an independent ballot supervisor for the purposes of sub-paragraph (2)(d) if the UK management reasonably believes that he will carry out any functions conferred on him in relation to the ballot competently and has no reasonable grounds for believing that his independence in relation to the ballot might reasonably be called into question.

(7) For the purposes of sub-paragraph (3), the arrangements for the ballot of the UK employees are defective if—

(a) any of the requirements specified in paragraphs (b) to (f) of sub-paragraph (2) is not satisfied; or

(b) in a case where the ballot is to comprise separate ballots, the constituencies determined by the UK management do not reflect adequately the interests of the UK employees as a whole.

5 Conduct of ballot

(1) The UK management must—

(a) ensure that a ballot supervisor appointed under paragraph 4(2)(d) carries out his functions under this paragraph and that there is no interference with his carrying out of those functions from the UK management, or the central management (where it is not also the UK management); and

(b) comply with all reasonable requests made by a ballot supervisor for the purposes of, or in connection with, the carrying out of those functions.

(2) A ballot supervisor's appointment shall require that he—

(a) supervises the conduct of the ballot, or the separate ballots he is being appointed to supervise, in accordance with the arrangements for the ballot of the UK employees published by the UK management under paragraph 4(2)(f) or, where appropriate, in accordance with the arrangements as required to be modified by an order made as a result of a complaint presented under paragraph 4(3);

(b) does not conduct the ballot or any of the separate ballots before the UK management has satisfied the requirement specified in paragraph 4(2)(e) and—

(i) where no complaint has been presented under paragraph 4(3), before the expiry of a period of 21 days beginning on the date on which the UK management published its arrangements under paragraph 4(2)(f); or

(ii) where a complaint has been presented under paragraph 4(3), before the complaint has been determined and, where appropriate, the arrangements have been modified as required by an order made as a result of the complaint;

(c) conducts the ballot, or each separate ballot, so as to secure that—

(i) so far as reasonably practicable, those entitled to vote are given the opportunity to vote,

(ii) so far as reasonably practicable, those entitled to stand as candidates are given the opportunity to stand,

(iii) so far as is reasonably practicable, those voting are able to do so in secret, and

(iv) the votes given in the ballot are fairly and accurately counted.

(3) As soon as reasonably practicable after the holding of the ballot, or each separate ballot, the ballot supervisor must publish the results of the ballot in such manner as to make them available to the UK management and, so far as reasonably practicable, the UK employees entitled to vote in the ballot or who stood as candidates in the ballot.

(4) A ballot supervisor shall publish an ineffective ballot report where he considers (whether or not on the basis of representations made to him by another person) that—

(a) any of the requirements referred to in sub-paragraph (2) was not satisfied with the result that the outcome of the ballot would have been different; or

(b) there was interference with the carrying out of his functions or a failure by management to comply with all reasonable requests made by him with the result that he was unable to form a proper judgment as to whether each of the requirements referred to in sub-paragraph (2) was satisfied in relation to the ballot.

(5) Where a ballot supervisor publishes an ineffective ballot report the report must be published within a period of one month commencing on the date on which the ballot supervisor publishes the results of the ballot under sub-paragraph (3).

(6) A ballot supervisor shall publish an ineffective ballot report in such manner as to make it available to the UK management and, so far as reasonably practicable, the UK employees entitled to vote in the ballot or who stood as candidates in the ballot.

(7) Where a ballot supervisor publishes an ineffective ballot report then—

(a) if there has been a single ballot or an ineffective ballot report has been published in respect of every separate ballot, the outcome of the ballot or ballots shall have no effect and the UK management shall again be under the obligation in paragraph 4(1);

(b) if there have been separate ballots and paragraph (a) does not apply—

(i) the UK management shall arrange for the separate ballot or ballots in respect of which an ineffective ballot report was issued to be reheld in accordance with paragraph 4 and this paragraph, and

(ii) no such ballot shall have effect until it has been so reheld and no ineffective ballot report has been published in respect of it.

(8) All costs relating to the holding of a ballot, including payments made to a ballot supervisor for supervising the conduct of the ballot, shall be borne by the central management (whether or not an ineffective ballot report has been made).

6 Competence of the European Works Council

(1) The competence of the European Works Council shall be limited to information and consultation on the matters which concern the Community-scale undertaking or Community-scale group of undertakings as a whole or at least two of its establishments or group undertakings situated in different Member States.

(2) In the case of a Community-scale undertaking or Community-scale group of undertakings falling within regulation 5(1)(b) or 5(1)(c), the competence of the European Works Council shall be limited to those matters concerning all of its establishments or group undertakings situated within the Member States or concerning at least two of its establishments or group undertakings situated in different Member States.

[(3) Information and consultation of employees shall take place between members of a European Works Council and the most appropriate level of management according to the matters under discussion.]

7 Information and consultation meetings

(1) Subject to paragraph 8, the European Works Council shall have the right to meet with the central management once a year in an information and consultation meeting, to be informed and consulted, on the basis of a report drawn up by the central management, on the progress of the business of the Community-scale undertaking or Community-scale group of undertakings and its prospects.

(2) The central management shall inform the local managements accordingly.

[(3) The information provided to the European Works Council shall relate in particular to the structure, economic and financial situation, the probable development of the business and of production and sales of the Community-scale undertaking or Community-scale group of undertakings.

(4) The information and consultation meeting shall relate in particular to the situation and probable trend of employment, investments, and substantial changes concerning organisation, introduction of new working methods or production processes, transfers of production, mergers, cut-backs or closures of undertakings, establishments or important parts of such undertakings or establishments, and collective redundancies.]

8 Exceptional information and consultation meetings

(1) Where there are exceptional circumstances affecting the employees' interests to a considerable extent, particularly in the event of relocations, the closure of establishments or undertakings or collective redundancies, the select committee or, where no such committee exists, the European Works Council shall have the right to be informed. It shall have the right to meet in an exceptional information and consultation meeting, at its request, the central management, or any other more appropriate level of management within the Community-scale undertaking or group of undertakings having its own powers of decision, so as to be informed and consulted . . .

(2) Those members of the European Works Council who have been elected or appointed by the establishments or undertakings which are directly concerned by the [circumstances] in question shall also have the right to participate in an exceptional information and consultation meeting referred to in sub-paragraph (1) of this paragraph organised with the select committee elected under sub-paragraph (6) of paragraph 2.

(3) The exceptional information and consultation meeting referred to in sub-paragraph (1) of this paragraph shall take place as soon as possible on the basis of a report drawn up by the central management or any other appropriate level of management of the Community-scale undertaking or Community-scale group of undertakings, on which an opinion may be delivered at the end of the meeting or within a reasonable time.

(4) The exceptional information and consultation meeting referred to in sub-paragraph (1) of this paragraph shall not affect the prerogatives of the central management.

[8A Use of agency workers

Where information is to be disclosed under paragraph 7 or 8 which includes information as to the employment situation in the Community-scale undertaking or, as the case may be, the Community-scale group of undertakings, this shall include suitable information relating to the use of agency workers (if any).]

9 Procedures

(1) Before an information and consultation meeting or exceptional information and consultation meeting with the central management, the European Works Council or the select committee, where necessary enlarged in accordance with sub-paragraph (2) of paragraph 8, shall be entitled to meet without the management concerned being present.

(2) Subject to regulation 23, the members of the European Works Council shall inform—

(a) the employees' representatives of the employees in the establishments of a Community-scale undertaking or in the undertakings of a Community-scale group of undertakings; or

(b) to the extent that any employees are not represented by employees' representatives, the employees themselves

of the content and outcome of the information and consultation procedure carried out in accordance with the provisions of this Schedule.

(3) The European Works Council shall adopt its own rules of procedure.

(4) The European Works Council or the select committee may be assisted by experts of its choice, in so far as this is necessary for it to carry out its tasks.

(5) The operating expenses of the European Works Council shall be borne by the central management; but where the European Works Council is assisted by more than one expert the central management is not required to pay such expenses in respect of more than one of them.

(6) The central management shall provide the members of the European Works Council [and its select committee] with such financial and material resources as enable them to perform their duties in an appropriate manner. In particular, the cost of organising meetings and arranging for interpretation facilities and the accommodation and travelling expenses of members of the European Works Council and its select committee shall be met by the central management unless the central management and European Works Council, or select committee, otherwise agree.

[(7) The employer must ensure that the consultation referred to in paragraphs 7(1) and 8(1) is conducted in such a way that the members of the European Works Council can, if they so request—

(a) meet with the central management; and

(b) obtain a reasoned response from the central management to any opinion expressed by those representatives on the reports referred to in paragraphs 7(1) and 8(3).

(8) Information and consultation carried out in accordance with this Schedule shall be carried out subject to regulation 23.]

10 The continuing application of the subsidiary requirements

(1) Four years after the European Works Council is established it shall examine whether to open negotiations for the conclusion of an agreement referred to in regulation 17 or to continue to apply the subsidiary requirements adopted in accordance with the provisions of this Schedule.

(2) If the European Works Council decides to negotiate an agreement in accordance with regulation 17, it shall notify the central management in writing to that effect, and

(a) such notification shall be treated as a valid request made under regulation 9; and

(b) regulations 16, 17 and 18 shall apply in respect of the negotiations for an agreement as if references in those regulations to the special negotiating body were references to the European Works Council.

NOTES

Para 2: substituted by the Transnational Information and Consultation of Employees (Amendment) Regulations 2010, SI 2010/1088, regs 2, 24.

Para 6: sub-para (3) added by SI 2010/1088, regs 2, 25.

Para 7: sub-paras (3), (4) substituted (for the original sub-para (3)) by SI 2010/1088, regs 2, 26.

Para 8: word omitted revoked, and word in square brackets substituted, by SI 2010/1088, regs 2, 27.

Para 8A: added by SI 2010/1088, regs 2, 28.

Para 9: words in square brackets in sub-para (6) inserted, and sub-paras (7), (8) added, by SI 2010/1088, regs 2, 29.

Para 10: revoked by the Employment Rights (Amendment) (EU Exit) Regulations 2019, SI 2019/535, reg 2(2), Sch 2, Pt 1, paras 1, 32, as from exit day (as defined in the European Union (Withdrawal) Act 2018, s 20) and subject to savings and transitional provisions in Sch 2, Pt 2 at **[2.2182]**.

DATA PROTECTION (PROCESSING OF SENSITIVE PERSONAL DATA) ORDER 2000 (NOTE)

(SI 2000/417)

[2.527]

NOTES

This Order was revoked by the Data Protection Act 2018, s 211, Sch 19, Pt 1, para 249, as from 25 May 2018 (for transitional provisions and savings relating to the repeal of the Data Protection Act 1998, see Sch 20 to the 2018 Act at **[1.2232]**).

TRADE UNION RECOGNITION (METHOD OF COLLECTIVE BARGAINING) ORDER 2000

(SI 2000/1300)

NOTES

Made: 11 May 2000.

Authority: Trade Union and Labour Relations (Consolidation) Act 1992, Sch A1, para 168(1).

Commencement: 6 June 2000.

See *Harvey* NI(7).

[2.528]

1 Citation and commencement

This Order may be cited as the Trade Union Recognition (Method of Collective Bargaining) Order 2000 and comes into force on 6th June 2000.

[2.529]
2 Specification of method

The method specified for the purposes of paragraphs 31(3) and 63(2) of Schedule A1 to the Trade Union and Labour Relations (Consolidation) Act 1992 is the method set out under the heading "the specified method" in the Schedule to this Order.

SCHEDULE

[2.530]
PREAMBLE

The method specified below ("the specified method") is one by which collective bargaining might be conducted in the particular, and possibly rare, circumstances discussed in the following paragraph. The specified method is not designed to be applied as a model for voluntary procedural agreements between employers and unions. Because most voluntary agreements are not legally binding and are usually concluded in a climate of trust and co-operation, they do not need to be as prescriptive as the specified method. However, the Central Arbitration Committee ("CAC") must take the specified method into account when exercising its powers to impose a method of collective bargaining under paragraphs 31(3) and 63(2) of Schedule A1 to the Trade Union and Labour Relations (Consolidation) Act 1992. In exercising those powers the CAC may depart from the specified method to such extent as it thinks appropriate in the circumstances of individual cases.

Paragraph 31(3) provides for the CAC to impose a method of collective bargaining in cases where a union (or unions, where two or more unions act jointly) has been recognised by an employer by means of an award of the CAC under Part I of Schedule A1, but the employer and union(s) have been unable to agree a method of bargaining between themselves, or have failed to follow an agreed method. Paragraph 63(2) provides for the CAC to impose a bargaining method in cases where an employer and a union (or unions) have entered an agreement for recognition, as defined by paragraph 52 of Part II of Schedule A1, but cannot agree a method of bargaining, or have failed to follow the agreed method.

The bargaining method imposed by the CAC has effect as if it were a legally binding contract between the employer and the union(s). If one party believes the other is failing to respect the method, the first party may apply to the court for an order of specific performance, ordering the other party to comply with the method. Failure to comply with such an order could constitute contempt of court.

Once the CAC has imposed a bargaining method, the parties can vary it, including the fact that it is legally binding, by agreement provided that they do so in writing.

The fact that the CAC has imposed a method does not affect the rights of individual workers under either statute or their contracts of employment. For example, it does not prevent or limit the rights of individual workers to discuss, negotiate or agree with their employer terms of their contract of employment, which differ from the terms of any collective agreement into which the employer and the union may enter as a result of collective bargaining conducted by this method. Nor does the imposed method affect an individual's statutory entitlement to time off for trade union activities or duties.

In cases where the CAC imposes a bargaining method on the parties, the employer is separately obliged, in accordance with Section 70B of the Trade Union and Labour Relations (Consolidation) Act 1992 (as inserted by section 5 of the Employment Relations Act 1999), to consult union representatives periodically on his policy, actions and plans on training. The specified method does not discuss how such consultations should be organised.

The law confers certain entitlements on independent trade unions which are recognised for collective bargaining purposes. For example, employers must disclose, on request, certain types of information to the representatives of the recognised unions. The fact that the CAC has imposed a bargaining method does not affect these existing statutory entitlements.

THE SPECIFIED METHOD

The Parties

1. The method shall apply in each case to two parties, who are referred to here as the "employer" and the "union". Unless the text specifies otherwise, the term "union" should be read to mean "unions" in cases where two or more unions are jointly recognised.

The Purpose

2. The purpose is to specify a method by which the employer and the union conduct collective bargaining concerning the pay, hours and holidays of the workers comprising the bargaining unit.

3. The employer shall not grant the right to negotiate pay, hours and holidays to any other union in respect of the workers covered by this method.

The Joint Negotiating Body

4. The employer and the union shall establish a Joint Negotiating Body (JNB) to discuss and negotiate the pay, hours and holidays of the workers comprising the bargaining unit. No other body or group shall undertake collective bargaining on the pay, hours and holidays of these workers, unless the employer and the union so agree.

JNB Membership

5. The membership of the JNB shall usually comprise three employer representatives (who together shall constitute the Employer Side of the JNB) and three union representatives (who together shall constitute the Union Side of the JNB). Each union recognised by the employer in respect of the bargaining unit shall be entitled to one seat at least. To meet this requirement, the Union Side may need to be larger than three and in this eventuality the employer shall be entitled to increase his representation on the JNB by the same number, if he wishes.

6. The employer shall select those individuals who comprise the Employer Side. The individuals must either be those who take the final decisions within the employer's organisation in respect of the pay, hours and holidays of the workers in the bargaining unit or who are expressly authorised by the employer to make recommendations directly to those who take such final decisions. Unless it would be unreasonable to do so, the employer shall select as a representative the most senior person responsible for employment relations in the bargaining unit.

7. The union shall select those individuals who comprise the Union Side in accordance with its own rules and procedures. The representatives must either be individuals employed by the employer or individuals employed by the union who are officials of the union within the meaning of sections 1 and 119 of the Trade Union and Labour Relations (Consolidation) Act 1992 ("the 1992 Act").

8. The JNB shall determine their own rules in respect of the attendance at JNB meetings of observers and substitutes who deputise for JNB members.

Officers

9. The Employer Side shall select one of its members to act as its Chairman and one to act as its Secretary. The Union Side shall select one of its members to act as its Chairman and one to act as its Secretary. The same person may perform the roles of Chairman and Secretary of a Side.

10. For the twelve months from the date of the JNB's first meeting, meetings of the JNB shall be chaired by the Chairman of the Employer Side. The Chairman of the Union Side shall chair the JNB's meetings for the following twelve months. The chairmanship of JNB meetings will alternate in the same way thereafter at intervals of twelve months. In the absence of the person who should chair JNB meetings, a JNB meeting shall be chaired by another member of that person's Side.

11. The Secretary of the Employer Side shall act as Secretary to the JNB. He shall circulate documentation and agendas in advance of JNB meetings, arrange suitable accommodation for meetings, notify members of meetings and draft the written record of JNB meetings. The Secretary of the Employer Side shall work closely with the Secretary of the Union Side in the discharge of these duties, disclosing full information about his performance of these tasks.

JNB Organisation

12. Draft agendas shall be circulated at least three working days in advance of JNB meetings. The draft record of JNB meetings shall be circulated within ten working days of the holding of meetings for approval at the next JNB meeting. The record does not need to be a verbatim account, but should fully describe the conclusions reached and the actions to be taken.

13. Subject to the timetable of meetings stipulated in paragraphs 15, 17, 20 and 28 below, the date, timing and location of meetings shall be arranged by the JNB's Secretary, in full consultation with the Secretary of the Union Side, to ensure maximum attendance at meetings. A meeting of the JNB shall be quorate if 50% or more of each Side's members (or, where applicable, their substitutes) are in attendance.

Bargaining Procedure

14 The union's proposals for adjustments to pay, hours and holidays shall be dealt with on an annual basis, unless the two Sides agree a different bargaining period.

15. The JNB shall conduct these negotiations for each bargaining round according to the following staged procedure.

Step 1— The union shall set out in writing, and send to the employer, its proposals (the "claim") to vary the pay, hours and holidays, specifying which aspects it wants to change. In its claim, the union shall set out the reasons for its proposals, together with the main supporting evidence at its disposal at the time. In cases where there is no established annual date when the employer reviews the pay, hours and holidays of all the workers in the bargaining unit, the union shall put forward its first claim within three months of this method being imposed (and by the same date in subsequent rounds). Where such a common review date is established, the union shall submit its first claim at least a month in advance of that date (and by the same date in subsequent rounds). In either case, the employer and the union may agree a different date by which the claim should be submitted each year. If the union fails to submit its claim by this date, then the procedure shall be ended for the bargaining round in question. Exceptionally, the union may submit a late claim without this penalty if its work on the claim was delayed while the Central Arbitration Committee considered a relevant complaint by the union of failure by the employer to disclose information for collective bargaining purposes.

Step 2— Within ten working days of the Employer Side's receipt of the union's letter, a quorate meeting of the JNB shall be held to discuss the claim. At this meeting, the Union Side shall explain its claim and answer any reasonable questions arising to the best of its ability.

Step 3—

(a) Within fifteen working days immediately following the Step 2 meeting, the employer shall either accept the claim in full or write to the union responding to its claim. If the Employer Side requests it, a quorate meeting of the JNB shall be held within the fifteen day period to enable the employer to present this written response directly to the Union Side. In explaining the basis of his response, the employer shall set out in this written communication all relevant information in his possession. In particular, the written communication shall contain information costing each element of the claim and describing the business consequences, particularly any staffing implications, unless the employer is not required to disclose such information for any of the reasons specified in section 182(1) of the 1992 Act. The basis of these estimated costs and effects, including the main assumptions that the employer has used, shall be set out in the communication. In determining what information is disclosed as relevant, the employer shall be under no greater obligation that he is under the general duty imposed on him by sections 181 and 182 of the 1992 Act to disclose information for the purposes of collective bargaining.

(b) If the response contains any counter-proposals, the written communication shall set out the reasons for making them, together with the supporting evidence. The letter shall provide information estimating the costs and staffing consequences of implementing each element of the counter-proposals, unless the employer is not required to disclose such information for any of the reasons specified in section 182(1) of the 1992 Act.

Step 4— Within ten working days of the Union Side's receipt of the employer's written communication, a further quorate meeting of the JNB shall be held to discuss the employer's response. At this meeting, the Employer Side shall explain its response and answer any reasonable questions arising to the best of its ability.

Step 5— If no agreement is reached at the Step 4 meeting (or the last of such meetings if more than one is held at that stage in the procedure), another quorate meeting of the JNB shall be held within ten working days. The union may bring to this meeting a maximum of two other individuals employed by the union who are officials within the meaning of the sections 1 and 119 of the 1992 Act. The employer may bring to the meeting a maximum of two other individuals who are employees or officials of an employer's organisation to which the employer belongs. These additional persons shall be allowed to contribute to the meeting, as if they were JNB members.

Step 6— If no agreement is reached at the Step 5 meeting (or the last of such meetings if more than one meeting is held at that stage in the procedure), within five working days the employer and the union shall consider, separately or jointly, consulting ACAS about the prospect of ACAS helping them to find a settlement of their differences through conciliation. In the event that both parties agree to invite ACAS to conciliate, both parties shall give such assistance to ACAS as is necessary to enable it to carry out the conciliation efficiently and effectively.

16. The parties shall set aside half a working day for each JNB meeting, unless the Employer Side Chairman and the Union Side Chairman agree a different length of time for the meeting. Unless it is essential to do otherwise, meetings shall be held during the normal working time of most union members of the JNB. Meetings may be adjourned, if both Sides agree. Additional meetings at any point in the procedure may be arranged, if both Sides agree. In addition, if the Employer Side requests it, a meeting of the JNB shall be held before the union has submitted its claim or before the employer is required to respond, enabling the Employer Side to explain the business context within which the employer shall assess the claim.

17. The employer shall not vary the contractual terms affecting the pay, hours or holidays of workers in the bargaining unit, unless he has first discussed his proposals with the union. Such proposals shall normally be made by the employer in the context of his consideration of the union's claim at Steps 3 or 4. If, however, the employer has not tabled his proposals during that process and he wishes to make proposals before the next bargaining round commences, he must write to the union setting out his proposals and the reasons for making them, together with the supporting evidence. The letter shall provide information estimating the costs and staffing consequences of implementing each element of the proposals, unless the employer is not required to disclose such information for any of the reasons specified in section 182(1) of the 1992 Act. A quorate meeting of the JNB shall be held within five working days of the Union Side's receipt of the letter. If there is a failure to resolve the issue at that meeting, then meetings shall be arranged, and steps shall be taken, in accordance with Steps 5 and 6 of the above procedure.

18. Paragraph 17 does not apply to terms in the contract of an individual worker where that worker has agreed that the terms may be altered only by direct negotiation between the worker and the employer.

Collective Agreements

19. Any agreements affecting the pay, hours and holidays of workers in the bargaining unit, which the employer and the union enter following negotiations, shall be set down in writing and signed by the Chairman of the Employer Side and by the Chairman of the Union Side or, in their absence, by another JNB member on their respective Sides.

20. If either the employer or union consider that there has been a failure to implement the agreement, then that party can request in writing a meeting of the JNB to discuss the alleged failure. A quorate meeting shall be held within five working days of the receipt of the request by the JNB Secretary. If there is a failure to resolve the issue at that meeting, then meetings shall be arranged, and steps shall be taken, in accordance with Steps 5 and 6 of the above procedure.

Facilities and Time Off

21. If they are employed by the employer, union members of the JNB:

— shall be given paid time off by the employer to attend JNB meetings;

— shall be given paid time off by the employer to attend a two hour pre-meeting of the Union Side before each JNB meeting; and

— shall be given paid time off by the employer to hold a day-long meeting to prepare the claim at Step 1 in the bargaining procedure.

The union members of the JNB shall schedule such meetings at times which minimise the effect on production and services. In arranging these meetings, the union members of the JNB shall provide the employer and their line management with as much notice as possible and give details of the purpose of the time off, the intended location of the meeting and the timing and duration of the time off. The employer shall provide adequate heating and lighting for these meetings, and ensure that they are held in private.

22. If they are not employed by the employer, union members of the JNB or other union officials attending JNB meetings shall be given sufficient access to the employer's premises to allow them to attend Union Side pre-meetings, JNB meetings and meetings of the bargaining unit as specified in paragraph 23.

23. The employer shall agree to the union's reasonable request to hold meetings with members of the bargaining unit on company premises to discuss the Step 1 claim, the employer's offer or revisions to either. The request shall be made at least three working days in advance of the proposed meeting. However, the employer is not required to provide such facilities, if the employer does not possess available premises which can be used for meetings on the scale suggested by the union. The employer shall provide adequate heating and lighting for meetings, and ensure that the meeting is held in private. Where such meetings are held in working time, the employer is under no obligation to pay individuals for the time off. Where meetings take place outside normal working hours, they should be arranged at a time which is otherwise convenient for the workers.

24. Where resources permit, the employer shall make available to the Union Side of the JNB such typing, copying and word-processing facilities as it needs to conduct its business in private.

25. Where resources permit, the employer shall set aside a room for the exclusive use of the Union Side of the JNB. The room shall possess a secure cabinet and a telephone.

26. In respect of issues which are not otherwise specified in this method, the employer and the union shall have regard to the guidance issued in the ACAS Code of Practice on Time Off for Trade Union Duties and Activities and ensure that there is no unwarranted or unjustified failure to abide by it.

Disclosure of Information

27. The employer and the union shall have regard to the ACAS Code of Practice on the Disclosure of Information to Trade Unions for Collective Bargaining Purposes and ensure that there is no unwarranted or unjustified failure to abide by it in relation to the bargaining arrangements specified by this method.

Revision of the Method

28. The employer or the union may request in writing a meeting of the JNB to discuss revising any element of this method, including its status as a legally binding contract. A quorate meeting of the JNB shall be held within ten working days of the receipt of the request by the JNB Secretary. This meeting shall be held in accordance with the same arrangements for the holding of other JNB meetings.

General

29. The employer and the union shall take all reasonable steps to ensure that this method to conduct collective bargaining is applied efficiently and effectively.

30. The definition of a "working day" used in this method is any day other than a Saturday or a Sunday, Christmas Day or Good Friday, or a day which is a bank holiday.

31. All time limits mentioned in this method may be varied on any occasion, if both the employer and the union agree.

RECOGNITION AND DERECOGNITION BALLOTS (QUALIFIED PERSONS) ORDER 2000

(SI 2000/1306)

NOTES

Made: 11 May 2000.
Authority: Trade Union and Labour Relations (Consolidation) Act 1992, Sch A1, paras 25(7)(a), 117(9)(a).
Commencement: 6 June 2000.

[2.531]

1 Citation, commencement and interpretation

(1) This Order may be cited as the Recognition and Derecognition Ballots (Qualified Persons) Order 2000 and shall come into force on 6th June 2000.

(2) In this Order "the relevant provisions" means paragraphs 25(7)(a) and 117(9)(a) of Schedule A1 to the Trade Union and Labour Relations (Consolidation) Act 1992.

Part 2 Statutory Instruments

[2.532]
2 Qualifications

In relation to an individual, the condition specified for the purposes of the relevant provisions is that he—

(a) has in force a practising certificate issued by the Law Society of England and Wales or the Law Society of Scotland; or

[(b) is eligible for appointment as a statutory auditor under Part 42 of the Companies Act 2006].

NOTES

Para (b): substituted by the Recognition and Derecognition Ballots (Qualified Persons) (Amendment) Order 2010, SI 2010/437, art 2(a).

[2.533]
3

In relation to a partnership, the condition specified for the purposes of the relevant provisions is that every member of the partnership is an individual who satisfies the condition specified in Article 2.

[2.534]
[4 Persons specified by name

The following persons are specified for the purpose of the relevant provisions—

Electoral Reform Services Limited;
Involvement and Participation Association;
Popularis Limited;
Print Image Network Limited (trading as UK Engage);
Democracy Technology Limited (trading as Mi-Voice);
Kanto Elect Limited.]

NOTES

Commencement: 1 October 2017.

Substituted by the Recognition and Derecognition Ballots (Qualified Persons) (Amendment) Order 2017, 2017/878, art 2, as from 1 October 2017.

PART-TIME WORKERS (PREVENTION OF LESS FAVOURABLE TREATMENT) REGULATIONS 2000

(SI 2000/1551)

NOTES

Made: 8 June 2000.

Authority: Employment Relations Act 1999, s 19.

Commencement: 1 July 2000.

These Regulations implement Council Directive 97/81/EC at **[3.187]**, as extended to the United Kingdom by Council Directive 98/23/EC.

Employment Appeal Tribunal: an appeal lies to the Employment Appeal Tribunal on any question of law arising from any decision of, or in any proceedings before, an employment tribunal under or by virtue of these Regulations; see the Employment Tribunals Act 1996, s 21(1)(j) at **[1.764]**.

Conciliation: employment tribunal proceedings under reg 8 are "relevant proceedings" for the purposes of the conciliation provisions contained in the Employment Tribunals Act 1996, ss 18–18C; see s 18(1)(l) of the 1996 Act at **[1.757]**.

See *Harvey* AI(2), DII.

ARRANGEMENT OF REGULATIONS

PART I
GENERAL AND INTERPRETATION

[2.535]

1 Citation, commencement and interpretation

(1) These Regulations may be cited as the Part-time Workers (Prevention of Less Favourable Treatment) Regulations 2000 and shall come into force on 1st July 2000.

(2) In these Regulations—

"the 1996 Act" means the Employment Rights Act 1996;

"contract of employment" means a contract of service or of apprenticeship, whether express or implied, and (if it is express) whether oral or in writing;

"employee" means an individual who has entered into or works under or (except where a provision of these Regulations otherwise requires) where the employment has ceased, worked under a contract of employment;

"employer", in relation to any employee or worker, means the person by whom the employee or worker is or (except where a provision of these Regulations otherwise requires) where the employment has ceased, was employed;

"pro rata principle" means that where a comparable full-time worker receives or is entitled to receive pay or any other benefit, a part-time worker is to receive or be entitled to receive not less than the proportion of that pay or other benefit that the number of his weekly hours bears to the number of weekly hours of the comparable full-time worker;

"worker" means an individual who has entered into or works under or (except where a provision of these Regulations otherwise requires) where the employment has ceased, worked under—

(a) a contract of employment; or

(b) any other contract, whether express or implied and (if it is express) whether oral or in writing, whereby the individual undertakes to do or perform personally any work or services for another party to the contract whose status is not by virtue of the contract that of a client or customer of any profession or business undertaking carried on by the individual.

(3) In the definition of the pro rata principle and in regulations 3 and 4 "weekly hours" means the number of hours a worker is required to work under his contract of employment in a week in which he has no absences from work and does not work any overtime or, where the number of such hours varies according to a cycle, the average number of such hours.

[2.536]

2 Meaning of full-time worker, part-time worker and comparable full-time worker

(1) A worker is a full-time worker for the purpose of these Regulations if he is paid wholly or in part by reference to the time he works and, having regard to the custom and practice of the employer in relation to workers employed by the worker's employer under the same type of contract, is identifiable as a full-time worker.

(2) A worker is a part-time worker for the purpose of these Regulations if he is paid wholly or in part by reference to the time he works and, having regard to the custom and practice of the employer in relation to workers employed by the worker's employer under the same type of contract, is not identifiable as a full-time worker.

[(3) For the purposes of paragraphs (1), (2) and (4), the following shall be regarded as being employed under different types of contract—

(a) employees employed under a contract that is not a contract of apprenticeship;

(b) employees employed under a contract of apprenticeship;

(c) workers who are not employees;

(d) any other description of worker that it is reasonable for the employer to treat differently from other workers on the ground that workers of that description have a different type of contract.]

(4) A full-time worker is a comparable full-time worker in relation to a part-time worker if, at the time when the treatment that is alleged to be less favourable to the part-time worker takes place—

(a) both workers are—

(i) employed by the same employer under the same type of contract, and

(ii) engaged in the same or broadly similar work having regard, where relevant, to whether they have a similar level of qualification, skills and experience; and

(b) the full-time worker works or is based at the same establishment as the part-time worker or, where there is no full-time worker working or based at that establishment who satisfies the requirements of sub-paragraph (a), works or is based at a different establishment and satisfies those requirements.

NOTES

Para (3): substituted by the Part-time Workers (Prevention of Less Favourable Treatment) Regulations 2000 (Amendment) Regulations 2002, SI 2002/2035, reg 2(a).

[2.537]

3 Workers becoming part-time

(1) This regulation applies to a worker who—

(a) was identifiable as a full-time worker in accordance with regulation 2(1); and

(b) following a termination or variation of his contract, continues to work under a new or varied contract, whether of the same type or not, that requires him to work for a number of weekly hours that is lower than the number he was required to work immediately before the termination or variation.

(2) Notwithstanding regulation 2(4), regulation 5 shall apply to a worker to whom this regulation applies as if he were a part-time worker and as if there were a comparable full-time worker employed under the terms that applied to him immediately before the variation or termination.

(3) The fact that this regulation applies to a worker does not affect any right he may have under these Regulations by virtue of regulation 2(4).

[2.538]

4 Workers returning part-time after absence

(1) This regulation applies to a worker who—

(a) was identifiable as a full-time worker in accordance with regulation 2(1) immediately before a period of absence (whether the absence followed a termination of the worker's contract or not);

(b) returns to work for the same employer within a period of less than twelve months beginning with the day on which the period of absence started;

(c) returns to the same job or to a job at the same level under a contract, whether it is a different contract or a varied contract and regardless of whether it is of the same type, under which he is required to work for a number of weekly hours that is lower than the number he was required to work immediately before the period of absence.

(2) Notwithstanding regulation 2(4), regulation 5 shall apply to a worker to whom this regulation applies ("the returning worker") as if he were a part-time worker and as if there were a comparable full-time worker employed under—

(a) the contract under which the returning worker was employed immediately before the period of absence; or

(b) where it is shown that, had the returning worker continued to work under the contract mentioned in sub-paragraph (a) a variation would have been made to its term during the period of absence, the contract mentioned in that sub-paragraph including that variation.

(3) The fact that this regulation applies to a worker does not affect any right he may have under these Regulations by virtue of regulation 2(4).

PART II
RIGHTS AND REMEDIES

[2.539]

5 Less favourable treatment of part-time workers

(1) A part-time worker has the right not to be treated by his employer less favourably than the employer treats a comparable full-time worker—

(a) as regards the terms of his contract; or

(b) by being subjected to any other detriment by any act, or deliberate failure to act, of his employer.

(2) The right conferred by paragraph (1) applies only if—

(a) the treatment is on the ground that the worker is a part-time worker, and

(b) the treatment is not justified on objective grounds.

(3) In determining whether a part-time worker has been treated less favourably than a comparable full-time worker the pro rata principle shall be applied unless it is inappropriate.

(4) A part-time worker paid at a lower rate for overtime worked by him in a period than a comparable full-time worker is or would be paid for overtime worked by him in the same period shall not, for that reason, be regarded as treated less favourably than the comparable full-time worker where, or to the extent that, the total number of hours worked by the part-time worker in the period, including overtime, does not exceed the number of hours the comparable full-time worker is required to work in the period, disregarding absences from work and overtime.

[2.540]

6 Right to receive a written statement of reasons for less favourable treatment

(1) If a worker who considers that his employer may have treated him in a manner which infringes a right conferred on him by regulation 5 requests in writing from his employer a written statement giving particulars of the reasons for the treatment, the worker is entitled to be provided with such a statement within twenty-one days of his request.

(2) A written statement under this regulation is admissible as evidence in any proceedings under these Regulations.

(3) If it appears to the tribunal in any proceedings under these Regulations—

(a) that the employer deliberately, and without reasonable excuse, omitted to provide a written statement, or

(b) that the written statement is evasive or equivocal,

it may draw any inference which it considers it just and equitable to draw, including an inference that the employer has infringed the right in question.

(4) This regulation does not apply where the treatment in question consists of the dismissal of an employee, and the employee is entitled to a written statement of reasons for his dismissal under section 92 of the 1996 Act.

[2.541]

7 Unfair dismissal and the right not to be subjected to detriment

(1) An employee who is dismissed shall be regarded as unfairly dismissed for the purposes of Part X of the 1996 Act if the reason (or, if more than one, the principal reason) for the dismissal is a reason specified in paragraph (3).

(2) A worker has the right not to be subjected to any detriment by any act, or any deliberate failure to act, by his employer done on a ground specified in paragraph (3).

(3) The reasons or, as the case may be, grounds are—

(a) that the worker has—

(i) brought proceedings against the employer under these Regulations;

(ii) requested from his employer a written statement of reasons under regulation 6;

(iii) given evidence or information in connection with such proceedings brought by any worker;

(iv) otherwise done anything under these Regulations in relation to the employer or any other person;

(v) alleged that the employer had infringed these Regulations; or
(vi) refused (or proposed to refuse) to forgo a right conferred on him by these Regulations, or

(b) that the employer believes or suspects that the worker has done or intends to do any of the things mentioned in sub-paragraph (a).

(4) Where the reason or principal reason for dismissal or, as the case may be, ground for subjection to any act or deliberate failure to act, is that mentioned in paragraph (3)(a)(v), or (b) so far as it relates thereto, neither paragraph (1) nor paragraph (2) applies if the allegation made by the worker is false and not made in good faith.

(5) Paragraph (2) does not apply where the detriment in question amounts to the dismissal of an employee within the meaning of Part X of the 1996 Act.

[2.542]

8 Complaints to employment tribunals etc

(1) Subject to regulation 7(5), a worker may present a complaint to an employment tribunal that his employer has infringed a right conferred on him by regulation 5 or 7(2).

(2) Subject to paragraph (3), an employment tribunal shall not consider a complaint under this regulation unless it is presented before the end of the period of three months (or, in a case to which regulation 13 applies, six months) beginning with the date of the less favourable treatment or detriment to which the complaint relates or, where an act or failure to act is part of a series of similar acts or failures comprising the less favourable treatment or detriment, the last of them.

[(2A) Regulation 8A (extension of time limits to facilitate conciliation before institution of proceedings) applies for the purposes of paragraph (2).]

(3) A tribunal may consider any such complaint which is out of time if, in all the circumstances of the case, it considers that it is just and equitable to do so.

(4) For the purposes of calculating the date of the less favourable treatment or detriment under paragraph (2)—

(a) where a term in a contract is less favourable, that treatment shall be treated, subject to paragraph (b), as taking place on each day of the period during which the term is less favourable;

(b) where an application relies on regulation 3 or 4 the less favourable treatment shall be treated as occurring on, and only on, in the case of regulation 3, the first day on which the applicant worked under the new or varied contract and, in the case of regulation 4, the day on which the applicant returned; and

(c) a deliberate failure to act contrary to regulation 5 or 7(2) shall be treated as done when it was decided on.

(5) In the absence of evidence establishing the contrary, a person shall be taken for the purposes of paragraph (4)(c) to decide not to act—

(a) when he does an act inconsistent with doing the failed act; or

(b) if he has done no such inconsistent act, when the period expires within which he might reasonably have been expected to have done the failed act if it was to be done.

(6) Where a worker presents a complaint under this regulation it is for the employer to identify the ground for the less favourable treatment or detriment.

(7) Where an employment tribunal finds that a complaint presented to it under this regulation is well founded, it shall take such of the following steps as it considers just and equitable—

(a) making a declaration as to the rights of the complainant and the employer in relation to the matters to which the complaint relates;

(b) ordering the employer to pay compensation to the complainant;

(c) recommending that the employer take, within a specified period, action appearing to the tribunal to be reasonable, in all the circumstances of the case, for the purpose of obviating or reducing the adverse effect on the complainant of any matter to which the complaint relates.

(8) . . .

(9) Where a tribunal orders compensation under paragraph (7)(b), the amount of the compensation awarded shall be such as the tribunal considers just and equitable in all the circumstances . . . having regard to—

(a) the infringement to which the complaint relates, and

(b) any loss which is attributable to the infringement having regard, in the case of an infringement of the right conferred by regulation 5, to the pro rata principle except where it is inappropriate to do so.

(10) The loss shall be taken to include—

(a) any expenses reasonably incurred by the complainant in consequence of the infringement, and

(b) loss of any benefit which he might reasonably be expected to have had but for the infringement.

(11) Compensation in respect of treating a worker in a manner which infringes the right conferred on him by regulation 5 shall not include compensation for injury to feelings.

(12) In ascertaining the loss the tribunal shall apply the same rule concerning the duty of a person to mitigate his loss as applies to damages recoverable under the common law of England and Wales or (as the case may be) Scotland.

(13) Where the tribunal finds that the act, or failure to act, to which the complaint relates was to any extent caused or contributed to by action of the complainant, it shall reduce the amount of the compensation by such proportion as it considers just and equitable having regard to that finding.

(14) If the employer fails, without reasonable justification, to comply with a recommendation made by an employment tribunal under paragraph (7)(c) the tribunal may, if it thinks it just and equitable to do so—

(a) increase the amount of compensation required to be paid to the complainant in respect of the complaint, where an order was made under paragraph (7)(b); or

(b) make an order under paragraph (7)(b).

NOTES

Para (2A): inserted by the Enterprise and Regulatory Reform Act 2013 (Consequential Amendments) (Employment) Order 2014, SI 2014/386, art 2, Schedule, paras 10, 11.

Para (8): revoked by the Part-time Workers (Prevention of Less Favourable Treatment) Regulations 2000 (Amendment) Regulations 2002, SI 2002/2035, reg 2(b)(i).

Para (9): words omitted revoked by SI 2002/2035, reg 2(b)(ii).

Conciliation: employment tribunal proceedings under this regulation are "relevant proceedings" for the purposes of the conciliation provisions contained in the Employment Tribunals Act 1996, ss 18–18C; see s 18(1)(l) of the 1996 Act at **[1.757]**.

[2.543]

[8A Extension of time limit to facilitate conciliation before institution of proceedings

(1) In this regulation—

(a) Day A is the day on which the worker concerned complies with the requirement in subsection (1) of section 18A of the Employment Tribunals Act 1996 (requirement to contact ACAS before instituting proceedings) in relation to the matter in respect of which the proceedings are brought, and

(b) Day B is the day on which the worker concerned receives or, if earlier, is treated as receiving (by virtue of regulations made under subsection (11) of that section) the certificate issued under subsection (4) of that section.

(2) In working out when the time limit set by regulation 8(2) expires the period beginning with the day after Day A and ending with Day B is not to be counted.

(3) If the time limit set by regulation 8(2) would (if not extended by this paragraph) expire during the period beginning with Day A and ending one month after Day B, the time limit expires instead at the end of that period.

(4) The power conferred on the employment tribunal by regulation 8(3) to extend the time limit set by paragraph (2) of that regulation is exercisable in relation to that time limit as extended by this regulation.]

NOTES

Inserted by the Enterprise and Regulatory Reform Act 2013 (Consequential Amendments) (Employment) Order 2014, SI 2014/386, art 2, Schedule, paras 10, 12.

[2.544]

9 Restrictions on contracting out

Section 203 of the 1996 Act (restrictions on contracting out) shall apply in relation to these Regulations as if they were contained in that Act.

PART III
MISCELLANEOUS

[2.545]

10 Amendments to primary legislation

The amendments in the Schedule to these Regulations shall have effect.

[2.546]

11 Liability of employers and principals

(1) Anything done by a person in the course of his employment shall be treated for the purposes of these Regulations as also done by his employer, whether or not it was done with the employer's knowledge or approval.

(2) Anything done by a person as agent for the employer with the authority of the employer shall be treated for the purposes of these Regulations as also done by the employer.

(3) In proceedings under these Regulations against any person in respect of an act alleged to have been done by a worker of his, it shall be a defence for that person to prove that he took such steps as were reasonably practicable to prevent the worker from—

(a) doing that act; or

(b) doing, in the course of his employment, acts of that description.

PART IV
SPECIAL CLASSES OF PERSON

[2.547]

12 Crown employment

(1) Subject to regulation 13, these Regulations have effect in relation to Crown employment and persons in Crown employment as they have effect in relation to other employment and other employees and workers.

(2) In paragraph (1) "Crown employment" means employment under or for the purposes of a government department or any officer or body exercising on behalf of the Crown functions conferred by a statutory provision.

(3) For the purposes of the application of the provisions of these Regulations in relation to Crown employment in accordance with paragraph (1)—

(a) references to an employee and references to a worker shall be construed as references to a person in Crown employment to whom the definition of employee or, as the case may be, worker is appropriate; and

(b) references to a contract in relation to an employee and references to a contract in relation to a worker shall be construed as references to the terms of employment of a person in Crown employment to whom the definition of employee or, as the case may be, worker is appropriate.

[2.548]
13 Armed forces

(1) These Regulations, shall have effect in relation—

(a) subject to paragraphs (2) and (3) and apart from regulation 7(1), to service as a member of the armed forces, and

(b) to employment by an association established for the purposes of Part XI of the Reserve Forces Act 1996.

(2) These Regulations shall not have effect in relation to service as a member of the reserve forces in so far as that service consists in undertaking training obligations—

(a) under section 38, 40 or 41 of the Reserve Forces Act 1980,

(b) under section 22 of the Reserve Forces Act 1996,

(c) pursuant to regulations made under section 4 of the Reserve Forces Act 1996,

or consists in undertaking voluntary training or duties under section 27 of the Reserve Forces Act 1996.

(3) No complaint concerning the service of any person as a member of the armed forces may be presented to an employment tribunal under regulation 8 unless—

(a) that person has made a complaint in respect of the same matter to an officer under the service redress procedures, and

(b) that complaint has not been withdrawn.

[(4) For the purpose of paragraph (3)(b), a person shall be treated as having withdrawn his complaint if, having made a complaint to an officer under the service redress procedures—

(a) where the service redress procedures are those referred to in section 334 of the Armed Forces Act 2006, neither that officer nor a superior officer has decided to refer the complaint to the Defence Council, and the person who made the complaint fails to apply for such a reference to be made;

(b) in any other case, the person who made the complaint fails to submit the complaint to the Defence Council under the service redress procedures.]

(5) Where a complaint of the kind referred to in paragraph (3) is presented to an employment tribunal, the service redress procedures may continue after the complaint is presented.

(6) In this regulation, "the service redress procedures" means the procedures, excluding those which relate to the making of a report to Her Majesty, referred to in section 180 of the Army Act 1955, section 180 of the Air Force Act 1955[, section 130 of the Naval Discipline Act 1957 or section 334 of the Armed Forces Act 2006].

NOTES

Para (4): substituted by the Armed Forces (Service Complaints) (Consequential Amendments) Order 2008, SI 2008/1696, art 3(1), (2).

Para (6): words in square brackets substituted by SI 2008/1696, art 3(1), (3).

[2.549]
14 House of Lords staff

(1) These Regulations have effect in relation to employment as a relevant member of the House of Lords staff as they have effect in relation to other employment.

(2) In this regulation "relevant member of the House of Lords staff" means any person who is employed under a contract with the Corporate Officer of the House of Lords by virtue of which he is a worker.

[2.550]
15 House of Commons staff

(1) These Regulations have effect in relation to employment as a relevant member of the House of Commons staff as they have effect in relation to other employment.

(2) In this regulation "relevant member of the House of Commons staff" means any person—

(a) who was appointed by the House of Commons Commission; or

(b) who is a member of the Speaker's personal staff.

[2.551]
16 Police service

(1) For the purposes of these Regulations, the holding, otherwise than under a contract of employment, of the office of constable or an appointment as a police cadet shall be treated as employment, under a contract of employment, by the relevant officer.

[(1A) [(1A) For the purposes of these Regulations, any constable who has been seconded to [NCA] to serve as a member of its staff shall be treated as employed by [NCA], in respect of actions taken by, or on behalf of, [NCA].

(1B) For the purposes of regulation 11 (liability of employers and principals),—

(a) the secondment of any constable to [NCA] to serve as a member of its staff shall be treated as employment by [NCA] (and not as being employment by any other person); and

(b) anything done by a constable so seconded in the performance, or purported performance, of his functions shall be treated as done in the course of that employment.]

(2) In this regulation "the relevant officer" means—

(a) in relation to a member of a police force or a special constable or police cadet appointed for a police area, the chief officer of police (or, in Scotland, the chief constable);

(b) . . . ; and

(c) in relation to any other person holding the office of constable or an appointment as a police cadet, the person who has the direction and control of the body of constables or cadets in question.

[(4) For the purposes of these Regulations the relevant officer, as defined by paragraph (3), shall be treated as a corporation sole.

(5) In the application of this regulation to Scotland paragraph (4) shall have effect as if for the words "corporation sole" there were substituted "distinct juristic person (that is to say, as a juristic person distinct from the individual who for the time being is the office-holder)".]

[(6) In this regulation ["NCA" means the National Crime Agency].]

NOTES

Paras (1A), (1B), (6): inserted and added respectively by the Serious Organised Crime and Police Act 2005 (Consequential and Supplementary Amendments to Secondary Legislation) Order 2006, SI 2006/594, art 2, Schedule, para 21(1), (2), (4); words in square brackets substituted by virtue of the Crime and Courts Act 2013, s 15(3), Sch 8, Pt 4, para 190 (for general transitional provisions and savings relating to the abolition of the Serious Organised Crime Agency, see s 15(3), Sch 8, Pt 1 thereto).

Para (2): sub-para (b) revoked by SI 2006/594, art 2, Schedule, para 21(1), (3).

Paras (4), (5): added by the Part-time Workers (Prevention of Less Favourable Treatment) Regulations 2000 (Amendment) Order 2005, SI 2005/2240, art 2. Note that art 2 provides that these paragraphs should be inserted "after paragraph (3)"; this appears to be an error, as does the reference in para (4) to "paragraph (3)", as the original Regulations did not contain a paragraph (3).

[2.552]

17 Holders of judicial offices

These Regulations do not apply to any individual in his capacity as the holder of a judicial office if he is remunerated on a daily fee-paid basis.

SCHEDULE

(The Schedule amends the Employment Tribunals Act 1996, ss 18, 21 at **[1.757]**, **[1.764]**, *the Employment Rights Act 1996, ss 105, 108 at* **[1.1023]**, **[1.1026]** *and amended s 109 of that Act (repealed).)*

FIXED-TERM EMPLOYEES (PREVENTION OF LESS FAVOURABLE TREATMENT) REGULATIONS 2002

(SI 2002/2034)

NOTES

Made: 30 July 2002.

Authority: Employment Act 2002, ss 45, 51(1).

Commencement: 1 October 2002.

These Regulations are the domestic implementation of Council Directive 99/70, and the framework agreement on fixed-term work embodied therein, at **[3.209]**.

Conciliation: employment tribunal proceedings under regs 7 or 9 are "relevant proceedings" for the purposes of the conciliation provisions contained in the Employment Tribunals Act 1996, ss 18–18C; see s 18(1)(m) of the 1996 Act at **[1.757]**.

Employment Appeal Tribunal: an appeal lies to the Employment Appeal Tribunal on any question of law arising from any decision of, or in any proceedings before, an employment tribunal under or by virtue of these Regulations; see the Employment Tribunals Act 1996, s 21(1)(k) at **[1.764]**.

See *Harvey* AI(3).

ARRANGEMENT OF REGULATIONS

PART 1
GENERAL AND INTERPRETATION

Part 2 Statutory Instruments

PART 2
RIGHTS AND REMEDIES

PART 3
MISCELLANEOUS

PART 4
SPECIAL CLASSES OF PERSON

PART 5
EXCLUSIONS

SCHEDULES

PART 1
GENERAL AND INTERPRETATION

[2.553]

1 Citation, commencement and interpretation

(1) These Regulations may be cited as the Fixed-term Employees (Prevention of Less Favourable Treatment) Regulations 2002 and shall come into force on 1st October 2002.

(2) In these Regulations—

"the 1996 Act" means the Employment Rights Act 1996;

"collective agreement" means a collective agreement within the meaning of section 178 of the Trade Union and Labour Relations (Consolidation) Act 1992; the trade union parties to which are independent trade unions within the meaning of section 5 of that Act;

"employer", in relation to any employee, means the person by whom the employee is (or, where the employment has ceased, was) employed;

"fixed-term contract" means a contract of employment that, under its provisions determining how it will terminate in the normal course, will terminate—

- (a) on the expiry of a specific term,
- (b) on the completion of a particular task, or
- (c) on the occurrence or non-occurrence of any other specific event other than the attainment by the employee of any normal and bona fide retiring age in the establishment for an employee holding the position held by him,

and any reference to "fixed-term" shall be construed accordingly;

"fixed-term employee" means an employee who is employed under a fixed-term contract;

"permanent employee" means an employee who is not employed under a fixed-term contract, and any reference to "permanent employment" shall be construed accordingly;

"pro rata principle" means that where a comparable permanent employee receives or is entitled to pay or any other benefit, a fixed-term employee is to receive or be entitled to such proportion of that pay or other benefit as is reasonable in the circumstances having regard to the length of his contract of employment and to the terms on which the pay or other benefit is offered;

"renewal" includes extension and references to renewing a contract shall be construed accordingly;

"workforce agreement" means an agreement between an employer and his employees or their representatives in respect of which the conditions set out in Schedule 1 to these Regulations are satisfied.

[2.554]
2 Comparable employees

(1) For the purposes of these Regulations, an employee is a comparable permanent employee in relation to a fixed-term employee if, at the time when the treatment that is alleged to be less favourable to the fixed-term employee takes place,

(a) both employees are—

(i) employed by the same employer, and

(ii) engaged in the same or broadly similar work having regard, where relevant, to whether they have a similar level of qualification and skills; and

(b) the permanent employee works or is based at the same establishment as the fixed-term employee or, where there is no comparable permanent employee working or based at that establishment who satisfies the requirements of sub-paragraph (a), works or is based at a different establishment and satisfies those requirements.

(2) For the purposes of paragraph (1), an employee is not a comparable permanent employee if his employment has ceased.

PART 2
RIGHTS AND REMEDIES

[2.555]
3 Less favourable treatment of fixed-term employees

(1) A fixed-term employee has the right not to be treated by his employer less favourably than the employer treats a comparable permanent employee—

(a) as regards the terms of his contract; or

(b) by being subjected to any other detriment by any act, or deliberate failure to act, of his employer.

(2) Subject to paragraphs (3) and (4), the right conferred by paragraph (1) includes in particular the right of the fixed-term employee in question not to be treated less favourably than the employer treats a comparable permanent employee in relation to—

(a) any period of service qualification relating to any particular condition of service,

(b) the opportunity to receive training, or

(c) the opportunity to secure any permanent position in the establishment.

(3) The right conferred by paragraph (1) applies only if—

(a) the treatment is on the ground that the employee is a fixed-term employee, and

(b) the treatment is not justified on objective grounds.

(4) Paragraph (3)(b) is subject to regulation 4.

(5) In determining whether a fixed-term employee has been treated less favourably than a comparable permanent employee, the pro rata principle shall be applied unless it is inappropriate.

(6) In order to ensure that an employee is able to exercise the right conferred by paragraph (1) as described in paragraph (2)(c) the employee has the right to be informed by his employer of available vacancies in the establishment.

(7) For the purposes of paragraph (6) an employee is "informed by his employer" only if the vacancy is contained in an advertisement which the employee has a reasonable opportunity of reading in the course of his employment or the employee is given reasonable notification of the vacancy in some other way.

[2.556]
4 Objective justification

(1) Where a fixed-term employee is treated by his employer less favourably than the employer treats a comparable permanent employee as regards any term of his contract, the treatment in question shall be regarded for the purposes of regulation 3(3)(b) as justified on objective grounds if the terms of the fixed-term employee's contract of employment, taken as a whole, are at least as favourable as the terms of the comparable permanent employee's contract of employment.

(2) Paragraph (1) is without prejudice to the generality of regulation 3(3)(b).

[2.557]
5 Right to receive a written statement of reasons for less favourable treatment

(1) If an employee who considers that his employer may have treated him in a manner which infringes a right conferred on him by regulation 3 requests in writing from his employer a written statement giving particulars of the reasons for the treatment, the employee is entitled to be provided with such a statement within twenty-one days of his request.

(2) A written statement under this regulation is admissible as evidence in any proceedings under these Regulations.

(3) If it appears to the tribunal in any proceedings under these Regulations—

(a) that the employer deliberately, and without reasonable excuse, omitted to provide a written statement, or

(b) that the written statement is evasive or equivocal,

it may draw any inference which it considers it just and equitable to draw, including an inference that the employer has infringed the right in question.

(4) This regulation does not apply where the treatment in question consists of the dismissal of an employee, and the employee is entitled to a written statement of reasons for his dismissal under section 92 of the 1996 Act.

[2.558]
6 Unfair dismissal and the right not to be subjected to detriment

(1) An employee who is dismissed shall be regarded as unfairly dismissed for the purposes of Part 10 of the 1996 Act if the reason (or, if more than one, the principal reason) for the dismissal is a reason specified in paragraph (3).

(2) An employee has the right not to be subjected to any detriment by any act, or any deliberate failure to act, of his employer done on a ground specified in paragraph (3).

(3) The reasons or, as the case may be, grounds are—

(a) that the employee—

(i) brought proceedings against the employer under these Regulations;
(ii) requested from his employer a written statement under regulation 5 or regulation 9;
(iii) gave evidence or information in connection with such proceedings brought by any employee;
(iv) otherwise did anything under these Regulations in relation to the employer or any other person;
(v) alleged that the employer had infringed these Regulations;
(vi) refused (or proposed to refuse) to forgo a right conferred on him by these Regulations;
(vii) declined to sign a workforce agreement for the purposes of these Regulations, or
(viii) being—

(aa) a representative of members of the workforce for the purposes of Schedule 1, or
(bb) a candidate in an election in which any person elected will, on being elected, become such a representative,

performed (or proposed to perform) any functions or activities as such a representative or candidate, or

(b) that the employer believes or suspects that the employee has done or intends to do any of the things mentioned in sub-paragraph (a).

(4) Where the reason or principal reason for dismissal or, as the case may be, ground for subjection to any act or deliberate failure to act, is that mentioned in paragraph (3)(a)(v), or (b) so far as it relates thereto, neither paragraph (1) nor paragraph (2) applies if the allegation made by the employee is false and not made in good faith.

(5) Paragraph (2) does not apply where the detriment in question amounts to dismissal within the meaning of Part 10 of the 1996 Act.

[2.559]
7 Complaints to employment tribunals etc

(1) An employee may present a complaint to an employment tribunal that his employer has infringed a right conferred on him by regulation 3, or (subject to regulation 6(5)), regulation 6(2).

(2) Subject to paragraph (3), an employment tribunal shall not consider a complaint under this regulation unless it is presented before the end of the period of three months beginning—

(a) in the case of an alleged infringement of a right conferred by regulation 3(1) or 6(2), with the date of the less favourable treatment or detriment to which the complaint relates or, where an act or failure to act is part of a series of similar acts or failures comprising the less favourable treatment or detriment, the last of them;
(b) in the case of an alleged infringement of the right conferred by regulation 3(6), with the date, or if more than one the last date, on which other individuals, whether or not employees of the employer, were informed of the vacancy.

[(2A) Regulation 7A (extension of time limits to facilitate conciliation before institution of proceedings) applies for the purposes of paragraph (2).]

(3) A tribunal may consider any such complaint which is out of time if, in all the circumstances of the case, it considers that it is just and equitable to do so.

(4) For the purposes of calculating the date of the less favourable treatment or detriment under paragraph (2)(a)—

(a) where a term in a contract is less favourable, that treatment shall be treated, subject to paragraph (b), as taking place on each day of the period during which the term is less favourable;
(b) a deliberate failure to act contrary to regulation 3 or 6(2) shall be treated as done when it was decided on.

(5) In the absence of evidence establishing the contrary, a person shall be taken for the purposes of paragraph (4)(b) to decide not to act—

(a) when he does an act inconsistent with doing the failed act; or
(b) if he has done no such inconsistent act, when the period expires within which he might reasonably have been expected to have done the failed act if it was to be done.

(6) Where an employee presents a complaint under this regulation in relation to a right conferred on him by regulation 3 or 6(2) it is for the employer to identify the ground for the less favourable treatment or detriment.

(7) Where an employment tribunal finds that a complaint presented to it under this regulation is well founded, it shall take such of the following steps as it considers just and equitable—

(a) making a declaration as to the rights of the complainant and the employer in relation to the matters to which the complaint relates;

(b) ordering the employer to pay compensation to the complainant;

(c) recommending that the employer take, within a specified period, action appearing to the tribunal to be reasonable, in all the circumstances of the case, for the purpose of obviating or reducing the adverse effect on the complainant of any matter to which the complaint relates.

(8) Where a tribunal orders compensation under paragraph (7)(b), the amount of the compensation awarded shall be such as the tribunal considers just and equitable in all the circumstances having regard to—

(a) the infringement to which the complaint relates, and

(b) any loss which is attributable to the infringement.

(9) The loss shall be taken to include—

(a) any expenses reasonably incurred by the complainant in consequence of the infringement, and

(b) loss of any benefit which he might reasonably be expected to have had but for the infringement.

(10) Compensation in respect of treating an employee in a manner which infringes the right conferred on him by regulation 3 shall not include compensation for injury to feelings.

(11) In ascertaining the loss the tribunal shall apply the same rule concerning the duty of a person to mitigate his loss as applies to damages recoverable under the common law of England and Wales or (as the case may be) the law of Scotland.

(12) Where the tribunal finds that the act, or failure to act, to which the complaint relates was to any extent caused or contributed to by action of the complainant, it shall reduce the amount of the compensation by such proportion as it considers just and equitable having regard to that finding.

(13) If the employer fails, without reasonable justification, to comply with a recommendation made by an employment tribunal under paragraph (7)(c) the tribunal may, if it thinks it just and equitable to do so—

(a) increase the amount of compensation required to be paid to the complainant in respect of the complaint, where an order was made under paragraph (7)(b); or

(b) make an order under paragraph (7)(b).

NOTES

Para (2A): inserted by the Enterprise and Regulatory Reform Act 2013 (Consequential Amendments) (Employment) Order 2014, SI 2014/386, art 2, Schedule, paras 13, 14.

Conciliation: employment tribunal proceedings under this regulation are "relevant proceedings" for the purposes of the conciliation provisions contained in the Employment Tribunals Act 1996, ss 18–18C; see s 18(1)(m) of the 1996 Act at **[1.757]**.

[2.560]

[7A Extension of time limit to facilitate conciliation before institution of proceedings

(1) In this regulation—

(a) Day A is the day on which the worker concerned complies with the requirement in subsection (1) of section 18A of the Employment Tribunals Act 1996 (requirement to contact ACAS before instituting proceedings) in relation to the matter in respect of which the proceedings are brought, and

(b) Day B is the day on which the worker concerned receives or, if earlier, is treated as receiving (by virtue of regulations made under subsection (11) of that section) the certificate issued under subsection (4) of that section.

(2) In working out when the time limit set by regulation 7(2) expires the period beginning with the day after Day A and ending with Day B is not to be counted.

(3) If the time limit set by regulation 7(2) would (if not extended by this paragraph) expire during the period beginning with Day A and ending one month after Day B, the time limit expires instead at the end of that period.

(4) The power conferred on the employment tribunal by regulation 7(3) to extend the time limit set by paragraph (2) of that regulation is exercisable in relation to that time limit as extended by this regulation.]

NOTES

Inserted by the Enterprise and Regulatory Reform Act 2013 (Consequential Amendments) (Employment) Order 2014, SI 2014/386, art 2, Schedule, paras 10, 12.

[2.561]

8 Successive fixed-term contracts

(1) This regulation applies where—

(a) an employee is employed under a contract purporting to be a fixed-term contract, and

(b) the contract mentioned in sub-paragraph (a) has previously been renewed, or the employee has previously been employed on a fixed-term contract before the start of the contract mentioned in sub-paragraph (a).

(2) Where this regulation applies then, with effect from the date specified in paragraph (3), the provision of the contract mentioned in paragraph (1)(a) that restricts the duration of the contract shall be of no effect, and the employee shall be a permanent employee, if—

(a) the employee has been continuously employed under the contract mentioned in paragraph 1(a), or under that contract taken with a previous fixed-term contract, for a period of four years or more, and

(b) the employment of the employee under a fixed-term contract was not justified on objective grounds—

(i) where the contract mentioned in paragraph (1)(a) has been renewed, at the time when it was last renewed;

(ii) where that contract has not been renewed, at the time when it was entered into.

(3) The date referred to in paragraph (2) is whichever is the later of—

(a) the date on which the contract mentioned in paragraph (1)(a) was entered into or last renewed, and

(b) the date on which the employee acquired four years' continuous employment.

(4) For the purposes of this regulation Chapter 1 of Part 14 of the 1996 Act shall apply in determining whether an employee has been continuously employed, and any period of continuous employment falling before the 10th July 2002 shall be disregarded.

(5) A collective agreement or a workforce agreement may modify the application of paragraphs (1) to (3) of this regulation in relation to any employee or specified description of employees, by substituting for the provisions of paragraph (2) or paragraph (3), or for the provisions of both of those paragraphs, one or more different provisions which, in order to prevent abuse arising from the use of successive fixed-term contracts, specify one or more of the following—

(a) the maximum total period for which the employee or employees of that description may be continuously employed on a fixed-term contract or on successive fixed-term contracts;

(b) the maximum number of successive fixed-term contracts and renewals of such contracts under which the employee or employees of that description may be employed; or

(c) objective grounds justifying the renewal of fixed-term contracts, or the engagement of the employee or employees of that description under successive fixed-term contracts,

and those provisions shall have effect in relation to that employee or an employee of that description as if they were contained in paragraphs (2) and (3).

[2.562]

9 Right to receive written statement of variation

(1) If an employee who considers that, by virtue of regulation 8, he is a permanent employee requests in writing from his employer a written statement confirming that his contract is no longer fixed-term or that he is now a permanent employee, he is entitled to be provided, within twenty-one days of his request, with either—

(a) such a statement, or

(b) a statement giving reasons why his contract remains fixed-term.

(2) If the reasons stated under paragraph (1)(b) include an assertion that there were objective grounds for the engagement of the employee under a fixed-term contract, or the renewal of such a contract, the statement shall include a statement of those grounds.

(3) A written statement under this regulation is admissible as evidence in any proceedings before a court, an employment tribunal and the Commissioners of the Inland Revenue.

(4) If it appears to the court or tribunal in any proceedings—

(a) that the employer deliberately, and without reasonable excuse, omitted to provide a written statement, or

(b) that the written statement is evasive or equivocal,

it may draw any inference which it considers it just and equitable to draw.

(5) An employee who considers that, by virtue of regulation 8, he is a permanent employee may present an application to an employment tribunal for a declaration to that effect.

(6) No application may be made under paragraph (5) unless—

(a) the employee in question has previously requested a statement under paragraph (1) and the employer has either failed to provide a statement or given a statement of reasons under paragraph (1)(b), and

(b) the employee is at the time the application is made employed by the employer.

NOTES

Conciliation: employment tribunal proceedings under this regulation are "relevant proceedings" for the purposes of the conciliation provisions contained in the Employment Tribunals Act 1996, ss 18–18C; see s 18(1)(m) of the 1996 Act at **[1.757]**.

Commissioners of Inland Revenue: a reference to the Commissioners of Inland Revenue is now to be taken as a reference to the Commissioners for Her Majesty's Revenue and Customs; see the Commissioners for Revenue and Customs Act 2005, s 50(1), (7).

PART 3
MISCELLANEOUS

[2.563]

10 Restrictions on contracting out

Section 203 of the 1996 Act (restrictions on contracting out) shall apply in relation to these Regulations as if they were contained in that Act.

[2.564]
11 Amendments to primary legislation

The amendments in Part 1 of Schedule 2 to these Regulations shall have effect subject to the transitional provisions in Part 2 of the Schedule.

[2.565]
12 Liability of employers and principals

(1) Anything done by a person in the course of his employment shall be treated for the purposes of these Regulations as also done by his employer, whether or not it was done with the employer's knowledge or approval.

(2) Anything done by a person as agent for the employer with the authority of the employer shall be treated for the purposes of these Regulations as also done by the employer.

(3) In proceedings under these Regulations against any person in respect of an act alleged to have been done by an employee of his, it shall be a defence for that person to prove that he took such steps as were reasonably practicable to prevent the employee from—

(a) doing that act, or
(b) doing, in the course of his employment, acts of that description.

PART 4
SPECIAL CLASSES OF PERSON

[2.566]
13 Crown employment

(1) Subject to regulation 14, these Regulations have effect in relation to Crown employment and persons in Crown employment as they have effect in relation to other employment and other employees.

(2) For the purposes of paragraphs (1) and (3) a person is to be regarded as being in Crown employment only if—

(a) he is in employment under or for the purposes of a government department or any officer or body exercising on behalf of the Crown functions conferred by a statutory provision, and
(b) having regard to the terms and conditions under which he works, he would be an employee if he was not in Crown employment.

(3) For the purposes of the application of the provisions of these Regulations in relation to Crown employment and persons in Crown employment in accordance with paragraph (1)—

(a) references to an employee shall be construed as references to a person in Crown employment;
(b) references to a contract of employment shall be construed, in relation to a person in Crown employment, as references to the terms and conditions mentioned in paragraph (2)(b); and
(c) references to dismissal shall be construed as references to the termination of Crown employment.

[2.567]
14 Armed forces

(1) These Regulations—

(a) do not apply to service as a member of the naval, military or air forces of the Crown, but
(b) do apply to employment by an association established for the purposes of Part 11 of the Reserve Forces Act 1996.

NOTES

Note: this regulation is reproduced as it appears in the Queen's Printer's copy of these Regulations, ie, with no para (2).

[2.568]
15 House of Lords staff

(1) These Regulations have effect in relation to employment as a relevant member of the House of Lords staff as they have effect in relation to other employment.

(2) In this regulation "relevant member of the House of Lords staff" means any person who is employed under a contract with the Corporate Officer of the House of Lords by virtue of which he is an employee.

[2.569]
16 House of Commons staff

(1) These Regulations have effect in relation to employment as a relevant member of the House of Commons staff as they have effect in relation to other employment.

(2) In this regulation "relevant member of the House of Commons staff" means any person—

(a) who was appointed by the House of Commons Commission; or
(b) who is a member of the Speaker's personal staff.

[2.570]
17 Police service

(1) For the purposes of these Regulations, the holding, otherwise than under a contract of employment, of the office of constable or an appointment as a police cadet shall be treated as employment, under a contract of employment, by the relevant officer.

[(1A) For the purposes of these Regulations, any constable or other person who has been seconded to SOCA to serve as a member of its staff shall be treated as employed by [NCA], in respect of actions taken by, or on behalf of, [NCA].

(1B) For the purposes of regulation 12 (liability of employers and principals),—

(a) the secondment of any constable or other person to [NCA] to serve as a member of its staff shall be treated as employment by [NCA] (and not as being employment by any other person); and

(b) anything done by a person so seconded in the performance, or purported performance, of his functions shall be treated as done in the course of that employment.]

(2) In this regulation "the relevant officer" means—

(a) in relation to a member of a police force or a special constable or police cadet appointed for a police area, the chief officer of police (or, in Scotland, the chief constable);

(b) . . . ; and

(c) in relation to any other person holding the office of constable or an appointment as a police cadet, the person who has the direction and control of the body of constables or cadets in question.

[(3) In this regulation ["NCA" means the National Crime Agency].]

NOTES

Paras (1A), (1B), (3): inserted and added respectively by the Serious Organised Crime and Police Act 2005 (Consequential and Supplementary Amendments to Secondary Legislation) Order 2006, SI 2006/594, art 2, Schedule, para 30(1), (2); words in square brackets substituted by virtue of the Crime and Courts Act 2013, s 15(3), Sch 8, Pt 4, para 190 (for general transitional provisions and savings relating to the abolition of SOCA, see s 15(3), Sch 8, Pt 1 thereto).

Para (2): sub-para (b) revoked by SI 2006/594, art 2, Schedule, para 30(1), (3).

PART 5
EXCLUSIONS

[2.571]

18 Government training schemes etc

(1) These Regulations shall not have effect in relation to a fixed-term employee who is employed on a scheme, designed to provide him with training or work experience for the purpose of assisting him to seek or obtain work, which is either—

(a) provided to him under arrangements made by the Government, or

(b) funded in whole or part by an Institution of the [European Union].

(2) These Regulations shall not have effect in relation to a fixed-term employee whose employment consists in attending a period of work experience not exceeding one year that he is required to attend as part of a higher education course.

(3) For the purpose of paragraph (2) "a higher education course" means—

(a) in England and Wales, a course of a description referred to in Schedule 6 to the Education Reform Act 1988;

(b) in Scotland, a course of a description falling within section 38 of the Further and Higher Education (Scotland) Act 1992; and

(c) in Northern Ireland, a course of a description referred to in Schedule 1 to the Further Education (Northern Ireland) Order 1997.

NOTES

Para (1): words in square brackets substituted by the Treaty of Lisbon (Changes in Terminology) Order 2011, SI 2011/1043, art 4(1).

[2.572]

19 Agency workers

[(1) Save in respect of paragraph 1 of Part 1 of Schedule 2, these Regulations shall not have effect in relation to employment under a fixed-term contract where the employee is an agency worker.]

(2) In this regulation "agency worker" means any person who is supplied by an employment business to do work for another person under a contract or other arrangements made between the employment business and the other person.

(3) In this regulation "employment business" means the business (whether or not carried on with a view to profit and whether or not carried on in conjunction with any other business) of supplying persons in the employment of the person carrying on the business, to act for, and under the control of, other persons in any capacity.

NOTES

Para (1): substituted by the Fixed-term Employees (Prevention of Less Favourable Treatment) (Amendment) Regulations 2008, SI 2008/2776, reg 2.

[2.573]

20 Apprentices

These Regulations shall not have effect in relation to employment under a fixed-term contract where the contract is a contract of apprenticeship [[,] an apprenticeship agreement (within the meaning of section 32 of the Apprenticeships, Skills, Children and Learning Act 2009) [or approved English apprenticeship agreement (within the meaning of section A1(3) of the Apprenticeships, Skills, Children and Learning Act 2009)]].

NOTES

Words in first (outer) pair of square brackets added by the Apprenticeships, Skills, Children and Learning Act 2009 (Consequential Amendments to Subordinate Legislation) (England and Wales) Order 2012, SI 2012/3112, art 3; comma in second (inner) pair of square brackets substituted, and words in third (inner) pair of square brackets inserted, by the Deregulation Act 2015 (Consequential Amendments) Order 2015, SI 2015/971, art 2, Sch 1, para 1, as from 26 May 2015.

SCHEDULES

SCHEDULE 1
WORKFORCE AGREEMENTS

Regulations 1 and 8

[2.574]

1. An agreement is a workforce agreement for the purposes of these Regulations if the following conditions are satisfied—

(a) the agreement is in writing;
(b) it has effect for a specified period not exceeding five years;
(c) it applies either—
  (i) to all of the relevant members of the workforce, or
  (ii) to all of the relevant members of the workforce who belong to a particular group;
(d) the agreement is signed—
  (i) in the case of an agreement of the kind referred to in sub-paragraph (c)(i), by the representatives of the workforce, and in the case of an agreement of the kind referred to in sub-paragraph (c)(ii) by the representatives of the group to which the agreement applies (excluding, in either case, any representative not a relevant member of the workforce on the date on which the agreement was first made available for signature), or
  (ii) if the employer employed 20 or fewer employees on the date referred to in sub-paragraph (d)(i), either by the appropriate representatives in accordance with that sub-paragraph or by the majority of the employees employed by him;
(e) before the agreement was made available for signature, the employer provided all the employees to whom it was intended to apply on the date on which it came into effect with copies of the text of the agreement and such guidance as those employees might reasonably require in order to understand it fully.

2. For the purposes of this Schedule—

"a particular group" is a group of the relevant members of a workforce who undertake a particular function, work at a particular workplace or belong to a particular department or unit within their employer's business;

"relevant members of the workforce" are all of the employees employed by a particular employer, excluding any employee whose terms and conditions of employment are provided for, wholly or in part, in a collective agreement;

"representatives of the workforce" are employees duly elected to represent the relevant members of the workforce, "representatives of the group" are employees duly elected to represent the members of a particular group, and representatives are "duly elected" if the election at which they were elected satisfied the requirements of paragraph 3 of this Schedule.

3. The requirements concerning elections referred to in paragraph 2 are that—

(a) the number of representatives to be elected is determined by the employer;
(b) the candidates for election as representatives of the workforce are relevant members of the workforce, and the candidates for election as representatives of a group are members of that group;
(c) no employee who is eligible to be a candidate is unreasonably excluded from standing for election;
(d) all the relevant members of the workforce are entitled to vote for representatives of the workforce, and all the members of a particular group are entitled to vote for representatives of the group;
(e) the employees entitled to vote may vote for as many candidates as there are representatives to be elected;
(f) the election is conducted so as to secure that—
  (i) so far as is reasonably practicable, those voting do so in secret, and
  (ii) the votes given at the election are fairly and accurately counted.

SCHEDULE 2

Regulation 11

(Sch 2, Pt 1 amends the Social Security Contributions and Benefits Act 1992, Sch 11 at **[1.262]***, the Employment Tribunals Act 1996, ss 18, 21 at* **[1.757]**, **[1.764]***, the Employment Rights Act 1996, ss 29, 65, 86, 92, 95, 97, 105, 108, 136, 145, 199, 203, 235 at* **[1.813]** *et seq, amended s 109 of that Act (repealed) and repeals s 197 of that Act.)*

PART 2
TRANSITIONAL PROVISIONS

[2.575]

4. Paragraph 1 of this Schedule applies where the relevant date (as defined in paragraph 3 of Schedule 11 to the Social Security Contributions and Benefits Act 1992) falls on or after 1st October 2002.

5. (1) This paragraph applies to the dismissal of an employee employed under a contract for a fixed term of two years or more which consists of the expiry of the term without its being renewed, where the employee has agreed in accordance with section 197 of the 1996 Act to exclude any right to a redundancy payment in that event.

(2) The repeal of sections 197, 199(6) and 203(2)(d) of the 1996 Act provided for by paragraph 3(k) of this Schedule shall have effect in relation to a dismissal to which this paragraph applies where the relevant date (within the meaning of section 145 of the 1996 Act) falls on or after 1st October 2002, unless both the following conditions are satisfied—

(a) that, where there has been no renewal of the contract, the contract was entered into before 1st October 2002 or, where there have been one or more renewals, the only or most recent renewal was agreed before that date, and

(b) that the agreement to exclude any right to a redundancy payment was entered into and took effect before 1st October 2002.

PATERNITY AND ADOPTION LEAVE REGULATIONS 2002

(SI 2002/2788)

NOTES

Made: 11 November 2002.

Authority: Employment Rights Act 1996, ss 47C(2), 75A(1)–(3), (6), (7), 75B(1), (2), (4), (8), 75C(1), (2), 75D(1), 80A(1), (2), (5), 80B(1), (2), (5), 80C(1), (6), 80D(1), 80E, 99(1).

Commencement: 8 December 2002; see reg 3 at **[2.578]** for detailed provision as to the application of particular regulations.

Adoption from overseas: as to the application of these Regulations, with certain modifications, to adoptions from overseas, see the Paternity and Adoption Leave (Adoption from Overseas) Regulations 2003, SI 2003/921.

Application to parental order parents: these Regulations, in so far as they apply to paternity leave (adoption) and statutory adoption leave, are applied to parental order parents with modifications, by the Paternity, Adoption and Shared Parental Leave (Parental Order Cases) Regulations 2014, SI 2014/3096; see **[2.1747]** et seq.

See *Harvey* J(8).

ARRANGEMENT OF REGULATIONS

PART 1
GENERAL

PART 2
PATERNITY LEAVE

PART 3
ADOPTION LEAVE

PART 4
PROVISIONS APPLICABLE IN RELATION TO BOTH PATERNITY AND ADOPTION LEAVE

PART 1
GENERAL

[2.576]

1 Citation and commencement

These Regulations may be cited as the Paternity and Adoption Leave Regulations 2002 and shall come into force on 8th December 2002.

[2.577]

2 Interpretation

(1) In these Regulations—

"the 1996 Act" means the Employment Rights Act 1996;

"additional adoption leave" means leave under section 75B of the 1996 Act;

"additional maternity leave" means leave under section 73 of the 1996 Act;

"adopter", in relation to a child, means a person who has been matched with the child for adoption, or, in a case where two people have been matched jointly, whichever of them has elected to be the child's adopter for the purposes of these Regulations;

"adoption agency" has the meaning given, in relation to England and Wales, by [section 2(1) of the Adoption and Children Act 2002] and, in relation to Scotland, by [section 119(1) of the Adoption and Children (Scotland) Act 2007];

"adoption leave" means ordinary or additional adoption leave;

"child" means a person who is, or when placed with an adopter for adoption was, under the age of 18;

"contract of employment" means a contract of service or apprenticeship, whether express or implied, and (if it is express) whether oral or in writing;

"employee" means an individual who has entered into or works under (or, where the employment has ceased, worked under) a contract of employment;

"employer" means the person by whom an employee is (or, where the employment has ceased, was) employed;

"expected week", in relation to the birth of a child, means the week, beginning with midnight between Saturday and Sunday, in which it is expected that the child will be born;

"ordinary adoption leave" means leave under section 75A of the 1996 Act;

"parental leave" means leave under regulation 13(1) of the Maternity and Parental Leave etc Regulations 1999;

"partner", in relation to a child's mother or adopter, means a person (whether of a different sex or the same sex) who lives with the mother or adopter and the child in an enduring family relationship but is not a relative of the mother or adopter of a kind specified in paragraph (2);

"paternity leave" means leave under regulation 4 or regulation 8 of these Regulations;

["placed for adoption" means—

(a) placed for adoption under the Adoption and Children Act 2002 or the Adoption and Children (Scotland) Act 2007; or

(b) placed in accordance with section 22C of the Children Act 1989 with a local authority foster parent who is also a prospective adopter;]

["prospective adopter" means a person who has been approved as suitable to adopt a child and has been notified of that decision in accordance with regulation 30B(4) of the Adoption Agencies Regulations 2005;]

["shared parental leave" means leave under section 75E or 75G of the 1996 Act;]

["statutory adoption leave" means ordinary adoption leave and additional adoption leave;

"statutory adoption leave period" means the period during which the adopter is on statutory adoption leave;]

"statutory leave" means leave provided for in Part 8 of the 1996 Act.

(2) The relatives of a child's mother or adopter referred to in the definition of "partner" in paragraph (1) are the mother's or adopter's parent, grandparent, sister, brother, aunt or uncle.

(3) References to relationships in paragraph (2)—

(a) are to relationships of the full blood or half blood or, in the case of an adopted person, such of those relationships as would exist but for the adoption, and

(b) include the relationship of a child with his adoptive, or former adoptive, parents,

but do not include any other adoptive relationships.

[(4) For the purposes of these Regulations—

(a) a person is matched with a child for adoption when an adoption agency decides that that person would be a suitable adoptive parent for the child either individually or jointly with another person;

(b) in a case where sub-paragraph (a) applies, a person is notified of having been matched with a child on the date on which the person receives notification of the agency's decision, under regulation 33(3)(a) of the Adoption Agencies Regulations 2005, regulation 28(3) of the Adoption Agencies (Wales) Regulations 2005, or regulation 8(5) of the Adoption Agencies (Scotland) Regulations 2009;

(c) a person is also matched with a child for adoption when a decision has been made in accordance with regulation 22A of the Care Planning, Placement and Case Review (England) Regulations 2010 and an adoption agency has identified that person with whom the child is to be placed in accordance with regulation 12B of the Adoption Agencies Regulations 2005;

(d) in a case where paragraph (c) applies, a person is notified of having been matched with a child on the date on which that person receives notification in accordance with regulation 12B(2)(a) of the Adoption Agencies Regulations 2005 of the decision to place for adoption the child with that person.

(4A) For the purposes of these Regulations, a person elects to be a child's adopter, in a case where the child is matched with him and another person jointly, if he and that person agree, at the time at which they are matched that he and not the other person will be the adopter.]

(5) A reference in any provision of these Regulations to a period of continuous employment is to a period computed in accordance with Chapter 1 of Part 14 of the 1996 Act, as if that provision were a provision of that Act.

(6) For the purposes of these Regulations, any two employers shall be treated as associated if—

(a) one is a company of which the other (directly or indirectly) has control; or

(b) both are companies of which a third person (directly or indirectly) has control;

and "associated employer" shall be construed accordingly.

NOTES

Para (1) is amended as follows:

In definition "adoption agency", words in first pair of square brackets substituted by the Paternity and Adoption Leave (Amendment) Regulations 2014, SI 2014/2112, regs 2, 3(a)(i), as from 1 December 2014; words in second pair of square brackets substituted by the Adoption and Children (Scotland) Act 2007 (Consequential Modifications) Order 2011, SI 2011/1740, art 2, Sch 1, Pt 2, para 30(1), (2)(a).

Definitions "placed for adoption" and "prospective adopter" inserted by the Paternity and Adoption Leave (Amendment) (No 2) Regulations 2014, SI 2014/3206, regs 2, 3, 4(1), (2), as from 5 April 2015, with effect in relation to children matched with a person who is notified of having been matched on or after that date.

Definition "shared parental leave" inserted by SI 2014/2112, regs 2, 3(a)(ii), as from 1 December 2014.

Definitions "statutory adoption leave" and "statutory adoption leave period" inserted by the Maternity and Parental Leave etc and the Paternity and Adoption Leave (Amendment) Regulations 2006, SI 2006/2014, regs 12, 13.

Paras (4), (4A): substituted, for the original para (4), by SI 2014/3206, regs 2, 3, 4(1), (3), as from 5 April 2015, with effect in relation to children matched with a person who is notified of having been matched on or after that date.

Adoption from overseas: as to the modification of this regulation in relation to adoptions from overseas, see the Paternity and Adoption Leave (Adoption from Overseas) Regulations 2003, SI 2003/921, reg 4.

Application to parental order parents: as to the modification of this regulation in relation to parental order parents, see the Paternity, Adoption and Shared Parental Leave (Parental Order Cases) Regulations 2014, SI 2014/3096, reg 6 at **[2.1752]**.

[2.578]

3 Application

(1) The provisions relating to paternity leave under regulation 4 below have effect only in relation to children—

(a) born on or after 6th April 2003, or

(b) whose expected week of birth begins on or after that date.

(2) The provisions relating to paternity leave under regulation 8 and adoption leave under regulation 15 below have effect only in relation to children—

(a) matched with a person who is notified of having been matched on or after 6th April 2003, or

(b) placed for adoption on or after that date.

(3) Regulation 28 (protection from detriment) has effect only in relation to an act or failure to act which takes place on or after 8th December 2002.

(4) For the purposes of paragraph (3)—

(a) where an act extends over a period, the reference to the date of the act is a reference to the last day of that period, and

(b) a failure to act is to be treated as done when it was decided on.

(5) For the purposes of paragraph (4), in the absence of evidence establishing the contrary an employer shall be taken to decide on a failure to act—

(a) when he does an act inconsistent with doing the failed act, or

(b) if he has done no such inconsistent act, when the period expires within which he might reasonably have been expected to do the failed act if it was to be done.

(6) Regulation 29 (unfair dismissal) has effect only in relation to dismissals where the effective date of termination (within the meaning of section 97 of the 1996 Act) falls on or after 8th December 2002.

NOTES

Adoption from overseas: as to the modification of this regulation in relation to adoptions from overseas, see the Paternity and Adoption Leave (Adoption from Overseas) Regulations 2003, SI 2003/921, reg 5.

Application to parental order parents: as to the modification of this regulation in relation to parental order parents, see the Paternity, Adoption and Shared Parental Leave (Parental Order Cases) Regulations 2014, SI 2014/3096, regs 7, 7A at **[2.1753]**, **[2.1754]**.

PART 2
PATERNITY LEAVE

[2.579]

4 Entitlement to paternity leave: birth

(1) [Subject to paragraph (1A), an] employee is entitled to be absent from work for the purpose of caring for a child or supporting the child's mother if he—

Part 2 Statutory Instruments

(a) satisfies the conditions specified in paragraph (2), and
(b) has complied with the notice requirements in regulation 6 and, where applicable, the evidential requirements in that regulation.

[(1A) An employee is not entitled to be absent from work under paragraph (1) if the employee has taken any shared parental leave in respect of the child.]

(2) The conditions referred to in paragraph (1) are that the employee—
(a) has been continuously employed for a period of not less than 26 weeks ending with the week immediately preceding the 14th week before the expected week of the child's birth;
(b) is either—
(i) the father of the child or;
(ii) married to[, the civil partner] or the partner of the child's mother, but not the child's father;
(c) has, or expects to have—
(i) if he is the child's father, responsibility for the upbringing of the child;
(ii) if he is the mother's husband[, civil partner] or partner but not the child's father, the main responsibility (apart from any responsibility of the mother) for the upbringing of the child.

(3) An employee shall be treated as having satisfied the condition in paragraph (2)(a) on the date of the child's birth notwithstanding the fact that he has not then been continuously employed for a period of not less than 26 weeks, where—
(a) the date on which the child is born is earlier than the 14th week before the week in which its birth is expected, and
(b) the employee would have been continuously employed for such a period if his employment had continued until that 14th week.

(4) An employee shall be treated as having satisfied the condition in paragraph (2)(b)(ii) if he would have satisfied it but for the fact that the child's mother has died.

(5) An employee shall be treated as having satisfied the condition in paragraph (2)(c) if he would have satisfied it but for the fact that the child was stillborn after 24 weeks of pregnancy or has died.

(6) An employee's entitlement to leave under this regulation shall not be affected by the birth, or expected birth, of more than one child as a result of the same pregnancy.

NOTES

Para (1): words in square brackets substituted by the Paternity and Adoption Leave (Amendment) Regulations 2014, SI 2014/2112, regs 2, 4(a), as from 1 December 2014.

Para (1A): inserted by SI 2014/2112, regs 2, 4(b), as from 1 December 2014.

Para (2): words in square brackets inserted by the Civil Partnership Act 2004 (Amendments to Subordinate Legislation) Order 2005, SI 2005/2114, art 2(17), Sch 17, para 1(1), (2).

Adoption from overseas: this regulation and regs 5–7 are disapplied in relation to adoptions from overseas, by the Paternity and Adoption Leave (Adoption from Overseas) Regulations 2003, SI 2003/921, reg 6.

Application to parental order parents: as to the modification of this regulation in relation to parental order parents, see the Paternity, Adoption and Shared Parental Leave (Parental Order Cases) Regulations 2014, SI 2014/3096, reg 8 at **[2.1755]**.

[2.580]

5 Options in respect of leave under regulation 4

(1) An employee may choose to take either one week's leave or two consecutive weeks' leave in respect of a child under regulation 4.

(2) The leave may only be taken during the period which begins with the date on which the child is born and ends—
(a) except in the case referred to in sub-paragraph (b), 56 days after that date;
(b) in a case where the child is born before the first day of the expected week of its birth, 56 days after that day.

(3) Subject to paragraph (2) and, where applicable, paragraph (4), an employee may choose to begin his period of leave on—
(a) the date on which the child is born;
(b) the date falling such number of days after the date on which the child is born as the employee may specify in a notice under regulation 6, or
(c) a predetermined date, specified in a notice under that regulation, which is later than the first day of the expected week of the child's birth.

(4) In a case where the leave is in respect of a child whose expected week of birth begins before 6th April 2003, an employee may choose to begin a period of leave only on a predetermined date, specified in a notice under regulation 6, which is at least 28 days after the date on which that notice is given.

NOTES

Adoption from overseas: disapplied as noted to reg 4 at **[2.579]**.

[2.581]

6 Notice and evidential requirements for leave under regulation 4

(1) An employee must give his employer notice of his intention to take leave in respect of a child under regulation 4, specifying—
(a) the expected week of the child's birth;
(b) the length of the period of leave that, in accordance with regulation 5(1), the employee has chosen to take, and

(c) the date on which, in accordance with regulation 5(3) or (4), the employee has chosen that his period of leave should begin.

(2) The notice provided for in paragraph (1) must be given to the employer—

(a) in or before the 15th week before the expected week of the child's birth, or

(b) in a case where it was not reasonably practicable for the employee to give the notice in accordance with sub-paragraph (a), as soon as is reasonably practicable.

(3) Where the employer requests it, an employee must also give his employer a declaration, signed by the employee, to the effect that the purpose of his absence from work will be that specified in regulation 4(1) and that he satisfies the conditions of entitlement in regulation 4(2)(b) and (c).

(4) An employee who has given notice under paragraph (1) may vary the date he has chosen as the date on which his period of leave will begin, subject to paragraph (5) and provided that he gives his employer notice of the variation—

(a) where the variation is to provide for the employee's period of leave to begin on the date on which the child is born, at least 28 days before the first day of the expected week of the child's birth;

(b) where the variation is to provide for the employee's period of leave to begin on a date that is a specified number of days (or a different specified number of days) after the date on which the child is born, at least 28 days before the date falling that number of days after the first day of the expected week of the child's birth;

(c) where the variation is to provide for the employee's period of leave to begin on a predetermined date (or a different predetermined date), at least 28 days before that date,

or, if it is not reasonably practicable to give the notice at least 28 days before whichever day or date is relevant, as soon as is reasonably practicable.

(5) In a case where regulation 5(4) applies, an employee may only vary the date which he has chosen as the date on which his period of leave will begin by substituting a different predetermined date.

(6) In a case where—

(a) the employee has chosen to begin his period of leave on a particular predetermined date, and

(b) the child is not born on or before that date,

the employee must vary his choice of date, by substituting a later predetermined date or (except in a case where regulation 5(4) applies) exercising an alternative option under regulation 5(3), and give his employer notice of the variation as soon as is reasonably practicable.

(7) An employee must give his employer a further notice, as soon as is reasonably practicable after the child's birth, of the date on which the child was born.

(8) Notice under paragraph (1), (4), (6) or (7) shall be given in writing, if the employer so requests.

NOTES

Adoption from overseas: disapplied as noted to reg 4 at **[2.579]**.

[2.582]

7 Commencement of leave under regulation 4

(1) Except in the case referred to in paragraph (2), an employee's period of paternity leave under regulation 4 begins on the date specified in his notice under regulation 6(1), or, where he has varied his choice of date under regulation 6(4) or (6), on the date specified in his notice under that provision (or the last such notice if he has varied his choice more than once).

(2) In a case where—

(a) the employee has chosen to begin his period of leave on the date on which the child is born, and

(b) he is at work on that date,

the employee's period of leave begins on the day after that date.

NOTES

Adoption from overseas: disapplied as noted to reg 4 at **[2.579]**.

[2.583]

8 Entitlement to paternity leave: adoption

(1) [Subject to paragraph (1A), an] employee is entitled to be absent from work for the purpose of caring for a child or supporting the child's adopter if he—

(a) satisfies the conditions specified in paragraph (2), and

(b) has complied with the notice requirements in regulation 10 and, where applicable, the evidential requirements in that regulation.

[(1A) An employee is not entitled to be absent from work under paragraph (1) if the employee—

(a) has taken any shared parental leave in respect of the child; . . .

(b) has exercised a right to take time off under section 57ZJ of the 1996 Act in respect of the child[; or

(c) has already taken paternity leave in relation to the child as a result of the child being placed with a prospective adopter who is at the time of the placement the employee's spouse, civil partner or partner.]]

(2) The conditions referred to in paragraph (1) are that the employee—

(a) has been continuously employed for a period of not less than 26 weeks ending with the week in which the child's adopter is notified of having been matched with the child;

(b) is either married to[, the civil partner] or the partner of the child's adopter, and

(c) has, or expects to have, the main responsibility (apart from the responsibility of the adopter) for the upbringing of the child.

(3) In paragraph (2)(a), "week" means the period of seven days beginning with Sunday.

(4) An employee shall be treated as having satisfied the condition in paragraph (2)(b) if he would have satisfied it but for the fact that the child's adopter died during the child's placement.

(5) An employee shall be treated as having satisfied the condition in paragraph (2)(c) if he would have satisfied it but for the fact that the child's placement with the adopter has ended.

(6) An employee's entitlement to leave under this regulation shall not be affected by the placement for adoption of more than one child as part of the same arrangement.

NOTES

Para (1): words in square brackets substituted by the Paternity and Adoption Leave (Amendment) Regulations 2014, SI 2014/2112, regs 2, 5(a), as from 1 December 2014.

Para (1A): inserted by SI 2014/2112, regs 2, 5(b), as from 1 December 2014 (in so far as relates to para (1A)(a)) and as from 5 April 2015 (in so far as relates to para (1A)(b)); word omitted from sub-para (a) revoked and sub-para (c) inserted together with word immediately preceding it, by the Paternity and Adoption Leave (Amendment) (No 2) Regulations 2014, SI 2014/3206, regs 2, 3, 5, as from 5 April 2015, with effect in relation to children matched with a person who is notified of having been matched on or after that date.

Para (2): words in square brackets in sub-para (b) inserted by the Civil Partnership Act 2004 (Amendments to Subordinate Legislation) Order 2005, SI 2005/2114, art 2(17), Sch 17, para 1(1), (3).

Adoption from overseas: as to the substitution of this regulation in relation to adoptions from overseas, see the Paternity and Adoption Leave (Adoption from Overseas) Regulations 2003, SI 2003/921, reg 7.

Application to parental order parents: as to the modification of this regulation in relation to parental order parents, see the Paternity, Adoption and Shared Parental Leave (Parental Order Cases) Regulations 2014, SI 2014/3096, reg 9 at **[2.1756]**.

[2.584]

9 Options in respect of leave under regulation 8

(1) An employee may choose to take either one week's leave or two consecutive weeks' leave in respect of a child under regulation 8.

(2) The leave may only be taken during the period of 56 days beginning with the date on which the child is placed with the adopter.

(3) Subject to paragraph (2) and, where applicable, paragraph (4), an employee may choose to begin a period of leave under regulation 8 on—

(a) the date on which the child is placed with the adopter;

(b) the date falling such number of days after the date on which the child is placed with the adopter as the employee may specify in a notice under regulation 10, or

(c) a predetermined date, specified in a notice under that regulation, which is later than the date on which the child is expected to be placed with the adopter.

(4) In a case where the adopter was notified of having been matched with the child before 6th April 2003, the employee may choose to begin a period of leave only on a predetermined date, specified in a notice under regulation 10, which is at least 28 days after the date on which that notice is given.

NOTES

Adoption from overseas: as to the substitution of this regulation in relation to adoptions from overseas, see the Paternity and Adoption Leave (Adoption from Overseas) Regulations 2003, SI 2003/921, reg 7.

Application to parental order parents: as to the modification of this regulation in relation to parental order parents, see the Paternity, Adoption and Shared Parental Leave (Parental Order Cases) Regulations 2014, SI 2014/3096, reg 10 at **[2.1757]**.

[2.585]

10 Notice and evidential requirements for leave under regulation 8

(1) An employee must give his employer notice of his intention to take leave in respect of a child under regulation 8, specifying—

(a) the date on which the adopter was notified of having been matched with the child;

(b) the date on which the child is expected to be placed with the adopter;

(c) the length of the period of leave that, in accordance with regulation 9(1), the employee has chosen to take, and

(d) the date on which, in accordance with regulation 9(3) or (4), the employee has chosen that his period of leave should begin.

(2) The notice provided for in paragraph (1) must be given to the employer—

(a) no more than seven days after the date on which the adopter is notified of having been matched with the child, or

(b) in a case where it was not reasonably practicable for the employee to give notice in accordance with sub-paragraph (a), as soon as is reasonably practicable.

(3) Where the employer requests it, an employee must also give his employer a declaration, signed by the employee, to the effect that the purpose of his absence from work will be that specified in regulation 8(1) and that he satisfies the conditions of entitlement in regulation 8(2)(b) and (c).

(4) An employee who has given notice under paragraph (1) may vary the date he has chosen as the date on which his period of leave will begin, subject to paragraph (5) and provided that he gives his employer notice of the variation—

(a) where the variation is to provide for the employee's period of leave to begin on the date on which the child is placed with the adopter, at least 28 days before the date specified in the employee's notice under paragraph (1) as the date on which the child is expected to be placed with the adopter;

(b) where the variation is to provide for the employee's period of leave to begin on a date that is a specified number of days (or a different specified number of days) after the date on which the child is placed with the adopter, at least 28 days before the date falling that number of days after the date specified in the employee's notice under paragraph (1) as the date on which the child is expected to be placed with the adopter;

(c) where the variation is to provide for the employee's period of leave to begin on a predetermined date, at least 28 days before that date,

or, if it is not reasonably practicable to give the notice at least 28 days before whichever date is relevant, as soon as is reasonably practicable.

(5) In a case where regulation 9(4) applies, an employee may only vary the date which he has chosen as the date on which his period of leave will begin by substituting a different predetermined date.

(6) In a case where—

(a) the employee has chosen to begin his period of leave on a particular predetermined date, and

(b) the child is not placed with the adopter on or before that date,

the employee must vary his choice of date, by substituting a later predetermined date or (except in a case where regulation 9(4) applies) exercising an alternative option under regulation 9(3), and give his employer notice of the variation as soon as is reasonably practicable.

(7) An employee must give his employer a further notice, as soon as is reasonably practicable after the child's placement, of the date on which the child was placed.

(8) Notice under paragraph (1), (4), (6) or (7) shall be given in writing, if the employer so requests.

NOTES

Adoption from overseas: as to the substitution of this regulation in relation to adoptions from overseas, see the Paternity and Adoption Leave (Adoption from Overseas) Regulations 2003, SI 2003/921, reg 7.

Application to parental order parents: as to the modification of this regulation in relation to parental order parents, see the Paternity, Adoption and Shared Parental Leave (Parental Order Cases) Regulations 2014, SI 2014/3096, reg 11 at **[2.1758]**.

[2.586]

11 Commencement of leave under regulation 8

(1) Except in the case referred to in paragraph (2), an employee's period of paternity leave under regulation 8 begins on the date specified in his notice under regulation 10(1), or, where he has varied his choice of date under regulation 10(4) or (6), on the date specified in his notice under that provision (or the last such date if he has varied his choice more than once).

(2) In a case where—

(a) the employee has chosen to begin his period of leave on the date on which the child is placed with the adopter, and

(b) he is at work on that date,

the employee's period of leave begins on the day after that date.

NOTES

Adoption from overseas: as to the modification of this regulation in relation to adoptions from overseas, see the Paternity and Adoption Leave (Adoption from Overseas) Regulations 2003, SI 2003/921, reg 8.

Application to parental order parents: as to the modification of this regulation in relation to parental order parents, see the Paternity, Adoption and Shared Parental Leave (Parental Order Cases) Regulations 2014, SI 2014/3096, reg 12 at **[2.1759]**.

[2.587]

12 Application of terms and conditions during paternity leave

(1) An employee who takes paternity leave—

(a) is entitled, during the period of leave, to the benefit of all of the terms and conditions of employment which would have applied if he had not been absent, and

(b) is bound, during that period, by any obligations arising under those terms and conditions, subject only to the exception in section 80C(1)(b) of the 1996 Act.

(2) In paragraph (1)(a), "terms and conditions of employment" has the meaning given by section 80C(5) of the 1996 Act, and accordingly does not include terms and conditions about remuneration.

(3) For the purposes of section 80C of the 1996 Act, only sums payable to an employee by way of wages or salary are to be treated as remuneration.

[2.588]

13 Right to return after paternity leave

(1) An employee who returns to work after a period of paternity leave which was—

(a) an isolated period of leave, or

[(b) the last of two or more consecutive periods of statutory leave which did not include any—

(i) period of parental leave of more than four weeks; or

(ii) period of statutory leave which when added to any other periods of statutory leave (excluding parental leave) taken in relation to the same child means that the total amount of statutory leave taken in relation to that child totals more than 26 weeks,] is entitled to return from leave to the job in which he was employed before his absence.

(2) An employee who returns to work after a period of paternity leave not falling within the description in paragraph (1)(a) or (b) above is entitled to return from leave to the job in which he was employed before his absence, or, if it is not reasonably practicable for the employer to permit him to return to that job, to another job which is both suitable for him and appropriate for him to do in the circumstances.

(3) The reference in paragraphs (1) and (2) to the job in which an employee was employed before his absence is a reference to the job in which he was employed—

(a) if his return is from an isolated period of paternity leave, immediately before that period began;

(b) if his return is from consecutive periods of statutory leave, immediately before the first such period.

NOTES

Para (1): sub-para (b) substituted by the Paternity and Adoption Leave (Amendment) Regulations 2014, SI 2014/2112, regs 2, 6, as from 1 December 2014.

[2.589]

14 Incidents of the right to return after paternity leave

(1) An employee's right to return under regulation 13 is a right to return—

(a) with his seniority, pension rights and similar rights—

(i) in a case where the employee is returning from consecutive periods of statutory leave which included a period of additional adoption leave or additional maternity leave, as they would have been if the period or periods of his employment prior to the additional adoption leave or (as the case may be) additional maternity leave were continuous with the period of employment following it;

(ii) in any other case, as they would have been if he had not been absent, and

(b) on terms and conditions not less favourable than those which would have applied if he had not been absent.

(2) The provision in paragraph (1)(a)(i) concerning the treatment of periods of additional maternity leave or additional adoption leave is subject to the requirements of [paragraphs 5, 5B and 6 of Schedule 5 to the Social Security Act 1989 (equal treatment under pension schemes: maternity absence, adoption leave and family leave)].

(3) The provisions in paragraph (1)(a)(ii) and (b) for an employee to be treated as if he had not been absent refer to his absence—

(a) if his return is from an isolated period of paternity leave, since the beginning of that period;

(b) if his return is from consecutive periods of statutory leave, since the beginning of the first such period.

NOTES

Para (2): words in square brackets substituted by the Pensions Act 2004 (Commencement No 2, Transitional Provisions and Consequential Amendments) Order 2005, SI 2005/275, art 5.

PART 3
ADOPTION LEAVE

[2.590]

15 Entitlement to ordinary adoption leave

(1) [Subject to paragraph (1A), an] employee is entitled to ordinary adoption leave in respect of a child if he—

(a) satisfies the conditions specified in paragraph (2), and

(b) has complied with the notice requirements in regulation 17 and, where applicable, the evidential requirements in that regulation.

[(1A) An employee is not entitled to be absent from work under paragraph (1) in relation to a child if the employee has already taken ordinary adoption leave as a result of that child being placed, or expected to be placed, with the employee under section 22C of the Children Act 1989.]

(2) The conditions referred to in paragraph (1) are that the employee—

(a) is the child's adopter; [and]

(b) . . .

(c) has notified the agency that he agrees that the child should be placed with him and on the date of placement.

(3) . . .

(4) An employee's entitlement to leave under this regulation shall not be affected by the placement for adoption of more than one child as part of the same arrangement.

NOTES

Para (1): words in square brackets substituted by the Paternity and Adoption Leave (Amendment) (No 2) Regulations 2014, SI 2014/3206, regs 2, 3, 6(1), (2), as from 5 April 2015, with effect in relation to children matched with a person who is notified of having been matched on or after that date.

Para (1A): inserted by SI 2014/3206, regs 2, 3, 6(1), (3), as from 5 April 2015, with effect in relation to children matched with a person who is notified of having been matched on or after that date.

Para (2): word in square brackets in sub-para (a) inserted and sub-para (b) revoked, by the Paternity and Adoption Leave (Amendment) Regulations 2014, SI 2014/2112, regs 2, 7(a), (b), as from 5 April 2015.

Para (3): revoked by SI 2014/2112, regs 2, 7(c), as from 5 April 2015.

Adoption from overseas: as to the substitution of this regulation in relation to adoptions from overseas, see the Paternity and Adoption Leave (Adoption from Overseas) Regulations 2003, SI 2003/921, reg 9.

Application to parental order parents: as to the modification of this regulation in relation to parental order parents, see the Paternity, Adoption and Shared Parental Leave (Parental Order Cases) Regulations 2014, SI 2014/3096, regs 13, 13A at **[2.1760]**, **[2.1761]**.

[2.591]

16 Options in respect of ordinary adoption leave

(1) Except in the case referred to in paragraph (2), an employee may choose to begin a period of ordinary adoption leave on—

(a) the date on which the child is placed with him for adoption, or

(b) a predetermined date, specified in a notice under regulation 17, which is no more than 14 days before the date on which the child is expected to be placed with the employee and no later than that date.

(2) In a case where the employee was notified of having been matched with the child before 6th April 2003, the employee may choose to begin a period of leave only on a predetermined date, specified in a notice under regulation 17, which is after 6th April 2003 and at least 28 days after the date on which that notice is given.

NOTES

Adoption from overseas: as to the substitution of this regulation in relation to adoptions from overseas, see the Paternity and Adoption Leave (Adoption from Overseas) Regulations 2003, SI 2003/921, reg 9.

Application to parental order parents: as to the modification of this regulation in relation to parental order parents, see the Paternity, Adoption and Shared Parental Leave (Parental Order Cases) Regulations 2014, SI 2014/3096, reg 14 at **[2.1762]**.

[2.592]

17 Notice and evidential requirements for ordinary adoption leave

(1) An employee must give his employer notice of his intention to take ordinary adoption leave in respect of a child, specifying—

(a) the date on which the child is expected to be placed with him for adoption, and

(b) the date on which, in accordance with regulation 16(1) or (2), the employee has chosen that his period of leave should begin.

(2) The notice provided for in paragraph (1) must be given to the employer—

(a) no more than seven days after the date on which the employee is notified of having been matched with the child for the purposes of adoption, or

(b) in a case where it was not reasonably practicable for the employee to give notice in accordance with sub-paragraph (a), as soon as is reasonably practicable.

(3) Where the employer requests it, an employee must also provide his employer with evidence, in the form of one or more documents issued by the adoption agency that matched the employee with the child, of—

(a) the name and address of the agency;

(b) . . .

(c) the date on which the employee was notified that he had been matched with the child, and

(d) the date on which the agency expects to place the child with the employee.

(4) An employee who has given notice under paragraph (1) may vary the date he has chosen as the date on which his period of leave will begin, subject to paragraph (5) and provided that he gives his employer notice of the variation—

(a) where the variation is to provide for the employee's period of leave to begin on the date on which the child is placed with him for adoption, at least 28 days before the date specified in his notice under paragraph (1) as the date on which the child is expected to be placed with him;

(b) where the variation is to provide for the employee's period of leave to begin on a predetermined date (or a different predetermined date), at least 28 days before that date,

or, if it is not reasonably practicable to give the notice 28 days before whichever date is relevant, as soon as is reasonably practicable.

(5) In a case where regulation 16(2) applies, an employee may only vary the date which he has chosen as the date on which his period of leave will begin by substituting a different predetermined date.

(6) Notice under paragraph (1) or (4) shall be given in writing, if the employer so requests.

(7) An employer who is given notice under paragraph (1) or (4) of the date on which an employee has chosen that his period of ordinary adoption leave should begin shall notify the employee, within 28 days of his receipt of the notice, of the date on which the period of additional adoption leave to which the employee will be entitled (if he satisfies the conditions in regulation 20(1)) after his period of ordinary adoption leave ends.

(8) The notification provided for in paragraph (7) shall be given to the employee—

(a) where the employer is given notice under paragraph (1), within 28 days of the date on which he received that notice;

(b) where the employer is given notice under paragraph (4), within 28 days of the date on which the employee's ordinary adoption leave period began.

NOTES

Para (3): sub-para (b) revoked by the Paternity and Adoption Leave (Amendment) Regulations 2004, SI 2004/923, regs 2, 3.

Adoption from overseas: as to the substitution of this regulation in relation to adoptions from overseas, see the Paternity and Adoption Leave (Adoption from Overseas) Regulations 2003, SI 2003/921, reg 9.

Application to parental order parents: as to the modification of this regulation in relation to parental order parents, see the Paternity, Adoption and Shared Parental Leave (Parental Order Cases) Regulations 2014, SI 2014/3096, reg 14 at **[2.1762]**.

[2.593]

18 Duration and commencement of ordinary adoption leave

(1) Subject to regulations 22 and 24, an employee's ordinary adoption leave period is a period of 26 weeks.

(2) Except in the case referred to in paragraph (3), an employee's ordinary adoption leave period begins on the date specified in his notice under regulation 17(1), or, where he has varied his choice of date under regulation 17(4), on the date specified in his notice under that provision (or the last such date if he has varied his choice more than once).

(3) In a case where—

(a) the employee has chosen to begin his period of leave on the date on which the child is placed with him, and

(b) he is at work on that date,

the employee's period of leave begins on the day after that date.

NOTES

Adoption from overseas: as to the modification of this regulation in relation to adoptions from overseas, see the Paternity and Adoption Leave (Adoption from Overseas) Regulations 2003, SI 2003/921, reg 10.

Application to parental order parents: as to the modification of this regulation in relation to parental order parents, see the Paternity, Adoption and Shared Parental Leave (Parental Order Cases) Regulations 2014, SI 2014/3096, reg 15 at **[2.1763]**.

[2.594]

19 Application of terms and conditions during ordinary adoption leave [and additional adoption leave]

(1) An employee who takes ordinary adoption leave [or additional adoption leave]—

(a) is entitled, during the period of leave, to the benefit of all of the terms and conditions of employment which would have applied if he had not been absent, and

(b) is bound, during that period, by any obligations arising under those terms and conditions, subject only to [the exceptions in sections 75A(3)(b) and 75B(4)(b)] of the 1996 Act.

(2) In paragraph (1)(a), "terms and conditions of employment" has the meaning given by [sections 75A(4) and 75B(5)] of the 1996 Act, and accordingly does not include terms and conditions about remuneration.

(3) For the purposes of [sections 75A and 75B] of the 1996 Act, only sums payable to an employee by way of wages or salary are to be treated as remuneration.

NOTES

The words in square brackets in the Regulation heading and the words in first pair of square brackets in para (1) were inserted, and the other words in square brackets in this regulation were substituted, by the Maternity and Parental Leave etc and the Paternity and Adoption Leave (Amendment) Regulations 2008, SI 2008/1966, regs 8, 9(1).

[2.595]

20 Additional adoption leave: entitlement, duration and commencement

(1) An employee is entitled to additional adoption leave in respect of a child if—

(a) the child was placed with him for adoption,

(b) he took ordinary adoption leave in respect of the child, and

(c) his ordinary adoption leave period did not end prematurely under regulation 22(2)(a) or 24.

(2) Subject to regulations 22 and 24, an employee's additional adoption leave period is a period of 26 weeks beginning on the day after the last day of his ordinary adoption leave period.

NOTES

Adoption from overseas: as to the modification of this regulation in relation to adoptions from overseas, see the Paternity and Adoption Leave (Adoption from Overseas) Regulations 2003, SI 2003/921, reg 11.

Application to parental order parents: as to the modification of this regulation in relation to parental order parents, see the Paternity, Adoption and Shared Parental Leave (Parental Order Cases) Regulations 2014, SI 2014/3096, regs 16, 16A at **[2.1764]**, **[2.1765]**.

21 *(Revoked by the Maternity and Parental Leave etc and the Paternity and Adoption Leave (Amendment) Regulations 2008, SI 2008/1966, regs 8, 9(1).)*

[2.596]

[21A Work during adoption leave period

(1) An employee may carry out up to 10 days' work for his employer during his statutory adoption leave period without bringing his statutory adoption leave to an end.

(2) For the purposes of this regulation, any work carried out on any day shall constitute a day's work.

(3) Subject to paragraph (4), for the purposes of this regulation, work means any work done under the contract of employment and may include training or any activity undertaken for the purposes of keeping in touch with the workplace.

(4) Reasonable contact from time to time between an employee and his employer which either party is entitled to make during an adoption leave period (for example to discuss an employee's return to work) shall not bring that period to an end.

(5) This regulation does not confer any right on an employer to require that any work be carried out during the statutory adoption leave period, nor any right on an employee to work during the statutory adoption leave period.

(6) Any days' work carried out under this regulation shall not have the effect of extending the total duration of the statutory adoption leave period.]

NOTES

Inserted by the Maternity and Parental Leave etc and the Paternity and Adoption Leave (Amendment) Regulations 2006, SI 2006/2014, regs 12, 14.

[2.597]

22 Disrupted placement in the course of adoption leave

(1) This regulation applies where—

(a) an employee has begun a period of adoption leave in respect of a child before the placement of the child with him, and the employee is subsequently notified that the placement will not be made, or

(b) during an employee's period of adoption leave in respect of a child placed with him—

(i) the child dies, or

[(ii) the child is returned after being placed for adoption.]

(2) Subject to regulation 24, in a case where this regulation applies—

(a) except in the circumstances referred to in sub-paragraphs (b) and (c), the employee's adoption leave period ends eight weeks after the end of the relevant week specified in paragraph (3);

(b) where the employee is taking ordinary adoption leave and the period of 26 weeks provided for in regulation 18 ends within eight weeks of the end of the relevant week—

(i) the employee's ordinary adoption leave period ends on the expiry of the 26-week period;

(ii) the employee is entitled to additional adoption leave, and

(iii) the employee's additional adoption leave period ends eight weeks after the end of the relevant week;

(c) where the employee is taking additional adoption leave and the period of 26 weeks provided for in regulation 20 ends within eight weeks of the end of the relevant week, the employee's additional adoption leave period ends on the expiry of the 26-week period.

(3) The relevant week referred to in paragraph (2) is—

(a) in a case falling within paragraph (1)(a), the week during which the person with whom the child was to be placed for adoption is notified that the placement will not be made;

(b) in a case falling within paragraph (1)(b)(i), the week during which the child dies;

(c) in a case falling within paragraph (1)(b)(ii), the week during which the child is returned.

[(3A) In paragraph (1) "returned after being placed for adoption" means—

(a) returned under sections 31 to 35 of the Adoption and Children Act 2002;

(b) in Scotland, returned to the adoption agency, adoption society or nominated person in accordance with section 25(6) of the Adoption and Children (Scotland) Act 2007; or

(c) where the child is placed in accordance with section 22C of the Children Act 1989, returned to the adoption agency following a termination of the placement.]

(4) In paragraph (3), "week" means the period of seven days beginning with Sunday.

NOTES

Para (1): sub-para (b)(ii) substituted by the Paternity and Adoption Leave (Amendment) (No 2) Regulations 2014, SI 2014/3206, regs 2, 3, 7(1), (2), as from 5 April 2015, with effect in relation to children matched with a person who is notified of having been matched on or after that date.

Para (3A): inserted by SI 2014/3206, regs 2, 3, 7(1), (3), as from 5 April 2015, with effect in relation to children matched with a person who is notified of having been matched on or after that date.

Adoption from overseas: as to the modification of this regulation in relation to adoptions from overseas, see the Paternity and Adoption Leave (Adoption from Overseas) Regulations 2003, SI 2003/921, reg 12.

Application to parental order parents: as to the modification of this regulation in relation to parental order parents, see the Paternity, Adoption and Shared Parental Leave (Parental Order Cases) Regulations 2014, SI 2014/3096, regs 17, 17A at **[2.1766]**, **[2.1767]**.

[2.598]

23 Redundancy during adoption leave

(1) This regulation applies where, during an employee's ordinary or additional adoption leave period, it is not practicable by reason of redundancy for his employer to continue to employ him under his existing contract of employment.

(2) Where there is a suitable available vacancy, the employee is entitled to be offered (before the end of his employment under his existing contract) alternative employment with his employer or his employer's successor, or an associated employer, under a new contract of employment which complies with paragraph (3) and takes effect immediately on the ending of his employment under the previous contract.

(3) The new contract of employment must be such that—

(a) the work to be done under it is of a kind which is both suitable in relation to the employee and appropriate for him to do in the circumstances, and

(b) its provisions as to the capacity and place in which he is to be employed, and as to the other terms and conditions of his employment, are not substantially less favourable to him than if he had continued to be employed under the previous contract.

[2.599]

24 Dismissal during adoption leave

Where an employee is dismissed after an ordinary or additional adoption leave period has begun but before the time when (apart from this regulation) that period would end, the period ends at the time of the dismissal.

[2.600]

25 Requirement to notify intention to return during adoption leave period

(1) An employee who intends to return to work earlier than the end of his additional adoption leave period must give his employer at least [8 weeks'] notice of the date on which he intends to return.

(2) If an employee attempts to return to work earlier than the end of his additional adoption leave period without complying with paragraph (1), his employer is entitled to postpone his return to a date such as will secure, subject to paragraph (3), that he has at least [8 weeks'] notice of the employee's return.

[(2A) An employee who complies with his obligations in paragraph (1) or whose employer has postponed his return in the circumstances described in paragraph (2), and who then decides to return to work—

(a) earlier than the original return date, must give his employer not less than 8 weeks' notice of the date on which he now intends to return;

(b) later than the original return date, must give his employer not less than 8 weeks' notice ending with the original return date.

(2B) In paragraph (2A) the "original return date" means the date which the employee notified to his employer as the date of his return to work under paragraph (1), or the date to which his return was postponed by his employer under paragraph (2).]

(3) An employer is not entitled under paragraph (2) to postpone an employee's return to work to a date after the end of the employee's additional adoption leave period.

(4) If an employee whose return has been postponed under paragraph (2) has been notified that he is not to return to work before the date to which his return was postponed, the employer is under no contractual obligation to pay him remuneration until the date to which his return was postponed if he returns to work before that date.

(5) This regulation does not apply in a case where the employer did not notify the employee in accordance with regulation 17(7) and (8) of the date on which the employee's additional adoption leave period would end.

(6) In a case where an employee's adoption leave is curtailed because regulation 22 applies, the references in this regulation to the end of an employee's additional adoption leave period are references to the date on which that period would have ended had that regulation not applied, irrespective of whether it was the employee's ordinary adoption leave period or his additional adoption leave period that was curtailed.

NOTES

Paras (1), (2): words in square brackets substituted by the Maternity and Parental Leave etc and the Paternity and Adoption Leave (Amendment) Regulations 2006, SI 2006/2014, regs 12, 15(a), (b).

Paras (2A), (2B): inserted by SI 2006/2014, regs 12, 15(c).

Modification: this regulation is modified in relation to an employee who is an 'employee shareholder', as if for "8 weeks' notice", in each place it occurs, there were substituted "16 weeks' notice"; see the Employment Rights Act 1996, s 205A(3) at **[1.1119]** (as inserted by the Growth and Infrastructure Act 2013, s 31(1)).

[2.601]

26 Right to return after adoption leave

(1) An employee who returns to work after a period of ordinary adoption leave which was—

(a) an isolated period of leave, or

[(b) the last of two or more consecutive periods of statutory leave which did not include any—

(i) period of parental leave of more than four weeks; or

(ii) period of statutory leave which when added to any other periods of statutory leave (excluding parental leave) taken in relation to the same child means that the total amount of statutory leave taken in relation to that child totals more than 26 weeks,]

is entitled to return from leave to the job in which he was employed before his absence.

(2) An employee who returns to work after—

(a) a period of additional adoption leave, whether or not preceded by another period of statutory leave, or

(b) a period of ordinary adoption leave not falling within the description in paragraph (1)(a) or (b) above,

is entitled to return from leave to the job in which he was employed before his absence, or, if it is not reasonably practicable for the employer to permit him to return to that job, to another job which is both suitable for him and appropriate for him to do in the circumstances.

(3) The reference in paragraphs (1) and (2) to the job in which an employee was employed before his absence is a reference to the job in which he was employed—

(a) if his return is from an isolated period of adoption leave, immediately before that period began;

(b) if his return is from consecutive periods of statutory leave, immediately before the first such period.

(4) This regulation does not apply where regulation 23 applies.

NOTES

Para (1): sub-para (b) substituted by the Paternity and Adoption Leave (Amendment) Regulations 2014, SI 2014/2112, regs 2, 9, as from 1 December 2014.

[2.602]

27 Incidents of the right to return from adoption leave

(1) An employee's right to return under regulation 26 is to return—

[(a) with his seniority, pension rights and similar rights as they would have been if he had not been absent, and]

(b) on terms and conditions . . . not less favourable than those which would have been applied to him if he had not been absent.

[(2) In the case of accrual of rights under an employment-related benefit scheme within the meaning given by Schedule 5 to the Social Security Act 1989, nothing in paragraph (1)(a) concerning the treatment of additional adoption leave shall be taken to impose a requirement which exceeds the requirements of paragraphs 5, 5B and 6 of that Schedule.]

(3) The provisions [in paragraph (1)] for an employee to be treated as if he had not been absent refer to his absence—

(a) if his return is from an isolated period of ordinary adoption leave, since the beginning of that period;

(b) if his return is from consecutive periods of statutory leave, since the beginning of the first such period.

NOTES

Para (1): sub-para (a) substituted by the Maternity and Parental Leave etc and the Paternity and Adoption Leave (Amendment) Regulations 2008, SI 2008/1966, regs 8, 10(a); words omitted from sub-para (b) revoked by the Paternity and Adoption Leave (Amendment) Regulations 2004, SI 2004/923, regs 2, 4.

Para (2): substituted by SI 2008/1966, regs 8, 10(b).

Para (3): words in square brackets substituted by SI 2008/1966, regs 8, 10(c).

PART 4
PROVISIONS APPLICABLE IN RELATION TO BOTH PATERNITY AND ADOPTION LEAVE

[2.603]

28 Protection from detriment

(1) An employee is entitled under section 47C of the 1996 Act not to be subjected to any detriment by any act, or any deliberate failure to act, by his employer because—

[(za) the employee took or sought to take time off under section 57ZE of the 1996 Act;

(zb) the employer believed that the employee was likely to take time off under section 57ZE of the 1996 Act;]

[(zc) the employee took or sought to take time off under section 57ZJ or 57ZL of the 1996 Act;

(zd) the employer believed that the employee was likely to take time off under section 57ZJ or 57ZL of the 1996 Act;]

(a) the employee took or sought to take paternity leave or ordinary or additional adoption leave;

(b) the employer believed that the employee was likely to take ordinary or additional adoption leave, . . .

[(bb) the employee undertook, considered undertaking or refused to undertake work in accordance with regulation 21A; or]

(c) the employee failed to return after a period of additional adoption leave in a case where—

(i) the employer did not notify him, in accordance with regulation 17(7) and (8) or otherwise, of the date on which that period ended, and he reasonably believed that the period had not ended, or

(ii) the employer gave him less than 28 days' notice of the date on which the period would end, and it was not reasonably practicable for him to return on that date.

(2) Paragraph (1) does not apply where the detriment in question amounts to dismissal within the meaning of Part 10 of the 1996 Act.

NOTES

Para (1): sub-paras (za), (zb) inserted by the Paternity and Adoption Leave (Amendment) Regulations 2014, SI 2014/2112, regs 2, 10, 14(1), as from 1 October 2014, in relation to an act or failure to act which takes place on or after that date; sub-paras (zc), (zd) inserted by SI 2014/2112, regs 2, 11, 14(2), as from 5 April 2015, in relation to an act or failure to act which takes place on or after that date; word omitted from sub-para (b) revoked, and sub-para (bb) inserted, by the Maternity and Parental Leave etc and the Paternity and Adoption Leave (Amendment) Regulations 2006, SI 2006/2014, regs 12, 16.

[2.604]
29 Unfair dismissal

(1) An employee who is dismissed is entitled under section 99 of the 1996 Act to be regarded for the purpose of Part 10 of that Act as unfairly dismissed if—

(a) the reason or principal reason for the dismissal is of a kind specified in paragraph (3), or
(b) the reason or principal reason for the dismissal is that the employee is redundant, and regulation 23 has not been complied with.

(2) An employee who is dismissed shall also be regarded for the purposes of Part 10 of the 1996 Act as unfairly dismissed if—

(a) the reason (or, if more than one, the principal reason) for the dismissal is that the employee was redundant;
(b) it is shown that the circumstances constituting the redundancy applied equally to one or more employees in the same undertaking who had positions similar to that held by the employee and who have not been dismissed by the employer, and
(c) it is shown that the reason (or, if more than one, the principal reason) for which the employee was selected for dismissal was a reason of a kind specified in paragraph (3).

(3) The kinds of reason referred to in paragraph (1) and (2) are reasons connected with the fact that—

[(za) the employee took or sought to take time off under section 57ZE of the 1996 Act;
(zb) the employer believed that the employee was likely to take time off under section 57ZE of the 1996 Act;]
[(zc) the employee took or sought to take time off under section 57ZJ or 57ZL of the 1996 Act;
(zd) the employer believed that the employee was likely to take time off under section 57ZJ or 57ZL of the 1996 Act;]
(a) the employee took, or sought to take, paternity or adoption leave;
(b) the employer believed that the employee was likely to take ordinary or additional adoption leave, . . .
[(bb) the employee undertook, considered undertaking or refused to undertake work in accordance with regulation 21A; or]
(c) the employee failed to return after a period of additional adoption leave in a case where—
 (i) the employer did not notify him, in accordance with regulation 17(7) and (8) or otherwise, of the date on which that period would end, and he reasonably believed that the period had not ended, or
 (ii) the employer gave him less than 28 days' notice of the date on which the period would end, and it was not reasonably practicable for him to return on that date.

(4) . . .

(5) Paragraph (1) does not apply in relation to an employee if—

(a) it is not reasonably practicable for a reason other than redundancy for the employer (who may be the same employer or a successor of his) to permit the employee to return to a job which is both suitable for the employee and appropriate for him to do in the circumstances;
(b) an associated employer offers the employee a job of that kind, and
(c) the employee accepts or unreasonably refuses that offer.

(6) Where, on a complaint of unfair dismissal, any question arises as to whether the operation of paragraph (1) is excluded by the provisions of paragraph . . . (5), it is for the employer to show that the provisions in question were satisfied in relation to the complainant.

NOTES

Para (3): sub-paras (za), (zb) inserted by the Paternity and Adoption Leave (Amendment) Regulations 2014, SI 2014/2112, regs 2, 12, 14(3), as from 1 October 2014, in relation to dismissals where the effective date of termination (within the meaning of the Employment Rights Act 1996, s 97) falls on or after that date; sub-paras (zc), (zd) inserted by SI 2014/2112, regs 2, 13, 14(4), as from 5 April 2015, in relation to dismissals where the effective date of termination (within the meaning of the Employment Rights Act 1996, s 97) falls on or after that date; word omitted from sub-para (b) revoked, and sub-para (bb) inserted, by the Maternity and Parental Leave etc and the Paternity and Adoption Leave (Amendment) Regulations 2006, SI 2006/2014, regs 12, 17(a).

Para (4): revoked by SI 2006/2014, regs 12, 17(b).

Para (6): words omitted revoked by SI 2006/2014, regs 12, 17(c).

[2.605]
30 Contractual rights to paternity or adoption leave

(1) This regulation applies where an employee is entitled to—

(a) paternity leave,
(b) ordinary adoption leave, or
(c) additional adoption leave,

(referred to in paragraph (2) as a "statutory right") and also to a right which corresponds to that right and which arises under the employee's contract of employment or otherwise.

(2) In a case where this regulation applies—

(a) the employee may not exercise the statutory right and the corresponding right separately but may, in taking the leave for which the two rights provide, take advantage of whichever right is, in any particular respect, the more favourable, and

(b) the provisions of the 1996 Act and of these Regulations relating to the statutory right apply, subject to any modifications necessary to give effect to any more favourable contractual terms, to the exercise of the composite right described in sub-paragraph (a) as they apply to the exercise of the statutory right.

[2.606]
31 Calculation of a week's pay

Where—

(a) under Chapter 2 of Part 14 of the 1996 Act, the amount of a week's pay of an employee falls to be calculated by reference to the average rate of remuneration, or the average amount of remuneration, payable to the employee in respect of a period of twelve weeks ending on a particular date (referred to as "the calculation date");

(b) during a week in that period, the employee was absent from work on paternity leave or ordinary or additional adoption leave, and

(c) remuneration is payable to the employee in respect of that week under his contract of employment, but the amount payable is less than the amount that would be payable if he were working,

that week shall be disregarded for the purpose of the calculation and account shall be taken of remuneration in earlier weeks so as to bring up to twelve the number of weeks of which account is taken.

STATUTORY PATERNITY PAY AND STATUTORY ADOPTION PAY (WEEKLY RATES) REGULATIONS 2002

(SI 2002/2818)

NOTES

Made: 11 November 2002.

Authority: Social Security Contributions and Benefits Act 1992, ss 171ZE(1), 171ZN(1); Social Security Administration Act 1992, s 5(1)(l).

Commencement: 8 December 2002.

Statutory paternity pay: as to the meaning of this, see the Children and Families Act 2014, s 126 at **[1.1894]**.

[2.607]
1 Citation and commencement

These Regulations may be cited as the Statutory Paternity Pay and Statutory Adoption Pay (Weekly Rates) Regulations and shall come into force on 8th December 2002.

[2.608]
[2 Weekly rate of payment of statutory paternity pay

The weekly rate of payment of statutory paternity pay shall be the smaller of the following two amounts—

(a) [£148.68];

(b) 90 per cent of the normal weekly earnings of the person claiming statutory paternity pay, determined in accordance with regulations 39 and 40 of the Statutory Paternity Pay and Statutory Adoption Pay (General) Regulations 2002.]

NOTES

Substituted by the Statutory Paternity Pay and Statutory Adoption Pay (Weekly Rates) (Amendment) Regulations 2004, SI 2004/925, reg 2.

Sum in square brackets in para (a) substituted by the Social Security Benefits Up-rating Order 2019, SI 2019/480, art 11(1)(a), as from 7 April 2019.

The previous amounts were: £135.45 (as from 1 April 2012, see the Social Security Benefits Up-rating Order 2012, SI 2012/780, art 11(1)(a)); £136.78 (as from 7 April 2013, see the Social Security Benefits Up-rating Order 2013, SI 2013/574, art 10(1)(a)); £138.18 (as from 6 April 2014, see the Welfare Benefits Up-rating Order 2014, SI 2014/147, art 5(1)(a)); £139.58 (as from 5 April 2015, see the Welfare Benefits Up-rating Order 2015, SI 2015/30, art 5(1)(a)); £140.98 (as from 2 April 2017, see the Social Security Benefits Up-rating Order 2017, SI 2017/260, art 11(a)); £145.18 (as from 1 April 2018, see the Social Security Benefits Up-rating Order 2018, SI 2018/281, art 11(1)(a)). Note that there was no increase in 2016.

[2.609]
3 Weekly rate of payment of statutory adoption pay

The weekly rate of payment of statutory adoption pay shall be the smaller of the following two amounts—

(a) [£148.68];

(b) 90 per cent of the normal weekly earnings of the person claiming statutory adoption pay, determined in accordance with regulations 39 and 40 of the Statutory Paternity Pay and Statutory Adoption Pay (General) Regulations 2002.

NOTES

Sum in square brackets in para (a) substituted by the Social Security Benefits Up-rating Order 2019, SI 2019/480, art 11(1)(b), as from 7 April 2019.

The previous amounts were as set out in the final note to reg 2 above.

[2.610]

[4 Rounding of fractional amounts

Where any payment of—

(a) statutory paternity pay is made on the basis of a calculation at—

 (i) the weekly rate specified in regulation 2(b); or

 (ii) the daily rate of one-seventh of the weekly rate specified in regulation 2(a) or (b); or

(b) statutory adoption pay is made on the basis of a calculation at—

 (i) the weekly rate specified in regulation 3(b); or

 (ii) the daily rate of one-seventh of the weekly rate specified in regulation 3(a) or (b),

and that amount includes a fraction of a penny, the payment shall be rounded up to the next whole number of pence.]

NOTES

Substituted by the Statutory Paternity Pay and Statutory Adoption Pay (General) and the Statutory Paternity Pay and Statutory Adoption Pay (Weekly Rates) (Amendment) Regulations 2006, SI 2006/2236, regs 6, 7.

STATUTORY PATERNITY PAY AND STATUTORY ADOPTION PAY (ADMINISTRATION) REGULATIONS 2002

(SI 2002/2820)

NOTES

Made: 13 November 2002.

Authority: Employment Act 2002, ss 7(1), (2)(a), (b), (4)(a)–(c), (5), 8(1), (2)(a)–(c), 10(1), (2), 51(1); Social Security Contributions (Transfer of Functions, etc) Act 1999, ss 8(1)(f), (ga), 25.

Commencement: 8 December 2002.

Statutory paternity pay: as to the meaning of this, see the Children and Families Act 2014, s 126 at **[1.1894]**

Adoption from overseas: as to the application of these Regulations to adoptions from overseas, see the Statutory Paternity Pay (Adoption) and Statutory Adoption Pay (Adoptions from Overseas) (Administration) Regulations 2003, SI 2003/1192.

Application to parental order cases: as to the application of these Regulations to parental order cases, see the Statutory Paternity Pay and Statutory Adoption Pay (Parental Orders and Prospective Adopters) Regulations 2014, SI 2014/2934, reg 26 at **[2.1576]**.

See *Harvey* J(8).

ARRANGEMENT OF REGULATIONS

[2.611]

1 Citation and commencement

These Regulations may be cited as the Statutory Paternity Pay and Statutory Adoption Pay (Administration) Regulations 2002 and shall come into force on 8th December 2002.

[2.612]

2 Interpretation

(1) In these Regulations—

"adopter", in relation to a child, means a person with whom the child is matched for adoption;

"adoption leave" means leave under section 75A of the Employment Rights Act 1996;

"adoption pay period" means the period prescribed under section 171ZN(2) of the Contributions and Benefits Act as the period in respect of which statutory adoption pay is payable to a person;

"the Board" means the Commissioners of Inland Revenue;

"the Contributions and Benefits Act" means the Social Security Contributions and Benefits Act 1992;

"contributions payments" has the same meaning as in section 7 of the Employment Act;
"the Contributions Regulations" means the Social Security (Contributions) Regulations 2001;
"the Employment Act" means the Employment Act 2002;
"income tax month" means the period beginning on the 6th day of any calendar month and ending on the 5th day of the following calendar month;
"income tax quarter" means the period beginning on the 6th day of April and ending on the 5th day of July, the period beginning on the 6th day of July and ending on the 5th day of October, the period beginning on the 6th day of October and ending on the 5th day of January or the period beginning on the 6th day of January and ending on the 5th day of April;
"paternity leave" means leave under section 80A or section 80B of the Employment Rights Act 1996;
"paternity pay period" means the period determined in accordance with section 171ZE(2) of the Contributions and Benefits Act as the period in respect of which statutory paternity pay is payable to a person;
"statutory adoption pay" means any payment under section 171ZL of the Contributions and Benefits Act;
"statutory paternity pay" means any payment under section 171ZA or section 171ZB of the Contributions and Benefits Act;
"tax year" means the 12 months beginning with 6th April in any year;
"writing" includes writing delivered by means of electronic communications approved by directions issued by the Board pursuant to regulations under section 132 of the Finance Act 1999.

(2) Any reference in these Regulations to the employees of an employer includes former employees of his.

NOTES

Adoption from overseas: as to the modification of this regulation in relation to adoptions from overseas, see the Statutory Paternity Pay (Adoption) and Statutory Adoption Pay (Adoptions from Overseas) (Administration) Regulations 2003, SI 2003/1192, reg 3(1)–(3).

Commissioners of Inland Revenue: a reference to the Commissioners of Inland Revenue is now to be taken as a reference to the Commissioners for Her Majesty's Revenue and Customs; see the Commissioners for Revenue and Customs Act 2005, s 50(1), (7).

[2.613]
3 Funding of employers' liabilities to make payments of statutory paternity or statutory adoption pay

(1) An employer who has made any payment of statutory paternity pay or statutory adoption pay shall be entitled—
- (a) to an amount equal to 92 per cent of such payment; or
- (b) if the payment qualifies for small employer's relief by virtue of section 7(3) of the Employment Act—
  - (i) to an amount equal to such payment; and
  - (ii) to an additional payment equal to the amount to which the employer would have been entitled under section 167(2)(b) of the Contributions and Benefits Act had the payment been a payment of statutory maternity pay.

(2) The employer shall be entitled in either case (a) or case (b) to apply for advance funding in respect of such payment in accordance with regulation 4, or to deduct it in accordance with regulation 5 from amounts otherwise payable by him.

[2.614]
4 Application for funding from the Board

(1) If an employer is entitled to a payment determined in accordance with regulation 3 in respect of statutory paternity pay or statutory adoption pay which he is required to pay to an employee or employees for an income tax month or income tax quarter, and the payment exceeds the aggregate of—
- (a) the total amount of tax which the employer is required to pay to the collector of taxes in respect of the deductions from the emoluments of his employees in accordance with the Income Tax (Employments) Regulations 1993 for the same income tax month or income tax quarter,
- (b) the total amount of the deductions made by the employer from the emoluments of his employees for the same income tax month or income tax quarter in accordance with regulations under section 22(5) of the Teaching and Higher Education Act 1998 or section 73B of the Education (Scotland) Act 1980 or in accordance with article 3(5) of the Education (Student Support) (Northern Ireland) Order 1998,
- (c) the total amount of contributions payments which the employer is required to pay to the collector of taxes in respect of the emoluments of his employees (whether by means of deduction or otherwise) in accordance with the Contributions Regulations for the same income tax month or income tax quarter, and
- (d) the total amount of payments which the employer is required to pay to the collector of taxes in respect of the deductions made on account of tax from payments to sub-contractors in accordance with section 559 of the Income and Corporation Taxes Act 1988 for the same income tax month or income tax quarter,

the employer may apply to the Board in accordance with paragraph (2) for funds to pay the statutory paternity pay or statutory adoption pay (or so much of it as remains outstanding) to the employee or employees.

(2) Where—

Part 2 Statutory Instruments

(a) the condition in paragraph (1) is satisfied, or
(b) the employer considers that the condition in paragraph (1) will be satisfied on the date of any subsequent payment of emoluments to one or more employees who are entitled to payment of statutory paternity pay or statutory adoption pay,

the employer may apply to the Board for funding in a form approved for that purpose by the Board.

(3) An application by an employer under paragraph (2) shall be for an amount up to, but not exceeding, the amount of the payment to which the employer is entitled in accordance with regulation 3 in respect of statutory paternity pay and statutory adoption pay which he is required to pay to an employee or employees for the income tax month or income tax quarter to which the payment of emoluments relates.

[2.615]
5 Deductions from payments to the Board

An employer who is entitled to a payment determined in accordance with regulation 3 may recover such payment by making one or more deductions from the aggregate of the amounts specified in sub-paragraphs (a) to (d) of regulation 4(1) except where and in so far as—

(a) those amounts relate to earnings paid before the beginning of the income tax month or income tax quarter in which the payment of statutory paternity pay or statutory adoption pay was made;
(b) those amounts are paid by him later than six years after the end of the tax year in which the payment of statutory paternity pay or statutory adoption pay was made;
(c) the employer has received payment from the Board under regulation 4; or
(d) the employer has made a request in writing under regulation 4 that the payment to which he is entitled in accordance with regulation 3 be paid to him and he has not received notification by the Board that the request is refused.

[2.616]
6 Payments to employers by the Board

If the total amount which an employer is or would otherwise be entitled to deduct under regulation 5 is less than the payment to which the employer is entitled in accordance with regulation 3 in an income tax month or income tax quarter, and the Board are satisfied that this is so, then provided that the employer has in writing requested them to do so, the Board shall pay the employer such amount as the employer was unable to deduct.

[2.617]
7 Date when certain contributions are to be treated as paid

Where an employer has made a deduction from a contributions payment under regulation 5, the date on which it is to be treated as having been paid for the purposes of section 7(5) of the Employment Act (when amount deducted from contributions payment to be treated as paid and received by the Board) is—

(a) in a case where the deduction did not extinguish the contributions payment, the date on which the remainder of the contributions payment or, as the case may be, the first date on which any part of the remainder of the contributions payment was paid; and
(b) in a case where the deduction extinguished the contributions payment, the 14th day after the end of the income tax month or income tax quarter during which there were paid the earnings in respect of which the contributions payment was payable.

[2.618]
8 Overpayments

(1) This regulation applies where funds have been provided to the employer pursuant to regulation 4 in respect of one or more employees and it appears to an officer of the Board that the employer has not used the whole or part of those funds to pay statutory paternity pay or statutory adoption pay.

(2) An officer of the Board shall decide to the best of his judgement the amount of funds provided pursuant to regulation 4 and not used to pay statutory paternity pay or statutory adoption pay and shall serve notice in writing of his decision on the employer.

(3) A decision under this regulation may cover funds provided pursuant to regulation 4—

(a) for any one income tax month or income tax quarter, or more than one income tax month or income tax quarter, in a tax year, and
(b) in respect of a class or classes of employees specified in the decision notice (without naming the individual employees), or in respect of one or more employees named in the decision notice.

(4) Subject to the following provisions of this regulation, Part 6 of the Taxes Management Act 1970 (collection and recovery) shall apply with any necessary modifications to a decision under this regulation as if it were an assessment and as if the amount of funds determined were income tax charged on the employer.

(5) Where an amount of funds determined under this regulation relates to more than one employee, proceedings may be brought for the recovery of that amount without distinguishing the amounts making up that sum which the employer is liable to repay in respect of each employee and without specifying the employee in question, and the amount determined under this regulation shall be one cause of action or one matter of complaint for the purposes of proceedings under section 65, 66 or 67 of the Taxes Management Act 1970.

(6) Nothing in paragraph (5) prevents the bringing of separate proceedings for the recovery of any amount which the employer is liable to repay in respect of each employee.

[2.619]

9 Records to be maintained by employers

Every employer shall maintain for three years after the end of a tax year in which he made payments of statutory paternity pay or statutory adoption pay to any employee of his a record of—

(a) if the employee's paternity pay period or adoption pay period began in that year—

(i) the date on which that period began, and

(ii) the evidence of entitlement to statutory paternity pay or statutory adoption pay provided by the employee pursuant to regulations made under section 171ZC(3)(c) or section 171ZL(8)(c) of the Contributions and Benefits Act;

(b) the weeks in that tax year in which statutory paternity pay or statutory adoption pay was paid to the employee and the amount paid in each week; and

(c) any week in that tax year which was within the employee's paternity pay period or adoption pay period but for which no payment of statutory paternity pay or statutory adoption pay was made to him and the reason no payment was made.

[2.620]

10 Inspection of employers' records

(1) Every employer, whenever called upon to do so by any authorised officer of the Board, shall produce the documents and records specified in paragraph (2) to that officer for inspection, at such time as that officer may reasonably require, at the prescribed place.

(2) The documents and records specified in this paragraph are—

(a) all wages sheets, deductions working sheets, records kept in accordance with regulation 9 and other documents and records whatsoever relating to the calculation or payment of statutory paternity pay or statutory adoption pay to his employees in respect of the years specified by such officer; or

(b) such of those wages sheets, deductions working sheets, or other documents and records as may be specified by the authorised officer.

(3) The "prescribed place" mentioned in paragraph (1) means—

(a) such place in Great Britain as the employer and the authorised officer may agree upon; or

(b) in default of such agreement, the place in Great Britain at which the documents and records referred to in paragraph (2)(a) are normally kept; or

(c) in default of such agreement and if there is no such place as is referred to in sub-paragraph (b) above, the employer's principal place of business in Great Britain.

(4) The authorised officer may—

(a) take copies of, or make extracts from, any document or record produced to him for inspection in accordance with paragraph (1);

(b) remove any document or record so produced if it appears to him to be necessary to do so, at a reasonable time and for a reasonable period.

(5) Where any document or record is removed in accordance with paragraph (4)(b), the authorised officer shall provide—

(a) a receipt for the document or record so removed; and

(b) a copy of the document or record, free of charge, within seven days, to the person by whom it was produced or caused to be produced where the document or record is reasonably required for the proper conduct of a business.

(6) Where a lien is claimed on a document produced in accordance with paragraph (1), the removal of the document under paragraph (4)(b) shall not be regarded as breaking the lien.

(7) Where records are maintained by computer, the person required to make them available for inspection shall provide the authorised officer with all facilities necessary for obtaining information from them.

[2.621]

11 Provision of information relating to entitlement to statutory paternity pay or statutory adoption pay

(1) Where an employer who has been given evidence of entitlement to statutory paternity pay or statutory adoption pay pursuant to regulations made under section 171ZC(3)(c) or section 171ZL(8)(c) of the Contributions and Benefits Act by a person who is or has been an employee decides that he has no liability to make payments of statutory paternity pay or statutory adoption pay to the employee, the employer shall furnish the employee with details of the decision and the reasons for it.

(2) Where an employer who has been given such evidence of entitlement to statutory adoption pay has made one or more payments of statutory adoption pay to the employee but decides, before the end of the adoption pay period, that he has no liability to make further payments to the employee because he has been detained in legal custody or sentenced to a term of imprisonment which was not suspended, the employer shall furnish the employee with—

(a) details of his decision and the reasons for it; and

(b) details of the last week in respect of which a liability to pay statutory adoption pay arose and the total number of weeks within the adoption pay period in which such a liability arose.

(3) The employer shall—

(a) return to the employee any evidence provided by him as referred to in paragraph (1) or (2); and

(b) comply with the requirements imposed by paragraph (1) within 28 days of—

(i) in the case of entitlement to statutory paternity pay under section 171ZA(1) of the Contributions and Benefits Act, the day the employee gave notice of his intended absence or the end of the fifteenth week before the expected week of birth, whichever is the later, or

(ii) in the case of entitlement to statutory paternity pay under section 171ZB(1) or of statutory adoption pay under section 171ZL(1) of the Contributions and Benefits Act, the end of the seven-day period that starts on the date on which the adopter is notified of having been matched with the child;

(c) comply with the requirements imposed by paragraph (2) within seven days of being notified of the employee's detention or sentence.

[(4) For the purposes of paragraph (3)(b)(ii), an adopter is notified as having been matched with a child—

(a) on the date that person receives notification of the adoption agency's decision under regulation 33(3)(a) of the Adoption Agencies Regulations 2005, regulation 28(3) of the Adoption Agencies (Wales) Regulations 2005 or regulation 8(5) of the Adoption Agencies (Scotland) Regulations 2009; or

(b) on the date on which that person receives notification in accordance with regulation 12B(2)(a) of the Adoption Agencies Regulations 2005.]

[(5) In this regulation "adoption agency" has the meaning given, in relation to England and Wales, by section 2 of the Adoption and Children Act 2002 and, in relation to Scotland, by section 119(1) of the Adoption and Children (Scotland) Act 2007.]

NOTES

Para (4): substituted by the Statutory Paternity Pay and Statutory Adoption Pay (Parental Orders and Prospective Adopters) Regulations 2014, SI 2014/2934, reg 25(a), as from 1 December 2014 (for effect see reg 3 thereof at **[2.1553]**).

Para (5): added by SI 2014/2934, reg 25(b), as from 1 December 2014 (for effect see reg 3 thereof at **[2.1553]**).

Adoption from overseas: as to the modification of this regulation in relation to adoptions from overseas, see the Statutory Paternity Pay (Adoption) and Statutory Adoption Pay (Adoptions from Overseas) (Administration) Regulations 2003, SI 2003/1192, reg 3(1), (4), (5).

Application to parental order cases: as to the modification of this regulation in relation to parental order cases, see the Statutory Paternity Pay and Statutory Adoption Pay (Parental Orders and Prospective Adopters) Regulations 2014, SI 2014/2934, reg 26 at **[2.1576]**.

[2.622]

12 Application for the determination of any issue arising as to, or in connection with, entitlement to statutory paternity pay or statutory adoption pay

(1) An application for the determination of any issue arising as to, or in connection with, entitlement to statutory paternity pay or statutory adoption pay may be submitted to an officer of the Board by the employee concerned.

(2) Such an issue shall be decided by an officer of the Board only on the basis of such an application or on his own initiative.

[2.623]

13 Applications in connection with statutory paternity pay or statutory adoption pay

(1) An application for the determination of any issue referred to in regulation 12 shall be made in a form approved for the purpose by the Board.

(2) Where such an application is made by an employee, it shall—

(a) be made to an officer of the Board within six months of the earliest day in respect of which entitlement to statutory paternity pay or statutory adoption pay is in issue;

(b) state the period in respect of which entitlement to statutory paternity pay or statutory adoption pay is in issue; and

(c) state the grounds (if any) on which the applicant's employer had denied liability for statutory paternity pay or statutory adoption pay in respect of the period specified in the application.

[2.624]

14 Provision of information

(1) Any person specified in paragraph (2) shall, where information or documents are reasonably required from him to ascertain whether statutory paternity pay or statutory adoption pay is or was payable, furnish that information or those documents within 30 days of receiving a notification from an officer of the Board requesting such information or documents.

(2) The requirement to provide such information or documents applies to—

(a) any person claiming to be entitled to statutory paternity pay or statutory adoption pay;

(b) any person who is, or has been, the spouse[, civil partner] or partner of such a person as is specified in paragraph (a);

(c) any person who is, or has been, an employer of such a person as is specified in paragraph (a);

(d) any person carrying on an agency or other business for the introduction or supply to persons requiring them of persons available to do work or to perform services; and

(e) any person who is a servant or agent of any such person as is specified in paragraphs (a) to (d).

NOTES

Para (2): words in square brackets in sub-para (b) inserted by the Civil Partnership Act 2004 (Amendments to Subordinate Legislation) Order 2005, SI 2005/2114, art 2(17), Sch 17, para 2.

STATUTORY PATERNITY PAY AND STATUTORY ADOPTION PAY (GENERAL) REGULATIONS 2002

(SI 2002/2822)

NOTES

Made: 13 November 2002.

Authority: Social Security Contributions and Benefits Act 1992, ss 171ZA(2)(a), 171ZB(2)(a), 171ZC(3)(a), (c), (d), (f), (g), 171ZD(2), (3), 171ZE(2)(a), (b)(i), (3), (7), (8), 171ZG(3), 171ZJ(1), (3), (4), (7), (8), 171ZL(8)(b)–(d), (f), (g), 171ZM(2), (3), 171ZN(2), (5), (6), 171ZP(6), 171ZS(1), (3), (4), (7), (8), 175(4); Social Security Administration Act 1992, s 5(1)(g), (i), (p).

Commencement: 8 December 2002.

Statutory paternity pay: as to the meaning of this, see the Children and Families Act 2014, s 126 at **[1.1894]**

Application to parental order parents: these Regulations are applied with modifications in relation to parental order parents, by the Statutory Paternity Pay and Statutory Adoption Pay (Parental Orders and Prospective Adopters) Regulations 2014, SI 2014/2934, regs 6–24 at **[2.1554]–[2.1575]**.

See *Harvey* J(8).

ARRANGEMENT OF REGULATIONS

PART 6
STATUTORY PATERNITY PAY AND STATUTORY ADOPTION PAY: PROVISIONS APPLICABLE TO BOTH STATUTORY PATERNITY PAY AND STATUTORY ADOPTION PAY

PART 1
INTRODUCTION

[2.625]
1 Citation and commencement

These Regulations may be cited as the Statutory Paternity Pay and Statutory Adoption Pay (General) Regulations 2002 and shall come into force on 8th December 2002.

[2.626]
2 Interpretation

(1) In these Regulations—

"the Act" means the Social Security Contributions and Benefits Act 1992;

"adopter", in relation to a child, means a person who has been matched with the child for adoption;

"adoption agency" has the meaning given, in relation to England and Wales, by section 1(4) of the Adoption Act 1976 and in relation to Scotland, by [section 119(1) of the Adoption and Children (Scotland) Act 2007];

"the Board" means the Commissioners of Inland Revenue;

"the Contributions Regulations" means the Social Security (Contributions) Regulations 2001;

"expected week", in relation to the birth of a child, means the week, beginning with midnight between Saturday and Sunday, in which it is expected that the child will be born;

"statutory paternity pay (adoption)" means statutory paternity pay payable in accordance with the provisions of Part 12ZA of the Act where the conditions specified in section 171ZB(2) of the Act are satisfied;

"statutory paternity pay (birth)" means statutory paternity pay payable in accordance with the provisions of Part 12ZA of the Act where the conditions specified in section 171ZA(2) of the Act are satisfied.

[(2) For the purposes of these Regulations—

(a) a person is matched with a child for adoption when an adoption agency decides that that person would be a suitable adoptive parent for the child;

(b) in a case where paragraph (a) applies, a person is notified as having been matched with a child on the date that person receives notification of the agency's decision, under regulation 33(3)(a) of the Adoption Agencies Regulations 2005, regulation 28(3) of the Adoption Agencies (Wales) Regulations 2005 or regulation 8(5) of the Adoption Agencies (Scotland) Regulations 2009;

(c) a person is also matched with a child for adoption when a decision is has been made in accordance with regulation 22A of the Care Planning, Placement and Case Review (England) Regulations 2010 and an adoption agency has identified that person with whom the child is to be placed in accordance with regulation 12B of the Adoption Agencies Regulations 2005.

(d) in a case where paragraph (c) applies, a person is notified as having been matched with a child on the date on which that person receives notification in accordance with regulation 12B(2)(a) of the Adoption Agencies Regulations 2005.]

[(3) A reference (however expressed) in these Regulations to "placed for adoption" means—

(a) placed for adoption under the Adoption and Children Act 2002 or the Adoption and Children (Scotland) Act 2007; or

(b) placed in accordance with section 22C of the Children Act 1989 with a local authority foster parent who is also a prospective adopter.

(4) The reference to "prospective adopter" in paragraph (3) means a person who has been approved as suitable to adopt a child and has been notified of that decision in accordance with regulation 30B(4) of the Adoption Agencies Regulations 2005.]

NOTES

Para (1): words in square brackets in the definition "adoption agency" substituted by the Adoption and Children (Scotland) Act 2007 (Consequential Modifications) Order 2011, SI 2011/1740, art 2, Sch 1, Pt 2, para 32(1), (2)(a).

Para (2): substituted by the Statutory Paternity Pay and Statutory Adoption Pay (Parental Orders and Prospective Adopters) Regulations 2014, SI 2014/2934, reg 4(1), (2), as from 1 December 2014 (for effect see reg 3 thereof at **[2.1553]**).

Paras (3), (4): added by SI 2014/2934, reg 4(1), (3), as from 1 December 2014 (for effect see reg 3 thereof at **[2.1553]**).

Commissioners of Inland Revenue: a reference to the Commissioners of Inland Revenue is now to be taken as a reference to the Commissioners for Her Majesty's Revenue and Customs; see the Commissioners for Revenue and Customs Act 2005, s 50(1), (7).

Modification in relation to parental order parents: as to the modification of this regulation, see the Statutory Paternity Pay and Statutory Adoption Pay (Parental Orders and Prospective Adopters) Regulations 2014, SI 2014/2934, regs 6, 7 at **[2.1554]**, **[2.1555]**.

[2.627]
3 Application

(1) Subject to the provisions of Part 12ZA of the Act (statutory paternity pay) and of these Regulations, there is entitlement to—
  (a) statutory paternity pay (birth) in respect of children—
    (i) born on or after 6th April 2003; or
    (ii) whose expected week of birth begins on or after that date;
  (b) statutory paternity pay (adoption) in respect of children—
    (i) matched with a person who is notified of having been matched on or after 6th April 2003; or
    (ii) placed for adoption on or after that date.

(2) Subject to the provisions of Part 12ZB of the Act (statutory adoption pay) and of these Regulations, there is entitlement to statutory adoption pay in respect of children—
  (a) matched with a person who is notified of having been matched on or after 6th April 2003; or
  (b) placed for adoption on or after that date.

NOTES

Modification in relation to parental order parents: as to the modification of this regulation, see the Statutory Paternity Pay and Statutory Adoption Pay (Parental Orders and Prospective Adopters) Regulations 2014, SI 2014/2934, regs 6, 8, 8A at **[2.1554]**, **[2.1556]**, **[2.1557]**.

PART 2
STATUTORY PATERNITY PAY (BIRTH)

[2.628]
4 Conditions of entitlement to statutory paternity pay (birth): relationship with newborn child and child's mother

The conditions prescribed under section 171ZA(2)(a) of the Act are those prescribed in regulation 4(2)(b) and (c) of the Paternity and Adoption Leave Regulations 2002.

[2.629]
5 Modification of entitlement conditions: early birth

Where a person does not meet the conditions specified in section 171ZA(2)(b) to (d) of the Act because the child's birth occurred earlier than the 14th week before the expected week of the birth, it shall have effect as if, for the conditions there set out, there were substituted the conditions that—
  (a) the person would, but for the date on which the birth occurred, have been in employed earner's employment with an employer for a continuous period of at least 26 weeks ending with the week immediately preceding the 14th week before the expected week of the child's birth;
  (b) his normal weekly earnings for the period of 8 weeks ending with the week immediately preceding the week in which the child is born are not less than the lower earnings limit in force under section 5(1)(a) of the Act immediately before the commencement of the week in which the child is born.

[2.630]
[5A Notice of entitlement to statutory paternity pay (birth)

The notice provided for in section 171ZC(1) of the Act must be given to the employer—
  (a) in or before the 15th week before the expected week of the child's birth, or
  (b) in a case where it was not reasonably practicable for the employee to give the notice in accordance with sub-paragraph (a), as soon as is reasonably practicable.]

NOTES

Commencement: 1 December 2014.

Inserted by the Statutory Paternity Pay and Statutory Adoption Pay (General) (Amendment) Regulations 2014, SI 2014/2862, regs 2(a), 3, 4, as from 1 December 2014, in relation to an entitlement to statutory paternity pay only in respect of children whose expected week of birth begins on or after 5 April 2015.

[2.631]
6 Period of payment of statutory paternity pay (birth)

(1) Subject to paragraph (2) and regulation 8, a person entitled to statutory paternity pay (birth) may choose the statutory paternity pay period to begin on—

(a) the date on which the child is born or, where he is at work on that day, the following day;
(b) the date falling such number of days after the date on which the child is born as the person may specify;
(c) a predetermined date, specified by the person, which is later than the first day of the expected week of the child's birth.

(2) In a case where statutory paternity pay (birth) is payable in respect of a child whose expected week of birth begins before 6th April 2003, the statutory paternity pay period shall begin on a predetermined date, specified by the person entitled to such pay in a notice under section 171ZC(1) of the Act, which is at least 28 days after the date on which that notice was given, unless the person liable to pay statutory paternity pay (birth) agrees to the period beginning earlier.

(3) A person may choose for statutory paternity pay (birth) to be paid in respect of a period of a week.

[(4) An employee who has made a choice in accordance with paragraph (1) may vary the date chosen provided that the employee gives the employer notice of the variation—

(a) where the variation is to provide for the employee's statutory paternity pay period to begin on the date on which the child is born, or where he is at work on that day, the following day, at least 28 days before the first day of the expected week of the child's birth;
(b) where the variation is to provide for the employee's statutory paternity pay period to begin on a date that is a specified number of days (or a different specified number of days) after the date on which the child is born, at least 28 days before the date falling that number of days after the first day of the expected week of the child's birth;
(c) where the variation is to provide for the employee's statutory paternity pay period to begin on a predetermined date (or a different predetermined date), at least 28 days before that date,

or, if it is not reasonably practicable to give the notice at least 28 days before whichever day or date is relevant, as soon as is reasonably practicable.]

NOTES

Para (4): substituted by the Statutory Paternity Pay and Statutory Adoption Pay (General) (Amendment) Regulations 2014, SI 2014/2862, regs 2(a), 3, 5, as from 1 December 2014, in relation to an entitlement to statutory paternity pay only in respect of children whose expected week of birth begins on or after 5 April 2015.

[2.632]
7 Additional notice requirements for statutory paternity pay (birth)

(1) Where the choice made by a person in accordance with paragraph (1) of regulation 6 and notified in accordance with section 171ZC(1) of the Act is that mentioned in sub-paragraph (a) or (b) of that paragraph, the person shall give further notice to the person liable to pay him statutory paternity pay, as soon as is reasonably practicable after the child's birth, of the date the child was born.

(2) Where the choice made by a person in accordance with paragraph (1) of regulation 6 and notified in accordance with section 171ZC(1) of the Act is that specified in sub-paragraph (c) of that paragraph, and the date of the child's birth is later than the date so specified, the person shall, if he wishes to claim statutory paternity pay (birth), give notice to the person liable to pay it, as soon as is reasonably practicable, that the period in respect of which statutory paternity pay is to be paid shall begin on a date different from that originally chosen by him.

(3) That date may be any date chosen in accordance with paragraph (1) of regulation 6.

[2.633]
8 Qualifying period for statutory paternity pay (birth)

The qualifying period for the purposes of section 171ZE(2) of the Act (period within which the statutory paternity pay period must occur) is a period which begins on the date of the child's birth and ends—

(a) except in the case referred to in paragraph (b), 56 days after that date;
(b) in a case where the child is born before the first day of the expected week of its birth, 56 days after that day.

[2.634]
9 Evidence of entitlement to statutory paternity pay (birth)

(1) A person shall provide evidence of his entitlement to statutory paternity pay (birth) by providing in writing to the person who will be liable to pay him statutory paternity pay (birth)—

(a) the information specified in paragraph (2);
(b) a declaration that he meets the conditions prescribed under section 171ZA(2)(a) of the Act and that it is not the case that statutory paternity pay (birth) is not payable to him by virtue of the provisions of section 171ZE(4) of the Act.

(2) The information referred to in paragraph (1)(a) is as follows—

(a) the name of the person claiming statutory paternity pay (birth);
(b) the expected week of the child's birth and, where the birth has already occurred, the date of birth;
(c) the date from which it is expected that the liability to pay statutory paternity pay (birth) will begin;

(d) whether the period chosen in respect of which statutory paternity pay (birth) is to be payable is a week.

[(3) The information and declaration referred to in paragraph (1) shall be provided—

(a) in or before the 15th week before the expected week of the child's birth, or

(b) in a case where it was not reasonably practicable for the employee to provide it in accordance with sub-paragraph (a), as soon as is reasonably practicable.]

(4) Where the person who will be liable to pay statutory paternity pay (birth) so requests, the person entitled to it shall inform him of the date of the child's birth within 28 days, or as soon as is reasonably practicable thereafter.

NOTES

Para (3): substituted by the Statutory Paternity Pay and Statutory Adoption Pay (General) (Amendment) Regulations 2014, SI 2014/2862, regs 2(a), 3, 6, as from 1 December 2014, in relation to an entitlement to statutory paternity pay only in respect of children whose expected week of birth begins on or after 5 April 2015.

[2.635]

10 Entitlement to statutory paternity pay (birth) where there is more than one employer

Statutory paternity pay (birth) shall be payable to a person in respect of a statutory pay week during any part of which he works only for an employer—

(a) who is not liable to pay him statutory paternity pay (birth); and

(b) for whom he has worked in the week immediately preceding the 14th week before the expected week of the child's birth.

PART 3
STATUTORY PATERNITY PAY (ADOPTION)

[2.636]

11 Conditions of entitlement to statutory paternity pay (adoption): relationship with child and with person with whom the child is placed for adoption

(1) The conditions prescribed under section 171ZB(2)(a) of the Act are that a person—

(a) is married to[, the civil partner] or the partner of a child's adopter (or in a case where there are two adopters, married to[, the civil partner] or the partner of the other adopter), and

(b) has, or expects to have, the main responsibility (apart from the responsibility of the child's adopter, or in a case where there two adopters, together with the other adopter) for the upbringing of the child.

(2) For the purposes of paragraph (1), "partner" means a person (whether of a different sex or the same sex) who lives with the adopter and the child in an enduring family relationship but is not a relative of the adopter of a kind specified in paragraph [(2A)].

[(2A) The relatives of the adopter referred to in paragraph (2) are the adopter's parent, grandparent, sister, brother, aunt or uncle.]

(3) References to relationships in paragraph [(2A)]—

(a) are to relationships of the full blood or half blood, or, in the case of an adopted person, such of those relationships as would exist but for the adoption, and

(b) include the relationship of a child with his adoptive, or former adoptive parents but do not include any other adoptive relationships.

NOTES

Para (1): words in square brackets in sub-para (a) inserted by the Civil Partnership Act 2004 (Amendments to Subordinate Legislation) Order 2005, SI 2005/2114, art 2(17), Sch 17, para 3.

Paras (2), (3): figures in square brackets substituted by the Statutory Paternity Pay and Statutory Adoption Pay (Amendment) Regulations 2004, SI 2004/488, reg 2(1), (2)(a), (c).

Para (2A): inserted by SI 2004/488, reg 2(1), (2)(b).

Modification in relation to parental order parents: as to the modification of this regulation, see the Statutory Paternity Pay and Statutory Adoption Pay (Parental Orders and Prospective Adopters) Regulations 2014, SI 2014/2934, regs 6, 9 at **[2.1554]**, **[2.1558]**.

[2.637]

[11A Notice of entitlement to statutory paternity pay (adoption)

The notice provided for in section 171ZC(1) of the Act must be given to the employer—

(a) no more than seven days after the date on which the adopter is notified of having been matched with the child, or

(b) in a case where it was not reasonably practicable for the employee to give notice in accordance with sub-paragraph (a), as soon as is reasonably practicable.]

NOTES

Commencement: 1 December 2014.

Inserted by the Statutory Paternity Pay and Statutory Adoption Pay (General) (Amendment) Regulations 2014, SI 2014/2862, regs 2(b), 3, 7, as from 1 December 2014, in relation to an entitlement to statutory paternity pay only in respect of children placed for adoption on or after 5 April 2015.

Modification in relation to parental order parents: as to the modification of this regulation, see the Statutory Paternity Pay and Statutory Adoption Pay (Parental Orders and Prospective Adopters) Regulations 2014, SI 2014/2934, regs 6, 10 at **[2.1554]**, **[2.1559]**.

[2.638]

12 Period of payment of statutory paternity pay (adoption)

(1) Subject to paragraph (2) and regulation 14, a person entitled to statutory paternity pay (adoption) may choose the statutory paternity pay period to begin on—

(a) the date on which the child is placed with the adopter or, where the person is at work on that day, the following day;

(b) the date falling such number of days after the date on which the child is placed with the adopter as the person may specify;

(c) a predetermined date, specified by the person, which is later than the date on which the child is expected to be placed with the adopter.

(2) In a case where statutory paternity pay (adoption) is payable in respect of a child matched with an adopter who is notified of having been matched before 6th April 2003, the statutory paternity pay period shall begin on a predetermined date, specified by the person entitled to such pay in a notice under section 171ZC(1) of the Act, which is at least 28 days after the date on which that notice was given, unless the person liable to pay statutory paternity pay (birth) agrees to the period beginning earlier.

(3) A person may choose for statutory paternity pay (adoption) to be paid in respect of a period of a week.

[(4) An employee who has made a choice in accordance with paragraph (1) may vary the date chosen provided that the employee gives the employer notice of the variation—

(a) where the variation is to provide for the employee's statutory paternity pay period to begin on the date on which the child is placed with the adopter or, where the person is at work on that day, the following day, at least 28 days before the date provided under regulation 15(2)(b) as the date on which the child is expected to be placed for adoption;

(b) where the variation is to provide for the employee's statutory paternity pay period to begin on a date that is a specified number of days (or a different specified number of days) after the date on which the child is placed with the adopter, at least 28 days before the date falling that number of days after the date provided under regulation 15(2)(b) as the date on which the child is expected to be placed for adoption;

(c) where the variation is to provide for the employee's statutory paternity pay period to begin on a predetermined date, at least 28 days before that date,

or, if it is not reasonably practicable to give the notice at least 28 days before whichever date is relevant, as soon as is reasonably practicable.]

NOTES

Para (4): substituted by the Statutory Paternity Pay and Statutory Adoption Pay (General) (Amendment) Regulations 2014, SI 2014/2862, regs 2(b), 3, 8, as from 1 December 2014, in relation to an entitlement to statutory paternity pay only in respect of children placed for adoption on or after 5 April 2015.

Modification in relation to parental order parents: as to the modification of this regulation, see the Statutory Paternity Pay and Statutory Adoption Pay (Parental Orders and Prospective Adopters) Regulations 2014, SI 2014/2934, regs 6, 11 at **[2.1554]**, **[2.1560]**.

[2.639]

13 Additional notice requirements for statutory paternity pay (adoption)

(1) Where the choice made by a person in accordance with paragraph (1) of regulation 12 and notified in accordance with section 171ZC(1) of the Act is that mentioned in sub-paragraph (a) or (b) of that paragraph, the person shall give further notice to the person liable to pay him statutory paternity pay as soon as is reasonably practicable of the date on which the placement occurred.

(2) Where the choice made by a person in accordance with paragraph (1) of regulation 12 and notified in accordance with section 171ZC(1) of the Act is that mentioned in sub-paragraph (c) of that paragraph, or a date is specified under paragraph (2) of that regulation, and the child is placed for adoption later than the date so specified, the person shall, if he wishes to claim statutory paternity pay (adoption), give notice to the person liable to pay it, as soon as is reasonably practicable, that the period in respect of which statutory paternity pay is to be paid shall begin on a date different from that originally chosen by him.

(3) That date may be any date chosen in accordance with paragraph (1) of regulation 12.

NOTES

Modification in relation to parental order parents: as to the modification of this regulation, see the Statutory Paternity Pay and Statutory Adoption Pay (Parental Orders and Prospective Adopters) Regulations 2014, SI 2014/2934, regs 6, 12 at **[2.1554]**, **[2.1561]**.

[2.640]

14 Qualifying period for statutory paternity pay (adoption)

The qualifying period for the purposes of section 171ZE(2) of the Act (period within which the statutory pay period must occur) is a period of 56 days beginning with the date of the child's placement for adoption.

NOTES

Modification in relation to parental order parents: as to the modification of this regulation, see the Statutory Paternity Pay and Statutory Adoption Pay (Parental Orders and Prospective Adopters) Regulations 2014, SI 2014/2934, regs 6, 13 at **[2.1554]**, **[2.1562]**.

[2.641]

15 Evidence of entitlement for statutory paternity pay (adoption)

(1) A person shall provide evidence of his entitlement to statutory paternity pay (adoption) by providing in writing to the person who will be liable to pay him statutory paternity pay (adoption)—

(a) the information specified in paragraph (2);

(b) a declaration that he meets the conditions prescribed under section 171ZB(2)(a) of the Act and that it is not the case that statutory paternity pay (adoption) is not payable to him by virtue of the provisions of section 171ZE(4) of the Act;

(c) a declaration that he has elected to receive statutory paternity pay (adoption), and not statutory adoption pay under Part 12ZB of the Act.

(2) The information referred to in paragraph (1) is as follows—

(a) the name of the person claiming statutory paternity pay (adoption);

(b) the date on which the child is expected to be placed for adoption or, where the child has already been placed for adoption, the date of placement of the child;

(c) the date from which it is expected that the liability to pay statutory paternity pay (adoption) will begin;

(d) whether the period chosen in respect of which statutory paternity pay (adoption) is to be payable is a week;

(e) the date the adopter was notified he had been matched with the child for the purposes of adoption.

[(3) The information and declaration referred to in paragraph (1) shall be provided—

(a) no more than seven days after the date on which the adopter is notified of having been matched with the child, or

(b) in a case where it was not reasonably practicable for the employee to provide it in accordance with sub-paragraph (a), as soon as is reasonably practicable.]

(4) Where the person who will be liable to pay statutory paternity pay (adoption) so requests, the person entitled to it shall inform him of the date of the child's placement within 28 days, or as soon as is reasonably practicable thereafter.

NOTES

Para (3): substituted by the Statutory Paternity Pay and Statutory Adoption Pay (General) (Amendment) Regulations 2014, SI 2014/2862, regs 2(b), 3, 9, as from 1 December 2014, in relation to an entitlement to statutory paternity pay only in respect of children placed for adoption on or after 5 April 2015.

Modification in relation to parental order parents: as to the modification of this regulation, see the Statutory Paternity Pay and Statutory Adoption Pay (Parental Orders and Prospective Adopters) Regulations 2014, SI 2014/2934, regs 6, 14 at **[2.1554]**, **[2.1563]**.

[2.642]

16 Entitlement to statutory paternity pay (adoption) where there is more than one employer

Statutory paternity pay (adoption) shall be payable to a person in respect of a statutory pay week during any part of which he works only for an employer—

(a) who is not liable to pay him statutory paternity pay (adoption); and

(b) for whom he has worked in the week in which the adopter is notified of being matched with the child.

NOTES

Modification in relation to parental order parents: as to the modification of this regulation, see the Statutory Paternity Pay and Statutory Adoption Pay (Parental Orders and Prospective Adopters) Regulations 2014, SI 2014/2934, regs 6, 15 at **[2.1554]**, **[2.1564]**.

PART 4
STATUTORY PATERNITY PAY: PROVISIONS APPLICABLE TO BOTH STATUTORY PATERNITY PAY (BIRTH) AND STATUTORY PATERNITY PAY (ADOPTION)

[2.643]

17 Work during a statutory paternity pay period

(1) Where, in a case where statutory paternity pay is being paid to a person who works during the statutory paternity pay period for an employer who is not liable to pay him statutory paternity pay and who does not fall within paragraph (b) of regulation 10 or, as the case may be, paragraph (b) of regulation 16, there shall be no liability to pay statutory paternity pay in respect of any remaining part of the statutory paternity pay period.

(2) In a case falling within paragraph (1), the person shall notify the person liable to pay statutory paternity pay within 7 days of the first day during which he works during the statutory pay period.

(3) The notification mentioned in paragraph (2) shall be in writing, if the person who has been liable to pay statutory paternity pay so requests.

[2.644]

18 Cases where there is no liability to pay statutory paternity pay

There shall be no liability to pay statutory paternity pay in respect of any week—

(a) during any part of which the person entitled to it is entitled to statutory sick pay under Part 11 of the Act;

(b) following that in which the person claiming it has died; or
(c) during any part of which the person entitled to it is detained in legal custody or sentenced to a term of imprisonment (except where the sentence is suspended), or which is a subsequent week within the same statutory paternity pay period.

[2.645]
19 Statutory paternity pay and contractual remuneration

For the purposes of section 171ZG(1) and (2) of the Act, the payments which are to be treated as contractual remuneration are sums payable under a contract of service—
(a) by way of remuneration;
(b) for incapacity for work due to sickness or injury;
(c) by reason of the birth or adoption of a child.

[2.646]
20 Avoidance of liability for statutory paternity pay

(1) A former employer shall be liable to make payments of statutory paternity pay to a former employee in any case where the employee had been employed for a continuous period of at least 8 weeks and his contract of service was brought to an end by the former employer solely, or mainly, for the purpose of avoiding liability for statutory paternity pay.

(2) In a case falling within paragraph (1)—
(a) the employee shall be treated as if he had been employed for a continuous period ending with the child's birth or, as the case may be, the placement of the child for adoption;
(b) his normal weekly earnings shall be calculated by reference to his normal weekly earnings for the period of 8 weeks ending with the last day in respect of which he was paid under his former contract of service.

NOTES

Modification in relation to parental order parents: as to the modification of this regulation, see the Statutory Paternity Pay and Statutory Adoption Pay (Parental Orders and Prospective Adopters) Regulations 2014, SI 2014/2934, regs 6, 16 at **[2.1554]**, **[2.1565]**.

PART 5
STATUTORY ADOPTION PAY

[2.647]
21 Adoption pay period

(1) Subject to paragraph (2), a person entitled to statutory adoption pay may choose the adoption pay period to begin—
(a) on the date on which the child is placed with him for adoption or, where he is at work on that day, on the following day;
(b) subject to paragraph (2), on a predetermined date, specified by him, which is no more than 14 days before the date on which the child is expected to be placed with him and no later than that date.

(2) In a case where statutory adoption pay is payable in respect of a child matched with an adopter who is notified of having been matched before 6th April 2003, the statutory adoption pay period shall begin on a predetermined date which is—
(a) on or after 6th April 2003, and
(b) no more than 14 days before the date on which the child is expected to be placed with the adopter.

(3) Subject to paragraph (4), where the choice made is that mentioned in sub-paragraph (b) of paragraph (1) or in a case where paragraph (2) applies, the adoption pay period shall, unless the employer agrees to the adoption pay period beginning earlier, begin no earlier than 28 days after notice under section 171ZL(6) of the Act has been given.

(4) Where the beginning of the adoption pay period determined in accordance with paragraph (3) is later than the date of placement, it shall be the date of placement.

(5) Subject to regulation 22, the duration of any adoption pay period shall be a continuous period of [39] weeks.

(6) A choice made under paragraph (1), or a date specified under paragraph (2), is not irrevocable, but where a person subsequently makes a different choice, section 171ZL(6) of the Act shall apply to it.

NOTES

Para (5): figure in square brackets substituted by the Statutory Paternity Pay and Statutory Adoption Pay (General) and the Statutory Paternity Pay and Statutory Adoption Pay (Weekly Rates) (Amendment) Regulations 2006, SI 2006/2236, regs 3, 4.

Modification in relation to parental order parents: as to the modification of this regulation, see the Statutory Paternity Pay and Statutory Adoption Pay (Parental Orders and Prospective Adopters) Regulations 2014, SI 2014/2934, regs 6, 17 at **[2.1554]**, **[2.1566]**.

[2.648]
22 Adoption pay period in cases where adoption is disrupted

(1) Where—

(a) after a child has been placed for adoption—
   (i) the child dies;
   [(ii) the child is returned after being placed, or]
(b) the adoption pay period has begun prior to the date the child has been placed for adoption, but the placement does not take place,

the adoption pay period shall terminate in accordance with the provisions of paragraph (2).

(2) The adoption pay period shall, in a case falling within paragraph (1), terminate 8 weeks after the end of the week specified in paragraph (3).

(3) The week referred to in paragraph (2) is—
(a) in a case falling within paragraph (1)(a)(i), the week during which the child dies;
(b) in a case falling within paragraph (1)(a)(ii), the week during which the child is returned;
(c) in a case falling within paragraph (1)(b), the week during which the person with whom the child was to be placed for adoption is notified that the placement will not be made.

(4) For the purposes of paragraph (3), "week" means a period of seven days beginning with Sunday.

[(5) In paragraph (1) "returned after being placed" means—
(a) returned to the adoption agency under sections 31 to 35 of the Adoption and Children Act 2002;
(b) in Scotland, returned to the adoption agency, adoption society or nominated person in accordance with section 25(6) of the Adoption and Children (Scotland) Act 2007; or
(c) where the child is placed in accordance with section 22C of the Children Act 1989, returned to the adoption agency following termination of the placement .]

NOTES

Para (1): sub-para (a)(ii) substituted by the Statutory Paternity Pay and Statutory Adoption Pay (Parental Orders and Prospective Adopters) Regulations 2014, SI 2014/2934, reg 5(1), (2), as from 1 December 2014 (for effect see reg 3 thereof at **[2.1553]**).

Para (5): added by SI 2014/2934, reg 5(1), (3), as from 1 December 2014 (for effect see reg 3 thereof at **[2.1553]**).

Modification in relation to parental order parents: as to the modification of this regulation, see the Statutory Paternity Pay and Statutory Adoption Pay (Parental Orders and Prospective Adopters) Regulations 2014, SI 2014/2934, regs 6, 18, 18A at **[2.1554]**, **[2.1567]**, **[2.1568]**.

[2.649]

23 Additional notice requirements for statutory adoption pay

(1) Where a person gives notice under section 171ZL(6) of the Act he shall at the same time give notice of the date on which the child is expected to be placed for adoption.

(2) Where the choice made in accordance with paragraph (1) of regulation 21 and notified in accordance with section 171ZL(6) of the Act is that mentioned in sub-paragraph (a) of that paragraph, the person shall give further notice to the person liable to pay him statutory adoption pay as soon as is reasonably practicable of the date the child is placed for adoption.

NOTES

Modification in relation to parental order parents: as to the modification of this regulation, see the Statutory Paternity Pay and Statutory Adoption Pay (Parental Orders and Prospective Adopters) Regulations 2014, SI 2014/2934, regs 6, 19 at **[2.1554]**, **[2.1569]**.

[2.650]

24 Evidence of entitlement to statutory adoption pay

(1) A person shall provide evidence of his entitlement to statutory adoption pay by providing to the person who will be liable to pay it—
(a) the information specified in paragraph (2), in the form of one or more documents provided to him by an adoption agency, containing that information;
(b) a declaration that he has elected to receive statutory adoption pay, and not statutory paternity pay (adoption) under Part 12ZA of the Act.

(2) The information referred to in paragraph (1) is—
(a) the name and address of the adoption agency and of the person claiming payment of statutory adoption pay;
(b) the date on which the child is expected to be placed for adoption or, where the child has already been placed for adoption, the date of placement; and
(c) the date on which the person claiming payment of statutory adoption pay was informed by the adoption agency that the child would be placed for adoption with him.

(3) The information and declaration referred to in paragraph (1) shall be provided to the person liable to pay statutory adoption pay at least 28 days before the date chosen as the beginning of the adoption pay period in accordance with paragraph (1) of regulation 21, or, if that is not reasonably practicable, as soon as is reasonably practicable thereafter.

NOTES

Modification in relation to parental order parents: as to the modification of this regulation, see the Statutory Paternity Pay and Statutory Adoption Pay (Parental Orders and Prospective Adopters) Regulations 2014, SI 2014/2934, regs 6, 20, 20A at **[2.1554]**, **[2.1570]**, **[2.1571]**.

[2.651]
25 Entitlement to statutory adoption pay where there is more than one employer

Statutory adoption pay shall be payable to a person in respect of a week during any part of which he works only for an employer—

(a) who is not liable to pay him statutory adoption pay; and

(b) for whom he has worked in the week in which he is notified of being matched with the child.

NOTES

Modification in relation to parental order parents: as to the modification of this regulation, see the Statutory Paternity Pay and Statutory Adoption Pay (Parental Orders and Prospective Adopters) Regulations 2014, SI 2014/2934, regs 6, 21 at **[2.1554]**, **[2.1572]**.

[2.652]
26 Work during an adoption pay period

(1) Where, in a case where statutory adoption pay is being paid to a person who works during the adoption pay period for an employer who is not liable to pay him statutory adoption pay and who does not fall within paragraph (b) of regulation 25, there shall be no liability to pay statutory adoption pay in respect of any remaining part of the adoption pay period.

(2) In a case falling within paragraph (1), the person shall notify the person liable to pay statutory adoption pay within 7 days of the first day during which he works during the adoption pay period.

(3) The notification contained in paragraph (2) shall be in writing if the person who has been liable to pay statutory adoption pay so requests.

[2.653]
27 Cases where there is no liability to pay statutory adoption pay

(1) There shall be no liability to pay statutory adoption pay in respect of any week—

(a) during any part of which the person entitled to it is entitled to statutory sick pay under Part 11 of the Act;

(b) following that in which the person claiming it has died; or

(c) subject to paragraph (2), during any part of which the person entitled to it is detained in legal custody or sentenced to a term of imprisonment (except where the sentence is suspended).

(2) There shall be liability to pay statutory adoption pay in respect of any week during any part of which the person entitled to it is detained in legal custody where that person—

(a) is released subsequently without charge;

(b) is subsequently found not guilty of any offence and is released; or

(c) is convicted of an offence but does not receive a custodial sentence.

[2.654]
[27A Working for not more than 10 days during an adoption pay period

In the case where an employee does any work under a contract of service with his employer on any day for not more than 10 such days during his adoption pay period, whether consecutive or not, statutory adoption pay shall continue to be payable to the employee by the employer.]

NOTES

Inserted by the Statutory Paternity Pay and Statutory Adoption Pay (General) and the Statutory Paternity Pay and Statutory Adoption Pay (Weekly Rates) (Amendment) Regulations 2006, SI 2006/2236, regs 3, 5.

[2.655]
28 Statutory adoption pay and contractual remuneration

For the purposes of section 171ZP(4) and (5) of the Act, the payments which are to be treated as contractual remuneration are sums payable under a contract of service—

(a) by way of remuneration;

(b) for incapacity for work due to sickness or injury;

(c) by reason of the adoption of a child.

[2.656]
29 Termination of employment before start of adoption pay period

(1) Where the employment of a person who satisfies the conditions of entitlement to statutory adoption pay terminates for whatever reason (including dismissal) before the adoption pay period chosen in accordance with regulation 21 has begun, the period shall begin 14 days before the expected date of placement or, where the termination occurs on, or within 14 days before, the expected date of placement, on the day immediately following the last day of his employment.

(2) In a case falling within paragraph (1), the notice requirements set out in section 171ZL(6) of the Act and these Regulations shall not apply.

NOTES

Modification in relation to parental order parents: as to the modification of this regulation, see the Statutory Paternity Pay and Statutory Adoption Pay (Parental Orders and Prospective Adopters) Regulations 2014, SI 2014/2934, regs 6, 22 at **[2.1554]**, **[2.1573]**.

[2.657]
30 Avoidance of liability for statutory adoption pay

(1) A former employer shall be liable to make payments of statutory adoption pay to a former employee in any case where the employee had been employed for a continuous period of at least 8 weeks and his contract of service was brought to an end by the former employer solely, or mainly, for the purpose of avoiding liability for statutory adoption pay.

(2) In a case falling within paragraph (1)—

(a) the employee shall be treated as if he had been employed for a continuous period ending with the week in which he was notified of having been matched with the child for adoption; and

(b) his normal weekly earnings shall be calculated by reference to his normal weekly earnings for the period of 8 weeks ending with the last day in respect of which he was paid under his former contract of service.

NOTES

Modification in relation to parental order parents: as to the modification of this regulation, see the Statutory Paternity Pay and Statutory Adoption Pay (Parental Orders and Prospective Adopters) Regulations 2014, SI 2014/2934, regs 6, 23 at **[2.1554]**, **[2.1574]**.

PART 6
STATUTORY PATERNITY PAY AND STATUTORY ADOPTION PAY: PROVISIONS APPLICABLE TO BOTH STATUTORY PATERNITY PAY AND STATUTORY ADOPTION PAY

[2.658]
31 Introductory

(1) Subject to paragraph (2), the provisions of regulations 32 to 47 below apply to statutory paternity pay payable under Part 12ZA of the Act and to statutory adoption pay payable under 12ZB of the Act.

(2) The provisions of regulation 44 only apply to statutory adoption pay.

[2.659]
32 Treatment of persons as employees

(1) [Subject to paragraph (1A),] in a case where, and in so far as, a person . . . is treated as an employed earner by virtue of the Social Security (Categorisation of Earners) Regulations 1978 he shall be treated as an employee for the purposes of Parts 12ZA and 12ZB of the Act, and in a case where, and in so far as, such a person is treated otherwise than as an employed earner by virtue of those regulations, he shall not be treated as an employee for the purposes of Parts 12ZA and 12ZB of the Act.

[(1A) Paragraph (1) shall have effect in relation to a person who—

(a) is under the age of 16; and

(b) would or, as the case may be, would not have been treated as an employed earner by virtue of the Social Security (Categorisation of Earners) Regulations 1978 had he been over that age,

as it has effect in relation to a person who is or, as the case may be, is not so treated.]

(2) A person who is in employed earner's employment within the meaning of the Act under a contract of apprenticeship shall be treated as an employee for the purposes of Parts 12ZA and 12ZB of the Act.

(3) A person who is in employed earner's employment within the meaning of the Act but whose employer—

(a) does not fulfil the conditions prescribed in regulation 145(1) of the Contributions Regulations in so far as that provision relates to residence or presence in Great Britain; or

(b) is a person who, by reason of any international treaty to which the United Kingdom is a party or of any international convention binding the United Kingdom—

(i) is exempt from the provisions of the Act; or

(ii) is a person against whom the provisions of the Act are not enforceable,

shall not be treated as an employee for the purposes of Parts 12ZA and 12ZB of the Act.

NOTES

Para (1): words in square brackets inserted, and words omitted revoked, by the Employment Equality (Age) Regulations 2006, SI 2006/1031, reg 49(1), Sch 8, Pt 2, paras 59, 60(1), (2).

Para (1A): inserted by SI 2006/1031, reg 49(1), Sch 8, Pt 2, paras 59, 60(1), (3); substituted by the Employment Equality (Age) (Consequential Amendments) Regulations 2007, SI 2007/825, reg 7.

[2.660]
33 Continuous employment

(1) Subject to the following provisions of this regulation, where in any week a person is, for the whole or part of the week—

(a) incapable of work in consequence of sickness or injury;

(b) absent from work on account of a temporary cessation of work;

(c) absent from work in circumstances such that, by arrangement or custom, he is regarded as continuing in the employment of his employer for all or any purposes,

and returns to work for his employer after the incapacity for or absence from work, that week shall be treated for the purposes of sections 171ZA, 171ZB and 171ZL of the Act as part of a continuous period of employment with that employer, notwithstanding that no contract of service exists with that employer in respect of that week.

(2) Incapacity for work which lasts for more than 26 consecutive weeks shall not count for the purposes of paragraph (1)(a).

(3) Where a person—

(a) is an employee in an employed earner's employment in which the custom is for the employer—

(i) to offer work for a fixed period of not more than 26 consecutive weeks;

(ii) to offer work for such period on two or more occasions in a year for periods which do not overlap; and

(iii) to offer the work available to those persons who had worked for him during the last or a recent such period, but

(b) is absent from work because of incapacity arising from some specific disease or bodily or mental disablement,

then in that case paragraph (1) shall apply as if the words "and returns to work for his employer after the incapacity for or absence from work," were omitted and paragraph (4) shall not apply.

(4) Where a person is employed under a contract of service for part only of the relevant week within the meaning of subsection (3) of section 171ZL of the Act (entitlement to statutory adoption pay), the whole of that week shall count in computing a period of continuous employment for the purposes of that section.

[2.661]
34 Continuous employment and unfair dismissal

(1) This regulation applies to a person in relation to whose dismissal an action is commenced which consists—

(a) of the presentation by him of a complaint under section 111(1) of the Employment Rights Act 1996;

(b) of his making a claim in accordance with a dismissals procedure agreement designated by an order under section 110 of that Act; . . .

(c) of any action taken by a conciliation officer under [any of sections 18A to 18C] of the Employment Tribunals Act 1996; [or

(d) of a decision arising out of the use of a statutory dispute resolution procedure contained in Schedule 2 to the Employment Act 2002 in a case where, in accordance with the Employment Act 2002 (Dispute Resolution) Regulations 2004, such a procedure applies].

(2) If, in consequence of an action of the kind specified in paragraph (1), a person is reinstated or re-engaged by his employer or by a successor or associated employer of that employer, the continuity of his employment shall be preserved for the purposes of Part 12ZA or, as the case may be, Part 12ZB of the Act, and any week which falls within the interval beginning with the effective date of termination and ending with the date of reinstatement or re-engagement, as the case may be, shall count in the computation of his period of continuous employment.

(3) In this regulation—

"successor" and "dismissal procedures agreement" have the same meanings as in section 235 of the Employment Rights Act 1996; and

"associated employer" shall be construed in accordance with section 231 of the Employment Rights Act 1996.

NOTES

Para (1): word omitted from sub-para (b) revoked, and sub-para (d) and the word immediately preceding it inserted, by the Statutory Maternity Pay (General) and Statutory Paternity Pay and Statutory Adoption Pay (General) (Amendment) Regulations 2005, SI 2005/358, reg 4; words in square brackets in sub-para (c) substituted by the Enterprise and Regulatory Reform Act 2013 (Consequential Amendments) (Employment) Order 2014, SI 2014/386, art 2, Schedule, para 19.

Note that Sch 2 to the 2002 Act (referred to in para (1)(d)) has been repealed, and the 2004 Regulations have lapsed, but no consequential amendments have been made to the paragraph.

[2.662]
35 Continuous employment and stoppages of work

(1) Where, for any week or part of a week a person does not work because there is a stoppage of work due to a trade dispute within the meaning of section 35(1) of the Jobseekers Act 1995 at his place of employment, the continuity of his employment shall, subject to paragraph (2), be treated as continuing throughout the stoppage but, subject to paragraph (3), no such week shall count in the computation of his period of employment.

(2) Subject to paragraph (3), where during the stoppage of work a person is dismissed from his employment, the continuity of his employment shall not be treated in accordance with paragraph (1) as continuing beyond the commencement of the day he stopped work.

(3) The provisions of paragraph (1), to the extent that they provide that a week in which the stoppage of work occurred shall not count in the computation of a period of employment, and paragraph (2) shall not apply to a person who proves that at no time did he have a direct interest in the trade dispute in question.

[2.663]
[35A Meaning of "week"

(1) This regulation applies where a person ("P") has been in employed earner's employment with the same employer in each of 26 consecutive weeks (but no more than 26 weeks), ending with—

(a) in relation to P's entitlement to statutory paternity pay (birth), the week immediately preceding the 14th week before the expected week of the child's birth, or

(b) in relation to P's entitlement to statutory paternity pay (adoption), the week in which P is notified that P has been matched with the child for the purposes of adoption.

(2) For the purpose of determining whether P's employment amounts to a continuous period of at least 26 weeks (see sections 171ZA(2)(b) and 171ZL(2)(b) of the Act) , the first of those 26 weeks is a period commencing on the first day of P's employment with the employer ("the start date") and ending at midnight on—

(a) the first Saturday after the start date, or
(b) where the start date is a Saturday, that day.]

NOTES

Commencement: 1 February 2016.

Inserted by the Statutory Paternity Pay, Statutory Adoption Pay and Statutory Shared Parental Pay (Amendment) Regulations 2015, SI 2015/2065, reg 2, as from 1 February 2016.

[2.664]
36 Change of employer

A person's employment shall, notwithstanding a change of employer, be treated as continuous employment with the second employer where—

(a) the employer's trade or business or an undertaking (whether or not it is an undertaking established by or under an Act of Parliament) is transferred from one person to another;
(b) by or under an Act of Parliament, whether public or local and whenever passed, a contract of employment between any body corporate and the person is modified and some other body corporate is substituted as his employer;
(c) on the death of his employer, the person is taken into employment of the personal representatives or trustees of the deceased;
(d) the person is employed by partners, personal representatives or trustees and there is a change in the partners, or, as the case may be, personal representatives or trustees;
(e) the person is taken into the employment of an employer who is, at the time he entered his employment, an associated employer of his previous employer, and for this purpose "associated employer" shall be construed in accordance with section 231 of the Employment Rights Act 1996;
(f) on the termination of his employment with an employer he is taken into the employment of another employer and those employers are governors of a school maintained by a [local authority] and that authority.

NOTES

Words in square brackets in para (f) substituted by the Local Education Authorities and Children's Services Authorities (Integration of Functions) (Local and Subordinate Legislation) Order 2010, SI 2010/1172, art 5, Sch 3, para 47.

[2.665]
37 Reinstatement after service with the armed forces etc

If a person who is entitled to apply to his employer under the Reserve Forces (Safeguard of Employment) Act 1985 enters the employment of that employer within the 6-month period mentioned in section 1(4)(b) of that Act, his previous period of employment with that employer (or if there was more than one such period, the last of those periods) and the period of employment beginning in that 6 month period shall be treated as continuous.

[2.666]
38 Treatment of two or more employers or two or more contracts of service as one

(1) In a case where the earnings paid to a person in respect of two or more employments are aggregated and treated as a single payment of earnings under regulation 15(1) of the Contributions Regulations, the employers of that person in respect of those employments shall be treated as one for the purposes of Part 12ZA or, as the case may be, Part 12ZB of the Act.

(2) Where two or more employers are treated as one under the provisions of paragraph (1), liability for statutory paternity pay or, as the case may be, statutory adoption pay, shall be apportioned between them in such proportions as they may agree or, in default of agreement, in the proportions which the person's earnings from each employment bear to the amount of the aggregated earnings.

(3) Where two or more contracts of service exist concurrently between one employer and one employee, they shall be treated as one for the purposes of Part 12ZA or, as the case may be, Part 12ZB of the Act, except where, by virtue of regulation 14 of the Contributions Regulations, the earnings from those contracts of service are not aggregated for the purposes of earnings-related contributions.

[2.667]
39 Meaning of "earnings"

(1) For the purposes of section 171ZJ(6) (normal weekly earnings for the purposes of Part 12ZA of the Act) and of section 171ZS(6) of the Act (normal weekly earnings for the purposes of Part 12ZB of the Act), the expression "earnings" shall be construed in accordance with the following provisions of this regulation.

(2) The expression "earnings" refers to gross earnings and includes any remuneration or profit derived from a person's employment except any payment or amount which is—

(a) excluded from the computation of a person's earnings under regulation 25 of and Schedule 3 to, and regulation 123 of, the Contributions Regulations (payments to be disregarded) and regulation 27 of those Regulations (payments to directors to be disregarded) [(or would have been so excluded had he not been under the age of 16)];

(b) a chargeable emolument under section 10A of the Act, except where, in consequence of such a chargeable emolument being excluded from earnings, a person would not be entitled to statutory paternity pay or, as the case may be, statutory adoption pay [(or where such a payment or amount would have been so excluded and in consequence he would not have been entitled to statutory paternity pay or, as the case may be, statutory adoption pay had he not been under the age of 16)].

(3) For the avoidance of doubt, "earnings" includes—

[(za) any amount retrospectively treated as earnings by regulations made by virtue of section 4B(2) of the Act;]

(a) any sum payable in respect of arrears of pay in pursuance of an order for reinstatement or re-engagement under the Employment Rights Act 1996;

(b) any sum payable by way of pay in pursuance of an order made under the Employment Rights Act 1996 for the continuation of a contract of employment;

(c) any sum payable by way of remuneration in pursuance of a protective award under section 189 of the Trade Union and Labour Relations (Consolidation) Act 1992;

(d) any sum payable by way of statutory sick pay, including sums payable in accordance with regulations made under section 151(6) of the Act;

(e) any sum payable by way of statutory maternity pay;

(f) any sum payable by way of statutory paternity pay;

(g) any sum payable by way of statutory adoption pay.

NOTES

Para (2): words in square brackets inserted by the Employment Equality (Age) Regulations 2006, SI 2006/1031, reg 49(1), Sch 8, Pt 2, paras 59, 61.

Para (3): sub-para (za) inserted by the Social Security, Occupational Pension Schemes and Statutory Payments (Consequential Provisions) Regulations 2007, SI 2007/1154, reg 6(1), (2).

[2.668]

40 Normal weekly earnings

(1) For the purposes of Part 12ZA and Part 12ZB of the Act, a person's normal weekly earnings shall be calculated in accordance with the following provisions of this regulation.

(2) In this regulation—

"the appropriate date" means—

(a) in relation to statutory paternity pay (birth), the first day of the 14th week before the expected week of the child's birth or the first day in the week in which the child is born, whichever is the earlier;

(b) in relation to statutory paternity pay (adoption) and statutory adoption pay, the first day of the week after the week in which the adopter is notified of being matched with the child for the purposes of adoption;

"normal pay day" means a day on which the terms of a person's contract of service require him to be paid, or the practice in his employment is for him to be paid, if any payment is due to him; and

"day of payment" means a day on which the person was paid.

(3) Subject to paragraph (4), the relevant period for the purposes of section 171ZJ(6) and 171ZS(6) is the period between—

(a) the last normal pay day to fall before the appropriate date; and

(b) the last normal pay day to fall at least 8 weeks earlier than the normal pay day mentioned in sub-paragraph (a),

including the normal pay day mentioned in sub-paragraph (a) but excluding that first mentioned in sub-paragraph (b).

(4) In a case where a person has no identifiable normal pay day, paragraph (3) shall have effect as if the words "day of payment" were substituted for the words "normal pay day" in each place where they occur.

(5) In a case where a person has normal pay days at intervals of or approximating to one or more calendar months (including intervals of or approximating to a year) his normal weekly earnings shall be calculated by dividing his earnings in the relevant period by the number of calendar months in that period (or, if it is not a whole number, the nearest whole number), multiplying the result by 12 and dividing by 52.

(6) In a case to which paragraph (5) does not apply and the relevant period is not an exact number of weeks, the person's normal weekly earnings shall be calculated by dividing his earnings in the relevant period by the number of days in the relevant period and multiplying the result by 7.

(7) In any case where a person receives a back-dated pay increase which includes a sum in respect of a relevant period, normal weekly earnings shall be calculated as if such a sum was paid in that relevant period even though received after that period.

NOTES

Modification in relation to parental order parents: as to the modification of this regulation, see the Statutory Paternity Pay and Statutory Adoption Pay (Parental Orders and Prospective Adopters) Regulations 2014, SI 2014/2934, regs 6, 24 at **[2.1554]**, **[2.1575]**.

[2.669]
41 Payment of statutory paternity pay and statutory adoption pay

Payments of statutory paternity pay and statutory adoption pay may be made in a like manner to payments of remuneration but shall not include payment in kind or by way of the provision of board or lodgings or of services or other facilities.

[2.670]
42 Time when statutory paternity pay and statutory adoption pay are to be paid

(1) In this regulation, "pay day" means a day on which it has been agreed, or it is the normal practice between an employer or former employer and a person who is or was an employee of his, that payments by way of remuneration are to be made, or, where there is no such agreement or normal practice, the last day of a calendar month.

(2) In any case where—

(a) a decision has been made by an officer of the Board under section 8(1) of the Social Security Contributions (Transfer of Functions, etc) Act 1999 as a result of which a person is entitled to an amount of statutory paternity pay or statutory adoption pay; and

(b) the time for bringing an appeal against the decision has expired and either—

(i) no such appeal has been brought; or

(ii) such an appeal has been brought and has been finally disposed of,

that amount of statutory paternity pay or statutory adoption pay shall be paid within the time specified in paragraph (3).

(3) Subject to paragraphs (4) and (5), the employer or former employer shall pay the amount not later than the first pay day after—

(a) where an appeal has been brought, the day on which the employer or former employer receives notification that it has been finally disposed of;

(b) where leave to appeal has been refused and there remains no further opportunity to apply for leave, the day on which the employer or former employer receives notification of the refusal; and

(c) in any other case, the day on which the time for bringing an appeal expires.

(4) Subject to paragraph (5), where it is impracticable, in view of the employer's or former employer's methods of accounting for and paying remuneration, for the requirement of payment referred to in paragraph (3) to be met by the pay day referred to in that paragraph, it shall be met not later than the next following pay day.

(5) Where the employer or former employer would not have remunerated the employee for his work in the week in question as early as the pay day specified in paragraph (3) or (if it applies) paragraph (4), the requirement of payment shall be met on the first day on which the employee would have been remunerated for his work in that week.

[2.671]
43 Liability of the Board to pay statutory paternity pay or statutory adoption pay

(1) Where—

(a) an officer of the Board has decided that an employer is liable to make payments of statutory paternity pay or, as the case may be, statutory adoption pay to a person;

(b) the time for appealing against the decision has expired; and

(c) no appeal against the decision has been lodged or leave to appeal against the decision is required and has been refused,

then for any week in respect of which the employer was liable to make payments of statutory paternity pay or, as the case may be, statutory adoption pay but did not do so, and for any subsequent weeks in the paternity pay period or, as the case may be, adoption pay period, the liability to make those payments shall, notwithstanding sections 171ZD and 171ZM of the Act, be that of the Board and not the employer.

(2) Liability to make payments of statutory paternity pay or, as the case may be, statutory adoption pay shall, notwithstanding sections 171ZD and 171ZM of the Act, be a liability of the Board and not the employer as from the week in which the employer first becomes insolvent until the end of the paternity pay or adoption pay period.

(3) For the purposes of paragraph (2) an employer shall be taken to be insolvent if, and only if—

(a) in England and Wales—

(i) he has been adjudged bankrupt or has made a composition or arrangement with his creditors;

(ii) he has died and his estate falls to be administered in accordance with an order made under section 421 of the Insolvency Act 1986; or

(iii) where an employer is a company or a limited liability partnership, a winding-up order . . . is made or a resolution for a voluntary winding-up is passed (or, in the case of a limited liability partnership, a determination for a voluntary winding-up has been made) with respect to it [or it enters administration], or a receiver or a manager of its undertaking is duly appointed, or possession is taken, by or on behalf of the holders of any debentures secured by a floating charge, of any property of the company or limited liability partnership comprised in or subject to the charge, or a voluntary arrangement proposed for the purposes of Part 1 of the Insolvency Act 1986 is approved under that Part of that Act;

(b) in Scotland—

(i) an award of sequestration is made on his estate or he executes a trust deed for his creditors or enters into a composition contract;

(ii) he has died and a judicial factor appointed under section 11A of the Judicial Factors (Scotland) Act 1889 is required by that section to divide his insolvent estate among his creditors; or

(iii) where the employer is a company or a limited liability partnership, a winding-up order . . . is made or a resolution for voluntary winding-up is passed (or, in the case of a limited liability partnership, a determination for a voluntary winding-up is made) with respect to it [or it enters administration], or a receiver of its undertaking is duly appointed, or a voluntary arrangement proposed for the purposes of Part 1 of the Insolvency Act 1986 is approved under that Part.

NOTES

Para (3): words omitted revoked, and words in square brackets inserted, by the Enterprise Act 2002 (Insolvency) Order 2003, SI 2003/2096, art 5, Schedule, Pt 2, para 79.

[2.672]
44 Liability of the Board to pay statutory adoption pay in cases of legal custody or imprisonment

Where—

(a) there is liability to pay statutory adoption pay in respect of a period which is subsequent to the last week falling within paragraph (1)(c) of regulation 27, or

(b) there is liability to pay statutory adoption pay during a period of detention in legal custody by virtue of the provisions of paragraph (2) of that regulation,

that liability shall, notwithstanding section 171ZM of the Act, be that of the Board and not the employer.

[2.673]
45 Payments by the Board

Where the Board become liable in accordance with regulation 43 or 44 to make payments of statutory paternity pay or, as the case may be, statutory adoption pay to a person, the first payment shall be made as soon as reasonably practicable after they become so liable, and payments thereafter shall be made at weekly intervals, by means of an instrument of payment or by such other means as appears to the Board to be appropriate in the circumstance of any particular case.

[2.674]
46 Persons unable to act

(1) Where in the case of any person—

(a) statutory paternity pay or, as the case may be, statutory adoption pay is payable to him or he is alleged to be entitled to it;

(b) he is unable for the time being to act; and

(c) either—

(i) no receiver has been appointed by the Court of Protection with power to receive statutory paternity pay or, as the case may be, statutory adoption pay on his behalf, or

(ii) in Scotland, his estate is not being administered by any tutor, curator or other guardian acting or appointed in terms of law,

the Board may, upon written application to them by a person who, if a natural person, is over the age of 18, appoint that person to exercise, on behalf of the person unable to act, any right to which he may be entitled under Part 12ZA or, as the case may be, Part 12ZB of the Act and to deal on his behalf with any sums payable to him.

(2) Where the Board have made an appointment under paragraph (1)—

(a) they may at any time in their absolute discretion revoke it;

(b) the person appointed may resign his office after having given one month's notice in writing to the Board of his intention to do so; and

(c) the appointment shall terminate when the Board are notified that a receiver or other person to whom paragraph (1)(c) applies has been appointed.

(3) Anything required by Part 12ZA or 12ZB of the Act to be done by or to any person who is unable to act may be done by or to the person appointed under this regulation to act on his behalf, and the receipt of the person so appointed shall be a good discharge to the person's employer or former employer for any sum paid.

[2.675]
47 Service of notices by post

A notice given in accordance with the provisions of these Regulations in writing contained in an envelope which is properly addressed and sent by prepaid post shall be treated as having been given on the day on which it is posted.

EMPLOYMENT TRIBUNALS (ENFORCEMENT OF ORDERS IN OTHER JURISDICTIONS) (SCOTLAND) REGULATIONS 2002

(SI 2002/2972)

ARRANGEMENT OF REGULATIONS

SCHEDULES

NOTES

Made: 2 December 2002.

Authority: Civil Jurisdiction and Judgments Act 1982, s 18(1)(a), Sch 6, paras 2(2), 4(1); Employment Tribunals Act 1996, s 7(1).

Commencement: 24 December 2002.

[2.676]

1 Citation, commencement and revocation

(1) These Regulations may be cited as the Employment Tribunals (Enforcement of Orders in Other Jurisdictions) (Scotland) Regulations 2002 and shall come into force on 24th December 2002.

(2) The Employment Tribunals (Enforcement of Orders under the Civil Jurisdiction and Judgments Act 1982) (Scotland) Regulations 1995 are hereby revoked.

[2.677]

2 Interpretation

In these Regulations—

"the Act of 1982" means the Civil Jurisdiction and Judgments Act 1982;

"Contracting State" has the meaning assigned in section 1(3) of the Act of 1982;

"Office of the Tribunals" means the Central Office of the Employment Tribunals (Scotland);

"order" means an order for the payment of one or more sums of money contained in a decision of an employment tribunal in Scotland;

"Register" means the register of applications, appeals and decisions kept in pursuance of regulation 12 of the Employment Tribunals (Constitution and Rules of Procedure) (Scotland) Regulations 2001;

"Regulation State" has the meaning assigned in section 1(3) of the Act of 1982; and

"Secretary" means the person for the time being appointed to act as the Secretary of the Office of the Tribunals.

NOTES

Definitions "Contracting State" and "Regulation State" revoked by the Civil Jurisdiction and Judgments (Amendment) (EU Exit) Regulations 2019, SI 2019/479, reg 76(1), (2), as from exit day (as defined in the European Union (Withdrawal) Act 2018, s 20).

[2.678]

3 Recognition or enforcement of tribunal decisions in another Contracting State

(1) An interested party who wishes to secure the recognition or enforcement, in another Contracting State, of an order, may apply for—

(a) a copy of the decision of the tribunal containing that order; and

(b) a certificate giving particulars relating to the decision and the proceedings in which it was given;

in accordance with paragraph (2).

(2) The application shall be in writing and shall state—

(a) the names of the parties to the proceedings in which the decision was given and, if known by the person applying, the case number of the originating application which relates to those proceedings;

(b) the date shown on the decision as being the date it was sent to the parties;

(c) if known by the person applying, whether enforcement of the order has been stayed or suspended; and

(d) that the application is made in pursuance of a wish on the part of the person applying to secure the recognition or enforcement of the order in another Contracting State.

(3) The application shall be presented to the Secretary at the Office of the Tribunals.

(4) If the Secretary is of the opinion that he is unable to issue a certificate under this regulation unless he is given further information, he shall, in writing, notify the person applying of that fact, specifying what further information is required.

[(5) Subject to paragraph (4), upon receiving an application which satisfies the requirements of this regulation, the Secretary shall issue to the person applying a certificate in the form of Annex V to the Convention on jurisdiction and the recognition and enforcement of judgments in civil and commercial matters, between the European Community and the Republic of Iceland, the Kingdom of Norway, the Swiss Confederation and the Kingdom of Denmark signed on behalf of the European Community on 30th October 2007.]

NOTES

Revoked by the Civil Jurisdiction and Judgments (Amendment) (EU Exit) Regulations 2019, SI 2019/479, reg 76(1), (3), as from exit day (as defined in the European Union (Withdrawal) Act 2018, s 20).

Para (5): substituted by the Civil Jurisdiction and Judgments Regulations 2009, SI 2009/3131, reg 45(a).

[2.679]

4 Recognition or enforcement of tribunal decisions in another Regulation State

(1) An interested party who wishes to secure recognition or apply for a declaration of enforceability of an order in another Regulation State may apply for—

(a) a copy of the decision of the tribunal containing that order; and

(b) a certificate giving particulars relating to the decision and the proceedings in which it was given;

in accordance with paragraph (2).

(2) The application shall be in writing and shall state—

(a) the names of the parties to the proceedings in which the decision containing the order was given and, if known by the person applying, the case number of the originating application which relates to those proceedings; and

(b) the date shown on the decision as being the date it was sent to the parties.

(3) The application shall be presented to the Secretary at the Office of the Tribunals.

(4) If the Secretary is of the opinion that he is unable to issue a certificate under this regulation unless he is given further information, he shall, in writing, notify the person applying of that fact, specifying the further information required.

(5) Subject to paragraph (4), upon receiving an application which satisfies the requirements of this regulation, the Secretary shall issue to the person applying—

(a) a certificate in the form of Annex V to the Council Regulation (EC) No 44/2001 of 22nd December 2000 on jurisdiction and the recognition and enforcement of judgments in civil and commercial matters[, as amended from time to time and as applied by the Agreement made on 19th October 2005 between the European Community and the Kingdom of Denmark on jurisdiction and the recognition and enforcement of judgments in civil and commercial matters]; and

(b) a copy of the decision as it appears on the Register.

NOTES

Revoked by the Civil Jurisdiction and Judgments (Amendment) (EU Exit) Regulations 2019, SI 2019/479, reg 76(1), (4), as from exit day (as defined in the European Union (Withdrawal) Act 2018, s 20).

Para (5): in sub-para (a) words in square brackets inserted by the Civil Jurisdiction and Judgments Regulations 2007, SI 2007/1655, reg 5, Schedule, Pt 2, para 36.

[2.680]

5 Enforcement of tribunal orders in other parts of the United Kingdom

(1) An interested party who wishes under Schedule 6 of the Act of 1982 to secure the enforcement, in another part of the United Kingdom, of an order made by a tribunal in Scotland, shall apply for a certificate in respect of that order, in accordance with paragraph (2).

(2) The application shall be in writing and shall—

(a) state—

(i) the names of the parties to the proceedings in which the decision containing the order was given and, if known by the person applying, the case number of the originating application which relates to those proceedings;

(ii) the date shown on the decision as being the date it was sent to the parties; and

(b) verify that enforcement of the order has not been stayed or suspended and that the time available for enforcement has not expired.

(3) The application shall be presented to the Secretary at the Office of the Tribunals.

(4) If the Secretary is of the opinion that he is unable to issue a certificate under this regulation unless he is given further information, he shall, in writing, notify the person applying of that fact, specifying the further information required.

(5) Subject to paragraph (4), upon receiving an application which satisfies the requirements of this regulation, the Secretary shall issue to the person applying—

(a) a certificate in the form set out in Schedule 2, or in a form substantially to the same effect, with such variation as circumstances may require; and

(b) a copy of the decision as it appears on the Register.

[2.681]
6 Miscellaneous

Any function of the Secretary may be performed by a person acting with the authority of the Secretary.

SCHEDULE 1

(Revoked by the Civil Jurisdiction and Judgments Regulations 2009, SI 2009/3131, reg 45(b).)

SCHEDULE 2
FORM

Regulation 5

[2.682]
Certificate under Paragraph 4(1) of Schedule 6 to the Civil Jurisdiction and Judgments Act 1982

The Central Office of the Employment Tribunals (Scotland)

. . . . *(applicant)* and

. . . . *(respondent)*

I , [the Secretary of the Central Office of the Employment Tribunals (Scotland)], hereby certify:—

1 That an employment tribunal sitting at [*place*] ordered, in a decision entered into the Register on [*date*], that the sum of £[*sum*] was payable by [*name*], [together with £[*sum*] expenses].

2 That the sum [excluding expenses] contained in the order carries interest at the rate of [ ] per cent per annum from [*date*] until payment.

3 That the time for appealing against the order contained in the decision has expired and [no appeal has been brought within that time or an appeal brought within that time has been finally disposed of].

4 That enforcement of the order has not for the time being been suspended and that the time available for its enforcement has not expired.

5 That this certificate is issued under paragraph 4(1) of Schedule 6 to the Civil Jurisdiction and Judgments Act 1982, in the form prescribed by regulation 5 of the Employment Tribunals (Enforcement of Orders in Other Jurisdictions) (Scotland) Regulations 2002.

Signed [*date*]

Secretary

Central Office of the Employment Tribunals (Scotland)

EDUCATION (MODIFICATION OF ENACTMENTS RELATING TO EMPLOYMENT) (ENGLAND) ORDER 2003

(SI 2003/1964)

NOTES

Made: 5 August 2003.

Authority: School Standards and Framework Act 1998, ss 81, 138(7).

Commencement: 1 September 2003.

Extent: this Order applies to England. The equivalent provisions for Wales are in the Education (Modification of Enactments Relating to Employment) (Wales) Order 2006, SI 2006/1073 at **[2.912]**. There is no equivalent provision for Scotland.

ARRANGEMENT OF ARTICLES

[2.683]
1 Citation, commencement, application and revocation

(1) This Order may be cited as the Education (Modification of Enactments Relating to Employment) (England) Order 2003 and shall come into force on 1st September 2003.

(2) These Regulations apply only in relation to England.

(3) The Education (Modification of Enactments Relating to Employment) Order 1999 is revoked, in relation to England.

[2.684]
2 Interpretation

(1) In this Order—

"the 1996 Act" means the Employment Rights Act 1996;

"the 1998 Act" means the School Standards and Framework Act 1998;

"the 2003 Regulations" mean the School Staffing (England) Regulations 2003;

"authority" means the [local authority] by which a maintained school is, or a proposed school is to be, maintained;

"governing body" means the governing body of a school which is maintained by an authority;

"governing body having a right to a delegated budget" and "school having a delegated budget" have the same meaning as in Part 2 of the 1998 Act.

(2) In this Order references to employment powers are references to the powers of appointment, suspension, conduct and discipline, capability and dismissal of staff conferred by the 2003 Regulations.

NOTES

Para (1): words in square brackets in definition "authority" substituted by the Local Education Authorities and Children's Services Authorities (Integration of Functions) (Local and Subordinate Legislation) Order 2010, SI 2010/1172, art 4(3)(a).

[2.685]
3 General modifications of employment enactments

(1) In their application to a governing body having a right to a delegated budget, the enactments set out in the Schedule have effect as if—

(a) any reference to an employer (however expressed) included a reference to the governing body acting in the exercise of its employment powers and as if that governing body had at all material times been such an employer;

(b) in relation to the exercise of the governing body's employment powers, employment by the authority at a school were employment by the governing body of the school;

(c) references to employees were references to employees at the school in question;

(d) references to dismissal by an employer included references to dismissal by the authority following notification of a determination by a governing body under regulation 18(1) of the 2003 Regulations; and

(e) references to trade unions recognised by an employer were references to trade unions recognised by the authority or the governing body.

(2) Paragraph (1) does not cause the exemption in respect of an employer with fewer employees than is specified in section 7(1) of the Disability Discrimination Act 1995 to apply (without prejudice to whether it applies irrespective of that paragraph).

[2.686]
4

Without prejudice to the generality of article 3, where an employee employed at a school having a delegated budget is dismissed by the authority following notification of such a determination as is mentioned in article 3(1)(d)—

(a) section 92 of the 1996 Act has effect as if the governing body had dismissed him and as if references to the employer's reasons for dismissing the employee were references to the reasons for which the governing body made its determination; and

(b) Part X of the 1996 Act has effect in relation to the dismissal as if the governing body had dismissed him, and the reason or principal reason for which the governing body did so had been the reason or principal reason for which it made its determination.

[2.687]
5 Trade disputes

(1) Subject to paragraph (2), a dispute between staff employed to work at a school having a delegated budget and the school's governing body, which relates wholly or mainly to one of the matters set out in section 244(1) of the Trade Union and Labour Relations (Consolidation) Act 1992 is a trade dispute within the meaning of that Act.

(2) In any case where there is a trade dispute only by virtue of this article, nothing in section 219 of that Act prevents an act from being actionable in tort where the inducement, interference or threat mentioned in that section relates to a contract the performance of which does not affect directly or indirectly the school over which the governing body in question exercises its functions.

[2.688]
6 Applications to Employment Tribunals

(1) Without prejudice to articles 3 and 4, and notwithstanding any provision in the Employment Tribunals Act 1996 and any regulations made under section 1(1) of that Act, this article applies in respect of any application to an employment tribunal, and any proceedings pursuant to such an application, in relation to which by virtue of article 3 or 4 a governing body is to be treated as if it were an employer (however expressed).

(2) The application must be made, and the proceedings must be carried on, against that governing body.

(3) Notwithstanding paragraph (2), any decision, declaration, order, recommendation or award made in the course of such proceedings except in so far as it requires reinstatement or re-engagement has effect as if made against the authority.

(4) Where any application is made against a governing body under paragraph (2)—

(a) the governing body must notify the authority within 14 days of receiving notification; and

(b) the authority, on written application to the employment tribunal, is entitled to be made an additional party to the proceedings and to take part in the proceedings accordingly.

SCHEDULE

Article 3

[2.689]

Sex Discrimination Act 1975
sections 6, 7, 9, 41 and 82(1A)

Race Relations Act 1976
sections 4, 5, 7 and 32

Trade Union and Labour Relations (Consolidation) Act 1992
sections 146, 147, 152–154 and 181–185

Disability Discrimination Act 1995
sections 4–6, 11, 12, 16, 55, 57 and 58

Employment Rights Act 1996
sections 66–68, 70, 71, 92, 93 and Part X

[Employment Act 2002
sections 29–32 and Schedules 2–4].

NOTES

Entry relating to the "Employment Act 2002" inserted by the Education (Modification of Enactments Relating to Employment) (England) (Amendment) Order 2004, SI 2004/2325, art 2. Note that these provisions of the 2002 Act were repealed by the Employment Act 2008.

Sex Discrimination Act 1975, Race Relations Act 1976, Disability Discrimination Act 1995: repealed by the Equality Act 2010, s 211(2), Sch 27, Pt 1.

CONDUCT OF EMPLOYMENT AGENCIES AND EMPLOYMENT BUSINESSES REGULATIONS 2003

(SI 2003/3319)

NOTES

Made: 17 December 2003.
Authority: Employment Agencies Act 1973, ss 5(1), 6(1), 12(3).
Commencement: 6 April 2004 (all except regs 26(7), 32); 6 July 2004 (regs 26(7), 32).

ARRANGEMENT OF REGULATIONS

PART I
GENERAL AND INTERPRETATION

PART II
GENERAL OBLIGATIONS

PART III
REQUIREMENTS TO BE SATISFIED BEFORE SERVICES ARE PROVIDED

PART I
GENERAL AND INTERPRETATION

[2.690]
1 Citation and commencement

(1) These Regulations may be cited as the Conduct of Employment Agencies and Employment Businesses Regulations 2003.

(2) With the exception of regulations 26(7) and 32, the Regulations shall come into force on 6th April 2004.

(3) Regulations 26(7) and 32 shall come into force on 6th July 2004.

[2.691]
2 Interpretation

In these Regulations, unless the context otherwise requires—

"the Act" means the Employment Agencies Act 1973;

"advertisement" includes every form of advertising by whatever means;

"agency" means an employment agency as defined in section 13(1) and (2) of the Act and includes a person carrying on an agency, and in the case of a person who carries on both an agency and an employment business means such a person in his capacity in carrying on the agency;

"business day" means a day other than a Saturday or a Sunday, Christmas Day or Good Friday, or a day which is a bank holiday under or by virtue of the Banking and Financial Dealings Act 1971 in that part of Great Britain;

"company" includes any body corporate (whether incorporated in Great Britain or elsewhere) and references to directors and other officers of a company and to voting power at any general meeting of a company have effect in the case of a company incorporated outside Great Britain with any necessary modifications;

"employment business" means an employment business as defined in section 13(1) and (3) of the Act and includes a person carrying on an employment business, and in the case of a person who carries on both an employment business and an agency means such a person in his capacity in carrying on the employment business;

"hirer" means a person (including an employment business) to whom an agency or employment business introduces or supplies or holds itself out as being capable of introducing or supplying a work-seeker;

"publication" means any publication whether in paper or electronic form other than a programme service within the meaning of the Broadcasting Act 1990;

["vulnerable person" means any person who by reason of age, infirmity, illness, disability or any other circumstance is in need of care or attention, and includes any person under the age of eighteen;]

"work-finding services" means services (whether by the provision of information or otherwise) provided—

(a) by an agency to a person for the purpose of finding that person employment or seeking to find that person employment;

(b) by an employment business to an employee of the employment business for the purpose of finding or seeking to find another person, with a view to the employee acting for and under the control of that other person;

(c) by an employment business to a person (the "first person") for the purpose of finding or seeking to find another person (the "second person"), with a view to the first person becoming employed by the employment business and acting for and under the control of the second person;

"work-seeker" means a person to whom an agency or employment business provides or holds itself out as being capable of providing work-finding services.

NOTES

Definition "vulnerable person" inserted by the Conduct of Employment Agencies and Employment Businesses (Amendment) Regulations 2010, SI 2010/1782, regs 2, 3.

[2.692]

3 The meaning of "connected"

(1) For the purposes of these Regulations a person is connected with—

(a) his spouse [or civil partner] or minor child or stepchild;

(b) any individual who employs him or is his employee;

(c) any person who is in partnership with him;

(d) any company of which he is a director or other officer and any company connected with that company;

(e) in the case of a company—

(i) any person who is a director or other officer of that company;

(ii) any subsidiary or holding company, both as defined in section 736 of the Companies Act 1985, of that company and any person who is a director or other officer, or an employee of any such subsidiary or holding company;

(iii) any company of which the same person or persons have control; and

(f) in the case of a trustee of a trust, a beneficiary of the trust, and any person to whom the terms of the trust confer a power that may be exercised for that person's benefit.

(2) For the purposes of paragraph (1)(e)(iii) a person is to be taken as having control of a company if—

(a) he or any person with whom he is connected is a director of that company or of another company which has control of it;

(b) the directors of that company or another company which has control of it (or any of them) are accustomed to act in accordance with his directions or instructions; or

(c) he is entitled to exercise, or control the exercise of, one third or more of the voting power at any general meeting of the company or of another company which has control of it.

NOTES

Para (1): words in square brackets in sub-para (a) inserted by the Civil Partnership Act 2004 (Amendments to Subordinate Legislation) Order 2005, SI 2005/2114, art 2(17), Sch 17, para 8.

Stepchild: as to the interpretation of the word "stepchild" in reg 3(1)(a), see the Civil Partnership Act 2004, s 246 and the Civil Partnership Act 2004 (Relationships Arising Through Civil Partnership) Order 2005, SI 2005/3137, art 3(1), Schedule, para 129.

Companies Act 1985, s 736: repealed by the Companies Act 2006, s 1295, Sch 16, as from 1 October 2009. The equivalent section of the 2006 Act is s 1159. There has been no amendment to this section to reflect the change.

[2.693]

4 Transitional and Saving Provisions and Revocation

(1) The transitional and saving provisions in Schedule 1 shall apply.

(2) Subject to the provisions of Schedule 1, the following statutory instruments are hereby revoked—

(a) the Conduct of Employment Agencies and Employment Businesses Regulations 1976;

(b) the Employment Agencies Act 1973 (Charging Fees to Workers) Regulations 1976; and

(c) the Employment Agencies Act 1973 (Charging Fees to Au Pairs) Regulations 1981.

PART II
GENERAL OBLIGATIONS

[2.694]

5 [Restriction on use of additional services]

[(1)] Neither an agency nor an employment business may make the provision to a work-seeker of work-finding services conditional upon the work-seeker—

(a) using other services for which the Act does not prohibit the charging of a fee, or

(b) hiring or purchasing goods,

whether provided by the agency or the employment business or by any person with whom the agency or employment business is connected.

[(2) Where the work-seeker uses services for which the Act does not prohibit the charging of a fee, an agency or employment business providing or making provision for such services shall ensure that the work-seeker is able to cancel or withdraw from those services at any time without incurring any detriment or penalty, subject to the work-seeker giving to the provider of those services in paper form or by electronic means notice of five business days or, for services relating to the provision of living accommodation, notice of ten business days.]

[(3) In addition, where the work-seeker is seeking employment as an actor, background artist, dancer, extra, musician, singer or other performer or as a photographic or fashion model and that work-seeker uses a service, for which the Act does not prohibit the charging of a fee, which includes the production of a photographic image or audio or video recording of the work-seeker, an agency or employment business providing or making provision for such service shall ensure that, for 30 days from the date of the agency or employment business entering into a contract for such a service whether written or oral—

(a) the agency or the employment business shall not charge a fee to a work-seeker for that part of the service which consists of providing or making provision for a photographic image or audio or video recording of the work-seeker; and

(b) the work-seeker shall be entitled without detriment or penalty to cancel or withdraw from any contract with the agency or employment business for such a service with immediate effect by informing the agency or employment business of cancellation or withdrawal and where the work-seeker informs the agency or employment business of cancellation or withdrawal the work-seeker has no obligation to make any payment under the contract.

(4) Paragraphs (2) and (3) do not apply to a service for which a fee may be charged by virtue of regulation 26(1).]

NOTES

Regulation heading substituted, para (1) numbered as such, and para (2) added, by the Conduct of Employment Agencies and Employment Businesses (Amendment) Regulations 2007, SI 2007/3575, regs 2, 3.

Paras (3), (4) added by the Conduct of Employment Agencies and Employment Businesses (Amendment) Regulations 2010, SI 2010/1782, regs 2, 4.

[2.695]

6 Restriction on detrimental action relating to work-seekers working elsewhere

(1) Neither an agency nor an employment business may (whether by the inclusion of a term in a contract with a relevant work-seeker or otherwise)—

(a) subject or threaten to subject a relevant work-seeker to any detriment on the ground that—

(i) the relevant work-seeker has terminated or given notice to terminate any contract between the work-seeker and the agency or employment business, or

(ii) in the case of an employment business, the relevant work-seeker has taken up or proposes to take up employment with any other person; or

(b) require the relevant work-seeker to notify the agency or the employment business, or any person with whom it is connected, of the identity of any future employer of the relevant work-seeker.

(2) For the avoidance of doubt, the following shall not constitute a detriment within the meaning of paragraph (1)(a)—

(a) the loss of any benefits to which the relevant work-seeker might have become entitled had he not terminated the contract;

(b) the recovery of losses incurred by an agency or employment business as a result of the failure of the relevant work-seeker to perform work he has agreed to perform; or

(c) a requirement in a contract with the agency or employment business for the work-seeker to give a period of notice which is reasonable to terminate the contract.

(3) In this regulation, "relevant work-seeker" means any work-seeker other than, in the case of an employment business, a work-seeker who is or will be employed by the employment business under a contract of service or apprenticeship.

[2.696]

7 Restriction on providing work-seekers in industrial disputes

(1) Subject to paragraph (2) an employment business shall not introduce or supply a work-seeker to a hirer to perform—

(a) the duties normally performed by a worker who is taking part in a strike or other industrial action ("the first worker"), or

(b) the duties normally performed by any other worker employed by the hirer and who is assigned by the hirer to perform the duties normally performed by the first worker,

unless in either case the employment business does not know, and has no reasonable grounds for knowing, that the first worker is taking part in a strike or other industrial action.

(2) Paragraph (1) shall not apply if, in relation to the first worker, the strike or other industrial action in question is an unofficial strike or other unofficial industrial action for the purposes of section 237 of the Trade Union and Labour Relations (Consolidation) Act 1992.

[2.697]

8 Restriction on paying work-seekers' remuneration

(1) Subject to paragraph (2), an agency shall not, in respect of a work-seeker whom the agency has introduced or supplied to a hirer—

(a) pay to;

(b) make arrangements for the payment to; or

(c) introduce or refer the hirer to any person with whom the agency is connected with a view to that person paying to, or making arrangements for the payment to,

the work-seeker, his remuneration arising from the employment with the hirer.

(2) Paragraph (1) shall not apply in the case of an introduction or supply of a work-seeker to a hirer where—

(a)

(i) the agency is permitted by regulation 26(1) to charge a fee to that work-seeker in respect of that introduction or supply; and

(ii) the agency complies with the provisions of regulation 25 and Schedule 2; or

(b) the hirer and the agency are connected.

9 (*Revoked by the Conduct of Employment Agencies and Employment Businesses (Amendment) Regulations 2016, SI 2016/510, reg 2(1), (2), as from 8 May 2016.*)

[2.698]

10 Restriction on charges to hirers

(1) Any term of a contract between an employment business and a hirer which is contingent on a work-seeker taking up employment with the hirer or working for the hirer pursuant to being supplied by another employment business is unenforceable by the employment business in relation to that work-seeker unless the contract provides that instead of a transfer fee the hirer may by notice to the employment business elect for a hire period of such length as is specified in the contract during which the work-seeker will be supplied to the hirer—

(a) in a case where there has been no supply, on the terms specified in the contract; or

(b) in any other case, on terms no less favourable to the hirer than those which applied immediately before the employment business received the notice.

(2) In paragraph (1), "transfer fee" means any payment in connection with the work-seeker taking up employment with the hirer or in connection with the work-seeker working for the hirer pursuant to being supplied by another employment business.

(3) Any term as mentioned in paragraph (1) is unenforceable where the employment business does not supply the work-seeker to the hirer, in accordance with the contract, for the duration of the hire period referred to in paragraph (1) unless the employment business is in no way at fault.

(4) Any term of a contract between an employment business and a hirer which is contingent on any of the following events, namely a work-seeker—

(a) taking up employment with the hirer;

(b) taking up employment with any person (other than the hirer) to whom the hirer has introduced him; or

(c) working for the hirer pursuant to being supplied by another employment business,

is unenforceable by the employment business in relation to the event concerned where the work-seeker begins such employment or begins working for the hirer pursuant to being supplied by another employment business, as the case may be, after the end of the relevant period.

(5) In paragraph (4), "the relevant period" means whichever of the following periods ends later, namely—

(a) the period of 8 weeks commencing on the day after the day on which the work-seeker last worked for the hirer pursuant to being supplied by the employment business; or

(b) subject to paragraph (6), the period of 14 weeks commencing on the first day on which the work-seeker worked for the hirer pursuant to the supply of that work-seeker to that hirer by the employment business.

(6) In determining for the purposes of paragraph (5)(b) the first day on which the work-seeker worked for the hirer pursuant to the supply of that work-seeker to that hirer by the employment business, no account shall be taken of any supply that occurred prior to a period of more than 42 days during which that work-seeker did not work for that hirer pursuant to being supplied by that employment business.

(7) An employment business shall not—

(a) seek to enforce against the hirer, or otherwise seek to give effect to, any term of a contract which is unenforceable by virtue of paragraph (1), (3) or (4); or

(b) otherwise directly or indirectly request a payment to which by virtue of this regulation the employment business is not entitled.

11 (*Revoked by the Conduct of Employment Agencies and Employment Businesses (Amendment) Regulations 2016, SI 2016/510, reg 2(1), (3), as from 8 May 2016.*)

[2.699]

12 Prohibition on employment businesses withholding payment to work-seekers on certain grounds

An employment business shall not, in respect of a work-seeker whom it supplies to a hirer, withhold or threaten to withhold from the work-seeker (whether by means of the inclusion of a term in a contract with the work-seeker or otherwise) the whole or any part of any payment in respect of any work done by the work-seeker on any of the following grounds—

(a) non-receipt of payment from the hirer in respect of the supply of any service provided by the employment business to the hirer;

(b) the work-seeker's failure to produce documentary evidence authenticated by the hirer of the fact that the work-seeker has worked during a particular period of time, provided that this provision shall not prevent the employment business from satisfying itself by other means that the work-seeker worked for the particular period in question;

(c) the work-seeker not having worked during any period other than that to which the payment relates; or

(d) any matter within the control of the employment business.

PART III
REQUIREMENTS TO BE SATISFIED BEFORE SERVICES ARE PROVIDED

[2.700]
13 Notification of charges and the terms of offers

(1) Subject to paragraph (2), on the first occasion that an agency or employment business offers to provide or arrange the provision of a service to a work-seeker, the agency or employment business shall give notice to the work-seeker stating—

(a) whether that service is a work-finding service for which the Act prohibits the agency or employment business from charging a fee; and

(b) whether any other services or goods which may be provided by the agency or employment business or any other person are services or goods for which the agency or employment business or other person providing them will or may charge a fee, together with details of any such fee including—

(i) the amount or method of calculation of the fee;

(ii) the identity of the person to whom the fee is or will be payable;

(iii) a description of the services or goods to which the fee relates [and a statement of the work-seeker's right to cancel or withdraw from the service [and, as the case may be, of the notice period required under paragraph (2) of regulation 5 or of the period during which the right under paragraph (3) of that regulation can be exercised]]; and

(iv) the circumstances, if any, in which refunds or rebates are payable to the work-seeker, the scale of such refunds or rebates, and if no refunds or rebates are payable, a statement to that effect.

(2) Paragraph (1) shall apply only where one or more services or goods referred to in paragraph (1)(b) for which the work-seeker will or may be charged a fee may be provided to the work-seeker.

(3) An agency or employment business shall give a further notice to a work-seeker stating the matters referred to in paragraph (1)(b) where, subsequent to the first occasion that it offers to provide or arrange the provision of a service to the work-seeker, the agency or employment business or the person providing to the work-seeker any services or goods referred to in paragraph 1(b), introduces or varies any fees in relation to any services or goods referred to in paragraph 1(b).

(4) Where an agency or employment business offers any gift or makes an offer of any benefit to a work-seeker, in order to induce him to engage the agency or employment business to provide him with services, the agency or employment business shall notify the work-seeker of the terms on which the gift or benefit is offered before the offer is open for acceptance by the work-seeker.

NOTES

Para (1): words in first (outer) pair of square brackets in sub-para (b)(iii) inserted by the Conduct of Employment Agencies and Employment Businesses (Amendment) Regulations 2007, SI 2007/3575, regs 2, 4; words in second (inner) pair of square brackets in that sub-paragraph substituted by the Conduct of Employment Agencies and Employment Businesses (Amendment) Regulations 2010, SI 2010/1782, regs 2, 5.

[2.701]
[13A Key information document: Employment businesses

(1) Before obtaining the agreement of the work-seeker to the terms which will apply as between the employment business and the work-seeker in accordance with regulation 14, an employment business must give the work-seeker and, where paragraph (6) applies, any person to be supplied by the work-seeker to carry out the work a key information document in accordance with this regulation.

(2) The key information document must be separate from any other documents provided to the work-seeker or any person to be supplied to carry out the work.

(3) The key information document must include—

(a) the title "Key Information Document" at the top of the first page;

(b) a statement immediately beneath the title that—

(i) the key information document specifies key information which relates to the relationship between the employment business and the work-seeker and, where paragraph (6) applies, any person to be supplied by the work-seeker to carry out the work;

(ii) where necessary, identifies documents where further related information may be found; and

(iii) includes contact details of the officers appointed or arranged to act under section 8A of the Employment Agencies Act 1973 and informs the work-seeker and, where paragraph (6) applies, any person to be supplied by the work-seeker to carry out the work that they may contact those officers if they are concerned about a breach by the employment business of obligations under that Act or these Regulations;

(c) except where paragraph (6) applies, details in respect of—

(i) whether the work-seeker is or will be employed by the employment business under a contract of service or apprenticeship, or a contract for services;
(ii) the identity of the employment business;
(iii) if not the employment business, the identity of the person who will normally pay the work-seeker in respect of the work done;
(iv) either—
(aa) the rate of remuneration payable to the work-seeker; or
(bb) the minimum rate of remuneration the employment business reasonably expects to achieve for the work-seeker;
(v) the intervals at which the remuneration will be paid;
(vi) the nature of any costs and deductions required by law and affecting the work-seeker's remuneration;
(vii) the nature and the amount (or, where the amount cannot be stated, the method of calculation) of any other costs and deductions affecting the work-seeker's remuneration;
(viii) the nature and the amount (or, where the amount cannot be stated, the method of calculation) of any fees for services or goods which may be provided by the employment business or any other person and for which the employment business or other person will or may charge a fee to the work-seeker;
(ix) any non-monetary benefits to which the work-seeker is entitled; and
(x) details of any entitlement to annual holidays and to payment in respect of such holidays; and
(d) except where paragraph (6) applies, a representative example statement which sets out as amounts, reasonably estimated where necessary and item by item, for a single prospective period based on the intervals at which remuneration will be paid—
(i) the gross remuneration payable to the work-seeker, as referred to at paragraph (c)(iv);
(ii) any costs and deductions affecting the remuneration which are required by law, as referred to at paragraph (c)(vi);
(iii) any other costs and deductions affecting the remuneration, as referred to at paragraph (c)(vii);
(iv) any fees for services or goods to be provided by the employment business or any other person and for which the employment business or any other person will or may charge a fee to the work-seeker, as referred to at paragraph (c)(viii); and
(v) the net remuneration payable to the work-seeker after taking account of all costs, deductions and fees.

(4) Paragraph (6) applies where—
(a) the work-seeker is not the person to be supplied to carry out the work;
(b) the work-seeker is not a company of which the person to be supplied to carry out the work or the spouse or civil partner of that person, either separately or together, has or have control; and
(c) either—
(i) the employment business arranges for the person to be supplied to carry out the work to be supplied by a work-seeker; or
(ii) the employment business is not the person who will normally pay the person to be supplied to carry out the work.

(5) For the purposes of sub-paragraph (4)(b), a person is to be taken to have control of a company if that person beneficially owns more than half of the issued share capital of the company or has the legal power to direct or cause the direction of the general management of the company.

(6) Where this paragraph applies, the key information document must include, instead of the information required by sub-paragraphs (3)(c) and (d)—
(a) details in respect of—
(i) the identity of the work-seeker;
(ii) whether the person to be supplied to carry out the work is or will be employed by their employer under a contract of service or apprenticeship, or a contract for services;
(iii) the identity of the employer of the person to be supplied to carry out the work;
(iv) if not the employer, the identity of the person who will normally pay the person to be supplied to carry out the work;
(v) where any of the employment business, the work-seeker, the employer of the person to be supplied to carry out the work and the person who will normally pay the person to be supplied to carry out the work is connected with any other such person, the nature of the connection;
(vi) either—
(aa) the rate of remuneration payable to the work-seeker in respect of the person to be supplied to carry out the work; or
(bb) the minimum rate of remuneration the employment business reasonably expects to achieve for the work-seeker in respect of the person to be supplied to carry out the work;
(vii) either—
(aa) the rate of remuneration payable to the person to be supplied to carry out the work; or
(bb) the minimum rate of remuneration the employment business reasonably expects to be achieved for the person to be supplied to carry out the work;

(viii) the intervals at which the remuneration will be paid to the work-seeker and the person to be supplied to carry out the work respectively;

(ix) the nature of any costs and deductions affecting the remuneration of the person to be supplied to carry out the work which are required by law, stating whether those costs and deductions will be applied to the remuneration stated in accordance with paragraph (vi) or to the remuneration stated in accordance with paragraph (vii);

(x) the nature and the amount (or, where the amount cannot be stated, the method of calculation) of any other costs and deductions affecting the remuneration of the person to be supplied to carry out the work, stating whether those costs and deductions will be applied to the remuneration stated in accordance with paragraph (vi) or to the remuneration stated in accordance with paragraph (vii);

(xi) the nature and the amount (or, where the amount cannot be stated, the method of calculation) of any fees for services or goods which may be provided by the employment business, the work-seeker or any other person and for which the employment business, the work-seeker or any other person will or may charge a fee to the person to be supplied to carry out the work;

(xii) an explanation of the difference between the rate of remuneration or minimum rate of remuneration payable to or expected to be achieved for the work-seeker as stated in accordance with paragraph (vi) and the net rate of remuneration payable to or expected to be achieved for the person to be supplied to carry out the work, if and to the extent that the difference is not fully explained by the information stated in accordance with paragraphs (ix), (x) and (xi);

(xiii) any non-monetary benefits to which the person to be supplied to carry out the work is entitled;

(xiv) details of any annual holidays to which the person to be supplied to carry out the work is entitled and of any entitlement to payment in respect of the same; and

(xv) where the work-seeker is a company and the work-seeker and the person to be supplied to carry out the work have made an agreement in accordance with paragraph (9) of regulation 32, details of that agreement; and

(b) a representative example statement which sets out as amounts, reasonably estimated where necessary and item by item, for a single prospective period based on the intervals at which remuneration will be paid to the person to be supplied to carry out the work—

(i) the gross remuneration payable to the work-seeker, as referred to at paragraph (a)(vi);

(ii) any costs and deductions affecting the remuneration of the person to be supplied to carry out the work which are required by law, as referred to at paragraph (a)(ix);

(iii) any other costs and deductions affecting the remuneration of the person to be supplied to carry out the work, as referred to at paragraph (a)(x);

(iv) any fees for services or goods to be provided by the employment business, the work-seeker or any other person and for which the employment business, the work-seeker or any other person will or may charge a fee to the person to be supplied to carry out the work, as referred to at paragraph (a)(xi);

(v) any other item referred to at paragraph (a)(xii); and

(vi) the net remuneration payable to the person to be supplied to carry out the work after taking account of all costs, deductions, fees and other items.

(7) Where information required by paragraph (6) is not directly within the knowledge of the employment business, the employment business may rely on information provided in writing to the employment business by the work-seeker, the employer of the person to be supplied to carry out the work or the person who will normally pay the person to be supplied to carry out the work, provided that any such information relates directly to the person providing it.

(8) The employment business must, by no later than the end of the fifth business day following a request by the work-seeker or the person who is or would be supplied to carry out the work, provide to the person requesting the information a copy of any information on which the employment business relies as permitted by paragraph (7).

(9) The key information document—

(a) may contain details of any other terms agreed under regulation 14 in respect of content required to be agreed under regulation 15; but

(b) may not contain any other items of additional information.

(10) The key information document must be—

(a) written in a clear and succinct manner;

(b) a maximum of two sides of A4-sized paper (being sides of paper with the dimensions 210 by 297 millimetres) when printed; and

(c) presented in a way that is easy to read, using characters of readable size.

(11) Where it is not possible to include all the information required under paragraph (3) and, where applicable, paragraph (6), together with any additional information included as permitted by sub-paragraph (9)(a), in a manner which complies with paragraph (10), the employment business may, to the extent necessary, provide a summary of that information in the key information document and a reference to where more details of that information may be found in another document, or documents, provided to the work-seeker and, where paragraph (6) applies, to the person to be supplied to carry out the work.

(12) The employment business—

(a) may (but is not required to) give the work-seeker and, where paragraph (6) applies, the person to be supplied to carry out the work more than one key information document where there are options or other variations which may apply to the details required to be included under paragraphs (3) and, where applicable, paragraph (6), or to any additional information included as permitted by sub-paragraph (9)(a), and therefore the document is not finalised; and

(b) must give the work-seeker and, where paragraph (6) applies, the person to be supplied to carry out the work a revised key information document where the details required to be included under paragraph (3) and, where applicable, paragraph (6), or included as additional information as permitted by sub-paragraph (9)(a), change after any key information document has been given in accordance with sub-paragraph (a) but before the agreement of the work-seeker to the terms which will apply as between the employment business and the work-seeker is obtained in accordance with regulation 14.

(13) Whether or not the employment business has previously given any key information document in accordance with paragraph (12), the employment business must at the appropriate time give a finalised key information document to the work-seeker and, where paragraph (6) applies, the person to be supplied to carry out the work.

(14) In paragraph (13), "the appropriate time" means any time after the content of the key information document is, subject only to the agreement of the work-seeker to the terms which will apply as between the employment business and the work-seeker being obtained in accordance with regulation 14, finalised (including, where relevant, by resolution of any options or variations), but before that agreement is obtained.

(15) If any of the details required to be included under paragraphs (3) or (6), or included as additional information as permitted by sub-paragraph (9)(a), change after the agreement of the work-seeker to the terms which will apply as between the employment business and the work-seeker is obtained in accordance with regulation 14, the employment business must, by no later than the end of the fifth business day following the day on which the change occurred, give to the work-seeker and, where paragraph (6) applies, to the person who is or would be supplied to carry out the work a revised key information document stating the date on or after which the revisions take effect.

(16) Paragraphs (2) to (11) apply to any revised key information document given in accordance with paragraph (15) in the same way as to a key information document given before any agreement of the work-seeker to the terms which will apply as between the employment business and the work-seeker in accordance with regulation 14, but as if references to the person to be supplied to do the work were references to the person who is or would be supplied to do the work.

(17) But paragraph (15) only applies—

(a) where the employment business first provided any work-finding services to a work-seeker on or after 6th April 2020 and, accordingly, was required to give a key information document in accordance with this regulation; and

(b) while the employment business continues to provide services in the course of its business as an employment business to the work-seeker or the person supplied to do the work.

(18) For the purposes of this regulation, a work-seeker includes a work-seeker which is a company, whether or not an agreement has been made in accordance with paragraph (9) of regulation 32.]

NOTES

Commencement: 6 April 2020.

Inserted by the Conduct of Employment Agencies and Employment Businesses (Amendment) Regulations 2019, SI 2019/725, regs 2, 3, as from 6 April 2020.

[2.702]

[14 Requirement to obtain agreement to terms with work-seekers: Employment Businesses

(1) Before first providing any work-finding services to a work-seeker, an employment business shall obtain the agreement of the work-seeker to the terms which apply or will apply as between the employment business and the work-seeker including—

(a) a statement that the employment business will operate as an employment business in relation to the work-seeker;

(b) the type of work the employment business will find or seek to find for the work-seeker; and

(c) the terms referred to in regulation 15.

(2) Subject to paragraph (3), an employment business shall ensure that—

(a) all terms in respect of which the employment business has obtained the work-seeker's agreement are recorded in a single document or, where this is not possible, in more than one document; and

(b) copies of all such documents are given at the same time as each other by the employment business to the work-seeker before the employment business provides any services to the work-seeker to which the terms contained in such documents relate.

(3) Paragraph (2) shall not apply in the case of an employment business where the work-seeker has been given a written statement of particulars of employment in accordance with Part I of the Employment Rights Act 1996.

(4) An employment business may not vary any terms set out in any document issued in accordance with paragraph (2), unless the work-seeker agrees to the variation.

(5) If the employment business and the work-seeker agree to any variation in the terms set out in any of the documents referred to in paragraph (2), the employment business shall as soon as possible, and in any event no later than the end of the fifth business day following the day on which the employment

business and the work-seeker agree to the variation, give to the work-seeker a single document or, where this is not possible, more than one document containing details of the terms as agreed to be varied and stating the date on or after which it is agreed that the varied terms are to take effect.

(6) An employment business may not make the continued provision of any services by it to a work-seeker conditional on the agreement by the work-seeker to any such variation.]

(7) This regulation shall not apply in the case of an agency where the only service provided by the agency to the work-seeker concerned is the provision of information to him in the form of a publication.

NOTES

Substituted by the Conduct of Employment Agencies and Employment Businesses (Amendment) Regulations 2010, SI 2010/1782, regs 2, 6.

[2.703]
15 Content of terms with work-seekers: Employment businesses

In the case of an employment business, the terms to be agreed in accordance with regulation 14 shall include—

(a) whether the work-seeker is or will be employed by the employment business under a contract of service or apprenticeship, or a contract for services, and in either case, the terms and conditions of employment of the work-seeker which apply, or will apply;
(b) an undertaking that the employment business will pay the work-seeker in respect of work done by him, whether or not it is paid by the hirer in respect of that work;
(c) the length of notice of termination which the work-seeker will be required to give the employment business, and which he will be entitled to receive from the employment business, in respect of particular assignments with hirers;
(d) either—
  (i) the rate of remuneration payable to the work-seeker; or
  (ii) the minimum rate of remuneration the employment business reasonably expects to achieve for the work-seeker;
(e) details of the intervals at which remuneration will be paid; and
(f) details of any entitlement to annual holidays and to payment in respect of such holidays.

[2.704]
[16 Requirement to obtain agreement to terms with work-seekers and content of terms with work-seekers: Agencies

(1) Before first providing any work-finding services to a work-seeker, for which it is permitted by regulation 26(1) to charge a fee, an agency shall obtain the agreement of the work-seeker to the terms which apply or will apply as between the agency and the work-seeker including—

(a) details of the work-finding services to be provided by the agency;
(b) details of the agency's authority, if any, to act on behalf of the work-seeker, including whether, and if so, upon what terms it is . . . authorised to enter into contracts with hirers on behalf of the work-seeker;
(c) a statement as to whether the agency is authorised to receive money on behalf of the work-seeker;
(d) details of any fee which may be payable by the work-seeker to the agency for work-finding services including—
  (i) the amount or method of calculation of the fee,
  (ii) a description of the particular work-finding service to which the fee relates,
  (iii) the circumstances, if any, in which refunds or rebates are payable to the work-seeker, the scale of such refunds or rebates, and if no refunds or rebates are payable, a statement to that effect, and
  (iv) the method of payment of the fee and, if the fee is to be deducted from the work-seeker's earnings received by the agency, the circumstances in which it is to be so deducted;
(e) a statement as to whether the work-seeker is required to give notice to terminate the contract between the work-seeker and the agency and, if so, a statement as to the length of the notice required; and
(f) a statement as to whether the work-seeker is entitled to receive notice of termination of the contract between the work-seeker and the agency and, if so, a statement of the length of the notice.

(2) In the case of an agency which is to provide the work-seeker with work-finding services to which regulation 26(5) applies, before first providing any such work-finding services to the work-seeker, the terms to be agreed, in addition to the terms in paragraph (1), are—

(a) that an agency shall not charge a fee permitted under regulation 26(5) to the work-seeker until the period referred to, as the case may be, in sub-paragraph (d) or (e) of regulation 26(5), during which the work-seeker may withdraw or cancel, has elapsed;
(b) that the work-seeker has the right without detriment or penalty to cancel or withdraw from the contract with immediate effect by informing the agency of such cancellation or withdrawal during the period referred to, as the case may be, in sub-paragraph (d) or (e) of regulation 26(5);
(c) that an agency shall not include information about the work-seeker in a publication until—
  (i) where sub-paragraph (d) of regulation 26(5) applies, the period referred to in that sub-paragraph has elapsed or,

(ii) where sub-paragraph (f) of regulation 26(5) applies, the later of, the date on which the period referred to in that sub-paragraph has elapsed or, following an objection, the date on which the reasonable requirements of the work-seeker have been addressed;

(d) in relation to a contract with a work-seeker seeking employment as an actor, background artist, dancer, extra, musician, singer or other performer, under which the agency proposes to include information about the work-seeker in a publication, that—

(i) the agency shall make a copy of the information available to the work-seeker;

(ii) at the same time, the agency shall inform the work-seeker of the right to object, its effect and the time limit for exercising that right; and

(iii) for the period referred to in paragraph (5)(f) of regulation 26, the work-seeker is entitled to object to any aspect of the information relating to the work-seeker by informing the agency of the objection;

(e) in a contract to which sub-paragraph (d) applies, that where the work-seeker informs the agency of an objection, the agency shall not charge a fee or include the information in a publication until the work-seeker's reasonable requirements have been addressed (even if addressing the requirements takes longer than the period referred to in paragraph (5)(f) of regulation 26);

(f) in a contract to which sub-paragraph (d) applies, that where an agency makes available to the work-seeker a copy of the information referred to in that sub-paragraph—

(i) during the period referred to in paragraph (5)(e) of regulation 26, where the period referred to in paragraph (5)(f) of regulation 26 has elapsed without an objection or where the reasonable requirements of the work-seeker have been addressed, paragraph (5)(e) of regulation 26 continues to apply; or

(ii) after the period referred to in paragraph (5)(e) of regulation 26 has elapsed, paragraph (5)(f) of regulation 26 applies from the expiry of that period until the later of, the date on which the period referred to in paragraph (5)(f) of regulation 26 has elapsed or, following an objection, the date on which the reasonable requirements of the work-seeker have been addressed; and

(g) that the work-seeker is entitled to receive a full refund of the fees paid if the publication including, or proposed to include, the work-seeker's information is not produced and made available to potential hirers within 60 days from the date on which payment is made by the work-seeker.

(3) Any reference in paragraph (2) to the inclusion of information about a work-seeker in a publication, includes the inclusion of a photographic image or audio or video recording of the work-seeker in a publication.

(4) Paragraph (3) shall not be construed, when read with paragraph (2), as preventing an agency producing a photographic image or audio or video recording for the purpose of providing a copy of the image or recording to the work-seeker.

(5) An agency shall ensure that—

(a) all terms in respect of which the agency has obtained the work-seeker's agreement are recorded in a single document or, where this is not possible, in more than one document; and

(b) copies of all such documents are given at the same time as each other by the agency to the work-seeker before the agency provides any services to the work-seeker to which the terms contained in such documents relate.

(6) An agency may not vary any terms set out in any document issued in accordance with paragraph (5), unless the work-seeker agrees to the variation.

(7) If the agency and the work-seeker agree to any variation in the terms set out in any of the documents referred to in paragraph (5), the agency shall as soon as possible, and in any event no later than the end of the fifth business day following the day on which the agency and the work- seeker agree to the variation, give to the work-seeker a single document or, where this is not possible, more than one document containing details of the terms as agreed to be varied and stating the date on or after which it is agreed that the varied terms are to take effect.

(8) An agency may not make the continued provision of any services by it to a work-seeker conditional on the agreement by the work-seeker to any such variation.]

NOTES

Substituted by the Conduct of Employment Agencies and Employment Businesses (Amendment) Regulations 2010, SI 2010/1782, regs 2, 7.

Para (1): words omitted from sub-para (b) revoked by the Conduct of Employment Agencies and Employment Businesses (Amendment) Regulations 2016, SI 2016/510, reg 2(1), (4), as from 8 May 2016.

17 *(Revoked by the Conduct of Employment Agencies and Employment Businesses (Amendment) Regulations 2016, SI 2016/510, reg 2(1), (5), as from 8 May 2016.)*

PART IV
REQUIREMENTS TO BE SATISFIED IN RELATION TO THE INTRODUCTION OR SUPPLY OF A WORK-SEEKER TO A HIRER

[2.705]

18 Information to be obtained from a hirer

Neither an agency nor an employment business may introduce or supply a work-seeker to a hirer unless the agency or employment business has obtained sufficient information from the hirer to select a suitable

Part 2 Statutory Instruments

work-seeker for the position which the hirer seeks to fill, including the following information—

(a) the identity of the hirer and, if applicable, the nature of the hirer's business;

(b) the date on which the hirer requires a work-seeker to commence work and the duration, or likely duration, of the work;

(c) the position which the hirer seeks to fill, including the type of work a work-seeker in that position would be required to do, the location at which and the hours during which he would be required to work and any risks to health or safety known to the hirer and what steps the hirer has taken to prevent or control such risks;

(d) the experience, training, qualifications and any authorisation which the hirer considers are necessary, or which are required by law, or by any professional body, for a work-seeker to possess in order to work in the position;

(e) any expenses payable by or to the work-seeker; and

(f) in the case of an agency—

(i) the minimum rate of remuneration and any other benefits which the hirer would offer to a person in the position which it seeks to fill, and the intervals at which the person would be paid; and

(ii) where applicable, the length of notice which a work-seeker in such a position would be required to give, and entitled to receive, to terminate the employment with the hirer.

[2.706]

[19 Confirmation to be obtained about a work-seeker

(1) An employment business may not introduce or supply a work-seeker to a hirer unless it has obtained confirmation—

(a) of the identity of the work-seeker, and

(b) that the work-seeker has the experience, training, qualifications and any authorisation which the hirer considers are necessary, or which are required by law or by any professional body, to work in the position which the hirer seeks to fill.

(2) An agency may not introduce or supply a work-seeker to a hirer with a view to the work-seeker taking up a position which involves working with, caring for or attending a vulnerable person, unless it has obtained confirmation—

(a) of the identity of the work-seeker, and

(b) that the work-seeker has the experience, training, qualifications and any authorisation which the hirer considers are necessary, or which are required by law or by any professional body, to work in the position which the hirer seeks to fill.

(3) Neither an agency nor an employment business may introduce or supply a work-seeker to a hirer unless it has obtained confirmation that the work-seeker is willing to work in the position which the hirer seeks to fill.]

NOTES

Substituted by the Conduct of Employment Agencies and Employment Businesses (Amendment) Regulations 2010, SI 2010/1782, regs 2, 9.

[2.707]

20 Steps to be taken for the protection of the work-seeker and the hirer

(1) Neither an agency nor an employment business may introduce or supply a work-seeker to a hirer unless the agency or employment business has—

(a) taken all such steps, as are reasonably practicable, to ensure that the work-seeker and the hirer are each aware of any requirements imposed by law, or by any professional body, which must be satisfied by the hirer or the work-seeker to enable the work-seeker to work for the hirer in the position which the hirer seeks to fill; and

(b) without prejudice to any of its duties under any enactment or rule of law in relation to health and safety at work, made all such enquiries, as are reasonably practicable, to ensure that it would not be detrimental to the interests of the work-seeker or the hirer for the work-seeker to work for the hirer in the position which the hirer seeks to fill.

(2) Where an employment business receives or obtains information, which gives it reasonable grounds to believe that a work-seeker is unsuitable for the position with a hirer for which the work-seeker is being supplied, it shall, without delay—

(a) inform the hirer of that information; and

(b) end the supply of that work-seeker to the hirer.

(3) Where an employment business receives or obtains information which indicates that a work-seeker may be unsuitable for the position with a hirer for which the work-seeker is being supplied, but where that information does not give it reasonable grounds to believe that the work-seeker is unsuitable, it shall, without delay—

(a) inform the hirer of that information; and

(b) commence making such further enquiries as are reasonably practicable as to the suitability of the work-seeker for the position concerned, and inform the hirer of the enquiries made and any further information it receives or obtains.

(4) Where, as a result of the enquiries made under paragraph (3) an employment business has reasonable grounds to believe that the work-seeker is unsuitable for the position concerned, it shall, without delay—

(a) inform the hirer of that information; and

(b) end the supply of that work-seeker to the hirer.

(5) Where an agency, having introduced a work-seeker to a hirer, receives or obtains information, which indicates that the work-seeker is or may be unsuitable for the position in which the work-seeker has been employed with that hirer, it shall inform the hirer of that information without delay.

(6) Paragraph (5) shall apply for a period of 3 months from the date of introduction of a work-seeker by an agency to a hirer.

(7) In this regulation, "without delay" means on the same day, or where that is not reasonably practicable, on the next business day.

[2.708]

21 Provision of information to work-seekers and hirers

(1) Subject to [paragraphs (3), (4) and (5)], an agency or employment business shall ensure that at the same time as—

(a) it proposes a particular work-seeker to a hirer—

(i) it gives to the hirer (whether orally or otherwise) all information it has been provided with about the matters referred to in regulation 19; and

(ii) in the case of an employment business, the information it gives to the hirer (whether orally or otherwise) includes whether the work-seeker to be supplied will be employed by it under a contract of service or apprenticeship or a contract for services;

(b) it offers a work-seeker a position with a hirer—

(i) it gives to the work-seeker (whether orally or otherwise) all information it has been provided with about the matters referred to in paragraphs (a) to (e) and, where applicable, paragraph (f) of regulation 18; and

(ii) in the case of an employment business that has not agreed a rate of remuneration in accordance with regulation 15(d)(i), it informs the work-seeker (whether orally or otherwise) of the rate of remuneration it will pay him to work in that position.

(2) Where any of the information referred to in paragraph (1) is not given to the work-seeker or hirer, as the case may be, in paper form or by electronic means at the time referred to in paragraph (1), the agency or employment business shall confirm such information in paper form or by electronic means to the work-seeker or hirer, as the case may be, as soon as possible and in any event no later than the end of the third business day following the day on which it was given to the work-seeker or hirer in accordance with paragraph (1).

(3) Paragraph (1) shall not apply where—

(a) an agency or employment business intends to introduce or supply a work-seeker to a hirer to work in the same position with that hirer as he has worked within the previous five business days; and

(b) the information which that agency or employment business would be required to give the work-seeker and hirer by virtue of this regulation (other than that required by regulation 18(b)), would be the same as the information which the work-seeker and hirer have already received,

unless the work-seeker or hirer requests otherwise.

[(4) Subject to paragraphs (3) and (5), where an employment business intends to introduce or supply a work-seeker to a hirer for an assignment of five consecutive business days' duration or less—

(a) paragraph (1)(a)(i) may be satisfied by the employment business giving to the hirer (whether orally or otherwise) the name of the work-seeker to be supplied and a written confirmation by the employment business that it has complied with regulation 19; and

(b) paragraph (1)(b) may be satisfied, where the employment business has previously provided the work-seeker with the information referred to under that paragraph and that information remains unchanged, by the employment business giving to the work-seeker in paper form or by electronic means the information referred to in regulation 18(a) and (b).

(5) Where, after it has started, an assignment to which paragraph (4) applies is extended beyond a duration of five business days, the information referred to in paragraph (1) which has not already been provided shall be provided in paper form or by electronic means by the end of the eighth business day of the assignment, or by the end of the assignment if sooner.]

NOTES

Para (1): words in square brackets substituted by the Conduct of Employment Agencies and Employment Businesses (Amendment) Regulations 2007, SI 2007/3575, regs 2, 5(a).

Paras (4), (5): added by SI 2007/3575, regs 2, 5(b).

[2.709]

[22 Additional requirements where professional qualifications or authorisation are required or where work-seekers are to work with vulnerable persons

(1) Where the work-seeker is to be supplied or introduced to a hirer with a view to taking up a position which involves working with, caring for or attending a vulnerable person, neither an agency nor an employment business may introduce or supply the work-seeker to a hirer unless, in addition to the requirements in regulations 18 to 21, the requirements in paragraph (2) are satisfied.

(2) The requirements referred to in paragraph (1) are that the agency or employment business has—

(a) subject to paragraph (3), obtained copies of any relevant qualifications or authorisations of the work-seeker and offered to provide copies of those documents to the hirer;

(b) subject to paragraph (3), obtained two references from persons who are not relatives of the work-seeker and who have agreed that the reference provided may be disclosed to the hirer, and the agency or employment business has offered to provide copies of those references to the hirer; and

(c) taken all other reasonably practicable steps to confirm that the work-seeker is suitable for the position concerned.

(3) Where the agency or employment business has taken all reasonably practicable steps to comply with the requirements in paragraph (2) and has been unable to do so fully, it may instead—

(a) comply with those requirements to the extent that it is able to do so;

(b) inform the hirer that it has taken all reasonably practicable steps to comply fully with those requirements and has been unable to do so; and

(c) inform the hirer of the details of the steps that it has taken in order to try and comply fully with those requirements.

(4) Where the work-seeker is required by law, or any professional body, to have any qualifications or authorisation to work in a position for which the work-seeker is to be supplied or introduced to a hirer, an employment business may not introduce or supply the work-seeker to a hirer unless, in addition to the requirements in regulations 18 to 21, the requirements in paragraph (5) are satisfied.

(5) The requirements referred to in paragraph (4) are that the employment business has—

(a) subject to paragraph (6), obtained copies of any relevant qualifications or authorisation of the work-seeker, and offered to provide copies of those documents to the hirer; and

(b) taken all other reasonably practicable steps to confirm that the work-seeker is suitable for the position concerned.

(6) Where the employment business has taken all reasonably practicable steps to comply with the requirements in paragraph (5) and has been unable to do so fully, it may instead—

(a) comply with those requirements to the extent that it is able to do so;

(b) inform the hirer that it has taken all reasonably practicable steps to comply fully with those requirements and has been unable to do so; and

(c) inform the hirer of the details of the steps that it has taken in order to try and comply fully with those requirements.

(7) In this regulation "relative" has the same meaning as it is given in section 63 the Family Law Act 1996.]

NOTES

Substituted by the Conduct of Employment Agencies and Employment Businesses (Amendment) Regulations 2010, SI 2010/1782, regs 2, 10.

23, 24 *((Pt V Special situations) outside the scope of this work.)*

PART VI
CLIENT ACCOUNTS AND CHARGES TO WORK-SEEKERS

25 *((Client accounts) outside the scope of this work.)*

[2.710]

26 Circumstances in which fees may be charged to work-seekers

(1) Subject to paragraphs (3) and (4), the restriction on charging fees to work-seekers contained in section 6(1)(a) of the Act shall not apply in respect of a fee charged by an agency for the service provided by it of finding or seeking to find a work-seeker employment in any of the occupations listed in Schedule 3.

(2) Where paragraph (1) applies, subject to paragraph (5), any fee charged by the agency may consist only of a charge or commission payable out of the work-seeker's earnings in any such employment which the agency has found for him.

(3) Paragraphs (1) and (7) shall not apply where the agency, or any person connected with it, charges a fee to the hirer in respect of the service of supplying or introducing that work-seeker to him.

(4) In any case in which the agency is connected with the hirer, paragraphs (1) and (7) only apply if, prior to the provision of the service in respect of which the fee is to be charged, the agency informs the work-seeker of the fact that it is connected with the hirer.

(5) Paragraph (2) shall not apply to any fee charged to a work-seeker[, who is not a work-seeker seeking employment as a photographic or fashion model,] by an agency in respect of the inclusion of information about the work-seeker in a publication provided that—

(a) the publication is wholly for one or both of the following purposes, namely the purpose of finding work-seekers employment in, or providing hirers with information about work-seekers in relation to, any of the occupations listed in Schedule 3[, other than photographic or fashion model]; and

(b) either—

(i) the only work-finding service provided by the agency or any person connected with it to the work-seeker is the service described in this paragraph; or

(ii) the fee charged to the work-seeker amounts to no more than a reasonable estimate of the cost of production and circulation of the publication attributable to the inclusion of information about that work-seeker in the publication; and

(c) in addition to the requirements in regulations 13 . . . and 16, in so far as they are applicable, the agency has, before it entered into the contract with the work-seeker by reference to which the fee is to be charged, made available to him a copy of a current edition of the publication (or, where the publication exists only in electronic form, given him access to a current edition of the publication) in which it is offering to include information about him[; and]

[(d) in relation to a work-seeker who is not seeking employment as an actor, background artist, dancer, extra, musician, singer or other performer, where an agency proposes to include information about the work-seeker in a publication, for 7 days from the date of the agency and the work-seeker entering into a contract for such a service, whether written or oral and whether or not expressly mentioning fees permitted under this paragraph—

(i) the agency shall not charge a fee permitted by this paragraph to a work-seeker;

(ii) the work-seeker shall be entitled without detriment or penalty to cancel or withdraw from any such contract with immediate effect by informing the agency of such cancellation or withdrawal; and

(iii) the agency shall not include the information in the publication,

and before entering into any such contract the agency shall inform the work-seeker of the right to cancel or withdraw from any such contract and the time limit for exercising that right;]]

[(e) where an agency proposes to include information about a work-seeker seeking employment as an actor, background artist, dancer, extra, musician, singer or other performer in a publication, for 30 days from the date of the agency and the work-seeker entering into a contract for such a service, whether written or oral and whether or not expressly mentioning fees permitted under this paragraph—

(i) the agency shall not charge a fee permitted by this paragraph to a work-seeker; and

(ii) the work-seeker shall be entitled without detriment or penalty to cancel or withdraw from any such contract with immediate effect by informing the agency of such cancellation or withdrawal,

and before entering into any such contract the agency shall inform the work-seeker of the right to cancel or withdraw from any such contract and the time limit for exercising that right;

(f) where an agency proposes to include information about a work-seeker referred to in sub-paragraph (e) in a publication, after the date of the agency and the work-seeker entering into the contract referred to in that sub-paragraph, the agency shall make available to the work-seeker a copy of the information and at the same time shall inform the work-seeker of the right to object, its effect and the time limit for exercising that right and for 7 days from the date on which the agency first makes available a copy of the information to the work-seeker—

(i) the agency shall not charge a fee permitted by this paragraph to a work-seeker;

(ii) the agency shall not include the information in the publication; and

(iii) the work-seeker is entitled to object to any aspect of the information relating to the work-seeker to be included in the publication by informing the agency of the objection;

(g) where sub-paragraph (f) applies and the work-seeker informs the agency of an objection, the agency shall not charge a fee or include the information in the publication until the work-seeker's reasonable requirements have been addressed (even if addressing the requirements takes longer than the period referred to in that sub-paragraph); and

(h) where an agency includes, or proposes to include, information about a work-seeker in a publication, the work-seeker is entitled to a full refund of the fees paid if the publication including that information is not produced and made available to potential hirers within 60 days from the date on which payment is made by the work-seeker].

[(5A) Where an agency makes available to the work-seeker a copy of the information referred to in paragraph (5)(f)—

(a) during the period referred to in paragraph (5)(e), where the period referred to in paragraph (5)(f) has elapsed without an objection or where the reasonable requirements of the work-seeker have been addressed, paragraph (5)(e) continues to apply; or

(b) after the period referred to in paragraph (5)(e) has elapsed, paragraph (5)(f) applies until the later of, the date on which the period referred to in paragraph (5)(f) has elapsed or, following an objection, the date on which the reasonable requirements of the work-seeker have been addressed.

(5B) Any reference in paragraph (5) to the inclusion of information about a work-seeker in a publication includes the inclusion of a photographic image or audio or video recording of the work-seeker in a publication.

(5C) Paragraph (5B) shall not be construed, when read with paragraph (5), as preventing an agency producing a photographic image or audio or video recording for the purpose of providing a copy of the image or recording to the work-seeker.]

(6) The restrictions on charging fees to work-seekers contained in section 6(1)(a) of the Act shall not apply to any fee consisting of a charge to a work-seeker in respect of the purchase of or subscription for a publication containing information about employers provided that—

(a) this is the only work-finding service provided by the agency or any person connected with it to the work-seeker; and

(b) the agency has made available to the work-seeker a copy of a current edition of the publication (or, where the publication exists only in electronic form, given him access to a current edition of the publication) in advance of the work-seeker purchasing or subscribing for it.

(7) The restriction on charging fees to work-seekers contained in section 6(1)(a) of the Act shall not apply in respect of a fee charged by an agency for the service provided by it of finding or seeking to find a work-seeker employment where—

(a) the work-seeker in question is a company; and

(b) the employment is in an occupation other than any of those occupations listed in Schedule 3.

NOTES

The word in square brackets at the end of sub-para (5)(c) was substituted, and sub-para (5)(d) was added, by the Conduct of Employment Agencies and Employment Businesses (Amendment) Regulations 2007, SI 2007/3575, regs 2, 7.

The first and second words in square brackets in para (5) were inserted, the number omitted from sub-para (5)(c) was revoked, sub-para (5)(d) was substituted, and sub-paras (5)(e)–(h) and paras (5A)–(5C) were inserted, by the Conduct of Employment Agencies and Employment Businesses (Amendment) Regulations 2010, SI 2010/1782, regs 2, 11.

PART VII
MISCELLANEOUS

[2.711]

27 Advertisements

(1) Every advertisement issued or caused to be issued by an agency or employment business shall mention in either audibly spoken words or easily legible characters the full name of the agency or employment business, and [in relation to each position it advertises whether it is for temporary or permanent work].

(2) Neither an agency nor an employment business may issue or cause to be issued an advertisement about positions which hirers seek to fill unless the agency or employment business has—

(a) information about specific positions of all types to which the advertisement relates; and

(b) in relation to each such position, the authority of the hirer concerned to find work-seekers for that position, or the authority of an agency or employment business, which has such authority to issue the advertisement or cause it to be issued.

(3) An agency or employment business shall, in every advertisement for work-seekers issued or caused to be issued by it in which rates of pay are given, state the nature of the work, the location at which the work-seeker would be required to work, and the minimum experience, training or qualifications which the work-seeker would be required to have in order to receive those rates of pay.

NOTES

Para (1): words in square brackets substituted by the Conduct of Employment Agencies and Employment Businesses (Amendment) Regulations 2010, SI 2010/1782, regs 2, 12.

[2.712]

[27A Advertising in *other* EEA states

(1) An agency or employment business must not publish a relevant recruitment advertisement in an EEA state *other than the United Kingdom* unless—

(a) it publishes the advertisement in English in Great Britain at the same time as it publishes the advertisement in the *other* EEA state; or

(b) it has published the advertisement in English in Great Britain for all or part of the period of 28 days ending with the day on which it publishes the advertisement in the *other* EEA state.

(2) Paragraph (1) does not apply if the relevant recruitment advertisement concerns a vacancy for a worker to act solely for, and under the control of, the agency or employment business itself.

(3) It is a defence in any proceedings under—

(a) section 5(2) of the Act, or

(b) regulation 30,

in respect of a contravention of paragraph (1) that the agency or employment business believes, on reasonable grounds, that publishing the relevant recruitment advertisement in English in Great Britain would be disproportionate having regard to the likelihood that doing so would bring the advertisement to the attention of a person with the skills sought by the agency or employment business.

(4) For the purposes of this regulation—

(a) "publish" means make, or cause to be made, available to the public or a section of the public,

(b) an advertisement on a website is taken to be published in all places from which the website can be accessed,

(c) "a relevant recruitment advertisement" means either—

(i) an advertisement in respect of a particular vacant position, the duties of which are ordinarily to be performed in Great Britain, or

(ii) an advertisement by which an agency or employment business seeks to identify worker-seekers who are looking for a position, the duties of which are ordinarily to be performed in Great Britain.]

NOTES

Commencement 8 May 2016.

Originally inserted by the Conduct of Employment Agencies and Employment Businesses (Amendment) Regulations 2014, SI 2014/3351, reg 2, as from 4 January 2015. Subsequently substituted by the Conduct of Employment Agencies and Employment Businesses (Amendment) Regulations 2016, SI 2016/510, reg 2(1), (7), as from 8 May 2016.

The words in italics in each place in the heading and para (1) are revoked by the Employment Rights (Amendment) (EU Exit) (No 2) Regulations 2019, SI 2019/536, reg 2, Schedule, Pt 2, para 3, as from exit day (as defined in the European Union (Withdrawal) Act 2018, s 20).

28, 29 *(Reg 28 (confidentiality), and reg 29 (records) are outside the scope of this work.)*

[2.713]
30 Civil liability

(1) Without prejudice to—
- (a) any right of action; and
- (b) any defence,

which exists or may be available apart from the provisions of the Act and these Regulations, contravention of, or failure to comply with, any of the provisions of the Act or of these Regulations by an agency or employment business shall, so far as it causes damage, be actionable.

(2) In this regulation, "damage" includes the death of, or injury to, any person (including any disease and any impairment of that person's physical or mental condition).

[2.714]
31 Effect of prohibited or unenforceable terms and recoverability of monies

(1) Where any term of a contract is prohibited or made unenforceable by these Regulations, the contract shall continue to bind the parties to it if it is capable of continuing in existence without that term.

(2) Where a hirer pays any money pursuant to a contractual term which is unenforceable by virtue of regulation 10, the hirer is entitled to recover that money.

32, 33 (*Reg 32 (application of the Regulations to work-seekers which are incorporated), and reg 33 (electronic and other communications) outside the scope of this work.*)

[2.715]
[34 Review

(1) The Secretary of State must from time to time carry out a review of the provisions listed in paragraph (2).

(2) The listed provisions are—
- (a) Part 2 (general obligations);
- (b) Part 3 (requirements to be satisfied before services are provided);
- (c) Part 5 (special situations); and
- (d) Part 7 (miscellaneous).

(3) The Secretary of State must—
- (a) set out the conclusions of the review carried out in accordance with paragraph (1) in a report; and
- (b) publish the report.

(4) The report must in particular—
- (a) set out the objectives intended to be achieved by the provisions listed in paragraph (2);
- (b) assess the extent to which those objectives are achieved; and
- (c) assess whether those objectives remain appropriate and, if so, the extent to which they could be achieved with a system that imposes less regulation.

(5) The first report under this regulation must be published before the end of the period of five years beginning with the day on which the Conduct of Employment Agencies and Employment Businesses (Amendment) Regulations 2016 come into force.

(6) Reports under this regulation are afterwards to be published at intervals not exceeding five years.]

NOTES

Commencement 8 May 2016.

Inserted by the Conduct of Employment Agencies and Employment Businesses (Amendment) Regulations 2016, SI 2016/510, reg 2(1), (12), as from 8 May 2016.

SCHEDULES

SCHEDULE 1 AND 2

(Sch 1 (transitional and saving provisions), and Sch 2 (client accounts) outside the scope of this work.)

SCHEDULE 3
OCCUPATIONS IN RESPECT OF WHICH EMPLOYMENT AGENCIES MAY CHARGE FEES TO WORK-SEEKERS

Regulation 26

[2.716]
Actor, musician, singer, dancer, [background artist, extra, walk-on] or other performer;

Composer, writer, artist, director, production manager, lighting cameraman, camera operator, make up artist, [clothes, hair or make up stylist,] film editor, action arranger or co-ordinator, stunt arranger, costume or production designer, recording engineer, property master, film continuity person, sound mixer, photographer, stage manager, producer, choreographer, theatre designer;

Photographic or fashion model;

Professional sports person.

NOTES

Words in first pair of square brackets inserted by the Conduct of Employment Agencies and Employment Businesses (Amendment) Regulations 2010, SI 2010/1782, regs 2, 14; words in second pair of square brackets inserted by the Conduct of Employment Agencies and Employment Businesses (Amendment) Regulations 2007, SI 2007/3575, regs 2, 10.

SCHEDULES 4–6

(Sch 4 (particulars to be included in an agency's or employment business's records relating to work-seekers), Sch 5 (particulars to be included in an agency's or employment business's records relating to hirers), and Sch 6 (particulars to be included in an agency's or employment business's records relating to other agencies or employment businesses) outside the scope of this work.)

ACAS ARBITRATION SCHEME (GREAT BRITAIN) ORDER 2004

(SI 2004/753)

NOTES

Made: 9 March 2004.
Authority: Trade Union and Labour Relations (Consolidation) Act 1992, s 212A(1), (3), (6), (7), (8), (9).
Commencement: 6 April 2004.
See *Harvey* PI(3).

ARRANGEMENT OF ARTICLES

[2.717]
1 Citation, commencement, interpretation and extent

(1) This Order may be cited as the ACAS Arbitration Scheme (Great Britain) Order 2004 and shall come into force on 6th April 2004.

(2) In this Order—

"the 1996 Act" means the Employment Rights Act 1996;

"basic amount" means such part of an award of compensation made by an arbitrator as comprises the basic amount, determined in accordance with paragraphs 139 to 146 of the Scheme;

"English/Welsh arbitration" means an arbitration under the Scheme, which the parties have agreed shall be determined under the laws of England and Wales;

"the Scheme" means the arbitration scheme set out in the Schedule with the exception of paragraphs 52EW, 110EW, 183EW, 187EW, 194EW, 200EW, 205EW, 209EW, 212EW, 217EW, 223EW and 224EW thereof;

"Scottish arbitration" means an arbitration under the Scheme, which the parties have agreed shall be determined according to the laws of Scotland.

(3) This Order extends to Great Britain.

(4) Paragraphs in the Schedule marked "EW" apply only to English/Welsh arbitrations.

(5) Paragraphs in the Schedule marked "S" apply only to Scottish arbitrations.

(6) Paragraphs in the Schedule not marked "EW" or "S" apply to both English/Welsh arbitrations and Scottish arbitrations.

[2.718]
2 Commencement of the Scheme

The Scheme shall come into effect on 6th April 2004.

[2.719]
3 Revocation

Subject to article 8, the ACAS Arbitration Scheme (England and Wales) Order 2001 is revoked.

[2.720]
4 Application of Part I of the Arbitration Act 1996

The provisions of Part I of the Arbitration Act 1996 referred to in the Schedule at paragraphs 52EW, 110EW, 183EW, 187EW, 194EW, 200EW, 205EW, 209EW, 212EW, 217EW, 223EW and 224EW and shown in italics shall, as modified in those paragraphs, apply to English/Welsh arbitrations conducted in accordance with the Scheme.

[2.721]
5

(1) section 46(1)(b) of the Arbitration Act 1996 shall apply to English/Welsh arbitrations conducted in accordance with the Scheme, subject to the following modification.

(2) For "such other considerations as are agreed by them or determined by the tribunal" in section 46(1)(b) substitute "the Terms of Reference in paragraph 17 of the arbitration scheme set out in the Schedule to the ACAS Arbitration Scheme (Great Britain) Order 2004".

[2.722]
6 Enforcement of re-employment orders

(1) Employment tribunals shall enforce re-employment orders made in arbitrations conducted in accordance with the Scheme in accordance with section 117 of the 1996 Act (enforcement by award of compensation), modified as follows.

(2) In subsection (1)(a), subsection (3) and subsection (8), for the words "section 113" substitute in each case "paragraph 123(i) of the Scheme".

(3) In subsection (2) for "section 124" substitute "section 124(1) and (5) and subsections (9) and (10)".

(4) In subsection (3)(a) for the words "sections 118 to 127A" substitute the words "sections 118 to 123, section 124(1) and (5), sections 126 and 127A and subsections (9) and (11)".

(5) After subsection (8) insert—

> "(9) section 124(1) shall not apply to compensation awarded, or to a compensatory award made, to a person in a case where the arbitrator finds the reason (or, if more than one, the principal reason) for the dismissal (or, in a redundancy case, for which the employee was selected for dismissal) to be a reason specified in any of the enactments mentioned in section 124(1)A.
>
> (10) In the case of compensation awarded to a person under section 117(1) and (2), the limit imposed by section 124(1) may be exceeded to the extent necessary to enable the award fully to reflect the amount specified as payable under the arbitrator's award in accordance with paragraphs 131(i) or 134(iv) of the Scheme.
>
> (11) Where—
>
> (a) a compensatory award is an award under subsection (3)(a) of section 117, and
>
> (b) an additional award falls to be made under subsection (3)(b) of that section, the limit imposed by section 124(1) on the compensatory award may be exceeded to the extent necessary to enable the aggregate of the compensatory award and additional awards fully to reflect the amount specified as payable under the arbitrator's award in accordance with paragraphs 131(i) or 134(iv) of the Scheme.
>
> (12) In this section "the Scheme" means the arbitration scheme set out in the Schedule to the ACAS Arbitration Scheme (Great Britain) Order 2004.".

[2.723]
7 Awards of compensation

An award of a basic amount shall be treated as a basic award of compensation for unfair dismissal for the purposes of section 184(1)(d) of the 1996 Act (which specifies such an award as a debt which the Secretary of State must satisfy if the employer has become insolvent).

[2.724]
8 Transitional provision

(1) The Scheme has effect in any case where the appropriate date falls on or after 6th April 2004.

(2) In a case where the appropriate date falls before 6th April 2004, the arbitration scheme set out in the Schedule to the ACAS Arbitration Scheme (England and Wales) Order 2001 continues to apply.

(3) In this article, the "appropriate date" means the date of the Arbitration Agreement. Where the parties sign the Arbitration Agreement on different dates, the appropriate date is the date of the first signature.

(4) In this article, "Arbitration Agreement" means an agreement to submit the dispute to arbitration, as defined in paragraph 26 of the Scheme.

SCHEDULE

(The Schedule (omitted for reasons of space) sets out the scheme, submitted to the Secretary of State by ACAS pursuant to the Trade Union and Labour Relations (Consolidation) Act 1992, s 212A, providing for arbitration in the case of disputes involving proceedings, or claims which could be the subject of

proceedings, before an employment tribunal arising out of a contravention, or alleged contravention, of the Employment Rights Act 1996, Pt X (unfair dismissal). The Scheme does not extend to other kinds of claim related to, or raised at the same time as, a claim of unfair dismissal, for example, sex discrimination cases, and claims for unpaid wages. The Scheme provides a voluntary alternative to the employment tribunal for the resolution by arbitration of such claims where both parties agree. The text is omitted for reasons of space.)

[SETTLEMENT] AGREEMENTS (DESCRIPTION OF PERSON) ORDER 2004

(SI 2004/754)

NOTES

Made: 12 March 2004.

Authority: Sex Discrimination Act 1975, s 77(4B)(d); Race Relations Act 1976, s 72(4B)(d); Trade Union and Labour Relations (Consolidation) Act 1992, s 288(4)(d); Disability Discrimination Act 1995, s 9(4)(d); Employment Rights Act 1996, s 203(3A)(d); National Minimum Wage Act 1998, s 49(5)(d). Note that the Sex Discrimination Act 1975, the Race Relations Act 1976 and the Disability Discrimination Act 1995 were repealed by the Equality Act 2010, s 211(2), Sch 27, Pt 1.

Commencement: 6 April 2004.

Title: word in square brackets substituted for original word "Compromise" by the Enterprise and Regulatory Reform Act 2013 (Consequential Amendments) (Employment) Order 2013, SI 2013/1956, art 2, Schedule, para 10(a).

[2.725]

1 Citation, commencement and interpretation

(1) This Order may be cited as the [Settlement] Agreements (Description of Person) Order 2004 and shall come into force on 6th April 2004.

(2) In this Order—

(a) "the 1975 Act" means the Sex Discrimination Act 1975;
(b) "the 1976 Act" means the Race Relations Act 1976;
(c) "the 1992 Act" means the Trade Union and Labour Relations (Consolidation) Act 1992;
(d) "the 1995 Act" means the Disability Discrimination Act 1995;
(e) "the 1996 Act" means the Employment Rights Act 1996; and
(f) "the 1998 Act" means the National Minimum Wage Act 1998.

NOTES

Para (1): word in square brackets substituted by the Enterprise and Regulatory Reform Act 2013 (Consequential Amendments) (Employment) Order 2013, SI 2013/1956, art 2, Schedule, para 10(b).

Sex Discrimination Act 1975, Race Relations Act 1976, Disability Discrimination Act 1995: repealed.

[2.726]

2 Person specified

For the purposes of section 77(4B)(d) of the 1975 Act, section 72(4B)(d) of the 1976 Act, section 288(4)(d) of the 1992 Act, section 9(4)(d) of the 1995 Act, section 203(3A)(d) of the 1996 Act and section 49(5)(d) of the 1998 Act, a Fellow of the Institute of Legal Executives [practising in a solicitor's practice (including a body recognised under section 9 of the Administration of Justice Act 1985)] is specified.

NOTES

Words in square brackets substituted by the Legal Services Act 2007 (Consequential Amendments) Order 2009, SI 2009/3348, art 22, Sch 1.

3 *(Revoked by the Compromise Agreements (Description of Person) Order 2004 (Amendment) Order 2004, SI 2004/2515, art 2.)*

CIVIL AVIATION (WORKING TIME) REGULATIONS 2004

(SI 2004/756)

NOTES

Made: 11 March 2004.

Authority: European Communities Act 1972, s 2(2).

Commencement: 13 April 2004.

Note: with regard to the authority for these Regulations, note that the European Communities Act 1972 is repealed by the European Union (Withdrawal) Act 2018, s 1, as from exit day (as defined in s 20 of that Act); but note also that provision is made for the continuation in force of any subordinate legislation made under the authority of s 2(2) of the 1972 Act by s 2 of the 2018 Act at **[1.2240]**, subject to the provisions of s 5 of, and Sch 1 to, the 2018 Act at **[1.2243]**, **[1.2253]**.

Conciliation: employment tribunal proceedings under reg 18 are "relevant proceedings" for the purposes of the conciliation provisions contained in the Employment Tribunals Act 1996, ss 18–18C; see s 18(1)(q) of the 1996 Act at **[1.757]**.

ARRANGEMENT OF REGULATIONS

SCHEDULES

[2.727]

1 Citation and commencement

These Regulations may be cited as the Civil Aviation (Working Time) Regulations 2004 and shall come into force on 13th April 2004.

[2.728]

[2 Scope

These Regulations apply to persons employed to act as crew members on board a civil aircraft flying for the purpose of—

(a) public transport; or
(b) the performance of a commercial air transport flight.]

NOTES

Substituted by the Civil Aviation (Working Time) (Amendment) Regulations 2010, SI 2010/1226, reg 2(1), (2).

[2.729]

3 Interpretation

In these Regulations—

"the 1974 Act" means the Health and Safety at Work Act 1974;

"block flying time" means the time between an aircraft first moving from its parking place for the purpose of taking off until it comes to rest on its designated parking position with all its engines stopped;

"the CAA" means the Civil Aviation Authority;

"cabin crew" means a person on board a civil aircraft, other than flight crew, who is carried for the purpose of performing in the interests of the safety of the passengers, duties that are assigned to him for that purpose by the operator or the commander of that aircraft;

"calendar year" means the period of 12 months beginning with 1st January in any year;

"collective agreement" means a collective agreement within the meaning of section 178 of the Trade Union and Labour Relations (Consolidation) Act 1992 the trade union parties to which are independent trade unions within the meaning of section 5 of that Act;

["commercial air transport flight" has the same meaning [paragraph 1 of Schedule 1 to the Air Navigation Order 2016];]

. . .

"crew member" means a person employed to act as a member of the cabin crew or flight crew on board a civil aircraft by an undertaking established in the United Kingdom;

"employer" means an undertaking established in the United Kingdom by whom a crew member is (or where the employment has ceased, was) employed;

"employment" in relation to a crew member, means employment under his contract, and "employed" shall be construed accordingly;

"the Executive" means both the Health and Safety Executive [referred to in section 10(1)] of the 1974 Act, and the Health and Safety Executive of Northern Ireland;

"flight crew" means a person employed to act as a pilot, flight navigator, flight engineer or flight radiotelephony operator on board a civil aircraft;

"inspector" means a person appointed by the CAA under paragraph 1 of Schedule 2;

["local mean time" means the time to which a crew member is acclimatised for the purposes of a scheme;]

. . .

"protection and prevention services or facilities" means those services or facilities that are designed to preserve the health and safety of the crew member from any hazards that may threaten his health or safety during the course of his undertaking his work and are capable of being provided by his employer;

["public transport" is to be construed in accordance with the conditions set out in [article 6(2) of the Air Navigation Order 2016] in relation to an aircraft that is flying on a public transport flight;]

"relevant agreement", in relation to a crew member, means a workforce agreement which applies to him, any provision of a collective agreement which forms part of a contract between him and his employer, or any other agreement in writing which is legally enforceable as between the crew member and his employer;

"the relevant requirements" means regulations 5(2), 6, 7(2)(a), 8, 9 and 10;

"relevant training" means the training required to enable a person to perform the duties of flight crew or cabin crew carried out or undertaken whilst employed by an employer;

"rest break" and "rest period", in relation to a crew member, means a period which is not working time;

"scheme" means a scheme operated by an employer and approved by the CAA pursuant to [article 175(1)(b) or 179(2)(a) of the Air Navigation Order 2016];;

"standby", in relation to a crew member, means a crew member who in accordance with the terms of his employment holds himself ready to act as a crew member if called upon to do so by his employer;

"workforce agreement" means an agreement between an employer and crew members employed by him or his representatives in respect of which the conditions set out in Schedule 1 to these Regulations are satisfied;

"working time", in relation to a crew member means—

(a) any period during which he is working at his employer's disposal and carrying out his activity or duties;

(b) any period during which he is receiving relevant training, . . .

(c) any additional period which is to be treated as working time for the purpose of these Regulations under a relevant agreement, [and

(d) subject to regulation 9A, any period during which he is on standby,]

and "work", "works" and "to work" shall be construed accordingly.

NOTES

Words in square brackets in the definitions "commercial air transport flight", "public transport" and "scheme" substituted by the Air Navigation Order 2016, SI 2016/765, reg 274(1), Sch 14, Pt 2, para 3(a), as from 25 August 2016.

Definition "the Commission" (omitted) revoked, and words in square brackets in the definition "the Executive" substituted, by the Legislative Reform (Health and Safety Executive) Order 2008, SI 2008/960, art 22, Sch 3.

All other amendments made by the Civil Aviation (Working Time) (Amendment) Regulations 2010, SI 2010/1226, reg 2(1), (3).

[2.730]

4 Entitlement to annual leave

(1) A crew member is entitled to paid annual leave of at least four weeks, or a proportion of four weeks in respect of a period of employment of less than one year.

(2) Leave to which a crew member is entitled under this regulation—

(a) may be taken in instalments;

(b) may not be replaced by a payment in lieu, except where the crew member's employment is terminated.

[2.731]

5 Health assessments

(1) An employer shall ensure that each crew member employed by him is entitled to a free health assessment before he commences his employment and thereafter at regular intervals of whatever duration may be appropriate in the case of the crew member.

(2) Subject to paragraph (3), no person shall disclose a health assessment referred to in paragraph (1) made in respect of a crew member to any person other than that crew member without that crew member's consent in writing.

(3) A registered medical practitioner who makes a health assessment referred to in paragraph (1) may advise the employer of the crew member in question that the crew member is suffering from health problems which the practitioner considers to be connected with the fact that the crew member works during night time.

(4) Where—

(a) a registered medical practitioner has advised an employer pursuant to paragraph (3); and

(b) it is possible for the employer to transfer the crew member to mobile or non-mobile work—

(i) for which the crew member is suited, and

(ii) which is to be undertaken during periods such that the crew member will cease to work during night time,

then the employer shall transfer the crew member accordingly.

(5) A health assessment referred to in paragraph (1)—

(a) may be conducted within the National Health Service, and

(b) is free if it is undertaken at no cost to the crew member to whom it relates.

(6) For the purposes of this regulation, a crew member works during night time when he works at any time between the hours of 2.00 am and 4.59 am local mean time; . . .

NOTES

Para (6): words omitted revoked by the Civil Aviation (Working Time) (Amendment) Regulations 2010, SI 2010/1226, reg 2(1), (4).

[2.732]

6 Health and safety protection at work

An employer shall ensure that each crew member employed by him is at all times during the course of that employment provided with adequate health and safety protection and prevention services or facilities appropriate to the nature of his employment.

[2.733]

7 Pattern of work

(1) Where an employer intends to organise work according to a certain pattern he shall take into account the general principle of adapting work to the worker to the extent that is relevant to the objective of protecting workers' health and safety.

(2) Without prejudice to the generality of paragraph (1), in a case where an employer intends to organise work according to a certain pattern he shall—

(a) ensure that pattern affords the crew member adequate rest breaks, and

(b) take into account the need to ensure, where practicable, that pattern offers the crew member work, within the scope of his duties, that alleviates monotony or working at a pre-determined rate.

[2.734]

8 Provision of information

(1) When requested to do so by the CAA, an employer shall provide the CAA with such information as it may specify relating to the working patterns of crew members in his employ.

(2) Any information which is generated by an employer relating to the working patterns of crew members shall be retained by the employer for a period of not less than two years.

[2.735]

9 Maximum annual working time

An employer shall ensure that in any month—

(a) no person employed by him shall act as a crew member during the course of his working time, if during the period of 12 months expiring at the end of the month before the month in question the aggregate block flying time of that person exceeds 900 hours; and

(b) no crew member employed by him shall have a total annual working time of more than 2,000 hours during the period of 12 months expiring at the end of the month before the month in question.

[2.736]

[9A Standby time

(1) For the purpose of calculating the total annual working time under regulation 9(b), time spent by a crew member on standby is to count in full as working time except where paragraph (2) or (3) applies, when it is to count as half the time spent.

(2) This paragraph applies where the period of notice given by the employer to the crew member before the crew member must report for duty is at least 2 hours 15 minutes.

(3) This paragraph applies where time spent by the crew on standby—

(a) is spent—

(i) at home,

(ii) in accommodation provided by the employer away from the place where the crew member is next required to report for duty, or

(iii) in other accommodation arranged by the crew member to stay in while temporarily deployed away from home; and

(b) is between the hours of 10.00 pm and 8.00 am local mean time, and during that time the crew member—

(i) can take undisturbed rest, and

(ii) is not called upon to report for duty.]

NOTES

Inserted by the Civil Aviation (Working Time) (Amendment) Regulations 2010, SI 2010/1226, reg 2(1), (5).

Part 2 Statutory Instruments

[2.737]

10 Rest days

(1) Without prejudice to regulation 4, an employer shall ensure that all crew members employed by him are notified in writing as soon as possible of their right to rest days which shall be free of all employment duties including acting as a standby.

(2) For the purposes of this regulation, rest days are—

(a) not less than 7 days in each month during which a crew member works for his employer, which may include any rest periods required under [a scheme referred to in article 175(1) or 179 of the Air Navigation Order 2016]; and

(b) not less than 96 days in each calendar year during which a crew member works for his employer, which may include any rest periods required under [a scheme referred to in article 175(1) or 179 of the Air Navigation Order 2016].

NOTES

Para (2): words in square brackets substituted by the Air Navigation Order 2016, SI 2016/765, reg 274(1), Sch 14, Pt 2, para 3(b), as from 25 August 2016.

[2.738]

11 Enforcement

The provisions of Schedule 2 to these Regulations shall apply in relation to the enforcement of the relevant requirements.

[2.739]

12 Offences

(1) Any person who fails to comply with any of the relevant requirements shall be guilty of an offence.

(2) The provisions of paragraph (3) shall apply where an inspector is exercising or has exercised any power conferred by Schedule 2.

(3) It is an offence for a person—

(a) to contravene any requirement imposed by an inspector under paragraph 2 of Schedule 2;

(b) to prevent or attempt to prevent any other person from appearing before an inspector or from answering any question to which an inspector may by virtue of paragraph 2(2)(e) of Schedule 2 require an answer;

(c) to contravene any requirement or prohibition imposed by an improvement notice or a prohibition notice referred to in paragraphs 3 and 4 of Schedule 2 (including any such notice as is modified on appeal);

(d) intentionally to obstruct an inspector in the exercise or performance of his powers;

(e) to use or disclose any information in contravention of paragraph 8 of Schedule 2;

(f) to make a statement which he knows to be false or recklessly to make a statement which is false where the statement is made in purported compliance with a requirement to furnish any information imposed by or under these Regulations.

(4) Any person guilty of an offence under paragraph (1) shall be liable—

(a) on summary conviction, to a fine not exceeding the statutory maximum;

(b) on conviction on indictment, to a fine.

(5) A person guilty of an offence under paragraph (3)(b) or (d) shall be liable on summary conviction to a fine not exceeding level 5 on the standard scale.

(6) A person guilty of an offence under paragraph (3)(c) shall be liable—

(a) on summary conviction, to imprisonment for a term not exceeding three months, or a fine not exceeding the statutory maximum;

(b) on conviction on indictment, to imprisonment for a term not exceeding two years, or a fine or both.

(7) A person guilty of an offence under paragraph (3)(a), (e) or (f) shall be liable—

(a) on summary conviction, to a fine not exceeding the statutory maximum;

(b) on conviction on indictment—

(i) if the offence is under paragraph (3)(e), to imprisonment for a term not exceeding two years or a fine or both,

(ii) if the offence is under paragraph (3)(a) or (f), to a fine.

(8) The provisions set out in regulations 13 to 17 shall apply in relation to the offences provided for in paragraphs (1) and (3).

[2.740]

13 Offences due to fault of other person

Where the commission by any person of an offence is due to the act or default of some other person, that other person shall be guilty of the offence, and a person may be charged with and convicted of the offence by virtue of this regulation whether or not proceedings are taken against the first mentioned person.

[2.741]
14 Offences by bodies corporate

(1) Where an offence committed by a body corporate is proved to have been committed with the consent or connivance of, or to have been attributable to any neglect on the part of, any director, manager, secretary or other similar officer of the body corporate or a person who was purporting to act in any such capacity, he as well as the body corporate shall be guilty of that offence and shall be liable to be proceeded against and punished accordingly.

(2) Where the affairs of a body corporate are managed by its members, the preceding paragraph shall apply in relation to the acts and defaults of a member in connection with his functions of management as if he were a director of the body corporate.

[2.742]
15 Restriction on institution of proceedings in England and Wales

Proceedings for an offence shall not be instituted in England or Wales except by an inspector or by, or with the consent of, the Director of Public Prosecutions.

[2.743]
16 Prosecution by inspectors

(1) If authorised in that behalf by the CAA, an inspector may prosecute proceedings for an offence before a magistrates' court even though the inspector is not of counsel or a solicitor.

(2) This regulation shall not apply in Scotland.

[2.744]
17 Power of court to order cause of offence to be remedied or, in certain cases, forfeiture

(1) This regulation applies where a person is convicted of an offence in respect of any matter which appears to the court to be a matter which it is in his power to remedy.

(2) In addition to or instead of imposing any punishment, the court may order the person in question to take such steps as may be specified in the order for remedying the said matters within such time as may be fixed by the order.

(3) The time fixed by an order under paragraph (2) may be extended or further extended by order of the court on an application made before the end of that time as originally fixed or as extended under this paragraph, as the case may be.

(4) Where a person is ordered under paragraph (2) to remedy any matters, that person shall not be liable under these Regulations in respect of that matter in so far as it continues during the time fixed by the order or any further time allowed under paragraph (3).

[2.745]
18 Remedies

(1) A crew member may present a complaint to an employment tribunal that his employer has refused to permit him to exercise any right he has under regulation 4, 5(1), (4), 7(1) or 7(2)(b).

(2) An employment tribunal shall not consider a complaint under this regulation unless it is presented—

(a) before the end of the period of three months beginning with the date on which it is alleged—

(i) that the exercise of the right should have been permitted (or in the case of a rest period or annual leave extending over more than one day, the date on which it should have been permitted to begin), or

(ii) the payment under regulation 4(2)(b) should have been made;

as the case may be; or

(b) within such further period as the tribunal considers reasonable in a case where it is satisfied that it was not reasonably practicable for the complaint to be presented before the end of that period of three months.

[(2A) Regulation 19 (extension of time limits to facilitate conciliation before institution of proceedings) applies for the purposes of paragraph (2)(a).]

(3) Where an employment tribunal finds a complaint under regulation 4, 5(1), (4), 7(1) or 7(2)(b) well-founded, the tribunal—

(a) shall make a declaration to that effect; and

(b) may make an award of compensation to be paid by the employer to the crew member.

(4) The amount of the compensation shall be such as the tribunal considers just and equitable in all the circumstances having regard to—

(a) the employer's default in refusing to permit the crew member to exercise his right; and

(b) any loss sustained by the crew member which is attributable to the matters complained of.

NOTES

Para (2A): inserted by the Employment Tribunals Act 1996 (Application of Conciliation Provisions) Order 2014, SI 2014/431, art 3, Schedule, paras 30, 31.

Conciliation: employment tribunal proceedings under this regulation are "relevant proceedings" for the purposes of the conciliation provisions contained in the Employment Tribunals Act 1996, ss 18–18C; see s 18(1)(q) of the 1996 Act at **[1.757]**.

[2.746]
[19 Extension of time limits to facilitate conciliation before institution of proceedings

(1) In this regulation—

Part 2 Statutory Instruments

(a) Day A is the day on which the worker concerned complies with the requirement in subsection (1) of section 18A of the Employment Tribunals Act 1996 (requirement to contact ACAS before instituting proceedings) in relation to the matter in respect of which the proceedings are brought, and

(b) Day B is the day on which the worker concerned receives or, if earlier, is treated as receiving (by virtue of regulations made under subsection (11) of that section) the certificate issued under subsection (4) of that section.

(2) In working out when the time limit set by regulation 18(2)(a) expires the period beginning with the day after Day A and ending with Day B is not to be counted.

(3) If the time limit set by regulation 18(2)(a) would (if not extended by this paragraph) expire during the period beginning with Day A and ending one month after Day B, the time limit expires instead at the end of that period.

(4) The power conferred on the employment tribunal by regulation 18(2)(b) to extend the time limit set by paragraph (2)(a) of that regulation is exercisable in relation to that time limit as extended by this regulation.]

NOTES

Added by the Employment Tribunals Act 1996 (Application of Conciliation Provisions) Order 2014, SI 2014/431, art 3, Schedule, paras 30, 32.

SCHEDULES

SCHEDULE 1
WORKFORCE AGREEMENTS

Regulation 3

[2.747]

1 An agreement is a workforce agreement for the purposes of these Regulations if the following conditions are satisfied—

(a) the agreement is in writing;

(b) it has effect for a specified period not exceeding five years;

(c) it applies either—

(i) to all of the relevant members of the workforce, or

(ii) to all of the relevant members of the workforce who belong to a particular group;

(d) the agreement is signed—

(i) in the case of an agreement of the kind referred to in sub-paragraph (c)(i), by the representatives of the workforce, and in the case of an agreement of the kind referred to in sub-paragraph (c)(ii), by the representatives of the group to which the agreement applies (excluding, in either case, any representative not a relevant member of the workforce on the date on which the agreement was first made available for signature), or

(ii) if the employer employed 20 or fewer individuals on the date referred to in sub-paragraph (d)(i), either by the appropriate representatives in accordance with that sub-paragraph or by the majority of the individuals employed by him; and

(e) before the agreement was made available for signature, the employer provided all the employees to whom it was intended to apply on the date on which it came into effect with copies of the text of the agreement and such guidance as those employees might reasonably require in order to understand it in full.

2 For the purposes of this Schedule—

"a particular group" is a group of the relevant members of a workforce who undertake a particular function, work at a particular workplace or belong to a particular department or unit within their employer's business;

"relevant members of the workforce" are all of the employees employed by a particular employer, excluding any employee whose terms and conditions of employment are provided for, wholly or in part, in a collective agreement;

"representatives of the group" are employees duly elected to represent the members of a particular group;

"representatives of the workforce" are employees duly elected to represent the relevant members of the workforce;

and representatives are "duly elected" if the election at which they were elected satisfied the requirements of paragraph 3.

3 The requirements concerning elections referred to in paragraph 2 are that—

(a) the number of representatives to be elected is determined by the employer;

(b) the candidates for election as representatives of the workforce are relevant members of the workforce, and candidates for election as representatives of the group are members of the group;

(c) no employee who is eligible to be a candidate is unreasonably excluded from standing for election;

(d) all the relevant members of the workforce are entitled to vote for representatives of the workforce, and all the members of a particular group are entitled to vote for representatives of the group;

(e) the employees entitled to vote may vote for as many candidates as there are representatives to be elected; and

(f) the election is conducted so as to secure that—

(i) so far as is reasonably practicable, those voting do so in secret, and

(ii) the votes given at the election are fairly and accurately counted.

4 In this Schedule "employee" means an individual who has entered into or works under a contract of employment.

SCHEDULE 2
ENFORCEMENT

Regulation 11

[2.748]

1 Appointment of inspectors

(1) The CAA may appoint as inspectors (under whatever title it may from time to time determine) such persons having suitable qualifications as it thinks necessary for carrying into effect these Regulations, and may terminate any appointment made under this paragraph.

(2) Every appointment of a person as an inspector under this paragraph shall be made by an instrument in writing specifying which of the powers conferred on inspectors by these Regulations are to be exercisable by the person appointed; and an inspector shall in right of his appointment under this paragraph—

(a) be entitled to exercise only such of those powers as are so specified; and

(b) be entitled to exercise the powers so specified only within the field of responsibility of the CAA.

(3) So much of an inspector's instrument of appointment as specifies the powers which he is entitled to exercise may be varied by the CAA.

(4) An inspector shall, if so required when exercising or seeking to exercise any power conferred on him by these Regulations, produce his instrument of appointment or a duly authenticated copy thereof.

2 Powers of inspectors

(1) Subject to the provisions of paragraph 1 and this paragraph, an inspector may for the purpose of carrying into effect these Regulations exercise the powers set out in sub-paragraph (2).

(2) The powers of an inspector are the following, namely—

(a) at any reasonable time (or in a situation which in his opinion may be dangerous, at any time) to enter any premises which he has reason to believe it is necessary for him to enter for the purposes mentioned in sub-paragraph (1);

(b) to take with him a constable if he has reasonable cause to apprehend any serious obstruction in the execution of his duty;

(c) without prejudice to paragraph (b), on entering any premises by virtue of paragraph (a) to take with him—

(i) any other person duly authorised by the CAA; and

(ii) any equipment or material required for any purpose for which the power of entry is being exercised;

(d) to make such examination and investigation as may in any circumstances be necessary for the purpose mentioned in sub-paragraph (1);

(e) to require any person whom he has reasonable cause to believe to be able to give any information relevant to any examination or investigation under paragraph (d) to answer (in the absence of persons other than a person nominated by him to be present and any persons whom the inspector may allow to be present) such questions as the inspector thinks fit to ask and to sign a declaration of the truth of his answers;

(f) to require the production of, inspect, and take copies of or of any entry in—

(i) any records which by virtue of these Regulations are required to be kept, and

(ii) any other books, records or documents which it is necessary for him to see for the purposes of any examination or investigation under paragraph (d);

(g) to require any person to afford him such facilities and assistance with respect to any matters or things within that person's control or in relation to which that person has responsibilities as are necessary to enable the inspector to exercise any of the powers conferred on him by this sub-paragraph;

(h) any other power which is necessary for the purpose mentioned in sub-paragraph (1).

(3) No answer given by a person in pursuance of a requirement imposed under sub-paragraph (2)(e) shall be admissible in evidence against that person or the husband or wife of that person in any proceedings.

(4) Nothing in this paragraph shall be taken to compel the production by any person of a document of which he would on grounds of legal professional privilege be entitled to withhold production on an order for discovery in an action in the High Court or, as the case may be, an order for the production of documents in an action in the Court of Session.

3 Improvement notices

If an inspector is of the opinion that a person—

(a) is contravening one or more of these Regulations; or

(b) has contravened one or more of these Regulations in circumstances that make it likely that the contravention will continue or be repeated,

he may serve on him a notice (in this Schedule referred to as "an improvement notice") stating that he is of that opinion, specifying the provision or provisions as to which he is of that opinion, giving particulars of the reasons why he is of that opinion, and requiring that person to remedy the contravention or, as the case may be, the matter occasioning it within such period (ending not earlier than the period within which an appeal against the notice can be brought under paragraph (6) as may be specified in the notice.

4 Prohibition notices

(1) This paragraph applies to any activities which are being or are likely to be carried on by or under the control of any person, being activities to or in relation to which any of these Regulations apply or will, if the activities are so carried on, apply.

(2) If as regards any activities to which this paragraph applies an inspector is of the opinion that, as carried on by or under the control of the person in question, the activities involve or, as the case may be, will involve a risk of serious personal injury, the inspector may serve on that person a notice (in this Schedule referred to as "a prohibition notice").

(3) A prohibition notice shall—

(a) state that the inspector is of the said opinion;

(b) specify the matters which in his opinion give or, as the case may be, will give rise to the said risk;

(c) where in his opinion any of those matters involves or, as the case may be, will involve a contravention of any of these Regulations, state that he is of that opinion, specify the regulation or regulations as to which he is of that opinion, and give particulars of the reasons why he is of that opinion; and

(d) direct that the activities to which the notice relates shall not be carried on by or under the control of the person on whom the notice is served unless the matters specified in the notice in pursuance of paragraph (b) and any associated contraventions of provisions so specified in pursuance of paragraph (c) have been remedied.

(4) A direction contained in a prohibition notice in pursuance of sub-paragraph (3)(d) shall take effect—

(a) at the end of the period specified in the notice; or

(b) if the notice so declares, immediately.

5 Provisions supplementary to paragraphs 3 and 4

(1) In this paragraph "a notice" means an improvement notice or a prohibition notice.

(2) A notice may (but need not) include directions as to the measures to be taken to remedy any contravention or matter to which the notice relates; and any such directions—

(a) may be framed to any extent by reference to any approved code of practice; and

(b) may be framed so as to afford the person on whom the notice is served a choice between different ways of remedying the contravention or matter.

(3) Where an improvement notice or prohibition notice which is not to take immediate effect has been served—

(a) the notice may be withdrawn by an inspector at any time before the end of the period specified therein in pursuance of paragraph 3 or paragraph 4(4) as the case may be; and

(b) the period so specified may be extended or further extended by an inspector at any time when an appeal against the notice is not pending.

6 Appeal against improvement or prohibition notice

(1) In this paragraph "a notice" means an improvement or prohibition notice.

(2) A person on whom a notice is served may within 21 days from the date of its service appeal to an employment tribunal; and on such an appeal the tribunal may either cancel or affirm the notice and, if it affirms it, may do so either in its original form or with such modifications as the tribunal may in the circumstances think fit.

(3) Where an appeal under this paragraph is brought against a notice within the period allowed under the preceding sub-paragraph, then—

(a) in the case of an improvement notice, the bringing of the appeal shall have the effect of suspending the operation of the notice until the appeal is finally disposed of or, if the appeal is withdrawn, until the withdrawal of the appeal;

(b) in the case of a prohibition notice, the bringing of the appeal shall have the like effect if, but only if, on the application of the appellant the tribunal so directs (and then only from the giving of the direction).

(4) One or more assessors may be appointed for the purposes of any proceedings brought before an employment tribunal under this paragraph.

7 Power of the CAA to indemnify inspectors

Where an action has been brought against an inspector in respect of an act done in the execution or purported execution of these Regulations and the circumstances are such that he is not legally entitled to require the CAA to indemnify him, then the CAA may, nevertheless, indemnify him against the whole or any part of any damages or costs or expenses which he may have been ordered to pay or may have incurred, if the CAA is satisfied that the inspector honestly believed that the act complained of was within his powers and that his duty as an inspector required or entitled him to do it.

8 Restrictions on disclosure of information

(1) In this paragraph—

"relevant information" means information obtained by an inspector in pursuance of a requirement imposed under paragraph 2; and

"the recipient", in relation to any relevant information, means the person by whom that information was so obtained or to whom that information was so furnished, as the case may be; and

"relevant statutory provisions" means—

(a) the provisions of the 1974 Act and any regulations made under powers contained in that Act; and

(b) while and to the extent that they remain in force, the provisions of the Acts mentioned in Schedule 1 to the 1974 Act and which are specified in the third column of that Schedule and the regulations, orders or other instruments of a legislative character made or having effect under a provision so specified.

(2) Subject to the following sub-paragraph, no relevant information shall be disclosed without the consent of the person by whom it was furnished.

(3) The preceding sub-paragraph shall not apply to—

(a) disclosure of information to . . . the Executive, a government department, or the CAA;

(b) without prejudice to paragraph (a), disclosure by the recipient of information to any person for the purpose of any function conferred on the recipient by or under any of the relevant statutory provisions or under these Regulations;

(c) without prejudice to paragraph (a), disclosure by the recipient of information to a constable authorised by a chief officer of police to receive it; or

(d) disclosure by the recipient of information in a form calculated to prevent it from being identified as relating to a particular person or case.

[(4) In the preceding paragraph, any reference to the Executive, the CAA or a government department includes respectively a reference to an officer of that body, and also, in the case of a reference to the Executive, includes a reference to—

(a) a person performing any of the functions of the Executive by virtue of section 13(3) of the 1974 Act;

(b) an officer of a body which is so performing any such functions; and

(c) an adviser appointed in pursuance of section 13(7) of the 1974 Act.]

(5) A person to whom information is disclosed in pursuance of sub-paragraph (3) shall not use the information for a purpose other than—

(a) in a case falling within sub-paragraph (3)(a), a purpose of . . . the Executive, a government department, or the CAA in question in connection with these Regulations or with the relevant statutory provisions, as the case may be;

(b) in the case of information given to a constable, the purposes of the police in connection with these Regulations, the relevant statutory provisions or any enactment whatsoever relating to working time.

(6) A person shall not disclose any information obtained by him as a result of the exercise of any power conferred by paragraph 2 (including in particular any information with respect to any trade secret obtained by him in any premises entered by him by virtue of any such power) except—

(a) for the purposes of his functions; or

(b) for the purposes of any legal proceedings; or

(c) with the relevant consent.

In this sub-paragraph "the relevant consent" means, in the case of information furnished in pursuance of a requirement imposed under paragraph 2, the consent of the person who furnished it, and, in any other case, the consent of a person having responsibilities in relation to the premises where the information was obtained.

(7) Notwithstanding anything in the preceding sub-paragraph an inspector shall, in circumstances in which it is necessary to do so for the purpose of assisting in keeping persons (or the representatives of persons) adequately informed about matters affecting their health, safety and welfare or working time, give to such persons or their representatives the following descriptions of information, that is to say—

(a) factual information obtained by him as mentioned in that sub-paragraph which relates to their working environment; and

(b) information with respect to any action which he has taken or proposes to take in or in connection with the performance of his functions in relation to their working environment;

and, where an inspector does as aforesaid, he shall give the like information to the employer of the first-mentioned persons.

(8) Notwithstanding anything in sub-paragraph (6), a person who has obtained such information as is referred to in that sub-paragraph may furnish to a person who appears to him to be likely to be a party to any civil proceedings arising out of any accident, occurrence, situation or other matter, a written statement of the relevant facts observed by him in the course of exercising any of the powers referred to in that sub-paragraph.

NOTES

Para 8: words omitted from sub-paras (3)(a), (5)(a) revoked, and sub-para (4) substituted, by the Legislative Reform (Health and Safety Executive) Order 2008, SI 2008/960, art 22, Sch 3.

Part 2 Statutory Instruments

FISHING VESSELS (WORKING TIME: SEA-FISHERMEN) REGULATIONS 2004

(SI 2004/1713)

NOTES

Made: 5 July 2004.

Authority: European Communities Act 1972, s 2(2); Merchant Shipping Act 1995, ss 85(1), (3), (5)(a), (6), (7), 86(1), (2).

Commencement: 16 August 2004.

Note: with regard to the authority for these Regulations, note that the European Communities Act 1972 is repealed by the European Union (Withdrawal) Act 2018, s 1, as from exit day (as defined in s 20 of that Act); but note also that provision is made for the continuation in force of any subordinate legislation made under the authority of s 2(2) of the 1972 Act by s 2 of the 2018 Act at **[1.2240]**, subject to the provisions of s 5 of, and Sch 1 to, the 2018 Act at **[1.2243]**, **[1.2253]**.

ARRANGEMENT OF REGULATIONS

PART 1
GENERAL

[2.749]

1 Citation and commencement

These Regulations may be cited as the Fishing Vessels (Working Time: Sea-fishermen) Regulations 2004 and shall come into force on 16th August 2004.

[2.750]

2 Interpretation

(1) In these Regulations—

"the Act" means the Merchant Shipping Act 1995;

"collective agreement" means a collective agreement within the meaning of section 178 of the Trade Union and Labour Relations (Consolidation) Act 1992, the trade union parties to which are independent trade unions within the meaning of section 5 of that Act;

"employer", in relation to a worker, means the person by whom the worker is (or, where the employment has ceased, was) employed;

"employment", in relation to a worker, means employment under his contract of employment, and "employed" shall be construed accordingly;

["fisherman" means every person employed, engaged or working in any capacity on board any fishing vessel, but does not include a person solely engaged as a pilot for the vessel;

"fishing vessel owner" means the owner of the fishing vessel or any other organisation or person such as the manager, agent or bareboat charterer, who has assumed the responsibility for the operation of the vessel from the owner;]

"MCA" means the Maritime and Coastguard Agency, an executive agency of the Department for Transport;

"Merchant Shipping Notice" means a notice described as such and issued by the MCA;

"night time" means a period—

(a) the duration of which is not less than seven hours, and

(b) which includes the period between midnight and 5 am (local time),

which is determined for the purposes of these Regulations by a relevant agreement, or, in default of such a determination, the period between 11pm and 6am (local time);

"night work" means work during night time;

"night worker" means a worker—

(a) who, as a normal course, works at least three hours of his daily working time during night time, or

(b) who is likely, during night time, to work at least such proportion of his annual working time as may be specified for the purposes of these Regulations in a collective agreement or a workforce agreement,

and, for the purpose of paragraph (a) of this definition, a person works hours as a normal course (without prejudice to the generality of that expression) if he works such hours on the majority of days on which he works;

"relevant agreement", in relation to a worker, means a workforce agreement which applies to him, any provision of a collective agreement which forms part of a contract between him and his employer, or any other agreement in writing which is legally enforceable as between the worker and his employer;

"relevant inspector" means a person mentioned in paragraph (a), (b) or (c) of section 258(1) of the Act;

"relevant training" means work experience provided pursuant to a training course or programme, training for employment, or both, other than work experience or training—

(a) the immediate provider of which is an educational institution or a person whose main business is the provision of training, and

(b) which is provided on a course run by that institution or person;

"rest period" means a period which is not working time, other than a rest break or leave to which the worker is entitled under these Regulations;

"United Kingdom fishing vessel" means a sea-going fishing vessel which is registered in the United Kingdom;

"worker" means a person employed (or, where the employment has ceased, who was employed) on board a fishing vessel;

"workforce agreement" means an agreement between an employer and workers employed by him or their representatives in respect of which the conditions set out in Schedule 1 to these Regulations are satisfied; and

"working time", in relation to a worker, means—

(a) any period during which he is working, at his employer's disposal and carrying out his activity or duties, and

(b) any period during which he is receiving relevant training,

and "work" shall be construed accordingly.

(2) Subject to paragraph (1), words and expressions used in these Regulations shall have the same meaning as in Council Directive 93/104/EC concerning certain aspects of the organisation of working time.

NOTES

Para (1): definitions "fisherman" and "fishing vessel owner" inserted by the Merchant Shipping (Work in Fishing Convention) (Consequential Provisions) Regulations 2018, SI 2018/1109, reg 8(1), (2), as from 31 December 2018.

[2.751]

3 Application

(1) These Regulations apply to United Kingdom fishing vessels wherever they may be.

(2) Regulations 7, 16 and 17 apply to fishing vessels registered in Member States other than the United Kingdom when they are within United Kingdom waters.

4 (*Outside the scope of this work.*)

PART 2
RIGHTS AND OBLIGATIONS CONCERNING WORKING TIME

[2.752]

5 General

The provisions of this Part have effect subject to the exceptions provided for in Part 3 of these Regulations.

[2.753]
6 Maximum weekly working time

(1) A worker's working time, including overtime, in any reference period which is applicable in his case shall not exceed an average of 48 hours for each seven days.

(2) An employer shall take all reasonable steps, in keeping with the need to protect the health and safety of workers, to ensure that the limit specified in paragraph (1) is complied with in the case of each worker employed by him in relation to whom it applies.

(3) Subject to paragraph (4) the reference period which applies in the case of a worker is any period of 52 weeks in the course of his employment.

(4) Where a worker has worked for his employer for less than 52 weeks, the reference period applicable in his case is the period that has elapsed since he started work for his employer.

(5) For the purposes of this regulation, a worker's average working time for each seven days during a reference period shall be determined according to the formula—

(A + B) / C

where—

A is the aggregate number of hours comprised in the worker's working time during the course of the reference period;

B is the aggregate number of hours comprised in his working time during the course of the period beginning immediately after the end of the reference period and ending when the number of days in that subsequent period on which he has worked equals the number of excluded days during the reference period; and

C is the number of weeks in the reference period.

(6) In paragraph (5), "excluded days" means days comprised in—

(a) any period of annual leave taken by the worker in exercise of his entitlement under regulation 11;
(b) any period of sick leave taken by the worker; and
(c) any period of maternity, paternity, adoption or parental leave taken by the worker.

[2.754]
7 Rest

(1) A worker is entitled to adequate rest.

(2) For the purposes of this regulation, "adequate rest" means that a worker has regular rest periods, the duration of which are expressed in units of time and which are sufficiently long and continuous to ensure that, as a result of fatigue or other irregular working patterns, he does not cause injury to himself, to fellow workers or to others and that he does not damage his health, either in the short term or in the longer term.

(3) Without prejudice to the generality of paragraph (2), a worker's minimum rest periods shall be—

(a) 10 hours in any 24-hour period, and
(b) 77 hours in any seven-day period.

(4) The rest periods referred to in paragraph (3)(a) above may be divided into no more than two periods, one of which shall be at least six hours in length; and the interval between consecutive rest periods shall not exceed 14 hours.

[(5) Paragraphs (1) to (3) also apply to fishermen.]

NOTES

Para (5): added by the Merchant Shipping (Work in Fishing Convention) (Consequential Provisions) Regulations 2018, SI 2018/1109, reg 8(1), (3), as from 31 December 2018.

[2.755]
8 Health assessment and transfer of night workers to day work

(1) An employer—

(a) shall not assign a worker to work which is to be undertaken during periods such that the worker will become a night worker unless—
  (i) the employer has ensured that the worker will have the opportunity of a free health assessment before he takes up the assignment; or
  (ii) the worker had a health assessment before being assigned to work to be undertaken during such periods on an earlier occasion, and the employer has no reason to believe that that assessment is no longer valid, and
(b) shall ensure that each night worker employed by him has the opportunity of a free health assessment at regular intervals of whatever duration may be appropriate in his case.

(2) For the purpose of paragraph (1), an assessment is free if it is at no cost to the worker to whom it relates.

(3) No person shall disclose an assessment made for the purposes of this regulation to any person other than the worker to whom it relates, unless—

(a) the worker makes the disclosure or has given his consent to it in writing, or
(b) the disclosure is confined to a statement that the assessment shows the worker to be fit—
  (i) in a case where paragraph (1)(a)(i) applies, to take up an assignment, or
  (ii) in a case where paragraph (1)(b) applies, to continue to undertake an assignment.

(4) Where—

(a) a registered medical practitioner has advised an employer that a worker employed by the employer is suffering from health problems which the practitioner considers to be connected with the fact that the worker performs night work, and
(b) it is possible for the employer to transfer the worker to work—
 (i) to which the worker is suited, and
 (ii) which is to be undertaken during periods such that the worker will cease to be a night worker,

the employer shall transfer the worker accordingly.

[2.756]
9 Pattern of work

Where the pattern according to which an employer organises work is such as to put the health and safety of a worker employed by him at risk, in particular because the work is monotonous or the work-rate is predetermined, the employer shall ensure that the worker is given reasonable rest breaks.

[2.757]
10 Records

An employer [or fishing vessel owner] shall—
(a) keep records which are adequate to show whether regulations 6(1), 7(1), (3) and (4) and 8(1) are being complied with in the case of each worker [or fisherman] employed by him in relation to whom they apply; and
(b) retain such records for two years from the date on which they are made.

NOTES

Words in square brackets inserted by the Merchant Shipping (Work in Fishing Convention) (Consequential Provisions) Regulations 2018, SI 2018/1109, reg 8(1), (4), as from 31 December 2018.

[2.758]
11 Entitlement to annual leave and payment for leave

(1) Subject to paragraph (2), a worker is entitled to at least four weeks' annual leave and to be paid in respect of any such leave at the rate of a week's pay in respect of each week of leave.

(2) In respect of a period of employment of less than one year, a worker is entitled to annual leave of a proportion of four weeks equal to the proportion the period of employment in question bears to one year; the proportion to be determined in days and any fraction of a day to be treated as a whole day.

(3) Leave to which a worker is entitled under this regulation—
(a) may be taken in instalments;
(b) may not be replaced by a payment in lieu, except where the worker's employment is terminated.

(4) Sections 221 to 224 of the Employment Rights Act 1996 shall apply for the purpose of determining the amount of a week's pay for the purposes of paragraph (1), subject to the modifications set out in paragraph (5).

(5) The provisions referred to in paragraph (4) shall apply as if—
(a) references to the employee were references to the worker;
(b) references to the employee's contract of employment were references to the worker's contract;
(c) the calculation date were the first day of the period of leave in question; and
(d) the references to sections 227 and 228 did not apply.

(6) A right to payment under paragraph (1) does not affect any right of a worker to remuneration under his contract ("contractual remuneration").

(7) Any contractual remuneration paid to a worker in respect of a period of leave goes towards discharging any liability of the employer to make payments under this regulation in respect of that period; and, conversely, any payment of remuneration under this regulation in respect of a period goes towards discharging any liability of the employer to pay contractual remuneration in respect of that period.

[2.759]
[11A

(1) Subject to paragraph (4), a worker is entitled in each leave year to a period of leave in addition to the entitlement under regulation 11 ("additional leave") determined in accordance with paragraph (2) and to be paid for any such leave at the rate of a week's pay in respect of each week of leave.

(2) The period of additional leave to which a worker is entitled under paragraph (1) is—
(a) in any leave year beginning on or after the coming into force of the Merchant Shipping (Work in Fishing Convention) (Consequential Provisions) Regulations 2018, 1.6 weeks in each leave year;
(b) in any leave year beginning before the coming into force of the Merchant Shipping (Work in Fishing Convention) (Consequential Provisions) Regulations 2018, a proportion of 1.6 weeks equivalent to the proportion of the year beginning on the date those regulations come into force which would have elapsed at the end of that leave year.

(3) In respect of a period of employment of less than one year, a worker is entitled to additional annual leave of a proportion of 1.6 weeks equal to the proportion the period of employment in question bears to one year; the proportion to be determined in days and any fraction of a day to be treated as a whole day.

(4) The aggregate entitlement provided for in paragraph (2) and regulation 11(1) is subject to a maximum of 28 days.

(5) A worker's leave year begins for the purposes of this regulation on the same date as a worker's leave year begins for the purposes of regulation 11.

(6) Regulation 11(3) to (7) shall apply as if the references to paragraph (1) of that regulation were to paragraph (1) of this regulation.]

NOTES

Commencement: 31 December 2018.

Inserted by the Merchant Shipping (Work in Fishing Convention) (Consequential Provisions) Regulations 2018, SI 2018/1109, reg 8(1), (5).

[2.760]

12 Entitlements under other provisions

Where during any period a worker is entitled to a rest period or annual leave both under a provision of these Regulations and under a separate provision (including a provision of his contract), he may not exercise the two rights separately, but may, in taking a rest period or annual leave during that period, take advantage of whichever right is, in any particular respect, the more favourable.

PART 3
EXCEPTIONS

[2.761]

13 Exceptions

(1) The Secretary of State may grant an exception from the limit in regulation 6(1) or the requirements of regulation 7(3) and 7(4) for objective or technical reasons or reasons concerning the organisation of work if—

- (a) he has first (so far as is possible) consulted representatives of the employers [fishing vessel owners, fishermen] and workers concerned, and
- (b) the exception is subject to such conditions and limitations as will protect the health and safety of workers [and fishermen].

(2) The Secretary of State may, on giving reasonable notice and after consulting such persons (if any) as he considers may be affected, alter or cancel any exception granted under paragraph (1).

(3) An exception granted in accordance with paragraph (1) above

- (a) shall be limited to the extent necessary for the reasons mentioned in that paragraph; and
- (b) may take account of the granting of compensatory leave periods to workers in place of the limit in regulation 6(1) and the rest periods required by regulation 7(3) and 7(4).

(4) An exception under paragraph (1) may relate to classes of cases (a "class exception") or to individual cases (an "individual exception").

(5) An individual exception granted under paragraph (1), and an alteration or cancellation of such an exception under paragraph (2), shall—

- (a) be given in writing,
- (b) specify the date on which it takes effect, and
- (c) in the case of the grant of an exemption, specify the conditions and limitations subject to which it is granted in accordance with paragraph (1)(b) of this regulation.

(6) A class exception granted under paragraph (1), and an alteration or cancellation of such an exception under paragraph (2)—

- (a) may relate to particular types of fishing vessel and methods of fishing, and
- (b) shall be specified by the Secretary of State in a Merchant Shipping Notice which is considered by him to be relevant from time to time.

NOTES

Para (1): words in square brackets inserted by the Merchant Shipping (Work in Fishing Convention) (Consequential Provisions) Regulations 2018, SI 2018/1109, reg 8(1), (6), as from 31 December 2018.

[2.762]

14 Emergencies

(1) Nothing in these Regulations prevents the master of a fishing vessel from requiring a worker [or fishermen] to work any hours of work necessary for the immediate safety of the fishing vessel, persons on board the fishing vessel or cargo or for the purpose of giving assistance to another ship or to a person in distress at sea.

(2) For the purposes of this regulation the word "vessel" includes her fishing gear and the word "cargo" includes the catch of a fishing vessel.

NOTES

Para (1): words in square brackets inserted by the Merchant Shipping (Work in Fishing Convention) (Consequential Provisions) Regulations 2018, SI 2018/1109, reg 8(1), (7), as from 31 December 2018.

PART 4
MISCELLANEOUS

15–18 (*Outside the scope of this work.*)

[2.763]
19 Remedies

(1) A worker may present a complaint to an employment tribunal that his employer—

(a) has refused to permit him to exercise any right he has under regulation 7(1), 7(3), or 7(4) or 11(1); or

(b) has failed to pay him the whole or any part of any amount due to him under regulation 11(1).

(2) An employment tribunal shall not consider a complaint under this regulation unless it is presented—

(a) before the end of the period of three months beginning with the date on which it is alleged that the exercise of the right should have been permitted (or in the case of a rest period or leave extending over more than one day, the date on which it should have been permitted to begin) or, as the case may be, the payment should have been made;

(b) within such further period as the tribunal considers reasonable in a case where it is satisfied that it was not reasonably practicable for the complaint to be presented before the end of that period of three months.

[(2A) Regulation 19A (extension of time limits to facilitate conciliation before institution of proceedings) applies for the purposes of paragraph (2).]

(3) Where an employment tribunal finds a complaint under paragraph (1)(a) well-founded, the tribunal—

(a) shall make a declaration to that effect, and

(b) may make an award of compensation to be paid by the employer to the worker.

(4) The amount of the compensation shall be such as the tribunal considers just and equitable in all the circumstances having regard to—

(a) the employer's default in refusing to permit the worker to exercise his right, and

(b) any loss sustained by the worker which is attributable to the matters complained of.

(5) Where on a complaint under paragraph (1)(b) an employment tribunal finds that an employer has failed to pay a worker in accordance with regulation 11(1), it shall order the employer to pay to the worker the amount which it finds to be due to him.

NOTES

Para (2A): inserted by the Enterprise and Regulatory Reform Act 2013 (Consequential Amendments) (Employment) Order 2014, SI 2014/386, art 2, Schedule, paras 26, 28.

[2.764]
[19A Extension of time limit to facilitate conciliation before institution of proceedings

(1) In this regulation—

(a) Day A is the day on which the worker concerned complies with the requirement in subsection (1) of section 18A of the Employment Tribunals Act 1996 (requirement to contact ACAS before instituting proceedings) in relation to the matter in respect of which the proceedings are brought, and

(b) Day B is the day on which the worker concerned receives or, if earlier, is treated as receiving (by virtue of regulations made under subsection (11) of that section) the certificate issued under subsection (4) of that section.

(2) In working out when the time limit set by regulation 19(2)(a) expires the period beginning with the day after Day A and ending with Day B is not to be counted.

(3) If the time limit set by regulation 19(2)(a) would (if not extended by this paragraph) expire during the period beginning with Day A and ending one month after Day B, the time limit expires instead at the end of that period.

(4) The power conferred on the employment tribunal by regulation 19(2)(b) to extend the time limit set by paragraph (2)(a) of that regulation is exercisable in relation to that time limit as extended by this regulation.]

NOTES

Inserted by the Enterprise and Regulatory Reform Act 2013 (Consequential Amendments) (Employment) Order 2014, SI 2014/386, art 2, Schedule, paras 26, 29.

[2.765]
20 Restriction on contracting out

(1) Any provision in an agreement (whether a contract of employment or not) is void in so far as it purports—

(a) to exclude or limit the operation of any provision of these Regulations, save in so far as these Regulations provide for an agreement to have that effect, or

(b) to preclude a person from bringing proceedings under these Regulations before an employment tribunal.

(2) Paragraph (1) does not apply to—

(a) any agreement to refrain from instituting or continuing proceedings where a conciliation officer has taken action under [any of sections 18A to 18C] of the Employment Tribunals Act 1996 (conciliation); or

(b) any agreement to refrain from instituting or continuing proceedings within [section 18(1)(r)] of the Employment Tribunals Act 1996 (proceedings under these Regulations where conciliation is available), if the conditions regulating [settlement] agreements under these Regulations are satisfied in relation to the agreement.

(3) For the purposes of paragraph (2)(b) the conditions regulating [settlement] agreements under these Regulations are that—

(a) the agreement must be in writing,
(b) the agreement must relate to the particular complaint,
(c) the worker must have received advice from a relevant independent adviser as to the terms and effect of the proposed agreement and, in particular, its effect on his ability to pursue his rights before an employment tribunal,
(d) there must be in force, when the adviser gives the advice, a contract of insurance, or an indemnity provided for members of a profession or a professional body, covering the risk of a claim by the worker in respect of loss arising in consequence of the advice,
(e) the agreement must identify the adviser, and
(f) the agreement must state that the conditions regulating [settlement] agreements under these Regulations are satisfied.

(4) A person is a relevant independent adviser for the purposes of paragraph (3)(c)—

(a) if he is a qualified lawyer,
(b) if he is an officer, official, employee or member of an independent trade union who has been certified in writing by the trade union as competent to give advice and as authorised to do so on behalf of the trade union, or
(c) if he works at an advice centre (whether as an employee or as a volunteer) and has been certified in writing by the centre as competent to give advice and as authorised to do so on behalf of the centre.

(5) But a person is not a relevant independent adviser for the purposes of paragraph (3)(c)—

(a) if he is, is employed by or is acting in the matter for the employer or an associated employer,
(b) in the case of a person within paragraph (4)(b), if the trade union is the employer or an associated employer, or
(c) in the case of a person within paragraph (4)(c), if the worker makes a payment for the advice received from him.

(6) In paragraph (4)(a), "qualified lawyer" means—

(a) as respects England and Wales, [a person who, for the purposes of the Legal Services Act 2007), is an authorised person in relation to an activity which constitutes the exercise of a right of audience or the conduct of litigation (within the meaning of that Act)];
(b) as respects Scotland, an advocate (whether in practice as such or employed to give legal advice), or a solicitor who holds a practising certificate; and
(c) as respects Northern Ireland, a barrister (whether in practice as such or employed to give legal advice), or a solicitor who holds a practising certificate.

(7) For the purposes of paragraph (5) any two employers shall be treated as associated if—

(a) one is a company of which the other (directly or indirectly) has control; or
(b) both are companies of which a third person (directly or indirectly) has control;

and "associated employer" shall be construed accordingly.

[(8) In the application of this regulation in relation to Northern Ireland, paragraphs (2) and (3) above shall have effect as if for "settlement agreements" (in each place where those words occur) there were substituted "compromise agreements.]

NOTES

Para (2): in sub-para (a) words in square brackets substituted by the Enterprise and Regulatory Reform Act 2013 (Consequential Amendments) (Employment) Order 2014, SI 2014/386, art 2, Schedule, paras 26, 30; in sub-para (b) words in first pair of square brackets substituted by the Employment Tribunals Act 1996 (Application of Conciliation Provisions) Order 2014, SI 2014/431, art 3, Schedule, para 33(b) and word in second pair of square brackets substituted by the Enterprise and Regulatory Reform Act 2013 (Consequential Amendments) (Employment) Order 2013, SI 2013/1956, art 2, Schedule, para 6(a).

Para (3): words in square brackets substituted by SI 2013/1956, art 2, Schedule, para 6(a).

Para (6): in sub-para (a) words in square brackets substituted by the Legal Services Act 2007 (Consequential Amendments) Order 2009, SI 2009/3348, art 23, Sch 2.

Para (8): added by SI 2013/1956, art 2, Schedule, para 6(b).

21 (*Introduces Schedule 2 (amendments to legislation).*)

SCHEDULE 1

Regulation 2(1)

[2.766]

1 The following are the conditions that must be satisfied for an agreement between an employer and workers employed by him or their representatives to constitute a workforce agreement for the purposes of these Regulations—

(a) the agreement is in writing;
(b) it has effect for a specified period not exceeding five years;
(c) it applies either—
 (i) to all of the relevant members of the workforce; or

(ii) to all of the members of the workforce who belong to a particular group;

(d) the agreement is signed—

(i) in the case of an agreement of the kind referred to in sub-paragraph (c)(i), by the representatives of the workforce, and in the case of an agreement of the kind referred to in sub-paragraph (c)(ii), by the representatives of the group to which the agreement applies (excluding, in either case, any representative not a relevant member of the workforce on the date on which the agreement was first made available for signature), or

(ii) if the employer employed 20 or fewer workers on the date referred to in sub-paragraph (d)(i), either by the appropriate representatives in accordance with that sub-paragraph or by the majority of the workers employed by him; and

(e) before the agreement was made available for signature, the employer provided all the workers to whom it was intended to apply on the date on which it came into effect with copies of the text of the agreement and such guidance as those workers may reasonably require in order to understand it fully.

2 For the purposes of this Schedule—

"a particular group" is a group of the relevant members of a workforce who undertake a particular function, work at a particular workplace or belong to a particular department or unit within their employer's business;

"relevant members of the workforce" are all of the workers employed by a particular employer, excluding any worker whose terms and conditions of employment are provided for, wholly or in part, in a collective agreement;

"representatives of the workforce" are workers duly elected to represent the relevant members of the workforce, "representatives of the group" are workers duly elected to represent the members of a particular group, and representatives are "duly elected" if the election at which they were elected satisfied the requirements of paragraph 3 of this Schedule.

3 The requirements concerning elections referred to in paragraph 2 are that—

(a) the number of representatives to be elected is determined by the employer;

(b) the candidates for election as representatives of the workforce are relevant members of the workforce, and the candidates for election as representatives of a group are members of the group;

(c) no worker who is eligible to be a candidate is unreasonably excluded from standing for election;

(d) all the relevant members of the workforce are entitled to vote for representatives of the workforce, and all members of a particular group are entitled to vote for representatives of the group;

(e) the workers entitled to vote may vote for as many candidates as there are representatives to be elected; and

(f) the election is conducted so as to secure that—

(i) so far as reasonably practicable, those voting do so in secret, and

(ii) the votes given at the election are fairly and accurately counted.

SCHEDULE 2

(*Sch 2 amends the Employment Tribunals Act 1996, s, 21 at* **[1.764]**, *the Employment Rights Act 1996, ss 45A, 101A, 104 at* **[1.883]**, **[1.1010]**, **[1.1015]**, *the Working Time Regulations 1998, SI 1998/1833, reg 18* **[2.295]** *and other legislation which is outside the scope of this work. It is effectively spent in so far as amended the Employment Tribunals Act 1996, s 18 at* **[1.757]** *following subsequent amendment of that section.*)

ACAS (FLEXIBLE WORKING) ARBITRATION SCHEME (GREAT BRITAIN) ORDER 2004 (NOTE)

(SI 2004/2333)

[2.767]

NOTES

Made: 6 September 2004.

Authority: Trade Union and Labour Relations (Consolidation) Act 1992, s 212A(3), (6), (7).

Commencement: 1 October 2004.

This Order sets out a revised scheme, submitted to the Secretary of State by ACAS pursuant to s 212A of the 1992 Act, providing for arbitration in the case of disputes involving proceedings, or claims which could be the subject of proceedings, before an employment tribunal arising out of a contravention or alleged contravention of ss 80G(1) or 80H(1)(b) of the Employment Rights Act 1996 (flexible working). This Order extends to Great Britain. The Scheme provides a voluntary alternative to the employment tribunal for the resolution of claims arising out of an application for flexible working made under s 80F(1) of the 1996 Act by arbitration where both parties agree. The Order also provides for certain provisions of the Arbitration Act 1996, as modified by the Order, to apply to arbitrations conducted in accordance with the Scheme, where the parties have agreed that the arbitration will be determined according to the law of England and Wales. The text of this Order has been omitted for reasons of space.

INFORMATION AND CONSULTATION OF EMPLOYEES REGULATIONS 2004

(SI 2004/3426)

NOTES

Made: 21 December 2004.

Authority: Employment Relations Act 2004, s 42.

Commencement: 6 April 2005 (subject to transitional provisions in Sch 1 at **[2.810]**).

These Regulations are the domestic implementation of European Parliament and Council Directive 2002/14/EC establishing a general framework for informing and consulting employees in the European Community at **[3.298]**.

Conciliation: employment tribunal proceedings under regs 29, 33 are "relevant proceedings" for the purposes of the conciliation provisions contained in the Employment Tribunals Act 1996, ss 18–18C; see s 18(1)(s) of the 1996 Act at **[1.757]**.

Employment Appeal Tribunal: an appeal lies to the Employment Appeal Tribunal on any question of law arising from any decision of, or in any proceedings before, an employment tribunal under or by virtue of these Regulations; see the Employment Tribunals Act 1996, s 21(1)(q) at **[1.764]**.

As to the application of these Regulations to undertakings with fewer than 150 employees, see regs 3, 4 at **[2.770]**, **[2.772]** and Sch 1 at **[2.810]**.

See *Harvey* CII(6), DII(9), NIII(2), PI(4).

ARRANGEMENT OF REGULATIONS

PART 1
GENERAL

PART II
EMPLOYEE NUMBERS AND ENTITLEMENT TO DATA

PART III
NEGOTIATED AGREEMENTS

PART IV
STANDARD INFORMATION AND CONSULTATION PROVISIONS

PART V
DUTY OF CO-OPERATION

PART VI
COMPLIANCE AND ENFORCEMENT

PART VII
CONFIDENTIAL INFORMATION

PART VIII
PROTECTIONS FOR INFORMATION AND CONSULTATION REPRESENTATIVES, ETC

PART IX
MISCELLANEOUS

SCHEDULES

PART 1
GENERAL

[2.768]

1 Citation, commencement and extent

(1) These Regulations may be cited as the Information and Consultation of Employees Regulations 2004 and shall come into force on 6th April 2005.

(2) These Regulations extend to Great Britain.

[2.769]

2 Interpretation

In these Regulations—

"the 1996 Act" means the Employment Rights Act 1996;

["agency worker" has the same meaning as in regulation 3 of the Agency Workers Regulations 2010;]

"Appeal Tribunal" means the Employment Appeal Tribunal;

"CAC" means the Central Arbitration Committee;

"consultation" means the exchange of views and establishment of a dialogue between—

(a) information and consultation representatives and the employer; or

(b) in the case of a negotiated agreement which provides as mentioned in regulation 16(1)(f)(ii), the employees and the employer;

"contract of employment" means a contract of service or apprenticeship, whether express or implied, and (if it is express) whether oral or in writing;

"date of the ballot" means the day or last day on which voting may take place and, where voting in different parts of the ballot is arranged to take place on different days or during periods ending on different days, the last of those days;

"employee" means an individual who has entered into or works under a contract of employment and in Part VIII and regulation 40 includes, where the employment has ceased, an individual who worked under a contract of employment;

"employee request" means a request by employees under regulation 7 for the employer to initiate negotiations to reach an agreement under these Regulations;

"employer notification" means a notification by an employer under regulation 11 that he wishes to initiate negotiations to reach an agreement under these Regulations;

"information" means data transmitted by the employer—

(a) to the information and consultation representatives; or

(b) in the case of a negotiated agreement which provides as mentioned in regulation 16(1)(f)(ii), directly to the employees,

in order to enable those representatives or those employees to examine and to acquaint themselves with the subject matter of the data;

"Information and Consultation Directive" means European Parliament and Council Directive 2002/14/EC of 11 March 2002 establishing a general framework for informing and consulting employees in the European Community;

"information and consultation representative" means—

(a) in the case of a negotiated agreement which provides as mentioned in regulation 16(1)(f)(i), a person appointed or elected in accordance with that agreement; or

(b) a person elected in accordance with regulation 19(1);

"negotiated agreement" means—

(a) an agreement between the employer and the negotiating representatives reached through negotiations as provided for in regulation 14 which satisfies the requirements of regulation 16(1); or

(b) an agreement between the employer and the information and consultation representatives referred to in regulation 18(2);

"negotiating representative" means a person elected or appointed pursuant to regulation 14(1)(a);

"parties" means the employer and the negotiating representatives or the information and consultation representatives, as the case may be;

["Pension Schemes Regulations" means the Occupational and Personal Pension Schemes (Consultation by Employers and Miscellaneous Amendment) Regulations 2006;]

"pre-existing agreement" means an agreement between an employer and his employees or their representatives which—

(a) is made prior to the making of an employee request; and

(b) satisfies the conditions set out in regulation 8(1)(a) to (d),

but does not include an agreement concluded in accordance with regulations 17 or 42 to 45 of the Transnational Information and Consultation of Employees Regulations 1999 or a negotiated agreement;

"standard information and consultation provisions" means the provisions set out in regulation 20;

["suitable information relating to the use of agency workers" means information as to—

(a) the number of agency workers working temporarily for and under the supervision and direction of the employer,

(b) the parts of the employer's undertaking in which those agency workers are working, and

(c) the type of work those agency workers are carrying out.]

"undertaking" means a public or private undertaking carrying out an economic activity, whether or not operating for gain;

"valid employee request" means an employee request made to their employer by the employees of an undertaking to which these Regulations apply (under regulation 3) that satisfies the requirements of regulation 7 and is not prevented from being valid by regulation 12.

NOTES

Definitions "agency worker" and "suitable information relating to the use of agency workers" inserted by the Agency Workers Regulations 2010, SI 2010/93, reg 25, Sch 2, Pt 2, paras 21, 22; definition "Pension Schemes Regulations" inserted by the Information and Consultation of Employees (Amendment) Regulations 2006, SI 2006/514, regs 2, 3.

[2.770]

3 Application

(1) These Regulations apply to undertakings—

(a) employing in the United Kingdom, in accordance with the calculation in regulation 4, at least the number of employees in column 1 of the table in Schedule 1 to these Regulations on or after the corresponding date in column 2 of that table; and

(b) subject to paragraph (2), whose registered office, head office or principal place of business is situated in Great Britain.

(2) Where the registered office is situated in Great Britain and the head office or principal place of business is situated in Northern Ireland or vice versa, these Regulations shall only apply where the majority of employees are employed to work in Great Britain.

(3) In these Regulations, an undertaking to which these Regulations apply is referred to, in relation to its employees, as "the employer".

[2.771]

[3A Agency Workers

(1) Paragraphs (2) and (3) apply to an agency worker whose contract within regulation 3(1)(b) of the Agency Workers Regulations 2010 (contract with the temporary work agency) is not a contract of employment.

(2) For the purposes of regulations 3, 4 and Schedule 1, any agency worker who has a contract with a temporary work agency shall be treated as being employed by that temporary work agency for the duration of that agency worker's assignment with the employer.

(3) In these Regulations "assignment" has the same meaning as in regulation 2 and "temporary work agency" has the same meaning as in regulation 4, of the Agency Workers Regulations 2010.]

NOTES

Inserted by the Agency Workers Regulations 2010, SI 2010/93, reg 25, Sch 2, Pt 2, paras 21, 23.

PART II
EMPLOYEE NUMBERS AND ENTITLEMENT TO DATA

[2.772]
4 Calculation of number of employees

(1) Subject to paragraph (4), the number of employees for the purposes of regulation 3(1) shall be determined by ascertaining the average number of employees employed in the previous twelve months, calculated in accordance with paragraph (2).

(2) Subject to paragraph (3), the average number of employees is to be ascertained by determining the number of employees employed in each month in the previous twelve months (whether they were employed throughout the month or not), adding together those monthly figures and dividing the number by 12.

(3) For the purposes of the calculation in paragraph (2) if, for the whole of a month within the twelve month period, an employee works under a contract by virtue of which he would have worked for 75 hours or less in that month—

(i) were the month to have contained 21 working days;
(ii) were the employee to have had no absences from work; and
(iii) were the employee to have worked no overtime,

the employee may be counted as representing half of a full-time employee for the month in question, if the employer so decides.

(4) If the undertaking has been in existence for less than twelve months, the references to twelve months in paragraphs (1), (2) and (3), and the divisor of 12 referred to in paragraph (2), shall be replaced by the number of months the undertaking has been in existence.

[2.773]
5 Entitlement to data

(1) An employee or an employees' representative may request data from the employer for the purpose of determining the number of people employed by the employer's undertaking in the United Kingdom.

(2) Any request for data made under paragraph (1) must be in writing and be dated.

(3) The employer must provide the employee or the employees' representative who made the request with data to enable him to—

(a) make the calculation of the numbers of employees referred to in regulation 4, and
(b) determine, for the purpose of regulation 7(2), what number of employees constitutes *10%* of the employees in the undertaking.

NOTES

Para (3): for the figure in italics in sub-para (b) there is substituted the figure "2%", by the Employment Rights (Miscellaneous Amendments) Regulations 2019, SI 2019/731, reg 16(1), (2), as from 6 April 2020.

[2.774]
6 Complaint of failure to provide data

(1) An employee or an employees' representative who has requested data under regulation 5 may present a complaint to the CAC that—

(a) the employer has failed to provide the data referred to in regulation 5(3); or
(b) the data which has been provided by the employer is false or incomplete in a material particular.

(2) Where the CAC finds the complaint to be well-founded it shall make an order requiring the employer to disclose data to the complainant which order shall specify—

(a) the data in respect of which the CAC finds that the complaint is well-founded and which is to be disclosed to the complainant;
(b) the date (or if more than one, the earliest date) on which the employer refused or failed to disclose data, or disclosed false or incomplete information;
(c) a date, not being less than one week from the date of the order, by which the employer must disclose the data specified in the order.

(3) The CAC shall not consider a complaint presented under this regulation unless it is made after the expiry of a period of one month beginning on the date on which the complainant made his request for data under regulation 5.

PART III
NEGOTIATED AGREEMENTS

[2.775]
7 Employee request to negotiate an agreement in respect of information and consultation

(1) On receipt of a valid employee request, the employer shall, subject to paragraphs (8) and (9), initiate negotiations by taking the steps set out in regulation 14(1).

(2) Subject to paragraph (3), an employee request is not a valid employee request unless it consists of—

(a) a single request made by at least *10%* of the employees in the undertaking; or
(b) a number of separate requests made on the same or different days by employees which when taken together mean that at least *10%* of the employees in that undertaking have made requests, provided that the requests are made within a period of six months.

Part 2 Statutory Instruments

(3) Where the figure of *10%* in paragraph (2) would result in less than 15 or more than 2,500 employees being required in order for a valid employee request to be made, that paragraph shall have effect as if, for the figure of *10%*, there were substituted the figure of 15, or as the case may be, 2,500.

(4) An employee request is not a valid employee request unless the single request referred to in paragraph (2)(a) or each separate request referred to in paragraph (2)(b)—

(a) is in writing;

(b) is sent to—

(i) the registered office, head office or principal place of business of the employer; or

(ii) the CAC; and

(c) specifies the names of the employees making it and the date on which it is sent.

(5) Where a request is sent to the CAC under paragraph (4)(b)(ii), the CAC shall—

(a) notify the employer that the request has been made as soon as reasonably practicable;

(b) request from the employer such information as it needs to verify the number and names of the employees who have made the request; and

(c) inform the employer and the employees who have made the request how many employees have made the request on the basis of the information provided by the employees and the employer.

(6) Where the CAC requests information from the employer under paragraph (5)(b), the employer shall provide the information requested as soon as reasonably practicable.

(7) The date on which an employee request is made is—

(a) where the request consists of a single request satisfying paragraph (2)(a) or of separate requests made on the same day satisfying paragraph (2)(b), the date on which the request is or requests are sent to the employer by the employees or the date on which the CAC informs the employer and the employees in accordance with paragraph (5)(c) of how many employees have made the request; and

(b) where the request consists of separate requests made on different days, the date on which—

(i) the request which results in paragraph (2)(b) being satisfied is sent to the employer by the employees; or

(ii) the CAC informs the employer and the employees in accordance with paragraph (5)(c) of how many employees have made the request where that request results in paragraph (2)(b) being satisfied.

(8) If the employer decides to hold a ballot under regulation 8 or 9, the employer shall not be required to initiate negotiations unless and until the outcome of the ballot is that in regulation 8(5)(b).

(9) If an application is made to the CAC under regulation 13, the employer shall not be required to initiate negotiations unless and until if the CAC declares that there was a valid employee request or that the employer's notification was valid.

NOTES

Paras (2), (3): for the figure "10%" in italics in each place there is substituted the figure "2%", by the Employment Rights (Miscellaneous Amendments) Regulations 2019, SI 2019/731, reg 16(1), (3), as from 6 April 2020.

[2.776]

8 Pre-existing agreements: ballot for endorsement of employee request

(1) Subject to regulation 9, this regulation applies where a valid employee request has been made under regulation 7 by fewer than 40% of employees employed in the undertaking on the date that request was made and where there exists one or more pre-existing agreements which—

(a) are in writing;

(b) cover all the employees of the undertaking;

(c) have been approved by the employees; and

(d) set out how the employer is to give information to the employees or their representatives and seek their views on such information.

(2) Where this regulation applies, the employer may, instead of initiating negotiations in accordance with regulation 7(1), hold a ballot to seek the endorsement of the employees of the undertaking for the employee request in accordance with paragraphs (3) and (4).

(3) The employer must—

(a) inform the employees in writing within one month of the date of the employee request that he intends to hold a ballot under this regulation; and

(b) arrange for the ballot to be held as soon as reasonably practicable thereafter, provided that the ballot does not take place before a period of 21 days has passed since the employer informed the employees under sub-paragraph (a).

(4) A ballot must satisfy the following requirements—

(a) the employer must make such arrangements as are reasonably practicable to ensure that the ballot is fair;

(b) all employees of the undertaking on the day on which the votes may be cast in the ballot, or if the votes may be cast on more than one day, on the first day of those days, must be given an entitlement to vote in the ballot;

(c) the ballot must be conducted so as to secure that—

(i) so far as is reasonably practicable, those voting do so in secret; and

(ii) the votes given in the ballot are accurately counted.

(5) Where the employer holds a ballot under this regulation—

(a) he must, as soon as reasonably practicable after the date of the ballot, inform the employees of the result; and
(b) if the employees endorse the employee request, the employer is under the obligation in regulation 7(1) to initiate negotiations; and
(c) if the employees do not endorse the employee request, the employer is no longer under the obligation in regulation 7(1) to initiate negotiations.

(6) For the purposes of paragraph (5), the employees are to be regarded as having endorsed the employee request if—
(a) at least 40% of the employees employed in the undertaking; and
(b) the majority of the employees who vote in the ballot,
have voted in favour of endorsing the request.

(7) An employee or an employees' representative who believes that an employer has not, pursuant to paragraph (3)(a), informed his employees that he intends to hold a ballot within the period specified in that paragraph may apply to the CAC for a declaration that the employer is under the duty in regulation 7(1) to initiate negotiations.

(8) Where an employer, acting pursuant to paragraph (3)(a), has informed the employees that he intends to hold a ballot, any employee or employees' representative who believes that the employer has not complied with paragraph (3)(b) may present a complaint to the CAC

(9) Where the CAC finds a complaint under paragraph (8) well-founded it shall make an order requiring the employer to hold the ballot within such period as the order may specify.

[2.777]
[8A Pre-existing agreements: agency workers

Where information about the employment situation is to be provided under a pre-existing agreement by an employer, such information must include suitable information relating to the use of agency workers (if any) in that undertaking.]

NOTES

Inserted by the Agency Workers Regulations 2010, SI 2010/93, reg 25, Sch 2, Pt 2, paras 21, 24.

[2.778]
9 Pre-existing agreements covering groups of undertakings

(1) This regulation applies where—
(a) the requirements of regulation 8(1) are satisfied in relation to an undertaking;
(b) the pre-existing agreement or one of the pre-existing agreements covers employees in one or more undertakings other than the undertaking mentioned in sub-paragraph (a); and
(c) the other undertaking or each of the other undertakings mentioned in sub-paragraph (b) is one in respect of which there is an agreement that satisfied, or are agreements that taken together satisfied, the requirements in sub-paragraphs (a) to (d) of regulation 8(1) on the date on which the valid employee request was made in respect of the undertaking mentioned in sub-paragraph (a); and
(d) the valid employee request in relation to the undertaking mentioned in sub-paragraph (a) either—
(i) alone, or
(ii) aggregated with any requests made by employees in the undertakings mentioned in sub-paragraph (b) within the period of six months preceding the date of the valid employee request mentioned in regulation 8(1),

is made by fewer than 40% of the employees in the undertakings mentioned in paragraph (1)(a) and (b).

(2) Where this regulation applies the employers may hold a combined ballot for endorsement of the employee request in accordance with this regulation and in that event regulation 8 shall apply to the ballot with the modification that references to employees shall be treated as referring to the employees employed in all of the undertakings referred to in paragraph (1)(a) and (b).

(3) Notwithstanding paragraph (2), the undertaking mentioned in paragraph (1)(a) may choose to hold the ballot for endorsement of the employee request in accordance with regulation 8 rather than under this regulation.

[2.779]
10 Complaint about ballot for endorsement of employee request

(1) Any employee in the undertaking referred to in regulation 8(1) or employee in one of the undertakings referred to in regulation 9(1), or representative of such employees, who believes that a requirement has not been satisfied that has to be satisfied in order to entitle either the employer, in accordance with regulation 8(2), to hold a ballot, or the employers, in accordance with regulation 9(2), to hold a combined ballot may, within 21 days of the employer informing the employees of the relevant undertaking under regulation 8(3)(a), present a complaint to the CAC

(2) Any employee or employees' representative who believes that the arrangements for a ballot held under regulation 8 or 9, as the case may be, did not satisfy one or more of the requirements set out in regulation 8(4) may, within 21 days of the date of the ballot, present a complaint to the CAC

(3) Where the CAC finds a complaint under paragraph (1) or (2) well-founded it shall—

(a) in the case of a finding on a complaint under paragraph (1) that any requirement set out in sub-paragraphs (a) to (d) of regulation 8(1) was not satisfied in relation to the undertaking referred to in regulation 8(1) or 9(1)(a), make an order requiring the employer to whom regulation 8(1) or 9(1)(a) relates to initiate negotiations in accordance with regulation 7(1);

(b) in the case of a finding on a complaint under paragraph (1) that any requirement set out in sub-paragraphs (b) to (d) of regulation 9(1) has not been satisfied, make an order that no combined ballot shall take place and requiring the employer to whom regulation 9(1)(a) relates, according to the preference he has expressed, to initiate negotiations in accordance with regulation 7(1) or, within such period as the order may specify, to conduct a ballot under regulation 8; and

(c) in the case of a complaint under paragraph (2)—

(i) where prior to the order being made, the employer referred to in regulation 8(1) or 9(1)(a) makes representations to the CAC that he would prefer to initiate negotiations under regulation 7, make an order requiring that employer to do so; or

(ii) in the absence of such representations, order the employer or employers to hold the ballot under regulation 8 or 9, as the case may be, again within such period as the order may specify.

[2.780]
11 Employer notification of decision to initiate negotiations

(1) The employer may start the negotiation process set out in regulation 14(1) on his own initiative by issuing a written notification satisfying the requirements of paragraph (2), and where the employer issues such a notification regulations 14 to 17 shall apply.

(2) The notification referred to in paragraph (1) must—

(a) state that the employer intends to start the negotiating process and that the notification is given for the purpose of these Regulations;

(b) state the date on which it is issued; and

(c) be published in such a manner as to bring it to the attention of, so far as reasonably practicable, all the employees of the undertaking.

[2.781]
12 Restrictions on employee request and employer notification

(1) Subject to paragraph (2), no employee request or employer notification is valid if it is made or issued, as the case may be,—

(a) where a negotiated agreement applies, within a period of three years from the date of the agreement or, where the agreement is terminated within that period, before the date on which the termination takes effect;

(b) where the standard information and consultation provisions apply within a period of three years from the date on which they started to apply; and

(c) where the employer has held a ballot under regulation 8, or was one of the employers who held a ballot under regulation 9 and the result was that the employees did not endorse the valid employee request referred to in regulation 8(1), within a period of three years from the date of that request.

(2) Paragraph (1) does not apply where there are material changes in the undertaking during the applicable period having the result—

(a) where a ballot held under regulation 8 or 9 had the result that the employees did not endorse the valid employee request, that there is no longer a pre-existing agreement which satisfies paragraph (1)(b) and (c) of regulation 8 or in the case of a ballot held under regulation 9, that there is no longer an agreement satisfying paragraph (1)(b) of that regulation; or

(b) where a negotiated agreement exists, that the agreement no longer complies with the requirement in regulation 16(1) that it must cover all the employees of the undertaking.

[2.782]
13 Dispute about employee request, employer notification or whether obligation in regulation 7(1) applies

(1) If the employer considers that there was no valid employee request—

(a) because the employee request did not satisfy any requirement of regulation 7(2) to (4) or was prevented from being valid by regulation 12, or

(b) because the undertaking was not one to which these Regulations applied (under Regulation 3) on the date on which the employee request was made,

the employer may apply to the CAC for a declaration as to whether there was a valid employee request.

(2) If an employee or an employees' representative considers that an employer notification was not valid because it did not comply with one or more of the requirements in regulation 11(2) or was prevented from being valid by regulation 12, he may apply to the CAC for a declaration as to whether the notification was valid.

(3) The CAC shall only consider an application for a declaration made under paragraph (1) or (2) if the application is made within a one month period beginning on the date of the employee request or the date on which the employer notification is made.

[2.783]
14 Negotiations to reach an agreement

(1) In order to initiate negotiations to reach an agreement under these Regulations the employer must as soon as reasonably practicable—

(a) make arrangements, satisfying the requirements of paragraph (2), for the employees of the undertaking to elect or appoint negotiating representatives; and thereafter
(b) inform the employees in writing of the identity of the negotiating representatives; and
(c) invite the negotiating representatives to enter into negotiations to reach a negotiated agreement.

(2) The requirements for the election or appointment of negotiating representatives under paragraph (1)(a) are that—
(a) the election or appointment of the representatives must be arranged in such a way that, following their election or appointment, all employees of the undertaking are represented by one or more representatives; and
(b) all employees of the undertaking must be entitled to take part in the election or appointment of the representatives and, where there is an election, all employees of the undertaking on the day on which the votes may be cast in the ballot, or if the votes may be cast on more than one day, on the first day of those days, must be given an entitlement to vote in the ballot.

(3) The negotiations referred to in paragraph (1)(c) shall last for a period not exceeding six months commencing at the end of the period of three months beginning with the date on which the valid employee request was made or the valid employer notification was issued; but the following periods shall not count towards the three month period—
(a) where the employer holds a ballot pursuant to regulation 8 or 9, the period between the employer notifying the employees of his decision to hold such a ballot and whichever of the following dates is applicable—
(i) where there is no complaint to the CAC under regulation 10, the date of the ballot;
(ii) where there is a complaint to the CAC under regulation 10 and the complaint is dismissed by the CAC or on appeal, the date on which it is finally dismissed;
(iii) where there is a complaint to the CAC and the outcome, whether of the complaint or of any appeal from it, is an order to hold the ballot under regulation 8 or 9 again, the date of the ballot that most recently took place;
(iv) where there is a complaint to the CAC under regulation 10 and the outcome, whether of the complaint or of any appeal from it, is an order requiring the employer to initiate negotiations in accordance with regulation 7(1), the date on which the order is made;
(b) where an application for a declaration is made to the CAC pursuant to regulation 13, the period between the date of that application and the final decision of the CAC or any appeal from that decision; and
(c) where a complaint about the election or appointment of negotiating representatives is presented pursuant to regulation 15, the time between the date of the complaint and the determination of the complaint, including any appeal and, where the complaint is upheld, the further period until the negotiating representatives are re-elected or re-appointed.

(4) Where a complaint about the ballot for employee approval of a negotiated agreement is presented pursuant to regulation 17, the time between the date the complaint is presented to the CAC and the determination of the complaint (including any appeal and, where the complaint is upheld, the further period until the re-holding of the ballot) shall not count towards the six month period mentioned in paragraph (3).

(5) If, before the end of the six month period referred to in paragraph (3), the employer and a majority of the negotiating representatives agree that that period should be extended, it may be extended by such period as the parties agree and thereafter may be further extended by such period or periods as the parties agree.

(6) Where one or more employers wish to initiate negotiations to reach an agreement to cover employees in more than one undertaking, any employer whose employees have not made a valid employee request and who has not issued a valid employer notification, shall issue such a notification.

(7) Where paragraph (6) applies, the provisions of paragraphs (1) to (5) of this regulation and regulations 15 and 16 apply with the following modifications—
(a) the references to the employees of the undertaking refer to the employees of all the undertakings to be covered by any agreement negotiated; and
(b) references to employees refer to employees of all the undertakings to be covered by any agreement negotiated.

[2.784]
15 Complaints about election or appointment of negotiating representatives

(1) If an employee or an employees' representative considers that one or both of the requirements for the appointment or election of negotiating representatives set out in regulation 14(2) have not been complied with, he may, within 21 days of the election or appointment, present a complaint to the CAC.

(2) Where the CAC finds the complaint well-founded it shall make an order requiring the employer to arrange for the process of election or appointment of negotiating representatives referred to in regulation 14 to take place again within such period as the order shall specify.

[2.785]
16 Negotiated agreements

(1) A negotiated agreement must cover all employees of the undertaking and may consist either of a single agreement or of different parts (each being approved in accordance with paragraph (4)) which, taken together, cover all the employees of the undertaking. The single agreement or each part must—
(a) set out the circumstances in which the employer must inform and consult the employees to which it relates;

(b) be in writing;
(c) be dated;
(d) be approved in accordance with paragraphs (3) to (5);
(e) be signed by or on behalf of the employer;
(f) either—
(i) provide for the appointment or election of information and consultation representatives to whom the employer must provide the information and whom the employer must consult in the circumstances referred to in sub-paragraph (a); or
(ii) provide that the employer must provide information directly to the employees to which it relates and consult those employees directly in the circumstances referred to in sub-paragraph (a); [and
(g) provide that where an employer is to provide information about the employment situation, under that agreement or under any part, such information shall include suitable information relating to the use of agency workers (if any) in that undertaking.]

(2) Where a negotiated agreement consist of different parts they may provide differently in relation to the matters referred to in paragraph (1)(a) and (f).

(3) A negotiated agreement consisting of a single agreement shall be treated as being approved for the purpose of paragraph (1)(d) if—
(a) it has been signed by all the negotiating representatives; or
(b) it has been signed by a majority of negotiating representatives and either—
(i) approved in writing by at least 50% of employees employed in the undertaking, or
(ii) approved by a ballot of those employees, the arrangements for which satisfied the requirements set out in paragraph (5), in which at least 50% of the employees voting, voted in favour of approval.

(4) A part shall be treated as being approved for the purpose of paragraph (1)(d) if the part—
(a) has been signed by all the negotiating representatives involved in negotiating the part; or
(b) has been signed by a majority of those negotiating representatives and either—
(i) approved in writing by at least 50% of employees (employed in the undertaking) to which the part relates, or
(ii) approved by a ballot of those employees, the arrangements for which satisfied the requirements set out in paragraph (5), in which at least 50% of the employees voting, voted in favour of approving the part.

(5) The ballots referred to in paragraphs (3) and (4) must satisfy the following requirements—
(a) the employer must make such arrangements as are reasonably practicable to ensure that the ballot is fair;
(b) all employees of the undertaking or, as the case may be, to whom the part of the agreement relates, on the day on which the votes may be cast in the ballot, or if the votes may be cast on more than one day, on the first day of those days, must be given an entitlement to vote in the ballot; and
(c) the ballot must be conducted so as to secure that—
(i) so far as is reasonably practicable, those voting do so in secret; and
(ii) the votes given in the ballot are accurately counted.

(6) Where the employer holds a ballot under this regulation he must, as soon as reasonably practicable after the date of the ballot, inform the employees entitled to vote of the result.

NOTES

Para (1): word omitted from sub-para (e) revoked and sub-para (g), together with word preceding it, inserted by the Agency Workers Regulations 2010, SI 2010/93, reg 25, Sch 2, Pt 2, paras 21, 25, 26.

[2.786]
17 Complaints about ballot for employee approval of negotiated agreement

(1) Any negotiating representative who believes that the arrangements for a ballot held under regulation 16 did not satisfy one or more of the requirements set out in paragraph (5) of that regulation, may, within 21 days of the date of the ballot, present a complaint to the CAC.

(2) Where the CAC finds the complaint well-founded it shall make an order requiring the employer to hold the ballot referred to in regulation 16 again within such period as the order may specify.

[2.787]
[17A Negotiated agreements and listed changes to pension schemes

(1) A requirement in any negotiated agreement or any part of such an agreement made before 6th April 2006 to inform and consult employees or their representatives about a listed change shall cease to apply once—
(a) the employer is under a duty under any of regulations 7(3) and 11 to 13 of the Pension Schemes Regulations; and
(b) he has notified the information and consultation representatives or, where he must consult employees directly, the employees in writing that he will be complying with his duty under the provisions of the Pension Schemes Regulations referred to in sub-paragraph (a), instead of his obligations under the negotiated agreement, provided that the notification is given on each occasion on which the employer has become or is about to become subject to the duty.

(2) For the purposes of this regulation "listed change" has the meaning given by regulation 6(2) of the Pension Schemes Regulations.]

NOTES

Inserted by the Information and Consultation of Employees (Amendment) Regulations 2006, SI 2006/514, regs 2, 4.

PART IV
STANDARD INFORMATION AND CONSULTATION PROVISIONS

[2.788]

18 Application of standard information and consultation provisions

(1) Subject to paragraph (2)—

(a) where the employer is under a duty, following the making of a valid employee request or issue of a valid employer notification, to initiate negotiations in accordance with regulation 14 but does not do so, the standard information and consultation provisions shall apply from the date—

(i) which is six months from the date on which the valid employee request was made or the valid employer notification was issued, or

(ii) information and consultation representatives are elected under regulation 19,

whichever is the sooner; and

(b) if the parties do not reach a negotiated agreement within the time limit referred to in regulation 14(3) (or that period as extended by agreement under paragraph (5) of that regulation) the standard information and consultation provisions shall apply from the date—

(i) which is six months from the date on which that time limit expires; or

(ii) information and consultation representatives are elected under regulation 19,

whichever is the sooner.

(2) Where the standard information and consultation provisions apply, the employer and the information and consultation representatives elected pursuant to regulation 19 may, at any time, reach an agreement that provisions other than the standard information and consultation provisions shall apply.

(3) An agreement referred to in paragraph (2) shall only have effect if it covers all the employees of the undertaking, complies with the requirements listed in regulation 16(1)(a) to (c), (e) and (f), and is signed by a majority of the information and consultation representatives.

[2.789]

19 Election of information and consultation representatives

(1) Where the standard information and consultation provisions are to apply, the employer shall, before the standard information and consultation provisions start to apply, arrange for the holding of a ballot of its employees to elect the relevant number of information and consultation representatives.

(2) The provisions in Schedule 2 to these Regulations apply in relation to the arrangements for and conduct of any such ballot.

(3) In this regulation the "relevant number of information and consultation representatives" means one representative per fifty employees or part thereof, provided that that number is at least 2 and does not exceed 25.

(4) An employee or an employee's representative may complain to the CAC that the employer has not arranged for the holding of a ballot in accordance with paragraph (1).

(5) Where the CAC finds the complaint well-founded, it shall make an order requiring the employer to arrange, or re-arrange, and hold the ballot.

(6) Where the CAC finds a complaint under paragraph (4) well-founded, the employee or the employee's representative may make an application to the Appeal Tribunal under regulation 22(6) and paragraphs (7) and (8) of that regulation shall apply to any such application.

[2.790]

20 Standard information and consultation provisions

(1) Where the standard information and consultation provisions apply pursuant to regulation 18, the employer must provide the information and consultation representatives with information on—

(a) the recent and probable development of the undertaking's activities and economic situation;

(b) the situation, structure and probable development of employment within the undertaking [(and such information must include suitable information relating to the use of agency workers (if any) in that undertaking)] and on any anticipatory measures envisaged, in particular, where there is a threat to employment within the undertaking; and

(c) subject to paragraph (5), decisions likely to lead to substantial changes in work organisation or in contractual relations, including those referred to in—

(i) sections 188 to 192 of the Trade Union and Labour Relations (Consolidation) Act 1992; and

[(ii) regulations 13 to 16 of the Transfer of Undertakings (Protection of Employment) Regulations 2006].

(2) The information referred to in paragraph (1) must be given at such time, in such fashion and with such content as are appropriate to enable, in particular, the information and consultation representatives to conduct an adequate study and, where necessary, to prepare for consultation.

(3) The employer must consult the information and consultation representatives on the matters referred to in paragraph (1)(b) and (c).

(4) The employer must ensure that the consultation referred to in paragraph (3) is conducted—

(a) in such a way as to ensure that the timing, method and content of the consultation are appropriate;
(b) on the basis of the information supplied by the employer to the information and consultation representatives and of any opinion which those representatives express to the employer;
(c) in such a way as to enable the information and consultation representatives to meet the employer at the relevant level of management depending on the subject under discussion and to obtain a reasoned response from the employer to any such opinion; and
(d) in relation to matters falling within paragraph (1)(c), with a view to reaching agreement on decisions within the scope of the employer's powers.

(5) The duties in this regulation to inform and consult the information and consultation representatives on decisions falling within paragraph (1)(c) cease to apply once the employer is under a duty under—
(a) section 188 of the Act referred to in paragraph (1)(c)(i) (duty of employer to consult representatives); . . .
(b) [regulation 13] of the Regulations referred to in paragraph (1)(c)(ii) (duty to inform and consult representatives), [or
(c) any of regulations 11 to 13 of the Pension Schemes Regulations,]
and he has notified the information and consultation representatives in writing that he will be complying with his duty under the legislation referred to in [sub-paragraph (a), (b) or (c)], as the case may be, instead of under these Regulations, provided that the notification is given on each occasion on which the employer has become or is about to become subject to the duty.

(6) Where there is an obligation in these Regulations on the employer to inform and consult his employees, a failure on the part of a person who controls the employer (either directly or indirectly) to provide information to the employer shall not constitute a valid reason for the employer failing to inform and consult.

NOTES

Para (1): words in square brackets in sub-para (b) inserted by the Agency Workers Regulations 2010, SI 2010/93, reg 25, Sch 2, Pt 2, paras 21, 27; sub-para (c)(ii) substituted by the Transfer of Undertakings (Protection of Employment) (Consequential Amendments) Regulations 2006, SI 2006/2405, reg 2.

Para (5): word omitted from sub-para (a) revoked, sub-para (c) and the word immediately preceding it inserted, and final words in square brackets substituted, by the Information and Consultation of Employees (Amendment) Regulations 2006, SI 2006/514, regs 2, 5(a); words in square brackets in sub-para (b) substituted by SI 2006/2405.

PART V
DUTY OF CO-OPERATION

[2.791]
21 Co-operation

The parties are under a duty, when negotiating or implementing a negotiated agreement or when implementing the standard information and consultation provisions, to work in a spirit of co-operation and with due regard for their reciprocal rights and obligations, taking into account the interests of both the undertaking and the employees.

PART VI
COMPLIANCE AND ENFORCEMENT

[2.792]
22 Disputes about operation of a negotiated agreement or the standard information and consultation provisions

(1) Where—
(a) a negotiated agreement has been agreed; or
(b) the standard information and consultation provisions apply,
a complaint may be presented to the CAC by a relevant applicant who considers that the employer has failed to comply with the terms of the negotiated agreement or, as the case may be, one or more of the standard information and consultation provisions.

(2) A complaint brought under paragraph (1) must be brought within a period of three months commencing with the date of the alleged failure.

(3) In this regulation—
"failure" means an act or omission; and
"relevant applicant" means—
(a) in a case where information and consultation representatives have been elected or appointed, an information and consultation representative, or
(b) in a case where no information and consultation representatives have been elected or appointed, an employee or an employees' representative.

(4) Where the CAC finds the complaint well-founded it shall make a declaration to that effect and may make an order requiring the employer to take such steps as are necessary to comply with the terms of the negotiated agreement or, as the case may be, the standard information and consultation provisions.

(5) An order made under paragraph (4) shall specify—
(a) the steps which the employer is required to take; and
(b) the period within which the order must be complied with.

(6) If the CAC makes a declaration under paragraph (4) the relevant applicant may, within the period of three months beginning with the date on which the declaration is made, make an application to the Appeal Tribunal for a penalty notice to be issued.

(7) Where such an application is made, the Appeal Tribunal shall issue a written penalty notice to the employer requiring him to pay a penalty to the Secretary of State in respect of the failure unless satisfied, on hearing representations from the employer, that the failure resulted from a reason beyond the employer's control or that he has some other reasonable excuse for his failure.

(8) Regulation 23 shall apply in respect of a penalty notice issued under this regulation.

(9) No order of the CAC under this regulation shall have the effect of suspending or altering the effect of any act done or of any agreement made by the employer or of preventing or delaying any act or agreement which the employer proposes to do or to make.

[2.793]
23 Penalties

(1) A penalty notice issued under regulation 22 shall specify—
- (a) the amount of the penalty which is payable;
- (b) the date before which the penalty must be paid; and
- (c) the failure and period to which the penalty relates.

(2) No penalty set by the Appeal Tribunal under this regulation may exceed £75,000.

(3) Matters to be taken into account by the Appeal Tribunal when setting the amount of the penalty shall include—
- (a) the gravity of the failure;
- (b) the period of time over which the failure occurred;
- (c) the reason for the failure;
- (d) the number of employees affected by the failure; and
- (e) the number of employees employed by the undertaking or, where a negotiated agreement covers employees in more than one undertaking, the number of employees employed by both or all of the undertakings.

(4) The date specified under paragraph (1)(b) must not be earlier than the end of the period within which an appeal against a declaration or order made by the CAC under regulation 22 may be made.

(5) If the specified date in a penalty notice has passed and—
- (a) the period during which an appeal may be made has expired without an appeal having been made; or
- (b) such an appeal has been made and determined,

the Secretary of State may recover from the employer, as a civil debt due to him, any amount payable under the penalty notice which remains outstanding.

(6) The making of an appeal suspends the effect of a penalty notice.

(7) Any sums received by the Secretary of State under regulation 22 or this regulation shall be paid into the Consolidated Fund.

[2.794]
24 Exclusivity of remedy

The remedy for infringement of the rights conferred by Parts I to VI of these Regulations is by way of complaint to the CAC, and not otherwise.

PART VII
CONFIDENTIAL INFORMATION

[2.795]
25 Breach of statutory duty

(1) A person to whom the employer, pursuant to his obligations under these Regulations, entrusts any information or document on terms requiring it to be held in confidence shall not disclose that information or document except, where the terms permit him to do so, in accordance with those terms.

(2) In this regulation a person referred to in paragraph (1) to whom information or a document is entrusted is referred to as a "recipient".

(3) The obligation to comply with paragraph (1) is a duty owed to the employer, and a breach of the duty is actionable accordingly (subject to the defences and other incidents applying to actions for breaches of statutory duty).

(4) Paragraph (3) shall not affect any legal liability which any person may incur by disclosing the information or document, or any right which any person may have in relation to such disclosure otherwise than under this regulation.

(5) No action shall lie under paragraph (3) where the recipient reasonably believed the disclosure to be a "protected disclosure" within the meaning given to that expression by section 43A of the 1996 Act.

(6) A recipient to whom the employer has entrusted any information or document on terms requiring it to be held in confidence may apply to the CAC for a declaration as to whether it was reasonable for the employer to require the recipient to hold the information or document in confidence.

(7) If the CAC considers, on an application under paragraph (6), that the disclosure of the information or document by the recipient would not, or would not be likely to, harm the legitimate interests of the undertaking, it shall make a declaration that it was not reasonable for the employer to require the recipient to hold the information or document in confidence.

(8) If a declaration is made under paragraph (7), the information or document shall not at any time thereafter be regarded as having been entrusted to the recipient who made the application under paragraph (6), or to any other recipient, on terms requiring it to be held in confidence.

[2.796]

26 Withholding of information by the employer

(1) The employer is not required to disclose any information or document to a person for the purposes of these Regulations where the nature of the information or document is such that, according to objective criteria, the disclosure of the information or document would seriously harm the functioning of, or would be prejudicial to, the undertaking.

(2) If there is a dispute between the employer and—

(a) where information and consultation representatives have been elected or appointed, such a representative; or

(b) where no information and consultation representatives have been elected or appointed, an employee or an employees' representative,

as to whether the nature of the information or document which the employer has failed to provide is such as is described in paragraph (1), the employer or a person referred to in sub-paragraph (a) or (b) may apply to the CAC for a declaration as to whether the information or document is of such a nature.

(3) If the CAC makes a declaration that the disclosure of the information or document in question would not, according to objective criteria, be seriously harmful or prejudicial as mentioned in paragraph (1), the CAC shall order the employer to disclose the information or document.

(4) An order under paragraph (3) shall specify—

(a) the information or document to be disclosed;

(b) the person or persons to whom the information or document is to be disclosed;

(c) any terms on which the information or document is to be disclosed; and

(d) the date before which the information or document is to be disclosed.

PART VIII
PROTECTIONS FOR INFORMATION AND CONSULTATION REPRESENTATIVES, ETC

[2.797]

27 Right to time off for information and consultation representatives, etc

(1) An employee who is—

(a) a negotiating representative; or

(b) an information and consultation representative,

is entitled to be permitted by his employer to take reasonable time off during the employee's working hours in order to perform his functions as such a representative.

(2) For the purposes of this regulation, the working hours of an employee shall be taken to be any time when, in accordance with his contract of employment, the employee is required to be at work.

[2.798]

28 Right to remuneration for time off under regulation 27

(1) An employee who is permitted to take time off under regulation 27 is entitled to be paid remuneration by his employer for the time taken off at the appropriate hourly rate.

(2) Chapter II of Part XIV of the 1996 Act (a week's pay) shall apply in relation to this regulation as it applies in relation to section 62 of the 1996 Act.

(3) The appropriate hourly rate, in relation to an employee, is the amount of one week's pay divided by the number of normal working hours in a week for that employee when employed under the contract of employment in force on the day when time is taken.

(4) But where the number of normal working hours differs from week to week or over a longer period, the amount of one week's pay shall be divided instead by—

(a) the average number of normal working hours calculated by dividing by twelve the total number of the employee's normal working hours during the period of twelve weeks ending with the last complete week before the day on which the time is taken off; or

(b) where the employee has not been employed for a sufficient period to enable the calculations to be made under sub-paragraph (a), a number which fairly represents the number of normal working hours in a week having regard to such of the considerations specified in paragraph (5) as are appropriate in the circumstances.

(5) The considerations referred to in paragraph (4)(b) are—

(a) the average number of normal working hours in a week which the employee could expect in accordance with the terms of his contract; and

(b) the average number of normal working hours of other employees engaged in relevant comparable employment with the same employer.

(6) A right to any amount under paragraph (1) does not affect any right of an employee in relation to remuneration under his contract of employment ("contractual remuneration").

(7) Any contractual remuneration paid to an employee in respect of a period of time off under regulation 27 goes towards discharging any liability of the employer to pay remuneration under paragraph (1) in respect of that period, and, conversely, any payment of remuneration under paragraph (1) in respect of a period goes towards discharging any liability of the employer to pay contractual remuneration in respect of that period.

[2.799]
29 Right to time off: complaint to tribunals

(1) An employee may present a complaint to an employment tribunal that his employer—
- (a) has unreasonably refused to permit him to take time off as required by regulation 27; or
- (b) has failed to pay the whole or part of any amount to which the employee is entitled under regulation 28.

(2) A tribunal shall not consider a complaint under this regulation unless it is presented—
- (a) before the end of the period of three months beginning with the day on which the time off was taken or on which it is alleged the time off should have been permitted; or
- (b) within such further period as the tribunal considers reasonable in a case where it is satisfied that it was not reasonably practicable for the complaint to be presented before the end of that period of three months.

[(2A) Regulation 29A (extension of time limits to facilitate conciliation before institution of proceedings) applies for the purposes of paragraph (2).]

(3) Where a tribunal finds a complaint under this regulation well-founded, the tribunal shall make a declaration to that effect.

(4) If the complaint is that the employer has unreasonably refused to permit the employee to take time off, the tribunal shall also order the employer to pay to the employee an amount equal to the remuneration to which he would have been entitled under regulation 28 if the employer had not refused.

(5) If the complaint is that the employer has failed to pay the employee the whole or part of any amount to which he is entitled under regulation 28, the tribunal shall also order the employer to pay to the employee the amount it finds due to him.

NOTES

Para (2A): inserted by the Enterprise and Regulatory Reform Act 2013 (Consequential Amendments) (Employment) Order 2014, SI 2014/386, art 2, Schedule, paras 32, 33.

Conciliation: employment tribunal proceedings under this regulation are "relevant proceedings" for the purposes of the conciliation provisions contained in the Employment Tribunals Act 1996, ss 18–18C; see s 18(1)(s) of the 1996 Act at **[1.757]**.

[2.800]
[29A Extension of time limit to facilitate conciliation before institution of proceedings

(1) In this regulation—
- (a) Day A is the day on which the worker concerned complies with the requirement in subsection (1) of section 18A of the Employment Tribunals Act 1996 (requirement to contact ACAS before instituting proceedings) in relation to the matter in respect of which the proceedings are brought, and
- (b) Day B is the day on which the worker concerned receives or, if earlier, is treated as receiving (by virtue of regulations made under subsection (11) of that section) the certificate issued under subsection (4) of that section.

(2) In working out when the time limit set by regulation 29(2)(a) expires the period beginning with the day after Day A and ending with Day B is not to be counted.

(3) If the time limit set by regulation 29(2)(a) would (if not extended by this paragraph) expire during the period beginning with Day A and ending one month after Day B, the time limit expires instead at the end of that period.

(4) The power conferred on the employment tribunal by regulation 29(2)(b) to extend the time limit set by paragraph (2)(a) of that regulation is exercisable in relation to that time limit as extended by this regulation.]

NOTES

Inserted by the Enterprise and Regulatory Reform Act 2013 (Consequential Amendments) (Employment) Order 2014, SI 2014/386, art 2, Schedule, paras 32, 34.

[2.801]
30 Unfair dismissal

(1) An employee who is dismissed and to whom paragraph (2) or (5) applies shall be regarded, if the reason (or, if more than one, the principal reason) for the dismissal is a reason specified in, respectively, paragraph (3) or (6), as unfairly dismissed for the purposes of Part 10 of the 1996 Act.

(2) This paragraph applies to an employee who is—
- (a) an employees' representative;
- (b) a negotiating representative;
- (c) an information and consultation representative; or
- (d) a candidate in an election in which any person elected will, on being elected, be such a representative.

(3) The reasons are that—

(a) the employee performed or proposed to perform any functions or activities as such a representative or candidate;
(b) the employee exercised or proposed to exercise an entitlement conferred on the employee by regulation 27 or 28; or
(c) the employee (or a person acting on his behalf) made or proposed to make a request to exercise such an entitlement.

(4) Paragraph (1) does not apply in the circumstances set out in paragraph (3)(a) where the reason (or principal reason) for the dismissal is that in the performance, or purported performance, of the employee's functions or activities he has disclosed any information or document in breach of the duty in regulation 25, unless the employee reasonably believed the disclosure to be a "protected disclosure" within the meaning given to that expression by section 43A of the 1996 Act.

(5) This paragraph applies to any employee whether or not he is an employee to whom paragraph (2) applies.

(6) The reasons are that the employee—
(a) took, or proposed to take, any proceedings before an employment tribunal to enforce a right or secure an entitlement conferred on him by these Regulations;
(b) exercised, or proposed to exercise, any entitlement to apply or complain to the CAC or the Appeal Tribunal conferred by these Regulations or to exercise the right to appeal in connection with any rights conferred by these Regulations;
(c) requested, or proposed to request, data in accordance with regulation 5;
(d) acted with a view to securing that an agreement was or was not negotiated or that the standard information and consultation provisions did or did not become applicable;
(e) indicated that he supported or did not support the coming into existence of a negotiated agreement or the application of the standard information and consultation provisions;
(f) stood as a candidate in an election in which any person elected would, on being elected, be a negotiating representative or an information and consultation representative;
(g) influenced or sought to influence by lawful means the way in which votes were to be cast by other employees in a ballot arranged under these Regulations;
(h) voted in such a ballot;
(i) expressed doubts, whether to a ballot supervisor or otherwise, as to whether such a ballot had been properly conducted; or
(j) proposed to do, failed to do, or proposed to decline to do, any of the things mentioned in sub-paragraphs (d) to (i).

(7) It is immaterial for the purpose of paragraph (6)(a)—
(a) whether or not the employee has the right or entitlement; or
(b) whether or not the right has been infringed;
but for that sub-paragraph to apply, the claim to the right and, if applicable, the claim that it has been infringed must be made in good faith.

31 (*Amends the Employment Rights Act 1996, ss 105, 108 at* **[1.1023]**, **[1.1026]**, *and amended s 109 (repealed).*)

[2.802]
32 Detriment

(1) An employee to whom paragraph (2) or (5) applies has the right not to be subjected to any detriment by any act, or deliberate failure to act, by his employer, done on a ground specified in, respectively, paragraph (3) or (6).

(2) This paragraph applies to an employee who is—
(a) an employees' representative;
(b) a negotiating representative;
(c) an information and consultation representative; or
(d) a candidate in an election in which any person elected will, on being elected, be such a representative.

(3) The ground is that—
(a) the employee performed or proposed to perform any functions or activities as such a representative or candidate;
(b) the employee exercised or proposed to exercise an entitlement conferred on the employee by regulation 27 or 28; or
(c) the employee (or a person acting on his behalf) made or proposed to make a request to exercise such an entitlement.

(4) Paragraph (1) does not apply in the circumstances set out in paragraph (3)(a) where the ground (or principal ground) for the subjection to detriment is that in the performance, or purported performance, of the employee's functions or activities he has disclosed any information or document in breach of the duty in regulation 25, unless the employee reasonably believed the disclosure to be a "protected disclosure" within the meaning given to that expression by section 43A of the 1996 Act.

(5) This paragraph applies to any employee whether or not he is an employee to whom paragraph (2) applies.

(6) The grounds are that the employee—
(a) took, or proposed to take, any proceedings before an employment tribunal to enforce a right or secure an entitlement conferred on him by these Regulations;

(b) exercised, or proposed to exercise, any entitlement to apply or complain to the CAC or the Appeal Tribunal conferred by these Regulations or to exercise the right to appeal in connection with any rights conferred by these Regulations;

(c) requested, or proposed to request, data in accordance with regulation 5;

(d) acted with a view to securing that an agreement was or was not negotiated or that the standard information and consultation provisions did or did not become applicable;

(e) indicated that he supported or did not support the coming into existence of a negotiated agreement or the application of the standard information and consultation provisions;

(f) stood as a candidate in an election in which any person elected would, on being elected, be a negotiating representative or an information and consultation representative;

(g) influenced or sought to influence by lawful means the way in which votes were to be cast by other employees in a ballot arranged under these Regulations;

(h) voted in such a ballot;

(i) expressed doubts, whether to a ballot supervisor or otherwise, as to whether such a ballot had been properly conducted; or

(j) proposed to do, failed to do, or proposed to decline to do, any of the things mentioned in sub-paragraphs (d) to (i).

(7) It is immaterial for the purpose of paragraph (6)(a)—

(a) whether or not the employee has the right or entitlement; or

(b) whether or not the right has been infringed,

but for that sub-paragraph to apply, the claim to the right and, if applicable, the claim that it has been infringed must be made in good faith.

(8) This regulation does not apply where the detriment in question amounts to dismissal.

[2.803]

33 Detriment: enforcement and subsidiary provisions

(1) An employee may present a complaint to an employment tribunal that he has been subjected to a detriment in contravention of regulation 32.

(2) The provisions of sections 48(2) to (4) and 49(1) to (5) of the 1996 Act (complaints to employment tribunals and remedies) shall apply in relation to a complaint under this regulation as they apply in relation to a complaint under section 48 of the Act but taking references to the employer as references to the employer within the meaning of regulation 32(1) above.

NOTES

Conciliation: employment tribunal proceedings under this regulation are "relevant proceedings" for the purposes of the conciliation provisions contained in the Employment Tribunals Act 1996, ss 18–18C; see s 18(1)(s) of the 1996 Act at **[1.757]**.

Tribunal jurisdiction: the Employment Act 2002, s 38 applies to proceedings before the employment tribunal relating to a claim under this regulation; see s 38(1) of, and Sch 5 to, the 2002 Act at **[1.1279]**, **[1.1287]**. See also the Trade Union and Labour Relations (Consolidation) Act 1992, s 207A at **[1.524]** (as inserted by the Employment Act 2008). That section provides that in proceedings before an employment tribunal relating to a claim by an employee under any of the jurisdictions listed in Sch A2 to the 1992 Act at **[1.704]** (which includes this regulation) the tribunal may adjust any award given if the employer or the employee has unreasonably failed to comply with a relevant Code of Practice as defined by s 207A(4). See also the revised Acas Code of Practice 1 – Disciplinary and Grievance Procedures (2015) at **[4.1]**, and the Acas Code of Practice 4 – Settlement Agreements (2013) at **[4.54]**.

34 (*Amended the Employment Tribunals Act 1996, s 18 at* **[1.757]**, *but is now effectively spent following the further amendment of s 18 by the Employment Tribunals Act 1996 (Application of Conciliation Provisions) Order 2014, SI 2014/431.*)

PART IX
MISCELLANEOUS

[2.804]

35 CAC proceedings

(1) Where under these Regulations a person presents a complaint or makes an application to the CAC the complaint or application must be in writing and in such form as the CAC may require.

(2) In its consideration of a complaint or application under these Regulations, the CAC shall make such enquiries as it sees fit and so far as reasonably practicable give any person whom it considers has a proper interest in the complaint or application an opportunity to be heard.

(3) The CAC may draw an adverse inference from a party's failure to comply with any reasonable request to provide information or documents relevant to a complaint presented to it or an application made to it.

(4) A declaration or order made by the CAC under these Regulations may be relied on—

(a) in relation to an employer whose registered office, head office or principal place of business is in England or Wales, as if it were a declaration or order made by the High Court, and

(b) in relation to an employer whose registered office, head office or principal place of business is in Scotland as if it were a declaration or order made by the Court of Session.

(5) A declaration or order made by the CAC under these Regulations must be in writing and state the reasons for the CAC's findings.

(6) An appeal lies to the Appeal Tribunal on any question of law arising from any declaration or order of, or arising in any proceedings before, the CAC under these Regulations.

[2.805]
36 Appeal Tribunal: location of certain proceedings under these Regulations

(1) Any proceedings before the Appeal Tribunal arising under these Regulations, other than appeals under paragraph (n) of section 21(1) of the Employment Tribunals Act 1996 (appeals from employment tribunals on questions of law), shall—

(a) where the registered office or, where there is no registered office, the head office or principal place of business is situated in England and Wales, be held in England and Wales; and

(b) where the registered office or, where there is no registered office, the head office or principal place of business is situated in Scotland, be held in Scotland.

(2) . . .

NOTES

Para (2): amends the Employment Tribunals Act 1996, s 20 at **[1.763]**.

37 (*Amends the Employment Tribunals Act 1996, s 21 at* **[1.764]**.)

[2.806]
38 ACAS

(1) If on receipt of an application or complaint under these Regulations the CAC is of the opinion that it is reasonably likely to be settled by conciliation or other assistance provided by the Advisory, Conciliation and Arbitration Service ('ACAS') in accordance with paragraph (2), it shall refer the application or complaint to ACAS and shall notify the applicant or complainant and any persons whom it considers have a proper interest in the application or complaint accordingly.

(2) Where the CAC refers an application or complaint to ACAS under paragraph (1), section 210 of the Trade Union and Labour Relations (Consolidation) Act 1992 (power of ACAS to offer assistance to settle disputes) shall apply, and ACAS may offer the parties to the application or complaint its assistance under that section with a view to bringing about a settlement, as if—

(a) the dispute or difference between the parties amounted to a trade dispute as defined in section 218 of that Act; and

(b) the parties to the application or complaint had requested the assistance of ACAS under section 210.

(3) If ACAS does not consider it appropriate to offer its assistance in accordance with paragraph (2) it shall inform the CAC.

(4) If ACAS has offered the parties its assistance in accordance with paragraph (2), the application or complaint referred has not thereafter been settled or withdrawn, and ACAS is of the opinion that no provision or further provision of its assistance is likely to result in a settlement or withdrawal, it shall inform the CAC of its opinion.

(5) If—

(a) an application or complaint is not referred to ACAS, or

(b) it is so referred, but ACAS informs the CAC as mentioned in paragraph (3) or (4),

the CAC shall proceed to hear and determine the application or complaint.

[2.807]
39 Restrictions on contracting out: general

(1) Any provision in any agreement (whether an employee's contract or not) is void in so far as it purports—

(a) to exclude or limit the operation of any provision of these Regulations other than a provision of Part VIII; or

(b) to preclude a person from bringing any proceedings before the CAC or the Appeal Tribunal under any provision of these Regulations other than a provision of Part VIII.

(2) Paragraph (1) does not apply to any agreement to refrain from continuing any proceedings referred to in sub-paragraph (b) of that paragraph made after the proceedings have been instituted.

[2.808]
40 Restrictions on contracting out: Part VIII

(1) Any provision in any agreement (whether an employee's contract or not) is void in so far as it purports—

(a) to exclude or limit the operation of any provision of Part VIII; or

(b) to preclude a person from bringing any proceedings before an employment tribunal under that Part.

(2) Paragraph (1) does not apply to any agreement to refrain from instituting or continuing proceedings before an employment tribunal where a conciliation officer has taken action under [any of sections 18A to 18C] of the Employment Tribunals Act 1996 (conciliation).

(3) Paragraph (1) does not apply to any agreement to refrain from instituting or continuing before an employment tribunal proceedings within section 18(1) of the Employment Tribunals Act 1996 (proceedings under these Regulations where conciliation is available) if the conditions regulating [settlement] agreements under these Regulations are satisfied in relation to the agreement.

(4) For the purposes of paragraph (3) the conditions regulating [settlement] agreements are that—

(a) the agreement must be in writing;

(b) the agreement must relate to the particular proceedings;

(c) the employee must have received advice from a relevant independent adviser as to the terms and effect of the proposed agreement and, in particular, its effect on his ability to pursue his rights before an employment tribunal;
(d) there must be in force, when the adviser gives the advice, a contract of insurance, or an indemnity provided for members of a profession or a professional body, covering the risk of a claim by the employee in respect of loss arising in consequence of the advice;
(e) the agreement must identify the adviser; and
(f) the agreement must state that the conditions in sub-paragraphs (a) to (e) are satisfied.

(5) A person is a relevant independent adviser for the purposes of paragraph (4)(c)—
(a) if he is a qualified lawyer;
(b) if he is an officer, official, employee or member of an independent trade union who has been certified in writing by the trade union as competent to give advice and as authorised to do so on behalf of the trade union; or
(c) if he works at an advice centre (whether as an employee or as a volunteer) and has been certified in writing by the centre as competent to give advice and as authorised to do so on behalf of the centre.

(6) But a person is not a relevant independent adviser for the purposes of paragraph (4)(c)—
(a) if he is, is employed by or is acting in the matter for the employer or an associated employer;
(b) in the case of a person within paragraph (5)(b) or (c), if the trade union or advice centre is the employer or an associated employer; or
(c) in the case of a person within (5)(c), if the employee makes a payment for the advice received from him.

(7) In paragraph (5)(a), "qualified lawyer" means—
(a) as respects England and Wales, [a person who, for the purposes of the Legal Services Act 2007), is an authorised person in relation to an activity which constitutes the exercise of a right of audience or the conduct of litigation (within the meaning of that Act)]; and
(b) as respects Scotland, an advocate (whether in practice as such or employed to give legal advice) or a solicitor who holds a practising certificate.

(8) A person shall be treated as being a qualified lawyer within the meaning of paragraph (7)(a) if he is a Fellow of the Institute of Legal Executives [practising in a solicitor's practice (including a body recognised under section 9 of the Administration of Justice Act 1985)].

(9) For the purposes of paragraph (6) any two employers shall be treated as associated if—
(a) one is a company of which the other (directly or indirectly) has control; or
(b) both are companies of which a third person (directly or indirectly) has control;
and "associated employer" shall be construed accordingly.

NOTES

Para (2): words in square brackets substituted by the Enterprise and Regulatory Reform Act 2013 (Consequential Amendments) (Employment) Order 2014, SI 2014/386, art 2, Schedule, paras 32, 35.

Paras (3), (4): word in square brackets substituted by the Enterprise and Regulatory Reform Act 2013 (Consequential Amendments) (Employment) Order 2013, SI 2013/1956, art 2, Schedule, para 9.

Para (7): words in square brackets substituted by the Legal Services Act 2007 (Consequential Amendments) Order 2009, SI 2009/3348, art 23, Sch 2.

Para (8): words in square brackets in sub-para (5) substituted by SI 2009/3348, art 22, Sch 1.

41 (*Amends the Employment Appeal Tribunal Rules 1993, SI 1993/2854, rr 2–5, 7, 16AA, 26, 31, Schedule at* **[2.146]–[2.150]**, **[2.152]**, **[2.162]**, **[2.177]**, **[2.183]**, **[2.198]** *et seq.*)

[2.809]

42 Crown employment

(1) These Regulations have effect in relation to Crown employment and persons in Crown employment as they have effect in relation to other employment and other employees.

(2) In these Regulations "Crown employment" means employment in an undertaking to which these Regulations apply and which is under or for the purposes of a government department or any officer or body exercising on behalf of the Crown functions conferred by a statutory provision.

(3) For the purposes of the application of these Regulations in relation to Crown employment in accordance with paragraph (1)—
(a) references to an employee shall be construed as references to a person in Crown employment; and
(b) references to a contract of employment shall be construed as references to the terms of employment of a person in Crown employment.

43 (*Revoked by the Seafarers (Insolvency, Collective Redundancies and Information and Consultation Miscellaneous Amendments) Regulations 2018, SI 2018/407, reg 4, as from 13 April 2018.*)

Part 2 Statutory Instruments

SCHEDULES

SCHEDULE 1
APPLICATION OF REGULATIONS

Regulation 3

[2.810]

Number of employees	Date Regulations apply
At least 150	6 April 2005
At least 100	6 April 2007
At least 50	6 April 2008

SCHEDULE 2
REQUIREMENTS FOR BALLOTS HELD UNDER REGULATION 19

Regulation 19

Ballot Arrangements

[2.811]

1. Ballots held under regulation 19 must comply with the requirements specified in paragraph 2.

2. The requirements referred to in paragraph 1 are that—

(a) the ballot must comprise a single ballot but may instead, if the employer so decides, comprise separate ballots of employees in such constituencies as the employer may decide where the employer considers that if separate ballots were to be held for those constituencies, the information and consultation representatives to be elected would better reflect the interests of the employees as a whole than if a single ballot were held;

(b) if, at any point, it becomes clear that the number of people standing as candidates in the ballot is equal to or fewer than the relevant number of information and consultation representatives (as defined in regulation 19(3)), the obligation on the employer to hold the ballot in regulation 19 will cease and the candidates referred to above will become the information and consultation representatives;

(c) all employees of the undertaking on the day on which the votes may be cast in the ballot, or if the votes may be cast on more than one day, on the first day of those days, must be given an entitlement to vote in the ballot;

(d) any employee who is an employee of the undertaking at the latest time at which a person may become a candidate in the ballot is entitled to stand in the ballot as a candidate as an information and consultation representative;

(e) the employer must, in accordance with paragraph 6, appoint an independent ballot supervisor to supervise the conduct of the ballot;

(f) after the employer has formulated proposals as to the arrangements for the ballot and before he has published the final arrangements under sub-paragraph (g) he must, so far as reasonably practicable, consult with employees' representatives or, if no such representatives exist, the employees, on the proposed arrangements for the ballot; and

(g) the employer must publish the final arrangements for the ballot in such manner as to bring them to the attention of, so far as reasonably practicable, his employees and, where they exist, the employees' representatives.

3. Any employee or an employees' representative who believes that the arrangements for the ballot are defective may, within a period of 21 days beginning on the date on which the employer published the final arrangements under paragraph 2(g), present a complaint to the CAC.

4. Where the CAC finds the complaint well-founded it shall make a declaration to that effect and may make an order requiring the employer to modify the arrangements he has made for the ballot or to satisfy the requirements in sub-paragraphs (a) to (f) of paragraph 2.

5. An order under paragraph 4 shall specify the modifications to the arrangements which the employer is required to make and the requirements he must satisfy.

6. A person is an independent ballot supervisor for the purposes of paragraph 2(e) if the employer reasonably believes that he will carry out any functions conferred on him in relation to the ballot competently and has no reasonable grounds for believing that his independence might reasonably be called into question.

7. For the purposes of paragraph 3 the arrangements for the ballot are defective if any of the requirements specified in sub-paragraphs (a) to (f) of paragraph 2 is not satisfied.

Conduct of the Ballot

8. The employer must—

(a) ensure that a ballot supervisor appointed under paragraph 2(e) carries out his functions under this Schedule and that there is no interference with his carrying out of those functions; and

(b) comply with all reasonable requests made by a ballot supervisor for the purposes of or in connection with the carrying out of those functions.

9. A ballot supervisor's appointment shall require that he—

(a) supervises the conduct of the ballot he is being appointed to supervise, in accordance with the arrangements for the ballot published by the employer under paragraph 2(g) or, where appropriate, in accordance with the arrangements as required to be modified by an order made under paragraph 4;

(b) does not conduct the ballot before the employer has satisfied the requirement specified in paragraph 2(g) and—

(i) where no complaint has been presented under paragraph 3, before the expiry of 21 days beginning with the date on which the employer published his arrangements under paragraph 2(g); or

(ii) where a complaint has been presented under paragraph 3, before the complaint has been determined and, where appropriate, the arrangements have been modified as required by an order made as a result of the complaint;

(c) conducts the ballot so as to secure that—

(i) so far as reasonably practicable, those entitled to vote are given the opportunity to do so;

(ii) so far as reasonably practicable, those entitled to stand as candidates are given the opportunity to stand;

(iii) so far as reasonably practicable, those voting are able to do so in secret; and

(iv) the votes given in the ballot are fairly and accurately counted.

10. As soon as reasonably practicable after the date of the ballot, the ballot supervisor must publish the results of the ballot in such manner as to make them available to the employer and, so far as reasonably practicable, the employees entitled to vote in the ballot and the persons who stood as candidates in the ballot.

11. A ballot supervisor shall publish a report ("an ineffective ballot report") where he considers (whether or not on the basis of representations made to him by another person) that—

(a) any of the requirements referred to in paragraph 2 was not satisfied with the result that the outcome of the ballot would have been different; or

(b) there was interference with the carrying out of his functions or a failure by the employer to comply with all reasonable requests made by him with the result that he was unable to form a proper judgement as to whether each of the requirements referred to in paragraph 2 was satisfied in the ballot.

12. Where a ballot supervisor publishes an ineffective ballot report the report must be published within a period of one month commencing on the date on which the ballot supervisor publishes the results of the ballot under paragraph 10.

13. A ballot supervisor must publish an ineffective ballot report in such manner as to make it available to the employer and, so far as reasonably practicable, the employees entitled to vote in the ballot and the persons who stood as candidates in the ballot.

14. Where a ballot supervisor publishes an ineffective ballot report, the outcome of the ballot shall be of no effect and—

(a) if there has been a single ballot or an ineffective ballot report has been published in respect of every separate ballot, the outcome of the ballot or ballots shall be of no effect and the employer shall again be under the obligation in regulation 19;

(b) if there have been separate ballots and sub-paragraph (a) does not apply—

(i) the employer shall arrange for the separate ballot or ballots in respect of which an ineffective ballot report has been issued to be reheld in accordance with regulation 19, and

(ii) no such ballot shall have effect until it has been reheld and no ineffective ballot report has been published in respect of it.

15. All costs relating to the holding of the ballot, including payments made to a ballot supervisor for supervising the conduct of the ballot, shall be borne by the employer (whether or not an ineffective ballot report has been made).

ROAD TRANSPORT (WORKING TIME) REGULATIONS 2005

(SI 2005/639)

NOTES

Made: 10 March 2005.

Authority: European Communities Act 1972, s 2(2).

Commencement: 4 April 2005.

Note: with regard to the authority for these Regulations, note that the European Communities Act 1972 is repealed by the European Union (Withdrawal) Act 2018, s 1, as from exit day (as defined in s 20 of that Act); but note also that provision is made for the continuation in force of any subordinate legislation made under the authority of s 2(2) of the 1972 Act by s 2 of the 2018 Act at **[1.2240]**, subject to the provisions of s 5 of, and Sch 1 to, the 2018 Act at **[1.2243]**, **[1.2253]**.

These Regulations are the domestic implementation of European Parliament and Council Directive 2002/15/EC on the organisation of working time of persons performing mobile transport activities at **[3.313]**.

Regulatory functions: the regulatory functions conferred by these Regulations are subject to the Legislative and Regulatory Reform Act 2006, ss 21, 22; see the Legislative and Regulatory Reform (Regulatory Functions) Order 2007, SI 2007/3544 (made under s 24(2) of the 2006 Act) for details.

See *Harvey* CI(1).

ARRANGEMENT OF REGULATIONS

[2.812]
1 Citation, commencement and extent

(1) These Regulations may be cited as the Road Transport (Working Time) Regulations 2005 and shall come into force on 4th April 2005.

(2) These Regulations extend to Great Britain only.

[2.813]
2 Interpretation

In these Regulations—

"AETR" means the European agreement concerning the work of crews of vehicles engaged in international road transport of 1st July 1970;

"collective agreement" means a collective agreement within the meaning of section 178 of the Trade Union and Labour Relations (Consolidation) Act 1992, the trade union parties to which are independent trade unions within the meaning of section 5 of that Act;

["the Community Drivers' Hours Regulation" means Regulation (EC) No 561/2006 of the European Parliament and of the Council of 15 March 2006 on the harmonisation of certain social legislation relating to road transport (and amending and repealing certain Council Regulations);]

"employer" in relation to a worker, means the person by whom the worker is (or, where the employment has ceased, was) employed;

"employment" in relation to a worker, means employment under his contract, and "employed" shall be construed accordingly;

"goods" includes goods or burden of any description;

"goods vehicle" means a motor vehicle constructed or adapted for use for the carriage of goods, or a trailer so constructed or adapted;

"inspector" means a person appointed under paragraph 1 of Schedule 2;

"mobile worker" means any worker forming part of the travelling staff, including trainees and apprentices, who is in the service of an undertaking which operates transport services for passengers or goods by road for hire or reward or on its own account;

"night time" means in respect of goods vehicles the period between midnight and 4am and in respect of passenger vehicles the period between 1am and 5am;

"motor vehicle" means a mechanically propelled vehicle intended or adapted for use on roads;

"night work" means any work performed during night time;

"passenger vehicle" means a motor vehicle which is constructed or adapted to carry more than eight seated passengers in addition to the driver;

"period of availability" means a period during which the mobile worker [or self-employed driver] is not required to remain at his workstation, [but—

(a) in the case of a mobile worker, is required to be available, or

(b) in the case of a self-employed driver, makes himself available,]

to answer any calls to start or resume driving or to carry out other work, including periods during which the mobile worker [or self-employed driver] is accompanying a vehicle being transported by a ferry or by a train as well as periods of waiting at frontiers and those due to traffic prohibitions;

"reference period" means the period for calculation of the average maximum weekly working time;

"relevant requirements" means regulations 4(8), [4(9)], 7(5), [7(6)], 8(2), [8(3)], 9(4), [9(5)], 10, 11, [11A] and 12;

"self-employed driver" means anyone whose main occupation is to transport passengers or goods by road for hire or reward within the meaning of [EU] legislation under cover of a Community licence or any other professional authorisation to carry out such transport, who is entitled to work for himself and who is not tied to an employer by an employment contract or by any other type of working hierarchical relationship, who is free to organise the relevant working activities, whose income depends directly on the profits made and who has the freedom, individually or through a co-operation between self-employed drivers, to have commercial relations with several customers;

"vehicle" means a goods vehicle or a passenger vehicle;

"week" means a period of seven days beginning at midnight between Sunday and Monday;

"worker" means an individual [who is not a self-employed driver and] who has entered into or works under (or, where employment has ceased, worked under)—

(a) a contract of employment; or

(b) any other contract, whether express or implied and (if it is express) whether oral or in writing, whereby the individual undertakes to do or perform personally any work or services for another party to the contract;

and any reference to a worker's contract shall be construed accordingly;

"workforce agreement" means an agreement between an employer and mobile workers employed by him or their representatives in respect of which the conditions set out in Schedule 1 to these Regulations are satisfied;

["working time" means the time from the beginning to the end of work during which—

(a) the mobile worker or self-employed driver is at his workstation;

(b) the mobile worker is at the disposal of his employer, or (as applicable) the self employed driver is at the disposal of the client; and

(c) the mobile worker or self-employed driver is exercising his functions or activities, being:

(i) time devoted to all road transport activities, including, in particular—

(aa) driving;

(bb) loading and unloading;

(cc) assisting passengers boarding and disembarking from the vehicle;

(dd) cleaning and technical maintenance;

(ee) all other work intended to ensure the safety of the vehicle, its cargo and passengers or to fulfil the legal or regulatory obligations directly linked to the specific transport operation under way, including monitoring of loading and unloading and dealing with administrative formalities with police, customs, immigration officers and others; or

(ii) time during which the mobile worker or self-employed driver cannot dispose freely of his time and is required (or, in relation to a self-employed driver, chooses) to be at his workstation, ready to take up normal work, with certain tasks associated with being on duty, in particular during periods awaiting loading or unloading where their foreseeable duration is not known in advance, that is to say either before departure or just before the actual start of the period in question, or under collective agreements or workforce agreements;

but, in relation to self-employed drivers, general administrative work that is not directly linked to the specific transport operation under way is excluded from working time;]

"workstation" means

(a) [in relation to a mobile worker] the location of the main place of business of the undertaking for which the person performing mobile transport activities carries out duties, together with its various subsidiary places of business, regardless of whether they are located in the same place as its head office or its main place of business; [or]

(b) [in relation to a mobile worker or self-employed driver] the vehicle which the person performing mobile road transport activities uses when he carries out duties; or

(c) [in relation to a mobile worker or self-employed driver] any other place in which activities connected with transport are carried out.

NOTES

Definition "the Community Drivers' Hours Regulation" substituted by the Road Transport (Working Time) (Amendment) Regulations 2007, SI 2007/853, reg 2(1), (2).

Reference in square brackets in definition "self-employed driver" substituted by the Treaty of Lisbon (Changes in Terminology) Order 2011, SI 2011/1043, art 6(2)(b).

All other amendments to this regulation were made by the Road Transport (Working Time) (Amendment) Regulations 2012, SI 2012/991, regs 2, 3.

[2.814]
3 Application

(1) These Regulations apply to mobile workers who are employed by, or who do work for, undertakings established in a Member State of the European Union, and to whom paragraph (2) or paragraph (3) applies.

[(1A) These Regulations also apply to self-employed drivers who are established in, or who do work for undertakings established in, a Member State of the European Union, and to whom paragraph (2) or paragraph (3) applies.]

[(2) This paragraph applies to mobile workers [or self-employed drivers] who, in the course of [their employment or working activities], drive or travel in or on vehicles—

(a) which are vehicles within the meaning of Article 4(b) of the Community Drivers' Hours Regulation,

(b) which are not vehicles described in Article 3 of that Regulation, and

(c) [which are not vehicles exempted from the provisions of that Regulation under regulation 2 of the Community Drivers' Hours and Recording Equipment Regulations 2007].]

(3) This paragraph applies to mobile workers [or self-employed drivers], to whom paragraph (2) does not apply, who in the course of [their employment or working activities] drive, or travel in, vehicles

(a) which fall within the meaning of a "vehicle" in Article 1 of the AETR;

(b) which are not referred to in [Article 2(2)] of the AETR; and

(c) which are performing international transport.

(4) These Regulations do not apply to—

(a) . . .

(b) any [mobile worker or self-employed driver] who does work which is included in the calculation of working time—

(i) where the reference period is shorter than 26 weeks, on fewer than 11 days in a reference period applicable to that [mobile worker or self-employed driver], or

(ii) in any other case on fewer than 16 days in a reference period applicable to that [mobile worker or self-employed driver].

NOTES

Para (2) was substituted by the Road Transport (Working Time) (Amendment) Regulations 2007, SI 2007/853, reg 2(1), (3).

The words in square brackets in para (3)(b) were substituted by the Drivers' Hours and Tachographs (Amendment etc) (EU Exit) Regulations 2019, SI 2019/453, reg 26, as from 26 March 2019.

All other amendments to this regulation were made by the Road Transport (Working Time) (Amendment) Regulations 2012, SI 2012/991, regs 2, 4.

[2.815]
[3A Duty to Review Regulation 3(1A)

(1) The Secretary of State must from time to time—

(a) carry out a review of regulation 3(1A),

(b) set out the conclusions of the review in a report, and

(c) publish the report.

(2) In carrying out the review the Secretary of State must, so far as is reasonable, have regard to how Directive 2002/15/EC, in so far as it applies to self-employed drivers (which is implemented by means of regulation 3(1A)), is implemented in other Member States.

(3) The report must in particular—

(a) set out the objectives intended to be achieved by the regulatory system established by regulation 3(1A),

(b) assess the extent to which those objectives are achieved, and

(c) assess whether those objectives remain appropriate and, if so, the extent to which they could be achieved with a system that imposes less regulation.

(4) The first report under this regulation must be published before the end of the period of five years beginning with the day on which regulation 3(1A) comes into force.

(5) Reports under this regulation are afterwards to be published at intervals not exceeding five years.]

NOTES

Inserted by the Road Transport (Working Time) (Amendment) Regulations 2012, SI 2012/991, regs 2, 5.

[2.816]
4 Working time

(1) Subject to paragraph (2) below, the working time, including overtime, of a mobile worker [or self-employed driver] shall not exceed 60 hours in a week.

(2) In any reference period which is applicable to his case, [the working time of a mobile worker or self-employed driver] shall not exceed an average of 48 hours for each week.

(3) The reference periods which apply . . . shall be—

[(a) in the case of a mobile worker—

(i) where a collective agreement or a workforce agreement provides for the application of this regulation in relation to successive periods of 17 weeks, each such period, or

(ii) in a case where there is no such provision, and the employer gives written notice to the mobile worker in writing that he intends to apply this subparagraph, any period of 17 weeks in the course of the worker's employment,]

[(b) in the case of a self-employed driver who elects to apply this subparagraph in relation to any period of 17 weeks or to successive periods of 17 weeks, each such period,]

(c) in any other case [for a mobile worker or self-employed driver,] the period ending at midnight between Sunday 31st July 2005 and Monday 1st August 2005 and thereafter, in each year, the successive periods beginning at midnight at the beginning of the Monday which falls on, or is the first Monday after, a date in column 1 below and ending at midnight at the beginning of the Monday which falls on, or is the first Monday after, the date on the same line in column 2 below.

Column 1 (beginning)	**Column 2 (end)**
1st December	1st April
1st April	1st August
1st August	1st December

(4) The reference period may be extended in relation to particular mobile workers or groups of mobile workers for objective or technical reasons or reasons concerning the organisation of work, by a collective agreement or a workforce agreement, by the substitution for 17 weeks of a period not exceeding 26 weeks in the application of paragraphs (2) and (3)(a) above.

[(4A) The reference period may be extended in relation to self-employed drivers for objective or technical reasons or reasons concerning the organisation of work, by the substitution for 17 weeks of a period not exceeding 26 weeks in the application of paragraphs (2) and (3)(b) above.]

(5) [The] average weekly working time during a reference period shall be determined according to the formula—

[**(A + B) ÷ C** for mobile workers, or

A ÷ C for self-employed drivers]

where—

A is the aggregate number of hours comprised in . . . working time during the course of the reference period;

B is the number of excluded hours during the reference period; and

C is the number of weeks in the reference period.

(6) In paragraph (5), "excluded hours" means hours comprised in—

(a) any period of annual leave taken by the mobile worker in exercise of entitlement under regulation 13 of the Working Time Regulations 1998;

(b) any period of sick leave taken by the mobile worker;

(c) any period of maternity, paternity, adoption or parental leave taken by the mobile worker;

(7) For the purposes of paragraph (5), the number of hours in a whole day shall be eight and the number of hours in a whole week shall be forty-eight.

(8) An employer shall take all reasonable steps, in keeping with the need to protect the health and safety of the mobile worker, to ensure that the limits specified above are complied with in the case of each mobile worker employed by him.

[(9) A self-employed driver must take all reasonable steps, in keeping with the need to protect his health and safety, to comply with the limits specified above.]

NOTES

All amendments to this regulation were made by the Road Transport (Working Time) (Amendment) Regulations 2012, SI 2012/991, regs 2, 6.

[2.817]

5

The times of breaks, rests and periods of availability shall not be included in the calculation of working time.

[2.818]

6 Periods of availability

(1) A period shall not be treated as a period of availability unless the mobile worker [or self-employed driver] knows before the start of the relevant period about that period of availability and its reasonably foreseeable duration.

(2) The time spent by a mobile worker [or self-employed driver], who is working as part of a team, travelling in, but not driving, a moving vehicle as part of that team shall be a period of availability for that mobile worker [or self-employed driver].

(3) Subject to paragraph (4) a period of availability shall not include a period of rest or a break.

(4) A period of availability may include a break taken by a mobile worker [or self-employed driver] during waiting time or time which is not devoted to driving by the mobile worker [or self-employed driver] and is spent in a moving vehicle, a ferry or a train.

NOTES

All amendments to this regulation were made by the Road Transport (Working Time) (Amendment) Regulations 2012, SI 2012/991, regs 2, 7.

[2.819]
7 Breaks

(1) No mobile worker [or self-employed driver] shall work for more than six hours without a break.

[(2) Where the working time of a mobile worker or self-employed driver exceeds six hours but does not exceed nine hours, the mobile worker or self-employed driver must take a break lasting at least 30 minutes and interrupting that period.]

[(3) Where the working time of a mobile worker or self-employed driver exceeds nine hours, the mobile worker or self-employed driver must take a break lasting at least 45 minutes and interrupting that period.]

(4) Each break may be made up of separate periods of not less than 15 minutes each.

(5) An employer shall take all reasonable steps, in keeping with the need to protect the health and safety of the mobile worker, to ensure that the limits specified above are complied with in the case of each mobile worker employed by him.

[(6) A self-employed driver must take all reasonable steps, in keeping with the need to protect his health and safety, to comply with the limits specified above.]

NOTES

All amendments to this regulation were made by the Road Transport (Working Time) (Amendment) Regulations 2012, SI 2012/991, regs 2, 8.

[2.820]
8 Rest periods

(1) In the application of these Regulations, the provisions of the Community Drivers' Hours Regulation relating to daily and weekly rest shall apply to all mobile workers [and self-employed drivers] to whom they do not apply under that Regulation as they apply to other mobile workers under that Regulation.

(2) An employer shall take all reasonable steps, in keeping with the need to protect the health and safety of the mobile worker, to ensure that those provisions are complied with in the case of each mobile worker employed by him, to whom they are applied by paragraph (1).

[(3) A self-employed driver must take all reasonable steps, in keeping with the need to protect his health and safety, to ensure that he complies with the provisions applied by paragraph (1).]

NOTES

All amendments to this regulation were made by the Road Transport (Working Time) (Amendment) Regulations 2012, SI 2012/991, regs 2, 9.

[2.821]
9 Night work

(1) The working time of a mobile worker [or self-employed driver], who performs night work in any period of 24 hours, shall not exceed 10 hours during that period.

(2) The period of 10 hours may be extended in relation to particular mobile workers or groups of mobile workers for objective or technical reasons or reasons concerning the organisation of work, by a collective agreement or a workforce agreement.

[(2A) A self-employed driver may elect to extend the period of 10 hours for objective or technical reasons or reasons concerning the organisation of work.

(3) Compensation for night work shall not be given to a mobile worker [or to a self-employed driver] in any manner which is liable to endanger road safety.

(4) An employer shall take all reasonable steps in keeping with the need to protect the health and safety of mobile workers to ensure that the limit specified in paragraph (1), or extended in accordance with paragraph (2), is complied with in the case of each mobile worker employed by him.

[(5) A self-employed driver must take all reasonable steps, in keeping with the need to protect his health and safety, to ensure that the limit specified in paragraph (1), or extended in accordance with paragraph (2A), is complied with.]

NOTES

All amendments to this regulation were made by the Road Transport (Working Time) (Amendment) Regulations 2012, SI 2012/991, regs 2, 10.

[2.822]
10 Information and records

An employer of mobile workers shall notify each worker of the provisions of these Regulations and the provisions of any collective or workforce agreement which is capable of application to that worker.

[2.823]
11

An employer of a mobile worker shall

(a) request from each mobile worker details of any time worked by that worker for another employer;
(b) include time worked for another employer in the calculation of the mobile worker's working time;
(c) keep records which are adequate to show whether the requirements of these Regulations are being complied with in the case of each mobile worker employed by him to whom they apply;
(d) retain such records for at least two years after the end of the period covered by those records;
(e) provide, at the request of a mobile worker, a copy of the record of hours worked by that worker;
(f) provide to an enforcement officer copies of such records relating to mobile workers as the officer may require;
(g) provide to a mobile worker or enforcement officer copies of such documentary evidence in the employer's possession as may be requested by the worker or officer in relation to records provided to him in accordance with paragraph (e) or (f) above.

[2.824]
[11A

A self-employed driver must—

(a) keep records which are adequate to show whether he is complying with the requirements of these Regulations;
(b) retain such records for at least two years after the end of the period covered by those records;
(c) provide to an enforcement officer copies of such records as the officer may require.]

NOTES

Inserted by the Road Transport (Working Time) (Amendment) Regulations 2012, SI 2012/991, regs 2, 11.

[2.825]
12

A mobile worker shall, at the request of his employer under regulation 11(a), notify his employer in writing of time worked by the worker for another employer for inclusion in the calculation of the mobile worker's working time.

[2.826]
13

(1) The Secretary of State shall arrange for the publication, in such form and manner as he considers appropriate, of information and advice concerning the operation of these Regulations.

(2) The information and advice shall be such as appear to him best calculated to enable [employers, workers and self-employed drivers] affected by these Regulations to understand their respective rights and obligations.

NOTES

Words in square brackets in para (2) substituted by the Road Transport (Working Time) (Amendment) Regulations 2012, SI 2012/991, regs 2, 12.

[2.827]
14 Agency workers not otherwise mobile workers

(1) This regulation applies in any case where an individual ("the agency worker")—

(a) is supplied by a person ("the agent") to do the work of a mobile worker for another ("the principal") under a contract or other arrangements made between the agent and the principal; but
(b) is not, as respects that work, a worker, because of the absence of a worker's contract between the individual and the agent or the principal; and
(c) is not a party to a contract under which he undertakes to do the work for another party to the contract whose status is, by virtue of the contract, that of a client or customer or any profession or business undertaking carried on by the individual.

(2) In a case where this regulation applies, the other provisions of these Regulations shall have effect as if there were a contract for the doing of the work by the agency worker made between the agency worker and—

(a) whichever of the agent and the principal is responsible for paying the agency worker in respect of the work; or
(b) if neither the agent nor the principal is so responsible, whichever of them pays the agency worker in respect of the work,
(c) and as if that person were the agency worker's employer.

[2.828]
[15 Individual carrying on trade or business

(1) This regulation applies to an individual who—

(a) for the purpose of a trade or business carried on by him, drives a vehicle described in paragraph (2) or (3) of regulation 3, and
(b) is neither—

Part 2 Statutory Instruments

(i) a self-employed driver, nor
(ii) an agency worker within the meaning of regulation 14.

(2) Where this regulation applies, these Regulations shall have effect as if—
(a) the individual were both a mobile worker and the employer of that mobile worker, and
(b) regulations 10, 11(a) and (e) and 12 were omitted.]

NOTES

Substituted by the Road Transport (Working Time) (Amendment) Regulations 2007, SI 2007/853, reg 2(1), (4).

[2.829]
16 Enforcement

(1) It shall be the duty of the Secretary of State to enforce the requirements of these Regulations.

(2) Schedule 2 shall apply in relation to the enforcement of the relevant requirements.

[2.830]
17

(1) Any person who fails to comply with any of the relevant requirements shall be guilty of an offence.

(2) The provisions of paragraph (3) shall apply where an inspector is exercising or has exercised any power conferred by Schedule 2.

(3) It is an offence for a person—
(a) to contravene any requirement imposed by an inspector under paragraph 2 of Schedule 2;
(b) to prevent or attempt to prevent any other person from appearing before an inspector or from answering any question to which an inspector may by virtue of paragraph 2(2)(e) of Schedule 2 require an answer;
(c) to contravene any requirement or prohibition imposed by an improvement notice or a prohibition notice referred to in paragraphs 3 and 4 of Schedule 2 (including any such notice as is modified on appeal);
(d) intentionally to obstruct an inspector in the exercise or performance of his powers;
(e) to use or disclose any information in contravention of paragraph 7 of Schedule 2;
(f) to make a statement which he knows to be false or recklessly to make a statement which is false where the statement is made in purported compliance with a requirement to furnish any information imposed by or under these Regulations.

(4) Any person guilty of an offence under paragraph (1) shall be liable—
(a) on summary conviction, to a fine not exceeding the statutory maximum;
(b) on conviction on indictment, to a fine.

(5) A person guilty of an offence under paragraph (3)(b) or (d) shall be liable on summary conviction to a fine not exceeding level 5 on the standard scale.

(6) A person guilty of an offence under paragraph (3)(c) shall be liable—
(a) on summary conviction, to imprisonment for a term not exceeding three months, or a fine not exceeding the statutory maximum;
(b) on conviction on indictment, to imprisonment for a term not exceeding two years, or a fine or both.

(7) A person guilty of an offence under paragraph (3)(a), (e) or (f) shall be liable—
(a) on summary conviction, to a fine not exceeding the statutory maximum;
(b) on conviction on indictment—
(i) if the offence is under paragraph (3)(e), to imprisonment for a term not exceeding two years or a fine or both,
(ii) if the offence is under paragraph (3)(a) or (f), to a fine.

(8) The provisions set out in regulations 18 to 22 shall apply in relation to the offences provided for in paragraphs (1) and (3).

[2.831]
18 Offences due to fault of other person

Where the commission by any person of an offence is due to the act or default of some other person, that other person shall be guilty of the offence, and a person may be charged with the conviction of the offence by virtue of this regulation whether or not proceedings are taken against the first-mentioned person.

[2.832]
19 Offences by bodies corporate

(1) Where an offence committed by a body corporate is proved to have been committed with the consent or connivance of, or to have been attributable to any neglect on the part of, any director, manager, secretary or other similar officer of the body corporate or a person who was purporting to act in any such capacity, he as well as the body corporate shall be guilty of that offence and shall be liable to be proceeded against and punished accordingly.

(2) Where the affairs of a body corporate are managed by its members, the preceding paragraph shall apply in relation to the acts and defaults of a member in connection with his functions of management as if he were a director of the body corporate.

[2.833]
20 Restriction on institution of proceedings in England and Wales

Proceedings for an offence shall not be instituted in England or Wales except by an inspector or by, or with the consent of, the Director of Public Prosecutions.

[2.834]
21 Prosecution by inspectors

(1) If authorised in that behalf by the Secretary of State an inspector may prosecute proceedings for an offence before a magistrates court even though the inspector is not of counsel or a solicitor.

(2) This regulation shall not apply in Scotland.

[2.835]
22 Power of court to order cause of offence to be remedied

(1) This regulation applies where a person is convicted of an offence in respect of any matter which appears to the court to be a matter which it is in his power to remedy.

(2) In addition to or instead of imposing any punishment, the court may order the person in question to take such steps as may be specified in the order for remedying the said matters within such time as may be fixed by the order.

(3) The time fixed by an order under paragraph (2) may be extended or further extended by order of the court on an application made before the end of that time as originally fixed or as extended under this paragraph, as the case may be.

(4) Where a person is ordered under paragraph (2) to remedy any matters, that person shall not be liable under these Regulations in respect of that matter in so far as it continues during the time fixed by the order or any further time allowed under paragraph (3).

SCHEDULES

SCHEDULE 1
WORKFORCE AGREEMENTS

Regulation 2

[2.836]
1. An agreement is a workforce agreement for the purposes of these Regulations if the following conditions are satisfied—

(a) the agreement is in writing;

(b) it has effect for a specified period not exceeding five years;

(c) it applies either—

 (i) to all of the relevant members of the workforce, or

 (ii) to all of the relevant members of the workforce who belong to a particular group;

(d) the agreement is signed—

 (i) in the case of an agreement of the kind referred to in sub-paragraph (c)(i), by the representatives of the workforce, and in the case of an agreement of the kind referred to in sub-paragraph (c)(ii), by the representatives of the group to which the agreement applies (excluding, in either case, any representative not a relevant member of the workforce on the date on which the agreement was first made available for signature), or

 (ii) if the employer employed 20 or fewer workers on the date referred to in sub-paragraph (d)(i), either by the appropriate representatives in accordance with that sub-paragraph or by the majority of the workers employed by him; and

(e) before the agreement was made available for signature, the employer provided all the workers to whom it was intended to apply on the date on which it came into effect with copies of the text of the agreement and such guidance as those employees might reasonably require in order to understand it in full.

2. For the purposes of this Schedule—

"a particular group" is a group of the relevant members of a workforce who undertake a particular function, work at a particular workplace or belong to a particular department or unit within their employer's business;

"relevant members of the workforce" are all of the workers employed by a particular employer, excluding any worker whose terms and conditions of employment are provided for, wholly or in part, in a collective agreement;

"representatives of the group" are workers duly elected to represent the members of a particular group;

"representatives of the workforce" are workers duly elected to represent the relevant members of the workforce;

and representatives are "duly elected" if the election at which they were elected satisfied the requirements of paragraph 3.

3. The requirements concerning elections referred to in paragraph 2 are that—

(a) the number of representatives to be elected is determined by the employer;

(b) the candidates for election as representatives of the workforce are relevant members of the workforce, and candidates for election as representatives of the group are members of the group;

(c) no worker who is eligible to be a candidate is unreasonably excluded from standing for election;

(d) all the relevant members of the workforce are entitled to vote for representatives of the workforce, and all the members of a particular group are entitled to vote for representatives of the group;

(e) the workers entitled to vote may vote for as many candidates as there are representatives to be elected; and

(f) the election is conducted so as to secure that—

(i) so far as is reasonably practicable, those voting do so in secret, and

(ii) the votes given at the election are fairly and accurately counted.

SCHEDULE 2
ENFORCEMENT

Regulation 16(2)

[2.837]

1 Appointment of inspectors

(1) The Secretary of State may appoint as inspectors (under whatever title he may from time to time determine) such persons having suitable qualifications as he thinks necessary for carrying into effect these Regulations, and may terminate any appointment made under this paragraph.

(2) Every appointment of a person as an inspector under this paragraph shall be made by an instrument in writing specifying which of the powers conferred on inspectors by these Regulations are to be exercisable by the person appointed; and an inspector shall in right of his appointment under this paragraph be entitled to exercise only such of those powers as are so specified.

(3) So much of an inspector's instrument of appointment as specifies the powers which he is entitled to exercise may be varied by the Secretary of State.

(4) An inspector shall, if so required when exercising or seeking to exercise any power conferred on him by these Regulations, produce his instrument of appointment or a duly authenticated copy thereof.

2 Powers of inspectors

(1) Subject to the provisions of paragraph 1 and this paragraph, an inspector may for the purpose of carrying into effect these Regulations exercise the powers set out in sub-paragraph (2).

(2) The powers of an inspector are the following, namely—

(a) at any reasonable time (or in a situation which in his opinion may be dangerous, at any time) to enter any premises which he has reason to believe it is necessary for him to enter for the purposes mentioned in sub-paragraph (1);

(b) to take with him a constable if he has reasonable cause to apprehend any serious obstruction in the execution of his duty;

(c) without prejudice to paragraph (b), on entering any premises by virtue of paragraph (a) to take with him—

(i) any other person duly authorised by the Secretary of State; and

(ii) any equipment or material required for any purpose for which the power of entry is being exercised;

(d) to make such examination and investigation as may in any circumstances be necessary for the purpose mentioned in sub-paragraph (1);

(e) to require any person whom he has reasonable cause to believe to be able to give any information relevant to any examination or investigation under paragraph (d) to answer (in the absence of persons other than a person nominated by him to be present and any persons whom the inspector may allow to be present) such questions as the inspector thinks fit to ask and to sign a declaration of the truth of his answers;

(f) to require the production of, inspect, and take copies of, or of any entry in—

(i) any records which by virtue of these Regulations are required to be kept, and

(ii) any other books, records or documents which it is necessary for him to see for the purposes of any examination or investigation under paragraph (d);

(g) to require any person to afford him such facilities and assistance with respect to any matters or things within that person's control or in relation to which that person has responsibilities as are necessary to enable the inspector to exercise any of the powers conferred on him by this sub-paragraph;

(h) any other power which is necessary for the purpose mentioned in sub-paragraph (1).

(3) No answer given by a person in pursuance of a requirement imposed under sub-paragraph (2)(e) shall be admissible in evidence against that person or the husband or wife of that person in any proceedings.

(4) Nothing in this paragraph shall be taken to compel the production by any person of a document of which he would on grounds of legal professional privilege be entitled to withhold production on an order for discovery in an action in the High Court or, as the case may be, an order for the production of documents in an action in the Court of Session.

3 Improvement notices

If an inspector is of the opinion that a person—

(a) is contravening one or more of these Regulations; or

(b) has contravened one or more of these Regulations in circumstances that make it likely that the contravention will continue or be repeated,

he may serve on him a notice (in this Schedule referred to as "an improvement notice") stating that he is of that opinion, specifying the provision or provisions as to which he is of that opinion, giving particulars of the reasons why he is of that opinion, and requiring that person to remedy the contravention or, as the case may be, the matter occasioning it within such period (ending not earlier than the period within which an appeal against the notice can be brought under paragraph (6)) as may be specified in the notice.

4 Prohibition notices

(1) This paragraph applies to any activities which are being, or are likely to be, carried on by or under the control of any person, being activities to or in relation to which any of these Regulations apply or will, if the activities are so carried on, apply.

(2) If as regards any activities to which this paragraph applies an inspector is of the opinion that, as carried on by or under the control of the person in question, the activities involve or, as the case may be, will involve a risk of serious personal injury, the inspector may serve on that person a notice (in this Schedule referred to as "a prohibition notice").

(3) A prohibition notice shall—

(a) state that the inspector is of the said opinion;

(b) specify the matters which in his opinion give or, as the case may be, will give rise to the said risk;

(c) where in his opinion any of those matters involves or, as the case may be, will involve a contravention of any of these Regulations, state that he is of that opinion, specify the regulation or regulations as to which he is of that opinion, and give particulars of the reasons why he is of that opinion; and

(d) direct that the activities to which the notice relates shall not be carried on by or under the control of the person on whom the notice is served unless the matters specified in the notice in pursuance of paragraph (b) and any associated contraventions of provisions so specified in pursuance of paragraph (c) have been remedied.

(4) A direction contained in a prohibition notice in pursuance of sub-paragraph (3)(d) shall take effect—

(a) at the end of the period specified in the notice; or

(b) if the notice so declares, immediately.

5 Provisions supplementary to paragraphs 3 and 4

(1) In this paragraph "a notice" means an improvement notice or a prohibition notice.

(2) A notice may (but need not) include directions as to the measures to be taken to remedy any contravention or matter to which the notice relates; and any such directions—

(a) may be framed to any extent by reference to any approved code of practice; and

(b) may be framed so as to afford the person on whom the notice is served a choice between different ways of remedying the contravention or matter.

(3) Where an improvement notice or prohibition notice which is not to take immediate effect has been served—

(a) the notice may be withdrawn by an inspector at any time before the end of the period specified therein in pursuance of paragraph 3 or paragraph 4(4) as the case may be; and

(b) the period so specified may be extended or further extended by an inspector at any time when an appeal against the notice is not pending.

6 Appeal against improvement or prohibition notice

(1) In this paragraph "a notice" means an improvement or prohibition notice.

(2) A person on whom a notice is served may within 21 days from the date of its service appeal to an employment tribunal; and on such an appeal the tribunal may either cancel or affirm the notice and, if it affirms it, may do so either in its original form or with such modifications as the tribunal may in the circumstances think fit.

(3) Where an appeal under this paragraph is brought against a notice within the period allowed under the preceding sub-paragraph, then—

(a) in the case of an improvement notice, the bringing of the appeal shall have the effect of suspending the operation of the notice until the appeal is finally disposed of or, if the appeal is withdrawn, until the withdrawal of the appeal;

(b) in the case of a prohibition notice, the bringing of the appeal shall have the like effect if, but only if, on the application of the appellant the tribunal so directs (and then only from the giving of the direction).

(4) One or more assessors may be appointed for the purposes of any proceedings brought before an employment tribunal under this paragraph.

7 Restrictions on disclosure of information

(1) In this paragraph—

"relevant information" means information obtained by an inspector in pursuance of a requirement imposed under paragraph 2;

"relevant statutory provisions" means the provisions of Part 6 of the Transport Act 1968 and of any orders or regulations made under powers contained in that Part; and

"the recipient", in relation to any relevant information, means the person by whom that information was so obtained or to whom that information was so furnished, as the case may be.

(2) Subject to the following sub-paragraph, no relevant information shall be disclosed without the consent of the person by whom it was furnished.

(3) The preceding sub-paragraph shall not apply to—

(a) disclosure of information to a government department;
(b) without prejudice to paragraph (a), disclosure by the recipient of information to any person for the purpose of any function conferred on the recipient by or under any of the relevant statutory provisions or under these Regulations;
(c) without prejudice to paragraph (a), disclosure by the recipient of information to—
(i) an officer of a local authority who is authorised by that authority to receive it: or
(ii) a constable authorised by a chief officer of police to receive it; or
(d) disclosure by the recipient of information in a form calculated to prevent it from being identified as relating to a particular person or case.

(4) A person to whom information is disclosed in pursuance of sub-paragraph (3) shall not use the information for a purpose other than—
(a) in a case falling within sub-paragraph (3)(a), a purpose of a government department or local authority in connection with these Regulations or with the relevant statutory provisions, or any enactment whatsoever relating to working time;
(b) in the case of information given to a constable, the purposes of the police in connection with these Regulations, the relevant statutory provisions or any enactment relating to working time.

(5) A person shall not disclose any information obtained by him as a result of the exercise of any power conferred by paragraph 2 (including in particular any information with respect to any trade secret obtained by him in any premises entered by him by virtue of any such power) except—
(a) for the purposes of his functions; or
(b) for the purposes of any legal proceedings; or
(c) with the relevant consent.

In this sub-paragraph "the relevant consent" means, in the case of information furnished in pursuance of a requirement imposed under paragraph 2, the consent of the person who furnished it, and, in any other case, the consent of a person having responsibilities in relation to the premises where the information was obtained.

(6) Notwithstanding anything in sub-paragraph (5) an inspector shall, in circumstances in which it is necessary to do so for the purpose of assisting in keeping persons (or the representatives of persons) adequately informed about matters affecting their health, safety and welfare or working time, give to such persons or their representatives the following descriptions of information, that is to say—
(a) factual information obtained by him as mentioned in that sub-paragraph which relates to their working environment; and
(b) information with respect to any action which he has taken or proposes to take in or in connection with the performance of his functions in relation to their working environment;

and, where an inspector does as aforesaid, he shall give the like information to the employer of the first-mentioned persons.

(7) Notwithstanding anything in sub-paragraph (5), a person who has obtained such information as is referred to in that sub-paragraph may furnish to a person who appears to him to be likely to be a party to any civil proceedings arising out of any accident, occurrence, situation or other matter, a written statement of the relevant facts observed by him in the course of exercising any of the powers referred to in that sub-paragraph.

TRANSFER OF EMPLOYMENT (PENSION PROTECTION) REGULATIONS 2005

(SI 2005/649)

NOTES

Made: 10 March 2005.
Authority: Pensions Act 2004, ss 258(2)(c)(ii), (7), 315(2), 318(1).
Commencement: 6 April 2005.
See *Harvey* F(6).

[2.838]

1 Citation, commencement, application and interpretation

(1) These Regulations may be cited as the Transfer of Employment (Pension Protection) Regulations 2005 and shall come into force on 6th April 2005.

(2) These Regulations apply in the case of a person ("the employee") in relation to whom section 257 of the Act (conditions for pension protection) applies, that is to say a person who, in the circumstances described in subsection 9(1) of that section, ceases to be employed by the transferor of an undertaking or part of an undertaking and becomes employed by the transferee.

[(3) In these Regulations—
"the Act" means the Pensions Act 2004;
"remuneration period" means a period in respect of which the employee is paid remuneration.

(4) In calculating the amount of the employee's remuneration for the purposes of these Regulations—
(a) only payments made in respect of basic pay shall be taken into account and bonus, commission, overtime and similar payments shall be disregarded; and

(b) no account shall be taken of any deductions which are made in respect of tax, national insurance or pension contributions.

(5) In calculating the amount of a transferee's pension contributions for the purposes of these Regulations in the case of a scheme which is contracted-out by virtue of section 9 of the Pension Schemes Act 1993, minimum payments within the meaning of that Act shall be disregarded.]

NOTES

Paras (3)–(5): substituted (for the original para (3)) by the Occupational Pension Schemes (Miscellaneous Amendments) Regulations 2014, SI 2014/540, reg 4(1), (2).

[2.839]

2 [Requirements where the transferee's pension scheme is not a money purchase scheme]

(1) In a case where these Regulations apply, and the transferee is the employer in relation to a pension scheme which is not a money purchase scheme, that scheme complies with section [258(2)(c)] of the Act (alternative standard for a scheme which is not a money purchase scheme) if it provides either—

(a) for members to be entitled to benefits the value of which equals or exceeds 6 per cent of pensionable pay for each year of employment together with the total amount of any contributions made by them, and, where members are required to make contributions to the scheme, for them to contribute at a rate which does not exceed 6 per cent of their pensionable pay; or

(b) for the transferee to make relevant contributions to the scheme on behalf of each employee of his who is an active member of it.

(2) In this regulation—

"pensionable pay" means that part of the remuneration payable to a member of a scheme by reference to which the amount of contributions and benefits are determined under the rules of the scheme;

["relevant contributions" means contributions—

(a) made by the transferee in respect of each remuneration period in respect of which the employee contributes to the scheme; and

(b) the amount of which is—

(i) where the employee's contributions are less than 6 per cent. of the employee's remuneration, not less than the contributions made by the employee; or

(ii) where the employee's contributions equal or exceed 6 per cent. of the employee's remuneration, not less than 6 per cent. of that remuneration.]

NOTES

Provision heading: substituted by the Occupational Pension Schemes (Miscellaneous Amendments) Regulations 2014, SI 2014/540, reg 4(1), (3).

Para (1): figure in square brackets substituted by the Pensions Act 2014 (Abolition of Contracting-out for Salary Related Pension Schemes) (Consequential Amendments and Savings) Order 2016, SI 2016/200, art 21, as from 6 April 2016.

Para (2): definition "relevant contributions" inserted by SI 2014/540, reg 4(1), (4).

[2.840]

[3 Requirements where the transferee's pension scheme is a money purchase scheme or stakeholder pension scheme

(1) In a case where these Regulations apply, the transferee's contributions are relevant contributions for the purposes of subsection (2)(b) (money purchase scheme) and subsections (3) to (5) (stakeholder pension scheme) of section 258 of the Act if—

(a) the contributions are made in respect of each remuneration period in respect of which the employee contributes to the scheme; and

(b) paragraph (2) or (3) is satisfied.

(2) This paragraph is satisfied if the amount contributed by the transferee in respect of each remuneration period is—

(a) where the employee's contributions are less than 6 per cent. of the employee's remuneration, an amount not less than the contributions made by the employee;

(b) where the employee's contributions equal or exceed 6 per cent. of the employee's remuneration, an amount not less than 6 per cent. of that remuneration.

(3) This paragraph is satisfied if—

(a) in respect of the remuneration period immediately before the relevant time—

(i) the transferor had been required to make contributions; and

(ii) those contributions had been solely for the purpose of producing money purchase benefits for the employee; and

(b) the amount contributed by the transferee is not less than the amount the transferor had been required to contribute.]

NOTES

Substituted by the Occupational Pension Schemes (Miscellaneous Amendments) Regulations 2014, SI 2014/540, reg 4(1), (5).

Part 2 Statutory Instruments

REGISTER OF JUDGMENTS, ORDERS AND FINES REGULATIONS 2005

(SI 2005/3595)

NOTES

Made: 29 December 2005.

Authority: Courts Act 2003, ss 98(1)–(3), 108(6).

Commencement: 30 December 2005 (for the purposes of regs 1, 2, 4); 6 April 2006 (otherwise).

These Regulations are included in this work because they have been amended to apply, inter alia, to judgments of employment tribunals and the Employment Appeal Tribunal; see regs 8, 9A at **[2.847]**, **[2.848]**. The Regulations apply only to England and Wales (see the Courts Act 2003, s 111).

ARRANGEMENT OF REGULATIONS

[2.841]

1 Citation, commencement and duration

These Regulations may be cited as the Register of Judgments, Orders and Fines Regulations 2005.

[2.842]

2

These Regulations shall come into force—

(a) for the purposes of this regulation and regulations 1 and 4, on the day after the day on which these Regulations are made; and

(b) for all other purposes, on 6th April 2006.

NOTES

Note: despite the heading preceding reg 1 there is no indication in this regulation or in reg 1 that these Regulations have a specified duration. Cf the Register of Fines Regulations 2003, SI 2003/3184 which (by reg 1(2) thereof as amended by reg 4 of these Regulations) expired on 6 April 2006.

[2.843]

3 Interpretation

In these Regulations—

"the 1998 Rules" means the Civil Procedure Rules 1998;

"the Act" means the Courts Act 2003;

"Administrative Court" has the same meaning as in Part 54 of the 1998 Rules;

"amendment notice" means the notice given to the Registrar in accordance with regulation 21;

"applicable charge" means the charge fixed by the Lord Chancellor in accordance with section 98(4) of the Act, or in accordance with section 98(4) as applied by section 98(7)(b) of the Act;

"appropriate officer" means—

(a) in the case of the High Court or a county court, an officer of the court in which the judgment is entered [or with which a tribunal decision is filed];

(b) in the case of a registration under paragraph 38(1)(b) of Schedule 5 to the Act—

(i) where a fines officer exercises the power to register following service of a notice under paragraph 37(6)(b) of that Schedule, that officer; or

(ii) where a court exercises the power to register by virtue of paragraph 39(3) or (4) of that Schedule, an officer of that court;

(c) in respect of a liability order designated for the purposes of section 33(5) of the Child Support Act 1991, the Secretary of State;

"appropriate fee" means the fee prescribed under section 92(1) of the Act;

"certificate of satisfaction" means the certificate applied for under regulation 17;

["data protection principles" means the principles set out in Article 5(1) of the *GDPR*;]

"debt" means the sum of money owed by virtue of a judgment, [administration order, fine or tribunal decision], and "debtor" means the individual, incorporated or unincorporated body liable to pay that sum;

"family proceedings" has the same meaning as in section 63 (interpretation) of the Family Law Act 1996;

["the GDPR" has the same meaning as in Parts 5 to 7 of the Data Protection Act 2018 (see section 3(10), (11) and (14) of that Act);]

"judgment" means any judgment or order of the court for a sum of money and, in respect of a county court, includes a liability order designated by the Secretary of State for the purposes of section 33(5) of the Child Support Act 1991;

"Local Justice Area" means the area specified in an order made under section 8(2) of the Act;

"Registrar" means—

(a) where the Register is kept by a body corporate in accordance with section 98(6) of the Act, that body corporate; or

(b) otherwise, the Lord Chancellor;

"the Register" means the register kept in accordance with section 98(1) of the Act;

"satisfied", in relation to a debt, means that the debt has been paid in full, and "satisfaction" is to be construed accordingly;

"Technology and Construction Court" has the same meaning as in Part 60 of the 1998 Rules;

["tribunal decision" includes an award];

["the UK GDPR" has the same meaning as in Parts 5 to 7 of the Data Protection Act 2018 (see section 3(10) and (14) of that Act)].

NOTES

Words in square brackets in definition "appropriate officer" inserted, words in square brackets in definition "debt" substituted, and definition "tribunal decision" inserted, by the Register of Judgments, Orders and Fines (Amendment) Regulations 2009, SI 2009/474, regs 2, 3.

Definition "data protection principles" substituted by the Data Protection Act 2018, s 211(1)(b), Sch 19, Pt 2, para 318(a), as from 25 May 2018 (for transitional provisions and savings relating to the repeal of the Data Protection Act 1998, see Sch 20 to the 2018 Act at **[1.2232]**).

Definition "the GDPR" inserted by the Data Protection Act 2018, s 211(1)(b), Sch 19, Pt 2, para 318(b), as from 25 May 2018 (for transitional provisions and savings relating to the repeal of the Data Protection Act 1998, see Sch 20 to the 2018 Act at **[1.2232]**).

For the reference to "GDPR" in the definition "data protection principles" there is substituted "UK GDPR", the definition "the GDPR" is revoked and the definition "the UK GDPR" is inserted, by the Data Protection, Privacy and Electronic Communications (Amendments etc) (EU Exit) Regulations 2019, SI 2019/419, reg 6(c), Sch 3, Pt 3, para 62, as from exit day (as defined in the European Union (Withdrawal) Act 2018, s 20); for transitional provisions etc, see the 2019 Regulations at **[2.2122]**.

4 *(Amended the Register of Fines Regulations 2003, SI 2003/3184 (expired on 6 April 2006 in accordance with reg 1(2) thereof as amended by this regulation).)*

[2.844]

5 Performance of steps under these Regulations

Any step to be taken under these Regulations by the appropriate officer or the Registrar shall be taken—

(a) in respect of—

(i) the registration of judgments to which regulation 8(1)(a) applies; . . .

(ii) the registration of administration orders to which regulation 8(1)(b) applies; [and

(iii) the registration of tribunal decisions to which regulation 8(1)(d) applies],

within one working day;

(b) in respect of the registration of sums to which regulation 8(1)(c) applies, as soon as may be reasonably practicable.

NOTES

Word omitted from para (a)(i) revoked, and para (a)(iii) and the word immediately preceding it inserted, by the Register of Judgments, Orders and Fines (Amendment) Regulations 2009, SI 2009/474, regs 2, 4.

[2.845]

6 Manner, etc, in which the Register is to be kept

(1) Where the Registrar is a body corporate, the Register shall be kept in accordance with the terms of the agreement between the Lord Chancellor and that body.

(2) The terms of the agreement between the Lord Chancellor and the body corporate shall specify—

(a) the manner in which the Register is to be kept;

(b) the form of the Register; and

(c) the place at which the Register is to be kept.

[2.846]
7
Where the Registrar is not a body corporate, the Register shall be kept by the Lord Chancellor in such a manner and at such a place as he shall determine.

[2.847]
8 Registration of judgments, [administration orders, fines and tribunal decisions]
(1) The appropriate officer shall send to the Registrar a return of—
(a) subject to regulation 9, every judgment entered in—
(i) the High Court; and
(ii) a county court;
(b) every administration order made under section 112 of the County Courts Act 1984 (power of county courts to make administration orders);
(c) every sum to be registered by virtue of paragraph 38(1)(b) of Schedule 5 to the Act (further steps available against defaulters)[;
(d) subject to regulation 9A, every tribunal decision made by—
(i) the First-tier Tribunal;
(ii) the Upper Tribunal;
(iii) an employment tribunal; or
(iv) the Employment Appeal Tribunal,
in pursuance of which a sum of money is payable].
(2) Following receipt of a return sent in accordance with paragraph (1), the Registrar shall record the details of the return as an entry in the Register.

NOTES
Regulation heading: words in square brackets substituted by the Register of Judgments, Orders and Fines (Amendment) Regulations 2009, SI 2009/474, regs 2, 5.
Para (1): sub-para (d) inserted by SI 2009/474, regs 2, 6.

9 *(Reg 9 (Exempt judgments—High Court and county courts) outside the scope of this work.)*

[2.848]
[9A Exempt tribunal decisions
Regulation 8(1)(d) does not apply until, pursuant to rule 70.5(2A)(a) of the 1998 Rules—
(a) in the case of a tribunal decision made by the First-tier Tribunal or the Upper Tribunal, a copy of the tribunal decision is filed with the High Court or a county court; or
(b) in the case of a tribunal decision made by an employment tribunal or the Employment Appeal Tribunal, a copy of the tribunal decision is filed with a county court.]

NOTES
Inserted by the Register of Judgments, Orders and Fines (Amendment) Regulations 2009, SI 2009/474, regs 2, 7.

[2.849]
10 Information contained in the appropriate officer's return
The return sent by virtue of regulation 8(1) shall contain details of—
(a) the full name and address of the debtor in respect of whom the entry in the Register is to be made;
(b) if the entry is to be in respect of an individual, that individual's date of birth (where known);
(c) the amount of the debt;
(d) the case number;
(e) in respect of a return sent by virtue of regulation 8(1)(a) regarding a liability order designated under section 33(5) of the Child Support Act 1991, the date of the judgment;
(f) in respect of all other returns sent by virtue of regulation 8(1)(a)—
(i) the name of the court which made the judgment; and
(ii) the date of the judgment;
(g) in respect of a return sent by virtue of regulation 8(1)(b)—
(i) the name of the court which made the administration order; and
(ii) the date of the order;
(h) in respect of a return sent by virtue of regulation 8(1)(c)—
(i) the Local Justice Area which imposed the fine; and
(ii) the date of conviction;
[(i) in respect of a return sent by virtue of regulation 8(1)(d)—
(i) the name of the court with which the tribunal decision was filed in accordance with regulation 9A; and
(ii) the date on which the tribunal decision was filed with the court].

NOTES
Para (i) inserted by the Register of Judgments, Orders and Fines (Amendment) Regulations 2009, SI 2009/474, regs 2, 8.

[2.850]

11 Cancellation or endorsement of entries relating to judgments of the High Court or a county court [or tribunal decisions]

(1) This regulation applies where an entry in the Register is one to which regulation 8(1)(a) applies (judgments entered in the High Court or a county court) [or to which regulation 8(1)(d) applies (tribunal decisions)].

(2) Where it comes to the attention of the appropriate officer that—

(a) the debt to which the entry relates has been satisfied one month or less from the date of the judgment [or the date on which the tribunal decision was filed with the court in accordance with regulation 9A;]

(b) the judgment to which the entry relates has been set aside or reversed[; or

(c) the tribunal decision to which the entry relates has been set aside],

that officer shall send a request to the Registrar to cancel the entry.

(3) Where it comes to the attention of the appropriate officer that the debt has been satisfied more than one month from the date of the judgment [or the date on which the tribunal decision was filed with the court in accordance with regulation 9A], that officer shall send a request to the Registrar to endorse the entry as to the satisfaction of the debt.

NOTES

Regulation heading, paras (1), (3): words in square brackets inserted by the Register of Judgments, Orders and Fines (Amendment) Regulations 2009, SI 2009/474, regs 2, 9, 10(a), (c).

Para (2): words in first pair of square brackets substituted, and words in second pair of square brackets inserted, by SI 2009/474, regs 2, 10(b).

12, 13 *(Reg 12 (Endorsement of entries relating to county court administration orders) and reg 13 (Cancellation or endorsement of entries relating to fines) outside the scope of this work.)*

[2.851]

14 Cancellation of entries in the Register—additional provisions

Where an entry in the Register is endorsed in accordance with regulations 11(3) or 13(3) and the appropriate officer is later of the opinion that the debt was satisfied one month or less from—

(a) the date of the judgment or administration order; . . .

(b) the date on which the fine was registered[; or

(c) the date on which the tribunal decision was filed with the court in accordance with regulation 9A],

that officer shall send a request to the Registrar to cancel the relevant entry.

NOTES

Word omitted from para (a) revoked, and para (c) and the word immediately preceding it inserted, by the Register of Judgments, Orders and Fines (Amendment) Regulations 2009, SI 2009/474, regs 2, 11.

[2.852]

15

Where—

(a) it comes to the attention of the appropriate officer that an administrative error has been made; and

(b) he is of the opinion that the error is such to require the cancellation of an entry in the Register,

that officer shall send a request to the Registrar to cancel the relevant entry.

[2.853]

16 Cancellation and endorsement of entries in the Register by the Registrar

Following receipt of a request under—

(a) regulation 11(2), 13(2), 14 or 15 (debt due satisfied in one month or less, etc), the Registrar shall cancel the relevant entry;

(b) regulation 11(3) or 13(3) (debt due satisfied in more than one month), the Registrar shall endorse the relevant entry as to the satisfaction of the debt;

(c) regulation 12(2) (administration order has been varied, revoked or debt has been satisfied), the Registrar shall endorse the relevant entry accordingly.

[2.854]

17 Application for, and issue of, a certificate of satisfaction

(1) A registered debtor may apply to the appropriate officer for a certificate ("certificate of satisfaction") as to the satisfaction of the debt.

(2) An application under paragraph (1) shall be—

(a) made in writing; and

(b) accompanied by the appropriate fee.

[2.855]
18

(1) In the case of an application for a certificate of satisfaction in respect of an entry in the Register to which regulation 8(1)(a) applies (judgments entered in the High Court or a county court) [or to which regulation 8(1)(d) applies (tribunal decisions)], the application under regulation 17(1) shall be accompanied by—

(a) sufficient evidence that the debt has been satisfied;
(b) a statement that the registered debtor has taken reasonable steps to obtain such evidence, but has been unable to do so; or
(c) a statement that the registered debtor believes such evidence is already in the possession of the appropriate officer.

(2) For the purposes of paragraph (1)(a), sufficient evidence that the debt has been satisfied includes a signed statement by the creditor to that effect.

(3) Where paragraph (1)(b) applies, the appropriate officer shall send notice of the registered debtor's application under regulation 17(1) to the creditor together with a request that the creditor confirms within one month of the date of the notice whether the debt has been satisfied.

(4) For the purposes of paragraph (1)(c), evidence which is already in the possession of the appropriate officer includes where—

(a) the debt has been paid as the result of court enforcement proceedings taken under Part 70 of the 1998 Rules;
(b) payment of the debt has otherwise been made to the court.

NOTES

Para (1): words in square brackets inserted by the Register of Judgments, Orders and Fines (Amendment) Regulations 2009, SI 2009/474, regs 2, 12.

[2.856]
19

Where an application has been made under regulation 17(1) and—

(a) the appropriate officer is of the opinion that the debt has been satisfied; or
(b) a notice has been sent in accordance with regulation 18(3) and the creditor has not responded within the time limit provided,

the appropriate officer shall issue a certificate of satisfaction to the registered debtor.

[2.857]
20 Amendment of the Register in respect of the amount registered

(1) Where it comes to the attention of the appropriate officer that the amount liable to be paid differs from the amount entered in the Register, due to—

(a) the issue of a final costs certificate; . . .
(b) an increase in the amount of the debt[; or
(c) in the case of an entry to which regulation 8(1)(d) applies, a tribunal decision on appeal],

the appropriate officer shall send a return to the Registrar to amend the Register to reflect the revised amount.

(2) The return sent in accordance with paragraph (1) shall contain the same information as prescribed by regulation 10 in respect of the return sent in accordance with regulation 8(1).

(3) Following receipt of a return sent in accordance with this regulation, the Registrar shall amend the Register accordingly.

NOTES

Para (1): word omitted from sub-para (a) revoked, and sub-para (c) and the word immediately preceding it inserted, by the Register of Judgments, Orders and Fines (Amendment) Regulations 2009, SI 2009/474, regs 2, 13.

[2.858]
21 Correction of registered details of the judgment, [administration order, fine or tribunal decision]

(1) Where it comes to the attention of a registered debtor that the entry in the Register relating to his debt is inaccurate with respect to the details of the judgment, [administration order, fine or tribunal decision], that debtor may give notice to the Registrar requiring an amendment to be made ("amendment notice").

(2) The amendment notice shall—

(a) identify the entry which is alleged to be inaccurate; and
(b) state the amendment which is required.

NOTES

The words in square brackets in the heading preceding this regulation, and in para (1), were substituted by the Register of Judgments, Orders and Fines (Amendment) Regulations 2009, SI 2009/474, regs 2, 14, 15.

[2.859]
22

Following receipt of an amendment notice in respect of an entry in the Register, the Registrar shall request that the appropriate officer verify the details of that entry.

[2.860]
23
Following receipt of a request for verification under regulation 22, the appropriate officer shall—
(a) check the information contained in the entry against the official records; and
(b) reply to the request, where applicable stating any necessary amendment.

[2.861]
24
(1) Where the appropriate officer informs the Registrar that the entry is inaccurate and requests an amendment, the Registrar shall amend the Register to rectify the inaccuracy.

(2) Following an amendment to the Register in accordance with paragraph (1), the Registrar shall inform the registered debtor of the action taken and the reasons for having taken that action.

[2.862]
25
Where the appropriate officer informs the Registrar that the entry is accurate, the Registrar shall inform the registered debtor that no action is to be taken and the reasons for not taking any action.

[2.863]
26 Removal of entries in the Register
The Registrar shall remove any entry in the Register registered—
(a) by virtue of regulation 8(1)(a) or (b), six years from the date of the judgment;
(b) by virtue of regulation 8(1)(c), five years from the date of conviction[;
(c) by virtue of regulation 8(1)(d), six years from the date on which the tribunal decision was filed with the court in accordance with regulation 9A].

NOTES
Para (c) inserted by the Register of Judgments, Orders and Fines (Amendment) Regulations 2009, SI 2009/474, regs 2, 16.

[2.864]
27 Searches of the Register
(1) Subject to regulation 29, searches of a section of the Register may be carried out on payment of the applicable charge relevant to the type and method of search.

(2) The types of search which may be carried out are—
(a) at a stated address, against a named individual or unincorporated body;
(b) against a named incorporated body;
(c) a periodical search—
(i) relating to a named court;
(ii) within a named county; or
(iii) with the agreement of the Registrar, against such other criteria as may be requested.

[2.865]
28 Certified copies
On receipt of—
(a) a written request for a certified copy of an entry in the Register; and
(b) the applicable charge for such a request,
the Registrar shall provide a copy of that entry, certified by him as a true and complete copy of the entry in the Register.

[2.866]
29 Refusal of access to the Register and appeals
(1) The Registrar may—
(a) refuse a person access to the Register, or to a part of the Register; and
(b) refuse to carry out a search of the Register,
if he believes that the purpose for which access has been requested or for which the results of the search will be used contravenes—
(i) any of the data protection principles; or
(ii) the provisions of any other enactment.

(2) Where a refusal is made under paragraph (1), the person who has been denied access to, or has been denied a search of, the Register may appeal to a county court against the decision of the Registrar.

TRANSFER OF UNDERTAKINGS (PROTECTION OF EMPLOYMENT) REGULATIONS 2006

(SI 2006/246)

NOTES
Made: 6 February 2006.
Authority: European Communities Act 1972, s 2(2); Employment Relations Act 1999, s 38.
Commencement: 6 April 2006 (subject to the transitional provisions in reg 21 at **[2.889]**).

Note: with regard to the authority for these Regulations, note that the European Communities Act 1972 is repealed by the European Union (Withdrawal) Act 2018, s 1, as from exit day (as defined in s 20 of that Act); but note also that provision is made for the continuation in force of any subordinate legislation made under the authority of s 2(2) of the 1972 Act by s 2 of the 2018 Act at **[1.2240]**, subject to the provisions of s 5 of, and Sch 1 to, the 2018 Act at **[1.2243]**, **[1.2253]**.

These Regulations represent the current domestic implementation of Council Directive 2001/23/EC at **[3.259]**, re-enacting the original Directive 77/187/EEC together with later amendments. They revoke and replace the Transfer of Undertakings (Protection of Employment) Regulations 1981, SI 1981/1794, subject to transitional provisions and savings in reg 21 *post*.

Employment Appeal Tribunal: an appeal lies to the Employment Appeal Tribunal on a question of law arising from any decision of, or arising in any proceedings before, an employment tribunal under or by virtue of these Regulations; see reg 16(2) of these Regulations at **[2.884]**.

The rights conferred by these Regulations are "relevant statutory rights" for the purposes of the Employment Rights Act 1996, s 104 (dismissal on grounds of assertion of statutory right); see s 104(4)(e) of that Act at **[1.1015]**.

These Regulations have been applied with modifications in a variety of specific circumstances by the following (in the case of the pre-2006 enactments listed below, as amended by these Regulations):

(a) the Industrial Training Act 1982, s 3B (application to the transfer of the activities of an industrial training board);
(b) the Ordnance Factories and Military Services Act 1984, s 4, Sch 2, para 2 (application to personnel transferred as a result of a transfer scheme made under s 1(1) of that Act);
(c) the Dockyard Services Act 1986, s 1(4)–(9) (application to transfers of dockyard undertakings under that Act);
(d) the Dartford-Thurrock Crossing Act 1988, Sch 5 (application to any transfer of an undertaking effected, or treated as effected, by s 14 of that Act);
(e) the Atomic Weapons Establishment Act 1991, s 2 (application to the transfer of certain staff employed in the Atomic Weapons Establishment);
(f) the Export and Investment Guarantees Act 1991, s 9 (application to transfers of property, rights or liabilities under a scheme under s 8 of the 1991 Act);
(g) the Ports Act 1991, Sch 1, para 5 (application to certain transfers of port undertakings made under s 2 of that Act);
(h) the Energy Act 2004, s 38(8), Sch 5, para 10 (application to a transfer of an undertaking or part of an undertaking in accordance with a nuclear transfer scheme or a modification agreement under that Act);
(i) the Criminal Proceedings etc (Reform) (Scotland) Act 2007, s 65(4) (application to a scheme for the transfer of the employment to the Scottish Administration of clerks, assessors and other staff of the district court to which an order under s 64(1) of that Act applies);
(j) the Personal Accounts Delivery Authority Winding Up Order 2010, SI 2010/911 (application to the transfer of property, rights and liabilities from the Personal Accounts Delivery Authority to the National Employment Savings Trust Corporation);
(k) the Office of the Renewable Fuels Agency (Dissolution and Transfer of Functions) Order 2011, SI 2011/493, art 6 (application to the transfer of functions of the Office of the Renewable Fuels Agency);
(l) the Local Government (Wales) Measure 2011, s 166(6) (application to transfers of staff etc as a result of local authority amalgamation orders made under that Measure);
(m) Postal Services Act 2011, ss 8(7), 64(4), 73(2), Schs 1, 11 (application to transfer schemes made under the 2011 Act);
(n) the Local Better Regulation Office (Dissolution and Transfer of Functions, Etc) Order 2012, SI 2012/246, art 6 (application to the dissolution of the LBRO and the transfer of functions etc to the Secretary of State);
(o) the Transfer of Undertakings (Protection of Employment) (RCUK Shared Services Centre Limited) Regulations 2012, SI 2012/2413 (transfer of employees of the Department for Business, Innovation and Skills to RCUK Shared Services Centre Limited);
(p) the Transfer of Undertakings (Protection of Employment) (Transfers of Public Health Staff) Regulations 2013, SI 2013/278 (transfers from bodies listed in the Schedule to the Regulations);
(q) the Transfer of Undertakings (Protection of Employment) (Transfer of Staff to the Department for Work and Pensions) Regulations 2014, SI 2014/1139;
(r) the Transfer of Undertakings (Protection of Employment) (Transfer of Police Staff to the National Crime Agency) Regulations 2019, SI 2019/267 (transfer of police staff to the National Crime Agency).

As to the application of these Regulations to certain individual financial institutions, see the Orders made under the Banking (Special Provisions) Act 2008 and the Banking Act 2009.

See *Harvey* F.

ARRANGEMENT OF REGULATIONS

[2.867]
1 Citation, commencement and extent

(1) These Regulations may be cited as the Transfer of Undertakings (Protection of Employment) Regulations 2006.

(2) These Regulations shall come into force on 6 April 2006.

(3) These Regulations shall extend to Northern Ireland, except where otherwise provided.

[2.868]
2 Interpretation

(1) In these Regulations—

"assigned" means assigned other than on a temporary basis;

"collective agreement", "collective bargaining" and "trade union" have the same meanings respectively as in the 1992 Act;

"contract of employment" means any agreement between an employee and his employer determining the terms and conditions of his employment;

references to "contractor" in regulation 3 shall include a sub-contractor;

"employee" means any individual who works for another person whether under a contract of service or apprenticeship or otherwise but does not include anyone who provides services under a contract for services and references to a person's employer shall be construed accordingly;

"insolvency practitioner" has the meaning given to the expression by Part XIII of the Insolvency Act 1986;

references to "organised grouping of employees" shall include a single employee;

"recognised" has the meaning given to the expression by section 178(3) of the 1992 Act;

"relevant transfer" means a transfer or a service provision change to which these Regulations apply in accordance with regulation 3 and "transferor" and "transferee" shall be construed accordingly and in the case of a service provision change falling within regulation 3(1)(b), "the transferor" means the person who carried out the activities prior to the service provision change and "the transferee" means the person who carries out the activities as a result of the service provision change;

"the 1992 Act" means the Trade Union and Labour Relations (Consolidation) Act 1992;

"the 1996 Act" means the Employment Rights Act 1996;

"the 1996 Tribunals Act" means the Employment Tribunals Act 1996;

"the 1981 Regulations" means the Transfer of Undertakings (Protection of Employment) Regulations 1981.

(2) For the purposes of these Regulations the representative of a trade union recognised by an employer is an official or other person authorised to carry on collective bargaining with that employer by that trade union.

(3) In the application of these Regulations to Northern Ireland the Regulations shall have effect as set out in Schedule 1.

[2.869]
3 A relevant transfer

(1) These Regulations apply to—

(a) a transfer of an undertaking, business or part of an undertaking or business situated immediately before the transfer in the United Kingdom to another person where there is a transfer of an economic entity which retains its identity;

(b) a service provision change, that is a situation in which—

(i) activities cease to be carried out by a person ("a client") on his own behalf and are carried out instead by another person on the client's behalf ("a contractor");

(ii) activities cease to be carried out by a contractor on a client's behalf (whether or not those activities had previously been carried out by the client on his own behalf) and are carried out instead by another person ("a subsequent contractor") on the client's behalf; or

(iii) activities cease to be carried out by a contractor or a subsequent contractor on a client's behalf (whether or not those activities had previously been carried out by the client on his own behalf) and are carried out instead by the client on his own behalf,

and in which the conditions set out in paragraph (3) are satisfied.

(2) In this regulation "economic entity" means an organised grouping of resources which has the objective of pursuing an economic activity, whether or not that activity is central or ancillary.

[(2A) References in paragraph (1)(b) to activities being carried out instead by another person (including the client) are to activities which are fundamentally the same as the activities carried out by the person who has ceased to carry them out.]

(3) The conditions referred to in paragraph (1)(b) are that—
(a) immediately before the service provision change—
(i) there is an organised grouping of employees situated in Great Britain which has as its principal purpose the carrying out of the activities concerned on behalf of the client;
(ii) the client intends that the activities will, following the service provision change, be carried out by the transferee other than in connection with a single specific event or task of short-term duration; and
(b) the activities concerned do not consist wholly or mainly of the supply of goods for the client's use.

(4) Subject to paragraph (1), these Regulations apply to—
(a) public and private undertakings engaged in economic activities whether or not they are operating for gain;
(b) a transfer or service provision change howsoever effected notwithstanding—
(i) that the transfer of an undertaking, business or part of an undertaking or business is governed or effected by the law of a country or territory outside the United Kingdom or that the service provision change is governed or effected by the law of a country or territory outside Great Britain;
(ii) that the employment of persons employed in the undertaking, business or part transferred or, in the case of a service provision change, persons employed in the organised grouping of employees, is governed by any such law;
(c) a transfer of an undertaking, business or part of an undertaking or business (which may also be a service provision change) where persons employed in the undertaking, business or part transferred ordinarily work outside the United Kingdom.

(5) An administrative reorganisation of public administrative authorities or the transfer of administrative functions between public administrative authorities is not a relevant transfer.

(6) A relevant transfer—
(a) may be effected by a series of two or more transactions; and
(b) may take place whether or not any property is transferred to the transferee by the transferor.

(7) Where, in consequence (whether directly or indirectly) of the transfer of an undertaking, business or part of an undertaking or business which was situated immediately before the transfer in the United Kingdom, a ship within the meaning of the Merchant Shipping Act 1995 registered in the United Kingdom ceases to be so registered, these Regulations shall not affect the right conferred by section 29 of that Act (right of seamen to be discharged when ship ceases to be registered in the United Kingdom) on a seaman employed in the ship.

NOTES

Para (2A): inserted by the Collective Redundancies and Transfer of Undertakings (Protection of Employment) (Amendment) Regulations 2014, SI 2014/16, regs 4, 5.

[2.870]

4 Effect of relevant transfer on contracts of employment

(1) Except where objection is made under paragraph (7), a relevant transfer shall not operate so as to terminate the contract of employment of any person employed by the transferor and assigned to the organised grouping of resources or employees that is subject to the relevant transfer, which would otherwise be terminated by the transfer, but any such contract shall have effect after the transfer as if originally made between the person so employed and the transferee.

(2) Without prejudice to paragraph (1), but subject to paragraph (6), and regulations 8 and 15(9), on the completion of a relevant transfer—
(a) all the transferor's rights, powers, duties and liabilities under or in connection with any such contract shall be transferred by virtue of this regulation to the transferee; and
(b) any act or omission before the transfer is completed, of or in relation to the transferor in respect of that contract or a person assigned to that organised grouping of resources or employees, shall be deemed to have been an act or omission of or in relation to the transferee.

(3) Any reference in paragraph (1) to a person employed by the transferor and assigned to the organised grouping of resources or employees that is subject to a relevant transfer, is a reference to a person so employed immediately before the transfer, or who would have been so employed if he had not been dismissed in the circumstances described in regulation 7(1), including, where the transfer is effected by a series of two or more transactions, a person so employed and assigned or who would have been so employed and assigned immediately before any of those transactions.

[(4) Subject to regulation 9, any purported variation of a contract of employment that is, or will be, transferred by paragraph (1), is void if the sole or principal reason for the variation is the transfer.

(5) Paragraph (4) does not prevent a variation of the contract of employment if—
(a) the sole or principal reason for the variation is an economic, technical, or organisational reason entailing changes in the workforce, provided that the employer and employee agree that variation; or
(b) the terms of that contract permit the employer to make such a variation.

(5A) In paragraph (5), the expression "changes in the workforce" includes a change to the place where employees are employed by the employer to carry on the business of the employer or to carry out work of a particular kind for the employer (and the reference to such a place has the same meaning as in section 139 of the 1996 Act).

(5B) Paragraph (4) does not apply in respect of a variation of the contract of employment in so far as it varies a term or condition incorporated from a collective agreement, provided that—

(a) the variation of the contract takes effect on a date more than one year after the date of the transfer; and

(b) following that variation, the rights and obligations in the employee's contract, when considered together, are no less favourable to the employee than those which applied immediately before the variation.

(5C) Paragraphs (5) and (5B) do not affect any rule of law as to whether a contract of employment is effectively varied.]

(6) Paragraph (2) shall not transfer or otherwise affect the liability of any person to be prosecuted for, convicted of and sentenced for any offence.

(7) Paragraphs (1) and (2) shall not operate to transfer the contract of employment and the rights, powers, duties and liabilities under or in connection with it of an employee who informs the transferor or the transferee that he objects to becoming employed by the transferee.

(8) Subject to paragraphs (9) and (11), where an employee so objects, the relevant transfer shall operate so as to terminate his contract of employment with the transferor but he shall not be treated, for any purpose, as having been dismissed by the transferor.

(9) Subject to regulation 9, where a relevant transfer involves or would involve a substantial change in working conditions to the material detriment of a person whose contract of employment is or would be transferred under paragraph (1), such an employee may treat the contract of employment as having been terminated, and the employee shall be treated for any purpose as having been dismissed by the employer.

(10) No damages shall be payable by an employer as a result of a dismissal falling within paragraph (9) in respect of any failure by the employer to pay wages to an employee in respect of a notice period which the employee has failed to work.

(11) Paragraphs (1), (7), (8) and (9) are without prejudice to any right of an employee arising apart from these Regulations to terminate his contract of employment without notice in acceptance of a repudiatory breach of contract by his employer.

NOTES

Paras (4)–(5C): substituted for the original paras (4), (5) by the Collective Redundancies and Transfer of Undertakings (Protection of Employment) (Amendment) Regulations 2014, SI 2014/16, regs 4, 6(1).

[2.871]

[4A Effect of relevant transfer on contracts of employment which incorporate provisions of collective agreements

(1) Where a contract of employment, which is transferred by regulation 4(1), incorporates provisions of collective agreements as may be agreed from time to time, regulation 4(2) does not transfer any rights, powers, duties and liabilities in relation to any provision of a collective agreement if the following conditions are met—

(a) the provision of the collective agreement is agreed after the date of the transfer; and

(b) the transferee is not a participant in the collective bargaining for that provision.

(2) For the purposes of regulation 4(1), the contract of employment has effect after the transfer as if it does not incorporate provisions of a collective agreement which meet the conditions in paragraph (1).]

NOTES

Inserted by the Collective Redundancies and Transfer of Undertakings (Protection of Employment) (Amendment) Regulations 2014, SI 2014/16, regs 4, 7.

[2.872]

5 Effect of relevant transfer on collective agreements

Where at the time of a relevant transfer there exists a collective agreement made by or on behalf of the transferor with a trade union recognised by the transferor in respect of any employee whose contract of employment is preserved by regulation 4(1) above, then—

(a) without prejudice to sections 179 and 180 of the 1992 Act (collective agreements presumed to be unenforceable in specified circumstances) that agreement, in its application in relation to the employee, shall, after the transfer, have effect as if made by or on behalf of the transferee with that trade union, and accordingly anything done under or in connection with it, in its application in relation to the employee, by or in relation to the transferor before the transfer, shall, after the transfer, be deemed to have been done by or in relation to the transferee; and

(b) any order made in respect of that agreement, in its application in relation to the employee, shall, after the transfer, have effect as if the transferee were a party to the agreement.

[2.873]

6 Effect of relevant transfer on trade union recognition

(1) This regulation applies where after a relevant transfer the transferred organised grouping of resources or employees maintains an identity distinct from the remainder of the transferee's undertaking.

(2) Where before such a transfer an independent trade union is recognised to any extent by the transferor in respect of employees of any description who in consequence of the transfer become employees of the transferee, then, after the transfer—

(a) the trade union shall be deemed to have been recognised by the transferee to the same extent in respect of employees of that description so employed; and
(b) any agreement for recognition may be varied or rescinded accordingly.

[2.874]
7 Dismissal of employee because of relevant transfer

[(1) Where either before or after a relevant transfer, any employee of the transferor or transferee is dismissed, that employee is to be treated for the purposes of Part 10 of the 1996 Act (unfair dismissal) as unfairly dismissed if the sole or principal reason for the dismissal is the transfer.

(2) This paragraph applies where the sole or principal reason for the dismissal is an economic, technical or organisational reason entailing changes in the workforce of either the transferor or the transferee before or after a relevant transfer.

(3) Where paragraph (2) applies—
(a) paragraph (1) does not apply;
(b) without prejudice to the application of section 98(4) of the 1996 Act (test of fair dismissal), for the purposes of sections 98(1) and 135 of that Act (reason for dismissal)—
(i) the dismissal is regarded as having been for redundancy where section 98(2)(c) of that Act applies; or
(ii) in any other case, the dismissal is regarded as having been for a substantial reason of a kind such as to justify the dismissal of an employee holding the position which that employee held.

(3A) In paragraph (2), the expression "changes in the workforce" includes a change to the place where employees are employed by the employer to carry on the business of the employer or to carry out work of a particular kind for the employer (and the reference to such a place has the same meaning as in section 139 of the 1996 Act).]

(4) The provisions of this regulation apply irrespective of whether the employee in question is assigned to the organised grouping of resources or employees that is, or will be, transferred.

(5) Paragraph (1) shall not apply in relation to the dismissal of any employee which was required by reason of the application of section 5 of the Aliens Restriction (Amendment) Act 1919 to his employment.

(6) Paragraph (1) shall not apply in relation to a dismissal of an employee if the application of section 94 of the 1996 Act to the dismissal of the employee is excluded by or under any provision of the 1996 Act, the 1996 Tribunals Act or the 1992 Act.

NOTES

Paras (1)–(3A): substituted, for the original paras (1)–(3), by the Collective Redundancies and Transfer of Undertakings (Protection of Employment) (Amendment) Regulations 2014, SI 2014/16, regs 4, 8(1).

Aliens Restriction (Amendment) Act 1919: s 5 was repealed by the Merchant Shipping Act 1970, Sch 5, as from 1 August 1995 (see the Merchant Shipping Act 1970 (Commencement No 12) Order 1995, SI 1995/1426).

[2.875]
8 Insolvency

(1) If at the time of a relevant transfer the transferor is subject to relevant insolvency proceedings paragraphs (2) to (6) apply.

(2) In this regulation "relevant employee" means an employee of the transferor—
(a) whose contract of employment transfers to the transferee by virtue of the operation of these Regulations; or
(b) whose employment with the transferor is terminated before the time of the relevant transfer in the circumstances described in regulation 7(1).

(3) The relevant statutory scheme specified in paragraph (4)(b) (including that sub-paragraph as applied by paragraph 5 of Schedule 1) shall apply in the case of a relevant employee irrespective of the fact that the qualifying requirement that the employee's employment has been terminated is not met and for those purposes the date of the transfer shall be treated as the date of the termination and the transferor shall be treated as the employer.

(4) In this regulation the "relevant statutory schemes" are—
(a) Chapter VI of Part XI of the 1996 Act;
(b) Part XII of the 1996 Act.

(5) Regulation 4 shall not operate to transfer liability for the sums payable to the relevant employee under the relevant statutory schemes.

(6) In this regulation "relevant insolvency proceedings" means insolvency proceedings which have been opened in relation to the transferor not with a view to the liquidation of the assets of the transferor and which are under the supervision of an insolvency practitioner.

(7) Regulations 4 and 7 do not apply to any relevant transfer where the transferor is the subject of bankruptcy proceedings or any analogous insolvency proceedings which have been instituted with a view to the liquidation of the assets of the transferor and are under the supervision of an insolvency practitioner.

[2.876]

9 Variations of contract where transferors are subject to relevant insolvency proceedings

(1) If at the time of a relevant transfer the transferor is subject to relevant insolvency proceedings these Regulations shall not prevent the transferor or transferee (or an insolvency practitioner) and appropriate representatives of assigned employees agreeing to permitted variations.

(2) For the purposes of this regulation "appropriate representatives" are—

(a) if the employees are of a description in respect of which an independent trade union is recognised by their employer, representatives of the trade union; or

(b) in any other case, whichever of the following employee representatives the employer chooses—

(i) employee representatives appointed or elected by the assigned employees (whether they make the appointment or election alone or with others) otherwise than for the purposes of this regulation, who (having regard to the purposes for, and the method by which they were appointed or elected) have authority from those employees to agree permitted variations to contracts of employment on their behalf;

(ii) employee representatives elected by assigned employees (whether they make the appointment or election alone or with others) for these particular purposes, in an election satisfying requirements identical to those contained in regulation 14 except those in regulation 14(1)(d).

(3) An individual may be an appropriate representative for the purposes of both this regulation and regulation 13 provided that where the representative is not a trade union representative he is either elected by or has authority from assigned employees (within the meaning of this regulation) and affected employees (as described in regulation 13(1)).

(4) . . .

(5) Where assigned employees are represented by non-trade union representatives—

(a) the agreement recording a permitted variation must be in writing and signed by each of the representatives who have made it or, where that is not reasonably practicable, by a duly authorised agent of that representative; and

(b) the employer must, before the agreement is made available for signature, provide all employees to whom it is intended to apply on the date on which it is to come into effect with copies of the text of the agreement and such guidance as those employees might reasonably require in order to understand it fully.

(6) A permitted variation shall take effect as a term or condition of the assigned employee's contract of employment in place, where relevant, of any term or condition which it varies.

(7) In this regulation—

"assigned employees" means those employees assigned to the organised grouping of resources or employees that is the subject of a relevant transfer;

"permitted variation" is a variation to the contract of employment of an assigned employee where—

[(a) the sole or principal reason for the variation is the transfer and not a reason referred to in regulation 4(5)(a); and]

(b) it is designed to safeguard employment opportunities by ensuring the survival of the undertaking, business or part of the undertaking or business that is the subject of the relevant transfer;

"relevant insolvency proceedings" has the meaning given to the expression by regulation 8(6).

NOTES

Para (4): amends the Trade Union and Labour Relations (Consolidation) Act 1992, s 168 at **[1.477]**.

Para (7): in definition "permitted variation" sub-para (a) substituted by the Collective Redundancies and Transfer of Undertakings (Protection of Employment) (Amendment) Regulations 2014, SI 2014/16, regs 4, 9.

[2.877]

10 Pensions

(1) Regulations 4 and 5 shall not apply—

(a) to so much of a contract of employment or collective agreement as relates to an occupational pension scheme within the meaning of the Pension Schemes Act 1993; or

(b) to any rights, powers, duties or liabilities under or in connection with any such contract or subsisting by virtue of any such agreement and relating to such a scheme or otherwise arising in connection with that person's employment and relating to such a scheme.

(2) For the purposes of paragraphs (1) and (3), any provisions of an occupational pension scheme which do not relate to benefits for old age, invalidity or survivors shall not be treated as being part of the scheme.

(3) An employee whose contract of employment is transferred in the circumstances described in regulation 4(1) shall not be entitled to bring a claim against the transferor for—

(a) breach of contract; or

(b) constructive unfair dismissal under section 95(1)(c) of the 1996 Act,

arising out of a loss or reduction in his rights under an occupational pension scheme in consequence of the transfer, save insofar as the alleged breach of contract or dismissal (as the case may be) occurred prior to the date on which these Regulations took effect.

[2.878]

11 Notification of Employee Liability Information

(1) The transferor shall notify to the transferee the employee liability information of any person employed by him who is assigned to the organised grouping of resources or employees that is the subject of a relevant transfer—

(a) in writing; or

(b) by making it available to him in a readily accessible form.

(2) In this regulation and in regulation 12 "employee liability information" means—

(a) the identity and age of the employee;

(b) those particulars of employment that an employer is obliged to give to an employee pursuant to section 1 of the 1996 Act;

(c) information of any—

(i) disciplinary procedure taken against an employee;

(ii) grievance procedure taken by an employee,

within the previous two years, in circumstances where [a Code of Practice issued under Part IV of the Trade Union and Labour Relations Act 1992 which relates exclusively or primarily to the resolution of disputes applies];

(d) information of any court or tribunal case, claim or action—

(i) brought by an employee against the transferor, within the previous two years;

(ii) that the transferor has reasonable grounds to believe that an employee may bring against the transferee, arising out of the employee's employment with the transferor; and

(e) information of any collective agreement which will have effect after the transfer, in its application in relation to the employee, pursuant to regulation 5(a).

(3) Employee liability information shall contain information as at a specified date not more than fourteen days before the date on which the information is notified to the transferee.

(4) The duty to provide employee liability information in paragraph (1) shall include a duty to provide employee liability information of any person who would have been employed by the transferor and assigned to the organised grouping of resources or employees that is the subject of a relevant transfer immediately before the transfer if he had not been dismissed in the circumstances described in regulation 7(1), including, where the transfer is effected by a series of two or more transactions, a person so employed and assigned or who would have been so employed and assigned immediately before any of those transactions.

(5) Following notification of the employee liability information in accordance with this regulation, the transferor shall notify the transferee in writing of any change in the employee liability information.

(6) A notification under this regulation shall be given not less than [28 days] before the relevant transfer or, if special circumstances make this not reasonably practicable, as soon as reasonably practicable thereafter.

(7) A notification under this regulation may be given—

(a) in more than one instalment;

(b) indirectly, through a third party.

NOTES

Para (2): words in square brackets in sub-para (c) substituted by the Transfer of Undertakings (Protection of Employment) (Amendment) Regulations 2009, SI 2009/592, reg 2(1), (2).

Para (6): words in square brackets substituted by the Collective Redundancies and Transfer of Undertakings (Protection of Employment) (Amendment) Regulations 2014, SI 2014/16, regs 4, 10.

[2.879]

12 Remedy for failure to notify employee liability information

(1) On or after a relevant transfer, the transferee may present a complaint to an employment tribunal that the transferor has failed to comply with any provision of regulation 11.

(2) An employment tribunal shall not consider a complaint under this regulation unless it is presented—

(a) before the end of the period of three months beginning with the date of the relevant transfer;

(b) within such further period as the tribunal considers reasonable in a case where it is satisfied that it was not reasonably practicable for the complaint to be presented before the end of that period of three months.

[(2A) Regulation 16A (extension of time limits to facilitate conciliation before institution of proceedings) applies for the purposes of paragraph (2).]

(3) Where an employment tribunal finds a complaint under paragraph (1) well-founded, the tribunal—

(a) shall make a declaration to that effect; and

(b) may make an award of compensation to be paid by the transferor to the transferee.

(4) The amount of the compensation shall be such as the tribunal considers just and equitable in all the circumstances, subject to paragraph (5), having particular regard to—

(a) any loss sustained by the transferee which is attributable to the matters complained of; and

(b) the terms of any contract between the transferor and the transferee relating to the transfer under which the transferor may be liable to pay any sum to the transferee in respect of a failure to notify the transferee of employee liability information.

(5) Subject to paragraph (6), the amount of compensation awarded under paragraph (3) shall be not less than £500 per employee in respect of whom the transferor has failed to comply with a provision of regulation 11, unless the tribunal considers it just and equitable, in all the circumstances, to award a lesser sum.

(6) In ascertaining the loss referred to in paragraph (4)(a) the tribunal shall apply the same rule concerning the duty of a person to mitigate his loss as applies to any damages recoverable under the common law of England and Wales, Northern Ireland or Scotland, as applicable.

(7) [Sections 18A to 18C] of the 1996 Tribunals Act (conciliation) shall apply to the right conferred by this regulation and to proceedings under this regulation as it applies to the rights conferred by that Act and the employment tribunal proceedings mentioned in that Act.

NOTES

Para (2A): inserted by the Enterprise and Regulatory Reform Act 2013 (Consequential Amendments) (Employment) (No 2) Order 2014, SI 2014/853, arts 2(1), (2), 3.

Para (7): words in square brackets substituted by the Enterprise and Regulatory Reform Act 2013 (Consequential Amendments) (Employment) Order 2014, SI 2014/386, art 2, Schedule, paras 36, 37.

[2.880]

13 Duty to inform and consult representatives

(1) In this regulation and regulations [13A,] 14 and 15 references to affected employees, in relation to a relevant transfer, are to any employees of the transferor or the transferee (whether or not assigned to the organised grouping of resources or employees that is the subject of a relevant transfer) who may be affected by the transfer or may be affected by measures taken in connection with it; and references to the employer shall be construed accordingly.

(2) Long enough before a relevant transfer to enable the employer of any affected employees to consult the appropriate representatives of any affected employees, the employer shall inform those representatives of—

(a) the fact that the transfer is to take place, the date or proposed date of the transfer and the reasons for it;

(b) the legal, economic and social implications of the transfer for any affected employees;

(c) the measures which he envisages he will, in connection with the transfer, take in relation to any affected employees or, if he envisages that no measures will be so taken, that fact; and

(d) if the employer is the transferor, the measures, in connection with the transfer, which he envisages the transferee will take in relation to any affected employees who will become employees of the transferee after the transfer by virtue of regulation 4 or, if he envisages that no measures will be so taken, that fact.

[(2A) Where information is to be supplied under paragraph (2) by an employer—

(a) this must include suitable information relating to the use of agency workers (if any) by that employer; and

(b) "suitable information relating to the use of agency workers" means—

(i) the number of agency workers working temporarily for and under the supervision and direction of the employer;

(ii) the parts of the employer's undertaking in which those agency workers are working; and

(iii) the type of work those agency workers are carrying out.]

(3) For the purposes of this regulation the appropriate representatives of any affected employees are—

(a) if the employees are of a description in respect of which an independent trade union is recognised by their employer, representatives of the trade union; or

(b) in any other case, whichever of the following employee representatives the employer chooses—

(i) employee representatives appointed or elected by the affected employees otherwise than for the purposes of this regulation, who (having regard to the purposes for, and the method by which they were appointed or elected) have authority from those employees to receive information and to be consulted about the transfer on their behalf;

(ii) employee representatives elected by any affected employees, for the purposes of this regulation, in an election satisfying the requirements of regulation 14(1).

(4) The transferee shall give the transferor such information at such a time as will enable the transferor to perform the duty imposed on him by virtue of paragraph (2)(d).

(5) The information which is to be given to the appropriate representatives shall be given to each of them by being delivered to them, or sent by post to an address notified by them to the employer, or (in the case of representatives of a trade union) sent by post to the trade union at the address of its head or main office.

(6) An employer of an affected employee who envisages that he will take measures in relation to an affected employee, in connection with the relevant transfer, shall consult the appropriate representatives of that employee with a view to seeking their agreement to the intended measures.

(7) In the course of those consultations the employer shall—

(a) consider any representations made by the appropriate representatives; and

(b) reply to those representations and, if he rejects any of those representations, state his reasons.

(8) The employer shall allow the appropriate representatives access to any affected employees and shall afford to those representatives such accommodation and other facilities as may be appropriate.

(9) If in any case there are special circumstances which render it not reasonably practicable for an employer to perform a duty imposed on him by any of paragraphs (2) to (7), he shall take all such steps towards performing that duty as are reasonably practicable in the circumstances.

(10) Where—

(a) the employer has invited any of the affected employee to elect employee representatives; and
(b) the invitation was issued long enough before the time when the employer is required to give information under paragraph (2) to allow them to elect representatives by that time,

the employer shall be treated as complying with the requirements of this regulation in relation to those employees if he complies with those requirements as soon as is reasonably practicable after the election of the representatives.

(11) If, after the employer has invited any affected employees to elect representatives, they fail to do so within a reasonable time, he shall give to any affected employees the information set out in paragraph (2).

(12) The duties imposed on an employer by this regulation shall apply irrespective of whether the decision resulting in the relevant transfer is taken by the employer or a person controlling the employer.

NOTES

Para (1): figure in square brackets inserted by the Collective Redundancies and Transfer of Undertakings (Protection of Employment) (Amendment) Regulations 2014, SI 2014/16, regs 4, 11(1), (5), in relation to a TUPE transfer which takes place on or after 31 July 2014.

Para (2A): inserted by the Agency Workers Regulations 2010, SI 2010/93, reg 25, Sch 2, Pt 2, paras 28, 29.

[2.881]

[13A Micro-business's duty to inform and consult where no appropriate representatives

(1) This regulation applies if, at the time when the employer is required to give information under regulation 13(2)—

(a) the employer employs fewer than 10 employees;
(b) there are no appropriate representatives within the meaning of regulation 13(3); and
(c) the employer has not invited any of the affected employees to elect employee representatives.

(2) The employer may comply with regulation 13 by performing any duty which relates to appropriate representatives as if each of the affected employees were an appropriate representative.]

NOTES

Inserted by the Collective Redundancies and Transfer of Undertakings (Protection of Employment) (Amendment) Regulations 2014, SI 2014/16, regs 4, 11(2), (5), in relation to a TUPE transfer which takes place on or after 31 July 2014.

[2.882]

14 Election of employee representatives

(1) The requirements for the election of employee representatives under regulation 13(3) are that—

(a) the employer shall make such arrangements as are reasonably practicable to ensure that the election is fair;
(b) the employer shall determine the number of representatives to be elected so that there are sufficient representatives to represent the interests of all affected employees having regard to the number and classes of those employees;
(c) the employer shall determine whether the affected employees should be represented either by representatives of all the affected employees or by representatives of particular classes of those employees;
(d) before the election the employer shall determine the term of office as employee representatives so that it is of sufficient length to enable information to be given and consultations under regulation 13 to be completed;
(e) the candidates for election as employee representatives are affected employees on the date of the election;
(f) no affected employee is unreasonably excluded from standing for election;
(g) all affected employees on the date of the election are entitled to vote for employee representatives;
(h) the employees entitled to vote may vote for as many candidates as there are representatives to be elected to represent them or, if there are to be representatives for particular classes of employees, may vote for as many candidates as there are representatives to be elected to represent their particular class of employee;
(i) the election is conducted so as to secure that—
   (i) so far as is reasonably practicable, those voting do so in secret; and
   (ii) the votes given at the election are accurately counted.

(2) Where, after an election of employee representatives satisfying the requirements of paragraph (1) has been held, one of those elected ceases to act as an employee representative and as a result any affected employees are no longer represented, those employees shall elect another representative by an election satisfying the requirements of paragraph (1)(a), (e), (f) and (i).

[2.883]

15 Failure to inform or consult

(1) Where an employer has failed to comply with a requirement of regulation 13 or regulation 14, a complaint may be presented to an employment tribunal on that ground—

(a) in the case of a failure relating to the election of employee representatives, by any of his employees who are affected employees;

(b) in the case of any other failure relating to employee representatives, by any of the employee representatives to whom the failure related;

(c) in the case of failure relating to representatives of a trade union, by the trade union; and

(d) in any other case, by any of his employees who are affected employees.

(2) If on a complaint under paragraph (1) a question arises whether or not it was reasonably practicable for an employer to perform a particular duty or as to what steps he took towards performing it, it shall be for him to show—

(a) that there were special circumstances which rendered it not reasonably practicable for him to perform the duty; and

(b) that he took all such steps towards its performance as were reasonably practicable in those circumstances.

(3) If on a complaint under paragraph (1) a question arises as to whether or not an employee representative was an appropriate representative for the purposes of regulation 13, it shall be for the employer to show that the employee representative had the necessary authority to represent the affected employees [except where the question is whether or not regulation 13A applied].

[(3A) If on a complaint under paragraph (1), a question arises as to whether or not regulation 13A applied, it is for the employer to show that the conditions in sub-paragraphs (a) and (b) of regulation 13A(1) applied at the time referred to in regulation 13A(1).]

(4) On a complaint under paragraph (1)(a) it shall be for the employer to show that the requirements in regulation 14 have been satisfied.

(5) On a complaint against a transferor that he had failed to perform the duty imposed upon him by virtue of regulation 13(2)(d) or, so far as relating thereto, regulation 13(9), he may not show that it was not reasonably practicable for him to perform the duty in question for the reason that the transferee had failed to give him the requisite information at the requisite time in accordance with regulation 13(4) unless he gives the transferee notice of his intention to show that fact; and the giving of the notice shall make the transferee a party to the proceedings.

(6) In relation to any complaint under paragraph (1), a failure on the part of a person controlling (directly or indirectly) the employer to provide information to the employer shall not constitute special circumstances rendering it not reasonably practicable for the employer to comply with such a requirement.

(7) Where the tribunal finds a complaint against a transferee under paragraph (1) well-founded it shall make a declaration to that effect and may order the transferee to pay appropriate compensation to such descriptions of affected employees as may be specified in the award.

(8) Where the tribunal finds a complaint against a transferor under paragraph (1) well-founded it shall make a declaration to that effect and may—

(a) order the transferor, subject to paragraph (9), to pay appropriate compensation to such descriptions of affected employees as may be specified in the award; or

(b) if the complaint is that the transferor did not perform the duty mentioned in paragraph (5) and the transferor (after giving due notice) shows the facts so mentioned, order the transferee to pay appropriate compensation to such descriptions of affected employees as may be specified in the award.

(9) The transferee shall be jointly and severally liable with the transferor in respect of compensation payable under sub-paragraph (8)(a) or paragraph (11).

(10) An employee may present a complaint to an employment tribunal on the ground that he is an employee of a description to which an order under paragraph (7) or (8) relates and that—

(a) in respect of an order under paragraph (7), the transferee has failed, wholly or in part, to pay him compensation in pursuance of the order;

(b) in respect of an order under paragraph (8), the transferor or transferee, as applicable, has failed, wholly or in part, to pay him compensation in pursuance of the order.

(11) Where the tribunal finds a complaint under paragraph (10) well-founded it shall order the transferor or transferee as applicable to pay the complainant the amount of compensation which it finds is due to him.

(12) An employment tribunal shall not consider a complaint under paragraph (1) or (10) unless it is presented to the tribunal before the end of the period of three months beginning with—

(a) in respect of a complaint under paragraph (1), the date on which the relevant transfer is completed; or

(b) in respect of a complaint under paragraph (10), the date of the tribunal's order under paragraph (7) or (8),

or within such further period as the tribunal considers reasonable in a case where it is satisfied that it was not reasonably practicable for the complaint to be presented before the end of the period of three months.

[(13) Regulation 16A (extension of time limits to facilitate conciliation before institution of proceedings) applies for the purposes of paragraph (12).]

NOTES

Para (3): words in square brackets added by the Collective Redundancies and Transfer of Undertakings (Protection of Employment) (Amendment) Regulations 2014, SI 2014/16, regs 4, 11(3), (5), in relation to a TUPE transfer which takes place on or after 31 July 2014.

Para (3A): inserted by SI 2014/16, regs 4, 11(4), (5), in relation to a TUPE transfer which takes place on or after 31 July 2014.

Para (13): added by the Enterprise and Regulatory Reform Act 2013 (Consequential Amendments) (Employment) (No 2) Order 2014, SI 2014/853, arts 2(1), (3), 3.

[2.884]

16 Failure to inform or consult: supplemental

(1) Section 205(1) of the 1996 Act (complaint to be sole remedy for breach of relevant rights) and [sections 18A to 18C] of the 1996 Tribunals Act (conciliation) shall apply to the rights conferred by regulation 15 and to proceedings under this regulation as they apply to the rights conferred by those Acts and the employment tribunal proceedings mentioned in those Acts.

(2) An appeal shall lie and shall lie only to the Employment Appeal Tribunal on a question of law arising from any decision of, or arising in any proceedings before, an employment tribunal under or by virtue of these Regulations; and section 11(1) of the Tribunals and Inquiries Act 1992 (appeals from certain tribunals to the High Court) shall not apply in relation to any such proceedings.

(3) "Appropriate compensation" in regulation 15 means such sum not exceeding thirteen weeks' pay for the employee in question as the tribunal considers just and equitable having regard to the seriousness of the failure of the employer to comply with his duty.

(4) Sections 220 to 228 of the 1996 Act shall apply for calculating the amount of a week's pay for any employee for the purposes of paragraph (3) and, for the purposes of that calculation, the calculation date shall be—

- (a) in the case of an employee who is dismissed by reason of redundancy (within the meaning of sections 139 and 155 of the 1996 Act) the date which is the calculation date for the purposes of any entitlement of his to a redundancy payment (within the meaning of those sections) or which would be that calculation date if he were so entitled;
- (b) in the case of an employee who is dismissed for any other reason, the effective date of termination (within the meaning of sections 95(1) and (2) and 97 of the 1996 Act) of his contract of employment;
- (c) in any other case, the date of the relevant transfer.

NOTES

Para (1): words in square brackets substituted by the Enterprise and Regulatory Reform Act 2013 (Consequential Amendments) (Employment) Order 2014, SI 2014/386, art 2, Schedule, paras 36, 38.

[2.885]

[16A Extension of time limit to facilitate conciliation before institution of proceedings

(1) This regulation applies where these Regulations provide for it to apply for the purposes of a provision in these Regulations ("a relevant provision").

(2) In this regulation—

- (a) Day A is the day on which the worker concerned complies with the requirement in subsection (1) of section 18A of the Employment Tribunals Act 1996 (requirement to contact ACAS before instituting proceedings) in relation to the matter in respect of which the proceedings are brought, and
- (b) Day B is the day on which the worker concerned receives or, if earlier, is treated as receiving (by virtue of regulations made under subsection (11) of that section) the certificate issued under subsection (4) of that section.

(3) In working out when the time limit set by a relevant provision expires the period beginning with the day after Day A and ending with Day B is not to be counted.

(4) If the time limit set by a relevant provision would (if not extended by this paragraph) expire during the period beginning with Day A and ending one month after Day B, the time limit expires instead at the end of that period.

(5) Where an employment tribunal has power under these Regulations to extend the time limit set by a relevant provision, the power is exercisable in relation to that time limit as extended by this regulation.]

NOTES

Inserted by the Enterprise and Regulatory Reform Act 2013 (Consequential Amendments) (Employment) (No 2) Order 2014, SI 2014/853, arts 2(1), (4), 3.

[2.886]

17 Employers' Liability Compulsory Insurance

(1) Paragraph (2) applies where—

- (a) by virtue of section 3(1)(a) or (b) of the Employers' Liability (Compulsory Insurance) Act 1969 ("the 1969 Act"), the transferor is not required by that Act to effect any insurance; or
- (b) by virtue of section 3(1)(c) of the 1969 Act, the transferor is exempted from the requirement of that Act to effect insurance.

(2) Where this paragraph applies, on completion of a relevant transfer the transferor and the transferee shall be jointly and severally liable in respect of any liability referred to in section 1(1) of the 1969 Act, in so far as such liability relates to the employee's employment with the transferor.

[2.887]
18 Restriction on contracting out

Section 203 of the 1996 Act (restrictions on contracting out) shall apply in relation to these Regulations as if they were contained in that Act, save for that section shall not apply in so far as these Regulations provide for an agreement (whether a contract of employment or not) to exclude or limit the operation of these Regulations.

19 (*Amends the Employment Rights Act 1996, s 104 at* **[1.1015]**.)

[2.888]
20 Repeals, revocations and amendments

(1) Subject to regulation 21, the 1981 Regulations are revoked.

(2) Section 33 of, and paragraph 4 of Schedule 9 to, the Trade Union Reform and Employment Rights Act 1993 are repealed.

(3) Schedule 2 (consequential amendments) shall have effect.

[2.889]
21 Transitional provisions and savings

(1) These Regulations shall apply in relation to—
- (a) a relevant transfer that takes place on or after 6 April 2006;
- (b) a transfer or service provision change, not falling within sub-paragraph (a), that takes place on or after 6 April 2006 and is regarded by virtue of any enactment as a relevant transfer.

(2) The 1981 Regulations shall continue to apply in relation to—
- (a) a relevant transfer (within the meaning of the 1981 Regulations) that took place before 6 April 2006;
- (b) a transfer, not falling within sub-paragraph (a), that took place before 6 April 2006 and is regarded by virtue of any enactment as a relevant transfer (within the meaning of the 1981 Regulations).

(3) In respect of a relevant transfer that takes place on or after 6 April 2006, any action taken by a transferor or transferee to discharge a duty that applied to them under regulation 10 or 10A of the 1981 Regulations shall be deemed to satisfy the corresponding obligation imposed by regulations 13 and 14 of these Regulations, insofar as that action would have discharged those obligations had the action taken place on or after 6 April 2006.

(4) The duty on a transferor to provide a transferee with employee liability information shall not apply in the case of a relevant transfer that takes place on or before 19 April 2006.

(5) Regulations 13, 14, 15 and 16 shall not apply in the case of a service provision change that is not also a transfer of an undertaking, business or part of an undertaking or business that takes place on or before 4 May 2006.

(6) The repeal of paragraph 4 of Schedule 9 to the Trade Union Reform and Employment Rights Act 1993 does not affect the continued operation of that paragraph so far as it remains capable of having effect.

SCHEDULES 1, 2

(Sch 1 (Application of the Regulations to Northern Ireland) outside the scope of this work; Sch 2 contains consequential amendments only and, in so far as relevant to this work, these have been incorporated at the appropriate place.)

OCCUPATIONAL AND PERSONAL PENSION SCHEMES (CONSULTATION BY EMPLOYERS AND MISCELLANEOUS AMENDMENT) REGULATIONS 2006

(SI 2006/349)

NOTES

Made: 15 February 2006.

Authority: Pensions Act 2004, ss 10(5)(a), 259(1), (2), 260(1), 261(2), (4), 286(1), (3)(g), 315(2), (3), (5), 318(1), (4)(a), (5).

Commencement: 6 February 2006 (reg 22); 6 April 2006 (otherwise).

Conciliation: employment tribunal proceedings under paras 4 or 8 of the Schedule are "relevant proceedings" for the purposes of the conciliation provisions contained in the Employment Tribunals Act 1996, ss 18–18C; see s 18(1)(t) of the 1996 Act at **[1.757]**.

Employment Appeal Tribunal: an appeal lies to the Employment Appeal Tribunal on any question of law arising from any decision of, or in any proceedings before, an employment tribunal under or by virtue of the Schedule to these Regulations; see the Employment Tribunals Act 1996, s 21(1)(r) at **[1.764]**.

See *Harvey* CII(6).

ARRANGEMENT OF REGULATIONS

Introductory

Introductory

[2.890]

1 Citation, commencement and extent

(1) These Regulations may be cited as the Occupational and Personal Pension Schemes (Consultation by Employers and Miscellaneous Amendment) Regulations 2006.

(2) Subject to paragraph (3), these Regulations shall come into force on 6th April 2006.

(3) Regulation 22 shall come into force on the day after the day on which these Regulations are made.

(4) Regulation 22 extends to Northern Ireland.

[2.891]

2 Interpretation

In these Regulations—

"active member"—

(a) in relation to an occupational pension scheme, has the meaning given by section 124 of the Pensions Act 1995 (interpretation), and

(b) in relation to a personal pension scheme, means any member in respect of whom employer contributions fall to be paid;

"affected members" has the meaning given by regulation 7(4);

"employer contributions", in relation to an occupational or personal pension scheme, means contributions payable by or on behalf of the employer in relation to the scheme on his own account (but in respect of one or more employees);

"member contributions", in relation to an occupational or personal pension scheme, means contributions, other than voluntary contributions, by or on behalf of active members of the scheme which are payable out of deductions from the member's earnings;

"listed change" has the meaning given by regulation 6(2);

"multi-employer scheme" has the meaning given by section 307 of the Pensions Act 2004 (modification of Act in relation to certain categories of schemes);

"personal pension scheme" has the meaning given by regulation 3(3);

"prospective member"—

(a) in relation to an occupational pension scheme, means any person who, under the terms of his contract of service or the rules of the scheme—

(i) is able, at his own option, to become a member of the scheme,

(ii) will become so able if he continues in the same employment for a sufficiently long period,

(iii) will be admitted to the scheme automatically unless he makes an election not to become a member, or

(iv) may be admitted to it subject to the consent of his employer;

(b) in relation to a personal pension scheme, means any person who, under the terms of his contract of service, is eligible if he becomes a member of the scheme for employer contributions to be paid in respect of him;

"the Regulator" means the Pensions Regulator established under section 1 of the Pensions Act 2004 (the Pensions Regulator); and

"relevant employer" has the meaning given by regulation 3(2).

Application of Regulations

[2.892]

3 Application

(1) These Regulations apply to—

(a) in the case of an occupational pension scheme which is not a multi-employer scheme—

(i) any relevant employer, and

(ii) if there is a relevant employer, the trustees or managers of the scheme;

(b) in the case of a multi-employer scheme in relation to which there are one or more relevant employers—

(i) each relevant employer,

(ii) the trustees or managers of the scheme, and

(iii) any other person who, under the rules of the scheme, has the power to make a listed change affecting the scheme; and

(c) in the case of a personal pension scheme where direct payment arrangements exist in respect of one or more members of the scheme who are his employees, a relevant employer.

[(2) For the purposes of these Regulations "relevant employer" means—

(a) an employer employing in Great Britain at least the number of employees specified in paragraph (2A); and

(b) in the case of—

(i) an occupational pension scheme, an employer in relation to the scheme other than one who is excluded by regulation 4, and

(ii) a personal pension scheme, an employer in relation to the scheme other than one who is excluded by regulation 5.

(2A) The number of employees referred to in paragraph (2)(a) is—

(a) 150 from 6th April 2006 to 5th April 2007,

(b) 100 from 6th April 2007 to 5th April 2008, and

(c) 50 from 6th April 2008 onwards.

(2B) For the purposes of paragraph (2)(a)—

(a) the number of people employed by an employer is to be determined using the same method of calculation as is set out in regulation 4 of the Information and Consultation of Employees Regulations 2004 (calculation of number of employees), but

(b) references in that regulation to the previous twelve months are to be taken as references to the period of twelve months ending with the date of the proposal to make a listed change to which regulation 6 of these Regulations applies.]

(3) In these Regulations references to a personal pension scheme are to a personal pension scheme falling within paragraph (1)(c).

NOTES

Paras (2), (2A), (2B): substituted (for the original para (2)) by the Occupational and Personal Pension Schemes (Miscellaneous Amendments) Regulations 2006, SI 2006/778, reg 10(1), (2).

[2.893]

4 Excluded employers: occupational pension schemes

(1) This regulation excludes—

(a) any employer in relation to a public service pension scheme;

(b) any employer in relation to a small occupational pension scheme;

(c) any employer in relation to an occupational pension scheme with fewer than two members;

(d) any employer in relation to an occupational pension scheme which is an employer-financed retirement benefits scheme;

(e) any employer in relation to an unregistered occupational pension scheme which has its main administration outside the *[EEA states]*; and

(f) . . .

(2), (3) . . .

(4) In this regulation—

"employer-financed retirement benefits scheme" has the meaning given by section 393A of the Income Tax (Earnings and Pensions) Act 2003 (employer-financed retirement benefits scheme);

"public service pension scheme" has the meaning given by section 1(1) of the Pension Schemes Act 1993;

"small occupational pension scheme" means—

(a) a scheme with fewer than twelve members where all of the members are trustees of the scheme and either—

Part 2 Statutory Instruments

(i) the provisions of the scheme provide that [any decision made by the trustees is made by the unanimous agreement of] the trustees who are members of the scheme, or

(ii) the scheme has a trustee who is independent in relation to the scheme for the purposes of section 23 of the Pensions Act 1995 (power to appoint independent trustees) and is registered in the register maintained by the Regulator in accordance with regulations made under subsection 9(4) of that section;

(b) a scheme with fewer than twelve members [where a company is the sole trustee] of the scheme, and all the members of the scheme are directors of the company and either—

(i) the provisions of the scheme provide that any decision made by the company in its capacity as trustee [is made by the unanimous agreement of the directors] who are members of the scheme, or

(ii) [one of the directors of the company] is independent in relation to the scheme for the purposes of section 23 of the Pensions Act 1995 and is registered in the register maintained by the Regulator in accordance with regulations made under subsection 9(4) of that section; and

"unregistered occupational pension scheme" means an occupational pension scheme which is not registered under section 153 of the Finance Act 2004 (registration of pension schemes).

NOTES

Para (1): words in square brackets and italics in sub-para (e) substituted by the Occupational Pension Schemes (EEA States) Regulations 2007, SI 2007/3014, reg 2(b), Schedule, para 9 and further substituted by the words "United Kingdom", by the Occupational and Personal Pension Schemes (Amendment etc) (EU Exit) Regulations 2019, SI 2019/192, reg 31, as from exit day (as defined in the European Union (Withdrawal) Act 2018, s 20). Sub-para (f) revoked by the Occupational and Personal Pension Schemes (Miscellaneous Amendments) Regulations 2006, SI 2006/778, reg 10(1), (3).

Paras (2), (3): revoked by SI 2006/778, reg 10(3).

Para (4): words in square brackets in definition "small occupational pension scheme" substituted by the Occupational and Personal Pension Schemes (Miscellaneous Amendments) Regulations 2007, SI 2007/814, reg 19.

[2.894]

[5 Excluded employers: personal pension schemes

This regulation excludes any employer in relation to a personal pension scheme where no employer contributions fall to be paid towards the scheme.]

NOTES

Substituted by the Occupational and Personal Pension Schemes (Miscellaneous Amendments) Regulations 2006, SI 2006/778, reg 10(1), (4).

Restriction on Decision-Making Pending Completion of Consultation

[2.895]

6 Consultation required before decisions to make listed changes affecting schemes

(1) No person falling within regulation 3(1) may decide to make a listed change that affects an occupational or personal pension scheme unless such consultation as is required by regulation 7(3) has been carried out.

(2) For the purposes of these Regulations, a change affecting an occupational or personal pension scheme is a "listed change" if—

(a) in relation to an occupational pension scheme, it is listed in regulation 8, or

(b) in relation to a personal pension scheme, it is listed in regulation 9,

and it is not excluded by virtue of regulation 10.

(3) Paragraph (1) does not require consultation to be carried out in any of the four cases described in paragraphs (4) to (7).

[(4) The first case is where the active or prospective members of the scheme to whom—

(a) a listed change mentioned in regulation 8(1)(h) relates were notified before 6th April 2012 of the proposal to make that change, or

(b) any other listed change relates were notified before 6th April 2006 of the proposal to make that change.]

(5) The second case is where, in relation to an occupational pension scheme—

(a) consultation has already been carried out under these Regulations in respect of a proposal to prevent the future accrual of benefits, as described in regulation 8(1)(c), and

(b) there is a further proposal as a result of that consultation to make a decision to reduce the rate of such accrual, as described in regulation 8(3)(d).

(6) The third case is where, in relation to an occupational pension scheme—

(a) consultation has already been carried out under these Regulations in respect of a proposal to remove the liability to make employer contributions, as described in regulation 8(1)(d), and

(b) there is a further proposal as a result of that consultation to make a decision to reduce such contributions, as described in regulation 8(2).

(7) The fourth case is where, in relation to a personal pension scheme—

(a) consultation has already been carried out under these Regulations in respect of a proposal to cease employer contributions, as described in regulation 9(a), and

(b) there is a further proposal as a result of that consultation to make a decision to reduce such contributions, as described in regulation 9(b).

NOTES

Para (4): substituted by the Pensions (Institute and Faculty of Actuaries and Consultation by Employers—Amendment) Regulations 2012, SI 2012/692, reg 2(1), (2).

[2.896]

7 Notifications to employers and duty to consult

(1) Any person falling within regulation 3(1) who proposes to make a listed change affecting an occupational or personal pension scheme must give written notice of that change to each employer in relation to the scheme.

(2) Paragraph (1) does not apply—

(a) in any of the four cases described in regulation 6(4) to (7), or

(b) where the person proposing the change is a relevant employer in relation to—

(i) an occupational pension scheme which is not a multi-employer scheme, or

(ii) a personal pension scheme[, or

(c) where the person proposing the change employs all the affected members].

[(3) A relevant employer must consult about the listed change in accordance with regulations 11 to 16 if—

(a) it employs all the affected members, or

(b) its employees appear to it to include affected members and it is a relevant employer who—

(i) has been notified under paragraph (1), or

(ii) falls within paragraph (2)(b).]

(4) For the purposes of these Regulations "affected members", in relation to a proposal to make a listed change affecting an occupational or personal pension scheme, means the active or prospective members of the scheme to whom the listed change relates.

NOTES

Para (2): sub-para (c) and the word immediately preceding it inserted by the Occupational and Personal Pension Schemes (Miscellaneous Amendments) Regulations 2011, SI 2011/672, reg 7(a).

Para (3): substituted by SI 2011/672, reg 7(b).

[2.897]

8 Listed changes: occupational pension schemes

(1) Listed changes that affect occupational pension schemes are—

(a) to increase the normal pension age specified in the scheme rules for members or members of a particular description;

(b) to prevent new members, or new members of a particular description, from being admitted to the scheme;

(c) to prevent the future accrual of benefits under the scheme for or in respect of members or members of a particular description;

(d) to remove the liability to make employer contributions towards the scheme in respect of members or members of a particular description;

(e) to introduce member contributions in any circumstances in which no such contributions were previously payable;

(f) to make any increase in member contributions by or on behalf of members or members of a particular description;

(g) to make any change specified in paragraph (2) or (3);

[(h) to change the rate at which—

(i) pensions in payment under the scheme are increased, or

(ii) pensions or other benefits payable under the scheme are revalued,

but only where that change would be, or would be likely to be, less generous to members or members of a particular description].

(2) A listed change affecting only money purchase benefits is to make any reduction in the amount of employer contributions towards the scheme in respect of members or members of a particular description.

(3) Listed changes affecting only benefits which are not money purchase benefits are—

(a) to change to money purchase benefits some or all of the benefits that may be provided under the scheme to or in respect of members or members of a particular description;

(b) to change, in whole or in part, the basis for determining the rate of future accrual of benefits under the scheme for or in respect of members or members of a particular description;

(c) to modify the scheme under section 229(2) of the Pensions Act 2004 (matters requiring agreement of the employer) so as to reduce the rate of future accrual of benefits under the scheme for or in respect of members or members of a particular description;

(d) to make any other reduction in the rate of future accrual of benefit under the scheme for or in respect of members or members of a particular description.

[(e) to change what elements of pay constitute pensionable earnings, or to change the proportion of or limit the amount of any element of pay that forms part of pensionable earnings, for or in respect of members or members of a particular description].

(4) "Normal pension age" has the meaning given by section 180 of the Pension Schemes Act 1993 (normal pension age).

[(5) "Pensionable earnings" means the earnings by reference to which pension benefits are calculated, and an "element of pay" includes basic salary, a pay rise, an overtime payment, and a bonus payment.]

NOTES

Para (1): sub-para (h) inserted by the Pensions (Institute and Faculty of Actuaries and Consultation by Employers—Amendment) Regulations 2012, SI 2012/692, reg 2(1), (3).

Para (3): sub-para (e) added by the Occupational and Personal Pension Schemes (Miscellaneous Amendments) Regulations 2010, SI 2010/499, reg 7(1), (2).

Para (5): added by SI 2010/499, reg 7(1), (3).

[2.898]

9 Listed changes: personal pension schemes

Listed changes that affect personal pension schemes are—

(a) to cease employer contributions towards the scheme in respect of members or members of a particular description;

(b) to make any reduction in the amount of employer contributions towards the scheme in respect of members or members of a particular description;

(c) to make any increase in member contributions by or on behalf of members or members of a particular description.

[2.899]

10 Listed changes: exclusions

(1) For the purposes of regulations 8 and 9, no account is to be taken of any change which—

(a) is made for the purposes of complying with a statutory provision,

[(aa) is made for the purposes of implementing an adjustment measure within regulation 10 of the Occupational Pension Scheme (Charges and Governance) Regulations 2015,]

[(ab) is made for either or both of the purposes referred to in regulation 7C(1) (modification of schemes: revaluation of guaranteed minimum pensions) of the Occupational Pension Schemes (Modification of Schemes) Regulations 2006,]

(b) is made for the purposes of complying with a determination made by the Regulator, or

(c) has no lasting effect on a person's rights to be admitted to a scheme or on the benefits that may be provided under it.

(2) No change which is—

(a) a regulated modification within the meaning of the subsisting rights provisions, and

(b) subject to the requirements of those provisions,

falls within regulation 8.

(3) "Statutory provision" means a provision comprised in—

(a) an Act of Parliament or subordinate legislation made under such an Act, whenever passed or made,

(b) an Act of the Scottish Parliament or subordinate legislation made under such an Act, whenever passed or made.

(4) "Subsisting rights provisions" has the meaning given by section 67 of the Pensions Act 1995 (the subsisting rights provisions).

NOTES

Para (1): sub-para (aa) inserted by the Occupational Pension Schemes (Charges and Governance) Regulations 2015, SI 2015/879, reg 13(1), as from 6 April 2015.

Para (1): sub-para (ab) inserted by the Occupational and Personal Pension Schemes (Modification of Schemes—Miscellaneous Amendments) Regulations 2016, SI 2016/231, reg 3, as from 6 April 2016.

Information Provision and Consultation

[2.900]

11 Requirement to provide information

(1) In relation to a proposal to make a listed change affecting an occupational or personal pension scheme, each relevant employer to whom regulation 7(3) applies must provide information about the proposal to—

(a) such of his employees as appear to him to be affected members of the scheme, and

(b) any representatives of such members who are to be consulted under regulation 12(2)(a) or (3) or 13(2).

(2) The information provided under paragraph (1) must—

(a) be in writing,

(b) be provided before the start of consultation under regulation 12 or 13,

(c) describe the listed change and state what effects it would (or would be likely to) have on the scheme and its members,

(d) be accompanied by any relevant background information,

(e) indicate the timescale on which measures giving effect to the change are proposed to be introduced, and

(f) be given in such fashion and with such content as are appropriate to enable, in particular, representatives of affected members to consider, conduct a study of, and give their views to the employer on, the impact of the listed change on such members.

[(3) Information provided under this regulation may be provided in accordance with regulations 26 to 28 of the Occupational and Personal Pension Schemes (Disclosure of Information) Regulations 2013 (giving information and documents).]

NOTES

Para (3): added by the Occupational and Personal Pension Schemes (Disclosure of Information) Regulations 2013, SI 2013/2734, reg 1(4), Sch 9, para 15.

[2.901]

12 Consultation under existing arrangements

(1) If arrangements specified in paragraph (2) or (3) exist in relation to his employees, each relevant employer to whom regulation 7(3) applies must consult about a listed change in accordance with such one or more of those arrangements as he may choose.

(2) The specified arrangements are arrangements under which employees appearing to the employer to be affected members—

(a) are represented by—

(i) in the case of employees of a description in respect of which an independent trade union is recognised by the employer, the representatives of the trade union,

(ii) in the case of employees of a description which has elected or appointed information and consultation representatives, those representatives, or

(iii) where there exists one or more pre-existing agreements which apply to any of the employees, any representatives identified in accordance with such agreement or agreements; or

(b) are to be consulted directly in accordance with the terms of a negotiated agreement or a pre-existing agreement.

(3) In any case where—

(a) an election of representatives as described in regulation 13(2) has taken place before any arrangements referred to in paragraph (2) are made, and

(b) the interests of affected members are represented by such representatives,

the specified arrangements also include arrangements for consultation of those representatives.

(4) "Independent trade union" and "recognised", in relation to an independent trade union, have the same meaning as in the Trade Union and Labour Relations (Consolidation) Act 1992.

(5) "Information and consultation representatives" and "negotiated agreement" have the same meaning as in the Information and Consultation of Employees Regulations 2004.

(6) "Pre-existing agreement"—

(a) means an agreement between an employer and his employees or their representatives which satisfies the conditions set out in regulation 8(1)(a) to (d) of the Information and Consultation of Employees Regulations 2004 and which has not been superseded, but

(b) does not include an agreement concluded in accordance with regulations 17 or 42 to 45 of the Transnational Information and Consultation of Employees Regulations 1999 or a negotiated agreement.

[2.902]

13 Consultation in cases not covered by regulation 12

(1) This regulation applies to a relevant employer to whom regulation 7(3) applies if (and only if) any of the employees who appear to the employer to be affected members are not covered by consultation arrangements referred to in regulation 12.

(2) Where, for the purposes of engaging in consultations under these Regulations, representatives of any affected members have been elected in an election which satisfies the requirements of regulation 14(1), the relevant employer must consult with those representatives about a listed change.

(3) If the interests of any affected members are not represented by representatives who are consulted under paragraph (2), the relevant employer must also consult directly with those members.

(4) If no representatives have been elected as described in paragraph (2), the relevant employer must consult directly with the affected members about a listed change.

(5) Consultation under this regulation—

(a) is required only in relation to the affected members falling within paragraph (1), and

(b) is additional to any consultation in relation to other affected members which is required by regulation 12.

[2.903]

14 Election of representatives

(1) The requirements of this paragraph are that—

(a) the employer must make such arrangements as are reasonably practical to ensure that the election is fair;

(b) the employer must determine the number of representatives to be elected so that there are sufficient representatives to represent the interests of active members and the interests of prospective members;

(c) the employer must determine whether the active and prospective members should be represented by representatives of all such members or by representatives of particular descriptions of such members;

Part 2 Statutory Instruments

(d) before the election the employer must determine the term of office as representative of active and prospective members;
(e) the candidates for election must be active or prospective members of the scheme on the date of the election;
(f) no active or prospective member may unreasonably be excluded from standing for election;
(g) all active or prospective members on the date of the election are entitled to vote for member representatives;
(h) the members entitled to vote may vote for as many candidates as there are representatives to be elected to represent them or, if there are to be classes of representative for particular descriptions of member, may vote for as many candidates as there are representatives to be elected to represent their particular description of member;
(i) the election is conducted so as to secure that—
    (i) so far as is reasonably practicable, those voting do so in secret, and
    (ii) the votes given at the election are accurately counted.

(2) Where, after an election of representatives satisfying the requirements of paragraph (1) has been held—
(a) one of those elected ceases to act as a representative, and
(b) the active or prospective members (or any description of them) are no longer represented,
those members must elect another representative by an election satisfying the requirements of paragraph (1)(a), (e), (f) and (i).

(3) The relevant employer must from time to time review the number of representatives determined under paragraph (1)(b) and the number of representatives elected must be adjusted accordingly (whether by members electing one or more other representatives by an election satisfying the requirements of paragraph (1)(a), (e), (f) and (i), by not holding an election under paragraph (2) or otherwise).

[2.904]
15 Conduct of consultation

(1) Each relevant employer who carries out a consultation must make such arrangements with respect to the persons to be consulted as appear to him to secure that, so far as is reasonably practicable, the consultation covers all affected members.

(2) In the course of consultation, the relevant employer and any person consulted are under a duty to work in a spirit of co-operation, taking into account the interests of both sides.

(3) At the start of any consultation required by these Regulations, the relevant employer must notify the persons to be consulted of any date set for the end of the consultation or for the submission of written comments.

(4) An appropriate period must be allowed for carrying out the consultation which in any event must not be less than 60 days.

(5) If no responses to the consultation are received before the end of the period allowed for the consultation in accordance with paragraphs (3) and (4), the consultation is to be regarded as complete.

[2.905]
16 End of consultation

(1) Where the relevant employer who carries out a consultation is not the person who proposed the listed change ("P"), the relevant employer must, as soon as reasonably practicable after the consultation is complete—
(a) report to P on the views (if any) which were expressed to the relevant employer otherwise than in writing,
(b) where the responses include written comments, forward those comments to P, and
(c) in any case where no responses were received, notify P accordingly.

(2) In a case falling within paragraph (1), P must take reasonable steps to satisfy himself that each consultation required by these Regulations in relation to the scheme was carried out in accordance with regulations 11 to 15.

(3) After the end of the period allowed for the consultation, the person who proposed the listed change must consider the responses (if any) received in the course of consultation before making his decision as to whether or not to make a listed change.

Miscellaneous

[2.906]
17 Employment rights and protections in connection with consultation

The Schedule to these Regulations contains provision as to employment rights and protections which, in connection with consultation under these Regulations, apply to the employees of an employer in relation to an occupational or personal pension scheme.

[2.907]
[18 Remedies for failure to comply]

[(1) The only remedies for a failure to comply with any obligations under regulations 6 to 16 in respect of any proposal or decision to make a listed change are—
(a) making a complaint to the Regulator,
(b) an improvement notice issued under section 13 of the Pensions Act 2004 (improvement notices), and
(c) a penalty imposed under regulation 18A.]

(2) A complaint [under paragraph (1)(a)] may be made by—
(a) any representative of affected members who falls within regulation 12(2)(a) or (3) or 13(2) (including any such representative who is not consulted), and
(b) any active or prospective member of an occupational or personal pension scheme who considers that he is or may be an affected member.

NOTES

Regulation heading, and para (1), substituted, and words in square brackets in para (2) inserted, by the Occupational, Personal and Stakeholder Pensions (Miscellaneous Amendments) Regulations 2009, SI 2009/615, reg 20(1), (2).

[2.908]
[18A Penalties

(1) Where a person fails, without reasonable excuse, to comply with a requirement to consult under regulation 7(3), the Regulator may by notice in writing require that person to pay a penalty.

(2) Any such penalty must be paid within 28 days and must not exceed—
(a) in the case of an individual, £5,000; and
(b) in any other case, £50,000.]

NOTES

Inserted by the Occupational, Personal and Stakeholder Pensions (Miscellaneous Amendments) Regulations 2009, SI 2009/615, reg 20(1), (3).

[2.909]
19 Powers of the Regulator to waive or relax requirements

(1) The Regulator may by order waive or relax any of the requirements of regulations 6 to 16.

(2) The power under paragraph (1) may be exercised only if the Regulator is satisfied that it is necessary to do so in order to protect the interests of the generality of the members of the scheme.

20 (*Adds the Pensions Act 2004, Sch 2, Pt 5.*)

[2.910]
21 Waiver or relaxation of requirements: prescribed regulatory function

The Regulator's power to make an order under regulation 19 to waive or relax any of the requirements of regulations 6 to 16 is prescribed for the purposes of section 97(5)(u) of the Pensions Act 2004 (special procedure: applicable cases).

22 (*Amends the Financial Assistance Scheme (Internal Review) Regulations 2005, SI 2005/1994, reg 5.*)

SCHEDULE
EMPLOYMENT RIGHTS AND PROTECTIONS IN CONNECTION WITH CONSULTATION

Regulation 17

[2.911]

1. In this Schedule—

"the 1996 Act" means the Employment Rights Act 1996;

"consulted representative" has the meaning given by paragraph 2(2);

"contract of employment" means a contract of service or apprenticeship whether express or implied and (if it is express) whether oral or in writing;

"employee" means an individual who has entered into or works under a contract of employment and includes, where the employment has ceased, an individual who worked under a contract of employment;

"employment", in relation to an employee, means employment under a contract of employment (and "employed" has a corresponding meaning);

"employer", in relation to an employee, means the person by whom the employee is (or where employment has ceased, was) employed.

Right to Time Off and Remuneration

2. (1) An employee who—
(a) is a representative falling within regulation 12(2)(a) or (3) or 13(2), and
(b) is consulted under these Regulations about a listed change by a relevant employer,

is entitled to be permitted by his employer to take reasonable time off during the employee's working hours in order to perform his functions as such a representative.

(2) In this Schedule "consulted representative" means an employee who satisfies the conditions specified in sub-paragraph (1)(a) and (b).

(3) For the purposes of this paragraph, the working hours of an employee shall be taken to be any time when, in accordance with his contract of employment, the employee is required to be at work.

3. (1) An employee who is permitted to take time off under paragraph 2 is entitled to be paid remuneration by his employer for the time taken off at the appropriate hourly rate.

(2) Chapter 2 of Part 14 of the 1996 Act (a week's pay) shall apply in relation to this paragraph as it applies in relation to section 62 of the 1996 Act (right to remuneration of certain representatives).

(3) The appropriate hourly rate, in relation to an employee, is the amount of one week's pay divided by the number of normal working hours in a week for that employee when employed under the contract of employment in force on the day when the time is taken off.

(4) But where the number of normal working hours differs from week to week or over a longer period, the amount of one week's pay shall be divided instead by—

(a) the average number of normal working hours calculated by dividing by twelve the total number of the employee's normal working hours during the period of twelve weeks ending with the last complete week before the day when the time is taken off, or

(b) where the employee has not been employed for a sufficient period to enable the calculations to be made under paragraph (a), a number which fairly represents the number of normal working hours in a week having regard to such of the considerations specified in sub-paragraph (5) as are appropriate in the circumstances.

(5) The considerations referred to in sub-paragraph (4)(b) are—

(a) the average number of normal working hours in a week which the employee could expect in accordance with the terms of his contract, and

(b) the average number of normal working hours of other employees engaged in relevant comparable employment with the same employer.

(6) A right to any amount under sub-paragraph (1) does not affect any right of an employee in relation to remuneration under his contract of employment ("contractual remuneration").

(7) Any contractual remuneration paid to an employee in respect of a period of time off under paragraph 2 goes towards discharging any liability of the employer to pay remuneration under sub-paragraph (1) in respect of that period, and, conversely, any payment of remuneration under sub-paragraph (1) in respect of a period goes towards discharging any liability of the employer to pay contractual remuneration in respect of that period.

4. (1) An employee may present a complaint to an employment tribunal that his employer—

(a) has unreasonably refused to permit him to take time off as required by paragraph 2, or

(b) has failed to pay the whole or part of any amount to which the employee is entitled under paragraph 3.

(2) A tribunal shall not consider a complaint under this paragraph unless it is presented—

(a) before the end of the period of three months beginning with the day on which the time off was taken or on which it is alleged the time off should have been permitted, or

(b) within such further period as the tribunal considers reasonable in a case where it is satisfied that it was not reasonably practicable for the complaint to be presented before the end of that period of three months.

[(2A) Paragraph 4A (extension of time limits to facilitate conciliation before institution of proceedings) applies for the purposes of sub-paragraph (2).]

(3) Where a tribunal finds a complaint under this paragraph well-founded, the tribunal shall make a declaration to that effect.

(4) If the complaint is that the employer has unreasonably refused to permit the employee to take time off, the tribunal shall also order the employer to pay to the employee an amount equal to the remuneration to which he would have been entitled under paragraph 3 if the employer had not refused.

(5) If the complaint is that the employer has failed to pay the employee the whole or part of any amount to which he is entitled under paragraph 3, the tribunal shall also order the employer to pay to the employee the amount it finds due to him.

[Extension of time limit to facilitate conciliation before institution of proceedings

4A. (1) In this paragraph—

(a) Day A is the day on which the worker concerned complies with the requirement in subsection (1) of section 18A of the Employment Tribunals Act 1996 (requirement to contact ACAS before instituting proceedings) in relation to the matter in respect of which the proceedings are brought, and

(b) Day B is the day on which the worker concerned receives or, if earlier, is treated as receiving (by virtue of regulations made under subsection (11) of that section) the certificate issued under subsection (4) of that section.

(2) In working out when the time limit set by paragraph 4(2)(a) expires the period beginning with the day after Day A and ending with Day B is not to be counted.

(3) If the time limit set by paragraph 4(2)(a) would (if not extended by this paragraph) expire during the period beginning with Day A and ending one month after Day B, the time limit expires instead at the end of that period.

(4) The power conferred on the employment tribunal by paragraph 4(2)(b) to extend the time limit set by paragraph 4(2)(a) is exercisable in relation to that time limit as extended by this regulation.]

Protections against Unfair Dismissal

5. (1) An employee who is dismissed and to whom sub-paragraph (2) or (4) applies shall be regarded, if the reason (or if more than one, the principal reason) for the dismissal is a reason specified in, respectively, sub-paragraph (3) or (5), as unfairly dismissed for the purposes of Part 10 of the 1996 Act (which makes provision as to rights and remedies relating to unfair dismissal).

(2) This sub-paragraph applies to an employee who is—

(a) a consulted representative, or
(b) a candidate in an election in which any person elected will, on being elected, be a representative of such description as is referred to in regulation 13(2).

(3) The reasons are that—
(a) the employee performed or proposed to perform any functions or activities under these Regulations in his capacity as such a representative or candidate,
(b) the employee exercised or proposed to exercise an entitlement conferred on the employee by paragraph 2 or 3, or
(c) the employee (or a person acting on his behalf) made or proposed to make a request to exercise such an entitlement.

(4) This sub-paragraph applies to any employee who is an active or prospective member of an occupational or personal pension scheme, whether or not he is an employee to whom sub-paragraph (2) applies.

(5) The reasons are that the employee—
(a) took, or proposed to take, any proceedings before an employment tribunal to enforce a right or secure an entitlement conferred on him by this Schedule,
(b) complained or proposed to complain to the Regulator that any person falling within regulation 3(1)—
  (i) has decided to make a listed change affecting an occupational or personal pension scheme in contravention of regulation 6(1), or
  (ii) has failed to comply with the requirements of regulation 16(2) or (3),
(c) complained or proposed to complain to the Regulator that any consultation required by these Regulations was not carried out in accordance with the requirements of these Regulations,
(d) stood as a candidate in an election in which any person elected would, on being elected, be a representative of such description as is referred to in regulation 13(2),
(e) influenced or sought to influence by lawful means the way in which votes were to be cast by other employees in an election arranged under regulation 14,
(f) voted in such an election,
(g) expressed doubts, whether to an election supervisor or otherwise, as to whether such an election had been properly conducted, or
(h) proposed to do, failed to do, or proposed to decline to do any of the things mentioned in paragraphs (d) to (g).

(6) It is immaterial for the purpose of sub-paragraph (5)(a)—
(a) whether or not the employee has the right or entitlement, or
(b) whether or not the right has been infringed,

but for that provision to apply, the claim to the right and, if applicable, the claim that it has been infringed must be made in good faith.

6. . . .

Protections from Suffering other Detriment in Employment

7. (1) An employee to whom sub-paragraph (2) or (4) applies has the right not to be subjected to any detriment by any act, or deliberate failure to act, by his employer done on a ground specified in, respectively, sub-paragraph (3) or (5).

(2) This sub-paragraph applies to an employee who is—
(a) a consulted representative, or
(b) a candidate in an election in which any person elected will, on being elected, be a representative of such description as is referred to in regulation 13(2).

(3) The grounds are that—
(a) the employee performed or proposed to perform any functions or activities under these Regulations in his capacity as such a representative or candidate,
(b) the employee exercised or proposed to exercise an entitlement conferred on the employee by paragraph 2 or 3, or
(c) the employee (or a person acting on his behalf) made or proposed to make a request to exercise such an entitlement.

(4) This sub-paragraph applies to any employee who is an active or prospective member of an occupational or personal pension scheme, whether or not he is an employee to whom sub-paragraph (2) applies.

(5) The grounds are that the employee—
(a) took, or proposed to take, any proceedings before an employment tribunal to enforce a right or secure an entitlement conferred on him by this Schedule,
(b) complained or proposed to complain to the Regulator that any person falling within regulation 3(1)—
  (i) has decided to make a listed change affecting an occupational or personal pension scheme in contravention of regulation 6(1), or
  (ii) has failed to comply with the requirements of regulation 16(2) or (3),
(c) complained or proposed to complain to the Regulator that any consultation required by these Regulations was not carried out in accordance with the requirements of these Regulations,
(d) stood as a candidate in an election in which any person elected would, on being elected, be a representative of such description as is referred to in regulation 13(2),

(e) influenced or sought to influence by lawful means the way in which votes were to be cast by other employees in an election arranged under regulation 14,

(f) voted in such a election,

(g) expressed doubts, whether to an election supervisor or otherwise, as to whether such an election had been properly conducted, or

(h) proposed to do, failed to do, or proposed to decline to do any of the things mentioned in paragraphs (d) to (g).

(6) It is immaterial for the purpose of sub-paragraph (5)(a)—

(a) whether or not the employee has the right or entitlement, or

(b) whether or not the right has been infringed,

but for that provision to apply, the claim to the right and, if applicable, the claim that it has been infringed must be made in good faith.

(7) This paragraph does not apply where the detriment in question amounts to dismissal.

8. (1) An employee may present a complaint to an employment tribunal that he has been subjected to a detriment in contravention of paragraph 7.

(2) The provisions of sections 48(2) to (4) and 49(1) to (5) of the 1996 Act (complaints to employment tribunals and remedies) shall apply in relation to a complaint under this paragraph as they apply in relation to a complaint under section 48 of that Act.

Conciliation and Appeals

9, 10. . . .

Miscellaneous

11. Any provision in any agreement (whether an employee's contract or not) is void in so far as it purports to exclude or limit the operation of any provision of regulations 6 to 16.

12. (1) Any provision in any agreement (whether an employee's contract or not) is void in so far as it purports—

(a) to exclude or limit the operation of any provision of this Schedule, or

(b) to preclude a person from bringing any proceedings before an employment tribunal under this Schedule.

(2) Sub-paragraph (1) does not apply to any agreement to refrain from instituting or continuing proceedings before an employment tribunal where a conciliation officer has taken action under [any of sections 18A to 18C] of the Employment Tribunals Act 1996 (conciliation).

(3) Sub-paragraph (1) does not apply to any agreement to refrain from instituting or continuing before an employment tribunal proceedings within section 18(1) of the Employment Tribunals Act 1996 (which specifies proceedings under these Regulations as being proceedings where conciliation is available) if the conditions specified in paragraph 13 regulating [settlement] agreements are satisfied in relation to the agreement.

13. (1) For the purposes of paragraph 12(3) the conditions regulating [settlement] agreements are that—

(a) the agreement must be in writing,

(b) the agreement must relate to the particular proceedings,

(c) the employee must have received advice from a relevant independent adviser as to the terms and effect of the proposed agreement and, in particular, its effect on his ability to pursue his rights before an employment tribunal,

(d) there must be in force, when the adviser gives the advice, a contract of insurance, or an indemnity provided for members of a profession or a professional body, covering the risk of a claim by the employee in respect of loss arising in consequence of the advice,

(e) the agreement must identify the adviser, and

(f) the agreement must state that the conditions in paragraphs (a) to (e) are satisfied.

(2) A person is a relevant independent adviser for the purposes of sub-paragraph (1)(c)—

(a) if he is a qualified lawyer,

(b) if he is an officer, official, employee or member of an independent trade union who has been certified in writing by the trade union as competent to give advice and as authorised to do so on behalf of the trade union, or

(c) if he works at an advice centre (whether as an employee or as a volunteer) and has been certified in writing by the centre as competent to give advice and as authorised to do so on behalf of the centre.

(3) But a person is not a relevant independent adviser for the purposes of sub-paragraph (1)(c)—

(a) if he is, is employed by or is acting in the matter for the employer or an associated employer,

(b) in the case of a person within sub-paragraph (2)(b) or (c), if the trade union or advice centre is the employer or an associated employer, or

(c) in the case of a person within sub-paragraph (2)(c), if the employee makes a payment for the advice received from him.

(4) In sub-paragraph (2)(a) "qualified lawyer" means—

(a) as respects England and Wales, [a person who, for the purposes of the Legal Services Act 2007), is an authorised person in relation to an activity which constitutes the exercise of a right of audience or the conduct of litigation (within the meaning of that Act)];

(b) as respects Scotland, an advocate (whether in practice as such or employed to give legal advice) or a solicitor who holds a practising certificate.

(5) A person shall be treated as being a qualified lawyer within the meaning of sub-paragraph (4)(a) if he is a Fellow of the Institute of Legal Executives [practising in a solicitor's practice (including a body recognised under section 9 of the Administration of Justice Act 1985)].

(6) In this paragraph—

(a) "independent trade union" has the same meaning as in the Trade Union and Labour Relations (Consolidation) Act 1992; and

(b) for the purposes of sub-paragraph (3) any two employers shall be treated as associated if—

(i) one is a company of which the other (directly or indirectly) has control, or

(ii) both are companies of which a third person (directly or indirectly) has control,

and "associated employer" shall be construed accordingly.

NOTES

Para 4: sub-para (2A) inserted by the Enterprise and Regulatory Reform Act 2013 (Consequential Amendments) (Employment) Order 2014, SI 2014/386, art 2, Schedule, paras 40, 41.

Para 4A: inserted by SI 2014/386, art 2, Schedule, paras 40, 42.

Para 6: amends the Employment Rights Act 1996, ss 105, 108 at **[1.1023]**, **[1.1026]**, and amended s 109 (repealed).

Paras 9, 10: amend the Employment Tribunals Act 1996, ss 18, 21 at **[1.757]**, **[1.764]**.

Para 12: words in square brackets in sub-para (2) substituted by SI 2014/386, art 2, Schedule, paras 40, 43; word in square brackets in sub-para (3) substituted by the Enterprise and Regulatory Reform Act 2013 (Consequential Amendments) (Employment) Order 2013, SI 2013/1956, art 2, Schedule, para 11.

Para 13: word in square brackets in sub-para (1) substituted by SI 2013/1956, art 2, Schedule, para 11; words in square brackets in sub-para (4) substituted by the Legal Services Act 2007 (Consequential Amendments) Order 2009, SI 2009/3348, art 23, Sch 2; words in square brackets in sub-para (5) substituted by SI 2009/3348, art 22, Sch 1.

Conciliation: employment tribunal proceedings under paras 4 or 8 of this Schedule are "relevant proceedings" for the purposes of the conciliation provisions contained in the Employment Tribunals Act 1996, ss 18–18C; see s 18(1)(t) of the 1996 Act at **[1.757]**.

Tribunal jurisdiction: the Employment Act 2002, s 38 applies to proceedings before the employment tribunal relating to a claim under para 8 of this Schedule; see s 38(1) of, and Sch 5 to, the 2002 Act at **[1.1279]**, **[1.1287]**. See also the Trade Union and Labour Relations (Consolidation) Act 1992, s 207A at **[1.524]** (as inserted by the Employment Act 2008). That section provides that in proceedings before an employment tribunal relating to a claim by an employee under any of the jurisdictions listed in Sch A2 to the 1992 Act at **[1.704]** (which includes para 8 of this Schedule) the tribunal may adjust any award given if the employer or the employee has unreasonably failed to comply with a relevant Code of Practice as defined by s 207A(4). See also the revised Acas Code of Practice 1 – Disciplinary and Grievance Procedures (2015) at **[4.1]**, and the Acas Code of Practice 4 – Settlement Agreements (2013) at **[4.54]**.

Employment Appeal Tribunal: see the introductory notes to these Regulations.

EDUCATION (MODIFICATION OF ENACTMENTS RELATING TO EMPLOYMENT) (WALES) ORDER 2006

(SI 2006/1073)

NOTES

Made: 5 April 2006.

Authority: School Standards and Framework Act 1998, ss 81(1), 138(7).

Commencement: 12 May 2006.

Extent: this Order applies to Wales; the equivalent provisions for England are in SI 2003/1964 at **[2.683]**. There is no equivalent Order applying to Scotland.

ARRANGEMENT OF ARTICLES

[2.912]

1 Citation, commencement, application and revocation

(1) This Order may be cited as the Education (Modification of Enactments Relating to Employment) (Wales) Order 2006 and shall come into force on 12th May 2006.

(2) This Order applies in relation to Wales.

(3) The Education (Modification of Enactments Relating to Employment) Order 1999 is revoked.

[2.913]
2 Interpretation

(1) In this Order—

"the 1996 Act" means the Employment Rights Act 1996;

"the 1998 Act" means the School Standards and Framework Act 1998;

"the 2006 Regulations" mean the Staffing of Maintained Schools (Wales) Regulations 2006;

"authority" means the [local authority] by which a maintained school is, or a proposed school is to be, maintained;

"governing body" means the governing body of a school which is maintained by a local education authority;

"governing body" means the governing body of a school which is maintained by a [local authority];

(2) In this Order references to employment powers are references to the powers of appointment, suspension, conduct and discipline, capability and dismissal of staff conferred by the 2006 Regulations.

NOTES

Para (1): words in square brackets in definitions "authority" and "governing body" substituted by the Local Education Authorities and Children's Services Authorities (Integration of Functions) (Subordinate Legislation) (Wales) Order 2010, SI 2010/1142, art 2(3).

[2.914]
3 General modifications of employment enactments

(1) In their application to a governing body having a right to a delegated budget, the enactments set out in the Schedule have effect as if—

(a) any reference to an employer (however expressed) included a reference to the governing body acting in the exercise of its employment powers and as if that governing body had at all material times been such an employer;

(b) in relation to the exercise of the governing body's employment powers, employment by the authority at a school were employment by the governing body of the school;

(c) references to employees were references to employees at the school in question;

(d) references to dismissal by an employer included references to dismissal by the authority following notification of a determination by a governing body under regulation 17(1) of the 2006 Regulations; and

(e) references to trade unions recognised by an employer were references to trade unions recognised by the authority or the governing body.

(2) Paragraph (1) does not cause the exemption in respect of an employer with fewer employees than is specified in section 7(1) of the Disability Discrimination Act 1995 to apply (without prejudice to whether it applies irrespective of that paragraph).

[2.915]
4

Without prejudice to the generality of article 3, where an employee employed at a school having a delegated budget is dismissed by the authority following notification of such a determination as is mentioned in article 3(1)(d)—

(a) section 92 of the 1996 Act has effect as if the governing body had dismissed him and as if references to the employer's reasons for dismissing the employee were references to the reasons for which the governing body made its determination; and

(b) Part X of the 1996 Act has effect in relation to the dismissal as if the governing body had dismissed him, and the reason or principal reason for which the governing body did so had been the reason or principal reason for which it made its determination.

[2.916]
5 Trade disputes

(1) Subject to paragraph (2), a dispute between staff employed to work at a school having a delegated budget and the school's governing body, which relates wholly or mainly to one of the matters set out in section 244(1) of the Trade Union and Labour Relations (Consolidation) Act 1992 is a trade dispute within the meaning of that Act.

(2) In any case where there is a trade dispute only by virtue of this article, nothing in section 219 of that Act prevents an act from being actionable in tort where the inducement, interference or threat mentioned in that section relates to a contract the performance of which does not affect directly or indirectly the school over which the governing body in question exercises its functions.

[2.917]
6 Applications to Employment Tribunals

(1) Without prejudice to articles 3 and 4, and despite any provision in the Employment Tribunals Act 1996 and any regulations made under section 1(1) of that Act, this article applies in respect of any application to an employment tribunal, and any proceedings pursuant to such an application, in relation to which by virtue of article 3 or 4 a governing body is to be treated as if it were an employer (however expressed).

(2) The application must be made, and the proceedings must be carried on, against that governing body.

(3) Despite paragraph (2), any decision, declaration, order, recommendation or award made in the course of such proceedings except in so far as it requires reinstatement or re-engagement has effect as if made against the authority.

(4) Where any application is made against a governing body under paragraph (2)—

(a) the governing body must notify the authority within 14 days of receiving notification; and

(b) the authority, on written application to the employment tribunal, is entitled to be made an additional party to the proceedings and to take part in the proceedings accordingly.

SCHEDULE

Article 3

[2.918]

Sex Discrimination Act 1975
sections 6, 7, 9, 41 and 82(1A)

Race Relations Act 1976
sections 4, 5, 7 and 32

Trade Union and Labour Relations (Consolidation) Act 1992
sections 146, 147, 152–154 and 181–185

Disability Discrimination Act 1995
sections 4–6, 11, 12, 16, 55, 57 and 58

Employment Rights Act 1996
sections 66–68, 70, 71, 92, 93 and Part X

Employment Act 2002
sections 29–32 and Schedules 2–4

NOTES

Note that the Employment Act 2002, ss 29–32, Schs 2–4 were repealed by the Employment Act 2008. The Sex Discrimination Act 1975, the Race Relations Act 1976, and the Disability Discrimination Act 1995 were repealed by the Equality Act 2010, s 211(2), Sch 27, Pt 1. As to the application of this Order to provisions of the Equality Act 2010 that replace the listed provisions of the 1975, 1976 and 1995 Acts, see the Interpretation Act 1978, s 17(2)(a).

LOCAL GOVERNMENT (EARLY TERMINATION OF EMPLOYMENT) (DISCRETIONARY COMPENSATION) (ENGLAND AND WALES) REGULATIONS 2006

(SI 2006/2914)

NOTES

Made: 6 November 2006.
Authority: Superannuation Act 1972, s 24.
Commencement: 29 November 2006 (with effect from 1 October 2006).
These Regulations apply to England and Wales only (see **[2.919]**).

ARRANGEMENT OF REGULATIONS

SCHEDULES

[2.919]

1 Citation, commencement and extent

(1) These Regulations may be cited as the Local Government (Early Termination of Employment) (Discretionary Compensation) (England and Wales) Regulations 2006.

(2) They shall come into force on 29th November 2006 but shall have effect from 1st October 2006 and extend to England and Wales.

[2.920]
2 Interpretation

(1) In these Regulations—

"the 1996 Act" means the Employment Rights Act 1996;

"the 2000 Regulations" means the Local Government (Early Termination of Employment) (Discretionary Compensation) (England and Wales) Regulations 2000;

["the Benefits Regulations" means the Local Government Pension Scheme (Benefits, Membership and Contributions) Regulations 2007;

"the Administration Regulations" means the Local Government Pension Scheme (Administration) Regulations 2008;]

"employing authority", in relation to a person, means—

[(a) a body listed in Part 1 of Schedule 2 (Scheme employers) to the Administration Regulations by whom the person is employed immediately before the termination date;

(b) a body listed in Part 2 of that Schedule by whom the person is employed immediately before the termination date and who has been designated by the body as being eligible for membership of the Scheme under regulation 4(3) of those Regulations; or

(c) in the case of a person who is eligible to be a Scheme member under [regulation 8(1) of the Administration Regulations], the [local authority] by whom the person is deemed to be employed under regulation 8(2) of those Regulations].

"employment" includes office but does not include a period as—

(a) the Mayor of London,

(b) a member of the London Assembly, or

(c) a councillor member;

. . .

["Scheme member" means a member of the Local Government Pension Scheme constituted by the Benefits Regulations and the Administration Regulations;]

"termination date" in relation to a person means the final day of his employment.

[(2) Expressions not defined in paragraph (1) but used in these Regulations and in the Benefits Regulations or the Administration Regulations or both have the same meaning as in the Benefits Regulations or the Administration Regulations, as the case may be.]

NOTES

In para (c) of the definition "employing authority" words in first pair of square brackets substituted by the Local Government Pension Scheme (Miscellaneous) Regulations 2012, SI 2012/1989, regs 2, 3, and words in second pair of square brackets substituted by the Local Education Authorities and Children's Services Authorities (Integration of Functions) (Local and Subordinate Legislation) Order 2010, SI 2010/1172, art 5, Sch 3, para 67.

All other amendments to this regulation were made by the Local Government Pension Scheme (Miscellaneous) Regulations 2009, SI 2009/3150, regs 2, 3.

[2.921]
3 Application to the Isles of Scilly

These Regulations apply to the Isles of Scilly as if they were a district in the county of Cornwall and the Council of the Isles of Scilly were a council of that district.

[2.922]
4 Application of the Regulations

(1) Subject to regulation 11(2), these Regulations apply in relation to a person—

(a) whose employment is terminated—

(i) by reason of redundancy,

(ii) in the interests of the efficient exercise of the employing authority's functions, or

(iii) in the case of a joint appointment, because the other holder of the appointment has left it;

(b) who, on the termination date, is—

(i) employed by an employing authority, and

[(ii) eligible to be a Scheme member (whether or not the person is such a member) or would be so eligible but for the giving of a notification under regulation 14 of the Administration Regulations; and]

(c) whose termination date is on or after 1st October 2006,

and in the following provisions of these Regulations, "person" shall be construed accordingly, unless the context indicates that it has a different meaning.

(2) Where an additional requirement is specified in any provision of regulations 5 and 6 in relation to a person, that provision does not apply in relation to him unless he satisfies that additional requirement.

NOTES

Para (1): sub-para (b)(ii) substituted by the Local Government Pension Scheme (Miscellaneous) Regulations 2009, SI 2009/3150, regs 2, 4.

[2.923]
5 Power to increase statutory redundancy payments

(1) Compensation may be paid in accordance with this regulation to a person who is entitled to a redundancy payment under the 1996 Act on the termination of his employment.

(2) The amount which may be paid must not be more than the difference between—

(a) the redundancy payment to which he is entitled under Part 11 of the 1996 Act; and

(b) the payment to which he would have been entitled if there had been no limit on the amount of a week's pay used in the calculation of his redundancy payment.

(3) The power to pay compensation is exercisable by the employing authority.

[2.924]
6 Discretionary compensation

(1) This regulation applies where a person—

(a) ceases to hold his employment with an employing authority, and

[(b) in respect of that cessation is not awarded—

(i) an additional period of membership under regulation 12 (power of employing authority to increase total membership of active members); or

(ii) an additional pension under regulation 13 (power of employing authority to award additional pension)

of the Benefits Regulations].

(2) Where this regulation applies, the employing authority may, not later than six months after the termination date, decide to pay compensation under this regulation and in that event shall, as soon as reasonably practicable after the decision, notify the person in whose favour it has been made, giving details of the amount of the compensation.

(3) The amount of compensation must not exceed 104 weeks' pay.

[(4) Chapter 2 (a week's pay) of Part 14 (Interpretation) of the 1996 Act shall apply for the purpose of calculating a person's week's pay as it applies for the purpose of calculating redundancy payments but without the limit on a week's pay imposed by section 227 of that Act.]

(5) If the person in whose favour a decision under paragraph (2) has been made receives a redundancy payment under Part 11 of the 1996 Act or compensation under regulation 5 of these Regulations, the equivalent amount shall be deducted from the compensation otherwise payable to him under this regulation.

(6) Compensation under this regulation shall be paid by the employing authority as soon as practicable after the decision under paragraph (2).

(7) The compensation shall be payable in the form of a lump sum.

NOTES

Para (1): sub-para (b) substituted by the Local Government Pension Scheme (Miscellaneous) Regulations 2009, SI 2009/3150, regs 2, 5(a).

Para (4): substituted by SI 2009/3150, regs 2, 5(b).

[2.925]
7 Policy Statements

(1) Each employing authority must formulate, publish and keep under review the policy that they apply in the exercise of their discretionary powers under regulations 5 and 6.

(2) If the authority decide to change their policy, they must publish a statement of the amended policy and may not give effect to any policy change until one month after the date of publication.

(3) In formulating and reviewing their policy the authority must—

(a) have regard to the extent to which the exercise of their discretionary powers (in accordance with the policy), unless properly limited, could lead to a serious loss of confidence in the public service; and

(b) be satisfied that the policy is workable, affordable and reasonable having regard to the foreseeable costs.

[2.926]
8 Payments and repayments

(1) Any compensation payable under these Regulations is payable to or in trust for the person entitled to receive it.

(2) Where any compensation is paid in error to any person—

(a) the employing authority must, as soon as possible after the discovery of the error—

(i) inform the person concerned, by notice in writing, giving details of the relevant calculation,

(ii) where there has been an underpayment, make a further payment,

(iii) where there has been an overpayment, specify a reasonable period for repayment;

(b) a person who has received a notice under sub-paragraph (a) must repay any overpayment within the specified period; and

(c) the employing authority may take such steps as they consider appropriate to recover from the person to whom it was paid any overpayment which has not been repaid within the specified period.

(3) The employing authority shall take into account the person's circumstances (so far as known or reasonably ascertainable) before taking steps under paragraph (2)(c).

[2.927]
9 Finance

The cost of any payment to be made under these Regulations must not be met out of any pension fund maintained under [the Local Government Pension Scheme (Management and Investment of Funds) Regulations 1998, the Benefits Regulations and the Administration Regulations].

NOTES

Words in square brackets substituted by the Local Government Pension Scheme (Miscellaneous) Regulations 2009, SI 2009/3150, regs 2, 6.

[2.928]
10 Consequential amendments

Schedule 1 shall have effect for the purpose of making amendments which are consequential on the making of these Regulations.

[2.929]
11 Revocation of Regulations, transitional provisions and savings

(1) The following are revoked but subject to the transitional provision in paragraph (2) and the savings in Schedule 2—

- (a) the 2000 Regulations,
- (b) regulation 598 of the Financial Services and Markets Act 2000 (Consequential Amendments and Repeals) Order 2001,
- (c) the Local Government (Early Termination of Employment) (Discretionary Compensation) (England and Wales) (Miscellaneous) Regulations 2002,
- (d) regulation 9(2) of the Local Government Pension Scheme and Discretionary Compensation (Local Authority Members in England) Regulations 2003, and
- (e) regulation 5 of the Local Government Pension Scheme (Civil Partnership) (Amendment) (England and Wales) Regulations 2005

(2) An employing authority may decide to pay compensation under the 2000 Regulations to a person whose employment with them commenced before 1st October 2006 and whose termination date is after 30th September 2006 and before 1st April 2007.

(3) An employing authority may decide to pay compensation under regulation 6 of these Regulations to a person—

- (a) whose employment with them terminated after 30th September 2006 and before the date on which these Regulations come into force, and
- (b) in respect of whom a decision to pay lump sum compensation has been made and notified under Part 3 of the 2000 Regulations before the date on which these Regulations come into force ("the 2000 lump sum").

(4) The amount that an employing authority may decide to pay under paragraph (3) may not exceed the difference between—

- (a) 104 weeks' pay, and
- (b) the 2000 lump sum

but if the person in whose favour a decision under paragraph (3) has been made receives a redundancy payment under Part 11 of the 1996 Act or compensation under regulation 5 of the 2000 Regulations or regulation 5 of these Regulations, the equivalent amount shall be deducted from the compensation otherwise payable to him under paragraph (3) if no such adjustment has already been made.

(5) Nothing in these Regulations shall place any individual who is eligible to participate in the benefits for which the 2000 Regulations provide in a worse position than he would have been in if all the provisions of these Regulations had been framed so as to have effect only from the date of their making.

SCHEDULE 1

(Sch 1 contains various amendments to statutory instruments that are outside the scope of this work.)

SCHEDULE 2
SAVINGS

Regulation 11

[2.930]

1. The revocation of the 2000 Regulations does not affect—

- (a) any person whose termination date is before 1st October 2006 and who is eligible for compensation under the provisions of those Regulations,
- (b) any person to whom an employing authority have decided that compensation shall be paid under those Regulations in accordance with regulation 11(2) of these Regulations, or
- (c) the rights of any person who is entitled to benefits under those Regulations in consequence of the death of such a person

and in relation to such persons those Regulations shall continue to apply.

2. Where—

(a) any provision continues to have effect in relation to any person by virtue of paragraph 1, and
(b) immediately before 1st October 2006 it has effect in relation to him subject to any saving, transitional provision or modification

nothing in these Regulations affects the operation of that saving, transitional provision or modification.

3. The revocation by these Regulations of any provision which previously revoked any provision subject to savings does not affect the continued operation of those savings, in so far as they remain capable of having effect.

IMMIGRATION (RESTRICTIONS ON EMPLOYMENT) ORDER 2007

(SI 2007/3290)

NOTES

Made: 15 November 2007.
Authority: Immigration, Asylum and Nationality Act 2006, ss 15(3), (7), 16(3), (5), 19(2), 23(3), 25(d).
Commencement: 29 February 2008.
See *Harvey* AI(5).

ARRANGEMENT OF ARTICLES

Citation, commencement and interpretation

[2.931]
1

This order may be cited as the Immigration (Restrictions on Employment) Order 2007 and shall come into force on 29 February 2008.

[2.932]
2

In this order—
"the 2006 Act" means the Immigration, Asylum and Nationality Act 2006; and
"document" means an original document;
["employee", except in articles 4(3) and 4B(3), includes a reference to a prospective employee].

NOTES

Definition "employee" inserted by the Immigration (Restrictions on Employment) (Code of Practice and Miscellaneous Amendments) Order 2018, SI 2018/1340, art 2(1), (2), as from 28 January 2019.

Excuse from paying civil penalty

[2.933]
3

(1) [Subject to article 5,] an employer is excused from paying a penalty under section 15 of the 2006 Act if—
(a) the employee . . . produces to the employer any of the documents or combinations of documents described in list A in the Schedule to this Order; and
(b) the employer complies with the requirements set out in article 6 of this order.

(2) . . .

NOTES

Para (1): words in square brackets substituted, and words omitted revoked, by the Immigration (Restrictions on Employment) (Code of Practice and Miscellaneous Amendments) Order 2018, SI 2018/1340, art 2(1), (3)(a), (b), as from 28 January 2019.
Para (2): revoked by SI 2018/1340, art 2(1), (3)(c), as from 28 January 2019.

[2.934]
[4

(1) To the extent provided for by paragraphs (2) and (3) an employer is excused from paying a penalty under section 15 of the 2006 Act if—
(a) the employee . . . produces to the employer any of the documents or combination of documents described in part 1 of list B in the Schedule to this Order; and
(b) the employer complies with the requirements set out in article 6 of this Order.

(2) Subject to article 5 an employer will be excused under this article from paying a penalty under section 15 of the 2006 Act for the period for which a document produced under paragraph (1)(a) provides that the employment is permitted.

(3) If, on the date on which the period specified in paragraph (2) expires, the employer is reasonably satisfied that the employee has an outstanding application to vary his leave to enter or remain in the United Kingdom or the employee has an appeal [or administrative review] pending against a decision on that application, the employer will be excused from paying that penalty for a further period beginning with the date on which the period specified in paragraph (2) expires and ending—

(a) after 28 days, or

(b) if earlier, on the date on which the Secretary of State gives the employer written notice that the employee does not have the right to undertake the employment in question.]

NOTES

Articles 4, 4A were substituted (for the original art 4) by the Immigration (Restrictions on Employment) (Codes of Practice and Amendment) Order 2014, SI 2014/1183, arts 2, 3.

Para (1): words omitted from sub-para (a) revoked by the Immigration (Restrictions on Employment) (Code of Practice and Miscellaneous Amendments) Order 2018, SI 2018/1340, art 2(1), (4)(a), as from 28 January 2019.

Para (3): words in square brackets inserted by SI 2018/1340, art 2(1), (4)(b), as from 28 January 2019.

[2.935]
[4A

(1) To the extent provided for by paragraph (2) an employer is excused from paying a penalty under section 15 of the 2006 Act if—

(a) either—

(i) the employee . . . produces to the employer a document described in paragraph 1 or 2 of part 2 of list B in the Schedule to this Order and the employer obtains a Positive Verification Notice issued by the Home Office Employer Checking Service which indicates that the person named in it is allowed to stay in the United Kingdom and is allowed to do the work in question; or

(ii) the employer obtains a Positive Verification Notice issued by the Home Office Employer Checking Service which indicates that the person named in it is allowed to stay in the United Kingdom and is allowed to do the work in question; and

(b) the employer complies with the requirements set out in article 6 of this Order.

(2) Subject to article 5 an employer will be excused under this article from paying a penalty under section 15 of the 2006 Act for a period of six months, beginning with the date of the Positive Verification Notice obtained under paragraph (1)(a).]

NOTES

Substituted as noted to art 4 at **[2.934]**.

Para (1): words omitted from sub-para (a) revoked by the Immigration (Restrictions on Employment) (Code of Practice and Miscellaneous Amendments) Order 2018, SI 2018/1340, art 2(1), (5), as from 28 January 2019.

[2.936]
[4B Excusal from paying civil penalty: Home Office online right to work checking service

(1) To the extent provided for by paragraphs (2) and (3), an employer is excused from paying a penalty under section 15 of the 2006 Act if—

(a) the employer uses the Home Office online right to work checking service in respect of an employee;

(b) the online right to work check confirms that the employee named in it is allowed to work in the United Kingdom and is allowed to do the work in question;

(c) the employer has satisfied himself that any photograph on the online right to work check is of the employee;

(d) the employer retains a clear copy of the online right to work check for a period of not less than two years after the employment has come to an end; and

(e) the employer complies, if applicable, with the requirement in article 6(2).

(2) Subject to article 5, an employer will be excused under this article from paying a penalty under section 15 of the 2006 Act for the period for which the online right to work check confirmed that the person named in it was permitted to carry out the work in question.

(3) If, on the date on which the period specified in paragraph (2) expires, the employer is reasonably satisfied that the employee has an outstanding application to vary his leave to enter or remain in the United Kingdom or the employee has an appeal or administrative review pending against a decision on that application, the employer will be excused from paying that penalty for a further period beginning with the date on which the period specified in paragraph (2) expires and ending—

(a) after 28 days, or

(b) if earlier, on the date on which the Secretary of State gives the employer written notice that the employee does not have the right to undertake the employment in question.

(4) In this article—

"online right to work check" means the response generated by the Home Office online right to work checking service in relation to a person;

"Home Office online right to work checking service" means the electronic system allowing employers to check whether a person is allowed to work in the United Kingdom and, if so, the nature of any restrictions on that person's right to do so.]

NOTES

Commencement: 28 January 2019.

Inserted by the Immigration (Restrictions on Employment) (Code of Practice and Miscellaneous Amendments) Order 2018, SI 2018/1340, art 2(1), (6), as from 28 January 2019.

[2.937]
5

An employer is excused from paying a penalty under section 15 of the 2006 Act by virtue of [article 3(1)][, article 4(2)[, article 4A(2) or article 4B(2)]] [only if the employee produces the relevant documents to the employer[, or the employer obtains an online right to work check which confirms that the employee named in it is allowed to work in the United Kingdom and is allowed to do the work in question,] prior to the commencement of employment].

NOTES

Words in first and third (inner) pairs of square brackets substituted, and words in fifth (inner) pair of square brackets inserted, by the Immigration (Restrictions on Employment) (Code of Practice and Miscellaneous Amendments) Order 2018, SI 2018/1340, art 2(1), (7), as from 28 January 2019. Words in second and fourth (outer) pairs of square brackets substituted by the Immigration (Restrictions on Employment) (Codes of Practice and Amendment) Order 2014, SI 2014/1183, arts 2, 4.

[2.938]
6

[(1)] The requirements in relation to any documents or combinations of documents produced by an employee pursuant to [article 3, 4 or 4A] of this order are that—

(a) the employer takes all reasonable steps to check the validity of the document [and retains a record of the date on which any check was made];

(b) the [clear] copy or copies are retained securely by the employer for a period of not less than two years after the employment has come to an end;

(c) if a document contains a photograph, the employer has satisfied himself that the photograph is of the . . . employee;

(d) if a document contains a date of birth, the employer has satisfied himself that the date of birth is consistent with the appearance of the . . . employee;

(e) the employer takes all other reasonable steps to check that the . . . employee is the rightful owner of the document;

(f) if the document is not a passport . . . the employer retains a [clear] copy of whole of the document in a format which cannot be subsequently altered, . . .

[(g) if the document is a passport . . . , the employer retains a [clear] copy of the following pages of that document in a format which cannot be subsequently altered—

(i) . . .

(ii) any page containing the holder's personal details including nationality;

(iii) any page containing the holder's photograph;

(iv) any page containing the holder's signature;

(v) any page containing the date of expiry; and

(vi) any page containing information indicating the holder has an entitlement to enter or remain in the UK and undertake the work in question.

(h) . . .].

[(2) A further requirement, if the employee . . . is a student who has permission to work for a limited number of hours per week during term time whilst studying in the United Kingdom, is that the employer must obtain and retain details of the term and vacation dates of the course that the employee . . . is undertaking.]

NOTES

Para (1): numbered as such, first words in square brackets inserted, words in square brackets in sub-para (a) substituted, first words omitted from sub-para (f) revoked, words omitted from sub-para (g) and the whole of sub-para (h) revoked, by the Immigration (Restrictions on Employment) (Codes of Practice and Amendment) Order 2014, SI 2014/1183, arts 2, 5(1), (2)(a)–(f).

Word in square brackets in sub-paras (b), (f), (g) inserted, and words omitted from sub-paras (c), (d), (e) revoked, by the Immigration (Restrictions on Employment) (Code of Practice and Miscellaneous Amendments) Order 2018, SI 2018/1340, art 2(1), (8)(a), as from 28 January 2019.

Second word omitted from sub-para (1)(f) revoked, and paras (1)(g), (h) substituted (for the original sub-para (g)) by the Immigration (Restrictions on Employment) (Amendment) Order 2009, SI 2009/2908, arts 2, 3.

Para (2): added by SI 2014/1183, arts 2, 5(1), (2)(g); words omitted revoked by SI 2018/1340, art 2(1), (8)(b), as from 28 January 2019.

[2.939]
7

Nothing in this Order permits employers to retain documents produced by an employee [or the Home Office] for the purposes of [article 3, [4, 4A or 4B]] for any period longer than is necessary for the purposes of ensuring compliance with article 6.

NOTES

Words in first pair of square brackets inserted, and words in third (inner) pair of square brackets substituted, by the Immigration (Restrictions on Employment) (Code of Practice and Miscellaneous Amendments) Order 2018, SI 2018/1340, art 2(1), (9), as from 28 January 2019.

Words in second (outer) pair of square brackets substituted by the Immigration (Restrictions on Employment) (Codes of Practice and Amendment) Order 2014, SI 2014/1183, arts 2, 6.

Objections

[2.940]
8
The manner prescribed in which the notice of objection must be given is that it must contain—
(a) the reference number of the notice given under section 15(2) of the 2006 Act;
(b) the name and contact address of the employer;
(c) the name and contact address of the employee in respect of whom the penalty was issued;
(d) the full grounds of objection;
(e) where the employer requests permission to pay by instalments, full details of the employer's ability to pay the penalty;
(f) confirmation and details of any appeal made by the employer to a County Court or Sheriff Court on the basis that the employer is not liable to the penalty, he is excused payment by virtue of section 15(3) of the 2006 Act, or that the amount of the penalty is too high; and
(g) any documents to be relied upon in support of the objection.

[2.941]
9
The prescribed period within which a notice of objection must be given for the purposes of section 16(3)(d) of the 2006 Act is 28 days, beginning with the date specified in the penalty notice as the date upon which it is given.

[2.942]
10
The period prescribed for the purposes of section 16(5)(b) of the 2006 Act within which the Secretary of State must inform the objector of his decision is 28 days, beginning with the date on which the notice of objection was given to the Secretary of State.

Codes of Practice

[2.943]
11
The code of practice entitled "Civil Penalties for Employers", issued by the Secretary of State under section 19(1) of the 2006 Act shall come into force on 29 February 2008.

NOTES

The Code of Practice brought into force by this article was replaced by a new Code of Practice in May 2014, which came into force on 16 May 2014. Note, however, that where the employment commenced on or after 29 February 2008 and the breach occurred before 16 May 2014, the Code published in February 2008 still applies.

The 2014 Code of Practice was subsequently replaced by a new Code of Practice, which came into force on 28 January 2019. Note however, that where the employment commenced on or after 29 February 2008 and the breach occurred on or after 16 May 2014 and before 28 January 2019, the Code published in May 2014 applies. See further the 2019 Code at **[4.108]**.

[2.944]
12
The code of practice entitled "Guidance for Employers on the Avoidance of Unlawful Discrimination in Employment Practice While Seeking to Prevent Illegal Working", issued by the Secretary of State under section 23(1) of the 2006 Act shall come into force on 29 February 2008.

NOTES

The Code of Practice brought into force by this article was replaced by a new Code of Practice in May 2014 (at **[4.79]**). Note that the 2014 Code of Practice applies where employment commenced on or after 16 May 2014. It also applies where a repeat check on an existing worker is required to be carried out on or after 16 May 2014 to retain a statutory excuse (see **[4.80]**). The 2008 Code still applies in other cases.

SCHEDULE

Articles 3 and 4

List A

[2.945]
1. [. . .] A passport showing that the holder, or a person named in the passport as the child of the holder, is a British citizen or a citizen of the United Kingdom and Colonies having the right of abode in the United Kingdom.

[**2.** A passport or national identity card showing that the holder, or a person named in the passport as the child of the holder, is a national of a European Economic Area country or Switzerland.]

3. A . . . registration certificate or document certifying . . . permanent residence issued by the Home Office or the Border and Immigration Agency to a national of a European Economic Area country or Switzerland.

4. A permanent residence card issued by the Home Office or the Border and Immigration Agency to the family member of a national of a European Economic Area country or Switzerland.

5. [A current biometric immigration document issued by the Home Office] to the holder which indicates that the person named in it is allowed to stay indefinitely in the United Kingdom, or has no time limit on their stay in the United Kingdom.

6. [A current passport] endorsed to show that the holder is exempt from immigration control, is allowed to stay indefinitely in the United Kingdom, has the right of abode in the United Kingdom, or has no time limit on their stay in the United Kingdom.

7. [A current immigration status document] issued by the Home Office or the Border and Immigration Agency to the holder with an endorsement indicating that the person named in it is allowed to stay indefinitely in the United Kingdom or has no time limit on their stay in the United Kingdom, when produced in combination with an official document giving the person's permanent National Insurance Number and their name issued by a Government agency or a previous employer.

8. A . . . birth certificate issued in the United Kingdom . . . , when produced in combination with an official document giving the person's permanent National Insurance Number and their name issued by a Government agency or a previous employer.

9. [An] adoption certificate issued in the United Kingdom . . . when produced in combination with an official document giving the person's permanent National Insurance Number and their name issued by a Government agency or a previous employer.

10. A birth certificate issued in the Channel Islands, the Isle of Man or Ireland, when produced in combination with an official document giving the person's permanent National Insurance Number and their name issued by a Government agency or a previous employer.

11. An adoption certificate issued in the Channel Islands, the Isle of Man or Ireland, when produced in combination with an official document giving the person's permanent National Insurance Number and their name issued by a Government agency or a previous employer.

12. A certificate of registration or naturalisation as a British citizen, when produced in combination with an official document giving the person's permanent National Insurance Number and their name issued by a Government agency or a previous employer.

13. . . .

[List B—Part 1

1. A current passport endorsed to show that the holder is allowed to stay in the United Kingdom and is allowed to do the type of work in question.

2. A current biometric immigration document issued by the Home Office to the holder which indicates that the person named in it is allowed to stay in the United Kingdom and is allowed to do the work in question.

3. A current residence card (including an accession residence card or a derivative residence card) issued by the Home Office to a non-European Economic Area national who is a family member of a national of a European Economic Area country or Switzerland or who has a derivative right of residence.

4. A current immigration status document containing a photograph issued by the Home Office to the holder with an endorsement indicating that the person named in it is allowed to stay in the United Kingdom and is allowed to do the work in question, when produced in combination with an official document giving the person's permanent National Insurance Number and their name issued by a Government agency or previous employer.

List B—Part 2

1. A certificate of application issued by the Home Office under [regulation 18(3) or 20(2) of the Immigration (European Economic Area) Regulations 2016], to a family member of a national of a European Economic Area country or Switzerland stating that the holder is permitted to take employment which is less than 6 months old.

2. An application registration card issued by the Home Office stating that the holder is permitted to take the employment in question.]

NOTES

In List A, the words omitted from paras 8, 9 are revoked and the word "An" in para 9 is substituted, by the Immigration (Restrictions on Employment) (Code of Practice and Miscellaneous Amendments) Order 2018, SI 2018/1340, art 2(1), (10), as from 28 January 2019.

All other words in square brackets in List A were substituted, and all other words omitted were revoked, by the Immigration (Restrictions on Employment) (Codes of Practice and Amendment) Order 2014, SI 2014/1183, arts 2, 8; note that the words omitted from para 1 were originally inserted by the Immigration (Restrictions on Employment) (Amendment) Order 2009, SI 2009/2908, arts 2, 4.

List B was substituted by SI 2014/1183, arts 2, 9. In Part 2, para 1, the words in square brackets were substituted by SI 2018/1340, art 2(1), (11), as from 28 January 2019.

IMMIGRATION (EMPLOYMENT OF ADULTS SUBJECT TO IMMIGRATION CONTROL) (MAXIMUM PENALTY) ORDER 2008

(SI 2008/132)

NOTES

Made: 22 January 2008.
Authority: Immigration, Asylum and Nationality Act 2006, s 15(2).
Commencement: 29 February 2008.

[2.946]
1 Citation and Commencement
This Order may be cited as the Immigration (Employment of Adults Subject to Immigration Control) (Maximum Penalty) Order 2008 and shall come into force on 29th February 2008.

[2.947]
2 Maximum Penalty
For the purposes of section 15(2) of the Immigration, Asylum and Nationality Act 2006 (employment of adults subject to immigration control: penalty notice) the prescribed maximum is [£20,000].

NOTES

Sum in square brackets substituted by the Immigration (Employment of Adults Subject to Immigration Control) (Maximum Penalty) (Amendment) Order 2014, SI 2014/1262, art 2(1), except in respect of a penalty notice issued to an employer who has acted contrary to s 15(1) of the 2006 Act if, in respect of any employment to which the notice relates, the contravention occurred solely before 16 May 2014. The previous sum was £10,000.

GANGMASTERS (LICENSING CONDITIONS) RULES 2009

(SI 2009/307)

NOTES

Made: 16 February 2009.
Authority: Gangmasters (Licensing) Act 2004, ss 8, 25(2).
Commencement: 6 April 2009.

ARRANGEMENT OF RULES

[2.948]
1 Citation and commencement
These Rules may be cited as the Gangmasters (Licensing Conditions) Rules 2009; they come into force on 6th April 2009.

[2.949]
2 Interpretation
(1) In these Rules—
"business" includes a sole trader, a company, an unincorporated association and a partnership;
"labour user" means a person to whom workers or services are supplied;
"licence holder" means the business granted a licence;
"principal authority" means the individual responsible for the day-to-day management of a business;
"working day" means a day other than a Saturday or a Sunday, Christmas Day or Good Friday, or a date which is a bank holiday under or by virtue of the Banking and Financial Dealings Act 1971.

[2.950]
3 Application for a licence

(1) An application for a licence must be made on the form provided by the Authority and contain such information as the Authority requires for the purposes of determining the application.

(2) The form must be signed by the principal authority of the applicant.

(3) For the purposes of determining the application, the Authority may require the applicant—

(a) to permit an inspection of the applicant's business by the Authority or any person acting on its behalf; and

(b) to supply or make available to the Authority or any person acting on its behalf any document or information.

(4) In paragraph (3)(a), "inspection" includes conducting interviews with such persons as the Authority considers appropriate.

(5) A licence may be renewed before it expires.

[2.951]
4 Licence conditions

(1) The Schedule (licence conditions) has effect.

(2) A licence is granted subject to the conditions set out in Part 2 of the Schedule.

(3) The Authority may grant a licence subject to such additional conditions as it thinks fit.

[2.952]
5 Expiry of licences on change of information

A licence expires if the licence holder's registered number (if it is a company), Unique Tax Reference or Value Added Tax number change.

[2.953]
6 Fees

(1) All fees are payable to the Authority.

(2) An applicant for a licence must, at the time of making the application, pay the application fee specified in the table appropriate to its annual turnover.

(3) If an inspection is required under rule 3(3)(a), the applicant must, on demand, pay the fee specified in the table appropriate to its annual turnover.

(4) A licence holder who wishes to renew its licence must, before the licence expires, pay the fee specified in the table appropriate to its annual turnover.

(5) In this rule, "annual turnover" means the turnover in the work sector regulated by the Gangmasters (Licensing) Act 2004 for the previous financial year or, if there has been no such trading in that sector, on the expected turnover in that sector for the forthcoming financial year, as placed in fee band A, B, C or D in the table.

Table

Annual turnover	*Fee Band*	*Application or renewal fee*	*Inspection fee*
£10 million or more	A	£2,600	£2,900
From £5 million to less than £10 million	B	£2,000	£2,400
From £1 million to less than £5 million	C	£1,200	£2,150
Less than £1 million	D	£400	£1,850

[2.954]
7 Civil liability

(1) Any contravention of, or failure to comply with, any provision of these Rules (including the conditions in the Schedule) by a licence holder is, so far as it causes damage, actionable.

(2) Paragraph (1) is without prejudice to any right of action or defence which exists or may be available apart from the provisions of the Gangmasters (Licensing) Act 2004 and these Rules.

(3) In paragraph (1), "damage" includes the death of, or injury to, any person (including any disease and any impairment of that person's physical or mental condition).

[2.955]
8 Effect of prohibited or unenforceable terms and recoverability of money

(1) Where any term of a contract is prohibited or made unenforceable under these Rules the contract continues to bind the parties if it is capable of continuing in existence without that term.

(2) Where a labour user pays any money pursuant to a contractual term which is unenforceable by virtue of paragraph 10 of the Schedule, the labour user is entitled to recover that money.

[2.956]

9 Requirements relating to information and notices

(1) Any notification, notice or document (including a record) required to be given, sent or made under these Rules must be in writing.

(2) Any notification, notice or document required or authorised by these Rules to be given or sent to any person ("the recipient") may be given to or sent—

(a) by delivering it to the recipient;

(b) by leaving it at the recipient's last known address;

(c) by sending it by post to the recipient at that address; or

(d) by transmitting it by means of an electronic communication, providing that the conditions in paragraph (2) are met.

(3) The conditions are that—

(a) the recipient has stated a willingness to receive the document by means of an electronic communication;

(b) the statement has not been withdrawn; and

(c) the document was transmitted to an electronic address specified by the recipient.

(4) A statement may be—

(a) limited to documents of a specified description;

(b) require a document to be in a specified electronic form;

(c) modified or withdrawn—

(i) in a case where the statement was made by being published, by publishing the modification or withdrawal in the same or in a similar manner;

(ii) in any other case, by giving a notice to the person to whom the statement was made.

(5) In this rule—

"electronic address" includes any number or address used for the purposes of receiving electronic communications;

"electronic communication" means an electronic communication within the meaning of the Electronic Communications Act 2000;

"specified" means specified in a statement made for the purposes of paragraph (2)(a)."

[2.957]

10 Revocations

The Gangmasters (Licensing Conditions) (No 2) Rules 2006 and the Gangmasters (Licensing Conditions) (No 2) (Amendment) Rules 2008 are revoked.

SCHEDULE
LICENCE CONDITIONS

Rule 4

PART 1
INTERPRETATION

[2.958]

1 Meaning of connected person

(1) For the purposes of this Schedule a person ("A") is considered to be connected with—

(a) the members of A's family;

(b) any individual who employs A or A's employee;

(c) any person who is in partnership with A;

(d) any company of which A is an officer and any company connected with that company;

(e) in the case of a company—

(i) any person who is an officer of that company;

(ii) any subsidiary or holding company both as defined in section 1159 of the Companies Act 2006, of that company and any person who is an officer or an employee of any such subsidiary or holding company; and

(iii) any company of which the same person or persons have control; and

(f) in the case of a trustee of a trust, a beneficiary of the trust and any person to whom the terms of the trust confer a power that may be exercised for that person's benefit.

(2) In sub-paragraph (1), the members of A's family are—

(a) A's spouse or civil partner;

(b) any other person (whether of a different sex or the same sex) with whom A lives as partner in an enduring family relationship;

(c) any child, step-child, parent, grandchild, grandparent, brother, sister, cousin, uncle or aunt of A;

(d) any child or step-child of a person within paragraph (b) (and who is not a child or step-child of A) who lives with A and has not attained the age of 18.

2 Meaning of employee

In this Schedule, "employee" has the same meaning as in section 230(1) of the Employment Rights Act 1996.

3 Meaning of 'work-finding services'

In this Schedule, "work-finding services" means services (whether by the provision of information or otherwise) provided by a licence holder—

(a) to a person for the purpose of finding that person employment or seeking to find that person employment;

(b) to an employee of the licence holder for the purpose of finding or seeking to find another person, with a view to the employee acting for and under the control of that other person;

(c) to a person ("B") for the purpose of finding or seeking to find another person ("C"), with a view to B becoming employed by the licence holder and acting for and under the control of C.

PART 2
CONDITIONS

[2.959]

4 Obligation to act in a fit and proper manner

(1) The licence holder, principal authority and any person named or otherwise specified in the licence must at all times act in a fit and proper manner.

(2) If the licence holder or any person named or otherwise specified in the licence is a body corporate, an unincorporated association or partnership—

(a) every director, manager, secretary or other similar officer of the body corporate,

(b) every officer of the association or any member of its governing body, and

(c) every partner,

including any person purporting to act in any such capacity, must at all times act in a fit and proper manner.

5 Obligation to provide information

(1) The licence holder must notify the Authority within 20 working days of commencing an activity authorised by the licence.

(2) The licence holder must notify the Authority within 20 working days if there are significant changes to the details submitted with the holder's application, including any changes to the persons named or the positions otherwise specified in the licence.

(3) The licence holder must notify the Authority as soon as reasonably practicable if the holder knows or suspects the holder's licence has been used by someone not authorised to act on behalf of that holder.

(4) The licence holder must, on request, provide details of the holder's licence to any constable, enforcement officer or compliance officer.

6 Inspection of the business

A licence holder must permit the Authority to inspect the business at any reasonable time.

7 Prohibition on charging fees

A licence holder must not charge a fee to a worker for any work-finding services.

8 Restriction on pre-conditions

(1) A licence holder must not make the provision of work-finding services conditional upon the worker—

(a) using other services or hiring or purchasing goods provided by the licence holder or any person with whom the licence holder is connected; or

(b) giving or not withdrawing consent to the disclosure of information relating to the worker.

(2) Where a worker uses services for which these Rules do not prohibit the charging of a fee, a licence holder providing or making provision for such services must ensure that the worker is able to cancel or withdraw from those services at any time without incurring any detriment or penalty, subject to the worker giving to the provider of those services notice of five working days or, for services relating to the provision of living accommodation, notice of ten working days.

9 Restriction on detrimental action relating to workers working elsewhere

(1) A licence holder must not subject or threaten to subject a worker to any detriment on the ground that the worker has—

(a) terminated or given notice to terminate any contract between the worker and the licence holder; or

(b) taken up or proposes to take up employment with any other person.

(2) A licence holder must not require the worker to notify the licence holder, or any person with whom the holder is connected, of the identity of any future employer.

(3) However, in sub-paragraph (1), "detriment" does not include—

(a) the loss of any benefits to which the worker might have become entitled had the worker not terminated the contract;

(b) the recovery of losses incurred by the licence holder as a result of the failure of the worker to perform agreed work; or

(c) a requirement in a contract with the licence holder for the worker to give a reasonable period of notice to terminate the contract.

10 Restriction on providing workers in industrial disputes

(1) A licence holder must not introduce or supply a worker to a labour user to perform the duties normally performed—

(a) by a worker who is taking part in a strike or other industrial action ("the first worker"), or

(b) by any other worker employed by the labour user and who is assigned by the labour user to perform the duties normally performed by the first worker.

(2) However, sub-paragraph (1) does not apply if—

(a) the licence holder does not know, and had no reasonable grounds for knowing, that the first worker is taking part in a strike or other industrial action, or

(b) in relation to the first worker, the strike or other industrial action is an unofficial strike or other unofficial industrial action for the purposes of section 237 of the Trade Union and Labour Relations (Consolidation) Act 1992.

11 Restriction on paying workers' remuneration

(1) A licence holder must not in respect of a worker whom the holder has introduced or supplied to a labour user who has then employed the worker—

(a) pay or make arrangements to pay to the worker the worker's remuneration arising from the employment with the labour user, or

(b) introduce or refer the labour user to any person with whom the licence holder is connected with a view to that person paying, or making arrangements to pay the remuneration to the worker.

(2) However, sub-paragraph (1) does not apply where the labour user and the licence holder are connected.

12 Restriction on charges to labour users

(1) Any term of a contract between a licence holder and a labour user which is contingent on a worker taking up employment with the labour user or working for the labour user pursuant to being supplied by another licence holder is unenforceable by the licence holder in relation to that worker, unless the contract provides that instead of a transfer fee the labour user may by notice to the licence holder elect for a hire period of such length as is specified in the contract during which the worker will be supplied to the labour user—

(a) in a case where there has been no supply, on the terms specified in the contract; or

(b) in any other case, on terms no less favourable to the labour user than those which applied immediately before the licence holder received the notice.

(2) In sub-paragraph (1), "transfer fee" means any payment in connection with the worker taking up employment with the labour user or in connection with the worker working for the labour user pursuant to being supplied by another licence holder.

(3) Any term as mentioned in sub-paragraph (1) is unenforceable where the licence holder does not supply the worker to the labour user, in accordance with the contract, for the duration of the hire period referred to in sub-paragraph (1) unless the licence holder is in no way at fault.

(4) Any term of a contract between a licence holder and a labour user which is contingent on a worker—

(a) taking up employment with the labour user or any other person to whom the labour user has introduced the worker, or

(b) working for the labour user pursuant to being supplied by another licence holder,

is unenforceable by the licence holder in relation to the event concerned where the worker takes up such employment or begins working pursuant to being supplied by another licence holder (as the case may be) after the end of the relevant period.

(5) In sub-paragraph (4), "the relevant period" means the period of—

(a) eight weeks starting on the day after the day on which the worker last worked for the labour user pursuant to being supplied by the licence holder, or

(b) 14 weeks starting on the first day on which the worker worked for the labour user pursuant to the supply of that worker to that labour user by the licence holder,

whichever period ends later.

(6) In determining the "first day" for the purposes of sub-paragraph (5)(b), no account is taken of any supply that occurred prior to a period of more than 42 days during which that worker did not work for that labour user pursuant to being supplied by that licence holder.

(7) A licence holder must not—

(a) seek to enforce against the labour user, or otherwise seek to give effect to, any term of a contract which is unenforceable by virtue of sub-paragraph (1), (3) or (4); or

(b) otherwise directly or indirectly request a payment to which by virtue of this paragraph the licence holder is not entitled.

13 Prohibition on withholding payment to workers

A licence holder must not withhold or threaten to withhold the whole or any part of any payment due to the worker in respect of any work done on any of the following grounds—

(a) non-receipt of payment from the labour user;

(b) the worker's failure to prove that the worker has worked during a particular period of time (but this does not prevent the licence holder from satisfying itself by other means that the worker worked for the particular period in question);

(c) the worker not having worked during any period other than that to which the payment relates; or

(d) any matter within the control of the licence holder.

14 Notification of charges and terms of offers

(1) Subject to sub-paragraph (2), on the first occasion that a licence holder offers to provide or arrange the provision of a service to a worker, the holder must give notice to the worker stating—

(a) whether that service is a work-finding service for which these Rules prohibit the licence holder from charging a fee; and

(b) whether any other services or goods which may be provided by the licence holder or any other person are services or goods for which the holder or other person providing them will or may charge a fee, together with details of any such fee including—

(i) the amount or method of calculation of the fee;

(ii) the identity of the person to whom the fee is or will be payable;

(iii) a description of the services or goods to which the fee relates and a statement of the worker's right to cancel or withdraw from the service and the notice period required; and

(iv) the circumstances in which refunds or rebates are payable to the worker, the scale of such refunds or rebates, and if no refunds or rebates are payable, a statement to that effect.

(2) Sub-paragraph (1) only applies where one or more services or goods referred to in sub-paragraph (1)(b) for which the worker will or may be charged a fee may be provided to the worker.

(3) A licence holder must give a further notice to a worker stating the matters referred to in sub-paragraph (1)(b) where, subsequent to the first occasion that it offers to provide or arrange the provision of a service to the worker, the licence holder or the person providing to the worker any services or goods referred to in sub-paragraph 1(b), introduces or varies any fees in relation to any services or goods referred to in sub-paragraph 1(b).

(4) Where a licence holder offers any gift or makes an offer of any benefit to a worker, in order to induce the worker to engage the licence holder to provide the worker with services, the holder must notify the worker of the terms on which the gift or benefit is offered before the offer is open for acceptance by the worker.

15 Requirement to agree terms with workers

(1) Before supplying a worker to a labour user, a licence holder must agree the terms which will apply between the licence holder and the worker.

(2) The terms must include—

(a) the type of work the licence holder will find or seek to find for the worker;

(b) whether the worker is or will be supplied by the licence holder under a contract of service or a contract for services, and in either case, the terms and conditions which will apply;

(c) an undertaking that the licence holder will pay the worker in respect of work done by the worker, whether or not the licence holder is paid by the labour user in respect of that work;

(d) the length of notice of termination which the worker is obliged to give the licence holder, and entitled to receive from the holder, in respect any particular assignment;

(e) the rate of remuneration payable, or the minimum rate the licence holder reasonably expects to achieve for the worker;

(f) details of the intervals at which remuneration will be paid; and

(g) details of any entitlement to annual holidays and to payment in respect of such holidays.

(3) A licence holder must record all the terms, where possible in one document, and give the worker the written terms before the holder provides any services to the worker.

(4) Those terms may only be varied by written agreement, a copy of which must be provided to the worker as soon as possible and in any event no later than the end of the fifth working day following the day the variation was agreed.

(5) However, sub-paragraph (3) does not apply if the worker has been given a written statement of particulars of employment in accordance with Part I of the Employment Rights Act 1996.

(6) A licence holder must not make the continued provision of any services by it to a worker conditional on the agreement by the worker to any variation.

16 Requirement to agree terms with labour users

(1) Before first providing services (other than providing information in the form of a publication) to a labour user, a licence holder must agree the terms which will apply between the licence holder and labour user.

(2) The terms must include—

(a) details of any fee which may be payable by the labour user to the licence holder including—

(i) the amount or method of calculation of such fee; and

(ii) the circumstances in which refunds or rebates are payable, and their scale, or, if no refunds or rebates are payable, a statement to that effect; and

(b) details of the procedure to be followed if a worker introduced or supplied to the labour user proves unsatisfactory.

(3) The licence holder must record the terms in a single document and send a copy to the labour user as soon as reasonably practicable.

(4) If any variation to those terms is agreed, the licence holder must provide the labour user with a document containing details and the date of the variation as soon as reasonably practicable.

Part 2 Statutory Instruments

17 Information to be obtained from a labour user

A licence holder must not supply a worker to a labour user unless the holder has obtained the following information—

(a) the identity of the labour user and, if applicable, the nature of the labour user's business;
(b) the date on which the labour user requires a worker to commence work and the duration, or likely duration, of the work;
(c) the position which the labour user seeks to fill, including the type of work a worker in that position would be required to do, the location at which and the hours during which the worker would be required to work;
(d) any risks to health or safety known to the licence holder or labour user and the steps the licence holder or labour user has taken to prevent or control such risks;
(e) the experience, training, qualifications and any authorisation which the licence holder or labour user considers are necessary, or which are required by law or by any professional body, for a worker to possess in order to work in the position; and
(f) any expenses payable by or to the worker.

18 Confirmation to be obtained about a worker

A licence holder must not supply a worker to a labour user unless the holder has obtained confirmation—

(a) of the identity of the worker;
(b) that the worker has the experience, training, qualifications and any authorisation which the licence holder or labour user considers are necessary, or which are required by law or by any professional body, to work in the position which the labour user seeks to fill; and
(c) that the worker is willing to work in the position which the labour user seeks to fill.

19 Steps to be taken for the protection of the worker and the labour user

(1) Before any work is commenced, a licence holder must have—

(a) taken all reasonably practicable steps to ensure that the worker and the labour user are each aware of any requirements imposed by law, or by any professional body, which must be satisfied; and
(b) made all reasonably practicable enquiries to ensure that it would not be detrimental to the interests of the worker or the labour user for the worker to work in the position which the labour user seeks to fill.

(2) Sub-paragraph (1)(a) is without prejudice to any of the licence holder's duties under any enactment or rule of law in relation to health and safety at work.

(3) Where a licence holder receives or obtains information which—

(a) gives the holder reasonable grounds to believe that a worker is unsuitable for the position with a labour user for which the worker is being supplied, or
(b) does not give such reasonable grounds but otherwise indicates that the worker may be unsuitable for that position,

the holder must without delay inform the labour user and any intermediaries of that information.

(4) If sub-paragraph (3)(a) applies, the licence holder must also end the supply of that worker to the labour user.

(5) If sub-paragraph (3)(b) applies, the licence holder must also make such further enquiries as are reasonably practicable as to the suitability of the worker for the position concerned.

(6) The licence holder must inform the labour user and any intermediaries about those enquiries and any further information obtained.

(7) Where information resulting from those enquiries gives the licence holder reasonable grounds to believe that the worker is unsuitable for the position concerned, the holder must without delay inform the labour user and any intermediaries of that information and end the supply of that worker to the labour user.

(8) In this paragraph "without delay" means on the same day, or where not reasonably practicable, the next working day.

(9) Nothing in this paragraph authorises the making of a disclosure in contravention of the Data Protection Act 1998.

20 Provision of information to workers and labour users

(1) A licence holder must ensure that at the same time as the holder supplies or proposes to supply a particular worker to a labour user, the holder—

(a) gives to the labour user the information about the worker obtained in accordance with paragraph 18; and
(b) informs the worker whether the worker will be supplied under a contract of service or a contract for services;

(2) A licence holder must ensure that at the same time as it offers a worker a position with a labour user—

(a) the holder gives to the worker (orally or otherwise) all information it has been provided with under paragraph 17; and
(b) if a rate of remuneration has not been agreed with the labour user, the holder informs the worker (orally or otherwise) of the rate of remuneration it will pay the worker to work in that position.

(3) Where any of the information referred to in sub-paragraph (1) was given orally, the licence holder must afterwards provide it in writing as soon as possible and in any event within three working days.

(4) Sub-paragraph (1) does not apply where—

(a) the worker has performed the same type of work with the labour user during the previous five working days, and

(b) the information required is the same as the information which the worker and labour user have already received,

unless the worker or labour user request otherwise.

(5) Subject to sub-paragraphs (4) and (6), where a licence holder intends to introduce or supply a worker to a labour user for an assignment of five consecutive working days' duration or less—

(a) sub-paragraph (1)(a) may be satisfied by the holder giving to the labour user (orally or otherwise) the name of the worker to be supplied and a written confirmation by the holder that the holder has complied with paragraph 18; and

(b) sub-paragraph (1)(b) may be satisfied, where the holder has previously provided the worker with the information referred to under that sub-paragraph and that information remains unchanged, by the employment business giving to the worker in writing the information referred to in paragraph 17(a) and (b).

(6) Where, after it has started, an assignment to which sub-paragraph (5) applies is extended beyond a duration of five working days, the information referred to in sub-paragraph (1) which has not already been provided must be provided in writing by the end of the eighth working day of the assignment, or by the end of the assignment if sooner.

21 Situations where workers are provided with travel or required to live away from home

(1) A licence holder must not arrange for a worker to take up a position other than as a labour user's employee if, in order to take up that position, the worker has to occupy accommodation other than the worker's home, unless the conditions in sub-paragraph (2) are satisfied.

(2) The conditions are that the licence holder has taken all reasonably practicable steps to ensure that—

(a) suitable accommodation will be available for the worker and details have been provided to the worker, including the terms on which it is offered and any cost; and

(b) suitable arrangements have been made for the worker to travel to such accommodation.

(3) Where a worker is—

(a) to be supplied to a labour user other than as the labour user's employee, or is under the age of 18; and

(b) the licence holder, labour user or any intermediary has arranged free travel or payment of fares for the worker's journey to the place of work,

the licence holder must, if the work does not start or upon it ending, either arrange free travel for the worker's return journey, pay the worker's return fare or obtain an undertaking from the labour user or any intermediary to arrange free travel or pay the return fare.

(4) The licence holder must give notice to the worker setting out the details of the free travel or payment of fares including any conditions on which the same are offered.

(5) If a labour user or intermediary does not comply with an undertaking given under sub-paragraph (3), the licence holder must either arrange free travel for the return journey of the worker or pay the worker's fare.

(6) A licence holder must not arrange for a worker who is under the age of 18 to take up a position which will require the worker to live away from home unless the parent or guardian of the worker has consented in writing.

(7) If a worker is loaned money by the licence holder, the labour user or any intermediary to meet travel or other expenses in order to take up a position—

(a) the worker must be provided with details in writing of the amount loaned and repayment terms; and

(b) the worker must not be asked to repay a greater sum than the amount loaned.

22 Records relating to workers

Every licence holder must record, as soon as reasonably practicable, the following details in relation to every application received from a worker—

(a) the date terms are agreed between the licence holder and the worker;

(b) the worker's name, address and, if under 22, date of birth;

(c) any terms which apply or will apply between the licence holder and the worker, and any document recording any variation;

(d) any relevant details of the worker's training, experience or qualifications and any authorisation to undertake particular work (and copies of any documentary evidence of the same obtained by the licence holder);

(e) details of any requirements specified by the worker in relation to taking up employment;

(f) the names of labour users or sub-contractors to whom the worker is supplied;

(g) details of any resulting engagement and the date from which it takes effect;

(h) the date the contract was terminated (where applicable); and

(i) details of any enquiries made under paragraphs 18 and 19 about the worker and the position concerned, with copies of all relevant documents and dates they were received or sent.

23 Records relating to labour user

Every licence holder must record, as soon as reasonably practicable, the following details relating to labour users—

(a) the date terms are agreed between the licence holder and the labour user;

Part 2 Statutory Instruments

(b) the labour user's name and address, and location of the place of work if different;
(c) details of any sub-contractors;
(d) details of the position the labour user seeks to fill;
(e) the duration or likely duration of the work;
(f) any experience, training, ability, qualifications, or authorisation required by the licence holder or labour user by law, or by any professional body; and any other conditions attaching to the position the labour user seeks to fill;
(g) the terms offered in respect of the position the labour user seeks to fill;
(h) a copy of the terms between the licence holder and the labour user, and any document recording any variation;
(i) the names of workers supplied;
(j) details of enquiries under paragraphs 17 and 19 about the labour user and the position the labour user seeks to fill, with copies of all relevant documents and dates of their receipt;
(k) the details of each resulting engagement and date from which it takes effect; and
(l) dates of requests by the licence holder for fees or other payment from the labour user and of receipt of such fees or other payments, and copies of statements or invoices.

24 Records relating to dealings with other licence holders

(1) Every licence holder must record, as soon as reasonably practicable, the names of any other licence holders whose services the licence holder uses, and details of enquiries made to ascertain that the other licence holder is licensed.

(2) A licence holder who has assigned or sub-contracted any of its obligations under any contract or arrangement with a worker or labour user to another licence holder must ensure that the terms upon which those obligations are assigned or sub-contracted are recorded, where possible in a single document.

25 General provisions relating to records

(1) A licence holder must keep all records for at least one year from creation or, where they have been supplied by another person, from last supply.

(2) If the records are kept other than at premises a licence holder uses for or in connection with the carrying on of its business, the licence holder must ensure that they are readily accessible and capable of being delivered to the licence holder's premises in the United Kingdom or to the Authority within two working days.

26 Conditions which apply to gathering shellfish

(1) This paragraph applies to licences granted in relation to shellfish gathering.

(2) The licence holder must ensure that there is a competent supervisor for each individual group of workers.

(3) The supervisor must be named on the licence.

(4) The supervisor must—
(a) accompany the workers at all times to the work area;
(b) be familiar with the use of any equipment or procedures used when gathering shellfish or accessing the work area; and
(c) be able to communicate directly with every one of the group of workers.

(5) The licence holder or the supervisor must notify the Maritime and Coastguard Agency Rescue and Coordination Centre of—
(a) the licence holder's licence number;
(b) contact details for the licence holder or supervisor;
(c) the number of workers in the group;
(d) the location of the work area; and
(e) the times the group is going out and returning from the work area.

(6) In this paragraph, the "work area" means the place where the shellfish are gathered.

(7) If a fisheries permit or licence is required to gather shellfish the licence holder must ensure that workers comply with the provisions of that permit or licence.

ECCLESIASTICAL OFFICES (TERMS OF SERVICE) REGULATIONS 2009

(SI 2009/2108)

NOTES

Made: 29 July 2009.
Authority: Ecclesiastical Offices (Terms of Service) Measure 2009, s 2.
Commencement: 1 January 2010.
Conciliation: employment tribunal proceedings under reg 9 are "relevant proceedings" for the purposes of the conciliation provisions contained in the Employment Tribunals Act 1996, ss 18–18C; see s 18(1)(x) of the 1996 Act at [**1.757**].

ARRANGEMENT OF REGULATIONS

PART I
INTRODUCTORY

PART II
PARTICULARS OF OFFICE

Right to statement of particulars of office

Enforcement

PART III
RIGHT TO STIPEND AND PROVISION OF ACCOMMODATION

Entitlement to stipend

PART V
TIME OFF WORK, TIME SPENT ON OTHER DUTIES AND SICKNESS

Time off and annual leave

Maternity, paternity, parental and adoption leave and time spent on public duties

Sickness

PART VI
DURATION AND TERMINATION OF APPOINTMENTS AND COMPENSATION

Limited appointments and termination of appointments

Compensation for loss of certain offices

PART VII
CAPABILITY AND GRIEVANCE PROCEDURES

Capability procedures

Grievance procedures

PART VIII
UNFAIR DISMISSAL

Rights on unfair dismissal

PART I
INTRODUCTORY

[2.960]
1 Citation and coming into force

These Regulations may be cited as the Ecclesiastical Offices (Terms of Service) Regulations 2009 and shall come into force on 1st January 2010.

[2.961]
2 Interpretation

(1) In these Regulations—

"capability procedures" means the procedures described in regulation 31 below;

"grievance procedures" means the procedures described in regulation 32 below;

"working day" means any day which is not a rest day or part of a rest period or which is not taken as part of annual or special leave or any such leave as is referred to in regulation 23(1) below and cognate expressions shall be construed accordingly;

"the Measure" means the Ecclesiastical Offices (Terms of Service) Measure 2009.

(2) [Subject to paragraph (3) below,] these Regulations apply to all office holders holding office subject to Common Tenure, whenever appointed to their office, and the following provisions of these Regulations (except regulation 33(3) below) shall apply to an office holder who becomes subject to Common Tenure whilst holding his or her office as if he or she had taken up that office on the day on which he or she became subject to Common Tenure.

[(3) Where an office holder holds an office in pursuance of a contract of employment, these Regulations shall not apply to the office holder in respect of that office, without prejudice to the application of the Regulations in respect of any other office held by that office holder.]

NOTES

Words in square brackets in para (2) inserted, and para (3) added, by the Ecclesiastical Offices (Terms of Service) (Amendment) (No 2) Regulations 2010, SI 2010/2848, reg 2.

PART II
PARTICULARS OF OFFICE

Right to statement of particulars of office

[2.962]
3 Statement of initial particulars of office

(1) An office holder shall be given a written statement of particulars of office by—

(a) an officer of the diocese nominated for that purpose by the diocesan bishop, or

(b) in the case of an office holder who is an archbishop or a diocesan bishop, by an officer of the province nominated by the registrar of the province in which the diocese is situated.

(2) The statement may be given in instalments and (whether or not given in instalments) shall be given not later than the relevant date.

(3) The relevant date for the purposes of paragraph (2) above shall be the expiry of the period of one month from the date on which the office holder took up the office.

(4) The statement shall contain particulars of—

(a) the name of the office holder and the title or description of the officer nominated by the bishop or registrar under paragraph (1) above and the body which is to be treated, for the purpose of these Regulations, as the respondent in any proceedings brought by the office holder before an employment tribunal,

(b) the title of the office to which the office holder has been appointed, and

(c) the date when the appointment took effect.

(5) The statement shall also contain particulars, as at a specified date not more than seven days before the statement (or the instalment containing them) is given, of—

(a) whether the office holder is entitled to a stipend and, if so, the amount of the stipend or the method of calculating it,

(b) the person or body responsible for the payment of the stipend,

(c) the intervals at which any stipend is payable (that is, weekly, monthly or other specified intervals),

(d) whether the office holder is entitled to receive parochial fees and the relationship, if any, of the receipt of such fees to any stipend,

(e) any terms and conditions relating to the reimbursement of expenses incurred in connection with the exercise of the office,

(f) whether the office is full-time or part-time and, in the case of part-time posts, and of posts for which special provision has been made for hours of work, any terms and conditions relating to hours of work (including any terms and conditions relating to normal working hours),

(g) any terms and conditions relating to any of the following—

(i) entitlement to rest periods and holidays, including public holidays,

(ii) incapacity for work due to sickness or injury, including any provision for sick pay,

(iii) pensions and pensions schemes, including, where the office holder comes within either the Church of England Pensions Scheme or the Church of England Funded Pensions Scheme, or both, a statement to that effect, and

(iv) entitlements to maternity, paternity, parental and adoption leave [and time off work to care for dependants] in accordance with regulation 23 below,

(h) where the office holder is required, for the better performance of his or her duties, to occupy any particular residence, details of the address of the property concerned, the person or body to whom or which it belongs, the terms of occupation and any contents to be provided by the relevant housing provider,

(i) the length of notice which the office holder is required to give and, if applicable, receive to terminate the appointment, and

(j) where the appointment is not intended to be permanent, the circumstances in which it may be terminated or, if it is for a fixed term, the date when it is to end.

NOTES

Para (5): words in square brackets in sub-para (g)(iv) inserted by the Ecclesiastical Offices (Terms of Service) (Amendment) Regulations 2010, SI 2010/2407, reg 2.

[2.963]

4 Statement of initial particulars: supplementary

(1) If, in the case of a statement under regulation 3 above, there are no particulars to be entered under any of the paragraphs of that regulation or any of the heads of any such paragraph, that fact shall be stated.

(2) A statement under regulation 3 above may refer the office holder for particulars of any of the matters mentioned in it to these Regulations, to any Measure or Canon, to other regulations of the General Synod or specified provisions thereof or to the provisions of some other document which is reasonably accessible to the office holder.

(3) A statement shall be given to an office holder even if his or her appointment ends before the end of the period within which the statement is required to be given.

[2.964]

5 Note about disciplinary, capability and grievance procedures and pensions

(1) A statement under regulation 3 above shall include a note—

(a) in the case of office holders to whom the provisions of the Ecclesiastical Jurisdiction Measure 1963 relating to offences or of the Clergy Discipline Measure 2003 relating to misconduct apply specifying those provisions,

(b) in the case of office holders other than those referred to in paragraph (a) above, specifying any disciplinary rules or procedures applicable to the office held by the office holder, and

(c) in the case of all office holders, specifying any capability or grievance procedures relating to office holders.

(2) A note included in a statement under paragraph (1) above may comply with that paragraph by referring the office holder to any such laws or documents as are referred to in regulation 4(2) above.

(3) . . .

NOTES

Para (3): revoked by the Church of England (Miscellaneous Provisions) Measure 2018, s 6(9), as from 1 March 2019.

[2.965]

6 Statement of changes

(1) If, after the material date, there is a change in any of the matters particulars of which are required by regulations 3 to 5 above to be included or referred to in a statement under regulation 3, the officer nominated by the bishop or registrar under regulation 3(1) shall give to the office holder a written statement containing particulars of the change.

(2) For the purposes of paragraph (1) above—

(a) in relation to a matter particulars of which are included or referred to in a statement given under regulation 3 other than in instalments, the material date is the date to which the statement relates,

(b) in relation to a matter particulars of which are included or referred to in an instalment of a statement given under regulation 3, the material date is the date to which the instalment relates, and

(c) in relation to any other matter, the material date is the date by which a statement under regulation 3 is required to be given.

(3) A statement under paragraph (1) above shall be given at the earliest opportunity and, in any event, not later than one month after the change in question.

(4) A statement under paragraph (1) may refer the office holder to any such laws or documents as are referred to in regulation 4(2) above.

[2.966]

7 Reasonably accessible document

In regulation 4 above the reference to a document which is reasonably accessible to an office holder is a reference to a document which—

(a) the office holder has reasonable opportunities of reading in the course of the exercise of his or her office, or

(b) where details of a website have been provided to the office holder, the office holder can gain access to without incurring unreasonable expense, or

(c) is made reasonably accessible to the office holder in some other way.

[2.967]

8 Right to itemised statement of stipend

(1) An office holder to whom a stipend is payable has the right to receive from the person or body who or which is responsible for the payment of the stipend, at or before the time at which any payment of stipend is made to him or her, a written itemised statement of stipend.

(2) The statement shall contain particulars of—

(a) the gross amount of the stipend,

(b) the amounts of any deductions from that gross amount and the purposes for which they are made, and

(c) the net amount of stipend payable.

Enforcement

[2.968]

9 References to employment tribunals

(1) Where the officer nominated under regulation 3 above does not give an office holder a statement as required by regulation 3 or 6 or where the office holder is not given a statement as required by regulation 8 (either because the person or body concerned gives no statement or because the statement which is given does not comply with what is required), the office holder may require a reference to be made to an employment tribunal to determine what particulars ought to have been included or referred to in a statement so as to comply with the requirements of the provision concerned.

(2) Where—

(a) a statement purporting to be a statement under regulation 3 or 6 above, or a statement of stipend purporting to comply with regulation 8, has been given to an office holder, and

(b) a question arises as to the particulars which ought to have been included or referred to in the statement so as to comply with the requirements of this Part of these Regulations,

either the person or body concerned or the office holder may require the question to be referred to and determined by an employment tribunal.

(3) For the purposes of this paragraph—

(a) a question as to the particulars which ought to have been included in the note required by regulation 5 above to be included in the statement under regulation 3 does not include any question whether the office is, has been or will be treated as contracted-out employment (for the purposes of Part III of the Pensions Schemes Act 1993), and

(b) a question as to the particulars which ought to have been included in a statement of stipend does not include a question solely as to the accuracy of an amount stated in any such particulars.

(4) An employment tribunal shall not consider a reference under this section in a case where the appointment to which the reference relates has ended unless an application requiring the reference to be made was made—

(a) before the end of the period of three months beginning with the date on which the appointment ended, or

(b) within such period as the tribunal considers reasonable in a case where it is satisfied that it was not reasonably practicable for the application to be made before the end of that period of three months.

[(5) Regulation 9A (extension of time limits to facilitate conciliation before institution of proceedings) applies for the purposes of paragraph (4)(a).]

NOTES

Para (5): added by the Employment Tribunals Act 1996 (Application of Conciliation Provisions) Order 2014, SI 2014/431, art 3, Schedule, paras 35, 36.

Conciliation: employment tribunal proceedings under this regulation are "relevant proceedings" for the purposes of the conciliation provisions contained in the Employment Tribunals Act 1996, ss 18–18C; see s 18(1)(x) of the 1996 Act at **[1.757]**.

[2.969]

[9A Extension of time limit to facilitate conciliation before institution of proceedings

(1) In this regulation—

(a) Day A is the day on which the office holder concerned complies with the requirement in subsection (1) of section 18A of the Employment Tribunals Act 1996 (requirement to contact ACAS before instituting proceedings) in relation to the matter in respect of which the proceedings are brought, and

(b) Day B is the day on which the office holder concerned receives or, if earlier, is treated as receiving (by virtue of regulations made under subsection (11) of that section) the certificate issued under subsection (4) of that section.

(2) In working out when the time limit set by regulation 9(4)(a) expires the period beginning with the day after Day A and ending with Day B is not to be counted.

(3) If the time limit set by regulation 9(4)(a) would (if not extended by this paragraph) expire during the period beginning with Day A and ending one month after Day B, the time limit expires instead at the end of that period.

(4) The power conferred on the employment tribunal by regulation 9(4)(b) to extend the time limit set by paragraph (4)(a) of that regulation is exercisable in relation to that time limit as extended by this regulation.]

NOTES

Inserted by the Employment Tribunals Act 1996 (Application of Conciliation Provisions) Order 2014, SI 2014/431, art 3, Schedule, paras 35, 37.

[2.970]
10 Determination of references

(1) Where, on a reference under regulation 9 above, an employment tribunal determines particulars as being those which ought to have been included or referred to in a statement given under regulation 3 or 6 above, the officer nominated under regulation 3 shall be deemed to have given the office holder a statement in which those particulars were included, or referred to, as specified in the decision of the tribunal.

(2) On determining a reference under regulation 9(2) above relating to a statement purporting to be a statement under regulation 3 or 6, an employment tribunal may—

(a) confirm the particulars as included or referred to in the statement given by the person nominated under regulation 3,
(b) amend those particulars, or
(c) substitute other particulars for them,

as the tribunal may determine to be appropriate; and the statement shall be deemed to have been given by that person to the office holder in accordance with the decision of the tribunal.

(3) Where on a reference under regulation 9 above an employment tribunal finds—

(a) that the person or body responsible has failed to give an office holder a statement of stipend in accordance with regulation 8, or
(b) that a statement of stipend does not, in relation to any deduction, contain the particulars required to be included in that statement by that regulation,

the tribunal shall make a declaration to that effect.

(4) Where on a reference in a case to which paragraph (3) above applies the tribunal further finds that any un-notified deductions have been made from the stipend of the office holder during the period of thirteen weeks immediately preceding the date of the application for the reference (whether or not the deductions were made in breach of the terms and conditions of the appointment), the tribunal may order the person or body who or which is responsible for the payment of the stipend to pay the office holder a sum not exceeding the aggregate of the un-notified deductions so made.

(5) For the purposes of paragraph (4) above a deduction is an un-notified deduction if it is made without the person or body concerned giving the office holder, in any statement of stipend, the particulars of the deduction required by regulation 8.

PART III
RIGHT TO STIPEND AND PROVISION OF ACCOMMODATION

Entitlement to stipend

[2.971]
11 Entitlement to stipend of office holders

(1) Subject to paragraph (3), an office holder who is occupying a full-time stipendiary post which is stated to be such in his or her terms of appointment shall be entitled to receive an annual stipend of an amount—

(a) which is not less than the National Minimum Stipend, or
(b) which, together with any income received by the office holder from other sources which is related to or derived from the duties of the office, is not less than the National Minimum Stipend.

(2) In sub-paragraph (1) above "National Minimum Stipend" means the amount specified from time to time by the Archbishops' Council, in exercise of its functions as the Central Stipends Authority, as the National Minimum Stipend, and the circumstances in which income is treated, for the purposes of paragraph (1)(b) above, as to be taken into account for the purpose of calculating an office holder's entitlement, shall be specified from time to time by the Council in the exercise of those functions.

(3) An office holder who is occupying a part-time post shall be entitled to such stipend as may be specified in the statement of particulars of office given under regulation 3 above.

(4) Paragraphs (1) and (3) above do not apply to an office holder who is serving a sentence of imprisonment following a conviction for a criminal offence.

(5) Any directions given by a diocesan bishop under section 5(2) of the Diocesan Stipends Funds Measure 1953 with respect to providing or augmenting the stipends of the office holders mentioned in that section shall be consistent with the provisions of this regulation.

12–20 *(Regs 12–17 (Provision of accommodation, etc) and regs 18–20 (Part IV: Ministerial development review, education and training) outside the scope of this work.)*

Part 2 Statutory Instruments

PART V
TIME OFF WORK, TIME SPENT ON OTHER DUTIES AND SICKNESS

Time off and annual leave

[2.972]
21 Weekly rest period

(1) An office holder shall be entitled to an uninterrupted rest period of not less than 24 hours in any period of seven days, but the statement of particulars of office issued under regulation 3 above may specify that any rest period may not be taken on or include a Sunday or any or all of the principal Feasts of the Church of England or Ash Wednesday or Good Friday.

[2.973]
22 Annual leave

(1) An office holder occupying a full-time post shall be entitled to thirty six days annual leave or such greater amount as may be specified in the statement of particulars of office in any calendar year without any deduction of any stipend to which the office holder is entitled, but the statement of particulars may specify particular days on which annual leave shall or may not be taken and may, in particular, specify the maximum number of Sundays on which annual leave may be taken.

(2) During the first calendar year of the appointment, the amount of leave which an office holder may take at any time in exercise of the entitlement under paragraph (1) above is limited to the amount which is deemed to have accrued in his or her case at that time under paragraph (3) below, as modified by paragraph (4) where that paragraph applies, less the amount of leave (if any) that he or she has already taken during that year.

(3) For the purposes of paragraph (2) above leave is deemed to accrue over the course of the first year of the appointment at a rate which is proportionate to the proportion of the calendar year remaining after the date on which the appointment begins.

(4) Where the amount of leave that has accrued in a particular case includes a fraction of a day the fraction shall be treated as a whole day.

(5) For the purposes of paragraph (1) above, the amount of leave allowed by that paragraph shall exclude any period of special leave allowed by the diocesan bishop (or in the case of an office holder who is a diocesan bishop, the archbishop of the province in which the diocese is situated), including any such leave granted for the purposes of removal and re-settlement.

(6) Paragraphs (3) and (4) above shall apply during the final calendar year of the appointment as they apply during the first such year.

(7) An office holder occupying a part-time post shall be entitled to such period of annual leave as may be specified in the statement of particulars of office given to the office holder under regulation 3 above and paragraphs (2) to (5) above shall apply accordingly.

Maternity, paternity, parental and adoption leave and time spent on public duties

[2.974]
[23 Maternity, parental, adoption etc leave and time off for carers

(1) An office holder is entitled to maternity, paternity, parental, adoption or shared parental leave for the same periods and subject to the same conditions as for the time being apply in the case of an employee under the Employment Rights Act 1996 or regulations made under it.

(2) Before exercising an entitlement under paragraph (1), an office holder must, in consultation with a responsible person or authority, use all reasonable endeavours to make arrangements for the duties of the office to be performed by one or more other persons during the period of leave.

(3) An office holder may request the appropriate authority to give him or her time off work or to make adjustments to the duties of the office to allow him or her to care for a dependant; and for this purpose, "the appropriate authority" is—

- (a) unless the office holder holds office in a cathedral, the bishop of the diocese;
- (b) if the office holder is the dean of a cathedral, the bishop of the diocese;
- (c) if the office holder holds another office in a cathedral, the dean of the cathedral.

(4) A request under paragraph (3) must be in writing; and the Archbishops' Council may impose other conditions as to the manner in which the request is to be made, including as to the supply of information with the request.

(5) The appropriate authority must consider a request under paragraph (3); and when doing so in the case of an office holder who does not hold office in a cathedral, it must consult the parochial church council of each parish belonging to the benefice concerned.

(6) Where the appropriate authority decides to grant a request under paragraph (3), it may—

- (a) give such time off work or make such adjustments to the duties of the office as appear to it to be reasonable, and
- (b) impose reasonable conditions on the grant of the request, including appropriate variations in the stipend which would otherwise be payable to the office holder.

(7) In this regulation—

"dependant", in relation to an office-holder, means any person who would, if the office-holder were an employee for the purposes of the Employment Rights Act 1996, be a dependant within the meaning of section 57A of that Act, and

"shared parental leave" means leave under section 75E or 75G of that Act.]

NOTES

Commencement: 1 March 2019.

Substituted by the Church of England (Miscellaneous Provisions) Measure 2018, s 6(10), as from 1 March 2019 and subject to s 6(14) thereof, which provides as follows—

"(14) The amendment made by subsection (10) does not affect the power to make further regulations amending or revoking the provision made by that amendment.".

[2.975]

24 Right to time spent on public duties

(1) An office holder may, subject to paragraph (2) below, spend time on public duties other than the duties of his or her office.

(2) The amount of time which an office holder may spend on public duties under this regulation, the occasions on which and any conditions subject to which the time may be spent, are those that are reasonable in all the circumstances, having regard, in particular, to—

(a) how much time is required for the performance of the particular public duty;

(b) how much time has already been spent on public duties under this regulation;

(c) the nature of the office and its duties and the effect of the absence of the office holder on the performance of the duties of the office; and

(d) any remuneration which the office holder is entitled to receive in connection with the duties of the office.

(3) In the event of any dispute as to any of the matters referred to in sub-paragraph (2) above, the matter shall be determined by the diocesan bishop or, in the case of an office holder who is a diocesan bishop, the archbishop of the province in which the diocese is situated.

(4) In this regulation "public duties" means—

(a) any work done for a public authority, including membership of a court or tribunal, or for a charity within the meaning of the Charities Act 2006 or an incorporated or a registered friendly society, and

(b) any work done in connection with the activities of an independent trade union representing office holders of a description which includes the person in question.

[2.976]

25 Right to time off for ante-natal care

(1) An office holder who—

(a) is pregnant, and

(b) has, on the advice of a registered medical practitioner, registered midwife or registered health visitor, made an appointment to attend at any place for the purpose of receiving ante-natal care,

is entitled to take time off during her working hours in order to enable her to keep the appointment.

(2) As soon as is reasonably practicable after the office holder's pregnancy is confirmed, she shall notify the officer of the diocese nominated under regulation 3(1)(a) above.

[2.977]

26 Payment of stipend during time off or time spent on public duties

(1) An office holder who takes any time off or spends time on public duties to which he or she is entitled under regulations 24 or 25 above and who is, under the terms of his or her service, entitled to the payment of a stipend, shall not suffer any reduction in his or her stipend during the time off or time spent on public duties, as the case may be, except, in the case of time spent on public duties, such reduction, if any, as may be specified in the statement of particulars of office given under regulation 3 above (including any statement of changes given under regulation 6 above).

Sickness

[2.978]

27 Sickness

(1) If an office holder who is in receipt of a stipend is unable to perform the duties of his or her office because of illness for a period of one working day or longer he or she must report the absence to the person nominated for the purposes of [this regulation], who shall inform the Commissioners and, if the report is in writing, send them a copy thereof.

[(1A) The person nominated under paragraph (1) above shall be nominated—

(a) in the case of an office holder other than the diocesan bishop, by the diocesan bishop, and

(b) in the case of an office holder who is a diocesan bishop, by the registrar of the province in which the diocese is situated.]

(2) If an office holder [who is in receipt of a stipend] is absent from work because of illness for a continuous period of more than seven days he or she must supply the person nominated as aforesaid with a certificate signed by a qualified medical practitioner and that person shall send a copy of the certificate to the Commissioners.

(3) An office holder who is absent from work because of illness must use all reasonable endeavours to make arrangements for the duties of the office to be performed by another person during the absence which may, where appropriate, consist of notifying a responsible person or authority of the absence.

(4) If an office holder is entitled to receive statutory sick pay under Part XI of the Social Security and Contributions and Benefits Act 1992 for any period of absence from work, the office holder shall be entitled during that period to receive in full any stipend which is payable in respect of the office.

(5) The diocesan bishop or, in the case of an office holder who is a diocesan bishop, the archbishop of the province in which the diocese is situated, may, if he is satisfied that the office holder is, by reason of illness, unable adequately to discharge the duties of his or her office, permit the office holder to be absent from work for such period as he thinks appropriate and may make provision for the discharge of those duties during the period of absence of the office holder.

(6) When giving any directions under section 5(2) of the Diocesan Stipends Funds Measure 1953 in relation to the payment of a stipend to an office holder who is absent from work for illness for any period after the date on which he or she is entitled to receive statutory sick pay under the said Part XI, a diocesan bishop shall have regard to any guidance issued by the Archbishops' Council in the exercise of its functions as the Central Stipends Authority.

NOTES

Words in square brackets in para (1) substituted, and para (1A) inserted, by the Ecclesiastical Offices (Terms of Service) (Amendment) Regulations 2010, SI 2010/2407, reg 4.

Words in square brackets in para (2) inserted by the Ecclesiastical Offices (Terms of Service) (Amendment) Regulations 2015, SI 2015/1654, reg 2, as from 15 November 2015.

[2.979]

28 Medical examination

(1) The diocesan bishop or, in the case of an office holder who is a diocesan bishop, the archbishop of the province in which the diocese is situated may, if he has reasonable grounds for concern about the physical or mental health of an office holder, direct that the office holder shall undergo a medical examination by a medical practitioner selected by agreement between the bishop (or archbishop) and the office holder or, in default of agreement, by medical practitioners consisting of a practitioner chosen by each party.

[(1A) The archbishop of either province may, if he has reasonable grounds for concern about the physical or mental health of the archbishop of the other province, direct that that archbishop shall undergo a medical examination by a medical practitioner selected by agreement between both archbishops or, in default of agreement, by medical practitioners consisting of a practitioner chosen by each archbishop.]

(2) If an office holder fails to comply with a direction given under paragraph (1) [or (1A)] above or fails to disclose or authorise the disclosure of any relevant medical records, when requested to do so, any person or body responsible for operating any capability procedures in respect of the office holder may draw such inferences as appear to that person or body to be appropriate having regard to all the circumstances.

NOTES

Para (1A) inserted, and words in square brackets in para (2) inserted, by the Ecclesiastical Offices (Terms of Service) (Amendment) Regulations 2010, SI 2010/2407, reg 5.

PART VI
DURATION AND TERMINATION OF APPOINTMENTS AND COMPENSATION

Limited appointments and termination of appointments

[2.980]

29 Fixed and other limited term appointments

(1) A person who holds or is to hold office under Common Tenure may be appointed for a fixed term or under terms which provide for the appointment to be terminated on the occurrence of a specified event if—

(a) the office holder occupies a post which is designated as a post created in order to cover an office holder's authorised absence from work,
(b) . . .
(c) the office is designated as a training post,
(d) the office is designated as a post subject to sponsorship funding,
(e) the office is designated as a probationary office,
(f) the office is created by a bishop's mission order made under [section 80 or 83 of the Mission and Pastoral Measure 2011], . . .
(g) the office holder holds a post which is designated as a post which is held in connection or conjunction with another office or employment,
[(h) the office holder does not have the right of abode, or unlimited leave to enter or remain, in the United Kingdom; . . .
(i) the office holder occupies a post which is designated as a Locally Supported Ministry Post,] [or
(j) the office is designated as an interim post,]

. . .

(2) Where a person holds office in any circumstances mentioned in paragraph (1) above the statement of particulars of office required to be given to the office holder under regulation 3 above shall, in addition, contain particulars of any relevant term mentioned in that paragraph.

(3) An office may be designated as a training post if the office holder is required by the diocesan bishop to undertake initial ministerial education.

[(3A) An office designated as a training post may continue to be designated as such for a period of no more than one year following the completion by the office holder of the initial ministerial education.]

(4) An office may be designated as a post subject to sponsorship funding if—

(a) the holder of the post is a person referred to in section 1(1)(g) or (h) of the Measure (other than a vicar in a team ministry), and

(b) any part of the cost of the holder's stipend or other remuneration, pension, housing accommodation or other expenses is defrayed by a person or body other than a diocesan board of finance, parsonages board, parochial church council or the Commissioners.

(5) An office may be designated as a probationary office if, on the date of the appointment of the office holder to the office, the office holder has not held any ecclesiastical office in any place during the period of twelve months immediately preceding that date.

(6) An office may be designated as a probationary office if the office holder has been removed from a previous office by a final adjudication under the capability procedures and the office designated as a probationary office under this paragraph is the first office occupied by the office holder after his or her removal from office.

(7) An office may be designated as a probationary office if—

(a) the office holder has been the subject of a complaint under the Ecclesiastical Jurisdiction Measure 1963 and has had a censure of prohibition, inhibition or suspension imposed on him or her or he or she has resigned, or

(b) the office holder has had imposed on him or her a penalty of removal from office, prohibition for a limited term or revocation of his or her licence under the Clergy Discipline Measure 2003 or he or she has resigned in accordance with that Measure,

and appointment to the office is made on the recommendation of the diocesan bishop with a view to facilitating his or her return to the ministry.

[(7A) An office may be designated as a Locally Supported Ministry Post if—

[(a) the post is held by an assistant curate who is not the priest-in-charge of the benefice to which the parish in which he or she serves belongs,]

(b) the parochial church council of that parish has entered into a legally binding agreement with the diocesan board of finance of the diocese in which the parish is situated to pay the whole cost of the office holder's stipend or other remuneration and expenses, including any pension and housing accommodation and other expenses, and

(c) the designation is in writing, signed by the bishop of the diocese, acting with the consent of the office holder and the parochial church council.]

[(7B) An office (other than an office in a cathedral) may be designated as an interim post if the designation is in writing, signed by the bishop of the diocese in which the office is situated acting with the consent of—

[(a) the office holder, and

(b) the mission and pastoral committee of the diocese.

[(7C) An office in a cathedral may be designated as an interim post if the designation is in writing, signed by the bishop of the diocese in which the cathedral is situated acting with the consent of—

[(a) the office holder,

(b) the dean of the cathedral, and

(c) the Chapter of the cathedral.

[(7D) In deciding whether to designate an office as an interim post, the bishop shall have regard to any guidance issued by the Archbishops' Council.

[(7E) The term of an office designated as an interim post may not exceed three years.

[(7F) An office designated as an interim post may be designated as such again for a further period of up to three years; but an office may not be designated as an interim post if it was designated as such on the two immediately preceding appointments.]

(8) The term of office of any office holder appointed for a fixed term or until the occurrence of a specified event shall terminate on the expiry of the fixed term (unless that term is extended for a further period or periods) or on the occurrence of the event, as the case may be.

NOTES

Sub-para (1)(b), and the final words omitted from para (1), were revoked by the Ecclesiastical Offices (Terms of Service) (Amendment) Regulations 2017, SI 2017/316, reg 2(3), as from 1 July 2017. Note that the Mission and Pastoral etc (Amendment) Measure 2018, s 13 also provided that the final words omitted from para (1) should be revoked, as from a day to be appointed, but the said s 13 was itself repealed by the Church of England (Miscellaneous Provisions) Measure 2018, s 6(15), as from 1 March 2019.

Words in square brackets in sub-para (1)(f) substituted, word omitted from sub-para (1)(h) revoked, sub-para (1)(j) (and the preceding word) inserted, paras (3A), (7B)–(7F) inserted, and sub-para (7A)(a) substituted, by the Ecclesiastical Offices (Terms of Service) (Amendment) Regulations 2015, SI 2015/1654, regs 3, 4(1)–(3), as from 1 November 2015.

Word omitted from sub-para (1)(f) revoked, sub-paras (1)(h), (i) inserted, and para (7A) inserted, by the Ecclesiastical Offices (Terms of Service) (Amendment) Regulations 2010, SI 2010/2407, reg 6.

[2.981]
[29A Holding office beyond the age of 70

(1) A person who holds or is to hold office under Common Tenure and has attained the age of 70 years may be appointed, or may have his or her appointment continued, for a fixed term or under terms which provide for the appointment to be terminated on the occurrence of a specified event if the person occupies a post by virtue of a direction given under this regulation.

(2) An archbishop may give a direction for a person holding the office of diocesan bishop in the archbishop's province who has attained the age of 70 years to continue to hold that office for the period specified in the direction.

(3) A diocesan bishop may, with the concurrence of the archbishop in whose province the diocese is situated, give a direction for a person holding the office of suffragan bishop or dean in the diocese who has attained the age of 70 years to continue to hold that office for the period specified in the direction.

(4) A diocesan bishop may give a direction for a person holding the office of residentiary canon or archdeacon in the diocese who has attained the age of 70 years to continue to hold that office for the period specified in the direction.

(5) A diocesan bishop may give a direction for a person who has attained the age of 70 years to hold or to continue to hold the office of incumbent of a benefice in the diocese, or to hold or to continue to hold an office in the diocese under a licence granted by the bishop, for the period specified in the direction (including in a case where the person was holding the office immediately before attaining that age).

(6) The power to give a direction under a paragraph of this regulation includes, in the case of a person holding office by virtue of a previous direction under that paragraph, a power to give one or more further directions under that paragraph.

(7) The period specified in a direction given under paragraph (2), (3) or (4)—
- (a) must begin with the day on which the person attains the age of 70 years or, where the person is holding the office by virtue of a previous direction given under that paragraph, immediately after the end of the period specified in that previous direction, and
- (b) must end on the date, or on the occurrence of an event, specified in the direction but must not extend beyond the day on which the person attains the age of 75 years.

(8) The period specified in a direction given under paragraph (5)—
- (a) must begin on or after the day on which the person attains the age of 70 years or, where the person is holding the office by virtue of a previous direction given under that paragraph, immediately after the end of the period specified in that previous direction, and
- (b) must end on the date, or on the occurrence of an event, specified in the direction (and may extend beyond the day on which the person attains the age of 75 years),

(9) An archbishop or diocesan bishop may not give a direction under this regulation unless he or she considers that the person in question will be capable of performing the duties of the office throughout the period for which the person is to hold the office.

(10) A diocesan bishop may not give a direction under paragraph (5) in the case of a person holding the office of incumbent or priest in charge of, or vicar in a team ministry for, a benefice in the diocese or the office of assistant curate in the diocese unless the bishop—
- (a) considers that the pastoral needs of the parish or parishes concerned or of the diocese make it desirable to give the direction, and
- (b) has obtained the consent of the parochial church council of the parish or each of the parishes concerned.

(11) In deciding whether to give a direction under this regulation, an archbishop or diocesan bishop shall have regard to any guidance issued by the Archbishops' Council.

(12) A direction given under this regulation must be in writing.]

NOTES

Commencement: 1 July 2017.

Inserted by the Ecclesiastical Offices (Terms of Service) (Amendment) Regulations 2017, SI 2017/316, reg 2(1), as from 1 July 2017.

Compensation for loss of certain offices

[2.982]
30 Posts subject to potential pastoral reorganisation and priests-in-charge

(1) Where—
- (a) an office holder is appointed to hold office as an archdeacon or incumbent or a vicar in a team ministry or a deacon in a team ministry . . .
- (b) at the time when the appointment is made, the mission and pastoral committee of the diocese in which the office is situated has invited the views of the interested parties before submitting proposals to the diocesan bishop in accordance with [section 6 of the Mission and Pastoral Measure 2011] for inclusion in a draft pastoral scheme or order which might affect the office,

the diocesan bishop may designate the office as an office which is subject to potential pastoral reorganisation and the statement of particulars required to be given to the office holder under regulation 3 above shall contain a declaration of that designation.

[(2) If an office designated under paragraph (1) above ceases to exist in consequence of a pastoral scheme or order and the office holder is in receipt of a stipend or other emoluments, the office holder shall be entitled to compensation under Schedule 4 to the Mission and Pastoral Measure 2011.

(2A) For that purpose, any periodical payments or lump sum payable under paragraph 5(1) of Schedule 4 to that Measure, and any entitlement in respect of a period of service deemed by paragraph 11(1)(a) of that Schedule to be a period of pensionable service for the purposes of that Measure, shall be calculated on the basis of the loss of one year's service.]

(3) If, following the designation of an office under paragraph (1) above, no pastoral scheme or order is made affecting the office within such period not exceeding five years immediately following the appointment of the office holder as may be specified by the bishop, the bishop shall notify the office holder that the office is no longer designated under that paragraph.

(4) Where notification is given to the office holder under paragraph (3) above, [section 40 of and Schedule 4 to the Mission and Pastoral Measure 2011] shall apply to the office holder [(and paragraph (2A) above shall not)].

(5) [Paragraphs (2) and (2A)] above shall also apply to any other office holder whose office ceases to exist in consequence of a pastoral scheme or order and who is not otherwise entitled to compensation under [section 40 of and Schedule 4 to the Mission and Pastoral Measure 2011].

(6) Where the licence of a priest-in-charge appointed to a benefice during a vacancy is revoked, in accordance with section 3(4) of the Measure, the priest-in-charge shall be entitled to compensation calculated on the same basis as that on which compensation is calculated under [paragraphs (2) and (2A)] above.

NOTES

Para (1): words omitted from sub-para (a) revoked by the Ecclesiastical Offices (Terms of Service) (Amendment) Regulations 2010, SI 2010/2407, reg 7; words in square brackets in sub-para (b) substituted by the Ecclesiastical Offices (Terms of Service) (Amendment) Regulations 2014, SI 2014/2083, reg 2(1), (2), as from 30 November 2014.

Paras (2), (2A): substituted (for the original para (2)) by SI 2014/2083, reg 2(1), (3), as from 30 November 2014.

Paras (4)–(6): words in square brackets substituted by SI 2014/2083, reg 2(1), (4)–(6), as from 30 November 2014.

PART VII
CAPABILITY AND GRIEVANCE PROCEDURES

Capability procedures

[2.983]

31 Capability procedures to be conducted in accordance with Codes of Practice

(1) The diocesan bishop may, if he considers that the performance of an office holder affords grounds for concern, instigate an inquiry into the capability of an office holder to perform the duties of his or her office in accordance with the following provisions of this regulation.

[(1A) Where the office holder is a diocesan bishop or an archbishop an inquiry may be instigated under paragraph (1)above—

(a) in the case of an office holder who is a diocesan bishop, by the archbishop of the province in which the diocese is situated, and

(b) in the case of an office holder who is an archbishop, by the archbishop of the other province.]

(2) An office holder who is the subject of an inquiry under paragraph (1) above shall be entitled, before the inquiry begins, to be informed in writing of—

(a) any matters relating to the office holder's performance which are to be taken into account in assessing his or her performance;

(b) the procedure which is to be followed in assessing his or her performance, which shall include the opportunity of a meeting between the office holder and the person or authority which is to carry out the procedure and the appointment of a panel or other body to adjudicate on issues concerning the officer holder's capability;

(c) the identity of the person or authority who or which is to carry out the procedure;

(d) any action which may be taken following the completion of the procedure; and

(e) the office holder's rights of appeal against the decision to take any action against the office holder.

(3) Any inquiry instituted under paragraph (1) above shall be conducted in accordance with a Code of Practice issued under section 8 of the Measure.

(4) Any Code of Practice issued under paragraph (3) above may provide for different procedures for different circumstances and may make provision for any other matters which the Archbishops' Council considers appropriate.

(5) When issuing any Code of Practice under paragraph (3) above the Archbishops' Council shall endeavour to ensure that an office holder who is the subject of the capability procedures under this regulation is placed in a position which is no less favourable than that in which an employee would be placed under a Code of Practice issued under Chapter III of Part IV of the Trade Union and Labour Relations (Consolidation) Act 1992.

NOTES

Para (1A): inserted by the Ecclesiastical Offices (Terms of Service) (Amendment) Regulations 2010, SI 2010/2407, reg 8.

Grievance procedures

[2.984]
32 Archbishops' Council to issue Codes of Practice concerning grievance procedures

(1) The Archbishops' Council shall issue a Code of Practice under section 8 of the Measure containing procedures for enabling an office holder to seek redress for grievances.

(2) Any Code of Practice issued under paragraph (1) above shall make provision for—

(a) the office holder to state his or her grievance in writing;
(b) informing the office holder of the person or authority to whom or to which the office holder is to address the grievance;
(c) informing the office holder of the procedures to be followed in discussing the grievance and for taking any action to redress it, including the opportunity for a meeting between the office holder and the person or authority to whom or to which the grievance is to be addressed;
(d) rights of appeal against the decision relating to the grievance and informing the office holder of such rights; and
(e) informing the office holder of any action which may be taken following the completion of the procedure.

(3) Any Code of Practice issued under paragraph (1) above may provide for different procedures for different circumstances and may make provision for any other matters which the Archbishops' Council considers appropriate.

(4) When issuing a Code of Practice under paragraph (1) above the Archbishops' Council shall endeavour to ensure that an office holder who seeks redress under this regulation is placed in a position which is no less favourable than that in which an employee would be placed under a Code of Practice issued under Chapter III of Part IV of the Trade Union and Labour Relations (Consolidation) Act 1992.

PART VIII
UNFAIR DISMISSAL

Rights on unfair dismissal

[2.985]
33 Right to apply to employment tribunal

(1) Where the appointment of an office holder has been terminated by notice given under section 3(6) of the Measure following adjudication under procedures carried out under regulation 31 above, the office holder shall have the right not to be unfairly dismissed.

(2) Subject to paragraph (3) and (4) below Part X of the Employment Rights Act 1996 (in this regulation referred to as "the 1996 Act") shall apply in relation to an office holder who is dismissed in the circumstances described in paragraph (1) above as it applies to an employee who is dismissed for a reason relating to the capability of the employee in accordance with section 98(2) of the 1996 Act and as if in that Act—

(a) any reference to an employee were a reference to the office holder;
(b) except in the case of a person holding office in a cathedral, any reference to an employer were a reference to the Diocesan Board of Finance for the diocese in which, on the date on which the office was terminated, the office holder exercised his office;
(c) in the case of a person holding office in a cathedral, any reference to an employer were a reference to the Chapter of the cathedral; and
(d) any reference to employment were a reference to the holding of an office;

and as if the office holder had been dismissed by that Diocesan Board of Finance or that Chapter, as the case may be, and the reason or principal reason stated in the notice referred to in paragraph (1) above were the reason or principal reason for the dismissal.

(3) Section 108 of the 1996 Act shall not apply in relation to an office holder who has the right not to be unfairly dismissed under this regulation and for the purposes of Part X of that Act the office holder shall be treated as if the period of continuous holding of the office were the period beginning with the date on which the office holder was appointed and ending with the date of the notice referred to in paragraph (1) above.

(4) This regulation shall not apply to any office holder who has attained the retirement age specified in relation to the office holder's office in section 1 of the Ecclesiastical Offices (Age Limit) Measure 1975.

EUROPEAN PUBLIC LIMITED-LIABILITY COMPANY (EMPLOYEE INVOLVEMENT) (GREAT BRITAIN) REGULATIONS 2009

(SI 2009/2401)

NOTES

Made: 9 September 2009.

Authority: European Communities Act 1972, s 2(2).

Commencement: 1 October 2009.

Note: with regard to the authority for these Regulations, note that the European Communities Act 1972 is repealed by the European Union (Withdrawal) Act 2018, s 1, as from exit day (as defined in s 20 of that Act); but note also that provision is made for the continuation in force of any subordinate legislation made under the authority of s 2(2) of the 1972 Act by s 2 of the 2018 Act at **[1.2240]**, subject to the provisions of s 5 of, and Sch 1 to, the 2018 Act at **[1.2243]**, **[1.2253]**.

Employment Appeal Tribunal: an appeal lies to the Employment Appeal Tribunal on any question of law arising from any decision of, or in any proceedings before, an employment tribunal under or by virtue of these Regulations; see the Employment Tribunals Act 1996, s 21(1)(w) at **[1.764]**.

Conciliation: employment tribunal proceedings under regs 28 or 32 are "relevant proceedings" for the purposes of the conciliation provisions contained in the Employment Tribunals Act 1996, ss 18–18C; see s 18(1)(y) of the 1996 Act at **[1.757]**.

See *Harvey* NIII(4).

ARRANGEMENT OF REGULATIONS

PART 1
INTRODUCTORY PROVISIONS

[2.986]

1 Citation, commencement and extent

(1) These Regulations may be cited as the European Public Limited-Liability Company (Employee Involvement) (Great Britain) Regulations 2009.

(2) These Regulations come into force on 1st October 2009.

(3) These Regulations extend to the whole of Great Britain.

[2.987]

2 EC Directive and EC Regulation

(1) In these Regulations—

"the EC Directive" means Council Directive 2001/86/EC of 8 October 2001 supplementing the Statute for a European Company with regard to the involvement of employees;

"the EC Regulation" means Council Regulation 2157/2001/EC of 8 October 2001 on the Statute for a European Company.

(2) References in these Regulations to numbered Articles are, unless otherwise specified, references to Articles in the EC Regulation.

[2.988]

3 Interpretation

(1) In these Regulations—

"absolute majority vote" means a vote passed by a majority of the total membership of the special negotiating body where the members voting with that majority represent the majority of the employees of the participating companies and their concerned subsidiaries and establishments employed in the EEA states;

["agency worker" has the same meaning as in regulation 3 of the Agency Workers Regulations 2010;]

"Appeal Tribunal" means the Employment Appeal Tribunal;

"CAC" means the Central Arbitration Committee;

"dismissed" and "dismissal", in relation to an employee, have the same meaning as in Part 10 of the Employment Rights Act 1996;

"employee" means an individual who has entered into or works under a contract of employment and includes, where the employment has ceased, an individual who worked under a contract of employment;

"employee involvement agreement" means an agreement reached between the special negotiating body and the competent organs of the participating companies governing the arrangements for the involvement of employees within the SE;

"employees' representatives" means—

(a) if the employees are of a description in respect of which an independent trade union is recognised by their employer for the purpose of collective bargaining, representatives of the trade union who normally take part as negotiators in the collective bargaining process, and

(b) any other employees of their employer who are elected or appointed as employee representatives to positions in which they are expected to receive, on behalf of the employees, information—

(i) which is relevant to the terms and conditions of employment of the employees, or

(ii) about the activities of the undertaking which may significantly affect the interests of the employees,

but excluding representatives who are expected to receive information relevant only to a specific aspect of the terms and conditions or interests of the employees, such as health and safety or collective redundancies;

"information and consultation representative" has the meaning given to it in regulation 15(5);

"participation" means the influence of the representative body and the employees' representatives in the SE or a participating company by way of the right to—

(a) elect or appoint some of the members of the SE's or the participating company's supervisory or administrative organ, or

(b) recommend or oppose the appointment of some or all of the members of the SE's or the participating company's supervisory or administrative organ;

["Relevant State" means an EEA State or the United Kingdom;]

"representative body" means the persons elected or appointed under the employee involvement agreement or under the standard rules on employee involvement;

"SE" means a European Public Limited-Liability Company (or Societas Europaea) within the meaning of the EC Regulation;

"SE established by merger" means an SE established in accordance with Article 2(1);

"SE established by formation of a holding company or subsidiary company" means an SE established in accordance with Article 2(2) or 2(3), as the case may be;

"SE established by transformation" means an SE established in accordance with Article 2(4);

"standard rules on employee involvement" means the rules in the Schedule to these Regulations;

["suitable information relating to the use of agency workers" means—

(a) the number of agency workers working temporarily for and under the supervision and direction of the undertaking;

(b) the parts of the undertaking in which those agency workers are working; and

(c) the type of work those agency workers are carrying out;]

"two thirds majority vote" means a vote passed by a majority of at least two thirds of the total membership of the special negotiating body where the members voting with that majority—

(a) represent at least two thirds of the employees of the participating companies and their concerned subsidiaries and establishments employed in the EEA states, and

(b) include members representing employees employed in at least two EEA states;

"UK employee" means an employee employed to work in the United Kingdom;

"UK members of the special negotiating body" means members of the special negotiating body elected or appointed by UK employees,

["UK Societas" means a European Public Limited-Liability Company (or Societas Europaea) within the meaning of the EC Regulation, as it had effect immediately before exit day, which on exit day converted to a United Kingdom Societas within the meaning of the EC Regulation.]

(2) In these Regulations the following expressions have the meaning given by Article 2 of the EC Directive[, subject to the stated modifications]—

"participating companies",

"subsidiary",

"special negotiating body",

"involvement of employees",

["information", read as if—

(a) for "Member State" there were substituted "Relevant State",

(b) after each occurrence of "SE" there were inserted "or the UK Societas"],

"consultation"[, read as if after each occurrence of "SE" there were inserted "or the UK Societas"], and references to a "concerned subsidiary" or a "concerned establishment" are to be construed in accordance with the definition of "concerned subsidiary or establishment" in the EC Directive.

[(2A) Where an employee involvement agreement was reached before exit day for a UK Societas, or where the standard rules on employee involvement apply in respect of that UK Societas, on and after exit day any reference to an "EEA State" in that agreement or those rules, insofar as they apply to that UK Societas, must, where appropriate, be read as if they were to "an EEA State and the United Kingdom.".]

(3) Except as otherwise provided, words and expressions used in the EC Regulation or the EC Directive have the same meaning in these Regulations as they have in that Regulation or Directive.

(4) Except as otherwise provided, references in these Regulations to an SE are to an SE that is to be, or is, registered in Great Britain.

NOTES

Para (1): definitions "agency worker" and "suitable information relating to the use of agency workers" inserted by the Agency Workers Regulations 2010, SI 2010/93, reg 25, Sch 2, Pt 2, paras 47, 48.

definitions "absolute majority vote", "agency worker", "participation", "SE established by merger", "SE established by formation of a holding company or subsidiary company", "SE established by transformation", "suitable information relating to the use of agency workers", "two thirds majority vote" and "UK members of the special negotiating body" revoked, definitions "Relevant State" and "UK Societas" inserted, and definitions "employee involvement agreement", "information and consultation representative", "SE" and "standard rules on employee involvement" substituted as follows, by the European

Public Limited-Liability Company (Amendment etc) (EU Exit) Regulations 2018, SI 2018/1298, regs 48, 49(a), as from exit day (as defined in the European Union (Withdrawal) Act 2018, s 20) (for transitional provisions and savings, see regs 146–152A of the 2018 Regulations at **[2.2102]** et seq).

""employee involvement agreement" means—

(a) an agreement reached before exit day between the special negotiating body and the competent organs of the participating companies which governs the arrangements for the involvement of employees within the UK Societas,

(b) an agreement reached before or after exit day between the special negotiating body and the competent organs of the participating companies which governs the arrangements for the involvement of employees within the SE,

(c) an agreement reached after exit day following a special negotiating body having been reconvened under regulation 17 of these Regulations, which governs the arrangements for the involvement of employees within the UK Societas;

"information and consultation representatives" means representatives elected or appointed to act pursuant to information and consultation procedures established in an employee involvement agreement instead of a representative body;

"SE" means a European Public Limited-Liability Company (or Societas Europaea) within the meaning of the EC Regulation, as it has effect in EU law as amended from time to time;

"standard rules on employee involvement" means—

(a) in respect of a UK Societas the rules on employee involvement which apply by virtue of regulation 19, as it had effect immediately before exit day,".

(b) in respect of an SE the rules laid down by the EEA State in which it has its registered office;".

Para (2): words in first and third pairs of square brackets inserted and words in second pair of square brackets substituted (for original word "information") by SI 2018/1298, regs 48, 49(b), as from exit day (as defined in the European Union (Withdrawal) Act 2018, s 20) (for transitional provisions and savings, see regs 146–152A of the 2018 Regulations at **[2.2102]** et seq).

Para (2A): inserted by SI 2018/1298, regs 48, 49(c), as from exit day (as defined in the European Union (Withdrawal) Act 2018, s 20) (for transitional provisions and savings, see regs 146–152A of the 2018 Regulations at **[2.2102]** et seq).

Para (4): revoked by SI 2018/1298, regs 48, 49(d), as from exit day (as defined in the European Union (Withdrawal) Act 2018, s 20) (for transitional provisions and savings, see regs 146–152A of the 2018 Regulations at **[2.2102]** et seq).

[2.989]

4 Application of these Regulations

(1) These Regulations apply where—

(a) a participating company intends to establish an SE whose registered office is to be in Great Britain, or

(b) an SE has its registered office in Great Britain.

(2) Where there are UK employees, Part 3 also applies (regardless of where the registered office is to be situated) in relation to the election or appointment of UK members of the special negotiating body, unless the majority of those employees is employed to work in Northern Ireland.

(3) Parts 6 to 9 also apply (regardless of where the registered office of the SE is, or is intended to be situated) if any of the following is registered or, as the case may be, situated in Great Britain—

(a) a participating company, its concerned subsidiaries or establishments;

(b) a subsidiary of an SE;

(c) an establishment of an SE;

(d) an employee or an employees' representative.

NOTES

Para (1): substituted by the European Public Limited-Liability Company (Amendment etc) (EU Exit) Regulations 2018, SI 2018/1298, regs 48, 50(a), as from exit day (as defined in the European Union (Withdrawal) Act 2018, s 20) (for transitional provisions and savings, see regs 146–152A of the 2018 Regulations at **[2.2102]** et seq), as follows—

"(1) These Regulations apply in respect of a UK Societas.".

Para (2): revoked by SI 2018/1298, regs 48, 50(b), as from exit day (as defined in the European Union (Withdrawal) Act 2018, s 20) (for transitional provisions and savings, see regs 146–152A of the 2018 Regulations at **[2.2102]** et seq).

Para (3): sub-para (d) substituted by SI 2018/1298, regs 48, 50(c), as from exit day (as defined in the European Union (Withdrawal) Act 2018, s 20) (for transitional provisions and savings, see regs 146–152A of the 2018 Regulations at **[2.2102]** et seq), as follows—

"(d) an employee of an SE or a representative of such an employee.".

PART 2
PARTICIPATING COMPANIES AND THE SPECIAL NEGOTIATING BODY

[2.990]

5 Duty on participating company to provide information

(1) When the competent organ of a participating company decides to form an SE, that organ must, as soon as possible after—

(a) publishing the draft terms of merger,

(b) creating a holding company, or

(c) agreeing a plan to form a subsidiary or to transform into an SE,

provide information to the employees' representatives of the participating company, its concerned subsidiaries and establishments or, if no such representatives exist, the employees themselves.

(2) The information referred to in paragraph (1) must include, as a minimum, information—

(a) identifying the participating companies, concerned subsidiaries and establishments,

(b) *giving the number of employees employed by each participating company and concerned subsidiary and at each concerned establishment, . . .*

(c) *giving the number of employees employed to work in each EEA State;*

[(d) *the number of agency workers working temporarily for and under the supervision and direction of the undertaking;*

(e) *the parts of the undertaking in which those agency workers are working; and*

(f) *the type of work those agency workers are carrying out].*

(3) When a special negotiating body has been formed in accordance with regulation 8, the competent organs of each participating company must provide that body with such information as is necessary to keep it informed of the plan and progress of establishing the SE up to the time the SE has been registered.

NOTES

Revoked, together with regs 6–16, by the European Public Limited-Liability Company (Amendment etc) (EU Exit) Regulations 2018, SI 2018/1298, regs 48, 51, as from exit day (as defined in the European Union (Withdrawal) Act 2018, s 20) (for transitional provisions and savings, see regs 146–152A of the 2018 Regulations at **[2.2102]** et seq).

Para (2): word omitted from sub-para (b) revoked, and sub-paras (d)–(f) added, by the Agency Workers Regulations 2010, SI 2010/93, reg 25, Sch 2, Pt 2, paras 47, 49.

[2.991]

6 Complaint of failure to provide information

(1) An employees' representative, or an employee for whom there is no such representative, may present a complaint to the CAC that—

(a) *the competent organ of a participating company has failed to provide the information referred to in regulation 5, or*

(b) *the information provided by the competent organ of a participating company for the purpose of complying with regulation 5 is false or incomplete in a material particular.*

(2) If the CAC finds the complaint well-founded, it must make an order requiring the competent organ to disclose information to the complainant.

(3) The order must specify—

(a) *the information in respect of which the CAC finds that the complaint is well-founded and which is to be disclosed to the complainant, and*

(b) *a date (not less than one week after the date of the order) by which the competent organ must disclose the information specified in the order.*

NOTES

Revoked as noted to reg 5 at **[2.990]**.

[2.992]

7 Function of the special negotiating body

The special negotiating body and the competent organs of the participating companies have the task of reaching an employee involvement agreement.

NOTES

Revoked as noted to reg 5 at **[2.990]**.

[2.993]

8 Composition of the special negotiating body

(1) The competent organs of the participating companies must make arrangements for the establishment of a special negotiating body constituted in accordance with the following provisions of this regulation.

(2) In each EEA state in which employees of a participating company or concerned subsidiary are employed to work, those employees must be given an entitlement to elect or appoint one member of the special negotiating body for each 10%, or fraction of 10%, which those employees represent of the total workforce. These members are the "ordinary members".

(3) If, in the case of an SE to be established by merger, following an election or appointment under paragraph (2), the members elected or appointed to the special negotiating body do not include at least one eligible member in respect of each relevant company, the employees of any relevant company in respect of which there is no eligible member must be given an entitlement, subject to paragraph (4), to elect or appoint an additional member to the special negotiating body.

(4) The number of additional members which the employees are entitled to elect or appoint under paragraph (3) must not exceed 20% of the number of ordinary members elected or appointed under paragraph (2). If the number of additional members under paragraph (3) would exceed that percentage, the employees who are entitled to appoint or elect the additional members are—

(a) *if one additional member is to be appointed or elected, those employed by the company not represented under paragraph (3) having the highest number of employees;*

(b) *if more than one additional member is to be appointed or elected, those employed by the companies in each EEA state that are not represented under paragraph (3) having the highest number of employees in descending order, starting with the company with the highest number, followed by those employed by the companies in each EEA state that are not so represented having the second highest number of employees in descending order, starting with the company (among those companies) with the highest number.*

(5) The competent organs of the participating companies must, as soon as reasonably practicable and in any event no later than one month after the establishment of the special negotiating body, inform their employees and those of their concerned subsidiaries of the identity of the members of the special negotiating body.

(6) If, following the appointment or election of members to the special negotiating body in accordance with this regulation, changes to the participating companies, concerned subsidiaries or concerned establishments result in the number of ordinary or additional members which employees would be entitled to elect or appoint under this regulation either increasing or decreasing—

(a) the original appointment or election of members of the special negotiating body ceases to have effect, and

(b) those employees are entitled to elect or appoint the new number of members in accordance with the provisions of these Regulations.

(7) If a member of the special negotiating body is no longer willing or able to continue serving as such a member, the employees whom the member represents are entitled to elect or appoint a new member in place of that member.

(8) In this regulation—

"eligible member" means a person who is—

(a) in the case of a relevant company registered in an EEA state whose legislation allows representatives of trade unions who are not employees to be elected to the special negotiating body, an employee of the relevant company or a trade union representative;

(b) in the case of a relevant company not registered in such an EEA state, an employee of the relevant company;

"relevant company" means a participating company which has employees in the EEA state in which it is registered and which it is proposed will cease to exist on or following the registration of the SE;

"the total workforce" means the total number of employees employed by all participating companies and concerned subsidiaries throughout all EEA states.

NOTES

Revoked as noted to reg 5 at **[2.990]**.

[2.994]

9 Complaint about establishment of special negotiating body

(1) An application may be presented to the CAC for a declaration that the special negotiating body has not been established at all or has not been established properly in accordance with regulation 8.

(2) An application may be presented under this regulation by any of the following—

(a) a person elected or appointed to be a member of the special negotiating body;

(b) an employees' representative;

(c) where there is no employees' representative in respect of a participating company or concerned subsidiary, an employee of that participating company or concerned subsidiary;

(d) the competent organ of a participating company or concerned subsidiary.

(3) The CAC may only consider an application made under paragraph (1) if it is made within a period of one month following the date or, if more than one, the last date on which the participating companies complied or should have complied with the obligation to inform their employees under regulation 8(5).

(4) If the CAC finds the application well-founded—

(a) it must make a declaration that the special negotiating body has not been established at all or has not been established properly, and

(b) the competent organs of the participating companies continue to be under the obligation in regulation 8(1).

NOTES

Revoked as noted to reg 5 at **[2.990]**.

PART 3
ELECTION OR APPOINTMENT OF UK MEMBERS OF THE SPECIAL NEGOTIATING BODY

[2.995]

10 Ballot arrangements

(1) Subject to regulation 11, the UK members of the special negotiating body must be elected by balloting the UK employees.

(2) The management of the participating companies that employ UK employees ("the management") must arrange for the holding of a ballot or ballots of those employees in accordance with the requirements specified in paragraph (3).

(3) The requirements are—

(a) in relation to the election of ordinary members under regulation 8(2), that—

(i) if the number of members which UK employees are entitled to elect to the special negotiating body is equal to the number of participating companies which have UK employees, there must be separate ballots of the UK employees in each participating company;

(ii) *if the number of members which the UK employees are entitled to elect to the special negotiating body is greater than the number of participating companies which have UK employees, there must be separate ballots of the UK employees in each participating company and the management must ensure, as far as practicable, that at least one member representing each such participating company is elected to the special negotiating body and that the number of members representing each company is proportionate to the number of employees in that company;*

(iii) *if the number of members which the UK employees are entitled to elect to the special negotiating body is smaller than the number of participating companies which have employees in the United Kingdom—*

(aa) *the number of ballots held must be equivalent to the number of members to be elected,*

(bb) *a separate ballot must be held in respect of each of the participating companies with the higher or highest number of employees, and*

(cc) *it must be ensured that any employees of a participating company in respect of which a ballot does not have to be held are entitled to vote in a ballot held in respect of one of the other participating companies;*

(iv) *if there are any UK employees employed by a concerned subsidiary or establishment of non-UK participating companies, the management must ensure that those employees are entitled to vote in a ballot held pursuant to this regulation;*

(b) *that in relation to the ballot of additional members under regulation 8(3) the management must hold a separate ballot in respect of each participating company entitled to elect an additional member;*

(c) *that, in a ballot in respect of a particular participating company, all UK employees employed by that participating company or by its concerned subsidiaries or at its concerned establishments are entitled to vote;*

(d) *that a person is entitled to stand as a candidate for election as a member of the special negotiating body in a ballot in respect of a particular participating company if, immediately before the latest time at which a person may become a candidate, the person is—*

(i) *a UK employee employed by that participating company, by any of its concerned subsidiaries or at any of its concerned establishments, or*

(ii) *if the management of that participating company so permits, a representative of a trade union who is not an employee of that participating company or any of its concerned subsidiaries;*

(e) *that the management must appoint in accordance with paragraph (7) a person (a "ballot supervisor")—*

(i) *to supervise the conduct of the ballot of UK employees, or*

(ii) *where there is to be more than one ballot, to supervise the conduct of each of the separate ballots,*

and, in a case falling within paragraph (ii), may appoint different persons to supervise the conduct of such different separate ballots as the management may determine;

(f) *that after the management has formulated proposals as to the arrangements for the ballot of UK employees and before it has published the final arrangements under sub-paragraph (g) it must, so far as reasonably practicable, consult the UK employees' representatives on the proposed arrangements for the ballot of UK employees; and*

(g) *that the management must publish the final arrangements for the ballot of UK employees in such manner as to bring them to the attention of, so far as reasonably practicable, all UK employees and the UK employees' representatives.*

(4) *Any UK employee or UK employees' representative who believes that the arrangements for the ballot of the UK employees do not comply with the requirements of paragraph (3) may, within a period of 21 days beginning on the date on which the management published the final arrangements under sub-paragraph (g) of that paragraph, present a complaint to the CAC.*

(5) *If the CAC finds the complaint well-founded, it must make a declaration to that effect and may make an order requiring the management to modify the arrangements it has made for the ballot of UK employees or to satisfy the requirements in sub-paragraph (f) or (g) of paragraph (3).*

(6) *An order under paragraph (5) must specify—*

(a) *the modifications to the arrangements which the management is required to make, and*

(b) *the requirements it must satisfy.*

(7) *The management may appoint a person to be a ballot supervisor for the purposes of paragraph (3)(e) only if the management—*

(a) *reasonably believes that the person will carry out competently any functions conferred on the person in relation to the ballot, and*

(b) *has no reasonable grounds for believing that the person's independence in relation to the ballot might reasonably be called into question.*

NOTES

Revoked as noted to reg 5 at **[2.990]**.

[2.996]

11 Conduct of the ballot

(1) *The management must—*

(a) ensure that a ballot supervisor appointed under regulation 10(3)(e) carries out the functions conferred or imposed on the ballot supervisor under this regulation;

(b) ensure that there is no interference from the management with the ballot supervisor's carrying out of those functions;

(c) comply with all reasonable requests made by a ballot supervisor for the purposes of, or in connection with, the carrying out of those functions.

(2) A ballot supervisor's appointment must require that the ballot supervisor—

(a) supervises the conduct of the ballot, or the separate ballots, that the ballot supervisor is being appointed to supervise, in accordance with the arrangements for the ballot of UK employees published by the management under regulation 10(3)(g) or, where appropriate, in accordance with the arrangements as required to be modified by an order made as a result of a complaint presented under regulation 10(4);

(b) does not conduct the ballot or any of the separate ballots before the management has satisfied the requirement specified in regulation 10(3)(g) and—

(i) where no complaint has been presented under regulation 10(4), before the expiry of a period of 21 days beginning on the date on which the management published its arrangements under regulation 10(3)(g), or

(ii) where a complaint has been presented under regulation 10(4), before the complaint has been determined and, where appropriate, the arrangements have been modified as required by an order made as a result of that complaint;

(c) conducts the ballot, or each separate ballot, so as to secure that—

(i) so far as reasonably practicable, those entitled to vote are given the opportunity to vote,

(ii) so far as reasonably practicable, those entitled to stand as candidates are given the opportunity to stand,

(iii) so far as reasonably practicable, those voting are able to do so in secret, and

(iv) the votes given in the ballot are fairly and accurately counted.

(3) As soon as reasonably practicable after the holding of the ballot, the ballot supervisor must publish the results of the ballot in such manner as to make them available to the management and, so far as reasonably practicable, to the UK employees entitled to vote in the ballot and the persons who stood as candidates.

(4) If a ballot supervisor considers (whether on the basis of representations made to the ballot supervisor by another person or otherwise)—

(a) that any of the requirements referred to in paragraph (2) was not satisfied, with the result that the outcome of the ballot would have been different, or

(b) that there was interference with the carrying out of the ballot supervisor's functions, or a failure by the management to comply with all reasonable requests made by the ballot supervisor, with the result that the ballot supervisor was unable to form a proper judgement as to whether each of the requirements referred to in paragraph (2) was satisfied in the ballot,

the ballot supervisor must publish a report ("an ineffective ballot report").

(5) Where a ballot supervisor publishes an ineffective ballot report, the report must be published within a period of one month commencing on the date on which the ballot supervisor publishes the results of the ballot under paragraph (3).

(6) A ballot supervisor must publish an ineffective ballot report in such manner as to make it available to the management and, so far as reasonably practicable, to the UK employees entitled to vote in the ballot and the persons who stood as candidates in the ballot.

(7) Where a ballot supervisor publishes an ineffective ballot report, then—

(a) if there has been a single ballot, or if an ineffective ballot report has been published in respect of every separate ballot, the outcome of the ballot or ballots has no effect and the management is again under the obligation in regulation 10(2);

(b) if there have been separate ballots and sub-paragraph (a) does not apply—

(i) the management must arrange for the separate ballot or ballots in respect of which an ineffective ballot report was published to be re-held in accordance with regulation 10 and this regulation, and

(ii) no such ballot has effect until it has been re-held and no ineffective ballot report has been published in respect of it.

(8) All costs relating to the holding of a ballot, including payments made to a ballot supervisor for supervising the conduct of the ballot, must be borne by the management (whether or not an ineffective ballot report has been published).

NOTES

Revoked as noted to reg 5 at **[2.990]**.

[2.997]

12 Appointment of UK members by a consultative committee

(1) This regulation applies where—

(a) regulation 10(3)(a)(i) or (ii) or (b) would (apart from this regulation) require a ballot to be held, but

(b) there exists in the participating company in respect of which a ballot would be held under regulation 10, a consultative committee.

(2) Where this regulation applies—

(a) the election provided for in regulation 10 must not take place;

(b) the consultative committee is entitled to appoint the UK member or members of the special negotiating body who would otherwise be elected pursuant to regulation 10;

(c) any such appointment by the consultative committee must comply with paragraph (3).

(3) The consultative committee may appoint as a member of the special negotiating body—

(a) one of their number, or

(b) if the management of the participating company in respect of which the consultative committee exists so permits, a trade union representative who is not an employee of that company.

(4) In this regulation a "consultative committee" means a body of persons—

(a) whose normal functions include or comprise the carrying out of an information and consultation function,

(b) which is able to carry out its information and consultation function without interference from the management of the participating company,

(c) which, in carrying out its information and consultation function, represents all the employees of the participating company, and

(d) which consists wholly of persons who are employees of the participating company or its concerned subsidiaries.

(5) In paragraph (4) "information and consultation function" means the function of—

(a) receiving, on behalf of all the employees of the participating company, information which may significantly affect the interests of the employees of that company, but excluding information which is relevant only to a specific aspect of the interests of the employees, such as health and safety or collective redundancies, and

(b) being consulted by the management of the participating company on the information referred to in sub-paragraph (a).

(6) The consultative committee must publish the names of the persons whom it has appointed to be members of the special negotiating body in such a manner as to bring them to the attention of the management of the participating company and, so far as reasonably practicable, the employees and the employees' representatives of that company and its concerned subsidiaries.

(7) Where the management of the participating company, or an employee or an employees' representative, believes that—

(a) the consultative committee does not satisfy the requirements in paragraph (4), or

(b) any of the persons appointed by the consultative committee is not entitled to be appointed,

the management of the participating company or, as the case may be, the employee or the employees' representative may present a complaint to the CAC within a period of 21 days beginning on the date on which the consultative committee published under paragraph (6) the names of the persons appointed.

(8) If the CAC finds the complaint well-founded it must make a declaration to that effect.

(9) Where the CAC has made a declaration under paragraph (8)—

(a) any appointment made by the consultative committee is ineffective, and

(b) the members of the special negotiating body must be elected by a ballot of the employees in accordance with regulation 10.

(10) Where the consultative committee appoints any person to be a member of the special negotiating body, that appointment has effect—

(a) where no complaint has been presented under paragraph (7), after the expiry of a period of 21 days beginning on the date on which the consultative committee published under paragraph (6) the names of the persons appointed;

(b) where a complaint has been presented under paragraph (7), as from the day on which the complaint has been determined without a declaration under paragraph (8) being made.

NOTES

Revoked as noted to reg 5 at **[2.990]**.

[2.998]

13 Representation of employees

(1) A member elected in a ballot in accordance with regulation 8(2) is treated as representing the employees for the time being of the participating company and of any concerned subsidiary or establishment whose employees were entitled to vote in the ballot in which the member was elected.

(2) If an additional member is elected in accordance with regulation 8(3) and (4), that additional member, and not any member elected in accordance with regulation 8(2), is treated as representing the employees for the time being of the participating company and of any concerned subsidiary or establishment whose employees were entitled to vote in the ballot in which the additional member was elected.

(3) When a member of the special negotiating body is appointed by a consultative committee in accordance with regulation 12, the employees whom the consultative committee represents and the employees of any concerned subsidiary are treated as being represented by the member so appointed.

NOTES

Revoked as noted to reg 5 at **[2.990]**.

PART 4
NEGOTIATION OF THE EMPLOYEE INVOLVEMENT AGREEMENT

[2.999]

14 Negotiations to reach an employee involvement agreement

(1) In this regulation and in regulation 15 the competent organs of the participating companies and the special negotiating body are referred to as "the parties".

(2) The parties are under a duty to negotiate in a spirit of cooperation with a view to reaching an employee involvement agreement.

(3) The duty referred to in paragraph (2) commences one month after the date or, if more than one, the last date on which the members of the special negotiating body were elected or appointed and applies—

- *(a) for the period of six months starting with the day on which the duty commenced or, where an employee involvement agreement is successfully negotiated within that period, until the completion of the negotiations;*
- *(b) where the parties agree before the end of that six month period that it is to be extended, for the period of twelve months starting with the day on which the duty commenced or, where an employee involvement agreement is successfully negotiated within the twelve month period, until the completion of the negotiations.*

NOTES

Revoked as noted to reg 5 at **[2.990]**.

[2.1000]

15 The employee involvement agreement

(1) The employee involvement agreement must be in writing.

(2) The employee involvement agreement must specify each of the following—

- *(a) the scope of the agreement;*
- *(b) the composition, number of members and allocation of seats on the representative body;*
- *(c) the functions and the procedure for the information and consultation of the representative body;*
- *(d) the frequency of meetings of the representative body;*
- *(e) the financial and material resources to be allocated to the representative body;*
- *(f) if, during negotiations, the parties decide to establish one or more information and consultation procedures instead of a representative body, the arrangements for implementing those procedures;*
- *(g) if, during negotiations, the parties decide to establish arrangements for participation, the substance of those arrangements including (if applicable) the number of members in the SE's administrative or supervisory body which the employees will be entitled to elect, appoint, recommend or oppose, the procedures as to how these members may be elected, appointed, recommended or opposed by the employees, and their rights;*
- *(h) the date of entry into force of the agreement and its duration, the circumstances, if any, in which the agreement is required to be re-negotiated and the procedure for its re-negotiation.*

This paragraph is without prejudice to the autonomy of the parties and is subject to paragraph (4).

(3) The employee involvement agreement is not subject to the standard rules on employee involvement, unless it contains a provision to the contrary.

[(3A) Where under the employee involvement agreement the competent organ of the SE is to provide information on the employment situation in that company, such information must include suitable information relating to the use of agency workers (if any) in that company.]

(4) In relation to an SE to be established by way of transformation, the employee involvement agreement must provide for the elements of employee involvement at all levels to be at least as favourable as those which exist in the company to be transformed into an SE.

(5) If—

- *(a) the parties decide, in accordance with paragraph (2)(f), to establish one or more information and consultation procedures instead of a representative body, and*
- *(b) those procedures include a provision for representatives to be elected or appointed to act in relation to information and consultation,*

those representatives are "information and consultation representatives".

NOTES

Revoked as noted to reg 5 at **[2.990]**.

Para (3A): inserted by the Agency Workers Regulations 2010, SI 2010/93, reg 25, Sch 2, Pt 2, paras 47, 50.

[2.1001]

16 Decisions of the special negotiating body

(1) Each member of the special negotiating body has one vote.

(2) The special negotiating body must take decisions by an absolute majority vote, except in those cases where paragraph (3) or regulation 17 provides otherwise.

(3) In the following circumstances any decision which would result in a reduction of participation rights must be taken by a two thirds majority vote—

(a) *where an SE is to be established by merger and at least 25% of the employees employed to work in the EEA states by the participating companies which are due to merge have participation rights;*

(b) *where an SE is to be established by formation of a holding company or of a subsidiary company and at least 50% of the total number of employees employed to work in the EEA states by the participating companies have participation rights.*

In this paragraph, "reduction of participation rights" means that the body representative of the employees has participation rights in relation to a smaller proportion of members of the supervisory or administrative organs of the SE than the employees' representatives had in the participating company which gave participation rights in relation to the highest proportion of such members in that company.

(4) Where the special negotiating body takes a decision under this regulation or under regulation 17—

(a) *it must publish the details of the decision in such a manner as to bring the decision, so far as reasonably practicable, to the attention of the employees whom it represents, and*

(b) *such publication must take place as soon as reasonably practicable and, in any event, no later than 14 days after the decision has been taken.*

(5) For the purpose of negotiations, the special negotiating body may be assisted by experts of its choice.

(6) The participating company or companies must pay for—

(a) *any reasonable expenses of the functioning of the special negotiating body, and*

(b) *any reasonable expenses relating to the negotiations that are necessary to enable the special negotiating body to carry out its functions in an appropriate manner,*

but where the special negotiating body is assisted by more than one expert the participating company is not required to pay such expenses in respect of more than one of them.

NOTES

Revoked as noted to reg 5 at **[2.990]**.

[2.1002]

17 Decision not to open, or to terminate, negotiations

(1) The special negotiating body may decide, by a two thirds majority vote,—

(a) *not to open negotiations with the competent organs of the participating companies, or*

(b) *to terminate any such negotiations.*

(2) The special negotiating body cannot take the decision referred to in paragraph (1) in relation to an SE to be established by transformation if any employees of the company to be transformed have participation rights.

(3) Any decision made under paragraph (1) has the following effects—

(a) *the duty in regulation 14(2) to negotiate with a view to reaching an employee involvement agreement ceases as from the date of the decision;*

(b) *any rules relating to the information and consultation of employees in an EEA state in which employees of the SE are employed apply to the employees of the SE in that EEA state;*

(c) *the special negotiating body* is to be reconvened only if a request that meets the conditions in paragraph (4) is made by employees or employees' representatives.

(4) The conditions are that the request is made—

(a) in writing;

(b) *by at least 10% of the employees of—*

(i) *the participating companies and their concerned subsidiaries, or*

(ii) *where the SE has been registered, the SE and its subsidiaries,*

or by employees' representatives representing at least that percentage of those employees;

(c) no earlier than two years after the decision made under paragraph (1) was or should have been published in accordance with regulation 16(4) unless—

(i) the special negotiating body, and

(ii) the competent organs of *every participating company or, where the SE has been registered,* the *SE*,

agree to the special negotiating body being reconvened earlier;

[(d) references in this regulation to paragraph (1) and regulation 16(4) are to those provisions in these Regulations, as they had effect at the time of that decision and publication.]

NOTES

Paras (1), (2), (3)(a), (b) are revoked, for the words in italics in para (3)(c) there are substituted the words "a special negotiating body", para (4)(b) is substituted as follows, in para (4)(c)(ii) the first words in italics are revoked and for the second words in italics there are substituted the words "UK Societas", and para (4)(d) is added, by the European Public Limited-Liability Company (Amendment etc) (EU Exit) Regulations 2018, SI 2018/1298, regs 48, 52, as from exit day (as defined in the European Union (Withdrawal) Act 2018, s 20) (for transitional provisions and savings, see regs 146–152A of the 2018 Regulations at **[2.2102]** et seq)—

"(b) by at least 10% of the employees of the UK Societas and its subsidiaries, or by employees' representatives representing at least that percentage of those employees;".

Note: it appears that the retention in para (3) of the words "Any decision made under paragraph (1) has the following effects—" is a drafting error, as para (1) is prospectively revoked as set out above.

[2.1003]
18 Complaint about decisions of special negotiating body

(1) If a person who is a member of the special negotiating body, or who is an employees' representative or an employee for whom there is no such representative, believes that the special negotiating body has taken a decision referred to in regulation 16 or 17 and—

(a) that the decision was not taken by the majority required by regulation 16 or 17, as the case may be, or

(b) that the special negotiating body failed to publish the decision in accordance with regulation 16(4),

the person may present a complaint to the CAC within 21 days after the date on which the special negotiating body published their decision in accordance with regulation 16(4) or, if they have not done so, the date by which they should have so published their decision.

(2) Where the CAC finds the complaint well-founded, it must make a declaration that the decision was not taken properly and that it is of no effect.

NOTES

Revoked, together with reg 19, by the European Public Limited-Liability Company (Amendment etc) (EU Exit) Regulations 2018, SI 2018/1298, regs 48, 53, as from exit day (as defined in the European Union (Withdrawal) Act 2018, s 20) (for transitional provisions and savings, see regs 146–152A of the 2018 Regulations at **[2.2102]** et seq).

PART 5
STANDARD RULES ON EMPLOYEE INVOLVEMENT

[2.1004]
19 Standard rules on employee involvement

(1) Where this regulation applies, the competent organ of the SE and its subsidiaries and establishments must make arrangements for the involvement of employees of the SE and its subsidiaries and establishments in accordance with the standard rules on employee involvement.

This paragraph is without prejudice to paragraph (3).

(2) This regulation applies in the following circumstances—

(a) where the parties agree that the standard rules on employee involvement are to apply; or

(b) where the period specified in regulation 14(3)(a) or, where applicable, (b) has expired without the parties reaching an employee involvement agreement and—

(i) the competent organs of each of the participating companies agree that the standard rules on employee involvement are to apply and so continue with the registration of the SE, and

(ii) the special negotiating body has not taken any decision under regulation 17(1) either not to open, or to terminate, the negotiations referred to in that regulation.

(3) The standard rules set out in Part 3 of the Schedule to these Regulations (standard rules on participation) apply only in the following circumstances—

(a) in the case of an SE established by merger if, before registration of the SE, one or more forms of participation existed in at least one of the participating companies and either—

(i) that participation applied to at least 25% of the total number of employees of the participating companies employed in the EEA states, or

(ii) that participation applied to less than 25% of the total number of employees of the participating companies employed in the EEA states but the special negotiating body has decided that the standard rules on participation will apply to the employees of the SE; or

(b) in the case of an SE established by formation of a holding company or subsidiary company if, before registration of the SE, one or more forms of employee participation existed in at least one of the participating companies and either—

(i) that participation applied to at least 50% of the total number of employees of the participating companies employed in the EEA states, or

(ii) that participation applied to less than 50% of the total number of employees of the participating companies employed in the EEA states but the special negotiating body has decided that the standard rules on participation will apply to the employees of the SE.

[(3A) This paragraph applies to an agency worker whose contract within regulation 3(1)(b) of the Agency Workers Regulations 2010 (contract with the temporary work agency) is not a contract of employment—

(a) for the purposes of paragraph (3)(a) and (b), any agency worker who has a contract with a temporary work agency, which was at the relevant time a participating company, is to be treated as having been employed by that temporary work agency for the duration of their assignment with a hirer, and

(b) in this paragraph "assignment" and "hirer" have the same meaning as in regulation 2, and "temporary work agency" has the same meaning as in regulation 4, of the Agency Workers Regulations 2010.]

(4) Where—

(a) the standard rules on participation apply, and

(b) more than one form of employee participation exists in the participating companies,

the special negotiating body must decide which of the existing forms of participation is to exist in the SE and must inform the competent organs of the participating companies accordingly.

NOTES

Revoked as noted to reg 18 at **[2.1003]**.

Para (3A): inserted by the Agency Workers Regulations 2010, SI 2010/93, reg 25, Sch 2, Pt 2, paras 47, 51.

PART 6
COMPLIANCE AND ENFORCEMENT

[2.1005]

20 Disputes about the operation of an employee involvement agreement or the standard rules on employee involvement

(1) Where—

(a) an employee involvement agreement has been agreed, or

(b) the standard rules on employee involvement apply,

a complaint may be presented to the CAC by a relevant applicant who considers that the competent organ of a participating company *or of the SE* has failed to comply with the terms of the employee involvement agreement or, as the case may be, one or more of the standard information and consultation provisions.

(2) A complaint brought under paragraph (1) must be brought within the period of 3 months commencing with—

(a) the date of the alleged failure, or

(b) where the failure takes place over a period, the last day of that period.

(3) In this regulation—

"failure" means an act or omission;

"relevant applicant" means—

(a) in a case where a representative body has been appointed or elected, a member of that body;

(b) in a case where no representative body has been elected or appointed, an information and consultation representative or an employee of the SE [or the UK Societas].

(4) Where it finds the complaint well-founded, the CAC—

(a) must make a declaration to that effect, and

(b) may make an order requiring the SE [or the UK Societas] to take such steps as are necessary to comply with the terms of the employee involvement agreement or, as the case may be, the standard rules on employee involvement.

(5) An order made under paragraph (4) must specify—

(a) the steps which the SE [or the UK Societas] is required to take;

(b) the date of the failure;

(c) the period within which the order must be complied with.

(6) If the CAC makes a declaration under paragraph (4), the relevant applicant may, within the period of three months beginning with the day on which the decision is made, make an application to the Appeal Tribunal for a penalty notice to be issued.

(7) Where such an application is made, the Appeal Tribunal must issue a written penalty notice to the SE [or the UK Societas] requiring it to pay a penalty to the Secretary of State in respect of the failure, unless the Appeal Tribunal is satisfied, on hearing representations from the SE [or the UK Societas],—

(a) that the failure resulted from a reason beyond its control, or

(b) that it has some other reasonable excuse for its failure.

(8) Regulation 21 applies in respect of a penalty notice issued under this regulation.

(9) No order of the CAC under this regulation has the effect of suspending or altering the effect of any act done or of any agreement made by the participating company *or the SE*.

NOTES

For the words in italics in paras (1), (9) there are substituted the words ", the SE or the UK Societas" and words in square brackets in paras (3), (4), (5), (7) inserted, by the European Public Limited-Liability Company (Amendment etc) (EU Exit) Regulations 2018, SI 2018/1298, regs 48, 54, as from exit day (as defined in the European Union (Withdrawal) Act 2018, s 20) (for transitional provisions and savings, see regs 146–152A of the 2018 Regulations at **[2.2102]** et seq).

[2.1006]

21 Penalties

(1) A penalty notice issued under regulation 20 must specify—

(a) the amount of the penalty which is payable;

(b) the date before which the penalty must be paid;

(c) the failure and period to which the penalty relates.

(2) No penalty set by the Appeal Tribunal under this regulation may exceed £75,000.

(3) When setting the amount of the penalty, the Appeal Tribunal must take into account—

(a) the gravity of the failure;

(b) the period of time over which the failure occurred;

(c) the reason for the failure;

(d) the number of employees affected by the failure;

(e) the number of employees employed by the undertaking.

(4) The date specified under paragraph (1)(b) must not be earlier than the end of the period within which an appeal against a decision or order made by the CAC under regulation 20 may be made.

(5) If the specified date in a penalty notice has passed and —

(a) the period during which an appeal may be made has expired without an appeal having been made, or

(b) such an appeal has been made and determined,

the Secretary of State may recover from the SE [or the UK Societas], as a civil debt due to the Secretary of State, any amount payable under the penalty notice which remains outstanding.

(6) The making of an appeal suspends the effect of the penalty notice.

(7) Any sums received by the Secretary of State under regulation 20 or this regulation must be paid into the Consolidated Fund.

NOTES

Para (5): words in square brackets inserted by the European Public Limited-Liability Company (Amendment etc) (EU Exit) Regulations 2018, SI 2018/1298, regs 48, 55, as from exit day (as defined in the European Union (Withdrawal) Act 2018, s 20) (for transitional provisions and savings, see regs 146–152A of the 2018 Regulations at **[2.2102]** et seq).

[2.1007]

22 Misuse of procedures

(1) If an employees' representative, or an employee for whom there is no such representative, believes that a participating company *or an SE* is misusing or intending to misuse the SE [or the UK Societas] or the powers in these Regulations for the purpose of—

(a) depriving the employees of that participating company or of any of its concerned subsidiaries or, as the case may be, of the SE [or the UK Societas] or of any of *its* subsidiaries of their rights to employee involvement, or

(b) withholding rights from any of the employees referred to in sub-paragraph (a),

the representative or, as the case may be, the employee may make a complaint to the CAC.

(2) Where a complaint is made to the CAC under paragraph (1)—

(a) before registration of the SE, or

(b) within the period of 12 months following the date of its registration [as an SE (including registration as an SE which subsequently converted to a UK Societas on exit day);],

the CAC must uphold the complaint unless the respondent proves that it did not misuse or intend to misuse the SE or the powers in these Regulations for a purpose specified in sub-paragraph (a) or (b) of paragraph (1).

(3) If it finds the complaint to be well founded, the CAC—

(a) must make a declaration to that effect, and

(b) may make an order requiring the participating company or the SE [or the UK Societas], as the case may be, to take such action as is specified in the order to ensure that the employees referred to in paragraph (1)(a) are not deprived of their rights to employee involvement or that such rights are not withheld from them,

and the provisions of regulations 20(6) to (9) and 21 apply where the CAC makes a declaration or order under this paragraph as they apply where it makes a declaration or order under regulation 20(4).

NOTES

For the words "or an SE" and "its" in italics in para (1) there are substituted the words ", an SE or a UK Societas" and "their" respectively, and words in square brackets in paras (1)–(3) inserted, by the European Public Limited-Liability Company (Amendment etc) (EU Exit) Regulations 2018, SI 2018/1298, regs 48, 56, as from exit day (as defined in the European Union (Withdrawal) Act 2018, s 20) (for transitional provisions and savings, see regs 146–152A of the 2018 Regulations at **[2.2102]** et seq).

[2.1008]

23 Exclusivity of remedy

The remedy for infringement of the rights conferred by these Regulations is by way of complaint to the CAC in accordance with these Regulations and not otherwise.

PART 7
CONFIDENTIAL INFORMATION

[2.1009]

24 Breach of statutory duty

(1) Where a body which is—

(a) an SE,

[(aa) a UK Societas,]

(b) a subsidiary of an SE [or a UK Societas],

(c) a participating company, or

(d) a concerned subsidiary,

entrusts a person, pursuant to the provisions of these Regulations, with any information or document on terms requiring it to be held in confidence, the person must not disclose that information or document except in accordance with the terms on which it was disclosed to the person.

(2) In this regulation a person referred to in paragraph (1) to whom information or a document is entrusted is referred to as a "recipient".

(3) Where paragraph (1) applies—

(a) the obligation to comply with that paragraph is a duty owed to the body that disclosed the information or document to the recipient, and
(b) a breach of the duty is actionable accordingly (subject to the defences and other incidents applying to actions for breach of statutory duty).

(4) Paragraph (3) does not affect—
(a) any legal liability which any person may incur otherwise than under this regulation by disclosing the information or document, or
(b) any right which any person may have in relation to such disclosure otherwise than under this regulation.

(5) No action lies under paragraph (3) where the recipient reasonably believed the disclosure to be a "protected disclosure" within the meaning given by section 43A of the Employment Rights Act 1996.

(6) A recipient to whom a body mentioned in paragraph (1) has, pursuant to the provisions of these Regulations, entrusted any information or document on terms requiring it to be held in confidence may apply to the CAC for a declaration as to whether it was reasonable for the body to require the recipient to hold the information or document in confidence.

(7) If the CAC considers that the disclosure of the information or the document by the recipient would not, or would not be likely to, harm the legitimate interests of the undertaking, it must make a declaration that it was not reasonable for the body to require the recipient to hold the information or document in confidence.

(8) If a declaration is made under paragraph (7), the information or document is not at any time after the making of the declaration to be regarded as having been entrusted to the recipient who made the application under paragraph (6), or to any other recipient, on terms requiring it to be held in confidence.

NOTES

Para (1): sub-para (aa) and words in square brackets in para (b) inserted by the European Public Limited-Liability Company (Amendment etc) (EU Exit) Regulations 2018, SI 2018/1298, regs 48, 57, as from exit day (as defined in the European Union (Withdrawal) Act 2018, s 20) (for transitional provisions and savings, see regs 146–152A of the 2018 Regulations at **[2.2102]** et seq).

[2.1010]
25 Withholding of information

(1) Neither an SE[, nor a UK Societas,] nor a participating company is required to disclose any information or document to a person for the purposes of these Regulations where the nature of the information or document is such that, according to objective criteria, the disclosure of the information or document would seriously harm the functioning of, or would be prejudicial to,—
(a) the SE [or the UK Societas,] or any subsidiary or establishment of the SE [or the UK Societas,], or
(b) the participating company or any subsidiary or establishment of the participating company.

(2) Where there is a dispute between the SE[, the UK Societas] or a participating company and—
(a) where a representative body has been appointed or elected, a member of that body, or
(b) where a representative body has not been appointed or elected, an information and consultation representative or an employee,

and the dispute is as to whether the nature of the information or document which the SE[, UK Societas] or the participating company has failed to provide is such as is described in paragraph (1), the SE[, UK Societas] or participating company, or a person referred to in sub-paragraph (a) or (b), may apply to the CAC for a declaration as to whether the information or document is of such a nature.

(3) If the CAC makes a declaration that the disclosure of the information or document in question would not, according to objective criteria, be seriously harmful or prejudicial as mentioned in paragraph (1), the CAC must order the company to disclose the information or document.

(4) An order under paragraph (3) must specify—
(a) the information or document to be disclosed;
(b) the person or persons to whom the information or document is to be disclosed;
(c) any terms on which the information or document is to be disclosed;
(d) the date before which the information or document is to be disclosed.

NOTES

Paras (1), (2): words in square brackets inserted by the European Public Limited-Liability Company (Amendment etc) (EU Exit) Regulations 2018, SI 2018/1298, regs 48, 58, as from exit day (as defined in the European Union (Withdrawal) Act 2018, s 20) (for transitional provisions and savings, see regs 146–152A of the 2018 Regulations at **[2.2102]** et seq).

PART 8
PROTECTION FOR MEMBERS OF SPECIAL NEGOTIATING BODY ETC

[2.1011]
26 Right to time off for members of special negotiating body etc

(1) Where an employee is any of the following—
(a) a member of a special negotiating body [reconvened under regulation 17, in a UK Societas,]
(b) a member of a representative body,
(c) an information and consultation representative,
(d) an employee member on a supervisory or administrative organ,

Part 2 Statutory Instruments

(e) a candidate in an election in which any person elected will, on being elected, be such a member or a representative,

the employee is entitled to be permitted by the employer to take reasonable time off during working hours in order to perform functions as such a member, representative or candidate.

(2) In this regulation "working hours" means any time when, in accordance with the employee's contract of employment, the employee is required to be at work.

NOTES

Para (1): words in square brackets in sub-para (a) inserted by the European Public Limited-Liability Company (Amendment etc) (EU Exit) Regulations 2018, SI 2018/1298, regs 48, 59, as from exit day (as defined in the European Union (Withdrawal) Act 2018, s 20) (for transitional provisions and savings, see regs 146–152A of the 2018 Regulations at **[2.2102]** et seq).

[2.1012]

27 Right to remuneration for time off under regulation 26

(1) An employee who is permitted to take time off under regulation 26 is entitled to be paid remuneration by the employer for the time taken off at the appropriate hourly rate.

(2) Chapter 2 of Part 14 of the Employment Rights Act 1996 (a week's pay) applies in relation to this regulation as it applies in relation to section 62 of that Act.

(3) The appropriate hourly rate, in relation to an employee, is the amount of one week's pay divided by the number of normal working hours in a week for that employee when employed under the contract of employment in force on the day when the time is taken.

(4) But where the number of normal working hours differs from week to week or over a longer period, the amount of one week's pay is to be divided instead by—

(a) the average number of normal working hours calculated by dividing by twelve the total number of the employee's normal working hours during the period of twelve weeks ending with the last complete week before the day on which the time off is taken, or

(b) where the employee has not been employed for a sufficient period to enable the calculation to be made under sub-paragraph (a), a number which fairly represents the number of normal working hours in a week having regard to such of the considerations specified in paragraph (5) as are appropriate in the circumstances.

(5) The considerations are—

(a) the average number of normal working hours in a week which the employee could expect in accordance with the terms of the contract;

(b) the average number of normal working hours of other employees engaged in relevant comparable employment with the same employer.

(6) A right to any amount under paragraph (1) does not affect any right of an employee in relation to remuneration under the employee's contract of employment.

(7) But—

(a) any contractual remuneration paid to an employee in respect of a period of time off under regulation 26 goes towards discharging any liability of the employer to pay remuneration under paragraph (1) in respect of that period, and

(b) conversely, any payment of remuneration under paragraph (1) in respect of a period goes towards discharging any liability of the employer to pay contractual remuneration in respect of that period.

[2.1013]

28 Right to time off: complaints to tribunals

(1) An employee may present a complaint to an employment tribunal that the employer—

(a) has unreasonably refused to permit the employee to take time off as required under regulation 26, or

(b) has failed to pay the whole or any part of any amount to which the employee is entitled under regulation 27.

(2) A tribunal must not consider a complaint under this regulation unless it is presented—

(a) before the end of the period of three months beginning with the day on which the time off was taken or on which it is alleged the time off should have been permitted, or

(b) within such further period as the tribunal considers reasonable in a case where it is satisfied that it was not reasonably practicable for the complaint to be presented before the end of that period of three months.

[(2A) Regulation 28A (extension of time limits to facilitate conciliation before institution of proceedings) applies for the purposes of paragraph (2).]

(3) Where a tribunal finds a complaint under this regulation well-founded, the tribunal must make a declaration to that effect.

(4) If the complaint is that the employer has unreasonably refused to permit the employee to take time off, the tribunal must also order the employer to pay to the employee an amount equal to the remuneration to which the employee would have been entitled under regulation 27 if the employer had not refused.

(5) If the complaint is that the employer has failed to pay the employee the whole or part of any amount to which the employee is entitled under regulation 27, the tribunal must also order the employer to pay to the employee the amount which it finds is due to the employee.

NOTES

Para (2A): added by the Employment Tribunals Act 1996 (Application of Conciliation Provisions) Order 2014, SI 2014/431, art 3, Schedule, paras 57, 58.

Conciliation: employment tribunal proceedings under this regulation are "relevant proceedings" for the purposes of the conciliation provisions contained in the Employment Tribunals Act 1996, ss 18–18C; see s 18(1)(y) of the 1996 Act at **[1.757]**.

[2.1014]

[28A Extension of time limit to facilitate conciliation before institution of proceedings

(1) In this regulation—

(a) Day A is the day on which the office holder concerned complies with the requirement in subsection (1) of section 18A of the Employment Tribunals Act 1996 (requirement to contact ACAS before instituting proceedings) in relation to the matter in respect of which the proceedings are brought, and

(b) Day B is the day on which the worker concerned receives or, if earlier, is treated as receiving (by virtue of regulations made under subsection (11) of that section) the certificate issued under subsection (4) of that section.

(2) In working out when the time limit set by regulation 28(2)(a) expires the period beginning with the day after Day A and ending with Day B is not to be counted.

(3) If the time limit set by regulation 28(2)(a) would (if not extended by this paragraph) expire during the period beginning with Day A and ending one month after Day B, the time limit expires instead at the end of that period.

(4) The power conferred on the employment tribunal by regulation 28(2)(b) to extend the time limit set by paragraph (2)(a) of that regulation is exercisable in relation to that time limit as extended by this regulation.]

NOTES

Inserted by the Enterprise and Regulatory Reform Act 2013 (Consequential Amendments) (Employment) Order 2014, SI 2014/386, art 2, Schedule, paras 57, 59.

[2.1015]

29 Unfair dismissal

(1) An employee who is dismissed is to be regarded as unfairly dismissed for the purposes of Part 10 of the Employment Rights Act 1996 if—

(a) paragraph (2) applies to the employee and the reason (or, if more than one, the principal reason) for the dismissal is a reason specified in paragraph (3), or

(b) paragraph (5) applies to the employee and the reason (or, if more than one, the principal reason) for the dismissal is a reason specified in paragraph (6).

(2) This paragraph applies to an employee who is any of the following—

(a) a member of a special negotiating body [reconvened under regulation 17, in a UK Societas];

(b) a member of a representative body;

(c) an information and consultation representative;

(d) an employee member in a supervisory or administrative organ;

(e) a candidate in an election in which any person elected will, on being elected, be such a member or a representative.

(3) The reasons are—

(a) that the employee performed, or proposed to perform, any functions or activities as such a member, representative or candidate (but see paragraph (4));

(b) that the employee, or a person acting on behalf of the employee, made or proposed to make a request to exercise an entitlement conferred on the employee by regulation 26 or 27.

(4) Paragraph (3)(a) does not apply if—

(a) the reason (or principal reason) for the dismissal is that, in the performance or purported performance of the employee's functions or activities, the employee has disclosed any information or document in breach of the duty in regulation 24, and

(b) the case is not one where the employee reasonably believed the disclosure to be a "protected disclosure" within the meaning given by section 43A of the Employment Rights Act 1996.

(5) This paragraph applies to any employee (whether or not paragraph (2) also applies).

(6) The reasons are that the employee did any of the following—

(a) took, or proposed to take, any proceedings before an employment tribunal to enforce any right conferred on the employee by these Regulations;

(b) exercised, or proposed to exercise, any entitlement to apply or complain to the CAC or the Appeal Tribunal conferred by these Regulations or exercised, or proposed to exercise, the right to appeal in connection with any rights conferred by these Regulations;

(c) acted with a view to securing that a special negotiating body [(including one reconvened under regulation 17, in a UK Societas)], a representative body or an information and consultation procedure did or did not come into existence;

(d) indicated that the employee did or did not support the coming into existence of a special negotiating body [(including one reconvened under regulation 17, in a UK Societas)], a representative body or an information and consultation procedure;

(e) stood as a candidate in an election in which any person elected would, on being elected, be a member of a special negotiating body [reconvened under regulation 17, in a UK Societas] or a representative body, an employee member on a supervisory or administrative organ, or an information and consultation representative;
(f) influenced, or sought to influence, by lawful means the way in which votes were to be cast by other employees in a ballot arranged under these Regulations;
(g) voted in such a ballot;
(h) expressed doubts, whether to a ballot supervisor or otherwise, as to whether such a ballot had been properly conducted;
(i) proposed to do, failed to do, or proposed to decline to do, any of the things mentioned in sub-paragraphs (d) to (h).

(7) It is immaterial for the purposes of sub-paragraph (a) of paragraph (6)—
(a) whether or not the employee has the right, or
(b) whether or not the right has been infringed,

but for that sub-paragraph to apply, the claim to the right and, if applicable, the claim that it has been infringed must be made in good faith.

NOTES

Words in square brackets in paras (2), (6) inserted by the European Public Limited-Liability Company (Amendment etc) (EU Exit) Regulations 2018, SI 2018/1298, regs 48, 60, as from exit day (as defined in the European Union (Withdrawal) Act 2018, s 20) (for transitional provisions and savings, see regs 146–152A of the 2018 Regulations at **[2.2102]** et seq).

30 (*Amends the Employment Rights Act 1996, ss 105, 108 at* **[1.1023]**, **[1.1026]**.)

[2.1016]
31 Detriment

(1) An employee to whom paragraph (2) or (5) applies has the right not to be subjected to any detriment by any act, or deliberate failure to act, by the employer, done on a ground specified in, respectively, paragraph (3) or (6).

(2) This paragraph applies to an employee who is any of the following—
(a) a member of a special negotiating body [reconvened under regulation 17, in a UK Societas];
(b) a member of a representative body;
(c) an information and consultation representative;
(d) an employee member on a supervisory or administrative organ;
(e) a candidate in an election in which any person elected will, on being elected, be such a member or representative.

(3) The grounds are—
(a) that the employee performed or proposed to perform any functions or activities as such a member, representative or candidate (but see paragraph (4));
(b) that the employee, or a person acting on behalf of the employee, made or proposed to make a request to exercise an entitlement conferred on the employee by regulation 26 or 27.

(4) Paragraph (3)(a) does not apply if—
(a) the ground for the subjection to detriment is that in the performance, or purported performance, of the employee's functions or activities the employee has disclosed any information or document in breach of the duty in regulation 24, and
(b) the case is not one where the employee reasonably believed the disclosure to be a "protected disclosure" within the meaning given by section 43A of the Employment Rights Act 1996.

(5) This paragraph applies to any employee (whether or not paragraph (2) also applies).

(6) The grounds are that the employee did any of the following—
(a) took, or proposed to take, any proceedings before an employment tribunal to enforce any right conferred on the employee by these Regulations;
(b) exercised, or proposed to exercise, any entitlement to apply or complain to the CAC or the Appeal Tribunal conferred by these Regulations or exercised, or proposed to exercise, the right to appeal in connection with any rights conferred by these Regulations;
(c) acted with a view to securing that a special negotiating body [(including one reconvened under regulation 17, in a UK Societas)], a representative body or an information and consultation procedure did or did not come into existence;
(d) indicated that the employee did or did not support the coming into existence of a special negotiating body [(including one reconvened under regulation 17, in a UK Societas)], a representative body or an information and consultation procedure;
(e) stood as a candidate in an election in which any person elected would, on being elected, be a member of a special negotiating body [reconvened under regulation 17, in a UK Societas] or a representative body, an employee member on a supervisory or administrative organ, or an information and consultation representative;
(f) influenced, or sought to influence, by lawful means the way in which votes were to be cast by other employees in a ballot arranged under these Regulations;
(g) voted in such a ballot;
(h) expressed doubts, whether to a ballot supervisor or otherwise, as to whether such a ballot had been properly conducted;
(i) proposed to do, failed to do, or proposed to decline to do, any of the things mentioned in sub-paragraphs (d) to (h).

(7) It is immaterial for the purposes of sub-paragraph (a) of paragraph (6)—

(a) whether or not the employee has the right, or

(b) whether or not the right has been infringed,

but for that sub-paragraph to apply, the claim to the right and, if applicable, the claim that it has been infringed must be made in good faith.

(8) This regulation does not apply where the detriment in question amounts to dismissal.

NOTES

Paras (2), (6): words in square brackets inserted by the European Public Limited-Liability Company (Amendment etc) (EU Exit) Regulations 2018, SI 2018/1298, regs 48, 61, as from exit day (as defined in the European Union (Withdrawal) Act 2018, s 20) (for transitional provisions and savings, see regs 146–152A of the 2018 Regulations at **[2.2102]** et seq).

[2.1017]

32 Detriment: enforcement and subsidiary provisions

(1) An employee may present a complaint to an employment tribunal that the employee has been subjected to a detriment in contravention of regulation 31.

(2) The provisions of section 48(2) to (4) of the Employment Rights Act 1996 (complaints to employment tribunals) apply in relation to a complaint under this regulation as they apply in relation to a complaint under section 48 of that Act but taking references in those provisions to the employer as references to the employer within the meaning of regulation 31(1).

(3) The provisions of section 49(1) to (5) of the Employment Rights Act 1996 (remedies) apply in relation to a complaint under this regulation.

NOTES

Conciliation: employment tribunal proceedings under this regulation are "relevant proceedings" for the purposes of the conciliation provisions contained in the Employment Tribunals Act 1996, ss 18–18C; see s 18(1)(y) of the 1996 Act at **[1.757]**.

33 (*Amended the Employment Tribunals Act 1996, s 18 at* **[1.757]** *and is now effectively spent due to subsequent amendments to that section.*)

PART 9
MISCELLANEOUS

[2.1018]

34 CAC proceedings

(1) Where under these Regulations a person presents a complaint or makes an application to the CAC, the complaint or application must be in writing and in such form as the CAC may require.

(2) In its consideration of a complaint or application under these Regulations, the CAC must—

(a) make such enquiries as it sees fit, and

(b) give any person whom it considers has a proper interest in the complaint or application an opportunity to be heard.

(3) Where the *participating company,* concerned subsidiary or establishment or the *SE* has its registered office in England and Wales—

(a) a declaration made by the CAC under these Regulations may be relied on as if it were a declaration or order made by the High Court in England and Wales, and

(b) an order made by the CAC under these Regulations may be enforced in the same way as an order of the High Court in England and Wales.

(4) Where a *participating company or* concerned subsidiary or *an SE* has its registered office in Scotland—

(a) a declaration or order made by the CAC under these Regulations may be relied on as if it were a declaration or order made by the Court of Session, and

(b) an order made by the CAC under these Regulations may be enforced in the same way as an order of the Court of Session.

(5) A declaration or order made by the CAC under these Regulations must be in writing and state the reasons for the CAC's findings.

(6) An appeal lies to the Appeal Tribunal on any question of law arising from any declaration or order of, or arising in any proceedings before, the CAC under these Regulations.

NOTES

Para (3): first words in italics revoked and for the word "SE" in italics there are substituted the words "UK Societas", by the European Public Limited-Liability Company (Amendment etc) (EU Exit) Regulations 2018, SI 2018/1298, regs 48, 62(a), as from exit day (as defined in the European Union (Withdrawal) Act 2018, s 20) (for transitional provisions and savings, see regs 146–152A of the 2018 Regulations at **[2.2102]** et seq).

Para (4): first words in italics revoked and for the words "an SE" in italics there are substituted the words "a UK Societas", by SI 2018/1298, regs 48, 62(b), as from exit day (as defined in the European Union (Withdrawal) Act 2018, s 20) (for transitional provisions and savings, see regs 146–152A of the 2018 Regulations at **[2.2102]** et seq).

[2.1019]
35 Appeal Tribunal: location of certain proceedings under these Regulations

(1) Any proceedings before the Appeal Tribunal under these Regulations, other than appeals under paragraph (w) of section 21(1) of the Employment Tribunals Act 1996 (appeals from employment tribunals on questions of law), must—

(a) where the registered office of the *participating company*, concerned subsidiary or the *SE* is situated in England and Wales, be held in England and Wales, and

(b) where the registered office of the *participating company*, concerned subsidiary or the *SE* is situated in Scotland, be held in Scotland.

(2) (*Amends the Employment Tribunals Act 1996, s 20 at* **[1.763]**.)

NOTES

Para (1): words "participating company," in italics in both places revoked and for the word "SE" in italics in both places there are substituted the words "UK Societas", by the European Public Limited-Liability Company (Amendment etc) (EU Exit) Regulations 2018, SI 2018/1298, regs 48, 63, as from exit day (as defined in the European Union (Withdrawal) Act 2018, s 20) (for transitional provisions and savings, see regs 146–152A of the 2018 Regulations at **[2.2102]** et seq).

36 (*Amends the Employment Tribunals Act 1996, s 21 at* **[1.764]**.)

[2.1020]
37 ACAS

(1) If, on receipt of an application or complaint under these Regulations, the CAC is of the opinion that it is reasonably likely to be settled by conciliation, it must—

(a) refer the application or complaint to the Advisory, Conciliation and Arbitration Service ("ACAS"), and

(b) notify the applicant or complainant and any persons whom it considers have a proper interest in the application or complaint accordingly,

and ACAS must seek to promote a settlement of the matter.

(2) If—

(a) an application or complaint so referred is not settled or withdrawn, and

(b) ACAS is of the opinion that further attempts at conciliation are unlikely to result in a settlement,

ACAS must inform the CAC of that opinion.

(3) If—

(a) the application or complaint is not referred to ACAS, or

(b) it is so referred, but ACAS informs the CAC of its opinion that further attempts at conciliation are unlikely to result in a settlement,

the CAC must proceed to hear and determine the application or complaint.

[2.1021]
38 Restrictions on contracting out: general

(1) Any provision in any agreement (whether an employee's contract or not) is void in so far as it purports—

(a) to exclude or limit the operation of any provision of these Regulations, other than a provision of Part 8, or

(b) to preclude a person from bringing any proceedings before the CAC under any provision of these Regulations other than a provision of that Part.

(2) Paragraph (1) does not apply to any agreement to refrain from continuing any proceedings referred to in sub-paragraph (b) of that paragraph made after the proceedings have been instituted.

[2.1022]
39 Restrictions on contracting out: Part 8

(1) Any provision in any agreement (whether an employee's contract or not) is void in so far as it purports—

(a) to exclude or limit the operation of any provision of Part 8 of these Regulations, or

(b) to preclude a person from bringing any proceedings before an employment tribunal under that Part.

(2) Paragraph (1) does not apply to any agreement to refrain from instituting or continuing proceedings before an employment tribunal where a conciliation officer has taken action under [any of sections 18A to 18C] of the Employment Tribunals Act 1996 (conciliation).

(3) Paragraph (1) does not apply to any agreement to refrain from instituting or continuing before an employment tribunal proceedings within [section 18(1)(y)] of the Employment Tribunals Act 1996 (proceedings under these Regulations where conciliation is available) if the conditions regulating [settlement] agreements under these Regulations are satisfied in relation to the agreement.

(4) For the purposes of paragraph (3) the conditions regulating [settlement] agreements are as follows—

(a) the agreement must be in writing;

(b) the agreement must relate to the particular proceedings;

(c) the employee must have received advice from a relevant independent adviser as to the terms and effect of the proposed agreement and, in particular, its effect on the ability of the employee to pursue the employee's rights before an employment tribunal;

(d) there must be in force, when the adviser gives the advice, a contract of insurance, or an indemnity provided for members of a profession or professional body, covering the risk of a claim by the employee in respect of loss arising in consequence of the advice;
(e) the agreement must identify the adviser;
(f) the agreement must state that the conditions in sub-paragraphs (a) to (e) are satisfied.

(5) For the purposes of paragraph (4)(c) a "relevant independent adviser" is a person who is any of the following—
(a) a qualified lawyer;
(b) an officer, official, employee or member of an independent trade union who has been certified in writing by the trade union as competent to give advice and authorised to do so on behalf of the trade union;
(c) a person who works at an advice centre (whether as an employee or as a volunteer) and has been certified in writing by the centre as competent to give advice and authorised to do so on behalf of the centre;

but this is subject to paragraph (6).

(6) A person is not a relevant independent adviser for the purposes of paragraph (4)(c) in relation to the employee in any of the following cases—
(a) if the person is, is employed by, or is acting in the matter for, the employer or an associated employer;
(b) in the case of a person within paragraph (5)(b) or (c), if the trade union or advice centre is the employer or an associated employer;
(c) in the case of a person within paragraph (5)(c), if the employee makes a payment for the advice received.

(7) In paragraph (5)(a) "qualified lawyer" means any of the following—
(a) as respects England and Wales—
(i) a barrister (whether in practice as such or employed to give legal advice);
(ii) a solicitor who holds a practising certificate;
(iii) a person, other than a barrister or solicitor, who is an authorised advocate or authorised litigator (within the meaning of the Courts and Legal Services Act 1990);
(b) as respects Scotland—
(i) an advocate (whether in practice as such or employed to give legal advice); or
(ii) a solicitor who holds a practising certificate.

(8) For the purposes of paragraph (6) any two employers are "associated" if—
(a) one is a company of which the other (directly or indirectly) has control, or
(b) both are companies of which a third person (directly or indirectly) has control,

and "associated employer" is to be construed accordingly.

NOTES

Para (2): words in square brackets substituted by the Enterprise and Regulatory Reform Act 2013 (Consequential Amendments) (Employment) Order 2014, SI 2014/386, art 2, Schedule, para 60.

Para (3): words in first pair of square brackets substituted by the Employment Tribunals Act 1996 (Application of Conciliation Provisions) Order 2014, SI 2014/431, art 3, Schedule, para 38; word in second pair of square brackets substituted by the Enterprise and Regulatory Reform Act 2013 (Consequential Amendments) (Employment) Order 2013, SI 2013/1956, art 2, Schedule, para 15.

Para (4): word in square brackets substituted by SI 2013/1956, art 2, Schedule, para 15.

40 (*Substitutes the Transnational Information and Consultation of Employees Regulations 1999, SI 1999/3323, reg 46A at* **[2.522]**.)

[2.1023]

41 Existing employee involvement rights

(1) Nothing in these Regulations affects involvement rights of employees of an SE, *its* subsidiaries or establishments provided for by law or practice in the *EEA state* in which they were employed immediately prior to the registration of the SE [(including an SE which converted to a UK Societas on exit day)].

(2) Paragraph (1) does not apply to rights to participation.

[(2A) In this regulation "participation" means the influence of the representative body and the employees' representatives in the SE or the UK Societas by way of the right to—
(a) elect or appoint some of the members of the SE or the UK Societas's supervisory or administrative organ, or
(b) recommend or oppose the appointment of some or all of the members of the SE or the UK Societas's supervisory or administrative organ.]

NOTES

For the first and second words in italics in para (1) there are substituted the words "or a UK Societas, or their" and "Relevant State" respectively, words in square brackets in para (1) inserted and para (2A) added, by the European Public Limited-Liability Company (Amendment etc) (EU Exit) Regulations 2018, SI 2018/1298, regs 48, 64, as from exit day (as defined in the European Union (Withdrawal) Act 2018, s 20) (for transitional provisions and savings, see regs 146–152A of the 2018 Regulations at **[2.2102]** et seq).

Part 2 Statutory Instruments

SCHEDULE
STANDARD RULES ON EMPLOYEE INVOLVEMENT

Regulation 19(3)

PART 1
COMPOSITION OF THE REPRESENTATIVE BODY

[2.1024]

1. (1) The management of the SE must arrange for the establishment of a representative body in accordance with the following provisions.

(2) The representative body must be composed of employees of the SE and its subsidiaries and establishments.

(3) The representative body must be composed of one member for each 10%, or fraction of 10%, of employees of the SE, its subsidiaries and establishments employed for the time being in each EEA state.

(4) The members of the representative body must be elected or appointed by the members of the special negotiating body.

(5) The election or appointment is to be carried out by whatever method the special negotiating body decides.

2. Where its size so warrants, the representative body must elect a select committee from among its members comprising at most 3 members.

3. The representative body must adopt rules of procedure.

4. The representative body must inform the competent organ of the SE of the composition of the representative body and any changes in its composition.

5. (1) Four years after its establishment, the representative body must decide—

(a) whether to open negotiations with the competent organ of the SE to reach an employee involvement agreement, or

(b) whether the standard rules in Part 2 of this Schedule and, where applicable, Part 3 of this Schedule are to continue to apply.

(2) Where a decision is taken under sub-paragraph (1) to open negotiations, regulations 14 to 16 and 18 apply to the representative body as they apply to the special negotiating body.

NOTES

Schedule revoked by the European Public Limited-Liability Company (Amendment etc) (EU Exit) Regulations 2018, SI 2018/1298, regs 48, 65, as from exit day (as defined in the European Union (Withdrawal) Act 2018, s 20) (for transitional provisions and savings, see regs 146–152A of the 2018 Regulations at **[2.2102]** et seq).

PART 2
STANDARD RULES FOR INFORMATION AND CONSULTATION

[2.1025]

6. (1) The competence of the representative body is limited to—

(a) questions which concern the SE itself and any of its subsidiaries or establishments in another EEA state, and

(b) questions which exceed the powers of the decision-making organ in a single EEA state.

(2) For the purpose of informing and consulting under sub-paragraph (1), the competent organ of the SE must—

(a) prepare and provide to the representative body regular reports on the progress of the business of the SE and the SE's prospects;

(b) provide the representative body with the agenda for meetings of the administrative or, where appropriate, the management or supervisory organs and copies of all documents submitted to the general meeting of its shareholders;

(c) inform the representative body when there are exceptional circumstances affecting the employees' interests to a considerable extent, particularly in the event of relocations, transfers, the closure of establishments or undertakings or collective redundancies.

7. (1) The competent organ must, if the representative body so desires, meet with that body at least once a year to discuss the reports referred to in paragraph 6(2)(a).

This sub-paragraph is without prejudice to paragraph 8.

(2) The meetings must relate in particular to the structure, economic and financial situation, the probable development of business and of production and sales, the situation and probable trend of employment, investments and substantial changes concerning organisation, introduction of new working methods or production processes, transfers of production, mergers, cut-backs or closures of undertakings or establishments, or important parts of undertakings or establishments, and collective redundancies.

8. (1) In the circumstances set out in paragraph 6(2)(c), the representative body may decide, for reasons of urgency, to allow the select committee to meet the competent organ and it has the right to meet a more appropriate level of management within the SE rather than the competent organ itself.

(2) In the event of the competent organ not acting in accordance with the opinion expressed by the representative body, the two bodies must meet again to seek an agreement, if the representative body so wishes.

(3) In the circumstances set out in sub-paragraph (1), if the select committee attends the meeting, any other members of the representative body who represent employees who are directly concerned by the measures being discussed also have the right to participate in the meeting.

(4) Before any meeting referred to in this paragraph, the members of the representative body or the select committee, as the case may be, are entitled to meet without the representatives of the competent organ being present.

*[**8A.** Where under the provisions of this Part, the competent organ of the SE is to provide information on the employment situation in that company, such information must include suitable information relating to the use of agency workers (if any) in that company.]*

***9.** Without prejudice to regulations 24 and 25, the members of the representative body must inform the employees' representatives or, if no such representatives exist, the employees of the SE and its subsidiaries and establishments, of the content and outcome of the information and consultation procedures.*

***10.** The representative body and the select committee may each be assisted by experts of its choice.*

***11.** (1) The costs of the representative body must be borne by the SE which must also provide the members of that body with financial and material resources needed to enable them to perform their duties in an appropriate manner, including (unless agreed otherwise) the cost of organising meetings, providing interpretation facilities and accommodation and travelling expenses.*

(2) However, where the representative body or the select committee is assisted by more than one expert, the SE is not required to pay the expenses of more than one of them.

NOTES

Revoked as noted to Pt 1 of this Schedule at **[2.1024]**.

Para 8A: inserted by the Agency Workers Regulations 2010, SI 2010/93, reg 25, Sch 2, Pt 2, paras 47, 52.

PART 3
STANDARD RULES FOR PARTICIPATION

[2.1026]

***12.** (1) In the case of an SE established by transformation, if the rules of a Member State relating to employee participation in the administrative or supervisory body applied before registration, all aspects of employee participation continue to apply to the SE.*

(2) Paragraph 13 applies to that end with the necessary modifications.

***13.** (1) In the case where—*

(a) an SE is established otherwise than by transformation, and

(b) the employees or their representatives of at least one of the participating companies had participation rights,

the representative body has the right to elect, appoint, recommend or oppose the appointment of a number of members of the administrative or supervisory body of the SE.

(2) Their number must be equal to the highest proportion in force in the participating companies concerned before the registration of the SE.

***14.** (1) The representative body must decide on the allocation of seats within the administrative or supervisory body.*

(2) In doing so, the representative body must take into account the proportion of employees of the SE employed in each EEA state.

(3) If the employees of one or more EEA states are not covered by that proportional criterion, the representative body, in making its decision under sub-paragraph (1), must appoint a member from one of those EEA states including one from the EEA state in which the SE is registered, if appropriate.

(4) Every member of the administrative body or, where appropriate, the supervisory body of the SE who has been elected, appointed or recommended by the representative body or the employees is to be a full member with the same rights and obligations as the members representing shareholders, including the right to vote.

NOTES

Revoked as noted to Pt 1 of this Schedule at **[2.1024]**.

SCHOOL STAFFING (ENGLAND) REGULATIONS 2009

(SI 2009/2680)

NOTES

Made: 2 October 2009.

Authority: School Standards and Framework Act 1998, ss 72, 138(7); Education Act 2002, ss 19(3), 26, 34(5), 35(4), (5), 36(4), (5), 210(7).

Commencement: 2 November 2009.

These Regulations apply only to England.

In relation to the application of these Regulations, with modifications, to the staffing of federations, see the School Governance (Federations) (England) Regulations 2012, SI 2012/1035, reg 25, Sch 7.

ARRANGEMENT OF REGULATIONS

PART 1
GENERAL

PART 2
PROVISIONS RELATING TO COMMUNITY, VOLUNTARY CONTROLLED, COMMUNITY SPECIAL AND MAINTAINED NURSERY SCHOOLS

PART 3
PROVISIONS RELATING TO FOUNDATION, VOLUNTARY AIDED AND FOUNDATION SPECIAL SCHOOLS

PART 4
COLLABORATION BETWEEN SCHOOLS

PART 5
STAFFING OF NEW SCHOOLS

PART 1
GENERAL

[2.1027]
1 Citation, commencement and application

(1) These Regulations may be cited as the School Staffing (England) Regulations 2009 and they come into force on 2nd November 2009.

(2) These Regulations apply only in relation to England.

[2.1028]
2 Revocations and amendments

The Regulations specified in Schedule 1 are revoked to the extent specified in the third column of that Schedule.

[2.1029]
3 Interpretation

(1) In these Regulations—

"PA 1997" means the Police Act 1997;

"EA 2002" means the Education Act 2002;

"authority" means the [local authority] by which a maintained school is, or a proposed school is to be, maintained;

"dismissal" is to be interpreted in accordance with sections 95 and 136 of the Employment Rights Act 1996;

"employment business" has the meaning given by section 13(3) of the Employment Agencies Act 1973;

"enhanced criminal record certificate" means an enhanced criminal record certificate [issued under] section 113B of PA 1997 which includes[, in such cases as are from time to time prescribed under section 113BA(1) of that Act,] suitability information relating to children within the meaning of section 113BA(2) of that Act;

["interim prohibition order" means an order made by virtue of paragraph 3 of Schedule 11A to EA 2002;

["negative up-date information" means up-date information of a kind falling within section 116A(8)(b)(i) or (c)(i) of PA 1997;]

"prohibition order" has the meaning given by section 141B of EA 2002;]

["relevant activity" means any activity which is a regulated activity relating to children within the meaning of—

(a) Part 1 of Schedule 4 to the Safeguarding Vulnerable Groups Act 2006; or

(b) Part 1 of Schedule 4 to that Act as it had effect immediately before the coming into force of section 64 of the Protection of Freedoms Act 2012;]

"safer recruitment training" means training provided . . . for the purpose of ensuring that those who undertake it know how to take proper account of the need to safeguard [and promote the welfare of] children when recruiting staff;

"support staff" means any member of a school's staff other than a teacher;

"teacher" means—

(a) a person who is a school teacher for the purposes of section 122 of EA 2002 Act; and

(b) a person who would fall within paragraph (a) but for the fact that the other party to the contract is not an authority or a governing body of a school falling within Part 3 of these Regulations;

["up-date information" has the meaning given by section 116A(8) of PA 1997.]

(2) References to a vacancy in any post include a prospective vacancy in the post.

(3) A person is to be treated as meeting any staff qualification requirements if the person—

(a) fulfils any requirements with respect to qualifications or registration which apply to the person as a result of regulations made under sections 132 to 135 of EA 2002 and regulations made under section 19 of the Teaching and Higher Education Act 1998;

(b) meets any conditions with respect to health and physical capacity which apply to the person as a result of regulations made under section 141 of the 2002 Act; . . .

[(c) is not barred from regulated activity relating to children in accordance with section 3(2) of the Safeguarding Vulnerable Groups Act 2006 in any case where it is intended that the person will engage in any activity which is a regulated activity relating to children within the meaning of Part 1 of Schedule 4 to that Act; and

(d) is not subject to a prohibition order or interim prohibition order or subject to any direction made under section 142 of EA 2002 or any prohibition, restriction or order having effect as such a direction.]

(4) References to support staff include support staff employed, or engaged otherwise than under a contract of employment, to provide community facilities and services under section 27 of EA 2002.

(5) For the purposes of these Regulations a person applies for an enhanced criminal record certificate if—

(a) the person countersigns an application for the certificate as a registered person, within the meaning of section 120 of PA 1997, or an application is countersigned on the person's behalf; and

(b) the application is submitted . . . in accordance with Part 5 of that Act.

[(6) For the purposes of these Regulations an enhanced criminal record certificate is subject to up-date arrangements in the circumstances set out in section 116A(3) of PA 1997.

(7) References to the giving of negative up-date information are references to the giving of such information under section 116A(1) of PA 1997.]

NOTES

Para (1) is amended as follows:

Words in square brackets in definition "authority" substituted by the Local Education Authorities and Children's Services Authorities (Integration of Functions) (Local and Subordinate Legislation) Order 2010, SI 2010/1172, art 4(3)(a).

In definition "enhanced criminal record certificate" words in first pair of square brackets substituted, words in second pair of square brackets inserted, and definitions "negative up-date information", "relevant activity" and "up-date information" inserted, by the School Staffing (England) (Amendment) Regulations 2015, SI 2015/887, regs 2, 3(1), as from 29 June 2015.

Definitions "interim prohibition order" and "prohibition order" inserted by the School Staffing (England) (Amendment) Regulations 2013, SI 2013/1940, reg 2(1), (2).

In definition "safer recruitment training" words omitted revoked, and words in square brackets inserted, by the School Staffing (England) (Amendment) Regulations 2014, SI 2014/798, reg 2, as from 1 September 2014.

Para (3): word omitted from sub-para (b) revoked, and sub-paras (c), (d) substituted (for the original para (c)), by SI 2015/887, regs 2, 3(2), as from 29 June 2015.

Para (5): words omitted from sub-para (b) revoked by SI 2015/887, regs 2, 3(3), as from 29 June 2015.

Paras (6), (7): added by SI 2015/887, regs 2, 3(4), as from 29 June 2015.

[2.1030]

4 Delegation of authority

(1) The governing body may delegate—

(a) any of the functions conferred upon it by these Regulations other than those conferred by [regulations 5 to 8 and 9], 15(3) and (5) and 27(3) and (5); and

(b) its power to appoint or dismiss any member of staff at a school to which Part 3 applies.

(2) Subject to paragraph (4), any delegation under paragraph (1) may be to—

(a) the head teacher,

(b) one or more governors; or

[(ba) a committee established by the governing body; or]

(c) one or more governors acting together with the head teacher.

(3) Where the governing body has made any delegation under paragraph (1) to one or more governors and the function being delegated does not directly concern the head teacher—

(a) the head teacher may attend and offer advice at all relevant proceedings; and

(b) the governor or governors to whom the delegation has been made must consider any such advice.

(4) Any delegation under paragraph (1) of—

(a) the determination that the head teacher should cease to work at the school; or

(b) the power to appoint or dismiss the head teacher,

may be to one or more governors, other than a governor who is the head teacher.

[(5) Paragraph (2)(ba) does not authorise delegation to a committee that includes an associate member who is a pupil or a member of staff at the school.]

NOTES

Para (1): words in square brackets in sub-para (a) substituted by the School Staffing (England) (Amendment) Regulations 2012, SI 2012/1740, reg 2(1), (2).

Para (2): sub-para (ba) inserted by the School Governance (Miscellaneous Amendments) (England) Regulations 2015, SI 2015/883, reg 5(1), (2)(a), as from 1 September 2015.

Para (5): added by SI 2015/883, reg 5(1), (2)(b), as from 1 September 2015.

[2.1031]

5 Head teacher duties and entitlements

(1) The governing body must ensure that the head teacher at the school—

(a) complies with the duties imposed upon the head teacher; and

(b) benefits from any entitlement conferred upon the head teacher,

by any order under section 122 of the EA 2002 (teachers' pay and conditions).

(2) In discharging its duty under paragraph (1)(a), the governing body must have regard to the desirability of the head teacher being able to achieve a satisfactory balance between the time spent discharging the professional duties of a head teacher and the time spent by the head teacher pursuing personal interests outside work.

[2.1032]
6 Performance of head teacher

(1) Where the authority has any serious concerns about the performance of the head teacher of a school it must—
- (a) make a written report of its concerns to the governing body of the school; and
- (b) at the same time, send a copy of the report to the head teacher.

(2) The governing body must notify the authority in writing of the action it proposes to take in the light of the authority's report.

[2.1033]
7 Conduct and discipline of staff

(1) The governing body must establish procedures—
- (a) for the regulation of the conduct and discipline of staff at the school; and
- (b) by which staff may seek redress for any grievance relating to their work at the school.

(2) Where the implementation of any determination made by the governing body in operation of the procedures requires any action which—
- (a) is not within the functions exercisable by the governing body by or under EA 2002; but
- (b) is within the power of the authority,

the authority must take that action at the request of the governing body.

[2.1034]
8 Capability of staff

The governing body must establish procedures for dealing with lack of capability on the part of staff at the school.

[2.1035]
[8A Provision of information about staff capability

(1) This regulation applies where a member of the teaching staff at a school (School A) applies for a teaching post at another school (School B), where School B is a maintained school or an Academy school.

(2) The governing body of School A must, at the request of the governing body or proprietor (as the case may be) of School B—
- (a) advise in writing whether or not that member of staff has, in the preceding two years, been the subject of the procedures established by the governing body in accordance with regulation 8 and, if so,
- (b) provide written details of the concerns which gave rise to this, the duration of the proceedings and their outcome.]

NOTES

Inserted by the School Staffing (England) (Amendment) Regulations 2012, SI 2012/1740, reg 2(1), (3).

[2.1036]
9 Safer recruitment training

With effect from 1st January 2010, the governing body must ensure that—
- (a) any person who interviews an applicant for any post under these Regulations has completed the safer recruitment training; or
- (b) in the case where—
  - (i) a selection panel is appointed for that purpose under regulation 15 or 26; or
  - (ii) the governing body delegates the appointment of a member of staff to two or more governors or one or more governors and the head teacher under regulation 4(1),

  at least one member of that panel or group has completed the safer recruitment training.

10 *(Amends the School Governance (Procedures) (England) Regulations 2003, SI 2003/1377 (outside the scope of this work).)*

PART 2
PROVISIONS RELATING TO COMMUNITY, VOLUNTARY CONTROLLED, COMMUNITY SPECIAL AND MAINTAINED NURSERY SCHOOLS

[2.1037]
11 Application of Part 2

This Part applies to community, voluntary controlled, community special and maintained nursery schools.

[2.1038]
12 Manner of appointment

(1) Where a governing body approves, identifies, selects or recommends a person for appointment under regulation 15(5), 15(7), 16(3) or 17(1), it must determine whether that person is to be appointed—

(a) under a contract of employment with the authority;
(b) by the authority otherwise than under a contract of employment; or
(c) by the governing body otherwise than under a contract of employment.

(2) The governing body must check—
(a) the identity of any such person;
(b) that the person meets all relevant staff qualification requirements; and
(c) that the person has a right to work in the United Kingdom.

(3) [Where it is intended that the person will engage in relevant activity, the] governing body must obtain an enhanced criminal record certificate in respect of any such person before, or as soon as practicable after, the person's appointment.

[(3A) Where a governing body obtains an enhanced criminal record certificate in respect of any such person and that certificate is subject to up-date arrangements, it must consider whether to request up-date information in relation to the certificate under section 116A(1) of PA 1997.]

(4) In the case of any such person for whom, by reason of having lived outside the United Kingdom, obtaining such a certificate is not sufficient to establish that person's suitability to work in a school, the governing body must make such further checks as the authority consider appropriate, having regard to any guidance issued by the Secretary of State.

(5) The governing body must complete the checks referred to in paragraphs (2) and (4) before a person is appointed.

(6) Paragraphs (3) and (4) do not apply to a person who has worked in—
(a) a school in England in a post—
(i) which brought the person regularly into contact with children or young persons; or
(ii) to which the person was appointed on or after 12th May 2006 and which did not bring the person regularly into contact with children or young persons; or
(b) an institution within the further education sector in England[, or in a 16 to 19 Academy,] in a post which involved the provision of education which brought the person regularly into contact with children or young persons,

during a period which ended not more than three months before the person's appointment.

(7) The governing body must keep a register containing the information specified in Schedule 2.

NOTES

Para (3): words in square brackets substituted by the School Staffing (England) (Amendment) Regulations 2015, SI 2015/887, regs 2, 4(1), as from 29 June 2015.

Para (3A): inserted by SI 2015/887, regs 2, 4(2), as from 29 June 2015.

Para (6): words in square brackets in sub-para (b) inserted by the Alternative Provision Academies and 16 to 19 Academies (Consequential Amendments to Subordinate Legislation) (England) Order 2012, SI 2012/979, art 2, Schedule, para 26.

[2.1039]

13 Application of regulation 12 to other appointments

Regulation 12(2) to (6) and (7) (insofar as it relates to paragraphs 2 to [4A], 7 and 8 of Schedule 2) also applies in relation to—
(a) any person appointed by an authority for the purpose of working at a school to which this Part applies in the temporary absence of a member of staff of the school; and
(b) any person appointed by an authority to work at a school as a member of the school meals staff.

NOTES

Figure "4A" in square brackets substituted by the School Staffing (England) (Amendment) Regulations 2013, SI 2013/1940, reg 2(1), (4).

[2.1040]

14 Authority's entitlement to offer advice

(1) A representative of the authority may attend and offer advice at all proceedings relating to the selection or dismissal of any teacher.

(2) The governing body must consider any advice offered by the authority pursuant to paragraph (1).

[2.1041]

15 Appointment of head teacher and deputy head teacher

(1) The governing body must notify the authority in writing of—
(a) any vacancy for the head teacher; and
(b) any post for a deputy head teacher which it has identified as one to be filled.

(2) The governing body must advertise any such vacancy or post in such manner as it considers appropriate unless it has good reason not to.

(3) Where the governing body advertises any such vacancy or post, it must appoint a selection panel, consisting of at least three of its members, other than a governor who is the head teacher or (as the case may be) a deputy head teacher, to—
(a) select for interview such applicants for the post as it thinks fit and, where the post is that of head teacher, notify the authority in writing of the names of the applicants selected;
(b) interview those applicants who attend for that purpose; and
(c) where it considers it appropriate, recommend to the governing body for appointment one of the applicants interviewed.

(4) If, within a period of seven days beginning with the date when it receives notification under paragraph (3)(a), the authority makes written representations to the selection panel that any applicant is not a suitable person for the post, the selection panel must—

- (a) consider those representations; and
- (b) where it decides to recommend for appointment any person about whom representations have been made, notify the governing body and authority in writing of its reasons.

(5) Subject to regulation 12(2) and, where appropriate, regulation 12(4), where the person recommended by the selection panel is approved by the governing body for appointment, the authority must appoint that person, unless the governing body has determined that the person is to be appointed by the governing body otherwise than under a contract of employment pursuant to regulation 12(1)(c).

(6) If—

- (a) the selection panel does not recommend a person to the governing body;
- (b) the governing body declines to approve the person recommended by the selection panel; or
- (c) the authority declines to appoint the person that the governing body approves,

the selection panel may recommend another person for appointment in accordance with this regulation (but this does not prevent it from recommending an existing applicant).

(7) Subject to regulation 12(2) and, where appropriate, regulation 12(4), where the governing body decides for good reason not to advertise and conduct a selection process to fill the vacancy or post in accordance with paragraphs (2) to (4), the authority must appoint the person identified by the governing body to fill the vacancy or post, unless the governing body has determined that the person is to be appointed by the governing body otherwise than under a contract of employment pursuant to regulation 12(1)(c).

[2.1042]
16 Appointment of other teachers

(1) This regulation applies to any post of teacher, other than a post of head teacher or deputy head teacher.

(2) Where the governing body identifies any such post to be filled for a period of more than four months, it must provide the authority with a specification for the post.

(3) Subject to regulation 12(2) and, where appropriate, regulation 12(4), where a person is selected by the governing body for appointment, the authority must appoint that person, unless the governing body has determined that the person is to be appointed by the governing body otherwise than under a contract of employment pursuant to regulation 12(1)(c).

(4) If the authority declines to appoint a person that the governing body selects, the governing body may select another person for appointment in accordance with this regulation (but this does not prevent it from selecting an existing applicant).

[2.1043]
17 Appointment of support staff

(1) Subject to regulation 21, where the governing body identifies a support staff post to be filled, it may recommend a person to the authority for appointment.

(2) Where the governing body recommends a person to the authority for appointment under paragraph (1) it must provide the authority with—

- (a) the name of any person it recommends pursuant to paragraph (1); and
- (b) a job specification for the post, which must include the governing body's recommendations as to—
  - (i) the duties to be performed,
  - (ii) the hours of work (where the post is part-time),
  - (iii) the duration of the appointment,
  - (iv) the grade; and
  - (v) the remuneration.

(3) The grade must be on the scale of grades applicable in relation to employment with the authority and such as the governing body considers appropriate.

(4) Where the authority has discretion with respect to remuneration, it must exercise that discretion in accordance with the governing body's recommendation.

(5) The authority may be regarded as having discretion with respect to remuneration if any provisions regulating the rates of remuneration or allowances payable to persons in the authority's employment—

- (a) do not apply in relation to that appointment; or
- (b) leave to the authority any degree of discretion as to the rate of remuneration.

(6) If, within a period of seven days after receiving the job specification, the authority makes written representations to the governing body relating to the grade or remuneration to be paid, the governing body must—

- (a) consider those representations; and
- (b) where it decides not to change the grade or remuneration to be paid, notify the authority in writing of its reasons.

(7) Subject to regulation 12(2) and, where appropriate, regulation 12(4), the authority must appoint the person recommended by the governing body to the post, unless the governing body has determined that the person is to be appointed by the governing body otherwise than under a contract of employment pursuant to regulation 12(1)(c).

[2.1044]
18 Supply staff

(1) The governing body must ensure that no person supplied by an employment business to a school is allowed to begin work as a teacher or member of support staff at the school unless the authority or (as the case may be) the governing body has received—

(a) written notification from the employment business in relation to that person—

(i) that it has made the checks referred to in [paragraphs 5(a)(i)[, (iii) and (iv)] and 5A] of Schedule 2;

(ii) [where it is intended that the person will engage in relevant activity,] that it or another employment business has applied for an enhanced criminal record certificate or has obtained such a certificate in response to an application made by that or another employment business; . . .

(iii) whether, if the employment business has obtained such a certificate before the person is due to begin work at the school, it disclosed any matter or information, or any information was provided to the employment business in accordance with section 113B(6) of PA 1997; and

[(iv) whether, if the employment business or another employment business has obtained such a certificate before the person is due to begin work at the school and the certificate is or has been subject to up-date arrangements, the employment business or another employment business has been given negative up-date information in relation to the certificate not more than three months before the person is due to begin work at the school; and]

(b) where the employment business has obtained an enhanced criminal record certificate before the person is due to begin work at the school which disclosed any matter or information or any information was provided to the employment business in accordance with section 113B(6) of PA 1997, a copy of the certificate[; and

(c) where an enhanced criminal record certificate is or has been subject to up-date arrangements and the employment business has been given negative up-date information in relation to the certificate not more than three months before the person is due to begin work at the school, a copy of the information].

(2) Subject to paragraph (3), the certificate referred to in paragraph (1)(a)(ii) must have been [issued and] obtained not more than three months before the person is due to begin work at the school [unless that certificate is or has been subject to up-date arrangements and the employment business or another employment business has been given negative up-date information in relation to the certificate not more than three months before the person is due to begin work at the school].

(3) Paragraph (2) does not apply in relation to a person who has worked in—

(a) a school in England in a post—

(i) which brought the person regularly into contact with children or young persons; or

(ii) to which the person was appointed on or after 12th May 2006 and which did not bring the person regularly into contact with children or young persons; or

(b) an institution within the further education sector in England[, or in a 16 to 19 Academy,] in a post which involved the provision of education which brought the person regularly into contact with children or young persons,

during a period which ended not more than three months before the person is due to begin work at the school.

(4) Before a person offered for supply by an employment business may begin work at the school the governing body must check the person's identity (whether or not the employment business made such a check before the person was offered for supply).

(5) The authority or (as the case may be) the governing body must, either in the contract or in other arrangements which it makes with any employment business, require it, in respect of any person whom the employment business supplies to the school—

(a) to provide the notification referred to in paragraph (1)(a); . . .

(b) if any enhanced criminal record certificate which the employment business obtains contains any matter or information, or if any information was provided to the employment business in accordance with section 113B(6) of PA 1997, to provide a copy of the certificate[; and

(c) if any such certificate is or has been subject to up-date arrangements and the employment business has been given negative up-date information in relation to the certificate not more than three months before the person is due to begin work at the school, to provide a copy of the information].

NOTES

Para (1): words in first (outer) pair of square brackets in sub-para (a)(i) substituted by the School Staffing (England) (Amendment) Regulations 2013, SI 2013/1940, reg 2(1), (5); words in second (inner) pair of square brackets in sub-para (a)(i) inserted, words in square brackets in sub-para (a)(ii) inserted, word omitted from sub-para (a)(ii) revoked, sub-para (a)(iv) inserted, and sub-para (c) inserted together with word immediately preceding it, by the School Staffing (England) (Amendment) Regulations 2015, SI 2015/887, regs 2, 5(1), (3), as from 29 June 2015.

Para (2): words in first and second pairs of square brackets inserted and added respectively by SI 2015/887, regs 2, 5(4), as from 29 June 2015.

Para (3): words in square brackets in sub-para (b) inserted by the Alternative Provision Academies and 16 to 19 Academies (Consequential Amendments to Subordinate Legislation) (England) Order 2012, SI 2012/979, art 2, Schedule, para 26.

Para (5): word omitted from sub-para (a) revoked, and sub-para (c) inserted together with word immediately preceding it, by SI 2015/887, regs 2, 5(5), as from 29 June 2015.

[2.1045]
19 Suspension of staff

(1) Subject to regulation 21, the governing body or the head teacher may suspend any person employed or engaged otherwise than under a contract of employment to work at the school where, in the opinion of the governing body or (as the case may be) the head teacher, such suspension is required.

(2) The governing body or (as the case may be) the head teacher must immediately inform the authority and the head teacher or (as the case may be) the governing body when a person is suspended under paragraph (1).

(3) Only the governing body may end a suspension under paragraph (1).

(4) On ending such a suspension, the governing body must immediately inform the authority and the head teacher.

(5) In this regulation "suspend" means suspend without loss of emoluments.

[2.1046]
20 Dismissal of staff

(1) Subject to regulation 21, where the governing body determines that any person employed or engaged by the authority to work at the school should cease to work there, it must notify the authority in writing of its determination and the reasons for it.

(2) If the person concerned is employed or engaged to work solely at the school (and does not resign), the authority must, before the end of the period of fourteen days beginning with the date of the notification under paragraph (1), either—

(a) terminate the person's contract with the authority, giving such notice as is required under that contract; or

(b) terminate such contract without notice if the circumstances are such that it is entitled to do so by reason of the person's conduct.

(3) If the person concerned is not employed or engaged by the authority to work solely at the school, the authority must require the person to cease to work at the school.

[2.1047]
21 School meals staff

(1) Subject to paragraphs (2) to (5), the authority is responsible for the appointment, discipline, suspension and dismissal of school meals staff who work or are to work at a school.

(2) Before exercising any such function the authority must consult the school's governing body to such extent as the authority thinks fit.

(3) Where an order is in force under section 512A(1) of the Education Act 1996 imposing on the governing body of a school a duty corresponding to a duty of the authority mentioned in section 512(3) and (4) of that Act (duty to provide school lunches) or section 512ZB(1) of that Act (duty to provide school lunches free of charge), paragraph (4) or (5) applies as appropriate.

(4) Where the governing body and the authority have agreed that the authority will provide lunches at the school and the governing body determines that any member of the school meals staff should cease to work at the school—

(a) the governing body must notify the authority in writing of its determination and the reasons for it; and

(b) the authority must require the person to cease to work at the school.

(5) Where no such agreement has been made, regulations 7, 17, 19 and 20 apply in relation to school meals staff.

[2.1048]
22 Checks on change of post

Where a member of the school staff who was appointed before 12th May 2006 moves from a post which did not bring the person regularly into contact with children or young persons to a post which does, the governing body must obtain an enhanced criminal record certificate in respect of the person before, or as soon as practicable after the move.

PART 3
PROVISIONS RELATING TO FOUNDATION, VOLUNTARY AIDED AND FOUNDATION SPECIAL SCHOOLS

[2.1049]
23 Application of Part 3

This Part applies to foundation, voluntary aided and foundation special schools.

[2.1050]
24 Manner of appointment

(1) Where the governing body has selected a person for appointment it may appoint that person either—

(a) under a contract of employment; or

(b) otherwise than under a contract of employment.

(2) The governing body must check—

(a) the identity of any such person;

Part 2 Statutory Instruments

(b) that the person meets all relevant staff qualification requirements; and
(c) that the person has a right to work in the United Kingdom.

(3) [Where it is intended that the person will engage in relevant activity, the] governing body must obtain an enhanced criminal record certificate in respect of any such person, before, or as soon as practicable after, the person's appointment.

[(3A) Where a governing body obtains an enhanced criminal record certificate in respect of any such person and that certificate is subject to up-date arrangements, it must consider whether to request up-date information in relation to the certificate under section 116A(1) of PA 1997.]

(4) In the case of any such person for whom, by reason of having lived outside the United Kingdom, obtaining such a certificate is not sufficient to establish the person's suitability to work in a school, the governing body must make such further checks as it considers appropriate, having regard to any guidance issued by the Secretary of State.

(5) The governing body must complete the checks referred to in paragraphs (2) and (4) before a person is appointed.

(6) Paragraphs (3) and (4) do not apply to a person who has worked in—
(a) a school in England in a post—
(i) which brought the person regularly into contact with children or young persons; or
(ii) to which the person was appointed on or after 12th May 2006 and which did not bring the person regularly into contact with children or young persons; or
(b) an institution within the further education sector in England[, or in a 16 to 19 Academy,] in a post which involved the provision of education which brought the person regularly into contact with children or young persons,

during a period which ended not more than three months before the person's appointment.

(7) The governing body must keep a separate register which contains the information specified in Schedule 2.

NOTES

Para (3): words in square brackets substituted by the School Staffing (England) (Amendment) Regulations 2015, SI 2015/887, regs 2, 4(1), as from 29 June 2015.

Para (3A): inserted by SI 2015/887, regs 2, 4(2), as from 29 June 2015.

Para (6): words in square brackets in sub-para (b) inserted by the Alternative Provision Academies and 16 to 19 Academies (Consequential Amendments to Subordinate Legislation) (England) Order 2012, SI 2012/979, art 2, Schedule, para 26.

[2.1051]
25 Application of regulation 24 to other appointments

Regulation 24(2) to (6) and (7) (insofar as it relates to paragraphs 2 to [4A], 7 and 8 of Schedule 2) also applies in relation to any person appointed by an authority for the purpose of working at a school to which this Part applies in the temporary absence of a member of staff of the school.

NOTES

Figure "4A" in square brackets substituted by the School Staffing (England) (Amendment) Regulations 2013, SI 2013/1940, reg 2(1), (6).

[2.1052]
26 Authority's entitlement to offer advice

(1) The authority may offer advice to the governing body in relation to the exercise of the governing body's functions of appointment and dismissal of any teacher, to the extent provided by, and subject to, any relevant agreement.

(2) A "relevant agreement" is an agreement in writing between the authority and the governing body which entitles the authority to offer advice to the governing body in relation to the exercise of any such function to the extent provided, and which has not been terminated by the governing body by notice in writing to the authority.

(3) The governing body must consider any advice offered by the authority pursuant to paragraph (1).

[2.1053]
27 Appointment of head teacher and deputy head teacher

(1) The governing body must notify the authority in writing of—
(a) any vacancy for the head teacher; and
(b) any post of deputy head teacher which it has identified as one to be filled.

(2) The governing body must advertise any such vacancy or post in such manner as it considers appropriate unless it has good reason not to.

(3) Where the governing body advertises any such vacancy or post, it must appoint a selection panel, consisting of at least three of its members, other than a governor who is the head teacher or (as the case may be) a deputy head teacher, to—
(a) select for interview such applicants for the post as it thinks fit and, where the post is that of head teacher, notify the authority in writing of the names of the applicants so selected;
(b) interview those applicants who attend for that purpose; and
(c) where it considers it appropriate to do so, recommend to the governing body for appointment one of the applicants interviewed.

(4) If, within a period of seven days beginning with the date when it receives notification under paragraph (3)(a), the authority makes written representations to the selection panel that any of the applicants is not a suitable person for the post, the selection panel must—

(a) consider those representations; and

(b) where it decides to recommend for appointment the person about whom the representations have been made, notify the authority in writing of its reasons.

(5) Subject to regulation 24(2) and, where appropriate, regulation 12(4), the governing body may appoint the person recommended by the selection panel to the vacancy or the post to be filled.

(6) If—

(a) the selection panel does not recommend a person to the governing body; or

(b) the governing body declines to appoint the person recommended by the selection panel,

the selection panel may recommend another person for appointment in accordance with this regulation (but this does not prevent it from recommending an existing applicant).

(7) Subject to regulation 24(2) and, where appropriate, regulation 12(4), if the governing body decides, for good reason, not to advertise and conduct a selection process to fill the vacancy or post in accordance with paragraphs (2) to (4), it may appoint the person it has identified to the vacancy or post to be filled.

(8) Paragraphs (2) to (7) are subject to regulation 34.

[2.1054]
28 Appointment of other teachers

Where the governing body identifies any post of teacher (other than head teacher or deputy head teacher) which is to be filled for a period of more than four months, it must send a specification for the post to the authority.

[2.1055]
29 Appointment of support staff

The governing body is responsible for the appointment of support staff unless the governing body and the authority agree that the authority will make such appointments.

[2.1056]
30 Supply staff

(1) The governing body must ensure that no person supplied by an employment business to a school is allowed to begin work as a teacher or member of support staff at the school unless the governing body has received—

(a) written notification from the employment business in relation to that person—

(i) that it has made the checks referred to in [paragraphs 5(a)(i), (iii) and (iv) and 5A] of Schedule 2;

(ii) [where it is intended that the person will engage in relevant activity,] that it or another employment business has applied for an enhanced criminal record certificate or has obtained such a certificate in response to an application made by that or another employment business; . . .

(iii) whether, if the employment business has obtained such a certificate before the person is due to begin work at the school, it disclosed any matter or information, or any information was provided to the employment business in accordance with section 113B(6) of PA 1997; and

[(iv) whether, if the employment business or another employment business has obtained such a certificate before the person is due to begin work at the school and the certificate is or has been subject to up-date arrangements, the employment business or another employment business has been given negative up-date information in relation to the certificate not more than three months before the person is due to begin work at the school; and]

(b) where the employment business has obtained such a certificate before the person is due to begin work at the school which disclosed any matter or information, or any information was provided to the employment business in accordance with section 113B(6) of PA 1997, a copy of the certificate[; and

(c) where an enhanced criminal record certificate is or has been subject to up-date arrangements and the employment business has been given negative up-date information in relation to the certificate not more than three months before the person is due to begin work at the school, a copy of the information].

(2) Subject to paragraph (3), the certificate referred to in paragraph (1)(a)(ii) must have been [issued and] obtained not more than three months before the person is due to begin work at the school [unless that certificate is or has been subject to up-date arrangements and the employment business or another employment business has been given negative up-date information in relation to the certificate not more than three months before the person is due to begin work at the school].

(3) Paragraph (2) does not apply in relation to a person who has worked in—

(a) a school in England in a post—

(i) which brought the person regularly into contact with children or young persons; or

(ii) to which the person was appointed on or after 12th May 2006 and which did not bring the person regularly into contact with children or young persons; or

(b) an institution within the further education sector in England[, or in a 16 to 19 Academy,] in a post which involved the provision of education which brought the person regularly into contact with children or young persons,

Part 2 Statutory Instruments

during a period which ended not more than three months before the person is due to begin work at the school.

(4) Before a person offered for supply by an employment business may begin work at the school the governing body must check the person's identity (whether or not the employment business made such a check before the person was offered for supply).

(5) The governing body must, either in the contract or in other arrangements which it makes with any employment business, require it, in respect of any person whom the employment business supplies to the school—

(a) to provide the notification referred to in paragraph (1)(a); . . .

(b) where the employment business obtains an enhanced criminal record certificate which discloses any matter or information, or if any information is provided to the employment business in accordance with section 113B(6) of PA 1997, to provide a copy of the certificate[; and

(c) if any such certificate is or has been subject to up-date arrangements and the employment business has been given negative up-date information in relation to the certificate not more than three months before the person is due to begin work at the school, to provide a copy of the information].

NOTES

Para (1): words in square brackets in sub-para (a)(i) substituted, in sub-para (a)(ii) words in square brackets inserted and word omitted revoked, sub-para (a)(iv) inserted, and sub-para (c) inserted together with word immediately preceding it, by the School Staffing (England) (Amendment) Regulations 2015, SI 2015/887, regs 2, 5(2), (3), as from 29 June 2015.

Para (2): words in first and second pairs of square brackets inserted and added respectively, by SI 2015/887, regs 2, 5(4), as from 29 June 2015.

Para (3): words in square brackets in sub-para (b) inserted by the Alternative Provision Academies and 16 to 19 Academies (Consequential Amendments to Subordinate Legislation) (England) Order 2012, SI 2012/979, art 2, Schedule, para 26.

Para (5): word omitted from sub-para (a) revoked, and sub-para (c) inserted together with word immediately preceding it, by SI 2015/887, regs 2, 5(5), as from 29 June 2015.

[2.1057]

31 Suspension of staff

(1) The governing body or the head teacher may suspend any person employed or engaged otherwise than under a contract of employment to work at the school where, in the opinion of the governing body or (as the case may be) the head teacher, the person's suspension from the school is required.

(2) The governing body or (as the case may be) head teacher must immediately inform the head teacher or (as the case may be) the governing body when a person is suspended under paragraph (1).

(3) Only the governing body may end a suspension under paragraph (1).

(4) On ending such a suspension, the governing body must inform the head teacher.

(5) In this regulation "suspend" means suspend without loss of emoluments.

[2.1058]

32 Suspension and dismissal of authority staff

In the case of staff employed, or engaged otherwise than under a contract of employment, by the authority in accordance with regulation 29, regulation 19 (in place of regulation 31) and regulation 20 apply as they apply to schools referred to in regulation 11.

[2.1059]

33 Checks on change of post

Where a member of the school staff who was appointed before 12th May 2006 moves from a post which did not bring the person regularly into contact with children or young persons to a post which does, the governing body must obtain an enhanced criminal record certificate in respect of the person before, or as soon as practicable after, the move.

[2.1060]

34 Appointment of head teachers for schools of Roman Catholic Religious Orders

(1) This regulation applies in relation to a voluntary aided school if the trustees under a trust deed relating to the school are also trustees of a Roman Catholic Religious Order ("the Order").

(2) Subject to paragraph (5), paragraphs (3) and (4) have effect in relation to the filling of a vacancy in the post of head teacher of the school, in place of regulation 27(2) to (7).

(3) The governing body must notify the Major Superior of the vacancy in writing.

(4) The governing body must—

(a) interview such persons who are members of the Order as are proposed as candidates for appointment to the post by the Major Superior; and

(b) appoint to the post one of the persons so interviewed unless, by virtue of regulation 24(2) or otherwise, the governing body has good reason for not making any such appointment.

(5) If the governing body does not make an appointment under paragraph (4)(b), regulation 27(2) to (7), has effect in relation to the filling of the vacancy.

(6) In this regulation—

"the Major Superior" means the Major Superior of the Order;

"Roman Catholic Religious Order" means a Roman Catholic religious institute or society of apostolic life.

PART 4
COLLABORATION BETWEEN SCHOOLS

[2.1061]
35 General

(1) Where two or more governing bodies agree to collaborate on the discharge of any function relating to individual members of the school staff, these Regulations apply, subject to this Part.

(2) In this Part—

"collaborating governing bodies" means two or more governing bodies which arrange for any of their functions to be discharged jointly;

"relevant school" means the school or schools to which any member of staff is, or is to be, appointed.

[2.1062]
36 Appointment of head teacher and deputy head teacher

(1) In relation to the appointment of a head teacher or a deputy head teacher under regulation 15 or 27—

(a) the collaborating governing bodies may delegate the notification to the authority and the advertisement of any vacancy or post to—

(i) the head teacher of one or more of the collaborating schools;

(ii) one or more governors from any of the collaborating schools;

(iii) one or more head teachers acting together with one or more governors from any of the collaborating schools;

(b) the selection panel must consist of at least three governors taken from any of the collaborating governing bodies other than a governor who is the head teacher or (as the case may be) a deputy head teacher of the relevant school; and

(c) the selection panel must make its recommendation to the governing body of the relevant school.

(2) If the governing body does not approve the recommendation the selection panel of the collaborating governing bodies must repeat the selection process unless the relevant school's governing body withdraws from the agreement to collaborate.

[2.1063]
37 Appointment of other teachers and support staff

(1) The collaborating governing bodies may delegate the appointment of any teacher (other than the head teacher and deputy head teacher) and the appointment of any member of the support staff to—

(a) the head teacher of one or more of the collaborating schools;

(b) one or more governors from any of the collaborating schools;

(c) one or more head teachers acting together with one or more governors from any of the collaborating schools.

(2) Where the collaborating governing bodies have delegated the appointment of a member of staff, other than to the head teacher of the relevant school—

(a) the head teacher of the relevant school may attend all relevant proceedings and offer advice; and

(b) the person or persons to whom the delegation has been made must consider any such advice.

[2.1064]
38 Dismissal of staff

(1) The collaborating governing bodies may delegate—

(a) the determination that a member of staff (other than the head teacher) should cease to work at a relevant school; or

(b) the power to dismiss a member of staff (other than the head teacher) from a relevant school.

(2) Any such delegation may be to—

(a) the head teacher of one or more of the collaborating schools;

(b) one or more governors from any of the collaborating schools;

(c) one or more head teachers acting together with one or more governors from any of the collaborating schools.

(3) The collaborating governing bodies may delegate—

(a) the determination that the head teacher should cease to work at a relevant school; or

(b) the power to dismiss the head teacher from a relevant school,

to one or more governors.

[2.1065]
39 Authority's entitlement to offer advice

(1) Where the authority is entitled to offer advice to any individual governing body in relation to the exercise of any function under regulation 14 or 26, it is also entitled to offer advice to any other collaborating governing bodies in relation to the exercise of any such function.

(2) The collaborating governing bodies must consider any advice offered by the authority pursuant to paragraph (1).

PART 5
STAFFING OF NEW SCHOOLS

[2.1066]
40 Interpretation of provisions applied by Part 5

Any provision of these Regulations or Schedule 2 to EA 2002 which applies in relation to a proposed school as a result of this Part has effect for that purpose as if—

(a) any reference to a "governing body" were a reference to a temporary governing body; and
(b) any reference to a "governor" were a reference to a temporary governor.

[2.1067]
41 Staffing of proposed community, voluntary controlled, community special and maintained nursery schools having delegated budgets

Where a proposed community, voluntary controlled, community special or maintained nursery school has a delegated budget, regulations 4 to 9 and 12 to 22 apply.

[2.1068]
42 Staffing of proposed foundation, voluntary aided and foundation special schools having delegated budgets

Where a proposed foundation, voluntary aided or foundation special school has a delegated budget, regulations 4 to 9 and 24 to 34 apply.

[2.1069]
43 Staffing of proposed community, voluntary controlled, community special and maintained nursery schools without delegated budgets

Where a proposed community, voluntary controlled, community special or maintained nursery school does not have a delegated budget, the provisions of Part 1 of Schedule 2 to EA 2002 apply.

[2.1070]
44 Staffing of proposed foundation, voluntary aided or foundation special schools without delegated budgets

Where a proposed foundation, voluntary aided or foundation special school does not have a delegated budget, the provisions of Part 2 of Schedule 2 to EA 2002 apply.

SCHEDULES
SCHEDULE 1

(Sch 1 (Revocations) outside the scope of this work.)

SCHEDULE 2
INFORMATION TO BE RECORDED IN THE REGISTER

Regulations 12(7) and 24(7)

[2.1071]
1. The register referred to in regulations 12(7) and 24(7) must contain the following information.

2. In relation to each member of staff appointed on or after 1st January 2007, whether—

(a) a check was made to establish the person's identity;
(b) a check was made to establish that the person is not barred from regulated activity relating to children in accordance with section 3(2) of the Safeguarding Vulnerable Groups Act 2006 or subject to any direction made under section 142 of EA 2002 or any prohibition, restriction or order having effect as such a direction;
(c) checks were made to establish that the person meets the requirements with respect to qualifications or registration mentioned in regulation 3(3)(a);
(d) an enhanced criminal record certificate was obtained in respect of the person;
(e) further checks were made pursuant to regulation 12(4) or 24(4), as the case may be;
(f) a check was made to establish the person's right to work in the United Kingdom and
(g) the date on which each such check was completed or the certificate obtained.

3. Subject to paragraph 4, in relation to each member of staff in post on 1st April 2007 who was appointed at any time before 1st January 2007—

(a) whether each check referred to in paragraph 2 was made;
(b) whether an enhanced criminal record certificate was obtained; and
(c) the date on which each such check was completed or certificate obtained.

4. Paragraph 3 applies, in the case of a member of staff who was appointed at any time before 12th May 2006, only if the work brings the person regularly into contact with children or young persons.

[**4A.** In relation to each member of staff appointed on or after 2nd September 2013, whether a check was made to establish that the person is not subject to a prohibition order or interim prohibition order.]

5. [(1)] In relation to any person supplied by an employment business to work at the school—

(a) whether written notification has been received from the employment business that—

(i) it has made checks corresponding to those which paragraph 2(a) . . . (c), (e) and (f) requires to be recorded in relation to a member of staff of a school; . . .

(ii) it or another employment business has applied for an enhanced criminal record certificate or has obtained such a certificate in response to an application made by that or another employment business; . . .

[(iii) it has made a check to establish that the person is not subject to any direction under section 142 of EA 2002 or any prohibition, restriction or order having effect as such a direction; and

(iv) subject to sub-paragraph (2), it has made a check to establish that the person is not barred from regulated activity relating to children in accordance with section 3(2) of the Safeguarding Vulnerable Groups Act 2006; and]

(b) the date on which such notification was received.

[(2) In the case of a person supplied on or after 29th June 2015, sub-paragraph (1)(a)(iv) applies only if it is intended that the person will engage in any activity which is a regulated activity relating to children within the meaning of Part 1 of Schedule 4 to the Safeguarding Vulnerable Groups Act 2006.]

[**5A.** In relation to any person supplied by an employment business on or after 2nd September 2013, whether a check was made to establish that the person is not subject to a prohibition order or interim prohibition order.]

6. Where written notification has been received from the employment business in accordance with a contract or other arrangements made pursuant to regulation 18(5) [or 30(5)] that it has obtained an enhanced criminal record certificate which disclosed any matter or information, or that information was provided to it in accordance with section 113B(6) of PA 1997, whether the employment business provided a copy of the certificate to the school.

[**6A.** In relation to any person supplied by an employment business on or after 29th June 2015, where written notification has been received from the employment business in accordance with a contract or other arrangements made pursuant to regulation 18(5) or 30(5) that it has been given negative up-date information in relation to an enhanced criminal record certificate not more than three months before the person was due to begin work at the school, whether the employment business provided a copy of the information.]

7. It is immaterial for the purposes of paragraphs 2 and 3 whether the check was made or certificate obtained pursuant to a legal obligation.

8. The register may be kept in electronic form, provided that the information so recorded is capable of being reproduced in legible form.

NOTES

Paras 4A, 5A: inserted by the School Staffing (England) (Amendment) Regulations 2013, SI 2013/1940, reg 2(1), (7).

Para 5: existing provision numbered as sub-para (1), in sub-para (1) words omitted revoked and words in square brackets inserted, and sub-para (2) added, by the School Staffing (England) (Amendment) Regulations 2015, SI 2015/887, regs 2, 6(1), (2), as from 29 June 2015.

Para 6: words in square brackets inserted by SI 2015/887, regs 2, 6(1), (3), as from 29 June 2015.

Para 6A: inserted by SI 2015/887, regs 2, 6(1), (4), as from 29 June 2015.

LAW APPLICABLE TO CONTRACTUAL OBLIGATIONS (ENGLAND AND WALES AND NORTHERN IRELAND) REGULATIONS 2009

(SI 2009/3064)

NOTES

Made: 15 November 2009.

Authority: European Communities Act 1972, s 2(2).

Commencement: 17 December 2009.

Note: with regard to the authority for these Regulations, note that the European Communities Act 1972 is repealed by the European Union (Withdrawal) Act 2018, s 1, as from exit day (as defined in s 20 of that Act); but note also that provision is made for the continuation in force of any subordinate legislation made under the authority of s 2(2) of the 1972 Act by s 2 of the 2018 Act at **[1.2240]**, subject to the provisions of s 5 of, and Sch 1 to, the 2018 Act at **[1.2243]**, **[1.2253]**.

[2.1072]

1 Citation, commencement and extent

(1) These Regulations may be cited as the Law Applicable to Contractual Obligations (England and Wales and Northern Ireland) Regulations 2009, and shall come into force on 17 December 2009.

(2) Regulation 3 extends to England and Wales only.

(3) Regulation 4 extends to Northern Ireland only.

(4) Otherwise, these Regulations extend to England and Wales and Northern Ireland.

2–4 *(Reg 2 inserts the Contracts (Applicable Law) Act 1990, s 4A at* **[1.195]***; reg 3 amends the Foreign Limitation Periods Act 1984, s 8; reg 4 amends the Foreign Limitation Periods (Northern Ireland) Order 1985, art 9.)*

[2.1073]

5 Application of the Regulation (EC) No 593/2008*: conflicts falling within Article 22(2)*

(1) *Notwithstanding Article 22(2) of* Regulation (EC) No 593/2008 of the European Parliament and of the Council on the law applicable to contractual obligations, *that Regulation* shall apply in the case of conflicts between—

(a) the laws of different parts of the United Kingdom, or

(b) the laws of one or more parts of the United Kingdom and Gibraltar,

as it applies in the case of conflicts between the laws of other countries.

(2) Paragraph (1) shall not apply to contracts falling within Article 7 of Regulation (EC) No 593/2008 (insurance contracts).

NOTES

The words in italics in each place are revoked by the Law Applicable to Contractual Obligations and Non-Contractual Obligations (Amendment etc) (EU Exit) Regulations 2019, SI 2019/834, reg 6, as from exit day (as defined in the European Union (Withdrawal) Act 2018, s 20).

LAW APPLICABLE TO CONTRACTUAL OBLIGATIONS (SCOTLAND) REGULATIONS 2009

(SSI 2009/410)

NOTES

Made: 23 November 2009.

Authority: European Communities Act 1972, s 2(2).

Commencement: 17 December 2009.

Note: with regard to the authority for these Regulations, note that the European Communities Act 1972 is repealed by the European Union (Withdrawal) Act 2018, s 1, as from exit day (as defined in s 20 of that Act); but note also that provision is made for the continuation in force of any subordinate legislation made under the authority of s 2(2) of the 1972 Act by s 2 of the 2018 Act at **[1.2240]**, subject to the provisions of s 5 of, and Sch 1 to, the 2018 Act at **[1.2243]**, **[1.2253]**.

[2.1074]

1 Citation, commencement and extent

(1) These Regulations may be cited as the Law Applicable to Contractual Obligations (Scotland) Regulations 2009 and come into force on 17th December 2009.

(2) These Regulations extend to Scotland only.

2, 3 *(Reg 2 inserts the Contracts (Applicable Law) Act 1990, s 4B at* **[1.196]***, and amends s 8 of that Act; reg 3 amends the Prescription and Limitation (Scotland) Act 1973, s 23A.)*

[2.1075]

4 *Conflicts falling within Article 22(2) of Regulation (EC) No 593/2008*

Notwithstanding Article 22(2) of Regulation (EC) No 593/2008 of the European Parliament and of the Council on the law applicable to contractual obligations (Rome I), *that Regulation* shall, with the exception of Article 7 (insurance contracts), apply in the case of conflicts between—

(a) the laws of different parts of the United Kingdom, or

(b) the laws of one or more parts of the United Kingdom and Gibraltar,

as it applies in the case of conflicts between the laws of other countries.

NOTES

For the heading in italics there are substituted the words "Application of Regulation (EC) No 593/2008", and the other words in italics are revoked, by the Law Applicable to Contractual Obligations and Non-Contractual Obligations (Amendment etc) (EU Exit) Regulations 2019, SI 2019/834, reg 9, as from exit day (as defined in the European Union (Withdrawal) Act 2018, s 20).

EMPLOYERS' DUTIES (IMPLEMENTATION) REGULATIONS 2010

(SI 2010/4)

NOTES

Made: 5 January 2010.

Authority: Pensions Act 2008, ss 12, 29(2), (4), 30(8), 99, 144(2), (4).

Commencement: 1 June 2012. Note that, as originally enacted, these Regulations were due to come into force on 1 September 2012. Regulation 1 of these Regulations (Citation, commencement and interpretation) was amended by the Automatic Enrolment (Miscellaneous Amendments) Regulations 2012, SI 2012/215, reg 3(a) with the effect that the commencement date became 1 June 2012. Note also that other amendments made to these Regulations by the 2012 Regulations also came into force on 1 June 2012 (immediately before the commencement of these Regulations by virtue of the amendment made by reg 3(a)).

ARRANGEMENT OF REGULATIONS

[2.1076]

1 Citation, commencement and interpretation

(1) These Regulations may be cited as the Employers' Duties (Implementation) Regulations 2010 and shall come into force on [1st June 2012, immediately after the time when the amendments to these Regulations made by the Automatic Enrolment (Miscellaneous Amendments) Regulations 2012 come into force].

(2) In these Regulations—

"the Act" means the Pensions Act 2008;

["deferral date" means the date specified in a notice given by an employer under regulation 4B(1) or (2);]

"employer"[, except in regulations 4B and 4C,] has the meaning given by—

(a) section 88(7) of the Act; and

(b) regulation 2(2);

"the employers' duties" means sections 2 to 9 of the Act;

"HMRC" means Her Majesty's Revenue and Customs;

"PAYE income" has the same meaning as in section 683 of the Income Tax (Earnings and Pensions) Act 2003;

"PAYE reference number" means a number issued by HMRC to a corresponding PAYE scheme, enabling an employer to pay over amounts deducted to HMRC;

"PAYE scheme" means the HMRC record [applicable] to an employer who—

(a) employs; or

(b) intends to employ,

a worker or workers to whom PAYE income is payable;

"scheme administrator" has the same meaning as in section 270 of the Finance Act 2004; and

["staging date" means the date prescribed in accordance with regulation 2(1) on which the employers' duties apply to employers.]

NOTES

Para (1): words in square brackets substituted by the Automatic Enrolment (Miscellaneous Amendments) Regulations 2012, SI 2012/215, regs 2, 3(a).

Para (2): definition "deferral date" inserted, and words in square brackets in definition "employer" inserted, by the Employers' Duties (Implementation) (Amendment) Regulations 2017, SI 2017/347, regs 2, 3(1), as from 1 April 2017. Word in square brackets in definition "PAYE scheme" substituted by SI 2012/215, regs 2, 3(b). Definition "staging date" substituted by the Employers' Duties (Implementation) (Amendment) Regulations 2012, SI 2012/1813, reg 2(1), (2).

[2.1077]

2 Application of the employers' duties to employers

[(1) Except where an employer satisfies the conditions for early automatic enrolment in regulation 3, the employers' duties do not apply to employers described in the first column of the table in regulation 4 until—

(a) the corresponding staging date prescribed in the final column of that table; or

(b) in a case to which paragraph (1A) applies—

(i) the corresponding staging date prescribed in the final column of that table in regulation 4; or

(ii) where the employer so chooses, the corresponding staging date prescribed in the final column of the table as modified by regulation 4A.]

[(1A) This paragraph applies in a case where, on 1st April 2012, the employer—

(a) had less than 50 workers; and

(b) had, or was part of, one or more PAYE schemes in which there were 50 or more persons.]

(2) For the purposes of these Regulations [(except for regulations 4B and 4C)], an employer is a person within the meaning of section 88(7) of the Act who—

(a) has[, or is part of,] a PAYE scheme of any size, determined by the Regulator in accordance with paragraphs (3) and (4); or

(b) meets any other description contained in the first column of the table in regulation 4 (including having no PAYE scheme).

(3) The size of an employer's PAYE scheme means the number of persons within that scheme.

(4) The number of persons within a PAYE scheme is based on the latest information available to the Regulator, as at 1st April 2012.

(5) Where—

(a) the employers' duties first apply to an employer in accordance with the table in regulation 4; and

(b) for any reason, an employer has another PAYE scheme (or schemes),

the employers' duties apply to that employer in respect of the scheme (or schemes) mentioned in subparagraph (b) from the staging date applicable in relation to subparagraph (a) (and this is so even where the staging date mentioned in the table for any such scheme (or schemes) is later than the staging date referred to in subparagraph (a)).

(6) Any employer who first pays PAYE income in respect of a worker between—

(a) 1st April 2012; and

(b) up to (but not including) [1st October 2017],

is to be treated as a new employer in accordance with the relevant entry in the first column of the table in regulation 4.

(7) Where paragraph (6) applies, the employers' duties do not apply to such an employer until PAYE income is first payable in respect of any worker and then only in accordance with the table in regulation 4.

[(8) Where—

(a) an employer first pays PAYE income in respect of any worker on or after 1st October 2017; and

(b) the employers' duties do not already apply to that employer,

the employers' duties apply to that employer from the day on which the employer's first worker begins to be employed by the employer.]

[(9) This paragraph applies in the case of an employer who does not have a PAYE scheme in respect of any worker after 1st April 2017.

(10) Where paragraph (9) applies and the employers' duties do not already apply to that employer, the employers' duties apply to that employer from the date on which [the employer's first worker begins to be employed by the employer].]

NOTES

Para (1): substituted by the Employers' Duties (Implementation) (Amendment) Regulations 2012, SI 2012/1813, reg 2(1), (3)(a).

Para (1A): inserted by SI 2012/1813, reg 2(1), (3)(b).

Para (2): words in first pair of square brackets inserted by the Employers' Duties (Implementation) (Amendment) Regulations 2017, SI 2017/347, regs 2, 3(2)(a), as from 1 April 2017; words in square brackets in sub-para (a) inserted by the Automatic Enrolment (Miscellaneous Amendments) Regulations 2012, SI 2012/215, regs 2, 4.

Para (6): words in square brackets substituted by SI 2012/1813, reg 2(1), (3)(c).

Para (8): substituted by SI 2017/347, regs 2, 3(2)(b), as from 1 April 2017.

Paras (9), (10): added by SI 2012/1813, reg 2(1), (3)(e). Words in square brackets in para (10) substituted by SI 2017/347, regs 2, 3(2)(c), as from 1 April 2017.

[2.1078]

3 Early automatic enrolment

[(1) Where the conditions in paragraphs (3) and (4) are both satisfied, the employers' duties apply to an employer from the early automatic enrolment date referred to in paragraph (5).]

[(1A) This regulation does not apply where the employer has chosen a staging date in accordance with regulation 2(1)(b)(ii).]

(2) Where the condition in paragraph (3) is satisfied but the condition in paragraph (4) is not satisfied, the employers' duties apply to an employer from the staging date corresponding to that employer's description . . . .

(3) The first condition is that an employer must fall within any description in the first column of the table in regulation 4.

(4) The second condition is that an employer has chosen an early automatic enrolment date [referred to in paragraph (5)] for the employers' duties to apply, which is earlier than the date mentioned in the final column of that table corresponding to that employer, and has—

(a) . . .

(b) [where, on the date the employer notifies the Regulator in accordance with sub-paragraph (c), the duty in section 3(2) of the Act (automatic enrolment) applies in relation to at least one of that employer's jobholders,] secured the agreement of the [trustees or managers] (or scheme administrator or provider) of [a pension scheme] that that scheme [is] to be used by the employer to comply with those duties from that early automatic enrolment date; and

[(c) notified the Regulator accordingly in writing, at any time—

[(i) where paragraph (5)(a) or (d) applies, on or before the early automatic enrolment date;]

(ii) where paragraph (5)(b) applies, before 1st November 2012; or

(iii) where paragraph (5)(c) applies, no later than the first day of the period of one month before the date specified in that sub-paragraph.]

[(5) The early automatic enrolment date is—

(a) any date in the final column of the table in regulation 4 which is earlier than the staging date corresponding to that employers' description;

(b) 1st December 2012; . . .

(c) in the case of an employer of 50,000 or more persons by PAYE scheme size or any other description, one of the following dates to be chosen by the employer—
 (i) 1st July 2012;
 (ii) 1st August 2012; or
 (iii) 1st September 2012[; or

(d) in the case of an employer who has no jobholder to whom the duty in section 3(2) of the Act applies on the date the employer notifies the Regulator in accordance with paragraph (4)(c)(i), any date which is earlier than the staging date corresponding to that employer's description].]

NOTES

Para (1): substituted by the Automatic Enrolment (Miscellaneous Amendments) Regulations 2012, SI 2012/215, regs 2, 5(a).

Para (1A): inserted by the Employers' Duties (Implementation) (Amendment) Regulations 2012, SI 2012/1813, reg 2(1), (4)(a).

Para (2): words omitted revoked by SI 2012/215, regs 2, 5(b).

Para (4) is amended as follows:

Words "referred to in paragraph (5)" in square brackets substituted, sub-para (a) revoked, words "trustees or managers" in square brackets in sub-para (b) substituted, and sub-para (c) substituted, by SI 2012/215, regs 2, 5(c).

Words in first pair of square brackets in sub-para (b) inserted, word "is" in square brackets in that sub-paragraph substituted, and sub-para (c)(i) substituted, by the Occupational and Personal Pension Schemes (Automatic Enrolment) (Miscellaneous Amendments) Regulations 2016, SI 2016/311, reg 2(1), (2)(a), as from 6 April 2016.

Words "a pension scheme" in square brackets in sub-para (b) substituted by SI 2012/1813, reg 2(1), (4)(b).

Para (5): added by SI 2012/215, regs 2, 5(d); word omitted from sub-para (b) revoked, and sub-para (d) (and the preceding word) added, by SI 2016/311, reg 2(1), (2)(b), as from 6 April 2016.

[2.1079]

4 Staging of the employers' duties

(1) The table in this regulation sets out the application of the employers' duties.

(2), (3) . . .

Table

Employer (by PAYE scheme size or other description)	. . .	*Staging date*
120,000 or more	. . .	1st October 2012
50,000–119,999	. . .	1st November 2012
30,000–49,999	. . .	1st January 2013
20,000–29,999	. . .	1st February 2013
10,000–19,999	. . .	1st March 2013
6,000–9,999	. . .	1st April 2013
4,100–5,999	. . .	1st May 2013
4,000–4,099	. . .	1st June 2013
3,000–3,999	. . .	1st July 2013
2,000–2,999	. . .	1st August 2013
1,250–1,999	. . .	1st September 2013
800–1,249	. . .	1st October 2013
500–799	. . .	1st November 2013
350–499	. . .	1st January 2014
250–349	. . .	1st February 2014
[160–249	. . .	1st April 2014
90–159	. . .	1st May 2014
62–89	. . .	1st July 2014
61	. . .	1st August 2014
60	. . .	1st October 2014
59	. . .	1st November 2014
58	. . .	1st January 2015
54–57	. . .	1st March 2015
50–53	. . .	1st April 2015
Less than 30 with the last 2 characters in their PAYE reference numbers 92, A1-A9, B1-B9, AA-AZ, BA-BW, M1-M9, MA-MZ, Z1-Z9, ZA-ZZ, 0A-0Z, 1A-1Z or 2A-2Z	. . .	1st June 2015

Employer (by PAYE scheme size or other description)	. . .	*Staging date*
Less than 30 with the last 2 characters in their PAYE reference numbers BX	. . .	1st July 2015
40–49	. . .	1st August 2015
Less than 30 with the last 2 characters in their PAYE reference numbers BY	. . .	1st September 2015
30–39	. . .	1st October 2015
Less than 30 with the last 2 characters in their PAYE reference numbers BZ	. . .	1st November 2015
Less than 30 with the last 2 characters in their PAYE reference numbers 02-04, C1-C9, D1-D9, CA-CZ, or DA-DZ	. . .	1st January 2016
Less than 30 with the last 2 characters in their PAYE reference numbers 00, 05-07, E1-E9 or EA-EZ	. . .	1st February 2016
Less than 30 with the last 2 characters in their PAYE reference numbers 01, 08-11, F1-F9, G1-G9, FA-FZ or GA-GZ	. . .	1st March 2016
Less than 30 with the last 2 characters in their PAYE reference numbers 12-16, 3A-3Z, H1-H9 or HA-HZ	. . .	1st April 2016
Less than 30 with the last 2 characters in their PAYE reference numbers I1-I9 or IA-IZ	. . .	1st May 2016
Less than 30 with the last 2 characters in their PAYE reference numbers 17-22, 4A-4Z, J1-J9 or JA-JZ	. . .	1st June 2016
Less than 30 with the last 2 characters in their PAYE reference numbers 23-29, 5A-5Z, K1-K9 or KA-KZ	. . .	1st July 2016
Less than 30 with the last 2 characters in their PAYE reference numbers 30-37, 6A-6Z, L1-L9 or LA-LZ	. . .	1st August 2016
Less than 30 with the last 2 characters in their PAYE reference numbers N1-N9 or NA-NZ	. . .	1st September 2016
Less than 30 with the last 2 characters in their PAYE reference numbers 38-46, 7A-7Z, O1-O9 or OA-OZ	. . .	1st October 2016
Less than 30 with the last 2 characters in their PAYE reference numbers 47-57, 8A-8Z, Q1-Q9, R1-R9, S1-S9, T1-T9, QA-QZ, RA-RZ, SA-SZ or TA-TZ	. . .	1st November 2016
Less than 30 with the last 2 characters in their PAYE reference numbers 58-69, 9A-9Z, U1-U9, V1-V9, W1-W9, UA-UZ, VA-VZ or WA-WZ	. . .	1st January 2017
Less than 30 with the last 2 characters in their PAYE reference numbers 70-83, X1-X9, Y1-Y9, XA-XZ, or YA-YZ	. . .	1st February 2017
Less than 30 with the last 2 characters in their PAYE reference numbers P1-P9 or PA-PZ	. . .	1st March 2017
Less than 30 with the last 2 characters in their PAYE reference numbers 84-91 or 93-99	. . .	1st April 2017
Less than 30 persons in the PAYE scheme not meeting any other description contained in the first column of this table	. . .	1st April 2017

Employer (by PAYE scheme size or other description)	. . .	*Staging date*
Employer who does not have a PAYE scheme	. . .	1st April 2017
New employer (PAYE income first payable between 1st April 2012 and 31st March 2013)	. . .	1st May 2017
New employer (PAYE income first payable between 1st April 2013 and 31st March 2014)	. . .	1st July 2017
New employer (PAYE income first payable between 1st April 2014 and 31st March 2015)	. . .	1st August 2017
New employer (PAYE income first payable between 1st April 2015 and 31st December 2015)	. . .	1st October 2017
New employer (PAYE income first payable between 1st January 2016 and 30th September 2016)	. . .	1st November 2017
New employer (PAYE income first payable between 1st October 2016 and 30th June 2017)	. . .	1st January 2018
New employer (PAYE income first payable between 1st July 2017 and 30th September 2017)	. . .	1st February 2018]

NOTES

Paras (2), (3) and column 2 of the table were revoked by the Occupational and Personal Pension Schemes (Automatic Enrolment) (Miscellaneous Amendments) Regulations 2016, SI 2016/311, reg 2(1), (3), as from 6 April 2016.

Entries in square brackets in the Table substituted by the Employers' Duties (Implementation) (Amendment) Regulations 2012, SI 2012/1813, reg 2(1), (5).

[2.1080]
[4A

(1) For the purposes of regulation 2(1)(b)(ii), the date in the final column of the table in regulation 4 is modified in accordance with paragraph (2).

(2) Where the staging date in the final column of the table in regulation 4 is in the period—

(a) beginning with 1st October 2012 and ending on 1st November 2012, the modified date is 1st August 2015;

(b) beginning with 1st January 2013 and ending on 1st February 2013, the modified date is 1st October 2015;

(c) beginning with 1st March 2013 and ending on 1st April 2013, the modified date is 1st January 2016;

(d) beginning with 1st May 2013 and ending on 1st June 2013, the modified date is 1st February 2016;

(e) beginning with 1st July 2013 and ending on 1st August 2013, the modified date is 1st March 2016;

(f) beginning with 1st September 2013 and ending on 1st October 2013, the modified date is 1st April 2016;

(g) beginning with 1st November 2013 and ending on 1st January 2014, the modified date is 1st May 2016;

(h) beginning with 1st February 2014 and ending on 1st April 2014, the modified date is 1st July 2016;

(i) beginning with 1st May 2014 and ending on 1st July 2014, the modified date is 1st September 2016;

(j) beginning with 1st August 2014 and ending on 1st October 2014, the modified date is 1st November 2016;

(k) beginning with 1st November 2014 and ending on 1st January 2015, the modified date is 1st February 2017; or

(l) beginning with 1st March 2015 and ending on 1st April 2015, the modified date is 1st April 2017.]

NOTES

Inserted by the Employers' Duties (Implementation) (Amendment) Regulations 2012, SI 2012/1813, reg 2(1), (6).

[2.1081]
[4B Deferral of automatic enrolment for post-staging employers

(1) Where—

(a) an employer ("E") gives to a worker, on the day on which the worker begins to be employed by E, notice that E intends to defer automatic enrolment for the worker until the deferral date; and

(b) the requirements in regulation 4C in relation to the notice are met,

the worker's automatic enrolment date is the deferral date if on that date section 3 of the Act (automatic enrolment) applies to the worker as a jobholder of E.

(2) Where—

(a) a worker employed by E becomes a jobholder to whom section 3 of the Act applies;

(b) E gives the worker notice that E intends to defer automatic enrolment until the deferral date; and

(c) the requirements in regulation 4C in relation to the notice are met,

the worker's automatic enrolment date is the deferral date if on that date section 3 of the Act applies to the worker as a jobholder of E.

(3) If section 3 of the Act does not apply to a worker falling within paragraph (1)(a) and (b) or (2)(a) to (c) on the deferral date, arrangements prescribed under section 3(2) of the Act do not apply in relation to any employment of the worker by E in the period beginning with the starting day and ending with the deferral date.

(4) A notice under paragraph (1) or (2) may be given on the starting day or within the period of six weeks beginning with the day after the starting day.

(5) The deferral date may be any date in the period of three months [after] the starting day.

(6) If E gives a worker a notice under paragraph (1), E may not give the worker a notice under paragraph (2) in relation to any occasion on or before the deferral date on which the worker becomes a jobholder to whom section 3 applies.

(7) In this regulation—

(a) references to "E" (or to an "employer") are to a person falling within the meaning of "employer" in section 88(7) of the Act—

[(i) who first pays PAYE income in respect of any worker on or after 1st October 2017; or]

(ii) who does not have a PAYE scheme, where E's first worker begins to be employed by E after 1st April 2017,

where the employers' duties did not apply before that date;

(b) "starting day" means—

(i) in the case of a notice under paragraph (1), the day on which the worker begins to be employed by E; or

(ii) in the case of a notice under paragraph (2), the day on which the worker becomes a jobholder to whom section 3 of the Act applies.]

NOTES

Commencement: 1 April 2017.

Inserted, together with reg 4C, by the Employers' Duties (Implementation) (Amendment) Regulations 2017, SI 2017/347, regs 2, 3(2)(a), as from 1 April 2017.

The word in square brackets in para (5), and all of sub-para (7)(a)(i), were substituted by the Employers' Duties (Miscellaneous Amendments) Regulations 2017, SI 2017/868, reg 2, as from 1 October 2017.

[2.1082]

[4C Deferral of automatic enrolment: notice requirements

(1) A notice (referred to in this regulation as "the notice") under regulation 4B(1) or (2) must be in writing.

(2) In the case of workers who are jobholders and who are not active members of a qualifying scheme, the notice must include the information described in paragraph (4) or (6) and the information described in paragraphs (7) to (9).

(3) In the case of workers who are not jobholders and who are not active members of a qualifying scheme, the notice must include the information described in paragraph (5) or (6) and the information described in paragraphs (7) to (9).

(4) A statement that the jobholder may, by giving written notice to the employer, require the employer to make arrangements for the jobholder to become an active member of an automatic enrolment scheme and that the jobholder is entitled to employer's contributions.

(5) A statement that the worker may, where he or she is working, or ordinarily works, in Great Britain and is aged at least 16 and under 75 and is not a member of a pension scheme that satisfies the requirements of section 9 of the Act, by giving written notice to the employer, require the employer to make arrangements for the worker to become an active member of such a pension scheme.

(6) A statement—

(a) that sets out the amount of the lower qualifying earnings limit ("the lower qualifying earnings limit") specified in section 13(1)(a) of the Act; and

(b) that by giving written notice to the employer, the worker who is aged at least 16 and under 75 and—

(i) who earns more than the lower qualifying earnings limit and is not an active member of a qualifying scheme, may require the employer to arrange for that worker to become an active member of an automatic enrolment scheme and is entitled to employer's contributions; or

(ii) who earns no more than the lower qualifying earnings limit and is not a member of a pension scheme that satisfies the requirements of section 9 of the Act, may require the employer to arrange for that worker to become an active member of such a pension scheme but is not entitled to employer's contributions.

(7) A statement that the employer has deferred automatic enrolment until the deferral date and which specifies that date.

(8) A statement—

(a) that sets out the amount of earnings ("the specified amount") that are payable as specified in section 3(1)(c) of the Act; and

(b) that the employer will automatically enrol the worker into an automatic enrolment scheme on the deferral date if, on that date—

(i) the worker is aged 22 or more but under state pension age;

(ii) the worker is working, or is ordinarily working, in Great Britain;

(iii) earnings of more than the specified amount are payable to the worker; and

(iv) the worker is not already an active member of a qualifying scheme.

(9) A statement that a written notice from the worker must be signed by the worker or, if it is given by means of an electronic communication, must include a statement that the worker personally submitted the notice.

(10) In this regulation, "employer" has the meaning given in regulation 4B(7).]

NOTES

Commencement: 1 April 2017.

Inserted as noted to reg 4B at **[2.1081]**.

[2.1083]

5 Transitional periods for money purchase and personal pension schemes

For the purposes of section 29 of the Act (transitional periods for money purchase and personal pension schemes)—

(a) the first transitional period . . . , beginning with the coming into force of section 20 (quality requirement: UK money purchase schemes)[, ends on, but includes, 5th April 2018]; and

(b) the second transitional period is one year, [beginning with 6th April 2018 and ending on, but including, 5th April 2019].

NOTES

Words omitted revoked, words in square brackets in para (a) inserted, and words in square brackets in para (b) substituted, by the Employers' Duties (Implementation) (Amendment) Regulations 2016, SI 2016/719, reg 2(1), (2), as from 1 October 2016.

[2.1084]

6 Transitional period for defined benefits and hybrid schemes

For the purposes of section 30 of the Act (transitional period for defined benefits and hybrid schemes), the transitional period for defined benefits and hybrid schemes . . . , beginning with the day on which section 3 (automatic enrolment) comes into force[, ends on, but includes, 30th September 2017].

NOTES

Words omitted revoked, and words in square brackets inserted, by the Employers' Duties (Implementation) (Amendment) Regulations 2016, SI 2016/719, reg 2(1), (3), as from 1 October 2016.

AGENCY WORKERS REGULATIONS 2010

(SI 2010/93)

NOTES

Made: 20 January 2010.

Authority: European Communities Act 1972, s 2(2); Health and Safety at Work etc Act 1974, ss 5(1), (2), (5), 82(3), Sch 3, paras 7, 8, 15(1).

Commencement: 1 October 2011.

Note: with regard to the authority for these Regulations, note that the European Communities Act 1972 is repealed by the European Union (Withdrawal) Act 2018, s 1, as from exit day (as defined in s 20 of that Act); but note also that provision is made for the continuation in force of any subordinate legislation made under the authority of s 2(2) of the 1972 Act by s 2 of the 2018 Act at **[1.2240]**, subject to the provisions of s 5 of, and Sch 1 to, the 2018 Act at **[1.2243]**, **[1.2253]**.

These Regulations are the domestic implementation of Council Directive 2008/104/EC on temporary agency work (at **[3.476]**).

Employment Appeal Tribunal: an appeal lies to the Employment Appeal Tribunal on any question of law arising from any decision of, or in any proceedings before, an employment tribunal under or by virtue of these Regulations; see the Employment Tribunals Act 1996, s 21(1)(y) at **[1.764]**.

Conciliation: employment tribunal proceedings under reg 18 are "relevant proceedings" for the purposes of the conciliation provisions contained in the Employment Tribunals Act 1996, ss 18–18C; see s 18(1)(z) of the 1996 Act at **[1.757]**.

See *Harvey* AI(4).

ARRANGEMENT OF REGULATIONS

PART 1
GENERAL AND INTERPRETATION

PART 1
GENERAL AND INTERPRETATION

[2.1085]
1 Citation, commencement and extent

(1) These Regulations may be cited as the Agency Workers Regulations 2010 and shall come into force on 1st October 2011.

(2) These Regulations extend to England and Wales and Scotland only, save as provided for in Schedule 1 (provisions extending to England and Wales, Scotland and Northern Ireland).

[2.1086]
2 Interpretation

In these Regulations—

"the 1996 Act" means the Employment Rights Act 1996;

"assignment" means a period of time during which an agency worker is supplied by one or more temporary work agencies to a hirer to work temporarily for and under the supervision and direction of the hirer;

"contract of employment" means a contract of service or of apprenticeship, whether express or implied, and (if it is express) whether oral or in writing;

"employee" means an individual who has entered into or works under or, where the employment has ceased, worked under a contract of employment;

"employer", in relation to an employee or worker, means the person by whom the employee or worker is (or where the employment has ceased, was) employed;

"employment"—

(a) in relation to an employee, means employment under a contract of employment, and
(b) in relation to a worker, means employment under that worker's contract,

and "employed" shall be construed accordingly;

"hirer" means a person engaged in economic activity, public or private, whether or not operating for profit, to whom individuals are supplied, to work temporarily for and under the supervision and direction of that person; and "worker" means an individual who is not an agency worker but who has entered into or works under (or where the employment has ceased, worked under)—

(a) a contract of employment, or

(b) any other contract, whether express or implied and (if it is express) whether oral or in writing, whereby the individual undertakes to do or perform personally any work or services for another party to the contract whose status is not by virtue of the contract that of a client or customer of any profession or business undertaking carried on by the individual,

and any reference to a worker's contract shall be construed accordingly.

[2.1087]

3 The meaning of agency worker

(1) In these Regulations "agency worker" means an individual who—

(a) is supplied by a temporary work agency to work temporarily for and under the supervision and direction of a hirer; and

(b) has a contract with the temporary work agency which is—

(i) a contract of employment with the agency, or

[(ii) any other contract with the agency to perform work or services personally].

(2) But an individual is not an agency worker if—

(a) the contract the individual has with the temporary work agency has the effect that the status of the agency is that of a client or customer of a profession or business undertaking carried on by the individual; or

(b) there is a contract, by virtue of which the individual is available to work for the hirer, having the effect that the status of the hirer is that of a client or customer of a profession or business undertaking carried on by the individual.

(3) For the purposes of paragraph (1)(a) an individual shall be treated as having been supplied by a temporary work agency to work temporarily for and under the supervision and direction of a hirer if—

(a) the temporary work agency initiates or is involved as an intermediary in the making of the arrangements that lead to the individual being supplied to work temporarily for and under the supervision and direction of the hirer, and

(b) the individual is supplied by an intermediary, or one of a number of intermediaries, to work temporarily for and under the supervision and direction of the hirer.

(4) An individual treated by virtue of paragraph (3) as having been supplied by a temporary work agency, shall be treated, for the purposes of paragraph (1)(b), as having a contract with the temporary work agency.

(5) An individual is not prevented from being an agency worker—

(a) because the temporary work agency supplies the individual through one or more intermediaries;

(b) because one or more intermediaries supply that individual;

(c) because the individual is supplied pursuant to any contract or other arrangement between the temporary work agency, one or more intermediaries and the hirer;

(d) because the temporary work agency pays for the services of the individual through one or more intermediaries; or

(e) because the individual is employed by or otherwise has a contract with one or more intermediaries.

(6) Paragraph (5) does not prejudice the generality of paragraphs (1) to (4).

NOTES

Para (1): sub-para (b)(ii) substituted by the Agency Workers (Amendment) Regulations 2011, SI 2011/1941, reg 2(1), (2).

[2.1088]

4 The meaning of temporary work agency

(1) In these Regulations "temporary work agency" means a person engaged in the economic activity, public or private, whether or not operating for profit, and whether or not carrying on such activity in conjunction with others, of—

(a) supplying individuals to work temporarily for and under the supervision and direction of hirers; or

(b) paying for, or receiving or forwarding payment for, the services of individuals who are supplied to work temporarily for and under the supervision and direction of hirers.

(2) Notwithstanding paragraph (1)(b) a person is not a temporary work agency if the person is engaged in the economic activity of paying for, or receiving or forwarding payments for, the services of individuals regardless of whether the individuals are supplied to work for hirers.

PART 2
RIGHTS

[2.1089]

5 Rights of agency workers in relation to the basic working and employment conditions

(1) Subject to regulation 7, an agency worker (A) shall be entitled to the same basic working and employment conditions as A would be entitled to for doing the same job had A been recruited by the hirer—

(a) other than by using the services of a temporary work agency; and

(b) at the time the qualifying period commenced.

(2) For the purposes of paragraph (1), the basic working and employment conditions are—

(a) where A would have been recruited as an employee, the relevant terms and conditions that are ordinarily included in the contracts of employees of the hirer;

(b) where A would have been recruited as a worker, the relevant terms and conditions that are ordinarily included in the contracts of workers of the hirer,

whether by collective agreement or otherwise, including any variations in those relevant terms and conditions made at any time after the qualifying period commenced.

(3) Paragraph (1) shall be deemed to have been complied with where—

(a) an agency worker is working under the same relevant terms and conditions as an employee who is a comparable employee, and

(b) the relevant terms and conditions of that comparable employee are terms and conditions ordinarily included in the contracts of employees, who are comparable employees of the hirer, whether by collective agreement or otherwise.

(4) For the purposes of paragraph (3) an employee is a comparable employee in relation to an agency worker if at the time when the breach of paragraph (1) is alleged to take place—

(a) both that employee and the agency worker are—

(i) working for and under the supervision and direction of the hirer, and

(ii) engaged in the same or broadly similar work having regard, where relevant, to whether they have a similar level of qualification and skills; and

(b) the employee works or is based at the same establishment as the agency worker or, where there is no comparable employee working or based at that establishment who satisfies the requirements of sub-paragraph (a), works or is based at a different establishment and satisfies those requirements.

(5) An employee is not a comparable employee if that employee's employment has ceased.

(6) This regulation is subject to regulation 10.

NOTES

Para (6): revoked by the Agency Workers (Amendment) Regulations 2019, SI 2019/724, reg 3(1), (2), as from 6 April 2020 and subject to regs 4–7 of the 2019 Regulations at **[2.2188]–[2.2191]**.

[2.1090]

6 Relevant terms and conditions

(1) In regulation 5(2) and (3) "relevant terms and conditions" means terms and conditions relating to—

(a) pay;

(b) the duration of working time;

(c) night work;

(d) rest periods;

(e) rest breaks; and

(f) annual leave.

(2) For the purposes of paragraph (1)(a), "pay" means any sums payable to a worker of the hirer in connection with the worker's employment, including any fee, bonus, commission, holiday pay or other emolument referable to the employment, whether payable under contract or otherwise, but excluding any payments or rewards within paragraph (3).

(3) Those payments or rewards are—

(a) any payment by way of occupational sick pay;

(b) any payment by way of a pension, allowance or gratuity in connection with the worker's retirement or as compensation for loss of office;

(c) any payment in respect of maternity, paternity or adoption leave;

(d) any payment referable to the worker's redundancy;

(e) any payment or reward made pursuant to a financial participation scheme;

(f) any bonus, incentive payment or reward which is not directly attributable to the amount or quality of the work done by a worker, and which is given to a worker for a reason other than the amount or quality of work done such as to encourage the worker's loyalty or to reward the worker's long-term service;

(g) any payment for time off under Part 6 of the 1996 Act or section 169 of the Trade Union and Labour Relations (Consolidation) Act 1992 (payment for time off for carrying out trade union duties etc);

(h) a guarantee payment under section 28 of the 1996 Act;

(i) any payment by way of an advance under an agreement for a loan or by way of an advance of pay (but without prejudice to the application of section 13 of the 1996 Act to any deduction made from the worker's wages in respect of any such advance);

(j) any payment in respect of expenses incurred by the worker in carrying out the employment; and

(k) any payment to the worker otherwise than in that person's capacity as a worker.

(4) For the purposes of paragraphs (2) and (3) any monetary value attaching to any payment or benefit in kind furnished to a worker by the hirer shall not be treated as pay of the worker except any voucher or stamp which is—

(a) of fixed value expressed in monetary terms, and

(b) capable of being exchanged (whether on its own or together with other vouchers, stamps or documents, and whether immediately or only after a time) for money, goods or services (or for any combination of two or more of those things).

(5) In this regulation—

"financial participation scheme" means any scheme that offers workers of the hirer—

(a) a distribution of shares or options, or

(b) a share of profits in cash or in shares;

"night time", in relation to an individual, means—

(a) a period—

(i) the duration of which is not less than seven hours, and

(ii) which includes the period between midnight and 5 am,

which is determined for the purposes of these Regulations by a working time agreement, or

(b) in default of such a determination, the period between 11 pm and 6 am;

"night work" means work during night time;

"relevant training" means work experience provided pursuant to a training course or programme, training for employment, or both, other than work experience or training—

(a) the immediate provider of which is an educational institution or a person whose main business is the provision of training, and

(b) which is provided on a course run by that institution or person;

"rest period", in relation to an individual, means a period which is not working time, other than a rest break or leave to which that individual is entitled either under the Working Time Regulations 1998 or under the contract between that individual and the employer of that individual;

"working time", in relation to an individual means—

(a) any period during which that individual is working, at the disposal of the employer of that individual and carrying out the activity or duties of that individual,

(b) any period during which that individual is receiving relevant training, and

(c) any additional period which is to be treated as working time for the purposes of the Working Time Regulations 1998 under a working time agreement; and

"working time agreement", in relation to an individual, means a workforce agreement within the meaning of regulation 2(1) of the Working Time Regulations 1998, which applies to the individual any provision of—

(a) a collective agreement which forms part of a contract between that individual and the employer of that individual, or

(b) any other agreement in writing which is legally enforceable as between the individual and the employer of that individual.

[2.1091]

7 Qualifying period

(1) Regulation 5 does not apply unless an agency worker has completed the qualifying period.

(2) To complete the qualifying period the agency worker must work in the same role with the same hirer for 12 continuous calendar weeks, during one or more assignments.

(3) For the purposes of this regulation and regulations 8 and 9, the agency worker works in "the same role" unless—

(a) the agency worker has started a new role with the same hirer, whether supplied by the same or by a different temporary work agency;

(b) the work or duties that make up the whole or the main part of that new role are substantively different from the work or duties that made up the whole or the main part of the previous role; and

(c) the temporary work agency has informed the agency worker in writing of the type of work the agency worker will be required to do in the new role.

(4) For the purposes of this regulation *and regulation 10*, any week during the whole or part of which an agency worker works during an assignment is counted as a calendar week.

(5) For the purposes of this regulation and regulations 8 and 9, when calculating whether any weeks completed with a particular hirer are continuous, where—

(a) the agency worker has started working during an assignment, and there is a break, either between assignments or during an assignment, when the agency worker is not working,

(b) paragraph (8) applies to that break, and

(c) the agency worker returns to work in the same role with the same hirer,

any continuous weeks during which the agency worker worked for that hirer before the break shall be carried forward and treated as continuous with any weeks during which the agency worker works for that hirer after the break.

(6) For the purposes of this regulation and regulation 8, when calculating the number of weeks during which the agency worker has worked, where the agency worker has—

(a) started working in a role during an assignment, and

(b) is unable to continue working for a reason described in paragraph (8)(c) or (8)(d)(i), (ii) or (iii),

for the period that is covered by one or more such reasons, that agency worker shall be deemed to be working in that role with the hirer, for the original intended duration, or likely duration of the assignment, whichever is the longer.

(7) Where—

(a) an assignment ends on grounds which are maternity grounds within the meaning of section 68A of the 1996 Act, and

(b) the agency worker is deemed to be working in that role in accordance with paragraph (6), the fact that an agency worker is actually working in another role, whether for the same or a different hirer during the period mentioned in paragraph (6) or any part of that period, does not affect the operation of that paragraph.

(8) This paragraph applies where there is a break between assignments, or during an assignment, when the agency worker is not working, and the break is—

- (a) for any reason and the break is not more than six calendar weeks;
- (b) wholly due to the fact that the agency worker is incapable of working in consequence of sickness or injury, and the requirements of paragraph (9) are satisfied;
- (c) related to pregnancy, childbirth or maternity and is at a time in a protected period;
- (d) wholly for the purpose of taking time off or leave, whether statutory or contractual, to which the agency worker is otherwise entitled which is—
  - (i) ordinary, compulsory or additional maternity leave;
  - (ii) ordinary or additional adoption leave;
  - (iii) paternity leave;
  - (iv) time off or other leave not listed in sub-paragraph (d)(i), (ii) or (iii); or
  - (v) for more than one of the reasons listed in sub-paragraph (d)(i) to (iv);
- (e) wholly due to the fact that the agency worker is required to attend at any place in pursuance of being summoned for service as a juror under the Juries Act 1974, the Coroners Act 1988, the Court of Session Act 1988 or the Criminal Procedure (Scotland) Act 1995, and the break is 28 calendar weeks or less;
- (f) wholly due to a temporary cessation in the hirer's requirement for any worker to be present at the establishment and work in a particular role, for a pre-determined period of time according to the established custom and practices of the hirer; or
- (g) wholly due to a strike, lock-out or other industrial action at the hirer's establishment; or
- (h) wholly due to more than one of the reasons listed in sub-paragraphs (b), (c), (d), (e), (f) or (g).

(9) Paragraph (8)(b) only applies where—

- (a) the break is 28 calendar weeks or less;
- (b) paragraph (8)(c) does not apply; and
- (c) if required to do so by the temporary work agency, the agency worker has provided such written medical evidence as may reasonably be required.

(10) For the purposes of paragraph (8)(c), a protected period begins at the start of the pregnancy, and the protected period associated with any particular pregnancy ends at the end of the 26 weeks beginning with childbirth or, if earlier, when the agency worker returns to work.

(11) For the purposes of paragraph (10) "childbirth" means the birth of a living child or the birth of a child whether living or dead after 24 weeks of pregnancy.

(12) Time spent by an agency worker working during an assignment before 1st October 2011 does not count for the purposes of this regulation.

NOTES

Para (4): words in italics revoked by the Agency Workers (Amendment) Regulations 2019, SI 2019/724, reg 3(1), (3), as from 6 April 2020 and subject to regs 4–7 of the 2019 Regulations at **[2.2188]–[2.2191]**.

[2.1092]

8 Completion of the qualifying period and continuation of the regulation 5 rights

Where an agency worker has completed the qualifying period with a particular hirer, the rights conferred by regulation 5 shall apply and shall continue to apply to that agency worker in relation to that particular hirer unless—

- (a) that agency worker is no longer working in the same role, within the meaning of regulation 7(3), with that hirer; or
- (b) there is a break between assignments, or during an assignment, when the agency worker is not working, to which regulation 7(8) does not apply.

[2.1093]

9 Structure of assignments

(1) Notwithstanding paragraphs (1) and (2) of regulation 7, and regulation 8, if paragraphs (3) and (4) apply an agency worker shall be treated as having completed the qualifying period from the time at which the agency worker would have completed the qualifying period but for the structure of the assignment or assignments mentioned in paragraph (3).

(2) Notwithstanding paragraphs (1) and (2) of regulation 7, and regulation 8, if paragraphs (3) and (4) apply an agency worker who has completed the qualifying period and—

- (a) is no longer entitled to the rights conferred by regulation 5, but
- (b) would be so entitled but for the structure of the assignment or assignments mentioned in paragraph (3),

shall be treated as continuing to be entitled to those rights from the time at which the agency worker completed that period.

(3) This paragraph applies when an agency worker has—

- (a) completed two or more assignments with a hirer (H),
- (b) completed at least one assignment with H and one or more earlier assignments with hirers connected to H, or

(c) worked in more than two roles during an assignment with H, and on at least two occasions has worked in a role that was not the "same role" as the previous role within the meaning of regulation 7(3).

(4) This paragraph applies where—

(a) the most likely explanation for the structure of the assignment, or assignments, mentioned in paragraph (3) is that H, or the temporary work agency supplying the agency worker to H, or, where applicable, H and one or more hirers connected to H, intended to prevent the agency worker from being entitled to, or from continuing to be entitled to, the rights conferred by regulation 5; and

(b) the agency worker would be entitled to, or would continue to be entitled to, the rights conferred by regulation 5 in relation to H, but for that structure.

(5) The following matters in particular shall be taken into account in determining whether the structure of the assignment or assignments mentioned in paragraph (3) shows that the most likely explanation for it is that mentioned in paragraph (4)(a)—

(a) the length of the assignments;

(b) the number of assignments with H and, where applicable, hirers connected to H;

(c) the number of times the agency worker has worked in a new role with H and, where applicable, hirers connected to H, and that new role is not the "same role" within the meaning of regulation 7(3);

(d) the number of times the agency worker has returned to work in the same role within the meaning of regulation 7(3) with H and, where applicable, hirers connected to H;

(e) the period of any break between assignments with H and, where applicable, hirers connected to H.

(6) For the purposes of this regulation hirers are connected to a hirer if one hirer (directly or indirectly) has control of the other hirer or a third person (directly or indirectly) has control of both hirers.

[2.1094]

10 Permanent contracts providing for pay between assignments

(1) To the extent to which it relates to pay, regulation 5 does not have effect in relation to an agency worker who has a permanent contract of employment with a temporary work agency if—

(a) the contract of employment was entered into before the beginning of the first assignment under that contract and includes terms and conditions in writing relating to—

(i) the minimum scale or rate of remuneration or the method of calculating remuneration,

(ii) the location or locations where the agency worker may be expected to work,

(iii) the expected hours of work during any assignment,

(iv) the maximum number of hours of work that the agency worker may be required to work each week during any assignment,

(v) the minimum hours of work per week that may be offered to the agency worker during any assignment provided that it is a minimum of at least one hour, and

(vi) the nature of the work that the agency worker may expect to be offered including any relevant requirements relating to qualifications or experience;

(b) the contract of employment contains a statement that the effect of entering into it is that the employee does not, during the currency of the contract, have any entitlement to the rights conferred by regulation 5 insofar as they relate to pay;

(c) during any period under the contract [after the end of the first assignment under that contract] in which the agency worker is not working temporarily for and under the supervision and direction of a hirer but is available to do so—

(i) the temporary work agency takes reasonable steps to seek suitable work for the agency worker,

(ii) if suitable work is available, the temporary work agency offers the agency worker to be proposed to a hirer who is offering such work, and

(iii) the temporary work agency pays the agency worker a minimum amount of remuneration in respect of that period ("the minimum amount"); and

(d) the temporary work agency does not terminate the contract of employment until it has complied with its obligations in sub-paragraph (c) for an aggregate of not less than four calendar weeks during the contract.

(2) For work to be suitable for the purposes of paragraph (1)(c) the nature of the work, and the terms and conditions applicable to the agency worker whilst performing the work, must not differ from the nature of the work and the terms and conditions included in the contract of employment under paragraph (1)(a).

NOTES

Revoked by the Agency Workers (Amendment) Regulations 2019, SI 2019/724, reg 3(1), (4), as from 6 April 2020 and subject to regs 4–7 of the 2019 Regulations at **[2.2188]–[2.2191]**.

Para (1): words in square brackets in sub-para (c) inserted by the Agency Workers (Amendment) Regulations 2011, SI 2011/1941, reg 2(1), (3).

[2.1095]

11 Calculating the minimum amount of pay

(1) Subject to paragraph (3), the minimum amount to be paid to the agency worker during a pay reference period falling within a period to which regulation 10(1)(c) applies shall not be less than 50% of the pay paid to the agency worker in the relevant pay reference period.

(2) For the purposes of paragraph (1), the relevant pay reference period shall be the pay reference period in which the agency worker received the highest level of pay which fell—

(a) within the 12 weeks immediately preceding the end of the previous assignment, where the assignment lasted for longer than 12 weeks, or

(b) during the assignment, where the assignment lasted for 12 or fewer weeks.

[(3) The minimum amount shall be not less than the amount that the agency worker would have been entitled to for the hours worked in the relevant pay reference period if the provisions of the National Minimum Wage Regulations 1999 . . . applied.]

(4) For the purposes of calculating the minimum amount as set out in paragraph (1), only payments in respect of basic pay whether by way of annual salary, payments for actual time worked or by reference to output or otherwise shall be taken into account.

(5) For the purposes of this regulation, "pay reference period" is a month or, in the case of a worker who is paid wages by reference to a period shorter than a month, that period.

NOTES

Revoked by the Agency Workers (Amendment) Regulations 2019, SI 2019/724, reg 3(1), (4), as from 6 April 2020 and subject to regs 4–7 of the 2019 Regulations at **[2.2188]–[2.2191]**.

Para (3): substituted by the National Minimum Wage Regulations 1999 (Amendment) Regulations 2010, SI 2010/1901, reg 8; words omitted revoked by the National Minimum Wage (Amendment) Regulations 2012, SI 2012/2397, reg 3.

Note that the National Minimum Wage Regulations 1999, SI 1999/584 were revoked and replaced by the National Minimum Wage Regulations 2015, SI 2015/621 but that this regulation has not been amended accordingly.

[2.1096]

12 Rights of agency workers in relation to access to collective facilities and amenities

(1) An agency worker has during an assignment the right to be treated no less favourably than a comparable worker in relation to the collective facilities and amenities provided by the hirer.

(2) The rights conferred by paragraph (1) apply only if the less favourable treatment is not justified on objective grounds.

(3) "Collective facilities and amenities" includes, in particular—

(a) canteen or other similar facilities;

(b) child care facilities; and

(c) transport services.

(4) For the purposes of paragraph (1) an individual is a comparable worker in relation to an agency worker if at the time when the breach of paragraph (1) is alleged to take place—

(a) both that individual and the agency worker are—

(i) working for and under the supervision and direction of the hirer, and

(ii) engaged in the same or broadly similar work having regard, where relevant, to whether they have a similar level of qualification and skills;

(b) that individual works or is based at the same establishment as the agency worker or, where there is no comparable worker working or based at that establishment who satisfies the requirements of sub-paragraph (a), works or is based at a different establishment and satisfies those requirements; and

(c) that individual is an employee of the hirer or, where there is no employee satisfying the requirements of sub-paragraphs (a) and (b), is a worker of the hirer and satisfies those requirements.

[2.1097]

13 Rights of agency workers in relation to access to employment

(1) An agency worker has during an assignment the right to be informed by the hirer of any relevant vacant posts with the hirer, to give that agency worker the same opportunity as a comparable worker to find permanent employment with the hirer.

(2) For the purposes of paragraph (1) an individual is a comparable worker in relation to an agency worker if at the time when the breach of paragraph (1) is alleged to take place—

(a) both that individual and the agency worker are—

(i) working for and under the supervision and direction of the hirer, and

(ii) engaged in the same or broadly similar work having regard, where relevant, to whether they have a similar level of qualification and skills;

(b) that individual works or is based at the same establishment as the agency worker; and

(c) that individual is an employee of the hirer or, where there is no employee satisfying the requirements of sub-paragraphs (a) and (b), is a worker of the hirer and satisfies those requirements.

(3) For the purposes of paragraph (1), an individual is not a comparable worker if that individual's employment with the hirer has ceased.

(4) For the purposes of paragraph (1) the hirer may inform the agency worker by a general announcement in a suitable place in the hirer's establishment.

PART 3
LIABILITY, PROTECTIONS AND REMEDIES

[2.1098]

14 Liability of temporary work agency and hirer

(1) [Subject to paragraph (3),] a temporary work agency shall be liable for any breach of regulation 5, to the extent that it is responsible for that breach.

(2) . . . The hirer shall be liable for any breach of regulation 5, to the extent that it is responsible for that breach.

(3) A temporary work agency shall not be liable for a breach of regulation 5 where it is established that the temporary work agency—

[(a) obtained, or has taken reasonable steps to obtain, relevant information from the hirer—

(i) about the basic working and employment conditions in force in the hirer;

(ii) if needed to assess compliance with regulation 5, about the relevant terms and conditions under which an employee of the hirer is working where—

(aa) that employee is considered to be a comparable employee in relation to that agency worker for the purposes of regulation 5(4), and

(bb) those terms and conditions are ordinarily included in the contract of such a comparable employee;

and

(iii) which explains the basis on which it is considered that the employee referred to in sub-paragraph (ii)(aa) is a comparable employee;]

(b) where it has received such information, has acted reasonably in determining what the agency worker's basic working and employment conditions should be at the end of the qualifying period and during the period after that until, in accordance with regulation 8, the agency worker ceases to be entitled to the rights conferred by regulation 5; and

(c) ensured that where it has responsibility for applying those basic working and employment conditions to the agency worker, that agency worker has been treated in accordance with the determination described in sub-paragraph (b),

and to the extent that the temporary work agency is not liable under this provision, the hirer shall be liable.

(4) . . .

(5) Where more than one temporary work agency is a party to the proceedings, when deciding whether or not each temporary work agency is responsible in full or in part, the employment tribunal shall have regard to the extent to which each agency was responsible for the determination, or application, of any of the agency worker's basic working and employment conditions.

(6) The hirer shall be liable for any breach of regulation 12 or 13.

(7) In relation to the rights conferred by regulation 17—

(a) a temporary work agency shall be liable for any act, or any deliberate failure to act, of that temporary work agency; and

(b) the hirer shall be liable for any act, or any deliberate failure to act, of the hirer.

NOTES

The words in square brackets in para (1) were inserted, the words omitted from para (2) were revoked, sub-para (3)(a) was substituted, and para (4) was revoked, by the Agency Workers (Amendment) Regulations 2011, SI 2011/1941, reg 2(1), (4).

[2.1099]

15 Restrictions on contracting out

Section 203 of the 1996 Act (restrictions on contracting out) shall apply in relation to these Regulations as if they were contained in that Act.

[2.1100]

16 Right to receive information

(1) An agency worker who considers that the hirer or a temporary work agency may have treated that agency worker in a manner which infringes a right conferred by regulation 5, may make a written request to the temporary work agency for a written statement containing information relating to the treatment in question.

(2) A temporary work agency that receives such a request from an agency worker shall, within 28 days of receiving it, provide the agency worker with a written statement setting out—

(a) relevant information relating to the basic working and employment conditions of the workers of the hirer,

(b) the factors the temporary work agency considered when determining the basic working and employment conditions which applied to the agency worker at the time when the breach of regulation 5 is alleged to have taken place, and

(c) where the temporary work agency seeks to rely on regulation 5(3), relevant information which—

(i) explains the basis on which it is considered that an individual is a comparable employee, and

(ii) describes the relevant terms and conditions, which apply to that employee.

(3) If an agency worker has made a request under paragraph (1) and has not been provided with such a statement within 30 days of making that request, the agency worker may make a written request to the hirer for a written statement containing information relating to the relevant basic working and employment conditions of the workers of the hirer.

(4) A hirer that receives a request made in accordance with paragraph (3) shall, within 28 days of receiving it, provide the agency worker with such a statement.

(5) An agency worker who considers that the hirer may have treated that agency worker in a manner which infringes a right conferred by regulation 12 or 13, may make a written request to the hirer for a written statement containing information relating to the treatment in question.

(6) A hirer that receives such a request from an agency worker shall, within 28 days of receiving it, provide the agency worker with a written statement setting out—

(a) all relevant information relating to the rights of a comparable worker in relation to the rights mentioned in regulation 12 or, as the case may be, regulation 13, and

(b) the particulars of the reasons for the treatment of the agency worker in respect of the right conferred by regulation 12 or, as the case may be, regulation 13.

(7) Paragraphs (1) and (3) apply only to an agency worker who at the time that worker makes such a request is entitled to the right conferred by regulation 5.

(8) Information provided under this regulation, whether in the form of a written statement or otherwise, is admissible as evidence in any proceedings under these Regulations.

(9) If it appears to the tribunal in any proceedings under these Regulations—

(a) that a temporary work agency or the hirer (as the case may be) deliberately, and without reasonable excuse, failed to provide information, whether in the form of a written statement or otherwise, or

(b) that any written statement supplied is evasive or equivocal,

it may draw any inference which it considers it just and equitable to draw, including an inference that that temporary work agency or hirer (as the case may be) has infringed the right in question.

[2.1101]

17 Unfair dismissal and the right not to be subjected to detriment

(1) An agency worker who is an employee and is dismissed shall be regarded as unfairly dismissed for the purposes of Part 10 of the 1996 Act if the reason (or, if more than one, the principal reason) for the dismissal is a reason specified in paragraph (3).

(2) An agency worker has the right not to be subjected to any detriment by, or as a result of, any act, or any deliberate failure to act, of a temporary work agency or the hirer, done on a ground specified in paragraph (3).

(3) The reasons or, as the case may be, grounds are—

(a) that the agency worker—

(i) brought proceedings under these Regulations;

(ii) gave evidence or information in connection with such proceedings brought by any agency worker;

(iii) made a request under regulation 16 for a written statement;

(iv) otherwise did anything under these Regulations in relation to a temporary work agency, hirer, or any other person;

(v) alleged that a temporary work agency or hirer has breached these Regulations;

(vi) refused (or proposed to refuse) to forgo a right conferred by these Regulations; or

(b) that the hirer or a temporary work agency believes or suspects that the agency worker has done or intends to do any of the things mentioned in sub-paragraph (a).

(4) Where the reason or principal reason for subjection to any act or deliberate failure to act is that mentioned in paragraph (3)(a)(v), or paragraph 3(b) so far as it relates to paragraph (3)(a)(v), neither paragraph (1) nor paragraph (2) applies if the allegation made by the agency worker is false and not made in good faith.

(5) Paragraph (2) does not apply where the detriment in question amounts to a dismissal of an employee within the meaning of Part 10 of the 1996 Act.

[2.1102]

18 Complaints to employment tribunals etc

(1) In this regulation "respondent" includes the hirer and any temporary work agency.

(2) Subject to regulation 17(5), an agency worker may present a complaint to an employment tribunal that a temporary work agency or the hirer has infringed a right conferred on the agency worker by regulation 5, 12, 13 or 17 (2).

(3) An agency worker may present a complaint to an employment tribunal that a temporary work agency has—

(a) breached a term of the contract of employment described in regulation 10(1)(a); or

(b) breached a duty under regulation 10(1)(b), (c) or (d).

(4) Subject to paragraph (5), an employment tribunal shall not consider a complaint under this regulation unless it is presented before the end of the period of three months beginning—

(a) in the case of an alleged infringement of a right conferred by regulation 5, 12 or 17(2) *or a breach of a term of the contract described in regulation 10(1)(a) or of a duty under regulation 10(1)(b), (c) or (d)*, with the date of the infringement, detriment or breach to which the complaint relates or, where an act or failure to act is part of a series of similar acts or failures comprising the infringement, detriment or breach, the last of them;

(b) in the case of an alleged infringement of the right conferred by regulation 13, with the date, or if more than one the last date, on which other individuals, whether or not employed by the hirer, were informed of the vacancy.

[(4A) Regulation 18A (extension of time limits to facilitate conciliation before institution of proceedings) applies for the purposes of paragraph (4).]

(5) A tribunal may consider any such complaint which is out of time if, in all the circumstances of the case, it considers that it is just and equitable to do so.

(6) For the purposes of calculating the date of the infringement, detriment or breach, under paragraph (4)(a)—

(a) where a term in a contract infringes a right conferred by regulation 5, 12 or 17(2), *or breaches regulation 10(1)*, that infringement or breach shall be treated, subject to sub-paragraph (b), as taking place on each day of the period during which the term infringes that right or breaches that duty;

(b) a deliberate failure to act that is contrary to regulation 5, 12 or 17(2) *or 10(1)* shall be treated as done when it was decided on.

(7) In the absence of evidence establishing the contrary, a person (P) shall be taken for the purposes of paragraph (6)(b) to decide not to act—

(a) when P does an act inconsistent with doing the failed act; or

(b) if P has done no such inconsistent act, when the period expires within which P might reasonably have been expected to have done the failed act if it was to be done.

(8) Where an employment tribunal finds that a complaint presented to it under this regulation is well founded, it shall take such of the following steps as it considers just and equitable—

(a) making a declaration as to the rights of the complainant in relation to the matters to which the complaint relates;

(b) ordering the respondent to pay compensation to the complainant;

(c) recommending that the respondent take, within a specified period, action appearing to the tribunal to be reasonable, in all the circumstances of the case, for the purpose of obviating or reducing the adverse effect on the complainant of any matter to which the complaint relates.

(9) Where a tribunal orders compensation under paragraph (8)(b), and there is more than one respondent, the amount of compensation payable by each or any respondent shall be such as may be found by the tribunal to be just and equitable having regard to the extent of each respondent's responsibility for the infringement to which the complaint relates.

(10) Subject to paragraphs (12) and (13), where a tribunal orders compensation under paragraph (8)(b), the amount of the compensation awarded shall be such as the tribunal considers just and equitable in all the circumstances having regard to—

(a) the infringement or breach to which the complaint relates; and

(b) any loss which is attributable to the infringement.

(11) The loss shall be taken to include—

(a) any expenses reasonably incurred by the complainant in consequence of the infringement or breach; and

(b) loss of any benefit which the complainant might reasonably be expected to have had but for the infringement or breach.

(12) Subject to paragraph (13), where a tribunal orders compensation under paragraph (8)(b), any compensation which relates to an infringement or breach of the rights—

(a) conferred by regulation 5 *or 10*; or

(b) conferred by regulation 17(2) to the extent that the infringement or breach relates to regulation 5 *or 10*,

shall not be less than two weeks' pay, calculated in accordance with regulation 19.

(13) Paragraph (12) does not apply where the tribunal considers that in all the circumstances of the case, taking into account the conduct of the claimant and respondent, two weeks' pay is not a just and equitable amount of compensation, and the amount shall be reduced as the tribunal consider appropriate.

(14) Where a tribunal finds that regulation 9(4) applies and orders compensation under paragraph (8)(b), the tribunal may make an additional award of compensation under paragraph 8(b), which shall not be more than £5,000, and where there is more than one respondent the proportion of any additional compensation awarded that is payable by each of them shall be such as the tribunal considers just and equitable having regard to the extent to which it considers each to have been responsible for the fact that regulation 9(4)(a) applies.

[(14A) In relation to an infringement or breach for which a tribunal orders a respondent to pay compensation under paragraph (8)(b), the tribunal may order the respondent also to pay a penalty under section 12A of the Employment Tribunals Act 1996 only if the tribunal decides not to exercise the power under paragraph (14) to make an additional award of compensation against the respondent.]

(15) Compensation in respect of treating an agency worker in a manner which infringes the right conferred by regulation 5, 12 or 13 *or breaches regulation 10(1)(b), (c) or (d), or breaches a term of the contract described in regulation 10(1)(a)*, shall not include compensation for injury to feelings.

(16) In ascertaining the loss the tribunal shall apply the same rule concerning the duty of a person to mitigate loss as applies to damages recoverable under the common law of England and Wales or (as the case may be) the law of Scotland.

(17) Where the tribunal finds that the act, or failure to act, to which the complaint relates was to any extent caused or contributed to by action of the complainant, it shall reduce the amount of the compensation by such proportion as it considers just and equitable having regard to that finding.

(18) If a temporary work agency or the hirer fails, without reasonable justification, to comply with a recommendation made by an employment tribunal under paragraph (8)(c) the tribunal may, if it thinks it just and equitable to do so—

(a) increase the amount of compensation required to be paid to the complainant in respect of the complaint, where an order was made under paragraph (8)(b); or

(b) make an order under paragraph (8)(b).

NOTES

Para (3) and the words in italics in paras (4), (6), (12), (15) are revoked by the Agency Workers (Amendment) Regulations 2019, SI 2019/724, reg 3(1), (5), as from 6 April 2020 and subject to regs 4–7 of the 2019 Regulations at **[2.2188]–[2.2191]**.

Para (4A): inserted by the Enterprise and Regulatory Reform Act 2013 (Consequential Amendments) (Employment) Order 2014, SI 2014/386, art 2, Schedule, paras 61, 62.

Para (14A): inserted by the Enterprise and Regulatory Reform Act 2013, s 16(2), Sch 3, para 6.

Conciliation: employment tribunal proceedings under this regulation are "relevant proceedings" for the purposes of the conciliation provisions contained in the Employment Tribunals Act 1996, ss 18–18C; see s 18(1)(z) of the 1996 Act at **[1.757]**.

[2.1103]

[18A Extension of time limit to facilitate conciliation before institution of proceedings

(1) In this regulation—

(a) Day A is the day on which the worker concerned complies with the requirement in subsection (1) of section 18A of the Employment Tribunals Act 1996 (requirement to contact ACAS before instituting proceedings) in relation to the matter in respect of which the proceedings are brought, and

(b) Day B is the day on which the worker concerned receives or, if earlier, is treated as receiving (by virtue of regulations made under subsection (11) of that section) the certificate issued under subsection (4) of that section.

(2) In working out when the time limit set by regulation 18(4) expires the period beginning with the day after Day A and ending with Day B is not to be counted.

(3) If the time limit set by regulation 18(4) would (if not extended by this paragraph) expire during the period beginning with Day A and ending one month after Day B, the time limit expires instead at the end of that period.

(4) The power conferred on the employment tribunal by regulation 18(5) to extend the time limit set by paragraph (4) of that regulation is exercisable in relation to that time limit as extended by this regulation.]

NOTES

Inserted by the Enterprise and Regulatory Reform Act 2013 (Consequential Amendments) (Employment) Order 2014, SI 2014/386, art 2, Schedule, paras 61, 63.

[2.1104]

19 Calculating a week's pay

(1) For the purposes of regulation 18(12)—

(a) a week's pay shall be the higher of—

(i) the average weekly pay received by the agency worker, in relation to the assignment to which the claim relates, in the relevant period; and

(ii) the average weekly pay the agency worker should have been receiving by virtue of regulation 5, in relation to the assignment to which the claim relates, in the relevant period; and

(b) for the purposes of this paragraph, only payments in respect of basic pay whether by way of annual salary, payments for actual time worked or by reference to output or otherwise shall be taken into account.

(2) The relevant period is—

(a) where the assignment has ended on or before the date the complaint was presented to the tribunal under regulation 18(2), the four week period (or in a case where the assignment was shorter than four weeks, that period) ending with the last day of the assignment to which the claim relates; or

(b) where the assignment has not so ended the four week period (or in the case where that assignment was shorter than four weeks, that period) ending with the date of the complaint.

[2.1105]

20 Liability of employers and principals

(1) Anything done by a person in the course of employment shall be treated for the purposes of these Regulations as also done by their employer, whether or not it was done with that employer's knowledge or approval.

(2) Anything done by a person as agent for the employer with the authority of the employer shall be treated for the purposes of these Regulations as also done by the employer.

(3) In proceedings under these Regulations against any person in respect of an act alleged to have been done by an employee of that person, it shall be a defence for that person to prove that he or she took such steps as were reasonably practicable to prevent the employee from—

(a) doing that act; or

(b) doing, in the course of his or her employment, acts of that description.

PART 4
SPECIAL CLASSES OF PERSON

[2.1106]

21 Crown employment and service as a member of the armed forces

(1) These Regulations have effect in relation to—

(a) Crown employment,

(b) service as a member of the armed forces of the Crown,

(c) persons in Crown employment, and

(d) persons in service as a member of the armed forces of the Crown,

as they have effect in relation to other employment and other employees.

(2) In paragraph (1) "Crown employment" means employment under or for the purposes of a government department or any officer or body exercising on behalf of the Crown functions conferred by a statutory provision but subject to paragraph (4).

(3) For the purposes of the application of the provisions of these Regulations in relation to Crown employment and service as a member of the armed forces of the Crown in accordance with paragraph (1)—

(a) references to an employee shall be construed as references to a person in Crown employment or in service as a member of the armed forces of the Crown to whom the definition of employee is appropriate; and

(b) references to a contract in relation to an employee shall be construed as references to the terms of employment of a person in Crown employment or in service as a member of the armed forces of the Crown to whom the definition of employee is appropriate.

(4) Crown employment—

(a) does not include service as a member of the armed forces of the Crown, but

(b) does include employment by an association established for the purposes of Part 11 of the Reserve Forces Act 1996.

[2.1107]

22 House of Lords staff

(1) These Regulations have effect in relation to employment as a relevant member of the House of Lords staff as they have effect in relation to other employment.

(2) In this regulation "relevant member of the House of Lords staff" means any person who is employed under a contract with the Corporate Officer of the House of Lords by virtue of which he is a worker.

[2.1108]

23 House of Commons staff

(1) These Regulations have effect in relation to employment as a relevant member of the House of Commons staff as they have effect in relation to other employment.

(2) In this regulation "relevant member of the House of Commons staff" means any person—

(a) who was appointed by the House of Commons Commission; or

(b) who is a member of the Speaker's personal staff.

[2.1109]

24 Police service

(1) For the purposes of these Regulations, the holding, otherwise than under a contract of employment, of the office of constable or an appointment as a police cadet shall be treated as employment, under a contract of employment, by the relevant officer.

(2) For the purposes of these Regulations, any constable or other person who has been seconded to [NCA] to serve as a member of its staff shall be treated as employed by [NCA], in respect of actions taken by, or on behalf of, [NCA].

(3) For the purposes of regulation 20—

(a) the secondment of any constable or other person to [NCA] to serve as a member of its staff shall be treated as employment by [NCA] (and not as being employment by any other person); and

(b) anything done by a person so seconded in the performance, or purported performance, of his functions shall be treated as done in the course of that employment.

(4) In this regulation "the relevant officer" means—

(a) in relation to a member of the police force or a special constable or police cadet appointed for a police area, the chief officer of police (or, in Scotland, the chief constable); and

(b) in relation to any other person holding the office of constable or an appointment as a police cadet, the person who has the direction and control of the body of constables or cadets in question.

(5) In this regulation ["NCA" means the National Crime Agency].

NOTES

Words in square brackets substituted by virtue of the Crime and Courts Act 2013, s 15(3), Sch 8, Pt 4, para 190 (for general transitional provisions and savings relating to the abolition of the Serious Organised Crime Agency (SOCA), see s 15(3), Sch 8, Pt 1 thereto).

25 *(Introduces Sch 2 (Consequential Amendments).)*

SCHEDULES 1 AND 2

(Sch 1 (Provisions Extending to England and Wales, Scotland and Northern Ireland) outside the scope of this work; Sch 2 contains consequential amendments which, in so far as relevant to this Handbook, have been incorporated at the appropriate place. Note that Sch 2, para 16 (which amends the Employment Rights Act 1996, s 108) was amended by the Agency Workers (Amendment) Regulations 2011, SI 2011/1941, reg 2(1), (5) to correct a drafting error in the original paragraph – see that section ante.)

EMPLOYEE STUDY AND TRAINING (PROCEDURAL REQUIREMENTS) REGULATIONS 2010

(SI 2010/155)

NOTES

Made: 25 January 2010.

Authority: Employment Rights Act 1996, ss 63F(3), (4), 63H(3).

Commencement: 6 April 2010.

Note that the enabling provisions under which these Regulations are made have (as at 15 May 2019) only been brought into force with regard to employers with at least 250 employees; see the note to s 63D of the 1996 Act at **[1.937]**.

Conciliation: employment tribunal proceedings under reg 17 are "relevant proceedings" for the purposes of the conciliation provisions contained in the Employment Tribunals Act 1996, ss 18–18C; see s 18(1)(z1) of the 1996 Act at **[1.757]**.

See *Harvey* CII(8).

ARRANGEMENT OF REGULATIONS

[2.1110]

1 Citation and commencement

These Regulations may be cited as The Employee Study and Training (Procedural Requirements) Regulations 2010 and come into force on 6th April 2010.

[2.1111]

2 Interpretation

(1) In these Regulations—

"the 1996 Act" means the Employment Rights Act 1996;

"companion" means a person who satisfies the requirements in regulation 16(2);

"electronic communication" means an electronic communication within the meaning of section 15(1) of the Electronic Communications Act 2000;

"employee" means an individual who has entered into or works under (or, where the employment has ceased, worked under) a contract of employment;

"employer" means the person by whom an employee is (or, where the employment has ceased, was) employed;

"worker" means an individual who has entered into or works under (or where the employment has ceased, worked under)—

(a) a contract of employment; or

(b) any other contract, whether express or implied and (if it is express) whether oral or in writing, whereby the individual undertakes to do or perform personally any work or services for another party to the contract whose status is not by virtue of the contract that of a client or customer of any profession or business undertaking carried on by the individual:

"writing" includes writing delivered by means of electronic communication.

(2) A section 63D application is taken as having been received—

(a) in relation to an application transmitted by electronic communication, on the day on which it is transmitted; and

(b) in relation to an application sent by post, on the day on which the application would be delivered in the ordinary course of post.

(3) A notice is taken as being given—

(a) in relation to a notice transmitted by electronic communication, on the day on which it is transmitted; and

(b) in relation to a notice sent by post, on the day on which the section 63D application would be delivered in the ordinary course of post.

[2.1112]

3 Circumstances in which employer must ignore earlier application

(1) For the purposes of section 63F(1) of the 1996 Act, at an employee's request, an employer must ignore an earlier application if paragraphs (2) or (4) apply.

(2) This paragraph applies where the employee failed to start the agreed study or training due to—

(a) an emergency or unforeseen circumstance beyond the employee's control; or

(b) cancellation of the study or training by—

(i) the employer;

(ii) the institution at which the employee was due to undertake a course;

(iii) the person whom it was agreed would supervise the training; or

(iv) any other proposed provider or facilitator of the proposed study or training.

(3) Paragraph (2)(b) does not apply where the cancellation of the study or training is attributable to the employee's own conduct in relation to the study or training.

(4) This paragraph applies where the employee—

(a) by mistake, submitted a section 63D application ("the earlier application") too soon after a previous section 63D application for the employer to be required to consider it under section 63F of the 1996 Act;

(b) submits a further section 63D application ("the current application") which the employer would be required to consider but for the earlier application; and

(c) at the time of making the current application, notifies the employer that—

(i) the earlier application was submitted too early by mistake; and

(ii) the employee wishes to withdraw the earlier application.

[2.1113]

4 Meeting to discuss application

(1) Subject to paragraph (2) and regulation 15, an employer to whom a section 63D application is submitted shall hold a meeting to discuss the application within 28 days after the date on which the application is received.

(2) Paragraph (1) does not apply where the employer agrees to the section 63D application and notifies the employee accordingly in writing within the period referred to in that paragraph.

[2.1114]

5 Notice of employer's decision following meeting

Where a meeting is held to discuss a section 63D application, the employer must give the employee notice of the employer's decision on the application within 14 days after the date of the meeting.

[2.1115]

6 Form of decision notice

(1) A notice under regulation 5 must—

(a) be in writing; and

(b) be dated.

(2) Where the employer's decision is to agree the section 63D application, a notice under regulation 5 must—

(a) give the following details of the agreed study or training—

(i) the subject of the study or training;

(ii) where and when it will take place;

(iii) who will provide or supervise it; and

(iv) what qualification (if any) it will lead to; and

(b) make clear—

(i) whether any remuneration under the employee's contract of employment will be paid for the time spent undertaking the agreed study or training;

(ii) any changes to the employee's working hours in order to accommodate the agreed study or training; and
(iii) how any tuition fees or other direct costs of the agreed study or training will be met.

(3) Where the decision is to refuse the section 63D application, a notice under regulation 5 must—
(a) state which of the grounds for refusal specified in section 63F(7) of the 1996 Act are considered by the employer to apply;
(b) contain a sufficient explanation as to why those grounds apply; and
(c) set out the appeal procedure.

(4) Where the employer's decision is to agree part of a section 63D application and refuse part of a section 63D application, a notice under regulation 5 must—
(a) make clear which part of the application is agreed to;
(b) make clear which part of the application is refused;
(c) give, in respect of the part which is agreed to, the information required under paragraph (2); and
(d) include, in respect of the part which is refused, the details required under paragraph (3).

[2.1116]
7 Variation by agreement

(1) An employer and employee may agree to dispose of a section 63D application, or part of a section 63D application, by the employer granting a varied form of it.

(2) Where agreement is reached by the employer and employee to a varied form of the application, the notice of the employer's decision under regulation 5 must—
(a) make clear the variation agreed to;
(b) be supported by written evidence of the employee's agreement to that variation; and
(c) make clear—
(i) whether any remuneration under the employee's contract of employment will be paid for the time spent undertaking the agreed study or training;
(ii) any changes to the employee's working hours in order to accommodate the agreed study or training; and
(iii) how any tuition fees or other direct costs of the agreed study or training will be met.

[2.1117]
8 Appeals

An employee is entitled to appeal against the employer's decision to refuse a section 63D application, or part of a section 63D application, by giving notice in accordance with regulation 9 within 14 days after the date on which notice of the decision is given.

[2.1118]
9

A notice of appeal under regulation 8 must—
(a) be in writing;
(b) set out the grounds of appeal; and
(c) be dated.

[2.1119]
10

(1) Subject to paragraph (2), the employer must hold a meeting with the employee to discuss the appeal within 14 days after the date on which notice under regulation 8 is given.

(2) Paragraph (1) does not apply where, within 14 days after the date on which notice under regulation 8 is given, the employer—
(a) upholds the appeal; and
(b) notifies the employee in writing of the employer's decision, specifying the information required by regulation 6(2).

[2.1120]
11

Where a meeting is held to discuss the appeal, the employer must notify the employee of the employer's decision on the appeal within 14 days after the date of the meeting.

[2.1121]
12

(1) Notice under regulation 11 must—
(a) be in writing; and
(b) be dated.

(2) Where the employer upholds the appeal, notice under regulation 11 must specify the information required by regulation 6(2).

(3) Where the employer dismisses the appeal, notice under regulation 11 must—
(a) state the grounds for the decision; and
(b) contain a sufficient explanation as to why those grounds apply.

[2.1122]
13 Time and place of meetings

The time and place of a meeting under regulation 4(1) or 10(1) must be convenient to the employer and the employee.

[2.1123]
14 Extension of periods

(1) An employer and employee may agree to an extension of any of the time periods referred to in regulations 4, 5, 8, 10, 11 and 15.

(2) An agreement under paragraph (1) must be recorded in writing by the employer.

(3) The employer's record referred to in paragraph (2) must—
- (a) specify what period the extension relates to;
- (b) specify the date on which the extension is to end;
- (c) be dated; and
- (d) be given to the employee.

[2.1124]
15

Where the individual who would ordinarily consider a section 63D application is absent from work on annual leave or on sick leave on the day on which the application is received, the period referred to in regulation 4(1) commences on the day the individual returns to work or 28 days after the application is received, whichever is the sooner.

[2.1125]
16 Right to be accompanied

(1) This regulation applies where—
- (a) a meeting is held under regulation 4(1) or 10(1); and
- (b) the employee reasonably requests to be accompanied at the meeting.

(2) Where this regulation applies, the employer must permit the employee to be accompanied at the meeting by a single companion who—
- (a) is chosen by the employee to attend the relevant meeting; and
- (b) is a worker employed by the same employer as the employee.

(3) A companion may—
- (a) address the meeting;
- (b) confer with the employee during the meeting.

(4) When addressing a meeting, a companion may not answer questions independently of the employee.

(5) If—
- (a) an employee has a right under this regulation to be accompanied at a meeting;
- (b) his chosen companion will not be available at the time proposed for the meeting by the employer; and
- (c) the employee proposes an alternative time which satisfies paragraph (6),

the employer must postpone the meeting to the time proposed by the employee.

(6) An alternative time must—
- (a) be convenient for employer, employee and companion; and
- (b) fall before the end of the period of seven days beginning with the first day after the day proposed by the employer.

(7) An employer shall permit a worker to take time off during working hours for the purpose of accompanying an employee in accordance with a request under paragraph (1)(b).

(8) Sections 168(3) and (4), 169 and 171 to 173 of the Trade Union and Labour Relations (Consolidation) Act 1992 (time off for carrying out trade union duties) apply in relation to paragraph (7) above as they apply in relation to section 168(1) of that Act.

[2.1126]
17 Complaint to employment tribunal

(1) An employee may present a complaint to an employment tribunal that the employer has failed, or threatened to fail, to comply with regulation 16(2), (3), or (5).

(2) A tribunal must not consider a complaint under this regulation in relation to a failure or threat unless the complaint is presented—
- (a) before the end of the period of three months beginning with the date of the failure or threat; or
- (b) within such further period as the tribunal considers reasonable in a case where it is satisfied that it was not reasonably practicable for the complaint to be presented before the end of that period of three months.

[(2A) Regulation 17A (extension of time limits to facilitate conciliation before institution of proceedings) applies for the purposes of paragraph (2)(a).]

(3) Where a tribunal finds that a complaint under this regulation is well-founded, it must order the employer to pay compensation to the worker of an amount not exceeding two weeks' pay.

(4) In applying Chapter 2 of Part 14 of the 1996 Act (calculation of a week's pay) for the purposes of paragraph (3), the calculation date shall be taken to be the date on which the relevant meeting took place (or was to have taken place).

(5) The limit in section 227(1) of the 1996 Act (maximum amount of a week's pay) shall apply for the purposes of paragraph (3).

NOTES

Para (2A): inserted by the Employment Tribunals Act 1996 (Application of Conciliation Provisions) Order 2014, SI 2014/431, art 3, Schedule, paras 39, 40.

Conciliation: employment tribunal proceedings under this regulation are "relevant proceedings" for the purposes of the conciliation provisions contained in the Employment Tribunals Act 1996, ss 18–18C; see s 18(1)(z1) of the 1996 Act at **[1.757]**.

[2.1127]

[17A Extension of time limit to facilitate conciliation before institution of proceedings

(1) In this regulation—

(a) Day A is the day on which the worker concerned complies with the requirement in subsection (1) of section 18A of the Employment Tribunals Act 1996 (requirement to contact ACAS before instituting proceedings) in relation to the matter in respect of which the proceedings are brought, and

(b) Day B is the day on which the worker concerned receives or, if earlier, is treated as receiving (by virtue of regulations made under subsection (11) of that section) the certificate issued under subsection (4) of that section.

(2) In working out when the time limit set by regulation 17(2)(a) expires the period beginning with the day after Day A and ending with Day B is not to be counted.

(3) If the time limit set by regulation 17(2)(a) would (if not extended by this paragraph) expire during the period beginning with Day A and ending one month after Day B, the time limit expires instead at the end of that period.

(4) The power conferred on the employment tribunal by regulation 17(2)(b) to extend the time limit set by paragraph (2)(a) of that regulation is exercisable in relation to that time limit as extended by this regulation.]

NOTES

Inserted by the Employment Tribunals Act 1996 (Application of Conciliation Provisions) Order 2014, SI 2014/431, art 3, Schedule, paras 39, 41.

[2.1128]

18 Detriment and dismissal

(1) A person has the right not to be subjected to any detriment by any act, or any deliberate failure to act, by the person's employer done on the ground that the person—

(a) exercised or sought to exercise the right under regulation 16(2) or (5); or

(b) at the employee's request, accompanied or sought to accompany an employee at a meeting held under regulation 4(1) or 10(1).

(2) Section 48 of the 1996 Act applies in relation to contraventions of paragraph (1) as it applies in relation to contraventions of certain sections of that Act.

(3) A person who is dismissed is to be treated for the purposes of Part 10 of the 1996 Act as unfairly dismissed if the reason (or, if more than one, the principal reason) for the dismissal is that the person—

(a) exercised or sought to exercise his right under regulation 16(2) or (5); or

(b) at the employee's request, accompanied or sought to accompany an employee at a meeting held under regulation 4(1) or 10(1).

(4) Section 108 of the 1996 Act (qualifying period of employment) does not apply in relation to paragraph (3).

(5) Sections 128 to 132 of the 1996 Act (interim relief) apply in relation to dismissal for the reason specified in paragraph (3)(a) or (b) as they apply in relation to dismissal for a reason specified in section 128(1)(b) of that Act.

(6) In the application of Chapter 2 of Part 10 of the 1996 Act in relation to paragraph (3), a reference to an employee is to be treated as a reference to a worker.

[2.1129]

19 Withdrawal of application by the employee

(1) An employer must treat a section 63D application as withdrawn where the employee has—

(a) notified the employer either orally or in writing that the employee is withdrawing the application;

(b) without reasonable cause, failed to attend a meeting under regulation 4(1) or 10(1) more than once; or

(c) without reasonable cause, refused to provide the employer with information the employer requires in order to assess whether the application should be agreed to.

(2) An employer must confirm the withdrawal of the section 63D application to the employee in writing unless the employee has provided him with written notice of the withdrawal under paragraph (1)(a).

[2.1130]
20 Employee's duties to inform employer

(1) An employee must inform the employee's employer within 14 days of an event listed in s 63H(2) of the 1996 Act occurring.

(2) Notice under paragraph (1) must—
- (a) be in writing; and
- (b) be dated.

EMPLOYEE STUDY AND TRAINING (ELIGIBILITY, COMPLAINTS AND REMEDIES) REGULATIONS 2010

(SI 2010/156)

NOTES

Made: 25 January 2010.
Authority: Employment Rights Act 1996, ss 63E(4)(c), (5)(a), 63I(3)(b), 63J(3).
Commencement: 6 April 2010.
Note that the enabling provisions under which these Regulations are made have (as of 15 May 2019) only been brought into force with regard to employers with at least 250 employees; see the note to s 63D of the 1996 Act at **[1.937]**.
See *Harvey* CII(8).

ARRANGEMENT OF REGULATIONS

[2.1131]
1 Citation and commencement

These Regulations may be cited as the Employee Study and Training (Eligibility, Complaints and Remedies) Regulations 2010 and come into force on 6th April 2010.

[2.1132]
2 Interpretation

(1) In these Regulations—

"the 1996 Act" means the Employment Rights Act 1996;

"the Procedure Regulations" means The Employee Study and Training (Procedural Requirements) Regulations 2010.

[2.1133]
3 Further information which the application must contain

(1) An employee must set out in the section 63D application—
- (a) the date on which the employee's last section 63D application (if any) was submitted to their employer; and
- (b) the method by which that application was submitted.

(2) For the purposes of paragraph (1) an employee submits a section 63D application by sending, delivering or otherwise transmitting it to their employer.

[2.1134]
4 Form of the application

A section 63D application must—
- (a) be made in writing; and
- (b) be dated.

[2.1135]
5 Breaches of the Procedure Regulations by the employer entitling an employee to make a complaint to an employment tribunal

The breaches of the Procedure Regulations which entitle an employee to make a complaint to an employment tribunal under section 63I of the 1996 Act notwithstanding the fact that the employee's section 63D application has not been disposed of by agreement or withdrawn are—
- (a) failure to hold a meeting in accordance with regulation 4(1) and 10(1) of the Procedure Regulations;
- (b) failure to notify a decision in accordance with regulations 5 or 11 of the Procedure Regulations.

[2.1136]
6 Compensation

(1) The maximum amount of compensation that an employment tribunal may award under section 63J of the 1996 Act where it finds a complaint by an employee under section 63I of the Act well-founded is 8 weeks' pay.

EMPLOYMENT RELATIONS ACT 1999 (BLACKLISTS) REGULATIONS 2010

(SI 2010/493)

NOTES

Made: 1 March 2010.

Authority: Employment Relations Act 1999, s 3.

Commencement: 2 March 2010.

Employment Appeal Tribunal: an appeal lies to the Employment Appeal Tribunal on any question of law arising from any decision of, or in any proceedings before, an employment tribunal under or by virtue of these Regulations; see the Employment Tribunals Act 1996, s 21(1)(x) at **[1.764]**.

Conciliation: employment tribunal proceedings under regs 5, 6 or 9 are "relevant proceedings" for the purposes of the conciliation provisions contained in the Employment Tribunals Act 1996, ss 18–18C; see s 18(1)(z2) of the 1996 Act at **[1.757]**.

Tribunal jurisdiction: the Trade Union and Labour Relations (Consolidation) Act 1992, s 207A at **[1.524]** (as inserted by the Employment Act 2008) provides that in proceedings before an employment tribunal relating to a claim by an employee under any of the jurisdictions listed in Sch A2 to the 1992 Act at **[1.704]** (which includes reg 9 of these Regulations) the tribunal may adjust any award given if the employer or the employee has unreasonably failed to comply with a relevant Code of Practice as defined by s 207A(4). See also the revised Acas Code of Practice 1 – Disciplinary and Grievance Procedures at **[4.1]**, and the Acas Code of Practice 4 – Settlement Agreements at **[4.54]**.

See *Harvey* NI(4)(H).

ARRANGEMENT OF REGULATIONS

Introductory provisions

Introductory provisions

[2.1137]
1 Citation, commencement and extent

These Regulations—

(a) may be cited as the Employment Relations Act 1999 (Blacklists) Regulations 2010,
(b) come into force on the day after the day on which they are made, and
(c) extend to Great Britain.

[2.1138]

2 Interpretation

(1) In these Regulations—

"'employment agency'" means a person who, for profit or not, provides services for the purposes of finding employment for workers or supplying employers with workers, and does not include a trade union by reason only of the services a trade union provides only for and in relation to its members;

"'office'", in relation to a trade union, means any position—

(a) by virtue of which the holder is an official of the trade union, or

(b) to which Chapter 4 of Part 1 of the Trade Union and Labour Relations (Consolidation) Act 1992 (duty to hold elections) applies,

and "'official'" has the meaning given by section 119 of that Act;

"'prohibited list'" has the meaning given by regulation 3(2);

"'services'", in relation to an employment agency, means services for the purposes of finding employment for workers or supplying employers with workers;

"'use'", in relation to a prohibited list, includes use of information contained in the list.

(2) References in these regulations to information supplied by a person who contravenes regulation 3 include information supplied by a person who would contravene that regulation if that person's actions took place in Great Britain.

General prohibition

[2.1139]

3 General prohibition

(1) Subject to regulation 4, no person shall compile, use, sell or supply a prohibited list.

(2) A "'prohibited list'" is a list which—

(a) contains details of persons who are or have been members of trade unions or persons who are taking part or have taken part in the activities of trade unions, and

(b) is compiled with a view to being used by employers or employment agencies for the purposes of discrimination in relation to recruitment or in relation to the treatment of workers.

(3) "'Discrimination'" means treating a person less favourably than another on grounds of trade union membership or trade union activities.

(4) In these Regulations references to membership of a trade union include references to—

(a) membership of a particular branch or section of a trade union, and

(b) membership of one of a number of particular branches or sections of a trade union;

and references to taking part in the activities of a trade union have a corresponding meaning.

[2.1140]

4 Exceptions to general prohibition

(1) A person does not contravene regulation 3 in the following cases.

(2) The first case is where a person supplies a prohibited list, but—

(a) does not know they are supplying a prohibited list, and

(b) could not reasonably be expected to know they are supplying a prohibited list.

(3) The second case is where a person compiles, uses or supplies a prohibited list, but—

(a) in doing so, that person's sole or principal purpose is to make known a contravention of regulation 3 or the possibility of such a contravention,

(b) no information in relation to a person whose details are included in the prohibited list is published without the consent of that person, and

(c) in all the circumstances compiling, using or supplying the prohibited list is justified in the public interest.

(4) The third case is where a person compiles, uses, sells or supplies a prohibited list, but in doing so that person's sole or principal purpose is to apply a requirement either—

(a) that a person may not be considered for appointment to an office or for employment unless that person has experience or knowledge of trade union matters, and in all the circumstances it is reasonable to apply such a requirement, or

(b) that a person may not be considered for appointment or election to an office in a trade union unless he is a member of the union.

(5) The fourth case is where a person compiles, uses, sells or supplies a prohibited list, but the compilation, use, sale or supply of the prohibited list is required or authorised—

(a) under an enactment,

(b) by any rule of law, or

(c) by an order of the court.

(6) The fifth case is where a person uses or supplies a prohibited list—

(a) for the purpose of, or in connection with, legal proceedings (including prospective legal proceedings), or

(b) for the purpose of giving or obtaining legal advice,

where the use or supply is necessary in order to determine whether these regulations have been, are being or will be complied with.

Refusal of employment or employment agency services

[2.1141]

5 Refusal of employment

(1) A person (P) has a right of complaint to an employment tribunal against another (R) if R refuses to employ P for a reason which relates to a prohibited list, and either—

(a) R contravenes regulation 3 in relation to that list, or

(b) R—

(i) relies on information supplied by a person who contravenes that regulation in relation to that list, and

(ii) knows or ought reasonably to know that the information relied on is supplied in contravention of that regulation.

(2) R shall be taken to refuse to employ P if P seeks employment of any description with R and R—

(a) refuses or deliberately omits to entertain and process P's application or enquiry;

(b) causes P to withdraw or cease to pursue P's application or enquiry;

(c) refuses or deliberately omits to offer P employment of that description;

(d) makes P an offer of such employment the terms of which are such as no reasonable employer who wished to fill the post would offer and which is not accepted; or

(e) makes P an offer of such employment but withdraws it or causes P not to accept it.

(3) If there are facts from which the tribunal could conclude, in the absence of any other explanation, that R contravened regulation 3 or relied on information supplied in contravention of that regulation, the tribunal must find that such a contravention or reliance on information occurred unless R shows that it did not.

NOTES

Conciliation: employment tribunal proceedings under this regulation are "relevant proceedings" for the purposes of the conciliation provisions contained in the Employment Tribunals Act 1996, ss 18–18C; see s 18(1)(z2) of the 1996 Act at **[1.757]**.

[2.1142]

6 Refusal of employment agency services

(1) A person (P) has a right of complaint to an employment tribunal against an employment agency (E) if E refuses P any of its services for a reason which relates to a prohibited list, and either—

(a) E contravenes regulation 3 in relation to that list, or

(b) E—

(i) relies on information supplied by a person who contravenes that regulation in relation to that list, and

(ii) knows or ought reasonably to know that information relied on is supplied in contravention of that regulation.

(2) E shall be taken to refuse P a service if P seeks to make use of the service and E—

(a) refuses or deliberately omits to make the service available to P;

(b) causes P not to make use of the service or to cease to make use of it; or

(c) does not provide P the same service, on the same terms, as is provided to others.

(3) If there are facts from which the tribunal could conclude, in the absence of any other explanation, that E contravened regulation 3 or relied on information supplied in contravention of that regulation, the tribunal must find that such a contravention or reliance on information occurred unless E shows that it did not.

NOTES

Conciliation: employment tribunal proceedings under this regulation are "relevant proceedings" for the purposes of the conciliation provisions contained in the Employment Tribunals Act 1996, ss 18–18C; see s 18(1)(z2) of the 1996 Act at **[1.757]**.

[2.1143]

7 Time limit for proceedings under regulation 5 or 6

(1) Subject to paragraph (2), an employment tribunal shall not consider a complaint under regulation 5 or 6 unless it is presented to the tribunal before the end of the period of three months beginning with the date of the conduct to which the complaint relates.

[(1A) Regulation 18 (extension of time limits to facilitate conciliation before institution of proceedings) applies for the purposes of paragraph (1).]

(2) An employment tribunal may consider a complaint under regulation 5 or 6 that is otherwise out of time if, in all the circumstances of the case, it considers that it is just and equitable to do so.

(3) The date of the conduct to which a complaint under regulation 5 relates shall be taken to be—

(a) in the case of an actual refusal, the date of the refusal;

(b) in the case of a deliberate omission—

(i) to entertain and process P's application or enquiry, or

(ii) to offer employment,

the end of the period within which it was reasonable to expect R to act;

(c) in the case of conduct causing P to withdraw or cease to pursue P's application or enquiry, the date of that conduct;

(d) in a case where R made but withdrew an offer, the date R withdrew the offer;

(e) in any other case where R made an offer which was not accepted, the date on which R made the offer.

(4) The date of the conduct to which a complaint under regulation 6 relates shall be taken to be—

(a) in the case of an actual refusal, the date of the refusal;

(b) in the case of a deliberate omission to make a service available, the end of the period within which it was reasonable to expect E to act;

(c) in the case of conduct causing P not make use of a service or to cease to make use of it, the date of that conduct;

(d) in the case of failure to provide the same service, on the same terms, as is provided to others, the date or last date on which the service in fact was provided.

NOTES

Para (1A): inserted by the Enterprise and Regulatory Reform Act 2013 (Consequential Amendments) (Employment) Order 2014, SI 2014/386, art 2, Schedule, paras 64, 65.

[2.1144]

8 Remedies in proceedings under regulation 5 or 6

(1) Where an employment tribunal finds that a complaint under regulation 5 or 6 is well-founded, it shall make a declaration to that effect and may make such of the following as it considers just and equitable—

(a) an order requiring the respondent to pay compensation;

(b) a recommendation that the respondent take within a specified period action appearing to the tribunal to be practicable for the purpose of obviating or reducing the adverse effect on the complainant of any conduct to which the complaint relates.

(2) Compensation shall be assessed on the same basis as damages for breach of statutory duty and may include compensation for injury to feelings.

(3) Where an award of compensation is made, the amount of compensation before any increase or reduction is made under paragraph (4), (5) or (6) shall not be less than £5,000.

(4) If the respondent fails without reasonable justification to comply with a recommendation under paragraph (1)(b), the tribunal may increase its award of compensation or, if it has not made such an award, make one.

(5) Where the tribunal considers that any conduct of the complainant before the refusal to which the complaint under regulation 5 or 6 relates was such that it would be just and equitable to reduce the award of compensation, the tribunal shall reduce that amount accordingly.

(6) The amount of compensation shall be reduced or further reduced by the amount of any compensation awarded by the tribunal under section 140 of the Trade Union and Labour Relations (Consolidation) Act 1992 in respect of the same refusal.

(7) The total amount of compensation shall not exceed £65,300.

Detriment

[2.1145]

9 Detriment

(1) A person (P) has a right of complaint to an employment tribunal against P's employer (D) if D, by any act or any deliberate failure to act, subjects P to a detriment for a reason which relates to a prohibited list, and either—

(a) D contravenes regulation 3 in relation to that list, or

(b) D—

(i) relies on information supplied by a person who contravenes that regulation in relation to that list, and

(ii) knows or ought reasonably to know that information relied on is supplied in contravention of that regulation.

(2) If there are facts from which the tribunal could conclude, in the absence of any other explanation, that D contravened regulation 3 or relied on information supplied in contravention of that regulation, the tribunal must find that such a contravention or reliance on information occurred unless D shows that it did not.

(3) This regulation does not apply where the detriment in question amounts to the dismissal of an employee within the meaning in Part 10 of the Employment Rights Act 1996.

NOTES

Conciliation: employment tribunal proceedings under this regulation are "relevant proceedings" for the purposes of the conciliation provisions contained in the Employment Tribunals Act 1996, ss 18–18C; see s 18(1)(z2) of the 1996 Act at **[1.757]**.

Tribunal jurisdiction: the Trade Union and Labour Relations (Consolidation) Act 1992, s 207A at **[1.524]** (as inserted by the Employment Act 2008) provides that in proceedings before an employment tribunal relating to a claim by an employee under any of the jurisdictions listed in Sch A2 of the 1992 Act at **[1.704]** (which includes this regulation) the tribunal may adjust any award given if the employer or the employee has unreasonably failed to comply with a relevant Code of Practice issued for the purposes of Chapter III of the 1992 Act. See also the revised Acas Code of Practice 1 – Disciplinary and Grievance Procedures at **[4.1]**, and the Acas Code of Practice 4 – Settlement Agreements at **[4.54]**.

[2.1146]
10 Time limit for proceedings under regulation 9

(1) Subject to paragraph (2), an employment tribunal shall not consider a complaint under regulation 9 unless it is presented before the end of the period of three months beginning with the date of the act or failure to which the complaint relates or, where that act or failure is part of a series of similar acts or failures (or both) the last of them.

[(1A) Regulation 18 (extension of time limits to facilitate conciliation before institution of proceedings) applies for the purposes of paragraph (1).]

(2) An employment tribunal may consider a complaint under regulation 9 that is otherwise out of time if, in all the circumstances of the case, it considers that it is just and equitable to do so.

(3) For the purposes of paragraph (1)—

(a) where an act extends over a period, the reference to the date of the act is a reference to the last day of the period;

(b) a failure to act shall be treated as done when it was decided on.

(4) For the purposes of paragraph (3), in the absence of evidence establishing the contrary D shall be taken to decide on a failure to act—

(a) when D does an act which is inconsistent with doing the failed act, or

(b) if D has done no such inconsistent act, when the period expires within which D might reasonably have been expected to do the failed act if it was done.

NOTES

Para (1A): inserted by the Enterprise and Regulatory Reform Act 2013 (Consequential Amendments) (Employment) Order 2014, SI 2014/386, art 2, Schedule, paras 64, 65.

[2.1147]
11 Remedies in proceedings under regulation 9

(1) Where the employment tribunal finds that a complaint under regulation 9 is well-founded, it shall make a declaration to that effect and may make an award of compensation to be paid by D to P in respect of the act or failure complained of.

(2) Subject to the following paragraphs, the amount of the compensation awarded shall be such as the tribunal considers just and equitable in all the circumstances having regard to the act or failure complained of and to any loss sustained by P which is attributable to D's act or failure.

(3) The loss shall be taken to include—

(a) any expenses P reasonably incurred in consequence of the act or failure complained of; and

(b) loss of any benefit which P might reasonably be expected to have had but for that act or failure.

(4) In ascertaining the loss, the tribunal shall apply the same rule concerning the duty of a person to mitigate his loss as applies to damages recoverable under the common law of England and Wales or Scotland.

(5) Where an award of compensation is made, the amount of compensation before any increase or reduction is made under paragraphs (6), (7) and (8) of this regulation and section 207A of the Trade Union and Labour Relations (Consolidation) Act 1992 shall not be less than £5,000.

(6) Where the conduct of P before the act or failure complained of was such that it would be just and equitable to reduce the amount of compensation, the tribunal shall reduce that amount accordingly.

(7) Where the tribunal finds that the act or failure complained of was to any extent caused or contributed to by action of P, it shall reduce or further reduce the amount of the compensation by such proportion as it considers just and equitable having regard to that finding.

(8) The amount of compensation shall be reduced or further reduced by the amount of any compensation awarded by the tribunal under section 149 of the Trade Union and Labour Relations (Consolidation) Act 1992 in respect of the same act or failure.

(9) In determining the amount of compensation to be awarded no account shall be taken of any pressure exercised on D by calling, organising, procuring or financing a strike or other industrial action, or by threatening to do so; and that question shall be determined as if no such pressure had been exercised.

(10) Where P is a worker and the detriment to which P is subjected is the termination of P's contract, and that contract is not a contract of employment, the compensation awarded to P under this regulation shall not exceed £65,300.

12 *(Reg 12 inserts the Employment Rights Act 1996, s 104F at* **[1.1021]**, *and amends ss 105, 108, 111, 120, 122, 128 and 129 in Part X of that Act (see Part X (Unfair dismissal) at* **[1.1001]** *et seq).)*

Action for breach of statutory duty

[2.1148]
13 Action for breach of statutory duty

(1) A contravention of regulation 3 is actionable as a breach of statutory duty.

(2) If there are facts from which the court could conclude, in the absence of any other explanation, that the defendant has contravened, or is likely to contravene, regulation 3, the court must find that such a contravention occurred, or is likely to occur, unless the defendant shows that it did not, or is not likely to, occur.

(3) In proceedings brought by virtue of this regulation, the court may (without prejudice to any of its other powers)—

(a) make such order as it considers appropriate for the purpose of restraining or preventing the defendant from contravening regulation 3; and

(b) award damages, which may include compensation for injured feelings.

(4) A person may complain to an employment tribunal under regulation 5, 6 or 9, or under Part 10 of the Employment Rights Act 1996 (unfair dismissal) as it applies by virtue of these Regulations and bring an action for breach of statutory duty in respect of the same conduct for the purpose of restraining or preventing the defendant from contravening regulation 3.

(5) Except as mentioned in paragraph (4), a person may not bring an action for breach of statutory duty and complain to an employment tribunal under regulation 5, 6 or 9, or under Part 10 of the Employment Rights Act 1996 (unfair dismissal) as it applies by virtue of these Regulations, in respect of the same conduct.

Supplementary provisions

[2.1149]

14 Complaint against employer and employment agency

(1) Where P has a right of complaint under regulation 5 or 6 against R and E arising out of the same facts, P may present a complaint against either R or E or against R and E jointly.

(2) If P presents a complaint against only one party, that party or P may request the tribunal to join or sist the other as a party to the proceedings.

(3) The request shall be granted if it is made before the hearing of the complaint begins, but may be refused if it is made after that time; and no such request may be made after the tribunal has made its decision as to whether the complaint is well-founded.

(4) Where P brings a complaint against R and E jointly, or where P brings a complaint against one of them and the other is joined or sisted as a party to the proceedings, and the tribunal—

(a) finds that the complaint is well-founded as against R and E, and

(b) awards compensation,

the tribunal may order that the compensation shall be paid by R, by E, or partly by R and partly by E, as the tribunal may consider just and equitable in all the circumstances.

[2.1150]

15 Awards against third parties in tribunal proceedings

(1) If in proceedings on a complaint under regulation 5, 6 or 9, or under Part 10 of the Employment Rights Act 1996 as it applies by virtue of these regulations, either the respondent or complainant claims that another person contravened regulation 3 in respect of the prohibited list to which the complaint relates, the complainant or respondent may request the tribunal to direct that other person be joined or sisted as a party to the proceedings.

(2) The request shall be granted if it is made before the hearing of the complaint begins, but may be refused if it is made after that time; and no such request may be made if it is made after the tribunal has made a decision as to whether the complaint is well-founded.

(3) Where a person has been so joined or sisted as a party to the proceedings and the tribunal—

(a) finds that the complaint is well-founded,

(b) awards compensation, and

(c) finds the claim in paragraph (1) is well-founded,

the tribunal shall make a declaration to that effect and may award such of the remedies mentioned in paragraph (4) as it considers just and equitable.

(4) The remedies the tribunal may award are—

(a) an order that compensation shall be paid by the person joined (or sisted) instead of by the respondent, or partly by that person and partly by the respondent;

(b) a recommendation that within a specified period the person joined (or sisted) takes action appearing to the tribunal to be practicable for the purpose of obviating or reducing the adverse effect on the complainant of any conduct to which the complaint relates.

(5) If the person joined (or sisted) fails without reasonable justification to comply with a recommendation to take action, the tribunal may increase its award of compensation or, if it has not made such an award, make one.

(6) Where by virtue of regulation 14 (complaint against employer and employment agency) there is more than one respondent, the above provisions apply to either or both of them.

[2.1151]

16 Restrictions on contracting out

Section 288 of the Trade Union and Labour Relations (Consolidation) Act 1992 (restrictions on contracting out) applies in relation to regulations 5, 6 and 9 as if they were contained in that Act.

17 *(Reg 17 amends the Employment Tribunals Act 1996, ss 10, 16, 18, 21 at* **[1.745]**, **[1.755]**, **[1.757]**, **[1.764]**, *and the Trade Union and Labour Relations (Consolidation) Act 1992, Sch A2 at* **[1.704]**.*)*

[2.1152]

[18 Extension of time limit to facilitate conciliation before institution of proceedings

(1) This regulation applies where these Regulations provide for it to apply for the purposes of a provision of these Regulations ("a relevant provision").

(2) In this regulation—

(a) Day A is the day on which the worker concerned complies with the requirement in subsection (1) of section 18A of the Employment Tribunals Act 1996 (requirement to contact ACAS before instituting proceedings) in relation to the matter in respect of which the proceedings are brought, and

(b) Day B is the day on which the worker concerned receives or, if earlier, is treated as receiving (by virtue of regulations made under subsection (11) of that section) the certificate issued under subsection (4) of that section.

(3) In working out when the time limit set by a relevant provision expires the period beginning with the day after Day A and ending with Day B is not to be counted.

(4) If the time limit set by a relevant provision would (if not extended by this paragraph) expire during the period beginning with Day A and ending one month after Day B, the time limit expires instead at the end of that period.

(5) Where an employment tribunal has power under these Regulations to extend the time limit set by a relevant provision, the power is exercisable in relation to that time limit as extended by this regulation.]

NOTES

Inserted by the Enterprise and Regulatory Reform Act 2013 (Consequential Amendments) (Employment) Order 2014, SI 2014/386, art 2, Schedule, paras 64, 66.

OCCUPATIONAL AND PERSONAL PENSION SCHEMES (AUTOMATIC ENROLMENT) REGULATIONS 2010

(SI 2010/772)

NOTES

Made: 11 March 2010.

Authority: Pension Schemes Act 1993, ss 111A(15)(b), 181, 182(2), (3); Pensions Act 1995, ss 49(8), 124(1), 174(2), (3); Pensions Act 2008, ss 2(3), 3(2), (5), (6), 4(1), (3), 5(2), (4), (6), (7), (8), 6(1)(b), (2), 7(4), (5), (6), 8(2)(b), (3), (4), (5), (6), 9(3), 10, 15, 16(2), (3)(c), 18(c), 22(4)–(7), 23(1)(b), (3), 24(1)(a), (b), 25, 27, 30(6)(c), 33(2), 37(3), 99, 144(2), (4).

Commencement: 1 July 2012 (see reg 1 at **[2.1153]**).

Only certain regulations of relevance to employment law are reproduced here. For reasons of space, the subject matter of regulations not printed is not annotated.

ARRANGEMENT OF REGULATIONS

PART 1
CITATION, COMMENCEMENT AND INTERPRETATION

PART 1A
EXEMPTION AND EXCEPTIONS

PART 2
AUTOMATIC ENROLMENT, OPT OUT AND REFUNDS

PART 3
AUTOMATIC RE-ENROLMENT

SCHEDULES

PART 1
CITATION, COMMENCEMENT AND INTERPRETATION

[2.1153]
1 Citation, commencement[, expiry] and interpretation

(1) These Regulations may be cited as the Occupational and Personal Pension Schemes (Automatic Enrolment) Regulations 2010 and shall come into force on [1st July 2012, immediately after the time when the amendments made by the Occupational and Personal Pension Schemes (Automatic Enrolment) (Amendment) Regulations 2012 come into force].

[(1A), (1B) . . .]

(2) In these Regulations—

"the Act" means the Pensions Act 2008;

"the 1993 Act" means the Pension Schemes Act 1993;

"the 1995 Act" means the Pensions Act 1995;

"applicable pay reference period" means—

(a) a period of one week; or

(b) in the case of a jobholder who is paid their regular wage or salary by reference to a period longer than a week, that period;

"automatic enrolment date" has the meaning given by section 3(7) (automatic enrolment) of the Act;

"automatic re-enrolment date" means the date determined in accordance with regulation 12;

"enrolment date" means the date determined in accordance with regulation 18(6);

"enrolment information" has the meaning given by regulation 2;

"jobholder information" has the meaning given by regulation 3;

"joining notice" means a notice given under section 9(2) (workers without qualifying earnings) of the Act;

"opt in" means the jobholder's right under section 7(3) of the Act (jobholder's right to opt in) by notice to require the employer to arrange for the jobholder to become an active member of an automatic enrolment scheme;

"opt in notice" means a notice given under section 7(3) (jobholder's right to opt in) of the Act;

"opt out" means the jobholder's right to give notice under section 8 (jobholder's right to opt out) of the Act;

"opt out notice" means a notice in the form set out in [Schedule 1];

"opt out period" means the period determined in accordance with regulation 9(2) or (3);

"staging date" means the date on which sections 2 to 8 of the Act first apply in relation to the employer.

NOTES

Regulation heading: word in square brackets inserted by the Occupational and Personal Pension Schemes (Automatic Enrolment) (Amendment) Regulations 2012, SI 2012/1257, regs 2, 3(a).

Para (1): words in square brackets substituted by SI 2012/1257, regs 2, 3(b).

Paras (1A), (1B): inserted by SI 2012/1257, regs 2, 3(c). These paras relate to the expiry of reg 52 of these Regulations, which is outside the scope of this work.

Para (2): words in square brackets in the definition "opt out notice" substituted by the Automatic Enrolment (Miscellaneous Amendments) Regulations 2012, SI 2012/215, regs 17, 43(1).

[2.1154]
[2 Enrolment information

In these Regulations "enrolment information" means the information described in paragraphs 1–15, [and 24] of Schedule 2.]

NOTES

Substituted by the Automatic Enrolment (Miscellaneous Amendments) Regulations 2012, SI 2012/215, regs 17, 18.

Words in square brackets substituted by the Occupational and Personal Pension Schemes (Automatic Enrolment) (Amendment) Regulations 2015, SI 2015/501, regs 2, 3, as from 1 April 2015.

[2.1155]
3 Jobholder information

(1) In these Regulations "jobholder information" is the jobholder's—

(a) name;

(b) date of birth;

(c) postal residential address;

(d) gender;

(e) automatic enrolment date, automatic re-enrolment date or enrolment date, as the case may be, or for a jobholder to whom regulation 28 or 29 applies, the date mentioned in regulation 7(1) as modified by regulation 28 or 29, as the case may be;

(f) national insurance number;

(g) the gross earnings due to the jobholder in any applicable pay reference period;
(h) the value of any contributions payable to the scheme by the employer and the jobholder in any applicable pay reference period, where this information is available to the employer;
(i) postal work address;
(j) individual work e-mail address, where an individual work e-mail address is allocated to that jobholder; and
(k) personal e-mail address, where the employer holds this information.

(2) For the purposes of paragraph (1)(h), "the value" of contributions may be expressed as a fixed amount or a percentage of any qualifying earnings or pensionable pay due to the jobholder in any applicable pay reference period.

[2.1156]
[4 Pay reference periods for the purposes of sections 1(1)(c), 3(1)(c) and 5(1)(c) of the Act

(1) This regulation applies for the purposes of sections 1(1)(c), 3(1)(c) and 5(1)(c) of the Act (jobholders, automatic enrolment and automatic re-enrolment).

(2) The pay reference period in respect of a person is determined in accordance with paragraph (3) or paragraphs (4) and (5), whichever the employer may decide.

(3) For the purposes of this paragraph, the pay reference period is—
(a) in the case of a person who is paid their regular wage or salary by reference to a period of a week, the period of one week;
(b) in the case of a person who is paid their regular wage or salary by reference to a period longer than a week, that period.

(4) For the purposes of this paragraph, subject to paragraph (6)(b), a pay reference period is—
(a) a period equal in length to the usual interval between payments of the person's regular wage or salary; or
(b) the period of a week,
whichever is the longer.

(5) For the purposes of paragraph (4), pay reference periods commence—
(a) where the person is paid monthly, on the first day of a tax month;
(b) where the person is paid weekly or the pay reference period is a week, on the first day of a tax week;
(c) where the person is paid at intervals of multiple weeks, on—
(i) 6th April; and
(ii) the first day of the tax week which commences immediately after the expiry of a pay interval period beginning on 6th April, unless paragraph (6) applies; and
(d) where the person is paid at intervals of multiple months, on—
(i) 6th April; and
(ii) the first day of the tax month which commences immediately after the expiry of a pay interval period beginning on 6th April, unless paragraph (6) applies.

(6) Where paragraphs (4) and (5) apply and a pay reference period includes the last day of a tax year—
(a) the next pay reference period commences on 6th April; and
(b) if the qualifying earnings which, but for this sub-paragraph, would fall in that pay reference period, are paid or payable on or after 6th April, the pay reference period ends on 5th April.

(7) In this regulation—
"pay interval period" means a period which is equal in length to the usual interval between payments and each whole multiple of that period;
"tax month" means the period beginning with the sixth day of the month and ending on the fifth day of the following month; and
"tax week" means one of the successive periods in a tax year beginning with the first day of that year and every seventh day after that (so that the last day of a tax year or, in the case of a tax year ending in a leap year, the last two days is treated as a separate week).]

NOTES

Substituted by the Automatic Enrolment (Miscellaneous Amendments) Regulations 2013, SI 2013/2556, reg 5(1), (2).

[2.1157]
[5 Pay reference periods for the purposes of section 20(1)(b) and (c) and section 26(4)(b) and (5)(b) of the Act

(1) The pay reference periods for the purposes of section 20(1)(b) and (c) (quality requirement: UK money purchase schemes) and section 26(4)(b) and (5)(b) (quality requirement: UK personal pension schemes) of the Act are as follows.

(2) A pay reference period may be either—
(a) subject to paragraph (10), a period of a year, ending on the day before an anniversary of the employer's staging date;
(b) a period which is equal in length to the period by reference to which the jobholder is paid their regular wage or salary, commencing on the first day of that period; or
(c) subject to paragraph (4)(b), a period which is equal in length to the usual interval between payments of the jobholder's regular wage or salary, commencing on the date determined in accordance with paragraph (3).

(3) Where paragraph (2)(c) applies, pay reference periods in respect of a person commence—

(a) where the person is paid monthly, on the first day of a tax month;
(b) where the person is paid weekly, on the first day of a tax week;
(c) where the person is paid at intervals of multiple weeks, on—
(i) 6th April; and
(ii) the first day of the tax week which commences immediately after the expiry of a pay interval period beginning on 6th April, unless paragraph (4) applies; and
(d) where the person is paid at intervals of multiple months, on—
(i) 6th April; and
(ii) the first day of the tax month which commences immediately after the expiry of a pay interval period beginning on 6th April, unless paragraph (4) applies.

(4) Where paragraph (2)(c) applies and a pay reference period includes the last day of a tax year—
(a) the next pay reference period commences on 6th April; and
(b) if the qualifying earnings which, but for this sub-paragraph, would fall in that pay reference period, are paid or payable on or after 6th April, the pay reference period ends on 5th April.

(5) Where paragraph (2)(a) applies, the first pay reference period in respect of a person commences—
(a) on the relevant day; or
(b) where there has been a period beginning after the relevant day, during which the requirements of section 1(1)(a) or (c) of the Act were not met but the person remained an active member of a qualifying scheme, on the day following the last day of that period.

(6) Where paragraph (2)(b) applies, the first pay reference period in respect of a person commences on the first day determined in accordance with that paragraph which falls on or after the relevant day.

(7) Where paragraph (2)(c) applies, the first pay reference period in respect of a person commences on the first day determined in accordance with paragraph (3) which falls on or after the relevant day.

(8) Subject to paragraph (2)(c), a pay reference period in relation to any person ends on the day before the day on which the next pay reference period begins.

(9) Where a person ceases to be a jobholder of the employer or ceases to be an active member of a qualifying scheme the last pay reference period—
(a) ends on the day on which the person's status so changes, where paragraph (2)(a) applies; or
(b) is the pay reference period which includes the day on which the person's status so changes, where paragraph (2)(b) or (c) applies.

(10) A pay reference period under paragraph (2)(a) may be less than a year if it either commences or ends within the period of a year ending on the day before an anniversary of the employer's staging date.

(11) In this regulation—
"relevant day" means the first day on or after the staging date on which the person is both a jobholder and an active member of a qualifying scheme; and
"pay interval period", "tax week" and "tax month" have the same meaning as in regulation 4.]

NOTES

Substituted by the Automatic Enrolment (Miscellaneous Amendments) Regulations 2013, SI 2013/2556, reg 5(1), (3).

[PART 1A
EXEMPTION [AND EXCEPTIONS]

NOTES

Part heading: words in square brackets inserted by the Occupational and Personal Pension Schemes (Automatic Enrolment) (Amendment) Regulations 2015, SI 2015/501, regs 2, 4, as from 1 April 2015.

[2.1158]
5A Exemption of European employers

Sections 2(1), 3(2), 5(2), 7(3), 9(2) and 54 of the Act (employer's obligations regarding membership of a qualifying scheme) do not apply in relation to a person's employment of an individual in relation to whom the person is a European employer.]

NOTES

Part 1A (originally reg 5A only) inserted by the Occupational and Personal Pension Schemes (Automatic Enrolment) (Amendment) (No 2) Regulations 2012, SI 2012/1477, reg 2.

[2.1159]
[5B Notice of termination of employment

(1) This regulation applies, subject to paragraph (3), where notice of termination of a worker's employment is given before the end of the period of six weeks beginning with the automatic enrolment date or automatic re-enrolment date, as the case may be.

(2) Where this regulation applies—
(a) sections 3(2) (automatic enrolment) and 5(2) (automatic re-enrolment) of the Act are to be read as if for "must" there were substituted "may";
(b) section 7(3) (jobholder's right to opt in) of the Act is to be read as if there were inserted at the end—

"unless notice of termination of employment of that jobholder has been given (and the jobholder and the employer have not agreed that such notice is withdrawn)".

Part 2 Statutory Instruments

(c) section 9(2) (workers without qualifying earnings) of the Act is to be read as if there were inserted at the end—

"unless notice of termination of employment of that worker has been given (and the worker and the employer have not agreed that such notice is withdrawn)".

(3) Where a jobholder and employer agree that the notice of termination of the jobholder's employment referred to in this regulation is withdrawn, paragraphs (1) and (2) cease to apply on the date of that agreement and, subject to paragraph (4), for the purposes of sections 3(2) and 5(2) of the Act, as the case may be—

(a) the automatic enrolment date; or

(b) the automatic re-enrolment date,

is the date of that agreement.

(4) Where, on the date referred to in paragraph (3), section 3 or 5, as the case may be, does not apply to the jobholder, the next date on which one of those sections applies to that jobholder is to be taken as the automatic enrolment date or automatic re-enrolment date, as the case may be, in relation to that jobholder.]

NOTES

Commencement: 1 April 2015.

Regs 5B–5F inserted by the Occupational and Personal Pension Schemes (Automatic Enrolment) (Amendment) Regulations 2015, SI 2015/501, regs 2, 5, as from 1 April 2015.

[2.1160]

[5C Former members

(1) This regulation applies where a person (P) is a jobholder and—

(a) P ceased to be an active member of a qualifying scheme because of an action or omission by P or an action by the employer at P's request; or

(b) at a time when P was a worker, but not a jobholder, ceased to be an active member of a scheme which would have been a qualifying scheme in relation to P, had P been a jobholder, because of an action or omission by P or an action by the employer at P's request.

(2) This regulation also applies where a jobholder gives notice under section 8 of the Act (jobholder's right to opt out).

(3) Where this regulation applies in relation to the jobholder mentioned in paragraphs (1) or (2)—

(a) during the period of 12 months beginning with the date that jobholder ceased to be an active member or gives notice, sections 3(2) and 5(2) of the Act are to be read as if for "must" there were substituted "may"; and

(b) after the expiry of that period, section 3(2) of the Act does not apply.]

NOTES

Commencement: 1 April 2015.

Inserted as noted to reg 5B at **[2.1159]**.

[2.1161]

[5D Tax protection

(1) This regulation applies where an employer has reasonable grounds to believe that one of the following provisions applies in relation to a jobholder—

(a) paragraph 7 (primary protection) or 12 (enhanced protection) of Schedule 36 (pension schemes etc: transitional provisions and savings) to the Finance Act 2004;

(b) paragraph 14 of Schedule 18 to the Finance Act 2011(fixed protection 2012);

(c) paragraph 1 of Schedule 22 to the Finance Act 2013 (fixed protection 2014);

(d) paragraph 1 of Schedule 6 to the Finance Act 2014 (individual protection 2014);

[(e) paragraph 1 (fixed protection 2016) or 9 (individual protection 2016) of Schedule 4 to the Finance Act 2016].

(2) Where this regulation applies, in relation to the jobholder referred to in paragraph (1), sections 3(2) and 5(2) of the Act are to be read as if for "must" there were substituted "may".]

NOTES

Commencement: 1 April 2015.

Inserted as noted to reg 5B at **[2.1159]**.

Para (1): sub-para (e) added by the Occupational and Personal Pension Schemes (Automatic Enrolment) (Amendment) Regulations 2017, SI 2017/79, reg 2, as from 6 March 2017.

[2.1162]

[5E Winding-up lump sum

(1) This regulation applies to a worker where—

(a) that worker has received a winding-up lump sum as defined in paragraph 10 of Schedule 29 to the Finance Act 2004 (winding-up lump sums) ("paragraph 10");

(b) at the time the winding-up lump sum was paid, the worker was employed by the person mentioned in sub-paragraph (1)(c) of paragraph 10; and

(c) during the period of 12 months beginning with the date on which the winding-up lump sum was paid—

(i) the worker has ceased to be employed and been re-employed by that person; and
(ii) after re-employment, either section 3(1) (automatic enrolment) or 5(1A) or (1B) (automatic re-enrolment) of the Act applies to the worker.]

(2) In relation to the worker to whom this regulation applies—
(a) during the period of 12 months beginning with the date on which the winding-up lump sum was paid—
(i) sections 3(2) and 5(2) of the Act are to be read as if for "must" there were substituted "may"; and
(ii) sections 7 and 9 of the Act do not apply; and
(b) after the expiry of that period, section 3(2) of the Act does not apply.]

NOTES

Commencement: 1 April 2015.

Inserted as noted to reg 5B at **[2.1159]**.

Para (1): sub-para (c) substituted by the Occupational and Personal Pension Schemes (Automatic Enrolment) (Miscellaneous Amendments) Regulations 2016, SI 2016/311, reg 4(1), (2), as from 6 April 2016.

[2.1163]
[5EA Company directors

(1) This regulation applies to a jobholder who holds office as a director of the company by which that jobholder is employed.

(2) In relation to the jobholder to whom this regulation applies, sections 3(2) (automatic enrolment) and 5(2) (automatic re-enrolment) of the Act are to be read as if for "must" there were substituted "may".]

NOTES

Commencement: 6 April 2016.

Inserted, together with reg 5EB, by the Occupational and Personal Pension Schemes (Automatic Enrolment) (Miscellaneous Amendments) Regulations 2016, SI 2016/311, reg 4(1), (3), as from 6 April 2016.

[2.1164]
[5EB Limited liability partnerships

(1) This regulation applies where a person (P) is a jobholder and—
(a) P is a member of a limited liability partnership;
(b) qualifying earnings are payable to P by that limited liability partnership; and
(c) P is not treated for income tax purposes as being employed by that limited liability partnership under section 863A of the Income Tax (Trading and other Income) Act 2005 (limited liability partnerships: salaried members).

(2) Where this regulation applies, in relation to the jobholder referred to in paragraph (1), sections 3(2) and 5(2) of the Act are to be read as if for "must" there were substituted "may".]

NOTES

Commencement: 6 April 2016.

Inserted as noted to reg 5EA at **[2.1163]**.

[2.1165]
[5F Effect of exercise of discretion

(1) This regulation applies to an employer who—
(a) exercises a discretion under section 3(2) or 5(2) of the Act, as conferred by regulations 5B, 5C, 5D[, 5E, 5EA or 5EB], so that the prescribed arrangements are made whereby the jobholder will become an active member of an automatic enrolment scheme;
(b) makes the arrangements referred to in section 7(3) of the Act for a jobholder, unless notice of termination of employment of that jobholder has been given (and the jobholder and the employer have not agreed that such notice is withdrawn); or
(c) makes the arrangements referred to in section 9(2) of the Act for a worker, unless notice of termination of employment of that worker has been given (and the worker and the employer have not agreed that such notice is withdrawn).

(2) In relation to the employer to whom this regulation applies, the employer is to be treated for all purposes as if the employer were acting under the duty which would apply by virtue of section 3(2) or 5(2) of the Act or were required to make the arrangements in section 7(3) or 9(2) of the Act but for the provisions of this Part.]

NOTES

Commencement: 1 April 2015.

Inserted as noted to reg 5B at **[2.1159]**.

Para (1): words in square brackets substituted by the Occupational and Personal Pension Schemes (Automatic Enrolment) (Miscellaneous Amendments) Regulations 2016, SI 2016/311, reg 4(1), (4), as from 6 April 2016.

PART 2
AUTOMATIC ENROLMENT, OPT OUT AND REFUNDS

[2.1166]

6 Arrangements to achieve active membership

(1) The arrangements the employer must make in accordance with section 3(2) (automatic enrolment) of the Act are to enter into arrangements with—

(a) the trustees or managers of an automatic enrolment scheme which is an occupational pension scheme, so that before the end of a period of [six weeks] beginning with the automatic enrolment date the jobholder to whom section 3 of the Act applies becomes an active member of that scheme with effect from the automatic enrolment date; or

(b) the provider of an automatic enrolment scheme which is a personal pension scheme, so that before the end of a period of [six weeks] beginning with the automatic enrolment date the jobholder to whom section 3 of the Act applies is given information about the terms and conditions of the agreement to be deemed to exist under paragraph (2).

(2) Where the employer enters into arrangements with a personal pension scheme provider under paragraph (1)(b), the jobholder is deemed to have entered into an agreement to be an active member of that scheme with effect from the automatic enrolment date, on the later of—

(a) the date on which the personal pension scheme provider gives the information required by paragraph (1)(b); or

(b) the date on which the employer gives the jobholder the enrolment information in accordance with regulation 7(1)(a).

(3) The terms and conditions of an agreement deemed to exist under paragraph (2) must, as a minimum—

(a) explain the purpose of the personal pension scheme;

(b) specify the services to be provided by the personal pension scheme provider;

(c) specify the value of any contributions payable by the jobholder, where this information is available to the personal pension scheme provider;

(d) specify the charges which may be payable to the personal pension scheme provider; and

(e) in the absence of a choice made by the jobholder, explain the investment strategy adopted by the personal pension scheme provider in relation to any contributions payable to the scheme by or in respect of the jobholder.

(4) In paragraph (1)(b) the reference to "terms and conditions" is a reference to the terms and conditions mentioned in paragraph (3).

NOTES

Para (1): words in square brackets substituted by the Automatic Enrolment (Miscellaneous Amendments) Regulations 2013, SI 2013/2556, reg 5(1), (4).

[2.1167]

7

(1) Subject to paragraph (2), for the purposes of the arrangements under section 3(2) of the Act, at any time before the end of a period of [six weeks] beginning with the automatic enrolment date, the employer must give—

(a) the jobholder the enrolment information in writing; and

(b) the trustees or managers of the occupational pension scheme or the personal pension scheme provider the jobholder information in writing.

(2) The requirement in paragraph (1)(b) does not apply in relation to the information specified in regulation 3(1)(g), (h), (i), (j) or (k), where the trustees or managers of the occupational pension scheme notify, or the personal pension scheme provider notifies, the employer that they do not require that piece of information for the purposes of arrangements under section 3(2) of the Act.

(3) Where the information referred to in regulation 3(1)(f) is not available to the employer on the automatic enrolment date, the employer must give the trustees or managers of the occupational pension scheme or the personal pension scheme provider that information within [six weeks] from the date on which the employer receives it.

NOTES

Words in square brackets substituted by the Automatic Enrolment (Miscellaneous Amendments) Regulations 2013, SI 2013/2556, reg 5(1), (4).

[2.1168]

8

An employer must, on or after the automatic enrolment date, deduct any contributions payable by the jobholder to the scheme, from . . . qualifying earnings or pensionable pay due to the jobholder . . .

NOTES

Words omitted revoked by the Automatic Enrolment (Miscellaneous Amendments) Regulations 2013, SI 2013/2556, reg 5(1), (5).

[2.1169]
9 Opting Out

(1) A jobholder who has become an active member of an occupational pension scheme or a personal pension scheme in accordance with arrangements under section 3(2) of the Act, may opt out by giving their employer a valid opt out notice obtained and given in accordance with this regulation.

(2) Where the jobholder has become an active member of an occupational pension scheme, the jobholder must give their employer a valid opt out notice within a period of one month beginning with the later of—

(a) the date on which the jobholder became an active member of the scheme in accordance with regulation 6(1)(a), or

(b) the date on which the jobholder was given the enrolment information.

(3) Where the jobholder has become an active member of a personal pension scheme, the jobholder must give their employer a valid opt out notice within a period of one month beginning with the date on which the agreement was deemed to exist under regulation 6(2).

(4) Subject to paragraph (5), the jobholder may only obtain an opt out notice from the scheme in which the jobholder is an active member.

(5) Where the jobholder is an active member of a scheme which is an occupational pension scheme and that scheme has, in its trust instrument, expressly delegated its administrative functions to the employer, the jobholder may obtain an opt out notice from that employer.

(6) An opt out notice is valid if—

[(a) it includes the wording set out in Schedule 1;

(aa) it includes statements from the jobholder to the effect that the jobholder wishes to opt out of pension saving and understands that, in so doing, the jobholder will lose the right to pension contributions from the employer and may have a lower income upon retirement;]

(b) it includes the jobholder's name;

(c) it includes the jobholder's national insurance number or date of birth;

(d) it is signed by the jobholder or, where the notice is in an electronic format, it must include a statement confirming that the jobholder personally submitted the notice; and

(e) it is dated.

(7) Where the employer is given an opt out notice which is not valid—

(a) the employer must inform the jobholder of the reason for the invalidity, and

(b) paragraphs (2) and (3) are modified so that for the reference to "one month" there is substituted "6 weeks".

[(8) Where an employer has accepted as valid an opt out notice prior to the coming into force of the 2013 Regulations, the notice is deemed to be valid on the coming into force of the 2013 Regulations.

(9) In this regulation "the 2013 Regulations" means the Automatic Enrolment (Miscellaneous Amendments) Regulations 2013.]

NOTES

Para (6): sub-paras (a), (aa) substituted (for the original para (a)) by the Automatic Enrolment (Miscellaneous Amendments) Regulations 2013, SI 2013/2556, reg 5(1), (6)(a).

Paras (8), (9): added by SI 2013/2556, reg 5(1), (6)(b).

[2.1170]
10

Where an employer is given a valid opt out notice, the employer must inform the scheme in which the jobholder is an active member that a valid opt out notice has been received.

[2.1171]
11 Refunds

(1) Where an employer receives a valid opt out notice, that employer must refund to the jobholder before the refund date any contributions paid to the scheme by the jobholder and any contributions made on behalf of the jobholder, except where any of those refunds are required to be paid as tax.

(2) Where a scheme receives the information required by regulation 10, the trustees or managers of the occupational pension scheme or the provider of the personal pension scheme, as the case may be, must refund to the employer before the refund date any contributions made to the scheme by the jobholder and any contributions made to the scheme by the employer on behalf or in respect of the jobholder.

(3) For the purposes of this regulation "the refund date" is—

(a) the date one month from the date on which the employer is given a valid opt out notice; or

(b) where the opt out notice is given to the employer after the employer's payroll arrangements have closed, the last day of the second applicable pay reference period following the date on which a valid opt out notice is given.

PART 3
AUTOMATIC RE-ENROLMENT

[2.1172]
12 Automatic re-enrolment dates

(1) Subject to paragraphs . . . (3) and (4), the automatic re-enrolment date for the purposes of section 5 (automatic re-enrolment) of the Act—

(a) is the date chosen at the discretion of the employer, within a period [beginning 3 months before, and ending at the end of the period of 3 months beginning with,] the third anniversary of the staging date; and
(b) thereafter, is the date chosen at the discretion of the employer, within a period [beginning 3 months before, and ending at the end of the period of 3 months beginning with,] the third anniversary of the date chosen for the previous automatic re-enrolment date.

(2) . . .

(3) In a case under section 6(4) of the Act, the automatic re-enrolment date for the purposes of section 5 is the day after the day on which [the jobholder ceases to be an active member of the scheme].

(4) In a case under section 6(5) of the Act, the automatic re-enrolment date for the purposes of section 5 is the first day on which all the requirements of section 1(1) (jobholders) of the Act are met (so that the person is a jobholder from that date).

NOTES

Words omitted revoked, and words in square brackets substituted, by the Automatic Enrolment (Miscellaneous Amendments) Regulations 2012, SI 2012/215, regs 17, 21.

[2.1173]
13 Arrangements to achieve active membership

(1) Except where the jobholder becomes an active member of an automatic enrolment scheme under paragraph (2), the arrangements in regulations 6, 7 and 8 are the arrangements prescribed to achieve active membership for the purposes of section 5 of the Act, but with the following modifications—
(a) in regulation 6 for all references to "section 3" substitute "section 5";
(b) in regulations 6, 7 and 8 for all references to "section 3(2)" substitute "section 5(2)"; and
(c) in regulations 6, 7 and 8 for all references to "the automatic enrolment date" substitute "the automatic re-enrolment date".

(2) Subject to paragraph (3), where before the jobholder's automatic re-enrolment date, the jobholder is a member of a personal pension scheme, or in a case under section 6(5) of the Act a member of a personal pension scheme or an occupational pension scheme, the employer may meet the obligation in section 5(2) of the Act by—
(a) before the end of a period of [six weeks] beginning with the automatic re-enrolment date, entering into arrangements with the provider or the trustees or managers of the scheme of which the jobholder is a member so that—
(i) the scheme is an automatic enrolment scheme; and
(ii) the jobholder is an active member of that scheme; and
(b) satisfying the requirements of regulation 7, as if for all references in regulation 7 to "section 3(2)" there was substituted "section 5(2)" and for all references to "the automatic enrolment date" there was substituted "the automatic re-enrolment date".

(3) Paragraph (2)(b) does not apply in a case under section 6(5) of the Act.

NOTES

Para (2): words in square brackets substituted by the Automatic Enrolment (Miscellaneous Amendments) Regulations 2013, SI 2013/2556, reg 5(1), (4).

14 *(Revoked by the Occupational and Personal Pension Schemes (Automatic Enrolment) (Amendment) Regulations 2015, SI 2015/501, regs 2, 6, as from 1 April 2015.)*

[2.1174]
15 Opting out

The arrangements in regulations 9 and 10 are the arrangements for the purposes of section 8 (jobholder's right to opt out) of the Act in relation to a jobholder who has become an active member of an automatic enrolment scheme under section 5 of the Act, but with the modification that in paragraph (1) of regulation 9 for "section 3(2)" substitute "section 5(2)".

[2.1175]
16 Refunds

The arrangements in regulation 11 are the arrangements for the purposes of section 8 of the Act in relation to a jobholder who has become an active member of an automatic enrolment scheme under section 5 of the Act.

17–53 *(The following Parts have been omitted for reasons of space: Part 4 (Jobholders Opting in to Pension Saving); Part 5 (Workers Joining Pension Saving); Part 6 (Postponement of Automatic Enrolment); Part 7 (Automatic Enrolment Following the Transitional Period for Defined Benefit and Hybrid Schemes); Part 7A (Certification that a Quality or Alternative Requirement is Satisfied); Part 8 (Existing Members of Qualifying Schemes); Part 9 (Automatic Enrolment Schemes); Part 10 (Exclusion as a Qualifying Scheme); Part 11 (Test Scheme); Part 12 (Hybrid Schemes); Part 13 (Non-UK Pension Schemes); Part 14 (Due Dates); Part 15 (Special Occupations); Part 16 (Review).)*

SCHEDULES

[SCHEDULE 1
INFORMATION FOR WORKERS

Regulation 9(6)(a)

[2.1176]

WHAT YOU NEED TO KNOW

Your employer cannot ask you or force you to opt out.

If you are asked or forced to opt out you can tell the Pensions Regulator—see www.thepensionsregulator.gov.uk

If you change your mind you may be able to opt back in—write to your employer if you want to do this.

If you stay opted out your employer will normally put you back into pension saving in around 3 years.

If you change job your new employer will normally put you back into pension saving straight away.

If you have another job your other employer might also put you into pension saving, now or in the future. This notice only opts you out of pension saving with the employer you name above. A separate notice must be filled out and given to any other employer you work for if you wish to opt out of that pension saving as well.]

NOTES

This Schedule was numbered as Schedule 1 by the Automatic Enrolment (Miscellaneous Amendments) Regulations 2012, SI 2012/215, regs 17, 43(2).

It was substituted by the Automatic Enrolment (Miscellaneous Amendments) Regulations 2013, SI 2013/2556, reg 5(1), (12).

[SCHEDULE 2
INFORMATION

Regulation 2, . . . 21, 24 [and 27]

NOTES

In the words above, reference omitted revoked and words in square brackets substituted, by the Occupational and Personal Pension Schemes (Automatic Enrolment) (Amendment) Regulations 2015, SI 2015/501, regs 2, 15(a), as from 1 April 2015.

[2.1177]

[**1.** A statement that the jobholder has been, or will be, enrolled into a pension scheme.]

2. The jobholder's automatic enrolment date, automatic re-enrolment date or enrolment date, as the case may be or, for a jobholder to whom regulation 28 or 29 applies, the day or date mentioned in regulation 6 as modified by regulation 28 or 29, as the case may be.

3. . . .

4. (1) The value of any contributions payable to the scheme by the employer and the jobholder in any applicable pay reference period.

(2) The information to be given to the jobholder under sub-paragraph (1) includes information on any change in the value of any contributions payable to the scheme by the employer or jobholder in any applicable pay reference period which will occur as the result of any changes to contributions brought about by the transitional periods for money purchase and personal pension schemes under section 29 of the Act (transitional periods for money purchase and personal pension schemes).

(3) The "value" of contributions may be expressed as a fixed amount or a percentage of any qualifying earnings or pensionable pay due to the jobholder in any applicable pay reference period.

5. A statement that any contributions payable to the scheme by the jobholder have been or will be deducted from any qualifying earnings or pensionable pay due to the jobholder.

6. Confirmation as to whether tax relief is or will be given [on employee contributions].

7. . . .

8. A statement that the jobholder has the right to opt out of the scheme during the opt out period.

9. A statement indicating the start and end dates of the opt out period applicable to the jobholder if that information is known to the employer but if not, a statement that the opt out period is the period determined in accordance with regulation 9(2) or (3) of the Occupational and Personal Pension Schemes (Automatic Enrolment) Regulations 2010.

10. Where the opt out notice may be obtained.

11. A statement that opting out means that the jobholder will be treated for all purposes as not having become an active member of the scheme on that occasion.

Part 2 Statutory Instruments

12. A statement that after a valid opt out notice is given to the employer in accordance with regulation 9(2) or (3) any contributions paid by the jobholder will be refunded to the jobholder by the employer.

13. A statement that where the jobholder opts out the jobholder may opt in, in which case the employer will be required to arrange for that jobholder to become an active member of an automatic enrolment scheme once in any 12 month period.

14. A statement that, after the opt out period, the jobholder may cease to make contributions in accordance with scheme rules.

15. A statement that a jobholder who opts out or who ceases active membership of the scheme will normally be automatically re-enrolled into an automatic enrolment scheme by the employer in accordance with regulations made under section 5 of the Act (automatic re-enrolment).

16. A statement that the jobholder may, by giving written notice to the employer, require the employer to make arrangements for the jobholder to become an active member of an automatic enrolment scheme and that the jobholder will be entitled to employer's contributions.

17. A statement that the worker may, where they are working or ordinarily work in Great Britain and are aged at least 16 and under 75 and are not a member of a pension scheme that satisfies the requirements of section 9 of the Act, by giving written notice to the employer, require the employer to make arrangements for the worker to become an active member of such a pension scheme.

[**18.** A statement that by giving written notice to the employer, the worker who is aged at least 16 and under 75 and—

(a) who earns more than the lower qualifying earnings limit as specified in section 13(1)(a) of the Act (and the amount must be specified in the statement) and is not an active member of a qualifying scheme, may require the employer to arrange for that worker to become an active member of an automatic enrolment scheme and will be entitled to employer's contributions; or

(b) who earns no more than the lower qualifying earnings limit as specified in section 13(1)(a) of the Act (and the amount must be specified in the statement) and is not a member of a pension scheme that satisfies the requirements of section 9 of the Act, may require the employer to arrange for that worker to become an active member of such a pension scheme but will not be entitled to employer's contributions.]

19. . . .

20. A statement that the employer has deferred automatic enrolment until the deferral date (and the date must be given).

21. A statement that the employer will automatically enrol the worker into an automatic enrolment scheme if, on the deferral date, the worker is aged 22 or more but less than state pension age, is working or ordinarily works in Great Britain, earnings of more than the amount specified in section 3(1)(c) of the Act (and the amount must be given) are payable to the worker and the worker is not already an active member of a qualifying scheme.

22. A statement that the employer intends to defer automatic enrolment in respect of that jobholder until the end of the transitional period for defined benefit and hybrid schemes.

23. . . .

24. A statement that a written notice from the worker must be signed by the worker or, if it is given by means of an electronic communication, must include a statement that the worker personally submitted the notice.

25. . . .]

NOTES

Added by the Automatic Enrolment (Miscellaneous Amendments) Regulations 2012, SI 2012/215, regs 17, 43(3), Schedule.

Paras 1, 18 substituted, paras 3, 7, 19, 23, 25 revoked, and words in square brackets in para 6 substituted, by the Occupational and Personal Pension Schemes (Automatic Enrolment) (Amendment) Regulations 2015, SI 2015/501, regs 2, 15(b)–(e), as from 1 April 2015.

EMPLOYEE STUDY AND TRAINING (QUALIFYING PERIOD OF EMPLOYMENT) REGULATIONS 2010

(SI 2010/800)

NOTES

Made: 15 March 2010.

Authority: Employment Rights Act 1996, s 63D(6)(a).

Commencement: 6 April 2010.

Note that the enabling provisions under which these Regulations are made have (as at 15 May 2019) only been brought into force with regard to employers with at least 250 employees; see the note to s 63D of the 1996 Act at **[1.937]**.

[2.1178]
1 Citation, commencement and interpretation

(1) These Regulations may be cited as the Employee Study and Training (Qualifying Period of Employment) Regulations 2010 and come into force on 6th April 2010.

(2) In these Regulations, "the 1996 Act" means the Employment Rights Act 1996.

[2.1179]
2 Duration of employment

(1) For the purposes of section 63D(6) of the 1996 Act, in order to be a qualifying employee, an employee must have been continuously employed for a period of not less than 26 weeks.

(2) In paragraph (1), a period of continuous employment means a period computed in accordance with Chapter 1 of Part 14 of the 1996 Act, as if that paragraph were a provision of that Act.

EQUALITY ACT 2010 (OFFSHORE WORK) ORDER 2010

(SI 2010/1835)

NOTES

Made: 21 July 2010.
Authority: Equality Act 2010, ss 82, 207(8).
Commencement: 1 October 2010.

[2.1180]
1 Citation, commencement, interpretation and extent

(1) This Order may be cited as the Equality Act 2010 (Offshore Work) Order 2010 and shall come into force on 1st October 2010.

(2) In this Order—

"the Equality Act" means the Equality Act 2010;
"Renewable Energy Zone" has the meaning given in section 84(4) of the Energy Act 2004.

(3) This Order does not extend to Northern Ireland.

[2.1181]
2 Application of provisions

(1) Part 5 of the Equality Act applies to offshore work as if the work were taking place in Great Britain unless it—

(a) takes place in the Northern Irish Area as defined by the Civil Jurisdiction (Offshore Activities) Order 1987; or
(b) is in connection with a ship which is in the course of navigation or a ship which is engaged in dredging or fishing.

(2) In paragraph (1)(b), "dredging" does not include the excavation of the sea-bed or its subsoil in the course of pipe laying.

[2.1182]
3 Jurisdiction over complaints arising in relation to offshore work within section 82(3)(a) and (b) of the Equality Act

In relation to offshore work within section 82(3)(a) and (b) of the Equality Act—

(1) The employment tribunal in England and Wales shall have jurisdiction to determine a complaint arising from an act taking place in the English area as defined in the Civil Jurisdiction (Offshore Activities) Order 1987, as it would have if that act had taken place in England and Wales.
(2) The employment tribunal in Scotland shall have jurisdiction to determine a complaint arising from an act taking place in the Scottish area as defined in the Civil Jurisdiction (Offshore Activities) Order 1987, as it would have if that act had taken place in Scotland.

[2.1183]
4 Jurisdiction over claims arising in relation to offshore work within section 82(3)(c) of the Equality Act

In relation to offshore work within section 82(3)(c) of the Equality Act—

(1) The High Court shall have jurisdiction to determine a claim arising from an act taking place in the English area as it would have if that act had taken place in England or Wales.
(2) The Court of Session shall have jurisdiction to determine a claim arising from an act taking place in the Scottish area as it would have if that act had taken place in Scotland.
(3) For purposes of this Article—

"offshore area" means—

(a) tidal waters and parts of the sea in or adjacent to Great Britain up to the seaward limits of the territorial sea;
(b) waters in the Renewable Energy Zone as designated by the Renewable Energy Zone (Designation of Area) Order 2004;

"the English area" means such of the offshore area adjacent to England and Wales which lies to the south of the Scottish border;

"the Scottish area" means such of the offshore area adjacent to Scotland which lies to the north of the Scottish border;

"the Scottish border" has the meaning in the Schedule to this Order.

SCHEDULE

(Definition of the Scottish border by means of points of longitude and latitude: outside the scope of this work.)

EQUALITY ACT 2010 (DISABILITY) REGULATIONS 2010

(SI 2010/2128)

NOTES

Made: 25 August 2010.
Authority: Equality Act 2010, ss 22(2)(a), (e), 207(1), (2), (4), 212(1), Sch 1, paras 1, 2(4), 3(2), 4, 7(1), Sch 21, para 6.
Commencement: 1 October 2010.
See *Harvey* L(1), (2)(B).

ARRANGEMENT OF REGULATIONS

PART 1
INTRODUCTORY

[2.1184]
1 Citation and Commencement

These Regulations may be cited as the Equality Act 2010 (Disability) Regulations 2010 and shall come into force on 1st October 2010.

[2.1185]
2 Interpretation

In these Regulations—

"the Act" means the Equality Act 2010;

"addiction" includes a dependency;

"building" means an erection or structure of any kind;

"consultant ophthalmologist" means a consultant or honorary consultant appointed in the medical speciality of ophthalmology, who is employed for the purposes of providing any service as part of the health service continued under section 1(1) and (2) of the National Health Service Act

2006, section 1(1) and (2) of the National Health Service (Wales) Act 2006, section 1(1) of the National Health Service (Scotland) Act 1978 or section 2(1)(a) of the Health and Social Care (Reform) Act (Northern Ireland) 2009;

"a second requirement duty" means a duty to comply with the second requirement contained in any of the following provisions of the Act—

(a) paragraph 2 of Schedule 2;
(b) paragraph 2 of Schedule 8;
(c) paragraph 3 of Schedule 13;
(d) paragraph 2 of Schedule 15.

PART 2
DETERMINATION OF DISABILITY

[2.1186]
3 Addictions

(1) Subject to paragraph (2) below, addiction to alcohol, nicotine or any other substance is to be treated as not amounting to an impairment for the purposes of the Act.

(2) Paragraph (1) above does not apply to addiction which was originally the result of administration of medically prescribed drugs or other medical treatment.

[2.1187]
4 Other conditions not to be treated as impairments

(1) For the purposes of the Act the following conditions are to be treated as not amounting to impairments:—

(a) a tendency to set fires,
(b) a tendency to steal,
(c) a tendency to physical or sexual abuse of other persons,
(d) exhibitionism, and
(e) voyeurism.

(2) Subject to paragraph (3) below, for the purposes of the Act the condition known as seasonal allergic rhinitis shall be treated as not amounting to an impairment.

(3) Paragraph (2) above shall not prevent that condition from being taken into account for the purposes of the Act where it aggravates the effect of any other condition.

[2.1188]
5 Tattoos and piercings

For the purposes of paragraph 3 of Schedule 1 to the Act, a severe disfigurement is not to be treated as having a substantial adverse effect on the ability of the person concerned to carry out normal day-to-day activities if it consists of—

(a) a tattoo (which has not been removed), or
(b) a piercing of the body for decorative or other non-medical purposes, including any object attached through the piercing for such purposes.

[2.1189]
6 Babies and young children

For the purposes of the Act, where a child under six years of age has an impairment which does not have a substantial and long-term adverse effect on the ability of that child to carry out normal day-to-day activities, the impairment is to be taken to have a substantial and long-term adverse effect on the ability of that child to carry out normal day-to-day activities where it would normally have that effect on the ability of a person aged 6 years or over to carry out normal day-to-day activities.

[2.1190]
7 Persons deemed to have a disability

A person is deemed to have a disability, and hence to be a disabled person, for the purposes of the Act where that person is certified as blind, severely sight impaired, sight impaired or partially sighted by a consultant ophthalmologist.

PART 3
AUXILIARY AIDS OR SERVICES

[2.1191]
8 Auxiliary aids or services

(1) The following are to be treated as auxiliary aids or services for the purposes of paragraphs 2 to 4 of Schedule 4 to the Act—

(a) the removal, replacement or (subject to paragraph (2)) provision of any furniture, furnishings, materials, equipment and other chattels;
(b) the replacement or provision of any signs or notices;
(c) the replacement of any taps or door handles;
(d) the replacement, provision or adaptation of any door bell, or any door entry system;
(e) changes to the colour of any surface (such as, for example, a wall or door).

(2) Paragraph (1)(a) does not include the provision of any item which would be a fixture when installed.

(3) It is reasonable to regard a request for a matter falling within paragraph (1) as a request for a controller of premises to take steps in order to provide an auxiliary aid or service.

(4) In paragraph (3), the "controller of premises" means—

(a) in relation to paragraph 2 of Schedule 4 to the Act, the controller of let premises;

(b) in relation to paragraph 3 of Schedule 4 to the Act, the controller of premises that are to let; and,

(c) in relation to paragraph 4 of Schedule 4 to the Act, the commonhold association.

PART 4
REASONABLE ADJUSTMENTS TO PHYSICAL FEATURES

[2.1192]
9 Reasonableness and design standards

(1) This regulation prescribes particular circumstances, for the purposes of paragraph 2 of Schedule 2 and paragraph 2 of Schedule 15 to the Act, in which it is not reasonable for a provider of services, a public authority carrying out its functions or an association to have to take the steps specified in this regulation.

(2) It is not reasonable for a provider of services, a public authority carrying out its functions or an association to have to remove or alter a physical feature where the feature concerned—

(a) was provided in or in connection with a building for the purpose of assisting people to have access to the building or to use facilities provided in the building; and

(b) satisfies the relevant design standard.

(3) Whether a physical feature satisfies the relevant design standard shall be determined in accordance with the Schedule.

[2.1193]
10 Landlord withholding consent

(1) This regulation prescribes particular circumstances in which a relevant landlord (L) is to be taken, for the purposes of Schedule 21 to the Act, to have withheld consent for alterations to premises.

(2) Subject to paragraph (3), L is to be taken to have withheld such consent where, within the period of 42 days beginning with the date on which L receives the application for consent, L—

(a) fails to reply consenting to or refusing the alteration; or

(b)

(i) replies consenting to the alteration subject to obtaining the consent of another person required under a superior leave or pursuant to a binding obligation, but

(ii) fails to seek that consent.

(3) L is not to be taken to have withheld consent for the purposes of paragraph (2) where—

(a) the applicant fails to submit with the application such plans and specifications as it is reasonable for L to require before consenting to the alteration, and

(b) within the period of 21 days beginning with the date on which he receives the application, L replies requesting the applicant to submit such plans and specifications.

(4) However, where such plans and specifications are submitted to L in response to a request made in accordance with paragraph (3)(b), L shall be taken to have withheld consent to the alteration where, within the period of 42 days beginning with the date on which he receives those plans and specifications L—

(a) fails to reply consenting or refusing the alteration; or

(b)

(i) replies consenting to the alteration subject to obtaining the consent of another person required under a superior lease or pursuant to a binding obligation, but

(ii) fails to seek that consent.

(5) L, who having sought the consent of the other person referred to in paragraphs (2)(b) or (4)(b), receives that consent, shall be taken to have withheld consent to the alteration where, within the period of 14 days beginning with the day on which he receives the consent, L fails to inform the applicant in writing that it has been received.

(6) L who, but for the requirements as to time, complies with the requirements of paragraphs (2), (4) or (5) shall be taken to have withheld consent until such time as he so complies.

(7) For the purposes of this regulation—

(a) L is to be treated as not having sought another's consent unless he—

(i) has applied in writing to that person indicating that—

(aa) the occupier has applied for consent to the alteration of the premises in order to comply with a second requirement duty; and

(bb) L has given his consent conditionally upon obtaining the other person's consent; and

(ii) submits to that other person any plans and specifications which have been submitted to L;

(b) "to reply" means to reply in writing.

[2.1194]
11 Landlord withholding consent unreasonably

(1) This regulation prescribes particular circumstances in which a relevant landlord (L) is to be taken, for the purposes of Schedule 21 to the Act, to have acted unreasonably in withholding consent for alterations to the premises.

(2) The circumstances so prescribed are that the lease provides that L shall give his consent to an alteration of the kind in question and L has withheld his consent to that alteration.

[2.1195]
12 Landlord withholding consent reasonably

(1) This regulation prescribes particular circumstances in which a relevant landlord (L) is to be taken, for the purposes of Schedule 21 to the Act, to have acted reasonably in withholding consent for alterations to premises.

(2) The circumstances so prescribed are where—

(a)

(i) there is a binding obligation requiring the consent of any person to the alteration;

(ii) L has taken steps to obtain that consent; and

(iii) that consent has not been given, or has been given subject to a condition making it reasonable for L to withhold consent; or

(b) L does not know, and could not reasonably be expected to know, that the alteration is one which the occupier proposes to make to comply with a second requirement duty.

[2.1196]
13 Landlord's consent subject to conditions

(1) This regulation prescribes particular circumstances in which a condition, subject to which a relevant landlord (L) has given consent to alterations to premises, is to be taken, for the purposes of Schedule 21 to the Act, to be reasonable.

(2) The circumstances so prescribed are where the condition is to the effect that—

(a) the occupier must obtain any necessary planning permission and any other consent or permission required by or under any enactment;

(b) the work must be carried out in accordance with any plans or specifications approved by the L;

(c) L must be permitted a reasonable opportunity to inspect the work (whether before or after it is completed);

(d) the consent of another person required under a superior lease or a binding agreement must be obtained;

(e) the occupier must repay to the L the costs reasonably incurred in connection with the giving of the consent.

[2.1197]
14 Modification of Schedule 21

(1) In relation to any case where the occupier occupies premises under a sub-tenancy, the provisions of Schedule 21 to the Act shall have effect as if they contained the following modifications.

(2) In paragraph 3(3) and (4) and 4(1), for "the landlord" substitute "the immediate landlord" in each place it occurs.

(3) After paragraph 3(3), insert the following sub-paragraph—

"(3A) Except to the extent to which it expressly so provides, any superior lease in respect of the premises shall have effect in relation to the landlord and tenant who are parties to that superior lease as if it provided—

(a) for the tenant to be entitled to give his consent to the alteration with the written consent of the landlord;

(b) for the tenant to have to make a written application to the landlord for consent if he wishes to give his consent to the alteration;

(c) if such an application is made, for the landlord not to withhold his consent unreasonably; and

(d) for the landlord to be entitled to make his consent subject to reasonable conditions.".

(4) After paragraph 4(2), insert the following sub-paragraph—

"(2A) Where the tenant of any superior lease in relation to the premises has applied in writing to his landlord for consent to the alteration and—

(a) That consent has been refused, or

(b) The landlord has made his consent subject to one or more conditions,

the occupier, tenant or a disabled person who has an interest in the alteration being made may refer the matter to a county court or, in Scotland, the sheriff.".

(5) In paragraph 5—

(a) In sub-paragraph (2), for 'the landlord' substitute "any landlord (including any superior landlord)";

(b) In sub-paragraph (3), for paragraph (a), substitute—

"(a) must grant the request if it is made before the hearing of the complaint or claim begins, unless it considers that another landlord should be joined or sisted as a party to the proceedings.".

Part 2 Statutory Instruments

[2.1198]
15 Revocation

(1) The Regulations listed in paragraph (2) are revoked.

(2) The Regulations referred to in paragraph (1) are—

(i) the Disability Discrimination (Meaning of Disability) Regulations 1996;
(ii) the Disability Discrimination (Providers of Services) (Adjustment of Premises) Regulations 2001;
(iii) the Disability Discrimination (Blind and Partially Sighted Persons) Regulations 2003;
(iv) the Disability Discrimination (Employment Field) (Leasehold Premises) Regulations 2004;
(v) the Disability Discrimination (Educational Institutions) (Alteration of Leasehold Premises) Regulations 2005;
(vi) the Disability Discrimination (Service Providers and Public Authorities Carrying Out Functions) Regulations 2005;
(vii) the Disability Discrimination (Private Clubs etc) Regulations 2005;
(viii) the Disability Discrimination (Premises) Regulations 2006.

SCHEDULE
REMOVAL OR ALTERATION OF PHYSICAL FEATURES: DESIGN STANDARDS

Regulation 9(3)

[2.1199]
1. Definition of "relevant design standard"

(1) Subject to sub-paragraph (3), a physical feature, in relation to a building situated in England or Wales, satisfies the relevant design standard for the purpose of regulation 9(2) where it accords with the relevant objectives, design considerations and provisions in Approved Document M.

(2) Subject to sub-paragraph (3), a physical feature, in relation to a building situated in Scotland, satisfies the relevant design standard for the purposes of regulation 9(2) where—

(a) it was provided in or in connection with the building on or after 30th June 1994 and before 1st May 2005 in accordance with the Technical Standards relevant in relation to that feature; or
(b) it was provided in or in connection with the building on or after 1st May 2005 in accordance with the relevant functional standards and guidance in the Technical Handbook.

(3) A physical feature does not satisfy the relevant design standard where more than 10 years have elapsed since—

(a) the day on which construction or installation of the feature was completed; or
(b) in the case of a physical feature provided as part of a larger building project, the day on which the works in relation to that project were completed.

2. Buildings in England and Wales

(1) For the purposes of this paragraph and paragraph 1(1)—

(a) "Approved Document M" means—
  (i) the 1992 edition of the document of that title approved by the Secretary of State as practical guidance on meeting the requirements of Part M of Schedule 1 to the Building Regulations 1991, first published for the Department of the Environment by Her Majesty's Stationery Office in 1991 (ISBN 011 752447 6); or
  (ii) the 1999 edition of the document of that title approved by the Secretary of State as practical guidance on meeting the requirements of Part M of Schedule 1 to the Building Regulations 1991, first published for the Department of the Environment, Transport and the Regions by The Stationery Office under licence from the Controller of Her Majesty's Stationery Office in 1998 (ISBN 011 753469 2); or
  (iii) the 2004 edition of the document of that title approved by the Secretary of State as practical guidance on meeting the requirements of Part M of Schedule 1 to the Building Regulations 2000, first published for the Office of the Deputy Prime Minister by the Stationery Office under licence from the Controller of Her Majesty's Stationery Office 2003 (ISBN 011 753901 5);
(b) "the Building Regulations" means the Building Regulations 1991 or the Building Regulations 2000.

(2) In the case of a physical feature provided as part of building works to which the Building Regulations applied, for the purposes of paragraph 1(1) Approved Document M is whichever edition is the practical guidance which was relevant in relation to meeting the requirements of the Building Regulations which applied to those building works.

(3) In any other case, for the purposes of paragraph 1(1) Approved Document M is whichever edition was the last edition published at the time when the physical feature was provided either in or in connection with the building.

(4) For the purposes of sub-paragraph (3), a physical feature is deemed to be provided in or in connection with the building on—

(a) the day upon which the works to install or construct the feature were commenced; or
(b) in the case of a physical feature provided as part of a larger building project, the day upon which the works in relation to that project were commenced.

(5) Where in relation to the physical feature in question any provision of Approved Document M refers to a standard or specification (in whole or in part), that standard or specification shall be construed as referring to any equivalent standard or specification recognised for use in any EEA state.

3. Buildings in Scotland

(1) For the purposes of this paragraph and paragraph 1(2)—

(a) "Technical standards" means the Technical Standards defined by regulation 2(1) of the Building Standards (Scotland) Regulations 1990 in effect at the time when the physical feature was provided in or in connection with the building;

(b) "Technical Handbook" means the following Technical Handbooks for non-domestic buildings issued by the Scottish Ministers as guidance meeting the requirements of the Building (Scotland) Regulations 2004:

(i) the 2004 edition of the document of that title published by Astron (ISBN 09546292 3 X); or

(ii) the 2007 edition of the document of that title published by The Stationery Office (ISBN 9780114973384); or

(iii) the 2010 edition of the document of that title published by The Stationery Office (ISBN 9780114973568).

(2) For the purposes of paragraph 1(2) and sub-paragraph (1)(a), and subject to sub-paragraph (3), a physical feature is deemed to be provided in or in connection with the building on—

(a) the day upon which the works to install or construct the feature was commenced; or

(b) in the case of a physical feature provided as part of a larger building project, the day upon which the works in relation to that project were commenced.

(3) In a case where the physical feature is provided as part of building works in relation to which an application for a warrant for the construction or conversion of the building has been made and granted, the works are deemed to have been commenced on the day upon which the application for the warrant was granted.

(4) Where in relation to the physical feature in question any provision of the Technical Standards or Technical Handbook refers to a standard or specification (in whole or in part), that standard or specification shall be construed as referring to any equivalent standard or specification recognised for use in any EEA state.

EQUALITY ACT 2010 (SEX EQUALITY RULE) (EXCEPTIONS) REGULATIONS 2010

(SI 2010/2132)

NOTES

Made: 25 August 2010.
Authority: Equality Act 2010, ss 207(1), 212(1), Sch 7, paras 4, 5.
Commencement: 1 October 2010.
See *Harvey* BI(9)(B)(11).

[2.1200]

1 Citation, commencement and interpretation

(1) These Regulations may be cited as the Equality Act 2010 (Sex Equality Rule) (Exceptions) Regulations 2010 and shall come into force on 1st October 2010.

(2) In these Regulations—

"the Act" means the Equality Act 2010;

"the additional pension of a Category A retirement pension" has the same meaning as in Part II of the Contributions and Benefits Act;

"Category A retirement pension" has the same meaning as in Part II of the Contributions and Benefits Act;

"the Contributions and Benefits Act" means the Social Security Contributions and Benefits Act 1992;

"normal pension age" has the meaning given in section 180 of the Pensions Schemes Act 1993;

"pensionable age" shall be construed in accordance with section 122(1) of the Contributions and Benefits Act;

"pensionable service" includes any service in respect of which transfer credits have been allowed by the scheme;

"personal pension scheme" has the meaning given in section 1(1) of the Pension Schemes Act 1993;

"salary-related contracted-out scheme" means an occupational pension scheme which is contracted-out by virtue of satisfying section 9(2) of the Pension Schemes Act 1993 and includes a scheme which was formerly a salary-related contracted-out scheme which is subject to supervision in accordance with section 53 of that Act;

"scheme" means an occupational pension scheme;

"transfer credits" has the meaning given in section 124(1) of the Pensions Act 1995.

[2.1201]

2 Exceptions to the sex equality rule: bridging pensions

The following circumstances are prescribed for the purposes of paragraph 4 of Part 2 of Schedule 7 to the Act (State retirement pensions)—

(a) the man is in receipt of a pension from the scheme and has not attained pensionable age but would have attained pensionable age if he were a woman; and [either]

(b) an additional amount of pension is paid to the man which does not exceed the amount of Category A retirement pension that would be payable to a woman with earnings the same as the man's earnings in respect of his period of pensionable service under the scheme (assuming that the requirements for entitlement to Category A retirement pension were satisfied and a claim made)[; or

(c) an additional amount of pension is paid to the man which does not exceed the amount of any state pension under Part 1 of the Pensions Act 2014 that would be payable to a woman with earnings the same as the man's earnings in respect of his period of pensionable service under the scheme (assuming that the requirements for entitlement to a state pension under Part 1 of the Pensions Act 2014 were satisfied and a claim made)].

NOTES

Words in square brackets inserted by the Pensions Act 2014 (Consequential, Supplementary and Incidental Amendments) Order 2015, SI 2015/1985, art 34(b), as from 6 April 2016.

[2.1202]

3 Exceptions to the sex equality rule: effect of indexation

(1) The following circumstances are prescribed for the purposes of paragraph 4 of Part 2 of Schedule 7 to the Act (state retirement pensions)—

(a) the scheme is a salary-related contracted-out scheme under which the annual rate of a pension payable to or in respect of a member is increased by more than it would have been increased had the recipient been of the other sex; and

(b) the amount by which the pension increase exceeds any increase that would have applied had the member been of the other sex, does not exceed the relevant amount.

(2) In this regulation, the relevant amount means the amount by which X exceeds Y where—

X is the amount by which the additional pension of a Category A retirement pension attributable to the member's earnings factors during the member's period of pensionable service under the scheme would have been increased following an order made under section 150(9) of the Social Security Administration Act 1992 if the member had been of the other sex; and

Y is the amount (if any) by which the member's entitlement to the additional pension of a Category A retirement pension attributable to the member's earnings factors during the member's period of pensionable service under the scheme is increased following an order made under section 150(9) of that Act.

[2.1203]

4 Exceptions to the sex equality rule: use of actuarial factors which differ for men and women

(1) The factors prescribed for the purposes of paragraph 5(1) of Part 2 of Schedule 7 to the Act (actuarial factors) are actuarial factors which differ for men and women in respect of the differences in the average life expectancy of men and women and which are determined with a view to providing equal periodical pension benefits for men and women.

(2) The following benefits are prescribed for the purposes of paragraph 5(2) of Part 2 of Schedule 7 to the Act—

(a) a lump sum payment which consists of a commuted periodical pension or part of such a pension;

(b) a periodical pension granted in exchange for a lump sum payment;

(c) [a pension which is derived from] money purchase benefits within the meaning of section 181(1) of the Pension Schemes Act 1993;

[(ca) a pension which is derived from cash balance benefits within the meaning of regulation 2 of the Pensions Act 2011 (Transitional, Consequential and Supplementary Provisions) Regulations 2014;]

(d) transfer credits and any rights allowed to a member by reference to a transfer from a personal pension scheme;

(e) a transfer payment including a cash equivalent within the meaning of section 94 of the Pension Schemes Act 1993;

(f) a periodical pension payable in respect of a member who opts to take such benefits before normal pension age or in respect of a member who defers taking such benefits until after normal pension age;

(g) benefits payable to another person in exchange for part of a member's benefits and the part of the member's benefits given up for that purpose.

NOTES

Para (2): words in square bracket inserted by the Pensions Act 2011 (Transitional, Consequential and Supplementary Provisions) Regulations 2014, SI 2014/1711, reg 75, with retrospective effect (see further the note below).

Note that SI 2014/1711, reg 74 provides as follows—

"(1) Regulation 4(2)(c) (exceptions to the sex equality rule: use of actuarial factors which differ for men and women) of the Equality Act 2010 (Sex Equality Rule) (Exceptions) Regulations 2010 ("the Sex Equality Exceptions Regulations") has effect as if the amendments made by regulation 75(a) of these Regulations came into force on 1st October 2010.

(2) Where the conditions specified in paragraph (3) are satisfied, regulation 4 of the Sex Equality Exceptions Regulations has effect as if the amendments made by regulation 75(b) of these Regulations came into force on 1st October 2010.

(3) The conditions specified in this paragraph are that on or after 1st October 2010 and before the appointed day the trustees or managers of an occupational pension scheme—

(a) treated benefits specified in regulation 73(3)(a) as if they were money purchase benefits; and

(b) applied different actuarial factors for men and for women in determining the rate of a pension derived from those benefits.".

EQUALITY ACT (AGE EXCEPTIONS FOR PENSION SCHEMES) ORDER 2010

(SI 2010/2133)

NOTES

Made: 25 August 2010.

Authority: Equality Act 2010, ss 61(8), 207(1), (2), (4)(a), Sch 9, para 16.

Commencement: 1 October 2010.

Note that the title is as printed in the Queen's Printers' copy of this Order, ie. without the year "2010" after the words "Equality Act". This appears to be a drafting oversight.

See *Harvey* BI(9)(B)(11), L(4)(c).

ARRANGEMENT OF ARTICLES

SCHEDULES

[2.1204]

1 Citation and commencement

This Order may be cited as the Equality Act (Age Exceptions for Pension Schemes) Order 2010 and shall come into force on 1st October 2010.

[2.1205]

2 Interpretation

(1) In this Order, subject to paragraph (2), "occupational pension scheme" means an occupational pension scheme within the meaning of section 1 of the Pension Schemes Act 1993.

(2) In relation to rules, practices, actions or decisions identified at paragraph 1(a) of Schedule 1, "occupational pension scheme" means an occupational pension scheme within the meaning of section 1 of the Pension Schemes Act 1993 under which only retirement-benefit activities within the meaning of section 255(4) of the Pensions Act 2004 are carried out.

(3) In this Order, "schemes" means an occupational pension scheme, construed in accordance with paragraphs (1) and (2).

(4) In this Order, in relation to a scheme—

["abolition date" means the day appointed for the commencement of section 15(1) of the Pensions Act 2007;]

"active member" has the meaning given by section 124 of the Pensions Act 1995, but in paragraph 8 of Schedule 1 also includes an active member within the meaning of section 151(2) of the Finance Act;

"additional state retirement pension" means the additional pension in the Category A retirement pension within the meaning of sections 44 and 45 of the Social Security Contributions and Benefits Act 1992;

"age related benefit" means benefit provided from a scheme to a member—

(a) on or following the member's retirement (including early retirement on grounds of ill health or otherwise),
(b) on the member reaching a particular age, or
(c) on termination of the member's service in an employment;

"basic [state] retirement pension" means the basic pension in the Category A retirement pension within the meaning of section 44 of the Social Security Contributions and Benefits Act 1992;

"block transfer" means a transfer in a single transaction or series of transactions from a scheme of all the sums or assets held for the purposes of, or representing, or derived from—

(a) all accrued rights under a scheme,
(b) contracted-out rights, or
(c) rights which are not contracted-out rights,

relating to a period of continuous pensionable service (or pensionable service which is treated as continuous) or one or more of a number of separate periods of such pensionable service which relate to a member and at least one other member;

["contracted-out rights" are such rights under, or derived from, an occupational pension scheme as fall within the following categories—

(a) entitlement to payment of, or accrued rights to, guaranteed minimum pensions; or

(b) section 9(2B) rights;]

"death benefit" means benefit payable from a scheme in respect of a member, in consequence of that member's death;

"defined benefits arrangement" has the meaning given by section 152(6) of the Finance Act, but the reference in that section to an arrangement shall be read as referring to an arrangement in respect of a member under a scheme as defined in section 1 of the Pension Schemes Act 1993 rather than in respect of a member under a pension scheme as defined in section 150(1) of the Finance Act;

"dependant" means a widow, widower or surviving civil partner, or a dependant as defined in the scheme rules;

"early retirement pivot age" means, in relation to age related benefit provided under a scheme, an age specified in the scheme rules (or otherwise determined) as the earliest age at which entitlement arises—

(a) without consent (whether of an employer, trustee or managers of the scheme or otherwise), and

(b) without an actuarial reduction,

but disregarding any special provision as to early payment on grounds of ill health or otherwise;

"the Finance Act" means the Finance Act 2004;

"guaranteed minimum pension" has the meaning given in section 8(2) of the Pension Schemes Act 1993;

"late retirement pivot age" means an age specified in the scheme rules (or otherwise determined) above which benefit becomes payable with actuarial enhancement;

"lower earnings limit" means the amount specified for the tax year in question in regulations made under section 5(1)(a)(i) of the Social Security Contributions and Benefits Act 1992 (earnings limits and thresholds for Class 1 contributions);

"member" means any active member, deferred member, or pensioner member, but in paragraph 7 includes any active, deferred or pensioner member within the meaning of section 151(2) to (4) of the Finance Act;

"money purchase arrangement" has the meaning given by section 152(2) of the Finance Act, but the reference in that section to an arrangement shall be read as referring to an arrangement in respect of a member under a scheme as defined in section 1 of the Pension Schemes Act 1993 rather than in respect of a member under a pension scheme as defined in section 150(1) of the Finance Act;

"non-discrimination rule" means the rule in section 61 of the Equality Act 2010 as it applies to the protected characteristic of age under that Act;

"normal pension age" has the meaning given by section 180 of the Pension Schemes Act 1993;

"normal retirement age", in relation to a member, means the age at which workers in the undertaking for which the member worked at the time of the member's retirement, and who held the same kind of position as the member held at retirement, were normally required to retire;

"pensionable pay" means that part of a member's pay which counts as pensionable pay under the scheme rules;

"prospective member" means any person who, under the terms of the person's employment, or the scheme rules, or both—

(a) is able, at the person's option, to become a member of the scheme,

(b) shall become so able if the person continues in the same employment for a sufficient period of time,

(c) shall be so admitted to it automatically unless the person makes an election not to become a member, or

(d) may be admitted to it subject to the consent of any person;

"protected rights" has the meaning given in section 10 of the Pension Schemes Act 1993 [as it had effect immediately prior to the abolition date];

"redundancy" means being dismissed by reason of redundancy for the purposes of the Employment Rights Act 1996;

"relevant transfer" has the meaning given in—

(a) regulation 2(1) of the Transfer of Undertakings (Protection of Employment) Regulations 1981 (a relevant transfer), or as the case may be,

(b) regulation 2(1) of the Transfer of Undertakings (Protection of Employment) Regulations 2006 (a relevant transfer);

"section 9(2B) rights" are—

(a) rights to the payment of pensions and accrued rights to pension (other than rights attributable to voluntary contributions) under a scheme contracted-out by virtue of section 9(2B) of the Pension Schemes Act 1993, so far as attributable to an earner's service in contracted-out employment on or after 6th April 1997; and

(b) where a transfer payment has been made to such a scheme, any rights arising under the scheme as a consequence of that payment which are derived directly or indirectly from—

(i) such rights as are referred to in sub-paragraph (a) under another scheme contracted-out by virtue of section 9(2B) of that Act; or

(ii) protected rights under another occupational pension scheme or under a personal pension scheme attributable to payments or contributions in respect of employment on or after 6th April 1997 [where the transfer took place before the abolition date];

"upper earnings limit" means the amount specified for the tax year in question in regulations made under section 5(1)(a)(iii) of the Social Security Contributions and Benefits Act 1992 (earnings limits and thresholds for Class 1 contributions).

(5) In this Order, "registered pension scheme" has the meaning given by section 150(2) of the Finance Act, and references to contributions under a money purchase arrangement shall be construed as including amounts credited to a member's account whether or not they reflect payments actually made under the scheme.

NOTES

Para (4): definition "abolition date" inserted, definition "contracted-out rights" substituted, and words in square brackets in definitions "protected rights" and "section 9(2B) rights" inserted, by the Pensions Act 2008 (Abolition of Protected Rights) (Consequential Amendments) Order 2011, SI 2011/1246, art 24. Word in square brackets in definition "basic state retirement pension" substituted by the Pensions Act 2014 (Consequential, Supplementary and Incidental Amendments) Order 2015, SI 2015/1985, art 35(1), (2), as from 6 April 2016.

[2.1206]

3 Occupational pension schemes: excepted rules, practices, actions and decisions

It is not a breach of the non-discrimination rule for the employer, or the trustees or managers of a scheme, to maintain or use in relation to the scheme,

[(a)] those rules, practices, actions or decisions set out in Schedule 1[; or

(b) rules, practices, actions or decisions as they relate to rights accrued, or benefits payable, in respect of periods of pensionable service prior to 1st December 2006 that would breach the non-discrimination rule but for this paragraph].

NOTES

Words in square brackets inserted by the Equality Act (Age Exceptions for Pension Schemes) (Amendment) Order 2010, SI 2010/2285, art 2(1), (2).

[2.1207]

4 Contributions by employers to personal pension schemes: excepted practices, actions and decisions

It is not an age contravention for the employer, in relation to the payment of contributions to any personal pension scheme in respect of a worker, to maintain or use those practices, actions or decisions set out in Schedule 2.

[2.1208]

5 Unlawfulness of rules, practices, actions or decisions

(1) The inclusion of a rule, practice, action or decision in Schedule 1 (Occupational Pension Schemes: excepted rules, practices, actions or decisions) shall not be taken to mean that, but for the exemption in Schedule 1, the use or maintenance by an employer or the trustees or managers of a scheme of the rule, practice, action or decision in relation to the scheme, would be unlawful.

(2) The inclusion of a practice, action or decision in Schedule 2 (Contributions by Employers to Personal Pension Schemes: excepted practices, actions or decisions) shall not be taken to mean that, but for the exemption in Schedule 2, the use or maintenance by an employer of the practice, action or decision in relation to the payment of contributions to a personal pension scheme in respect of a worker, would be unlawful.

[2.1209]

[6 Length of service exceptions

(1) Paragraph (2) is subject to paragraph (3).

(2) In addition to the excepted rules, practices, actions or decisions contained in Schedules 1 and 2, none of the following is a breach of the non-discrimination rule or is an age contravention, as applicable—

(a) any rule, practice, action or decision of the trustees or managers ("A") of an occupational pension scheme regarding—

(i) admission to that scheme ("admission terms"); or

(ii) the accrual of, or eligibility for, any benefit under the scheme ("benefit terms"),

where the admission terms or the benefit terms put a member ("B") of the scheme at a disadvantage when compared with another member ("C") if and to the extent that the disadvantage suffered by B is because B's length of service with an employer ("D") in relation to the scheme is less than that of C;

(b) any rule, practice, action or decision of an employer ("E") in relation to an occupational pension scheme regarding the admission terms or benefit terms where it puts a member ("F") of that scheme at a disadvantage when compared with another member ("G") if and to the extent that the disadvantage suffered by F is because F's length of service with E is less than that of G; or

(c) any practice, action or decision of an employer ("H") regarding payment of contributions in respect of a worker ("I") to a personal pension scheme or to a money purchase arrangement ("contribution terms") where it puts I at a disadvantage when compared with another worker ("J") if and to the extent that the disadvantage suffered by I is because I's length of service with H is less than that of J.

(3) Where B's, or as the case may be, F's or I's, length of service exceeds 5 years and a length of service criterion in the admission terms or, as the case may be, the benefit terms or contribution terms, puts B or F or I at a disadvantage—

(a) where paragraph (2)(a) applies, A—
 (i) must ask D to confirm whether the length of service criterion reasonably appears to D to fulfil a business need of D's undertaking (for example by encouraging the loyalty or motivation, or rewarding the experience, of some or all of his workers); and
 (ii) may rely on D's confirmation;

(b) for the purposes of sub-paragraph (a)(i), D must—
 (i) calculate B's length of service;
 (ii) provide A with details of B's length of service; and
 (iii) respond to A's request within a reasonable time;

(c) where paragraph (2)(a) or (b) or (c) applies, it must reasonably appear to D or, as the case may be, E or H, that the length of service criterion applies in such a way that it fulfils a business need of his undertaking (for example by encouraging the loyalty or motivation, or rewarding the experience, of some or all of his workers).

(4) When calculating B's or, as the case may be, F's or I's, length of service, D or, as the case may be, E or H, must calculate—

(a) the length of time the member or worker has been working for that employer doing work which that employer reasonably considers to be at or above a particular level (assessed by reference to the demands made on the member or worker, for example, in terms of effort, skills and decision making); or

(b) the length of time the member or worker has been working for that employer in total,

and it is for D or, as the case may be, E or H to decide which of sub-paragraphs (a) or (b) to use.

(5) For the purposes of paragraph (4), D or, as the case may be, E or H, shall calculate the length of time a member or worker has been working for that employer in accordance with sub-paragraphs (4) to (6) of paragraph 10 of Schedule 9 to the Equality Act 2010 (benefits based on length of service) and any reference in those sub-paragraphs to—

(a) "A" shall be read as if it were a reference to "D" or, as the case may be, "E" or "H"; and

(b) "person" (except in the phrase "person other than A") shall, where paragraph (2)(a) or (b) applies, be read as if it were a reference to "member".

(6) For the purposes of this article, a "member" shall include a "prospective member".]

NOTES

Inserted by the Equality Act (Age Exceptions for Pension Schemes) (Amendment) Order 2010, SI 2010/2285, art 2(1), (3).

SCHEDULES

SCHEDULE 1
OCCUPATIONAL PENSION SCHEMES: EXCEPTED RULES, PRACTICES, ACTIONS AND DECISIONS

Article 3

Admission to schemes

[2.1210]

1. In relation to admission to a scheme—

(a) a minimum or maximum age for admission, including different ages for admission for different groups or categories of worker;

(b) a minimum level of pensionable pay for admission where that minimum—
 (i) does not exceed one and a half times the lower earnings limit;
 (ii) does not exceed an amount calculated by reference to the lower earnings limit where the aim is more or less to reflect the amount of the basic state retirement pension; or
 (iii) does not exceed an amount calculated more or less to reflect the amount of the basic state retirement pension plus the additional state retirement pension[; or
 (iv) does not exceed an amount calculated more or less to reflect the amount of the state pension under Part 1 of the Pensions Act 2014].

The use of age criteria in actuarial calculations

2. The use of age criteria in actuarial calculations in a scheme, for example in the actuarial calculation of—

(a) any age related benefit commencing before any early retirement pivot age or enhancement of such benefit commencing after any late retirement pivot age;

(b) member or employer contributions by or in respect of a member to a scheme; or

(c) any age related benefit commuted in exchange for the payment of any lump sum.

Contributions

3. Any difference in the rate of member or employer contributions, to a scheme, by or in respect of different members to the extent that this is attributable to any differences in the pensionable pay or, where paragraph 18 applies, different accrual rates of those members.

Contributions under money purchase arrangements

4. Under a money purchase arrangement—

(a) different rates of member or employer contributions according to the age of the members by or in respect of whom contributions are made where the aim in setting the different rates is—

(i) to equalise the amount of age related benefit in respect of comparable aggregate periods of pensionable service to which members of different ages who are otherwise in a comparable situation will become entitled under the arrangement, or

(ii) to make more nearly equal the amount of the age related benefit, in respect of comparable aggregate periods of pensionable service, to which members of different ages who are otherwise in a comparable situation will become entitled under the arrangement;

(b) equal rates of member or employer contributions irrespective of the age of the members by or in respect of whom contributions are made;

(c) any limitation on any employer contributions in respect of a member or member contributions by reference to a maximum level of pensionable pay.

Contributions under defined benefits arrangements

5. Under a defined benefits arrangement, different rates of member or employer contributions according to the age of the members by or in respect of whom contributions are made, to the extent that—

(a) each year of pensionable service entitles members in a comparable situation to accrue a right to defined benefits based on the same fraction of pensionable pay, and

(b) the aim in setting the different rates is to reflect the increasing cost of providing the defined benefits in respect of members as they get older.

6. Any limitation on employer contributions in respect of a member or member contributions to a defined benefit arrangement by reference to a maximum level of pensionable pay.

Rules, practices, actions and decisions relating to benefit

7. (1) Subject to sub-paragraph (4), a minimum age for any member of a scheme to be entitled to a particular age related benefit that is paid in accordance with sub-paragraph (2) and is paid—

(a) either with or without consent (whether of an employer, the trustees or managers of the scheme or otherwise), and

(b) before the early retirement pivot age relevant to that age related benefit.

(2) The age related benefit must—

(a) be actuarially reduced on the basis that the aim is to reflect that it is paid on a date before the applicable early retirement pivot age; and

(b) not be enhanced by crediting the member with any additional periods of pensionable service or additional benefits.

(3) Sub-paragraph (1) shall also apply to different minimum ages for different groups or categories of members.

(4) Sub-paragraph (1) shall not apply to any member who retires on the grounds to which paragraph 8, 9 or 12 apply.

8. (1) A minimum age for any active or prospective members of a scheme for payment of or entitlement to a particular age related benefit before the early retirement pivot age relevant to that age related benefit where—

(a) the entitlement to the age related benefit at a minimum age applies to a member who is an active or prospective member of the scheme on 1st December 2006;

(b) the age related benefit may be paid, at a minimum age, to the active or prospective member either with or without consent (whether of an employer, the trustees or managers of the scheme or otherwise); and

(c) the age related benefit is enhanced in one or more of the ways specified in sub-paragraph (2).

(2) For the purposes of sub-paragraph (1)(c) the specified ways are the enhancement of any age related benefit payable to or in respect of the member calculated in one or more of the following ways—

(a) by reference to some or all of the years of prospective pensionable service a member would have completed if that member had remained in pensionable service until normal pension age;

(b) by reference to a fixed number of years of prospective pensionable service;

(c) by making an actuarial reduction which is smaller than if early retirement had been on grounds to which paragraph 7 applies; or

(d) by not making any actuarial reduction for early retirement.

(3) Sub-paragraph (1) shall also apply to different minimum ages for different groups or categories of active or prospective members.

9. Paragraph 8 shall continue to apply to any member who after 1st December 2006—

(a) joins a scheme as a result of a block transfer or relevant transfer;

(b) joins a scheme as a result of a block transfer or relevant transfer from a scheme to which paragraph (a) applied; or

(c) joins a scheme on the basis that it will provide the same benefits as those provided by the scheme to which paragraph 8 applied.

10. (1) A minimum age for any member of a scheme for payment of or entitlement to a particular age related benefit on the grounds of redundancy where it is enhanced in accordance with sub-paragraph (2) and paid either with or without consent (whether of an employer, the trustees or managers of the scheme or otherwise).

(2) The enhancement of any age related benefit payable to or in respect of a member on the grounds of redundancy where the enhancement is calculated in one or more of the following ways—

(a) by reference to the years of prospective pensionable service a member would have completed if that member had remained in pensionable service until normal pension age;

(b) by reference to a fixed number of years of prospective pensionable service;

(c) by making an actuarial reduction which is smaller than if early retirement had been on grounds to which paragraph 7 applies; or

(d) by not making any actuarial reduction for early retirement.

(3) Sub-paragraph (1) shall also apply to different minimum ages for different groups or categories of members.

11. An early retirement pivot age or a late retirement pivot age including—

(a) different such ages for different groups or categories of member, and

(b) any early retirement pivot age or late retirement pivot age for deferred members which is different than for active members.

12. (1) A minimum age for any member of a scheme for payment of or entitlement to a particular age related benefit on the grounds of ill health where the age related benefit is enhanced in accordance with sub-paragraph (2) and paid either with or without consent (whether of an employer, the trustees or managers of the scheme or otherwise).

(2) The enhancement of any age related benefit payable to or in respect of a member on the grounds of ill health where the enhancement is calculated in one or more of the following ways—

(a) by reference to some or all of the years of prospective pensionable service a member would have completed if he had remained in pensionable service until normal pension age;

(b) by reference to a fixed number of years of prospective pensionable service;

(c) by making an actuarial reduction which is smaller than if early retirement had been on the grounds to which paragraph 7 applies; or

(d) by not making any actuarial reduction for early retirement.

(3) Sub-paragraph (1) shall also apply to different minimum ages for different groups or categories of members.

13. (1) The calculation of any death benefit payable in respect of a member—

(a) by reference to some or all of the years of prospective pensionable service a member would have completed if that member had remained in service until normal pension age; or

(b) by reference to a fixed number of years of prospective pensionable service.

(2) Payment after a member's death of a death benefit calculated by reference to the period remaining in a pension guarantee period.

(3) For the purposes of sub-paragraph (2), a pension guarantee period means a fixed period specified in or permitted by the scheme rules beginning on—

(a) the date on which the payment of pension to or in respect of the member began, or

(b) if specified in the scheme rules, the date of the member's death on or after normal pension age where payment of pension to or in respect of that member had not begun.

(4) Any difference between the death benefits payable in respect of deferred members who die before normal pension age and the death benefits payable in respect of deferred members who die on or after normal pension age.

14. (1) Any rule, practice, action or decision where—

(a) the rate of pension to which a pensioner member is entitled is reduced at any time between age 60 and [that member's state pension age] ("the reduction date"), by either—

(i) an amount not exceeding the relevant state retirement pension rate at the reduction date, or

(ii) the rate of the pension in payment where on the reduction date the relevant state retirement pension rate is greater than the rate of that pension;

(b) from the date a member is entitled to present payment of a pension from a scheme that member is entitled to an additional amount of pension which does not exceed the amount of the basic state retirement pension plus the additional state retirement pension [or the state pension under Part 1 of the Pensions Act 2014] that would be payable at state pension age; or

(c) a member who reaches his state pension age is not entitled to, or no longer entitled to, an additional amount of pension which does not exceed the amount of the basic state retirement pension plus the additional state retirement pension [or the state pension under Part 1 of the Pensions Act 2014] that would be payable at state pension age.

(2) For the purposes of paragraph (1)—

"relevant state retirement pension rate" has the same meaning as in [regulation 4(3)(b) (pensions bridging: pensionable age on or after 6th April 2016) of the Registered Pension Schemes (Bridging Pensions) and Appointed Day Regulations 2016];

"state pension age" means the pensionable age specified in the rules in paragraph 1 of Schedule 4 to the Pensions Act 1995.

15. The actuarial reduction of any pension payable from a scheme in consequence of a member's death to any dependant of the member where that dependant is more than a specified number of years younger than the member.

16. In relation to pensioner members who have retired from a scheme on ill health grounds, discontinuation of any life assurance cover once any such members reach the normal retirement age which applied to them at the time they retired, or in relation to members to whom no such normal retirement age applied, once such members reach the age of 65.

Other rules, practices, actions and decisions relating to benefit

17. Any difference in the amount of any age related benefit or death benefit payable under a scheme to or in respect of members with different lengths of pensionable service to the extent that the difference in amount is attributable to their differing lengths of service, provided that, for each year of pensionable service, members in a comparable situation are entitled to accrue a right to benefit based upon the same fraction of pensionable pay.

18. (1) Any differences in—

(a) the fraction of pensionable pay at which any age related benefit accrues, or

(b) the amount of death benefit,

to or in respect of active or prospective members of a scheme where the differences are attributable to the aim specified in sub-paragraph (2).

(2) The aim referred to in sub-paragraph (1) is that members in a comparable situation will have the right to age related benefit or death benefit equal to the same fraction, proportion or multiple of pensionable pay—

(a) without regard to each member's length of pensionable service under the scheme, and

(b) provided that each member continues in pensionable service under the scheme until normal pension age.

(3) Any differences in age related benefits which accrue, or entitlement to any death benefits which arises, to or in respect of active or prospective members of a scheme who are in a comparable situation where—

(a) those differences are attributable to the aim specified in sub-paragraph (2), and

(b) the member's pensionable service under the arrangement ceases before normal pension age.

(4) Where sub-paragraph (1) applies, any limitation on the amount of any age related benefit or death benefit payable from a scheme where the limitation arises from imposing one or both of the following—

(a) a maximum amount on the age related benefit or death benefit which is equal to a fraction, proportion or multiple of the member's pensionable pay, or

(b) a minimum period of pensionable service.

19. Where paragraph 18 applies, different rates of member or employer contributions according to the age of the members by, or in respect of whom, contributions are made, where for each year of pensionable service members in comparable situations accrue different fractions of pensionable pay.

20. Any difference in the amount of any age related benefit or death benefit payable from a scheme to or in respect of different members to the extent that the difference in amount is attributable to differences over time in the pensionable pay of those members.

21. (1) Any limitation on the amount of any age related benefit or death benefit payable from a scheme where either or both sub-paragraphs (2) and (3) apply.

(2) The limitation results from imposing a maximum number of years of pensionable service by reference to which the age related benefit or death benefit may be calculated.

(3) The limitation arises from imposing a maximum amount on the age related benefit or death benefit which is equal to a fraction, proportion or multiple of a member's pensionable pay.

22. Any rule, practice, action or decision where any age related benefit or death benefit is only payable from a scheme where a member is entitled to short service benefit under section 71 of the Pension Schemes Act 1993 (basic principles as to short service benefit).

23. When determining a member's pensionable pay by reference to which any age related benefit or death benefit payable to or in respect of a member is calculated, to exclude from the member's remuneration an amount which—

(a) does not exceed one and a half times the lower earnings limit;

(b) does not exceed an amount calculated by reference to the lower earnings limit where the aim is more or less to reflect the amount of the basic state retirement pension; or

(c) does not exceed an amount calculated more or less to reflect the amount of the basic state retirement pension plus the additional state retirement pension[; or

(d) does not exceed an amount calculated more or less to reflect the amount of the state pension under Part 1 of the Pensions Act 2014].

Part 2 Statutory Instruments

24. Any difference in the amount of age related benefit or death benefit payable under a scheme to or in respect of members where the difference is attributable to accrual of age related benefit at a higher fraction of pensionable pay for pensionable pay over the upper earnings limit (and a lower fraction of pensionable pay for pensionable pay under the upper earnings limit) where the aim is to reflect the additional state retirement pension.

25. Any limitation on the amount of any age related benefit or death benefit payable from a scheme where the limitation—

(a) relates to—

(i) all members who joined or who became eligible to join the scheme on, after or before a particular date; or

(ii) any group or category of members who joined or who became eligible to join the scheme on, after or before a particular date; and

(b) results from imposing a maximum level of pensionable pay by reference to which the age related benefit or death benefit may be calculated.

Closure of schemes

26. The closure of a scheme, from a particular date, to workers who have not already joined it.

Closure of sections of schemes

27. (1) The closure of any section of a scheme, from a particular date, to workers who have not already joined it.

(2) For the purposes of paragraph (1)—

(a) a scheme may be divided into two or more sections, and

(b) a section of a scheme shall mean any of the groups in sub-paragraph (3).

(3) A section of a scheme shall mean any of the following—

(a) any group of members who became eligible to join, or who joined, the scheme on, after or before a particular date on the basis that particular benefits will be provided to or in respect of those members or that a particular level of contributions will be paid in respect of those members; or

(b) any group of members who became eligible to join, or who joined, the scheme as a result of a block transfer or relevant transfer.

Other rules, practices, actions and decisions

28. Increases of pensions in payment which are made to members over 55 but not to members below that age.

29. Any difference in the rate of increase of pensions in payment for members of different ages to the extent that the aim in setting the different rates is to maintain or more nearly maintain the relative value of members' pensions.

30. Any difference in the rate of increase of pensions in payment for members whose pensions have been in payment for different lengths of time to the extent that the aim in setting the different rates is to maintain or more nearly maintain the relative value of members' pensions.

31. The application of an age limit for transfer of the value of a member's accrued rights into or out of a scheme, provided that any such age limit is not more than one year before the member's normal pension age.

Registered pension schemes

32. Any rules, practices, actions or decisions relating to entitlement to or payment of benefits under a scheme which is a registered pension scheme insofar as compliance is necessary to secure any tax relief or exemption available under Part 4 of the Finance Act or to prevent any charge to tax arising under that Part of that Act, whoever is liable in relation to such charge.

33 . . .

NOTES

Para 1: sub-para (b)(iv) (and the preceding word) inserted by the Pensions Act 2014 (Consequential, Supplementary and Incidental Amendments) Order 2015, SI 2015/1985, art 35(1), (3)(a), as from 6 April 2016.

Para 14: words in square brackets in sub-paras (1)(a), (2) substituted by the Equality Act (Age Exceptions for Pension Schemes) (Amendment) Order 2019, SI 2019/879, art 2, as from 15 May 2019; words in square brackets in sub-para (1)(b), (c) inserted by SI 2015/1985, art 35(1), (3)(b), (c), as from 6 April 2016.

Para 23: sub-para (d) (and the preceding word) inserted by SI 2015/1985, art 35(1), (3)(d), as from 6 April 2016.

Para 33: revoked by the Equality Act (Age Exceptions for Pension Schemes) (Amendment) Order 2010, SI 2010/2285, art 2(1), (4).

SCHEDULE 2
CONTRIBUTIONS BY EMPLOYERS TO PERSONAL PENSION SCHEMES: EXCEPTED PRACTICES, ACTIONS OR DECISIONS

Article 4

Contributions by employers

[2.1211]
1. Different rates of contributions by an employer to a personal pension scheme according to the age of the workers in respect of whom the contributions are made where the aim in setting the different rates is—

(a) to equalise the amount of age related benefit, derived from contributions made each year by the employer, to which workers of different ages who are otherwise in a comparable situation will become entitled under their personal pension schemes, or

(b) to make more nearly equal the amount of the age related benefit, derived from contributions made each year by the employer, to which workers of different ages who are otherwise in a comparable situation will become entitled under their personal pension schemes.

2. Any difference in the rate of contributions by an employer to a personal pension scheme in respect of different workers to the extent that this is attributable to any differences in remuneration payable to those workers.

3. Any limitation on any contributions by an employer, to a personal pension scheme, by reference to a maximum level of remuneration.

4. A minimum age for commencement of payment of contributions by an employer to a personal pension scheme in respect of a worker.

5. Different minimum ages for commencement of payment of contributions by an employer to a personal pension scheme in respect of different groups or categories of workers.

6. Equal rates of contributions by an employer to a personal pension scheme irrespective of the age of the workers in respect of whom contributions are made.

EQUALITY ACT 2010 (QUALIFYING [SETTLEMENT AGREEMENT] SPECIFIED PERSON) ORDER 2010

(SI 2010/2192)

NOTES

Made: 2 September 2010.
Authority: Equality Act 2010, ss 147(4)(d), 207(1).
Commencement: 1 October 2010.
Words in square brackets in the Order title substituted by virtue of the Enterprise and Regulatory Reform Act 2013 (Consequential Amendments) (Employment) Order 2013, SI 2013/1956, art 2, Schedule, para 17(a).

[2.1212]
1 Citation and commencement

This Order may be cited as the Equality Act 2010 (Qualifying [Settlement Agreement] Specified Person) Order 2010 and comes into force on 1st October 2010.

NOTES

Words in square brackets substituted by the Enterprise and Regulatory Reform Act 2013 (Consequential Amendments) (Employment) Order 2013, SI 2013/1956, art 2, Schedule, para 17(n).

[2.1213]
2 Person specified

For the purpose of section 147(4)(d) of the Equality Act 2010, a Fellow of the Institute of Legal Executives practising in a solicitor's practice (including a recognised body under section 9(1) of the Administration of Justice Act 1985) is specified.

EQUALITY ACT 2010 (GENERAL QUALIFICATIONS BODIES REGULATOR AND RELEVANT QUALIFICATIONS) (WALES) REGULATIONS 2010

(SI 2010/2217)

NOTES

Made: 6 September 2010.
Authority: Equality Act 2010, ss 96(10), 97(3).
Commencement: 1 October 2010.

These Regulations apply to Wales only; see reg 1(2) at **[2.1214]**.

[2.1214]
1 Title, commencement and application

(1) The title of these Regulations is the Equality Act 2010 (General Qualifications Bodies Regulator and Relevant Qualifications) (Wales) Regulations 2010.

(2) These Regulations come into force on 1 October 2010 and apply in relation to Wales.

[2.1215]
2 The appropriate regulator

The Welsh Ministers are prescribed as the appropriate regulator in relation to a qualifications body that confers qualifications in Wales.

[2.1216]
3 Relevant Qualifications

The qualifications listed in the Schedule are prescribed as relevant qualifications in relation to conferments of qualifications in Wales.

SCHEDULE

regulation 3

[2.1217]

1. Advanced Extension Awards
2. Entry level certificate qualifications
3. Free Standing Maths Qualifications
4. Functional Skills
5. General Certificate of Education Advanced level (A and AS levels)
6. General Certificate of Secondary Education
7. The International Baccalaureate
8. Key Skills and Essential Skills Wales
9. Principal Learning and Project Qualifications
10. The Welsh Baccalaureate Qualification Core Certificate

EQUALITY ACT 2010 (QUALIFICATIONS BODY REGULATOR AND RELEVANT QUALIFICATIONS) (SCOTLAND) REGULATIONS 2010

(SSI 2010/315)

NOTES

Made: 6 September 2010.
Authority: Equality Act 2010, ss 96(10)(a), 97(3)(a).
Commencement: 1 October 2010.

[2.1218]
1 Citation and commencement

These Regulations may be cited as the Equality Act 2010 (Qualifications Body Regulator and Relevant Qualifications) (Scotland) Regulations 2010 and come into force on 1st October 2010.

[2.1219]
2 Appropriate Regulator

The Scottish Qualifications Authority is prescribed for the purposes of section 96(10)(c) as appropriate regulator in relation to a qualifications body that confers qualifications in Scotland.

[2.1220]
3 Relevant Qualification

Those qualifications known as "National Qualifications in Scotland" are prescribed for the purposes of section 97(3)(c) as relevant qualifications in relation to conferments in Scotland.

EQUALITY ACT 2010 (GENERAL QUALIFICATIONS BODIES) (APPROPRIATE REGULATOR AND RELEVANT QUALIFICATIONS) REGULATIONS 2010

(SI 2010/2245)

NOTES

Made: 9 September 2010.
Authority: Equality Act 2010, ss 96(10)(a), 97(3)(a).
Commencement: 1 October 2010.

[2.1221]
1 Citation, commencement and application

(1) These Regulations may be cited as the Equality Act 2010 (General Qualifications Bodies) (Appropriate Regulator and Relevant Qualifications) Regulations 2010 and come into force on 1st October 2010.

(2) Regulations 3 and 4 apply in relation to England only.

[2.1222]
2 Manner of publishing matters specified under section 96(7) of the Equality Act 2010

An appropriate regulator must publish any matter specified under section 96(7) of the Equality Act 2010 on the regulator's website.

[2.1223]
3 The appropriate regulator

The appropriate regulator in relation to a qualifications body that confers qualifications in England is the Office of Qualifications and Examinations Regulation.

[2.1224]
4 Relevant qualifications

Relevant qualifications in relation to conferments in England are those qualifications listed in the Schedule.

SCHEDULE 1

Regulation 4

[2.1225]
14–19 Diploma Principal Learning

Advanced Extension Awards

[Cambridge IGCSE]

Cambridge International Certificate

Cambridge Pre-University qualification

. . .

. . .

[English for Speakers of Other Languages (ESOL)]

Entry level certificates in GCSE subjects

Extended projects

Foundation Projects

Free Standing Maths Qualifications

Functional Skills

General Certificate of Education Advanced level (Advanced and Advanced Subsidiary levels)

General Certificate of Secondary Education

. . .

Higher projects

International Baccalaureate Diploma

[International GCSEs (level 1/2 certificates)]

. . .

. . .

NOTES

Entries in square brackets inserted, and entries omitted revoked, by the Equality Act 2010 (General Qualifications Bodies) (Appropriate Regulator and Relevant Qualifications) (Amendment) (England) Regulations 2017, SI 2017/705, reg 2(2), as from 1 September 2017.

Note: despite this Schedule being numbered as Schedule 1, these Regulations do not contain a Schedule 2.

EQUALITY ACT 2010 (STATUTORY DUTIES) (WALES) REGULATIONS 2011

(SI 2011/1064)

NOTES

Made: 3 April 2011.
Authority: Equality Act 2006, ss 153(2), 207(4).
Commencement: 6 April 2011.

ARRANGEMENT OF REGULATIONS

[2.1226]
1 Title, commencement and application

(1) The title of these Regulations is the Equality Act 2010 (Statutory Duties) (Wales) Regulations 2011.

(2) These Regulations come into force on 6 April 2011.

[2.1227]
2 Interpretation

In these Regulations—

"authority" ("*awdurdod*") means an authority specified in Part 2 of Schedule 19 to the Equality Act 2010 and "authorities" ("*awdurdodau*") is to be construed accordingly;

"employment" ("*cyflogaeth*"), "employees" ("*cyflogeion*") and "persons employed" ("*personau a gyflogir*") are to be construed in accordance with section 83 of the Equality Act 2010;

"gender pay difference" ("*gwahaniaeth cyflog rhwng y rhywiau*") means any difference between the pay of—

(a) a woman and a man; or
(b) women and men,

who are employed by an authority and where either the first or second condition is met.

The first condition is that the difference is for a reason that is related to the protected characteristic of sex.

The second condition is that it appears to the authority to be reasonably likely that the difference is for a reason that is related to the protected characteristic of sex;

"the general duty" ("*y ddyletswydd gyffredinol*") means the duty in section 149(1) of the Equality Act 2010;

"gender pay equality objective" ("*amcan cyflog cyfartal rhwng y rhywiau*") means an equality objective—

(i) that relates to the need to address the causes of any gender pay difference; and
(ii) which the authority has published;

"relevant date" ("*dyddiad perthnasol*") means 31 March;

"relevant information" ("*gwybodaeth berthnasol*") means information that relates to compliance (or otherwise) by the authority with the general duty; and

"reporting period" ("*cyfnod adrodd*") means the period 1 April to 31 March except in relation to the reporting period ending 31 March 2012 in which case "reporting period" means the period 6 April 2011 to 31 March 2012.

[2.1228]

3 Equality objectives

(1) An authority must publish objectives that are designed to enable it to better perform the general duty.

(2) The authority must also—

(a) publish a statement setting out—

(i) the steps that it has taken or intends to take in order to fulfil each objective; and

(ii) how long the authority expects it will take in order to fulfil each objective;

(b) make such arrangements as it considers appropriate for monitoring the progress that it makes and the effectiveness of the steps that it takes in order to fulfil its equality objectives.

In these Regulations such objectives are referred to as "equality objectives".

(3) If an authority does not publish an equality objective in respect of one or more of the protected characteristics it must publish reasons for its decision not to do so.

(4) Paragraph (3) applies even if an authority publishes an equality objective for the purpose referred to in regulation 11(1) (and for that reason such an objective is to be ignored for the purpose of paragraph (3)).

[2.1229]

4 Preparation and review etc of equality objectives

(1) When considering what its equality objectives should be and when designing any equality objective (or any revision to such an objective) the authority must—

(a) comply with the engagement provisions (*see* regulation 5); and

(b) have due regard to relevant information that it holds.

(2) An authority must comply with regulation 3(1) by publishing equality objectives—

(a) not later than 2 April 2012; and

(b) subsequently as it considers appropriate.

(3) An authority must review each of its equality objectives—

(a) not later than the end of the period of four years beginning with the date that the objective was first published; and

(b) subsequently at intervals not later than the end of the period of four years beginning with the date of the last review of the objective.

(4) An authority may carry out a review of any of its equality objectives at any other time.

(5) An authority may revise or remake an equality objective at any time.

(6) If an authority revises an objective without remaking it then the authority must, as soon as possible after making the revision, publish the revision or the objective as revised (as it considers appropriate).

(7) If an authority does any of the things referred to in paragraph (5) it must either amend the statement published by it under regulation 3(2) or publish a new statement.

[2.1230]

5 Engagement provisions

(1) The provisions in paragraph (2) are referred to in these Regulations as "the engagement provisions".

(2) Where any provision of these Regulations requires an authority to comply with the engagement provisions in carrying out any activity (see for example regulation 4(1)(a)), compliance with those provisions means that in carrying out that activity the authority—

(a) must involve such persons as the authority considers—

(i) represent the interests of persons who share one or more of the protected characteristics; and

(ii) have an interest in the way that the authority carries out its functions;

(b) may involve such other persons as the authority considers appropriate;

(c) may consult such persons as the authority considers appropriate.

(3) In reaching a decision under paragraph (2)(b) or (c) the authority must have regard to the need to involve or consult (as the case may be), so far as is reasonably practicable to do so, persons who—

(a) share one or more of the protected characteristics; and

(b) have an interest in the way that the authority carries out its functions.

[2.1231]

6 Accessibility of published information

(1) This regulation applies to any document or information that an authority is required by these Regulations to publish.

(2) The authority must take all reasonable steps to ensure that the document or information is accessible by persons who share one or more protected characteristics.

[2.1232]

7 Arrangements for collection etc of information about compliance with the general duty

(1) An authority must make such arrangements as it considers appropriate to ensure that, from time to time, it—

(a) identifies relevant information that it holds;

(b) identifies and collects relevant information that it does not hold; and

(c) publishes relevant information that it holds and which it considers appropriate to publish.

For further provision about what the arrangements must contain see also regulation 11(2).

(2) For the purposes of these Regulations an authority holds relevant information if—

(a) it is held by the authority, otherwise than on behalf of another person;

(b) it is held by another person on behalf of the authority; or

(c) it is held by the authority on behalf of another person and—

(i) that person has consented to the authority using the information for the purpose of compliance by the authority with the general duty and the duties under these Regulations; or

(ii) use of the information by the authority for the purpose of compliance by it with those duties meets the conditions in paragraph (3).

(3) The conditions referred to in paragraph (2)(c)(ii) are that the use of the information by the authority—

(a) is not contrary to law; and

(b) is reasonable, having regard to all the circumstances including, in particular, the nature of the information and the circumstances in which it was obtained by the authority.

(4) The identification of relevant information includes identifying such information by means of carrying out an assessment of whether there are—

(a) things done by the authority that contribute to the authority complying (or otherwise) with the general duty; and

(b) things that it could do that would be likely to contribute to compliance by the authority with that duty.

(5) When carrying out an assessment referred to in paragraph (4), the authority must—

(a) comply with the engagement provisions; and

(b) have due regard to relevant information that it holds.

(6) The arrangements referred to in paragraph (1) must ensure that, not later than 2 April 2012, the authority—

(a) carries out an assessment referred to in paragraph (4); and

(b) publishes relevant information that it holds and which it considers appropriate to publish.

[2.1233]

8 Impact and monitoring of policies and practices

(1) An authority must make such arrangements as it considers appropriate for—

(a) assessing the likely impact of its proposed policies and practices on its ability to comply with the general duty;

(b) assessing the impact of any—

(i) policy or practice that the authority has decided to review,

(ii) revision that the authority proposes to make to a policy or practice,

on its ability to comply with that duty;

(c) monitoring the impact of its policies and practices on its ability to comply with that duty; and

(d) publishing reports in respect of any assessment that—

(i) is referred to in sub-paragraph (a) or (b); and

(ii) shows that the impact or likely impact (as the case may be) on the authority's ability to comply with that duty is substantial.

(2) Reports under paragraph (1)(d) must set out, in particular—

(a) the purpose of—

(i) the proposed policy or practice;

(ii) the policy or practice; or

(iii) the proposed revision to a policy or practice,

that has been assessed;

(b) a summary of the steps that the authority has taken to carry out the assessment;

(c) a summary of the information that the authority has taken into account in the assessment;

(d) the results of the assessment; and

(e) any decisions taken by the authority in relation to those results.

(3) When carrying out an assessment referred to in paragraph (1)(a) or (b) the authority must—

(a) comply with the engagement provisions; and

(b) have due regard to relevant information that it holds.

[2.1234]

9 Training and collection of employment information

(1) An authority must, in each year, collect the following information—

(a) the number of persons employed by the authority at the relevant date in that year;

(b) the number of persons employed by the authority at that date broken down by—

(i) job;

(ii) grade but only where an authority operates a grade system in respect of its employees;
(iii) pay;
(iv) contract type (including, but not limited to permanent and fixed-term contracts); and
(v) working pattern (including, but not limited to full-time, part-time and other flexible working arrangements).

(c) the number, during the reporting period ending with the relevant date in that year, of—
(i) persons who have applied for employment with the authority (excluding persons already employed by the authority);
(ii) the authority's employees who have changed position within the authority including the number who applied to change position and the number who were successful (or otherwise) in their application;
(iii) the authority's employees who have applied for training and the number who were successful (or otherwise) in their application;
(iv) the authority's employees who completed the training;
(v) the authority's employees who were or are involved in grievance procedures by reason of either being the person who made an accusation against another or being the person against whom an accusation was made;
(vi) the authority's employees who were or are the subject of disciplinary proceedings; and
(vii) the authority's employees who left the employment of the authority.

(2) In paragraph (1) (other than paragraph (1)(b)) any reference to the number of persons or employees includes, in respect of each protected characteristic, the numbers who share the protected characteristic.

(3) In paragraph (1)(b) the reference to the number of persons employed includes, in respect of the protected characteristic of sex, the number who are women and the number who are men.

(4) The authority must publish the information it has collected in accordance with paragraphs (1), (2) and (3).

(5) Nothing in this regulation is to be relied upon by an authority so as to require any person to whom this paragraph applies to provide information to the authority.

(6) Paragraph (5) applies to—
(a) any employee of the authority; and
(b) any person who applies for employment with the authority.

[2.1235]
10

An authority must make such arrangements as it considers appropriate for—
(a) promoting amongst its employees knowledge and understanding of the general duty and the duties in these Regulations; and
(b) for using its performance assessment procedures (if any) to identify and address the training needs of its employees in relation to those duties.

[2.1236]
11 Pay and action plans

(1) An authority must, when considering what its equality objectives should be, have due regard to the need to have equality objectives that address the causes of any differences between the pay of any person or persons employed by the authority ("P") who (as the case may be)—
(a) has a protected characteristic;
(b) share a protected characteristic,

and those who do not where either the first or second condition is met.

The first condition is that the difference is for a reason that is related to the fact that P has or share that protected characteristic (as the case may be).

The second condition is that it appears to the authority to be reasonably likely that the difference is for a reason that is related to the fact that P has or share that protected characteristic (as the case may be).

(2) The arrangements referred to in regulation 7(1) must also contain arrangements for identifying and collecting information about—
(a) any differences between the pay of persons referred to in paragraph (1); and
(b) the causes of any such differences.

(3) Where an authority—
(a) has, in accordance with paragraph (1), identified any gender pay difference; and
(b) has not published an equality objective to address the causes of that difference,

the authority must publish reasons for its decision not to publish such an objective.

[2.1237]
12

(1) An authority must publish an action plan setting out—
(a) any policy of the authority that relates to the need to address the causes of any gender pay difference;
(b) any gender pay equality objective published by it;
(c) any revision to a gender pay equality objective or any revised gender pay equality objective it is required to publish in accordance with regulation 4(6);
(d) information it is required to publish in accordance with regulation 3(2)(a) in respect of any gender pay equality objective;

(e) any reasons it is required to publish in accordance with regulation 11(3).

(2) If, in respect of a gender pay equality objective, an authority does any of the things referred to in regulation 4(5) it must either amend the action plan published by it or publish a new action plan.

[2.1238]

13 Review etc of arrangements

(1) An authority must keep the arrangements to which this regulation applies under review.

(2) An authority may, at any time, revise or remake the arrangements to which this regulation applies.

(3) This regulation applies to arrangements that the authority has made to comply with—

(i) regulation 3(2)(b);
(ii) regulation 7(1);
(iii) regulation 8(1); and
(iv) regulation 10.

[2.1239]

14 Strategic Equality Plans

(1) Not later than 2 April 2012, an authority must make a Strategic Equality Plan (SEP).

(2) The SEP must contain a statement setting out—

(a) a description of the authority;
(b) the authority's equality objectives;
(c) in respect of each of those objectives—
(i) the steps that the authority has taken or intends to take in order to fulfil the objective; and
(ii) how long the authority expects it will take in order to fulfil the objective;
(d) the arrangements that it has made or intends to make to comply with—
(i) regulation 3(2)(b);
(ii) regulation 7(1);
(iii) regulation 8(1);
(iv) regulation 10, and
(e) the authority's action plan referred to in regulation 12.

(3) The SEP may contain such other matters that are relevant to compliance with the general duty as the authority considers appropriate.

(4) The authority may revise or remake its SEP at any time.

[2.1240]

15 Preparation, publication and review of SEPs

(1) In making, remaking or revising a SEP the authority must—

(a) comply with the engagement provisions; and
(b) have due regard to relevant information that it holds.

(2) An authority must publish its SEP as soon as possible after the SEP is made or remade.

(3) If an authority revises its SEP without remaking it then the authority must, as soon as possible after making the revisions, publish the revisions or the SEP as revised (as it considers appropriate).

(4) An authority may comply with the duty to publish its SEP by setting out the SEP as part of another published document or within a number of other published documents.

For the purpose of this paragraph "SEP" includes any revisions to the SEP.

(5) The authority must keep under review—

(a) its SEP; and
(b) any revisions made to the SEP.

(6) In complying with the duty in paragraph (5) the authority must have due regard to—

(i) relevant information that it holds; and
(ii) any other information that the authority considers would be likely to assist it in the review.

[2.1241]

16 Reports by authorities on compliance with the general duty

(1) An authority must, in respect of each reporting period, publish a report not later than the relevant date in the year following the year in which that reporting period ends.

(2) The report must set out—

(a) the steps that the authority has taken to identify and collect relevant information;
(b) in respect of relevant information that it holds, how the authority has used that information for the purpose of complying with the general duty and the duties in these Regulations;
(c) the authority's reasons for not collecting any relevant information that it has identified but does not hold;
(d) the progress that the authority has made in order to fulfil each of its equality objectives;
(e) a statement by the authority of the effectiveness of—
(i) its arrangements for identifying and collecting relevant information; and
(ii) the steps it has taken in order to fulfil each of its equality objectives; and
(f) the information that the authority is required to publish by regulation 9(4) unless the authority has already published that information.

(3) The authority may, if it considers it appropriate to do so, include in a report any other matter that is relevant to compliance by the authority with the general duty and the duties in these Regulations.

(4) The authority may comply with the duty to publish a report under paragraph (1) by setting out its report (including any matter referred to in paragraph (3)) as part of another published document or within a number of other published documents.

[2.1242]
17 Reports by Welsh Ministers on compliance with the general duty etc by authorities

(1) The Welsh Ministers must, in accordance with paragraph (2), publish reports that set out an overview of the progress made by authorities towards compliance by those authorities with the general duty.

(2) Reports under paragraph (1) must—

(a) be published—

(i) not later than 31 December 2014; and

(ii) subsequently at intervals not later than the end of each successive period of four years beginning with the date that the last report was published in accordance with this sub-paragraph; and

(b) be published—

(i) not later than 31 December 2016; and

(ii) subsequently at intervals not later than the end of each successive period of four years beginning with the date that the last report was published in accordance with this sub-paragraph.

(3) Reports under paragraph (1), other than the first reports in accordance with paragraph (2)(a)(i) and (b)(i), must cover the period since the date that the last report under paragraph (2)(b) was published.

(4) The Welsh Ministers must publish a report, not later than 31 December 2011, setting out—

(a) an overview of the progress made by authorities towards compliance by them with the general duty so far as it relates to persons who share the protected characteristic of disability; and

(b) information relating to the period 2 December 2008 to 5 April 2011 that the Welsh Ministers would have been required to include in a report under regulation 5 of the Disability Discrimination (Public Authorities) (Statutory Duties) Regulations 2005 by virtue of regulation 5(2)(a) of those regulations if those regulations were in force.

(5) Reports under this regulation must also set out the Welsh Ministers' proposals for the coordination of action by authorities so as to bring about further progress towards compliance by those authorities with the general duty.

[2.1243]
18 Public procurement

(1) Where an authority that is a contracting authority proposes to enter into a relevant agreement on the basis of an offer which is the most economically advantageous it must have due regard to whether the award criteria should include considerations relevant to its performance of the general duty.

(2) Where an authority that is a contracting authority proposes to stipulate conditions relating to the performance of a relevant agreement it must have due regard to whether the conditions should include considerations relevant to its performance of the general duty.

(3) In this regulation—

"contracting authority" ("*awdurdod contractio*"), "framework agreement" ("*cytundeb fframwaith*") and "public contracts" ("*contractau cyhoeddus*") have the same meaning as in *the Public Sector Directive*; and

"relevant agreement" ("*cytundeb perthnasol*") means the award of a public contract or the conclusion of a framework agreement that is regulated by *the Public Sector Directive*.

NOTES

Para (3): for the words "the Public Sector Directive" in both places they appear, there are substituted the words "the Public Contracts Regulations 2015", by the Equality Act 2010 (Statutory Duties) (Wales) (Amendment) (EU Exit) Regulations 2019, SI 2019/120, reg 2, as from exit day (as defined in the European Union (Withdrawal) Act 2018, s 20).

[2.1244]
19 Compliance with duties by Welsh Ministers etc

Where the Welsh Ministers, the First Minister for Wales and the Counsel General to the Welsh Assembly Government are required by these Regulations to prepare a SEP, publish a report or do any other thing, they may comply with the duty by acting jointly.

NOTES

Welsh Assembly Government: see the Wales Act 2014, s 4 which provides that, unless the context requires otherwise, any reference to the Welsh Assembly Government is to be read as, or as including, a reference to the Welsh Government.

[2.1245]
20 Disclosure of information

Nothing in these Regulations is to be taken to require an authority to publish information if—

(a) to do so would constitute a breach—

(i) of confidence actionable by any person; or

(ii) of the Data Protection Act 1998; or

(b) the authority would be entitled to refuse to produce the information in or for the purposes of proceedings in a court or tribunal in England and Wales.

EQUALITY ACT 2010 (WORK ON SHIPS AND HOVERCRAFT) REGULATIONS 2011

(SI 2011/1771)

NOTES

Made: 18 July 2011.
Authority: Equality Act 2010, ss 81, 207(1), (4)(b), 212(1).
Commencement: 1 August 2011.

ARRANGEMENT OF REGULATIONS

[2.1246]
1 Citation and commencement

These Regulations may be cited as the Equality Act 2010 (Work on Ships and Hovercraft) Regulations 2011 and come into force fourteen days after the day on which they are made.

[2.1247]
2 Interpretation

(1) In these Regulations—

"the Act" means the Equality Act 2010;

"British citizen" has the same meaning as in the British Nationality Act 1981;

"designated state" means the countries of the African, Caribbean and Pacific Group of States, the Kingdom of Morocco, Montenegro, the Most Serene Republic of San Marino, the People's Democratic Republic of Algeria, the Principality of Andorra, the Republic of Albania, the Republic of Croatia, the Republic of Macedonia, the Republic of Tunisia, the Republic of Turkey, the Russian Federation or the Swiss Confederation;

"United Kingdom ship" means a ship registered in the United Kingdom under Part II of the Merchant Shipping Act 1995, and

"United Kingdom waters" means the sea or other waters within the seaward limits of the territorial sea of the United Kingdom.

(2) For the purposes of regulations 3(3)(c) and 4(2)(b)—

(a) the legal relationship of the seafarer's employment is located within Great Britain if the contract under which the seafarer is employed—
 (i) was entered into in Great Britain; or
 (ii) takes effect in Great Britain,

(b) whether the legal relationship of the seafarer's employment retains a sufficiently close link with Great Britain is to be determined by reference to all relevant factors including—
 (i) where the seafarer is subject to tax;
 (ii) where the employer or principal is incorporated;
 (iii) where the employer or principal is established;
 (iv) where the ship or hovercraft on which the seafarer works is registered.

[2.1248]
3 Application of Part 5 of the Act to seafarers working wholly or partly in Great Britain and adjacent waters

(1) Part 5 of the Act applies to a seafarer who works wholly or partly within Great Britain (including United Kingdom waters adjacent to Great Britain) if the seafarer is on—

(a) a United Kingdom ship and the ship's entry in the register maintained under section 8 of the Merchant Shipping Act 1995 specifies a port in Great Britain as the ship's port of choice, or

(b) a hovercraft registered in the United Kingdom and operated by a person whose principal place of business, or ordinary residence, is in Great Britain.

(2) Part 5 of the Act, except in relation to the protected characteristic of marriage and civil partnership, also applies to a seafarer who works wholly or partly within Great Britain (including United Kingdom waters adjacent to Great Britain) and who is on—

(a) a ship registered in or entitled to fly the flag of an EEA State *other than the United Kingdom*, or

(b) a hovercraft registered in an EEA State *other than the United Kingdom*,

if paragraph (3) applies.

(3) This paragraph applies if—

(a) the ship or hovercraft is in United Kingdom waters adjacent to Great Britain,
(b) the seafarer is a British citizen, or a national of an EEA State *other than the United Kingdom* or of a designated state, and
(c) the legal relationship of the seafarer's employment is located within Great Britain or retains a sufficiently close link with Great Britain.

NOTES

Paras (2), (3): the words "other than the United Kingdom" in each place they appear in italics are revoked by the Merchant Shipping (Miscellaneous Provisions) (Amendments etc) (EU Exit) Regulations 2018, SI 2018/1221, reg 4, Schedule, para 22(1), (2), as from exit day (as defined in the European Union (Withdrawal) Act 2018, s 20).

[2.1249]
4 Application of Part 5 of the Act to seafarers working wholly outside Great Britain and adjacent waters

(1) Part 5 of the Act applies to a seafarer who works wholly outside Great Britain and United Kingdom waters adjacent to Great Britain if the seafarer is on—
(a) a United Kingdom ship and the ship's entry in the register maintained under section 8 of the Merchant Shipping Act 1995 specifies a port in Great Britain as the ship's port of choice, or
(b) a hovercraft registered in the United Kingdom and operated by a person whose principal place of business, or ordinary residence, is in Great Britain,
and paragraph (2) applies.

(2) This paragraph applies if—
(a) the seafarer is a British citizen, or a national of an EEA State *other than the United Kingdom* or of a designated state, and
(b) the legal relationship of the seafarer's employment is located within Great Britain or retains a sufficiently close link with Great Britain.

NOTES

Para (2): the words in italics are revoked by the Merchant Shipping (Miscellaneous Provisions) (Amendments etc) (EU Exit) Regulations 2018, SI 2018/1221, reg 4, Schedule, para 22(1), (3), as from exit day (as defined in the European Union (Withdrawal) Act 2018, s 20).

[2.1250]
5 Differentiation in relation to pay

It is not a contravention of section 39(1)(b) or (2)(a) or 41(1)(a) of the Act, as applied by regulations 3 and 4, for an employer or principal to offer to pay or to pay a person (A) at a lower rate than that at which the employer or principal offers to pay or pays another person (B) because A is of a different nationality from B, if—
(a) A—
(i) applied for work as a seafarer, or
(ii) was recruited as a seafarer,
outside Great Britain, and
(b) A is not—
(i) a British Citizen,
(ii) a national of *another* EEA State, or
(iii) a national of a designated state.

NOTES

For the word in italics in para (b)(ii) there is substituted the word "an", by the Merchant Shipping (Miscellaneous Provisions) (Amendments etc) (EU Exit) Regulations 2018, SI 2018/1221, reg 4, Schedule, para 22(1), (4), as from exit day (as defined in the European Union (Withdrawal) Act 2018, s 20).

[2.1251]
6 Review

(1) Before the end of each review period, the Secretary of State must—
(a) carry out a review of regulations 3 to 5,
(b) set out the conclusions of the review in a report, and
(c) publish the report.

(2) In carrying out the review the Secretary of State must, so far as is reasonable, have regard to how—
(a) Council Directive 2000/43/EC of 29 June 2000 implementing the principle of equal treatment between persons irrespective of racial or ethnic origin,
(b) Council Directive 2000/78/EC of 27 November 2000 establishing a general framework of equal treatment in employment and occupation, and
(c) Directive 2006/54/EC of the European Parliament and of the Council of 5 July 2006 on the implementation of the principle of equal opportunities and equal treatment of men and women in matters of employment and occupation (recast),
are implemented in other member States in relation to work on ships and hovercraft and seafarers.

(3) The report must in particular—
(a) set out the objectives intended to be achieved by applying Part 5 of the Act to work on ships and hovercraft and seafarers,
(b) assess the extent to which those objectives are achieved, and

(c) assess whether those objectives remain appropriate and, if so, the extent to which they could be achieved by imposing less regulation.

(4) "Review period" means—

(a) the period of five years beginning with the day on which these Regulations come into force, and

(b) subject to paragraph (5), each successive period of five years.

(5) If a report under this regulation is published before the last day of the review period to which it relates, the following review period is to begin with the day on which that report is published.

TEACHERS' DISCIPLINARY (ENGLAND) REGULATIONS 2012

(SI 2012/560)

NOTES

Made: 28 February 2012.
Authority: Education Act 2002, ss 141A(2), 141D(3), 141E(3), 210(7), Sch 11A.
Commencement: 1 April 2012.
These Regulations apply only to England.

ARRANGEMENT OF REGULATIONS

[2.1252]

1 Citation and commencement

These Regulations may be cited as the Teachers' Disciplinary (England) Regulations 2012 and come into force on 1st April 2012.

[2.1253]

2 Interpretation

In these Regulations—

"professional conduct panel" means a panel appointed by the Secretary of State in accordance with regulation 6;

"teacher" means a person who is employed or engaged to carry out teaching work at—

(a) a school in England;

(b) a sixth form college in England;

(c) relevant youth accommodation in England;

(d) a children's home in England; or

(e) when section 53 of the Education Act 2011 is fully in force, a 16 to 19 Academy; and

"the prohibited list" means the list maintained by the Secretary of State under section 141C (1) of the Education Act 2002.

[2.1254]

3 Teaching work

(1) Subject to paragraph (3), each of the following activities is teaching work for the purposes of these Regulations—

(a) planning and preparing lessons and courses for pupils;

(b) delivering lessons to pupils;

(c) assessing the development, progress and attainment of pupils; and
(d) reporting on the development, progress and attainment of pupils.

(2) In paragraph (1)(b) "delivering" includes delivering lessons through distance learning or computer aided techniques.

(3) The activities specified in paragraph (1) are not teaching work for the purposes of these Regulations if the person carrying out the activity does so (other than for the purposes of induction) subject to the direction and supervision of a qualified teacher or other person nominated by the head teacher to provide such direction and supervision.

[2.1255]
4 Teachers' standards

Any decision made under these Regulations may take into account any failure by a teacher to comply with the personal and professional conduct standards set out in part two of "Teachers' Standards" published by the Secretary of State in July 2011.

[2.1256]
5 Consideration of cases

(1) This paragraph applies where the Secretary of State considers that a teacher—
(a) may be guilty of unacceptable professional conduct or conduct that may bring the teaching profession into disrepute; or
(b) has been convicted (at any time) of a relevant offence.

(2) Where paragraph (1) applies the Secretary of State must—
(a) inform the teacher of the allegation that has been made against the teacher; and
(b) give the teacher an opportunity to—
(i) submit evidence and make representations in writing; and
(ii) comment on any other relevant evidence.

(3) The Secretary of State may require any person to produce documents or other material evidence for the purposes of making the decision referred to in paragraph (4).

(4) The Secretary of State must consider all relevant evidence, representations and comments and decide whether the case should be—
(a) discontinued; or
(b) considered by a professional conduct panel,
and must inform the teacher of such decision.

(5) Where the Secretary of State decides that the case should be discontinued, the Secretary of State must at the request of the teacher publish a statement to that effect.

[2.1257]
6 Appointment and membership of a professional conduct panel

(1) Where the Secretary of State decides under regulation 5(4) that a case should be considered by a professional conduct panel, the Secretary of State must appoint such a panel in accordance with paragraph (2) to consider the case.

(2) A professional conduct panel must include at least three persons, comprising—
(a) one or more teachers or persons who have been teachers in the past five years; and
(b) one or more other persons.

[(3) In this regulation, "persons who have been teachers in the past five years" means persons who were teachers in the five years immediately before the date they were appointed by the Secretary of State as suitable to be a member of a professional conduct panel.]

NOTES

Para (3): added by the Teachers' Disciplinary (Amendment) (England) Regulations 2014, SI 2014/1685, reg 2(1), (2), as from 1 September 2014.

[2.1258]
7 Proceedings of a professional conduct panel

(1) A professional conduct panel must consider cases referred to it by the Secretary of State in accordance with paragraphs (2) to (5) and regulations 9 to 11.

(2) Subject to paragraph (3), a professional conduct panel must determine all cases following a hearing.

(3) A professional conduct panel may determine a case without a hearing at the written request of the teacher who is the subject of the case.

(4) Where the professional conduct panel does not find the case proved, the Secretary of State must at the request of the teacher publish a statement to that effect.

(5) Where a professional conduct panel finds the teacher—
(a) to have been guilty of unacceptable professional conduct or conduct that may bring the teaching profession into disrepute; or
(b) to have been convicted (at any time) of a relevant offence,
the panel must make a recommendation to the Secretary of State as to whether a prohibition order should be made.

[2.1259]
8 Decision of the Secretary of State

(1) The Secretary of State must consider any recommendation made by a professional conduct panel before deciding whether to make a prohibition order.

(2) Where the Secretary of State decides to make a prohibition order, the Secretary of State must decide—

(a) whether an application may be made for a review of the order under regulation 16; and

(b) if the Secretary of State decides such an application may be made, the minimum period before the end of which no such application may be made.

(3) The minimum period under paragraph (2) must not be less than two years from the date on which the prohibition order takes effect.

(4) Where the Secretary of State decides not to make a prohibition order, the Secretary of State must notify the teacher in writing of the decision, giving reasons for the decision.

(5) The decision of the Secretary of State following the determination of a professional conduct panel must be published.

[2.1260]
9 Entitlement to appear and be represented at hearings

A teacher who is the subject of a case may appear and make oral representations, and be represented by any person, at any hearing at which the case is considered.

[2.1261]
10 Attendance of witnesses

The Secretary of State may require, or authorise the professional conduct panel to require, any person to attend and give evidence or to produce documents or other material evidence at any hearing.

[2.1262]
11 Requirement for hearings to be held in public

(1) Subject to paragraphs (2) and (3), a hearing of a professional conduct panel must take place in public.

(2) A professional conduct panel may deliberate at any time and for any purpose in private, during or after a hearing.

(3) A professional conduct panel may exclude the public from a hearing or any part of a hearing—

(a) where it appears to the panel to be in the interests of justice or the public interest to do so; or

(b) where the teacher who is the subject of the case requests that the hearing or part of the hearing should be in private and the panel does not consider it to be contrary to the public interest to do so.

[2.1263]
12 Administration of oaths and affirmations

A professional conduct panel may require any witness at a hearing to give evidence on oath or affirmation.

[2.1264]
12A Limits of evidence requirements

[Nothing in these Regulations shall be taken to require any person to give evidence or produce any document or other material evidence which the person could not be compelled to give or produce in civil proceedings in any court in England and Wales.]

NOTES

Commencement: 1 September 2014.

Inserted by the Teachers' Disciplinary (Amendment) (England) Regulations 2014, SI 2014/1685, reg 2(1), (3), as from 1 September 2014.

[2.1265]
13 Prohibition orders

(1) A prohibition order must record the decision of the Secretary of State, the date on which the order is made, and the date on which the order takes effect.

(2) A prohibition order must in addition record—

(a) whether an application for a review of the order by the Secretary of State may be made under regulation 16, and

(b) if such an application may be made, the minimum period before the end of which no such application may be made and the procedure for making such an application.

(3) A prohibition order takes effect on the date on which notice of the order is served on the teacher to whom the order relates.

(4) The Secretary of State must—

(a) serve notice of the prohibition order on the teacher to whom the order relates;

(b) serve notice of the order on the teacher's employer [(or, as the case may be, the person by whom the teacher was engaged to carry out teaching work)] and, where arrangements have been made by a person for the teacher to carry out work at the request of or with the consent of a relevant employer, that person.

(5) The notice referred to in paragraph (4)(a) must contain the following information:

(a) the text of the order;

(b) a description of the effect of the order;

(c) the reasons for making the order; and

(d) notification of the right to appeal to the High Court against the order within 28 days of service of notice of the order.

NOTES

Para (4): words in square brackets in sub-para (b) inserted by the Teachers' Disciplinary (Amendment) (England) Regulations 2014, SI 2014/1685, reg 2(1), (3), as from 1 September 2014.

[2.1266]

14 Interim prohibition orders

(1) Subject to paragraph (2), the Secretary of State may make an interim prohibition order at any time pending a decision as to whether to make a prohibition order, if the Secretary of State considers that it is necessary in the public interest to do so.

(2) The Secretary of State must give the teacher to whom the interim prohibition order relates seven days' notice of the intention to make such an order.

(3) The Secretary of State must review an interim prohibition order—

(a) within six months of the order being made; and

(b) thereafter at intervals of six months,

if the teacher to whom the order relates makes an application to the Secretary of State for such a review.

(4) An application under paragraph (3) must be made in writing and must specify the grounds upon which it is made.

(5) An interim prohibition order ceases to have effect if the case is discontinued or found not to be proved, or a decision has been made in relation to the teacher by the Secretary of State under regulation 8.

(6) No application for a review under regulation 16 or an appeal under regulation 17 may be made in relation to an interim prohibition order.

[2.1267]

15 Publication of prohibition orders

(1) The Secretary of State must publish the information set out in paragraph (2) in relation to a teacher to whom a prohibition order relates—

(a) on a website which the Secretary of State maintains on the internet; or

(b) in such other manner as the Secretary of State sees fit.

(2) The information to be published is—

(a) the teacher's name, date of birth and Teacher Reference Number;

(b) the name of the institution at which the teacher was last employed or engaged to carry out teaching work or if the teacher was employed by a local authority, the name of the local authority;

(c) the dates on which the prohibition order was made and takes effect; and

(d) the reasons for making the order.

[2.1268]

16 Review of prohibition orders

(1) Subject to regulation 8(2), a teacher in relation to whom a prohibition order has been made may apply to the Secretary of State for the order to be set aside.

(2) An application under paragraph (1) must be made in writing and must specify the grounds upon which it is made.

(3) The Secretary of State may require any person to produce documents or other material evidence for the purposes of an application under paragraph (1).

(4) The Secretary of State must decide whether the application should be—

(a) allowed; or

(b) referred to a professional conduct panel for a recommendation as to whether it should be allowed.

(5) If the Secretary of State refuses an application under paragraph (1), the Secretary of State must specify the period before the end of which no further application may be made for a review of the order.

(6) The period in paragraph (5) must not be less than one year from the date on which the application was refused.

(7) Where the Secretary of State decides that the application should be referred to a professional conduct panel, the Secretary of State must—

(a) appoint such a panel in accordance with regulation 6(2); and

(b) consider any recommendation made by the panel before deciding whether to set aside the prohibition order.

(8) Paragraphs (2) and (3) of regulation 7, and regulations 9 to 12, apply to any reference made by the Secretary of State under paragraph (7) as they apply in relation to a reference to a professional conduct panel under regulation 5(4).

[2.1269]
17 Appeals

A person in relation to whom a prohibition order is made may appeal to the High Court within 28 days of the date on which notice of the order is served on that person.

[2.1270]
18 Persons prohibited from teaching in Wales, Scotland or Northern Ireland

Regulations 16 and 17 do not apply in relation to persons who are included on the prohibited list under section 141C(2) of the Education Act 2002.

[2.1271]
19 Service of notices and orders

(1) Anything required to be served on a teacher for the purposes of these Regulations may be—

- (a) delivered to the teacher personally;
- (b) sent to or left at the teacher's last known address; or
- (c) where the teacher requests in writing that documents be served by such a method, sent by facsimile or electronic mail or similar means which are capable of producing a document containing the text of the communication.

(2) For the purposes of regulation 13(3) notice of a prohibition order shall be taken to have been served—

- (a) where it was delivered to the teacher personally, on the day of delivery;
- (b) where it was sent to the teacher by post or left at the teacher's last known address, on the fourth day after the day on which it was sent or left;
- (c) where the teacher requests in writing that documents be served by such a method, where it was sent by facsimile or electronic mail or similar means which are capable of producing a document containing the text of the communication, on the second day after the day on which it was transmitted.

[2.1272]
20 Provision of information by employer

(1) The information prescribed for the purposes of sections 141D(3) and 141E(3) of the Education Act 2002 is the information set out in paragraph (2).

(2) The information referred to in paragraph (1) is—

- (a) information (including copies of relevant documents) relating to the teacher and the teacher's conduct; and
- (b) details (including copies of relevant documents) of any investigation into the teacher's conduct, including details of any disciplinary proceedings and the outcome of such proceedings.

APPRENTICESHIPS (FORM OF APPRENTICESHIP AGREEMENT) REGULATIONS 2012

(SI 2012/844)

NOTES

Made: 15 March 2012.
Authority: Apprenticeships, Skills, Children and Learning Act 2009, ss 32(2)(b), 36(4), 262(1).
Commencement: 6 April 2012.

[2.1273]
1 Citation, commencement and interpretation

(1) These Regulations may be cited as the Apprenticeships (Form of Apprenticeship Agreement) Regulations 2012 and come into force on 6th April 2012.

(2) In these Regulations—

"the Act" means the Apprenticeships, Skills, Children and Learning Act 2009; and
"the 1996 Act" means the Employment Rights Act 1996.

[2.1274]
2 Form of the apprenticeship agreement

(1) The prescribed form of an apprenticeship agreement for the purposes of section 32(2)(b) of the Act is—

- (a) a written statement of particulars of employment given to an employee for the purposes of section 1 of the 1996 Act; or
- (b) a document in writing in the form of a contract of employment or letter of engagement where the employer's duty under section 1 of the 1996 Act is treated as met for the purposes of section 7A of the 1996 Act.

(2) An apprenticeship agreement must include a statement of the skill, trade or occupation for which the apprentice is being trained under the apprenticeship framework.

(3) This regulation does not apply where regulation 4 applies.

[2.1275]

3 Form of the apprenticeship agreement for Crown servants and Parliamentary staff

(1) For the purposes of persons falling within section 36(1)(a) and (c)(ii) of the Act, regulation 2 applies, subject to the following provisions.

(2) In relation to an apprenticeship agreement under which a person undertakes Crown employment, a reference to—

(a) a contract of service shall be construed as a reference to the terms of employment of an apprentice in Crown employment;

(b) an apprentice shall be construed as a reference to an apprentice in Crown employment.

(3) In relation to an apprenticeship agreement under which a person undertakes employment as a relevant member of the House of Commons staff, a reference to—

(a) a contract of service shall be construed as including a reference to the terms of employment of a relevant member of the House of Commons staff;

(b) an apprentice shall be construed as a reference to a relevant member of the House of Commons staff;

(c) an employer will be to—

(i) the House of Commons Commission, for a person appointed by the Commission; or

(ii) the Speaker, for a member of the Speaker's personal staff and any person employed in the refreshment department, where that person was not appointed by the Commission.

[2.1276]

4 Form of the apprenticeship agreement for persons who are members of the naval, military or air forces of the Crown

For the purposes of persons falling within section 36(1)(b) of the Act, the prescribed form of an apprenticeship agreement for the purposes of section 32(2)(b) is the agreement signed by the member of the naval, military or air forces of the Crown which specifies the name of the apprenticeship framework.

EQUALITY ACT 2010 (SPECIFIC DUTIES) (SCOTLAND) REGULATIONS 2012

(SSI 2012/162)

NOTES

Made: 23 May 2012.
Authority: Equality Act 2010, ss 153(3), 155(1)(c), (2), 207(4).
Commencement: 27 May 2012.
These Regulations apply only to Scotland.

ARRANGEMENT OF REGULATIONS

[2.1277]

1 Citation and commencement

These Regulations may be cited as the Equality Act 2010 (Specific Duties) (Scotland) Regulations 2012 and come into force on 27th May 2012.

[2.1278]

2 Interpretation

In these Regulations—

"the Act" means the Equality Act 2010;

"employee" is to be construed in accordance with section 83 of the Act except that it is also to include a constable (including a chief constable) and a police cadet of a police force maintained under section 1 of the Police (Scotland) Act 1967;

"listed authority" means a public authority listed in [regulation 2A(1) [or 2B(1)] of or] the Schedule to these Regulations;

"relevant protected characteristic" is to be construed in accordance with section 149(7) of the Act; and

"the equality duty" means the duty of the listed authority to have, in the exercise of its functions, due regard to the needs mentioned in section 149(1) of the Act.

NOTES

In definition "listed authority" words in first (outer) pair of square brackets inserted by the Equality Act 2010 (Specific Duties) (Scotland) Amendment Regulations 2015, SSI 2015/254, regs 2, 3, as from 11 June 2015; words in second (inner) pair of square brackets inserted by the Equality Act 2010 (Specific Duties) (Scotland) Amendment Regulations 2018, SSI 2018/220, regs 2, 3, as from 29 June 2018.

[2.1279]

[2A Further listed authorities

(1) The following public authorities are, in addition to those listed in [regulation 2B(1) and in] the Schedule, listed authorities—

(a) Children's Hearings Scotland;
(b) Food Standards Scotland;
(c) Historic Environment Scotland;
(d) an integration joint board established by order under section 9(2) of the Public Bodies (Joint Working) (Scotland) Act 2014;
(e) a regional board (within the meaning of section 35(1) of the Further and Higher Education (Scotland) Act 2005);
(f) Revenue Scotland.

(2) These Regulations apply to the authorities listed in sub-paragraphs (a), (b) and (d) to (f) of paragraph (1) subject to the modifications set out in paragraphs (3) [and (4)].

(3) In regulation 3(a), for "2013" substitute "2016".

(4) In regulation 4—

(a) in paragraph (1)(a), for "2013" substitute "2016"; and
(b) in paragraph (4)(a), for "2015" substitute "2018".

(5), (6) . . .

(7) These Regulations apply to Historic Environment Scotland subject to—

(a) . . .
(b) the modifications that—
(i) in each of regulations 3(a) [and 4(1)(a)], "2017" is to be substituted for "2013"; and
(ii) in regulation 4(4)(a), "2019" is to be substituted for "2015".]

NOTES

Commencement: 11 June 2015.

Inserted by the Equality Act 2010 (Specific Duties) (Scotland) Amendment Regulations 2015, SSI 2015/254, regs 2, 4, as from 11 June 2015.

Words in square brackets in para (1) inserted by the Equality Act 2010 (Specific Duties) (Scotland) Amendment Regulations 2018, SSI 2018/220, regs 2, 4, as from 29 June 2018.

Words in square brackets in paras (2), (7) substituted, paras (5) and (6) revoked, and sub-para (7)(a) revoked, by the Equality Act 2010 (Specific Duties) (Scotland) Amendment Regulations 2016, SSI 2016/159, regs 2, 3, as from 18 March 2016.

[2.1280]

[2B Further listed authority: ILF Scotland

(1) ILF Scotland is, in addition to the public authorities listed in regulation 2A(1) and in the schedule, a listed authority.

(2) These Regulations apply to ILF Scotland subject to the modifications set out in paragraphs (3) and (4).

(3) In regulation 3(a), for "2013" substitute "2020".

(4) In regulation 4—

(a) in paragraph (1)(a), for "2013" substitute "2020"; and
(b) in paragraph (4)(a), for "2015" substitute "2022".]

NOTES

Commencement: 29 June 2018.

Inserted by the Equality Act 2010 (Specific Duties) (Scotland) Amendment Regulations 2018, SSI 2018/220, regs 2, 5, as from 29 June 2018.

[2.1281]
3 Duty to report progress on mainstreaming the equality duty

A listed authority must publish a report on the progress it has made to make the equality duty integral to the exercise of its functions so as to better perform that duty—

(a) not later than 30th April 2013; and
(b) subsequently, at intervals of not more than 2 years, beginning with the date on which it last published a report under this regulation.

[2.1282]
4 Duty to publish equality outcomes and report progress

(1) A listed authority must publish a set of equality outcomes which it considers will enable it to better perform the equality duty—

(a) not later than 30th April 2013; and
(b) subsequently, at intervals of not more than 4 years, beginning with the date on which it last published a set of equality outcomes under this paragraph.

(2) In preparing a set of equality outcomes under paragraph (1), a listed authority must—

(a) take reasonable steps to involve persons who share a relevant protected characteristic and any person who appears to the authority to represent the interests of those persons; and
(b) consider relevant evidence relating to persons who share a relevant protected characteristic.

(3) If a set of equality outcomes published by a listed authority does not seek to further the needs mentioned in section 149(1) of the Act in relation to every relevant protected characteristic, the authority must publish its reasons for proceeding in this way.

(4) A listed authority must publish a report on the progress made to achieve the equality outcomes published by it under paragraph (1)—

(a) not later than 30th April 2015; and
(b) subsequently, at intervals of not more than 2 years, beginning with the date on which it last published a report under this paragraph.

(5) In this regulation, "equality outcome" means a result that the listed authority aims to achieve in order to further one or more of the needs mentioned in section 149(1) of the Act.

[2.1283]
5 Duty to assess and review policies and practices

(1) A listed authority must, where and to the extent necessary to fulfil the equality duty, assess the impact of applying a proposed new or revised policy or practice against the needs mentioned in section 149(1) of the Act.

(2) In making the assessment, a listed authority must consider relevant evidence relating to persons who share a relevant protected characteristic (including any received from those persons).

(3) A listed authority must, in developing a policy or practice, take account of the results of any assessment made by it under paragraph (1) in respect of that policy or practice.

(4) A listed authority must publish, within a reasonable period, the results of any assessment made by it under paragraph (1) in respect of a policy or practice that it decides to apply.

(5) A listed authority must make such arrangements as it considers appropriate to review and, where necessary, revise any policy or practice that it applies in the exercise of its functions to ensure that, in exercising those functions, it complies with the equality duty.

(6) For the purposes of this regulation, any consideration by a listed authority as to whether or not it is necessary to assess the impact of applying a proposed new or revised policy or practice under paragraph (1) is not to be treated as an assessment of its impact.

[2.1284]
6 Duty to gather and use employee information

(1) A listed authority must take steps to gather information on—

(a) the composition of the authority's employees (if any); and
(b) the recruitment, development and retention of persons as employees of the authority,

with respect to, in each year, the number and relevant protected characteristics of such persons.

(2) The authority must use this information to better perform the equality duty.

(3) A report published by the listed authority in accordance with regulation 3 must include—

(a) an annual breakdown of information gathered by it in accordance with paragraph (1) which has not been published previously in such a report; and
(b) details of the progress that the authority has made in gathering and using that information to enable it to better perform the equality duty.

[2.1285]
[6A Use of member information

(1) The Scottish Ministers must from time to time take steps to—

(a) gather information on the relevant protected characteristics of members of a listed authority; and
(b) provide information gathered by them to the listed authority in question.

(2) A listed authority in receipt of information provided to it under paragraph (1) must use the information to better perform the equality duty.

(3) Each relevant listed authority is to include in any report published by it in accordance with regulation 3 details of—

(a) the number of men and of women who have been members of the authority during the period covered by the report; and

(b) the way in which—

(i) the information provided to it under paragraph (1) has been used; and

(ii) the authority proposes to use the information,

in taking steps towards there being diversity amongst the authority's members so far as relevant protected characteristics are concerned.

(4) Paragraph (3) does not apply in relation to a report published before 1st May 2016 by an authority listed in sub-paragraphs (a), (b) and (d) to (f) of regulation 2A(1).

(5) In paragraph (3), a "relevant listed authority" means any listed authority the members of which, or the board of management of which, include or includes at least one appointed member, but none of the following is a "relevant listed authority"—

(a) the Scottish Ministers;

(b) a council;

(c) a joint board;

(d) a licensing board;

(e) an education authority;

(f) an individual holder of a public office.

(6) Where a listed authority is not made up of members but has a board of management, paragraphs (1)(a) and (3) have effect as if a member of the board of management were a member of the authority.]

NOTES

Commencement: 18 March 2016.

Inserted by the Equality Act 2010 (Specific Duties) (Scotland) Amendment Regulations 2016, SSI 2016/159, regs 2, 4, as from 18 March 2016.

[2.1286]

7 Duty to publish gender pay gap information

(1) A listed authority must[, in accordance with regulation 8A,] publish information on the percentage difference among its employees between men's average hourly pay (excluding overtime) and women's average hourly pay (excluding overtime).

(2) . . .

(3) The information published must be based on the most recent data available for a date when the authority had at least [20] employees.

(4), (5) . . .

NOTES

Words in square brackets in para (1) inserted, paras (2), (4), (5) revoked, and figure in square brackets in para (3) substituted, by the Equality Act 2010 (Specific Duties) (Scotland) Amendment Regulations 2016, SSI 2016/159, regs 2, 5, as from 18 March 2016.

[2.1287]

8 Duty to publish statements on equal pay, etc

(1) A listed authority must[, in accordance with regulation 8A,] publish a statement containing the information specified in paragraph (2) . . .

(2) The statement must specify—

(a) the authority's policy on equal pay among its employees between—

(i) men and women;

(ii) persons who are disabled and persons who are not; and

(iii) persons who fall into a minority racial group and persons who do not; and

(b) occupational segregation among its employees, being the concentration of—

(i) men and women;

(ii) persons who are disabled and persons who are not; and

(iii) persons who fall into a minority racial group and persons who do not,

in particular grades and in particular occupations.

(3) The information published must be based on the most recent data available for a date when the authority had at least [20] employees.

(4) . . .

(5) Paragraphs (2)(a)(ii) and (iii) and (2)(b)(ii) and (iii) apply only in relation to the second and subsequent statements published by a listed authority under [this regulation].

(6) In paragraph (2), "racial group" is to be construed in accordance with section 9 of the Act.

(7) The Scottish Ministers must review from time to time whether the matters specified in paragraph (2) . . . should be amended.

NOTES

All words in square brackets in this regulation were substituted or inserted, and all words omitted were revoked, by the Equality Act 2010 (Specific Duties) (Scotland) Amendment Regulations 2016, SSI 2016/159, regs 2, 6, as from 18 March 2016.

[2.1288]

[8A Publication under regulations 7 and 8

(1) Publication under regulations 7(1) and 8(1) is to take place no later than—

(a) 30th April 2016 in the case of Food Standards Scotland;

(b) 30th April 2017 in the case of Historic Environment Scotland or an authority listed in the Schedule;

(c) 30th April 2018 in the case of an authority listed in sub-paragraphs (a) and (d) to (f) of regulation 2A(1).

[(d) 30th April 2020 in the case of ILF Scotland.]

(2) Publication is also to take place—

(a) under regulation 7(1), no later than 30th April in each second year after the year specified in paragraph (1) in relation to the authority in question;

(b) under regulation 8(1), no later than 30th April in each fourth year after the year specified in paragraph (1) in relation to the authority in question.

(3) An authority need not effect publication under regulations 7(1) and 8(1) by the end of a relevant period if, during that period, the authority has at no time had 20 or more employees.

(4) Each of the following is a "relevant period" for the purposes of paragraph (3)—

(a) in relation to publication under regulation 7(1) by an authority listed in the Schedule, the period from 1st May 2015 to 30th April 2017;

(b) in relation to publication under regulation 8(1) by an authority listed in the Schedule, the period from 1st May 2013 to 30th April 2017;

(c) in relation to publication by Food Standards Scotland, the period from 11th June 2015 to 30th April 2016;

(d) in relation to publication by Historic Environment Scotland, the period from 11th June 2015 to 30th April 2017;

(e) in relation to publication by an authority listed in sub-paragraphs (a) and (d) to (f) of regulation 2A(1), the period from 11th June 2015 to 30th April 2018;

[(ea) n relation to publication by ILF Scotland, the period from 1st May 2018 to 30th April 2020;]

(f) in relation to any listed authority, the period from the day after publication by that authority is due under paragraph (1) (ignoring paragraph (3)) to the day by which publication is next due under paragraph (2);

(g) in relation to any listed authority, the period from the day after publication by that authority is due under paragraph (2) (ignoring paragraph (3)) to the day by which publication is next due under that paragraph.]

NOTES

Commencement: 18 March 2016.

Inserted by the Equality Act 2010 (Specific Duties) (Scotland) Amendment Regulations 2016, SSI 2016/159, regs 2, 7, as from 18 March 2016.

Para (1): sub-para (d) added by the Equality Act 2010 (Specific Duties) (Scotland) Amendment Regulations 2018, SSI 2018/220, regs 2, 6(a), as from 29 June 2018.

Para (4): sub-para (ea) inserted by SSI 2018/220, regs 2, 6(b), as from 29 June 2018.

[2.1289]

9 Duty to consider award criteria and conditions in relation to public procurement

(1) Where a listed authority is a contracting authority and proposes to enter into a relevant agreement on the basis of an offer which is the most economically advantageous, it must have due regard to whether the award criteria should include considerations to enable it to better perform the equality duty.

(2) Where a listed authority is a contracting authority and proposes to stipulate conditions relating to the performance of a relevant agreement, it must have due regard to whether the conditions should include considerations to enable it to better perform the equality duty.

(3) Nothing in this regulation imposes any requirement on a listed authority where in all the circumstances such a requirement would not be related to and proportionate to the subject matter of the proposed agreement.

(4) In this regulation—

"contracting authority", "framework agreement" and "public contract" have the same meaning as in the [Public Contracts (Scotland) Regulations 2015]; and

"relevant agreement" means a public contract or a framework agreement that is regulated by the [Public Contracts (Scotland) Regulations 2015].

NOTES

Para (4): words in square brackets in the definitions "contracting authority" and "relevant agreement" substituted by the Public Contracts (Scotland) Regulations 2015, SSI 2015/446, reg 97(2), Sch 6, Pt 2, para 7, as from 18 April 2016.

[2.1290]

10 Duty to publish in a manner that is accessible, etc

(1) A listed authority must comply with its duty to publish under regulations 3, 4, 7 and 8 in a manner that makes the information published accessible to the public.

(2) A listed authority must, so far as practicable, comply with its duty to publish under regulations 3, 4, 7 and 8 by employing an existing means of public performance reporting.

[2.1291]
11 Duty to consider other matters

In carrying out its duties under these Regulations, a listed authority may be required to consider such matters as may be specified from time to time by the Scottish Ministers.

[2.1292]
12 Duty of the Scottish Ministers to publish proposals to enable better performance

(1) The Scottish Ministers must publish proposals for activity to enable a listed authority to better perform the equality duty—

(a) not later than 31st December 2013; and

(b) subsequently, at intervals of not more than 4 years, beginning with the date on which it last published proposals under this paragraph.

(2) The Scottish Ministers must publish a report on progress in relation to the activity—

(a) not later than 31st December 2015; and

(b) subsequently, at intervals of not more than 4 years, beginning with the date on which it last published a report under this paragraph.

SCHEDULE
LIST OF PUBLIC AUTHORITIES

Regulation 2

[2.1293]
Scottish Administration

The Scottish Ministers.

Keeper of the Records of Scotland.

Keeper of the Registers of Scotland.

Registrar General of Births, Deaths and Marriages for Scotland.

Scottish Court Service.

National Health Service

A Health Board constituted under section 2 of the National Health Service (Scotland) Act 1978.

A Special Health Board constituted under that section.

Local government

A council constituted under section 2 of the Local Government etc (Scotland) Act 1994.

A joint board within the meaning of section 235(1) of the Local Government (Scotland) Act 1973.

. . .

A licensing board established under section 5 of the Licensing (Scotland) Act 2005, or continued in being by virtue of that section.

A National Park authority established by a designation order made under section 6 of the National Parks (Scotland) Act 2000.

Scottish Enterprise and Highlands and Islands Enterprise, established under the Enterprise and New Towns (Scotland) Act 1990.

Other educational bodies

An education authority in Scotland (within the meaning of section 135(1) of the Education (Scotland) Act 1980).

The managers of a grant-aided school (within the meaning of that section).

The board of management of a college of further education (within the meaning of section 36(1) of the Further and Higher Education (Scotland) Act 1992) which is a [post-16 education body (within the meaning of section 35(1)] of the Further and Higher Education (Scotland) Act 2005).

In the case of such a college of further education not under the management of a board of management, the board of governors of the college or any person responsible for the management of the college, whether or not formally constituted as a governing body or board of governors.

The governing body of an institution within the higher education sector (within the meaning of Part 2 of the Further and Higher Education (Scotland) Act 1992) which is a [post-16 education body (within the meaning of section 35(1)] of the Further and Higher Education (Scotland) Act 2005).

[Police and Fire]

[The Scottish Police Authority.

The chief constable of the Police Service of Scotland.

The Scottish Fire and Rescue Service.

The Chief Officer of the Scottish Fire and Rescue Service.]

Other bodies and offices

Accounts Commission for Scotland.

Audit Scotland.

Board of Trustees for the National Galleries of Scotland.

Board of Trustees of the National Museums of Scotland.

Bòrd na Gáidhlig.

. . .

A chief officer of a community justice authority.

. . .

Commissioner for Children and Young People in Scotland.

The Common Services Agency for the Scottish Health Service.

A community justice authority.

Creative Scotland.

Healthcare Improvement Scotland.

The Mental Welfare Commission for Scotland.

A regional Transport Partnership created by an order under section 1(1) of the Transport (Scotland) Act 2005.

Scottish Children's Reporter Administration.

The Scottish Criminal Cases Review Commission.

Scottish Environment Protection Agency.

Scottish Further and Higher Education Funding Council

The Scottish Legal Aid Board.

Scottish Natural Heritage.

Scottish Qualifications Authority.

The Scottish Social Services Council.

The Scottish Sports Council.

Scottish Water.

Skills Development Scotland.

Social Care and Social Work Improvement Scotland.

[National Library of Scotland.]

VisitScotland.

NOTES

Local government: entry "A joint fire and rescue board constituted by a scheme under section 2(1) of the Fire (Scotland) Act 2005" (omitted) revoked by the Police and Fire Reform (Scotland) Act 2012 (Consequential Modifications and Savings) Order 2013, SSI 2013/119, art 4, Sch 3, Pt 2, para 10(a).

Other educational bodies: words in square brackets in the third and final entries substituted by the Equality Act 2010 (Specific Duties) (Scotland) Amendment Regulations 2015, SSI 2015/254, regs 2, 5, as from 11 June 2015.

Police and Fire: the heading "Police and Fire" was substituted (for the original heading "Police"), and the entries "The Scottish Police Authority", "The chief constable of the Police Service of Scotland", "The Scottish Fire and Rescue Service" and The Chief Officer of the Scottish Fire and Rescue Service" were substituted (for the original entry "A police authority established under section 2 of the Police (Scotland) Act 1967"), by SSI 2013/119, art 4, Sch 3, Pt 2, para 10(b), (c).

Other bodies and offices: entries "A Chief Constable of a police force maintained under section 1 of the Police (Scotland) Act 1967" and "A Chief Officer of a relevant authority appointed under section 7 of the Fire (Scotland) Act 2005" (omitted) revoked by SSI 2013/119, art 4, Sch 3, Pt 2, para 10(d).

Other bodies and offices: entry "National Library of Scotland" substituted (for the original entry "The Trustees of the National Library of Scotland") by the National Library of Scotland Act 2012 (Consequential Modifications) Order 2013, SSI 2013/169, art 5.

OFFERS TO SETTLE IN CIVIL PROCEEDINGS ORDER 2013

(SI 2013/93)

NOTES

Made: 21 January 2013.
Authority: Legal Aid, Sentencing and Punishment of Offenders Act 2012, s 55.
Commencement: 12 February 2013.
This Order applies to England and Wales only; see ss 55 and 152 of the 2012 Act.

[2.1294]

1 Citation and commencement

This Order may be cited as the Offers to Settle in Civil Proceedings Order 2013 and shall come into force on 12th February 2013.

[2.1295]

2 Additional amount to be paid where a claim is only for an amount of money

Where rules of court make provision for a court to order a defendant in civil proceedings to pay an additional amount to a claimant in those proceedings and the claim is for (and only for) an amount of money then, for the purposes of section 55(3) of the Legal Aid, Sentencing and Punishment of Offenders Act 2012, the prescribed percentage shall be—

Amount awarded by the court	*Prescribed percentage*
Up to £500,000	10% of the amount awarded.
Above £500,000, up to £1,000,000	10% of the first £500,000 and 5% of the amount awarded above that figure.
Above £1,000,000	7.5% of the first £1,000,000 and 0.001% of the amount awarded above that figure.

[2.1296]

3 Amount to be paid where a claim is or includes a non-monetary claim

(1) Rules of court may make provision for a court to order a defendant in civil proceedings to pay an amount to a claimant ("the amount to be paid") in those proceedings where—

(a) the claim is or includes a non-monetary claim;
(b) judgment is given in favour of the claimant; and
(c) the judgment in respect of the claim is at least as advantageous as an offer to settle the claim which the claimant made in accordance with rules of court and has not withdrawn in accordance with those rules.

(2) The amount to be paid shall be calculated as prescribed in paragraph (4).

(3) Rules made under paragraph (1) may—

(a) include provision as to the assessment of whether a judgment is at least as advantageous as an offer to settle; and
(b) make provision as to the calculation of the value of a non-monetary benefit awarded to a claimant.

(4) Subject to subparagraph (5), the amount to be paid shall be—

(a) if a claim includes both a claim for an amount of money and a non-monetary claim, the following percentages of the amount awarded to the claimant by the court (excluding any amount awarded in respect of the claimant's costs)—

Amount awarded by the court	*Amount to be paid by the defendant*
Up to £500,000	10% of the amount awarded.
Above £500,000, up to £1,000,000	10% of the first £500,000 and 5% of the amount awarded above that figure; and

(b) in a non-monetary claim only, the following percentages of any costs ordered by the court to be paid to the claimant by the defendant—

Costs ordered to be paid to the claimant	*Amount to be paid by the defendant*
Up to £500,000	10% of the costs ordered to be paid.
Above £500,000, up to £1,000,000	10% of the first £500,000 and 5% of any costs ordered to be paid above that figure.

Costs ordered to be paid to the claimant	***Amount to be paid by the defendant***

(5) The amount to be paid shall not exceed £75,000.

DAMAGES-BASED AGREEMENTS REGULATIONS 2013

(SI 2013/609)

NOTES

Made: 13 March 2013.
Authority: Courts and Legal Services Act 1990, ss 58AA(4), (5), 120(3).
Commencement: 1 April 2013.
These Regulations apply to England and Wales only (the extent of the enabling provisions of the 1990 Act).

ARRANGEMENT OF REGULATIONS

[2.1297]

1 Citation, commencement, interpretation and application

(1) These Regulations may be cited as the Damages-Based Agreements Regulations 2013 and come into force on 1st April 2013.

(2) In these Regulations—

"the Act" means the Courts and Legal Services Act 1990;

"claim for personal injuries" has the same meaning as in Rule 2.3 of the Civil Procedure Rules 1998;

"client" means the person who has instructed the representative to provide advocacy services, litigation services (within section 119 of the Act) or claims management services (within the meaning of [section 419A of the Financial Services and Markets Act 2000]) and is liable to make a payment for those services;

"costs" means the total of the representative's time reasonably spent, in respect of the claim or proceedings, multiplied by the reasonable hourly rate of remuneration of the representative;

"employment matter" means a matter that is, or could become, the subject of proceedings before an employment tribunal;

"expenses" means disbursements incurred by the representative, including the expense of obtaining an expert's report and, in an employment matter only, counsel's fees;

"payment" means that part of the sum recovered in respect of the claim or damages awarded that the client agrees to pay the representative, and excludes expenses but includes, in respect of any claim or proceedings to which these regulations apply other than an employment matter, any disbursements incurred by the representative in respect of counsel's fees;

"representative" means the person providing the advocacy services, litigation services or claims management services to which the damages-based agreement relates.

(3) Subject to paragraphs (4), (5) and (6), these Regulations shall apply to all damages-based agreements entered into on or after the date on which these Regulations come into force.

(4) Subject to paragraph (6), these Regulations shall not apply to any damages-based agreement to which section 57 of the Solicitors Act 1974 (non-contentious business agreements between solicitor and client) applies.

(5) In these Regulations—

(a) regulation 4 does not apply; and
(b) regulations 5, 6, 7 and 8 only apply,

to any damages-based agreement in respect of an employment matter.

(6) Where these Regulations relate to an employment matter, they apply to all damages-based agreements signed on or after the date on which these Regulations come into force.

NOTES

Para (2): in the definition of "client", words in square brackets substituted for original words "section 4(2)(b) of the Compensation Act 2006", by the Financial Services and Markets Act 2000 (Claims Management Activity) Order 2018, SI 2018/1253, art 102, as from 1 April 2019, subject to art 112 thereof, which provides that this amendment does not have effect in relation to any damages-based agreement made before 1 April 2019.

[2.1298]

2 Revocation of 2010 Regulations and transitional provision

(1) Subject to paragraph (2), the Damages-Based Agreements Regulations 2010 ("the 2010 Regulations") are revoked.

(2) The 2010 Regulations shall continue to have effect in respect of any damages-based agreement to which those Regulations applied and which was signed before the date on which these Regulations come into force.

[2.1299]

3 Requirements of an agreement in respect of all damages-based agreements

The requirements prescribed for the purposes of section 58AA(4)(c) of the Act are that the terms and conditions of a damages-based agreement must specify—

(a) the claim or proceedings or parts of them to which the agreement relates;

(b) the circumstances in which the representative's payment, expenses and costs, or part of them, are payable; and

(c) the reason for setting the amount of the payment at the level agreed, which, in an employment matter, shall include having regard to, where appropriate, whether the claim or proceedings is one of several similar claims or proceedings.

4 (*(Payment in respect of claims or proceedings other than an employment matter) is outside the scope of this work.*)

[2.1300]

5 Information required to be given before an agreement is made in an employment matter

(1) In an employment matter, the requirements prescribed for the purposes of section 58AA(4)(d) of the Act are to provide—

(a) information to the client in writing about the matters in paragraph (2); and

(b) such further explanation, advice or other information about any of those matters as the client may request.

(2) Those matters are—

(a) the circumstances in which the client may seek a review of costs and expenses of the representative and the procedure for doing so;

(b) the dispute resolution service provided by the Advisory, Conciliation and Arbitration Service (ACAS) in regard to actual and potential claims;

(c) whether other methods of pursuing the claim or financing the proceedings, including—

(i) advice under [arrangements made for the purposes of Part 1 (legal aid) of the Legal Aid, Sentencing and Punishment of Offenders Act 2012],

(ii) legal expenses insurance,

(iii) pro bono representation, or

(iv) trade union representation,

are available, and, if so, how they apply to the client and the claim or proceedings in question; and

(d) the point at which expenses become payable; and

(e) a reasonable estimate of the amount that is likely to be spent upon expenses, inclusive of VAT.

NOTES

Para (2): words in square brackets in sub-para (c)(i) substituted by the Legal Aid, Sentencing and Punishment of Offenders Act 2012 (Consequential, Transitional and Saving Provisions) Regulations 2013, SI 2013/534, reg 14(1), Schedule, Pt 2, para 26.

[2.1301]

6 Additional causes of action in an employment matter

In an employment matter, any amendment to a damages-based agreement to cover additional causes of action must be in writing and signed by the client and the representative.

[2.1302]

7 Payment in an employment matter

In an employment matter, a damages-based agreement must not provide for a payment above an amount which, including VAT, is equal to 35% of the sums ultimately recovered by the client in the claim or proceedings.

[2.1303]

8 Terms and conditions of termination in an employment matter

(1) In an employment matter, the additional requirements prescribed for the purposes of section 58AA(4)(c) of the Act are that the terms and conditions of a damages-based agreement must be in accordance with paragraphs (2), (3) and (4).

(2) If the agreement is terminated, the representatives may not charge the client more than the representative's costs and expenses for the work undertaken in respect of the client's claim or proceedings.

(3) The client may not terminate the agreement—

(a) after settlement has been agreed; or

(b) within seven days before the start of the tribunal hearing.

(4) The representative may not terminate the agreement and charge costs unless the client has behaved or is behaving unreasonably.

(5) Paragraphs (3) and (4) are without prejudice to any right of either party under general law of contract to terminate the agreement.

CONDITIONAL FEE AGREEMENTS ORDER 2013

(SI 2013/689)

NOTES

Made: 19 March 2013.

Authority: Courts and Legal Services Act 1990, ss 58(4)(a), (c), 58(4A)(b), (4B)(c), (d), 120(3).

Commencement: 1 April 2013.

These Regulations apply to England and Wales only (the extent of the enabling provisions of the 1990 Act).

ARRANGEMENT OF ARTICLES

[2.1304]

1 Citation, commencement, interpretation and application

(1) This Order may be cited as the Conditional Fee Agreements Order 2013 and will come into force on 1st April 2013.

(2) In this Order—

"the 1986 Act" means the Insolvency Act 1986;

"the 1990 Act" means the Courts and Legal Services Act 1990;

"claim for personal injuries" has the same meaning as in Rule 2.3 of the Civil Procedure Rules 1998;

"company" means a company within the meaning of section 1 of the Companies Act 2006 or a company which may be wound up under Part V of the 1986 Act;

"diffuse mesothelioma" has the same meaning as in section 48(2) of the Legal Aid, Sentencing and Punishment of Offenders Act 2012;

"news publisher" means a person who publishes a newspaper, magazine or website containing news or information about or comment on current affairs;

"publication and privacy proceedings" means proceedings for—

(a) defamation;
(b) malicious falsehood;
(c) breach of confidence involving publication to the general public;
(d) misuse of private information; or
(e) harassment, where the defendant is a news publisher.

"representative" means the person or persons providing the advocacy services or litigation services to which the conditional fee agreement relates.

[2.1305]

2 Agreements providing for a success fee

All proceedings which, under section 58 of the Act, can be the subject of an enforceable conditional fee agreement, except proceedings under section 82 of the Environmental Protection Act 1990, are proceedings specified for the purpose of section 58(4)(a) of the Act.

[2.1306]

3 Amount of success fee

In relation to all proceedings specified in article 2, the percentage specified for the purposes of section 58(4)(c) of the Act is 100%.

[2.1307]

4 Specified proceedings

A claim for personal injuries shall be proceedings specified for the purpose of section 58(4A)(b) of the Act.

[2.1308]

5 Amount of success fee in specified proceedings

(1) In relation to the proceedings specified in article 4, the percentage prescribed for the purposes of section 58(4B)(c) of the Act is—

(a) in proceedings at first instance, 25%; and

Part 2 Statutory Instruments

(b) in all other proceedings, 100%.

(2) The descriptions of damages specified for the purposes of section 58(4B)(d) of the Act are—

(a) general damages for pain, suffering, and loss of amenity; and

(b) damages for pecuniary loss, other than future pecuniary loss,

net of any sums recoverable by the Compensation Recovery Unit of the Department for Work and Pensions.

[2.1309]

6 Transitional and saving provisions

(1) Articles 4 and 5 do not apply to a conditional fee agreement which is entered into before the date upon which this Order comes into force if—

(a) the agreement was entered into specifically for the purposes of the provision to a person ("P") of advocacy or litigation services in connection with the matter which is the subject of the proceedings; or

(b) advocacy or litigation services were provided to P under the agreement in connection with those proceedings before that date.

(2) Articles 4 and 5 do not apply to any conditional fee agreement entered into in relation to—

(a) proceedings relating to a claim for damages in respect of diffuse mesothelioma;

(b) publication and privacy proceedings;

(c) proceedings in England and Wales brought by a person acting in the capacity of—

(i) a liquidator of a company which is being wound up in England and Wales or Scotland under Parts IV or V of the 1986 Act; or

(ii) a trustee of a bankrupt's estate under Part IX of the 1986 Act;

(d) proceedings brought by a person acting in the capacity of an administrator appointed pursuant to the provisions of Part II of the 1986 Act;

(e) proceedings in England and Wales brought by a company which is being wound up in England and Wales or Scotland under Parts IV or V of the 1986 Act; or

(f) proceedings brought by a company which has entered administration under Part II of the 1986 Act.

7 (*Revokes the Conditional Fee Agreements Order 2000, SI 2000/823.*)

REHABILITATION OF OFFENDERS ACT 1974 (EXCLUSIONS AND EXCEPTIONS) (SCOTLAND) ORDER 2013

(SSI 2013/50)

NOTES

Made: 13 February 2013.

Authority: Rehabilitation of Offenders Act 1974, ss 4(4), 7(4), 10(1).

Commencement: 14 February 2013.

This Order extends to Scotland only and, in so far as it extends beyond Scotland, it does so only as a matter of Scots law (see art 1 at **[2.1310]**). The equivalent English and Welsh Order is at **[2.15]**.

ARRANGEMENT OF ARTICLES

SCHEDULES

[2.1310]

1 Citation, commencement and extent

(1) This Order may be cited as the Rehabilitation of Offenders Act 1974 (Exclusions and Exceptions) (Scotland) Order 2013, and comes into force the day after the day on which it is made.

(2) This Order extends to Scotland and, in so far as it extends beyond Scotland, it does so only as a matter of Scots law.

[2.1311]

2 Interpretation

(1) In this Order—

["the 1997 Act" means the Police Act 1997;]

"the 2000 Act" means the Financial Services and Markets Act 2000;

"the 2001 Act" means the Regulation of Care (Scotland) Act 2001;

"the 2007 Act" means the Protection of Vulnerable Groups (Scotland) Act 2007;

"the 2010 Act" means the Public Services Reform (Scotland) Act 2010;

"the Act" means the Rehabilitation of Offenders Act 1974;

"actuary" means a member of the Institute and Faculty of Actuaries;

"accountant" means a member of—

(a) the Association of Chartered Certified Accountants;

(b) the Institute of Chartered Accountants of Scotland;

(c) the Institute of Chartered Accountants in England and Wales;

(d) the Chartered Institute of Public Finance and Accountancy; or

(e) the Chartered Institute of Management Accountants;

"adopt" includes any arrangements to adopt a child, including arrangements for adoption where the proposed adopter is a relative of the child, whether under the Adoption and Children (Scotland) Act 2007 or the Adoptions with a Foreign Element (Scotland) Regulations 2009;

"approved regulator" has the meaning given in Part 2 of the Legal Services (Scotland) Act 2010;

"associate", in relation to a person ("A"), means someone who is a controller, director or a manager of A or, where A is a partnership, any partner of A;

"authorised electronic money institution" has the meaning given by regulation 2(1) of the Electronic Money Regulations 2011;

"authorised payment institution" has the meaning given by regulation 2(1) of the [Payment Services Regulations 2017];

"care service" has the meaning given in section 47 of the 2010 Act;

"collective investment scheme" has the meaning given in section 235 of the 2000 Act;

. . .

"contracting authority" means a contracting authority within the meaning of Article 1(9) of Directive 2004/18/EC;

"contracting entity" means a contracting entity within the meaning of Article 2(2) of Directive 2004/17/EC;

"controller" has the meaning given in section 422 of the 2000 Act;

"Council of Lloyd's" means the council constituted by section 3 of the Lloyd's Act 1982;

["depositary", in relation to an authorised contractual scheme, has the meaning given in section 237(2) of the 2000 Act;]

"Directive 2004/17/EC" means Directive 2004/17/EC of the European Parliament and of the Council of 31st March 2004;

"Directive 2004/18/EC" means Directive 2004/18/EC of the European Parliament and of the Council of 31st March 2004;

"director" has the meaning given in section 417 of the 2000 Act;

"electronic money institution" has the meaning given in regulation 2(1) of the Electronic Money Regulations 2011;

"enactment" includes an Act of the Scottish Parliament and any order, regulation or other instrument having effect by virtue of such an Act;

["the FCA" means the Financial Conduct Authority;]

"firearms dealer" has the meaning given in section 57(4) of the Firearms Act 1968;

"Head of Practice" has the meaning given in Part 2 of the Legal Services Act;

"health services" means services provided under the National Health Service (Scotland) Act 1978 and similar services provided otherwise than under the National Health Service;

"Her Majesty's Inspectors" has the meaning given in section 135 of the Education (Scotland) Act 1980;

["higher level disclosure" means—

(a) a criminal record certificate issued under section 113A(1) or section 114(1) of the 1997 Act;

(b) an enhanced criminal record certificate issued under section 113B(1) or section 116(1) of that Act; or

(c) a scheme record disclosed under section 52(3) or (7) of the 2007 Act;]

"judicial appointment" means an appointment to any office by virtue of which the holder has power (whether alone or with others) under any enactment or rule of law to determine any question affecting the rights, privileges, obligations or liabilities of any person;

["key worker" means—

(a) any individual who is likely, in the course of exercising the duties of that individual's office or employment, to play a significant role in the decision making process of the FCA, the PRA or the Bank of England in relation to the exercise of its public functions (within the meaning of section 349(5) of the 2000 Act); or

(b) any individual who is likely, in the course of exercising the duties of that individual's office or employment, to support directly an individual mentioned in paragraph (a);]

["lay representative" means a person who—

(a) is representing a party in civil proceedings in the sheriff court or proceedings in the Court of Session; and

(b) is not—

(i) a solicitor or an advocate; or

(ii) someone having the right to conduct litigation, or a right of audience, by virtue of section 27 of the Law Reform (Miscellaneous Provisions) (Scotland) Act 1990;]

"the Legal Services Act" means the Legal Services (Scotland) Act 2010;

"licensed legal services provider" has the meaning given in Part 2 of the Legal Services Act;

"manager" has the meaning given in section 423 of the 2000 Act;

"non-solicitor investor" has the meaning given in Part 2 of the Legal Services Act;

"open-ended investment company" has the meaning given in section 236 of the 2000 Act;

["operator", in relation to an authorised contractual scheme, has the meaning given in section 237(2) of the 2000 Act;]

["the PRA" means the Prudential Regulation Authority;]

["Part 4A permission" has the meaning given by section 55A(5) of the 2000 Act;]

"payment services" has the meaning given in regulation 2(1) of the [Payment Services Regulations 2017];

"personal information" means any information (in any form) which relates to a living individual who can be identified from that data, which is of a confidential nature and is not in the public domain;

"Practice Committee" has the meaning given in Part 2 of the Legal Services Act;

"private hire driver" means a driver of a private hire car, as defined by section 23(1) of the Civic Government (Scotland) Act 1982, who is required to be licensed by a licensing authority under the provisions of that Act;

"prosecutor" has the meaning given in section 307 of the Criminal Procedure (Scotland) Act 1995;

["protected conviction" means a spent conviction of a kind mentioned in article 2A(1);]

["recognised clearing house" means a recognised clearing house as defined in section 285 of the 2000 Act;]

["registered account information service provider" has the meaning given by regulation 2(1) of the Payment Services Regulations 2017;]

"registered chiropractor" has the meaning given in section 43 of the Chiropractors Act 1994;

"registered European lawyer" has the meaning given in section 65 of the Solicitors (Scotland) Act 1980;

"registered foreign lawyer" has the meaning given in section 65 of the Solicitors (Scotland) Act 1980;

"registered osteopath" has the meaning given in section 41 of the Osteopaths Act 1993;

"registered pharmacist" means a person who is registered as a pharmacist in Part 1 or 4 of the register maintained under article 19 of the Pharmacy Order 2010;

"registered pharmacy technician" means a person who is registered in Part 2 or 5 of the register maintained under article 19 of the Pharmacy Order 2010;

"registered teacher" means a teacher registered under the Public Services Reform (General Teaching Council for Scotland) Order 2011;

"regulated work with adults" has the meaning given in section 91(3) of the 2007 Act;

"regulated work with children" has the meaning given in section 91(2) of the 2007 Act;

"relevant collective investment scheme" means a collective investment scheme which is recognised under section *264 (schemes constituted in other EEA States),* 270 (schemes authorised in designated countries or territories) or 272 (individually recognised overseas schemes) of the 2000 Act;

"Scottish Social Services Council" has the meaning given in section 43 of the 2001 Act;

["sent" means—

(a) in relation to a criminal record certificate or an enhanced criminal record certificate issued under section 113A(1) or 113B(1) of the 1997 Act, sent in accordance with section 116ZA(2) or (4) of that Act to the registered person who countersigned the application for that certificate under section [113A(2)(a)] or, as the case may be, 113B(2)(a) of that Act;

(b) in relation to a criminal record certificate or enhanced criminal record certificate issued under section 114(1) or 116(1) of the 1997 Act, sent in accordance with section 116ZA(2) or (4) of that Act to the person who made the statement under section 114(2) or, as the case may be, 116(2) of that Act; and

(c) in relation to a scheme record disclosed under section 52(3) or (7) of the 2007 Act, disclosed to the registered person who made the declaration mentioned in condition C in section 55 of that Act;]

"small electronic money institution" has the meaning given in regulation 2(1) of the Electronic Money Regulations 2011;

"small payment institution" has the meaning given in regulation 2(1) of the [Payment Services Regulations 2017];

"Social Care and Social Work Improvement Scotland" has the meaning given in section 44 of the 2010 Act;

"social service worker" has the meaning given in section 77 of the 2001 Act;

"social worker" has the meaning given in section 77 of the 2001 Act;

"taxi driver" means a driver of a taxi as defined by section 23(1) of the Civic Government (Scotland) Act 1982, who is required to be licensed by a licensing authority under the provisions of that Act;

"trustee", in relation to a unit trust scheme, has the meaning given in section 237(2) of the 2000 Act;

. . .

"UK recognised investment exchange" means an investment exchange in relation to which a recognition order under section 290 of the 2000 Act, otherwise than by virtue of section 292(2) (overseas investment exchanges) of that Act, is in force;

"work" includes work of any kind, whether paid or unpaid and whether under a contract of service or apprenticeship, under a contract for services, or otherwise than under a contract.

[(1A) In this Order references to the Bank of England do not include the Bank acting in its capacity as the Prudential Regulation Authority.]

(2) Any reference in this Order to a numbered article or Schedule is, unless the context otherwise requires, a reference to the article or Schedule so numbered in this Order.

NOTES

Para (1) is amended as follows:

Definitions "the 1997 Act", "higher level disclosure", "protected conviction", and "sent" inserted, and definition "lay representative" substituted, by the Rehabilitation of Offenders Act 1974 (Exclusions and Exceptions) (Scotland) Amendment Order 2015, SSI 2015/329, art 2(1), as from 10 September 2015.

The words in square brackets in the definitions definition "authorised payment institution", "payment services", and "small payment institution" were inserted, and the definition "registered account information service provider" was inserted, by the Payment Systems and Services and Electronic Money (Miscellaneous Amendments) Regulations 2017, SI 2017/1173, reg 6(a), s from 22 December 2017 (for the purposes of the determination by the FCA of applications for authorisation or registration made under Part 2 of the Payment Services Regulations 2017), and as from 13 January 2018 (otherwise).

Definition "the competent authority for listing" (omitted) revoked, definitions "the FCA" and "the PRA" inserted, definition "key worker" substituted, and definition "Part 4A permission" substituted (for the original definition "Part IV permission"), by the Financial Services Act 2012 (Consequential Amendments and Transitional Provisions) Order 2013, SI 2013/472, art 3, Sch 2, para 250(1), (2).

Definitions "depositary" and "operator" inserted by the Collective Investment in Transferable Securities (Contractual Scheme) Regulations 2013, SI 2013/1388, reg 15(1), (2).

Definition "recognised clearing house" inserted, and definition "UK recognised clearing house" (omitted) revoked, by the Financial Services and Markets Act 2000 (Over the Counter Derivatives, Central Counterparties and Trade Repositories) Regulations 2013, SI 2013/504, reg 48(1), (2).

In definition "relevant collective investment scheme" words in italics revoked by the Collective Investment Schemes (Amendment etc) (EU Exit) Regulations 2019, SI 2019/325, reg 57, as from exit day (as defined in the European Union (Withdrawal) Act 2018, s 20).

Figure in square brackets in definition "sent" substituted by the Rehabilitation of Offenders Act 1974 (Exclusions and Exceptions) (Scotland) Amendment Order 2016, SSI 2016/91, art 2, as from 8 February 2016.

Para (1A): inserted by the Bank of England and Financial Services (Consequential Amendments) Regulations 2017, SI 2017/80, reg 2, Schedule, Pt 2, para 39, as from 1 March 2017.

[2.1312]

[2A Protected convictions

(1) For the purposes of this Order, a person's conviction is a protected conviction if—

(a) it is a spent conviction; and

(b) either—

(i) it is not a conviction for an offence listed in Schedule A1 or B1; or

(ii) it is a conviction for an offence listed in Schedule B1 and at least one of the conditions specified in paragraph (2) is satisfied.

(2) The conditions are—

(a) the sentence imposed in respect of the conviction was an admonition or an absolute discharge;

(b) the person was aged under 18 on the date of conviction and at least 7 years and 6 months have passed since the date of conviction; and

(c) the person was aged 18 or over on the date of conviction and at least 15 years have passed since the date of conviction.

(3) In [paragraph] (2)(a), the reference to an absolute discharge includes a reference to the discharge of the referral of a child's case to a children's hearing under—

(a) section 69(1)(b) and (12) of the Children (Scotland) Act 1995; or

(b) section 91(3)(b), 93(2)(b), 108(3)(b) or 119(3)(b) of the Children's Hearings (Scotland) Act 2011.]

NOTES

Commencement: 10 September 2015.

Inserted by the Rehabilitation of Offenders Act 1974 (Exclusions and Exceptions) (Scotland) Amendment Order 2015, SSI 2015/329, art 2(2), as from 10 September 2015.

Para (3): word in square brackets substituted by the Rehabilitation of Offenders Act 1974 (Exclusions and Exceptions) (Scotland) Amendment Order 2016, SSI 2016/91, art 3, as from 8 February 2016.

[2.1313]

3 Exclusion of section 4(1) of the Act

[(1)] The application of section 4(1) of the Act is excluded in relation to—

(a) any proceedings specified in Schedule 1; and
(b) any proceedings with respect to a decision or a proposed decision specified in Part 1 of Schedule 2—
(i) to the extent that there falls to be determined in those proceedings any issue relating to a spent conviction or to circumstances ancillary thereto; and
(ii) to the extent that section 4(1) renders inadmissible any evidence relating to the conviction or circumstances or removes the requirement to answer any question relating to the conviction or circumstances.

[(2) But the application of section 4(1) of the Act is not excluded in relation to any protected conviction, or any circumstances ancillary to such a conviction, in relation to—
(a) proceedings specified in paragraphs 1, 2, 6, 8, 9, 13, 15, 16, 18, 20, 25 or 28 of Schedule 1; or
(b) proceedings specified in paragraph (1)(b).]

NOTES

Para (1) numbered as such, and para (2) added, by the Rehabilitation of Offenders Act 1974 (Exclusions and Exceptions) (Scotland) Amendment Order 2015, SSI 2015/329, art 3, as from 10 September 2015.

[2.1314]

4 Exclusion of section 4(2)(a) and (b) of the Act

[(1)] The application of section 4(2)(a) and (b) of the Act is excluded in relation to questions put in the circumstances to which Schedule 3 applies.

[(2) But the application of section 4(2)(a) and (b) of the Act is not excluded in relation to any question relating to a spent conviction, or any circumstances ancillary to that conviction, if that conviction is—
(a) a protected conviction; or
[(b) a conviction which—
(i) falls within paragraph (2A); and
(ii) is not included in a higher level disclosure sent in connection with the purpose for which the question is put.]

[(2A) A spent conviction falls within this paragraph if it is—
(a) a conviction for an offence listed in schedule A1 and either—
(i) the person was aged under 18 on the date of conviction and at least 7 years and 6 months have passed since the date of conviction; or
(ii) the person was aged 18 or over on the date of conviction and at least 15 years have passed since the date of conviction; or
(b) a conviction for an offence listed in schedule B1 which is not a protected conviction.]

(3) Paragraph (2) does not apply to—
(a) any question put to assess the suitability of a person to hold—
(i) any certificate or permit mentioned in paragraph 3(3)(a) [or (aa)] of Schedule 3;
(ii) a certificate mentioned in paragraph 3(3)(c) of that Schedule;
(iii) a licence mentioned in paragraph 3(3)(ca) of that Schedule;
(b) any question mentioned in paragraph 6(1) of Schedule 3; or
(c) any question put to assess the suitability of a person to hold an occupation mentioned in paragraph 1 or 4 of Part 3 of Schedule 4.

(4) If a spent conviction [which falls within paragraph (2A)] for an offence listed in Schedule B1 is included in a higher level disclosure, the application of section 4(2)(a) and (b) of the Act is not excluded in relation to any failure to disclose that conviction, or any circumstances ancillary to that conviction, which occurred before that higher level disclosure was sent.]

[(5) Paragraph (4) does not apply if the failure to disclose the conviction related to a question asked when the conviction did not fall within paragraph (2A).]

NOTES

Para (1) numbered as such, and paras (2)–(4) added, by the Rehabilitation of Offenders Act 1974 (Exclusions and Exceptions) (Scotland) Amendment Order 2015, SSI 2015/329, art 4, as from 10 September 2015.

Sub-para (2)(b) was substituted, paras (2A) and (5) were inserted and added respectively, and the words in square brackets in para (4) were substituted, by the Rehabilitation of Offenders Act 1974 (Exclusions and Exceptions) (Scotland) Amendment Order 2018, SSI 2018/51, art 2(1), (2), as from 17 February 2018.

Para (3): words in square brackets in sub-para (a)(i) inserted by the Rehabilitation of Offenders Act 1974 (Exclusions and Exceptions) (Scotland) Amendment (No 2) Order 2016, SSI 2016/147, arts 2, 3(1), as from 1 July 2016.

[2.1315]

5 Exceptions from section 4(3) of the Act

[(1)] There is excepted from the provisions of section 4(3)(b) of the Act—
(a) any profession, office, employment or occupation specified in Schedule 4;
(b) any action taken for the purpose of safeguarding national security; and
(c) any decision or proposed decision taken by a person specified in Part 1 of Schedule 2 to do or to refuse to do anything specified in that Part.

[(2) But the exceptions in paragraph (1)(a) and (c) do not apply in relation to a spent conviction, or any circumstances ancillary to that conviction, if that conviction is—
(a) a protected conviction; or
[(b) a conviction which—
(i) falls within paragraph (2A); and

(ii) is not included in a higher level disclosure sent in connection with the profession, office, employment, occupation, decision or proposed decision to which the exception would otherwise apply.]

[(2A) A spent conviction falls within this paragraph if it is—

(a) a conviction for an offence listed in Schedule A1 and either—

(i) the person was aged under 18 on the date of conviction and at least 7 years and 6 months have passed since the date of conviction; or

(ii) the person was aged 18 or over on the date of conviction and at least 15 years have passed since the date of conviction; or

(b) a conviction for an offence listed in schedule B1 which is not a protected conviction.]

(3) Paragraph (2) does not apply in relation to an occupation listed in paragraph 1 or 4 of Part 3 of Schedule 4.

(4) If a spent conviction [which falls within paragraph (2A)] for an offence listed in Schedule B1 is included in a higher level disclosure, the exceptions in paragraph (1)(a) and (c) do not apply to any failure to disclose that conviction, or any circumstances ancillary to that conviction, which occurred before that higher level disclosure was sent.]

[(5) Paragraph (4) does not apply if the failure to disclose the conviction related to a question asked when the conviction did not fall within paragraph (2A).]

NOTES

Para (1) numbered as such, and paras (2)–(4) added, by the Rehabilitation of Offenders Act 1974 (Exclusions and Exceptions) (Scotland) Amendment Order 2015, SSI 2015/329, art 5, as from 10 September 2015.

Sub-para (2)(b) was substituted, paras (2A) and (5) were inserted and added respectively, and the words in square brackets in para (4) were substituted, by the Rehabilitation of Offenders Act 1974 (Exclusions and Exceptions) (Scotland) Amendment Order 2018, SSI 2018/51, art 2(1), (3), as from 17 February 2018.

6 (*Introduces Sch 5 (Revocations).*)

SCHEDULES

[SCHEDULE A1
[OFFENCES WHICH MUST BE DISCLOSED SUBJECT TO EXCEPTIONS]

Article 2A

Common law offences

[2.1316]

1 Abduction.

2 Abortion.

3 Assault to the danger of life.

4 Assault to severe injury.

5 Assault with intent to rape or ravish.

6 Assault with intent to commit the statutory offence of rape.

7 Bestiality.

8 Cruel and unnatural treatment of persons.

9 Culpable homicide.

10 Drugging.

11 Extortion.

12 Hamesucken.

13 Hijacking.

14 Piracy.

15 Plagium.

16 Reset of plagium.

17 Treason.

18 Uttering threats.

Statutory offences

Armed forces

19 An offence under section 42 of the Armed Forces Act 2006 (criminal conduct) where the corresponding offence under the law of England and Wales is, or corresponds to, an offence listed in this Schedule.

Aviation and maritime

20 An offence under the Piracy Act 1837.

21 An offence under any of the following provisions of the Aviation Security Act 1982—
(a) section 1 (hijacking);
(b) section 2 (destroying, damaging or endangering safety of aircraft);
(c) section 3 (other acts endangering or likely to endanger safety of aircraft); and
(d) section 4 (offences in relation to certain dangerous articles).

22 An offence under section 9 of the Aviation and Maritime Security Act 1990 (hijacking of ships).

[**23** An offence under article 265 of the Air Navigation Order 2016 in respect of a contravention of article 240 of that Order (endangering safety of aircraft).]

Children

24 An offence under section 12 of the Children and Young Persons (Scotland) Act 1937 (cruelty to persons under 16).

Explosives

25 An offence under the Explosive Substances Act 1883.

Firearms and other weapons

26 An offence under any of the following provisions of the Firearms Act 1968—
(a) section 4 (conversion of weapons);
(b) section 5 (weapons subject to a general prohibition);
(c) section 16 (possession of firearm with intent to injure);
(d) section 16A (possession of firearm with intent to cause fear or violence);
(e) section 17 (use of firearm to resist arrest);
(f) section 18 (carrying firearm with criminal intent);
(g) section 19 (carrying firearm in a public place);
(h) section 20 (trespassing with firearm);
(i) section 21 (possession of firearm by persons previously convicted of crime);
(j) section 24 (supplying firearms to minors);
(k) section 25 (supplying firearm to person drunk or insane);
(l) section 28A(7) (certificates: supplementary);
(m) section 29 (variation of firearm certificates);
(n) section 30D(3) (revocation of certificates: supplementary);
(o) section 39 (offences in connection with registration);
(p) section 40 (compulsory register of transactions in firearms);
(q) section 46(5) (power of search with warrant);
(r) section 47 (powers of constables to stop and search); and
(s) section 48 (production of certificates).

27 An offence under the Chemical Weapons Act 1996.

Forced marriage

28 An offence under section 122 of the Anti-social Behaviour, Crime and Policing Act 2014 (offence of forced marriage: Scotland).

Human trafficking and exploitation

29 An offence under section 22 of the Criminal Justice (Scotland) Act 2003 (traffic in prostitution etc).

30 An offence under section 4 of the Asylum and Immigration (Treatment of Claimants, etc) Act 2004 (trafficking people for exploitation).

31 An offence under section 47 of the Criminal Justice and Licensing (Scotland) Act 2010 (slavery, servitude and forced or compulsory labour).

32 An offence under the Prohibition of Female Genital Mutilation (Scotland) Act 2005.

Medical professions etc

33 An offence under section 10Z9 of the National Health Service (Scotland) Act 1978 (offences in relation to registration).

34 An offence under any of the following provisions of the Medical Act 1983—
(a) section 49 (penalty for pretending to be registered); and
(b) section 49A (penalty for pretending to hold a licence to practise) .

35 An offence under article 38 (offences relating to the Register) of the Pharmacy Order 2010.

Medicines

36 An offence under any of the following provisions of the Medicines Act 1968—
(a) section 67(1A) and (1B) (offences under Part III); and
(b) section 78 (restrictions on use of titles, descriptions and emblems).

Official Secrets

37 An offence under the Official Secrets Act 1911.

Prostitution

38 An offence under any of the following provisions of the Criminal Law (Consolidation) (Scotland) Act 1995—

(a) section 7 (procuring);
(b) section 11 (trading in prostitution and brothel-keeping); and
(c) section 12 (allowing child to be in brothel).

Road traffic

39 An offence under any of the following provisions of the Road Traffic Act 1988—

(a) section 1 (causing death by dangerous driving);
(b) section 3ZC (causing death by driving: disqualified drivers); and
(c) section 3A (causing death by careless driving when under influence of drink or drugs).

Serious organised crime

40 An offence under any of the following provisions of the Criminal Justice and Licensing (Scotland) Act 2010—

(a) section 28 (involvement in serious organised crime);
(b) section 30 (directing serious organised crime); and
(c) section 31 (failure to report serious organised crime).

Sexual offences

41 An offence under section 50(3) of the Customs and Excise Management Act 1979 (penalty for improper importation of goods) in relation to goods prohibited to be imported under section 42 of the Customs Consolidation Act 1876, but only where the prohibited goods include indecent photographs of persons.

42 A sexual offence within the meaning given by section 210A(10) of the Criminal Procedure (Scotland) Act 1995 other than an offence mentioned in paragraph (xxvii)(ZF) or (ZG) of that section (engaging while an older child in sexual conduct with or towards another older child).

43 An offence under section 113 of the Sexual Offences Act 2003 (breach of sexual offences prevention order or interim sexual offences prevention order, etc).

44 An offence under section 7 of the Protection of Children and Prevention of Sexual Offences (Scotland) Act 2005 (offence: breach of RSHO or interim RSHO etc).

Stalking and harassment

45 An offence under section 50A of the Criminal Law (Consolidation) (Scotland) Act 1995 (racially aggravated harassment).

46 An offence under any of the following provisions of the Criminal Justice and Licensing (Scotland) Act 2010—

(a) section 38 (threatening or abusive behaviour); and
(b) section 39 (offence of stalking).

Terrorism

47 An offence under any of the following provisions of the Terrorism Act 2000—

(a) section 11 (membership);
(b) section 12 (support);
(c) section 15 (fund-raising);
(d) section 16 (use and possession);
(e) section 17 (funding arrangements);
(f) section 17A(2) or (4) (insurance payments made in response to terrorist demands);
(g) section 18 (money laundering);
(h) section 19 (disclosure of information: duty);
(i) section 21A (failure to disclose: regulated sector);
(j) section 21D (tipping off: regulated sector);
(k) section 38B (information about acts of terrorism);
(l) section 39 (disclosure of information, &c);
(m) section 54 (weapons training);
(n) section 56 (directing terrorist organisation);
(o) section 57 (possession for terrorist purposes);
(p) section 58 (collection of information);
(q) section 58A (eliciting, publishing or communicating); and
(r) section 61 (inciting terrorism overseas).

48 An offence under any of the following provisions of the Anti-terrorism, Crime and Security Act 2001—

(a) section 47 (use etc of nuclear weapons);
(b) section 50 (assisting or inducing certain weapons-related acts overseas);

(c) section 52 (powers of entry);
(d) section 54 (offences);
(e) section 67 (offences);
(f) section 79 (prohibition of disclosures relating to nuclear security);
(g) section 80 (prohibition of disclosures of uranium enrichment technology);
(h) section 113 (use of noxious substances or things to cause harm and intimidate);
(i) section 114 (hoaxes involving noxious substances or things); and
(j) paragraph 7 of Schedule 3 (offences).

49 An offence under the Terrorism Act 2006.

50 An offence under any of the following provisions of the Counter-Terrorism Act 2008—
(a) section 2 (offence of obstruction);
(b) section 54 (offences relating to notification);
(c) paragraph 15 of Schedule 5 (breach of foreign travel restriction order and offence);
(d) paragraph 30 of Schedule 7 (offences: failure to comply with requirement imposed by direction);
(e) paragraph 30A of Schedule 7 (offences: relevant person circumventing requirements); and
(f) paragraph 31 of Schedule 7 (offences in connection with licences).

Violent offender orders

51 An offence under section 113(1) of the Criminal Justice and Immigration Act 2008 (breach of violent offender order or interim violent offender order).

Vulnerable persons

52 An offence under section 83 of the Adults with Incapacity (Scotland) Act 2000 (offence of ill-treatment and wilful neglect).

53 An offence under section 315 of the Mental Health (Care and Treatment) (Scotland) Act 2003 (ill-treatment and wilful neglect of mentally disordered person).

54 An offence under any of the following provisions of the Protection of Vulnerable Groups (Scotland) Act 2007—
(a) section 34 (barred individuals not to do regulated work);
(b) section 35 (organisations not to use barred individuals for regulated work); and
(c) section 36 (personnel suppliers not to supply barred individuals for regulated work).

55 Any offence where the conduct in respect of which the person was convicted also constituted a breach of a banning order granted under section 19 of the Adult Support and Protection (Scotland) Act 2007 (banning orders).

Witness protection

56 An offence under any of the following provisions of the Serious Organised Crime and Police Act 2005—
(a) section 86 (offence of disclosing information about protection arrangements); and
(b) section 88 (offences of disclosing information relating to persons assuming new identity).

Statutory aggravations

57 An offence in relation to which either of the following provisions applies—
(a) section 29(1) of the Criminal Justice and Licensing (Scotland) Act 2010 (offences aggravated by connection with serious organised crime); or
(b) section 31 of the Counter-Terrorism Act 2008 (offences aggravated by terrorism).

Other

Common law aggravations

58 An offence the conviction for which indicates that it was committed against a child.

59 An offence the conviction for which indicates that it included a sexual element.

Inchoate offences

60 An offence committed by aiding, abetting, counselling, procuring or inciting the commission of the offence of murder or any offence listed in paragraphs 1 to 59 of this Schedule.

61 An offence committed by attempting or conspiring to commit the offence of murder or any offence listed in paragraphs 1 to 59 of this Schedule.

Superseded offences

62 An offence superseded (whether directly or indirectly) by any offence listed in paragraphs 1 to 61 of this Schedule (and any qualification in relation to a listed offence applies to the superseded offence as it applies to the listed offence).

Combined offences

63 An offence which was charged, and the conviction for which was received, in conjunction with any offence listed in paragraphs 1 to 62 of this Schedule.

Corresponding offences elsewhere in the UK or abroad

64 An offence under the law of England and Wales or Northern Ireland, or any country or territory outside the United Kingdom, which corresponds to any offence listed in paragraphs 1 to 63 of this Schedule.]

NOTES

Commencement: 8 February 2016.

Inserted by the Rehabilitation of Offenders Act 1974 (Exclusions and Exceptions) (Scotland) Amendment Order 2015, SSI 2015/329, art 6, as from 10 September 2015.

Substituted by the Rehabilitation of Offenders Act 1974 (Exclusions and Exceptions) (Scotland) Amendment Order 2016, SSI 2016/91, art 4, as from 8 February 2016.

The Schedule heading was substituted by the Rehabilitation of Offenders Act 1974 (Exclusions and Exceptions) (Scotland) Amendment Order 2018, SSI 2018/51, art 2(1), (4), as from 17 February 2018.

Para 23: substituted by the Air Navigation Order 2016, SI 2016/765, art 274(1), Sch 14, Pt 2, para 11, as from 25 August 2016.

[SCHEDULE B1
OFFENCES WHICH ARE TO BE DISCLOSED SUBJECT TO RULES

Articles 2A, 4 and 5

Common law offences

[2.1317]

1 An offence of perverting, or attempting to pervert, the course of justice (by whatever means and however the offence is described), including in particular—
- (a) perjury;
- (b) prevarication on oath;
- (c) prison breaking; and
- (d) subornation of perjury.

2 Assault excluding any assault of a kind listed in Schedule A1.

3 Breach of the peace.

4 Clandestinely taking possession.

5 Culpable and reckless conduct.

6 Culpable and reckless endangering of the public.

7 Culpable and reckless fireraising.

8 Embezzlement.

9 False accusation of a crime.

10 Fraud.

11 Housebreaking with intent to steal.

12 Mobbing and rioting.

13 Opening a lockfast place with intent to steal.

14 Public indecency.

15 Reset (excluding reset of plagium).

16 Robbery.

17 Theft (excluding plagium).

18 Uttering.

19 Wilful fireraising.

Statutory offences

Adult support and protection

20 An offence under section 49 of the Adult Support and Protection (Scotland) Act 2007 (obstruction).

Animals

21 An offence under the Rabies (Importation of Dogs, Cats and Other Mammals) Order 1974.

22 An offence under any of the following provisions of the Wildlife and Countryside Act 1981—
- (a) section 1 (protection of wild birds, their nests and eggs and prevention of poaching);
- (b) section 5 (prohibition of certain methods of killing or taking wild birds);
- (c) section 9 (protection of other wild animals and prevention of poaching);
- (d) section 11 (prohibition of certain methods of killing or taking wild animals);
- (e) section 11A, 11B and 11C (offences in relation to snares);

(f) section 14ZC (prohibition on keeping etc of invasive animals or plants);
(g) section 15A (possession of pesticides); and
(h) section 18 (attempts to commit offences etc), but only in relation to an offence listed in sub-paragraphs (a) to (g) of this paragraph.

23 An offence under the Dangerous Dogs Act 1991.

24 An offence under the Protection of Badgers Act 1992.

25 An offence under any of the following provisions of the Conservation (Natural Habitats, &c) Regulations 1994—
(a) regulation 39 (protection of certain wild animals); and
(b) regulation 41 (prohibition of certain methods of taking or killing wild animals).

26 An offence under the Welfare of Animals (Slaughter or Killing) Regulations 1995.

27 An offence under the Wild Mammals Protection Act 1996.

28 An offence under the Protection of Wild Mammals (Scotland) Act 2002.

29 An offence under the Animal Health and Welfare (Scotland) Act 2006.

Armed forces

30 An offence under section 42 of the Armed Forces Act 2006 (criminal conduct) where the corresponding offence under the law of England and Wales is, or corresponds to, an offence listed in this Schedule.

Assaulting or hindering public officials

31 An offence under section 89 of the Police Act 1996 (assaults on constables).

32 An offence under section 32 of the Commissioners for Revenue and Customs Act 2005 (assault).

33 An offence under the Emergency Workers (Scotland) Act 2005.

34 An offence under section 85 of the Fire (Scotland) Act 2005 (false alarms).

35 An offence under section 90 of the Police and Fire Reform (Scotland) Act 2012 (assaulting or impeding police).

Aviation

36 An offence under any of the following provisions of the Aviation Security Act 1982—
(a) section 20B (detention direction); and
(b) section 21FA (air cargo agents: documents).

Bomb hoaxes

37 An offence under section 51 of the Criminal Law Act 1977 (bomb hoaxes).

Bribery

38 An offence under the Bribery Act 2010.

Care services

39 An offence under any of the following provisions of the Regulation of Care (Scotland) Act 2001—
(a) section 45 (application for registration under Part 3); and
(b) section 52 (use of title "social worker" etc).

40 An offence under any of the following provisions of the Public Services Reform (Scotland) Act 2010—
(a) section 80(1) (offences in relation to registration under Chapter 3);
(b) section 81 (false statements in application under Chapter 3); and
(c) section 90 (offences under Chapter 4).

41 An offence under article 27 of the Public Services Reform (General Teaching Council for Scotland) Order 2011 (offences).

42 An offence under regulation 19 of the Social Care and Social Work Improvement (Scotland) (Requirements for Care Services) Regulations 2011 (offences).

Charities

43 An offence under the Charities and Trustee Investment (Scotland) Act 2005.

Child Support

44 An offence under section 50 of the Child Support Act 1991 (unauthorised disclosure of information).

Children

45 An offence under section 6 of the Child Abduction Act 1984 (offence in Scotland of parent, etc taking or sending child out of United Kingdom).

Crossbows

46 An offence under section 1 of the Crossbows Act 1987 (sale and letting on hire).

Domestic abuse

47 An offence under section 2 of the Domestic Abuse (Scotland) Act 2011 (breach of domestic abuse interdict with power of arrest).

Drugs

48 An offence under any of the following provisions of the Misuse of Drugs Act 1971—

(a) section 3 (restriction of importation and exportation of controlled drugs);
(b) section 4 (restriction of production and supply of controlled drugs);
(c) section 4A (aggravation of offence of supply of controlled drug);
(d) section 5(3) (restriction of possession of controlled drugs);
(e) section 6 (restriction of cultivation of cannabis plant);
(f) section 8(a) and (b) (occupiers etc of premises to be punishable for certain activities taking place there);
(g) section 12 (directions prohibiting prescribing, supply etc of controlled drugs by practitioners etc convicted of certain offences);
(h) section 13 (directions prohibiting prescribing, supply etc of controlled drugs by practitioners in other cases);
(i) section 17 (power to obtain information from doctors, pharmacists etc in certain circumstances);
(j) section 19 (attempts etc to commit offences), but only in relation to an offence listed in sub-paragraphs (a) to (i) of this paragraph; and
(k) section 20 (assisting in or inducing commission outside United Kingdom of offence punishable under corresponding law).

49 An offence under any of the following provisions of the Customs and Excise Management Act 1979 in relation to goods prohibited to be imported or exported under section 3(1) of the Misuse of Drugs Act 1971 (restriction of importation and exportation of controlled drugs)—

(a) section 50(2) or (3) (penalty for improper importation of goods);
(b) section 68(2) (offences in relation to exportation of prohibited or restricted goods); and
(c) section 170 (fraudulent evasion of duty).

50 An offence under the Criminal Justice (International Co-operation) Act 1990.

Escape from custody etc

51 An offence under section 316 of the Mental Health (Care and Treatment) (Scotland) Act 2003 (inducing and assisting absconding etc).

52 An offence under section 91 of the Police and Fire Reform (Scotland) Act 2012 (escape from custody).

Financial Services

53 An offence under the Financial Services and Markets Act 2000.

54 An offence under the Financial Services Act 2012.

Fire safety

55 An offence under section 72(1) or (3) of the Fire (Scotland) Act 2005 (offences).

Firearms

56 An offence under any of the following provisions of the Firearms Act 1968—

(a) section 1 (requirement of firearms certificate);
(b) section 2 (requirement of certificate for possession of shot guns);
(c) section 3 (business and other transactions with firearms and ammunition);
(d) section 22 (acquisition and possession of firearms by minors); and
(e) section 23 (exceptions from section 22(4)).

57 An offence under section 50(5) of the Civic Government (Scotland) Act 1982 (drunk in possession of firearm).

58 An offence under the Firearms (Amendment) Act 1997.

59 An offence under any of the following provisions of the Violent Crime Reduction Act 2006—

(a) section 28 (using someone to mind a weapon);
(b) section 32 (sales of air weapons by way of trade or business to be face to face);
(c) section 35 (restriction on sale and purchase of primers); and
(d) section 36 (manufacture, import and sale of realistic imitation firearms).

Food safety and standards

60 An offence under any of the following provisions of the Food Safety Act 1990—

(a) section 7 (rendering food injurious to health); and
(b) section 9 (inspection and seizure of suspected food).

61 An offence under regulation 4(b) of the General Food Regulations 2004.

Forced marriage

62 An offence under section 9 of the Forced Marriage etc (Protection and Jurisdiction) (Scotland) Act 2011 (offence of breaching order).

Fraud and forgery

63 An offence under the Forgery and Counterfeiting Act 1981.

64 An offence under section 46A of the Criminal Law (Consolidation) (Scotland) Act 1995 (false monetary instruments).

65 An offence under section 49 of the Criminal Justice and Licensing (Scotland) Act 2010 (articles for use in fraud).

66 An offence under section 92 of the Police and Fire Reform (Scotland) Act 2012 (impersonation etc).

Harassment

67 An offence under section 234A of the Criminal Procedure (Scotland) Act 1995 (non-harassment orders).

68 An offence under section 9 of the Protection from Harassment Act 1997 (breach of non-harassment order).

Immigration, etc

69 An offence under any of the following provisions of the Immigration Act 1971—

(a) section 24 (illegal entry and similar offences);
(b) section 24A (deception);
(c) section 25 (assisting unlawful immigration to member State);
(d) section 25A (helping asylum-seeker to enter United Kingdom);
(e) section 25B (assisting entry to United Kingdom in breach of deportation or exclusion order);
(f) section 26 (general offences in connection with administration of Act);
(g) section 26A (registration card);
(h) section 26B (possession of immigration stamp); and
(i) section 27 (offences by captains, owners or agents of ships or aircraft).

70 An offence under any of the following provisions of the Immigration and Asylum Act 1999—

(a) section 105 (false representations);
(b) section 106 (dishonest representations);
(c) any of the following paragraphs of Schedule 11—
  (i) paragraph 1 (obtaining certificates of authorisation by false pretences);
  (ii) paragraph 4 (assaulting a detainee custody officer); and
  (iii) paragraph 5 (obstructing detainee custody officer); and
(d) any of the following paragraphs of Schedule 12—
  (i) paragraph 3 (failure to submit to a medical examination);
  (ii) paragraph 4 (assisting detained persons to escape);
  (iii) paragraph 5 (bringing alcohol into a detention centre); and
  (iv) paragraph 6 (conveying articles into or out of a detention centre).

71 An offence under section 35 of the Asylum and Immigration (Treatment of Claimants, etc) Act 2004 (deportation or removal: cooperation).

72 An offence under section 21 of the Immigration, Asylum and Nationality Act 2006 (offence).

Insolvency

73 An offence under any of the following provisions of the Insolvency Act 1986—

(a) section 131 (company's statement of affairs);
(b) section 206 (fraud, etc in anticipation of winding up);
(c) section 208 (misconduct in course of winding up);
(d) section 216 (restriction on re-use of company names); and
(e) section 235 (duty to co-operate with office-holder).

Landmines

74 An offence under section 2 of the Landmines Act 1998 (prohibited conduct).

Medicines

75 An offence under section 67(2) [or] (3) (offences under Part III) of the Medicines Act 1968.

76 An offence under any of the following provisions of the Human Medicines Regulations 2012—

(a) regulation 34(1) (offences: breach of regulations and false information and defence concerning starting materials); and
(b) regulation 255(1)(a), (b), (c) or (d) (offences relating to dealings with medicinal products).

Mental health

77 An offence under section 318 of the Mental Health (Care and Treatment) (Scotland) Act 2003 (false statements).

Neglect of duty

78 An offence under Part 4 (shipping: alcohol and drugs) or Part 5 (aviation: alcohol and drugs) of the Railways and Transport Safety Act 2003.

79 An offence under section 22 of the Police and Fire Reform (Scotland) Act 2012 (failure to perform duty).

Obscene material etc

80 An offence under section 1(1) of the Indecent Displays Act 1981 (indecent displays).

81 An offence under any of the following provisions of the Civic Government (Scotland) Act 1982—
(a) section 51 (obscene material);
(b) section 51A (extreme pornography); . . .
(c) . . .

82 An offence under section 85(3) of the Postal Services Act 2000 (prohibition on sending certain articles by post).

83 An offence under section 127(1) of the Communications Act 2003 (improper use of public electronic communications network).

Offences in relation to children

84 An offence under any of the following provisions of the Children and Young Persons (Scotland) Act 1937—
(a) section 15 (causing or allowing persons under 16 to be used for begging);
(b) section 22 (exposing children under seven to risk of burning);
(c) section 31(1) (penalties and legal proceedings in respect of general provisions as to employment);
(d) section 33 (prohibition of persons under sixteen taking part in performances endangering life or limb); and
(e) section 34 (restrictions on training for performances of a dangerous nature).

85 An offence under section 40(1) of the Children and Young Persons Act 1963 (offences).

86 An offence under section 50(2) of the Civic Government (Scotland) Act 1982 (drunk in charge of a child).

87 An offence under section 81 of the Children (Scotland) Act 1995 (offences in connection with orders etc for the protection of children).

88 An offence under any of the following provisions of the Children's Hearings (Scotland) Act 2011—
(a) section 59 (offences); and
(b) section 171 (offences related to absconding).

Offensive behaviour etc

89 An offence under the Offensive Behaviour at Football and Threatening Communications (Scotland) Act 2012.

Offensive weapons

90 An offence under the Restriction of Offensive Weapons Act 1959.

91 An offence under section 50(3) (penalty for improper importation of goods) or section 170 (fraudulent evasion of duty) of the Customs and Excise Management Act 1979 in relation to goods prohibited to be imported under—
(a) section 1(2) of the Restriction of Offensive Weapons Act 1959 (penalties for offences in connection with dangerous weapons); or
(b) section 141(4) of the Criminal Justice Act 1988 (offensive weapons).

92 An offence under any of the following provisions of the Criminal Justice Act 1988—
(a) section 141 (offensive weapons); and
(b) section 141A (sale of knives and certain articles with blade or point to persons under eighteen).

93 An offence under any of the following provisions of the Criminal Law (Consolidation) (Scotland) Act 1995—
(a) section 47 (prohibition of the carrying of offensive weapons);
(b) section 48 (search for offensive weapons);
(c) section 49 (offence of having in a public place an article with a blade or point);
(d) section 49A (offence of having article with blade or point (or offensive weapon) on school premises);
(e) section 49C (offence of having offensive weapon etc in prison); and
(f) section 50 (extension of constable's power to stop, search and arrest without warrant).

Official Secrets Acts

94 An offence under the Official Secrets Act 1920.

95 An offence under the Official Secrets Act 1989.

Prisons

96 An offence under section 41 of the Prisons (Scotland) Act 1989 (unlawful introduction of tobacco, etc, into prison).

Proceeds of crime and money laundering

97 An offence under any of the following provisions of the Proceeds of Crime Act 2002—
(a) Part 7 (money laundering);
(b) Part 8 (investigations); and
(c) section 453A (certain offences in relation to financial investigators).

98 An offence under the Proceeds of Crime Act 2002 (External Investigations) Order 2013.

99 An offence under the Proceeds of Crime Act 2002 (External Investigations) (Scotland) Order 2015.

Prostitution

100 An offence under any of the following provisions of the Criminal Law (Consolidation) (Scotland) Act 1995—
(a) section 9 (permitting girl to use premises for intercourse); and
(b) section 13(9) (living on earnings of another from male prostitution).

101 An offence under the Prostitution (Public Places) (Scotland) Act 2007.

Public order

102 An offence under any of the following provisions of the Public Order Act 1986—
(a) section 1 (riot);
(b) section 2 (violent disorder);
(c) section 3 (affray);
(d) section 4 (fear or provocation of violence);
(e) section 4A (intentional harassment, alarm or distress);
(f) section 5 (harassment alarm or distress);
(g) section 18 (use of words or behaviour or display of written material);
(h) section 19 (publishing or distributing written material);
(i) section 20 (public performance of play);
(j) section 21 (distributing, showing or playing a recording);
(k) section 22 (broadcasting or including programme in cable programme service);
(l) section 23 (possession of racially inflammatory material);
(m) section 29B (use of words or behaviour or display of written material);
(n) section 29C (publishing or distributing written material);
(o) section 29D (public performance of play);
(p) section 29E (distributing, showing or playing recording);
(q) section 29F (broadcasting or including programme in programme service); and
(r) section 29G (possession of inflammatory material).

Road traffic

103 An offence under any of the following provisions of the Road Traffic Act 1988—
(a) section 1A (causing serious injury by dangerous driving);
(b) section 2 (dangerous driving);
(c) section 2B (causing death by careless, or inconsiderate, driving);
(d) section 3ZB (causing death by driving: unlicensed or uninsured drivers);
(e) section 3ZD (causing serious injury by driving: disqualified drivers);
(f) section 4(1) (driving, or being in charge, when under the influence of drink or drugs);
(g) section 5(1)(a) (driving or being in charge of a motor vehicle with alcohol concentration above prescribed limit); and
(h) section 178 (taking motor vehicle without authority, etc).

Sexual offences

104 An offence under section 37(1) or (4) of the Sexual Offences (Scotland) Act 2009 (older children engaging in sexual conduct with each other).

Solicitors

105 An offence under the Solicitors (Scotland) Act 1980.

Terrorism

106 An offence under any of the following provisions of the Terrorism Act 2000—
(a) section 13 (uniform);
(b) section 36 (police powers);
(c) section 51 (offences);
(d) section 116 (powers to stop and search);

(e) paragraph 32 of Schedule 5 (urgent cases); and
(f) paragraph 18 of Schedule 7 (offences).

Vets

107 An offence under any of the following provisions of the Veterinary Surgeons Act 1966—
(a) section 19 (restriction of practice of veterinary surgery by unqualified persons); and
(b) section 20 (prohibition of use of practitioners' titles by unqualified persons).

Miscellaneous statutory offences

108 An offence under any of the following provisions of the Civic Government (Scotland) Act 1982—
(a) section 57 (being in or on building etc with intent to commit theft);
(b) section 58 (convicted thief in possession); and
(c) section 60 (powers of search and seizure).

109 An offence under section 22 of the Rent (Scotland) Act 1984 (unlawful eviction and harassment of occupier).

110 An offence under section 85(1) of the Postal Services Act 2000 (prohibition on sending certain articles by post).

111 An offence under any of the following provisions of the Serious Organised Crime and Police Act 2005—
(a) section 67 (offences in connection with disclosure notices or search warrants);
(b) section 129 (corresponding Scottish offence);
(c) section 145 (interference with contractual relationships so as to harm animal research organisation); and
(d) section 146 (intimidation of persons connected with animal research organisation).

Statutory aggravations

112 An offence (other than an offence listed in Schedule A1) in relation to which either of the following provisions applies—
(a) section 96 of the Crime and Disorder Act 1998 (offences racially aggravated); or
(b) section 74 of the Criminal Justice (Scotland) Act 2003 (offences aggravated by religious prejudice).

113 An offence (other than an offence listed in Schedule A1) to which either of the following provisions of the Offences (Aggravation by Prejudice) (Scotland) Act 2009 applies—
(a) section 1(1) (prejudice relating to disability); or
(b) section 2(1) (prejudice relating to sexual orientation or transgender identity).

Other

Common law aggravations

114 An offence (other than an offence listed in Schedule A1 or in paragraph 112 of this Schedule), the conviction for which indicates that it included an element of racial prejudice or was racially motivated.

115 An offence (other than an offence listed in Schedule A1 or in paragraph 112 of this schedule), the conviction for which indicates that it included an element of religious prejudice or was motivated by religious prejudice.

Inchoate offences

116 An offence committed by aiding, abetting, counselling, procuring or inciting the commission of any offence listed in paragraphs 1 to 115 of this Schedule.

117 An offence committed by attempting or conspiring to commit any offence listed in paragraphs 1 to 115 of this Schedule.

Superseded offences

118 An offence superseded (whether directly or indirectly) by any offence listed in paragraphs 1 to 117 of this Schedule (and any qualification in relation to a listed offence applies to the superseded offence as it applies to the listed offence).

Combined offences

119 An offence which was charged, and the conviction for which was received, in conjunction with any offence listed in paragraphs 1 to 118 of this Schedule.

Corresponding offences elsewhere in the UK or abroad

120 An offence under the law of England and Wales or Northern Ireland, or any country or territory outside the United Kingdom, which corresponds to any offence listed in paragraphs 1 to 119 of this Schedule.]

NOTES

Commencement: 8 February 2016.

Inserted by the Rehabilitation of Offenders Act 1974 (Exclusions and Exceptions) (Scotland) Amendment Order 2015, SSI 2015/329, art 6, as from 10 September 2015.

Part 2 Statutory Instruments

Substituted by the Rehabilitation of Offenders Act 1974 (Exclusions and Exceptions) (Scotland) Amendment Order 2016, SSI 2016/91, art 5, as from 8 February 2016.

The word in square brackets in para 75 was substituted, and the words omitted from para 81 were revoked, by the Rehabilitation of Offenders Act 1974 (Exclusions and Exceptions) (Scotland) Amendment Order 2018, SSI 2018/51, art 2(1), (5), as from 17 February 2018.

SCHEDULE 1
PROCEEDINGS

Article 3(a)

[2.1318]

1. Proceedings in respect of a person's admission to, or disciplinary proceedings against a member of, any profession specified in Part 1 of Schedule 4 to this Order.

2. Disciplinary proceedings against a constable.

3–10A. . . .

11. Proceedings by way of appeal against, or review of, any decision taken, by virtue of any of the provisions of this Order, on consideration of a spent conviction.

12. Proceedings held for the receipt of evidence affecting the determination of any question arising in any proceedings specified in this Schedule.

13–29. . . .

NOTES

Paras 3–10A, 13–29: outside the scope of this work.

SCHEDULE 2

(*Sch 2 (Financial Services) outside the scope of this work.*)

SCHEDULE 3
EXCLUSIONS OF SECTION 4(2)(A) AND (B) OF THE ACT

Article 4

[2.1319]

1 **Application**

Subject to paragraph 2, this Schedule applies, for the purposes of article 4, to the circumstances set out in paragraphs 3 to 15.

2 **Requirements to inform**

(1) This Schedule applies only where the person questioned is informed at the time the question is asked that, by virtue of this Order, spent convictions are to be disclosed.

(2) In the case of questions put in the circumstances to which paragraph 6 applies, the person questioned is also to be informed at that time that spent convictions are to be disclosed in the interests of national security.

3 **Specified professions etc**

(1) Any question asked in order to assess the suitability—

(a) of the person to whom the question relates for a profession specified in Part 1 of Schedule 4;

(b) of the person to whom the question relates for any office or employment specified in Part 2 of Schedule 4;

(c) of the person to whom the question relates or of any other person to pursue any occupation specified in Part 3 of Schedule 4 or to pursue it subject to a particular condition or restriction; and

(d) of the person to whom the question relates or of any other person to be placed on a register or to hold a licence, certificate or permit specified in sub-paragraph (3) or to be placed on it or hold it subject to a particular condition or restriction.

(2) For the avoidance of doubt, references in sub-paragraph (1) to the suitability of a person for any profession or for any office, employment or occupation include the suitability of that person for training for such profession or, as the case may be, for training for such office, employment or occupation.

(3) The register, licences, certificates or permits referred to in sub-paragraph (1)(d) are—

(a) firearm certificates and shot gun certificates issued under the Firearms Act 1968, and permits issued under section 7(1), 9(2) or 13(1)(c) of that Act;

[(aa) air weapon certificates granted or renewed under section 5 of the Air Weapons and Licensing (Scotland) Act 2015(e), and permits granted under section 12, 13 or 17 of that Act;]

(b) licences issued under section 25 (restrictions on persons under eighteen going abroad for the purpose of performing for profit) of the Children and Young Persons Act 1933;

(c) explosives certificates issued by a chief officer of police pursuant to [regulation 11 of the Explosives Regulations 2014] as to the fitness of a person to acquire or acquire and keep explosives;

[(ca) licences granted under [section 4A of the Poisons Act 1972;]]
(d) licences granted under section 8 of the Private Security Industry Act 2001; or
(e) licences issued under, and the register of approved instructors referred to in, Part V (driving instruction) of the Road Traffic Act 1988.

4, 5 . . .

6 National Security

(1) Any question asked by or on behalf of—
(a) the Crown, the United Kingdom Atomic Energy Authority, [the FCA, the PRA, the Bank of England] or a universal service provider within the meaning of section 65 of the Postal Services Act 2011, in order to assess, for the purpose of safeguarding national security, the suitability of the person to whom the question relates or of any other person for any office or employment;
(b) the Civil Aviation Authority;
(c) any other person authorised to provide air traffic services under section 4 or 5 of the Transport Act 2000 (in any case where such person is a company, an "authorised company"); or
(d) subject to sub-paragraph (3)—
(i) any company which is a subsidiary, within the meaning given by section 1159(1) of the Companies Act 2006, of an authorised company; and
(ii) any company of which an authorised company is a subsidiary,

in the circumstances set out in sub-paragraph (2).

(2) The circumstances are that the question is put in order to assess, for the purpose of safeguarding national security, the suitability of the person to whom the question relates or of any other person for any office or employment.

(3) Where the question is put on behalf of a company mentioned in sub-paragraph (1)(d), this paragraph applies only where the question is put in relation to the provision of air traffic services.

7–15 . . .

NOTES

Para 3: sub-para (3)(aa) inserted by the Rehabilitation of Offenders Act 1974 (Exclusions and Exceptions) (Scotland) Amendment (No 2) Order 2016, SSI 2016/147, arts 2, 3(2), as from 1 July 2016; words in square brackets in sub-para (3)(c) substituted by the Explosives Regulations 2014, SI 2014/1638, reg 48(1), Sch 13, Pt 2, para 30(b), as from 1 October 2014; sub-para (3)(ca) inserted by the Control of Explosives Precursors Regulations 2014, SI 2014/1942, reg 18(1), (3), as from 2 September 2014; words in square brackets in sub-para (3)(ca) substituted by the Deregulation Act 2015 (Poisons and Explosives Precursors) (Consequential Amendments, Revocations and Transitional Provisions) Order 2015, SI 2015/968, art 3, Schedule, para 16(1), (3), as from 26 May 2015.

Paras 4, 5, 7–15: outside the scope of this work.

Para 6: words in square brackets in sub-para (1)(a) substituted by the Financial Services Act 2012 (Consequential Amendments and Transitional Provisions) Order 2013, SI 2013/472, art 3, Sch 2, para 250(1), (5).

SCHEDULE 4
EXCEPTED PROFESSIONS, OFFICES, EMPLOYMENTS AND OCCUPATIONS

Article 5(a)

PART 1
PROFESSIONS

[2.1320]

1. Medical practitioner.

2. Advocate, solicitor.

3. Accountant.

4. Dentist or any profession complementary to dentistry for which a title is specified in regulations under section 36A(2) of the Dentists Act 1984 (professions complementary to dentistry) by virtue of section 36A(3) of that Act.

5. Veterinary surgeon.

6. Nurse or midwife.

7. Ophthalmic optician, dispensing optician.

8. Registered pharmacist.

9. Registered pharmacy technician.

10. Registered teacher.

11. Any profession to which the Health Professions Order 2001 applies and which is undertaken following registration under that Order.

12. Registered osteopath.

13. Registered chiropractor.

14. Actuary.

15. Registered European lawyer, registered foreign lawyer.

16. Social worker.

17. Social service worker.

PART 2
OFFICES AND EMPLOYMENTS

[2.1321]
1. Judicial appointments.

2. Prosecutors, officers assisting prosecutors, and officers assisting in the work of the Crown Office.

3. Justices of the Peace and members of local authorities with signing functions under section 76 of the Criminal Proceedings etc (Reform) (Scotland) Act 2007.

4. Clerks (including depute and assistant clerks) and officers of the High Court of Justiciary, the Court of Session and the justice of the peace court, sheriff clerks (including sheriff clerks depute) and their clerks and assistants and other support officers assisting in the work of the Scottish Court Service.

5. Precognition agents.

6. Constables, police custody and security officers, persons appointed as police cadets to undergo training with a view to becoming constables, persons employed for the purposes of a police force established under any enactment, persons appointed to assist in the carrying out of police functions and naval, military and air force police.

[**7.** Any office, employment or work which is concerned with the administration of, or is otherwise normally carried out wholly or partly within the precincts of, a prison, remand centre, young offenders institution, detention centre or removal centre, prison monitoring co-ordinators appointed under section 7A(2) of the Prisons (Scotland) Act 1989 and independent prison monitors appointed under section 7B(2)(a) of that Act.]

8. Traffic wardens appointed under or in accordance with section 95 of the Road Traffic Regulation Act 1984.

9. Any employment or work which is concerned with the provision of a care service.

10. Any employment or work which is concerned with the provision of health services and which is of such a kind as to enable the holder to have access to persons in receipt of such services in the course of that person's normal duties.

11. Any regulated work with children.

12. Any employment or work in the Scottish Society for the Prevention of Cruelty to Animals where the person employed or working, as part of his or her duties, may carry out the killing of animals.

13. Any office, employment or work in the Serious Fraud Office.

14. Any office, employment or work in [the National Crime Agency].

15. Any office, employment or work in Her Majesty's Revenue and Customs.

16. Any employment which is concerned with the monitoring, for the purposes of child protection, of communications by means of the internet.

17. Any office or employment in the Scottish Social Services Council.

18. Her Majesty's Inspectors, or any person appointed by the Scottish Ministers for the purposes of section 66 of the Education (Scotland) Act 1980 or section 9 of the Standards in Scotland's Schools etc Act 2000, or members of any Management Board established to assist either Her Majesty's Inspectors or any such person, or any individual undertaking employment or work for Her Majesty's Inspectors or any such person in relation to the carrying out of inspections under section 66 of the Education (Scotland) Act 1980, section 9 of the Standards in Scotland's Schools etc Act 2000 or section 115 of the 2010 Act, or otherwise in regard to matters associated with such inspections.

19. . . .

20. Members of a panel established by virtue of section 101(1) of the Children (Scotland) Act 1995 (panels for curators *ad litem*, reporting officers and safeguarders).

21. Any office or employment in the Risk Management Authority.

22. Any office or employment in the Scottish Criminal Cases Review Commission.

23. Any office or employment in [the Scottish Fire and Rescue Service].

24. Any employment or work in a body concerned primarily with the provision of counselling or other support to individuals who are or appear to be victims of, or witnesses to, offences, and which involves having access to personal information about such individuals.

25. Any regulated work with adults.

26. Members mentioned in section 35(4)(c) of the Judiciary and Courts (Scotland) Act 2008 of a tribunal constituted under section 35(1) of that Act to consider the fitness for judicial office of a person holding a judicial office mentioned in section 35(2) of that Act.

[**27.** Members mentioned in section 21(4)(d) of the Courts Reform (Scotland) Act 2014 of a tribunal constituted under section 21(1) or (2) of that Act to consider the fitness for office of a person holding a judicial office mentioned in section 21(3) of that Act.]

28. Lay members of the Judicial Appointments Board for Scotland appointed by the Scottish Ministers under paragraph 2 of schedule 1 to the Judiciary and Courts (Scotland) Act 2008.

29. Non-judicial members of the Scottish Court Service mentioned in paragraph 2(3)(d) of schedule 3 to the Judiciary and Courts (Scotland) Act 2008.

30. Any office or employment in Social Care and Social Work Improvement Scotland.

31. Any office or employment in the General Teaching Council for Scotland.

32. A Head of Practice or a member of a Practice Committee of a licensed legal services provider.

NOTES

Para 7: substituted by the Public Services Reform (Inspection and Monitoring of Prisons) (Scotland) Order 2015, SSI 2015/39, art 6, Schedule, Pt 2, para 12, as from 31 August 2015.

Para 14: words in square brackets substituted by virtue of the Crime and Courts Act 2013, s 15(3), Sch 8, Pt 4, para 190.

Para 19: revoked by the Rehabilitation of Offenders Act 1974 (Exclusions and Exceptions) (Scotland) Amendment Order 2013, SSI 2013/204, arts 2, 4.

Para 23: words in square brackets substituted by the Police and Fire Reform (Scotland) Act 2012 (Consequential Modifications and Savings) Order 2013, SSI 2013/119, art 4, Sch 2, para 28.

Para 27: substituted by the Courts Reform (Scotland) Act 2014 (Consequential Provisions) Order 2015, SSI 2015/150, art 2, Schedule, Pt 2, para 10, as from 1 April 2015.

PART 3
OCCUPATIONS

[2.1322]

1. Firearms dealer.

2. Any occupation in respect of which an application to the Gambling Commission for a licence, certificate or registration is required by or under any enactment.

3. Any occupation which is concerned with the management of a place in respect of which the approval of the Scottish Ministers is required by section 1 of the Abortion Act 1967.

4. Any occupation in respect of which the holder is required pursuant to [regulations 4, 5 and 11 of the Explosives Regulations 2014] to obtain from the chief officer of police an explosives certificate certifying that person to be a fit person to acquire or acquire and keep explosives.

5. Taxi driver or private hire driver.

6. Any occupation in respect of which an application to the Security Industry Authority for a licence is required by the Private Security Industry Act 2001.

7. Any occupation which is concerned with visiting persons detained in police stations, for the purposes of examining and reporting on the conditions under which they are held.

8. Any occupation in respect of which a licence or registration is required by or under Part V (driving instruction) of the Road Traffic Act 1988.

NOTES

Para 4: words in square brackets substituted by the Explosives Regulations 2014, SI 2014/1638, reg 48(1), Sch 13, Pt 2, para 30(c), as from 1 October 2014.

SCHEDULE 5

(Sch 5 (Revocations) outside the scope of this work.)

EMPLOYMENT TRIBUNALS (CONSTITUTION AND RULES OF PROCEDURE) REGULATIONS 2013

(SI 2013/1237)

NOTES

Made: 28 May 2013.

Authority: Health and Safety at Work etc Act 1974, s 24(2); Employment Tribunals Act 1996, ss 1(1), 4(6), (6A), 7(1), (3), (3ZA), (3A), (3AA), (3AB), (3B), (3C), (5), 7A(1), (2), 7B(1), (2), 9(1), (2), 10(2), (5)–(7), 10A(1), 11(1), 12(2), 13, 13A, 19, 41(4); Scotland Act 1998, Sch 6, para 37; Government of Wales Act 2006, Sch 9, para 32.

Commencement: 1 July 2013 (regs 1, 3 11) and 29 July 2013 (otherwise); see reg 1(2) below.

Note: for transitional provisions see reg 15 at **[2.1337]**.

ARRANGEMENT OF REGULATIONS

SCHEDULES

[2.1323]

1 Citation and commencement

(1) These Regulations may be cited as the Employment Tribunals (Constitution and Rules of Procedure) Regulations 2013 and the Rules of Procedure contained in Schedules 1, 2 and 3 may be referred to, respectively, as—

(a) the Employment Tribunals Rules of Procedure 2013;
(b) the Employment Tribunals (National Security) Rules of Procedure 2013; and
(c) the Employment Tribunals (Equal Value) Rules of Procedure 2013.

(2) This regulation and regulations 3 and 11 come into force on 1st July 2013 and the remainder of these Regulations (including the Schedules) come into force on 29th July 2013.

[2.1324]

2 Revocation

Subject to the savings in regulation 15 the Employment Tribunals (Constitution and Rules of Procedure) Regulations 2004 are revoked.

[2.1325]

3 Interpretation

Except in the Schedules which are subject to the definitions contained in the Schedules, in these Regulations—

"2004 Regulations" means the Employment Tribunals (Constitution and Rules of Procedure) Regulations 2004;

"appointing office holder" means, in England and Wales, the Lord Chancellor, and in Scotland, the Lord President;

"Employment Tribunals Act" means the Employment Tribunals Act 1996;

"Lord President" means the Lord President of the Court of Session;

"national security proceedings" means proceedings in relation to which a direction is given, or an order is made, under rule 94 of Schedule 1;

"President" means either of the two presidents appointed from time to time in accordance with regulation 5(1);

"Regional Employment Judge" means a person appointed or nominated in accordance with regulation 6(1) or (2);

"Senior President of Tribunals" means the person appointed in accordance with section 2 of the Tribunals, Courts and Enforcement Act 2007;

"Tribunal" means an employment tribunal established in accordance with regulation 4 and, in relation to any proceedings, means the Tribunal responsible for the proceedings in question, whether performing administrative or judicial functions;

"Vice President" means a person appointed or nominated in accordance with regulation 6(3) or (4).

[2.1326]

4 Establishment of employment tribunals

There are to be tribunals known as employment tribunals.

[2.1327]

5 President of Employment Tribunals

(1) There shall be a President of Employment Tribunals, responsible for Tribunals in England and Wales, and a President of Employment Tribunals, responsible for Tribunals in Scotland, appointed by the appointing office holder.

(2) A President shall be—

(a) a person who satisfies the judicial-appointment eligibility condition within the meaning of section 50 of the Tribunals, Courts and Enforcement Act 2007 on a 5-year basis;

(b) an advocate or solicitor admitted in Scotland of at least five years standing; or

(c) a member of the Bar of Northern Ireland or solicitor of the Supreme Court of Northern Ireland of at least five years standing.

(3) A President may at any time resign from office by giving the appointing officer holder notice in writing to that effect.

(4) The appointing officer holder may remove a President from office on the ground of inability or misbehaviour, or if the President is [made] bankrupt or makes a composition or arrangement with his creditors.

(5) Where a President is unable to carry out the functions set out in these Regulations, those functions may be discharged by a person nominated by the appointing office holder (save that any nomination in relation to England and Wales shall be made by the Lord Chief Justice following consultation with the Senior President of Tribunals, rather than by the Lord Chancellor).

(6) The Lord Chief Justice may nominate a judicial office holder (as defined in section 109(4) of the Constitutional Reform Act 2005) to exercise his functions under this regulation.

NOTES

Para (4): word in square brackets substituted by the Enterprise and Regulatory Reform Act 2013 (Consequential Amendments) (Bankruptcy) and the Small Business, Enterprise and Employment Act 2015 (Consequential Amendments) Regulations 2016, SI 2016/481, reg 2(2), Sch 2, para 12, as from 6 April 2016.

[2.1328]

6 Regional Employment Judges and the Vice President

(1) The Lord Chancellor may appoint Regional Employment Judges.

(2) The President (England and Wales) or the Regional Employment Judge for an area may nominate an Employment Judge to discharge the functions of the Regional Employment Judge for that area.

(3) The Lord President may appoint a Vice President.

(4) The President (Scotland) or the Vice President may nominate an Employment Judge to discharge the functions of the Vice President.

(5) Appointments and nominations under this regulation shall be from the [salaried] Employment Judges on the panel referred to in regulation 8(2)(a).

NOTES

Para (5): word in square brackets substituted by the Employment Tribunals (Constitution and Rules of Procedure) (Amendment) Regulations 2014, SI 2014/271, reg 2.

[2.1329]

7 Responsibilities of the Presidents, Regional Employment Judges and Vice President

(1) The President shall, in relation to the area for which the President is responsible, use the resources available to—

(a) secure, so far as practicable, the speedy and efficient disposal of proceedings;

(b) determine the allocation of proceedings between Tribunals; and

(c) determine where and when Tribunals shall sit.

(2) The President (England and Wales) may direct Regional Employment Judges, and the President (Scotland) may direct the Vice President, to take action in relation to the fulfilment of the responsibilities in paragraph (1) and the Regional Employment Judges and Vice President shall follow such directions.

[2.1330]

8 Panels of members for tribunals

(1) There shall be three panels of members for the Employment Tribunals (England and Wales) and three panels of members for the Employment Tribunals (Scotland).

(2) The panels of members shall be—

(a) a panel of [Employment Judges] who satisfy the criteria set out in regulation 5(2) and are appointed by the appointing office holder . . .

(b) a panel of persons appointed by the Lord Chancellor after consultation with organisations or associations representative of employees; and

(c) a panel of persons appointed by the Lord Chancellor after consultation with organisations or associations representative of employers.

(3) Members of the panels shall hold and vacate office in accordance with the terms of their appointment, but may resign from office by written notice to the person who appointed them under paragraph (2), and any member who ceases to hold office shall be eligible for reappointment.

(4) The President may establish further specialist panels of members referred to in paragraph (2) and may select persons from those panels to deal with proceedings in which particular specialist knowledge would be beneficial.

NOTES

Para (2): words in square brackets substituted, and words omitted revoked, by the Employment Tribunals (Constitution and Rules of Procedure) (Amendment) Regulations 2014, SI 2014/271, reg 3.

[2.1331]

9 Composition of tribunals

(1) Where proceedings are to be determined by a Tribunal comprising an Employment Judge and two other members, the President, Vice President or a Regional Employment Judge shall select—

(a) an Employment Judge; and

(b) one member from each of the panels referred to in regulation 8(2)(b) and (c),

and for all other proceedings shall select an Employment Judge.

(2) The President, Vice President or a Regional Employment Judge may select him or herself as the Employment Judge required under paragraph (1).

(3) The President, Vice President or a Regional Employment Judge may select from the appropriate panel a substitute for a member previously selected to hear any proceedings.

(4) This regulation does not apply in relation to national security proceedings (see regulation 10(2)).

[2.1332]

10 National security proceedings—panel of members and composition of tribunals

(1) The President shall select—

(a) a panel of persons from the panel referred to in regulation 8(2)(a);

(b) a panel of persons from the panel referred to in regulation 8(2)(b); and

(c) a panel of persons from the panel referred to in regulation 8(2)(c),

who may act in national security proceedings.

(2) Where proceedings become national security proceedings, the President, Vice President or a Regional Employment Judge shall—

(a) select an Employment Judge from the panel referred to in paragraph (1)(a) and may select him or herself; and

(b) where the proceedings are to be determined by a Tribunal comprising an Employment Judge and two other members, select in addition one member from each of the panels referred to in sub-paragraphs (b) and (c) of paragraph (1).

[2.1333]

11 Practice directions

(1) The President may make, vary or revoke practice directions about the procedure of the Tribunals in the area for which the President is responsible, including—

(a) practice directions about the exercise by Tribunals of powers under these Regulations (including the Schedules); and

(b) practice directions about the provision by Employment Judges of mediation, in relation to disputed matters in a case that is the subject of proceedings, and may permit an Employment Judge to act as mediator in a case even though they have been selected to decide matters in that case.

(2) Practice directions may make different provision for different cases, different areas, or different types of proceedings.

(3) Any practice direction made, varied or revoked shall be published by the President in an appropriate manner to bring it to the attention of the persons to whom it is addressed.

NOTES

Practice Directions: see Part 5, Section B of this Handbook *post*.

[2.1334]

12 Power to prescribe

(1) The Secretary of State may prescribe—

(a) one or more versions of a form which shall be used by claimants to start proceedings in a Tribunal;

(b) one or more versions of a form which shall be used by respondents to respond to a claim before a Tribunal; and

(c) that the provision of certain information on the prescribed forms is mandatory.

(2) It is not necessary to use a form prescribed under paragraph (1) if the proceedings are—

(a) referred to a Tribunal by a court;
(b) proceedings in which a Tribunal will be exercising its appellate jurisdiction; or
(c) proceedings brought by an employer under section 11 of the Employment Rights Act 1996.

(3) The Secretary of State shall publish the prescribed forms in an appropriate manner to bring them to the attention of prospective claimants, respondents and their advisers.

[2.1335]
13 Application of Schedules 1 to 3

(1) Subject to paragraph (2), Schedule 1 applies to all proceedings before a Tribunal except where separate rules of procedure made under the provisions of any enactment are applicable.

(2) Schedules 2 and 3 apply to modify the rules in Schedule 1 in relation, respectively, to proceedings which are—

(a) national security proceedings; or
(b) proceedings which involve an equal value claim (as defined in rule 1 of Schedule 3).

[2.1336]
14 Register and proof of judgments

(1) The Lord Chancellor shall maintain a register containing a copy of all judgments and written reasons issued by a Tribunal which are required to be entered in the register under Schedules 1 to 3.

(2) . . .

(3) A document purporting to be certified by a member of staff of a Tribunal to be a true copy of an entry of a judgment in the register shall, unless the contrary is proved, be sufficient evidence of the document and its contents.

NOTES

Para (2): revoked by the Employment Tribunals (Constitution and Rules of Procedure) (Amendment) (No 2) Regulations 2014, SI 2014/611, reg 2.

[2.1337]
15 Transitional provisions

(1) Subject to paragraphs (2) and (3), these Regulations and the Rules of Procedure contained in Schedules 1 to 3 apply in relation to all proceedings to which they relate.

(2) Where a respondent receives from a Tribunal a copy of the claim form before 29th July 2013, rules 23 to 25 of Schedule 1 do not apply to the proceedings and rule 7 of Schedule 1 to the 2004 Regulations continues to apply.

(3) Where in accordance with Schedules 3 to 5 of the 2004 Regulations, a notice of appeal was presented to a Tribunal before 29th July 2013, Schedule 1 does not apply to the proceedings and Schedule 3, 4 or 5, as appropriate, of the 2004 Regulations continues to apply.

SCHEDULES

SCHEDULE 1
THE EMPLOYMENT TRIBUNALS RULES OF PROCEDURE

NOTES

All rules in this Schedule came into force on 29 July 2013.

For transitional provisions (affecting in particular rules 23–25 below and proceedings to which Schs 3, 4 or 5 to the previous (2004) Rules of Procedure apply) see reg 15 at **[2.1337]**.

Regulation 13(1)

INTRODUCTORY AND GENERAL

[2.1338]
1 Interpretation

(1) In these Rules—

"ACAS" means the Advisory, Conciliation and Arbitration Service referred to in section 247 of the Trade Union and Labour Relations (Consolidation) Act 1992;

"claim" means any proceedings before an Employment Tribunal making a complaint;

"claimant" means the person bringing the claim;

"Commission for Equality and Human Rights" means the body established under section 1 of the Equality Act 2006;

"complaint" means anything that is referred to as a claim, complaint, reference, application or appeal in any enactment which confers jurisdiction on the Tribunal;

["early conciliation certificate" means a certificate issued by ACAS in accordance with the Employment Tribunals (Early Conciliation: Exemptions and Rules of Procedure) Regulations 2013;]

["early conciliation exemption" means an exemption contained in regulation 3(1) of the Employment Tribunals (Early Conciliation: Exemptions and Rules of Procedure) Regulations 2014;]

["early conciliation number" means the unique reference number which appears on an early conciliation certificate;]

"Employment Appeal Tribunal" means the Employment Appeal Tribunal established under section 87 of the Employment Protection Act 1975 and continued in existence under section 135 of the Employment Protection (Consolidation) Act 1978 and section 20(1) of the Employment Tribunals Act;

"electronic communication" has the meaning given to it by section 15(1) of the Electronic Communications Act 2000;

"employee's contract claim" means a claim brought by an employee in accordance with articles 3 and 7 of the Employment Tribunals Extension of Jurisdiction (England and Wales) Order 1994 or articles 3 and 7 of the Employment Tribunals Extension of Jurisdiction (Scotland) Order 1994;

"employer's contract claim" means a claim brought by an employer in accordance with articles 4 and 8 of the Employment Tribunals Extension of Jurisdiction (England and Wales) Order 1994 or articles 4 and 8 of the Employment Tribunals Extension of Jurisdiction (Scotland) Order 1994;

"Employment Tribunal" or "Tribunal" means an employment tribunal established in accordance with regulation 4, and in relation to any proceedings means the Tribunal responsible for the proceedings in question, whether performing administrative or judicial functions;

"Employment Tribunals Act" means the Employment Tribunals Act 1996;

["Energy Act IN" means a notice given by an inspector under paragraph 3 of Schedule 8 to the Energy Act 2013;]

["Energy Act PN" means a notice given by an inspector under paragraph 4 of Schedule 8 to the Energy Act 2013;]

"Equality Act" means the Equality Act 2010;

"full tribunal" means a Tribunal constituted in accordance with section 4(1) of the Employment Tribunals Act;

"Health and Safety Act" means the Health and Safety at Work etc Act 1974;

"improvement notice" means a notice under section 21 of the Health and Safety Act;

"levy appeal" means an appeal against an assessment to a levy imposed under section 11 of the Industrial Training Act 1982;

"Minister" means Minister of the Crown;

"prescribed form" means any appropriate form prescribed by the Secretary of State in accordance with regulation 12;

"present" means deliver (by any means permitted under rule 85) to a tribunal office;

"President" means either of the two presidents appointed from time to time in accordance with regulation 5(1);

"prohibition notice" means a notice under section 22 of the Health and Safety Act;

"Regional Employment Judge" means a person appointed or nominated in accordance with regulation 6(1) or (2);

"Register" means the register of judgments and written reasons kept in accordance with regulation 14;

["relevant proceedings" means those proceedings listed in section 18(1) of the Employment Tribunals Act 1996;]

"remission application" means any application which may be made under any enactment for remission or part remission of a Tribunal fee;

"respondent" means the person or persons against whom the claim is made;

"Tribunal fee" means any fee which is payable by a party under any enactment in respect of a claim, employer's contract claim, application or judicial mediation in an Employment Tribunal;

"tribunal office" means any office which has been established for any area in either England and Wales or Scotland and which carries out administrative functions in support of the Tribunal, and in relation to particular proceedings it is the office notified to the parties as dealing with the proceedings;

"unlawful act notice" means a notice under section 21 of the Equality Act 2006;

"Vice President" means a person appointed or nominated in accordance with regulation 6(3) or (4);

"writing" includes writing delivered by means of electronic communication.

(2) Any reference in the Rules to a Tribunal applies to both a full tribunal and to an Employment Judge acting alone (in accordance with section 4(2) or (6) of the Employment Tribunals Act).

(3) An order or other decision of the Tribunal is either—

(a) a "case management order", being an order or decision of any kind in relation to the conduct of proceedings, not including the determination of any issue which would be the subject of a judgment; or

(b) a "judgment", being a decision, made at any stage of the proceedings (but not including a decision under rule 13 or 19), which finally determines—

(i) a claim, or part of a claim, as regards liability, remedy or costs (including preparation time and wasted costs); . . .

(ii) any issue which is capable of finally disposing of any claim, or part of a claim, even if it does not necessarily do so (for example, an issue whether a claim should be struck out or a jurisdictional issue);

[(iii) the imposition of a financial penalty under section 12A of the Employment Tribunals Act].

NOTES

The definitions "early conciliation certificate", "early conciliation exemption", "early conciliation number", and "relevant proceedings" in para (1) were inserted, the word omitted from sub-para (3)(b)(i) was revoked, and sub-para (3)(b)(iii) was inserted, by the Employment Tribunals (Constitution and Rules of Procedure) (Amendment) Regulations 2014, SI 2014/271, regs 4–6.

Definitions "Energy Act IN" and "Energy Act PN" inserted by the Energy Act 2013 (Improvement and Prohibition Notices Appeals) Regulations 2014, SI 2014/468, reg 2(1), (2).

[2.1339]
2 Overriding objective

The overriding objective of these Rules is to enable Employment Tribunals to deal with cases fairly and justly. Dealing with a case fairly and justly includes, so far as practicable—

(a) ensuring that the parties are on an equal footing;
(b) dealing with cases in ways which are proportionate to the complexity and importance of the issues;
(c) avoiding unnecessary formality and seeking flexibility in the proceedings;
(d) avoiding delay, so far as compatible with proper consideration of the issues; and
(e) saving expense.

A Tribunal shall seek to give effect to the overriding objective in interpreting, or exercising any power given to it by, these Rules. The parties and their representatives shall assist the Tribunal to further the overriding objective and in particular shall co-operate generally with each other and with the Tribunal.

[2.1340]
3 Alternative dispute resolution

A Tribunal shall wherever practicable and appropriate encourage the use by the parties of the services of ACAS, judicial or other mediation, or other means of resolving their disputes by agreement.

[2.1341]
4 Time

(1) Unless otherwise specified by the Tribunal, an act required by these Rules, a practice direction or an order of a Tribunal to be done on or by a particular day may be done at any time before midnight on that day. If there is an issue as to whether the act has been done by that time, the party claiming to have done it shall prove compliance.

(2) If the time specified by these Rules, a practice direction or an order for doing any act ends on a day other than a working day, the act is done in time if it is done on the next working day. "Working day" means any day except a Saturday or Sunday, Christmas Day, Good Friday or a bank holiday under section 1 of the Banking and Financial Dealings Act 1971.

(3) Where any act is required to be, or may be, done within a certain number of days of or from an event, the date of that event shall not be included in the calculation. (For example, a response shall be presented within 28 days of the date on which the respondent was sent a copy of the claim: if the claim was sent on 1st October the last day for presentation of the response is 29th October.)

(4) Where any act is required to be, or may be, done not less than a certain number of days before or after an event, the date of that event shall not be included in the calculation. (For example, if a party wishes to present representations in writing for consideration by a Tribunal at a hearing, they shall be presented not less than 7 days before the hearing: if the hearing is fixed for 8th October, the representations shall be presented no later than 1st October.)

(5) Where the Tribunal imposes a time limit for doing any act, the last date for compliance shall, wherever practicable, be expressed as a calendar date.

(6) Where time is specified by reference to the date when a document is sent to a person by the Tribunal, the date when the document was sent shall, unless the contrary is proved, be regarded as the date endorsed on the document as the date of sending or, if there is no such endorsement, the date shown on the letter accompanying the document.

[2.1342]
5 Extending or shortening time

The Tribunal may, on its own initiative or on the application of a party, extend or shorten any time limit specified in these Rules or in any decision, whether or not (in the case of an extension) it has expired.

[2.1343]
6 Irregularities and non-compliance

A failure to comply with any provision of these Rules (except rule 8(1), 16(1), 23 or 25) or any order of the Tribunal (except for an order under rules 38 or 39) does not of itself render void the proceedings or any step taken in the proceedings. In the case of such non-compliance, the Tribunal may take such action as it considers just, which may include all or any of the following—

(a) waiving or varying the requirement;
(b) striking out the claim or the response, in whole or in part, in accordance with rule 37;
(c) barring or restricting a party's participation in the proceedings;
(d) awarding costs in accordance with rules 74 to 84.

[2.1344]
7 Presidential Guidance

The Presidents may publish guidance for England and Wales and for Scotland, respectively, as to matters of practice and as to how the powers conferred by these Rules may be exercised. Any such guidance shall be published by the Presidents in an appropriate manner to bring it to the attention of claimants, respondents and their advisers. Tribunals must have regard to any such guidance, but they shall not be bound by it.

NOTES

Presidential Guidance: see Part 5, Section B of this Handbook *post*.

STARTING A CLAIM

[2.1345]

8 Presenting the claim

(1) A claim shall be started by presenting a completed claim form (using a prescribed form) in accordance with any practice direction made under regulation 11 which supplements this rule.

(2) A claim may be presented in England and Wales if—

(a) the respondent, or one of the respondents, resides or carries on business in England and Wales;
(b) one or more of the acts or omissions complained of took place in England and Wales;
(c) the claim relates to a contract under which the work is or has been performed partly in England and Wales; or
(d) the Tribunal has jurisdiction to determine the claim by virtue of a connection with Great Britain and the connection in question is at least partly a connection with England and Wales.

(3) A claim may be presented in Scotland if—

(a) the respondent, or one of the respondents, resides or carries on business in Scotland;
(b) one or more of the acts or omissions complained of took place in Scotland;
(c) the claim relates to a contract under which the work is or has been performed partly in Scotland; or
(d) the Tribunal has jurisdiction to determine the claim by virtue of a connection with Great Britain and the connection in question is at least partly a connection with Scotland.

[2.1346]

9 Multiple claimants

Two or more claimants may make their claims on the same claim form if their claims are based on the same set of facts. Where two or more claimants wrongly include claims on the same claim form, this shall be treated as an irregularity falling under rule 6.

[2.1347]

10 Rejection: form not used or failure to supply minimum information

(1) The Tribunal shall reject a claim if—

(a) it is not made on a prescribed form; . . .
(b) it does not contain all of the following information—
 (i) each claimant's name;
 (ii) each claimant's address;
 (iii) each respondent's name;
 (iv) each respondent's address[; or
(c) it does not contain all of the following information—
 (i) an early conciliation number;
 (ii) confirmation that the claim does not institute any relevant proceedings; or
 (iii) confirmation that one of the early conciliation exemptions applies].

(2) The form shall be returned to the claimant with a notice of rejection explaining why it has been rejected. The notice shall contain information about how to apply for a reconsideration of the rejection.

NOTES

The word omitted from sub-para (1)(a) was revoked, and sub-para (1)(c) (and the preceding word) was inserted, by the Employment Tribunals (Constitution and Rules of Procedure) (Amendment) Regulations 2014, SI 2014/271, regs 4, 7.

[2.1348]

11 Rejection: absence of Tribunal fee or remission application

(1) The Tribunal shall reject a claim if it is not accompanied by a Tribunal fee or a remission application.

(2) Where a claim is accompanied by a Tribunal fee but the amount paid is lower than the amount payable for the presentation of that claim, the Tribunal shall send the claimant a notice specifying a date for payment of the additional amount due and the claim, or part of it in respect of which the relevant Tribunal fee has not been paid, shall be rejected by the Tribunal if the amount due is not paid by the date specified.

(3) If a remission application is refused in part or in full, the Tribunal shall send the claimant a notice specifying a date for payment of the Tribunal fee and the claim shall be rejected by the Tribunal if the Tribunal fee is not paid by the date specified.

(4) If a claim, or part of it, is rejected, the form shall be returned to the claimant with a notice of rejection explaining why it has been rejected.

[2.1349]

12 Rejection: substantive defects

(1) The staff of the tribunal office shall refer a claim form to an Employment Judge if they consider that the claim, or part of it, may be—

(a) one which the Tribunal has no jurisdiction to consider; . . .

(b) in a form which cannot sensibly be responded to or is otherwise an abuse of the process;
[(c) one which institutes relevant proceedings and is made on a claim form that does not contain either an early conciliation number or confirmation that one of the early conciliation exemptions applies;
(d) one which institutes relevant proceedings, is made on a claim form which contains confirmation that one of the early conciliation exemptions applies, and an early conciliation exemption does not apply;
(e) one which institutes relevant proceedings and the name of the claimant on the claim form is not the same as the name of the prospective claimant on the early conciliation certificate to which the early conciliation number relates; or
(f) one which institutes relevant proceedings and the name of the respondent on the claim form is not the same as the name of the prospective respondent on the early conciliation certificate to which the early conciliation number relates].

(2) The claim, or part of it, shall be rejected if the Judge considers that the claim, or part of it, is of a kind described in sub-paragraphs (a)[, (b), (c) or (d)] of paragraph (1).

[(2A) The claim, or part of it, shall be rejected if the Judge considers that the claim, or part of it, is of a kind described in sub-paragraph (e) or (f) of paragraph (1) unless the Judge considers that the claimant made a minor error in relation to a name or address and it would not be in the interests of justice to reject the claim.]

(3) If the claim is rejected, the form shall be returned to the claimant together with a notice of rejection giving the Judge's reasons for rejecting the claim, or part of it. The notice shall contain information about how to apply for a reconsideration of the rejection.

NOTES

The word omitted from sub-para (1)(a) was revoked, sub-paras (1)(c)–(f) were inserted, the words in square brackets in para (2) were substituted, and para (2A) was inserted, by the Employment Tribunals (Constitution and Rules of Procedure) (Amendment) Regulations 2014, SI 2014/271, regs 4, 8.

[2.1350]

13 Reconsideration of rejection

(1) A claimant whose claim has been rejected (in whole or in part) under rule 10 or 12 may apply for a reconsideration on the basis that either—
(a) the decision to reject was wrong; or
(b) the notified defect can be rectified.

(2) The application shall be in writing and presented to the Tribunal within 14 days of the date that the notice of rejection was sent. It shall explain why the decision is said to have been wrong or rectify the defect and if the claimant wishes to request a hearing this shall be requested in the application.

(3) If the claimant does not request a hearing, or an Employment Judge decides, on considering the application, that the claim shall be accepted in full, the Judge shall determine the application without a hearing. Otherwise the application shall be considered at a hearing attended only by the claimant.

(4) If the Judge decides that the original rejection was correct but that the defect has been rectified, the claim shall be treated as presented on the date that the defect was rectified.

[2.1351]

14 Protected disclosure claims: notification to a regulator

If a claim alleges that the claimant has made a protected disclosure, the Tribunal may, with the consent of the claimant, send a copy of any accepted claim to a regulator listed in Schedule 1 to the Public Interest Disclosure (Prescribed Persons) Order 1999. "Protected disclosure" has the meaning given to it by section 43A of the Employment Rights Act 1996.

THE RESPONSE TO THE CLAIM

[2.1352]

15 Sending claim form to respondents

Unless the claim is rejected, the Tribunal shall send a copy of the claim form, together with a prescribed response form, to each respondent with a notice which includes information on—
(a) whether any part of the claim has been rejected; and
(b) how to submit a response to the claim, the time limit for doing so and what will happen if a response is not received by the Tribunal within that time limit.

[2.1353]

16 Response

(1) The response shall be on a prescribed form and presented to the tribunal office within 28 days of the date that the copy of the claim form was sent by the Tribunal.

(2) A response form may include the response of more than one respondent if they are responding to a single claim and either they all resist the claim on the same grounds or they do not resist the claim.

(3) A response form may include the response to more than one claim if the claims are based on the same set of facts and either the respondent resists all of the claims on the same grounds or the respondent does not resist the claims.

[2.1354]
17 Rejection: form not used or failure to supply minimum information

(1) The Tribunal shall reject a response if—
  (a) it is not made on a prescribed form; or
  (b) it does not contain all of the following information—
    (i) the respondent's full name;
    (ii) the respondent's address;
    (iii) whether the respondent wishes to resist any part of the claim.

(2) The form shall be returned to the respondent with a notice of rejection explaining why it has been rejected. The notice shall explain what steps may be taken by the respondent, including the need (if appropriate) to apply for an extension of time, and how to apply for a reconsideration of the rejection.

[2.1355]
18 Rejection: form presented late

(1) A response shall be rejected by the Tribunal if it is received outside the time limit in rule 16 (or any extension of that limit granted within the original limit) unless an application for extension has already been made under rule 20 or the response includes or is accompanied by such an application (in which case the response shall not be rejected pending the outcome of the application).

(2) The response shall be returned to the respondent together with a notice of rejection explaining that the response has been presented late. The notice shall explain how the respondent can apply for an extension of time and how to apply for a reconsideration.

[2.1356]
19 Reconsideration of rejection

(1) A respondent whose response has been rejected under rule 17 or 18 may apply for a reconsideration on the basis that the decision to reject was wrong or, in the case of a rejection under rule 17, on the basis that the notified defect can be rectified.

(2) The application shall be in writing and presented to the Tribunal within 14 days of the date that the notice of rejection was sent. It shall explain why the decision is said to have been wrong or rectify the defect and it shall state whether the respondent requests a hearing.

(3) If the respondent does not request a hearing, or the Employment Judge decides, on considering the application, that the response shall be accepted in full, the Judge shall determine the application without a hearing. Otherwise the application shall be considered at a hearing attended only by the respondent.

(4) If the Judge decides that the original rejection was correct but that the defect has been rectified, the response shall be treated as presented on the date that the defect was rectified (but the Judge may extend time under rule 5).

[2.1357]
20 Applications for extension of time for presenting response

(1) An application for an extension of time for presenting a response shall be presented in writing and copied to the claimant. It shall set out the reason why the extension is sought and shall, except where the time limit has not yet expired, be accompanied by a draft of the response which the respondent wishes to present or an explanation of why that is not possible and if the respondent wishes to request a hearing this shall be requested in the application.

(2) The claimant may within 7 days of receipt of the application give reasons in writing explaining why the application is opposed.

(3) An Employment Judge may determine the application without a hearing.

(4) If the decision is to refuse an extension, any prior rejection of the response shall stand. If the decision is to allow an extension, any judgment issued under rule 21 shall be set aside.

[2.1358]
21 Effect of non-presentation or rejection of response, or case not contested

(1) Where on the expiry of the time limit in rule 16 no response has been presented, or any response received has been rejected and no application for a reconsideration is outstanding, or where the respondent has stated that no part of the claim is contested, paragraphs (2) and (3) shall apply.

(2) An Employment Judge shall decide whether on the available material (which may include further information which the parties are required by a Judge to provide), a determination can properly be made of the claim, or part of it. To the extent that a determination can be made, the Judge shall issue a judgment accordingly. Otherwise, a hearing shall be fixed before a Judge alone.

(3) The respondent shall be entitled to notice of any hearings and decisions of the Tribunal but, unless and until an extension of time is granted, shall only be entitled to participate in any hearing to the extent permitted by the Judge.

[2.1359]
22 Notification of acceptance

Where the Tribunal accepts the response it shall send a copy of it to all other parties.

EMPLOYER'S CONTRACT CLAIM

[2.1360]
23 Making an employer's contract claim

Any employer's contract claim shall be made as part of the response, presented in accordance with rule 16, to a claim which includes an employee's contract claim. An employer's contract claim may be rejected on the same basis as a claimant's claim may be rejected under rule 12, in which case rule 13 shall apply.

[2.1361]
24 Notification of employer's contract claim

When the Tribunal sends the response to the other parties in accordance with rule 22 it shall notify the claimant that the response includes an employer's contract claim and include information on how to submit a response to the claim, the time limit for doing so, and what will happen if a response is not received by the Tribunal within that time limit.

[2.1362]
25 Responding to an employer's contract claim

A claimant's response to an employer's contract claim shall be presented to the tribunal office within 28 days of the date that the response was sent to the claimant. If no response is presented within that time limit, rules 20 and 21 shall apply.

INITIAL CONSIDERATION OF CLAIM FORM AND RESPONSE

[2.1363]
26 Initial consideration

(1) As soon as possible after the acceptance of the response, the Employment Judge shall consider all of the documents held by the Tribunal in relation to the claim, to confirm whether there are arguable complaints and defences within the jurisdiction of the Tribunal (and for that purpose the Judge may order a party to provide further information).

(2) Except in a case where notice is given under rule 27 or 28, the Judge conducting the initial consideration shall make a case management order (unless made already), which may deal with the listing of a preliminary or final hearing, and may propose judicial mediation or other forms of dispute resolution.

[2.1364]
27 Dismissal of claim (or part)

(1) If the Employment Judge considers either that the Tribunal has no jurisdiction to consider the claim, or part of it, or that the claim, or part of it, has no reasonable prospect of success, the Tribunal shall send a notice to the parties—

(a) setting out the Judge's view and the reasons for it; and
(b) ordering that the claim, or the part in question, shall be dismissed on such date as is specified in the notice unless before that date the claimant has presented written representations to the Tribunal explaining why the claim (or part) should not be dismissed.

(2) If no such representations are received, the claim shall be dismissed from the date specified without further order (although the Tribunal shall write to the parties to confirm what has occurred).

(3) If representations are received within the specified time they shall be considered by an Employment Judge, who shall either permit the claim (or part) to proceed or fix a hearing for the purpose of deciding whether it should be permitted to do so. The respondent may, but need not, attend and participate in the hearing.

(4) If any part of the claim is permitted to proceed the Judge shall make a case management order.

[2.1365]
28 Dismissal of response (or part)

(1) If the Employment Judge considers that the response to the claim, or part of it, has no reasonable prospect of success the Tribunal shall send a notice to the parties—

(a) setting out the Judge's view and the reasons for it;
(b) ordering that the response, or the part in question, shall be dismissed on such date as is specified in the notice unless before that date the respondent has presented written representations to the Tribunal explaining why the response (or part) should not be dismissed; and
(c) specifying the consequences of the dismissal of the response, in accordance with paragraph (5) below.

(2) If no such representations are received, the response shall be dismissed from the date specified without further order (although the Tribunal shall write to the parties to confirm what has occurred).

(3) If representations are received within the specified time they shall be considered by an Employment Judge, who shall either permit the response (or part) to stand or fix a hearing for the purpose of deciding whether it should be permitted to do so. The claimant may, but need not, attend and participate in the hearing.

(4) If any part of the response is permitted to stand the Judge shall make a case management order.

(5) Where a response is dismissed, the effect shall be as if no response had been presented, as set out in rule 21 above.

CASE MANAGEMENT ORDERS AND OTHER POWERS

[2.1366]
29 Case management orders

The Tribunal may at any stage of the proceedings, on its own initiative or on application, make a case management order. [Subject to rule 30A(2) and (3)] the particular powers identified in the following rules do not restrict that general power. A case management order may vary, suspend or set aside an earlier case management order where that is necessary in the interests of justice, and in particular where a party affected by the earlier order did not have a reasonable opportunity to make representations before it was made.

NOTES

Words in square brackets inserted by the Employment Tribunals (Constitution and Rules of Procedure) (Amendment) Regulations 2016, SI 2016/271, reg 2(1), (2), as from 6 April 2016, in relation to proceedings which are presented to an employment tribunal on or after that date (see reg 3 of the 2016 Regulations).

[2.1367]
30 Applications for case management orders

(1) An application by a party for a particular case management order may be made either at a hearing or presented in writing to the Tribunal.

(2) Where a party applies in writing, they shall notify the other parties that any objections to the application should be sent to the Tribunal as soon as possible.

(3) The Tribunal may deal with such an application in writing or order that it be dealt with at a preliminary or final hearing.

[2.1368]
[30A Postponements

(1) An application by a party for the postponement of a hearing shall be presented to the Tribunal and communicated to the other parties as soon as possible after the need for a postponement becomes known.

(2) Where a party makes an application for a postponement of a hearing less than 7 days before the date on which the hearing begins, the Tribunal may only order the postponement where—

(a) all other parties consent to the postponement and—

(i) it is practicable and appropriate for the purposes of giving the parties the opportunity to resolve their disputes by agreement; or

(ii) it is otherwise in accordance with the overriding objective;

(b) the application was necessitated by an act or omission of another party or the Tribunal; or

(c) there are exceptional circumstances.

(3) Where a Tribunal has ordered two or more postponements of a hearing in the same proceedings on the application of the same party and that party makes an application for a further postponement, the Tribunal may only order a postponement on that application where—

(a) all other parties consent to the postponement and—

(i) it is practicable and appropriate for the purposes of giving the parties the opportunity to resolve their disputes by agreement; or

(ii) it is otherwise in accordance with the overriding objective;

(b) the application was necessitated by an act or omission of another party or the Tribunal; or

(c) there are exceptional circumstances.

(4) For the purposes of this rule—

(a) references to postponement of a hearing include any adjournment which causes the hearing to be held or continued on a later date;

(b) "exceptional circumstances" may include ill health relating to an existing long term health condition or disability.]

NOTES

Inserted by the Employment Tribunals (Constitution and Rules of Procedure) (Amendment) Regulations 2016, SI 2016/271, reg 2(1), (3), as from 6 April 2016, in relation to proceedings which are presented to an employment tribunal on or after that date (see reg 3 of the 2016 Regulations).

[2.1369]
31 Disclosure of documents and information

The Tribunal may order any person in Great Britain to disclose documents or information to a party (by providing copies or otherwise) or to allow a party to inspect such material as might be ordered by a county court or, in Scotland, by a sheriff.

[2.1370]
32 Requirement to attend to give evidence

The Tribunal may order any person in Great Britain to attend a hearing to give evidence, produce documents, or produce information.

[2.1371]

33 *Evidence from other EU Member States*

The Tribunal may use the procedures for obtaining evidence prescribed in Council Regulation (EC) No [1206/2001] of 28 May 2001 on cooperation between the courts of the Member States in the taking of evidence in civil or commercial matters.

NOTES

Revoked by the Employment Rights (Amendment) (EU Exit) Regulations 2019, SI 2019/535, reg 2(1), Sch 1, Pt 2, para 14(a), as from exit day (as defined in the European Union (Withdrawal) Act 2018, s 20).

The reference to "1206/2001" in square brackets was substituted by the Employment Tribunals (Constitution and Rules of Procedure) (Amendment) Regulations 2014, SI 2014/271, regs 4, 9.

[2.1372]

34 Addition, substitution and removal of parties

The Tribunal may on its own initiative, or on the application of a party or any other person wishing to become a party, add any person as a party, by way of substitution or otherwise, if it appears that there are issues between that person and any of the existing parties falling within the jurisdiction of the Tribunal which it is in the interests of justice to have determined in the proceedings; and may remove any party apparently wrongly included.

[2.1373]

35 Other persons

The Tribunal may permit any person to participate in proceedings, on such terms as may be specified, in respect of any matter in which that person has a legitimate interest.

[2.1374]

36 Lead cases

(1) Where a Tribunal considers that two or more claims give rise to common or related issues of fact or law, the Tribunal or the President may make an order specifying one or more of those claims as a lead case and staying, or in Scotland sisting, the other claims ("the related cases").

(2) When the Tribunal makes a decision in respect of the common or related issues it shall send a copy of that decision to each party in each of the related cases and, subject to paragraph (3), that decision shall be binding on each of those parties.

(3) Within 28 days after the date on which the Tribunal sent a copy of the decision to a party under paragraph (2), that party may apply in writing for an order that the decision does not apply to, and is not binding on the parties to, a particular related case.

(4) If a lead case is withdrawn before the Tribunal makes a decision in respect of the common or related issues, it shall make an order as to—
- (a) whether another claim is to be specified as a lead case; and
- (b) whether any order affecting the related cases should be set aside or varied.

[2.1375]

37 Striking out

(1) At any stage of the proceedings, either on its own initiative or on the application of a party, a Tribunal may strike out all or part of a claim or response on any of the following grounds—
- (a) that it is scandalous or vexatious or has no reasonable prospect of success;
- (b) that the manner in which the proceedings have been conducted by or on behalf of the claimant or the respondent (as the case may be) has been scandalous, unreasonable or vexatious;
- (c) for non-compliance with any of these Rules or with an order of the Tribunal;
- (d) that it has not been actively pursued;
- (e) that the Tribunal considers that it is no longer possible to have a fair hearing in respect of the claim or response (or the part to be struck out).

(2) A claim or response may not be struck out unless the party in question has been given a reasonable opportunity to make representations, either in writing or, if requested by the party, at a hearing.

(3) Where a response is struck out, the effect shall be as if no response had been presented, as set out in rule 21 above.

[2.1376]

38 Unless orders

(1) An order may specify that if it is not complied with by the date specified the claim or response, or part of it, shall be dismissed without further order. If a claim or response, or part of it, is dismissed on this basis the Tribunal shall give written notice to the parties confirming what has occurred.

(2) A party whose claim or response has been dismissed, in whole or in part, as a result of such an order may apply to the Tribunal in writing, within 14 days of the date that the notice was sent, to have the order set aside on the basis that it is in the interests of justice to do so. Unless the application includes a request for a hearing, the Tribunal may determine it on the basis of written representations.

(3) Where a response is dismissed under this rule, the effect shall be as if no response had been presented, as set out in rule 21.

[2.1377]
39 Deposit orders

(1) Where at a preliminary hearing (under rule 53) the Tribunal considers that any specific allegation or argument in a claim or response has little reasonable prospect of success, it may make an order requiring a party ("the paying party") to pay a deposit not exceeding £1,000 as a condition of continuing to advance that allegation or argument.

(2) The Tribunal shall make reasonable enquiries into the paying party's ability to pay the deposit and have regard to any such information when deciding the amount of the deposit.

(3) The Tribunal's reasons for making the deposit order shall be provided with the order and the paying party must be notified about the potential consequences of the order.

(4) If the paying party fails to pay the deposit by the date specified the specific allegation or argument to which the deposit order relates shall be struck out. Where a response is struck out, the consequences shall be as if no response had been presented, as set out in rule 21.

(5) If the Tribunal at any stage following the making of a deposit order decides the specific allegation or argument against the paying party for substantially the reasons given in the deposit order—

(a) the paying party shall be treated as having acted unreasonably in pursuing that specific allegation or argument for the purpose of rule 76, unless the contrary is shown; and

(b) the deposit shall be paid to the other party (or, if there is more than one, to such other party or parties as the Tribunal orders),

otherwise the deposit shall be refunded.

(6) If a deposit has been paid to a party under paragraph (5)(b) and a costs or preparation time order has been made against the paying party in favour of the party who received the deposit, the amount of the deposit shall count towards the settlement of that order.

[2.1378]
40 Non-payment of fees

(1) Subject to rule 11, where a party has not paid a relevant Tribunal fee or presented a remission application in respect of that fee the Tribunal will send the party a notice specifying a date for payment of the Tribunal fee or presentation of a remission application.

(2) If at the date specified in a notice sent under paragraph (1) the party has not paid the Tribunal fee and no remission application in respect of that fee has been presented—

(a) where the Tribunal fee is payable in relation to a claim, the claim shall be dismissed without further order;

(b) where the Tribunal fee is payable in relation to an employer's contract claim, the employer's contract claim shall be dismissed without further order;

(c) where the Tribunal fee is payable in relation to an application, the application shall be dismissed without further order;

(d) where the Tribunal fee is payable in relation to judicial mediation, the judicial mediation shall not take place.

(3) Where a remission application is refused in part or in full, the Tribunal shall send the claimant a notice specifying a date for payment of the Tribunal fee.

(4) If at the date specified in a notice sent under paragraph (3) the party has not paid the Tribunal fee, the consequences shall be those referred to in sub-paragraphs (a) to (d) of paragraph (2).

(5) In the event of a dismissal under paragraph (2) or (4) a party may apply for the claim or response, or part of it, which was dismissed to be reinstated and the Tribunal may order a reinstatement. A reinstatement shall be effective only if the Tribunal fee is paid, or a remission application is presented and accepted, by the date specified in the order.

NOTES

This rule has not been revoked, as of 15 May 2019, despite the quashing by the Supreme Court in *R (UNISON) v Lord Chancellor* [2017] UKSC 51, [2017] ICR 1037 of the Employment Tribunals and the Employment Appeal Tribunal Fees Order 2013, SI 2013/1893, the statutory authority for the charging of fees in relation to employment tribunal claims.

RULES COMMON TO ALL KINDS OF HEARING

[2.1379]
41 General

The Tribunal may regulate its own procedure and shall conduct the hearing in the manner it considers fair, having regard to the principles contained in the overriding objective. The following rules do not restrict that general power. The Tribunal shall seek to avoid undue formality and may itself question the parties or any witnesses so far as appropriate in order to clarify the issues or elicit the evidence. The Tribunal is not bound by any rule of law relating to the admissibility of evidence in proceedings before the courts.

[2.1380]
42 Written representations

The Tribunal shall consider any written representations from a party, including a party who does not propose to attend the hearing, if they are delivered to the Tribunal and to all other parties not less than 7 days before the hearing.

[2.1381]
43 Witnesses

Where a witness is called to give oral evidence, any witness statement of that person ordered by the Tribunal shall stand as that witness's evidence in chief unless the Tribunal orders otherwise. Witnesses shall be required to give their oral evidence on oath or affirmation. The Tribunal may exclude from the hearing any person who is to appear as a witness in the proceedings until such time as that person gives evidence if it considers it in the interests of justice to do so.

[2.1382]
44 Inspection of witness statements

Subject to rules 50 and 94, any witness statement which stands as evidence in chief shall be available for inspection during the course of the hearing by members of the public attending the hearing unless the Tribunal decides that all or any part of the statement is not to be admitted as evidence, in which case the statement or that part shall not be available for inspection.

[2.1383]
45 Timetabling

A Tribunal may impose limits on the time that a party may take in presenting evidence, questioning witnesses or making submissions, and may prevent the party from proceeding beyond any time so allotted.

[2.1384]
46 Hearings by electronic communication

A hearing may be conducted, in whole or in part, by use of electronic communication (including by telephone) provided that the Tribunal considers that it would be just and equitable to do so and provided that the parties and members of the public attending the hearing are able to hear what the Tribunal hears and see any witness as seen by the Tribunal.

[2.1385]
47 Non-attendance

If a party fails to attend or to be represented at the hearing, the Tribunal may dismiss the claim or proceed with the hearing in the absence of that party. Before doing so, it shall consider any information which is available to it, after any enquiries that may be practicable, about the reasons for the party's absence.

[2.1386]
48 Conversion from preliminary hearing to final hearing and vice versa

A Tribunal conducting a preliminary hearing may order that it be treated as a final hearing, or vice versa, if the Tribunal is properly constituted for the purpose and if it is satisfied that neither party shall be materially prejudiced by the change.

[2.1387]
49 Majority decisions

Where a Tribunal is composed of three persons any decision may be made by a majority and if it is composed of two persons the Employment Judge has a second or casting vote.

[2.1388]
50 Privacy and restrictions on disclosure

(1) A Tribunal may at any stage of the proceedings, on its own initiative or on application, make an order with a view to preventing or restricting the public disclosure of any aspect of those proceedings so far as it considers necessary in the interests of justice or in order to protect the Convention rights of any person or in the circumstances identified in section 10A of the Employment Tribunals Act.

(2) In considering whether to make an order under this rule, the Tribunal shall give full weight to the principle of open justice and to the Convention right to freedom of expression.

(3) Such orders may include—

- (a) an order that a hearing that would otherwise be in public be conducted, in whole or in part, in private;
- (b) an order that the identities of specified parties, witnesses or other persons referred to in the proceedings should not be disclosed to the public, by the use of anonymisation or otherwise, whether in the course of any hearing or in its listing or in any documents entered on the Register or otherwise forming part of the public record;
- (c) an order for measures preventing witnesses at a public hearing being identifiable by members of the public;
- (d) a restricted reporting order within the terms of section 11 or 12 of the Employment Tribunals Act.

(4) Any party, or other person with a legitimate interest, who has not had a reasonable opportunity to make representations before an order under this rule is made may apply to the Tribunal in writing for the order to be revoked or discharged, either on the basis of written representations or, if requested, at a hearing.

(5) Where an order is made under paragraph (3)(d) above—

- (a) it shall specify the person whose identity is protected; and may specify particular matters of which publication is prohibited as likely to lead to that person's identification;

(b) it shall specify the duration of the order;
(c) the Tribunal shall ensure that a notice of the fact that such an order has been made in relation to those proceedings is displayed on the notice board of the Tribunal with any list of the proceedings taking place before the Tribunal, and on the door of the room in which the proceedings affected by the order are taking place; and
(d) the Tribunal may order that it applies also to any other proceedings being heard as part of the same hearing.

(6) "Convention rights" has the meaning given to it in section 1 of the Human Rights Act 1998.

WITHDRAWAL

[2.1389]
51 End of claim

Where a claimant informs the Tribunal, either in writing or in the course of a hearing, that a claim, or part of it, is withdrawn, the claim, or part, comes to an end, subject to any application that the respondent may make for a costs, preparation time or wasted costs order.

[2.1390]
52 Dismissal following withdrawal

Where a claim, or part of it, has been withdrawn under rule 51, the Tribunal shall issue a judgment dismissing it (which means that the claimant may not commence a further claim against the respondent raising the same, or substantially the same, complaint) unless—
(a) the claimant has expressed at the time of withdrawal a wish to reserve the right to bring such a further claim and the Tribunal is satisfied that there would be legitimate reason for doing so; or
(b) the Tribunal believes that to issue such a judgment would not be in the interests of justice.

PRELIMINARY HEARINGS

[2.1391]
53 Scope of preliminary hearings

(1) A preliminary hearing is a hearing at which the Tribunal may do one or more of the following—
(a) conduct a preliminary consideration of the claim with the parties and make a case management order (including an order relating to the conduct of the final hearing);
(b) determine any preliminary issue;
(c) consider whether a claim or response, or any part, should be struck out under rule 37;
(d) make a deposit order under rule 39;
(e) explore the possibility of settlement or alternative dispute resolution (including judicial mediation).

(2) There may be more than one preliminary hearing in any case.

(3) "Preliminary issue" means, as regards any complaint, any substantive issue which may determine liability (for example, an issue as to jurisdiction or as to whether an employee was dismissed).

[2.1392]
54 Fixing of preliminary hearings

A preliminary hearing may be directed by the Tribunal on its own initiative following its initial consideration (under rule 26) or at any time thereafter or as the result of an application by a party. The Tribunal shall give the parties reasonable notice of the date of the hearing and in the case of a hearing involving any preliminary issues at least 14 days notice shall be given and the notice shall specify the preliminary issues that are to be, or may be, decided at the hearing.

[2.1393]
55 Constitution of tribunal for preliminary hearings

Preliminary hearings shall be conducted by an Employment Judge alone, except that where notice has been given that any preliminary issues are to be, or may be, decided at the hearing a party may request in writing that the hearing be conducted by a full tribunal in which case an Employment Judge shall decide whether that would be desirable.

[2.1394]
56 When preliminary hearings shall be in public

Preliminary hearings shall be conducted in private, except that where the hearing involves a determination under rule 53(1)(b) or (c), any part of the hearing relating to such a determination shall be in public (subject to rules 50 and 94) and the Tribunal may direct that the entirety of the hearing be in public.

FINAL HEARING

[2.1395]
57 Scope of final hearing

A final hearing is a hearing at which the Tribunal determines the claim or such parts as remain outstanding following the initial consideration (under rule 26) or any preliminary hearing. There may be different final hearings for different issues (for example, liability, remedy or costs).

[2.1396]
58 Notice of final hearing

The Tribunal shall give the parties not less than 14 days' notice of the date of a final hearing.

[2.1397]
59 When final hearing shall be in public

Any final hearing shall be in public, subject to rules 50 and 94.

DECISIONS AND REASONS

[2.1398]
60 Decisions made without a hearing

Decisions made without a hearing shall be communicated in writing to the parties, identifying the Employment Judge who has made the decision.

[2.1399]
61 Decisions made at or following a hearing

(1) Where there is a hearing the Tribunal may either announce its decision in relation to any issue at the hearing or reserve it to be sent to the parties as soon as practicable in writing.

(2) If the decision is announced at the hearing, a written record (in the form of a judgment if appropriate) shall be provided to the parties (and, where the proceedings were referred to the Tribunal by a court, to that court) as soon as practicable. (Decisions concerned only with the conduct of a hearing need not be identified in the record of that hearing unless a party requests that a specific decision is so recorded.)

(3) The written record shall be signed by the Employment Judge.

[2.1400]
62 Reasons

(1) The Tribunal shall give reasons for its decision on any disputed issue, whether substantive or procedural (including any decision on an application for reconsideration or for orders for costs, preparation time or wasted costs).

(2) In the case of a decision given in writing the reasons shall also be given in writing. In the case of a decision announced at a hearing the reasons may be given orally at the hearing or reserved to be given in writing later (which may, but need not, be as part of the written record of the decision). Written reasons shall be signed by the Employment Judge.

(3) Where reasons have been given orally, the Employment Judge shall announce that written reasons will not be provided unless they are asked for by any party at the hearing itself or by a written request presented by any party within 14 days of the sending of the written record of the decision. The written record of the decision shall repeat that information. If no such request is received, the Tribunal shall provide written reasons only if requested to do so by the Employment Appeal Tribunal or a court.

(4) The reasons given for any decision shall be proportionate to the significance of the issue and for decisions other than judgments may be very short.

(5) In the case of a judgment the reasons shall: identify the issues which the Tribunal has determined, state the findings of fact made in relation to those issues, concisely identify the relevant law, and state how that law has been applied to those findings in order to decide the issues. Where the judgment includes a financial award the reasons shall identify, by means of a table or otherwise, how the amount to be paid has been calculated.

[2.1401]
63 Absence of Employment Judge

If it is impossible or not practicable for the written record or reasons to be signed by the Employment Judge as a result of death, incapacity or absence, it shall be signed by the other member or members (in the case of a full tribunal) or by the President, Vice President or a Regional Employment Judge (in the case of a Judge sitting alone).

[2.1402]
64 Consent orders and judgments

If the parties agree in writing or orally at a hearing upon the terms of any order or judgment a Tribunal may, if it thinks fit, make such order or judgment, in which case it shall be identified as having been made by consent.

[2.1403]
65 When a judgment or order takes effect

A judgment or order takes effect from the day when it is given or made, or on such later date as specified by the Tribunal.

[2.1404]
66 Time for compliance

A party shall comply with a judgment or order for the payment of an amount of money within 14 days of the date of the judgment or order, unless—

(a) the judgment, order, or any of these Rules, specifies a different date for compliance; or
(b) the Tribunal has stayed (or in Scotland sisted) the proceedings or judgment.

[2.1405]
67 The Register

Subject to rules 50 and 94, a copy shall be entered in the Register of any judgment and of any written reasons for a judgment.

[2.1406]
68 Copies of judgment for referring court

Where the proceedings were referred to the Tribunal by a court a copy of any judgment and of any written reasons shall be provided to that court.

[2.1407]
69 Correction of clerical mistakes and accidental slips

An Employment Judge may at any time correct any clerical mistake or other accidental slip or omission in any order, judgment or other document produced by a Tribunal. If such a correction is made, any published version of the document shall also be corrected. If any document is corrected under this rule, a copy of the corrected version, signed by the Judge, shall be sent to all the parties.

RECONSIDERATION OF JUDGMENTS

[2.1408]
70 Principles

A Tribunal may, either on its own initiative (which may reflect a request from the Employment Appeal Tribunal) or on the application of a party, reconsider any judgment where it is necessary in the interests of justice to do so. On reconsideration, the decision ("the original decision") may be confirmed, varied or revoked. If it is revoked it may be taken again.

[2.1409]
71 Application

Except where it is made in the course of a hearing, an application for reconsideration shall be presented in writing (and copied to all the other parties) within 14 days of the date on which the written record, or other written communication, of the original decision was sent to the parties or within 14 days of the date that the written reasons were sent (if later) and shall set out why reconsideration of the original decision is necessary.

[2.1410]
72 Process

(1) An Employment Judge shall consider any application made under rule 71. If the Judge considers that there is no reasonable prospect of the original decision being varied or revoked (including, unless there are special reasons, where substantially the same application has already been made and refused), the application shall be refused and the Tribunal shall inform the parties of the refusal. Otherwise the Tribunal shall send a notice to the parties setting a time limit for any response to the application by the other parties and seeking the views of the parties on whether the application can be determined without a hearing. The notice may set out the Judge's provisional views on the application.

(2) If the application has not been refused under paragraph (1), the original decision shall be reconsidered at a hearing unless the Employment Judge considers, having regard to any response to the notice provided under paragraph (1), that a hearing is not necessary in the interests of justice. If the reconsideration proceeds without a hearing the parties shall be given a reasonable opportunity to make further written representations.

(3) Where practicable, the consideration under paragraph (1) shall be by the Employment Judge who made the original decision or, as the case may be, chaired the full tribunal which made it; and any reconsideration under paragraph (2) shall be made by the Judge or, as the case may be, the full tribunal which made the original decision. Where that is not practicable, the President, Vice President or a Regional Employment Judge shall appoint another Employment Judge to deal with the application or, in the case of a decision of a full tribunal, shall either direct that the reconsideration be by such members of the original Tribunal as remain available or reconstitute the Tribunal in whole or in part.

[2.1411]
73 Reconsideration by the Tribunal on its own initiative

Where the Tribunal proposes to reconsider a decision on its own initiative, it shall inform the parties of the reasons why the decision is being reconsidered and the decision shall be reconsidered in accordance with rule 72(2) (as if an application had been made and not refused).

COSTS ORDERS, PREPARATION TIME ORDERS AND WASTED COSTS ORDERS

[2.1412]
74 Definitions

(1) "Costs" means fees, charges, disbursements or expenses incurred by or on behalf of the receiving party (including expenses that witnesses incur for the purpose of, or in connection with, attendance at a Tribunal hearing). In Scotland all references to costs (except when used in the expression "wasted costs") shall be read as references to expenses.

(2) "Legally represented" means having the assistance of a person (including where that person is the receiving party's employee) who—

(a) has a right of audience in relation to any class of proceedings in any part of the Senior Courts of England and Wales, or all proceedings in county courts or magistrates' courts;

(b) is an advocate or solicitor in Scotland; or

(c) is a member of the Bar of Northern Ireland or a solicitor of the Court of Judicature of Northern Ireland.

(3) "Represented by a lay representative" means having the assistance of a person who does not satisfy any of the criteria in paragraph (2) and who charges for representation in the proceedings.

[2.1413]

75 Costs orders and preparation time orders

(1) A costs order is an order that a party ("the paying party") make a payment to—

(a) another party ("the receiving party") in respect of the costs that the receiving party has incurred while legally represented or while represented by a lay representative;

(b) the receiving party in respect of a Tribunal fee paid by the receiving party; or

(c) another party or a witness in respect of expenses incurred, or to be incurred, for the purpose of, or in connection with, an individual's attendance as a witness at the Tribunal.

(2) A preparation time order is an order that a party ("the paying party") make a payment to another party ("the receiving party") in respect of the receiving party's preparation time while not legally represented. "Preparation time" means time spent by the receiving party (including by any employees or advisers) in working on the case, except for time spent at any final hearing.

(3) A costs order under paragraph (1)(a) and a preparation time order may not both be made in favour of the same party in the same proceedings. A Tribunal may, if it wishes, decide in the course of the proceedings that a party is entitled to one order or the other but defer until a later stage in the proceedings deciding which kind of order to make.

[2.1414]

76 When a costs order or a preparation time order may or shall be made

(1) A Tribunal may make a costs order or a preparation time order, and shall consider whether to do so, where it considers that—

(a) a party (or that party's representative) has acted vexatiously, abusively, disruptively or otherwise unreasonably in either the bringing of the proceedings (or part) or the way that the proceedings (or part) have been conducted; or

(b) any claim or response had no reasonable prospect of success; [or

(c) a hearing has been postponed or adjourned on the application of a party made less than 7 days before the date on which the relevant hearing begins.]

(2) A Tribunal may also make such an order where a party has been in breach of any order or practice direction or where a hearing has been postponed or adjourned on the application of a party.

(3) Where in proceedings for unfair dismissal a final hearing is postponed or adjourned, the Tribunal shall order the respondent to pay the costs incurred as a result of the postponement or adjournment if—

(a) the claimant has expressed a wish to be reinstated or re-engaged which has been communicated to the respondent not less than 7 days before the hearing; and

(b) the postponement or adjournment of that hearing has been caused by the respondent's failure, without a special reason, to adduce reasonable evidence as to the availability of the job from which the claimant was dismissed or of comparable or suitable employment.

(4) A Tribunal may make a costs order of the kind described in rule 75(1)(b) where a party has paid a Tribunal fee in respect of a claim, employer's contract claim or application and that claim, counterclaim or application is decided in whole, or in part, in favour of that party.

(5) A Tribunal may make a costs order of the kind described in rule 75(1)(c) on the application of a party or the witness in question, or on its own initiative, where a witness has attended or has been ordered to attend to give oral evidence at a hearing.

NOTES

Para (1): sub-para (c) (and the preceding word) inserted by the Employment Tribunals (Constitution and Rules of Procedure) (Amendment) Regulations 2016, SI 2016/271, reg 2(1), (4), as from 6 April 2016, in relation to proceedings which are presented to an employment tribunal on or after that date (see reg 3 of the 2016 Regulations).

[2.1415]

77 Procedure

A party may apply for a costs order or a preparation time order at any stage up to 28 days after the date on which the judgment finally determining the proceedings in respect of that party was sent to the parties. No such order may be made unless the paying party has had a reasonable opportunity to make representations (in writing or at a hearing, as the Tribunal may order) in response to the application.

[2.1416]

78 The amount of a costs order

(1) A costs order may—

(a) order the paying party to pay the receiving party a specified amount, not exceeding £20,000, in respect of the costs of the receiving party;

(b) order the paying party to pay the receiving party the whole or a specified part of the costs of the receiving party, with the amount to be paid being determined, in England and Wales, by way of detailed assessment carried out either by a county court in accordance with the Civil Procedure

Rules 1998, or by an Employment Judge applying the same principles; or, in Scotland, by way of taxation carried out either by the auditor of court in accordance with the Act of Sederunt (Fees of Solicitors in the Sheriff Court)(Amendment and Further Provisions) 1993, or by an Employment Judge applying the same principles;

(c) order the paying party to pay the receiving party a specified amount as reimbursement of all or part of a Tribunal fee paid by the receiving party;

(d) order the paying party to pay another party or a witness, as appropriate, a specified amount in respect of necessary and reasonably incurred expenses (of the kind described in rule 75(1)(c)); or

(e) if the paying party and the receiving party agree as to the amount payable, be made in that amount.

(2) Where the costs order includes an amount in respect of fees charged by a lay representative, for the purposes of the calculation of the order, the hourly rate applicable for the fees of the lay representative shall be no higher than the rate under rule 79(2).

(3) For the avoidance of doubt, the amount of a costs order under sub-paragraphs (b) to (e) of paragraph (1) may exceed £20,000.

[2.1417]
79 The amount of a preparation time order

(1) The Tribunal shall decide the number of hours in respect of which a preparation time order should be made, on the basis of—

(a) information provided by the receiving party on time spent falling within rule 75(2) above; and

(b) the Tribunal's own assessment of what it considers to be a reasonable and proportionate amount of time to spend on such preparatory work, with reference to such matters as the complexity of the proceedings, the number of witnesses and documentation required.

(2) The hourly rate is £33 and increases on 6 April each year by £1.

(3) The amount of a preparation time order shall be the product of the number of hours assessed under paragraph (1) and the rate under paragraph (2).

[2.1418]
80 When a wasted costs order may be made

(1) A Tribunal may make a wasted costs order against a representative in favour of any party ("the receiving party") where that party has incurred costs—

(a) as a result of any improper, unreasonable or negligent act or omission on the part of the representative; or

(b) which, in the light of any such act or omission occurring after they were incurred, the Tribunal considers it unreasonable to expect the receiving party to pay.

Costs so incurred are described as "wasted costs".

(2) "Representative" means a party's legal or other representative or any employee of such representative, but it does not include a representative who is not acting in pursuit of profit with regard to the proceedings. A person acting on a contingency or conditional fee arrangement is considered to be acting in pursuit of profit.

(3) A wasted costs order may be made in favour of a party whether or not that party is legally represented and may also be made in favour of a representative's own client. A wasted costs order may not be made against a representative where that representative is representing a party in his or her capacity as an employee of that party.

[2.1419]
81 Effect of a wasted costs order

A wasted costs order may order the representative to pay the whole or part of any wasted costs of the receiving party, or disallow any wasted costs otherwise payable to the representative, including an order that the representative repay to its client any costs which have already been paid. The amount to be paid, disallowed or repaid must in each case be specified in the order.

[2.1420]
82 Procedure

A wasted costs order may be made by the Tribunal on its own initiative or on the application of any party. A party may apply for a wasted costs order at any stage up to 28 days after the date on which the judgment finally determining the proceedings as against that party was sent to the parties. No such order shall be made unless the representative has had a reasonable opportunity to make representations (in writing or at a hearing, as the Tribunal may order) in response to the application or proposal. The Tribunal shall inform the representative's client in writing of any proceedings under this rule and of any order made against the representative.

[2.1421]
83 Allowances

Where the Tribunal makes a costs, preparation time, or wasted costs order, it may also make an order that the paying party (or, where a wasted costs order is made, the representative) pay to the Secretary of State, in whole or in part, any allowances (other than allowances paid to members of the Tribunal) paid by the Secretary of State under section 5(2) or (3) of the Employment Tribunals Act to any person for the purposes of, or in connection with, that person's attendance at the Tribunal.

[2.1422]
84 Ability to pay

In deciding whether to make a costs, preparation time, or wasted costs order, and if so in what amount, the Tribunal may have regard to the paying party's (or, where a wasted costs order is made, the representative's) ability to pay.

DELIVERY OF DOCUMENTS

[2.1423]
85 Delivery to the Tribunal

(1) Subject to paragraph (2), documents may be delivered to the Tribunal—
- (a) by post;
- (b) by direct delivery to the appropriate tribunal office (including delivery by a courier or messenger service); or
- (c) by electronic communication.

(2) A claim form may only be delivered in accordance with the practice direction made under regulation 11 which supplements rule 8.

(3) The Tribunal shall notify the parties following the presentation of the claim of the address of the tribunal office dealing with the case (including any fax or email or other electronic address) and all documents shall be delivered to either the postal or the electronic address so notified. The Tribunal may from time to time notify the parties of any change of address, or that a particular form of communication should or should not be used, and any documents shall be delivered in accordance with that notification.

[2.1424]
86 Delivery to parties

(1) Documents may be delivered to a party (whether by the Tribunal or by another party)—
- (a) by post;
- (b) by direct delivery to that party's address (including delivery by a courier or messenger service);
- (c) by electronic communication; or
- (d) by being handed personally to that party, if an individual and if no representative has been named in the claim form or response; or to any individual representative named in the claim form or response; or, on the occasion of a hearing, to any person identified by the party as representing that party at that hearing.

(2) For the purposes of sub-paragraphs (a) to (c) of paragraph (1), the document shall be delivered to the address given in the claim form or response (which shall be the address of the party's representative, if one is named) or to a different address as notified in writing by the party in question.

(3) If a party has given both a postal address and one or more electronic addresses, any of them may be used unless the party has indicated in writing that a particular address should or should not be used.

[2.1425]
87 Delivery to non-parties

Subject to the special cases which are the subject of rule 88, documents shall be sent to non-parties at any address for service which they may have notified and otherwise at any known address or place of business in the United Kingdom or, if the party is a corporate body, at its registered or principal office in the United Kingdom or, if permitted by the President, at an address outside the United Kingdom.

[2.1426]
88 Special cases

Addresses for serving the Secretary of State, the Law Officers, and the Counsel General to the Welsh Assembly Government, in cases where they are not parties, shall be issued by practice direction.

NOTES

Welsh Assembly Government: see the Wales Act 2014, s 4 which provides that, unless the context requires otherwise, any reference to the Welsh Assembly Government is to be read as, or as including, a reference to the Welsh Government.

[2.1427]
89 Substituted service

Where no address for service in accordance with the above rules is known or it appears that service at any such address is unlikely to come to the attention of the addressee, the President, Vice President or a Regional Employment Judge may order that there shall be substituted service in such manner as appears appropriate.

[2.1428]
90 Date of delivery

Where a document has been delivered in accordance with rule 85 or 86, it shall, unless the contrary is proved, be taken to have been received by the addressee—
- (a) if sent by post, on the day on which it would be delivered in the ordinary course of post;
- (b) if sent by means of electronic communication, on the day of transmission;
- (c) if delivered directly or personally, on the day of delivery.

[2.1429]
91 Irregular service

A Tribunal may treat any document as delivered to a person, notwithstanding any non-compliance with rules 86 to 88, if satisfied that the document in question, or its substance, has in fact come to the attention of that person.

[2.1430]
92 Correspondence with the Tribunal: copying to other parties

Where a party sends a communication to the Tribunal (except an application under rule 32) it shall send a copy to all other parties, and state that it has done so (by use of "cc" or otherwise). The Tribunal may order a departure from this rule where it considers it in the interests of justice to do so.

MISCELLANEOUS

[2.1431]
93 ACAS

(1) Where proceedings concern an enactment which provides for conciliation, the Tribunal shall—
- (a) send a copy of the claim form and the response to an ACAS conciliation officer; and
- (b) inform the parties that the services of an ACAS conciliation officer are available to them.

(2) Subject to rules 50 and 94, a representative of ACAS may attend any preliminary hearing.

[2.1432]
94 National security proceedings

(1) Where in relation to particular Crown employment proceedings a Minister considers that it would be expedient in the interests of national security, the Minister may direct a Tribunal to—
- (a) conduct all or part of the proceedings in private;
- (b) exclude a person from all or part of the proceedings;
- (c) take steps to conceal the identity of a witness in the proceedings.

(2) Where the Tribunal considers it expedient in the interests of national security, it may order—
- (a) in relation to particular proceedings (including Crown employment proceedings), anything which can be required to be done under paragraph (1);
- (b) a person not to disclose any document (or the contents of any document), where provided for the purposes of the proceedings, to any other person (save for any specified person).

Any order made must be kept under review by the Tribunal.

(3) Where the Tribunal considers that it may be necessary to make an order under paragraph (2) in relation to particular proceedings (including Crown employment proceedings), the Tribunal may consider any material provided by a party (or where a Minister is not a party, by a Minister) without providing that material to any other person. Such material shall be used by the Tribunal solely for the purposes of deciding whether to make that order (unless that material is subsequently used as evidence in the proceedings by a party).

(4) Where a Minister considers that it would be appropriate for the Tribunal to make an order under paragraph (2), the Minister may make an application for such an order.

(5) Where a Minister has made an application under paragraph (4), the Tribunal may order—
- (a) in relation to the part of the proceedings preceding the outcome of the application, anything which can be required to be done under paragraph (1);
- (b) a person not to disclose any document (or the contents of any document) to any other person (save for any specified person), where provided for the purposes of the proceedings preceding the outcome of the application.

(6) Where a Minister has made an application under paragraph (4) for an order to exclude any person from all or part of the proceedings, the Tribunal shall not send a copy of the response to that person, pending the decision on the application.

(7) If before the expiry of the time limit in rule 16 a Minister makes a direction under paragraph (1) or makes an application under paragraph (4), the Minister may apply for an extension of the time limit in rule 16.

(8) A direction under paragraph (1) or an application under paragraph (4) may be made irrespective of whether or not the Minister is a party.

(9) Where the Tribunal decides not to make an order under paragraph (2), rule 6 of Schedule 2 shall apply to the reasons given by the Tribunal under rule 62 for that decision, save that the reasons will not be entered on the Register.

(10) The Tribunal must ensure that in exercising its functions, information is not disclosed contrary to the interests of national security.

[2.1433]
95 Interim relief proceedings

When a Tribunal hears an application for interim relief (or for its variation or revocation) under section 161 or section 165 of the Trade Union and Labour Relations (Consolidation) Act 1992 or under section 128 or section 131 of the Employment Rights Act 1996, rules 53 to 56 apply to the hearing and the Tribunal shall not hear oral evidence unless it directs otherwise.

[2.1434]
96 Proceedings involving the National Insurance Fund

The Secretary of State shall be entitled to appear and be heard at any hearing in relation to proceedings which may involve a payment out of the National Insurance Fund and shall be treated as a party for the purposes of these Rules.

[2.1435]
97 Collective agreements

Where a claim includes a complaint under section 146(1) of the Equality Act relating to a term of a collective agreement, the following persons, whether or not identified in the claim, shall be regarded as the persons against whom a remedy is claimed and shall be treated as respondents for the purposes of these Rules—

(a) the claimant's employer (or prospective employer); and
(b) every organisation of employers and organisation of workers, and every association of or representative of such organisations, which, if the terms were to be varied voluntarily, would be likely, in the opinion of an Employment Judge, to negotiate the variation.

An organisation or association shall not be treated as a respondent if the Judge, having made such enquiries of the claimant and such other enquiries as the Judge thinks fit, is of the opinion that it is not reasonably practicable to identify the organisation or association.

[2.1436]
98 Devolution issues

(1) Where a devolution issue arises, the Tribunal shall as soon as practicable send notice of that fact and a copy of the claim form and response to the Advocate General for Scotland and the Lord Advocate, where it is a Scottish devolution issue, or to the Attorney General and the Counsel General to the Welsh Assembly Government, where it is a Welsh devolution issue, unless they are a party to the proceedings.

(2) A person to whom notice is sent may be treated as a party to the proceedings, so far as the proceedings relate to the devolution issue, if that person sends notice to the Tribunal within 14 days of receiving a notice under paragraph (1).

(3) Any notices sent under paragraph (1) or (2) must at the same time be sent to the parties.

(4) "Devolution issue" has the meaning given to it in paragraph 1 of Schedule 6 to the Scotland Act 1998 (for the purposes of a Scottish devolution issue), and in paragraph 1 of Schedule 9 to the Government of Wales Act 2006 (for the purposes of a Welsh devolution issue).

NOTES

Welsh Assembly Government: see the Wales Act 2014, s 4 which provides that, unless the context requires otherwise, any reference to the Welsh Assembly Government is to be read as, or as including, a reference to the Welsh Government.

[2.1437]
99 Transfer of proceedings between Scotland and England & Wales

(1) The President (England and Wales) or a Regional Employment Judge may at any time, on their own initiative or on the application of a party, with the consent of the President (Scotland), transfer to a tribunal office in Scotland any proceedings started in England and Wales which could (in accordance with rule 8(3)) have been started in Scotland and which in that person's opinion would more conveniently be determined there.

(2) The President (Scotland) or the Vice President may at any time, on their own initiative or on the application of a party, with the consent of the President (England and Wales), transfer to a tribunal office in England and Wales any proceedings started in Scotland which could (in accordance with rule 8(2)) have been started in England and Wales and in that person's opinion would more conveniently be determined there.

[2.1438]
100 *References to the Court of Justice of the European Union*

Where a Tribunal decides to refer a question to the Court of Justice of the European Union for a preliminary ruling under Article 267 of the Treaty on the Functioning of the European Union, a copy of that decision shall be sent to the registrar of that court.

NOTES

Revoked by the Employment Rights (Amendment) (EU Exit) Regulations 2019, SI 2019/535, reg 2(1), Sch 1, Pt 2, para 14(b), as from exit day (as defined in the European Union (Withdrawal) Act 2018, s 20).

[2.1439]
101 Transfer of proceedings from a court

Where proceedings are referred to a Tribunal by a court, these Rules apply as if the proceedings had been presented by the claimant.

[2.1440]
102 Vexatious litigants

The Tribunal may provide any information or documents requested by the Attorney General, the Solicitor General or the Lord Advocate for the purpose of preparing an application or considering whether to make an application under section 42 of the Senior Courts Act 1981, section 1 of the Vexatious Actions (Scotland) Act 1898[, section 100 of the Courts Reform (Scotland) Act 2014] or section 33 of the Employment Tribunals Act.

NOTES

Words in square brackets inserted by the Courts Reform (Scotland) Act 2014 (Relevant Officer and Consequential Provisions) Order 2016, SSI 2016/387, art 3, Sch 2, Pt 2, para 3, as from 28 November 2016.

[2.1441]
103 Information to the Commission for Equality and Human Rights

The Tribunal shall send to the Commission for Equality and Human Rights copies of all judgments and written reasons relating to complaints under section 120, 127 or 146 of the Equality Act. That obligation shall not apply in any proceedings where a Minister of the Crown has given a direction, or a Tribunal has made an order, under rule 94; and either the Security Service, the Secret Intelligence Service or the Government Communications Headquarters is a party to the proceedings.

[2.1442]
104 Application of this Schedule to levy appeals

For the purposes of a levy appeal, references in this Schedule to a claim or claimant shall be read as references to a levy appeal or to an appellant in a levy appeal respectively.

[2.1443]
105 Application of this Schedule to appeals against improvement and prohibition notices

(1) A person ("the appellant") may appeal an improvement notice or a prohibition notice by presenting a claim to a tribunal office—
- (a) before the end of the period of 21 days beginning with the date of the service on the appellant of the notice which is the subject of the appeal; or
- (b) within such further period as the Tribunal considers reasonable where it is satisfied that it was not reasonably practicable for an appeal to be presented within that time.

(2) For the purposes of an appeal against an improvement notice or a prohibition notice, this Schedule shall be treated as modified in the following ways—
- (a) references to a claim or claimant shall be read as references to an appeal or to an appellant in an appeal respectively;
- (b) references to a respondent shall be read as references to the inspector appointed under section 19(1) of the Health and Safety Act who issued the notice which is the subject of the appeal.

[2.1444]
[105A Application of this Schedule to appeals against notices given under the Energy Act 2013

(1) A person ("the appellant") may appeal an Energy Act IN or Energy Act PN by presenting a claim to a tribunal office—
- (a) before the end of the period of 21 days beginning with the date on which the notice which is the subject of the appeal is given to the appellant; or
- (b) within such further period as the Tribunal considers reasonable where it is satisfied that it was not reasonably practicable for an appeal to be presented within that period.

(2) For the purposes of an appeal against an Energy Act IN or Energy Act PN, this Schedule shall be treated as modified in the following ways—
- (a) references to a claim or claimant shall be read as references to an appeal or to an appellant in an appeal respectively;
- (b) references to a respondent shall be read as references to the inspector appointed under paragraph 1 of Schedule 8 to the Energy Act 2013 who issued the notice which is the subject of the appeal.]

NOTES

Inserted by the Energy Act 2013 (Improvement and Prohibition Notices Appeals) Regulations 2014, SI 2014/468, reg 2(1), (3).

[2.1445]
106 Application of this Schedule to appeals against unlawful act notices

For the purposes of an appeal against an unlawful act notice, this Schedule shall be treated as modified in the following ways—
- (a) references in this Schedule to a claim or claimant shall be read as references to a notice of appeal or to an appellant in an appeal against an unlawful act notice respectively;
- (b) references to a respondent shall be read as references to the Commission for Equality and Human Rights.

SCHEDULE 2
THE EMPLOYMENT TRIBUNALS (NATIONAL SECURITY) RULES OF PROCEDURE

Regulation 13(2)

[2.1446]

1 Application of Schedule 2

(1) This Schedule applies to proceedings in relation to which a direction is given, or order is made, under rule 94 and modifies the rules in Schedule 1 in relation to such proceedings.

(2) References in this Schedule to rule numbers are to those in Schedule 1.

(3) The definitions in rule 1 apply to terms in this Schedule and in this Schedule—
"excluded person" means, in relation to any proceedings, a person who has been excluded from all or part of the proceedings by virtue of a direction under rule 94(1)(b) or an order under rule 94(2)(a) (read with rule 94(1)(b)).

2 Serving of documents

The Tribunal shall not send a copy of the response to any excluded person.

3 Witness orders and disclosure of documents

(1) Where a person or their representative has been excluded under rule 94 from all or part of the proceedings and a Tribunal is considering whether to make an order under rule 31 or 32, a Minister (whether or not he is a party to the proceedings) may make an application to the Tribunal objecting to that order. If such an order has been made, the Minister may make an application to vary or set aside the order.

(2) The Tribunal shall hear and determine the Minister's application in private and the Minister shall be entitled to address the Tribunal.

4 Special advocate

(1) The Tribunal shall inform the relevant Law Officer if a party becomes an excluded person. For the purposes of this rule, "relevant Law Officer" means, in relation to England and Wales, the Attorney General, and, in relation to Scotland, the Advocate General.

(2) The relevant Law Officer may appoint a special advocate to represent the interests of a person in respect of those parts of the proceedings from which—
- (a) a person's representative is excluded;
- (b) a person and their representative are excluded;
- (c) a person is excluded and is unrepresented.

(3) A special advocate shall be a person who has a right of audience in relation to any class of proceedings in any part of the Senior Courts or all proceedings in county courts or magistrates' courts, or shall be an advocate or a solicitor admitted in Scotland.

(4) An excluded person (where that person is a party) may make a statement to the Tribunal before the commencement of the proceedings or the relevant part of the proceedings.

(5) The special advocate may communicate, directly or indirectly, with an excluded person at any time before receiving material from a Minister in relation to which the Minister states an objection to disclosure to the excluded person ("closed material").

(6) After receiving closed material, the special advocate must not communicate with any person about any matter connected with the proceedings, except in accordance with paragraph (7) or (9) or an order of the Tribunal.

(7) The special advocate may communicate about the proceedings with—
- (a) the Tribunal;
- (b) the Minister, or their representative;
- (c) the relevant Law Officer, or their representative;
- (d) any other person, except for an excluded person or his representative, with whom it is necessary for administrative purposes to communicate about matters not connected with the substance of the proceedings.

(8) The special advocate may apply for an order from the Tribunal to authorise communication with an excluded person or with any other person and if such an application is made—
- (a) the Tribunal must notify the Minister of the request; and
- (b) the Minister may, within a period specified by the Tribunal, present to the Tribunal and serve on the special advocate notice of any objection to the proposed communication.

(9) After the special advocate has received closed material, an excluded person may only communicate with the special advocate in writing and the special advocate must not reply to the communication, except that the special advocate may send a written acknowledgment of receipt to the legal representative.

(10) References in these Regulations and Schedules 1 and 2 to a party shall include any special advocate appointed in particular proceedings, save that the references to "party" or "parties" in rules 3, 6(c), 22, 26, 34, 36(2), 36(3), the first reference in rule 37, 38, 39, 40, 41, 45, 47, 64, 74 to 84, 86, 96 and 98(3) shall not include the special advocate.

5 Hearings

(1) Subject to any order under rule 50 or any direction or order under rule 94, any hearing shall take place in public, and any party may attend and participate in the hearing.

(2) . . .

6 Reasons in national security proceedings

(1) The Tribunal shall send a copy of the written reasons given under rule 62 to the Minister and allow 42 days for the Minister to make a direction under paragraph (3) below before sending them to any party or entering them onto the Register.

(2) If the Tribunal considers it expedient in the interests of national security, it may by order take steps to keep secret all or part of the written reasons.

(3) If the Minister considers it expedient in the interests of national security, the Minister may direct that the written reasons—

(a) shall not be disclosed to specified persons and require the Tribunal to prepare a further document which sets out the reasons for the decision, but omits specified information ("the edited reasons");

(b) shall not be disclosed to specified persons and that no further document setting out the reasons for the decision should be prepared.

(4) Where the Minister has directed the Tribunal to prepare edited reasons, the Employment Judge shall initial each omission.

(5) Where a direction has been made under paragraph (3)(a), the Tribunal shall—

(a) send the edited reasons to the specified persons;

(b) send the edited reasons and the written reasons to the relevant persons listed in paragraph (7); and

(c) where the written reasons relate to a judgment, enter the edited reasons on the Register but not enter the written reasons on the Register.

(6) Where a direction has been made under paragraph (3)(b), the Tribunal shall send the written reasons to the relevant persons listed in paragraph (7), but not enter the written reasons on the Register.

(7) The relevant persons are—

(a) the respondent or the respondent's representative, provided that they were not specified in the direction made under paragraph (3);

(b) the claimant or the claimant's representative, provided that they were not specified in the direction made under paragraph (3);

(c) any special advocate appointed in the proceedings; and

(d) where the proceedings were referred to the Tribunal by a court, to that court.

(8) Where written reasons or edited reasons are corrected under rule 69, the Tribunal shall send a copy of the corrected reasons to the same persons who had been sent the reasons.

NOTES

Rule 5: para (2) revoked by the Employment Tribunals (Constitution and Rules of Procedure) (Amendment) Regulations 2014, SI 2014/271, reg 10.

SCHEDULE 3
THE EMPLOYMENT TRIBUNALS (EQUAL VALUE) RULES OF PROCEDURE

Regulation 13(2)

[2.1447]

1 Application of Schedule 3

(1) This Schedule applies to proceedings involving an equal value claim and modifies the rules in Schedule 1 in relation to such proceedings.

(2) The definitions in rule 1 of Schedule 1 apply to terms in this Schedule and in this Schedule—

"comparator" means the person of the opposite sex to the claimant in relation to whom the claimant alleges that his or her work is of equal value;

"equal value claim" means a claim relating to a breach of a sex equality clause or rule within the meaning of the Equality Act in a case involving work within section 65(1)(c) of that Act;

"the facts relating to the question" has the meaning in rule 6(1)(a);

"independent expert" means a member of the panel of independent experts mentioned in section 131(8) of the Equality Act;

"the question" means whether the claimant's work is of equal value to that of the comparator; and

"report" means a report required by a Tribunal to be prepared in accordance with section 131(2) of the Equality Act.

(3) A reference in this Schedule to a rule, is a reference to a rule in this Schedule unless otherwise provided.

(4) A reference in this Schedule to "these rules" is a reference to the rules in Schedules 1 and 3 unless otherwise provided.

2 General power to manage proceedings

(1) The Tribunal may (subject to rules 3(1) and 6(1)) order—

(a) that no new facts shall be admitted in evidence by the Tribunal unless they have been disclosed to all other parties in writing before a date specified by the Tribunal (unless it was not reasonably practicable for a party to have done so);

(b) the parties to send copies of documents or provide information to the independent expert;

(c) the respondent to grant the independent expert access to the respondent's premises during a period specified in the order to allow the independent expert to conduct interviews with persons identified as relevant by the independent expert;

(d) when more than one expert is to give evidence in the proceedings, that those experts present to the Tribunal a joint statement of matters which are agreed between them and matters on which they disagree.

(2) In managing the proceedings, the Tribunal shall have regard to the indicative timetable in the Annex to this Schedule.

3 Conduct of stage 1 equal value hearing

(1) Where there is a dispute as to whether one person's work is of equal value to another's (equal value being construed in accordance with section 65(6) of the Equality Act), the Tribunal shall conduct a hearing, which shall be referred to as a "stage 1 equal value hearing", and at that hearing shall—

(a) strike out the claim (or the relevant part of it) if in accordance with section 131(6) of the Equality Act the Tribunal must determine that the work of the claimant and the comparator are not of equal value;

(b) determine the question or require an independent expert to prepare a report on the question;

(c) if the Tribunal has decided to require an independent expert to prepare a report on the question, fix a date for a further hearing, which shall be referred to as a "stage 2 equal value hearing"; and

(d) if the Tribunal has not decided to require an independent expert to prepare a report on the question, fix a date for the final hearing.

(2) Before a claim or part is struck out under sub-paragraph (1)(a), the Tribunal shall send notice to the claimant and allow the claimant to make representations to the Tribunal as to whether the evaluation contained in the study in question falls within paragraph (a) or (b) of section 131(6) of the Equality Act. The Tribunal shall not be required to send a notice under this paragraph if the claimant has been given an opportunity to make such representations orally to the Tribunal.

(3) The Tribunal may, on the application of a party, hear evidence and submissions on the issue contained in section 69 of the Equality Act before determining whether to require an independent expert to prepare a report under paragraph (1)(b).

(4) The Tribunal shall give the parties reasonable notice of the date of the stage 1 equal value hearing and the notice shall specify the matters that are to be, or may be, considered at the hearing and give notice of the standard orders in rule 4.

4 Standard orders for stage 1 equal value hearing

(1) At a stage 1 equal value hearing a Tribunal shall, unless it considers it inappropriate to do so, order that—

(a) before the end of the period of 14 days the claimant shall—

(i) disclose in writing to the respondent the name of any comparator, or, if the claimant is not able to name the comparator, disclose information which enables the respondent to identify the comparator; and

(ii) identify to the respondent in writing the period in relation to which the claimant considers that the claimant's work and that of the comparator are to be compared;

(b) before the end of the period of 28 days—

(i) where the claimant has not disclosed the name of the comparator to the respondent under sub-paragraph (a) and the respondent has been provided with sufficient detail to be able to identify the comparator, the respondent shall disclose in writing the name of the comparator to the claimant;

(ii) the parties shall provide each other with written job descriptions for the claimant and any comparator;

(iii) the parties shall identify to each other in writing the facts which they consider to be relevant to the question;

(c) the respondent shall grant access to the respondent's premises during a period specified in the order to allow the claimant and his or her representative to interview any comparator;

(d) the parties shall before the end of the period of 56 days present to the Tribunal an agreed written statement specifying—

(i) job descriptions for the claimant and any comparator;

(ii) the facts which both parties consider are relevant to the question;

(iii) the facts on which the parties disagree (as to the fact or as to the relevance to the question) and a summary of their reasons for disagreeing;

(e) the parties shall, at least 56 days before the final hearing, disclose to each other, to any independent or other expert and to the Tribunal written statements of any facts on which they intend to rely in evidence at the final hearing; and

(f) the parties shall, at least 28 days before the final hearing, present to the Tribunal a statement of facts and issues on which the parties are in agreement, a statement of facts and issues on which the parties disagree and a summary of their reasons for disagreeing.

(2) The Tribunal may add to, vary or omit any of the standard orders in paragraph (1).

5 Involvement of independent expert in fact finding

Where the Tribunal has decided to require an independent expert to prepare a report on the question, it may at any stage of the proceedings, on its own initiative or on the application of a party, order the independent expert to assist the Tribunal in establishing the facts on which the independent expert may rely in preparing the report.

6 Conduct of stage 2 equal value hearing

(1) Any stage 2 equal value hearing shall be conducted by a full tribunal and at the hearing the Tribunal shall—

(a) make a determination of facts on which the parties cannot agree which relate to the question and shall require the independent expert to prepare the report on the basis of facts which have (at any stage of the proceedings) either been agreed between the parties or determined by the Tribunal (referred to as "the facts relating to the question"); and

(b) fix a date for the final hearing.

(2) Subject to paragraph (3), the facts relating to the question shall, in relation to the question, be the only facts on which the Tribunal shall rely at the final hearing.

(3) At any stage of the proceedings the independent expert may make an application to the Tribunal for some or all of the facts relating to the question to be amended, supplemented or omitted.

(4) The Tribunal shall give the parties reasonable notice of the date of the stage 2 equal value hearing and the notice shall draw the attention of the parties to this rule and give notice of the standard orders in rule 7.

7 Standard orders for stage 2 equal value hearing

(1) At a stage 2 equal value hearing a Tribunal shall, unless it considers it inappropriate to do so, order that—

(a) by a specified date the independent expert shall prepare his report on the question and shall (subject to rule 13) send copies of it to the parties and to the Tribunal; and

(b) the independent expert shall prepare his report on the question on the basis only of the facts relating to the question.

(2) The Tribunal may add to, vary or omit any of the standard orders in paragraph (1).

8 Final hearing

(1) Where an independent expert has prepared a report, unless the Tribunal determines that the report is not based on the facts relating to the question, the report of the independent expert shall be admitted in evidence.

(2) If the Tribunal does not admit the report of an independent expert in accordance with paragraph (1), it may determine the question itself or require another independent expert to prepare a report on the question.

(3) The Tribunal may refuse to admit evidence of facts or hear submissions on issues which have not been disclosed to the other party as required by these rules or any order (unless it was not reasonably practicable for a party to have done so).

9 Duties and powers of the independent expert

(1) When a Tribunal makes an order under rule 3(1)(b) or 5, it shall inform that independent expert of the duties and powers under this rule.

(2) The independent expert shall have a duty to the Tribunal to—

(a) assist it in furthering the overriding objective set out in rule 2 of Schedule 1;
(b) comply with the requirements of these rules and any orders made by the Tribunal;
(c) keep the Tribunal informed of any delay in complying with any order (with the exception of minor or insignificant delays in compliance);
(d) comply with any timetable imposed by the Tribunal in so far as this is reasonably practicable;
(e) when requested, inform the Tribunal of progress in the preparation of the report;
(f) prepare a report on the question based on the facts relating to the question and (subject to rule 13) send it to the Tribunal and the parties; and
(g) attend hearings.

(3) The independent expert may make an application for any order or for a hearing to be held as if he were a party to the proceedings.

(4) At any stage of the proceedings the Tribunal may, after giving the independent expert the opportunity to make representations, withdraw the requirement on the independent expert to prepare a report. If it does so, the Tribunal may itself determine the question, or it may require a different independent expert to prepare the report.

(5) When paragraph (4) applies the independent expert who is no longer required to prepare the report shall provide the Tribunal with all documentation and work in progress relating to the proceedings by a specified date. Such documentation and work in progress must be in a form which the Tribunal is able to use and may be used in relation to those proceedings by the Tribunal or by another independent expert.

10 Use of expert evidence

(1) The Tribunal shall restrict expert evidence to that which it considers is reasonably required to resolve the proceedings.

(2) An expert shall have a duty to assist the Tribunal on matters within the expert's expertise. This duty overrides any obligation to the person from whom the expert has received instructions or by whom the expert is paid.

(3) No party may call an expert or put in evidence an expert's report without the permission of the Tribunal. No expert report shall be put in evidence unless it has been disclosed to all other parties and any independent expert at least 28 days before the final hearing.

(4) In proceedings in which an independent expert has been required to prepare a report on the question, the Tribunal shall not admit evidence of another expert on the question unless such evidence is based on the facts relating to the question. Unless the Tribunal considers it inappropriate to do so, any such expert report shall be disclosed to all parties and to the Tribunal on the same date on which the independent expert is required to send his report to the parties and to the tribunal.

(5) If an expert (other than an independent expert) does not comply with these rules or an order made by the Tribunal, the Tribunal may order that the evidence of that expert shall not be admitted.

(6) Where two or more parties wish to submit expert evidence on a particular issue, the Tribunal may order that the evidence on that issue is to be given by one joint expert only and if the parties wishing to instruct the joint expert cannot agree an expert, the Tribunal may select an expert.

11 Written questions to experts (including independent experts)

(1) When an expert has prepared a report, a party or any other expert involved in the proceedings may put written questions about the report to the expert who has prepared the report.

(2) Unless the Tribunal agrees otherwise, written questions under paragraph (1)—

(a) may be put once only;
(b) must be put within 28 days of the date on which the parties were sent the report;
(c) must be for the purpose only of clarifying the factual basis of the report; and
(d) must be copied to all other parties and experts involved in the proceedings at the same time as they are sent to the expert who prepared the report.

(3) An expert shall answer written questions within 28 days of receipt and the answers shall be treated as part of the expert's report.

(4) Where a party has put a written question to an expert instructed by another party and the expert does not answer that question within 28 days, the Tribunal may order that the party instructing that expert may not rely on the evidence of that expert.

12 Procedural matters

(1) Where an independent expert has been required to prepare a report, the Tribunal shall send that expert notice of any hearing, application, order or judgment in the proceedings as if the independent expert were a party to those proceedings and when these rules or an order requires a party to provide information to another party, such information shall also be provided to the independent expert.

(2) There may be more than one stage 1 or stage 2 equal value hearing in any case.

(3) Any power conferred on an Employment Judge by Schedule 1 may (subject to the provisions of this Schedule) in an equal value claim be carried out by a full tribunal or an Employment Judge.

13 National security proceedings

Where in an equal value claim a direction is given, or order is made, under rule 94 of Schedule 1—

(a) any independent expert appointed shall send a copy of any report and any responses to written questions to the Tribunal only; and

(b) before the Tribunal sends the parties a copy of a report or answers which have been received from an independent expert, it shall follow the procedure set out in rule 6 of Schedule 2 as if that rule referred to the independent expert's report or answers (as the case may be) instead of written reasons, except that the independent expert's report or answers shall not be entered on the Register.

ANNEX
THE INDICATIVE TIMETABLE

[2.1448]

Claims not involving an independent expert

Claim → 28 days → Response → 3 weeks → Stage 1 equal value hearing → 18 weeks → Hearing → Total 25 weeks

Claims involving an independent expert

Claim → 28 days → Response → 3 weeks → Stage 1 equal value hearing → 10 weeks → Stage 2 equal value hearing → 8 weeks → Independent expert's report → 4 weeks → written questions → 8 weeks →Hearing → →Total 37 weeks

HEALTH AND SAFETY AT WORK ETC ACT 1974 (CIVIL LIABILITY) (EXCEPTIONS) REGULATIONS 2013

(SI 2013/1667)

NOTES

Made: 4 July 2013.

Authority: European Communities Act 1972, s 2(2); Health and Safety at Work etc Act 1974, ss 15(1), (2), 47(2), (2B)(b), (7), 50(1)(a).

Commencement: 1 October 2013.

Note: with regard to the authority for these Regulations, note that the European Communities Act 1972 is repealed by the European Union (Withdrawal) Act 2018, s 1, as from exit day (as defined in s 20 of that Act); but note also that provision is made for the continuation in force of any subordinate legislation made under the authority of s 2(2) of the 1972 Act by s 2 of the 2018 Act at **[1.2240]**, subject to the provisions of s 5 of, and Sch 1 to, the 2018 Act at **[1.2243]**, **[1.2253]**.

[2.1449]

1 Citation and commencement

(1) These Regulations may be cited as the Health and Safety at Work etc Act 1974 (Civil Liability) (Exceptions) Regulations 2013.

(2) These Regulations come into force on 1st October 2013.

[2.1450]

2 Exception relating to compulsory maternity leave

(1) Breach of a duty imposed by section 72(1) of the Employment Rights Act 1996 (which by virtue of section 72(4) of that Act is for these purposes treated as imposed by health and safety regulations) shall, so far as it causes damage, be actionable.

(2) Any term of an agreement which purports to exclude or restrict any liability for such a breach is void.

3 (*This Regulation substitutes the Management of Health and Safety at Work Regulations 1999, SI 1992/3242, reg 22 at* **[2.442]**.)

[2.1451]

4 Revocations

The Management of Health and Safety at Work (Amendment) Regulations 2006 are revoked.

[2.1452]

5 Review

(1) The Secretary of State must from time to time—

(a) carry out a review of these Regulations;

(b) set out the conclusions of the review in a report; and

(c) publish the report.

(2) In carrying out the review the Secretary of State must, so far as is reasonable, have regard to the measures taken to implement rules on the enforcement of obligations imposed by Directive 92/85/EEC in other Member States.

(3) The report must in particular—

(a) set out the objectives intended to be achieved by the measures taken to implement rules on enforcement in relation to that Directive,

(b) assess the extent to which those objectives are achieved, and

(c) assess whether those objectives remain appropriate and, if so, the extent to which they could be achieved with a system that imposes less regulation.

(4) The first report under this regulation must be published before 1st October 2018.

(5) Reports under this regulation are afterwards to be published at intervals not exceeding five years.

ADDED TRIBUNALS (EMPLOYMENT TRIBUNALS AND EMPLOYMENT APPEAL TRIBUNAL) ORDER 2013

(SI 2013/1892)

NOTES

Made: 28 July 2013.

Authority: Tribunals, Courts and Enforcement Act 2007, s 42(3).

Commencement: 28 July 2013.

[2.1453]

1 Citation and commencement

This Order may be cited as the Added Tribunals (Employment Tribunals and Employment Appeal Tribunal) Order 2013.

NOTES

Note: despite the name of this Article, it makes no provision for commencement.

[2.1454]

2 Employment tribunals and the Employment Appeal Tribunal to be "added tribunals"

Employment tribunals and the Employment Appeal Tribunal are "added tribunals" for the purpose of section 42 of the 2007 Act.

EMPLOYMENT TRIBUNALS AND THE EMPLOYMENT APPEAL TRIBUNAL FEES ORDER 2013 (NOTE)

(SI 2013/1893)

[2.1455]

NOTES

Made: 28 July 2013.

Authority: Tribunals, Courts and Enforcement Act 2007, ss 42(1)(d), (2), 49(3).

Commencement: 29 July 2013.

This Order was quashed by the Supreme Court in *R (UNISON) v Lord Chancellor* [2017] UKSC 51, [2017] ICR 1037 and has, therefore, been omitted from this work. The Order has not, however, been formally revoked.

GANGMASTERS LICENSING (EXCLUSIONS) REGULATIONS 2013

(SI 2013/2216)

NOTES

Made: 3 September 2013.

Authority: Gangmasters (Licensing) Act 2004, s 6(2).

Commencement: 1 October 2013.

[2.1456]

1 Citation, commencement and extent

(1) These Regulations may be cited as the Gangmasters Licensing (Exclusions) Regulations 2013 and come into force on 1st October 2013.

(2) They do not extend to Northern Ireland.

[2.1457]

2 Circumstances in which a licence is not required

A person does not require a licence to act as a gangmaster under section 6(1) of the Gangmasters (Licensing) Act 2004 in the circumstances specified in the Schedule.

[2.1458]

3 Revocation

The Gangmasters Licensing (Exclusions) Regulations 2010 are revoked.

SCHEDULE
CIRCUMSTANCES IN WHICH A LICENCE IS NOT REQUIRED

Regulation 2

PART 1
PRODUCE WORKERS

[2.1459]

1. The supply of a worker to process or pack produce if the worker is supplied to—

(a) a catering establishment;
(b) a shop or other retail establishment;
(c) a wholesale market;
(d) a wholesale establishment;
(e) a distribution warehouse.

2. The supply of a worker to process or pack a product which includes a derivative of produce but where the product concerned is not a food product, pet food product or a product which is primarily an agricultural, fish or shellfish product.

3. In this Part—

"catering establishment" means—

(a) a restaurant, canteen, club, public house, school kitchen, prison kitchen, hospital kitchen or similar establishment (including a vehicle or a fixed or mobile stall) where—
  (i) food is cooked or made ready for consumption without further preparation; and
  (ii) food is prepared for service to the consumer;
(b) other premises where—
  (i) food is cooked or made ready for consumption without further preparation;
  (ii) food is prepared for service to the consumer; and
  (iii) there is no change of ownership of the food concerned between preparation and delivery to the consumer;

"distribution warehouse" means premises where produce is received prior to onward distribution to a wholesale or retail establishment and—
(a) there is no change in the ownership of the produce concerned between receipt and onward distribution;
(b) the wholesale or retail establishment to which delivery is made is excluded under paragraph 1 of this Schedule; and
(c) the premises are owned by the same person that owns the retail or wholesale establishment to which the produce is delivered;

"produce" means produce derived from agricultural work, shellfish, fish or products derived from shellfish or fish;

"wholesale establishment" means a facility operated solely for the purpose of selling produce for the purposes of resale or to a catering establishment, and includes a cash and carry warehouse but excludes a food processing or packaging facility.

"to process or pack" includes to carry out the daily cleaning and maintenance of machinery used for the processing or packing.

PART 2
AGRICULTURAL WORKERS

[2.1460]

4. (1) The supply of a worker for agricultural work by a farmer (A) to another farmer (B) where—
(a) the supply is to do work on a farm which is the subject of a share-farming agreement between A and B; or
(b) the total hours the worker works for B are not more than thirty per cent of the total hours the worker worked for A in the twelve months immediately preceding the commencement of the period of work undertaken for B; or
(c) the worker has been supplied to A by a person (C) who acts as a gangmaster in making that supply, and the supply by A—
  (i) is made with C's agreement to the nature of the work to be undertaken for B; and
  (ii) is a one-off arrangement of less than two weeks.

(2) In this paragraph—

"share-farming agreement" means an agreement entered into between two or more persons to share the net receipts of—
(a) their separate business assets, or
(b) services for carrying out specified farming operations,

as divided between them and paid to the businesses in agreed proportions.

5. The use of a worker for agricultural work by a farmer (A) to provide a service to another farmer (B) where the service provided involves a one-off arrangement of less than four weeks and—
(a) the total hours the worker works delivering services to B are not more than thirty per cent of the total hours the worker worked for A in the twelve months immediately preceding the commencement of the delivery of services to B; or
(b) the worker has been supplied to A by a person (C) who acts as a gangmaster in making that supply, and the use of the worker to deliver services by A is made with C's agreement to the nature of the services to be provided to B.

6. The supply of a worker by a farmer to a person (A) to operate machinery supplied by A for the purpose of undertaking agricultural work for that farmer.

7. (1) The supply of a worker by a sole operator in the Seasonal Agricultural Workers Scheme to another Seasonal Agricultural Workers Scheme operator.

(2) In this paragraph "Seasonal Agricultural Workers Scheme" means a scheme operated by the Home Office, which allows farmers and growers in the United Kingdom to recruit overseas workers to undertake work that is both seasonal and agricultural.

8. The use of a worker for agricultural work by a person (A) to provide a service to a farmer where—
(a) the service involves the use of machinery owned or hired by A; and
(b) the worker is employed by A to operate or to support the operation of that machinery.

9. The use of a worker for agricultural work by a person (A) to provide a service to a farmer where—
(a) A enters into an arrangement with another person (B) to deliver the service;
(b) the service involves the use of machinery owned or hired by B; and
(c) the worker is employed by B to operate or to support the operation of that machinery.

10. The use of a worker by a person (A) to provide a food and drink processing and packaging service where A—
(a) is the worker's employer;
(b) owns, hires or leases any equipment, tools or machinery used by the worker which are necessary to carry out the service; and
(c) owns or leases the premises where the work is carried out.

11. The use of a worker to harvest crops by a person who has transferred title to the land on which the crops are grown, but has retained title to the crops.

[**12.** The supply of a worker for the purpose of killing an animal where the worker has—
(a) a certificate of competence or licence to kill animals under the Welfare of Animals at the Time of Killing (England) Regulations 2015;
(b) a certificate of competence or licence to kill animals under the Welfare of Animals at the Time of Killing (Wales) Regulations 2014; or
(c) a certificate of competence to kill animals under the Welfare of Animals at the Time of Killing (Scotland) Regulations 2012.]

13. The supply of a worker by an educational establishment to undertake agricultural work solely in furtherance of education or training provided to the worker by that establishment leading to an agricultural qualification which—
(a) in relation to England, is a qualification to which Part 7 of the Apprenticeships, Skills, Children and Learning Act 2009 applies;
[(b) in relation to Wales, is a qualification within the meaning of section 56 of the Qualifications Wales Act 2015;]
(c) in relation to Scotland, is an SQA qualification within the meaning of section 21 of the Education (Scotland) Act 1996 or an accredited qualification under section 3 of that Act.

14. The supply of an apprentice by an Apprentice Training Agency—
(a) recognised by the Skills Funding Agency or the Welsh Government; or
(b) registered with the National Apprenticeship Service or the Welsh Government as an Apprentice Training Agency in development.

15. The supply by a person (A) to a farmer of a worker to undertake agricultural work in which that worker is specialised where—
(a) the worker holds a specific qualification at or above National Vocational Qualification Level 2 or Scottish National Vocational Qualification Level 2, or an equivalent qualification, which is relevant and necessary to ensure the worker can effectively discharge the responsibilities that the worker will be required to undertake; and
(b) the farmer employs the worker following the worker's supply by A; and
(c) no more than four such workers are supplied to the farmer by A at any one time.

16. (1) The use of a worker for agricultural work by a person (A) to provide a service to a farmer where the worker is a member of A's family.
(2) In this paragraph the members of A's family are—
(a) A's spouse or civil partner;
(b) any other person (whether of a different sex or the same sex) with whom A lives as partner in an enduring family relationship;
(c) any child, step-child, parent, grandchild, grandparent, brother or sister of A; and
(d) any child or step-child of a person within paragraph (b) (and who is not a child or stepchild of A) who lives with A and has not attained the age of 18.

17. The use of a worker by a land agent where—
(a) the land agent is a member of the Royal Institute of Chartered Surveyors;
(b) the land agent is contracted to manage the land on which the workers will be employed; and
(c) the use of that worker is incidental to the fulfilment of the land agent's contract to manage that land.

18. The use of a worker by a farmer to plant, raise, care for or harvest crops or animals which are—
(a) the property of a third party;
(b) managed by the farmer under the terms of a written agreement; and
(c) grown or kept on land owned or occupied by the farmer.

19. The supply of volunteers to undertake conservation work.

20. The use of a worker by A for forestry work where A uses the worker to do work in connection with services provided by A to another person.

21. The use of a worker by a member of the Royal College of Veterinarians, or an incorporated veterinary practice, to carry out work incidental to the supply of veterinary services.

22. The use of a worker by a supplier of vaccines to perform vaccinations.

23. The supply or use of a worker to determine the sex of chickens and other poultry.

24. The supply of a worker by a person authorised to carry out functions of, or under contract to provide services to, the Secretary of State for Work and Pensions in connection with employment related support designed to assist the worker to obtain or remain in work or be able to do so.

25. In this Part "farmer" means a person who—

(a) occupies land which the person uses for agriculture; or

(b) is employed by a person with title to land to manage the use of that land for agriculture.

NOTES

Para 12: substituted by the Welfare of Animals at the Time of Killing (England) Regulations 2015, SI 2015/1782, reg 43, Sch 6, para 5, as from 5 November 2015.

Para 13: sub-para (b) substituted by the Qualifications Wales Act 2015 (Consequential Amendments) Regulations 2016, SI 2016/236, reg 16, as from 1 May 2016.

PART 3
SHELLFISH GATHERERS

[2.1461]

26. (1) The use of a worker—

(a) to dive with the aid of breathing apparatus to gather shellfish from the sea bed; or

(b) to operate a net, dredge or other machinery used to gather shellfish from the sea bed, other than a hand net or hand-held rake, where the worker is using the net, dredge or other machinery on board a fishing vessel which is operating at sea.

(2) The use by shellfish cultivators with an exclusive right to cultivate shellfish on an area of the seabed of a worker to gather—

(a) shellfish from the shore for cultivation; or

(b) shellfish cultivated on the areas to which they have exclusive access.

(3) The use of a worker by the owner or operator of a shellfish hatchery to gather shellfish.

PART 4

[2.1462]

27 Bodies corporate

The supply of a worker by a body corporate (A) to another body corporate (B) or the use of a worker by A to provide a service to B where—

(a) the worker is employed by A under a contract of service, and—

(b) either—

(i) A and B are wholly-owned subsidiaries of the same body corporate;

(ii) A is a wholly-owned subsidiary of B; or

(iii) B is a wholly-owned subsidiary of A.

28 Scottish partnerships

The use of a worker by a Scottish partnership where the worker is a partner in that partnership.

COLLECTIVE REDUNDANCIES AND TRANSFER OF UNDERTAKINGS (PROTECTION OF EMPLOYMENT) (AMENDMENT) REGULATIONS 2014

(SI 2014/16)

NOTES

Made: 8 January 2014.

Authority: European Communities Act 1972, s 2(2); Employment Relations Act 1999, s 38.

Commencement: 31 January 2014.

Note: with regard to the authority for these Regulations, note that the European Communities Act 1972 is repealed by the European Union (Withdrawal) Act 2018, s 1, as from exit day (as defined in s 20 of that Act); but note also that provision is made for the continuation in force of any subordinate legislation made under the authority of s 2(2) of the 1972 Act by s 2 of the 2018 Act at **[1.2240]**, subject to the provisions of s 5 of, and Sch 1 to, the 2018 Act at **[1.2243]**, **[1.2253]**.

ARRANGEMENT OF REGULATIONS

Part 2 Statutory Instruments

[2.1463]
1 Citation, commencement and extent

(1) These Regulations may be cited as the Collective Redundancies and Transfer of Undertakings (Protection of Employment) (Amendment) Regulations 2014.

(2) These Regulations come into force on 31st January 2014.

(3) These Regulations do not extend to Northern Ireland.

[2.1464]
2 Interpretation

For the purposes of these Regulations—

"TUPE transfer" means—

(a) a relevant transfer under the Transfer of Undertakings (Protection of Employment) Regulations 2006, or
(b) anything else regarded, by virtue of an enactment, as a relevant transfer for the purposes of those Regulations.

[2.1465]
3 Amendment of the Trade Union and Labour Relations (Consolidation) Act 1992

(*Reg 3 inserts the Trade Union and Labour Relations (Consolidation) Act 1992, ss 198A, 198B at* **[1.513]**, **[1.514]** *and amends s 299 of that Act at* **[1.633]**.)

[2.1466]
4 Amendment of the Transfer of Undertakings (Protection of Employment) Regulations 2006

The Transfer of Undertakings (Protection of Employment) Regulations 2006 are amended as set out in regulations 5 to 11.

[2.1467]
5 Activities carried out by another person

(1) (*Inserts reg 3(2A) of the 2006 Regulations at* **[2.869]**.)

(2) The amendment made by paragraph (1) applies in relation to a TUPE transfer which takes place on or after 31st January 2014.

[2.1468]
6 Restrictions on varying contracts

(1) (*Amends reg 4 of the 2006 Regulations at* **[2.870]**.)

(2) The amendment made by paragraph (1) applies in relation to any purported variation of a contract of employment that is transferred by a TUPE transfer if—

(a) the TUPE transfer takes place on or after 31st January 2014, and
(b) that purported variation is agreed on or after 31st January 2014, or, in a case where the variation is not agreed, it starts to have effect on or after that date.

[2.1469]
7 Effect of relevant transfer on contracts of employment which incorporate provisions of collective agreements

(1) (*Inserts reg 4A of the 2006 Regulations at* **[2.871]**.)

(2) The amendment made by paragraph (1) applies in relation to a TUPE transfer which takes place on or after 31st January 2014.

[2.1470]
8 Dismissal of employee because of relevant transfer

(1) (*Amends reg 7 of the 2006 Regulations at* **[2.874]**.)

(2) The amendment made by paragraph (1) applies in relation to any case where—

(a) the TUPE transfer takes place on or after 31st January 2014, and
(b) the date when any notice of termination is given by an employer or an employee in respect of any dismissal is 31st January 2014 or later, or, in a case where no notice is given, the date on which the termination takes effect is 31st January 2014 or later.

[2.1471]
9 Definition of "permitted variation"

(1) (*Amends reg 9 of the 2006 Regulations at* **[2.875]**.)

(2) The amendment made by paragraph (1) applies in relation to any case where—

(a) the TUPE transfer takes place on or after 31st January 2014, and
(b) the permitted variation is agreed on or after 31st January 2014.

[2.1472]
10 Deadline for notification of employee liability information

(1) (*Amends reg 11 of the 2006 Regulations at* **[2.878]**.)

(2) The amendment made by paragraph (1) applies in relation to a TUPE transfer which takes place on or after 1st May 2014.

[2.1473]
11 Micro-business's duty to inform and consult where no appropriate representatives

(1)–(4) (*Amend regs 13, 15 of the 2006 Regulations at* **[2.880]**, **[2.883]**, *and inserts reg 13A at* **[2.881]**.)

(5) The amendments made by this regulation apply in relation to a TUPE transfer which takes place on or after 31st July 2014.

EMPLOYMENT TRIBUNALS (EARLY CONCILIATION: EXEMPTIONS AND RULES OF PROCEDURE) REGULATIONS 2014

(SI 2014/254)

NOTES

Made: 11 February 2014.
Authority: Employment Tribunals Act 1996, ss 18A(7), (11), (12), 41(4).
Commencement: 6 March 2014 (reg 4); 6 April 2014 (otherwise).

[2.1474]
1 Citation and commencement

(1) These Regulations may be cited as the Employment Tribunals (Early Conciliation: Exemptions and Rules of Procedure) Regulations 2014 and the Rules of Procedure contained in the Schedule may be referred to as the Early Conciliation Rules of Procedure.

(2) Regulation 4 comes into force on 6th March 2014 and the remainder of the regulations come into force on 6th April 2014.

[2.1475]
2 Interpretation

In these Regulations and in the Schedule—

"ACAS" means the Advisory, Conciliation and Arbitration Service referred to in section 247 of the Trade Union and Labour Relations (Consolidation) Act 1992;

"claim form" means the form prescribed by the Secretary of State in accordance with regulation 12(1)(a) of the Employment Tribunals Regulations;

"conciliation officer" means an officer designated by ACAS under section 211 of the Trade Union and Labour Relations (Consolidation) Act 1992;

"early conciliation certificate" means the certificate prescribed by the Secretary of State in accordance with regulation 4(b);

"early conciliation form" means a form prescribed by the Secretary of State in accordance with regulation 4(a);

"Employment Tribunal" means an employment tribunal established in accordance with regulation 4 of the Employment Tribunals Regulations;

"Employment Tribunals Act" means the Employment Tribunals Act 1996;

"Employment Tribunals Regulations" means the Employment Tribunals (Constitution and Rules of Procedure) Regulations 2013;

"prospective claimant" means a person who is considering presenting a claim form to an Employment Tribunal in relation to relevant proceedings;

"prospective respondent" means the person who would be the respondent on the claim form which the prospective claimant is considering presenting to an Employment Tribunal;

"relevant proceedings" are those proceedings listed in section 18(1) of the Employment Tribunals Act;

"respondent" means the person against whom proceedings are brought in the Employment Tribunal; and

"requirement for early conciliation" means the requirement set out in section 18A(1) of the Employment Tribunals Act.

[2.1476]
3 Exemptions from early conciliation

(1) A person ("A") may institute relevant proceedings without complying with the requirement for early conciliation where—

(a) another person ("B") has complied with that requirement in relation to the same dispute and A wishes to institute proceedings on the same claim form as B;

(b) A institutes those relevant proceedings on the same claim form as proceedings which are not relevant proceedings;

Part 2 Statutory Instruments

(c) A is able to show that the respondent has contacted ACAS in relation to a dispute, ACAS has not received information from A under section 18A(1) of the Employment Tribunals Act in relation to that dispute, and the proceedings on the claim form relate to that dispute;

(d) the proceedings are proceedings under Part X of the Employment Rights Act 1996 and the application to institute those proceedings is accompanied by an application under section 128 of that Act or section 161 of the Trade Union and Labour Relations (Consolidation) Act 1992; or

(e) A is instituting proceedings against the Security Service, the Secret Intelligence Service or the Government Communications Headquarters.

(2) Where A benefits from the exemption in paragraph (1)(a), the requirement for early conciliation shall be treated as complied with for the purposes of any provision extending the time limit for instituting relevant proceedings in relation to that matter.

[2.1477]

4 Power to prescribe

(1) The Secretary of State may prescribe—

(a) one or more forms to be used by all prospective claimants for the purpose of complying with the early conciliation requirement; and

(b) a certificate to be issued by ACAS if rule 7 of the Schedule applies.

(2) The Secretary of State must publish any forms prescribed under paragraph (1)(a) in a manner which the Secretary of State considers appropriate to bring them to the attention of prospective claimants and their advisers.

[2.1478]

5 Application of the Schedule

The Schedule to these Regulations has effect and the rules of procedure contained in the Schedule may be referred to as the Early Conciliation Rules of Procedure.

SCHEDULE
THE EARLY CONCILIATION RULES OF PROCEDURE

Regulation 5

Starting early conciliation

[2.1479]

1 Satisfying the requirement for early conciliation

To satisfy the requirement for early conciliation, a prospective claimant must—

(a) present a completed early conciliation form to ACAS in accordance with rule 2; or

(b) telephone ACAS in accordance with rule 3.

2. (1) An early conciliation form which is presented to ACAS must be—

(a) submitted using the online form on the ACAS website; or

(b) sent by post to the ACAS address set out on the early conciliation form.

(2) An early conciliation form must contain—

(a) the prospective claimant's name and address; and

(b) the prospective respondent's name and address.

(3) ACAS may reject a form that does not contain the information specified in paragraph (2) or may contact the prospective claimant to obtain any missing information.

(4) If ACAS rejects a form under paragraph (3), it must return the form to the prospective claimant.

3. (1) A prospective claimant telephoning ACAS for early conciliation must call the telephone number set out on the early conciliation form and tell ACAS—

(a) the prospective claimant's name and address; and

(b) the prospective respondent's name and address.

(2) ACAS must insert the information provided under paragraph (1) on to an early conciliation form.

[**4.** If there is more than one prospective respondent, the prospective claimant must present a separate early conciliation form under rule 2 in respect of each respondent or, in the case of a telephone call made under rule 3, must name each prospective respondent.]

The early conciliation process

5 Contact between ACAS and the parties

(1) ACAS must make reasonable attempts to contact the prospective claimant.

(2) If the prospective claimant consents to ACAS contacting the prospective respondent, ACAS must make reasonable attempts to contact the prospective respondent.

(3) If ACAS is unable to make contact with the prospective claimant or prospective respondent it must conclude that settlement is not possible.

6 Period for early conciliation

(1) For up to one calendar month starting on the date—

(a) of receipt by ACAS of the early conciliation form presented in accordance with rule 2; or

(b) the prospective claimant telephoned ACAS in accordance with rule 3, the conciliation officer must endeavour to promote a settlement between the prospective claimant and the prospective respondent.

(2) The period for early conciliation may be extended by a conciliation officer, provided that the prospective claimant and prospective respondent consent to the extension and the conciliation officer considers that there is a reasonable prospect of achieving a settlement before the expiry of the extended period.

(3) An extension under paragraph (2) of the period for early conciliation may only occur once and may be for up to a maximum of 14 days.

7 Early conciliation certificate

(1) If at any point during the period for early conciliation, or during any extension of that period, the conciliation officer concludes that a settlement of a dispute, or part of it, is not possible, ACAS must issue an early conciliation certificate.

(2) If the period for early conciliation, including any extension of that period, expires without a settlement having been reached, ACAS must issue an early conciliation certificate.

8. An early conciliation certificate must contain—

(a) the name and address of the prospective claimant;

(b) the name and address of the prospective respondent;

(c) the date of receipt by ACAS of the early conciliation form presented in accordance with rule 2 or the date that the prospective claimant telephoned ACAS in accordance with rule 3;

(d) the unique reference number given by ACAS to the early conciliation certificate; and

(e) the date of issue of the certificate, which will be the date that the certificate is sent by ACAS, and a statement indicating the method by which the certificate is to be sent.

9. (1) Where ACAS issues an early conciliation certificate, it must send a copy to the prospective claimant and, if ACAS has had contact with the prospective respondent during the period for early conciliation, to the prospective respondent.

(2) If the prospective claimant or prospective respondent has provided an email address to ACAS, ACAS must send the early conciliation certificate by email and in any other case must send the early conciliation certificate by post.

(3) An early conciliation certificate will be deemed received—

(a) if sent by email, on the day it is sent; or

(b) if sent by post, on the day on which it would be delivered in the ordinary course of the post.

NOTES

Para 4: substituted by the Employment Tribunals (Early Conciliation: Exemptions and Rules of Procedure) (Amendment) Regulations 2014, SI 2014/847, reg 2.

IMMIGRATION (RESTRICTIONS ON EMPLOYMENT) (CODES OF PRACTICE AND AMENDMENT) ORDER 2014 (NOTE)

(SI 2014/1183)

[2.1480]

NOTES

This Order was made on 6 May 2014 under the powers conferred by the Immigration, Asylum and Nationality Act 2006, ss 15(3), (7), 19(2), 20(1), 23(3), 25(d). It came into force on 16 May 2014.

This Order amends the Immigration (Restrictions on Employment) Order 2007, SI 2007/3290 at **[2.931]** et seq. This Order does not contain any transitional provisions or savings.

Article 10 provides: "The revised code of practice entitled "Code of practice on preventing illegal working: Civil penalty scheme for employers", issued by the Secretary of State under section 19(1) of the 2006 Act, shall come into force on 16th May 2014". Note that the 2014 Code has been replaced by a 2019 Code at **[4.107]**.

Article 11 provides: "The revised code of practice entitled "Code of practice for employers: Avoiding unlawful discrimination while preventing illegal working", issued by the Secretary of State under section 23(1) of the 2006 Act, shall come into force on 16th May 2014". This Code of Practice is at **[4.79]**.

FLEXIBLE WORKING REGULATIONS 2014

(SI 2014/1398)

NOTES

Made: 2 June 2014.

Authority: Employment Rights Act 1996, ss 80F(1)(b), (5), (8)(a), 80G(2), (3), 80H(3)(b), 80I(3), 236(5). Note that, following the repeal of s 80G(2), (3) (as noted at **[1.990]**) and the substitution of s 80H(3)(b) (as noted at **[1.991]**), these Regulations have lapsed in so far as made under those provisions.

Commencement: 30 June 2014.

ARRANGEMENT OF REGULATIONS

[2.1481]
1 Citation, commencement and interpretation

(1) These Regulations may be cited as the Flexible Working Regulations 2014 and come into force on 30th June 2014.

(2) In these Regulations—

"the 1996 Act" means the Employment Rights Act 1996;

"flexible working application" means an application made under section 80F of the 1996 Act (statutory right to request contract variation).

NOTES

Commencement: 30 June 2014.

[2.1482]
2 Application, revocation and saving

(1) These Regulations apply to a flexible working application made on or after 30th June 2014.

(2) The Flexible Working (Eligibility, Complaints and Remedies) Regulations 2002 are revoked but continue to apply to a flexible working application made before 30th June 2014.

NOTES

Commencement: 30 June 2014.

[2.1483]
3 Entitlement to make an application

An employee who has been continuously employed for a period of at least 26 weeks is entitled to make a flexible working application.

NOTES

Commencement: 30 June 2014.

[2.1484]
4 Form of application

A flexible working application must—

(a) be in writing;

(b) state whether the employee has previously made any such application to the employer and, if so, when; and

(c) be dated.

NOTES

Commencement: 30 June 2014.

[2.1485]
5 Date when application is taken as made

(1) A flexible working application is taken as made on the day it is received.

(2) Any such application is received, unless the contrary is proved—

(a) Where paragraph (3) applies and the application is sent by electronic transmission, on the day of transmission;

(b) if sent by post, on the day on which it would have been delivered in the ordinary course of post; and

(c) if it is delivered personally, on the day of delivery.

(3) This paragraph applies where the employer has agreed that the application can be sent by electronic transmission and has specified an electronic address to which the application can be sent and the electronic form to be used by the employee.

NOTES

Commencement: 30 June 2014.

[2.1486]
6 Compensation

For the purposes of section 80I of the 1996 Act (remedies) the maximum amount of compensation is 8 weeks' pay of the employee who presented the complaint under section 80H of the 1996 Act (complaints to employment tribunals).

NOTES

Commencement: 30 June 2014.

MERCHANT SHIPPING (MARITIME LABOUR CONVENTION) (MINIMUM REQUIREMENTS FOR SEAFARERS ETC) REGULATIONS 2014

(SI 2014/1613)

NOTES

Made: 9 July 2014.

Authority: European Communities Act 1972, s 2(2); Merchant Shipping Act 1995, ss 85(1)(a), (b), (3), (5)–(7), 86(1), (2).

Commencement: 7 August 2014.

Note: with regard to the authority for these Regulations, note that the European Communities Act 1972 is repealed by the European Union (Withdrawal) Act 2018, s 1, as from exit day (as defined in s 20 of that Act); but note also that provision is made for the continuation in force of any subordinate legislation made under the authority of s 2(2) of the 1972 Act by s 2 of the 2018 Act at **[1.2240]**, subject to the provisions of s 5 of, and Sch 1 to, the 2018 Act at **[1.2243]**, **[1.2253]**.

ARRANGEMENT OF REGULATIONS

SCHEDULES

PART 1
GENERAL MATTERS

[2.1487]

1 Citation and commencement

(1) These Regulations may be cited as the Merchant Shipping (Maritime Labour Convention) (Minimum Requirements for Seafarers etc) Regulations 2014.

(2) These Regulations come into force on 7th August 2014.

NOTES

Commencement: 7 August 2014.

[2.1488]

2 Interpretation

(1) In these Regulations—

"the Act" means the Merchant Shipping Act 1995;

"Declaration of Maritime Labour Compliance" means, in relation to a ship, the Part 1 and Part 2 documents drawn up and issued in accordance with the MLC, in the forms corresponding to the relevant models given in Appendix A5-II of the MLC and having the contents, duration and validity specified in Regulation 5.1.3 and Standard A5.1.3 of the MLC;

"employee" means an individual who is employed under a contract of employment;

"fishing vessel" has the meaning given in section 313(1) of the Act;

"Maritime Labour Certificate" and "interim Maritime Labour Certificate" mean, in relation to a ship, a certificate of that name issued in accordance with the MLC, in a form corresponding to the relevant model given in Appendix A5-II of the MLC and having the contents, duration and validity specified in Regulation 5.1.3 and Standard A5.1.3 of the MLC;

"the MCA" means the Maritime and Coastguard Agency, an executive agency of the Department for Transport;

"the MLC" means the Maritime Labour Convention, which was adopted on 23rd February 2006 by the General Conference of the International Labour Organization;

"Merchant Shipping Notice" means a notice described as such and issued by the MCA, and any reference to a particular Merchant Shipping Notice includes a reference to a Merchant Shipping Notice amending or replacing that Notice which is considered by the Secretary of State to be relevant from time to time;

["personal representative", in relation to a seafarer who has died, means—

(a) a person responsible for administering the seafarer's estate under the law of England and Wales, Scotland or Northern Ireland; or

(b) a person who, under the law of another country or territory, has functions equivalent to those of administering the seafarer's estate;]

"pleasure vessel" means—

(a) any vessel which at the time it is being used is—

[(i) in the case of a vessel wholly owned by—

(aa) an individual or individuals, used only for the sport or pleasure of the owner or the immediate family or friends of the owner; or

(bb) a body corporate, used only for sport or pleasure and on which the persons on board are employees or officers of the body corporate, or their immediate family or friends; and]

(ii) on a voyage or excursion which is one for which the owner does not receive money for or in connection with operating the vessel or carrying any person, other than as a contribution to the direct expenses of the operation of the vessel incurred during the voyage or excursion; or

(b) any vessel wholly owned by or on behalf of a members' club formed for the purpose of sport or pleasure which, at the time it is being used, is used only for the sport or pleasure of members of that club or their immediate family, and for the use of which any charges levied are paid into club funds and applied for the general use of the club,

where, in the case of any vessel referred to in [paragraph] (a) or (b), no other payments are made by or on behalf of users of the vessel, other than by the owner; and in this definition "immediate family" means, in relation to an individual, the spouse or civil partner of the individual, and a relative of the individual or the individual's spouse or civil partner; and "relative" means brother, sister, ancestor or lineal descendant;

"proper officer" has the meaning given in section 313(1) of the Act;

"relevant inspector" means any of the persons mentioned in section 258(1) of the Act;

"seafarer" means any person, including the master of a ship, who is employed or engaged or works in any capacity on board a ship and whose normal place of work is on board a ship;

"seafarer employment agreement" means a written agreement between a seafarer and another person in respect of the seafarer's work on board a ship;

"sea-going" in relation to a United Kingdom ship means—

(a) a ship which operates outside the waters specified as Category A, B, C and D waters in Merchant Shipping Notice 1837(M);

(b) a ship to which the Merchant Shipping (Survey and Certification) Regulations 1995 apply and in respect of which no exemption granted under regulation 2(2) of those Regulations applies;

(c) a ship to which regulation 4 of the Merchant Shipping (Vessels in Commercial Use for Sport or Pleasure) Regulations 1998 applies and which falls within the description given in paragraph (3) of that regulation; or

(d) a high speed craft in respect of which a permit to operate outside waters of Categories A, B, C or D has been issued in accordance with regulation 8 of the Merchant Shipping (High Speed Craft) Regulations 2004;

"ship" includes hovercraft;

"shipowner" means—

(a) in relation to a ship which has a valid Maritime Labour Certificate or interim Maritime Labour Certificate, the person identified as the shipowner on that Certificate;

(b) in relation to any other ship, the owner of the ship or, if different, any other organisation or person such as the manager, or the bareboat charterer, that has assumed the responsibility for the operation of the ship from the owner;

"United Kingdom ship" means a ship which is—

(a) a United Kingdom ship within the meaning of section 85(2) of the Act;

(b) a Government ship within the meaning of section 308(4) of the Act which is ordinarily engaged in commercial maritime operations; or

(c) a hovercraft registered under the Hovercraft Act 1968; and

"United Kingdom waters" has the meaning given in section 313(2) of the Act.

(2) In the application of these Regulations to a hovercraft, a reference to the master of a ship includes a reference to the captain of that hovercraft.

NOTES

Commencement: 7 August 2014.

Para (1): definition "personal representative" inserted by the Merchant Shipping (Maritime Labour Convention) (Compulsory Financial Security) (Amendment) Regulations 2018, SI 2018/667, reg 2(1), (2), as from 12 July 2018; words in square brackets in definition "pleasure vessel" substituted by the Merchant Shipping (Maritime Labour Convention) (Miscellaneous Amendments) Regulations 2018, SI 2018/242, reg 5(1), (2), as from 6 April 2018.

[2.1489]

3 Application

(1) Subject to paragraph (5) and regulations 37(1) and 44(2), the provisions specified in paragraph (2) apply to—

(a) a sea-going United Kingdom ship wherever it may be; and

(b) a sea-going ship which is not a United Kingdom ship, while that ship is in United Kingdom waters, if—

(i) the MLC has not come into force for the State whose flag the ship is entitled to fly; or

(ii) the MLC has come into force for the State whose flag the ship is entitled to fly, but the ship does not carry—

(aa) a Maritime Labour Certificate to which a Declaration of Maritime Labour Compliance is attached; or

(bb) an interim Maritime Labour Certificate.

(2) The provisions referred to in paragraph (1) are as follows—

(a) all of the provisions in Parts 2 to [10B], other than those referred to in sub-paragraph (4)(b); and

(b) all of the provisions in Part 11, other than regulations 55 and 57.

(3) Subject to paragraph (5) and regulation 46(4), the provisions specified in paragraph (4) apply to a sea-going ship which is not a United Kingdom ship, while that ship is in United Kingdom waters, if—

(a) the MLC has come into force for the State whose flag the ship is entitled to fly; and

(b) the ship carries—

(i) a Maritime Labour Certificate to which a Declaration of Maritime Labour Compliance is attached; or

(ii) an interim Maritime Labour Certificate.

(4) The provisions referred to in paragraph (3) are as follows—

(a) [regulation 26] and all of the provisions in Parts 3 and 11 (other than regulation 54); and

(b) the following provisions—

(i) regulation 6;

(ii) regulation 15;

(iii) regulation 18;

(iv) regulation 28;

(v) regulation 33;

(vi) regulation 41; . . .

Part 2 Statutory Instruments

(vii) regulation 46;
[(viii) regulation 53B(1)(b); and
(ix) regulation 53M(1)(b).]

(5) These Regulations do not apply to—
(a) pleasure vessels;
(b) fishing vessels;
(c) ships of traditional build;
(d) warships or naval auxiliaries; or
(e) vessels which are not ordinarily engaged in commercial activities.

NOTES

Commencement: 7 August 2014.

Para (2): figure in square brackets substituted by the Merchant Shipping (Maritime Labour Convention) (Compulsory Financial Security) (Amendment) Regulations 2018, SI 2018/667, reg 2(1), (3)(a), as from 12 July 2018.

Para (4): words in square brackets in sub-para (a) substituted, word omitted from sub-para (b)(vi) revoked and sub-para (b)(viii), (ix) added, by SI 2018/667, reg 2(1), (3)(b), as from 12 July 2018.

PART 2
MINIMUM AGE

[2.1490]

4 Seafarer to be of minimum age

(1) A person under 16 years of age must not be employed, engaged or work on board a ship.

(2) A breach of paragraph (1) is an offence by the shipowner, the master of the ship and the employer of the person under the age of 16.

NOTES

Commencement: 7 August 2014.

[2.1491]

5 Young persons on night duty

(1) Subject to paragraph (2), a seafarer under 18 years of age must not be employed, engaged or work on board a ship at night.

(2) Paragraph (1) does not apply where—
(a) the effective training of the seafarer, in accordance with established programmes and schedules, would be impaired by its application; or
(b) the specific nature of the duty or of a recognised training programme requires that the seafarer performs duties at night and the work to be carried out is specified in Merchant Shipping Notice 1838(M) as not being detrimental to the health and well-being of seafarers under the age of 18.

(3) In this regulation, "night" means a period—
(a) the duration of which is not less than nine consecutive hours; and
(b) which starts no later than midnight and ends no earlier than 5 am (local time).

(4) A breach of paragraph (1) is an offence by the shipowner, the master of the ship and the employer of the person under the age of 18.

NOTES

Commencement: 7 August 2014.

[2.1492]

6 Part 2 requirements for non-United Kingdom ships with MLC documentation

(1) A ship must not be operated in breach of the prohibitions in paragraphs 1 and 2 of Standard A1.1 (minimum age) of the MLC, subject to any exceptions made by the State whose flag the ship is entitled to fly in accordance with paragraph 3 of that Standard.

(2) A breach of paragraph (1) is an offence by the shipowner, the master of the ship and the employer of a seafarer under the age prescribed in Regulation 1.1 of the MLC or, in the case of night work, the age prescribed in paragraph 2 of Standard A1.1 of the MLC.

NOTES

Commencement: 7 August 2014.

[2.1493]

7 Meaning of "employer" etc

In this Part—

"employer" means the person by whom a person under 16 years of age or, as the case may be, a seafarer under 18 years of age is employed or engaged in breach of regulation 4, 5 or 6;

"employed" means employed under a contract of employment; and

"engaged" means engaged under a contract, whether express or implied and (if it is express) whether oral or in writing, whereby the person or seafarer so engaged undertakes to do or perform personally any work or services for the employer, or another party to the contract, whose status is not by virtue of the contract that of a client or customer of any profession or business undertaking carried out by the person or seafarer.

NOTES

Commencement: 7 August 2014.

PART 3
RECRUITMENT AND PLACEMENT

[2.1494]

8 Duty on shipowner in respect of recruitment and placement services

(1) A shipowner must not use a recruitment and placement service to recruit a person as a seafarer to work on board a ship unless it is a service falling within paragraph (2).

(2) A recruitment and placement service falls within this paragraph if it—

(a) is based—

(i) in the United Kingdom;

(ii) in a country which has ratified the MLC; or

(iii) in a country to which another country's ratification of the MLC has been extended; or

(b) is based in another country and conforms to the requirements relating to recruitment and placement services referred to in paragraph 5 of Standard A1.4 of the MLC, whether or not those requirements are obligations under the law of the country in which it is based.

(3) A breach of paragraph (1) is an offence by the shipowner.

(4) In this regulation, "recruitment and placement service" means any person or organisation which is engaged in recruiting seafarers on behalf of shipowners or placing seafarers with shipowners.

NOTES

Commencement: 7 August 2014.

PART 4
SEAFARERS' EMPLOYMENT AGREEMENTS

[2.1495]

9 Duty to enter into seafarer employment agreement

(1) A seafarer must have a seafarer employment agreement which complies with this regulation.

(2) Subject to paragraph (4), if the seafarer is an employee but is not an employee of the shipowner—

(a) the employer of the seafarer must be a party to the seafarer employment agreement; and

(b) the seafarer employment agreement must include provision under which the shipowner guarantees to the seafarer the performance of the employer's obligations under the agreement insofar as they relate to the matters specified in—

(i) paragraphs 5 to 11 of Part 1 of Schedule 1; and

(ii) Part 2 of Schedule 1.

(3) Subject to paragraph (4), if the seafarer is not an employee or if the seafarer is an employee of the shipowner, the shipowner must be a party to the seafarer employment agreement.

(4) Paragraphs (2)(b) and (3) do not apply if the parties to a seafarer employment agreement are—

(a) a seafarer who is on board the ship for the principal purpose of receiving training; and

(b) an approved training provider.

(5) A breach of paragraphs (1) to (3) is an offence by the shipowner.

(6) In this Part—

"approved training provider" means a person who provides or secures the provision of seafarer training pursuant to an agreement with the Secretary of State; and

"employer" means a person by whom the seafarer is employed under a contract of employment.

NOTES

Commencement: 7 August 2014.

[2.1496]

10 Content of seafarer employment agreement

(1) Subject to paragraph (2), a seafarer employment agreement must include provision about the following matters—

(a) if the seafarer is an employee of the shipowner or of any other person, the matters in Part 1 and Part 2 of Schedule 1;

(b) if the seafarer is not an employee, the matters in Part 1 and Part 3 of Schedule 1,

and where the seafarer employment agreement is one which falls within regulation 9(4), the name and address of the approved training provider must be set out in the agreement.

(2) Such provision may be achieved by way of reference to another document which includes provision about those matters.

(3) A breach of paragraph (1) is an offence by the shipowner.

(4) Prior to entering into a seafarer employment agreement, the shipowner or, in the case of an agreement falling within regulation 9(4), the approved training provider must take reasonable steps to satisfy itself with regard to the following requirements—

(a) the seafarer must have had a sufficient opportunity to review and take advice on the terms and conditions of the agreement;
(b) the seafarer must have received an explanation of the rights and responsibilities of the seafarer under the agreement; and
(c) the seafarer must be entering into the agreement freely.

(5) Where a shipowner—
(a) fails to take such reasonable steps; or
(b) in relevant cases, fails to take reasonable steps to ensure that the approved training provider has complied with paragraph (4),

the shipowner commits an offence.

(6) A seafarer employment agreement must contain a declaration by the shipowner and the seafarer or, in the case of an agreement falling within regulation 9(4), by the approved training provider and the seafarer confirming that the requirements in paragraph (4)(a) to (c) have been met.

(7) A breach of paragraph (6) is an offence by the shipowner.

NOTES
Commencement: 7 August 2014.

[2.1497]
11 Minimum notice period

(1) Subject to paragraph (3), the minimum period of notice which must be given before terminating a seafarer employment agreement is seven days or such longer period as may be specified in the agreement.

(2) The minimum period of notice which must be given by a seafarer before terminating a seafarer employment agreement must not be longer than the minimum period of notice which must be given by the shipowner or, as the case may be, the approved training provider.

(3) Nothing in this regulation prevents the earlier termination of a seafarer employment agreement without penalty where this is requested by the seafarer on compassionate grounds or where the seafarer is dismissed for reasons of gross misconduct.

NOTES
Commencement: 7 August 2014.

[2.1498]
12 Documents

(1) As soon as is practicable after entering into a seafarer employment agreement, the shipowner must provide to the seafarer an original of the agreement signed by each party and a copy of any document referred to in that agreement.

(2) A breach of paragraph (1) is an offence by the shipowner.

(3) The shipowner must—
(a) ensure that a copy of the seafarer employment agreement (and a copy of any document referred to in that agreement) for each seafarer on a ship is held on board; and
(b) allow each seafarer to see the copy of the seafarer employment agreement to which the seafarer is a party (and a copy of any document referred to in that agreement) on request.

(4) A breach of paragraph (3) is an offence by the shipowner.

(5) Subject to paragraph (7), as soon as is practicable after a seafarer's work on board a ship comes to an end, the shipowner must provide to the seafarer a written record of the seafarer's work on that ship.

(6) For the purposes of paragraph (5), the record—
(a) must contain provision about the matters set out in Schedule 2;
(b) must not contain provision about the quality of the seafarer's work; and
(c) must not contain provision about the seafarer's wages.

(7) Paragraph (5) does not apply if regulation 25 of the Merchant Shipping (Crew Agreements, Lists of Crew and Discharge of Seamen) Regulations 1991 applies in respect of the seafarer.

(8) A breach of paragraph (5) or (6) is an offence by the shipowner.

NOTES
Commencement: 7 August 2014.

[2.1499]
13 Foreign language seafarer employment agreement

(1) This regulation applies where a seafarer has a seafarer employment agreement which is not in the English language.

(2) The shipowner must ensure that an English translation of the provisions of the seafarer employment agreement (including any provisions which are contained in another document referred to in the agreement) is held on board.

(3) A breach of paragraph (2) is an offence by the shipowner.

NOTES
Commencement: 7 August 2014.

[2.1500]

14 Duty of master to produce seafarer employment agreement

(1) The master of a ship must produce to the Secretary of State, the Registrar-General of Shipping and Seamen or the Commissioners for Her Majesty's Revenue and Customs (or any person acting on their behalf) on demand copies of any documentation held on board pursuant to regulations 12(3)(a) and 13(2).

(2) A breach of paragraph (1) is an offence by the master of the ship.

NOTES

Commencement: 7 August 2014.

[2.1501]

15 Part 4 requirements for non-United Kingdom ships with MLC documentation

(1) A ship must not be operated unless it complies with the requirements in—

(a) paragraph 1 of Standard A2.1 (seafarers' employment agreements) of the MLC; and

(b) paragraph 4 of Standard A2.1 of the MLC regarding the particulars to be contained in seafarers' employment agreements,

whether or not the State whose flag the ship is entitled to fly has adopted any relevant laws or regulations.

(2) A breach of paragraph (1) (other than a breach of the requirement referred to in paragraph (3)) is an offence by the shipowner.

(3) A breach of the requirement in sub-paragraph 1(d) of Standard A2.1 of the MLC is an offence by the master of the ship.

NOTES

Commencement: 7 August 2014.

PART 5
WAGES

[2.1502]

16 Late payment of wages etc

(1) Subject to paragraph (2), if any amount in respect of wages or other remuneration payable to a seafarer under a seafarer employment agreement is not paid on the due date, interest must be paid on the unpaid amount at the rate of 20 per cent per annum from the date on which the amount was due until the date of payment.

(2) Paragraph (1) does not apply to the extent that the failure to make such payment on the required date was due to—

(a) a mistake;

(b) a reasonable dispute as to liability;

(c) the act or default of the seafarer; or

(d) any other cause not being the wrongful act or default of the persons liable to make the payment or of their servants or agents.

NOTES

Commencement: 7 August 2014.

[2.1503]

17 Account of seafarer's wages etc

(1) The shipowner must ensure that an account of the seafarer's wages or other remuneration under a seafarer employment agreement is prepared and delivered to the seafarer—

(a) periodically during the term of the seafarer employment agreement, at intervals not exceeding one month; and

(b) within one month of the agreement terminating.

(2) Where the seafarer is an employee, such account must include the following information—

(a) the name of the seafarer;

(b) the date of birth of the seafarer (if known);

(c) the number of the seafarer's current discharge book (if any);

(d) the capacity in which the seafarer worked on board the ship;

(e) the period covered by the account;

(f) the amounts payable for the period covered by the account; and

(g) the type and amount of any deductions made during the period covered by the account.

(3) Where, pursuant to paragraph (2), the account includes information of amounts which have been determined by reference to a currency exchange rate, the account must include details of the relevant exchange rate and any commission paid.

(4) Where the seafarer is not an employee, such account must include the following information—

(a) payments due;

(b) payments made (including any not falling within sub-paragraph (a)); and

(c) any rates of exchange and any commissions paid which are relevant to those payments.

(5) A breach of paragraphs (1) to (4) is an offence by the shipowner.

NOTES

Commencement: 7 August 2014.

[2.1504]

18 Part 5 requirements for non-United Kingdom ships with MLC documentation

(1) A ship must not be operated unless the shipowner complies with the requirements in paragraph 2 of Standard A2.2 (wages).

(2) A breach of paragraph (1) is an offence by the shipowner.

NOTES

Commencement: 7 August 2014.

PART 6
REPATRIATION

19–22 *(Outside the scope of this work.)*

[2.1505]

23 Prohibition on recovering costs from seafarer

(1) Subject to paragraph (2), a shipowner must not enter into an agreement with a seafarer under which the seafarer must make payment in respect of either—

(a) repatriation costs; or
(b) relief and maintenance costs.

(2) A seafarer employment agreement may provide that the seafarer must reimburse repatriation costs where the agreement is terminated because of the seafarer's serious misconduct.

(3) If a seafarer employment agreement contains provision described in paragraph (2) and that obligation arises, a deduction equivalent to those costs may be made from the wages due to the seafarer under that agreement.

(4) If a seafarer employment agreement does not contain provision such as that described in paragraph (2), the shipowner may only recover the costs described in paragraph (1) (or damages in respect of such costs) where the agreement is terminated because of the seafarer's serious misconduct.

(5) A breach of paragraph (1) is an offence by the shipowner.

(6) An agreement is void to the extent it provides that a seafarer must make a payment to the shipowner in respect of either repatriation costs or relief and maintenance costs in breach of paragraph (1).

NOTES

Commencement: 7 August 2014.

24–58 *(Regs 24–28, 29–58 (Pts 7–11) outside the scope of this work.)*

PART 12
OFFENCES AND PENALTIES

[2.1506]

59 Penalties

(1) Subject to paragraphs (2) to (5) [and regulation 59A], offences under these Regulations are punishable on summary conviction by a fine not exceeding level 5 on the standard scale.

(2) Offences under the following provisions are punishable on summary conviction by a fine not exceeding level 4 on the standard scale—

(a) regulation 10(3) and (7);
(b) regulation 12(4);
(c) regulation 15(2), but only in relation to an offence consisting of a breach of regulation 15(1)(b);
(d) regulation 36(3);
(e) regulation 45(2); . . .
(f) regulation 46(2);
[(g) regulation 53G(3);
(h) regulation 53I(3); and
(i) regulation 53Q(3).]

(3) Offences under the following provisions are punishable on summary conviction by a fine not exceeding level 3 on the standard scale—

(a) regulation 12(8);
(b) regulation 13(3);
(c) regulation 24(5), (9) and (12);
(d) regulation 25(3);
(e) regulation 28(4), but only in relation to an offence consisting of a breach of regulation 28(3)(b);
(f) regulation 29(5);
(g) regulation 33(5), but only in relation to an offence consisting of a breach of regulation 33(4)(a);
(h) regulation 36(5); . . .
(i) regulation 41(4), but only in relation to an offence consisting of a breach of regulation 41(3)(b).
[(j) regulation 53G(5); and

(k) regulation 53Q(5).]

(4) Offences under the following provisions are punishable on summary conviction by a fine not exceeding level 2 on the standard scale—

(a) regulation 17(5);
(b) regulation 18(2);
(c) regulation 24(3);
(d) regulation 29(7); and
(e) regulation 33(5), but only in relation to an offence consisting of a breach of regulation 33(4)(b).

(5) (*Outside the scope of this work.*)

NOTES

Commencement: 7 August 2014.

Para (1): words in square brackets inserted by the Merchant Shipping (Maritime Labour Convention) (Compulsory Financial Security) (Amendment) Regulations 2018, SI 2018/667, reg 2(1), (9)(a), as from 12 July 2018.

Para (2): word omitted from sub-para (e) revoked, and sub-paras (g), (h), (i) added, by SI 2018/667, reg 2(1), (9)(b), as from 12 July 2018.

Para (2): word omitted from sub-para (h) revoked, and sub-paras (j), (k) added, by SI 2018/667, reg 2(1), (9)(c), as from 12 July 2018.

59A (*Outside the scope of this work.*)

[2.1507]

60 Defence

In any proceedings for an offence under these Regulations (other than an offence under regulation 10(5)) it is a defence for the person charged to show that all reasonable steps had been taken by that person to ensure compliance with the provision concerned.

NOTES

Commencement: 7 August 2014.

PART 13
REVIEW

[2.1508]

61 Review

(1) The Secretary of State must from time to time—

(a) carry out a review of these Regulations;
(b) set out the conclusions of the review in a report; and
(c) publish the report.

(2) In carrying out the review the Secretary of State must, so far as is reasonable, have regard to how the MLC is implemented in other member States.

(3) The report must in particular—

(a) set out the objectives intended to be achieved by these Regulations;
(b) assess the extent to which those objectives are achieved; and
(c) assess whether those objectives remain appropriate and, if so, the extent to which they could be achieved with a system that imposes less regulation.

(4) The first report under this regulation must be published before the end of the period of five years beginning with the day on which these Regulations come into force.

(5) Reports under this regulation are afterwards to be published at intervals not exceeding five years.

NOTES

Commencement: 7 August 2014.

SCHEDULES

SCHEDULE 1
PROVISION TO BE INCLUDED IN A SEAFARER EMPLOYMENT AGREEMENT

Regulation 10(1)

PART 1
PROVISION TO BE INCLUDED IN ALL AGREEMENTS

[2.1509]

1. The full name, birthplace and date of birth (or age at the time of entering into the agreement) of the seafarer.

2. The name and address of the shipowner.

3. The place where the agreement is entered into.

4. The date on which the agreement is entered into.

5. The capacity in which the seafarer is to work.

6. If the agreement has been made for a definite period, the termination date.

7. If the agreement has been made for an indefinite period, the period of notice of termination required and the circumstances in which such notice may be given.

8. If the agreement has been made for a particular voyage, the destination port and the period following arrival after which the agreement terminates.

9. The health and social security protection benefits to be provided to the seafarer under the agreement.

10. The maximum period of service on board following which the seafarer is entitled to repatriation (which must not exceed a period of 12 months less the number of days statutory paid leave to which the seafarer is entitled).

11. The seafarer's entitlement to repatriation (including the mode of transport and destination of repatriation).

12. The circumstances in which the seafarer is required to meet or reimburse the shipowner for the costs of repatriation.

13. The maximum sum which the shipowner will pay to the seafarer in respect of compensation for any loss of personal property arising from the loss or foundering of the ship.

14. Details of any collective bargaining agreement which is incorporated (in whole or in part) into the agreement or is otherwise relevant to it.

NOTES

Commencement: 7 August 2014.

PART 2
PROVISION TO BE INCLUDED WHERE SEAFARER IS AN EMPLOYEE

[2.1510]

1. The wages (either the amount or the formula to be used in determining them).

2. The manner in which wages must be paid, including payment dates (the first of which must be no more than one month after the date on which the agreement is entered into, with all subsequent dates being no more than one month apart) and the circumstances (if any) in which wages may or must be paid in a different currency.

3. The hours of work.

4. The paid leave (either the amount or the formula to be used in determining it).

5. Any pension arrangements, including any entitlement to participate in a pension scheme.

6. The grievance and disciplinary procedures.

NOTES

Commencement: 7 August 2014.

PART 3
PROVISION TO BE INCLUDED WHERE SEAFARER IS NOT AN EMPLOYEE

[2.1511]

1. The remuneration (either the amount or the formula to be used in determining it).

2. The manner in which the remuneration must be paid, including payment dates (the first of which must be no more than one month after the date on which the agreement is entered into, with all subsequent dates being no more than one month apart) and the circumstances (if any) in which the remuneration may or must be paid in a different currency.

NOTES

Commencement: 7 August 2014.

SCHEDULES 2–4

(Schs 2–4 outside the scope of this work.)

PATERNITY AND ADOPTION LEAVE (AMENDMENT) REGULATIONS 2014 (NOTE)

(SI 2014/2112)

[2.1512]

NOTES

Made: 5 August 2014.

Authority: Employment Rights Act 1996, ss 47C(2)(aa), (ab), 75A(1), (3)(c), 75D(2), 80A(4A), 80B(4A), (5)(ba), 80C(1)(c), 80D(1), 99(1), (2), (3)(aa), (ab).

Commencement: 1 October 2014 (regs 1, 2, 10, 12, 14(1), (3)); 1 December 2014 (regs 3, 4, 5(a), reg 5(b) (so far as it relates to the inserted para (1A)(a)), regs 6, 8, 9); 5 April 2015 (reg 5(b) (so far as it relates to the inserted para (1A)(b)), regs 7, 11, 13, 14(2), (4)).

These Regulations amend the Paternity and Adoption Leave Regulations 2002, SI 2002/2788 at **[2.576]** et seq. Regulation 1 provides for citation and commencement and reg 2 introduces the amendments in regs 3–13.

Regulation 3 amends reg 2 of the 2002 Regulations; reg 4 amends reg 4 at; reg 5 amends reg 8(1) and inserts reg 8(1A); reg 6 substitutes reg 13(1)(b); reg 7 amends reg 15; reg 8 amends reg 22; reg 9 substitutes reg 26(1)(b); reg 10 inserts reg 28(1)(za), (zb); reg 11 inserts reg 28(1)(zc), (zd); reg 12 inserts reg 29(3)(za), (zb); reg 13 inserts reg 29(3)(zc), (zd).

Regulation 14 provides for the following transitional provisions:

Regulation 10 (insertion of reg 28(1)(za), (zb)) has effect only in relation to an act or failure to act which takes place on or after 1 October 2014.

Regulation 11 (insertion of reg 28(1)(zc), (zd)) has effect only in relation to an act or failure to act which takes place on or after 5 April 2015.

Regulation 12 (insertion of reg 29(3)(za), (zb)) has effect only in relation to dismissals where the effective date of termination (within the meaning of the Employment Rights Act 1996, s 97) falls on or after 1 October 2014.

Regulation 13 (insertion of reg 29(3)(zc), (zd)) has effect only in relation to dismissals where the effective date of termination (within the meaning of the Employment Rights Act 1996, s 97) falls on or after 5 April 2015.

PUBLIC INTEREST DISCLOSURE (PRESCRIBED PERSONS) ORDER 2014

(SI 2014/2418)

NOTES

Made: 8 September 2014.

Authority: Employment Rights Act 1996, ss 43F, 236(5).

Commencement: 1 October 2014.

See also the Prescribed Persons (Reports on Disclosures of Information) Regulations 2017, SI 2017/507 at **[2.2019]**. The 2017 Regulations specify requirements for prescribed persons (as to which, see the Schedule to this Order) to report annually on disclosures of information that they receive from workers.

[2.1513]

1 Citation and commencement

(1) This Order may be cited as the Public Interest Disclosure (Prescribed Persons) Order 2014 and comes into force on 1st October 2014.

(2) This Order applies to a disclosure made on or after 1st October 2014.

NOTES

Commencement: 1 October 2014.

[2.1514]

2 Revocation and Transitional Provision

(1) The Public Interest Disclosure (Prescribed Persons) Order 1999 is revoked except as provided for in paragraph (2).

(2) The Public Interest Disclosure (Prescribed Persons) Order 1999 continues to apply in relation to a disclosure made before 1st October 2014.

NOTES

Commencement: 1 October 2014.

[2.1515]

3 Prescribed Persons

(1) The persons and descriptions of persons specified in the first column of the Schedule are prescribed for the purposes of section 43F of the Employment Rights Act 1996.

(2) Each of the descriptions of matters in the second column of the Schedule is prescribed for the purposes of section 43F of the Employment Rights Act 1996 in relation to the entry specified in the first column opposite that description of matters.

Part 2 Statutory Instruments

NOTES

Commencement: 1 October 2014.

SCHEDULE

Article 3(1) and (2)

[2.1516]

First Column *Persons and descriptions of people*	*Second Column* *Description of matters*
Accounts Commission for Scotland and auditors appointed by the Commission to audit the accounts of local government bodies.	The proper conduct of public business; value for money, fraud and corruption in local government bodies.
. . .	. . .
[Audit Scotland.	The proper conduct of public business; value for money, fraud and corruption in public bodies.]
Auditor General for Wales.	The proper conduct of public business; value for money, fraud and corruption in relation to the provision of public services.
Auditor General for Scotland and persons appointed by or on his behalf under the Public Finance and Accountability (Scotland) Act 2000 to act as auditors or examiners for the purposes of sections 21 to 24 of that Act.	The proper conduct of public business; value for money, fraud and corruption in relation to the provision of public services.
[Auditors appointed to audit the accounts of bodies listed in Schedule 2 to the Local Audit and Accountability Act 2014.]	The proper conduct of public business; value for money, fraud and corruption in public bodies.
Auditors appointed by NHS foundation trusts to audit the accounts of those trusts.	The proper conduct of public business; value for money, fraud and corruption in public bodies.
The Bank of England.	[Matters relating to— (a) the functioning of clearing houses (including central-counterparties) [and central securities depositories]; (b) . . . payment systems; [(ba) the provision of services relating to payment systems;] (c) securities settlement systems [and the internalised settlement of securities]; (d) the treatment, holding and issuing of banknotes by the authorised banks (and their agents) under Part 6 of the Banking Act 2009; (e) the custody, distribution and processing of Bank of England banknotes under the Bank of England's Note Circulation Scheme.]
. . .	. . .
Care Inspectorate.	Matters relating to the provision of care services, as defined in the Public Services Reform (Scotland) Act 2010.
Care Quality Commission.	Matters relating to— (a) the registration and provision of a regulated activity as defined in section 8 of the Health and Social Care Act 2008 and the carrying out of any reviews and investigations under Part 1 of that Act; or [(b)the functions exercised by the Healthwatch England committee, including any functions of the Care Quality Commission exercised by that committee on its behalf; or (c) any activities not covered by (a) or (b) in relation to which the Care Quality Commission exercises its functions].
Certification Officer.	Fraud, and other irregularities, relating to the financial affairs of trade unions and employers' associations.
Charity Commission for England and Wales.	The proper administration of charities and of funds given or held for charitable purposes.
Chief Executive of the Criminal Cases Review Commission.	Actual or potential miscarriages of justice.
Chief Executive of the Scottish Criminal Cases Review Commission.	Actual or potential miscarriages of justice.
Children's Commissioner.	Matters relating to the rights, welfare and interests of children.
Children's Commissioner for Wales.	Matters relating to the rights, welfare and interests of children.

First Column ***Persons and descriptions of people***	***Second Column*** ***Description of matters***
Civil Aviation Authority.	Compliance with the requirements of civil aviation legislation, including aviation safety and aviation security.
Commissioner for Children and Young People in Scotland.	Matters relating to promoting and safeguarding the rights of children and young people.
[Commissioner for Ethical Standards in Public Life in Scotland.	Breaches by a councillor or a member of a devolved public body (as defined in section 28 of the Ethical Standards in Public Life etc (Scotland) Act 2000) of the code of conduct applicable to that councillor or member under that Act.]
Commissioners for Her Majesty's Revenue and Customs.	Matters relating to the functions of the Commissioners for Her Majesty's Revenue and Customs as set out in the Commissioners for Revenue and Customs Act 2005, including— (a) the administration of the UK's taxes, including income tax, inheritance tax, corporation tax, capital gains tax, VAT and the excise duties; (b) the administration of the national insurance and tax credits systems; (c) Customs and border-related functions; and (d) criminal investigations.
[Commissioners nominated under section 15(6) of the Local Government Act 1999.	Matters relating to the exercise of specified functions of a best value authority as directed by the Secretary of State.]
Competition and Markets Authority.	Matters concerning the sale of goods or the supply of services, which adversely affect the interests of consumers. Competition affecting markets in the United Kingdom.
Comptroller and Auditor General.	The proper conduct of public business; value for money, fraud and corruption in relation to the provision of public services.
Director of the Serious Fraud Office.	Matters relating to— (a) serious or complex fraud within the meaning of section 1(3) of the Criminal Justice Act 1987; or (b) civil recovery of the proceeds of unlawful conduct, civil recovery investigations and disclosure orders in relation to confiscation investigations as set out in Part 5 or 8 of the Proceeds of Crime Act 2002.
Elected local policing bodies.	Matters relating to any report made in accordance with section 114 of the Local Government Finance Act 1988 in relation to— (a) the chief constable for the elected local policing body's area; or (b) the Commissioner of Police of the Metropolis, where the elected local policing body is the Mayor's Office for Policing and Crime.
Environment Agency.	Acts or omissions which have an actual or potential effect on the environment or the management or regulation of the environment, including those relating to pollution, abstraction of water, flooding, the flow in rivers, inland fisheries and migratory salmon or trout.
[The European Securities and Markets Authority	Matters relating to compliance with Directive 2009/65/EC of the European Parliament and of the Council of 13th July 2009 on the coordination of laws, regulations and administrative provisions relating to undertakings for collective investment in transferable securities, as amended by Directive 2014/91/EU of the European Parliament and of the Council of 23rd July 2014.]
Financial Conduct Authority.	Matters relating to— (a) the carrying on of investment business, of insurance business or of deposit taking business or of any business related to or constituting a regulated activity as defined in section 22 of the Financial Services and Markets Act 2000 and wholesale money market regimes; (b) the conduct of persons authorised for the purposes of section 31 of the Financial Services and Markets Act 2000 including banks, building societies established under the Building Societies Act 1986, consumer credit firms and credit unions within the meaning of the Credit Unions Act 1979 or registered under the Credit Unions (Northern Ireland) Order 1985, or the Industrial and Provident Societies Act (Northern Ireland) 1969, friendly societies within the meaning of the Friendly Societies Act 1974 and the Friendly Societies Act 1992, insurers, the Society of Lloyd's incorporated by the Lloyd's Act 1871 and Lloyd's managing agents; (c) the conduct of persons who are subject to Part 18 of the Financial Services and Markets Act 2000; (d) the conduct of persons who are electronic money issuers for the purposes of the electronic money regulations 2011;

Part 2 Statutory Instruments

First Column *Persons and descriptions of people*	*Second Column* *Description of matters*
	(e) the conduct of persons who are payment service providers for the purposes of the payment services regulations 2009; (f) the operation of small UK Alternative Investment Fund Managers registered under regulation 10 of the Alternative Investment Fund Managers Regulations 2013; (g) the operation of societies registered under the Friendly Societies Act 1974 and the Friendly Societies Act 1992, including friendly societies, benevolent societies, working men's clubs, specially authorised societies; (h) the operation of "registered societies" within the meaning of the Co-operative and Community Benefit Societies Act 2014; (i) the conduct of persons subject to rules made under Part 6 of the Financial Services and Markets Act 2000; (j) competition in relation to the provision of financial services and the financial services markets; (k) the functioning of financial markets; . . . (l) money laundering, financial crime, and other serious financial misconduct, in connection with activities regulated by the Financial Conduct Authority. [(m) the conduct of persons who are subject to— (i) Part 3 and 4 of the Financial Services and Markets Act 2000 (Markets in Financial Instruments) Regulations 2017; (ii) the Data Reporting Services Regulations 2017; or (iii) Regulation (EU) No 600/2014 of the European Parliament and of the Council of 15 May 2014 on markets in financial instruments][; and (n) the conduct of PRIIP manufacturers and persons advising on or selling a PRIIP referred to in regulation (EU) No 1286/2014 of the European Parliament and of the Council of 26th November 2014 on key information documents for packaged retail and insurance-based investment products, for the purposes of that regulation][; and (o) the conduct of persons regulated under Regulation (EU) 2017/2402 of the European Parliament and of the Council of 12 December 2017 laying down a general framework for securitisation and creating a specific framework for simple, transparent and standardised securitisation, and amending Directives 2009/65/EC, 2009/138/EC and 2011/61/EU and Regulations (EC) No 1060/2009 and (EU) No 648/2012.]
The Financial Reporting Council Limited and its [Conduct Committee].	Matters relating to— [(za) exercising the functions of the competent authority under the Statutory Auditors and Third Country Auditors Regulations 2016 and under Regulation (EU) 537/2014 of the European Parliament and of the Council on specific requirements regarding statutory audit of public-interest entities;] (a) the independent oversight of the regulation of the accountancy, . . . and actuarial professions; (b) the independent supervision of Auditors General (as defined in section 1226 of the Companies Act 2006); (c) the monitoring of . . . major local audits (as defined in [paragraph 13(10) of Schedule 10 to the Companies Act 2006] as applied by paragraph 28 of Schedule 5 to the Local Audit and Accountability Act 2014); [(d) exercising, in relation to third country auditors (as defined by section 1261 of the Companies Act 2006), functions— (i) of the Secretary of State under Part 42 of that Act, delegated under that Part, (ii) under the arrangements within Schedule 12 to that Act, and (iii) of the designated body under the Statutory Auditors and Third Country Auditors Regulations 2013;] (e) compliance with the requirements of legislation relating to accounting and reporting; and [(f) the investigation of, and enforcement action in relation to, conduct of members of the accountancy and actuarial professions in matters which raise or appear to raise important issues affecting the public interest;]

First Column Persons and descriptions of people	***Second Column Description of matters***
	[(g) the investigation of, and enforcement action in relation to, the conduct of local auditors (as defined by section 4(1)(b) of the Local Audit and Accountability Act 2014), . . . in public interest cases (as defined in paragraph 24 of Schedule 10 to the Companies Act 2006 as applied by paragraph 28 of Schedule 5 of the Local Audit and Accountability Act 2014).]
Food Standards Agency.	Matters which may affect the health of any member of the public in relation to the consumption of food and matters which concern the protection of the interests of consumers in relation to food [in England, Wales or Northern Ireland].
[Food Standards Scotland.	Matters which affect the health of any member of the public in Scotland in relation to the consumption of food and matters which concern the protection of consumers in relation to food.]
Gas and Electricity Markets Authority.	Matters relating to— (a) the generation, transmission, distribution and supply of electricity, participation in the operation of an electricity interconnector (as defined in section 4(3E) of the Electricity Act 1989); (b) providing a smart meter communication service (as defined in section 4(3G) of that Act) and activities ancillary to these matters; (c) the transportation, shipping and supply of gas through pipes, participation in the operation of a gas interconnector (as defined in section 5(8) of the Gas Act 1986); (d) providing a smart meter communication service (as defined in section 5(11) of that Act) and activities ancillary to these matters; and (e) the renewable generation of heat (as defined in section 100(3) of the Energy Act 2008) and activities ancillary to that matter.
General Chiropractic Council.	Matters relating to— (a) the registration and fitness to practise of a member of a profession regulated by the Council; and (b) any activities not covered by (a) in relation to which the Council has functions.
General Dental Council.	Matters relating to— (a) the registration and fitness to practise of a member of a profession regulated by the Council; and (b) any activities not covered by (a) in relation to which the Council has functions.
General Medical Council.	Matters relating to— (a) the registration and fitness to practise of a member of a profession regulated by the Council; and (b) any activities not covered by (a) in relation to which the Council has functions.
General Optical Council.	Matters relating to— (a) the registration and fitness to practise of a member of a profession regulated by the Council; and (b) any activities not covered by (a) in relation to which the Council has functions.
General Osteopathic Council.	Matters relating to— (a) the registration and fitness to practise of a member of a profession regulated by the Council; and (b) any activities not covered by (a) in relation to which the Council has functions.
[General Pharmaceutical Council.	Matters relating to— (a) the registration and fitness to practise of a member of a profession regulated by the Council; (b) regulated activities at or from pharmacy premises registered by the Council; and (c) any activities not covered by (a) or (b) in relation to which the Council has functions.]
Health and Care Professions Council.	Matters relating to— (a) the registration and fitness to practise of a member of a profession regulated by the Council; and (b) any activities not covered by (a) in relation to which the Council has functions.

First Column *Persons and descriptions of people*	*Second Column* *Description of matters*
[Health Education England.	Matters relating to— (a) Health Education England's functions under sections 97(1) and 98(1) of the Care Act 2014 (which relate to planning and delivering education and training for health care workers and to ensuring sufficient skilled and trained health care workers are available for the health service throughout England); (b) the functions exercised by Local Education and Training Boards, including any functions of Health Education England exercised by Local Education and Training Boards on its behalf; or (c) any activities not covered by (a) or (b) in relation to which Health Education England exercises its functions.]
Health and Safety Executive.	[Matters relating to those industries and work activities for which the Health and Safety Executive is the enforcing authority under the Health and Safety (Enforcing Authority) Regulations 1998 and which are about the health and safety of individuals at work, or the health and safety of the public arising out of or in connection with the activities of persons at work.]
Healthcare Improvement Scotland.	Matters relating to— (a) furthering the improvement in the quality of health care (within the meaning of section 10A of the National Health Service (Scotland) Act 1978); and (b) any activities not covered by (a) in relation to which Healthcare Improvement Scotland has functions.
Her Majesty's Chief Inspector of Education, Children's Services and Skills ("the Chief Inspector").	Matters relating to— (a) the regulation and inspection of establishments and agencies under Part 2 of the Care Standards Act 2000; (b) the inspection of the functions of local authorities in England referred to in section 135 (c) to (e) of the Education and Inspections Act 2006; (c) the inspection of children's services under section 20 of the Children Act 2004; (d) the review of Local Safeguarding Children Boards under section 15A of the Children Act 2004; (e) the inspection, under section 87 of the Children Act 1989, of the welfare of children provided with accommodation by boarding schools and further education colleges; (f) the inspection of the Children and Family Court Advisory and Support Service under section 143 of the Education and Inspections Act 2006; and (g) any other activities falling within the remit of the Chief Inspector as defined in section 117(6) of the Education and Inspections Act 2006 and any other functions which may be assigned to the Chief Inspector under section 118(4) of that Act but only in so far as they relate to one of the functions set out in (a) to (f) above.
Homes and Communities Agency.	[Matters relating to the proper conduct of the business of registered providers of social housing.]
Independent Police Complaints Commission.	Matters relating to the conduct of a person serving with the police (as defined in section 12(7) of the Police Reform Act 2002) or of any other person in relation to whose conduct the Independent Police Complaints Commission exercises functions in or under any legislation.
Information Commissioner.	Compliance with the requirements of legislation relating to data protection and to freedom of information.
[The Keeper of the Registers of Scotland	Land and buildings transaction tax.]
Local authorities which are responsible for the enforcement of food standards in accordance with sections 5 and 6 of the Food Safety Act 1990.	Compliance with the requirements of food safety legislation.
Local authorities which are responsible for the enforcement of health and safety legislation.	Matters which may affect the health or safety of any individual at work; matters, which may affect the health and safety of any member of the public, arising out of or in connection with the activities of persons at work.
Local weights and measures authorities as defined by section 69 of the Weights and Measures Act 1985 which are responsible for the enforcement of consumer protection legislation.	Compliance with the requirements of consumer protection legislation.

First Column *Persons and descriptions of people*	*Second Column* *Description of matters*
Lord Advocate, Scotland.	Serious or complex fraud within the meaning of section 27 of the Criminal Law (Consolidation) (Scotland) Act 1995.
A member of the House of Commons.	Any matter specified in this column.
Monitor.	Matters relating to— (a) the regulation and performance of NHS foundation trusts; and (b) any activities not covered by (a) in relation to which Monitor exercises its functions.
[National Health Service Commissioning Board.	Matters relating to the provision of services pursuant to a contract, agreement or arrangement under Part 4 (which relates to primary medical services), Part 5 (which relates to primary dental services), Part 6 (which relates to primary ophthalmic services) or Part 7 (pharmaceutical services and local pharmaceutical services) of the National Health Service Act 2006.]
National Crime Agency.	[Matters relating to— (a) corrupt individuals or companies offering or receiving bribes to secure a benefit for themselves or others; (b) compliance with— (i) the Terrorism Act 2000; (ii) the Proceeds of Crime Act 2002; or (iii) the Money Laundering, Terrorist Financing and Transfer of Funds (Information on the Payer) Regulations 2017.]
National Health Service Trust Development Authority.	The performance of English NHS trusts, including clinical quality, governance and management of risk.
The National Society for the Prevention of Cruelty to Children (NSPCC) and any of its officers.	Matters relating to child welfare and protection.
NHS Counter Fraud Authority (being a special health authority established under section 28 of the National Health Service Act 2006).	Matters relating to fraud, corruption or other such unlawful activity in relation to the health service in England.]
Nursing and Midwifery Council.	Matters relating to— (a) the registration and fitness to practise of a member of a profession regulated by the Council; and (b) any activities not covered by (a) in relation to which the Council has functions.
Office for Nuclear Regulation.	Matters which may affect the health and safety of any individual at work wholly or mainly on premises which are, or are on— (a) a GB nuclear site (within the meaning given in section 68 of the Energy Act 2013); (b) an authorised defence site (within the meaning given in regulation 2(1) of the Health and Safety (Enforcing Authority) Regulations 1998; or (c) a new nuclear build site (within the meaning given in regulation 2A of those Regulations). Matters which may affect the health and safety of any member of the public, arising out of or in connection with the activities of persons at work on premises which are, or are on, such sites.
Office of Communications.	Matters relating to— (a) the provision of electronic communications networks and services and the use of the electro-magnetic spectrum; (b) broadcasting and the provision of television and radio services; (c) media ownership and control; and (d) competition in communications markets.
Office of Qualifications and Examinations Regulation.	Matters in relation to which the Office of Qualifications and Examinations Regulation exercises functions under the Apprenticeships, Skills, Children and Learning Act 2009.
[Office of Rail and Road.]	Matters relating to— (a) the provision and supply of railway services; and (b) any activities not covered by (a) in relation to which [the Office of Rail and Road] has functions.
Office of the Scottish Charity Regulator.	The proper administration of charities and of funds given or held for charitable purposes.
[Older People's Commissioner.	Matters relating to the rights and wellbeing of older people in Wales.]
Payment Systems Regulator.	Payment systems (within the meaning given by section 41 of the Financial Services (Banking Reform) Act 2013) and the services provided by them.

Part 2 Statutory Instruments

First Column ***Persons and descriptions of people***	*Second Column* ***Description of matters***
Pensions Regulator.	Matters relating to occupational pension schemes and . . . private pension arrangements including matters relating to the Pensions Regulator's objective of maximising compliance with the duties under Chapter 1 of Part 1 (and the safeguards in sections 50 and 54) of the Pensions Act 2008.
Police and Crime Panels.	Matters relating to— (a) any complaint about the conduct of a relevant office holder, within the meaning of section 31 of the Police Reform and Social Responsibility Act 2011; and (b) any report made in accordance with section 114 of the Local Government Finance Act 1988 or section 4 or 5 of the Local Government and Housing Act 1989 in relation to the elected local policing body for the Police and Crime Panel's area.
Prudential Regulation Authority.	Matters relating to— (a) the carrying on of deposit-taking business or insurance business or investment business or any business related to or constituting a regulated activity as designated pursuant to section 22A of the Financial Services and Markets Act 2000; (b) the safety and soundness of persons authorised for the purposes of section 31 of the Financial Services and Markets Act 2000, including banks, insurers, the Society of Lloyd's incorporated by the Lloyd's Act 1871, Lloyds managing agents, building societies established under the Building Societies Act 1986, designated investment firms, societies registered under the Friendly Societies Act 1974 and the Friendly Societies Act 1992, including friendly societies, benevolent societies, working men's clubs and specially authorised societies, and credit unions within the meaning [of the] Credit Unions Act 1979 or registered under the Credit Unions (Northern Ireland) Order 1985 or under the Industrial and Provident Societies Act (Northern Ireland) 1969, in connection with matters regulated by the Prudential Regulation Authority[; and (c) he conduct of persons regulated under Regulation (EU) 2017/2402 of the European Parliament and of the Council of 12 December 2017 laying down a general framework for securitisation and creating a specific framework for simple, transparent and standardised securitisation, and amending Directives 2009/65/EC, 2009/138/EC and 2011/61/EU and Regulations (EC) No 1060/2009 and (EU) No 648/2012.]
Public Services Ombudsman for Wales.	Breaches by a member or co-opted member of a relevant authority (as defined in section 49(6) of the Local Government Act 2000) of that authority's code of conduct.
[Qualifications Wales.	Matters in respect of which Qualifications Wales exercises functions under the Qualifications Wales Act 2015.]
[Revenue Scotland	Devolved taxes (within the meaning of section 80A(4) of the Scotland Act 1998).]
Scottish Environment Protection Agency.	Acts or omissions which have an actual or potential effect on the environment or the management or regulation of the environment, including those relating to flood warning systems and pollution. [Scottish landfill tax.]
Scottish Housing Regulator.	Social landlords' performance of housing activities; the registration of Registered Social Landlords in accordance with Part 2 of the Housing (Scotland) Act 2010; and the financial well-being and standards of governance of Registered Social Landlords.
Scottish Information Commissioner.	Compliance with the requirements of legislation relating to freedom of information.
Scottish Social Services Council.	Matters relating to the registration of the social services workforce by the Scottish Social Services Council under the Regulation of Care (Scotland) Act 2001.
[Secretary of State for Business, Energy and Industrial Strategy.]	Fraud, and other misconduct, in relation to companies. Consumer safety.
[Secretary of State for Education.	Matters relating to the following educational institutions in England— (a) a maintained school (as defined in section 20(7) of the School Standards and Framework Act 1998); (b) a maintained nursery school (as defined in section 22(9) of the School Standards and Framework Act 1998);

First Column *Persons and descriptions of people*	*Second Column* *Description of matters*
	(c) an independent educational institution (as defined in section 92(1) of the Education and Skills Act 2008) entered on a register of independent educational institutions kept under section 95 of the Education and Skills Act 2008; (d) a school approved under section 342 of the Education Act 1996 (non-maintained special schools); (e) a pupil referral unit (as defined in section 19(2B) of the Education Act 1996); (f) an alternative provision Academy (as defined in section 1C(3) of the Academies Act 2010); (g) a 16-19 Academy (as defined in section 1B(3) of the Academies Act 2010); [(h) an institution within the further education sector (as defined in section 91(3) of the Further and Higher Education Act 1992);] (i) a special post-16 institution (as defined in section 83(2) of the Children and Families Act 2014).]
[Secretary of State for Health [and Social Care].	Matters relating to— (a) protecting the public in England from disease or other dangers to health under section 2A of the National Health Service Act 2006; (b) improving the health of the people of England under section 2B of the National Health Service Act 2006; or (c) any other public health functions exercised by or on behalf of the Secretary of State for Health [and Social Care] in relation to the people of England and not covered by (a) or (b), including those exercised by Public Health England.]
[Secretary of State for Transport.	Matter relating to— (a) compliance with the requirements of merchant shipping law, including maritime safety; (b) motoring services with respect to driver and vehicle standards, the testing and certification of vehicles, their systems and components; and (c) road, rail and maritime transport security.]
[The Single Source Regulations Office.	Matters relating to single source defence procurement, including the application of and compliance with Part 2 of the Defence Reform Act 2014 and the Single Source Contract Regulations 2014.]
[Social Care Wales.	Matters relating to the registration of social care workers under the Regulation and Inspection of Social Care (Wales) Act 2016.]
. . .	. . .
[. . .	
Water Services Regulation Authority.	The supply of water and the provision of sewerage services.
Water Industry Commission for Scotland.	The supply of water and the provision of sewerage services.
Water Industry Commission for Scotland.	The supply of water and the provision of sewerage services.
Water Industry Commission for Scotland.	The supply of water and the provision of sewerage services.
[Welsh Revenue Authority	Matters relating to devolved taxes (within the meaning of section 116A(4) of the Government of Wales Act 2006)]
Welsh Ministers.	Matters relating to the provision of Part II services as defined in section 8 of the Care Standards Act 2000 and the Children Act 1989. Matters relating to the inspection and performance assessment of Welsh local authority social services as defined in section 148 of the Health and Social Care (Community Heath and Standards) Act 2003 Matters relating to the review of, and investigation into, the provision of health care by and for Welsh NHS bodies as defined under the Health and Social Care (Community Health and Standards) Act 2003. The regulation of registered social landlords in accordance with Part 1 of the Housing Act 1996 (as amended by the Housing (Wales) Measure 2011). [Matters relating to the environment and natural resources as set out in the Natural Resources Body for Wales (Establishment) Order 2012.] [Matters relating to regulated services as defined in section 2 of the Regulation and Inspection of Social Care (Wales) Act 2016.]

NOTES

Commencement: 1 October 2014.

Entry relating to "Audit Scotland" inserted by the Public Interest Disclosure (Prescribed Persons) (Amendment) Order 2018, SI 2018/795, art 2(a), as from 1 August 2018.

In the entry relating to "The Bank of England" the whole of column 2 was substituted by the Public Interest Disclosure (Prescribed Persons) (Amendment) Order 2016, SI 2016/968, art 2, Schedule, as from 1 November 2016. The words in square brackets in paras (a) and (c) were inserted by the Central Securities Depositories Regulations 2017, SI 2017/1064, reg 10, Schedule, Pt 2, para 42, as from 28 November 2017. The words omitted from para (b) were revoked by SI 2017/880, art 2(c), as from 1 October 2017. Para (ba) was inserted by SI 2018/795, art 2(b), as from 1 August 2018

Entry relating to "Care Council for Wales" (omitted) revoked by SI 2017/880, art 2(a), as from 1 October 2017.

Entries relating to "Commissioners nominated under section 15(6) of the Local Government Act 1999", "Food Standards Scotland", "Older People's Commissioner", "and Qualifications Wales" inserted, words in square brackets in the entry relating to "Food Standards Agency" inserted, and the words "Secretary of State for Business, Energy and Industrial Strategy" substituted, by SI 2016/968, art 2, Schedule, as from 1 November 2016.

Entry "The European Securities and Markets Authority" inserted by the Undertakings for Collective Investment in Transferable Securities Regulations 2016, SI 2016/225, as from 18 March 2016.

In the entry relating to the "Financial Conduct Authority" the word omitted from para (k) was revoked, and para (m) was added, by the Financial Services and Markets Act 2000 (Markets in Financial Instruments) Regulations 2017, SI 2017/701, reg 50(4), Sch 5, para 21, as from 3 January 2018. Para (n) and the preceding word were added by the Packaged Retail and Insurance-based Investment Products Regulations 2017, SI 2017/1127, reg 12, Sch 2, para 9, as from 1 January 2018. Para (o) and the preceding word were added by the Securitisation Regulations 2018, SI 2018/1288, reg 28, Sch 2, para 6(1), (2), as from 1 January 2019.

In the entry relating to the "The Financial Reporting Council Limited", the words omitted from paras (a), (g) were revoked and para (f) was substituted, by SI 2018/795, art 2(c), as from 1 August 2018; all other amendments were made by the Statutory Auditors and Third Country Auditors Regulations 2017, SI 2017/516, reg 17, as from 1 May 2017.

Entries "General Pharmaceutical Council" and "Secretary of State for Transport" substituted by SI 2018/795, art 2(d), (e), as from 1 August 2018

Entries relating to "The Keeper of the Registers of Scotland" and "Revenue Scotland" inserted, and in entry relating to "Scottish Environment Protection Agency" words "Scottish landfill tax" in square brackets inserted, by the Revenue Scotland and Tax Powers Act 2014 (Consequential Provisions and Modifications) Order 2014, SI 2014/3294, art 6, as from 1 January 2015.

In the entry relating to "National Crime Agency" the whole of column 2 was substituted by the Money Laundering, Terrorist Financing and Transfer of Funds (Information on the Payer) Regulations 2017, SI 2017/692, reg 109, Sch 7, Pt 2, para 31, as from 26 June 2017.

Entry relating to "NHS Counter Fraud Authority (being a special health authority established under section 28 of the National Health Service Act 2006)" substituted (for the original entry relating to "NHS Business Services Authority") by the NHS Counter Fraud Authority (Investigatory Powers and Other Miscellaneous Amendments) Order 2017, SI 2017/960, art 5, as from 1 November 2017.

In the entry relating to "Office of Rail and Road" words in square brackets substituted by the Office of Rail Regulation (Change of Name) Regulations 2015, SI 2015/1682, reg 2(2), Schedule, Pt 2, para 10(kk), as from 16 October 2015.

In entry "Prudential Regulation Authority" words in square brackets inserted by SI 2018/1288, reg 28, Sch 2, para 6(1), (3), as from 1 January 2019.

Entry relating to "Secretary of State for Education" inserted by the Public Interest Disclosure (Prescribed Persons) (Amendment) Order 2015, SI 2015/1407, art 2, as from 21 July 2015. Para (h) substituted by SI 2017/880, art 2(b), as from 1 October 2017.

Entry relating to "Secretary of State for Health": words "and Social Care" in square brackets in both places they appear inserted by the Secretaries of State for Health and Social Care and for Housing, Communities and Local Government and Transfer of Functions (Commonhold Land) Order 2018, SI 2018/378, art 15, Schedule, Pt 2, para 21(r), as from 11 April 2018.

Entry relating to "Social Care Wales" inserted by SI 2017/880, art 2(e), as from 1 October 2017.

Entry relating to "Wales Audit Office" originally inserted by SI 2016/968, art 2, Schedule, as from 1 November 2016. Subsequently revoked by SI 2017/880, art 2(a), as from 1 October 2017.

In the entry relating to "Welsh Ministers" the final words in square brackets were added by SI 2017/880, art 2(d). as from 1 October 2017.

Entry "Welsh Revenue Authority" inserted by the Tax Collection and Management (Wales) Act 2016 and the Land Transaction Tax and Anti-avoidance of Devolved Taxes (Wales) Act 2017 (Consequential Amendments) Order 2018, SI 2018/1237, art 4, as from 22 November 2018.

All other amendments to this Schedule were made by the Public Interest Disclosure (Prescribed Persons) (Amendment) (No 2) Order 2015, SI 2015/1981, art 2, Schedule, as from 1 February 2016.

EQUALITY ACT 2010 (EQUAL PAY AUDITS) REGULATIONS 2014

(SI 2014/2559)

NOTES

Made: 22 September 2014.

Authority: Equality Act 2010, ss 139A, 207(1), (4).

Commencement: 1 October 2014.

ARRANGEMENT OF REGULATIONS

[2.1517]

1 Citation, commencement and interpretation

(1) These Regulations may be cited as the Equality Act 2010 (Equal Pay Audits) Regulations 2014 and come into force on 1st October 2014.

(2) In these Regulations—

"the Act" means the Equality Act 2010;

"audit" means an equal pay audit;

"date of complaint" means the date on which a complaint in respect of an equal pay breach is presented to a tribunal;

"date of judgment" means the date on which a tribunal finds that there has been an equal pay breach;

"relevant gender pay information" means information relating to the pay of men and women (including the maternity-related pay of women to whom section 74 of the Act applies (maternity equality clause: pay))—

(a) who are employed by the respondent;

(b) who are appointed to a personal or public office by the respondent;

(c) for whom the respondent is the relevant person in relation to the terms of appointment to a personal or public office;

"relevant person" has the same meaning as in section 52(6) of the Act;

"tribunal" means an employment tribunal.

NOTES

Commencement: 1 October 2014.

[2.1518]

2 Requirement for a tribunal to order an audit

(1) This regulation applies to a complaint presented on or after 1st October 2014 where a tribunal finds that there has been an equal pay breach.

(2) Subject to regulations 3 and 4, the tribunal must order the respondent to carry out an audit.

NOTES

Commencement: 1 October 2014.

[2.1519]

3 Circumstances in which an audit must not be ordered

(1) A tribunal must not order the respondent to carry out an audit where it considers that—

(a) the information which would be required to be included in the audit under regulation 6 were the tribunal to make an order, is already available from an audit which has been completed by the respondent in the previous 3 years;

(b) it is clear without an audit whether any action is required to avoid equal pay breaches occurring or continuing;

(c) the breach which the tribunal has found gives no reason to think that there may be other breaches; or

(d) the disadvantages of an audit would outweigh its benefits.

(2) In paragraph (1), "previous 3 years" means the 3 years preceding the date on which the tribunal issues a judgment, orally or in writing, stating that there has been an equal pay breach.

NOTES

Commencement: 1 October 2014.

[2.1520]

4 Exemption for existing micro-businesses and new businesses

(1) A tribunal must not, within the applicable exemption period, order a respondent to carry out an audit in relation to persons employed for the purposes of a business where the respondent is carrying on that business and the business is—

(a) an existing micro-business, or

(b) a new business.

(2) The Schedule defines "micro-business" and "new business" and the exemption period applicable for each.

NOTES

Commencement: 1 October 2014.

[2.1521]

5 Content of the tribunal's order

(1) An order made by a tribunal under regulation 2 must—

(a) specify descriptions of persons in relation to whom relevant gender pay information must be included in the audit and the period of time to which the audit must relate; and

(b) specify the date by which the audit must be received by the tribunal.

(2) The date specified for the purposes of paragraph (1)(b) must not be sooner than 3 months after the date on which the order is made.

NOTES

Commencement: 1 October 2014.

[2.1522]

6 Content of an audit

An audit must—

(a) include the relevant gender pay information related to the descriptions of persons specified by the tribunal for the purposes of regulation 5(1)(a);

(b) identify any differences in pay between the descriptions of men and women specified for the purposes of regulation 5(1)(a) and the reasons for those differences;

(c) include the reasons for any potential equal pay breach identified by the audit; and

(d) include the respondent's plan to avoid equal pay breaches occurring or continuing.

NOTES

Commencement: 1 October 2014.

[2.1523]

7 Determining compliance with an order to carry out an audit on the papers

(1) Where an audit has been received by a tribunal by the date specified in relation to it for the purpose of regulation 5(1)(b), the tribunal must determine whether the audit complies with the requirements in regulation 6.

(2) Where the tribunal determines that the audit complies with the requirements in regulation 6, it must make an order to that effect and provide a copy of that order to the respondent.

(3) Where the tribunal is not satisfied that the audit complies with the requirements in regulation 6 or where the audit was not received by the tribunal by the date specified for the purposes of regulation 5(1)(b), the tribunal must—

(a) fix a hearing;

(b) notify the respondent of—

(i) the reasons why it is not satisfied that the audit complies with the requirements in regulation 6 (where an audit was received by the tribunal by the date specified for the purposes of regulation 5(1)(b)) and the powers available to the tribunal;

(ii) the date of the hearing; and

(iii) the right of the respondent to make representations at the hearing; and

(c) where an audit has not been received by the date specified for the purposes of regulation 5(1)(b), make an order specifying the new date by which the audit must be received by the tribunal, which must be no later than the date specified in paragraph (b)(ii).

NOTES

Commencement: 1 October 2014.

[2.1524]

8 Determining compliance with an order to carry out an audit at a hearing

(1) This regulation applies where a tribunal has held a hearing fixed under regulation 7(3) and considered any representations made by the respondent.

(2) Where an audit has been received by a tribunal by the date of the hearing, it must determine whether the audit complies with the requirements in regulation 6.

(3) Where the tribunal determines that the audit complies with the requirements in regulation 6, it must—

(a) make an order to that effect and provide a copy of that order to the respondent; and

(b) where the audit was not received by the tribunal by the date specified for the purposes of regulation 5(1)(b) or (as the case may be) regulation 7(3)(c), paragraph (4)(a) below or paragraph 5(a) below, consider whether to make an order under regulation 11.

(4) Where the tribunal determines that the audit does not comply with the requirements in regulation 6, it must—

(a) make an order requiring the respondent to amend the audit so that it does so comply and specifying the date by which the tribunal must receive the amended audit;

(b) notify the respondent of the reasons for its determination;

(c) provide a copy of that order to the respondent; and
(d) consider whether to make an order under regulation 11.

(5) Where the audit has not been received by the tribunal by the date of the hearing, the tribunal must—
(a) make an order specifying a new date by which the tribunal must receive the audit;
(b) provide a copy of that order to the respondent; and
(c) consider whether to make an order under regulation 11.

(6) Where the respondent fails to comply with an order under paragraph (4) or (5), the tribunal must—
(a) fix a further hearing; and
(b) notify the respondent of—
(i) the date of the hearing; and
(ii) the right of the respondent to make representations.

(7) The preceding provisions of this regulation apply to a hearing fixed under paragraph (6) as they apply to a hearing fixed under regulation 7(3).

NOTES

Commencement: 1 October 2014.

[2.1525]
9 Publishing an audit

(1) This regulation applies where a tribunal makes an order under regulation 7(2) or 8(3).

(2) Subject to paragraph (3), the respondent must, not later than 28 days after the date of the order, publish the audit—
(a) if the respondent has a website, by placing it on the respondent's website for a period of at least 3 years starting with the date on which it is placed on the website; and
(b) by informing all persons about whom relevant gender pay information was included in the audit where they can obtain a copy.

(3) Where the respondent considers that publication under paragraph (2) would result in a breach of a legal obligation, the respondent—
(a) must, so far as possible, publish the audit in accordance with paragraph (2) with such revisions as it considers necessary to ensure compliance with that obligation while still ensuring compliance with regulation 6; or
(b) where it is satisfied that it is not possible to comply with sub-paragraph (a), need not publish the audit.

(4) Where the respondent publishes the audit under paragraph (2), it must send to the tribunal evidence of this not later than 28 days after the date of publication of the audit.

(5) Where the respondent publishes the audit under paragraph (3)(a), it must send to the tribunal—
(a) evidence that the audit has been published; and
(b) adequate written reasons why it considers that publication under paragraph (2) would result in a breach of a legal obligation,

not later than 28 days after the date of publication of the audit.

(6) Where the respondent, in reliance on paragraph (3)(b), does not publish the audit, it must send to the tribunal, not later than 28 days after the date on which the tribunal makes an order under regulation 7(2) or 8(3), adequate reasons in writing explaining why it considers that publication would result in a breach of a legal obligation and why it is satisfied that it is not possible to comply with paragraph (3)(a).

NOTES

Commencement: 1 October 2014.

[2.1526]
10 Determining compliance with an order to publish an audit

(1) This regulation applies where a tribunal makes an order under regulation 7(2) or 8(3).

(2) The tribunal must, no sooner than 56 days after the date of that order, consider whether the respondent has complied with the publication requirements.

(3) Where the tribunal determines that the respondent—
(a) has complied with the publication requirements; or
(b) is not required to do so by virtue of regulation 9(3)(b),

the tribunal must issue a decision in writing to the respondent stating that the respondent has so complied or that the respondent is not required to do so.

(4) Where the tribunal is not satisfied that the respondent has complied with the publication requirements and is required to do so, it must—
(a) fix a hearing to determine whether the respondent has complied with the publication requirements; and
(b) notify the respondent of—
(i) the reasons why it is not satisfied that the respondent has complied with the publication requirements;
(ii) the date of the hearing; and
(iii) the right of the respondent to make representations.

(5) Paragraphs (6) to (8) apply where the tribunal has held a hearing under paragraph (4) and considered any representations made by the respondent.

(6) Where the tribunal determines that the respondent—

(a) has complied with the publication requirements; or

(b) is not required to do so by virtue of regulation 9(3)(b),

it must issue a decision in writing stating that the respondent has so complied, or is not required to do so.

(7) Where the tribunal determines that the respondent has not complied with the publication requirements and is not exempt from doing so by virtue of regulation 9(3)(b), it must make an order specifying a new date by which the respondent must comply with the publication requirements, in so far as the respondent has not done so.

(8) Where the respondent fails to comply with an order under paragraph (7), the tribunal must—

(a) fix a further hearing; and

(b) notify the respondent of—

(i) the date of the hearing; and

(ii) the right of the respondent to make further representations.

(9) The preceding provisions of this regulation apply to a hearing fixed under paragraph (8) as they apply to a hearing fixed under paragraph (4).

(10) In this regulation, "publication requirements" means the requirement to—

(a) publish the audit; and

(b) provide evidence of publication to the tribunal,

in accordance with regulation 9.

NOTES

Commencement: 1 October 2014.

[2.1527]

11 Power to order a penalty

(1) Where a tribunal—

(a) determines that a respondent has failed to comply with an order made under regulation 2 or 8; and

(b) is of the opinion that the respondent has no reasonable excuse for failing to comply with the order,

the tribunal may order the respondent to pay a penalty to the Secretary of State.

(2) Where the respondent fails to comply with an order made following a hearing fixed in accordance with regulation 8(6), the tribunal may order the respondent to pay—

(a) an additional penalty or a further additional penalty, if the tribunal previously ordered the respondent to pay a penalty or an additional penalty; or

(b) a penalty, if the tribunal previously decided not to order the respondent to pay a penalty, because the tribunal was then of the opinion that there was a reasonable excuse for not complying with an earlier order or otherwise.

(3) The tribunal must have regard to the respondent's ability to pay—

(a) in deciding whether to order the respondent to pay a penalty or an additional penalty under this regulation; and

(b) in deciding the amount of a penalty or an additional penalty.

(4) The amount of each penalty or additional penalty ordered under this regulation must not exceed £5,000.

NOTES

Commencement: 1 October 2014.

SCHEDULE
EXEMPTION FOR EXISTING MICRO-BUSINESSES AND NEW BUSINESSES

Regulation 4

[2.1528]

1. Micro-businesses

A micro-business is a business that has fewer than 10 employees.

2. Existing micro-businesses

An existing micro-business is a business that was a micro-business immediately before the date of judgment.

3. New businesses

(1) A new business is a business which a person, or a number of persons, ("P") begins to carry on during the period of 12 months ending with the date of complaint.

(2) But a business is not a new business if—

(a) P has, at any time during the period of 6 months ending immediately before the date on which P begins to carry on the business, carried on another business consisting of the activities of which the business consists (or most of them); or

(b) P carries on the business as a result of a transfer (within the meaning of sub-paragraph (4)).

(3) Sub-paragraph (2)(a) does not apply if the other business referred to in that paragraph was a new business (within the meaning of this Schedule).

(4) P carries on a business as a result of a transfer if P begins to carry on the business on another person ceasing to carry on the activities of which it consists (or most of them) in consequence of arrangements involving P and the other person.

(5) For this purpose, P is to be taken to begin to carry on a business on another person ceasing to carry on such activities if—

(a) the business begins to be carried on by P otherwise than in partnership on such activities ceasing to be carried on by persons in partnership; or

(b) P is a number of persons in partnership who begin to carry on the business on such activities ceasing to be carried on—

(i) by a person, or a number of persons, otherwise than in partnership;

(ii) by persons in partnership who do not consist only of all the persons who constitute P; or

(iii) partly as mentioned in paragraph (i) and partly as mentioned in paragraph (ii).

(6) Sub-paragraph (2)(b) does not apply if the activities referred to in sub-paragraph (4) were, when carried on by the person who is not P referred to in that paragraph, activities of a new business (within the meaning of this Schedule).

(7) P is not to be regarded as beginning to carry on a business for the purposes of sub-paragraph (1) if—

(a) before P begins to carry on the business, P is a party to arrangements under which P may (at any time during the period of 5 years beginning with the commencement date) carry on, as part of the business, activities carried on by any other person; and

(b) the business would have been prevented by sub-paragraph (2)(b) from being a new business if—

(i) P had begun to carry on the activities when beginning to carry on the business; and

(ii) the other person had at that time ceased to carry them on.

(8) "Arrangements" includes an agreement, understanding, scheme, transaction or series of transactions (whether or not legally enforceable).

4. The exemption period: existing micro-businesses

(1) The exemption period, in relation to an existing micro-business, is the period beginning with the commencement date and ending when the business is treated as ceasing to be a micro-business for the purpose of this paragraph or (if sooner) the day 10 years after the commencement date.

(2) A business is treated as ceasing to be a micro-business for the purpose of this paragraph on the day after the assessment period if, during an assessment period, the number of days when the business is not a micro-business is greater than the number of days when the business is a micro-business.

(3) An "assessment period", in relation to an existing micro-business, is a period of 6 months beginning with—

(a) the first day after the commencement date on which the business ceases to be a micro-business; or

(b) where, during an earlier assessment period, the number of days when the business is not a micro-business is less than or equal to the number of days when the business is a micro-business—

(i) the day after the end of the earlier assessment period, if on that day the business is not a micro-business; or

(ii) the first day after the end of the earlier assessment period on which the business ceases to be a micro-business, in any other case.

5. The exemption period: new businesses

(1) The exemption period, in relation to a new business, is the period beginning with the commencement date and ending with the date on which P ceases to carry on the business or (if sooner) the day 10 years after the commencement date.

(2) If P is a number of persons in partnership, P is not to be taken for this purpose to cease to carry on the business if—

(a) the members of the partnership change, or the partnership is dissolved; and

(b) after the change or dissolution, the business is carried on by at least one of the persons who constituted P.

6. Number of employees of a business

(1) For the purposes of this Schedule, the number of employees of a business is taken to be the number of its full-time equivalent employees.

(2) The number of full-time equivalent employees of a business is calculated as follows—

TH/37.5

where TH is the total number of hours per week for which all the employees of the business are contracted to work.

7. Employees of a business

For the purposes of this Schedule, the employees of a business are all persons who are employed for the purposes of the business.

8. Employees

(1) In this Schedule, "employee" means an individual who has entered into or works under a contract of employment.

(2) In sub-paragraph (1) "contract of employment" means a contract of service, whether express or implied, and (if it is express) whether oral or in writing.

9. The commencement date

For the purposes of this Schedule, "commencement date" means the date on which these Regulations come into force.

NOTES

Commencement: 1 October 2014.

SOCIAL SECURITY CONTRIBUTIONS AND BENEFITS ACT 1992 (APPLICATION OF PARTS 12ZA, 12ZB AND 12ZC TO PARENTAL ORDER CASES) REGULATIONS 2014

(SI 2014/2866)

NOTES

Made: 20 October 2014.

Authority: Social Security Contributions and Benefits Act 1992, ss 171ZK(2), 171ZT(2), 171ZZ5(2).

Commencement: 19 November 2014 (certain purposes); to be appointed (otherwise) (see reg 1 at **[2.1529]**).

[2.1529]

1 Citation, commencement and application

(1) These Regulations may be cited as the Social Security Contributions and Benefits Act 1992 (Application of Parts 12ZA, 12ZB and 12ZC to Parental Order Cases) Regulations 2014.

(2) Subject to paragraphs (3) and (4), these Regulations come into force on 19th November 2014.

(3) The modification of section 171ZB of the Social Security Contributions and Benefits Act 1992 by the insertion of subsection (3C) as set out in Schedule 1 to these Regulations comes into force on the date that section 171ZB(2)(ba) comes into force.

(4) The modification of section 171ZL of the Social Security Contributions and Benefits Act 1992 by the insertion of subsection (3B) as set out in Schedule 2 to these Regulations comes into force on the date that section 171ZL(2)(ba) comes into force.

(5) Regulation 4 does not have effect in cases involving children whose expected week of birth ends on or before 4th April 2015.

NOTES

Commencement: 19 November 2014.

Note: as of 15 May 2019, no date had been appointed for the commencement of the Welfare Reform Act 2012, s 63 which inserts s 171ZB(2)(ba) and s 171ZL(2)(ba) of the Social Security Contributions and Benefits Act 1992 (and amends various other provisions of that Act).

[2.1530]

2 Interpretation

In these Regulations—

"the Act" means the Social Security Contributions and Benefits Act 1992;

["intended parent", in relation to a child, means a person who, on the day of the child's birth—

(a) applies, or intends to apply during the period of 6 months beginning with that day—

(i) with another person for an order under section 54 of the Human Fertilisation and Embryology Act 2008 in respect of the child; or

(ii) as the sole applicant for an order under section 54A of that Act in respect of the child; and

(b) expects the court to make such an order in respect of the child;]

. . .

["section 54 parental order parent" means a person—

(a) on whose application the court has made an order under section 54 of the Human Fertilisation and Embryology Act 2008 in respect of a child; or

(b) who is an intended parent of a child by reference to an application or intended application for such an order;

"section 54A parental order parent" means a person—

(a) on whose application the court has made an order under section 54A of the Human Fertilisation and Embryology Act 2008 in respect of a child; or

(b) who is an intended parent of a child by reference to an application or intended application for such an order.]

NOTES

Commencement: 19 November 2014.

Definition "intended parent" substituted, definitions "parental order" and "parental order parent" (omitted) revoked, and definitions "section 54 parental order parent" and "section 54A parental order parent" inserted, by the Human Fertilisation and Embryology Act 2008 (Remedial) Order 2018, SI 2018/1413, art 3(2), Sch 2, para 6(1), (2), as from 3 January 2019.

[2.1531]

3 Application of Part 12ZA of the Act to parental order parents

Part 12ZA of the Act (statutory paternity pay) has effect in relation to [section 54 parental order parents] with the modifications of sections 171ZA, 171ZB and 171ZE of the Act specified in the second column of Schedule 1 to these Regulations.

NOTES

Commencement: 19 November 2014 (certain purposes); to be appointed (otherwise) (see further reg 1 and Sch 1 at **[2.1529]** and **[2.1534]**).

Words in square brackets substituted by the Human Fertilisation and Embryology Act 2008 (Remedial) Order 2018, SI 2018/1413, art 3(2), Sch 2, para 6(1), (3), as from 3 January 2019.

[2.1532]

4 Application of Part 12ZB of the Act to parental order parents

Part 12ZB of the Act (statutory adoption pay) has effect in relation to [section 54 parental order parents and section 54A parental order parents] with the modifications of sections 171ZL and 171ZN of the Act specified in the second column of Schedule 2 to these Regulations.

NOTES

Commencement: 19 November 2014 (certain purposes); to be appointed (otherwise) (see further reg 1 and Sch 2 at **[2.1529]** and **[2.1535]**).

Words in square brackets substituted by the Human Fertilisation and Embryology Act 2008 (Remedial) Order 2018, SI 2018/1413, art 3(2), Sch 2, para 6(1), (4), as from 3 January 2019.

[2.1533]

5 Application of Part 12ZC of the Act to parental order parents

Part 12ZC of the Act (statutory shared parental pay) has effect in relation to [section 54 parental order parents] with the modifications of section 171ZV of the Act specified in the second column of Schedule 3 to these Regulations.

NOTES

Commencement: 19 November 2014.

Words in square brackets substituted by the Human Fertilisation and Embryology Act 2008 (Remedial) Order 2018, SI 2018/1413, art 3(2), Sch 2, para 6(1), (5), as from 3 January 2019.

SCHEDULES

SCHEDULE 1
APPLICATION OF PART 12ZA OF THE ACT TO PARENTAL ORDER CASES

Regulation 3

[2.1534]

Provision	***Modification***
Section 171ZA	After subsection (4) insert— "(4A) A person who satisfies the conditions in section 171ZB(2)(a) to (d) in relation to a child is not entitled to statutory paternity pay under this section in respect of that child.".
Section 171ZB	For paragraph (a) of subsection (2) substitute— "(a) that he satisfies prescribed conditions as to being a person— (i) on whose application the court has made a parental order in respect of a child, or (ii) who is an intended parent of a child; (ab) that he satisfies prescribed conditions as to relationship with the other person on whose application the parental order was made or who is an intended parent of the child;". In paragraph (d) of subsection (2), for "placed for adoption" substitute "born". In paragraph (e) of subsection (2), omit "where he is a person with whom the child is placed for adoption,". For subsection (3) substitute— "(3) The references in this section to the relevant week are to the week immediately preceding the 14th week before the expected week of the child's birth.".

Provision	Modification
	After subsection (3) insert— "(3B) In a case where a child is born earlier than the 14th week before the expected week of the child's birth— (a) subsection (2)(b) shall be treated as satisfied in relation to a person if, had the birth occurred after the end of the relevant week, the person would have been in employed earner's employment with an employer for a continuous period of at least 26 weeks ending with the relevant week; (b) subsection (2)(c) shall be treated as satisfied in relation to a person if the person's normal weekly earnings for the period of 8 weeks ending with the week immediately preceding the week in which the child is born are not less than the lower earnings limit in force under section 5(1)(a) immediately before the commencement of the week in which the child is born; and (c) subsection (2)(d) shall not apply. (3C) In a case where a child is born before the end of the relevant week, subsection (2)(ba) shall be treated as satisfied in relation to a person if, had the birth occurred after the end of the relevant week, the person would have been entitled to be in the relevant employment at the end of the relevant week. In this subsection "the relevant employment" means the employment by reference to which the person satisfies the condition in subsection (2)(b).". In subsection (6), for "placement for adoption of more than one child as part of the same arrangement" substitute "birth, or expected birth, of more than one child as a result of the same pregnancy". For subsection (7) substitute— "(7) In this section— "intended parent", in relation to a child, means a person who, on the day of the child's birth— (a) applies, or intends to apply during the period of 6 months beginning with that day, with another person for a parental order in respect of the child, and (b) expects the court to make a parental order on that application in respect of the child; and "parental order" means an order under section 54(1) of the Human Fertilisation and Embryology Act 2008.". Omit subsection (8). Omit subsection (9).
Section 171ZE	In paragraph (b) of subsection (3), for "placement for adoption" substitute "birth". In subsection (4)— (a) in paragraph (a), for "sub-paragraph (i) of section 171ZA(2)(a)" substitute "section 171ZA(2)(a)(i)"; (b) in paragraph (b), for "sub-paragraph (ii) of that provision" substitute "section 171ZA(2)(a)(ii) or 171ZB(2)(ab)". In subsection (9), for "the reference in subsection (3)(a) to the date of the child's birth shall be read as a reference" substitute "the references in subsection (3)(a) and (b) to the date of the child's birth shall be read as references". Omit subsection (10). Omit subsection (12).

NOTES

Commencement: 19 November 2014 (except for the purpose of the insertion of s 171ZB(3C) above); to be appointed (otherwise; being the date on which s 171ZB(2)(ba) of the 1992 Act (as inserted by the Welfare Reform Act 2012, s 63(1), (4)(a)) comes into force).

SCHEDULE 2
APPLICATION OF PART 12ZB OF THE ACT TO PARENTAL ORDER CASES

Regulation 4

[2.1535]

Provision	*Modification*
Section 171ZL	For paragraph (a) of subsection (2) substitute— "(a) that he is— (i) a person on whose application the court has made a [an order under section 54 or 54A of the Human Fertilisation and Embryology Act 2008] in respect of a child, or (ii) an intended parent of a child;". [At the beginning of paragraph (e) of subsection (2) insert "in the case of a person on whose application the court has made an order under section 54 of the Human Fertilisation and Embryology Act 2008 or who is an intended parent of a child by reference to an application or intended application for such an order,"]. For subsection (3) substitute— "(3) The references in this section to the relevant week are to the week immediately preceding the 14th week before the expected week of the child's birth.". After subsection (3) insert— "(3A) In a case where a child is born earlier than the 14th week before the expected week of the child's birth— (a) subsection (2)(b) shall be treated as satisfied in relation to a person if, had the birth occurred after the end of the relevant week, the person would have been in employed earner's employment with an employer for a continuous period of at least 26 weeks ending with the relevant week; and (b) subsection (2)(d) shall be treated as satisfied in relation to a person if the person's normal weekly earnings for the period of 8 weeks ending with the week immediately preceding the week in which the child is born are not less than the lower earnings limit in force under section 5(1)(a) immediately before the commencement of the week in which the child is born. (3B) In a case where a child is born before the end of the relevant week, subsection (2)(ba) shall be treated as satisfied in relation to a person if, had the birth occurred after the end of the relevant week, the person would have been entitled to be in the relevant employment at the end of the relevant week. In this subsection "the relevant employment" means the employment by reference to which the person satisfies the condition in subsection (2)(b).". For paragraph (b) of subsection (4), substitute— "(b) the other person on whose application the court has made a [an order under section 54 of the Human Fertilisation and Embryology Act 2008] in respect of the child or who is an intended parent of the child— (i) is a person to whom the conditions in subsection (2) above apply, and (ii) has elected to receive statutory adoption pay.". Omit subsection (4A). Omit subsection (4B). In subsection (5), for "placement, or expected placement, for adoption of more than one child as part of the same arrangement" substitute "birth, or expected birth, of more than one child as a result of the same pregnancy". After subsection (8) insert— ["(8A) In this section— "intended parent", in relation to a child, means a person who, on the day of the child's birth— (a) applies, or intends to apply during the period of 6 months beginning with that day— (i) with another person for an order under section 54 of the Human Fertilisation and Embryology Act 2008 in respect of the child; or (ii) as the sole applicant for an order under section 54A of that Act in respect of the child; and (b) expects the court to make such an order in respect of the child.".] Omit subsection (9). Omit subsection (10).
Section 171ZN	In subsection (2F) , for "in which the person is notified that the person has been matched with a child for the purposes of adoption" substitute "immediately preceding the 14th week before the expected week of the child's birth".

Part 2 Statutory Instruments

Provision	Modification
	Omit subsection (9).

NOTES

Commencement: 19 November 2014 (except for the purpose of the insertion of s 171ZL(3B) above); to be appointed (otherwise; being the date on which s 171ZL(2)(ba) of the 1992 Act (as inserted by the Welfare Reform Act 2012, s 63(1), (8)(a)) comes into force).

In the modifications relating to s 171ZL, words in square brackets inserted or substituted by the Human Fertilisation and Embryology Act 2008 (Remedial) Order 2018, SI 2018/1413, art 3(2), Sch 2, para 6(1), (6), (7), as from 3 January 2019.

SCHEDULE 3
APPLICATION OF PART 12ZC OF THE ACT TO PARENTAL ORDER CASES

Regulation 5

[2.1536]

Provision	Modification
Section 171ZV	In subsection (1), for "with whom a child is, or is expected to be, placed for adoption under the law of any part of the United Kingdom" substitute "on whose application the court has made a parental order in respect of a child or who is an intended parent of a child". In paragraph (a) of subsection (2), for "another person" substitute "the other person on whose application the court has made a parental order in respect of the child or who is an intended parent of the child". In paragraph (g) of subsection (2), for "the placement for adoption of the child" substitute "being a person on whose application the court has made a parental order in respect of the child or being an intended parent of the child". In paragraph (a) of subsection (4), for "with whom a child is, or is expected to be, placed for adoption under the law of any part of the United Kingdom" substitute "on whose application the court has made a parental order in respect of a child or who is an intended parent of a child". In paragraph (h) of subsection (4), for "the placement for adoption of the child" substitute "being a person on whose application the court has made a parental order in respect of the child or being an intended parent of the child". In subsection (16), for "the placement for adoption of more than one child as part of the same arrangement" substitute "the birth of more than one child as a result of the same pregnancy". After subsection (16) insert— "(16A) In this section— "intended parent", in relation to a child, means a person who, on the day of the child's birth— (a) applies, or intends to apply during the period of 6 months beginning with that day, with another person for a parental order in respect of the child, and (b) expects the court to make a parental order on that application in respect of the child; and "parental order" means an order under section 54(1) of the Human Fertilisation and Embryology Act 2008.". Omit subsection (17). Omit subsection (18).

NOTES

Commencement: 19 November 2014.

STATUTORY SHARED PARENTAL PAY (ADMINISTRATION) REGULATIONS 2014

(SI 2014/2929)

NOTES

Made: 5 November 2014.

Authority: Social Security Contributions (Transfer of Functions, etc) Act 1999, ss 8(1)(f), (ga), 25(3), (6); Employment Act 2002, ss 7, 8, 10, 51(1).

Commencement: 1 December 2014.

ARRANGEMENT OF REGULATIONS

[2.1537]

1 Citation and commencement

These Regulations may be cited as the Statutory Shared Parental Pay (Administration) Regulations 2014 and come into force on 1st December 2014.

NOTES

Commencement: 1 December 2014.

[2.1538]

2 Interpretation

(1) In these Regulations—

"the 1992 Act" means the Social Security Contributions and Benefits Act 1992;

"the Commissioners" means the Commissioners for Her Majesty's Revenue and Customs;

"contributions payments" has the same meaning as in section 7 of the Employment Act 2002;

"the Contributions Regulations" means the Social Security (Contributions) Regulations 2001;

"income tax month" means the period beginning on the 6th day of any calendar month and ending on the 5th day of the following calendar month;

"income tax quarter" means the period beginning on—

(a) the 6th day of April and ending on the 5th day of July;
(b) the 6th day of July and ending on the 5th day of October;
(c) the 6th day of October and ending on the 5th day of January;
(d) the 6th day of January and ending on the 5th day of April;

"period of payment of statutory shared parental pay" means each week during which statutory shared parental pay is payable to a person under section 171ZY(2) of the 1992 Act;

"statutory shared parental pay" means statutory shared parental pay payable in accordance with the provisions of Part 12ZC of the 1992 Act;

"tax year" means the 12 months beginning with 6th April in any year;

"writing" includes writing delivered by means of electronic communications to the extent that the electronic communications are approved by directions issued by the Commissioners pursuant to regulations under section 132 of the Finance Act 1999.

(2) Any reference in these Regulations to the employees of an employer includes the employer's former employees.

NOTES

Commencement: 1 December 2014.

[2.1539]

3 Funding of employers' liabilities to make payments of statutory shared parental pay

(1) An employer who has made any payment of statutory shared parental pay shall be entitled—

(a) to an amount equal to 92% of such payment; or
(b) if the payment qualifies for small employer's relief by virtue of section 7(3) of the Employment Act 2002—
  (i) to an amount equal to such payment; and
  (ii) to an additional payment equal to the amount to which the employer would have been entitled under section 167(2)(b) of the 1992 Act had the payment been a payment of statutory maternity pay.

(2) The employer shall be entitled in either case (a) or case (b) to apply for advance funding in respect of such payment in accordance with regulation 4, or to deduct it in accordance with regulation 5 from amounts otherwise payable by the employer.

NOTES

Commencement: 1 December 2014.

[2.1540]

4 Applications for funding from the Commissioners

(1) An employer may apply to the Commissioners for funds to pay the statutory shared parental pay (or so much of it as remains outstanding) to the employee or employees in a form approved for that purpose by the Commissioners where—

(a) the conditions in paragraph (2) are satisfied; or

(b) the condition in paragraph (2)(a) is satisfied and the employer considers that the condition in paragraph (2)(b) will be satisfied on the date of any subsequent payment of emoluments to one or more employees who are entitled to payment of statutory shared parental pay.

(2) The conditions in this paragraph are—

(a) the employer is entitled to a payment determined in accordance with regulation 3 in respect of statutory shared parental pay which the employer is required to pay to an employee or employees for an income tax month or income tax quarter; and

(b) the payment exceeds the aggregate of—

(i) the total amount of tax which the employer is required to pay to the collector of taxes in respect of the deduction from the emoluments of employees in accordance with the Income Tax (Pay as You Earn) Regulations 2003 for the same income tax month or income tax quarter;

(ii) the total amount of the deductions made by the employer from the emoluments of employees for the same income tax month or income tax quarter in accordance with regulations under section 22(5) of the Teaching and Higher Education Act 1998 or under section 73B of the Education (Scotland) Act 1980 or in accordance with article 3(5) of the Education (Student Support) (Northern Ireland) Order 1998;

(iii) the total amount of contributions payments which the employer is required to pay to the collector of taxes in respect of the emoluments of employees (whether by means of deduction or otherwise) in accordance with the Contributions Regulations for the same income tax month or income tax quarter; and

(iv) the total amount of payments which the employer is required to pay to the collector of taxes in respect of the deductions made on account of tax from payments to sub-contractors in accordance with section 61 of the Finance Act 2004 for the same income tax month or income quarter.

(3) An application by an employer under paragraph (1) shall be for an amount up to, but not exceeding, the amount of the payment to which the employer is entitled in accordance with regulation 3 in respect of statutory shared parental pay which the employer is required to pay to an employee or employees for the income tax month or income tax quarter to which the payment of emoluments relates.

NOTES

Commencement: 1 December 2014.

[2.1541]

5 Deductions from payments to the Commissioners

An employer who is entitled to a payment determined in accordance with regulation 3 may recover such payment by making one or more deductions from the aggregate of the amounts specified in sub-paragraphs (i) to (iv) of regulation 4(2)(b) except where and in so far as—

(a) those amounts relate to earnings paid before the beginning of the income tax month or income tax quarter in which the payment of statutory shared parental pay was made;

(b) those amounts are paid by the employer later than six years after the end of the tax year in which the payment of statutory shared parental pay was made;

(c) the employer has received payment from the Commissioners under regulation 4; or

(d) the employer has made a request in writing under regulation 4 that the payment to which the employer is entitled in accordance with regulation 3 be paid and the employer has not received notification by the Commissioners that the request is refused.

NOTES

Commencement: 1 December 2014.

[2.1542]

6 Payments to employers by the Commissioners

The Commissioners shall pay the employer such amount as the employer was unable to deduct where—

(a) the Commissioners are satisfied that the total amount which the employer is or would otherwise be entitled to deduct under regulation 5 is less than the payment to which the employer is entitled in accordance with regulation 3 in an income tax month or income tax quarter; and

(b) the employer has in writing requested the Commissioners to do so.

NOTES

Commencement: 1 December 2014.

[2.1543]
7 Date when certain contributions are to be treated as paid

Where an employee has made a deduction from a contributions payment under regulation 5, the date on which it is to be treated as having been paid for the purposes of subsection (5) of section 7 (funding of employers' liabilities) of the Employment 2002 is—

(a) in a case where the deduction did not extinguish the contributions payment, the date on which the remainder of the contributions payment or, as the case may be, the first date on which any part of the remainder of the contributions payment was paid; and

(b) in a case where deduction extinguished the contributions payment, the 14th day after the end of the income tax month or income tax quarter during which there were paid the earnings in respect of which the contributions payment was payable.

NOTES

Commencement: 1 December 2014.

[2.1544]
8 Overpayments

(1) This regulation applies where funds have been provided to the employer pursuant to regulation 4 in respect of one or more employees and it appears to an officer of Revenue and Customs that the employer has not used the whole or part of those funds to pay statutory shared parental pay.

(2) An officer of Revenue and Customs shall decide to the best of the officer's judgement the amount of funds provided pursuant to regulation 4 and not used to pay statutory shared parental pay and shall serve notice in writing of this decision on the employer.

(3) A decision under this regulation may cover funds provided pursuant to regulation 4—

(a) for any one income tax month or income tax quarter, or more than one income tax month or income tax quarter, in a tax year; and

(b) in respect of a class or classes of employees specified in the decision notice (without naming the individual employees), or in respect of one or more employees named in the decision notice.

(4) Subject to the following provisions of this regulation, Part 6 of the Taxes Management Act 1970 (collection and recovery) shall apply with any necessary modifications to a decision under this regulation as if it were an assessment and as if the amount of funds determined were income tax charged on the employer.

(5) Where an amount of funds determined under this regulation relates to more than one employee, proceedings may be brought for the recovery of that amount without distinguishing the amounts making up that sum which the employer is liable to repay in respect of each employee and without specifying the employee in question, and the amount determined under this regulation shall be one cause of action or one matter of complaint for the purposes of proceedings under section 65, 66 or 67 of the Taxes Management Act 1970.

(6) Nothing in paragraph (5) prevents the bringing of separate proceedings for the recovery of any amount which the employer is liable to repay in respect of each employee.

NOTES

Commencement: 1 December 2014.

[2.1545]
9 Records to be maintained by employers

Every employer shall maintain for three years after the end of a tax year in which the employer made payments of statutory shared parental pay to any employee a record of—

(a) if the employee's period of payment of statutory shared parental pay began in that year—

(i) the date of which that period began; and

(ii) the evidence of entitlement to statutory shared parental pay provided by the employee pursuant to regulations made under section 171ZW(1)(b) of the 1992 Act;

(b) the weeks in that tax year in which statutory shared parental pay was paid to the employee and the amount paid in each week;

(c) any week in that tax year which was within the employee's period of payment of statutory shared parental pay but for which no payment of statutory shared parental pay was made to the employee and the reason no payment was made.

NOTES

Commencement: 1 December 2014.

[2.1546]
10 Inspection of employers' records

(1) Every employer, whenever called upon to do so by any authorised officer of Revenue and Customs, shall produce the documents and records specified in paragraph (2) to that officer for inspection, at such time as that officer may reasonably require, at the prescribed place.

(2) The documents and records specified in this paragraph are—

(a) all wage sheets, deductions working sheets, records kept in accordance with regulation 9 and other documents relating to the calculation or payment of statutory shared parental pay to employees in respect of the years specified by such officer; or

(b) such of those wages sheets, deductions working sheets, or other documents and records as may be specified by the authorised officer.

(3) The "prescribed place" mentioned in paragraph (1) means—

(a) such place in Great Britain as the employer and the authorised officer may agree upon; or

(b) in default of such agreement, the place in Great Britain at which the documents and records referred to in paragraph (2)(a) are normally kept; or

(c) in default of such agreement and if there is no such place as it referred to in sub-paragraph (b), the employer's principal place of business in Great Britain.

(4) The authorised officer may—

(a) take copies of, or make extracts from, any document or record produced to the authorised officer for inspection in accordance with paragraph (1); and

(b) remove any document or record so produced if it appears to the authorised officer to be necessary to do so, at a reasonable time and for a reasonable period.

(5) Where any document or record is removed in accordance with paragraph (4)(b), the authorised officer shall provide—

(a) a receipt for the document or record so removed; and

(b) a copy of the document or record, free of charge, within seven days, to the person by whom it was produced or caused to be produced where the document or record is reasonably required for the proper conduct of business.

(6) Where a lien is claimed on a document produced in accordance with paragraph (1), the removal of the document under paragraph (4)(b) shall not be regarded as breaking the lien.

(7) Where records are maintained by computer, the person required to make them available for inspection shall provide the authorised officer with all facilities necessary for obtaining information from them.

NOTES

Commencement: 1 December 2014.

[2.1547]

11 Provision of information relating to entitlement to statutory shared parental pay

(1) An employer shall furnish the employee with details of a decision that the employer has no liability to make payments of statutory shared parental pay to the employee and the reason for it where the employer—

(a) has been given evidence of entitlement to statutory shared parental pay pursuant to regulations made under section 171ZW(1)(b) of the 1992 Act; and

(b) decides that they have no liability to make payments of statutory shared parental pay to the employee.

(2) An employer who has been given such evidence of entitlement to statutory shared parental pay shall furnish the employee with the information specified in paragraph (3) where the employer—

(a) has made one or more payments of statutory shared parental pay to the employee but,

(b) decides, before the end of the period of payment of statutory shared parental pay, that they have no liability to make further payments to the employee because the employee has been detained in legal custody or sentenced to a term of imprisonment which was not suspended.

(3) The information specified in this paragraph is—

(a) details of the employer's decision and the reasons for it; and

(b) details of the last week in respect of which a liability to pay statutory shared parental pay arose and the total number of weeks within the period of payment of statutory shared parental pay in which such liability arose.

(4) The employer shall—

(a) return to the employee any evidence provided by the employee as referred to in paragraph (1) or (2);

(b) comply with the requirements imposed by paragraph (1) within 28 days of the day the employee gave evidence of entitlement to statutory shared parental pay pursuant to regulations made under section 171ZW(1)(b) of the 1992 Act; and

(c) comply with the requirements imposed by paragraph (2) within seven days of being notified of the employee's detention or sentence.

NOTES

Commencement: 1 December 2014.

[2.1548]

12 Application for the determination of any issue arising as to, or in connection with, entitlement to statutory shared parental pay

(1) An application for the determination of any issue arising as to, or in connection with, entitlement to statutory shared parental pay may be submitted to an officer of Revenue and Customs by the employee concerned.

(2) Such an issue shall be decided by an officer of Revenue and Customs only on the basis of such an application or on their own initiative.

NOTES

Commencement: 1 December 2014.

[2.1549]

13 Applications in connection with statutory shared parental pay

(1) An application for the determination of any issue referred to in regulation 12 shall be made in a form approved for the purpose by the Commissioners.

(2) Where such an application is made by an employee, it shall—

(a) be made to an officer of Revenue and Customs within six months of the earliest day in respect of which entitlement to statutory shared parental pay is an issue;

(b) state the period in respect of which entitlement to statutory shared parental pay is in issue; and

(c) state the grounds (if any) on which the applicant's employer had denied liability for statutory shared parental pay in respect of the period specified in the application.

NOTES

Commencement: 1 December 2014.

[2.1550]

14 Provision of information

(1) Where an officer of Revenue and Customs—

(a) reasonably requires information or documents from a person specified in paragraph (2) to ascertain whether statutory shared parental pay is or was payable, and

(b) gives notification to that person requesting such information or documents,

that person shall furnish that information within 30 days of receiving the notification.

(2) The requirement to provide such information or documents applies to—

(a) any person claiming to be entitled to statutory shared parental pay;

(b) any person who is, or has been, the spouse, civil partner or partner of such a person as is specified in sub-paragraph (a);

(c) any person who is, or has been, an employer of such a person as is specified in sub-paragraph (a);

(d) any person carrying on an agency or other business for the introduction or supply of persons available to do work or to perform services to persons requiring them; and

(e) any person who is a servant or agent of any such person as is specified in sub-paragraphs (a) to (d).

NOTES

Commencement: 1 December 2014.

STATUTORY PATERNITY PAY AND STATUTORY ADOPTION PAY (PARENTAL ORDERS AND PROSPECTIVE ADOPTERS) REGULATIONS 2014

(SI 2014/2934)

NOTES

Made: 5 November 2014.

Authority: Social Security Contributions and Benefits Act 1992, ss 171ZB(2)(a), 171ZC(1A), (3)(a), (c), (d), (f), (g), 171ZD(2), (3), 171ZE(2), (3), (7), (8), 171ZG(3), 171ZJ(1), (3), (4), (7), (8), 171ZL(8)(b)–(d), (f), (g), 171ZM(2), (3), 171ZN(2), (5), (6), 171ZP(6), 171ZS(1), (3), (4), (7), (8), 175(4); Social Security Administration Act 1992, s 5(1)(g), (i), (p); Employment Act 2002, ss 8(1), (2)(c), 51(1).

Commencement: 1 December 2014.

PART 1
GENERAL

[2.1551]

1 Citation and commencement

These Regulations may be cited as the Statutory Paternity Pay and Statutory Adoption Pay (Parental Orders and Prospective Adopters) Regulations 2014 and come into force on 1st December 2014.

NOTES

Commencement: 1 December 2014.

[2.1552]

2 Interpretation

In these Regulations—

"Administration Regulations" means the Statutory Paternity Pay and Statutory Adoption Pay (Administration) Regulations 2002;

["intended parent", in relation to a child, means a person who, on the day of the child's birth—

(a) applies, or intends to apply during the period of 6 months beginning with that day—

(i) with another person for an order under section 54 of the Human Fertilisation and Embryology Act 2008 in respect of the child; or

(ii) as the sole applicant for an order under section 54A of that Act in respect of the child; and

(b) expects the court to make such an order in respect of the child;]

. . .

"Pay Regulations" means the Statutory Paternity Pay and Statutory Adoption Pay (General) Regulations 2002;

["section 54 parental order parent" means a person—

(a) on whose application the court has made an order under section 54 of the Human Fertilisation and Embryology Act 2008 in respect of a child; or

(b) who is an intended parent of a child by reference to an application or intended application for such an order;

"section 54A parental order parent" means a person—

(a) on whose application the court has made an order under section 54A of the Human Fertilisation and Embryology Act 2008 in respect of a child; or

(b) who is an intended parent of a child by reference to an application or intended application for such an order.]

NOTES

Commencement: 1 December 2014.

Definitions "intended parent", "section 54 parental order parent", "section 54A parental order parent" inserted and definition "parental order parent" (omitted) revoked, by the Human Fertilisation and Embryology Act 2008 (Remedial) Order 2018, SI 2018/1413, art 3(2), Sch 2, para 7(1), (2), as from 3 January 2019.

[2.1553]

3

(1) The amendments made in Part 2 and 4 of these Regulations have effect only in relation to children matched with a person who is notified of having been matched on or after 5th April 2015.

(2) For the purposes of paragraph (1)—

(a) a person is matched with a child for adoption when an adoption agency decides that that person would be a suitable adoptive parent for the child;

(b) in a case where paragraph (a) applies, a person is notified as having been matched with a child on the date that person receives notification of the agency's decision, under regulation 33(3)(a) of the Adoption Agencies Regulations 2005, regulation 28(3) of the Adoption Agencies (Wales) Regulations 2005 or regulation 8(5) of the Adoption Agencies (Scotland) Regulations 2009;

(c) a person is also matched with a child for adoption when a decision has been made in accordance with regulation 22A of the Care Planning, Placement and Case Review (England) Regulations 2010 and an adoption agency has identified that person with whom the child is to be placed in accordance with regulation 12B of the Adoption Agencies Regulations 2005;

(d) in a case where paragraph (c) applies, a person is notified as having been matched with a child on the date on which that person receives notification in accordance with regulation 12B(2)(a) of the Adoption Agencies Regulations 2005.

(3) In paragraph (2) "adoption agency" has the meaning given, in relation to England and Wales, by section 2 of the Adoption and Children Act 2002 and in relation to Scotland, by section 119(1) of the Adoption and Children (Scotland) Act 2007.

NOTES

Commencement: 1 December 2014.

4, 5 *((Pt 2) Amends the Statutory Paternity Pay and Statutory Adoption Pay (General) Regulations 2002, SI 2002/2822, regs 2, 22 at* **[2.626]**, **[2.648]**.

PART 3
APPLICATION AND MODIFICATION OF THE PAY REGULATIONS IN PARENTAL ORDER CASES

[2.1554]

6 Application of the Pay Regulations to intended parents and parental order parents

[(1) The provisions of the Pay Regulations, in so far as they apply to statutory paternity pay (adoption), shall apply to a section 54 parental order parent with the modifications set out in this Part of these Regulations.

(1A) The provisions of the Pay Regulations, in so far as they apply to statutory adoption pay, shall apply to—

(a) a section 54 parental order parent; and

(b) a section 54A parental order parent,

with the modifications set out in this Part of these Regulations.]

(2) In this regulation—

"statutory adoption pay" means statutory adoption pay payable in accordance with the provisions of Part 12ZB of the Social Security Contributions and Benefits Act 1992;

"statutory paternity pay (adoption)" means statutory paternity pay payable in accordance with the provisions of Part 12ZA of the Social Security Contributions and Benefits Act 1992 where the conditions specified in section 171ZB(2) of that Act are satisfied.

NOTES

Commencement: 1 December 2014.

Paras (1), (1A): substituted for original para (1), by the Human Fertilisation and Embryology Act 2008 (Remedial) Order 2018, SI 2018/1413, art 3(2), Sch 2, para 7(1), (3), as from 3 January 2019.

[2.1555]
7

In regulation 2 (interpretation) of the Pay Regulations as they apply to an intended parent or a parental order parent—

(a) paragraph (1) shall read as if—
  (i) the definition of "adopter" were omitted;
  (ii) there were the following definitions—

"["intended parent", in relation to a child, means a person who, on the day of the child's birth—
  (a) applies, or intends to apply during the period of 6 months beginning with that day—
    (i) with another person for an order under section 54 of the Human Fertilisation and Embryology Act 2008 in respect of the child; or
    (ii) as the sole applicant for an order under section 54A of that Act in respect of the child; and
  (b) expects the court to make such an order in respect of the child;]

"Parent A" in relation to a child means [the section 54 parental order parent] who has elected to be Parent A;

. . .

["section 54 parental order parent" means a person—
  (a) on whose application the court has made an order under section 54 of the Human Fertilisation and Embryology Act 2008 in respect of a child; or
  (b) who is an intended parent of a child by reference to an application or intended application for such an order;

"section 54A parental order parent" means a person—
  (a) on whose application the court has made an order under section 54A of the Human Fertilisation and Embryology Act 2008 in respect of a child; or
  (b) who is an intended parent of a child by reference to an application or intended application for such an order;]

"statutory shared parental pay" means statutory shared parental pay payable in accordance with Part 12ZC of the Act;";

(b) paragraph (2) shall apply as if that paragraph read—

"(2) [A section 54 parental order parent] elects to be Parent A in relation to a child if that person (A) agrees with [the other section 54 parental order parent] of the child (B) that A and not B will be parent A.".

NOTES

Commencement: 1 December 2014.

Words in square brackets inserted or substituted and words omitted revoked, by the Human Fertilisation and Embryology Act 2008 (Remedial) Order 2018, SI 2018/1413, art 3(2), Sch 2, para 7(1), (4), as from 3 January 2019.

[2.1556]
8

In regulation 3 (application) of the Pay Regulations [as they apply to a section 54 parental order parent]—

(a) paragraph (1)(b) shall read as if sub-paragraphs (i) and (ii) were omitted and replaced by—

"whose expected week of birth begins on or after 5th April 2015".

(b) paragraph (2) shall read as if sub-paragraphs (a) and (b) were omitted and replaced by—

"whose expected week of birth begins on or after 5th April 2015".

NOTES

Commencement: 1 December 2014.

Words in square brackets substituted by the Human Fertilisation and Embryology Act 2008 (Remedial) Order 2018, SI 2018/1413, art 3(2), Sch 2, para 7(1), (5), as from 3 January 2019.

[2.1557]
[8A

Regulation 3 (application) of the Pay Regulations as they apply to a section 54A parental order parent shall read as if—

(a) paragraph (1) were omitted; and
(b) for paragraph (2) there were substituted—

"(2) Subject to the provisions of Part 12ZB of the Act (statutory adoption pay) and of these Regulations, there is entitlement to statutory adoption pay in respect of children whose expected week of birth begins on or after the day which follows the last day of the period of 120 days beginning with the day on which the Human Fertilisation and Embryology Act 2008 (Remedial) Order 2018 comes into force.".]

NOTES

Commencement: 3 January 2019.

Inserted by the Human Fertilisation and Embryology Act 2008 (Remedial) Order 2018, SI 2018/1413, art 3(2), Sch 2, para 7(1), (6), as from 3 January 2019.

[2.1558]
9

In regulation 11 (conditions of entitlement) of the Pay Regulations [as they apply to a section 54 parental order parent]—

(a) paragraph (1) shall apply as if sub-paragraphs (a) and (b) were omitted and replaced by—

"(a) is [a section 54] parental order parent in relation to the child;

(b) is married to, the civil partner or the partner of Parent A; and

(c) has or expects to have the main responsibility for the upbringing of the child (apart from the responsibility of Parent A)."

(b) paragraph (2) shall read as if the words "the adopter" in both places where those words occur were "Parent A";

(c) paragraph (2A) shall read as if the words "the adopter" in both places where those words occur were "Parent A".

NOTES

Commencement: 1 December 2014.

Words in square brackets substituted by the Human Fertilisation and Embryology Act 2008 (Remedial) Order 2018, SI 2018/1413, art 3(2), Sch 2, para 7(1), (7), as from 3 January 2019.

[2.1559]
10

Regulation 11A (notice of entitlement to statutory paternity pay (adoption)) of the Pay Regulations [as they apply to a section 54 parental order parent] shall apply as if paragraphs (a) and (b) read—

"(a) in or before the 15th week before the expected week of the child's birth; or

(b) in a case where it was not reasonably practicable for the employee to give the notice in accordance with paragraph (a), as soon as reasonably practicable.".

NOTES

Commencement: 1 December 2014.

Words in square brackets substituted by the Human Fertilisation and Embryology Act 2008 (Remedial) Order 2018, SI 2018/1413, art 3(2), Sch 2, para 7(1), (8), as from 3 January 2019.

[2.1560]
11

In regulation 12 (period of payment of statutory paternity pay (adoption)) of the Pay Regulations [as they apply to a section 54 parental order parent]—

(a) paragraph (1) shall apply as if that paragraph read—

"(1) Subject to regulation 14, a person entitled to statutory paternity pay (adoption) may choose the statutory pay period to begin—

(a) on the date on which the child is born or, where the person is at work on that day, the following day;

(b) the date falling such number of days after the date on which the child is born as the person may specify; or

(c) a predetermined date, specified by the person which is later than the expected week of the child's birth.";

(b) paragraph (2) shall not apply;

(c) paragraph (4) shall apply as if sub-paragraphs (a) to (c) read—

"(a) where the variation is to provide for the employee's statutory paternity pay period to begin on the date on which the child is born, or where the employee is at work on that day, the following day, at least 28 days before the first day of the expected week of the child's birth,

(b) where the variation is to provide for the employee's statutory paternity pay period to begin on a date that is a specified number of days (or a different specified number of days) after the date on which the child is born, at least 28 days before the date falling that number of days after the first day of the expected week of the child's birth,

(c) where the variation is to provide for the employee's statutory paternity pay period to begin on a predetermined date (or a different predetermined date), at least 28 days before that date,".

NOTES

Commencement: 1 December 2014.

Words in square brackets substituted by the Human Fertilisation and Embryology Act 2008 (Remedial) Order 2018, SI 2018/1413, art 3(2), Sch 2, para 7(1), (9), as from 3 January 2019.

[2.1561]
12

In regulation 13 (additional notice requirements for statutory paternity pay (adoption)) of the Pay Regulations [as they apply to a section 54 parental order parent]—

(a) paragraph (1) shall read as if the words "the date on which the placement occurred" were "the date on which the child was born";

(b) paragraph (2) shall read as if the words "is placed for adoption" were "is born".

NOTES

Commencement: 1 December 2014.

Words in square brackets substituted by the Human Fertilisation and Embryology Act 2008 (Remedial) Order 2018, SI 2018/1413, art 3(2), Sch 2, para 7(1), (10), as from 3 January 2019.

[2.1562]
13

In regulation 14 (qualifying period for statutory paternity pay (adoption)) of the Pay Regulations [as they apply to a section 54 parental order parent] shall read as if the words "of 56 days" to the end were omitted and replaced by—

"which begins on the date of the child's birth and ends—

(a) except in the case referred to in paragraph (b), 56 days after that date;

(b) in a case where the child is born before the first day of the expected week of its birth, 56 days after that day.".

NOTES

Commencement: 1 December 2014.

Words in square brackets substituted by the Human Fertilisation and Embryology Act 2008 (Remedial) Order 2018, SI 2018/1413, art 3(2), Sch 2, para 7(1), (11), as from 3 January 2019.

[2.1563]
14

In regulation 15 (evidence of entitlement for statutory paternity pay (adoption)) of the Pay Regulations [as they apply to a section 54 parental order parent]—

(a) paragraph (2)(b) shall apply as if that paragraph read—

"(b) the expected week of the child's birth;";

(b) paragraph (2)(e) shall apply as if that paragraph read—

"(e) the date on which the child was born";

(c) paragraph (3) shall apply as if sub-paragraphs (a) and (b) read—

"(a) in or before the 15th week before the expected week of the child's birth;

(b) in a case where it was not reasonably practicable for the employee to provide it in accordance with sub-paragraph (a), as soon as reasonably practicable.";

(d) paragraph (4) shall read as if the words "child's placement" were "child's birth".

NOTES

Commencement: 1 December 2014.

Words in square brackets substituted by the Human Fertilisation and Embryology Act 2008 (Remedial) Order 2018, SI 2018/1413, art 3(2), Sch 2, para 7(1), (12), as from 3 January 2019.

[2.1564]
15

In regulation 16 (entitlement to statutory paternity pay (adoption) where there is more than one employer) of the Pay Regulations [as they apply to a section 54 parental order parent], paragraph (b) shall read as if the words "in which the adopter is notified of being matched with the child" were "immediately preceding the 14th week before the expected week of the child's birth".

NOTES

Commencement: 1 December 2014.

Words in square brackets substituted by the Human Fertilisation and Embryology Act 2008 (Remedial) Order 2018, SI 2018/1413, art 3(2), Sch 2, para 7(1), (13), as from 3 January 2019.

[2.1565]
16

In regulation 20 (avoidance of liability for statutory paternity pay) of the Pay Regulations [as they apply to a section 54 parental order parent], paragraph (2)(a) shall read as if the words "or, as the case may be, the placement of the child for adoption" were omitted.

NOTES

Commencement: 1 December 2014.

Words in square brackets substituted by the Human Fertilisation and Embryology Act 2008 (Remedial) Order 2018, SI 2018/1413, art 3(2), Sch 2, para 7(1), (14), as from 3 January 2019.

[2.1566]
17

(1) In regulation 21 (adoption pay period) of the Pay Regulations [as they apply to a section 54 parental order parent or a section 54A parental order parent], paragraph (1) shall read as if that paragraph read—

"(1) The adoption pay period in respect of a person entitled to statutory adoption pay shall begin on the day on which the child is born or, where the person is at work on that day, the following day.".

(2) Paragraph (2), (3), (4) and (6) shall not apply.

NOTES

Commencement: 1 December 2014.

Words in square brackets substituted by the Human Fertilisation and Embryology Act 2008 (Remedial) Order 2018, SI 2018/1413, art 3(2), Sch 2, para 7(1), (15), as from 3 January 2019.

[2.1567]
18

In regulation 22 (adoption pay period in cases where adoption is disrupted) of the Pay Regulations [as they apply to a section 54 parental order parent]—

(a) paragraph (1) shall apply as if that paragraph read—

"(1) The adoption pay period shall terminate in accordance with the provisions of paragraph (2) where—

(a) the child dies;

[(b) the section 54 parental order parent who is entitled to statutory adoption pay does not apply for an order under section 54 of the Human Fertilisation and Embryology Act 2008 in respect of the child within the time limit set by subsection (3) of that section;] or

(c) the that person's application for [an order under that section] in respect of the child is refused, withdrawn or otherwise terminated and any time limit for an appeal or a new application has expired;";

(b) in paragraph (3)—

(i) sub-paragraph (a) shall apply as if the reference to paragraph (1)(a)(i) were a reference to paragraph (1)(a);

(ii) sub-paragraph (b) shall apply as if that sub-paragraph read—

"(b) in a case falling within paragraph (1)(b) the week during which the time limit in section 54(3) of the Human Fertilisation and Embryology Act 2008 for an application for [an order under that section] for the child expires;";

(iii) sub-paragraph (c) shall apply as if that sub-paragraph read—

"(c) in a case falling within paragraph (1)(c) the week during which the person's application for [an order under that section] is refused, withdrawn or otherwise terminated without the order being granted.".

NOTES

Commencement: 1 December 2014.

Words in square brackets substituted by the Human Fertilisation and Embryology Act 2008 (Remedial) Order 2018, SI 2018/1413, art 3(2), Sch 2, para 7(1), (16), as from 3 January 2019.

[2.1568]
[18A

In regulation 22 (adoption pay period in cases where adoption is disrupted) of the Pay Regulations as they apply to a section 54A parental order parent—

(a) paragraph (1) shall apply as if that paragraph read—

"(1) The adoption pay period shall terminate in accordance with the provisions of paragraph (2) where—

(a) the child dies;

(b) the section 54A parental order parent does not apply for an order under section 54A of the Human Fertilisation and Embryology Act 2008 in respect of the child within the time limit set by subsection (2) of that section; or

(c) the section 54A parental order parent's application for an order under that section in respect of the child is refused, withdrawn or otherwise terminated and any time limit for an appeal or a new application has expired."; and

(b) in paragraph (3)—

(i) sub-paragraph (a) shall apply as if the reference to paragraph (1)(a)(i) were a reference to paragraph (1)(a);

(ii) sub-paragraph (b) shall apply as if that sub-paragraph read—

"(b) in a case falling within paragraph (1)(b) the week during which the time limit in section 54A(2) of the Human Fertilisation and Embryology Act 2008 for an application for an order under that section for the child expires;"; and

(iii) sub-paragraph (c) shall apply as if that sub-paragraph read—

"(c) in a case falling within paragraph (1)(c) the week during which the section 54A parental order parent's application for an order under that section is refused, withdrawn or otherwise terminated without the order being granted.".]

NOTES

Commencement: 3 January 2019.

Inserted by the Human Fertilisation and Embryology Act 2008 (Remedial) Order 2018, SI 2018/1413, art 3(2), Sch 2, para 7(1), (17), as from 3 January 2019.

[2.1569]
19

In regulation 23 (additional notice requirements for statutory adoption pay) of the Pay Regulations [as they apply to a section 54 parental order parent or a section 54A parental order parent]—

(a) paragraph (1) shall read as if the words "the date on which the child is expected to be placed for adoption" were "the expected week of the child's birth";

(b) paragraph (2) shall read as if—

(i) the words from "Where the choice" to "sub-paragraph (a) of that paragraph," were omitted;

(ii) the words "the date the child is placed for adoption" were "the date on which the child is born".

NOTES

Commencement: 1 December 2014.

Words in square brackets substituted by the Human Fertilisation and Embryology Act 2008 (Remedial) Order 2018, SI 2018/1413, art 3(2), Sch 2, para 7(1), (18), as from 3 January 2019.

[2.1570]
20

In regulation 24 (evidence of entitlement to statutory adoption pay) of the Pay Regulations [as they apply to a section 54 parental order parent]—

(a) in paragraph (1), sub-paragraph (a) shall apply as if that sub-paragraph read—

"(a) a statutory declaration specified in paragraph (2) where the person who will be liable to pay the statutory adoption pay requests it in accordance with paragraph (3)";

(b) paragraph (2) shall apply as if that paragraph read—

"(2) The statutory declaration referred to in paragraph (1)(a) is a statutory declaration stating that the person making the declaration—

(a) has applied, or intends to apply, under section 54 of the Human Fertilisation and Embryology Act 2008 with another person for [an order under that section] in respect of the child within the time limit for making such an application; and

(b) expects the court to make [an order under that section] on that application in respect of the child.";

(c) paragraph (3) shall apply as if that paragraph read—

"(3) The declaration in referred to—

(a) in paragraph (1)(a) shall be provided to the person liable to pay statutory adoption pay within 14 days of that person requesting that declaration where the person requests it within 14 days of receiving the notice under section 171ZL(6) of the Act;

(b) in paragraph (1)(b) shall be provided to the person liable to pay statutory adoption pay at least 28 days before the beginning of the adoption pay period, or if that is not reasonably practicable , as soon as reasonably practicable after that date.".

NOTES

Commencement: 1 December 2014.

Words in square brackets substituted by the Human Fertilisation and Embryology Act 2008 (Remedial) Order 2018, SI 2018/1413, art 3(2), Sch 2, para 7(1), (19), as from 3 January 2019.

[2.1571]
[20A

In regulation 24 (evidence of entitlement to statutory adoption pay) of the Pay Regulations as they apply to a section 54A parental order parent—

"24

(1) A section 54A parental order parent shall provide evidence of his or her entitlement to statutory adoption pay by providing to the person who will be liable to pay it ("E") a statutory declaration specified in paragraph (2) where E requests it in accordance with paragraph (3).

(2) The statutory declaration referred to in paragraph (1) is a statutory declaration stating that the person making the declaration—

(a) has applied, or intends to apply, under section 54A of the Human Fertilisation and Embryology Act 2008 for an order under that section in respect of the child within the time limit for making such an application; and

(b) expects the court to make an order under that section on that application in respect of the child.

(3) The declaration referred to in paragraph (1) shall be provided to E within 14 days of E requesting that declaration where E requests it within 14 days of receiving the notice under section 171ZL(6) of the Act.".]

NOTES

Commencement: 3 January 2019.

Inserted by the Human Fertilisation and Embryology Act 2008 (Remedial) Order 2018, SI 2018/1413, art 3(2), Sch 2, para 7(1), (20), as from 3 January 2019.

[2.1572]
21

In regulation 25 (entitlement to statutory adoption pay where there is more than one employer) of the Pay Regulations [as they apply to a section 54 parental order parent or a section 54A parental order parent], paragraph (b) shall read as if the words "in which he is notified of being matched with the child" were "immediately preceding the 14th week before the expected week of the child's birth".

NOTES

Commencement: 1 December 2014.

Words in square brackets substituted by the Human Fertilisation and Embryology Act 2008 (Remedial) Order 2018, SI 2018/1413, art 3(2), Sch 2, para 7(1), (21), as from 3 January 2019.

[2.1573]
22

In regulation 29 (termination of employment before start of adoption pay period) of the Pay Regulations [as they apply to a section 54 parental order parent or a section 54A parental order parent], paragraph (1) shall apply as if—

(a) the words "chosen in accordance with regulation 21" were omitted;

(b) the words "14 days before the expected date of placement" to the end were "on the day on which the child is born".

NOTES

Commencement: 1 December 2014.

Words in square brackets substituted by the Human Fertilisation and Embryology Act 2008 (Remedial) Order 2018, SI 2018/1413, art 3(2), Sch 2, para 7(1), (22), as from 3 January 2019.

[2.1574]
23

In regulation 30 (avoidance of liability for statutory adoption pay) of the Pay Regulations [as they apply to a section 54 parental order parent or a section 54A parental order parent], in paragraph (2), sub-paragraph (a) shall read as if the words "in which he was notified of having been matched with the child for adoption" read "immediately preceding the 14th week before the expected week of the child's birth".

NOTES

Commencement: 1 December 2014.

Words in square brackets substituted by the Human Fertilisation and Embryology Act 2008 (Remedial) Order 2018, SI 2018/1413, art 3(2), Sch 2, para 7(1), (23), as from 3 January 2019.

[2.1575]
24

In regulation 40 (normal weekly earnings) of the Pay Regulations [as they apply to a section 54 parental order parent or a section 54A parental order parent], in paragraph (2), the definition of "the appropriate date" shall read—

""the appropriate date" means in relation to statutory paternity pay (adoption) and statutory adoption pay , the first day of the 14th week before the expected week of the child's birth or the first day in the week in which the child is born, whichever is earlier;".

NOTES

Commencement: 1 December 2014.

Words in square brackets substituted by the Human Fertilisation and Embryology Act 2008 (Remedial) Order 2018, SI 2018/1413, art 3(2), Sch 2, para 7(1), (24), as from 3 January 2019.

25 *((Pt 4) Amends the Statutory Paternity Pay and Statutory Adoption Pay (Administration) Regulations 2002, SI 2002/2820, reg 11 at* **[2.621]**.

PART 5
MODIFICATION OF THE ADMINISTRATION REGULATIONS IN PARENTAL ORDER CASES

[2.1576]
26

In the case of entitlement to statutory paternity pay or statutory adoption pay under section 171ZB or 171ZL of the Social Security Contributions and Benefits Act 1992 [as those sections apply to a section 54 parental order parent or a section 54A parental order parent]—

(a) paragraph (3)(b)(ii) of regulation 11 (provision of information) of the Administration Regulations shall read as if the words from "the end of the seven day period that starts on the date on which the adopter is notified of having been matched with the child" were—

"the day the employee gave notice of the employee's intended absence or the end of the fifteenth week before the expected week of birth, whichever is later;";

(b) paragraph (4) and (5) of that regulation shall not apply.

NOTES

Commencement: 1 December 2014.

Words in square brackets substituted by the Human Fertilisation and Embryology Act 2008 (Remedial) Order 2018, SI 2018/1413, art 3(2), Sch 2, para 7(1), (25), as from 3 January 2019.

SHARED PARENTAL LEAVE REGULATIONS 2014

(SI 2014/3050)

NOTES

Made: 18 November 2014.

Authority: Employment Rights Act 1996, ss 47C(2), 75E, 75F(1), (4), (7)–(14), (16), 75G(1)–(6), 75H(1), (4), (7)–(14), (16), 75I(1), (4), (5), 75J, 75K(1), (6), 99.

Commencement: 1 December 2014.

Application: as to the application of these Regulations to parental order cases under the Human Fertilisation and Embryology Act 2008, ss 54, 54A with modifications, see the Paternity, Adoption and Shared Parental Leave (Parental Order Cases) Regulations 2014, SI 2014/3096, regs 5, 20–33 at **[2.1751]**, **[2.1770]–[2.1783]**. As to the application of these Regulations to adoptions from overseas, see the Shared Parental Leave and Paternity and Adoption Leave (Adoptions from Overseas) Regulations 2014, SI 2014/3092 at **[2.1704]** et seq.

ARRANGEMENT OF REGULATIONS

PART 1
GENERAL

PART 2
ENTITLEMENT TO SHARED PARENTAL LEAVE (BIRTH)

CHAPTER 1
ENTITLEMENT TO LEAVE—GENERAL

CHAPTER 2
ENTITLEMENT TO PARTICULAR PERIODS OF LEAVE

Part 2 Statutory Instruments

PART 1
GENERAL

[2.1577]

1 Citation and commencement

These Regulations may be cited as the Shared Parental Leave Regulations 2014 and come into force on 1st December 2014.

NOTES

Commencement: 1 December 2014.

[2.1578]

2 Application

(1) The provisions relating to shared parental leave in Part 2 have effect only in relation to children whose expected week of birth begins on or after 5th April 2015.

(2) The provisions relating to shared parental leave in Part 3 have effect only in relation to children placed for adoption on or after 5th April 2015.

(3) Regulation 42 (protection from detriment) has effect only in relation to an act or failure to act which takes place on or after 1st December 2014.

(4) Regulation 43 (unfair dismissal) has effect only in relation to dismissals where the effective date of termination (within the meaning of section 97 of the 1996 Act) falls on or after 1st December 2014.

NOTES

Commencement: 1 December 2014.

Modification: this regulation is applied with modifications in relation to parental order cases under the Human Fertilisation and Embryology Act 2008, s 54, by the Paternity, Adoption and Shared Parental Leave (Parental Order Cases) Regulations 2014, SI 2014/3096, reg 20 at **[2.1770]**, and in relation to adoptions from overseas by the Shared Parental Leave and Paternity and Adoption Leave (Adoptions from Overseas) Regulations 2014, SI 2014/3092, regs 7–9 at **[2.1710]**–**[2.1712]**.

[2.1579]

3 Interpretation

(1) In these Regulations—

"1992 Act" means the Social Security Contributions and Benefits Act 1992;

"1996 Act" means the Employment Rights Act 1996;

"A", in relation to C, means the person with whom C is, or is expected to be, placed for adoption, or, in a case where two people have been matched jointly, whichever of them has elected to be the child's adopter for the purposes of the Paternity and Adoption Leave Regulations 2002;

"adoption agency" has the meaning given, in relation to England and Wales, by section 2(1) of the Adoption and Children Act 2002 and, in relation to Scotland, by section 119(1) of the Adoption and Children (Scotland) Act 2007;

"adoption pay period" means the period in which statutory adoption pay may be payable in respect of C;

"allowance curtailment date" means the last day of M's maternity allowance period where that period has been reduced under section 35(3A) of the 1992 Act;

"AP" means the person who at the date that C is placed for adoption is married to, or the civil partner or the partner of, A;

"C" means the child in relation to whom an entitlement to shared parental leave arises;

"expected week of birth" means the week, beginning with midnight between Saturday and Sunday, in which it is expected that C will be born;

"leave curtailment date" means—

(a) in Part 2, the last day of M's statutory maternity leave period where that period has been curtailed under section 71(3)(ba) or 73(3)(a) of the 1996 Act;

(b) in Part 3, the last day of A's statutory adoption leave period where that period has been curtailed under section 75A(2A)(a) or 75B(3)(aa) of the 1996 Act;

"M" means the mother (or expectant mother) of C;

"maternity allowance" means a maternity allowance under section 35(1) of the 1992 Act;

"maternity allowance period" means the period referred to in section 35(2) of the 1992 Act;

"maternity pay period" has the meaning given by regulation 2 of the Statutory Maternity Pay (General) Regulations 1986;

"P" means the father of C, or the person who at the date of C's birth is married to, or the civil partner or the partner of, M;

"partner" in relation to M or A, means a person (whether of a different sex or the same sex) who lives with M or A and with C in an enduring family relationship but is not M's or A's child, parent, grandchild, grandparent, sibling, aunt, uncle, niece or nephew;

"pay curtailment date" means—

(a) in Part 2, the last day of M's maternity pay period where that period has been reduced under section 165(3A) of the 1992 Act;

(b) in Part 3, the last day of A's adoption pay period where that period has been reduced under section 171ZN(2A);

"period of leave notice" means a notice given in accordance with regulation 12 or 28;

"placed for adoption" means—

(a) placed for adoption under the Adoption and Children Act 2002 or the Adoption and Children (Scotland) Act 2007; or

(b) placed in accordance with section 22C of the Children Act 1989 with a local authority foster parent who is also a prospective adopter;

"processing", in relation to information, has the meaning given by section 1(1) of the Data Protection Act 1998;

"returned after being placed for adoption" means—

(a) returned under sections 31 to 35 of the Adoption and Children Act 2002,
(b) in Scotland, returned to the adoption agency, adoption society or nominated person in accordance with section 25(6) of the Adoption and Children (Scotland) Act 2007, or
(c) where the child is placed in accordance with section 22C of the Children Act 1989, returned to the adoption agency following a termination of the placement;

"revocation notice" means a notice given under section 71(3)(bb), 73(3)(aa), 75A(2A)(b), or 75B(3)(aa) of the 1996 Act or section 35(3D), 165(3D), or 171ZN(2D) of the 1992 Act, as the case may be, which revokes a notice previously given under that section;

"shared parental leave" means leave under section 75E or 75G of the 1996 Act;

"statutory adoption leave" means ordinary adoption leave under section 75A of the 1996 Act or additional adoption leave under section 75B of that Act;

"statutory adoption pay" has the meaning given in section 171ZL of the 1992 Act;

"statutory maternity leave" means ordinary maternity leave under section 71 of the 1996 Act or additional maternity leave under section 73 of that Act;

"statutory maternity pay" has the meaning given in section 164(1) of the 1992 Act; and

"statutory shared parental pay" means any pay payable in accordance with the provisions of Part 12ZC of the 1992 Act.

(2) References to relationships in the definition of "partner" in paragraph (1)—
(a) are to relationships of the full blood or half blood or, in the case of an adopted person, such of those relationships as would exist but for the adoption, and
(b) include the relationship of a child with adoptive, or former adoptive, parents, but do not include other adoptive relationships.

(3) For the purposes of these Regulations—
(a) a person is matched with a child for adoption when an adoption agency decides that that person would be a suitable adoptive parent for the child either individually or jointly with another person;
(b) in a case where sub-paragraph (a) applies, a person is notified of having been matched with a child on the date on which the person receives notification of the agency's decision, under regulation 33(3)(a) of the Adoption Agencies Regulations 2005, regulation 28(3) of the Adoption Agencies (Wales) Regulations 2005, or regulation 8(5) of the Adoption Agencies (Scotland) Regulations 2009;
(c) a person is also matched with a child for adoption when a decision has been made in accordance with regulation 22A of the Care Planning, Placement and Case Review (England) Regulations 2010 and an adoption agency has identified that person with whom the child is to be placed in accordance with regulation 12B of the Adoption Agencies Regulations 2005;
(d) in a case where paragraph (c) applies, a person is notified of having been matched with a child on the date on which that person receives notification in accordance with regulation 12B(2)(a) of the Adoption Agencies Regulations 2005 of the decision to place for adoption the child with that person.

(4) The reference to "local authority foster parent" in the definition of "placed for adoption" in paragraph (1) means a person approved as a local authority foster parent in accordance with regulations made by virtue of paragraph 12F of Schedule 2 to the Children Act 1989.

(5) The reference to "prospective adopter" in the definition of "placed for adoption" in paragraph (1) means a person who has been approved as suitable to adopt a child and has been notified of that decision in accordance with regulation 30B(4) of the Adoption Agencies Regulations 2005.

NOTES

Commencement: 1 December 2014.

Modification: this regulation is applied with modifications in relation to parental order cases under the Human Fertilisation and Embryology Act 2008, s 54, by the Paternity, Adoption and Shared Parental Leave (Parental Order Cases) Regulations 2014, SI 2014/3096, reg 21 at **[2.1771]**, and in relation to adoptions from overseas by the Shared Parental Leave and Paternity and Adoption Leave (Adoptions from Overseas) Regulations 2014, SI 2014/3092, regs 7, 8, 10 at **[2.1710]**, **[2.1711]**, **[2.1713]**.

PART 2
ENTITLEMENT TO SHARED PARENTAL LEAVE (BIRTH)

CHAPTER 1 ENTITLEMENT TO LEAVE—GENERAL

[2.1580]
4 Mother's entitlement to shared parental leave

(1) M is entitled to be absent from work to take shared parental leave in accordance with Chapter 2 to care for C if she satisfies the conditions specified in paragraph (2) and P satisfies the conditions specified in paragraph (3).

(2) The conditions are that—
(a) M satisfies the continuity of employment test (see regulation 35);
(b) M has, at the date of C's birth, the main responsibility for the care of C (apart from the responsibility of P);
(c) M is entitled to statutory maternity leave in respect of C;

(d) M has ended any entitlement to statutory maternity leave by curtailing that leave under section 71(3)(ba) or 73(3)(a) of the 1996 Act (and that leave remains curtailed) or, where M has not curtailed in that way, M has returned to work before the end of her statutory maternity leave;
(e) M has complied with regulation 8 (notice to employer of entitlement to shared parental leave);
(f) M has complied with regulation 10(3) to (5) (evidence for employer); and
(g) M has given a period of leave notice in accordance with regulation 12.

(3) The conditions are that—
(a) P satisfies the employment and earnings test (see regulation 36); and
(b) P has, at the date of C's birth, the main responsibility for the care of C (apart from the responsibility of M).

(4) Entitlement under paragraph (1) is not affected by the number of children born or expected as a result of the same pregnancy.

NOTES

Commencement: 1 December 2014.

[2.1581]
5 Father's or partner's entitlement to shared parental leave

(1) P is entitled to be absent from work to take shared parental leave in accordance with Chapter 2 to care for C if P satisfies the conditions specified in paragraph (2) and M satisfies the conditions specified in paragraph (3).

(2) The conditions are that—
(a) P satisfies the continuity of employment test (see regulation 35);
(b) P has, at the date of C's birth, the main responsibility for the care of C (apart from the responsibility of M);
(c) P has complied with regulation 9 (notice to employer of entitlement to shared parental leave);
(d) P has complied with regulation 10(3) to (5) (evidence for employer); and
(e) P has given a period of leave notice in accordance with regulation 12.

(3) The conditions are that—
(a) M satisfies the employment and earnings test (see regulation 36);
(b) M has, at the date of C's birth, the main responsibility for the care of C (apart from the responsibility of P);
(c) M is entitled to statutory maternity leave, statutory maternity pay, or maternity allowance in respect of C; and
(d) where—
(i) M is entitled to statutory maternity leave, she has ended any entitlement to statutory maternity leave by curtailing that leave under section 71(3)(ba) or section 73(3)(a) of the 1996 Act (and that leave remains curtailed) or, where M has not curtailed in that way, M has returned to work before the end of her statutory maternity leave,
(ii) M is not entitled to statutory maternity leave but is entitled to statutory maternity pay, she has curtailed the maternity pay period under section 165(3A) of the 1992 Act (and that period remains curtailed), or
(iii) M is not entitled to statutory maternity leave but is entitled to maternity allowance, she has curtailed the maternity allowance period under section 35(3A) of that Act (and that period remains curtailed).

(4) Entitlement under paragraph (1) is not affected by the number of children born or expected as a result of the same pregnancy.

NOTES

Commencement: 1 December 2014.

[2.1582]
6 Calculation of total amount of shared parental leave available (birth)

(1) Where M is entitled to statutory maternity leave, subject to paragraph (10), the total amount of shared parental leave available to M and P in relation to C is 52 weeks less—
(a) where there is a leave curtailment date, the number of weeks of statutory maternity leave beginning with the first day of statutory maternity leave taken by M and ending with the leave curtailment date (irrespective of whether or not M returns to work before that date), or
(b) where M's statutory maternity leave ends without her curtailing that leave under section 71(3) or section 73(3) of the 1996 Act, the number of weeks of statutory maternity leave taken.

(2) Where M is not entitled to statutory maternity leave, but is entitled to statutory maternity pay, subject to paragraph (11), the total amount of shared parental leave available to P in relation to C is 52 weeks less—
(a) where M returns to work without reducing her statutory maternity pay period under section 165(3A) of the 1992 Act, the number of weeks of statutory maternity pay payable to M in respect of C before M returns to work, or
(b) in any other case, the number of weeks of statutory maternity pay payable to M in respect of C up to the pay curtailment date.

(3) Where M is not entitled to statutory maternity leave, but is entitled to maternity allowance, the total amount of shared parental leave available to P in relation to C is 52 weeks less—

(a) where M returns to work without reducing her maternity allowance period under section 35(3A) of the 1992 Act, the number of weeks of maternity allowance payable to M in respect of C before M returns to work, or

(b) in any other case, the number of weeks of maternity allowance payable to M in respect of C up to the allowance curtailment date.

(4) The total amount of shared parental leave which M is entitled to take in relation to C is the product of the calculation in paragraph (1) less—

(a) any shared parental leave which P has notified under regulation 12 (as varied by any notice under regulation 15),

(b) any period of leave which is required to be taken in accordance with paragraph (2) of regulation 18, and

(c) any weeks of statutory shared parental pay to which P is entitled and during which P is not absent on shared parental leave.

(5) The total amount of shared parental leave which P is entitled to take in relation to C is the product of the calculation in paragraph (1), (2) or (3), as the case may be, less—

(a) any shared parental leave which M has notified under regulation 12 (as varied by any notice under regulation 15),

(b) any period of leave which is required to be taken in accordance with paragraph (1) of regulation 18, and

(c) any weeks of statutory shared parental pay to which [M] is entitled and during which [M] is not absent on shared parental leave.

(6) For the purposes of paragraphs (4)(a) and (5)(a), any leave notified but, as a result of M giving a revocation notice, not taken must be disregarded.

(7) For the purposes of paragraph (1), a part of a week in which maternity leave is taken is to be treated as a whole week.

(8) For the purposes of paragraph (2) and (3)—

(a) a part of a week in respect of which statutory maternity pay or maternity allowance is payable is to be treated as a whole week, and

(b) "week" has the meaning given by section 165(8) of the 1992 Act, in relation to statutory maternity pay, and the meaning given by section 122(1) of that Act, in relation to maternity allowance.

(9) For the purposes of paragraphs (4) and (5), any week of leave or pay notified by M or P, as the case may be, to be taken concurrently from more than one employer is to be treated as one week.

(10) Where M is entitled to take statutory maternity leave from more than one employment, any calculation under paragraph (1) of the total amount of shared parental leave available must be calculated using—

(a) the first day of statutory maternity leave taken by M in relation to C from any employment; and

(b) the later of—

(i) the leave curtailment date, or

(ii) the last day of statutory maternity leave taken by M from any employment in relation to C where that leave ends without her curtailing it under section 71(3) or section 73(3) of the 1996 Act.

(11) Where M is not entitled to statutory maternity leave, but has more than one entitlement to statutory maternity pay—

(a) paragraph (2)(a) is to apply as though it read—

"(a) where M returns to work for all of her employers without reducing her statutory maternity pay periods under section 165(3A) of the 1992 Act, the number of weeks of statutory maternity pay payable to M in respect of C before the last date on which M returns to work, or", and

(b) paragraph (2)(b) is to apply as though it read—

"(b) in any other case, the number of weeks of statutory maternity pay payable to M in respect of C up to the latest pay curtailment date.".

NOTES

Commencement: 1 December 2014.

Para (5): letters in square brackets in sub-para (c) substituted by the Shared Parental Leave and Leave Curtailment (Amendment) Regulations 2015, SI 2015/552, reg 2(1), (2), as from 5 April 2015.

[2.1583]

7 Periods when shared parental leave may be taken

(1) Shared parental leave may be taken at any time within the period which begins on the date C is born (or, where more than one child is born as the result of the same pregnancy, the date on which the first child is born) and ends the day before C's first birthday.

(2) Shared parental leave must be taken in complete weeks.

(3) Shared parental leave may be taken as one continuous period or in discontinuous periods.

(4) The minimum period of shared parental leave which may be taken is one week.

(5) An employee may be absent on shared parental leave in relation to C at the same time that another employee is—

(a) absent on leave provided for in Part 8 of the 1996 Act in relation to C;
(b) in receipt of pay under section 35 or Part 12, 12ZA, or 12ZC of the 1992 Act in relation to C.

NOTES

Commencement: 1 December 2014.

[2.1584]

8 Mother's notice of entitlement and intention to take shared parental leave

(1) M must, not less than eight weeks before the start date of the first period of shared parental leave to be taken by M, give her employer a written notice which contains the information specified in paragraph (2) and is accompanied by the declarations specified in paragraph (3).

(2) The specified information is—
(a) M's name;
(b) P's name;
(c) the start and end dates of any period of statutory maternity leave taken or to be taken by M;
(d) the total amount of shared parental leave available (in accordance with regulation 6(1));
(e) C's expected week of birth and C's date of birth (except as provided for in paragraph (5));
(f) how much shared parental leave M and P each intend to take;
(g) an indication as to when M intends to take shared parental leave (including the start and end dates for each period of leave).

(3) The specified declarations are—
(a) a declaration signed by M that—
(i) M satisfies, or will satisfy, the conditions in regulation 4(2);
(ii) the information given by M in the notice is accurate;
(iii) M will immediately inform her employer if she ceases to care for C;
(b) a declaration signed by P—
(i) specifying P's name, address, and national insurance number (or a declaration that P does not have a national insurance number);
(ii) that P satisfies, or will satisfy, the conditions in regulation 4(3);
(iii) that P is the father of C, or the person who is married to, or the civil partner or the partner of, M;
(iv) that P consents to the amount of leave which M intends to take (as set out in the notice for the purposes of paragraph (2)(f));
(v) that P consents to M's employer processing the information in P's declaration.

(4) The references to P in paragraphs (2) and (3) are references to the individual who satisfies paragraph (3) of regulation 4.

(5) Where a notice is given under paragraph (1) before C is born, M must give C's date of birth to her employer as soon as reasonably practicable after the birth of C and, in any event, before the first period of shared parental leave to be taken by M.

(6) The indication provided in accordance with paragraph (2)(g) is non-binding and must not be treated as a period of leave notice unless otherwise indicated in the notice.

NOTES

Commencement: 1 December 2014.

[2.1585]

9 Father's or partner's notice of entitlement and intention to take shared parental leave

(1) P must, not less than eight weeks before the start date of the first period of shared parental leave to be taken by P, give P's employer a written notice which contains the information specified in paragraph (2) and is accompanied by the declarations specified in paragraph (3).

(2) The specified information is—
(a) P's name;
(b) M's name;
(c) the start and end dates of any—
(i) period of statutory maternity leave taken or to be taken by M;
(ii) period in respect of which statutory maternity pay received or to be received by M (where statutory maternity leave was not taken or is not be taken in relation to that period) is payable; or
(iii) period in respect of which maternity allowance received or to be received by M (where statutory maternity leave was not taken or is not be taken in relation to that period) is payable;
(d) the total amount of shared parental leave available (in accordance with regulation 6(1), (2) or (3));
(e) C's expected week of birth and C's date of birth (except as provided for in paragraph (4));
(f) how much shared parental leave P and M each intend to take;
(g) an indication as to when P intends to take shared parental leave (including the start and end dates for each period of leave).

(3) The specified declarations are—
(a) a declaration signed by P that—
(i) P satisfies, or will satisfy, the conditions in regulation 5(2);
(ii) the information given by P in the notice is accurate;

(iii) that P is the father of C, or the person who is married to, or the civil partner or the partner of, M;
(iv) P will immediately inform P's employer if P ceases to care for C or if M informs P that she has ceased to satisfy the condition in regulation 5(3)(d);

(b) a declaration signed by M—
(i) specifying M's name, address, and national insurance number (or a declaration that M does not have a national insurance number);
(ii) that M satisfies, or will satisfy, the conditions in regulation 5(3);
(iii) that M consents to the amount of leave which P intends to take (as set out in the notice for the purposes of paragraph (2)(f));
(iv) that M will immediately inform P if she ceases to satisfy the conditions in regulation 5(3)(d);
(v) that M consents to P's employer processing the information in M's declaration.

(4) Where a notice is given under paragraph (1) before C is born, P must give C's date of birth to P's employer as soon as reasonably practicable after the birth of C and, in any event, before the first period of shared parental leave to be taken by P.

(5) The indication provided in accordance with paragraph (2)(g) is non-binding and must not be treated as a period of leave notice unless otherwise indicated in the notice.

NOTES

Commencement: 1 December 2014.

[2.1586]

10 Supplementary evidence requirements (birth)

(1) Where M gives a notice under regulation 8 (excluding any notice given under regulation 8(5)), her employer may request within 14 days beginning with the date on which that notice was given—
(a) a copy of C's birth certificate;
(b) the name and address of P's employer.

(2) Where P gives a notice under regulation 9 (excluding any notice given under regulation 9(4)), P's employer may request within 14 days beginning with the date on which that notice was given—
(a) a copy of C's birth certificate;
(b) the name and address of M's employer.

(3) Where an employer makes a request under paragraph (1)(a) or (2)(a) after C's birth, M or P, as the case may be, must, within 14 days beginning with the date on which that request was made, send the employer—
(a) a copy of C's birth certificate, where one has been issued, or
(b) if the birth certificate has yet to be issued, a declaration signed by M or P, as the case may be, which states the date and location of C's birth and states that a birth certificate has not yet been issued.

(4) Where an employer makes a request under paragraph (1)(a) or (2)(a) before C's birth, M or P, as the case may be, must, within 14 days beginning on the date on which C is born, send the employer—
(a) a copy of C's birth certificate, where one has been issued, or
(b) if the birth certificate has yet to be issued, a declaration signed by M or P, as the case may be, which states the date and location of C's birth and states that a birth certificate has not yet been issued.

(5) Where an employer makes a request under paragraph (1)(b) or (2)(b), M or P, as the case may be, must, within 14 days beginning on the date on which that request was made, send the employer—
(a) the name and address requested, or
(b) a declaration that M or P, as the case may be, has no employer.

NOTES

Commencement: 1 December 2014.

[2.1587]

11 Variation of notice of intention to take shared parental leave (birth)

(1) M may give M's employer a written notice to vary a notice given under regulation 8 to vary how much shared parental leave M and P each intend to take.

(2) P may give P's employer a written notice to vary a notice given under regulation 9 to vary how much shared parental leave M and P each intend to take.

(3) A notice under paragraph (1) or (2) must contain—
(a) an indication as to when M or P, as the case may be, intends to take shared parental leave (including the start and end dates for each period of leave);
(b) a description of the periods of shared parental leave that have been notified by M and P under regulation 12 or 15 in relation to C;
(c) a description of the periods of statutory shared parental pay that have been notified by M and P under Regulations made under Part 12ZC of the 1992 Act in relation to C (where that pay was notified in relation to a period in which shared parental leave was not to be taken);
(d) a declaration signed by M and P that they agree the variation.

(4) The indication provided in accordance with paragraph (3)(a) is non-binding and must not be treated as a period of leave notice unless otherwise indicated in the notice.

(5) For the purposes of any notices given by M, the reference to P in paragraph (3)(d) is a reference to the individual who satisfies paragraph (3) of regulation 4.

(6) There is no limit on the number of notices that may be given under this regulation.

NOTES

Commencement: 1 December 2014.

CHAPTER 2 ENTITLEMENT TO PARTICULAR PERIODS OF LEAVE

[2.1588]

12 Period of leave notice (birth)

(1) M may only be absent from work to take a period of shared parental leave if she gives her employer a written notice which sets out the start and end dates of each period of shared parental leave requested in that notice.

(2) P may only be absent from work to take a period of shared parental leave if P gives P's employer a written notice which sets out the start and end dates of each period of shared parental leave requested in that notice.

(3) A notice given under paragraph (1) or (2) must be given not less than eight weeks before the start date of the first period of shared parental leave requested in the notice.

(4) A notice under this regulation may—

(a) be given at the same time as a notice under regulation 8, 9 or 11 is given to the employer;

(b) provide notice of more than one period of leave;

(c) if given before C is born—

(i) contain a start date for the leave which is the day on which C is born or which is expressed as a number of days following the date of C's birth;

(ii) contain an end date expressed as a number of days following the date of C's birth.

(5) A notice under this regulation may not—

(a) be given before a notice is given to the employer under regulation 8 or 9, as the case may be;

(b) request leave with a start or end date which is outside of the period in which shared parental leave may be taken (see regulation 7(1)).

NOTES

Commencement: 1 December 2014.

[2.1589]

13 Continuous period of shared parental leave (birth)

Where an employee gives a notice under regulation 12 which requests one continuous period of shared parental leave, the employee is entitled to take that period of leave.

NOTES

Commencement: 1 December 2014.

[2.1590]

14 Discontinuous periods of shared parental leave (birth)

(1) This regulation applies where an employee gives a notice under regulation 12 which requests discontinuous periods of shared parental leave.

(2) In the two weeks beginning with the date the notice was given the employer who received the notice may—

(a) consent to the periods of leave requested;

(b) propose alternative dates for the periods of leave; or

(c) refuse the periods of leave requested without proposing alternative dates.

(3) Where in the two weeks beginning with the date the notice was given the employer—

(a) agrees to the periods of leave requested in that notice, or

(b) agrees with the employee alternative dates for the periods of leave,

the employee is entitled to take the leave on the dates agreed.

(4) Where in the two weeks beginning with the date the notice was given no agreement has been reached, the employee is entitled to take the total amount of leave requested in the notice as a continuous period of leave.

(5) Where the employee is entitled to take a continuous period of leave under paragraph (4)—

(a) the employee must choose a start date for that leave which is a date after the period of eight weeks beginning with the date on which the period of leave notice was given and must notify the employer of that date within 5 days of the end of the two week period referred to in paragraph (4); or

(b) if the employee does not choose a start date under sub-paragraph (a), that leave must start on the start date of the first period of leave requested in the period of leave notice.

(6) An employee may withdraw a notice which requests discontinuous periods of shared parental leave on or before the 15th day after the notice was given unless the employee and employer have agreed to periods of leave.

NOTES

Commencement: 1 December 2014.

[2.1591]

15 Variation of period of leave (birth)

(1) Where an employee is entitled to a period of leave under regulation 13 or 14, the employee may give a written notice to request a variation of that period of leave.

(2) A notice under paragraph (1) may—

(a) vary the start date or the end date of any period of shared parental leave provided that the notice is given not less than eight weeks before both the date varied and the new date;

(b) request that a single period of leave become discontinuous periods of leave or vice versa;

[(c) cancel the leave requested provided that the notice is given not less than eight weeks before the leave cancelled by the notice is due to commence.]

(3) A notice under paragraph (1) must state what periods of shared parental leave the employee is entitled to under regulation 13 or 14.

(4) A notice under paragraph (1) may not request leave with a start or end date which is outside of the period in which shared parental leave may be taken (see regulation 7(1)).

[(5) Regulations 13 and 14 apply to a notice under paragraph (1) as they apply to a period of leave notice given in accordance with regulation 12; and for these purposes a reference in those regulations to a notice under regulation 12 (however expressed) is to be read as a reference to a notice under paragraph (1).]

NOTES

Commencement: 1 December 2014.

Para (2): sub-para (c) substituted by the Shared Parental Leave and Leave Curtailment (Amendment) Regulations 2015, SI 2015/552, reg 2(1), (3)(a), as from 5 April 2015.

Para (5): substituted by SI 2015/552, reg 2(1), (3)(b), as from 5 April 2015.

[2.1592]

16 Limit on number of period of leave notices or variations (birth)

(1) An employee may give a combined total of up to three notices under regulations 12 and 15.

(2) Any notice which is—

(a) withdrawn under regulation 14(6),

(b) given under regulation 15 as a result of C being born earlier or later than the expected week of birth, or

(c) given under regulation 15 in response to a request from the employer that the employee vary a period of leave,

is to be disregarded for the purposes of paragraph (1).

(3) Where an employee has more than one employer, the limit in paragraph (1) applies in respect of each employer.

(4) The limit in paragraph (1) may be waived by agreement between the employee and the employer.

NOTES

Commencement: 1 December 2014.

[2.1593]

17 Modification of eight week requirement for notices where child born early

(1) This paragraph applies where—

(a) M or P, as the case may be, is entitled to take a period of shared parental leave with a start date in the eight weeks following the expected week of birth;

(b) C is born before the first day of the expected week of birth; and

(c) M or P, as the case may be, gives a notice under regulation 15 to vary the start date of the period of leave referred to in sub-paragraph (a) so that the period starts the same length of time following C's date of birth as the period would have started after the first day of the expected week of birth.

(2) Where paragraph (1) applies—

(a) the requirement in regulation 15(2)(a) to give not less than eight weeks' notice is satisfied if the notice is given as soon as reasonably practicable after C's date of birth; and

(b) M or P, as the case may be, is entitled to the period of leave requested in the notice referred to in paragraph (1)(c) above (provided that the notice did not also request a variation of the length of the period of leave).

(3) This paragraph applies where—

(a) M has given a notice under regulation 8, but not given a notice under regulation 12; and

(b) C is born eight or more weeks before the first day of the expected week of birth.

(4) Where paragraph (3) applies—

(a) in regulation 8(1) omit "not less than eight weeks";

(b) the requirement in regulation 12 for a notice to be given not less than eight weeks before the start date of a period of leave is to be treated as satisfied if the notice requests a period of leave with a start date in the eight weeks beginning with the date on which C is born and the notice is given as soon as reasonably practicable after C's date of birth; and

(c) where an employer—

(i) has made a request under regulation 10 and the 14 day period in paragraph (3), (4) or (5) has not ended, or

(ii) has not made a request under regulation 10,

regulations 4(2)(f) and 10 do not apply to M.

(5) This paragraph applies where—

(a) M has not given a notice under regulation 8; and

(b) C is born eight or more weeks before the first day of the expected week of birth.

(6) Where paragraph (5) applies—

(a) the requirement in regulation 8 for the notice to be given not less than eight weeks before the start date of a period of leave is to be treated as satisfied if the notice is given as soon as reasonably practicable after C's date of birth;

(b) the requirement in regulation 12 for a notice to be given not less than eight weeks before the start date of a period of leave is to be treated as satisfied if the notice requests a period of leave with a start date in the eight weeks beginning with the date on which C is born and the notice is given as soon as reasonably practicable after C's date of birth; and

(c) regulations 4(2)(f) and 10 do not apply to M.

(7) This paragraph applies where—

(a) P has given a notice under regulation 9, but not given a notice under regulation 12; and

(b) C is born eight or more weeks before the first day of the expected week of birth.

(8) Where paragraph (7) applies—

(a) in regulation 9(1) omit "not less than eight weeks";

(b) the requirement in regulation 12 for a notice to be given not less than eight weeks before the start date of a period of leave is to be treated as satisfied if the notice requests a period of leave with a start date in the eight weeks beginning with the date on which C is born and the notice is given as soon as reasonably practicable after C's date of birth; and

(c) where an employer—

(i) has made a request under regulation 10 and the 14 day period in paragraph (3), (4) or (5) has not ended, or

(ii) has not made a request under regulation 10,

regulations 5(2)(d) and 10 do not apply to P.

(9) This paragraph applies where—

(a) P has not given a notice under regulation 9; and

(b) C is born eight of more weeks before the first day of the expected week of birth.

(10) Where paragraph (9) applies—

(a) the requirement in regulation 9 for the notice to be given not less than eight weeks before the start date of a period of leave is to be treated as satisfied if the notice is given as soon as reasonably practicable after C's date of birth;

(b) the requirement in regulation 12 for a notice to be given not less than eight weeks before the start date of a period of leave is to be treated as satisfied if the notice requests a period of leave with a start date in the eight weeks beginning with the date on which C is born and the notice is given as soon as reasonably practicable after C's date of birth; and

(c) regulations 5(2)(d) and 10 do not apply to P.

NOTES

Commencement: 1 December 2014.

[2.1594]

18 Change of circumstances (birth)

(1) Where less than 8 weeks before M is due to take a period of shared parental leave or during a period of such leave—

(a) M informs M's employer that M has ceased to care for C (and therefore M will not be absent from work on shared parental leave), and

(b) it is not reasonably practicable for M's employer to accommodate the change in circumstances by allowing M to work during the planned period of shared parental leave,

M's employer may require M to take a period of leave.

(2) Where less than 8 weeks before P is due to take a period of shared parental leave or during a period of such leave—

(a) P informs P's employer that P has ceased to care for C or that M has informed P that M has ceased to satisfy the condition in regulation 5(3)(d) (and therefore P will not be absent from work on shared parental leave), and

(b) it is not reasonably practicable for P's employer to accommodate the change in circumstances by allowing P to work during the planned period of shared parental leave,

P's employer may require P to take a period of leave.

(3) This regulation does not apply where regulation 19 applies.

(4) Leave that is required to be taken under paragraph (1) or (2) must be treated as shared parental leave for the purposes of these Regulations.

(5) Where M or P, as the case may be, is not on a period of shared parental leave at the time that the employer is informed of the change of circumstances, any leave that is required to be taken under paragraph (1) or (2) must—

(a) start on the date on which the next period of shared parental leave was due to start; and

(b) end as soon as it is reasonably practicable for the employer to accommodate the change in circumstances by allowing M or P, as the case may be, to work and, in any event, must end no later than—

(i) the date on which the next period of shared parental leave was due to end, or

(ii) eight weeks after the employer is informed of the change in circumstances,

whichever is the earlier.

(6) Where M or P, as the case may be, is on a period of shared parental leave at the time that the employer is informed of the change of circumstances, any leave that is required to be taken under paragraph (1) or (2) must—

(a) start on the date that the employer was informed of the change of circumstances; and

(b) end as soon as it is reasonably practicable for the employer to accommodate the change in circumstances by allowing M or P, as the case may be, to work and, in any event, must end no later than—

(i) the date on which that period of shared parental leave was due to end, or

(ii) eight weeks after the employer is informed of the change in circumstances,

whichever is the earlier.

NOTES

Commencement: 1 December 2014.

[2.1595]

19 Entitlement to shared parental leave in the event of the death of mother, father or partner, or child

Part 1 of the Schedule applies where M, P or C dies before the end of the period during which shared parental leave may be taken (see regulation 7(1)).

NOTES

Commencement: 1 December 2014.

PART 3
ENTITLEMENT TO SHARED PARENTAL LEAVE (ADOPTION)
CHAPTER 1 ENTITLEMENT TO LEAVE—GENERAL

[2.1596]

20 Adopter's entitlement to shared parental leave

(1) A is entitled to be absent from work to take shared parental leave in accordance with Chapter 2 to care for C if A satisfies the conditions specified in paragraph (2) and AP satisfies the conditions specified in paragraph (3).

(2) The conditions are that—

(a) A satisfies the continuity of employment test (see regulation 35);

(b) A has, at the date of the placement for adoption of C, the main responsibility for the care of C (apart from the responsibility of AP);

(c) A is entitled to statutory adoption leave in respect of C;

(d) A has ended any entitlement to statutory adoption leave by curtailing that leave under section 75A(2A) or 75B(3)(a) of the 1996 Act (and that leave remains curtailed) or, where A has not curtailed in that way, A has returned to work before the end of the statutory adoption leave;

(e) A has complied with regulation 24 (notice to employer of entitlement to shared parental leave);

(f) A has complied with regulation 26(3) and (4) (evidence for employer); and

(g) A has given a period of leave notice in accordance with regulation 28.

(3) The conditions are that—

(a) AP satisfies the employment and earnings test (see regulation 36); and

(b) AP has, at the date of the placement for adoption of C, the main responsibility for the care of C (apart from the responsibility of A).

(4) The entitlement under paragraph (1) is not affected by the number of children placed for adoption through a single placement.

NOTES

Commencement: 1 December 2014.

Modification: this regulation is applied with modifications in relation to parental order cases under the Human Fertilisation and Embryology Act 2008, s 54, by the Paternity, Adoption and Shared Parental Leave (Parental Order Cases) Regulations 2014, SI 2014/3096, reg 22 at **[2.1772]**, and in relation to adoptions from overseas by the Shared Parental Leave and Paternity and Adoption Leave (Adoptions from Overseas) Regulations 2014, SI 2014/3092, regs 7, 8, 11 at **[2.1710]**, **[2.1711]**, **[2.1714]**.

[2.1597]

21 Adopter's partner's entitlement to shared parental leave

(1) AP is entitled to be absent from work to take shared parental leave in accordance with Chapter 2 to care for C if AP satisfies the conditions specified in paragraph (2) and A satisfies the conditions specified in paragraph (3).

(2) The conditions are that—

(a) AP satisfies the continuity of employment test (see regulation 35);

(b) AP has, at the date of the placement for adoption of C, the main responsibility for the care of C (apart from the responsibility of A);

(c) AP has complied with regulation 25 (notice to employer of entitlement to shared parental leave);

(d) AP has complied with regulation 26(3) and (4) (evidence for employer); and

(e) AP has given a period of leave notice in accordance with regulation 28.

(3) The conditions are that—

(a) A satisfies the employment and earnings test (see regulation 36);

(b) A has, at the date of the placement for adoption of C, the main responsibility for the care of C (apart from the responsibility of AP);

(c) A is entitled to statutory adoption leave or statutory adoption pay in respect of C; and

(d) where—

(i) A is entitled to statutory adoption leave, A has ended any entitlement to statutory adoption leave by curtailing that leave under section 75A(2A) or 75B(3)(a) of the 1996 Act (and that leave remains curtailed) or, where A has not curtailed in that way, A has returned to work before the end of the statutory adoption leave, or

(ii) where A is not entitled to statutory adoption leave but is entitled to statutory adoption pay, A has curtailed the adoption pay period under section 171ZN(2A) of the 1992 Act (and that period remains curtailed).

(4) The entitlement under paragraph (1) is not affected by the number of children placed for adoption through a single placement.

NOTES

Commencement: 1 December 2014.

Modification: this regulation is applied with modifications in relation to parental order cases under the Human Fertilisation and Embryology Act 2008, s 54, by the Paternity, Adoption and Shared Parental Leave (Parental Order Cases) Regulations 2014, SI 2014/3096, reg 23 at **[2.1773]**, and in relation to adoptions from overseas by the Shared Parental Leave and Paternity and Adoption Leave (Adoptions from Overseas) Regulations 2014, SI 2014/3092, regs 7, 8, 12 at **[2.1710]**, **[2.1711]**, **[2.1715]**.

[2.1598]

22 Calculation of total amount of shared parental leave available (adoption)

(1) Where A is entitled to statutory adoption leave, subject to paragraph (9), the total amount of shared parental leave available to A and AP in relation to C is 52 weeks less—

(a) where there is a leave curtailment date, the number of weeks of statutory adoption leave beginning with the first day of statutory adoption leave taken by A and ending with the leave curtailment date (irrespective of whether or not A returns to work before that date), or

(b) where A's statutory adoption leave ends without A curtailing that leave under section 75A(2A) or section 75B(3) of the 1996 Act, either—

(i) the number of weeks of statutory adoption leave taken; or

(ii) 2 weeks,

whichever is greater.

(2) Where A is not entitled to statutory adoption leave, but is entitled to statutory adoption pay, subject to paragraph (10), the total amount of shared parental leave available to AP in relation to C is 52 weeks less—

(a) where A returns to work without reducing A's statutory adoption pay period under section 171ZN(2A) of the 1992 Act, the number of weeks of statutory adoption pay payable to A in respect of C before A returns to work, or

(b) in any other case, the number of weeks of statutory adoption pay payable to A in respect of C up to the pay curtailment date.

(3) The total amount of shared parental leave which A is entitled to take is the product of the calculation in (1) less—

(a) any shared parental leave which AP has notified under regulation 28 (as varied by any notice under regulation 31),

(b) any period of leave which is required to be taken in accordance with paragraph (2) of regulation 33, and

(c) any weeks of statutory shared parental pay to which AP is entitled and during which AP is not absent on shared parental leave.

(4) The total amount of shared parental leave which AP is entitled to take is the product of the calculation in (1) or (2), as the case may be, less—

(a) any shared parental leave which A has notified under regulation 28 (as varied by any notice under regulation 31),

(b) any period of leave which is required to be taken in accordance with paragraph (1) of regulation 33, and

(c) any weeks of statutory shared parental pay to which AP is entitled and during which AP is not absent on shared parental leave.

(5) For the purposes of paragraphs (3)(a) and (4)(a), any leave notified but, as a result of A giving a revocation notice, not taken must be disregarded.

(6) For the purposes of paragraph (1), a part of a week in which statutory adoption leave is taken is to be treated as a whole week.

(7) For the purposes of paragraph (2)—

(a) a part of a week in respect of which statutory adoption pay is payable is to be treated as a whole week, and

(b) "week" has the meaning given by section 171ZN(8) of the 1992 Act.

(8) For the purposes of paragraphs (3) and (4), any week of leave or pay notified by A or AP, as the case may be, to be taken concurrently from more than one employer is to be treated as one week.

(9) Where A is entitled to take statutory adoption leave from more than one employment, any calculation under paragraph (1) of the total amount of shared parental leave available must be calculated using—

(a) the first day of statutory adoption leave taken by A in relation to C from any employment; and

(b) the later of—

(i) the leave curtailment date, or

(ii) the last day of statutory adoption leave taken by [A] from any employment in relation to C where that leave ends without A curtailing it under section 75A(2A) or section 75B(3) of the 1996 Act.

(10) Where A is not entitled to statutory adoption leave, but has more than one entitlement to statutory adoption pay—

(a) paragraph (2)(a) is to apply as though it read—

"(a) where A returns to work for all of A's employers without reducing the statutory adoption pay periods under section 171ZN(2A) of the 1992 Act, the number of weeks of statutory adoption pay payable to [A] in respect of C before the last date on which A returns to work, or", and

(b) paragraph (2)(b) is to apply as though it read—

"(b) in any other case, the number of weeks of statutory adoption pay payable to A in respect of C up to the latest pay curtailment date.".

NOTES

Commencement: 1 December 2014.

Paras (9), (10): letters in square brackets substituted by the Shared Parental Leave and Leave Curtailment (Amendment) Regulations 2015, SI 2015/552, reg 2(1), (4), as from 5 April 2015.

[2.1599]

23 Periods when shared parental leave may be taken (adoption)

(1) Shared parental leave may be taken at any time within the period which begins on the date C is placed for adoption with A (or, where more than one child is placed for adoption through a single placement, the date of the placement of the first child) and ends the day before the first anniversary of the date on which C was placed for adoption.

(2) Shared parental leave must be taken in complete weeks.

(3) Shared parental leave may be taken as one continuous period or in discontinuous periods.

(4) The minimum period of shared parental leave which may be taken is one week.

(5) An employee may be absent on shared parental leave in relation to C at the same time that another employee is—

(a) absent on leave provided for in Part 8 of the 1996 Act in relation to C;

(b) in receipt of pay under section 35 or Part 12, 12ZA, 12ZB, or 12ZC of the 1992 Act in relation to C.

NOTES

Commencement: 1 December 2014.

Modification: this regulation is applied with modifications in relation to parental order cases under the Human Fertilisation and Embryology Act 2008, s 54, by the Paternity, Adoption and Shared Parental Leave (Parental Order Cases) Regulations 2014, SI 2014/3096, reg 24 at **[2.1774]**, and in relation to adoptions from overseas by the Shared Parental Leave and Paternity and Adoption Leave (Adoptions from Overseas) Regulations 2014, SI 2014/3092, regs 7, 8, 13 at **[2.1710]**, **[2.1711]**, **[2.1716]**.

[2.1600]

24 Adopter's notice of entitlement and intention to take shared parental leave

(1) A must, not less than eight weeks before the start date of the first period of shared parental leave to be taken by A, give A's employer a written notice which contains the information specified in paragraph (2) and is accompanied by the declarations specified in paragraph (3).

(2) The specified information is—

(a) A's name;

(b) AP's name;

(c) the date that A was notified of having been matched for adoption with C;

(d) the date that C is expected to be placed for adoption with A and the date of the placement (except as provided for in paragraph (5));
(e) the start and end dates of any period of statutory adoption leave taken or to be taken by A;
(f) the total amount of shared parental leave available (in accordance with the regulation 22(1));
(g) how much shared parental leave A and AP each intend to take;
(h) an indication as to when A intends to take shared parental leave (including the start and end dates for each period of leave).

(3) The specified declarations are—
(a) a declaration signed by A that—
(i) A satisfies, or will satisfy, the conditions in regulation 20(2);
(ii) the information given by A in the notice is accurate;
(iii) A will immediately inform A's employer if A ceases to care for C;
(b) a declaration signed by AP—
(i) specifying AP's name, address, and national insurance number (or a declaration that AP does not have a national insurance number);
(ii) that AP satisfies, or will satisfy the conditions in regulation 20(3);
(iii) that AP is married to, or the civil partner or partner of, A;
(iv) that AP consents to the amount of leave which A intends to take (as set out in the notice for the purposes of paragraph (2)(g));
(v) that AP consents to A's employer processing the information in AP's declaration.

(4) The references to AP in paragraphs (2) and (3) are references to the individual who satisfies paragraph (3) of regulation 20.

(5) Where a notice is given under paragraph (1) before the date that C is placed for adoption, A must give the date of placement for adoption to A's employer as soon as reasonably practicable after the placement and, in any event, before the first period of shared parental leave to be taken by A.

(6) The indication in the notice provided in accordance with paragraph (2)(h) is non-binding and must not be treated as a period of leave notice unless otherwise indicated in the notice.

NOTES

Commencement: 1 December 2014.

Modification: this regulation is applied with modifications in relation to parental order cases under the Human Fertilisation and Embryology Act 2008, s 54, by the Paternity, Adoption and Shared Parental Leave (Parental Order Cases) Regulations 2014, SI 2014/3096, reg 25 at **[2.1775]**, and in relation to adoptions from overseas by the Shared Parental Leave and Paternity and Adoption Leave (Adoptions from Overseas) Regulations 2014, SI 2014/3092, regs 7, 8, 14 at **[2.1710]**, **[2.1711]**, **[2.1717]**.

[2.1601]

25 Adopter's partner's notice of entitlement and intention to take shared parental leave

(1) AP must, not less than eight weeks before the start date of the first period of shared parental leave to be taken by AP, give AP's employer a written notice which contains the information specified in paragraph (2) and is accompanied by the declarations specified in paragraph (3).

(2) The specified information is—
(a) AP's name;
(b) A's name;
(c) the date that A was notified of having been matched for adoption with C;
(d) the date that C is expected to be placed for adoption with A and the date of the placement (except as provided for in paragraph (4));
(e) the start and end dates of any—
(i) period of statutory adoption leave taken or to be taken by A; or
(ii) period in respect of which statutory adoption pay received or to be received by A (where statutory adoption leave was not taken or is not be taken in relation to that period) is payable;
(f) the total amount of shared parental leave available (in accordance with the regulation 22(1) or (2));
(g) how much shared parental leave AP and A each intend to take;
(h) an indication as to when AP intends to take shared parental leave (including the start and end dates for each period of leave).

(3) The specified declarations are—
(a) a declaration signed by AP that—
(i) AP satisfies, or will satisfy, the conditions in regulation 21(2);
(ii) the information given by AP in the notice is accurate;
(iii) that AP is married to, or the civil partner or partner of, A;
(iv) AP will immediately inform AP's employer if AP ceases to care for C or if A informs AP that A has ceased to satisfy the condition in regulation 21(3)(d);
(b) a declaration signed by A—
(i) specifying A's name, address, and national insurance number (or a declaration that A does not have a national insurance number);
(ii) that A satisfies, or will satisfy, the conditions in regulation 21(3);
(iii) that A consents to the amount of leave which AP intends to take (as set out in the notice for the purposes of paragraph (2)(g));
(iv) that A will immediately inform AP if A ceases to satisfy the conditions in regulation 21(3)(d);

(v) that A consents to AP's employer processing the information in A's declaration.

(4) Where a notice is given under paragraph (1) before the date that C is placed for adoption, AP must give the date of placement for adoption to AP's employer as soon as reasonably practicable after the placement and, in any event, before the first period of shared parental leave to be taken by AP.

(5) The indication provided in accordance with paragraph (2)(h) is non-binding and must not be treated as a period of leave notice unless otherwise indicated in the notice.

NOTES

Commencement: 1 December 2014.

Modification: this regulation is applied with modifications in relation to parental order cases under the Human Fertilisation and Embryology Act 2008, s 54, by the Paternity, Adoption and Shared Parental Leave (Parental Order Cases) Regulations 2014, SI 2014/3096, reg 26 at **[2.1776]**, and in relation to adoptions from overseas by the Shared Parental Leave and Paternity and Adoption Leave (Adoptions from Overseas) Regulations 2014, SI 2014/3092, regs 7, 8, 15 at **[2.1710]**, **[2.1711]**, **[2.1718]**.

[2.1602]

26 Supplementary evidence (adoption)

(1) Where A gives a notice under regulation 24 (excluding any notice given under regulation 24(5)), A's employer may request within 14 days beginning with the date on which that notice was given—

(a) evidence, in the form of one or more documents issued by the adoption agency that matched A with C, of—

(i) the name and address of the adoption agency;

(ii) the date that A was notified of having been matched for adoption with C;

(iii) the date on which the adoption agency expects to place C with A; and

(b) the name and address of AP's employer.

(2) Where AP gives a notice under regulation 25 (excluding any notice given under regulation 25(4)), AP's employer may request within 14 days beginning with the date on which that notice was given—

(a) evidence, in the form of one or more documents issued by the adoption agency that matched A with C, of—

(i) the name and address of the adoption agency;

(ii) the date that A was notified of having been matched for adoption with C;

(iii) the date on which the adoption agency expects to place C with A; and

(b) the name and address of A's employer.

(3) Where an employer makes a request under paragraph (1)(a) or (2)(a), A or AP, as the case may be, must send the employer the evidence requested within 14 days beginning with the date on which that request was made.

(4) Where an employer makes a request under paragraph (1)(b) or (2)(b), A or AP, as the case may be, must, within 14 days beginning with the date on which that request was made, send the employer—

(a) the name and address requested, or

(b) a declaration that A or AP, as the case may be, has no employer.

NOTES

Commencement: 1 December 2014.

Modification: this regulation is applied with modifications in relation to parental order cases under the Human Fertilisation and Embryology Act 2008, s 54, by the Paternity, Adoption and Shared Parental Leave (Parental Order Cases) Regulations 2014, SI 2014/3096, reg 27 at **[2.1777]**, and in relation to adoptions from overseas by the Shared Parental Leave and Paternity and Adoption Leave (Adoptions from Overseas) Regulations 2014, SI 2014/3092, regs 7, 8, 16 at **[2.1710]**, **[2.1711]**, **[2.1719]**.

[2.1603]

27 Variation of notice of intention to take shared parental leave (adoption)

(1) A may give A's employer a written notice to vary a notice given under regulation 24 to vary how much shared parental leave A and AP each intend to take.

(2) AP may give AP's employer a written notice to vary a notice given under regulation 25 to vary how much shared parental leave AP and A each intend to take.

(3) A notice under paragraph (1) or (2) must contain—

(a) an indication as to when A or AP, as the case may be, intends to take shared parental leave (including the start and end dates for each period of leave);

(b) a description of the periods of shared parental leave that have been notified by A and AP under regulation 28 or 31 in relation to C;

(c) a description of the periods of statutory shared parental pay that have been notified by A and AP under Regulations made under Part 12ZC of the 1992 Act in relation to C (where that pay was notified in relation to a period in which shared parental leave was not to be taken);

(d) a declaration signed by A and AP that they agree the variation.

(4) The indication in the notice provided in accordance with paragraph (3)(a) is non-binding and must not to be treated as a period of leave notice unless otherwise indicated in the notice.

(5) For the purposes of any notices given by A, the reference to AP in paragraph (3)(d) is a reference to the individual who satisfies paragraph (3) of regulation 20.

(6) There is no limit on the number of notices that may be given under this regulation.

NOTES

Commencement: 1 December 2014.

CHAPTER 2 ENTITLEMENT TO PARTICULAR PERIODS OF LEAVE

[2.1604]
28 Period of leave notice (adoption)

(1) A may only be absent from work to take a period of shared parental leave if A gives A's employer a written notice which sets out the start and end dates of each period of shared parental leave requested in that notice.

(2) AP may only be absent from work to take a period of shared parental leave if AP gives AP's employer a written notice which sets out the start and end dates of each period of shared parental leave requested in that notice.

(3) A notice given under paragraph (1) or (2) must be given not less than eight weeks before the start date of the first period of shared parental leave requested in the notice.

(4) A notice under this regulation may—
- (a) be given at the same time as a notice under regulation 24, 25 or 27 is given to the employer;
- (b) provide notice of more than one period of leave;
- (c) if given before C is placed for adoption—
  - (i) contain a start date for the leave which is the day on which C is placed for adoption or which is expressed as a number of days following the date of C's placement for adoption;
  - (ii) contain an end date expressed as a number of days following the date of C's placement for adoption.

(5) A notice under this regulation may not—
- (a) be given before a notice is given to the employer under regulation 24 or 25, as the case may be;
- (b) request leave with a start or end date which is outside of the period in which shared parental leave may be taken (see regulation 23(1)).

NOTES

Commencement: 1 December 2014.

Modification: this regulation is applied with modifications in relation to parental order cases under the Human Fertilisation and Embryology Act 2008, s 54, by the Paternity, Adoption and Shared Parental Leave (Parental Order Cases) Regulations 2014, SI 2014/3096, reg 28 at **[2.1778]**, and in relation to adoptions from overseas by the Shared Parental Leave and Paternity and Adoption Leave (Adoptions from Overseas) Regulations 2014, SI 2014/3092, regs 7, 8, 17 at **[2.1710]**, **[2.1711]**, **[2.1720]**.

[2.1605]
29 Continuous period of shared parental leave (adoption)

Where an employee gives a notice under regulation 28 which requests one continuous period of shared parental leave, the employee is entitled to take that period of leave.

NOTES

Commencement: 1 December 2014.

[2.1606]
30 Discontinuous periods of shared parental leave (adoption)

(1) This regulation applies where an employee gives a notice under regulation 28 which requests discontinuous periods of shared parental leave.

(2) In the two weeks beginning with the date the notice was given the employer who received the notice may—
- (a) consent to the periods of leave requested;
- (b) propose alternative dates for the periods of leave; or
- (c) refuse the periods of leave requested without proposing alternative dates.

(3) Where in the two weeks beginning with the date the notice was given the employer—
- (a) agrees to the periods of leave requested in that notice, or
- (b) agrees with the employee alternative dates for the periods of leave,

the employee is entitled to take the leave on the dates agreed.

(4) Where in the two weeks beginning with the date that notice was given no agreement has been reached, the employee is entitled to take the total amount of leave requested in the notice as a continuous period of leave.

(5) Where the employee is entitled to take a continuous period of leave under paragraph (4)—
- (a) the employee must choose a start date for that leave which is a date after the period of eight weeks beginning with the date on which the period of leave notice was given and must notify the employer of that date within 5 days of the end of the two week period referred to in paragraph (4); or
- (b) if the employee does not choose a start date under sub-paragraph (a), that leave must start on the start date of the first period of leave requested in the period of leave notice.

(6) An employee may withdraw a notice which requests discontinuous periods of shared parental leave on or before the 15th day after the notice was given unless the employee and employer have agreed to periods of leave.

NOTES

Commencement: 1 December 2014.

[2.1607]

31 Variation of period of leave (adoption)

(1) Where an employee is entitled to a period of leave under regulation 29 or 30, the employee may give a written notice to request a variation of that period of leave.

(2) A notice under paragraph (1) may—

(a) vary the start date or end date of any period of shared parental leave provided that the notice is given not less than eight weeks before the date varied and the new date;

(b) request that a single period of leave become discontinuous periods of leave or vice versa;

[(c) cancel the leave requested provided that the notice is given not less than eight weeks before the leave cancelled by the notice is due to commence.]

(3) A notice under paragraph (1) must state what periods of shared parental leave the employee is entitled to under regulation 29 or 30.

(4) A notice under paragraph (1) may not request leave with a start or end date which is outside of the period in which shared parental leave may be taken (see regulation 23(1)).

[(5) Regulations 29 and 30 apply to a notice under paragraph (1) as they apply to a period of leave notice given in accordance with regulation 28; and for these purposes a reference in those regulations to a notice under regulation 28 (however expressed) is to be read as a reference to a notice under paragraph (1).]

NOTES

Commencement: 1 December 2014.

Para (2): sub-para (c) substituted by the Shared Parental Leave and Leave Curtailment (Amendment) Regulations 2015, SI 2015/552, reg 2(1), (5)(a), as from 5 April 2015.

Para (5): substituted by SI 2015/552, reg 2(1), (5)(b), as from 5 April 2015.

[2.1608]

32 Limit on number of period of leave notices or variations (adoption)

(1) An employee may give a combined total of up to three notices under regulations 28 and 31.

(2) Any notice which is—

(a) withdrawn under regulation 30(6),

(b) given under regulation 31 as a result of C being placed earlier or later than the date expected,

(c) given under regulation 31 in response to a request from the employer that the employee vary a period of leave,

is to be disregarded for the purposes of paragraph (1).

(3) Where an employee has more than one employer, the limit in paragraph (1) applies in respect of each employer.

(4) The limit in paragraph (1) may be waived by agreement between the employee and the employer.

NOTES

Commencement: 1 December 2014.

Modification in relation to parental order cases: this regulation is applied with modifications in relation to parental order cases under the Human Fertilisation and Embryology Act 2008, s 54, by the Paternity, Adoption and Shared Parental Leave (Parental Order Cases) Regulations 2014, SI 2014/3096, reg 29 at **[2.1779]**.

[2.1609]

33 Change of circumstances (adoption)

(1) Where less than 8 weeks before A is due to take a period of shared parental leave or during a period of such leave—

(a) A informs A's employer that A has ceased to care for C (and therefore A will not be absent from work on shared parental leave); and

(b) it is not reasonably practicable for A's employer to accommodate the change in circumstances by allowing A to work during the planned period of shared parental leave,

A's employer may require A to take a period of leave.

(2) Where less than 8 weeks before AP is due to take a period of shared parental leave or during a period of such leave—

(a) AP informs AP's employer that AP has ceased to care for C or that A has informed AP that A has ceased to satisfy the condition in regulation 21(3)(d) (and therefore AP will not be absent from work on shared parental leave); and

(b) it is not reasonably practicable for AP's employer to accommodate the change in circumstances by allowing AP to work during the planned period of shared parental leave,

AP's employer may require AP to take a period of leave.

(3) This regulation does not apply where regulation 34 applies.

(4) Leave that is required to be taken under paragraph (1) or (2) must be treated as shared parental leave for the purposes of these Regulations.

(5) Where A or AP, as the case may be, is not on a period of shared parental leave at the time the employer is informed of the change of circumstances, any leave that is required to be taken under paragraph (1) or (2) must—

(a) start on the date on which the next period of shared parental leave was due to start; and

(b) end as soon as it is reasonably practicable for the employer to accommodate the change in circumstances by allowing A or AP, as the case may be, to work and, in any event, end no later than—
  (i) the date on which the next period of shared parental leave was due to end, or
  (ii) eight weeks after the employer is informed of the change in circumstances,
whichever is the earlier.

(6) Where A or AP, as the case may be, is on a period of shared parental leave at the time the employer is informed of the change of circumstances, any leave that is required to be taken under paragraph (1) or (2) must—

(a) start on the date that the employer is informed of the change of circumstances; and
(b) end as soon as it is reasonably practicable for the employer to accommodate the change in circumstances by allowing A or AP, as the case may be, to work and, in any event, end no later than—
  (i) the date on which that period of shared parental leave was due to end, or
  (ii) eight weeks after the employer is informed of the change in circumstances,
whichever is the earlier.

NOTES

Commencement: 1 December 2014.

[2.1610]

34 Entitlement to shared parental leave in the event of a disrupted placement or the death of adopter, adopter's partner or child

Part 2 of the Schedule applies where before the end of the period during which shared parental leave may be taken (see regulation 23(1))—

(a) A, AP or C dies, or
(b) C is returned after being placed for adoption.

NOTES

Commencement: 1 December 2014.

Modification: this regulation is applied with modifications in relation to parental order cases under the Human Fertilisation and Embryology Act 2008, s 54, by the Paternity, Adoption and Shared Parental Leave (Parental Order Cases) Regulations 2014, SI 2014/3096, reg 30 at **[2.1780]**, and in relation to adoptions from overseas by the Shared Parental Leave and Paternity and Adoption Leave (Adoptions from Overseas) Regulations 2014, SI 2014/3092, regs 7, 8, 18 at **[2.1710]**, **[2.1711]**, **[2.1721]**.

PART 4
CONDITIONS OF ENTITLEMENT RELATING TO EMPLOYMENT AND EARNINGS

[2.1611]

35 Continuity of employment test

(1) For the purposes of entitlement to shared parental leave (see regulations 4, 5, 20 and 21), an employee satisfies the continuity of employment test if the employee—

(a) has been continuously employed with an employer for a period of not less than 26 weeks ending with the relevant week (see paragraph (3)); and
(b) remains in continuous employment with that employer until the week before any period of shared parental leave taken by the employee.

(2) Where Part 2 applies and C is born earlier than the relevant week and an employee would have satisfied the condition in sub-paragraph (a) of paragraph (1) if the employee's employment had continued until the end of the week immediately preceding that week, the employee must be treated as having satisfied that condition.

(3) In this regulation—

"relevant week" means—

  (a) where Part 2 applies, the week immediately preceding the 14th week before the expected week of birth;
  (b) where Part 3 applies, the week in which A was notified of having been matched for adoption with C.

NOTES

Commencement: 1 December 2014.

Modification: this regulation is applied with modifications in relation to parental order cases under the Human Fertilisation and Embryology Act 2008, s 54, by the Paternity, Adoption and Shared Parental Leave (Parental Order Cases) Regulations 2014, SI 2014/3096, reg 31 at **[2.1781]**, and in relation to adoptions from overseas by the Shared Parental Leave and Paternity and Adoption Leave (Adoptions from Overseas) Regulations 2014, SI 2014/3092, regs 7, 8, 19 at **[2.1710]**, **[2.1711]**, **[2.1722]**.

[2.1612]

36 Employment and earnings test

(1) An individual satisfies the employment and earnings test if that individual—

(a) has been engaged in employment as an employed or self-employed earner for any part of the week in the case of at least 26 of the 66 weeks immediately preceding the calculation week; and
(b) has average weekly earnings (determined in accordance with paragraph (2)) of not less than the amount set out in section 35(6A) of the 1992 Act in relation to the tax year preceding the tax year containing the calculation week.

(2) An individual's average weekly earnings are determined by dividing by 13 the specified payments made, or treated as being made, to or for the benefit of that individual, in the 13 weeks (whether or not consecutive) in the period of 66 weeks immediately preceding the calculation week in which the payments are greatest.

(3) Where an individual receives any pay after the end of the period in paragraph (2) in respect of any week falling within that period, the average weekly amount is to be determined as if such sum had been paid in that period.

(4) Where an individual is not paid weekly, the payments made, or treated as made, to or for the benefit of that individual or for that individual's benefit for the purposes of paragraph (2), must be determined by dividing the total sum paid to that individual by the nearest whole number of weeks in respect of which that sum is paid.

(5) In this regulation—

"calculation week" means—

(a) where Part 2 applies, the expected week of birth;

(b) where Part 3 applies, the week in which A was notified of having been matched for adoption with C.

"employed earner" has the meaning given by section 2 of the 1992 Act, subject for these purposes to the effect of regulations made under section 2(2)(b) of that Act;

"self-employed earner" has the meaning given by section 2 of the 1992 Act, subject for these purposes to the effect of regulations made under section 2(2)(b) of that Act;

"specified payments"—

(a) in relation to a self-employed earner who satisfies the conditions in paragraph (6), are to be treated as made to the self-employed earner at an amount per week equal to the amount set out in section 35(6A) of the 1992 Act that is in force at the end of the week;

(b) in relation to an employed earner, are all payments made to the employed earner or for the employed earner's benefit as an employed earner specified in regulation 2 (specified payments for employed earners) of the Social Security (Maternity Allowance) (Earnings) Regulations 2000; and

"tax year" means the 12 months beginning with the 6th April in any year.

(6) The conditions referred to in paragraph (a) of the definition of "specified payments" are that, in respect of any week, the self-employed earner—

(a) does not hold a certificate of exception issued pursuant to regulation 44(1) of the Social Security (Contributions) Regulations 2001 and has paid a Class 2 contribution (within the meaning of section 1 of the 1992 Act), or

(b) holds such a certificate of exception.

NOTES

Commencement: 1 December 2014.

Modification: this regulation is applied with modifications in relation to parental order cases under the Human Fertilisation and Embryology Act 2008, s 54, by the Paternity, Adoption and Shared Parental Leave (Parental Order Cases) Regulations 2014, SI 2014/3096, reg 32 at **[2.1782]**, and in relation to adoptions from overseas by the Shared Parental Leave and Paternity and Adoption Leave (Adoptions from Overseas) Regulations 2014, SI 2014/3092, regs 7, 8, 20 at **[2.1710]**, **[2.1711]**, **[2.1723]**.

PART 5
TAKING SHARED PARENTAL LEAVE

[2.1613]

37 Work during shared parental leave

(1) An employee may carry out work for the employer during a period of shared parental leave without bringing the period of leave to an end.

(2) An employee may work no more than 20 days under paragraph (1) for each employer during the period in which shared parental leave may be taken (see regulations 7(1) and 23(1)).

(3) For the purposes of this regulation, any work carried out on any day constitutes a day's work.

(4) Subject to paragraph (5), for the purposes of this regulation, "work" means any work done under the contract of employment and includes training or any activity undertaken for the purposes of keeping in touch with the workplace.

(5) Contact to discuss an employee's return to work or any other reasonable contact from time to time between an employer and an employee does not constitute work for the purposes of this regulation.

(6) This regulation does not confer any right on an employer to require that any work be carried out during a period of shared parental leave, nor any right on an employee to work during a period of leave.

(7) Any day's work carried out under this regulation does not have the effect of extending the total duration of a period of shared parental leave.

NOTES

Commencement: 1 December 2014.

[2.1614]

38 Application of terms and conditions during shared parental leave

(1) An employee who takes shared parental leave is, during any period of leave—

(a) entitled to the benefit of all of the terms and conditions of employment which would have applied if the employee had not been absent, and

(b) bound by any obligations arising under those terms and conditions, subject only to the exception in section 75I(1)(b) of the 1996 Act.

(2) In paragraph (1), "terms and conditions of employment" has the meaning given by section 75I(2) of the 1996 Act, and accordingly does not include terms and conditions about remuneration.

(3) For the purposes of section 75I of the 1996 Act, only sums payable to the employee by way of wages or salary are to be treated as remuneration.

(4) In the case of accrual of rights under an employment-related benefit scheme within the meaning given by paragraph 7 of Schedule 5 to the Social Security Act 1989, nothing in paragraph (1)(a) above imposes a requirement which exceeds the requirements of paragraph 5C of that Schedule.

NOTES

Commencement: 1 December 2014.

[2.1615]

39 Redundancy during shared parental leave

(1) This regulation applies where, during a period in which an employee is taking shared parental leave, it is not practicable by reason of redundancy for an employer to continue to employ that employee under the existing contract of employment.

(2) Where there is a suitable alternative vacancy, the employee is entitled to be offered (before the end of the employee's employment under the contract of employment) alternative employment with the employer, the employer's successor, or an associated employer, under a new contract of employment which complies with paragraph (3) and takes effect immediately on the ending of the employee's employment under the previous contract.

(3) The new contract of employment must be such that—

(a) the work to be done under it is of a kind which is both suitable in relation to the employee and appropriate for the employee to do in the circumstances, and

(b) its provisions as to the capacity and place in which the employee is to be employed, and as to the other terms and conditions of the employee's employment, are not substantially less favourable to the employee than if the employee had continued to be employed under the previous contract.

NOTES

Commencement: 1 December 2014.

[2.1616]

40 Right to return after shared parental leave

(1) Where an employee returns to work after a period of shared parental leave which, when added to any other period of relevant statutory leave (see paragraph (3)) taken by the employee in relation to C, means that the total amount of relevant statutory leave taken by the employee in relation to C is 26 weeks or less, the employee is entitled to return from leave to the job in which the employee was employed before the absence, except where paragraph (2)(b) applies.

(2) Where an employee returns to work after a period of shared parental leave which—

(a) when added to any other period of relevant statutory leave taken by the employee in relation to C, means that the total amount of relevant statutory leave taken by the employee in relation to C is more than 26 weeks; or

(b) was the last of two or more consecutive periods of relevant statutory leave which included a period of parental leave of more than four weeks, a period of additional maternity leave, or a period of additional adoption leave,

the employee is entitled to return from leave to the job in which the employee was employed before the absence, or, if it is not reasonably practicable for the employer to permit the employee to return to that job, to another job which is both suitable for the employee and appropriate for the employee to do in the circumstances.

(3) In this regulation—

"additional adoption leave" means leave under section 75B of the 1996 Act;

"additional maternity leave" means leave under section 73 of the 1996 Act;

"parental leave" means leave under section 76 of the 1996 Act;

"relevant statutory leave" means leave provided for in Part 8 of the 1996 Act except any period of parental leave.

(4) This regulation does not apply where it is not practicable by reason of redundancy for the employer to continue to employ the employee under the existing contract of employment.

NOTES

Commencement: 1 December 2014.

[2.1617]

41 Right to return after shared parental leave: supplementary

(1) For the purposes of regulation 40 a job is—

Part 2 Statutory Instruments

(a) the nature of the work which the employee is employed to do under the contract of employment; and
(b) the capacity and place the employee was employed in before the absence.

(2) References in regulation 40 to the job in which the employee was employed before the absence are references to the job in which the employee was employed—
(a) if the return is from an isolated period of shared parental leave, immediately before that period, or
(b) if the return is from consecutive periods of leave provided for in Part 8 of the 1996 Act, immediately before the first such period.

(3) The right to return under regulation 40 is a right to return—
(a) with the employee's seniority, pension rights and similar rights as they would have been if there had been no absence, and
(b) on terms and conditions not less favourable than those which would have applied if there had been no absence.

(4) In the case of accrual of rights under an employment-related benefit scheme within the meaning given by paragraph 7 of Schedule 5 to the Social Security Act 1989, nothing in paragraph (3)(a) above imposes a requirement which exceeds the requirements of paragraphs 5A to 6 of that Schedule.

NOTES

Commencement: 1 December 2014.

[2.1618]

42 Protection from detriment

(1) An employee is entitled under section 47C of the 1996 Act not to be subjected to any detriment by any act, or any deliberate failure to act, by an employer because—
(a) the employee took, sought to take, or made use of the benefits of, shared parental leave;
(b) the employer believed that the employee was likely to take shared parental leave; or
(c) the employee undertook, considered undertaking, or refused to undertake work in accordance with regulation 37.

(2) For the purposes of paragraph (1)(a), the employee makes use of the benefits of shared parental leave if, during a period of shared parental leave, the employee benefits from any of the terms and conditions of employment preserved by regulation 38 during that period.

(3) Paragraph (1) does not apply where the detriment in question amounts to dismissal within the meaning of Part 10 of the 1996 Act.

NOTES

Commencement: 1 December 2014.

[2.1619]

43 Unfair dismissal

(1) An employee who is dismissed is entitled under section 99 of the 1996 Act to be regarded for the purposes of Part 10 of that Act as unfairly dismissed if—
(a) the reason or principal reason for the dismissal is of a kind specified in paragraph (3), or
(b) the reason or principal reason for the dismissal is that the employee is redundant and regulation 39 has not been complied with.

(2) An employee who is dismissed is to be regarded for the purposes of Part 10 of the 1996 Act as unfairly dismissed if—
(a) the reason or principal reason for the dismissal is that the employee was redundant,
(b) it is shown that the circumstances constituting the redundancy applied equally to one or more employees in the same undertaking who had positions similar to that held by the dismissed employee and who have not been dismissed by an employer, and
(c) it is shown that the reason or principal reason for which the employee was selected for dismissal was a reason of a kind specified in paragraph (3).

(3) The reasons referred to in paragraphs (1) and (2) are reasons connected with any of the following facts—
(a) that the employee took, sought to take, or made use of the benefits of, shared parental leave;
(b) that the employer believed that the employee was likely to take shared parental leave; or
(c) that the employee undertook, considered undertaking, or refused to undertake work in accordance with regulation 37.

(4) For the purposes of paragraph (3)(a), the employee makes use of the benefits of shared parental leave if, during a period of shared parental leave, the employee benefits from any of the terms and conditions of employment preserved by regulation 38 during that period.

NOTES

Commencement: 1 December 2014.

[2.1620]

44 Calculation of a week's pay for the purposes of Chapter 2 of Part 14 of the 1996 Act

Where—

(a) under Chapter 2 of Part 14 of the 1996 Act, the amount of a week's pay of an employee falls to be calculated by reference to the average rate of remuneration, or the average amount of remuneration, payable to the employee in respect of a period of 12 weeks ending on a particular date (referred to as the "calculation date"),

(b) during a week in that period, the employee was absent from work on shared parental leave, and

(c) remuneration is payable to the employee in respect of that week under the employee's contract of employment, but the amount payable is less than the amount that would be payable if the employee were working,

that week shall be disregarded for the purpose of the calculation and account must be taken of remuneration in earlier weeks so as to bring up to 12 the number of weeks of which account is taken.

NOTES

Commencement: 1 December 2014.

PART 6
CONTRACTUAL RIGHTS AND SERVICE OF NOTICES

[2.1621]

45 Contractual rights to shared parental leave

Where an employee is entitled to shared parental leave (referred to in this regulation as "the statutory right") and also to a right which corresponds to that right and which arises under the employee's contract of employment or otherwise—

(a) the employee may not exercise the statutory right and the corresponding right separately but may, in taking the leave for which the two rights provide, take advantage of whichever right is, in any particular respect, the more favourable, and

(b) the provisions of the 1996 Act and of these Regulations relating to the statutory right apply, subject to any modifications necessary to give effect to any more favourable contractual terms, to the exercise of the composite right described in sub-paragraph (a) as they apply to the exercise of the statutory right.

NOTES

Commencement: 1 December 2014.

[2.1622]

46 Service of notices

(1) Where a notice is to be given under these Regulations, it may be given—

(a) where paragraph (2) applies, by electronic communication;

(b) by post; or

(c) by personal delivery.

(2) This paragraph applies where the person who is to receive the notice has agreed that the notice may be given to the person by being transmitted to an electronic address and in an electronic form specified by the person for the purpose.

(3) Where a notice is to be given under these Regulations it is to be taken to have been given—

(a) if sent by electronic communication, on the day of transmission;

(b) if sent by post in an envelope which is properly addressed and sent by prepaid post, on the day on which it is posted;

(c) if delivered personally, on the day of delivery.

NOTES

Commencement: 1 December 2014.

SCHEDULE
SHARED PARENTAL LEAVE IN SPECIAL CIRCUMSTANCES

Regulations 19 and 34

PART 1
SHARED PARENTAL LEAVE (BIRTH)

Entitlement of father or partner to shared parental leave in the event of death of mother before curtailment

[2.1623]

1. (1) Where before P has given a notice under regulation 9 M dies—

(a) without curtailing her statutory maternity leave under section 71(3) or 73(3) of the 1996 Act;

(b) before the end of her maternity pay period and without curtailing that period under section 165(3A) of the 1992 Act; or

(c) before the end of her maternity allowance period and without curtailing that period under section 35(3A) of the 1992 Act,

sub-paragraph (2) applies in relation to the entitlement of P to shared parental leave.

(2) The provisions of the Regulations apply in respect of any period after M dies with the modifications specified in paragraphs (a) to (l)—

(a) a person is to be regarded as falling within the definition of "P" in regulation 3(1) if that person fell within that definition immediately before M died;

(b) regulation 5(2)(d) does not have effect;
(c) in regulation 5(3)(a) for "M satisfies" substitute "immediately before her death M satisfied";
(d) in regulation 5(3)(c) for "M is entitled" substitute "immediately before her death, M was entitled";
(e) regulation 5(3)(d) does not have effect;
(f) in regulation 6—
(i) for paragraph (1) substitute—

"(1) Where M was entitled to statutory maternity leave, subject to paragraph (10), the total amount of shared parental leave available in relation to C is 52 weeks less the number of weeks of statutory maternity leave taken by M before M died.";

(ii) for paragraph (2) substitute—

"(2) Where M was not entitled to statutory maternity leave, but was entitled to statutory maternity pay, subject to paragraph (11), the total amount of shared parental leave available in relation to C is 52 weeks less the number of weeks of statutory maternity pay payable to M in respect of C before M died.";

(iii) for paragraph (3) substitute—

"(3) Where M was not entitled to statutory maternity leave, but was entitled to maternity allowance, the total amount of shared parental leave available in relation to C is 52 weeks less the number of weeks of maternity allowance payable to M in respect of C before M died.";

(g) in regulation 9(2)(f) for "and M each intend" substitute "intends";
(h) in regulation 9(2) after sub-paragraph (g) insert—
"(h) the date of M's death.";
(i) regulation 9(3)(b) is omitted;
(j) regulation 10 is omitted;
(k) regulation 11(3)(d) is omitted;
(l) where under regulation 9 or 12 a notice is required to be given not less than eight weeks before a start date and it is not reasonably practicable for P to satisfy that requirement, the notice may be given as soon as is reasonably practicable after the death of M and before the start date of the leave. The modification of regulation 12 applies only to the first notice given under regulation 12 following the death of M.

Entitlement of father or partner to shared parental leave in the event of death of mother after curtailment and before notice of entitlement given

2. Where M dies after curtailing her statutory maternity leave under section 71(3) or 73(3) of the 1996 Act or her statutory maternity pay period under section 165(3A) of the 1992 Act or her maternity allowance period under section 35(3A) of that Act, or after returning to work, as the case may be, and before P gives a notice under regulation 9, sub-paragraphs (2)(a) to (e) and (g) to (l) in paragraph 1 of this Schedule apply in relation to the entitlement of P to shared parental leave.

Entitlement of father or partner to shared parental leave in the event of death of mother after notice of entitlement given

3. (1) Where M dies after P has given a notice under regulation 9, the provisions of the Regulations apply in respect of any period after M dies with the modifications in sub-paragraphs (2) (on entitlement), (3) to (6) (on the provision of notices), and (7) (on evidence) in relation to the entitlement of P to shared parental leave.

(2) Sub-paragraphs (2)(a) to (e) in paragraph 1 of this Schedule apply.

(3) Regulation 11(3)(d) does not have effect.

(4) Where by reason of M's death it is not reasonably practicable for P to satisfy a requirement under regulation 9, 12 or 15 for a notice to be given not less than eight weeks before the date on which a period of shared parental leave begins, that regulation is to have effect as if it required P to give the notice as soon as reasonably practicable before the date on which the period of leave begins. The modification of regulations 12 and 15 applies only to the first notice given under either regulation 12 or 15 following the death M.

(5) The first notice given under either regulation 12 or 15 following the death of M must include the date of M's death.

(6) Where at the time of M's death P has given a combined total of three notices under regulations 12 and 15, in regulation 16(1) for "three" substitute "four".

(7) Where an employer—
(a) has made a request under regulation 10 and the 14 day period in paragraph (3), (4) or (5) has not ended, or
(b) has not made a request under regulation 10,

before M dies, regulation 5(2)(d) does not have effect and regulation 10 is omitted.

Entitlement of mother to shared parental leave in the event of death of father or partner

4. (1) Where P dies after M has given a notice under regulation 8, the provisions of the Regulations apply in respect of any period after P dies with the modifications in sub-paragraphs (2) (on entitlement), (3) to (6) (on the provision of notices), and (7) (on evidence) apply.

(2) The following modifications apply—

(a) a person is to be regarded as falling within the definition of "P" in regulation 3(1) if that person fell within that definition immediately before that person died;

(b) regulation 4(2)(f) does not have effect;

(c) in regulation 4(3)(a) for "P satisfies" substitute "immediately before P's death P satisfied".

(3) Regulation 11(3)(d) does not have effect.

(4) Where by reason of P's death it is not reasonably practicable for M to satisfy a requirement under regulation 8, 12 or 15 for a notice to be given not less than eight weeks before the date on which a period of shared parental leave begins, that regulation is to have effect as if it required M to give the notice as soon as reasonably practicable before the date on which the period of leave begins. The modification of regulation 12 or 15 applies only to the first notice given under either regulation 12 or 15 following the death P.

(5) The first notice given under either regulation 12 or 15 following the death of P must include the date of P's death.

(6) Where at the time of P's death M has given a combined total of three notices under regulations 12 and 15, in regulation 16(1) for "three" substitute "four".

(7) Where an employer—

(a) has made a request under regulation 10 and the 14 day period in paragraph (3), (4) or (5) has not ended, or

(b) has not made a request under regulation 10,

before P dies, regulation 4(2)(f) does not have effect and regulation 10 is omitted.

Entitlement to shared parental leave in the event of death of child (birth)

5. (1) Where after a notice of entitlement has been given under regulation 8 C dies following birth, the modifications set out in paragraphs (3), (5) and (6) below apply in relation to the entitlement of M to shared parental leave after C's death.

(2) Where after a notice of entitlement has been given under regulation 9 C dies following birth, the modifications set out in paragraphs (4) to (6) below apply in relation to the entitlement of P to shared parental leave after C's death.

(3) In regulation 4(1) omit "to care for C".

(4) In regulation 5(1) omit "to care for C".

(5) In regulation 15 for paragraph (2) substitute—

"(2) A notice under paragraph (1) may—

(a) vary the end date of any period of shared parental leave to reduce the period of leave to be taken provided that the notice is given at least eight weeks before the new end date;

(b) cancel a period or periods of leave."

(6) In regulation 16 for paragraph (1) substitute—

"(1) After C dies, no notice may be given under regulation 12 and only one notice may be given under regulation 15.".

(7) Where more than one child is born of the same pregnancy, a reference in this paragraph relating to the death of C must be construed as a reference to the last of those children to die.

NOTES

Commencement: 1 December 2014.

PART 2
SHARED PARENTAL LEAVE (ADOPTION)

Entitlement of adopter's partner to shared parental leave in the event of death of adopter before curtailment

[2.1624]

6. (1) Where before AP has given a notice under regulation 25 A dies—

(a) without curtailing A's statutory adoption leave under section 75A(2A) or 75B(3) of the 1996 Act; or

(b) before the end of the adoption pay period and without curtailing that period under section 171ZN(2A) of the 1992 Act,

sub-paragraph (2) applies in relation to the entitlement of AP to shared parental leave.

(2) The provisions of the Regulations apply in respect of any period after A dies with the modifications specified in paragraphs (a) to (l)—

(a) a person is to be regarded as falling within the definition of P in regulation 3(1) if that person fell within that definition immediately before A died;

(b) regulation 21(2)(d) does not have effect;

(c) in regulation 21(3)(a) for "A satisfies" substitute "immediately before A's death A satisfied";
(d) in regulation 21(3)(c) for "A is entitled" substitute "immediately before A's death, A was entitled";
(e) regulation 21(3)(d) does not have effect.
(f) in regulation 22—
   (i) for paragraph (1) substitute—

"(1) Where A was entitled to statutory adoption leave, subject to paragraph (9), the total amount of shared parental leave available in relation to C is 52 weeks less the number of weeks of statutory adoption leave taken by A before A died.";

   (ii) for paragraph (2) substitute—

"(2) Where A was not entitled to statutory adoption leave, but was entitled to statutory adoption pay, subject to paragraph (10), the total amount of shared parental leave available in relation to C is 52 weeks less the number of weeks of statutory adoption pay payable to A before A died.";

(g) in regulation 25(2)(g) for "and A each intend" substitute "intends";
(h) in regulation 25(2) after sub-paragraph (h) insert—

"(i) the date of A's death.";

(i) regulation 25(3)(b) is omitted;
(j) regulation 26 is omitted;
(k) regulation 27(3)(d) is omitted;
(l) where under regulation 25 or 28 a notice is required to be given not less than eight weeks before a start date and it is not reasonably practicable for P to satisfy that requirement, the notice may be given as soon as is reasonably practicable after the death of A and before the start date of the leave. The modification of regulation 28 applies only to the first notice given under regulation 28 following the death of A.

Entitlement of adopter's partner to shared parental leave in the event of death of adopter after curtailment and before notice of entitlement given

7. Where A dies after curtailing A's statutory adoption leave under section 75A(2A) or 75B(3) of the 1996 Act, or after curtailing the statutory adoption pay period under section 171ZN(2A) of the 1992 Act, or after returning to work, as the case may be, and before AP has given a notice under regulation 25, sub-paragraph (2)(a) to (e) and (g) to (l) in paragraph 6 of this Schedule apply in relation to the entitlement of AP to shared parental leave.

Entitlement of adopter's partner to shared parental leave in the event of death of adopter after notice of entitlement given

8. (1) Where A dies after AP has given a notice of entitlement under regulation 25, the provisions of the Regulations apply in respect of any period after A dies with the modifications in paragraphs (2) (on entitlement), (3) to (6) (on the provision of notices), and (7) (on evidence) in relation to the entitlement of AP to shared parental leave.

(2) Sub-paragraphs (2)(a) to (e) in paragraph 6 of this Schedule apply.

(3) Regulation 27(3)(d) does not have effect.

(4) Where by reason of A's death it is not reasonably practicable for AP to satisfy a requirement under regulation 25, 28 or 31 for a notice to be given not less than eight weeks before the date on which a period of shared parental leave begins, that regulation is to have effect as if it required AP to give the notice as soon as reasonably practicable before the date on which the period of leave begins. The modification of regulations 28 and 31 applies only to the first notice given under either regulation 28 or 31 following the death A.

(5) The first notice given under either regulation 28 or 31 following the death of A must include the date of A's death.

(6) Where at the time of A's death AP has given a combined total of three notices under regulations 28 and 31, in regulation 32(1) for "three" substitute "four".

(7) Where an employer—
(a) has made a request under regulation 26 and the 14 day period in paragraph (3) or (4) has not ended, or
(b) has not made a request under regulation 26,

before A dies, regulation 21(2)(d) does not have effect and regulation 26 is omitted.

Entitlement of adopter to shared parental leave in the event of death of adopter's partner

9. (1) Where AP dies after A has given a notice of entitlement under regulation 24, the provisions of the Regulations apply in respect of any period after AP dies with the modifications in sub-paragraphs (2) (on entitlement), (3) to (6) (on the provision of notices), and (7) (on evidence) apply.

(2) The following modifications apply—
(a) a person is to be regarded as falling within the definition of "AP" in regulation 3(1) if that person fell within that definition immediately before that person died;
(b) regulation 20(2)(f) does not have effect;
(c) in regulation 20(3)(a) for "AP satisfies" substitute "immediately before AP's death AP satisfied".

(3) Regulation 27(3)(d) does not have effect.

(4) Where by reason of AP's death it is not reasonably practicable for A to satisfy a requirement under regulation 24, 28 or 31 for a notice to be given not less than eight weeks before the date on which a period of shared parental leave begins, that regulation is to have effect as if it required A to give the notice as soon as reasonably practicable before the date on which the period of leave begins. The modification of regulations 28 and 31 applies only to the first notice given under either regulation 28 or 31 following the death AP.

(5) The first notice given under either regulation 28 or 31 following the death of AP must include the date of AP's death.

(6) Where at the time of AP's death A has given a combined total of three notices under regulations 28 and 31, in regulation 32(1) for "three" substitute "four".

(7) Where an employer—

(a) has made a request under regulation 26 and the 14 day period in paragraph (3) or (4) has not ended, or

(b) has not made a request under regulation 26,

before AP dies, regulation 20(2)(f) does not have effect and regulation 26 is omitted.

Entitlement to shared parental leave in the event of a disrupted placement or the death of child

10. (1) Where after a notice of entitlement has been given under regulation 24 C dies or is returned after being placed for adoption, the modifications set out in paragraphs (3), (5) and (6) below apply in relation to the entitlement of A to shared parental leave after C's return or death.

(2) Where after a notice of entitlement has been given under regulation 25 C dies or is returned after being placed for adoption, the modifications set out in paragraphs (4) to (6) below apply in relation to the entitlement of AP to shared parental leave after C's return or death.

(3) In regulation 20(1) omit "to care for C".

(4) In regulation 21(1) omit "to care for C".

(5) In regulation 31 for paragraph (2) substitute—

"(2) A notice under paragraph (1) may—

(a) vary the end date of any period of shared parental leave to reduce the period of leave to be taken provided that the notice is given at least eight weeks before the new end date;

(b) cancel a period or periods of leave."

(6) In regulation 32 for paragraph (1) substitute—

"(1) After C dies or is returned after being placed for adoption, no notice may be given under regulation 28 and only one notice may be given under regulation 31.".

(7) Where more than one child is placed for adoption as a result of the same placement, a reference in this paragraph to the death of C or to the return of C after being placed for adoption must be construed as a reference to the last of those children to die or to the last of those children to be returned after being placed for adoption.

NOTES

Commencement: 1 December 2014.

Modification: para 10 above is applied with modifications in relation to parental order cases under the Human Fertilisation and Embryology Act 2008, s 54, by the Paternity, Adoption and Shared Parental Leave (Parental Order Cases) Regulations 2014, SI 2014/3096, reg 33 at **[2.1783]**, and in relation to adoptions from overseas by the Shared Parental Leave and Paternity and Adoption Leave (Adoptions from Overseas) Regulations 2014, SI 2014/3092, regs 7, 8, 21 at **[2.1710]**, **[2.1711]**, **[2.1724]**.

STATUTORY SHARED PARENTAL PAY (GENERAL) REGULATIONS 2014

(SI 2014/3051)

NOTES

Made: 18 November 2014.

Authority: Social Security Contributions and Benefits Act 1992, ss 171ZU(1)–(5), (12)–(15), 171ZV(1)–(5), (12)–(15), (17), 171ZW(1)(a)–(f), 171ZX(2), (3), 171ZY(1), (3)–(5), 171ZZ1(3), 171ZZ4(3), (4), (7), (8), 175(3); Social Security Administration Act 1992, s 5(1)(g), (i), (l), (p).

Commencement: 1 December 2014.

Application: as to the application of these Regulations to parental order cases under the Human Fertilisation and Embryology Act 2008, s 54, see the Statutory Shared Parental Pay (Parental Order Cases) Regulations 2014, SI 2014/3097 at **[2.1784]** et seq. As to the application of these Regulations to adoptions from overseas, see the Statutory Shared Parental Pay (Adoption from Overseas) Regulations 2014, SI 2014/3093 at **[2.1725]** et seq.

ARRANGEMENT OF REGULATIONS

PART 1
GENERAL

PART 2
ENTITLEMENT TO STATUTORY SHARED PARENTAL PAY (BIRTH)

PART 3
ENTITLEMENT TO STATUTORY SHARED PARENTAL PAY (ADOPTION)

PART 4
CONDITIONS OF ENTITLEMENT RELATING TO EMPLOYMENT AND EARNINGS

PART 5
PAYMENT OF STATUTORY SHARED PARENTAL PAY

SCHEDULES

PART 1
GENERAL

[2.1625]
1 Citation and commencement

These Regulations may be cited as the Statutory Shared Parental Pay (General) Regulations 2014 and come into force on 1st December 2014.

NOTES

Commencement: 1 December 2014.

[2.1626]
2 Definitions

(1) In these Regulations—

"1992 Act" means the Social Security Contributions and Benefits Act 1992;

"A" means a person with whom C is, or is expected to be, placed for adoption under the law of any part of the United Kingdom;

"AP" means a person who at the date C is placed for adoption is married to, or is the civil partner of, or is the partner of A;

"C" means the child in relation to whom entitlement to statutory shared parental pay arises;

"M" means the mother (or expectant mother) of C;

"P" means the father of C or a person who at the date of C's birth is married to, or is the civil partner of, or is the partner of M;

"actual week of birth", in relation to a child, means the week beginning with midnight between Saturday and Sunday, in which the child was born;

"adoption agency" has the meaning given, in relation to England and Wales, by section 2 of the Adoption and Children Act 2002 and in relation to Scotland, by section 119(1) of the Adoption and Children (Scotland) Act 2007;

"child", in relation to A, means a person who is, or when placed with A for adoption was, under the age of 18;

"the Commissioners" means the Commissioners for Her Majesty's Revenue and Customs;

"expected week of birth", in relation to a child, means the week, beginning with midnight between Saturday and Sunday, in which, as appropriate, it is expected that the child will be born, or was expected that the child would be born;

"partner", in relation to M or A, means a person (whether of a different sex or the same sex) who lives with, as the case may be, M or A as well as C in an enduring family relationship but is not a relative of M or A of a kind specified in paragraph (2);

"placed for adoption" means—

(a) placed for adoption under the Adoption and Children Act 2002 or the Adoption and Children (Scotland) Act 2007; or

(b) placed in accordance with section 22C of the Children Act 1989 with a local authority foster parent who is also a prospective adopter;

"processing", in relation to information, has the meaning given by section 1(1) of the Data Protection Act 1998;

"shared parental leave" means leave under section 75E or 75G of the Employment Rights Act 1996;

"statutory shared parental pay" means statutory shared parental pay payable in accordance with Part 12ZC of the 1992 Act;

"statutory shared parental pay (adoption)" means statutory shared parental pay payable where entitlement to that pay arises under regulation 17 or 18;

"statutory shared parental pay (birth)" means statutory shared parental pay payable where entitlement to that pay arises under regulation 4 or 5;

"week" in Parts 2, 3 and 5 means a period of seven days.

(2) The relatives of M or A referred to in the definition of "partner" in paragraph (1) are M's, or, A's parent, grandparent, sister, brother, aunt, uncle, child, grandchild, niece or nephew.

(3) References to relationships in paragraph (2)—

(a) are to relationships of the full-blood or half-blood or, in the case of an adopted person, such of those relationships as would exist but for the adoption; and

(b) include the relationship of a child with his adoptive, or former adoptive parents, but do not include any other adoptive relationship.

(4) For the purpose of these Regulations—

(a) a person is matched with a child for adoption when an adoption agency decides that that person would be a suitable adoptive parent for the child;

(b) in a case where paragraph (a) applies, a person is notified as having been matched with a child on the date that person receives notification of the agency's decision, under regulation 33(3)(a) of the Adoption Agencies Regulations 2005, regulation 28(3) of the Adoption Agencies (Wales) Regulations 2005 or regulation 8(5) of the Adoption Agencies (Scotland) Regulations 2009;

(c) a person is also matched with a child for adoption when a decision has been made in accordance with regulation 22A of the Care Planning, Placement and Case Review (England) Regulations 2010 and an adoption agency has identified that person with whom the child is to be placed in accordance with regulation 12B of the Adoption Agencies Regulations 2005;

(d) in a case where paragraph (c) applies, a person is notified as having been matched with a child on the date on which that person receives notification in accordance with regulation 12B(2)(a) of the Adoption Agencies Regulations 2005.

(5) The reference to "local authority foster parent" in the definition of "placed for adoption" in paragraph (1) means a person approved as a local authority foster parent in accordance with regulations made by virtue of paragraph 12F of Schedule 2 to the Children Act 1989.

(6) The reference to "prospective adopter" in the definition of "placed for adoption" in paragraph (1) means a person who has been approved as suitable to adopt a child and has been notified of that decision in accordance with regulation 30B(4) of the Adoption Agencies Regulations 2005.

NOTES

Commencement: 1 December 2014.

Modification: this regulation is applied with modifications in relation to parental order cases, by the Statutory Shared Parental Pay (Parental Order Cases) Regulations 2014, SI 2014/3097, reg 4 at **[2.1787]**, and in relation to adoptions from overseas, by the Statutory Shared Parental Pay (Adoption from Overseas) Regulations 2014, SI 2014/3093, regs 3–5 at **[2.1727]–[2.1729]**.

[2.1627]

3 Application

These Regulations apply in relation to—

(a) statutory shared parental pay (birth) in respect of children whose expected week of birth begins on or after 5th April 2015;

(b) statutory shared parental pay (adoption) in respect of children placed for adoption on or after 5th April 2015.

NOTES

Commencement: 1 December 2014.

Modification: this regulation is applied with modifications in relation to parental order cases, by the Statutory Shared Parental Pay (Parental Order Cases) Regulations 2014, SI 2014/3097, reg 5 at **[2.1788]**, and in relation to adoptions from overseas, by the Statutory Shared Parental Pay (Adoption from Overseas) Regulations 2014, SI 2014/3093, regs 3, 4, 6 at **[2.1727]**, **[2.1728]**, **[2.1730]**.

PART 2
ENTITLEMENT TO STATUTORY SHARED PARENTAL PAY (BIRTH)

[2.1628]

4 Entitlement of mother to statutory shared parental pay (birth)

(1) M is entitled to statutory shared parental pay (birth) if M satisfies the conditions specified in paragraph (2) and if P satisfies the conditions specified in paragraphs (3).

(2) The conditions referred to in paragraph (1) are that—

(a) M satisfies the conditions as to continuity of employment and normal weekly earnings specified in regulation 30;

(b) M has at the date of C's birth the main responsibility for the care of C (apart from the responsibility of P);

(c) M has complied with the requirements specified in regulation 6 (notification and evidential requirements of M);

(d) M became entitled by reference to the birth or expected birth of C to statutory maternity pay in respect of C;

(e) the maternity pay period that applies as a result of M's entitlement to statutory maternity pay is, and continues to be, reduced under section 165(3A) of the 1992 Act;

(f) it is M's intention to care for C during each week in respect of which statutory shared parental pay (birth) is paid to her;

(g) M is absent from work during each week in respect of which statutory shared parental pay (birth) is paid to her (except in the cases referred to in regulation 15 (entitlement to shared parental pay: absence from work)); and

(h) where M is an employee (within the meaning of the Employment Rights Act 1996) M's absence from work as an employee during each week that statutory shared parental pay (birth) is paid to her is absence on shared parental leave in respect of C;

(3) The conditions referred to in paragraph (1) are that—

(a) P has at the date of C's birth the main responsibility for the care of C (apart from the responsibility of M); and

(b) P satisfies the conditions relating to employment and earnings in regulation 29 (conditions as to employment and earnings of claimant's partner).

NOTES

Commencement: 1 December 2014.

[2.1629]

5 Entitlement of father or partner to statutory shared parental pay (birth)

(1) P is entitled to statutory shared parental pay (birth) if P satisfies the conditions specified in paragraph (2) and M satisfies the conditions specified in paragraph (3).

(2) The conditions specified in paragraph (1) are that—

(a) P satisfies the conditions as to continuity of employment and normal weekly earnings specified in regulation 30;

(b) P has at the date of C's birth the main responsibility for the care of C (apart from the responsibility of M);

(c) P has complied with the requirements specified in regulation 7 (notification and evidential requirements of P);

(d) it is P's intention to care for C during each week in respect of which statutory shared parental pay (birth) is paid to P;

(e) P is absent from work during each week in respect of which statutory shared parental pay (birth) is paid to P (except in the cases referred to in regulation 15 (entitlement to statutory shared parental pay: absence from work)); and

(f) where P is an employee (within the meaning of the Employment Rights Act 1996 P's absence from work as an employee during each week that statutory shared parental pay (birth) is paid to P is absence on shared parental leave in respect of C.

(3) The conditions specified in paragraph (1) are—

(a) M has at the date of C's birth the main responsibility for the care of C (apart from the responsibility of P);

(b) M meets the conditions as to employment and earnings in regulation 29 (conditions as to employment and earnings of claimant's partner);

(c) M became entitled by reference to the birth, or expected birth, of C to statutory maternity pay or maternity allowance; and

(d) the maternity pay period or the maternity allowance period which applies to M as a result of her entitlement to statutory maternity pay or maternity allowance is, and continues to be, reduced under sections 35(3A) or 165(3A) of the 1992 Act.

NOTES

Commencement: 1 December 2014.

[2.1630]

6 Notification and evidential requirements relating to the mother

(1) The notice and evidential requirements referred to in regulation 4(2)(c) are that M gives the employer who will be liable to pay statutory shared parental pay (birth) to M the notice and information specified in—

(a) paragraphs (2) and (3)(a), (b), (d) and (e) at least 8 weeks before the beginning of the first period specified by M pursuant to paragraph (2)(d);

(b) paragraph (3)(c) at least 8 weeks before the beginning of the first period specified by M pursuant to paragraph (2)(d) or, where C is not born by that time, as soon as reasonably practicable after the birth of C but in any event before the beginning of that first period; and

(c) paragraph (4) within 14 days of that employer requesting that information where the employer requests it within 14 days of receiving the notice and information specified in paragraph (2) and (3)(a),(b),(d) and (e).

(2) The notice specified in this paragraph is notice of—

(a) the number of weeks in respect of which M would be entitled to claim statutory shared parental pay (birth) in respect of C if entitlement were fully exercised disregarding any intention of P to claim statutory shared parental pay in respect of C;

(b) the number of weeks out of those specified under sub-paragraph (a) in respect of which M intends to claim statutory shared parental pay (birth) in respect of C;

(c) the number of weeks out of those specified under sub-paragraph (a) in respect of which P intends to claim statutory shared parental pay (birth) in respect of C;

(d) the period or periods during which M intends to claim statutory shared parental pay (birth) in respect of C.

(3) The information specified in this paragraph is—

(a) a written declaration signed by P who in connection with M's claim is required to satisfy the conditions specified in regulation 4(3)—

(i) that P consents to M's intended claim for statutory shared parental pay;

(ii) that P meets, or will meet, the conditions in regulation 4(3) (conditions to be satisfied by P);

(iii) specifying P's name, address and national insurance number or, if P has no national insurance number, stating that P has no such number; and

(iv) providing P's consent as regards the processing by the employer who will be liable to pay statutory shared parental pay (birth) to M of the information in the written declaration;

(b) C's expected week of birth;

(c) C's date of birth;
(d) M's name;
(e) a written declaration signed by M—
(i) that the information given by M under paragraphs (2) and (3) is correct;
(ii) that M meets, or will meet, the conditions in regulation 4(2);
(iii) that M will immediately inform the person who will be liable to pay statutory shared parental pay (birth) if M ceases to meet the condition in regulation 4(2)(e); and
(iv) specifying the date on which M's maternity pay period or maternity allowance period in respect of C began and the number of weeks by which it is, or will be, reduced.

(4) The information specified in this paragraph is—
(a) a copy of C's birth certificate or, if one has not been issued, a declaration signed by M which states that it has not been issued; and
(b) the name and address of P's employer or, if P has no employer, a written declaration signed by M that P has no employer.

NOTES

Commencement: 1 December 2014.

[2.1631]

7 Notification and evidential requirements relating to the father or partner

(1) The notification and evidential requirements referred to in regulation 5(2)(c), are that P gives the employer who will be liable to pay statutory shared parental pay (birth) to P the notice and information specified in—
(a) paragraphs (2) and (3)(a), (b), (d) and (e) at least 8 weeks before the beginning of the first period specified by P pursuant to paragraph (2)(d);
(b) paragraph 3(c) at least 8 weeks before the beginning of the first period specified by P pursuant to paragraph (2)(d) or, where C is not born by that time, as soon as reasonably practicable after the birth of C but in any event before the beginning of that first period; and
(c) paragraph (4) within 14 days of that employer requesting that information where the employer requests it within 14 days of receiving all the notices and information specified in paragraphs (2) and (3)(a), (b), (d) and (e).

(2) The notice specified in this paragraph is notice of—
(a) the number of weeks in respect of which P would be entitled to claim statutory shared parental pay (birth) in respect of C if entitlement were fully exercised disregarding any intention of M to claim statutory shared parental pay in respect of C;
(b) the number of weeks out of those specified under sub-paragraph (a) in respect of which P intends to claim statutory shared parental pay (birth) in respect of C;
(c) the number of weeks out of those specified under sub-paragraph (a) in respect of which M intends to claim statutory shared parental pay (birth) in respect of C;
(d) the period or periods during which P intends to claim statutory shared parental pay (birth) in respect of C.

(3) The information specified in this paragraph is—
(a) a written declaration signed by M who in connection with P's claim is required to satisfy the conditions specified in regulation 5(3)—
(i) that M consents to P's intended claim for statutory shared parental pay;
(ii) that M meets, or will meet, the conditions in regulation 5(3) (conditions to be satisfied by M);
(iii) that M will immediately inform P if M ceases to meet the condition in regulation 5(3)(d);
(iv) specifying M's name, address and national insurance number or, if M has no national insurance number, stating that M has no such number;
(v) specifying the date on which M's maternity pay period or maternity allowance period in respect of C began and the number of weeks by which it is, or will be, reduced; and
(vi) providing M's consent as regards the processing by the person who is, or will be, liable to pay statutory shared parental pay (birth) to P under section 171ZX(1) of the 1992 Act of the information in the written declaration;
(b) C's expected week of birth;
(c) C's date of birth;
(d) P's name;
(e) a written declaration signed by P—
(i) that the information given by P is correct;
(ii) that P meets, or will meet, the conditions in regulation 5(2); and
(iii) that P will immediately inform the person who will be liable to pay statutory shared parental pay (birth) if M ceases to meet the condition in regulation 5(3)(d).

(4) The information specified in this paragraph is—
(a) a copy of C's birth certificate or, if one has not been issued, a declaration signed by P which states that it has not been issued; and
(b) the name and address of M's employer (or, if M has no employer a written declaration signed by P that M has no employer.

NOTES

Commencement: 1 December 2014.

[2.1632]

8 Variation of number of weeks of pay to be claimed and of periods when pay is to be claimed

(1) M or, as the case may be, P may vary the period or periods during which they intend to claim statutory shared parental pay (birth) by notice in writing given to the employer who will be liable to pay that pay to M or P at least 8 weeks before the beginning of the first period specified in that notice.

(2) M may vary the number of weeks in respect of which M intends to claim statutory shared parental pay (birth) by notice in writing given to the employer who will be liable to pay statutory shared parental pay (birth) to M—

(a) of the number of weeks during which M and P have exercised, or intend to exercise, an entitlement to statutory shared parental pay (birth) in respect of C; and

(b) which is accompanied by a written declaration signed by P who in connection with M's claim is required to satisfy the conditions specified in regulation 4(3) that P consents to that variation.

(3) P may vary the number of weeks in respect of which P intends to claim statutory shared parental pay (birth) by notice in writing given to the employer who will be liable to pay statutory shared parental pay (birth) to P—

(a) of the number of weeks during which P and M have exercised, or intend to exercise, an entitlement to statutory shared parental pay (birth) in respect of C; and

(b) which is accompanied by a written declaration by M who in connection with P's claim is required to satisfy the conditions specified in regulation 5(3) that M consents to that variation.

NOTES

Commencement: 1 December 2014.

[2.1633]

9 Modification of notice conditions in case of early birth

(1) This paragraph applies where—

(a) one or more of the periods specified in a notice given under regulation 6, 7, or 8 during which M or, as the case may be, P intends to claim statutory shared parental pay (birth) start in the 8 weeks following the first day of C's expected week of birth;

(b) C's date of birth is before the first day of the expected week of birth; and

(c) M or, as the case may be, P varies by notice under regulation 8(1) the period or periods referred to in sub-paragraph (a) so that that period or those periods start the same length of time following C's date of birth as that period or those periods would have started after the first day of the expected week of birth.

(2) Where paragraph (1) applies the requirement in regulation 8(1) to give notice at least 8 weeks before the first period specified in the notice is satisfied if such notice is given as soon as reasonably practicable after C's date of birth.

(3) This paragraph applies where—

(a) C is born more than 8 weeks before the first day of the expected week of birth; and

(b) M or, as the case may be, P has not given the notice and information under regulations 6 or 7 before the date of C's birth.

(4) Where paragraph (3) applies and M, or as the case may be, P specifies in a notice under regulation 6 or 7 a period or periods of statutory shared parental pay (birth) which start in the 8 weeks following C's date of birth, then the following modifications apply—

(a) in regulation 6—

(i) paragraph (1)(a) shall apply as if it read—

"(a) paragraphs (2) and (3) as soon as reasonably practicable after the date of C's birth but in any event before the first period specified by M pursuant to paragraph (2)(d);";

(ii) paragraph (1)(b) and (c) shall not apply;

(iii) paragraph (4) shall not apply.

(b) in regulation 7—

(i) paragraph (1)(a) shall apply as if it read—

"(a) paragraphs (2) and (3) as soon as reasonably practicable after the date of C's birth but in any event before the first period specified by P pursuant to paragraph (2)(d).";

(ii) paragraph (1)(b) and (c) shall not apply;

(iii) paragraph (4) shall not apply.

NOTES

Commencement: 1 December 2014.

[2.1634]

10 Extent of entitlement to statutory shared parental pay (birth)

(1) The number of weeks in respect of which M or P is entitled to payments of statutory shared parental pay (birth) in respect of C is 39 weeks less—

(a) the number of weeks—

(i) in respect of which maternity allowance or statutory maternity pay is payable to M in respect of C up to the time M has returned to work (where M has returned to work without satisfying the condition in regulations 4(2)(e) or 5(3)(d) (condition as to reduction of the maternity pay period or the maternity allowance period)); or

Part 2 Statutory Instruments

(ii) in any other case, to which the maternity allowance period is reduced by virtue of section 35(3A) of the 1992 Act or, as the case may be, the maternity pay period is reduced by virtue of section 165(3A); and

(b) the number of weeks of statutory shared parental pay in respect of C which—

(i) in the case of M, P has notified P's intention to claim under regulation 7 or 8; or

(ii) in the case of P, M has notified M's intention to claim under regulation 6 or 8.

(2) In a case where—

(a) P was entitled to payments of statutory shared parental pay (birth) in respect of C; and

(b) P ceases to be so entitled because M ceases to satisfy the condition in regulation 5(3)(d); and

(c) P becomes entitled again to such payments as a result of M satisfying the condition in regulation 5(3)(d);

the number of weeks in which P claimed statutory shared parental pay (birth) up to the time P ceases to be so entitled is also to be deducted from the number of weeks specified in paragraph (1).

(3) Where paragraph (2) applies the number of weeks of statutory shared parental pay (birth) which P notified P's intention to claim under regulation 7(2)(b) (as varied under regulation 8(3)) before P ceases to be entitled to statutory shared parental pay (birth) is to be disregarded for the purposes of this regulation.

(4) In the case where M has more than one entitlement to statutory maternity pay in respect of C and in relation to all those entitlements she returns to work without satisfying the conditions in regulation 4(2)(e) or (5)(3)(d), paragraph (1)(a)(i) shall apply as though it read—

"(i) in respect of which statutory maternity pay is payable to M in respect of C up to the last day M returns to work;".

(5) In the case where M has more than one entitlement to statutory maternity pay in respect of C and the maternity pay periods which apply as a result of those entitlements are all reduced by virtue of section 165(3A) of the 1992 Act before she returns to work, paragraph (1)(a)(ii) shall apply as though it read—

"(ii) falling in the period beginning with the first day of the maternity pay period which is the earliest to begin and ending on the last day of the maternity pay period which is the last to end;".

(6) In the case where M has more than one entitlement to statutory maternity pay in respect of C and—

(a) M returns to work in relation to one or more of those entitlements without satisfying the condition regulation 4(2)(e) or 5(3)(d), and

(b) in relation to one or more of the maternity pay periods which apply as a result of those entitlements that period or those periods are reduced by virtue of section 165(3A) before M returns to work,

paragraph (1)(a) shall apply as though it read—

"(a) the number of weeks falling within the period beginning with the first day of the maternity pay period which is the earliest to begin and ending with the later of—

(i) the last day of the maternity pay period which is reduced by virtue of section 165(3A) before M returns to work (or, where there is more than one such period, the last of those periods); and

(ii) the day on which M returned to work without satisfying the condition in regulation 4(2)(e) or 5(3)(d) in relation to that period (or, where there is more than one such period, the last of those periods);".

(7) In a case where P has more than one entitlement to statutory shared parental pay in respect of C, paragraph (1)(b)(i) shall apply as though it read—

"(i) in the case of M, P has notified P's intention to claim under regulation 7 or 8 falling within the period beginning with the first day of the earliest period so notified and ending with the last day of the latest period so notified;".

(8) In a case where M has more than one entitlement to statutory shared parental pay in respect of C, paragraph (1)(b)(ii) shall apply as though it read—

"(ii) in the case of P, M has notified M's intention to claim under regulations 6 or 8 falling within the period beginning with the first day of the earliest period so notified and ending with the last day of the latest period so notified;".

(9) In a case where P has more than one entitlement to statutory shared parental pay in respect of C, paragraph (2) shall apply as though the number of weeks referred to were the number of weeks which P claimed statutory shared parental pay in respect of C falling within the period beginning with the first day of the earliest period P claimed statutory shared parental pay and ending with the time P ceases to be so entitled.

(10) In this regulation a person is treated as returning to work if one of the following situations apply—

(a) in a case where the person is entitled to maternity allowance, the allowance is not payable to her by virtue of regulations made under section 35(3)(a)(i) of the 1992 Act;

(b) in a case where the person is entitled to statutory maternity pay, that payment is not payable to her in accordance with section 165(4) or (6) of the 1992 Act.

(11) In determining in paragraph (1)(a)(i) the number of weeks in respect of which maternity allowance is payable to M in respect of C up to the time M has returned to work, part of a week in respect of which maternity allowance is payable is to be treated as a whole week.

(12) In paragraph (1)(a)(ii), (6), (7), (8) and (9) part of a week is to be treated as a whole week.

(13) In paragraph (1)(a) "week" has the meaning given by section 122(1) of the 1992 Act, in relation to maternity allowance, or the meaning given by section 165(8) in relation to statutory maternity pay.

NOTES

Commencement: 1 December 2014.

[2.1635]
11 When statutory shared parental pay (birth) is not to be paid

(1) Statutory shared parental pay (birth) is not payable after the day before C's first birthday (or where more than one child is born as a result of the same pregnancy the first birthday of the first child so born).

(2) Statutory shared parental pay (birth) is not payable to M before the end of M's maternity pay period.

NOTES

Commencement: 1 December 2014.

[2.1636]
12 Work during period of payment of statutory shared parental pay (birth)

(1) Despite section 171ZY(4) of the 1992 Act (statutory shared parental pay not payable to a person in respect of a week during any part of which the person works for any employer) statutory shared parental pay (birth) is payable to M or, as the case may be, P—

- (a) in respect of a statutory pay week during any part of which M or, as the case may be, P works only for an employer—
  - (i) who is not liable to pay that person statutory shared parental pay; and
  - (ii) for whom that person worked in the week immediately preceding the 14th week before the expected week of birth; or,
- (b) where M or, as the case may be, P does any work on any day under a contract of service with an employer during a statutory pay week during which that employer is liable to pay that person statutory shared parental pay (birth) in respect of C and where that day and any previous days so worked do not exceed 20.

(2) Where statutory shared parental pay (birth) is paid to M or P in respect of any week falling within a period specified in a notice under regulation 6, 7, and 8 during which M or P works for an employer falling within paragraph (1)(a)(i) but not paragraph (1)(a)(ii), M or, as the case may be, P shall notify the employer liable to pay statutory shared parental pay (birth) within seven days of the first day during which the former does such work.

(3) The notification mentioned in paragraph (2) shall be in writing, if the employer who has been liable to pay statutory shared parental pay (birth) so requests.

(4) In this regulation "statutory pay week" means a week in respect of which that person has chosen to exercise an entitlement to statutory shared parental pay (birth).

NOTES

Commencement: 1 December 2014.

[2.1637]
13 Care of child during period of payment of statutory shared parental pay

Despite section 171ZY(3) of the 1992 Act (statutory shared parental pay not payable to a person in respect of a week if it is not the person's intention at the beginning of the week to care for C) statutory shared parental pay (birth) is payable in the cases referred to in paragraph 6 of the Schedule (death of child).

NOTES

Commencement: 1 December 2014.

[2.1638]
14 Other cases where there is no liability to pay statutory shared parental pay

(1) There is no liability to pay statutory shared parental pay (birth) to M or, as the case may be, P in respect of any week—

- (a) during any part of which the person who is entitled to that pay is entitled to statutory sick pay under Part 11 of the 1992 Act;
- (b) following that in which the person who is claiming that pay has died; or
- (c) during any part of which the person who is entitled to that pay is detained in legal custody or sentenced to a term of imprisonment except where the sentence is suspended (but see paragraph (2)).

(2) There is liability to pay statutory shared parental pay (birth) to M or, as the case may be, P in respect of any week during any part of which the person who is entitled to that pay is detained in legal custody where that person—

- (a) is released subsequently without charge;

(b) is subsequently found not guilty of any offence and is released; or
(c) is convicted of an offence but does not receive a custodial sentence.

NOTES
Commencement: 1 December 2014.

[2.1639]
15 Conditions of entitlement to statutory shared parental pay: absence from work

(1) The condition in regulation 4(2)(g) and 5(2)(e) does not apply where M or, as the case may be, P—
(a) during any part of a statutory pay week works other than for an employer;
(b) during any part of a statutory pay week works only for an employer who falls within paragraph (1)(a) of regulation 12 (work during period payment of statutory shared parental pay);
(c) works in circumstance where paragraph (1)(b) of regulation 12 applies.

(2) In this regulation "statutory pay week" means a week in respect of which that person has chosen to exercise an entitlement to statutory shared parental pay (birth).

NOTES
Commencement: 1 December 2014.

[2.1640]
16 Entitlement to statutory shared parental pay (birth) in cases relating to death

The Part 1 of the Schedule (statutory shared parental pay in special circumstances) has effect.

NOTES
Commencement: 1 December 2014.

PART 3
ENTITLEMENT TO STATUTORY SHARED PARENTAL PAY (ADOPTION)

[2.1641]
17 Entitlement of adopter to statutory shared parental pay (adoption)

(1) A is entitled to statutory shared parental pay (adoption) if A satisfies the conditions specified in paragraph (2) and AP satisfies the conditions specified in paragraph (3).

(2) The conditions referred to in paragraph (1) are that—
(a) A satisfies the conditions as to continuity of employment and normal weekly earnings specified in regulation 31 (conditions as to claimant's continuity of employment and normal weekly earnings);
(b) A has at the date of C's placement for adoption the main responsibility for the care of C (apart from the responsibility of AP);
(c) A has complied with the requirements specified in regulation 19 (notification and evidential requirements);
(d) A became entitled to statutory adoption pay by reference to the placement for adoption of C;
(e) the adoption pay period that applies as a result of A's entitlement to statutory adoption pay is, and continues to be, reduced under section 171ZN(2A) of the 1992 Act;
(f) it is A's intention to care for C during each week in respect of which statutory shared parental pay (adoption) is paid to A;
(g) A is absent from work during each week in respect of which statutory shared parental pay is paid to A (except in the cases referred to in regulation 27 (entitlement to statutory shared parental pay (adoption): absence from work); and
(h) where A is an employee (within the meaning of the Employment Rights Act 1996) A's absence from work as an employee during each week that statutory shared parental pay is paid to A is absence on shared parental leave in respect of C.

(3) The conditions referred to in paragraph (1) are that—
(a) AP has at the date of C's placement for adoption the main responsibility for the care of C (apart from the responsibility of A); and
(b) AP satisfies the employment and earnings conditions in regulation 29 (conditions relating to employment and earnings of claimant's partner).

NOTES
Commencement: 1 December 2014.
Modification: this regulation is applied with modifications in relation to parental order cases, by the Statutory Shared Parental Pay (Parental Order Cases) Regulations 2014, SI 2014/3097, reg 6 at **[2.1789]**, and in relation to adoptions from overseas, by the Statutory Shared Parental Pay (Adoption from Overseas) Regulations 2014, SI 2014/3093, regs 3, 4, 7 at **[2.1727]**, **[2.1728]**, **[2.1731]**.

[2.1642]
18 Entitlement of partner to statutory shared parental pay (adoption)

(1) AP is entitled to statutory shared parental pay (adoption) if AP satisfies the conditions specified in paragraph (2) and A satisfies the conditions specified in paragraph (3).

(2) The conditions specified in paragraph (1) are that—

(a) AP satisfies the conditions as to continuity of employment and normal weekly earnings specified in regulation 31 (conditions as to continuity of employment and normal weekly earnings);
(b) AP has at the date of C's placement for adoption the main responsibility for the care of C (apart from the responsibility of A);
(c) AP has complied with the requirements specified in regulation 20 (notification and evidential requirements);
(d) it is AP's intention to care for C during each week in respect of which statutory shared parental pay (adoption) is paid to AP;
(e) AP is absent from work during each week in respect of which statutory shared parental pay (adoption) is paid to AP (except in the cases referred to in regulation 27 (entitlement to statutory shared parental pay: absence from work)); and
(f) where AP is an employee (within the meaning of the Employment Rights Act 1996) AP's absence from work as an employee during each week that statutory shared parental pay is paid to AP is absence on shared parental leave in respect of C.

(3) The conditions specified in paragraph (1) are that—
(a) A has at the date of C's placement for adoption the main responsibility for the care of C (apart from any responsibility of AP);
(b) A satisfies the employment and earnings conditions in regulation 29;
(c) A became entitled to statutory adoption pay by reference to the placement for adoption of C; and
(d) the adoption pay period that applies as a result A's entitlement to statutory adoption pay is, and continues to be, reduced under section 171ZN(2A) of the 1992 Act.

NOTES

Commencement: 1 December 2014.

Modification: this regulation is applied with modifications in relation to parental order cases, by the Statutory Shared Parental Pay (Parental Order Cases) Regulations 2014, SI 2014/3097, reg 7 at **[2.1790]**, and in relation to adoptions from overseas, by the Statutory Shared Parental Pay (Adoption from Overseas) Regulations 2014, SI 2014/3093, regs 3, 4, 8 at **[2.1727]**, **[2.1728]**, **[2.1732]**.

[2.1643]

19 Notification and evidential requirements relating to the adopter

(1) The notification and evidential requirements referred to in regulation 17(2)(c) are that A gives the employer who will be liable to pay statutory shared parental pay (adoption) to A the notice and information specified in—
(a) paragraphs (2) and (3)(a), (b), (d) and (e) at least 8 weeks before the beginning of the first period specified by A pursuant to paragraph (2)(d);
(b) paragraph (3)(c) at least 8 weeks before the beginning of the first period specified by A pursuant to paragraph (2)(d) or, if C is not placed for adoption by that time, as soon as reasonably practicable after the placement of C but in any event before the beginning of that first period; and
(c) paragraph (4) within 14 days of that employer requesting that information where the employer requests it within 14 days of receiving the notice and information specified in paragraph (2) and (3)(a), (b), (d) and (e).

(2) The notice specified in this paragraph is notice of—
(a) the number of weeks in respect of which A would be entitled to claim statutory shared parental pay (adoption) in respect of C if entitlement were fully exercised disregarding any intention of AP to claim statutory shared parental pay (adoption) in respect of C;
(b) the number of weeks (out of those specified under paragraph (2)(a)) in respect of which A intends to claim statutory shared parental pay (adoption) in respect of C;
(c) the number of weeks (out of those specified under paragraph (2)(a)) in respect of which AP intends to claim statutory shared parental pay (adoption) in respect of C; and
(d) the period or periods during which A intends to claim statutory shared parental pay (adoption) in respect of C.

(3) The information specified in this paragraph is—
(a) a written declaration signed by AP who in connection with A's claim is required to satisfy the conditions specified in regulation 17(3)—
(i) that AP consents to A's intended claim for statutory shared parental pay;
(ii) that AP meets or will meet the conditions in regulation 17(3) (conditions to be satisfied by AP);
(iii) specifying AP's name, address and national insurance number or, if AP has no national insurance number, stating that AP has no such number; and
(iv) providing AP's consent as regards the processing by the employer who will be liable to pay statutory shared parental pay (adoption) to A of the information in the written declaration;
(b) the date on which A was notified that A had been matched with C;
(c) the date of C's placement for adoption;
(d) A's name; and
(e) a written declaration signed by A—
(i) that the information given by A under paragraph (2) and (3) is correct;
(ii) that A meets or will meet the conditions in regulation 17(2); and

Part 2 Statutory Instruments

(iii) that A will immediately inform the person who will be liable to pay statutory shared parental pay (adoption) if A ceases to meet the condition in regulation 17(2)(e); and

(iv) specifying the date on which A's adoption pay period in respect of C began and the number of weeks by which it is, or will be, reduced.

(4) The information specified in this paragraph is—

(a) evidence, in the form of one or more documents issued by the adoption agency that matched A with C, of—

(i) the name and address of the adoption agency;

(ii) the date on which A was notified that A had been matched with C; and

(iii) the date on which the adoption agency was expecting to place C with A; and

(b) the name and address of AP's employer or, if AP has no employer, a written declaration signed by A that AP has no employer.

NOTES

Commencement: 1 December 2014.

Modification: this regulation is applied with modifications in relation to parental order cases, by the Statutory Shared Parental Pay (Parental Order Cases) Regulations 2014, SI 2014/3097, regs 8, 10 at **[2.1791]**, **[2.1793]**, and in relation to adoptions from overseas, by the Statutory Shared Parental Pay (Adoption from Overseas) Regulations 2014, SI 2014/3093, regs 3, 4, 9 at **[2.1727]**, **[2.1728]**, **[2.1733]**.

[2.1644]

20 Notification and evidential requirements relating to the partner

(1) The notification and evidential conditions referred to in regulation 18(2)(c) are that AP gives the employer who will be liable to pay statutory shared parental pay (adoption) to AP the notice and information specified in—

(a) paragraphs (2) and (3)(a), (b), (d) and (e) at least 8 weeks before the beginning of the first period specified by AP pursuant to paragraph (2)(d);

(b) paragraph (3)(c) at least 8 weeks before the beginning of the first period specified by AP pursuant to paragraph (2)(d) or if C is not placed for adoption by that time, as soon as reasonably practicable after the placement of C but in any event before that first period; and

(c) paragraph (4) (where applicable) within 14 days of that employer requesting this information where the employer requests it within 14 days of receiving all the notice and information specified in paragraph (2) and (3)(a), (b), (d) and (e).

(2) The notice specified in this paragraph is notice of—

(a) the number of weeks in respect of which AP would be entitled to claim statutory shared parental pay (adoption) in respect of C if entitlement were fully exercised disregarding any intention of A to claim statutory shared parental pay (adoption) in respect of C;

(b) the number of weeks (out of those specified under paragraph (2)(a)) in respect of which AP intends to claim statutory shared parental pay (adoption) in respect of C;

(c) the number of weeks (out of those specified under paragraph (2)(a)) in respect of which A intends to claim statutory shared parental pay (adoption) in respect of C;

(d) the period or periods during which AP intends to claim statutory shared parental pay (adoption) in respect of C.

(3) The information specified in this paragraph is—

(a) a written declaration signed by A who in connection with AP's claim is required to satisfy the conditions in regulation 18(3)—

(i) that A consents to AP's intended claim for statutory shared parental pay (adoption);

(ii) that A meets, or will meet, the conditions in regulation 18(3) (conditions to be satisfied by A);

(iii) that A will immediately inform AP if A ceases to meet the conditions in regulation 18(3)(d);

(iv) specifying A's name, address and national insurance number or, if A has no national insurance number, stating that A has no such number;

(v) specifying the date on which A's adoption pay period in respect of C began and the number of weeks by which it is, or will be, reduced; and

(vi) providing A's consent as regards the processing by the employer who is, or will be, liable to pay statutory shared parental pay (adoption) to AP of the information in the written declaration;

(b) the date on which A was notified that A had been matched with C;

(c) the date of C's placement for adoption;

(d) AP's name;

(e) a written declaration signed by AP—

(i) that the information given by AP is correct;

(ii) that AP meets, or will meet, the conditions in regulation 18(2); and

(iii) that AP will immediately inform the person who will be liable to pay statutory shared parental pay (adoption) if A ceases to meet the condition 18(3)(d) .

(4) The information specified in this paragraph is—

(a) evidence, in the form of one or more documents issued by the adoption agency that matched A with C, of—

(i) the name and address of the adoption agency;

(ii) the date on which A was notified that A had been matched with C; and

(iii) the date on which the adoption agency was expecting to place C for adoption with A; and

(b) the name and address of A's employer or, if A has no employer, a written declaration signed by AP that A has no employer.

NOTES

Commencement: 1 December 2014.

Modification: this regulation is applied with modifications in relation to parental order cases, by the Statutory Shared Parental Pay (Parental Order Cases) Regulations 2014, SI 2014/3097, regs 9, 10 at **[2.1792]**, **[2.1793]**, and in relation to adoptions from overseas, by the Statutory Shared Parental Pay (Adoption from Overseas) Regulations 2014, SI 2014/3093, regs 3, 4, 10 at **[2.1727]**, **[2.1728]**, **[2.1734]**.

[2.1645]

21 Variation of number of weeks of pay to be claimed and of periods when pay is to be claimed

(1) A or, as the case may be, AP may vary the period or periods during which they intend to claim statutory shared parental pay (adoption) by notice in writing given to the employer who will be liable to pay that pay to A or AP at least 8 weeks before the beginning of the first period specified in that notice.

(2) A may vary the number of weeks in respect of which A intends to claim statutory shared parental pay (adoption) by notice in writing given to the employer who will be liable to pay that pay to A—

(a) of the number of weeks during which A and AP have exercised, or intend to exercise, an entitlement to statutory shared parental pay in respect of C; and

(b) which contains a written declaration signed by AP who in connection with A's claim is required to satisfy the conditions in regulation 17(3) that AP consents to that variation.

(3) AP may vary the number of weeks in respect of which AP intends to claim statutory shared parental pay (adoption) by notice in writing given to the employer who will be liable to pay that pay to AP—

(a) of the number of weeks during which AP and A have exercised, or intend to exercise, an entitlement to statutory shared parental pay (adoption) in respect of C; and

(b) which is accompanied by a written declaration by A who in connection with AP's claim is requires to satisfy the conditions in regulation 18(3) that A consents to that variation.

NOTES

Commencement: 1 December 2014.

[2.1646]

22 Extent of entitlement to statutory shared parental pay (adoption)

(1) The number of weeks in respect of which A or, as the case may be, AP is entitled to payments of statutory shared parental pay (adoption) in respect of C is 39 weeks less—

(a) the number of weeks—

(i) in respect of which statutory adoption pay is payable to A in respect of C up to the time that person has returned to work (where that person has returned to work without satisfying the conditions in regulations 17(2)(e) or 18(3)(d)) (condition as to reduction in adoption pay period); or

(ii) in any other case, to which the adoption pay period is reduced by virtue of section 171ZN(2A) of the 1992 Act; and

(b) the number of weeks of statutory shared parental pay (adoption) in respect of C which—

(i) in the case of A, AP has notified AP's intention to claim under regulation 20 or 21; or

(ii) in the case of AP, A has notified A's intention to claim under regulation 19 or 21.

(2) In the case where A has more than one entitlement to statutory adoption pay in respect of C and in relation to all those entitlements A returns to work without satisfying the conditions in regulation 17(2)(e) or 18(3)(d), paragraph (1)(a)(i) shall apply as though it read—

"(i) in respect of which statutory adoption pay is payable to A in respect of C up to the last day A returns to work;".

(3) In the case where A has more than one entitlement to statutory adoption pay in respect of C and the adoption pay periods which apply as a result of those entitlements are all reduced by virtue of section 171ZN(2A) of the 1992 Act before A returns to work, paragraph (1)(a)(ii) shall apply as though it read—

"(ii) falling in the period beginning with the first day of the adoption pay period which is the earliest to begin and ending with the last day of the adoption pay period which is the last to end;".

(4) In a case where A has more than one entitlement to statutory adoption pay in respect of C and—

(a) A returns to work in relation to one or more of those entitlements without satisfying the conditions in regulation 17(2)(e) or 18(3)(d), and

(b) in relation to one or more of the adoption pay periods which apply as a result of those entitlements that period or those periods are reduced by virtue of section 171ZN(2A) of the 1992 Act before A returns to work,

paragraph (1)(a) shall apply as though it read—

"(a) the number of weeks falling within the period beginning with the first day of the adoption pay period which is the earliest to begin and ending with the later of—

(i) the last day of the adoption pay period which is reduced by virtue of section 171ZN(2A) of the 1992 Act before A returns to work (or, where there is more than one such period, the last of those periods); and

(ii) the day on which A returned to work without satisfying the conditions in regulation 17(2)(e) or 18(3)(d) in relation to that period (or, where there is more than one such period, the last of those periods);".

(5) In the case where AP has more than one entitlement to statutory shared parental pay in respect of C, paragraph (1)(b)(i) shall apply as though it read—

"(i) in the case of A, AP has notified AP's intention to claim under regulation 20 or 21 falling within the period beginning with the first day of the earliest period so notified and ending with the last day of the latest period so notified;".

(6) In the case where A has more than one entitlement to statutory shared parental pay in respect of C, paragraph (1)(b)(ii) shall apply as though it read—

"(ii) in the case of AP, A has notified A's intention to claim under regulation 19 or 21 falling within the period beginning with the first day of the earliest period so notified and ending with the last day of the latest period so notified;".

(7) In this regulation a person is treated as returning to work if statutory adoption pay is not payable to A in accordance with section 171ZN(3) or (5) of the 1992 Act.

(8) In paragraph (1)(a)(ii), (4), (5) and (6) part of a week is to be treated as a whole week.

(9) In paragraph (1)(a) "week" has the meaning given by section 171ZN(8) of the 1992 Act.

NOTES

Commencement: 1 December 2014.

[2.1647]

23 When statutory shared parental pay (adoption) is not to be paid

(1) Statutory shared parental pay (adoption) is not payable after the day before the first anniversary of the date on which C was placed for adoption (or where more than one child is placed for adoption through a single placement, the first anniversary of the date of placement of the first child).

(2) Statutory shared parental pay (adoption) is not payable to A before the end of A's adoption pay period.

NOTES

Commencement: 1 December 2014.

Modification: this regulation is applied with modifications in relation to parental order cases, by the Statutory Shared Parental Pay (Parental Order Cases) Regulations 2014, SI 2014/3097, reg 11 at **[2.1794]**, and in relation to adoptions from overseas, by the Statutory Shared Parental Pay (Adoption from Overseas) Regulations 2014, SI 2014/3093, regs 3, 4, 11 at **[2.1727]**, **[2.1728]**, **[2.1735]**.

[2.1648]

24 Work during period of payment of statutory shared parental pay (adoption)

(1) Despite section 171ZY(4) of the 1992 Act (statutory shared parental pay not payable to a person in respect of a week during any part of which person works for any employer) statutory shared parental pay (adoption) is payable to A or, as the case may be, AP—

(a) in respect of a statutory pay week during any part of which A or, as the case may be, AP works only for an employer—

(i) who is not liable to pay that person statutory shared parental pay; and

(ii) for whom that person worked in the week immediately preceding the 14th week before the expected week of the placement for adoption; or

(b) where A or, as the case may be, AP does any work on any day under a contract of service with an employer during a statutory pay week during which that employer is liable to pay that person statutory shared parental pay (adoption) in respect of C and where that day and any previous days so worked do not exceed 20.

(2) Where statutory shared parental pay (adoption) is paid to A or AP in respect of any week falling within a period specified in a notice under regulation 19, 20 or 21 during which A or AP works for an employer falling within paragraph (1)(a)(i) but not paragraph (1)(a)(ii) A or, as the case may be, AP shall notify the employer liable to pay statutory shared parental pay within seven days of the first day during which the former does such work.

(3) The notification mentioned in paragraph (2) shall be in writing, if the employer who has been liable to pay statutory shared parental pay so requests.

(4) In this regulation "statutory pay week" means a week in respect of which that person has chosen to exercise an entitlement to statutory shared parental pay (adoption).

NOTES

Commencement: 1 December 2014.

Modification: this regulation is applied with modifications in relation to parental order cases, by the Statutory Shared Parental Pay (Parental Order Cases) Regulations 2014, SI 2014/3097, reg 12 at **[2.1795]**, and in relation to adoptions from overseas, by the Statutory Shared Parental Pay (Adoption from Overseas) Regulations 2014, SI 2014/3093, regs 3, 4, 12 at **[2.1727]**, **[2.1728]**, **[2.1736]**.

[2.1649]

25 Care of child during period of payment of statutory shared parental pay

Despite section 171ZY(3) of the 1992 Act (statutory shared parental pay not payable to a person in respect of a week if it is not the person's intention at the beginning of the week to care for C) statutory shared parental pay (adoption) is payable in the cases set out in paragraph 12 of the Schedule (disrupted placement or death of child).

NOTES

Commencement: 1 December 2014.

[2.1650]

26 Other cases where there is no liability to pay statutory shared parental pay

(1) There is no liability to pay statutory shared parental pay (adoption) to A or, as the case may be, AP in respect of any week—

(a) during any part of which the person who is entitled to that pay is entitled to statutory sick pay under Part 11 of the 1992 Act;

(b) following that in which the person who is claiming that has died; or

(c) during any part of which the person who is entitled to it is detained in legal custody or sentenced to a term of imprisonment except where the sentence is suspended (but see paragraph (2)).

(2) There is liability to pay statutory shared parental pay to A or, as the case may be, AP in respect of any week during any part of which the person entitled to that pay is detained in legal custody where that person—

(a) is released subsequently without charge;

(b) is subsequently found not guilty of any offence and is released; or

(c) is convicted of an offence but does not receive a custodial sentence.

NOTES

Commencement: 1 December 2014.

[2.1651]

27 Conditions of entitlement to statutory shared parental pay: absence from work

(1) The condition in regulations 17(2)(g) and 18(2)(e) does not apply are where A or, as the case may be, AP—

(a) during any part of a statutory pay week works other than for an employer;

(b) during any part of a statutory pay week works only for an employer who falls within paragraph (1)(a) of regulation 24 (work during period payment of statutory shared parental pay);

(c) works in circumstances where paragraph (1)(b) of regulation 24 applies.

(2) In this regulation "statutory pay week" means a week in respect of which that person has chosen to exercise an entitlement to statutory shared parental pay (adoption).

NOTES

Commencement: 1 December 2014.

[2.1652]

28 Entitlement to statutory shared parental pay (adoption) in cases relating to death

Part 2 of the Schedule (statutory shared parental pay in special circumstances) has effect.

NOTES

Commencement: 1 December 2014.

PART 4
CONDITIONS OF ENTITLEMENT RELATING TO EMPLOYMENT AND EARNINGS

[2.1653]

29 Conditions relating to employment and earnings of a claimant's partner

(1) In relation to the entitlement of M, P, A or AP to statutory shared parental pay a person satisfies the conditions as to earnings and employment specified in regulations 4(3)(b), 5(3)(b), 17(3)(b) and 18(3)(b) if that person—

(a) has been engaged in employment as an employed or self-employed earner for any part of the week in the case of at least 26 of the 66 weeks immediately preceding the calculation week; and

(b) has average weekly earnings (determined in accordance with paragraph (2)) of not less than the amount set out in section 35A(6A) (state maternity allowance) of the 1992 Act in relation to the tax year before the tax year containing the calculation week.

(2) A person's average weekly earnings are determined by dividing by 13 the specified payments made, or treated as being made, to or for the benefit of that person in the 13 weeks (whether or not consecutive) in the period of 66 weeks immediately preceding the calculation week in which the payments are greatest.

(3) Where a person receives any pay after the end of the period in [paragraph (2)] in respect of any week falling [within] that period, the average weekly amount is to be determined as if such sum had been paid in that period.

(4) Where a person is not paid weekly, the payments made or treated as made for that person's benefit for the purposes of [paragraph (2)], are to be determined by dividing the total sum paid to that individual by the nearest whole number of weeks in respect of which that sum is paid.

(5) In this regulation—

"calculation week" means in relation to—

(a) statutory shared parental pay (birth) the expected week of birth of C; and

(b) statutory shared parental pay (adoption), the week in which A was notified as having been matched for adoption with C;

"employed earner" has the meaning given by section 2 of the 1992 Act, subject for these purposes to the effect of regulations made under section 2(2)(b) of that Act;

"self-employed earner" has the meaning given by section 2 of the 1992 Act, subject for these purposes to the effect of regulations made under section 2(2)(b) of that Act;

"specified payments"—

(a) in relation to a self-employed earner who satisfies the conditions in paragraph (6), are to be treated as made to the self-employed earner at an amount per week equal to the amount set out in section 35(6A) of the 1992 Act that is in force at the end of the week;

(b) in relation to an employed earner, are all payments made to the employed earner or for that employed earner's benefit as an employed earner specified in regulation 2 (specified payments for employed earners) of the Social Security (Maternity Allowance) (Earnings) Regulations 2000;

"tax year" means the 12 months beginning with the 6th April in any year.

(6) The conditions referred to in paragraph (a) of the definition of "specified payments" are that, in respect of any week, the self-employed earner—

(a) does not hold a certificate of exception issued pursuant to regulation 44(1) of the Social Security (Contributions) Regulations 2001 and has paid a Class 2 contribution (within the meaning of section 1 of the 1992 Act), or

(b) holds such a certificate of exception.

NOTES

Commencement: 1 December 2014.

Paras (3), (4): words in square brackets substituted by the Statutory Shared Parental Pay (General) (Amendment) Regulations 2015, SI 2015/189, reg 2(1), (2), as from 8 March 2015.

Modification: this regulation is applied with modifications in relation to parental order cases, by the Statutory Shared Parental Pay (Parental Order Cases) Regulations 2014, SI 2014/3097, reg 13 at **[2.1796]**, and in relation to adoptions from overseas, by the Statutory Shared Parental Pay (Adoption from Overseas) Regulations 2014, SI 2014/3093, regs 3, 4, 13 at **[2.1727]**, **[2.1728]**, **[2.1737]**.

[2.1654]

30 Conditions as to continuity of employment and normal weekly earnings relating to a claimant for statutory shared parental pay (birth)

(1) The conditions as to continuity of employment and normal weekly earnings referred to in regulation 4(2)(a) and 5(2)(a) are—

(a) the person has been in employed earner's employment with an employer for a continuous period of at least 26 weeks ending with the relevant week;

(b) the person's normal weekly earnings (see regulation 32) with the employer by reference to which the condition in sub-paragraph (a) is satisfied for the period of eight weeks ending with the relevant week are not less than the lower earnings limit in force under subsection (1)(a) of section 5 (earnings limits and thresholds for class 1 contributions) of the 1992 Act at the end of the relevant week;

(c) the person continues in employed earner's employment with the employer by reference to which the condition in sub-paragraph (a) is satisfied for a continuous period beginning with the relevant week and ending with the week before the first week falling within the relevant period relating to that person under section 171ZY(2) of the 1992 Act.

[(1A) Paragraph (1B) applies where a person has been in employed earner's employment with the same employer in each of 26 consecutive weeks (but no more than 26 weeks), ending with the relevant week.

(1B) For the purpose of determining whether a person meets the condition in paragraph (1)(a), the first of those 26 weeks is a period commencing on the first day of the person's employment with the employer ("the start date") and ending at midnight on—

(a) the first Saturday after the start date, or

(b) where the start date is a Saturday, that day.]

(2) Where C's birth occurs earlier than the 14th week before C's expected week of birth paragraph (1) shall have effect as if, for the conditions set out there, there were substituted conditions that—

(a) the person would have been in employed earner's employment for a continuous period of at least 26 weeks ending with the relevant week had C been born after the relevant week;

(b) the person's normal weekly earnings for the period of eight weeks ending with the week immediately preceding C's actual week of birth are not less than the lower earnings limit in force under section 5(1)(a) of the 1992 Act immediately before the commencement of C's actual week of birth; and

(c) the person continues in employed earner's employment with the employer by reference to whom the condition in sub-paragraph (a) is satisfied for a continuous period beginning with the date of C's birth and ending with the week before the first week falling within the relevant period relating to that person under section 171ZY(2) of the 1992 Act.

(3) The references in this regulation to the relevant week are to the week immediately preceding the 14th week before C's expected week of birth.

(4) Where more than one child is born as a result of the same pregnancy the date the first child is born is to be used to determine C's actual week of birth or the date of C's birth.

NOTES

Commencement: 1 December 2014.

Paras (1A), (1B): inserted by the Statutory Paternity Pay, Statutory Adoption Pay and Statutory Shared Parental Pay (Amendment) Regulations 2015, SI 2015/2065, reg 3(1), (2), as from 1 February 2016.

[2.1655]

31 Conditions as to continuity of employment and normal weekly earnings in relation to a claimant for statutory shared parental pay (adoption)

(1) The conditions as to continuity of employment and normal weekly earnings referred to in regulations 17(2)(a) and 18(2)(a) relating to the entitlement of A and AP to statutory shared parental pay (adoption) are—

(a) the person has been in employed earner's employment with an employer for a continuous period of at least 26 weeks ending with the relevant week;

(b) the person's normal weekly earnings (see regulation 32) with the employer by reference to which the condition in sub-paragraph (a) is satisfied for the period of eight weeks ending with the relevant week are not less than the lower earnings limit in force under subsection (1)(a) of section 5 (earnings limits and thresholds for class 1 contributions) of the 1992 Act at the end of the [relevant week];

(c) the person continues in employed earner's employment with the employer by reference to which the condition in sub-paragraph (a) is satisfied for a continuous period beginning with the relevant week and ending with the week before the first week falling within the relevant period relating to that person under section 171ZY(2) of the 1992 Act.

[(1A) Paragraph (1B) applies where a person has been in employed earner's employment with the same employer in each of 26 consecutive weeks (but no more than 26 weeks), ending with the relevant week.

(1B) For the purpose of determining whether a person meets the condition in paragraph (1)(a), the first of those 26 weeks is a period commencing on the first day of the person's employment with the employer ("the start date") and ending at midnight on—

(a) the first Saturday after the start date, or

(b) where the start date is a Saturday, that day.]

(2) The references in paragraph (1) to the relevant week are to the week in which A was notified of having been matched with C.

NOTES

Commencement: 1 December 2014.

Para (1): words in square brackets substituted by the Statutory Shared Parental Pay (General) (Amendment) Regulations 2015, SI 2015/189, reg 2(1), (3), as from 8 March 2015.

Paras (1A), (1B): inserted by the Statutory Paternity Pay, Statutory Adoption Pay and Statutory Shared Parental Pay (Amendment) Regulations 2015, SI 2015/2065, reg 3(1), (3), as from 1 February 2016.

Modification: this regulation is applied with modifications in relation to parental order cases, by the Statutory Shared Parental Pay (Parental Order Cases) Regulations 2014, SI 2014/3097, reg 14 at **[2.1797]**, and in relation to adoptions from overseas, by the Statutory Shared Parental Pay (Adoption from Overseas) Regulations 2014, SI 2014/3093, regs 3, 4, 14 at **[2.1727]**, **[2.1728]**, **[2.1738]**.

[2.1656]

32 Normal weekly earnings of a claimant for statutory shared parental pay

(1) For the purpose of section 171ZZ4(6) (which defines normal weekly earnings for the purposes of Part 12ZC of the 1992 Act) "earnings" and "relevant period" have the meanings given in this regulation.

(2) The relevant period is the period—

(a) ending on the last normal pay day to fall before the appropriate date; and

(b) beginning with the day following the last normal pay day to fall at least eight weeks earlier than the normal pay day mentioned in sub-paragraph (a).

(3) In a case where a person has no identifiable normal pay day, paragraph (2) shall have effect as if the words "day of payment" were substituted for the words "normal pay day" in each place where they occur.

(4) In a case where a person has normal pay days at intervals of or approximating to one or more calendar months (including intervals of or approximating to a year) that person's normal weekly earnings shall be calculated by dividing their earnings in the relevant period by the number of calendar months in that period (or, if it is not a whole number, the nearest whole number), multiplying the result by 12 and dividing by 52.

(5) In a case to which paragraph (4) does not apply and the relevant period is not an exact number of weeks, the person's normal weekly earnings shall be calculated by dividing their earnings in the relevant period by the number of days in the relevant period and multiplying the result by seven.

(6) In any case where a person receives a back-dated pay increase which includes a sum in respect of a relevant period, normal weekly earnings shall be calculated as if such a sum was paid in that relevant period even though received after that period.

(7) The expression "earnings" refers to gross earnings and includes any remuneration or profit derived from a person's employment except any amount which is—

(a) excluded from the computation of a person's earnings under regulation 25 (payments to be disregarded) of, and Schedule 3 to, the Social Security (Contributions) Regulations 2001 and regulation 27 (payments to directors to be disregarded) of those Regulations (or would have been so excluded had they not been made under the age of 16);

(b) a chargeable emolument under section 10A (class 1B contributions) of the 1992 Act except where, in consequence of such a chargeable emolument being excluded from earnings, a person would not be entitled to statutory shared parental pay (or where such a payment or amount would have been so excluded and in consequence the person would not have been entitled to statutory shared parental pay had they not been aged under the age of 16).

(8) The expression "earnings" includes—

(a) any amount retrospectively treated as earnings by regulations made by virtue of section 4B(2) of the 1992 Act;

(b) any sum payable in respect of arrears of pay in pursuance of an order for reinstatement or re-engagement under the Employment Rights Act 1996;

(c) any sum payable by way of pay in pursuance of an order made under the Employment Rights Act 1996 for the continuation of a contract of employment;

(d) any sum payable by way of remuneration in pursuance of a protective award under section 189 of the Trade Union and Labour Relations (Consolidation) Act 1992;

(e) any sum payable by way of statutory sick pay, including sums payable in accordance with regulations made under section 151(6) of the 1992 Act;

(f) any sum payable by way of statutory maternity pay;

(g) any sum payable by way of statutory paternity pay;

(h) any sum payable by way of statutory shared parental pay; and

(i) any sum payable by way of statutory adoption pay.

(9) In paragraphs (2) to (4)—

(a) "the appropriate date" means—

(i) in relation to statutory shared parental pay (birth), the first day of the 14th week before the expected week of the child's birth or the first day in the week in which the child is born, whichever is earlier (but see paragraph (10)),

(ii) in relation to statutory shared parental pay (adoption) the first day of the week after the week in which A is notified of being matched with the child for the purposes of adoption;

(b) "day of payment" means a day on which the person was paid; and

(c) "normal pay day" means a day on which the terms of a person's contract of service require the person to be paid, or the practice in that person's employment is for that person to be paid if any payment is due to them.

(10) Where more than one child is born as a result of the same pregnancy, the date the first child is born is to be used to determine the week in which the child is born.

NOTES

Commencement: 1 December 2014.

Modification: this regulation is applied with modifications in relation to parental order cases, by the Statutory Shared Parental Pay (Parental Order Cases) Regulations 2014, SI 2014/3097, reg 15 at **[2.1798]**, and in relation to adoptions from overseas, by the Statutory Shared Parental Pay (Adoption from Overseas) Regulations 2014, SI 2014/3093, regs 3, 4, 15 at **[2.1727]**, **[2.1728]**, **[2.1739]**.

[2.1657]

33 Treatment of persons as employees

(1) A person is treated as an employee for the purposes of Part 12ZC of the 1992 Act (even though not falling within the definition of 'employee' in section 171ZZ4(2) of that Act) where, and in so far as, that person is treated as an employed earner by virtue of the Social Security (Categorisation of Earners) Regulations 1978 (but see paragraph (3)).

(2) A person shall not be treated as an employee for the purposes of Part 12ZC of the 1992 Act (even though falling within the definition of 'employee' in section 171ZZ4(2) of that Act) where, and in so far as, that person is not treated as an employed earner by virtue of those Regulations (but see paragraph (3)).

(3) Paragraphs (1) and (2) shall have effect in relation to a person who—

(a) is under the age of 16; and

(b) would, or as the case may be, would not have been treated as an employed earner by virtue of those Regulations had they been over that age;

as they have effect in relation to a person who is, or as the case may be, is not treated as an employed earner by virtue of those Regulations.

(4) A person is treated as an employee for the purpose of Part 12ZC of the 1992 Act (even though not falling within the definition of 'employee' in section 171ZZ4(2) of that Act) where that person is in employed earner's employment under a contract of apprenticeship.

(5) A person is not to be treated as an employee for the purposes of Part 12ZC of the 1992 Act (even though falling within the definition of 'employee' in section 171ZZ4(2) of that Act) where that person is in employed earner's employment but that person's employer—

(a) does not fulfil the conditions prescribed in regulation 145(1) (conditions as to residence or presence) of the Social Security (Contributions) Regulations 2001 in so far as that provision relates to residence or presence in Great Britain; or

(b) is a person who, by reason of any international treaty to which the United Kingdom is a party or of any international convention binding the United Kingdom—

(i) is exempt from the provisions of the 1992 Act; or
(ii) is a person against whom the provisions of the 1992 Act are not enforceable.

NOTES

Commencement: 1 December 2014.

[2.1658]

34 Continuous employment

(1) A week is to be treated for the purposes of sections 171ZU and 171ZV of the 1992 Act (see also regulations 30 and 31) as part of a period of continuous employment with the employer even though no contract of service exists with that employer in respect of that week in the circumstances mentioned in paragraph (2) and subject to paragraphs (3) and (4).

(2) The circumstances mentioned in paragraphs (1) are that in any week the person is, for the whole or part of the week—

(a) incapable of work in consequence of sickness or injury;
(b) absent from work on account of a temporary cessation of work; or
(c) absent from work in circumstances such that, by arrangement or custom, that person is regarded as continuing in the employment of their employer for all or any purposes;

and returns to work for their employer after the incapacity for or absence from work.

(3) Incapacity for work which lasts for more than 26 consecutive weeks shall not count for the purposes of paragraph (2)(a).

(4) Where a person—

(a) is an employee in employed earner's employment in which the custom is for the employer—
(i) to offer work for a fixed period of not more than 26 consecutive weeks;
(ii) to offer work for such period on two or more occasions in a year for periods which do not overlap; and
(iii) to offer the work available to those persons who had worked for the employer during the last or a recent such period; but
(b) is absent from work because of incapacity arising from some specific disease or bodily or mental disablement;

then in that case paragraph (2) shall apply as if the words "and returns to work for their employment for their employer after the incapacity for or absence from work" were omitted.

NOTES

Commencement: 1 December 2014.

[2.1659]

35 Continuous employment and unfair dismissal

(1) Where in consequence of specified action in relation to a person's dismissal, the person is reinstated or re-engaged by their employer or by a successor or associated employer of that employer then—

(a) the continuity of their employment shall be preserved for the purposes of sections 171ZU and [171ZV] of the 1992 Act (see also regulations 30 and 31) for the period beginning with the effective date of termination and ending with the date of reinstatement or re-engagement; and
(b) any week which falls within the interval beginning with the effective date of termination and ending with the date of reinstatement or re-engagement, as the case may be, shall count in the computation of their period of continuous employment.

(2) In this regulation—

(a) "associated employer" shall be construed in accordance with section 231 of the Employment Rights Act 1996;
(b) "dismissal procedures agreement" and "successor" have the same meanings as in section 235 of the Employment Rights Act 1996;
(c) "specified action in relation to a person's dismissal" means action which consists of—
(i) the presentation by that person of a complaint under section 111(1) (complaints to employment tribunal) of the Employment Rights Act 1996;
(ii) that person making a claim in accordance with a dismissal procedure agreement designated by an order under section 110 of that Act; or
(iii) any action taken by a conciliation officer under section 18 (conciliation) of the Employment Tribunals Act 1996.

NOTES

Commencement: 1 December 2014.

Para (1): figure in square brackets substituted by virtue of the Statutory Shared Parental Pay (General) (Amendment) Regulations 2015, SI 2015/189, reg 2(1), (4), as from 8 March 2015.

[2.1660]

36 Continuous employment and stoppages of work

(1) Where a person does not work for any week or part of a week because there is a stoppage of work at that person's place of employment due to a trade dispute within the meaning of section 35(1) of the Jobseekers Act 1995 then—

Part 2 Statutory Instruments

(a) that person's continuity of employment shall be treated as continuing throughout the stoppage (but see paragraph (2)) for the purposes of sections 171ZU and [171ZV] of the 1992 Act (see also regulations 30 and 31); and
(b) no such week shall count in the computation of their period of continuous employment (but see paragraph(3)).

(2) Where during the stoppage of work a person is dismissed from their employment, that person's continuity of employment shall not be treated under paragraph (1) as continuing beyond the commencement of the day that person stopped work (but see paragraph (3)).

(3) Paragraph (1)(b) and paragraph (2) do not apply to a person who proves that at no time did they have a direct interest in the trade dispute in question.

NOTES

Commencement: 1 December 2014.

Para (1): figure in square brackets substituted by virtue of the Statutory Shared Parental Pay (General) (Amendment) Regulations 2015, SI 2015/189, reg 2(1), (5)(a), as from 8 March 2015. Note that the closing round bracket following the words "paragraph (2)" in sub-para (1)(a) was inserted by reg 2(1), (5)(b) of the 2015 Regulations.

[2.1661]

37 Change of employer

(1) Where a person's employer changes, a person's employment is to be treated for the purposes of sections 171ZU and 171ZV of the 1992 Act (see also regulations 30 and 31) as continuous employment with the second employer in the following circumstances—

(a) the employer's trade or business or an undertaking (whether or not it is an undertaking established by or under an Act of Parliament) is transferred from one person to another;
(b) a contract of employment between any body corporate and the person is modified by or under an Act of Parliament, whether public or local and whenever passed and some other body corporate is substituted as that person's employer;
(c) on the death of the employer, the person is taken into the employment of the personal representatives or trustees of the deceased;
(d) the person is employed by partners, personal representatives or trustees and there is a change in the partners, or as the case may be, personal representatives or trustees;
(e) the person is taken into the employment of an employer who is, at the time the person entered into to the employer's employment, an associated employer of the person's previous employer; or
(f) on the termination of the person's employment with an employer that person is taken into the employment of another employer and those employers are governors of a school maintained by a local education authority.

(2) In paragraph (1)(e) "associated employer" shall be construed in accordance with section 231 of the Employment Rights Act 1996.

NOTES

Commencement: 1 December 2014.

[2.1662]

38 Reinstatement after service with the armed forces etc

Where a person—

(a) is entitled to apply to their employer under the Reserve Forces (Safeguard of Employment) Act 1985; and
(b) enters the employment of that employer within the six month period mentioned in section 1(4)(b) (obligation to reinstate) of that Act;

that person's previous period of employment with that employer (or if there was more than one such period, the last of those periods) and the period of employment beginning in that six month period shall be treated as continuous for the purposes of sections 171ZU and 171ZV of the 1992 Act (see also regulations 30 and 31).

NOTES

Commencement: 1 December 2014.

[2.1663]

39 Treatment of two or more employers or two or more contracts of service as one

(1) In a case where the earnings paid to a person in respect of two or more employments are aggregated and treated as a single payment of earnings under regulation 15(1) (aggregation of earnings paid in respect of different employed earner's employments by different persons) of the Social Security (Contributions) Regulations 2001, the employers of that person in respect of those employments shall be treated as one for the purposes of Part 12ZC of the 1992 Act (and these Regulations).

(2) Where two or more employers are treated as one under the provisions of paragraph (1), liability for statutory shared parental pay shall be apportioned between them in such proportions as they may agree, or in default of agreement, in the proportions which the person's normal weekly earnings from each employment bear to the amount of the aggregated normal weekly earnings over the relevant period as defined in regulation 32(2).

(3) Where two or more contracts of service exist concurrently between one employer and one employee, they shall be treated as one for the purposes of Part 12ZC of the 1992 Act (and these Regulations) except where, by virtue of regulation 14 (aggregation of earnings paid in respect of separate employed earner's employments under the same employer) of the Social Security (Contributions) Regulations 2001, the earnings from those contracts of service are not aggregated for the purpose of earnings-related contributions.

NOTES

Commencement: 1 December 2014.

PART 5
PAYMENT OF STATUTORY SHARED PARENTAL PAY

[2.1664]

40 Weekly rate of payment of statutory shared parental pay

(1) The weekly rate of payment of statutory shared parental pay is the smaller of the following two amounts—

(a) [£148.68];

(b) 90% of the normal weekly earnings of the individual claiming statutory shared parental pay determined in accordance with section 171ZZ4(6) of the 1992 Act and regulation 32).

(2) Where the amount of any payment of statutory shared parental pay is calculated by reference to—

(a) the weekly rate specified in paragraph (1)(b), or

(b) the daily rate of one-seventh of the weekly rate specified in paragraph (1)(a) or (b),

and that amount includes a fraction of a penny, the payment shall be rounded up to the nearest whole number of pence.

NOTES

Commencement: 1 December 2014.

Para (1): sum in square brackets in sub-para (a) substituted by the Social Security Benefits Up-rating Order 2019, SI 2019/480, art 11(2), as from 7 April 2019. Previous sums were: £145.18 (from 1 April 2018, see SI 2018/281, art 11(2)); £140.98 (from 2 April 2017, see SI 2017/260); £139.58 (from 5 April 2015, see SI 2015/30, art 5(3)). Note that there was no increase in 2016.

[2.1665]

41 Statutory shared parental pay and contractual remuneration

For the purposes of section 171ZZ1(1) and (2) (payment of contractual remuneration to go towards discharging liability to pay statutory shared parental pay and payment of statutory shared parental pay to go towards discharging liability to pay contractual remuneration) the payments which are to be treated as contractual remuneration are sums payable under a contract of service—

(a) by way of remuneration;

(b) for incapacity for work due to sickness or injury; and

(c) by reason of birth, adoption or care of a child.

NOTES

Commencement: 1 December 2014.

[2.1666]

42 Avoidance of liability for statutory shared parental pay

(1) A former employer is liable to make payments of statutory shared parental pay to a former employee in any case where the employee has been employed for a continuous period of at least eight weeks and the employee's contract of service was brought to an end by the former employer solely, or mainly, for the purpose of avoiding liability for statutory shared parental pay.

(2) In a case falling within paragraph (1)—

(a) the employee shall be treated as if the employee had been employed for a continuous period ending with the period of seven days beginning with Sunday before the first week falling within the relevant period relating to that employee under section 171ZY(2) of the 1992 Act; and

(b) regulation 32(2) (relevant period for the purpose of the calculation of normal weekly earnings) shall apply as if it read—

"(2) The relevant period is the period—

(a) ending on the last day of payment under the former contract of employment; and

(b) beginning with the day following the day of payment under that contract to fall at least 8 weeks earlier than the day of payment mentioned in sub-paragraph (a).".

NOTES

Commencement: 1 December 2014.

[2.1667]

43 Payment of statutory shared parental pay

Payments of statutory shared parental pay may be made in like manner to payments of remuneration but shall not include payment in kind or by way of the provision of board and lodgings.

NOTES

Commencement: 1 December 2014.

[2.1668]

44 Time when statutory shared parental pay is to be paid

(1) In any case where—

(a) a decision has been made by an officer of Revenue and Customs under section 8(1) (decisions by officers) of the Social Security Contributions (Transfer of Functions, etc) Act 1999 as a result of which a person is entitled to an amount of statutory shared parental pay; and

(b) the time for bringing an appeal against the decision has expired and either—

(i) no such appeal has been brought; or

(ii) such appeal has been brought and has been finally disposed of;

that amount of statutory shared parental pay shall be paid within the time specified in paragraph (2).

(2) The employer or former employer shall pay the amount not later than the first pay day after the following days (but see paragraphs (3) and (4))—

(a) where an appeal has been brought, the day on which the employer or former employer receives notification that it has been finally disposed of;

(b) where leave to appeal has been refused, and there remains no further opportunity to apply for leave, the day on which the employer or former employer receives notification of the refusal; and

(c) in any other case, the day on which the time for bringing an appeal expires.

(3) Where it is impracticable, in view of the employer's or former employer's methods of accounting for and paying remuneration, for the requirement of payment referred to in paragraph (2) to be met by the pay day referred to in that paragraph, it shall be met not later than the next following pay day (but see paragraph (4)).

(4) Where the employer or former employer would not have remunerated the employee for their work in the week in respect of which statutory shared parental pay is payable as early as the pay day specified in paragraph (2) or (if it applies) paragraph (3), the requirement of payment shall be met on the first day on which the employee would have been remunerated for his work in that week.

(5) In this regulation "pay day" means a day on which it has been agreed, or it is the normal practice between an employer or former employer to agree and a person who is or was an employee of theirs, that payments by way of remuneration are to be made, or, where there is no such agreement or normal practice, the last day of a calendar month.

NOTES

Commencement: 1 December 2014.

[2.1669]

45 Liability of the Commissioners to pay statutory shared parental pay

(1) Despite section 171ZX(1) of the 1992 Act (liability to make payments of statutory shared parental pay is liability of the employer) where the conditions in paragraph (2) are satisfied, liability to make payments of statutory shared parental pay to a person is to be liability of the Commissioners and not the employer for—

(a) any week in respect of which the employer was liable to pay statutory shared parental pay to that person but did not do so; and

(b) for any subsequent weeks that person is entitled to payments of statutory shared parental pay.

(2) The conditions in this paragraph are that—

(a) an officer of the Revenue and Customs has decided under section 8(1) of the Social Security Contributions (Transfer of Functions, etc) Act 1999 that an employer is liable to make payments of statutory shared parental pay;

(b) the time for appealing against the decision has expired; and

(c) no appeal against the decision has been lodged or leave to appeal against the decision is required and has been refused.

(3) Despite section 171ZX(1) of the 1992 Act, liability to make payments of statutory shared parental pay to a person is to be a liability of the Commissioners and not the employer as from the week in which the employer first becomes insolvent (see paragraphs 4 and 5) until the last week that person is entitled to payment of statutory shared parental pay.

(4) For the purposes of paragraph (3) an employer shall be taken to be insolvent if, and only if, in England and Wales—

(a) the employer has been adjudged bankrupt or has made a composition or arrangement with its creditors;

(b) the employer has died and the employer's estate falls to be administered in accordance with an order made under section 421 Insolvency Act 1986; or

(c) where an employer is a company or a limited liability partnership—

(i) a winding-up order is made or a resolution for a voluntary winding-up is passed (or, in the case of a limited liability partnership, a determination for voluntary winding-up has been made) with respect to it,

(ii) it enters administration,

(iii) a receiver or manager of its undertaking is duly appointed,

(iv) possession is taken, by or on behalf of the holders of any debentures secured by a floating charge, of any property of the company or limited liability partnership comprised in or subject to the charge, or

(v) a voluntary arrangement proposed for the purposes of Part 1 of the Insolvency Act 1986 is approved under that Part.

(5) For the purposes of paragraph (3) an employer shall be taken to be insolvent if, and only if, in Scotland—

(a) an award of sequestration is made on the employer's estate;

(b) the employer executes a trust deed for its creditors;

(c) the employer enters into a composition contract;

(d) the employer has died and a judicial factor appointed under section 11A of the Judicial Factors (Scotland) Act 1889 is required by that section to divide the employer's insolvent estate among the employer's creditors; or

(e) where the employer is a company or a limited liability partnership—

(i) a winding-up order is made or a resolution for voluntary winding-up is passed (or in the case of a limited liability partnership, a determination for a voluntary winding-up is made) with respect to it,

(ii) it enters administration,

(iii) a receiver of its undertaking is duly appointed, or

(iv) a voluntary arrangement proposed for the purposes of Part I of the Insolvency Act 1986 is approved under that Part.

NOTES

Commencement: 1 December 2014.

[2.1670]

46 Liability of the Commissioners to pay statutory shared parental pay in case of legal custody or imprisonment

Where there is liability to pay statutory shared parental pay—

(a) in respect of a period which is subsequent to the last week falling within paragraph (1)(c) of regulations 14 and 26 (cases where there is no liability to pay statutory shared parental pay); or

(b) during a period of detention in legal custody by virtue of paragraph (2) of those regulations;

that liability, despite section 171ZX(1) of the 1992 Act, shall be that of the Commissioners and not the employer.

NOTES

Commencement: 1 December 2014.

[2.1671]

47 Payments by the Commissioners

Where the Commissioners become liable in accordance with regulation 45 (liability of the Commissioners to pay statutory shared parental pay) or regulation 46 (liability of the Commissioners to pay statutory shared parental pay in case of legal custody or imprisonment) then—

(a) the first payment is to be made as soon as reasonably practicable after they become so liable; and

(b) subsequent payments are to be made at weekly intervals;

by means of an instrument of payment or by such other means as appear to the Commissioners to be appropriate in the circumstances of any particular case.

NOTES

Commencement: 1 December 2014.

[2.1672]

48 Persons unable to act

(1) This regulation applies where—

(a) statutory shared parental pay is payable to a person or it is alleged that statutory shared parental pay is payable to a person;

(b) that person is unable for the time being to act;

(c) no deputy has been appointed by the Court of Protection with power to receive [statutory shared parental pay] on their behalf or, in Scotland, their estate is not being administered by a guardian acting or appointed under the Adults with Incapacity (Scotland) Act 2000; and

(d) a written application has been made to the Commissioners by a person, who, if a natural person, is over the age of 18 to exercise any right, or deal with any sums payable, under Part 12ZC of the 1992 Act on behalf of the person unable to act.

(2) Where this regulation applies the Commissioners may appoint the person referred to in paragraph (1)(d)—

(a) to exercise, on behalf of the person unable to act, any right which the person unable to act may be entitled under Part 12ZC of the 1992 Act; and

(b) to deal, on behalf of the person unable to act, with any sums payable to the person unable to act under Part 12ZC of the 1992 Act.

(3) Where the Commissioners have made an appointment under paragraph (2)—

(a) they may at any time revoke it;

(b) the person appointed may resign their office after having given one month's notice in writing to the Commissioners of that person's intention to do so; and

(c) the appointment shall end when the Commissioners are notified that a deputy or other person to whom paragraph (1)(c) applies has been appointed.

(4) Anything required by Part 12ZC of the 1992 Act to be done by or to the person who is unable to act may be done by or to the person appointed under this regulation to act on behalf of the person unable to act, and the receipt of the person so appointed shall be a good discharge to the employer or former employer of the person unable to act for any sum paid.

NOTES

Commencement: 1 December 2014.

Para (1): words in square brackets substituted by the Statutory Shared Parental Pay (General) (Amendment) Regulations 2015, SI 2015/189, reg 2(1), (6), as from 8 March 2015.

[2.1673]
49 Service of notices

(1) Where a notice is to be given under these Regulations, it may be given—

(a) where paragraph (2) applies, by electronic communication;

(b) by post; or

(c) by personal delivery.

(2) This paragraph applies where the person who is to receive the notice has agreed that the notice may be given to the person by being transmitted to an electronic address and in an electronic form specified by the person for that purpose.

(3) Where a notice is to be given under these Regulations it is to be taken to have been given—

(a) if sent by electronic communication, on the day of transmission;

(b) if sent by post in an envelope which is properly addressed and sent by prepaid post, on the day on which it is posted;

(c) if delivered personally, on the day of delivery.

NOTES

Commencement: 1 December 2014.

SCHEDULE
STATUTORY SHARED PARENTAL PAY IN SPECIAL CIRCUMSTANCES

Regulations 16 and 28

PART 1
STATUTORY SHARED PARENTAL PAY (BIRTH)

Entitlement of father or partner to statutory shared parental pay (birth) in the event of the death of M before curtailment

[2.1674]

1. (1) In a case where M dies—

(a) before the end of her maternity allowance period in respect of C and without reducing that period under section 35(3A) of the 1992 Act, or

(b) before the end of her maternity pay period in respect of C and without reducing that period under section 165(3A) of the 1992 Act,

then these Regulations shall apply, in respect of any period after M dies, subject to the modifications in the following provisions of this paragraph.

(2) In regulation 2(1) a person is to be regarded as falling within the definition of P it that person would have done so but for the fact that M had died.

(3) In regulation 5 (entitlement of father or partner)—

(a) paragraph (3)(d) shall not apply;

(b) in a case where M dies before her maternity allowance period or maternity pay period in respect of C starts then the condition in paragraph (3)(c) shall be taken to be satisfied if it would have been satisfied but for the fact that M had died.

(4) In regulation 7 (notification and evidential requirements relating to father or mother's partner)—

(a) paragraph (1)(a) shall apply as if it read—

"(a) paragraphs (2) and (3) at least 8 weeks before the beginning of the first period specified by P pursuant to paragraph (2)(d) or, where it is not reasonably practicable for P to satisfy this requirement, as soon as reasonably practicable after the death of M, but in any event before that period;";

(b) paragraph (1)(b) and (c) shall not apply;

(c) in paragraph (2)—

(i) sub-paragraph (a) shall apply as if the words "disregarding any intention of M to claim statutory shared parental pay (birth) in respect of C" were omitted; and

(ii) sub-paragraph (c) shall not apply;

(d) in paragraph (3)—

(i) sub-paragraph (a) shall not apply;

(ii) sub-paragraph (d) shall apply as if it read—

"(d) the following information relating to P and M—
(i) P's name, M's name and national insurance number (where this number is known to P), M's address immediately before she died and the date of M's death; and
(ii) the start date of M's maternity pay period or maternity allowance period in respect of C or, where M's death occurred before her maternity allowance period or maternity pay period in respect of C started, the date that period would have started but for the fact that M had died;"; and
(iii) sub-paragraph (e)(iii) shall not apply;
(e) paragraph (4) shall not apply.

(5) In regulation 8(3) (variation)—
(a) sub-paragraph (a) shall apply as if the reference to M were omitted; and
(b) sub-paragraph (b) shall not apply.

(6) In regulation 10 (extent of entitlement), paragraph (1)(a) shall apply as if the number of weeks referred to is the number of weeks in which maternity allowance or statutory maternity pay was payable to M in respect of C up to the time of M's death.

Notification and variation: death of mother or partner after curtailment

2. (1) In the case where—
(a) P, who in connection with a claim by M would be required to satisfy the conditions specified in regulation 4(3), dies after M has reduced her maternity allowance period in respect of C under section 35(3A) of the 1992 Act or her maternity pay period in respect of C under section 165(3A) of the 1992 Act; and
(b) before P dies M has not given the notices and information specified in regulation 6 (notice and evidential requirements relation to the mother),

then these Regulations apply in respect of any period after P dies, subject to the modifications in the following provisions of this paragraph.

(2) In regulation 6 (notification and evidential requirements relating to the mother)—
(a) paragraph (1)(a) shall apply as if it read—

"(a) paragraphs (2) and (3) at least 8 weeks before the beginning of the first period specified by M pursuant to paragraph (2)(d) or where it is not reasonably practicable for M to satisfy this requirement as soon as reasonably practicable after the death of P, but in any event before that period;";

(b) paragraph (1)(b) and (c) shall not apply;
(c) in paragraph (2)—
(i) sub-paragraph (a) shall apply as if the words "disregarding any intention of P to claim statutory shared parental pay in respect of C" were omitted;
(ii) sub-paragraph (c) shall not apply;
(d) in paragraph (3)—
(i) sub-paragraph (a) shall not apply;
(ii) sub-paragraph (d) shall apply as if it read—

"(d) M's name, P's name and national insurance number (where this number is known to M), P's address immediately before P died and the date of P's death";

(e) paragraph (4) shall not apply.

(3) In regulation 8 (variation)—
(a) paragraph (2)(a) shall apply as if it read—

"(a) of the number of weeks during which M and P have exercised, and the number of weeks M intends to exercise, an entitlement to statutory shared parental pay (birth) in respect of C";

(b) paragraph (2)(b) shall not apply.

(4) In regulation 10 (extent of entitlement)—
(a) paragraph (1)(b)(i) shall apply as if the words "P has notified P's intention to claim" to the end read "the number of weeks in which P claimed statutory shared parental pay (birth) in respect of C up to the time of P's death.";
(b) paragraph (7) shall apply as if the words "the last day of the latest period so notified" were "the time of P's death".

3. (1) In the case where—
(a) P, who in connection with M's claim is required to satisfy the conditions specified in regulation 4(3), dies after M has reduced her maternity allowance period in respect of C under section 35(3A) of the 1992 Act or her maternity pay period in respect of C under section 165(3A) of the 1992 Act, and
(b) before P dies M has given the notices and information specified in regulation 6 (notification and evidential requirements relating to the mother),

then these Regulations apply in respect of any period after P dies, subject to the modifications in the following provisions of this paragraph.

(2) In regulation 8 (variation)—

(a) paragraph (1) shall apply in relation to the first notice made under that paragraph following P's death as if at the end of that paragraph there is added—
"or, where it is not reasonably practicable for M to satisfy this requirement, by notice in writing given to that employer as soon as reasonably practicable after the death of P, but in any event before that period and which states the date of P's death";
(b) paragraph (2)(a) shall apply as if it read—
"(a) of the number of weeks during which M and P have exercised, and the number of weeks M intends to exercise, an entitlement to statutory shared parental pay (birth) in respect of C";
(c) paragraph (2)(b) shall not apply.

(3) In regulation 10—
(a) paragraph (1)(b)(i) shall apply as if the words "P has notified P's intention to claim" to the end read—
"the number of weeks in which P claimed statutory shared parental pay (birth) in respect of C up to the time of P's death;";
(b) paragraph (7) shall apply as if the words "the last day of the latest period so notified" were "the time of P's death".

4. (1) In the case where—
(a) M dies after she has reduced her maternity allowance period in respect of C under section 35(3A) of the 1992 Act or her maternity pay period in respect of C under section 165(3A) of the 1992 Act, and
(b) before M dies P has not given the notices and information specified in regulation 7 (notification and evidential requirements relating to father or partner),
then these Regulations apply in respect of any period after M dies, subject to the modifications in the following provisions of this paragraph.

(2) In regulation 2(1) (definitions) a person is to be regarded as falling within the definition of P if that person would have done so but for the fact that M has died.

(3) In regulation 7 (notification and evidential requirements relating to P)—
(a) in paragraph (1)—
(i) sub-paragraph (a) shall apply as if it read—
"(a) paragraphs (2) and (3) at least 8 weeks before the beginning of the first period specified by P pursuant to paragraph (2)(d) or where it is not reasonably practicable for P to satisfy this requirement as soon as reasonably practicable after the death of M, but in any event before that period;";
(ii) sub-paragraphs (b) and (c) shall not apply;
(b) in paragraph (2)—
(i) sub-paragraph (a) shall apply as if the words "disregarding any intention of M to claim statutory shared parental pay in respect of C" were omitted;
(ii) sub-paragraph (c) shall not apply;
(c) in paragraph (3)—
(i) sub-paragraph (a) shall not apply;
(ii) sub-paragraph (d) shall apply as if it read—
"(d) P's name, M's name and national insurance number (where this number is known to P), M's address immediately before she died and the date of M's death";
(iii) sub-paragraph (e)(iii) shall not apply;
(d) paragraph (4) shall not apply.

(4) In regulation 8 (variation), in paragraph (3)—
(a) sub-paragraph (a) shall apply as if it read—
"(a) of the number of weeks during which P and M have exercised, and the number of weeks P intends to exercise, an entitlement to statutory shared parental pay (birth) in respect of C";
(b) sub-paragraph (b) shall not apply.

(5) In regulation 10 (extent of entitlement)—
(a) paragraph (1)(b)(ii) shall apply as if the words "M has notified M's intention to claim" to the end read—
"the number of weeks in which M claimed statutory shared parental pay (birth) in respect of C up to the time of M's death;";
(b) paragraph (8) shall apply as if the words "the last day of the latest period" were "the time of M's death".

5. (1) In the case where—
(a) M dies after she has reduced her maternity allowance period in respect of C under section 35(3A) of the 1992 Act or her maternity pay period in respect of C under section 165(3A) of the 1992 Act, and
(b) before M dies P has given the notice and information specified in regulation 7 (notification and evidential requirements relating to father or mother's partner),

then these Regulations apply in respect of any period after M dies subject to the modifications in the following provisions of this paragraph.

(2) In regulation 8 (variation)—

(a) paragraph (1) shall apply in relation to the first notice made under that regulation following M's death as if at the end of that paragraph there is added—

"or, where it is not reasonably practicable for P to satisfy this requirement, by notice in writing given to that employer as soon as reasonably practicable after the death of M, but in any event before that period and which states the date of M's death";

(b) paragraph (3)(a) shall apply as if it read—

"(a) of the number of weeks during which P and M have exercised, and the number of weeks P intends to exercise, an entitlement to statutory shared parental pay (birth) in respect of C";

(c) paragraph (3)(b) shall not apply.

(3) In regulation 10 (extent of entitlement)—

(a) paragraph (1)(b)(ii) shall apply as if the words "M has notified M's intention to claim" to the end read—

"the number of weeks in which M claimed statutory shared parental pay (birth) in respect of C up to the time of M's death";

(b) paragraph (8) shall apply as if the words "the last day of the latest period" were "the time of M's death".

Death of child

6. (1) In the case where M has given the notice and information in accordance with regulation 6(1) and then C dies, then in respect of any period after C dies paragraph (2)(f) of regulation 4 (entitlement of mother to statutory shared parental pay), shall not apply, and regulation 8 shall apply in accordance with sub-paragraph (3).

(2) In the case where P has given the notices and information in accordance with regulation 7(1) and then C dies, then in respect of any period after C dies paragraph (2)(d) of regulation 5 (entitlement of father or partner to statutory shared parental pay) shall not apply and regulation 8 shall apply in accordance with sub-paragraph (3).

(3) Where paragraph (1) or (2) applies, regulation 8 (variation) shall apply as if it read—

"(1) M, or as the case may be, P may cancel the period or periods during which they intend to claim statutory shared parental pay (birth) by notice in writing which is given at least 8 weeks before the first period to be cancelled, or, if this is not reasonably practicable, as soon as reasonably practicable after the death of C, but in any event before that period to the employer who will be liable to pay statutory shared parental pay (birth) to M or P.

(2) M and P may each only give one notice under paragraph (1).".

(4) Where more than one child is born of the same pregnancy—

(a) sub-paragraphs (2) and (3) only apply where all the children die; and

(b) a reference in this paragraph relating to the death of C (however expressed) is to the death of the last of those children to die.

NOTES

Commencement: 1 December 2014.

PART 2
STATUTORY SHARED PARENTAL PAY (ADOPTION)

Entitlement of adopter's partner to statutory shared parental pay (adoption) in the event of the death of adopter before curtailment

[2.1675]

7. (1) In a case where A dies before the end of A's adoption pay period in respect of C and without reducing that period under section 171ZN(2A) of the 1992 Act then these Regulations apply in respect of any period after A dies, subject to the modifications in the following provisions of this paragraph.

(2) In regulation 2 a person is to be regarded as falling within the definition of AP if that person would have done so but for the fact that A had died.

(3) In regulation 18 (entitlement of partner to statutory shared parental pay (adoption))—

(a) paragraph (3)(d) shall not apply;

(b) in the case where A dies before A's adoption pay period in respect of C starts, then the condition in paragraph (3)(c) shall be taken to be satisfied if it would have been satisfied but for the fact that A had died.

(4) In regulation 20 (notification and evidential requirements relating to partner)—

(a) paragraph (1)(a) shall apply as if it read—

"(a) paragraphs (2) and (3) at least 8 weeks before the beginning of the first period specified by AP pursuant to paragraph (2)(d) or, where it is not reasonably practicable for AP to satisfy this requirement, as soon as reasonably practicable after the death of A, but in any event before that week";

(b) paragraph (1)(b) and (c) shall not apply;

(c) in paragraph (2)—

(i) sub-paragraph (a) shall apply as if the words "disregarding any intention of A to claim statutory shared parental pay (adoption) in respect of C" were omitted,

(ii) sub-paragraph (c) shall not apply;

(d) in paragraph (3)—

(i) sub-paragraph (a) shall not apply,

(ii) sub-paragraph (d) shall apply as if it read—

"(d) the following information about AP and A—

(i) AP's name, A's name and national insurance number (where this number is known to AP), A's address immediately before she died and the date of A's death; and

(ii) the start date of A's adoption pay period in respect of C;",

(iii) sub-paragraph (e)(iii) shall not apply;

(e) paragraph (4) shall not apply.

(5) In regulation 21(variation), in paragraph (3)—

(a) sub-paragraph (a) shall apply as if the reference to A were omitted;

(b) sub-paragraph (b) shall not apply.

(6) In regulation 22 (extent of entitlement), paragraph (1)(a) shall apply as if the number of weeks referred to is the number of weeks in which statutory adoption pay was payable to A in respect of C up to the time of A's death.

Notification or variation: death of adopter or adopter's partner after curtailment

8. (1) In the case where—

(a) AP who in connection with a claim by A would be required to satisfy the conditions in regulation 17(3), dies after A has reduced A's adoption pay period in respect of C under section 171ZN(2A) of the 1992 Act, and

(b) before AP dies A has not given the notice and information specified in regulation 19 (notification and evidential requirements relating to the adopter),

then these Regulations apply in respect of any period after AP dies, subject to the modifications in the following provisions of this paragraph.

(2) In regulation 19 (notification and evidential requirements relating to the adopter)—

(a) paragraph (1)(a) shall apply as if it read—

"(a) paragraphs (2) and (3) at least 8 weeks before the beginning of the first period specified by A pursuant to paragraph (2)(d) or, where it is not reasonably practicable for A to satisfy this requirement, as soon as reasonably practicable after the death of AP but in any event before that period;";

(b) paragraph (1)(b) and (c) shall not apply;

(c) paragraph (2)(a) shall apply as if the words "disregarding any intention of AP to claim statutory shared parental pay (adoption) in respect of C" were omitted;

(d) paragraph (2)(c) shall not apply;

(e) paragraph (3)(a) shall not apply;

(f) paragraph (3)(d) shall apply as if it read—

"(d) A's name, AP's name and national insurance number (where this number is known to A), AP's address immediately before AP died and the date of AP's death";

(g) paragraph (4) shall not apply.

(3) In regulation 21 (variation), in paragraph (3) sub-paragraph (a) shall apply as if it read—

"(a) of the number of weeks during which A and AP have exercised, and the number of weeks A intends to exercise, an entitlement to statutory shared parental pay (adoption) in respect of C;";

(a) paragraph (b) shall not apply.

(4) In regulation 22 (extent of entitlement to statutory shared parental pay (adoption))—

(a) paragraph (1)(b)(i) shall apply as if the words "AP has notified AP's intention to claim" to the end read—

"the number of weeks in which AP claimed statutory shared parental pay (adoption) in respect of C up to the time of AP's death;";

(b) paragraph (5) shall apply as if the words "the last day of the latest period so notified" were "the time of AP's death".

9. (1) In the case where—

(a) AP, who in connection with A's claim is required to satisfy the conditions specified in regulation 17(3), dies after A has reduced A's adoption pay period under section 171ZN(2A) of the 1992 Act, and

(b) before AP dies A has given the notices and information specified in regulation 19 (notification and evidential requirements relating to the adopter),

then these Regulations apply in respect of any period after AP dies, subject to the modifications in the following provisions of this paragraph.

(2) In regulation 21 (variation)—

(a) paragraph (1) shall apply in relation to the first notice made under that paragraph following AP's death as if at the end of that paragraph there is added—

"or, where it is not reasonably practicable for A to satisfy this requirement, by notice in writing given to that employer as soon as reasonably practicable after the death of AP, but in any event before that period and which states the date of AP's death";

(b) paragraph (2)(a) shall apply as if it read—

"(a) of the number of weeks during which A and AP have exercised, and the number of weeks A intends to exercise, an entitlement to statutory shared parental pay (adoption) in respect of C;";

(c) paragraph (2)(b) shall not apply.

(3) In regulation 22 (extent of entitlement)—

(a) paragraph (1)(b)(i) shall apply as if the words "AP has notified AP's intention to claim" to the end read "the number of weeks in which AP claimed statutory shared parental pay (adoption) in respect of C up to the time of AP's death;";

(b) paragraph (5) shall apply as if the words "the last day of the latest period so notified" were "the time of AP's death".

10. (1) In the case where—

(a) A dies after A has reduced A's adoption pay period in respect of C under section 171ZN(2A) of the 1992 Act, and

(b) before A dies AP has not given the notice and information specified in regulation 20 (notification and evidential requirements relating to adopter's partner);

then the Regulations apply in respect of any period after A dies subject to the modifications in the following provisions of this paragraph.

(2) In regulation 2(1) (definitions) a person is to be regarded as falling within the definition of AP if that person would have done so but for the fact that A has died.

(3) In regulation 20 (notification and evidential requirements relating to partner)—

(a) paragraph (1)(a) shall apply as if it read—

"(a) paragraphs (2) and (3) at least 8 weeks before the beginning of the first period specified by AP pursuant to paragraph (2)(d) or if it is not reasonably practicable for AP to satisfy this requirement as soon as reasonably practicable after the death of A, but in any event before that period;";

(b) paragraph (1)(b) and (c) shall not apply;

(c) paragraph (2)(a) shall apply as if the words "disregarding any intention of A to claim statutory shared parental pay (adoption) in respect of C" were omitted;

(d) paragraph (2)(c) shall not apply;

(e) paragraph (3)(a) shall not apply;

(f) paragraph (3)(d) shall apply as if it read—

"(d) AP's name, A's name and national insurance number (where this number is known to AP), A's address immediately before A died and the date of A's death;";

(g) paragraph (4) shall not apply.

(4) In regulation 21 (variation), in paragraph (3)—

(a) sub-paragraph (a) shall apply as if it read—

"(a) of the number of weeks during which AP and A have exercised, and the number of weeks AP intends to exercise, an entitlement to statutory shared parental pay (adoption) in respect of C";

(b) sub-paragraph (b) shall not apply.

(5) In regulation 22 (extent of entitlement)—

(a) paragraph (1)(b)(ii) shall apply as if the words "A has notified A's intention to claim" to the end read—

"the number of weeks in which A claimed statutory shared parental pay (adoption) in respect of C up to the time of A's death;".

(b) paragraph (6) shall apply as if the words "the last day of the latest period so notified" were "the time of A's death".

11. (1) In the case where—

(a) A dies after A has reduced A's adoption pay period in respect of C under section 171ZN(2A) of the 1992 Act; and

(b) before A dies AP has given the notice and information specified in regulation 20 (notification and evidential requirements relating to the partner);

then these Regulations apply in respect of any period after A dies subject to the modifications in the following provisions of this paragraph.

(2) In regulation 21 (variation)—

(a) paragraph (1) shall apply in relation to the first notice made under that regulation following A's death as if at the end of that paragraph there is added—

"or, where is it not reasonably practicable for AP to satisfy this requirement, by notice in writing given to that employer as soon as reasonably practicable after the death of A, but in any event before that period and which states the date of A's death;";

(b) paragraph (3)(a) shall apply as it is read—

"(a) of the number of weeks during which AP and A have exercised, and the number of weeks AP intends to exercise, an entitlement to statutory shared parental pay (adoption) in respect of C";

(c) paragraph (3)(b) shall not apply.

(3) In regulation 22 (extent of entitlement)—

(a) paragraph (1)(b)(ii) shall apply as if the words "A has notified A's intention to claim" to the end read—

"the number of weeks in which A claimed statutory shared parental pay (adoption) in respect of C up to the time of A's death.".

(b) paragraph (6) shall apply as if the words "the last day of the latest period so notified" were "the time of A's death".

Death of child or disrupted placement

12. (1) In the case where A has given the notices and information specified in regulation 19(1) and then C dies or is returned after being placed then in respect of any period after C dies or is returned after being placed paragraph (2)(f) of regulation 17 (entitlement of adopter to statutory shared parental pay) shall not apply and regulation 21 shall apply in accordance with sub-paragraph (3).

(2) In the case where AP has given the notices and information specified in regulation 20(1) and then C dies or is returned after being placed then in respect of any period after C dies or is returned after being placed paragraph (2)(d) of regulation 18 (entitlement of adopter to statutory shared parental pay) shall not apply and regulation 21 shall apply in accordance with sub-paragraph (3).

(3) Where paragraph (1) or (2) applies, regulation 21 (variation) shall apply as if it read—

"(1) A or, as the case may be, AP may cancel the period or periods during which they intend to claim statutory shared parental pay (adoption) by notice in writing which is given at least 8 weeks before the first period to be cancelled or, if this is not reasonably practicable, as soon as reasonably practicable after the death of C or after C is returned after being placed, but in any event before that period to the employer who will be liable to pay statutory shared parental pay (adoption) to A or AP.
(2) A and AP may each only give one notice under paragraph (1).".

(4) Where more than one child is placed for adoption as a result of the same placement—

(a) sub-paragraphs (1) and (2) only apply where all the children die or, as the case may be, all the children are returned after being placed;

(b) a reference in this paragraph to the death of C or to the return of C after being placed (however expressed) is to the death of the last of those children to die or is to the last of those children to be returned after being placed.

(5) In this paragraph "returned after being placed" means—

(a) returned to the adoption agency under sections 31 to 35 of the Adoption and Children Act 2002;

(b) in Scotland, returned to the adoption agency, adoption society or nominated person in accordance with section 25(6) of the Adoption and Children (Scotland) Act 2007; or

(c) where the child is placed in accordance with section 22C of the Children Act 1989, returned to the adoption agency following termination of the placement.

NOTES

Commencement: 1 December 2014.

Modification: para 12 above is applied with modifications in relation to parental order cases, by the Statutory Shared Parental Pay (Parental Order Cases) Regulations 2014, SI 2014/3097, reg 16 at **[2.1799]**, and in relation to adoptions from overseas, by the Statutory Shared Parental Pay (Adoption from Overseas) Regulations 2014, SI 2014/3093, regs 3, 4, 16 at **[2.1727]**, **[2.1728]**, **[2.1740]**.

MATERNITY AND ADOPTION LEAVE (CURTAILMENT OF STATUTORY RIGHTS TO LEAVE) REGULATIONS 2014

(SI 2014/3052)

NOTES

Made: 18 November 2014.

Authority: Employment Rights Act 1996, ss 71(2), (3)(ba), (bb), (3A), 73(2), (3)(a), (aa), (3A), 75(1)(a), (2), 75A(1A), (2), (2A), (2B), 75B(2), (3)(a), (aa), (3A), 75D(1)(a), (2).

Commencement: 1 December 2014.

Application: as to the application of these Regulations to parental order cases under the Human Fertilisation and Embryology Act 2008, ss 54, 54A with modifications, see the Paternity, Adoption and Shared Parental Leave (Parental Order Cases) Regulations 2014, SI 2014/3096, regs 4, 18, 19 at **[2.1750]**, **[2.1768]**, **[2.1769]**. As to the application of these Regulations to adoptions from overseas, see the Shared Parental Leave and Paternity and Adoption Leave (Adoptions from Overseas) Regulations 2014, SI 2014/3092 at **[2.1704]** et seq.

ARRANGEMENT OF REGULATIONS

PART 1
GENERAL

PART 2
CURTAILMENT OF STATUTORY MATERNITY LEAVE

PART 3
CURTAILMENT OF STATUTORY ADOPTION LEAVE

PART 1
GENERAL

[2.1676]
1 Citation and commencement

These Regulations may be cited as the Maternity and Adoption Leave (Curtailment of Statutory Rights to Leave) Regulations 2014 and come into force on 1st December 2014.

NOTES

Commencement: 1 December 2014.

[2.1677]
2 Application

(1) Part 2 of these Regulations has effect only in relation to children whose expected week of birth begins on or after 5th April 2015.

(2) Part 3 of these Regulations has effect only in relation to children placed for adoption on or after 5th April 2015.

NOTES

Commencement: 1 December 2014.

Modification: this regulation is applied with modifications in relation to parental order cases under the Human Fertilisation and Embryology Act 2008, s 54, by the Paternity, Adoption and Shared Parental Leave (Parental Order Cases) Regulations 2014, SI 2014/3096, reg 18 at **[2.1768]**, and in relation to adoptions from overseas by the Shared Parental Leave and Paternity and Adoption Leave (Adoptions from Overseas) Regulations 2014, SI 2014/3092, regs 3–5 at **[2.1706]–[2.1708]**.

[2.1678]
3 Interpretation

(1) In these Regulations—

"the 1996 Act" means the Employment Rights Act 1996;

"A", in relation to C, means the person with whom C is, or is expected to be, placed for adoption, or, in the case where two people have been matched jointly, whichever of them has elected to be C's adopter for the purposes of the Paternity and Adoption Leave Regulations 2002;

"AP" means the person who is married to or is the civil partner or the partner of A;

"C" means—

(a) in Part 2 of the Regulations, the child in relation to whom M has an entitlement to statutory maternity leave;

(b) in Part 3 of the Regulations, the child in relation to whom A has an entitlement to statutory adoption leave;

"declaration of consent and entitlement" means—

(a) in Part 2 of the Regulations, a written declaration signed by M stating that—

(i) P has given a notice to his employer in accordance with regulations made under section 75E(4)(d) of the 1996 Act; and

(ii) M has consented to the amount of leave that P intends to take in accordance with regulations made under section 75E(4)(e) of the 1996 Act;

(b) in Part 3 of the Regulations, a written declaration by A stating that—

(i) AP has given notice to AP's employer in accordance with regulations made under section 75G(4)(d) of the 1996 Act; and

(ii) AP has consented to the amount of leave that AP intends to take in accordance with regulations made under section 75G(4)(e) of the 1996 Act;

"expected week of birth" means the week, beginning with midnight between Saturday and Sunday, in which it is expected that the child will be born;

"leave curtailment date" means the date specified in a leave curtailment notice;

"leave curtailment notice" means—

(a) in Part 2, a notice which complies with the requirements of regulation 6;

(b) in Part 3, a notice which complies with the requirements of regulation 10;

"local authority foster parent" means a person approved as a local authority foster parent in accordance with regulations made by virtue of paragraph 12F of Schedule 2 to the Children Act 1989";

"M" means the mother (or expectant mother) of C;

"notice of entitlement" means—

(a) in Part 2 of the Regulations, a notice given by M in accordance with regulations made under section 75E(1)(f) of the 1996 Act;

(b) in Part 3 of the Regulations, a notice given by A in accordance with regulations made under section 75G(1)(f) of the 1996 Act;

"P" means the father of C, or the person who is married to, or is the civil partner or partner of M;

"partner" in relation to M or A means a person (whether of a different sex or the same sex) who lives with M or A and with C in an enduring family relationship but is not M or A's child, parent, grandchild, grandparent, sibling, aunt, uncle, niece or nephew;

"placed for adoption" means—

(a) placed for adoption under the Adoption and Children Act 2002 or the Adoption and Children (Scotland) Act 2007; or

(b) placed in accordance with section 22C of the Children Act 1989 with a local authority foster parent who is also a prospective adopter;

"prospective adopter" means a person who has been approved as suitable to adopt a child and has been notified of that decision in accordance with regulation 30B(4) of the Adoption Agencies Regulations 2005;

"revocation notice"—

(a) in Part 2, is a notice which complies with the requirements of regulation 8(3);

(b) in Part 3, is a notice which complies with the requirements of regulation 12(2);

"shared parental leave" means leave under section 75E or 75G of the 1996 Act;

"shared parental pay" means shared parental pay payable in accordance with the provisions of Part 12ZC of the Social Security Contributions and Benefits Act 1992;

"statutory adoption leave" means leave under section 75A of the 1996 Act (ordinary adoption leave) and leave under section 75B of the 1996 Act (additional adoption leave);

"statutory maternity leave" means leave under section 71 of the 1996 Act (ordinary maternity leave) and leave under section 73 of the 1996 Act (additional maternity leave);

"week" means any period of seven consecutive days.

(2) References to relationships in the definition of "partner" in paragraph (1)—

(a) are to relationships of the full blood or half blood or, in the case of an adopted person, such of those relationships as would exist but for the adoption, and

(b) include the relationship of a child with his adoptive, or former adoptive, parents but do not include other adoptive relationships.

(3) For the purposes of these Regulations a person is matched with a child for adoption when—

(a) an adoption agency decides that that person would be a suitable adoptive parent for the child, either individually or jointly with another person; or

(b) a decision has been made in accordance with regulation 22A of the Care Planning, Placement and Case Review (England) Regulations 2010 and an adoption agency has identified that person as the person with whom the child is to be placed in accordance with regulation 12B of the Adoption Agencies Regulations 2005.

NOTES

Commencement: 1 December 2014.

Modification: this regulation is applied with modifications in relation to parental order cases under the Human Fertilisation and Embryology Act 2008, s 54, by the Paternity, Adoption and Shared Parental Leave (Parental Order Cases) Regulations 2014, SI 2014/3096, reg 19 at **[2.1769]**, and in relation to adoptions from overseas by the Shared Parental Leave and Paternity and Adoption Leave (Adoptions from Overseas) Regulations 2014, SI 2014/3092, regs 3, 4, 6 at **[2.1706]**, **[2.1707]**, **[2.1709]**.

[2.1679]
4 Notices

(1) Where a notice is to be given under these Regulations, it may be given—

(a) where paragraph (2) applies, by electronic communication;

(b) by post; or

(c) by personal delivery.

(2) This paragraph applies where the person who is to receive the notice has agreed that the notice may be given to the person by being transmitted to an electronic address and in an electronic form specified by the person for the purpose.

(3) Where a notice is to be given under these Regulations it is to be taken to have been given—

(a) if sent by electronic communication, on the day of transmission;

(b) if sent by post in an envelope which is properly addressed and sent by prepaid post, on the day on which it is posted;

(c) if delivered personally, on the day of delivery.

NOTES

Commencement: 1 December 2014.

PART 2
CURTAILMENT OF STATUTORY MATERNITY LEAVE

[2.1680]

5 Entitlement to curtail statutory maternity leave

(1) M may bring forward the date on which her ordinary maternity leave period or additional maternity leave period ends by giving her employer a leave curtailment notice and either—

(a) a notice of entitlement; or

(b) a declaration of consent and entitlement.

(2) M must give her employer her leave curtailment notice at the same time as she gives her employer either a notice of entitlement or a declaration of consent and entitlement.

(3) If M has an entitlement to statutory maternity leave with more than one employer in relation to C, she must curtail her ordinary maternity leave period or additional maternity leave period in accordance with paragraphs (1) and (2) with each of those employers at the same time.

(4) M's obligation in paragraph (3) does not apply in relation to any employer with which she has returned to work on or before the date on which she gives notices in accordance with paragraphs (1) and (2).

NOTES

Commencement: 1 December 2014.

[2.1681]

6 Leave curtailment notice

(1) A leave curtailment notice must be in writing and must state—

(a) where M curtails her ordinary maternity leave period, the date on which M's ordinary maternity leave period is to end;

(b) where M curtails her additional maternity leave period, the date on which M's statutory additional maternity leave period is to end.

(2) The date specified in the leave curtailment notice must be—

(a) at least one day after the end of the compulsory maternity leave period;

(b) at least eight weeks after the date on which M gave the leave curtailment notice to her employer; and

(c) where M curtails her additional maternity leave period, at least one week before the last day of M's additional maternity leave period.

(3) In paragraph (2) "the end of the compulsory maternity leave period" means whichever is the later of—

(a) the last day of the compulsory maternity leave period provided for in regulations under section 72(2) of the 1996 Act; or

(b) where section 205 of the Public Health Act 1936 (women not to be employed in factories or workshops within four weeks after birth of child) applies to M's employment, the last day of the period in which an occupier of a factory is prohibited from knowingly allowing M to be employed in that factory.

NOTES

Commencement: 1 December 2014.

[2.1682]

7 Effect of the leave curtailment notice

(1) Where M has brought forward the date on which her ordinary maternity leave period or additional maternity leave period ends in accordance with regulation 5, her statutory maternity leave period will end on the leave curtailment date.

(2) In this regulation "statutory maternity leave period" means the period during which M is on statutory maternity leave.

NOTES

Commencement: 1 December 2014.

[2.1683]

8 Revocation

(1) M may revoke a leave curtailment notice by giving a revocation notice if—

(a) neither M nor P are entitled to shared parental leave or statutory shared parental pay;

(b) M served her leave curtailment notice before the birth of C; or

(c) P dies.

(2) A revocation notice must be given to M's employer before the leave curtailment date and—

(a) if given in accordance with paragraph (1)(a), within 8 weeks of the date on which M gave her leave curtailment notice to her employer in accordance with regulation 5(1);
(b) if given in accordance with paragraph (1)(b), within six weeks of the date of C's birth; or
(c) if given in accordance with paragraph (1)(c), within a reasonable time of the date of P's death.

(3) A revocation notice must—
(a) be in writing;
(b) state that M revokes her leave curtailment notice; and
(c) if given in accordance with paragraph (1)(c), must state the date of P's death.

(4) If M has given a leave curtailment notice to more than one employer, she must give revocation notices to each of those employers.

(5) The obligation in paragraph (4) does not apply to any employer with which M has returned to work on or before the date on which she gives the revocation notice.

(6) M may not give her employer a leave curtailment notice subsequent to giving a revocation notice unless the revocation was made in accordance with paragraph (1)(b).

NOTES
Commencement: 1 December 2014.

PART 3
CURTAILMENT OF STATUTORY ADOPTION LEAVE

[2.1684]
9 Entitlement to curtail statutory adoption leave

(1) A may bring forward the date on which A's ordinary adoption leave period or additional adoption leave period ends by giving A's employer a leave curtailment notice and either—
(a) a notice of entitlement; or
(b) a declaration of consent and entitlement.

(2) A must give A's employer the leave curtailment notice at the same time as A gives the employer either a notice of entitlement or a declaration of consent and entitlement.

(3) If A has an entitlement to statutory adoption leave in relation to C with more than one employer, A must curtail the ordinary adoption leave period or additional adoption leave period in accordance with paragraphs (1) and (2) with each of those employers at the same time.

(4) A's obligation in paragraph (3) does not apply in relation to any employer with which A has returned to work on or before the date on which A gives notices in accordance with paragraphs (1) and (2).

NOTES
Commencement: 1 December 2014.

[2.1685]
10 Leave curtailment notice: adoption

(1) A leave curtailment notice must be in writing and must state -
(a) where A curtails A's ordinary adoption leave period, the date on which A's ordinary adoption leave period is to end; or
(b) where A curtails A's additional adoption leave period, the date on which A's additional adoption leave period is to end.

(2) The date specified in the leave curtailment notice must be—
(a) at least eight weeks after the date on which A gives the leave curtailment notice to A's employer;
(b) at least two weeks after the first day of A's ordinary adoption leave period; and
(c) where A curtails A's additional adoption leave period, at least one week before the last day of A's additional adoption leave period.

NOTES
Commencement: 1 December 2014.

[2.1686]
11 Effect of the leave curtailment notice: adoption

(1) Where A has brought forward the date on which A's ordinary adoption leave period or additional adoption leave period ends in accordance with regulation 9, A's statutory adoption leave period will end on the leave curtailment date.

(2) In this Regulation "statutory adoption leave period" means the period during which A is on statutory adoption leave.

NOTES
Commencement: 1 December 2014.

[2.1687]
12 Revocation: adoption

(1) A may revoke a leave curtailment notice by giving a revocation notice if—
(a) neither A nor AP are eligible for shared parental leave or statutory shared parental pay; or

(b) AP dies.

(2) A revocation notice must be given to A's employer before the leave curtailment date and—

(a) if given in accordance with paragraph (1)(a), within 8 weeks of the date on which A gave the leave curtailment notice to A's employer in accordance with regulation 9(1);

(b) if given in accordance with paragraph (1)(b), within a reasonable time of the date of [AP's] death.

(3) A revocation notice—

(a) must be in writing;

(b) must state that A revokes the leave curtailment notice; and

(c) if given in accordance with paragraph (1)(b), must state the date of [AP's] death.

(4) If A has given a leave curtailment notice to more than one employer, A must give revocation notices to each of those employers.

(5) The obligation in paragraph (4) does not apply to any employer with which A has returned to work on or before the date on which A gives the revocation notice.

(6) A may not give A's employer a leave curtailment notice subsequent to giving a revocation notice.

NOTES

Commencement: 1 December 2014.

Paras (2), (3): words in square brackets substituted by the Shared Parental Leave and Leave Curtailment (Amendment) Regulations 2015, SI 2015/552, reg 3, as from 5 April 2015.

STATUTORY MATERNITY PAY AND STATUTORY ADOPTION PAY (CURTAILMENT) REGULATIONS 2014

(SI 2014/3054)

NOTES

Made: 19 November 2014.

Authority: Social Security Contributions and Benefits Act 1992, ss 165(3A)–(3D), 171ZN(2A)–(2D), 175(1), (3), (4).

Commencement: 1 December 2014.

ARRANGEMENT OF REGULATIONS

PART 1
GENERAL

[2.1688]

1 Citation and commencement

These Regulations may be cited as the Statutory Maternity Pay and Statutory Adoption Pay (Curtailment) Regulations 2014 and come into force on 1st December 2014.

NOTES

Commencement: 1 December 2014.

[2.1689]
2 Interpretation

In these Regulations—

"the 1992 Act" means the Social Security Contributions and Benefits Act 1992;

"the 1996 Act" means the Employment Rights Act 1996;

"A" means a person who is entitled to statutory adoption pay;

"adoption pay curtailment date" means, subject to regulation 12(4), the date specified in an adoption pay period curtailment notice;

"adoption pay period curtailment notice" means a notice given in accordance with regulation 12;

"AP" means the person who is married to, or the civil partner or the partner of, A;

"C" means the child in respect of whom an entitlement to—

(a) shared parental leave arises under section 75E (entitlement to shared parental leave: birth) or 75G (entitlement to shared parental leave: adoption) of the 1996 Act;

(b) statutory shared parental pay arises under section 171ZU (entitlement: birth) or 171ZV (entitlement: adoption) of the 1992 Act;

"calendar week" means a period of seven days beginning with a Sunday;

"M" means the mother (or expectant mother) of C;

"maternity pay period curtailment date" means, subject to regulation 7(5), the date specified in a maternity pay period curtailment notice;

"maternity pay period curtailment notice" means a notice given in accordance with regulation 7 and regulation 8(5);

"P" means the father of C, or the person who is married to, or the civil partner or the partner of, M;

"partner" in relation to M or A, means a person (whether of a different sex or the same sex) who lives with M or A and with C in an enduring family relationship but is not M's or A's child, parent, grandchild, grandparent, sibling, aunt, uncle, niece or nephew;

"SPL Regulations" means the Shared Parental Leave Regulations 2014;

"ShPP Regulations" means the Statutory Shared Parental Pay (General) Regulations 2014;

"statutory adoption pay" has the meaning given in section 171ZL (entitlement) of the 1992 Act;

"statutory maternity pay" has the meaning given in section 164(1) (statutory maternity pay—entitlement and liability to pay) of the 1992 Act.

NOTES

Commencement: 1 December 2014.

[2.1690]
3 Notices

(1) Where a notice is to be given under these Regulations, it may be given—

(a) where paragraph (2) applies, by electronic communication;

(b) by post; or

(c) by personal delivery.

(2) This paragraph applies where the person who is to receive the notice has agreed that the notice may be given to the person by being transmitted to an electronic address and in an electronic form specified by the person for the purpose.

(3) Where a notice is to be given under these Regulations it is to be taken to have been given—

(a) if sent by electronic communication, on the day of transmission;

(b) if sent by post in an envelope which is properly addressed and sent by prepaid post, on the day on which it is posted;

(c) if delivered personally, on the day of delivery.

NOTES

Commencement: 1 December 2014.

PART 2
CURTAILMENT OF MATERNITY PAY PERIOD

[2.1691]
4 Curtailment of maternity pay period (statutory shared parental pay: M)

M's maternity pay period shall end on the maternity pay period curtailment date if—

(a) M gives a maternity pay period curtailment notice (unless the notice is revoked under regulation 8);

(b) M satisfies the conditions in sub-paragraphs (a) and (d) of regulation 4(2) (entitlement of mother to statutory shared parental pay (birth)) of the ShPP Regulations; and

(c) P satisfies the conditions in sub-paragraph (b) of regulation 4(3) of the ShPP Regulations.

NOTES

Commencement: 1 December 2014.

[2.1692]
5 Curtailment of maternity pay period (statutory shared parental pay: P)

M's maternity pay period shall end on the maternity pay period curtailment date if—

(a) M gives a maternity pay period curtailment notice (unless the notice is revoked under regulation 8);
(b) P satisfies the conditions in sub-paragraph (a) of regulation 5(2) (entitlement of father or partner to statutory shared parental pay (birth)) of the ShPP Regulations; and
(c) M satisfies the conditions in sub-paragraphs (b) and (c) of regulation 5(3) of the ShPP Regulations.

NOTES

Commencement: 1 December 2014.

[2.1693]

6 Curtailment of maternity pay period (shared parental leave: P)

M's maternity pay period shall end on the maternity pay period curtailment date if—
(a) M gives a maternity pay period curtailment notice (unless the notice is revoked under regulation 8);
(b) P satisfies the condition in sub-paragraph (a) of regulation 5(2) (father's or partner's entitlement to shared parental leave) of the SPL Regulations; and
(c) M satisfies the conditions in sub-paragraphs (a) and (c) of regulation 5(3) of the SPL Regulations.

NOTES

Commencement: 1 December 2014.

[2.1694]

7 Maternity pay period curtailment notice

(1) A maternity pay period curtailment notice must—
(a) be in writing;
(b) specify the date on which M's statutory maternity pay period is to end; and
(c) be given to the person who is liable to pay M's statutory maternity pay.

(2) The date specified in accordance with paragraph (1)(b) must be—
(a) the last day of a week;
(b) if M has the right to maternity leave under section 71 (ordinary maternity leave) of the 1996 Act, at least one day after the end of the compulsory maternity leave period, or, if M does not have that right, at least two weeks after the end of the pregnancy;
(c) at least eight weeks after the date on which M gave the maternity pay period curtailment notice; and
(d) at least one week before the last day of the maternity pay period.

(3) In paragraph (2) "the end of the compulsory maternity leave period" means whichever is the later of—
(a) the last day of the compulsory maternity leave period provided for in regulations under section 72(2) (compulsory maternity leave) of the 1996 Act; or
(b) where section 205 of the Public Health Act 1936 (women not to be employed in factories or workshops within four weeks after birth of a child) applies to M's employment, the last day of the period in which an occupier of a factory is prohibited from knowingly allowing M to be employed in that factory.

(4) If M has more than one entitlement to statutory maternity pay in relation to C, M must curtail the maternity pay period in relation to each (or none) of those entitlements, and in relation to each of those entitlements M must specify a maternity pay period curtailment date which falls in the same calendar week.

(5) Where M—
(a) returns to work before giving a notice in accordance with paragraph (1); and
(b) subsequently gives such a notice;

the "maternity pay period curtailment date" shall be the last day of the week in which that notice is given (irrespective of the date given in that notice under paragraph (1)).

(6) For the purposes of paragraphs (2)(a) and (5), "week" has the meaning given in section 165(8) (the maternity pay period) of the 1992 Act.

(7) In this regulation, M is treated as returning to work where statutory maternity pay is not payable to her in accordance with section 165(4) or (6) of the 1992 Act.

NOTES

Commencement: 1 December 2014.

[2.1695]

8 Revocation (maternity pay period curtailment notice)

(1) Subject to paragraph (2), M may revoke a maternity pay period curtailment notice by giving a notice ("a revocation notice") before the maternity pay period curtailment date if—
(a) she gave the maternity pay period curtailment notice before the birth of C; or
(b) P dies.

(2) Revocation is effective under paragraph (1) where M gives a revocation notice to the person who is liable to pay M's statutory maternity pay that—
(a) if given under paragraph (1)(a), is given within six weeks of the date of C's birth; or

Part 2 Statutory Instruments

(b) if given under paragraph (1)(b), is given within a reasonable period from the date of P's death.

(3) A revocation notice must—

(a) be in writing;

(b) state that M revokes the maternity pay period curtailment notice; and

(c) if given under paragraph (1)(b), state the date of P's death.

(4) Where in accordance with regulation 7(4) M has given a maternity pay period curtailment notice to more than one person, M must give a revocation notice to each of those persons.

(5) M may not give a maternity pay period curtailment notice in respect of the same maternity pay period subsequent to giving a revocation notice unless the revocation was made in accordance with paragraph (1)(a).

NOTES

Commencement: 1 December 2014.

PART 3
CURTAILMENT OF ADOPTION PAY PERIOD

[2.1696]

9 Curtailment of adoption pay period (statutory shared parental pay: A)

A's adoption pay period shall end on the adoption pay curtailment date if—

(a) A gives an adoption pay period curtailment notice (unless the notice is revoked under regulation 13);

(b) A satisfies the conditions in sub-paragraphs (a) and (d) of regulation 17(2) (entitlement of adopter to statutory shared parental pay (adoption)) of the ShPP Regulations; and

(c) AP satisfies the condition in sub-paragraph (b) of regulation 17(3) of the ShPP Regulations.

NOTES

Commencement: 1 December 2014.

[2.1697]

10 Curtailment of adoption pay period (statutory shared parental pay: AP)

A's adoption pay period shall end on the adoption pay curtailment date if—

(a) A gives an adoption pay period curtailment notice (unless the notice is revoked under regulation 13);

(b) AP satisfies the conditions in sub-paragraph (a) of regulation 18(2) (entitlement of adopter's partner to statutory shared parental pay (adoption)) of the ShPP Regulations; and

(c) A satisfies the conditions in sub-paragraphs (b) and (c) of regulation 18(3) of the ShPP Regulations.

NOTES

Commencement: 1 December 2014.

[2.1698]

11 Curtailment of adoption pay period (shared parental leave: AP)

A's adoption pay period shall end on the adoption pay curtailment date if—

(a) A gives an adoption pay period curtailment notice (unless the notice is revoked under regulation 13);

(b) AP satisfies the condition in sub-paragraph (a) of regulation 21(2) (adopter's partner's entitlement to shared parental leave) of the SPL Regulations; and

(c) A satisfies the conditions in sub-paragraphs (a) and (c) of regulation 21(3) of the SPL Regulations.

NOTES

Commencement: 1 December 2014.

[2.1699]

12 Adoption pay period curtailment notice

(1) An adoption pay period curtailment notice must—

(a) be in writing;

(b) specify the date on which A's statutory adoption pay period is to end; and

(c) be given to the person who is liable to pay A's statutory adoption pay.

(2) The date specified in accordance with paragraph (1)(b) must be—

(a) the last day of a week;

(b) at least eight weeks after the date on which A gave the adoption pay period curtailment notice;

(c) at least two weeks after the first day of the adoption pay period; and

(d) at least one week before the last day of the adoption pay period.

(3) If A has more than one entitlement to statutory adoption pay in relation to C, A must curtail the adoption pay period in relation to each (or none) of those entitlements, and in relation to each of those entitlements A must specify an adoption pay curtailment date which falls in the same calendar week.

(4) Where A—

(a) returns to work before giving a notice in accordance with paragraph (1); and

(b) subsequently gives such a notice;

the adoption pay curtailment date shall be the last day of the week in which that notice is submitted (irrespective of the date given in that notice under paragraph (1)).

(5) For the purposes of paragraph (2)(a) and (4), "week" has the meaning given in section 171ZN(8) of the 1992 Act.

(6) In this regulation, A is treated as returning to work where statutory adoption pay is not payable to A in accordance with section 171ZN(3) or (5) of the 1992 Act.

NOTES

Commencement: 1 December 2014.

[2.1700]

13 Revocation (adoption pay period curtailment notice)

(1) Where AP dies before the adoption pay curtailment date, A may revoke an adoption pay period curtailment notice by giving a notice ("a revocation notice") in accordance with paragraph (2).

(2) A revocation notice must be given to the person who is liable to pay A statutory adoption pay within a reasonable period from the date of AP's death and before the adoption pay curtailment date.

(3) A revocation notice must—

(a) be in writing;

(b) state that A revokes the adoption pay period curtailment notice; and

(c) state the date of AP's death.

(4) Where in accordance with regulation 12(3) A has given an adoption pay period curtailment notice to more than one person, A must give a revocation notice to each of those persons.

(5) A may not give an adoption pay period curtailment notice subsequent to giving a revocation notice.

NOTES

Commencement: 1 December 2014.

EMPLOYMENT RIGHTS ACT 1996 (APPLICATION OF SECTIONS 75G AND 75H TO ADOPTIONS FROM OVERSEAS) REGULATIONS 2014

(2014/3091)

NOTES

Made: 24 November 2014.
Authority: Employment Rights Act 1996, s 75H(17).
Commencement: 25 November 2014.

[2.1701]

1 Citation and commencement

These Regulations may be cited as the Employment Rights Act 1996 (Application of Sections 75G and 75H to Adoptions from Overseas) Regulations 2014 and come into force on 25th November 2014.

NOTES

Commencement: 25 November 2014.

[2.1702]

2 Application of sections 75G and 75H of the Employment Rights Act 1996 to adoptions from overseas

(1) Sections 75G and 75H of the Employment Rights Act 1996 have effect in relation to adoptions from overseas with the modifications specified in the second column of the Schedule to these Regulations.

(2) In this regulation "adoption from overseas" means the adoption of a child who enters Great Britain from outside the United Kingdom in connection with or for the purposes of adoption which does not involve the placement of the child for adoption under the law of any part of the United Kingdom.

NOTES

Commencement: 25 November 2014.

SCHEDULE

Regulation 2

[2.1703]

Provision	***Modification***
Section 75G	For paragraph (b) of subsection (1) substitute— "(b) as to being a person by whom a child is, or is expected to be, adopted from overseas,".

Provision	Modification
	For paragraph (b) of subsection (4) substitute— "(b) as to relationship with a child adopted, or expected to be adopted, from overseas or with a person ("A") by whom the child is, or is expected to be, so adopted,". After subsection (6) insert— "(6A) For the purposes of this section and section 75H, a person adopts a child from overseas if the person adopts a child who enters Great Britain from outside the United Kingdom in connection with or for the purposes of adoption which does not involve the placement of the child for adoption under the law of any part the United Kingdom.". Omit subsection (7). Omit subsection (8).
Section 75H	In paragraph (a) of subsection (2), for "with whom the child is, or is expected to be, placed for adoption" substitute "by whom the child is, or is expected to be, adopted from overseas". In paragraph (b) of subsection (2), for "with whom the child is, or is expected to be, placed for adoption" substitute "by whom the child is, or is expected to be, adopted from overseas". In paragraph (b) of subsection (14), for "placed for adoption" substitute "adopted from overseas".

NOTES

Commencement: 25 November 2014.

SHARED PARENTAL LEAVE AND PATERNITY AND ADOPTION LEAVE (ADOPTIONS FROM OVERSEAS) REGULATIONS 2014

(SI 2014/3092)

NOTES

Made: 26 November 2014.

Authority: Employment Rights Act 1996, ss 47C(2), 75A(1), (2A), (2B), 75B(3)(a), (aa), (3A), 75D(1)(a), (2), 75G(1)–(6), 75H(1), (4), (7)–(14), (16), (17), 75I(1), (4), (5), 75J, 75K(1), (6), 80B(2), (4A), 99.

Commencement: 5 April 2015.

PART 1
GENERAL

[2.1704]

1 Citation and commencement

These Regulations may be cited as the Shared Parental Leave and Paternity and Adoption Leave (Adoptions from Overseas) Regulations 2014 and come into force on 5th April 2015.

NOTES

Commencement: 5 April 2015.

[2.1705]

2 Interpretation

In these Regulations—

"the Application Regulations" means the Employment Rights Act 1996 (Application of Sections 75G and 75H to Adoptions from Overseas) Regulations 2014;

"adoption from overseas" means the adoption of a child who enters Great Britain from outside the United Kingdom in connection with or for the purposes of adoption which does not involve the placement of the child for adoption under the law of any part of the United Kingdom, and references to a child adopted from overseas shall be construed accordingly;

"enter Great Britain" means enter Great Britain from outside the United Kingdom in connection with or for the purposes of adoption.

NOTES

Commencement: 5 April 2015.

PART 2
APPLICATION OF THE MATERNITY AND ADOPTION LEAVE (CURTAILMENT) REGULATIONS 2014

[2.1706]
3 Application of the Maternity and Adoption Leave (Curtailment) Regulations 2014 to adoptions from overseas

(1) The provisions of the Maternity and Adoption Leave (Curtailment) Regulations 2014, insofar as they provide for the curtailment of statutory adoption leave, apply to adoptions from overseas, subject to the modifications set out in paragraph (2) and regulations 4 to 6 below.

(2) Any references in the provisions of the Maternity and Adoption Leave (Curtailment) Regulations 2014 to the provisions in Chapter 1B of Part 8 of the Employment Rights Act 1996 Act must be construed as references to the provisions of Chapter 1B as modified by the Application Regulations.

NOTES
Commencement: 5 April 2015.

[2.1707]
4 Modifications to the Maternity and Adoption Leave (Curtailment) Regulations 2014

The Maternity and Adoption Leave (Curtailment) Regulations 2014 are modified as follows.

NOTES
Commencement: 5 April 2015.

[2.1708]
5

In regulation 2 (application) for paragraph (2) substitute—

"(2) Part 3 of these Regulations has effect only in relation to children who enter Great Britain on or after 5th April 2015.".

NOTES
Commencement: 5 April 2015.

[2.1709]
6

(1) Regulation 3 (interpretation) is modified as follows.

(2) In paragraph (1)—

(a) for the definition of "A" substitute—

""A", in relation to C, means the person by whom C has been or is to be adopted, or, in a case where two people have adopted C jointly, whichever of them has elected to be the adopter for the purposes of the Parental and Adoption Leave Regulations 2002;";

(b) for the definition of "AP" substitute—

""AP" means the person who at the date on which C enters Great Britain is married to, or the civil partner or the partner of, A;"; and

(c) after the definition of "declaration of consent and entitlement", insert—

""enter Great Britain" means enter Great Britain from outside the United Kingdom in connection with or for the purposes of adoption;".

NOTES
Commencement: 5 April 2015.

PART 3
APPLICATION OF THE SHARED PARENTAL LEAVE REGULATIONS 2014

[2.1710]
7 Application of the Shared Parental Leave Regulations 2014 to adoptions from overseas

(1) The provisions of the Shared Parental Leave Regulations 2014 mentioned in paragraph (2), insofar as they apply to shared parental leave (adoption), apply to adoptions from overseas, subject to the modifications set out in paragraphs (3) and (4) and regulations 8 to 21 below.

(2) The relevant provisions are—

(a) regulation 2;
(b) regulation 3;
(c) Parts 3 to 6;
(d) Part 2 of the Schedule.

(3) Any references in the provisions of the Shared Parental Leave Regulations 2014 mentioned in paragraph (2) to the provisions in Chapter 1B of Part 8 of the Employment Rights Act 1996 Act must be construed as references to the provisions of Chapter 1B as modified by the Application Regulations.

(4) Any references in the provisions of the Shared Parental Leave Regulations 2014 mentioned in paragraph (2) to other provisions of those Regulations must be construed as references to those provisions as modified by these Regulations.

NOTES

Commencement: 5 April 2015.

[2.1711]

8 Modifications to the Shared Parental Leave Regulations 2014 for the purposes of adoptions from overseas

The Shared Parental Leave Regulations 2014 are modified as follows.

NOTES

Commencement: 5 April 2015.

[2.1712]

9

In regulation 2 (application) for paragraph (2) substitute—

"(2) The provisions relating to shared parental leave in Part 3 have effect only in relation to children who enter Great Britain on or after 5th April 2015.".

NOTES

Commencement: 5 April 2015.

[2.1713]

10

(1) Regulation 3 (interpretation) is modified as follows.

(2) In paragraph (1)—

(a) for the definition of "A" substitute—

""A", in relation to C, means the person by whom C has been or is to be adopted, or, in a case where two people have adopted C jointly, whichever of them has elected to be the adopter for the purposes of the Parental and Adoption Leave Regulations 2002;";

(b) for the definition of "AP" substitute—

""AP" means the person who at the date on which C enters Great Britain is married to, or the civil partner or the partner of, A;"; and

(c) insert the following definitions in the appropriate places alphabetically—

""enter Great Britain" means enter Great Britain from outside the United Kingdom in connection with or for the purposes of adoption;

"official notification" means written notification, issued by or on behalf of the relevant central authority, that it is prepared to issue a certificate to the overseas authority concerned with the adoption of C, or that it has issued a certificate and sent it to that authority, confirming, in either case, that A is eligible to adopt, and has been assessed and approved as being a suitable adoptive parent;

"relevant central authority" means—

(a) where Part 3 of the Adoptions with a Foreign Element Regulations 2005 applies to A and A is habitually resident in Wales, the Welsh Ministers;

(b) where the Adoptions with a Foreign Element (Scotland) Regulations 2009 apply to A and A is habitually resident in Scotland, the Scottish Ministers; and

(c) in any other case, the Secretary of State.".

NOTES

Commencement: 5 April 2015.

[2.1714]

11

(1) Regulation 20 (adopter's entitlement to shared parental leave) is modified as follows.

(2) In paragraphs (2)(b) and (3)(b) for "of the placement for adoption of C" substitute "on which C enters Great Britain".

(3) In paragraph (4) for "placed for adoption through a single placement" substitute "adopted as part of the same arrangement".

NOTES

Commencement: 5 April 2015.

[2.1715]

12

(1) Regulation 21 (adopter's partner's entitlement to shared parental leave) is modified as follows.

(2) In paragraphs (2)(b) and (3)(b) for "of the placement for adoption of C" substitute "on which C enters Great Britain".

(3) In paragraph (4) for "placed for adoption through a single placement" substitute "adopted as part of the same arrangement".

NOTES

Commencement: 5 April 2015.

[2.1716]
13

In regulation 23 (periods when shared parental leave may be taken), for paragraph (1) substitute—

"(1) Shared parental leave may be taken at any time within the period which begins on the date on which C enters Great Britain (or where more than one child is adopted as a result of the same arrangement, the date on which the first child entered Great Britain) and ends on the day before the first anniversary of that date.".

NOTES

Commencement: 5 April 2015.

[2.1717]
14

(1) Regulation 24 (adopter's notice of entitlement) is modified as follows.

(2) For sub-paragraph (c) in paragraph (2) substitute—

"(c) the date that A received the official notification;".

(3) For sub-paragraph (d) in paragraph (2) substitute—

"(d) the date on which C is expected to enter Great Britain (except as provided for in paragraph (5));".

(4) For paragraph (5) substitute—

"(5) Where a notice is given under paragraph (1) before the date that C enters Great Britain and C enters Great Britain less than eight weeks before the start of the first period of shared parental leave, A must give the date of C's entry into Great Britain to A's employer as soon as reasonably practicable and, in any event, before the first period of shared parental leave to be taken by A.".

NOTES

Commencement: 5 April 2015.

[2.1718]
15

(1) Regulation 25 (adopter's partner's notice of entitlement) is modified as follows.

(2) For sub-paragraph (c) in paragraph (2) substitute—

"(c) the date that A received the official notification;".

(3) For sub-paragraph (d) in paragraph (2) substitute—

"(d) the date that C is expected to enter Great Britain (except as provided for in paragraph (4));".

(4) For paragraph (4) substitute—

"(4) Where a notice is given under paragraph (1) before the date that C enters Great Britain, AP must give the date of C's entry into Great Britain to AP's employer as soon as reasonably practicable after the entry and, in any event, before the first period of shared parental leave to be taken by AP.".

NOTES

Commencement: 5 April 2015.

[2.1719]
16

(1) Regulation 26 (supplementary evidence) is modified as follows.

(2) For sub-paragraph (a) of paragraph (1) substitute—

"(a) a copy of the official notification; and".

(3) For sub-paragraph (a) of paragraph (2) substitute—

"(a) a copy of the official notification; and".

NOTES

Commencement: 5 April 2015.

[2.1720]
17

In regulation 28 (period of leave notice), for sub-paragraph (c) of paragraph (4) substitute—

"(c) if given before C enters Great Britain—
(i) contain a start for the leave which is the day on which C enters Great Britain or which is expressed as a number of days following the date of C's entry into Great Britain;
(ii) contain an end date expressed as a number of days following the date of C's entry into Great Britain.".

NOTES

Commencement: 5 April 2015.

[2.1721]
18

In regulation 34 (entitlement in the event of disrupted placement or death), for paragraph (b) substitute—

"(b) regulation 28 of the Adoptions with a Foreign Element Regulations 2005 or regulation 31 of the Adoptions with a Foreign Element (Scotland) Regulations 2009 applies.".

NOTES

Commencement: 5 April 2015.

[2.1722]
19

In regulation 35 (continuity of employment test), in sub-paragraph (b) of paragraph (3), for "A was notified of having been matched for adoption with C" substitute "A received the official notification".

NOTES

Commencement: 5 April 2015.

[2.1723]
20

In regulation 36 (employment and earnings test), in paragraph (5), for the definition of "calculation week" substitute—

""calculation week" means the week during which C enters Great Britain;".

NOTES

Commencement: 5 April 2015.

[2.1724]
21

(1) Paragraph 10 (entitlement in the event of disrupted placement or death) of the Schedule is modified as follows.

(2) For sub-paragraph (1) substitute—

"(1) Where after a notice of entitlement has been given under regulation 24—
(a) C dies, or
(b) regulation 28 of the Adoptions with a Foreign Element Regulations 2005 or regulation 31 of the Adoptions with a Foreign Element (Scotland) Regulations 2009 applies,

the modifications set out in paragraphs (3), (5) and (6) below apply in relation to the entitlement of A to shared parental leave after C dies or either of those regulations apply.".

(3) For sub-paragraph (2) substitute—

"(2) Where after a notice of entitlement has been given under regulation 25—
(a) C dies, or
(b) regulation 28 of the Adoptions with a Foreign Element Regulations 2005 or regulation 31 of the Adoptions with a Foreign Element (Scotland) Regulations 2009 applies,

the modifications set out in paragraphs (4) to (6) below apply in relation to the entitlement of AP to shared parental leave after C dies or either of those regulations apply.".

(4) For sub-paragraph (6) substitute—

"(6) In regulation 32, for paragraph (1) substitute—

"(1) After the date on which C dies or regulation 28 of the Adoptions with a Foreign Element Regulations 2005 or regulation 31 of the Adoptions with a Foreign Element (Scotland) Regulations 2009 applies, only one notice may be given under regulation 31.".

(5) For sub-paragraph (7) substitute—

"(7) Where more than one child is adopted as a result of the same arrangement, a reference in this paragraph to the death of C or to the application of regulation 28 of the Adoptions with a Foreign Element Regulations 2005 or regulation 31 of the Adoptions with a Foreign Element (Scotland) Regulations 2009 must be construed as a reference to the last of those children to die or to the last of those children in relation to whom those regulations applied.".

NOTES

Commencement: 5 April 2015.

22–25 *(((Pt 4) Amends the Paternity and Adoption Leave (Adoption from Overseas) Regulations 2003, SI 2003/921 (outside the scope of this work)).*

STATUTORY SHARED PARENTAL PAY (ADOPTION FROM OVERSEAS) REGULATIONS 2014

(SI 2014/3093)

NOTES

Made: 26 November 2014.

Authority: Social Security Contributions and Benefits Act 1992, ss 171ZV(1)–(5), (12)–(15), 171ZW(1), 171ZX(2), (3), 171ZY(1), (3)–(5), 171ZZ1(3), 171ZZ4(3), (4), (7) (8), 175(3); Social Security Administration Act 1992, s 5(1)(g), (i), (l), (p).

Commencement: 5 April 2015.

[2.1725]

1 Citation and commencement

These Regulations may be cited as the Statutory Shared Parental Pay (Adoption from Overseas) Regulations 2014 and come into force on 5th April 2015.

NOTES

Commencement: 5 April 2015.

[2.1726]

2 Interpretation

In these Regulations—

"1992 Act" means the Social Security Contributions and Benefits Act 1992;

"the Application Regulations" means the Social Security Contributions and Benefits Act 1992 (Application of Parts 12ZA, 12ZB and 12ZC to Adoptions from Overseas) Regulations 2003;

"the General Regulations" means the Statutory Shared Parental Pay (General) Regulations 2014; and

"statutory shared parental pay (adoption)" means any pay payable in accordance with the provisions of Part 12ZC of the 1992 Act where the conditions in section 171ZV of that Act are satisfied.

NOTES

Commencement: 5 April 2015.

[2.1727]

3 Application of the General Regulations to adoptions from overseas

(1) The provisions of the General Regulations mentioned in paragraph (2), in so far as they apply to statutory shared parental pay (adoption), apply to adoptions from overseas, subject to paragraphs (3) and (4) and the modifications set out in regulations 4 to 16 below.

(2) The relevant provisions are—

(a) regulation 2;

(b) regulation 3(b);

(c) Parts 3 to 5;

(d) Part 2 of the Schedule.

(3) Any references in the provisions of the General Regulations mentioned in paragraph (2) to the provisions of Part 12ZC of the 1992 Act must be construed as references to the provisions of Part 12ZC as modified by the Application Regulations.

(4) Any references in the provisions of the General Regulations mentioned in paragraph (2) to other provisions of the General Regulations must be construed as references to those provisions as modified by these Regulations.

NOTES

Commencement: 5 April 2015.

[2.1728]

4 Modifications to the General Regulations for the purposes of adoptions from overseas

The General Regulations are modified as follows.

NOTES
Commencement: 5 April 2015.

[2.1729]
5

(1) Regulation 2 (definitions) is modified as follows.

(2) In paragraph (1)—

(a) for the definition of "A" substitute—

""A", in relation to C, means the person by whom C has been or is to be adopted;" and

(b) insert the following definitions in the appropriate places alphabetically—

""enter Great Britain" means enter Great Britain from outside the United Kingdom in connection with or for the purposes of adoption;";

""official notification" means written notification, issued by or on behalf of the relevant central authority, that it is prepared to issue a certificate to the overseas authority concerned with the adoption of C, or that it has issued a certificate and sent it to that authority, confirming, in either case, that A is eligible to adopt, and has been assessed and approved as being a suitable adoptive parent;";

""relevant central authority" means—

(a) in the case of an adopter to whom Part 3 of the Adoptions with a Foreign Element Regulations 2005 applies and who is habitually resident in Wales, the Welsh Ministers;

(b) in the case of an adopter to whom the Adoptions with a Foreign Element (Scotland) Regulations 2009 apply and who is habitually resident in Scotland, the Scottish Ministers; and

(c) in any other case, the Secretary of State.".

NOTES
Commencement: 5 April 2015.

[2.1730]
6

In regulation 3 (application), for paragraph (b) substitute—

"(b) statutory shared parental pay (adoption) in respect of children who enter Great Britain on or after 5th April 2015.".

NOTES
Commencement: 5 April 2015.

[2.1731]
7

(1) Regulation 17 (entitlement of adopter to statutory shared parental pay (adoption)) is modified as follows.

(2) In paragraphs (2)(b) and (3)(a) for "date of C's placement for adoption" substitute "date C enters Great Britain".

(3) In paragraph (2)(d) for "the placement for adoption of C" substitute "the adoption of C".

NOTES
Commencement: 5 April 2015.

[2.1732]
8

(1) Regulation 18 (entitlement of partner to statutory shared parental pay (adoption)) is modified as follows.

(2) In paragraphs (2)(b) and (3)(a) for "date of C's placement for adoption" substitute "date C enters Great Britain".

(3) In paragraph 3(c) for "the placement for adoption of C" substitute "the adoption of C".

NOTES
Commencement: 5 April 2015.

[2.1733]
9

(1) Regulation 19 (notification and evidential requirements relating to the adopter) is modified as follows.

(2) In paragraph (1)(b)—

(a) for "if C is not placed for adoption by that time" substitute "if C has not entered Great Britain by that time";

(b) for "placement of C" substitute "date of C's entry into Great Britain".

(3) In paragraph (3)(b) for "A was notified that A had been matched with C" substitute "A received the official notification".

(4) In paragraph (3)(c) for "date of C's placement for adoption" substitute "date of C's entry into Great Britain".

(5) For paragraph (4)(a) substitute—

"(a) the date on which A expects C to enter Great Britain; and".

NOTES

Commencement: 5 April 2015.

[2.1734]
10

(1) Regulation 20 (notification and evidential requirements relating to the partner) is modified as follows.

(2) In paragraph (1)(b)—

(a) for "if C is not placed for adoption by that time" substitute "if C has not entered Great Britain by that time";

(b) for "placement of C" substitute "date of C's entry into Great Britain".

(3) In paragraph (3)(b) for "A was notified that A had been matched with C" substitute "A received the official notification".

(4) In paragraph (3)(c) for "date of C's placement for adoption" substitute "date of C's entry into Great Britain".

(5) For paragraph (4)(a) substitute—

"(a) the date on which A expects C to enter Great Britain; and".

NOTES

Commencement: 5 April 2015.

[2.1735]
11

In regulation 23 (period of payment of statutory shared parental pay), in paragraph (1), for "C was placed for adoption (or where more than one child is placed for adoption as a result of the same arrangement, the date of placement of the first child to be placed as part of the arrangement)" substitute "C entered Great Britain (or where more than one child is adopted as a result of the same arrangement, the date on which the first child entered Great Britain)".

NOTES

Commencement: 5 April 2015.

[2.1736]
12

In regulation 24 (work during a period of statutory shared parental pay), in paragraph (1)(a)(ii), for "immediately preceding the 14th week before the expected week of the placement for adoption" substitute "in which A received the official notification".

NOTES

Commencement: 5 April 2015.

[2.1737]
13

In regulation 29 (conditions relating to employment and earnings of claimant's partner), in paragraph (5), for the definition of "calculation week" substitute—

""calculation week" means the week in which A received the official notification;".

NOTES

Commencement: 5 April 2015.

[2.1738]
14

In regulation 31 (conditions as to continuity of employment and earnings), in paragraph (2), for "A was notified of having been matched with C" substitute "A received the official notification".

NOTES

Commencement: 5 April 2015.

[2.1739]
15

In regulation 32 (normal weekly earnings of a claimant), in paragraph (9), in the definition of "appropriate date" for "the week in which A is notified of being matched with the child for the purposes of adoption" substitute "the week in which the official notification is sent to A".

NOTES

Commencement: 5 April 2015.

[2.1740]
16

(1) Paragraph 12 (death of child) of the Schedule is modified as follows.

(2) In sub-paragraphs (1) and (2) for "or is returned after being placed" substitute "or regulation 28 of the Adoptions with a Foreign Element Regulations 2005 or regulation 31 of the Adoptions with a Foreign Element (Scotland) Regulations 2009 applies,".

(3) In sub-paragraph (3) for "the death of C or after C is returned after being placed" substitute "the date on which C dies or regulation 28 of the Adoptions with a Foreign Element Regulations 2005 or regulation 31 of the Adoptions with a Foreign Element (Scotland) Regulations 2009 applies".

(4) In sub-paragraph (4)—

(a) for "placed for adoption as a result of the same placement" substitute "adopted as a result of the same arrangement";

(b) for "all the children are returned after being placed" substitute "regulation 28 of the Adoptions with a Foreign Element Regulations 2005 or regulation 31 of the Adoptions with a Foreign Element (Scotland) Regulations 2009 applies in relation to all of the children";

(c) for paragraph (b) substitute—

"(b) a reference in this paragraph to the death of C or to the application of regulation 28 of the Adoptions with a Foreign Element Regulations 2005 or regulation 31 of the Adoptions with a Foreign Element (Scotland) Regulations 2009 (however expressed) is to the death of the last of those children to die or is to the last of those children in relation to whom those regulations applied.".

(5) Omit sub-paragraph (5).

NOTES

Commencement: 5 April 2015.

EMPLOYMENT RIGHTS ACT 1996 (APPLICATION OF SECTIONS 75A, 75B, 75G, 75H, 80A AND 80B TO PARENTAL ORDER CASES) REGULATIONS 2014

(SI 2014/3095)

NOTES

Made: 24 November 2014.
Authority: Employment Rights Act 1996, ss 75A(8), 75B(9), 75H(18), 80B(9), 236(5).
Commencement: 25 November 2014.

[2.1741]
1 Citation, commencement and interpretation

(1) These Regulations may be cited as the Employment Rights Act 1996 (Application of Sections 75A, 75B, 75G, 75H, 80A and 80B to Parental Order Cases) Regulations 2014 and come into force on 25th November 2014.

(2) In these Regulations—

"the Act" means the Employment Rights Act 1996;

["intended parent", in relation to a child, means a person who, on the day of the child's birth—

(a) applies, or intends to apply during the period of 6 months beginning with that day—

(i) with another person for an order under section 54 of the Human Fertilisation and Embryology Act 2008 in respect of the child; or

(ii) as the sole applicant for an order under section 54A of that Act in respect of the child; and

(b) expects the court to make such an order in respect of the child;]

. . .

. . .

["section 54 parental order parent" means a person—

(a) on whose application the court has made an order under section 54 of the Human Fertilisation and Embryology Act 2008 in respect of a child; or

(b) who is an intended parent of a child by reference to an application or intended application for such an order;

"section 54A parental order parent" means a person—

(a) on whose application the court has made an order under section 54A of the Human Fertilisation and Embryology Act 2008 in respect of a child; or

(b) who is an intended parent of a child by reference to an application or intended application for such an order.]

NOTES

Commencement: 25 November 2014.

Para (2): definition "intended parent" substituted, definitions "parental order" and "parental order parent" (omitted) revoked, and definitions "section 54 parental order parent" and "section 54A parental order parent" inserted, by the Human Fertilisation and Embryology Act 2008 (Remedial) Order 2018, SI 2018/1413, art 3(2), Sch 2, para 8(1), (2), as from 3 January 2019.

[2.1742]

2 Application of sections 75A and 75B of the Act to parental order parents

Sections 75A and 75B of the Act have effect in relation to [section 54 parental order parents and section 54A parental order parents].

NOTES

Commencement: 25 November 2014.

Words in square brackets substituted by the Human Fertilisation and Embryology Act 2008 (Remedial) Order 2018, SI 2018/1413, art 3(2), Sch 2, para 8(1), (3), as from 3 January 2019.

[2.1743]

3 Application of sections 75G and 75H of the Act to parental order parents

Sections 75G and 75H of the Act have effect in relation to [section 54 parental order parents] with the modifications specified in the second column of Schedule 1 to these Regulations.

NOTES

Commencement: 25 November 2014.

Words in square brackets substituted by the Human Fertilisation and Embryology Act 2008 (Remedial) Order 2018, SI 2018/1413, art 3(2), Sch 2, para 8(1), (4), as from 3 January 2019.

[2.1744]

4 Application of sections 80A and 80B of the Act to parental order parents

Sections 80A and 80B of the Act have effect in relation to [section 54 parental order parents] with the modifications specified in the second column of Schedule 2 to these Regulations.

NOTES

Commencement: 25 November 2014.

Words in square brackets substituted by the Human Fertilisation and Embryology Act 2008 (Remedial) Order 2018, SI 2018/1413, art 3(2), Sch 2, para 8(1), (5), as from 3 January 2019.

SCHEDULES

SCHEDULE 1

Regulation 3

[2.1745]

Provision	*Modification*
Section 75G	For paragraph (b) of subsection (1) substitute— "(b) as to being a person— (i) on whose application the court has made a parental order in respect of a child, or (ii) who is an intended parent of a child,". For paragraph (b) of subsection (4) substitute— "(b) as to being a person— (i) on whose application the court has made a parental order in respect of a child, or (ii) who is an intended parent of a child, (ba) as to relationship with the other person ("A") on whose application the parental order was made or who is an intended parent of the child,". After subsection (6) insert— "(6A) In this section and section 75H— ["intended parent", in relation to a child, means a person who, on the day of the child's birth—

Provision	Modification
	(a) applies, or intends to apply during the period of 6 months beginning with that day (i) with another person for an order under section 54 of the Human Fertilisation and Embryology Act 2008 in respect of the child; or (ii) as the sole applicant for an order under section 54A of that Act in respect of the child; and (b) expects the court to make such an order in respect of the child; and "parental order" means an order under section 54 or 54A of the Human Fertilisation and Embryology Act 2008.] Omit subsection (7). Omit subsection (8).
Section 75H	In paragraph (a) of subsection (2), for "with whom the child is, or is expected to be placed for adoption" substitute "on whose application the court has made a parental order in respect of the child or who is an intended parent of the child". In paragraph (b) of subsection (2), for "with whom the child is, or is expected to be placed for adoption" substitute "on whose application the court has made a parental order in respect of the child or who is an intended parent of the child". In paragraph (b) of subsection (14), for "placed for adoption as part of the same arrangement" substitute "born as a result of the same pregnancy".

NOTES

Commencement: 25 November 2014.

Words in square brackets substituted by the Human Fertilisation and Embryology Act 2008 (Remedial) Order 2018, SI 2018/1413, art 3(2), Sch 2, para 8(1), (6), as from 3 January 2019.

SCHEDULE 2

Regulation 4

[2.1746]

Provision	Modification
Section 80A	After paragraph (a) in subsection (5) insert— "(aa) make provision excluding the right to be absent on leave under this section in the case of an employee who satisfies— (i) the conditions specified in regulations under section 75A(1) or 80B(1), or (ii) such of those conditions as are specified in regulations under subsection (1);".
Section 80B	For paragraph (b) of subsection (1) (and the following "and") substitute— "(b) as to being a person— (i) on whose application the court has made a parental order in respect of a child, or (ii) who is an intended parent of a child, and". For paragraph (c) of subsection (1) substitute— "(c) as to relationship with the other person on whose application the parental order was made or who is an intended parent of the child,". In subsection (4), for "placement for adoption" substitute "birth". In paragraph (a) of subsection (5), for "a person with whom a child is placed for adoption" substitute "the other person on whose application the court has made a parental order in respect of a child or who is an intended parent of a child". Omit paragraph (aa) of subsection (5). In paragraph (c) of subsection (5), for "placed for adoption as part of the same arrangement" substitute "born as a result of the same pregnancy". For subsection (6) substitute— "(6) Where more than one child is born as a result of the same pregnancy, the reference in subsection (4) to the date of the child's birth shall be read as a reference to the date of birth of the first child born as a result of the pregnancy.". Omit subsection (6A). Omit subsection (6B).

Provision	*Modification*
	After subsection (7) insert— "(7A) In this section— ["intended parent", in relation to a child, means a person who, on the day of the child's birth— (a) applies, or intends to apply during the period of 6 months beginning with that day (i) with another person for an order under section 54 of the Human Fertilisation and Embryology Act 2008 in respect of the child; or (ii) as the sole applicant for an order under section 54A of that Act in respect of the child; and (b) expects the court to make such an order in respect of the child; and "parental order" means an order under section 54 or 54A of the Human Fertilisation and Embryology Act 2008.]

NOTES

Commencement: 25 November 2014.

Words in square brackets substituted by the Human Fertilisation and Embryology Act 2008 (Remedial) Order 2018, SI 2018/1413, art 3(2), Sch 2, para 8(1), (7), as from 3 January 2019.

PATERNITY, ADOPTION AND SHARED PARENTAL LEAVE (PARENTAL ORDER CASES) REGULATIONS 2014

(SI 2014/3096)

NOTES

Made: 28 November 2014.

Authority: Employment Rights Act 1996, ss 47C(2), 75A(1), (2), (2A), (2B), (3), (6), (7), 75B(1), (2), (3), (3A), (4), (7), (8), 75C(1), (2), 75D, 75G(1)–(6), 75H(1), (4), (7)–(14), (16), 75I(1), (4), (5), 75J, 75K(1), (6), (7), 80A(5)(aa), 80B(1), (2), (4A), (5), 80C(1), (6), 80D(1), 80E, 99.

Commencement: 1 December 2014.

PART 1
GENERAL

[2.1747]

1 Citation and commencement

These Regulations may be cited as the Paternity, Adoption and Shared Parental Leave (Parental Order Cases) Regulations 2014 and come into force on 1st December 2014.

NOTES

Commencement: 1 December 2014.

[2.1748]

2 Interpretation

In these Regulations—

"Curtailment Regulations" means the Maternity and Adoption Leave (Curtailment of Statutory Rights to Leave) Regulations 2014;

["intended parent", in relation to a child, means a person who, on the day of the child's birth—

(a) applies, or intends to apply during the period of 6 months beginning with that day—

(i) with another person for an order under section 54 of the Human Fertilisation and Embryology Act 2008 in respect of the child; or

(ii) as the sole applicant for an order under section 54A of that Act in respect of the child; and

(b) expects the court to make such an order in respect of the child;]

"Leave Regulations" means the Paternity and Adoption Leave Regulations 2002;

. . .

"paternity leave (adoption)" means paternity leave under regulation 8 of the Leave Regulations;

["section 54 parental order parent" means a person—

(a) on whose application the court has made an order under section 54 of the Human Fertilisation and Embryology Act 2008 in respect of a child; or

(b) who is an intended parent of a child by reference to an application or intended application for such an order;

"section 54A parental order parent" means a person—

(a) on whose application the court has made an order under section 54A of the Human Fertilisation and Embryology Act 2008 in respect of a child; or

(b) who is an intended parent of a child by reference to an application or intended application for such an order;]

"statutory adoption leave" means ordinary adoption leave under section 75A of the Employment Rights Act 1996 or additional adoption leave under section 75B of that Act;

"SPL Regulations" means the Shared Parental Leave Regulations 2014.

NOTES

Commencement: 1 December 2014.

Definition "intended parent" substituted, definitions "parental order" and "parental order parent" (omitted) revoked, and definitions "section 54 parental order parent" and "section 54A parental order parent" inserted, by the Human Fertilisation and Embryology Act 2008 (Remedial) Order 2018, SI 2018/1413, art 3(2), Sch 2, para 9(1), (2), as from 3 January 2019.

[2.1749]

[3 Application of the Leave Regulations to Parental Order Parents

(1) The provisions of the Leave Regulations, in so far as they apply to paternity leave (adoption) apply to section 54 parental order parents with the modifications set out in Part 2 of these Regulations.

(2) The provisions of the Leave Regulations, in so far as they apply to statutory adoption leave, apply to—

(a) section 54 parental order parents; and

(b) section 54A parental order parents,

with the modifications set out in Part 2 of these Regulations.]

NOTES

Commencement: 3 January 2019.

Substituted by the Human Fertilisation and Embryology Act 2008 (Remedial) Order 2018, SI 2018/1413, art 3(2), Sch 2, para 9(1), (3), as from 3 January 2019.

[2.1750]

4 Application of the Curtailment Regulations to Parental Order Parents

The provisions of the Curtailment Regulations in so far as they apply to the curtailment of statutory adoption leave, apply to [section 54] parental order parents with the modifications set out in Part 3 of these Regulations.

NOTES

Commencement: 1 December 2014.

Words in square brackets inserted by the Human Fertilisation and Embryology Act 2008 (Remedial) Order 2018, SI 2018/1413, art 3(2), Sch 2, para 9(1), (4), as from 3 January 2019.

[2.1751]

5 Application of the SPL Regulations to Parental Order Parents

The provisions of the SPL Regulations in so far as they apply to shared parental leave (adoption), apply to [section 54] parental order parents with the modifications set out in Part 4 of these Regulations.

NOTES

Commencement: 1 December 2014.

Words in square brackets inserted by the Human Fertilisation and Embryology Act 2008 (Remedial) Order 2018, SI 2018/1413, art 3(2), Sch 2, para 9(1), (5), as from 3 January 2019.

PART 2
PARENTAL ORDER PARENTS: PATERNITY AND ADOPTION LEAVE

[2.1752]

6

Regulation 2 (interpretation) of the Leave Regulations as they apply to [section 54 parental order parents and section 54A parental order parents] shall read as if—

(a) in paragraph (1)—

(i) the definitions of "adopter" and "child" were omitted;

(ii) in the definition of "partner", the words "a child's mother or adopter" were "Parent A" and the words "mother or adopter", in both places, were "Parent A";

(iii) there were, in the appropriate places alphabetically, the following definitions—

"["intended parent", in relation to a child, means a person who, on the day of the child's birth—

(a) applies, or intends to apply during the period of 6 months beginning with that day—

(i) with another person for an order under section 54 of the Human Fertilisation and Embryology Act 2008 in respect of the child; or

(ii) as the sole applicant for an order under section 54A of that Act in respect of the child; and

(b) expects the court to make such an order in respect of the child;]

"Parent A" in relation to a child, means the [section 54] parental order parent who has elected to be Parent A;

. . .

. . .

["parental statutory declaration" means a statutory declaration stating that the person making the declaration—
(a) has applied, or intends to apply—
(i) under section 54 of the Human Fertilisation and Embryology Act 2008 with another person; or
(ii) under section 54A of that Act, alone,
for a parental order under that section in respect of the child within the time limit for making such an application; and
(b) expects the court to make such an order in respect of the child;]
"shared parental leave" means leave under section 75E or 75G of the Employment Rights Act 1996;"
["section 54 parental order parent" means a person—
(a) on whose application the court has made an order under section 54 of the Human Fertilisation and Embryology Act 2008 in respect of a child; or
(b) who is an intended parent of a child by reference to an application or intended application for such an order;
"section 54A parental order parent" means a person—
(a) on whose application the court has made an order under section 54A of the Human Fertilisation and Embryology Act 2008 in respect of a child; or
(b) who is an intended parent of a child by reference to an application or intended application for such an order;]
(b) in paragraph (2)—
(i) the words "a child's mother or adopter" were "Parent A";
(ii) the words "the mother's or adopter's" were "Parent A's";
(c) the words of paragraph (4) were—

"a [section 54] parental order parent elects to be Parent A in relation to a child if he agrees with the other [section 54] parental order parent of the child that he, and not the other [section 54] parental order parent, will be Parent A".

NOTES

Commencement: 1 December 2014.

Words in square brackets inserted or substituted, and words omitted revoked, by the Human Fertilisation and Embryology Act 2008 (Remedial) Order 2018, SI 2018/1413, art 3(2), Sch 2, para 9(1), (6), as from 3 January 2019.

[2.1753]
7

Regulation 3 (application) of the Leave Regulations as they apply to [section 54] parental order parents shall read as if—
(a) paragraph (1) were omitted;
(b) the words of paragraph (2) were—

"The provisions in relation to paternity leave under regulation 8 and in relation to adoption leave under regulation 15 have effect in relation to children whose expected week of birth begins on or after 5th April 2015."

(c) in paragraphs (3) and (6), the words "8th December 2002" were "1st December 2014".

NOTES

Commencement: 1 December 2014.

Words in square brackets inserted by the Human Fertilisation and Embryology Act 2008 (Remedial) Order 2018, SI 2018/1413, art 3(2), Sch 2, para 9(1), (7), as from 3 January 2019.

[2.1754]
[7A

Regulation 3 (application) of the Leave Regulations as they apply to section 54A parental order parents shall read as if—
(a) paragraph (1) were omitted;
(b) the words of paragraph (2) were—

"The provisions in relation to adoption leave under regulation 15 have effect in relation to children whose expected week of birth begins on or after the last day of the period of 120 days beginning with the day on which the Human Fertilisation and Embryology Act 2008 (Remedial) Order 2018 comes into force."; and

(c) in paragraphs (3) and (6), the words "8th December 2002" were "on or after the day on which the Human Fertilisation and Embryology Act 2008 (Remedial) Order 2018 comes into force".]

NOTES

Commencement: 3 January 2019.

Inserted by the Human Fertilisation and Embryology Act 2008 (Remedial) Order 2018, SI 2018/1413, art 3(2), Sch 2, para 9(1), (8), as from 3 January 2019.

[2.1755]
8

In regulation 4 (entitlement to paternity leave: birth), paragraph (1A) of the Leave Regulations, as they apply to [section 54] parental order parents, shall read as if the words of that paragraph were—

"An employee is not entitled to be absent from work under paragraph (1) if the employee—
- (a) has taken any shared parental leave in respect of the child;
- (b) meets the criteria for entitlement to paternity leave under regulation 8; or
- (c) meets the criteria for entitlement to adoption leave under regulation 15."

NOTES

Commencement: 1 December 2014.

Words in square brackets inserted by the Human Fertilisation and Embryology Act 2008 (Remedial) Order 2018, SI 2018/1413, art 3(2), Sch 2, para 9(1), (9), as from 3 January 2019.

[2.1756]
9

In regulation 8 (entitlement to paternity leave: adoption) of the Leave Regulations as they apply to [section 54] parental order parents—
- (a) paragraph (1) shall read as if the words "the child's adopter" were "Parent A";
- (b) paragraph (2)(a) shall read as if the words after "the week" to the end were "immediately preceding the 14th week before the expected week of the child's birth";
- (c) paragraph (2)(b) shall read as if—
  - (i) the words "the child's adopter" were "Parent A";
  - (ii) the word "and" were omitted;
- (d) paragraph (2)(c) shall read as if—
  - (i) the words "the adopter" were "Parent A";
  - (ii) the full stop were omitted;
  - (iii) there were inserted after that paragraph—

  "and
  - (d) is a section 54 parental order parent] of the child.";
- (e) paragraph (4) shall read as if the words of that paragraph were—

  "An employee shall be treated as having satisfied the condition in paragraph (2)(b) if he would have satisfied it but for the fact that Parent A has died.";
- (f) paragraph (5) shall read as if the words of that paragraph were—

  "An employee shall be treated as having satisfied the condition in paragraph (2)(c) if he would have satisfied it but for the fact that the child was stillborn after 24 weeks of pregnancy or has died."
- (g) paragraph (6) shall read as if the words of that paragraph were—

  "An employee's entitlement to leave under this regulation shall not be affected by the birth or expected birth of more than one child as a result of the same pregnancy.";
- (h) it shall read as if the following paragraph were inserted after paragraph (6)—

  "(7) An employee shall be treated as having satisfied the condition in paragraph (2)(a) on the date of the child's birth notwithstanding the fact that he has not then been continuously employed for a period of not less than 26 weeks, where—
  - (a) the date on which the child is born is earlier than the 14th week before the week in which its birth is expected, and
  - (b) the employee would have been continuously employed for such a period if his employment had continued until that 14th week.".

NOTES

Commencement: 1 December 2014.

Words in square brackets inserted by the Human Fertilisation and Embryology Act 2008 (Remedial) Order 2018, SI 2018/1413, art 3(2), Sch 2, para 9(1), (10), as from 3 January 2019.

[2.1757]
10

In regulation 9 (options in respect of leave under regulation 8) of the Leave Regulations as they apply to [section 54] parental order parents—
- (a) paragraph (2) shall read as if the words "the child is placed with the adopter" were "the child is born";
- (b) paragraph (3) shall read as if the words of that paragraph were—

  "Subject to paragraph (2), an employee may choose to begin a period of leave under regulation 8 on—
  - (a) the date on which the child is born;
  - (b) the date falling such number of days after the date on which the child is born as the employee may specify in a notice under regulation 10; or

(c) a predetermined date, specified in a notice under that regulation, which is later than the first day of the expect week of the child's birth.".

NOTES

Commencement: 1 December 2014.

Words in square brackets inserted by the Human Fertilisation and Embryology Act 2008 (Remedial) Order 2018, SI 2018/1413, art 3(2), Sch 2, para 9(1), (11), as from 3 January 2019.

[2.1758]

11

Regulation 10 (notice and evidential requirements for leave under regulation 8) of the Leave Regulations as they apply to [section 54] parental order parents shall read as if the words of that regulation were—

"10

(1) An employee must give his employer notice of his intention to take leave in respect of a child under regulation 8, specifying—

(a) the expected week of the child's birth;

(b) the length of the period of leave that the employee has chosen to take in accordance with regulation 9(1); and

(c) the date on which, in accordance with regulation 9(3), the employee has chosen as the date on which the period of paternity leave should begin.

(2) The notice provided for in paragraph (1) must be given to the employer in or before the 15th week before the expected week of the child's birth.

(3) Where the employer requests it, an employee must give the employer, within 14 days of receipt of a request, a written declaration, signed by the employee, to the effect that—

(a) the purpose of the employee's absence from work will be that specified in regulation 8(1);

(b) the employee satisfies the conditions of entitlement in sub-paragraphs (b) and (c) of regulation 8(2); and

(c) the employee and Parent A are the [section 54] parental order parents of the child.

(4) An employee who has given notice under paragraph (1) may vary the date chosen as the date on which the period of leave will begin provided that the employee has given the employer notice of the variation—

(a) where the variation is to provide for the employee's period of leave to begin on the date on which the child is born, at least 28 days before the first day of the expected week of the child's birth;

(b) where the variation is to provide for the employee's period of leave to begin on the date that is a specified number of days (or a different specified number of days), after the date on which the child is born, at least 28 days before that date falling that number of days after the first day of the expected week of the child's birth;

(c) where the variation is to provide for the employee's period of leave to begin on a predetermined date (or a different predetermined date) at least 28 days before that date.

(5) The employee must vary the choice of date by substituting a later predetermined date or exercising an alternative option under paragraph (3)(a) or (3)(b) of regulation 9 in a case where—

(a) the employee has chosen to begin the period of leave on a particular predetermined date, and

(b) the child is not born on or before that date.

(6) Where an employee varies the date on which the period of paternity leave is to begin in accordance with paragraph (5) above the employee must give the employer notice of the variation as soon as is reasonably practicable.

(7) An employee must give his employer a further notice, as soon as reasonably practicable after the child's birth, of the date on which the child was born.

(8) Any notice under paragraph (1), (4), (6) or (7) must be given in writing, if the employer so requests.".

NOTES

Commencement: 1 December 2014.

Words in square brackets inserted by the Human Fertilisation and Embryology Act 2008 (Remedial) Order 2018, SI 2018/1413, art 3(2), Sch 2, para 9(1), (12), as from 3 January 2019.

[2.1759]

12

In regulation 11 (commencement of leave under regulation 8) of the Leave Regulations, as they apply to [section 54] parental order parents—

(a) paragraph (1) shall read as if the words "10(4) or (6)" were "10(4) or (5)";

(b) paragraph (2)(a) shall read as if the words "the child is placed with the adopter" were "the child is born".

NOTES

Commencement: 1 December 2014.

Words in square brackets inserted by the Human Fertilisation and Embryology Act 2008 (Remedial) Order 2018, SI 2018/1413, art 3(2), Sch 2, para 9(1), (13), as from 3 January 2019.

[2.1760]
13

In regulation 15 (entitlement to ordinary adoption leave) of the Leave Regulations, as they apply to [section 54] parental order parents—

(a) paragraph (2) shall read as if the words of that paragraph were—

"The conditions referred to in paragraph (1) are that the employee—

(a) is one of the child's [section 54] parental order parents; and

(b) has elected to be Parent A."

(b) paragraph (4) shall read as if the words of that paragraph were—

"An employee's entitlement to leave under this regulation shall not be affected by the birth or expected birth of more than one child as a result of the same pregnancy.".

NOTES

Commencement: 1 December 2014.

Words in square brackets inserted by the Human Fertilisation and Embryology Act 2008 (Remedial) Order 2018, SI 2018/1413, art 3(2), Sch 2, para 9(1), (14), as from 3 January 2019.

[2.1761]
[13A

In regulation 15 (entitlement to ordinary adoption leave) of the Leave Regulations, as they apply to section 54A parental order parents—

(a) paragraph (1)(a) shall read as if the word "conditions" were "condition";

(b) paragraph (2) shall read as if the words of that paragraph were—

"The condition referred to in paragraph (1) is that the employee is a child's section 54A parental order parent.";

(c) paragraph (4) shall read as if the words of that paragraph were—

"An employee's entitlement to leave under this regulation shall not be affected by the birth or expected birth of more than one child as a result of the same pregnancy."]

NOTES

Commencement: 3 January 2019.

Inserted by the Human Fertilisation and Embryology Act 2008 (Remedial) Order 2018, SI 2018/1413, art 3(2), Sch 2, para 9(1), (15), as from 3 January 2019.

[2.1762]
14

Regulations 16 (options in respect of ordinary adoption leave) and 17 (notice and evidential requirements for ordinary adoption leave) of the Leave Regulations as they apply to [section 54 parental order parents and section 54A parental order parents] shall read as if the wording of those regulations were—

16 "Commencement of ordinary adoption leave

(1) Except in a case referred to in paragraph (2), an employee's period of ordinary adoption leave begins on the day on which the child is born.

(2) In a case where the employee is at work on the date on which the child is born the employee's leave begins on the day after that date.

17 Notice and evidential requirements for ordinary adoption leave

(1) An employee must give the employer notice of their intention to take ordinary adoption leave in respect of a child specifying the expected week of the child's birth.

(2) The notice provided for in paragraph (1) must be given to the employer in or before the 15th week before the expected week of the child's birth.

(3) Where an employer requests it, an employee must also provide the employer with a parental statutory declaration.

(4) An employer who is given notice under paragraph (1) of the employee's intention to take ordinary adoption leave must notify the employee within 28 days of the receipt of the notice of the date on which the period of additional adoption leave to which the employee will be entitled (if the employee satisfies the conditions in regulation 20(1)) after the employee's period of ordinary adoption leave ends.

(5) The notification provided for in paragraph (4) must be given to the employee within 28 days of the date on which the employer received that notice.

(6) An employee must give the employer a further notice, as soon as reasonably practicable after the child's birth, of the date on which the child was born.

(7) Notices under paragraphs (1) and (6) must be given in writing, if the employer so requests.".

NOTES

Commencement: 1 December 2014.

Words in square brackets substituted by the Human Fertilisation and Embryology Act 2008 (Remedial) Order 2018, SI 2018/1413, art 3(2), Sch 2, para 9(1), (16), as from 3 January 2019.

[2.1763]
15

In regulation 18 (duration and commencement of ordinary adoption leave) of the Leave Regulations as they apply to [section 54 parental order parents and section 54A parental order parents]—

(a) The heading shall read as if the words "commencement of" were omitted;
(b) Paragraph (1) is unnumbered; and
(c) paragraphs (2) and (3) were omitted.

NOTES

Commencement: 1 December 2014.

Words in square brackets substituted by the Human Fertilisation and Embryology Act 2008 (Remedial) Order 2018, SI 2018/1413, art 3(2), Sch 2, para 9(1), (17), as from 3 January 2019.

[2.1764]
16

In regulation 20 (additional adoption leave: entitlement, duration and commencement) of the Leave Regulations as they apply to [section 54] parental order parents, paragraph (1)(a) shall read as if the words of that sub-paragraph were "the employee is Parent A".

NOTES

Commencement: 1 December 2014.

Words in square brackets inserted by the Human Fertilisation and Embryology Act 2008 (Remedial) Order 2018, SI 2018/1413, art 3(2), Sch 2, para 9(1), (18), as from 3 January 2019.

[2.1765]
[16A

In regulation 20 (additional adoption leave: entitlement duration and commencement) of the Leave Regulations as they apply to section 54A parental order parents, paragraph (1)(a) shall read as if the words of that sub-paragraph were "the employee is a section 54A parental order parent in respect of that child.".]

NOTES

Commencement: 3 January 2019.

Inserted by the Human Fertilisation and Embryology Act 2008 (Remedial) Order 2018, SI 2018/1413, art 3(2), Sch 2, para 9(1), (19), as from 3 January 2019.

[2.1766]
17

In regulation 22 (disrupted placement in the course of adoption leave) of the Leave Regulations as they apply to [section 54] parental order parents—

(a) paragraph (1) shall read as if the words of that paragraph were—

"This regulation applies where—

[(a) the employee does not apply for an order under section 54 of the Human Fertilisation and Embryology Act 2008 within the time limit set by subsection (3) of that section;
(b) the employee's application for an order under that section for the child is refused, withdrawn or otherwise terminated without the order being granted and any time for an appeal or a new application has expired; or
(c) the child dies.";]

(b) paragraph (3) shall read as if—
(i) in paragraph (a) the words from "the person with whom" to the end were "the time limit in section 54(3) of the Human Fertilisation and Embryology Act 2008 for an application for [an order under that section] for the child expires;";
(ii) in paragraph (b) the words "paragraph (1)(b)(i)" to the end were "paragraph (1)(b), the week in which the employee's application for [an order under that section] is refused, withdrawn or otherwise terminated without the order being granted;";
(iii) in paragraph (c) the words "paragraph (1)(b)(ii)" to the end were "paragraph (1)(c), the week during which the child dies";

(c) paragraph (3A) is omitted in relation to any time on or after the date on which that paragraph comes into force.

NOTES

Commencement: 1 December 2014.

Words in square brackets inserted or substituted by the Human Fertilisation and Embryology Act 2008 (Remedial) Order 2018, SI 2018/1413, art 3(2), Sch 2, para 9(1), (20), as from 3 January 2019.

[2.1767]
[17A

In regulation 22 (disrupted placement in the course of adoption leave) of the Leave Regulations as they apply to section 54A parental order parents—

(a) paragraph (1) shall read as if the words of that paragraph were—

"This regulation applies where—

Part 2 Statutory Instruments

(a) the employee does not apply for an order under section 54A of the Human Fertilisation and Embryology Act 1998 within the time limit set by subsection (2) of that section;
(b) the employee's application for an order under that section for the child is refused, withdrawn or otherwise terminated without the order being granted and any time limit for an appeal or new application has expired; or
(c) the child dies.";
(b) paragraph (3) shall read as if—
(i) in paragraph (a), the words from "the person with whom" to the end were "the time limit in section 54A(2) of the Human Fertilisation and Embryology Act 2008 for an application for an order under that section for the child expires;";
(ii) in paragraph (b), the words "paragraph (1)(b)(i)" to the end were "paragraph (1)(b), the week in which the employee's application for an order under that section is refused, withdrawn or otherwise terminated without the order being granted;";
(iii) in paragraph (c), the words "paragraph (1)(b)(ii)" to the end were "paragraph (1)(c), the week during which the child dies"; and
(c) paragraph (3A) shall be treated as omitted.]

NOTES

Commencement: 3 January 2019.

Inserted by the Human Fertilisation and Embryology Act 2008 (Remedial) Order 2018, SI 2018/1413, art 3(2), Sch 2, para 9(1), (21), as from 3 January 2019.

PART 3
PARENTAL ORDER PARENTS: CURTAILMENT

[2.1768]
18

Regulation 2(2) (application) of the Curtailment Regulations as they apply to [section 54] parental order parents shall read as if the words in that regulation were—

"Part 3 of these Regulations has effect only in relation to children whose expected week of birth begins on or after 5th April 2015.".

NOTES

Commencement: 1 December 2014.

Words in square brackets inserted by the Human Fertilisation and Embryology Act 2008 (Remedial) Order 2018, SI 2018/1413, art 3(2), Sch 2, para 9(1), (22), as from 3 January 2019.

[2.1769]
19

Regulation 3 (interpretation) of the Curtailment Regulations as they apply to [section 54] parental order parents shall read as if in paragraph (1)—
(a) the definition of "A" read—

"means in relation to C, the parental order parent of C who has elected to be Parent A in respect of C in accordance with regulation 2(4) of the Paternity and Adoption Leave Regulations 2002;"

(b) the definition of "AP" read—

"means the parental order parent of C who is married to, or is the civil partner or partner of, A;"

(c) there were, in the appropriate places alphabetically, the following definitions—
""intended parent", in relation to a child, means a person who, on the day of the child's birth—
(a) applies, or intends to apply during the period of 6 months beginning with that day, with another person for a parental order in respect of the child, and
(b) expects the court to make a parental order on that application in respect of the child;
"parental order" means an order under section 54(1) of the Human Fertilisation and Embryology Act 2008;
"parental order parent" means a person—
(a) on whose application the court has made a parental order in respect of the child, or
(b) who is an intended parent of a child;".

NOTES

Commencement: 1 December 2014.

Words in square brackets inserted by the Human Fertilisation and Embryology Act 2008 (Remedial) Order 2018, SI 2018/1413, art 3(2), Sch 2, para 9(1), (23), as from 3 January 2019.

PART 4
PARENTAL ORDER PARENTS: SHARED PARENTAL LEAVE

[2.1770]
20

In regulation 2 (application) of the SPL Regulations as they apply to [section 54] parental order parents—

(a) paragraph (1) is omitted;
(b) paragraph (2) shall read as if the words in that paragraph were—
(c) "The provisions relating to shared parental leave in Part 3 have effect only in relation to children whose expected week of birth begins on or after 5th April 2015.".

NOTES

Commencement: 1 December 2014.

Words in square brackets inserted by the Human Fertilisation and Embryology Act 2008 (Remedial) Order 2018, SI 2018/1413, art 3(2), Sch 2, para 9(1), (24), as from 3 January 2019.

[2.1771]
21

Regulation 3 (interpretation) of the SPL Regulations as they apply to [section 54] parental order parents shall read as if in paragraph (1)—

(a) the definition of "A" read—

"means in relation to C, the parental order parent of C who has elected be Parent A in respect of C in accordance with regulation 2(4) of the Paternity and Adoption Leave Regulations 2002 ;";

(b) the definition of "AP" read—

"means the parental order parent of C who at the date of C's birth is married to, or the civil partner or the partner of, A;";

(c) there were, in the appropriate places alphabetically, the following definitions—

"["intended parent", in relation to a child, means a person who, on the day of the child's birth—

(a) applies, or intends to apply during the period of 6 months beginning with that day, with another person for a parental order in respect of the child; and
(b) expects the court to make a parental order on that application in respect of the child;";

""parental order" means an order under section 54(1) of the Human Fertilisation and Embryology Act 2008;]

"parental order parent" means a person—

(a) on whose application the court has made a parental order in respect of the child, or
(b) who is an intended parent of a child;

"parental statutory declaration" means a statutory declaration stating that the person making the declaration—

(a) has applied, or intends to apply, under section 54 of the Human Fertilisation and Embryology Act 2008 with another person for a parental order in respect of the child within the time limit for making such an application; and
(b) expects the court to make a parental order on that application in respect of the child;".

NOTES

Commencement: 1 December 2014.

Words in square brackets inserted by the Human Fertilisation and Embryology Act 2008 (Remedial) Order 2018, SI 2018/1413, art 3(2), Sch 2, para 9(1), (25), as from 3 January 2019.

Shared Parental Leave (Adoption)

[2.1772]
22

In regulation 20 (adopter's entitlement to shared parental leave) of the SPL Regulations as they apply to [section 54] parental order parents—

(a) paragraphs (2)(b) and (3)(b) shall read as if the words "at the date of the placement for adoption of C" were "at the date of C's birth";
(b) paragraph (4) shall read as if the words of that paragraph were—

"Entitlement under paragraph (1) is not affected by the number of children born or expected as a result of the same pregnancy.".

NOTES

Commencement: 1 December 2014.

Words in square brackets inserted by the Human Fertilisation and Embryology Act 2008 (Remedial) Order 2018, SI 2018/1413, art 3(2), Sch 2, para 9(1), (26), as from 3 January 2019.

[2.1773]
23

In regulation 21 (adopter's partner's entitlement to shared parental leave) of the SPL Regulations as they apply to [section 54] parental order parents—

(a) paragraphs (2)(b) and (3)(b) shall read as if the words "at the date of the placement for adoption of C" were "at the date of C's birth";

(b) paragraph (4) shall read as if the words of that paragraph were—

"Entitlement under paragraph (1) is not affected by the number of children born or expected as a result of the same pregnancy.".

NOTES

Commencement: 1 December 2014.

Words in square brackets inserted by the Human Fertilisation and Embryology Act 2008 (Remedial) Order 2018, SI 2018/1413, art 3(2), Sch 2, para 9(1), (27), as from 3 January 2019.

[2.1774]
24

Regulation 23 (periods when shared parental leave may be taken (adoption)) of the SPL Regulations as they apply to [section 54] parental order parents shall read as if the words of paragraph (1) were—

"Shared parental leave may be taken at any time within the period which begins on the date C is born (or where more than one child is born as a result of the same pregnancy, the date on which the first child is born) and ends on the day before C's first birthday.".

NOTES

Commencement: 1 December 2014.

Words in square brackets inserted by the Human Fertilisation and Embryology Act 2008 (Remedial) Order 2018, SI 2018/1413, art 3(2), Sch 2, para 9(1), (28), as from 3 January 2019.

[2.1775]
25

In regulation 24 (adopter's notice of entitlement and intention to take shared parental leave) of the SPL Regulations as they apply to [section 54] parental order parents—

(a) paragraph (2) shall read as if—

(i) the words of sub-paragraph (c) were—

"the expected week of birth for C and C's date of birth (except as provided for in paragraph (5));";

(ii) the words of sub-paragraph (d) were—

"if the parental order has been granted, the date on which it was granted";

(b) paragraph (3) shall read as if there were inserted after sub-paragraph (b)—

"(c) a parental statutory declaration signed by A.";

(c) paragraph (5) shall read as if the words in that paragraph were—

"(5) Where a notice is given under paragraph (1) before C is born, A must give notice of C's date of birth as soon as reasonably practicable after the birth of C and in any event before the first period of shared parental leave to be taken by A.";

(d) it shall read as if after paragraph (6) there were inserted—

"(7) A is only required to supply a parental statutory declaration in accordance with paragraph (3)(c) if—

(a) A has not obtained a parental order for C, and

(b) A has not already supplied such a declaration to his employer.".

NOTES

Commencement: 1 December 2014.

Words in square brackets inserted by the Human Fertilisation and Embryology Act 2008 (Remedial) Order 2018, SI 2018/1413, art 3(2), Sch 2, para 9(1), (29), as from 3 January 2019.

[2.1776]
26

In regulation 25 (adopter's partner's notice of entitlement and intention to take shared parental leave) of the SPL Regulations, as they apply to [section 54] parental order parents—

(a) paragraph (2) shall read as if—

(i) the words in sub-paragraph (c) were—

"C's expected week of birth and, where known, C's date of birth (except as provided for in paragraph (4));";

(ii) the words of sub-paragraph (d) were—

"if the parental order has been granted, the date on which it was granted";

(b) paragraph (3) shall read as if there were inserted after sub-paragraph (a)(iv)—

"(v) A and AP are the parental order parents of the child";

(c) paragraph (4) shall read as if the words of that paragraph were—

"(4) Where a notice is given under paragraph (1) before C is born, AP must give C's date of birth to AP's employer as soon as reasonably practicable after the birth of C and, in any event, before the first period of shared parental leave to be taken by AP.".

NOTES

Commencement: 1 December 2014.

Words in square brackets inserted by the Human Fertilisation and Embryology Act 2008 (Remedial) Order 2018, SI 2018/1413, art 3(2), Sch 2, para 9(1), (30), as from 3 January 2019.

[2.1777]
27

In regulation 26 (supplementary evidence (adoption)) of the SPL Regulations as they apply to [section 54 parental order] parents—

(a) paragraph (1)(a) shall read as if the words in that paragraph were replaced by—

"if available, evidence in the form of a parental order;";

(b) paragraph (2)(a) shall read as if the words of that paragraph were replaced by—

"if available, evidence in the form of a parental order;";

NOTES

Commencement: 1 December 2014.

Words in square brackets substituted by the Human Fertilisation and Embryology Act 2008 (Remedial) Order 2018, SI 2018/1413, art 3(2), Sch 2, para 9(1), (31), as from 3 January 2019.

[2.1778]
28

In regulation 28 (period of leave notice (adoption)) of the SPL Regulations as they apply to [section 54] parental order parents, paragraph (4)(c) shall read as if the words in that paragraph were—

"if given before C is born—

(i) contain a start date for the leave which is the day on which C is born or which is expressed as a number of days following the date of C's birth;

(ii) contain an end date expressed as a number of days following the date of C's birth.".

NOTES

Commencement: 1 December 2014.

Words in square brackets inserted by the Human Fertilisation and Embryology Act 2008 (Remedial) Order 2018, SI 2018/1413, art 3(2), Sch 2, para 9(1), (32), as from 3 January 2019.

[2.1779]
29

In regulation 32 (limit on number of period of leave notices or variations (adoption)) of the SPL Regulations as they apply to [section 54] parental order parents, paragraph (2)(b) shall read as if the words "being placed earlier or later than the date expected" in that paragraph were "being born earlier or later than the expected week of birth".

NOTES

Commencement: 1 December 2014.

Words in square brackets inserted by the Human Fertilisation and Embryology Act 2008 (Remedial) Order 2018, SI 2018/1413, art 3(2), Sch 2, para 9(1), (33), as from 3 January 2019.

[2.1780]
30

In regulation 34 (entitlement to shared parental leave in the event of a disrupted placement or the death of adopter, adopter's partner or child) of the SPL Regulations as they apply to [section 54] parental order parents—

(a) paragraph (a) shall read as if the word "or" were omitted;

(b) paragraph (b) shall read as if the words of that paragraph were—

"A and AP do not apply for a parental order for C within the time limit in section 54(3) of the Human Fertilisation and Embryology Act 2008 for making such an application;";

(c) it shall read as if after paragraph (b) there were inserted—

"or

(c) A and AP's application for a parental order for C is refused, withdrawn or otherwise terminated without the order being granted and any time limit for an appeal or new application has expired.".

NOTES

Commencement: 1 December 2014.

Words in square brackets inserted by the Human Fertilisation and Embryology Act 2008 (Remedial) Order 2018, SI 2018/1413, art 3(2), Sch 2, para 9(1), (34), as from 3 January 2019.

[2.1781]
31

In regulation 35 (continuity of employment test) of the SPL Regulations as they apply to [section 54] parental order parents—

(a) shall read as if after paragraph (2) there were inserted—

"(2A) Where Part 3 applies and C is born earlier than the relevant week and an employee would have satisfied the condition in sub-paragraph (a) of paragraph (1) if the employee's employment had continued until the end of the week immediately preceding that week, the employee must be treated as having satisfied that condition.";

(b) paragraph (3) shall read as if the words of that paragraph were—

"In this regulation "relevant week" means the week immediately preceding the 14th week before the expected week of birth.".

NOTES

Commencement: 1 December 2014.

Words in square brackets inserted by the Human Fertilisation and Embryology Act 2008 (Remedial) Order 2018, SI 2018/1413, art 3(2), Sch 2, para 9(1), (35), as from 3 January 2019.

[2.1782]
32

Regulation 36 (employment and earnings test) of the SPL Regulations as they apply to [section 54] parental order parents shall read as if the definition of "calculation week" in paragraph (5) were—

""calculation week" means the expected week of birth.".

NOTES

Commencement: 1 December 2014.

Words in square brackets inserted by the Human Fertilisation and Embryology Act 2008 (Remedial) Order 2018, SI 2018/1413, art 3(2), Sch 2, para 9(1), (36), as from 3 January 2019.

[2.1783]
33

In the Schedule (shared parental leave in special circumstances) of the SPL Regulations as they apply to [section 54] parental order parents—

(a) paragraph 10 (entitlement to shared parental leave in the event of a disrupted placement or the death of a child) shall read as if—

(i) in sub-paragraphs (1) and (2) the words "is returned after being placed for adoption" were "the parental order does not proceed";

(ii) the words "C's return or" were omitted;

(iii) in the amendment of regulation 32(1) set out in paragraph (6), the words "is returned after being placed for adoption" were replaced by "the parental order does not proceed";

(b) it shall read as if after paragraph (6) there is inserted—

"(6A) In this paragraph a parental order does not proceed if—

(a) A and AP have not made an application for a parental order for C within the time limit for such an application under section 54(3) of the Human Fertilisation and Embryology Act 2008; or

(b) an application made for a parental order in respect of C is refused, withdrawn or otherwise terminated and any time limit for an appeal or new application has expired.";

(c) paragraph (7) shall read as if the words of that sub-paragraph were—

"Where more than one child is born of the same pregnancy, a reference in this paragraph relating to the death of C must be construed as a reference to the last of those children to die.".

NOTES

Commencement: 1 December 2014.

Words in square brackets inserted by the Human Fertilisation and Embryology Act 2008 (Remedial) Order 2018, SI 2018/1413, art 3(2), Sch 2, para 9(1), (37), as from 3 January 2019.

STATUTORY SHARED PARENTAL PAY (PARENTAL ORDER CASES) REGULATIONS 2014

(SI 2014/3097)

NOTES

Made: 26 November 2014.

Authority: Social Security Contributions and Benefits Act 1992, ss 171ZV(1)–(5), (12)–(15), 171ZW(1)(a)–(f), 171ZX(2), (3), 171ZY(1), (3), (4), (5), 171ZZ1(3), 171ZZ4(3), (4), (7), (8), 175(3); Social Security Administration Act 1992, s 5(1)(g), (i), (l), (p).

Commencement: 1 December 2014.

PART 1 INTRODUCTION

[2.1784]

1 Citation and commencement

These Regulations may be cited as the Statutory Shared Parental Pay (Parental Order Cases) Regulations 2014 and come into force on 1st December 2014.

NOTES

Commencement: 1 December 2014.

[2.1785]

2 Interpretation

In these Regulations—

"A" and "AP" have the same meanings as in the Pay Regulations as modified by these Regulations;

"C", "expected week of birth" and "statutory shared parental pay (adoption)" have the same meanings as under the Pay Regulations;

"parental order parent" means a person on whose application the court has made a parental order in respect of C;

"parental statutory declaration" means a statutory declaration stating that the person making the declaration—

(a) has applied, or intends to apply, under section 54 of the Human Fertilisation and Embryology Act 2008 with another person for a parental order in respect of C within the time limit for making such an application; and

(b) expects the court to make a parental order on that application in respect of C;

"Pay Regulations" means the Statutory Shared Parental Pay (General) Regulations 2014.

NOTES

Commencement: 1 December 2014.

[2.1786]

3 Application of the Pay Regulations to an intended parent or a parental order parent

The provisions of the Pay Regulations in so far as they apply to statutory shared parental pay (adoption) shall apply to an intended parent or a parental order parent with the modifications set out in Part 2 of these Regulations.

NOTES

Commencement: 1 December 2014.

PART 2 MODIFICATIONS OF THE PAY REGULATIONS AS THEY APPLY TO AN INTENDED PARENT OR A PARENTAL ORDER PARENT

[2.1787]

4

Regulation 2 (interpretation) of the Pay Regulations as they apply to an intended parent or a parental order parent shall read as if—

(a) in paragraph (1)—

(i) the definition of "A" read "means the intended parent or parental order parent in relation to C who has elected to receive statutory adoption pay under section 171ZL(2)(e) of the 1992 Act and to whom the conditions in that subsection apply;";

(ii) the definition of "AP" read "means the intended parent or parental order parent in relation to C who at the date of C's birth is married to, or is the civil partner of, or is the partner of A;";

(iii) the definition of "child" were omitted;

(iv) there was the following definition—

""parental order parent" means a person on whose application the court has made an order in respect of C under section 54(1) of the Human Fertilization and Embryology Act 2008;";

(v) the definitions of "placed for adoption" and "adoption agency" were omitted;

(b) paragraphs (4), (5) and (6) were omitted.

NOTES

Commencement: 1 December 2014.

[2.1788]
5

In regulation 3 (application) of the Pay Regulations as they apply to an intended parent or a parental order parent paragraph (b) shall read as if the words in that paragraph were—

"statutory shared parental pay (adoption) in respect of children whose expected week of birth begins on or after 5th April 2015.".

NOTES

Commencement: 1 December 2014.

[2.1789]
6

In regulation 17 (entitlement of adopter to statutory shared parental pay (adoption)) of the Pay Regulations as they apply to an intended parent or a parental order parent—

(a) in paragraph (2)—

(i) sub-paragraph (b) shall read as if the words in that sub-paragraph were—

"A has, or expects to have, at the date of C's birth the main responsibility for the care of C (apart from the responsibility of AP);";

(ii) sub-paragraph (d) shall read as if the words "to the placement for adoption of C" read "to being the intended parent or parental order parent of C";

(b) in paragraph (3), sub-paragraph (a) shall read as if the words in that sub-paragraph were—

"AP has, or expects to have, at the date of C's birth the main responsibility for the care of C (apart from the responsibility of A);".

NOTES

Commencement: 1 December 2014.

[2.1790]
7

In regulation 18 (entitlement of partner to statutory shared parental pay (adoption)) of the Pay Regulations as they apply to an intended parent or a parental order parent—

(a) in paragraph (2), sub-paragraph (b) shall read as if the words in that sub-paragraph were—

"AP has, or expects to have, at the date of C's birth the main responsibility for the care of C (apart from the responsibility of A)";

(b) in paragraph (3)—

(i) sub-paragraph (a) shall read as if the words in that sub-paragraph were—

"A has, or expects to have, at the date of C's birth the main responsibility for the care of C (apart from the responsibility of A);";

(ii) sub-paragraph (c) shall read as if the words "to the placement for adoption of C" read "to being the intended parent or parental order parent of C".

NOTES

Commencement: 1 December 2014.

[2.1791]
8

(1) In regulation 19 (notification and evidential requirements relating to the adopter) of the Pay Regulations as they apply to an intended parent or a parental order parent—

(a) paragraph (1)(b) shall read as if the words "if C is not placed for adoption by that time as soon as reasonably practicable after the placement of C " were "if C is not born by that time as soon as reasonably practicable after the birth of C";

(b) in paragraph (3)—

(i) sub-paragraph (b) shall read as if the words in that sub-paragraph were "the expected week of birth of C";

(ii) sub-paragraph (c) shall read as if the words in that sub-paragraph were "C's date of birth";

(iii) that paragraph shall apply as if there were also specified a parental statutory declaration by A unless the condition in paragraph (2)(a) or (b) of this regulation is satisfied;

(c) paragraph (4) shall apply as if—

(i) sub-paragraph (a) were omitted;

(ii) there were also specified a copy of C's birth certificate or, if one has not been issued, a written declaration signed by A which states that it has not been issued;

(iii) where A has not provided a parental statutory declaration as a result of the condition in paragraph (2)(a) of this regulation being satisfied, there were specified a parental statutory declaration.

(2) The conditions referred to in paragraph (1)(b)(iii) and (c)(iii) are—

(a) that A has given the employer who will be liable to pay statutory shared parental pay (adoption) to A a statutory declaration as evidence of A's entitlement to statutory adoption pay in respect of C in accordance with regulation 24 of the Statutory Paternity Pay and Statutory Adoption Pay (General) Regulations 2002;

(b) that A is a parental order parent and has given the employer a copy of the order in respect of C made under section 54(1) of the Human Fertilisation and Embryology Act 2008.

NOTES

Commencement: 1 December 2014.

[2.1792]
9

In regulation 20 (notification and evidential requirements relating to the partner) of the Pay Regulations as they apply to an intended parent or a parental order parent—

(a) paragraph (1)(b) shall read as if the words "if C is not placed for adoption by that time as soon as reasonably practicable after the placement of C " were "if C is not born by that time as soon as reasonably practicable after the birth of C";

(b) in paragraph (3)—

(i) sub-paragraph (b) shall read as if the words in that sub-paragraph were "the expected week of birth of C";

(ii) sub-paragraph (c) shall read as if the words in that sub-paragraph were "C's date of birth";

(iii) sub-paragraph (e) shall read as if the written declaration signed by AP was also required to contain the statement that A and AP are the intended parents or the parental order parents of C;

(c) paragraph (4) shall apply as if—

(i) sub-paragraph (a) were omitted; and

(ii) there were specified a copy of C's birth certificate or, if one has not been issued, a written declaration signed by AP which states that it has not been issued.

NOTES

Commencement: 1 December 2014.

[2.1793]
10

(1) The Pay Regulations apply to an intended parent or a parental order parent with the modification provided for in paragraph (2) where—

(a) one or more of the periods specified in a notice under regulation 19, 20 or 21 of the Pay Regulations during which A or, as the case may be, AP intends to claim statutory shared parental pay (adoption) start in the 8 weeks following the first day of C's expected week of birth;

(b) C's date of birth is before the first day of the expected week of birth; and

(c) A or, as the case may be, AP varies by notice under regulation 21(1) the period or periods referred to in sub-paragraph (a) so that that period or those periods start the same length of time following C's date of birth as that period or those periods would have started after the first day of the expected week of birth.

(2) The modification in this paragraph is that the requirement in regulation 21(1) to give notice at least 8 weeks before the first period specified in the notice is satisfied if such notice is given as soon as reasonably practicable after C's date of birth.

(3) The Pay Regulations apply to an intended parent or a parental order parent with the modifications provided for in paragraph (4) where—

(a) C is born more than 8 weeks before the first day of the expected week of birth;

(b) A or, as the case may be, AP has not given the notice and information under regulations 19 or 20 of the Pay Regulations before the date of C's birth; and

(c) A or, as the case may be, AP specifies in a notice under regulations 19 or 20 a period or periods of statutory shared parental pay (adoption) which start in the 8 weeks following C's date of birth.

(4) The modifications in this paragraph are—

(a) in regulation 19—

(i) paragraph (1)(a) shall read as if the words in that sub-paragraph were—

"paragraphs (2) and (3) as soon as reasonably practicable after the date of C's birth but in any event before the first period specified by A pursuant to paragraph (2)(d)";

(ii) paragraph (1)(b) and (c) shall not apply;

(iii) paragraph (4) shall not apply.

(b) in regulation 20—

(i) paragraph (1)(a) shall read as if the words in that sub-paragraph were—

"paragraphs (2) and (3) as soon as reasonably practicable after the date of C's birth but in any event before the first period specified by AP pursuant to paragraph (2)(d)";

(ii) paragraph (1)(b) and (c) shall not apply;

(iii) paragraph (4) shall not apply.

NOTES

Commencement: 1 December 2014.

[2.1794]
11

In regulation 23 (when statutory shared parental pay (adoption) is not to be paid) of the Pay Regulations as they apply to an intended parent or a parental order parent, paragraph (1) shall read—

"Statutory shared parental pay (adoption) is not payable after the day before the date of C's first birthday (or, where more than one child is born of the same pregnancy, the birthday of the first child so born).".

NOTES

Commencement: 1 December 2014.

[2.1795]
12

In regulation 24 (work during period of payment of statutory shared parental pay) of the Pay Regulations as they apply to an intended parent or a parental order parent, paragraph (1)(a)(ii) shall read as if the words "the expected week of placement for adoption" read "the expected week of birth".

NOTES

Commencement: 1 December 2014.

[2.1796]
13

In regulation 29 (conditions relating to employment and earnings of a claimant's partner) of the Pay Regulations as they apply to an intended parent or a parental order parent, in paragraph (5), the definition of "calculation week" shall read—

""calculation week" means the expected week of birth of C;".

NOTES

Commencement: 1 December 2014.

[2.1797]
14

Regulation 31 (conditions as to continuity of employment and normal weekly earnings in relation to a claimant) of the Pay Regulations as they apply to an intended parent or a parental order parent, shall read as if—

(a) the words in paragraph (2) were—

"Where C's birth occurs earlier than the 14th week before C's expected week of birth paragraph (1) shall have effect as if, for the conditions set out there, there were substituted conditions that—

(a) the person would have been in employer earner's employment for a continuous period of at least 26 weeks ending with the relevant week had C been born after the relevant week;

(b) the person's normal weekly earnings for the period of eight weeks ending with the week immediately preceding C's actual week of birth are not less than the lower earnings limit in force under section 5(1)(a) of the 1992 Act immediately before the commencement of C's actual week of birth; and

(c) the person continues in employed earner's employment with the employer by reference to whom the condition in sub-paragraph (a) is satisfied for a continuous period beginning with the date of C's birth and ending with the week before the first week falling within the relevant period relating to that person under section 171ZY(2) of the 1992 Act.".

(b) the following paragraphs were added—

"(3) The references in this regulation to the relevant week are to the week immediately preceding the 14th week before C's expected week of birth.

(4) Where more than one child is born as a result of the same pregnancy the date the first child is born is to be used to determine C's actual week of birth or the date of C's birth.".

NOTES

Commencement: 1 December 2014.

[2.1798]
15

In regulation 32 (normal weekly earnings of a claimant for statutory shared parental pay) of the Pay Regulations as they apply to an intended parent or a parental order parent, in paragraph (9), sub-paragraph (a), the definition of "the appropriate date" shall read—

""the appropriate date" means the first day of the 14th week before the expected week of the child's birth or the first day in the week in which the child is born, whichever is earlier (but see paragraph (10)).".

NOTES

Commencement: 1 December 2014.

[2.1799]
16

In the Schedule (statutory shared parental pay in special circumstances) to the Pay Regulations as they apply to an intended parent or a parental order parent, in paragraph 12—

(a) sub-paragraphs (1) and (2) shall read as if the words "is returned after being placed" (in each place where they occur) read "the parental order does not proceed";

(b) sub-paragraph (4) shall read as if the words in that sub-paragraph were—

"Where more than one child is born of the same pregnancy—

(a) sub-paragraphs (1) and (2) only apply where all the children die or the parental order does not proceed in respect of all the children; and

(b) a reference in this paragraph relating to the death of C (however expressed) is to the death of the last of those children to die.".

(c) sub-paragraph (5) shall read as if the words in that sub-paragraph were—

"For the purpose of this paragraph a parental order does not proceed if—

(a) A and AP have not made an application for an order in respect of C under section 54(1) of the Human Fertilisation and Embryology Act 2008 within the time limit for such an application under section 54(3) of that Act; or

(b) an application made for such an order in respect of C is refused, withdrawn or otherwise terminated and any time limit for an appeal or a new application has expired.".

NOTES

Commencement: 1 December 2014.

STATUTORY SHARED PARENTAL PAY (PERSONS ABROAD AND MARINERS) REGULATIONS 2014

(SI 2014/3134)

NOTES

Made: 24 November 2014.
Authority: Social Security Contributions and Benefits Act 1992, ss 171ZZ3(1), 171ZZ4(3)(b).
Commencement: 1 December 2014.

ARRANGEMENT OF REGULATIONS

PART 1
GENERAL

PART 2
STATUTORY SHARED PARENTAL PAY

SCHEDULES

PART 1
GENERAL

[2.1800]
1 Citation and commencement

These Regulations may be cited as the Statutory Shared Parental Pay (Persons Abroad and Mariners) Regulations 2014 and come into force on 1st December 2014.

NOTES

Commencement: 1 December 2014.

PART 2
STATUTORY SHARED PARENTAL PAY

[2.1801]
2 Interpretation

(1) In these Regulations—

"the Act" means the Social Security Contributions and Benefits Act 1992;

"adopter", in relation to a child, means the person with whom a child is, or is expected to be, placed for adoption under the law of the United Kingdom;

"adoption from overseas" means the adoption of a child who enters Great Britain from outside the United Kingdom in connection with or for the purposes of adoption which does not involve the placement of the child for adoption under the law of any part of the United Kingdom;

"EEA" means European Economic Area;

"foreign-going ship" means any ship or vessel which is not a home-trade ship;

"General Regulations" means the Statutory Shared Parental Pay (General) Regulations 2014;

"home-trade ship" includes—

(a) every ship or vessel employed in trading or going within the following limits—
  (i) the United Kingdom (including for this purpose the Republic of Ireland),
  (ii) the Channel Islands,
  (iii) the Isle of Man, and
  (iv) the continent of Europe between the river Elbe and Brest inclusive;

(b) every fishing vessel not proceeding beyond the following limits—
  (i) on the South, Latitude 48°30'N,
  (ii) on the West, Longitude 12°W, and
  (iii) on the North, Latitude 61°N;

"mariner" means a person who is or has been in employment under a contract of service either as a master or member of the crew of any ship or vessel, or in any other capacity on board any ship or vessel where—

(a) the employment in that other capacity is for the purposes of that ship or vessel or her crew or any passengers or cargo or mails carried by the ship or vessel; and

(b) the contract is entered into in the United Kingdom with a view to its performance (in whole or in part) while the ship or vessel is on her voyage,

but does not include a person in so far as their employment is as a serving member of the forces;

"placed for adoption" means—

(a) placed for adoption under the Adoption and Children Act 2002 or the Adoption and Children (Scotland) Act 2007; or

(b) placed in accordance with section 22C of the Children Act 1989 with a local authority foster parent who is also a prospective adopter;

"serving member of the forces" means a person, other than one mentioned in Part 2 of Schedule 1, who, being over the age of 16, is a member of any establishment or organisation specified in Part 1 of that Schedule (being a member who gives full pay service) but does not include any such person while absent on desertion;

"statutory shared parental pay (adoption)" means statutory shared parental pay payable where entitlement to that pay arises under regulation 17 or 18 of the General Regulations;

"statutory shared parental pay (birth)" means statutory shared parental pay payable where entitlement to that pay arises under regulation 4 or 5 of the General Regulations.

(2) For the purposes of these regulations, the expressions "ship" and "ship or vessel" include hovercraft, except in regulation 9(2).

(3) For the purposes of these Regulations—

(a) a person is matched with a child for adoption when an adoption agency decides that that person would be a suitable adoptive parent for the child;

(b) in a case where paragraph (a) applies, a person is notified as having been matched with a child on the date that person receives notification of the agency's decision, under regulation 33(3)(a) of the Adoption Agencies Regulations 2005, regulation 28(3) of the Adoption Agencies (Wales) Regulations 2005 or regulation 8(5) of the Adoption Agencies (Scotland) Regulations 2009;

(c) a person is also matched with a child for adoption when a decision has been made in accordance with regulation 22A of the Care Planning, Placement and Case Review (England) Regulations 2010 and an adoption agency has identified that person with whom the child is to be placed in accordance with regulation 12B of the Adoption Agencies Regulations 2005;

(d) in a case where paragraph (c) applies, a person is notified as having been matched with a child on the date on which that person receives notification in accordance with regulation 12B(2)(a) of the Adoption Agencies Regulations 2005.

(4) The reference to "prospective adopter" in the definition of "placed for adoption" in paragraph (1) means a person who has been approved as suitable to adopt a child and has been notified of that decision in accordance with regulation 30B(4) of the Adoption Agencies Regulations 2005.

(5) The reference to "adoption agency" in paragraph (3) has the meaning given, in relation to England and Wales, by section 2 of the Adoption and Children Act 2002 and in relation to Scotland, by section 119(1) of the Adoption and Children (Scotland) Act 2007.

NOTES

Commencement: 1 December 2014.

[2.1802]

3 Application

These Regulations apply in relation to—

(a) statutory shared parental pay (birth) in respect of children whose expected week of birth begins on or after 5th April 2015;

(b) statutory shared parental pay (adoption) in respect of children placed for adoption on or after 5th April 2015.

NOTES

Commencement: 1 December 2014.

[2.1803]

4 Restriction on scope

A person who would not be treated under regulation 33 (treatment of persons as employees) of the General Regulations as an employee for the purposes of Part 12ZC (statutory shared parental pay) of the Act if that person's employment were in Great Britain shall not be treated as an employee under these Regulations.

NOTES

Commencement: 1 December 2014.

[2.1804]

5 Treatment of persons in *other* EEA states as employees

A person who is—

(a) gainfully employed in an EEA state *other than the United Kingdom* in such circumstances that, if the employment were in Great Britain, the person would be an employee for the purposes of Part 12ZC of the Act, or a person treated as such an employee under regulation 33 of the General Regulations; and

(b) subject to the legislation of the United Kingdom under Council Regulation (EEC) No1408/71 [as amended from time to time or Regulation (EC) 883/2004 of the European Parliament and of the Council of 29 April 2004 as amended from time to time on the coordination of social security systems],

notwithstanding that person not being employed in Great Britain, shall be treated as an employee for the purposes of Parts 12ZC of the Act.

NOTES

Commencement: 1 December 2014.

Words in italics revoked (as from exit day, as defined in the European Union (Withdrawal) Act 2018, s 20) and words in square brackets in para (b) inserted (as from 5 March 2019) by the Employment Rights (Amendment) (EU Exit) Regulations 2019, SI 2019/535, reg 2(1), Sch 1, Pt 2, paras 15, 16.

[2.1805]

6 Treatment of certain persons absent from Great Britain as employees

Subject to regulation 9(2), where a person, while absent from Great Britain for any purpose, is gainfully employed by an employer who is liable to pay secondary Class 1 contributions (within the meaning of section 1(2) of the Act) in respect of that person's employment under section 6 of the Act or regulation 146 of the Social Security Contributions Regulations 2001, that person shall be treated as an employee for the purposes of Part 12ZC of the Act.

NOTES

Commencement: 1 December 2014.

[2.1806]
7 Entitlement to statutory shared parental pay where person has worked in an EEA state

(1) A person who—

(a) is an employee or treated as an employee under regulation 5;

(b) in the week immediately preceding the 14th week before the expected week of the child's birth was in employed earner's employment with an employer in Great Britain; and

(c) had in any week within the period of 26 weeks immediately preceding that week been employed by the same employer in *another* EEA state,

shall be treated for the purposes of section 171ZU of the Act (entitlement to shared parental pay: birth) as having been employed in employed earner's employment with an employer in those weeks in which the person was so employed in *the other EEA* state.

(2) A person who—

(a) is an employee or treated as an employee under regulation 5;

(b) in the week in which the adopter is notified of having been matched with the child for the purposes of adoption was in employed earner's employment with an employer in Great Britain; and

(c) had in any week within the period of 26 weeks immediately preceding that week been employed by the same employer in *another* EEA State,

shall be treated for the purposes of section 171ZV of the Act (entitlement to shared parental pay: adoption) as having been employed in employed earner's employment in those weeks in which the person was so employed in *the other EEA* State.

NOTES

Commencement: 1 December 2014.

For the words "another" and "the other EEA" in italics there are substituted the words "an" and "the EEA" respectively, by the Employment Rights (Amendment) (EU Exit) Regulations 2019, SI 2019/535, reg 2(1), Sch 1, Pt 2, paras 15, 17, as from exit day (as defined in the European Union (Withdrawal) Act 2018, s 20).

[2.1807]
8 Time for compliance with Part 12ZC of the Act or regulations made under it

Where—

(a) a person is outside the United Kingdom;

(b) Part 12ZC of the Act or regulations made under it require any act to be done forthwith or on the happening of a certain event or within a specified time; and

(c) because the person is outside the United Kingdom that person or that person's employer cannot comply with the requirement,

the person or the employer, as the case may be, shall be deemed to have complied with the requirement if the act is performed as soon as reasonably practicable.

NOTES

Commencement: 1 December 2014.

[2.1808]
9 Mariners

(1) A mariner engaged in employment on board a home-trade ship with an employer who has a place of business within the United Kingdom shall be treated as an employee for the purposes of Part 12ZC of the Act, notwithstanding that he may not be employed in Great Britain.

(2) A mariner who is engaged in employment—

(a) on a foreign-going ship; or

(b) on a home-trade ship with an employer who does not have a place of business within the United Kingdom,

shall not be treated as an employee for the purposes of Part 12ZC of the Act, notwithstanding that the mariner may have been employed in Great Britain.

NOTES

Commencement: 1 December 2014.

[2.1809]
10 Continental shelf

(1) In this regulation—

"designated area" means any area which may from time to time be designated by Order in Council under section 1(7) of the Continental Shelf Act 1964 as an area within which the rights of the United Kingdom with respect to the seabed and subsoil and their natural resources may be exercised;

"prescribed employment" means any employment (whether under a contract of service or not) in a designated area in connection with continental shelf operations, as defined in section 120(2) of the Act.

(2) A person in prescribed employment shall be treated as an employee for the purposes of Part 12ZC of the Act notwithstanding that that person may not be employed in Great Britain.

NOTES

Commencement: 1 December 2014.

[2.1810]
11 Adoptions from overseas
Schedule 2 applies to adoptions from overseas.

NOTES
Commencement: 1 December 2014.

12–14 *(Regs 12–14 (Part 3) amend the Statutory Paternity Pay and Statutory Adoption Pay (Persons Abroad and Mariners) Regulations 2002, SI 2002/2821 (outside the scope of this work).*

SCHEDULES

SCHEDULE 1

Regulation 2(1)

PART 1
ESTABLISHMENTS AND ORGANISATIONS

[2.1811]
1. Any of the regular, naval, military or air forces of the Crown.

2. Royal Fleet Reserve.

3. Royal Naval Reserve

4. Royal Marines Reserve.

5. Army Reserve.

6. Territorial Army.

7. Royal Air Force Reserve.

8. Royal Auxiliary Air Force.

9. The Royal Irish Regiment, to the extent that its members are not members of any force falling within paragraph 1.

NOTES
Commencement: 1 December 2014.

PART 2
ESTABLISHMENTS AND ORGANISATIONS OF WHICH HER MAJESTY'S FORCES SHALL NOT CONSIST

[2.1812]
10. Her Majesty's forces shall not be taken to consist of any of the establishments or organisations specified in Part 1 of this Schedule by virtue only of the employment in such establishment or organisation of the following persons—

(a) any person who is serving as a member of any naval force of Her Majesty's forces and who (not having been an insured person under the National Insurance Act 1965 and not being a contributor under the Social Security Act 1975 or the Social Security Contributions and Benefits Act 1992) locally entered that force at an overseas base;

(b) any person who is serving as a member of any military force of Her Majesty's forces and who entered that force, or was recruited for that force outside the United Kingdom, and the depot of whose unit is situated outside the United Kingdom;

(c) any person who is serving as a member of any air force of Her Majesty's forces and who entered that force, or was recruited for that force, outside the United Kingdom, and is liable under the terms of his engagement to serve only in a specified part of the world outside the United Kingdom.

NOTES
Commencement: 1 December 2014.

SCHEDULE 2
ADOPTIONS FROM OVERSEAS

Regulation 11

Interpretation

[2.1813]
1. In this Schedule "the Application Regulations" means the Social Security Contributions and Benefits Act 1992 (Application of Parts 12ZA, 12ZB and 12ZC to Adoptions from Overseas) Regulations 2003.

Application to adoptions from overseas

2. (1) The provisions of these Regulations, in so far as they apply to statutory shared parental pay (adoption) apply to adoptions from overseas with the modifications set out in paragraphs 3 to 6 and subject to sub-paragraphs (2) and (3).

(2) Any references in these Regulations to the provisions of Part 12ZC of the Act must be construed as references to the provisions of Part 12ZC as modified by the Application Regulations.

Modifications of the Regulations for the purposes of adoptions from overseas

3. The Regulations are modified as follows.

4. (1) Regulation 2 (interpretation) is modified as follows.

(2) In paragraph 1—

(a) for the definition of "adopter" substitute—

""adopter", in relation to C, means the person by whom C has been or is to be adopted;";

(b) for the definition of "statutory shared parental pay (adoption)" substitute—

""statutory shared parental pay (adoption)" means statutory shared parental pay payable where entitlement to that pay arises under regulation 17 or 18 of the General Regulations as modified by the Statutory Shared Parental Pay (Adoption from Overseas) Regulations 2014;";

(c) insert the following definitions in the appropriate places alphabetically—

""enter Great Britain" means enter Great Britain from outside the United Kingdom in connection with or for the purposes of adoption;";

""official notification" means written notification, issued by or on behalf of the relevant central authority, that it is prepared to issue a certificate to the overseas authority concerned with the adoption of the child, or that it has issued a certificate and sent it to that authority, confirming, in either case, that the adopter is eligible to adopt, and has been assessed and approved as being a suitable adoptive parent;";

""relevant central authority" means—

(a) in the case of an adopter to whom Part 3 of the Adoptions with a Foreign Element Regulations 2005 apply and who is habitually resident in Wales, the Welsh Ministers;

(b) in the case of an adopter to whom the Adoptions with a Foreign Element (Scotland) Regulations 2009 apply and who is habitually resident in Scotland, the Scottish Ministers; and

(c) in any other case, the Secretary of State;".

5. In Regulation 3 (application), for paragraph (1)(b) substitute—

"(b) statutory shared parental pay (adoption) in respect of children who enter Great Britain on or after 5th April 2015.".

6. (1) In regulation 7 (entitlement to shared parental pay where person has worked in an EEA State), for paragraph (2) substitute—

"(2) A person who—

(a) is an employee or treated as an employee under regulation 5;

(b) in the week in which the adopter received the official notification was in employed earner's employment with an employer in Great Britain; and

(c) had in any week within the period of 26 weeks immediately preceding that week been employed by the same employer in *another* EEA State,

shall be treated for the purposes of section 171ZV of the Act (entitlement to shared parental pay: adoption) as modified by the Application Regulations as having been employed in employed earner's employment in those weeks in which the person was so employed in *the other EEA* State.".

NOTES

Commencement: 1 December 2014.

For the words "another" and "the other EEA" in italics there are substituted the words "an" and "the EEA" respectively, by the Employment Rights (Amendment) (EU Exit) Regulations 2019, SI 2019/535, reg 2(1), Sch 1, Pt 2, paras 15, 18, as from exit day (as defined in the European Union (Withdrawal) Act 2018, s 20).

DEDUCTION FROM WAGES (LIMITATION) REGULATIONS 2014 (NOTE)

(SI 2014/3322)

[2.1814]

NOTES

Made: 17 December 2014.

Authority: European Communities Act 1972, s 2(2).

Commencement: 8 January 2015.

Note: with regard to the authority for these Regulations, note that the European Communities Act 1972 is repealed by the European Union (Withdrawal) Act 2018, s 1, as from exit day (as defined in s 20 of that Act); but note also that provision is made for the continuation in force of any subordinate legislation made under the authority of s 2(2) of the 1972 Act by s 2 of the 2018 Act at **[1.2240]**, subject to the provisions of s 5 of, and Sch 1 to, the 2018 Act at **[1.2243]**, **[1.2253]**.

These Regulations insert the Employment Rights Act 1996, s 23(4A), (4B) at **[1.837]** and amend the Working Time Regulations 1998, SI 1998/1833, reg 16 at **[2.293]**. Regulation 4 provides that the amendment made to the Employment Rights Act 1996, s 23 only applies in relation to complaints presented to an employment tribunal on or after 1 July 2015.

TEACHERS (COMPENSATION FOR REDUNDANCY AND PREMATURE RETIREMENT) REGULATIONS 2015

(SI 2015/601)

NOTES

Made: 5 March 2015.

Authority: Public Service Pensions Act 2013, ss 1, 3, Sch 3.

Commencement: 1 April 2015.

ARRANGEMENT OF REGULATIONS

PART 1
GENERAL

PART 2
DISCRETIONARY COMPENSATION FOR REDUNDANCY

PART 3
DISCRETIONARY COMPENSATION FOR TERMINATION

PART 4
MANDATORY COMPENSATION FOR PREMATURE RETIREMENT

PART 5
DISCRETIONARY COMPENSATION FOR PREMATURE RETIREMENT

PART 1
GENERAL

[2.1815]
1 Citation and commencement

These Regulations may be cited as the Teachers (Compensation for Redundancy and Premature Retirement) Regulations 2015 and come into force on 1st April 2015.

NOTES

Commencement: 1 April 2015.

[2.1816]
2 Interpretation

(1) In these Regulations—

(a) any expression for which there is an entry in the first column of Schedule 1 to the 2010 Regulations has the meaning given in the second column; and

(b) any expression for which there is an entry in regulation 3 of the 2014 Regulations has the meaning given to it in that regulation.

(2) In these Regulations—

"the 1996 Act" means the Employment Rights Act 1996;
"the 1998 Act" means the School Standards and Framework Act 1998;
"the 2002 Act" means the Education Act 2002;
"the 2010 Regulations" means the Teachers' Pensions Regulations 2010;
"the 2014 Regulations" means the Teachers' Pension Scheme Regulations 2014;
"the 2015 scheme" means the scheme established by the 2014 Regulations;
"adult compensation" has the meaning given in regulation 23;
"appropriate person" means—

(a) before 1st September 1999—

(i) in the case of a person employed at a maintained school within the meaning of section 20 of the 1998 Act or at a grant-maintained or grant-maintained special school, the local authority;

(ii) in the case of any other employee, the person by whom the employee was employed;

(b) on or after 1st September 1999—

(i) in the case of a person employed at a foundation or voluntary aided school or a foundation special school within the meaning of section 20 of the 1998 Act, the local authority;

(ii) in the case of any other employee, the person by whom the employee was employed;

"compensating authority" is to be construed in accordance with regulation 35 and Schedule 2;

"credited teacher" has the meaning given in regulation 17;

"credited period" has the meaning given in regulation 17;

"deciding authority" is to be construed in accordance with regulation 34 and Schedule 2;

"effective service" has the meaning given in regulation 17(5);

"eligible teacher" has the meaning given in regulation 14(2);

"former employment" in relation to an eligible teacher or a credited teacher means relevant employment in relation to which the conditions in regulation 14(3) are satisfied, and "former employer" means the person who employed the teacher in that employment;

"local authority" has the same meaning as in section 579 of the Education Act 1996;

"long-term compensation" has the meaning given in regulation 21;

"material date" in relation to an eligible teacher or a credited teacher means the date on which the teacher ceased to hold a former employment;

"new employment" means employment mentioned in regulation 64A of the 2010 regulations;

"notional annual compensation rate" has the meaning given in regulation 15;

"redundancy payment" in relation to a person's former employment means the aggregate of the amounts paid in respect of its cessation by way of—

(a) the redundancy payment to which the person became entitled under the Redundancy Payments Act 1965 or under Part 11 of the 1996 Act;

(b) any increase paid by the former employer before 11th August 1983 so that the payment, as increased, corresponded to that which would have been payable had the Redundancy Payments (Local Government) (Modification) Order 1983 been in force on the material date; and

(c) any compensation which was paid by the former employer under regulation 6 or was of an amount corresponding to that which would have been payable under that regulation if it had been in force on the material date;

"short-term compensation" has the meaning given in regulation 21;

"termination payment" has the meaning given in regulation 28;

"transition member" has the meaning assigned to it by paragraph 20 of Schedule 3 to the 2014 Regulations;

"a week's pay" is to be calculated in accordance with Chapter 2 of Part 14 of the 1996 Act but, for the purposes of these Regulations, the calculation date is the date that the person in question ceased to hold the relevant employment in question and that Chapter is to be applied as if section 227(1)(c) of the 1996 Act had been repealed.

(3) If these Regulations require anything to be done within a specified period after or from a specified day or event, the period begins immediately after the specified day or, as the case may be, the day on which the specified event occurs.

(4) For the purposes of these Regulations, a grant-maintained or grant-maintained special school is, in respect of any period before 1st September 1999, to be treated as a school maintained by a local authority.

NOTES

Commencement: 1 April 2015.

[2.1817]

3 Relevant employment

(1) Subject to paragraph (3), relevant employment is employment falling within paragraphs 1, 2, 4, 6 or 7 of Schedule 2 to the 2010 Regulations or paragraphs 9, 10, 12, 14 or 15 of Schedule 1 to the 2014 Regulations.

(2) Employment is also relevant employment if a person who has made an election under regulation B1A(4) of the Teachers' Pensions Regulations 1997 remains employed by—

(a) a local authority; or

(b) a function provider in connection with the performance of a function in respect of which the function provider is accepted in accordance with regulation 14 of the 2010 Regulations or paragraph 3 of Schedule 1 to the 2014 Regulations,

to undertake the same, or substantially the same, functions as the person was undertaking immediately before the date of the election, under either the same contract of employment or under a contract of employment which has effect by virtue of regulation 4 of the Transfer of Undertakings (Protection of Employment) Regulations 2006.

(3) Employment falling within paragraph 6 or 7 of Schedule 2 to the 2010 Regulations or paragraph 14 or 15 of Schedule 1 to the 2014 Regulations is only relevant employment if it is at an institution which is within the further education sector as defined in section 91(3) of the Further and Higher Education Act 1992

NOTES

Commencement: 1 April 2015.

[2.1818]
4 Normal pension age

(1) Subject to paragraphs (2) and (3), a person's normal pension age is to be determined in accordance with Part 7 of the 2010 Regulations and regulation 3 of the 2014 Regulations.

(2) A person who is a member of the existing scheme with a normal pension age of 60 is, for the purposes of these Regulations, to be treated as having a normal pension age of 65.

(3) The normal pension age of a transition member is—

(i) in relation to reckonable service under the existing scheme which is taken into account in calculating mandatory compensation under Part 4, 65;

(ii) in relation to accrued pension under the 2015 scheme which is taken into account in calculating mandatory compensation under Part 4 or discretionary compensation under Part 5, the state pension age.

(4) A person who attains normal pension age in relation to the existing scheme but has not attained normal pension age in relation to the 2015 scheme is eligible to receive benefits under the existing scheme which are payable by reason of the person having attained normal pension age under that scheme and benefits under the 2015 scheme which are payable by reason of the person not having attained normal pension age under that scheme.

NOTES

Commencement: 1 April 2015.

PART 2
DISCRETIONARY COMPENSATION FOR REDUNDANCY

[2.1819]
5 Application of this Part

This Part applies to any person (P) who has become entitled to a redundancy payment under Part 11 of the 1996 Act in consequence of P having ceased to be employed in relevant employment.

NOTES

Commencement: 1 April 2015.

[2.1820]
6 Discretionary compensation for redundancy

The appropriate person may pay to a person to whom this Part applies compensation which does not exceed the difference between—

(a) the redundancy payment to which the person is entitled under Part 11 of the 1996 Act; and

(b) the redundancy payment to which the person would have been so entitled if section 227(1)(c) of the 1996 Act had been repealed.

NOTES

Commencement: 1 April 2015.

PART 3
DISCRETIONARY COMPENSATION FOR TERMINATION

[2.1821]
7 Application of this Part

This Part applies to any person (P) who has ceased on or after 1st April 1997 to be employed in relevant employment by reason of P's redundancy or in the interests of the efficient discharge of P's employer's functions.

NOTES

Commencement: 1 April 2015.

[2.1822]
8 Discretionary compensation for termination

Subject to section 37(1) to (3) of the 2002 Act the appropriate person may pay to a person to whom this Part applies compensation which does not exceed A-B where—

A is a sum equivalent to 104 weeks' pay;

B is the aggregate of—

(a) any redundancy payment to which the person is entitled under Part 11 of the 1996 Act; and

(b) any compensation which is paid to the person under Part 2.

NOTES

Commencement: 1 April 2015.

PART 4
MANDATORY COMPENSATION FOR PREMATURE RETIREMENT

[2.1823]

9 Entitlement to mandatory compensation

(1) A person to whom paragraphs (3) and (5) or paragraphs (4) and (5) apply is eligible for annual compensation under these Regulations.

(2) A person to whom paragraph (3) and regulation 62(6) of the 2010 Regulations apply is eligible for lump sum compensation under these Regulations.

(3) This paragraph applies to a person (P) if—

- (a) P ceases to be in pensionable or excluded employment because P's employment is terminated by reason of P's redundancy or in the interests of the efficient discharge of P's employer's functions;
- (b) P has attained normal minimum pension age on or before the date that P falls within sub-paragraph (a);
- (c) P's employer gives written notice to the scheme manager that—
  - (i) P's employment was terminated by reason of P's redundancy or in the interests of the efficient discharge of the employer's functions; and
  - (ii) P's employer agrees that a premature retirement pension should become payable;
- (d) P has not received or is not to receive compensation under Part 3 as a result of the termination of the employment; and
- (e) P either—
  - (i) makes an application under regulation 107 of the 2010 Regulations for retirement benefits on the basis that P satisfies the requirements of this paragraph and that no Case in Schedule 7 to the 2010 Regulations other than Case A applies to P's reckonable service; or
  - (ii) is entitled to payment of a premature retirement pension under regulation 101 of the 2014 Regulations.

(4) This paragraph applies to a person (P) if—

- (a) P has attained normal minimum pension age and—
  - (i) if P is a member of the existing scheme, has not attained the age of 65;
  - (ii) if P is a transition member or a member of the 2015 scheme, has not attained normal pension age;
- (b) P is qualified or re-qualified for retirement benefits within the meaning of—
  - (i) regulation 54 of the 2010 Regulations; or
  - (ii) regulation 82 or 83 of the 2014 Regulations;
- (c) P's pensionable service in relation to an employment is terminated by reason of P's redundancy or in the interests of the efficient discharge of the functions of P's employer;
- (d) P's employer gives written notice to the scheme manager that—
  - (i) P's pensionable service was terminated by reason of P's redundancy or in the interests of the efficient discharge of the employer's functions; and
  - (ii) the employer agrees that a premature retirement pension should become payable to P;
- (e) P has not received and is not to receive compensation under Part 3 as a result of P's pensionable service being terminated;
- (f) P has left all eligible employment;
- (g) P has applied under regulation 162 of the 2014 Regulations for payment of a premature retirement pension; and
- (h) P has not applied under that regulation for payment of any other retirement pension.

(5) This paragraph applies to a person to whom—

- (i) paragraph (6) or (7) of regulation 61 of the 2010 Regulations applies;
- (ii) regulation 96 or 102 of the 2014 Regulations applies.

(6) A transition member who is eligible for annual compensation in respect of pension accrued in the 2015 scheme is also eligible for annual compensation in respect of pension accrued in the existing scheme.

NOTES

Commencement: 1 April 2015.

[2.1824]

10 Calculation of annual compensation

(1) Subject to paragraph 2, a person (P)'s rate of annual compensation under regulation 9(1) is—

- (a) if P was accruing pensionable service under the 2010 Regulations immediately before the termination of P's employment, the difference between—
  - (i) the annual rate of P's retirement pension calculated in accordance with regulation 61(5) of the 2010 Regulations or, if higher, the annual rate calculated in accordance with regulation 70(2) of those Regulations; and
  - (ii) the annual rate of P's retirement pension calculated in accordance with regulation 61(6) or (7) of those Regulations, whichever is applicable;

(b) if P was accruing pensionable service under the 2014 Regulations immediately before the termination of P's employment, the total amount of any standard reduction and actuarial adjustment to which the annual rate of P's retirement pension is subject in accordance with regulation 102(b) of the 2014 Regulations.

(2) If a person (P) in receipt of annual compensation under regulation 9(1) attains state pension age and the annual rate of P's retirement pension under the 2010 Regulations is increased by virtue of regulation 120 of those regulations then from the date on which P attained state pension age P's annual compensation under paragraph (1) is to be reduced by the difference between—

(a) the annual rate of P's retirement pension calculated subject to regulation 120 of the 2010 Regulations; and

(b) the annual rate of P's retirement pension calculated without reference to that regulation.

NOTES

Commencement: 1 April 2015.

[2.1825]
11 Calculation of lump sum compensation

The lump sum compensation payable to a person under regulation 9(2) is the amount of any reduction made under regulation 62(6) of the 2010 Regulations to the person's retirement lump sum.

NOTES

Commencement: 1 April 2015.

[2.1826]
12 Further death grants

(1) This regulation applies if a death grant is payable under regulation 87 of the 2010 Regulations or regulation 141 of the 2014 Regulations, whether or not such a grant is paid.

(2) If this regulation applies the compensating authority may pay a further death grant of A-B where—
A is 5 times the rate of annual compensation payable under regulation 10(1) at the date of the member's death;
B is the amount of compensation paid to the person since the compensation became payable.

(3) If regulation 31 applies any amount by which the annual rate of compensation is reduced under that regulation is treated as being payable for the purposes of the calculation in paragraph (2).

NOTES

Commencement: 1 April 2015.

[2.1827]
13 Entitlement to short-term family benefits

(1) This regulation applies if—

(a) the amount of a person's pension at the short-term rate payable under regulation 95 or 98 of the 2010 Regulations is reduced by the combined effect of—
(i) regulation 61(6) or (7); and
(ii) regulation 95(2)(d) or 98(3)(d)
of the 2010 Regulations;

(b) the amount of a person's pension at the short-term rate payable under regulation 143 or 150 of the 2014 Regulations is reduced by the combined effect of—
(i) regulation 96 or 102; and
(ii) regulation 143(2)(b) or 150(2)(b)
of the 2014 Regulations.

(2) If this regulation applies the person to whom a pension is payable at the short-term rate is eligible for compensation, for each month during which the short-term compensation is payable, which is equal to the amount by which the short-term pension is reduced for that month.

NOTES

Commencement: 1 April 2015.

PART 5
DISCRETIONARY COMPENSATION FOR PREMATURE RETIREMENT

[2.1828]
14 Application of this Part

(1) This Part applies to eligible teachers.

(2) An eligible teacher is a person (P)—

(a) to whom Part 4 applies, or would apply but for the fact that the member is a protected member;

(b) who immediately before the material date was employed in relevant employment whether or not in a single post and, if in more than one post, had left all such posts on the material date; and

(c) in relation to whom the conditions in paragraph (3) are satisfied.

(3) The conditions are that—

(a) retirement benefits have not become payable to P by virtue of Case C applying to P's reckonable service, and P has not applied for an ill-health pension or a total incapacity pension under regulation 162 of the 2014 Regulations;

(b) there is no entitlement for P's case to be considered or further considered for the payment of long-term or retirement compensation under the Colleges of Education (Compensation) Regulations 1975 (whether or not by way of review under regulation 32 of those Regulations) in respect of the termination of employment;

(c) P has not received, and is not entitled to receive, a payment under section 37(1) to (3) of the 2002 Act.

NOTES

Commencement: 1 April 2015.

[2.1829]

15 Interpretation of this Part

(1) In this part, "notional annual compensation rate" means the rate at which annual compensation would have been payable under regulation 19(1) immediately before the recipient's death if there had been left out of account any reduction under regulation 27(4)(b), 28, 30 or 31.

(2) For the purposes of paragraph (1), if the deceased died in new employment which was pensionable employment the deceased is to be taken to have ceased to be in that employment immediately before death.

NOTES

Commencement: 1 April 2015.

[2.1830]

16 Adjustments

Adjustments to compensation payable under this Part may be made under Part 6.

NOTES

Commencement: 1 April 2015.

[2.1831]

17 Discretion to credit an additional period of service

(1) The deciding authority may credit an eligible teacher, including an eligible teacher who has since died, ("a credited teacher") with a period of service ("the credited period").

(2) Schedule 1 makes provision for a deduction to be made from the credited period in the circumstances set out in paragraph 1 of that Schedule.

(3) The credited period is not to exceed the shortest of—

(a) the period beginning on the day following the material date and ending on the date the member attains normal pension age less, if paragraph 1 of Schedule 1 applies, any period required by paragraph 2 to be deducted;

(b) the length of effective service;

(c) 10 years.

(4) Any credit by the deciding authority must be within 6 months after the material date.

(5) Effective service is the sum of—

(a) any period or periods which the member is entitled to count as reckonable service under the 2010 Regulations or pensionable service under the 2014 Regulations; and

(b) if the member's employment was not pensionable service, any period which the member would have been entitled so to count if it had been.

NOTES

Commencement: 1 April 2015.

[2.1832]

18 Entitlement of credited teacher to compensation

(1) A credited teacher is eligible for annual compensation.

(2) A credited teacher who is eligible for lump sum compensation under regulation 9(2) is eligible for lump sum compensation under this Part.

NOTES

Commencement: 1 April 2015.

[2.1833]

19 Calculation of annual compensation

(1) Subject to regulations 27 and 28, the rate of annual compensation payable to a member of the existing scheme is calculated in accordance with the formula—

A x B/C

where A is the member's period of credited service, B is the member's average salary and C is the accrual rate used to determine the annual rate of the member's premature retirement pension.

Part 2 Statutory Instruments

(2) Subject to regulations 27 and 28, the rate of annual compensation payable to a member of the 2015 scheme, including a transition member, is calculated in accordance with the formula—

D x E/57

where D is the member's salary on the material date or, if the member was not a full time employee on the material date, the salary that would have been payable had the member been a full time employee on the material date and E is the period of credited service under regulation 17.

NOTES

Commencement: 1 April 2015.

[2.1834]

20 Calculation of lump sum compensation

Subject to regulations 27 and 28, the amount of lump sum compensation under regulation 18(2) is the difference between—

(a) the lump sum which would be payable under regulation 62 of the 2010 Regulations if the member's credited service under regulation 17 were added to the member's reckonable service under the 2010 Regulations; and

(b) the lump sum which would be payable under regulation 62 of the 2010 Regulations if no such addition were made.

NOTES

Commencement: 1 April 2015.

[2.1835]

21 Short-term compensation on death

(1) This regulation applies if a credited teacher (C) dies and a pension—

(a) becomes payable at the short-term rate under regulation 95 or 98 of the 2010 Regulations or regulation 143 or 150 of the 2014 Regulations; or

(b) would have become so payable but for an election under regulation 9 of the 2010 Regulations or regulation 28 or 31 of the 2014 Regulations.

(2) Subject to regulation 25, compensation ("short-term compensation") is to be paid to or, as the case may be, for the benefit of every person who is or would have been entitled to payment of the short-term pension.

(3) Subject to paragraph (4) and to regulation 29, the rate of the short-term compensation is the rate at which C's annual compensation payable under regulation 19 would have been payable immediately before C's death if any reduction under regulation 28 or 30 had not been made.

(4) If C died in new employment which was pensionable employment, C is for the purposes of paragraph (3) to be taken to have ceased to be in that employment immediately before C's death.

(5) If the rate calculated in accordance with paragraph (3) is less than that of long-term compensation to which there is prospective entitlement under regulation 22, the rate of the short-term compensation is the same as that of the long-term compensation.

NOTES

Commencement: 1 April 2015.

[2.1836]

22 Long-term compensation on death

Subject to regulation 25, compensation ("long-term compensation") is to be paid to or, as the case may be, for the benefit of every person who became or would have become entitled to payment of a long-term pension if a credited teacher dies and a pension—

(a) becomes payable at the long-term rate under regulation 96 or 99 of the 2010 Regulations or regulation 144 or 151 of the 2014 Regulations; or

(b) would have become so payable but for an election under regulation 9 of the 2010 Regulations or regulation 28 or 31 of the 2014 Regulations.

NOTES

Commencement: 1 April 2015.

[2.1837]

23 Adult Compensation

Subject to regulation 29, the rate of the long-term compensation payable to a person (P) who is not a child ("adult compensation") is—

(a) if P is a member of the existing scheme with a normal pension age of 60, one half of the notional annual compensation rate;

(b) if P is a member of the existing scheme with a normal pension age of 65, 1/160 of MxN, where
M is P's average salary;
N is P's family benefit service;

(c) if P is a transition member or a member of the 2015 scheme, 37.5% of P's annual pension.

NOTES

Commencement: 1 April 2015.

[2.1838]
24 Child compensation

(1) Subject to regulation 29, the rate of long-term compensation payable to or for the benefit of a child or children while adult compensation is payable is—

(a) one quarter of the notional annual compensation rate if compensation is payable to one child;
(b) one half of the notional annual compensation rate if compensation is payable to two or more children.

(2) Subject to regulation 29, the rate of long-term compensation payable to or for the benefit of a child or children if adult compensation did not become payable, or ceased to be payable, is—

(a) one third of the notional annual compensation rate if compensation is payable to one child;
(b) two thirds of the notional annual compensation rate if compensation is payable to two or more children.

NOTES
Commencement: 1 April 2015.

[2.1839]
25 Duration of compensation on death

(1) Subject to paragraph (3), a person's short-term compensation is payable from the day after that of the death, and the duration of the short-term compensation payable is to be ascertained from the table below.

Table

Category	*Person entitled to short-term compensation*	*Duration of compensation (months)*
1	Spouse, civil partner, surviving nominated partner or nominated beneficiary	3
2	One child or more and adult compensation is payable	3
3	One child or more and no adult compensation is payable	6

In the table above "adult compensation" means short-term compensation payable to a spouse, civil partner, surviving nominated partner or nominated beneficiary.

(2) Subject to paragraph (3), a person's long-term compensation is payable for life—

(a) from the day following that on which the person's short-term compensation ceases to be payable; or
(b) if no short-term compensation was payable, from the day after that of the death.

(3) Short-term or long-term compensation payable to or for the benefit of a child ceases to be payable when the child ceases to be an eligible child.

NOTES
Commencement: 1 April 2015.

PART 6
ADJUSTMENTS

[2.1840]
26 Application of this Part

This Part applies to eligible teachers.

NOTES
Commencement: 1 April 2015.

[2.1841]
27 Redundancy payments

(1) This regulation applies to a credited teacher (C) where—

(a) C's credited period exceeds 6 2/3rds years; and
(b) C has received, or is to receive, compensation under regulation 6 in respect of the cessation of C's former employment.

(2) If C's lump sum compensation payable under regulation 20 would exceed the relevant amount, it is to be reduced by the relevant amount.

(3) If C's lump sum compensation payable under regulation 20 would equal the relevant amount, it is not to be paid.

(4) If C's lump sum compensation payable under regulation 20 would be less than the relevant amount—

(a) it is not to be paid; and
(b) the rate of C's annual compensation payable under regulation 19 is to be determined by the scheme manager on advice from the scheme actuary.

Part 2 Statutory Instruments

(5) The relevant amount is—

(3 x A / 10) x B

where—

A is the amount of the redundancy payment;

B is the length of time, expressed in years and any fraction of a year, by which the credited period exceeds 6 2/3rds years.

NOTES

Commencement: 1 April 2015.

[2.1842]

28 Termination payments

(1) This regulation applies to a credited teacher (C) who receives a termination payment.

(2) A termination payment is the aggregate of any lump sum payments made to C by C's former employer which—

(a) are made in consequence of, or as compensation for, the loss of C's former employment;

(b) are made in pursuance of any contract or arrangement or any provision contained in, or made under, any enactment, whenever made or enacted;

(c) are not made by way of an excepted payment.

(3) The excepted payments are—

(a) a redundancy payment in respect of the cessation of C's former employment;

(b) so much of any payment in lieu of notice of termination of that employment as does not exceed the remuneration which C would, but for its termination, have received for the three months following the material date;

(c) compensation paid under regulation 8, 10, 11, 19 or 20.

(4) If C's lump sum compensation under regulation 20 would exceed the termination payment, it is to be reduced by the amount of the termination payment.

(5) If C's lump sum compensation under regulation 20 would be equal to the termination payment, it is not to be paid.

(6) If C's lump sum compensation under regulation 20 would be less than the termination payment—

(a) it is not to be paid; and

(b) C's annual compensation under regulation 19 is to be reduced by the difference.

(7) C's annual compensation under regulation 19 is to be reduced by the amount of the termination payment if—

(a) by reason of regulation 27(3) or (4) no lump sum compensation is payable under regulation 20; or

(b) lump sum compensation was paid under regulation 20 before the termination payment became payable.

(8) The reduction under paragraph (6)(b) in annual compensation payable under regulation 19 is a reduction in the total amount payable, and accordingly payment is to be suspended until the full reduction has been achieved

NOTES

Commencement: 1 April 2015.

[2.1843]

29 Periodic payments

(1) This regulation applies if—

(a) relevant periodic payments are payable to a credited teacher or to a person to whom compensation is payable under regulation 21 or 22; and

(b) the material date is later than 31st August 1985.

(2) Relevant periodic payments are payments made by the credited teacher's former employer which—

(a) are in respect neither of a lump sum nor of a return of contributions;

(b) are made as mentioned in regulation 28(2); and

(c) are not made under regulation 13.

(3) If the relevant periodic payments in respect of any period equal or exceed the annual or other compensation that would be payable in respect of that period, excluding any compensation paid under regulation 9 or 13, the compensation is not to be paid.

(4) If the relevant periodic payments in respect of any period are less than the compensation referred to in paragraph (3), that compensation is to be reduced by the amount of those payments.

NOTES

Commencement: 1 April 2015.

[2.1844]

30 Cessation of discretionary annual compensation during new employment

(1) If a credited teacher (C) enters further employment, compensation payable under regulation 18(1) is to be reduced in accordance with this regulation.

(2) The reduction mentioned in paragraph (1) is to be made if the result of the calculation in paragraph (3) exceeds F, where F is the total, in years and any fraction of a year, of C's reckonable service assuming that C had remained in the former employment until, being an existing scheme member, C attained the age of 65 or, being a 2015 scheme member, C attained normal pension age.

(3) The calculation is as follows—

A + B + (C – D) + E

where—

A is C's effective service;

B is the period, in years and any fraction of a year, between the material date and the later of the date of completion of the further employment and the date C, being an existing scheme member, attains the age of 65 or, being a 2015 scheme member, attains normal pension age;

C is the credited period;

D is the total period in respect of which any previous reductions were made to compensation payable under regulation 31(1) as a result of C entering further employment;

E is the total, in years and any fraction of a year, of any additional periods of service credited to C in respect of termination or redundancy under the provisions referred to in paragraph 1 of Schedule 2.

(4) The reduction mentioned in paragraph (1) is to be calculated in accordance with the following formula—

G x ((H x J) / 80)

where—

G is the period, in years and any fraction of a year, by which the result of the calculation in paragraph (3) exceeds F;

H is the shorter of B and C–D;

J is the lower of C's average salary in the former employment and the figure produced by applying the formula K – (K x L) / (L + 100) where K is C's average salary in the new employment and L is the PIA index adjustment.

NOTES

Commencement: 1 April 2015.

PART 7
ABATEMENT

[2.1845]

31 Abatement of annual compensation during further employment

(1) This regulation applies if the amount of retirement pension paid to a person (P) is reduced under regulations 64A and 64B of the 2010 Regulations.

(2) If this regulation applies—

(a) and by virtue of sub-paragraph (1)(a) or (2)(a) of regulation 64B of the 2010 Regulations no retirement pension is paid during a tax year, no compensation is to be paid under regulation 10 or 19 in that tax year;

(b) and in any other case the compensation to which P is entitled under regulation 10 and the compensation to which P is entitled under regulation 19 in any tax year is each to be reduced if necessary so as to secure that the total compensation paid under regulation 10 and 19 during that tax year does not exceed Ax(R/S) where—

A has the same meaning as in regulation 64B of the 2010 Regulations;

R is the full annual rate of P's compensation under regulation 10 during the tax year in question;

S is the total, for the tax year in question, of—

(i) the full annual rate of P's retirement pension including, in the case of a transition member, any pension under the 2014 Regulations;

(ii) the full annual rate of compensation payable under regulation 10; and

(iii) the full annual rate of all compensation payable under regulation 19.

(3) If compensation under regulations 10 and 19 falls to be reduced under paragraph (2)(b) in any tax year—

(a) the compensating authority is to pay the compensation under each regulation in accordance with regulation 41—

(i) at the rate which is appropriate without taking account of the reduction;

(ii) until the amount to which the compensation is to be reduced, on the assumption that P will remain in employment at the same salary for the rest of the tax year, has been paid; and

(b) no further payment is to be made during that tax year.

(4) If there is a change in circumstances which results in a change to any of the conditions for calculating a reduction in annual compensation under paragraph (2) in any tax year, the compensating authority is to recalculate the amount of compensation which is payable in order to secure the result described in paragraph (2).

(5) For the purposes of paragraph (2)—

(a) regulation 64B of the 2010 Regulations is to be construed as if the former employment were pensionable employment;

(b) if P had more than one entitlement to annual compensation under regulation 19, R comprises the total annual compensation under regulation 19 but each component is to be reduced under paragraph (2)(b) only in the proportion which it bears to the total.

NOTES

Commencement: 1 April 2015.

[2.1846]

32 Abatement of discretionary annual compensation following termination or redundancy payment

(1) The annual compensation under regulation 19 is to be reduced by the amount of the termination or redundancy payment if—

(a) lump sum compensation was paid under regulation 20 before a termination payment or a redundancy payment became payable; and—

(b) either—

(i) the termination payment, if paid before the lump sum compensation became payable, would have resulted in the lump sum compensation being reduced or not paid under regulation 28; or

(ii) the redundancy payment, if paid before the lump sum compensation became payable, would have resulted in the lump sum compensation being reduced or not paid under regulation 27.

(2) The reduction under paragraph (1) in annual compensation payable under regulation 19 is a reduction in the total amount payable, and accordingly payment is to be suspended until the full reduction has been achieved.

NOTES

Commencement: 1 April 2015.

PART 8
MISCELLANEOUS

[2.1847]

33 Deciding and compensating authorities

(1) Schedule 2 makes provision concerning the deciding authority and the compensating authority.

(2) The deciding authority is determined from the first and second columns of the table in Schedule 2.

(3) The compensating authority is determined from the first and third columns of the table in Schedule 2.

NOTES

Commencement: 1 April 2015.

[2.1848]

34 Categories of employment

For the purposes of regulation 33—

(1) Category A comprises relevant employment at a single school or institution maintained by a local authority which for the time being had a delegated budget as defined in section 139(5) of the Education Reform Act 1988 or section 49(7) of the 1998 Act.

(2) Category B comprises relevant employment at a school or institution maintained by a local authority which did not have a delegated budget, relevant employment by a local authority otherwise than at a school or institution and relevant employment at a maintained school or institution with a delegated budget which was concurrent with employment of either of those kinds or with relevant employment at another school or institution.

(3) Category C comprises relevant employment at an institution in respect of which the Secretary of State has entered into an Academy arrangement as defined in section 1 of the Academies Act 2010.

(4) Category D comprises relevant employment as a teacher by a function provider in connection with the performance of a function in respect of which the function provider is accepted in accordance with regulation 14 of the 2010 Regulations or paragraph 3 of Schedule 1 to the 2014 Regulations.

(5) Category E comprises relevant employment at an institution within the further education sector as defined in section 91(3) of the Further and Higher Education Act 1992.

NOTES

Commencement: 1 April 2015.

[2.1849]

35 Liability for compensation

(1) The cost of compensation to which a person is entitled under Parts 4 and 5 is to be met by the compensating authority.

(2) If—

(a) the former employer fell within category E; and

(b) in consequence of any amalgamation, merger or other arrangement the institution becomes part of another (the "successor establishment") and ceases to have a separate governing body

the governing body of the successor establishment becomes the compensating authority.

(3) The Secretary of State becomes the compensating authority if—
- (a) the former employer fell within category E; and
- (b) the institution closes and there is no successor establishment

(4) If the former employment did not fall within any of the categories A to E the compensating authority is—
- (a) the person or body of persons responsible for the management of the institution;
- (b) if the institution has amalgamated or merged with another institution or has closed, the institution with which it has amalgamated or merged or by which it has been succeeded ("the successor establishment");
- (c) if there is no successor establishment, the Secretary of State.

(5) References in paragraphs (2) to (4) above to an institution include references to a successor establishment.

(6) If the former employment fell within category D the function provider is to pay to the Secretary of State on receipt of a written demand a sum equal to the actuarial value of the total compensation payable.

(7) If the former employment did not fall within any of the categories A to E and the compensating authority as determined under paragraph (4) is not the Secretary of State the compensating authority is to pay to the Secretary of State on receipt of a written demand a sum equal to the actuarial value of the total compensation payable.

NOTES

Commencement: 1 April 2015.

[2.1850]
36 Arrangements for payout

(1) A compensating authority may—
- (a) pay any compensation under these Regulations for which it is liable; or
- (b) arrange for the compensation to be paid by any suitable person and for its reimbursement by the compensating authority.

(2) Arrangements for reimbursement may provide—
- (a) for the periodical repayment by the compensating authority of amounts paid on its behalf;
- (b) for a single payment by the compensating authority of a sum equal to the actuarial value of the total compensation payable; or
- (c) for the payment of such a sum by not more than five annual instalments.

NOTES

Commencement: 1 April 2015.

[2.1851]
37 Notification

(1) The compensating authority is to give a written notification to every person to whom compensation has become payable or whose compensation is affected as soon as is reasonably practicable after—
- (a) an eligible teacher has been credited with a period of service under regulation 17;
- (b) a credited teacher has died;
- (c) a person becomes eligible for compensation under regulation 9;
- (d) any adjustment has been made under regulation 31 or Part 6.

(2) The notification is to state—
- (a) if paragraph (1)(a), (b) or (c) applies, what compensation is payable and how this has been calculated;
- (b) if paragraph (1)(d) applies, what adjustment has been made and how this has been calculated.

NOTES

Commencement: 1 April 2015.

[2.1852]
38 Supply of information

(1) A credited teacher or a person eligible for compensation under regulation 9 who enters or leaves new employment is, within one month after doing so, to notify the compensating authority in writing of that fact.

(2) A person to whom compensation is payable must provide the compensating authority with such information, and produce such documents, as the compensating authority may reasonably require for the purposes of its functions under these Regulations.

NOTES

Commencement: 1 April 2015.

[2.1853]
39 Payment of compensation

(1) Compensation, other than lump sum compensation payable under regulation 11 or 20, is to be paid in arrears—

Part 2 Statutory Instruments

(a) at intervals of one month; or
(b) at such longer intervals as may be agreed between the compensating authority and the recipient.

(2) If compensation ceases to be payable before the next date on which a payment would be due, a proportionate payment is to be made for the period beginning on the day after the period in respect of which the previous payment (if any) was payable ended and ending on the date of cessation ("the period").

(3) A proportionate payment is a payment of—

((A/12) x B + ((A/12) x (C/D))

where—

A is the annual rate of the compensation;
B is the number of complete months, if any, in the period;
C is the number of days remaining in the period after deducting B;
D is the number of days in the month in which the period ended.

(4) If a person eligible for payment of compensation ("P") has not attained the age of 18, or is incapable by reason of infirmity of mind or body of managing P's affairs, the compensating authority may—

(a) pay it to any person having the care of P; or
(b) apply it for the benefit of P or P's dependents.

NOTES

Commencement: 1 April 2015.

[2.1854]

40 Compensation not assignable

(1) Any assignment of, or charge on, or agreement to assign or charge, any compensation payable under these Regulations is void.

(2) On the bankruptcy of a person eligible for such compensation no part of the compensation is to pass to any trustee or other person acting on behalf of the creditors except in accordance with an income payments order made by a court under section 310 of the Insolvency Act 1986.

NOTES

Commencement: 1 April 2015.

[2.1855]

41 Modified application in relation to persons entitled to admitted service benefits

In relation to a person with admitted service these Regulations have effect subject to the modifications set out in Schedule 3.

NOTES

Commencement: 1 April 2015.

PART 9
CONSEQUENTIAL AMENDMENTS, REVOCATION AND TRANSITIONAL PROVISIONS

42, 43 *(Regs 42 and 43 amend the Teachers' Pensions Regulations 2010, SI 2010/990 and the Teachers' Pension Scheme Regulations 2014, SI 2014/512 (both outside the scope of this work).)*

[2.1856]

44 Revocation and transitional provisions

(1) The Regulations specified in Schedule 4 are revoked.

(2) Anything done or having effect as if done under or for the purposes of a provision of the Teachers (Compensation for Redundancy and Premature Retirement) Regulations 1997 has effect, if it could have been done under or for the purpose of the corresponding provision of these Regulations, as if done under or for the purposes of that corresponding provision.

(3) If a period of time specified in, or applying by virtue of, a provision of the Teachers (Compensation for Redundancy and Premature Retirement) Regulations 1997 is current at the commencement of these Regulations, these Regulations have effect as if the corresponding provision of these Regulations had been in force when that period began to run.

NOTES

Commencement: 1 April 2015.

SCHEDULES

SCHEDULE 1
PREVIOUS COMPENSATION

Regulation 17(2)

[2.1857]

1. This paragraph applies if, before the cessation of the former employment of a credited teacher (C), C has been credited with a period of additional service, or C's period of service has been increased, for the purpose of calculating—

(a) retirement compensation under regulations made under section 259 of the Local Government Act on account of loss of employment;
(b) benefit under regulations made under section 260 of the Local Government Act1972;
(c) compensation under any scheme made under section 1 of the Superannuation Act 1972 on account of C's retirement in the public interest, or for loss of office;
(d) compensation under these Regulations or any regulations made under section 24 of the Superannuation Act 1972 on account of the termination of C's employment by reason of redundancy or in the interests of the efficient discharge of C's employer's functions;
(e) compensation under any contract or arrangement made before 31st August 1985 in the expectation that regulations would be made under that section providing for compensation for such termination of employment.

2. The period to be deducted, if paragraph 1 applies, from the first period mentioned in regulation 17(3)(a) is A – B – C, where—

A is the period with which C has been credited, or by which C's service has been increased, as mentioned in paragraph 1;

B is any period by which A has been reduced in consequence of the cessation of subsequent employment;

C is the aggregate of any periods falling between the cessation of employment that gave rise to A and the material date during which C was neither in pensionable employment nor in employment which would have been pensionable employment but for an election under regulation 9 of the 2010 Regulations or regulation 28 or 31 of the 2014 Regulations.

NOTES

Commencement: 1 April 2015.

SCHEDULE 2
DECIDING AND COMPENSATING AUTHORITIES

Regulation 33

[2.1858]

Table

Employment category	*Deciding authority*	*Compensating authority*
A	Governing body	Local authority
B	Local authority	Local authority
C	Academy trust	Academy trust
D	Function provider	Function provider
E	Governing body	Governing body

NOTES

Commencement: 1 April 2015.

SCHEDULE 3
MODIFIED APPLICATION IN RELATION TO PERSONS ENTITLED TO ADMITTED SERVICE BENEFITS

Regulation 41

[2.1859]

1. A person who is entitled to an annual pension in respect of admitted service and to whom regulation 81(4) of the 2010 Regulations applies by virtue of Case D applying to the person's reckonable service is entitled to annual compensation and to lump sum compensation under this Schedule.

2. The rate of annual compensation is the difference between the rate of annual pension in respect of admitted service if calculated in accordance with regulation 81(2)(a) of the 2010 Regulations without any reduction under paragraph (4) of that regulation and the actual rate of annual pension.

3. The amount of lump sum compensation is the amount by which the lump sum in respect of admitted service is reduced by virtue of regulation 81 of the 2010 Regulations.

4. Regulations 35, 36, 37, 38, 39 and 40 are to apply in relation to compensation payable under this Schedule as they apply in relation to compensation payable under regulation 9.

NOTES

Commencement: 1 April 2015.

SCHEDULE 4

(Schedule 4 contains revocations of instruments outside the scope of this work.)

NATIONAL MINIMUM WAGE REGULATIONS 2015

(SI 2015/621)

NOTES

Made: 9 March 2015.
Authority: National Minimum Wage Act 1998, ss 1(3), (4), 2, 3, 9, 51(1)(b).
Commencement: 6 April 2015.

ARRANGEMENT OF REGULATIONS

Part 2 Statutory Instruments

PART 1
GENERAL AND INTERPRETATION

[2.1860]

1 Citation and commencement

These Regulations may be cited as the National Minimum Wage Regulations 2015 and come into force on 6th April 2015.

NOTES

Commencement: 6 April 2015.

[2.1861]

2 Revocations

The instruments specified in the Schedule are revoked.

NOTES

Commencement: 6 April 2015.

[2.1862]

3 General interpretative provisions

In these Regulations—

"the Act" means the National Minimum Wage Act 1998;

"basic hours" has the meaning given in regulation 21(5);

"compulsory school age" has the meaning given in section 8 of the Education Act 1996;

"days" includes a fraction of a day, other than as specified in regulation 16(2) (amount for provision of living accommodation);

"further education course" means—

(a) in England, a course of education, other than a higher education course, that is suitable to the requirements of persons who are over compulsory school age and that—

(i) is funded by the Secretary of State under section 14 of the Education Act 2002 [or section 100 of the Apprenticeships, Skills, Children and Learning Act 2009],

(ii) . . .

(iii) is funded by a local authority,

(iv) leads to a qualification to which Part 7 of the Apprenticeships, Skills, Children and Learning Act 2009 applies which is awarded or authenticated by a body which is recognised by the Office of Qualifications and Examinations Regulation under section 132 of that Act in respect of the qualification, or

(v) leads to a qualification that is approved pursuant to section 98 of the Learning and Skills Act 2000;

(b) in Wales, a course of education, other than a higher education course, that is suitable to the requirements of persons who are over compulsory school age and that—

(i) is funded by the Welsh Ministers,

[(ii) is funded by a local authority, or

(iii) leads to a qualification awarded by a body in respect of the award of which it is recognised by Qualifications Wales under Part 3 of the Qualifications Wales Act 2015;]

(c) in Scotland, a course of "fundable further education" as defined in section 5(1) and (2) of the Further and Higher Education (Scotland) Act 2005;

(d) in Northern Ireland, a course of education or training as defined in article 3(1) and (2) of the Further Education (Northern Ireland) Order 1997;

"higher education course" means—

(a) in England and Wales, a course of a description referred to in Schedule 6 to the Education Reform Act 1988;

(b) in Scotland, a course of "fundable higher education" as defined in section 5(3), (4) and (5) of the Further and Higher Education (Scotland) Act 2005;

(c) in Northern Ireland, a course of a description referred to in Schedule 1 to the Further Education (Northern Ireland) Order 1997;

"hours" includes a fraction of an hour;

"hours of work" has the meaning given in regulation 17;

"output work" has the meaning given in regulation 36;

"pay reference period" has the meaning given in regulation 6;

"performance bonus" has the meaning given in regulation 21(6);

"remuneration" has the meaning given in regulation 8;

"salaried hours work" has the meaning given in regulation 21;

"time work" has the meaning given in regulation 30;

"unmeasured work" has the meaning given in regulation 44;

"work" is to be construed subject to regulations 57 and 58.

NOTES

Commencement: 6 April 2015.

First words in square brackets in definition "further education course" inserted, and words omitted from that definition revoked, by the Deregulation Act 2015 (Consequential Amendments) Order 2015, SI 2015/971, art 2, Sch 3, para 33(1), (2), as from 26 May 2015.

Sub-paras (b)(ii), (iii) of the definition "further education course" substituted (for the original sub-paras (b)(ii)–(iv)) by the Qualifications Wales Act 2015 (Consequential Amendments) Regulations 2016, SI 2016/236, reg 19, as from 1 May 2016. See also the Qualifications Wales Act 2015 (Consequential Provision) Order 2017, SI 2017/121, art 3 which provides (as from 1 April 2017) as follows—

"(1) Paragraph (b) of the definition of "further education course" in regulation 3 of the National Minimum Wage Regulations 2015 is amended as follows.

(2) The sub-paragraphs (ii) and (iii) that extend to England and Wales also extend to Scotland and Northern Ireland (consequently omit the sub-paragraphs (ii) and (iii) that immediately before the coming into force of this Order extended to Scotland and Northern Ireland).

(3) Omit the sub-paragraph (iv) that immediately before the coming into force of this Order extended to Scotland and Northern Ireland.".

PART 2
RATES OF THE NATIONAL MINIMUM WAGE AND PAY REFERENCE PERIOD

[2.1863]

[4 The national living wage

The single hourly rate of the national minimum wage for the purposes of section 1(3) of the Act ("the national living wage rate") is [£8.21].]

NOTES

Commencement: 1 April 2016.

Regulations 4, 4A, 4B substituted (for the original reg 4) by the National Minimum Wage (Amendment) Regulations 2016, SI 2016/68, reg 3, as from 1 April 2016.

Sum in square brackets substituted by the National Minimum Wage (Amendment) Regulations 2019, SI 2019/603, reg 2(1), (2), as from 1 April 2019. The previous sum was £7.83 (from 1 April 2018; see SI 2018/455). As to previous hourly rates, see the notes to the National Minimum Wage Act 1998, s 1 at **[1.1171]**.

[2.1864]

[4A Workers who qualify for the national minimum wage at a different rate

(1) The hourly rate of the national minimum wage is—

(a) [£7.70] for a worker who is aged 21 years or over (but is not yet aged 25 years);

(b) [£6.15] for a worker who is aged 18 years or over (but is not yet aged 21 years);

(c) [£4.35] for a worker who is aged under 18 years;

(d) [£3.90] for a worker to whom the apprenticeship rate applies, as determined in accordance with regulation 5.

(2) If the rate in paragraph (1)(d) applies to a worker, the national living wage rate and the rates in paragraph (1)(a), (b) and (c) of this regulation do not apply to that worker.]

NOTES

Commencement: 1 April 2016.

Regulations 4, 4A, 4B substituted (for the original reg 4) by the National Minimum Wage (Amendment) Regulations 2016, SI 2016/68, reg 3, as from 1 April 2016.

Sums in square brackets substituted by the National Minimum Wage (Amendment) Regulations 2019, SI 2019/603, reg 2(1), (3), as from 1 April 2019. The previous sums in sub-paras (1)(a)–(d) were: £7.38; £5.90; £4.20; and £3.70 respectively (from 1 April 2018; see SI 2018/455). See further the notes to the National Minimum Wage Act 1998, s 1 at **[1.1171]**.

[2.1865]

[4B Determining the applicable national minimum wage rate

The hourly rate of the national minimum wage at which a worker is entitled to be remunerated as respects work, in a pay reference period, is the rate which applies to the worker on the first day of that period.]

NOTES

Commencement: 1 April 2016.

Regulations 4, 4A, 4B substituted (for the original reg 4) by the National Minimum Wage (Amendment) Regulations 2016, SI 2016/68, reg 3, as from 1 April 2016.

[2.1866]

5 Determining whether the apprenticeship rate applies

(1) The apprenticeship rate applies to a worker—

(a) who is employed under a contract of apprenticeship[,] apprenticeship agreement (within the meaning of section 32 of the Apprenticeships, Skills, Children and Learning Act 2009) [or approved English apprenticeship agreement (within the meaning of section A1(3) of the Apprenticeships, Skills, Children and Learning Act 2009)], or is treated as employed under a contract of apprenticeship, and

(b) who is within the first 12 months after the commencement of that employment or under 19 years of age.

(2) A worker is treated as employed under a contract of apprenticeship if the worker is engaged—

(a) in England, under Government arrangements known as Apprenticeships, Advanced Apprenticeships, Intermediate Level Apprenticeships, Advanced Level Apprenticeships or under a Trailblazer Apprenticeship;

(b) in Scotland, under Government arrangements known as Modern Apprenticeships;

(c) in Northern Ireland, under Government arrangements known as Apprenticeships NI; or

(d) in Wales, under Government arrangements known as Foundation Apprenticeships, Apprenticeships or Higher Apprenticeships.

(3) In paragraph (1)(b), a worker does not commence employment with an employer where that worker has previously been employed by another employer and the continuity of employment is preserved between the two employments by or under any enactment.

(4) In this regulation—

(a) "Government arrangements" means—

(i) in England, arrangements made by the Secretary of State under section 2 of the Employment and Training Act 1973 or section 17B of the Jobseekers Act 1995,

(ii) in Wales, arrangements made by the Secretary of State or the Welsh Ministers under section 2 of the Employment and Training Act 1973 or the Secretary of State under section 17B of the Jobseekers Act 1995,

(iii) in Scotland, arrangements made by the Secretary of State or the Scottish Ministers under section 2 of the Employment and Training Act 1973 or by Scottish Enterprise or Highlands and Islands Enterprise under section 2 of the Enterprise and New Towns (Scotland) Act 1990,

(iv) in Northern Ireland, arrangements made by the Department for Employment and Learning under section 1 of the Employment and Training Act (Northern Ireland) 1950;

(b) "Trailblazer Apprenticeship" means an agreement between an employer and a worker which provides for the worker to perform work for that employer and for the employer, or another person, to provide training in order to assist the worker to achieve the apprenticeship standard in the work done under the agreement;

(c) "apprenticeship standard" means the standard published by the Secretary of State in connection with the Government arrangements known as Trailblazer Apprenticeships, which applies as respects the work done under the agreement.

NOTES

Commencement: 6 April 2015.

Para (1): the comma in square brackets was substituted (for the original word "or"), and the words in square brackets were inserted, by the Deregulation Act 2015 (Consequential Amendments) Order 2015, SI 2015/971, art 2, Sch 1, para 3(1), (2), as from 26 May 2015.

[2.1867]

6 Pay reference period

A "pay reference period" is a month, or in the case of a worker who is paid wages by reference to a period shorter than a month, that period.

NOTES

Commencement: 6 April 2015.

PART 3
CALCULATION OF THE HOURLY RATE

[2.1868]

7 Calculation to determine whether the national minimum wage has been paid

A worker is to be treated as remunerated by the employer in a pay reference period at the hourly rate determined by the calculation—

R/H

where—

"R" is the remuneration in the pay reference period determined in accordance with Part 4;

"H" is the hours of work in the pay reference period determined in accordance with Part 5.

NOTES

Commencement: 6 April 2015.

PART 4
REMUNERATION FOR THE PURPOSES OF THE NATIONAL MINIMUM WAGE

[2.1869]

8 Remuneration in a pay reference period

The remuneration in the pay reference period is the payments from the employer to the worker as respects the pay reference period, determined in accordance with Chapter 1, less reductions determined in accordance with Chapter 2.

NOTES

Commencement: 6 April 2015.

CHAPTER 1 PAYMENTS FROM THE EMPLOYER TO THE WORKER

[2.1870]

9 Payments as respects the pay reference period

(1) The following payments and amounts, except as provided in regulation 10, are to be treated as payments by the employer to the worker as respects the pay reference period—

(a) payments paid by the employer to the worker in the pay reference period (other than payments required to be included in an earlier pay reference period in accordance with sub-paragraphs (b) or (c));

(b) payments paid by the employer to the worker in the following pay reference period as respects the pay reference period (whether as respects work or not);

(c) payments paid by the employer to the worker later than the following pay reference period where the requirements in paragraph (2) are met;

(d) where a worker's contract terminates then as respects the worker's final pay reference period, payments paid by the employer to the worker in the period of a month beginning with the day after that on which the contract was terminated;

(e) amounts determined in accordance with regulation 16 (amount for provision of living accommodation) where—

(i) the employer has provided the worker with living accommodation during the pay reference period, and

(ii) as respects that provision of living accommodation, the employer is not entitled to make a deduction from the worker's wages or to receive a payment from the worker.

(2) The requirements are that as respects the work in the pay reference period—

(a) the worker is under an obligation to complete a record of the amount of work done,

(b) the worker is not entitled to payment until the completed record has been given to the employer,

(c) the worker has failed to give the record to the employer before the fourth working day before the end of that following pay reference period, and

(d) the payment is paid in either the pay reference period in which the record is given to the employer or the pay reference period after that.

NOTES

Commencement: 6 April 2015.

[2.1871]

10 Payments and benefits in kind which do not form part of a worker's remuneration

The following payments and benefits in kind do not form part of a worker's remuneration—

(a) payments by way of an advance under an agreement for a loan or by way of an advance of wages;

(b) payment of a pension, allowance or gratuity in connection with the worker's retirement or as compensation for loss of office;

(c) payment of an award made by a court or tribunal or a payment to settle proceedings which have been or might be brought before a court or tribunal, other than the payment of an amount due under the worker's contract;

(d) payments referable to the worker's redundancy;

(e) payment of an award for a suggestion made by the worker under a scheme established by the employer to reward suggestions made by workers;

(f) benefits in kind provided to the worker, whether or not a monetary value is attached to the benefit, other than living accommodation;

(g) a voucher, stamp or similar document capable of being exchanged for money, goods or services (or for any combination of those things);

(h) payments as respects hours which are not, or not treated as—

(i) hours of time work in accordance with regulation 35 (absences, industrial action, rest breaks),

(ii) hours of output work in accordance with regulation 40 (industrial action), or

(iii) hours of unmeasured work in accordance with regulation 48 (industrial action);

(i) payments, in the context of salaried hours work, attributable to the hours to be reduced under regulation 23 (worker entitled to less than normal proportion of annual salary because of absence) whether directly or by reason of regulation 28(3) (where the worker works more than the basic hours);

(j) payments paid by the employer to the worker as respects hours of time work or output work in the pay reference period if—

(i) there is a lower rate per hour which could be payable under the contract as respects that work (including if the work was done at a different time or in different circumstances), and

(ii) to the extent that such payments exceed the lowest rate;

(k) payments paid by the employer to the worker attributable to a particular aspect of the working arrangements or to working or personal circumstances that are not consolidated into the worker's standard pay unless the payments are attributable to the performance of the worker in carrying out the work;

(l) payments paid by the employer to the worker as respects the worker's expenditure in connection with the employment;

(m) payments paid by the employer to the worker representing amounts paid by customers by way of a service charge, tip, gratuity or cover charge;

(n) payments paid by the employer to the worker as respects travelling expenses that are allowed as deductions from earnings under section 338 of the Income Tax (Earnings and Pensions) Act 2003.

NOTES

Commencement: 6 April 2015.

CHAPTER 2 REDUCTIONS

[2.1872]
11 Determining the reductions which reduce the worker's remuneration

(1) In regulation 8, the reductions in the pay reference period are determined by adding together all of the payments or deductions treated as reductions in that period in accordance with this Chapter.

(2) To the extent that any payment or deduction is required to be subtracted by virtue of more than one provision in this Chapter, it is to be subtracted only once.

NOTES

Commencement: 6 April 2015.

[2.1873]
12 Deductions or payments for the employer's own use and benefit

(1) Deductions made by the employer in the pay reference period, or payments due from the worker to the employer in the pay reference period, for the employer's own use and benefit are treated as reductions except as specified in paragraph (2) and regulation 14 (deductions or payments as respects living accommodation).

(2) The following deductions and payments are not treated as reductions—

(a) deductions, or payments, in respect of the worker's conduct, or any other event, where the worker (whether together with another worker or not) is contractually liable;

(b) deductions, or payments, on account of an advance under an agreement for a loan or an advance of wages;

(c) deductions, or payments, as respects an accidental overpayment of wages made by the employer to the worker;

(d) deductions, or payments, as respects the purchase by the worker of shares, other securities or share options, or of a share in a partnership;

(e) payments as respects the purchase by the worker of goods or services from the employer, unless the purchase is made in order to comply with a requirement imposed by the employer in connection with the worker's employment.

NOTES

Commencement: 6 April 2015.

[2.1874]
13 Deductions or payments as respects a worker's expenditure

The following deductions and payments are to be treated as reductions if the deduction or payment is paid by or due from the worker in the pay reference period—

(a) deductions made by the employer, or payments paid by or due from the worker to the employer, as respects the worker's expenditure in connection with the employment;

(b) payments to any person (other than the employer) on account of the worker's expenditure in connection with the employment unless the expenditure is met, or intended to be met, by a payment paid to the worker by the employer.

NOTES

Commencement: 6 April 2015.

[2.1875]
14 Deductions or payments as respects living accommodation

(1) The amount of any deduction the employer is entitled to make, or payment the employer is entitled to receive from the worker, as respects the provision of living accommodation by the employer to the worker in the pay reference period, as adjusted, where applicable, in accordance with regulation 15, is treated as a reduction to the extent that it exceeds the amount determined in accordance with regulation 16, unless the payment or deduction falls within paragraph (2).

(2) The following payments and deductions are not treated as reductions—

(a) payments made to or deductions by a Higher Education Institution, Further Education Institution or a 16 to 19 Academy in respect of the provision of living accommodation where the living accommodation is provided to a worker who is enrolled on a full-time higher education course or a full-time further education course at that Higher Education Institution or Further Education Institution or on a full-time course provided by that 16 to 19 Academy;

(b) payments made to or deductions by a local housing authority or a registered social landlord in respect of the provision of living accommodation, except where the living accommodation is provided to the worker in connection with the worker's employment with the local housing authority or registered social landlord.

(3) For the purposes of this regulation—

"further education institution" means an institution within the further education sector as defined by section 91(3) of the Further and Higher Education Act 1992;

"higher education institution" means an institution within the higher education sector as defined by section 91(5) of the Further and Higher Education Act 1992;

"local housing authority" means—

(a) in England and Wales, a local housing authority, as defined in Part 1 of the Housing Act 1985, or a county council in England;
(b) in Scotland, a local authority landlord as defined in section 11(3) of the Housing (Scotland) Act 2001;
(c) in Northern Ireland, the Northern Ireland Housing Executive;

"registered social landlord" means—

(d) in England and Wales—
(i) a private registered provider of social housing or a subsidiary or associate of such a provider, as defined in Part 2 of the Housing and Regeneration Act 2008, or
(ii) a social landlord registered under Part 1 of the Housing Act 1996 or a subsidiary or associate of such a person as defined in that Act;
(e) in Scotland, a body registered in the register maintained under section 20(1) of the Housing (Scotland) Act 2010;
(f) in Northern Ireland, a housing association registered under Chapter II of Part II of the Housing (Northern Ireland) Order 1992.

NOTES

Commencement: 6 April 2015.

[2.1876]

15 Deductions or payments as respects living accommodation adjusted for absences

(1) The amount referred to in regulation 14 is to be adjusted in accordance with paragraph (2) if, in the pay reference period, a worker is absent from work and all of the following conditions are met—

(a) the worker would be required to do time work but for the absence;
(b) the worker is paid, for the hours of work during which the worker was absent, an amount not less than that which the worker would have been entitled to under these Regulations but for the absence;
(c) the hours of work in the pay reference period are, by reason of the absence, less than they would be in a pay reference period containing the same number of working days in which the worker worked without reduced hours and for no additional hours;
(d) the amount of the deduction or payment the employer is entitled to make or receive in respect of the provision of living accommodation to the worker during the pay reference period does not increase by reason of the worker's absence from work.

(2) The amount is adjusted by the formula—

(A x B) / C

where—

"A" is the amount of the deduction thc employer is entitled to make or payment the employer is entitled to receive in respect of the provision of living accommodation by the employer to the worker during the pay reference period;

"B" is the number of hours of time work determined in accordance with Part 5;

"C" is the number of hours of work the worker would have worked in the pay reference period (including the hours of work actually worked) but for the absence.

NOTES

Commencement: 6 April 2015.

CHAPTER 3 ACCOMMODATION OFFSET AMOUNT

[2.1877]

16 Amount for provision of living accommodation

(1) In regulations 9(1)(e), 14 and 15, the amount as respects the provision of living accommodation is the amount resulting from multiplying the number of days in the pay reference period for which accommodation was provided by [£7.55].

(2) Living accommodation is provided for a day only if it is provided for the whole of a day.

(3) Amounts required to be determined in accordance with paragraph (1) as respects a pay reference period are to be determined in accordance with the regulations as they are in force on the first day of that period.

NOTES

Commencement: 6 April 2015.

Para (1): sum in square brackets substituted by the National Minimum Wage (Amendment) Regulations 2019, SI 2019/603, reg 2(1), (4), as from 1 April 2019. The previous sums were: £7.00 (as from 1 April 2018); £6.40 (as from 1 April 2017); £6.00 (as from 1 October 2016); £5.35 (as from 1 October 2015); £5.08 (as from 1 October 2014); £4.91 (as from 1 October 2013); £4.82 (as from 1 October 2012); £4.73 (as from 1 October 2011); and £4.61 (as from 1 October 2010).

PART 5
HOURS WORKED FOR THE PURPOSES OF THE NATIONAL MINIMUM WAGE
CHAPTER 1 DETERMINING THE HOURS OF WORK

[2.1878]
17 Hours of work for determining whether the national minimum wage has been paid

In regulation 7 (calculation to determine whether the national minimum wage has been paid), the hours of work in the pay reference period are the hours worked or treated as worked by the worker in the pay reference period as determined—

(a) for salaried hours work, in accordance with Chapter 2;
(b) for time work, in accordance with Chapter 3;
(c) for output work, in accordance with Chapter 4;
(d) for unmeasured work, in accordance with Chapter 5.

NOTES
Commencement: 6 April 2015.

[2.1879]
18 Hours where payment due on submission of a record

If the worker is only entitled to payment for hours of work when a record of the hours has been given to the employer, then the hours of work in the pay reference period do not include hours of work in respect of which that record has not been submitted.

NOTES
Commencement: 6 April 2015.

[2.1880]
19 Hours spent training

(1) In this Part, references to "training" include hours when the worker is—
(a) attending at a place other than the worker's normal place of work, when the worker would otherwise be working, for the purpose of receiving training that has been approved by the employer;
(b) travelling, when the worker would otherwise be working, between a place of work and a place where the worker receives such training;
(c) receiving such training at the worker's normal place of work.

(2) In paragraph (1), hours when the worker would "otherwise be working" include any hours when the worker is attending at a place or travelling where it is uncertain whether the worker would otherwise be working because the worker's hours of work vary either as to their length or in respect of the time at which they are performed.

NOTES
Commencement: 6 April 2015.

[2.1881]
20 Hours spent travelling

In this Part, references to "travelling" include hours when the worker is—
(a) in the course of a journey by a mode of transport or is making a journey on foot;
(b) waiting at a place of departure to begin a journey by a mode of transport;
(c) waiting at a place of departure for a journey to re-commence either by the same or another mode of transport, except for any time the worker spends taking a rest break; or
(d) waiting at the end of a journey for the purpose of carrying out duties, or to receive training, except for any time the worker spends taking a rest break.

NOTES
Commencement: 6 April 2015.

CHAPTER 2 SALARIED HOURS WORK

[2.1882]
21 The meaning of salaried hours work

(1) "Salaried hours work" is work which is done under a worker's contract and which meets the conditions in paragraphs (2) to (5) of this regulation.

(2) The first condition is that the worker is entitled under their contract to be paid an annual salary or an annual salary and performance bonus.

(3) The second condition is that the worker is entitled under their contract to be paid that salary or salary and performance bonus in respect of a number of hours in a year, whether those hours are specified in or ascertained in accordance with their contract ("the basic hours").

(4) The third condition is that the worker is not entitled under their contract to a payment in respect of the basic hours other than an annual salary or an annual salary and performance bonus.

(5) The fourth condition is that the worker is entitled under their contract to be paid, where practicable and regardless of the number of hours actually worked in a particular week or month—

(a) in equal weekly or monthly instalments, or

(b) in monthly instalments that vary but have the result that the worker is entitled to be paid an equal amount in each quarter.

(6) Circumstances where it may not be practicable to pay a worker by equal instalments, or by an equal amount in each quarter, include where—

(a) a performance bonus is awarded;

(b) the annual salary is varied;

(c) a payment is made in respect of hours in addition to basic hours; or

(d) the employment starts or terminates during a week or month with the result that the worker is paid a proportionate amount of their annual salary for that week or month.

(7) Work may be salaried hours work whether or not—

(a) all the basic hours are working hours;

(b) the worker works hours in excess of the basic hours (whether the worker is entitled to be paid for those additional hours or not);

(c) the annual salary may be reduced due to an absence from work.

(8) A "performance bonus" is a payment paid to a worker on merit attributable to the quality or amount of work done in the course of more than one pay reference period.

NOTES

Commencement: 6 April 2015.

[2.1883]

22 Determining hours of salaried hours work in a pay reference period

(1) The hours of salaried hours work in a pay reference period are to be calculated in accordance with the following paragraphs.

(2) Where the pay reference period is a week, the hours of salaried hours work in that period are the basic hours divided by 52.

(3) Where the pay reference period is a month, the hours of salaried hours work in that period are the basic hours divided by 12.

(4) Where the pay reference period is any other period, the hours of salaried hours work in that period are the basic hours divided by the figure obtained by dividing 365 by the number of days in the pay reference period.

(5) The basic hours are to be ascertained in accordance with the worker's contract on the first day of the pay reference period in question unless paragraphs (6) or (7) apply.

(6) The hours of salaried hours work in a pay reference period are to be ascertained in accordance with regulations 24 to 28 if the worker—

(a) during or before the payment reference period, works additional hours in excess of the basic hours in the calculation year, and

(b) is not entitled to be paid more than annual salary and a performance bonus for those additional hours.

(7) The hours of salaried hours work in a pay reference period are to be determined in accordance with regulation 29 if the employment terminates before the end of the calculation year or the contract is varied before the end of the calculation year so that it is no longer a contract for salaried hours work.

NOTES

Commencement: 6 April 2015.

[2.1884]

23 Absences from work to be reduced from the salaried hours work in a pay reference period

(1) The hours a worker is absent from work are to be subtracted from the hours of salaried hours work in a pay reference period if all of the following conditions are met—

(a) the employer is entitled under the worker's contract to reduce the annual salary due to the absence;

(b) the employer pays the worker less than the normal proportion of annual salary in the pay reference period as a result of the absence.

(2) The hours during which a worker takes industrial action are to be subtracted from the hours of salaried hours work in a pay reference period if an annual salary was payable for those hours, or would have been payable but for the industrial action.

NOTES

Commencement: 6 April 2015.

[2.1885]

24 The meaning of the calculation year

(1) In this Chapter, "the calculation year" has the meaning given in the following paragraphs.

(2) For a worker who commenced the employment before 1st April 1999, then for so long as the worker continues in that employment the calculation year is a year beginning on an anniversary of the commencement of that employment.

(3) For a worker whose annual salary is payable monthly and who commenced the employment after 31st March 1999, then for so long as the worker continues in that employment—

(a) if the worker commenced employment on the first day of a month, the calculation year is—

(i) the year beginning with that day;

(ii) in each subsequent year, a year beginning on an anniversary of that day;

(b) if the worker commenced employment on any other day of a month, the calculation year is—

(i) the period beginning with that day and ending with the day before the first anniversary of the first day of the next month;

(ii) in each subsequent year, a year beginning on an anniversary of the first day of that month.

(4) For a worker whose annual salary is payable weekly and who commenced the employment after 31st March 1999, then for so long as the worker continues in that employment the calculation year is—

(a) the year beginning with the first day of employment;

(b) in each subsequent year, a year beginning on an anniversary of that day.

NOTES

Commencement: 6 April 2015.

[2.1886]

25 Determining the basic hours in the calculation year

(1) In this Chapter, the basic hours in a calculation year are determined in accordance with the following paragraphs.

(2) The basic hours in the calculation year are the basic hours ascertained in accordance with the contract at the start of the calculation year, unless there is a variation to the basic hours which takes effect in the calculation year.

(3) Where a variation to the basic hours takes effect in the calculation year, the basic hours in the calculation year are determined by adding together—

(a) the proportion of basic hours in the calculation year in the period starting before the day during which the variation takes effect, and

(b) the proportion of basic hours in the calculation year in the period after the day during which the variation takes effect until the end of the calculation year.

(4) If more than one contractual variation takes effect in the calculation year, the "basic hours in the calculation year" are determined by adding together—

(a) the proportion of basic hours in the calculation year in the period starting before the day during which the first variation takes effect, and

(b) for each variation, the proportion of basic hours in the calculation year in the period after the day during which the variation takes effect and before the day during which the next variation takes effect or, in the case of the final variation, the end of the calculation year.

(5) The proportion of basic hours in the calculation year for each of the periods in paragraphs (3) and (4) is calculated using the formula—

(D / 365) x H

where—

"D" means the number of days in the period;

"H" means the basic hours in the calculation year which have effect in that period.

NOTES

Commencement: 6 April 2015.

[2.1887]

26 Determining whether the worker works more than the basic hours in the calculation year

(1) For the purposes of this regulation and regulations 22(6) and 28, a worker works more than the basic hours in a calculation year if all of the following hours added together are more than the basic hours in a calculation year—

(a) hours worked which form part of the basic hours in the calculation year;

(b) hours when the worker was absent from work which form part of the basic hours in the calculation year;

(c) hours worked in the calculation year which do not form part of the basic hours in the calculation year in respect of which the worker had no entitlement under their contract to a payment other than annual salary or annual salary and a performance bonus;

(d) hours treated as worked in accordance with regulation 27 to the extent that such hours consist of hours in respect of which the worker had no entitlement under their contract to a payment other than annual salary or annual salary and a performance bonus.

(2) Hours during which the worker was taking part in industrial action are not to be included in sub-paragraphs (a) to (d).

NOTES

Commencement: 6 April 2015.

[2.1888]

27 Hours treated as worked for the purpose of determining whether the worker works more than the basic hours in the calculation year and, where the worker does, the number of salaried hours work in that year

(1) The hours listed in sub-paragraphs (a) to (c) are treated as worked for the purposes of determining whether the worker works more than the basic hours in the calculation year (in accordance with regulation 26(1)(d)) and, where the worker does, the number of hours of salaried hours work in that year (in accordance with regulation 28)—

(a) hours a worker spends training when the worker would otherwise be working;

(b) hours a worker is available at or near a place of work for the purposes of working, unless the worker is at home;

(c) hours a worker spends travelling for the purposes of working, when the worker would otherwise be working, unless the travelling is between—

(i) the worker's home, or a place where the worker is temporarily residing other than for the purposes of working, and

(ii) a place of work or a place where an assignment is carried out.

(2) In paragraph (1)(b), hours when a worker is available only includes hours when the worker is awake for the purposes of working, even if a worker is required to sleep at or near a place of work and the employer provides suitable facilities for sleeping.

(3) In paragraph (1)(c), hours treated as hours when the worker would otherwise be working include—

(a) hours when the worker is travelling for the purpose of carrying out assignments to be carried out at different places between which the worker is obliged to travel, and which are not places occupied by the employer;

(b) hours when the worker is travelling where it is uncertain whether the worker would otherwise be working because the worker's hours of work vary either as to their length or in respect of the time at which they are performed.

NOTES

Commencement: 6 April 2015.

[2.1889]

28 Determining hours of salaried hours work if the worker works more than the basic hours in the calculation year

(1) If, in a pay reference period, a worker has worked more than the basic hours in the calculation year, the hours of salaried hours work in that pay reference period are calculated by adding together all of the following hours—

(a) the proportion of basic hours attributable to the part of the pay reference period starting before the day during which the worker worked more than the basic hours in the calculation year;

(b) the proportion of basic hours attributable to the part of the pay reference period starting on the day during which the worker worked more than the basic hours in the calculation year;

(c) the number of hours actually worked in the pay reference period starting on the day during which the worker worked more than the basic hours in the calculation year;

(d) the number of hours treated as worked, in accordance with regulation 27, in the pay reference period starting on the day during which the worker worked more than the basic hours in the calculation year.

(2) In paragraph (1)(a) and (b), each proportion of basic hours in the pay reference period is calculated using the formula—

$(D / 365) \times H$

where—

"D" means the number of days in the part of the pay reference period referred to in paragraph (1)(a) or (b);

"H" means the basic hours in the calculation year.

(3) Reductions from the basic hours in the calculation year for absences, in accordance with regulation 23, must only be made from the proportion of basic hours determined under paragraph (1)(a).

(4) For each pay reference period in the calculation year after the pay reference period in which the worker worked more than the basic hours, the number of hours of salaried hours work are calculated by adding together all of the following hours—

(a) the number of hours of salaried hours work in the pay reference period determined in accordance with regulation 22(2) to (4);

(b) the number of hours actually worked in the pay reference period;

(c) the number of hours treated as worked in the pay reference period in accordance with regulation 27.

(5) Regulation 23 (absences from work to be reduced from the hours of salaried hours work in a pay reference period) does not apply to the calculation in paragraph (4)(a).

NOTES

Commencement: 6 April 2015.

[2.1890]

29 Hours of salaried hours work if the employment terminates before the end of the calculation year (or contract is varied so it is no longer a contract for salaried hours work)

(1) Where the employment terminates before the end of a calculation year the hours of salaried hours work in the final pay reference period are calculated in accordance with the following paragraphs.

(2) Where the worker does not work more than basic hours in the calculation year, the hours of salaried hours work in the final pay reference period are the sum of the following—

(a) the number of hours of salaried hours work in the pay reference period calculated in accordance with regulation 22(2) to (4), and

(b) the number of hours (if any) by which A exceeds B where—

"A" is the number of hours determined in accordance with regulation 26; and

"B" is the total of the number of hours of salaried hours work determined in accordance with regulation 22(2) to (4) in respect of all pay reference periods (including the final pay reference period) since the beginning of the calculation year.

(3) Where the worker works more than the basic hours in the calculation year, the hours of salaried hours work in the final pay reference period are the sum of the following—

(a) the number of hours determined in accordance with regulation 28, and

(b) the number of hours of salaried hours work calculated in accordance with regulation 22(2) to (4) for the period beginning on the day following the last day of the final pay reference period and ending at the end of the calculation year as if—

(i) it was a single pay reference period (containing that number of days), and

(ii) the worker had remained employed until the end of the calculation year without any absences.

(4) If a contract for salaried hours work is varied with the effect that it is no longer a contract for salaried hours work, this regulation is to apply as if the employment of the worker had been terminated and the last day of the worker's final pay reference period had fallen on the day before the day on which the variation took effect.

NOTES

Commencement: 6 April 2015.

CHAPTER 3 TIME WORK

[2.1891]

30 The meaning of time work

Time work is work, other than salaried hours work, in respect of which a worker is entitled under their contract to be paid—

(a) by reference to the time worked by the worker;

(b) by reference to a measure of output in a period of time where the worker is required to work for the whole of that period; or

(c) for work that would fall within sub-paragraph (b) but for the worker having an entitlement to be paid by reference to the period of time alone when the output does not exceed a particular level.

NOTES

Commencement: 6 April 2015.

[2.1892]

31 Determining hours of time work in a pay reference period

The hours of time work in a pay reference period are the total number of hours of time work worked by the worker or treated under this Chapter as hours of time work in that period.

NOTES

Commencement: 6 April 2015.

[2.1893]

32 Time work where worker is available at or near a place of work

(1) Time work includes hours when a worker is available, and required to be available, at or near a place of work for the purposes of working unless the worker is at home.

(2) In paragraph (1), hours when a worker is "available" only includes hours when the worker is awake for the purposes of working, even if a worker by arrangement sleeps at or near a place of work and the employer provides suitable facilities for sleeping.

NOTES

Commencement: 6 April 2015.

[2.1894]

33 Training treated as hours of time work

The hours a worker spends training, when the worker would otherwise be doing time work, are treated as hours of time work.

NOTES

Commencement: 6 April 2015.

[2.1895]

34 Travelling treated as hours of time work

(1) The hours when a worker is travelling for the purposes of time work, where the worker would otherwise be working, are treated as hours of time work unless the travelling is between—

(a) the worker's home, or a place where the worker is temporarily residing other than for the purposes of working, and

(b) a place of work or a place where an assignment is carried out.

(2) In paragraph (1), hours treated as hours when the worker would "otherwise be working" include—

(a) hours when the worker is travelling for the purpose of carrying out assignments to be carried out at different places between which the worker is obliged to travel, and which are not places occupied by the employer;

(b) hours when the worker is travelling where it is uncertain whether the worker would otherwise be working because the worker's hours of work vary either as to their length or in respect of the time at which they are performed.

NOTES

Commencement: 6 April 2015.

[2.1896]

35 Hours not treated as time work

(1) The hours a worker is absent from work are not treated as hours of time work, except as specified in regulations 32 to 34.

(2) The hours a worker spends taking part in industrial action are not hours of time work.

(3) The hours a worker spends taking a rest break are not hours of time work.

(4) A worker is not to be treated as taking a rest break during hours which, in accordance with regulation 34, are treated as hours of time work.

NOTES

Commencement: 6 April 2015.

CHAPTER 4 OUTPUT WORK

[2.1897]

36 The meaning of output work

Output work is work, other than time work, in respect of which a worker is entitled under their contract to be paid by reference to a measure of output by the worker, including a number of pieces made or processed, or a number of tasks performed.

NOTES

Commencement: 6 April 2015.

[2.1898]

37 Determining hours of output work in a pay reference period

The hours of output work in a pay reference period are the total number of hours—

(a) of rated output work which the worker is treated as working in that period as determined in accordance with regulation 43.

(b) of output work in that period which is not rated output work; and

(c) treated as hours of output work in that period as determined in accordance with regulations 38 and 39.

NOTES

Commencement: 6 April 2015.

[2.1899]

38 Training treated as hours of output work

The hours when a worker is training, if the worker would otherwise be doing output work, are treated as hours of output work.

NOTES

Commencement: 6 April 2015.

[2.1900]

39 Travelling treated as hours of output work

(1) The hours when a worker is travelling for the purposes of output work are treated as hours of output work unless the travelling is between—

(a) the worker's home, or place where the worker is temporarily residing, and

(b) the place of work or, except as mentioned in paragraph (2), premises at which the worker reports.

(2) If a worker does output work at home or a place where the worker is temporarily residing the hours when a worker is travelling between that place and premises at which the worker reports are to be treated as hours of output work.

NOTES

Commencement: 6 April 2015.

[2.1901]

40 Industrial action not treated as output work

The hours when a worker is taking part in industrial action are not to be treated as hours of output work.

NOTES

Commencement: 6 April 2015.

[2.1902]

41 Requirements for rated output work

(1) In this Chapter, output work is "rated output work" if all of the following requirements are met—

(a) there are no minimum or maximum working hours in the worker's contract in relation to the output work;

(b) the employer does not determine or control the hours actually worked in relation to the output work;

(c) the employer has determined the average hourly output rate in accordance with regulation 42;

(d) a notice which satisfies the requirements in paragraph (2) is given to the worker.

(2) The requirements are—

(a) the notice was given to the worker before the beginning of the pay reference period (whether or not it was given before or had effect in relation to earlier pay reference periods), and

(b) the notice conveys all of the following information in writing—

(i) that for the purposes of these Regulations the worker is to be treated as working for a certain period of time;

(ii) the employer has conducted a test or made an estimate of the average speed at which workers do the work to determine the period of time the worker is to be treated as working;

(iii) what the average hourly output rate is for the output;

(iv) the rate to be paid to the worker for a single measure of output;

(v) the telephone number for the Secretary of State's helpline for workers and employers on workers' pay and rights at work as published, from time to time, by the Secretary of State.

NOTES

Commencement: 6 April 2015.

[2.1903]

42 The meaning of average hourly output rate (rated output work)

(1) In this Chapter, the "average hourly output rate" is the mean number (including any fraction) of the measure of output per hour.

(2) To determine the average hourly output rate the employer must either—

(a) conduct a test which satisfies the requirements in paragraph (3); or

(b) make an estimate of the mean speed the output work is done which satisfies the requirements in paragraph (4).

(3) The requirements are—

(a) the test is conducted on—

(i) all the employer's workers who do the output work, or

(ii) a sample of those workers which, as respects the speed, is representative of the worker's work as respects that measure of output;

(b) the test is conducted in similar physical conditions to those in which the worker will be doing the work; and

(c) the total output per hour during the test is divided by the number of workers tested.

(4) The requirements are—

(a) a test is conducted on a sample of the employer's workers which is, so far as reasonably practicable, representative as respects the speed at which they work, of the speed at which the workers who produce the measure of output work;

(b) that test is carried out in relation to work which—

(i) is reasonably similar to the output work and was done in similar physical conditions to those of the worker, or

(ii) is the same as the output work but was done in different physical conditions to those of the worker; and

(c) the average speed is reasonably adjusted to take into account the likely difference in time involved in the worker doing the output work in the worker's physical conditions in comparison to the test which was carried out.

(5) If there are changes in the number or identity of workers who do the output work, the employer is not required to conduct a further test or make a further estimate unless the employer has reason to believe that the changes materially affect the average hourly output rate.

NOTES

Commencement: 6 April 2015.

[2.1904]

43 Determining hours of rated output work in a pay reference period

Where output work is rated output work, the time spent by the worker doing the output work during the pay reference period is 120 per cent of the number of hours that a worker, doing the work at the average hourly output rate, would have taken to produce the same measure of output in that period.

NOTES

Commencement: 6 April 2015.

CHAPTER 5 UNMEASURED WORK

[2.1905]

44 The meaning of unmeasured work

Unmeasured work is any other work that is not time work, salaried hours work or output work.

NOTES

Commencement: 6 April 2015.

[2.1906]

45 Determining hours of unmeasured work in a pay reference period

The hours of unmeasured work in a pay reference period are the total number of hours—

(a) which are worked (or treated as hours of unmeasured work in accordance with regulations 46 and 47) by the worker in that period; or

(b) which the worker is treated as working under a daily average agreement in that period, as determined in accordance with regulation 50.

NOTES

Commencement: 6 April 2015.

[2.1907]

46 Training treated as hours of unmeasured work

The hours when a worker is training, where the worker would otherwise be doing unmeasured work, are to be treated as hours of unmeasured work.

NOTES

Commencement: 6 April 2015.

[2.1908]

47 Travelling treated as hours of unmeasured work

The hours when a worker is travelling for the purposes of unmeasured work are to be treated as hours of unmeasured work.

NOTES

Commencement: 6 April 2015.

[2.1909]

48 Industrial action not to be unmeasured work

The hours when a worker takes part in industrial action are not to be treated as hours of unmeasured work.

NOTES

Commencement: 6 April 2015.

[2.1910]

49 The daily average agreement

(1) A "daily average agreement" is an agreement between a worker and employer—

(a) which specifies the average daily number of hours the worker is likely to spend working where the worker is available to work for the full amount of time contemplated by the contract, and

(b) is made in writing before the beginning of the pay reference period to which it relates.

(2) The requirement in paragraph (1)(a) is not satisfied unless the employer can show that the average daily number of hours specified is a reasonable estimate.

(3) Unless the worker and employer agree otherwise, the daily average agreement has effect solely for the purpose of determining the amount of unmeasured work the worker is to be treated as having worked for the purposes of these Regulations.

NOTES

Commencement: 6 April 2015.

[2.1911]

50 Determining the hours treated as worked under a daily average agreement

The hours treated as worked under a daily average agreement for each day on which the worker worked in the pay reference period are—

(a) where the worker was available to work for at least the full amount of time contemplated under the contract, the average daily number of hours specified in the daily average agreement;

(b) where the worker was available to work for only part of the time contemplated by the contract, the proportion of the average daily number of hours specified in the daily average agreement which that part bears to the full amount of time contemplated under the contract.

NOTES

Commencement: 6 April 2015.

PART 6
EXCLUSIONS

[2.1912]

51 Schemes for training, work experience, temporary work or for seeking or obtaining work

(1) A person who is participating in a scheme which meets the requirements in paragraph (2) does not qualify for the national minimum wage for work done as part of that scheme.

(2) The requirements are that the scheme—

(a) is designed to provide training, work experience or temporary work, or to assist in the seeking or obtaining of work, and

(b) is, in whole or in part, made or funded by—

(i) the Secretary of State under section 2 of the Employment and Training Act 1973[,] section 17B of the Jobseekers Act 1995 [or section 100 of the Apprenticeships, Skills, Children and Learning Act 2009];

(ii) the Scottish Ministers or the Welsh Ministers under section 2 of the Employment and Training Act 1973;

(iii) . . .

(iv) Scottish Enterprise or Highlands and Islands Enterprise under section 2 of the Enterprise and New Towns (Scotland) Act 1990;

(v) the Department for Employment and Learning under section 1 of the Employment and Training Act (Northern Ireland) 1950; or

(vi) the European Social Fund established under Article 162 of the Treaty on the Functioning of the European Union .

NOTES

Commencement: 6 April 2015.

Para (2): the comma in square brackets was substituted (for the original word "or"), the words in square brackets were inserted, and sub-para (b)(iii) was revoked, by the Deregulation Act 2015 (Consequential Amendments) Order 2015, SI 2015/971, art 2, Sch 3, para 33(1), (3), as from 26 May 2015.

[2.1913]

52 Schemes for trial periods of work

(1) A person who is participating in a trial period of work with an employer for a period of six weeks or less, as part of a scheme which meets the requirements in paragraph (2), does not qualify for the national minimum wage for the work done for that employer in that period.

(2) The requirements are that the scheme—

(a) is designed to provide training, work experience or temporary work, or to assist in the seeking or obtaining of work, and

(b) is, in whole or in part, made or funded by—

(i) the Secretary of State under section 2 of the Employment and Training Act 1973[,] section 17B of the Jobseekers Act 1995 [or section 100 of the Apprenticeships, Skills, Children and Learning Act 2009];

(ii) the Scottish Ministers or the Welsh Ministers under section 2 of the Employment and Training Act 1973;

(iii) . . .

(iv) Scottish Enterprise or Highlands and Islands Enterprise under section 2 of the Enterprise and New Towns (Scotland) Act 1990;

(v) the Department for Employment and Learning under section 1 of the Employment and Training Act (Northern Ireland) 1950; or

(vi) the European Social Fund established under Article 162 of the Treaty on the Functioning of the European Union.

NOTES

Commencement: 6 April 2015.

Para (2): the comma in square brackets was substituted (for the original word "or"), the words in square brackets were inserted, and sub-para (b)(iii) was revoked, by the Deregulation Act 2015 (Consequential Amendments) Order 2015, SI 2015/971, art 2, Sch 3, para 33(1), (4), as from 26 May 2015.

[2.1914]
53 Work experience as part of a higher or further education course

A person who undertakes a higher education course or further education course, and before the course ends is required, as part of that course, to attend a period of work experience not exceeding one year, does not qualify for the national minimum wage as respects work done for the employer as part of that course.

NOTES

Commencement: 6 April 2015.

[2.1915]
54 Traineeships in England

(1) A worker does not qualify for the national minimum wage for work done as part of that worker's participation in a traineeship in England to which paragraph (2) applies.

(2) This paragraph applies to a traineeship consisting of a skills programme which meets the following conditions—

(a) the programme includes a work experience placement and work preparation training;
(b) the programme lasts no more than six months;
(c) the programme is government funded; and
(d) the programme is open to persons who on the first day of the traineeship have attained the age of 16 but not 25 years old.

NOTES

Commencement: 6 April 2015.

[2.1916]
55 Work schemes for provision of accommodation to the homeless

(1) A worker, who meets the requirements in paragraph (2), does not qualify for the national minimum wage for work done for an employer, under a scheme which meets the requirements in paragraph (3), if the worker is provided with accommodation and other benefits (which may include money) under that scheme.

(2) The requirements are that immediately before entry into the scheme the worker was homeless or residing in a hostel for homeless persons and—

(a) was in receipt of, or entitled to any of the following benefits—
  (i) universal credit (payable under Part 1 of the Welfare Reform Act 2012),
  (ii) income support (payable under Part VII of the Social Security Contributions and Benefits Act 1992),
  (iii) income-based jobseeker's allowance (payable under Part I of the Jobseekers Act 1995),
  (iv) income-related employment and support allowance (payable under Part 1 of the Welfare Reform Act 2007 or Part 1 of the Welfare Reform Act (Northern Ireland) 2007); or
(b) was not entitled to receive any of those benefits only because the worker was not habitually resident in the United Kingdom.

(3) The requirements for the scheme are as follows—

(a) no one makes a profit out of the scheme other than—
  (i) a profit only applied to running the scheme or other qualifying schemes, or
  (ii) where the person operating the scheme is a charity, for a purpose of the charity relating to the alleviation of poverty;
(b) every person participating in the scheme satisfies the same requirements as for workers in paragraph (2) (although they need not all be workers);
(c) the accommodation available under the scheme is provided by the person operating the scheme or under arrangements made between that person and another person; and
(d) the work done under the scheme is both provided by, and performed for, the person operating the scheme.

NOTES

Commencement: 6 April 2015.

[2.1917]
56 European Union programmes

A worker does not qualify for the national minimum wage for work that is done as a participant in any of the following programmes—

(a) the second phase of the European Community Leonardo da Vinci programme (established pursuant to Council Decision 99/382/EC);
(b) the European Community Leonardo da Vinci programme (established pursuant to Decision No 1720/2006/EC of the European Parliament and the Council of the European Union establishing an action programme in the field of lifelong learning);
(c) the European Community Youth in Action Programme (established pursuant to Decision No 1719/2006/EC of the European Parliament and the Council of the European Union);

(d) the European Community Erasmus Programme or Comenius Programme (both established pursuant to Decision No 1720/2006/EC of the European Parliament and the Council of the European Union establishing an action programme in the field of lifelong learning);

(e) Erasmus+ established pursuant to Regulation (EU) No1288/2013 of the European Parliament and of the Council of 11th December 2013 establishing 'Erasmus+': the Union programme for education, training, youth and sport.

NOTES

Commencement: 6 April 2015.

[2.1918]

57 Work does not include work relating to family household

(1) In these Regulations, "work" does not include any work done by a worker in relation to an employer's family household if the requirements in paragraphs (2) or (3) are met.

(2) The requirements are all of the following—

(a) the worker is a member of the employer's family;

(b) the worker resides in the family home of the employer;

(c) the worker shares in the tasks and activities of the family.

(3) The requirements are all of the following—

(a) the worker resides in the family home of the worker's employer;

(b) the worker is not a member of that family, but is treated as such, in particular as regards to the provision of living accommodation and meals and the sharing of tasks and leisure activities;

(c) the worker is neither liable to any deduction, nor to make any payment to the employer, or any other person, as respects the provision of the living accommodation or meals;

(d) if the work had been done by a member of the employer's family, it would not be treated as work or as performed under a worker's contract because the requirements in paragraph (2) would be met.

NOTES

Commencement: 6 April 2015.

[2.1919]

58 Work does not include work relating to family business

"Work" does not include any work done by a worker in relation to an employer's family business if the worker—

(a) is a member of the employer's family,

(b) resides in the family home of the employer, and

(c) participates in the running of the family business.

NOTES

Commencement: 6 April 2015.

PART 7
RECORDS

[2.1920]

59 Records to be kept by an employer

(1) The employer of a worker who qualifies for the national minimum wage must keep in respect of that worker records sufficient to establish that the employer is remunerating the worker at a rate at least equal to the national minimum wage.

(2) The records required to be kept under paragraph (1) are to be in a form which enables the information kept about a worker in respect of a pay reference period to be produced in a single document.

(3) The employer of a worker who does unmeasured work, and with whom the employer has entered into a daily average agreement in accordance with regulation 49, must keep a copy of that agreement.

(4) The employer of a worker who does output work, and has given the worker a notice in accordance with regulation 41(1)(d), must keep a copy of that notice and a copy of such data as is necessary to show how the average hourly output rate has been determined.

(5) The employer of a worker who qualifies for an agricultural minimum rate of wages must, in addition to the records the employer is required to keep under paragraphs (1), (3), and (4), keep as respects that worker sufficient records to establish that the employer is remunerating the worker at a rate at least equal to the agricultural minimum rate of wages applicable to the worker.

(6) In paragraph (5), "agricultural minimum rate of wages" means—

(a) in Wales, a minimum rate of wages fixed under section 4 of the Agricultural Sector (Wales) Act 2014;

(b) in Scotland, a minimum rate of wages fixed under section 3(1)(a) of the Agricultural Wages (Scotland) Act 1949;

(c) in Northern Ireland, a minimum rate of wages fixed under Article 4(1) of the Agricultural Wages (Regulation) (Northern Ireland) Order 1977.

(7) Where under paragraph (5) an employer is required to keep records in respect of a worker in addition to those the employer is required to keep under paragraph (1), those additional records are to be in a form which enables the information kept under paragraph (5) about a worker in respect of a pay reference period to be produced in a single document.

(8) The records required to be kept by this regulation must be kept by the employer for a period of three years beginning with the day upon which the pay reference period immediately following that to which they relate ends.

(9) The records required to be kept by this regulation may be kept by means of a computer.

NOTES

Commencement: 6 April 2015.

SCHEDULE
REVOCATIONS

(*This Schedule revokes the National Minimum Wage Regulations 1999, SI 1999/584 and subsequent Regulations that amended it.*)

HEALTH AND SAFETY AT WORK ETC ACT 1974 (GENERAL DUTIES OF SELF-EMPLOYED PERSONS) (PRESCRIBED UNDERTAKINGS) REGULATIONS 2015

(SI 2015/1583)

NOTES

Made: 3 August 2015.
Authority: Health and Safety at Work etc Act 1974, ss 3(2), (2A), 53(1), 82(3)(a).
Commencement: 1 October 2015.

[2.1921]
1 Citation and commencement

(1) These Regulations may be cited as the Health and Safety at Work etc Act 1974 (General Duties of Self-Employed Persons) (Prescribed Undertakings) Regulations 2015.

(2) These Regulations come into force on 1st October 2015.

NOTES

Commencement: 1 October 2015.

[2.1922]
2 Prescribed descriptions of undertakings

An undertaking is of a prescribed description for the purposes of section 3(2) of the Health and Safety at Work etc Act 1974 if it involves the carrying out of any activity which—

(a) is listed in the Schedule; or
(b) where not listed in the Schedule, may pose a risk to the health and safety of another person (other than the self-employed person carrying it out or their employees).

NOTES

Commencement: 1 October 2015.

[2.1923]
3 Review

(1) Before the end of each review period, the Secretary of State must—

(a) carry out a review of these Regulations;
(b) set out the conclusions of the review in a report; and
(c) publish the report.

(2) The report must in particular—

(a) set out the objectives intended to be achieved by the regulatory system established by these Regulations;
(b) assess the extent to which those objectives are achieved; and
(c) assess whether those objectives remain appropriate, and, if so, the extent to which they could be achieved with a system that imposes less regulation.

(3) "Review period" means the period of five years beginning with the day on which these Regulations come into force.

NOTES

Commencement: 1 October 2015.

SCHEDULE
ACTIVITIES

Regulation 2

[2.1924]

1 Agriculture (including forestry)

Any work which is an agricultural activity (which is to be read in accordance with regulation 2(1) of the Health and Safety (Enforcing Authority) Regulations 1998).

2 Asbestos

(1) Any work with asbestos.

(2) Any work which—

(a) involves a sampling activity; but

(b) is not work with asbestos.

(3) Any activity carried out by a dutyholder under regulation 4 of the Control of Asbestos Regulations 2012 (the "2012 Regulations") (duty to manage asbestos in non-domestic premises).

(4) In this paragraph—

(a) "asbestos" has the meaning given in regulation 2 of the 2012 Regulations;

(b) "dutyholder" has the meaning given in regulation 4(1) of the 2012 Regulations;

(c) "sampling activity" means—

(i) air monitoring;

(ii) the collection of air samples; or

(iii) the analysis of air samples,

to ascertain whether asbestos fibres are present in the air, or to measure the concentration of such fibres; and

(d) "work with asbestos" is to be read in accordance with regulation 2(2) of the 2012 Regulations.

3 Construction

(1) Any work which is carried out on a construction site.

(2) Any work in relation to a project carried out by a designer, a client, a contractor, a principal contractor or a principal designer which gives rise to a duty under the Construction (Design and Management) Regulations 2015 ("the 2015 Regulations").

(3) In this paragraph—

(a) "client", "contractor", "designer", "principal contractor", "principal designer" and "project" have the meanings given in regulation 2(1) of the 2015 Regulations; and

(b) "construction site" is to be read in accordance with that regulation.

4 Gas

Any activity to which the Gas Safety (Installation and Use) Regulations 1998 apply.

5 Genetically modified organisms

Contained use within the meaning of regulation 2(1) of the Genetically Modified Organisms (Contained Use) Regulations 2014.

6 Railways

The operation of a railway (which is to be read in accordance with regulation 2 of the Health and Safety (Enforcing Authority for Railways and Other Guided Transport Systems) Regulations 2006).

NOTES

Commencement: 1 October 2015.

EXCLUSIVITY TERMS IN ZERO HOURS CONTRACTS (REDRESS) REGULATIONS 2015

(SI 2015/2021)

NOTES

Made: 14 December 2015.

Authority: Employment Rights Act 1996, ss 27B(1), (5), 209(1).

Commencement: 10 January 2016.

Conciliation: employment tribunal proceedings under reg 3 are "relevant proceedings" for the purposes of the conciliation provisions contained in the Employment Tribunals Act 1996, ss 18–18C; see s 18(1)(z3) of the 1996 Act at **[1.757]**.

ARRANGEMENT OF REGULATIONS

[2.1925]

1 Citation, commencement and interpretation

(1) These Regulations may be cited as the Exclusivity Terms in Zero Hours Contracts (Redress) Regulations 2015.

(2) These Regulations come into force at the end of the period of 28 days beginning with the day on which they are made.

(3) In these Regulations "the 1996 Act" means the Employment Rights Act 1996.

NOTES

Commencement: 10 January 2016.

[2.1926]

2 Unfair dismissal and the right not to be subjected to detriment

(1) An employee who works under a zero hours contract is to be regarded for the purposes of Part 10 of the 1996 Act as unfairly dismissed if the reason (or, if more than one, the principal reason) for the dismissal is the reason specified in paragraph (3).

(2) A worker who works under a zero hours contract has the right not to be subjected to any detriment by, or as a result of, any act, or any deliberate failure to act, of an employer done for the reason specified in paragraph (3).

(3) The reason is that the worker breached a provision or purported provision of the zero hours contract to which section 27A(3) of the 1996 Act applies.

(4) Paragraph (2) does not apply where the detriment in question amounts to a dismissal of an employee within the meaning of Part 10 of the 1996 Act.

(5) Section 108 of the 1996 Act (qualifying period of employment) does not apply in relation to a dismissal to which paragraph (1) applies.

NOTES

Commencement: 10 January 2016.

[2.1927]

3 Complaints to employment tribunals

(1) Subject to regulation 2(4), a worker may present a complaint to an employment tribunal that an employer has infringed the right conferred on the worker by regulation 2(2).

(2) Subject to paragraph (3), an employment tribunal must not consider a complaint under this regulation unless it is presented before the end of the period of three months beginning with the date of the act or failure to act to which the complaint relates or, where that act or failure is part of a series of similar acts or failures, the last of them.

[(2A) Regulation 3A (extension of time limit to facilitate conciliation before institution of proceedings) applies for the purposes of paragraph (2).]

(3) A tribunal may consider any such complaint which is out of time if, in all the circumstances of the case, it considers that it is just and equitable to do so.

(4) For the purposes of paragraph (2)—

(a) where an act extends over a period, the "date of the act" means the last day of that period; and

(b) failure to do something is to be treated as occurring when the person in question decided on it.

(5) In the absence of evidence to the contrary, a person (P) is to be taken to decide on failure to do something—

(a) when P does an act inconsistent with doing it, or

(b) if P does no inconsistent act, on the expiry of the period in which P might reasonably have been expected to do it.

(6) Where a worker presents a complaint under this regulation it is for the employer to identify the ground on which any act, or deliberate failure to act, was done.

NOTES

Commencement: 10 January 2016.

Para (2A): inserted by the Employment Tribunals Act 1996 (Application of Conciliation Provisions) Order 2015, SI 2015/2054, art 3(1), (2), as from 11 January 2016.

Conciliation: employment tribunal proceedings under this regulation are "relevant proceedings" for the purposes of the conciliation provisions contained in the Employment Tribunals Act 1996, ss 18–18C; see s 18(1), (z3) of the 1996 Act at **[1.757]**.

[2.1928]

[3A Extension of time limit to facilitate conciliation before institution of proceedings]

[(1) In this regulation—

(a) Day A is the day on which the worker concerned complies with the requirement in subsection (1) of section 18A of the Employment Tribunals Act 1996 (requirement to contact ACAS before instituting proceedings) in relation to the matter in respect of which the proceedings are brought, and

(b) Day B is the day on which the worker concerned receives or, if earlier, is treated as receiving (by virtue of regulations made under subsection (11) of that section) the certificate issued under subsection (4) of that section.

(2) In working out when the time limit set by regulation 3(2) expires the period beginning with the day after Day A and ending with Day B is not to be counted.

(3) If the time limit set by regulation 3(2) would (if not extended by this paragraph) expire during the period beginning with Day A and ending one month after Day B, the time limit expires instead at the end of that period.

(4) The power conferred on the employment tribunal by regulation 3(3) to extend the time limit set by paragraph (2) of that regulation is exercisable in relation to that time limit as extended by this regulation.]

NOTES

Commencement: 11 January 2016.

Inserted by the Employment Tribunals Act 1996 (Application of Conciliation Provisions) Order 2015, SI 2015/2054, art 3(1), (3), as from 11 January 2016.

[2.1929]

4 Remedies

(1) Where an employment tribunal finds that a complaint presented to it under regulation 3 is well founded, it must take such of the following steps as it considers just and equitable—

(a) making a declaration as to the rights of the complainant and the employer in relation to the matters to which the complaint relates; and

(b) ordering the employer to pay compensation to the complainant.

(2) Subject to paragraphs (5) and (6), where a tribunal orders compensation under paragraph (1)(b), the amount of the compensation awarded must be such as the tribunal considers just and equitable in all the circumstances having regard to—

(a) the infringement to which the complaint relates; and

(b) any loss which is attributable to the act, or failure to act, which infringed the complainant's right.

(3) The loss must be taken to include—

(a) any expenses reasonably incurred by the complainant in consequence of the act, or failure to act, to which the complaint relates; and

(b) loss of any benefit which the complainant might reasonably be expected to have had but for that act or failure to act.

(4) In ascertaining the loss the tribunal must apply the same rule concerning the duty of a person to mitigate loss as applies to damages recoverable under the common law of England and Wales or (as the case may be) the law of Scotland.

(5) Where—

(a) the detriment to which the worker is subjected is the termination of the worker's contract, but

(b) that contract is not a contract of employment,

any compensation awarded under paragraph (1)(b) must not exceed the limit specified in paragraph (6).

(6) The limit is the total of—

(a) the sum which would be the basic award for unfair dismissal, calculated in accordance with section 119 of the 1996 Act, if the worker had been an employee and the contract terminated had been a contract of employment; and

(b) the sum for the time being specified in section 124(1ZA) of the 1996 Act which is the limit for a compensatory award to a person calculated in accordance with section 123 of the 1996 Act.

(7) Where the tribunal finds that the act, or failure to act, to which the complaint relates was to any extent caused or contributed to by action of the complainant, it must reduce the amount of the compensation by such proportion as it considers just and equitable having regard to that finding.

NOTES

Commencement: 10 January 2016.

[2.1930]

5 Review

(1) The Secretary of State must from time to time—

(a) carry out a review of regulations 2 to 4;

(b) set out the conclusions of the review in a report; and

(c) publish the report.

(2) The report must in particular—

(a) set out the objectives intended to be achieved by the regulatory system established by those regulations;

(b) assess the extent to which those objectives are achieved; and

(c) assess whether those objectives remain appropriate and, if so, the extent to which they could be achieved with a system that imposes less regulation.

(3) The first report under this regulation must be published before the end of the period of five years beginning with the day on which regulations 2 to 4 come into force.

(4) Reports under this regulation are afterwards to be published at intervals not exceeding five years.

NOTES

Commencement: 10 January 2016.

HEALTH AND SAFETY AND NUCLEAR (FEES) REGULATIONS 2016

(SI 2016/253)

NOTES

Made: 2 March 2016.

Authority: European Communities Act 1972, s 2(2); Health and Safety at Work etc Act 1974, ss 43(2), (4), (5), (6), 82(3)(a); Energy Act 2013, ss 101(1), (2), (3), 113(1), (6), (7).

Commencement: 6 April 2016.

Note: with regard to the authority for these Regulations, note that the European Communities Act 1972 is repealed by the European Union (Withdrawal) Act 2018, s 1, as from exit day (as defined in s 20 of that Act); but note also that provision is made for the continuation in force of any subordinate legislation made under the authority of s 2(2) of the 1972 Act by s 2 of the 2018 Act at **[1.2240]**, subject to the provisions of s 5 of, and Sch 1 to, the 2018 Act at **[1.2243]**, **[1.2253]**.

Only those provisions of these Regulations relevant to employment law are reproduced.

ARRANGEMENT OF REGULATIONS

[2.1931]

1 Citation, commencement and extent

(1) These Regulations may be cited as the Health and Safety and Nuclear (Fees) Regulations 2016 and come into force on 6th April 2016.

(2) These Regulations cease to have effect at the end of the period of five years beginning on 6th April 2016.

(3) These Regulations extend to Great Britain.

NOTES

Commencement: 6 April 2016.

[2.1932]

2 Interpretation

(1) In these Regulations—

"the 1974 Act" means the Health and Safety at Work etc Act 1974;

"the 2013 Act" means the Energy Act 2013;

["the 2017 Regulations" means the Ionising Radiations Regulations 2017 (SI 2017/1075);]

"the 2012 Asbestos Regulations" means the Control of Asbestos Regulations 2012;

"the 2013 Biocidal Products and Chemicals Regulations" means the Biocidal Products and Chemicals (Appointment of Authorities and Enforcement) Regulations 2013;

"the 2014 GMO Regulations" means the Genetically Modified Organisms (Contained Use) Regulations 2014;

"approval" includes the amendment of an approval, and "amendment of an approval" includes the issue of a new approval replacing the original and incorporating one or more amendments;

"employment medical adviser" means an employment medical adviser appointed under section 56(1) of the 1974 Act;

"the ONR" means the Office for Nuclear Regulation;

"original approval" and "original type approval" do not include an amendment of an approval; and

"working days" does not include weekends or public holidays.

(2) Any reference in these Regulations to the renewal of an approval, explosives certificate or licence (each referred to in this paragraph as an "authorisation") means the granting of the authorisation concerned to follow a previous authorisation of the same kind without any amendment or gap in time.

NOTES

Commencement: 6 April 2016.

Para (1): definition "the 2017 Regulations" substituted (for the original definition "the 1999 Regulations") by the Ionising Radiations Regulations 2017, SI 2017/1075, reg 42(1), Sch 9, para 16(1), (2), as from 1 January 2018.

3-21A (*Outside the scope of this work.*)

[2.1933]
22 Fees for intervention

(1) Subject to regulation 23, if—

(a) a person is contravening or has contravened one or more of the relevant statutory provisions for which the Executive is the enforcing authority; and

(b) an inspector is of the opinion that that person is doing so or has done so, and notifies that person in writing of that opinion,

a fee is payable by that person to the Executive for its performance of the functions described in paragraphs (2) and (3).

(2) The fee referred to in paragraph (1) is payable for the performance by the Executive of any function conferred on it by the relevant statutory provisions, in consequence of any contravention referred to in the opinion notified to that person pursuant to paragraph (1)(b).

(3) Where, during a site-visit, an inspector forms the opinion that a person is contravening or has contravened one or more of the relevant statutory provisions, the fee referred to in paragraph (1) is payable for the performance by the Executive, during that site-visit, of any function conferred on it by the relevant statutory provisions for which no fee is payable by virtue of paragraph (2).

(4) For the purposes of paragraphs (6) and (7) and regulations 23 and 24, "fee for intervention" means the fee described in paragraphs (1) to (3).

(5) An inspector of the opinion that a person is contravening or has contravened one or more of the relevant statutory provisions must have regard, when deciding whether to notify that person in writing of that opinion, to the guidance entitled "HSE 47—Guidance on the application of Fee for Intervention" (1st edition) approved by the Executive on 11th June 2012.

(6) A written notification under paragraph (1) must—

(a) specify the provision or provisions to which that inspector's opinion relates;

(b) give particulars of the reasons for that opinion; and

(c) inform the person to whom it is given that fee for intervention is payable to the Executive in accordance with this regulation and regulation 23.

(7) Fee for intervention is payable by a person in respect of the functions described in paragraph (3) only to the extent that the performance of any such function by the Executive is reasonably attributable to that person.

NOTES

Commencement: 6 April 2016.

[2.1934]
23 Provisions supplementary to regulation 22

(1) Fee for intervention is not to exceed the sum of the costs reasonably incurred by the Executive for its performance of the functions referred to in paragraphs (2) and (3) of regulation 22.

(2) Fee for intervention is payable within 30 days from the date of each invoice that the Executive has sent or given to the person who must pay that fee, and such invoices must include a statement of the work done and the costs incurred, including the period to which the statement relates.

(3) No fee for intervention is payable by a person to the extent that an opinion of an inspector that that person is contravening or has contravened one or more of the relevant statutory provisions relates to any contravention which, having regard to the guidance specified in regulation 22(5), should not have been notified in writing to that person.

(4) No fee for intervention is payable in relation to any contravention of the relevant statutory provisions in consequence of which the Executive performed any function prior to the day on which the Health and Safety (Fees) Regulations 2012 came into force.

(5) No fee for intervention is payable for the performance by any inspector not employed by the Executive of any function conferred on it by the relevant statutory provisions.

(6) No fee for intervention payable for or in connection with any contravention of the relevant statutory provisions is to include any costs connected with—

(a) in England and Wales, any criminal investigation or prosecution, incurred (in either case) from the date on which any information is laid or, as the case may be, any written charge is issued;

(b) in Scotland, any criminal investigation or prosecution, incurred (in either case) after such time as the Executive submits a report to the Procurator Fiscal for a decision as to whether a prosecution should be brought;

(c) any appeal pursuant to section 24 of the 1974 Act (appeal against improvement or prohibition notice) and Schedule 1 to the Employment Tribunals (Constitution and Rules of Procedure) Regulations 2013; or

(d) any functions performed from the date on which the Executive formally notifies a person that, but for section 48(1) of the 1974 Act, it would have commenced a criminal prosecution against that person in relation to any such contravention.

(7) No fee for intervention is payable by a person in respect of any contravention of the relevant statutory provisions by that person in his or her capacity as an employee.

(8) No fee for intervention is payable by a self-employed person in respect of any contravention by that self-employed person of the relevant statutory provisions which does not and did not expose any other person to a health or safety risk.

(9) No fee for intervention is payable for the performance by the Executive of any function conferred on it by the relevant statutory provisions to the extent that, in respect of any such function, another fee is payable or has been paid.

(10) No fee for intervention is payable for the performance by the Executive of any function conferred on it by the relevant statutory provisions in respect of which fee for intervention is payable or has been paid in consequence of an opinion previously notified in accordance with paragraphs (1), (5) and (6) of regulation 22.

(11) No fee for intervention is payable in respect of any contravention of the relevant statutory provisions which relates to any contained use.

(12) In paragraph (11), "contained use" has the same meaning as in the 2014 GMO Regulations.

(13) No fee for intervention is payable in respect of any contravention of the relevant statutory provisions which relates to any of the activities specified in paragraph 3(3) of Part 1 of Schedule 3 to the Control of Substances Hazardous to Health Regulations 2002.

(14) No fee for intervention is payable by a person who holds a licence to undertake work with asbestos in respect of any contravention of the relevant statutory provisions which relates to licensable work with asbestos.

(15) In paragraph (14), "licensable work with asbestos" has the same meaning as in the 2012 Asbestos Regulations, and "work with asbestos" is to be construed in accordance with regulation 2(2) of those Regulations.

(16) No fee for intervention is payable for the performance by the Executive of any function conferred on the Executive by—

(a) the Control of Major Accident Hazards Regulations 2015;
(b) the Chemicals (Hazard Information and Packaging for Supply) Regulations 2009;
(c) the 2013 Biocidal Products and Chemicals Regulations; and
(d) the 2014 GMO Regulations.

NOTES

Commencement: 6 April 2016.

[2.1935]
24 Repayments and disputes

(1) Subject to paragraph (2), if a person is—

(a) charged with, but not convicted of, a criminal offence; or
(b) served with an enforcement notice that is subsequently cancelled,

the Executive must repay such part of any fee for intervention paid as is wholly and exclusively attributable to the performance by the Executive of functions relating only to that criminal offence or, as the case may be, that enforcement notice.

(2) If—

(a) a person is charged with, but not convicted of, more than one criminal offence; or
(b) two or more enforcement notices served on a person are subsequently cancelled,

the Executive must repay such part of any fee for intervention paid as is wholly and exclusively attributable to the performance by the Executive of functions relating only to the criminal offences of which that person is not convicted or, as the case may be, the enforcement notices that are cancelled.

(3) Where all or part of any fee for intervention paid to the Executive was paid in error, the Executive must repay that fee for intervention or, as the case may be, that part of that fee for intervention.

(4) Where a person has been charged with one or more criminal offences or served with one or more enforcement notices, that person is not obliged to pay fee for intervention to the extent that that fee, when paid, would be repayable in accordance with paragraph (1) or (2) because—

(a) that person has not been convicted of one or more of those criminal offences; or
(b) one or more of those enforcement notices has been cancelled.

(5) The Executive must provide a procedure by which disputes relating to fee for intervention will be considered.

(6) If a dispute relating to fee for intervention is not upheld, the fee for intervention payable is to include costs reasonably incurred by the Executive in handling the dispute.

(7) For the purposes of this regulation, "enforcement notice" means an improvement notice or a prohibition notice.

NOTES

Commencement: 6 April 2016.

[2.1936]
25 Review

(1) Before the end of the review period, the Secretary of State must—

(a) carry out a review of these Regulations;
(b) set out the conclusions in a report; and
(c) publish the report.

(2) The report must in particular—
(a) set out the objectives intended to be achieved by the regulatory system established by these Regulations;
(b) assess the extent to which those objectives are achieved; and
(c) assess whether those objectives remain appropriate and, if so, the extent to which they could be achieved with a system that imposes less regulation.

(3) For the purposes of this regulation "review period" means the period of three years beginning with the 6th April 2016.

NOTES

Commencement: 6 April 2016.

26 (*Revokes the Health and Safety and Nuclear (Fees) Regulations 2015, SI 2015/363 and contains other provision that is outside the scope of this work.*)

SCHEDULES 1–16

(*Schedules 1–16 contain fees tables for applications under various sets of Regulations etc, and are outside the scope of this work.*)

POSTED WORKERS (ENFORCEMENT OF EMPLOYMENT RIGHTS) REGULATIONS 2016

(SI 2016/539)

NOTES

Made: 25 April 2016.

Authority: Employment Tribunals Act 1996, s 18(8), (9); European Communities Act 1972, s 2(2).

Commencement: 18 June 2016.

Note: with regard to the authority for these Regulations, note that the European Communities Act 1972 is repealed by the European Union (Withdrawal) Act 2018, s 1, as from exit day (as defined in s 20 of that Act); but note also that provision is made for the continuation in force of any subordinate legislation made under the authority of s 2(2) of the 1972 Act by s 2 of the 2018 Act at **[1.2240]**, subject to the provisions of s 5 of, and Sch 1 to, the 2018 Act at **[1.2243]**, **[1.2253]**.

Conciliation: employment tribunal proceedings under reg 6 are "relevant proceedings" for the purposes of the conciliation provisions contained in the Employment Tribunals Act 1996, ss 18–18C; see s 18(1), (z4) of the 1996 Act at **[1.757]**.

ARRANGEMENT OF REGULATIONS

PART 1
GENERAL

PART 1
GENERAL

[2.1937]

1 Citation, commencement and extent

(1) These Regulations may be cited as the Posted Workers (Enforcement of Employment Rights) Regulations 2016 and come into force on 18th June 2016.

(2) These Regulations extend to England, Wales and Scotland.

NOTES

Commencement: 18 June 2016.

[2.1938]

2 Interpretation

In these Regulations—

"Directive 96/71/EC" means Council Directive 96/71/EC of 16 December 1996 concerning the posting of workers in the framework of the provision of services;

"Directive 2014/67/EU" means Council Directive 2014/67/EU of the European Parliament and the Council on the enforcement of Directive 96/71/EC concerning the posting of workers in the framework of the provision of services and amending Regulation (EU) No 1024/2012 on administrative cooperation through the Internal Market Information System ('the IMI Regulation').

NOTES

Commencement: 18 June 2016.

[2.1939]

3 Review

(1) The Secretary of State must from time to time—

(a) carry out a review of these Regulations,

(b) set out the conclusions of the review in a report, and

(c) publish the report.

(2) In carrying out the review the Secretary of State must, so far as is reasonable, have regard to what is done in other Member States to implement Directive 2014/67/EU.

(3) The report must in particular—

(a) set out the objectives intended to be achieved by the regulatory system established by those Regulations,

(b) assess the extent to which those objectives are achieved, and

(c) assess whether those objectives remain appropriate and, if so, the extent to which they could be achieved with a system that imposes less regulation.

(4) The first report under this regulation must be published before the end of the period of five years beginning with the day on which these Regulations come into force.

(5) Reports under this regulation are afterwards to be published at intervals not exceeding five years.

NOTES

Commencement: 18 June 2016.

PART 2
POSTED WORKERS IN THE CONSTRUCTION SECTOR

[2.1940]

4 Scope of application of this Part

(1) This regulation and regulations 5 to 9 apply to a posted worker in the construction sector who—

(a) is working or has worked in Great Britain; and

(b) is working or has worked for the employer to perform services that relate to the employer's contractual obligations to the contractor.

(2) For the purposes of this regulation and regulations 5 to 9—

"contractor" means a person with whom the employer has contracted to provide services;

"employer" means a service provider established in a Member State which posts or hires out workers in accordance with paragraph 3 of Article 1 of Directive 96/71/EC;

"posted worker in the construction sector" means a worker who—

(a) normally works in a Member State *other than the United Kingdom* but, for a limited period, carries out work on behalf of the employer in Great Britain; and

(b) undertakes building work relating to the construction, repair, upkeep, alteration or demolition of buildings including any of the following—

(i) excavation;

(ii) earthmoving;

(iii) actual building work;

(iv) assembly and dismantling of prefabricated elements;

(v) fitting out or installations;

(vi) alterations;

(vii) renovation;

(viii) repairs;

(ix) dismantling;

(x) demolition;

(xi) maintenance;

(xii) upkeep, painting and cleaning work; and

(xiii) improvements.

[(3) For the purposes of the definition of "employer" in paragraph (2), paragraph 3 of Article 1 of Directive 96/71/EC is to be read as if—

(a) in point (a)—

(i) after "post workers to" there were inserted "the United Kingdom or";
(ii) after "operating in" there were inserted "the United Kingdom or";
(b) in point (b), after "by the group in" there were inserted "the United Kingdom or";
(c) in point (c), after "operating in" there were inserted "the United Kingdom or".]

NOTES

Commencement: 18 June 2016.

Para (2): definition "employer" substituted as follows, and words in italics in definition "posted worker in the construction sector" revoked, by the Employment Rights (Amendment) (EU Exit) Regulations 2019, SI 2019/535, reg 2(1), Sch 1, Pt 2, paras 19, 20(1), (2), as from exit day (as defined in the European Union (Withdrawal) Act 2018, s 20)—

""employer" means a service provider established in the United Kingdom or a Member State which posts or hires out workers in a manner described by paragraph 3 of Article 1 of Directive 96/71/EC;".

Para (3): added by SI 2019/535, reg 2(1), Sch 1, Pt 2, paras 19, 20(1), (3), as from exit day (as defined in the European Union (Withdrawal) Act 2018, s 20).

[2.1941]

5 Right not to suffer unauthorised deductions

(1) This regulation applies if a posted worker in the construction sector is remunerated by the employer for any pay reference period commencing on or after the date these Regulations come into force at a rate that is less than the national minimum wage.

(2) The contractor is to be treated for the purpose of these Regulations as having made an unauthorised deduction of the relevant sum from the worker's wages.

(3) In this regulation and in regulation 6 the "relevant sum" means the proportion of the amount due to the worker as additional remuneration in respect of the pay reference period, calculated in accordance with section 17 of the National Minimum Wage Act 1998 (non-compliance: worker entitled to additional remuneration), which is the same as the proportion of the pay reference period during which the worker carried out work relating to the employer's obligations to the contractor.

(4) In this regulation—

"national minimum wage" has the same meaning as in the National Minimum Wage Act 1998;

"pay reference period" has the meaning given by regulation 6 of the National Minimum Wage Regulations 2015.

NOTES

Commencement: 18 June 2016.

[2.1942]

6 Complaints to employment tribunals

(1) A posted worker in the construction sector may present a complaint against a contractor to an employment tribunal that the contractor is to be treated as having made an unauthorised deduction of the relevant sum from the worker's wages by virtue of regulation 5(2).

(2) Paragraph (1) does not apply to a posted worker in the construction sector who has—
(a) presented a claim against the employer under section 23(1)(a) of the Employment Rights Act 1996 (deductions from worker's wages in contravention of section 13 of that Act) to an employment tribunal in respect of the sum due; or
(b) commenced other civil proceedings against the employer for the recovery, on a claim in contract, of the sum due.

(3) In any complaint brought under paragraph (1), it is a defence for the contractor to show that it exercised all due diligence to ensure that the worker's employer would remunerate the worker in respect of the relevant sum due to the worker.

(4) Subject to paragraph (6) and regulation 7 (extension of time limit to facilitate conciliation), an employment tribunal must not consider a complaint under this regulation unless it is presented before the end of the period of three months beginning with the date of payment of the relevant wages from which the deduction was made.

(5) Where a complaint is brought under this regulation in respect of a series of deductions, the reference in paragraph (4) to the deduction is to the last deduction in the series.

(6) Where the employment tribunal is satisfied that it was not reasonably practicable for a complaint under this regulation to be presented before the end of the relevant period of three months, the tribunal may consider the complaint if it is presented within such further period as the tribunal considers reasonable.

(7) An employment tribunal is not (despite paragraphs (5) and (6)) to consider so much of a complaint brought under this regulation as relates to a deduction where the date of payment of the relevant sum from which the deduction was made was before the period of two years ending with the date of presentation of the complaint.

(8) A posted worker in the construction sector who presents a complaint under this regulation is prohibited from—
(a) presenting a complaint against the employer under section 23(1)(a) of the Employment Rights Act 1996 (deductions from worker's wages in contravention of section 13 of that Act) to an employment tribunal in respect of the sum due; or

(b) commencing other civil proceedings against the employer for the recovery, on a claim in contract, of the sum due,

unless the tribunal dismisses the complaint under this regulation in accordance with paragraph (3).

NOTES

Commencement: 18 June 2016.

Conciliation: employment tribunal proceedings under this regulation are "relevant proceedings" for the purposes of the conciliation provisions contained in the Employment Tribunals Act 1996, ss 18–18C; see s 18(1), (z4) of the 1996 Act at [1.757].

[2.1943]

7 Extension of time limits to facilitate conciliation before institution of proceedings

(1) In this regulation—

(a) Day A is the day on which the posted worker in the construction sector complies with the requirement in subsection (1) of section 18A of the Employment Tribunals Act 1996 (requirement to contact ACAS before instituting proceedings) in relation to the matter in respect of which the proceedings are brought, and

(b) Day B is the day on which that worker receives or, if earlier, is treated as receiving (by virtue of regulations made under subsection (11) of that section) the certificate issued under subsection (4) of that section.

(2) In working out when the time limit set by regulation 6(4) expires, the period beginning with the day after Day A and ending with Day B is not to be counted.

(3) If the time limit set by regulation 6(4) would (if not extended by this paragraph) expire during the period beginning with Day A and ending one month after Day B, the time limit expires instead at the end of that period.

(4) The power conferred on the employment tribunal by regulation 6(6) to extend the time limit set by paragraph (4) of that regulation is exercisable in relation to that time limit as extended by this regulation.

NOTES

Commencement: 18 June 2016.

[2.1944]

8 Determination of complaints

(1) Where a tribunal finds a complaint under regulation 6 well-founded, it must make a declaration to that effect and must order the contractor to pay to the worker the relevant sum treated as deducted by the contractor from the worker's wages.

(2) Where a tribunal makes a declaration under paragraph (1), it may order the contractor to pay to the worker (in addition to any amount ordered to be paid under that paragraph) such amount as the tribunal considers appropriate in all the circumstances to compensate the worker for any financial loss sustained by the worker which is attributable to the matter complained of.

(3) Where, in the case of a complaint made under regulation 6, a tribunal finds that, although neither of the conditions set out in section 13(1)(a) and (b) of the Employment Rights Act 1996 was satisfied with respect to the whole amount of the deduction, one of those conditions was satisfied with respect to any lesser amount, the amount of the deduction must for the purposes of paragraph (1) be treated as reduced by the amount with respect to which that condition was satisfied.

(4) A tribunal may not order a contractor to pay or to repay to the worker any amount in respect of a deduction, or in respect of any combination of deductions, in so far as it appears to the tribunal that the contractor or the worker's employer has already paid or repaid any such amount to the worker.

NOTES

Commencement: 18 June 2016.

[2.1945]

9 Restrictions on contracting out

(1) Any provision in an agreement (whether a contract of employment or not) is void in so far as it purports—

(a) to exclude or limit the operation of any provision of these Regulations, or

(b) to preclude a person from bringing proceedings under these Regulations before an employment tribunal.

(2) Paragraph (1) does not apply to—

(a) any agreement to refrain from instituting or continuing proceedings where a conciliation officer has taken action under any of sections 18A to 18C of the Employment Tribunals Act 1996 (conciliation); or

(b) any agreement to refrain from instituting or continuing proceedings if the conditions regulating settlement agreements under these Regulations are satisfied in relation to the agreement.

(3) For the purposes of paragraph (2)(b) the conditions regulating settlement agreements under these Regulations are that—

(a) the agreement must be in writing;

(b) the agreement must relate to the particular complaint;

(c) the worker must have received advice from a relevant independent adviser as to the terms and effect of the proposed agreement and, in particular, its effect on the ability of the worker to pursue the worker's rights before an employment tribunal;
(d) there must be in force, when the adviser gives the advice, a contract of insurance, or an indemnity provided for members of a profession or professional body, covering the risk of a claim by the worker in respect of loss arising in consequence of the advice;
(e) the agreement must identify the adviser; and
(f) the agreement must state that the conditions regulating settlement agreements under these Regulations are satisfied.

(4) For the purposes of paragraph (3)(c) a "relevant independent adviser" is a person who is any of the following—
(a) a qualified lawyer;
(b) an officer, official, employee or member of an independent trade union who has been certified in writing by the trade union as competent to give advice and as authorised to do so on behalf of the trade union;
(c) an advice centre worker (including a volunteer) who has been certified in writing by the centre as competent to give advice and as authorised to do so on behalf of the centre,

but this is subject to paragraph (5).

(5) A person is not a relevant independent adviser for the purposes of paragraph (3)(c) in relation to the worker in any of the following cases—
(a) if the person is, is employed by, or is acting in the matter for, the employer or an associated employer;
(b) in the case of a person within paragraph (4)(b) or (c), if the trade union or advice centre is the employer or an associated employer;
(c) in the case of a person within paragraph (4)(c), if the worker makes a payment for the advice received.

(6) In paragraph (4)(a) "qualified lawyer" means any of the following—
(a) as respects England and Wales a person who, for the purposes of the Legal Services Act 2007, is an authorised person in relation to an activity which constitutes the exercise of a right of audience or the conduct of litigation (within the meaning of that Act), and
(b) as respects Scotland, an advocate (whether in practice as such or employed to give legal advice) or a solicitor who holds a practising certificate.

(7) In paragraph (4)(b) "independent trade union" means a trade union (within the meaning given by section 1 of the Trade Union and Labour Relations (Consolidation) Act 1992) which—
(a) is not under the domination or control of an employer or a group of employers or of one or more employers' associations, and
(b) is not liable to interference by an employer or any such group or association (arising out of the provision of financial or material support or by any other means whatever) tending towards such control.

(8) For the purposes of paragraph (5) any two employers are "associated" if—
(a) one is a company of which the other (directly or indirectly) has control; or
(b) both are companies of which a third person (directly or indirectly) has control.

NOTES

Commencement: 18 June 2016.

10 (*Amends the Employment Tribunals Act 1996, s 18(1) at* **[1.757]**.)

PART 3
CROSS-BORDER ENFORCEMENT AND DISCLOSURE OF INFORMATION

[2.1946]

11 Cross-border enforcement of financial administrative penalties and fines

(1) An amount payable in pursuance of an EU penalty is recoverable—
(a) in England and Wales, if the county court so orders, under section 85 of the County Courts Act 1984 or otherwise as if the sum were payable under an order of that court;
(b) in Scotland, by diligence as if the sum were an extract registered decree arbitral bearing a warrant for execution issued by the sheriff court of any sheriffdom in Scotland.

(2) Where a competent authority in a Member State *other than the United Kingdom* requests that the Secretary of State recover an EU penalty, the Secretary of State is entitled to recover the amount of any sum owing as part of that EU penalty.

(3) For the purposes of this regulation—

"EU penalty" means a financial administrative penalty or fine including fees and surcharges relating to non-compliance with Directive 96/71/EC or Directive 2014/67/EU—
(a) imposed on a service provider established in the United Kingdom by a competent authority in a Member State *other than the United Kingdom*; or
(b) confirmed by an administrative or judicial body in a Member State other than the United Kingdom as payable by a service provider established in the United Kingdom;

"competent authority" means a competent authority designated by a Member State *other than the United Kingdom* for the purposes of Directive 2014/67/EU.

(4) Any amount received by the Secretary of State under this Part is to be paid into the Consolidated Fund.

NOTES

Commencement: 18 June 2016.

Words in italics revoked by the Employment Rights (Amendment) (EU Exit) Regulations 2019, SI 2019/535, reg 2(1), Sch 1, Pt 2, paras 19, 21, as from exit day (as defined in the European Union (Withdrawal) Act 2018, s 20).

[2.1947]

12 Disclosure of information held by Revenue and Customs

(1) This regulation applies to information which is held by or on behalf of the Revenue and Customs, including information obtained before the coming into force of this regulation.

(2) No obligation of secrecy imposed by statute or otherwise prevents the disclosure, in accordance with this regulation, of information if the disclosure is made for the purposes of replying to reasoned requests for information made by a competent authority of another Member State in accordance with Article 6 of Directive 2014/67/EU.

(3) The information must not be disclosed except by the Revenue and Customs as defined in section 17(3) of the Commissioners for Revenue and Customs Act 2005.

(4) Information obtained by means of a disclosure authorised by paragraph (2) must not be further disclosed except for the purpose mentioned in that paragraph.

(5) Nothing in this regulation authorises the making of any disclosure which is prohibited by any provision of the Data Protection Act 1998.

(6) Nothing in this regulation must be taken to prejudice any power to disclose information which exists apart from this regulation.

NOTES

Commencement: 18 June 2016.

ILLEGAL WORKING COMPLIANCE ORDERS REGULATIONS 2016

(SI 2016/1058)

NOTES

Made: 2 November 2016.

Authority: Immigration Act 2016, Sch 6, para 5(6).

Commencement: 1 December 2016.

ARRANGEMENT OF REGULATIONS

SCHEDULES

[2.1948]

1 Citation and commencement

(1) These Regulations may be cited as the Illegal Working Compliance Orders Regulations 2016.

(2) These Regulations come into force on 1st December 2016.

NOTES

Commencement: 1 December 2016.

[2.1949]
2 Interpretation

In these Regulations—

"administrative review" means review conducted under the immigration rules;

"biometric immigration document" has the same meaning as in section 5 of the UK Borders Act 2007;

"derivative right of residence" has the same meaning as in regulation 15A of the Immigration (European Economic Area) Regulations 2006;

"document" means an original document;

["employee", except in regulations 4(2), 4(3), 5A(2) and 5A(3), includes a reference to a prospective employee;]

["Home Office online right to work checking service" means the electronic system allowing employers to check whether a person is allowed to work in the United Kingdom and, if so, the nature of any restrictions on that person's right to do so;]

"immigration rules" has the same meaning as in section 33 of the Immigration Act 1971;

["online right to work check" means the response generated by the Home Office online right to work checking service in relation to a person;]

"Positive Verification Notice" means a document issued by the Home Office Employer Checking Service which indicates that the person named in it is allowed to stay in the United Kingdom and is allowed to do the work in question;

"registration certificate" means a certificate issued to a national of an EEA state or Switzerland as proof of the holder's right of residence in the United Kingdom as at the date of issue;

"relevant person" means a person required to comply with these Regulations by virtue of an illegal working compliance order;

"residence card" means a card issued to a person who is not a national of an EEA state or Switzerland as proof of the holder's right of residence in the United Kingdom as at the date of issue.

NOTES

Commencement: 1 December 2016.

Definition "employee" substituted and definitions "Home Office online right to work checking service" and "online right to work check" inserted, by the Immigration (Restrictions on Employment) (Code of Practice and Miscellaneous Amendments) Order 2018, SI 2018/1340, art 3(1), (2), as from 28 January 2019.

[2.1950]
3 Obligation to conduct right to work checks

Where an illegal working compliance order requires a person to carry out checks relating to the right to work in accordance with these Regulations, the person must comply with [any of regulations 4, 5 or 5A] in respect of each of their employees within the scope of the order.

NOTES

Commencement: 1 December 2016.

Words in square brackets substituted by the Immigration (Restrictions on Employment) (Code of Practice and Miscellaneous Amendments) Order 2018, SI 2018/1340, art 3(1), (3), as from 28 January 2019.

[2.1951]
4 Right to work checks: prescribed documents

(1) A relevant person must—

(a) require the employee to produce to them a document or combination of documents relating to the employee described in Schedule 1 or 2; and

(b) comply with the requirements in regulation 6.

(2) Where a document or combination of documents described in Schedule 2 provides that the employment is permitted for a limited period, a relevant person is deemed to comply with this regulation for a further period if the relevant person is satisfied on reasonable grounds that—

(a) the employee has an outstanding application to vary his or her leave to enter or remain in the United Kingdom; or

(b) the employee has an appeal or administrative review pending against a decision on that application.

(3) In paragraph (2), the further period begins on the date on which the limited period expires and ends—

(a) after 28 days; or

(b) if earlier, on the date on which the Secretary of State gives the relevant person written notice that the employee does not have the right to undertake the employment in question.

NOTES

Commencement: 1 December 2016.

[2.1952]
5 Right to work checks: Positive Verification Notice

(1) A relevant person must—

(a) obtain a Positive Verification Notice in respect of the employee (subject to paragraph (2)); and

(b) comply, if applicable, with the requirement in regulation 6(2).

(2) A relevant person does not comply with this regulation if a period of more than six months has elapsed beginning with the date the Positive Verification Notice was obtained under paragraph (1)(a).

NOTES

Commencement: 1 December 2016.

[2.1953]

[5A Right to work checks: Home Office online right to work checking service

(1) A relevant person must—

(a) use the Home Office online right to work checking service in respect of an employee;

(b) obtain an online right to work check confirming that the employee named in it is allowed to work in the United Kingdom and is allowed to do the work in question;

(c) be satisfied that any photograph on the online right to work check is of the employee;

(d) retain a clear copy of the online right to work check for a period of not less than two years after the employment has come to an end; and

(e) comply, if applicable, with the requirement in regulation 6(2).

(2) Where the online right to work check provides that the employment is permitted for a limited period, a relevant person is deemed to comply with this regulation for a further period if the relevant person is satisfied on reasonable grounds that—

(a) the employee has an outstanding application to vary his or her leave to enter or remain in the United Kingdom; or

(b) the employee has an appeal or administrative review pending against a decision on that application.

(3) In paragraph (2), the further period begins on the date on which the limited period expires and ends—

(a) after 28 days; or

(b) if earlier, on the date on which the Secretary of State gives the relevant person written notice that the employee does not have the right to undertake the employment in question.]

NOTES

Commencement: 28 January 2019.

Inserted by the Immigration (Restrictions on Employment) (Code of Practice and Miscellaneous Amendments) Order 2018, SI 2018/1340, art 3(1), (4), as from 28 January 2019.

[2.1954]

6 Right to work checks: general requirements

(1) The requirements of this regulation are that—

(a) the relevant person takes all reasonable steps to check the validity of the document and retains a record of the date on which any check was made;

(b) a [clear] copy of that document or combination of documents is retained securely by the relevant person for the period during which the illegal working compliance order is in force;

(c) if a document contains a photograph purporting to be of the employee, the relevant person has satisfied himself that the photograph is of the employee;

(d) if a document contains a date of birth purporting to relate to the employee, the relevant person has satisfied himself that the date of birth is consistent with the appearance of the employee;

(e) the relevant person takes all other reasonable steps to verify that the employee is the rightful holder of the document;

(f) if the document is not a passport, the relevant person retains a [clear] copy of the whole of the document;

(g) if the document is a passport, the relevant person retains a [clear] copy of the following pages of that document—

(i) any page containing the holder's personal details including nationality;

(ii) any page containing the holder's photograph;

(iii) any page containing the holder's signature;

(iv) any page containing the date of expiry; and

(v) any page containing information indicating the holder has an entitlement to enter or remain in the United Kingdom and undertake the work in question.

(2) A further requirement, if the employee is a student who has permission to work for a limited number of hours per week during term time whilst studying in the United Kingdom, is that the relevant person must—

(a) require the employee to provide details of the term and vacation dates of the course that the employee is undertaking; and

(b) retain a record of these details.

NOTES

Commencement: 1 December 2016.

Para (1): word in square brackets in sub-paras (b), (f), (g) inserted by the Immigration (Restrictions on Employment) (Code of Practice and Miscellaneous Amendments) Order 2018, SI 2018/1340, art 3(1), (5), as from 28 January 2019.

[2.1955]

7 Obligation to produce documents to an immigration officer

Where an illegal working compliance order requires a person to produce documents relating to the right to work to an immigration officer in accordance with these Regulations, the person must comply with [any of regulations 8, 9 or 9A] in respect each of their employees within the scope of the order.

NOTES

Commencement: 1 December 2016.

Words in square brackets substituted by the Immigration (Restrictions on Employment) (Code of Practice and Miscellaneous Amendments) Order 2018, SI 2018/1340, art 3(1), (6), as from 28 January 2019.

[2.1956]

8 Documents to be produced to an immigration officer: general

(1) A relevant person must produce—

(a) a [clear] copy of a document or a [clear] copy of a combination of documents relating to the employee described in Schedule 1 or 2 in accordance with paragraphs (2) and (3); and

(b) if the employee is a student who has permission to work for a limited number of hours per week during term time whilst studying in the United Kingdom, a document or [clear] copy of a document which records the details of the term and vacation dates of the course that the employee is undertaking.

(2) In respect of a passport, the relevant person must produce a [clear] copy of the following pages of that document—

(a) any page containing the holder's personal details including nationality;

(b) any page containing the holder's photograph;

(c) any page containing the holder's signature;

(d) any page containing the date of expiry; and

(e) any page containing information indicating the holder has an entitlement to enter or remain in the United Kingdom and undertake the work in question.

(3) In respect of a document which is not a passport, the relevant person must produce a [clear] copy of the whole of the document.

NOTES

Commencement: 1 December 2016.

All words in square brackets inserted by the Immigration (Restrictions on Employment) (Code of Practice and Miscellaneous Amendments) Order 2018, SI 2018/1340, art 3(1), (7), as from 28 January 2019.

[2.1957]

9 Documents to be produced to an immigration officer: Positive Verification Notice

A relevant person must produce—

(a) a Positive Verification Notice which has been obtained in respect of the employee within the preceding period of six months from the date on which it is produced to an immigration officer; and

(b) if the employee is a student who has permission to work for a limited number of hours per week during term time whilst studying in the United Kingdom, a document or copy of a document which records the details of the term and vacation dates of the course that the employee is undertaking.

NOTES

Commencement: 1 December 2016.

[2.1958]

[9A Documents to be produced to an immigration officer: Home Office online right to work checking service

A relevant person must produce—

(a) a clear copy of the online right to work check; and

(b) if the employee is a student who has permission to work for a limited number of hours per week during term time whilst studying in the United Kingdom, a document or clear copy of a document which records the details of the term and vacation dates of the course that the employee is undertaking.]

NOTES

Commencement: 28 January 2019.

Inserted by the Immigration (Restrictions on Employment) (Code of Practice and Miscellaneous Amendments) Order 2018, SI 2018/1340, art 3(1), (8), as from 28 January 2019.

[2.1959]

10 Restriction on retention of documents

Nothing in these Regulations permits a relevant person to retain documents produced by an employee [or the Home Office] for the purposes of these Regulations for any period longer than is necessary for the purposes of ensuring compliance with regulation [6, 8, 9 or 9A].

NOTES

Commencement: 1 December 2016.

Words in first pair of square brackets inserted, and words in second pair of square brackets substituted, by the Immigration (Restrictions on Employment) (Code of Practice and Miscellaneous Amendments) Order 2018, SI 2018/1340, art 3(1), (9), as from 28 January 2019.

SCHEDULES

SCHEDULE 1

Regulations 4 and 8

[2.1960]
1. An expired or current passport showing that the holder, or a person named in the passport as the child of the holder, is a British citizen or a citizen of the United Kingdom and Colonies having the right of abode in the United Kingdom.

2. An expired or current passport or national identity card showing that the holder, or a person named in the passport as the child of the holder, is a national of an EEA state or Switzerland.

3. A registration certificate or document certifying permanent residence issued by the Home Office to a national of an EEA state or Switzerland.

4. A permanent residence card issued by the Home Office to the family member of a national of an EEA state or Switzerland.

5. A current biometric immigration document issued by the Home Office to the holder which indicates that the person named in it is allowed to stay indefinitely in the United Kingdom, or has no time limit on their stay in the United Kingdom.

6. A current passport endorsed to show that the holder is exempt from immigration control, is allowed to stay indefinitely in the United Kingdom, has the right of abode in the United Kingdom, or has no time limit on their stay in the United Kingdom.

7. A current immigration status document issued by the Home Office to the holder with an endorsement indicating that the person named in it is allowed to stay indefinitely in the United Kingdom or has no time limit on their stay in the United Kingdom, when produced in combination with an official document giving the person's permanent National Insurance Number and their name issued by a Government agency or a previous employer.

8. A . . . birth certificate issued in the United Kingdom . . . , when produced in combination with an official document giving the person's permanent National Insurance Number and their name issued by a Government agency or a previous employer.

9. [An] adoption certificate issued in the United Kingdom . . . when produced in combination with an official document giving the person's permanent National Insurance Number and their name issued by a Government agency or a previous employer.

10. A birth certificate issued in the Channel Islands, the Isle of Man or Ireland, when produced in combination with an official document giving the person's permanent National Insurance Number and their name issued by a Government agency or a previous employer.

11. An adoption certificate issued in the Channel Islands, the Isle of Man or Ireland, when produced in combination with an official document giving the person's permanent National Insurance Number and their name issued by a Government agency or a previous employer.

12. A certificate of registration or naturalisation as a British citizen, when produced in combination with an official document giving the person's permanent National Insurance Number and their name issued by a Government agency or a previous employer.

NOTES

Commencement: 1 December 2016.

Words omitted from paras 8, 9 revoked, and word in square brackets in para 9 substituted, by the Immigration (Restrictions on Employment) (Code of Practice and Miscellaneous Amendments) Order 2018, SI 2018/1340, art 3(1), (10), as from 28 January 2019.

SCHEDULE 2

Regulations 4 and 8

[2.1961]
1. A current passport endorsed to show that the holder is allowed to stay in the United Kingdom and is allowed to do the work in question.

2. A current biometric immigration document issued by the Home Office to the holder which indicates that the person named in it is allowed to stay in the United Kingdom and is allowed to do the work in question.

3. A current residence card issued by the Home Office to a person who is not a national of an EEA state or Switzerland, but who is a family member of such a national or who has a derivative right of residence.

4. A current immigration status document containing a photograph issued by the Home Office to the holder with an endorsement indicating that the person named in it is allowed to stay in the United Kingdom and is allowed to do the work in question, when produced in combination with an official document giving the person's permanent National Insurance Number and their name issued by a Government agency or previous employer.

NOTES

Commencement: 1 December 2016.

TRADE UNION ACT 2016 (POLITICAL FUNDS) (TRANSITION PERIOD) REGULATIONS 2017

(SI 2017/130)

NOTES

Made: 9 February 2017.
Authority: Trade Union Act 2016, s 11(6).
Commencement: 10 February 2017.

[2.1962]

1 Citation and commencement

(1) These Regulations may be cited as the Trade Union Act 2016 (Political Funds) (Transition Period) Regulations 2017.

(2) These Regulations come into force on the day after the day on which they are made.

NOTES

Commencement: 10 February 2017.

[2.1963]

2 Transition period

The transition period referred to in section 11(5) of the Trade Union Act 2016 is the period of 12 months beginning on 1st March 2017.

NOTES

Commencement: 10 February 2017.

IMPORTANT PUBLIC SERVICES (HEALTH) REGULATIONS 2017

(SI 2017/132)

NOTES

Made: 9 February 2017.
Authority: Trade Union and Labour Relations (Consolidation) Act 1992, s 226(2D).
Commencement: 2 March 2017.

[2.1964]

1 Citation, commencement and interpretation

(1) These Regulations may be cited as the Important Public Services (Health) Regulations 2017.

(2) These Regulations come into force on—

(a) 1st March 2017, or

(b) if later, at the end of the period of 21 days beginning with the day on which they are made.

NOTES

Commencement: 2 March 2017.

[2.1965]

2 Health services

(1) The following health services are important public services for the purposes of section 226 of the Trade Union and Labour Relations (Consolidation) Act 1992—

(a) the ambulance services listed in paragraph (3) provided in an emergency;

(b) accident and emergency services in a hospital;

(c) services which are provided in high-dependency units and intensive care in a hospital;

(d) psychiatric services provided in a hospital for conditions which require immediate attention in order to prevent serious injury, serious illness or loss of life; and

(e) obstetric and midwifery services provided in a hospital for conditions which require immediate attention in order to prevent serious injury, serious illness or loss of life.

(2) A service referred to in paragraph (1) is not an important public service for the purposes of section 226 if it is provided in a private hospital or by a private ambulance service.

(3) The ambulance services referred to in paragraph (1)(a) are—

(a) dealing with, and organising a response to, a call made by telephone or another device to an emergency telephone number and received by a provider of ambulance services;

(b) the diagnosis or treatment of a person in response to such a call, irrespective of whether the person is subsequently transferred to a hospital, or another place where further health services may be provided; and

(c) the conveyance of a person to a hospital or another place where further health services may be provided in response to such a call.

(4) For the purposes of this regulation—

(a) "emergency telephone number" means the telephone numbers 112 and 999;

(b) a "private hospital" is a hospital whose primary purpose is not the provision of publicly funded health services; and

(c) a "private ambulance service" is an ambulance or associated transport service whose primary purpose is not the provision of publicly funded ambulance services.

NOTES

Commencement: 2 March 2017.

IMPORTANT PUBLIC SERVICES (EDUCATION) REGULATIONS 2017

(SI 2017/133)

NOTES

Made: 9 February 2017.
Authority: Trade Union and Labour Relations (Consolidation) Act 1992, s 226(2D).
Commencement: 2 March 2017.

[2.1966]

1 Citation, commencement and interpretation

(1) These Regulations may be cited as the Important Public Services (Education) Regulations 2017.

(2) These Regulations come into force on—

(a) 1st March 2017, or

(b) if later, at the end of the period of 21 days beginning with the day on which they are made.

(3) In these Regulations "a further education institution"—

(a) in relation to England and Wales, means an institution that provides further education as defined in section 2(3) of the Education Act 1996; and

(b) in relation to Scotland, means a college of further education as defined in section 36(1) of the Further and Higher Education (Scotland) Act 1992.

NOTES

Commencement: 2 March 2017.

[2.1967]

2 Education of those aged under 17

(1) Teaching and other services provided by teachers and persons appointed to fulfil the role of a head teacher or principal at—

(a) a school other than a fee-paying school;

(b) a 16–19 Academy; or

(c) a further education institution other than one whose services to persons of compulsory school age are not publicly funded,

are important public services for the purposes of section 226 of the Trade Union and Labour Relations (Consolidation) Act 1992.

(2) A school is a fee-paying school if a majority of the pupils at the school have fees for their attendance paid for them by individuals.

(3) A further education institution provides services to persons of compulsory school age which are not publicly funded if a majority of those persons have fees for their attendance paid for them by individuals.

(4) Paragraph (1) does not include services to persons who are not of compulsory school age.

NOTES

Commencement: 2 March 2017.

IMPORTANT PUBLIC SERVICES (FIRE) REGULATIONS 2017

(SI 2017/134)

NOTES

Made: 9 February 2017.
Authority: Trade Union and Labour Relations (Consolidation) Act 1992, s 226(2D).
Commencement: 2 March 2017.

[2.1968]
1 Citation, commencement and interpretation

(1) These Regulations may be cited as the Important Public Services (Fire) Regulations 2017.

(2) These Regulations come into force on—

(a) 1st March 2017, or

(b) if later, at the end of the period of 21 days beginning with the day on which they are made.

NOTES

Commencement: 2 March 2017.

[2.1969]
2 Fire services

The following fire services are important public services for the purposes of section 226 of the Trade Union and Labour Relations (Consolidation) Act 1992—

(a) services provided by firefighters in extinguishing fires and protecting life and property in the event of fires; and

(b) services provided by fire and rescue authority personnel in dealing with, and organising a response to, a call made from a telephone or other device to request the services provided by firefighters as mentioned in paragraph (a).

NOTES

Commencement: 2 March 2017.

IMPORTANT PUBLIC SERVICES (TRANSPORT) REGULATIONS 2017

(SI 2017/135)

NOTES

Made: 9 February 2017.
Authority: Trade Union and Labour Relations (Consolidation) Act 1992, s 226(2D).
Commencement: 2 March 2017.

[2.1970]
1 Citation, commencement and interpretation

(1) These Regulations may be cited as the Important Public Services (Transport) Regulations 2017.

(2) These Regulations come into force on—

(a) 1st March 2017, or

(b) if later, at the end of the period of 21 days beginning with the day on which they are made.

NOTES

Commencement: 2 March 2017.

[2.1971]
2 Transport services

(1) The following transport services are important public services for the purposes of section 226 of the Trade Union and Labour Relations (Consolidation) Act 1992—

(a) any bus service which is a London local service as defined in section 179(1) of the Greater London Authority Act 1999;

(b) passenger railway services;

(c) civil air traffic control services provided by persons licensed by virtue of requirements in Commission Regulation (EU) 2015/340 laying down technical requirements and administrative procedures relating to air traffic controllers' licences and certificates pursuant to Regulation (EC) No 216/2008 of the European Parliament and of the Council, amending Commission Implementing Regulation (EU) No 923/2012 and repealing Commission Regulation (EU) No 805/2011;

(d) airport security services provided by workers at airports who—

(i) control access to a secure area of an airport;

(ii) screen persons entering a secure area;

(iii) screen items or vehicles entering a secure area;

(iv) search secure areas; or

(v) patrol secure areas;

(e) port security services provided by workers at ports who—

(i) control access to a restricted area of a port;

(ii) screen persons entering a restricted area;

(iii) screen items or vehicles entering a restricted area;

(iv) search restricted areas; or

(v) patrol restricted areas.

(2) In this regulation—

"heritage vehicle" means an historical or special type of railway vehicle exclusively or primarily used for tourist, educational or recreational purposes;

"network", "railway vehicle", "station services" and "train" have the meanings given by section 83 of the Railways Act 1993;

"passenger railway services" means any of the following—

(a) services for the carriage of passengers by railway or tramway;

(b) services for the maintenance of passenger trains or of the network;

(c) signalling or controlling the operation of the network;

(d) any station services that are essential to enable passenger trains to operate safely and securely;

but does not include any service for the carriage of passengers—

(i) using a heritage vehicle;

(ii) on a railway which the Office of Rail and Road determines in accordance with regulation 2A(1) of the Railways and Other Guided Transport Systems (Safety) Regulations 2006 is a heritage, museum or tourist railway that operates on its own network; or

(iii) that starts or terminates outside Great Britain.

"railway" and "tramway" have the meanings given by section 67 of the Transport and Works Act 1992.

NOTES

Commencement: 2 March 2017.

IMPORTANT PUBLIC SERVICES (BORDER SECURITY) REGULATIONS 2017

(SI 2017/136)

NOTES

Made: 9 February 2017.

Authority: Trade Union and Labour Relations (Consolidation) Act 1992, s 226(2D).

Commencement: 2 March 2017.

[2.1972]

1 Citation, commencement and interpretation

(1) These Regulations may be cited as the Important Public Services (Border Security) Regulations 2017.

(2) These Regulations come into force on—

(a) 1st March 2017, or

(b) if later, at the end of the period of 21 days beginning with the day on which they are made.

NOTES

Commencement: 2 March 2017.

[2.1973]

2 Border Security

(1) The following border security functions are important public services for the purposes of section 226 of the Trade Union and Labour Relations (Consolidation) Act 1992—

(a) the examination by a Border Force officer of persons arriving in or leaving the United Kingdom;

(b) the examination by a Border Force officer of goods—

(i) imported to or exported from the United Kingdom, or

(ii) entered for exportation or brought to any place in the United Kingdom for exportation;

(c) the patrol by a Border Force officer of the sea and other waters within the seaward limits of the territorial sea adjacent to the United Kingdom;

(d) the collection and dissemination of intelligence by a Border Force officer for the purposes of the functions set out in sub-paragraph (a), (b) or (c);

(e) the direction and control by a Border Force officer of the functions set out in sub-paragraph (a), (b), (c) or (d).

(2) In this regulation "Border Force officer" means a person who is appointed as such by the Secretary of State.

NOTES

Commencement: 2 March 2017.

TRADE UNION ACT 2016 (COMMENCEMENT NO 3 AND TRANSITIONAL) REGULATIONS 2017

(SI 2017/139)

NOTES

Made: 9 February 2017.
Authority: Trade Union Act 2016, s 25.

[2.1974]
1 Citation
These Regulations may be cited as the Trade Union Act 2016 (Commencement No 3 and Transitional) Regulations 2017.

[2.1975]
2 Provisions coming into force on 1st March 2017
The following provisions of the Trade Union Act 2016 come into force on 1st March 2017—

(a) section 2 (ballots: 50% turnout requirement);
(b) section 3 (40% support requirement for industrial action ballots in important public services), to the extent that it is not already in force;
(c) section 5 (information to be included on the voting paper);
(d) section 6 (information to members etc about result of the ballot);
(e) section 7 (information to Certification Officer about industrial action etc);
(f) section 8 (two weeks' notice to be given to employers of industrial action);
(g) section 9 (expiry of mandate for industrial action);
(h) section 10 (union supervision of picketing);
(i) section 11 (opting in by union members to contribute to political funds), to the extent that it is not already in force;
(j) section 12 (union's annual return to include details of political expenditure);
(k) section 13 (publication requirements in relation to facility time);
(l) section 15 (restriction on deduction of union subscriptions from wages in public sector) for the purpose of making regulations under section 116B of the Trade Union and Labour Relations (Consolidation) Act 1992 (as inserted by section 15);
(m) section 18 (enforcement by Certification Officer of new annual return requirements);
(n) section 22 (minor and consequential amendments), in so far as it relates to the following paragraphs of Schedule 4—
 (i) paragraphs 4 to 14;
 (ii) paragraphs 17 to 20; and
 (iii) paragraph 21(a) and (c).

[2.1976]
3 Transitional Provisions
The amendments made by section 10 apply in relation to a trade union organising or encouraging members after 1st March 2017 to take part in picketing (in accordance with section 220A(1) of the Trade Union and Labour Relations (Consolidation) Act 1992).

[2.1977]
4
The amendments made by paragraphs 5 to 11 and paragraph 20 of Schedule 4 apply only after the end of the transition period of 12 months beginning on 1st March 2017 specified under section 11(6) of the Trade Union Act 2016, and only in relation to a person—

(a) who after the end of that period joins a trade union that has a political fund, or
(b) who is a member of a trade union that has a political fund but did not have one immediately before the end of that period.

EQUALITY ACT 2010 (GENDER PAY GAP INFORMATION) REGULATIONS 2017

(SI 2017/172)

NOTES

Made: 6 February 2017.
Authority: Equality Act 2010, ss 78, 207(1), (4).
Commencement: 6 April 2017.

ARRANGEMENT OF REGULATIONS

[2.1978]

1 Citation, commencement and interpretation

(1) These Regulations may be cited as the Equality Act 2010 (Gender Pay Gap Information) Regulations 2017 and come into force on 6th April 2017.

(2) In these Regulations—

"bonus pay" has the meaning given in regulation 4;

"full-pay relevant employee" means a relevant employee who is not, during the relevant pay period, being paid at a reduced rate or nil as a result of the employee being on leave;

"hourly rate of pay" has the meaning given in regulation 6;

"ITEPA 2003" means the Income Tax (Earnings and Pensions) Act 2003;

"leave" includes—

(a) annual leave;
(b) maternity, paternity, adoption, parental or shared parental leave;
(c) sick leave; and
(d) special leave;

"ordinary pay" has the meaning given in regulation 3;

"pay period" has the meaning given in regulation 5(1);

"piecework" means work in respect of which an employee is entitled to be paid by reference to a number of pieces made or processed, or a number of tasks performed, instead of by reference to a period of time worked;

"relevant employee" means (subject to paragraph (4)) a person who is employed by the relevant employer on the snapshot date;

"relevant employer" means (subject to paragraph (6)) an employer who has 250 or more employees on the snapshot date;

"relevant pay period" has the meaning given in regulation 5(2);

"snapshot date" means the 5th April in the year to which the information required by regulation 2 relates.

(3) For the purposes of these Regulations, the amount of an employee's ordinary pay or bonus pay is to be calculated before deductions made at source (for example deductions in relation to income tax).

(4) In paragraph (2), a "relevant employee" does not include a partner in a firm.

(5) For the purposes of paragraph (4)—

(a) "firm" has the same meaning as in the Income Tax (Trading and Other Income) Act 2005, and
(b) "partner" includes a member of a limited liability partnership to which section 863(1) of the Income Tax (Trading and Other Income) Act 2005 applies.

(6) In paragraph (2), a "relevant employer" does not include—

(a) a person specified in Schedule 19 to the Equality Act 2010; or
(b) a government department or part of the armed forces not specified in that Schedule.

NOTES

Commencement: 6 April 2017.

[2.1979]

2 Duty to publish annual information relating to pay

(1) A relevant employer must publish, for 2017 and each subsequent year, the following information—

(a) the difference between the mean hourly rate of pay of male full-pay relevant employees and that of female full-pay relevant employees (see regulation 8);
(b) the difference between the median hourly rate of pay of male full-pay relevant employees and that of female full-pay relevant employees (see regulation 9);
(c) the difference between the mean bonus pay paid to male relevant employees and that paid to female relevant employees (see regulation 10);
(d) the difference between the median bonus pay paid to male relevant employees and that paid to female relevant employees (see regulation 11);

(e) the proportions of male and female relevant employees who were paid bonus pay (see regulation 12); and
(f) the proportions of male and female full-pay relevant employees in the lower, lower middle, upper middle and upper quartile pay bands (see regulation 13).

(2) The relevant employer must publish the information required by paragraph (1) within the period of 12 months beginning with the snapshot date.

(3) In compiling the information required by paragraph (1), the relevant employer is not required to include data relating to a relevant employee if—
(a) the employee is employed under a contract personally to do work, and
(b) the employer does not have, and it is not reasonably practicable for the employer to obtain, the data.

NOTES

Commencement: 6 April 2017.

[2.1980]
3 Meaning of "ordinary pay"

(1) In these Regulations, "ordinary pay" means (subject to paragraph (2))—
(a) basic pay;
(b) allowances;
(c) pay for piecework;
(d) pay for leave;
(e) shift premium pay.

(2) "Ordinary pay" does not include—
(a) remuneration referable to overtime,
(b) remuneration referable to redundancy or termination of employment,
(c) remuneration in lieu of leave, or
(d) remuneration provided otherwise than in money.

(3) In paragraph (1)—
(a) "allowances" includes any sum paid with respect to—
(i) any duty of the employee, such as a duty in connection with the role of fire or bomb warden, that is ancillary to the main duties of the employee's employment;
(ii) the location of the employment in a particular area;
(iii) the purchase, lease or maintenance of a vehicle;
(iv) the recruitment and retention of an employee; and
(v) the purchase, lease or maintenance of an item;
but excludes any payment to reimburse expenditure wholly and necessarily incurred by the employee in the course of his or her employment.
(b) "shift premium pay" means the difference between basic pay and any higher rate paid by the employer for work during different times of the day or night.

NOTES

Commencement: 6 April 2017.

[2.1981]
4 Meaning of "bonus pay"

(1) In these Regulations, "bonus pay" means (subject to paragraph (2)) any remuneration that—
(a) is in the form of money, vouchers, securities, securities options, or interests in securities,
(b) relates to profit sharing, productivity, performance, incentive or commission.

(2) "Bonus pay" does not include—
(a) ordinary pay,
(b) remuneration referable to overtime, or
(c) remuneration referable to redundancy or termination of employment.

(3) For the purpose of paragraph (1), remuneration in the form of securities, securities options and interests in securities is to be treated as paid to the employee at the time, and in the amounts in respect of which, the securities, securities options and interests in securities give rise to (or would give rise to, if the employee were an employee for the purposes of Part 2 of ITEPA 2003 (employment income))—
(a) any taxable earnings within the meaning of section 10(2) of ITEPA 2003; or
(b) any taxable specific income within the meaning of section 10(3) of ITEPA 2003.

(4) In this regulation, "securities", "securities options" and "interests in securities" have the same meaning as in section 420 of ITEPA 2003.

NOTES

Commencement: 6 April 2017.

[2.1982]
5 Meaning of the "pay period" and the "relevant pay period"

(1) In these Regulations, the "pay period", in relation to a relevant employee, means—
(a) the period in respect of which the relevant employer pays the employee basic pay, whether weekly, fortnightly, monthly or any other period, or

(b) if the relevant employer does not pay the employee basic pay, the period in respect of which the employer most frequently pays the employee one of the elements of ordinary pay mentioned in regulation 3(1)(b) to (e).

(2) In these Regulations, the "relevant pay period" means the pay period within which the snapshot date falls.

NOTES

Commencement: 6 April 2017.

[2.1983]

6 Meaning of "hourly rate of pay"

(1) The "hourly rate of pay", in relation to a relevant employee, is to be determined as follows—

Step 1

Identify all amounts of ordinary pay and bonus pay paid to the employee during the relevant pay period.

Step 2

Where an amount identified under Step 1 is an amount of ordinary pay, exclude any amount that would normally fall to be paid in a different pay period.

Step 3

Where an amount identified under Step 1 is an amount of bonus pay, and is paid in respect of a period ("the bonus period") which is not the same length as the relevant pay period, divide the amount by the length of the bonus period (in days) and multiply it by the length of the relevant pay period (in days).

Step 4

Add together the amounts identified under Step 1 (as adjusted, where necessary, under Steps 2 and 3).

Step 5

Multiply the amount found under Step 4 by the appropriate multiplier (see paragraphs (2) and (3)).

Step 6

Divide the amount found under Step 5 by the number of working hours in a week for that employee (see regulation 7).

(2) In this regulation, "the appropriate multiplier" means 7 divided by the number of days in the relevant pay period.

(3) In determining for the purposes of this regulation the number of days in the relevant pay period or bonus period where those periods are (or are determined by reference to) a month or a year—

(a) a month is treated as having 30.44 days;

(b) a year is treated as having 365.25 days.

NOTES

Commencement: 6 April 2017.

[2.1984]

7 Employee's working hours in a week

(1) The number of working hours in a week for a relevant employee, for the purposes of Step 6 in regulation 6, is to be determined as follows.

(2) Subject to paragraph (6), where an employee has normal working hours that do not differ from week to week or over a longer period, the number of working hours in a week for a relevant employee is the number of the normal working hours in a week for that employee under the employee's contract of employment, or terms of employment, in force on the snapshot date.

(3) Subject to paragraph (6), where the employee has no normal working hours, or the number of the normal working hours differs from week to week or over a longer period, the number of working hours in a week for the employee is—

(a) the average number of working hours calculated by dividing by twelve the total number of the employee's working hours during the period of twelve weeks ending with the last complete week of the relevant pay period, or

(b) where the employee has not been at work for a sufficient period, or for some other reason the employer is not reasonably able to make the calculation under paragraph (a), a number which fairly represents the number of working hours in a week having regard to such of the considerations specified in paragraph (5) as are appropriate in the circumstances.

(4) In calculating the average number of working hours for the purposes of paragraph (3)(a), no account is to be taken of a week in which no hours were worked by the employee, and hours worked in earlier weeks must be brought in so as to bring up to twelve the number of weeks of which account is taken.

(5) The considerations referred to in paragraph (3)(b) are—

(a) the average number of working hours in a week which the employee could expect under the employee's contract of employment, or terms of employment; and

(b) the average number of working hours of other employees engaged in comparable employment with the same employer.

(6) Where the employee is paid on the basis of piecework, the number of working hours in a week for the employee is the number of hours of output work for that employee in the week during the relevant pay period within which the snapshot date falls, determined in accordance with Chapter 4 of Part 5 of the National Minimum Wage Regulations 2015.

(7) In its application by virtue of paragraph (6), Chapter 4 of Part 5 of the National Minimum Wage Regulations 2015 has effect as if—

(a) references to a worker were references to an employee, and

(b) references to a pay reference period were references to a week.

(8) In this regulation, "working hours"—

(a) includes hours when an employee is available, and required to be available, at or near a place of work for the purposes of working unless the employee is at home, and

(b) excludes any hours for which an employee is entitled to overtime pay.

(9) In paragraph (8), hours when a worker is "available" only includes hours when the worker is awake for the purposes of working, even if a worker by arrangement sleeps at or near a place of work and the employer provides suitable facilities for sleeping.

NOTES

Commencement: 6 April 2017.

[2.1985]

8 Difference in mean hourly rate of pay

The difference between the mean hourly rate of pay of male full-pay relevant employees and that of female full-pay relevant employees must be expressed as a percentage of the mean hourly rate of pay of male full pay relevant employees and is to be determined as follows—

$((A - B) / A) \times 100$

where—

A is the mean hourly rate of pay of all male full-pay relevant employees; and
B is the mean hourly rate of pay of all female full-pay relevant employees.

NOTES

Commencement: 6 April 2017.

[2.1986]

9 Difference in median hourly rate of pay

The difference between the median hourly rate of pay of male full-pay relevant employees and that of female full-pay relevant employees must be expressed as a percentage of the median pay of male full-pay relevant employees and is to be determined as follows—

$((A - B) / A) \times 100$

where—

A is the median hourly rate of pay of all male full-pay relevant employees; and
B is the median hourly rate of pay of all female full-pay relevant employees.

NOTES

Commencement: 6 April 2017.

[2.1987]

10 Difference in mean bonus pay

(1) The difference between the mean bonus pay paid to male relevant employees and that paid to female relevant employees must be expressed as a percentage of the mean bonus pay paid to male relevant employees and is to be determined as follows—

$((A - B) / A) \times 100$

where—

A is the mean bonus pay paid during the relevant period to male relevant employees who were paid bonus pay during that period; and

B is the mean bonus pay paid during the relevant period to female relevant employees who were paid bonus pay during that period.

(2) In this regulation "the relevant period" means the period of 12 months ending with the snapshot date.

NOTES

Commencement: 6 April 2017.

[2.1988]

11 Difference in median bonus pay

(1) The difference between the median bonus pay paid to male relevant employees and that paid to female relevant employees must be expressed as a percentage of the median bonus pay paid to male relevant employees and is to be determined as follows—

$((A - B) / A) \times 100$

where—

A is the median bonus pay paid during the relevant period to male relevant employees who were paid bonus pay during that period; and

B is the median bonus pay paid during the relevant period to female relevant employees who were paid bonus pay during that period.

(2) In this regulation "the relevant period" means the period of 12 months ending with the snapshot date.

NOTES

Commencement: 6 April 2017.

[2.1989]

12 Proportion of male and female employees who received bonus pay

(1) The proportion of male relevant employees who were paid bonus pay must be expressed as a percentage of male relevant employees and is to be determined as follows—

$(A / B) \times 100$

where—

A is the number of male relevant employees who were paid bonus pay during the relevant period; and

B is the number of male relevant employees.

(2) The proportion of female relevant employees who were paid bonus pay must be expressed as a percentage of female relevant employees and is to be determined as follows—

$(A / B) \times 100$

where—

A is the number of female relevant employees who were paid bonus pay during the relevant period; and

B is the number of female relevant employees.

(3) In this regulation "the relevant period" means the period of 12 months ending with the snapshot date.

NOTES

Commencement: 6 April 2017.

[2.1990]

13 Proportion of male and female employees according to quartile pay bands

(1) The proportions of male and female full-pay relevant employees in the lower, lower middle, upper middle and upper quartile pay bands is to be determined as follows.

Step 1

Determine the hourly rate of pay for each male and female full-pay relevant employee and then rank those employees in order from lowest paid to highest paid.

Step 2

Divide the employees, as ranked under Step 1, into four sections, each comprising (so far as possible) an equal number of employees, to determine the lower, lower middle, upper middle and upper quartile pay bands.

Step 3

The proportion of male full-pay relevant employees within each quartile pay band must be expressed as a percentage of the full-pay relevant employees within that band as follows—

$(A / B) \times 100$

where—

A is the number of male full-pay relevant employees in a quartile pay band; and

B is the number of full-pay relevant employees in that quartile pay band.

Step 4

The proportion of female full-pay relevant employees within each quartile pay band must be expressed as a percentage of the full-pay relevant employees within that band as follows—

$(A / B) \times 100$

where—

A is the number of female full-pay relevant employees in a quartile pay band; and

B is the number of full-pay relevant employees in that quartile pay band.

(2) Where employees receiving the same hourly rate of pay fall within more than one quartile pay band, the employer must (so far as possible) ensure that, when ranking the employees under Step 1, the relative proportion of male and female employees receiving that rate of pay is the same in each of those pay bands.

NOTES

Commencement: 6 April 2017.

[2.1991]
14 Information to be accompanied by signed statement

(1) The information published under regulation 2 must be accompanied by a written statement which—
(a) confirms that the information is accurate; and
(b) is signed in accordance with paragraph (2).

(2) Where the relevant employer is—
(a) a body corporate other than a limited liability partnership within the meaning of the Limited Liability Partnerships Act 2000, the written statement must be signed by a director (or equivalent);
(b) a limited liability partnership, the written statement must be signed by a designated member (see section 8 of that Act);
(c) the partners in a limited partnership registered under the Limited Partnerships Act 1907, the written statement must be signed by a general partner (see section 3 of that Act);
(d) the partners in any other kind of partnership, the written statement must be signed by a partner;
(e) the members or officers of an unincorporated body of persons other than a partnership, the written statement must be signed by a member of the governing body or a senior officer;
(f) any other type of body, the written statement must be signed by the most senior employee.

(3) In this regulation, "partnership" means—
(a) a partnership within the Partnership Act 1890;
(b) a limited partnership registered under the Limited Partnerships Act 1907; or
(c) a firm, or an entity of a similar character, formed under the law of a country outside the United Kingdom.

NOTES
Commencement: 6 April 2017.

[2.1992]
15 Form and manner of publication

(1) The requirement in regulation 2 to publish information, and the requirement in regulation 14 for the information to be accompanied by a written statement, are requirements that that information and statement be published on the employer's website—
(a) in a manner that is accessible to all its employees and to the public; and
(b) for a period of at least three years beginning with the date of publication.

(2) A relevant employer must also publish on a website designated for that purpose by the Secretary of State—
(a) the information required by regulation 2, and
(b) the name and job title of the person who signed the statement required by regulation 14.

NOTES
Commencement: 6 April 2017.

[2.1993]
16 Review

(1) The Secretary of State must from time to time—
(a) carry out a review of these Regulations;
(b) set out the conclusion of the review in a report; and
(c) publish the report.

(2) The report must in particular—
(a) set out the objectives intended to be achieved by these Regulations;
(b) assess the extent to which those objectives are achieved; and
(c) assess whether those objectives remain appropriate and, if so, the extent to which they could be achieved with a system that imposes less regulation.

(3) The first report under this regulation must be published before the end of the period of five years beginning with the day on which these Regulations come into force.

(4) Reports under this regulation are afterwards to be published at intervals not exceeding five years.

NOTES
Commencement: 6 April 2017.

TRADE UNION (FACILITY TIME PUBLICATION REQUIREMENTS) REGULATIONS 2017

(SI 2017/328)

NOTES
Made: 8 March 2017.
Authority: Trade Union and Labour Relations (Consolidation) Act 1992, s 172A(1), (2), (3), (5), (6), (10).
Commencement: 1 April 2017.

ARRANGEMENT OF REGULATIONS

SCHEDULES

[2.1994]

1 Citation and commencement

These Regulations may be cited as the Trade Union (Facility Time Publication Requirements) Regulations 2017 and come into force on 1st April 2017.

NOTES

Commencement: 1 April 2017.

[2.1995]

2 Interpretation: general

In these Regulations—

"the 1992 Act" means the Trade Union and Labour Relations (Consolidation) Act 1992;

"paid facility time hours" means the number of hours spent on facility time by an employee who is a relevant union official during a relevant period (excluding hours attributable to time taken off under section 170(1)(b) of the 1992 Act in respect of which a relevant union official does not receive wages from the relevant public sector employer) and "total paid facility time hours" means the total of all such hours spent during that period by all such employees;

"paid trade union activities" means time taken off under section 170(1)(b) of the 1992 Act in respect of which a relevant union official receives wages from the relevant public sector employer;

"relevant period" means a period of 12 months beginning with 1st April, and the first relevant period begins on 1st April 2017;

"wages" (and "gross amount" in relation to wages) has the meaning given in section 27 of the Employment Rights Act 1996;

"working hours" has the meaning given in section 173(1) of the 1992 Act.

NOTES

Commencement: 1 April 2017.

[2.1996]

3 Crown employees: person or entity to be treated as an employer

For the purposes of section 172A of the 1992 Act, a public authority that is an emanation of the Crown is to be treated as the employer of a relevant union official who is employed by the Crown under or for the purposes of that authority (and a reference in these Regulations to an employee is, in the case of such a public authority, to a person employed by the Crown under or for the purposes of that authority).

NOTES

Commencement: 1 April 2017.

[2.1997]

4 Meaning of total cost of facility time

(1) For the purposes of these Regulations, the total cost of facility time for a relevant period is calculated by taking the following steps—

(a) Step 1—determine the hourly cost of each employee who was a relevant union official during that period;

(b) Step 2—multiply the hourly cost for each such employee by the number of paid facility time hours spent by that employee on facility time during the period (if there is only one employee who was a relevant union official, this amount is the total cost of facility time);

(c) Step 3—if there is more than one employee who was a relevant union official, add together each of the amounts produced by the calculations at step 2.

(2) The hourly cost for the purposes of step 1 is calculated by—

(a) adding—

(i) the gross amount spent on wages by the employer in respect of the employee during the period;

(ii) the amount spent on pension contributions by the employer in respect of that employee during the period; and

(iii) the amount of national insurance contributions paid by the employer in respect of the employee during the period; then

(b) dividing that amount by the working hours of the employee during the period.

(3) But a notional hourly cost must be used at step 2, instead of the actual hourly cost determined under step 1, where the employee is identifiable.

(4) An employee is identifiable if the employer considers that the use of the actual hourly cost will lead, when the information required to be published under these Regulations is published, to another person being able to identify the employee's wages during the relevant period.

(5) The notional hourly cost referred to in paragraph (3) must be reasonable having regard to the type of work the identifiable employee ordinarily did for the employer during the relevant period.

NOTES

Commencement: 1 April 2017.

[2.1998]

5 Meaning of total pay bill

For the purposes of these Regulations, the total pay bill for a relevant period is calculated by adding—

(a) the total gross amount spent on wages by the employer in respect of its employees during the period;

(b) the total amount spent on pension contributions by the employer in respect of its employees during the period; and

(c) the total amount of national insurance contributions paid by the employer in respect of its employees during the period.

NOTES

Commencement: 1 April 2017.

[2.1999]

6 Meaning of full-time equivalent employee number

For the purposes of these Regulations, the full-time equivalent employee number is calculated by—

(a) establishing the number of full-time employees; and

(b) adding to that number such fraction as is just and reasonable in respect of those employees who are not full-time.

NOTES

Commencement: 1 April 2017.

[2.2000]

7 Relevant public sector employer

(1) Subject to paragraph (3), a public authority referred to in paragraph (2) is specified for the purposes of section 172A(2)(a) of the 1992 Act.

(2) The public authorities are—

(a) any department of the Government of the United Kingdom (excluding the Secret Intelligence Service, the Security Service and the Government Communications Headquarters);

(b) the Scottish Ministers; and

(c) an authority listed, or of a description, in Schedule 1.

(3) An authority of a description in Schedule 1 which is a devolved Welsh authority is not specified for the purposes of section 172A(2)(a).

(4) In paragraph (3), "devolved Welsh authority" has the same meaning as in section 157A of the Government of Wales Act 2006 (inserted into that Act by section 4 of the Wales Act 2017).

NOTES

Commencement: 1 April 2017.

[2.2001]

8 Requirement to publish information

(1) If the employee number condition is met in respect of a relevant period, a relevant public sector employer must publish the information that comprises the response to the questions, or request for information, set out in Schedule 2 in respect of that period as it applies to that employer.

(2) The employee number condition is met if the relevant public sector employer has a full-time equivalent employee number of more than 49 throughout the entirety of any seven of the months within the relevant period.

(3) The information must be published, together with the questions, or request for information, in the form indicated in Schedule 2.

(4) The information must be published by being—
  (a) placed on a website maintained by or on behalf of the employer before 31st July in the calendar year in which the relevant period to which the information relates ends; and
  (b) included in the employer's annual report which covers the relevant period, where the employer produces an annual report.

(5) If the information is not, by virtue of paragraph (4), placed on a website maintained by or on behalf of the Government of the United Kingdom, the employer must also cause it to be placed on such a website before 31st July in the calendar year in which the relevant period to which the information relates ends.

(6) Paragraph (7) applies to a local authority, the Common Council of the City of London and the Council of the Isles of Scilly if the authority or Council is required to publish information under this regulation in respect of a relevant period.

(7) The authority or Council must comply with the requirements of this regulation separately in relation to—
  (a) its central function employees;
  (b) its education function employees;
  (c) its fire and rescue function employees,

to the extent it has employees within those categories.

(8) The reference in paragraph (7) to "separately" means publishing the information, and carrying out such calculations as are necessary for the purposes of determining the information to be published, as if the employer were a separate employer for each category of employees.

(9) In paragraph (7)—

"central function employees" means employees of the authority or Council other than—
  (a) its fire and rescue function employees; and
  (b) its education function employees;

"education function employees" means persons employed by virtue of section 35(2) of the Education Act 2002 (staffing of community, voluntary controlled, community special and maintained nursery schools);

"fire and rescue function employees" means employees employed to carry out functions that the authority or Council has because it is a fire and rescue authority (see section 1 of the Fire and Rescue Services Act 2004).

NOTES

Commencement: 1 April 2017.

SCHEDULES

SCHEDULE 1
PUBLIC AUTHORITIES

Regulation 7

PART 1
LOCAL AUTHORITIES

[2.2002]

1. A local authority within the meaning of the Local Government Act 1972.

2. The Council of the Isles of Scilly.

3. The Common Council of the City of London.

4. The Greater London Authority as established under section 1 of the Greater London Authority Act 1999.

5. An economic prosperity board established under section 88 of the Local Democracy, Economic Development and Construction Act 2009.

6. A combined authority established under section 103 of the Local Democracy, Economic Development and Construction Act 2009.

7. A council constituted under section 2 of the Local Government etc (Scotland) Act 1994.

8. A joint board, within the meaning of section 235(1) of the Local Government (Scotland) Act 1973.

9. A fire and rescue authority constituted by a scheme under section 2 of the Fire and Rescue Services Act 2004 or a scheme to which section 4 of that Act applies.

[**9A.** A fire and rescue authority created by an order under section 4A of the Fire and Rescue Services Act 2004.]

10. A joint fire authority established under Part 4 of the Local Government Act 1985 (police, fire services, civil defence and transport).

11. Any body established pursuant to an order under section 67 of the Local Government Act 1985 (successors to residuary bodies).

[12. The London Fire Commissioner.]

13. The Scottish Fire and Rescue Service established under section 1A of the Fire (Scotland) Act 2005.

14. An internal drainage board which is being continued by virtue of section 1 of the Land Drainage Act 1991.

15. Transport for London as established under section 154 of the Greater London Authority Act 1999.

16. The London Transport Users' Committee as established under section 247 of the Greater London Authority Act 1999.

17. A Passenger Transport Executive for an integrated transport area or a passenger transport area within the meaning of Part 2 of the Transport Act 1968.

18. The Passengers' Council as established by section 19 of the Railways Act 2005.

19. A Transport Partnership established under section 1 of the Transport (Scotland) Act 2005.

20. A sub-national transport body established under section 102E of the Local Transport Act 2008.

21. A National Park Authority established by an order under section 63 of the Environment Act 1995.

22. A National Park Authority established by virtue of Schedule 1 to the National Parks (Scotland) Act 2000.

23. The Broads Authority established by section 1 of the Norfolk and Suffolk Broads Act 1988.

24. A Conservation Board established under section 86 of the Countryside and Rights of Way Act 2000.

NOTES

Commencement: 1 April 2017.

Para 9A: inserted, in relation to England only, by the Fire and Rescue Authority (Police and Crime Commissioner) (Application of Local Policing Provisions, Inspection, Powers to Trade and Consequential Amendments) Order 2017, SI 2017/863, art 29, Sch 2, para 10, as from 1 October 2017.

Para 12: substituted by the London Government (London Fire Commissioner and Policing) (Amendment) Regulations 2018, SI 2018/269, reg 2, Schedule, para 19, as from 1 April 2018.

PART 2
THE NATIONAL HEALTH SERVICE

[2.2003]

25. A clinical commissioning group established under section 14D of the National Health Service Act 2006.

26. A National Health Service Foundation Trust established under section 35 of the National Health Service Act 2006.

27. A National Health Service Trust established under section 25 of the National Health Service Act 2006.

28. A special health authority established under section 28 of the National Health Service Act 2006 or section 22 of the National Health Service (Wales) Act 2006.

29. The Common Services Agency for the Scottish Health Service established under section 10 of the National Health Service (Scotland) Act 1978.

30. A Health Board, or Special Health Board, constituted under section 2 of the National Health Service (Scotland) Act 1978.

31. Healthcare Improvement Scotland established under section 10A of the National Health Service (Scotland) Act 1978.

32. The National Health Service Commissioning Board established under section 1H of the National Health Service Act 2006.

33. Monitor.

NOTES

Commencement: 1 April 2017.

PART 3
MAINTAINED SCHOOLS AND OTHER EDUCATIONAL INSTITUTIONS

[2.2004]

34. The governing body of a foundation school, voluntary aided school or foundation special school.

35. The proprietor (as defined in section 579(1) of the Education Act 1996) of—

(a) an Academy school within the meaning of section 1A of the Academies Act 2010;

(b) a 16 to 19 Academy within the meaning of section 1B of that Act;

(c) an alternative provision Academy within the meaning of section 1C of that Act.

36. The governing body (as defined in section 90 of the Further and Higher Education Act 1992) of—

(a) an institution in the further education sector within the meaning of section 91(3) and (3A) of that Act;

(b) an institution conducted by a higher education corporation within the meaning of section 90(1) of that Act;

(c) a designated institution for the purposes of Part 2 of that Act, as defined by section 72(3) of that Act.

37. A university, including any college, school, hall or other institution of that university, receiving financial support under section 65 of the Further and Higher Education Act 1992.

38. A manager (as defined by section 135 of the Education (Scotland) Act 1980) of a central institution within the meaning of that Act.

39. The governing body (as defined by section 35 of the Further and Higher Education (Scotland) Act 2005) of an institution in receipt of funding from the Scottish Further and Higher Education Funding Council or a regional strategic body within the meaning of that Act.

NOTES

Commencement: 1 April 2017.

PART 4
POLICE STAFF

[2.2005]

40. A police and crime commissioner as established by section 1 of the Police Reform and Social Responsibility Act 2011.

41. A chief officer of a police force in England or Wales.

42. The British Transport Police Authority as established by section 18 of the Railway and Transport Safety Act 2003.

43. The Civil Nuclear Police Authority as established by section 51 of the Energy Act 2004.

44. The Scottish Police Authority established under section 1 of the Police and Fire Reform (Scotland) Act 2012.

NOTES

Commencement: 1 April 2017.

PART 5
OTHER BODIES

[2.2006]

45. Accountant in Bankruptcy.

46. The Advisory, Conciliation and Arbitration Service.

47. The Arts Council England.

48. The Arts and Humanities Research Council.

49. The Big Lottery Fund.

50. The Biotechnology and Biological Sciences Research Council.

51. The Board of Commissioners of the Royal Hospital at Chelsea.

52. The Board of Governors of the Museum of London.

53. The Board of Trustees of the Armouries.

54. The Board of Trustees of the National Gallery.

55. The Board of Trustees of the National Galleries of Scotland.

56. The Board of Trustees of the National Museums and Galleries on Merseyside.

57. The Board of Trustees of the National Museums Scotland.

58. The Board of Trustees of the National Portrait Gallery.

59. The Board of Trustees of the Royal Botanic Garden, Edinburgh.

60. The Board of Trustees of the Royal Botanic Gardens, Kew.

61. The Board of Trustees of the Science Museum.

62. The Board of Trustees of the Tate Gallery.

63. The Board of Trustees of the Victoria and Albert Museum.

64. The Board of Trustees of the Wallace Collection.

65. The Britain-Russia Centre and the British East-West Centre.

66. The British Broadcasting Corporation.

67. The British Council.

68. The British Library Board.

69. The British Tourist Authority.

70. The Children and Family Court Advisory and Support Service.

71. The Care Quality Commission.

72. The Children's Commissioner.

73. Children's Hearings Scotland.

74. The Civil Service Commission.

75. The Coal Authority.

76. College of Policing Limited.

77. The Commission for Equality and Human Rights.

78. The Commission for Local Administration in England.

79. The Commissioner for Children and Young People in Scotland.

80. The Commissioner for Ethical Standards in Public Life in Scotland.

81. The Commissioner for Public Appointments.

82. The Commissioner for Victims and Witnesses.

83. The Committee on Climate Change.

84. The Community Development Foundation.

85. The Community Justice Authority.

86. The Covent Garden Market Authority.

87. Creative Scotland.

88. The Criminal Cases Review Commission.

89. The Crofting Commission.

90. Design Council.

91. The Director of Fair Access to Higher Education.

92. The Disclosure and Barring Service.

93. The Doncaster Children's Services Trust.

94. Ebbsfleet Development Corporation.

95. The Economic and Social Research Council.

96. The Engineering and Physical Sciences Research Council.

97. The Engineering Construction Industry Training Board.

98. The English Sports Council.

99. The Environment Agency.

100. Food Standards Scotland.

101. The Gaelic Media Service.

102. Gangmasters and Labour Abuse Authority.

103. The Great Britain-China Centre.

104. The Health and Safety Executive.

105. The Health and Social Care Information Centre.

106. Health Education England.

107. The Health Research Authority.

108. Her Majesty's Chief Inspector of Prisons.

109. Her Majesty's Inspectorate of Probation for England and Wales.

110. Higher Education Funding Council for England.

111. Highlands and Islands Enterprise.

112. The Historic Buildings and Monuments Commission for England.

113. Historic Environment Scotland.

114. The Homes and Communities Agency.

115. The Human Fertilisation and Embryology Authority.

116. The Human Tissue Authority.

117. The Independent Police Complaints Commission.

118. The Information Commissioner.

119. The Institute for Apprenticeships.

120. The Joint Nature Conservation Committee.

121. The Judicial Appointments and Conduct Ombudsman.

122. The Judicial Appointments Commission.

123. The Marine Management Organisation.

124. The Marshall Aid Commemoration Commission.

125. The Medical Research Council.

126. Mental Welfare Commission for Scotland.

127. The National Army Museum.

128. The National Forest Company.

129. The National Institute for Health and Care Excellence.

130. The National Library of Scotland.

131. The National Museum of the Royal Navy.

132. The National Non-Foods Crops Centre Limited.

133. National Records of Scotland.

134. Natural England.

135. Natural Environment Research Council.

136. Nuclear Decommissioning Authority.

137. The Office for Budget Responsibility.

138. The Office of Manpower Economics.

139. The Office of the Scottish Charity Regulator.

140. The Oil and Pipeline Agency.

141. The Parole Board for England and Wales.

142. The Parole Board for Scotland.

143. The Police Investigations and Review Commissioner.

144. The Prisons and Probation Ombudsman for England and Wales.

145. The Registrar of Independent Schools.

146. Registers of Scotland.

147. Revenue Scotland.

148. Risk Management Authority.

149. The Royal Air Force Museum.

150. The Science and Technology Facilities Council.

151. The Scottish Ambulance Service Board.

152. The Scottish Children's Reporter Administration.

153. The Scottish Commission for Human Rights.

154. The Scottish Courts and Tribunals Service.

155. The Scottish Criminal Cases Review Commission.

156. Scottish Enterprise.

157. The Scottish Environment Protection Agency.

158. The Scottish Fiscal Commission.

159. The Scottish Further and Higher Education Funding Council.

160. The Scottish Housing Regulator.

161. The Scottish Information Commissioner.

162. The Scottish Legal Aid Board.

163. The Scottish Natural Heritage.

164. The Scottish Public Services Ombudsman.

165. The Scottish Qualifications Authority.

166. The Scottish Road Works Commissioner.

167. The Scottish Social Services Council.

168. The Scottish Sports Council.

169. The Sea Fish Industry Authority.

170. The Security Industry Authority.

171. Sianel Pedwar Cymru (S4C).

172. The Single Source Regulations Office.

173. The Slough Children's Services Trust.

174. Social Care and Social Work Improvement Scotland.

175. The Social Care Institute for Excellence.

176. The Sports Grounds Safety Authority.

177. The Standards Commission for Scotland.

178. The Technology Strategy Board.

179. The Trustees of the British Museum.

180. The Trustees of the Imperial War Museum.

181. The Trustees of National Heritage Memorial Fund.

182. The Trustees of the National Maritime Museum.

183. The Trustees of the Natural History Museum.

184. The Trustees of the Sir John Soane's Museum.

185. The UK Atomic Energy Authority.

186. The UK Commission for Employment and Skills.

187. The United Kingdom Anti-Doping Limited.

188. The United Kingdom Sports Council.

189. VisitScotland.

190. The Westminster Foundation for Democracy Limited.

191. The Youth Justice Board for England and Wales.

NOTES

Commencement: 1 April 2017.

SCHEDULE 2
INFORMATION TO BE PUBLISHED

Regulation 8

[2.2007]

Table 1

Relevant union officials

What was the total number of your employees who were relevant union officials during the relevant period?

Number of employees who were relevant union officials during the relevant period	Full-time equivalent employee number

Table 2

Percentage of time spent on facility time

How many of your employees who were relevant union officials employed during the relevant period spent a) 0%, b) 1%–50%, c) 51%–99% or d) 100% of their working hours on facility time?

Percentage of time	Number of employees
0%	
1–50%	
51%–99%	
100%	

Table 3

Percentage of pay bill spent on facility time

Provide the figures requested in the first column of the table below to determine the percentage of your total pay bill spent on paying employees who were relevant union officials for facility time during the relevant period.

First Column	Figures
Provide the total cost of facility time	
Provide the total pay bill	
Provide the percentage of the total pay bill spent on facility time, calculated as: (total cost of facility time / total pay bill) x 100	

Table 4

Paid trade union activities

As a percentage of total paid facility time hours, how many hours were spent by employees who were relevant union officials during the relevant period on paid trade union activities?

Time spent on paid trade union activities as a percentage of total paid facility time hours calculated as: (total hours spent on paid trade union activities by relevant union officials during the relevant period / total paid facility time hours) x 100	

NOTES

Commencement: 1 April 2017.

EQUALITY ACT 2010 (SPECIFIC DUTIES AND PUBLIC AUTHORITIES) REGULATIONS 2017

(SI 2017/353)

NOTES

Made: 9 March 2017.
Authority: Equality Act 2010, ss 151(1), 153(1), 154(2), 207(4).
Commencement: 31 March 2017.

ARRANGEMENT OF REGULATIONS

SCHEDULES

[2.2008]
1 Citation, commencement and interpretation

(1) These Regulations may be cited as the Equality Act 2010 (Specific Duties and Public Authorities) Regulations 2017 and come into force on 31st March 2017.

(2) In these Regulations—
"the Act" means the Equality Act 2010;
"the 1996 Act" means the Employment Rights Act 1996;
"the 2011 Regulations" means the Equality Act 2010 (Specific Duties) Regulations 2011;
"employment" and related expressions have the meaning given in regulation 2;
"English local authority" has the same meaning as in section 162 of the Education and Inspections Act 2006;
"maintained school" has the same meaning as in section 20(7) of the School Standards and Framework Act 1998.

NOTES

Commencement: 31 March 2017.

[2.2009]
2 Meaning of "employment"

(1) In these Regulations, "employment" means—
(a) employment under a contract of employment, a contract of apprenticeship or a contract personally to do work, and
(b) Crown employment (within the meaning of section 191(3) of the 1996 Act).

(2) Section 191(4) of the 1996 Act applies for the purposes of these Regulations as it applies for the purposes set out in that subsection.

(3) For the purposes of these Regulations, an employee of an English local authority at a maintained school is to be treated as an employee of the governing body of that school.

(4) These Regulations apply to service in the armed forces as they apply to employment by, (or in the case of Crown employment, under or for the purposes of) a public authority, and for that purpose, references to terms of employment, or to a contract of employment, are to be read as including references to terms of service.

(5) For the purposes of these Regulations, the holding, otherwise than under a contract of employment, of the office of constable, or of an appointment as a police cadet, is to be treated as employment by the relevant officer (and for that purpose, references to terms of employment, or to a contract of employment, are to be read as including references to terms of service).

(6) In paragraph (4)—
(a) "constable" does not include a special constable;
(b) "police cadet" means a person appointed to undergo training with a view to becoming a constable;
(c) "relevant officer" means—

(i) in relation to a member of a police force or a police cadet appointed for a police area, the chief officer of police;

(ii) in relation to any other person holding the office of constable or an appointment as a police cadet, the person who has the direction and control of the body of constables or cadets in question.

NOTES

Commencement: 31 March 2017.

[2.2010]

3 Gender pay gap reporting

Schedule 1 to these Regulations (which imposes obligations on public authorities to publish gender pay gap information relating to employees) has effect.

NOTES

Commencement: 31 March 2017.

[2.2011]

4 Publication of information

(1) Each public authority listed in Schedule 2 to these Regulations must publish information to demonstrate its compliance with the duty imposed by section 149(1) of the Act.

(2) The public authority must publish the information required by paragraph (1)—

(a) not later than 30th March 2018; and

(b) subsequently at intervals of not greater than one year beginning with the date of last publication.

(3) The information a public authority publishes in compliance with paragraph (1) must include, in particular, information relating to persons who share a relevant protected characteristic who are—

(a) its employees;

(b) other persons affected by its policies and practices.

(4) Paragraph (3)(a) does not apply to a public authority with fewer than 150 employees.

NOTES

Commencement: 31 March 2017.

[2.2012]

5 Equality objectives

(1) Each public authority listed in Schedule 2 to these Regulations must prepare and publish one or more objectives it thinks it should achieve to do any of the things mentioned in paragraphs (a) to (c) of section 149(1) of the Act.

(2) The objectives must be published—

(a) not later than 30th March 2018 (subject to regulation 9(2)); and

(b) subsequently at intervals of not greater than four years beginning with the date of last publication.

(3) An objective published by a public authority in compliance with paragraph (1) must be specific and measurable.

NOTES

Commencement: 31 March 2017.

[2.2013]

6 Manner of publication

(1) The requirements in regulations 4 and 5 to publish information are requirements to publish the information in a manner that is accessible to the public.

(2) A public authority may comply with the requirements to publish information in regulation 4 or 5 by publishing the information within another published document.

NOTES

Commencement: 31 March 2017.

[2.2014]

7 Monitor and the NHS Trust Development Authority

Monitor and the NHS Trust Development Authority may jointly comply with the obligations imposed by these Regulations as if they were a single public authority.

NOTES

Commencement: 31 March 2017.

[2.2015]

8 Amendment of Schedule 19 to the Act

Schedule 3 to these Regulations (which amends Parts 1 and 2 of Schedule 19 to the Act) has effect.

NOTES

Commencement: 31 March 2017.

[2.2016]

9 Revocation, saving and transitional provision

(1) The 2011 Regulations are revoked (subject to paragraph (3)).

(2) Where a public authority has, within the period of four years ending with 30th March 2018, published equality objectives in compliance with regulation 3(1) of the 2011 Regulations—

(a) regulation 5(2)(a) does not apply; and

(b) regulation 5(2)(b) is to be read as if—

(i) the word "subsequently" were omitted, and

(ii) the "date of last publication" referred to the date of last publication under regulation 3 of the 2011 Regulations.

(3) Where—

(a) immediately before the commencement date a public authority is required by regulation 2 of the 2011 Regulations to publish the information referred to in paragraph (1) of that regulation,

(b) that information is required to be published on or before 6 April 2017, and

(c) the information is not published before the commencement date in a form and manner that complies with regulations 2 and 4 of those Regulations,

regulations 2 and 4 are to continue to have effect on and after the commencement date in so far as they relate to the publication of that information by that authority.

NOTES

Commencement: 31 March 2017.

SCHEDULES

SCHEDULE 1
GENDER PAY GAP REPORTING

Regulation 3

[2.2017]

1 (1) In this Schedule—

"bonus pay" has the meaning given in paragraph 4;

"full-pay relevant employee" means a relevant employee who is not, during the relevant pay period, being paid at a reduced rate or nil as a result of the employee being on leave;

"hourly rate of pay" has the meaning given in paragraph 6;

"ITEPA 2003" means the Income Tax (Earnings and Pensions) Act 2003;

"leave" includes—

(a) annual leave;

(b) maternity, paternity, adoption, parental or shared parental leave;

(c) sick leave; and

(d) special leave;

"ordinary pay" has the meaning given in paragraph 3;

"pay period" has the meaning given in paragraph 5(1);

"piecework" means work in respect of which an employee is entitled to be paid by reference to a number of pieces made or processed, or a number of tasks performed, instead of by reference to a period of time worked;

"relevant employee" means a person who is employed by, (or in the case of Crown employment, under or for the purposes of) the relevant public authority on the snapshot date;

"relevant pay period" has the meaning given in paragraph 5(2);

"relevant public authority" means a public authority listed in Schedule 2 to these Regulations which has 250 or more employees on the snapshot date;

"snapshot date" means the 31st March in the year to which the information required by paragraph 2 relates.

(2) For the purposes of this Schedule, the amount of an employee's ordinary pay or bonus pay is to be calculated before deductions made at source (for example deductions in relation to income tax).

Duty to publish annual information relating to pay

2 (1) A relevant public authority must publish, for 2017 and each subsequent year, the following information—

(a) the difference between the mean hourly rate of pay of male full-pay relevant employees and that of female full-pay relevant employees (see paragraph 8);

(b) the difference between the median hourly rate of pay of male full-pay relevant employees and that of female full-pay relevant employees (see paragraph 9);

(c) the difference between the mean bonus pay paid to male relevant employees and that paid to female relevant employees (see paragraph 10);

(d) the difference between the median bonus pay paid to male relevant employees and that paid to female relevant employees (see paragraph 11);

(e) the proportions of male and female relevant employees who were paid bonus pay (see paragraph 12); and

(f) the proportions of male and female full-pay relevant employees in the lower, lower middle, upper middle and upper quartile pay bands (see paragraph 13).

(2) The relevant public authority must publish the information required by sub-paragraph (1) within the period of 12 months beginning with the snapshot date.

(3) In compiling the information required by sub-paragraph (1), a relevant public authority is not required to include data relating to a relevant employee if—

(a) the employee is employed under a contract personally to do work, and

(b) the public authority does not have, and it is not reasonably practicable for the public authority to obtain, the data.

Meaning of "ordinary pay"

3 (1) In this Schedule, "ordinary pay" means (subject to sub-paragraph (2))—

(a) basic pay;

(b) allowances;

(c) pay for piecework;

(d) pay for leave; and

(e) shift premium pay.

(2) "Ordinary pay" does not include—

(a) remuneration referable to overtime;

(b) remuneration referable to redundancy or termination of employment;

(c) remuneration in lieu of leave; or

(d) remuneration provided otherwise than in money.

(3) In sub-paragraph (1)—

(a) "allowances" includes any sum paid with respect to—

(i) any duty of the employee, such as a duty in connection with the role of fire or bomb warden, that is ancillary to the main duties of the employee's employment;

(ii) the location of the employment in a particular area;

(iii) the purchase, lease or maintenance of a vehicle;

(iv) the recruitment and retention of an employee; or

(v) the purchase, lease or maintenance of an item;

but excludes any payment to reimburse expenditure wholly and necessarily incurred by the employee in the course of his or her employment;

(b) "shift premium pay" means the difference between basic pay and any higher rate paid by the public authority for work during different times of the day or night.

Meaning of "bonus pay"

4 (1) In this Schedule, "bonus pay" means (subject to sub-paragraph (2)) any remuneration that—

(a) is in the form of money, vouchers, securities, securities options or interests in securities, and

(b) relates to profit sharing, productivity, performance, incentive or commission.

(2) "Bonus pay" does not include—

(a) ordinary pay;

(b) remuneration referable to overtime; or

(c) remuneration referable to redundancy or termination of employment.

(3) For the purpose of sub-paragraph (1), remuneration in the form of securities, securities options and interests in securities, is to be treated as paid to the employee at the time, and in the amounts in respect of which, the securities, securities options and interests in securities give rise to (or would give rise to, if the employee were an employee for the purposes of Part 2 of ITEPA 2003 (employment income))—

(a) any taxable earnings within the meaning of section 10(2) of ITEPA 2003; or

(b) any taxable specific income within the meaning of section 10(3) of ITEPA 2003.

(4) In this paragraph "securities", "securities options" and "interests in securities" have the same meaning as in section 420 of ITEPA 2003.

Meaning of the "pay period" and the "relevant pay period"

5 (1) In this Schedule, "pay period", in relation to a relevant employee, means—

(a) the period in respect of which the relevant public authority pays the employee basic pay, whether weekly, fortnightly, monthly or any other period, or

(b) if the relevant public authority does not pay the employee basic pay, the period in respect of which the public authority most frequently pays the employee one of the elements of ordinary pay mentioned in paragraph 3(1)(b) to (e).

(2) In this Schedule, the "relevant pay period" means the pay period within which the snapshot date falls.

Meaning of "hourly rate of pay"

6 (1) The "hourly rate of pay" in relation to a relevant employee, is to be determined as follows—

Step 1

Identify all amounts of ordinary pay and bonus pay paid to the employee during the relevant pay period.

Step 2

Where an amount identified under Step 1 is an amount of ordinary pay, exclude any amount that would normally fall to be paid in a different pay period.

Step 3

Where an amount identified under Step 1 is an amount of bonus pay, and is paid in respect of a period ("the bonus period") which is not the same length as the relevant pay period, divide the amount by the length of the bonus period (in days) and multiply it by the length of the relevant pay period (in days).

Step 4

Add together the amounts identified under Step 1 (as adjusted, where necessary, under Steps 2 and 3).

Step 5

Multiply the amount found under Step 4 by the appropriate multiplier (see sub-paragraphs (2) and (3)).

Step 6

Divide the amount found under Step 5 by the number of working hours in a week for that employee (see paragraph 7).

(2) In this paragraph, "the appropriate multiplier" means 7 divided by the number of days in the relevant pay period.

(3) In determining for the purposes of this paragraph the number of days in the relevant pay period or bonus period where those periods are (or are determined by reference to) a month or a year—

- (a) a month is treated as having 30.44 days;
- (b) a year is treated as having 365.25 days.

Employee's working hours in a week

7 (1) The number of working hours in a week for a relevant employee, for the purposes of Step 6 in paragraph 6, is to be determined as follows.

(2) Subject to sub-paragraph (6), where an employee has normal working hours that do not differ from week to week or over a longer period, the number of working hours in a week for a relevant employee is the number of the normal working hours in a week for that employee under the employee's contract of employment, or terms of employment, in force on the snapshot date.

(3) Subject to sub-paragraph (6), where the employee has no normal working hours, or the number of the normal working hours differs from week to week or over a longer period, the number of working hours in a week for the employee is—

- (a) the average number of working hours calculated by dividing by twelve the total number of the employee's working hours during the period of twelve weeks ending with the last complete week of the relevant pay period, or
- (b) where the employee has not been at work for a sufficient period, or for some other reason the public authority is not reasonably able to make the calculation under paragraph (a), a number which fairly represents the number of working hours in a week having regard to such of the considerations specified in sub-paragraph (5) as are appropriate in the circumstances.

(4) In calculating the average number of working hours for the purposes of sub-paragraph (3)(a), no account is to be taken of a week in which no hours were worked by the employee, and hours worked in earlier weeks must be brought in so as to bring up to twelve the number of weeks of which account is taken.

(5) The considerations referred to in sub-paragraph (3)(b) are—

- (a) the average number of working hours in a week which the employee could expect under the employee's contract of employment, or terms of employment; and
- (b) the average number of working hours of other employees engaged in comparable employment with the same public authority.

(6) Where the employee is paid on the basis of piecework, the number of working hours in a week for the employee is the number of hours of output work for that employee in the week during the relevant pay period within which the snapshot date falls, determined in accordance with Chapter 4 of Part 5 of the National Minimum Wage Regulations 2015.

(7) In its application by virtue of sub-paragraph (6), Chapter 4 of Part 5 of the National Minimum Wage Regulations 2015 has effect as if—

- (a) references to a worker were references to an employee, and
- (b) references to a pay reference period were references to a week.

(8) In this paragraph, "working hours"—

- (a) includes hours when an employee is available, and required to be available, at or near a place of work for the purposes of working unless the employee is at home, and
- (b) excludes any hours for which an employee is entitled to overtime pay.

(9) In sub-paragraph (8), hours when an employee is "available" only includes hours when the employee is awake for the purposes of working, even if an employee by arrangement sleeps at or near a place of work and the employer provides suitable facilities for sleeping.

Difference in mean hourly rate of pay

8 The difference between the mean hourly rate of pay of male full-pay relevant employees and that of female full-pay relevant employees must be expressed as a percentage of the mean hourly rate of pay of male full-pay relevant employees and is to be determined as follows—

(A - B) / A x 100

where—

A is the mean hourly rate of pay of all male full-pay relevant employees; and

B is the mean hourly rate of pay of all female full-pay relevant employees.

Difference in median hourly rate of pay

9 The difference between the median hourly rate of pay of male full-pay relevant employees and that of female full-pay relevant employees must be expressed as a percentage of the median pay of male full-pay relevant employees and is to be determined as follows—

(A - B) / A x 100

where—

A is the median hourly rate of pay of all male full-pay relevant employees; and

B is the median hourly rate of pay of all female full-pay relevant employees.

Difference in mean bonus pay

10 (1) The difference between the mean bonus pay paid to male relevant employees and that paid to female relevant employees must be expressed as a percentage of the mean bonus pay paid to male relevant employees and is to be determined as follows—

(A - B) / A x 100

where—

A is the mean bonus pay paid during the relevant period to male relevant employees who were paid bonus pay during that period; and

B is the mean bonus pay paid during the relevant period to female relevant employees who were paid bonus pay during that period.

(2) In this paragraph, "the relevant period" means the period of 12 months ending with the snapshot date.

Difference in median bonus pay

11 (1) The difference between the median bonus pay paid to male relevant employees and that paid to female relevant employees must be expressed as a percentage of the median bonus pay paid to male relevant employees and is to be determined as follows—

(A - B) / A x 100

where—

A is the median bonus pay paid during the relevant period to male relevant employees who were paid bonus pay during that period; and

B is the median bonus pay paid during the relevant period to female relevant employees who were paid bonus pay during that period.

(2) In this paragraph, "the relevant period" means the period of 12 months ending with the snapshot date.

Proportion of male and female employees who were paid bonus pay

12 (1) The proportion of male relevant employees who were paid bonus pay must be expressed as a percentage of male relevant employees and as is to be determined as follows—

(A / B) x 100

where—

A is the number of male relevant employees who were paid bonus pay during the relevant period; and

B is the number of male relevant employees.

(2) The proportion of female relevant employees who were paid bonus pay must be expressed as a percentage of female relevant employees and is to be determined as follows—

(A / B) x 100

where—

A is the number of female relevant employees who were paid bonus pay during the relevant period; and

B is the number of female relevant employees.

(3) In this paragraph, "the relevant period" means the period of 12 months ending with the snapshot date.

Proportion of male and female employees according to quartile pay bands

13 (1) The proportions of male and female full-pay relevant employees in the lower, lower middle, upper middle and upper quartile pay bands is to be determined as follows.

Step 1

Determine the hourly rate of pay for each full-pay relevant employee and then rank those employees in order from lowest paid to highest paid.

Step 2
Divide the employees, as ranked under Step 1, into four sections, each comprising (so far as possible) an equal number of employees, to determine the lower, lower middle, upper middle and upper quartile pay bands.
Step 3
The proportion of male full-pay relevant employees within each quartile pay band must be expressed as a percentage of the full-pay relevant employees within that band as follows—

(A / B) x 100

where—
A is the number of male full-pay relevant employees in a quartile pay band; and
B is the number of full-pay relevant employees in that quartile pay band.
Step 4
The proportion of female full-pay relevant employees within each quartile pay band must be expressed as a percentage of the full-pay relevant employees within that band as follows—

(A / B) x 100

where—
A is the number of female full-pay relevant employees in a quartile pay band; and
B is the number of full-pay relevant employees in that quartile pay band.

(2) Where employees receiving the same hourly rate of pay fall within more than one quartile pay band, the public authority must (so far as possible) ensure that, when ranking the employees under Step 1, the relative proportion of male and female employees receiving that rate of pay is the same in each of those pay bands.

Manner of publication

14 (1) The requirement in paragraph 2(1) to publish information is a requirement that that information be published on the public authority's website—
- (a) in a manner that is accessible to all its employees and to the public; and
- (b) for a period of at least three years beginning with the date of publication.

(2) A relevant public authority must also publish the information required by paragraph 2(1) on a website designated for that purpose by the Secretary of State.

(3) Where the relevant public authority comprises one of the armed forces, the information required by paragraph 2(1) may be published by a government department on its behalf.

(4) Where a government department publishes information by virtue of sub-paragraph (3), the reference in sub-paragraph (1) to the public authority's website is to be read as a reference to that government department's website.

NOTES

Commencement: 31 March 2017.

SCHEDULE 2
PUBLIC AUTHORITIES REQUIRED TO PUBLISH INFORMATION

Regulation 4(2)

[2.2018]

Armed Forces

Any of the armed forces other than any part of the armed forces which is, in accordance with a requirement of the Secretary of State, assisting the Government Communications Headquarters.

Broadcasting

The British Broadcasting Corporation ("BBC"), except in respect of functions relating to the provision of a content service (within the meaning given by section 32(7) of the Communications Act 2003); and the reference to the BBC includes a reference to a body corporate which—
- (a) is a wholly owned subsidiary of the BBC,
- (b) is not operated with a view to generating a profit, and
- (c) undertakes activities primarily in order to promote the BBC's public purposes.

The Channel Four Television Corporation, except in respect of—
- (a) functions relating to the provision of a content service (within the meaning given by section 32(7) of the Communications Act 2003), and
- (b) the function of carrying on the activities referred to in section 199 of that Act.

The Welsh Authority (as defined by section 56(1) of the Broadcasting Act 1990), except in respect of functions relating to the provision of a content service (within the meaning given by section 32(7) of the Communications Act 2003).

Civil liberties

The Commission for Equality and Human Rights.

The Information Commissioner.

Court services and legal services

The Children and Family Court Advisory and Support Service.

The Judicial Appointments Commission.

The Legal Services Board.

Criminal justice

The Criminal Cases Review Commission.

Her Majesty's Chief Inspector of Constabulary.

Her Majesty's Chief Inspector of the Crown Prosecution Service.

Her Majesty's Chief Inspector of Prisons.

Her Majesty's Chief Inspector of Probation for England and Wales.

The Parole Board for England and Wales.

A probation trust established by an order made under section 5(1) of the Offender Management Act 2007.

The Youth Justice Board for England and Wales.

Education

The governing body of an educational establishment maintained by an English local authority (within the meaning of section 162 of the Education and Inspections Act 2006).

The governing body of an institution in England within the further education sector (within the meaning of section 91(3) of the Further and Higher Education Act 1992).

The governing body of an institution in England within the higher education sector (within the meaning of section 91(5) of that Act).

The Higher Education Funding Council for England.

A local authority in England with respect to the pupil referral units it establishes and maintains by virtue of section 19 of the Education Act 1996.

The proprietor of a City Technology College, City College for Technology of the Arts, or an Academy.

The Student Loans Company Limited.

Environment, housing and development

The Environment Agency.

The Homes and Communities Agency.

Natural England.

Health, social care and social security

The Care Quality Commission.

A clinical commissioning group established under section 14D of the National Health Service Act 2006.

Health Education England.

The Health Research Authority.

The Health and Social Care Information Centre.

Monitor.

An NHS foundation trust within the meaning given by section 30 of the National Health Service Act 2006.

An NHS trust established under section 25 of that Act.

The National Health Service Commissioning Board.

The National Institute for Health and Care Excellence.

A Special Health Authority established under section 28 of the National Health Service Act 2006.

Industry, business, finance etc

The Advisory, Conciliation and Arbitration Service.

The Bank of England, in respect of its public functions.

The Board of the Pension Protection Fund.

The Civil Aviation Authority.

The Coal Authority.

The Construction Industry Training Board.

The Engineering Construction Industry Training Board.

The Financial Conduct Authority.

The National Audit Office.

The Nuclear Decommissioning Authority.

The Office for Budget Responsibility.

The Office of Communications.

The Oil and Gas Authority.

The Prudential Regulation Authority.

Local government

A body corporate established pursuant to an order under section 67 of the Local Government Act 1985.

A combined authority established by an order made under section 103(1) of the Local Democracy, Economic Development and Construction Act 2009.

The Common Council of the City of London in its capacity as a local authority or port health authority.

The Council of the Isles of Scilly.

A county council or district council in England.

An economic prosperity board established by an order made under section 88(1) of the Local Democracy, Economic Development and Construction Act 2009.

A fire and rescue authority constituted by a scheme under section 2 of the Fire and Rescue Services Act 2004, or a scheme to which section 4 of that Act applies, for an area in England.

[A fire and rescue authority created by an order under section 4A of the Fire and Rescue Services Act 2004.]

The Greater London Authority.

A joint committee constituted in accordance with section 102(1)(b) of the Local Government Act 1972 for an area in England.

A London borough council.

[The London Fire Commissioner.]

A National Park authority established by an order under section 63 of the Environment Act 1995 for an area in England.

A Passenger Transport Executive for an integrated transport area in England (within the meaning of Part 2 of the Transport Act 1968).

Transport for London.

Ministers of the Crown and government departments

A government department other than the Security Service, the Secret Intelligence Service or the Government Communications Headquarters.

A Minister of the Crown.

Parliamentary and devolved bodies

The National Assembly for Wales Commission (Comisiwn Cynulliad Cenedlaethol Cymru).

The Scottish Parliamentary Corporate Body.

Police

The British Transport Police Force.

A chief constable of a police force maintained under section 2 of the Police Act 1996.

The Chief Inspector of the UK Border Agency.

The Civil Nuclear Police Authority.

The College of Policing.

The Commissioner of Police for the City of London.

The Commissioner of Police of the Metropolis.

The Common Council of the City of London in its capacity as a police authority.

The Independent Police Complaints Commission.

The Mayor's Office for Policing and Crime established under section 3 of the Police Reform and Social Responsibility Act 2011.

A police and crime commissioner established under section 1 of that Act.

Regulators

The Disclosure and Barring Service.

The Gambling Commission.

The Gangmasters and Labour Abuse Authority.

The General Council of the Bar, in respect of its public functions.

The Health and Safety Executive.

The Law Society of England and Wales, in respect of its public functions.

The Office for Nuclear Regulation.

The Pensions Regulator.

[The Regulator of Social Housing.]

The Security Industry Authority.

[Social Work England.]

Transport

High Speed Two (HS2) Limited.

Highways England Company Limited.

Network Rail Limited.

NOTES

Commencement: 31 March 2017.

Local government:

Entry "A fire and rescue authority created by an order under section 4A of the Fire and Rescue Services Act 2004" inserted, in relation to England only, by the Fire and Rescue Authority (Police and Crime Commissioner) (Application of Local Policing Provisions, Inspection, Powers to Trade and Consequential Amendments) Order 2017, SI 2017/863, art 29, Sch 2, para 11, as from 1 October 2017.

Entry "The London Fire Commissioner" substituted (for the original entry "The London Fire and Emergency Planning Authority") by the London Government (London Fire Commissioner and Policing) (Amendment) Regulations 2018, SI 2018/269, reg 2, Schedule, para 20, as from 1 April 2018.

Regulators:

Entry "The Regulator of Social Housing." inserted, in relation to England only, by the Legislative Reform (Regulator of Social Housing) (England) Order 2018, SI 2018/1040, art 2, Schedule, Pt 2, para 44, as from 1 October 2018.

Entry "Social Work England" inserted by the Social Workers Regulations 2018, SI 2018/893, reg 46, as from a day to be appointed.

SCHEDULE 3
AMENDMENTS TO SCHEDULE 19 OF THE ACT

(*Sch 3 amends the Equality Act 2010, Sch 19 at* **[1.1782]**.)

PRESCRIBED PERSONS (REPORTS ON DISCLOSURES OF INFORMATION) REGULATIONS 2017

(SI 2017/507)

NOTES

Made: 30 March 2017.
Authority: Employment Rights Act 1996, s 43FA.
Commencement: 1 April 2017.

[2.2019]

1 Citation and commencement

(1) These Regulations may be cited as the Prescribed Persons (Reports on Disclosures of Information) Regulations 2017.

(2) These Regulations come into force on 1st April 2017.

(3) These Regulations apply in relation to reporting periods beginning on or after—

(a) 1st April 2017 for relevant prescribed persons except auditors appointed to audit the accounts of larger authorities;

(b) 1st April 2018 for auditors appointed to audit the accounts of larger authorities.

NOTES

Commencement: 1 April 2017.

[2.2020]

2 Interpretation

In these Regulations—

"larger authority" means a person listed in Schedule 2 to the Local Audit and Accountability Act 2014 which is not a smaller authority;

"relevant prescribed person" means a person prescribed for the purposes of section 43F of the Employment Rights Act 1996 other than—

(a) a member of the House of Commons,
(b) a Minister of the Crown,
(c) a Welsh Minister,
(d) a Scottish Minister,
(e) the European Securities and Markets Authority, or
(f) an auditor appointed to audit smaller authorities;

"smaller authority" has the meaning given by section 6 of the Local Audit and Accountability Act 2014;

"workers' disclosures" means disclosures of information made to a relevant prescribed person other than those which the relevant prescribed person has reason to believe—

(a) were not made by a worker; or
(b) were made by a worker on behalf of the worker's employer.

NOTES

Commencement: 1 April 2017.

[2.2021]

3 Annual report on disclosures of information

(1) In relation to each reporting period, each relevant prescribed person must report in writing on the workers' disclosures that it has received.

(2) The reporting period is 12 months beginning on 1st April of each year.

(3) A relevant prescribed person is not required to report on disclosures that it reasonably believes do not fall within the description of matters in respect of which that person is so prescribed.

NOTES

Commencement: 1 April 2017.

[2.2022]

4 Manner of publication of report

(1) The relevant prescribed person must publish the report mentioned in regulation 3—

(a) by placing the report on its website, or

(b) in such other manner as the relevant prescribed person considers appropriate for bringing the report to the attention of the public.

(2) The report must be published within 6 months of the end of the reporting period.

NOTES

Commencement: 1 April 2017.

[2.2023]
5 Content of report

The report must contain, without including any information in the report that would identify a worker who has made a disclosure of information, or an employer or other person in respect of whom a disclosure of information has been made—

(a) the number of workers' disclosures received during the reporting period that the relevant prescribed person reasonably believes are—
  (i) qualifying disclosures within the meaning of section 43B of the Employment Rights Act 1996; and
  (ii) which fall within the matters in respect of which that person is so prescribed;

(b) the number of those disclosures in relation to which the relevant prescribed person decided during the reporting period to take further action;

(c) a summary of—
  (i) the action that the relevant prescribed person has taken during the reporting period in respect of the workers' disclosures; and
  (ii) how workers' disclosures have impacted on the relevant prescribed person's ability to perform its functions and meet its objectives during the reporting period;

(d) an explanation of the functions and objectives of the relevant prescribed person.

NOTES

Commencement: 1 April 2017.

MERCHANT SHIPPING (MARITIME LABOUR CONVENTION) (HOURS OF WORK) REGULATIONS 2018

(SI 2018/58)

NOTES

Made: 29 January 2018.

Authority: European Communities Act 1972, s 2(2); Merchant Shipping Act 1995, ss 85(1)(a), (b), (3), (5), (7), 86(1), (2).

Commencement: 6 April 2018.

Note: with regard to the authority for these Regulations, note that the European Communities Act 1972 is repealed by the European Union (Withdrawal) Act 2018, s 1, as from exit day (as defined in s 20 of that Act); but note also that provision is made for the continuation in force of any subordinate legislation made under the authority of s 2(2) of the 1972 Act by s 2 of the 2018 Act at **[1.2240]**, subject to the provisions of s 5 of, and Sch 1 to, the 2018 Act at **[1.2243]**, **[1.2253]**.

Only the provisions of the Regulations most relevant to this work are reproduced.

Conciliation: employment tribunal proceedings under reg 26 are "relevant proceedings" for the purposes of the conciliation provisions contained in the Employment Tribunals Act 1996, ss 18–18C; see s 18(1)(n) of the 1996 Act at **[1.757]**.

Employment Appeal Tribunal: an appeal lies to the Employment Appeal Tribunal on any question of law arising from any decision of, or in any proceedings before, an employment tribunal under or by virtue of these Regulations; see the Employment Tribunals Act 1996, s 21(1)(z) at **[1.764]**.

ARRANGEMENT OF REGULATIONS

SCHEDULES

[2.2024]

1 Citation and commencement

These Regulations may be cited as the Merchant Shipping (Maritime Labour Convention) (Hours of Work) Regulations 2018 and come into force on 6th April 2018.

NOTES

Commencement: 6 April 2018.

[2.2025]

2 Interpretation

(1) In these Regulations—

"collective agreement" means a collective agreement within the meaning of section 178 of the Trade Union and Labour Relations (Consolidation) Act 1992, the trade union parties to which are independent trade unions within the meaning of section 5 of that Act;

"Declaration of Maritime Labour Compliance" means, in relation to a ship, the Part 1 and Part 2 documents drawn up and issued in accordance with the Maritime Labour Convention, in the forms corresponding to the relevant models given in appendix A5-II of the Convention and having the contents, duration and validity specified in Regulation 5.1.3 and Standard A5.1.3 of the Convention;

"hours of rest" means time outside hours of work and does not include short breaks;

"hours of work" means time during which a seafarer is required to do work on the business of the ship;

"Maritime Labour Certificate" and "interim Maritime Labour Certificate" mean, in relation to a ship, a certificate of that name issued in accordance with the Maritime Labour Convention, in a form corresponding to the relevant model given in appendix A5-II of the Convention and having the contents, duration and validity specified in Regulation 5.1.3 and Standard A5.1.3 of the Convention;

"the Maritime Labour Convention" means the Convention adopted on 23rd February 2006 by the General Conference of the International Labour Organization;

"master" in the application of these Regulations to a hovercraft includes the captain of a hovercraft;

"MCA" means the Maritime and Coastguard Agency;

"Merchant Shipping Notice" means a notice described as such and issued by the MCA; and any reference to a particular Merchant Shipping Notice includes a reference to a Merchant Shipping Notice amending or replacing that notice which is considered by the Secretary of State to be relevant from time to time;

"MLC ship" means a sea-going ship which is not a United Kingdom ship if—

(a) the Maritime Labour Convention has come into force for the State whose flag the ship is entitled to fly; and

(b) the ship carries—

(i) a Maritime Labour Certificate to which a Declaration of Maritime Labour Compliance is attached; or

(ii) an interim Maritime Labour Certificate;

"non-MLC ship" means a sea-going ship which is neither a United Kingdom ship nor an MLC ship;

"pleasure vessel" means—

(a) any vessel which at the time it is being used is—

(i) in the case of a vessel wholly owned by—

(aa) an individual or individuals, used only for the sport or pleasure of the owner or the immediate family or friends of the owner; or

(bb) a body corporate, used only for sport or pleasure and on which the persons on board are employees or officers of the body corporate, or their immediate [family or friends]; and

(ii) on a voyage or excursion which is one for which the owner does not receive money for or in connection with operating the vessel or carrying any person, other than as a contribution to the direct expenses of the operation of the vessel incurred during the voyage or excursion; or

(b) any vessel wholly owned by or on behalf of a members club formed for the purpose of sport or pleasure which, at the time it is being used, is used only for the sport or pleasure of members of that club or their immediate family, and for the use of which any charges levied are paid into club funds and applied for the general use of the club,

where, in the case of any vessel referred to in paragraph (a) or (b), no other payments are made by or on behalf of users of the vessel, other than by the owner; and in this definition "immediate family" means, in relation to an individual, the spouse or civil partner of the individual, and a relative of the individual or the individual's spouse or civil partner; and "relative" means brother, sister, ancestor or lineal descendant;

"relevant inspector" means any of the persons mentioned in section 258(1) of the Merchant Shipping Act 1995;

"sea-going" in relation to a United Kingdom ship means—

(a) a ship which operates outside the waters specified as category A, B, C and D waters in Merchant Shipping Notice 1837(M);
(b) a ship to which the Merchant Shipping (Survey and Certification) Regulations 2015 apply and in respect of which no exemption granted under regulation 5(3) of those regulations applies;
(c) a ship to which regulation 4 of the Merchant Shipping (Vessels in Commercial Use for Sport or Pleasure) Regulations 1998 applies and which falls within the description given in paragraph (3) of that regulation; or
(d) a high speed craft in respect of which a permit to operate outside waters of Categories A, B, C or D has been issued in accordance with regulation 8 of the Merchant Shipping (High Speed Craft) Regulations 2004;

"ship" includes hovercraft;

"shipowner" means—

(a) in relation to a ship which has a valid Maritime Labour Certificate or interim Maritime Labour Certificate, the person identified as the shipowner on that certificate;
(b) in relation to any other ship, the owner of the ship or, if different, any other organisation or person such as the manager, or the bareboat charterer, that has assumed responsibility for the operation of the ship from the owner;

"United Kingdom ship" means a ship which is—

(a) a United Kingdom ship within the meaning of section 85(2) of the Merchant Shipping Act 1995;
(b) a Government ship within the meaning given by section 308(4) of the Merchant Shipping Act 1995 which is ordinarily engaged in commercial maritime operations; or
(c) a hovercraft registered under the Hovercraft Act 1968;

"workforce agreement" means an agreement between an employer and persons employed by that employer or their representatives in respect of which the conditions set out in Schedule 1 to these Regulations are satisfied.

(2) For the purposes of these Regulations—

(a) "seafarer" means any person, including a master, who is employed or engaged or who works in any capacity on board a ship and whose normal place of work is on a ship, other than a seafarer who is subject to any requirement contained in the Merchant Shipping (Working Time: Inland Waterways) Regulations 2003;
(b) "engaged", in the application of these Regulations to a seafarer, means engaged under a contract, whether express or implied, and (if it is express) whether oral or in writing, whereby the seafarer undertakes to do or perform personally any work or services for another party to the contract whose status is not by virtue of the contract that of a client or customer of any profession or business undertaking carried out by the seafarer;
(c) "employed seafarer" means a seafarer who is employed under a contract of employment or engaged (or where the employment has ceased, was employed or engaged);
(d) "employer" in relation to an employed seafarer means the person by whom the employed seafarer is or was employed or engaged; and
(e) "employment" in relation to an employed seafarer is to be construed accordingly.

NOTES

Commencement: 6 April 2018.

Para (1): words in square brackets in definition "pleasure vessel" substituted by the Merchant Shipping (Maritime Labour Convention) (Miscellaneous Amendments) Regulations 2018, SI 2018/242, reg 7, as from 6 April 2018.

[2.2026]

3 Application to ships

(1) The following regulations apply to a sea-going United Kingdom ship wherever it may be and a non-MLC ship while it is in United Kingdom waters—

(a) regulation 5 (general duty of shipowner, master, employer to provide hours of rest);
(b) regulation 9 (requirement to post up table);
(c) regulation 11 (exception to hours of rest in emergencies);
(d) regulation 12 (requirement to keep records of hours of rest);
(e) regulation 14 (provision of information on request);
(f) regulation 15 (annual and additional leave);
(g) regulation 17 (shore leave) (but see paragraph (3));
(h) regulation 19 (inspection);
(i) regulation 21 (detention);
(j) regulation 22 (release of ships).

(2) The following regulations apply to an MLC ship while that ship is in United Kingdom waters—

(a) regulation 8 (general duty of shipowner, master, employer to provide hours of rest);
(b) regulation 10 (requirement to post up table);
(c) regulation 11 (exception to hours of rest in emergencies);
(d) regulation 13 (requirement to keep records of hours of rest);
(e) regulation 16 (annual leave);
(f) regulation 17 (shore leave) (but see paragraph (3));
(g) regulation 20 (inspection);
(h) regulation 21 (detention);
(i) regulation 22 (release of ships).

Part 2 Statutory Instruments

(3) Regulation 17 (shore leave) does not apply to ships of traditional build.

(4) These Regulations do not apply to—

(a) pleasure vessels;

(b) fishing vessels;

(c) warships or naval auxiliaries;

(d) vessels which are not ordinarily engaged in commercial activities.

NOTES

Commencement: 6 April 2018.

4 (*Application to Northern Ireland – outside the scope of this work.*)

[2.2027]

5 General duty of shipowner, master, employer

(1) It is the duty of the persons mentioned in paragraph (2) to ensure that a seafarer in relation to a ship to which this regulation applies is provided with at least the minimum hours of rest.

(2) The persons are—

(a) the shipowner in relation to the ship;

(b) the master of the ship; and

(c) where the seafarer is an employed seafarer, the seafarer's employer.

(3) A muster, drill or training session held pursuant to the Merchant Shipping (Musters, Training and Decision Support Systems) Regulations 1999—

(a) may require the participation of a seafarer during the seafarer's hours of rest, but

(b) must be conducted in a manner which minimises disturbance of the seafarer's hours of rest and does not induce fatigue.

(4) A seafarer who is on-call on board ship—

(a) may be required to do call-outs during hours of rest, but

(b) must be provided with an adequate compensatory rest period for any call-out work done during hours of rest.

(5) Nothing in this regulation restricts the operation of regulation 6 of the Merchant Shipping and Fishing Vessels (Health and Safety at Work) (Employment of Young Persons Regulations 1998 (rest periods for young persons).

(6) This regulation is subject to regulation 11.

NOTES

Commencement: 6 April 2018.

[2.2028]

6 Minimum hours of rest

(1) The minimum hours of rest are—

(a) 10 hours in any 24-hour period; and

(b) 77 hours in any 7-day period.

(2) The 10 hours of rest mentioned in paragraph (1)(a) may be divided into no more than 2 periods, one of which is to be at least 6 hours in length.

(3) This regulation is subject to regulation 7.

NOTES

Commencement: 6 April 2018.

[2.2029]

7 Authorised exceptions to minimum hours of rest

(1) The MCA may authorise collective agreements or workforce agreements which—

(a) provide exceptions to the minimum hours of rest mentioned in regulation 6(1)(b);

(b) provide for exceptions to regulation 6(2).

(2) A collective agreement or workforce agreement under paragraph (1)(a) must require that—

(a) there are at least 70 hours total rest in any period of 7 days;

(b) the exceptions provided for in the agreement do not apply in relation to a period of more than two consecutive weeks; and

(c) where the exceptions apply in relation to two periods separated by an interval, the interval is at least twice the duration of the longer of the two periods.

(3) A collective agreement or workforce agreement under paragraph (1)(b) must require that the 10 minimum hours of rest mentioned in regulation 6(1)(a) are divided into three periods—

(a) one of the three periods is at least 6 hours long and neither of the two other periods are less than one hour long;

(b) intervals between consecutive periods do not exceed 14 hours each; and

(c) the exceptions provided for in the agreement do not apply in relation to more than two 24 hour periods in any 7 day period.

(4) Paragraphs (2) and (3) do not apply in relation to ships which—

(a) operate only within 60 miles of a safe haven;

(b) are not engaged in the transport of cargo or passengers; and

(c) do not operate to or from, or call at, any port in a country other than the United Kingdom.

(5) A "safe haven" is a harbour of shelter of any kind which affords entry and protection from the weather.

NOTES

Commencement: 6 April 2018.

[2.2030]

8 Hours of rest requirement for MLC ships

(1) It is the duty of the persons mentioned in paragraph (2) to ensure that a seafarer in relation to a ship to which this regulation applies is provided with hours of work or hours of rest in accordance with the provisions of Standard A2.3 of the Maritime Labour Convention.

(2) The persons are—

(a) the shipowner in relation to the ship;

(b) the master of the ship; and

(c) where the seafarer is an employed seafarer, the seafarer's employer.

NOTES

Commencement: 6 April 2018.

[2.2031]

9 Posting up of table

(1) The master of a ship to which this regulation applies, or a person authorised by the master, must ensure that the following tables are posted up in a prominent and easily accessible place in the ship—

(a) a table of scheduled watchkeeping; and

(b) a table of scheduled hours of rest.

(2) A table under paragraph (1) is to—

(a) contain the information specified in Merchant Shipping Notice 1877(M);

(b) be in the format specified in that Merchant Shipping Notice, or in a format substantially like it; and

(c) be in English and in the working language of the ship, if that is not English.

NOTES

Commencement: 6 April 2018.

[2.2032]

10 Requirement to post up table in relation to MLC ships

The master of a ship to which this regulation applies, or a person authorised by the master, must post a table of the working shipboard arrangements in accordance with the provisions of paragraphs 10 and 11 of Standard A2.3 of the Maritime Labour Convention.

NOTES

Commencement: 6 April 2018.

[2.2033]

11 Exception for emergencies

(1) The master of a ship to which this regulation applies may require a seafarer to work any hours of work necessary for the immediate safety of the ship, persons on board or cargo, or for the purpose of giving assistance to another ship or to a person in distress at sea.

(2) As soon as practicable after the normal situation has been restored the master must ensure that any seafarer who has performed work in hours of rest scheduled in the table under regulation 9 is provided with an adequate rest period.

NOTES

Commencement: 6 April 2018.

[2.2034]

12 Records

(1) The master of a ship to which this regulation applies, or a person authorised by the master, must maintain records of each seafarer's daily hours of rest in accordance with the requirements of Merchant Shipping Notice 1877(M).

(2) Records under paragraph (1) must be in a format which complies with the requirements specified in Merchant Shipping Notice 1877(M).

(3) Records under paragraph (1) must be in English and in the working language of the ship if that is not English.

(4) The records kept under paragraph (1) must be endorsed by—

(a) the master, or the person authorised by the master; and

(b) the seafarer to whom the record relates.

(5) The master, or a person authorised by the master, must give a copy of the endorsed record to the seafarer to whom the record relates.

(6) A relevant inspector must examine and endorse, at appropriate intervals, records kept under paragraph (1).

(7) The shipowner and the master must ensure that a copy of these Regulations, Merchant Shipping Notice 1877(M) and any collective agreements or workforce agreements relevant to the ship which are authorised under regulation 7 (exceptions to minimum hours of rest) are carried at all times on board ship in an easily accessible place.

NOTES

Commencement: 6 April 2018.

[2.2035]

13 Records requirement for MLC ships

The master of a ship to which this regulation applies, or a person authorised by the master, must maintain records of seafarers' daily hours of rest or work and provide copies of such records to seafarers in accordance with the provisions of paragraph 12 of Standard A2.3 of the Maritime Labour Convention.

NOTES

Commencement: 6 April 2018.

[2.2036]

14 Power to require information

A shipowner in relation to a ship to which this regulation applies must provide the MCA with such information as the MCA may specify on watchkeepers and other seafarers working at night.

NOTES

Commencement: 6 April 2018.

[2.2037]

15 Entitlement to annual and additional leave

(1) An employed seafarer on a ship to which this regulation applies is entitled to—

(a) paid annual leave that is to be calculated on the basis of two and a half days for each month of employment in the leave year and pro rata for incomplete months; and

(b) additional paid leave of eight days in each leave year and pro rata for incomplete years.

(2) Leave to which a seafarer is entitled under this regulation—

(a) may be taken in instalments; and

(b) may not be replaced by payment in lieu, except where the seafarer's employment is terminated.

(3) Justified absences from work are not to be considered annual leave for the purposes of paragraph (1)(a).

(4) For the purposes of this regulation, "justified absences from work" include any absence authorised by—

(a) any enactment;

(b) any contract between the seafarer's employer and the seafarer;

(c) any collective agreement or workplace agreement; or

(d) custom and practice.

NOTES

Commencement: 6 April 2018.

[2.2038]

16 Annual leave requirement for MLC ships

The employer of a seafarer in relation to a ship to which this regulation applies must ensure that the seafarer is given paid annual leave in accordance with Regulation 2.4 of the Maritime Labour Convention.

NOTES

Commencement: 6 April 2018.

[2.2039]

17 Shore leave

The shipowner and the master of a ship to which this regulation applies must ensure that shore leave is granted to seafarers who work on the ship to benefit their health and well-being where consistent with the operational requirements of their positions.

NOTES

Commencement: 6 April 2018.

[2.2040]

18 Entitlements under other provisions

Where during any period a seafarer is entitled to hours of rest or paid leave both under a provision of these Regulations and under a separate provision (including a provision of the seafarer's contract), the seafarer may not exercise the two rights separately, but may, in taking hours of rest or paid leave during that period, take advantage of whichever right is, in any particular respect, the more favourable.

NOTES

Commencement: 6 April 2018.

19–24 (*Inspection of ships, and detention & release of ships, etc – outside the scope of this work.*)

[2.2041]

25 Offences, penalties and defence

(1) It is an offence for—

(a) the master of the ship to breach regulation 5(1), (3)(b) or (4)(b), 8(1), 9(1), 10, 11(2), 12(1), (4)(a), (5) or (7), 13 or 17;

(b) the employer of an employed seafarer to breach regulation 5(1), 8(1) or 16;

(c) the person authorised by the master of the ship to breach regulation 9(1), 10, 12(1), (4)(a) or (5) or 13;

(d) the shipowner to breach regulation 5(1), 8(1), 12(7), 14 or 17.

(2) Where there is a contravention of regulation 15(1)(a) or (b), the employer of the seafarer is guilty of an offence.

(3) A person guilty of an offence under these Regulations is liable on summary conviction—

(a) in England and Wales, to a fine;

(b) in Scotland or Northern Ireland, to a fine not exceeding level 5 on the standard scale.

(4) In any proceedings for an offence under these Regulations it is a defence for the defendant to show that all reasonable steps had been taken by the defendant to ensure compliance with these Regulations.

NOTES

Commencement: 6 April 2018.

[2.2042]

26 Remedies

(1) An employed seafarer may present a complaint to an employment tribunal that the seafarer's employer—

(a) has refused to permit the exercise of any right that the seafarer has under regulation 15(1)(a) or (b) (entitlement to annual leave etc); or

(b) has failed to pay the seafarer the whole or any part of any amount due to the seafarer under regulation 15(1)(a) or (b).

(2) An employment tribunal must not consider a complaint under this regulation unless it is presented—

(a) before the end of the complaint period; or

(b) within such further period as the tribunal considers reasonable in a case where it is satisfied that it was not reasonably practicable for the complaint to be presented before the end of the complaint period.

(3) Where an employment tribunal finds a complaint under paragraph (1)(a) to be well-founded, the tribunal—

(a) must make a declaration to that effect; and

(b) may make an award of compensation to be paid by the employer to the seafarer.

(4) The amount of the compensation is to be such amount as the tribunal considers just and equitable in all the circumstances having regard to—

(a) the employer's default in refusing to permit the seafarer to exercise the seafarer's right; and

(b) any loss sustained by the seafarer which is attributable to the matters complained of.

(5) Where on complaint under paragraph (1)(b) an employment tribunal finds that an employer has failed to pay a seafarer in accordance with regulation 15(1)(a) or (b), it must order the employer to pay the seafarer the amount which it finds to be due to the seafarer.

(6) The "complaint period" is the period of three months beginning with the date on which it is alleged that the exercise of the right should have been permitted (or in the case of a period of annual leave or additional leave extending over more than one day, the date on which it should have been permitted to begin) or, as the case may be, the payment should have been made.

NOTES

Commencement: 6 April 2018.

Conciliation: employment tribunal proceedings under this regulation are "relevant proceedings" for the purposes of the conciliation provisions contained in the Employment Tribunals Act 1996, ss 18–18C; see s 18(1)(n) of the 1996 Act at **[1.757]**.

[2.2043]

27 Extension of complaint period to facilitate conciliation before institution of proceedings

(1) In working out when the complaint period expires, the period beginning with the day after Day A and ending with Day B is not to be counted.

(2) If the complaint period would (if not extended by this paragraph) expire during the period beginning with Day A and ending one month after Day B, the time limit expires instead at the end of that period.

(3) In this regulation—

(a) "complaint period" has the meaning given in regulation 26(6);

Part 2 Statutory Instruments

(b) "Day A" is the day on which the seafarer concerned complies with the requirement in section 18A(1) of the Employment Tribunals Act 1996 (requirement to contact ACAS before instituting proceedings) in relation to the matter in respect of which the proceedings are brought; and

(c) "Day B" is the day on which the seafarer concerned receives or, if earlier, is treated as receiving (by virtue of regulations made under section 18A(11) of the Employment Tribunals Act 1996) the certificate issued under subsection (4) of that section.

NOTES

Commencement: 6 April 2018.

[2.2044]

28 Restriction on contracting out

(1) Any provision in an agreement (whether a contract of employment or not) is void in so far as it purports to—

(a) exclude or limit the operation of any provision of these Regulations; or

(b) preclude a person from bringing proceedings under these Regulations before an employment tribunal.

(2) Paragraph (1) does not apply to—

(a) any agreement to refrain from instituting or continuing proceedings where a conciliation officer has taken action under sections 18A to 18C of the Employment Tribunals Act 1996 (conciliation); or

(b) any agreement to refrain from instituting or continuing proceedings under regulation 26, if the following conditions are met.

(3) For the purposes of paragraph (2)(b) the conditions are—

(a) the agreement is in writing;

(b) the agreement relates to the particular complaint;

(c) the seafarer has received advice from a relevant independent adviser as to the terms and effect of the proposed agreement and, in particular, its effect on the seafarer's ability to pursue the seafarer's rights before an employment tribunal;

(d) there is in force, when the adviser gives the advice, a contract of insurance, or an indemnity provided for members of a profession or a professional body, covering the risk of a claim by the seafarer in respect of loss arising in consequence of the advice; and

(e) the agreement states that the conditions in sub-paragraphs (a) to (d) are satisfied.

(4) A person is a relevant independent adviser for the purposes of paragraph (3)(c) if the person—

(a) is a qualified lawyer;

(b) is an officer, official, employee or member of an independent trade union who has been certified in writing by the trade union as competent to give advice and as authorised to do so on behalf of the trade union; or

(c) works at an advice centre (whether as an employee or a volunteer) and has been certified in writing by the centre as competent to give advice and as authorised to do so on behalf of the centre.

(5) But a person is not a relevant independent adviser for the purposes of paragraph (3)(c)—

(a) if the person is, is employed by or is acting in the matter for the employer or an associated employer;

(b) in the case of a person within paragraph (4)(b), if the trade union is the employer or an associated employer; or

(c) in the case of a person within paragraph (4)(c), if the seafarer makes a payment for the advice received from the person.

(6) In paragraph (4)(a), "qualified lawyer" means—

(a) as respects England and Wales, a person who, for the purposes of the Legal Services Act 2007, is an authorised person in relation to an activity which constitutes the exercise of a right of audience or the conduct of litigation (within the meaning of that Act);

(b) as respects Scotland, an advocate (whether in practice as such or employed to give legal advice), or a solicitor who holds a practising certificate; and

(c) as respects Northern Ireland, a barrister (whether in practice as such or employed to give legal advice), or a solicitor who holds a practising certificate.

(7) For the purposes of paragraph (5) any two employers are to be treated as associated if—

(a) one is a company of which the other (directly or indirectly) has control; or

(b) both are companies of which a third person (directly or indirectly) has control,

and "associated employer" is to be construed accordingly.

NOTES

Commencement: 6 April 2018.

[2.2045]

29 Review

(1) The Secretary of State must from time to time—

(a) carry out a review of the regulatory provision contained in these Regulations; and

(b) publish a report setting out the conclusions of the review.

(2) The first report must be published before 5th April 2020.

(3) Subsequent reports must be published at intervals not exceeding 5 years.

(4) Section 30(3) of the Small Business, Enterprise and Employment Act 2015 requires that a review carried out under this regulation must, so far as is reasonable, have regard to how other member States have implemented—

(a) Council Directive 1999/63/EC of 21st June 1999 concerning the Agreement on the organisation of working time of seafarers concluded by the European Communities Shipowners' Association (ECSA) and the Federation of Transport Workers' Unions in the European Union (FST), as amended by Council Directive 2009/13/EC of 16th February 2009 implementing the Agreement concluded by the European Community Shipowners' Associations (ECSA) and the European Transport Workers' Federation (ETF) on the Maritime Labour Convention, 2006;

(b) article 15 of Council Directive 2008/106/EC of 19th November 2008 on the minimum level of training of seafarers (recast), as amended by article 1(14) of Council Directive 2012/35/EU of 21st November 2012;

(c) article 19 of Directive 2009/16/EC of 23rd April 2009 on port state control, as amended by article 1 of Council Directive 2013/38/EU of 12th August 2013; and

(d) article 3 of Council Directive 2013/54/EU of 20th November 2013 concerning certain flag state responsibilities for compliance with and enforcement of the Maritime Labour Convention, 2006.

(5) Section 30(3) of the Small Business, Enterprise and Employment Act 2015 requires that a report published under this regulation must, in particular—

(a) set out the objectives intended to be achieved by the regulatory provision contained in these Regulations;

(b) assess the extent to which those objectives are achieved;

(c) assess whether those objectives remain appropriate; and

(d) if those objectives remain appropriate, assess the extent to which they could be achieved in another way which involves less onerous regulatory provision.

(6) In this regulation "regulatory provision" has the same meaning as in sections 28 to 32 of the Small Business, Enterprise and Employment Act 2015 (see section 32 of that Act).

NOTES

Commencement: 6 April 2018.

[2.2046]

30 Revocations and savings

The following Regulations are revoked—

(a) the Merchant Shipping (Hours of Work) Regulations 2002, except for regulation 21 and Schedule 2;

(b) the Merchant Shipping (Hours of Work) (Amendment) Regulations 2004; and

(c) the Merchant Shipping (Maritime Labour Convention) (Hours of Work) (Amendments) Regulations 2014, except for regulation 3 and the Schedule.

NOTES

Commencement: 6 April 2018.

31 (*Introduces Schedule 2 – Consequential amendments.*)

SCHEDULES

SCHEDULE 1
WORKFORCE AGREEMENTS

Regulation 2(1)

[2.2047]

1. An agreement is a workforce agreement for the purposes of these Regulations if the following conditions are satisfied—

(a) the agreement is in writing;

(b) the agreement has effect for a specified period not exceeding five years;

(c) the agreement applies either—

(i) to all of the relevant members of the workforce, or

(ii) to all of the relevant members of the workforce who belong to a particular group;

(d) the agreement is signed—

(i) in the case of an agreement of the kind referred to in sub-paragraph (c)(i)—

(aa) by the representatives of the workforce, or

(bb) if the employer employed 20 or fewer individuals on the date on which the agreement was first made available for signature, the majority of the individuals employed by the employer; or

(ii) in the case of an agreement of the kind referred to in sub-paragraph (c)(ii)—

(aa) by the representatives of the group to which the agreement applies (excluding, in either case, any representative not a relevant member of the workforce on the date on which the agreement was first made available for signature), or (bb) if the employer employed 20 or fewer individuals on the date on which the agreement was first made available for signature, the majority of the individuals employed by the employer; and

(e) before the agreement was made available for signature, the employer provided all the employees to whom it was intended to apply on the date on which it came into effect with copies of the text of the agreement and such guidance as those employees might reasonably require in order to understand it in full.

2. "A particular group" is a group of the relevant members of a workforce who undertake a particular function, work at a particular workplace or belong to a particular department or unit within their employer's business;

"employee" means an individual who has entered into or works under a contract of employment;

"relevant members of the workforce" are all of the employees employed by a particular employer, excluding any employee whose terms and conditions of employment are provided for, wholly or in part, in a collective agreement;

"representatives of the workforce" are employees duly elected to represent the relevant members of the workforce, "representatives of the group" are employees duly elected to represent the members of a particular group, and representatives are "duly elected" if the election at which they were elected satisfies the requirements of paragraph 3 of this Schedule.

3. The requirements concerning elections referred to in the definition of "representatives of the workforce" are that—

(a) the number of representatives to be elected is determined by the employer;

(b) the candidates for election as representatives of the workforce are relevant members of the workforce, and the candidates for election as representatives of a group are members of the group;

(c) no employee who is eligible to be a candidate is unreasonably excluded from standing in the election;

(d) all the relevant members of the workforce are entitled to vote for representatives of the workforce, and all the members of a particular group are entitled to vote for representatives of the group;

(e) the employees entitled to vote may vote for as many candidates as there are representatives to be elected; and

(f) the election is conducted so as to ensure that—

(i) so far as practicable, those voting do so in secret; and

(ii) the votes given at the election are fairly and accurately counted.

NOTES

Commencement: 6 April 2018.

SCHEDULE 2

(*This Schedule contains consequential amendments which, in so far as relevant, have been incorporated.*)

EMPLOYMENT RIGHTS ACT 1996 (ITEMISED PAY STATEMENT) (AMENDMENT) ORDER 2018

(SI 2018/147)

NOTES

Made: 7 February 2018.
Authority: Employment Rights Act 1996, ss 10, 236(5).
Commencement: 6 April 2019.

[2.2048]

1 Citation and commencement

This Order may be cited as the Employment Rights Act 1996 (Itemised Pay Statement) (Amendment) Order 2018 and comes into force on 6th April 2019.

NOTES

Commencement: 6 April 2019.

2 (*Amends the Employment Rights Act 1996, s 8 at* **[1.822]**.)

[2.2049]

3 Application

The amendments made by this Order do not apply in relation to wages or salary paid in respect of a period of work which commences before this Order comes into force.

NOTES

Commencement: 6 April 2019.

SEAFARERS (INSOLVENCY, COLLECTIVE REDUNDANCIES AND INFORMATION AND CONSULTATION MISCELLANEOUS AMENDMENTS) REGULATIONS 2018

(SI 2018/407)

NOTES

Made: 22 March 2018.

Authority: Employment Rights Act 1996, s 209(1)(c); Trade Union and Labour Relations (Consolidation) Act 1992, s 286(2), (3); Employment Relations Act 2004, s 42(1).

Commencement: 13 April 2018.

[2.2050]

1 Citation, commencement and extent

(1) These Regulations may be cited as the Seafarers (Insolvency, Collective Redundancies and Information and Consultation Miscellaneous Amendments) Regulations 2018 and come into force on the 22nd day after the day on which they are made.

(2) These Regulations extend to England and Wales and Scotland.

NOTES

Commencement: 13 April 2018.

[2.2051]

2 Amendment of the Employment Rights Act 1996

(1)–(3) (*Amend the Employment Rights Act 1996, s 199 at* **[1.1112]**.)

(4) The amendment made by paragraph (2), insofar as it relates to Part XI of the Employment Rights Act 1996, only has effect in relation to employees who on or after the date on which these Regulations come into force—

(a) are dismissed by reason of redundancy, or

(b) become eligible for a redundancy payment by reason of being laid off or kept on short-time.

(5) The amendment made by paragraph (2), insofar as it relates to Part XII of the Employment Rights Act 1996, and the amendment made by paragraph (3) only have effect in relation to employees whose employer has become insolvent on or after the date on which these Regulations come into force.

NOTES

Commencement: 13 April 2018.

[2.2052]

3 Amendment of the Trade Union and Labour Relations (Consolidation) Act 1992

(1), (2) (*Amend the Trade Union and Labour Relations (Consolidation) Act 1992, s 284 at* **[1.618]**.)

(3) The amendment made by paragraph (2) only has effect in relation to dismissals which are first proposed by an employer on or after the date on which these Regulations come into force.

NOTES

Commencement: 13 April 2018.

4 (*Revokes the Information and Consultation of Employees Regulations 2004, SI 2004/3426, reg 43.*)

[2.2053]

5 Review of Regulations

(1) The Secretary of State must from time to time—

(a) carry out a review of the regulatory provision contained in regulation 4, and

(b) publish a report setting out the conclusions of the review.

(2) The first report must be published before the end of the period of five years beginning with the date on which these Regulations come into force.

(3) Subsequent reports must be published at intervals not exceeding five years.

(4) Section 30(3) of the Small Business, Enterprise and Employment Act 2015 requires that a review carried out under this regulation must, so far as is reasonable, have regard to how Article 3(3) of Directive 2002/14/EC, which is amended by Article 3 of Directive 2015/1794/EC, is implemented in other member States.

(5) Section 30(4) of the Small Business, Enterprise and Employment Act 2015 requires that a report published under this regulation must, in particular—

(a) set out the objectives intended to be achieved by the regulatory provision referred to in paragraph (1)(a),
(b) assess the extent to which those objectives are achieved,
(c) assess whether those objectives remain appropriate, and
(d) if those objectives remain appropriate, assess the extent to which they could be achieved in another way which involves less onerous regulatory provision.

(6) In this regulation, "regulatory provision" has the same meaning as in sections 28 to 32 of the Small Business, Enterprise and Employment Act 2015 (see section 32 of that Act).

NOTES

Commencement: 13 April 2018.

EMPLOYMENT RIGHTS ACT 1996 (ITEMISED PAY STATEMENT) (AMENDMENT) (NO 2) ORDER 2018

(SI 2018/529)

NOTES

Made: 25 April 2018.
Authority: Employment Relations Act 1999, s 23.
Commencement: 6 April 2019.

[2.2054]
1 Citation and commencement

This Order may be cited as the Employment Rights Act 1996 (Itemised Pay Statement) (Amendment) (No 2) Order 2018 and comes into force on 6th April 2019.

NOTES

Commencement: 6 April 2019.

2 (*Amends the Employment Rights Act 1996, ss 8, 9, 11, 12 at* **[1.822]** *et seq.*)

[2.2055]
3 Application

The amendments made by this Order do not apply in relation to wages or salary paid in respect of a period of work which commences before this Order comes into force.

NOTES

Commencement: 6 April 2019.

EMPLOYMENT RIGHTS ACT 1996 (NHS RECRUITMENT—PROTECTED DISCLOSURE) REGULATIONS 2018

(SI 2018/579)

NOTES

Made: 2 May 2018.
Authority: Employment Rights Act 1996, ss 49B(1), (4), (6), 236(5).
Commencement: 23 May 2018.
Conciliation: employment tribunal proceedings under reg 4 are "relevant proceedings" for the purposes of the conciliation provisions contained in the Employment Tribunals Act 1996, ss 18–18C; see s 18(1)(z5) of the 1996 Act at **[1.757]**.

ARRANGEMENT OF REGULATIONS

[2.2056]

1 Citation, commencement and extent

(1) These Regulations may be cited as the Employment Rights Act 1996 (NHS Recruitment—Protected Disclosure) Regulations 2018.

(2) These Regulations come into force 21 days after the day on which they are made.

(3) These Regulations extend to England and Wales and Scotland.

NOTES

Commencement: 23 May 2018.

[2.2057]

2 NHS public bodies prescribed for the purposes of the definition of "NHS employer"

The NHS public bodies prescribed for the purposes of section 49B(6) of the Employment Rights Act 1996 (which defines "NHS employer" by reference to those NHS public bodies that are prescribed by regulations) are the bodies listed in paragraphs (a) to (p) of subsection (7) of that section.

NOTES

Commencement: 23 May 2018.

[2.2058]

3 Prohibition of discrimination because of protected disclosure

An NHS employer must not discriminate against an applicant because it appears to the NHS employer that the applicant has made a protected disclosure.

NOTES

Commencement: 23 May 2018.

[2.2059]

4 Right of complaint to an employment tribunal

(1) An applicant has a right of complaint to an employment tribunal against an NHS employer if the NHS employer contravenes regulation 3.

(2) If there are facts from which the employment tribunal could decide, in the absence of any other explanation, that an NHS employer contravened regulation 3, the tribunal must find that such a contravention occurred unless the NHS employer shows that it did not contravene regulation 3.

NOTES

Commencement: 23 May 2018.

Conciliation: employment tribunal proceedings under this regulation are "relevant proceedings" for the purposes of the conciliation provisions contained in the Employment Tribunals Act 1996, ss 18–18C; see s 18(1)(z5) of the 1996 Act at **[1.757]**.

[2.2060]

5 Time limit for proceedings under regulation 4

(1) Subject to paragraph (4), an employment tribunal must not consider a complaint under regulation 4 unless it is presented to the tribunal before the end of the period of three months beginning with the date of the conduct to which the complaint relates.

(2) An employment tribunal may consider a complaint under regulation 4 that is otherwise out of time if, in all the circumstances of the case, it considers it just and equitable to do so.

(3) In the cases specified in paragraphs (a) to (e), the date of the conduct to which a complaint under regulation 4 relates is—

- (a) in the case of a decision by an NHS employer not to employ or appoint an applicant, the date that decision was communicated to the applicant;
- (b) in the case of a deliberate omission—
  - (i) to entertain and process an applicant's application or enquiry, or
  - (ii) to offer a contract of employment, a contract to do work personally, or an appointment to an office or post,

  the end of the period within which it was reasonable to expect the NHS employer to act;
- (c) in the case of conduct which causes an applicant to withdraw or no longer pursue an application or enquiry, the date of that conduct;
- (d) in a case where the NHS employer withdrew an offer, the date when the offer was withdrawn;
- (e) in any other case where the NHS employer made an offer which was not accepted, the date when the NHS employer made the offer.

(4) Where a complaint under regulation 4 relates to conduct extending over a period, the conduct is to be treated as done at the end of the period.

NOTES

Commencement: 23 May 2018.

Part 2 Statutory Instruments

[2.2061]
6 Remedies in proceedings under regulation 4

Where an employment tribunal finds in proceedings under regulation 4 that there has been a contravention of regulation 3—

(a) it must make a declaration to that effect;
(b) it may order the NHS employer to pay compensation to the applicant in respect of the conduct complained of; and
(c) it may recommend that, within a specified period, the NHS employer takes specified steps for the purpose of obviating or reducing the adverse effect on the applicant of the discrimination to which the proceedings relate.

NOTES

Commencement: 23 May 2018.

[2.2062]
7 Amount of compensation

(1) Subject to the following paragraphs, the amount of compensation which the employment tribunal may award must be such as the tribunal considers just and equitable in all the circumstances.

(2) When considering the amount of compensation to award, if any, the tribunal must have regard to the conduct complained of and to any loss sustained by the applicant which was caused by that conduct.

(3) The reference in paragraph (2) to loss sustained by the applicant includes—

(a) expenses which the applicant reasonably incurred because of the discriminatory conduct of the NHS employer; and
(b) the loss of any benefit which the applicant might reasonably be expected to have had but for that conduct.

(4) In ascertaining the loss, the tribunal must apply the same rule concerning the duty to mitigate loss as applies to damages recoverable under the common law of England and Wales or (as the case may be) Scotland.

(5) When considering the amount of compensation, if any, to award, the tribunal may also have regard to—

(a) the actions of the applicant before the conduct complained of; and
(b) whether the applicant acted so as to contribute to or cause, to any extent, that conduct.

(6) If the NHS employer fails without reasonable justification to comply with a recommendation under regulation 6(c), the tribunal may increase its award or, if it has not made such an award, make one.

NOTES

Commencement: 23 May 2018.

[2.2063]
8 Action for breach of statutory duty

(1) A contravention of regulation 3 is actionable as a breach of statutory duty.

(2) If there are facts from which the court could conclude, in the absence of any other explanation, that the defendant has contravened, or is likely to contravene, regulation 3, the court must find that such a contravention has occurred, or is likely to occur, unless the defendant shows that it did not, or is not likely to occur.

(3) In proceedings brought by virtue of this regulation, the court may (without prejudice to any of its other powers)—

(a) make such order as it considers appropriate for the purpose of restraining or preventing the defendant from contravening regulation 3; and
(b) award damages, which may include compensation for injured feelings.

(4) Except as provided in paragraph (5), an applicant may not complain to an employment tribunal under regulation 4 and bring an action for breach of statutory duty in respect of the same conduct.

(5) An applicant may complain to an employment tribunal under regulation 4 and bring an action for breach of statutory duty in respect of the same conduct for the purpose of restraining or preventing the defendant from contravening regulation 3.

NOTES

Commencement: 23 May 2018.

[2.2064]
9 Discrimination by worker or agent of NHS employer

(1) Discrimination by a worker of an NHS employer is to be treated, for the purposes of these Regulations, as discrimination by the NHS employer where the discriminatory conduct occurs in the course of the worker's employment.

(2) It does not matter whether the NHS employer knows about or approves the conduct of the worker.

(3) Discrimination by an agent of an NHS employer is to be treated, for the purposes of these Regulations, as discrimination by the NHS employer where the discriminatory conduct occurs with the authority of the NHS employer.

(4) In proceedings under regulation 4 or 8, in respect of anything alleged to have been done in the course of employment by a worker of an NHS employer, or anything alleged to have been done by an agent acting with the authority of the NHS employer, it is a defence for the NHS employer to show that it took all reasonable steps to prevent the worker or agent—

(a) from doing that thing; or
(b) from doing anything of that description.

NOTES

Commencement: 23 May 2018.

10 (*Amends the Employment Tribunals Act 1996, ss 10, 16 and 18 at* **[1.745]**, **[1.755]** and **[1.757]**.)

TRADE SECRETS (ENFORCEMENT, ETC) REGULATIONS 2018

(SI 2018/597)

NOTES

Made: 15 May 2018.
Authority: European Communities Act 1972, s 2(2).
Commencement: 9 June 2018.
Note: with regard to the authority for these Regulations, note that the European Communities Act 1972 is repealed by the European Union (Withdrawal) Act 2018, s 1, as from exit day (as defined in s 20 of that Act); but note also that provision is made for the continuation in force of any subordinate legislation made under the authority of s 2(2) of the 1972 Act by s 2 of the 2018 Act at **[1.2240]**, subject to the provisions of s 5 of, and Sch 1 to, the 2018 Act at **[1.2243]**, **[1.2253]**.
These Regulations are the domestic implementation of Directive (2016/943/EU) on the protection of undisclosed know-how and business information (trade secrets) against their unlawful acquisition, use and disclosure (the Trade Secrets Directive) at **[3.659]**.

ARRANGEMENT OF REGULATIONS

[2.2065]
1 Citation, commencement and extent

(1) These Regulations may be cited as the Trade Secrets (Enforcement, etc) Regulations 2018 and come into force on 9th June 2018.

(2) These Regulations extend to England and Wales, Scotland and Northern Ireland.

NOTES

Commencement: 9 June 2018.

[2.2066]
2 Interpretation

For the purposes of these Regulations—

"court" means—

(a) in England and Wales, a County Court hearing centre where there is also a Chancery District Registry or the High Court (as provided for in rule 63.13 of the Civil Procedure Rules 1998),
(b) in Scotland, the sheriff or the Court of Session, and
(c) (*applies to Northern Ireland only*).

Part 2 Statutory Instruments

"infringer" means a person who has unlawfully acquired, used or disclosed a trade secret;

"infringing goods" means goods, the design, functioning, production process, marketing or a characteristic of which significantly benefits from a trade secret unlawfully acquired, used or disclosed;

"trade secret" means information which—

(a) is secret in the sense that it is not, as a body or in the precise configuration and assembly of its components, generally known among, or readily accessible to, persons within the circles that normally deal with the kind of information in question,

(b) has commercial value because it is secret, and

(c) has been subject to reasonable steps under the circumstances, by the person lawfully in control of the information, to keep it secret;

"trade secret holder" means any person lawfully controlling a trade secret.

NOTES

Commencement: 9 June 2018.

[2.2067]

3 Wider protection

(1) The acquisition, use or disclosure of a trade secret is unlawful where the acquisition, use or disclosure constitutes a breach of confidence in confidential information.

(2) A trade secret holder may apply for and a court may grant measures, procedures, and remedies available in an action for breach of confidence where the measures, procedures and remedies—

(a) provide wider protection to the trade secret holder than that provided under these Regulations in respect of the unlawful acquisition, use or disclosure of a trade secret, and

(b) comply with the safeguards referred to in Article 1 of Directive (EU) 2016/943 of the European Parliament and of the Council of 8 June 2016 on the protection of undisclosed know-how and business information (trade secrets) against their unlawful acquisition, use and disclosure.

(3) A trade secret holder may apply for and a court may grant the measures, procedures and remedies referred to in paragraph (2) in addition, or as an alternative, to the measures procedures and remedies provided for in these Regulations in respect of the unlawful acquisition, use or disclosure of a trade secret.

NOTES

Commencement: 9 June 2018.

[2.2068]

4 Time limits for bringing proceedings

(1) Proceedings may not be brought before a court in respect of a claim for the unlawful acquisition, use or disclosure of a trade secret and for the application of measures, procedures and remedies provided for under these Regulations—

(a) in England and Wales and Northern Ireland, after the end of the limitation period for the claim, and

(b) in Scotland, after the end of the prescriptive period for the claim, except where the subsistence of the obligation in relation to which the claim is made was relevantly acknowledged before the end of that period.

(2) The limitation period referred to in paragraph 1(a) is to be determined in accordance with this regulation and regulations 5 to 7 and 9.

(3) Section 36 of the Limitation Act 1980 (equitable jurisdiction and remedies) does not apply in relation to proceedings in respect of a claim for the unlawful acquisition, use or disclosure of a trade secret.

(4) The prescriptive period referred to in paragraph 1(b) is to be determined in accordance with this regulation and regulations 5, 6 and 8.

(5) Section 6 of the Prescription and Limitation (Scotland) Act 1973 (extinction of obligations by prescriptive periods of five years) does not apply in relation to an obligation arising from a claim for the unlawful acquisition, use or disclosure of a trade secret.

(6) The following provisions of the Prescription and Limitation (Scotland) Act 1973 apply for the purposes of, or in relation to, paragraph (1)(b) as they apply for the purposes of, or in relation to, section 6 of that Act—

(a) section 10 (relevant acknowledgment);

(b) section 13 (prohibition of contracting out);

(c) section 14(1)(c) and (d) (computation of prescriptive periods).

NOTES

Commencement: 9 June 2018.

[2.2069]

5 Length of limitation or prescriptive period

(1) The limitation period is six years.

(2) The prescriptive period is five years.

(3) The limitation or prescriptive period begins with the day specified in regulation 6.

NOTES

Commencement: 9 June 2018.

[2.2070]

6 Beginning of limitation or prescriptive period

(1) The limitation or prescriptive period for a claim for the unlawful acquisition, use or disclosure of a trade secret against an infringer begins with the later of—

(a) the day on which the unlawful acquisition, use or disclosure that is the subject of the claim ceases, and

(b) the day of knowledge of the trade secret holder.

(2) In paragraph (1)(b), "the day of knowledge of the trade secret holder" is the day on which the trade secret holder first knows or could reasonably be expected to know—

(a) of the infringer's activity,

(b) that the activity constitutes an unlawful acquisition, use or disclosure of a trade secret, and

(c) the identity of the infringer.

(3) The reference in paragraph (2) to the trade secret holder knowing something is to the trade secret holder having sufficient knowledge of it to bring a claim for the unlawful acquisition, use or disclosure of a trade secret.

(4) Where a person has acquired the liability of an infringer from another person (whether by operation of law or otherwise)—

(a) the reference to an infringer in paragraph (1) is to be read as a reference to the person who has acquired the liability, but

(b) the references to the infringer in paragraph (2) are to be read as references to the original infringer.

(5) This regulation has effect subject to—

(a) regulation 7 in relation to the limitation period, and

(b) regulation 8 in relation to the prescriptive period.

NOTES

Commencement: 9 June 2018.

[2.2071]

7 Effect of disability on limitation period

(1) If, in relation to a claim in England and Wales and Northern Ireland for the unlawful acquisition, use or disclosure of a trade secret, the trade secret holder is under a disability during the whole or any part of the limitation period, the limitation period for the claim begins with the earlier of—

(a) the day on which the trade secret holder ceases to be under a disability, and

(b) the day on which the trade secret holder dies.

(2) In England and Wales, references in paragraph (1) to a person being "under a disability" have the same meaning as in section 38(2) of the Limitation Act 1980 (interpretation).

(3) (*Applies to Northern Ireland only*).

NOTES

Commencement: 9 June 2018.

[2.2072]

8 Suspension of prescriptive period during period of disability

(1) If, in relation to a claim in Scotland for the unlawful acquisition, use or disclosure of a trade secret, the trade secret holder is under legal disability for a period at any time, the period during which the trade secret holder is under legal disability—

(a) is not to be counted when calculating whether the prescriptive period for the claim has expired, and

(b) is not to be regarded as separating the time immediately before it from the time immediately after it.

(2) In paragraph (1), "legal disability" has the same meaning as in section 15(1) of the Prescription and Limitation (Scotland) Act 1973 (interpretation).

NOTES

Commencement: 9 June 2018.

[2.2073]

9 New claims in pending actions: England and Wales and Northern Ireland

For the purposes of regulations 4 to 7—

(a) section 35 of the Limitation Act 1980 (new claims in pending action) applies in relation to a claim for the unlawful acquisition, use or disclosure of a trade secret that is a new claim and to proceedings for the unlawful acquisition, use or disclosure of a trade secret as it applies in relation to new claims and proceedings for the purposes of that Act; and

(b) (*applies to Northern Ireland only*).

NOTES

Commencement: 9 June 2018.

[2.2074]

10 Preservation of confidentiality of trade secrets in the course of proceedings

(1) A participant, or a participant who has access to documents which form part of the proceedings, must not use or disclose any trade secret or alleged trade secret—

(a) which, on a duly reasoned application by an interested party or on a court's own initiative, a court by order identifies as confidential, and

(b) of which a participant has become aware as a result of participation in the proceedings or the access.

(2) The obligation referred to in paragraph (1) remains in force after the proceedings have ended, subject to paragraph (3).

(3) The obligation in paragraph (1) ceases to exist—

(a) where a court, by final decision, finds that the alleged trade secret does not meet the requirements of a trade secret, or

(b) where over time the information in question becomes generally known among, or readily accessible to, persons within the circles that normally deal with that kind of information.

(4) On a duly reasoned application by a party or on a court's own initiative, a court may order any of the measures set out in paragraph (5) as may be necessary to preserve the confidentiality of any trade secret or alleged trade secret used or referred to in the course of proceedings.

(5) A court may—

(a) restrict access to any document containing a trade secret or alleged trade secret submitted by the parties or third parties, in whole or in part, to a limited number of persons,

(b) restrict access to hearings, when trade secrets or alleged trade secrets may be disclosed, and to the record or transcript of those hearings to a limited number of persons, and

(c) make available to a person, who is not one of the limited number of persons referred to in sub-paragraph (a) or (b), a non-confidential version of any judicial decision, in which the passages containing trade secrets have been removed or redacted.

(6) The number of persons referred to in paragraph 5(a) or (b) must be no greater than necessary to ensure compliance with the right of the parties to the legal proceedings to an effective remedy and to a fair trial, and must include, at least, one individual from each party and the lawyers or other representatives of those parties to the proceedings.

(7) In deciding whether or not to grant the measures in paragraph (5) in accordance with paragraphs (4) and (6) and which of the measures to order and in assessing the proportionality of the measures, a court must take into account—

(a) the need to ensure the right to an effective remedy and to a fair trial,

(b) the legitimate interests of the parties, and

(c) any potential harm for the parties.

(8) In this regulation—

"participant" means a party, a lawyer or other representative of a party, a court official, a witness, an expert or any other person participating in proceedings;

"parties", in paragraph (7), includes, where appropriate, third parties;

"proceedings" means legal proceedings relating to the unlawful acquisition, use or disclosure of a trade secret.

NOTES

Commencement: 9 June 2018.

[2.2075]

11 Interim measures

(1) On the application of a trade secret holder, a court may order any of the following measures against the alleged infringer—

(a) the cessation of, or (as the case may be) the prohibition of, the use or disclosure of the trade secret on a provisional basis;

(b) the prohibition of the production, offering, placing on the market or use of infringing goods, or the importation, export or storage of infringing goods for those purposes;

(c) the seizure or delivery up of the suspected infringing goods, including imported goods, so as to prevent the goods entering into, or circulating on, the market.

(2) A person to whom the suspected infringing goods are delivered up under paragraph (1)(c) must retain the infringing goods pending a decision to make or not to make an order under regulation 14(2).

(3) A court making an order under paragraph (1) may set a reasonable period within which a trade secret holder must bring proceedings for a decision on the merits of the case before a court.

(4) Where no period is set under paragraph (3), a trade secret holder must bring proceedings before a court within a period not exceeding 20 working days or 31 calendar days after the day on which the order under paragraph (1) has been made, whichever is the longer.

(5) For the purposes of paragraph (4)—

(a) if the period of 20 working days ends on a day other than a working day, the proceedings are in time if they are brought on the next working day, and
(b) "working day" means any day except a Saturday or Sunday, Christmas Day, Good Friday or a day which is a bank holiday in any part of the United Kingdom under section 1 of the Banking and Financial Dealings Act 1971 (bank holidays).

(6) As an alternative to the measures referred to in paragraph (1), a court may make an order making the continuation of the alleged unlawful use conditional upon the lodging by the alleged infringer of guarantees intended to ensure the compensation of the trade secret holder.

(7) An order under paragraph (6) must not permit disclosure of a trade secret in return for the lodging of guarantees.

(8) A court may make an order under paragraph (1) or (6) conditional upon the lodging by the trade secret holder of adequate security or an equivalent assurance intended to ensure compensation for any prejudice suffered by the alleged infringer and, where appropriate, by any other person affected by the order.

NOTES

Commencement: 9 June 2018.

[2.2076]

12 Matters to be considered before making an order under regulation 11(1)

(1) Before making an order under regulation 11(1), a court may require the trade secret holder to provide evidence that may reasonably be considered available to satisfy the court with a sufficient degree of certainty that—
(a) a trade secret exists,
(b) the trade secret holder is making the application, and
(c) the alleged infringer—
(i) has acquired the trade secret unlawfully,
(ii) is unlawfully using or disclosing the trade secret, or
(iii) is about to unlawfully use or disclose the trade secret.

(2) In considering whether to make an order under regulation 11(1) and in assessing the proportionality of such an order, a court must take into account the specific circumstances of the case, including where appropriate—
(a) the value and other specific features of the trade secret,
(b) the measures taken to protect the trade secret,
(c) the conduct of the alleged infringer in acquiring, using or disclosing the trade secret,
(d) the impact of the unlawful use or disclosure of the trade secret,
(e) the legitimate interests of the parties and the impact which the granting or rejection of the measures could have on the parties,
(f) the legitimate interests of third parties,
(g) the public interest, and
(h) the safeguard of fundamental rights.

NOTES

Commencement: 9 June 2018.

[2.2077]

13 Revocation of order under regulation 11(1)

(1) Where a court makes an order under regulation 11(1), the court may, on the application of the alleged infringer, revoke the order—
(a) if the trade secret holder does not bring proceedings leading to a decision on the merits of the case before a court within the period set under regulation 11(3) or in regulation 11(4), or
(b) if the information in question is no longer a trade secret for reasons that cannot be attributed to the alleged infringer.

(2) A court may, on the application of the alleged infringer or an injured third party, order the trade secret holder to provide the alleged infringer, or the injured third party, appropriate compensation for any injury caused by a measure ordered under regulation 11(1)—
(a) where a court revokes an order under paragraph (1)(a),
(b) where the measure lapses due to any act or omission by the trade secret holder, or
(c) where it is subsequently found that there has been no unlawful acquisition, use or disclosure of a trade secret or threat of such conduct.

NOTES

Commencement: 9 June 2018.

[2.2078]

14 Injunctions or interdicts and corrective measures

(1) Where a court finds on the merits of the case that there has been an unlawful acquisition, use or disclosure of a trade secret, the court may, on application by the trade secret holder, order one or more of the following measures against the infringer—
(a) the cessation of, or (as the case may be) the prohibition of, the use or disclosure of the trade secret;

(b) the prohibition of the production, offering, placing on the market or use of infringing goods, or the importation, export or storage of infringing goods for those purposes;

(c) the adoption of corrective measures with regard to the infringing goods, including where appropriate—

(i) recall of the infringing goods from the market;

(ii) depriving the infringing goods of their infringing quality;

(iii) destruction of the infringing goods or their withdrawal from the market, provided that the withdrawal does not undermine the protection of the trade secret in question;

(d) the destruction of all or part of any document, object, material, substance or electronic file containing or embodying the trade secret, or where appropriate, the delivery up to the applicant of all or part of that document, object, material, substance or electronic file.

(2) Where a court orders that infringing goods be withdrawn from the market, the court may order, on the application of the trade secret holder, that the infringing goods be delivered up and forfeited to the trade secret holder together with all or part of any document, object, material, substance or electronic file containing or embodying the trade secret.

(3) Where a court makes an order for a measure under paragraph (1)(c) or (d) or paragraph (2), the court must—

(a) order that the measure be carried out at the expense of the infringer, unless there are particular reasons for not doing so, and

(b) ensure the measure is without prejudice to any damages that may be due to the trade secret holder by reason of the unlawful acquisition, use or disclosure of the trade secret.

NOTES

Commencement: 9 June 2018.

[2.2079]

15 Matters to be considered when making an order under regulation 14

(1) In considering an application for an order under regulation 14 and assessing the proportionality of such an order, the court must take into account the specific circumstances of the case, including where appropriate—

(a) the value or other specific features of the trade secret,

(b) the measures taken to protect the trade secret,

(c) the conduct of the infringer in acquiring, using or disclosing the trade secret,

(d) the impact of the unlawful use or disclosure of the trade secret,

(e) the legitimate interests of the parties and the impact which the granting or rejection of the measures could have on the parties,

(f) the legitimate interests of third parties,

(g) the public interest, and

(h) the safeguard of fundamental rights.

(2) Where a court makes an order limiting the duration of a measure ordered under regulation 14(1)(a) or (b), the duration must be sufficient to eliminate any commercial or economic advantage that the infringer could have derived from the unlawful acquisition, use or disclosure of the trade secret.

(3) On the application of the defendant, the court must revoke a measure ordered under regulation 14(1)(a) or (b) if the information in question no longer constitutes a trade secret for reasons that cannot be attributed directly or indirectly to the defendant.

(4) In the application of paragraph (3) to Scotland, "defendant" means defender.

NOTES

Commencement: 9 June 2018.

[2.2080]

16 Compensation instead of order under regulation 14

(1) A person liable to the imposition of an order under regulation 14 may apply for, and a court may make, an order for compensation to be paid to the injured party instead of an order under regulation 14—

(a) if at the time of use or disclosure the person neither knew nor ought, under the circumstances, to have known that the trade secret was obtained from another person who was using or disclosing the trade secret unlawfully,

(b) if the execution of the measures in question would cause disproportionate harm to the person liable to the measures, and

(c) if it appears reasonably satisfactory to pay compensation to the injured party.

(2) Where a court makes an order for the payment of compensation instead of an order under regulation 14(1)(a) or (b), the compensation must not exceed the amount of royalties or fees which would have been due, had that person obtained a licence to use the trade secret in question, for the period for which use of the trade secret could have been prohibited.

NOTES

Commencement: 9 June 2018.

[2.2081]
17 Assessment of damages

(1) On the application of an injured party, a court must order an infringer, who knew or ought to have known that unlawful acquisition, use or disclosure of a trade secret was being engaged in, to pay the trade secret holder damages appropriate to the actual prejudice suffered as a result of the unlawful acquisition, use or disclosure of the trade secret.

(2) A court may award damages under paragraph (1) on the basis of either paragraph (3) or (4).

(3) When awarding damages under paragraph (1) on the basis of this paragraph, a court must take into account all appropriate factors, including in particular—

(i) the negative economic consequences, including any lost profits, which the trade secret holder has suffered, and any unfair profits made by the infringer, and

(ii) elements other than economic factors, including the moral prejudice caused to the trade secret holder by the unlawful acquisition, use or disclosure of the trade secret.

(4) When awarding damages under paragraph (1) on the basis of this paragraph, a court may, where appropriate, award damages on the basis of the royalties or fees which would have been due had the infringer obtained a licence to use the trade secret in question.

NOTES

Commencement: 9 June 2018.

[2.2082]
18 Publication of judicial decisions

(1) In proceedings for the unlawful acquisition, use or disclosure of a trade secret, a court may order, on the application of the trade secret holder and at the expense of the infringer, appropriate measures for the dissemination of information concerning the judgment, including its publication in whole or in part.

(2) Any measure a court may order under paragraph (1) must preserve the confidentiality of trade secrets as provided for in regulation 10.

(3) In deciding whether to order a measure under paragraph (1) and when assessing whether such measure is proportionate, the court must take into account where appropriate—

(a) the value of the trade secret,

(b) the conduct of the infringer in acquiring, using or disclosing the trade secret,

(c) the impact of the unlawful use or disclosure of the trade secret,

(d) the likelihood of further unlawful use, or disclosure of the trade secret by the infringer, and

(e) whether the information on the infringer would be such as to allow an individual to be identified and, if so, whether publication of that information would be justified, in particular in the light of the possible harm that such measure may cause to the privacy and reputation of the infringer.

NOTES

Commencement: 9 June 2018.

[2.2083]
19 Proceedings to which these Regulations apply

These Regulations apply only to proceedings—

(a) brought before a court after the coming into force of these Regulations,

(b) in respect a claim for the unlawful acquisition, use or disclosure of a trade secret, and

(c) for the application of measures, procedures and remedies provided for under these Regulations.

NOTES

Commencement: 9 June 2018.

MERCHANT SHIPPING (WORK IN FISHING CONVENTION) REGULATIONS 2018

(SI 2018/1106)

NOTES

Made: 24 October 2018.

Authority: European Communities Act 1972, s 2(2); Merchant Shipping Act 1995, ss 85(1)(a), (b), (3), (5), (7), 86.

Commencement: 30 November 2019 (reg 26); 31 December 2018 (otherwise).

Note: with regard to the authority for these Regulations, note that the European Communities Act 1972 is repealed by the European Union (Withdrawal) Act 2018, s 1, as from exit day (as defined in s 20 of that Act); but note also that provision is made for the continuation in force of any subordinate legislation made under the authority of s 2(2) of the 1972 Act by s 2 of the 2018 Act at **[1.2240]**, subject to the provisions of s 5 of, and Sch 1 to, the 2018 Act at **[1.2243]**, **[1.2253]**.

PART 1
GENERAL MATTERS

[2.2084]
1 Citation and commencement

(1) These Regulations may be cited as the Merchant Shipping (Work in Fishing Convention) Regulations 2018.

(2) These Regulations, other than regulation 26, come into force on 31st December 2018; regulation 26 comes into force on 30th November 2019.

NOTES

Commencement: 31 December 2018.

[2.2085]
2 Interpretation

In these Regulations—

"the Act" means the Merchant Shipping Act 1995;

"Convention" or "Work in Fishing Convention" means the convention adopted at Geneva on 14th June 2007 by the International Labour Organisation;

"fisherman" means a person, including the skipper, employed, engaged or working in any capacity on board any fishing vessel, but does not include a person solely engaged as a pilot for the vessel;

"fisherman's work agreement" means a written agreement between a fisherman and another person in respect of the fisherman's work on board a fishing vessel;

"fishing vessel owner" means the owner of a fishing vessel or any other person such as the manager, agent or bareboat charterer, who has assumed the responsibility for the operation of the vessel from the owner and who, on assuming such responsibility, has agreed to take over the duties and responsibilities imposed on fishing vessel owners in accordance with the Convention, regardless of whether any other organisation or person fulfils certain of the duties or responsibilities on behalf of the fishing vessel owner;

"Merchant Shipping Notice" means a notice described as such and issued by the Secretary of State, and any reference to a particular Merchant Shipping Notice includes a reference to a Merchant Shipping Notice amending or replacing that Notice which is considered by the Secretary of State to be relevant from time to time;

"skipper" means the person having command of a fishing vessel;

"United Kingdom fishing vessel" means a fishing vessel which is—

(a) a United Kingdom ship within the meaning of section 85(2) of the Act; or

(b) a hovercraft registered under the Hovercraft Act 1968.

NOTES

Commencement: 31 December 2018.

[2.2086]
3 Application

These Regulations apply to—

(a) a United Kingdom fishing vessel wherever it may be; and

(b) a fishing vessel which is not a United Kingdom fishing vessel while that ship is in United Kingdom waters.

NOTES

Commencement: 31 December 2018.

[2.2087]
4 Obligation to comply with orders

(1) A fisherman must comply with the lawful orders of the skipper regarding health and safety.

(2) A fisherman who fails to comply with paragraph (1) commits an offence.

NOTES

Commencement: 31 December 2018.

[2.2088]
5 Competent authority

The Secretary of State is the competent authority for the purposes of the Convention.

NOTES

Commencement: 31 December 2018.

PART 2
MINIMUM AGE

[2.2089]
6 Minimum age for fishermen

(1) Subject to paragraphs (2) and (3), a person under 16 years of age must not be employed or engaged to work on board a fishing vessel.

(2) Paragraph (1) does not apply where—

(a) the person is 15 years of age or older;

(b) the employment or engagement is limited to light work during school holidays;

(c) the purpose of the employment or engagement is to facilitate work experience and shadowing; and

(d) the person is able to demonstrate that they have completed a course of training regarding basic survival at sea which satisfied the requirements specified in Merchant Shipping Notice 1882 (F).

(3) A person under 18 years of age must not be employed or engaged to work on board a fishing vessel where the nature of the activities, or the circumstances in which they are carried out, are likely to jeopardize that person's health, safety or morals.

(4) A breach of paragraph (1) or (3) is an offence by the fishing vessel owner, the skipper and the employer of the person.

NOTES

Commencement: 31 December 2018.

[2.2090]
7 Young persons on night duty

(1) Subject to paragraph (2) a person under the age of 18 years must not be employed or engaged to work on a fishing vessel at night.

(2) Paragraph (1) does not apply where—

(a) the effective training of the person, in accordance with established programmes and schedules, would be impaired by its application; or

(b) the specific nature of the duty or a recognized training programme requires that the fisherman performs duties at night and the training and the nature of the duties conform to the requirements set out in Merchant Shipping Notice 1882 (F) as not being of detrimental impact to the person's health or well-being.

(3) In this regulation "night" means a period—

(a) the duration of which is at least 9 consecutive hours; and

(b) which starts no later than midnight and ends no earlier than 5 am (local time).

(4) A breach of paragraph (1) is an offence by the fishing vessel owner, the skipper and the employer of the person under the age of 18.

NOTES

Commencement: 31 December 2018.

PART 3
FISHERMEN'S WORK AGREEMENTS

[2.2091]
8 Duty to enter into a fisherman's work agreement

(1) Subject to paragraph (2), a fisherman must have a fisherman's work agreement which complies with paragraphs (1) and (2) of regulation 9.

(2) Paragraph (1) does not apply to a fishing vessel owner who is single-handedly operating a vessel.

(3) A breach of paragraph (1) is an offence by the fishing vessel owner.

NOTES

Commencement: 31 December 2018.

[2.2092]
9 Content of fisherman's work agreement

(1) Subject to paragraph (2), a fisherman's work agreement must—

(a) be comprehensible to the fisherman and consistent with the provisions of the Convention; and

(b) include provision about the matters in the Schedule.

(2) Such provision may be achieved by way of reference to another document which includes provision about those matters.

(3) Prior to entering into a fisherman's work agreement, the fishing vessel owner must take reasonable steps to satisfy itself with regard to the following requirements—

(a) the fisherman must have had sufficient opportunity to review and take advice on the terms of and conditions of the agreement;

(b) the fisherman must have received an explanation of the rights and responsibilities of the fisherman under the agreement; and

(c) the fisherman must be entering into the agreement freely.

Part 2 Statutory Instruments

(4) Where a fishing vessel owner fails to take such reasonable steps the fishing vessel owner commits an offence.

NOTES

Commencement: 31 December 2018.

[2.2093]

10 Documents

(1) As soon as is practicable after entering into a fisherman's work agreement, the fishing vessel owner must provide to the fisherman an original of the agreement signed by each party and a copy of any document referred to in that agreement.

(2) A breach of paragraph (1) is an offence by the fishing vessel owner.

(3) The fishing vessel owner must—

(a) ensure that—

(i) a copy of the fisherman's work agreement;

(ii) a copy of any document referred to in that agreement; and

(iii) any translation of such document required by regulation 11,

for each fisherman on the fishing vessel is held on board; and

(b) allow each fisherman to see the copy of the fisherman's work agreement to which the fisherman is a party (and any document referred to in paragraph (a)) on request.

(4) A breach of paragraph (3) is an offence by the fishing vessel owner.

NOTES

Commencement: 31 December 2018.

[2.2094]

11 Foreign language fisherman's work agreement

(1) This regulation applies where a fisherman has a fisherman's work agreement which is not in the English language.

(2) The fishing vessel owner must ensure that an English translation of the provisions of the fisherman's work agreement (including any provisions that are contained in another document) is made and made available to the fisherman.

NOTES

Commencement: 31 December 2018.

[2.2095]

12 Payments under a fisherman's work agreement

(1) Subject to paragraph (2), where a fisherman's work agreement provides that—

(a) the fisherman is entitled to receive wages, the wages must be paid monthly, or at other regular intervals as are set out in the fisherman's work agreement;

(b) the fisherman is entitled to receive any other remuneration, such payment of the remuneration must be made within a reasonable time or as otherwise set out in the fisherman's work agreement.

(2) Paragraph (1) does not apply to the extent that the failure to make such payment at the required time was due to—

(a) a mistake;

(b) a reasonable dispute as to liability;

(c) the act or default of the fisherman; or

(d) any other cause not being the wrongful act or default of the person liable to make the payment or of that person's servants or agents.

NOTES

Commencement: 31 December 2018.

[2.2096]

13 Account of payments

(1) The fishing vessel owner must ensure that an account of the fisherman's wages or other remuneration under a fisherman's work agreement is prepared and delivered to the fisherman—

(a) periodically during the term of the fisherman's work agreement, at intervals not exceeding one month; and

(b) within one month of the date on which the agreement terminated.

(2) Where the fisherman is not an employee, such account must include the following information—

(a) payments due;

(b) payments made (including any not falling within sub-paragraph (a)); and

(c) any rates of exchange and any commissions paid which are relevant to those payments.

(3) A breach of paragraph (1) is an offence by the fishing vessel owner.

NOTES

Commencement: 31 December 2018.

14–28 (*Regs 14–28 (Pts 4–8) outside the scope of this work.*)

PART 9
PENALTIES

[2.2097]
29 Penalties

(1) Subject to paragraphs (2) and (3), offences under these Regulations are punishable on summary conviction—
- (a) in England and Wales by a fine; or
- (b) in Scotland or Northern Ireland by a fine not exceeding level 5 on the standard scale.

(2) An offence under regulation 10(4) is punishable on summary conviction by a fine not exceeding level 4 on the standard scale.

(3) An offence under regulation 13(3) is punishable on summary conviction by a fine not exceeding level 2 on the standard scale.

(4) An offence under regulation 21(4) is punishable—
- (a) on summary conviction—
  - (i) in England and Wales by a fine; or
  - (ii) in Scotland and Northern Ireland by a fine not exceeding the statutory maximum, or
- (b) on conviction on indictment to imprisonment for a term not exceeding two years or to a fine, or to both.

NOTES
Commencement: 31 December 2018.

[2.2098]
30 Defence

In any proceedings for an offence under these Regulations it is a defence for the person charged to show that all reasonable steps had been taken by that person to ensure compliance with the provision concerned.

NOTES
Commencement: 31 December 2018.

31 (*Reg 31 (Pt 10) revokes the Merchant Shipping (Provisions and Water) Regulations 1989, SI 1989/102 (outside the scope of this work).*)

PART 11
REVIEW

[2.2099]
32 Review

(1) The Secretary of State must from time to time—
- (a) carry out a review of the regulatory provision contained in regulations 3 to 30, and
- (b) publish a report setting out the conclusions of the review.

(2) The first report must be published before 25th October 2023.

(3) Subsequent reports must be published at intervals not exceeding 5 years.

(4) Section 30(3) of the Small Business, Enterprise and Employment Act 2015 requires that a review carried out under this regulation must, so far as is reasonable, have regard to how the obligations under the Work in Fishing Convention are implemented in other countries which are subject to the obligations.

(5) Section 30(4) of the Small Business, Enterprise and Employment Act 2015 requires that a report published under this regulation must, in particular—
- (a) set out the objectives intended to be achieved by the regulatory provision referred to in paragraph (1)(a),
- (b) assess the extent to which those objectives are achieved,
- (c) assess whether those objectives remain appropriate, and
- (d) if those objectives remain appropriate, assess the extent to which they could be achieved in another way which involves less onerous regulatory provision.

(6) In this regulation, "regulatory provision" has the same meaning as in sections 28 to 32 of the Small Business, Enterprise and Employment Act 2015 (see section 32 of that Act).

NOTES
Commencement: 31 December 2018.

SCHEDULE
FISHERMAN'S WORK AGREEMENT

Regulation 9(1)

[2.2100]
1 The fisherman's family name and other names, date of birth or age and birthplace.

Part 2 Statutory Instruments

2 The place at which and date on which the agreement was concluded.

3 The name of the fishing vessel or vessels and the registration number of the vessel or vessels on board which the fisherman undertakes to work.

4 The name of the employer, or fishing vessel owner, or other party to the fisherman's work agreement.

5 The voyage or voyages to be undertaken, if this can be determined at the time of making the agreement.

6 The capacity in which the fisherman is to be employed or engaged.

7 If possible, the place at which and date on which the fisherman is required to report on board for service.

8 The provisions to be supplied to the fisherman.

9 The amount of wages, or the amount of the share and the method of calculating such share if remuneration is to be on a share basis, or the amount of the wage and share and the method of calculating the latter if remuneration is to be on a combined basis, and any agreed minimum wage.

10 The termination of the agreement and the conditions thereof, namely—
- (a) if the agreement has been made for a definite period, the date fixed for its expiry,
- (b) if the agreement has been made for a voyage, the port of destination and the time which has to expire after arrival before the fisherman is to be discharged,
- (c) if the agreement has been made for an indefinite period, the conditions which will entitle either party to rescind it, as well as the required period of notice for rescission, provided that such period must not be less for the employer, or fishing vessel owner or other party to the agreement than for the fisherman.

11 The protection that will cover the fisherman in the event of sickness, injury or death in connection with service.

12 The amount of paid annual leave or the formula used for calculating leave, where applicable;

13 The health and social security coverage and benefits to be provided to the fisherman by the employer, fishing vessel owner, or other party or parties to the fisherman's work agreement, as applicable.

14 The fisherman's entitlement to repatriation.

15 A reference to the collective bargaining agreement, where applicable.

16 The minimum periods of rest.

17 A declaration by the fishing vessel owner and the fisherman confirming that the requirements in regulation 9(4) (a) to (c) have been met.

NOTES

Commencement: 31 December 2018.

EUROPEAN PUBLIC LIMITED-LIABILITY COMPANY (AMENDMENT ETC) (EU EXIT) REGULATIONS 2018

(SI 2018/1298)

NOTES

Made: 3 December 2018.
Authority: European Union (Withdrawal) Act 2018, s 8(1).
Commencement: exit day (as defined in the European Union (Withdrawal) Act 2018, s 20).

PART 1
INTRODUCTION

[2.2101]
1 Citation and commencement

These Regulations may be cited as the European Public Limited-Liability Company (Amendment etc) (EU Exit) Regulations 2018 and come into force on exit day.

NOTES

Commencement: exit day (as defined in the European Union (Withdrawal) Act 2018, s 20).

2–139 *(In Part 2 (regs 2–95), regs 2–47, 66–95 amend legislation outside the scope of this work and regs 48–65 amend the European Public Limited-Liability Company (Employee Involvement) (Great Britain) Regulations 2009, SI 2009/2401 at* **[2.986]**. *Part 3 (regs 96–139) is outside the scope of this work.)*

PART 4
TRANSITIONAL AND SAVINGS PROVISIONS

140–145 *(Regs 140–145 are outside the scope of this work.)*

[2.2102]
146 Provisions in Respect of Amendments Made to the European Public Limited-Liability Company (Employee Involvement) (Great Britain) Regulations 2009

(1) Despite the revocations and amendments made by these Regulations, an employee who was a member of a special negotiating body before exit day—

(a) may after exit day present a complaint to an employment tribunal under regulation 28 (right to time off: complaints to tribunals) of the European Public Limited-Liability Company (Employee Involvement) (Great Britain) Regulations 2009, and regulation 28A (extension of time limit to facilitate conciliation before institution of proceedings) applies accordingly, that the employer—

(i) has unreasonably refused to permit the employee to take time off as required under regulation 26 (right to time off for members of special negotiating body etc), or

(ii) has failed to pay the whole or any part of any amount to which the employee is entitled under regulation 27 (right to remuneration for time off under regulation 26),

provided the complaint is in respect of a time off before exit day;

(b) who is dismissed, is to be regarded as unfairly dismissed within the terms of regulation 29(2) and (3) (unfair dismissal), and regulation 30 (subsidiary provisions relating to unfair dismissal) applies accordingly, provided the reason (or, if more than one, the principal reason) for the dismissal occurred before exit day;

(c) has the right not to be subjected to any detriment within the terms of regulation 31(2) and (3) (detriment), and regulation 32 (detriment: enforcement and subsidiary provisions) applies accordingly, provided the grounds for the detriment occurred before exit day.

NOTES

Commencement: exit day (as defined in the European Union (Withdrawal) Act 2018, s 20).

[2.2103]
147

In regulations 148 to [152A]—

"the pre-exit 2009 GB Regulations" means the European Public Limited-Liability Company (Employee Involvement) (Great Britain) Regulations 2009, as they had effect immediately before exit day;

"the 2009 GB Regulations" means the European Public Limited-Liability Company (Employee Involvement) (Great Britain) Regulations 2009;

"SE" means a European Public Limited-Liability Company (or Societas Europaea) within the meaning of the EC Regulation, as it had effect immediately before exit day.

NOTES

Commencement: exit day (as defined in the European Union (Withdrawal) Act 2018, s 20).

Figure in square brackets substituted by the International Accounting Standards and European Public Limited-Liability Company (Amendment etc) (EU Exit) Regulations 2019, SI 2019/685, reg 21, Sch 3, Pt 2, paras 13, 14, as from exit day (as defined in the European Union (Withdrawal) Act 2018, s 20).

[2.2104]
148

Despite the amendments and revocations made by these Regulations, regulations 3 and 7 to 18 of the pre-exit 2009 GB Regulations continue, on and after exit day, to have effect in relation to a special negotiating body reconvened under regulation 17 (decision not to open, or to terminate, negotiations) of the 2009 GB Regulations, as appropriate and practicable and subject to the modifications in regulation 149.

NOTES

Commencement: exit day (as defined in the European Union (Withdrawal) Act 2018, s 20).

[2.2105]
149

The modifications to the pre-exit 2009 Regulations are as follows—

(a) references to "EEA State", "an EEA State" or "EEA States" are to be read as though they were references to "Relevant State", "a Relevant State" or "Relevant States";

(b) references to "SE" or "SE's" are to be read as if they were references to "UK Societas" or "UK Societas's"—

(i) in regulation 3 (interpretation)—

(aa) in paragraph (1), in the definitions of "employee involvement agreement" and "participation";

(bb) in paragraph (2), in the definitions of "information" and "consultation";

(ii) in regulation 15(2)(g) and (3A);

(iii) in the definition of "reduction of participation rights" in regulation 16(3); and

(iv) in regulation 17(3)(b), (4)(b)(ii) and (c)(ii);

(c) otherwise, regulation 3 (interpretation) is to be read as if amended by these Regulations, save as if—

(i) in paragraph (1) the following definitions were not omitted—

(aa) "absolute majority vote";

(bb) "agency worker";

(cc) "participation";

(dd) "SE established by merger";

(ee) "SE established by formation of a holding company or subsidiary company";

(ff) "SE established by transformation";

(gg) "suitable information relating to the use of agency workers";

(hh) "two thirds majority vote";

(ii) "UK members of the special negotiating body";

(ii) the definition of "information and consultation representative" were omitted;

(iii) after "participation" there were inserted—

""Relevant State" means an EEA State or the United Kingdom;";

(iv) for the definition of "SE" there were substituted—

""SE" means a European Public Limited Liability Company (or Societas Europaea) within the meaning of the EC Regulation, as it had effect immediately before exit day;";

(v) in paragraph (2), the definition of "special negotiating body" were to a special negotiating body reconvened after exit day under regulation 17 (decision not to open, or to terminate, negotiations) of these Regulations, as they have effect after exit day;

(d) regulation 14 (negotiations to reach an employee involvement agreement) is to be read as if paragraphs (2) and (3) were omitted.

NOTES

Commencement: exit day (as defined in the European Union (Withdrawal) Act 2018, s 20).

[2.2106]
150

Regulations 146 to 149 are without prejudice to the application otherwise, in these circumstances, of the remaining regulations of the 2009 GB Regulations.

NOTES

Commencement: exit day (as defined in the European Union (Withdrawal) Act 2018, s 20).

[2.2107]
151

If an employee involvement agreement is not agreed following the reconvening of a special negotiating body, the standard rules on employee involvement in the Schedule to the pre-exit 2009 GB Regulations do not apply.

NOTES

Commencement: exit day (as defined in the European Union (Withdrawal) Act 2018, s 20).

[2.2108]
152

If an employee involvement agreement is agreed following the reconvening of a special negotiating body, the provisions of the 2009 GB Regulations apply thereafter.

NOTES

Commencement: exit day (as defined in the European Union (Withdrawal) Act 2018, s 20).

[2.2109]
[152A

(1) Despite the amendments and revocations made by these Regulations, paragraph 5(1) of the Schedule to the pre-exit 2009 GB Regulations applies to a UK Societas whose representative body was established less than four years before exit day.

(2) Where paragraph 5(1) applies—

(a) regulations 14 to 16 and 18 of the pre-exit 2009 GB Regulations apply, to the representative body as they apply to the special negotiating body, and the date referred to in regulation 14(3) is the date of the decision;

(b) Parts 2 and 3 of the Schedule to the pre-exit 2009 GB Regulations apply, where appropriate, and

(c) the following modifications to the pre-exit 2009 GB Regulations have effect—

(i) references to "EEA State" are to be read as though they were references to "Relevant State";

(ii) references to "SE" are to be read as if they were references to "UK Societas".]

NOTES

Commencement: exit day (as defined in the European Union (Withdrawal) Act 2018, s 20).

Inserted by the International Accounting Standards and European Public Limited-Liability Company (Amendment etc) (EU Exit) Regulations 2019, SI 2019/685, reg 21, Sch 3, Pt 2, paras 13, 15, as from exit day (as defined in the European Union (Withdrawal) Act 2018, s 20).

153–159 *(Regs 153–159 are outside the scope of this work.)*

IMMIGRATION (RESTRICTIONS ON EMPLOYMENT) (CODE OF PRACTICE AND MISCELLANEOUS AMENDMENTS) ORDER 2018 (NOTE)

(SI 2018/1340)

[2.2110]

NOTES

This Order was made on 6 December 2018 under the powers conferred by the Immigration, Asylum and Nationality Act 2006, ss 15(3), (7)(b)–(e), 19(2), (3), 25, and the Immigration Act 2016, s 38, Sch 6, para 5(6)(b), (c). It came into force on 28 January 2019.

This Order amends the Immigration (Restrictions on Employment) Order 2007, SI 2007/3290 at **[2.931]** et seq and the Illegal Working Compliance Orders Regulations 2016, SI 2016/1058 at **[2.1948]** et seq. This Order does not contain any transitional provisions or savings.

Article 4 provides: "The revised code of practice entitled "Code of practice on preventing illegal working: Civil penalty scheme for employers", issued by the Secretary of State under section 19(1) of the Immigration, Asylum and Nationality Act 2006 and laid in draft before Parliament on 10th December 2018, comes into force on 28th January 2019.". The 2019 Code is reproduced at **[4.107]**.

EMPLOYMENT RIGHTS (EMPLOYMENT PARTICULARS AND PAID ANNUAL LEAVE) (AMENDMENT) REGULATIONS 2018

(SI 2018/1378)

NOTES

Made: 17 December 2018.

Authority: European Communities Act 1972, s 2(2); Employment Rights Act 1996, ss 7, 236(5).

Commencement: 6 April 2020.

Note: with regard to the authority for these Regulations, note that the European Communities Act 1972 is repealed by the European Union (Withdrawal) Act 2018, s 1, as from exit day (as defined in s 20 of that Act); but note also that provision is made for the continuation in force of any subordinate legislation made under the authority of s 2(2) of the 1972 Act by s 2 of the 2018 Act at **[1.2240]**, subject to the provisions of s 5 of, and Sch 1 to, the 2018 Act at **[1.2243]**, **[1.2253]**.

PART 1
CITATION AND COMMENCEMENT

[2.2111]

1 Citation and commencement

These Regulations may be cited as The Employment Rights (Employment Particulars and Paid Annual Leave) (Amendment) Regulations 2018 and come into force on 6th April 2020.

NOTES

Commencement: 6 April 2020.

PART 2
EMPLOYMENT PARTICULARS

[2.2112]

2 Amendment to the Employment Rights Act 1996

The Employment Rights Act 1996 is amended as follows.

NOTES

Commencement: 6 April 2020.

3–7 *(Reg 3 amends the Employment Rights Act 1996, s 1 at* **[1.813]** *and regs 4–6 amend ss 2, 4, 7A thereof at* **[1.814]**, **[1.816]**, **[1.820]** *respectively. Reg 7 repeals s 198 of the 1996 Act at* **[1.1111]**.*)*

Part 2 Statutory Instruments

[2.2113]
8 Application

Subject to regulation 9, the amendments made by regulations 2 to 6 only apply in relation to a written statement required by section 1 or 4 of the Employment Rights Act 1996 where the worker to whom the statement must be given begins employment with the employer on or after 6 April 2020.

NOTES

Commencement: 6 April 2020.

9, 10 (*Reg 9 amends the Employment Rights Act 1996, Sch 2 at* **[1.1157]**; *reg 10 (Pt 3) amends the Working Time Regulations 1998, reg 16 at* **[2.293]**.)

EMPLOYMENT RIGHTS (INCREASE OF LIMITS) ORDER 2019

(SI 2019/324)

NOTES

Made: 20 February 2019.
Authority: Employment Relations Act 1999, s 34.
Commencement: 6 April 2019.

[2.2114]
1 Citation, commencement and interpretation

(1) This Order may be cited as the Employment Rights (Increase of Limits) Order 2019 and shall come into force on 6th April 2019.

(2) In this Order—

"the 1992 Act" means the Trade Union and Labour Relations (Consolidation) Act 1992; and
"the 1996 Act" means the Employment Rights Act 1996.

NOTES

Commencement: 6 April 2019.

[2.2115]
2 Revocation

The Employment Rights (Increase of Limits) Order 2018 is revoked.

NOTES

Commencement: 6 April 2019.

[2.2116]
3 Increase of limits

In the provisions set out in column 1 of the Schedule to this Order (generally described in column 2), for the sums specified in column 3 substitute the sums specified in column 4.

NOTES

Commencement: 6 April 2019.

[2.2117]
4 Transitional provisions

(1) The revocation in article 2 and the substitution made in article 3 do not have effect in relation to a case where the appropriate date falls before 6th April 2019.

(2) In this article "the appropriate date" means—

(a) in the case of an application made under section 67(1) of the 1992 Act (compensation for unjustifiable discipline by a trade union), the date of the determination infringing the applicant's right;

(b) in the case of a complaint presented under section 70C(1) of the 1992 Act (failure by an employer to consult with a trade union on training matters), the date of the failure;

(c) in the case of a complaint presented under section 137(2) of the 1992 Act (refusal of employment on grounds related to union membership) or section 138(2) of that Act (refusal of service of employment agency on grounds related to union membership), the date of the conduct to which the complaint relates, as determined under section 139 of that Act;

(d) in the case of an award under section 145E(2)(b) of the 1992 Act (award to worker in respect of offer made by employer in contravention of section 145A or 145B of that Act), the date of the offer;

(e) in the case of an application for an award of compensation under section 176(2) of the 1992 Act (compensation for exclusion or expulsion from a trade union), the date of the exclusion or expulsion from the union;

(f) in the case of an award under paragraph 159(1) of Schedule A1 to the 1992 Act, where a worker has suffered a detriment that is the termination of the worker's contract, the date of the termination;

(g) in the case of a guarantee payment to which an employee is entitled under section 28(1) of the 1996 Act (right to guarantee payment in respect of workless day), the day in respect of which the payment is due;

(h) in the case of an award of compensation under section 49(1)(b) of the 1996 Act by virtue of section 24(2) of the National Minimum Wage Act 1998, where a worker has suffered a detriment that is the termination of the worker's contract, the date of the termination;

(i) in the case of an award of compensation under section 63J(1)(b) of the 1996 Act (employer's failure, refusal or part refusal following request in relation to study or training), the date of the failure, or the date on which the employer notified the employee of a decision to refuse the application (or part of it) on appeal (as the case may be);

(j) in the case of an award of compensation under section 80I(1)(b) of the 1996 Act (complaint to an employment tribunal relating to an application for contract variation), the date of the failure in relation to the application or of the decision to reject the application or of the notification by the employer under section 80G(1D) of the 1996 Act;

(k) in the case of an award under section 112(4) of the 1996 Act (award in relation to unfair dismissal), the effective date of termination as defined by section 97 of that Act;

(l) in the case of an award under section 117(1) or (3) of the 1996 Act, where an employer has failed to comply fully with the terms of an order for reinstatement or re-engagement or has failed to reinstate or re-engage the complainant in accordance with such an order, the date by which the order for reinstatement (specified under section 114(2)(c) of that Act) or re-engagement (specified under section 115(2)(f) of that Act), should have been complied with;

(m) in the case of entitlement to a redundancy payment by virtue of section 135(1)(a) of the 1996 Act (dismissal by reason of redundancy), the relevant date as defined by section 145 of that Act;

(n) in the case of entitlement to a redundancy payment by virtue of section 135(1)(b) of the 1996 Act (eligibility for a redundancy payment by reason of being laid off or kept on short-time), the relevant date as defined by section 153 of that Act;

(o) in the case of entitlement to a payment under section 182 of the 1996 Act (payments by the Secretary of State), the appropriate date as defined by section 185 of that Act;

(p) in the case of a complaint presented under section 11(1) of the Employment Relations Act 1999 (failure or threatened failure to allow the worker to be accompanied at the disciplinary or grievance hearing, to allow the companion to address the hearing or confer with the worker, or to postpone the hearing), the date of the failure or threat;

(q) in the case of an award made under section 38(2) of the Employment Act 2002 (failure to give statement of employment particulars etc), the date the proceedings to which that section applies were begun;

(r) in the case of an increase in an award in pursuance of section 38(3) of the Employment Act 2002 (failure to give statement of employment particulars etc), the date the proceedings to which that section applies were begun; and

(s) in the case of a complaint presented under regulation 15 of the Flexible Working (Procedural Requirements) Regulations 2002 (failure or threatened failure to allow an employee to be accompanied at a meeting, to allow the companion to address the meeting or confer with the employee, or to postpone the meeting), the date of the failure or threat.

NOTES

Commencement: 6 April 2019.

SCHEDULE

Article 3

[2.2118]

Column 1		*Column 2*	*Column 3*	*Column 4*
Relevant statutory provision		*Subject of provision*	*Old limit*	*New limit*
1	Section 145E(3) of the 1992 Act	Amount of award for unlawful inducement relating to trade union membership or activities or for unlawful inducement relating to collective bargaining.	£4,059	£4,193
2	Section 156(1) of the 1992 Act	Minimum amount of basic award of compensation where dismissal is unfair by virtue of sections 152(1) or 153 of the 1992 Act.	£6,203	£6,408
3	Section 176(6A) of the 1992 Act	Minimum amount of compensation where individual excluded or expelled from union in contravention of section 174 of the 1992 Act and not admitted or re-admitted by date of tribunal application.	£9,474	£9,787

Part 2 Statutory Instruments

4	Section 31(1) of the 1996 Act	Limit on amount of guarantee payment payable to an employee in respect of any day.	£28	£29
5	Section 120(1) of the 1996 Act	Minimum amount of basic award of compensation where dismissal is unfair by virtue of section 100(1)(a) and (b), 101A(d), 102(1) or 103 of the 1996 Act.	£6,203	£6,408
6	Section 124(1ZA)(a) of the 1996 Act	Limit on amount of compensatory award for unfair dismissal.	£83,682	£86,444
7	Paragraphs (a) and (b) of section 186(1) of the 1996 Act	Limit on amount in respect of any one week payable to an employee in respect of a debt to which Part XII of the 1996 Act applies and which is referable to a period of time.	£508	£525
8	Section 227(1) of the 1996 Act	Maximum amount of "a week's pay" for the purpose of calculating a redundancy payment or for various awards including the basic or additional award of compensation for unfair dismissal.	£508	£525

NOTES

Commencement: 6 April 2019.

AUTOMATIC ENROLMENT (EARNINGS TRIGGER AND QUALIFYING EARNINGS BAND) ORDER 2019

(SI 2019/374)

NOTES

Made: 26 February 2019.
Authority: Pensions Act 2008, ss 14(2), 15A(1), 144(4).
Commencement: 6 April 2019.

[2.2119]
1 Citation, commencement and interpretation

(1) This Order may be cited as the Automatic Enrolment (Earnings Trigger and Qualifying Earnings Band) Order 2019.

(2) This Order comes into force on 6th April 2019.

(3) In this Order, "the Act" means the Pensions Act 2008.

NOTES

Commencement: 6 April 2019.

2 (*Amends the Pensions Act 2008, s 13 at* **[1.1577]**.)

[2.2120]
3 Rounded figures

For a pay reference period referred to in an entry in column 1 of the table—

(a) the amount of a jobholder's earnings which triggers the automatic enrolment, or as the case may be, the automatic re-enrolment of the jobholder pursuant to sections 3 and 5 respectively of the Act, is the rounded figure in the corresponding entry in column 2 of the table;

(b) the lower amount of qualifying earnings (see section 13(1)(a) of the Act), is the rounded figure in the corresponding entry in column 3 of the table;

(c) the upper amount of qualifying earnings (see section 13(1)(b) of the Act), is the rounded figure in the corresponding entry in column 4 of the table.

Table

Column 1	*Column 2*	*Column 3*	*Column 4*
Pay Reference Period	*Automatic enrolment and automatic re-enrolment earnings trigger: Rounded figure*	*Lower amount of qualifying earnings: Rounded figure*	*Upper amount of qualifying earnings: Rounded figure*
1 week	£192	£118	£962
2 weeks	£384	£236	£1,924
4 weeks	£768	£472	£3,847
1 month	£833	£512	£4,167
3 months	£2,499	£1,534	£12,500
6 months	£4,998	£3,068	£25,000

NOTES

Commencement: 6 April 2019.

[2.2121]

4 Revocation

The Automatic Enrolment (Earnings Trigger and Qualifying Earnings Band) Order 2018 is revoked.

NOTES

Commencement: 6 April 2019.

DATA PROTECTION, PRIVACY AND ELECTRONIC COMMUNICATIONS (AMENDMENTS ETC) (EU EXIT) REGULATIONS 2019

(SI 2019/419)

NOTES

Made: 28 February 2019.

Authority: European Communities Act 1972, s 2(2); Data Protection Act 2018, s 211(2); European Union (Withdrawal) Act 2018, ss 8(1), 23(1), Sch 4, para 1(1), Sch 7, para 21.

Commencement: see reg 1(2), (3).

Note: with regard to the authority for these Regulations, note that the European Communities Act 1972 is repealed by the European Union (Withdrawal) Act 2018, s 1, as from exit day (as defined in s 20 of that Act); but note also that provision is made for the continuation in force of any subordinate legislation made under the authority of s 2(2) of the 1972 Act by s 2 of the 2018 Act at **[1.2240]**, subject to the provisions of s 5 of, and Sch 1 to, the 2018 Act at **[1.2243]**, **[1.2253]**.

[2.2122]

1 Citation, commencement and extent

(1) These Regulations may be cited as the Data Protection, Privacy and Electronic Communications (Amendments etc) (EU Exit) Regulations 2019.

(2) Subject to paragraph (3), they come into force on exit day.

(3) Regulations 7 and 8 and Schedule 4 come into force on 29th March 2019.

(4) An amendment, repeal or revocation made by these Regulations has the same extent in the United Kingdom as the provision to which it relates.

NOTES

Commencement: exit day (as defined in the European Union (Withdrawal) Act 2018, s 20).

[2.2123]

2 Interpretation

In these Regulations—

"the 2018 Act" means the Data Protection Act 2018;

"the UK GDPR" means Regulation (EU) 2016/679 of the European Parliament and of the Council of 27th April 2016 on the protection of natural persons with regard to the processing of personal data and on the free movement of such data (General Data Protection Regulation) as it forms part of the law of England and Wales, Scotland and Northern Ireland by virtue of section 3 of the European Union (Withdrawal) Act 2018.

NOTES

Commencement: exit day (as defined in the European Union (Withdrawal) Act 2018, s 20).

[2.2124]
3 Amendment of the UK GDPR

Schedule 1 amends the UK GDPR.

NOTES

Commencement: exit day (as defined in the European Union (Withdrawal) Act 2018, s 20).

[2.2125]
4 Amendment of the Data Protection Act 2018

Schedule 2 amends the 2018 Act.

NOTES

Commencement: exit day (as defined in the European Union (Withdrawal) Act 2018, s 20).

[2.2126]
5 GDPR merger modifications

(1) Schedules 1 and 2 include modifications ("the GDPR merger modifications") that merge the provisions relating to the processing of personal data that, immediately before exit day, are found in the EU GDPR and the applied GDPR, read with the 2018 Act.

(2) Retained case law and retained general principles of EU law falling within paragraph (3) are not, by virtue of the GDPR merger modifications, to be treated as relevant to the UK GDPR or the 2018 Act as they apply to applied GDPR processing on and after exit day.

(3) Retained case law and retained general principles of EU law fall within this paragraph so far as they are, or are derived from, principles or decisions that are not relevant to any of the following immediately before exit day—

(a) the applied GDPR,
(b) the applied Chapter 2, or
(c) Parts 5 to 7 of the 2018 Act so far as they apply to applied GDPR processing,

having regard (among other things) to the limits of EU competence immediately before exit day.

(4) In this regulation—

"the applied Chapter 2" means Chapter 2 of Part 2 of the 2018 Act as applied by Chapter 3 of that Part immediately before exit day (see section 22 of that Act);

"the applied GDPR" means the EU GDPR as applied by Chapter 3 of Part 2 of the 2018 Act as it has effect immediately before exit day (see section 22 of that Act);

"applied GDPR processing" means the processing of personal data to which the applied GDPR applied immediately before exit day (see section 21 of the 2018 Act);

"the EU GDPR" means Regulation (EU) 2016/679 of the European Parliament and of the Council of 27th April 2016 on the protection of natural persons with regard to the processing of personal data and on the free movement of such data (General Data Protection Regulation) as it has effect in EU law immediately before exit day;

"retained case law" and "retained general principles of EU law" have the same meaning as in the European Union (Withdrawal) Act 2018 (see section 6(7) of that Act).

NOTES

Commencement: exit day (as defined in the European Union (Withdrawal) Act 2018, s 20).

[2.2127]
6 Consequential amendments of other legislation

In Schedule 3—

(a) Part 1 revokes certain retained EU law;
(b) Part 2 contains amendments of primary legislation (as defined in section 211(7) of the 2018 Act) that are consequential on Schedules 1 and 2;
(c) Part 3 contains amendments of other legislation that are consequential on those Schedules;
(d) Part 4 contains modifications of legislation that are consequential on those Schedules;
(e) Part 5 contains supplementary provision.

NOTES

Commencement: exit day (as defined in the European Union (Withdrawal) Act 2018, s 20).

7 Amendments consequential on provisions of the 2018 Act

Schedule 4 contains amendments consequential on provisions of the 2018 Act.

NOTES

Commencement: 29 March 2019.

8 *(Amends the Privacy and Electronic Communications (EC Directive) Regulations 2003, SI 2003/2426, which are outside the scope of this work.)*

SCHEDULES 1, 2

(Sch 1 sets out amendments to the UK GDPR at **[3.598]** *et seq. Note that para 80 of Sch 1 provides that it is not to be presumed, by virtue of the repeal of a provision by that Schedule, that the provision was applicable to the UK immediately before exit day (and so would, but for that Schedule, be part of the UK GDPR). Sch 2 sets out amendments to the Data Protection Act 2018 at* **[1.2111]** *et seq.)*

SCHEDULE 3
CONSEQUENTIAL AMENDMENTS OF OTHER LEGISLATION

Regulation 6

PARTS 1–3

(Pt 1 of Sch 3 concerns the revocation of retained EU Law; Parts 2, 3 of Sch 3 contain amendments which, in so far as relevant to this work, have been incorporated at the appropriate place in this work.)

PART 4
MODIFICATION

[2.2128]
References to the GDPR

111. (1) Legislation described in sub-paragraph (2) has effect on and after exit day as if it were modified in accordance with sub-paragraphs (3) and (4) (but see sub-paragraph (5)).

(2) That legislation is—
- (a) subordinate legislation made on or before exit day;
- (b) primary legislation passed or made on or before exit day.

(3) The following have effect as references to the UK GDPR—
- (a) references to the GDPR as defined in section 3(10) of the 2018 Act or as defined for the purposes of Parts 5 to 7 of the 2018 Act;
- (b) other references to Regulation (EU) 2016/679 of the European Parliament and of the Council of 27th April 2016 on the protection of natural persons with regard to the processing of personal data and on the free movement of such data (General Data Protection Regulation).

(4) References described in sub-paragraph (3) which are references to the GDPR or the Regulation read with Chapter 2 of Part 2 of the 2018 Act have effect as references to the UK GDPR read with Part 2 of that Act.

(5) Sub-paragraphs (1) to (4) have effect unless the context otherwise requires and, in particular, do not affect references to the Regulation mentioned in sub-paragraph (3)(b) as it has effect in EU law.

(6) Paragraph 2 of Schedule 21 to the 2018 Act (inserted by these Regulations) has effect in relation to references to the UK GDPR arising as a result of this paragraph as it has effect in relation of other references to the UK GDPR.

(7) In this paragraph—

"primary legislation" has the meaning given in section 211 of the 2018 Act;

"references" includes any references, however expressed;

"subordinate legislation" has the meaning given in the Interpretation Act 1978.

PART 5
SUPPLEMENTARY

[2.2129]
Interpretation of references to enactments

112. Nothing in Parts 2 to 4 of this Schedule is to be read as implying anything about whether references to an enactment or statutory provision (whether in Acts or instruments amended by those Parts of this Schedule or elsewhere) include the UK GDPR or other retained direct EU legislation.

SCHEDULE 4

(Sch 4 sets out amendments consequential on provisions of the Data Protection Act 2018; in so far as relevant to this work they have been incorporated at the appropriate place.)

CROSS-BORDER MEDIATION (EU DIRECTIVE) (EU EXIT) REGULATIONS 2019

(SI 2019/469)

NOTES

Made: 1 March 2019.

Authority: European Union (Withdrawal) Act 2018, s 8(1), Sch 7, para 21.

Commencement: exit day (as defined in the European Union (Withdrawal) Act 2018, s 20).

[2.2130]

1 Citation, commencement and extent

(1) These Regulations may be cited as the Cross-Border Mediation (EU Directive) (EU Exit) Regulations 2019 and come into force on exit day.

(2) Any amendment, revocation or modification made by these Regulations has the same extent as the provision amended, revoked or modified.

NOTES

Commencement: exit day (as defined in the European Union (Withdrawal) Act 2018, s 20).

2–4 (*Regs 2, 3 revoke, subject to savings, the Cross-Border Mediation (EU Directive) Regulations 2011, SI 2011/1133 and the Cross-Border Mediation Regulations (Northern Ireland) 2011, SR 2011/157, which are both outside the scope of this work. Reg 4 introduces Sch 1 to the Regulations (amendments to enactments).*)

[2.2131]

5 Mediations begun before exit day: saving and transitional provision

(1) This regulation applies to a mediation in respect of which any enactment which is amended by Schedule 1 applied immediately before exit day.

(2) The enactments amended by Schedule 1 apply to that mediation, on and after exit day—

(a) as if the amendments made by that Schedule do not have effect; and

(b) with the modifications specified in Schedule 2.

NOTES

Commencement: exit day (as defined in the European Union (Withdrawal) Act 2018, s 20).

SCHEDULE 1

(*Sch 1, Pt 1 amends the Limitation Act 1980 at* **[1.119]**, *the Employment Rights Act 1996 at* **[1.813]**, *the Employment Relations Act 1999, 11 at* **[1.1248]**, *the Equality Act 2010 at* **[1.1620]**, *and other legislation which is outside the scope of this work. Sch 1, Pt 2 amends the Employment Tribunals Extension of Jurisdiction (England and Wales) Order 1994, SI 1994/1623 at* **[2.215]**, *the Employment Tribunals Extension of Jurisdiction (Scotland) Order 1994, SI 1994/1624 at* **[2.227]**, *the Working Time Regulations 1998, SI 1998/1833 at* **[2.274]**, *and other legislation which is outside the scope of this work.*)

SCHEDULE 2

Regulation 5

PART 1
MODIFICATION OF PRIMARY LEGISLATION

[2.2132]

1–7 . . .

8 Modification of the Limitation Act 1980

(1) Section 33A of the Limitation Act 1980 (extension of time limits because of mediation in certain cross-border disputes) is modified as follows.

(2) Subsection (1) is to be read as if for it there were substituted—

"(1) In this section—

(a) "Mediation Directive" means Directive 2008/52/EC of the European Parliament and of the Council of 21 May 2008 on certain aspects of mediation in civil and commercial matters,

(b) "mediation" and "mediator" have the meanings given by Article 3 of the Mediation Directive, except that for the purpose of construing those expressions—

(i) Article 3(a) is to be read as if for "the law of a Member State" there were substituted "law", and

(ii) Article 3(b) is to be read as if for "Member State concerned" there were substituted "United Kingdom or the Member State concerned", and

(c) "relevant dispute" means a dispute within Article 8(1) of the Mediation Directive (certain cross-border disputes), reading Article 8 as if—
(i) the obligation imposed on Member States by paragraph (1) were also imposed in relation to the United Kingdom, and
(ii) in paragraph (2), for "Member States" there were substituted "the United Kingdom and Member States".

(1A) In construing the definition of "relevant dispute" in subsection (1)(c), Article 2 of the Mediation Directive (which defines cross-border disputes for the purposes of the Mediation Directive) is to be read as if—
(a) in paragraph 1 for "in a Member State other than that of any other party" there were substituted "in the United Kingdom, and at least one other party is domiciled or habitually resident in a Member State", and
(b) in paragraph 2 for "in a Member State" there were substituted "in a country ("country" for these purposes being limited to the United Kingdom or a Member State)", and
(c) for paragraph 3 there were substituted—

"**3** For the purposes of paragraphs 1 and 2, domicile is to be determined in accordance with paragraphs 4 to 8.

4 In order to determine whether a party is domiciled in the country ("country" for these purposes being limited to the United Kingdom or a Member State) whose courts are seised of a matter, the court shall apply its internal law.

5 If a party is not domiciled in the country whose courts are seised of the matter, then, in order to determine whether the party is domiciled in another country, the court shall apply the law of that country.

6 For the purposes of paragraphs 1 and 2, a company or other legal person or association of natural or legal persons is domiciled at the place where it has its—
(a) statutory seat;
(b) central administration; or
(c) principal place of business.

7 For the purposes of Ireland, Cyprus and the United Kingdom, "statutory seat" means the registered office or, where there is no such office anywhere, the place of incorporation or, where there is no such place anywhere, the place under the law of which the formation took place.

8 In order to determine whether a trust is domiciled in the country whose courts are seised of the matter, the court shall apply its rules of private international law.".

9–12 . . .

13 Modification of the Employment Rights Act 1996

(1) Section 207A of the Employment Rights Act 1996 (extension of time limits because of mediation in certain cross-border disputes) is modified as follows.

(2) Subsection (1) is to be read as if for it there were substituted—

"(1) In this section—
(a) "Mediation Directive" means Directive 2008/52/EC of the European Parliament and of the Council of 21 May 2008 on certain aspects of mediation in civil and commercial matters,
(b) "mediation and "mediator" have the meanings given by Article 3 of the Mediation Directive, except that for the purpose of construing those expressions—
(i) Article 3(a) is to be read as if for "the law of a Member State" there were substituted "law", and
(ii) Article 3(b) is to be read as if for "Member State concerned" there were substituted "United Kingdom or the Member State concerned", and
(c) "relevant dispute" means a dispute within Article 8(1) of the Mediation Directive (certain cross-border disputes), reading Article 8 as if—
(i) the obligation imposed on Member States by paragraph (1) were also imposed in relation to the United Kingdom; and
(ii) in paragraph (2), for "Member States" there were substituted "the United Kingdom and Member States".

(1A) In construing the definition of "relevant dispute" in subsection (1)(c), Article 2 of the Mediation Directive (which defines cross-border disputes for the purposes of the Mediation Directive) is to be read as if—
(a) in paragraph 1 for "in a Member State other than that of any other party" there were substituted "in the United Kingdom, and at least one other party is domiciled or habitually resident in a Member State";
(b) in paragraph 2 for "in a Member State" there were substituted "in a country ("country" for these purposes being limited to the United Kingdom or a Member State)"; and
(c) for paragraph 3 there were substituted—

"**3** For the purposes of paragraphs 1 and 2, domicile is to be determined in accordance with paragraphs 4 to 8.

4 In order to determine whether a party is domiciled in the country ("country" for these purposes being limited to the United Kingdom or a Member State) whose courts are seised of a matter, the court shall apply its internal law.

5 If a party is not domiciled in the country whose courts are seised of the matter, then, in order to determine whether the party is domiciled in another country, the court shall apply the law of that country.

6 For the purposes of paragraphs 1 and 2, a company or other legal person or association of natural or legal persons is domiciled at the place where it has its—

(a) statutory seat;
(b) central administration; or
(c) principal place of business.

7 For the purposes of Ireland, Cyprus and the United Kingdom, "statutory seat" means the registered office or, where there is no such office anywhere, the place of incorporation or, where there is no such place anywhere, the place under the law of which the formation took place.

8 In order to determine whether a trust is domiciled in the country whose courts are seised of the matter, the court shall apply its rules of private international law.".

14–16 . . .

17 Modification of the Equality Act 2010

(1) Section 140A of the Equality Act 2010 (extension of time limits because of mediation in certain cross-border disputes) is modified as follows.

(2) Subsection (1) is to be read as if for it there were substituted—

"(1) In this section—

(a) "Mediation Directive" means Directive 2008/52/EC of the European Parliament and of the Council of 21 May 2008 on certain aspects of mediation in civil and commercial matters,

(b) "mediation and "mediator" have the meanings given by Article 3 of the Mediation Directive, except that for the purpose of construing those expressions—

(i) Article 3(a) is to be read as if for "the law of a Member State" there were substituted "law", and

(ii) Article 3(b) is to be read as if for "Member State concerned" there were substituted "United Kingdom or the Member State concerned", and

(c) "relevant dispute" means a dispute within Article 8(1) of the Mediation Directive (certain cross-border disputes), reading Article 8 as if—

(i) the obligation imposed on Member States by paragraph (1) were also imposed in relation to the United Kingdom, and

(ii) in paragraph (2), for "Member States" there were substituted "the United Kingdom and Member States".

(1A) In construing the definition of "relevant dispute" in subsection (1)(c), Article 2 of the Mediation Directive (which defines cross-border disputes for the purposes of the Mediation Directive) is to be read as if—

(a) in paragraph 1 for "in a Member State other than that of any other party" there were substituted "in the United Kingdom, and at least one other party is domiciled or habitually resident in a Member State", and

(b) in paragraph 2 for "in a Member State" there were substituted "in a country ("country" for these purposes being limited to the United Kingdom or a Member State)", and

(c) for paragraph 3 there were substituted—

"**3** For the purposes of paragraphs 1 and 2, domicile is to be determined in accordance with paragraphs 4 to 8.

4 In order to determine whether a party is domiciled in the country ("country" for these purposes being limited to the United Kingdom or a Member State) whose courts are seised of a matter, the court shall apply its internal law.

5 If a party is not domiciled in the country whose courts are seised of the matter, then, in order to determine whether the party is domiciled in another country, the court shall apply the law of that country.

6 For the purposes of paragraphs 1 and 2, a company or other legal person or association of natural or legal persons is domiciled at the place where it has its—

(a) statutory seat;
(b) central administration; or
(c) principal place of business.

7 For the purposes of Ireland, Cyprus and the United Kingdom, "statutory seat" means the registered office or, where there is no such office anywhere, the place of incorporation or, where there is no such place anywhere, the place under the law of which the formation took place.

8 In order to determine whether a trust is domiciled in the country whose courts are seised of the matter, the court shall apply its rules of private international law.".

NOTES

Commencement: exit day (as defined in the European Union (Withdrawal) Act 2018, s 20).

Paras 1–7, 9–12, 14–16: outside the scope of this work.

PART 2
MODIFICATION OF SUBORDINATE LEGISLATION

[2.2133]

18 Modification of the Employment Tribunals Extension of Jurisdiction (England and Wales) Order 1994

(1) Article 8A of the Employment Tribunals Extension of Jurisdiction (England and Wales) Order 1994 (extension of time limits because of mediation in certain cross-border disputes) is modified as follows.

(2) Paragraph (1) is to be read as if for it there were substituted—

"(1) In this article—

(a) "Mediation Directive" means Directive 2008/52/EC of the European Parliament and of the Council of 21 May 2008 on certain aspects of mediation in civil and commercial matters;

(b) "mediation" and "mediator" have the meanings given by Article 3 of the Mediation Directive, except that for the purpose of construing those expressions—

(i) Article 3(a) is to be read as if for "the law of a Member State" there were substituted "law"; and

(ii) Article 3(b) is to be read as if for "Member State concerned" there were substituted "United Kingdom or the Member State concerned";

(c) "relevant dispute" means a dispute within Article 8(1) of the Mediation Directive (certain cross-border disputes), reading Article 8 as if—

(i) the obligation imposed on Member States by paragraph (1) were also imposed in relation to the United Kingdom; and

(ii) in paragraph (2), for "Member States" there were substituted "the United Kingdom and Member States".

(1A) In construing the definition of "relevant dispute" in paragraph (1)(c), Article 2 of the Mediation Directive (which defines cross-border disputes for the purposes of the Mediation Directive) is to be read as if—

(a) in paragraph 1 for "in a Member State other than that of any other party" there were substituted "in the United Kingdom, and at least one other party is domiciled or habitually resident in a Member State";

(b) in paragraph 2 for "in a Member State" there were substituted "in a country ("country" for these purposes being limited to the United Kingdom or a Member State)"; and

(c) for paragraph 3 there were substituted—

"**3** For the purposes of paragraphs 1 and 2, domicile is to be determined in accordance with paragraphs 4 to 8.

4 In order to determine whether a party is domiciled in the country ("country" for these purposes being limited to the United Kingdom or a Member State) whose courts are seised of a matter, the court shall apply its internal law.

5 If a party is not domiciled in the country whose courts are seised of the matter, then, in order to determine whether the party is domiciled in another country, the court shall apply the law of that country.

6 For the purposes of paragraphs 1 and 2, a company or other legal person or association of natural or legal persons is domiciled at the place where it has its—

(a) statutory seat;

(b) central administration; or

(c) principal place of business.

7 For the purposes of Ireland, Cyprus and the United Kingdom, "statutory seat" means the registered office or, where there is no such office anywhere, the place of incorporation or, where there is no such place anywhere, the place under the law of which the formation took place.

8 In order to determine whether a trust is domiciled in the country whose courts are seised of the matter, the court shall apply its rules of private international law.".

19 Modification of the Employment Tribunals Extension of Jurisdiction (Scotland) Order 1994

(1) Article 8A of the Employment Tribunals Extension of Jurisdiction (Scotland) Order 1994 (extension of time limits because of mediation in certain cross-border disputes) is modified as follows.

(2) Paragraph (1) is to be read as if for it there were substituted—

"(1) In this article—

(a) "Mediation Directive" means Directive 2008/52/EC of the European Parliament and of the Council of 21 May 2008 on certain aspects of mediation in civil and commercial matters;

(b) "mediation" and "mediator" have the meanings given by Article 3 of the Mediation Directive, except that for the purpose of construing those expressions—

(i) Article 3(a) is to be read as if for "the law of a Member State" there were substituted "law";

(ii) Article 3(b) is to be read as if for "Member State concerned" there were substituted "United Kingdom or the Member State concerned";

(c) "relevant dispute" means a dispute within Article 8(1) of the Mediation Directive (certain cross-border disputes), reading Article 8 as if—

(i) the obligation imposed on Member States by paragraph (1) were also imposed in relation to the United Kingdom; and

(ii) in paragraph (2), for "Member States" there were substituted "the United Kingdom and Member States".

(1A) In construing the definition of "relevant dispute" in paragraph (1)(c), Article 2 of the Mediation Directive (which defines cross-border disputes for the purposes of the Mediation Directive) is to be read as if—

(a) in paragraph 1 for "in a Member State other than that of any other party" there were substituted "in the United Kingdom, and at least one other party is domiciled or habitually resident in a Member State";

(b) in paragraph 2 for "in a Member State" there were substituted "in a country ("country" for these purposes being limited to the United Kingdom or a Member State)"; and

(c) for paragraph 3 there were substituted—

"**3** For the purposes of paragraphs 1 and 2, domicile is to be determined in accordance with paragraphs 4 to 8.

4 In order to determine whether a party is domiciled in the country ("country" for these purposes being limited to the United Kingdom or a Member State) whose courts are seised of a matter, the court shall apply its internal law.

5 If a party is not domiciled in the country whose courts are seised of the matter, then, in order to determine whether the party is domiciled in another country, the court shall apply the law of that country.

6 For the purposes of paragraphs 1 and 2, a company or other legal person or association of natural or legal persons is domiciled at the place where it has its—

(a) statutory seat;

(b) central administration; or

(c) principal place of business.

7 For the purposes of Ireland, Cyprus and the United Kingdom, "statutory seat" means the registered office or, where there is no such office anywhere, the place of incorporation or, where there is no such place anywhere, the place under the law of which the formation took place.

8 In order to determine whether a trust is domiciled in the country whose courts are seised of the matter, the court shall apply its rules of private international law.".

20 Modification of the Working Time Regulations 1998

(1) Regulation 30A of the Working Time Regulations 1998 (extension of time limits because of mediation in certain cross-border disputes) is modified as follows.

(2) Paragraph (1) is to be read as if for it there were substituted—

"(1) In this regulation—

(a) "Mediation Directive" means Directive 2008/52/EC of the European Parliament and of the Council of 21 May 2008 on certain aspects of mediation in civil and commercial matters;

(b) "mediation" and "mediator" have the meanings given by Article 3 of the Mediation Directive, except that for the purpose of construing those expressions—

(i) Article 3(a) is to be read as if for "the law of a Member State" there were substituted "law";

(ii) Article 3(b) is to be read as if for "Member State concerned" there were substituted "United Kingdom or the Member State concerned"; and

(c) "relevant dispute" means a dispute within Article 8(1) of the Mediation Directive (certain cross-border disputes), reading Article 8 as if—

(i) the obligation imposed on Member States by paragraph (1) were also imposed in relation to the United Kingdom; and

(ii) in paragraph (2), for "Member States" there were substituted "the United Kingdom and Member States".

(1A) In construing the definition of "relevant dispute" in paragraph (1)(c), Article 2 of the Mediation Directive (which defines cross-border disputes for the purposes of the Mediation Directive) is to be read as if—

(a) in paragraph 1 for "in a Member State other than that of any other party" there were substituted "in the United Kingdom, and at least one other party is domiciled or habitually resident in a Member State";

(b) in paragraph 2 for "in a Member State" there were substituted "in a country ("country" for these purposes being limited to the United Kingdom or a Member State)"; and

(c) for paragraph 3 there were substituted—

"**3** For the purposes of paragraphs 1 and 2, domicile is to be determined in accordance with paragraphs 4 to 8.

4 In order to determine whether a party is domiciled in the country ("country" for these purposes being limited to the United Kingdom or a Member State) whose courts are seised of a matter, the court shall apply its internal law.

5 If a party is not domiciled in the country whose courts are seised of the matter, then, in order to determine whether the party is domiciled in another country, the court shall apply the law of that country.

6 For the purposes of paragraphs 1 and 2, a company or other legal person or association of natural or legal persons is domiciled at the place where it has its—

(a) statutory seat;
(b) central administration; or
(c) principal place of business.

7 For the purposes of Ireland, Cyprus and the United Kingdom, "statutory seat" means the registered office or, where there is no such office anywhere, the place of incorporation or, where there is no such place anywhere, the place under the law of which the formation took place.

8 In order to determine whether a trust is domiciled in the country whose courts are seised of the matter, the court shall apply its rules of private international law.".

21, 22 . . .

NOTES

Commencement: exit day (as defined in the European Union (Withdrawal) Act 2018, s 20).
Paras 21, 22: outside the scope of this work.

CIVIL JURISDICTION AND JUDGMENTS (AMENDMENT) (EU EXIT) REGULATIONS 2019

(SI 2019/479)

NOTES

Made: 4 March 2019.
Authority: European Union (Withdrawal) Act 2018, s 8(1), Sch 7, para 21.
Commencement: exit day (as defined in the European Union (Withdrawal) Act 2018, s 20).

PART 1
INTRODUCTION

[2.2134]

1 Citation, commencement and extent

(1) These Regulations may be cited as the Civil Jurisdiction and Judgments (Amendment) (EU Exit) Regulations 2019 and come into force on exit day.

(2) Subject to paragraph (3), these Regulations extend to England and Wales, Scotland and Northern Ireland.

(3) Any amendment made by these Regulations has the same extent as the provision it amends.

NOTES

Commencement: exit day (as defined in the European Union (Withdrawal) Act 2018, s 20).

PART 2
AMENDMENT OF PRIMARY LEGISLATION

2–69 (*Regs 2, 3, 63–69 amend legislation outside the scope of this work; regs 4–62 amend the Civil Jurisdiction and Judgments Act 1982 at* **[1.135]** *et seq.*)

PART 3
AMENDMENT OF SUBORDINATE LEGISLATION

70–81 (*Regs 70–75, 77–81 amend legislation outside the scope of this work; reg 76 amends the Employment Tribunals (Enforcement of Orders in Other Jurisdictions) (Scotland) Regulations 2002, SI 2002/2792 at* **[2.676]** *et seq.*)

PART 4
TREATY RIGHTS AND OBLIGATIONS

[2.2135]
82 The 1968 Convention, the Lugano Conventions and the EC-Denmark Agreement

(1) Any rights, powers, liabilities, obligations, restrictions, remedies and procedures which—

(a) continue by virtue of section 4(1) of the European Union (Withdrawal) Act 2018; and

(b) are derived from—

(i) the Brussels Conventions;

(ii) the Convention on jurisdiction and the recognition and enforcement of judgments in civil and commercial matters, between the member States of the European Communities and the Republic of Iceland, the Kingdom of Norway and the Swiss Confederation, signed by the member States on 16 September 1988;

(iii) the Agreement between the European Community and the Kingdom of Denmark on jurisdiction and the recognition and enforcement of judgments in civil and commercial matters, of 19 October 2005; or

(iv) the Convention on jurisdiction and the recognition and enforcement of judgments in civil and commercial matters, between the European Community and the Republic of Iceland, the Kingdom of Norway, the Swiss Confederation and the Kingdom of Denmark, signed on behalf of the Community on 30 October 2007,

cease to be recognised and available in domestic law (and to be enforced, allowed and followed accordingly) on exit day.

(2) In this regulation, "the Brussels Conventions" means—

(i) the Convention on jurisdiction and the enforcement of judgments in civil and commercial matters (including the Protocol annexed to that Convention), signed at Brussels on 27 September 1968;

(ii) the Protocol on the interpretation of the 1968 Convention by the European Court, signed at Luxembourg on 3 June 1971;

(iii) the Convention on the accession to the 1968 Convention and the 1971 Protocol of Denmark, the Republic of Ireland and the United Kingdom, signed at Luxembourg on 9 October 1968;

(iv) the Convention on the accession of the Hellenic Republic to the 1968 Convention and the 1971 Protocol, with the adjustments made to them by the Accession Convention, signed at Luxembourg on 25 October 1982;

(v) the Convention on the Accession of the Kingdom of Spain and the Portuguese Republic to the 1968 Convention and the 1971 Protocol, with the adjustments made to them by the Accession Convention and the 1982 Accession Convention, signed at Donostia, San Sebastián on 26 May 1989; and

(vi) the Convention on the Accession of the Republic of Austria, the Republic of Finland and the Kingdom of Sweden to the 1968 Convention and the 1971 Protocol, with the adjustments made to them by the Accession Convention, the 1982 Accession Convention and the 1989 Accession Convention, signed at Brussels on 29 November 1996.

NOTES

Commencement: exit day (as defined in the European Union (Withdrawal) Act 2018, s 20).

PART 5
REVOCATION OF RETAINED DIRECT EU LEGISLATION

83 (*Outside the scope of this work.*)

[2.2136]
84 Council regulation (EC) No 44/2001

Council Regulation (EC) No 44/2001 of 22 December 2000 on jurisdiction and the recognition and enforcement of judgments in civil and commercial matters is revoked.

NOTES

Commencement: exit day (as defined in the European Union (Withdrawal) Act 2018, s 20).

85–88 (*Outside the scope of this work.*)

[2.2137]
89 Regulation (EU) No 1215/2012

Regulation (EU) No 1215/2012 of the European Parliament and of the Council of 12 December 2012 on jurisdiction and the recognition and enforcement of judgments in civil and commercial matters (recast) is revoked.

NOTES

Commencement: exit day (as defined in the European Union (Withdrawal) Act 2018, s 20).

90, 91 (*Outside the scope of this work.*)

PART 6
SAVINGS

[2.2138]

92 Savings Relating to Jurisdiction, Recognition and Enforcement

(1) Subject to paragraph (5) and to regulation 93, this regulation applies—

(a) where one of the relevant instruments applies immediately before exit day to determine questions relating to the jurisdiction of a court in any part of the United Kingdom to hear proceedings of which that court was seised before exit day and which are not concluded before exit day;

(b) in relation to recognition or enforcement by a court in any part of the United Kingdom of—

(i) a judgment or decision given in proceedings of which a court in a State bound by a relevant instrument was seised before exit day;

(ii) a court settlement concluded, or authentic instrument registered, before exit day in a State bound by a relevant instrument,

where the question of recognition or enforcement has not arisen for consideration by the first mentioned court before exit day, or having so arisen, that court has not concluded its consideration before that day.

(2) The relevant instruments referred to in paragraph (1) are—

(a) the Convention on Jurisdiction and the Enforcement of Judgments in Civil and Commercial matters, signed at Brussels on 27 September 1968;

(b) the Convention on Jurisdiction and the Recognition and Enforcement of Judgments in Civil and Commercial matters, between the member States of the European Communities and the Republic of Iceland, the Kingdom of Norway and the Swiss Confederation, signed by the member States on 16 September 1988;

(c) the Agreement between the European Community and the Kingdom of Denmark on Jurisdiction and the Recognition and Enforcement of Judgments in Civil and Commercial matters, of 19 October 2005;

(d) the 2007 Lugano Convention;

(e) Regulation (EC) No 44/2001;

(f) Regulation (EU) No 1215/2012.

(3) Notwithstanding the provision made by these Regulations, and subject to regulation 93, on and after exit day—

(a) the relevant instruments, as they are incorporated or saved by sections 3 and 4 of the European Union (Withdrawal) Act 2018, continue to have effect in relation to questions of jurisdiction, or recognition or enforcement, mentioned in paragraph (1) as if those instruments had not been revoked by these Regulations and the United Kingdom remained a member State;

(b) EU-derived domestic legislation relating to the relevant instruments, as it is saved by section 2 of the European Union (Withdrawal) Act 2018, continues to have effect in relation to questions of jurisdiction, or recognition or enforcement, mentioned in paragraph (1) as if the provision made by these Regulations in respect of that legislation had not been made and the United Kingdom remained a member State.

(4) In this regulation, a reference to "recognition" includes non-recognition if the context so requires.

(5) This regulation does not apply to a maintenance obligation or request to which the International Recovery of Maintenance (Hague Convention on the International Recovery of Child Support and Other Forms of Family Maintenance 2007) (EU Exit) Regulations 2018 apply.

NOTES

Commencement: exit day (as defined in the European Union (Withdrawal) Act 2018, s 20).

[2.2139]

93 Modifications of Relevant Instruments and EU-Derived Domestic Legislation Saved by regulation 92

(1) In any case where regulation 92 applies, the relevant instruments and EU-derived domestic legislation saved by regulation 92 apply with the following modifications.

(2) Where before exit day a court in any part of the United Kingdom (the UK court) was seised of proceedings to which a relevant instrument applies, and a court in a State bound by that relevant instrument is subsequently seised of proceedings involving the same cause of action and between the same parties, the UK court may after exit day decline jurisdiction if, and only if, it considers that it would be unjust not to do so.

(3) If before exit day a court in any part of the United Kingdom was seised of proceedings against a defendant domiciled in a State bound by a relevant instrument, and it has not been possible to transmit the document instituting the proceedings in accordance with Regulation (EC) No 1393/2007 by reason of the exit of the United Kingdom from the European Union, then, if the defendant does not appear before the court, the court may apply whichever of the following provisions of that relevant instrument listed below as appears just—

(a) Article 26(2) or (4) of Regulation (EC) No 44/2001;

(b) Article 26(2) or (4) of the 2007 Lugano Convention;

(c) Article 28(2) or (4) of Regulation (EU) No 1215/2012.

Part 2 Statutory Instruments

(4) Where regulation 92(1)(b) applies, any obligation to provide or serve a certificate under any of the following provisions does not apply—

(a) Articles 54, 57 and 58 of Regulation (EC) No 44/2001;

(b) Articles 54, 57 and 58 of the 2007 Lugano Convention;

(c) Articles 53 and 60 of Regulation (EU) No 1215/2012.

(5) In this regulation, "Regulation (EC) No 1393/2007" means Regulation (EC) No 1393/2007 of the European Parliament and of the Council of 13 November 2007 on the service in the Member States of judicial and extrajudicial documents in civil or commercial matters (service of documents) and repealing Council Regulation (EC) No 1348/2000.

(6) In this regulation, references to "defendant" include "defender".

NOTES

Commencement: exit day (as defined in the European Union (Withdrawal) Act 2018, s 20).

[2.2140]

94 Savings for European Enforcement Orders and European Orders for Payment Applied for, and European Small Claims Procedures Commenced, before Exit Day

(1) This regulation applies in relation to the provisions of Regulation (EU) No 1215/2012 (including those provisions as applied to references to Regulation (EC) No 44/2001 by Article 80 of the first mentioned Regulation) which are referred to by, or applied for the purposes of, the following instruments—

(a) Regulation (EC) No 805/2004 of the European Parliament and of the Council of 21 April 2004 creating a European Enforcement Order for uncontested claims;

(b) Regulation (EC) No 1896/2006 of the European Parliament and of the Council of 12 December 2006 creating a European order for payment procedure;

(c) Regulation (EC) No 861/2007 of the European Parliament and of the Council of 11 July 2007 establishing a European Small Claims Procedure.

(2) The provisions of Regulation (EU) No 1215/2012 mentioned in paragraph (1), as incorporated by section 3 of the European Union (Withdrawal) Act 2018, continue to have effect in relation to European Enforcement Orders and European orders for payment applied for, and European Small Claims procedures commenced, before exit day to which regulations 16, 17 and 18 of the European Enforcement Order, European Order for Payment and European Small Claims Procedures (Amendment etc) (EU Exit) Regulations 2018 apply, as if the revocation of those provisions by these Regulations had not occurred and the UK remained a member State.

(3) Where a statement of opposition is lodged after exit day in accordance with regulation 17 of the European Enforcement Order, European Order for Payment and European Small Claims Procedure (Amendment etc) (EU Exit) Regulations 2018 in relation to an application for a European Order for Payment made before exit day, regulation 92(3) of these Regulations applies to the proceedings transferred in accordance with regulation 17 of the first mentioned Regulations as if the court to which they are transferred had been seised of those proceedings before exit day.

NOTES

Commencement: exit day (as defined in the European Union (Withdrawal) Act 2018, s 20).

[2.2141]

95 Interpretation of this Part

(1) In this Part—

"relevant instrument" means an instrument mentioned in paragraph (2) of regulation 92;

"Regulation (EU) No 1215/2012" means Regulation (EU) No 1215/2012 of the European Parliament and of the Council of 12 December 2012 on Jurisdiction and the Recognition and Enforcement of Judgments in Civil and Commercial matters, including as applied by virtue of the Agreement between the European Community and the Kingdom of Denmark on Jurisdiction and the Recognition and Enforcement of Judgments in Civil and Commercial matters, of 19 October 2005;

"Regulation (EC) No 44/2001" means Council Regulation (EC) No 44/2001 on Jurisdiction and the Recognition and Enforcement of Judgments in Civil and Commercial matters, including as applied by virtue of the Agreement between the European Community and the Kingdom of Denmark on Jurisdiction and the Recognition and Enforcement of Judgments in Civil and Commercial matters, of 19 October 2005;

"the 2007 Lugano Convention" means the Convention on Jurisdiction and the Recognition and Enforcement of Judgments in Civil and Commercial matters, between the European Community and the Republic of Iceland, the Kingdom of Norway, the Swiss Confederation and the Kingdom of Denmark, signed on behalf of the Community on 30 October 2007.

(2) In this Part, a court shall be deemed to be seised—

(a) at the time when the document instituting the proceedings or an equivalent document is lodged with the court, provided that the applicant has not subsequently failed to take the steps the applicant was required to take to have service effected on the respondent; or

(b) if the document has to be served before being lodged with the court, at the time when it is received by the authority responsible for service (being the first authority receiving the document to be served), provided that the applicant has not subsequently failed to take the steps the applicant was required to take to have the document lodged with the court.

(3) In paragraph (2), references to "applicant" include "claimant" or "pursuer", and references to "respondent" include "defendant" or "defender".

(4) Nothing in this Part shall be interpreted as saving any obligation upon the United Kingdom under any of the relevant instruments to notify the Depository or the European Commission, as the case may be, of any matter, or update any such notification after exit day.

NOTES

Commencement: exit day (as defined in the European Union (Withdrawal) Act 2018, s 20).

AGRICULTURAL WAGES (WALES) ORDER 2019

(SI 2019/511)

NOTES

Made: 6 March 2019.
Authority: Agricultural Sector (Wales) Act 2014, ss 3, 4(1), 17.
Commencement: 1 April 2019.
Only the provisions of the Order most relevant to this work are reproduced.

ARRANGEMENT OF ARTICLES

PART 1 PRELIMINARY

PART 2 AGRICULTURAL WORKERS

PART 3 AGRICULTURAL MINIMUM WAGE

PART 4 ENTITLEMENT TO AGRICULTURAL SICK PAY

PART 5 ENTITLEMENT TO TIME OFF

PART 1
PRELIMINARY

[2.2142]

1 Title and commencement

The title of this Order is the Agricultural Wages (Wales) Order 2019 and it comes into force on 1 April 2019.

NOTES

Commencement: 1 April 2019.

[2.2143]

2 Interpretation

(1) In this Order—

"basic hours" ("*oriau sylfaenol*") means 39 hours of work per week, excluding overtime, worked in accordance with either an agricultural worker's contract of service or an apprenticeship;

"birth and adoption grant" ("*grant geni a mabwysiadu*") means a payment that an agricultural worker is entitled to receive from their employer on the birth of their child or upon the adoption of a child and is payable—

(a) where the agricultural worker has given their employer a copy of the child's Birth Certificate or Adoption Order (naming the worker as the child's parent or adoptive parent) within 3 months of the child's birth or adoption; and

(b) in circumstances where both parents or adoptive parents are agricultural workers with the same employer, to each agricultural worker;

"compulsory school age" ("*oedran ysgol gorfodol*") has the meaning given in section 8 of the Education Act 1996;

"guaranteed overtime" ("*goramser gwarantedig*") means overtime which an agricultural worker is obliged to work either under their contract of service or their apprenticeship and in respect of which the agricultural worker's employer guarantees payment, whether or not there is work for the agricultural worker to do;

"hours" ("*oriau*") includes a fraction of an hour;

"house" ("*ty*") means a whole dwelling house or self-contained accommodation that by virtue of the agricultural worker's contract of service the agricultural worker is required to live in for the proper or better performance of their duties and includes any garden within the curtilage of such a dwelling house or self-contained accommodation;

"night work" ("*gwaith nos*") means work (apart from overtime hours) undertaken by an agricultural worker between 7 pm on one evening and 6 am the following morning, but excluding the first two hours of work that an agricultural worker does in that period;

"on-call" ("*ar alwad*") means a formal arrangement between the agricultural worker and their employer where an agricultural worker who is not at work agrees with their employer to be contactable by an agreed method and able to reach the place where they may be required to work within an agreed time;

"other accommodation" ("*llety arall*") means any living accommodation other than a house which—

(a) is fit for human habitation;

(b) is safe and secure;

(c) provides a bed for the sole use of each individual agricultural worker; and

(d) provides clean drinking water, suitable and sufficient sanitary conveniences and washing facilities for agricultural workers in accordance with regulations 20 to 22 of the Workplace (Health, Safety and Welfare) Regulations 1992 as if the accommodation was a workplace to which regulations 20 to 22 of those Regulations applied;

"overtime" ("*goramser*") means—

(a) in relation to an agricultural worker who began their employment prior to 1 October 2006, time that is not guaranteed overtime worked by the agricultural worker—

(i) in addition to an 8 hour working day;

(ii) in addition to the agreed hours of work in their contract of service;

(iii) on a public holiday,

(iv) on a Sunday; or

(v) in any period commencing on a Sunday and continuing to the following Monday up until the time that worker would normally start their working day;

(b) in relation to all other agricultural workers, time that is not guaranteed overtime worked by the agricultural worker—

(i) in addition to an 8 hour working day;

(ii) in addition to the agreed hours of work in their contract of service; or

(iii) on a public holiday;

"output work" ("*gwaith allbwn*") means work which, for the purposes of remuneration, is measured by the number of pieces made or processed or the number of tasks performed by an agricultural worker;

"qualifying days" ("*diwrnodau cymwys*") means days on which the agricultural worker would normally be required to be available for work including days on which the agricultural worker—

(a) was taking annual leave;

(b) was taking bereavement leave;

(c) was taking statutory maternity, paternity, shared parental or adoption leave; or

(d) was on a period of sickness absence;

"sickness absence" ("*absenoldeb salwch*") means the absence of an agricultural worker from work due to incapacity by reason of—

(a) any illness suffered by the agricultural worker;

(b) illness or incapacity caused by the agricultural worker's pregnancy or suffered as a result of childbirth;

(c) an injury that occurs to the agricultural worker at the agricultural worker's place of work;

(d) an injury that occurs to the agricultural worker when travelling to or from their place of work;

(e) time spent by the agricultural worker recovering from an operation caused by an illness; or

(f) time spent by the agricultural worker recovering from an operation in consequence of an injury suffered at their place of work or an injury suffered whilst travelling to or from their place of work,

but does not include any injury suffered by the agricultural worker when not at their place of work nor any injury suffered when the agricultural worker is not travelling to or from their place of work;

"travelling" ("*teithio*") means a journey by a mode of transport or a journey on foot and includes—

(a) waiting at a place of departure to begin a journey by a mode of transport;

(b) waiting at a place of departure for a journey to re-commence either by the same or another mode of transport, except for any time the agricultural worker spends taking a rest break; and

(c) waiting at the end of a journey for the purpose of carrying out duties, or to receive training, except for any time the agricultural worker spends taking a rest break;

"working time" ("*amser gweithio*") means any period during which an agricultural worker is working at their employer's disposal and carrying out activities or duties in accordance with either their contract of service or their apprenticeship and includes—

(a) any period during which an agricultural worker is receiving relevant training;

(b) any time spent travelling by an agricultural worker for the purposes of their employment but does not include time spent commuting between their home and their place of work;

(c) any period during which an agricultural worker is prevented from carrying out activities or duties in accordance with their contract of service or their apprenticeship due to bad weather; and

(d) any additional period which the employer and the agricultural worker agree is to be treated as working time,

and references to "work" ("*gwaith*") are to be construed accordingly.

(2) In this article the reference to agricultural workers who began their employment prior to the 1 October 2006 includes agricultural workers—

(a) whose contract terms have since been subject to any variation; or

(b) who have since been employed by a new employer pursuant to the Transfer of Undertakings (Protection of Employment) Regulations 2006.

(3) References in this Order to a period of continuous employment are to be construed as a period of continuous employment computed in accordance with sections 210 to 219 of the Employment Rights Act 1996.

NOTES

Commencement: 1 April 2019.

PART 2
AGRICULTURAL WORKERS

[2.2144]

3 Terms and conditions of employment

An agricultural worker's employment is subject to the terms and conditions set out in this Part and Parts 3, 4 and 5 of this Order.

NOTES

Commencement: 1 April 2019.

4–11 (*Arts 4–11 concern the grades and categories of agricultural workers and are outside the scope of this work.*)

PART 3
AGRICULTURAL MINIMUM WAGE

[2.2145]

12 Minimum rates of pay

(1) Subject to the operation of section 1 of the National Minimum Wage Act 1998, agricultural workers must be remunerated by their employer in respect of their work at a rate which is not less than the agricultural minimum wage.

(2) The agricultural minimum wage is the minimum hourly rate specified in the Table in Schedule 4 as being applicable to each grade of agricultural worker and to apprentices.

NOTES

Commencement: 1 April 2019.

[2.2146]

13 Minimum rates of pay for overtime

Agricultural workers must be remunerated by their employer in respect of overtime worked at a rate which is not less than 1.5 times the agricultural minimum wage specified in article 12 of, and Schedule 4 to, this Order which is applicable to their grade or category.

NOTES

Commencement: 1 April 2019.

[2.2147]

14 Minimum rates of pay for output work

Agricultural workers must be remunerated by their employer in respect of output work at a rate which is not less than the agricultural minimum wage specified in article 12 of, and Schedule 4 to, this Order which is applicable to their grade or category.

NOTES

Commencement: 1 April 2019.

[2.2148]

15 Accommodation offset allowance

(1) Where in any week an employer provides an agricultural worker with a house for the whole of that week, the employer may deduct the sum of £1.50 from the agricultural worker's minimum wage payable under article 12 of this Order for that week.

(2) Subject to paragraphs (3) and (4), where in any week an employer provides an agricultural worker with other accommodation, the employer may deduct the sum of £4.82 from the agricultural worker's minimum wage payable under article 12 of this Order for each day in the week that the other accommodation is provided to the worker.

(3) The deduction in paragraph (2) may only be made when the agricultural worker has worked for a minimum of 15 hours in that week.

(4) Any time during that week when the agricultural worker is on annual leave or bereavement leave must count towards those 15 hours.

NOTES

Commencement: 1 April 2019.

[2.2149]

16 Payments which do not form part of an agricultural worker's remuneration

The following allowances and payments do not form part of an agricultural worker's remuneration—

(a) a dog allowance of £8.17 per dog to be paid weekly where an agricultural worker is required by their employer to keep one or more dogs;

(b) on-call allowance of a sum which is equivalent to two times the hourly overtime rate set out in article 13 of this Order;

(c) a night work allowance of £1.55 for each hour of night work; and

(d) a birth and adoption grant of £64.29 for each child.

NOTES

Commencement: 1 April 2019.

[2.2150]

17 Training costs

(1) Where an agricultural worker attends a training course with the prior agreement of their employer, the employer must pay—

(a) any fees for the course; and

(b) any travelling and accommodation expenses incurred by the agricultural worker attending the course.

(2) An agricultural worker who has been continuously employed at Grade 1 by the same employer for not less than 30 weeks is deemed to have received the approval of their employer to undertake training with a view to attaining the necessary qualifications required of a Grade 2 worker.

(3) Any training undertaken by an agricultural worker in accordance with paragraph (2), is to be paid for by the employer.

NOTES

Commencement: 1 April 2019.

PART 4
ENTITLEMENT TO AGRICULTURAL SICK PAY

[2.2151]

18 Entitlement to agricultural sick pay

Subject to the provisions in this Part, an agricultural worker is entitled to receive agricultural sick pay from their employer in respect of their sickness absence.

NOTES

Commencement: 1 April 2019.

[2.2152]

19 Qualifying conditions for agricultural sick pay

An agricultural worker qualifies for agricultural sick pay under this Order provided that the agricultural worker has—

(a) been continuously employed by their employer for a period of at least 52 weeks prior to the sickness absence;

(b) notified their employer of the sickness absence in a way previously agreed with their employer or, in the absence of any such agreement, by any reasonable means;

(c) in circumstances where the sickness absence has continued for a period of 8 or more consecutive days, provided their employer with a certificate from a registered medical practitioner which discloses the diagnosis of the worker's medical disorder and states that the disorder has caused the agricultural worker's sickness absence.

NOTES

Commencement: 1 April 2019.

[2.2153]

20 Periods of sickness absence

Any 2 periods of sickness absence which are separated by a period of not more than 14 days must be treated as a single period of sickness absence.

NOTES

Commencement: 1 April 2019.

[2.2154]

21 Limitations on entitlement to agricultural sick pay

(1) Agricultural sick pay will not be payable for the first 3 days sickness absence in circumstances where the duration of the sickness absence is less than 14 days.

(2) During each period of entitlement, the maximum number of weeks that an agricultural worker is entitled to agricultural sick pay is—

(a) 13 weeks where the agricultural worker has been employed by the same employer for at least 12 months but not more than 24 months;

(b) 16 weeks where the agricultural worker has been employed by the same employer for at least 24 months but not more than 36 months;

(c) 19 weeks where the agricultural worker has been employed by the same employer for at least 36 months but not more than 48 months;

(d) 22 weeks where the agricultural worker has been employed by the same employer for at least 48 months but not more than 59 months;

(e) 26 weeks where the agricultural worker has been employed by the same employer for 59 months or more.

(3) Where an agricultural worker works basic hours or, where applicable any guaranteed overtime, on a fixed number of days each week, the maximum number of days of agricultural sick pay that the agricultural worker is entitled to is calculated by multiplying the maximum number of weeks relevant to the agricultural worker by the number of qualifying days worked each week.

(4) Where an agricultural worker works basic hours or, where applicable any guaranteed overtime, on a varying number of days each week, the maximum number of days of agricultural sick pay that the agricultural worker is entitled to is calculated by multiplying the maximum number of weeks relevant to that worker by the number of relevant days.

(5) The number of relevant days is calculated by dividing the number of qualifying days worked during a period of 12 months leading up to the period of sickness absence by 52.

(6) An agricultural worker's maximum entitlement to agricultural sick pay applies regardless of the number of occasions of sickness absence during any period of entitlement.

(7) Subject to paragraph (8), in this article, "a period of entitlement" is a period beginning with the commencement of a sickness absence and ending 12 months later.

(8) If the agricultural worker has a period of sickness absence which commences at any time during the period of entitlement described in paragraph (7), but which continues beyond the end of that period of entitlement, the period of entitlement must be extended so as to end on whichever of the following first occurs—

(a) the date when the agricultural worker's sickness absence ends and the agricultural worker returns to work; or

(b) the day on which the agricultural worker reaches the maximum entitlement to agricultural sick pay applicable to the 12 month period referred to in paragraph (7) (had it not been extended).

NOTES

Commencement: 1 April 2019.

[2.2155]

22 Determining the amount of agricultural sick pay

(1) Agricultural sick pay is payable at a rate which is equivalent to the minimum hourly rate of pay prescribed in article 12 of, and Schedule 4 to, this Order as applicable to that grade or category of agricultural worker.

(2) The amount of agricultural sick pay payable to an agricultural worker is determined by calculating the number of daily contractual hours that would have been worked during a period of sickness absence.

(3) The number of daily contractual hours are determined—

(a) in circumstances where an agricultural worker works a fixed number of hours each week by dividing the total number of hours worked during any week by the number of days worked in that week;

(b) in circumstances where an agricultural worker works a varying number of hours each week, by applying the formula—

(QH / 8) / DWEW

where for the purposes of this article:

QH is the total number of qualifying hours in the period, and

DWEW is the number of days worked each week by the agricultural worker when taken as an average during a period of 8 weeks immediately preceding the commencement of the sickness absence.

(4) In this article "qualifying hours" are hours where—

(a) the agricultural worker worked basic hours or guaranteed overtime;

(b) the agricultural worker took annual leave or bereavement leave;

(c) the agricultural worker had sickness absence qualifying for agricultural sick pay under this Order; or

(d) the agricultural worker had sickness absence not qualifying for agricultural sick pay under this Order; and

"qualifying days" are any days within the period on which there were qualifying hours relating to the agricultural worker.

(5) For the purposes of calculations under this article, where an agricultural worker has been employed by their employer for less than 8 weeks, account must be taken of qualifying hours and qualifying days in the actual number of weeks of the agricultural worker's employment with their employer.

NOTES

Commencement: 1 April 2019.

[2.2156]

23 Agricultural sick pay to take account of statutory sick pay

An amount equal to any payment of statutory sick pay made in accordance with Part XI of the Social Security Contributions and Benefits Act 1992 in respect of a period of an agricultural worker's sickness absence may be deducted from that worker's agricultural sick pay.

NOTES

Commencement: 1 April 2019.

[2.2157]
24 Payment of agricultural sick pay

Agricultural sick pay must be paid to the agricultural worker on their normal pay day in accordance with either their contract of service or their apprenticeship.

NOTES

Commencement: 1 April 2019.

[2.2158]
25 Employment ending during sickness absence

(1) Subject to paragraph (2), if during a period of sickness absence, either an agricultural worker's contract of service or their apprenticeship is terminated or the agricultural worker is given notice that either their contract of service or their apprenticeship is to be terminated, any entitlement which the agricultural worker has to agricultural sick pay continues after that contract ends as if the agricultural worker was still employed by their employer, until one of the following occurs—

- (a) the agricultural worker's sickness absence ends;
- (b) the agricultural worker starts work for another employer; or
- (c) the maximum entitlement to agricultural sick pay in accordance with article 21 is exhausted.

(2) An agricultural worker whose contract has been terminated is not entitled to any agricultural sick pay after the end of their employment in accordance with paragraph (1) if the agricultural worker was given notice that their employer intended to terminate their contract of service or their apprenticeship before the period of sickness absence commenced.

NOTES

Commencement: 1 April 2019.

[2.2159]
26 Overpayments of agricultural sick pay

(1) Subject to the provisions of paragraph (2), if an agricultural worker who is entitled to agricultural sick pay under this Part is paid more agricultural sick pay than their entitlement, their employer can recover the overpayment of such agricultural sick pay by deduction from that agricultural worker's wages.

(2) If an overpayment of agricultural sick pay under this Order is deducted as mentioned in paragraph (1), the employer must not deduct more than 20% of the agricultural worker's gross wage unless notice has been given to terminate the employment or the employment has already been terminated in which case more than 20% of the agricultural worker's gross wage may be deducted by the employer from payment of the agricultural worker's final wages.

NOTES

Commencement: 1 April 2019.

[2.2160]
27 Damages recovered for loss of earnings

(1) This article applies to an agricultural worker whose entitlement to agricultural sick pay arises because of the actions or omissions of a person other than their employer and damages are recovered by the agricultural worker in respect of loss of earnings suffered during the period in respect of which the agricultural worker received agricultural sick pay from their employer.

(2) Where paragraph (1) applies—

- (a) the agricultural worker must immediately notify their employer of all the relevant circumstances and of any claim and of any damages recovered under any compromise, settlement or judgment;
- (b) all agricultural sick pay paid by the employer to that agricultural worker in respect of the sickness absence for which damages for loss of earnings are recovered must constitute a loan to the worker; and
- (c) the agricultural worker must refund to their employer a sum not exceeding the lesser of—
  - (i) the amount of damages recovered for loss of earnings in the period for which agricultural sick pay was paid; and
  - (ii) the sums advanced to the agricultural worker from their employer under this Part by way of agricultural sick pay.

NOTES

Commencement: 1 April 2019.

PART 5
ENTITLEMENT TO TIME OFF

[2.2161]
28 Rest breaks

(1) An agricultural worker who is aged 18 or over and who has a daily working time of more than 5 and a half hours is entitled to a rest break.

Part 2 Statutory Instruments

(2) The rest break provided for in paragraph (1) is an uninterrupted period of not less than 30 minutes and the agricultural worker is entitled to spend it away from their workstation (if they have one) or other place of work.

(3) Subject to paragraph (4), the provisions relating to rest breaks as specified in paragraphs (1) and (2) do not apply to an agricultural worker where—

(a) due to the specific characteristics of the activity in which the agricultural worker is engaged, the duration of their working time is not measured or predetermined;

(b) the agricultural worker's activities involve the need for continuity of service or production;

(c) there is a foreseeable surge of activity;

(d) the agricultural worker's activities are affected by—

(i) an occurrence due to unusual and unforeseeable circumstances, beyond the control of their employer;

(ii) exceptional events, the consequences of which could not have been avoided despite the exercise of all due care by the employer; or

(iii) an accident or the imminent risk of an accident; or

(e) the employer and agricultural worker agree to modify or exclude the application of paragraphs (1) and (2) in the manner and to the extent permitted by or under the Working Time Regulations 1998.

(4) Where paragraph (3) applies and an agricultural worker is accordingly required by their employer to work during a period which would otherwise be a rest break—

(a) the employer must, unless sub-paragraph (b) applies, allow the agricultural worker to take an equivalent period of compensatory rest; and

(b) in exceptional cases in which it is not possible, for objective reasons, to grant such a period of rest, the agricultural worker's employer must afford them such protection as may be appropriate in order to safeguard the agricultural worker's health and safety.

NOTES

Commencement: 1 April 2019.

[2.2162]

29 Annual leave year

The annual leave year for all agricultural workers is the period of 12 months beginning on 1 October and ending on 30 September.

NOTES

Commencement: 1 April 2019.

[2.2163]

30 Amount of annual leave for agricultural workers with fixed working days employed throughout the annual leave year

(1) An agricultural worker who is employed by the same employer throughout the annual leave year is entitled to the amount of annual leave prescribed in the Table in Schedule 5.

(2) Where an agricultural worker works their basic hours and, where applicable any guaranteed overtime, on a fixed number of qualifying days each week, the number of days worked each week for the purposes of the Table in Schedule 5 is that fixed number of days.

NOTES

Commencement: 1 April 2019.

[2.2164]

31 Amount of annual leave for agricultural workers with variable working days employed throughout the annual leave year

(1) Where an agricultural worker works their basic hours on a varying number of days each week, the number of days worked each week for the purposes of the Table in Schedule 5, is to be taken as an average of the number of qualifying days worked each week during the period of 12 weeks immediately preceding the commencement of the agricultural worker's annual leave and that average number of qualifying days must, where appropriate, be rounded to the nearest whole day.

(2) At the end of the annual leave year the employer must calculate the agricultural worker's actual entitlement for the purposes of the Table in Schedule 5, based upon the number of qualifying days worked each week, taken as an average of the number of qualifying days worked each week during the annual leave year ($21 over a period of 52 weeks) and the average number of qualifying days must be, where appropriate, rounded to the nearest whole day.

(3) If at the end of the annual leave year, the agricultural worker has accrued but untaken holiday entitlement, the agricultural worker is entitled to carry forward any accrued but untaken holiday to the following annual leave year in accordance with article 33(3) of this Order or the agricultural worker and the employer may agree to a payment in lieu of any accrued but untaken holiday in accordance with article 36 of this Order.

(4) If at the end of the annual leave year, the agricultural worker has taken more holiday days than they were entitled to under this Order, based on the average number of qualifying days worked per week (calculated in accordance with paragraph (2)), the employer is entitled to deduct any pay for holiday days taken in excess of the agricultural worker's entitlement or, in the alternative, deduct the holiday days

taken in excess of the agricultural worker's entitlement from their entitlement for the following annual leave year (provided any such deduction does not result in the agricultural worker receiving less than their statutory annual leave entitlement under regulations 13 and 13A of the Working Time Regulations 1998).

NOTES

Commencement: 1 April 2019.

[2.2165]

32 Amount of annual leave for agricultural workers employed for part of the leave year

(1) An agricultural worker employed by the same employer for part of the annual leave year is entitled to accrue annual leave at a rate of 1/52nd of the annual leave entitlement specified in the Table in Schedule 5 for each completed week of service with the same employer.

(2) Where the amount of annual leave accrued in a particular case includes a fraction of a day other than a half day, that fraction is to be—

(a) rounded down to the next whole day if it is less than half a day; and

(b) rounded up to the next whole day if it is more than half a day.

NOTES

Commencement: 1 April 2019.

[2.2166]

33 Timing of annual leave

(1) An agricultural worker may take annual leave to which they are entitled under this Order at any time within the annual leave year subject to the approval of their employer.

(2) An agricultural worker is not entitled to carry forward from one leave year to the next leave year any untaken annual leave entitlement without the approval of their employer.

(3) Where an employer has agreed that an agricultural worker may carry forward any unused annual leave entitlement, the balance carried forward may only be taken in the leave year to which it is carried forward.

(4) During the period from 1 October to 31 March in any annual leave year an employer may require an agricultural worker to take up to 2 weeks of their annual leave entitlement under this Order and may direct that the worker takes one of those 2 weeks of annual leave on days in the same week.

(5) During the period from 1 April to 30 September in any annual leave year an employer must permit an agricultural worker to take 2 weeks of the worker's annual leave entitlement under this Order in consecutive weeks.

(6) For the purpose of this article, 1 week of an agricultural worker's annual leave is equivalent to the number of days worked each week by the agricultural worker as determined in accordance with articles 30 and 31.

NOTES

Commencement: 1 April 2019.

[2.2167]

34 Holiday pay

(1) An agricultural worker is entitled to be remunerated in respect of each day of annual leave taken by them.

(2) The amount of holiday pay to which an agricultural worker is entitled under paragraph (1) is to be determined by dividing the agricultural worker's weekly wage as determined in accordance with paragraph (3), or as the case may be paragraph (4), by the number of qualifying days worked each week by that agricultural worker.

(3) Where the agricultural worker's normal working hours under either their contract of service or apprenticeship do not vary (subject to paragraph (4)), the amount of the agricultural worker's weekly pay for the purposes of paragraph (2) is the agricultural worker's normal weekly pay payable by the employer.

(4) Where the agricultural worker's normal working hours vary from week to week, or where an agricultural worker with normal working hours (as in paragraph (3)) works overtime in addition to those hours, the amount of the agricultural worker's normal weekly pay for the purposes of paragraph (2) is calculated by adding together the amount of the agricultural worker's normal weekly pay in each of the 12 weeks immediately preceding the commencement of the worker's annual leave and dividing the total by 12.

(5) For the purposes of this article "normal weekly pay" means—

(a) the agricultural worker's basic pay under their contract of service or apprenticeship; and

(b) any overtime pay and any allowance paid to the agricultural worker on a consistent basis.

(6) Where an agricultural worker has been employed by their employer for less than 12 weeks, account must be taken only of weeks in which pay was due to the agricultural worker.

(7) For the purposes of paragraph (2), the number of qualifying days worked is determined in accordance with the provisions in articles 30 and 31 of this Order.

(8) Any pay due to an agricultural worker under this article must be made not later than the agricultural worker's last working day before the commencement of the period of annual leave to which the payment relates.

NOTES

Commencement: 1 April 2019.

[2.2168]

35 Public holidays and bank holidays

(1) This article applies where a public holiday or bank holiday in Wales falls on a day when an agricultural worker is normally required to work either under their contract of service or their apprenticeship.

(2) An agricultural worker required by their employer to work on the public holiday or bank holiday is entitled to be paid not less than the overtime rate specified in article 13.

(3) An agricultural worker who is not required by their employer to work on the public holiday or bank holiday is to have the balance of their accrued annual leave for that leave year under this Order reduced by 1 day in respect of the public holiday or bank holiday on which the agricultural worker is not required to work.

NOTES

Commencement: 1 April 2019.

[2.2169]

36 Payment in lieu of annual leave

(1) Subject to the conditions in paragraph (2), an agricultural worker and their employer may agree that the agricultural worker is to receive payment in lieu of a day of the agricultural worker's annual leave entitlement.

(2) The conditions referred to in paragraph (1) are—

(a) the maximum number of days for which an agricultural worker can receive a payment in lieu of annual leave during any annual leave year is prescribed in the Table in Schedule 6;

(b) a written record is to be kept by the employer of any agreement that an agricultural worker will receive payment in lieu of a day's annual leave for a minimum of 3 years commencing at the end of that annual leave year;

(c) in circumstances where the agricultural worker does not work on a day as agreed in accordance with paragraph (1), that day is to remain part of the agricultural worker's annual leave entitlement;

(d) payment in lieu of annual leave is to be paid at a rate which comprises both the overtime rate specified in article 13 and holiday pay calculated in accordance with article 34 as if the day for which a payment in lieu of annual leave is made is a day on which the agricultural worker is taking annual leave.

NOTES

Commencement: 1 April 2019.

[2.2170]

37 Payment of holiday pay on termination of employment

(1) Where an agricultural worker's employment is terminated and the agricultural worker has not taken all of the annual leave entitlement which has accrued to them at the date of termination, the agricultural worker is entitled in accordance with paragraph (2) to be paid in lieu of that accrued but untaken annual leave.

(2) The amount of payment to be made to the agricultural worker in lieu of each day of their accrued but untaken holiday as at the date of termination is to be calculated in accordance with article 34 as if the date of termination was the first day of a period of the agricultural worker's annual leave.

NOTES

Commencement: 1 April 2019.

[2.2171]

38 Recovery of holiday pay

(1) If an agricultural worker's employment terminates before the end of the annual leave year and the agricultural worker has taken more annual leave than they were entitled to under the provisions of this Order or otherwise, their employer is entitled to recover the amount of holiday pay which has been paid to the agricultural worker in respect of annual leave taken in excess of their entitlement.

(2) Where under paragraph (1) an employer is entitled to recover holiday pay from an agricultural worker, the employer may do so by means of a deduction from the final payment of wages to the agricultural worker.

NOTES

Commencement: 1 April 2019.

[2.2172]

39 Bereavement leave

(1) An agricultural worker is entitled to paid bereavement leave in circumstances where the bereavement relates to a person in Category A or Category B.

(2) For the purposes of paragraph (1), persons in Category A are—

(a) a parent of the agricultural worker;

(b) a son or daughter of the agricultural worker;

(c) the agricultural worker's spouse or civil partner; or

(d) someone with whom the agricultural worker lives as husband and wife without being legally married or someone with whom the agricultural worker lives as if they were in a civil partnership.

(3) For the purposes of paragraph (1), persons in Category B are—

(a) a brother or sister of the agricultural worker;

(b) a grandparent of the agricultural worker; or

(c) a grandchild of the agricultural worker.

(4) Bereavement leave for the purposes of paragraph (1) is in addition to any other leave entitlements under this Order.

NOTES

Commencement: 1 April 2019.

[2.2173]

40 Determining the amount of bereavement leave

(1) The amount of bereavement leave to which an agricultural worker is entitled following the death of a person within Category A is—

(a) 4 days where the agricultural worker works their basic hours on 5 days or more each week for the same employer; or

(b) where the agricultural worker works their basic hours on 4 days a week or less for the same employer, the number of days calculated in accordance with paragraph (2).

(2) Subject to paragraph (6), the amount of an agricultural worker's entitlement to bereavement leave following the death of a person within Category A is to be calculated according to the following formula—

(DWEW x 4) / 5

(3) The amount of bereavement leave to which an agricultural worker is entitled following the death of a person in Category B is—

(a) 2 days where the agricultural worker works their basic hours on 5 days or more each week for the same employer; or

(b) where the agricultural worker works their basic hours on 4 days a week or less for the same employer, the number of days calculated in accordance with paragraph (4).

(4) Subject to paragraph (6), where this article applies the amount of an agricultural worker's entitlement to bereavement leave following the death of a person within Category B is to be calculated according to the following formula—

(DWEW x 2) / 5

(5) For the purposes of the formula in paragraphs (2) and (4), DWEW is the number of days worked each week by the agricultural worker calculated in accordance with article 30 or 31 (as appropriate).

(6) Where the calculation in either paragraph (2) or (4) results in an entitlement to bereavement leave of less than 1 day, the entitlement is to be rounded up to one whole day.

(7) In circumstances where an agricultural worker has more than one employment (whether with the same employer or with different employers), paid bereavement leave may be taken in respect of more than one employment but must not exceed, in respect of any one occasion of bereavement, the maximum amount of bereavement leave specified for a single employment in this article.

NOTES

Commencement: 1 April 2019.

[2.2174]

41 Amount of pay for bereavement leave

The amount of pay in respect of bereavement leave is to be determined in accordance with the provisions in article 34 as if the first day of the agricultural worker's bereavement leave was the first day of that worker's annual leave.

NOTES

Commencement: 1 April 2019.

[2.2175]

42 Unpaid leave

An agricultural worker may, with their employer's consent, take a period of unpaid leave.

NOTES

Commencement: 1 April 2019.

PART 6
REVOCATION AND TRANSITIONAL PROVISION

[2.2176]

43 Revocation and transitional provision

(1) The Agricultural Wages (Wales) Order 2018 ("the 2018 Order") is revoked.

(2) An agricultural worker employed as a worker at a Grade or as an apprentice, and subject to the terms and conditions prescribed in the 2018 Order or any previous Orders continue to be employed in that Grade or as an apprentice and are, from the date this Order comes into force, subject to the terms and conditions prescribed in this Order.

(3) In this article "previous Orders" means the Agricultural Wages (Wales) Order 2017 , the Agricultural Wages (Wales) Order 2016 , the Agricultural Wages (England and Wales) Order 2012 and every order revoked by article 70 of that Order.

NOTES

Commencement: 1 April 2019.

SCHEDULES 1–3

(*Awards and Certificates of Competence for Grades 2–4 workers (outside the scope of this work).*)

SCHEDULE 4
MINIMUM RATES OF PAY

Article 12

[2.2177]

Table

Grade or category of workers	Minimum hourly rate of pay
Grade 1 worker under compulsory school age	£3.54
Grade 1 worker (16–24 years of age)	£7.70
Grade 1 worker (aged 25+)	£8.21
Grade 2 worker	£8.45
Grade 3 worker	£8.70
Grade 4 worker	£9.36
Grade 5 worker	£9.88
Grade 6 worker	£10.64
Year 1 Apprentice	£4.00
Year 2 Apprentice (aged 16–17)	£4.29
Year 2 Apprentice (aged 18–20)	£6.15
Year 2 Apprentice (aged 21–24)	£7.70
Year 2 Apprentice (aged 25+)	£8.21

NOTES

Commencement: 1 April 2019.

SCHEDULE 5
ANNUAL LEAVE ENTITLEMENT

Articles 30 and 31

[2.2178]

Table

Number of days worked each week by an agricultural worker	More than 6	More than 5 but not more than 6	More than 4 but not more than 5	More than 3 but not more than 4	More than 2 but not more than 3	More than 1 but not more than 2	1 or less

Annual leave entitlement (days)	38	35	31	25	20	13	7.5

NOTES

Commencement: 1 April 2019.

SCHEDULE 6
PAYMENT IN LIEU OF ANNUAL LEAVE

Article 36

[2.2179]
Table

Maximum number of annual leave days that may be paid in lieu

Days worked each week	More than 6	More than 5 but not more than 6	More than 4 but not more than 5	More than 3 but not more than 4	More than 2 but not more than 3	More than 1 but not more than 2	1 or less
Maximum number of annual leave days under this Order that may be paid in lieu	10	7	3	2.5	2.5	1.5	1.5

NOTES

Commencement: 1 April 2019.

EMPLOYMENT RIGHTS (AMENDMENT) (EU EXIT) REGULATIONS 2019

(SI 2019/535)

NOTES

Made: 4 March 2019.

Authority: European Communities Act 1972, s 2(2), Sch 2, para 1A; European Union (Withdrawal) Act 2018, s 8(1), Sch 7, para 21.

Commencement: see reg 1.

Note: with regard to the authority for these Regulations, note that the European Communities Act 1972 is repealed by the European Union (Withdrawal) Act 2018, s 1, as from exit day (as defined in s 20 of that Act); but note also that provision is made for the continuation in force of any subordinate legislation made under the authority of s 2(2) of the 1972 Act by s 2 of the 2018 Act at **[1.2240]**, subject to the provisions of s 5 of, and Sch 1 to, the 2018 Act at **[1.2243]**, **[1.2253]**.

[2.2180]
1 Citation, commencement and extent

(1) These Regulations may be cited as the Employment Rights (Amendment) (EU Exit) Regulations 2019 and come into force on exit day, subject to paragraph (2).

(2) The following provisions of these Regulations come into force the day after the day on which these Regulations are made—

- (a) this regulation;
- (b) in Schedule 1—
  - (i) paragraph 9,
  - (ii) paragraph 11(c), and
  - (iii) paragraph 16(c);

  and regulation 2(1), as it relates to those provisions.

(3) Any amendment by these Regulations of an enactment has the same extent as the enactment amended.

NOTES

Commencement: 5 March 2019.

[2.2181]

2 Amendments to employment rights legislation

(1) Schedule 1 (which amends employment rights legislation extending to England and Wales and Scotland, and contains a saving provision) has effect.

(2) Schedule 2 (which amends the Transnational Information and Consultation of Employees Regulations 1999 which extend to the whole of the United Kingdom, and contains saving and transitional provisions) has effect.

NOTES

Commencement: 5 March 2019 (para (1) in so far as it relates to Sch 1, paras 9, 11(c), 16(c)); otherwise as from exit day (as defined in the European Union (Withdrawal) Act 2018, s 20).

SCHEDULE 1
AMENDMENTS TO EMPLOYMENT RIGHTS LEGISLATION EXTENDING TO ENGLAND AND WALES, AND SCOTLAND

(Pts 1, 3 of Sch 1 amend the Employment Rights Act 1996, s 79, Sch 2 at **[1.977]**, **[1.1157]**, *the Employment Relations Act 1999, s 19 at* **[1.1253]**, *the Employment Act 2002, s 45 at* **[1.1281]**, *and the Employment Relations Act 2004, s 42 at* **[1.1415]**, *subject to savings as noted to those provisions. Pt 2 of Sch 1 amends the Working Time Regulations 1998, SI 1998/1833 at* **[2.274]**, *the Employment Tribunals (Constitution and Rules of Procedure) Regulations 2013, SI 2013/1237 at* **[2.1323]**, *the Statutory Shared Parental Pay (Persons Abroad and Mariners) Regulations 2014, SI 2014/3134 at* **[2.1800]**, *the Posted Workers (Enforcement of Employment Rights) Regulations 2016, SI 2016/539 at* **[2.1937]** *and other legislation outside the scope of this work.)*

SCHEDULE 2
AMENDMENTS TO THE TRANSNATIONAL INFORMATION AND CONSULTATION OF EMPLOYEES REGULATIONS 1999

Regulation 2(2)

PART 1

1–32 *(Paras 1–32 amend the Transnational Information and Consultation of Employees Regulations 1999, SI 1999/3323 at* **[2.472]**.)

PART 2
SAVING AND TRANSITIONAL PROVISIONS

Interpretation

[2.2182]

33 In this Part—

(a) "the 1999 Regulations" means the Transnational Information and Consultation of Employees Regulations 1999;

(b) "the modifications" means the following modifications to the 1999 Regulations—

(i) any reference to a "Member State" or "Member States" is to be read as a reference to a "Relevant State" or "Relevant States" (as the case may be);

(ii) regulation 2 is to be read as if—

(aa) the definition of "Member State" were omitted; and

(bb) the following were inserted at the appropriate place—

""Relevant State" means—

(a) a state which is a Contracting Party to the Agreement on the European Economic Area signed at Oporto on 2nd May 1992 as adjusted by the Protocol signed at Brussels on 17th March 1993; and

(b) the United Kingdom;"

(iii) regulation 3(4) is to be read as if—

(aa) for the words "referred to" there were substituted "described";

(bb) at the end there were inserted the words "(whether or not the Regulation applies to that company)";

(c) terms used which are defined in the 1999 Regulations have the same meanings in this Part as in those Regulations, as they had effect before exit day or as they have effect on and after exit day, as the context requires.

Information requests

34 Despite the amendments and revocations made by Part 1 of this Schedule, the 1999 Regulations continue, on and after exit day, to have effect in relation to a request for information made under regulation 7(1) before exit day as they had effect immediately before that day, but subject to the modifications.

Ongoing negotiations

35 Despite the amendments and revocations made by Part 1 of this Schedule, the 1999 Regulations continue, on and after exit day, to have effect in relation to ongoing negotiations as they had effect immediately before that day, but subject to the modifications.

36 The reference in paragraph 35 to ongoing negotiations is a reference to any case in which the negotiation process for the establishment of a European Works Council or an information and consultation procedure was commenced, but not concluded, before exit day.

37 For the purposes of paragraph 36—
- (a) the negotiation process for the establishment of a European Works Council or an information and consultation is commenced on the date on which either—
  - (i) a valid request is made by employees or employees' representatives under regulation 9(1) of the 1999 Regulations; or
  - (ii) the central management initiates negotiations in accordance with regulation 9(5) of the 1999 Regulations; and
- (b) the negotiation process is concluded on the date on which either—
  - (i) the special negotiating body makes a decision under regulation 16(3) of the 1999 Regulations not to open negotiations with central management or to terminate negotiations;
  - (ii) the central management and the special negotiating body reach a written agreement on the detailed arrangements for the information and consultation of employees in accordance with regulation 17(1) of the 1999 Regulations; or
  - (iii) the provisions of the Schedule to the 1999 Regulations first apply by virtue of regulation 18(1)(b) or (c) of those Regulations.

38 The 1999 Regulations (as amended by Part 1 of this Schedule) apply in relation to a European Works Council or an information and consultation procedure established pursuant to this Part of this Schedule on or after exit day as if it had been established before exit day.

39 The 1999 Regulations (as amended by Part 1 of this Schedule) apply in relation to an agreement on the establishment of a European Works Council or an information and consultation procedure reached pursuant to this Part of this Schedule on or after exit day as if the agreement had been reached before exit day.

40 The 1999 Regulations (as amended by Part 1 of this Schedule) apply in relation to a case where the negotiation process is concluded as mentioned in paragraph 37(b)(iii) on or after exit day as if the case is within regulation 18 of those Regulations.

Complaints and proceedings

41 Despite the amendments and revocations made by Part 1 of this Schedule, the 1999 Regulations continue, on and after exit day, to have effect, in relation to any complaint or application presented under those Regulations before exit day to the Central Arbitration Committee or the Employment Appeal Tribunal, as they had effect immediately before that day but subject to the modifications.

NOTES

Commencement: exit day (as defined in the European Union (Withdrawal) Act 2018, s 20).

EMPLOYMENT RIGHTS (AMENDMENT) (EU EXIT) (NO 2) REGULATIONS 2019

(SI 2019/536)

NOTES

Made: 4 March 2019.

Authority: Employment Agencies Act 1973, s 5(1); European Union (Withdrawal) Act 2018, s 8(1), Sch 7, para 21.

Commencement: exit day (as defined in the European Union (Withdrawal) Act 2018, s 20).

[2.2183]

1 Citation, commencement and extent

(1) These Regulations may be cited as the Employment Rights (Amendment) (EU Exit) (No 2) Regulations 2019 and come into force on exit day.

(2) Any amendment by these Regulations of an enactment has the same extent as the enactment amended.

NOTES

Commencement: exit day (as defined in the European Union (Withdrawal) Act 2018, s 20).

[2.2184]

2 Amendments to employment rights legislation

The Schedule (which amends employment rights legislation extending to England and Wales and Scotland, and contains a saving provision) has effect.

NOTES

Commencement: exit day (as defined in the European Union (Withdrawal) Act 2018, s 20).

SCHEDULE
AMENDMENTS TO EMPLOYMENT RIGHTS LEGISLATION EXTENDING TO ENGLAND AND WALES, AND SCOTLAND

Regulation 2

Pt 1 (paras 1, 2) of this Schedule amends the Employment Relations Act 1999, s 38 at **[1.1260]** *and the Work and Families Act 2006, s 13 at* **[1.1486]**. *Pt 2 (para 3) amends the Conduct of Employment Agencies and Employment Businesses Regulations 2003, SI 2003/3319, reg 27A* **[2.712]**.)

PART 3
SAVING PROVISION

[2.2185]

4 The amendments made by Part 1 of this Schedule do not affect the validity of any regulations that came into force before exit day and were made under any of the Acts amended by that Part.

AGENCY WORKERS (AMENDMENT) REGULATIONS 2019

(SI 2019/724)

NOTES

Made: 28 March 2019.

Authority: European Communities Act 1972, s 2(2).

Commencement: 6 April 2020.

Note: with regard to the authority for these Regulations, note that the European Communities Act 1972 is repealed by the European Union (Withdrawal) Act 2018, s 1, as from exit day (as defined in s 20 of that Act); but note also that provision is made for the continuation in force of any subordinate legislation made under the authority of s 2(2) of the 1972 Act by s 2 of the 2018 Act at **[1.2240]**, subject to the provisions of s 5 of, and Sch 1 to, the 2018 Act at **[1.2243]**, **[1.2253]**.

[2.2186]

1 Citation, commencement and extent

(1) These Regulations may be cited as the Agency Workers (Amendment) Regulations 2019 and come into force on 6th April 2020.

(2) These Regulations extend to England and Wales and Scotland only.

NOTES

Commencement: 6 April 2020.

[2.2187]

2 Interpretation

In these Regulations—

"the 1996 Act" means the Employment Rights Act 1996;

"the 2010 Regulations" means the Agency Workers Regulations 2010; and

"contract of employment", "agency worker" and "temporary work agency" have the meanings respectively given in regulations 2, 3 and 4 of the 2010 Regulations.

NOTES

Commencement: 6 April 2020.

3 (*Amends the Agency Workers Regulations 2010, SI 2010/93 at* **[2.1085]**.)

[2.2188]

4 Requirement to provide written statement

(1) Where a contract of employment which is in effect when these Regulations come into force contains a statement for the purposes of regulation 10(1)(b) of the 2010 Regulations ("the original statement"), the temporary work agency which is party to that contract of employment must, in accordance with paragraph (2), provide a written statement to the agency worker that, with effect from 6th April 2020—

(a) the agency worker is entitled to rights relating to pay as part of the rights conferred by regulation 5 of the 2010 Regulations, subject to completion of the qualifying period as stated in regulation 7 of those regulations; and

(b) the original statement no longer has effect.

(2) A written statement under paragraph (1) must be provided on or before 30th April 2020, unless the contract of employment is terminated on or before that date.

(3) An agency worker may present a complaint to an employment tribunal that a temporary work agency has infringed the right to be provided with a written statement conferred on the agency worker by this regulation.

(4) Paragraphs (4)(a), (4A), (5), (6), (7), (8), (10), (11), (12), (13), (15), (16), (17) and (18) of regulation 18 and regulations 18A, 19 and 20 of the 2010 Regulations apply to a complaint under paragraph (3) in the same way as to a complaint under regulation 18(2) of the 2010 Regulations but with the modification that references to rights conferred by regulation 5 of the 2010 Regulations are to be treated as references to the right to be provided with a written statement conferred by this regulation.

NOTES

Commencement: 6 April 2020.

[2.2189]

5 Unfair dismissal and the right not to be subjected to detriment

(1) An agency worker who is an employee and is dismissed shall be regarded as unfairly dismissed for the purposes of Part 10 of the 1996 Act if the reason (or, if more than one, the principal reason) for the dismissal is a reason specified in paragraph (3).

(2) An agency worker has the right not to be subjected to any detriment by, or as a result of, any act, or deliberate failure to act, of the temporary work agency which is the employer of the agency worker, done on a ground specified in paragraph (3).

(3) The reasons or, as the case may be, grounds are—

- (a) that the agency worker—
  - (i) brought proceedings under these Regulations;
  - (ii) gave evidence or information in connection with such proceedings brought by any agency worker;
  - (iii) otherwise did anything under these Regulations in relation to a temporary work agency or other person;
  - (iv) alleged that the temporary work agency which is the employer of the agency worker has breached these Regulations;
  - (v) refused (or proposed to refuse) to forgo a right conferred by these Regulations; or
- (b) that the temporary work agency believes or suspects that the agency worker has done or intends to do any of the things mentioned in sub-paragraph (a).

(4) Where the reason or principal reason for subjection to any act or deliberate failure to act is that mentioned in paragraph (3)(a)(iv), or paragraph (3)(b) so far as it relates to paragraph (3)(a)(iv), neither paragraph (1) nor paragraph (2) applies if the allegation made by the agency worker is false and not made in good faith.

(5) Paragraph (2) does not apply where the detriment in question amounts to a dismissal of an employee within the meaning of Part 10 of the 1996 Act.

(6) Subject to paragraph (5), an agency worker may present a complaint to an employment tribunal that a temporary work agency has infringed a right conferred on the agency worker by this regulation.

(7) Paragraphs (4)(a), (4A), (5), (6), (7), (8), (10), (11), (12), (13), (16), (17) and (18) of regulation 18 and regulations 18A, 19 and 20 of the 2010 Regulations apply to a complaint under paragraph (6) in the same way as to a complaint under regulation 18(2) of the 2010 Regulations, but with the modification that references to rights conferred by regulation 17(2) of the 2010 Regulations are to be treated as references to rights conferred by this regulation.

NOTES

Commencement: 6 April 2020.

[2.2190]

6 Special classes of person

(1) Regulations 21 to 24 of the 2010 Regulations apply for the purposes of giving effect to these Regulations in the case of the persons referred to in regulations 21 to 24 in the same way and to the same extent as the 2010 Regulations apply to those persons.

(2) Accordingly, for those purposes—

- (a) references in regulations 21 to 24 to the 2010 Regulations are to be treated as references to these Regulations; and
- (b) the reference in regulation 24 to regulation 20 of the 2010 Regulations is to be treated as a reference to regulation 20 as it applies to these Regulations in accordance with regulations 4 and 5.

NOTES

Commencement: 6 April 2020.

[2.2191]

7 Saving provision

Nothing in these Regulations affects the application of the 2010 Regulations to complaints which relate to breaches of the 2010 Regulations which occurred prior to these Regulations coming into force.

NOTES

Commencement: 6 April 2020.

8 (*Amends the Employment Tribunals Act 1996, s 18 at* **[1.757]** *and the Employment Rights Act 1996, s 105 at* **[1.1023]**.)

[2.2192]

9 Review

(1) The Secretary of State must from time to time—

(a) carry out a review of the regulatory provisions contained in—

(i) regulations 4 and 5; and

(ii) the 2010 Regulations, to the extent only of the effect of the amendments made by regulation 3 of these Regulations; and

(b) publish a report setting out the conclusions of the review.

(2) The first report must be published before 6th April 2025. Subsequent reports must be published at intervals not exceeding 5 years. Section 30(4) of the Small Business, Enterprise and Employment Act 2015 requires that a report published under this regulation must, in particular—

(a) set out the objectives intended to be achieved by the regulatory provisions referred to in sub-paragraph (1)(a);

(b) assess the extent to which those objectives are achieved;

(c) assess whether those objectives remain appropriate; and

(d) if those objectives remain appropriate, assess the extent to which they could be achieved in another way which involves less onerous regulatory provision.

(3) In this regulation, "regulatory provision" has the same meaning as in sections 28 to 32 of the Small Business, Enterprise and Employment Act 2015 (see section 32 of that Act).

NOTES

Commencement: 6 April 2020.

CONDUCT OF EMPLOYMENT AGENCIES AND EMPLOYMENT BUSINESSES (AMENDMENT) REGULATIONS 2019

(SI 2019/725)

NOTES

Made: 28 March 2019.

Authority: Employment Agencies Act 1973, ss 5(1), 12(3).

Commencement: 6 April 2020.

[2.2193]

1 Citation and commencement

These Regulations may be cited as the Conduct of Employment Agencies and Employment Businesses (Amendment) Regulations 2019 and come into force on 6th April 2020.

NOTES

Commencement: 6 April 2020.

2–6 (*Regs 2–6 insert the Conduct of Employment Agencies and Employment Businesses Regulations 2003, SI 2003/3319, reg 13A at* **[2.701]** *and amend regs 29, 32 of, and Sch 4, to those Regulations (all outside the scope of this work).*)

[2.2194]

7 Review

(1) The Secretary of State must from time to time—

(a) carry out a review of the regulatory provisions contained in the Conduct of Employment Agencies and Employment Businesses Regulations 2003 to the extent only of the effect of the amendments made by these Regulations; and

(b) publish a report setting out the conclusions of the review.

(2) The first report must be published before 6th April 2025.

(3) Subsequent reports must be published at intervals not exceeding 5 years.

(4) A report published under this regulation must, in particular—

(a) set out the objectives intended to be achieved by the regulatory provisions referred to in paragraph (1)(a);

(b) assess the extent to which those objectives are achieved;

(c) assess whether those objectives remain appropriate; and

(d) if those objectives remain appropriate, assess the extent to which they could be achieved in another way which involves less onerous regulatory provision.

(5) In this regulation, "regulatory provision" has the same meaning as in sections 28 to 32 of the Small Business, Enterprise and Employment Act 2015 (see section 32 of that Act).

NOTES

Commencement: 6 April 2020.

EMPLOYMENT RIGHTS (MISCELLANEOUS AMENDMENTS) REGULATIONS 2019

(SI 2019/731)

NOTES

Made: 28 March 2019.

Authority: Employment Tribunals Act 1996, s 12A(12)(a); Employment Relations Act 1999, s 23(2), (4)(c), (d), (5A); Employment Relations Act 2004, s 42(1), (3)(a), (b).

Commencement: 6 April 2019 (regs 1–3); 6 April 2020 (regs 4–18).

PART 1 CITATION AND COMMENCEMENT

[2.2195]

1 Citation and commencement

(1) These Regulations may be cited as the Employment Rights (Miscellaneous Amendments) Regulations 2019.

(2) Parts 1 and 2 of these Regulations come into force on 6th April 2019 and all other parts come into force on 6th April 2020.

NOTES

Commencement: 6 April 2019.

PART 2 FINANCIAL PENALTIES

2 (*Amends the Employment Tribunals Act 1996, s 12A at* **[1.750]**.)

[2.2196]

3 Application of regulation 2

The substitutions made by regulation 2 only apply in relation to a penalty payable in respect of a breach of a worker's rights which begins on or after the date when regulation 2 comes into force.

NOTES

Commencement: 6 April 2019.

PART 3 STATEMENTS OF EMPLOYMENT PARTICULARS

4–14 (*Regs 4–14 amend the Employment Rights Act 1996, ss 1–6, 7A, 7B, 11, 12 at* **[1.813]–[1.818]**, **[1.820]**, **[1.821]**, **[1.825]**, **[1.826]**.)

[2.2197]

15 Application of regulations 4 to 14

The amendments made by regulations 4 to 14 only apply in relation to a written statement required by section 1 or 4 of The Employment Rights Act 1996 where the worker to whom the statement must be given begins employment with the employer on or after the date those regulations come into force.

NOTES

Commencement: 6 April 2020.

16–18 *Reg 16 (Pt 4) amends the Information and Consultation of Employees Regulations 2004, SI 2004/3426 at* **[2.768]**; *regs 17, 18 (Pt 5) amend the Employment Act 2002, ss 38, 40 at* **[1.1279]**, **[1.1280]**.

COMPANIES (DIRECTORS' REMUNERATION POLICY AND DIRECTORS' REMUNERATION REPORT) REGULATIONS 2019

(SI 2019/970)

NOTES

Made: 22 May 2019.

Authority: European Communities Act 1972, s 2(2); Companies Act 2006, ss 421(1), 468(1), (2), 1292(1).

Commencement: 10 June 2019.

Note: with regard to the authority for these Regulations, note that the European Communities Act 1972 is repealed by the European Union (Withdrawal) Act 2018, s 1, as from exit day (as defined in s 20 of that Act); but note also that provision is made for the continuation in force of any subordinate legislation made under the authority of s 2(2) of the 1972 Act by s 2 of the 2018 Act at **[1.2240]**, subject to the provisions of s 5 of, and Sch 1 to, the 2018 Act at **[1.2243]**, **[1.2253]**.

These Regulations implement Articles 9A and 9B of Directive 2007/36/EC of the European Parliament and of the Council on the exercise of certain rights of shareholders in listed companies (the Shareholders' Rights Directive). Articles 9A and 9B were inserted by Directive (EU) 2017/828 of the European Parliament and of the Council amending Directive 2007/36/EC as regards the encouragement of long-term shareholder engagement.

PART 1
INTRODUCTORY

[2.2198]

1 Citation and commencement

(1) These Regulations may be cited as the Companies (Directors' Remuneration Policy and Directors' Remuneration Report) Regulations 2019.

(2) These Regulations come into force on 10th June 2019.

NOTES

Commencement: 10 June 2019.

[2.2199]

2 Application, transitional provisions and interpretation

(1) The amendments made by—

(a) regulations 6 to 10 apply to a quoted company from the first date on or after 10th June 2019 on which a relevant directors' remuneration policy for the company approved under section 439A of the Companies Act 2006 takes effect;

(b) regulation 15 apply in relation to—

(i) a directors' remuneration report or directors' remuneration policy of a quoted company first required to be made available under section 430 of the Companies Act 2006 on or after 10th June 2019;

(ii) annual accounts and reports of an unquoted traded company for a financial year of the company beginning on or after 10th June 2019;

(c) regulation 31 apply in relation to a directors' remuneration report for a financial year of a company beginning on or after 10th June 2019;

(d) regulation 32 apply in relation to a relevant directors' remuneration policy that was approved under section 439A of the Companies Act 2006 on or after 10th June 2019.

(2) Where a company is an unquoted traded company immediately before the day on which these Regulations come into force and paragraph (4) does not apply—

(a) section 226D(6)of the Companies Act 2006 (as amended by regulation 9) applies as if—

(i) in the opening words "the earlier of" were omitted; and

(ii) paragraph (a) was omitted;

(b) section 439A(1)(a) of the Companies Act 2006 (as amended by regulation 20) applies to the company as if for "the day on which the company becomes a quoted company or (as the case may be) an unquoted traded company" there were substituted "1st January 2020 or at an earlier general meeting".

(3) Paragraph (4) applies if, immediately before the day on which these Regulations come into force, an unquoted traded company has a relevant directors' remuneration policy in effect which—

(a) was approved by a resolution passed by the members of the company at an accounts or other general meeting before 10th June 2019, and

(b) complied with the requirements of the Companies Act 2006 in relation to such policies.

(4) Where this paragraph applies—

(a) section 439A(1)(a) of the Companies Act 2006 does not apply to the company;

(b) the notice that was given of the intention to move a resolution to approve the policy is to be treated as having been given under section 439A(1) for the purpose of determining the period within which the next notice under that section must be given;

(c) regulation 2(1)(a) applies to the company as if it were a quoted company.

(5) In this regulation—

"directors' remuneration policy", "quoted company" and "unquoted traded company" have the same meanings as in section 226A(1) of the Companies Act 2006;

"directors' remuneration report" has the same meaning as in section 420 of the Companies Act 2006;

"relevant directors' remuneration policy" has the same meaning as in section 439A(7) of the Companies Act 2006.

NOTES

Commencement: 10 June 2019.

PARTS 2, 3

3–33 *(Part 2 (regs 3–27) amends Parts 10, 15 and 16 of, and Sch 8 to, the Companies Act 2006 (at* **[1.1490]** *et seq). Part 3 (regs 28–33) amends the Large and Medium-sized Companies and Groups (Accounts and Reports) Regulations 2008, SI 2008/410 (outside the scope of this work).)*

PART 3
EU MATERIALS

A. CONSTITUTIONAL MATERIALS

CONSOLIDATED VERSION OF THE TREATY ON EUROPEAN UNION

NOTES

Date of publication in OJ: OJ C326, 26.10.2012, p 13. Note that the Treaty is also reproduced in OJ C202, 7.6.2016.

Commencement: 1 December 2009.

This is the Treaty on European Union as consolidated following the amendments made by the Treaty of Lisbon, which came into force on 1 December 2009. Only those Articles of particular relevance to employment law are printed here.

Cross-references to the equivalent article in the pre-Lisbon Treaty version of the Treaty are given at the beginning of each of the Articles reproduced which have such equivalents; these cross-references are part of the official text. For further information on the derivation of Articles reproduced here see the Table of Equivalences at **[3.13]**.

UK withdrawal from the European Union: for the legal status of the Treaty after exit day (as defined by the European Union Withdrawal Act 2018, s 20), see the European Union Withdrawal Act 2018, ss 4, 5, Sch 1 at **[1.2242]**, **[1.2243]**, **[1.2253]**.

TITLE I COMMON PROVISIONS

[3.1]
Article 1
(ex Article 1 TEU)

By this Treaty, the HIGH CONTRACTING PARTIES establish among themselves a EUROPEAN UNION, hereinafter called "the Union", on which the Member States confer competences to attain objectives they have in common.

This Treaty marks a new stage in the process of creating an ever closer union among the peoples of Europe, in which decisions are taken as openly as possible and as closely as possible to the citizen.

The Union shall be founded on the present Treaty and on the Treaty on the Functioning of the European Union (hereinafter referred to as "the Treaties"). Those two Treaties shall have the same legal value. The Union shall replace and succeed the European Community.

[3.2]
Article 2

The Union is founded on the values of respect for human dignity, freedom, democracy, equality, the rule of law and respect for human rights, including the rights of persons belonging to minorities. These values are common to the Member States in a society in which pluralism, non-discrimination, tolerance, justice, solidarity and equality between women and men prevail.

[3.3]
Article 3
(ex Article 2 TEU)

1. The Union's aim is to promote peace, its values and the well-being of its peoples.
2. The Union shall offer its citizens an area of freedom, security and justice without internal frontiers, in which the free movement of persons is ensured in conjunction with appropriate measures with respect to external border controls, asylum, immigration and the prevention and combating of crime.
3. The Union shall establish an internal market. It shall work for the sustainable development of Europe based on balanced economic growth and price stability, a highly competitive social market economy, aiming at full employment and social progress, and a high level of protection and improvement of the quality of the environment. It shall promote scientific and technological advance.

It shall combat social exclusion and discrimination, and shall promote social justice and protection, equality between women and men, solidarity between generations and protection of the rights of the child.

It shall promote economic, social and territorial cohesion, and solidarity among Member States.

It shall respect its rich cultural and linguistic diversity, and shall ensure that Europe's cultural heritage is safeguarded and enhanced.

4. The Union shall establish an economic and monetary union whose currency is the euro.
5. In its relations with the wider world, the Union shall uphold and promote its values and interests and contribute to the protection of its citizens. It shall contribute to peace, security, the sustainable development of the Earth, solidarity and mutual respect among peoples, free and fair trade, eradication of poverty and the protection of human rights, in particular the rights of the child, as well as to the strict observance and the development of international law, including respect for the principles of the United Nations Charter.
6. The Union shall pursue its objectives by appropriate means commensurate with the competences which are conferred upon it in the Treaties.

[3.4]
Article 4
1. In accordance with Article 5, competences not conferred upon the Union in the Treaties remain with the Member States.
2. The Union shall respect the equality of Member States before the Treaties as well as their national identities, inherent in their fundamental structures, political and constitutional, inclusive of regional and local self-government. It shall respect their essential State functions, including ensuring the territorial integrity of the State, maintaining law and order and safeguarding national security. In particular, national security remains the sole responsibility of each Member State.
3. Pursuant to the principle of sincere cooperation, the Union and the Member States shall, in full mutual respect, assist each other in carrying out tasks which flow from the Treaties.

The Member States shall take any appropriate measure, general or particular, to ensure fulfilment of the obligations arising out of the Treaties or resulting from the acts of the institutions of the Union.

The Member States shall facilitate the achievement of the Union's tasks and refrain from any measure which could jeopardise the attainment of the Union's objectives.

[3.5]
Article 5
(ex Article 5 TEC)
1. The limits of Union competences are governed by the principle of conferral. The use of Union competences is governed by the principles of subsidiarity and proportionality.
2. Under the principle of conferral, the Union shall act only within the limits of the competences conferred upon it by the Member States in the Treaties to attain the objectives set out therein. Competences not conferred upon the Union in the Treaties remain with the Member States.
3. Under the principle of subsidiarity, in areas which do not fall within its exclusive competence, the Union shall act only if and in so far as the objectives of the proposed action cannot be sufficiently achieved by the Member States, either at central level or at regional and local level, but can rather, by reason of the scale or effects of the proposed action, be better achieved at Union level.

The institutions of the Union shall apply the principle of subsidiarity as laid down in the Protocol on the application of the principles of subsidiarity and proportionality. National Parliaments ensure compliance with the principle of subsidiarity in accordance with the procedure set out in that Protocol.
4. Under the principle of proportionality, the content and form of Union action shall not exceed what is necessary to achieve the objectives of the Treaties.

The institutions of the Union shall apply the principle of proportionality as laid down in the Protocol on the application of the principles of subsidiarity and proportionality.

[3.6]
Article 6
(ex Article 6 TEU)
1. The Union recognises the rights, freedoms and principles set out in the Charter of Fundamental Rights of the European Union of 7 December 2000, as adapted at Strasbourg, on 12 December 2007, which shall have the same legal value as the Treaties.

The provisions of the Charter shall not extend in any way the competences of the Union as defined in the Treaties.

The rights, freedoms and principles in the Charter shall be interpreted in accordance with the general provisions in Title VII of the Charter governing its interpretation and application and with due regard to the explanations referred to in the Charter, that set out the sources of those provisions.
2. The Union shall accede to the European Convention for the Protection of Human Rights and Fundamental Freedoms. Such accession shall not affect the Union's competences as defined in the Treaties.
3. Fundamental rights, as guaranteed by the European Convention for the Protection of Human Rights and Fundamental Freedoms and as they result from the constitutional traditions common to the Member States, shall constitute general principles of the Union's law.

TITLE III PROVISIONS ON THE INSTITUTIONS

[3.7]
Article 13
1. The Union shall have an institutional framework which shall aim to promote its values, advance its objectives, serve its interests, those of its citizens and those of the Member States, and ensure the consistency, effectiveness and continuity of its policies and actions.

The Union's institutions shall be:

— the European Parliament,
— the European Council,
— the Council,
— the European Commission (hereinafter referred to as "the Commission"),
— the Court of Justice of the European Union,
— the European Central Bank,
— the Court of Auditors.

2. Each institution shall act within the limits of the powers conferred on it in the Treaties, and in conformity with the procedures, conditions and objectives set out in them. The institutions shall practice mutual sincere cooperation.

3. The provisions relating to the European Central Bank and the Court of Auditors and detailed provisions on the other institutions are set out in the Treaty on the Functioning of the European Union.
4. The European Parliament, the Council and the Commission shall be assisted by an Economic and Social Committee and a Committee of the Regions acting in an advisory capacity.

[3.8]
Article 14
1. The European Parliament shall, jointly with the Council, exercise legislative and budgetary functions. It shall exercise functions of political control and consultation as laid down in the Treaties. It shall elect the President of the Commission.
2. The European Parliament shall be composed of representatives of the Union's citizens. They shall not exceed seven hundred and fifty in number, plus the President. Representation of citizens shall be degressively proportional, with a minimum threshold of six members per Member State. No Member State shall be allocated more than ninety-six seats.

The European Council shall adopt by unanimity, on the initiative of the European Parliament and with its consent, a decision establishing the composition of the European Parliament, respecting the principles referred to in the first subparagraph.
3. The members of the European Parliament shall be elected for a term of five years by direct universal suffrage in a free and secret ballot.
4. The European Parliament shall elect its President and its officers from among its members.

[3.9]
Article 15
1. The European Council shall provide the Union with the necessary impetus for its development and shall define the general political directions and priorities thereof. It shall not exercise legislative functions.
2. The European Council shall consist of the Heads of State or Government of the Member States, together with its President and the President of the Commission. The High Representative of the Union for Foreign Affairs and Security Policy shall take part in its work.
3. The European Council shall meet twice every six months, convened by its President. When the agenda so requires, the members of the European Council may decide each to be assisted by a minister and, in the case of the President of the Commission, by a member of the Commission. When the situation so requires, the President shall convene a special meeting of the European Council.
4. Except where the Treaties provide otherwise, decisions of the European Council shall be taken by consensus.
5. The European Council shall elect its President, by a qualified majority, for a term of two and a half years, renewable once. In the event of an impediment or serious misconduct, the European Council can end the President's term of office in accordance with the same procedure.
6. The President of the European Council:
- (a) shall chair it and drive forward its work;
- (b) shall ensure the preparation and continuity of the work of the European Council in cooperation with the President of the Commission, and on the basis of the work of the General Affairs Council;
- (c) shall endeavour to facilitate cohesion and consensus within the European Council;
- (d) shall present a report to the European Parliament after each of the meetings of the European Council.

The President of the European Council shall, at his level and in that capacity, ensure the external representation of the Union on issues concerning its common foreign and security policy, without prejudice to the powers of the High Representative of the Union for Foreign Affairs and Security Policy.

The President of the European Council shall not hold a national office.

[3.10]
Article 16
1. The Council shall, jointly with the European Parliament, exercise legislative and budgetary functions. It shall carry out policy-making and coordinating functions as laid down in the Treaties.
2. The Council shall consist of a representative of each Member State at ministerial level, who may commit the government of the Member State in question and cast its vote.
3. The Council shall act by a qualified majority except where the Treaties provide otherwise.
4. As from 1 November 2014, a qualified majority shall be defined as at least 55% of the members of the Council, comprising at least fifteen of them and representing Member States comprising at least 65% of the population of the Union.

A blocking minority must include at least four Council members, failing which the qualified majority shall be deemed attained.

The other arrangements governing the qualified majority are laid down in Article 238(2) of the Treaty on the Functioning of the European Union.
5. The transitional provisions relating to the definition of the qualified majority which shall be applicable until 31 October 2014 and those which shall be applicable from 1 November 2014 to 31 March 2017 are laid down in the Protocol on transitional provisions.
6–9. . . .

NOTES

Paras 6–9: outside the scope of this work.

[3.11]
Article 19

1. The Court of Justice of the European Union shall include the Court of Justice, the General Court and specialised courts. It shall ensure that in the interpretation and application of the Treaties the law is observed.

Member States shall provide remedies sufficient to ensure effective legal protection in the fields covered by Union law.

2. The Court of Justice shall consist of one judge from each Member State. It shall be assisted by Advocates-General.

The General Court shall include at least one judge per Member State.

The Judges and the Advocates-General of the Court of Justice and the Judges of the General Court shall be chosen from persons whose independence is beyond doubt and who satisfy the conditions set out in Articles 253 and 254 of the Treaty on the Functioning of the European Union. They shall be appointed by common accord of the governments of the Member States for six years. Retiring Judges and Advocates-General may be reappointed.

3. The Court of Justice of the European Union shall, in accordance with the Treaties:

(a) rule on actions brought by a Member State, an institution or a natural or legal person;
(b) give preliminary rulings, at the request of courts or tribunals of the Member States, on the interpretation of Union law or the validity of acts adopted by the institutions;
(c) rule in other cases provided for in the Treaties.

TITLE VI FINAL PROVISIONS

[3.12]
Article 50

1. Any Member State may decide to withdraw from the Union in accordance with its own constitutional requirements.

2. A Member State which decides to withdraw shall notify the European Council of its intention. In the light of the guidelines provided by the European Council, the Union shall negotiate and conclude an agreement with that State, setting out the arrangements for its withdrawal, taking account of the framework for its future relationship with the Union. That agreement shall be negotiated in accordance with Article 218(3) of the Treaty on the Functioning of the European Union. It shall be concluded on behalf of the Union by the Council, acting by a qualified majority, after obtaining the consent of the European Parliament.

3. The Treaties shall cease to apply to the State in question from the date of entry into force of the withdrawal agreement or, failing that, two years after the notification referred to in paragraph 2, unless the European Council, in agreement with the Member State concerned, unanimously decides to extend this period.

4. For the purposes of paragraphs 2 and 3, the member of the European Council or of the Council representing the withdrawing Member State shall not participate in the discussions of the European Council or Council or in decisions concerning it.

A qualified majority shall be defined in accordance with Article 238(3)(b) of the Treaty on the Functioning of the European Union.

5. If a State which has withdrawn from the Union asks to rejoin, its request shall be subject to the procedure referred to in Article 49.

TREATY ON EUROPEAN UNION TABLE OF EQUIVALENCES

[3.13]

NOTES

Date of publication in OJ: OJ C326, 26.10.2012, p 363.

This table shows in column (1) provisions of the Treaty on European Union prior to consolidation, and in column (2) the new numbering of relevant provisions of the Treaty as reproduced in this work.

The abbreviations used in this Table and thc related notes are as follows:

— "TEC" means the Treaty establishing the European Community;

— "TEU" means the Treaty on European Union;

— "TFEU" means the Treaty on the Functioning of the European Union.

(1) **Old numbering of the Treaty on European Union**	(2) **New numbering of the Treaty on European Union**
Title I Common Provisions	Title I Common Provisions
Article 1	Article 1
—	Article 2
Article 2	Article 3
Article 3 (repealed)[1]	—
—	Article 4
—	Article 5[2]
Article 4 (repealed)[3]	—
Article 5 (repealed)[4]	—
Article 6	Article 6
Title III Provisions amending the Treaty establishing the European Coal and Steel Community	Title III Provisions on the Institutions
Article 9 (repealed)[5]	Article 13
—	Article 14[6]
—	Article 15[7]
—	Article 16[8]
—	Article 19[9]
Title VIII Final Provisions	Title VI Final Provisions
—	Article 50

[1] Replaced, in substance, by Article 7 TFEU and by Articles 13(1) and 21, para 3, second subparagraph of TEU.

[2] Replaces Article 5 TEC.

[3] Replaced, in substance, by Article 15.

[4] Replaced, in substance, by Article 13, paragraph 2.

[5] The current Article 9 TEU amended the Treaty establishing the European Coal and Steel Community. This latter expired on 23 July 2002. Article 9 is repealed and the number thereof is used to insert another provision.

[6] Paras 1 and 2 replace, in substance, Article 189 TEC; paras 1 to 3 replace, in substance, paras 1 to 3 of Article 190 TEC; para 1 replaces, in substance, the first sub-para of Article 192 TEC; para 4 replaces, in substance, the first sub-para of Article 197 TEC.

[7] Replaces, in substance, Article 4.

[8] Para 1 replaces, in substance, the first and second indents of Article 202 TEC; paras 2 and 9 replace, in substance, Article 203 TEC; paras 4 and 5 replace, in substance, paras 2 and 4 of Article 205 TEC.

[9] Replaces, in substance, Article 220 TEC. The first sub-para of para 2 replaces, in substance, the first sub-para of Article 221 TEC.

CONSOLIDATED VERSION OF THE TREATY ON THE FUNCTIONING OF THE EUROPEAN UNION

NOTES

Date of publication in OJ: OJ C326, 26.10.2012, p 47. Note that the Treaty is also reproduced in OJ C202, 7.6.2016.

Commencement: 1 December 2009.

Formerly titled the "Treaty Establishing the European Community" (Treaty of Rome).

This is the Treaty currently in force which is the successor to the Treaty of Rome, as consolidated following the amendments to and the renaming of the Treaty by the Treaty of Lisbon, which came into force on 1 December 2009.

Only those Articles of particular relevance to employment law are printed here. These include those relating to the free movement of persons and the right of establishment; social policy; the legislative powers of the European Union; and the powers of the Court of Justice of the European Union.

Cross-references to the equivalent article in the pre-Lisbon Treaty version of the Treaty are given at the beginning of each of the Articles reproduced which have such equivalents; these cross-references are part of the official text. A Table of Equivalences showing derivation of the provisions included in this work is at **[3.61]**.

UK withdrawal from the European Union: for the legal status of the Treaty after exit day (as defined by the European Union Withdrawal Act 2018, s 20), see the European Union Withdrawal Act 2018, ss 4, 5, Sch 1 at **[1.2242]**, **[1.2243]**, **[1.2253]**.

PART ONE PRINCIPLES

TITLE II PROVISIONS HAVING GENERAL APPLICATION

[3.14]
Article 7
The Union shall ensure consistency between its policies and activities, taking all of its objectives into account and in accordance with the principle of conferral of powers.

[3.15]
Article 8
(ex Article 3(2) TEC)
In all its activities, the Union shall aim to eliminate inequalities, and to promote equality, between men and women.

[3.16]
Article 9
In defining and implementing its policies and activities, the Union shall take into account requirements linked to the promotion of a high level of employment, the guarantee of adequate social protection, the fight against social exclusion, and a high level of education, training and protection of human health.

[3.17]
Article 10
In defining and implementing its policies and activities, the Union shall aim to combat discrimination based on sex, racial or ethnic origin, religion or belief, disability, age or sexual orientation.

PART TWO NON-DISCRIMINATION AND CITIZENSHIP OF THE UNION

[3.18]
Article 18
(ex Article 12 TEC)
Within the scope of application of the Treaties, and without prejudice to any special provisions contained therein, any discrimination on grounds of nationality shall be prohibited.

The European Parliament and the Council, acting in accordance with the ordinary legislative procedure, may adopt rules designed to prohibit such discrimination.

[3.19]
Article 19
(ex Article 13 TEC)
1. Without prejudice to the other provisions of the Treaties and within the limits of the powers conferred by them upon the Union, the Council, acting unanimously in accordance with a special legislative procedure and after obtaining the consent of the European Parliament, may take appropriate action to combat discrimination based on sex, racial or ethnic origin, religion or belief, disability, age or sexual orientation.
2. By way of derogation from paragraph 1, the European Parliament and the Council, acting in accordance with the ordinary legislative procedure, may adopt the basic principles of Union incentive measures, excluding any harmonisation of the laws and regulations of the Member States, to support action taken by the Member States in order to contribute to the achievement of the objectives referred to in paragraph 1.

PART THREE UNION POLICIES AND INTERNAL ACTIONS

TITLE I THE INTERNAL MARKET

[3.20]
Article 26
(ex Article 14 TEC)
1. The Union shall adopt measures with the aim of establishing or ensuring the functioning of the internal market, in accordance with the relevant provisions of the Treaties.
2. The internal market shall comprise an area without internal frontiers in which the free movement of goods, persons, services and capital is ensured in accordance with the provisions of the Treaties.
3. The Council, on a proposal from the Commission, shall determine the guidelines and conditions necessary to ensure balanced progress in all the sectors concerned.

TITLE IV FREE MOVEMENT OF PERSONS, SERVICES AND CAPITAL

CHAPTER 1
WORKERS

[3.21]
Article 45
(ex Article 39 TEC)
1. Freedom of movement for workers shall be secured within the Union.
2. Such freedom of movement shall entail the abolition of any discrimination based on nationality between workers of the Member States as regards employment, remuneration and other conditions of work and employment.
3. It shall entail the right, subject to limitations justified on grounds of public policy, public security or public health:
   (a) to accept offers of employment actually made;
   (b) to move freely within the territory of Member States for this purpose;
   (c) to stay in a Member State for the purpose of employment in accordance with the provisions governing the employment of nationals of that State laid down by law, regulation or administrative action;
   (d) to remain in the territory of a Member State after having been employed in that State, subject to conditions which shall be embodied in regulations to be drawn up by the Commission.
4. The provisions of this Article shall not apply to employment in the public service.

CHAPTER 2
RIGHT OF ESTABLISHMENT

[3.22]
Article 49
(ex Article 43 TEC)
Within the framework of the provisions set out below, restrictions on the freedom of establishment of nationals of a Member State in the territory of another Member State shall be prohibited. Such prohibition shall also apply to restrictions on the setting-up of agencies, branches or subsidiaries by nationals of any Member State established in the territory of any Member State.

Freedom of establishment shall include the right to take up and pursue activities as self-employed persons and to set up and manage undertakings, in particular companies or firms within the meaning of the second paragraph of Article 54, under the conditions laid down for its own nationals by the law of the country where such establishment is effected, subject to the provisions of the Chapter relating to capital.

CHAPTER 3
SERVICES

[3.23]
Article 56
(ex Article 49 TEC)
Within the framework of the provisions set out below, restrictions on freedom to provide services within the Union shall be prohibited in respect of nationals of Member States who are established in a Member State other than that of the person for whom the services are intended.

The European Parliament and the Council, acting in accordance with the ordinary legislative procedure, may extend the provisions of the Chapter to nationals of a third country who provide services and who are established within the Union.

[3.24]
Article 57
(ex Article 50 TEC)
Services shall be considered to be 'services' within the meaning of the Treaties where they are normally provided for remuneration, in so far as they are not governed by the provisions relating to freedom of movement for goods, capital and persons.
'Services' shall in particular include:
   (a) activities of an industrial character;

(b) activities of a commercial character;
(c) activities of craftsmen;
(d) activities of the professions.

Without prejudice to the provisions of the Chapter relating to the right of establishment, the person providing a service may, in order to do so, temporarily pursue his activity in the Member State where the service is provided, under the same conditions as are imposed by that State on its own nationals.

TITLE V AREA OF FREEDOM, SECURITY AND JUSTICE

CHAPTER 3
JUDICIAL COOPERATION IN CIVIL MATTERS

[3.25]
Article 81
(ex Article 65 TEC)

1. The Union shall develop judicial cooperation in civil matters having cross-border implications, based on the principle of mutual recognition of judgments and of decisions in extrajudicial cases. Such cooperation may include the adoption of measures for the approximation of the laws and regulations of the Member States.

2. For the purposes of paragraph 1, the European Parliament and the Council, acting in accordance with the ordinary legislative procedure, shall adopt measures, particularly when necessary for the proper functioning of the internal market, aimed at ensuring:
(a) the mutual recognition and enforcement between Member States of judgments and of decisions in extrajudicial cases;
(b) the cross-border service of judicial and extrajudicial documents;
(c) the compatibility of the rules applicable in the Member States concerning conflict of laws and of jurisdiction;
(d) cooperation in the taking of evidence;
(e) effective access to justice;
(f) the elimination of obstacles to the proper functioning of civil proceedings, if necessary by promoting the compatibility of the rules on civil procedure applicable in the Member States;
(g) the development of alternative methods of dispute settlement;
(h) support for the training of the judiciary and judicial staff.

3. . . .

NOTES

Para 3: outside the scope of this work.

TITLE VII COMMON RULES ON COMPETITION, TAXATION AND APPROXIMATION OF LAWS

CHAPTER 3
APPROXIMATION OF LAWS

[3.26]
Article 114
(ex Article 95 TEC)

1. Save where otherwise provided in the Treaties, the following provisions shall apply for the achievement of the objectives set out in Article 26. The European Parliament and the Council shall, acting in accordance with the ordinary legislative procedure and after consulting the Economic and Social Committee, adopt the measures for the approximation of the provisions laid down by law, regulation or administrative action in Member States which have as their object the establishment and functioning of the internal market.

2. Paragraph 1 shall not apply to fiscal provisions, to those relating to the free movement of persons nor to those relating to the rights and interests of employed persons.

3. The Commission, in its proposals envisaged in paragraph 1 concerning health, safety, environmental protection and consumer protection, will take as a base a high level of protection, taking account in particular of any new development based on scientific facts. Within their respective powers, the European Parliament and the Council will also seek to achieve this objective.

4. If, after the adoption of a harmonisation measure by the European Parliament and the Council, by the Council or by the Commission, a Member State deems it necessary to maintain national provisions on grounds of major needs referred to in Article 36, or relating to the protection of the environment or the working environment, it shall notify the Commission of these provisions as well as the grounds for maintaining them.

5. Moreover, without prejudice to paragraph 4, if, after the adoption of a harmonisation measure by the European Parliament and the Council, by the Council or by the Commission, a Member State deems it necessary to introduce national provisions based on new scientific evidence relating to the protection of the environment or the working environment on grounds of a problem specific to that Member State arising after the adoption of the harmonisation measure, it shall notify the Commission of the envisaged provisions as well as the grounds for introducing them.

6. The Commission shall, within six months of the notifications as referred to in paragraphs 4 and 5, approve or reject the national provisions involved after having verified whether or not they are a means of arbitrary discrimination or a disguised restriction on trade between Member States and whether or not they shall constitute an obstacle to the functioning of the internal market.

In the absence of a decision by the Commission within this period the national provisions referred to in paragraphs 4 and 5 shall be deemed to have been approved.

When justified by the complexity of the matter and in the absence of danger for human health, the Commission may notify the Member State concerned that the period referred to in this paragraph may be extended for a further period of up to six months.

7. When, pursuant to paragraph 6, a Member State is authorised to maintain or introduce national provisions derogating from a harmonisation measure, the Commission shall immediately examine whether to propose an adaptation to that measure.

8. When a Member State raises a specific problem on public health in a field which has been the subject of prior harmonisation measures, it shall bring it to the attention of the Commission which shall immediately examine whether to propose appropriate measures to the Council.

9. By way of derogation from the procedure laid down in Articles 258 and 259, the Commission and any Member State may bring the matter directly before the Court of Justice of the European Union if it considers that another Member State is making improper use of the powers provided for in this Article.

10. The harmonisation measures referred to above shall, in appropriate cases, include a safeguard clause authorising the Member States to take, for one or more of the non-economic reasons referred to in Article 36, provisional measures subject to a Union control procedure.

[3.27]
Article 115
(ex Article 94 TEC)
Without prejudice to Article 114, the Council shall, acting unanimously in accordance with a special legislative procedure and after consulting the European Parliament and the Economic and Social Committee, issue directives for the approximation of such laws, regulations or administrative provisions of the Member States as directly affect the establishment or functioning of the internal market.

TITLE X SOCIAL POLICY

[3.28]
Article 151
(ex Article 136 TEC)
The Union and the Member States, having in mind fundamental social rights such as those set out in the European Social Charter signed at Turin on 18 October 1961 and in the 1989 Community Charter of the Fundamental Social Rights of Workers, shall have as their objectives the promotion of employment, improved living and working conditions, so as to make possible their harmonisation while the improvement is being maintained, proper social protection, dialogue between management and labour, the development of human resources with a view to lasting high employment and the combating of exclusion.

To this end the Union and the Member States shall implement measures which take account of the diverse forms of national practices, in particular in the field of contractual relations, and the need to maintain the competitiveness of the Union's economy.

They believe that such a development will ensue not only from the functioning of the internal market, which will favour the harmonisation of social systems, but also from the procedures provided for in the Treaties and from the approximation of provisions laid down by law, regulation or administrative action.

[3.29]
Article 152
The Union recognises and promotes the role of the social partners at its level, taking into account the diversity of national systems. It shall facilitate dialogue between the social partners, respecting their autonomy.

The Tripartite Social Summit for Growth and Employment shall contribute to social dialogue.

[3.30]
Article 153
(ex Article 137 TEC)
1. With a view to achieving the objectives of Article 151, the Union shall support and complement the activities of the Member States in the following fields:

(a) improvement in particular of the working environment to protect workers' health and safety;
(b) working conditions;
(c) social security and social protection of workers;
(d) protection of workers where their employment contract is terminated;
(e) the information and consultation of workers;
(f) representation and collective defence of the interests of workers and employers, including co-determination, subject to paragraph 5;
(g) conditions of employment for third-country nationals legally residing in Union territory;
(h) the integration of persons excluded from the labour market, without prejudice to Article 166;
(i) equality between men and women with regard to labour market opportunities and treatment at work;
(j) the combating of social exclusion;

(k) the modernisation of social protection systems without prejudice to point (c).

2. To this end, the European Parliament and the Council:

(a) may adopt measures designed to encourage cooperation between Member States through initiatives aimed at improving knowledge, developing exchanges of information and best practices, promoting innovative approaches and evaluating experiences, excluding any harmonisation of the laws and regulations of the Member States;

(b) may adopt, in the fields referred to in paragraph 1(a) to (i), by means of directives, minimum requirements for gradual implementation, having regard to the conditions and technical rules obtaining in each of the Member States. Such directives shall avoid imposing administrative, financial and legal constraints in a way which would hold back the creation and development of small and medium-sized undertakings.

The European Parliament and the Council shall act in accordance with the ordinary legislative procedure after consulting the Economic and Social Committee and the Committee of the Regions.

In the fields referred to in paragraph 1(c), (d), (f) and (g), the Council shall act unanimously, in accordance with a special legislative procedure, after consulting the European Parliament and the said Committees.

The Council, acting unanimously on a proposal from the Commission, after consulting the European Parliament, may decide to render the ordinary legislative procedure applicable to paragraph 1(d), (f) and (g).

3. A Member State may entrust management and labour, at their joint request, with the implementation of directives adopted pursuant to paragraph 2, or, where appropriate, with the implementation of a Council decision adopted in accordance with Article 155.

In this case, it shall ensure that, no later than the date on which a directive or a decision must be transposed or implemented, management and labour have introduced the necessary measures by agreement, the Member State concerned being required to take any necessary measure enabling it at any time to be in a position to guarantee the results imposed by that directive or that decision.

4. The provisions adopted pursuant to this Article:

— shall not affect the right of Member States to define the fundamental principles of their social security systems and must not significantly affect the financial equilibrium thereof,

— shall not prevent any Member State from maintaining or introducing more stringent protective measures compatible with the Treaties.

5. The provisions of this Article shall not apply to pay, the right of association, the right to strike or the right to impose lock-outs.

[3.31]
Article 154
(ex Article 138 TEC)

1. The Commission shall have the task of promoting the consultation of management and labour at Union level and shall take any relevant measure to facilitate their dialogue by ensuring balanced support for the parties.

2. To this end, before submitting proposals in the social policy field, the Commission shall consult management and labour on the possible direction of Union action.

3. If, after such consultation, the Commission considers Union action advisable, it shall consult management and labour on the content of the envisaged proposal. Management and labour shall forward to the Commission an opinion or, where appropriate, a recommendation.

4. On the occasion of the consultation referred to in paragraphs 2 and 3, management and labour may inform the Commission of their wish to initiate the process provided for in Article 155. The duration of this process shall not exceed nine months, unless the management and labour concerned and the Commission decide jointly to extend it.

[3.32]
Article 155
(ex Article 139 TEC)

1. Should management and labour so desire, the dialogue between them at Union level may lead to contractual relations, including agreements.

2. Agreements concluded at Union level shall be implemented either in accordance with the procedures and practices specific to management and labour and the Member States or, in matters covered by Article 153, at the joint request of the signatory parties, by a Council decision on a proposal from the Commission. The European Parliament shall be informed.

The Council shall act unanimously where the agreement in question contains one or more provisions relating to one of the areas for which unanimity is required pursuant to Article 153(2).

[3.33]
Article 156
(ex Article 140 TEC)

With a view to achieving the objectives of Article 151 and without prejudice to the other provisions of the Treaties, the Commission shall encourage cooperation between the Member States and facilitate the coordination of their action in all social policy fields under this Chapter, particularly in matters relating to:

— employment,
— labour law and working conditions,
— basic and advanced vocational training,
— social security,

— prevention of occupational accidents and diseases,
— occupational hygiene,
— the right of association and collective bargaining between employers and workers.

To this end, the Commission shall act in close contact with Member States by making studies, delivering opinions and arranging consultations both on problems arising at national level and on those of concern to international organisations, in particular initiatives aiming at the establishment of guidelines and indicators, the organisation of exchange of best practice, and the preparation of the necessary elements for periodic monitoring and evaluation. The European Parliament shall be kept fully informed.

Before delivering the opinions provided for in this Article, the Commission shall consult the Economic and Social Committee.

[3.34]
Article 157
(ex Article 141 TEC)

1. Each Member State shall ensure that the principle of equal pay for male and female workers for equal work or work of equal value is applied.

2. For the purpose of this Article, 'pay' means the ordinary basic or minimum wage or salary and any other consideration, whether in cash or in kind, which the worker receives directly or indirectly, in respect of his employment, from his employer.

Equal pay without discrimination based on sex means:

(a) that pay for the same work at piece rates shall be calculated on the basis of the same unit of measurement;
(b) that pay for work at time rates shall be the same for the same job.

3. The European Parliament and the Council, acting in accordance with the ordinary legislative procedure, and after consulting the Economic and Social Committee, shall adopt measures to ensure the application of the principle of equal opportunities and equal treatment of men and women in matters of employment and occupation, including the principle of equal pay for equal work or work of equal value.

4. With a view to ensuring full equality in practice between men and women in working life, the principle of equal treatment shall not prevent any Member State from maintaining or adopting measures providing for specific advantages in order to make it easier for the under-represented sex to pursue a vocational activity or to prevent or compensate for disadvantages in professional careers.

[3.35]
Article 158
(ex Article 142 TEC)

Member States shall endeavour to maintain the existing equivalence between paid holiday schemes.

PART 5 THE UNION'S EXTERNAL ACTION

TITLE V INTERNATIONAL AGREEMENTS

[3.36]
Article 218
(ex Article 300 TEC)

1. Without prejudice to the specific provisions laid down in Article 207, agreements between the Union and third countries or international organisations shall be negotiated and concluded in accordance with the following procedure.

2. The Council shall authorise the opening of negotiations, adopt negotiating directives, authorise the signing of agreements and conclude them.

3. The Commission, or the High Representative of the Union for Foreign Affairs and Security Policy where the agreement envisaged relates exclusively or principally to the common foreign and security policy, shall submit recommendations to the Council, which shall adopt a decision authorising the opening of negotiations and, depending on the subject of the agreement envisaged, nominating the Union negotiator or the head of the Union's negotiating team.

4. The Council may address directives to the negotiator and designate a special committee in consultation with which the negotiations must be conducted.

5. The Council, on a proposal by the negotiator, shall adopt a decision authorising the signing of the agreement and, if necessary, its provisional application before entry into force.

6. The Council, on a proposal by the negotiator, shall adopt a decision concluding the agreement.

Except where agreements relate exclusively to the common foreign and security policy, the Council shall adopt the decision concluding the agreement:

(a) after obtaining the consent of the European Parliament in the following cases:
  (i) association agreements;
  (ii) agreement on Union accession to the European Convention for the Protection of Human Rights and Fundamental Freedoms;
  (iii) agreements establishing a specific institutional framework by organising cooperation procedures;
  (iv) agreements with important budgetary implications for the Union;
  (v) agreements covering fields to which either the ordinary legislative procedure applies, or the special legislative procedure where consent by the European Parliament is required.

  The European Parliament and the Council may, in an urgent situation, agree upon a time-limit for consent.

(b) after consulting the European Parliament in other cases. The European Parliament shall deliver its opinion within a time-limit which the Council may set depending on the urgency of the matter. In the absence of an opinion within that time-limit, the Council may act.

7. When concluding an agreement, the Council may, by way of derogation from paragraphs 5, 6 and 9, authorise the negotiator to approve on the Union's behalf modifications to the agreement where it provides for them to be adopted by a simplified procedure or by a body set up by the agreement. The Council may attach specific conditions to such authorisation.

8. The Council shall act by a qualified majority throughout the procedure.

However, it shall act unanimously when the agreement covers a field for which unanimity is required for the adoption of a Union act as well as for association agreements and the agreements referred to in Article 212 with the States which are candidates for accession. The Council shall also act unanimously for the agreement on accession of the Union to the European Convention for the Protection of Human Rights and Fundamental Freedoms; the decision concluding this agreement shall enter into force after it has been approved by the Member States in accordance with their respective constitutional requirements.

9. The Council, on a proposal from the Commission or the High Representative of the Union for Foreign Affairs and Security Policy, shall adopt a decision suspending application of an agreement and establishing the positions to be adopted on the Union's behalf in a body set up by an agreement, when that body is called upon to adopt acts having legal effects, with the exception of acts supplementing or amending the institutional framework of the agreement.

10. The European Parliament shall be immediately and fully informed at all stages of the procedure.

11. A Member State, the European Parliament, the Council or the Commission may obtain the opinion of the Court of Justice as to whether an agreement envisaged is compatible with the Treaties. Where the opinion of the Court is adverse, the agreement envisaged may not enter into force unless it is amended or the Treaties are revised.

PART SIX INSTITUTIONAL AND FINANCIAL PROVISIONS

TITLE I INSTITUTIONAL PROVISIONS

CHAPTER 1
THE INSTITUTIONS

Section 3
The Council

[3.37]
Article 238
(ex Article 205(1) and (2) TEC)

1. Where it is required to act by a simple majority, the Council shall act by a majority of its component members.

2. By way of derogation from Article 16(4) of the Treaty on European Union, as from 1 November 2014 and subject to the provisions laid down in the Protocol on transitional provisions, where the Council does not act on a proposal from the Commission or from the High Representative of the Union for Foreign Affairs and Security Policy, the qualified majority shall be defined as at least 72% of the members of the Council, representing Member States comprising at least 65% of the population of the Union.

3. As from 1 November 2014 and subject to the provisions laid down in the Protocol on transitional provisions, in cases where, under the Treaties, not all the members of the Council participate in voting, a qualified majority shall be defined as follows:

(a) A qualified majority shall be defined as at least 55% of the members of the Council representing the participating Member States, comprising at least 65% of the population of these States.

A blocking minority must include at least the minimum number of Council members representing more than 35% of the population of the participating Member States, plus one member, failing which the qualified majority shall be deemed attained;

(b) By way of derogation from point (a), where the Council does not act on a proposal from the Commission or from the High Representative of the Union for Foreign Affairs and Security Policy, the qualified majority shall be defined as at least 72% of the members of the Council representing the participating Member States, comprising at least 65% of the population of these States.

4. Abstentions by Members present in person or represented shall not prevent the adoption by the Council of acts which require unanimity.

Section 5
The Court Of Justice Of The European Union

[3.38]
Article 251
(ex Article 221 TEC)

The Court of Justice shall sit in chambers or in a Grand Chamber, in accordance with the rules laid down for that purpose in the Statute of the Court of Justice of the European Union.

When provided for in the Statute, the Court of Justice may also sit as a full Court.

[3.39]
Article 252
(ex Article 222 TEC)
The Court of Justice shall be assisted by eight Advocates-General. Should the Court of Justice so request, the Council, acting unanimously, may increase the number of Advocates-General.

It shall be the duty of the Advocate-General, acting with complete impartiality and independence, to make, in open court, reasoned submissions on cases which, in accordance with the Statute of the Court of Justice of the European Union, require his involvement.

[3.40]
Article 253
(ex Article 223 TEC)
The Judges and Advocates-General of the Court of Justice shall be chosen from persons whose independence is beyond doubt and who possess the qualifications required for appointment to the highest judicial offices in their respective countries or who are jurisconsults of recognised competence; they shall be appointed by common accord of the governments of the Member States for a term of six years, after consultation of the panel provided for in Article 255.

Every three years there shall be a partial replacement of the Judges and Advocates-General, in accordance with the conditions laid down in the Statute of the Court of Justice of the European Union.

The Judges shall elect the President of the Court of Justice from among their number for a term of three years. He may be re-elected.

Retiring Judges and Advocates-General may be reappointed.

The Court of Justice shall appoint its Registrar and lay down the rules governing his service.

The Court of Justice shall establish its Rules of Procedure. Those Rules shall require the approval of the Council.

[3.41]
Article 254
(ex Article 224 TEC)
The number of Judges of the General Court shall be determined by the Statute of the Court of Justice of the European Union. The Statute may provide for the General Court to be assisted by Advocates-General.

The members of the General Court shall be chosen from persons whose independence is beyond doubt and who possess the ability required for appointment to high judicial office. They shall be appointed by common accord of the governments of the Member States for a term of six years, after consultation of the panel provided for in Article 255. The membership shall be partially renewed every three years. Retiring members shall be eligible for reappointment.

The Judges shall elect the President of the General Court from among their number for a term of three years. He may be re-elected.

The General Court shall appoint its Registrar and lay down the rules governing his service.

The General Court shall establish its Rules of Procedure in agreement with the Court of Justice. Those Rules shall require the approval of the Council.

Unless the Statute of the Court of Justice of the European Union provides otherwise, the provisions of the Treaties relating to the Court of Justice shall apply to the General Court.

[3.42]
Article 258
(ex Article 226 TEC)
If the Commission considers that a Member State has failed to fulfil an obligation under the Treaties, it shall deliver a reasoned opinion on the matter after giving the State concerned the opportunity to submit its observations.

If the State concerned does not comply with the opinion within the period laid down by the Commission, the latter may bring the matter before the Court of Justice of the European Union.

[3.43]
Article 259
(ex Article 227 TEC)
A Member State which considers that another Member State has failed to fulfil an obligation under the Treaties may bring the matter before the Court of Justice of the European Union.

Before a Member State brings an action against another Member State for an alleged infringement of an obligation under the Treaties, it shall bring the matter before the Commission.

The Commission shall deliver a reasoned opinion after each of the States concerned has been given the opportunity to submit its own case and its observations on the other party's case both orally and in writing.

If the Commission has not delivered an opinion within three months of the date on which the matter was brought before it, the absence of such opinion shall not prevent the matter from being brought before the Court.

[3.44]
Article 260
(ex Article 228 TEC)
1. If the Court of Justice of the European Union finds that a Member State has failed to fulfil an obligation under the Treaties, the State shall be required to take the necessary measures to comply with the judgment of the Court.

2. If the Commission considers that the Member State concerned has not taken the necessary measures to comply with the judgment of the Court, it may bring the case before the Court after giving that State the opportunity to submit its observations. It shall specify the amount of the lump sum or penalty payment to be paid by the Member State concerned which it considers appropriate in the circumstances.

If the Court finds that the Member State concerned has not complied with its judgment it may impose a lump sum or penalty payment on it.

This procedure shall be without prejudice to Article 259.

3. When the Commission brings a case before the Court pursuant to Article 258 on the grounds that the Member State concerned has failed to fulfil its obligation to notify measures transposing a directive adopted under a legislative procedure, it may, when it deems appropriate, specify the amount of the lump sum or penalty payment to be paid by the Member State concerned which it considers appropriate in the circumstances.

If the Court finds that there is an infringement it may impose a lump sum or penalty payment on the Member State concerned not exceeding the amount specified by the Commission. The payment obligation shall take effect on the date set by the Court in its judgment.

[3.45]
Article 263
(ex Article 230 TEC)

The Court of Justice of the European Union shall review the legality of legislative acts, of acts of the Council, of the Commission and of the European Central Bank, other than recommendations and opinions, and of acts of the European Parliament and of the European Council intended to produce legal effects vis-à-vis third parties. It shall also review the legality of acts of bodies, offices or agencies of the Union intended to produce legal effects vis-à-vis third parties.

It shall for this purpose have jurisdiction in actions brought by a Member State, the European Parliament, the Council or the Commission on grounds of lack of competence, infringement of an essential procedural requirement, infringement of the Treaties or of any rule of law relating to their application, or misuse of powers.

The Court shall have jurisdiction under the same conditions in actions brought by the Court of Auditors, by the European Central Bank and by the Committee of the Regions for the purpose of protecting their prerogatives.

Any natural or legal person may, under the conditions laid down in the first and second paragraphs, institute proceedings against an act addressed to that person or which is of direct and individual concern to them, and against a regulatory act which is of direct concern to them and does not entail implementing measures.

Acts setting up bodies, offices and agencies of the Union may lay down specific conditions and arrangements concerning actions brought by natural or legal persons against acts of these bodies, offices or agencies intended to produce legal effects in relation to them.

The proceedings provided for in this Article shall be instituted within two months of the publication of the measure, or of its notification to the plaintiff, or, in the absence thereof, of the day on which it came to the knowledge of the latter, as the case may be.

[3.46]
Article 264
(ex Article 231 TEC)

If the action is well founded, the Court of Justice of the European Union shall declare the act concerned to be void.

However, the Court shall, if it considers this necessary, state which of the effects of the act which it has declared void shall be considered as definitive.

[3.47]
Article 267
(ex Article 234 TEC)

The Court of Justice of the European Union shall have jurisdiction to give preliminary rulings concerning:

(a) the interpretation of the Treaties;

(b) the validity and interpretation of acts of the institutions, bodies, offices or agencies of the Union;

Where such a question is raised before any court or tribunal of a Member State, that court or tribunal may, if it considers that a decision on the question is necessary to enable it to give judgment, request the Court to give a ruling thereon.

Where any such question is raised in a case pending before a court or tribunal of a Member State against whose decisions there is no judicial remedy under national law, that court or tribunal shall bring the matter before the Court.

If such a question is raised in a case pending before a court or tribunal of a Member State with regard to a person in custody, the Court of Justice of the European Union shall act with the minimum of delay.

[3.48]
Article 270
(ex Article 236 TEC)

The Court of Justice of the European Union shall have jurisdiction in any dispute between the Union and its servants within the limits and under the conditions laid down in the Staff Regulations of Officials and the Conditions of Employment of other servants of the Union.

[3.49]
Article 278
(ex Article 242 TEC)
Actions brought before the Court of Justice of the European Union shall not have suspensory effect. The Court may, however, if it considers that circumstances so require, order that application of the contested act be suspended.

[3.50]
Article 279
(ex Article 243 TEC)
The Court of Justice of the European Union may in any cases before it prescribe any necessary interim measures.

CHAPTER 2
LEGAL ACTS OF THE UNION, ADOPTION PROCEDURES AND OTHER PROVISIONS

Section 1
The Legal Acts Of The Union

[3.51]
Article 288
(ex Article 249 TEC)
To exercise the Union's competences, the institutions shall adopt regulations, directives, decisions, recommendations and opinions.

A regulation shall have general application. It shall be binding in its entirety and directly applicable in all Member States.

A directive shall be binding, as to the result to be achieved, upon each Member State to which it is addressed, but shall leave to the national authorities the choice of form and methods.

A decision shall be binding in its entirety. A decision which specifies those to whom it is addressed shall be binding only on them.

Recommendations and opinions shall have no binding force.

[3.52]
Article 289
1. The ordinary legislative procedure shall consist in the joint adoption by the European Parliament and the Council of a regulation, directive or decision on a proposal from the Commission. This procedure is defined in Article 294.
2. In the specific cases provided for by the Treaties, the adoption of a regulation, directive or decision by the European Parliament with the participation of the Council, or by the latter with the participation of the European Parliament, shall constitute a special legislative procedure.
3. Legal acts adopted by legislative procedure shall constitute legislative acts.
4. In the specific cases provided for by the Treaties, legislative acts may be adopted on the initiative of a group of Member States or of the European Parliament, on a recommendation from the European Central Bank or at the request of the Court of Justice or the European Investment Bank.

Section 2
Procedures For The Adoption Of Acts And Other Provisions

[3.53]
Article 293
(ex Article 250 TEC)
1. Where, pursuant to the Treaties, the Council acts on a proposal from the Commission, it may amend that proposal only by acting unanimously, except in the cases referred to in paragraphs 10 and 13 of Article 294, in Articles 310, 312 and 314 and in the second paragraph of Article 315.
2. As long as the Council has not acted, the Commission may alter its proposal at any time during the procedures leading to the adoption of a Union act.

[3.54]
Article 294
(ex Article 251 TEC)
1. Where reference is made in the Treaties to the ordinary legislative procedure for the adoption of an act, the following procedure shall apply.
2. The Commission shall submit a proposal to the European Parliament and the Council.

First reading

3. The European Parliament shall adopt its position at first reading and communicate it to the Council.
4. If the Council approves the European Parliament's position, the act concerned shall be adopted in the wording which corresponds to the position of the European Parliament.
5. If the Council does not approve the European Parliament's position, it shall adopt its position at first reading and communicate it to the European Parliament.
6. The Council shall inform the European Parliament fully of the reasons which led it to adopt its position at first reading. The Commission shall inform the European Parliament fully of its position.

Second reading

7. If, within three months of such communication, the European Parliament:

(a) approves the Council's position at first reading or has not taken a decision, the act concerned shall be deemed to have been adopted in the wording which corresponds to the position of the Council;
(b) rejects, by a majority of its component members, the Council's position at first reading, the proposed act shall be deemed not to have been adopted;
(c) proposes, by a majority of its component members, amendments to the Council's position at first reading, the text thus amended shall be forwarded to the Council and to the Commission, which shall deliver an opinion on those amendments.

8. If, within three months of receiving the European Parliament's amendments, the Council, acting by a qualified majority:
(a) approves all those amendments, the act in question shall be deemed to have been adopted;
(b) does not approve all the amendments, the President of the Council, in agreement with the President of the European Parliament, shall within six weeks convene a meeting of the Conciliation Committee.

9. The Council shall act unanimously on the amendments on which the Commission has delivered a negative opinion.

Conciliation

10. The Conciliation Committee, which shall be composed of the members of the Council or their representatives and an equal number of members representing the European Parliament, shall have the task of reaching agreement on a joint text, by a qualified majority of the members of the Council or their representatives and by a majority of the members representing the European Parliament within six weeks of its being convened, on the basis of the positions of the European Parliament and the Council at second reading.

11. The Commission shall take part in the Conciliation Committee's proceedings and shall take all necessary initiatives with a view to reconciling the positions of the European Parliament and the Council.

12. If, within six weeks of its being convened, the Conciliation Committee does not approve the joint text, the proposed act shall be deemed not to have been adopted.

Third reading

13. If, within that period, the Conciliation Committee approves a joint text, the European Parliament, acting by a majority of the votes cast, and the Council, acting by a qualified majority, shall each have a period of six weeks from that approval in which to adopt the act in question in accordance with the joint text. If they fail to do so, the proposed act shall be deemed not to have been adopted.

14. The periods of three months and six weeks referred to in this Article shall be extended by a maximum of one month and two weeks respectively at the initiative of the European Parliament or the Council.

Special provisions

15. Where, in the cases provided for in the Treaties, a legislative act is submitted to the ordinary legislative procedure on the initiative of a group of Member States, on a recommendation by the European Central Bank, or at the request of the Court of Justice, paragraph 2, the second sentence of paragraph 6, and paragraph 9 shall not apply.

In such cases, the European Parliament and the Council shall communicate the proposed act to the Commission with their positions at first and second readings. The European Parliament or the Council may request the opinion of the Commission throughout the procedure, which the Commission may also deliver on its own initiative. It may also, if it deems it necessary, take part in the Conciliation Committee in accordance with paragraph 11.

[3.55]
Article 295

The European Parliament, the Council and the Commission shall consult each other and by common agreement make arrangements for their cooperation. To that end, they may, in compliance with the Treaties, conclude interinstitutional agreements which may be of a binding nature.

[3.56]
Article 296
(ex Article 253 TEC)

Where the Treaties do not specify the type of act to be adopted, the institutions shall select it on a case-by-case basis, in compliance with the applicable procedures and with the principle of proportionality.

Legal acts shall state the reasons on which they are based and shall refer to any proposals, initiatives, recommendations, requests or opinions required by the Treaties.

When considering draft legislative acts, the European Parliament and the Council shall refrain from adopting acts not provided for by the relevant legislative procedure in the area in question.

[3.57]
Article 297
(ex Article 254 TEC)

1. Legislative acts adopted under the ordinary legislative procedure shall be signed by the President of the European Parliament and by the President of the Council.

Legislative acts adopted under a special legislative procedure shall be signed by the President of the institution which adopted them.

Legislative acts shall be published in the Official Journal of the European Union. They shall enter into force on the date specified in them or, in the absence thereof, on the twentieth day following that of their publication.

2. Non-legislative acts adopted in the form of regulations, directives or decisions, when the latter do not specify to whom they are addressed, shall be signed by the President of the institution which adopted them.

Regulations and directives which are addressed to all Member States, as well as decisions which do not specify to whom they are addressed, shall be published in the Official Journal of the European Union. They shall enter into force on the date specified in them or, in the absence thereof, on the twentieth day following that of their publication.

Other directives, and decisions which specify to whom they are addressed, shall be notified to those to whom they are addressed and shall take effect upon such notification.

PART SEVEN GENERAL AND FINAL PROVISIONS

[3.58]
Article 352
(ex Article 308 TEC)

1. If action by the Union should prove necessary, within the framework of the policies defined in the Treaties, to attain one of the objectives set out in the Treaties, and the Treaties have not provided the necessary powers, the Council, acting unanimously on a proposal from the Commission and after obtaining the consent of the European Parliament, shall adopt the appropriate measures. Where the measures in question are adopted by the Council in accordance with a special legislative procedure, it shall also act unanimously on a proposal from the Commission and after obtaining the consent of the European Parliament.
2. Using the procedure for monitoring the subsidiarity principle referred to in Article 5(3) of the Treaty on European Union, the Commission shall draw national Parliaments' attention to proposals based on this Article.
3. Measures based on this Article shall not entail harmonisation of Member States' laws or regulations in cases where the Treaties exclude such harmonisation.
4. This Article cannot serve as a basis for attaining objectives pertaining to the common foreign and security policy and any acts adopted pursuant to this Article shall respect the limits set out in Article 40, second paragraph, of the Treaty on European Union.

PROTOCOL (NO 30) ON THE APPLICATION OF THE CHARTER OF FUNDAMENTAL RIGHTS OF THE EUROPEAN UNION TO POLAND AND TO THE UNITED KINGDOM

[3.59]
THE HIGH CONTRACTING PARTIES,

WHEREAS in Article 6 of the Treaty on European Union, the Union recognises the rights, freedoms and principles set out in the Charter of Fundamental Rights of the European Union,

WHEREAS the Charter is to be applied in strict accordance with the provisions of the aforementioned Article 6 and Title VII of the Charter itself,

WHEREAS the aforementioned Article 6 requires the Charter to be applied and interpreted by the courts of Poland and of the United Kingdom strictly in accordance with the explanations referred to in that Article,

WHEREAS the Charter contains both rights and principles,

WHEREAS the Charter contains both provisions which are civil and political in character and those which are economic and social in character,

WHEREAS the Charter reaffirms the rights, freedoms and principles recognised in the Union and makes those rights more visible, but does not create new rights or principles,

RECALLING the obligations devolving upon Poland and the United Kingdom under the Treaty on European Union, the Treaty on the Functioning of the European Union, and Union law generally,

NOTING the wish of Poland and the United Kingdom to clarify certain aspects of the application of the Charter,

DESIROUS therefore of clarifying the application of the Charter in relation to the laws and administrative action of Poland and of the United Kingdom and of its justiciability within Poland and within the United Kingdom,

REAFFIRMING that references in this Protocol to the operation of specific provisions of the Charter are strictly without prejudice to the operation of other provisions of the Charter,

REAFFIRMING that this Protocol is without prejudice to the application of the Charter to other Member States,

REAFFIRMING that this Protocol is without prejudice to other obligations devolving upon Poland and the United Kingdom under the Treaty on European Union, the Treaty on the Functioning of the European Union, and Union law generally,

HAVE AGREED UPON the following provisions, which shall be annexed to the Treaty on European Union and to the Treaty on the Functioning of the European Union:

Article 1

1. The Charter does not extend the ability of the Court of Justice of the European Union, or any court or tribunal of Poland or of the United Kingdom, to find that the laws, regulations or administrative provisions, practices or action of Poland or of the United Kingdom are inconsistent with the fundamental rights, freedoms and principles that it reaffirms.

2. In particular, and for the avoidance of doubt, nothing in Title IV of the Charter creates justiciable rights applicable to Poland or the United Kingdom except in so far as Poland or the United Kingdom has provided for such rights in its national law.

Article 2
To the extent that a provision of the Charter refers to national laws and practices, it shall only apply to Poland or the United Kingdom to the extent that the rights or principles that it contains are recognised in the law or practices of Poland or of the United Kingdom.

PROTOCOL (NO 36) ON TRANSITIONAL PROVISIONS

[3.60]
THE HIGH CONTRACTING PARTIES,

WHEREAS, in order to organise the transition from the institutional provisions of the Treaties applicable prior to the entry into force of the Treaty of Lisbon to the provisions contained in that Treaty, it is necessary to lay down transitional provisions,

HAVE AGREED UPON the following provisions, which shall be annexed to the Treaty on European Union, to the Treaty on the Functioning of the European Union and to the Treaty establishing the European Atomic Energy Community:

Article 1
In this Protocol, the words "the Treaties" shall mean the Treaty on European Union, the Treaty on the Functioning of the European Union and the Treaty establishing the European Atomic Energy Community.

Article 2
(*Outside the scope of this work.*)

Article 3
1. In accordance with Article 16(4) of the Treaty on European Union, the provisions of that paragraph and of Article 238(2) of the Treaty on the Functioning of the European Union relating to the definition of the qualified majority in the European Council and the Council shall take effect on 1 November 2014.
2. Between 1 November 2014 and 31 March 2017, when an act is to be adopted by qualified majority, a member of the Council may request that it be adopted in accordance with the qualified majority as defined in paragraph 3. In that case, paragraphs 3 and 4 shall apply.
[3. Until 31 October 2014, the following provisions shall remain in force, without prejudice to the second subparagraph of Article 235(1) of the Treaty on the Functioning of the European Union.

For acts of the European Council and of the Council requiring a qualified majority, members' votes shall be weighted as follows:

Belgium	12	**Lithuania**	7
Bulgaria	10	**Luxembourg**	4
Czech Republic	12	**Hungary**	12
Denmark	7	**Malta**	3
Germany	29	**Netherlands**	13
Estonia	4	**Austria**	10
Ireland	7	**Poland**	27
Greece	12	**Portugal**	12
Spain	27	**Romania**	14
France	29	**Slovenia**	4
Croatia	7	**Slovakia**	7
Italy	29	**Finland**	7
Cyprus	4	**Sweden**	10
Latvia	4	**United Kingdom**	29

Acts shall be adopted if there are at least 260 votes in favour representing a majority of the members where, under the Treaties, they must be adopted on a proposal from the Commission. In other cases decisions shall be adopted if there are at least 260 votes in favour representing at least two thirds of the members.

A member of the European Council or the Council may request that, where an act is adopted by the European Council or the Council by a qualified majority, a check is made to ensure that the Member States comprising the qualified majority represent at least 62% of the total population of the Union. If that proves not to be the case, the act shall not be adopted.]

4. Until 31 October 2014, the qualified majority shall, in cases where, under the Treaties, not all the members of the Council participate in voting, namely in the cases where reference is made to the qualified majority as defined in Article 238(3) of the Treaty on the Functioning of the European Union, be defined as the same proportion of the weighted votes and the same proportion of the number of the Council members and, if appropriate, the same percentage of the population of the Member States concerned as laid down in paragraph 3 of this Article.

NOTES

Article 3(3) was substituted by Article 19 of the Treaty on the Accession of Croatia (OJ L112, 24.4.2012).

Articles 4–10

(*Outside the scope of this work.*)

TREATY ON THE FUNCTIONING OF THE EUROPEAN UNION TABLE OF EQUIVALENCES

[3.61]

NOTES

Date of publication in OJ: OJ C326, 26.10.2012, p 368.

This table shows in column (1) the provisions of the Treaty establishing the European Community which were reproduced in previous editions of this Handbook, and in column (2) the new numbering of provisions of that Treaty as consolidated and renamed the "Treaty on the Functioning of the European Union".

The abbreviations used in this Table and the related notes are as follows:

(i) "TEU" means the Treaty on European Union;
(ii) "TFEU" means the Treaty on the Functioning of the European Union.

(1) **Old numbering of the Treaty establishing the European Community**	(2) **New numbering of the Treaty on the Functioning of the European Union**
PART ONE	PART ONE
PRINCIPLES	PRINCIPLES
Article 1 (repealed)	—
—	Article 1
Article 2 (repealed)[1]	—
—	Title I Categories and areas of union competence
—	Article 2
—	Article 3
—	Article 4
—	Article 5
—	Article 6
—	Title II Provisions having general application
—	Article 7
Article 3, paragraph 1 (repealed)[2]	—
Article 3, paragraph 2	Article 8
—	Article 9
—	Article 10
PART TWO	PART TWO
CITIZENSHIP OF THE UNION	NON-DISCRIMINATION AND CITIZENSHIP OF THE UNION
Article 12 (moved)	Article 18
Article 13 (moved)	Article 19
PART THREE	PART THREE
COMMUNITY POLICIES	POLICIES AND INTERNAL ACTIONS OF THE UNION
—	Title I The internal market
Article 14 (moved)	Article 26
Title III	Title IV
Free movement of persons, services and capital	Free movement of persons, services and capital
Chapter 1	Chapter 1
Workers	Workers
Article 39	Article 45
Article 40	Article 46
Article 41	Article 47
Article 42	Article 48
Chapter 2	Chapter 2
Right of establishment	Right of establishment
Article 43	Article 49
Chapter 3	Chapter 3
Services	Services
Article 49	Article 56
Article 50	Article 57

(1) **Old numbering of the Treaty establishing the European Community**	(2) **New numbering of the Treaty on the Functioning of the European Union**
Article 54	Article 61
Title IV	Title V
Visas, asylum, immigration and other policies related to free movement of persons	Area of freedom, security and justice
—	Chapter 3
	Judicial cooperation in civil matters
Article 65	Article 81
Title VI	Title VII
Common rules on competition, taxation and approximation of laws	Common rules on competition, taxation and approximation of laws
Chapter 3	Chapter 3
Approximation of laws	Approximation of laws
Article 95 (moved)	Article 114
Article 94 (moved)	Article 115
Title VIII	Title IX
Employment	Employment
Article 125	Article 145
Article 126	Article 146
Article 127	Article 147
Article 128	Article 148
Article 129	Article 149
Article 130	Article 150
Title XI	Title X
Social policy, education, vocational training and youth	Social policy
Chapter 1	
social provisions (repealed)	—
Article 136	Article 151
—	Article 152
Article 137	Article 153
Article 138	Article 154
Article 139	Article 155
Article 140	Article 156
Article 141	Article 157
Article 142	Article 158
Article 143	Article 159
Article 144	Article 160
Article 145	Article 161
	PART FIVE
	THE UNION'S EXTERNAL ACTION
	Title V
	International Agreements
Article 300	Article 218
PART FIVE	PART SIX
INSTITUTIONS OF THE COMMUNITY	INSTITUTIONAL AND FINANCIAL PROVISIONS
Title I	Title I
Institutional provisions	Institutional provisions
Chapter 1	Chapter 1
The institutions	The institutions
Section 2	Section 3
The Council	The Council
Article 205, paragraphs 1 and 3	Article 238
Section 4	Section 5
The Court of Justice	The Court of Justice of the European Union

(1) **Old numbering of the Treaty establishing the European Community**	(2) **New numbering of the Treaty on the Functioning of the European Union**
Article 220 (repealed)[3]	—
Article 221, first paragraph (repealed)[4]	—
Article 221, second and third paragraphs	Article 251
Article 222	Article 252
Article 223	Article 253
Article 224[5]	Article 254
Article 226	Article 258
Article 227	Article 259
Article 228	Article 260
Article 229	Article 261
Article 229a	Article 262
Article 230	Article 263
Article 231	Article 264
Article 234	Article 267
Article 236	Article 270
Article 242	Article 278
Article 243	Article 279
Chapter 2	Chapter 2
Provisions common to several institutions	Legal acts of the Union, adoption procedures and other provisions
—	Section 1
	The legal acts of the Union
Article 249	Article 288
—	Article 289
—	Section 2
	Procedures for the adoption of acts and other provisions
Article 250	Article 293
Article 251	Article 294
Article 252 (repealed)	—
—	Article 295
Article 253	Article 296
Article 254	Article 297
PART SIX	PART SEVEN
GENERAL AND FINAL PROVISIONS	GENERAL AND FINAL PROVISIONS
Article 308	Article 352

1 Replaced, in substance, by Article 3 TEU.

2 Replaced, in substance, by Articles 3 to 6 TFEU.

3 Replaced, in substance, by Article 19 TEU.

4 Replaced, in substance, by Article 19, paragraph 2, first subparagraph, of the TEU.

5 The first sentence of the first subparagraph is replaced, in substance, by Article 19, paragraph 2, second subparagraph of the TEU.

CHARTER OF FUNDAMENTAL RIGHTS OF THE EUROPEAN UNION

NOTES

Date of publication in OJ: OJ C326, 26.10.2012, p 391. Note that the Charter is also reproduced in OJ C202, 7.6.2016.

Commencement: 1 December 2009.

This Charter, originally adopted in 2001, is printed as amended by the Treaty of Lisbon, to which it is annexed. As to the legal status of the Charter whilst the United Kingdom remains a member of the European Union, see Protocol No 30 to the Treaty on the Functioning of the European Union, at **[3.59]**.

Only those Articles potentially relevant to matters within the scope of this work are included. Articles omitted are not annotated.

UK withdrawal from the European Union: the European Union Withdrawal Act 2018, s 5(4) provides that this Charter will cease to form part of domestic law exit day (as defined by s 20 of the Act).

[3.62]

THE EUROPEAN PARLIAMENT, THE COUNCIL AND THE COMMISSION SOLEMNLY PROCLAIM THE FOLLOWING TEXT AS THE CHARTER OF FUNDAMENTAL RIGHTS OF THE EUROPEAN UNION.

PREAMBLE

The peoples of Europe, in creating an ever closer union among them, are resolved to share a peaceful future based on common values.

Conscious of its spiritual and moral heritage, the Union is founded on the indivisible, universal values of human dignity, freedom, equality and solidarity; it is based on the principles of democracy and the rule of law. It places the individual at the heart of its activities, by establishing the citizenship of the Union and by creating an area of freedom, security and justice.

The Union contributes to the preservation and to the development of these common values while respecting the diversity of the cultures and traditions of the peoples of Europe as well as the national identities of the Member States and the organisation of their public authorities at national, regional and local levels; it seeks to promote balanced and sustainable development and ensures free movement of persons, services, goods and capital, and the freedom of establishment.

To this end, it is necessary to strengthen the protection of fundamental rights in the light of changes in society, social progress and scientific and technological developments by making those rights more visible in a Charter.

This Charter reaffirms, with due regard for the powers and tasks of the Union and for the principle of subsidiarity, the rights as they result, in particular, from the constitutional traditions and international obligations common to the Member States, the European Convention for the Protection of Human Rights and Fundamental Freedoms, the Social Charters adopted by the Union and by the Council of Europe and the case-law of the Court of Justice of the European Union and of the European Court of Human Rights. In this context the Charter will be interpreted by the courts of the Union and the Member States with due regard to the explanations prepared under the authority of the Praesidium of the Convention which drafted the Charter and updated under the responsibility of the Praesidium of the European Convention.

Enjoyment of these rights entails responsibilities and duties with regard to other persons, to the human community and to future generations.

The Union therefore recognises the rights, freedoms and principles set out hereafter.

TITLE I DIGNITY

[3.63]

Article 1

Human dignity

Human dignity is inviolable. It must be respected and protected.

[3.64]

Article 5

Prohibition of slavery and forced labour

1. No one shall be held in slavery or servitude.
2. No one shall be required to perform forced or compulsory labour.
3. Trafficking in human beings is prohibited.

TITLE II FREEDOMS

[3.65]

Article 6

Right to liberty and security

Everyone has the right to liberty and security of person.

[3.66]

Article 7

Respect for private and family life

Everyone has the right to respect for his or her private and family life, home and communications.

[3.67]
Article 8
Protection of personal data

1. Everyone has the right to the protection of personal data concerning him or her.
2. Such data must be processed fairly for specified purposes and on the basis of the consent of the person concerned or some other legitimate basis laid down by law. Everyone has the right of access to data which has been collected concerning him or her, and the right to have it rectified.
3. Compliance with these rules shall be subject to control by an independent authority.

[3.68]
Article 9
Right to marry and right to found a family

The right to marry and the right to found a family shall be guaranteed in accordance with the national laws governing the exercise of these rights.

[3.69]
Article 10
Freedom of thought, conscience and religion

1. Everyone has the right to freedom of thought, conscience and religion. This right includes freedom to change religion or belief and freedom, either alone or in community with others and in public or in private, to manifest religion or belief, in worship, teaching, practice and observance.
2. The right to conscientious objection is recognised, in accordance with the national laws governing the exercise of this right.

[3.70]
Article 11
Freedom of expression and information

1. Everyone has the right to freedom of expression. This right shall include freedom to hold opinions and to receive and impart information and ideas without interference by public authority and regardless of frontiers.
2. The freedom and pluralism of the media shall be respected.

[3.71]
Article 12
Freedom of assembly and of association

1. Everyone has the right to freedom of peaceful assembly and to freedom of association at all levels, in particular in political, trade union and civic matters, which implies the right of everyone to form and to join trade unions for the protection of his or her interests.
2. Political parties at Union level contribute to expressing the political will of the citizens of the Union.

[3.72]
Article 13
Freedom of the arts and sciences

The arts and scientific research shall be free of constraint. Academic freedom shall be respected.

[3.73]
Article 14
Right to education

1. Everyone has the right to education and to have access to vocational and continuing training.
2. This right includes the possibility to receive free compulsory education.
3. The freedom to found educational establishments with due respect for democratic principles and the right of parents to ensure the education and teaching of their children in conformity with their religious, philosophical and pedagogical convictions shall be respected, in accordance with the national laws governing the exercise of such freedom and right.

[3.74]
Article 15
Freedom to choose an occupation and right to engage in work

1. Everyone has the right to engage in work and to pursue a freely chosen or accepted occupation.
2. Every citizen of the Union has the freedom to seek employment, to work, to exercise the right of establishment and to provide services in any Member State.
3. Nationals of third countries who are authorised to work in the territories of the Member States are entitled to working conditions equivalent to those of citizens of the Union.

[3.75]
Article 16
Freedom to conduct a business

The freedom to conduct a business in accordance with Union law and national laws and practices is recognised.

TITLE III EQUALITY

[3.76]
Article 20
Equality before the law
Everyone is equal before the law.

[3.77]
Article 21
Non-discrimination
1. Any discrimination based on any ground such as sex, race, colour, ethnic or social origin, genetic features, language, religion or belief, political or any other opinion, membership of a national minority, property, birth, disability, age or sexual orientation shall be prohibited.
2. Within the scope of application of the Treaties and without prejudice to any of their specific provisions, any discrimination on grounds of nationality shall be prohibited.

[3.78]
Article 22
Cultural, religious and linguistic diversity
The Union shall respect cultural, religious and linguistic diversity.

[3.79]
Article 23
Equality between women and men
Equality between women and men must be ensured in all areas, including employment, work and pay.

The principle of equality shall not prevent the maintenance or adoption of measures providing for specific advantages in favour of the under-represented sex.

[3.80]
Article 26
Integration of persons with disabilities
The Union recognises and respects the right of persons with disabilities to benefit from measures designed to ensure their independence, social and occupational integration and participation in the life of the community.

TITLE IV SOLIDARITY

[3.81]
Article 27
Workers' right to information and consultation within the undertaking
Workers or their representatives must, at the appropriate levels, be guaranteed information and consultation in good time in the cases and under the conditions provided for by Union law and national laws and practices.

[3.82]
Article 28
Right of collective bargaining and action
Workers and employers, or their respective organisations, have, in accordance with Union law and national laws and practices, the right to negotiate and conclude collective agreements at the appropriate levels and, in cases of conflicts of interest, to take collective action to defend their interests, including strike action.

[3.83]
Article 29
Right of access to placement services
Everyone has the right of access to a free placement service.

[3.84]
Article 30
Protection in the event of unjustified dismissal
Every worker has the right to protection against unjustified dismissal, in accordance with Union law and national laws and practices.

[3.85]
Article 31
Fair and just working conditions
1. Every worker has the right to working conditions which respect his or her health, safety and dignity.
2. Every worker has the right to limitation of maximum working hours, to daily and weekly rest periods and to an annual period of paid leave.

[3.86]
Article 32
Prohibition of child labour and protection of young people at work
The employment of children is prohibited. The minimum age of admission to employment may not be lower than the minimum school-leaving age, without prejudice to such rules as may be more favourable

to young people and except for limited derogations.

Young people admitted to work must have working conditions appropriate to their age and be protected against economic exploitation and any work likely to harm their safety, health or physical, mental, moral or social development or to interfere with their education.

[3.87]
Article 33
Family and professional life

1. The family shall enjoy legal, economic and social protection.
2. To reconcile family and professional life, everyone shall have the right to protection from dismissal for a reason connected with maternity and the right to paid maternity leave and to parental leave following the birth or adoption of a child.

TITLE VI JUSTICE

[3.88]
Article 47
Right to an effective remedy and to a fair trial

Everyone whose rights and freedoms guaranteed by the law of the Union are violated has the right to an effective remedy before a tribunal in compliance with the conditions laid down in this Article.

Everyone is entitled to a fair and public hearing within a reasonable time by an independent and impartial tribunal previously established by law. Everyone shall have the possibility of being advised, defended and represented.

Legal aid shall be made available to those who lack sufficient resources in so far as such aid is necessary to ensure effective access to justice.

TITLE VII GENERAL PROVISIONS GOVERNING THE INTERPRETATION AND APPLICATION OF THE CHARTER

[3.89]
Article 51
Field of application

1. The provisions of this Charter are addressed to the institutions, bodies, offices and agencies of the Union with due regard for the principle of subsidiarity and to the Member States only when they are implementing Union law. They shall therefore respect the rights, observe the principles and promote the application thereof in accordance with their respective powers and respecting the limits of the powers of the Union as conferred on it in the Treaties.
2. The Charter does not extend the field of application of Union law beyond the powers of the Union or establish any new power or task for the Union, or modify powers and tasks as defined in the Treaties.

[3.90]
Article 52
Scope and interpretation of rights and principles

1. Any limitation on the exercise of the rights and freedoms recognised by this Charter must be provided for by law and respect the essence of those rights and freedoms. Subject to the principle of proportionality, limitations may be made only if they are necessary and genuinely meet objectives of general interest recognised by the Union or the need to protect the rights and freedoms of others.
2. Rights recognised by this Charter for which provision is made in the Treaties shall be exercised under the conditions and within the limits defined by those Treaties.
3. In so far as this Charter contains rights which correspond to rights guaranteed by the Convention for the Protection of Human Rights and Fundamental Freedoms, the meaning and scope of those rights shall be the same as those laid down by the said Convention. This provision shall not prevent Union law providing more extensive protection.
4. In so far as this Charter recognises fundamental rights as they result from the constitutional traditions common to the Member States, those rights shall be interpreted in harmony with those traditions.
5. The provisions of this Charter which contain principles may be implemented by legislative and executive acts taken by institutions, bodies, offices and agencies of the Union, and by acts of Member States when they are implementing Union law, in the exercise of their respective powers. They shall be judicially cognisable only in the interpretation of such acts and in the ruling on their legality.
6. Full account shall be taken of national laws and practices as specified in this Charter.
7. The explanations drawn up as a way of providing guidance in the interpretation of this Charter shall be given due regard by the courts of the Union and of the Member States.

[3.91]
Article 53
Level of protection

Nothing in this Charter shall be interpreted as restricting or adversely affecting human rights and fundamental freedoms as recognised, in their respective fields of application, by Union law and international law and by international agreements to which the Union or all the Member States are party, including the European Convention for the Protection of Human Rights and Fundamental Freedoms, and by the Member States' constitutions.

[3.92]
Article 54
Prohibition of abuse of rights

Nothing in this Charter shall be interpreted as implying any right to engage in any activity or to perform any act aimed at the destruction of any of the rights and freedoms recognised in this Charter or at their limitation to a greater extent than is provided for herein.

B. REGULATIONS AND DIRECTIVES

NOTES

For the status and effect of Regulations and Directives printed in this section after exit day (as defined by the European Union Withdrawal Act 2018, s 20), see ss 2–5 of, and Sch 1 to, the 2018 Act at **[1.2240]–[1.2243]** and **[1.2253]**.

COUNCIL DIRECTIVE

(79/7/EEC)

of 19 December 1978

on the progressive implementation of the principle of equal treatment for men and women in matters of social security

[3.93]

NOTES

Date of publication in OJ: OJ L6, 10.1.1979, p 24.

This Order was implemented in the UK by the Social Security (Severe Disablement Allowance) Amendment Regulations 1993, SI 1993/3194 and the Social Security (Severe Disablement Allowance and Invalid Care Allowance) Amendment Regulations 1994, SI 1994/2556.

THE COUNCIL OF THE EUROPEAN COMMUNITIES,

Having regard to the Treaty establishing the European Economic Community, and in particular Article 235 thereof;

Having regard to the proposal from the Commission;[1]

Having regard to the opinion of the European Parliament;[2]

Having regard to the opinion of the Economic and Social Committee;[3]

Whereas Article 1(2) of Council Directive 76/207/EEC of 9 February 1976 on the implementation of the principle of equal treatment for men and women as regards access to employment, vocational training and promotion, and working conditions[4] provides that, with a view to ensuring the progressive implementation of the principle of equal treatment in matters of social security, the Council, acting on a proposal from the Commission, will adopt provisions defining its substance, its scope and the arrangements for its application; whereas the Treaty does not confer the specific powers required for this purpose;

Whereas the principle of equal treatment in matters of social security should be implemented in the first place in the statutory schemes which provide protection against the risks of sickness, invalidity, old age, accidents at work, occupational diseases and unemployment, and in social assistance in so far as it is intended to supplement or replace the abovementioned schemes;

Whereas the implementation of the principle of equal treatment in matters of social security does not prejudice the provisions relating to the protection of women on the ground of maternity; whereas, in this respect, Member States may adopt specific provisions for women to remove existing instances of unequal treatment,

NOTES

1 OJ C34, 11.2.77, p 3.

2 OJ C299, 12.12.77, p 13.

3 OJ C180, 28.7.77, p 36.

4 OJ L39, 14.2.76, p 40.

HAS ADOPTED THIS DIRECTIVE—

[3.94]
Article 1

The purpose of this Directive is the progressive implementation, in the field of social security and other elements of social protection provided for in Article 3, of the principle of equal treatment for men and women in matters of social security, hereinafter referred to as 'the principle of equal treatment'.

[3.95]
Article 2

This Directive shall apply to the working population—including self-employed persons, workers and self-employed persons whose activity is interrupted by illness, accident or involuntary unemployment and persons seeking employment—and to retired or invalided workers and self-employed persons.

[3.96]
Article 3

1. This Directive shall apply to—
   (a) statutory schemes which provide protection against the following risks—

— sickness,
— invalidity,
— old age,
— accidents at work and occupational diseases,
— unemployment;

(b) social assistance, in so far as it is intended to supplement or replace the schemes referred to in (a).

2. This Directive shall not apply to the provisions concerning survivors' benefits nor to those concerning family benefits, except in the case of family benefits granted by way of increases of benefits due in respect of the risks referred to in paragraph 1(a).

3. With a view to ensuring implementation of the principle of equal treatment in occupational schemes, the Council, acting on a proposal from the Commission, will adopt provisions defining its substance, its scope and the arrangements for its application.

[3.97]
Article 4

1. The principle of equal treatment means that there shall be no discrimination whatsoever on ground of sex either directly, or indirectly by reference in particular to marital or family status, in particular as concerns—

— the scope of the schemes and the conditions of access thereto,
— the obligation to contribute and the calculation of contributions,
— the calculation of benefits including increases due in respect of a spouse and for dependants and the conditions governing the duration and retention of entitlement to benefits.

2. The principle of equal treatment shall be without prejudice to the provisions relating to the protection of women on the grounds of maternity.

[3.98]
Article 5

Member States shall take the measures necessary to ensure that any laws, regulations and administrative provisions contrary to the principle of equal treatment are abolished.

[3.99]
Article 6

Member States shall introduce into their national legal systems such measures as are necessary to enable all persons who consider themselves wronged by failure to apply the principle of equal treatment to pursue their claims by judicial process, possibly after recourse to other competent authorities.

[3.100]
Article 7

1. This Directive shall be without prejudice to the right of Member States to exclude from its scope—

(a) the determination of pensionable age for the purposes of granting old-age and retirement pensions and the possible consequences thereof for other benefits;

(b) advantages in respect of old-age pension schemes granted to persons who have brought up children; the acquisition of benefit entitlements following periods of interruption of employment due to the bringing up of children;

(c) the granting of old-age or invalidity benefit entitlements by virtue of the derived entitlements of a wife;

(d) the granting of increases of long-term invalidity, old-age, accidents at work and occupational disease benefits for a dependent wife;

(e) the consequences of the exercise, before the adoption of this Directive, of a right of option not to acquire rights to incur obligations under a statutory scheme.

2. Member States shall periodically examine matters excluded under paragraph 1 in order to ascertain, in the light of social developments in the matter concerned, whether there is justification for maintaining the exclusions concerned.

[3.101]
Article 8

1. Member States shall bring into force the laws, regulations and administrative provisions necessary to comply with this Directive within six years of its notification. They shall immediately inform the Commission thereof.

2. Member States shall communicate to the Commission the text of laws, regulations and administrative provisions which they adopt in the field covered by this Directive, including measures adopted pursuant to Article 7(2).

They shall inform the Commission of their reasons for maintaining any existing provisions on the matters referred to in Article 7(1) and of the possibilities for reviewing them at a later date.

[3.102]
Article 9

Within seven years of notification of this Directive, Member States shall forward all information necessary to the Commission to enable it to draw up a report on the application of this Directive for submission to the Council and to propose such further measures as may be required for the implementation of the principle of equal treatment.

[3.103]
Article 10
This Directive is addressed to the Member States.

COUNCIL DIRECTIVE

(89/391/EEC)

of 12 June 1989

on the introduction of measures to encourage improvements in the safety and health of workers at work

[3.104]

NOTES

Date of publication in OJ: OJ L183, 29.6.1989, p 1. The text of this Directive incorporates the corrigendum published in OJ L275, 5.10.1990, p 42.

For the domestic implementation of this Directive see, in particular, the Management of Health and Safety at Work Regulations 1999, SI 1999/3242 at **[2.417]**, the Employment Rights Act 1996, ss 44, 100 at **[1.880]**, **[1.1007]**, and the Health and Safety (Consultation with Employees) Regulations 1996, SI 1996/1513 at **[2.239]**.

THE COUNCIL OF THE EUROPEAN COMMUNITIES,

Having regard to the Treaty establishing the European Economic Community, and in particular Article 118a thereof,

Having regard to the proposal from the Commission,[1] drawn up after consultation with the Advisory Committee on Safety, Hygiene and Health Protection at Work,

In cooperation with the European Parliament,[2]

Having regard to the opinion of the Economic and Social Committee,[3]

Whereas Article 118a of the Treaty provides that the Council shall adopt, by means of Directives, minimum requirements for encouraging improvements, especially in the working environment, to guarantee a better level of protection of the safety and health of workers;

Whereas this Directive does not justify any reduction in levels of protection already achieved in individual Member States, the Member State being committed, under the Treaty, to encouraging improvements in conditions in this area and to harmonising conditions while maintaining the improvements made;

Whereas it is known that workers can be exposed to the effects of dangerous environmental factors at the work place during the course of their working life;

Whereas, pursuant to Article 118a of the Treaty, such Directives must avoid imposing administrative, financial and legal constraints which would hold back the creation and development of small and medium-sized undertakings;

Whereas the communication from the Commission on its programme concerning safety, hygiene and health at work[4] provides for the adoption of Directives designed to guarantee the safety and health of workers;

Whereas the Council, in its resolution of 21 December 1987 on safety, hygiene and health at work,[5] took note of the Commission's intention to submit to the Council in the near future a Directive on the organisation of the safety and health of workers at the work place;

Whereas in February 1988 the European Parliament adopted four resolutions following the debate on the internal market and worker protection; whereas these resolutions specifically invited the Commission to draw up a framework Directive to serve as a basis for more specific Directives covering all the risks connected with safety and health at the work place;

Whereas Member States have a responsibility to encourage improvements in the safety and health of workers on their territory; whereas taking measures to protect the health and safety of workers at work also helps, in certain cases, to preserve the health and possibly the safety of persons residing with them;

Whereas Member States' legislative systems covering safety and health at the work place differ widely and need to be improved; whereas national provisions on the subject, which often include technical specifications and/or self-regulatory standards, may result in different levels of safety and health protection and allow competition at the expense of safety and health;

Whereas the incidence of accidents at work and occupational diseases is still too high; whereas preventive measures must be introduced or improved without delay in order to safeguard the safety and health of workers and ensure a higher degree of protection;

Whereas, in order to ensure an improved degree of protection, workers and/or their representatives must be informed of the risks to their safety and health and of the measures required to reduce or eliminate these risks; whereas they must also be in a position to contribute, by means of balanced participation in accordance with national laws and/or practices, to seeing that the necessary protective measures are taken;

Whereas information, dialogue and balanced participation on safety and health at work must be developed between employers and workers and/or their representatives by means of appropriate procedures and instruments, in accordance with national laws and/or practices;

Whereas the improvement of workers' safety, hygiene and health at work is an objective which should not be subordinated to purely economic considerations;

Whereas employers shall be obliged to keep themselves informed of the latest advances in technology and scientific findings concerning work-place design, account being taken of the inherent dangers in their undertaking, and to inform accordingly the workers' representatives exercising participation rights under this Directive, so as to be able to guarantee a better level of protection of workers' health and safety;

Whereas the provisions of this Directive apply, without prejudice to more stringent present or future Community provisions, to all risks, and in particular to those arising from the use at work of chemical, physical and biological agents covered by Directive 80/1107/EEC,[6] as last amended by Directive 88/642/EEC;[7]

Whereas, pursuant to Decision 74/325/EEC,[8] the Advisory Committee on Safety, Hygiene and Health Protection at Work is consulted by the Commission on the drafting of proposals in this field;

Whereas a Committee composed of members nominated by the Member States needs to be set up to assist the Commission in making the technical adaptations to the individual Directives provided for in this Directive.

NOTES

[1] OJ C141, 30.5.88, p 1.

[2] OJ C326, 19.12.88, p 102 and OJ C158, 26.6.89.

[3] OJ C175, 4.7.88, p 22.

[4] OJ C28, 3.2.88, p 3.

[5] OJ C28, 3.2.88, p 1.

[6] OJ L327, 3.12.80, p 8.

[7] OJ L356, 24.12.88, p 74.

[8] OJ L185, 9.7.74, p 15.

HAS ADOPTED THIS DIRECTIVE—

SECTION I GENERAL PROVISIONS

[3.105]
Article 1
Object

1. The object of this Directive is to introduce measures to encourage improvements in the safety and health of workers at work.

2. To that end it contains general principles concerning the prevention of occupational risks, the protection of safety and health, the elimination of risk and accident factors, the informing, consultation, balanced participation in accordance with national laws and/or practices and training of workers and their representatives, as well as general guidelines for the implementation of the said principles.

3. This Directive shall be without prejudice to existing or future national and Community provisions which are more favourable to protection of the safety and health of workers at work.

[3.106]
Article 2
Scope

1. This Directive shall apply to all sectors of activity, both public and private (industrial, agricultural, commercial, administrative, service, educational, cultural, leisure, etc).

2. This Directive shall not be applicable where characteristics peculiar to certain specific service activities, such as the armed forces or the police, or to certain specific activities in the civil protection services inevitably conflict with it.

In that event, the safety and health of workers must be ensured as far as possible in the light of the objectives of this Directive.

[3.107]
Article 3
Definitions

For the purposes of this Directive, the following terms shall have the following meanings—

(a) worker: any person employed by an employer, including trainees and apprentices but excluding domestic servants;

(b) employer: any natural or legal person who has an employment relationship with the worker and has responsibility for the undertaking and/or establishment;

(c) workers' representative with specific responsibility for the safety and health of workers: any person elected, chosen or designated in accordance with national laws and/or practices to represent workers where problems arise relating to the safety and health protection of workers at work;

(d) prevention: all the steps or measures taken or planned at all stages of work in the undertaking to prevent or reduce occupational risks.

[3.108]
Article 4

1. Member States shall take the necessary steps to ensure that employers, workers and workers' representatives are subject to the legal provisions necessary for the implementation of this Directive.

2. In particular, Member States shall ensure adequate controls and supervision.

SECTION II EMPLOYERS' OBLIGATIONS

[3.109]
Article 5
General provision

1. The employer shall have a duty to ensure the safety and health of workers in every aspect related to the work.
2. Where, pursuant to Article 7(3), an employer enlists competent external services or persons, this shall not discharge him from his responsibilities in this area.
3. The workers' obligations in the field of safety and health at work shall not affect the principle of the responsibility of the employer.
4. This Directive shall not restrict the option of Member States to provide for the exclusion or the limitation of employers' responsibility where occurrences are due to unusual and unforeseeable circumstances, beyond the employers' control, or to exceptional events, the consequences of which could not have been avoided despite the exercise of all due care.

Member States need not exercise the option referred to in the first sub-paragraph.

[3.110]
Article 6
General obligations on employers

1. Within the context of his responsibilities, the employer shall take the measures necessary for the safety and health protection of workers, including prevention of occupational risks and provision of information and training, as well as provision of the necessary organisation and means.

The employer shall be alert to the need to adjust these measures to take account of changing circumstances and aim to improve existing situations.

2. The employer shall implement the measures referred to in the first subparagraph of paragraph 1 on the basis of the following general principles of prevention—
   (a) avoiding risks;
   (b) evaluating the risks which cannot be avoided;
   (c) combating the risk at source;
   (d) adapting the work to the individual, especially as regards the design of work places, the choice of work equipment and the choice of working and production methods, with a view, in particular, to alleviating monotonous work and work at a predetermined work-rate and to reducing their effect on health;
   (e) adapting to technical progress;
   (f) replacing the dangerous by the non-dangerous or the less dangerous;
   (g) developing a coherent overall prevention policy which covers technology, organisation of work, working conditions, social relationships and the influence of factors related to the working environment;
   (h) giving collective protective measures priority over individual protective measures;
   (i) giving appropriate instructions to the workers.
3. Without prejudice to the other provisions of this Directive, the employers shall, taking into account the nature of the activities of the enterprise and/or establishment—
   (a) evaluate the risks to the safety and health of workers, *inter alia* in the choice of work equipment, the chemical substances or preparations used, and the fitting-out of work places.

   Subsequent to this evaluation and as necessary, the preventive measures and the working and production methods implemented by the employer must—
   — assure an improvement in the level of protection afforded to workers with regard to safety and health,
   — be integrated into all the activities of the undertaking and/or establishment and at all hierarchical levels;

   (b) where he entrusts tasks to a worker, take into consideration the worker's capabilities as regards health and safety;
   (c) ensure that the planning and introduction of new technologies are the subject of consultation with the workers and/or their representatives, as regards the consequences of the choice of equipment, the working conditions and the working environment for the safety and health of workers;
   (d) take appropriate steps to ensure that only workers who have received adequate instructions may have access to areas where there is serious and specific danger.
4. Without prejudice to the other provisions of this Directive, where several undertakings share a work place, the employers shall co-operate in implementing the safety, health and occupational hygiene provisions and, taking into account the nature of the activities, shall coordinate their actions in matters of the protection and prevention of occupational risks, and shall inform one another and their respective workers and/or workers' representatives of these risks.
5. Measures related to safety, hygiene and health at work may in no circumstances involve the workers in financial cost.

[3.111]
Article 7
Protective and preventive services

1. Without prejudice to the obligations referred to in Articles 5 and 6, the employer shall designate one or more workers to carry out activities related to the protection and prevention of occupational risks for the undertaking and/or establishment.

2. Designated workers may not be placed at any disadvantage because of their activities related to the protection and prevention of occupational risks.

Designated workers shall be allowed adequate time to enable them to fulfil their obligations arising from this Directive.

3. If such protective and preventive measures cannot be organised for lack of competent personnel in the undertaking and/or establishment, the employer shall enlist competent external services or persons.

4. Where the employer enlists such services or persons, he shall inform them of the factors known to affect, or suspected of affecting, the safety and health of the workers and they must have access to the information referred to in Article 10(2).

5. In all cases—

— the workers designated must have the necessary capabilities and the necessary means,

— the external services or persons consulted must have the necessary aptitudes and the necessary personal and professional means, and

— the workers designated and the external services or persons consulted must be sufficient in number

to deal with the organisation of protective and preventive measures, taking into account the size of the undertaking and/or establishment and/or the hazards to which the workers are exposed and their distribution throughout the entire undertaking and/or establishment.

6. The protection from, and prevention of, the health and safety risks which form the subject of this Article shall be the responsibility of one or more workers, of one service or of separate services whether from inside or outside the undertaking and/or establishment.

The worker(s) and/or agency(ies) must work together whenever necessary.

7. Member States may define, in the light of the nature of the activities and size of the undertakings, the categories or undertakings in which the employer, provided he is competent, may himself take responsibility for the measures referred to in paragraph 1.

8. Member States shall define the necessary capabilities and aptitudes referred to in paragraph 5.

They may determine the sufficient number referred to in paragraph 5.

[3.112]
Article 8
First aid, fire-fighting and evacuation of workers, serious and imminent danger

1. The employer shall—

— take the necessary measures for first aid, fire-fighting and evacuation of workers, adapted to the nature of the activities and the size of the undertaking and/or establishment and taking into account other persons present;

— arrange any necessary contacts with external services, particularly as regards first aid, emergency medical care, rescue work and fire-fighting.

2. Pursuant to paragraph 1, the employer shall, *inter alia*, for first aid, fire-fighting and the evacuation of workers, designate the workers required to implement such measures.

The number of such workers, their training and the equipment available to them shall be adequate, taking account of the size and/or specific hazards of the undertaking and/or establishment.

3. The employer shall—

(a) as soon as possible, inform all workers who are, or may be, exposed to serious and imminent danger of the risk involved and of the steps taken or to be taken as regards protection;

(b) take action and give instructions to enable workers in the event of serious, imminent and unavoidable danger to stop work and/or immediately to leave the work place and proceed to a place of safety;

(c) save in exceptional cases for reasons duly substantiated, refrain from asking workers to resume work in a working situation where there is still a serious and imminent danger.

4. Workers who, in the event of serious, imminent and unavoidable danger, leave their workstation and/or a dangerous area may not be placed at any disadvantage because of their action and must be protected against any harmful and unjustified consequences, in accordance with national laws and/or practices.

5. The employer shall ensure that all workers are able, in the event of serious and imminent danger to their own safety and/or that of other persons, and where the immediate superior responsible cannot be contacted, to take the appropriate steps in the light of their knowledge and the technical means at their disposal, to avoid the consequences of such danger.

Their actions shall not place them at any disadvantage, unless they acted carelessly or there was negligence on their part.

[3.113]
Article 9
Various obligations on employers

1. The employer shall—

(a) be in possession of an assessment of the risks to safety and health at work, in including those facing groups of workers exposed to particular risks;

(b) decide on the protective measures to be taken and, if necessary, the protective equipment to be used;

(c) keep a list of occupational accidents resulting in a worker being unfit for work for more than three working days;

(d) draw up, for the responsible authorities and in accordance with national laws and/or practices, reports on occupational accidents suffered by his workers.

2. Member States shall define, in the light of the nature of the activities and size of the undertaking, the obligations to be met by the different categories of undertakings in respect of the drawing-up of the documents provided for in paragraph 1(a) and (b) and when preparing the documents provided for in paragraph 1(c) and (d).

[3.114]
Article 10
Worker information

1. The employer shall take appropriate measures so that workers and/or their representatives in the undertaking and/or establishment receive in accordance with national laws and/or practices which may take account, *inter alia*, of the size of the undertaking and/or establishment, all the necessary information concerning—

(a) the safety and health risks and protective and preventive measures and activities in respect of both the undertaking and/or establishment in general and each type of workstation and/or job;
(b) the measures taken pursuant to Article 8(2).

2. The employer shall take appropriate measures so that employers of workers from any outside undertakings and/or establishments engaged in work in his undertaking and/or establishment receive, in accordance with national laws and/or practices, adequate information concerning the points referred to in paragraph 1(a) and (b) which is to be provided to the workers in question.
3. The employer shall take appropriate measures so that workers with specific functions in protecting the safety and health of workers, or workers' representatives with specific responsibility for the safety and health of workers shall have access, to carry out their functions and in accordance with national laws and/or practices, to—

(a) the risk assessment and protective measures referred to in Article 9(1)(a) and (b);
(b) the list and reports referred to in Article 9(1)(c) and (d);
(c) the information yielded by protective and preventive measures, inspection agencies and bodies responsible for safety and health.

[3.115]
Article 11
Consultation and participation of workers

1. Employers shall consult workers and/or their representatives and allow them to take part in discussions on all questions relating to safety and health at work.

This presupposes—

— the consultation of workers,
— the right of workers and/or their representatives to make proposals,
— balanced participation in accordance with national laws and/or practices.

2. Workers or workers' representatives with specific responsibility for the safety and health of workers shall take part in a balanced way, in accordance with national laws and/or practices, or shall be consulted in advance and in good time by the employer with regard to—

(a) any measure which may substantially affect safety and health;
(b) the designation of workers referred to in Articles 7(1) and 8(2) and the activities referred to in Article 7(1);
(c) the information referred to in Articles 9(1) and 10;
(d) the enlistment, where appropriate, of the competent services or persons outside the undertaking and/or establishment, as referred to in Article 7(3);
(e) the planning and organisation of the training referred to in Article 12.

3. Workers' representatives with specific responsibility for the safety and health of workers shall have the right to ask the employer to take appropriate measures and to submit proposals to him to that end to mitigate hazards for workers and/or to remove sources of danger.
4. The workers referred to in paragraph 2 and the workers' representatives referred to in paragraphs 2 and 3 may not be placed at a disadvantage because of their respective activities referred to in paragraphs 2 and 3.
5. Employers must allow workers' representatives with specific responsibility for the safety and health of workers adequate time off work, without loss of pay, and provide them with the necessary means to enable such representatives to exercise their rights and functions deriving from this Directive.
6. Workers and/or their representatives are entitled to appeal, in accordance with national law and/or practice, to the authority responsible for safety and health protection at work if they consider that the measures taken and the means employed by the employer are inadequate for the purposes of ensuring safety and health at work.

Workers' representatives must be given the opportunity to submit their observations during inspection visits by the competent authority.

[3.116]
Article 12
Training of workers

1. The employer shall ensure that each worker receives adequate safety and health training, in particular in the form of information and instructions specific to his workstation or job—

— on recruitment,
— in the event of a transfer or a change of job,
— in the event of the introduction of new work equipment or a change in equipment,
— in the event of the introduction of any new technology.

The training shall be—

— adapted to take account of new or changed risks, and
— repeated periodically if necessary.

2. The employer shall ensure that workers from outside undertakings and/or establishments engaged in work in his undertaking and/or establishment have in fact received appropriate instructions regarding health and safety risks during their activities in his undertaking and/or establishment.

3. Workers' representatives with a specific role in protecting the safety and health of workers shall be entitled to appropriate training.

4. The training referred to in paragraphs 1 and 3 may not be at the workers' expense or at that of the workers' representatives.

The training referred to in paragraph 1 must take place during working hours.

The training referred to in paragraph 3 must take place during working hours or in accordance with national practice either within or outside the undertaking and/or the establishment.

SECTION III WORKERS' OBLIGATIONS

[3.117]
Article 13

1. It shall be the responsibility of each worker to take care as far as possible of his own safety and health and that of other persons affected by his acts or omissions at work in accordance with his training and the instructions given by his employer.

2. To this end, workers must in particular, in accordance with their training and the instructions given by their employer—

(a) make correct use of machinery, apparatus, tools, dangerous substances, transport equipment and other means of production;
(b) make correct use of the personal protective equipment supplied to them and, after use, return it to its proper place;
(c) refrain from disconnecting, changing or removing arbitrarily safety devices fitted, eg to machinery, apparatus, tools, plant and buildings, and use such safety devices correctly;
(d) immediately inform the employer and/or the workers with specific responsibility for the safety and health of workers of any work situation they have reasonable grounds for considering represents a serious and immediate danger to safety and health and of any shortcomings in the protection arrangements;
(e) co-operate, in accordance with national practice, with the employer and/or workers with specific responsibility for the safety and health of workers, for as long as may be necessary to enable any tasks or requirements imposed by the competent authority to protect the safety and health of workers at work to be carried out;
(f) co-operate, in accordance with national practice, with the employer and/or workers with specific responsibility for the safety and health of workers, for as long as may be necessary to enable the employer to ensure that the working environment and working conditions are safe and pose no risk to safety and health within their field of activity.

SECTION IV MISCELLANEOUS PROVISIONS

[3.118]
Article 14
Health surveillance

1. To ensure that workers receive health surveillance appropriate to the health and safety risks they incur at work, measures shall be introduced in accordance with national law and/or practices.

2. The measures referred to in paragraph 1 shall be such that each worker, if he so wishes, may receive health surveillance at regular intervals.

3. Health surveillance may be provided as part of a national health system.

[3.119]
Article 15
Risk groups

Particularly sensitive risk groups must be protected against the dangers which specifically affect them.

[3.120]
Article 16
Individual Directives—Amendments—General scope of this Directive

1. The Council, acting on a proposal from the Commission based on Article 118a of the Treaty, shall adopt individual Directives, *inter alia*, in the areas listed in the Annex.

2. This Directive and, without prejudice to the procedure referred to in Article 17 concerning technical adjustments, the individual Directives may be amended in accordance with the procedure provided for in Article 118a of the Treaty.

3. The provisions of this Directive shall apply in full to all the areas covered by the individual Directives, without prejudice to more stringent and/or specific provisions contained in these individual Directives.

NOTES

Article 118a: see now Art 154 at **[3.31]**.

[3.121]
[Article 17
Committee procedure

1. The Commission shall be assisted by a committee to make purely technical adjustments to the individual directives provided for in Article 16(1) in order to take account of:

(a) the adoption of directives in the field of technical harmonisation and standardisation;

(b) technical progress, changes in international regulations or specifications and new findings.

Those measures, designed to amend non-essential elements of the individual directives, shall be adopted in accordance with the regulatory procedure with scrutiny referred to in paragraph 2. On imperative grounds of urgency, the Commission may have recourse to the urgency procedure referred to in paragraph 3.

2. Where reference is made to this paragraph, Article 5a(1) to (4) and Article 7 of Decision 1999/468/EC shall apply, having regard to the provisions of Article 8 thereof.

3. Where reference is made to this paragraph, Article 5a(1), (2), (4) and (6) and Article 7 of Decision 1999/468/EC shall apply, having regard to the provisions of Article 8 thereof.]

NOTES

Substituted by European Parliament and Council Regulation 1137/2008/EC, Art 1, Annex, para 2.

[3.122]
[Article 17a
Implementation reports

1. Every five years, the Member States shall submit a single report to the Commission on the practical implementation of this Directive and individual Directives within the meaning of Article 16(1), indicating the points of view of the social partners. The report shall assess the various points related to the practical implementation of the different Directives and, where appropriate and available, provide data disaggregated by gender.

2. The structure of the report, together with a questionnaire specifying its content, shall be defined by the Commission, in cooperation with the Advisory Committee on Safety and Health at Work.

The report shall include a general part on the provisions of this Directive relating to the common principles and points applicable to all of the Directives referred to in paragraph 1.

To complement the general part, specific chapters shall deal with implementation of the particular aspects of each Directive, including specific indicators, where available.

3. The Commission shall submit the structure of the report, together with the above-mentioned questionnaire specifying its content, to the Member States at least six months before the end of the period covered by the report. The report shall be transmitted to the Commission within 12 months of the end of the five-year period that it covers.

4. Using these reports as a basis, the Commission shall evaluate the implementation of the Directives concerned in terms of their relevance, of research and of new scientific knowledge in the various fields in question. It shall, within 36 months of the end of the five-year period, inform the European Parliament, the Council, the European Economic and Social Committee and the Advisory Committee on Safety and Health at Work of the results of this evaluation and, if necessary, of any initiatives to improve the operation of the regulatory framework.

5. The first report shall cover the period 2007 to 2012.]

NOTES

Inserted by European Parliament and Council Directive 2007/30/EC, Art 1.

[3.123]
Article 18
Final provisions

1. Member States shall bring into force the laws, regulations and administrative provisions necessary to comply with this Directive by 31 December 1992.

They shall forthwith inform the Commission thereof.

2. Member States shall communicate to the Commission the texts of the provisions of rational law which they have already adopted or adopt in the field covered by this Directive.

3, 4. . . .

NOTES

Paras 3, 4: repealed by European Parliament and Council Directive 2007/30/EC, Art 3(1).

[3.124]
Article 19

This Directive is addressed to the Member States.

ANNEX
LIST OF AREAS REFERRED TO IN ARTICLE 16(1)

[3.125]

— Work places

— Work equipment

— Personal protective equipment

— Work with visual display units

— Handling of heavy loads involving risk of back injury

— Temporary or mobile work sites

— Fisheries and agriculture.

COUNCIL DIRECTIVE

(91/533/EEC)

of 14 October 1991

on an employer's obligation to inform employees of the conditions applicable to the contract or employment relationship

[3.126]

NOTES

Date of publication in OJ: OJ L288, 18.10.1991, p 32.

There is no specific domestic legislation introduced to implement this Directive as its provisions were already reflected in what is now Part I of the Employment Rights Act 1996 (qv, at **[1.813]**–**[1.826]**).

See also *Harvey* AII(3).

THE COUNCIL OF THE EUROPEAN COMMUNITIES,

Having regard to the Treaty establishing the European Economic Community, and in particular Article 100 thereof,

Having regard to the proposal from the Commission,[1]

Having regard to the opinion of the European Parliament,[2]

Having regard to the opinion of the Economic and Social Committee,[3]

Whereas the development, in the Member States, of new forms of work has led to an increase in the number of types of employment relationship;

Whereas, faced with this development, certain Member States have considered it necessary to subject employment relationships to formal requirements; whereas these provisions are designed to provide employees with improved protection against possible infringements of their rights and to create greater transparency on the labour market;

Whereas the relevant legislation of the Member States differs considerably on such fundamental points as the requirement to inform employees in writing of the main terms of the contract or employment relationship;

Whereas differences in the legislation of Member States may have a direct effect on the operation of the common market;

Whereas Article 117 of the Treaty provides for the Member States to agree upon the need to promote improved working conditions and an improved standard of living for workers, so as to make possible their harmonisation while the improvement is being maintained;

Whereas point 9 of the Community Charter of Fundamental Social Rights for Workers, adopted at the Strasbourg European Council on 9 December 1989 by the Heads of State and Government of 11 Member States, states—

'The conditions of employment of every worker of the European Community shall be stipulated in laws, a collective agreement or a contract of employment, according to arrangements applying in each country.';

Whereas it is necessary to establish at Community level the general requirement that every employee must be provided with a document containing information on the essential elements of his contract or employment relationship;

Whereas, in view of the need to maintain a certain degree of flexibility in employment relationships, Member States should be able to exclude certain limited cases of employment relationship from this Directive's scope of application;

Whereas the obligation to provide information may be met by means of a written contract, a letter of appointment or one or more other documents or, if they are lacking, a written statement signed by the employer;

Whereas, in the case of expatriation of the employee, the latter must, in addition to the main terms of this contract or employment relationship, be supplied with relevant information connected with his secondment;

Whereas, in order to protect the interests of employees with regard to obtaining a document, any change in the main terms of the contract or employment relationship must be communicated to them in writing;

Whereas it is necessary for Member States to guarantee that employees can claim the rights conferred on them by this Directive;

Whereas Member States are to adopt the laws, regulations and legislative provisions necessary to comply with this Directive or are to ensure that both sides of industry set up the necessary provisions by agreement, with Member States being obliged to take the necessary steps enabling them at all times to guarantee the results imposed by this Directive,

NOTES

[1] OJ C24, 31.1.1991, p 3.

[2] OJ C240, 16.9.1991, p 21.

[3] OJ C159, 17.6.1991, p 32.

HAS ADOPTED THIS DIRECTIVE—

[3.127]
Article 1
Scope

1. This Directive shall apply to every paid employee having a contract or employment relationship defined by the law in force in a Member State and/or governed by the law in force in a Member State.

2. Member States may provide that this Directive shall not apply to employees having a contract or employment relationship—

(a) with a total duration not exceeding one month, and/or
with a working week not exceeding eight hours; or

(b) of a casual and/or specific nature provided, in these cases, that its non-application is justified by objective considerations.

[3.128]
Article 2
Obligation to provide information

1. An employer shall be obliged to notify an employee to whom this Directive applies, hereinafter referred to as 'the employee', of the essential aspects of the contract or employment relationship.

2. The information referred to in paragraph 1 shall cover at least the following—

(a) the identities of the parties;

(b) the place of work; where there is no fixed or main place of work, the principle that the employee is employed at various places and the registered place of business or, where appropriate, the domicile of the employer;

(c)

(i) the title, grade, nature or category of the work for which the employee is employed; or

(ii) a brief specification or description of the work;

(d) the date of commencement of the contract or employment relationship;

(e) in the case of a temporary contract or employment relationship, the expected duration thereof;

(f) the amount of paid leave to which the employee is entitled or, where this cannot be indicated when the information is given, the procedures for allocating and determining such leave;

(g) the length of the periods of notice to be observed by the employer and the employee should their contract or employment relationship be terminated or, where this cannot be indicated when the information is given, the method for determining such periods of notice;

(h) the initial basic amount, the other component elements and the frequency of payment of the remuneration to which the employee is entitled;

(i) the length of the employee's normal working day or week;

(j) where appropriate—

(i) the collective agreements governing the employee's conditions of work; or

(ii) in the case of collective agreements concluded outside the business by special joint bodies or institutions, the name of the competent body or joint institution within which the agreements were concluded.

3. The information referred to in paragraph 2(f), (g), (h) and (i) may, where appropriate, be given in the form of a reference to the laws, regulations and administrative or statutory provisions or collective agreements governing those particular points.

[3.129]
Article 3
Means of information

1. The information referred to in Article 2(2) may be given to the employee, not later than two months after the commencement of employment, in the form of—

(a) a written contract of employment; and/or

(b) a letter of engagement; and/or

(c) one or more other written documents, where one of these documents contains at least all the information referred to in Article 2(2)(a), (b), (c), (d), (h) and (i).

2. Where none of the documents referred to in paragraph 1 is handed over to the employee within the prescribed period, the employer shall be obliged to give the employee, not later than two months after the commencement of employment, a written declaration signed by the employer and containing at least the information referred to in Article 2(2).

Where the document(s) referred to in paragraph 1 contain only part of the information required, the written declaration provided for in the first subparagraph of this paragraph shall cover the remaining information.

3. Where the contract or employment relationship comes to an end before expiry of a period of two months as from the date of the start of work, the information provided for in Article 2 and in this Article must be made available to the employee by the end of this period at the latest.

[3.130]
Article 4
Expatriate employees

1. Where an employee is required to work in a country or countries other than the Member State whose law and/or practice governs the contract or employment relationship, the document(s) referred to in Article 3 must be in his/her possession before his/her departure and must include at least the following additional information—

(a) the duration of the employment abroad;
(b) the currency to be used for the payment of remuneration;
(c) where appropriate, the benefits in cash or kind attendant on the employment abroad;
(d) where appropriate, the conditions governing the employee's repatriation.

2. The information referred to in paragraph 1(b) and (c) may, where appropriate, be given in the form of a reference to the laws, regulations and administrative or statutory provisions or collective agreements governing those particular points.

3. Paragraphs 1 and 2 shall not apply if the duration of the employment outside the country whose law and/or practice governs the contract or employment relationship is one month or less.

[3.131]
Article 5
Modification of aspects of the contract or employment relationship

1. Any change in the details referred to in Articles 2(2) and 4(1) must be the subject of a written document to be given by the employer to the employee at the earliest opportunity and not later than one month after the date of entry into effect of the change in question.

2. The written document referred to in paragraph 1 shall not be compulsory in the event of a change in the laws, regulations and administrative or statutory provisions or collective agreements cited in the documents referred to in Article 3, supplemented, where appropriate, pursuant to Article 4(1).

[3.132]
Article 6
Form and proof of the existence of a contract or employment relationship and procedural rules

This Directive shall be without prejudice to national law and practice concerning—

— the form of the contract or employment relationship,
— proof as regards the existence and content of a contract or employment relationship,
— the relevant procedural rules.

[3.133]
Article 7
More favourable provisions

This Directive shall not affect Member States' prerogative to apply or to introduce laws, regulations or administrative provisions which are more favourable to employees or to encourage or permit the application of agreements which are more favourable to employees.

[3.134]
Article 8
Defence of rights

1. Member States shall introduce into their national legal systems such measures as are necessary to enable all employees who consider themselves wronged by failure to comply with the obligations arising from this Directive to pursue their claims by judicial process after possible recourse to other competent authorities.

2. Member States may provide that access to the means of redress referred to in paragraph 1 are subject to the notification of the employer by the employee and the failure by the employer to reply within 15 days of notification.

However, the formality of prior notification may in no case be required in the cases referred to in Article 4, neither for workers with a temporary contract or employment relationship, nor for employees not covered by a collective agreement or by collective agreements relating to the employment relationship.

[3.135]
Article 9
Final provisions

1. Member States shall adopt the laws, regulations and administrative provisions necessary to comply with this Directive no later than 30 June 1993 or shall ensure by that date that the employers' and workers' representatives introduce the required provisions by way of agreement, the Member States being obliged to take the necessary steps enabling them at all times to guarantee the results imposed by this Directive.

They shall forthwith inform the Commission thereof.

2. Member States shall take the necessary measures to ensure that, in the case of employment relationships in existence upon entry into force of the provisions that they adopt, the employer gives the employee, on request, within two months of receiving that request; any of the documents referred to in Article 3, supplemented, where appropriate, pursuant to Article 4(1).

3. When Member States adopt the measures referred to in paragraph 1, such measures shall contain a reference to this Directive or shall be accompanied by such reference on the occasion of their official publication. The methods of making such a reference shall be laid down by the Member States.
4. Member States shall forthwith inform the Commission of the measures they take to implement this Directive.

[3.136]
Article 10
This Directive is addressed to the Member States.

COUNCIL DIRECTIVE

(92/85/EEC)

of 19 October 1992

on the introduction of measures to encourage improvements in the safety and health of pregnant workers and workers who have recently given birth or are breastfeeding (tenth individual Directive within the meaning of Article 16(1) of Directive 89/391)

[3.137]
NOTES

Date of publication in OJ: OJ L348, 28.11.1992, p 1.

For the domestic implementation of this Directive see, in particular, the Employment Rights Act 1996, ss 66–75 at **[1.947]** et seq; the Management of Health and Safety at Work Regulations 1999, SI 1999/3242, regs 16–18 at **[2.432]**–**[2.436]**; and the Social Security Contributions and Benefits Act 1992, Pt XII, at **[1.212]**, and Regulations made thereunder.

See also *Harvey* J(2), (3), (4), (5), (6).

THE COUNCIL OF THE EUROPEAN COMMUNITIES,

Having regard to the Treaty establishing the European Economic Community, and in particular Article 118a thereof,

Having regard to the proposal from the Commission, drawn up after consultation with the Advisory Committee on Safety, Hygiene and Health Protection at work,[1]

In cooperation with the European Parliament,[2]

Having regard to the opinion of the Economic and Social Committee,[3]

Whereas Article 118a of the Treaty provides that the Council shall adopt, by means of directives, minimum requirements for encouraging improvements, especially in the working environment, to protect the safety and health of workers;

Whereas this Directive does not justify any reduction in levels of protection already achieved in individual Member States, the Member States being committed, under the Treaty, to encouraging improvements in conditions in this area and to harmonizing conditions while maintaining the improvements made;

Whereas, under the terms of Article 118a of the Treaty, the said directives are to avoid imposing administrative, financial and legal constraints in a way which would hold back the creation and development of small and medium-sized undertakings;

Whereas, pursuant to Decision 74/325/EEC,[4] as last amended by the 1985 Act of Accession, the Advisory Committee on Safety, Hygiene and Health Protection at Work is consulted by the Commission on the drafting of proposals in this field;

Whereas the Community Charter of the fundamental social rights of workers, adopted at the Strasbourg European Council on 9 December 1989 by the Heads of State or Government of 11 Member States, lays down, in paragraph 19 in particular, that—

'Every worker must enjoy satisfactory health and safety conditions in his working environment. Appropriate measures must be taken in order to achieve further harmonization of conditions in this area while maintaining the improvements made';

Whereas the Commission, in its action programme for the implementation of the Community Charter of the fundamental social rights of workers, has included among its aims the adoption by the Council of a Directive on the protection of pregnant women at work;

Whereas Article 15 of Council Directive 89/391/EEC of 12 June 1989 on the introduction of measures to encourage improvements in the safety and health of workers at work[5] provides that particularly sensitive risk groups must be protected against the dangers which specifically affect them;

Whereas pregnant workers, workers who have been recently given birth or who are breastfeeding must be considered a specific risk group in many respects, and measures must be taken with regard to their safety and health;

Whereas the protection of the safety and health of pregnant workers, workers who have recently given birth or workers who are breastfeeding should not treat women on the labour market unfavourably nor work to the detriment of directives concerning equal treatment for men and women;

Whereas some types of activities may pose a specific risk, for pregnant workers, workers who have recently given birth or workers who are breastfeeding, of exposure to dangerous agents, processes or working conditions; whereas such risks must therefore be assessed and the result of such assessment communicated to female workers and/or their representatives;

Whereas, further, should the result of this assessment reveal the existence of a risk to the safety or health of the female worker, provision must be made for such worker to be protected;

Whereas pregnant workers and workers who are breastfeeding must not engage in activities which have been assessed as revealing a risk of exposure, jeopardising safety and health, to certain particularly dangerous agents or working conditions;

Whereas provision should be made for pregnant workers, workers who have recently given birth or workers who are breastfeeding not to be required to work at night where such provision is necessary from the point of view of their safety and health;

Whereas the vulnerability of pregnant workers, workers who have recently given birth or who are breastfeeding makes it necessary for them to be granted the right to maternity leave of at least 14 continuous weeks, allocated before and/or after confinement, and renders necessary the compulsory nature of maternity leave of at least two weeks, allocated before and/or after confinement;

Whereas the risk of dismissal for reasons associated with their condition may have harmful effects on the physical and mental state of pregnant workers, workers who have recently given birth or who are breastfeeding; whereas provision should be made for such dismissal to be prohibited;

Whereas measures for the organization of work concerning the protection of the health of pregnant workers, workers who have recently given birth or workers who are breastfeeding would serve no purpose unless accompanied by the maintenance of rights linked to the employment contract, including maintenance of payment and/or entitlement to an adequate allowance;

Whereas, moreover, provision concerning maternity leave would also serve no purpose unless accompanied by the maintenance of rights linked to the employment contract and/or entitlement to an adequate allowance;

Whereas the concept of an adequate allowance in the case of maternity leave must be regarded as a technical point of reference with a view to fixing the minimum level of protection and should in no circumstances be interpreted as suggesting an analogy between pregnancy and illness,

NOTES

1 OJ C281, 9.11.90, p 3; and OJ C25, 1.2.91, p 9.

2 OJ C19, 28.1.91, p 177; and OJ C150, 15.6.92, p 99.

3 OJ C41, 18.2.91, p 29.

4 OJ L185, 9.7.74, p 15.

5 OJ L183, 29.6.89, p 1.

HAS ADOPTED THIS DIRECTIVE—

SECTION I PURPOSE AND DEFINITIONS

[3.138]
Article 1
Purpose

1. The purpose of this Directive, which is the tenth individual Directive within the meaning of Article 16(1) of Directive 89/391/EEC, is to implement measures to encourage improvements in the safety and health at work of pregnant workers and workers who have recently given birth or who are breastfeeding.

2. The provisions of Directive 89/391/EEC, except for Article 2(2) thereof, shall apply in full to the whole area covered by paragraph 1, without prejudice to any more stringent and/or specific provisions contained in this Directive.

3. This Directive may not have the effect of reducing the level of protection afforded to pregnant workers, workers who have recently given birth or who are breastfeeding as compared with the situation which exists in each Member State on the date on which this Directive is adopted.

[3.139]
Article 2
Definitions

For the purposes of this Directive—

(a) *pregnant worker* shall mean a pregnant worker who informs her employer of her condition, in accordance with national legislation and/or national practice;

(b) *worker who has recently given birth* shall mean a worker who has recently given birth within the meaning of national legislation and/or national practice and who informs her employer of her condition, in accordance with that legislation and/or practice;

(c) *worker who is breastfeeding* shall mean a worker who is breastfeeding within the meaning of national legislation and/or national practice and who informs her employer of her condition, in accordance with that legislation and/or practice.

SECTION II GENERAL PROVISIONS

[3.140]
Article 3
Guidelines

1. In consultation with the Member States and assisted by the Advisory Committee on Safety, Hygiene and Health Protection at Work, the Commission shall draw up guidelines on the assessment of the chemical, physical and biological agents and industrial process considered hazardous for the safety or health of workers within the meaning of Article 2.

The guidelines referred to in the first subparagraph shall also cover movements and postures, mental and physical fatigue and other types of physical and mental stress connected with the work done by workers within the meaning of Article 2.

2. The purpose of the guidelines referred to in paragraph 1 is to serve as a basis for the assessment referred to in Article 4(1).

To this end, Member States shall bring these guidelines to the attention of all employers and all female workers and/or their representatives in the respective Member State.

[3.141]
Article 4
Assessment and information

1. For all activities liable to involve a specific risk of exposure to the agents, processes or working conditions of which a non-exhaustive list is given in Annex 1, the employer shall assess the nature, degree and duration of exposure, in the undertaking and/or establishment concerned, or workers within the meaning of Article 2, either directly or by way of the protective and preventative services referred to in Article 7 of Directive 89/391/EEC, in order to—

— assess any risks to the safety or health and any possible effect on the pregnancies or breastfeeding of workers within the meaning of Article 2,
— decide what measures should be taken.

2. Without prejudice to Article 10 of Directive 89/391/EEC, workers within the meaning of Article 2 and workers likely to be in one of the situations referred to in Article 2 in the undertaking and/or establishment concerned and/or their representatives shall be informed of the results of the assessment referred to in paragraph 1 and of all measures to be taken concerning health and safety at work.

[3.142]
Article 5
Action further to the results of the assessment

1. Without prejudice to Article 6 of Directive 89/391/EEC, if the results of the assessment referred to in Article 4(1) reveal a risk to the safety or health or an effect on the pregnancy or breastfeeding of a worker within the meaning of Article 2, the employer shall take the necessary measures to ensure that, by temporarily adjusting the working conditions and/or the working hours of the worker concerned, the exposure of that worker to such risks is avoided.

2. If the adjustment of her working conditions and/or working hours is not technically and/or objectively feasible, or cannot reasonably be required on duly substantiated grounds, the employer shall take the necessary measures to move the worker concerned to another job.

3. If moving her to another job is not technically and/or objectively feasible or cannot reasonably be required on duly substantiated grounds, the worker concerned shall be granted leave in accordance with national legislation and/or national practice for the whole of the period necessary to protect her safety or health.

4. The provisions of this Article shall apply *mutatis mutandis* to the case where a worker pursuing an activity which is forbidden pursuant to Article 6 becomes pregnant or starts breastfeeding and informs her employer thereof.

[3.143]
Article 6
Cases in which exposure is prohibited

In addition to the general provisions concerning the protection of workers, in particular those relating to the limit values for occupational exposure—

1. pregnant workers within the meaning of Article 2(a) may under no circumstances be obliged to perform duties for which the assessment has revealed a risk of exposure, which would jeopardize safety or health, to the agents and working conditions listed in Annex II, Section A;
2. workers who are breastfeeding, within the meaning of Article 2(c), may under no circumstances be obliged to perform duties for which the assessment has revealed a risk of exposure, which would jeopardize safety or health, to the agents and working conditions listed in Annex II, Section B.

[3.144]
Article 7
Night work

1. Member States shall take the necessary measures to ensure that workers referred to in Article 2 are not obliged to perform night work during their pregnancy and for a period following childbirth which shall be determined by the national authority competent for safety and health, subject to submission, in accordance with the procedures laid down by the Member States, of a medical certificate stating that this is necessary for the safety or health of the worker concerned.

2. The measures referred to in paragraph 1 must entail the possibility, in accordance with national legislation and/or national practice, of

(a) transfer to daytime work; or

(b) leave from work or extension of maternity leave where such a transfer is not technically and/or objectively feasible or cannot reasonably be required on duly substantiated grounds.

[3.145]
Article 8
Maternity leave

1. Member States shall take the necessary measures to ensure that workers within the meaning of Article 2 are entitled to a continuous period of maternity leave of at least 14 weeks allocated before and/or after confinement in accordance with national legislation and/or practice.

2. The maternity leave stipulated in paragraph 1 must include compulsory maternity leave of at least two weeks allocated before and/or after confinement in accordance with national legislation and/or practice.

[3.146]
Article 9
Time off for ante-natal examinations

Member States shall take the necessary measures to ensure that pregnant workers within the meaning of Article 2(a) are entitled to, in accordance with national legislation and/or practice, time off, without loss of pay, in order to attend ante-natal examinations, if such examinations have to take place during working hours.

[3.147]
Article 10
Prohibition of dismissal

In order to guarantee workers, within the meaning of Article 2, the exercise of their health and safety protection rights as recognized under this Article, it shall be provided that—

1. Member States shall take the necessary measures to prohibit the dismissal of workers, within the meaning of Article 2, during the period from the beginning of their pregnancy to the end of the maternity leave referred to in Article 8(1) save in exceptional cases not connected with their condition which are permitted under national legislation and/or practice and, where applicable, provided that the competent authority has given its consent;
2. if a worker, within the meaning of Article 2, is dismissed during the period referred to in point 1, the employer must cite duly substantiated grounds for her dismissal in writing;
3. Member States shall take the necessary measures to protect workers, within the meaning of Article 2, from consequences of dismissal which is unlawful by virtue of point 1.

[3.148]
Article 11
Employment rights

In order to guarantee workers within the meaning of Article 2 the exercise of their health and safety protection rights as recognized in this Article, it shall be provided that—

1. in the cases referred to in Articles 5, 6 and 7, the employment rights relating to the employment contract, including the maintenance of a payment to, and/or entitlement to an adequate allowance for, workers within the meaning of Article 2, must be ensured in accordance with national legislation and/or national practice;
2. in the case referred to in Article 8, the following must be ensured—
   (a) the rights connected with the employment contract of workers within the meaning of Article 2, other than those referred to in point (b) below;
   (b) maintenance of a payment to, and/or entitlement to an adequate allowance for, workers within the meaning of Article 2;
3. the allowance referred to in point 2(b) shall be deemed adequate if it guarantees income at least equivalent to that which the worker concerned would receive in the event of a break in her activities on grounds connected with her state of health, subject to any ceiling laid down under national legislation;
4. Member States may make entitlement to pay or the allowance referred to in points 1 and 2(b) conditional upon the worker concerned fulfilling the conditions of eligibility for such benefits laid down under national legislation.

These conditions may under no circumstances provide for periods of previous employment in excess of 12 months immediately prior to the presumed date of confinement.

NOTES

The Council and Commission issued the following formal statement at the 1608th meeting of the Council on 19 October 1992 (OJ L348/92, p 8)—

THE COUNCIL AND THE COMMISSION stated that—

"In determining the level of the allowances referred to in Article 11(2)(b) and (3), reference shall be made, for purely technical reasons, to the allowance which a worker would receive in the event of a break in her activities on grounds connected with her state of health. Such a reference is not intended in any way to imply that pregnancy and childbirth be equated with sickness. The national social security legislation of all Member States provides for an allowance to be paid during an absence from work due to sickness. The link with such allowance in the chosen formulation is simply intended to serve as a concrete, fixed reference amount in all Member States for the determination of the minimum amount of maternity allowance payable. In so far as allowances are paid in individual Member States which exceed those provided for in the Directive, such allowances are, of course, retained. This is clear from Article 1(3) of the Directive.".

[3.149]
Article 12
Defence of rights

Member States shall introduce into their national legal systems such measures as are necessary to enable all workers who should themselves wronged by failure to comply with the obligations arising from this Directive to pursue their claims by judicial process (and/or, in accordance with national laws and/or practices) by recourse to other competent authorities.

NOTE

This Article is printed as in the *Official Journal*: presumably the word "consider" ought to have been inserted after the word "should".

[3.150]
Article 13
Amendments to the Annexes

1. Strictly technical adjustments to Annex I as a result of technical progress, changes in international regulations or specifications and new findings in the area covered by this Directive shall be adopted in accordance with the procedure laid down in Article 17 of Directive 89/391/EEC.
2. Annex II may be amended only in accordance with the procedure laid down in Article 118a of the Treaty.

NOTES

Article 118a: see now Art 154 at **[3.31]**.

[3.151]
Article 14
Final provisions

1. Member States shall bring into force the laws, regulations and administrative provisions necessary to comply with this Directive not later than two years after the adoption thereof or ensure, at the latest two years after the adoption of this Directive, that the two sides of industry introduce the requisite provisions by means of collective agreements, with Member States being required to make all the necessary provisions to enable them at all times to guarantee the results laid down by this Directive. They shall forthwith inform the Commission thereof.
2. When Member States adopt the measure referred to in paragraph 1, they shall contain a reference of this Directive or shall be accompanied by such reference on the occasion of their official publication. The methods of making such a reference shall be laid down by the Member States.
3. Member States shall communicate to the Commission the texts of the essential provisions of national law which they have already adopted or adopt in the field governed by this Directive.
4–6. . . .

NOTES

Paras 4–6: repealed by European Parliament and Council Directive 2007/30/EC, Art 3(11).

[3.152]
Article 15

The Directive is addressed to the Member States.

ANNEX I
NON-EXHAUSTIVE LIST OF AGENTS, PROCESSES AND WORKING CONDITIONS

(referred to in Article 4(1))

[3.153]
A. Agents

1. Physical agents where these are regarded as agents causing foetal lesions and/or likely to disrupt placental attachment, and in particular—

(a) shocks, vibration or movement;
(b) handling of loads entailing risks, particularly of a dorsolumbar nature;
(c) noise;
(d) ionising radiation;[1]
(e) non-ionising radiation;
(f) extremes of cold or heat;
(g) movements and postures, travelling—either inside or outside the establishment— mental and physical fatigue and other physical burdens connected with the activity of the worker within the meaning of Article 2 of the Directive.

[2. *Biological agents*

Biological agents of risk groups 2, 3 and 4 within the meaning of points 2, 3 and 4 of second paragraph of Article 2 of Directive 2000/54/EC of the European Parliament and of the Council,[2] in so far as it is known that such agents or the therapeutic measures necessitated by them endanger the health of pregnant women and the unborn child, and in so far as they do not yet appear in Annex II.]

3. Chemical agents

The following chemical agents in so far as it is known that they endanger the health of pregnant women and the unborn child and in so far as they do not yet appear in Annex II—

[(a) substances and mixtures which meet the criteria for classification under Regulation (EC) No 1272/2008 of the European Parliament and of the Council[3] in one or more of the following hazard classes and hazard categories with one or more of the following hazard statements, in so far as they do not yet appear in Annex II;

— germ cell mutagenicity, category 1A, 1B or 2 (H340, H341);

— carcinogenicity, category 1A, 1B or 2 (H350, H350i, H351);

— reproductive toxicity, category 1A, 1B or 2 or the additional category for effects on or via lactation (H360, H360D, H360FD, H360Fd, H360Df, H361, H361d, H361fd, H362);

— specific target organ toxicity after single exposure, category 1 or 2 (H370, H371).

(b) chemical agents in Annex I to Directive 2004/37/EC of the European Parliament and of the Council;[4]]

(c) mercury and mercury derivatives;

(d) antimitotic drugs;

(e) carbon monoxide;

(f) chemical agents of known and dangerous percutaneous absorption.

[B. Processes

Industrial processes listed in Annex I to Directive 2004/37/EC.]

C. Working Conditions

Underground mining work.

NOTES

Section A, point 2: substituted by European Parliament and Council Directive 2014/27/EU, Art 2(1)(a).

Section A, point 3: paras (a), (b) substituted by European Parliament and Council Directive 2014/27/EU, Art 2(1)(b).

Section B: substituted by European Parliament and Council Directive 2014/27/EU, Art 2(2).

1 See Directive 80/836/Euratom (OJ L246, 17.9.80, p 1).

2 Directive 2000/54/EC of the European Parliament and of the Council of 18 September 2000 on the protection of workers from risks related to exposure to biological agents at work (seventh individual directive within the meaning of Article 16(1) of Directive 89/391/EEC) (OJ L262, 17.10.2000, p 21).

3 Regulation (EC) No 1272/2008 of the European Parliament and of the Council of 16 December 2008 on classification, labelling and packaging of substances and mixtures, amending and repealing Directives 67/548/EEC and 1999/45/EC, and amending Regulation (EC) No 1907/2006 (OJ L353, 31.12.2008, p 1).

4 Directive 2004/37/EC of the European Parliament and of the Council of 29 April 2004 on the protection of workers from the risks related to exposure to carcinogens or mutagens at work (Sixth individual Directive within the meaning of Article 16(1) of Council Directive 89/391/EEC) (OJ L158, 30.4.2004, p 50).

ANNEX II
NON-EXHAUSTIVE LIST OF AGENTS AND WORKING CONDITIONS

(referred to in Article 6)

[3.154]

A. Pregnant workers within the meaning of Article 2(A)

1. Agents

(a) Physical agents

Work in hyperbaric atmosphere, eg pressurized enclosures and underwater diving.

(b) Biological agents

The following biological agents—

— toxoplasma,

— rubella virus,

unless the pregnant workers are proved to be adequately protected against such agents by immunization.

(c) Chemical agents

Lead and lead derivatives in so far as these agents are capable of being absorbed by the human organism.

2. Working conditions

Underground mining work.

B. Workers who are breastfeeding within the meaning of Article 2(C)

1. Agents

(a) Chemical agents

Lead and lead derivatives in so far as these agents are capable of being absorbed by the human organism.

2. Working conditions

Underground mining work.

COUNCIL DIRECTIVE

(94/33/EC)

of 22 June 1994

on the protection of young people at work

[3.155]

NOTES

Date of publication in OJ: OJ L 216, 20.8.1994, p 12.

For the domestic implementation of those parts of this Directive within the scope of this work see, in particular, the Working Time Regulations 1998, SI 1998/1833, at **[2.274]** et seq.

See *Harvey* AI(6), CI(1).

THE COUNCIL OF THE EUROPEAN UNION,

Having regard to the Treaty establishing the European Community, and in particular Article 118a thereof,

Having regard to the proposal from the Commission,[1]

Having regard to the opinion, of the Economic and Social Committee,[2]

Acting in accordance with the procedure referred to in Article 189c of the Treaty,[3]

Whereas Article 118a of the Treaty provides that the Council shall adopt, by means of directives, minimum requirements to encourage improvements, especially in the working environment, as regards the health and safety of workers;

Whereas, under that Article, such directives must avoid imposing administrative, financial and legal constraints in a way which would hold back the creation and development of small and medium-sized undertakings;

Whereas points 20 and 22 of the Community Charter of the Fundamental Social Rights of Workers, adopted by the European Council in Strasbourg on 9 December 1989, state that—

'20. Without prejudice to such rules as may be more favourable to young people, in particular those ensuring their preparation for work through vocational training, and subject to derogations limited to certain light work, the minimum employment age must not be lower than the minimum school-leaving age and, in any case, not lower than 15 years;

22. Appropriate measures must be taken to adjust labour regulations applicable to young workers so that their specific development and vocational training and access to employment needs are met.

The duration of work must, in particular, be limited—without it being possible to circumvent this limitation through recourse to overtime—and night work prohibited in the case of workers of under eighteen years of age, save in the case of certain jobs laid down in national legislation or regulations.';

Whereas account should be taken of the principles of the International Labour Organisation regarding the protection of young people at work, including those relating to the minimum age for access to employment or work;

Whereas, in its Resolution on child labour,[4] the European Parliament summarised the various aspects of work by young people and stressed its effects on their health, safety and physical and intellectual development, and pointed to the need to adopt a Directive harmonising national legislation in the field;

Whereas Article 15 of Council Directive 89/391/EEC of 12 June 1989 on the introduction of measures to encourage improvements in the safety and health of workers at work[5] provides that particularly sensitive risk groups must be protected against the dangers which specifically affect them;

Whereas children and adolescents must be considered specific risk groups, and measures must be taken with regard to their safety and health;

Whereas the vulnerability of children calls for Member States to prohibit their employment and ensure that the minimum working or employment age is not lower than the minimum age at which compulsory schooling as imposed by national law ends or 15 years in any event; whereas derogations from the prohibition on child labour may be admitted only in special cases and under the conditions stipulated in this Directive; whereas, under no circumstances, may such derogations be detrimental to regular school attendance or prevent children benefiting fully from their education;

Whereas, in view of the nature of the transition from childhood to adult life, work by adolescents should be strictly regulated and protected;

Whereas every employer should guarantee young people working conditions appropriate to their age;

Whereas employers should implement the measures necessary to protect the safety and health of young people on the basis on an assessment of work-related hazards to the young;

Whereas Member States should protect young people against any specific risks arising from their lack of experience, absence of awareness of existing or potential risks, or from their immaturity;

Whereas Member States should therefore prohibit the employment of young people for the work specified by this Directive;

Whereas the adoption of specific minimal requirements in respect of the organisation of working time is likely to improve working conditions for young people;

Whereas the maximum working time of young people should be strictly limited and night work by young people should be prohibited, with the exception of certain jobs specified by national legislation or rules;

Part 3 EU Materials

Whereas Member States should take the appropriate measures to ensure that the working time of adolescents receiving school education does not adversely affect their ability to benefit from that education;

Whereas time spent on training by young persons working under a theoretical and/or practical combined work/training scheme or an in-plant work-experience should be counted as working time;

Whereas, in order to ensure the safety and health of young people, the latter should be granted minimum daily, weekly and annual periods of rest and adequate breaks;

Whereas, with respect to the weekly rest period, due account should be taken of the diversity of cultural, ethnic, religious and other factors prevailing in the Member States; whereas in particular, it is ultimately for each Member State to decide whether Sunday should be included in the weekly rest period, and if so to what extent;

Whereas appropriate work experience may contribute to the aim of preparing young people for adult working and social life, provided it is ensured that any harm to their safety, health and development is avoided;

Whereas, although derogations from the bans and limitations imposed by this Directive would appear indispensable for certain activities or particular situations, applications thereof must not prejudice the principles underlying the established protection system;

Whereas this Directive constitutes a tangible step towards developing the social dimension of the internal market;

Whereas the application in practice of the system of protection laid down by this Directive will require that Member States implement a system of effective and proportionate measures;

Whereas the implementation of some provisions of this Directive poses particular problems for one Member State with regard to its system of protection for young people at work; whereas that Member State should therefore be allowed to refrain from implementing the relevant provisions for a suitable period,

NOTES

[1] OJ C84, 4.4.92, p 7.

[2] OJ C313, 30.11.92, p 70.

[3] Opinion of the European Parliament of 17 December 1992 (OJ C21, 25.1.93, p 167). Council Common Position of 23 November 1993 (not yet published in the Official Journal) and Decision of the European Parliament of 9 March 1994 (OJ C 91, 28.3.94, p 89).

[4] OJ C190, 20.7.87, p 44.

[5] OJ L183, 29.6.89, p 1.

HAS ADOPTED THIS DIRECTIVE—

SECTION I

[3.156]
Article 1
Purpose

1. Member States shall take the necessary measures to prohibit work by children.

They shall ensure, under the conditions laid down by this Directive, that the minimum working or employment age is not lower than the minimum age at which compulsory full-time schooling as imposed by national law ends or 15 years in any event.

2. Member States ensure that work by adolescents is strictly regulated and protected under the conditions laid down in this Directive.

3. Member States shall ensure in general that employers guarantee that young people have working conditions which suit their age.

They shall ensure that young people are protected against economic exploitation and against any work likely to harm their safety, health or physical, mental, moral or social development or to jeopardise their education.

[3.157]
Article 2
Scope

1. This Directive shall apply to any person under 18 years of age having an employment contract or an employment relationship defined by the law in force in a Member State and/or governed by the law in force in a Member State.

2. Member States may make legislative or regulatory provision for this Directive not to apply, within the limits and under the conditions which they set by legislative or regulatory provision, to occasional work or short-term work involving—

(a) domestic service in a private household, or

(b) work regarded as not being harmful, damaging or dangerous to young people in a family undertaking.

[3.158]
Article 3
Definitions

For the purposes of this Directive—

(a) 'young person' shall mean any person under 18 years of age referred to in Article 2(1);

(b) 'child' shall mean any young person of less than 15 years of age or who is still subject to compulsory full-time schooling under national law;

(c) 'adolescent' shall mean any young person of at least 15 years of age but less than 18 years of age who is no longer subject to compulsory full-time schooling under national law;

(d) 'light work' shall mean all work which, on account of the inherent nature of the tasks which it involves and the particular conditions under which they are performed—

(i) is not likely to be harmful to the safety, health or development of children, and

(ii) is not such as to be harmful to their attendance at school, their participation in vocational guidance or training programmes approved by the competent authority or their capacity to benefit from the instruction received;

(e) 'working time' shall mean any period during which the young person is at work, at the employer's disposal and carrying out his activity or duties in accordance with national legislation and/or practice;

(f) 'rest period' shall mean any period which is not working time.

[3.159]
Article 4
Prohibition of work by children

1. Member States shall adopt the measures necessary to prohibit work by children.

2. Taking into account the objectives set out in Article 1, Member States may make legislative or regulatory provision for the prohibition of work by children not to apply to—

(a) children pursuing the activities set out in Article 5;

(b) children of at least 14 years of age working under a combined work/ training scheme or an in-plant work-experience scheme, provided that such work is done in accordance with the conditions laid down by the competent authority;

(c) children of at least 14 years of age performing light work other than that covered by Article 5; light work other than that covered by Article 5 may, however, be performed by children of 13 years of age for a limited number of hours per week in the case of categories of work determined by national legislation.

3. Member States that make use of the opinion referred to in paragraph 2(c) shall determine, subject to the provisions of this Directive, the working conditions relating to the light work in question.

[3.160]
Article 5
Cultural or similar activities

1. The employment of children for the purposes of performance in cultural, artistic, sports or advertising activities shall be subject to prior authorisation to be given by the competent authority in individual cases.

2. Member States shall by legislative or regulatory provision lay down the working conditions for children in the cases referred to in paragraph 1 and the details of the prior authorisation procedure, on condition that the activities—

(i) are not likely to be harmful to the safety, health or development of children, and

(ii) are not such as to be harmful to their attendance at school, their participation in vocational guidance or training programmes approved by the competent authority or their capacity to benefit from the instruction received.

3. By way of derogation from the procedure laid down in paragraph 1, in the case of children of at least 13 years of age, Member States may authorise, by legislative or regulatory provision, in accordance with conditions which they shall determine, the employment of children for the purposes of performance in cultural, artistic, sports or advertising activities.

4. The Member States which have a specific authorisation system for modelling agencies with regard to the activities of children may retain that system.

SECTION II

[3.161]
Article 6
General obligations on employers

1. Without prejudice to Article 4 (1), the employer shall adopt the measures necessary to protect the safety and health of young people, taking particular account of the specific risks referred to in Article 7(1).

2. The employer shall implement the measures provided for in paragraph 1 on the basis of an assessment of the hazards to young people in connection with their work.

The assessment must be made before young people begin work and when there is any major change in working conditions and must pay particular attention to the following points—

(a) the fitting-out and layout of the workplace and the workstation;

(b) the nature, degree and duration of exposure to physical, biological and chemical agents;

(c) the form, range and use of work equipment, in particular agents, machines, apparatus and devices, and the way in which they are handled;

(d) the arrangement of work processes and operations and the way in which these are combined (organisation of work);

(e) the level of training and instruction given to young people.

Where this assessment shows that there is a risk to the safety, the physical or mental health or development of young people, an appropriate free assessment and monitoring of their health shall be provided at regular intervals without prejudice to Directive 89/391/EEC.

The free health assessment and monitoring may form part of a national health system.

3. The employer shall inform young people of possible risks and of all measures adopted concerning their safety and health.

Furthermore, he shall inform the legal representatives of children of possible risks and of all measures adopted concerning children's safety and health.

4. The employer shall involve the protective and preventive services referred to in Article 7 of Directive 89/391/EEC in the planning, implementation and monitoring of the safety and health conditions applicable to young people.

[3.162]
Article 7
Vulnerability of young people—Prohibition of work

1. Member States shall ensure that young people are protected from any specific risks to their safety, health and development which are a consequence of their lack of experience, of absence of awareness of existing or potential risks or of the fact that young people have not yet fully matured.

2. Without prejudice to Article 4(1), Member States shall to this end prohibit the employment of young people for—

(a) work which is objectively beyond their physical or psychological capacity;

(b) work involving harmful exposure to agents which are toxic, carcinogenic, cause heritable genetic damage, or harm to the unborn child or which in any other way chronically affect human health;

(c) work involving harmful exposure to radiation;

(d) work involving the risk of accidents which it may be assumed cannot be recognised or avoided by young persons owing to their insufficient attention to safety or lack of experience or training; or

(e) work in which there is a risk to health from extreme cold or heat, or from noise or vibration.

Work which is likely to entail specific risks for young people within the meaning of paragraph I includes—

— work involving harmful exposure to the physical, biological and chemical agents referred to in point I of the Annex, and

— processes and work referred to in point II of the Annex.

3. Member States may, by legislative or regulatory provision, authorise derogations from paragraph 2 in the case of adolescents where such derogations are indispensable for their vocational training, provided that protection of their safety and health is ensured by the fact that the work is performed under the supervision of a competent person within the meaning of Article 7 of Directive 89/391/EEC and provided that the protection afforded by that Directive is guaranteed.

SECTION III

[3.163]
Article 8
Working time

1. Member States which make use of the option in Article 4(2)(b) or (c) shall adopt the measures necessary to limit the working time of children to—

(a) eight hours a day and 40 hours a week for work performed under a combined work/training scheme or an in-plant work-experience scheme;

(b) two hours on a school day and 12 hours a week for work performed in term-time outside the hours fixed for school attendance, provided that this is not prohibited by national legislation and/or practice;

in no circumstances may the daily working time exceed seven hours; this limit may be raised to eight hours in the case of children who have reached the age of 15;

(c) seven hours a day and 35 hours a week for work performed during a period of at least a week when school is not operating; these limits may be raised to eight hours a day and 40 hours a week in the case of children who have reached the age of 15;

(d) seven hours a day and 35 hours a week for light work performed by children no longer subject to compulsory full-time schooling under national law.

2. Member States shall adopt the measures necessary to limit the working time of adolescents to eight hours a day and 40 hours a week.

3. The time spent on training by a young person working under a theoretical and/or practical combined work/training scheme or an in-plant work-experience scheme shall be counted as working time.

4. Where a young person is employed by more than one employer, working days and working time shall be cumulative.

5. Member States may, by legislative or regulatory provision, authorise derogations from paragraph 1(a) and paragraph 2 either by way of exception or where there are objective grounds for so doing.

Member States shall, by legislative or regulatory provision, determine the conditions, limits and procedure for implementing such derogations.

[3.164]
Article 9
Night work

1.

(a) Member States which make use of the option in Article 4(2)(b) or (c) shall adopt the measures necessary to prohibit work by children between 8 pm and 6 am.

(b) Member States shall adopt the measures necessary to prohibit work by adolescents either between 10 pm and 6 am or between 11 pm and 7 am.

2.

(a) Member States may, by legislative or regulatory provision, authorise work by adolescents in specific areas of activity during the period in which night work is prohibited as referred to in paragraph 1(b).

In that event, Member States shall take appropriate measures to ensure that the adolescent is supervised by an adult where such supervision is necessary for the adolescent's protection.

(b) If point (a) is applied, work shall continue to be prohibited between midnight and 4 am.

However, Member States may, by legislative or regulatory provision, authorise work by adolescents during the period in which night work is prohibited in the following cases, where there are objective grounds for so doing and provided that adolescents are allowed suitable compensatory rest time and that the objectives set out in Article 1 are not called into question—

— work performed in the shipping or fisheries sectors;
— work performed in the context of the armed forces or the police;
— work performed in hospitals or similar establishments;
— cultural, artistic, sports or advertising activities.

3. Prior to any assignment to night work and at regular intervals thereafter, adolescents shall be entitled to a free assessment of their health and capacities, unless the work they do during the period during which work is prohibited is of an exceptional nature.

[3.165]
Article 10
Rest period

1.

(a) Member States which make use of the option in Article 4(2), (b) or (c) shall adopt the measures necessary to ensure that, for each 24 hour period, children are entitled to a minimum rest period of 14 consecutive hours.

(b) Member States shall adopt the measures necessary to ensure that, for each 24-hour period, adolescents are entitled to a minimum rest period of 12 consecutive hours.

2. Member States shall adopt the measures necessary to ensure that, for each seven-day period—

— children in respect of whom they have made use of the option in Article 4(2)(b) or (c), and
— adolescents

are entitled to a minimum rest period of two days, which shall be consecutive if possible.

Where justified by technical or organisation reasons, the minimum rest period may be reduced, but may in no circumstances be less than 36 consecutive hours.

The minimum rest period referred to in the first and second subparagraphs shall in principle include Sunday.

3. Member States may, by legislative or regulatory provision, provide for the minimum rest periods referred to in paragraphs 1 and 2 to be interrupted in the case of activities involving periods of work that are split up over the day or are of short duration.

4. Member States may make legislative or regulatory provision for derogations from paragraph 1(b) and paragraph 2 in respect of adolescents in the following cases, where there are objective grounds for so doing and provided that they are granted appropriate compensatory rest time and that the objectives set out in Article 1 are not called into question—

(a) work performed in the shipping or fisheries sectors;
(b) work performed in the context of the armed forces or the police;
(c) work performed in hospitals or similar establishments;
(d) work performed in agriculture;
(e) work performed in the tourism industry or in the hotel, restaurant and café sector;
(f) activities involving periods of work split up over the day.

[3.166]
Article 11
Annual rest

Member States which make use of the option referred to in Article 4(2)(b) or (c) shall see to it that a period free of any work is included, as far as possible, in the school holidays of children subject to compulsory full-time schooling under national law.

[3.167]
Article 12
Breaks

Member States shall adopt the measures necessary to ensure that, where daily working time is more than four and a half hours, young people are entitled to a break of at least 30 minutes, which shall be consecutive if possible.

[3.168]
Article 13
Work by adolescents in the event of *force majeure*
Member States may, by legislative or regulatory provision, authorise derogations from Article 8(2), Article 9(l)(b), Article 10(1)(b) and, in the case of adolescents, Article 12, for work in the circumstances referred to in Article 5(4) of Directive 89/391/EEC, provided that such work is of a temporary nature and must be performed immediately, that adult workers are not available and that the adolescents are allowed equivalent compensatory rest time within the following three weeks.

SECTION IV

[3.169]
Article 14
Measures
Each Member State shall lay down any necessary measures to be applied in the event of failure to comply with the provisions adopted in order to implement this Directive; such measures must be effective and proportionate.

[3.170]
Article 15
Adaptation of the Annex
Adaptations of a strictly technical nature to the Annex in the light of technical progress, changes in international rules or specifications and advances in knowledge in the field covered by this Directive shall be adopted in accordance with the procedure provided for in Article 17 of Directive 89/391/EEC.

[3.171]
Article 16
Non-reducing clause
Without prejudice to the right of Member States to develop, in the light of changing circumstances, different provisions on the protection of young people, as long as the minimum requirements provided for by this Directive are complied with, the implementation of this Directive shall not constitute valid grounds for reducing the general level of protection afforded to young people.

[3.172]
Article 17
Final provisions
1.
(a) Member States shall bring into force the laws, regulations and administrative provisions necessary to comply with this Directive not later than 22 June 1996 or ensure, by that date at the latest, that the two sides of industry introduce the requisite provisions by means of collective agreements, with Member States being required to make all the necessary provisions to enable them at all times to guarantee the results laid down by this Directive.
(b) The United Kingdom may refrain from implementing the first subparagraph of Article 8(1)(b) with regard to the provision relating to the maximum weekly working time, and also Article 8(2) and Article 9(1)(b) and (2) for a period of four years from the date specified in subparagraph (a).
The Commission shall submit a report on the effects of this provision.
The Council, acting in accordance with the conditions laid down by the Treaty, shall decide whether this period should be extended.
(c) Member States shall forthwith inform the Commission thereof.
2. When Member States adopt the measures referred to in paragraph 1, such measures shall contain a reference to this Directive or shall be accompanied by such reference on the occasion of their official publication. The methods of making such reference shall be laid down by Member States.
3. Member States shall communicate to the Commission the texts of the main provisions of national law which they have already adopted or adopt in the field governed by this Directive.
4, 5. . . .

NOTES
Paras 4, 5: repealed by European Parliament and Council Directive 2007/30/EC, Art 3(15).

[3.173]
[Article 17a
Implementation report
Every five years, the Member States shall submit to the Commission a report on the practical implementation of this Directive in the form of a specific chapter of the single report referred to in Article 17a(1), (2) and (3) of Directive 89/391/EEC, which serves as a basis for the Commission's evaluation, in accordance with Article 17a(4) of that Directive.]

NOTES
Inserted by European Parliament and Council Directive 2007/30/EC, Art 2(4).

[3.174]
Article 18
This Directive is addressed to the Member States.

ANNEX
NON-EXHAUSTIVE LIST OF AGENTS, PROCESSES AND WORK (ARTICLE 7(2), SECOND SUBPARAGRAPH)

[3.175]
I. Agents
1. *Physical agents*
 (a) Ionising radiation;
 (b) Work in a high-pressure atmosphere, eg in pressurised containers, diving.
2. *Biological agents*
 [(a) Biological agents of risk groups 3 and 4 within the meaning of points 3 and 4 of second paragraph of Article 2 of Directive 2000/54/EC of the European Parliament and of the Council.[1]]
3. *Chemical agents*
 [(a) Substances and mixtures which meet the criteria for classification under Regulation (EC) No 1272/2008 of the European Parliament and of the Council[2] in one or more of the following hazard classes and hazard categories with one or more of the following hazard statements:
 — acute toxicity, category 1, 2 or 3 (H300, H310, H330, H301, H311, H331);
 — skin corrosion, category 1A, 1B or 1C (H314);
 — flammable gas, category 1 or 2 (H220, H221);
 — flammable aerosols, category 1 (H222);
 — flammable liquid, category 1 or 2 (H224, H225);
 — explosives, categories 'Unstable explosive', or explosives of Divisions 1.1, 1.2, 1.3, 1.4, 1.5 (H200, H201, H202, H203, H204, H205);
 — self-reactive substances and mixtures, type A, B, C or D (H240, H241, H242);
 — organic peroxides, type A or B (H240, H241);
 — specific target organ toxicity after single exposure, category 1 or 2 (H370, H371);
 — specific target organ toxicity after repeated exposure, category 1 or 2 (H372, H373);
 — respiratory sensitisation, category 1, subcategory 1A or 1B (H334);
 — skin sensitisation, category 1, subcategory 1A or 1B (H317);
 — carcinogenicity, category 1A, 1B or 2 (H350, H350i, H351);
 — germ cell mutagenicity, category 1A, 1B or 2 (H340, H341);
 — reproductive toxicity, category 1A or 1B (H360, H360F, H360FD, H360Fd, H360D, H360Df).]
 (b) . . .
 (c) . . .
 [(d) Substances and mixtures referred to in point (ii) of point (a) of Article 2 of Directive 2004/37/EC of the European Parliament and of the Council;[3]]
 (e) Lead and compounds thereof, inasmuch as the agents in question are absorbable by the human organism;
 (f) Asbestos.

II. Processes and work
[1. Processes at work referred to in Annex I to Directive 2004/37/EC.]
2. Manufacture and handling of devices, fireworks or other objects containing explosives.
3. Work with fierce or poisonous animals.
4. Animal slaughtering on an industrial scale.
5. Work involving the handling of equipment for the production, storage or application of compressed, liquefied or dissolved gases.
6. Work with vats, tanks, reservoirs or carboys containing chemical agents referred to in 1.3.
7. Work involving a risk of structural collapse.
8. Work involving high-voltage electrical hazards.
9. Work the pace of which is determined by machinery and involving payment by results.

NOTES
Section I, point 2: para (a) substituted by European Parliament and Council Directive 2014/27/EU, Art 3(1)(a).
Section I, point 3: paras (a), (d) substituted, and paras (b), (c) repealed, by European Parliament and Council Directive 2014/27/EU, Art 3(1)(b).
Section II, point 1: substituted by European Parliament and Council Directive 2014/27/EU, Art 3(2).

[1] Directive 2000/54/EC of the European Parliament and of the Council of 18 September 2000 on the protection of workers from risks related to exposure to biological agents at work (seventh individual directive within the meaning of Article 16(1) of Directive 89/391/EEC) (OJ L262, 17.10.2000, p 21).

[2] Regulation (EC) No 1272/2008 of the European Parliament and of the Council of 16 December 2008 on classification, labelling and packaging of substances and mixtures, amending and repealing Directives 67/548/EEC and 1999/45/EC, and amending Regulation (EC) No 1907/2006 (OJ L353, 31.12.2008, p 1).

[3] Directive 2004/37/EC of the European Parliament and of the Council of 29 April 2004 on the protection of workers from the risks related to exposure to carcinogens or mutagens at work (Sixth individual Directive within the meaning of Article 16(1) of Council Directive 89/391/EEC) (OJ L158, 30.4.2004, p 50).

DIRECTIVE OF THE EUROPEAN PARLIAMENT AND OF THE COUNCIL

(96/71/EC)

of 16 December 1996

concerning the posting of workers in the framework of the provision of services

[3.176]

NOTES

Date of publication in OJ: OJ L18, 21.1.1997, p 1.

This Directive was implemented in the UK by the Equal Opportunities (Employment Legislation) (Territorial Limits) Regulations 1999, SI 1999/3163. The Regulations amended the Sex Discrimination Act 1975, the Race Relations Act 1976, and the Disability Discrimination Act 1995 (all of which have been repealed).

THE EUROPEAN PARLIAMENT AND THE COUNCIL OF THE EUROPEAN UNION,

Having regard to the Treaty establishing the European Community, and in particular Articles 57(2) and 66 thereof,

Having regard to the proposal from the Commission,[1]

Having regard to the opinion of the Economic and Social Committee,[2]

Acting in accordance with the procedure laid down in Article 189b of the Treaty,[3]

(1) Whereas, pursuant to Article 3(c) of the Treaty, the abolition, as between Member States, of obstacles to the free movement of persons and services constitutes one of the objectives of the Community;

(2) Whereas, for the provision of services, any restrictions based on nationality or residence requirements are prohibited under the Treaty with effect from the end of the transitional period;

(3) Whereas the completion of the internal market offers a dynamic environment for the transnational provision of services, prompting a growing number of undertakings to post employees abroad temporarily to perform work in the territory of a Member State other than the State in which they are habitually employed;

(4) Whereas the provision of services may take the form either of performance of work by an undertaking on its account and under its direction, under a contract concluded between that undertaking and the party for whom the services are intended, or of the hiring-out of workers for use by an undertaking in the framework of a public or a private contract;

(5) Whereas any such promotion of the transnational provision of services requires a climate of fair competition and measures guaranteeing respect for the rights of workers;

(6) Whereas the transnationalization of the employment relationship raises problems with regard to the legislation applicable to the employment relationship; whereas it is in the interests of the parties to lay down the terms and conditions governing the employment relationship envisaged;

(7) Whereas the Rome Convention of 19 June 1980 on the law applicable to contractual obligations,[4] signed by 12 Member States, entered into force on 1 April 1991 in the majority of Member States;

(8) Whereas Article 3 of that Convention provides, as a general rule, for the free choice of law made by the parties; whereas, in the absence of choice, the contract is to be governed, according to Article 6(2), by the law of the country, in which the employee habitually carries out his work in performance of the contract, even if he is temporarily employed in another country, or, if the employee does not habitually carry out his work in any one country, by the law of the country in which the place of business through which he was engaged is situated, unless it appears from the circumstances as a whole that the contract is more closely connected with another country, in which case the contract is to be governed by the law of that country;

(9) Whereas, according to Article 6(1) of the said Convention, the choice of law made by the parties is not to have the result of depriving the employee of the protection afforded to him by the mandatory rules of the law which would be applicable under paragraph 2 of that Article in the absence of choice;

(10) Whereas Article 7 of the said Convention lays down, subject to certain conditions, that effect may be given, concurrently with the law declared applicable, to the mandatory rules of the law of another country, in particular the law of the Member State within whose territory the worker is temporarily posted;

(11) Whereas, according to the principle of precedence of Community law laid down in its Article 20, the said Convention does not affect the application of provisions which, in relation to a particular matter, lay down choice-of-law rules relating to contractual obligations and which are or will be contained in acts of the institutions of the European Communities or in national laws harmonized in implementation of such acts;

(12) Whereas Community law does not preclude Member States from applying their legislation, or collective agreements entered into by employers and labour, to any person who is employed, even temporarily, within their territory, although his employer is established in another Member State; whereas Community law does not forbid Member Stares to guarantee the observance of those rules by the appropriate means;

(13) Whereas the laws of the Member States must be coordinated in order to lay down a nucleus of mandatory rules for minimum protection to be observed in the host country by employers who post workers to perform temporary work in the territory of a Member State where the services are provided; whereas such coordination can be achieved only by means of Community law;

(14) Whereas a 'hard core' of clearly defined protective rules should be observed by the provider of the services notwithstanding the duration of the worker's posting;

(15) Whereas it should be laid down that, in certain clearly defined cases of assembly and/or installation of goods, the provisions on minimum rates of pay and minimum paid annual holidays do nor apply;

(16) Whereas there should also be some flexibility in application of the provisions concerning minimum rates of pay and the minimum length of paid annual holidays; whereas, when the length of the posting is not more than one month, Member States may, under certain conditions, derogate from the provisions concerning minimum rates of pay or provide for the possibility of derogation by means of collective agreements; whereas, where the amount of work to be done is not significant, Member States may derogate from the provisions concerning minimum rates of pay and the minimum length of paid annual holidays;

(17) Whereas the mandatory rules for minimum protection in force in the host country must not prevent the application of terms and conditions of employment which are more favourable to workers;

(18) Whereas the principle that undertakings established outside the Community must not receive more favourable treatment than undertakings established in the territory of a Member State should be upheld;

(19) Whereas, without prejudice to other provisions of Community law, this Directive does not entail the obligation to give legal recognition to the existence of temporary employment undertakings, nor does it prejudice the application by Member States of their laws concerning the hiring-out of workers and temporary employment undertakings to undertakings not established in their territory but operating therein in the framework of the provision of services;

(20) Whereas this Directive does not affect either the agreements concluded by the Community with third countries or the laws of Member States concerning the access to their territory of third-country providers of services; whereas this Directive is also without prejudice to national laws relating to the entry, residence and access to employment of third-country workers;

(21) Whereas Council Regulation (EEC) No 1408/71 of 14 June 1971 on the application of social security schemes to employed persons and their families moving within the Community[5] lays down the provisions applicable with regard to social security benefits and contributions;

(22) Whereas this Directive is without prejudice to the law of the Member States concerning collective action to defend the interests of trades and professions;

(23) Whereas competent bodies in different Member States must cooperate with each other in the application of this Directive; whereas Member States must provide for appropriate remedies in the event of failure to comply with this Directive;

(24) Whereas it is necessary to guarantee proper application of this Directive and to that end to make provision for close collaboration between the Commission and the Member States;

(25) Whereas five years after adoption of this Directive at the latest the Commission must review the detailed rules for implementing this Directive with a view to proposing, where appropriate, the necessary amendments,

NOTES

1 OJ C225, 30.8.91, p 6 and OJ C187, 9.7.93, p 5.

2 OJ C49, 24.2.92, p 41.

3 Opinion of the European Parliament of 10 February 1993 (OJ C72, 15.3.93, p 78), Council common position of 3 June 1996 (OJ C220, 29.7.96, p 1) and Decision of the European Parliament of 18 September 1996 (not yet published in the Official Journal). Council Decision of 24 September 1996.

4 OJ L266, 9.10.80, p 1.

5 OJ L149, 5.7.71, p 2; Special Edition 1971 (II), p 416. Regulation as last amended by Regulation 3096/95/EC (OJ L335, 30.12.95, p 10).

HAVE ADOPTED THIS DIRECTIVE—

[3.177]
Article 1
[Subject-matter and scope]

[–1. This Directive shall ensure the protection of posted workers during their posting in relation to the freedom to provide services, by laying down mandatory provisions regarding working conditions and the protection of workers' health and safety that must be respected.

–1a. This Directive shall not in any way affect the exercise of fundamental rights as recognised in the Member States and at Union level, including the right or freedom to strike or to take other action covered by the specific industrial relations systems in Member States, in accordance with national law and/or practice. Nor does it affect the right to negotiate, to conclude and enforce collective agreements, or to take collective action in accordance with national law and/or practice.]

1. This Directive shall apply to undertakings established in a Member State which, in the framework of the transnational provision of services, post workers, in accordance with paragraph 3, to the territory of a Member State.
2. This Directive shall not apply to merchant navy undertakings as regards seagoing personnel.
3. This Directive shall apply to the extent that the undertakings referred to in paragraph 1 take one of the following transnational measures—
(a) post workers to the territory of a Member State on their account and under their direction, under a contract concluded between the undertaking making the posting and the party for whom the services are intended, operating in that Member State, provided there is an employment relationship between the undertaking making the posting and the worker during the period of posting; or
(b) post workers to an establishment or to an undertaking owned by the group in the territory of a Member State, provided there is an employment relationship between the undertaking making the posting and the worker during the period of posting; or
[(c) being a temporary employment undertaking or placement agency, hire out a worker to a user undertaking established or operating in the territory of a Member State, provided that there is an employment relationship between the temporary employment undertaking or placement agency and the worker during the period of posting.]

[Where a worker who has been hired out by a temporary employment undertaking or placement agency to a user undertaking as referred to in point (c) is to carry out work in the framework of the transnational provision of services within the meaning of point (a), (b) or (c) by the user undertaking in the territory of a Member State other than where the worker normally works for the temporary employment undertaking or placement agency, or for the user undertaking, the worker shall be considered to be posted to the territory of that Member State by the temporary employment undertaking or placement agency with which the worker is in an employment relationship. The temporary employment undertaking or placement agency shall be considered to be an undertaking as referred to in paragraph 1 and shall fully comply with the relevant provisions of this Directive and Directive 2014/67/EU of the European Parliament and of the Council.[1]

The user undertaking shall inform the temporary employment undertaking or placement agency which hired out the worker in due time before commencement of the work referred to in the second subparagraph.]

4. Undertakings established in a non-member State must not be given more favourable treatment than undertakings established in a Member State.

NOTES

Article heading: substituted for original word "Scope", by European Parliament and Council Directive 2018/957/EU, Art 1(1)(a), as from 29 July 2018. Note that Directive 2018/957/EU has a transposition date of 30 July 2020 (see reg 3 thereof at **[3.683]**).

Paras –1, –1a: inserted by European Parliament and Council Directive 2018/957/EU, Art 1(1)(b), as from 29 July 2018. Note that Directive 2018/957/EU has a transposition date of 30 July 2020 (see reg 3 thereof at **[3.683]**).

Para 3: point (c) is substituted, and the words in square brackets following point (c) are inserted, by European Parliament and Council Directive 2018/957/EU, Art 1(1)(c), as from 29 July 2018. Note that Directive 2018/957/EU has a transposition date of 30 July 2020 (see reg 3 thereof at **[3.683]**) and point (c) originally read as follows—

"(c) being a temporary employment undertaking or placement agency, hire out a worker to a user undertaking established or operating in the territory of a Member State, provided there is an employment relationship between the temporary employment undertaking or placement agency and the worker during the period of posting.".

[1] Directive 2014/67/EU of the European Parliament and of the Council of 15 May 2014 on the enforcement of Directive 96/71/EC concerning the posting of workers in the framework of the provision of services and amending Regulation (EU) No 1024/2012 on administrative cooperation through the Internal Market Information System ("the IMI Regulation") (OJ L159, 28.5.2014, p 11).

[3.178]
Article 2
Definition

1. For the purposes of this Directive, 'posted worker' means a worker who, for a limited period, carries out his work in the territory of a Member State other than the State in which he normally works.
2. For the purposes of this Directive, the definition of a worker is that which applies in the law of the Member State to whose territory the worker is posted.

[3.179]
Article 3
Terms and conditions of employment

[1. Member States shall ensure, irrespective of which law applies to the employment relationship, that undertakings as referred to in Article 1(1) guarantee, on the basis of equality of treatment, workers who are posted to their territory the terms and conditions of employment covering the following matters which are laid down in the Member State where the work is carried out:
— by law, regulation or administrative provision, and/or
— by collective agreements or arbitration awards which have been declared universally applicable or otherwise apply in accordance with paragraph 8:
(a) maximum work periods and minimum rest periods;
(b) minimum paid annual leave;
(c) remuneration, including overtime rates; this point does not apply to supplementary occupational retirement pension schemes;

(d) the conditions of hiring-out of workers, in particular the supply of workers by temporary employment undertakings;
(e) health, safety and hygiene at work;
(f) protective measures with regard to the terms and conditions of employment of pregnant women or women who have recently given birth, of children and of young people;
(g) equality of treatment between men and women and other provisions on non-discrimination;
(h) the conditions of workers' accommodation where provided by the employer to workers away from their regular place of work;
(i) allowances or reimbursement of expenditure to cover travel, board and lodging expenses for workers away from home for professional reasons.

Point (i) shall apply exclusively to travel, board and lodging expenditure incurred by posted workers where they are required to travel to and from their regular place of work in the Member State to whose territory they are posted, or where they are temporarily sent by their employer from that regular place of work to another place of work.

For the purposes of this Directive, the concept of remuneration shall be determined by the national law and/or practice of the Member State to whose territory the worker is posted and means all the constituent elements of remuneration rendered mandatory by national law, regulation or administrative provision, or by collective agreements or arbitration awards which, in that Member State, have been declared universally applicable or otherwise apply in accordance with paragraph 8.

Without prejudice to Article 5 of Directive 2014/67/EU, Member States shall publish the information on the terms and conditions of employment, in accordance with national law and/or practice, without undue delay and in a transparent manner, on the single official national website referred to in that Article, including the constituent elements of remuneration as referred to in the third subparagraph of this paragraph and all the terms and conditions of employment in accordance with paragraph 1a of this Article.

Member States shall ensure that the information provided on the single official national website is accurate and up to date. The Commission shall publish on its website the addresses of the single official national websites.

Where, contrary to Article 5 of Directive 2014/67/EU, the information on the single official national website does not indicate which terms and conditions of employment are to be applied, that circumstance shall be taken into account, in accordance with national law and/or practice, in determining penalties in the event of infringements of the national provisions adopted pursuant to this Directive, to the extent necessary to ensure the proportionality thereof.]

[1a. Where the effective duration of a posting exceeds 12 months, Member States shall ensure, irrespective of which law applies to the employment relationship, that undertakings as referred to in Article 1(1) guarantee, on the basis of equality of treatment, workers who are posted to their territory, in addition to the terms and conditions of employment referred to in paragraph 1 of this Article, all the applicable terms and conditions of employment which are laid down in the Member State where the work is carried out:

— by law, regulation or administrative provision, and/or
— by collective agreements or arbitration awards which have been declared universally applicable or otherwise apply in accordance with paragraph 8.

The first subparagraph of this paragraph shall not apply to the following matters:

(a) procedures, formalities and conditions of the conclusion and termination of the employment contract, including non-competition clauses;
(b) supplementary occupational retirement pension schemes.

Where the service provider submits a motivated notification, the Member State where the service is provided shall extend the period referred to in the first subparagraph to 18 months.

Where an undertaking as referred to in Article 1(1) replaces a posted worker by another posted worker performing the same task at the same place, the duration of the posting shall, for the purposes of this paragraph, be the cumulative duration of the posting periods of the individual posted workers concerned.

The concept of "the same task at the same place" referred to in the fourth subparagraph of this paragraph shall be determined taking into consideration, inter alia, the nature of the service to be provided, the work to be performed and the address(es) of the workplace.

1b. Member States shall provide that the undertakings referred to in point (c) of Article 1(3) guarantee posted workers the terms and conditions of employment which apply pursuant to Article 5 of Directive 2008/104/EC of the European Parliament and of the Council[1] to temporary agency workers hired-out by temporary-work agencies established in the Member State where the work is carried out.

The user undertaking shall inform the undertakings referred to in point (c) of Article 1(3) of the terms and conditions of employment that it applies regarding the working conditions and remuneration to the extent covered by the first subparagraph of this paragraph.]

2. In the case of initial assembly and/or first installation of goods where this is an integral part of a contract for the supply of goods and necessary for taking the goods supplied into use and carried out by the skilled and/or specialist workers of the supplying undertaking, the first subparagraph of paragraph 1(b) and (c) shall not apply, if the period of posting does not exceed eight days.

This provision shall not apply to activities in the field of building work listed in the Annex.

3. Member States may, after consulting employers and labour, in accordance with the traditions and practices of each Member State, decide not to apply the first subparagraph of paragraph 1(c) in the cases referred to in Article 1(3)(a) and (b) when the length of the posting does not exceed one month.

4. Member States may, in accordance with national laws and/or practices, provide that exemptions may be made from the first subparagraph of paragraph 1(c) in the cases referred to in Article 1(3)(a) and (b) and from a decision by a Member State within the meaning of paragraph 3 of this Article, by means of collective agreements within the meaning of paragraph 8 of this Article, concerning one or more sectors of activity, where the length of the posting does not exceed one month.

5. Member States may provide for exemptions to be granted from the first subparagraph of paragraph 1(b) and (c) in the cases referred to in Article 1(3)(a) and (b) on the grounds that the amount of work to be done is not significant.

Member States availing themselves of the option referred to in the first subparagraph shall lay down the criteria which the work to be performed must meet in order to be considered as 'non-significant'.

6. The length of the posting shall be calculated on the basis of a reference period of one year from the beginning of the posting.

For the purpose of such calculations, account shall be taken of any previous periods for which the post has been filled by a posted worker.

[7. Paragraphs 1 to 6 shall not prevent the application of terms and conditions of employment which are more favourable to workers.

Allowances specific to the posting shall be considered to be part of remuneration, unless they are paid in reimbursement of expenditure actually incurred on account of the posting, such as expenditure on travel, board and lodging. The employer shall, without prejudice to point (h) of the first subparagraph of paragraph 1, reimburse the posted worker for such expenditure in accordance with the national law and/or practice applicable to the employment relationship.

Where the terms and conditions of employment applicable to the employment relationship do not determine whether and, if so, which elements of the allowance specific to the posting are paid in reimbursement of expenditure actually incurred on account of the posting or which are part of remuneration, then the entire allowance shall be considered to be paid in reimbursement of expenditure.]

8. 'Collective agreements or arbitration awards which have been declared universally applicable' means collective agreements or arbitration awards which must be observed by all undertakings in the geographical area and in the profession or industry concerned.

[In the absence of, or in addition to, a system for declaring collective agreements or arbitration awards to be of universal application within the meaning of the first subparagraph, Member States may, if they so decide, base themselves on:

— collective agreements or arbitration awards which are generally applicable to all similar undertakings in the geographical area and in the profession or industry concerned, and/or
— collective agreements which have been concluded by the most representative employers' and labour organisations at national level and which are applied throughout national territory,

provided that their application to undertakings as referred to in Article 1(1) ensures equality of treatment on matters listed in the first subparagraph of paragraph 1 of this Article and, where applicable, with regard to the terms and conditions of employment to be guaranteed posted workers in accordance with paragraph 1a of this Article, between those undertakings and the other undertakings referred to in this subparagraph which are in a similar position.

Equality of treatment, within the meaning of this Article, shall be deemed to exist where national undertakings in a similar position:

— are subject, in the place in question or in the sector concerned, to the same obligations as undertakings as referred to in Article 1(1) as regards the matters listed in the first subparagraph of paragraph 1 of this Article and, where applicable, as regards the terms and conditions of employment to be guaranteed posted workers in accordance with paragraph 1a of this Article, and
— are required to fulfil such obligations with the same effects.]

[9. Member States may require undertakings as referred to in Article 1(1) to guarantee workers referred to in point (c) of Article 1(3), in addition to the terms and conditions of employment referred to in paragraph 1b of this Article, other terms and conditions that apply to temporary agency workers in the Member State where the work is carried out.

10. This Directive shall not preclude the application by Member States, in compliance with the Treaties, to national undertakings and to the undertakings of other Member States, on the basis of equality of treatment, of terms and conditions of employment on matters other than those referred to in the first subparagraph of paragraph 1 in the case of public policy provisions.]

NOTES

Paras 1, 7, 9, 10: substituted by European Parliament and Council Directive 2018/957/EU, Art 1(2)(a), (c), (e), as from 29 July 2018. Note that Directive 2018/957/EU has a transposition date of 30 July 2020 (see reg 3 thereof at **[3.683]**) and paras 1, 7, 9, 10 originally read as follows—

"1. Member States shall ensure that, whatever the law applicable to the employment relationship, the undertakings referred to in Article 1(1) guarantee workers posted to their territory the terms and conditions of employment covering the following matters which, in the Member State where the work is carried out, are laid down—

— by law, regulation or administrative provision, and/or
— by collective agreements or arbitration awards which have been declared universally applicable within the meaning of paragraph 8, insofar as they concern the activities referred to in the Annex—

(a) maximum work periods and minimum rest periods;
(b) minimum paid annual holidays;
(c) the minimum rates of pay, including overtime rates; this point does not apply to supplementary occupational retirement pension schemes;
(d) the conditions of hiring-out of workers, in particular the supply of workers by temporary employment undertakings;

(e) health, safety and hygiene at work;
(f) protective measures with regard to the terms and conditions of employment of pregnant women or women who have recently given birth, of children and of young people;
(g) equality of treatment between men and women and other provisions on non-discrimination.

For the purposes of this Directive, the concept of minimum rates of pay referred to in paragraph 1(c) is defined by the national law and/or practice of the Member State to whose territory the worker is posted.

7. Paragraphs 1 to 6 shall not prevent application of terms and conditions of employment which are more favourable to workers.

Allowances specific to the posting shall be considered to be part of the minimum wage, unless they are paid in reimbursement of expenditure actually incurred on account of the posting, such as expenditure on travel, board and lodging.

9. Member States may provide that the undertakings referred to in Article 1(1) must guarantee workers referred to in Article 1(3)(c) the terms and conditions which apply to temporary workers in the Member State where the work is carried out.

10. This Directive shall not preclude the application by Member States, in compliance with the Treaty, to national undertakings and to the undertakings of other States, on a basis of equality of treatment, of—

— terms and conditions of employment on matters other than those referred to in the first subparagraph of paragraph 1 in the case of public policy provisions,
— terms and conditions of employment laid down in the collective agreements or arbitration awards within the meaning of paragraph 8 and concerning activities other than those referred to in the Annex.".

Paras 1a, 1b: inserted by European Parliament and Council Directive 2018/957/EU, Art 1(2)(b), as from 29 July 2018. Note that Directive 2018/957/EU has a transposition date of 30 July 2020 (see reg 3 thereof at **[3.683]**).

Para 8: second and third subparagraphs in square brackets substituted by European Parliament and Council Directive 2018/957/EU, Art 1(2)(d), as from 29 July 2018. Note that Directive 2018/957/EU has a transposition date of 30 July 2020 (see reg 3 thereof at **[3.683]**) and the original wording read as follows—

"In the absence of a system for declaring collective agreements or arbitration awards to be of universal application within the meaning of the first subparagraph, Member States may, if they so decide, base themselves on—

— collective agreements or arbitration awards which are generally applicable to all similar undertakings in the geographical area and in the profession or industry concerned, and/or
— collective agreements which have been concluded by the most representative employers' and labour organizations at national level and which are applied throughout national territory,

provided that their application to the undertakings referred to in Article 1(1) ensures equality of treatment on matters listed in the first subparagraph of paragraph 1 of this Article between those undertakings and the other undertakings referred to in this subparagraph which are in a similar position.

Equality of treatment, within the meaning of this Article, shall be deemed to exist where national undertakings in a similar position—

— are subject, in the place in question or in the sector concerned, to the same obligations as posting undertakings as regards the matters listed in the first subparagraph of paragraph 1, and
— are required to fulfil such obligations with the same effects."

[1] Directive 2008/104/EC of the European Parliament and of the Council of 19 November 2008 on temporary agency work (OJ L327, 5.12.2008, p 9)..

[3.180]
Article 4
Cooperation on information

1. For the purposes of implementing this Directive, Member States shall, in accordance with national legislation and/or practice, designate one or more liaison offices or one or more competent national bodies.

2. [Member States shall make provision for cooperation between the competent authorities or bodies, including public authorities, which, in accordance with national law, are responsible for monitoring the terms and conditions of employment referred to in Article 3, including at Union level. Such cooperation shall in particular consist in replying to reasoned requests from those authorities or bodies for information on the transnational hiring-out of workers, and in tackling manifest abuses or possible cases of unlawful activities, such as transnational cases of undeclared work and bogus self-employment linked to the posting of workers. Where the competent authority or body in the Member State from which the worker is posted does not possess the information requested by the competent authority or body of the Member State to whose territory the worker is posted, it shall seek to obtain that information from other authorities or bodies in that Member State. In the event of persistent delays in the provision of such information to the Member State to whose territory the worker is posted, the Commission shall be informed and shall take appropriate measures.]

The Commission and the public authorities referred to in the first subparagraph shall cooperate closely in order to examine any difficulties which might arise in the application of Article 3(10).

Mutual administrative assistance shall be provided free of charge.

3. Each Member State shall take the appropriate measures to make the information on the terms and conditions of employment referred to in Article 3 generally available.

4. Each Member State shall notify the other Member States and the Commission of the liaison offices and/or competent bodies referred to in paragraph 1.

NOTES

Para 2: words in square brackets substituted by European Parliament and Council Directive 2018/957/EU, Art 1(3), as from 29 July 2018. Note that Directive 2018/957/EU has a transposition date of 30 July 2020 (see reg 3 thereof at **[3.683]**) and the original wording read as follows—

"Member States shall make provision for cooperation between the public authorities which, in accordance with national legislation, are responsible for monitoring the terms and conditions of employment referred to in Article 3. Such cooperation shall in particular consist in replying to reasoned requests from those authorities for information on the transnational hiring-out of workers, including manifest abuses or possible cases of unlawful transnational activities.".

[3.181]
[Article 5
Monitoring, control and enforcement
The Member State to whose territory the worker is posted and the Member State from which the worker is posted shall be responsible for the monitoring, control and enforcement of the obligations laid down in this Directive and in Directive 2014/67/EU and shall take appropriate measures in the event of failure to comply with this Directive.
Member States shall lay down the rules on penalties applicable to infringements of national provisions adopted pursuant to this Directive and shall take all measures necessary to ensure that they are implemented. The penalties provided for shall be effective, proportionate and dissuasive.
Member States shall in particular ensure that adequate procedures are available to workers and/or workers' representatives for the enforcement of obligations under this Directive.
Where, following an overall assessment made pursuant to Article 4 of Directive 2014/67/EU by a Member State, it is established that an undertaking is improperly or fraudulently creating the impression that the situation of a worker falls within the scope of this Directive, that Member State shall ensure that the worker benefits from relevant law and practice.
Member States shall ensure that this Article does not lead to the worker concerned being subject to less favourable conditions than those applicable to posted workers.]

NOTES
Substituted by European Parliament and Council Directive 2018/957/EU, Art 1(4), as from 29 July 2018. Note that Directive 2018/957/EU has a transposition date of 30 July 2020 (see reg 3 thereof at **[3.683]**) and Art 5 originally read as follows—

"Article 5
Measures
Member States shall take appropriate measures in the event of failure to comply with this Directive.
They shall in particular ensure that adequate procedures are available to workers and/or their representatives for the enforcement of obligations under this Directive.".

[3.182]
Article 6
Jurisdiction
In order to enforce the right to the terms and conditions of employment guaranteed in Article 3, judicial proceedings may be instituted in the Member State in whose territory the worker is or was posted, without prejudice, where applicable, to the right, under existing international conventions on jurisdiction, to institute proceedings in another State.

[3.183]
Article 7
Implementation
Member States shall adopt the laws, regulations and administrative provisions necessary to comply with this Directive by 16 December 1999 at the latest. They shall forthwith inform the Commission thereof.
When Member States adopt these provisions, they shall contain a reference to this Directive or shall be accompanied by such reference on the occasion of their official publication. The methods of making such reference shall be laid down by Member States.

[3.184]
Article 8
Commission review
By 16 December 2001 at the latest, the Commission shall review the operation of this Directive with a view to proposing the necessary amendments to the Council where appropriate.

[3.185]
Article 9
This Directive is addressed to the Member States.

ANNEX

[3.186]
[The activities referred to in Article 3(2) include all building work related to the construction, repair, upkeep, alteration or demolition of buildings, and in particular the following work—]

1. excavation
2. earthmoving
3. actual building work
4. assembly and dismantling of prefabricated elements

5. fitting out or installation
6. alterations
7. renovation
8. repairs
9. dismantling
10. demolition
11. maintenance
12. upkeep, painting and cleaning work
13. improvements.

NOTES

Substituted by European Parliament and Council Directive 2018/957/EU, Art 1(5), as from 29 July 2018. Note that Directive 2018/957/EU has a transposition date of 30 July 2020 (see reg 3 thereof at **[3.683]**) and the original wording read as follows—

"The activities mentioned in Article 3(1), second indent, include all building work relating to the construction, repair, upkeep, alteration or demolition of buildings, and in particular the following work—".

COUNCIL DIRECTIVE

(97/81/EC)
of 15 December 1997

concerning the Framework Agreement on part-time work concluded by UNICE, CEEP and the ETUC

[3.187]

NOTES

Date of publication in OJ: OJ L14, 20.1.1998, p 9.

This Directive implements a Framework Agreement made by the Social Partners (the Union of Industrial and Employers' Confederations of Europe (UNICE), since renamed Business Europe, the European Centre of Enterprises with Public Participation (CEEP), and the European Trade Union Confederation (ETUC)) in accordance with Art 4 of the Agreement on Social Policy annexed to Protocol 14 to the Treaty of Union 1992 and, therefore, did not bind the United Kingdom. It was subsequently extended to the UK by Directive 98/23/EC with a required date of transposition of 7 April 2000 (see Art 2(1A) of this Directive at **[3.189]**). For the domestic implementation of this Directive as extended to the UK by Directive 98/23/EC, see the Employment Relations Act 1999, ss 19–21 at **[1.1253]–[1.1255]** and the Part-time Workers (Prevention of Less Favourable Treatment) Regulations 2000, SI 2000/1551 at **[2.535]** (as amended by the Part-time Workers (Prevention of Less Favourable Treatment) Regulations 2000 (Amendment) Regulations 2002, SI 2002/2035).

THE COUNCIL OF THE EUROPEAN UNION,

Having regard to the Agreement on social policy annexed to the Protocol (No 14) on social policy, annexed to the Treaty establishing the European Community, and in particular Article 4(2) thereof,

Having regard to the proposal from the Commission,

(1) Whereas on the basis of the Protocol on social policy annexed to the Treaty establishing the European Community, the Member States, with the exception of the United Kingdom of Great Britain and Northern Ireland (hereinafter referred to as 'the Member States'), wishing to continue along the path laid down in the 1989 Social Charter, have concluded an agreement on social policy;

(2) Whereas management and labour (the social partners) may, in accordance with Article 4(2) of the Agreement on social policy, request jointly that agreements at Community level be implemented by a Council decision on a proposal from the Commission;

(3) Whereas point 7 of the Community Charter of the Fundamental Social Rights of Workers provides, *inter alia*, that 'the completion of the internal market must lead to an improvement in the living and working conditions of workers in the European Community. This process must result from an approximation of these conditions while the improvement is being maintained, as regards in particular (. . .) forms of employment other than open-ended contracts, such as fixed-term contracts, part-time working, temporary work and seasonal work';

(4) Whereas the Council has not reached a decision on the proposal for a Directive on certain employment relationships with regard to distortions of competition,[1] as amended,[2] nor on the proposal for a Directive on certain employment relationships with regard to working conditions;[3]

(5) Whereas the conclusions of the Essen European Council stressed the need to take measures to promote employment and equal opportunities for women and men, and called for measures with a view to increasing the employment-intensiveness of growth, in particular by a more flexible organization of work in a way which fulfils both the wishes of employees and the requirements of competition;

Part 3 EU Materials

(6) Whereas the Commission, in accordance with Article 3(2) of the Agreement on social policy, has consulted management and labour on the possible direction of Community action with regard to flexible working time and job security;

(7) Whereas the Commission, considering after such consultation that Community action was desirable, once again consulted management and labour at Community level on the substance of the envisaged proposal in accordance with Article 3(3) of the said Agreement;

(8) Whereas the general cross-industry organizations, the Union of Industrial and Employer's Confederations of Europe (UNICE), the European Centre of Enterprises with Public Participation (CEEP) and the European Trade Union Confederation (ETUC) informed the Commission in their joint letter of 19 June 1996 of their desire to initiate the procedure provided for in Article 4 of the Agreement on social policy; whereas they asked the Commission, in a joint letter dated 12 March 1997, for a further three months; whereas the Commission complied with this request;

(9) Whereas the said cross-industry organizations concluded, on 6 June 1997, a Framework Agreement on part-time work; whereas they forwarded to the Commission their joint request to implement this Framework Agreement by a Council decision on a proposal from the Commission, in accordance with Article 4(2) of the said Agreement;

(10) Whereas the Council, in its Resolution of 6 December 1994 on prospects for a European Union social policy: contribution to economic and social convergence in the Union,[4] asked management and labour to make use of the opportunities for concluding agreements, since they are as a rule closer to social reality and to social problems;

(11) Whereas the signatory parties wished to conclude a framework agreement on part-time work setting out the general principles and minimum requirements for part-time working; whereas they have demonstrated their desire to establish a general framework for eliminating discrimination against part-time workers and to contribute to developing the potential for part-time work on a basis which is acceptable for employers and workers alike;

(12) Whereas the social partners wished to give particular attention to part-time work, while at the same time indicating that it was their intention to consider the need for similar agreements for other flexible forms of work;

(13) Whereas, in the conclusions of the Amsterdam European Council, the Heads of State and Government of the European Union strongly welcomed the agreement concluded by the social partners on part-time work;

(14) Whereas the proper instrument for implementing the Framework Agreement is a Directive within the meaning of Article 189 of the Treaty; whereas it therefore binds the Member States as to the result to be achieved, whilst leaving national authorities the choice of form and methods;

(15) Whereas, in accordance with the principles of subsidiarity and proportionality as set out in Article 3(b) of the Treaty, the objectives of this Directive cannot be sufficiently achieved by the Member States and can therefore be better achieved by the Community; whereas this Directive does not go beyond what is necessary for the attainment of those objectives;

(16) Whereas, with regard to terms used in the Framework Agreement which are not specifically defined therein, this Directive leaves Member States free to define those terms in accordance with national law and practice, as is the case for other social policy Directives using similar terms, providing that the said definitions respect the content of the Frame-work Agreement;

(17) Whereas the Commission has drafted its proposal for a Directive, in accordance with its Communication of 14 December 1993 concerning the application of the Protocol (No 14) on social policy and its Communication of 18 September 1996 concerning the development of the social dialogue at Community level, taking into account the representative status of the signatory parties and the legality of each clause of the Framework Agreement;

(18) Whereas the Commission has drafted its proposal for a Directive in compliance with Article 2(2) of the Agreement on social policy which provides that Directives in the social policy domain 'shall avoid imposing administrative, financial and legal constraints in a way which would hold back the creation and development of small and medium-sized undertakings';

(19) Whereas the Commission, in accordance with its Communication of 14 December 1993 concerning the application of the Protocol (No 14) on social policy, informed the European Parliament by sending it the text of its proposal for a Directive containing the Framework Agreement;

(20) Whereas the Commission also informed the Economic and Social Committee;

(21) Whereas Clause 6.1 of the Framework Agreement provides that Member States and/or the social partners may maintain or introduce more favourable provisions;

(22) Whereas Clause 6.2 of the Framework Agreement provides that implementation of this Directive may not serve to justify any regression in relation to the situation which already exists in each Member State;

(23) Whereas the Community Charter of the Fundamental Social Rights of Workers recognizes the importance of the fight against all forms of discrimination, especially based on sex, colour, race, opinion and creed;

(24) Whereas Article F(2) of the Treaty on European Union states that the Union shall respect fundamental rights, as guaranteed by the European Convention for the Protection of Human Rights and Fundamental Freedoms and as they result from the constitutional traditions common to the Member States, as general principles of Community law;

(25) Whereas the Member States may entrust the social partners, at their joint request, with the implementation of this Directive, provided that the Member States take all the necessary steps to ensure that they can at all times guarantee the results imposed by this Directive;

(26) Whereas the implementation of the Framework Agreement contributes to achieving the objectives under Article 1 of the Agreement on social policy,

NOTES

[1] OJ C224, 8.9.90, p 6.

[2] OJ C305, 5.12.90, p 8.

[3] OJ C224, 8.9.90, p 4.

[4] OJ C368, 23.12.94, p 6.

HAS ADOPTED THIS DIRECTIVE—

[3.188]
Article 1
The purpose of this Directive is to implement the Framework Agreement on part-time work concluded on 6 June 1997 between the general cross-industry organizations (UNICE, CEEP and the ETUC) annexed hereto.

[3.189]
Article 2
1. Member States shall bring into force the laws, regulations and administrative provisions necessary to comply with this Directive not later than 20 January 2000, or shall ensure that, by that date at the latest, the social partners have introduced the necessary measures by agreement, the Member States being required to take any necessary measures to enable them at any time to be in a position to guarantee the results imposed by this Directive. They shall forthwith inform the Commission thereof.

Member States may have a maximum of one more year, if necessary, to take account of special difficulties or implementation by a collective agreement.

They shall inform the Commission forthwith in such circumstances.

When Member States adopt the measures referred to in the first subparagraph, they shall contain a reference to this Directive or shall be accompanied by such reference on the occasion of their official publication. The methods of making such a reference shall be laid down by the Member States.

[1A. As regards the United Kingdom of Great Britain and Northern Ireland, the date of 20 January 2000 in paragraph 1 shall be replaced by the date of 7 April 2000.]

2. Member States shall communicate to the Commission the text of the main provisions of domestic law which they have adopted or which they adopt in the field governed by this Directive.

NOTES

Para 1A: inserted by Council Directive 98/23/EC, Art 2.

[3.190]
Article 3
This Directive shall enter into force on the day of its publication in the *Official Journal of the European Communities*.

[3.191]
Article 4
This Directive is addressed to the Member States.

ANNEX
UNION OF INDUSTRIAL AND EMPLOYERS' CONFEDERATIONS OF EUROPE
EUROPEAN TRADE UNION CONFEDERATION
EUROPEAN CENTRE OF ENTERPRISES WITH PUBLIC PARTICIPATION

FRAMEWORK AGREEMENT ON PART-TIME WORK

[3.192]
Preamble
This Framework Agreement is a contribution to the overall European strategy on employment. Part-time work has had an important impact on employment in recent years. For this reason, the parties to this agreement have given priority attention to this form of work. It is the intention of the parties to consider the need for similar agreements relating to other forms of flexible work.

Recognizing the diversity of situations in Member States and acknowledging that part-time work is a feature of employment in certain sectors and activities, this Agreement sets out the general principles and minimum requirements relating to part-time work. It illustrates the willingness of the social partners to establish a general framework for the elimination of discrimination against part-time workers and to assist the development of opportunities for part-time working on a basis acceptable to employers and workers.

This Agreement relates to employment conditions of part-time workers recognizing that matters concerning statutory social security are for decision by the Member States. In the context of the principle of non-discrimination, the parties to this Agreement have noted the Employment Declaration of the Dublin European Council of December 1996, wherein the Council inter alia emphasized the need to make social security systems more employment-friendly by 'developing social protection systems capable of adapting to new patterns of work and of providing appropriate protection to people engaged in such work'. The parties to this Agreement consider that effect should be given to this Declaration.

ETUC, UNICE and CEEP request the Commission to submit this Framework Agreement to the Council for a decision making these requirements binding in the Member States which are party to the Agreement on social policy annexed to the Protocol (No 14) on social policy annexed to the Treaty establishing the European Community.

The parties to this Agreement ask the Commission, in its proposal to implement this Agreement, to request that Member States adopt the laws, regulations and administrative provisions necessary to comply with the Council decision within a period of two years from its adoption or ensure[1] that the social partners establish the necessary measures by way of agreement by the end of this period. Member States may, if necessary to take account of particular difficulties or implementation by collective agreement, have up to a maximum of one additional year to comply with this provision.

Without prejudice to the role of national courts and the Court of Justice, the parties to this agreement request that any matter relating to the interpretation of this agreement at European level should, in the first instance, be referred by the Commission to them for an opinion.

NOTES

[1] Within the meaning of Article 2(4) of the agreement on social policy of the Treaty establishing the European Community.

[3.193]

General considerations

1. Having regard to the Agreement on social policy annexed to the Protocol (No 14) on social policy annexed to the Treaty establishing the European Community, and in particular Articles 3(4) and 4(2) thereof;

2. Whereas Article 4(2) of the Agreement on social policy provides that agreements concluded at Community level may be implemented, at the joint request of the signatory parties, by a Council decision on a proposal from the Commission.

3. Whereas, in its second consultation document on flexibility of working time and security for workers, the Commission announced its intention to propose a legally binding Community measure;

4. Whereas the conclusions of the European Council meeting in Essen emphasized the need for measures to promote both employment and equal opportunities for women and men, and called for measures aimed at 'increasing the employment intensiveness of growth, in particular by more flexible organization of work in a way which fulfils both the wishes of employees and the requirements of competition';

5. Whereas the parties to this agreement attach importance to measures which would facilitate access to part-time work for men and women in order to prepare for retirement, reconcile professional and family life, and take up education and training opportunities to improve their skills and career opportunities for the mutual benefit of employers and workers and in a manner which would assist the development of enterprises;

6. Whereas this Agreement refers back to Member States and social partners for the arrangements for the application of these general principles, minimum requirements and provisions, in order to take account of the situation in each Member State;

7. Whereas this Agreement takes into consideration the need to improve social policy requirements, to enhance the competitiveness of the Community economy and to avoid imposing administrative, financial and legal constraints in a way which would hold back the creation and development of small and medium-sized undertakings;

8. Whereas the social partners are best placed to find solutions that correspond to the needs of both employers and workers and must therefore be given a special role in the implementation and application of this Agreement.

THE SIGNATORY PARTIES HAVE AGREED THE FOLLOWING:

[3.194]

Clause 1: Purpose

The purpose of this Framework Agreement is—

(a) to provide for the removal of discrimination against part-time workers and to improve the quality of part-time work;

(b) to facilitate the development of part-time work on a voluntary basis and to contribute to the flexible organization of working time in a manner which takes into account the needs of employers and workers.

Clause 2: Scope

1. This Agreement applies to part-time workers who have an employment contract or employment relationship as defined by the law, collective agreement or practice in force in each Member State.

2. Member States, after consultation with the social partners in accordance with national law, collective agreements or practice, and/or the social partners at the appropriate level in conformity with national industrial relations practice may, for objective reasons, exclude wholly or partly from the terms of this Agreement part-time workers who work on a casual basis. Such exclusions should be reviewed periodically to establish if the objective reasons for making them remain valid.

Clause 3: Definitions

For the purpose of this agreement—

1. The term 'part-time worker' refers to an employee whose normal hours of work, calculated on a weekly basis or on average over a period of employment of up to one year, are less than the normal hours of work of a comparable full-time worker.
2. The term 'comparable full-time worker' means a full-time worker in the same establishment having the same type of employment contract or relationship, who is engaged in the same or a similar work/occupation, due regard being given to other considerations which may include seniority and qualification/skills.

Where there is no comparable full-time worker in the same establishment, the comparison shall be made by reference to the applicable collective agreement or, where there is no applicable collective agreement, in accordance with national law, collective agreements or practice.

Clause 4: Principle of non-discrimination

1. In respect of employment conditions, part-time workers shall not be treated in a less favourable manner than comparable full-time workers solely because they work part time unless different treatment is justified on objective grounds.

2. Where appropriate, the principle of *pro rata temporis* shall apply.

3. The arrangements for the application of this clause shall be defined by the Member States and/or social partners, having regard to European legislation, national law, collective agreements and practice.

4. Where justified by objective reasons, Member States after consultation of the social partners in accordance with national law, collective agreements or practice and/or social partners may, where appropriate, make access to particular conditions of employment subject to a period of service, time worked or earnings qualification. Qualifications relating to access by part-time workers to particular conditions of employment should be reviewed periodically having regard to the principle of non-discrimination as expressed in Clause 4.1.

Clause 5: Opportunities for part-time work

1. In the context of Clause 1 of this Agreement and of the principle of non-discrimination between part-time and full-time workers—

(a) Member States, following consultations with the social partners in accordance with national law or practice, should identify and review obstacles of a legal or administrative nature which may limit the opportunities for part-time work and, where appropriate, eliminate them;

(b) the social partners, acting within their sphere of competence and through the procedures set out in collective agreements, should identify and review obstacles which may limit opportunities for part-time work and, where appropriate, eliminate them.

2. A worker's refusal to transfer from full-time to part-time work or vice-versa should not in itself constitute a valid reason for termination of employment, without prejudice to termination in accordance with national law, collective agreements and practice, for other reasons such as may arise from the operational requirements of the establishment concerned.

3. As far as possible, employers should give consideration to—

(a) requests by workers to transfer from full-time to part-time work that becomes available in the establishment;

(b) requests by workers to transfer from part-time to full-time work or to increase their working time should the opportunity arise;

(c) the provision of timely information on the availability of part-time and full-time positions in the establishment in order to facilitate transfers from full-time to part-time or vice versa;

(d) measures to facilitate access to part-time work at all levels of the enterprise, including skilled and managerial positions, and where appropriate, to facilitate access by part-time workers to vocational training to enhance career opportunities and occupational mobility;

(e) the provision of appropriate information to existing bodies representing workers about part-time working in the enterprise.

Clause 6: Provisions on implementation

1. Member States and/or social partners may maintain or introduce more favourable provisions than set out in this agreement.

2. Implementation of the provisions of this Agreement shall not constitute valid grounds for reducing the general level of protection afforded to workers in the field of this agreement. This does not prejudice the right of Member States and/or social partners to develop different legislative, regulatory or contractual provisions, in the light of changing circumstances, and does not prejudice the application of Clause 5.1 as long as the principle of non-discrimination as expressed in Clause 4.1 is complied with.

3. This Agreement does not prejudice the right of the social partners to conclude, at the appropriate level, including European level, agreements adapting and/or complementing the provisions of this Agreement in a manner which will take account of the specific needs of the social partners concerned.

4. This Agreement shall be without prejudice to any more specific Community provisions, and in particular Community provisions concerning equal treatment or opportunities for men and women.

5. The prevention and settlement of disputes and grievances arising from the application of this Agreement shall be dealt with in accordance with national law, collective agreements and practice.

6. The signatory parties shall review this Agreement, five years after the date of the Council decision, if requested by one of the parties to this Agreement.

COUNCIL DIRECTIVE

(98/59/EC)

of 20 July 1998

on the approximation of the laws of the Member States relating to collective redundancies

[3.195]

NOTES

Date of publication in OJ: OJ L225, 12.8.1998, p 16. The text of this Directive incorporates the corrigendum published in OJ L59, 27.2.2007, p 84. Note that the Recitals are reproduced as they appear in the official OJ version of this Directive.

This Directive is essentially a consolidation of Directive 75/129/EEC as amended by Directive 92/56/EEC. For the domestic implementation of those Directives, see the Trade Union and Labour Relations (Consolidation) Act 1992, ss 188–198 at **[1.500]**–**[1.512]**.

See *Harvey* E(17).

THE COUNCIL OF THE EUROPEAN UNION,

Having regard to the Treaty establishing the European Community, and in particular Article 100 thereof,

Having regard to the proposal from the Commission,

Having regard to the opinion of the European Parliament,[1]

Having regard to the opinion of the Economic and Social Committee,[2]

(1) Whereas for reasons of clarity and rationality Council Directive 75/129/EEC of 17 February 1975 on the approximation of the laws of the Member States relating to collective redundancies[3] should be consolidated;

(2) Whereas it is important that greater protection should be afforded to workers in the event of collective redundancies while taking into account the need for balanced economic and social development within the Community;

(3) Whereas, despite increasing convergence, differences still remain between the provisions in force in the Member States concerning the practical arrangements and procedures for such redundancies and the measures designed to alleviate the consequences of redundancy for workers;

(4) Whereas these differences can have a direct effect on the functioning of the internal market;

(5) Whereas the Council resolution of 21 January 1974 concerning a social action programme[4] made provision for a directive on the approximation of Member States' legislation on collective redundancies;

(6) Whereas the Community Charter of the fundamental social rights of workers, adopted at the European Council meeting held in Strasbourg on 9 December 1989 by the Heads of State or Government of 11 Member States, states, *inter alia*, in point 7, first paragraph, first sentence, and second paragraph; in point 17, first paragraph; and in point 18, third indent—

"7. The completion of the internal market must lead to an improvement in the living and working conditions of workers in the European Community (. . .).

The improvement must cover, where necessary, the development of certain aspects of employment regulations such as procedures for collective redundancies and those regarding bankruptcies.

(. . .)

17. Information, consultation and participation for workers must be developed along appropriate lines, taking account of the practices in force in the various Member States.

(. . .)

18. Such information, consultation and participation must be implemented in due time, particularly in the following cases—

(. . .)

(. . .)

— in cases of collective redundancy procedures;

(. . .)";

(7) Whereas this approximation must therefore be promoted while the improvement is being maintained within the meaning of Article 117 of the Treaty;

(8) Whereas, in order to calculate the number of redundancies provided for in the definition of collective redundancies within the meaning of this Directive, other forms of termination of employment contracts on the initiative of the employer should be equated to redundancies, provided that there are at least five redundancies;

(9) Whereas it should be stipulated that this Directive applies in principle also to collective redundancies resulting where the establishment's activities are terminated as a result of a judicial decision;

(10) Whereas the Member States should be given the option of stipulating that workers' representatives may call on experts on grounds of the technical complexity of the matters which are likely to be the subject of the informing and consulting;

(11) Whereas it is necessary to ensure that employers' obligations as regards information, consultation and notification apply independently of whether the decision on collective redundancies emanates from the employer or from an undertaking which controls that employer;

(12) Whereas Member States should ensure that workers' representatives and/or workers have at their disposal administrative and/or judicial procedures in order to ensure that the obligations laid down in this Directive are fulfilled;

(13) Whereas this Directive must not affect the obligations of the Member States concerning the deadlines for transposition of the Directives set out in Annex I, Part B,

NOTES

[1] OJ C210, 6.7.98.

[2] OJ C158, 26.5.97, p 11.

[3] OJ L48, 22.2.75, p 29. Directive as amended by Directive 92/56/EEC (OJ L245, 26.8.92, p 3).

[4] OJ C13, 12.2.74, p 1.

HAS ADOPTED THIS DIRECTIVE—

SECTION I DEFINITIONS AND SCOPE

[3.196]

Article 1

1. For the purposes of this Directive—

(a) 'collective redundancies' means dismissals effected by an employer for one or more reasons not related to the individual workers concerned where, according to the choice of the Member States, the number of redundancies is—

(i) either, over a period of 30 days—

— at least 10 in establishments normally employing more than 20 and less than 100 workers,

— at least 10% of the number of workers in establishments normally employing at least 100 but less than 300 workers,

— at least 30 in establishments normally employing 300 workers or more,

(ii) or, over a period of 90 days, at least 20, whatever the number of workers normally employed in the establishments in question;

(b) 'workers' representatives' means the workers' representatives provided for by the laws or practices of the Member States.

For the purpose of calculating the number of redundancies provided for in the first subparagraph of point (a), terminations of an employment contract which occur on the employer's initiative for one or more reasons not related to the individual workers concerned shall be assimilated to redundancies, provided that there are at least five redundancies.

2. This Directive shall not apply to—

(a) collective redundancies effected under contracts of employment concluded for limited periods of time or for specific tasks except where such redundancies take place prior to the date of expiry or the completion of such contracts;

(b) workers employed by public administrative bodies or by establishments governed by public law (or, in Member States where this concept is unknown, by equivalent bodies);

(c) the crews of seagoing vessels.

NOTES

Para 2: sub-para (c) repealed by Directive 2015/1794/EU, Art 4(1), as from 9 October 2015.

SECTION II INFORMATION AND CONSULTATION

[3.197]

Article 2

1. Where an employer is contemplating collective redundancies, he shall begin consultations with the workers' representatives in good time with a view to reaching an agreement.

2. These consultations shall, at least, cover ways and means of avoiding collective redundancies or reducing the number of workers affected, and of mitigating the consequences by recourse to accompanying social measures aimed, *inter alia*, at aid for redeploying or retraining workers made redundant.

Member States may provide that the workers' representatives may call on the services of experts in accordance with national legislation and/or practice.

3. To enable workers' representatives to make constructive proposals, the employers shall in good time during the course of the consultations—

(a) supply them with all relevant information and

(b) in any event notify them in writing of—

(i) the reasons for the projected redundancies;

(ii) the number and categories of workers to be made redundant;

(iii) the number and categories of workers normally employed;

(iv) the period over which the projected redundancies are to be effected;

(v) the criteria proposed for the selection of the workers to be made redundant in so far as national legislation and/or practice confers the power therefore upon the employer;

(vi) the method for calculating any redundancy payments other than those arising out of national legislation and/or practice.

The employer shall forward to the competent public authority a copy of, at least, the elements of the written communication which are provided for in the first subparagraph, point (b), sub-points (i) to (v).

4. The obligations laid down in paragraphs 1, 2 and 3 shall apply irrespective of whether the decision regarding collective redundancies is being taken by the employer or by an undertaking controlling the employer.

In considering alleged breaches of the information, consultation and notification requirements laid down by this Directive, account shall not be taken of any defence on the part of the employer on the ground that the necessary information has not been provided to the employer by the undertaking which took the decision leading to collective redundancies.

SECTION III PROCEDURE FOR COLLECTIVE REDUNDANCIES

[3.198]
Article 3

1. Employers shall notify the competent public authority in writing of any projected collective redundancies.

However, Member States may provide that in the case of planned collective redundancies arising from termination of the establishment's activities as a result of a judicial decision, the employer shall be obliged to notify the competent public authority in writing only if the latter so requests.

This notification shall contain all relevant information concerning the projected collective redundancies and the consultations with workers' representatives provided for in Article 2, and particularly the reasons for the redundancies, the number of workers to be made redundant, the number of workers normally employed and the period over which the redundancies are to be effected.

[Where the projected collective redundancy concerns members of the crew of a seagoing vessel, the employer shall notify the competent authority of the State of the flag which the vessel flies.]

2. Employers shall forward to the workers' representatives a copy of the notification provided for in paragraph 1.

The workers' representatives may send any comments they may have to the competent public authority.

NOTES

Para 1: words in square brackets inserted by Directive 2015/1794/EU, Art 4(2), as from 9 October 2015.

[3.199]
Article 4

1. Projected collective redundancies notified to the competent public authority shall take effect not earlier than 30 days after the notification referred to in Article 3(1) without prejudice to any provisions governing individual rights with regard to notice of dismissal.

Member States may grant the competent public authority the power to reduce the period provided for in the preceding subparagraph.

2. The period provided for in paragraph 1 shall be used by the competent public authority to seek solutions to the problems raised by the projected collective redundancies.

3. Where the initial period provided for in paragraph 1 is shorter than 60 days, Member States may grant the competent public authority the power to extend the initial period to 60 days following notification where the problems raised by the projected collective redundancies are not likely to be solved within the initial period.

Member States may grant the competent public authority wider powers of extension.

The employer must be informed of the extension and the grounds for it before expiry of the initial period provided for in paragraph 1.

4. Member States need not apply this Article to collective redundancies arising from termination of the establishment's activities where this is the result of a judicial decision.

SECTION IV FINAL PROVISIONS

[3.200]
Article 5

This Directive shall not affect the right of Member States to apply or to introduce laws, regulations or administrative provisions which are more favourable to workers or to promote or to allow the application of collective agreements more favourable to workers.

[3.201]
Article 6

Member States shall ensure that judicial and/or administrative procedures for the enforcement of obligations under this Directive are available to the workers' representatives and/or workers.

[3.202]
Article 7

Member States shall forward to the Commission the text of any fundamental provisions of national law already adopted or being adopted in the area governed by this Directive.

[3.203]
Article 8
1. The Directives listed in Annex I, Part A, are hereby repealed without prejudice to the obligations of the Member States concerning the deadlines for transposition of the said Directive set out in Annex I, Part B.
2. References to the repealed Directives shall be construed as references to this Directive and shall be read in accordance with the correlation table in Annex II.

[3.204]
Article 9
This Directive shall enter into force on the 20th day following its publication in the *Official Journal of the European Communities*.

[3.205]
Article 10
This Directive is addressed to the Member States.

ANNEX I

PART A

REPEALED DIRECTIVES
(REFERRED TO BY ARTICLE 8)

[3.206]
Council Directive 75/129/EEC and its following amendment:

Council Directive 92/56/EEC.

PART B

DEADLINES FOR TRANSPOSITION INTO NATIONAL LAW
(REFERRED TO BY ARTICLE 8)

[3.207]

Directive	*Deadline for transposition*
75/129/EEC (OJ L48, 22.2.1975, p 29)	19 February 1977
92/56/EEC (OJ L245, 26.8.1992, p 3)	24 June 1994

ANNEX II

CORRELATION TABLE

[3.208]

Directive 75/129/EEC	*This Directive*
Article 1(1), first subparagraph, point (a), first indent, point 1	Article 1(1), first subparagraph, point (a)(i), first indent
Article 1(1), first subparagraph, point (a), first indent, point 2	Article 1(1), first subparagraph, point (a)(i), second indent
Article 1(1), first subparagraph, point (a), first indent, point 3	Article 1(1), first subparagraph, point (a)(i), third indent
Article 1(1), first subparagraph, point (a), second indent	Article 1(1), first subparagraph, point (a)(ii)
Article 1(1), first subparagraph, point (b)	Article 1(1), first subparagraph, point (b)
Article 1(1), second subparagraph	Article 1(1), second subparagraph
Article 1(2)	Article 1(2)
Article 2	Article 2
Article 3	Article 3
Article 4	Article 4
Article 5	Article 5
Article 5a	Article 6
Article 6(1)	—
Article 6(2)	Article 7
Article 7	—
—	Article 8
—	Article 9

Directive 75/129/EEC	*This Directive*
—	Article 10
—	Annex I
—	Annex II

COUNCIL DIRECTIVE

(99/70/EC)

of 28 June 1999

concerning the framework agreement on fixed-term work concluded by ETUC, UNICE and CEEP

[3.209]

NOTES

Date of publication in OJ: OJ L175, 10.7.1999, p 43. The text of this Directive incorporates the corrigendum published in OJ L244, 16.9.1999, p 64 (see further Article 2 below).

For the domestic implementation of this Directive, see the Fixed-term Employees (Prevention of Less Favourable Treatment) Regulations 2002, SI 2002/2034 at **[2.553]**.

THE COUNCIL OF THE EUROPEAN UNION,

Having regard to the Treaty establishing the European Community, and in particular Article 139(2) thereof,

Having regard to the proposal from the Commission,

Whereas:

(1) Following the entry into force of the Treaty of Amsterdam the provisions of the Agreement on social policy annexed to the Protocol on social policy, annexed to the Treaty establishing the European Community have been incorporated into Articles 136 to 139 of the Treaty establishing the European Community;

(2) Management and labour (the social partners) may, in accordance with Article 139(2) of the Treaty, request jointly that agreements at Community level be implemented by a Council decision on a proposal from the Commission;

(3) Point 7 of the Community Charter of the Fundamental Social Rights of Workers provides, *inter alia*, that 'the completion of the internal market must lead to an improvement in the living and working conditions of workers in the European Community. This process must result from an approximation of these conditions while the improvement is being maintained, as regards in particular forms of employment other than open-ended contracts, such as fixed-term contracts, part-time working, temporary work and seasonal work';

(4) The Council has been unable to reach a decision on the proposal for a Directive on certain employment relationships with regard to distortions of competition,[1] nor on the proposal for a Directive on certain employment relationships with regard to working conditions;[2]

(5) The conclusions of the Essen European Council stressed the need to take measures with a view to 'increasing the employment-intensiveness of growth, in particular by a more flexible organisation of work in a way which fulfils both the wishes of employees and the requirements of competition';

(6) The Council Resolution of 9 February 1999 on the 1999 Employment Guidelines invites the social partners at all appropriate levels to negotiate agreements to modernise the organisation of work, including flexible working arrangements, with the aim of making undertakings productive and competitive and achieving the required balance between flexibility and security;

(7) The Commission, in accordance with Article 3(2) of the Agreement on social policy, has consulted management and labour on the possible direction of Community action with regard to flexible working time and job security;

(8) The Commission, considering after such consultation that Community action was desirable, once again consulted management and labour on the substance of the envisaged proposal in accordance with Article 3(3) of the said Agreement;

(9) The general cross-industry organisations, namely the Union of Industrial and Employers' Confederations of Europe (UNICE), the European Centre of Enterprises with Public Participation (CEEP) and the European Trade Union Confederation (ETUC), informed the Commission in a joint letter dated 23 March 1998 of their desire to initiate the procedure provided for in Article 4 of the said Agreement; they asked the Commission, in a joint letter, for a further period of three months; the Commission complied with this request extending the negotiation period to 30 March 1999;

(10) The said cross-industry organisations on 18 March 1999 concluded a framework agreement on fixed-term work; they forwarded to the Commission their joint request to implement the framework agreement by a Council Decision on a proposal from the Commission, in accordance with Article 4(2) of the Agreement on social policy;

(11) The Council, in its Resolution of 6 December 1994 on 'certain aspects for a European Union social policy: a contribution to economic and social convergence in the Union',[3] asked management and labour to make use of the opportunities for concluding agreements, since they are as a rule closer to social reality and to social problems;

(12) The signatory parties, in the preamble to the framework agreement on part-time work concluded on 6 June 1997, announced their intention to consider the need for similar agreements relating to other forms of flexible work;

(13) Management and labour wished to give particular attention to fixed-term work, while at the same time indicating that it was their intention to consider the need for a similar agreement relating to temporary agency work;

(14) The signatory parties wished to conclude a framework agreement on fixed-term work setting out the general principles and minimum requirements for fixed-term employment contracts and employment relationships; they have demonstrated their desire to improve the quality of fixed-term work by ensuring the application of the principle of non-discrimination, and to establish a framework to prevent abuse arising from the use of successive fixed-term employment contracts or relationships;

(15) The proper instrument for implementing the framework agreement is a directive within the meaning of Article 249 of the Treaty; it therefore binds the Member States as to the result to be achieved, whilst leaving them the choice of form and methods;

(16) In accordance with the principles of subsidiarity and proportionality as set out in Article 5 of the Treaty, the objectives of this Directive cannot be sufficiently achieved by the Member States and can therefore be better achieved by the Community; this Directive limits itself to the minimum required for the attainment of those objectives and does not go beyond what is necessary for that purpose;

(17) As regards terms used in the framework agreement but not specifically defined therein, this Directive allows Member States to define such terms in conformity with national law or practice as is the case for other Directives on social matters using similar terms, provided that the definitions in question respect the content of the framework agreement;

(18) The Commission has drafted its proposal for a Directive, in accordance with its Communication of 14 December 1993 concerning the application of the agreement on social policy and its Communication of 20 May 1998 on adapting and promoting the social dialogue at Community level, taking into account the representative status of the contracting parties, their mandate and the legality of each clause of the framework agreement; the contracting parties together have a sufficiently representative status;

(19) The Commission informed the European Parliament and the Economic and Social Committee by sending them the text of the agreement, accompanied by its proposal for a Directive and the explanatory memorandum, in accordance with its communication concerning the implementation of the Protocol on social policy;

(20) On 6 May 1999 the European Parliament adopted a Resolution on the framework agreement between the social partners;

(21) The implementation of the framework agreement contributes to achieving the objectives in Article 136 of Treaty,

NOTES

1 OJ C224, 8.9.90, p 6 and OJ C305, 5.12.90, p 8.

2 OJ C224, 8.9.90, p 4.

3 OJ C368, 23.12.94, p 6.

HAS ADOPTED THIS DIRECTIVE—

[3.210]
Article 1
The purpose of the Directive is to put into effect the framework agreement on fixed-term contracts concluded on 18 March 1999 between the general cross-industry organisations (ETUC, UNICE and CEEP) annexed hereto.

[3.211]
Article 2
Member States shall bring into force the laws, regulations and administrative provisions necessary to comply with this Directive by 10 July 2001, or shall ensure that, by that date at the latest, management and labour have introduced the necessary measures by agreement, the Member States being required to take any necessary measures to enable them at any time to be in a position to guarantee the results imposed by this Directive. They shall forthwith inform the Commission thereof.

Member States may have a maximum of one more year, if necessary, and following consultation with management and labour, to take account of special difficulties or implementation by a collective agreement. They shall inform the Commission forthwith in such circumstances.

When Member States adopt the provisions referred to in the first paragraph, these shall contain a reference to this Directive or shall be accompanied by such reference at the time of their official publication. The procedure for such reference shall be adopted by the Member States.

NOTES

The date of 10 July 2001 in the first paragraph is by virtue of the Corrigendum to Council Directive 1999/70/EC of 28 June 1999 concerning the framework agreement on fixed-term work concluded by ETUC, UNICE and CEEP. The original date (as published in the Official Journal) was 10 July 1999.

[3.212]
Article 3

This Directive shall enter into force on the day of its publication in the *Official Journal of the European Communities*.

[3.213]
Article 4

This Directive is addressed to the Member States.

ANNEX
ETUC-UNICE-CEEP

FRAMEWORK AGREEMENT ON FIXED-TERM WORK

[3.214]
Preamble

This framework agreement illustrates the role that the social partners can play in the European employment strategy agreed at the 1997 Luxembourg extra-ordinary summit and, following the framework agreement on part-time work, represents a further contribution towards achieving a better balance between "flexibility in working time and security for workers".

The parties to this agreement recognise that contracts of an indefinite duration are, and will continue to be, the general form of employment relationship between employers and workers. They also recognise that fixed-term employment contracts respond, in certain circumstances, to the needs of both employers and workers.

This agreement sets out the general principles and minimum requirements relating to fixed-term work, recognising that their detailed application needs to take account of the realities of specific national, sectoral and seasonal situations. It illustrates the willingness of the Social Partners to establish a general framework for ensuring equal treatment for fixed-term workers by protecting them against discrimination and for using fixed-term employment contracts on a basis acceptable to employers and workers.

This agreement applies to fixed-term workers with the exception of those placed by a temporary work agency at the disposition of a user enterprise. It is the intention of the parties to consider the need for a similar agreement relating to temporary agency work.

This agreement relates to the employment conditions of fixed-term workers, recognising that matters relating to statutory social security are for decision by the Member States. In this respect the Social Partners note the Employment Declaration of the Dublin European Council in 1996 which emphasised *inter alia*, the need to develop more employment-friendly social security systems by "developing social protection systems capable of adapting to new patterns of work and providing appropriate protection to those engaged in such work". The parties to this agreement reiterate the view expressed in the 1997 part-time agreement that Member States should give effect to this Declaration without delay.

In addition, it is also recognised that innovations in occupational social protection systems are necessary in order to adapt them to current conditions, and in particular to provide for the transferability of rights.

The ETUC, UNICE and CEEP request the Commission to submit this framework agreement to the Council for a decision making these requirements binding in the Member States which are party to the Agreement on social policy annexed to the Protocol (No 14) on social policy annexed to the Treaty establishing the European Community.

The parties to this agreement ask the Commission, in its proposal to implement the agreement, to request Member States to adopt the laws, regulations and administrative provisions necessary to comply with the Council decision within two years from its adoption or ensure[1] that the social partners establish the necessary measures by way of agreement by the end of this period. Member States may, if necessary and following consultation with the social partners, and in order to take account of particular difficulties or implementation by collective agreement have up to a maximum of one additional year to comply with this provision.

The parties to this agreement request that the social partners are consulted prior to any legislative, regulatory or administrative initiative taken by a Member State to conform to the present agreement.

Without prejudice to the role of national courts and the Court of Justice, the parties to this agreement request that any matter relating to the interpretation of this agreement at European level, should in the first instance, be referred by the Commission to them for an opinion.

NOTES

[1] Within the meaning of Article 2.4 of the Agreement on social policy annexed to the Protocol (No 14) on social policy annexed to the Treaty establishing the European Community.

[3.215]

General considerations

1. Having regard to the Agreement on social policy annexed to the Protocol (No 14) on social policy annexed to the Treaty establishing the European Community, and in particular Article 3.4 and 4.2 thereof;

2. Whereas Article 4.2 of the Agreement on social policy provides that agreements concluded at Community level may be implemented, at the joint request of the signatory parties, by a Council decision on a proposal from the Commission;

3. Whereas, in its second consultation document on flexibility in working time and security for workers, the Commission announced its intention to propose a legally-binding Community measure;

4. Whereas in its opinion on the proposal for a directive on part-time work, the European Parliament invited the Commission to submit immediately proposals for directives on other forms of flexible work, such as fixed-term work and temporary agency work;

5. Whereas in the conclusions of the extraordinary summit on employment adopted in Luxembourg, the European Council invited the social partners to negotiate agreements to "modernise the organisation of work, including flexible working arrangements, with the aim of making undertakings productive and competitive and achieving the required balance between flexibility and security";

6. Whereas employment contracts of an indefinite duration are the general form of employment relationships and contribute to quality of life of the workers concerned and improve performance;

7. Whereas the use of fixed-term employment contracts based on objective reasons is a way to prevent abuse;

8. Whereas fixed-term employment contracts are a feature of employment in certain sectors, occupations and activities which can suit both employers and workers;

9. Whereas more than half of fixed-term workers in the European Union are women and this agreement can therefore contribute to improving equality of opportunities between women and men;

10. Whereas this agreement refers back to Member States and social partners for the arrangements for the application of its general principles, minimum requirements and provisions, in order to take account of the situation in each Member State and the circumstances of particular sectors and occupations, including the activities of a seasonal nature;

11. Whereas this agreement takes into consideration the need to improve social policy requirements, to enhance the competitiveness of the Community economy and to avoid imposing administrative, financial and legal constraints in a way which would hold back the creation and development of small and medium-sized undertakings;

12. Whereas the social partners are best placed to find solutions that correspond to the needs of both employers and workers and shall therefore be given a special role in the implementation and application of this agreement.

The signatory parties have agreed the following

[3.216]

Purpose (clause 1)

The purpose of this framework agreement is to—

(1) improve the quality of fixed-term work by ensuring the application of the principle of non-discrimination;

(2) establish a framework to prevent abuse arising from the use of successive fixed-term employment contracts or relationships.

Scope (clause 2)

1. This agreement applies to fixed-term workers who have an employment contract or employment relationship as defined in law, collective agreements or practice in each Member State.

2. Member States after consultation with the social partners and/or the social partners may provide that this agreement does not apply to—

(a) initial vocational training relationships and apprenticeship schemes;

(b) employment contracts and relationships which have been concluded within the framework of a specific public or publicly-supported training, integration and vocational retraining programme.

Definitions (clause 3)

1. For the purpose of this agreement the term "fixed-term worker" means a person having an employment contract or relationship entered into directly between an employer and a worker where the end of the employment contract or relationship is determined by objective conditions such as reaching a specific date, completing a specific task, or the occurrence of a specific event.

2. For the purpose of this agreement, the term "comparable permanent worker" means a worker with an employment contract or relationship of an indefinite duration, in the same establishment, engaged in the same or similar work/occupation, due regard being given to qualifications/skills.

Where there is no comparable permanent worker in the same establishment, the comparison shall be made by reference to the applicable collective agreement, or where there is no applicable collective agreement, in accordance with national law, collective agreements or practice.

Principle of non-discrimination (clause 4)

1. In respect of employment conditions, fixed-term workers shall not be treated in a less favourable manner than comparable permanent workers solely because they have a fixed-term contract or relation unless justified on objective grounds.

2. Where appropriate, the principle of *pro rata temporis* shall apply.

3. The arrangements for the application of this clause shall be defined by the Member States after consultation with the social partners and/or the social partners, having regard to Community law, national law, collective agreements and practice.

4. Period of service qualifications relating to particular conditions of employment shall be the same for fixed term workers as for permanent workers except where different length of service qualifications are justified on objective grounds.

Measures to prevent abuse (clause 5)

1. To prevent abuse arising from the use of successive fixed-term employment contracts or relationships, Member States, after consultation with social partners in accordance with national law, collective agreements or practice, and/or the social partners, shall, where there are no equivalent legal measures to prevent abuse, introduce in a manner which takes account of the needs of specific sectors and/or categories of workers, one or more of the following measures—

(a) objective reasons justifying the renewal of such contracts or relationships;

(b) the maximum total duration of successive fixed-term employment contracts or relationships;

(c) the number of renewals of such contracts or relationships.

2. Member States after consultation with the social partners and/or the social partners, shall, where appropriate, determine under what conditions fixed-term employment contracts or relationships—

(a) shall be regarded as "successive";

(b) shall be deemed to be contracts or relationships of indefinite duration.

Information and employment opportunities (clause 6)

1. Employers shall inform fixed-term workers about vacancies which become available in the undertaking or establishment to ensure that they have the same opportunity to secure permanent positions as other workers. Such information may be provided by way of a general announcement at a suitable place in the undertaking or establishment.

2. As far as possible, employers should facilitate access by fixed-term workers to appropriate training opportunities to enhance their skills, career development and occupational mobility.

Information and consultation (clause 7)

1. Fixed-term workers shall be taken into consideration in calculating the threshold above which workers' representative bodies provided for in national and Community law may be constituted in the undertaking as required by national provisions.

2. The arrangements for the application of clause 7.1 shall be defined by Member States after consultation with the social partners and/or the social partners in accordance with national law, collective agreements or practice and having regard to clause 4.1.

3. As far as possible, employers should give consideration to the provision of appropriate information to existing workers' representative bodies about fixed-term work in the undertaking.

Provisions on implementation (clause 8)

1. Member States and/or the social partners can maintain or introduce more favourable provisions for workers than set out in this agreement.

2. This agreement shall be without prejudice to any more specific Community provisions, and in particular Community provisions concerning equal treatment or opportunities for men and women.

3. Implementation of this agreement shall not constitute valid grounds for reducing the general level of protection afforded to workers in the field of the agreement.

4. The present agreement does not prejudice the right of the social partners to conclude at the appropriate level, including European level, agreements adapting and/or complementing the provisions of this agreement in a manner which will take account of the specific needs of the social partners concerned.

5. The prevention and settlement of disputes and grievances arising from the application of this agreement shall be dealt with in accordance with national law, collective agreements and practice.

6. The signatory parties shall review the application of this agreement five years after the date of the Council decision if requested by one of the parties to this agreement.

18 March 1999

COUNCIL DIRECTIVE

(2000/43/EC)

of 29 June 2000

implementing the principle of equal treatment between persons irrespective of racial or ethnic origin

[3.217]

NOTES

Date of publication in OJ: OJ L180, 19.7.2000, p 22.

For the domestic implementation of this Directive, see now the Equality Act 2010, s 9, Part 2, Chapter 2, and Part 5 (the 2010 Act is at **[1.1620]**).

See *Harvey* L(2)(e), (3), (4), (5).

THE COUNCIL OF THE EUROPEAN UNION,

Having regard to the Treaty establishing the European Community and in particular Article 13 thereof,

Having regard to the proposal from the Commission,[1]

Having regard to the opinion of the European Parliament,[2]

Having regard to the opinion of the Economic and Social Committee,[3]

Having regard to the opinion of the Committee of the Regions,[4]

Whereas:

(1) The Treaty on European Union marks a new stage in the process of creating an ever closer union among the peoples of Europe.

(2) In accordance with Article 6 of the Treaty on European Union, the European Union is founded on the principles of liberty, democracy, respect for human rights and fundamental freedoms, and the rule of law, principles which are common to the Member States, and should respect fundamental rights as guaranteed by the European Convention for the protection of Human Rights and Fundamental Freedoms and as they result from the constitutional traditions common to the Member States, as general principles of Community Law.

(3) The right to equality before the law and protection against discrimination for all persons constitutes a universal right recognised by the Universal Declaration of Human Rights, the United Nations Convention on the Elimination of all forms of Discrimination Against Women, the International Convention on the Elimination of all forms of Racial Discrimination and the United Nations Covenants on Civil and Political Rights and on Economic, Social and Cultural Rights and by the European Convention for the Protection of Human Rights and Fundamental Freedoms, to which all Member States are signatories.

(4) It is important to respect such fundamental rights and freedoms, including the right to freedom of association. It is also important, in the context of the access to and provision of goods and services, to respect the protection of private and family life and transactions carried out in this context.

(5) The European Parliament has adopted a number of Resolutions on the fight against racism in the European Union.

(6) The European Union rejects theories which attempt to determine the existence of separate human races. The use of the term "racial origin" in this Directive does not imply an acceptance of such theories.

(7) The European Council in Tampere, on 15 and 16 October 1999, invited the Commission to come forward as soon as possible with proposals implementing Article 13 of the EC Treaty as regards the fight against racism and xenophobia.

(8) The Employment Guidelines 2000 agreed by the European Council in Helsinki, on 10 and 11 December 1999, stress the need to foster conditions for a socially inclusive labour market by formulating a coherent set of policies aimed at combating discrimination against groups such as ethnic minorities.

(9) Discrimination based on racial or ethnic origin may undermine the achievement of the objectives of the EC Treaty, in particular the attainment of a high level of employment and of social protection, the raising of the standard of living and quality of life, economic and social cohesion and solidarity. It may also undermine the objective of developing the European Union as an area of freedom, security and justice.

(10) The Commission presented a communication on racism, xenophobia and anti-Semitism in December 1995.

(11) The Council adopted on 15 July 1996 Joint Action (96/443/JHA) concerning action to combat racism and xenophobia[5] under which the Member States undertake to ensure effective judicial cooperation in respect of offences based on racist or xenophobic behaviour.

(12) To ensure the development of democratic and tolerant societies which allow the participation of all persons irrespective of racial or ethnic origin, specific action in the field of discrimination based on racial or ethnic origin should go beyond access to employed and self-employed activities and cover areas such as education, social protection including social security and healthcare, social advantages and access to and supply of goods and services.

(13) To this end, any direct or indirect discrimination based on racial or ethnic origin as regards the areas covered by this Directive should be prohibited throughout the Community. This prohibition of discrimination should also apply to nationals of third countries, but does not cover differences of treatment based on nationality and is without prejudice to provisions governing the entry and residence of third-country nationals and their access to employment and to occupation.

(14) In implementing the principle of equal treatment irrespective of racial or ethnic origin, the Community should, in accordance with Article 3(2) of the EC Treaty, aim to eliminate inequalities, and to promote equality between men and women, especially since women are often the victims of multiple discrimination.

(15) The appreciation of the facts from which it may be inferred that there has been direct or indirect discrimination is a matter for national judicial or other competent bodies, in accordance with rules of national law or practice. Such rules may provide in particular for indirect discrimination to be established by any means including on the basis of statistical evidence.

(16) It is important to protect all natural persons against discrimination on grounds of racial or ethnic origin. Member States should also provide, where appropriate and in accordance with their national traditions and practice, protection for legal persons where they suffer discrimination on grounds of the racial or ethnic origin of their members.

(17) The prohibition of discrimination should be without prejudice to the maintenance or adoption of measures intended to prevent or compensate for disadvantages suffered by a group of persons of a particular racial or ethnic origin, and such measures may permit organisations of persons of a particular racial or ethnic origin where their main object is the promotion of the special needs of those persons.

(18) In very limited circumstances, a difference of treatment may be justified where a characteristic related to racial or ethnic origin constitutes a genuine and determining occupational requirement, when the objective is legitimate and the requirement is proportionate. Such circumstances should be included in the information provided by the Member States to the Commission.

(19) Persons who have been subject to discrimination based on racial and ethnic origin should have adequate means of legal protection. To provide a more effective level of protection, associations or legal entities should also be empowered to engage, as the Member States so determine, either on behalf or in support of any victim, in proceedings, without prejudice to national rules of procedure concerning representation and defence before the courts.

(20) The effective implementation of the principle of equality requires adequate judicial protection against victimisation.

(21) The rules on the burden of proof must be adapted when there is a prima facie case of discrimination and, for the principle of equal treatment to be applied effectively, the burden of proof must shift back to the respondent when evidence of such discrimination is brought.

(22) Member States need not apply the rules on the burden of proof to proceedings in which it is for the court or other competent body to investigate the facts of the case. The procedures thus referred to are those in which the plaintiff is not required to prove the facts, which it is for the court or competent body to investigate.

(23) Member States should promote dialogue between the social partners and with non-governmental organisations to address different forms of discrimination and to combat them.

(24) Protection against discrimination based on racial or ethnic origin would itself be strengthened by the existence of a body or bodies in each Member State, with competence to analyse the problems involved, to study possible solutions and to provide concrete assistance for the victims.

(25) This Directive lays down minimum requirements, thus giving the Member States the option of introducing or maintaining more favourable provisions. The implementation of this Directive should not serve to justify any regression in relation to the situation which already prevails in each Member State.

(26) Member States should provide for effective, proportionate and dissuasive sanctions in case of breaches of the obligations under this Directive.

(27) The Member States may entrust management and labour, at their joint request, with the implementation of this Directive as regards provisions falling within the scope of collective agreements, provided that the Member States take all the necessary steps to ensure that they can at all times guarantee the results imposed by this Directive.

(28) In accordance with the principles of subsidiarity and proportionality as set out in Article 5 of the EC Treaty, the objective of this Directive, namely ensuring a common high level of protection against discrimination in all the Member States, cannot be sufficiently achieved by the Member States and can therefore, by reason of the scale and impact of the proposed action, be better achieved by the Community. This Directive does not go beyond what is necessary in order to achieve those objectives,

NOTES

1 Not yet published in the Official Journal.

2 Opinion delivered on 18.5.2000 (not yet published in the Official Journal).

3 Opinion delivered on 12.4.2000 (not yet published in the Official Journal).

4 Opinion delivered on 31.5.2000 (not yet published in the Official Journal).

5 OJ L185, 24.7.96, p 5.

HAS ADOPTED THIS DIRECTIVE—

CHAPTER I GENERAL PROVISIONS

[3.218]
Article 1
Purpose

The purpose of this Directive is to lay down a framework for combating discrimination on the grounds of racial or ethnic origin, with a view to putting into effect in the Member States the principle of equal treatment.

[3.219]
Article 2
Concept of discrimination

1. For the purposes of this Directive, the principle of equal treatment shall mean that there shall be no direct or indirect discrimination based on racial or ethnic origin.

2. For the purposes of paragraph 1—

(a) direct discrimination shall be taken to occur where one person is treated less favourably than another is, has been or would be treated in a comparable situation on grounds of racial or ethnic origin;

(b) indirect discrimination shall be taken to occur where an apparently neutral provision, criterion or practice would put persons of a racial or ethnic origin at a particular disadvantage compared with other persons, unless that provision, criterion or practice is objectively justified by a legitimate aim and the means of achieving that aim are appropriate and necessary.

3. Harassment shall be deemed to be discrimination within the meaning of paragraph 1, when an unwanted conduct related to racial or ethnic origin takes place with the purpose or effect of violating the dignity of a person and of creating an intimidating, hostile, degrading, humiliating or offensive environment. In this context, the concept of harassment may be defined in accordance with the national laws and practice of the Member States.
4. An instruction to discriminate against persons on grounds of racial or ethnic origin shall be deemed to be discrimination within the meaning of paragraph 1.

[3.220]
Article 3
Scope
1. Within the limits of the powers conferred upon the Community, this Directive shall apply to all persons, as regards both the public and private sectors, including public bodies, in relation to—
- (a) conditions for access to employment, to self-employment and to occupation, including selection criteria and recruitment conditions, whatever the branch of activity and at all levels of the professional hierarchy, including promotion;
- (b) access to all types and to all levels of vocational guidance, vocational training, advanced vocational training and retraining, including practical work experience;
- (c) employment and working conditions, including dismissals and pay;
- (d) membership of and involvement in an organisation of workers or employers, or any organisation whose members carry on a particular profession, including the benefits provided for by such organisations;
- (e) social protection, including social security and healthcare;
- (f) social advantages;
- (g) education;
- (h) access to and supply of goods and services which are available to the public, including housing.

2. This Directive does not cover difference of treatment based on nationality and is without prejudice to provisions and conditions relating to the entry into and residence of third-country nationals and stateless persons on the territory of Member States, and to any treatment which arises from the legal status of the third-country nationals and stateless persons concerned.

[3.221]
Article 4
Genuine and determining occupational requirements
Notwithstanding Article 2(1) and (2), Member States may provide that a difference of treatment which is based on a characteristic related to racial or ethnic origin shall not constitute discrimination where, by reason of the nature of the particular occupational activities concerned or of the context in which they are carried out, such a characteristic constitutes a genuine and determining occupational requirement, provided that the objective is legitimate and the requirement is proportionate.

[3.222]
Article 5
Positive action
With a view to ensuring full equality in practice, the principle of equal treatment shall not prevent any Member State from maintaining or adopting specific measures to prevent or compensate for disadvantages linked to racial or ethnic origin.

[3.223]
Article 6
Minimum requirements
1. Member States may introduce or maintain provisions which are more favourable to the protection of the principle of equal treatment than those laid down in this Directive.
2. The implementation of this Directive shall under no circumstances constitute grounds for a reduction in the level of protection against discrimination already afforded by Member States in the fields covered by this Directive.

CHAPTER II REMEDIES AND ENFORCEMENT

[3.224]
Article 7
Defence of rights
1. Member States shall ensure that judicial and/or administrative procedures, including where they deem it appropriate conciliation procedures, for the enforcement of obligations under this Directive are available to all persons who consider themselves wronged by failure to apply the principle of equal treatment to them, even after the relationship in which the discrimination is alleged to have occurred has ended.
2. Member States shall ensure that associations, organisations or other legal entities, which have, in accordance with the criteria laid down by their national law, a legitimate interest in ensuring that the provisions of this Directive are complied with, may engage, either on behalf or in support of the complainant, with his or her approval, in any judicial and/or administrative procedure provided for the enforcement of obligations under this Directive.
3. Paragraphs 1 and 2 are without prejudice to national rules relating to time limits for bringing actions as regards the principle of equality of treatment.

[3.225]
Article 8
Burden of proof

1. Member States shall take such measures as are necessary, in accordance with their national judicial systems, to ensure that, when persons who consider themselves wronged because the principle of equal treatment has not been applied to them establish, before a court or other competent authority, facts from which it may be presumed that there has been direct or indirect discrimination, it shall be for the respondent to prove that there has been no breach of the principle of equal treatment.
2. Paragraph 1 shall not prevent Member States from introducing rules of evidence which are more favourable to plaintiffs.
3. Paragraph 1 shall not apply to criminal procedures.
4. Paragraphs 1, 2 and 3 shall also apply to any proceedings brought in accordance with Article 7(2).
5. Member States need not apply paragraph 1 to proceedings in which it is for the court or competent body to investigate the facts of the case.

[3.226]
Article 9
Victimisation

Member States shall introduce into their national legal systems such measures as are necessary to protect individuals from any adverse treatment or adverse consequence as a reaction to a complaint or to proceedings aimed at enforcing compliance with the principle of equal treatment.

[3.227]
Article 10
Dissemination of information

Member States shall take care that the provisions adopted pursuant to this Directive, together with the relevant provisions already in force, are brought to the attention of the persons concerned by all appropriate means throughout their territory.

[3.228]
Article 11
Social dialogue

1. Member States shall, in accordance with national traditions and practice, take adequate measures to promote the social dialogue between the two sides of industry with a view to fostering equal treatment, including through the monitoring of workplace practices, collective agreements, codes of conduct, research or exchange of experiences and good practices.
2. Where consistent with national traditions and practice, Member States shall encourage the two sides of the industry without prejudice to their autonomy to conclude, at the appropriate level, agreements laying down anti-discrimination rules in the fields referred to in Article 3 which fall within the scope of collective bargaining. These agreements shall respect the minimum requirements laid down by this Directive and the relevant national implementing measures.

[3.229]
Article 12
Dialogue with non-governmental organisations

Member States shall encourage dialogue with appropriate non-governmental organisations which have, in accordance with their national law and practice, a legitimate interest in contributing to the fight against discrimination on grounds of racial and ethnic origin with a view to promoting the principle of equal treatment.

CHAPTER III BODIES FOR THE PROMOTION OF EQUAL TREATMENT

[3.230]
Article 13

1. Member States shall designate a body or bodies for the promotion of equal treatment of all persons without discrimination on the grounds of racial or ethnic origin. These bodies may form part of agencies charged at national level with the defence of human rights or the safeguard of individuals' rights.
2. Member States shall ensure that the competences of these bodies include—
   — without prejudice to the right of victims and of associations, organisations or other legal entities referred to in Article 7(2), providing independent assistance to victims of discrimination in pursuing their complaints about discrimination,
   — conducting independent surveys concerning discrimination,
   — publishing independent reports and making recommendations on any issue relating to such discrimination.

CHAPTER IV FINAL PROVISIONS

[3.231]
Article 14
Compliance

Member States shall take the necessary measures to ensure that—
(a) any laws, regulations and administrative provisions contrary to the principle of equal treatment are abolished;

(b) any provisions contrary to the principle of equal treatment which are included in individual or collective contracts or agreements, internal rules of undertakings, rules governing profit-making or non-profit-making associations, and rules governing the independent professions and workers' and employers' organisations, are or may be declared, null and void or are amended.

[3.232]
Article 15
Sanctions
Member States shall lay down the rules on sanctions applicable to infringements of the national provisions adopted pursuant to this Directive and shall take all measures necessary to ensure that they are applied. The sanctions, which may comprise the payment of compensation to the victim, must be effective, proportionate and dissuasive. The Member States shall notify those provisions to the Commission by 19 July 2003 at the latest and shall notify it without delay of any subsequent amendment affecting them.

[3.233]
Article 16
Implementation
Member States shall adopt the laws, regulations and administrative provisions necessary to comply with this Directive by 19 July 2003 or may entrust management and labour, at their joint request, with the implementation of this Directive as regards provisions falling within the scope of collective agreements. In such cases, Member States shall ensure that by 19 July 2003, management and labour introduce the necessary measures by agreement, Member States being required to take any necessary measures to enable them at any time to be in a position to guarantee the results imposed by this Directive. They shall forthwith inform the Commission thereof.

When Member States adopt these measures, they shall contain a reference to this Directive or be accompanied by such a reference on the occasion of their official publication. The methods of making such a reference shall be laid down by the Member States.

[3.234]
Article 17
Report
1. Member States shall communicate to the Commission by 19 July 2005, and every five years thereafter, all the information necessary for the Commission to draw up a report to the European Parliament and the Council on the application of this Directive.
2. The Commission's report shall take into account, as appropriate, the views of the European Monitoring Centre on Racism and Xenophobia, as well as the viewpoints of the social partners and relevant non-governmental organisations. In accordance with the principle of gender mainstreaming, this report shall, inter alia, provide an assessment of the impact of the measures taken on women and men. In the light of the information received, this report shall include, if necessary, proposals to revise and update this Directive.

[3.235]
Article 18
Entry into force
This Directive shall enter into force on the day of its publication in the *Official Journal of the European Communities*.

[3.236]
Article 19
Addressees
This Directive is addressed to the Member States.

COUNCIL DIRECTIVE

(2000/78/EC)

of 27 November 2000

establishing a general framework for equal treatment in employment and occupation

[3.237]

NOTES

Date of publication in OJ: OJ L303, 2.12.2000, p 16.

For the domestic implementation of this Directive, see now the Equality Act 2010, Parts 2, 5 and 9 (the 2010 Act is at **[1.1620]**).

See *Harvey* L.

THE COUNCIL OF THE EUROPEAN UNION,

Having regard to the Treaty establishing the European Community, and in particular Article 13 thereof,

Having regard to the proposal from the Commission,[1]

Part 3 EU Materials

Having regard to the Opinion of the European Parliament,[2]
Having regard to the Opinion of the Economic and Social Committee,[3]
Having regard to the Opinion of the Committee of the Regions,[4]
Whereas—

(1) In accordance with Article 6 of the Treaty on European Union, the European Union is founded on the principles of liberty, democracy, respect for human rights and fundamental freedoms, and the rule of law, principles which are common to all Member States and it respects fundamental rights, as guaranteed by the European Convention for the Protection of Human Rights and Fundamental Freedoms and as they result from the constitutional traditions common to the Member States, as general principles of Community law.

(2) The principle of equal treatment between women and men is well established by an important body of Community law, in particular in Council Directive 76/207/EEC of 9 February 1976 on the implementation of the principle of equal treatment for men and women as regards access to employment, vocational training and promotion, and working conditions.[5]

(3) In implementing the principle of equal treatment, the Community should, in accordance with Article 3(2) of the EC Treaty, aim to eliminate inequalities, and to promote equality between men and women, especially since women are often the victims of multiple discrimination.

(4) The right of all persons to equality before the law and protection against discrimination constitutes a universal right recognised by the Universal Declaration of Human Rights, the United Nations Convention on the Elimination of All Forms of Discrimination against Women, United Nations Covenants on Civil and Political Rights and on Economic, Social and Cultural Rights and by the European Convention for the Protection of Human Rights and Fundamental Freedoms, to which all Member States are signatories. Convention No 111 of the International Labour Organisation (ILO) prohibits discrimination in the field of employment and occupation.

(5) It is important to respect such fundamental rights and freedoms. This Directive does not prejudice freedom of association, including the right to establish unions with others and to join unions to defend one's interests.

(6) The Community Charter of the Fundamental Social Rights of Workers recognises the importance of combating every form of discrimination, including the need to take appropriate action for the social and economic integration of elderly and disabled people.

(7) The EC Treaty includes among its objectives the promotion of coordination between employment policies of the Member States. To this end, a new employment chapter was incorporated in the EC Treaty as a means of developing a coordinated European strategy for employment to promote a skilled, trained and adaptable workforce.

(8) The Employment Guidelines for 2000 agreed by the European Council at Helsinki on 10 and 11 December 1999 stress the need to foster a labour market favourable to social integration by formulating a coherent set of policies aimed at combating discrimination against groups such as persons with disability. They also emphasise the need to pay particular attention to supporting older workers, in order to increase their participation in the labour force.

(9) Employment and occupation are key elements in guaranteeing equal opportunities for all and contribute strongly to the full participation of citizens in economic, cultural and social life and to realising their potential.

(10) On 29 June 2000 the Council adopted Directive 2000/43/EC[6] implementing the principle of equal treatment between persons irrespective of racial or ethnic origin. That Directive already provides protection against such discrimination in the field of employment and occupation.

(11) Discrimination based on religion or belief, disability, age or sexual orientation may undermine the achievement of the objectives of the EC Treaty, in particular the attainment of a high level of employment and social protection, raising the standard of living and the quality of life, economic and social cohesion and solidarity, and the free movement of persons.

(12) To this end, any direct or indirect discrimination based on religion or belief, disability, age or sexual orientation as regards the areas covered by this Directive should be prohibited throughout the Community. This prohibition of discrimination should also apply to nationals of third countries but does not cover differences of treatment based on nationality and is without prejudice to provisions governing the entry and residence of third-country nationals and their access to employment and occupation.

(13) This Directive does not apply to social security and social protection schemes whose benefits are not treated as income within the meaning given to that term for the purpose of applying Article 141 of the EC Treaty, nor to any kind of payment by the State aimed at providing access to employment or maintaining employment.

(14) This Directive shall be without prejudice to national provisions laying down retirement ages.

(15) The appreciation of the facts from which it may be inferred that there has been direct or indirect discrimination is a matter for national judicial or other competent bodies, in accordance with rules of national law or practice. Such rules may provide, in particular, for indirect discrimination to be established by any means including on the basis of statistical evidence.

(16) The provision of measures to accommodate the needs of disabled people at the workplace plays an important role in combating discrimination on grounds of disability.

(17) This Directive does not require the recruitment, promotion, maintenance in employment or training of an individual who is not competent, capable and available to perform the essential functions of the post concerned or to undergo the relevant training, without prejudice to the obligation to provide reasonable accommodation for people with disabilities.

(18) This Directive does not require, in particular, the armed forces and the police, prison or emergency services to recruit or maintain in employment persons who do not have the required capacity to carry out the range of functions that they may be called upon to perform with regard to the legitimate objective of preserving the operational capacity of those services.

(19) Moreover, in order that the Member States may continue to safeguard the combat effectiveness of their armed forces, they may choose not to apply the provisions of this Directive concerning disability and age to all or part of their armed forces. The Member States which make that choice must define the scope of that derogation.

(20) Appropriate measures should be provided, ie effective and practical measures to adapt the workplace to the disability, for example adapting premises and equipment, patterns of working time, the distribution of tasks or the provision of training or integration resources.

(21) To determine whether the measures in question give rise to a disproportionate burden, account should be taken in particular of the financial and other costs entailed, the scale and financial resources of the organisation or undertaking and the possibility of obtaining public funding or any other assistance.

(22) This Directive is without prejudice to national laws on marital status and the benefits dependent thereon.

(23) In very limited circumstances, a difference of treatment may be justified where a characteristic related to religion or belief, disability, age or sexual orientation constitutes a genuine and determining occupational requirement, when the objective is legitimate and the requirement is proportionate. Such circumstances should be included in the information provided by the Member States to the Commission.

(24) The European Union in its Declaration No 11 on the status of churches and non-confessional organisations, annexed to the Final Act of the Amsterdam Treaty, has explicitly recognised that it respects and does not prejudice the status under national law of churches and religious associations or communities in the Member States and that it equally respects the status of philosophical and non-confessional organisations. With this in view, Member States may maintain or lay down specific provisions on genuine, legitimate and justified occupational requirements which might be required for carrying out an occupational activity.

(25) The prohibition of age discrimination is an essential part of meeting the aims set out in the Employment Guidelines and encouraging diversity in the workforce. However, differences in treatment in connection with age may be justified under certain circumstances and therefore require specific provisions which may vary in accordance with the situation in Member States. It is therefore essential to distinguish between differences in treatment which are justified, in particular by legitimate employment policy, labour market and vocational training objectives, and discrimination which must be prohibited.

(26) The prohibition of discrimination should be without prejudice to the maintenance or adoption of measures intended to prevent or compensate for disadvantages suffered by a group of persons of a particular religion or belief, disability, age or sexual orientation, and such measures may permit organisations of persons of a particular religion or belief, disability, age or sexual orientation where their main object is the promotion of the special needs of those persons.

(27) In its Recommendation 86/379/EEC of 24 July 1986 on the employment of disabled people in the Community,[7] the Council established a guideline framework setting out examples of positive action to promote the employment and training of disabled people, and in its Resolution of 17 June 1999 on equal employment opportunities for people with disabilities,[8] affirmed the importance of giving specific attention inter alia to recruitment, retention, training and lifelong learning with regard to disabled persons.

(28) This Directive lays down minimum requirements, thus giving the Member States the option of introducing or maintaining more favourable provisions. The implementation of this Directive should not serve to justify any regression in relation to the situation which already prevails in each Member State.

(29) Persons who have been subject to discrimination based on religion or belief, disability, age or sexual orientation should have adequate means of legal protection. To provide a more effective level of protection, associations or legal entities should also be empowered to engage in proceedings, as the Member States so determine, either on behalf or in support of any victim, without prejudice to national rules of procedure concerning representation and defence before the courts.

(30) The effective implementation of the principle of equality requires adequate judicial protection against victimisation.

(31) The rules on the burden of proof must be adapted when there is a prima facie case of discrimination and, for the principle of equal treatment to be applied effectively, the burden of proof must shift back to the respondent when evidence of such discrimination is brought. However, it is not for the respondent to prove that the plaintiff adheres to a particular religion or belief, has a particular disability, is of a particular age or has a particular sexual orientation.

(32) Member States need not apply the rules on the burden of proof to proceedings in which it is for the court or other competent body to investigate the facts of the case. The procedures thus referred to are those in which the plaintiff is not required to prove the facts, which it is for the court or competent body to investigate.

(33) Member States should promote dialogue between the social partners and, within the framework of national practice, with non-governmental organisations to address different forms of discrimination at the workplace and to combat them.

(34) The need to promote peace and reconciliation between the major communities in Northern Ireland necessitates the incorporation of particular provisions into this Directive.

(35) Member States should provide for effective, proportionate and dissuasive sanctions in case of breaches of the obligations under this Directive.

(36) Member States may entrust the social partners, at their joint request, with the implementation of this Directive, as regards the provisions concerning collective agreements, provided they take any necessary steps to ensure that they are at all times able to guarantee the results required by this Directive.

(37) In accordance with the principle of subsidiarity set out in Article 5 of the EC Treaty, the objective of this Directive, namely the creation within the Community of a level playing-field as regards equality in employment and occupation, cannot be sufficiently achieved by the Member States and can therefore, by reason of the scale and impact of the action, be better achieved at Community level. In accordance with the principle of proportionality, as set out in that Article, this Directive does not go beyond what is necessary in order to achieve that objective.

NOTES

1 OJ C177 E, 27.6.2000, p 42.

2 Opinion delivered on 12 October 2000 (not yet published in the Official Journal).

3 OJ C204, 18.7.2000, p 82.

4 OJ C226, 8.8.2000, p 1.

5 OJ L9, 14.2.1976, p 40.

6 OJ L180, 19.7.2000, p 22.

7 OJ L225, 12.8.1986, p 43.

8 OJ C186, 2.7.1999, p 3.

HAS ADOPTED THIS DIRECTIVE—

CHAPTER I GENERAL PROVISIONS

[3.238]
Article 1
Purpose

The purpose of this Directive is to lay down a general framework for combating discrimination on the grounds of religion or belief, disability, age or sexual orientation as regards employment and occupation, with a view to putting into effect in the Member States the principle of equal treatment.

[3.239]
Article 2
Concept of discrimination

1. For the purposes of this Directive, the "principle of equal treatment" shall mean that there shall be no direct or indirect discrimination whatsoever on any of the grounds referred to in Article 1.

2. For the purposes of paragraph 1—
 (a) direct discrimination shall be taken to occur where one person is treated less favourably than another is, has been or would be treated in a comparable situation, on any of the grounds referred to in Article 1;
 (b) indirect discrimination shall be taken to occur where an apparently neutral provision, criterion or practice would put persons having a particular religion or belief, a particular disability, a particular age, or a particular sexual orientation at a particular disadvantage compared with other persons unless—
  (i) that provision, criterion or practice is objectively justified by a legitimate aim and the means of achieving that aim are appropriate and necessary, or
  (ii) as regards persons with a particular disability, the employer or any person or organisation to whom this Directive applies, is obliged, under national legislation, to take appropriate measures in line with the principles contained in Article 5 in order to eliminate disadvantages entailed by such provision, criterion or practice.

3. Harassment shall be deemed to be a form of discrimination within the meaning of paragraph 1, when unwanted conduct related to any of the grounds referred to in Article 1 takes place with the purpose or effect of violating the dignity of a person and of creating an intimidating, hostile, degrading, humiliating or offensive environment. In this context, the concept of harassment may be defined in accordance with the national laws and practice of the Member States.

4. An instruction to discriminate against persons on any of the grounds referred to in Article 1 shall be deemed to be discrimination within the meaning of paragraph 1.

5. This Directive shall be without prejudice to measures laid down by national law which, in a democratic society, are necessary for public security, for the maintenance of public order and the prevention of criminal offences, for the protection of health and for the protection of the rights and freedoms of others.

[3.240]
Article 3
Scope

1. Within the limits of the areas of competence conferred on the Community, this Directive shall apply to all persons, as regards both the public and private sectors, including public bodies, in relation to—

(a) conditions for access to employment, to self-employment or to occupation, including selection criteria and recruitment conditions, whatever the branch of activity and at all levels of the professional hierarchy, including promotion;

(b) access to all types and to all levels of vocational guidance, vocational training, advanced vocational training and retraining, including practical work experience;

(c) employment and working conditions, including dismissals and pay;

(d) membership of, and involvement in, an organisation of workers or employers, or any organisation whose members carry on a particular profession, including the benefits provided for by such organisations.

2. This Directive does not cover differences of treatment based on nationality and is without prejudice to provisions and conditions relating to the entry into and residence of third-country nationals and stateless persons in the territory of Member States, and to any treatment which arises from the legal status of the third-country nationals and stateless persons concerned.

3. This Directive does not apply to payments of any kind made by state schemes or similar, including state social security or social protection schemes.

4. Member States may provide that this Directive, in so far as it relates to discrimination on the grounds of disability and age, shall not apply to the armed forces.

[3.241]
Article 4
Occupational requirements

1. Notwithstanding Article 2(1) and (2), Member States may provide that a difference of treatment which is based on a characteristic related to any of the grounds referred to in Article 1 shall not constitute discrimination where, by reason of the nature of the particular occupational activities concerned or of the context in which they are carried out, such a characteristic constitutes a genuine and determining occupational requirement, provided that the objective is legitimate and the requirement is proportionate.

2. Member States may maintain national legislation in force at the date of adoption of this Directive or provide for future legislation incorporating national practices existing at the date of adoption of this Directive pursuant to which, in the case of occupational activities within churches and other public or private organisations the ethos of which is based on religion or belief, a difference of treatment based on a person's religion or belief shall not constitute discrimination where, by reason of the nature of these activities or of the context in which they are carried out, a person's religion or belief constitute a genuine, legitimate and justified occupational requirement, having regard to the organisation's ethos. This difference of treatment shall be implemented taking account of Member States' constitutional provisions and principles, as well as the general principles of Community law, and should not justify discrimination on another ground.

Provided that its provisions are otherwise complied with, this Directive shall thus not prejudice the right of churches and other public or private organisations, the ethos of which is based on religion or belief, acting in conformity with national constitutions and laws, to require individuals working for them to act in good faith and with loyalty to the organisation's ethos.

[3.242]
Article 5
Reasonable accommodation for disabled persons

In order to guarantee compliance with the principle of equal treatment in relation to persons with disabilities, reasonable accommodation shall be provided. This means that employers shall take appropriate measures, where needed in a particular case, to enable a person with a disability to have access to, participate in, or advance in employment, or to undergo training, unless such measures would impose a disproportionate burden on the employer. This burden shall not be disproportionate when it is sufficiently remedied by measures existing within the framework of the disability policy of the Member State concerned.

[3.243]
Article 6
Justification of differences of treatment on grounds of age

1. Notwithstanding Article 2(2), Member States may provide that differences of treatment on grounds of age shall not constitute discrimination, if, within the context of national law, they are objectively and reasonably justified by a legitimate aim, including legitimate employment policy, labour market and vocational training objectives, and if the means of achieving that aim are appropriate and necessary.

Such differences of treatment may include, among others—

(a) the setting of special conditions on access to employment and vocational training, employment and occupation, including dismissal and remuneration conditions, for young people, older workers and persons with caring responsibilities in order to promote their vocational integration or ensure their protection;

(b) the fixing of minimum conditions of age, professional experience or seniority in service for access to employment or to certain advantages linked to employment;

(c) the fixing of a maximum age for recruitment which is based on the training requirements of the post in question or the need for a reasonable period of employment before retirement.

2. Notwithstanding Article 2(2), Member States may provide that the fixing for occupational social security schemes of ages for admission or entitlement to retirement or invalidity benefits, including the fixing under those schemes of different ages for employees or groups or categories of employees, and the use, in the context of such schemes, of age criteria in actuarial calculations, does not constitute discrimination on the grounds of age, provided this does not result in discrimination on the grounds of sex.

[3.244]
Article 7
Positive action

1. With a view to ensuring full equality in practice, the principle of equal treatment shall not prevent any Member State from maintaining or adopting specific measures to prevent or compensate for disadvantages linked to any of the grounds referred to in Article 1.
2. With regard to disabled persons, the principle of equal treatment shall be without prejudice to the right of Member States to maintain or adopt provisions on the protection of health and safety at work or to measures aimed at creating or maintaining provisions or facilities for safeguarding or promoting their integration into the working environment.

[3.245]
Article 8
Minimum requirements

1. Member States may introduce or maintain provisions which are more favourable to the protection of the principle of equal treatment than those laid down in this Directive.
2. The implementation of this Directive shall under no circumstances constitute grounds for a reduction in the level of protection against discrimination already afforded by Member States in the fields covered by this Directive.

CHAPTER II REMEDIES AND ENFORCEMENT

[3.246]
Article 9
Defence of rights

1. Member States shall ensure that judicial and/or administrative procedures, including where they deem it appropriate conciliation procedures, for the enforcement of obligations under this Directive are available to all persons who consider themselves wronged by failure to apply the principle of equal treatment to them, even after the relationship in which the discrimination is alleged to have occurred has ended.
2. Member States shall ensure that associations, organisations or other legal entities which have, in accordance with the criteria laid down by their national law, a legitimate interest in ensuring that the provisions of this Directive are complied with, may engage, either on behalf or in support of the complainant, with his or her approval, in any judicial and/or administrative procedure provided for the enforcement of obligations under this Directive.
3. Paragraphs 1 and 2 are without prejudice to national rules relating to time limits for bringing actions as regards the principle of equality of treatment.

[3.247]
Article 10
Burden of proof

1. Member States shall take such measures as are necessary, in accordance with their national judicial systems, to ensure that, when persons who consider themselves wronged because the principle of equal treatment has not been applied to them establish, before a court or other competent authority, facts from which it may be presumed that there has been direct or indirect discrimination, it shall be for the respondent to prove that there has been no breach of the principle of equal treatment.
2. Paragraph 1 shall not prevent Member States from introducing rules of evidence which are more favourable to plaintiffs.
3. Paragraph 1 shall not apply to criminal procedures.
4. Paragraphs 1, 2 and 3 shall also apply to any legal proceedings commenced in accordance with Article 9(2).
5. Member States need not apply paragraph 1 to proceedings in which it is for the court or competent body to investigate the facts of the case.

[3.248]
Article 11
Victimisation

Member States shall introduce into their national legal systems such measures as are necessary to protect employees against dismissal or other adverse treatment by the employer as a reaction to a complaint within the undertaking or to any legal proceedings aimed at enforcing compliance with the principle of equal treatment.

[3.249]
Article 12
Dissemination of information

Member States shall take care that the provisions adopted pursuant to this Directive, together with the relevant provisions already in force in this field, are brought to the attention of the persons concerned by all appropriate means, for example at the workplace, throughout their territory.

[3.250]
Article 13
Social dialogue

1. Member States shall, in accordance with their national traditions and practice, take adequate measures to promote dialogue between the social partners with a view to fostering equal treatment, including through the monitoring of workplace practices, collective agreements, codes of conduct and through research or exchange of experiences and good practices.

2. Where consistent with their national traditions and practice, Member States shall encourage the social partners, without prejudice to their autonomy, to conclude at the appropriate level agreements laying down anti-discrimination rules in the fields referred to in Article 3 which fall within the scope of collective bargaining. These agreements shall respect the minimum requirements laid down by this Directive and by the relevant national implementing measures.

[3.251]
Article 14
Dialogue with non-governmental organisations

Member States shall encourage dialogue with appropriate non-governmental organisations which have, in accordance with their national law and practice, a legitimate interest in contributing to the fight against discrimination on any of the grounds referred to in Article 1 with a view to promoting the principle of equal treatment.

CHAPTER III PARTICULAR PROVISIONS

[3.252]
Article 15
Northern Ireland

1. In order to tackle the under-representation of one of the major religious communities in the police service of Northern Ireland, differences in treatment regarding recruitment into that service, including its support staff, shall not constitute discrimination insofar as those differences in treatment are expressly authorised by national legislation.

2. In order to maintain a balance of opportunity in employment for teachers in Northern Ireland while furthering the reconciliation of historical divisions between the major religious communities there, the provisions on religion or belief in this Directive shall not apply to the recruitment of teachers in schools in Northern Ireland in so far as this is expressly authorised by national legislation.

CHAPTER IV FINAL PROVISIONS

[3.253]
Article 16
Compliance

Member States shall take the necessary measures to ensure that—

(a) any laws, regulations and administrative provisions contrary to the principle of equal treatment are abolished;

(b) any provisions contrary to the principle of equal treatment which are included in contracts or collective agreements, internal rules of undertakings or rules governing the independent occupations and professions and workers' and employers' organisations are, or may be, declared null and void or are amended.

[3.254]
Article 17
Sanctions

Member States shall lay down the rules on sanctions applicable to infringements of the national provisions adopted pursuant to this Directive and shall take all measures necessary to ensure that they are applied. The sanctions, which may comprise the payment of compensation to the victim, must be effective, proportionate and dissuasive. Member States shall notify those provisions to the Commission by 2 December 2003 at the latest and shall notify it without delay of any subsequent amendment affecting them.

[3.255]
Article 18
Implementation

Member States shall adopt the laws, regulations and administrative provisions necessary to comply with this Directive by 2 December 2003 at the latest or may entrust the social partners, at their joint request, with the implementation of this Directive as regards provisions concerning collective agreements. In such cases, Member States shall ensure that, no later than 2 December 2003, the social partners introduce the necessary measures by agreement, the Member States concerned being required to take any necessary measures to enable them at any time to be in a position to guarantee the results imposed by this Directive. They shall forthwith inform the Commission thereof.

In order to take account of particular conditions, Member States may, if necessary, have an additional period of 3 years from 2 December 2003, that is to say a total of 6 years, to implement the provisions of this Directive on age and disability discrimination. In that event they shall inform the Commission forthwith Any Member State which chooses to use this additional period shall report annually to the Commission on the steps it is taking to tackle age and disability discrimination and on the progress it is making towards implementation. The Commission shall report annually to the Council.

When Member States adopt these measures, they shall contain a reference to this Directive or be accompanied by such reference on the occasion of their official publication. The methods of making such reference shall be laid down by Member States.

[3.256]
Article 19
Report

1. Member States shall communicate to the Commission, by 2 December 2005 at the latest and every five years thereafter, all the information necessary for the Commission to draw up a report to the European Parliament and the Council on the application of this Directive.

2. The Commission's report shall take into account, as appropriate, the viewpoints of the social partners and relevant non-governmental organisations. In accordance with the principle of gender mainstreaming, this report shall, inter alia, provide an assessment of the impact of the measures taken on women and men. In the light of the information received, this report shall include, if necessary, proposals to revise and update this Directive.

[3.257]
Article 20
Entry into force

This Directive shall enter into force on the day of its publication in the *Official Journal of the European Communities*.

[3.258]
Article 21
Addressees

This Directive is addressed to the Member States.

COUNCIL DIRECTIVE

(2001/23/EC)

of 12 March 2001

on the approximation of the laws of the Member States relating to the safeguarding of employees' rights in the event of transfers of undertakings, businesses or parts of undertakings or businesses

[3.259]

NOTES

Date of publication in OJ: OJ L82, 22.03.2001, p 16. The text of this Directive incorporates the corrigendum published in OJ L181, 9.7.2015, p 84.

This Directive consolidates Directive 77/187/EC ('the Acquired Rights Directive') as amended by Directive 98/50/EC. Annex II at **[3.276]** is a table correlating the provisions in the former and current Directives. For the domestic implementation of this Directive, see the Transfer of Undertakings (Protection of Employment) Regulations 2006, SI 2006/246 at **[2.867]**.

See *Harvey* F.

THE COUNCIL OF THE EUROPEAN UNION,

Having regard to the Treaty establishing the European Community, and in particular Article 94 thereof,

Having regard to the proposal from the Commission,

Having regard to the opinion of the European Parliament,[1]

Having regard to the opinion of the Economic and Social Committee,[2]

Whereas:

(1) Council Directive 77/187/EEC of 14 February 1977 on the approximation of the laws of the Member States relating to the safeguarding of employees' rights in the event of transfers of undertakings, businesses or parts of undertakings or businesses[3] has been substantially amended.[4] In the interests of clarity and rationality, it should therefore be codified.

(2) Economic trends are bringing in their wake, at both national and Community level, changes in the structure of undertakings, through transfers of undertakings, businesses or parts of undertakings or businesses to other employers as a result of legal transfers or mergers.

(3) It is necessary to provide for the protection of employees in the event of a change of employer, in particular, to ensure that their rights are safeguarded.

(4) Differences still remain in the Member States as regards the extent of the protection of employees in this respect and these differences should be reduced.

(5) The Community Charter of the Fundamental Social Rights of Workers adopted on 9 December 1989 ("Social Charter") states, in points 7, 17 and 18 in particular that: "The completion of the internal market must lead to an improvement in the living and working conditions of workers in the

European Community. The improvement must cover, where necessary, the development of certain aspects of employment regulations such as procedures for collective redundancies and those regarding bankruptcies. Information, consultation and participation for workers must be developed along appropriate lines, taking account of the practice in force in the various Member States. Such information, consultation and participation must be implemented in due time, particularly in connection with restructuring operations in undertakings or in cases of mergers having an impact on the employment of workers".

(6) In 1977 the Council adopted Directive 77/187/EEC to promote the harmonisation of the relevant national laws ensuring the safeguarding of the rights of employees and requiring transferors and transferees to inform and consult employees' representatives in good time.

(7) That Directive was subsequently amended in the light of the impact of the internal market, the legislative tendencies of the Member States with regard to the rescue of undertakings in economic difficulties, the case-law of the Court of Justice of the European Communities, Council Directive 75/129/EEC of 17 February 1975 on the approximation of the laws of the Member States relating to collective redundancies[5] and the legislation already in force in most Member States.

(8) Considerations of legal security and transparency required that the legal concept of transfer be clarified in the light of the case-law of the Court of Justice. Such clarification has not altered the scope of Directive 77/187/EEC as interpreted by the Court of Justice.

(9) The Social Charter recognises the importance of the fight against all forms of discrimination, especially based on sex, colour, race, opinion and creed.

(10) This Directive should be without prejudice to the time limits set out in Annex I Part B within which the Member States are to comply with Directive 77/187/EEC, and the act amending it,

NOTES

1 Opinion delivered on 25 October 2000 (not yet published in the Official Journal).
2 OJ C367, 20.12.2000, p 21.
3 OJ L61, 5.3.1977, p 26.
4 See Annex I, Part A.
5 OJ L48, 22.2.1975, p 29. Directive replaced by Directive 98/59/EC (OJ L225, 12.8.1998, p 16).

HAS ADOPTED THIS DIRECTIVE—

CHAPTER I SCOPE AND DEFINITIONS

[3.260]
Article 1

1.
(a) This Directive shall apply to any transfer of an undertaking, business, or part of an undertaking or business to another employer as a result of a legal transfer or merger.
(b) Subject to subparagraph (a) and the following provisions of this Article, there is a transfer within the meaning of this Directive where there is a transfer of an economic entity which retains its identity, meaning an organised grouping of resources which has the objective of pursuing an economic activity, whether or not that activity is central or ancillary.
(c) This Directive shall apply to public and private undertakings engaged in economic activities whether or not they are operating for gain. An administrative reorganisation of public administrative authorities, or the transfer of administrative functions between public administrative authorities, is not a transfer within the meaning of this Directive.

2. This Directive shall apply where and in so far as the undertaking, business or part of the undertaking or business to be transferred is situated within the territorial scope of the Treaty.

[3. This Directive shall apply to a transfer of a seagoing vessel that is part of a transfer of an undertaking, business or part of an undertaking or business within the meaning of paragraphs 1 and 2, provided that the transferee is situated, or the transferred undertaking, business, or part of an undertaking or business remains, within the territorial scope of the Treaty.

This Directive shall not apply where the object of the transfer consists exclusively of one or more seagoing vessels.]

NOTES

Para 3: substituted by Directive 2015/1794/EU, Art 5, as from 9 October 2015.

[3.261]
Article 2

1. For the purposes of this Directive—
(a) "transferor" shall mean any natural or legal person who, by reason of a transfer within the meaning of Article 1(1), ceases to be the employer in respect of the undertaking, business or part of the undertaking or business;
(b) "transferee" shall mean any natural or legal person who, by reason of a transfer within the meaning of Article 1(1), becomes the employer in respect of the undertaking, business or part of the undertaking or business;
(c) "representatives of employees" and related expressions shall mean the representatives of the employees provided for by the laws or practices of the Member States;

Part 3 EU Materials

(d) "employee" shall mean any person who, in the Member State concerned, is protected as an employee under national employment law.

2. This Directive shall be without prejudice to national law as regards the definition of contract of employment or employment relationship.

However, Member States shall not exclude from the scope of this Directive contracts of employment or employment relationships solely because—

(a) of the number of working hours performed or to be performed,

(b) they are employment relationships governed by a fixed-duration contract of employment within the meaning of Article 1(1) of Council Directive 91/383/EEC of 25 June 1991 supplementing the measures to encourage improvements in the safety and health at work of workers with a fixed-duration employment relationship or a temporary employment relationship, or

they are temporary employment relationships within the meaning of Article 1(2) of Directive 91/383/EEC, and the undertaking, business or part of the undertaking or business transferred is, or is part of, the temporary employment business which is the employer.

CHAPTER II SAFEGUARDING OF EMPLOYEES' RIGHTS

[3.262]
Article 3

1. The transferor's rights and obligations arising from a contract of employment or from an employment relationship existing on the date of a transfer shall, by reason of such transfer, be transferred to the transferee.

Member States may provide that, after the date of transfer, the transferor and the transferee shall be jointly and severally liable in respect of obligations which arose before the date of transfer from a contract of employment or an employment relationship existing on the date of the transfer.

2. Member States may adopt appropriate measures to ensure that the transferor notifies the transferee of all the rights and obligations which will be transferred to the transferee under this Article, so far as those rights and obligations are or ought to have been known to the transferor at the time of the transfer. A failure by the transferor to notify the transferee of any such right or obligation shall not affect the transfer of that right or obligation and the rights of any employees against the transferee and/or transferor in respect of that right or obligation.

3. Following the transfer, the transferee shall continue to observe the terms and conditions agreed in any collective agreement on the same terms applicable to the transferor under that agreement, until the date of termination or expiry of the collective agreement or the entry into force or application of another collective agreement.

Member States may limit the period for observing such terms and conditions with the proviso that it shall not be less than one year.

4.

(a) Unless Member States provide otherwise, paragraphs 1 and 3 shall not apply in relation to employees' rights to old-age, invalidity or survivors' benefits under supplementary company or intercompany pension schemes outside the statutory social security schemes in Member States.

(b) Even where they do not provide in accordance with subparagraph (a) that paragraphs 1 and 3 apply in relation to such rights, Member States shall adopt the measures necessary to protect the interests of employees and of persons no longer employed in the transferor's business at the time of the transfer in respect of rights conferring on them immediate or prospective entitlement to old age benefits, including survivors' benefits, under supplementary schemes referred to in subparagraph (a).

[3.263]
Article 4

1. The transfer of the undertaking, business or part of the undertaking or business shall not in itself constitute grounds for dismissal by the transferor or the transferee. This provision shall not stand in the way of dismissals that may take place for economic, technical or organisational reasons entailing changes in the workforce.

Member States may provide that the first subparagraph shall not apply to certain specific categories of employees who are not covered by the laws or practice of the Member States in respect of protection against dismissal.

2. If the contract of employment or the employment relationship is terminated because the transfer involves a substantial change in working conditions to the detriment of the employee, the employer shall be regarded as having been responsible for termination of the contract of employment or of the employment relationship.

[3.264]
Article 5

1. Unless Member States provide otherwise, Articles 3 and 4 shall not apply to any transfer of an undertaking, business or part of an undertaking or business where the transferor is the subject of bankruptcy proceedings or any analogous insolvency proceedings which have been instituted with a view to the liquidation of the assets of the transferor and are under the supervision of a competent public authority (which may be an insolvency practitioner authorised by a competent public authority).

2. Where Articles 3 and 4 apply to a transfer during insolvency proceedings which have been opened in relation to a transferor (whether or not those proceedings have been instituted with a view to the liquidation of the assets of the transferor) and provided that such proceedings are under the supervision of a competent public authority (which may be an insolvency practitioner determined by national law) a Member State may provide that—

(a) notwithstanding Article 3(1), the transferor's debts arising from any contracts of employment or employment relationships and payable before the transfer or before the opening of the insolvency proceedings shall not be transferred to the transferee, provided that such proceedings give rise, under the law of that Member State, to protection at least equivalent to that provided for in situations covered by Council Directive 80/987/EEC of 20 October 1980 on the approximation of the laws of the Member States relating to the protection of employees in the event of the insolvency of their employer, and, or alternatively, that,

(b) the transferee, transferor or person or persons exercising the transferor's functions, on the one hand, and the representatives of the employees on the other hand may agree alterations, in so far as current law or practice permits, to the employees' terms and conditions of employment designed to safeguard employment opportunities by ensuring the survival of the undertaking, business or part of the undertaking or business.

3. A Member State may apply paragraph 20(b) to any transfers where the transferor is in a situation of serious economic crisis, as defined by national law, provided that the situation is declared by a competent public authority and open to judicial supervision, on condition that such provisions already existed in national law on 17 July 1998.

The Commission shall present a report on the effects of this provision before 17 July 2003 and shall submit any appropriate proposals to the Council.

4. Member States shall take appropriate measures with a view to preventing misuse of insolvency proceedings in such a way as to deprive employees of the rights provided for in this Directive.

[3.265]
Article 6

1. If the undertaking, business or part of an undertaking or business preserves its autonomy, the status and function of the representatives or of the representation of the employees affected by the transfer shall be preserved on the same terms and subject to the same conditions as existed before the date of the transfer by virtue of law, regulation, administrative provision or agreement, provided that the conditions necessary for the constitution of the employee's representation are fulfilled.

The first subparagraph shall not apply if, under the laws, regulations, administrative provisions or practice in the Member States, or by agreement with the representatives of the employees, the conditions necessary for the reappointment of the representatives of the employees or for the reconstitution of the representation of the employees are fulfilled.

Where the transferor is the subject of bankruptcy proceedings or any analogous insolvency proceedings which have been instituted with a view to the liquidation of the assets of the transferor and are under the supervision of a competent public authority (which may be an insolvency practitioner authorised by a competent public authority), Member States may take the necessary measures to ensure that the transferred employees are properly represented until the new election or designation of representatives of the employees.

If the undertaking, business or part of an undertaking or business does not preserve its autonomy, the Member States shall take the necessary measures to ensure that the employees transferred who were represented before the transfer continue to be properly represented during the period necessary for the reconstitution or reappointment of the representation of employees in accordance with national law or practice.

2. If the term of office of the representatives of the employees affected by the transfer expires as a result of the transfer, the representatives shall continue to enjoy the protection provided by the laws, regulations, administrative provisions or practice of the Member States.

CHAPTER III INFORMATION AND CONSULTATION

[3.266]
Article 7

1. The transferor and transferee shall be required to inform the representatives of their respective employees affected by the transfer of the following—

— the date or proposed date of the transfer,
— the reasons for the transfer,
— the legal, economic and social implications of the transfer for the employees,
— any measures envisaged in relation to the employees.

The transferor must give such information to the representatives of his employees in good time, before the transfer is carried out.

The transferee must give such information to the representatives of his employees in good time, and in any event before his employees are directly affected by the transfer as regards their conditions of work and employment.

2. Where the transferor or the transferee envisages measures in relation to his employees, he shall consult the representatives of this employees in good time on such measures with a view to reaching an agreement.

3. Member States whose laws, regulations or administrative provisions provide that representatives of the employees may have recourse to an arbitration board to obtain a decision on the measures to be taken in relation to employees may limit the obligations laid down in paragraphs 1 and 2 to cases where the transfer carried out gives rise to a change in the business likely to entail serious disadvantages for a considerable number of the employees.

The information and consultations shall cover at least the measures envisaged in relation to the employees.

The information must be provided and consultations take place in good time before the change in the business as referred to in the first subparagraph is effected.

4. The obligations laid down in this Article shall apply irrespective of whether the decision resulting in the transfer is taken by the employer or an undertaking controlling the employer.

In considering alleged breaches of the information and consultation requirements laid down by this Directive, the argument that such a breach occurred because the information was not provided by an undertaking controlling the employer shall not be accepted as an excuse.

5. Member States may limit the obligations laid down in paragraphs 1, 2 and 3 to undertakings or businesses which, in terms of the number of employees, meet the conditions for the election or nomination of a collegiate body representing the employees.

6. Member States shall provide that, where there are no representatives of the employees in an undertaking or business through no fault of their own, the employees concerned must be informed in advance of—

— the date or proposed date of the transfer,
— the reason for the transfer,
— the legal, economic and social implications of the transfer for the employees,
— any measures envisaged in relation to the employees.

CHAPTER IV FINAL PROVISIONS

[3.267]
Article 8
This Directive shall not affect the right of Member States to apply or introduce laws, regulations or administrative provisions which are more favourable to employees or to promote or permit collective agreements or agreements between social partners more favourable to employees.

[3.268]
Article 9
Member States shall introduce into their national legal systems such measures as are necessary to enable all employees and representatives of employees who consider themselves wronged by failure to comply with the obligations arising from this Directive to pursue their claims by judicial process after possible recourse to other competent authorities.

[3.269]
Article 10
The Commission shall submit to the Council an analysis of the effect of the provisions of this Directive before 17 July 2006. It shall propose any amendment which may seem necessary.

[3.270]
Article 11
Member States shall communicate to the Commission the texts of the laws, regulations and administrative provisions which they adopt in the field covered by this Directive.

[3.271]
Article 12
Directive 77/187/EEC, as amended by the Directive referred to in Annex I, Part A, is repealed, without prejudice to the obligations of the Member States concerning the time limits for implementation set out in Annex I, Part B.

References to the repealed Directive shall be construed as references to this Directive and shall be read in accordance with the correlation table in Annex II.

[3.272]
Article 13
This Directive shall enter into force on the 20th day following its publication in the *Official Journal of the European Communities*.

[3.273]
Article 14
This Directive is addressed to the Member States.

ANNEX I

PART A REPEALED DIRECTIVE AND ITS AMENDING DIRECTIVE

(referred to in Article 12)

[3.274]
Council Directive 77/187/EEC (OJ L 61, 5.3.1977, p. 26)

Council Directive 98/50/EC (OJ L 201, 17.7.1998, p. 88)

PART B DEADLINES FOR TRANSPOSITION INTO NATIONAL LAW

(referred to in Article 12)

[3.275]

Directive	*Deadline for transposition*
77/187/EEC	16 February 1979
98/50/EC	17 July 2001

ANNEX II
CORRELATION TABLE

[3.276]

Directive 77/187/EEC	*This Directive*
Article 1	Article 1
Article 2	Article 2
Article 3	Article 3
Article 4	Article 4
Article 4a	Article 5
Article 5	Article 6
Article 6	Article 7
Article 7	Article 8
Article 7a	Article 9
Article 7b	Article 10
Article 8	Article 11
—	Article 12
—	Article 13
—	Article 14
—	Annex I
	Annex II

COUNCIL DIRECTIVE

(2001/86/EC)

of 8 October 2001

supplementing the Statute for a European company with regard to the involvement of employees

[3.277]

NOTES

Date of publication in OJ: OJ L294, 10.11.2001, p 22.

For the domestic implementation of this Directive see the European Public Limited-Liability Company (Employee Involvement) (Great Britain) Regulations 2009, SI 2009/2401 at **[2.986]**.

See *Harvey* NIII(4).

THE COUNCIL OF THE EUROPEAN UNION,

Having regard to the Treaty establishing the European Community, and in particular Article 308 thereof,

Having regard to the amended proposal from the Commission,[1]

Having regard to the opinion of the European Parliament,[2]

Having regard to the opinion of the Economic and Social Committee,[3]

Whereas:

(1) In order to attain the objectives of the Treaty, Council Regulation (EC) No 2157/2001[4] establishes a Statute for a European company (SE).

(2) That Regulation aims at creating a uniform legal framework within which companies from different Member States should be able to plan and carry out the reorganisation of their business on a Community scale.

(3) In order to promote the social objectives of the Community, special provisions have to be set, notably in the field of employee involvement, aimed at ensuring that the establishment of an SE does not entail the disappearance or reduction of practices of employee involvement existing within the companies participating in the establishment of an SE. This objective should be pursued through the establishment of a set of rules in this field, supplementing the provisions of the Regulation.

(4) Since the objectives of the proposed action, as outlined above, cannot be sufficiently achieved by the Member States, in that the object is to establish a set of rules on employee involvement applicable to the SE, and can therefore, by reason of the scale and impact of the proposed action, be better achieved at Community level, the Community may adopt measures, in accordance with the principle of subsidiarity as set out in Article 5 of the Treaty. In accordance with the principle of proportionality, as set out in that Article, this Directive does not go beyond what is necessary to achieve these objectives.

(5) The great diversity of rules and practices existing in the Member States as regards the manner in which employees' representatives are involved in decision-making within companies makes it inadvisable to set up a single European model of employee involvement applicable to the SE.

(6) Information and consultation procedures at transnational level should nevertheless be ensured in all cases of creation of an SE.

(7) If and when participation rights exist within one or more companies establishing an SE, they should be preserved through their transfer to the SE, once established, unless the parties decide otherwise.

(8) The concrete procedures of employee transnational information and consultation, as well as, if applicable, participation, to apply to each SE should be defined primarily by means of an agreement between the parties concerned or, in the absence thereof, through the application of a set of subsidiary rules.

(9) Member States should still have the option of not applying the standard rules relating to participation in the case of a merger, given the diversity of national systems for employee involvement. Existing systems and practices of participation where appropriate at the level of participating companies must in that case be maintained by adapting registration rules.

(10) The voting rules within the special body representing the employees for negotiation purposes, in particular when concluding agreements providing for a level of participation lower than the one existing within one or more of the participating companies, should be proportionate to the risk of disappearance or reduction of existing systems and practices of participation. That risk is greater in the case of an SE established by way of transformation or merger than by way of creating a holding company or a common subsidiary.

(11) In the absence of an agreement subsequent to the negotiation between employees' representatives and the competent organs of the participating companies, provision should be made for certain standard requirements to apply to the SE, once it is established. These standard requirements should ensure effective practices of transnational information and consultation of employees, as well as their participation in the relevant organs of the SE if and when such participation existed before its establishment within the participating companies.

(12) Provision should be made for the employees' representatives acting within the framework of the Directive to enjoy, when exercising their functions, protection and guarantees which are similar to those provided to employees' representatives by the legislation and/or practice of the country of employment. They should not be subject to any discrimination as a result of the lawful exercise of their activities and should enjoy adequate protection as regards dismissal and other sanctions.

(13) The confidentiality of sensitive information should be preserved even after the expiry of the employees' representatives terms of office and provision should be made to allow the competent organ of the SE to withhold information which would seriously harm, if subject to public disclosure, the functioning of the SE.

(14) Where an SE and its subsidiaries and establishments are subject to Council Directive 94/45/EC of 22 September 1994 on the establishment of a European Works Council or a procedure in Community-scale undertakings and Community-scale groups of undertakings for the purposes of informing and consulting employees,[5] the provisions of that Directive and the provision transposing it into national legislation should not apply to it nor to its subsidiaries and establishments, unless the special negotiating body decides not to open negotiations or to terminate negotiations already opened.

(15) This Directive should not affect other existing rights regarding involvement and need not affect other existing representation structures, provided for by Community and national laws and practices.

(16) Member States should take appropriate measures in the event of failure to comply with the obligations laid down in this Directive.

(17) The Treaty has not provided the necessary powers for the Community to adopt the proposed Directive, other than those provided for in Article 308.

(18) It is a fundamental principle and stated aim of this Directive to secure employees' acquired rights as regards involvement in company decisions. Employee rights in force before the establishment of SEs should provide the basis for employee rights of involvement in the SE (the "before and after" principle). Consequently, that approach should apply not only to the initial establishment of an SE but also to structural changes in an existing SE and to the companies affected by structural change processes.

(19) Member States should be able to provide that representatives of trade unions may be members of a special negotiating body regardless of whether they are employees of a company participating in the establishment of an SE. Member States should in this context in particular be able to introduce this right in cases where trade union representatives have the right to be members of, and to vote in, supervisory or administrative company organs in accordance with national legislation.

(20) In several Member States, employee involvement and other areas of industrial relations are based on both national legislation and practice which in this context is understood also to cover collective agreements at various national, sectoral and/or company levels,

NOTES

[1] OJ C138, 29.5.1991, p 8.

[2] OJ C342, 20.12.1993, p 15.

[3] OJ C124, 21.5.1990, p 34.

[4] See page 1 of this Official Journal.

[5] OJ L254, 30.9.1994, p 64. Directive as last amended by Directive 97/74/EC (OJ L10, 16.1.1998, p 22).

HAS ADOPTED THIS DIRECTIVE:

SECTION I GENERAL

[3.278]
Article 1
Objective

1. This Directive governs the involvement of employees in the affairs of European public limited-liability companies (Societas Europaea, hereinafter referred to as "SE"), as referred to in Regulation (EC) No 2157/2001.
2. To this end, arrangements for the involvement of employees shall be established in every SE in accordance with the negotiating procedure referred to in Articles 3 to 6 or, under the circumstances specified in Article 7, in accordance with the Annex.

[3.279]
Article 2
Definitions

For the purposes of this Directive—

(a) "SE" means any company established in accordance with Regulation (EC) No 2157/2001;

(b) "participating companies" means the companies directly participating in the establishing of an SE;

(c) "subsidiary" of a company means an undertaking over which that company exercises a dominant influence defined in accordance with Article 3(2) to (7) of Directive 94/45/EC;

(d) "concerned subsidiary or establishment" means a subsidiary or establishment of a participating company which is proposed to become a subsidiary or establishment of the SE upon its formation;

(e) "employees' representatives" means the employees' representatives provided for by national law and/or practice;

(f) "representative body" means the body representative of the employees set up by the agreements referred to in Article 4 or in accordance with the provisions of the Annex, with the purpose of informing and consulting the employees of an SE and its subsidiaries and establishments situated in the Community and, where applicable, of exercising participation rights in relation to the SE;

(g) "special negotiating body" means the body established in accordance with Article 3 to negotiate with the competent body of the participating companies regarding the establishment of arrangements for the involvement of employees within the SE;

(h) "involvement of employees" means any mechanism, including information, consultation and participation, through which employees' representatives may exercise an influence on decisions to be taken within the company;

(i) "information" means the informing of the body representative of the employees and/or employees' representatives by the competent organ of the SE on questions which concern the SE itself and any of its subsidiaries or establishments situated in another Member State or which exceed the powers of the decision-making organs in a single Member State at a time, in a manner and with a content which allows the employees' representatives to undertake an in-depth assessment of the possible impact and, where appropriate, prepare consultations with the competent organ of the SE;

(j) "consultation" means the establishment of dialogue and exchange of views between the body representative of the employees and/or the employees' representatives and the competent organ of the SE, at a time, in a manner, and with a content which allows the employees' representatives, on the basis of information provided, to express an opinion on measures envisaged by the competent organ which may be taken into account in the decision-making process within the SE;

(k) "participation" means the influence of the body representative of the employees and/or the employees' representatives in the affairs of a company by way of—

— the right to elect or appoint some of the members of the company's supervisory or administrative organ, or

— the right to recommend and/or oppose the appointment of some or all of the members of the company's supervisory or administrative organ.

SECTION II NEGOTIATING PROCEDURE

[3.280]
Article 3
Creation of a special negotiating body

1. Where the management or administrative organs of the participating companies draw up a plan for the establishment of an SE, they shall as soon as possible after publishing the draft terms of merger or creating a holding company or after agreeing a plan to form a subsidiary or to transform into an SE, take the necessary steps, including providing information about the identity of the participating companies, concerned subsidiaries or establishments, and the number of their employees, to start negotiations with the representatives of the companies' employees on arrangements for the involvement of employees in the SE.

2. For this purpose, a special negotiating body representative of the employees of the participating companies and concerned subsidiaries or establishments shall be created in accordance with the following provisions—

(a) in electing or appointing members of the special negotiating body, it must be ensured—

(i) that these members are elected or appointed in proportion to the number of employees employed in each Member State by the participating companies and concerned subsidiaries or establishments, by allocating in respect of a Member State one seat per portion of employees employed in that Member State which equals 10%, or a fraction thereof, of the number of employees employed by the participating companies and concerned subsidiaries or establishments in all the Member States taken together;

(ii) that in the case of an SE formed by way of merger, there are such further additional members from each Member State as may be necessary in order to ensure that the special negotiating body includes at least one member representing each participating company which is registered and has employees in that Member State and which it is proposed will cease to exist as a separate legal entity following the registration of the SE, in so far as—

— the number of such additional members does not exceed 20% of the number of members designated by virtue of point (i), and

— the composition of the special negotiating body does not entail a double representation of the employees concerned.

If the number of such companies is higher than the number of additional seats available pursuant to the first subparagraph, these additional seats shall be allocated to companies in different Member States by decreasing order of the number of employees they employ;

(b) Member States shall determine the method to be used for the election or appointment of the members of the special negotiating body who are to be elected or appointed in their territories. They shall take the necessary measures to ensure that, as far as possible, such members shall include at least one member representing each participating company which has employees in the Member State concerned. Such measures must not increase the overall number of members.

Member States may provide that such members may include representatives of trade unions whether or not they are employees of a participating company or concerned subsidiary or establishment.

Without prejudice to national legislation and/or practice laying down thresholds for the establishing of a representative body, Member States shall provide that employees in undertakings or establishments in which there are no employees' representatives through no fault of their own have the right to elect or appoint members of the special negotiating body.

3. The special negotiating body and the competent organs of the participating companies shall determine, by written agreement, arrangements for the involvement of employees within the SE.

To this end, the competent organs of the participating companies shall inform the special negotiating body of the plan and the actual process of establishing the SE, up to its registration.

4. Subject to paragraph 6, the special negotiating body shall take decisions by an absolute majority of its members, provided that such a majority also represents an absolute majority of the employees. Each member shall have one vote. However, should the result of the negotiations lead to a reduction of participation rights, the majority required for a decision to approve such an agreement shall be the votes of two thirds of the members of the special negotiating body representing at least two thirds of the employees, including the votes of members representing employees employed in at least two Member States—

— in the case of an SE to be established by way of merger, if participation covers at least 25% of the overall number of employees of the participating companies, or

— in the case of an SE to be established by way of creating a holding company or forming a subsidiary, if participation covers at least 50% of the overall number of employees of the participating companies.

Reduction of participation rights means a proportion of members of the organs of the SE within the meaning of Article 2(k), which is lower than the highest proportion existing within the participating companies.

5. For the purpose of the negotiations, the special negotiating body may request experts of its choice, for example representatives of appropriate Community level trade union organisations, to assist it with its work. Such experts may be present at negotiation meetings in an advisory capacity at the request of the

special negotiating body, where appropriate to promote coherence and consistency at Community level. The special negotiating body may decide to inform the representatives of appropriate external organisations, including trade unions, of the start of the negotiations.

6. The special negotiating body may decide by the majority set out below not to open negotiations or to terminate negotiations already opened, and to rely on the rules on information and consultation of employees in force in the Member States where the SE has employees. Such a decision shall stop the procedure to conclude the agreement referred to in Article 4. Where such a decision has been taken, none of the provisions of the Annex shall apply.

The majority required to decide not to open or to terminate negotiations shall be the votes of two thirds of the members representing at least two thirds of the employees, including the votes of members representing employees employed in at least two Member States.

In the case of an SE established by way of transformation, this paragraph shall not apply if there is participation in the company to be transformed.

The special negotiating body shall be reconvened on the written request of at least 10% of the employees of the SE, its subsidiaries and establishments, or their representatives, at the earliest two years after the abovementioned decision, unless the parties agree to negotiations being reopened sooner. If the special negotiating body decides to reopen negotiations with the management but no agreement is reached as a result of those negotiations, none of the provisions of the Annex shall apply.

7. Any expenses relating to the functioning of the special negotiating body and, in general, to negotiations shall be borne by the participating companies so as to enable the special negotiating body to carry out its task in an appropriate manner.

In compliance with this principle, Member States may lay down budgetary rules regarding the operation of the special negotiating body. They may in particular limit the funding to cover one expert only.

[3.281]
Article 4
Content of the agreement

1. The competent organs of the participating companies and the special negotiating body shall negotiate in a spirit of cooperation with a view to reaching an agreement on arrangements for the involvement of the employees within the SE.

2. Without prejudice to the autonomy of the parties, and subject to paragraph 4, the agreement referred to in paragraph 1 between the competent organs of the participating companies and the special negotiating body shall specify—

(a) the scope of the agreement;
(b) the composition, number of members and allocation of seats on the representative body which will be the discussion partner of the competent organ of the SE in connection with arrangements for the information and consultation of the employees of the SE and its subsidiaries and establishments;
(c) the functions and the procedure for the information and consultation of the representative body;
(d) the frequency of meetings of the representative body;
(e) the financial and material resources to be allocated to the representative body;
(f) if, during negotiations, the parties decide to establish one or more information and consultation procedures instead of a representative body, the arrangements for implementing those procedures;
(g) if, during negotiations, the parties decide to establish arrangements for participation, the substance of those arrangements including (if applicable) the number of members in the SE's administrative or supervisory body which the employees will be entitled to elect, appoint, recommend or oppose, the procedures as to how these members may be elected, appointed, recommended or opposed by the employees, and their rights;
(h) the date of entry into force of the agreement and its duration, cases where the agreement should be renegotiated and the procedure for its renegotiation.

3. The agreement shall not, unless provision is made otherwise therein, be subject to the standard rules referred to in the Annex.

4. Without prejudice to Article 13(3)(a), in the case of an SE established by means of transformation, the agreement shall provide for at least the same level of all elements of employee involvement as the ones existing within the company to be transformed into an SE.

[3.282]
Article 5
Duration of negotiations

1. Negotiations shall commence as soon as the special negotiating body is established and may continue for six months thereafter.

2. The parties may decide, by joint agreement, to extend negotiations beyond the period referred to in paragraph 1, up the total of one year from the establishment of the special negotiating body.

[3.283]
Article 6
Legislation applicable to the negotiation procedure

Except where otherwise provided in this Directive, the legislation applicable to the negotiation procedure provided for in Articles 3 to 5 shall be the legislation of the Member State in which the registered office of the SE is to be situated.

[3.284]
Article 7
Standard rules

1. In order to achieve the objective described in Article 1, Member States shall, without prejudice to paragraph 3 below, lay down standard rules on employee involvement which must satisfy the provisions set out in the Annex.

The standard rules as laid down by the legislation of the Member State in which the registered office of the SE is to be situated shall apply from the date of the registration of the SE where either—

(a) the parties so agree; or

(b) by the deadline laid down in Article 5, no agreement has been concluded, and—

— the competent organ of each of the participating companies decides to accept the application of the standard rules in relation to the SE and so to continue with its registration of the SE, and

— the special negotiating body has not taken the decision provided in Article 3(6).

2. Moreover, the standard rules fixed by the national legislation of the Member State of registration in accordance with part 3 of the Annex shall apply only—

(a) in the case of an SE established by transformation, if the rules of a Member State relating to employee participation in the administrative or supervisory body applied to a company transformed into an SE;

(b) in the case of an SE established by merger—

— if, before registration of the SE, one or more forms of participation applied in one or more of the participating companies covering at least 25% of the total number of employees in all the participating companies, or

— if, before registration of the SE, one or more forms of participation applied in one or more of the participating companies covering less than 25% of the total number of employees in all the participating companies and if the special negotiating body so decides,

(c) in the case of an SE established by setting up a holding company or establishing a subsidiary—

— if, before registration of the SE, one or more forms of participation applied in one or more of the participating companies covering at least 50% of the total number of employees in all the participating companies; or

— if, before registration of the SE, one or more forms of participation applied in one or more of the participating companies covering less than 50% of the total number of employees in all the participating companies and if the special negotiating body so decides.

If there was more than one form of participation within the various participating companies, the special negotiating body shall decide which of those forms must be established in the SE. Member States may fix the rules which are applicable in the absence of any decision on the matter for an SE registered in their territory. The special negotiating body shall inform the competent organs of the participating companies of any decisions taken pursuant to this paragraph.

3. Member States may provide that the reference provisions in part 3 of the Annex shall not apply in the case provided for in point (b) of paragraph 2.

SECTION III MISCELLANEOUS PROVISIONS

[3.285]
Article 8
Reservation and confidentiality

1. Member States shall provide that members of the special negotiating body or the representative body, and experts who assist them, are not authorised to reveal any information which has been given to them in confidence.

The same shall apply to employees' representatives in the context of an information and consultation procedure.

This obligation shall continue to apply, wherever the persons referred to may be, even after the expiry of their terms of office.

2. Each Member State shall provide, in specific cases and under the conditions and limits laid down by national legislation, that the supervisory or administrative organ of an SE or of a participating company established in its territory is not obliged to transmit information where its nature is such that, according to objective criteria, to do so would seriously harm the functioning of the SE (or, as the case may be, the participating company) or its subsidiaries and establishments or would be prejudicial to them.

A Member State may make such dispensation subject to prior administrative or judicial authorisation.

3. Each Member State may lay down particular provisions for SEs in its territory which pursue directly and essentially the aim of ideological guidance with respect to information and the expression of opinions, on condition that, on the date of adoption of this Directive, such provisions already exist in the national legislation.

4. In applying paragraphs 1, 2 and 3, Member States shall make provision for administrative or judicial appeal procedures which the employees' representatives may initiate when the supervisory or administrative organ of an SE or participating company demands confidentiality or does not give information.

Such procedures may include arrangements designed to protect the confidentiality of the information in question.

[3.286]
Article 9
Operation of the representative body and procedure for the information and consultation of employees
The competent organ of the SE and the representative body shall work together in a spirit of cooperation with due regard for their reciprocal rights and obligations.

The same shall apply to cooperation between the supervisory or administrative organ of the SE and the employees' representatives in conjunction with a procedure for the information and consultation of employees.

[3.287]
Article 10
Protection of employees' representatives
The members of the special negotiating body, the members of the representative body, any employees' representatives exercising functions under the information and consultation procedure and any employees' representatives in the supervisory or administrative organ of an SE who are employees of the SE, its subsidiaries or establishments or of a participating company shall, in the exercise of their functions, enjoy the same protection and guarantees provided for employees' representatives by the national legislation and/or practice in force in their country of employment.

This shall apply in particular to attendance at meetings of the special negotiating body or representative body, any other meeting under the agreement referred to in Article 4(2)(f) or any meeting of the administrative or supervisory organ, and to the payment of wages for members employed by a participating company or the SE or its subsidiaries or establishments during a period of absence necessary for the performance of their duties.

[3.288]
Article 11
Misuse of procedures
Member States shall take appropriate measures in conformity with Community law with a view to preventing the misuse of an SE for the purpose of depriving employees of rights to employee involvement or withholding such rights.

[3.289]
Article 12
Compliance with this Directive
1. Each Member State shall ensure that the management of establishments of an SE and the supervisory or administrative organs of subsidiaries and of participating companies which are situated within its territory and the employees' representatives or, as the case may be, the employees themselves abide by the obligations laid down by this Directive, regardless of whether or not the SE has its registered office within its territory.
2. Member States shall provide for appropriate measures in the event of failure to comply with this Directive; in particular they shall ensure that administrative or legal procedures are available to enable the obligations deriving from this Directive to be enforced.

[3.290]
Article 13
Link between this Directive and other provisions
1. Where an SE is a Community-scale undertaking or a controlling undertaking of a Community-scale group of undertakings within the meaning of Directive 94/45/EC or of Directive 97/74/EC[1] extending the said Directive to the United Kingdom, the provisions of these Directives and the provisions transposing them into national legislation shall not apply to them or to their subsidiaries.

However, where the special negotiating body decides in accordance with Article 3(6) not to open negotiations or to terminate negotiations already opened, Directive 94/45/EC or Directive 97/74/EC and the provisions transposing them into national legislation shall apply.
2. Provisions on the participation of employees in company bodies provided for by national legislation and/or practice, other than those implementing this Directive, shall not apply to companies established in accordance with Regulation (EC) No 2157/2001 and covered by this Directive.
3. This Directive shall not prejudice—
(a) the existing rights to involvement of employees provided for by national legislation and/or practice in the Member States as enjoyed by employees of the SE and its subsidiaries and establishments, other than participation in the bodies of the SE;
(b) the provisions on participation in the bodies laid down by national legislation and/or practice applicable to the subsidiaries of the SE.
4. In order to preserve the rights referred to in paragraph 3, Member States may take the necessary measures to guarantee that the structures of employee representation in participating companies which will cease to exist as separate legal entities are maintained after the registration of the SE.

NOTES
[1] OJ L10, 16.1.1998, p 22.

[3.291]
Article 14
Final provisions
1. Member States shall adopt the laws, regulations and administrative provisions necessary to comply with this Directive no later than 8 October 2004, or shall ensure by that date at the latest that management and labour introduce the required provisions by way of agreement, the Member States being obliged to take all necessary steps enabling them at all times to guarantee the results imposed by this Directive. They shall forthwith inform the Commission thereof.
2. When Member States adopt these measures, they shall contain a reference to this Directive or shall be accompanied by such reference on the occasion of their official publication. The methods of making such reference shall be laid down by the Member States.

[3.292]
Article 15
Review by the Commission
No later than 8 October 2007, the Commission shall, in consultation with the Member States and with management and labour at Community level, review the procedures for applying this Directive, with a view to proposing suitable amendments to the Council where necessary.

[3.293]
Article 16
Entry into force
This Directive shall enter into force on the day of its publication in the *Official Journal of the European Communities*.

[3.294]
Article 17
Addressees
This Directive is addressed to the Member States.

ANNEX
STANDARD RULES

(referred to in Article 7)

[3.295]
Part 1: Composition of the body representative of the employees
In order to achieve the objective described in Article 1, and in the cases referred to in Article 7, a representative body shall be set up in accordance with the following rules.

(a) The representative body shall be composed of employees of the SE and its subsidiaries and establishments elected or appointed from their number by the employees' representatives or, in the absence thereof, by the entire body of employees.
(b) The election or appointment of members of the representative body shall be carried out in accordance with national legislation and/or practice.

Member States shall lay down rules to ensure that the number of members of, and allocation of seats on, the representative body shall be adapted to take account of changes occurring within the SE and its subsidiaries and establishments.

(c) Where its size so warrants, the representative body shall elect a select committee from among its members, comprising at most three members.
(d) The representative body shall adopt its rules of procedure.
(e) The members of the representative body are elected or appointed in proportion to the number of employees employed in each Member State by the participating companies and concerned subsidiaries or establishments, by allocating in respect of a Member State one seat per portion of employees employed in that Member State which equals 10%, or a fraction thereof, of the number of employees employed by the participating companies and concerned subsidiaries or establishments in all the Member States taken together.
(f) The competent organ of the SE shall be informed of the composition of the representative body.
(g) Four years after the representative body is established, it shall examine whether to open negotiations for the conclusion of the agreement referred to in Articles 4 and 7 or to continue to apply the standard rules adopted in accordance with this Annex.

Articles 3(4) to (7) and 4 to 6 shall apply, mutatis mutandis, if a decision has been taken to negotiate an agreement according to Article 4, in which case the term "special negotiating body" shall be replaced by "representative body". Where, by the deadline by which the negotiations come to an end, no agreement has been concluded, the arrangements initially adopted in accordance with the standard rules shall continue to apply.

[3.296]
Part 2: Standard rules for information and consultation
The competence and powers of the representative body set up in an SE shall be governed by the following rules.

(a) The competence of the representative body shall be limited to questions which concern the SE itself and any of its subsidiaries or establishments situated in another Member State or which exceed the powers of the decision-making organs in a single Member State.

(b) Without prejudice to meetings held pursuant to point (c), the representative body shall have the right to be informed and consulted and, for that purpose, to meet with the competent organ of the SE at least once a year, on the basis of regular reports drawn up by the competent organ, on the progress of the business of the SE and its prospects. The local managements shall be informed accordingly.

The competent organ of the SE shall provide the representative body with the agenda for meetings of the administrative, or, where appropriate, the management and supervisory organ, and with copies of all documents submitted to the general meeting of its shareholders.

The meeting shall relate in particular to the structure, economic and financial situation, the probable development of the business and of production and sales, the situation and probable trend of employment, investments, and substantial changes concerning organisation, introduction of new working methods or production processes, transfers of production, mergers, cut-backs or closures of undertakings, establishments or important parts thereof, and collective redundancies.

(c) Where there are exceptional circumstances affecting the employees' interests to a considerable extent, particularly in the event of relocations, transfers, the closure of establishments or undertakings or collective redundancies, the representative body shall have the right to be informed. The representative body or, where it so decides, in particular for reasons of urgency, the select committee, shall have the right to meet at its request the competent organ of the SE or any more appropriate level of management within the SE having its own powers of decision, so as to be informed and consulted on measures significantly affecting employees' interests.

Where the competent organ decides not to act in accordance with the opinion expressed by the representative body, this body shall have the right to a further meeting with the competent organ of the SE with a view to seeking agreement.

In the case of a meeting organised with the select committee, those members of the representative body who represent employees who are directly concerned by the measures in question shall also have the right to participate.

The meetings referred to above shall not affect the prerogatives of the competent organ.

(d) Member States may lay down rules on the chairing of information and consultation meetings.

Before any meeting with the competent organ of the SE, the representative body or the select committee, where necessary enlarged in accordance with the third subparagraph of paragraph (c), shall be entitled to meet without the representatives of the competent organ being present.

(e) Without prejudice to Article 8, the members of the representative body shall inform the representatives of the employees of the SE and of its subsidiaries and establishments of the content and outcome of the information and consultation procedures.

(f) The representative body or the select committee may be assisted by experts of its choice.

(g) In so far as this is necessary for the fulfilment of their tasks, the members of the representative body shall be entitled to time off for training without loss of wages.

(h) The costs of the representative body shall be borne by the SE, which shall provide the body's members with the financial and material resources needed to enable them to perform their duties in an appropriate manner.

In particular, the SE shall, unless otherwise agreed, bear the cost of organising meetings and providing interpretation facilities and the accommodation and travelling expenses of members of the representative body and the select committee.

In compliance with these principles, the Member States may lay down budgetary rules regarding the operation of the representative body. They may in particular limit funding to cover one expert only.

[3.297]

Part 3: Standard rules for participation

Employee participation in an SE shall be governed by the following provisions.

(a) In the case of an SE established by transformation, if the rules of a Member State relating to employee participation in the administrative or supervisory body applied before registration, all aspects of employee participation shall continue to apply to the SE. Point (b) shall apply mutatis mutandis to that end.

(b) In other cases of the establishing of an SE, the employees of the SE, its subsidiaries and establishments and/or their representative body shall have the right to elect, appoint, recommend or oppose the appointment of a number of members of the administrative or supervisory body of the SE equal to the highest proportion in force in the participating companies concerned before registration of the SE.

If none of the participating companies was governed by participation rules before registration of the SE, the latter shall not be required to establish provisions for employee participation.

The representative body shall decide on the allocation of seats within the administrative or supervisory body among the members representing the employees from the various Member States or on the way in which the SE's employees may recommend or oppose the appointment of the members of these bodies according to the proportion of the SE's employees in each Member State. If the employees of one or more

Member States are not covered by this proportional criterion, the representative body shall appoint a member from one of those Member States, in particular the Member State of the SE's registered office where that is appropriate. Each Member State may determine the allocation of the seats it is given within the administrative or supervisory body.

Every member of the administrative body or, where appropriate, the supervisory body of the SE who has been elected, appointed or recommended by the representative body or, depending on the circumstances, by the employees shall be a full member with the same rights and obligations as the members representing the shareholders, including the right to vote.

DIRECTIVE OF THE EUROPEAN PARLIAMENT AND OF THE COUNCIL

(2002/14/EC)

of 11 March 2002

establishing a general framework for informing and consulting employees in the European Community

[3.298]

NOTES

Date of publication in OJ: OJ L80, 23.3.2002, p 29.

For the domestic implementation of this Directive, see the Information and Consultation of Employees Regulations 2004, SI 2004/3426 at **[2.768]**.

See *Harvey* CII(7), N(III)(2).

THE EUROPEAN PARLIAMENT AND THE COUNCIL OF THE EUROPEAN UNION,

Having regard to the Treaty establishing the European Community, and in particular Article 137(2) thereof,

Having regard to the proposal from the Commission,[1]

Having regard to the opinion of the Economic and Social Committee,[2]

Having regard to the opinion of the Committee of the Regions,[3]

Acting in accordance with the procedure referred to in Article 251,[4] and in the light of the joint text approved by the Conciliation Committee on 23 January 2002,

Whereas—

(1) Pursuant to Article 136 of the Treaty, a particular objective of the Community and the Member States is to promote social dialogue between management and labour.

(2) Point 17 of the Community Charter of Fundamental Social Rights of Workers provides, inter alia, that information, consultation and participation for workers must be developed along appropriate lines, taking account of the practices in force in different Member States.

(3) The Commission consulted management and labour at Community level on the possible direction of Community action on the information and consultation of employees in undertakings within the Community.

(4) Following this consultation, the Commission considered that Community action was advisable and again consulted management and labour on the contents of the planned proposal; management and labour have presented their opinions to the Commission.

(5) Having completed this second stage of consultation, management and labour have not informed the Commission of their wish to initiate the process potentially leading to the conclusion of an agreement.

(6) The existence of legal frameworks at national and Community level intended to ensure that employees are involved in the affairs of the undertaking employing them and in decisions which affect them has not always prevented serious decisions affecting employees from being taken and made public without adequate procedures having been implemented beforehand to inform and consult them.

(7) There is a need to strengthen dialogue and promote mutual trust within undertakings in order to improve risk anticipation, make work organisation more flexible and facilitate employee access to training within the undertaking while maintaining security, make employees aware of adaptation needs, increase employees' availability to undertake measures and activities to increase their employability, promote employee involvement in the operation and future of the undertaking and increase its competitiveness.

(8) There is a need, in particular, to promote and enhance information and consultation on the situation and likely development of employment within the undertaking and, where the employer's evaluation suggests that employment within the undertaking may be under threat, the possible anticipatory measures envisaged, in particular in terms of employee training and skill development, with a view to offsetting the negative developments or their consequences and increasing the employability and adaptability of the employees likely to be affected.

(9) Timely information and consultation is a prerequisite for the success of the restructuring and adaptation of undertakings to the new conditions created by globalisation of the economy, particularly through the development of new forms of organisation of work.

(10) The Community has drawn up and implemented an employment strategy based on the concepts of "anticipation", "prevention" and "employability", which are to be incorporated as key elements into all public policies likely to benefit employment, including the policies of individual undertakings, by strengthening the social dialogue with a view to promoting change compatible with preserving the priority objective of employment.

(11) Further development of the internal market must be properly balanced, maintaining the essential values on which our societies are based and ensuring that all citizens benefit from economic development.

(12) Entry into the third stage of economic and monetary union has extended and accelerated the competitive pressures at European level. This means that more supportive measures are needed at national level.

(13) The existing legal frameworks for employee information and consultation at Community and national level tend to adopt an excessively a posteriori approach to the process of change, neglect the economic aspects of decisions taken and do not contribute either to genuine anticipation of employment developments within the undertaking or to risk prevention.

(14) All of these political, economic, social and legal developments call for changes to the existing legal framework providing for the legal and practical instruments enabling the right to be informed and consulted to be exercised.

(15) This Directive is without prejudice to national systems regarding the exercise of this right in practice where those entitled to exercise it are required to indicate their wishes collectively.

(16) This Directive is without prejudice to those systems which provide for the direct involvement of employees, as long as they are always free to exercise the right to be informed and consulted through their representatives.

(17) Since the objectives of the proposed action, as outlined above, cannot be adequately achieved by the Member States, in that the object is to establish a framework for employee information and consultation appropriate for the new European context described above, and can therefore, in view of the scale and impact of the proposed action, be better achieved at Community level, the Community may adopt measures in accordance with the principle of subsidiarity as set out in Article 5 of the Treaty. In accordance with the principle of proportionality, as set out in that Article, this Directive does not go beyond what is necessary in order to achieve these objectives.

(18) The purpose of this general framework is to establish minimum requirements applicable throughout the Community while not preventing Member States from laying down provisions more favourable to employees.

(19) The purpose of this general framework is also to avoid any administrative, financial or legal constraints which would hinder the creation and development of small and medium-sized undertakings. To this end, the scope of this Directive should be restricted, according to the choice made by Member States, to undertakings with at least 50 employees or establishments employing at least 20 employees.

(20) This takes into account and is without prejudice to other national measures and practices aimed at fostering social dialogue within companies not covered by this Directive and within public administrations.

(21) However, on a transitional basis, Member States in which there is no established statutory system of information and consultation of employees or employee representation should have the possibility of further restricting the scope of the Directive as regards the numbers of employees.

(22) A Community framework for informing and consulting employees should keep to a minimum the burden on undertakings or establishments while ensuring the effective exercise of the rights granted.

(23) The objective of this Directive is to be achieved through the establishment of a general framework comprising the principles, definitions and arrangements for information and consultation, which it will be for the Member States to comply with and adapt to their own national situation, ensuring, where appropriate, that management and labour have a leading role by allowing them to define freely, by agreement, the arrangements for informing and consulting employees which they consider to be best suited to their needs and wishes.

(24) Care should be taken to avoid affecting some specific rules in the field of employee information and consultation existing in some national laws, addressed to undertakings or establishments which pursue political, professional, organisational, religious, charitable, educational, scientific or artistic aims, as well as aims involving information and the expression of opinions.

(25) Undertakings and establishments should be protected against disclosure of certain particularly sensitive information.

(26) The employer should be allowed not to inform and consult where this would seriously damage the undertaking or the establishment or where he has to comply immediately with an order issued to him by a regulatory or supervisory body.

(27) Information and consultation imply both rights and obligations for management and labour at undertaking or establishment level.

(28) Administrative or judicial procedures, as well as sanctions that are effective, dissuasive and proportionate in relation to the seriousness of the offence, should be applicable in cases of infringement of the obligations based on this Directive.

(29) This Directive should not affect the provisions, where these are more specific, of Council Directive 98/59/EC of 20 July 1998 on the approximation of the laws of the Member States relating to collective redundancies[5] and of Council Directive 2001/23/EC of 12 March 2001 on the approximation of the laws of the Member States relating to the safeguarding of employees' rights in the event of transfers of undertakings, businesses or parts of undertakings or businesses.[6]

(30) Other rights of information and consultation, including those arising from Council Directive 94/45/EEC of 22 September 1994 on the establishment of a European Works Council or a procedure in Community-scale undertakings and Community-scale groups of undertakings for the purposes of informing and consulting employees,[7] should not be affected by this Directive.

(31) Implementation of this Directive should not be sufficient grounds for a reduction in the general level of protection of workers in the areas to which it applies,

NOTES

1 OJ C2, 5.1.1999, p 3.

2 OJ C258, 10.9.1999, p 24.

3 OJ C144, 16.5.2001, p 58.

4 Opinion of the European Parliament of 14 April 1999 (OJ C219, 30.7.1999, p 223), confirmed on 16 September 1999 (OJ C54, 25.2.2000, p 55), Council Common Position of 27 July 2001 (OJ C307, 31.10.2001, p 16) and Decision of the European Parliament of 23 October 2001 (not yet published in the Official Journal). Decision of the European Parliament of 5 February 2002 and Decision of the Council of 18 February 2002.

5 OJ L225, 12.8.1998, p 16.

6 OJ L82, 22.3.2001, p 16.

7 OJ L254, 30.9.1994, p 64. Directive as amended by Directive 97/74/EC (OJ L10, 16.1.1998, p 22.

HAVE ADOPTED THIS DIRECTIVE:

[3.299]
Article 1
Object and principles

1. The purpose of this Directive is to establish a general framework setting out minimum requirements for the right to information and consultation of employees in undertakings or establishments within the Community.

2. The practical arrangements for information and consultation shall be defined and implemented in accordance with national law and industrial relations practices in individual Member States in such a way as to ensure their effectiveness.

3. When defining or implementing practical arrangements for information and consultation, the employer and the employees' representatives shall work in a spirit of cooperation and with due regard for their reciprocal rights and obligations, taking into account the interests both of the undertaking or establishment and of the employees.

[3.300]
Article 2
Definitions

For the purposes of this Directive—

(a) "undertaking" means a public or private undertaking carrying out an economic activity, whether or not operating for gain, which is located within the territory of the Member States;

(b) "establishment" means a unit of business defined in accordance with national law and practice, and located within the territory of a Member State, where an economic activity is carried out on an ongoing basis with human and material resources;

(c) "employer" means the natural or legal person party to employment contracts or employment relationships with employees, in accordance with national law and practice;

(d) "employee" means any person who, in the Member State concerned, is protected as an employee under national employment law and in accordance with national practice;

(e) "employees' representatives" means the employees' representatives provided for by national laws and/or practices;

(f) "information" means transmission by the employer to the employees' representatives of data in order to enable them to acquaint themselves with the subject matter and to examine it;

(g) "consultation" means the exchange of views and establishment of dialogue between the employees' representatives and the employer.

[3.301]
Article 3
Scope

1. This Directive shall apply, according to the choice made by Member States, to—

(a) undertakings employing at least 50 employees in any one Member State, or

(b) establishments employing at least 20 employees in any one Member State.

Member States shall determine the method for calculating the thresholds of employees employed.

2. In conformity with the principles and objectives of this Directive, Member States may lay down particular provisions applicable to undertakings or establishments which pursue directly and essentially political, professional organisational, religious, charitable, educational, scientific or artistic aims, as well as aims involving information and the expression of opinions, on condition that, at the date of entry into force of this Directive, provisions of that nature already exist in national legislation.

3. . . .

NOTES

Para 3: repealed by Directive 2015/1794/EU, Art 3, as from 9 October 2015.

[3.302]
Article 4
Practical arrangements for information and consultation

1. In accordance with the principles set out in Article 1 and without prejudice to any provisions and/or practices in force more favourable to employees, the Member States shall determine the practical arrangements for exercising the right to information and consultation at the appropriate level in accordance with this Article.

2. Information and consultation shall cover—

(a) information on the recent and probable development of the undertaking's or the establishment's activities and economic situation;

(b) information and consultation on the situation, structure and probable development of employment within the undertaking or establishment and on any anticipatory measures envisaged, in particular where there is a threat to employment;

(c) information and consultation on decisions likely to lead to substantial changes in work organisation or in contractual relations, including those covered by the Community provisions referred to in Article 9(1).

3. Information shall be given at such time, in such fashion and with such content as are appropriate to enable, in particular, employees' representatives to conduct an adequate study and, where necessary, prepare for consultation.

4. Consultation shall take place—

(a) while ensuring that the timing, method and content thereof are appropriate;

(b) at the relevant level of management and representation, depending on the subject under discussion;

(c) on the basis of information supplied by the employer in accordance with Article 2(f) and of the opinion which the employees' representatives are entitled to formulate;

(d) in such a way as to enable employees' representatives to meet the employer and obtain a response, and the reasons for that response, to any opinion they might formulate;

(e) with a view to reaching an agreement on decisions within the scope of the employer's powers referred to in paragraph 2(c).

[3.303]
Article 5
Information and consultation deriving from an agreement

Member States may entrust management and labour at the appropriate level, including at undertaking or establishment level, with defining freely and at any time through negotiated agreement the practical arrangements for informing and consulting employees. These agreements, and agreements existing on the date laid down in Article 11, as well as any subsequent renewals of such agreements, may establish, while respecting the principles set out in Article 1 and subject to conditions and limitations laid down by the Member States, provisions which are different from those referred to in Article 4.

[3.304]
Article 6
Confidential information

1. Member States shall provide that, within the conditions and limits laid down by national legislation, the employees' representatives, and any experts who assist them, are not authorised to reveal to employees or to third parties, any information which, in the legitimate interest of the undertaking or establishment, has expressly been provided to them in confidence. This obligation shall continue to apply, wherever the said representatives or experts are, even after expiry of their terms of office. However, a Member State may authorise the employees' representatives and anyone assisting them to pass on confidential information to employees and to third parties bound by an obligation of confidentiality.

2. Member States shall provide, in specific cases and within the conditions and limits laid down by national legislation, that the employer is not obliged to communicate information or undertake consultation when the nature of that information or consultation is such that, according to objective criteria, it would seriously harm the functioning of the undertaking or establishment or would be prejudicial to it.

3. Without prejudice to existing national procedures, Member States shall provide for administrative or judicial review procedures for the case where the employer requires confidentiality or does not provide the information in accordance with paragraphs 1 and 2. They may also provide for procedures intended to safeguard the confidentiality of the information in question.

[3.305]
Article 7
Protection of employees' representatives

Member States shall ensure that employees' representatives, when carrying out their functions, enjoy adequate protection and guarantees to enable them to perform properly the duties which have been assigned to them.

[3.306]
Article 8
Protection of rights

1. Member States shall provide for appropriate measures in the event of non-compliance with this Directive by the employer or the employees' representatives. In particular, they shall ensure that adequate administrative or judicial procedures are available to enable the obligations deriving from this Directive to be enforced.

2. Member States shall provide for adequate sanctions to be applicable in the event of infringement of this Directive by the employer or the employees' representatives. These sanctions must be effective, proportionate and dissuasive.

[3.307]
Article 9
Link between this Directive and other Community and national provisions

1. This Directive shall be without prejudice to the specific information and consultation procedures set out in Article 2 of Directive 98/59/EC and Article 7 of Directive 2001/23/EC.

2. This Directive shall be without prejudice to provisions adopted in accordance with Directives 94/45/EC and 97/74/EC.

3. This Directive shall be without prejudice to other rights to information, consultation and participation under national law.

4. Implementation of this Directive shall not be sufficient grounds for any regression in relation to the situation which already prevails in each Member State and in relation to the general level of protection of workers in the areas to which it applies.

[3.308]
Article 10
Transitional provisions

Notwithstanding Article 3, a Member State in which there is, at the date of entry into force of this Directive, no general, permanent and statutory system of information and consultation of employees, nor a general, permanent and statutory system of employee representation at the workplace allowing employees to be represented for that purpose, may limit the application of the national provisions implementing this Directive to—

(a) undertakings employing at least 150 employees or establishments employing at least 100 employees until 23 March 2007, and

(b) undertakings employing at least 100 employees or establishments employing at least 50 employees during the year following the date in point (a).

[3.309]
Article 11
Transposition

1. Member States shall adopt the laws, regulations and administrative provisions necessary to comply with this Directive not later than 23 March 2005 or shall ensure that management and labour introduce by that date the required provisions by way of agreement, the Member States being obliged to take all necessary steps enabling them to guarantee the results imposed by this Directive at all times. They shall forthwith inform the Commission thereof.

2. Where Member States adopt these measures, they shall contain a reference to this Directive or shall be accompanied by such reference on the occasion of their official publication. The methods of making such reference shall be laid down by the Member States.

[3.310]
Article 12
Review by the Commission

Not later than 23 March 2007, the Commission shall, in consultation with the Member States and the social partners at Community level, review the application of this Directive with a view to proposing any necessary amendments.

[3.311]
Article 13
Entry into force

This Directive shall enter into force on the day of its publication in the *Official Journal of the European Communities*.

[3.312]
Article 14
Addressees

This Directive is addressed to the Member States.

DIRECTIVE OF THE EUROPEAN PARLIAMENT AND OF THE COUNCIL

(2002/15/EC)

of 11 March 2002

on the organisation of the working time of persons performing mobile road transport activities

[3.313]

NOTES

Date of publication in OJ: OJ L80, 23.3.2002, p 35.

For the domestic implementation of this Directive, see the Road Transport (Working Time) Regulations 2005, SI 2005/639 at **[2.812]**.

See *Harvey* CI(1).

THE EUROPEAN PARLIAMENT AND THE COUNCIL OF THE EUROPEAN UNION,

Having regard to the Treaty establishing the European Community, and in particular Article 71 and Article 137(2) thereof,

Having regard to the proposal from the Commission,[1]

Having regard to the opinion of the Economic and Social Committee,[2]

Following consultation of the Committee of the Regions,

Acting in accordance with the procedure laid down in Article 251 of the Treaty,[3] and in the light of the joint text approved by the Conciliation Committee on 16 January 2002,

Whereas:

(1) Council Regulation (EEC) No 3820/85 of 20 December 1985 on the harmonisation of certain social legislation relating to road transport[4] laid down common rules on driving times and rest periods for drivers; that Regulation does not cover other aspects of working time for road transport.

(2) Council Directive 93/104/EC of 23 November 1993 concerning certain aspects of the organisation of working time[5] makes it possible to adopt more specific requirements for the organisation of working time. Bearing in mind the sectoral nature of this Directive, the provisions thereof take precedence over Directive 93/104/EC by virtue of Article 14 thereof.

(3) Despite intensive negotiations between the social partners, it has not been possible to reach agreement on the subject of mobile workers in road transport.

(4) It is therefore necessary to lay down a series of more specific provisions concerning the hours of work in road transport intended to ensure the safety of transport and the health and safety of the persons involved.

(5) Since the objectives of the proposed action cannot be sufficiently achieved by the Member States and can therefore, by reason of the scale and effects of the proposed action, be better achieved at Community level, the Community may adopt measures, in accordance with the principle of subsidiarity as set out in Article 5 of the Treaty. In accordance with the principle of proportionality, as set out in that Article, this Directive does not go beyond what is necessary in order to achieve those objectives.

(6) The scope of this Directive covers only mobile workers employed by transport undertakings established in a Member State participating in mobile road transport activities covered by Regulation (EEC) No 3820/85 or, failing that, by the European agreement concerning the work of crews of vehicles engaged in international road transport (AETR).

(7) It should be made clear that mobile workers excluded from the scope of this Directive, other than self-employed drivers, benefit from the basic protection provided for in Directive 93/104/EC. That basic protection includes the existing rules on adequate rest, the maximum average working week, annual leave and certain basic provisions for night workers including health assessment.

(8) As self-employed drivers are included within the scope of Regulation (EEC) No 3820/85 but excluded from that of Directive 93/104/EC, they should be excluded temporarily from the scope of this Directive in accordance with the provisions of Article 2(1).

(9) The definitions used in this Directive are not to constitute a precedent for other Community regulations on working time.

(10) In order to improve road safety, prevent the distortion of competition and guarantee the safety and health of the mobile workers covered by this Directive, the latter should know exactly which periods devoted to road transport activities constitute working time and which do not and are thus deemed to be break times, rest times or periods of availability. These workers should be granted minimum daily and weekly periods of rest, and adequate breaks. It is also necessary to place a maximum limit on the number of weekly working hours.

(11) Research has shown that the human body is more sensitive at night to environmental disturbances and also to certain burdensome forms of organisation and that long periods of night work can be detrimental to the health of workers and can endanger their safety and also road safety in general.

(12) As a consequence, there is a need to limit the duration of periods of night work and to provide that professional drivers who work at night should receive appropriate compensation for their activity and should not be disadvantaged as regards training opportunities.

Part 3 EU Materials

(13) Employers should keep records of instances when the maximum average working week applicable to mobile workers is exceeded.

(14) The provisions of Regulation (EEC) No 3820/85 on driving time in international and national passenger transport, other than regular services, should continue to apply.

(15) The Commission should monitor the implementation of this Directive and developments in this field in the Member States and submit to the European Parliament, the Council, the Economic and Social Committee and the Committee of the Regions a report on the application of the rules and the consequences of the provisions on night work.

(16) It is necessary to provide that certain provisions may be subject to derogations adopted, according to the circumstances, by the Member States or the two sides of industry. As a general rule, in the event of a derogation, the workers concerned must be given compensatory rest periods,

NOTES

1 OJ C43, 17.2.1999, p 4.

2 OJ C138, 18.5.1999, p 33.

3 Opinion of the European Parliament of 14 April 1999 (OJ C219, 30.7.1999, p 235), as confirmed on 6 May 1999 (OJ C279, 1.10.1999, p 270), Council Common Position of 23 March 2001 (OJ C142, 15.5.2001, p 24) and Decision of the European Parliament of 14 June 2001 (not yet published in the Official Journal). Decision of the European Parliament of 5 February 2002 and Council Decision of 18 February 2002.

4 OJ L370, 31.12.1985, p 1.

5 OJ L307, 13.12.1993, p 18. Directive as last amended by Directive 2000/34/EC of the European Parliament and of the Council (OJ L195, 1.8.2000, p 41).

HAVE ADOPTED THIS DIRECTIVE:

[3.314]
Article 1
Purpose

The purpose of this Directive shall be to establish minimum requirements in relation to the organisation of working time in order to improve the health and safety protection of persons performing mobile road transport activities and to improve road safety and align conditions of competition.

[3.315]
Article 2
Scope

1. This Directive shall apply to mobile workers employed by undertakings established in a Member State, participating in road transport activities covered by Regulation (EEC) No 3820/85 or, failing that, by the AETR Agreement.

Without prejudice to the provisions of following subparagraph, this Directive shall apply to self-employed drivers from 23 March 2009.

At the latest two years before this date, the Commission shall present a report to the European Parliament and the Council. This report shall analyse the consequences of the exclusion of self-employed drivers from the scope of the Directive in respect of road safety, conditions of competition, the structure of the profession as well as social aspects. The circumstances in each Member State relating to the structure of the transport industry and to the working environment of the road transport profession shall be taken into account. On the basis of this report, the Commission shall submit a proposal, the aim of which may be either, as appropriate

— to set out the modalities for the inclusion of the self-employed drivers within the scope of the Directive in respect of certain self-employed drivers who are not participating in road transport activities in other Member States and who are subject to local constraints for objective reasons, such as peripheral location, long internal distances and a particular competitive environment, or
— not to include self-employed drivers within the scope of the Directive.

2. The provisions of Directive 93/104/EC shall apply to mobile workers excluded from the scope of this Directive.

3. In so far as this Directive contains more specific provisions as regards mobile workers performing road transport activities it shall, pursuant to Article 14 of Directive 93/104/EC, take precedence over the relevant provisions of that Directive.

4. This Directive shall supplement the provisions of Regulation (EEC) No 3820/85 and, where necessary, of the AETR Agreement, which take precedence over the provisions of this Directive.

[3.316]
Article 3
Definitions

For the purposes of this Directive:

(a) "working time" shall mean:

1. in the case of mobile workers: the time from the beginning to the end of work, during which the mobile worker is at his workstation, at the disposal of the employer and exercising his functions or activities, that is to say:
   — the time devoted to all road transport activities. These activities are, in particular, the following:
      (i) driving;
      (ii) loading and unloading;

(iii) assisting passengers boarding and disembarking from the vehicle;
(iv) cleaning and technical maintenance;
(v) all other work intended to ensure the safety of the vehicle, its cargo and passengers or to fulfil the legal or regulatory obligations directly linked to the specific transport operation under way, including monitoring of loading and unloading, administrative formalities with police, customs, immigration officers etc,

— the times during which he cannot dispose freely of his time and is required to be at his workstation, ready to take up normal work, with certain tasks associated with being on duty, in particular during periods awaiting loading or unloading where their foreseeable duration is not known in advance, that is to say either before departure or just before the actual start of the period in question, or under the general conditions negotiated between the social partners and/or under the terms of the legislation of the Member States;

2. in the case of self-employed drivers, the same definition shall apply to the time from the beginning to the end of work, during which the self employed driver is at his workstation, at the disposal of the client and exercising his functions or activities other than general administrative work that is not directly linked to the specific transport operation under way.

The break times referred to in Article 5, the rest times referred to in Article 6 and, without prejudice to the legislation of Member States or agreements between the social partners providing that such periods should be compensated or limited, the periods of availability referred to in (b) of this Article, shall be excluded from working time;

(b) "periods of availability" shall mean:

— periods other than those relating to break times and rest times during which the mobile worker is not required to remain at his workstation, but must be available to answer any calls to start or resume driving or to carry out other work. In particular such periods of availability shall include periods during which the mobile worker is accompanying a vehicle being transported by ferryboat or by train as well as periods of waiting at frontiers and those due to traffic prohibitions.

These periods and their foreseeable duration shall be known in advance by the mobile worker, that is to say either before departure or just before the actual start of the period in question, or under the general conditions negotiated between the social partners and/or under the terms of the legislation of the Member States,

— for mobile workers driving in a team, the time spent sitting next to the driver or on the couchette while the vehicle is in motion;

(c) "workstation" shall mean:

— the location of the main place of business of the undertaking for which the person performing mobile road transport activities carries out duties, together with its various subsidiary places of business, regardless of whether they are located in the same place as its head office or main place of business,

— the vehicle which the person performing mobile road transport activities uses when he carries out duties, and

— any other place in which activities connected with transportation are carried out;

(d) "mobile worker" shall mean any worker forming part of the travelling staff, including trainees and apprentices, who is in the service of an undertaking which operates transport services for passengers or goods by road for hire or reward or on its own account;

(e) "self-employed driver" shall mean anyone whose main occupation is to transport passengers or goods by road for hire or reward within the meaning of Community legislation under cover of a Community licence or any other professional authorisation to carry out the aforementioned transport, who is entitled to work for himself and who is not tied to an employer by an employment contract or by any other type of working hierarchical relationship, who is free to organise the relevant working activities, whose income depends directly on the profits made and who has the freedom to, individually or through a cooperation between self-employed drivers, have commercial relations with several customers.

For the purposes of this Directive, those drivers who do not satisfy these criteria shall be subject to the same obligations and benefit from the same rights as those provided for mobile workers by this Directive;

(f) "person performing mobile road transport activities" shall mean any mobile worker or self-employed driver who performs such activities;

(g) "week" shall mean the period between 00.00 hours on Monday and 24.00 hours on Sunday;

(h) "night time" shall mean a period of at least four hours, as defined by national law, between 00.00 hours and 07.00 hours;

(i) "night work" shall mean any work performed during night time.

[3.317]
Article 4
Maximum weekly working time

Member States shall take the measures necessary to ensure that:

(a) the average weekly working time may not exceed 48 hours. The maximum weekly working time may be extended to 60 hours only if, over four months, an average of 48 hours a week is not exceeded. The fourth and fifth subparagraphs of Article 6(1) of Regulation (EEC) No 3820/85 or, where necessary, the fourth subparagraph of Article 6(1) of the AETR Agreement shall take precedence over this Directive, in so far as the drivers concerned do not exceed an average working time of 48 hours a week over four months;

(b) working time for different employers is the sum of the working hours. The employer shall ask the mobile worker concerned in writing for an account of time worked for another employer. The mobile worker shall provide such information in writing.

[3.318]
Article 5
Breaks

1. Member States shall take the measures necessary to ensure that, without prejudice to the level of protection provided by Regulation (EEC) No 3820/85 or, failing that, by the AETR Agreement, persons performing mobile road transport activities, without prejudice to Article 2(1), in no circumstances work for more than six consecutive hours without a break. Working time shall be interrupted by a break of at least 30 minutes, if working hours total between six and nine hours, and of at least 45 minutes, if working hours total more than nine hours.
2. Breaks may be subdivided into periods of at least 15 minutes each.

[3.319]
Article 6
Rest periods

For the purposes of this Directive, apprentices and trainees shall be covered by the same provisions on rest time as other mobile workers in pursuance of Regulation (EEC) No 3820/85 or, failing that, of the AETR Agreement.

[3.320]
Article 7
Night work

1. Member States shall take the measures necessary to ensure that:
— if night work is performed, the daily working time does not exceed ten hours in each 24 period,
— compensation for night work is given in accordance with national legislative measures, collective agreements, agreements between the two sides of industry and/or national practice, on condition that such compensation is not liable to endanger road safety.

2. By 23 March 2007, the Commission shall, within the framework of the report which it draws up in accordance with Article 13(2), assess the consequences of the provisions laid down in paragraph 1 above. The Commission shall, if necessary, submit appropriate proposals along with that report.
3. The Commission shall present a proposal for a Directive containing provisions relating to the training of professional drivers, including those who perform night work, and laying down the general principles of such training.

[3.321]
Article 8
Derogations

1. Derogations from Articles 4 and 7 may, for objective or technical reasons or reasons concerning the organisation of work, be adopted by means of collective agreements, agreements between the social partners, or if this is not possible, by laws, regulations or administrative provisions provided there is consultation of the representatives of the employers and workers concerned and efforts are made to encourage all relevant forms of social dialogue.
2. The option to derogate from Article 4 may not result in the establishment of a reference period exceeding six months, for calculation of the average maximum weekly working time of forty-eight hours.

[3.322]
Article 9
Information and records

Member States shall ensure that:

(a) mobile workers are informed of the relevant national requirements, the internal rules of the undertaking and agreements between the two sides of industry, in particular collective agreements and any company agreements, reached on the basis of this Directive, without prejudice to Council Directive 91/533/EEC of 14 October 1991 on an employer's obligation to inform employees of the conditions applicable to the contract or employment relationship;[1]
(b) without prejudice to Article 2(1), the working time of persons performing mobile road transport activities is recorded. Records shall be kept for at least two years after the end of the period covered. Employers shall be responsible for recording the working time of mobile workers. Employers shall upon request provide mobile workers with copies of the records of hours worked.

NOTES

[1] OJ L288, 18.10.1991, p 32.

[3.323]
Article 10
More favourable provisions

This Directive shall not affect Member States' right to apply or introduce laws, regulations or administrative provisions more favourable to the protection of the health and safety of persons performing mobile road transport activities, or their right to facilitate or permit the application of collective agreements or other agreements concluded between the two sides of industry which are more favourable to the protection of the health and safety of mobile workers. Implementation of this Directive shall not constitute valid grounds for reducing the general level of protection afforded to workers referred to in Article 2(1).

[3.324]
Article 11
Penalties
Member States shall lay down a system of penalties for breaches of the national provisions adopted pursuant to this Directive and shall take all the measures necessary to ensure that these penalties are applied. The penalties thus provided for shall be effective, proportional and dissuasive.

[3.325]
Article 12
Negotiations with third countries
Once this Directive has entered into force, the Community shall begin negotiations with the relevant third countries with a view to the application of rules equivalent to those laid down in this Directive to mobile workers employed by undertakings established in a third country.

[3.326]
Article 13
Reports
1. Member States shall report to the Commission every two years on the implementation of this Directive, indicating the views of the two sides of industry. The report must reach the Commission no later than 30 September following the date on which the two-year period covered by the report expires. The two-year period shall be the same as that referred to in Article 16(2) of Regulation (EEC) No 3820/85.
2. The Commission shall produce a report every two years on the implementation of this Directive by Member States and developments in the field in question. The Commission shall forward this report to the European Parliament, the Council, the Economic and Social Committee and the Committee of the Regions.

[3.327]
Article 14
Final provisions
1. Member States shall adopt the laws, regulations and administrative provisions necessary to comply with this Directive by 23 March 2005 or shall ensure by that date that the two sides of industry have established the necessary measures by agreement, the Member States being obliged to take any steps to allow them to be able at any time to guarantee the results required by this Directive. When Member States adopt the measures referred to in the first subparagraph, they shall contain a reference to this Directive or shall be accompanied by such reference on the occasion of their official publication. The methods of making such reference shall be laid down by Member States.
2. Member States shall communicate to the Commission the provisions of national law which they have already adopted or which they adopt in the field covered by this Directive.
3. Member States shall take care that consignors, freight forwarders, prime contractors, subcontractors and enterprises which employ mobile workers comply with the relevant provisions of this Directive.

[3.328]
Article 15
Entry into force
This Directive shall enter into force on the day of its publication in the *Official Journal of the European Communities*.

[3.329]
Article 16
Addressees
This Directive is addressed to the Member States.

DIRECTIVE OF THE EUROPEAN PARLIAMENT AND OF THE COUNCIL

(2003/88/EC)

of 4 November 2003

concerning certain aspects of the organisation of working time

[3.330]

NOTES

Date of publication in OJ: OJ L229, 18.11.2003, p 9.

This Directive is a consolidation of Directive 93/104/EEC, as amended by Council Directive 2000/34/EC ('the Working Time Directive' and 'the Horizontal Amending Directive'). A correlation table is in Annex II at **[3.362]**. For the domestic implementation of this Directive and its predecessor in the United Kingdom, see the Working Time Regulations 1998, SI 1998/1833 at **[2.274]**.

See *Harvey* CI(1).

THE EUROPEAN PARLIAMENT AND THE COUNCIL OF THE EUROPEAN UNION,

Having regard to the Treaty establishing the European Community, and in particular Article 137(2) thereof,

Having regard to the proposal from the Commission,

Having regard to the opinion of the European Economic and Social Committee,[1]

Having consulted the Committee of the Regions,

Acting in accordance with the procedure referred to in Article 251 of the Treaty,[2]

Whereas:

(1) Council Directive 93/104/EC of 23 November 1993, concerning certain aspects of the organisation of working time,[3] which lays down minimum safety and health requirements for the organisation of working time, in respect of periods of daily rest, breaks, weekly rest, maximum weekly working time, annual leave and aspects of night work, shift work and patterns of work, has been significantly amended. In order to clarify matters, a codification of the provisions in question should be drawn up.

(2) Article 137 of the Treaty provides that the Community is to support and complement the activities of the Member States with a view to improving the working environment to protect workers' health and safety. Directives adopted on the basis of that Article are to avoid imposing administrative, financial and legal constraints in a way which would hold back the creation and development of small and medium-sized undertakings.

(3) The provisions of Council Directive 89/391/EEC of 12 June 1989 on the introduction of measures to encourage improvements in the safety and health of workers at work[4] remain fully applicable to the areas covered by this Directive without prejudice to more stringent and/or specific provisions contained herein.

(4) The improvement of workers' safety, hygiene and health at work is an objective which should not be subordinated to purely economic considerations.

(5) All workers should have adequate rest periods. The concept of "rest" must be expressed in units of time, ie in days, hours and/or fractions thereof. Community workers must be granted minimum daily, weekly and annual periods of rest and adequate breaks. It is also necessary in this context to place a maximum limit on weekly working hours.

(6) Account should be taken of the principles of the International Labour Organisation with regard to the organisation of working time, including those relating to night work.

(7) Research has shown that the human body is more sensitive at night to environmental disturbances and also to certain burdensome forms of work organisation and that long periods of night work can be detrimental to the health of workers and can endanger safety at the workplace.

(8) There is a need to limit the duration of periods of night work, including overtime, and to provide for employers who regularly use night workers to bring this information to the attention of the competent authorities if they so request.

(9) It is important that night workers should be entitled to a free health assessment prior to their assignment and thereafter at regular intervals and that whenever possible they should be transferred to day work for which they are suited if they suffer from health problems.

(10) The situation of night and shift workers requires that the level of safety and health protection should be adapted to the nature of their work and that the organisation and functioning of protection and prevention services and resources should be efficient.

(11) Specific working conditions may have detrimental effects on the safety and health of workers. The organisation of work according to a certain pattern must take account of the general principle of adapting work to the worker.

(12) A European Agreement in respect of the working time of seafarers has been put into effect by means of Council Directive 1999/63/EC of 21 June 1999 concerning the Agreement on the organisation of working time of seafarers concluded by the European Community Shipowners' Association (ECSA) and the Federation of Transport Workers' Unions in the European Union (FST)[5] based on Article 139(2) of the Treaty. Accordingly, the provisions of this Directive should not apply to seafarers.

(13) In the case of those "share-fishermen" who are employees, it is for the Member States to determine, pursuant to this Directive, the conditions for entitlement to, and granting of, annual leave, including the arrangements for payments.

(14) Specific standards laid down in other Community instruments relating, for example, to rest periods, working time, annual leave and night work for certain categories of workers should take precedence over the provisions of this Directive.

(15) In view of the question likely to be raised by the organisation of working time within an undertaking, it appears desirable to provide for flexibility in the application of certain provisions of this Directive, whilst ensuring compliance with the principles of protecting the safety and health of workers.

(16) It is necessary to provide that certain provisions may be subject to derogations implemented, according to the case, by the Member States or the two sides of industry. As a general rule, in the event of a derogation, the workers concerned must be given equivalent compensatory rest periods.

(17) This Directive should not affect the obligations of the Member States concerning the deadlines for transposition of the Directives set out in Annex I, part B,

NOTES

1 OJ C61, 14.3.2003, p 123.

2 Opinion of the European Parliament of 17 December 2002 (not yet published in the Official Journal) and Council Decision of 22 September 2003.

3 OJ L307, 13.12.1993, p 18. Directive as amended by Directive 2000/34/EC of the European Parliament and of the Council (OJ L195, 1.8.2000, p 41).

4 OJ L183, 29.6.1989, p 1.

5 OJ L167, 2.7.1999, p 33.

HAVE ADOPTED THIS DIRECTIVE:

CHAPTER 1 SCOPE AND DEFINITIONS

[3.331]
Article 1
Purpose and scope

1. This Directive lays down minimum safety and health requirements for the organisation of working time.

2. This Directive applies to:
 (a) minimum periods of daily rest, weekly rest and annual leave, to breaks and maximum weekly working time; and
 (b) certain aspects of night work, shift work and patterns of work.

3. This Directive shall apply to all sectors of activity, both public and private, within the meaning of Article 2 of Directive 89/391/EEC, without prejudice to Articles 14, 17, 18 and 19 of this Directive.

This Directive shall not apply to seafarers, as defined in Directive 1999/63/EC without prejudice to Article 2(8) of this Directive.

4. The provisions of Directive 89/391/EEC are fully applicable to the matters referred to in paragraph 2, without prejudice to more stringent and/or specific provisions contained in this Directive.

[3.332]
Article 2
Definitions

For the purposes of this Directive, the following definitions shall apply:

1. "working time" means any period during which the worker is working, at the employer's disposal and carrying out his activity or duties, in accordance with national laws and/or practice;
2. "rest period" means any period which is not working time;
3. "night time" means any period of not less than seven hours, as defined by national law, and which must include, in any case, the period between midnight and 5.00;
4. "night worker" means:
 (a) on the one hand, any worker, who, during night time, works at least three hours of his daily working time as a normal course; and
 (b) on the other hand, any worker who is likely during night time to work a certain proportion of his annual working time, as defined at the choice of the Member State concerned:
  (i) by national legislation, following consultation with the two sides of industry; or
  (ii) by collective agreements or agreements concluded between the two sides of industry at national or regional level;
5. "shift work" means any method of organising work in shifts whereby workers succeed each other at the same work stations according to a certain pattern, including a rotating pattern, and which may be continuous or discontinuous, entailing the need for workers to work at different times over a given period of days or weeks;
6. "shift worker" means any worker whose work schedule is part of shift work;
7. "mobile worker" means any worker employed as a member of travelling or flying personnel by an undertaking which operates transport services for passengers or goods by road, air or inland waterway;
8. "offshore work" means work performed mainly on or from offshore installations (including drilling rigs), directly or indirectly in connection with the exploration, extraction or exploitation of mineral resources, including hydrocarbons, and diving in connection with such activities, whether performed from an offshore installation or a vessel;
9. "adequate rest" means that workers have regular rest periods, the duration of which is expressed in units of time and which are sufficiently long and continuous to ensure that, as a result of fatigue or other irregular working patterns, they do not cause injury to themselves, to fellow workers or to others and that they do not damage their health, either in the short term or in the longer term.

CHAPTER 2 MINIMUM REST PERIODS—OTHER ASPECTS OF THE ORGANISATION OF WORKING TIME

[3.333]
Article 3
Daily rest
Member States shall take the measures necessary to ensure that every worker is entitled to a minimum daily rest period of 11 consecutive hours per 24-hour period.

[3.334]
Article 4
Breaks
Member States shall take the measures necessary to ensure that, where the working day is longer than six hours, every worker is entitled to a rest break, the details of which, including duration and the terms on which it is granted, shall be laid down in collective agreements or agreements between the two sides of industry or, failing that, by national legislation.

[3.335]
Article 5
Weekly rest period
Member States shall take the measures necessary to ensure that, per each seven-day period, every worker is entitled to a minimum uninterrupted rest period of 24 hours plus the 11 hours' daily rest referred to in Article 3.

If objective, technical or work organisation conditions so justify, a minimum rest period of 24 hours may be applied.

[3.336]
Article 6
Maximum weekly working time
Member States shall take the measures necessary to ensure that, in keeping with the need to protect the safety and health of workers:

(a) the period of weekly working time is limited by means of laws, regulations or administrative provisions or by collective agreements or agreements between the two sides of industry;

(b) the average working time for each seven-day period, including overtime, does not exceed 48 hours.

[3.337]
Article 7
Annual leave
1. Member States shall take the measures necessary to ensure that every worker is entitled to paid annual leave of at least four weeks in accordance with the conditions for entitlement to, and granting of, such leave laid down by national legislation and/or practice.
2. The minimum period of paid annual leave may not be replaced by an allowance in lieu, except where the employment relationship is terminated.

CHAPTER 3 NIGHT WORK—SHIFT WORK—PATTERNS OF WORK

[3.338]
Article 8
Length of night work
Member States shall take the measures necessary to ensure that:

(a) normal hours of work for night workers do not exceed an average of eight hours in any 24-hour period;

(b) night workers whose work involves special hazards or heavy physical or mental strain do not work more than eight hours in any period of 24 hours during which they perform night work.

For the purposes of point (b), work involving special hazards or heavy physical or mental strain shall be defined by national legislation and/or practice or by collective agreements or agreements concluded between the two sides of industry, taking account of the specific effects and hazards of night work.

[3.339]
Article 9
Health assessment and transfer of night workers to day work
1. Member States shall take the measures necessary to ensure that:

(a) night workers are entitled to a free health assessment before their assignment and thereafter at regular intervals;

(b) night workers suffering from health problems recognised as being connected with the fact that they perform night work are transferred whenever possible to day work to which they are suited.

2. The free health assessment referred to in paragraph 1(a) must comply with medical confidentiality.
3. The free health assessment referred to in paragraph 1(a) may be conducted within the national health system.

[3.340]
Article 10
Guarantees for night-time working
Member States may make the work of certain categories of night workers subject to certain guarantees, under conditions laid down by national legislation and/or practice, in the case of workers who incur risks to their safety or health linked to night-time working.

[3.341]
Article 11
Notification of regular use of night workers
Member States shall take the measures necessary to ensure that an employer who regularly uses night workers brings this information to the attention of the competent authorities if they so request.

[3.342]
Article 12
Safety and health protection
Member States shall take the measures necessary to ensure that:
(a) night workers and shift workers have safety and health protection appropriate to the nature of their work;
(b) appropriate protection and prevention services or facilities with regard to the safety and health of night workers and shift workers are equivalent to those applicable to other workers and are available at all times.

[3.343]
Article 13
Pattern of work
Member States shall take the measures necessary to ensure that an employer who intends to organise work according to a certain pattern takes account of the general principle of adapting work to the worker, with a view, in particular, to alleviating monotonous work and work at a predetermined work-rate, depending on the type of activity, and of safety and health requirements, especially as regards breaks during working time.

CHAPTER 4 MISCELLANEOUS PROVISIONS

[3.344]
Article 14
More specific Community provisions
This Directive shall not apply where other Community instruments contain more specific requirements relating to the organisation of working time for certain occupations or occupational activities.

[3.345]
Article 15
More favourable provisions
This Directive shall not affect Member States' right to apply or introduce laws, regulations or administrative provisions more favourable to the protection of the safety and health of workers or to facilitate or permit the application of collective agreements or agreements concluded between the two sides of industry which are more favourable to the protection of the safety and health of workers.

[3.346]
Article 16
Reference periods
Member States may lay down:
(a) for the application of Article 5 (weekly rest period), a reference period not exceeding 14 days;
(b) for the application of Article 6 (maximum weekly working time), a reference period not exceeding four months.

The periods of paid annual leave, granted in accordance with Article 7, and the periods of sick leave shall not be included or shall be neutral in the calculation of the average;
(c) for the application of Article 8 (length of night work), a reference period defined after consultation of the two sides of industry or by collective agreements or agreements concluded between the two sides of industry at national or regional level.

If the minimum weekly rest period of 24 hours required by Article 5 falls within that reference period, it shall not be included in the calculation of the average.

CHAPTER 5 DEROGATIONS AND EXCEPTIONS

[3.347]
Article 17
Derogations
1. With due regard for the general principles of the protection of the safety and health of workers, Member States may derogate from Articles 3 to 6, 8 and 16 when, on account of the specific characteristics of the activity concerned, the duration of the working time is not measured and/or predetermined or can be determined by the workers themselves, and particularly in the case of:
(a) managing executives or other persons with autonomous decision-taking powers;
(b) family workers; or

(c) workers officiating at religious ceremonies in churches and religious communities.

2. Derogations provided for in paragraphs 3, 4 and 5 may be adopted by means of laws, regulations or administrative provisions or by means of collective agreements or agreements between the two sides of industry provided that the workers concerned are afforded equivalent periods of compensatory rest or that, in exceptional cases in which it is not possible, for objective reasons, to grant such equivalent periods of compensatory rest, the workers concerned are afforded appropriate protection.

3. In accordance with paragraph 2 of this Article derogations may be made from Articles 3, 4, 5, 8 and 16:

(a) in the case of activities where the worker's place of work and his place of residence are distant from one another, including offshore work, or where the worker's different places of work are distant from one another;

(b) in the case of security and surveillance activities requiring a permanent presence in order to protect property and persons, particularly security guards and caretakers or security firms;

(c) in the case of activities involving the need for continuity of service or production, particularly:

(i) services relating to the reception, treatment and/or care provided by hospitals or similar establishments, including the activities of doctors in training, residential institutions and prisons;

(ii) dock or airport workers;

(iii) press, radio, television, cinematographic production, postal and telecommunications services, ambulance, fire and civil protection services;

(iv) gas, water and electricity production, transmission and distribution, household refuse collection and incineration plants;

(v) industries in which work cannot be interrupted on technical grounds;

(vi) research and development activities;

(vii) agriculture;

(viii) workers concerned with the carriage of passengers on regular urban transport services;

(d) where there is a foreseeable surge of activity, particularly in:

(i) agriculture;

(ii) tourism;

(iii) postal services;

(e) in the case of persons working in railway transport:

(i) whose activities are intermittent;

(ii) who spend their working time on board trains; or

(iii) whose activities are linked to transport timetables and to ensuring the continuity and regularity of traffic;

(f) in the circumstances described in Article 5(4) of Directive 89/391/EEC;

(g) in cases of accident or imminent risk of accident.

4. In accordance with paragraph 2 of this Article derogations may be made from Articles 3 and 5:

(a) in the case of shift work activities, each time the worker changes shift and cannot take daily and/or weekly rest periods between the end of one shift and the start of the next one;

(b) in the case of activities involving periods of work split up over the day, particularly those of cleaning staff.

5. In accordance with paragraph 2 of this Article, derogations may be made from Article 6 and Article 16(b), in the case of doctors in training, in accordance with the provisions set out in the second to the seventh subparagraphs of this paragraph.

With respect to Article 6 derogations referred to in the first subparagraph shall be permitted for a transitional period of five years from 1 August 2004.

Member States may have up to two more years, if necessary, to take account of difficulties in meeting the working time provisions with respect to their responsibilities for the organisation and delivery of health services and medical care. At least six months before the end of the transitional period, the Member State concerned shall inform the Commission giving its reasons, so that the Commission can give an opinion, after appropriate consultations, within the three months following receipt of such information. If the Member State does not follow the opinion of the Commission, it will justify its decision. The notification and justification of the Member State and the opinion of the Commission shall be published in the *Official Journal of the European Union* and forwarded to the European Parliament.

Member States may have an additional period of up to one year, if necessary, to take account of special difficulties in meeting the responsibilities referred to in the third subparagraph. They shall follow the procedure set out in that subparagraph.

Member States shall ensure that in no case will the number of weekly working hours exceed an average of 58 during the first three years of the transitional period, an average of 56 for the following two years and an average of 52 for any remaining period.

The employer shall consult the representatives of the employees in good time with a view to reaching an agreement, wherever possible, on the arrangements applying to the transitional period. Within the limits set out in the fifth subparagraph, such an agreement may cover:

(a) the average number of weekly hours of work during the transitional period; and

(b) the measures to be adopted to reduce weekly working hours to an average of 48 by the end of the transitional period.

With respect to Article 16(b) derogations referred to in the first subparagraph shall be permitted provided that the reference period does not exceed 12 months, during the first part of the transitional period specified in the fifth subparagraph, and six months thereafter.

[3.348]

Article 18

Derogations by collective agreements

Derogations may be made from Articles 3, 4, 5, 8 and 16 by means of collective agreements or agreements concluded between the two sides of industry at national or regional level or, in conformity with the rules laid down by them, by means of collective agreements or agreements concluded between the two sides of industry at a lower level.

Member States in which there is no statutory system ensuring the conclusion of collective agreements or agreements concluded between the two sides of industry at national or regional level, on the matters covered by this Directive, or those Member States in which there is a specific legislative framework for this purpose and within the limits thereof, may, in accordance with national legislation and/or practice, allow derogations from Articles 3, 4, 5, 8 and 16 by way of collective agreements or agreements concluded between the two sides of industry at the appropriate collective level.

The derogations provided for in the first and second subparagraphs shall be allowed on condition that equivalent compensating rest periods are granted to the workers concerned or, in exceptional cases where it is not possible for objective reasons to grant such periods, the workers concerned are afforded appropriate protection.

Member States may lay down rules:

(a) for the application of this Article by the two sides of industry; and

(b) for the extension of the provisions of collective agreements or agreements concluded in conformity with this Article to other workers in accordance with national legislation and/or practice.

[3.349]

Article 19

Limitations to derogations from reference periods

The option to derogate from Article 16(b), provided for in Article 17(3) and in Article 18, may not result in the establishment of a reference period exceeding six months.

However, Member States shall have the option, subject to compliance with the general principles relating to the protection of the safety and health of workers, of allowing, for objective or technical reasons or reasons concerning the organisation of work, collective agreements or agreements concluded between the two sides of industry to set reference periods in no event exceeding 12 months.

Before 23 November 2003, the Council shall, on the basis of a Commission proposal accompanied by an appraisal report, re-examine the provisions of this Article and decide what action to take.

[3.350]

Article 20

Mobile workers and offshore work

1. Articles 3, 4, 5 and 8 shall not apply to mobile workers.

Member States shall, however, take the necessary measures to ensure that such mobile workers are entitled to adequate rest, except in the circumstances laid down in Article 17(3)(f) and (g).

2. Subject to compliance with the general principles relating to the protection of the safety and health of workers, and provided that there is consultation of representatives of the employer and employees concerned and efforts to encourage all relevant forms of social dialogue, including negotiation if the parties so wish, Member States may, for objective or technical reasons or reasons concerning the organisation of work, extend the reference period referred to in Article 16(b) to 12 months in respect of workers who mainly perform offshore work.

3. Not later than 1 August 2005 the Commission shall, after consulting the Member States and management and labour at European level, review the operation of the provisions with regard to offshore workers from a health and safety perspective with a view to presenting, if need be, the appropriate modifications.

[3.351]

Article 21

Workers on board seagoing fishing vessels

1. Articles 3 to 6 and 8 shall not apply to any worker on board a seagoing fishing vessel flying the flag of a Member State.

Member States shall, however, take the necessary measures to ensure that any worker on board a seagoing fishing vessel flying the flag of a Member State is entitled to adequate rest and to limit the number of hours of work to 48 hours a week on average calculated over a reference period not exceeding 12 months.

2. Within the limits set out in paragraph 1, second subparagraph, and paragraphs 3 and 4 Member States shall take the necessary measures to ensure that, in keeping with the need to protect the safety and health of such workers:

(a) the working hours are limited to a maximum number of hours which shall not be exceeded in a given period of time; or

(b) a minimum number of hours of rest are provided within a given period of time.

The maximum number of hours of work or minimum number of hours of rest shall be specified by law, regulations, administrative provisions or by collective agreements or agreements between the two sides of the industry.

3. The limits on hours of work or rest shall be either:

(a) maximum hours of work which shall not exceed:

(i) 14 hours in any 24-hour period; and

Part 3 EU Materials

(ii) 72 hours in any seven-day period; or

(b) minimum hours of rest which shall not be less than:

(i) 10 hours in any 24-hour period; and

(ii) 77 hours in any seven-day period.

4. Hours of rest may be divided into no more than two periods, one of which shall be at least six hours in length, and the interval between consecutive periods of rest shall not exceed 14 hours.

5. In accordance with the general principles of the protection of the health and safety of workers, and for objective or technical reasons or reasons concerning the organisation of work, Member States may allow exceptions, including the establishment of reference periods, to the limits laid down in paragraph 1, second subparagraph, and paragraphs 3 and 4. Such exceptions shall, as far as possible, comply with the standards laid down but may take account of more frequent or longer leave periods or the granting of compensatory leave for the workers. These exceptions may be laid down by means of:

(a) laws, regulations or administrative provisions provided there is consultation, where possible, of the representatives of the employers and workers concerned and efforts are made to encourage all relevant forms of social dialogue; or

(b) collective agreements or agreements between the two sides of industry.

6. The master of a seagoing fishing vessel shall have the right to require workers on board to perform any hours of work necessary for the immediate safety of the vessel, persons on board or cargo, or for the purpose of giving assistance to other vessels or persons in distress at sea.

7. Members States may provide that workers on board seagoing fishing vessels for which national legislation or practice determines that these vessels are not allowed to operate in a specific period of the calendar year exceeding one month, shall take annual leave in accordance with Article 7 within that period.

[3.352]
Article 22
Miscellaneous provisions

1. A Member State shall have the option not to apply Article 6, while respecting the general principles of the protection of the safety and health of workers, and provided it takes the necessary measures to ensure that:

(a) no employer requires a worker to work more than 48 hours over a seven-day period, calculated as an average for the reference period referred to in Article 16(b), unless he has first obtained the worker's agreement to perform such work;

(b) no worker is subjected to any detriment by his employer because he is not willing to give his agreement to perform such work;

(c) the employer keeps up-to-date records of all workers who carry out such work;

(d) the records are placed at the disposal of the competent authorities, which may, for reasons connected with the safety and/or health of workers, prohibit or restrict the possibility of exceeding the maximum weekly working hours;

(e) the employer provides the competent authorities at their request with information on cases in which agreement has been given by workers to perform work exceeding 48 hours over a period of seven days, calculated as an average for the reference period referred to in Article 16(b).

Before 23 November 2003, the Council shall, on the basis of a Commission proposal accompanied by an appraisal report, re-examine the provisions of this paragraph and decide on what action to take.

2. Member States shall have the option, as regards the application of Article 7, of making use of a transitional period of not more than three years from 23 November 1996, provided that during that transitional period:

(a) every worker receives three weeks' paid annual leave in accordance with the conditions for the entitlement to, and granting of, such leave laid down by national legislation and/or practice; and

(b) the three-week period of paid annual leave may not be replaced by an allowance in lieu, except where the employment relationship is terminated.

3. If Member States avail themselves of the options provided for in this Article, they shall forthwith inform the Commission thereof.

CHAPTER 6 FINAL PROVISIONS

[3.353]
Article 23
Level of Protection

Without prejudice to the right of Member States to develop, in the light of changing circumstances, different legislative, regulatory or contractual provisions in the field of working time, as long as the minimum requirements provided for in this Directive are complied with, implementation of this Directive shall not constitute valid grounds for reducing the general level of protection afforded to workers.

[3.354]
Article 24
Reports

1. Member States shall communicate to the Commission the texts of the provisions of national law already adopted or being adopted in the field governed by this Directive.

2. Member States shall report to the Commission every five years on the practical implementation of the provisions of this Directive, indicating the viewpoints of the two sides of industry.

The Commission shall inform the European Parliament, the Council, the European Economic and Social Committee and the Advisory Committee on Safety, Hygiene and Health Protection at Work thereof.

3. Every five years from 23 November 1996 the Commission shall submit to the European Parliament, the Council and the European Economic and Social Committee a report on the application of this Directive taking into account Articles 22 and 23 and paragraphs 1 and 2 of this Article.

[3.355]
Article 25
Review of the operation of the provisions with regard to workers on board seagoing fishing vessels
Not later than 1 August 2009 the Commission shall, after consulting the Member States and management and labour at European level, review the operation of the provisions with regard to workers on board seagoing fishing vessels, and, in particular examine whether these provisions remain appropriate, in particular, as far as health and safety are concerned with a view to proposing suitable amendments, if necessary.

[3.356]
Article 26
Review of the operation of the provisions with regard to workers concerned with the carriage of passengers
Not later than 1 August 2005 the Commission shall, after consulting the Member States and management and labour at European level, review the operation of the provisions with regard to workers concerned with the carriage of passengers on regular urban transport services, with a view to presenting, if need be, the appropriate modifications to ensure a coherent and suitable approach in the sector.

[3.357]
Article 27
Repeal
1. Directive 93/104/EC, as amended by the Directive referred to in Annex I, part A, shall be repealed, without prejudice to the obligations of the Member States in respect of the deadlines for transposition laid down in Annex I, part B.
2. The references made to the said repealed Directive shall be construed as references to this Directive and shall be read in accordance with the correlation table set out in Annex II.

[3.358]
Article 28
Entry into force
This Directive shall enter into force on 2 August 2004.

[3.359]
Article 29
Addressees
This Directive is addressed to the Member States.

ANNEX I

PART A REPEALED DIRECTIVE AND ITS AMENDMENT

(Article 27)

[3.360]

Council Directive 93/104/EC	(OJ L307, 13.12.1993, p 18)
Directive 2000/34/EC of the European Parliament and of the Council	(OJ L195, 1.8.2000, p 41)

PART B DEADLINES FOR TRANSPOSITION INTO NATIONAL LAW

(Article 27)

[3.361]

Directive	*Deadline for transposition*
93/104/EC	23 November 1996
2000/34/EC	1 August 2003[1]

NOTES

[1] 1 August 2004 in the case of doctors in training. See Article 2 of Directive 2000/34/EC.

ANNEX II
CORRELATION TABLE

[3.362]

Directive 93/104/EC	*This Directive*
Articles 1 to 5	Articles 1 to 5
Article 6, introductory words	Article 6, introductory words
Article 6(1)	Article 6(a)
Article 6(2)	Article 6(b)
Article 7	Article 7
Article 8, introductory words	Article 8, introductory words
Article 8(1)	Article 8(a)
Article 8(2)	Article 8(b)
Articles 9, 10 and 11	Articles 9, 10 and 11
Article 12, introductory words	Article 12, introductory words
Article 12(1)	Article 12(a)
Article 12(2)	Article 12(b)
Articles 13, 14 and 15	Articles 13, 14 and 15
Article 16, introductory words	Article 16, introductory words
Article 16(1)	Article 16(a)
Article 16(2)	Article 16(b)
Article 16(3)	Article 16(c)
Article 17(1)	Article 17(1)
Article 17(2), introductory words	Article 17(2)
Article 17(2)(1)	Article 17(3)(a) to (e)
Article 17(2)(2)	Article 17(3)(f) to (g)
Article 17(2)(3)	Article 17(4)
Article 17(2)(4)	Article 17(5)
Article 17(3)	Article 18
Article 17(4)	Article 19
Article 17a(1)	Article 20(1), first subparagraph
Article 17a(2)	Article 20(1), second subparagraph
Article 17a(3)	Article 20(2)
Article 17a(4)	Article 20(3)
Article 17b(1)	Article 21(1), first subparagraph
Article 17b(2)	Article 21(1), second subparagraph
Article 17b(3)	Article 21(2)
Article 17b(4)	Article 21(3)
Article 17b(5)	Article 21(4)
Article 17b(6)	Article 21(5)
Article 17b(7)	Article 21(6)
Article 17b(8)	Article 21(7)
Article 18(1)(a)	—
Article 18(1)(b)(i)	Article 22(1)
Article 18(1)(b)(ii)	Article 22(2)
Article 18(1)(c)	Article 22(3)
Article 18(2)	—
Article 18(3)	Article 23
Article 18(4)	Article 24(1)
Article 18(5)	Article 24(2)
Article 18(6)	Article 24(3)
—	Article 25[1]
—	Article 26[2]
—	Article 27

Directive 93/104/EC	This Directive
—	Article 28
Article 19	Article 29
—	Annex I
—	Annex II

NOTES

[1] Directive 2000/34/EC, Article 3.

[2] Directive 2000/34/EC, Article 4.

DIRECTIVE OF THE EUROPEAN PARLIAMENT AND OF THE COUNCIL

(2006/54/EC)

of 5 July 2006

on the implementation of the principle of equal opportunities and equal treatment of men and women in matters of employment and occupation (recast)

[3.363]

NOTES

Date of publication in OJ: OJ L204, 26.7.2006, p 23.

This Directive consolidates and updates the four major directives on gender equality, the Equal Pay Directive (75/117/EEC), the Equal Treatment Directive (76/207/EEC), the Directive on Equal Treatment in Occupational Social Security Schemes (86/378/EEC) and the Burden of Proof Directive (97/80/EC), in each case as subsequently amended. Those Directives are repealed by Art 34 of, and Annex I, Pt A to, this Directive, with effect from 15 August 2009 (see **[3.397]** and **[3.400]**). From that date, references in other EU legislation are to be read as references to the corresponding provisions in this Directive. Note that, apparently by oversight, Art 34 of this Directive does not list the amending Directives 96/97/EC, 98/52/EC or 2002/73/EC. However, it appears from Annex I, Pt A of this Directive that the amending Directives are also intended to be repealed.

For the domestic implementation of this Directive, see now the Equality Act 2010, Parts 2, 5, 9, 10 and 11 (the 2010 Act is at **[1.1620]**).

See *Harvey* K, L.

THE EUROPEAN PARLIAMENT AND THE COUNCIL OF THE EUROPEAN UNION,

Having regard to the Treaty establishing the European Community, and in particular Article 141(3) thereof,

Having regard to the proposal from the Commission,

Having regard to the opinion of the European Economic and Social Committee,[1]

Acting in accordance with the procedure laid down in Article 251 of the Treaty,[2]

Whereas:

(1) Council Directive 76/207/EEC of 9 February 1976 on the implementation of the principle of equal treatment for men and women as regards access to employment, vocational training and promotion, and working conditions[3] and Council Directive 86/378/EEC of 24 July 1986 on the implementation of the principle of equal treatment for men and women in occupational social security schemes[4] have been significantly amended.[5] Council Directive 75/117/EEC of 10 February 1975 on the approximation of the laws of the Member States relating to the application of the principle of equal pay for men and women[6] and Council Directive 97/80/EC of 15 December 1997 on the burden of proof in cases of discrimination based on sex[7] also contain provisions which have as their purpose the implementation of the principle of equal treatment between men and women. Now that new amendments are being made to the said Directives, it is desirable, for reasons of clarity, that the provisions in question should be recast by bringing together in a single text the main provisions existing in this field as well as certain developments arising out of the case-law of the Court of Justice of the European Communities (hereinafter referred to as the Court of Justice).

(2) Equality between men and women is a fundamental principle of Community law under Article 2 and Article 3(2) of the Treaty and the case-law of the Court of Justice. Those Treaty provisions proclaim equality between men and women as a "task" and an "aim" of the Community and impose a positive obligation to promote it in all its activities.

(3) The Court of Justice has held that the scope of the principle of equal treatment for men and women cannot be confined to the prohibition of discrimination based on the fact that a person is of one or other sex. In view of its purpose and the nature of the rights which it seeks to safeguard, it also applies to discrimination arising from the gender reassignment of a person.

(4) Article 141(3) of the Treaty now provides a specific legal basis for the adoption of Community measures to ensure the application of the principle of equal opportunities and equal treatment in matters of employment and occupation, including the principle of equal pay for equal work or work of equal value.

(5) Articles 21 and 23 of the Charter of Fundamental Rights of the European Union also prohibit any discrimination on grounds of sex and enshrine the right to equal treatment between men and women in all areas, including employment, work and pay.

(6) Harassment and sexual harassment are contrary to the principle of equal treatment between men and women and constitute discrimination on grounds of sex for the purposes of this Directive. These forms of discrimination occur not only in the workplace, but also in the context of access to employment, vocational training and promotion. They should therefore be prohibited and should be subject to effective, proportionate and dissuasive penalties.

(7) In this context, employers and those responsible for vocational training should be encouraged to take measures to combat all forms of discrimination on grounds of sex and, in particular, to take preventive measures against harassment and sexual harassment in the workplace and in access to employment, vocational training and promotion, in accordance with national law and practice.

(8) The principle of equal pay for equal work or work of equal value as laid down by Article 141 of the Treaty and consistently upheld in the case-law of the Court of Justice constitutes an important aspect of the principle of equal treatment between men and women and an essential and indispensable part of the *acquis communautaire*, including the case-law of the Court concerning sex discrimination. It is therefore appropriate to make further provision for its implementation.

(9) In accordance with settled case-law of the Court of Justice, in order to assess whether workers are performing the same work or work of equal value, it should be determined whether, having regard to a range of factors including the nature of the work and training and working conditions, those workers may be considered to be in a comparable situation.

(10) The Court of Justice has established that, in certain circumstances, the principle of equal pay is not limited to situations in which men and women work for the same employer.

(11) The Member States, in collaboration with the social partners, should continue to address the problem of the continuing gender-based wage differentials and marked gender segregation on the labour market by means such as flexible working time arrangements which enable both men and women to combine family and work commitments more successfully. This could also include appropriate parental leave arrangements which could be taken up by either parent as well as the provision of accessible and affordable child-care facilities and care for dependent persons.

(12) Specific measures should be adopted to ensure the implementation of the principle of equal treatment in occupational social security schemes and to define its scope more clearly.

(13) In its judgment of 17 May 1990 in Case C-262/88,[8] the Court of Justice determined that all forms of occupational pension constitute an element of pay within the meaning of Article 141 of the Treaty.

(14) Although the concept of pay within the meaning of Article 141 of the Treaty does not encompass social security benefits, it is now clearly established that a pension scheme for public servants falls within the scope of the principle of equal pay if the benefits payable under the scheme are paid to the worker by reason of his/her employment relationship with the public employer, notwithstanding the fact that such scheme forms part of a general statutory scheme. According to the judgments of the Court of Justice in Cases C-7/93[9] and C-351/00,[10] that condition will be satisfied if the pension scheme concerns a particular category of workers and its benefits are directly related to the period of service and calculated by reference to the public servant's final salary. For reasons of clarity, it is therefore appropriate to make specific provision to that effect.

(15) The Court of Justice has confirmed that whilst the contributions of male and female workers to a defined-benefit pension scheme are covered by Article 141 of the Treaty, any inequality in employers' contributions paid under funded defined-benefit schemes which is due to the use of actuarial factors differing according to sex is not to be assessed in the light of that same provision.

(16) By way of example, in the case of funded defined-benefit schemes, certain elements, such as conversion into a capital sum of part of a periodic pension, transfer of pension rights, a reversionary pension payable to a dependant in return for the surrender of part of a pension or a reduced pension where the worker opts to take earlier retirement, may be unequal where the inequality of the amounts results from the effects of the use of actuarial factors differing according to sex at the time when the scheme's funding is implemented.

(17) It is well established that benefits payable under occupational social security schemes are not to be considered as remuneration insofar as they are attributable to periods of employment prior to 17 May 1990, except in the case of workers or those claiming under them who initiated legal proceedings or brought an equivalent claim under the applicable national law before that date. It is therefore necessary to limit the implementation of the principle of equal treatment accordingly.

(18) The Court of Justice has consistently held that the Barber Protocol[11] does not affect the right to join an occupational pension scheme and that the limitation of the effects in time of the judgment in Case C-262/88 does not apply to the right to join an occupational pension scheme. The Court of Justice also ruled that the national rules relating to time limits for bringing actions under national law may be relied on against workers who assert their right to join an occupational pension scheme, provided that they are not less favourable for that type of action than for similar actions of a domestic nature and that they do not render the exercise of rights conferred by Community law impossible in practice. The Court of Justice has also pointed out that the fact that a worker can claim retroactively to join an occupational pension scheme does not allow the worker to avoid paying the contributions relating to the period of membership concerned.

(19) Ensuring equal access to employment and the vocational training leading thereto is fundamental to the application of the principle of equal treatment of men and women in matters of employment and occupation. Any exception to this principle should therefore be limited to those occupational activities which necessitate the employment of a person of a particular sex by reason of their nature or the context in which they are carried out, provided that the objective sought is legitimate and complies with the principle of proportionality.

(20) This Directive does not prejudice freedom of association, including the right to establish unions with others and to join unions to defend one's interests. Measures within the meaning of Article 141(4) of the Treaty may include membership or the continuation of the activity of organisations or unions whose main objective is the promotion, in practice, of the principle of equal treatment between men and women.

(21) The prohibition of discrimination should be without prejudice to the maintenance or adoption of measures intended to prevent or compensate for disadvantages suffered by a group of persons of one sex. Such measures permit organisations of persons of one sex where their main object is the promotion of the special needs of those persons and the promotion of equality between men and women.

(22) In accordance with Article 141(4) of the Treaty, with a view to ensuring full equality in practice between men and women in working life, the principle of equal treatment does not prevent Member States from maintaining or adopting measures providing for specific advantages in order to make it easier for the under-represented sex to pursue a vocational activity or to prevent or compensate for disadvantages in professional careers. Given the current situation and bearing in mind Declaration No 28 to the Amsterdam Treaty, Member States should, in the first instance, aim at improving the situation of women in working life.

(23) It is clear from the case-law of the Court of Justice that unfavourable treatment of a woman related to pregnancy or maternity constitutes direct discrimination on grounds of sex. Such treatment should therefore be expressly covered by this Directive.

(24) The Court of Justice has consistently recognised the legitimacy, as regards the principle of equal treatment, of protecting a woman's biological condition during pregnancy and maternity and of introducing maternity protection measures as a means to achieve substantive equality. This Directive should therefore be without prejudice to Council Directive 92/85/EEC of 19 October 1992 on the introduction of measures to encourage improvements in the safety and health at work of pregnant workers and workers who have recently given birth or are breastfeeding.[12] This Directive should further be without prejudice to Council Directive 96/34/EC of 3 June 1996 on the framework agreement on parental leave concluded by UNICE, CEEP and the ETUC.[13]

(25) For reasons of clarity, it is also appropriate to make express provision for the protection of the employment rights of women on maternity leave and in particular their right to return to the same or an equivalent post, to suffer no detriment in their terms and conditions as a result of taking such leave and to benefit from any improvement in working conditions to which they would have been entitled during their absence.

(26) In the Resolution of the Council and of the Ministers for Employment and Social Policy, meeting within the Council, of 29 June 2000 on the balanced participation of women and men in family and working life,[14] Member States were encouraged to consider examining the scope for their respective legal systems to grant working men an individual and non-transferable right to paternity leave, while maintaining their rights relating to employment.

(27) Similar considerations apply to the granting by Member States to men and women of an individual and non-transferable right to leave subsequent to the adoption of a child. It is for the Member States to determine whether or not to grant such a right to paternity and/or adoption leave and also to determine any conditions, other than dismissal and return to work, which are outside the scope of this Directive.

(28) The effective implementation of the principle of equal treatment requires appropriate procedures to be put in place by the Member States.

(29) The provision of adequate judicial or administrative procedures for the enforcement of the obligations imposed by this Directive is essential to the effective implementation of the principle of equal treatment.

(30) The adoption of rules on the burden of proof plays a significant role in ensuring that the principle of equal treatment can be effectively enforced. As the Court of Justice has held, provision should therefore be made to ensure that the burden of proof shifts to the respondent when there is a prima facie case of discrimination, except in relation to proceedings in which it is for the court or other competent national body to investigate the facts. It is however necessary to clarify that the appreciation of the facts from which it may be presumed that there has been direct or indirect discrimination remains a matter for the relevant national body in accordance with national law or practice. Further, it is for the Member States to introduce, at any appropriate stage of the proceedings, rules of evidence which are more favourable to plaintiffs.

(31) With a view to further improving the level of protection offered by this Directive, associations, organisations and other legal entities should also be empowered to engage in proceedings, as the Member States so determine, either on behalf or in support of a complainant, without prejudice to national rules of procedure concerning representation and defence.

(32) Having regard to the fundamental nature of the right to effective legal protection, it is appropriate to ensure that workers continue to enjoy such protection even after the relationship giving rise to an alleged breach of the principle of equal treatment has ended. An employee defending or giving evidence on behalf of a person protected under this Directive should be entitled to the same protection.

(33) It has been clearly established by the Court of Justice that in order to be effective, the principle of equal treatment implies that the compensation awarded for any breach must be adequate in relation to the damage sustained. It is therefore appropriate to exclude the fixing of any prior upper limit for such compensation, except where the employer can prove that the only damage suffered by an applicant as a result of discrimination within the meaning of this Directive was the refusal to take his/her job application into consideration.

(34) In order to enhance the effective implementation of the principle of equal treatment, Member States should promote dialogue between the social partners and, within the framework of national practice, with non-governmental organisations.

(35) Member States should provide for effective, proportionate and dissuasive penalties for breaches of the obligations under this Directive.

(36) Since the objectives of this Directive cannot be sufficiently achieved by the Member States and can therefore be better achieved at Community level, the Community may adopt measures in accordance with the principle of subsidiarity as set out in Article 5 of the Treaty. In accordance with the principle of proportionality, as set out in that Article, this Directive does not go beyond what is necessary in order to achieve those objectives.

(37) For the sake of a better understanding of the different treatment of men and women in matters of employment and occupation, comparable statistics disaggregated by sex should continue to be developed, analysed and made available at the appropriate levels.

(38) Equal treatment of men and women in matters of employment and occupation cannot be restricted to legislative measures. Instead, the European Union and the Member States should continue to promote the raising of public awareness of wage discrimination and the changing of public attitudes, involving all parties concerned at public and private level to the greatest possible extent. The dialogue between the social partners could play an important role in this process.

(39) The obligation to transpose this Directive into national law should be confined to those provisions which represent a substantive change as compared with the earlier Directives. The obligation to transpose the provisions which are substantially unchanged arises under the earlier Directives.

(40) This Directive should be without prejudice to the obligations of the Member States relating to the time limits for transposition into national law and application of the Directives set out in Annex I, Part B.

(41) In accordance with paragraph 34 of the Inter-institutional agreement on better law-making,[15] Member States are encouraged to draw up, for themselves and in the interest of the Community, their own tables, which will, as far as possible, illustrate the correlation between this Directive and the transposition measures and to make them public,

NOTES

1 OJ C157, 28.6.2005, p 83.

2 Opinion of the European Parliament of 6 July 2005 (not yet published in the Official Journal), Council Common Position of 10 March 2006 (OJ C126E, 30.5.2006, p 33) and Position of the European Parliament of 1 June 2006 (not yet published in the Official Journal).

3 OJ L39, 14.2.1976, p 40. Directive as amended by Directive 2002/73/EC of the European Parliament and of the Council (OJ L269, 5.10.2002, p 15).

4 OJ L225, 12.8.1986, p 40. Directive as amended by Directive 96/97/EC (OJ L46, 17.2.1997, p 20).

5 See Annex I Part A.

6 OJ L45, 19.2.1975, p 19.

7 OJ L14, 20.1.1998, p 6. Directive as amended by Directive 98/52/EC (OJ L205, 22.7.1998, p 66).

8 C-262/88: *Barber v Guardian Royal Exchange Assurance Group* (1990 ECR I-1889).

9 C-7/93: *Bestuur van het Algemeen Burgerlijk Pensioenfonds v G. A. Beune* (1994 ECR I-4471).

10 C-351/00: *Pirkko Niemi* (2002 ECR I-7007).

11 Protocol 17 concerning Article 141 of the Treaty establishing the European Community (1992).

12 OJ L348, 28.11.1992, p 1.

13 OJ L145, 19.6.1996, p 4. Directive as amended by Directive 97/75/EC (OJ L10, 16.1.1998, p 24).

14 OJ C218, 31.7.2000, p 5.

15 OJ C321, 31.12.2003, p 1.

HAVE ADOPTED THIS DIRECTIVE:

TITLE I GENERAL PROVISIONS

[3.364]
Article 1
Purpose

The purpose of this Directive is to ensure the implementation of the principle of equal opportunities and equal treatment of men and women in matters of employment and occupation.

To that end, it contains provisions to implement the principle of equal treatment in relation to:

(a) access to employment, including promotion, and to vocational training;
(b) working conditions, including pay;
(c) occupational social security schemes.

It also contains provisions to ensure that such implementation is made more effective by the establishment of appropriate procedures.

[3.365]
Article 2
Definitions

1. For the purposes of this Directive, the following definitions shall apply:
   (a) 'direct discrimination': where one person is treated less favourably on grounds of sex than another is, has been or would be treated in a comparable situation;
   (b) 'indirect discrimination': where an apparently neutral provision, criterion or practice would put persons of one sex at a particular disadvantage compared with persons of the other sex, unless that provision, criterion or practice is objectively justified by a legitimate aim, and the means of achieving that aim are appropriate and necessary;
   (c) 'harassment': where unwanted conduct related to the sex of a person occurs with the purpose or effect of violating the dignity of a person, and of creating an intimidating, hostile, degrading, humiliating or offensive environment;
   (d) 'sexual harassment': where any form of unwanted verbal, non-verbal or physical conduct of a sexual nature occurs, with the purpose or effect of violating the dignity of a person, in particular when creating an intimidating, hostile, degrading, humiliating or offensive environment;
   (e) 'pay': the ordinary basic or minimum wage or salary and any other consideration, whether in cash or in kind, which the worker receives directly or indirectly, in respect of his/her employment from his/her employer;
   (f) 'occupational social security schemes': schemes not governed by Council Directive 79/7/EEC of 19 December 1978 on the progressive implementation of the principle of equal treatment for men and women in matters of social security[1] whose purpose is to provide workers, whether employees or self-employed, in an undertaking or group of undertakings, area of economic activity, occupational sector or group of sectors with benefits intended to supplement the benefits provided by statutory social security schemes or to replace them, whether membership of such schemes is compulsory or optional.
2. For the purposes of this Directive, discrimination includes:
   (a) harassment and sexual harassment, as well as any less favourable treatment based on a person's rejection of or submission to such conduct;
   (b) instruction to discriminate against persons on grounds of sex;
   (c) any less favourable treatment of a woman related to pregnancy or maternity leave within the meaning of Directive 92/85/EEC.

NOTES

[1] OJ L6, 10.1.1979, p 24.

[3.366]
Article 3
Positive action

Member States may maintain or adopt measures within the meaning of Article 141(4) of the Treaty with a view to ensuring full equality in practice between men and women in working life.

TITLE II SPECIFIC PROVISIONS

CHAPTER 1 EQUAL PAY

[3.367]
Article 4
Prohibition of discrimination

For the same work or for work to which equal value is attributed, direct and indirect discrimination on grounds of sex with regard to all aspects and conditions of remuneration shall be eliminated.

In particular, where a job classification system is used for determining pay, it shall be based on the same criteria for both men and women and so drawn up as to exclude any discrimination on grounds of sex.

CHAPTER 2 EQUAL TREATMENT IN OCCUPATIONAL SOCIAL SECURITY SCHEMES

[3.368]
Article 5
Prohibition of discrimination

Without prejudice to Article 4, there shall be no direct or indirect discrimination on grounds of sex in occupational social security schemes, in particular as regards:
   (a) the scope of such schemes and the conditions of access to them;
   (b) the obligation to contribute and the calculation of contributions;
   (c) the calculation of benefits, including supplementary benefits due in respect of a spouse or dependants, and the conditions governing the duration and retention of entitlement to benefits.

[3.369]
Article 6
Personal scope

This Chapter shall apply to members of the working population, including self-employed persons, persons whose activity is interrupted by illness, maternity, accident or involuntary unemployment and persons seeking employment and to retired and disabled workers, and to those claiming under them, in accordance with national law and/or practice.

[3.370]
Article 7
Material scope

1. This Chapter applies to:
   (a) occupational social security schemes which provide protection against the following risks:
      (i) sickness,
      (ii) invalidity,
      (iii) old age, including early retirement,
      (iv) industrial accidents and occupational diseases,
      (v) unemployment;
   (b) occupational social security schemes which provide for other social benefits, in cash or in kind, and in particular survivors' benefits and family allowances, if such benefits constitute a consideration paid by the employer to the worker by reason of the latter's employment.

2. This Chapter also applies to pension schemes for a particular category of worker such as that of public servants if the benefits payable under the scheme are paid by reason of the employment relationship with the public employer. The fact that such a scheme forms part of a general statutory scheme shall be without prejudice in that respect.

[3.371]
Article 8
Exclusions from the material scope

1. This Chapter does not apply to:
   (a) individual contracts for self-employed persons;
   (b) single-member schemes for self-employed persons;
   (c) insurance contracts to which the employer is not a party, in the case of workers;
   (d) optional provisions of occupational social security schemes offered to participants individually to guarantee them:
      (i) either additional benefits,
      (ii) or a choice of date on which the normal benefits for self-employed persons will start, or a choice between several benefits;
   (e) occupational social security schemes in so far as benefits are financed by contributions paid by workers on a voluntary basis.

2. This Chapter does not preclude an employer granting to persons who have already reached the retirement age for the purposes of granting a pension by virtue of an occupational social security scheme, but who have not yet reached the retirement age for the purposes of granting a statutory retirement pension, a pension supplement, the aim of which is to make equal or more nearly equal the overall amount of benefit paid to these persons in relation to the amount paid to persons of the other sex in the same situation who have already reached the statutory retirement age, until the persons benefiting from the supplement reach the statutory retirement age.

[3.372]
Article 9
Examples of discrimination

1. Provisions contrary to the principle of equal treatment shall include those based on sex, either directly or indirectly, for:
   (a) determining the persons who may participate in an occupational social security scheme;
   (b) fixing the compulsory or optional nature of participation in an occupational social security scheme;
   (c) laying down different rules as regards the age of entry into the scheme or the minimum period of employment or membership of the scheme required to obtain the benefits thereof;
   (d) laying down different rules, except as provided for in points (h) and (j), for the reimbursement of contributions when a worker leaves a scheme without having fulfilled the conditions guaranteeing a deferred right to long-term benefits;
   (e) setting different conditions for the granting of benefits or restricting such benefits to workers of one or other of the sexes;
   (f) fixing different retirement ages;
   (g) suspending the retention or acquisition of rights during periods of maternity leave or leave for family reasons which are granted by law or agreement and are paid by the employer;
   (h) setting different levels of benefit, except in so far as may be necessary to take account of actuarial calculation factors which differ according to sex in the case of defined-contribution schemes; in the case of funded defined-benefit schemes, certain elements may be unequal where the inequality of the amounts results from the effects of the use of actuarial factors differing according to sex at the time when the scheme's funding is implemented;
   (i) setting different levels for workers' contributions;
   (j) setting different levels for employers' contributions, except:

(i) in the case of defined-contribution schemes if the aim is to equalise the amount of the final benefits or to make them more nearly equal for both sexes,

(ii) in the case of funded defined-benefit schemes where the employer's contributions are intended to ensure the adequacy of the funds necessary to cover the cost of the benefits defined;

(k) laying down different standards or standards applicable only to workers of a specified sex, except as provided for in points (h) and (j), as regards the guarantee or retention of entitlement to deferred benefits when a worker leaves a scheme.

2. Where the granting of benefits within the scope of this Chapter is left to the discretion of the scheme's management bodies, the latter shall comply with the principle of equal treatment.

[3.373]
Article 10
Implementation as regards self-employed persons

1. Member States shall take the necessary steps to ensure that the provisions of occupational social security schemes for self-employed persons contrary to the principle of equal treatment are revised with effect from 1 January 1993 at the latest or for Member States whose accession took place after that date, at the date that Directive 86/378/EEC became applicable in their territory.

2. This Chapter shall not preclude rights and obligations relating to a period of membership of an occupational social security scheme for self-employed persons prior to revision of that scheme from remaining subject to the provisions of the scheme in force during that period.

[3.374]
Article 11
Possibility of deferral as regards self-employed persons

As regards occupational social security schemes for self-employed persons, Member States may defer compulsory application of the principle of equal treatment with regard to:

(a) determination of pensionable age for the granting of old-age or retirement pensions, and the possible implications for other benefits:

(i) either until the date on which such equality is achieved in statutory schemes,

(ii) or, at the latest, until such equality is prescribed by a directive;

(b) survivors' pensions until Community law establishes the principle of equal treatment in statutory social security schemes in that regard;

(c) the application of Article 9(1)(i) in relation to the use of actuarial calculation factors, until 1 January 1999 or for Member States whose accession took place after that date until the date that Directive 86/378/EEC became applicable in their territory.

[3.375]
Article 12
Retroactive effect

1. Any measure implementing this Chapter, as regards workers, shall cover all benefits under occupational social security schemes derived from periods of employment subsequent to 17 May 1990 and shall apply retroactively to that date, without prejudice to workers or those claiming under them who have, before that date, initiated legal proceedings or raised an equivalent claim under national law. In that event, the implementation measures shall apply retroactively to 8 April 1976 and shall cover all the benefits derived from periods of employment after that date. For Member States which acceded to the Community after 8 April 1976, and before 17 May 1990, that date shall be replaced by the date on which Article 141 of the Treaty became applicable in their territory.

2. The second sentence of paragraph 1 shall not prevent national rules relating to time limits for bringing actions under national law from being relied on against workers or those claiming under them who initiated legal proceedings or raised an equivalent claim under national law before 17 May 1990, provided that they are not less favourable for that type of action than for similar actions of a domestic nature and that they do not render the exercise of rights conferred by Community law impossible in practice.

3. For Member States whose accession took place after 17 May 1990 and which were on 1 January 1994 Contracting Parties to the Agreement on the European Economic Area, the date of 17 May 1990 in the first sentence of paragraph 1 shall be replaced by 1 January 1994.

4. For other Member States whose accession took place after 17 May 1990, the date of 17 May 1990 in paragraphs 1 and 2 shall be replaced by the date on which Article 141 of the Treaty became applicable in their territory.

[3.376]
Article 13
Flexible pensionable age

Where men and women may claim a flexible pensionable age under the same conditions, this shall not be deemed to be incompatible with this Chapter.

CHAPTER 3 EQUAL TREATMENT AS REGARDS ACCESS TO EMPLOYMENT, VOCATIONAL TRAINING AND PROMOTION AND WORKING CONDITIONS

[3.377]
Article 14
Prohibition of discrimination

1. There shall be no direct or indirect discrimination on grounds of sex in the public or private sectors, including public bodies, in relation to:
   (a) conditions for access to employment, to self-employment or to occupation, including selection criteria and recruitment conditions, whatever the branch of activity and at all levels of the professional hierarchy, including promotion;
   (b) access to all types and to all levels of vocational guidance, vocational training, advanced vocational training and retraining, including practical work experience;
   (c) employment and working conditions, including dismissals, as well as pay as provided for in Article 141 of the Treaty;
   (d) membership of, and involvement in, an organisation of workers or employers, or any organisation whose members carry on a particular profession, including the benefits provided for by such organisations.

2. Member States may provide, as regards access to employment including the training leading thereto, that a difference of treatment which is based on a characteristic related to sex shall not constitute discrimination where, by reason of the nature of the particular occupational activities concerned or of the context in which they are carried out, such a characteristic constitutes a genuine and determining occupational requirement, provided that its objective is legitimate and the requirement is proportionate.

[3.378]
Article 15
Return from maternity leave

A woman on maternity leave shall be entitled, after the end of her period of maternity leave, to return to her job or to an equivalent post on terms and conditions which are no less favourable to her and to benefit from any improvement in working conditions to which she would have been entitled during her absence.

[3.379]
Article 16
Paternity and adoption leave

This Directive is without prejudice to the right of Member States to recognise distinct rights to paternity and/or adoption leave. Those Member States which recognise such rights shall take the necessary measures to protect working men and women against dismissal due to exercising those rights and ensure that, at the end of such leave, they are entitled to return to their jobs or to equivalent posts on terms and conditions which are no less favourable to them, and to benefit from any improvement in working conditions to which they would have been entitled during their absence.

TITLE III HORIZONTAL PROVISIONS

CHAPTER 1 REMEDIES AND ENFORCEMENT

SECTION 1
REMEDIES

[3.380]
Article 17
Defence of rights

1. Member States shall ensure that, after possible recourse to other competent authorities including where they deem it appropriate conciliation procedures, judicial procedures for the enforcement of obligations under this Directive are available to all persons who consider themselves wronged by failure to apply the principle of equal treatment to them, even after the relationship in which the discrimination is alleged to have occurred has ended.

2. Member States shall ensure that associations, organisations or other legal entities which have, in accordance with the criteria laid down by their national law, a legitimate interest in ensuring that the provisions of this Directive are complied with, may engage, either on behalf or in support of the complainant, with his/her approval, in any judicial and/or administrative procedure provided for the enforcement of obligations under this Directive.

3. Paragraphs 1 and 2 are without prejudice to national rules relating to time limits for bringing actions as regards the principle of equal treatment.

[3.381]
Article 18
Compensation or reparation

Member States shall introduce into their national legal systems such measures as are necessary to ensure real and effective compensation or reparation as the Member States so determine for the loss and damage sustained by a person injured as a result of discrimination on grounds of sex, in a way which is dissuasive and proportionate to the damage suffered. Such compensation or reparation may not be restricted by the fixing of a prior upper limit, except in cases where the employer can prove that the only damage suffered by an applicant as a result of discrimination within the meaning of this Directive is the refusal to take his/her job application into consideration.

SECTION 2
BURDEN OF PROOF

[3.382]
Article 19
Burden of proof
1. Member States shall take such measures as are necessary, in accordance with their national judicial systems, to ensure that, when persons who consider themselves wronged because the principle of equal treatment has not been applied to them establish, before a court or other competent authority, facts from which it may be presumed that there has been direct or indirect discrimination, it shall be for the respondent to prove that there has been no breach of the principle of equal treatment.
2. Paragraph 1 shall not prevent Member States from introducing rules of evidence which are more favourable to plaintiffs.
3. Member States need not apply paragraph 1 to proceedings in which it is for the court or competent body to investigate the facts of the case.
4. Paragraphs 1, 2 and 3 shall also apply to:
(a) the situations covered by Article 141 of the Treaty and, insofar as discrimination based on sex is concerned, by Directives 92/85/EEC and 96/34/EC;
(b) any civil or administrative procedure concerning the public or private sector which provides for means of redress under national law pursuant to the measures referred to in (a) with the exception of out-of-court procedures of a voluntary nature or provided for in national law.
5. This Article shall not apply to criminal procedures, unless otherwise provided by the Member States.

CHAPTER 2 PROMOTION OF EQUAL TREATMENT—DIALOGUE

[3.383]
Article 20
Equality bodies
1. Member States shall designate and make the necessary arrangements for a body or bodies for the promotion, analysis, monitoring and support of equal treatment of all persons without discrimination on grounds of sex. These bodies may form part of agencies with responsibility at national level for the defence of human rights or the safeguard of individuals' rights.
2. Member States shall ensure that the competences of these bodies include:
(a) without prejudice to the right of victims and of associations, organisations or other legal entities referred to in Article 17(2), providing independent assistance to victims of discrimination in pursuing their complaints about discrimination;
(b) conducting independent surveys concerning discrimination;
(c) publishing independent reports and making recommendations on any issue relating to such discrimination;
(d) at the appropriate level exchanging available information with corresponding European bodies such as any future European Institute for Gender Equality.

[3.384]
Article 21
Social dialogue
1. Member States shall, in accordance with national traditions and practice, take adequate measures to promote social dialogue between the social partners with a view to fostering equal treatment, including, for example, through the monitoring of practices in the workplace, in access to employment, vocational training and promotion, as well as through the monitoring of collective agreements, codes of conduct, research or exchange of experience and good practice.
2. Where consistent with national traditions and practice, Member States shall encourage the social partners, without prejudice to their autonomy, to promote equality between men and women, and flexible working arrangements, with the aim of facilitating the reconciliation of work and private life, and to conclude, at the appropriate level, agreements laying down anti-discrimination rules in the fields referred to in Article 1 which fall within the scope of collective bargaining. These agreements shall respect the provisions of this Directive and the relevant national implementing measures.
3. Member States shall, in accordance with national law, collective agreements or practice, encourage employers to promote equal treatment for men and women in a planned and systematic way in the workplace, in access to employment, vocational training and promotion.
4. To this end, employers shall be encouraged to provide at appropriate regular intervals employees and/or their representatives with appropriate information on equal treatment for men and women in the undertaking.

Such information may include an overview of the proportions of men and women at different levels of the organisation; their pay and pay differentials; and possible measures to improve the situation in cooperation with employees' representatives.

[3.385]
Article 22
Dialogue with non-governmental organisations
Member States shall encourage dialogue with appropriate non-governmental organisations which have, in accordance with their national law and practice, a legitimate interest in contributing to the fight against discrimination on grounds of sex with a view to promoting the principle of equal treatment.

CHAPTER 3 GENERAL HORIZONTAL PROVISIONS

[3.386]
Article 23
Compliance

Member States shall take all necessary measures to ensure that:

(a) any laws, regulations and administrative provisions contrary to the principle of equal treatment are abolished;

(b) provisions contrary to the principle of equal treatment in individual or collective contracts or agreements, internal rules of undertakings or rules governing the independent occupations and professions and workers' and employers' organisations or any other arrangements shall be, or may be, declared null and void or are amended;

(c) occupational social security schemes containing such provisions may not be approved or extended by administrative measures.

[3.387]
Article 24
Victimisation

Member States shall introduce into their national legal systems such measures as are necessary to protect employees, including those who are employees' representatives provided for by national laws and/or practices, against dismissal or other adverse treatment by the employer as a reaction to a complaint within the undertaking or to any legal proceedings aimed at enforcing compliance with the principle of equal treatment.

[3.388]
Article 25
Penalties

Member States shall lay down the rules on penalties applicable to infringements of the national provisions adopted pursuant to this Directive, and shall take all measures necessary to ensure that they are applied. The penalties, which may comprise the payment of compensation to the victim, must be effective, proportionate and dissuasive. The Member States shall notify those provisions to the Commission by 5 October 2005 at the latest and shall notify it without delay of any subsequent amendment affecting them.

[3.389]
Article 26
Prevention of discrimination

Member States shall encourage, in accordance with national law, collective agreements or practice, employers and those responsible for access to vocational training to take effective measures to prevent all forms of discrimination on grounds of sex, in particular harassment and sexual harassment in the workplace, in access to employment, vocational training and promotion.

[3.390]
Article 27
Minimum requirements

1. Member States may introduce or maintain provisions which are more favourable to the protection of the principle of equal treatment than those laid down in this Directive.
2. Implementation of this Directive shall under no circumstances be sufficient grounds for a reduction in the level of protection of workers in the areas to which it applies, without prejudice to the Member States' right to respond to changes in the situation by introducing laws, regulations and administrative provisions which differ from those in force on the notification of this Directive, provided that the provisions of this Directive are complied with.

[3.391]
Article 28
Relationship to Community and national provisions

1. This Directive shall be without prejudice to provisions concerning the protection of women, particularly as regards pregnancy and maternity.
2. This Directive shall be without prejudice to the provisions of Directive 96/34/EC and Directive 92/85/EEC.

[3.392]
Article 29
Gender mainstreaming

Member States shall actively take into account the objective of equality between men and women when formulating and implementing laws, regulations, administrative provisions, policies and activities in the areas referred to in this Directive.

[3.393]
Article 30
Dissemination of information

Member States shall ensure that measures taken pursuant to this Directive, together with the provisions already in force, are brought to the attention of all the persons concerned by all suitable means and, where appropriate, at the workplace.

TITLE IV FINAL PROVISIONS

[3.394]
Article 31
Reports
1. By 15 February 2011, the Member States shall communicate to the Commission all the information necessary for the Commission to draw up a report to the European Parliament and the Council on the application of this Directive.
2. Without prejudice to paragraph 1, Member States shall communicate to the Commission, every four years, the texts of any measures adopted pursuant to Article 141(4) of the Treaty, as well as reports on these measures and their implementation. On the basis of that information, the Commission will adopt and publish every four years a report establishing a comparative assessment of any measures in the light of Declaration No 28 annexed to the Final Act of the Treaty of Amsterdam.
3. Member States shall assess the occupational activities referred to in Article 14(2), in order to decide, in the light of social developments, whether there is justification for maintaining the exclusions concerned. They shall notify the Commission of the results of this assessment periodically, but at least every 8 years.

[3.395]
Article 32
Review
By 15 February 2011 at the latest, the Commission shall review the operation of this Directive and if appropriate, propose any amendments it deems necessary.

[3.396]
Article 33
Implementation
Member States shall bring into force the laws, regulations and administrative provisions necessary to comply with this Directive by 15 August 2008 at the latest or shall ensure, by that date, that management and labour introduce the requisite provisions by way of agreement. Member States may, if necessary to take account of particular difficulties, have up to one additional year to comply with this Directive. Member States shall take all necessary steps to be able to guarantee the results imposed by this Directive. They shall forthwith communicate to the Commission the texts of those measures.

When Member States adopt these measures, they shall contain a reference to this Directive or be accompanied by such reference on the occasion of their official publication. They shall also include a statement that references in existing laws, regulations and administrative provisions to the Directives repealed by this Directive shall be construed as references to this Directive. Member States shall determine how such reference is to be made and how that statement is to be formulated.

The obligation to transpose this Directive into national law shall be confined to those provisions which represent a substantive change as compared with the earlier Directives. The obligation to transpose the provisions which are substantially unchanged arises under the earlier Directives.

Member States shall communicate to the Commission the text of the main provisions of national law which they adopt in the field covered by this Directive.

[3.397]
Article 34
Repeal
1. With effect from 15 August 2009 Directives 75/117/EEC, 76/207/EEC, 86/378/EEC and 97/80/EC shall be repealed without prejudice to the obligations of the Member States relating to the time-limits for transposition into national law and application of the Directives set out in Annex I, Part B.
2. References made to the repealed Directives shall be construed as being made to this Directive and should be read in accordance with the correlation table in Annex II.

[3.398]
Article 35
Entry into force
This Directive shall enter into force on the 20th day following its publication in the *Official Journal of the European Union*.

[3.399]
Article 36
Addressees
This Directive is addressed to the Member States.

ANNEX I

PART A REPEALED DIRECTIVES WITH THEIR SUCCESSIVE AMENDMENTS

[3.400]

Council Directive 75/117/EEC	OJ L45, 19.2.1975, p 19
Council Directive 76/207/EEC	OJ L39, 14.2.1976, p 40
Directive 2002/73/EC of the European Parliament and of the Council	OJ L269, 5.10.2002, p 15

Council Directive 86/378/EEC	OJ L225, 12.8.1986, p 40
Council Directive 96/97/EC	OJ L46, 17.2.1997, p 20
Council Directive 97/80/EC	OJ L14, 20.1.1998, p 6
Council Directive 98/52/EC	OJ L205, 22.7.1998, p 66

PART B LIST OF TIME LIMITS FOR TRANSPOSITION INTO NATIONAL LAW AND APPLICATION DATES

(referred to in Article 34(1))

[3.401]

Directive	Time-limit for transposition	Date of application
Directive 75/117/EEC	19.2.1976	
Directive 76/207/EEC	14.8.1978	
Directive 86/378/EEC	1.1.1993	
Directive 96/97/EC	1.7.1997	17.5.1990 in relation to workers, except for those workers or those claiming under them who had before that date initiated legal proceedings or raised an equivalent claim under national law. Article 8 of Directive 86/378/EEC – 1.1.1993 at the latest. Article 6(1)(i), first indent of Directive 86/378/EEC – 1.1.1999 at the latest.
Directive 97/80/EC	1.1.2001	As regards the United Kingdom of Great Britain and Northern Ireland 22.7.2001
Directive 98/52/EC	22.7.2001	
Directive 2002/73/EC	5.10.2005	

ANNEX II
CORRELATION TABLE

[3.402]

Directive 75/117/EEC	Directive 76/207/EEC	Directive 86/378/EEC	Directive 97/80/EC	This Directive
—	Article 1(1)	Article 1	Article 1	Article 1
—	Article 1(2)	—	—	—
—	Article 2(2), first indent	—	—	Article 2(1)(a)
—	Article 2(2), second indent	—	Article 2(2)	Article 2(1)(b)
—	Article 2(2), third and fourth indents	—	—	Article 2(1)(c) and (d)
—	—	—	—	Article 2(1)(e)
—	—	Article 2(1)	—	Article 2(1)(f)
—	Article 2(3) and (4) and Article 2(7) third subparagraph	—	—	Article 2(2)
—	Article 2(8)	—	—	Article 3
Article 1	—	—	—	Article 4
—	—	Article 5(1)	—	Article 5
—	—	Article 3	—	Article 6
—	—	Article 4	—	Article 7(1)
—	—	—	—	Article 7(2)
—	—	Article 2(2)	—	Article 8(1)
—	—	Article 2(3)	—	Article 8(2)
—	—	Article 6	—	Article 9

Directive 75/117/EEC	Directive 76/207/EEC	Directive 86/378/EEC	Directive 97/80/EC	This Directive
—	—	Article 8	—	Article 10
—	—	Article 9	—	Article 11
—	—	(Article 2 of Directive 96/97/EC)	—	Article 12
—	—	Article 9a	—	Article 13
—	Articles 2(1) and 3(1)	—	Article 2(1)	Article 14(1)
—	Article 2(6)	—	—	Article 14(2)
—	Article 2(7), second subparagraph	—	—	Article 15
—	Article 2(7), fourth subparagraph, second and third sentence	—	—	Article 16
Article 2	Article 6(1)	Article 10	—	Article 17(1)
—	Article 6(3)	—	—	Article 17(2)
—	Article 6(4)	—	—	Article 17(3)
—	Article 6(2)	—	—	Article 18
—	—	—	Articles 3 and 4	Article 19
—	Article 8a	—	—	Article 20
—	Article 8b	—	—	Article 21
—	Article 8c	—	—	Article 22
Articles 3 and 6	Article 3(2)(a)	—	—	Article 23(a)
Article 4	Article 3(2)(b)	Article 7(a)	—	Article 23(b)
—	—	Article 7(b)	—	Article 23(c)
Article 5	Article 7	Article 11	—	Article 24
Article 6	—	—	—	—
—	Article 8d	—	—	Article 25
	Article 2(5)			Article 26
—	Article 8e(1)	—	Article 4(2)	Article 27(1)
—	Article 8e(2)	—	Article 6	Article 27(2)
—	Article 2(7) first subparagraph	Article 5(2)	—	Article 28(1)
—	Article 2(7) fourth subparagraph first sentence			Article 28(2)
—	Article 1(1a)			Article 29
Article 7	Article 8	—	Article 5	Article 30
Article 9	Article 10	Article 12(2)	Article 7, fourth subparagraph	Article 31(1) and (2)
—	Article 9(2)	—	—	Article 31(3)
—	—	—	—	Article 32
Article 8	Article 9(1), first subparagraph and 9(2) and (3)	Article 2(1)	Article 7, first, second and third subparagraphs	Article 33
—	Article 9(1), second subparagraph	—	—	—
—	—	—	—	Article 34
—	—	—	—	Article 35
—	—	—	—	Article 36
—	—	Annex	—	—

REGULATION OF THE EUROPEAN PARLIAMENT AND OF THE COUNCIL

(864/2007/EC)

of 11 July 2007

on the law applicable to non-contractual obligations (Rome II)

[3.403]

NOTES

Date of publication in OJ: OJ L199, 31.07.2007, p 40.

The provisions of the Regulation reproduced here came into force on 11 January 2009 (see Art 32 at **[3.429]**) but apply only in relation to events giving rise to damage which occur after the entry into force of the Regulation (see Art 31 at **[3.428]**).

This Regulation is included for the provisions it makes for determining the applicable law in disputes relating to employment issues, including in particular industrial action. Only those parts of the Regulation within the scope of this work are reproduced here.

See *Harvey* H(3).

THE EUROPEAN PARLIAMENT AND THE COUNCIL OF THE EUROPEAN UNION,

Having regard to the Treaty establishing the European Community, and in particular Articles 61(c) and 67 thereof,

Having regard to the proposal from the Commission,

Having regard to the opinion of the European Economic and Social Committee,[1]

Acting in accordance with the procedure laid down in Article 251 of the Treaty in the light of the joint text approved by the Conciliation Committee on 25 June 2007,[2]

Whereas:

(1) The Community has set itself the objective of maintaining and developing an area of freedom, security and justice. For the progressive establishment of such an area, the Community is to adopt measures relating to judicial cooperation in civil matters with a cross-border impact to the extent necessary for the proper functioning of the internal market.

(2) According to Article 65(b) of the Treaty, these measures are to include those promoting the compatibility of the rules applicable in the Member States concerning the conflict of laws and of jurisdiction.

(3) The European Council meeting in Tampere on 15 and 16 October 1999 endorsed the principle of mutual recognition of judgments and other decisions of judicial authorities as the cornerstone of judicial cooperation in civil matters and invited the Council and the Commission to adopt a programme of measures to implement the principle of mutual recognition.

(4) On 30 November 2000, the Council adopted a joint Commission and Council programme of measures for implementation of the principle of mutual recognition of decisions in civil and commercial matters.[3] The programme identifies measures relating to the harmonisation of conflict-of-law rules as those facilitating the mutual recognition of judgments.

(5) The Hague Programme,[4] adopted by the European Council on 5 November 2004, called for work to be pursued actively on the rules of conflict of laws regarding non-contractual obligations (Rome II).

(6) The proper functioning of the internal market creates a need, in order to improve the predictability of the outcome of litigation, certainty as to the law applicable and the free movement of judgments, for the conflict-of-law rules in the Member States to designate the same national law irrespective of the country of the court in which an action is brought.

(7) The substantive scope and the provisions of this Regulation should be consistent with Council Regulation (EC) No 44/2001 of 22 December 2000 on jurisdiction and the recognition and enforcement of judgments in civil and commercial matters[5] (Brussels I) and the instruments dealing with the law applicable to contractual obligations.

(8) This Regulation should apply irrespective of the nature of the court or tribunal seised.

(9) Claims arising out of *acta iure imperii* should include claims against officials who act on behalf of the State and liability for acts of public authorities, including liability of publicly appointed office-holders. Therefore, these matters should be excluded from the scope of this Regulation.

(10) Family relationships should cover parentage, marriage, affinity and collateral relatives. The reference in Article 1(2) to relationships having comparable effects to marriage and other family relationships should be interpreted in accordance with the law of the Member State in which the court is seised.

(11) The concept of a non-contractual obligation varies from one Member State to another. Therefore for the purposes of this Regulation non-contractual obligation should be understood as an autonomous concept. The conflict-of-law rules set out in this Regulation should also cover non-contractual obligations arising out of strict liability.

(12) The law applicable should also govern the question of the capacity to incur liability in tort/delict.

(13) Uniform rules applied irrespective of the law they designate may avert the risk of distortions of competition between Community litigants.

(14) The requirement of legal certainty and the need to do justice in individual cases are essential elements of an area of justice. This Regulation provides for the connecting factors which are the most appropriate to achieve these objectives. Therefore, this Regulation provides for a general rule but also for specific rules and, in certain provisions, for an "escape clause" which allows a departure from these rules where it is clear from all the circumstances of the case that the tort/delict is manifestly more closely connected with another country. This set of rules thus creates a flexible framework of conflict-of-law rules. Equally, it enables the court seised to treat individual cases in an appropriate manner.

(15) The principle of the *lex loci delicti commissi* is the basic solution for non-contractual obligations in virtually all the Member States, but the practical application of the principle where the component factors of the case are spread over several countries varies. This situation engenders uncertainty as to the law applicable.

(16) Uniform rules should enhance the foreseeability of court decisions and ensure a reasonable balance between the interests of the person claimed to be liable and the person who has sustained damage. A connection with the country where the direct damage occurred (lex loci damni) strikes a fair balance between the interests of the person claimed to be liable and the person sustaining the damage, and also reflects the modern approach to civil liability and the development of systems of strict liability.

(17) The law applicable should be determined on the basis of where the damage occurs, regardless of the country or countries in which the indirect consequences could occur. Accordingly, in cases of personal injury or damage to property, the country in which the damage occurs should be the country where the injury was sustained or the property was damaged respectively.

(18) The general rule in this Regulation should be the *lex loci damni* provided for in Article 4(1). Article 4(2) should be seen as an exception to this general principle, creating a special connection where the parties have their habitual residence in the same country. Article 4(3) should be understood as an 'escape clause' from Article 4(1) and (2), where it is clear from all the circumstances of the case that the tort/delict is manifestly more closely connected with another country.

(19) Specific rules should be laid down for special torts/delicts where the general rule does not allow a reasonable balance to be struck between the interests at stake.

(20)–(25) (*Outside the scope of this work.*)

(26) Regarding infringements of intellectual property rights, the universally acknowledged principle of the *lex loci protectionis* should be preserved. For the purposes of this Regulation, the term 'intellectual property rights' should be interpreted as meaning, for instance, copyright, related rights, the *sui generis* right for the protection of databases and industrial property rights.

(27) The exact concept of industrial action, such as strike action or lock-out, varies from one Member State to another and is governed by each Member State's internal rules. Therefore, this Regulation assumes as a general principle that the law of the country where the industrial action was taken should apply, with the aim of protecting the rights and obligations of workers and employers.

(28) The special rule on industrial action in Article 9 is without prejudice to the conditions relating to the exercise of such action in accordance with national law and without prejudice to the legal status of trade unions or of the representative organisations of workers as provided for in the law of the Member States.

(29) Provision should be made for special rules where damage is caused by an act other than a tort/delict, such as unjust enrichment, *negotiorum gestio* and *culpa in contrahendo*.

(30) *Culpa in contrahendo* for the purposes of this Regulation is an autonomous concept and should not necessarily be interpreted within the meaning of national law. It should include the violation of the duty of disclosure and the breakdown of contractual negotiations. Article 12 covers only non-contractual obligations presenting a direct link with the dealings prior to the conclusion of a contract. This means that if, while a contract is being negotiated, a person suffers personal injury, Article 4 or other relevant provisions of this Regulation should apply.

(31) To respect the principle of party autonomy and to enhance legal certainty, the parties should be allowed to make a choice as to the law applicable to a non-contractual obligation. This choice should be expressed or demonstrated with reasonable certainty by the circumstances of the case. Where establishing the existence of the agreement, the court has to respect the intentions of the parties. Protection should be given to weaker parties by imposing certain conditions on the choice.

(32) Considerations of public interest justify giving the courts of the Member States the possibility, in exceptional circumstances, of applying exceptions based on public policy and overriding mandatory provisions. In particular, the application of a provision of the law designated by this Regulation which would have the effect of causing non-compensatory exemplary or punitive damages of an excessive nature to be awarded may, depending on the circumstances of the case and the legal order of the Member State of the court seised, be regarded as being contrary to the public policy (*ordre public*) of the forum.

(33)–(35) (*Outside the scope of this work.*)

(36) Respect for international commitments entered into by the Member States means that this Regulation should not affect international conventions to which one or more Member States are parties at the time this Regulation is adopted. To make the rules more accessible, the Commission should publish the list of the relevant conventions in the *Official Journal of the European Union* on the basis of information supplied by the Member States.

(37) The Commission will make a proposal to the European Parliament and the Council concerning the procedures and conditions according to which Member States would be entitled to negotiate and conclude on their own behalf agreements with third countries in individual and exceptional cases, concerning sectoral matters, containing provisions on the law applicable to non-contractual obligations.

(38) Since the objective of this Regulation cannot be sufficiently achieved by the Member States, and can therefore, by reason of the scale and effects of this Regulation, be better achieved at Community level, the Community may adopt measures, in accordance with the principle of subsidiarity set out in Article 5 of the Treaty. In accordance with the principle of proportionality set out in that Article, this Regulation does not go beyond what is necessary to attain that objective.

(39) In accordance with Article 3 of the Protocol on the position of the United Kingdom and Ireland annexed to the Treaty on European Union and to the Treaty establishing the European Community, the United Kingdom and Ireland are taking part in the adoption and application of this Regulation.

(40) In accordance with Articles 1 and 2 of the Protocol on the position of Denmark, annexed to the Treaty on European Union and to the Treaty establishing the European Community, Denmark does not take part in the adoption of this Regulation, and is not bound by it or subject to its application,

NOTES

1 OJ C241, 28.9.2004, p 1.

2 Opinion of the European Parliament of 6 July 2005 (OJ C157 E, 6.7.2006, p 371), Council Common Position of 25 September 2006 (OJ C289 E, 28.11.2006, p 68) and Position of the European Parliament of 18 January 2007 (not yet published in the Official Journal). European Parliament Legislative Resolution of 10 July 2007 and Council Decision of 28 June 2007.

3 OJ C12, 15.1.2001, p 1.

4 OJ C53, 3.3.2005, p 1.

5 OJ L12, 16.1.2001, p 1. Regulation as last amended by Regulation (EC) No 1791/2006 (OJ L363, 20.12.2006, p 1).

HAVE ADOPTED THIS REGULATION:

CHAPTER I SCOPE

[3.404]
Article 1
Scope

1. This Regulation shall apply, in situations involving a conflict of laws, to non-contractual obligations in civil and commercial matters. It shall not apply, in particular, to revenue, customs or administrative matters or to the liability of the State for acts and omissions in the exercise of State authority (*acta iure imperii*).

2. The following shall be excluded from the scope of this Regulation:
- (a) non-contractual obligations arising out of family relationships and relationships deemed by the law applicable to such relationships to have comparable effects including maintenance obligations;
- (b) non-contractual obligations arising out of matrimonial property regimes, property regimes of relationships deemed by the law applicable to such relationships to have comparable effects to marriage, and wills and succession;
- (c) non-contractual obligations arising under bills of exchange, cheques and promissory notes and other negotiable instruments to the extent that the obligations under such other negotiable instruments arise out of their negotiable character;
- (d) non-contractual obligations arising out of the law of companies and other bodies corporate or unincorporated regarding matters such as the creation, by registration or otherwise, legal capacity, internal organisation or winding-up of companies and other bodies corporate or unincorporated, the personal liability of officers and members as such for the obligations of the company or body and the personal liability of auditors to a company or to its members in the statutory audits of accounting documents;
- (e) non-contractual obligations arising out of the relations between the settlors, trustees and beneficiaries of a trust created voluntarily;
- (f) non-contractual obligations arising out of nuclear damage;
- (g) non-contractual obligations arising out of violations of privacy and rights relating to personality, including defamation.

3. This Regulation shall not apply to evidence and procedure, without prejudice to Articles 21 and 22.

4. For the purposes of this Regulation, *"Member State" shall mean* any Member State other than Denmark.

NOTES

Para 4: for the words in italics there are substituted the words ""relevant state" means the United Kingdom or", by the Law Applicable to Contractual Obligations and Non-Contractual Obligations (Amendment etc) (EU Exit) Regulations 2019, SI

2019/834, reg 11(1), (2), as from exit day (as defined in the European Union (Withdrawal) Act 2018, s 20) and only in so far as this Regulation will apply in the UK after that date by virtue of s 3 of the 2018 Act.

[3.405]
Article 2
Non-contractual obligations

1. For the purposes of this Regulation, damage shall cover any consequence arising out of tort/delict, unjust enrichment, *negotiorum gestio* or *culpa in contrahendo*.
2. This Regulation shall apply also to non-contractual obligations that are likely to arise.
3. Any reference in this Regulation to:
   (a) an event giving rise to damage shall include events giving rise to damage that are likely to occur; and
   (b) damage shall include damage that is likely to occur.

[3.406]
Article 3
Universal application

Any law specified by this Regulation shall be applied whether or not it is the law of *a Member State*.

NOTES

For the words in italics there are substituted the words "the United Kingdom or a part of the United Kingdom", by the Law Applicable to Contractual Obligations and Non-Contractual Obligations (Amendment etc) (EU Exit) Regulations 2019, SI 2019/834, reg 11(1), (3), as from exit day (as defined in the European Union (Withdrawal) Act 2018, s 20) and only in so far as this Regulation will apply in the UK after that date by virtue of s 3 of the 2018 Act.

CHAPTER II TORTS/DELICTS

[3.407]
Article 4
General rule

1. Unless otherwise provided for in this Regulation, the law applicable to a non-contractual obligation arising out of a tort/delict shall be the law of the country in which the damage occurs irrespective of the country in which the event giving rise to the damage occurred and irrespective of the country or countries in which the indirect consequences of that event occur.
2. However, where the person claimed to be liable and the person sustaining damage both have their habitual residence in the same country at the time when the damage occurs, the law of that country shall apply.
3. Where it is clear from all the circumstances of the case that the tort/delict is manifestly more closely connected with a country other than that indicated in paragraphs 1 or 2, the law of that other country shall apply. A manifestly closer connection with another country might be based in particular on a pre-existing relationship between the parties, such as a contract, that is closely connected with the tort/delict in question.

Articles 5–7 (*Outside the scope of this work.*)

[3.408]
Article 8
Infringement of intellectual property rights

1. The law applicable to a non-contractual obligation arising from an infringement of an intellectual property right shall be the law of the country for which protection is claimed.
2. In the case of a non-contractual obligation arising from an infringement [which occurred before exit day] of a unitary Community intellectual property right, the law applicable [in any proceedings of which a court was seised before exit day and which are not concluded before exit day] shall, for any question that is not governed by *the relevant Community instrument*, be the law of the country in which the act of infringement was committed.

[2A. In paragraph 2, "unitary Community intellectual property right" refers to that right as it had effect immediately before exit day.]

3. The law applicable under this Article may not be derogated from by an agreement pursuant to Article 14.

NOTES

Para 2: words in square brackets inserted and for the words in italics there are substituted the words "retained EU law", by the Law Applicable to Contractual Obligations and Non-Contractual Obligations (Amendment etc) (EU Exit) Regulations 2019, SI 2019/834, reg 11(1), (5)(a), as from exit day (as defined in the European Union (Withdrawal) Act 2018, s 20) and only in so far as this Regulation will apply in the UK after that date by virtue of s 3 of the 2018 Act.

Para 2A: inserted by SI 2019/834, reg 11(1), (5)(b), as from exit day (as defined in the European Union (Withdrawal) Act 2018, s 20) and only in so far as this Regulation will apply in the UK after that date by virtue of s 3 of the 2018 Act.

[3.409]
Article 9
Industrial action
Without prejudice to Article 4(2), the law applicable to a non-contractual obligation in respect of the liability of a person in the capacity of a worker or an employer or the organisations representing their professional interests for damages caused by an industrial action, pending or carried out, shall be the law of the country where the action is to be, or has been, taken.

CHAPTER III UNJUST ENRICHMENT, *NEGOTIORUM GESTIO* AND *CULPA IN CONTRAHENDO*

[3.410]
Article 10
Unjust enrichment
1. If a non-contractual obligation arising out of unjust enrichment, including payment of amounts wrongly received, concerns a relationship existing between the parties, such as one arising out of a contract or a tort/delict, that is closely connected with that unjust enrichment, it shall be governed by the law that governs that relationship.
2. Where the law applicable cannot be determined on the basis of paragraph 1 and the parties have their habitual residence in the same country when the event giving rise to unjust enrichment occurs, the law of that country shall apply.
3. Where the law applicable cannot be determined on the basis of paragraphs 1 or 2, it shall be the law of the country in which the unjust enrichment took place.
4. Where it is clear from all the circumstances of the case that the non-contractual obligation arising out of unjust enrichment is manifestly more closely connected with a country other than that indicated in paragraphs 1, 2 and 3, the law of that other country shall apply.

[3.411]
Article 11
Negotiorum gestio
1. If a non-contractual obligation arising out of an act performed without due authority in connection with the affairs of another person concerns a relationship existing between the parties, such as one arising out of a contract or a tort/delict, that is closely connected with that non-contractual obligation, it shall be governed by the law that governs that relationship.
2. Where the law applicable cannot be determined on the basis of paragraph 1, and the parties have their habitual residence in the same country when the event giving rise to the damage occurs, the law of that country shall apply.
3. Where the law applicable cannot be determined on the basis of paragraphs 1 or 2, it shall be the law of the country in which the act was performed.
4. Where it is clear from all the circumstances of the case that the non-contractual obligation arising out of an act performed without due authority in connection with the affairs of another person is manifestly more closely connected with a country other than that indicated in paragraphs 1, 2 and 3, the law of that other country shall apply.

[3.412]
Article 12
Culpa in contrahendo
1. The law applicable to a non-contractual obligation arising out of dealings prior to the conclusion of a contract, regardless of whether the contract was actually concluded or not, shall be the law that applies to the contract or that would have been applicable to it had it been entered into.
2. Where the law applicable cannot be determined on the basis of paragraph 1, it shall be:
(a) the law of the country in which the damage occurs, irrespective of the country in which the event giving rise to the damage occurred and irrespective of the country or countries in which the indirect consequences of that event occurred; or
(b) where the parties have their habitual residence in the same country at the time when the event giving rise to the damage occurs, the law of that country; or
(c) where it is clear from all the circumstances of the case that the non-contractual obligation arising out of dealings prior to the conclusion of a contract is manifestly more closely connected with a country other than that indicated in points (a) and (b), the law of that other country.

[3.413]
Article 13
Applicability of Article 8
For the purposes of this Chapter, Article 8 shall apply to non-contractual obligations arising from an infringement of an intellectual property right.

CHAPTER IV FREEDOM OF CHOICE

[3.414]
Article 14
Freedom of choice
1. The parties may agree to submit non-contractual obligations to the law of their choice:
(a) by an agreement entered into after the event giving rise to the damage occurred; or

(b) where all the parties are pursuing a commercial activity, also by an agreement freely negotiated before the event giving rise to the damage occurred.

The choice shall be expressed or demonstrated with reasonable certainty by the circumstances of the case and shall not prejudice the rights of third parties.

2. Where all the elements relevant to the situation at the time when the event giving rise to the damage occurs are located in a country other than the country whose law has been chosen, the choice of the parties shall not prejudice the application of provisions of the law of that other country which cannot be derogated from by agreement.

3. Where all the elements relevant to the situation at the time when the event giving rise to the damage occurs are located in one or more of *the Member States*, the parties' choice of the law applicable other than that of a *Member State* shall not prejudice the application of *provisions of Community law, where appropriate as implemented in the Member State of the forum*, which cannot be derogated from by agreement.

NOTES

Para 3: for the words in italics in the first and second places there are substituted the words "relevant states" and "relevant state" respectively, and for the words in italics in the final place there are substituted the words "retained EU law", by the Law Applicable to Contractual Obligations and Non-Contractual Obligations (Amendment etc) (EU Exit) Regulations 2019, SI 2019/834, reg 11(1), (6), as from exit day (as defined in the European Union (Withdrawal) Act 2018, s 20) and only in so far as this Regulation will apply in the UK after that date by virtue of s 3 of the 2018 Act.

CHAPTER V COMMON RULES

[3.415]
Article 15
Scope of the law applicable

The law applicable to non-contractual obligations under this Regulation shall govern in particular:

(a) the basis and extent of liability, including the determination of persons who may be held liable for acts performed by them;
(b) the grounds for exemption from liability, any limitation of liability and any division of liability;
(c) the existence, the nature and the assessment of damage or the remedy claimed;
(d) within the limits of powers conferred on the court by its procedural law, the measures which a court may take to prevent or terminate injury or damage or to ensure the provision of compensation;
(e) the question whether a right to claim damages or a remedy may be transferred, including by inheritance;
(f) persons entitled to compensation for damage sustained personally;
(g) liability for the acts of another person;
(h) the manner in which an obligation may be extinguished and rules of prescription and limitation, including rules relating to the commencement, interruption and suspension of a period of prescription or limitation.

[3.416]
Article 16
Overriding mandatory provisions

Nothing in this Regulation shall restrict the application of the provisions of the law of the forum in a situation where they are mandatory irrespective of the law otherwise applicable to the non-contractual obligation.

[3.417]
Article 17
Rules of safety and conduct

In assessing the conduct of the person claimed to be liable, account shall be taken, as a matter of fact and in so far as is appropriate, of the rules of safety and conduct which were in force at the place and time of the event giving rise to the liability.

[3.418]
Article 18
Direct action against the insurer of the person liable

The person having suffered damage may bring his or her claim directly against the insurer of the person liable to provide compensation if the law applicable to the non-contractual obligation or the law applicable to the insurance contract so provides.

[3.419]
Article 19
Subrogation

Where a person (the creditor) has a non-contractual claim upon another (the debtor), and a third person has a duty to satisfy the creditor, or has in fact satisfied the creditor in discharge of that duty, the law which governs the third person's duty to satisfy the creditor shall determine whether, and the extent to which, the third person is entitled to exercise against the debtor the rights which the creditor had against the debtor under the law governing their relationship.

[3.420]
Article 20
Multiple liability

If a creditor has a claim against several debtors who are liable for the same claim, and one of the debtors has already satisfied the claim in whole or in part, the question of that debtor's right to demand compensation from the other debtors shall be governed by the law applicable to that debtor's non-contractual obligation towards the creditor.

[3.421]
Article 21
Formal validity

A unilateral act intended to have legal effect and relating to a non-contractual obligation shall be formally valid if it satisfies the formal requirements of the law governing the non-contractual obligation in question or the law of the country in which the act is performed.

[3.422]
Article 22
Burden of proof

1. The law governing a non-contractual obligation under this Regulation shall apply to the extent that, in matters of non-contractual obligations, it contains rules which raise presumptions of law or determine the burden of proof.
2. Acts intended to have legal effect may be proved by any mode of proof recognised by the law of the forum or by any of the laws referred to in Article 21 under which that act is formally valid, provided that such mode of proof can be administered by the forum.

CHAPTER VI OTHER PROVISIONS

[3.423]
Article 23
Habitual residence

1. For the purposes of this Regulation, the habitual residence of companies and other bodies, corporate or unincorporated, shall be the place of central administration.

Where the event giving rise to the damage occurs, or the damage arises, in the course of operation of a branch, agency or any other establishment, the place where the branch, agency or any other establishment is located shall be treated as the place of habitual residence.
2. For the purposes of this Regulation, the habitual residence of a natural person acting in the course of his or her business activity shall be his or her principal place of business.

[3.424]
Article 24
Exclusion of renvoi

The application of the law of any country specified by this Regulation means the application of the rules of law in force in that country other than its rules of private international law.

[3.425]
Article 25
States with more than one legal system

1. Where a State comprises several territorial units, each of which has its own rules of law in respect of non-contractual obligations, each territorial unit shall be considered as a country for the purposes of identifying the law applicable under this Regulation.
2. *A Member State within which different territorial units have their own rules of law in respect of non-contractual obligations shall not be required to apply this Regulation to conflicts solely between the laws of such units.*

NOTES

Para 2: repealed by the Law Applicable to Contractual Obligations and Non-Contractual Obligations (Amendment etc) (EU Exit) Regulations 2019, SI 2019/834, reg 11(1), (7), as from exit day (as defined in the European Union (Withdrawal) Act 2018, s 20) and only in so far as this Regulation will apply in the UK after that date by virtue of s 3 of the 2018 Act.

[3.426]
Article 26
Public policy of the forum

The application of a provision of the law of any country specified by this Regulation may be refused only if such application is manifestly incompatible with the public policy (*ordre public*) of the forum.

[3.427]
Article 27
Relationship with other provisions of *Community law*

This Regulation shall not prejudice the application of provisions of *Community law* which, in relation to particular matters, lay down conflict-of-law rules relating to non-contractual obligations.

NOTES

For the words "Community law" in italics in both places there are substituted the words "retained EU law", by the Law Applicable to Contractual Obligations and Non-Contractual Obligations (Amendment etc) (EU Exit) Regulations 2019, SI

2019/834, reg 11(1), (8), as from exit day (as defined in the European Union (Withdrawal) Act 2018, s 20) and only in so far as this Regulation will apply in the UK after that date by virtue of s 3 of the 2018 Act.

Article 28 *(Outside the scope of this work.)*

CHAPTER VII FINAL PROVISIONS

Articles 29, 30 *(Outside the scope of this work.)*

[3.428]
Article 31
Application in time

This Regulation shall apply to events giving rise to damage which occur after *its entry into force*.

NOTES

For the words in italics there are substituted the words "on or after 11 January 2009", by the Law Applicable to Contractual Obligations and Non-Contractual Obligations (Amendment etc) (EU Exit) Regulations 2019, SI 2019/834, reg 11(1), (11), as from exit day (as defined in the European Union (Withdrawal) Act 2018, s 20) and only in so far as this Regulation will apply in the UK after that date by virtue of s 3 of the 2018 Act.

[3.429]
Article 32
Date of application

This Regulation shall apply from 11 January 2009, except for Article 29, which shall apply from 11 July 2008.

This Regulation shall be binding in its entirety and directly applicable in the Member States in accordance with the Treaty establishing the European Community.

NOTES

Repealed by the Law Applicable to Contractual Obligations and Non-Contractual Obligations (Amendment etc) (EU Exit) Regulations 2019, SI 2019/834, reg 11(1), (12), as from exit day (as defined in the European Union (Withdrawal) Act 2018, s 20) and only in so far as this Regulation will apply in the UK after that date by virtue of s 3 of the 2018 Act.

(*Commission Statement on the review clause, Commission Statement on road accidents, Commission Statement on the treatment of foreign law; outside the scope of this work.*)

REGULATION OF THE EUROPEAN PARLIAMENT AND OF THE COUNCIL

(593/2008/EC)

of 17 June 2008

on the law applicable to contractual obligations (Rome I)

[3.430]

NOTES

Date of publication in OJ: OJ L177, 4.7.2008, p 6. The text of this Directive incorporates the corrigendum published in OJ L309, 24.11.2009, p 87.

Only those provisions within the scope of this work are reproduced.

Application to the United Kingdom: Commission Decision 2009/26/EC of 22 December 2008 (OJ L10, 15.1.2009, p 22) provides that:

> **"Article 1**
> Regulation (EC) No 593/2008 shall apply to the United Kingdom in accordance with Article 2.
> **Article 2** Regulation (EC) No 593/2008 shall enter into force in the United Kingdom from the date of notification of this Decision. It shall apply from 17 December 2009, except for Article 26 which shall apply from 17 June 2009.".

The Regulation applies to contracts concluded as from 17 December 2009: see Art 28 at **[3.453]**.
See also the Contracts (Applicable Law) Act 1990, ss 4A, 4B at **[1.195]** and **[1.196]**.
See *Harvey* H(3).

THE EUROPEAN PARLIAMENT AND THE COUNCIL OF THE EUROPEAN UNION,

Having regard to the Treaty establishing the European Community, and in particular Article 61(c) and the second indent of Article 67(5) thereof,

Having regard to the proposal from the Commission,

Having regard to the opinion of the European Economic and Social Committee,[1]

Acting in accordance with the procedure laid down in Article 251 of the Treaty,[2]

Whereas:

(1) The Community has set itself the objective of maintaining and developing an area of freedom, security and justice. For the progressive establishment of such an area, the Community is to adopt measures relating to judicial cooperation in civil matters with a cross-border impact to the extent necessary for the proper functioning of the internal market.

(2) According to Article 65, point (b) of the Treaty, these measures are to include those promoting the compatibility of the rules applicable in the Member States concerning the conflict of laws and of jurisdiction.

(3) The European Council meeting in Tampere on 15 and 16 October 1999 endorsed the principle of mutual recognition of judgments and other decisions of judicial authorities as the cornerstone of judicial cooperation in civil matters and invited the Council and the Commission to adopt a programme of measures to implement that principle.

(4) On 30 November 2000 the Council adopted a joint Commission and Council programme of measures for implementation of the principle of mutual recognition of decisions in civil and commercial matters.[3] The programme identifies measures relating to the harmonisation of conflict-of-law rules as those facilitating the mutual recognition of judgments.

(5) The Hague Programme,[4] adopted by the European Council on 5 November 2004, called for work to be pursued actively on the conflict-of-law rules regarding contractual obligations (Rome I).

(6) The proper functioning of the internal market creates a need, in order to improve the predictability of the outcome of litigation, certainty as to the law applicable and the free movement of judgments, for the conflict-of-law rules in the Member States to designate the same national law irrespective of the country of the court in which an action is brought.

(7) The substantive scope and the provisions of this Regulation should be consistent with Council Regulation (EC) No 44/2001 of 22 December 2000 on jurisdiction and the recognition and enforcement of judgments in civil and commercial matters[5] (Brussels I) and Regulation (EC) No 864/2007 of the European Parliament and of the Council of 11 July 2007 on the law applicable to non-contractual obligations (Rome II).[6]

(8) Family relationships should cover parentage, marriage, affinity and collateral relatives. The reference in Article 1(2) to relationships having comparable effects to marriage and other family relationships should be interpreted in accordance with the law of the Member State in which the court is seised.

(9) Obligations under bills of exchange, cheques and promissory notes and other negotiable instruments should also cover bills of lading to the extent that the obligations under the bill of lading arise out of its negotiable character.

(10) Obligations arising out of dealings prior to the conclusion of the contract are covered by Article 12 of Regulation (EC) No 864/2007. Such obligations should therefore be excluded from the scope of this Regulation.

(11) The parties' freedom to choose the applicable law should be one of the cornerstones of the system of conflict-of-law rules in matters of contractual obligations.

(12) An agreement between the parties to confer on one or more courts or tribunals of a Member State exclusive jurisdiction to determine disputes under the contract should be one of the factors to be taken into account in determining whether a choice of law has been clearly demonstrated.

(13) This Regulation does not preclude parties from incorporating by reference into their contract a non-State body of law or an international convention.

(14) Should the Community adopt, in an appropriate legal instrument, rules of substantive contract law, including standard terms and conditions, such instrument may provide that the parties may choose to apply those rules.

(15) Where a choice of law is made and all other elements relevant to the situation are located in a country other than the country whose law has been chosen, the choice of law should not prejudice the application of provisions of the law of that country which cannot be derogated from by agreement. This rule should apply whether or not the choice of law was accompanied by a choice of court or tribunal. Whereas no substantial change is intended as compared with Article 3(3) of the 1980 Convention on the Law Applicable to Contractual Obligations[7] (the Rome Convention), the wording of this Regulation is aligned as far as possible with Article 14 of Regulation (EC) No 864/2007.

(16) To contribute to the general objective of this Regulation, legal certainty in the European judicial area, the conflict-of-law rules should be highly foreseeable. The courts should, however, retain a degree of discretion to determine the law that is most closely connected to the situation.

(17) As far as the applicable law in the absence of choice is concerned, the concept of 'provision of services' and 'sale of goods' should be interpreted in the same way as when applying Article 5 of Regulation (EC) No 44/2001 in so far as sale of goods and provision of services are covered by that Regulation. Although franchise and distribution contracts are contracts for services, they are the subject of specific rules.

(18) As far as the applicable law in the absence of choice is concerned, multilateral systems should be those in which trading is conducted, such as regulated markets and multilateral trading facilities as referred to in Article 4 of Directive 2004/39/EC of the European Parliament and of the Council of 21 April 2004 on markets in financial instruments,[8] regardless of whether or not they rely on a central counterparty.

(19) Where there has been no choice of law, the applicable law should be determined in accordance with the rule specified for the particular type of contract. Where the contract cannot be categorised as being one of the specified types or where its elements fall within more than one of the specified types, it should be governed by the law of the country where the party required to effect the characteristic performance of the contract has his habitual residence. In the case of a contract consisting of a bundle of rights and obligations capable of being categorised as falling within more than one of the specified types of contract, the characteristic performance of the contract should be determined having regard to its centre of gravity.

(20) Where the contract is manifestly more closely connected with a country other than that indicated in Article 4(1) or (2), an escape clause should provide that the law of that other country is to apply. In order to determine that country, account should be taken, inter alia, of whether the contract in question has a very close relationship with another contract or contracts.

(21) In the absence of choice, where the applicable law cannot be determined either on the basis of the fact that the contract can be categorised as one of the specified types or as being the law of the country of habitual residence of the party required to effect the characteristic performance of the contract, the contract should be governed by the law of the country with which it is most closely connected. In order to determine that country, account should be taken, inter alia, of whether the contract in question has a very close relationship with another contract or contracts.

(22) (*Outside the scope of this work.*)

(23) As regards contracts concluded with parties regarded as being weaker, those parties should be protected by conflict-of-law rules that are more favourable to their interests than the general rules.

(24)–(33) (*Outside the scope of this work.*)

(34) The rule on individual employment contracts should not prejudice the application of the overriding mandatory provisions of the country to which a worker is posted in accordance with Directive 96/71/EC of the European Parliament and of the Council of 16 December 1996 concerning the posting of workers in the framework of the provision of services.[9]

(35) Employees should not be deprived of the protection afforded to them by provisions which cannot be derogated from by agreement or which can only be derogated from to their benefit.

(36) As regards individual employment contracts, work carried out in another country should be regarded as temporary if the employee is expected to resume working in the country of origin after carrying out his tasks abroad. The conclusion of a new contract of employment with the original employer or an employer belonging to the same group of companies as the original employer should not preclude the employee from being regarded as carrying out his work in another country temporarily.

(37) Considerations of public interest justify giving the courts of the Member States the possibility, in exceptional circumstances, of applying exceptions based on public policy and overriding mandatory provisions. The concept of 'overriding mandatory provisions' should be distinguished from the expression 'provisions which cannot be derogated from by agreement' and should be construed more restrictively.

(38) In the context of voluntary assignment, the term 'relationship' should make it clear that Article 14(1) also applies to the property aspects of an assignment, as between assignor and assignee, in legal orders where such aspects are treated separately from the aspects under the law of obligations. However, the term 'relationship' should not be understood as relating to any relationship that may exist between assignor and assignee. In particular, it should not cover preliminary questions as regards a voluntary assignment or a contractual subrogation. The term should be strictly limited to the aspects which are directly relevant to the voluntary assignment or contractual subrogation in question.

(39) For the sake of legal certainty there should be a clear definition of habitual residence, in particular for companies and other bodies, corporate or unincorporated. Unlike Article 60(1) of Regulation (EC) No 44/2001, which establishes three criteria, the conflict-of-law rule should proceed on the basis of a single criterion; otherwise, the parties would be unable to foresee the law applicable to their situation.

(40) A situation where conflict-of-law rules are dispersed among several instruments and where there are differences between those rules should be avoided. This Regulation, however, should not exclude the possibility of inclusion of conflict-of-law rules relating to contractual obligations in provisions of Community law with regard to particular matters.

This Regulation should not prejudice the application of other instruments laying down provisions designed to contribute to the proper functioning of the internal market in so far as they cannot be applied in conjunction with the law designated by the rules of this Regulation. The application of provisions of the applicable law designated by the rules of this Regulation should not restrict the free movement of goods and services as regulated by Community instruments, such as Directive 2000/31/EC of the European Parliament and of the Council of 8 June 2000 on certain legal aspects of information society services, in particular electronic commerce, in the Internal Market (Directive on electronic commerce).[10]

(41) Respect for international commitments entered into by the Member States means that this Regulation should not affect international conventions to which one or more Member States are parties at the time when this Regulation is adopted. To make the rules more accessible, the Commission should publish the list of the relevant conventions in the *Official Journal of the European Union* on the basis of information supplied by the Member States.

(42) The Commission will make a proposal to the European Parliament and to the Council concerning the procedures and conditions according to which Member States would be entitled to negotiate and conclude, on their own behalf, agreements with third countries in individual and exceptional cases, concerning sectoral matters and containing provisions on the law applicable to contractual obligations.

(43) Since the objective of this Regulation cannot be sufficiently achieved by the Member States and can therefore, by reason of the scale and effects of this Regulation, be better achieved at Community level, the Community may adopt measures, in accordance with the principle of subsidiarity as set out in Article 5 of the Treaty. In accordance with the principle of proportionality, as set out in that Article, this Regulation does not go beyond what is necessary to attain its objective.

(44) In accordance with Article 3 of the Protocol on the position of the United Kingdom and Ireland, annexed to the Treaty on European Union and to the Treaty establishing the European Community, Ireland has notified its wish to take part in the adoption and application of the present Regulation.

(45) In accordance with Articles 1 and 2 of the Protocol on the position of the United Kingdom and Ireland, annexed to the Treaty on European Union and to the Treaty establishing the European Community, and without prejudice to Article 4 of the said Protocol, the United Kingdom is not taking part in the adoption of this Regulation and is not bound by it or subject to its application.

(46) In accordance with Articles 1 and 2 of the Protocol on the position of Denmark, annexed to the Treaty on European Union and to the Treaty establishing the European Community, Denmark is not taking part in the adoption of this Regulation and is not bound by it or subject to its application,

NOTES

1 OJ C318, 23.12.2006, p 56.

2 Opinion of the European Parliament of 29 November 2007 (not yet published in the Official Journal) and Council Decision of 5 June 2008.

3 OJ C12, 15.1.2001, p 1.

4 OJ C53, 3.3.2005, p 1.

5 OJ L12, 16.1.2001, p 1. Regulation as last amended by Regulation (EC) No 1791/2006 (OJ L363, 20.12.2006, p 1).

6 OJ L199, 31.7.2007, p 40.

7 OJ C334, 30.12.2005, p 1.

8 OJ L145, 30.4.2004, p 1. Directive as last amended by Directive 2008/10/EC (OJ L76, 19.3.2008, p 33).

9 OJ L18, 21.1.1997, p 1.

10 OJ L178, 17.7.2000, p 1.

HAVE ADOPTED THIS REGULATION:

CHAPTER I SCOPE

[3.431]

Article 1 Material scope

1. This Regulation shall apply, in situations involving a conflict of laws, to contractual obligations in civil and commercial matters.

It shall not apply, in particular, to revenue, customs or administrative matters.

2. The following shall be excluded from the scope of this Regulation:

(a) questions involving the status or legal capacity of natural persons, without prejudice to Article 13;

(b) obligations arising out of family relationships and relationships deemed by the law applicable to such relationships to have comparable effects, including maintenance obligations;

(c) obligations arising out of matrimonial property regimes, property regimes of relationships deemed by the law applicable to such relationships to have comparable effects to marriage, and wills and succession;

(d) obligations arising under bills of exchange, cheques and promissory notes and other negotiable instruments to the extent that the obligations under such other negotiable instruments arise out of their negotiable character;

(e) arbitration agreements and agreements on the choice of court;

(f) questions governed by the law of companies and other bodies, corporate or unincorporated, such as the creation, by registration or otherwise, legal capacity, internal organisation or winding-up of companies and other bodies, corporate or unincorporated, and the personal liability of officers and members as such for the obligations of the company or body;

(g) the question whether an agent is able to bind a principal, or an organ to bind a company or other body corporate or unincorporated, in relation to a third party;

(h) the constitution of trusts and the relationship between settlors, trustees and beneficiaries;

(i) obligations arising out of dealings prior to the conclusion of a contract;

(j) insurance contracts arising out of operations carried out by organisations other than undertakings referred to in *Article 2 of Directive 2002/83/EC of the European Parliament and of the Council of 5 November 2002 concerning life assurance*[1] the object of which is to provide benefits for employed or self-employed persons belonging to an undertaking or group of undertakings, or to a trade or group of trades, in the event of death or survival or of discontinuance or curtailment of activity, or of sickness related to work or accidents at work.

3. This Regulation shall not apply to evidence and procedure, without prejudice to Article 18.

4. In this Regulation, the term 'Member State' shall mean Member States to which this Regulation applies. However, in Article 3(4) and Article 7 the term shall mean all the Member States.

NOTES

Para 2: for the words in italics in sub-para (j) there are substituted the words "Article 2(1) of Directive 2009/138/EU which carry on life assurance under Article 2(3) of that Directive", by the Law Applicable to Contractual Obligations and Non-Contractual Obligations (Amendment etc) (EU Exit) Regulations 2019, SI 2019/834, reg 10(1), (2)(a), as from exit day (as defined in the European Union (Withdrawal) Act 2018, s 20) and only in so far as this Regulation will apply in the UK after that date by virtue of s 3 of the 2018 Act.

Para 4: substituted by SI 2019/834, reg 10(1), (2)(b), as from exit day (as defined in the European Union (Withdrawal) Act 2018, s 20) and only in so far as this Regulation will apply in the UK after that date by virtue of s 3 of the 2018 Act, as follows—

"4. In this Regulation, "relevant state" means the United Kingdom and—
- (a) in Article 3(4) and Article 7, all the Member States;
- (b) in all other Articles, the Member States to which Regulation (EC) No 593/2008 of the European Parliament and of the Council of 17 June 2008 on the law applicable to contractual obligations (Rome I), as it has effect in EU law and as amended from time to time, applies.".

[1] OJ L345, 19.12.2002, p 1. Directive as last amended by Directive 2008/19/EC (OJ L76, 19.3.2008, p 44).

[3.432]
Article 2
Universal application

Any law specified by this Regulation shall be applied whether or not it is the law of *a Member State*.

NOTES

For the words in italics there are substituted the words "the United Kingdom or a part of the United Kingdom", by the Law Applicable to Contractual Obligations and Non-Contractual Obligations (Amendment etc) (EU Exit) Regulations 2019, SI 2019/834, reg 10(1), (3), as from exit day (as defined in the European Union (Withdrawal) Act 2018, s 20) and only in so far as this Regulation will apply in the UK after that date by virtue of s 3 of the 2018 Act.

CHAPTER II UNIFORM RULES

[3.433]
Article 3
Freedom of choice

1. A contract shall be governed by the law chosen by the parties. The choice shall be made expressly or clearly demonstrated by the terms of the contract or the circumstances of the case. By their choice the parties can select the law applicable to the whole or to part only of the contract.
2. The parties may at any time agree to subject the contract to a law other than that which previously governed it, whether as a result of an earlier choice made under this Article or of other provisions of this Regulation. Any change in the law to be applied that is made after the conclusion of the contract shall not prejudice its formal validity under Article 11 or adversely affect the rights of third parties.
3. Where all other elements relevant to the situation at the time of the choice are located in a country other than the country whose law has been chosen, the choice of the parties shall not prejudice the application of provisions of the law of that other country which cannot be derogated from by agreement.
4. Where all other elements relevant to the situation at the time of the choice are located in one or more *Member States*, the parties' choice of applicable law other than that of a *Member State* shall not prejudice the application of provisions of *Community law, where appropriate as implemented in the Member State of the forum,* which cannot be derogated from by agreement.
5. The existence and validity of the consent of the parties as to the choice of the applicable law shall be determined in accordance with the provisions of Articles 10, 11 and 13.

NOTES

For the words in italics in the first and second places there are substituted the words "relevant states" and "relevant state" respectively, and for the words in italics in the final place there are substituted the words "retained EU law", by the Law Applicable to Contractual Obligations and Non-Contractual Obligations (Amendment etc) (EU Exit) Regulations 2019, SI 2019/834, reg 10(1), (4), as from exit day (as defined in the European Union (Withdrawal) Act 2018, s 20) and only in so far as this Regulation will apply in the UK after that date by virtue of s 3 of the 2018 Act.

[3.434]
Article 4
Applicable law in the absence of choice

1. To the extent that the law applicable to the contract has not been chosen in accordance with Article 3 and without prejudice to Articles 5 to 8, the law governing the contract shall be determined as follows:
- (a) a contract for the sale of goods shall be governed by the law of the country where the seller has his habitual residence;
- (b) a contract for the provision of services shall be governed by the law of the country where the service provider has his habitual residence;
- (c) a contract relating to a right in rem in immovable property or to a tenancy of immovable property shall be governed by the law of the country where the property is situated;
- (d) notwithstanding point (c), a tenancy of immovable property concluded for temporary private use for a period of no more than six consecutive months shall be governed by the law of the country where the landlord has his habitual residence, provided that the tenant is a natural person and has his habitual residence in the same country;

(e) a franchise contract shall be governed by the law of the country where the franchisee has his habitual residence;

(f) a distribution contract shall be governed by the law of the country where the distributor has his habitual residence;

(g) a contract for the sale of goods by auction shall be governed by the law of the country where the auction takes place, if such a place can be determined;

(h) a contract concluded within a multilateral system which brings together or facilitates the bringing together of multiple third-party buying and selling interests in financial instruments, as defined *by Article 4(1), point (17) of Directive 2004/39/EC*, in accordance with non-discretionary rules and governed by a single law, shall be governed by that law.

2. Where the contract is not covered by paragraph 1 or where the elements of the contract would be covered by more than one of points (a) to (h) of paragraph 1, the contract shall be governed by the law of the country where the party required to effect the characteristic performance of the contract has his habitual residence.

3. Where it is clear from all the circumstances of the case that the contract is manifestly more closely connected with a country other than that indicated in paragraphs 1 or 2, the law of that other country shall apply.

4. Where the law applicable cannot be determined pursuant to paragraphs 1 or 2, the contract shall be governed by the law of the country with which it is most closely connected.

NOTES

Para 1: for the words in italics in sub-para (h) there are substituted the words "in Part 1 of Schedule 2 to the Financial Services and Markets Act 2000 (Regulated Activities) Order 2001", by the Law Applicable to Contractual Obligations and Non-Contractual Obligations (Amendment etc) (EU Exit) Regulations 2019, SI 2019/834, reg 10(1), (5), as from exit day (as defined in the European Union (Withdrawal) Act 2018, s 20) and only in so far as this Regulation will apply in the UK after that date by virtue of s 3 of the 2018 Act.

Articles 5–7 (*Outside the scope of this work.*)

[3.435]
Article 8
Individual employment contracts

1. An individual employment contract shall be governed by the law chosen by the parties in accordance with Article 3. Such a choice of law may not, however, have the result of depriving the employee of the protection afforded to him by provisions that cannot be derogated from by agreement under the law that, in the absence of choice, would have been applicable pursuant to paragraphs 2, 3 and 4 of this Article.

2. To the extent that the law applicable to the individual employment contract has not been chosen by the parties, the contract shall be governed by the law of the country in which or, failing that, from which the employee habitually carries out his work in performance of the contract. The country where the work is habitually carried out shall not be deemed to have changed if he is temporarily employed in another country.

3. Where the law applicable cannot be determined pursuant to paragraph 2, the contract shall be governed by the law of the country where the place of business through which the employee was engaged is situated.

4. Where it appears from the circumstances as a whole that the contract is more closely connected with a country other than that indicated in paragraphs 2 or 3, the law of that other country shall apply.

[3.436]
Article 9
Overriding mandatory provisions

1. Overriding mandatory provisions are provisions the respect for which is regarded as crucial by a country for safeguarding its public interests, such as its political, social or economic organisation, to such an extent that they are applicable to any situation falling within their scope, irrespective of the law otherwise applicable to the contract under this Regulation.

2. Nothing in this Regulation shall restrict the application of the overriding mandatory provisions of the law of the forum.

3. Effect may be given to the overriding mandatory provisions of the law of the country where the obligations arising out of the contract have to be or have been performed, in so far as those overriding mandatory provisions render the performance of the contract unlawful. In considering whether to give effect to those provisions, regard shall be had to their nature and purpose and to the consequences of their application or non-application.

[3.437]
Article 10
Consent and material validity

1. The existence and validity of a contract, or of any term of a contract, shall be determined by the law which would govern it under this Regulation if the contract or term were valid.

2. Nevertheless, a party, in order to establish that he did not consent, may rely upon the law of the country in which he has his habitual residence if it appears from the circumstances that it would not be reasonable to determine the effect of his conduct in accordance with the law specified in paragraph 1.

[3.438]
Article 11
Formal validity

1. A contract concluded between persons who, or whose agents, are in the same country at the time of its conclusion is formally valid if it satisfies the formal requirements of the law which governs it in substance under this Regulation or of the law of the country where it is concluded.

2. A contract concluded between persons who, or whose agents, are in different countries at the time of its conclusion is formally valid if it satisfies the formal requirements of the law which governs it in substance under this Regulation, or of the law of either of the countries where either of the parties or their agent is present at the time of conclusion, or of the law of the country where either of the parties had his habitual residence at that time.

3. A unilateral act intended to have legal effect relating to an existing or contemplated contract is formally valid if it satisfies the formal requirements of the law which governs or would govern the contract in substance under this Regulation, or of the law of the country where the act was done, or of the law of the country where the person by whom it was done had his habitual residence at that time.

4. Paragraphs 1, 2 and 3 of this Article shall not apply to contracts that fall within the scope of Article 6. The form of such contracts shall be governed by the law of the country where the consumer has his habitual residence.

5. Notwithstanding paragraphs 1 to 4, a contract the subject matter of which is a right in rem in immovable property or a tenancy of immovable property shall be subject to the requirements of form of the law of the country where the property is situated if by that law:

(a) those requirements are imposed irrespective of the country where the contract is concluded and irrespective of the law governing the contract; and
(b) those requirements cannot be derogated from by agreement.

[3.439]
Article 12
Scope of the law applicable

1. The law applicable to a contract by virtue of this Regulation shall govern in particular:

(a) interpretation;
(b) performance;
(c) within the limits of the powers conferred on the court by its procedural law, the consequences of a total or partial breach of obligations, including the assessment of damages in so far as it is governed by rules of law;
(d) the various ways of extinguishing obligations, and prescription and limitation of actions;
(e) the consequences of nullity of the contract.

2. In relation to the manner of performance and the steps to be taken in the event of defective performance, regard shall be had to the law of the country in which performance takes place.

[3.440]
Article 13
Incapacity

In a contract concluded between persons who are in the same country, a natural person who would have capacity under the law of that country may invoke his incapacity resulting from the law of another country, only if the other party to the contract was aware of that incapacity at the time of the conclusion of the contract or was not aware thereof as a result of negligence.

[3.441]
Article 14
Voluntary assignment and contractual subrogation

1. The relationship between assignor and assignee under a voluntary assignment or contractual subrogation of a claim against another person (the debtor) shall be governed by the law that applies to the contract between the assignor and assignee under this Regulation.

2. The law governing the assigned or subrogated claim shall determine its assignability, the relationship between the assignee and the debtor, the conditions under which the assignment or subrogation can be invoked against the debtor and whether the debtor's obligations have been discharged.

3. The concept of assignment in this Article includes outright transfers of claims, transfers of claims by way of security and pledges or other security rights over claims.

[3.442]
Article 15
Legal subrogation

Where a person (the creditor) has a contractual claim against another (the debtor) and a third person has a duty to satisfy the creditor, or has in fact satisfied the creditor in discharge of that duty, the law which governs the third person's duty to satisfy the creditor shall determine whether and to what extent the third person is entitled to exercise against the debtor the rights which the creditor had against the debtor under the law governing their relationship.

[3.443]
Article 16
Multiple liability

If a creditor has a claim against several debtors who are liable for the same claim, and one of the debtors has already satisfied the claim in whole or in part, the law governing the debtor's obligation towards the creditor also governs the debtor's right to claim recourse from the other debtors. The other debtors may rely on the defences they had against the creditor to the extent allowed by the law governing their obligations towards the creditor.

[3.444]
Article 17
Set-off

Where the right to set-off is not agreed by the parties, set-off shall be governed by the law applicable to the claim against which the right to set-off is asserted.

[3.445]
Article 18
Burden of proof

1. The law governing a contractual obligation under this Regulation shall apply to the extent that, in matters of contractual obligations, it contains rules which raise presumptions of law or determine the burden of proof.
2. A contract or an act intended to have legal effect may be proved by any mode of proof recognised by the law of the forum or by any of the laws referred to in Article 11 under which that contract or act is formally valid, provided that such mode of proof can be administered by the forum.

CHAPTER III OTHER PROVISIONS

[3.446]
Article 19
Habitual residence

1. For the purposes of this Regulation, the habitual residence of companies and other bodies, corporate or unincorporated, shall be the place of central administration.

The habitual residence of a natural person acting in the course of his business activity shall be his principal place of business.
2. Where the contract is concluded in the course of the operations of a branch, agency or any other establishment, or if, under the contract, performance is the responsibility of such a branch, agency or establishment, the place where the branch, agency or any other establishment is located shall be treated as the place of habitual residence.
3. For the purposes of determining the habitual residence, the relevant point in time shall be the time of the conclusion of the contract.

[3.447]
Article 20
Exclusion of renvoi

The application of the law of any country specified by this Regulation means the application of the rules of law in force in that country other than its rules of private international law, unless provided otherwise in this Regulation.

[3.448]
Article 21
Public policy of the forum

The application of a provision of the law of any country specified by this Regulation may be refused only if such application is manifestly incompatible with the public policy (*ordre public*) of the forum.

[3.449]
Article 22
States with more than one legal system

1. Where a State comprises several territorial units, each of which has its own rules of law in respect of contractual obligations, each territorial unit shall be considered as a country for the purposes of identifying the law applicable under this Regulation.
2. *A Member State where different territorial units have their own rules of law in respect of contractual obligations shall not be required to apply this Regulation to conflicts solely between the laws of such units.*

NOTES

Para 2: repealed by the Law Applicable to Contractual Obligations and Non-Contractual Obligations (Amendment etc) (EU Exit) Regulations 2019, SI 2019/834, reg 10(1), (8), as from exit day (as defined in the European Union (Withdrawal) Act 2018, s 20) and only in so far as this Regulation will apply in the UK after that date by virtue of s 3 of the 2018 Act.

[3.450]
Article 23
Relationship with other provisions of *Community law*

With the exception of Article 7, this Regulation shall not prejudice the application of provisions of *Community law* which, in relation to particular matters, lay down conflict-of-law rules relating to contractual obligations.

NOTES

For the words "Community law" in italics in both places there are substituted the words "retained EU law", by the Law Applicable to Contractual Obligations and Non-Contractual Obligations (Amendment etc) (EU Exit) Regulations 2019, SI 2019/834, reg 10(1), (9), as from exit day (as defined in the European Union (Withdrawal) Act 2018, s 20) and only in so far as this Regulation will apply in the UK after that date by virtue of s 3 of the 2018 Act.

[3.451]
Article 24
Relationship with the Rome Convention

1. This Regulation shall replace the Rome Convention in the Member States, except as regards the territories of the Member States which fall within the territorial scope of that Convention and to which this Regulation does not apply pursuant to Article 299 of the Treaty.

2. In so far as this Regulation replaces the *provisions of the Rome Convention*, any reference to *that* Convention shall be understood as a reference to this Regulation.

NOTES

Para 1: substituted by the Law Applicable to Contractual Obligations and Non-Contractual Obligations (Amendment etc) (EU Exit) Regulations 2019, SI 2019/834, reg 10(1), (10)(a), as from exit day (as defined in the European Union (Withdrawal) Act 2018, s 20) and only in so far as this Regulation will apply in the UK after that date by virtue of s 3 of the 2018 Act, as follows—

"1. This Regulation replaces the provision made by section 2 of, and Schedule 1 to, the Contracts (Applicable Law) Act 1990.".

Para 2: for the words in italics in the first and second places there are substituted the words "provision made by section 2 of, and Schedule 1 to, the Contracts (Applicable Law) Act 1990" and "the Rome" respectively, by SI 2019/834, reg 10(1), (10)(b), as from exit day (as defined in the European Union (Withdrawal) Act 2018, s 20) and only in so far as this Regulation will apply in the UK after that date by virtue of s 3 of the 2018 Act.

[3.452]
Article 25
Relationship with existing international conventions

1. This Regulation shall not prejudice the application of international conventions to which *one or more Member States are parties* at the time when this Regulation *is adopted* and which lay down conflict-of-law rules relating to contractual obligations.

2. However, this Regulation shall, as between *Member States*, take precedence over conventions concluded exclusively between two or more of them in so far as such conventions concern matters governed by this Regulation.

NOTES

Para 1: for the words in italics in the first and second places there are substituted the words "the United Kingdom was a party" and "was adopted" respectively, by the Law Applicable to Contractual Obligations and Non-Contractual Obligations (Amendment etc) (EU Exit) Regulations 2019, SI 2019/834, reg 10(1), (11)(a), as from exit day (as defined in the European Union (Withdrawal) Act 2018, s 20) and only in so far as this Regulation will apply in the UK after that date by virtue of s 3 of the 2018 Act.

Para 2: for the words in italics there are substituted the words "relevant states", by SI 2019/834, reg 10(1), (11)(b), as from exit day (as defined in the European Union (Withdrawal) Act 2018, s 20) and only in so far as this Regulation will apply in the UK after that date by virtue of s 3 of the 2018 Act.

Articles 26, 27 (*Spent.*)

[3.453]
Article 28
Application in time

This Regulation shall apply to contracts concluded as from 17 December 2009.

CHAPTER IV FINAL PROVISIONS

[3.454]
Article 29
Entry into force and application

This Regulation shall enter into force on the 20th day following its publication in the Official Journal of the European Union.

It shall apply from 17 December 2009 except for Article 26 which shall apply from 17 June 2009.

This Regulation shall be binding in its entirety and directly applicable in the Member States in accordance with the Treaty establishing the European Community.

NOTES

Repealed by the Law Applicable to Contractual Obligations and Non-Contractual Obligations (Amendment etc) (EU Exit) Regulations 2019, SI 2019/834, reg 10(1), (13), as from exit day (as defined in the European Union (Withdrawal) Act 2018, s 20) and only in so far as this Regulation will apply in the UK after that date by virtue of s 3 of the 2018 Act.

DIRECTIVE OF THE EUROPEAN PARLIAMENT AND OF THE COUNCIL

(2008/94/EC)

of 22 October 2008

on the protection of employees in the event of the insolvency of their employer

(Codified version) Text with EEA relevance

[3.455]

NOTES

Date of publication in OJ: OJ L283, 28.10.2008, p 36.

This Directive consolidates and replaces Directive 80/987/EC as amended. A correlation table for the provisions of Directive 80/987/EC is at Annex II (at **[3.475]**). For the domestic implementation of the provisions consolidated see the Employment Rights Act 1996, ss 166–170 at **[1.1081]–[1.1085]** and Part XII at **[1.1097]**. The Directive came into force on 17 November 2008 (20 days after publication in the *Official Journal*): see Art 17 at **[3.472]**.

See *Harvey* E(16), G.

THE EUROPEAN PARLIAMENT AND THE COUNCIL OF THE EUROPEAN UNION,

Having regard to the Treaty establishing the European Community, and in particular Article 137(2) thereof,

Having regard to the proposal from the Commission,

Having regard to the opinion of the European Economic and Social Committee,[1]

After consultation of the Committee of the Regions,

Acting in accordance with the procedure laid down in Article 251 of the Treaty,[2]

Whereas:

(1) Council Directive 80/987/EEC of 20 October 1980 on the protection of employees in the event of the insolvency of their employer[3] has been substantially amended several times.[4] In the interests of clarity and rationality the said Directive should be codified.

(2) The Community Charter of Fundamental Social Rights for Workers adopted on 9 December 1989 states, in point 7, that the completion of the internal market must lead to an improvement in the living and working conditions of workers in the Community and that this improvement must cover, where necessary, the development of certain aspects of employment regulations such as procedures for collective redundancies and those regarding bankruptcies.

(3) It is necessary to provide for the protection of employees in the event of the insolvency of their employer and to ensure a minimum degree of protection, in particular in order to guarantee payment of their outstanding claims, while taking account of the need for balanced economic and social development in the Community. To this end, the Member States should establish a body which guarantees payment of the outstanding claims of the employees concerned.

(4) In order to ensure equitable protection for the employees concerned, the state of insolvency should be defined in the light of the legislative trends in the Member States and that concept should also include insolvency proceedings other than liquidation. In this context, Member States should, in order to determine the liability of the guarantee institution, be able to lay down that where an insolvency situation results in several insolvency proceedings, the situation is to be treated as a single insolvency procedure.

(5) It should be ensured that the employees referred to in Council Directive 97/81/EC of 15 December 1997 concerning the Framework Agreement on part-time work concluded by UNICE, CEEP and the ETUC,[5] Council Directive 1999/70/EC of 28 June 1999 concerning the framework agreement on fixed-term work concluded by the ETUC, UNICE and CEEP[6] and Council Directive 91/383/EEC of 25 June 1991 supplementing the measures to encourage improvements in the safety and health at work of workers with a fixed-duration employment relationship or a temporary employment relationship[7] are not excluded from the scope of this Directive.

(6) In order to ensure legal certainty for employees in the event of insolvency of undertakings pursuing their activities in a number of Member States, and to strengthen employees' rights in line with the established case-law of the Court of Justice of the European Communities, provisions should be laid down which expressly state which institution is responsible for meeting pay claims in these cases and establish as the aim of cooperation between the competent administrative authorities of the Member States the early settlement of employees' outstanding claims. Furthermore it is necessary to ensure that the relevant arrangements are properly implemented by making provision for collaboration between the competent administrative authorities in the Member States.

(7) Member States may set limitations on the responsibility of the guarantee institutions. Those limitations must be compatible with the social objective of the Directive and may take into account the different levels of claims.

(8) In order to make it easier to identify insolvency proceedings, in particular in situations with a cross-border dimension, provision should be made for the Member States to notify the Commission and the other Member States about the types of insolvency proceedings which give rise to intervention by the guarantee institution.

(9) Since the objective of the action to be taken cannot be sufficiently achieved by the Member States and can therefore be better achieved at Community level, the Community may adopt measures, in accordance with the principle of subsidiarity as set out in Article 5 of the Treaty. In accordance with the principle of proportionality, as set out in that Article, this Directive does not go beyond what is necessary in order to achieve that objective.

(10) The Commission should submit to the European Parliament and the Council a report on the implementation and application of this Directive in particular as regards the new forms of employment emerging in the Member States.

(11) This Directive should be without prejudice to the obligations of the Member States relating to the time-limits for transposition into national law and application of the Directives set out in Annex I, Part C,

NOTES

1 OJ C161, 13.7.2007, p 75.

2 Opinion of the European Parliament of 19 June 2007 (OJ C146 E, 12.6.2008, p 71) and Council Decision of 25 September 2008.

3 OJ L283, 28.10.1980, p 23.

4 See Annex I, Parts A and B.

5 OJ L14, 20.1.1998, p 9.

6 OJ L175, 10.7.1999, p 43.

7 OJ L206, 29.7.1991, p 19.

HAVE ADOPTED THIS DIRECTIVE:

CHAPTER I SCOPE AND DEFINITIONS

[3.456]
Article 1

1. This Directive shall apply to employees' claims arising from contracts of employment or employment relationships and existing against employers who are in a state of insolvency within the meaning of Article 2(1).
2. Member States may, by way of exception, exclude claims by certain categories of employee from the scope of this Directive, by virtue of the existence of other forms of guarantee if it is established that these offer the persons concerned a degree of protection equivalent to that resulting from this Directive.
[3. Where such provision already applies in their national legislation, Member States may continue to exclude domestic servants employed by a natural person from the scope of this Directive.]

NOTES

Para 3: substituted by Directive 2015/1794/EU, Art 1, as from 9 October 2015.

[3.457]
Article 2

1. For the purposes of this Directive, an employer shall be deemed to be in a state of insolvency where a request has been made for the opening of collective proceedings based on insolvency of the employer, as provided for under the laws, regulations and administrative provisions of a Member State, and involving the partial or total divestment of the employer's assets and the appointment of a liquidator or a person performing a similar task, and the authority which is competent pursuant to the said provisions has:
   (a) either decided to open the proceedings; or
   (b) established that the employer's undertaking or business has been definitively closed down and that the available assets are insufficient to warrant the opening of the proceedings.
2. This Directive is without prejudice to national law as regards the definition of the terms "employee", "employer", "pay", "right conferring immediate entitlement" and "right conferring prospective entitlement".

However, the Member States may not exclude from the scope of this Directive:
   (a) part-time employees within the meaning of Directive 97/81/EC;
   (b) employees with a fixed-term contract within the meaning of Directive 1999/70/EC;
   (c) employees with a temporary employment relationship within the meaning of Article 1(2) of Directive 91/383/EEC.
3. Member States may not set a minimum duration for the contract of employment or the employment relationship in order for employees to qualify for claims under this Directive.

4. This Directive does not prevent Member States from extending employee protection to other situations of insolvency, for example where payments have been de facto stopped on a permanent basis, established by proceedings different from those mentioned in paragraph 1 as provided for under national law.

Such procedures shall not however create a guarantee obligation for the institutions of the other Member States in the cases referred to in Chapter IV.

CHAPTER II PROVISIONS CONCERNING GUARANTEE INSTITUTIONS

[3.458]
Article 3
Member States shall take the measures necessary to ensure that guarantee institutions guarantee, subject to Article 4, payment of employees' outstanding claims resulting from contracts of employment or employment relationships, including, where provided for by national law, severance pay on termination of employment relationships.

The claims taken over by the guarantee institution shall be the outstanding pay claims relating to a period prior to and/or, as applicable, after a given date determined by the Member States.

[3.459]
Article 4
1. Member States shall have the option to limit the liability of the guarantee institutions referred to in Article 3.
2. If Member States exercise the option referred to in paragraph 1, they shall specify the length of the period for which outstanding claims are to be met by the guarantee institution. However, this may not be shorter than a period covering the remuneration of the last three months of the employment relationship prior to and/or after the date referred to in the second paragraph of Article 3.

Member States may include this minimum period of three months in a reference period with a duration of not less than six months.

Member States having a reference period of not less than 18 months may limit the period for which outstanding claims are met by the guarantee institution to eight weeks. In this case, those periods which are most favourable to the employee shall be used for the calculation of the minimum period.
3. Member States may set ceilings on the payments made by the guarantee institution. These ceilings must not fall below a level which is socially compatible with the social objective of this Directive.

If Member States exercise this option, they shall inform the Commission of the methods used to set the ceiling.

[3.460]
Article 5
Member States shall lay down detailed rules for the organisation, financing and operation of the guarantee institutions, complying with the following principles in particular:

(a) the assets of the institutions must be independent of the employers' operating capital and be inaccessible to proceedings for insolvency;
(b) employers must contribute to financing, unless it is fully covered by the public authorities;
(c) the institutions' liabilities must not depend on whether or not obligations to contribute to financing have been fulfilled.

CHAPTER III PROVISIONS CONCERNING SOCIAL SECURITY

[3.461]
Article 6
Member States may stipulate that Articles 3, 4 and 5 shall not apply to contributions due under national statutory social security schemes or under supplementary occupational or inter-occupational pension schemes outside the national statutory social security schemes.

[3.462]
Article 7
Member States shall take the measures necessary to ensure that non-payment of compulsory contributions due from the employer, before the onset of his insolvency, to their insurance institutions under national statutory social security schemes does not adversely affect employees' benefit entitlement in respect of these insurance institutions in so far as the employees' contributions have been deducted at source from the remuneration paid.

[3.463]
Article 8
Member States shall ensure that the necessary measures are taken to protect the interests of employees and of persons having already left the employer's undertaking or business at the date of the onset of the employer's insolvency in respect of rights conferring on them immediate or prospective entitlement to old-age benefits, including survivors' benefits, under supplementary occupational or inter-occupational pension schemes outside the national statutory social security schemes.

CHAPTER IV PROVISIONS CONCERNING TRANSNATIONAL SITUATIONS

[3.464]
Article 9
1. If an undertaking with activities in the territories of at least two Member States is in a state of insolvency within the meaning of Article 2(l), the institution responsible for meeting employees' outstanding claims shall be that in the Member State in whose territory they work or habitually work.
2. The extent of employees' rights shall be determined by the law governing the competent guarantee institution.
3. Member States shall take the measures necessary to ensure that, in the cases referred to in paragraph 1 of this Article, decisions taken in the context of insolvency proceedings referred to in Article 2(1), which have been requested in another Member State, are taken into account when determining the employer's state of insolvency within the meaning of this Directive.

[3.465]
Article 10
1. For the purposes of implementing Article 9, Member States shall make provision for the sharing of relevant information between their competent administrative authorities and/or the guarantee institutions mentioned in the first paragraph of Article 3, making it possible in particular to inform the guarantee institution responsible for meeting the employees' outstanding claims.
2. Member States shall notify the Commission and the other Member States of the contact details of their competent administrative authorities and/or guarantee institutions. The Commission shall make that information publicly accessible.

CHAPTER V GENERAL AND FINAL PROVISIONS

[3.466]
Article 11
This Directive shall not affect the option of Member States to apply or introduce laws, regulations or administrative provisions which are more favourable to employees.

Implementation of this Directive shall not under any circumstances be sufficient grounds for a regression in relation to the current situation in the Member States and in relation to the general level of protection of employees in the area covered by it.

[3.467]
Article 12
This Directive shall not affect the option of Member States:
- (a) to take the measures necessary to avoid abuses;
- (b) to refuse or reduce the liability referred to in the first paragraph of Article 3 or the guarantee obligation referred to in Article 7 if it appears that fulfilment of the obligation is unjustifiable because of the existence of special links between the employee and the employer and of common interests resulting in collusion between them;
- (c) to refuse or reduce the liability referred to in the first paragraph of Article 3 or the guarantee obligation referred to in Article 7 in cases where the employee, on his or her own or together with his or her close relatives, was the owner of an essential part of the employer's undertaking or business and had a considerable influence on its activities.

[3.468]
Article 13
Member States shall notify the Commission and the other Member States of the types of national insolvency proceedings falling within the scope of this Directive, and of any amendments relating thereto.

The Commission shall publish these communications in the *Official Journal of the European Union*.

[3.469]
Article 14
Member States shall communicate to the Commission the text of the laws, regulations and administrative provisions which they adopt in the field covered by this Directive.

[3.470]
Article 15
By 8 October 2010 at the latest, the Commission shall submit to the European Parliament and to the Council a report on the implementation and application in the Member States of Articles 1 to 4, 9 and 10, Article 11, second paragraph, Article 12, point (c), and Articles 13 and 14.

[3.471]
Article 16
Directive 80/987/EEC, as amended by the acts listed in Annex I, is repealed, without prejudice to the obligations of the Member States relating to the time-limits for transposition into national law and application of the Directives set out in Annex I, Part C.

References to the repealed Directive shall be construed as references to this Directive and shall be read in accordance with the correlation table in Annex II.

[3.472]
Article 17
This Directive shall enter into force on the 20th day following its publication in the *Official Journal of the European Union*.

[3.473]
Article 18
This Directive is addressed to the Member States.

ANNEX I

PART A REPEALED DIRECTIVE WITH ITS SUCCESSIVE AMENDMENTS

(referred to in Article 16)
[3.474]

Council Directive 80/987/EEC	(OJ L283, 28.10.1980, p 23).
Council Directive 87/164/EEC	(OJ L66, 11.3.1987, p 11).
Directive 2002/74/EC of the European Parliament and of the Council	(OJ L270, 8.10.2002, p 10).

PART B NON-REPEALED AMENDING ACT

(referred to in Article 16)

1994 Act of Accession

PART C TIME-LIMITS FOR TRANSPOSITION INTO NATIONAL LAW AND APPLICATION

(referred to in Article 16)

Directive	*Time-limit for transposition*	*Date of application*
80/987/EEC	23 October 1983	
87/164/EEC		1 January 1986
2002/74/EC	7 October 2005	

ANNEX II
CORRELATION TABLE

[3.475]

Directive 80/987/EEC	*This Directive*
Article 1	Article 1
Article 2	Article 2
Article 3	Article 3
Article 4	Article 4
Article 5	Article 5
Article 6	Article 6
Article 7	Article 7
Article 8	Article 8
Article 8a	Article 9
Article 8b	Article 10
Article 9	Article 11
Article 10	Article 12
Article 10a	Article 13
Article 11(1)	—
Article 11(2)	Article 14
Article 12	
—	Article 15
—	Article 16
—	Article 17
Article 13	Article 18
—	Annex I
—	Annex II

DIRECTIVE OF THE EUROPEAN PARLIAMENT AND OF THE COUNCIL

(2008/104/EC)
of 19 November 2008

on temporary agency work

[3.476]

NOTES

Date of publication in OJ: OJ L327, 5.12.2008, p 9.

For the domestic implementation of this Directive see the Agency Workers Regulations 2010, SI 2010/93 at **[2.1085]**.

See *Harvey* AI(4).

THE EUROPEAN PARLIAMENT AND THE COUNCIL OF THE EUROPEAN UNION,

Having regard to the Treaty establishing the European Community, and in particular Article 137(2) thereof,

Having regard to the proposal from the Commission,

Having regard to the opinion of the European Economic and Social Committee,[1]

After consulting the Committee of the Regions,

Acting in accordance with the procedure laid down in Article 251 of the Treaty,[2]

Whereas:

(1) This Directive respects the fundamental rights and complies with the principles recognised by the Charter of Fundamental Rights of the European Union.[3] In particular, it is designed to ensure full compliance with Article 31 of the Charter, which provides that every worker has the right to working conditions which respect his or her health, safety and dignity, and to limitation of maximum working hours, to daily and weekly rest periods and to an annual period of paid leave.

(2) The Community Charter of the Fundamental Social Rights of Workers provides, in point 7 thereof, inter alia, that the completion of the internal market must lead to an improvement in the living and working conditions of workers in the European Community; this process will be achieved by harmonising progress on these conditions, mainly in respect of forms of work such as fixed-term contract work, part-time work, temporary agency work and seasonal work.

(3) On 27 September 1995, the Commission consulted management and labour at Community level in accordance with Article 138(2) of the Treaty on the course of action to be adopted at Community level with regard to flexibility of working hours and job security of workers.

(4) After that consultation, the Commission considered that Community action was advisable and on 9 April 1996, further consulted management and labour in accordance with Article 138(3) of the Treaty on the content of the envisaged proposal.

(5) In the introduction to the framework agreement on fixed-term work concluded on 18 March 1999, the signatories indicated their intention to consider the need for a similar agreement on temporary agency work and decided not to include temporary agency workers in the Directive on fixed-term work.

(6) The general cross-sector organisations, namely the Union of Industrial and Employers' Confederations of Europe (UNICE),[4] the European Centre of Enterprises with Public Participation and of Enterprises of General Economic Interest (CEEP) and the European Trade Union Confederation (ETUC), informed the Commission in a joint letter of 29 May 2000 of their wish to initiate the process provided for in Article 139 of the Treaty. By a further joint letter of 28 February 2001, they asked the Commission to extend the deadline referred to in Article 138(4) by one month. The Commission granted this request and extended the negotiation deadline until 15 March 2001.

(7) On 21 May 2001, the social partners acknowledged that their negotiations on temporary agency work had not produced any agreement.

(8) In March 2005, the European Council considered it vital to relaunch the Lisbon Strategy and to refocus its priorities on growth and employment. The Council approved the Integrated Guidelines for Growth and Jobs 2005–2008, which seek, inter alia, to promote flexibility combined with employment security and to reduce labour market segmentation, having due regard to the role of the social partners.

(9) In accordance with the Communication from the Commission on the Social Agenda covering the period up to 2010, which was welcomed by the March 2005 European Council as a contribution towards achieving the Lisbon Strategy objectives by reinforcing the European social model, the European Council considered that new forms of work organisation and a greater diversity of contractual arrangements for workers and businesses, better combining flexibility with security, would contribute to adaptability. Furthermore, the December 2007 European Council endorsed the agreed common principles of flexicurity, which strike a balance between flexibility and security in the labour market and help both workers and employers to seize the opportunities offered by globalisation.

(10) There are considerable differences in the use of temporary agency work and in the legal situation, status and working conditions of temporary agency workers within the European Union.

(11) Temporary agency work meets not only undertakings' needs for flexibility but also the need of employees to reconcile their working and private lives. It thus contributes to job creation and to participation and integration in the labour market.

(12) This Directive establishes a protective framework for temporary agency workers which is non-discriminatory, transparent and proportionate, while respecting the diversity of labour markets and industrial relations.

(13) Council Directive 91/383/EEC of 25 June 1991 supplementing the measures to encourage improvements in the safety and health at work of workers with a fixed-duration employment relationship or a temporary employment relationship[5] establishes the safety and health provisions applicable to temporary agency workers.

(14) The basic working and employment conditions applicable to temporary agency workers should be at least those which would apply to such workers if they were recruited by the user undertaking to occupy the same job.

(15) Employment contracts of an indefinite duration are the general form of employment relationship. In the case of workers who have a permanent contract with their temporary-work agency, and in view of the special protection such a contract offers, provision should be made to permit exemptions from the rules applicable in the user undertaking.

(16) In order to cope in a flexible way with the diversity of labour markets and industrial relations, Member States may allow the social partners to define working and employment conditions, provided that the overall level of protection for temporary agency workers is respected.

(17) Furthermore, in certain limited circumstances, Member States should, on the basis of an agreement concluded by the social partners at national level, be able to derogate within limits from the principle of equal treatment, so long as an adequate level of protection is provided.

(18) The improvement in the minimum protection for temporary agency workers should be accompanied by a review of any restrictions or prohibitions which may have been imposed on temporary agency work. These may be justified only on grounds of the general interest regarding, in particular the protection of workers, the requirements of safety and health at work and the need to ensure that the labour market functions properly and that abuses are prevented.

(19) This Directive does not affect the autonomy of the social partners nor should it affect relations between the social partners, including the right to negotiate and conclude collective agreements in accordance with national law and practices while respecting prevailing Community law.

(20) The provisions of this Directive on restrictions or prohibitions on temporary agency work are without prejudice to national legislation or practices that prohibit workers on strike being replaced by temporary agency workers.

(21) Member States should provide for administrative or judicial procedures to safeguard temporary agency workers' rights and should provide for effective, dissuasive and proportionate penalties for breaches of the obligations laid down in this Directive.

(22) This Directive should be implemented in compliance with the provisions of the Treaty regarding the freedom to provide services and the freedom of establishment and without prejudice to Directive 96/71/EC of the European Parliament and of the Council of 16 December 1996 concerning the posting of workers in the framework of the provision of services.[6]

(23) Since the objective of this Directive, namely to establish a harmonised Community-level framework for protection for temporary agency workers, cannot be sufficiently achieved by the Member States and can therefore, by reason of the scale or effects of the action, be better achieved at Community level by introducing minimum requirements applicable throughout the Community, the Community may adopt measures in accordance with the principle of subsidiarity as set out in Article 5 of the Treaty. In accordance with the principle of proportionality, as set out in that Article, this Directive does not go beyond what is necessary in order to achieve that objective,

NOTES

1 OJ 61, 14.3.2003, p 124.

2 Opinion of the European Parliament of 21 November 2002 (OJ C25E, 29.1.2004, p 368), Council Common Position of 15 September 2008 and Position of the European Parliament of 22 October 2008 (not yet published in the Official Journal).

3 OJ C303, 14.12.2007, p 1.

4 UNICE changed its name to BUSINESSEUROPE in January 2007.

5 OJ L206, 29.7.1991, p 19.

6 OJ L18, 21.1.1997, p 1.

HAVE ADOPTED THIS DIRECTIVE:

CHAPTER I GENERAL PROVISIONS

[3.477]
Article 1
Scope

1. This Directive applies to workers with a contract of employment or employment relationship with a temporary-work agency who are assigned to user undertakings to work temporarily under their supervision and direction.
2. This Directive applies to public and private undertakings which are temporary-work agencies or user undertakings engaged in economic activities whether or not they are operating for gain.
3. Member States may, after consulting the social partners, provide that this Directive does not apply to employment contracts or relationships concluded under a specific public or publicly supported vocational training, integration or retraining programme.

[3.478]
Article 2
Aim

The purpose of this Directive is to ensure the protection of temporary agency workers and to improve the quality of temporary agency work by ensuring that the principle of equal treatment, as set out in Article 5, is applied to temporary agency workers, and by recognising temporary-work agencies as employers, while taking into account the need to establish a suitable framework for the use of temporary agency work with a view to contributing effectively to the creation of jobs and to the development of flexible forms of working.

[3.479]
Article 3
Definitions

1. For the purposes of this Directive:
   (a) "worker" means any person who, in the Member State concerned, is protected as a worker under national employment law;
   (b) "temporary-work agency" means any natural or legal person who, in compliance with national law, concludes contracts of employment or employment relationships with temporary agency workers in order to assign them to user undertakings to work there temporarily under their supervision and direction;
   (c) "temporary agency worker" means a worker with a contract of employment or an employment relationship with a temporary-work agency with a view to being assigned to a user undertaking to work temporarily under its supervision and direction;
   (d) "user undertaking" means any natural or legal person for whom and under the supervision and direction of whom a temporary agency worker works temporarily;
   (e) "assignment" means the period during which the temporary agency worker is placed at the user undertaking to work temporarily under its supervision and direction;
   (f) "basic working and employment conditions" means working and employment conditions laid down by legislation, regulations, administrative provisions, collective agreements and/or other binding general provisions in force in the user undertaking relating to:
      (i) the duration of working time, overtime, breaks, rest periods, night work, holidays and public holidays;
      (ii) pay.
2. This Directive shall be without prejudice to national law as regards the definition of pay, contract of employment, employment relationship or worker.

Member States shall not exclude from the scope of this Directive workers, contracts of employment or employment relationships solely because they relate to part-time workers, fixed-term contract workers or persons with a contract of employment or employment relationship with a temporary-work agency.

[3.480]
Article 4
Review of restrictions or prohibitions

1. Prohibitions or restrictions on the use of temporary agency work shall be justified only on grounds of general interest relating in particular to the protection of temporary agency workers, the requirements of health and safety at work or the need to ensure that the labour market functions properly and abuses are prevented.
2. By 5 December 2011, Member States shall, after consulting the social partners in accordance with national legislation, collective agreements and practices, review any restrictions or prohibitions on the use of temporary agency work in order to verify whether they are justified on the grounds mentioned in paragraph 1.
3. If such restrictions or prohibitions are laid down by collective agreements, the review referred to in paragraph 2 may be carried out by the social partners who have negotiated the relevant agreement.
4. Paragraphs 1, 2 and 3 shall be without prejudice to national requirements with regard to registration, licensing, certification, financial guarantees or monitoring of temporary-work agencies.
5. The Member States shall inform the Commission of the results of the review referred to in paragraphs 2 and 3 by 5 December 2011.

CHAPTER II EMPLOYMENT AND WORKING CONDITIONS

[3.481]
Article 5
The principle of equal treatment

1. The basic working and employment conditions of temporary agency workers shall be, for the duration of their assignment at a user undertaking, at least those that would apply if they had been recruited directly by that undertaking to occupy the same job.

For the purposes of the application of the first subparagraph, the rules in force in the user undertaking on:

(a) protection of pregnant women and nursing mothers and protection of children and young people; and
(b) equal treatment for men and women and any action to combat any discrimination based on sex, race or ethnic origin, religion, beliefs, disabilities, age or sexual orientation;

must be complied with as established by legislation, regulations, administrative provisions, collective agreements and/or any other general provisions.

2. As regards pay, Member States may, after consulting the social partners, provide that an exemption be made to the principle established in paragraph 1 where temporary agency workers who have a permanent contract of employment with a temporary-work agency continue to be paid in the time between assignments.

3. Member States may, after consulting the social partners, give them, at the appropriate level and subject to the conditions laid down by the Member States, the option of upholding or concluding collective agreements which, while respecting the overall protection of temporary agency workers, may establish arrangements concerning the working and employment conditions of temporary agency workers which may differ from those referred to in paragraph 1.

4. Provided that an adequate level of protection is provided for temporary agency workers, Member States in which there is either no system in law for declaring collective agreements universally applicable or no such system in law or practice for extending their provisions to all similar undertakings in a certain sector or geographical area, may, after consulting the social partners at national level and on the basis of an agreement concluded by them, establish arrangements concerning the basic working and employment conditions which derogate from the principle established in paragraph 1. Such arrangements may include a qualifying period for equal treatment.

The arrangements referred to in this paragraph shall be in conformity with Community legislation and shall be sufficiently precise and accessible to allow the sectors and firms concerned to identify and comply with their obligations. In particular, Member States shall specify, in application of Article 3(2), whether occupational social security schemes, including pension, sick pay or financial participation schemes are included in the basic working and employment conditions referred to in paragraph 1. Such arrangements shall also be without prejudice to agreements at national, regional, local or sectoral level that are no less favourable to workers.

5. Member States shall take appropriate measures, in accordance with national law and/or practice, with a view to preventing misuse in the application of this Article and, in particular, to preventing successive assignments designed to circumvent the provisions of this Directive. They shall inform the Commission about such measures.

[3.482]
Article 6
Access to employment, collective facilities and vocational training

1. Temporary agency workers shall be informed of any vacant posts in the user undertaking to give them the same opportunity as other workers in that undertaking to find permanent employment. Such information may be provided by a general announcement in a suitable place in the undertaking for which, and under whose supervision, temporary agency workers are engaged.

2. Member States shall take any action required to ensure that any clauses prohibiting or having the effect of preventing the conclusion of a contract of employment or an employment relationship between the user undertaking and the temporary agency worker after his assignment are null and void or may be declared null and void.

This paragraph is without prejudice to provisions under which temporary agencies receive a reasonable level of recompense for services rendered to user undertakings for the assignment, recruitment and training of temporary agency workers.

3. Temporary-work agencies shall not charge workers any fees in exchange for arranging for them to be recruited by a user undertaking, or for concluding a contract of employment or an employment relationship with a user undertaking after carrying out an assignment in that undertaking.

4. Without prejudice to Article 5(1), temporary agency workers shall be given access to the amenities or collective facilities in the user undertaking, in particular any canteen, child-care facilities and transport services, under the same conditions as workers employed directly by the undertaking, unless the difference in treatment is justified by objective reasons.

5. Member States shall take suitable measures or shall promote dialogue between the social partners, in accordance with their national traditions and practices, in order to:

(a) improve temporary agency workers' access to training and to child-care facilities in the temporary-work agencies, even in the periods between their assignments, in order to enhance their career development and employability;
(b) improve temporary agency workers' access to training for user undertakings' workers.

[3.483]
Article 7
Representation of temporary agency workers

1. Temporary agency workers shall count, under conditions established by the Member States, for the purposes of calculating the threshold above which bodies representing workers provided for under Community and national law and collective agreements are to be formed at the temporary-work agency.
2. Member States may provide that, under conditions that they define, temporary agency workers count for the purposes of calculating the threshold above which bodies representing workers provided for by Community and national law and collective agreements are to be formed in the user undertaking, in the same way as if they were workers employed directly for the same period of time by the user undertaking.
3. Those Member States which avail themselves of the option provided for in paragraph 2 shall not be obliged to implement the provisions of paragraph 1.

[3.484]
Article 8
Information of workers' representatives

Without prejudice to national and Community provisions on information and consultation which are more stringent and/or more specific and, in particular, Directive 2002/14/EC of the European Parliament and of the Council of 11 March 2002 establishing a general framework for informing and consulting employees in the European Community,[1] the user undertaking must provide suitable information on the use of temporary agency workers when providing information on the employment situation in that undertaking to bodies representing workers set up in accordance with national and Community legislation.

NOTES

[1] OJ L80, 23.3.2002, p. 29.

CHAPTER III FINAL PROVISIONS

[3.485]
Article 9
Minimum requirements

1. This Directive is without prejudice to the Member States' right to apply or introduce legislative, regulatory or administrative provisions which are more favourable to workers or to promote or permit collective agreements concluded between the social partners which are more favourable to workers.
2. The implementation of this Directive shall under no circumstances constitute sufficient grounds for justifying a reduction in the general level of protection of workers in the fields covered by this Directive. This is without prejudice to the rights of Member States and/or management and labour to lay down, in the light of changing circumstances, different legislative, regulatory or contractual arrangements to those prevailing at the time of the adoption of this Directive, provided always that the minimum requirements laid down in this Directive are respected.

[3.486]
Article 10
Penalties

1. Member States shall provide for appropriate measures in the event of non-compliance with this Directive by temporary-work agencies or user undertakings. In particular, they shall ensure that adequate administrative or judicial procedures are available to enable the obligations deriving from this Directive to be enforced.
2. Member States shall lay down rules on penalties applicable in the event of infringements of national provisions implementing this Directive and shall take all necessary measures to ensure that they are applied. The penalties provided for must be effective, proportionate and dissuasive. Member States shall notify these provisions to the Commission by 5 December 2011. Member States shall notify to the Commission any subsequent amendments to those provisions in good time. They shall, in particular, ensure that workers and/or their representatives have adequate means of enforcing the obligations under this Directive.

[3.487]
Article 11
Implementation

1. Member States shall adopt and publish the laws, regulations and administrative provisions necessary to comply with this Directive by 5 December 2011, or shall ensure that the social partners introduce the necessary provisions by way of an agreement, whereby the Member States must make all the necessary arrangements to enable them to guarantee at any time that the objectives of this Directive are being attained. They shall forthwith inform the Commission thereof.
2. When Member States adopt these measures, they shall contain a reference to this Directive or shall be accompanied by such reference on the occasion of their official publication. The methods of making such reference shall be laid down by Member States.

[3.488]
Article 12
Review by the Commission
By 5 December 2013, the Commission shall, in consultation with the Member States and social partners at Community level, review the application of this Directive with a view to proposing, where appropriate, the necessary amendments.

[3.489]
Article 13
Entry into force
This Directive shall enter into force on the day of its publication in the *Official Journal of the European Union*.

[3.490]
Article 14
Addressees
This Directive is addressed to the Member States.

DIRECTIVE OF THE EUROPEAN PARLIAMENT AND OF THE COUNCIL

(2009/38/EC)

of 6 May 2009

on the establishment of a European Works Council or a procedure in Community-scale undertakings and Community-scale groups of undertakings for the purposes of informing and consulting employees

(Recast) (Text with EEA relevance)

[3.491]

NOTES
Date of publication in OJ: OJ L122, 16.05.2009, p 28.
This Directive is a recast replacement of Directive 94/45/EC which was repealed and replaced on 6 June 2011 following the coming into force of this Directive on 5 June 2011: see Art 16(1) at **[3.507]** and Art 17 at **[3.508]**. A Table of Correlations for the previous Directive is at Annex III (at **[3.514]**).
For the domestic implementation of this Directive see the Transnational Information and Consultation of Employees Regulations 1999, SI 1999/3323 (as amended to implement this Directive) at **[2.472]**.
See *Harvey* NIII(3).

THE EUROPEAN PARLIAMENT AND THE COUNCIL OF THE EUROPEAN UNION,
Having regard to the Treaty establishing the European Community, and in particular Article 137 thereof,
Having regard to the proposal from the Commission,
Having regard to the opinion of the European Economic and Social Committee,[1]
Having consulted the Committee of the Regions,
Acting in accordance with the procedure referred to in Article 251 of the Treaty,[2]
Whereas:

(1) A number of substantive changes are to be made to Council Directive 94/45/EC of 22 September 1994 on the establishment of a European Works Council or a procedure in Community-scale undertakings and Community-scale groups of undertakings for the purposes of informing and consulting employees.[3] In the interests of clarity, that Directive should be recast.

(2) Pursuant to Article 15 of Directive 94/45/EC, the Commission has, in consultation with the Member States and with management and labour at European level, reviewed the operation of that Directive and, in particular, examined whether the workforce size thresholds are appropriate, with a view to proposing suitable amendments where necessary.

(3) Having consulted the Member States and management and labour at European level, the Commission submitted, on 4 April 2000, a report on the application of Directive 94/45/EC to the European Parliament and to the Council.

(4) Pursuant to Article 138(2) of the Treaty, the Commission consulted management and labour at Community level on the possible direction of Community action in this area.

(5) Following this consultation, the Commission considered that Community action was advisable and again consulted management and labour at Community level on the content of the planned proposal, pursuant to Article 138(3) of the Treaty.

(6) Following this second phase of consultation, management and labour have not informed the Commission of their shared wish to initiate the process which might lead to the conclusion of an agreement, as provided for in Article 138(4) of the Treaty.

(7) It is necessary to modernise Community legislation on transnational information and consultation of employees with a view to ensuring the effectiveness of employees' transnational information and consultation rights, increasing the proportion of European Works Councils established while enabling the continuous functioning of existing agreements, resolving the problems encountered in the practical application of Directive 94/45/EC and remedying the lack of legal certainty resulting from some of its provisions or the absence of certain provisions, and ensuring that Community legislative instruments on information and consultation of employees are better linked.

(8) Pursuant to Article 136 of the Treaty, one particular objective of the Community and the Member States is to promote dialogue between management and labour.

(9) This Directive is part of the Community framework intended to support and complement the action taken by Member States in the field of information and consultation of employees. This framework should keep to a minimum the burden on undertakings or establishments while ensuring the effective exercise of the rights granted.

(10) The functioning of the internal market involves a process of concentrations of undertakings, cross-border mergers, take-overs, joint ventures and, consequently, a transnationalisation of undertakings and groups of undertakings. If economic activities are to develop in a harmonious fashion, undertakings and groups of undertakings operating in two or more Member States must inform and consult the representatives of those of their employees who are affected by their decisions.

(11) Procedures for informing and consulting employees as embodied in legislation or practice in the Member States are often not geared to the transnational structure of the entity which takes the decisions affecting those employees. This may lead to the unequal treatment of employees affected by decisions within one and the same undertaking or group of undertakings.

(12) Appropriate provisions must be adopted to ensure that the employees of Community-scale undertakings or Community-scale groups of undertakings are properly informed and consulted when decisions which affect them are taken in a Member State other than that in which they are employed.

(13) In order to guarantee that the employees of undertakings or groups of undertakings operating in two or more Member States are properly informed and consulted, it is necessary to set up European Works Councils or to create other suitable procedures for the transnational information and consultation of employees.

(14) The arrangements for informing and consulting employees need to be defined and implemented in such a way as to ensure their effectiveness with regard to the provisions of this Directive. To that end, informing and consulting the European Works Council should make it possible for it to give an opinion to the undertaking in a timely fashion, without calling into question the ability of undertakings to adapt. Only dialogue at the level where directions are prepared and effective involvement of employees' representatives make it possible to anticipate and manage change.

(15) Workers and their representatives must be guaranteed information and consultation at the relevant level of management and representation, according to the subject under discussion. To achieve this, the competence and scope of action of a European Works Council must be distinct from that of national representative bodies and must be limited to transnational matters.

(16) The transnational character of a matter should be determined by taking account of both the scope of its potential effects, and the level of management and representation that it involves. For this purpose, matters which concern the entire undertaking or group or at least two Member States are considered to be transnational. These include matters which, regardless of the number of Member States involved, are of importance for the European workforce in terms of the scope of their potential effects or which involve transfers of activities between Member States.

(17) It is necessary to have a definition of "controlling undertaking" relating solely to this Directive, without prejudice to the definitions of "group" or "control" in other acts.

(18) The mechanisms for informing and consulting employees in undertakings or groups of undertakings operating in two or more Member States must encompass all of the establishments or, as the case may be, the group's undertakings located within the Member States, regardless of whether the undertaking or the group's controlling undertaking has its central management inside or outside the territory of the Member States.

(19) In accordance with the principle of autonomy of the parties, it is for the representatives of employees and the management of the undertaking or the group's controlling undertaking to determine by agreement the nature, composition, the function, mode of operation, procedures and financial resources of European Works Councils or other information and consultation procedures so as to suit their own particular circumstances.

(20) In accordance with the principle of subsidiarity, it is for the Member States to determine who the employees' representatives are and in particular to provide, if they consider appropriate, for a balanced representation of different categories of employees.

(21) It is necessary to clarify the concepts of information and consultation of employees, in accordance with the definitions in the most recent Directives on this subject and those which apply within a national framework, with the objectives of reinforcing the effectiveness of dialogue at transnational level, permitting suitable linkage between the national and transnational levels of dialogue and ensuring the legal certainty required for the application of this Directive.

(22) The definition of "information" needs to take account of the goal of allowing employees representatives to carry out an appropriate examination, which implies that the information be provided at such time, in such fashion and with such content as are appropriate without slowing down the decision-making process in undertakings.

(23) The definition of "consultation" needs to take account of the goal of allowing for the expression of an opinion which will be useful to the decision-making process, which implies that the consultation must take place at such time, in such fashion and with such content as are appropriate.

(24) The information and consultation provisions laid down in this Directive must be implemented in the case of an undertaking or a group's controlling undertaking which has its central management outside the territory of the Member States by its representative agent, to be designated if necessary, in one of the Member States or, in the absence of such an agent, by the establishment or controlled undertaking employing the greatest number of employees in the Member States.

(25) The responsibility of undertakings or groups of undertakings in the transmission of the information required to commence negotiations must be specified in a way that enables employees to determine whether the undertaking or group of undertakings where they work is a Community-scale undertaking or group of undertakings and to make the necessary contacts to draw up a request to commence negotiations.

(26) The special negotiating body must represent employees from the various Member States in a balanced fashion. Employees' representatives must be able to cooperate to define their positions in relation to negotiations with the central management.

(27) Recognition must be given to the role that recognised trade union organisations can play in negotiating and renegotiating the constituent agreements of European Works Councils, providing support to employees' representatives who express a need for such support. In order to enable them to monitor the establishment of new European Works Councils and promote best practice, competent trade union and employers' organisations recognised as European social partners shall be informed of the commencement of negotiations. Recognised competent European trade union and employers' organisations are those social partner organisations that are consulted by the Commission under Article 138 of the Treaty. The list of those organisations is updated and published by the Commission.

(28) The agreements governing the establishment and operation of European Works Councils must include the methods for modifying, terminating, or renegotiating them when necessary, particularly where the make-up or structure of the undertaking or group of undertakings is modified.

(29) Such agreements must lay down the arrangements for linking the national and transnational levels of information and consultation of employees appropriate for the particular conditions of the undertaking or group of undertakings. The arrangements must be defined in such a way that they respect the competences and areas of action of the employee representation bodies, in particular with regard to anticipating and managing change.

(30) Those agreements must provide, where necessary, for the establishment and operation of a select committee in order to permit coordination and greater effectiveness of the regular activities of the European Works Council, together with information and consultation at the earliest opportunity where exceptional circumstances arise.

(31) Employees' representatives may decide not to seek the setting-up of a European Works Council or the parties concerned may decide on other procedures for the transnational information and consultation of employees.

(32) Provision should be made for certain subsidiary requirements to apply should the parties so decide or in the event of the central management refusing to initiate negotiations or in the absence of agreement subsequent to such negotiations.

(33) In order to perform their representative role fully and to ensure that the European Works Council is useful, employees' representatives must report to the employees whom they represent and must be able to receive the training they require.

(34) Provision should be made for the employees' representatives acting within the framework of this Directive to enjoy, when exercising their functions, the same protection and guarantees as those provided to employees' representatives by the legislation and/or practice of the country of employment. They must not be subject to any discrimination as a result of the lawful exercise of their activities and must enjoy adequate protection as regards dismissal and other sanctions.

(35) The Member States must take appropriate measures in the event of failure to comply with the obligations laid down in this Directive.

(36) In accordance with the general principles of Community law, administrative or judicial procedures, as well as sanctions that are effective, dissuasive and proportionate in relation to the seriousness of the offence, should be applicable in cases of infringement of the obligations arising from this Directive.

(37) For reasons of effectiveness, consistency and legal certainty, there is a need for linkage between the Directives and the levels of informing and consulting employees established by Community and national law and/or practice. Priority must be given to negotiations on these procedures for linking information within each undertaking or group of undertakings. If there are no agreements on this subject and where decisions likely to lead to substantial changes in work organisation or contractual relations are envisaged, the process must be conducted at both national and European level in such a way that it respects the competences and areas of action of the employee representation bodies. Opinions expressed by the

European Works Council should be without prejudice to the competence of the central management to carry out the necessary consultations in accordance with the schedules provided for in national legislation and/or practice. National legislation and/or practice may have to be adapted to ensure that the European Works Council can, where applicable, receive information earlier or at the same time as the national employee representation bodies, but must not reduce the general level of protection of employees.

(38) This Directive should be without prejudice to the information and consultation procedures referred to in Directive 2002/14/EC of the European Parliament and of the Council of 11 March 2002 establishing a general framework for informing and consulting employees in the European Community[4] and to the specific procedures referred to in Article 2 of Council Directive 98/59/EC of 20 July 1998 on the approximation of the laws of the Member States relating to collective redundancies[5] and Article 7 of Council Directive 2001/23/EC of 12 March 2001 on the approximation of the laws of the Member States relating to the safeguarding of employees' rights in the event of transfers of undertakings, businesses or parts of undertakings or businesses.[6]

(39) Special treatment should be accorded to Community-scale undertakings and groups of undertakings in which there existed, on 22 September 1996, an agreement, covering the entire workforce, providing for the transnational information and consultation of employees.

(40) Where the structure of the undertaking or group of undertakings changes significantly, for example, due to a merger, acquisition or division, the existing European Works Council(s) must be adapted. This adaptation must be carried out as a priority pursuant to the clauses of the applicable agreement, if such clauses permit the required adaptation to be carried out. If this is not the case and a request establishing the need is made, negotiations, in which the members of the existing European Works Council(s) must be involved, will commence on a new agreement. In order to permit the information and consultation of employees during the often decisive period when the structure is changed, the existing European Works Council(s) must be able to continue to operate, possibly with adaptations, until a new agreement is concluded. Once a new agreement is signed, the previously established councils must be dissolved, and the agreements instituting them must be terminated, regardless of their provisions on validity or termination.

(41) Unless this adaptation clause is applied, the agreements in force should be allowed to continue in order to avoid their obligatory renegotiation when this would be unnecessary. Provision should be made so that, as long as agreements concluded prior to 22 September 1996 under Article 13(1) of Directive 94/45/EC or under Article 3(1) of Directive 97/74/EC[7] remain in force, the obligations arising from this Directive should not apply to them. Furthermore, this Directive does not establish a general obligation to renegotiate agreements concluded pursuant to Article 6 of Directive 94/45/EC between 22 September 1996 and 5 June 2011.

(42) Without prejudice to the possibility of the parties to decide otherwise, a European Works Council set up in the absence of agreement between the parties must, in order to fulfil the objective of this Directive, be kept informed and consulted on the activities of the undertaking or group of undertakings so that it may assess the possible impact on employees' interests in at least two different Member States. To that end, the undertaking or controlling undertaking must be required to communicate to the employees' appointed representatives general information concerning the interests of employees and information relating more specifically to those aspects of the activities of the undertaking or group of undertakings which affect employees' interests. The European Works Council must be able to deliver an opinion at the end of the meeting.

(43) Certain decisions having a significant effect on the interests of employees must be the subject of information and consultation of the employees' appointed representatives as soon as possible.

(44) The content of the subsidiary requirements which apply in the absence of an agreement and serve as a reference in the negotiations must be clarified and adapted to developments in the needs and practices relating to transnational information and consultation. A distinction should be made between fields where information must be provided and fields where the European Works Council must also be consulted, which involves the possibility of obtaining a reasoned response to any opinions expressed. To enable the select committee to play the necessary coordinating role and to deal effectively with exceptional circumstances, that committee must be able to have up to five members and be able to consult regularly.

(45) Since the objective of this Directive, namely the improvement of the right to information and to consultation of employees in Community-scale undertakings and Community-scale groups of undertakings, cannot be sufficiently achieved by the Member States and can therefore be better achieved at Community level, the Community may adopt measures, in accordance with the principle of subsidiarity as set out in Article 5 of the Treaty. In accordance with the principle of proportionality as set out in that Article, this Directive does not go beyond what is necessary in order to achieve that objective.

(46) This Directive respects fundamental rights and observes in particular the principles recognised by the Charter of Fundamental Rights of the European Union. In particular, this Directive seeks to ensure full respect for the right of workers or their representatives to be guaranteed information and consultation in good time at the appropriate levels in the cases and under the conditions provided for by Community law and national laws and practices (Article 27 of the Charter of Fundamental Rights of the European Union).

(47) The obligation to transpose this Directive into national law should be confined to those provisions which represent a substantive change as compared with the earlier Directives. The obligation to transpose the provisions which are unchanged arises under the earlier Directives.

(48) In accordance with point 34 of the Interinstitutional Agreement on better law-making,[8] Member States are encouraged to draw up, for themselves and in the interests of the Community, tables illustrating, as far as possible, the correlation between this Directive and the transposition measures, and to make them public.

(49) This Directive should be without prejudice to the obligations of the Member States relating to the time limits set out in Annex II, Part B for transposition into national law and application of the Directives,

NOTES

[1] Opinion of 4 December 2008 (not yet published in the Official Journal).

[2] Opinion of the European Parliament of 16 December 2008 (not yet published in the Official Journal) and Council Decision of 17 December 2008.

[3] OJ L254, 30.9.1994, p 64.

[4] OJ L80, 23.3.2002, p 29.

[5] OJ L225, 12.8.1998, p 16.

[6] OJ L82, 22.3.2001, p 16.

[7] Council Directive 97/74/EC of 15 December 1997 extending, to the United Kingdom of Great Britain and Northern Ireland, Directive 94/45/EC on the establishment of a European Works Council or a procedure in Community-scale undertakings and Community-scale groups of undertakings for the purposes of informing and consulting employees (OJ L10, 16.1.1998, p 22).

[8] OJ C321, 31.12.2003, p 1.

HAVE ADOPTED THIS DIRECTIVE:

SECTION I GENERAL

[3.492]
Article 1
Objective

1. The purpose of this Directive is to improve the right to information and to consultation of employees in Community-scale undertakings and Community-scale groups of undertakings.
2. To that end, a European Works Council or a procedure for informing and consulting employees shall be established in every Community-scale undertaking and every Community-scale group of undertakings, where requested in the manner laid down in Article 5(1), with the purpose of informing and consulting employees. The arrangements for informing and consulting employees shall be defined and implemented in such a way as to ensure their effectiveness and to enable the undertaking or group of undertakings to take decisions effectively.
3. Information and consultation of employees must occur at the relevant level of management and representation, according to the subject under discussion. To achieve that, the competence of the European Works Council and the scope of the information and consultation procedure for employees governed by this Directive shall be limited to transnational issues.
4. Matters shall be considered to be transnational where they concern the Community-scale undertaking or Community-scale group of undertakings as a whole, or at least two undertakings or establishments of the undertaking or group situated in two different Member States.
5. Notwithstanding paragraph 2, where a Community-scale group of undertakings within the meaning of Article 2(1)(c) comprises one or more undertakings or groups of undertakings which are Community-scale undertakings or Community-scale groups of undertakings within the meaning of Article 2(1)(a) or (c), a European Works Council shall be established at the level of the group unless the agreements referred to in Article 6 provide otherwise.
6. Unless a wider scope is provided for in the agreements referred to in Article 6, the powers and competence of European Works Councils and the scope of information and consultation procedures established to achieve the purpose specified in paragraph 1 shall, in the case of a Community-scale undertaking, cover all the establishments located within the Member States and, in the case of a Community-scale group of undertakings, all group undertakings located within the Member States.
7. . . .

NOTES

Para 7: repealed by Directive 2015/1794/EU, Art 2(1), as from 9 October 2015.

[3.493]
Article 2
Definitions

1. For the purposes of this Directive:
   (a) "Community-scale undertaking" means any undertaking with at least 1000 employees within the Member States and at least 150 employees in each of at least two Member States;
   (b) "group of undertakings" means a controlling undertaking and its controlled undertakings;
   (c) "Community-scale group of undertakings" means a group of undertakings with the following characteristics:
      — at least 1000 employees within the Member States,
      — at least two group undertakings in different Member States, and
      — at least one group undertaking with at least 150 employees in one Member State and at least one other group undertaking with at least 150 employees in another Member State;

(d) "employees' representatives" means the employees' representatives provided for by national law and/or practice;
(e) "central management" means the central management of the Community-scale undertaking or, in the case of a Community-scale group of undertakings, of the controlling undertaking;
(f) "information" means transmission of data by the employer to the employees' representatives in order to enable them to acquaint themselves with the subject matter and to examine it; information shall be given at such time, in such fashion and with such content as are appropriate to enable employees' representatives to undertake an in-depth assessment of the possible impact and, where appropriate, prepare for consultations with the competent organ of the Community-scale undertaking or Community-scale group of undertakings;
(g) "consultation" means the establishment of dialogue and exchange of views between employees' representatives and central management or any more appropriate level of management, at such time, in such fashion and with such content as enables employees' representatives to express an opinion on the basis of the information provided about the proposed measures to which the consultation is related, without prejudice to the responsibilities of the management, and within a reasonable time, which may be taken into account within the Community-scale undertaking or Community-scale group of undertakings;
(h) "European Works Council" means a council established in accordance with Article 1(2) or the provisions of Annex I, with the purpose of informing and consulting employees;
(i) "special negotiating body" means the body established in accordance with Article 5(2) to negotiate with the central management regarding the establishment of a European Works Council or a procedure for informing and consulting employees in accordance with Article 1(2).

2. For the purposes of this Directive, the prescribed thresholds for the size of the workforce shall be based on the average number of employees, including part-time employees, employed during the previous two years calculated according to national legislation and/or practice.

[3.494]
Article 3
Definition of "controlling undertaking"

1. For the purposes of this Directive, "controlling undertaking" means an undertaking which can exercise a dominant influence over another undertaking (the controlled undertaking) by virtue, for example, of ownership, financial participation or the rules which govern it.
2. The ability to exercise a dominant influence shall be presumed, without prejudice to proof to the contrary, when an undertaking, in relation to another undertaking directly or indirectly:
(a) holds a majority of that undertaking's subscribed capital;
(b) controls a majority of the votes attached to that undertaking's issued share capital; or
(c) can appoint more than half of the members of that undertaking's administrative, management or supervisory body.
3. For the purposes of paragraph 2, a controlling undertaking's rights as regards voting and appointment shall include the rights of any other controlled undertaking and those of any person or body acting in his or its own name but on behalf of the controlling undertaking or of any other controlled undertaking.
4. Notwithstanding paragraphs 1 and 2, an undertaking shall not be deemed to be a "controlling undertaking" with respect to another undertaking in which it has holdings where the former undertaking is a company referred to in Article 3(5)(a) or (c) of Council Regulation (EC) No 139/2004 of 20 January 2004 on the control of concentrations between undertakings.[1]
5. A dominant influence shall not be presumed to be exercised solely by virtue of the fact that an office holder is exercising his functions, according to the law of a Member State relating to liquidation, winding up, insolvency, cessation of payments, compositions or analogous proceedings.
6. The law applicable in order to determine whether an undertaking is a controlling undertaking shall be the law of the Member State which governs that undertaking.

Where the law governing that undertaking is not that of a Member State, the law applicable shall be the law of the Member State within whose territory the representative of the undertaking or, in the absence of such a representative, the central management of the group undertaking which employs the greatest number of employees is situated.

7. Where, in the case of a conflict of laws in the application of paragraph 2, two or more undertakings from a group satisfy one or more of the criteria laid down in that paragraph, the undertaking which satisfies the criterion laid down in point (c) thereof shall be regarded as the controlling undertaking, without prejudice to proof that another undertaking is able to exercise a dominant influence.

NOTES

[1] OJ L24, 29.1.2004, p 1.

SECTION II ESTABLISHMENT OF A EUROPEAN WORKS COUNCIL OR AN EMPLOYEE INFORMATION AND CONSULTATION PROCEDURE

[3.495]
Article 4
Responsibility for the establishment of a European Works Council or an employee information and consultation procedure

1. The central management shall be responsible for creating the conditions and means necessary for the setting-up of a European Works Council or an information and consultation procedure, as provided for in Article 1(2), in a Community-scale undertaking and a Community-scale group of undertakings.

2. Where the central management is not situated in a Member State, the central management's representative agent in a Member State, to be designated if necessary, shall take on the responsibility referred to in paragraph 1.

In the absence of such a representative, the management of the establishment or group undertaking employing the greatest number of employees in any one Member State shall take on the responsibility referred to in paragraph 1.

3. For the purposes of this Directive, the representative or representatives or, in the absence of any such representatives, the management referred to in the second subparagraph of paragraph 2, shall be regarded as the central management.

4. The management of every undertaking belonging to the Community-scale group of undertakings and the central management or the deemed central management within the meaning of the second subparagraph of paragraph 2 of the Community-scale undertaking or group of undertakings shall be responsible for obtaining and transmitting to the parties concerned by the application of this Directive the information required for commencing the negotiations referred to in Article 5, and in particular the information concerning the structure of the undertaking or the group and its workforce. This obligation shall relate in particular to the information on the number of employees referred to in Article 2(1)(a) and (c).

[3.496]
Article 5
Special negotiating body

1. In order to achieve the objective set out in Article 1(1), the central management shall initiate negotiations for the establishment of a European Works Council or an information and consultation procedure on its own initiative or at the written request of at least 100 employees or their representatives in at least two undertakings or establishments in at least two different Member States.

2. For this purpose, a special negotiating body shall be established in accordance with the following guidelines:

(a) The Member States shall determine the method to be used for the election or appointment of the members of the special negotiating body who are to be elected or appointed in their territories.

Member States shall provide that employees in undertakings and/or establishments in which there are no employees' representatives through no fault of their own, have the right to elect or appoint members of the special negotiating body.

The second subparagraph shall be without prejudice to national legislation and/or practice laying down thresholds for the establishment of employee representation bodies.

(b) The members of the special negotiating body shall be elected or appointed in proportion to the number of employees employed in each Member State by the Community-scale undertaking or Community-scale group of undertakings, by allocating in respect of each Member State one seat per portion of employees employed in that Member State amounting to 10%, or a fraction thereof, of the number of employees employed in all the Member States taken together;

(c) The central management and local management and the competent European workers' and employers' organisations shall be informed of the composition of the special negotiating body and of the start of the negotiations.

3. The special negotiating body shall have the task of determining, with the central management, by written agreement, the scope, composition, functions, and term of office of the European Works Council(s) or the arrangements for implementing a procedure for the information and consultation of employees.

4. With a view to the conclusion of an agreement in accordance with Article 6, the central management shall convene a meeting with the special negotiating body. It shall inform the local managements accordingly.

Before and after any meeting with the central management, the special negotiating body shall be entitled to meet without representatives of the central management being present, using any necessary means for communication.

For the purpose of the negotiations, the special negotiating body may request assistance from experts of its choice which can include representatives of competent recognised Community-level trade union organisations. Such experts and such trade union representatives may be present at negotiation meetings in an advisory capacity at the request of the special negotiating body.

5. The special negotiating body may decide, by at least two-thirds of the votes, not to open negotiations in accordance with paragraph 4, or to terminate the negotiations already opened.

Such a decision shall stop the procedure to conclude the agreement referred to in Article 6. Where such a decision has been taken, the provisions in Annex I shall not apply.

A new request to convene the special negotiating body may be made at the earliest two years after the abovementioned decision unless the parties concerned lay down a shorter period.

6. Any expenses relating to the negotiations referred to in paragraphs 3 and 4 shall be borne by the central management so as to enable the special negotiating body to carry out its task in an appropriate manner.

In compliance with this principle, Member States may lay down budgetary rules regarding the operation of the special negotiating body. They may in particular limit the funding to cover one expert only.

[3.497]
Article 6
Content of the agreement

1. The central management and the special negotiating body must negotiate in a spirit of cooperation with a view to reaching an agreement on the detailed arrangements for implementing the information and consultation of employees provided for in Article 1(1).

2. Without prejudice to the autonomy of the parties, the agreement referred to in paragraph 1 and effected in writing between the central management and the special negotiating body shall determine:

(a) the undertakings of the Community-scale group of undertakings or the establishments of the Community-scale undertaking which are covered by the agreement;
(b) the composition of the European Works Council, the number of members, the allocation of seats, taking into account where possible the need for balanced representation of employees with regard to their activities, category and gender, and the term of office;
(c) the functions and the procedure for information and consultation of the European Works Council and the arrangements for linking information and consultation of the European Works Council and national employee representation bodies, in accordance with the principles set out in Article 1(3);
(d) the venue, frequency and duration of meetings of the European Works Council;
(e) where necessary, the composition, the appointment procedure, the functions and the procedural rules of the select committee set up within the European Works Council;
(f) the financial and material resources to be allocated to the European Works Council;
(g) the date of entry into force of the agreement and its duration, the arrangements for amending or terminating the agreement and the cases in which the agreement shall be renegotiated and the procedure for its renegotiation, including, where necessary, where the structure of the Community-scale undertaking or Community-scale group of undertakings changes.

3. The central management and the special negotiating body may decide, in writing, to establish one or more information and consultation procedures instead of a European Works Council.

The agreement must stipulate by what method the employees' representatives shall have the right to meet to discuss the information conveyed to them.

This information shall relate in particular to transnational questions which significantly affect workers' interests.

4. The agreements referred to in paragraphs 2 and 3 shall not, unless provision is made otherwise therein, be subject to the subsidiary requirements of Annex I.

5. For the purposes of concluding the agreements referred to in paragraphs 2 and 3, the special negotiating body shall act by a majority of its members.

[3.498]
Article 7
Subsidiary requirements

1. In order to achieve the objective set out in Article 1(1), the subsidiary requirements laid down by the legislation of the Member State in which the central management is situated shall apply:

— where the central management and the special negotiating body so decide,
— where the central management refuses to commence negotiations within six months of the request referred to in Article 5(1), or
— where, after three years from the date of this request, they are unable to conclude an agreement as laid down in Article 6 and the special negotiating body has not taken the decision provided for in Article 5(5).

2. The subsidiary requirements referred to in paragraph 1 as adopted in the legislation of the Member States must satisfy the provisions set out in Annex I.

SECTION III MISCELLANEOUS PROVISIONS

[3.499]
Article 8
Confidential information

1. Member States shall provide that members of special negotiating bodies or of European Works Councils and any experts who assist them are not authorised to reveal any information which has expressly been provided to them in confidence.

The same shall apply to employees' representatives in the framework of an information and consultation procedure.

That obligation shall continue to apply, wherever the persons referred to in the first and second subparagraphs are, even after the expiry of their terms of office.

2. Each Member State shall provide, in specific cases and under the conditions and limits laid down by national legislation, that the central management situated in its territory is not obliged to transmit information when its nature is such that, according to objective criteria, it would seriously harm the functioning of the undertakings concerned or would be prejudicial to them.

A Member State may make such dispensation subject to prior administrative or judicial authorisation.

3. Each Member State may lay down particular provisions for the central management of undertakings in its territory which pursue directly and essentially the aim of ideological guidance with respect to information and the expression of opinions, on condition that, at the date of adoption of this Directive such particular provisions already exist in the national legislation.

[3.500]
Article 9
Operation of the European Works Council and the information and consultation procedure for workers

The central management and the European Works Council shall work in a spirit of cooperation with due regard to their reciprocal rights and obligations.

The same shall apply to cooperation between the central management and employees' representatives in the framework of an information and consultation procedure for workers.

[3.501]
Article 10
Role and protection of employees' representatives

1. Without prejudice to the competence of other bodies or organisations in this respect, the members of the European Works Council shall have the means required to apply the rights arising from this Directive, to represent collectively the interests of the employees of the Community-scale undertaking or Community-scale group of undertakings.

2. Without prejudice to Article 8, the members of the European Works Council shall inform the representatives of the employees of the establishments or of the undertakings of a Community-scale group of undertakings or, in the absence of representatives, the workforce as a whole, of the content and outcome of the information and consultation procedure carried out in accordance with this Directive.

3. Members of special negotiating bodies, members of European Works Councils and employees' representatives exercising their functions under the procedure referred to in Article 6(3) shall, in the exercise of their functions, enjoy protection and guarantees similar to those provided for employees' representatives by the national legislation and/or practice in force in their country of employment.

This shall apply in particular to attendance at meetings of special negotiating bodies or European Works Councils or any other meetings within the framework of the agreement referred to in Article 6(3), and the payment of wages for members who are on the staff of the Community-scale undertaking or the Community-scale group of undertakings for the period of absence necessary for the performance of their duties.

[A member of a special negotiating body or of a European Works Council, or such a member's alternate, who is a member of the crew of a seagoing vessel, shall be entitled to participate in a meeting of the special negotiating body or of the European Works Council, or in any other meeting under any procedures established pursuant to Article 6(3), where that member or alternate is not at sea or in a port in a country other than that in which the shipping company is domiciled, when the meeting takes place.

Meetings shall, where practicable, be scheduled to facilitate the participation of members or alternates, who are members of the crews of seagoing vessels.

In cases where a member of a special negotiating body or of a European Works Council, or such a member's alternate, who is a member of the crew of a seagoing vessel, is unable to attend a meeting, the possibility of using, where possible, new information and communication technologies shall be considered.]

4. In so far as this is necessary for the exercise of their representative duties in an international environment, the members of the special negotiating body and of the European Works Council shall be provided with training without loss of wages.

NOTES

Para 3: words in square brackets inserted by Directive 2015/1794/EU, Art 2(2), as from 9 October 2015.

[3.502]
Article 11
Compliance with this Directive

1. Each Member State shall ensure that the management of establishments of a Community-scale undertaking and the management of undertakings which form part of a Community-scale group of undertakings which are situated within its territory and their employees' representatives or, as the case may be, employees abide by the obligations laid down by this Directive, regardless of whether or not the central management is situated within its territory.

2. Member States shall provide for appropriate measures in the event of failure to comply with this Directive; in particular, they shall ensure that adequate administrative or judicial procedures are available to enable the obligations deriving from this Directive to be enforced.

3. Where Member States apply Article 8, they shall make provision for administrative or judicial appeal procedures which the employees' representatives may initiate when the central management requires confidentiality or does not give information in accordance with that Article.

Such procedures may include procedures designed to protect the confidentiality of the information in question.

[3.503]
Article 12
Relationship with other Community and national provisions

1. Information and consultation of the European Works Council shall be linked to those of the national employee representation bodies, with due regard to the competences and areas of action of each and to the principles set out in Article 1(3).

2. The arrangements for the links between the information and consultation of the European Works Council and national employee representation bodies shall be established by the agreement referred to in Article 6. That agreement shall be without prejudice to the provisions of national law and/or practice on the information and consultation of employees.
3. Where no such arrangements have been defined by agreement, the Member States shall ensure that the processes of informing and consulting are conducted in the European Works Council as well as in the national employee representation bodies in cases where decisions likely to lead to substantial changes in work organisation or contractual relations are envisaged.
4. This Directive shall be without prejudice to the information and consultation procedures referred to in Directive 2002/14/EC and to the specific procedures referred to in Article 2 of Directive 98/59/EC and Article 7 of Directive 2001/23/EC.
5. Implementation of this Directive shall not be sufficient grounds for any regression in relation to the situation which already prevails in each Member State and in relation to the general level of protection of workers in the areas to which it applies.

[3.504]
Article 13
Adaptation

Where the structure of the Community-scale undertaking or Community-scale group of undertakings changes significantly, and either in the absence of provisions established by the agreements in force or in the event of conflicts between the relevant provisions of two or more applicable agreements, the central management shall initiate the negotiations referred to in Article 5 on its own initiative or at the written request of at least 100 employees or their representatives in at least two undertakings or establishments in at least two different Member States.

At least three members of the existing European Works Council or of each of the existing European Works Councils shall be members of the special negotiating body, in addition to the members elected or appointed pursuant to Article 5(2).

During the negotiations, the existing European Works Council(s) shall continue to operate in accordance with any arrangements adapted by agreement between the members of the European Works Council(s) and the central management.

[3.505]
Article 14
Agreements in force

1. Without prejudice to Article 13, the obligations arising from this Directive shall not apply to Community-scale undertakings or Community-scale groups of undertakings in which, either
(a) an agreement or agreements covering the entire workforce, providing for the transnational information and consultation of employees have been concluded pursuant to Article 13(1) of Directive 94/45/EC or Article 3(1) of Directive 97/74/EC, or where such agreements are adjusted because of changes in the structure of the undertakings or groups of undertakings; or
(b) an agreement concluded pursuant to Article 6 of Directive 94/45/EC is signed or revised between 5 June 2009 and 5 June 2011.

The national law applicable when the agreement is signed or revised shall continue to apply to the undertakings or groups of undertakings referred to in point (b) of the first subparagraph.
2. Upon expiry of the agreements referred to in paragraph 1, the parties to those agreements may decide jointly to renew or revise them. Where this is not the case, the provisions of this Directive shall apply.

[3.506]
Article 15
Report

No later than 5 June 2016, the Commission shall report to the European Parliament, the Council and the European Economic and Social Committee on the implementation of this Directive, making appropriate proposals where necessary.

[3.507]
Article 16
Transposition

1. Member States shall bring into force the laws, regulations and administrative provisions necessary to comply with Article 1(2), (3) and (4), Article 2(1), points (f) and (g), Articles 3(4), Article 4(4), Article 5(2), points (b) and (c), Article 5(4), Article 6(2), points (b), (c), (e) and (g), and Articles 10, 12, 13 and 14, as well as Annex I, point 1(a), (c) and (d) and points 2 and 3, no later than 5 June 2011 or shall ensure that management and labour introduce on that date the required provisions by way of agreement, the Member States being obliged to take all necessary steps enabling them at all times to guarantee the results imposed by this Directive.

When Member States adopt those provisions, they shall contain a reference to this Directive or be accompanied by such a reference on the occasion of their official publication. They shall also include a statement that references in existing laws, regulations and administrative provisions to the directive repealed by this Directive shall be construed as references to this Directive. Member States shall determine how such reference is to be made and how that statement is to be formulated.
2. Member States shall communicate to the Commission the text of the main provisions of national law which they adopt in the field covered by this Directive.

[3.508]
Article 17
Repeal

Directive 94/45/EC, as amended by the Directives listed in Annex II, Part A, is repealed with effect from 6 June 2011 without prejudice to the obligations of the Member States relating to the time limit for transposition into national law of the Directives set out in Annex II, Part B.

References to the repealed Directive shall be construed as references to this Directive and shall be read in accordance with the correlation table in Annex III.

[3.509]
Article 18
Entry into force

This Directive shall enter into force on the 20th day following its publication in the *Official Journal of the European Union.*

Article 1(1), (5), (6) and (7), Article 2(1), points (a) to (e), (h) and (i), Article 2(2), Articles 3(1), (2), (3), (5), (6) and (7), Article 4(1), (2) and (3), Article 5(1), (3), (5) and (6), Article 5(2), point (a), Article 6(1), Article 6(2), points (a), (d) and (f), and Article 6(3), (4) and (5), and Articles 7, 8, 9 and 11, as well as Annex I, point 1(b), (e) and (f), and points 4, 5 and 6, shall apply from 6 June 2011.

[3.510]
Article 19
Addressees

This Directive is addressed to the Member States.

ANNEX I
SUBSIDIARY REQUIREMENTS (REFERRED TO IN ARTICLE 7)

[3.511]

1. In order to achieve the objective set out in Article 1(1) and in the cases provided for in Article 7(1), the establishment, composition and competence of a European Works Council shall be governed by the following rules:

(a) The competence of the European Works Council shall be determined in accordance with Article 1(3).

The information of the European Works Council shall relate in particular to the structure, economic and financial situation, probable development and production and sales of the Community-scale undertaking or group of undertakings. The information and consultation of the European Works Council shall relate in particular to the situation and probable trend of employment, investments, and substantial changes concerning organisation, introduction of new working methods or production processes, transfers of production, mergers, cut-backs or closures of undertakings, establishments or important parts thereof, and collective redundancies. The consultation shall be conducted in such a way that the employees' representatives can meet with the central management and obtain a response, and the reasons for that response, to any opinion they might express;

(b) The European Works Council shall be composed of employees of the Community-scale undertaking or Community-scale group of undertakings elected or appointed from their number by the employees' representatives or, in the absence thereof, by the entire body of employees.

The election or appointment of members of the European Works Council shall be carried out in accordance with national legislation and/or practice;

(c) The members of the European Works Council shall be elected or appointed in proportion to the number of employees employed in each Member State by the Community-scale undertaking or Community-scale group of undertakings, by allocating in respect of each Member State one seat per portion of employees employed in that Member State amounting to 10%, or a fraction thereof, of the number of employees employed in all the Member States taken together;

(d) To ensure that it can coordinate its activities, the European Works Council shall elect a select committee from among its members, comprising at most five members, which must benefit from conditions enabling it to exercise its activities on a regular basis.

It shall adopt its own rules of procedure;

(e) The central management and any other more appropriate level of management shall be informed of the composition of the European Works Council;

(f) Four years after the European Works Council is established it shall examine whether to open negotiations for the conclusion of the agreement referred to in Article 6 or to continue to apply the subsidiary requirements adopted in accordance with this Annex.

Articles 6 and 7 shall apply, mutatis mutandis, if a decision has been taken to negotiate an agreement according to Article 6, in which case "special negotiating body" shall be replaced by "European Works Council".

2. The European Works Council shall have the right to meet with the central management once a year, to be informed and consulted, on the basis of a report drawn up by the central management, on the progress of the business of the Community-scale undertaking or Community-scale group of undertakings and its prospects. The local managements shall be informed accordingly.

3. Where there are exceptional circumstances or decisions affecting the employees' interests to a considerable extent, particularly in the event of relocations, the closure of establishments or undertakings or collective redundancies, the select committee or, where no such committee exists, the European Works Council shall have the right to be informed. It shall have the right to meet, at its request, the central management, or any other more appropriate level of management within the Community-scale undertaking or group of undertakings having its own powers of decision, so as to be informed and consulted.

Those members of the European Works Council who have been elected or appointed by the establishments and/or undertakings which are directly concerned by the circumstances or decisions in question shall also have the right to participate where a meeting is organised with the select committee.

This information and consultation meeting shall take place as soon as possible on the basis of a report drawn up by the central management or any other appropriate level of management of the Community-scale undertaking or group of undertakings, on which an opinion may be delivered at the end of the meeting or within a reasonable time.

This meeting shall not affect the prerogatives of the central management.

The information and consultation procedures provided for in the above circumstances shall be carried out without prejudice to Article 1(2) and Article 8.

4. The Member States may lay down rules on the chairing of information and consultation meetings.

Before any meeting with the central management, the European Works Council or the select committee, where necessary enlarged in accordance with the second paragraph of point 3, shall be entitled to meet without the management concerned being present.

5. The European Works Council or the select committee may be assisted by experts of its choice, in so far as this is necessary for it to carry out its tasks.

6. The operating expenses of the European Works Council shall be borne by the central management.

The central management concerned shall provide the members of the European Works Council with such financial and material resources as enable them to perform their duties in an appropriate manner.

In particular, the cost of organising meetings and arranging for interpretation facilities and the accommodation and travelling expenses of members of the European Works Council and its select committee shall be met by the central management unless otherwise agreed.

In compliance with these principles, the Member States may lay down budgetary rules regarding the operation of the European Works Council. They may in particular limit funding to cover one expert only.

ANNEX II

PART A REPEALED DIRECTIVE WITH ITS SUCCESSIVE AMENDMENTS (REFERRED TO IN ARTICLE 17)

[3.512]

Council Directive 94/45/EC	(OJ L254, 30.9.1994, p 64)
Council Directive 97/74/EC	(OJ L10, 16.1.1998, p 22)
Council Directive 2006/109/EC	(OJ L363, 20.12.2006, p 416)

PART B TIME LIMITS FOR TRANSPOSITION INTO NATIONAL LAW (REFERRED TO IN ARTICLE 17)

[3.513]

Directive	Time limit for transposition
94/45/EC	22.9.1996
97/74/EC	15.12.1999
2006/109/EC	1.1.2007

ANNEX III
CORRELATION TABLE

[3.514]

Directive 94/45/EC	This Directive
Article 1(1)	Article 1(1)
Article 1(2)	Article 1(2), first sentence
—	Article 1(2), second sentence
—	Article 1(3) and (4)
Article 1(3)	Article 1(5)
Article 1(4)	Article 1(6)
Article 1(5)	Article 1(7)
Article 2(1)(a) to (e)	Article 2(1)(a) to (e)

Part 3 EU Materials

Directive 94/45/EC	This Directive
—	Article 2(1)(f)
Article 2(1)(f)	Article 2(1)(g)
Article 2(1)(g) and (h)	Article 2(1)(h) and (i)
Article 2(2)	Article 2(2)
Article 3	Article 3
Article 4(1), (2) and (3)	Article 4(1), (2) and (3)
Article 11(2)	Article 4(4)
Article 5(1) and (2)(a)	Article 5(1) and (2)(a)
Article 5(2)(b) and (c)	Article 5(2)(b)
Article 5(2)(d)	Article 5(2)(c)
Article 5(3)	Article 5(3)
Article 5(4), first subparagraph	Article 5(4), first subparagraph
—	Article 5(4), second subparagraph
Article 5(4), second subparagraph	Article 5(4), third subparagraph
Article 5(5) and (6)	Article 5(5) and (6)
Article 6(1) and (2)(a)	Article 6(1) and (2)(a)
Article 6(2)(b)	Article 6(2)(b)
Article 6(2)(c)	Article 6(2)(c)
Article 6(2)(d)	Article 6(2)(d)
—	Article 6(2)(e)
Article 6(2)(e)	Article 6(2)(f)
Article 6(2)(f)	Article 6(2)(g)
Article 6(3), (4) and (5)	Article 6(3), (4) and (5)
Article 7	Article 7
Article 8	Article 8
Article 9	Article 9
—	Article 10(1) and (2)
Article 10	Article 10(3)
—	Article 10(4)
Article 11(1)	Article 11(1)
Article 11(2)	Article 4(4)
Article 11(3)	Article 11(2)
Article 11(4)	Article 11(3)
Article 12(1) and (2)	
—	Article 12(1) to (5)
—	Article 13
Article 13(1)	Article 14(1)
Article 13(2)	Article 14(2)
—	Article 15
Article 14	Article 16
—	Article 17
—	Article 18
Article 16	Article 19
Annex	Annex I
Point 1, introductory wording	Point 1, introductory wording
Point 1(a) (partly) and point 2, second paragraph (partly)	Point 1(a) (partly)
Point 1(b)	Point 1(b)
Point 1(c) (partly) and point 1(d)	Point 1(c)
Point 1(c) (partly)	Point 1(d)
Point 1(e)	Point 1(e)
Point 1(f)	Point 1(f)

Directive 94/45/EC	This Directive
Point 2, first paragraph	Point 2
Point 3	Point 3
Point 4	Point 4
Point 5	—
Point 6	Point 5
Point 7	Point 6
—	Annexes II and III

COUNCIL DIRECTIVE

(2010/18/EU)

of 8 March 2010

implementing the revised Framework Agreement on parental leave concluded by BUSINESSEUROPE, UEAPME, CEEP and ETUC and repealing Directive 96/34/EC

(Text with EEA relevance)

[3.515]

NOTES

Date of publication in OJ: OJ L68, 18.03.2010, p 13.

This Directive replaced Council Directive 96/34/EC with effect from 8 March 2012. For the domestic implementation of the provisions in the Directive replaced by this Directive see the Employment Rights Act 1996, ss 57A, 57B, 76–80 at **[1.926]**, **[1.927]**, **[1.974]**–**[1.978]**. See also the Maternity and Parental Leave etc Regulations 1999, SI 1999/3312 at **[2.447]**, and the Parental Leave (EU Directive) Regulations 2013, SI 2013/283.

See *Harvey* J(1), (7).

THE COUNCIL OF THE EUROPEAN UNION,

Having regard to the Treaty on the Functioning of the European Union, and in particular Article 155(2) thereof,

Having regard to the proposal from the European Commission,

Whereas:

(1) Article 153 of the Treaty on the Functioning of the European Union (the "TFEU") enables the Union to support and complement the activities of the Member States, inter alia in the field of equality between men and women with regard to labour market opportunities and treatment at work.

(2) Social dialogue at Union level may, in accordance with Article 155(1) of the TFEU, lead to contractual relations, including agreements, should management and labour (the "social partners") so desire. The social partners may, in accordance with Article 155(2) of the TFEU, request jointly that agreements concluded by them at Union level in matters covered by Article 153 of the TFEU be implemented by a Council decision on a proposal from the Commission.

(3) A Framework Agreement on parental leave was concluded by the European cross-industry social partner organisations (ETUC, UNICE and CEEP) on 14 December 1995 and was given legal effect by Council Directive 96/34/EC of 3 June 1996 on the framework agreement on parental leave concluded by UNICE, CEEP and the ETUC.[1] That Directive was amended and extended to the United Kingdom of Great Britain and Northern Ireland by Council Directive 97/75/EC.[2] Directive 96/34/EC contributed greatly to improving the opportunities available to working parents in the Member States to better reconcile their work and family responsibilities through leave arrangements.

(4) In accordance with Article 138(2) and (3) of the Treaty establishing the European Community (the "EC Treaty"),[3] the Commission consulted the European social partners in 2006 and 2007 on ways of further improving the reconciliation of work, private and family life and, in particular, the existing Community legislation on maternity protection and parental leave, and on the possibility of introducing new types of family-related leave, such as paternity leave, adoption leave and leave to care for family members.

(5) The three European general cross-industry social partner organisations (ETUC, CEEP and BUSINESSEUROPE, formerly named UNICE) and the European cross-industry social partner organisation representing a certain category of undertakings (UEAPME) informed the Commission on 11 September 2008 of their wish to enter into negotiations, in accordance with Article 138(4) and Article 139 of the EC Treaty,[4] with a view to revising the Framework Agreement on parental leave concluded in 1995.

(6) On 18 June 2009, those organisations signed the revised Framework Agreement on parental leave (the "revised Framework Agreement") and addressed a joint request to the Commission to submit a proposal for a Council decision implementing that revised Framework Agreement.

(7) In the course of their negotiations, the European social partners completely revised the 1995 Framework Agreement on parental leave. Therefore Directive 96/34/EC should be repealed and replaced by a new directive rather than being simply amended.

(8) Since the objectives of the Directive, namely to improve the reconciliation of work, private and family life for working parents and equality between men and women with regard to labour market opportunities and treatment at work across the Union, cannot be sufficiently achieved by the Member States and can therefore be better achieved at Union level, the Union may adopt measures, in accordance with the principle of subsidiarity as set out in Article 5 of the Treaty on European Union. In accordance with the principle of proportionality, as set out in that Article, this Directive does not go beyond what is necessary in order to achieve those objectives.

(9) When drafting its proposal for a Directive, the Commission took account of the representative status of the signatory parties to the revised Framework Agreement, their mandate and the legality of the clauses in that revised Framework Agreement and its compliance with the relevant provisions concerning small and medium-sized undertakings.

(10) The Commission informed the European Parliament and the European Economic and Social Committee of its proposal.

(11) Clause 1(1) of the revised Framework Agreement, in line with the general principles of Union law in the social policy area, states that the Agreement lays down minimum requirements.

(12) Clause 8(1) of the revised Framework Agreement states that the Member States may apply or introduce more favourable provisions than those set out in the Agreement.

(13) Clause 8(2) of the revised Framework Agreement states that the implementation of the provisions of the Agreement shall not constitute valid grounds for reducing the general level of protection afforded to workers in the field covered by the Agreement.

(14) Member States should provide for effective, proportionate and dissuasive penalties in the event of any breach of the obligations under this Directive.

(15) Member States may entrust the social partners, at their joint request, with the implementation of this Directive, as long as such Member States take all the steps necessary to ensure that they can at all times guarantee the results imposed by this Directive.

(16) In accordance with point 34 of the Interinstitutional agreement on better law-making,[5] Member States are encouraged to draw up, for themselves and in the interests of the Union, their own tables which will, as far as possible, illustrate the correlation between this Directive and the transposition measures, and to make them public,

NOTES

1 OJ L145, 19.6.1996, p 4.

2 OJ L10, 16.1.1998, p 24.

3 Renumbered: Article 154(2) and (3) of the TFEU.

4 Renumbered: Articles 154(4) and 155 of the TFEU.

5 OJ C321, 31.12.2003, p 1.

HAS ADOPTED THIS DIRECTIVE:

[3.516]
Article 1
This Directive puts into effect the revised Framework Agreement on parental leave concluded on 18 June 2009 by the European cross-industry social partner organisations (BUSINESSEUROPE, UEAPME, CEEP and ETUC), as set out in the Annex.

[3.517]
Article 2
Member States shall determine what penalties are applicable when national provisions enacted pursuant to this Directive are infringed. The penalties shall be effective, proportionate and dissuasive.

[3.518]
Article 3
1. Member States shall bring into force the laws, regulations and administrative provisions necessary to comply with this Directive or shall ensure that the social partners have introduced the necessary measures by agreement by 8 March 2012 at the latest. They shall forthwith inform the Commission thereof.

When those provisions are adopted by Member States, they shall contain a reference to this Directive or shall be accompanied by such reference on the occasion of their official publication. The methods of making such reference shall be laid down by Member States.

2. Member States may have a maximum additional period of one year to comply with this Directive, if this is necessary to take account of particular difficulties or implementation by collective agreement. They shall inform the Commission thereof by 8 March 2012 at the latest, stating the reasons for which an additional period is required.

[By way of derogation from the first subparagraph, the additional period referred to therein shall be extended to 31 December 2018 as regards Mayotte as an outermost region of the Union within the meaning of Article 349 TFEU.]

3. Member States shall communicate to the Commission the text of the main provisions of national law which they adopt in the field covered by this Directive.

NOTES

Para 2: words in square brackets inserted by Council Directive 2013/62/EU, Art 1.

[3.519]
Article 4
Directive 96/34/EC shall be repealed with effect from 8 March 2012. References to Directive 96/34/EC shall be construed as references to this Directive.

[3.520]
Article 5
This Directive shall enter into force on the 20th day following its publication in the *Official Journal of the European Union*.

[3.521]
Article 6
This Directive is addressed to the Member States.

ANNEX
FRAMEWORK AGREEMENT ON PARENTAL LEAVE (REVISED)
18 JUNE 2009

[3.522]
Preamble
This framework agreement between the European social partners, BUSINESSEUROPE, UEAPME, CEEP and ETUC (and the liaison committee Eurocadres/CEC) revises the framework agreement on parental leave, concluded on 14 December 1995, setting out the minimum requirements on parental leave, as an important means of reconciling professional and family responsibilities and promoting equal opportunities and treatment between men and women.
The European social partners request the Commission to submit this framework agreement to the Council for a Council decision making these requirements binding in the Member States of the European Union.

I. General considerations

1. Having regard to the EC Treaty and in particular Articles 138 and 139 thereof;[1]
2. Having regard to Articles 137(1)(c) and 141 of the EC Treaty[2] and the principle of equal treatment (Articles 2, 3 and 13 of the EC Treaty)[3] and the secondary legislation based on this, in particular Council Directive 75/117/EEC on the approximation of the laws of the Member States relating to the application of the principle of equal pay for men and women;[4] Council Directive 92/85/EEC on the introduction of measures to encourage improvements in the safety and health at work of pregnant workers and workers who have recently given birth or are breastfeeding;[5] Council Directive 96/97/EC amending Directive 86/378/EEC on the implementation of the principle of equal treatment for men and women in occupational social security schemes;[6] and Directive 2006/54/EC on the implementation of the principle of equal opportunities and equal treatment of men and women in matters of employment and occupation (recast);[7]
3. Having regard to the Charter of Fundamental Rights of the European Union of 7 December 2000 and Articles 23 and 33 thereof relating to equality between men and women and reconciliation of professional, private and family life;
4. Having regard to the 2003 Report from the Commission on the Implementation of Council Directive 96/34/EC of 3 June 1996 on the framework agreement on parental leave concluded by UNICE, CEEP and the ETUC;
5. Having regard to the objective of the Lisbon strategy on growth and jobs of increasing overall employment rates to 70%, women's employment rates to 60% and the employment rates of older workers to 50%; to the Barcelona targets on the provision of childcare facilities; and to the contribution of policies to improve reconciliation of professional, private and family life in achieving these targets;
6. Having regard to the European social partners' Framework of Actions on Gender Equality of 22 March 2005 in which supporting work-life balance is addressed as a priority area for action, while recognising that, in order to continue to make progress on the issue of reconciliation, a balanced, integrated and coherent policy mix must be put in place, comprising of leave arrangements, working arrangements and care infrastructures;
7. Whereas measures to improve reconciliation are part of a broader policy agenda to address the needs of employers and workers and improve adaptability and employability, as part of a flexicurity approach;
8. Whereas family policies should contribute to the achievement of gender equality and be looked at in the context of demographic changes, the effects of an ageing population, closing the generation gap, promoting women's participation in the labour force and the sharing of care responsibilities between women and men;
9. Whereas the Commission has consulted the European social partners in 2006 and 2007 in a first and second stage consultation on reconciliation of professional, private and family life, and, among other things, has addressed the issue of updating the regulatory framework at Community level, and has encouraged the European social partners to assess the provisions of their framework agreement on parental leave with a view to its review;

Part 3 EU Materials

10. Whereas the Framework agreement of the European social partners of 1995 on parental leave has been a catalyst for positive change, ensured common ground on work life balance in the Member States and played a significant role in helping working parents in Europe to achieve better reconciliation; however, on the basis of a joint evaluation, the European social partners consider that certain elements of the agreement need to be adapted or revised in order to better achieve its aims;
11. Whereas certain aspects need to be adapted, taking into account the growing diversity of the labour force and societal developments including the increasing diversity of family structures, while respecting national law, collective agreements and/or practice;
12. Whereas in many Member States encouraging men to assume an equal share of family responsibilities has not led to sufficient results; therefore, more effective measures should be taken to encourage a more equal sharing of family responsibilities between men and women;
13. Whereas many Member States already have a wide variety of policy measures and practices relating to leave facilities, childcare and flexible working arrangements, tailored to the needs of workers and employers and aiming to support parents in reconciling their professional, private and family life; these should be taken into account when implementing this agreement;
14. Whereas this framework agreement provides one element of European social partners' actions in the field of reconciliation;
15. Whereas this agreement is a framework agreement setting out minimum requirements and provisions for parental leave, distinct from maternity leave, and for time off from work on grounds of force majeure, and refers back to Member States and social partners for the establishment of conditions for access and modalities of application in order to take account of the situation in each Member State;
16. Whereas the right of parental leave in this agreement is an individual right and in principle non-transferable, and Member States are allowed to make it transferable. Experience shows that making the leave non-transferable can act as a positive incentive for the take up by fathers, the European social partners therefore agree to make a part of the leave non-transferable;
17. Whereas it is important to take into account the special needs of parents with children with disabilities or long term illness;
18. Whereas Member States should provide for the maintenance of entitlements to benefits in kind under sickness insurance during the minimum period of parental leave;
19. Whereas Member States should also, where appropriate under national conditions and taking into account the budgetary situation, consider the maintenance of entitlements to relevant social security benefits as they stand during the minimum period of parental leave as well as the role of income among other factors in the take-up of parental leave when implementing this agreement;
20. Whereas experiences in Member States have shown that the level of income during parental leave is one factor that influences the take up by parents, especially fathers;
21. Whereas the access to flexible working arrangements makes it easier for parents to combine work and parental responsibilities and facilitates the reintegration into work, especially after returning from parental leave;
22. Whereas parental leave arrangements are meant to support working parents during a specific period of time, aimed at maintaining and promoting their continued labour market participation; therefore, greater attention should be paid to keeping in contact with the employer during the leave or by making arrangements for return to work;
23. Whereas this agreement takes into consideration the need to improve social policy requirements, to enhance the competitiveness of the European Union economy and to avoid imposing administrative, financial and legal constraints in a way which would hold back the creation and development of small and medium sized undertakings;
24. Whereas the social partners are best placed to find solutions that correspond to the needs of both employers and workers and shall therefore play a special role in the implementation, application, monitoring and evaluation of this agreement, in the broader context of other measures to improve the reconciliation of professional and family responsibilities and to promote equal opportunities and treatment between men and women.

The signatory parties have agreed the following:

II. Content

Clause 1: Purpose and scope

1. This agreement lays down minimum requirements designed to facilitate the reconciliation of parental and professional responsibilities for working parents, taking into account the increasing diversity of family structures while respecting national law, collective agreements and/or practice.
2. This agreement applies to all workers, men and women, who have an employment contract or employment relationship as defined by the law, collective agreements and/or practice in force in each Member State.
3. Member States and/or social partners shall not exclude from the scope and application of this agreement workers, contracts of employment or employment relationships solely because they relate to part-time workers, fixed-term contract workers or persons with a contract of employment or employment relationship with a temporary agency.

Clause 2: Parental leave

1. This agreement entitles men and women workers to an individual right to parental leave on the grounds of the birth or adoption of a child to take care of that child until a given age up to eight years to be defined by Member States and/or social partners.
2. The leave shall be granted for at least a period of four months and, to promote equal opportunities and equal treatment between men and women, should, in principle, be provided on a non-transferable basis. To encourage a more equal take-up of leave by both parents, at least one of the four months shall

be provided on a non-transferable basis. The modalities of application of the non-transferable period shall be set down at national level through legislation and/or collective agreements taking into account existing leave arrangements in the Member States.

Clause 3: Modalities of application

1. The conditions of access and detailed rules for applying parental leave shall be defined by law and/or collective agreements in the Member States, as long as the minimum requirements of this agreement are respected. Member States and/or social partners may, in particular:

(a) decide whether parental leave is granted on a full-time or part-time basis, in a piecemeal way or in the form of a time-credit system, taking into account the needs of both employers and workers;

(b) make entitlement to parental leave subject to a period of work qualification and/or a length of service qualification which shall not exceed one year; Member States and/or social partners shall ensure, when making use of this provision, that in case of successive fixed term contracts, as defined in Council Directive 1999/70/EC on fixed-term work, with the same employer the sum of these contracts shall be taken into account for the purpose of calculating the qualifying period;

(c) define the circumstances in which an employer, following consultation in accordance with national law, collective agreements and/or practice, is allowed to postpone the granting of parental leave for justifiable reasons related to the operation of the organisation. Any problem arising from the application of this provision should be dealt with in accordance with national law, collective agreements and/or practice;

(d) in addition to (c), authorise special arrangements to meet the operational and organisational requirements of small undertakings.

2. Member States and/or social partners shall establish notice periods to be given by the worker to the employer when exercising the right to parental leave, specifying the beginning and the end of the period of leave. Member States and/or social partners shall have regard to the interests of workers and of employers in specifying the length of such notice periods.

3. Member States and/or social partners should assess the need to adjust the conditions for access and modalities of application of parental leave to the needs of parents of children with a disability or a long-term illness.

Clause 4: Adoption

1. Member States and/or social partners shall assess the need for additional measures to address the specific needs of adoptive parents.

Clause 5: Employment rights and non-discrimination

1. At the end of parental leave, workers shall have the right to return to the same job or, if that is not possible, to an equivalent or similar job consistent with their employment contract or employment relationship.

2. Rights acquired or in the process of being acquired by the worker on the date on which parental leave starts shall be maintained as they stand until the end of parental leave. At the end of parental leave, these rights, including any changes arising from national law, collective agreements and/or practice, shall apply.

3. Member States and/or social partners shall define the status of the employment contract or employment relationship for the period of parental leave.

4. In order to ensure that workers can exercise their right to parental leave, Member States and/or social partners shall take the necessary measures to protect workers against less favourable treatment or dismissal on the grounds of an application for, or the taking of, parental leave in accordance with national law, collective agreements and/or practice.

5. All matters regarding social security in relation to this agreement are for consideration and determination by Member States and/or social partners according to national law and/or collective agreements, taking into account the importance of the continuity of the entitlements to social security cover under the different schemes, in particular health care.

All matters regarding income in relation to this agreement are for consideration and determination by Member States and/or social partners according to national law, collective agreements and/or practice, taking into account the role of income – among other factors – in the take-up of parental leave.

Clause 6: Return to work

1. In order to promote better reconciliation, Member States and/or social partners shall take the necessary measures to ensure that workers, when returning from parental leave, may request changes to their working hours and/or patterns for a set period of time. Employers shall consider and respond to such requests, taking into account both employers' and workers' needs.

The modalities of this paragraph shall be determined in accordance with national law, collective agreements and/or practice.

2. In order to facilitate the return to work following parental leave, workers and employers are encouraged to maintain contact during the period of leave and may make arrangements for any appropriate reintegration measures, to be decided between the parties concerned, taking into account national law, collective agreements and/or practice.

Clause 7: Time off from work on grounds of force majeure

1. Member States and/or social partners shall take the necessary measures to entitle workers to time off from work, in accordance with national legislation, collective agreements and/or practice, on grounds of force majeure for urgent family reasons in cases of sickness or accident making the immediate presence of the worker indispensable.

2. Member States and/or social partners may specify the conditions of access and detailed rules for applying clause 7.1 and limit this entitlement to a certain amount of time per year and/or per case.

Clause 8: Final provisions

1. Member States may apply or introduce more favourable provisions than those set out in this agreement.
2. Implementation of the provisions of this agreement shall not constitute valid grounds for reducing the general level of protection afforded to workers in the field covered by this agreement. This shall not prejudice the right of Member States and/or social partners to develop different legislative, regulatory or contractual provisions, in the light of changing circumstances (including the introduction of non-transferability), as long as the minimum requirements provided for in the present agreement are complied with.
3. This agreement shall not prejudice the right of social partners to conclude, at the appropriate level including European level, agreements adapting and/or complementing the provisions of this agreement in order to take into account particular circumstances.
4. Member States shall adopt the laws, regulations and administrative provisions necessary to comply with the Council decision within a period of two years from its adoption or shall ensure that social partners introduce the necessary measures by way of agreement by the end of this period. Member States may, if necessary to take account of particular difficulties or implementation by collective agreements, have up to a maximum of one additional year to comply with this decision.
5. The prevention and settlement of disputes and grievances arising from the application of this agreement shall be dealt with in accordance with national law, collective agreements and/or practice.
6. Without prejudice to the respective role of the Commission, national courts and the European Court of Justice, any matter relating to the interpretation of this agreement at European level should, in the first instance, be referred by the Commission to the signatory parties who will give an opinion.
7. The signatory parties shall review the application of this agreement five years after the date of the Council decision if requested by one of the parties to this agreement.

NOTES

[1] Renumbered: Articles 154 and 155 of the TFEU.

[2] Renumbered: Articles 153(1)c and 157 of the TFEU.

[3] Article 2 of the EC Treaty is repealed and replaced, in substance, by Article 3 of the Treaty on the European Union. Article 3(1) of the EC Treaty is repealed and replaced, in substance, by Articles 3 to 6 of the TFEU. Article 3(2) of the EC Treaty is renumbered as Article 8 of the TFEU. Article 13 of the EC Treaty is renumbered as Article 19 of the TFEU.

[4] OJ L45, 19.2.1975, p 19–20.

[5] OJ L348, 28.11.1992, p 1–8.

[6] OJ L46, 17.2.1997, p 20–24.

[7] OJ L204, 26.7.2006, p 23–36.

DIRECTIVE OF THE EUROPEAN PARLIAMENT AND OF THE COUNCIL

(2010/41/EU)

of 7 July 2010

on the application of the principle of equal treatment between men and women engaged in an activity in a self-employed capacity and repealing Council Directive 86/613/EEC

[3.523]

NOTES

Date of publication in OJ: OJ L180, 15.7.2010, p 1.

The deadline for domestic implementation of this Directive was 5 August 2012 (see Article 16 at **[3.539]**). As to the domestic implementation of this Directive, see the Social Security (Maternity Allowance) (Participating Wife or Civil Partner of Self-employed Earner) Regulations 2014, SI 2014/606 (which amend the Social Security Contributions and Benefits Act 1992 and implement Article 8 of this Directive), and the Social Security (Maternity Allowance) (Miscellaneous Amendments) Regulations 2014, SI 2014/884 (which amend various statutory instruments and also implement Article 8). No other domestic implementing measures have been introduced, presumably because it was considered that the Directive was sufficiently implemented by existing law.

THE EUROPEAN PARLIAMENT AND THE COUNCIL OF THE EUROPEAN UNION,

Having regard to the Treaty on the Functioning of the European Union, and in particular Article 157(3) thereof,

Having regard to the proposal from the European Commission,

Having regard to the opinion of the European Economic and Social Committee,[1]

Acting in accordance with the ordinary legislative procedure,[2]

Whereas:

(1) Council Directive 86/613/EEC of 11 December 1986 on the application of the principle of equal treatment between men and women engaged in an activity, including agriculture, in a self-employed capacity, and on the protection of self-employed women during pregnancy and motherhood[3] ensures application in Member States of the principle of equal treatment as between men and women engaged in

an activity in a self-employed capacity, or contributing to the pursuit of such activity. As far as self-employed workers and spouses of self-employed workers are concerned, Directive 86/613/EEC has not been very effective and its scope should be reconsidered, as discrimination based on sex and harassment also occur in areas outside salaried work. In the interest of clarity, Directive 86/613/EEC should be replaced by this Directive.

(2) In its Communication of 1 March 2006 entitled 'Roadmap for equality between women and men', the Commission announced that in order to improve governance of gender equality, it would review the existing Union gender equality legislation not included in the 2005 recast exercise with a view to updating, modernising and recasting where necessary. Directive 86/613/EEC was not included in the recasting exercise.

(3) In its conclusions of 5 and 6 December 2007 on 'Balanced roles of women and men for jobs, growth and social cohesion', the Council called on the Commission to consider the need to revise, if necessary, Directive 86/613/EEC in order to safeguard the rights related to motherhood and fatherhood of self-employed workers and their helping spouses.

(4) The European Parliament has consistently called on the Commission to review Directive 86/613/EEC, in particular so as to boost maternity protection for self-employed women and to improve the situation of spouses of self-employed workers.

(5) The European Parliament has already stated its position on these matters in its resolution of 21 February 1997 on the situation of the assisting spouses of the self-employed.[4]

(6) In its Communication of 2 July 2008 entitled 'Renewed Social Agenda: Opportunities, access and solidarity in 21st century Europe', the Commission has affirmed the need to take action on the gender gap in entrepreneurship as well as to improve the reconciliation of private and professional life.

(7) There are already a number of existing legal instruments for the implementation of the principle of equal treatment which cover self-employment activities, in particular Council Directive 79/7/EEC of 19 December 1978 on the progressive implementation of the principle of equal treatment for men and women in matters of social security[5] and Directive 2006/54/EC of the European Parliament and of the Council of 5 July 2006 on the implementation of the principle of equal opportunities and equal treatment of men and women in matters of employment and occupation.[6] This Directive should therefore not apply to the areas already covered by other directives.

(8) This Directive is without prejudice to the powers of the Member States to organise their social protection systems. The exclusive competence of the Member States with regard to the organisation of their social protection systems includes, inter alia decisions on the setting up, financing and management of such systems and related institutions as well as on the substance and delivery of benefits, the level of contributions and the conditions for access.

(9) This Directive should apply to self-employed workers and to their spouses or, when and in so far as recognised by national law, their life partners, where they, under the conditions laid down by national law, habitually participate in the activities of the business. In order to improve the situation for these spouses and, when and in so far as recognised by national law, the life partners of self-employed workers, their work should be recognised.

(10) This Directive should not apply to matters covered by other Directives implementing the principle of equal treatment between men and women, notably Council Directive 2004/113/EC of 13 December 2004 implementing the principle of equal treatment between men and women in the access to and supply of goods and services,[7] inter alia, Article 5 of Directive 2004/113/EC on insurance and related financial services remains applicable.

(11) To prevent discrimination based on sex, this Directive should apply to both direct and indirect discrimination. Harassment and sexual harassment should be considered discrimination and therefore prohibited.

(12) This Directive should be without prejudice to the rights and obligations deriving from marital or family status as defined in national law.

(13) The principle of equal treatment should cover the relationships between the self-employed worker and third parties within the remit of this Directive, but not relationships between the self-employed worker and his or her spouse or life partner.

(14) In the area of self-employment, the application of the principle of equal treatment means that there must be no discrimination on grounds of sex, for instance in relation to the establishment, equipment or extension of a business or the launching or extension of any other form of self-employed activity.

(15) Member States may, under Article 157(4) of the Treaty on the Functioning of the European Union, maintain or adopt measures providing for specific advantages in order to make it easier for the under-represented sex to engage in self-employed activities or to prevent or compensate for disadvantages in their professional careers. In principle, measures such as positive action aimed at achieving gender equality in practice should not be seen as being in breach of the legal principle of equal treatment between men and women.

(16) It is necessary to ensure that the conditions for setting up a company between spouses or, when and in so far as recognised by national law, life partners, are not more restrictive than the conditions for setting up a company between other persons.

(17) In view of their participation in the activities of the family business, the spouses or, when and in so far as recognised by national law, the life partners of self-employed workers who have access to a system for social protection, should also be entitled to benefit from social protection. Member States

should be required to take the necessary measures to organise this social protection in accordance with national law. In particular, it is up to Member States to decide whether this social protection should be implemented on a mandatory or voluntary basis. Member States may provide that this social protection may be proportional to the participation in the activities of the self-employed worker and/or the level of contribution.

(18) The economic and physical vulnerability of pregnant self-employed workers and pregnant spouses and, when and in so far as recognised by national law, pregnant life partners of self-employed workers, makes it necessary for them to be granted the right to maternity benefits. The Member States remain competent to organise such benefits, including establishing the level of contributions and all the arrangements concerning benefits and payments, provided the minimum requirements of this Directive are complied with. In particular, they may determine in which period before and/or after confinement the right to maternity benefits is granted.

(19) The length of the period during which female self-employed workers and female spouses or, when and in so far as recognised by national law, female life partners of self-employed workers, are granted maternity benefits is similar to the duration of maternity leave for employees currently in place at Union level. In case the duration of maternity leave provided for employees is modified at Union level, the Commission should report to the European Parliament and the Council assessing whether the duration of maternity benefits for female self-employed workers and female spouses and life partners referred to in Article 2 should also be modified.

(20) In order to take the specificities of self-employed activities into account, female self-employed workers and female spouses or, when and in so far as recognised by national law, female life partners of self-employed workers should be given access to any existing services supplying temporary replacement enabling interruptions in their occupational activity owing to pregnancy or motherhood, or to any existing national social services. Access to those services can be an alternative to or a part of the maternity allowance.

(21) Persons who have been subject to discrimination based on sex should have suitable means of legal protection. To provide more effective protection, associations, organisations and other legal entities should be empowered to engage in proceedings, as Member States so determine, either on behalf or in support of any victim, without prejudice to national rules of procedure concerning representation and defence before the courts.

(22) Protection of self-employed workers and spouses of self-employed workers and, when and in so far as recognised by national law, the life partners of self-employed workers, from discrimination based on sex should be strengthened by the existence of a body or bodies in each Member State with competence to analyse the problems involved, to study possible solutions and to provide practical assistance to the victims. The body or bodies may be the same as those with responsibility at national level for the implementation of the principle of equal treatment.

(23) This Directive lays down minimum requirements, thus giving the Member States the option of introducing or maintaining more favourable provisions.

(24) Since the objective of the action to be taken, namely to ensure a common high level of protection from discrimination in all the Member States, cannot be sufficiently achieved by the Member States and can be better achieved at Union level, the Union may adopt measures, in accordance with the principle of subsidiarity as set out in Article 5 of the Treaty on European Union. In accordance with the principle of proportionality, as set out in that Article, this Directive does not go beyond what is necessary in order to achieve that objective,

NOTES

1 OJ C228, 22.9.2009, p 107.

2 Position of the European Parliament of 6 May 2009 (not yet published in the Official Journal), Position of the Council at first reading of 8 March 2010 (OJ C123 E, 12.5.2010, p 5), Position of the European Parliament of 18 May 2010.

3 OJ L359, 19.12.1986, p 56.

4 OJ C85, 17.3.1997, p 186.

5 OJ L6, 10.1.1979, p 24.

6 OJ L204, 26.7.2006, p 23.

7 OJ L373, 21.12.2004, p 37.

HAVE ADOPTED THIS DIRECTIVE:

[3.524]
Article 1
Subject matter

1. This Directive lays down a framework for putting into effect in the Member States the principle of equal treatment between men and women engaged in an activity in a self-employed capacity, or contributing to the pursuit of such an activity, as regards those aspects not covered by Directives 2006/54/EC and 79/7/EEC.

2. The implementation of the principle of equal treatment between men and women in the access to and supply of goods and services remains covered by Directive 2004/113/EC.

[3.525]
Article 2
Scope
This Directive covers:
(a) self-employed workers, namely all persons pursuing a gainful activity for their own account, under the conditions laid down by national law;
(b) the spouses of self-employed workers or, when and in so far as recognised by national law, the life partners of self-employed workers, not being employees or business partners, where they habitually, under the conditions laid down by national law, participate in the activities of the self-employed worker and perform the same tasks or ancillary tasks.

[3.526]
Article 3
Definitions
For the purposes of this Directive, the following definitions shall apply:
(a) 'direct discrimination': where one person is treated less favourably on grounds of sex than another is, has been or would be, treated in a comparable situation;
(b) 'indirect discrimination': where an apparently neutral provision, criterion or practice would put persons of one sex at a particular disadvantage compared with persons of the other sex, unless that provision, criterion or practice is objectively justified by a legitimate aim, and the means of achieving that aim are appropriate and necessary;
(c) 'harassment': where unwanted conduct related to the sex of a person occurs with the purpose, or effect, of violating the dignity of that person, and of creating an intimidating, hostile, degrading, humiliating or offensive environment;
(d) 'sexual harassment': where any form of unwanted verbal, non-verbal, or physical, conduct of a sexual nature occurs, with the purpose or effect of violating the dignity of a person, in particular when creating an intimidating, hostile, degrading, humiliating or offensive environment.

[3.527]
Article 4
Principle of equal treatment
1. The principle of equal treatment means that there shall be no discrimination whatsoever on grounds of sex in the public or private sectors, either directly or indirectly, for instance in relation to the establishment, equipment or extension of a business or the launching or extension of any other form of self-employed activity.
2. In the areas covered by paragraph 1, harassment and sexual harassment shall be deemed to be discrimination on grounds of sex and therefore prohibited. A person's rejection of, or submission to, such conduct may not be used as a basis for a decision affecting that person.
3. In the areas covered by paragraph 1, an instruction to discriminate against persons on grounds of sex shall be deemed to be discrimination.

[3.528]
Article 5
Positive action
Member States may maintain or adopt measures within the meaning of Article 157(4) of the Treaty on the Functioning of the European Union with a view to ensuring full equality in practice between men and women in working life, for instance aimed at promoting entrepreneurship initiatives among women.

[3.529]
Article 6
Establishment of a company
Without prejudice to the specific conditions for access to certain activities which apply equally to both sexes, the Member States shall take the measures necessary to ensure that the conditions for the establishment of a company between spouses, or between life partners when and in so far as recognised by national law, are not more restrictive than the conditions for the establishment of a company between other persons.

[3.530]
Article 7
Social protection
1. Where a system for social protection for self-employed workers exists in a Member State, that Member State shall take the necessary measures to ensure that spouses and life partners referred to in Article 2(b) can benefit from a social protection in accordance with national law.
2. The Member States may decide whether the social protection referred to in paragraph 1 is implemented on a mandatory or voluntary basis.

[3.531]
Article 8
Maternity benefits
1. The Member States shall take the necessary measures to ensure that female self-employed workers and female spouses and life partners referred to in Article 2 may, in accordance with national law, be granted a sufficient maternity allowance enabling interruptions in their occupational activity owing to pregnancy or motherhood for at least 14 weeks.

2. The Member States may decide whether the maternity allowance referred to in paragraph 1 is granted on a mandatory or voluntary basis.
3. The allowance referred to in paragraph 1 shall be deemed sufficient if it guarantees an income at least equivalent to:
(a) the allowance which the person concerned would receive in the event of a break in her activities on grounds connected with her state of health and/or;
(b) the average loss of income or profit in relation to a comparable preceding period subject to any ceiling laid down under national law and/or;
(c) any other family related allowance established by national law, subject to any ceiling laid down under national law.
4. The Member States shall take the necessary measures to ensure that female self-employed workers and female spouses and life partners referred to in Article 2 have access to any existing services supplying temporary replacements or to any existing national social services. The Member States may provide that access to those services is an alternative to or a part of the allowance referred to in paragraph 1 of this Article.

[3.532]
Article 9
Defence of rights
1. The Member States shall ensure that judicial or administrative proceedings, including, where Member States consider it appropriate, conciliation procedures, for the enforcement of the obligations under this Directive are available to all persons who consider they have sustained loss or damage as a result of a failure to apply the principle of equal treatment to them, even after the relationship in which the discrimination is alleged to have occurred has ended.
2. The Member States shall ensure that associations, organisations and other legal entities which have, in accordance with the criteria laid down by their national law, a legitimate interest in ensuring that this Directive is complied with may engage, either on behalf or in support of the complainant, with his or her approval, in any judicial or administrative proceedings provided for the enforcement of obligations under this Directive.
3. Paragraphs 1 and 2 shall be without prejudice to national rules on time limits for bringing actions relating to the principle of equal treatment.

[3.533]
Article 10
Compensation or reparation
The Member States shall introduce such measures into their national legal systems as are necessary to ensure real and effective compensation or reparation, as Member States so determine, for the loss or damage sustained by a person as a result of discrimination on grounds of sex, such compensation or reparation being dissuasive and proportionate to the loss or damage suffered. Such compensation or reparation shall not be limited by the fixing of a prior upper limit.

[3.534]
Article 11
Equality bodies
1. The Member States shall take the necessary measures to ensure that the body or bodies designated in accordance with Article 20 of Directive 2006/54/EC are also competent for the promotion, analysis, monitoring and support of equal treatment of all persons covered by this Directive without discrimination on grounds of sex.
2. The Member States shall ensure that the tasks of the bodies referred to in paragraph 1 include:
(a) providing independent assistance to victims of discrimination in pursuing their complaints of discrimination, without prejudice to the rights of victims and of associations, organisations and other legal entities referred to in Article 9(2);
(b) conducting independent surveys on discrimination;
(c) publishing independent reports and making recommendations on any issue relating to such discrimination;
(d) exchanging, at the appropriate level, the information available with the corresponding European bodies, such as the European Institute for Gender Equality.

[3.535]
Article 12
Gender mainstreaming
The Member States shall actively take into account the objective of equality between men and women when formulating and implementing laws, regulations, administrative provisions, policies and activities in the areas referred to in this Directive.

[3.536]
Article 13
Dissemination of information
The Member States shall ensure that the provisions adopted pursuant to this Directive, together with the relevant provisions already in force, are brought by all appropriate means to the attention of the persons concerned throughout their territory.

[3.537]
Article 14
Level of protection

The Member States may introduce or maintain provisions which are more favourable to the protection of the principle of equal treatment between men and women than those laid down in this Directive.

The implementation of this Directive shall under no circumstances constitute grounds for a reduction in the level of protection against discrimination already afforded by Member States in the fields covered by this Directive.

[3.538]
Article 15
Reports

1. Member States shall communicate all available information concerning the application of this Directive to the Commission by 5 August 2015.

The Commission shall draw up a summary report for submission to the European Parliament and to the Council no later than 5 August 2016. That report should take into account any legal change concerning the duration of maternity leave for employees. Where appropriate, that report shall be accompanied by proposals for amending this Directive.

2. The Commission's report shall take the viewpoints of the stakeholders into account.

[3.539]
Article 16
Implementation

1. The Member States shall bring into force the laws, regulations and administrative provisions necessary to comply with this Directive by 5 August 2012 at the latest. They shall forthwith communicate to the Commission the text of those provisions.

When the Member States adopt those provisions, they shall contain a reference to this Directive or be accompanied by such a reference on the occasion of their official publication. Member States shall determine how such reference is to be made.

2. Where justified by particular difficulties, the Member States may, if necessary, have an additional period of two years until 5 August 2014 in order to comply with Article 7, and in order to comply with Article 8 as regards female spouses and life partners referred to in Article 2(b).

3. The Member States shall communicate to the Commission the text of the main provisions of national law which they adopt in the field covered by this Directive.

[3.540]
Article 17
Repeal

Directive 86/613/EEC shall be repealed, with effect from 5 August 2012.

References to the repealed Directive shall be construed as references to this Directive.

[3.541]
Article 18
Entry into force

This Directive shall enter into force on the 20th day following its publication in the *Official Journal of the European Union*.

[3.542]
Article 19
Addressees

This Directive is addressed to the Member States.

EUROPEAN PARLIAMENT AND COUNCIL REGULATION

(1215/2012/EU)

of 12 December 2012

on jurisdiction and the recognition and enforcement of judgments in civil and commercial matters

(recast)

[3.543]

NOTES

Date of publication in OJ: OJ L351, 20.12.2012, p 1.

Only those parts of this Regulation of most relevance to this work are included.

This Regulation is a recast replacement of Council Regulation 44/2001/EC, which was repealed with effect from 10 January 2015, subject to transitional provisions: see Arts 66, 80, 81 of this Regulation at **[3.565]**, **[3.567]**, **[3.568]**. A Table of Correlations for the relevant parts of the 2001 Regulation is in Annex III (at **[3.569]**). Note that the provisions of this Regulation reproduced here came into effect from 10 January 2015 (see Art 81 at **[3.568]**).

Prospective repeal: this Regulation is repealed by the Civil Jurisdiction and Judgments (Amendment) (EU Exit) Regulations 2019, SI 2019/479, reg 89, as from exit day (as defined in the European Union (Withdrawal) Act 2018, s 20); for savings see regs 92–95 of the 2019 Regulations at **[2.2138]–[2.2141]**. Note that Council Regulation 44/2001/EC mentioned above, is also repealed by SI 2019/479, reg 84, as from exit day and subject to savings in regs 92–95 thereof.

THE EUROPEAN PARLIAMENT AND THE COUNCIL OF THE EUROPEAN UNION,

Having regard to the Treaty on the Functioning of the European Union, and in particular Article 67(4) and points (a), (c) and (e) of Article 81(2) thereof,

Having regard to the proposal from the European Commission,

After transmission of the draft legislative act to the national parliaments,

Having regard to the opinion of the European Economic and Social Committee,[1]

Acting in accordance with the ordinary legislative procedure,[2]

Whereas:

(1) On 21 April 2009, the Commission adopted a report on the application of Council Regulation (EC) No 44/2001 of 22 December 2000 on jurisdiction and the recognition and enforcement of judgments in civil and commercial matters.[3] The report concluded that, in general, the operation of that Regulation is satisfactory, but that it is desirable to improve the application of certain of its provisions, to further facilitate the free circulation of judgments and to further enhance access to justice. Since a number of amendments are to be made to that Regulation it should, in the interests of clarity, be recast.

(2) At its meeting in Brussels on 10 and 11 December 2009, the European Council adopted a new multiannual programme entitled "The Stockholm Programme – an open and secure Europe serving and protecting citizens".[4] In the Stockholm Programme the European Council considered that the process of abolishing all intermediate measures (the exequatur) should be continued during the period covered by that Programme. At the same time the abolition of the exequatur should also be accompanied by a series of safeguards.

(3) The Union has set itself the objective of maintaining and developing an area of freedom, security and justice, inter alia, by facilitating access to justice, in particular through the principle of mutual recognition of judicial and extra-judicial decisions in civil matters. For the gradual establishment of such an area, the Union is to adopt measures relating to judicial cooperation in civil matters having cross-border implications, particularly when necessary for the proper functioning of the internal market.

(4) Certain differences between national rules governing jurisdiction and recognition of judgments hamper the sound operation of the internal market. Provisions to unify the rules of conflict of jurisdiction in civil and commercial matters, and to ensure rapid and simple recognition and enforcement of judgments given in a Member State, are essential.

(5) Such provisions fall within the area of judicial cooperation in civil matters within the meaning of Article 81 of the Treaty on the Functioning of the European Union (TFEU).

(6) In order to attain the objective of free circulation of judgments in civil and commercial matters, it is necessary and appropriate that the rules governing jurisdiction and the recognition and enforcement of judgments be governed by a legal instrument of the Union which is binding and directly applicable.

(7) On 27 September 1968, the then Member States of the European Communities, acting under Article 220, fourth indent, of the Treaty establishing the European Economic Community, concluded the Brussels Convention on Jurisdiction and the Enforcement of Judgments in Civil and Commercial Matters, subsequently amended by conventions on the accession to that Convention of new Member States[5] ("the 1968 Brussels Convention"). On 16 September 1988, the then Member States of the European Communities and certain EFTA States concluded the Lugano Convention on Jurisdiction and the Enforcement of Judgments in Civil and Commercial Matters[6] ("the 1988 Lugano Convention"), which is a parallel convention to the 1968 Brussels Convention. The 1988 Lugano Convention became applicable to Poland on 1 February 2000.

(8) On 22 December 2000, the Council adopted Regulation (EC) No 44/2001, which replaces the 1968 Brussels Convention with regard to the territories of the Member States covered by the TFEU, as between the Member States except Denmark. By Council Decision 2006/325/EC,[7] the Community concluded an agreement with Denmark ensuring the application of the provisions of Regulation (EC) No 44/2001 in Denmark. The 1988 Lugano Convention was revised by the Convention on Jurisdiction and the Recognition and Enforcement of Judgments in Civil and Commercial Matters,[8] signed at Lugano on 30 October 2007 by the Community, Denmark, Iceland, Norway and Switzerland ("the 2007 Lugano Convention").

(9) The 1968 Brussels Convention continues to apply to the territories of the Member States which fall within the territorial scope of that Convention and which are excluded from this Regulation pursuant to Article 355 of the TFEU.

(10) The scope of this Regulation should cover all the main civil and commercial matters apart from certain well-defined matters, in particular maintenance obligations, which should be excluded from the scope of this Regulation following the adoption of Council Regulation (EC) No 4/2009 of 18 December 2008 on jurisdiction, applicable law, recognition and enforcement of decisions and cooperation in matters relating to maintenance obligations.[9]

(11) For the purposes of this Regulation, courts or tribunals of the Member States should include courts or tribunals common to several Member States, such as the Benelux Court of Justice when it exercises jurisdiction on matters falling within the scope of this Regulation. Therefore, judgments given by such courts should be recognised and enforced in accordance with this Regulation.

(12) This Regulation should not apply to arbitration. Nothing in this Regulation should prevent the courts of a Member State, when seised of an action in a matter in respect of which the parties have entered into an arbitration agreement, from referring the parties to arbitration, from staying or dismissing the proceedings, or from examining whether the arbitration agreement is null and void, inoperative or incapable of being performed, in accordance with their national law.

A ruling given by a court of a Member State as to whether or not an arbitration agreement is null and void, inoperative or incapable of being performed should not be subject to the rules of recognition and enforcement laid down in this Regulation, regardless of whether the court decided on this as a principal issue or as an incidental question.

On the other hand, where a court of a Member State, exercising jurisdiction under this Regulation or under national law, has determined that an arbitration agreement is null and void, inoperative or incapable of being performed, this should not preclude that court's judgment on the substance of the matter from being recognised or, as the case may be, enforced in accordance with this Regulation. This should be without prejudice to the competence of the courts of the Member States to decide on the recognition and enforcement of arbitral awards in accordance with the Convention on the Recognition and Enforcement of Foreign Arbitral Awards, done at New York on 10 June 1958 ("the 1958 New York Convention"), which takes precedence over this Regulation.

This Regulation should not apply to any action or ancillary proceedings relating to, in particular, the establishment of an arbitral tribunal, the powers of arbitrators, the conduct of an arbitration procedure or any other aspects of such a procedure, nor to any action or judgment concerning the annulment, review, appeal, recognition or enforcement of an arbitral award.

(13) There must be a connection between proceedings to which this Regulation applies and the territory of the Member States. Accordingly, common rules of jurisdiction should, in principle, apply when the defendant is domiciled in a Member State.

(14) A defendant not domiciled in a Member State should in general be subject to the national rules of jurisdiction applicable in the territory of the Member State of the court seised.

However, in order to ensure the protection of consumers and employees, to safeguard the jurisdiction of the courts of the Member States in situations where they have exclusive jurisdiction and to respect the autonomy of the parties, certain rules of jurisdiction in this Regulation should apply regardless of the defendant's domicile.

(15) The rules of jurisdiction should be highly predictable and founded on the principle that jurisdiction is generally based on the defendant's domicile. Jurisdiction should always be available on this ground save in a few well-defined situations in which the subject-matter of the dispute or the autonomy of the parties warrants a different connecting factor. The domicile of a legal person must be defined autonomously so as to make the common rules more transparent and avoid conflicts of jurisdiction.

(16) In addition to the defendant's domicile, there should be alternative grounds of jurisdiction based on a close connection between the court and the action or in order to facilitate the sound administration of justice. The existence of a close connection should ensure legal certainty and avoid the possibility of the defendant being sued in a court of a Member State which he could not reasonably have foreseen. This is important, particularly in disputes concerning non-contractual obligations arising out of violations of privacy and rights relating to personality, including defamation.

(17) The owner of a cultural object as defined in Article 1(1) of Council Directive 93/7/EEC of 15 March 1993 on the return of cultural objects unlawfully removed from the territory of a Member State[10] should be able under this Regulation to initiate proceedings as regards a civil claim for the recovery, based on ownership, of such a cultural object in the courts for the place where the cultural object is situated at the time the court is seised. Such proceedings should be without prejudice to proceedings initiated under Directive 93/7/EEC.

(18) In relation to insurance, consumer and employment contracts, the weaker party should be protected by rules of jurisdiction more favourable to his interests than the general rules.

(19) The autonomy of the parties to a contract, other than an insurance, consumer or employment contract, where only limited autonomy to determine the courts having jurisdiction is allowed, should be respected subject to the exclusive grounds of jurisdiction laid down in this Regulation.

(20) Where a question arises as to whether a choice-of-court agreement in favour of a court or the courts of a Member State is null and void as to its substantive validity, that question should be decided in accordance with the law of the Member State of the court or courts designated in the agreement, including the conflict-of-laws rules of that Member State.

(21) In the interests of the harmonious administration of justice it is necessary to minimise the possibility of concurrent proceedings and to ensure that irreconcilable judgments will not be given in different Member States. There should be a clear and effective mechanism for resolving cases of lis pendens and related actions, and for obviating problems flowing from national differences as to the determination of the time when a case is regarded as pending. For the purposes of this Regulation, that time should be defined autonomously.

(22) However, in order to enhance the effectiveness of exclusive choice-of-court agreements and to avoid abusive litigation tactics, it is necessary to provide for an exception to the general lis pendens rule in order to deal satisfactorily with a particular situation in which concurrent proceedings may arise. This is the situation where a court not designated in an exclusive choice-of-court agreement has been seised of proceedings and the designated court is seised subsequently of proceedings involving the same cause of action and between the same parties. In such a case, the court first seised should be required to stay its proceedings as soon as the designated court has been seised and until such time as the latter court declares

that it has no jurisdiction under the exclusive choice-of-court agreement. This is to ensure that, in such a situation, the designated court has priority to decide on the validity of the agreement and on the extent to which the agreement applies to the dispute pending before it. The designated court should be able to proceed irrespective of whether the non-designated court has already decided on the stay of proceedings.

This exception should not cover situations where the parties have entered into conflicting exclusive choice-of-court agreements or where a court designated in an exclusive choice-of-court agreement has been seised first. In such cases, the general lis pendens rule of this Regulation should apply.

(23) This Regulation should provide for a flexible mechanism allowing the courts of the Member States to take into account proceedings pending before the courts of third States, considering in particular whether a judgment of a third State will be capable of recognition and enforcement in the Member State concerned under the law of that Member State and the proper administration of justice.

(24) When taking into account the proper administration of justice, the court of the Member State concerned should assess all the circumstances of the case before it. Such circumstances may include connections between the facts of the case and the parties and the third State concerned, the stage to which the proceedings in the third State have progressed by the time proceedings are initiated in the court of the Member State and whether or not the court of the third State can be expected to give a judgment within a reasonable time.

That assessment may also include consideration of the question whether the court of the third State has exclusive jurisdiction in the particular case in circumstances where a court of a Member State would have exclusive jurisdiction.

(25)–(33) (*Outside the scope of this work.*)

(34) Continuity between the 1968 Brussels Convention, Regulation (EC) No 44/2001 and this Regulation should be ensured, and transitional provisions should be laid down to that end. The same need for continuity applies as regards the interpretation by the Court of Justice of the European Union of the 1968 Brussels Convention and of the Regulations replacing it.

(35) Respect for international commitments entered into by the Member States means that this Regulation should not affect conventions relating to specific matters to which the Member States are parties.

(36) Without prejudice to the obligations of the Member States under the Treaties, this Regulation should not affect the application of bilateral conventions and agreements between a third State and a Member State concluded before the date of entry into force of Regulation (EC) No 44/2001 which concern matters governed by this Regulation.

(37) In order to ensure that the certificates to be used in connection with the recognition or enforcement of judgments, authentic instruments and court settlements under this Regulation are kept up-to-date, the power to adopt acts in accordance with Article 290 of the TFEU should be delegated to the Commission in respect of amendments to Annexes I and II to this Regulation. It is of particular importance that the Commission carry out appropriate consultations during its preparatory work, including at expert level. The Commission, when preparing and drawing up delegated acts, should ensure a simultaneous, timely and appropriate transmission of relevant documents to the European Parliament and to the Council.

(38) This Regulation respects fundamental rights and observes the principles recognised in the Charter of Fundamental Rights of the European Union, in particular the right to an effective remedy and to a fair trial guaranteed in Article 47 of the Charter.

(39) Since the objective of this Regulation cannot be sufficiently achieved by the Member States and can be better achieved at Union level, the Union may adopt measures in accordance with the principle of subsidiarity as set out in Article 5 of the Treaty on European Union (TEU). In accordance with the principle of proportionality, as set out in that Article, this Regulation does not go beyond what is necessary in order to achieve that objective.

(40) The United Kingdom and Ireland, in accordance with Article 3 of the Protocol on the position of the United Kingdom and Ireland, annexed to the TEU and to the then Treaty establishing the European Community, took part in the adoption and application of Regulation (EC) No 44/2001. In accordance with Article 3 of Protocol No 21 on the position of the United Kingdom and Ireland in respect of the area of freedom, security and justice, annexed to the TEU and to the TFEU, the United Kingdom and Ireland have notified their wish to take part in the adoption and application of this Regulation.

(41) In accordance with Articles 1 and 2 of Protocol No 22 on the position of Denmark annexed to the TEU and to the TFEU, Denmark is not taking part in the adoption of this Regulation and is not bound by it or subject to its application, without prejudice to the possibility for Denmark of applying the amendments to Regulation (EC) No 44/2001 pursuant to Article 3 of the Agreement of 19 October 2005 between the European Community and the Kingdom of Denmark on jurisdiction and the recognition and enforcement of judgments in civil and commercial matters,[11]

NOTES

[1] OJ C218, 23.7.2011, p 78.

[2] Position of the European Parliament of 20 November 2012 (not yet published in the Official Journal) and decision of the Council of 6 December 2012.

[3] OJ L12, 16.1.2001, p 1.

[4] OJ C115, 4.5.2010, p 1.

[5] OJ L299, 31.12.1972, p 32, OJ L304, 30.10.1978, p 1, OJ L388, 31.12.1982, p 1, OJ L285, 3.10.1989, p 1, OJ C15,

15.1.1997, p 1. For a consolidated text, see OJ C27, 26.1.1998, p 1.

[6] OJ L319, 25.11.1988, p 9.

[7] OJ L120, 5.5.2006, p 22.

[8] OJ L147, 10.6.2009, p 5.

[9] OJ L7, 10.1.2009, p 1.

[10] OJ L74, 27.3.1993, p 74.

[11] OJ L299, 16.11.2005, p 62.

HAVE ADOPTED THIS REGULATION:

CHAPTER I SCOPE AND DEFINITIONS

[3.544]
Article 1

1. This Regulation shall apply in civil and commercial matters whatever the nature of the court or tribunal. It shall not extend, in particular, to revenue, customs or administrative matters or to the liability of the State for acts and omissions in the exercise of State authority (*acta iure imperii*).
2. The Regulation shall not apply to:
   (a) the status or legal capacity of natural persons, rights in property arising out of a matrimonial relationship or out of a relationship deemed by the law applicable to such relationship to have comparable effects to marriage;
   (b) bankruptcy, proceedings relating to the winding-up of insolvent companies or other legal persons, judicial arrangements, compositions and analogous proceedings;
   (c) social security;
   (d) arbitration;
   (e) maintenance obligations arising from a family relationship, parentage, marriage or affinity;
   (f) wills and succession, including maintenance obligations arising by reason of death.

[3.545]
Article 2

For the purposes of this Regulation:
   (a) "judgment" means any judgment given by a court or tribunal of a Member State, whatever the judgment may be called, including a decree, order, decision or writ of execution, as well as a decision on the determination of costs or expenses by an officer of the court.
   For the purposes of Chapter III, "judgment" includes provisional, including protective, measures ordered by a court or tribunal which by virtue of this Regulation has jurisdiction as to the substance of the matter. It does not include a provisional, including protective, measure which is ordered by such a court or tribunal without the defendant being summoned to appear, unless the judgment containing the measure is served on the defendant prior to enforcement;
   (b) "court settlement" means a settlement which has been approved by a court of a Member State or concluded before a court of a Member State in the course of proceedings;
   (c) "authentic instrument" means a document which has been formally drawn up or registered as an authentic instrument in the Member State of origin and the authenticity of which:
      (i) relates to the signature and the content of the instrument; and
      (ii) has been established by a public authority or other authority empowered for that purpose;
   (d) "Member State of origin" means the Member State in which, as the case may be, the judgment has been given, the court settlement has been approved or concluded, or the authentic instrument has been formally drawn up or registered;
   (e) "Member State addressed" means the Member State in which the recognition of the judgment is invoked or in which the enforcement of the judgment, the court settlement or the authentic instrument is sought;
   (f) "court of origin" means the court which has given the judgment the recognition of which is invoked or the enforcement of which is sought.

[3.546]
Article 3

For the purposes of this Regulation, "court" includes the following authorities to the extent that they have jurisdiction in matters falling within the scope of this Regulation:
   (a) in Hungary, in summary proceedings concerning orders to pay (fizetési meghagyásos eljárás), the notary (közjegyző);
   (b) in Sweden, in summary proceedings concerning orders to pay (betalningsföreläggande) and assistance (handräckning), the Enforcement Authority (Kronofogdemyndigheten).

CHAPTER II JURISDICTION

SECTION 1 GENERAL PROVISIONS

[3.547]
Article 4

1. Subject to this Regulation, persons domiciled in a Member State shall, whatever their nationality, be sued in the courts of that Member State.

2. Persons who are not nationals of the Member State in which they are domiciled shall be governed by the rules of jurisdiction applicable to nationals of that Member State.

[3.548]
Article 5
1. Persons domiciled in a Member State may be sued in the courts of another Member State only by virtue of the rules set out in Sections 2 to 7 of this Chapter.
2. In particular, the rules of national jurisdiction of which the Member States are to notify the Commission pursuant to point (a) of Article 76(1) shall not be applicable as against the persons referred to in paragraph 1.

[3.549]
Article 6
1. If the defendant is not domiciled in a Member State, the jurisdiction of the courts of each Member State shall, subject to Article 18(1), Article 21(2) and Articles 24 and 25, be determined by the law of that Member State.
2. As against such a defendant, any person domiciled in a Member State may, whatever his nationality, avail himself in that Member State of the rules of jurisdiction there in force, and in particular those of which the Member States are to notify the Commission pursuant to point (a) of Article 76(1), in the same way as nationals of that Member State.

SECTION 2 SPECIAL JURISDICTION

[3.550]
Article 7
A person domiciled in a Member State may be sued in another Member State:

(1)
- (a) in matters relating to a contract, in the courts for the place of performance of the obligation in question;
- (b) for the purpose of this provision and unless otherwise agreed, the place of performance of the obligation in question shall be:
  - — in the case of the sale of goods, the place in a Member State where, under the contract, the goods were delivered or should have been delivered,
  - — in the case of the provision of services, the place in a Member State where, under the contract, the services were provided or should have been provided;
- (c) if point (b) does not apply then point (a) applies;

(2) in matters relating to tort, delict or quasi-delict, in the courts for the place where the harmful event occurred or may occur;

(3) as regards a civil claim for damages or restitution which is based on an act giving rise to criminal proceedings, in the court seised of those proceedings, to the extent that that court has jurisdiction under its own law to entertain civil proceedings;

(4) as regards a civil claim for the recovery, based on ownership, of a cultural object as defined in point 1 of Article 1 of Directive 93/7/EEC initiated by the person claiming the right to recover such an object, in the courts for the place where the cultural object is situated at the time when the court is seised;

(5) as regards a dispute arising out of the operations of a branch, agency or other establishment, in the courts for the place where the branch, agency or other establishment is situated;

(6) as regards a dispute brought against a settlor, trustee or beneficiary of a trust created by the operation of a statute, or by a written instrument, or created orally and evidenced in writing, in the courts of the Member State in which the trust is domiciled;

(7) as regards a dispute concerning the payment of remuneration claimed in respect of the salvage of a cargo or freight, in the court under the authority of which the cargo or freight in question:
- (a) has been arrested to secure such payment; or
- (b) could have been so arrested, but bail or other security has been given;

provided that this provision shall apply only if it is claimed that the defendant has an interest in the cargo or freight or had such an interest at the time of salvage.

[3.551]
Article 8
A person domiciled in a Member State may also be sued:

(1) where he is one of a number of defendants, in the courts for the place where any one of them is domiciled, provided the claims are so closely connected that it is expedient to hear and determine them together to avoid the risk of irreconcilable judgments resulting from separate proceedings;

(2) as a third party in an action on a warranty or guarantee or in any other third-party proceedings, in the court seised of the original proceedings, unless these were instituted solely with the object of removing him from the jurisdiction of the court which would be competent in his case;

(3) on a counter-claim arising from the same contract or facts on which the original claim was based, in the court in which the original claim is pending;

(4) in matters relating to a contract, if the action may be combined with an action against the same defendant in matters relating to rights in rem in immovable property, in the court of the Member State in which the property is situated.

[3.552]
Article 9
Where by virtue of this Regulation a court of a Member State has jurisdiction in actions relating to liability from the use or operation of a ship, that court, or any other court substituted for this purpose by the internal law of that Member State, shall also have jurisdiction over claims for limitation of such liability.

Articles 10–19 (*Outside the scope of this work.*)

SECTION 5 JURISDICTION OVER INDIVIDUAL CONTRACTS OF EMPLOYMENT

[3.553]
Article 20
1. In matters relating to individual contracts of employment, jurisdiction shall be determined by this Section, without prejudice to Article 6, point 5 of Article 7 and, in the case of proceedings brought against an employer, point 1 of Article 8.
2. Where an employee enters into an individual contract of employment with an employer who is not domiciled in a Member State but has a branch, agency or other establishment in one of the Member States, the employer shall, in disputes arising out of the operations of the branch, agency or establishment, be deemed to be domiciled in that Member State.

[3.554]
Article 21
1. An employer domiciled in a Member State may be sued:
(a) in the courts of the Member State in which he is domiciled; or
(b) in another Member State:
(i) in the courts for the place where or from where the employee habitually carries out his work or in the courts for the last place where he did so; or
(ii) if the employee does not or did not habitually carry out his work in any one country, in the courts for the place where the business which engaged the employee is or was situated.
2. An employer not domiciled in a Member State may be sued in a court of a Member State in accordance with point (b) of paragraph 1.

[3.555]
Article 22
1. An employer may bring proceedings only in the courts of the Member State in which the employee is domiciled.
2. The provisions of this Section shall not affect the right to bring a counter-claim in the court in which, in accordance with this Section, the original claim is pending.

[3.556]
Article 23
The provisions of this Section may be departed from only by an agreement:
(1) which is entered into after the dispute has arisen; or
(2) which allows the employee to bring proceedings in courts other than those indicated in this Section.

Article 24 (*Outside the scope of this work.*)

SECTION 7 PROROGATION OF JURISDICTION

[3.557]
Article 25
1. If the parties, regardless of their domicile, have agreed that a court or the courts of a Member State are to have jurisdiction to settle any disputes which have arisen or which may arise in connection with a particular legal relationship, that court or those courts shall have jurisdiction, unless the agreement is null and void as to its substantive validity under the law of that Member State. Such jurisdiction shall be exclusive unless the parties have agreed otherwise. The agreement conferring jurisdiction shall be either:
(a) in writing or evidenced in writing;
(b) in a form which accords with practices which the parties have established between themselves; or
(c) in international trade or commerce, in a form which accords with a usage of which the parties are or ought to have been aware and which in such trade or commerce is widely known to, and regularly observed by, parties to contracts of the type involved in the particular trade or commerce concerned.
2. Any communication by electronic means which provides a durable record of the agreement shall be equivalent to 'writing'.
3. The court or courts of a Member State on which a trust instrument has conferred jurisdiction shall have exclusive jurisdiction in any proceedings brought against a settlor, trustee or beneficiary, if relations between those persons or their rights or obligations under the trust are involved.
4. Agreements or provisions of a trust instrument conferring jurisdiction shall have no legal force if they are contrary to Articles 15, 19 or 23, or if the courts whose jurisdiction they purport to exclude have exclusive jurisdiction by virtue of Article 24.

5. An agreement conferring jurisdiction which forms part of a contract shall be treated as an agreement independent of the other terms of the contract.

The validity of the agreement conferring jurisdiction cannot be contested solely on the ground that the contract is not valid.

[3.558]
Article 26

1. Apart from jurisdiction derived from other provisions of this Regulation, a court of a Member State before which a defendant enters an appearance shall have jurisdiction. This rule shall not apply where appearance was entered to contest the jurisdiction, or where another court has exclusive jurisdiction by virtue of Article 24.

2. In matters referred to in Sections 3, 4 or 5 where the policyholder, the insured, a beneficiary of the insurance contract, the injured party, the consumer or the employee is the defendant, the court shall, before assuming jurisdiction under paragraph 1, ensure that the defendant is informed of his right to contest the jurisdiction of the court and of the consequences of entering or not entering an appearance.

Articles 27, 28 (*Outside the scope of this work.*)

SECTION 9 *LIS PENDENS* — RELATED ACTIONS

[3.559]
Article 29

1. Without prejudice to Article 31(2), where proceedings involving the same cause of action and between the same parties are brought in the courts of different Member States, any court other than the court first seised shall of its own motion stay its proceedings until such time as the jurisdiction of the court first seised is established.

2. In cases referred to in paragraph 1, upon request by a court seised of the dispute, any other court seised shall without delay inform the former court of the date when it was seised in accordance with Article 32.

3. Where the jurisdiction of the court first seised is established, any court other than the court first seised shall decline jurisdiction in favour of that court.

[3.560]
Article 30

1. Where related actions are pending in the courts of different Member States, any court other than the court first seised may stay its proceedings.

2. Where the action in the court first seised is pending at first instance, any other court may also, on the application of one of the parties, decline jurisdiction if the court first seised has jurisdiction over the actions in question and its law permits the consolidation thereof.

3. For the purposes of this Article, actions are deemed to be related where they are so closely connected that it is expedient to hear and determine them together to avoid the risk of irreconcilable judgments resulting from separate proceedings.

[3.561]
Article 31

1. Where actions come within the exclusive jurisdiction of several courts, any court other than the court first seised shall decline jurisdiction in favour of that court.

2. Without prejudice to Article 26, where a court of a Member State on which an agreement as referred to in Article 25 confers exclusive jurisdiction is seised, any court of another Member State shall stay the proceedings until such time as the court seised on the basis of the agreement declares that it has no jurisdiction under the agreement.

3. Where the court designated in the agreement has established jurisdiction in accordance with the agreement, any court of another Member State shall decline jurisdiction in favour of that court.

4. Paragraphs 2 and 3 shall not apply to matters referred to in Sections 3, 4 or 5 where the policyholder, the insured, a beneficiary of the insurance contract, the injured party, the consumer or the employee is the claimant and the agreement is not valid under a provision contained within those Sections.

[3.562]
Article 32

1. For the purposes of this Section, a court shall be deemed to be seised:

(a) at the time when the document instituting the proceedings or an equivalent document is lodged with the court, provided that the claimant has not subsequently failed to take the steps he was required to take to have service effected on the defendant; or

(b) if the document has to be served before being lodged with the court, at the time when it is received by the authority responsible for service, provided that the claimant has not subsequently failed to take the steps he was required to take to have the document lodged with the court.

The authority responsible for service referred to in point (b) shall be the first authority receiving the documents to be served.

2. The court, or the authority responsible for service, referred to in paragraph 1, shall note, respectively, the date of the lodging of the document instituting the proceedings or the equivalent document, or the date of receipt of the documents to be served.

[3.563]
Article 33

1. Where jurisdiction is based on Article 4 or on Articles 7, 8 or 9 and proceedings are pending before a court of a third State at the time when a court in a Member State is seised of an action involving the same cause of action and between the same parties as the proceedings in the court of the third State, the court of the Member State may stay the proceedings if:

(a) it is expected that the court of the third State will give a judgment capable of recognition and, where applicable, of enforcement in that Member State; and

(b) the court of the Member State is satisfied that a stay is necessary for the proper administration of justice.

2. The court of the Member State may continue the proceedings at any time if:

(a) the proceedings in the court of the third State are themselves stayed or discontinued;

(b) it appears to the court of the Member State that the proceedings in the court of the third State are unlikely to be concluded within a reasonable time; or

(c) the continuation of the proceedings is required for the proper administration of justice.

3. The court of the Member State shall dismiss the proceedings if the proceedings in the court of the third State are concluded and have resulted in a judgment capable of recognition and, where applicable, of enforcement in that Member State.

4. The court of the Member State shall apply this Article on the application of one of the parties or, where possible under national law, of its own motion.

[3.564]
Article 34

1. Where jurisdiction is based on Article 4 or on Articles 7, 8 or 9 and an action is pending before a court of a third State at the time when a court in a Member State is seised of an action which is related to the action in the court of the third State, the court of the Member State may stay the proceedings if:

(a) it is expedient to hear and determine the related actions together to avoid the risk of irreconcilable judgments resulting from separate proceedings;

(b) it is expected that the court of the third State will give a judgment capable of recognition and, where applicable, of enforcement in that Member State; and

(c) the court of the Member State is satisfied that a stay is necessary for the proper administration of justice.

2. The court of the Member State may continue the proceedings at any time if

(a) it appears to the court of the Member State that there is no longer a risk of irreconcilable judgments;

(b) the proceedings in the court of the third State are themselves stayed or discontinued;

(c) it appears to the court of the Member State that the proceedings in the court of the third State are unlikely to be concluded within a reasonable time; or

(d) the continuation of the proceedings is required for the proper administration of justice.

3. The court of the Member State may dismiss the proceedings if the proceedings in the court of the third State are concluded and have resulted in a judgment capable of recognition and, where applicable, of enforcement in that Member State.

4. The court of the Member State shall apply this Article on the application of one of the parties or, where possible under national law, of its own motion.

Articles 35–65 (*Outside the scope of this work.*)

CHAPTER VI TRANSITIONAL PROVISIONS

[3.565]
Article 66

1. This Regulation shall apply only to legal proceedings instituted, to authentic instruments formally drawn up or registered and to court settlements approved or concluded on or after 10 January 2015.

2. Notwithstanding Article 80, Regulation (EC) No 44/2001 shall continue to apply to judgments given in legal proceedings instituted, to authentic instruments formally drawn up or registered and to court settlements approved or concluded before 10 January 2015 which fall within the scope of that Regulation.

CHAPTER VII RELATIONSHIP WITH OTHER INSTRUMENTS

Article 67 (*Outside the scope of this work.*)

[3.566]
Article 68

1. This Regulation shall, as between the Member States, supersede the 1968 Brussels Convention, except as regards the territories of the Member States which fall within the territorial scope of that Convention and which are excluded from this Regulation pursuant to Article 355 of the TFEU.

2. In so far as this Regulation replaces the provisions of the 1968 Brussels Convention between the Member States, any reference to that Convention shall be understood as a reference to this Regulation.

Articles 69–73 (*Outside the scope of this work.*)

CHAPTER VIII FINAL PROVISIONS

Articles 74–79 (*Outside the scope of this work.*)

[3.567]
Article 80
This Regulation shall repeal Regulation (EC) No 44/2001. References to the repealed Regulation shall be construed as references to this Regulation and shall be read in accordance with the correlation table set out in Annex III.

[3.568]
Article 81
This Regulation shall enter into force on the twentieth day following that of its publication in the *Official Journal of the European Union.*

It shall apply from 10 January 2015, with the exception of Articles 75 and 76, which shall apply from 10 January 2014.

This Regulation shall be binding in its entirety and directly applicable in the Member States in accordance with the Treaties.

ANNEXES I, II

(*Outside the scope of this work.*)

ANNEX III

CORRELATION TABLE

[3.569]

NOTES

Only those entries which relate to the provisions of Regulation 44/2001/EC and Regulation 1215/2012/EU reproduced in this work are listed below.

Regulation 44/2001/EC	*This Regulation*
Article 1(1)	Article 1(1)
Article 1(2), introductory words	Article 1(2), introductory words
Article 1(2) point (a)	Article 1(2), points (a) and (f)
Article 1(2), points (b) to (d)	Article 1(2), points (b) to (d)
—	Article 1(2), point (e)
Article 1(3)	—
—	Article 2
Article 2	Article 4
Article 3	Article 5
Article 4	Article 6
Article 5, introductory words	Article 7, introductory words
Article 5, point (1)	Article 7, point (1)
Article 5, point (2)	—
Article 5, points (3) and (4)	Article 7, points (2) and (3)
—	Article 7, point (4)
Article 5, points (5) to (7)	Article 7, points (5) to (7)
Article 6	Article 8
Article 7	Article 9
. . .	. . .
Article 18	Article 20
Article 19, points (1) and (2)	Article 21(1)
—	Article 21(2)
Article 20	Article 22
Article 21	Article 23
. . .	
Article 23(1) and (2)	Article 25(1) and (2)
Article 23(3)	—
Article 23(4) and (5)	Article 25(3) and (4)
—	Article 25(5)
Article 24	Article 26(1)
—	Article 26(2)

Regulation 44/2001/EC	***This Regulation***
Article 25	Article 27
Article 26	Article 28
Article 27(1)	Article 29(1)
—	Article 29(2)
Article 27(2)	Article 29(3)
Article 28	Article 30
Article 29	Article 31(1)
—	Article 31(2)
—	Article 31(3)
—	Article 31(4)
Article 30	Article 32(1), points (a) and (b)
—	Article 32(1), second subparagraph
—	Article 32(2)
—	Article 33
—	Article 34
Article 31	Article 35
Article 32	Article 2, point (a)
. . .	. . .
Article 59	Article 62
Article 60	Article 63
. . .	. . .
Article 76	Article 81
Annex I	Article 76(1), point (a)
. . .	. . .
—	Annex III

DIRECTIVE OF THE EUROPEAN PARLIAMENT AND OF THE COUNCIL

(2014/54/EU)

of 16 April 2014

on measures facilitating the exercise of rights conferred on workers in the context of freedom of movement for workers

(Text with EEA relevance)

[3.570]

NOTES

Date of publication in OJ: OJ L128, 30.4.2014, p 8.

The date for domestic implementation of the provisions of this Directive was 21 May 2016 (see Article 8 at **[3.578]**). As of 15 May 2019, no specific domestic implementing legislation had been made, presumably because the UK government considers that existing legislation (in particular, provisions of the Equality Acts 2006 and 2010) sufficiently implement this Directive.

THE EUROPEAN PARLIAMENT AND THE COUNCIL OF THE EUROPEAN UNION,

Having regard to the Treaty on the Functioning of the European Union, and in particular Article 46 thereof,

Having regard to the proposal from the European Commission,

After transmission of the draft legislative act to the national parliaments,

Having regard to the opinion of the European Economic and Social Committee,[1]

After consulting the Committee of the Regions,

Acting in accordance with the ordinary legislative procedure,[2]

Whereas:

(1) The free movement of workers is a fundamental freedom of Union citizens and one of the pillars of the internal market in the Union enshrined in Article 45 of the Treaty on the Functioning of the European Union (TFEU). Its implementation is further developed by Union law aiming to guarantee the

full exercise of rights conferred on Union citizens and the members of their family. 'Members of their family' should be understood as having the same meaning as the term defined in point (2) of Article 2 of Directive 2004/38/EC of the European Parliament and of the Council,[3] which applies also to family members of frontier workers.

(2) The free movement of workers is also a key element in the development of a genuine Union labour market, allowing workers to move to areas where there are labour shortages or more employment opportunities, helping more people find posts which are better suited to their skills and overcoming bottlenecks in the labour market.

(3) The free movement of workers gives every citizen of the Union, irrespective of his or her place of residence, the right to move freely to another Member State in order to work there and/or to reside there for work purposes. It protects them against discrimination on grounds of nationality as regards access to employment, conditions of employment and work, in particular with regard to remuneration, dismissal, and tax and social advantages, by ensuring their equal treatment, under national law, practice and collective agreements, in comparison to nationals of that Member State. Such rights should be enjoyed without discrimination by all Union citizens exercising their right to free movement, including permanent, seasonal and frontier workers. The free movement of workers needs to be distinguished from the freedom to provide services, which includes the right of undertakings to provide services in another Member State, for which they may post their own workers to another Member State temporarily in order for them to carry out the work necessary to provide services in that Member State.

(4) With respect to Union workers and members of their family exercising their right to free movement, Article 45 TFEU confers substantial rights for the exercise of this fundamental freedom, which are further specified in Regulation (EU) No 492/2011 of the European Parliament and of the Council.[4]

(5) The effective exercise of the freedom of movement of workers is, however, still a major challenge and many Union workers are very often unaware of their rights to free movement. Because of, inter alia, their potentially more vulnerable position, Union workers may still suffer from unjustified restrictions or obstacles to the exercise of their right to free movement, such as non-recognition of qualifications, discrimination on grounds of nationality and exploitation when they move to another Member State. There is, therefore, a gap between the law and its application in practice that needs to be addressed.

(6) In July 2010, in its Communication entitled 'Reaffirming the free movement of workers: rights and major developments' the Commission pointed out that it would explore ways of tackling the new needs and challenges, in particular in the light of new patterns of mobility, facing Union workers and members of their family. It also stated that, in the context of the new strategy for the internal market, it would consider how to promote and enhance mechanisms for the effective implementation of the principle of equal treatment for Union workers and members of their family exercising their right to free movement. The Commission also summarised developments in legislation and case-law, in particular with regard to the personal scope of the Union law on free movement of workers and the substance of the rights enjoyed by Union workers and members of their family.

(7) In the 2010 EU Citizenship Report entitled 'Dismantling the obstacles to EU citizens' rights' of 27 October 2010, the Commission identified the divergent and incorrect application of Union law on the right to free movement as one of the main obstacles that Union citizens are confronted with in the effective exercise of their rights under Union law. Accordingly, the Commission announced its intention to take action to facilitate free movement of EU citizens and their third-country national family members by enforcing EU rules strictly, including on non-discrimination, by promoting good practices and increased knowledge or EU rules on the ground and by stepping up the dissemination of information to EU citizens about their free movement rights (action 15 of the 2010 EU Citizenship Report). In addition in the 2013 EU Citizenship Report entitled 'EU citizens: your rights, your future', the Commission addressed the need to remove administrative hurdles and to simplify procedures for Union citizens living, working and travelling in other Member States.

(8) In the Commission Communication entitled 'Towards a job-rich recovery' of 18 April 2012 (the Employment Package), the Commission announced its intention to: present a legislative proposal (information and advice) in order to support mobile workers in the exercise of rights derived from the TFEU and Regulation (EU) No 492/2011, and urged Member States to: raise awareness of and access to rights conferred by Union law in relation to anti-discrimination, gender equality and free movement of workers and to open and facilitate access by Union citizens to public sector posts, in accordance with Union law, as interpreted by the Court of Justice of the European Union. In this context, the Court has consistently held that the restriction of access to certain posts in the public service to a Member State's own nationals is to be interpreted restrictively and that it covers only posts involving direct or indirect participation in the exercise of powers conferred by public law and duties designed to safeguard the general interests of the State or of other public authorities.

(9) Adequate and effective application and enforcement of Article 45 TFEU and Regulation (EU) No 492/2011, as well as awareness of rights, are key elements in protecting the rights and equal treatment of Union workers and members of their family, whereas poor enforcement undermines the effectiveness of Union rules applicable in this area and endangers the rights and protection of Union workers and members of their family.

(10) A more effective and uniform application of rights conferred by Union rules on the free movement of workers is also necessary for the proper functioning of the internal market.

(11) The application and monitoring of the Union rules on the free movement of workers should be improved to ensure that Union workers and members of their family as well as employers, public authorities, and other persons concerned are better informed about free movement rights and responsi-

bilities, to assist and to protect Union workers and members of their family in the exercise of those rights, and to combat circumvention of those rules by public authorities and public or private employers. In that context Member States may also take into consideration the effects of increased mobility, such as 'brain drain' or 'youth drain'.

(12) In order to ensure the correct application of, and to monitor compliance with, the substantive Union rules on free movement of workers, Member States should take the appropriate measures to protect Union workers and members of their family exercising their right to free movement against both discrimination on grounds of nationality and any unjustified restriction or obstacle to the exercise of that right.

(13) To that end, it is appropriate to provide specific rules for effective enforcement and to facilitate a better and more uniform application of the substantive rules governing the freedom of movement of workers under Article 45 TFEU and under Regulation (EU) No 492/2011. Enforcement of that fundamental freedom should take into consideration the principle of equality between women and men and the prohibition of discrimination of Union workers and members of their family on any ground set out in Article 21 of the Charter of Fundamental Rights of the European Union ('the Charter').

(14) In that context, Union workers and members of their family who have been subject to discrimination on the grounds of nationality, or to any unjustified restriction or obstacles to exercising their right to free movement, should be guaranteed real and effective judicial protection. Where Member States provide for administrative procedures as a means of legal redress, they should ensure that any administrative decision may be challenged before a tribunal within the meaning of Article 47 of the Charter. Taking into account the right to effective legal protection, Union workers should be protected from any adverse treatment or consequence resulting from a complaint or proceedings which aim to enforce the rights safeguarded under this Directive.

(15) In order to provide more effective levels of protection, associations and legal entities, including the social partners, should also be empowered to engage, as the Member States determine, either on behalf of or in support of any alleged victim, with his or her approval, in proceedings. This should be without prejudice to national rules of procedure concerning representation and defence before the courts and to other competences and collective rights of social partners, employees' and employers' representatives, such as those relating to the enforcement of collective agreements, where applicable, including actions on behalf of a collective interest, under national law or practice. With a view to ensuring effective legal protection, and without prejudice to the existing collective defence mechanisms available to the social partners and national law or practice, Member States are invited to examine the implementation of common principles for injunctive and compensatory collective redress mechanisms.

(16) In accordance with the case-law of the Court of Justice, national rules on time limits for the enforcement of rights under this Directive should be such that they cannot be regarded as capable of rendering virtually impossible or excessively difficult the exercise of those rights.

(17) Protection against discrimination based on the grounds of nationality would itself be strengthened by the existence of effective bodies with appropriate expertise in each Member State with competence to promote equal treatment, to analyse the problems faced by Union workers and members of their family, to study possible solutions and to provide specific assistance to them. The competence of those bodies should include, inter alia, the provision to Union workers and members of their family of independent legal and/or other assistance, such as the provision of legal advice on the application to them of the relevant Union and national rules on free movement of workers, of information about complaint procedures, and of help to protect the rights of workers and members of their family. It may also include assistance in legal proceedings.

(18) It should be up to each Member State to decide whether to attribute the tasks to be carried out under this Directive to the bodies referred to above or whether to attribute those tasks to existing bodies with similar objectives at national level, for example, the promotion of free movement of persons, the implementation of the principle of equal treatment or the safeguarding of individual rights. Should a Member State decide to expand the mandate of an existing body, it should ensure allocation of sufficient resources to the existing body for the effective and adequate performance of its existing and additional tasks. Where the tasks are allocated to more than one body, Member States should ensure that they are adequately coordinated.

(19) Member States should ensure that one or more of those bodies act as a contact point and that they cooperate and share information, such as the contact details of all the bodies, the means of redress and the contact details of the associations, organisations or other legal entities which provide information and services to Union workers and members of their family, with equivalent contact points in other Member States. The list of contact points should be made publicly available.

(20) Member States should promote cooperation between the bodies designated by them under this Directive and existing information and assistance services provided by the social partners, associations, organisations or other relevant legal entities, such as organisations with responsibility for coordination arrangements under Regulation (EC) No 883/2004 of the European Parliament and of the Council[5] and, where relevant, labour inspectorates.

(21) Member States should ensure the promotion of synergies with existing information and support tools at Union level and, to that end, should ensure that existing or newly created bodies work closely with the existing information and assistance services, such as Your Europe, SOLVIT, Enterprise Europe Network, the Points of Single Contact and EURES, including, where relevant, EURES cross-border partnerships.

(22) Member States should promote dialogue with the social partners and with appropriate non-governmental organisations to address and combat unjustified restrictions and obstacles to the right to free movement or different forms of discrimination on the grounds of nationality.

(23) Member States should establish how Union citizens, such as workers, students and recent graduates, as well as employers, the social partners and other interested parties can be provided with easily accessible, relevant information on the provisions of this Directive and of Regulation (EU) No 492/2011, including information about the bodies designated under this Directive and available means of redress and protection. Member States should take measures to make this information available in more than one official Union language taking into account demands in the labour market. This should not interfere with Member States' legislation on the use of languages. That information could be provided by individual counselling and should also be easily accessible through Your Europe and EURES.

(24) In order to facilitate the enforcement of the rights granted under Union law, Council Directive 91/533/EEC[6] should be implemented and monitored consistently.

(25) This Directive lays down minimum requirements, thus giving the Member States the option of introducing or maintaining more favourable provisions. Member States also have the possibility to extend the competences of the organisations entrusted with tasks related to the protection of Union workers against discrimination on grounds of nationality so as to cover the right to equal treatment without discrimination on grounds of nationality of all Union citizens exercising their right to free movement and the members of their family, as enshrined in Article 21 TFEU and in Directive 2004/38/EC. The implementation of this Directive should not serve to justify any regression in relation to the situation which already prevails in each Member State.

(26) The effective implementation of this Directive implies that Member States, when adopting the appropriate measures to comply with their obligations under this Directive, should provide a reference to this Directive or be accompanied by such a reference on the occasion of the official publication of implementing measures.

(27) In accordance with the Joint Political Declaration of Member States and the Commission on explanatory documents of 28 September 2011, Member States have undertaken to accompany, in justified cases, the notification of their transposition measures with one or more documents explaining the relationship between the components of a directive and the corresponding parts of national transposition instruments. With regard to this Directive, the legislator considers the transmission of such documents to be justified.

(28) After sufficient time for the implementation of this Directive has elapsed, the Commission should prepare a report on its implementation, evaluating in particular the opportunity to present any necessary proposal aiming to guarantee a better enforcement of Union law on free movement. In that report, the Commission should address the possible difficulties faced by young graduates looking for employment across the Union and by third-country spouses of Union workers.

(29) This Directive respects the fundamental rights and observes the principles recognised in the Charter in particular the freedom to choose an occupation and the right to engage in work, the right to non-discrimination, in particular on grounds of nationality, the right to collective bargaining and action, fair and just working conditions, the right to freedom of movement and residence and the right to an effective remedy and a fair trial. It has to be implemented in accordance with those rights and principles.

(30) This Directive respects the different labour market models of the Member States, including labour market models regulated by collective agreements.

(31) Since the objective of this Directive, namely to establish a general common framework of appropriate provisions, measures and mechanisms necessary for the better and more uniform application and enforcement in practice of the rights relating to free movement of workers conferred by the TFEU and by Regulation (EU) No 492/2011, cannot be sufficiently achieved by the Member States, but can rather, by reason of the scale and effect of the action, be better achieved at Union level, the Union may adopt measures in accordance with the principle of subsidiarity as set out in Article 5 of the Treaty on European Union. In accordance with the principle of proportionality, as set out in that Article, this Directive does not go beyond what is necessary in order to achieve that objective,

NOTES

1 OJ C341, 21.11.2013, p 54.

2 Position of the European Parliament of 12 March 2014 (not yet published in the Official Journal) and decision of the Council of 14 April 2014.

3 Directive 2004/38/EC of the European Parliament and of the Council of 29 April 2004 on the right of citizens of the Union and their family members to move and reside freely within the territory of the Member States, amending Regulation (EEC) No 1612/68 and repealing Directives 64/221/EEC, 68/360/EEC, 72/194/EEC, 73/148/EEC, 75/34/EEC, 75/35/EEC, 90/364/EEC, 90/365/EEC and 93/96/EEC (OJ L158, 30.4.2004, p 77).

4 Regulation (EU) No 492/2011 of the European Parliament and of the Council of 5 April 2011 on freedom of movement for workers within the Union (OJ L141, 27.5.2011, p 1).

5 Regulation (EC) No 883/2004 of the European Parliament and of the Council of 29 April 2004 on the coordination of social security systems (OJ L166, 30.4.2004, p 1).

6 Council Directive 91/533/EEC of 14 October 1991 on an employer's obligation to inform employees of the conditions applicable to the contract or employment relationship (OJ L288, 18.10.1991, p 32).

HAVE ADOPTED THIS DIRECTIVE:

[3.571]
Article 1
Subject matter
This Directive lays down provisions which facilitate the uniform application and enforcement in practice of the rights conferred by Article 45 TFEU and by Articles 1 to 10 of Regulation (EU) No 492/2011. This Directive applies to Union citizens exercising those rights and to members of their family ('Union workers and members of their family').

[3.572]
Article 2
Scope
1. This Directive applies to the following matters, as referred to in Articles 1 to 10 of Regulation (EU) No 492/2011, in the area of freedom of movement for workers:
- (a) access to employment;
- (b) conditions of employment and work, in particular as regards remuneration, dismissal, health and safety at work, and, if Union workers become unemployed, reinstatement or re-employment;
- (c) access to social and tax advantages;
- (d) membership of trade unions and eligibility for workers' representative bodies;
- (e) access to training;
- (f) access to housing;
- (g) access to education, apprenticeship and vocational training for the children of Union workers;
- (h) assistance afforded by the employment offices.

2. The scope of this Directive is identical to that of Regulation (EU) No 492/2011.

[3.573]
Article 3
Defence of rights
1. Member States shall ensure that after possible recourse to other competent authorities including, where they deem it to be appropriate, conciliation procedures, judicial procedures, for the enforcement of obligations under Article 45 TFEU and under Articles 1 to 10 of Regulation (EU) No 492/2011, are available to all Union workers and members of their family who consider that they have suffered or are suffering from unjustified restrictions and obstacles to their right to free movement or who consider themselves wronged by a failure to apply the principle of equal treatment to them, even after the relationship in which the restriction and obstacle or discrimination is alleged to have occurred has ended.
2. Member States shall ensure that associations, organisations, including the social partners, or other legal entities, which have, in accordance with the criteria laid down in their national law, practice or collective agreements, a legitimate interest in ensuring that this Directive is complied with, may engage, either on behalf of or in support of, Union workers and members of their family, with their approval, in any judicial and/or administrative procedure provided for the enforcement of the rights referred to in Article 1.
3. Paragraph 2 shall apply without prejudice to other competences and collective rights of the social partners, employees' and employers' representatives, where applicable, including the right to take action on behalf of a collective interest, under national law or practice.
4. Paragraph 2 shall apply without prejudice to national rules of procedure concerning representation and defence in court proceedings.
5. Paragraphs 1 and 2 of this Article shall apply without prejudice to national rules on time limits for enforcement of the rights referred to in Article 1. However, those national time-limits shall not render virtually impossible or excessively difficult the exercise of those rights.
6. Member States shall introduce in their national legal systems such measures as are necessary to protect Union workers from any adverse treatment or adverse consequence as a reaction to a complaint or proceedings aimed at enforcing compliance with the rights referred to in Article 1.

[3.574]
Article 4
Bodies to promote equal treatment and to support Union workers and members of their family
1. Each Member State shall designate one or more structures or bodies ('bodies') for the promotion, analysis, monitoring and support of equal treatment of Union workers and members of their family without discrimination on grounds of nationality, unjustified restrictions or obstacles to their right to free movement and shall make the necessary arrangements for the proper functioning of such bodies. Those bodies may form part of existing bodies at national level which have similar objectives.
2. Member States shall ensure that the competences of those bodies include:
- (a) providing or ensuring the provision of independent legal and/or other assistance to Union workers and members of their family, without prejudice to their rights, and to the rights of associations, organisations and other legal entities referred to in Article 3;
- (b) acting as a contact point *vis-à-vis* equivalent contact points in other Member States in order to cooperate and share relevant information;
- (c) conducting or commissioning independent surveys and analyses concerning unjustified restrictions and obstacles to the right to free movement, or discrimination on grounds of nationality, of Union workers and members of their family;
- (d) ensuring the publication of independent reports and making recommendations on any issue relating to such restrictions and obstacles or discrimination;

(e) publishing relevant information on the application at national level of Union rules on free movement of workers.

3. Member States shall communicate to the Commission the names and contact details of the contact points and any updated information or changes thereto. The Commission shall keep a list of contact points and shall make it available to the Member States.

4. Member States shall ensure that existing or newly created bodies are aware of, and are able to make use of, and cooperate with, the existing information and assistance services at Union level, such as Your Europe, SOLVIT, EURES, Enterprise Europe Network and the Points of Single Contact.

5. Where the tasks referred to in paragraph 2 are allocated to more than one body, Member States shall ensure that those tasks are adequately coordinated.

[3.575]
Article 5
Dialogue

Member States shall promote dialogue with the social partners and with relevant non-governmental organisations which have, in accordance with national law or practice, a legitimate interest in contributing to the fight against unjustified restrictions and obstacles to the right to free movement, and discrimination on grounds of nationality, of Union workers and members of their family with a view to promoting the principle of equal treatment.

[3.576]
Article 6
Access to and dissemination of information

1. Member States shall ensure that the provisions adopted pursuant to this Directive and to Articles 1 to 10 of Regulation (EU) No 492/2011, are brought to the attention of the persons concerned throughout their territory, in particular Union workers and employers, by all appropriate means.

2. Member States shall provide, in more than one official language of the institutions of the Union, information on the rights conferred by Union law concerning the free movement of workers that is clear, free of charge, easily accessible, comprehensive and up-to-date. This information should also be easily accessible through Your Europe and EURES.

[3.577]
Article 7
Minimum requirements

1. Member States may introduce or maintain provisions which are more favourable to the protection of the principle of equal treatment than those laid down in this Directive.

2. Member States may provide that the competences of the bodies referred to in Article 4 of this Directive for the promotion, analysis, monitoring and support of equal treatment of Union workers and members of their family without discrimination on grounds of nationality also cover the right to equal treatment without discrimination on grounds of nationality of all Union citizens exercising their right to free movement and the members of their family, in accordance with Article 21 TFEU and Directive 2004/38/EC.

3. The implementation of this Directive shall under no circumstances be sufficient grounds for a reduction in the level of protection of Union workers and members of their family, in the areas to which it applies, without prejudice to the Member States' right to respond to changes in the situation by introducing laws, regulations and administrative provisions which differ from those in force on 20 May 2014, provided that this Directive is complied with.

[3.578]
Article 8
Transposition

1. Member States shall bring into force the laws, regulations and administrative provisions necessary to comply with this Directive by 21 May 2016. They shall forthwith communicate to the Commission the text of those measures.

When Member States adopt those measures they shall contain a reference to this Directive or be accompanied by such a reference on the occasion of their official publication. Member States shall determine how such reference is to be made.

2. Member States shall communicate to the Commission the text of the main provisions of national law which they adopt in the field covered by this Directive.

[3.579]
Article 9
Report

By 21 November 2018, the Commission shall submit a report to the European Parliament, to the Council and to the European Economic and Social Committee on the implementation of this Directive, with a view to proposing, where appropriate, the necessary amendments.

[3.580]
Article 10
Entry into force

This Directive shall enter into force on the twentieth day following that of its publication in the *Official Journal of the European Union*.

[3.581]
Article 11
Addressees
This Directive is addressed to the Member States.

DIRECTIVE OF THE EUROPEAN PARLIAMENT AND OF THE COUNCIL

(2014/67/EU)

of 15 May 2014

on the enforcement of Directive 96/71/EC concerning the posting of workers in the framework of the provision of services and amending Regulation (EU) No 1024/2012 on administrative co-operation through the Internal Market Information System ('the IMI Regulation')

(Text with EEA relevance)

[3.582]

NOTES

Date of publication in OJ: OJ L159, 28.5.2014, p 11.

Only those provisions of this Directive relevant to employment law are reproduced here. Domestic implementation of this Directive was required by 18 June 2016 (see Article 23 at **[3.594]**). For the domestic implementation of those provisions of the Directive for which implementing legislation was considered necessary by the UK government, see the Posted Workers (Enforcement of Employment Rights) Regulations 2016, SI 2016/539 at **[2.1937]**.

THE EUROPEAN PARLIAMENT AND THE COUNCIL OF THE EUROPEAN UNION,

Having regard to the Treaty on the Functioning of the European Union, and in particular Article 53(1) and Article 62 thereof,

Having regard to the proposal from the European Commission,

After transmission of the draft legislative act to the national parliaments,

Having regard to the opinion of the European Economic and Social Committee,[1]

Having regard to the opinion of the Committee of the Regions,[2]

Acting in accordance with the ordinary legislative procedure,[3]

Whereas:

(1) The free movement of workers, freedom of establishment and freedom to provide services are fundamental principles of the internal market in the Union enshrined in the Treaty on the Functioning of the European Union (TFEU). The implementation of those principles is further developed by the Union aimed at guaranteeing a level playing field for businesses and respect for the rights of workers.

(2) The freedom to provide services includes the right of undertakings to provide services in another Member State, to which they may post their own workers temporarily in order to provide those services there. It is necessary for the purpose of the posting of workers to distinguish this freedom from the free movement of workers, which gives every citizen the right to move freely to another Member State to work and reside there for that purpose and protects them against discrimination as regards employment, remuneration and other conditions of work and employment in comparison to nationals of that Member State.

(3) With respect to workers temporarily posted to carry out work in order to provide services in another Member State than the one in which they habitually carry out their work, Directive 96/71/EC of the European Parliament and of the Council[4] establishes a core set of clearly defined terms and conditions of employment which are required to be complied with by the service provider in the Member State to which the posting takes place to ensure the minimum protection of the posted workers concerned.

(4) All measures introduced by this Directive should be justified and proportionate so as not to create administrative burdens or to limit the potential that undertakings, in particular small and medium-sized enterprises (SMEs), have to create new jobs, while protecting posted workers.

(5) In order to ensure compliance with Directive 96/71/EC, whilst not putting an unnecessary administrative burden on the service providers, it is essential that the factual elements referred to in the provisions on the identification of a genuine posting and preventing abuse and circumvention in this Directive are considered to be indicative and non-exhaustive. In particular, there should be no requirement that each element is to be satisfied in every posting case.

(6) Notwithstanding the fact that the assessment of the indicative factual elements should be adapted to each specific case and take account of the specificities of the situation, situations representing the same factual elements should not lead to a different legal appreciation or assessment by competent authorities in different Member States.

(7) In order to prevent, avoid and combat abuse and circumvention of the applicable rules by undertakings taking improper or fraudulent advantage of the freedom to provide services enshrined in the TFEU and/or of the application of Directive 96/71/EC, the implementation and monitoring of the notion of posting should be improved and more uniform elements, facilitating a common interpretation, should be introduced at Union level.

(8) Therefore, the constituent factual elements characterising the temporary nature inherent to the notion of posting, and the condition that the employer is genuinely established in the Member State from which the posting takes place, need to be examined by the competent authority of the host Member State and, where necessary, in close cooperation with the Member State of establishment.

(9) When considering the size of the turnover realised by an undertaking in the Member State of establishment for the purpose of determining whether that undertaking genuinely performs substantial activities, other than purely internal management and/or administrative activities, competent authorities should take into account differences in the purchasing power of currencies.

(10) The elements set out in this Directive relating to the implementation and monitoring of posting may also assist the competent authorities in identifying workers falsely declared as self-employed. According to Directive 96/71/EC, the relevant definition of a worker is that which applies in the law of the Member State to whose territory a worker is posted. Further clarification and improved monitoring of posting by relevant competent authorities would enhance legal certainty and provide a useful tool contributing to combating bogus self-employment effectively and ensuring that posted workers are not falsely declared as self-employed, thus helping prevent, avoid and combat circumvention of the applicable rules.

(11) Where there is no genuine posting situation and a conflict of law arises, due regard should be given to the provisions of Regulation (EC) No 593/2008 of the European Parliament and of the Council[5] ('Rome I') or the Rome Convention[6] that are aimed at ensuring that employees should not be deprived of the protection afforded to them by provisions which cannot be derogated from by an agreement or which can only be derogated from to their benefit. Member States should ensure that provisions are in place to adequately protect workers who are not genuinely posted.

(12) The lack of the certificate concerning the applicable social security legislation referred to in Regulation (EC) No 883/2004 of the European Parliament and of the Council[7] may be an indication that the situation should not be characterised as one of temporarily posting to a Member State other than the one in which the worker concerned habitually works in the framework of the provision of services.

(13) As is the case with Directive 96/71/EC, this Directive should not prejudice the application of Regulation (EC) No 883/2004 and Regulation (EC) No 987/2009 of the European Parliament and of the Council.[8]

(14) Respect for the diversity of national industrial relations systems as well as the autonomy of social partners is explicitly recognised by the TFEU.

(15) In many Member States, the social partners play an important role in the context of the posting of workers for the provision of services since they may, in accordance with national law and/or practice, determine the different levels, alternatively or simultaneously, of the applicable minimum rates of pay. The social partners should communicate and inform about those rates.

(16) Adequate and effective implementation and enforcement are key elements in protecting the rights of posted workers and in ensuring a level-playing field for the service providers, whereas poor enforcement undermines the effectiveness of the Union rules applicable in this area. Close cooperation between the Commission and the Member States, and where relevant, regional and local authorities, is therefore essential, without neglecting the important role of labour inspectorates and the social partners in this respect. Mutual trust, a spirit of cooperation, continuous dialogue and mutual understanding are essential in this respect.

(17) Effective monitoring procedures in Member States are essential for the enforcement of Directive 96/71/EC and of this Directive and therefore they should be established throughout the Union.

(18) Difficulties in accessing information on terms and conditions of employment are very often the reason why existing rules are not applied by service providers. Member States should therefore ensure that such information is made generally available, free of charge and that effective access to it is provided, not only to service providers from other Member States, but also to the posted workers concerned.

(19) Where terms and conditions of employment are laid down in collective agreements which have been declared to be universally applicable, Member States should ensure, while respecting the autonomy of social partners, that those collective agreements are made generally available in an accessible and transparent way.

(20) In order to improve accessibility of information, a single source of information should be established in Member States. Each Member State should provide for a single official national website, in accordance with web accessibility standards, and other suitable means of communication. The single official national website should, as a minimum, be in the form of a website portal and should serve as a gateway or main entry point and should provide in clear and precise way links to the relevant sources of the information as well as brief information on the content of the website and the links referred to. Such websites should include in particular any website put in place pursuant to Union legislation with a view to promoting entrepreneurship and/or the development of cross-border provision of services. Host Member States should provide information on the periods laid down in their national law for which the service providers have to retain documents after the period of posting.

(21) Posted workers should have the right to receive from the host Member State general information on national law and/or practice that is applicable to them.

(22) Administrative cooperation and mutual assistance between the Member States should comply with the rules on the protection of personal data laid down in Directive 95/46/EC of the European Parliament and of the Council,[9] and in accordance with national data protection rules implementing Union legislation. With regard to administrative cooperation through the Internal Market Information System (IMI), it should also comply with Regulation (EC) No 45/2001 of the European Parliament and of the Council[10] and Regulation (EU) No 1024/2012 of the European Parliament and of the Council.[11]

(23) In order to ensure the correct application of, and to monitor compliance with, the substantive rules on the terms and conditions of employment to be respected with regard to posted workers, Member States should apply only certain administrative requirements and control measures to undertakings that post workers in the framework of the provision of services. According to the case law of the Court of Justice of the European Union, such requirements and measures may be justified by overriding reasons of general interest, which include the effective protection of workers' rights, provided they are appropriate for securing the attainment of the objective pursued and do not go beyond what is necessary to attain it. Such requirements and measures may only be imposed provided that the competent authorities cannot carry out their supervisory task effectively without the requested information and/or less restrictive measures would not ensure that the objectives of the national control measures deemed necessary are attained

(24) A service provider should ensure that the identity of the posted workers included in the declaration made by the service provider in order to allow factual controls at the workplace is verifiable for the duration of the posting by the competent authorities.

(25) A service provider established in another Member State should inform the competent authorities in the host Member State without undue delay of any important changes to the information contained in the declaration made by the service provider in order to allow factual controls at the workplace.

(26) The obligation to communicate administrative requirements and control measures to the Commission should not constitute an ex-ante authorisation process.

(27) In order to ensure better and more uniform application of Directive 96/71/EC as well as its enforcement in practice and to reduce, as far as possible, differences in the level of application and enforcement across the Union, Member States should ensure that effective and adequate inspections are carried out on their territory, thus contributing, inter alia, to the fight against undeclared work in the context of posting, also taking into account other legal initiatives to address this issue better.

(28) Member States should provide, where applicable, in accordance with their national law and/or practice, the inspected undertaking with a post-inspection or control document which includes any relevant information.

(29) Member States should ensure that sufficient staff are available with the skills and qualifications needed to carry out inspections effectively and to enable requests for information as provided for in this Directive, from the host Member State or the Member State of establishment to be responded to without undue delay.

(30) Labour inspectorates, social partners and other monitoring bodies are of paramount importance in this respect and should continue to play a crucial role.

(31) In order to cope in a flexible way with the diversity of labour markets and industrial relations systems, by way of exception, the management and labour and/or other actors and/or bodies may monitor certain terms and conditions of employment of posted workers, provided they offer the persons concerned an equivalent degree of protection and exercise their monitoring in a non-discriminatory and objective manner.

(32) Member States' inspection authorities and other relevant monitoring and enforcement bodies should avail themselves of the cooperation and exchange of information provided for in the relevant law in order to verify whether the rules applicable to posted workers have been respected.

(33) Member States are particularly encouraged to introduce a more integrated approach to labour inspections. The need to develop common standards in order to establish comparable methods, practices and minimum standards at Union level should equally be examined. However, the development of common standards should not result in Member States being hampered in their efforts to combat undeclared work effectively.

(34) To facilitate the enforcement of Directive 96/71/EC and ensure its more effective application, effective complaint mechanisms should exist through which posted workers may lodge complaints or engage in proceedings either directly or, with their approval, through relevant designated third parties, such as trade unions or other associations as well as common institutions of social partners. This should be without prejudice to national rules of procedure concerning representation and defence before the courts and to the competences and other rights of trade unions and other employee representatives under national law and/or practice.

(35) For the purpose of ensuring that a posted worker receives the correct pay and provided that allowances specific to posting can be considered part of minimum rates of pay, such allowances should only be deducted from wages if national law, collective agreements and/or practice of the host Member State provide for this.

(36) Compliance with the applicable rules in the field of posting in practice and the effective protection of workers' rights in this respect is a matter of particular concern in subcontracting chains and should be ensured through appropriate measures in accordance with national law and/or practice and in compliance with Union law. Such measures may include the introduction on a voluntary basis, after consulting the relevant social partners, of a mechanism of direct subcontracting liability, in addition to or in place of the liability of the employer, in respect of any outstanding net remuneration corresponding to the minimum rates of pay and/or contributions due to common funds or institutions of social partners regulated by law or collective agreement in so far as these are covered by Article 3(1) of Directive 96/71/EC. However, Member States remain free to provide for more stringent liability rules under national law or to go further under national law on a non-discriminatory and proportionate basis.

(37) Member States that have introduced measures to ensure compliance with the applicable rules in subcontracting chains should have the possibility to provide that a (sub)contractor should not be liable in specific circumstances or that the liability may be limited in cases where due diligence obligations have been undertaken by that (sub)contractor. Those measures should be defined by national law, taking into account the specific circumstances of the Member State concerned, and they may include, inter alia, measures taken by the contractor concerning documentation of compliance with administrative requirements and control measures in order to ensure effective monitoring of compliance with the applicable rules on the posting of workers.

(38)–(45) (*Outside the scope of this work.*)

(46) This Directive does not aim to establish harmonised rules for judicial cooperation, jurisdiction, or the recognition and enforcement of decisions in civil and commercial matters, or to deal with applicable law.

(47) Member States should take appropriate measures in the event of failure to comply with the obligations laid down in this Directive, including administrative and judicial procedures, and should provide for effective, dissuasive and proportionate penalties for any breaches of the obligations under this Directive.

(48) This Directive respects the fundamental rights and observes the principles recognised in the Charter of Fundamental Rights of the European Union, notably protection of personal data (Article 8), the freedom to choose an occupation and right to engage in work (Article 15), the freedom to conduct a business (Article 16), the right to collective bargaining and action (Article 28), fair and just working conditions (Article 31), the right to an effective remedy and to a fair trial (Article 47), the presumption of innocence and right of defence (Article 48) and the right not to be tried twice for the same offence (*ne bis in idem*) (Article 50), and has to be implemented in accordance with those rights and principles.

(49) In order to facilitate better and more uniform application of Directive 96/71/EC, it is appropriate to provide for an electronic information exchange system to facilitate administrative cooperation and competent authorities should use the IMI as much as possible. However, that should not prevent the application of existing and future bilateral agreements or arrangements concerning administrative cooperation and mutual assistance.

(50) Since the objective of this Directive, namely to establish a common framework of a set of appropriate provisions, measures and control mechanisms necessary for better and more uniform implementation, application and enforcement in practice of Directive 96/71/EC, cannot be sufficiently achieved by the Member States, and can rather, by reason of the scale and effects of the action, be better achieved at Union level, the Union may adopt measures, in accordance with the principle of subsidiarity as set out in Article 5 of the TEU. In accordance with the principle of proportionality, as set out in that Article, this Directive does not go beyond what is necessary in order to achieve that objective.

(51) The European Data Protection Supervisor has been consulted in accordance with Article 28(2) of Regulation (EC) No 45/2001 and delivered an opinion on 19 July 2012,[12]

NOTES

1 OJ C351, 15.11.2012, p 61.

2 OJ C17, 19.1.2013, p 67.

3 Position of the European Parliament of 16 April 2014 (not yet published in the Official Journal) and decision of the Council of 13 May 2014.

4 Directive 96/71/EC of the European Parliament and of the Council of 16 December 1996 concerning the posting of workers in the framework of the provision of services (OJ L18, 21.1.1997, p 1).

5 Regulation (EC) No 593/2008 of the European Parliament and of the Council of 17 June 2008 on the law applicable to contractual obligations (Rome I) (OJ L177, 4.7.2008, p 6).

6 Rome Convention of 19 June 1980 on the law applicable to contractual obligations (80/934/EEC) (OJ L266, 9.10.1980, p 1).

7 Regulation (EC) No 883/2004 of the European Parliament and of the Council of 29 April 2004 on the coordination of social security systems (OJ L166, 30.4.2004, p 1).

8 Regulation (EC) No 987/2009 of the European Parliament and of the Council of 16 September 2009 laying down the procedure for implementing Regulation (EC) No 883/2004 on the coordination of social security systems (OJ L284, 30.10.2009, p 1)

9 Directive 95/46/EC of the European Parliament and of the Council of 24 October 1995 on the protection of individuals with regard to the processing of personal data and on the free movement of such data (OJ L281, 23.11.1995, p 31).

10 Regulation (EC) No 45/2001 of the European Parliament and of the Council of 18 December 2000 on the protection of individuals with regard to the processing of personal data by the Community institutions and bodies and on the free movement of such data (OJ L8, 12.1.2001, p 1).

[11] Regulation (EU) No 1024/2012 of the European Parliament and of the Council of 25 October 2012 on administrative cooperation through the Internal Market Information System and repealing Commission Decision 2008/49/EC ('the IMI Regulation') (OJ L316, 14.11.2012, p 1)

[12] OJ C27, 29.1.2013, p 4.

HAVE ADOPTED THIS DIRECTIVE:

CHAPTER I GENERAL PROVISIONS

[3.583]
Article 1
Subject matter

1. This Directive establishes a common framework of a set of appropriate provisions, measures and control mechanisms necessary for better and more uniform implementation, application and enforcement in practice of Directive 96/71/EC, including measures to prevent and sanction any abuse and circumvention of the applicable rules and is without prejudice to the scope of Directive 96/71/EC.

This Directive aims to guarantee respect for an appropriate level of protection of the rights of posted workers for the cross-border provision of services, in particular the enforcement of the terms and conditions of employment that apply in the Member State where the service is to be provided in accordance with Article 3 of Directive 96/71/EC, while facilitating the exercise of the freedom to provide services for service providers and promoting fair competition between service providers, and thus supporting the functioning of the internal market.

2. This Directive shall not affect in any way the exercise of fundamental rights as recognised in Member States and at Union level, including the right or freedom to strike or to take other action covered by the specific industrial relations systems in Member States, in accordance with national law and/or practice. Nor does it affect the right to negotiate, conclude and enforce collective agreements and to take collective action in accordance with national law and/or practice.

[3.584]
Article 2
Definitions

For the purposes of this Directive, the following definitions apply:

(a) 'competent authority' means an authority or body, which may include the liaison office(s) as referred to in Article 4 of Directive 96/71/EC, designated by a Member State to perform functions set out in Directive 96/71/EC and this Directive;

(b) 'requesting authority' means the competent authority of a Member State which makes a request for assistance, information, notification or recovery of a penalty and/or fine, as referred to in Chapter VI;

(c) 'requested authority' means the competent authority of a Member State to which a request for assistance, information, notification or recovery of a penalty and/or fine is made, as referred to in Chapter VI.

[3.585]
Article 3
Competent authorities and liaison offices

For the purposes of this Directive, Member States shall, in accordance with national law and/or practice, designate one or more competent authorities, which may include the liaison office(s) as referred to in Article 4 of Directive 96/71/EC. When designating their competent authorities Member States shall have due regard for the need to ensure data protection of exchanged information and the legal rights of natural and legal persons that may be affected. Member States shall remain ultimately responsible for safeguarding data protection and the legal rights of affected persons and shall put in place appropriate mechanisms in this respect.

Member States shall communicate the contact details of the competent authorities to the Commission and to the other Member States. The Commission shall publish and regularly update the list of the competent authorities and liaison offices.

Other Member States and Union institutions shall respect each Member State's choice of competent authorities.

[3.586]
Article 4
Identification of a genuine posting and prevention of abuse and circumvention

1. For the purpose of implementing, applying and enforcing Directive 96/71/EC, the competent authorities shall make an overall assessment of all factual elements that are deemed to be necessary, including, in particular, those set out in paragraphs 2 and 3 of this Article. Those elements are intended to assist competent authorities when carrying out checks and controls and where they have reason to believe that a worker may not qualify as a posted worker under Directive 96/71/EC. Those elements are indicative factors in the overall assessment to be made and therefore shall not be considered in isolation.

2. In order to determine whether an undertaking genuinely performs substantial activities, other than purely internal management and/or administrative activities, the competent authorities shall make an overall assessment of all factual elements characterising those activities, taking account of a wider timeframe, carried out by an undertaking in the Member State of establishment, and where necessary, in the host Member State. Such elements may include in particular:

(a) the place where the undertaking has its registered office and administration, uses office space, pays taxes and social security contributions and, where applicable, in accordance with national law has a professional licence or is registered with the chambers of commerce or professional bodies;
(b) the place where posted workers are recruited and from which they are posted;
(c) the law applicable to the contracts concluded by the undertaking with its workers, on the one hand, and with its clients, on the other;
(d) the place where the undertaking performs its substantial business activity and where it employs administrative staff;
(e) the number of contracts performed and/or the size of the turnover realised in the Member State of establishment, taking into account the specific situation of, inter alia, newly established undertakings and SMEs.

3. In order to assess whether a posted worker temporarily carries out his or her work in a Member State other than the one in which he or she normally works, all factual elements characterising such work and the situation of the worker shall be examined. Such elements may include in particular:
(a) the work is carried out for a limited period of time in another Member State;
(b) the date on which the posting starts;
(c) the posting takes place to a Member State other than the one in or from which the posted worker habitually carries out his or her work according to Regulation (EC) No 593/2008 (Rome I) and/or the Rome Convention;
(d) the posted worker returns to or is expected to resume working in the Member State from which he or she is posted after completion of the work or the provision of services for which he or she was posted;
(e) the nature of activities;
(f) travel, board and lodging or accommodation is provided or reimbursed by the employer who posts the worker and, if so, how this is provided or the method of reimbursement;
(g) any previous periods during which the post was filled by the same or by another (posted) worker.

4. The failure to satisfy one or more of the factual elements set out in paragraphs 2 and 3 shall not automatically preclude a situation from being characterised as one of posting. The assessment of those elements shall be adapted to each specific case and take account of the specificities of the situation.

5. The elements that are referred to in this Article used by the competent authorities in the overall assessment of a situation as a genuine posting may also be considered in order to determine whether a person falls within the applicable definition of a worker in accordance with Article 2(2) of Directive 96/71/EC. Member States should be guided, inter alia, by the facts relating to the performance of work, subordination and the remuneration of the worker, notwithstanding how the relationship is characterised in any arrangement, whether contractual or not, that may have been agreed between the parties.

CHAPTER II ACCESS TO INFORMATION

[3.587]
Article 5
Improved access to information

1. Member States shall take the appropriate measures to ensure that the information on the terms and conditions of employment referred to in Article 3 of Directive 96/71/EC which are to be applied and complied with by service providers is made generally available free of charge in a clear, transparent, comprehensive and easily accessible way at a distance and by electronic means, in formats and in accordance with web accessibility standards that ensure access to persons with disabilities and to ensure that the liaison offices or other competent national bodies referred to in Article 4 of Directive 96/71/EC are in a position to carry out their tasks effectively.

2. In order to bring about further improvements with respect to access to information, Member States shall:
(a) indicate clearly, in a detailed and user-friendly manner and in an accessible format on a single official national website and by other suitable means, which terms and conditions of employment and/or which parts of their national and/or regional law are to be applied to workers posted to their territory;
(b) take the necessary measures to make generally available on the single official national website and by other suitable means information on which collective agreements are applicable and to whom they are applicable, and which terms and conditions of employment are to be applied by service providers from other Member States in accordance with Directive 96/71/EC, including where possible, links to existing websites and other contact points, in particular the relevant social partners;
(c) make the information available to workers and service providers free of charge in the official language(s) of the host Member State and in the most relevant languages taking into account demands in its labour market, the choice being left to the host Member State. That information shall be made available if possible in summarised leaflet form indicating the main labour conditions applicable, including the description of the procedures to lodge complaints and upon requests in formats accessible to persons with disabilities; further detailed information on the labour and social conditions applicable to posted workers, including occupational health and safety, shall be made easily available and free of charge;
(d) improve the accessibility and clarity of the relevant information, in particular that provided on a single official national website, as referred to in point (a);
(e) indicate a contact person at the liaison office in charge of dealing with requests for information;

(f) keep the information provided for in the country fiches up to date.

3. The Commission shall continue to support the Member States in the area of access to information.

4. Where, in accordance with national law, traditions and practice, including respect for the autonomy of social partners, the terms and conditions of employment referred to in Article 3 of Directive 96/71/EC are laid down in collective agreements in accordance with Article 3(1) and (8) of that Directive, Member States shall ensure that those terms and conditions are made available in an accessible and transparent way to service providers from other Member States and to posted workers, and shall seek the involvement of the social partners in that respect. The relevant information should, in particular, cover the different minimum rates of pay and their constituent elements, the method used to calculate the remuneration due and, where relevant, the qualifying criteria for classification in the different wage categories.

5. Member States shall indicate the bodies and authorities to which workers and undertakings can turn for general information on national law and practice applicable to them concerning their rights and obligations within their territory.

Articles 6–8 *((Chapter III) outside the scope of this work.)*

CHAPTER IV MONITORING COMPLIANCE

[3.588]
Article 9
Administrative requirements and control measures

1. Member States may only impose administrative requirements and control measures necessary in order to ensure effective monitoring of compliance with the obligations set out in this Directive and Directive 96/71/EC, provided that these are justified and proportionate in accordance with Union law.

For these purposes Member States may in particular impose the following measures:

(a) an obligation for a service provider established in another Member State to make a simple declaration to the responsible national competent authorities at the latest at the commencement of the service provision, into (one of) the official language(s) of the host Member State, or into (an)other language(s) accepted by the host Member State, containing the relevant information necessary in order to allow factual controls at the workplace, including:
  (i) the identity of the service provider;
  (ii) the anticipated number of clearly identifiable posted workers;
  (iii) the persons referred to under points (e) and (f);
  (iv) the anticipated duration, envisaged beginning and end date of the posting;
  (v) the address(es) of the workplace; and
  (vi) the nature of the services justifying the posting;

(b) an obligation to keep or make available and/or retain copies, in paper or electronic form, of the employment contract or an equivalent document within the meaning of Council Directive 91/533/EEC,[1] including, where appropriate or relevant, the additional information referred to in Article 4 of that Directive, payslips, time-sheets indicating the beginning, end and duration of the daily working time and proof of payment of wages or copies of equivalent documents during the period of posting in an accessible and clearly identified place in its territory, such as the workplace or the building site, or for mobile workers in the transport sector the operations base or the vehicle with which the service is provided;

(c) an obligation to deliver the documents referred to under point (b), after the period of posting, at the request of the authorities of the host Member State, within a reasonable period of time;

(d) an obligation to provide a translation of the documents referred to under point (b) into (one of) the official language(s) of the host Member State, or into (an)other language(s) accepted by the host Member State;

(e) an obligation to designate a person to liaise with the competent authorities in the host Member State in which the services are provided and to send out and receive documents and/or notices, if need be;

(f) an obligation to designate a contact person, if necessary, acting as a representative through whom the relevant social partners may seek to engage the service provider to enter into collective bargaining within the host Member State, in accordance with national law and/or practice, during the period in which the services are provided. That person may be different from the person referred to under point (e) and does not have to be present in the host Member State, but has to be available on a reasonable and justified request;

2. Member States may impose other administrative requirements and control measures, in the event that situations or new developments arise from which it appears that existing administrative requirements and control measures are not sufficient or efficient to ensure effective monitoring of compliance with the obligations set out in Directive 96/71/EC and this Directive, provided that these are justified and proportionate.

3. Nothing in this Article shall affect other obligations deriving from the Union legislation, including those deriving from Council Directive 89/391/EEC[2] and the Regulation (EC) No 883/2004, and/or those under national law regarding the protection or employment of workers provided that the latter are equally applicable to undertakings established in the Member State concerned and that they are justified and proportionate.

4. Member States shall ensure that the procedures and formalities relating to the posting of workers pursuant to this Article can be completed in a user-friendly way by undertakings, at a distance and by electronic means as far as possible.

5. Member States shall communicate to the Commission and inform service providers of any measures referred to in paragraphs 1 and 2 that they apply or that have been implemented by them. The Commission shall communicate those measures to the other Member States. The information for the service providers shall be made generally available on a single national website in the most relevant language(s), as determined by the Member State.
The Commission shall monitor the application of the measures referred to in paragraphs 1 and 2 closely, evaluate their compliance with Union law and shall, where appropriate, take the necessary measures in accordance with its competences under the TFEU.
The Commission shall report regularly to the Council on measures communicated by Member States and, where appropriate, on the state of play of its analysis and/or assessment.

NOTES

[1] Council Directive 91/533/EEC of 14 October 1991 on an employer's obligation to inform employees of the conditions applicable to the contract or employment relationship (OJ L288, 18.10.1991, p 32).

[2] Council Directive 89/391/EEC of 12 June 1989 on the introduction of measures to encourage improvements in the safety and health of workers at work (OJ L183, 29.6.1989, p 1).

[3.589]
Article 10
Inspections

1. Member States shall ensure that appropriate and effective checks and monitoring mechanisms provided in accordance with national law and practice are put in place and that the authorities designated under national law carry out effective and adequate inspections on their territory in order to control and monitor compliance with the provisions and rules laid down in Directive 96/71/EC, taking into account the relevant provisions of this Directive and thus guarantee their proper application and enforcement. Notwithstanding the possibility of conducting random checks, inspections shall be based primarily on a risk assessment by the competent authorities. The risk assessment may identify the sectors of activity in which the employment of workers posted for the provision of services is concentrated on their territory. When making such a risk assessment, the carrying out of large infrastructural projects, the existence of long chains of subcontractors, geographic proximity, the special problems and needs of specific sectors, the past record of infringement, as well as the vulnerability of certain groups of workers may in particular be taken into account.
2. Member States shall ensure that inspections and controls of compliance under this Article are not discriminatory and/or disproportionate, whilst taking into account the relevant provisions of this Directive.
3. If information is needed in the course of the inspections and in the light of Article 4, the host Member State and the Member State of establishment shall act in accordance with the rules on administrative cooperation. In particular, the competent authorities shall cooperate pursuant to the rules and principles laid down in Articles 6 and 7.
4. In Member States where, in accordance with national law and/or practice, the setting of the terms and conditions of employment of posted workers referred to in Article 3 of Directive 96/71/EC, and in particular the minimum rates of pay, including working time, is left to management and labour they may, at the appropriate level and subject to the conditions laid down by the Member States, also monitor the application of the relevant terms and conditions of employment of posted workers, provided that an adequate level of protection equivalent to that resulting from Directive 96/71/EC and this Directive is guaranteed.
5. Member States where labour inspectorates have no competence with respect to the control and monitoring of the working conditions and/or terms and conditions of employment of posted workers may, in accordance with national law and/or practice, establish, modify or maintain arrangements, procedures and mechanisms guaranteeing the respect of these terms and conditions of employment, provided that the arrangements offer the persons concerned an adequate degree of protection equivalent to that resulting from Directive 96/71/EC and this Directive.

CHAPTER V ENFORCEMENT

[3.590]
Article 11
Defence of rights — facilitation of complaints — back-payments

1. For the enforcement of the obligations under Directive 96/71/EC, in particular Article 6 thereof, and this Directive, Member States shall ensure that there are effective mechanisms for posted workers to lodge complaints against their employers directly, as well as the right to institute judicial or administrative proceedings, also in the Member State in whose territory the workers are or were posted, where such workers consider they have sustained loss or damage as a result of a failure to apply the applicable rules, even after the relationship in which the failure is alleged to have occurred has ended.
2. Paragraph 1 shall apply without prejudice to the jurisdiction of the courts in the Member States as laid down, in particular, in the relevant instruments of Union law and/or international conventions.
3. Member States shall ensure that trade unions and other third parties, such as associations, organisations and other legal entities which have, in accordance with the criteria laid down under national law, a legitimate interest in ensuring that this Directive and Directive 96/71/EC are complied with, may engage, on behalf or in support of the posted workers or their employer, and with their approval, in any judicial or administrative proceedings with the objective of implementing this Directive and Directive 96/71/EC and/or enforcing the obligations under this Directive and Directive 96/71/EC.
4. Paragraphs 1 and 3 shall apply without prejudice to:

(a) national rules on prescription deadlines or time limits for bringing similar actions, provided that they are not regarded as capable of rendering virtually impossible or excessively difficult the exercise of those rights;
(b) other competences and collective rights of social partners, employees and employers representatives, where applicable, under national law and/or practice
(c) national rules of procedure concerning representation and defence before the courts.

5. Posted workers bringing judicial or administrative proceedings within the meaning of paragraph 1 shall be protected against any unfavourable treatment by their employer.

6. Member States shall ensure that the employer of the posted worker is liable for any due entitlements resulting from the contractual relationship between the employer and that posted worker.

Member States shall in particular ensure that the necessary mechanisms are in place to ensure that the posted workers are able to receive:
(a) any outstanding net remuneration which, under the applicable terms and conditions of employment covered by Article 3 of Directive 96/71/EC, would have been due;
(b) any back-payments or refund of taxes or social security contributions unduly withheld from their salaries;
(c) a refund of excessive costs, in relation to net remuneration or to the quality of the accommodation, withheld or deducted from wages for accommodation provided by the employer;
(d) where relevant, employer's contributions due to common funds or institutions of social partners unduly withheld from their salaries.

This paragraph shall also apply in cases where the posted workers have returned from the Member State to which the posting took place.

[3.591]
Article 12
Subcontracting liability

1. In order to tackle fraud and abuse, Member States may, after consulting the relevant social partners in accordance with national law and/or practice, take additional measures on a non–discriminatory and proportionate basis in order to ensure that in subcontracting chains the contractor of which the employer (service provider) covered by Article 1(3) of Directive 96/71/EC is a direct subcontractor can, in addition to or in place of the employer, be held liable by the posted worker with respect to any outstanding net remuneration corresponding to the minimum rates of pay and/or contributions due to common funds or institutions of social partners in so far as covered by Article 3 of Directive 96/71/EC.

2. As regards the activities mentioned in the Annex to Directive 96/71/EC, Member States shall provide for measures ensuring that in subcontracting chains, posted workers can hold the contractor of which the employer is a direct subcontractor liable, in addition to or in place of the employer, for the respect of the posted workers' rights referred to in para- graph 1 of this Article.

3. The liability referred to in paragraphs 1 and 2 shall be limited to worker's rights acquired under the contractual relationship between the contractor and his or her subcontractor.

4. Member States may, in conformity with Union law, equally provide for more stringent liability rules under national law on a non-discriminatory and proportionate basis with regard to the scope and range of subcontracting liability. Member States may also, in conformity with Union law, provide for such liability in sectors other than those referred to in the Annex to Directive 96/71/EC.

5. Member States may in the cases referred to in paragraphs 1, 2 and 4 provide that a contractor that has undertaken due diligence obligations as defined by national law shall not be liable.

6. Instead of the liability rules referred to in paragraph 2, Member States may take other appropriate enforcement measures, in accordance with Union and national law and/or practice, which enable, in a direct subcontracting relationship, effective and proportionate sanctions against the contractor, to tackle fraud and abuse in situations when workers have difficulties in obtaining their rights.

7. Member States shall inform the Commission about measures taken under this Article and shall make the information generally available in the most relevant language(s), the choice being left to Member States.

In the case of paragraph 2, the information provided to the Commission shall include elements setting out liability in subcontracting chains.

In the case of paragraph 6, the information provided to the Commission shall include elements setting out the effectiveness of the alternative national measures with regard to the liability rules referred to in paragraph 2.

The Commission shall make this information available to the other Member States.

8. The Commission shall closely monitor the application of this Article.

Articles 13–19 (*(Chapter VI) outside the scope of this work.*)

CHAPTER VII FINAL PROVISIONS

[3.592]
Article 20
Penalties

Member States shall lay down rules on penalties applicable in the event of infringements of national provisions adopted pursuant to this Directive and shall take all the necessary measures to ensure that they are implemented and complied with. The penalties provided for shall be effective, proportionate and dissuasive. Member States shall notify those provisions to the Commission by 18 June 2016. They shall notify without delay any subsequent amendments to them.

[3.593]
Article 21
Internal Market Information System

1. The administrative cooperation and mutual assistance between the competent authorities of the Member States provided for in Articles 6 and 7, Article 10(3), and Articles 14 to 18 shall be implemented through the Internal Market Information System (IMI), established by Regulation (EU) No 1024/2012.

2. Member States may apply bilateral agreements or arrangements concerning administrative cooperation and mutual assistance between their competent authorities as regards the application and monitoring of the terms and conditions of employment applicable to posted workers referred to in Article 3 of Directive 96/71/EC, in so far as these agreements or arrangements do not adversely affect the rights and obligations of the workers and undertakings concerned.

Member States shall inform the Commission of the bilateral agreements and/or arrangements they apply and shall make the text of those bilateral agreements generally available.

3. In the context of bilateral agreements or arrangements referred to in paragraph 2, competent authorities of the Member States shall use IMI as much as possible. In any event, where a competent authority in one of the Member States concerned has used IMI, it shall where possible be used for any follow-up required.

Article 22
Amendment to Regulation (EU) No 1024/2012
(This Article amends Regulation 1024/2012/EU (outside the scope of this work).)

[3.594]
Article 23
Transposition

1. Member States shall bring into force the laws, regulations and administrative provisions necessary to comply with this Directive by 18 June 2016. They shall immediately inform the Commission thereof. When Member States adopt those measures, they shall contain a reference to this Directive or shall be accompanied by such reference on the occasion of their official publication. The methods of making such reference shall be laid down by Member States.

2. Member States shall communicate to the Commission the text of the main measures of national law which they adopt in the field covered by this Directive.

[3.595]
Article 24
Review

1. The Commission shall review the application and implementation of this Directive.

No later than 18 June 2019, the Commission shall present a report on its application and implementation to the European Parliament, the Council and the European Economic and Social Committee and propose, where appropriate, necessary amendments and modifications.

2. In its review the Commission shall, after consultation of Member States and, where relevant, social partners at Union level, in particular assess:

(a) the necessity and appropriateness of the factual elements for identification of a genuine posting, including the possibilities to amend existing and defining possible new elements to be taken into account in order to determine whether the undertaking is genuine and a posted worker temporarily carries out his or her work, as referred to in Article 4;
(b) the adequacy of data available relating to the posting process;
(c) the appropriateness and adequacy of the application of national control measures in light of the experience with and effectiveness of the system for administrative cooperation and exchange of information, the development of more uniform, standardised documents, the establishment of common principles or standards for inspections in the field of the posting of workers and technological developments, as referred to in Article 9;
(d) liability and/or enforcement measures introduced to ensure compliance with the applicable rules and effective protection of workers' rights in subcontracting chains, as referred to Article 12;
(e) the application of the provisions on cross-border enforcement of financial administrative penalties and fines in particular in light of experience with and effectiveness of the system, as laid down in Chapter VI;
(f) the use of bilateral agreements or arrangements in relation to IMI, taking into account, where appropriate, the report referred to in Article 25(1) of Regulation (EU) No 1024/2012;
(g) the possibility to adjust the deadlines established in Article 6(6) for supplying the information requested by Member States or the Commission with a view to reducing those deadlines, taking into account the progress achieved in the functioning and use of IMI.

[3.596]
Article 25
Entry into force

This Directive shall enter into force on the twentieth day following that of its publication in the *Official Journal of the European Union*.

[3.597]
Article 26
Addressees

This Directive is addressed to the Member States.

EUROPEAN PARLIAMENT AND COUNCIL REGULATION

(2016/679/EU)

of 27 April 2016

on the protection of natural persons with regard to the processing of personal data and on the free movement of such data, *and repealing Directive 95/46/EC (General Data Protection Regulation)*

(Text with EEA relevance)

[3.598]

NOTES

Date of publication in OJ: OJ L119, 4.5.2016, p 1. The text of this Directive incorporates the corrigendum published in OJ L127, 23.5.2018, p 72.

Only those provisions of this Regulation that are relevant to employment law are reproduced. Provisions not reproduced are not annotated.

This Regulation came into force on 25 May 2018 (see Article 99 at **[3.658]**). This Regulation repeals Directive 95/46/EC as from that date (see Article 94 at **[3.657]**). For further domestic implementation of this Regulation (in so far as it does not take effect automatically), see the Data Protection Act 2018 at **[1.2111]**.

This Regulation will become Retained EU legislation in accordance with the European Union (Withdrawal) Act 2018, s 3, as from exit day, as defined in s 20 of the 2018 Act. Accordingly, the title of this Regulation is amended (as from exit day, as so defined) by the Data Protection, Privacy and Electronic Communications (Amendments etc) (EU Exit) Regulations 2019, SI 2019/419, reg 3, Sch 1, paras 1, 2, which provide that for the words in italics there shall be substituted the words "(United Kingdom General Data Protection Regulation)". For transitional provisions etc, see the 2019 Regulations at **[2.2122]**) See, in particular, para 80 of Sch 1 to the 2019 Regulations which provides that it is not to be presumed, by virtue of the repeal of a provision of this Regulation by that Schedule, that the provision was applicable to the United Kingdom immediately before exit day (and so would, but for that Schedule, be part of the UK GDPR).

The text of this Regulation is printed in its original (and current, as at 15 May 2019) format, with the text of any amendments made by SI 2019/419 set out separately in the notes to each Article to which there are prospective amendments. This has been done for clarity of presentation.

THE EUROPEAN PARLIAMENT AND THE COUNCIL OF THE EUROPEAN UNION,

Having regard to the Treaty on the Functioning of the European Union, and in particular Article 16 thereof, Having regard to the proposal from the European Commission,

After transmission of the draft legislative act to the national parliaments,

Having regard to the opinion of the European Economic and Social Committee,[1] Having regard to the opinion of the Committee of the Regions,[2]

Acting in accordance with the ordinary legislative procedure,[3] Whereas:

(1) The protection of natural persons in relation to the processing of personal data is a fundamental right. Article 8(1) of the Charter of Fundamental Rights of the European Union (the 'Charter') and Article 16(1) of the Treaty on the Functioning of the European Union (TFEU) provide that everyone has the right to the protection of personal data concerning him or her.

(2) The principles of, and rules on the protection of natural persons with regard to the processing of their personal data should, whatever their nationality or residence, respect their fundamental rights and freedoms, in particular their right to the protection of personal data. This Regulation is intended to contribute to the accomplishment of an area of freedom, security and justice and of an economic union, to economic and social progress, to the strengthening and the convergence of the economies within the internal market, and to the well-being of natural persons.

(3) Directive 95/46/EC of the European Parliament and of the Council[4] seeks to harmonise the protection of fundamental rights and freedoms of natural persons in respect of processing activities and to ensure the free flow of personal data between Member States.

(4) The processing of personal data should be designed to serve mankind. The right to the protection of personal data is not an absolute right; it must be considered in relation to its function in society and be balanced against other fundamental rights, in accordance with the principle of proportionality. This Regulation respects all fundamental rights and observes the freedoms and principles recognised in the Charter as enshrined in the Treaties, in particular the respect for private and family life, home and communications, the protection of personal data, freedom of thought, conscience and religion, freedom of expression and information, freedom to conduct a business, the right to an effective remedy and to a fair trial, and cultural, religious and linguistic diversity.

(5) The economic and social integration resulting from the functioning of the internal market has led to a substantial increase in cross-border flows of personal data. The exchange of personal data between public and private actors, including natural persons, associations and undertakings across the Union has increased. National authorities in the Member States are being called upon by Union law to cooperate and exchange personal data so as to be able to perform their duties or carry out tasks on behalf of an authority in another Member State.

(6) Rapid technological developments and globalisation have brought new challenges for the protection of personal data. The scale of the collection and sharing of personal data has increased significantly. Technology allows both private companies and public authorities to make use of personal data on an unprecedented scale in order to pursue their activities. Natural persons increasingly make personal information available publicly and globally. Technology has transformed both the economy and social life, and should further facilitate the free flow of personal data within the Union and the transfer to third countries and international organisations, while ensuring a high level of the protection of personal data.

(7) Those developments require a strong and more coherent data protection framework in the Union, backed by strong enforcement, given the importance of creating the trust that will allow the digital economy to develop across the internal market. Natural persons should have control of their own personal data. Legal and practical certainty for natural persons, economic operators and public authorities should be enhanced.

(8) Where this Regulation provides for specifications or restrictions of its rules by Member State law, Member States may, as far as necessary for coherence and for making the national provisions comprehensible to the persons to whom they apply, incorporate elements of this Regulation into their national law.

(9) The objectives and principles of Directive 95/46/EC remain sound, but it has not prevented fragmentation in the implementation of data protection across the Union, legal uncertainty or a widespread public perception that there are significant risks to the protection of natural persons, in particular with regard to online activity. Differences in the level of protection of the rights and freedoms of natural persons, in particular the right to the protection of personal data, with regard to the processing of personal data in the Member States may prevent the free flow of personal data throughout the Union. Those differences may therefore constitute an obstacle to the pursuit of economic activities at the level of the Union, distort competition and impede authorities in the discharge of their responsibilities under Union law. Such a difference in levels of protection is due to the existence of differences in the implementation and application of Directive 95/46/EC.

(10) In order to ensure a consistent and high level of protection of natural persons and to remove the obstacles to flows of personal data within the Union, the level of protection of the rights and freedoms of natural persons with regard to the processing of such data should be equivalent in all Member States. Consistent and homogenous application of the rules for the protection of the fundamental rights and freedoms of natural persons with regard to the processing of personal data should be ensured throughout the Union. Regarding the processing of personal data for compliance with a legal obligation, for the performance of a task carried out in the public interest or in the exercise of official authority vested in the controller, Member States should be allowed to maintain or introduce national provisions to further specify the application of the rules of this Regulation. In conjunction with the general and horizontal law on data protection implementing Directive 95/46/EC, Member States have several sector-specific laws in areas that need more specific provisions. This Regulation also provides a margin of manoeuvre for Member States to specify its rules, including for the processing of special categories of personal data ('sensitive data'). To that extent, this Regulation does not exclude Member State law that sets out the circumstances for specific processing situations, including determining more precisely the conditions under which the processing of personal data is lawful.

(11) Effective protection of personal data throughout the Union requires the strengthening and setting out in detail of the rights of data subjects and the obligations of those who process and determine the processing of personal data, as well as equivalent powers for monitoring and ensuring compliance with the rules for the protection of personal data and equivalent sanctions for infringements in the Member States.

(12) Article 16(2) TFEU mandates the European Parliament and the Council to lay down the rules relating to the protection of natural persons with regard to the processing of personal data and the rules relating to the free movement of personal data.

(13) In order to ensure a consistent level of protection for natural persons throughout the Union and to prevent divergences hampering the free movement of personal data within the internal market, a Regulation is necessary to provide legal certainty and transparency for economic operators, including micro, small and medium-sized enterprises, and to provide natural persons in all Member States with the same level of legally enforceable rights and obligations and responsibilities for controllers and processors, to ensure consistent monitoring of the processing of personal data, and equivalent sanctions in all Member States as well as effective cooperation between the supervisory authorities of different Member States. The proper functioning of the internal market requires that the free movement of personal data within the Union is not restricted or prohibited for reasons connected with the protection of natural persons with regard to the processing of personal data. To take account of the specific situation of micro, small and medium-sized enterprises, this Regulation includes a derogation for organisations with fewer than 250 employees with regard to record-keeping. In addition, the Union institutions and bodies, and Member States and their supervisory authorities, are encouraged to take account of the specific needs of micro, small and medium-sized enterprises in the application of this Regulation. The notion of micro, small and medium-sized enterprises should draw from Article 2 of the Annex to Commission Recommendation 2003/361/EC.[5]

(14) The protection afforded by this Regulation should apply to natural persons, whatever their nationality or place of residence, in relation to the processing of their personal data. This Regulation does not cover the processing of personal data which concerns legal persons and in particular undertakings established as legal persons, including the name and the form of the legal person and the contact details of the legal person.

(15) In order to prevent creating a serious risk of circumvention, the protection of natural persons should be technologically neutral and should not depend on the techniques used. The protection of natural persons should apply to the processing of personal data by automated means, as well as to manual processing, if the personal data are contained or are intended to be contained in a filing system. Files or sets of files, as well as their cover pages, which are not structured according to specific criteria should not fall within the scope of this Regulation.

(16) This Regulation does not apply to issues of protection of fundamental rights and freedoms or the free flow of personal data related to activities which fall outside the scope of Union law, such as activities concerning national security. This Regulation does not apply to the processing of personal data by the Member States when carrying out activities in relation to the common foreign and security policy of the Union.

(17) Regulation (EC) No 45/2001 of the European Parliament and of the Council[6] applies to the processing of personal data by the Union institutions, bodies, offices and agencies. Regulation (EC) No 45/2001 and other Union legal acts applicable to such processing of personal data should be adapted to the principles and rules established in this Regulation and applied in the light of this Regulation. In order to provide a strong and coherent data protection framework in the Union, the necessary adaptations of Regulation (EC) No 45/2001 should follow after the adoption of this Regulation, in order to allow application at the same time as this Regulation.

(18) This Regulation does not apply to the processing of personal data by a natural person in the course of a purely personal or household activity and thus with no connection to a professional or commercial activity. Personal or household activities could include correspondence and the holding of addresses, or social networking and online activity undertaken within the context of such activities. However, this Regulation applies to controllers or processors which provide the means for processing personal data for such personal or household activities.

(19) The protection of natural persons with regard to the processing of personal data by competent authorities for the purposes of the prevention, investigation, detection or prosecution of criminal offences or the execution of criminal penalties, including the safeguarding against and the prevention of threats to public security and the free movement of such data, is the subject of a specific Union legal act. This Regulation should not, therefore, apply to processing activities for those purposes. However, personal data processed by public authorities under this Regulation should, when used for those purposes, be governed by a more specific Union legal act, namely Directive (EU) 2016/680 of the European Parliament and of the Council.[7] Member States may entrust competent authorities within the meaning of Directive (EU) 2016/680 with tasks which are not necessarily carried out for the purposes of the prevention, investigation, detection or prosecution of criminal offences or the execution of criminal penalties, including the safeguarding against and prevention of threats to public security, so that the processing of personal data for those other purposes, in so far as it is within the scope of Union law, falls within the scope of this Regulation.

With regard to the processing of personal data by those competent authorities for purposes falling within scope of this Regulation, Member States should be able to maintain or introduce more specific provisions to adapt the application of the rules of this Regulation. Such provisions may determine more precisely specific requirements for the processing of personal data by those competent authorities for those other purposes, taking into account the constitutional, organisational and administrative structure of the respective Member State. When the processing of personal data by private bodies falls within the scope of this Regulation, this Regulation should provide for the possibility for Member States under specific conditions to restrict by law certain obligations and rights when such a restriction constitutes a necessary and proportionate measure in a democratic society to safeguard specific important interests including public security and the prevention, investigation, detection or prosecution of criminal offences or the execution of criminal penalties, including the safeguarding against and the prevention of threats to public security. This is relevant for instance in the framework of anti-money laundering or the activities of forensic laboratories.

(20) While this Regulation applies, inter alia, to the activities of courts and other judicial authorities, Union or Member State law could specify the processing operations and processing procedures in relation to the processing of personal data by courts and other judicial authorities. The competence of the supervisory authorities should not cover the processing of personal data when courts are acting in their judicial capacity, in order to safeguard the independence of the judiciary in the performance of its judicial tasks, including decision-making. It should be possible to entrust supervision of such data processing operations to specific bodies within the judicial system of the Member State, which should, in particular ensure compliance with the rules of this Regulation, enhance awareness among members of the judiciary of their obligations under this Regulation and handle complaints in relation to such data processing operations.

(21) This Regulation is without prejudice to the application of Directive 2000/31/EC of the European Parliament and of the Council,[8] in particular of the liability rules of intermediary service providers in Articles 12 to 15 of that Directive. That Directive seeks to contribute to the proper functioning of the internal market by ensuring the free movement of information society services between Member States.

(22) Any processing of personal data in the context of the activities of an establishment of a controller or a processor in the Union should be carried out in accordance with this Regulation, regardless of whether the processing itself takes place within the Union. Establishment implies the effective and real exercise of activity through stable arrangements. The legal form of such arrangements, whether through a branch or a subsidiary with a legal personality, is not the determining factor in that respect.

(23) In order to ensure that natural persons are not deprived of the protection to which they are entitled under this Regulation, the processing of personal data of data subjects who are in the Union by a controller or a processor not established in the Union should be subject to this Regulation where the processing activities are related to offering goods or services to such data subjects irrespective of whether connected to a payment. In order to determine whether such a controller or processor is offering goods or services to data subjects who are in the Union, it should be ascertained whether it is apparent that the controller or processor envisages offering services to data subjects in one or more Member States in the Union. Whereas the mere accessibility of the controller's, processor's or an intermediary's website in the Union, of an email address or of other contact details, or the use of a language generally used in the third country where the controller is established, is insufficient to ascertain such intention, factors such as the use of a language or a currency generally used in one or more Member States with the possibility of ordering goods and services in that other language, or the mentioning of customers or users who are in the Union, may make it apparent that the controller envisages offering goods or services to data subjects in the Union.

(24) The processing of personal data of data subjects who are in the Union by a controller or processor not established in the Union should also be subject to this Regulation when it is related to the monitoring of the behaviour of such data subjects in so far as their behaviour takes place within the Union. In order to determine whether a processing activity can be considered to monitor the behaviour of data subjects, it should be ascertained whether natural persons are tracked on the internet including potential subsequent use of personal data processing techniques which consist of profiling a natural person, particularly in order to take decisions concerning her or him or for analysing or predicting her or his personal preferences, behaviours and attitudes.

(25) Where Member State law applies by virtue of public international law, this Regulation should also apply to a controller not established in the Union, such as in a Member State's diplomatic mission or consular post.

(26) The principles of data protection should apply to any information concerning an identified or identifiable natural person. Personal data which have undergone pseudonymisation, which could be attributed to a natural person by the use of additional information should be considered to be information on an identifiable natural person. To determine whether a natural person is identifiable, account should be taken of all the means reasonably likely to be used, such as singling out, either by the controller or by another person to identify the natural person directly or indirectly. To ascertain whether means are reasonably likely to be used to identify the natural person, account should be taken of all objective factors, such as the costs of and the amount of time required for identification, taking into consideration the available technology at the time of the processing and technological developments. The principles of data protection should therefore not apply to anonymous information, namely information which does not relate to an identified or identifiable natural person or to personal data rendered anonymous in such a manner that the data subject is not or no longer identifiable. This Regulation does not therefore concern the processing of such anonymous information, including for statistical or research purposes.

(27) This Regulation does not apply to the personal data of deceased persons. Member States may provide for rules regarding the processing of personal data of deceased persons.

(28) The application of pseudonymisation to personal data can reduce the risks to the data subjects concerned and help controllers and processors to meet their data-protection obligations. The explicit introduction of 'pseudonymisation' in this Regulation is not intended to preclude any other measures of data protection.

(29) In order to create incentives to apply pseudonymisation when processing personal data, measures of pseudonymisation should, whilst allowing general analysis, be possible within the same controller when that controller has taken technical and organisational measures necessary to ensure, for the processing concerned, that this Regulation is implemented, and that additional information for attributing the personal data to a specific data subject is kept separately. The controller processing the personal data should indicate the authorised persons within the same controller.

(32) Consent should be given by a clear affirmative act establishing a freely given, specific, informed and unambiguous indication of the data subject's agreement to the processing of personal data relating to him or her, such as by a written statement, including by electronic means, or an oral statement. This could include ticking a box when visiting an internet website, choosing technical settings for information society services or another statement or conduct which clearly indicates in this context the data subject's acceptance of the proposed processing of his or her personal data. Silence, pre-ticked boxes or inactivity should not therefore constitute consent. Consent should cover all processing activities carried out for the same purpose or purposes. When the processing has multiple purposes, consent should be given for all of them. If the data subject's consent is to be given following a request by electronic means, the request must be clear, concise and not unnecessarily disruptive to the use of the service for which it is provided.

(33) It is often not possible to fully identify the purpose of personal data processing for scientific research purposes at the time of data collection. Therefore, data subjects should be allowed to give their consent to certain areas of scientific research when in keeping with recognised ethical standards for scientific research. Data subjects should have the opportunity to give their consent only to certain areas of research or parts of research projects to the extent allowed by the intended purpose.

(35) Personal data concerning health should include all data pertaining to the health status of a data subject which reveal information relating to the past, current or future physical or mental health status of the data subject. This includes information about the natural person collected in the course of the registration for, or the provision of, health care services as referred to in Directive 2011/24/EU of the European Parliament and of the Council[9] to that natural person; a number, symbol or particular assigned

to a natural person to uniquely identify the natural person for health purposes; information derived from the testing or examination of a body part or bodily substance, including from genetic data and biological samples; and any information on, for example, a disease, disability, disease risk, medical history, clinical treatment or the physiological or biomedical state of the data subject independent of its source, for example from a physician or other health professional, a hospital, a medical device or an in vitro diagnostic test.

(36) The main establishment of a controller in the Union should be the place of its central administration in the Union, unless the decisions on the purposes and means of the processing of personal data are taken in another establishment of the controller in the Union, in which case that other establishment should be considered to be the main establishment. The main establishment of a controller in the Union should be determined according to objective criteria and should imply the effective and real exercise of management activities determining the main decisions as to the purposes and means of processing through stable arrangements. That criterion should not depend on whether the processing of personal data is carried out at that location. The presence and use of technical means and technologies for processing personal data or processing activities do not, in themselves, constitute a main establishment and are therefore not determining criteria for a main establishment. The main establishment of the processor should be the place of its central administration in the Union or, if it has no central administration in the Union, the place where the main processing activities take place in the Union. In cases involving both the controller and the processor, the competent lead supervisory authority should remain the supervisory authority of the Member State where the controller has its main establishment, but the supervisory authority of the processor should be considered to be a supervisory authority concerned and that supervisory authority should participate in the cooperation procedure provided for by this Regulation. In any case, the supervisory authorities of the Member State or Member States where the processor has one or more establishments should not be considered to be supervisory authorities concerned where the draft decision concerns only the controller. Where the processing is carried out by a group of undertakings, the main establishment of the controlling undertaking should be considered to be the main establishment of the group of undertakings, except where the purposes and means of processing are determined by another undertaking.

(37) A group of undertakings should cover a controlling undertaking and its controlled undertakings, whereby the controlling undertaking should be the undertaking which can exert a dominant influence over the other undertakings by virtue, for example, of ownership, financial participation or the rules which govern it or the power to have personal data protection rules implemented. An undertaking which controls the processing of personal data in undertakings affiliated to it should be regarded, together with those undertakings, as a group of undertakings.

(39) Any processing of personal data should be lawful and fair. It should be transparent to natural persons that personal data concerning them are collected, used, consulted or otherwise processed and to what extent the personal data are or will be processed. The principle of transparency requires that any information and communication relating to the processing of those personal data be easily accessible and easy to understand, and that clear and plain language be used. That principle concerns, in particular, information to the data subjects on the identity of the controller and the purposes of the processing and further information to ensure fair and transparent processing in respect of the natural persons concerned and their right to obtain confirmation and communication of personal data concerning them which are being processed. Natural persons should be made aware of risks, rules, safeguards and rights in relation to the processing of personal data and how to exercise their rights in relation to such processing. In particular, the specific purposes for which personal data are processed should be explicit and legitimate and determined at the time of the collection of the personal data. The personal data should be adequate, relevant and limited to what is necessary for the purposes for which they are processed. This requires, in particular, ensuring that the period for which the personal data are stored is limited to a strict minimum. Personal data should be processed only if the purpose of the processing could not reasonably be fulfilled by other means. In order to ensure that the personal data are not kept longer than necessary, time limits should be established by the controller for erasure or for a periodic review. Every reasonable step should be taken to ensure that personal data which are inaccurate are rectified or deleted. Personal data should be processed in a manner that ensures appropriate security and confidentiality of the personal data, including for preventing unauthorised access to or use of personal data and the equipment used for the processing.

(40) In order for processing to be lawful, personal data should be processed on the basis of the consent of the data subject concerned or some other legitimate basis, laid down by law, either in this Regulation or in other Union or Member State law as referred to in this Regulation, including the necessity for compliance with the legal obligation to which the controller is subject or the necessity for the performance of a contract to which the data subject is party or in order to take steps at the request of the data subject prior to entering into a contract.

(41) Where this Regulation refers to a legal basis or a legislative measure, this does not necessarily require a legislative act adopted by a parliament, without prejudice to requirements pursuant to the constitutional order of the Member State concerned. However, such a legal basis or legislative measure should be clear and precise and its application should be foreseeable to persons subject to it, in accordance with the case-law of the Court of Justice of the European Union (the 'Court of Justice') and the European Court of Human Rights.

(42) Where processing is based on the data subject's consent, the controller should be able to demonstrate that the data subject has given consent to the processing operation. In particular in the context of a written declaration on another matter, safeguards should ensure that the data subject is aware of the fact that and the extent to which consent is given. In accordance with Council Directive 93/13/EEC[10] a declaration of consent pre-formulated by the controller should be provided in an intelligible and easily accessible form, using clear and plain language and it should not contain unfair

terms. For consent to be informed, the data subject should be aware at least of the identity of the controller and the purposes of the processing for which the personal data are intended. Consent should not be regarded as freely given if the data subject has no genuine or free choice or is unable to refuse or withdraw consent without detriment.

(43) In order to ensure that consent is freely given, consent should not provide a valid legal ground for the processing of personal data in a specific case where there is a clear imbalance between the data subject and the controller, in particular where the controller is a public authority and it is therefore unlikely that consent was freely given in all the circumstances of that specific situation. Consent is presumed not to be freely given if it does not allow separate consent to be given to different personal data processing operations despite it being appropriate in the individual case, or if the performance of a contract, including the provision of a service, is dependent on the consent despite such consent not being necessary for such performance.

(44) Processing should be lawful where it is necessary in the context of a contract or the intention to enter into a contract.

(47) The legitimate interests of a controller, including those of a controller to which the personal data may be disclosed, or of a third party, may provide a legal basis for processing, provided that the interests or the fundamental rights and freedoms of the data subject are not overriding, taking into consideration the reasonable expectations of data subjects based on their relationship with the controller. Such legitimate interest could exist for example where there is a relevant and appropriate relationship between the data subject and the controller in situations such as where the data subject is a client or in the service of the controller. At any rate the existence of a legitimate interest would need careful assessment including whether a data subject can reasonably expect at the time and in the context of the collection of the personal data that processing for that purpose may take place. The interests and fundamental rights of the data subject could in particular override the interest of the data controller where personal data are processed in circumstances where data subjects do not reasonably expect further processing. Given that it is for the legislator to provide by law for the legal basis for public authorities to process personal data, that legal basis should not apply to the processing by public authorities in the performance of their tasks. The processing of personal data strictly necessary for the purposes of preventing fraud also constitutes a legitimate interest of the data controller concerned. The processing of personal data for direct marketing purposes may be regarded as carried out for a legitimate interest.

(48) Controllers that are part of a group of undertakings or institutions affiliated to a central body may have a legitimate interest in transmitting personal data within the group of undertakings for internal administrative purposes, including the processing of clients' or employees' personal data. The general principles for the transfer of personal data, within a group of undertakings, to an undertaking located in a third country remain unaffected.

(49) The processing of personal data to the extent strictly necessary and proportionate for the purposes of ensuring network and information security, i.e. the ability of a network or an information system to resist, at a given level of confidence, accidental events or unlawful or malicious actions that compromise the availability, authenticity, integrity and confidentiality of stored or transmitted personal data, and the security of the related services offered by, or accessible via, those networks and systems, by public authorities, by computer emergency response teams (CERTs), computer security incident response teams (CSIRTs), by providers of electronic communications networks and services and by providers of security technologies and services, constitutes a legitimate interest of the data controller concerned. This could, for example, include preventing unauthorised access to electronic communications networks and malicious code distribution and stopping 'denial of service' attacks and damage to computer and electronic communication systems.

(50) The processing of personal data for purposes other than those for which the personal data were initially collected should be allowed only where the processing is compatible with the purposes for which the personal data were initially collected. In such a case, no legal basis separate from that which allowed the collection of the personal data is required. If the processing is necessary for the performance of a task carried out in the public interest or in the exercise of official authority vested in the controller, Union or Member State law may determine and specify the tasks and purposes for which the further processing should be regarded as compatible and lawful. Further processing for archiving purposes in the public interest, scientific or historical research purposes or statistical purposes should be considered to be compatible lawful processing operations. The legal basis provided by Union or Member State law for the processing of personal data may also provide a legal basis for further processing. In order to ascertain whether a purpose of further processing is compatible with the purpose for which the personal data are initially collected, the controller, after having met all the requirements for the lawfulness of the original processing, should take into account, inter alia: any link between those purposes and the purposes of the intended further processing; the context in which the personal data have been collected, in particular the reasonable expectations of data subjects based on their relationship with the controller as to their further use; the nature of the personal data; the consequences of the intended further processing for data subjects; and the existence of appropriate safeguards in both the original and intended further processing operations.

Where the data subject has given consent or the processing is based on Union or Member State law which constitutes a necessary and proportionate measure in a democratic society to safeguard, in particular, important objectives of general public interest, the controller should be allowed to further process the personal data irrespective of the compatibility of the purposes. In any case, the application of the principles set out in this Regulation and in particular the information of the data subject on those other purposes and on his or her rights including the right to object, should be ensured. Indicating possible criminal acts or threats to public security by the controller and transmitting the relevant personal data in individual cases or in several cases relating to the same criminal act or threats to public security to a competent authority should be regarded as being in the legitimate interest pursued by the controller. However, such transmission in the legitimate interest of the controller or further processing of personal data should be prohibited if the processing is not compatible with a legal, professional or other binding obligation of secrecy.

(51) Personal data which are, by their nature, particularly sensitive in relation to fundamental rights and freedoms merit specific protection as the context of their processing could create significant risks to the fundamental rights and freedoms. Those personal data should include personal data revealing racial or ethnic origin, whereby the use of the term 'racial origin' in this Regulation does not imply an acceptance by the Union of theories which attempt to determine the existence of separate human races. The processing of photographs should not systematically be considered to be processing of special categories of personal data as they are covered by the definition of biometric data only when processed through a specific technical means allowing the unique identification or authentication of a natural person. Such personal data should not be processed, unless processing is allowed in specific cases set out in this Regulation, taking into account that Member States law may lay down specific provisions on data protection in order to adapt the application of the rules of this Regulation for compliance with a legal obligation or for the performance of a task carried out in the public interest or in the exercise of official authority vested in the controller. In addition to the specific requirements for such processing, the general principles and other rules of this Regulation should apply, in particular as regards the conditions for lawful processing. Derogations from the general prohibition for processing such special categories of personal data should be explicitly provided, inter alia, where the data subject gives his or her explicit consent or in respect of specific needs in particular where the processing is carried out in the course of legitimate activities by certain associations or foundations the purpose of which is to permit the exercise of fundamental freedoms.

(52) Derogating from the prohibition on processing special categories of personal data should also be allowed when provided for in Union or Member State law and subject to suitable safeguards, so as to protect personal data and other fundamental rights, where it is in the public interest to do so, in particular processing personal data in the field of employment law, social protection law including pensions and for health security, monitoring and alert purposes, the prevention or control of communicable diseases and other serious threats to health. Such a derogation may be made for health purposes, including public health and the management of health-care services, especially in order to ensure the quality and cost-effectiveness of the procedures used for settling claims for benefits and services in the health insurance system, or for archiving purposes in the public interest, scientific or historical research purposes or statistical purposes. A derogation should also allow the processing of such personal data where necessary for the establishment, exercise or defence of legal claims, whether in court proceedings or in an administrative or out-of-court procedure.

(53) Special categories of personal data which merit higher protection should be processed for health-related purposes only where necessary to achieve those purposes for the benefit of natural persons and society as a whole, in particular in the context of the management of health or social care services and systems, including processing by the management and central national health authorities of such data for the purpose of quality control, management information and the general national and local supervision of the health or social care system, and ensuring continuity of health or social care and cross-border healthcare or health security, monitoring and alert purposes, or for archiving purposes in the public interest, scientific or historical research purposes or statistical purposes, based on Union or Member State law which has to meet an objective of public interest, as well as for studies conducted in the public interest in the area of public health. Therefore, this Regulation should provide for harmonised conditions for the processing of special categories of personal data concerning health, in respect of specific needs, in particular where the processing of such data is carried out for certain health-related purposes by persons subject to a legal obligation of professional secrecy. Union or Member State law should provide for specific and suitable measures so as to protect the fundamental rights and the personal data of natural persons. Member States should be allowed to maintain or introduce further conditions, including limitations, with regard to the processing of genetic data, biometric data or data concerning health. However, this should not hamper the free flow of personal data within the Union when those conditions apply to cross-border processing of such data.

(57) If the personal data processed by a controller do not permit the controller to identify a natural person, the data controller should not be obliged to acquire additional information in order to identify the data subject for the sole purpose of complying with any provision of this Regulation. However, the controller should not refuse to take additional information provided by the data subject in order to support the exercise of his or her rights. Identification should include the digital identification of a data subject, for example through authentication mechanism such as the same credentials, used by the data subject to log-in to the on-line service offered by the data controller.

(58) The principle of transparency requires that any information addressed to the public or to the data subject be concise, easily accessible and easy to understand, and that clear and plain language and, additionally, where appropriate, visualisation be used. Such information could be provided in electronic form, for example, when addressed to the public, through a website. This is of particular relevance in situations where the proliferation of actors and the technological complexity of practice make it difficult for the data subject to know and understand whether, by whom and for what purpose personal data relating to him or her are being collected, such as in the case of online advertising. Given that children merit specific protection, any information and communication, where processing is addressed to a child, should be in such a clear and plain language that the child can easily understand.

(59) Modalities should be provided for facilitating the exercise of the data subject's rights under this Regulation, including mechanisms to request and, if applicable, obtain, free of charge, in particular, access to and rectification or erasure of personal data and the exercise of the right to object. The controller

should also provide means for requests to be made electronically, especially where personal data are processed by electronic means. The controller should be obliged to respond to requests from the data subject without undue delay and at the latest within one month and to give reasons where the controller does not intend to comply with any such requests.

(60) The principles of fair and transparent processing require that the data subject be informed of the existence of the processing operation and its purposes. The controller should provide the data subject with any further information necessary to ensure fair and transparent processing taking into account the specific circumstances and context in which the personal data are processed. Furthermore, the data subject should be informed of the existence of profiling and the consequences of such profiling. Where the personal data are collected from the data subject, the data subject should also be informed whether he or she is obliged to provide the personal data and of the consequences, where he or she does not provide such data. That information may be provided in combination with standardised icons in order to give in an easily visible, intelligible and clearly legible manner, a meaningful overview of the intended processing. Where the icons are presented electronically, they should be machine-readable.

(61) The information in relation to the processing of personal data relating to the data subject should be given to him or her at the time of collection from the data subject, or, where the personal data are obtained from another source, within a reasonable period, depending on the circumstances of the case. Where personal data can be legitimately disclosed to another recipient, the data subject should be informed when the personal data are first disclosed to the recipient. Where the controller intends to process the personal data for a purpose other than that for which they were collected, the controller should provide the data subject prior to that further processing with information on that other purpose and other necessary information. Where the origin of the personal data cannot be provided to the data subject because various sources have been used, general information should be provided.

(62) However, it is not necessary to impose the obligation to provide information where the data subject already possesses the information, where the recording or disclosure of the personal data is expressly laid down by law or where the provision of information to the data subject proves to be impossible or would involve a disproportionate effort. The latter could in particular be the case where processing is carried out for archiving purposes in the public interest, scientific or historical research purposes or statistical purposes. In that regard, the number of data subjects, the age of the data and any appropriate safeguards adopted should be taken into consideration.

(63) A data subject should have the right of access to personal data which have been collected concerning him or her, and to exercise that right easily and at reasonable intervals, in order to be aware of, and verify, the lawfulness of the processing. This includes the right for data subjects to have access to data concerning their health, for example the data in their medical records containing information such as diagnoses, examination results, assessments by treating physicians and any treatment or interventions provided. Every data subject should therefore have the right to know and obtain communication in particular with regard to the purposes for which the personal data are processed, where possible the period for which the personal data are processed, the recipients of the personal data, the logic involved in any automatic personal data processing and, at least when based on profiling, the consequences of such processing. Where possible, the controller should be able to provide remote access to a secure system which would provide the data subject with direct access to his or her personal data. That right should not adversely affect the rights or freedoms of others, including trade secrets or intellectual property and in particular the copyright protecting the software. However, the result of those considerations should not be a refusal to provide all information to the data subject. Where the controller processes a large quantity of information concerning the data subject, the controller should be able to request that, before the information is delivered, the data subject specify the information or processing activities to which the request relates.

(64) The controller should use all reasonable measures to verify the identity of a data subject who requests access, in particular in the context of online services and online identifiers. A controller should not retain personal data for the sole purpose of being able to react to potential requests.

(65) A data subject should have the right to have personal data concerning him or her rectified and a 'right to be forgotten' where the retention of such data infringes this Regulation or Union or Member State law to which the controller is subject. In particular, a data subject should have the right to have his or her personal data erased and no longer processed where the personal data are no longer necessary in relation to the purposes for which they are collected or otherwise processed, where a data subject has withdrawn his or her consent or objects to the processing of personal data concerning him or her, or where the processing of his or her personal data does not otherwise comply with this Regulation. That right is relevant in particular where the data subject has given his or her consent as a child and is not fully aware of the risks involved by the processing, and later wants to remove such personal data, especially on the internet. The data subject should be able to exercise that right notwithstanding the fact that he or she is no longer a child. However, the further retention of the personal data should be lawful where it is necessary, for exercising the right of freedom of expression and information, for compliance with a legal obligation, for the performance of a task carried out in the public interest or in the exercise of official authority vested in the controller, on the grounds of public interest in the area of public health, for archiving purposes in the public interest, scientific or historical research purposes or statistical purposes, or for the establishment, exercise or defence of legal claims.

(66) To strengthen the right to be forgotten in the online environment, the right to erasure should also be extended in such a way that a controller who has made the personal data public should be obliged to inform the controllers which are processing such personal data to erase any links to, or copies or replications of those personal data. In doing so, that controller should take reasonable steps, taking into account available technology and the means available to the controller, including technical measures, to inform the controllers which are processing the personal data of the data subject's request.

(67) Methods by which to restrict the processing of personal data could include, inter alia, temporarily moving the selected data to another processing system, making the selected personal data unavailable to users, or temporarily removing published data from a website. In automated filing systems, the restriction of processing should in principle be ensured by technical means in such a manner that the personal data are not subject to further processing operations and cannot be changed. The fact that the processing of personal data is restricted should be clearly indicated in the system.

(68) To further strengthen the control over his or her own data, where the processing of personal data is carried out by automated means, the data subject should also be allowed to receive personal data concerning him or her which he or she has provided to a controller in a structured, commonly used, machine-readable and interoperable format, and to transmit it to another controller. Data controllers should be encouraged to develop interoperable formats that enable data portability. That right should apply where the data subject provided the personal data on the basis of his or her consent or the processing is necessary for the performance of a contract. It should not apply where processing is based on a legal ground other than consent or contract. By its very nature, that right should not be exercised against controllers processing personal data in the exercise of their public duties. It should therefore not apply where the processing of the personal data is necessary for compliance with a legal obligation to which the controller is subject or for the performance of a task carried out in the public interest or in the exercise of an official authority vested in the controller. The data subject's right to transmit or receive personal data concerning him or her should not create an obligation for the controllers to adopt or maintain processing systems which are technically compatible. Where, in a certain set of personal data, more than one data subject is concerned, the right to receive the personal data should be without prejudice to the rights and freedoms of other data subjects in accordance with this Regulation. Furthermore, that right should not prejudice the right of the data subject to obtain the erasure of personal data and the limitations of that right as set out in this Regulation and should, in particular, not imply the erasure of personal data concerning the data subject which have been provided by him or her for the performance of a contract to the extent that and for as long as the personal data are necessary for the performance of that contract. Where technically feasible, the data subject should have the right to have the personal data transmitted directly from one controller to another.

(69) Where personal data might lawfully be processed because processing is necessary for the performance of a task carried out in the public interest or in the exercise of official authority vested in the controller, or on grounds of the legitimate interests of a controller or a third party, a data subject should, nevertheless, be entitled to object to the processing of any personal data relating to his or her particular situation. It should be for the controller to demonstrate that its compelling legitimate interest overrides the interests or the fundamental rights and freedoms of the data subject.

(71) The data subject should have the right not to be subject to a decision, which may include a measure, evaluating personal aspects relating to him or her which is based solely on automated processing and which produces legal effects concerning him or her or similarly significantly affects him or her, such as automatic refusal of an online credit application or e-recruiting practices without any human intervention. Such processing includes 'profiling' that consists of any form of automated processing of personal data evaluating the personal aspects relating to a natural person, in particular to analyse or predict aspects concerning the data subject's performance at work, economic situation, health, personal preferences or interests, reliability or behaviour, location or movements, where it produces legal effects concerning him or her or similarly significantly affects him or her. However, decision-making based on such processing, including profiling, should be allowed where expressly authorised by Union or Member State law to which the controller is subject, including for fraud and tax-evasion monitoring and prevention purposes conducted in accordance with the regulations, standards and recommendations of Union institutions or national oversight bodies and to ensure the security and reliability of a service provided by the controller, or necessary for the entering or performance of a contract between the data subject and a controller, or when the data subject has given his or her explicit consent. In any case, such processing should be subject to suitable safeguards, which should include specific information to the data subject and the right to obtain human intervention, to express his or her point of view, to obtain an explanation of the decision reached after such assessment and to challenge the decision. Such measure should not concern a child.

In order to ensure fair and transparent processing in respect of the data subject, taking into account the specific circumstances and context in which the personal data are processed, the controller should use appropriate mathematical or statistical procedures for the profiling, implement technical and organisational measures appropriate to ensure, in particular, that factors which result in inaccuracies in personal data are corrected and the risk of errors is minimised, secure personal data in a manner that takes account of the potential risks involved for the interests and rights of the data subject, and prevent, inter alia, discriminatory effects on natural persons on the basis of racial or ethnic origin, political opinion, religion or beliefs, trade union membership, genetic or health status or sexual orientation, or processing that results in measures having such an effect. Automated decision-making and profiling based on special categories of personal data should be allowed only under specific conditions.

(74) The responsibility and liability of the controller for any processing of personal data carried out by the controller or on the controller's behalf should be established. In particular, the controller should be obliged to implement appropriate and effective measures and be able to demonstrate the compliance of processing activities with this Regulation, including the effectiveness of the measures. Those measures should take into account the nature, scope, context and purposes of the processing and the risk to the rights and freedoms of natural persons.

(75) The risk to the rights and freedoms of natural persons, of varying likelihood and severity, may result from personal data processing which could lead to physical, material or non-material damage, in particular: where the processing may give rise to discrimination, identity theft or fraud, financial loss,

damage to the reputation, loss of confidentiality of personal data protected by professional secrecy, unauthorised reversal of pseudonymisation, or any other significant economic or social disadvantage; where data subjects might be deprived of their rights and freedoms or prevented from exercising control over their personal data; where personal data are processed which reveal racial or ethnic origin, political opinions, religion or philosophical beliefs, trade union membership, and the processing of genetic data, data concerning health or data concerning sex life or criminal convictions and offences or related security measures; where personal aspects are evaluated, in particular analysing or predicting aspects concerning performance at work, economic situation, health, personal preferences or interests, reliability or behaviour, location or movements, in order to create or use personal profiles; where personal data of vulnerable natural persons, in particular of children, are processed; or where processing involves a large amount of personal data and affects a large number of data subjects.

(76) The likelihood and severity of the risk to the rights and freedoms of the data subject should be determined by reference to the nature, scope, context and purposes of the processing. Risk should be evaluated on the basis of an objective assessment, by which it is established whether data processing operations involve a risk or a high risk.

(77) Guidance on the implementation of appropriate measures and on the demonstration of compliance by the controller or the processor, especially as regards the identification of the risk related to the processing, their assessment in terms of origin, nature, likelihood and severity, and the identification of best practices to mitigate the risk, could be provided in particular by means of approved codes of conduct, approved certifications, guidelines provided by the Board or indications provided by a data protection officer. The Board may also issue guidelines on processing operations that are considered to be unlikely to result in a high risk to the rights and freedoms of natural persons and indicate what measures may be sufficient in such cases to address such risk.

(81) To ensure compliance with the requirements of this Regulation in respect of the processing to be carried out by the processor on behalf of the controller, when entrusting a processor with processing activities, the controller should use only processors providing sufficient guarantees, in particular in terms of expert knowledge, reliability and resources, to implement technical and organisational measures which will meet the requirements of this Regulation, including for the security of processing. The adherence of the processor to an approved code of conduct or an approved certification mechanism may be used as an element to demonstrate compliance with the obligations of the controller. The carrying-out of processing by a processor should be governed by a contract or other legal act under Union or Member State law, binding the processor to the controller, setting out the subject-matter and duration of the processing, the nature and purposes of the processing, the type of personal data and categories of data subjects, taking into account the specific tasks and responsibilities of the processor in the context of the processing to be carried out and the risk to the rights and freedoms of the data subject. The controller and processor may choose to use an individual contract or standard contractual clauses which are adopted either directly by the Commission or by a supervisory authority in accordance with the consistency mechanism and then adopted by the Commission. After the completion of the processing on behalf of the controller, the processor should, at the choice of the controller, return or delete the personal data, unless there is a requirement to store the personal data under Union or Member State law to which the processor is subject.

(82) In order to demonstrate compliance with this Regulation, the controller or processor should maintain records of processing activities under its responsibility. Each controller and processor should be obliged to cooperate with the supervisory authority and make those records, on request, available to it, so that it might serve for monitoring those processing operations.

(83) In order to maintain security and to prevent processing in infringement of this Regulation, the controller or processor should evaluate the risks inherent in the processing and implement measures to mitigate those risks, such as encryption. Those measures should ensure an appropriate level of security, including confidentiality, taking into account the state of the art and the costs of implementation in relation to the risks and the nature of the personal data to be protected. In assessing data security risk, consideration should be given to the risks that are presented by personal data processing, such as accidental or unlawful destruction, loss, alteration, unauthorised disclosure of, or access to, personal data transmitted, stored or otherwise processed which may in particular lead to physical, material or non-material damage.

(84) In order to enhance compliance with this Regulation where processing operations are likely to result in a high risk to the rights and freedoms of natural persons, the controller should be responsible for the carrying-out of a data protection impact assessment to evaluate, in particular, the origin, nature, particularity and severity of that risk. The outcome of the assessment should be taken into account when determining the appropriate measures to be taken in order to demonstrate that the processing of personal data complies with this Regulation. Where a data-protection impact assessment indicates that processing operations involve a high risk which the controller cannot mitigate by appropriate measures in terms of available technology and costs of implementation, a consultation of the supervisory authority should take place prior to the processing.

(85) A personal data breach may, if not addressed in an appropriate and timely manner, result in physical, material or non-material damage to natural persons such as loss of control over their personal data or limitation of their rights, discrimination, identity theft or fraud, financial loss, unauthorised reversal of pseudonymisation, damage to reputation, loss of confidentiality of personal data protected by professional secrecy or any other significant economic or social disadvantage to the natural person concerned. Therefore, as soon as the controller becomes aware that a personal data breach has occurred, the controller should notify the personal data breach to the supervisory authority without undue delay and, where feasible, not later than 72 hours after having become aware of it, unless the controller is able to demonstrate, in accordance with the accountability principle, that the personal data breach is unlikely

to result in a risk to the rights and freedoms of natural persons. Where such notification cannot be achieved within 72 hours, the reasons for the delay should accompany the notification and information may be provided in phases without undue further delay.

(86) The controller should communicate to the data subject a personal data breach, without undue delay, where that personal data breach is likely to result in a high risk to the rights and freedoms of the natural person in order to allow him or her to take the necessary precautions. The communication should describe the nature of the personal data breach as well as recommendations for the natural person concerned to mitigate potential adverse effects. Such communications to data subjects should be made as soon as reasonably feasible and in close cooperation with the supervisory authority, respecting guidance provided by it or by other relevant authorities such as law-enforcement authorities. For example, the need to mitigate an immediate risk of damage would call for prompt communication with data subjects whereas the need to implement appropriate measures against continuing or similar personal data breaches may justify more time for communication.

(87) It should be ascertained whether all appropriate technological protection and organisational measures have been implemented to establish immediately whether a personal data breach has taken place and to inform promptly the supervisory authority and the data subject. The fact that the notification was made without undue delay should be established taking into account in particular the nature and gravity of the personal data breach and its consequences and adverse effects for the data subject. Such notification may result in an intervention of the supervisory authority in accordance with its tasks and powers laid down in this Regulation.

(88) In setting detailed rules concerning the format and procedures applicable to the notification of personal data breaches, due consideration should be given to the circumstances of that breach, including whether or not personal data had been protected by appropriate technical protection measures, effectively limiting the likelihood of identity fraud or other forms of misuse. Moreover, such rules and procedures should take into account the legitimate interests of law-enforcement authorities where early disclosure could unnecessarily hamper the investigation of the circumstances of a personal data breach.

(89) Directive 95/46/EC provided for a general obligation to notify the processing of personal data to the supervisory authorities. While that obligation produces administrative and financial burdens, it did not in all cases contribute to improving the protection of personal data. Such indiscriminate general notification obligations should therefore be abolished, and replaced by effective procedures and mechanisms which focus instead on those types of processing operations which are likely to result in a high risk to the rights and freedoms of natural persons by virtue of their nature, scope, context and purposes. Such types of processing operations may be those which in, particular, involve using new technologies, or are of a new kind and where no data protection impact assessment has been carried out before by the controller, or where they become necessary in the light of the time that has elapsed since the initial processing.

(90) In such cases, a data protection impact assessment should be carried out by the controller prior to the processing in order to assess the particular likelihood and severity of the high risk, taking into account the nature, scope, context and purposes of the processing and the sources of the risk. That impact assessment should include, in particular, the measures, safeguards and mechanisms envisaged for mitigating that risk, ensuring the protection of personal data and demonstrating compliance with this Regulation.

(91) This should in particular apply to large-scale processing operations which aim to process a considerable amount of personal data at regional, national or supranational level and which could affect a large number of data subjects and which are likely to result in a high risk, for example, on account of their sensitivity, where in accordance with the achieved state of technological knowledge a new technology is used on a large scale as well as to other processing operations which result in a high risk to the rights and freedoms of data subjects, in particular where those operations render it more difficult for data subjects to exercise their rights. A data protection impact assessment should also be made where personal data are processed for taking decisions regarding specific natural persons following any systematic and extensive evaluation of personal aspects relating to natural persons based on profiling those data or following the processing of special categories of personal data, biometric data, or data on criminal convictions and offences or related security measures. A data protection impact assessment is equally required for monitoring publicly accessible areas on a large scale, especially when using optic-electronic devices or for any other operations where the competent supervisory authority considers that the processing is likely to result in a high risk to the rights and freedoms of data subjects, in particular because they prevent data subjects from exercising a right or using a service or a contract, or because they are carried out systematically on a large scale. The processing of personal data should not be considered to be on a large scale if the processing concerns personal data from patients or clients by an individual physician, other health care professional or lawyer. In such cases, a data protection impact assessment should not be mandatory.

(92) There are circumstances under which it may be reasonable and economical for the subject of a data protection impact assessment to be broader than a single project, for example where public authorities or bodies intend to establish a common application or processing platform or where several controllers plan to introduce a common application or processing environment across an industry sector or segment or for a widely used horizontal activity.

(103) The Commission may decide with effect for the entire Union that a third country, a territory or specified sector within a third country, or an international organisation, offers an adequate level of data protection, thus providing legal certainty and uniformity throughout the Union as regards the third country or international organisation which is considered to provide such level of protection. In such

cases, transfers of personal data to that third country or international organisation may take place without the need to obtain any further authorisation. The Commission may also decide, having given notice and a full statement setting out the reasons to the third country or international organisation, to revoke such a decision.

(104) In line with the fundamental values on which the Union is founded, in particular the protection of human rights, the Commission should, in its assessment of the third country, or of a territory or specified sector within a third country, take into account how a particular third country respects the rule of law, access to justice as well as international human rights norms and standards and its general and sectoral law, including legislation concerning public security, defence and national security as well as public order and criminal law. The adoption of an adequacy decision with regard to a territory or a specified sector in a third country should take into account clear and objective criteria, such as specific processing activities and the scope of applicable legal standards and legislation in force in the third country. The third country should offer guarantees ensuring an adequate level of protection essentially equivalent to that ensured within the Union, in particular where personal data are processed in one or several specific sectors. In particular, the third country should ensure effective independent data protection supervision and should provide for cooperation mechanisms with the Member States' data protection authorities, and the data subjects should be provided with effective and enforceable rights and effective administrative and judicial redress.

(141) Every data subject should have the right to lodge a complaint with a single supervisory authority, in particular in the Member State of his or her habitual residence, and the right to an effective judicial remedy in accordance with Article 47 of the Charter if the data subject considers that his or her rights under this Regulation are infringed or where the supervisory authority does not act on a complaint, partially or wholly rejects or dismisses a complaint or does not act where such action is necessary to protect the rights of the data subject. The investigation following a complaint should be carried out, subject to judicial review, to the extent that is appropriate in the specific case. The supervisory authority should inform the data subject of the progress and the outcome of the complaint within a reasonable period. If the case requires further investigation or coordination with another supervisory authority, intermediate information should be given to the data subject. In order to facilitate the submission of complaints, each supervisory authority should take measures such as providing a complaint submission form which can also be completed electronically, without excluding other means of communication.

(142) Where a data subject considers that his or her rights under this Regulation are infringed, he or she should have the right to mandate a not-for-profit body, organisation or association which is constituted in accordance with the law of a Member State, has statutory objectives which are in the public interest and is active in the field of the protection of personal data to lodge a complaint on his or her behalf with a supervisory authority, exercise the right to a judicial remedy on behalf of data subjects or, if provided for in Member State law, exercise the right to receive compensation on behalf of data subjects. A Member State may provide for such a body, organisation or association to have the right to lodge a complaint in that Member State, independently of a data subject's mandate, and the right to an effective judicial remedy where it has reasons to consider that the rights of a data subject have been infringed as a result of the processing of personal data which infringes this Regulation. That body, organisation or association may not be allowed to claim compensation on a data subject's behalf independently of the data subject's mandate.

(146) The controller or processor should compensate any damage which a person may suffer as a result of processing that infringes this Regulation. The controller or processor should be exempt from liability if it proves that it is not in any way responsible for the damage. The concept of damage should be broadly interpreted in the light of the case-law of the Court of Justice in a manner which fully reflects the objectives of this Regulation. This is without prejudice to any claims for damage deriving from the violation of other rules in Union or Member State law. Processing that infringes this Regulation also includes processing that infringes delegated and implementing acts adopted in accordance with this Regulation and Member State law specifying rules of this Regulation. Data subjects should receive full and effective compensation for the damage they have suffered. Where controllers or processors are involved in the same processing, each controller or processor should be held liable for the entire damage. However, where they are joined to the same judicial proceedings, in accordance with Member State law, compensation may be apportioned according to the responsibility of each controller or processor for the damage caused by the processing, provided that full and effective compensation of the data subject who suffered the damage is ensured. Any controller or processor which has paid full compensation may subsequently institute recourse proceedings against other controllers or processors involved in the same processing.

(147) Where specific rules on jurisdiction are contained in this Regulation, in particular as regards proceedings seeking a judicial remedy including compensation, against a controller or processor, general jurisdiction rules such as those of Regulation (EU) No 1215/2012 of the European Parliament and of the Council[11] should not prejudice the application of such specific rules.

(148) In order to strengthen the enforcement of the rules of this Regulation, penalties including administrative fines should be imposed for any infringement of this Regulation, in addition to, or instead of appropriate measures imposed by the supervisory authority pursuant to this Regulation. In a case of a minor infringement or if the fine likely to be imposed would constitute a disproportionate burden to a natural person, a reprimand may be issued instead of a fine. Due regard should however be given to the nature, gravity and duration of the infringement, the intentional character of the infringement, actions taken to mitigate the damage suffered, degree of responsibility or any relevant previous infringements, the manner in which the infringement became known to the supervisory authority, compliance with measures ordered against the controller or processor, adherence to a code of conduct and any other aggravating or

mitigating factor. The imposition of penalties including administrative fines should be subject to appropriate procedural safeguards in accordance with the general principles of Union law and the Charter, including effective judicial protection and due process.

(149) Member States should be able to lay down the rules on criminal penalties for infringements of this Regulation, including for infringements of national rules adopted pursuant to and within the limits of this Regulation. Those criminal penalties may also allow for the deprivation of the profits obtained through infringements of this Regulation. However, the imposition of criminal penalties for infringements of such national rules and of administrative penalties should not lead to a breach of the principle of *ne bis in idem*, as interpreted by the Court of Justice.

(150) In order to strengthen and harmonise administrative penalties for infringements of this Regulation, each supervisory authority should have the power to impose administrative fines. This Regulation should indicate infringements and the upper limit and criteria for setting the related administrative fines, which should be determined by the competent supervisory authority in each individual case, taking into account all relevant circumstances of the specific situation, with due regard in particular to the nature, gravity and duration of the infringement and of its consequences and the measures taken to ensure compliance with the obligations under this Regulation and to prevent or mitigate the consequences of the infringement. Where administrative fines are imposed on an undertaking, an undertaking should be understood to be an undertaking in accordance with Articles 101 and 102 TFEU for those purposes. Where administrative fines are imposed on persons that are not an undertaking, the supervisory authority should take account of the general level of income in the Member State as well as the economic situation of the person in considering the appropriate amount of the fine. The consistency mechanism may also be used to promote a consistent application of administrative fines. It should be for the Member States to determine whether and to which extent public authorities should be subject to administrative fines. Imposing an administrative fine or giving a warning does not affect the application of other powers of the supervisory authorities or of other penalties under this Regulation.

(152) Where this Regulation does not harmonise administrative penalties or where necessary in other cases, for example in cases of serious infringements of this Regulation, Member States should implement a system which provides for effective, proportionate and dissuasive penalties. The nature of such penalties, criminal or administrative, should be determined by Member State law.

(155) Member State law or collective agreements, including 'works agreements', may provide for specific rules on the processing of employees' personal data in the employment context, in particular for the conditions under which personal data in the employment context may be processed on the basis of the consent of the employee, the purposes of the recruitment, the performance of the contract of employment, including discharge of obligations laid down by law or by collective agreements, management, planning and organisation of work, equality and diversity in the workplace, health and safety at work, and for the purposes of the exercise and enjoyment, on an individual or collective basis, of rights and benefits related to employment, and for the purpose of the termination of the employment relationship.

(171) Directive 95/46/EC should be repealed by this Regulation. Processing already under way on the date of application of this Regulation should be brought into conformity with this Regulation within the period of two years after which this Regulation enters into force. Where processing is based on consent pursuant to Directive 95/46/EC, it is not necessary for the data subject to give his or her consent again if the manner in which the consent has been given is in line with the conditions of this Regulation, so as to allow the controller to continue such processing after the date of application of this Regulation. Commission decisions adopted and authorisations by supervisory authorities based on Directive 95/46/EC remain in force until amended, replaced or repealed.

NOTES

1 OJ C229, 31.7.2012, p 90.

2 OJ C391, 18.12.2012, p 127.

3 Position of the European Parliament of 12 March 2014 (not yet published in the Official Journal) and position of the Council at first reading of 8 April 2016 (not yet published in the Official Journal). Position of the European Parliament of 14 April 2016.

4 Directive 95/46/EC of the European Parliament and of the Council of 24 October 1995 on the protection of individuals with regard to the processing of personal data and on the free movement of such data (OJ L281, 23.11.1995, p 31).

5 Commission Recommendation of 6 May 2003 concerning the definition of micro, small and medium-sized enterprises (C(2003) 1422) (OJ L124, 20.5.2003, p 36).

6 Regulation (EC) No 45/2001 of the European Parliament and of the Council of 18 December 2000 on the protection of individuals with regard to the processing of personal data by the Community institutions and bodies and on the free movement of such data (OJ L8, 12.1.2001, p 1).

7 Directive (EU) 2016/680 of the European Parliament and of the Council of 27 April 2016 on the protection of natural persons with regard to the processing of personal data by competent authorities for the purposes of prevention, investigation, detection or prosecution of criminal offences or the execution of criminal penalties, and the free movement of such data and repealing Council Framework Decision 2008/977/JHA (see page 89 of this Official Journal).

8 Directive 2000/31/EC of the European Parliament and of the Council of 8 June 2000 on certain legal aspects of information society services, in particular electronic commerce, in the Internal Market ('Directive on electronic commerce') (OJ L178, 17.7.2000, p 1).

9 Directive 2011/24/EU of the European Parliament and of the Council of 9 March 2011 on the application of patients' rights in cross-border healthcare (OJ L88, 4.4.2011, p 45).

10 Council Directive 93/13/EEC of 5 April 1993 on unfair terms in consumer contracts (OJ L95, 21.4.1993, p 29).

11 Regulation (EU) No 1215/2012 of the European Parliament and of the Council of 12 December 2012 on jurisdiction and

the recognition and enforcement of judgments in civil and commercial matters (OJ L351, 20.12.2012, p 1).

HAVE ADOPTED THIS REGULATION:

CHAPTER I GENERAL PROVISIONS

[3.599]

Article 1 Subject-matter and objectives

1. This Regulation lays down rules relating to the protection of natural persons with regard to the processing of personal data and rules relating to the free movement of personal data.

2. This Regulation protects fundamental rights and freedoms of natural persons and in particular their right to the protection of personal data.

3. The free movement of personal data within the Union shall be neither restricted nor prohibited for reasons connected with the protection of natural persons with regard to the processing of personal data.

NOTES

This Article is amended by the Data Protection, Privacy and Electronic Communications (Amendments etc) (EU Exit) Regulations 2019, SI 2019/419, reg 3, Sch 1, paras 1, 3, as from exit day (as defined in the European Union (Withdrawal) Act 2018, s 20) and only in so far as this Regulation will apply in the UK after that date by virtue of s 3 of the 2018 Act, as follows (for transitional provisions etc, see the 2019 Regulations at **[2.2122]**)—

3.

In Article 1, omit paragraph 3.

[3.600]

Article 2

Material scope

1. This Regulation applies to the processing of personal data wholly or partly by automated means and to the processing other than by automated means of personal data which form part of a filing system or are intended to form part of a filing system.

2. This Regulation does not apply to the processing of personal data:

(a) in the course of an activity which falls outside the scope of Union law;

(b) by the Member States when carrying out activities which fall within the scope of Chapter 2 of Title V of the TEU;

(c) by a natural person in the course of a purely personal or household activity;

(d) by competent authorities for the purposes of the prevention, investigation, detection or prosecution of criminal offences or the execution of criminal penalties, including the safeguarding against and the prevention of threats to public security.

3. For the processing of personal data by the Union institutions, bodies, offices and agencies, Regulation (EC) No 45/2001 applies. Regulation (EC) No 45/2001 and other Union legal acts applicable to such processing of personal data shall be adapted to the principles and rules of this Regulation in accordance with Article 98.

4. This Regulation shall be without prejudice to the application of Directive 2000/31/EC, in particular of the liability rules of intermediary service providers in Articles 12 to 15 of that Directive.

NOTES

This Article is amended by the Data Protection, Privacy and Electronic Communications (Amendments etc) (EU Exit) Regulations 2019, SI 2019/419, reg 3, Sch 1, paras 1, 4, as from exit day (as defined in the European Union (Withdrawal) Act 2018, s 20) and only in so far as this Regulation will apply in the UK after that date by virtue of s 3 of the 2018 Act, as follows (for transitional provisions etc, see the 2019 Regulations at **[2.2122]**)—

4.

(1) Article 2 is amended as follows.

(2) For paragraph 1 substitute—

"1. This Regulation applies to the automated or structured processing of personal data, including—

(a) processing in the course of an activity which, immediately before exit day, fell outside the scope of EU law, and

(b) processing in the course of an activity which, immediately before exit day, fell within the scope of Chapter 2 of Title 5 of the Treaty on European Union (common foreign and security policy activities).

1A. This Regulation also applies to the manual unstructured processing of personal data held by an FOI public authority.".

(3) For paragraph 2 substitute—

"2. This Regulation does not apply to—

(a) the processing of personal data by an individual in the course of a purely personal or household activity;

(b) the processing of personal data by a competent authority for any of the law enforcement purposes (see Part 3 of the 2018 Act);

(c) the processing of personal data to which Part 4 of the 2018 Act (intelligence services processing) applies.".

(4) Omit paragraph 3.

(5) In paragraph 4, for "Directive 2000/31/EC" to the end substitute "the Electronic Commerce (EC Directive) Regulations 2002, in particular the provisions about mere conduits, caching and hosting (see regulations 17 to 19 of those Regulations).".

(6) After paragraph 4 insert—

"5. In this Article—

(a) 'the automated or structured processing of personal data' means—
(i) the processing of personal data wholly or partly by automated means, and
(ii) the processing otherwise than by automated means of personal data which forms part of a filing system or is intended to form part of a filing system;
(b) 'the manual unstructured processing of personal data' means the processing of personal data which is not the automated or structured processing of personal data;
(c) 'FOI public authority' has the same meaning as in Chapter 3 of Part 2 of the 2018 Act (see section 21(5) of that Act);
(d) references to personal data 'held' by an FOI public authority are to be interpreted in accordance with section 21(6) and (7) of the 2018 Act;
(e) 'competent authority' and 'law enforcement purposes' have the same meaning as in Part 3 of the 2018 Act (see sections 30 and 31 of that Act).".

[3.601]
Article 3
Territorial scope

1. This Regulation applies to the processing of personal data in the context of the activities of an establishment of a controller or a processor in the Union, regardless of whether the processing takes place in the Union or not.
2. This Regulation applies to the processing of personal data of data subjects who are in the Union by a controller or processor not established in the Union, where the processing activities are related to:
(a) the offering of goods or services, irrespective of whether a payment of the data subject is required, to such data subjects in the Union; or
(b) the monitoring of their behaviour as far as their behaviour takes place within the Union.
3. This Regulation applies to the processing of personal data by a controller not established in the Union, but in a place where Member State law applies by virtue of public international law.

NOTES

This Article is amended by the Data Protection, Privacy and Electronic Communications (Amendments etc) (EU Exit) Regulations 2019, SI 2019/419, reg 3, Sch 1, paras 1, 5, as from exit day (as defined in the European Union (Withdrawal) Act 2018, s 20) and only in so far as this Regulation will apply in the UK after that date by virtue of s 3 of the 2018 Act, as follows (for transitional provisions etc, see the 2019 Regulations at **[2.2122]**)—

5.
(1) Article 3 is amended as follows.
(2) In paragraph 1, for "the Union" (in both places) substitute "the United Kingdom".
(3) In paragraph 2—
(a) before "processing" (in the first place) insert "relevant";
(b) for "the Union" (in each place) substitute "the United Kingdom".
(4) After paragraph 2 insert—

"2A. In paragraph 2, "relevant processing of personal data" means processing to which this Regulation applies, other than processing described in Article 2(1)(a) or (b) or (1A).".

(5) In paragraph 3—
(a) for "the Union" substitute "the United Kingdom";
(b) for "Member State law" substitute "domestic law".

[3.602]
Article 4
Definitions

For the purposes of this Regulation:
(1) 'personal data' means any information relating to an identified or identifiable natural person ('data subject'); an identifiable natural person is one who can be identified, directly or indirectly, in particular by reference to an identifier such as a name, an identification number, location data, an online identifier or to one or more factors specific to the physical, physiological, genetic, mental, economic, cultural or social identity of that natural person;
(2) 'processing' means any operation or set of operations which is performed on personal data or on sets of personal data, whether or not by automated means, such as collection, recording, organisation, structuring, storage, adaptation or alteration, retrieval, consultation, use, disclosure by transmission, dissemination or otherwise making available, alignment or combination, restriction, erasure or destruction;
(3) 'restriction of processing' means the marking of stored personal data with the aim of limiting their processing in the future;
(4) 'profiling' means any form of automated processing of personal data consisting of the use of personal data to evaluate certain personal aspects relating to a natural person, in particular to analyse or predict aspects concerning that natural person's performance at work, economic situation, health, personal preferences, interests, reliability, behaviour, location or movements;
(5) 'pseudonymisation' means the processing of personal data in such a manner that the personal data can no longer be attributed to a specific data subject without the use of additional information, provided that such additional information is kept separately and is subject to technical and organisational measures to ensure that the personal data are not attributed to an identified or identifiable natural person;
(6) 'filing system' means any structured set of personal data which are accessible according to specific criteria, whether centralised, decentralised or dispersed on a functional or geographical basis;

(7) 'controller' means the natural or legal person, public authority, agency or other body which, alone or jointly with others, determines the purposes and means of the processing of personal data; where the purposes and means of such processing are determined by Union or Member State law, the controller or the specific criteria for its nomination may be provided for by Union or Member State law;
(8) 'processor' means a natural or legal person, public authority, agency or other body which processes personal data on behalf of the controller;
(9) 'recipient' means a natural or legal person, public authority, agency or another body, to which the personal data are disclosed, whether a third party or not. However, public authorities which may receive personal data in the framework of a particular inquiry in accordance with Union or Member State law shall not be regarded as recipients; the processing of those data by those public authorities shall be in compliance with the applicable data protection rules according to the purposes of the processing;
(10) 'third party' means a natural or legal person, public authority, agency or body other than the data subject, controller, processor and persons who, under the direct authority of the controller or processor, are authorised to process personal data;
(11) 'consent' of the data subject means any freely given, specific, informed and unambiguous indication of the data subject's wishes by which he or she, by a statement or by a clear affirmative action, signifies agreement to the processing of personal data relating to him or her;
(12) 'personal data breach' means a breach of security leading to the accidental or unlawful destruction, loss, alteration, unauthorised disclosure of, or access to, personal data transmitted, stored or otherwise processed;
(13) 'genetic data' means personal data relating to the inherited or acquired genetic characteristics of a natural person which give unique information about the physiology or the health of that natural person and which result, in particular, from an analysis of a biological sample from the natural person in question;
(14) 'biometric data' means personal data resulting from specific technical processing relating to the physical, physiological or behavioural characteristics of a natural person, which allow or confirm the unique identification of that natural person, such as facial images or dactyloscopic data;
(15) 'data concerning health' means personal data related to the physical or mental health of a natural person, including the provision of health care services, which reveal information about his or her health status;
(16) 'main establishment' means:

(a) as regards a controller with establishments in more than one Member State, the place of its central administration in the Union, unless the decisions on the purposes and means of the processing of personal data are taken in another establishment of the controller in the Union and the latter establishment has the power to have such decisions implemented, in which case the establishment having taken such decisions is to be considered to be the main establishment;
(b) as regards a processor with establishments in more than one Member State, the place of its central administration in the Union, or, if the processor has no central administration in the Union, the establishment of the processor in the Union where the main processing activities in the context of the activities of an establishment of the processor take place to the extent that the processor is subject to specific obligations under this Regulation;

(17) 'representative' means a natural or legal person established in the Union who, designated by the controller or processor in writing pursuant to Article 27, represents the controller or processor with regard to their respective obligations under this Regulation;
(18) 'enterprise' means a natural or legal person engaged in an economic activity, irrespective of its legal form, including partnerships or associations regularly engaged in an economic activity;
(19) 'group of undertakings' means a controlling undertaking and its controlled undertakings;
(20) 'binding corporate rules' means personal data protection policies which are adhered to by a controller or processor established on the territory of a Member State for transfers or a set of transfers of personal data to a controller or processor in one or more third countries within a group of undertakings, or group of enterprises engaged in a joint economic activity;
(21) 'supervisory authority' means an independent public authority which is established by a Member State pursuant to Article 51;
(22) 'supervisory authority concerned' means a supervisory authority which is concerned by the processing of personal data because:

(a) the controller or processor is established on the territory of the Member State of that supervisory authority;
(b) data subjects residing in the Member State of that supervisory authority are substantially affected or likely to be substantially affected by the processing; or
(c) a complaint has been lodged with that supervisory authority;

(23) 'cross-border processing' means either:

(a) processing of personal data which takes place in the context of the activities of establishments in more than one Member State of a controller or processor in the Union where the controller or processor is established in more than one Member State; or
(b) processing of personal data which takes place in the context of the activities of a single establishment of a controller or processor in the Union but which substantially affects or is likely to substantially affect data subjects in more than one Member State.

(24) 'relevant and reasoned objection' means an objection to a draft decision as to whether there is an infringement of this Regulation, or whether envisaged action in relation to the controller or processor complies with this Regulation, which clearly demonstrates the significance of the risks posed by the draft decision as regards the fundamental rights and freedoms of data subjects and, where applicable, the free flow of personal data within the Union;

(25) ''information society service' means a service as defined in point (b) of Article 1(1) of Directive (EU) 2015/1535 of the European Parliament and of the Council;[1]

(26) 'international organisation' means an organisation and its subordinate bodies governed by public international law, or any other body which is set up by, or on the basis of, an agreement between two or more countries.

NOTES

This Article is amended by the Data Protection, Privacy and Electronic Communications (Amendments etc) (EU Exit) Regulations 2019, SI 2019/419, reg 3, Sch 1, paras 1, 6, as from exit day (as defined in the European Union (Withdrawal) Act 2018, s 20) and only in so far as this Regulation will apply in the UK after that date by virtue of s 3 of the 2018 Act, as follows (for transitional provisions etc, see the 2019 Regulations at **[2.2122]**)—

6. (1) Article 4 is amended as follows.

(2) Before paragraph (1) insert—

"(A1) 'the 2018 Act' means the Data Protection Act 2018;

(A2) 'domestic law' means the law of the United Kingdom or of a part of the United Kingdom;

(A3) 'the Commissioner' means the Information Commissioner (see section 114 of the 2018 Act);".

(3) In paragraph (7), for "; where the purposes and means of such processing are determined by Union or Member State law, the controller or the specific criteria for its nomination may be provided for by Union or Member State law" substitute "(but see section 6 of the 2018 Act)".

(4) In paragraph (9), for "Union or Member State law" substitute "domestic law".

(5) After paragraph (10) insert—

"(10A) 'public authority' and 'public body' are to be interpreted in accordance with section 7 of the 2018 Act and provision made under that section;".

(6) Omit paragraph (16).

(7) In paragraph (17), for "the Union" substitute "the United Kingdom".

(8) In paragraph (20), for "on the territory of a Member State" substitute "in the United Kingdom".

(9) Omit paragraph (21).

(10) After paragraph (21) insert—

"(21A) 'foreign designated authority' means an authority designated for the purposes of Article 13 of the Data Protection Convention (as defined in section 3 of the 2018 Act) by a party, other than the United Kingdom, which is bound by that Convention;".

(11) Omit paragraphs (22), (23) and (24).

(12) In paragraph (25), at the end insert "as it has effect immediately before exit day".

(13) After paragraph (26) insert—

"(27) 'third country' means a country or territory outside the United Kingdom;

(28) references to a fundamental right or fundamental freedom (however expressed) are to a fundamental right or fundamental freedom which continues to form part of domestic law on and after exit day by virtue of section 4 of the European Union (Withdrawal) Act 2018, as the right or freedom is amended or otherwise modified by domestic law from time to time on or after exit day.".

[1] Directive (EU) 2015/1535 of the European Parliament and of the Council of 9 September 2015 laying down a procedure for the provision of information in the field of technical regulations and of rules on Information Society services (OJ L241, 17.9.2015, p 1).

CHAPTER II PRINCIPLES

[3.603]

Article 5

Principles relating to processing of personal data

1. Personal data shall be:

(a) processed lawfully, fairly and in a transparent manner in relation to the data subject ('lawfulness, fairness and transparency');

(b) collected for specified, explicit and legitimate purposes and not further processed in a manner that is incompatible with those purposes; further processing for archiving purposes in the public interest, scientific or historical research purposes or statistical purposes shall, in accordance with Article 89(1), not be considered to be incompatible with the initial purposes ('purpose limitation');

(c) adequate, relevant and limited to what is necessary in relation to the purposes for which they are processed ('data minimisation');

(d) accurate and, where necessary, kept up to date; every reasonable step must be taken to ensure that personal data that are inaccurate, having regard to the purposes for which they are processed, are erased or rectified without delay ('accuracy');

(e) kept in a form which permits identification of data subjects for no longer than is necessary for the purposes for which the personal data are processed; personal data may be stored for longer periods insofar as the personal data will be processed solely for archiving purposes in the public interest, scientific or historical research purposes or statistical purposes in accordance with Article 89(1) subject to implementation of the appropriate technical and organisational measures required by this Regulation in order to safeguard the rights and freedoms of the data subject ('storage limitation');

(f) processed in a manner that ensures appropriate security of the personal data, including protection against unauthorised or unlawful processing and against accidental loss, destruction or damage, using appropriate technical or organisational measures ('integrity and confidentiality').

2. The controller shall be responsible for, and be able to demonstrate compliance with, paragraph 1 ('accountability').

[3.604]
Article 6
Lawfulness of processing

1. Processing shall be lawful only if and to the extent that at least one of the following applies:
   (a) the data subject has given consent to the processing of his or her personal data for one or more specific purposes;
   (b) processing is necessary for the performance of a contract to which the data subject is party or in order to take steps at the request of the data subject prior to entering into a contract;
   (c) processing is necessary for compliance with a legal obligation to which the controller is subject;
   (d) processing is necessary in order to protect the vital interests of the data subject or of another natural person;
   (e) processing is necessary for the performance of a task carried out in the public interest or in the exercise of official authority vested in the controller;
   (f) processing is necessary for the purposes of the legitimate interests pursued by the controller or by a third party, except where such interests are overridden by the interests or fundamental rights and freedoms of the data subject which require protection of personal data, in particular where the data subject is a child.

Point (f) of the first subparagraph shall not apply to processing carried out by public authorities in the performance of their tasks.

2. Member States may maintain or introduce more specific provisions to adapt the application of the rules of this Regulation with regard to processing for compliance with points (c) and (e) of paragraph 1 by determining more precisely specific requirements for the processing and other measures to ensure lawful and fair processing including for other specific processing situations as provided for in Chapter IX.

3. The basis for the processing referred to in point (c) and (e) of paragraph 1 shall be laid down by:
   (a) Union law; or
   (b) Member State law to which the controller is subject.

The purpose of the processing shall be determined in that legal basis or, as regards the processing referred to in point (e) of paragraph 1, shall be necessary for the performance of a task carried out in the public interest or in the exercise of official authority vested in the controller. That legal basis may contain specific provisions to adapt the application of rules of this Regulation, inter alia: the general conditions governing the lawfulness of processing by the controller; the types of data which are subject to the processing; the data subjects concerned; the entities to, and the purposes for which, the personal data may be disclosed; the purpose limitation; storage periods; and processing operations and processing procedures, including measures to ensure lawful and fair processing such as those for other specific processing situations as provided for in Chapter IX. The Union or the Member State law shall meet an objective of public interest and be proportionate to the legitimate aim pursued.

4. Where the processing for a purpose other than that for which the personal data have been collected is not based on the data subject's consent or on a Union or Member State law which constitutes a necessary and proportionate measure in a democratic society to safeguard the objectives referred to in Article 23(1), the controller shall, in order to ascertain whether processing for another purpose is compatible with the purpose for which the personal data are initially collected, take into account, inter alia:
   (a) any link between the purposes for which the personal data have been collected and the purposes of the intended further processing;
   (b) the context in which the personal data have been collected, in particular regarding the relationship between data subjects and the controller;
   (c) the nature of the personal data, in particular whether special categories of personal data are processed, pursuant to Article 9, or whether personal data related to criminal convictions and offences are processed, pursuant to Article 10;
   (d) the possible consequences of the intended further processing for data subjects;
   (e) the existence of appropriate safeguards, which may include encryption or pseudonymisation.

NOTES

This Article is amended by the Data Protection, Privacy and Electronic Communications (Amendments etc) (EU Exit) Regulations 2019, SI 2019/419, reg 3, Sch 1, paras 1, 7, as from exit day (as defined in the European Union (Withdrawal) Act 2018, s 20) and only in so far as this Regulation will apply in the UK after that date by virtue of s 3 of the 2018 Act, as follows (for transitional provisions etc, see the 2019 Regulations at **[2.2122]**)—

7.
(1) Article 6 is amended as follows.
(2) Omit paragraph 2.
(3) In paragraph 3—
   (a) in the first subparagraph, for points (a) and (b) (and the colon before them) substitute "domestic law";
   (b) in the second subparagraph, for "The Union or Member State law" substitute "The domestic law".
(4) In paragraph 4—
   (a) for "a Union or Member State law" substitute "domestic law";
   (b) after "safeguard" insert "national security, defence or any of".

[3.605]
Article 7
Conditions for consent

1. Where processing is based on consent, the controller shall be able to demonstrate that the data subject has consented to processing of his or her personal data.
2. If the data subject's consent is given in the context of a written declaration which also concerns other matters, the request for consent shall be presented in a manner which is clearly distinguishable from the other matters, in an intelligible and easily accessible form, using clear and plain language. Any part of such a declaration which constitutes an infringement of this Regulation shall not be binding.
3. The data subject shall have the right to withdraw his or her consent at any time. The withdrawal of consent shall not affect the lawfulness of processing based on consent before its withdrawal. Prior to giving consent, the data subject shall be informed thereof. It shall be as easy to withdraw as to give consent.
4. When assessing whether consent is freely given, utmost account shall be taken of whether, inter alia, the performance of a contract, including the provision of a service, is conditional on consent to the processing of personal data that is not necessary for the performance of that contract.

[3.606]
Article 9
Processing of special categories of personal data

1. Processing of personal data revealing racial or ethnic origin, political opinions, religious or philosophical beliefs, or trade union membership, and the processing of genetic data, biometric data for the purpose of uniquely identifying a natural person, data concerning health or data concerning a natural person's sex life or sexual orientation shall be prohibited.
2. Paragraph 1 shall not apply if one of the following applies:
   (a) the data subject has given explicit consent to the processing of those personal data for one or more specified purposes, except where Union or Member State law provide that the prohibition referred to in paragraph 1 may not be lifted by the data subject;
   (b) processing is necessary for the purposes of carrying out the obligations and exercising specific rights of the controller or of the data subject in the field of employment and social security and social protection law in so far as it is authorised by Union or Member State law or a collective agreement pursuant to Member State law providing for appropriate safeguards for the fundamental rights and the interests of the data subject;
   (c) processing is necessary to protect the vital interests of the data subject or of another natural person where the data subject is physically or legally incapable of giving consent;
   (d) processing is carried out in the course of its legitimate activities with appropriate safeguards by a foundation, association or any other not-for-profit body with a political, philosophical, religious or trade union aim and on condition that the processing relates solely to the members or to former members of the body or to persons who have regular contact with it in connection with its purposes and that the personal data are not disclosed outside that body without the consent of the data subjects;
   (e) processing relates to personal data which are manifestly made public by the data subject;
   (f) processing is necessary for the establishment, exercise or defence of legal claims or whenever courts are acting in their judicial capacity;
   (g) processing is necessary for reasons of substantial public interest, on the basis of Union or Member State law which shall be proportionate to the aim pursued, respect the essence of the right to data protection and provide for suitable and specific measures to safeguard the fundamental rights and the interests of the data subject;
   (h) processing is necessary for the purposes of preventive or occupational medicine, for the assessment of the working capacity of the employee, medical diagnosis, the provision of health or social care or treatment or the management of health or social care systems and services on the basis of Union or Member State law or pursuant to contract with a health professional and subject to the conditions and safeguards referred to in paragraph 3;
   (i) processing is necessary for reasons of public interest in the area of public health, such as protecting against serious cross-border threats to health or ensuring high standards of quality and safety of health care and of medicinal products or medical devices, on the basis of Union or Member State law which provides for suitable and specific measures to safeguard the rights and freedoms of the data subject, in particular professional secrecy;
   (j) processing is necessary for archiving purposes in the public interest, scientific or historical research purposes or statistical purposes in accordance with Article 89(1) based on Union or Member State law which shall be proportionate to the aim pursued, respect the essence of the right to data protection and provide for suitable and specific measures to safeguard the fundamental rights and the interests of the data subject.
3. Personal data referred to in paragraph 1 may be processed for the purposes referred to in point (h) of paragraph 2 when those data are processed by or under the responsibility of a professional subject to the obligation of professional secrecy under Union or Member State law or rules established by national competent bodies or by another person also subject to an obligation of secrecy under Union or Member State law or rules established by national competent bodies.
4. Member States may maintain or introduce further conditions, including limitations, with regard to the processing of genetic data, biometric data or data concerning health.

NOTES

This Article is amended by the Data Protection, Privacy and Electronic Communications (Amendments etc) (EU Exit) Regulations 2019, SI 2019/419, reg 3, Sch 1, paras 1, 9, as from exit day (as defined in the European Union (Withdrawal) Act 2018, s 20) and only in so far as this Regulation will apply in the UK after that date by virtue of s 3 of the 2018 Act, as follows (for transitional provisions etc, see the 2019 Regulations at **[2.2122]**)—

9. (1) Article 9 is amended as follows.

(2) In paragraph 2(a), for "Union or Member State law provide" substitute "domestic law provides".

(3) In paragraph 2(b)—

(a) for "Union or Member State law" substitute "domestic law";

(b) for "to Member State law" substitute "to domestic law".

(4) In paragraph 2(g), for "Union or Member State law" substitute "domestic law".

(5) In paragraph 2(h), for "Union or Member State law" substitute "domestic law".

(6) In paragraph 2(i), for "Union or Member State law" substitute "domestic law".

(7) paragraph 2(j)—

(a) after "Article 89(1)" insert "(as supplemented by section 19 of the 2018 Act)";

(b) for "Union or Member State law" substitute "domestic law".

(8) In paragraph 3, for "Union or Member State law" (in both places) substitute "domestic law".

(9) After that paragraph insert—

"3A. In paragraph 3, 'national competent bodies' means competent bodies of the United Kingdom or a part of the United Kingdom.".

(10) Omit paragraph 4.

(11) After that paragraph insert—

"5. In the 2018 Act—

(a) section 10 makes provision about when the requirement in paragraph 2(b), (g), (h), (i) or (j) of this Article for authorisation by, or a basis in, domestic law is met;

(b) section 11(1) makes provision about when the processing of personal data is carried out in circumstances described in paragraph 3 of this Article.".

[3.607]

Article 10

Processing of personal data relating to criminal convictions and offences

Processing of personal data relating to criminal convictions and offences or related security measures based on Article 6(1) shall be carried out only under the control of official authority or when the processing is authorised by Union or Member State law providing for appropriate safeguards for the rights and freedoms of data subjects. Any comprehensive register of criminal convictions shall be kept only under the control of official authority.

NOTES

This Article is amended by the Data Protection, Privacy and Electronic Communications (Amendments etc) (EU Exit) Regulations 2019, SI 2019/419, reg 3, Sch 1, paras 1, 10, as from exit day (as defined in the European Union (Withdrawal) Act 2018, s 20) and only in so far as this Regulation will apply in the UK after that date by virtue of s 3 of the 2018 Act, as follows (for transitional provisions etc, see the 2019 Regulations at **[2.2122]**)—

10.

(1) Article 10 is amended as follows.

(2) The existing text becomes paragraph 1.

(3) In that paragraph, for "Union or Member State law" substitute "domestic law".

(4) After that paragraph insert—

"2. In the 2018 Act—

(a) section 10 makes provision about when the requirement in paragraph 1 of this Article for authorisation by domestic law is met;

(b) section 11(2) makes provision about the meaning of "personal data relating to criminal convictions and offences or related security measures".".

[3.608]

Article 11

Processing which does not require identification

1. If the purposes for which a controller processes personal data do not or do no longer require the identification of a data subject by the controller, the controller shall not be obliged to maintain, acquire or process additional information in order to identify the data subject for the sole purpose of complying with this Regulation.

2. Where, in cases referred to in paragraph 1 of this Article, the controller is able to demonstrate that it is not in a position to identify the data subject, the controller shall inform the data subject accordingly, if possible. In such cases, Articles 15 to 20 shall not apply except where the data subject, for the purpose of exercising his or her rights under those articles, provides additional information enabling his or her identification.

CHAPTER III RIGHTS OF THE DATA SUBJECT

SECTION 1 TRANSPARENCY AND MODALITIES

[3.609]

Article 12

Transparent information, communication and modalities for the exercise of the rights of the data subject

1. The controller shall take appropriate measures to provide any information referred to in Articles 13 and 14 and any communication under Articles 15 to 22 and 34 relating to processing to the data subject in a concise, transparent, intelligible and easily accessible form, using clear and plain language, in particular for any information addressed specifically to a child. The information shall be provided in writing, or by other means, including, where appropriate, by electronic means. When requested by the data subject, the information may be provided orally, provided that the identity of the data subject is proven by other means.

2. The controller shall facilitate the exercise of data subject rights under Articles 15 to 22. In the cases referred to in Article 11(2), the controller shall not refuse to act on the request of the data subject for exercising his or her rights under Articles 15 to 22, unless the controller demonstrates that it is not in a position to identify the data subject.

3. The controller shall provide information on action taken on a request under Articles 15 to 22 to the data subject without undue delay and in any event within one month of receipt of the request. That period may be extended by two further months where necessary, taking into account the complexity and number of the requests. The controller shall inform the data subject of any such extension within one month of receipt of the request, together with the reasons for the delay. Where the data subject makes the request by electronic form means, the information shall be provided by electronic means where possible, unless otherwise requested by the data subject.

4. If the controller does not take action on the request of the data subject, the controller shall inform the data subject without delay and at the latest within one month of receipt of the request of the reasons for not taking action and on the possibility of lodging a complaint with a supervisory authority and seeking a judicial remedy.

5. Information provided under Articles 13 and 14 and any communication and any actions taken under Articles 15 to 22 and 34 shall be provided free of charge. Where requests from a data subject are manifestly unfounded or excessive, in particular because of their repetitive character, the controller may either:

(a) charge a reasonable fee taking into account the administrative costs of providing the information or communication or taking the action requested; or

(b) refuse to act on the request.

The controller shall bear the burden of demonstrating the manifestly unfounded or excessive character of the request.

6. Without prejudice to Article 11, where the controller has reasonable doubts concerning the identity of the natural person making the request referred to in Articles 15 to 21, the controller may request the provision of additional information necessary to confirm the identity of the data subject.

7. The information to be provided to data subjects pursuant to Articles 13 and 14 may be provided in combination with standardised icons in order to give in an easily visible, intelligible and clearly legible manner a meaningful overview of the intended processing. Where the icons are presented electronically they shall be machine-readable.

8. The Commission shall be empowered to adopt delegated acts in accordance with Article 92 for the purpose of determining the information to be presented by the icons and the procedures for providing standardised icons.

NOTES

This Article is amended by the Data Protection, Privacy and Electronic Communications (Amendments etc) (EU Exit) Regulations 2019, SI 2019/419, reg 3, Sch 1, paras 1, 11, as from exit day (as defined in the European Union (Withdrawal) Act 2018, s 20) and only in so far as this Regulation will apply in the UK after that date by virtue of s 3 of the 2018 Act, as follows (for transitional provisions etc, see the 2019 Regulations at **[2.2122]**)—

11.

(1) Article 12 is amended as follows.

(2) In paragraph 4, for "a supervisory authority" substitute "the Commissioner".

(3) After paragraph 6 insert—

"6A. The Commissioner may publish (and amend or withdraw)—

(a) standardised icons for use in combination with information provided to data subjects under Articles 13 and 14;

(b) a notice stating that other persons may publish (and amend or withdraw) such icons, provided that the icons satisfy requirements specified in the notice as to the information to be presented by the icons and the procedures for providing the icons.

6B. The Commissioner must not publish icons or a notice under paragraph 6A unless satisfied (as appropriate) that the icons give a meaningful overview of the intended processing in an easily visible, intelligible and clearly legible manner or that the notice will result in icons that do so.".

(4) In paragraph 7—

(a) for "The information" substitute "If standardised icons are published as described in paragraph 6A (and not withdrawn), the information";

(b) for "standardised" to "processing" substitute "the icons".

(5) Omit paragraph 8.

SECTION 2 INFORMATION AND ACCESS TO PERSONAL DATA

[3.610]
Article 13
Information to be provided where personal data are collected from the data subject

1. Where personal data relating to a data subject are collected from the data subject, the controller shall, at the time when personal data are obtained, provide the data subject with all of the following information:
   (a) the identity and the contact details of the controller and, where applicable, of the controller's representative;
   (b) the contact details of the data protection officer, where applicable;
   (c) the purposes of the processing for which the personal data are intended as well as the legal basis for the processing;
   (d) where the processing is based on point (f) of Article 6(1), the legitimate interests pursued by the controller or by a third party;
   (e) the recipients or categories of recipients of the personal data, if any;
   (f) where applicable, the fact that the controller intends to transfer personal data to a third country or international organisation and the existence or absence of an adequacy decision by the Commission, or in the case of transfers referred to in Article 46 or 47, or the second subparagraph of Article 49(1), reference to the appropriate or suitable safeguards and the means by which to obtain a copy of them or where they have been made available.
2. In addition to the information referred to in paragraph 1, the controller shall, at the time when personal data are obtained, provide the data subject with the following further information necessary to ensure fair and transparent processing:
   (a) the period for which the personal data will be stored, or if that is not possible, the criteria used to determine that period;
   (b) the existence of the right to request from the controller access to and rectification or erasure of personal data or restriction of processing concerning the data subject or to object to processing as well as the right to data portability;
   (c) where the processing is based on point (a) of Article 6(1) or point (a) of Article 9(2), the existence of the right to withdraw consent at any time, without affecting the lawfulness of processing based on consent before its withdrawal;
   (d) the right to lodge a complaint with a supervisory authority;
   (e) whether the provision of personal data is a statutory or contractual requirement, or a requirement necessary to enter into a contract, as well as whether the data subject is obliged to provide the personal data and of the possible consequences of failure to provide such data;
   (f) the existence of automated decision-making, including profiling, referred to in Article 22(1) and (4) and, at least in those cases, meaningful information about the logic involved, as well as the significance and the envisaged consequences of such processing for the data subject.
3. Where the controller intends to further process the personal data for a purpose other than that for which the personal data were collected, the controller shall provide the data subject prior to that further processing with information on that other purpose and with any relevant further information as referred to in paragraph 2.
4. Paragraphs 1, 2 and 3 shall not apply where and insofar as the data subject already has the information.

NOTES

This Article is amended by the Data Protection, Privacy and Electronic Communications (Amendments etc) (EU Exit) Regulations 2019, SI 2019/419, reg 3, Sch 1, paras 1, 12, as from exit day (as defined in the European Union (Withdrawal) Act 2018, s 20) and only in so far as this Regulation will apply in the UK after that date by virtue of s 3 of the 2018 Act, as follows (for transitional provisions etc, see the 2019 Regulations at **[2.2122]**)—

12.
(1) Article 13 is amended as follows.
(2) In paragraph 1(f), for "an adequacy decision by the Commission" substitute "relevant adequacy regulations under section 17A of the 2018 Act".
(3) In paragraph 2(d), for "a supervisory authority" substitute "the Commissioner".

[3.611]
Article 14
Information to be provided where personal data have not been obtained from the data subject

1. Where personal data have not been obtained from the data subject, the controller shall provide the data subject with the following information:
   (a) the identity and the contact details of the controller and, where applicable, of the controller's representative;
   (b) the contact details of the data protection officer, where applicable;
   (c) the purposes of the processing for which the personal data are intended as well as the legal basis for the processing;
   (d) the categories of personal data concerned;
   (e) the recipients or categories of recipients of the personal data, if any;
   (f) where applicable, that the controller intends to transfer personal data to a recipient in a third country or international organisation and the existence or absence of an adequacy decision by

the Commission, or in the case of transfers referred to in Article 46 or 47, or the second subparagraph of Article 49(1), reference to the appropriate or suitable safeguards and the means to obtain a copy of them or where they have been made available.

2. In addition to the information referred to in paragraph 1, the controller shall provide the data subject with the following information necessary to ensure fair and transparent processing in respect of the data subject:

(a) the period for which the personal data will be stored, or if that is not possible, the criteria used to determine that period;
(b) where the processing is based on point (f) of Article 6(1), the legitimate interests pursued by the controller or by a third party;
(c) the existence of the right to request from the controller access to and rectification or erasure of personal data or restriction of processing concerning the data subject and to object to processing as well as the right to data portability;
(d) where processing is based on point (a) of Article 6(1) or point (a) of Article 9(2), the existence of the right to withdraw consent at any time, without affecting the lawfulness of processing based on consent before its withdrawal;
(e) the right to lodge a complaint with a supervisory authority;
(f) from which source the personal data originate, and if applicable, whether it came from publicly accessible sources;
(g) the existence of automated decision-making, including profiling, referred to in Article 22(1) and (4) and, at least in those cases, meaningful information about the logic involved, as well as the significance and the envisaged consequences of such processing for the data subject.

3. The controller shall provide the information referred to in paragraphs 1 and 2:

(a) within a reasonable period after obtaining the personal data, but at the latest within one month, having regard to the specific circumstances in which the personal data are processed;
(b) if the personal data are to be used for communication with the data subject, at the latest at the time of the first communication to that data subject; or
(c) if a disclosure to another recipient is envisaged, at the latest when the personal data are first disclosed.

4. Where the controller intends to further process the personal data for a purpose other than that for which the personal data were obtained, the controller shall provide the data subject prior to that further processing with information on that other purpose and with any relevant further information as referred to in paragraph 2.

5. Paragraphs 1 to 4 shall not apply where and insofar as:

(a) the data subject already has the information;
(b) the provision of such information proves impossible or would involve a disproportionate effort, in particular for processing for archiving purposes in the public interest, scientific or historical research purposes or statistical purposes, subject to the conditions and safeguards referred to in Article 89(1) or in so far as the obligation referred to in paragraph 1 of this Article is likely to render impossible or seriously impair the achievement of the objectives of that processing. In such cases the controller shall take appropriate measures to protect the data subject's rights and freedoms and legitimate interests, including making the information publicly available;
(c) obtaining or disclosure is expressly laid down by Union or Member State law to which the controller is subject and which provides appropriate measures to protect the data subject's legitimate interests; or
(d) where the personal data must remain confidential subject to an obligation of professional secrecy regulated by Union or Member State law, including a statutory obligation of secrecy.

NOTES

This Article is amended by the Data Protection, Privacy and Electronic Communications (Amendments etc) (EU Exit) Regulations 2019, SI 2019/419, reg 3, Sch 1, paras 1, 13, as from exit day (as defined in the European Union (Withdrawal) Act 2018, s 20) and only in so far as this Regulation will apply in the UK after that date by virtue of s 3 of the 2018 Act, as follows (for transitional provisions etc, see the 2019 Regulations at **[2.2122]**)—

13.

(1) Article 14 is amended as follows.

(2) In paragraph 1(f), for "an adequacy decision by the Commission" substitute "relevant adequacy regulations under section 17A of the 2018 Act".

(3) In paragraph 2(e), for "a supervisory authority" substitute "the Commissioner".

(4) In paragraph 5(c), for "Union or Member State law to which the controller is subject and" substitute "a provision of domestic law".

(5) In paragraph 5(d), for "Union or Member State law" substitute "domestic law".

[3.612]

Article 15

Right of access by the data subject

1. The data subject shall have the right to obtain from the controller confirmation as to whether or not personal data concerning him or her are being processed, and, where that is the case, access to the personal data and the following information:

(a) the purposes of the processing;
(b) the categories of personal data concerned;
(c) the recipients or categories of recipient to whom the personal data have been or will be disclosed, in particular recipients in third countries or international organisations;

(d) where possible, the envisaged period for which the personal data will be stored, or, if not possible, the criteria used to determine that period;
(e) the existence of the right to request from the controller rectification or erasure of personal data or restriction of processing of personal data concerning the data subject or to object to such processing;
(f) the right to lodge a complaint with a supervisory authority;
(g) where the personal data are not collected from the data subject, any available information as to their source;
(h) the existence of automated decision-making, including profiling, referred to in Article 22(1) and (4) and, at least in those cases, meaningful information about the logic involved, as well as the significance and the envisaged consequences of such processing for the data subject.

2. Where personal data are transferred to a third country or to an international organisation, the data subject shall have the right to be informed of the appropriate safeguards pursuant to Article 46 relating to the transfer.

3. The controller shall provide a copy of the personal data undergoing processing. For any further copies requested by the data subject, the controller may charge a reasonable fee based on administrative costs. Where the data subject makes the request by electronic means, and unless otherwise requested by the data subject, the information shall be provided in a commonly used electronic form.

4. The right to obtain a copy referred to in paragraph 3 shall not adversely affect the rights and freedoms of others.

NOTES

This Article is amended by the Data Protection, Privacy and Electronic Communications (Amendments etc) (EU Exit) Regulations 2019, SI 2019/419, reg 3, Sch 1, paras 1, 14, as from exit day (as defined in the European Union (Withdrawal) Act 2018, s 20) and only in so far as this Regulation will apply in the UK after that date by virtue of s 3 of the 2018 Act, as follows (for transitional provisions etc, see the 2019 Regulations at **[2.2122]**)—

14.
In Article 15(1)(f), for "a supervisory authority" substitute "the Commissioner".

SECTION 3 RECTIFICATION AND ERASURE

[3.613]
Article 16
Right to rectification

The data subject shall have the right to obtain from the controller without undue delay the rectification of inaccurate personal data concerning him or her. Taking into account the purposes of the processing, the data subject shall have the right to have incomplete personal data completed, including by means of providing a supplementary statement.

[3.614]
Article 17
Right to erasure ('right to be forgotten')

1. The data subject shall have the right to obtain from the controller the erasure of personal data concerning him or her without undue delay and the controller shall have the obligation to erase personal data without undue delay where one of the following grounds applies:
(a) the personal data are no longer necessary in relation to the purposes for which they were collected or otherwise processed;
(b) the data subject withdraws consent on which the processing is based according to point (a) of Article 6(1), or point (a) of Article 9(2), and where there is no other legal ground for the processing;
(c) the data subject objects to the processing pursuant to Article 21(1) and there are no overriding legitimate grounds for the processing, or the data subject objects to the processing pursuant to Article 21(2);
(d) the personal data have been unlawfully processed;
(e) the personal data have to be erased for compliance with a legal obligation in Union or Member State law to which the controller is subject;
(f) the personal data have been collected in relation to the offer of information society services referred to in Article 8(1).

2. Where the controller has made the personal data public and is obliged pursuant to paragraph 1 to erase the personal data, the controller, taking account of available technology and the cost of implementation, shall take reasonable steps, including technical measures, to inform controllers which are processing the personal data that the data subject has requested the erasure by such controllers of any links to, or copy or replication of, those personal data.

3. Paragraphs 1 and 2 shall not apply to the extent that processing is necessary:
(a) for exercising the right of freedom of expression and information;
(b) for compliance with a legal obligation which requires processing by Union or Member State law to which the controller is subject or for the performance of a task carried out in the public interest or in the exercise of official authority vested in the controller;
(c) for reasons of public interest in the area of public health in accordance with points (h) and (i) of Article 9(2) as well as Article 9(3);

(d) for archiving purposes in the public interest, scientific or historical research purposes or statistical purposes in accordance with Article 89(1) in so far as the right referred to in paragraph 1 is likely to render impossible or seriously impair the achievement of the objectives of that processing; or
(e) for the establishment, exercise or defence of legal claims.

NOTES

This Article is amended by the Data Protection, Privacy and Electronic Communications (Amendments etc) (EU Exit) Regulations 2019, SI 2019/419, reg 3, Sch 1, paras 1, 15, as from exit day (as defined in the European Union (Withdrawal) Act 2018, s 20) and only in so far as this Regulation will apply in the UK after that date by virtue of s 3 of the 2018 Act, as follows (for transitional provisions etc, see the 2019 Regulations at **[2.2122]**)—

15.
(1) Article 17 is amended as follows.
(2) In paragraph 1(e), for "in Union or Member State law to which the controller is subject" substitute "under domestic law".
(3) In paragraph 3(b), for "by Union or Member State law to which the controller is subject" substitute "under domestic law".

[3.615]
Article 18
Right to restriction of processing

1. The data subject shall have the right to obtain from the controller restriction of processing where one of the following applies:
(a) the accuracy of the personal data is contested by the data subject, for a period enabling the controller to verify the accuracy of the personal data;
(b) the processing is unlawful and the data subject opposes the erasure of the personal data and requests the restriction of their use instead;
(c) the controller no longer needs the personal data for the purposes of the processing, but they are required by the data subject for the establishment, exercise or defence of legal claims;
(d) the data subject has objected to processing pursuant to Article 21(1) pending the verification whether the legitimate grounds of the controller override those of the data subject.

2. Where processing has been restricted under paragraph 1, such personal data shall, with the exception of storage, only be processed with the data subject's consent or for the establishment, exercise or defence of legal claims or for the protection of the rights of another natural or legal person or for reasons of important public interest of the Union or of a Member State.
3. A data subject who has obtained restriction of processing pursuant to paragraph 1 shall be informed by the controller before the restriction of processing is lifted.

NOTES

This Article is amended by the Data Protection, Privacy and Electronic Communications (Amendments etc) (EU Exit) Regulations 2019, SI 2019/419, reg 3, Sch 1, paras 1, 16, as from exit day (as defined in the European Union (Withdrawal) Act 2018, s 20) and only in so far as this Regulation will apply in the UK after that date by virtue of s 3 of the 2018 Act, as follows (for transitional provisions etc, see the 2019 Regulations at **[2.2122]**)—

16.
In Article 18(2), omit "of the Union or of a Member State".

[3.616]
Article 19
Notification obligation regarding rectification or erasure of personal data or restriction of processing

The controller shall communicate any rectification or erasure of personal data or restriction of processing carried out in accordance with Article 16, Article 17(1) and Article 18 to each recipient to whom the personal data have been disclosed, unless this proves impossible or involves disproportionate effort. The controller shall inform the data subject about those recipients if the data subject requests it.

[3.617]
Article 20
Right to data portability

1. The data subject shall have the right to receive the personal data concerning him or her, which he or she has provided to a controller, in a structured, commonly used and machine-readable format and have the right to transmit those data to another controller without hindrance from the controller to which the personal data have been provided, where:
(a) the processing is based on consent pursuant to point (a) of Article 6(1) or point (a) of Article 9(2) or on a contract pursuant to point (b) of Article 6(1); and
(b) the processing is carried out by automated means.

2. In exercising his or her right to data portability pursuant to paragraph 1, the data subject shall have the right to have the personal data transmitted directly from one controller to another, where technically feasible.
3. The exercise of the right referred to in paragraph 1 of this Article shall be without prejudice to Article 17. That right shall not apply to processing necessary for the performance of a task carried out in the public interest or in the exercise of official authority vested in the controller.
4. The right referred to in paragraph 1 shall not adversely affect the rights and freedoms of others.

SECTION 4 RIGHT TO OBJECT AND AUTOMATED INDIVIDUAL DECISION-MAKING

[3.618]
Article 21
Right to object

1. The data subject shall have the right to object, on grounds relating to his or her particular situation, at any time to processing of personal data concerning him or her which is based on point (e) or (f) of Article 6(1), including profiling based on those provisions. The controller shall no longer process the personal data unless the controller demonstrates compelling legitimate grounds for the processing which override the interests, rights and freedoms of the data subject or for the establishment, exercise or defence of legal claims.
2. Where personal data are processed for direct marketing purposes, the data subject shall have the right to object at any time to processing of personal data concerning him or her for such marketing, which includes profiling to the extent that it is related to such direct marketing.
3. Where the data subject objects to processing for direct marketing purposes, the personal data shall no longer be processed for such purposes.
4. At the latest at the time of the first communication with the data subject, the right referred to in paragraphs 1 and 2 shall be explicitly brought to the attention of the data subject and shall be presented clearly and separately from any other information.
5. In the context of the use of information society services, and notwithstanding Directive 2002/58/EC, the data subject may exercise his or her right to object by automated means using technical specifications.
6. Where personal data are processed for scientific or historical research purposes or statistical purposes pursuant to Article 89(1), the data subject, on grounds relating to his or her particular situation, shall have the right to object to processing of personal data concerning him or her, unless the processing is necessary for the performance of a task carried out for reasons of public interest.

NOTES

This Article is amended by the Data Protection, Privacy and Electronic Communications (Amendments etc) (EU Exit) Regulations 2019, SI 2019/419, reg 3, Sch 1, paras 1, 17, as from exit day (as defined in the European Union (Withdrawal) Act 2018, s 20) and only in so far as this Regulation will apply in the UK after that date by virtue of s 3 of the 2018 Act, as follows (for transitional provisions etc, see the 2019 Regulations at **[2.2122]**)—

17.
In Article 21(5)—
(a) omit "and notwithstanding Directive 2002/58/EC,";
(b) at the end insert ", notwithstanding domestic law made before exit day implementing Directive 2002/58/EC of the European Parliament and of the Council of 12th July 2002 concerning the processing of personal data and the protection of privacy in the electronic communications sector".

[3.619]
Article 22
Automated individual decision-making, including profiling

1. The data subject shall have the right not to be subject to a decision based solely on automated processing, including profiling, which produces legal effects concerning him or her or similarly significantly affects him or her.
2. Paragraph 1 shall not apply if the decision:
   (a) is necessary for entering into, or performance of, a contract between the data subject and a data controller;
   (b) is authorised by Union or Member State law to which the controller is subject and which also lays down suitable measures to safeguard the data subject's rights and freedoms and legitimate interests; or
   (c) is based on the data subject's explicit consent.
3. In the cases referred to in points (a) and (c) of paragraph 2, the data controller shall implement suitable measures to safeguard the data subject's rights and freedoms and legitimate interests, at least the right to obtain human intervention on the part of the controller, to express his or her point of view and to contest the decision.
4. Decisions referred to in paragraph 2 shall not be based on special categories of personal data referred to in Article 9(1), unless point (a) or (g) of Article 9(2) applies and suitable measures to safeguard the data subject's rights and freedoms and legitimate interests are in place.

NOTES

This Article is amended by the Data Protection, Privacy and Electronic Communications (Amendments etc) (EU Exit) Regulations 2019, SI 2019/419, reg 3, Sch 1, paras 1, 18, as from exit day (as defined in the European Union (Withdrawal) Act 2018, s 20) and only in so far as this Regulation will apply in the UK after that date by virtue of s 3 of the 2018 Act, as follows (for transitional provisions etc, see the 2019 Regulations at **[2.2122]**)—

18.
(1) Article 22 is amended as follows.
(2) In paragraph 2(b), for "authorised by Union or Member State law to which the controller is subject and" substitute "required or authorised by domestic law".
(3) After paragraph 3 insert—

"3A. Section 14 of the 2018 Act, and regulations under that section, make provision to safeguard data subjects' rights, freedoms and legitimate interests in cases that fall within point (b) of paragraph 2 (but not within point (a) or (c) of that paragraph).".

SECTION 5 RESTRICTIONS

[3.620]
Article 23
Restrictions

1. Union or Member State law to which the data controller or processor is subject may restrict by way of a legislative measure the scope of the obligations and rights provided for in Articles 12 to 22 and Article 34, as well as Article 5 in so far as its provisions correspond to the rights and obligations provided for in Articles 12 to 22, when such a restriction respects the essence of the fundamental rights and freedoms and is a necessary and proportionate measure in a democratic society to safeguard:

(a) national security;
(b) defence;
(c) public security;
(d) the prevention, investigation, detection or prosecution of criminal offences or the execution of criminal penalties, including the safeguarding against and the prevention of threats to public security;
(e) other important objectives of general public interest of the Union or of a Member State, in particular an important economic or financial interest of the Union or of a Member State, including monetary, budgetary and taxation a matters, public health and social security;
(f) the protection of judicial independence and judicial proceedings;
(g) the prevention, investigation, detection and prosecution of breaches of ethics for regulated professions;
(h) a monitoring, inspection or regulatory function connected, even occasionally, to the exercise of official authority in the cases referred to in points (a) to (e) and (g);
(i) the protection of the data subject or the rights and freedoms of others;
(j) the enforcement of civil law claims.

2. In particular, any legislative measure referred to in paragraph 1 shall contain specific provisions at least, where relevant, as to:

(a) the purposes of the processing or categories of processing;
(b) the categories of personal data;
(c) the scope of the restrictions introduced;
(d) the safeguards to prevent abuse or unlawful access or transfer;
(e) the specification of the controller or categories of controllers;
(f) the storage periods and the applicable safeguards taking into account the nature, scope and purposes of the processing or categories of processing;
(g) the risks to the rights and freedoms of data subjects; and
(h) the right of data subjects to be informed about the restriction, unless that may be prejudicial to the purpose of the restriction.

NOTES

This Article is amended by the Data Protection, Privacy and Electronic Communications (Amendments etc) (EU Exit) Regulations 2019, SI 2019/419, reg 3, Sch 1, paras 1, 19, as from exit day (as defined in the European Union (Withdrawal) Act 2018, s 20) and only in so far as this Regulation will apply in the UK after that date by virtue of s 3 of the 2018 Act, as follows (for transitional provisions etc, see the 2019 Regulations at **[2.2122]**)—

19.

(1) Article 23 is amended as follows.

(2) In paragraph 1—

(a) for "Union or Member State law to which the data controller or processor is subject may restrict by way of legislative measure" substitute "The Secretary of State may restrict";
(b) omit points (a) and (b);
(c) in point (e)—
(i) omit "of the Union or of a Member State" in the first place it occurs;
(ii) for "of the Union or of a Member State", in the second place it occurs, substitute "of the United Kingdom".

(3) In paragraph 2, for "any legislative measure referred to in" substitute "provision made in exercise of the power under".

(4) After that paragraph insert—

"3. The Secretary of State may exercise the power under paragraph 1 only by making regulations under section 16 of the 2018 Act.".

CHAPTER IV CONTROLLER AND PROCESSOR

SECTION 1 GENERAL OBLIGATIONS

[3.621]
Article 24
Responsibility of the controller

1. Taking into account the nature, scope, context and purposes of processing as well as the risks of varying likelihood and severity for the rights and freedoms of natural persons, the controller shall implement appropriate technical and organisational measures to ensure and to be able to demonstrate that processing is performed in accordance with this Regulation. Those measures shall be reviewed and updated where necessary.

Part 3 EU Materials

2. Where proportionate in relation to processing activities, the measures referred to in paragraph 1 shall include the implementation of appropriate data protection policies by the controller.
3. Adherence to approved codes of conduct as referred to in Article 40 or approved certification mechanisms as referred to in Article 42 may be used as an element by which to demonstrate compliance with the obligations of the controller.

[3.622]
Article 25
Data protection by design and by default
1. Taking into account the state of the art, the cost of implementation and the nature, scope, context and purposes of processing as well as the risks of varying likelihood and severity for rights and freedoms of natural persons posed by the processing, the controller shall, both at the time of the determination of the means for processing and at the time of the processing itself, implement appropriate technical and organisational measures, such as pseudonymisation, which are designed to implement data-protection principles, such as data minimisation, in an effective manner and to integrate the necessary safeguards into the processing in order to meet the requirements of this Regulation and protect the rights of data subjects.
2. The controller shall implement appropriate technical and organisational measures for ensuring that, by default, only personal data which are necessary for each specific purpose of the processing are processed. That obligation applies to the amount of personal data collected, the extent of their processing, the period of their storage and their accessibility. In particular, such measures shall ensure that by default personal data are not made accessible without the individual's intervention to an indefinite number of natural persons.
3. An approved certification mechanism pursuant to Article 42 may be used as an element to demonstrate compliance with the requirements set out in paragraphs 1 and 2 of this Article.

[3.623]
Article 26
Joint controllers
1. Where two or more controllers jointly determine the purposes and means of processing, they shall be joint controllers. They shall in a transparent manner determine their respective responsibilities for compliance with the obligations under this Regulation, in particular as regards the exercising of the rights of the data subject and their respective duties to provide the information referred to in Articles 13 and 14, by means of an arrangement between them unless, and in so far as, the respective responsibilities of the controllers are determined by Union or Member State law to which the controllers are subject. The arrangement may designate a contact point for data subjects.
2. The arrangement referred to in paragraph 1 shall duly reflect the respective roles and relationships of the joint controllers vis-à-vis the data subjects. The essence of the arrangement shall be made available to the data subject.
3. Irrespective of the terms of the arrangement referred to in paragraph 1, the data subject may exercise his or her rights under this Regulation in respect of and against each of the controllers.

NOTES
This Article is amended by the Data Protection, Privacy and Electronic Communications (Amendments etc) (EU Exit) Regulations 2019, SI 2019/419, reg 3, Sch 1, paras 1, 20, as from exit day (as defined in the European Union (Withdrawal) Act 2018, s 20) and only in so far as this Regulation will apply in the UK after that date by virtue of s 3 of the 2018 Act, as follows (for transitional provisions etc, see the 2019 Regulations at **[2.2122]**)—

20.
In Article 26(1), for "Union or Member State law to which the controllers are subject" substitute "domestic law".

[3.624]
Article 30
Records of processing activities
1. Each controller and, where applicable, the controller's representative, shall maintain a record of processing activities under its responsibility. That record shall contain all of the following information:
- (a) the name and contact details of the controller and, where applicable, the joint controller, the controller's representative and the data protection officer;
- (b) the purposes of the processing;
- (c) a description of the categories of data subjects and of the categories of personal data;
- (d) the categories of recipients to whom the personal data have been or will be disclosed including recipients in third countries or international organisations;
- (e) where applicable, transfers of personal data to a third country or an international organisation, including the identification of that third country or international organisation and, in the case of transfers referred to in the second subparagraph of Article 49(1), the documentation of suitable safeguards;
- (f) where possible, the envisaged time limits for erasure of the different categories of data;
- (g) where possible, a general description of the technical and organisational security measures referred to in Article 32(1).

2. Each processor and, where applicable, the processor's representative shall maintain a record of all categories of processing activities carried out on behalf of a controller, containing:
- (a) the name and contact details of the processor or processors and of each controller on behalf of which the processor is acting, and, where applicable, of the controller's or the processor's representative, and the data protection officer;

(b) the categories of processing carried out on behalf of each controller;
(c) where applicable, transfers of personal data to a third country or an international organisation, including the identification of that third country or international organisation and, in the case of transfers referred to in the second subparagraph of Article 49(1), the documentation of suitable safeguards;
(d) where possible, a general description of the technical and organisational security measures referred to in Article 32(1).

3. The records referred to in paragraphs 1 and 2 shall be in writing, including in electronic form.
4. The controller or the processor and, where applicable, the controller's or the processor's representative, shall make the record available to the supervisory authority on request.
5. The obligations referred to in paragraphs 1 and 2 shall not apply to an enterprise or an organisation employing fewer than 250 persons unless the processing it carries out is likely to result in a risk to the rights and freedoms of data subjects, the processing is not occasional, or the processing includes special categories of data as referred to in Article 9(1) or personal data relating to criminal convictions and offences referred to in Article 10.

NOTES

This Article is amended by the Data Protection, Privacy and Electronic Communications (Amendments etc) (EU Exit) Regulations 2019, SI 2019/419, reg 3, Sch 1, paras 1, 24, as from exit day (as defined in the European Union (Withdrawal) Act 2018, s 20) and only in so far as this Regulation will apply in the UK after that date by virtue of s 3 of the 2018 Act, as follows (for transitional provisions etc, see the 2019 Regulations at **[2.2122]**)—

24.
(1) Article 30 is amended as follows.
(2) In paragraph 1(g), after "Article 32(1)" insert "or, as appropriate, the security measures referred to in section 28(3) of the 2018 Act".
(3) In paragraph 2(d), after "Article 32(1)" insert "or, as appropriate, the security measures referred to in section 28(3) of the 2018 Act".
(4) In paragraph 4, for "the supervisory authority" substitute "the Commissioner".

[3.625]
Article 31
Cooperation with the supervisory authority

The controller and the processor and, where applicable, their representatives, shall cooperate, on request, with the supervisory authority in the performance of its tasks.

NOTES

This Article is amended by the Data Protection, Privacy and Electronic Communications (Amendments etc) (EU Exit) Regulations 2019, SI 2019/419, reg 3, Sch 1, paras 1, 25, as from exit day (as defined in the European Union (Withdrawal) Act 2018, s 20) and only in so far as this Regulation will apply in the UK after that date by virtue of s 3 of the 2018 Act, as follows (for transitional provisions etc, see the 2019 Regulations at **[2.2122]**)—

25.
(1) Article 31 is amended as follows.
(2) In the heading, for "the supervisory authority" substitute "the Commissioner".
(3) For "the supervisory authority in the performance of its tasks" substitute "the Commissioner in the performance of the Commissioner's tasks".

SECTION 2 SECURITY OF PERSONAL DATA

[3.626]
Article 32
Security of processing

1. Taking into account the state of the art, the costs of implementation and the nature, scope, context and purposes of processing as well as the risk of varying likelihood and severity for the rights and freedoms of natural persons, the controller and the processor shall implement appropriate technical and organisational measures to ensure a level of security appropriate to the risk, including inter alia as appropriate:
(a) the pseudonymisation and encryption of personal data;
(b) the ability to ensure the ongoing confidentiality, integrity, availability and resilience of processing systems and services;
(c) the ability to restore the availability and access to personal data in a timely manner in the event of a physical or technical incident;
(d) a process for regularly testing, assessing and evaluating the effectiveness of technical and organisational measures for ensuring the security of the processing.

2. In assessing the appropriate level of security account shall be taken in particular of the risks that are presented by processing, in particular from accidental or unlawful destruction, loss, alteration, unauthorised disclosure of, or access to personal data transmitted, stored or otherwise processed.
3. Adherence to an approved code of conduct as referred to in Article 40 or an approved certification mechanism as referred to in Article 42 may be used as an element by which to demonstrate compliance with the requirements set out in paragraph 1 of this Article.
4. The controller and processor shall take steps to ensure that any natural person acting under the authority of the controller or the processor who has access to personal data does not process them except on instructions from the controller, unless he or she is required to do so by Union or Member State law.

NOTES

This Article is amended by the Data Protection, Privacy and Electronic Communications (Amendments etc) (EU Exit) Regulations 2019, SI 2019/419, reg 3, Sch 1, paras 1, 26, as from exit day (as defined in the European Union (Withdrawal) Act 2018, s 20) and only in so far as this Regulation will apply in the UK after that date by virtue of s 3 of the 2018 Act, as follows (for transitional provisions etc, see the 2019 Regulations at **[2.2122]**)—

26.

In Article 32(4), for "Union or Member State law" substitute "domestic law".

[3.627]
Article 33
Notification of a personal data breach to the supervisory authority

1. In the case of a personal data breach, the controller shall without undue delay and, where feasible, not later than 72 hours after having become aware of it, notify the personal data breach to the supervisory authority competent in accordance with Article 55, unless the personal data breach is unlikely to result in a risk to the rights and freedoms of natural persons. Where the notification to the supervisory authority is not made within 72 hours, it shall be accompanied by reasons for the delay.
2. The processor shall notify the controller without undue delay after becoming aware of a personal data breach.
3. The notification referred to in paragraph 1 shall at least:
   (a) describe the nature of the personal data breach including where possible, the categories and approximate number of data subjects concerned and the categories and approximate number of personal data records concerned;
   (b) communicate the name and contact details of the data protection officer or other contact point where more information can be obtained;
   (c) describe the likely consequences of the personal data breach;
   (d) describe the measures taken or proposed to be taken by the controller to address the personal data breach, including, where appropriate, measures to mitigate its possible adverse effects.
4. Where, and in so far as, it is not possible to provide the information at the same time, the information may be provided in phases without undue further delay.
5. The controller shall document any personal data breaches, comprising the facts relating to the personal data breach, its effects and the remedial action taken. That documentation shall enable the supervisory authority to verify compliance with this Article.

NOTES

This Article is amended by the Data Protection, Privacy and Electronic Communications (Amendments etc) (EU Exit) Regulations 2019, SI 2019/419, reg 3, Sch 1, paras 1, 27, as from exit day (as defined in the European Union (Withdrawal) Act 2018, s 20) and only in so far as this Regulation will apply in the UK after that date by virtue of s 3 of the 2018 Act, as follows (for transitional provisions etc, see the 2019 Regulations at **[2.2122]**)—

27.

(1) Article 33 is amended as follows.
(2) In the heading, for "the supervisory authority" substitute "the Commissioner".
(3) In paragraph 1—
   (a) for "the supervisory authority competent in accordance with Article 55" substitute "the Commissioner";
   (b) for "the notification to the supervisory authority" substitute "the notification under this paragraph".
(4) In paragraph 5, for "the supervisory authority" substitute "the Commissioner".

[3.628]
Article 34
Communication of a personal data breach to the data subject

1. When the personal data breach is likely to result in a high risk to the rights and freedoms of natural persons, the controller shall communicate the personal data breach to the data subject without undue delay.
2. The communication to the data subject referred to in paragraph 1 of this Article shall describe in clear and plain language the nature of the personal data breach and contain at least the information and measures referred to in points (b), (c) and (d) of Article 33(3).
3. The communication to the data subject referred to in paragraph 1 shall not be required if any of the following conditions are met:
   (a) the controller has implemented appropriate technical and organisational protection measures, and those measures were applied to the personal data affected by the personal data breach, in particular those that render the personal data unintelligible to any person who is not authorised to access it, such as encryption;
   (b) the controller has taken subsequent measures which ensure that the high risk to the rights and freedoms of data subjects referred to in paragraph 1 is no longer likely to materialise;
   (c) it would involve disproportionate effort. In such a case, there shall instead be a public communication or similar measure whereby the data subjects are informed in an equally effective manner.
4. If the controller has not already communicated the personal data breach to the data subject, the supervisory authority, having considered the likelihood of the personal data breach resulting in a high risk, may require it to do so or may decide that any of the conditions referred to in paragraph 3 are met.

NOTES

This Article is amended by the Data Protection, Privacy and Electronic Communications (Amendments etc) (EU Exit) Regulations 2019, SI 2019/419, reg 3, Sch 1, paras 1, 28, as from exit day (as defined in the European Union (Withdrawal) Act 2018, s 20) and only in so far as this Regulation will apply in the UK after that date by virtue of s 3 of the 2018 Act, as follows (for transitional provisions etc, see the 2019 Regulations at **[2.2122]**)—

28.

In Article 34(4), for "the supervisory authority" substitute "the Commissioner".

SECTION 3 DATA PROTECTION IMPACT ASSESSMENT AND PRIOR CONSULTATION

[3.629]

Article 35

Data protection impact assessment

1. Where a type of processing in particular using new technologies, and taking into account the nature, scope, context and purposes of the processing, is likely to result in a high risk to the rights and freedoms of natural persons, the controller shall, prior to the processing, carry out an assessment of the impact of the envisaged processing operations on the protection of personal data. A single assessment may address a set of similar processing operations that present similar high risks.

2. The controller shall seek the advice of the data protection officer, where designated, when carrying out a data protection impact assessment.

3. A data protection impact assessment referred to in paragraph 1 shall in particular be required in the case of:

(a) a systematic and extensive evaluation of personal aspects relating to natural persons which is based on automated processing, including profiling, and on which decisions are based that produce legal effects concerning the natural person or similarly significantly affect the natural person;

(b) processing on a large scale of special categories of data referred to in Article 9(1), or of personal data relating to criminal convictions and offences referred to in Article 10; or

(c) a systematic monitoring of a publicly accessible area on a large scale.

4. The supervisory authority shall establish and make public a list of the kind of processing operations which are subject to the requirement for a data protection impact assessment pursuant to paragraph 1. The supervisory authority shall communicate those lists to the Board referred to in Article 68.

5. The supervisory authority may also establish and make public a list of the kind of processing operations for which no data protection impact assessment is required. The supervisory authority shall communicate those lists to the Board.

6. Prior to the adoption of the lists referred to in paragraphs 4 and 5, the competent supervisory authority shall apply the consistency mechanism referred to in Article 63 where such lists involve processing activities which are related to the offering of goods or services to data subjects or to the monitoring of their behaviour in several Member States, or may substantially affect the free movement of personal data within the Union.

7. The assessment shall contain at least:

(a) a systematic description of the envisaged processing operations and the purposes of the processing, including, where applicable, the legitimate interest pursued by the controller;

(b) an assessment of the necessity and proportionality of the processing operations in relation to the purposes;

(c) an assessment of the risks to the rights and freedoms of data subjects referred to in paragraph 1; and

(d) the measures envisaged to address the risks, including safeguards, security measures and mechanisms to ensure the protection of personal data and to demonstrate compliance with this Regulation taking into account the rights and legitimate interests of data subjects and other persons concerned.

8. Compliance with approved codes of conduct referred to in Article 40 by the relevant controllers or processors shall be taken into due account in assessing the impact of the processing operations performed by such controllers or processors, in particular for the purposes of a data protection impact assessment.

9. Where appropriate, the controller shall seek the views of data subjects or their representatives on the intended processing, without prejudice to the protection of commercial or public interests or the security of processing operations.

10. Where processing pursuant to point (c) or (e) of Article 6(1) has a legal basis in Union law or in the law of the Member State to which the controller is subject, that law regulates the specific processing operation or set of operations in question, and a data protection impact assessment has already been carried out as part of a general impact assessment in the context of the adoption of that legal basis, paragraphs 1 to 7 shall not apply unless Member States deem it to be necessary to carry out such an assessment prior to processing activities.

11. Where necessary, the controller shall carry out a review to assess if processing is performed in accordance with the data protection impact assessment at least when there is a change of the risk represented by processing operations.

NOTES

This Article is amended by the Data Protection, Privacy and Electronic Communications (Amendments etc) (EU Exit) Regulations 2019, SI 2019/419, reg 3, Sch 1, paras 1, 29, as from exit day (as defined in the European Union (Withdrawal) Act 2018, s 20) and only in so far as this Regulation will apply in the UK after that date by virtue of s 3 of the 2018 Act, as follows

(for transitional provisions etc, see the 2019 Regulations at **[2.2122]**)—

29.

(1) Article 35 is amended as follows.

(2) In paragraph 4—

(a) in the first sentence, for "The supervisory authority" substitute "The Commissioner";

(b) omit the second sentence.

(3) In paragraph 5—

(a) in the first sentence, for "The supervisory authority" substitute "The Commissioner";

(b) omit the second sentence.

(4) Omit paragraph 6.

(5) For paragraph 10 substitute—

"10. In the case of processing pursuant to point (c) or (e) of Article 6(1), paragraphs 1 to 7 of this Article do not apply if a data protection impact assessment has already been carried out for the processing as part of a general impact assessment required by domestic law, unless domestic law provides otherwise.".

[3.630]
Article 36
Prior consultation

1. The controller shall consult the supervisory authority prior to processing where a data protection impact assessment under Article 35 indicates that the processing would result in a high risk in the absence of measures taken by the controller to mitigate the risk.

2. Where the supervisory authority is of the opinion that the intended processing referred to in paragraph 1 would infringe this Regulation, in particular where the controller has insufficiently identified or mitigated the risk, the supervisory authority shall, within period of up to eight weeks of receipt of the request for consultation, provide written advice to the controller and, where applicable to the processor, and may use any of its powers referred to in Article 58. That period may be extended by six weeks, taking into account the complexity of the intended processing. The supervisory authority shall inform the controller and, where applicable, the processor, of any such extension within one month of receipt of the request for consultation together with the reasons for the delay. Those periods may be suspended until the supervisory authority has obtained information it has requested for the purposes of the consultation.

3. When consulting the supervisory authority pursuant to paragraph 1, the controller shall provide the supervisory authority with:

(a) where applicable, the respective responsibilities of the controller, joint controllers and processors involved in the processing, in particular for processing within a group of undertakings;

(b) the purposes and means of the intended processing;

(c) the measures and safeguards provided to protect the rights and freedoms of data subjects pursuant to this Regulation;

(d) where applicable, the contact details of the data protection officer;

(e) the data protection impact assessment provided for in Article 35; and

(f) any other information requested by the supervisory authority.

4. Member States shall consult the supervisory authority during the preparation of a proposal for a legislative measure to be adopted by a national parliament, or of a regulatory measure based on such a legislative measure, which relates to processing.

5. Notwithstanding paragraph 1, Member State law may require controllers to consult with, and obtain prior authorisation from, the supervisory authority in relation to processing by a controller for the performance of a task carried out by the controller in the public interest, including processing in relation to social protection and public health.

NOTES

This Article is amended by the Data Protection, Privacy and Electronic Communications (Amendments etc) (EU Exit) Regulations 2019, SI 2019/419, reg 3, Sch 1, paras 1, 30, as from exit day (as defined in the European Union (Withdrawal) Act 2018, s 20) and only in so far as this Regulation will apply in the UK after that date by virtue of s 3 of the 2018 Act, as follows (for transitional provisions etc, see the 2019 Regulations at **[2.2122]**)—

30.

(1) Article 36 is amended as follows.

(2) In paragraph 1, for "the supervisory authority" substitute "the Commissioner".

(3) In paragraph 2—

(a) in the first sentence, for "the supervisory authority" (in both places) substitute "the Commissioner";

(b) in the third sentence, for "The supervisory authority" substitute "The Commissioner";

(c) in the last sentence, for "the supervisory authority has obtained information it" substitute "the Commissioner has obtained information the Commissioner".

(4) In paragraph 3—

(a) in the opening words, for "the supervisory authority" (in both places) substitute "the Commissioner";

(b) in point (f), for "the supervisory authority" substitute "the Commissioner".

(5) In paragraph 4—

(a) for "Members States shall consult the supervisory authority" substitute "The relevant authority must consult the Commissioner";

(b) for "a national parliament" substitute "Parliament, the National Assembly for Wales, the Scottish Parliament or the Northern Ireland Assembly".

(6) After that paragraph insert—

"4A. In paragraph 4, "the relevant authority" means—

(a) in relation to a legislative measure adopted by Parliament, or a regulatory measure based on such a legislative measure, the Secretary of State;

(b) in relation to a legislative measure adopted by the National Assembly for Wales, or a regulatory measure based on such a legislative measure, the Welsh Ministers;

(c) in relation to a legislative measure adopted by the Scottish Parliament, or a regulatory measure based on such a legislative measure, the Scottish Ministers;

(d) in relation to a legislative measure adopted by the Northern Ireland Assembly, or a regulatory measure based on such a legislative measure, the relevant Northern Ireland department.".

(7) Omit paragraph 5.

SECTION 4 DATA PROTECTION OFFICER

[3.631]
Article 37
Designation of the data protection officer

1. The controller and the processor shall designate a data protection officer in any case where:
   (a) the processing is carried out by a public authority or body, except for courts acting in their judicial capacity;
   (b) the core activities of the controller or the processor consist of processing operations which, by virtue of their nature, their scope and/or their purposes, require regular and systematic monitoring of data subjects on a large scale; or
   (c) the core activities of the controller or the processor consist of processing on a large scale of special categories of data pursuant to Article 9 or personal data relating to criminal convictions and offences referred to in Article 10.
2. A group of undertakings may appoint a single data protection officer provided that a data protection officer is easily accessible from each establishment.
3. Where the controller or the processor is a public authority or body, a single data protection officer may be designated for several such authorities or bodies, taking account of their organisational structure and size.
4. In cases other than those referred to in paragraph 1, the controller or processor or associations and other bodies representing categories of controllers or processors may or, where required by Union or Member State law shall, designate a data protection officer. The data protection officer may act for such associations and other bodies representing controllers or processors.
5. The data protection officer shall be designated on the basis of professional qualities and, in particular, expert knowledge of data protection law and practices and the ability to fulfil the tasks referred to in Article 39.
6. The data protection officer may be a staff member of the controller or processor, or fulfil the tasks on the basis of a service contract.
7. The controller or the processor shall publish the contact details of the data protection officer and communicate them to the supervisory authority.

NOTES

This Article is amended by the Data Protection, Privacy and Electronic Communications (Amendments etc) (EU Exit) Regulations 2019, SI 2019/419, reg 3, Sch 1, paras 1, 31, as from exit day (as defined in the European Union (Withdrawal) Act 2018, s 20) and only in so far as this Regulation will apply in the UK after that date by virtue of s 3 of the 2018 Act, as follows (for transitional provisions etc, see the 2019 Regulations at **[2.2122]**)—

31.
(1) Article 37 is amended as follows.
(2) In paragraph 4, omit "or, where required by Union or Member State law shall,".
(3) In paragraph 7, for "the supervisory authority" substitute "the Commissioner".

[3.632]
Article 38
Position of the data protection officer

1. The controller and the processor shall ensure that the data protection officer is involved, properly and in a timely manner, in all issues which relate to the protection of personal data.
2. The controller and processor shall support the data protection officer in performing the tasks referred to in Article 39 by providing resources necessary to carry out those tasks and access to personal data and processing operations, and to maintain his or her expert knowledge.
3. The controller and processor shall ensure that the data protection officer does not receive any instructions regarding the exercise of those tasks. He or she shall not be dismissed or penalised by the controller or the processor for performing his tasks. The data protection officer shall directly report to the highest management level of the controller or the processor.
4. Data subjects may contact the data protection officer with regard to all issues related to processing of their personal data and to the exercise of their rights under this Regulation.
5. The data protection officer shall be bound by secrecy or confidentiality concerning the performance of his or her tasks, in accordance with Union or Member State law.
6. The data protection officer may fulfil other tasks and duties. The controller or processor shall ensure that any such tasks and duties do not result in a conflict of interests.

NOTES

This Article is amended by the Data Protection, Privacy and Electronic Communications (Amendments etc) (EU Exit) Regulations 2019, SI 2019/419, reg 3, Sch 1, paras 1, 32, as from exit day (as defined in the European Union (Withdrawal) Act 2018, s 20) and only in so far as this Regulation will apply in the UK after that date by virtue of s 3 of the 2018 Act, as follows (for transitional provisions etc, see the 2019 Regulations at **[2.2122]**)—

32.

In Article 38(5), for "Union or Member State law" substitute "domestic law".

[3.633]
Article 39
Tasks of the data protection officer

1. The data protection officer shall have at least the following tasks:
   (a) to inform and advise the controller or the processor and the employees who carry out processing of their obligations pursuant to this Regulation and to other Union or Member State data protection provisions;
   (b) to monitor compliance with this Regulation, with other Union or Member State data protection provisions and with the policies of the controller or processor in relation to the protection of personal data, including the assignment of responsibilities, awareness-raising and training of staff involved in processing operations, and the related audits;
   (c) to provide advice where requested as regards the data protection impact assessment and monitor its performance pursuant to Article 35;
   (d) to cooperate with the supervisory authority;
   (e) to act as the contact point for the supervisory authority on issues relating to processing, including the prior consultation referred to in Article 36, and to consult, where appropriate, with regard to any other matter.

2. The data protection officer shall in the performance of his or her tasks have due regard to the risk associated with processing operations, taking into account the nature, scope, context and purposes of processing.

NOTES

This Article is amended by the Data Protection, Privacy and Electronic Communications (Amendments etc) (EU Exit) Regulations 2019, SI 2019/419, reg 3, Sch 1, paras 1, 33, as from exit day (as defined in the European Union (Withdrawal) Act 2018, s 20) and only in so far as this Regulation will apply in the UK after that date by virtue of s 3 of the 2018 Act, as follows (for transitional provisions etc, see the 2019 Regulations at **[2.2122]**)—

33.

(1) Article 39 is amended as follows.

(2) In paragraph 1(a) and (b), for "other Union or Member State data protection provisions" substitute "other domestic law relating to data protection".

(3) In paragraph 1(d) and (e), for "the supervisory authority" substitute "the Commissioner".

SECTION 5 CODES OF CONDUCT AND CERTIFICATION

[3.634]
Article 40
Codes of conduct

1. The Member States, the supervisory authorities, the Board and the Commission shall encourage the drawing up of codes of conduct intended to contribute to the proper application of this Regulation, taking account of the specific features of the various processing sectors and the specific needs of micro, small and medium-sized enterprises.

2. Associations and other bodies representing categories of controllers or processors may prepare codes of conduct, or amend or extend such codes, for the purpose of specifying the application of this Regulation, such as with regard to:
   (a) fair and transparent processing;
   (b) the legitimate interests pursued by controllers in specific contexts;
   (c) the collection of personal data;
   (d) the pseudonymisation of personal data;
   (e) the information provided to the public and to data subjects;
   (f) the exercise of the rights of data subjects;
   (g) the information provided to, and the protection of, children, and the manner in which the consent of the holders of parental responsibility over children is to be obtained;
   (h) the measures and procedures referred to in Articles 24 and 25 and the measures to ensure security of processing referred to in Article 32;
   (i) the notification of personal data breaches to supervisory authorities and the communication of such personal data breaches to data subjects;
   (j) the transfer of personal data to third countries or international organisations; or
   (k) out-of-court proceedings and other dispute resolution procedures for resolving disputes between controllers and data subjects with regard to processing, without prejudice to the rights of data subjects pursuant to Articles 77 and 79.

3. In addition to adherence by controllers or processors subject to this Regulation, codes of conduct approved pursuant to paragraph 5 of this Article and having general validity pursuant to paragraph 9 of this Article may also be adhered to by controllers or processors that are not subject to this Regulation

pursuant to Article 3 in order to provide appropriate safeguards within the framework of personal data transfers to third countries or international organisations under the terms referred to in point (e) of Article 46(2). Such controllers or processors shall make binding and enforceable commitments, via contractual or other legally binding instruments, to apply those appropriate safeguards including with regard to the rights of data subjects.

4. A code of conduct referred to in paragraph 2 of this Article shall contain mechanisms which enable the body referred to in Article 41(1) to carry out the mandatory monitoring of compliance with its provisions by the controllers or processors which undertake to apply it, without prejudice to the tasks and powers of supervisory authorities competent pursuant to Article 55 or 56.

5. Associations and other bodies referred to in paragraph 2 of this Article which intend to prepare a code of conduct or to amend or extend an existing code shall submit the draft code, amendment or extension to the supervisory authority which is competent pursuant to Article 55. The supervisory authority shall provide an opinion on whether the draft code, amendment or extension complies with this Regulation and shall approve that draft code, amendment or extension if it finds that it provides sufficient appropriate safeguards.

6. Where the draft code, or amendment or extension is approved in accordance with paragraph 5, and where the code of conduct concerned does not relate to processing activities in several Member States, the supervisory authority shall register and publish the code.

7. Where a draft code of conduct relates to processing activities in several Member States, the supervisory authority which is competent pursuant to Article 55 shall, before approving the draft code, amendment or extension, submit it in the procedure referred to in Article 63 to the Board which shall provide an opinion on whether the draft code, amendment or extension complies with this Regulation or, in the situation referred to in paragraph 3 of this Article, provides appropriate safeguards.

8. Where the opinion referred to in paragraph 7 confirms that the draft code, amendment or extension complies with this Regulation, or, in the situation referred to in paragraph 3, provides appropriate safeguards, the Board shall submit its opinion to the Commission.

9. The Commission may, by way of implementing acts, decide that the approved code of conduct, amendment or extension submitted to it pursuant to paragraph 8 of this Article have general validity within the Union. Those implementing acts shall be adopted in accordance with the examination procedure set out in Article 93(2).

10. The Commission shall ensure appropriate publicity for the approved codes which have been decided as having general validity in accordance with paragraph 9.

11. The Board shall collate all approved codes of conduct, amendments and extensions in a register and shall make them publicly available by way of appropriate means.

NOTES

This Article is amended by the Data Protection, Privacy and Electronic Communications (Amendments etc) (EU Exit) Regulations 2019, SI 2019/419, reg 3, Sch 1, paras 1, 34, as from exit day (as defined in the European Union (Withdrawal) Act 2018, s 20) and only in so far as this Regulation will apply in the UK after that date by virtue of s 3 of the 2018 Act, as follows (for transitional provisions etc, see the 2019 Regulations at **[2.2122]**)—

34.

(1) Article 40 is amended as follows.

(2) In paragraph 1, for "The Member States, the supervisory authorities, the Board and the Commission" substitute "The Commissioner".

(3) In paragraph 2(i), for "supervisory authorities" substitute "the Commissioner".

(4) In paragraph 3, omit "and having general validity pursuant to paragraph 9 of this Article".

(5) In paragraph 4, for "supervisory authorities competent pursuant to Article 55 or 56" substitute "the Commissioner".

(6) In paragraph 5—

(a) for "the supervisory authority which is competent pursuant to Article 55. The supervisory authority" substitute "the Commissioner, who";

(b) for "it finds" substitute "the Commissioner finds".

(7) In paragraph 6, for "and where the code of conduct concerned does not relate to processing activities in several Member States, the supervisory authority" substitute "the Commissioner".

(8) Omit paragraphs 7, 8, 9, 10 and 11.

[3.635]

Article 41

Monitoring of approved codes of conduct

1. Without prejudice to the tasks and powers of the competent supervisory authority under Articles 57 and 58, the monitoring of compliance with a code of conduct pursuant to Article 40 may be carried out by a body which has an appropriate level of expertise in relation to the subject-matter of the code and is accredited for that purpose by the competent supervisory authority.

2. A body as referred to in paragraph 1 may be accredited to monitor compliance with a code of conduct where that body has:

(a) demonstrated its independence and expertise in relation to the subject-matter of the code to the satisfaction of the competent supervisory authority;

(b) established procedures which allow it to assess the eligibility of controllers and processors concerned to apply the code, to monitor their compliance with its provisions and to periodically review its operation;

(c) established procedures and structures to handle complaints about infringements of the code or the manner in which the code has been, or is being, implemented by a controller or processor, and to make those procedures and structures transparent to data subjects and the public; and

(d) demonstrated to the satisfaction of the competent supervisory authority that its tasks and duties do not result in a conflict of interests.

3. The competent supervisory authority shall submit the draft requirements for accreditation of a body as referred to in paragraph 1 of this Article to the Board pursuant to the consistency mechanism referred to in Article 63.

4. Without prejudice to the tasks and powers of the competent supervisory authority and the provisions of Chapter VIII, a body as referred to in paragraph 1 of this Article shall, subject to appropriate safeguards, take appropriate action in cases of infringement of the code by a controller or processor, including suspension or exclusion of the controller or processor concerned from the code. It shall inform the competent supervisory authority of such actions and the reasons for taking them.

5. The competent supervisory authority shall revoke the accreditation of a body as referred to in paragraph 1 if the requirements for accreditation are not, or are no longer, met or where actions taken by the body infringe this Regulation.

6. This Article shall not apply to processing carried out by public authorities and bodies.

NOTES

This Article is amended by the Data Protection, Privacy and Electronic Communications (Amendments etc) (EU Exit) Regulations 2019, SI 2019/419, reg 3, Sch 1, paras 1, 35, as from exit day (as defined in the European Union (Withdrawal) Act 2018, s 20) and only in so far as this Regulation will apply in the UK after that date by virtue of s 3 of the 2018 Act, as follows (for transitional provisions etc, see the 2019 Regulations at **[2.2122]**)—

35. (1) Article 41 is amended as follows.

(2) In paragraph 1, for "the competent supervisory authority" (in both places) substitute "the Commissioner".

(3) In paragraph 2(a) and (d), for "the competent supervisory authority" substitute "the Commissioner".

(4) Omit paragraph 3.

(5) In paragraph 4, for "the competent supervisory authority" (in both places) substitute "the Commissioner".

(6) In paragraph 5, for "The competent supervisory authority" substitute "The Commissioner".

CHAPTER VI INDEPENDENT SUPERVISORY AUTHORITIES

NOTES

This heading is amended by the Data Protection, Privacy and Electronic Communications (Amendments etc) (EU Exit) Regulations 2019, SI 2019/419, reg 3, Sch 1, paras 1, 44, as from exit day (as defined in the European Union (Withdrawal) Act 2018, s 20) and only in so far as this Regulation will apply in the UK after that date by virtue of s 3 of the 2018 Act, as follows (for transitional provisions etc, see the 2019 Regulations at **[2.2122]**)—

44. For the heading of Chapter 6 substitute "The Commissioner".

SECTION 1 INDEPENDENT STATUS

[3.636]

Article 51 Supervisory authority

1. Each Member State shall provide for one or more independent public authorities to be responsible for monitoring the application of this Regulation, in order to protect the fundamental rights and freedoms of natural persons in relation to processing and to facilitate the free flow of personal data within the Union ('supervisory authority').

2. Each supervisory authority shall contribute to the consistent application of this Regulation throughout the Union. For that purpose, the supervisory authorities shall cooperate with each other and the Commission in accordance with Chapter VII.

3. Where more than one supervisory authority is established in a Member State, that Member State shall designate the supervisory authority which is to represent those authorities in the Board and shall set out the mechanism to ensure compliance by the other authorities with the rules relating to the consistency mechanism referred to in Article 63.

4. Each Member State shall notify to the Commission the provisions of its law which it adopts pursuant to this Chapter, by 25 May 2018 and, without delay, any subsequent amendment affecting them.

NOTES

This Article is amended by the Data Protection, Privacy and Electronic Communications (Amendments etc) (EU Exit) Regulations 2019, SI 2019/419, reg 3, Sch 1, paras 1, 45, as from exit day (as defined in the European Union (Withdrawal) Act 2018, s 20) and only in so far as this Regulation will apply in the UK after that date by virtue of s 3 of the 2018 Act, as follows (for transitional provisions etc, see the 2019 Regulations at **[2.2122]**)—

45.

(1) Article 51 is amended as follows.

(2) For the heading, substitute "Monitoring the application of this Regulation".

(3) In paragraph 1—

(a) for "Each Member State shall provide for one or more independent public authorities to be" substitute "The Commissioner is";

(b) omit "within the Union ("supervisory authority")".

(4) Omit paragraphs 2, 3 and 4.

[3.637]

Article 52

Independence

1. Each supervisory authority shall act with complete independence in performing its tasks and exercising its powers in accordance with this Regulation.

2. The member or members of each supervisory authority shall, in the performance of their tasks and exercise of their powers in accordance with this Regulation, remain free from external influence, whether direct or indirect, and shall neither seek nor take instructions from anybody.

3. Member or members of each supervisory authority shall refrain from any action incompatible with their duties and shall not, during their term of office, engage in any incompatible occupation, whether gainful or not.

4. Each Member State shall ensure that each supervisory authority is provided with the human, technical and financial resources, premises and infrastructure necessary for the effective performance of its tasks and exercise of its powers, including those to be carried out in the context of mutual assistance, cooperation and participation in the Board.

5. Each Member State shall ensure that each supervisory authority chooses and has its own staff which shall be subject to the exclusive direction of the member or members of the supervisory authority concerned.

6. Each Member State shall ensure that each supervisory authority is subject to financial control which does not affect its independence and that it has separate, public annual budgets, which may be part of the overall state or national budget.

NOTES

This Article is amended by the Data Protection, Privacy and Electronic Communications (Amendments etc) (EU Exit) Regulations 2019, SI 2019/419, reg 3, Sch 1, paras 1, 46, as from exit day (as defined in the European Union (Withdrawal) Act 2018, s 20) and only in so far as this Regulation will apply in the UK after that date by virtue of s 3 of the 2018 Act, as follows (for transitional provisions etc, see the 2019 Regulations at **[2.2122]**)—

46.

(1) Article 52 is amended as follows.

(2) In paragraph 1—

(a) for "Each supervisory authority" substitute "The Commissioner";

(b) omit "its" (in both places).

(3) In paragraph 2—

(a) for "The member or members of each supervisory authority" substitute "The Commissioner";

(b) omit "their" (in both places).

(4) In paragraph 3—

(a) for "Member or members of each supervisory authority" substitute "The Commissioner";

(b) for "their duties" substitute "the Commissioner's duties";

(c) for "during their term of office" substitute "while holding office".

(5) Omit paragraphs 4, 5 and 6.

[3.638]

Article 53

General conditions for the members of the supervisory authority

1. Member States shall provide for each member of their supervisory authorities to be appointed by means of a transparent procedure by:

— their parliament;

— their government;

— their head of State; or

— an independent body entrusted with the appointment under Member State law.

2. Each member shall have the qualifications, experience and skills, in particular in the area of the protection of personal data, required to perform its duties and exercise its powers.

3. The duties of a member shall end in the event of the expiry of the term of office, resignation or compulsory retirement, in accordance with the law of the Member State concerned.

4. A member shall be dismissed only in cases of serious misconduct or if the member no longer fulfils the conditions required for the performance of the duties.

NOTES

This Article is repealed by the Data Protection, Privacy and Electronic Communications (Amendments etc) (EU Exit) Regulations 2019, SI 2019/419, reg 3, Sch 1, paras 1, 47, as from exit day (as defined in the European Union (Withdrawal) Act 2018, s 20) and only in so far as this Regulation will apply in the UK after that date by virtue of s 3 of the 2018 Act, as follows (for transitional provisions etc, see the 2019 Regulations at **[2.2122]**).

[3.639]

Article 54

Rules on the establishment of the supervisory authority

1. Each Member State shall provide by law for all of the following:

(a) the establishment of each supervisory authority;

(b) the qualifications and eligibility conditions required to be appointed as member of each supervisory authority;

(c) the rules and procedures for the appointment of the member or members of each supervisory authority;

(d) the duration of the term of the member or members of each supervisory authority of no less than four years, except for the first appointment after 24 May 2016, part of which may take place for a shorter period where that is necessary to protect the independence of the supervisory authority by means of a staggered appointment procedure;

(e) whether and, if so, for how many terms the member or members of each supervisory authority is eligible for reappointment;

(f) the conditions governing the obligations of the member or members and staff of each supervisory authority, prohibitions on actions, occupations and benefits incompatible therewith during and after the term of office and rules governing the cessation of employment.

2. The member or members and the staff of each supervisory authority shall, in accordance with Union or Member State law, be subject to a duty of professional secrecy both during and after their term of office, with regard to any confidential information which has come to their knowledge in the course of the performance of their tasks or exercise of their powers. During their term of office, that duty of professional secrecy shall in particular apply to reporting by natural persons of infringements of this Regulation.

NOTES

This Article is repealed by the Data Protection, Privacy and Electronic Communications (Amendments etc) (EU Exit) Regulations 2019, SI 2019/419, reg 3, Sch 1, paras 1, 48, as from exit day (as defined in the European Union (Withdrawal) Act 2018, s 20) and only in so far as this Regulation will apply in the UK after that date by virtue of s 3 of the 2018 Act, as follows (for transitional provisions etc, see the 2019 Regulations at **[2.2122]**).

SECTION 2 COMPETENCE, TASKS AND POWERS

NOTES

This heading is amended by the Data Protection, Privacy and Electronic Communications (Amendments etc) (EU Exit) Regulations 2019, SI 2019/419, reg 3, Sch 1, paras 1, 49, as from exit day (as defined in the European Union (Withdrawal) Act 2018, s 20) and only in so far as this Regulation will apply in the UK after that date by virtue of s 3 of the 2018 Act, as follows (for transitional provisions etc, see the 2019 Regulations at **[2.2122]**)—

49.

In the heading of section 2 of Chapter 6, for "Competence, tasks" substitute "Tasks".

[3.640]

Article 55 Competence

1. Each supervisory authority shall be competent for the performance of the tasks assigned to and the exercise of the powers conferred on it in accordance with this Regulation on the territory of its own Member State.

2. Where processing is carried out by public authorities or private bodies acting on the basis of point (c) or (e) of Article 6(1), the supervisory authority of the Member State concerned shall be competent. In such cases Article 56 does not apply.

3. Supervisory authorities shall not be competent to supervise processing operations of courts acting in their judicial capacity.

NOTES

This Article is repealed by the Data Protection, Privacy and Electronic Communications (Amendments etc) (EU Exit) Regulations 2019, SI 2019/419, reg 3, Sch 1, paras 1, 50, as from exit day (as defined in the European Union (Withdrawal) Act 2018, s 20) and only in so far as this Regulation will apply in the UK after that date by virtue of s 3 of the 2018 Act, as follows (for transitional provisions etc, see the 2019 Regulations at **[2.2122]**).

[3.641]

Article 56

Competence of the lead supervisory authority

1. Without prejudice to Article 55, the supervisory authority of the main establishment or of the single establishment of the controller or processor shall be competent to act as lead supervisory authority for the cross-border processing carried out by that controller or processor in accordance with the procedure provided in Article 60.

2. By derogation from paragraph 1, each supervisory authority shall be competent to handle a complaint lodged with it or a possible infringement of this Regulation, if the subject matter relates only to an establishment in its Member State or substantially affects data subjects only in its Member State.

3. In the cases referred to in paragraph 2 of this Article, the supervisory authority shall inform the lead supervisory authority without delay on that matter. Within a period of three weeks after being informed the lead supervisory authority shall decide whether or not it will handle the case in accordance with the procedure provided in Article 60, taking into account whether or not there is an establishment of the controller or processor in the Member State of which the supervisory authority informed it.

4. Where the lead supervisory authority decides to handle the case, the procedure provided in Article 60 shall apply. The supervisory authority which informed the lead supervisory authority may submit to the lead supervisory authority a draft for a decision. The lead supervisory authority shall take utmost account of that draft when preparing the draft decision referred to in Article 60(3).

5. Where the lead supervisory authority decides not to handle the case, the supervisory authority which informed the lead supervisory authority shall handle it according to Articles 61 and 62.

6. The lead supervisory authority shall be the sole interlocutor of the controller or processor for the cross-border processing carried out by that controller or processor.

NOTES

This Article is repealed by the Data Protection, Privacy and Electronic Communications (Amendments etc) (EU Exit) Regulations 2019, SI 2019/419, reg 3, Sch 1, paras 1, 51, as from exit day (as defined in the European Union (Withdrawal) Act 2018, s 20) and only in so far as this Regulation will apply in the UK after that date by virtue of s 3 of the 2018 Act, as follows (for transitional provisions etc, see the 2019 Regulations at **[2.2122]**).

[3.642]
Article 57
Tasks

1. Without prejudice to other tasks set out under this Regulation, each supervisory authority shall on its territory:

(a) monitor and enforce the application of this Regulation;
(b) promote public awareness and understanding of the risks, rules, safeguards and rights in relation to processing. Activities addressed specifically to children shall receive specific attention;
(c) advise, in accordance with Member State law, the national parliament, the government, and other institutions and bodies on legislative and administrative measures relating to the protection of natural persons' rights and freedoms with regard to processing;
(d) promote the awareness of controllers and processors of their obligations under this Regulation;
(e) upon request, provide information to any data subject concerning the exercise of their rights under this Regulation and, if appropriate, cooperate with the supervisory authorities in other Member States to that end;
(f) handle complaints lodged by a data subject, or by a body, organisation or association in accordance with Article 80, and investigate, to the extent appropriate, the subject matter of the complaint and inform the complainant of the progress and the outcome of the investigation within a reasonable period, in particular if further investigation or coordination with another supervisory authority is necessary;
(g) cooperate with, including sharing information and provide mutual assistance to, other supervisory authorities with a view to ensuring the consistency of application and enforcement of this Regulation;
(h) conduct investigations on the application of this Regulation, including on the basis of information received from another supervisory authority or other public authority;
(i) monitor relevant developments, insofar as they have an impact on the protection of personal data, in particular the development of information and communication technologies and commercial practices;
(j) adopt standard contractual clauses referred to in Article 28(8) and in point (d) of Article 46(2);
(k) establish and maintain a list in relation to the requirement for data protection impact assessment pursuant to Article 35(4);
(l) give advice on the processing operations referred to in Article 36(2);
(m) encourage the drawing up of codes of conduct pursuant to Article 40(1) and provide an opinion and approve such codes of conduct which provide sufficient safeguards, pursuant to Article 40(5);
(n) encourage the establishment of data protection certification mechanisms and of data protection seals and marks pursuant to Article 42(1), and approve the criteria of certification pursuant to Article 42(5);
(o) where applicable, carry out a periodic review of certifications issued in accordance with Article 42(7);
(p) draft and publish the requirements for accreditation of a body for monitoring codes of conduct pursuant to Article 41 and of a certification body pursuant to Article 43;
(q) conduct the accreditation of a body for monitoring codes of conduct pursuant to Article 41 and of a certification body pursuant to Article 43;
(r) authorise contractual clauses and provisions referred to in Article 46(3);
(s) approve binding corporate rules pursuant to Article 47;
(t) contribute to the activities of the Board;
(u) keep internal records of infringements of this Regulation and of measures taken in accordance with Article 58(2); and
(v) fulfil any other tasks related to the protection of personal data.

2. Each supervisory authority shall facilitate the submission of complaints referred to in point (f) of paragraph 1 by measures such as a complaint submission form which can also be completed electronically, without excluding other means of communication.

3. The performance of the tasks of each supervisory authority shall be free of charge for the data subject and, where applicable, for the data protection officer.

4. Where requests are manifestly unfounded or excessive, in particular because of their repetitive character, the supervisory authority may charge a reasonable fee based on administrative costs, or refuse to act on the request. The supervisory authority shall bear the burden of demonstrating the manifestly unfounded or excessive character of the request.

NOTES

This Article is amended by the Data Protection, Privacy and Electronic Communications (Amendments etc) (EU Exit) Regulations 2019, SI 2019/419, reg 3, Sch 1, paras 1, 52, as from exit day (as defined in the European Union (Withdrawal) Act 2018, s 20) and only in so far as this Regulation will apply in the UK after that date by virtue of s 3 of the 2018 Act, as follows

(for transitional provisions etc, see the 2019 Regulations at **[2.2122]**)—

52.

(1) Article 57 is amended as follows.

(2) In paragraph 1—

(a) for "each supervisory authority shall on its territory" substitute "the Commissioner must";

(b) in point (c), for ", in accordance with Member State law, the national parliament" substitute "Parliament";

(c) in point (e), for "the supervisory authorities in other Member States" substitute "foreign designated authorities";

(d) in point (f), for "another supervisory authority" substitute "a foreign designated authority";

(e) omit point (g);

(f) in point (h), for "another supervisory authority" substitute "a foreign designated authority";

(g) in point (j), after "and" insert "issue standard data protection clauses referred to";

(h) after point (o) insert—

"(oa) maintain a public register of certification mechanisms and data protection seals and marks pursuant to Article 42(8) and of controllers or processors established in third countries and certified pursuant to Article 42(7);";

(i) omit point (t).

(3) In paragraph 2, for "Each supervisory authority" substitute "The Commissioner".

(4) In paragraph 3, for "the tasks of each supervisory authority shall be" substitute "the Commissioner's tasks is to be".

(5) In paragraph 4, for "supervisory authority" (in both places) substitute "Commissioner".

[3.643]

Article 58
Powers

1. Each supervisory authority shall have all of the following investigative powers:

(a) to order the controller and the processor, and, where applicable, the controller's or the processor's representative to provide any information it requires for the performance of its tasks;

(b) to carry out investigations in the form of data protection audits;

(c) to carry out a review on certifications issued pursuant to Article 42(7);

(d) to notify the controller or the processor of an alleged infringement of this Regulation;

(e) to obtain, from the controller and the processor, access to all personal data and to all information necessary for the performance of its tasks;

(f) to obtain access to any premises of the controller and the processor, including to any data processing equipment and means, in accordance with Union or Member State procedural law.

2. Each supervisory authority shall have all of the following corrective powers:

(a) to issue warnings to a controller or processor that intended processing operations are likely to infringe provisions of this Regulation;

(b) to issue reprimands to a controller or a processor where processing operations have infringed provisions of this Regulation;

(c) to order the controller or the processor to comply with the data subject's requests to exercise his or her rights pursuant to this Regulation;

(d) to order the controller or processor to bring processing operations into compliance with the provisions of this Regulation, where appropriate, in a specified manner and within a specified period;

(e) to order the controller to communicate a personal data breach to the data subject;

(f) to impose a temporary or definitive limitation including a ban on processing;

(g) to order the rectification or erasure of personal data or restriction of processing pursuant to Articles 16, 17 and 18 and the notification of such actions to recipients to whom the personal data have been disclosed pursuant to Article 17(2) and Article 19;

(h) to withdraw a certification or to order the certification body to withdraw a certification issued pursuant to Articles 42 and 43, or to order the certification body not to issue certification if the requirements for the certification are not or are no longer met;

(i) to impose an administrative fine pursuant to Article 83, in addition to, or instead of measures referred to in this paragraph, depending on the circumstances of each individual case;

(j) to order the suspension of data flows to a recipient in a third country or to an international organisation.

3. Each supervisory authority shall have all of the following authorisation and advisory powers:

(a) to advise the controller in accordance with the prior consultation procedure referred to in Article 36;

(b) to issue, on its own initiative or on request, opinions to the national parliament, the Member State government or, in accordance with Member State law, to other institutions and bodies as well as to the public on any issue related to the protection of personal data;

(c) to authorise processing referred to in Article 36(5), if the law of the Member State requires such prior authorisation;

(d) to issue an opinion and approve draft codes of conduct pursuant to Article 40(5);

(e) to accredit certification bodies pursuant to Article 43;

(f) to issue certifications and approve criteria of certification in accordance with Article 42(5);

(g) to adopt standard data protection clauses referred to in Article 28(8) and in point (d) of Article 46(2);

(h) to authorise contractual clauses referred to in point (a) of Article 46(3);

(i) to authorise administrative arrangements referred to in point (b) of Article 46(3);

(j) to approve binding corporate rules pursuant to Article 47.

4. The exercise of the powers conferred on the supervisory authority pursuant to this Article shall be subject to appropriate safeguards, including effective judicial remedy and due process, set out in Union and Member State law in accordance with the Charter.

5. Each Member State shall provide by law that its supervisory authority shall have the power to bring infringements of this Regulation to the attention of the judicial authorities and where appropriate, to commence or engage otherwise in legal proceedings, in order to enforce the provisions of this Regulation.

6. Each Member State may provide by law that its supervisory authority shall have additional powers to those referred to in paragraphs 1, 2 and 3. The exercise of those powers shall not impair the effective operation of Chapter VII.

NOTES

This Article is amended by the Data Protection, Privacy and Electronic Communications (Amendments etc) (EU Exit) Regulations 2019, SI 2019/419, reg 3, Sch 1, paras 1, 53, as from exit day (as defined in the European Union (Withdrawal) Act 2018, s 20) and only in so far as this Regulation will apply in the UK after that date by virtue of s 3 of the 2018 Act, as follows (for transitional provisions etc, see the 2019 Regulations at **[2.2122]**)—

53. (1) Article 58 is amended as follows.

(2) In paragraph 1—

(a) for "Each supervisory authority shall have" substitute "The Commissioner has";

(b) in point (e), for "its" substitute "the Commissioner's";

(c) in point (f), for "Union or Member State procedural law" substitute "domestic law".

(3) In paragraph 2, for "Each supervisory authority shall have" substitute "The Commissioner has".

(4) In paragraph 3—

(a) for "Each supervisory authority shall have" substitute "The Commissioner has";

(b) in point (b)—

(i) for "its" substitute "the Commissioner's";

(ii) for "the national parliament, the Member State government or, in accordance with Member State law, to" substitute "Parliament, the government or";

(c) omit point (c)

(5) After paragraph 3 insert—

"3A. In the 2018 Act, section 115(4) to (9) provide that the Commissioner's functions under this Article are subject to certain safeguards.".

(6) Omit paragraphs 4, 5 and 6.

[3.644]

Article 59

Activity reports

Each supervisory authority shall draw up an annual report on its activities, which may include a list of types of infringement notified and types of measures taken in accordance with Article 58(2). Those reports shall be transmitted to the national parliament, the government and other authorities as designated by Member State law. They shall be made available to the public, to the Commission and to the Board.

NOTES

This Article is amended by the Data Protection, Privacy and Electronic Communications (Amendments etc) (EU Exit) Regulations 2019, SI 2019/419, reg 3, Sch 1, paras 1, 54, as from exit day (as defined in the European Union (Withdrawal) Act 2018, s 20) and only in so far as this Regulation will apply in the UK after that date by virtue of s 3 of the 2018 Act, as follows (for transitional provisions etc, see the 2019 Regulations at **[2.2122]**)—

54.

In Article 59—

(a) for "Each supervisory authority" substitute "The Commissioner";

(b) for "its" substitute "the Commissioner's";

(c) for the second sentence substitute "The Commissioner must arrange for those reports to be laid before Parliament and send a copy to the Secretary of State.";

(d) omit ", to the Commission and to the Board".

CHAPTER VIII REMEDIES, LIABILITY AND PENALTIES

[3.645]

Article 77

Right to lodge a complaint with a supervisory authority

1. Without prejudice to any other administrative or judicial remedy, every data subject shall have the right to lodge a complaint with a supervisory authority, in particular in the Member State of his or her habitual residence, place of work or place of the alleged infringement if the data subject considers that the processing of personal data relating to him or her infringes this Regulation.

2. The supervisory authority with which the complaint has been lodged shall inform the complainant on the progress and the outcome of the complaint including the possibility of a judicial remedy pursuant to Article 78.

NOTES

This Article is amended by the Data Protection, Privacy and Electronic Communications (Amendments etc) (EU Exit) Regulations 2019, SI 2019/419, reg 3, Sch 1, paras 1, 56, as from exit day (as defined in the European Union (Withdrawal) Act 2018, s 20) and only in so far as this Regulation will apply in the UK after that date by virtue of s 3 of the 2018 Act, as follows

(for transitional provisions etc, see the 2019 Regulations at **[2.2122]**)—

56.

(1) Article 77 is amended as follows.

(2) In the heading, for "a supervisory authority" substitute "the Commissioner".

(3) In paragraph 1, for "a supervisory authority, in particular in the Member State of his or her habitual residence, place of work or place of the alleged infringement" substitute "the Commissioner".

(4) In paragraph 2, for "The supervisory authority with which the complaint has been lodged" substitute "The Commissioner".

[3.646]

Article 78

Right to an effective judicial remedy against a supervisory authority

1. Without prejudice to any other administrative or non-judicial remedy, each natural or legal person shall have the right to an effective judicial remedy against a legally binding decision of a supervisory authority concerning them.

2. Without prejudice to any other administrative or non-judicial remedy, each data subject shall have the right to a an effective judicial remedy where the supervisory authority which is competent pursuant to Articles 55 and 56 does not handle a complaint or does not inform the data subject within three months on the progress or outcome of the complaint lodged pursuant to Article 77.

3. Proceedings against a supervisory authority shall be brought before the courts of the Member State where the supervisory authority is established.

4. Where proceedings are brought against a decision of a supervisory authority which was preceded by an opinion or a decision of the Board in the consistency mechanism, the supervisory authority shall forward that opinion or decision to the court.

NOTES

This Article is amended by the Data Protection, Privacy and Electronic Communications (Amendments etc) (EU Exit) Regulations 2019, SI 2019/419, reg 3, Sch 1, paras 1, 57, as from exit day (as defined in the European Union (Withdrawal) Act 2018, s 20) and only in so far as this Regulation will apply in the UK after that date by virtue of s 3 of the 2018 Act, as follows (for transitional provisions etc, see the 2019 Regulations at **[2.2122]**)—

57.

(1) Article 78 is amended as follows.

(2) In the heading, for "a supervisory authority" substitute "the Commissioner".

(3) In paragraph 1, for "a supervisory authority" substitute "the Commissioner".

(4) In paragraph 2, for "the supervisory authority which is competent pursuant to Articles 55 and 56" substitute "the Commissioner".

(5) Omit paragraph 3.

(6) Omit paragraph 4.

[3.647]

Article 79

Right to an effective judicial remedy against a controller or processor

1. Without prejudice to any available administrative or non-judicial remedy, including the right to lodge a complaint with a supervisory authority pursuant to Article 77, each data subject shall have the right to an effective judicial remedy where he or she considers that his or her rights under this Regulation have been infringed as a result of the processing of his or her personal data in non-compliance with this Regulation.

2. Proceedings against a controller or a processor shall be brought before the courts of the Member State where the controller or processor has an establishment. Alternatively, such proceedings may be brought before the courts of the Member State where the data subject has his or her habitual residence, unless the controller or processor is a public authority of a Member State acting in the exercise of its public powers.

NOTES

This Article is amended by the Data Protection, Privacy and Electronic Communications (Amendments etc) (EU Exit) Regulations 2019, SI 2019/419, reg 3, Sch 1, paras 1, 58, as from exit day (as defined in the European Union (Withdrawal) Act 2018, s 20) and only in so far as this Regulation will apply in the UK after that date by virtue of s 3 of the 2018 Act, as follows (for transitional provisions etc, see the 2019 Regulations at **[2.2122]**)—

58.

(1) Article 79 is amended as follows.

(2) In paragraph 1, for "a supervisory authority" substitute "the Commissioner".

(3) Omit paragraph 2.

[3.648]

Article 80

Representation of data subjects

1. The data subject shall have the right to mandate a not-for-profit body, organisation or association which has been properly constituted in accordance with the law of a Member State, has statutory objectives which are in the public interest, and is active in the field of the protection of data subjects'

rights and freedoms with regard to the protection of their personal data to lodge the complaint on his or her behalf, to exercise the rights referred to in Articles 77, 78 and 79 on his or her behalf, and to exercise the right to receive compensation referred to in Article 82 on his or her behalf where provided for by Member State law.

2. Member States may provide that any body, organisation or association referred to in paragraph 1 of this Article, independently of a data subject's mandate, has the right to lodge, in that Member State, a complaint with the supervisory authority which is competent pursuant to Article 77 and to exercise the rights referred to in Articles 78 and 79 if it considers that the rights of a data subject under this Regulation have been infringed as a result of the processing.

NOTES

This Article is amended by the Data Protection, Privacy and Electronic Communications (Amendments etc) (EU Exit) Regulations 2019, SI 2019/419, reg 3, Sch 1, paras 1, 59, as from exit day (as defined in the European Union (Withdrawal) Act 2018, s 20) and only in so far as this Regulation will apply in the UK after that date by virtue of s 3 of the 2018 Act, as follows (for transitional provisions etc, see the 2019 Regulations at **[2.2122]**)—

59. (1) Article 80 is amended as follows.

(2) In paragraph 1—

(a) for the words from "a not-for profit" to "their personal data" substitute "a body or other organisation which meets the conditions in section 187(3) and (4) of the 2018 Act";

(b) omit "where provided for by Member State law".

(3) In paragraph 2—

(a) for "Member States" substitute "The Secretary of State";

(b) omit ", in that Member State,";

(c) for "the supervisory authority which is competent pursuant to Article 77" substitute "the Commissioner".

(4) After that paragraph insert—

"3. The Secretary of State may exercise the power under paragraph 2 of this Article only by making regulations under section 190 of the 2018 Act.".

[3.649]
Article 81
Suspension of proceedings

1. Where a competent court of a Member State has information on proceedings, concerning the same subject matter as regards processing by the same controller or processor, that are pending in a court in another Member State, it shall contact that court in the other Member State to confirm the existence of such proceedings.

2. Where proceedings concerning the same subject matter as regards processing of the same controller or processor are pending in a court in another Member State, any competent court other than the court first seized may suspend its proceedings.

3. Where those proceedings are pending at first instance, any court other than the court first seized may also, on the application of one of the parties, decline jurisdiction if the court first seized has jurisdiction over the actions in question and its law permits the consolidation thereof.

NOTES

This Article is repealed by the Data Protection, Privacy and Electronic Communications (Amendments etc) (EU Exit) Regulations 2019, SI 2019/419, reg 3, Sch 1, paras 1, 60, as from exit day (as defined in the European Union (Withdrawal) Act 2018, s 20) and only in so far as this Regulation will apply in the UK after that date by virtue of s 3 of the 2018 Act (for transitional provisions etc, see the 2019 Regulations at **[2.2122]**).

[3.650]
Article 82
Right to compensation and liability

1. Any person who has suffered material or non-material damage as a result of an infringement of this Regulation shall have the right to receive compensation from the controller or processor for the damage suffered.

2. Any controller involved in processing shall be liable for the damage caused by processing which infringes this Regulation. A processor shall be liable for the damage caused by processing only where it has not complied with obligations of this Regulation specifically directed to processors or where it has acted outside or contrary to lawful instructions of the controller.

3. A controller or processor shall be exempt from liability under paragraph 2 if it proves that it is not in any way responsible for the event giving rise to the damage.

4. Where more than one controller or processor, or both a controller and a processor, are involved in the same processing and where they are, under paragraphs 2 and 3, responsible for any damage caused by processing, each controller or processor shall be held liable for the entire damage in order to ensure effective compensation of the data subject.

5. Where a controller or processor has, in accordance with paragraph 4, paid full compensation for the damage suffered, that controller or processor shall be entitled to claim back from the other controllers or processors involved in the same processing that part of the compensation corresponding to their part of responsibility for the damage, in accordance with the conditions set out in paragraph 2.

6. Court proceedings for exercising the right to receive compensation shall be brought before the courts competent under the law of the Member State referred to in Article 79(2).

NOTES

This Article is amended by the Data Protection, Privacy and Electronic Communications (Amendments etc) (EU Exit) Regulations 2019, SI 2019/419, reg 3, Sch 1, paras 1, 61, as from exit day (as defined in the European Union (Withdrawal) Act 2018, s 20) and only in so far as this Regulation will apply in the UK after that date by virtue of s 3 of the 2018 Act, as follows (for transitional provisions etc, see the 2019 Regulations at **[2.2122]**)—

61.

In Article 82, omit paragraph 6.

[3.651]

Article 83

General conditions for imposing administrative fines

1. Each supervisory authority shall ensure that the imposition of administrative fines pursuant to this Article in respect of infringements of this Regulation referred to in paragraphs 4, 5 and 6 shall in each individual case be effective, proportionate and dissuasive.

2. Administrative fines shall, depending on the circumstances of each individual case, be imposed in addition to, or instead of, measures referred to in points (a) to (h) and (j) of Article 58(2). When deciding whether to impose an administrative fine and deciding on the amount of the administrative fine in each individual case due regard shall be given to the following:

(a) the nature, gravity and duration of the infringement taking into account the nature scope or purpose of the processing concerned as well as the number of data subjects affected and the level of damage suffered by them;

(b) the intentional or negligent character of the infringement;

(c) any action taken by the controller or processor to mitigate the damage suffered by data subjects;

(d) the degree of responsibility of the controller or processor taking into account technical and organisational measures implemented by them pursuant to Articles 25 and 32;

(e) any relevant previous infringements by the controller or processor;

(f) the degree of cooperation with the supervisory authority, in order to remedy the infringement and mitigate the possible adverse effects of the infringement;

(g) the categories of personal data affected by the infringement;

(h) the manner in which the infringement became known to the supervisory authority, in particular whether, and if so to what extent, the controller or processor notified the infringement;

(i) where measures referred to in Article 58(2) have previously been ordered against the controller or processor concerned with regard to the same subject-matter, compliance with those measures;

(j) adherence to approved codes of conduct pursuant to Article 40 or approved certification mechanisms pursuant to Article 42; and

(k) any other aggravating or mitigating factor applicable to the circumstances of the case, such as financial benefits gained, or losses avoided, directly or indirectly, from the infringement.

3. If a controller or processor intentionally or negligently, for the same or linked processing operations, infringes several provisions of this Regulation, the total amount of the administrative fine shall not exceed the amount specified for the gravest infringement.

4. Infringements of the following provisions shall, in accordance with paragraph 2, be subject to administrative fines up to 10,000,000 EUR, or in the case of an undertaking, up to 2% of the total worldwide annual turnover of the preceding financial year, whichever is higher:

(a) the obligations of the controller and the processor pursuant to Articles 8, 11, 25 to 39 and 42 and 43;

(b) the obligations of the certification body pursuant to Articles 42 and 43;

(c) the obligations of the monitoring body pursuant to Article 41(4).

5. Infringements of the following provisions shall, in accordance with paragraph 2, be subject to administrative fines up to 20,000,000 EUR, or in the case of an undertaking, up to 4% of the total worldwide annual turnover of the preceding financial year, whichever is higher:

(a) the basic principles for processing, including conditions for consent, pursuant to Articles 5, 6, 7 and 9;

(b) the data subjects' rights pursuant to Articles 12 to 22;

(c) the transfers of personal data to a recipient in a third country or an international organisation pursuant to Articles 44 to 49;

(d) any obligations pursuant to Member State law adopted under Chapter IX;

(e) non-compliance with an order or a temporary or definitive limitation on processing or the suspension of data flows by the supervisory authority pursuant to Article 58(2) or failure to provide access in violation of Article 58(1).

6. Non-compliance with an order by the supervisory authority as referred to in Article 58(2) shall, in accordance with paragraph 2 of this Article, be subject to administrative fines up to 20,000,000 EUR, or in the case of an undertaking, up to 4% of the total worldwide annual turnover of the preceding financial year, whichever is higher.

7. Without prejudice to the corrective powers of supervisory authorities pursuant to Article 58(2), each Member State may lay down the rules on whether and to what extent administrative fines may be imposed on public authorities and bodies established in that Member State.

8. The exercise by the supervisory authority of its powers under this Article shall be subject to appropriate procedural safeguards in accordance with Union and Member State law, including effective judicial remedy and due process.

9. Where the legal system of the Member State does not provide for administrative fines, this Article may be applied in such a manner that the fine is initiated by the competent supervisory authority and imposed by competent national courts, while ensuring that those legal remedies are effective and have an equivalent effect to the administrative fines imposed by supervisory authorities. In any event, the fines imposed shall be effective, proportionate and dissuasive. Those Member States shall notify to the Commission the provisions of their laws which they adopt pursuant to this paragraph by 25 May 2018 and, without delay, any subsequent amendment law or amendment affecting them.

NOTES

This Article is amended by the Data Protection, Privacy and Electronic Communications (Amendments etc) (EU Exit) Regulations 2019, SI 2019/419, reg 3, Sch 1, paras 1, 62, as from exit day (as defined in the European Union (Withdrawal) Act 2018, s 20) and only in so far as this Regulation will apply in the UK after that date by virtue of s 3 of the 2018 Act, as follows (for transitional provisions etc, see the 2019 Regulations at **[2.2122]**)—

62. (1) Article 83 is amended as follows.

(2) In paragraph 1, for "Each supervisory authority" substitute "The Commissioner".

(3) In paragraph 2—

(a) in point (f), for "the supervisory authority" substitute "the Commissioner";

(b) in point (h), for "the supervisory authority" substitute "the Commissioner".

(4) In paragraph 4, for "10 000 000 EUR" substitute "£8,700,000".

(5) In paragraph 5—

(a) for "20 000 000 EUR" substitute "£17,500,000";

(b) for point (d) substitute—

"(d) any obligations under Part 5 or 6 of Schedule 2 to the 2018 Act or regulations made under section 16(1)(c) of the 2018 Act;";

(c) in point (e), for "the supervisory authority" substitute "the Commissioner".

(6) In paragraph 6—

(a) for "the supervisory authority" substitute "the Commissioner";

(b) for "20 000 000 EUR" substitute "£17,500,000".

(7) Omit paragraphs 7, 8 and 9.

(8) After paragraph 9 insert—

"10. In the 2018 Act, section 115(9) makes provision about the exercise of the Commissioner's functions under this Article.".

[3.652]
Article 84
Penalties

1. Member States shall lay down the rules on other penalties applicable to infringements of this Regulation in particular for infringements which are not subject to administrative fines pursuant to Article 83, and shall take all measures necessary to ensure that they are implemented. Such penalties shall be effective, proportionate and dissuasive.

2. Each Member State shall notify to the Commission the provisions of its law which it adopts pursuant to paragraph 1, by 25 May 2018 and, without delay, any subsequent amendment affecting them.

NOTES

This Article is amended by the Data Protection, Privacy and Electronic Communications (Amendments etc) (EU Exit) Regulations 2019, SI 2019/419, reg 3, Sch 1, paras 1, 63, as from exit day (as defined in the European Union (Withdrawal) Act 2018, s 20) and only in so far as this Regulation will apply in the UK after that date by virtue of s 3 of the 2018 Act, as follows (for transitional provisions etc, see the 2019 Regulations at **[2.2122]**)—

63.
In Article 84, for paragraphs 1 and 2 substitute—

"Part 6 of the 2018 Act makes further provision about penalties applicable to infringements of this Regulation.".

CHAPTER IX PROVISIONS RELATING TO SPECIFIC PROCESSING SITUATIONS

[3.653]
Article 85
Processing and freedom of expression and information

1. Member States shall by law reconcile the right to the protection of personal data pursuant to this Regulation with the right to freedom of expression and information, including processing for journalistic purposes and the purposes of academic, artistic or literary expression.

2. For processing carried out for journalistic purposes or the purpose of academic artistic or literary expression, Member States shall provide for exemptions or derogations from Chapter II (principles), Chapter III (rights of the data subject), Chapter IV (controller and processor), Chapter V (transfer of personal data to third countries or international organisations), Chapter VI (independent supervisory authorities), Chapter VII (cooperation and consistency) and Chapter IX (specific data processing situations) if they are necessary to reconcile the right to the protection of personal data with the freedom of expression and information.

3. Each Member State shall notify to the Commission the provisions of its law which it has adopted pursuant to paragraph 2 and, without delay, any subsequent amendment law or amendment affecting them.

NOTES

This Article is amended by the Data Protection, Privacy and Electronic Communications (Amendments etc) (EU Exit) Regulations 2019, SI 2019/419, reg 3, Sch 1, paras 1, 64, as from exit day (as defined in the European Union (Withdrawal) Act 2018, s 20) and only in so far as this Regulation will apply in the UK after that date by virtue of s 3 of the 2018 Act, as follows (for transitional provisions etc, see the 2019 Regulations at **[2.2122]**)—

64.

(1) Article 85 is amended as follows.

(2) Omit paragraph 1.

(3) In paragraph 2—

(a) for "Members States shall" substitute "the Secretary of State may";

(b) for "independent supervisory authorities" substitute "the Commissioner";

(c) omit ", Chapter VII (cooperation and consistency)".

(4) After that paragraph insert—

"2A. The Secretary of State may exercise the power under paragraph 2 of this Article only by making regulations under section 16 of the 2018 Act.".

(5) Omit paragraph 3.

[3.654]
Article 86
Processing and public access to official documents

Personal data in official documents held by a public authority or a public body or a private body for the performance of a task carried out in the public interest may be disclosed by the authority or body in accordance with Union or Member State law to which the public authority or body is subject in order to reconcile public access to official documents with the right to the protection of personal data pursuant to this Regulation.

NOTES

This Article is amended by the Data Protection, Privacy and Electronic Communications (Amendments etc) (EU Exit) Regulations 2019, SI 2019/419, reg 3, Sch 1, paras 1, 65, as from exit day (as defined in the European Union (Withdrawal) Act 2018, s 20) and only in so far as this Regulation will apply in the UK after that date by virtue of s 3 of the 2018 Act, as follows (for transitional provisions etc, see the 2019 Regulations at **[2.2122]**)—

65.

(1) Article 86 is amended as follows.

(2) The existing text becomes paragraph 1.

(3) In that paragraph, for "Union or Member State law" substitute "domestic law".

(4) After that paragraph insert—

"2. Chapter 3 of Part 2 of the 2018 Act makes provision about the application of this Regulation to the manual unstructured processing of personal data held by an FOI public authority (as defined in Article 2).".

Note also that the following Article is added by para 66 of Sch 1 to the 2019 Regulations (as from the same date and subject to the same transitional provisions as noted above)—

66. After Article 86 insert—

"86A Processing and national security and defence

Chapter 3 of Part 2 of the 2018 Act makes provision about the application of this Regulation where processing is carried out, or exemption from a provision of this Regulation is required, for the purposes of safeguarding national security or for defence purposes.".

[3.655]
Article 87
Processing of the national identification number

Member States may further determine the specific conditions for the processing of a national identification number or any other identifier of general application. In that case the national identification number or any other identifier of general application shall be used only under appropriate safeguards for the rights and freedoms of the data subject pursuant to this Regulation.

NOTES

This Article is repealed by the Data Protection, Privacy and Electronic Communications (Amendments etc) (EU Exit) Regulations 2019, SI 2019/419, reg 3, Sch 1, paras 1, 67, as from exit day (as defined in the European Union (Withdrawal) Act 2018, s 20) and only in so far as this Regulation will apply in the UK after that date by virtue of s 3 of the 2018 Act (for transitional provisions etc, see the 2019 Regulations at **[2.2122]**).

[3.656]
Article 88
Processing in the context of employment

1. Member States may, by law or by collective agreements, provide for more specific rules to ensure the protection of the rights and freedoms in respect of the processing of employees' personal data in the employment context, in particular for the purposes of the recruitment, the performance of the contract of employment, including discharge of obligations laid down by law or by collective agreements, management, planning and organisation of work, equality and diversity in the workplace, health and

safety at work, protection of employer's or customer's property and for the purposes of the exercise and enjoyment, on an individual or collective basis, of rights and benefits related to employment, and for the purpose of the termination of the employment relationship.

2. Those rules shall include suitable and specific measures to safeguard the data subject's human dignity, legitimate interests and fundamental rights, with particular regard to the transparency of processing, the transfer of personal data within a group of undertakings, or a group of enterprises engaged in a joint economic activity and monitoring systems at the work place.

3. Each Member State shall notify to the Commission those provisions of its law which it adopts pursuant to paragraph 1, by 25 May 2018 and, without delay, any subsequent amendment affecting them.

NOTES

This Article is repealed by the Data Protection, Privacy and Electronic Communications (Amendments etc) (EU Exit) Regulations 2019, SI 2019/419, reg 3, Sch 1, paras 1, 68, as from exit day (as defined in the European Union (Withdrawal) Act 2018, s 20) and only in so far as this Regulation will apply in the UK after that date by virtue of s 3 of the 2018 Act (for transitional provisions etc, see the 2019 Regulations at **[2.2122]**).

CHAPTER XI FINAL PROVISIONS

[3.657]
Article 94
Repeal of Directive 95/46/EC

1. Directive 95/46/EC is repealed with effect from 25 May 2018.

2. References to the repealed Directive shall be construed as references to this Regulation. References to the Working Party on the Protection of Individuals with regard to the Processing of Personal Data established by Article 29 of Directive 95/46/EC shall be construed as references to the European Data Protection Board established by this Regulation.

NOTES

This Article is amended by the Data Protection, Privacy and Electronic Communications (Amendments etc) (EU Exit) Regulations 2019, SI 2019/419, reg 3, Sch 1, paras 1, 73, as from exit day (as defined in the European Union (Withdrawal) Act 2018, s 20) and only in so far as this Regulation will apply in the UK after that date by virtue of s 3 of the 2018 Act, as follows (for transitional provisions etc, see the 2019 Regulations at **[2.2122]**)—

73.
(1) Article 94 is amended as follows.
(2) Omit paragraph 1.
(3) In paragraph 2—
(a) in the first sentence, for "the repealed Directive" substitute "Directive 95/46/EC of the European Parliament and of the Council of 24th October 1995 on the protection of individuals with regard to the processing of personal data and on the free movement of such data (which ceased to have effect on 25th May 2018)";
(b) in the second sentence, for "by this Regulation" substitute "by the EU GDPR (as defined in section 3 of the 2018 Act)".

[3.658]
Article 99
Entry into force and application

1. This Regulation shall enter into force on the twentieth day following that of its publication in the *Official Journal of the European Union*.

2. It shall apply from 25 May 2018.

This Regulation shall be binding in its entirety and directly applicable in all Member States.

NOTES

This Article is repealed by the Data Protection, Privacy and Electronic Communications (Amendments etc) (EU Exit) Regulations 2019, SI 2019/419, reg 3, Sch 1, paras 1, 78, 79, as from exit day (as defined in the European Union (Withdrawal) Act 2018, s 20) and only in so far as this Regulation will apply in the UK after that date by virtue of s 3 of the 2018 Act (for transitional provisions etc, see the 2019 Regulations at **[2.2122]**).

DIRECTIVE OF THE EUROPEAN PARLIAMENT AND OF THE COUNCIL

(2016/943/EU)

of 8 June 2016

on the protection of undisclosed know-how and business information (trade secrets) against their unlawful acquisition, use and disclosure

(Text with EEA relevance)

[3.659]

NOTES

Date of publication in OJ: OJ L157, 15.6.2016, p 1.

Part 3 EU Materials

For the domestic implementation of this Directive, see the Trade Secrets (Enforcement, etc) Regulations 2018, SI 2018/597 at **[2.2065]**.

THE EUROPEAN PARLIAMENT AND THE COUNCIL OF THE EUROPEAN UNION,

Having regard to the Treaty on the Functioning of the European Union, and in particular Article 114 thereof,

Having regard to the proposal from the European Commission,

After transmission of the draft legislative act to the national parliaments,

Having regard to the opinion of the European Economic and Social Committee,[1]

Acting in accordance with the ordinary legislative procedure,[2]

Whereas:

(1) Businesses and non-commercial research institutions invest in acquiring, developing and applying know-how and information which is the currency of the knowledge economy and provides a competitive advantage. This investment in generating and applying intellectual capital is a determining factor as regards their competitiveness and innovation-related performance in the market and therefore their returns on investment, which is the underlying motivation for business research and development. Businesses have recourse to different means to appropriate the results of their innovation-related activities when openness does not allow for the full exploitation of their investment in research and innovation. Use of intellectual property rights, such as patents, design rights or copyright, is one such means. Another means of appropriating the results of innovation is to protect access to, and exploit, knowledge that is valuable to the entity and not widely known. Such valuable know-how and business information, that is undisclosed and intended to remain confidential, is referred to as a trade secret.

(2) Businesses, irrespective of their size, value trade secrets as much as patents and other forms of intellectual property right. They use confidentiality as a business competitiveness and research innovation management tool, and in relation to a diverse range of information that extends beyond technological knowledge to commercial data such as information on customers and suppliers, business plans, and market research and strategies. Small and medium-sized enterprises (SMEs) value and rely on trade secrets even more. By protecting such a wide range of know-how and business information, whether as a complement or as an alternative to intellectual property rights, trade secrets allow creators and innovators to derive profit from their creation or innovation and, therefore, are particularly important for business competitiveness as well as for research and development, and innovation-related performance.

(3) Open innovation is a catalyst for new ideas which meet the needs of consumers and tackle societal challenges, and allows those ideas to find their way to the market. Such innovation is an important lever for the creation of new knowledge, and underpins the emergence of new and innovative business models based on the use of co-created knowledge. Collaborative research, including cross-border cooperation, is particularly important in increasing the levels of business research and development within the internal market. The dissemination of knowledge and information should be considered as being essential for the purpose of ensuring dynamic, positive and equal business development opportunities, in particular for SMEs. In an internal market in which barriers to cross-border collaboration are minimised and cooperation is not distorted, intellectual creation and innovation should encourage investment in innovative processes, services and products. Such an environment conducive to intellectual creation and innovation, and in which employment mobility is not hindered, is also important for employment growth and for improving the competitiveness of the Union economy. Trade secrets have an important role in protecting the exchange of knowledge between businesses, including in particular SMEs, and research institutions both within and across the borders of the internal market, in the context of research and development, and innovation. Trade secrets are one of the most commonly used forms of protection of intellectual creation and innovative know-how by businesses, yet at the same time they are the least protected by the existing Union legal framework against their unlawful acquisition, use or disclosure by other parties.

(4) Innovative businesses are increasingly exposed to dishonest practices aimed at misappropriating trade secrets, such as theft, unauthorised copying, economic espionage or the breach of confidentiality requirements, whether from within or from outside of the Union. Recent developments, such as globalisation, increased outsourcing, longer supply chains, and the increased use of information and communication technology contribute to increasing the risk of those practices. The unlawful acquisition, use or disclosure of a trade secret compromises legitimate trade secret holders' ability to obtain first-mover returns from their innovation-related efforts. Without effective and comparable legal means for protecting trade secrets across the Union, incentives to engage in innovation-related cross-border activity within the internal market are undermined, and trade secrets are unable to fulfil their potential as drivers of economic growth and jobs. Thus, innovation and creativity are discouraged and investment diminishes, thereby affecting the smooth functioning of the internal market and undermining its growth-enhancing potential.

(5) International efforts made in the framework of the World Trade Organisation to address this problem led to the conclusion of the Agreement on Trade-related Aspects of Intellectual Property Rights (the TRIPS Agreement). The TRIPS Agreement contains, inter alia, provisions on the protection of trade secrets against their unlawful acquisition, use or disclosure by third parties, which are common international standards. All Member States, as well as the Union itself, are bound by this Agreement which was approved by Council Decision 94/800/EC.[3]

(6) Notwithstanding the TRIPS Agreement, there are important differences in the Member States' legislation as regards the protection of trade secrets against their unlawful acquisition, use or disclosure by other persons. For example, not all Member States have adopted national definitions of a trade secret

or the unlawful acquisition, use or disclosure of a trade secret, therefore knowledge on the scope of protection is not readily accessible and that scope differs across the Member States. Furthermore, there is no consistency as regards the civil law remedies available in the event of unlawful acquisition, use or disclosure of trade secrets, as cease and desist orders are not always available in all Member States against third parties who are not competitors of the legitimate trade secret holder. Divergences also exist across the Member States with respect to the treatment of a third party who has acquired the trade secret in good faith but subsequently learns, at the time of use, that the acquisition derived from a previous unlawful acquisition by another party.

(7) National rules also differ as to whether legitimate trade secret holders are allowed to seek the destruction of goods produced by third parties who use trade secrets unlawfully, or the return or destruction of any documents, files or materials containing or embodying the unlawfully acquired or used trade secret. Furthermore, applicable national rules on the calculation of damages do not always take account of the intangible nature of trade secrets, which makes it difficult to demonstrate the actual profits lost or the unjust enrichment of the infringer where no market value can be established for the information in question. Only a few Member States allow for the application of abstract rules on the calculation of damages based on the reasonable royalty or fee which could have been due had a licence for the use of the trade secret existed. Additionally, many national rules do not provide for appropriate protection of the confidentiality of a trade secret where the trade secret holder introduces a claim for alleged unlawful acquisition, use or disclosure of the trade secret by a third party, thereby reducing the attractiveness of the existing measures and remedies and weakening the protection offered.

(8) The differences in the legal protection of trade secrets provided for by the Member States imply that trade secrets do not enjoy an equivalent level of protection throughout the Union, thus leading to fragmentation of the internal market in this area and a weakening of the overall deterrent effect of the relevant rules. The internal market is affected in so far as such differences lower the incentives for businesses to undertake innovation-related cross-border economic activity, including research cooperation or production cooperation with partners, outsourcing or investment in other Member States, which depends on the use of information that enjoys protection as trade secrets. Cross-border network research and development, as well as innovation-related activities, including related production and subsequent cross-border trade, are rendered less attractive and more difficult within the Union, thus also resulting in Union-wide innovation-related inefficiencies.

(9) In addition, there is a higher risk for businesses in Member States with comparatively lower levels of protection, due to the fact that trade secrets may be stolen or otherwise unlawfully acquired more easily. This leads to inefficient allocation of capital to growth-enhancing innovation within the internal market because of the higher expenditure on protective measures to compensate for the insufficient legal protection in some Member States. It also favours the activity of unfair competitors who, subsequent to the unlawful acquisition of trade secrets, could spread goods resulting from such acquisition across the internal market. Differences in legislative regimes also facilitate the importation of goods from third countries into the Union through entry points with weaker protection, when the design, production or marketing of those goods rely on stolen or otherwise unlawfully acquired trade secrets. On the whole, such differences hinder the proper functioning of the internal market.

(10) It is appropriate to provide for rules at Union level to approximate the laws of the Member States so as to ensure that there is a sufficient and consistent level of civil redress in the internal market in the event of unlawful acquisition, use or disclosure of a trade secret. Those rules should be without prejudice to the possibility for Member States of providing for more far-reaching protection against the unlawful acquisition, use or disclosure of trade secrets, as long as the safeguards explicitly provided for in this Directive for protecting the interests of other parties are respected.

(11) This Directive should not affect the application of Union or national rules that require the disclosure of information, including trade secrets, to the public or to public authorities. Nor should it affect the application of rules that allow public authorities to collect information for the performance of their duties, or rules that allow or require any subsequent disclosure by those public authorities of relevant information to the public. Such rules include, in particular, rules on the disclosure by the Union's institutions and bodies or national public authorities of business-related information they hold pursuant to Regulation (EC) No 1049/2001 of the European Parliament and of the Council,[4] Regulation (EC) No 1367/2006 of the European Parliament and of the Council[5] and Directive 2003/4/EC of the European Parliament and of the Council, [6] or pursuant to other rules on public access to documents or on the transparency obligations of national public authorities.

(12) This Directive should not affect the right of social partners to enter into collective agreements, where provided for under labour law, as regards any obligation not to disclose a trade secret or to limit its use, and the consequences of a breach of such an obligation by the party subject to it. This should be on the condition that any such collective agreement does not restrict the exceptions laid down in this Directive when an application for measures, procedures or remedies provided for in this Directive for alleged acquisition, use or disclosure of a trade secret is to be dismissed.

(13) This Directive should not be understood as restricting the freedom of establishment, the free movement of workers or the mobility of workers as provided for in Union law. Nor is it intended to affect the possibility of concluding non-competition agreements between employers and employees, in accordance with applicable law.

(14) It is important to establish a homogenous definition of a trade secret without restricting the subject matter to be protected against misappropriation. Such definition should therefore be constructed so as to cover know-how, business information and technological information where there is both a legitimate interest in keeping them confidential and a legitimate expectation that such confidentiality will be

preserved. Furthermore, such know-how or information should have a commercial value, whether actual or potential. Such know-how or information should be considered to have a commercial value, for example, where its unlawful acquisition, use or disclosure is likely to harm the interests of the person lawfully controlling it, in that it undermines that person's scientific and technical potential, business or financial interests, strategic positions or ability to compete. The definition of trade secret excludes trivial information and the experience and skills gained by employees in the normal course of their employment, and also excludes information which is generally known among, or is readily accessible to, persons within the circles that normally deal with the kind of information in question.

(15) It is also important to identify the circumstances in which legal protection of trade secrets is justified. For this reason, it is necessary to establish the conduct and practices which are to be regarded as unlawful acquisition, use or disclosure of a trade secret.

(16) In the interest of innovation and to foster competition, the provisions of this Directive should not create any exclusive right to know-how or information protected as trade secrets. Thus, the independent discovery of the same know-how or information should remain possible. Reverse engineering of a lawfully acquired product should be considered as a lawful means of acquiring information, except when otherwise contractually agreed. The freedom to enter into such contractual arrangements can, however, be limited by law.

(17) In some industry sectors, where creators and innovators cannot benefit from exclusive rights and where innovation has traditionally relied upon trade secrets, products can nowadays be easily reverse-engineered once in the market. In such cases, those creators and innovators can be victims of practices such as parasitic copying or slavish imitations that free-ride on their reputation and innovation efforts. Some national laws dealing with unfair competition address those practices. While this Directive does not aim to reform or harmonise the law on unfair competition in general, it would be appropriate that the Commission carefully examine the need for Union action in that area.

(18) Furthermore, the acquisition, use or disclosure of trade secrets, whenever imposed or permitted by law, should be treated as lawful for the purposes of this Directive. This concerns, in particular, the acquisition and disclosure of trade secrets in the context of the exercise of the rights of workers' representatives to information, consultation and participation in accordance with Union law and national laws and practices, and the collective defence of the interests of workers and employers, including co-determination, as well as the acquisition or disclosure of a trade secret in the context of statutory audits performed in accordance with Union or national law. However, such treatment of the acquisition of a trade secret as lawful should be without prejudice to any obligation of confidentiality as regards the trade secret or any limitation as to its use that Union or national law imposes on the recipient or acquirer of the information. In particular, this Directive should not release public authorities from the confidentiality obligations to which they are subject in respect of information passed on by trade secret holders, irrespective of whether those obligations are laid down in Union or national law. Such confidentiality obligations include, inter alia, the obligations in respect of information forwarded to contracting authorities in the context of procurement procedures, as laid down, for example, in Directive 2014/23/EU of the European Parliament and of the Council,[7] Directive 2014/24/EU of the European Parliament and of the Council[8] and Directive 2014/25/EU of the European Parliament and of the Council.[9]

(19) While this Directive provides for measures and remedies which can consist of preventing the disclosure of information in order to protect the confidentiality of trade secrets, it is essential that the exercise of the right to freedom of expression and information which encompasses media freedom and pluralism, as reflected in Article 11 of the Charter of Fundamental Rights of the European Union ('the Charter'), not be restricted, in particular with regard to investigative journalism and the protection of journalistic sources.

(20) The measures, procedures and remedies provided for in this Directive should not restrict whistleblowing activity. Therefore, the protection of trade secrets should not extend to cases in which disclosure of a trade secret serves the public interest, insofar as directly relevant misconduct, wrongdoing or illegal activity is revealed. This should not be seen as preventing the competent judicial authorities from allowing an exception to the application of measures, procedures and remedies in a case where the respondent had every reason to believe in good faith that his or her conduct satisfied the appropriate criteria set out in this Directive.

(21) In line with the principle of proportionality, measures, procedures and remedies intended to protect trade secrets should be tailored to meet the objective of a smooth-functioning internal market for research and innovation, in particular by deterring the unlawful acquisition, use and disclosure of a trade secret. Such tailoring of measures, procedures and remedies should not jeopardise or undermine fundamental rights and freedoms or the public interest, such as public safety, consumer protection, public health and environmental protection, and should be without prejudice to the mobility of workers. In this respect, the measures, procedures and remedies provided for in this Directive are aimed at ensuring that competent judicial authorities take into account factors such as the value of a trade secret, the seriousness of the conduct resulting in the unlawful acquisition, use or disclosure of the trade secret and the impact of such conduct. It should also be ensured that the competent judicial authorities have the discretion to weigh up the interests of the parties to the legal proceedings, as well as the interests of third parties including, where appropriate, consumers.

(22) The smooth-functioning of the internal market would be undermined if the measures, procedures and remedies provided for were used to pursue illegitimate intents incompatible with the objectives of this Directive. Therefore, it is important to empower judicial authorities to adopt appropriate measures with

regard to applicants who act abusively or in bad faith and submit manifestly unfounded applications with, for example, the aim of unfairly delaying or restricting the respondent's access to the market or otherwise intimidating or harassing the respondent.

(23) In the interest of legal certainty, and considering that legitimate trade secret holders are expected to exercise a duty of care as regards the preservation of the confidentiality of their valuable trade secrets and the monitoring of their use, it is appropriate to restrict substantive claims or the possibility of initiating actions for the protection of trade secrets to a limited period. National law should also specify, in a clear and unambiguous manner, from when that period is to begin to run and under what circumstances that period is to be interrupted or suspended.

(24) The prospect of losing the confidentiality of a trade secret in the course of legal proceedings often deters legitimate trade secret holders from instituting legal proceedings to defend their trade secrets, thus jeopardising the effectiveness of the measures, procedures and remedies provided for. For this reason, it is necessary to establish, subject to appropriate safeguards ensuring the right to an effective remedy and to a fair trial, specific requirements aimed at protecting the confidentiality of the litigated trade secret in the course of legal proceedings instituted for its defence. Such protection should remain in force after the legal proceedings have ended and for as long as the information constituting the trade secret is not in the public domain.

(25) Such requirements should include, as a minimum, the possibility of restricting the circle of persons entitled to have access to evidence or hearings, bearing in mind that all such persons should be subject to the confidentiality requirements set out in this Directive, and of publishing only the non-confidential elements of judicial decisions. In this context, considering that assessing the nature of the information which is the subject of a dispute is one of the main purposes of legal proceedings, it is particularly important to ensure both the effective protection of the confidentiality of trade secrets and respect for the right of the parties to those proceedings to an effective remedy and to a fair trial. The restricted circle of persons should therefore consist of at least one natural person from each of the parties as well as the respective lawyers of the parties and, where applicable, other representatives appropriately qualified in accordance with national law in order to defend, represent or serve the interests of a party in legal proceedings covered by this Directive, who should all have full access to such evidence or hearings. In the event that one of the parties is a legal person, that party should be able to propose a natural person or natural persons who ought to form part of that circle of persons so as to ensure proper representation of that legal person, subject to appropriate judicial control to prevent the objective of the restriction of access to evidence and hearings from being undermined. Such safeguards should not be understood as requiring the parties to be represented by a lawyer or another representative in the course of legal proceedings where such representation is not required by national law. Nor should they be understood as restricting the competence of the courts to decide, in conformity with the applicable rules and practices of the Member State concerned, whether and to what extent relevant court officials should also have full access to evidence and hearings for the exercise of their duties.

(26) The unlawful acquisition, use or disclosure of a trade secret by a third party could have devastating effects on the legitimate trade secret holder, as once publicly disclosed, it would be impossible for that holder to revert to the situation prior to the loss of the trade secret. As a result, it is essential to provide for fast, effective and accessible provisional measures for the immediate termination of the unlawful acquisition, use or disclosure of a trade secret, including where it is used for the provision of services. It is essential that such relief be available without having to await a decision on the merits of the case, while having due respect for the right of defence and the principle of proportionality, and having regard to the characteristics of the case. In certain instances, it should be possible to permit the alleged infringer, subject to the lodging of one or more guarantees, to continue to use the trade secret, in particular where there is little risk that it will enter the public domain. It should also be possible to require guarantees of a level sufficient to cover the costs and the injury caused to the respondent by an unjustified application, particularly where any delay would cause irreparable harm to the legitimate trade secret holder.

(27) For the same reasons, it is also important to provide for definitive measures to prevent unlawful use or disclosure of a trade secret, including where it is used for the provision of services. For such measures to be effective and proportionate, their duration, when circumstances require a limitation in time, should be sufficient to eliminate any commercial advantage which the third party could have derived from the unlawful acquisition, use or disclosure of the trade secret. In any event, no measure of this type should be enforceable if the information originally covered by the trade secret is in the public domain for reasons that cannot be attributed to the respondent.

(28) It is possible that a trade secret could be used unlawfully to design, produce or market goods, or components thereof, which could be spread across the internal market, thus affecting the commercial interests of the trade secret holder and the functioning of the internal market. In such cases, and when the trade secret in question has a significant impact on the quality, value or price of the goods resulting from that unlawful use or on reducing the cost of, facilitating or speeding up their production or marketing processes, it is important to empower judicial authorities to order effective and appropriate measures with a view to ensuring that those goods are not put on the market or are withdrawn from it. Considering the global nature of trade, it is also necessary that such measures include the prohibition of the importation of those goods into the Union or their storage for the purposes of offering or placing them on the market. Having regard to the principle of proportionality, corrective measures should not necessarily entail the destruction of the goods if other viable options are present, such as depriving the good of its infringing quality or the disposal of the goods outside the market, for example, by means of donations to charitable organisations.

(29) A person could have originally acquired a trade secret in good faith, but only become aware at a later stage, including upon notice served by the original trade secret holder, that that person's knowledge of the trade secret in question derived from sources using or disclosing the relevant trade secret in an unlawful manner. In order to avoid, under those circumstances, the corrective measures or injunctions provided for causing disproportionate harm to that person, Member States should provide for the possibility, in appropriate cases, of pecuniary compensation being awarded to the injured party as an alternative measure. Such compensation should not, however, exceed the amount of royalties or fees which would have been due had that person obtained authorisation to use the trade secret in question, for the period of time for which use of the trade secret could have been prevented by the original trade secret holder. Nevertheless, where the unlawful use of the trade secret would constitute an infringement of law other than that provided for in this Directive or would be likely to harm consumers, such unlawful use should not be allowed.

(30) In order to avoid a person who knowingly, or with reasonable grounds for knowing, unlawfully acquires, uses or discloses a trade secret being able to benefit from such conduct, and to ensure that the injured trade secret holder, to the extent possible, is placed in the position in which he, she or it would have been had that conduct not taken place, it is necessary to provide for adequate compensation for the prejudice suffered as a result of that unlawful conduct. The amount of damages awarded to the injured trade secret holder should take account of all appropriate factors, such as loss of earnings incurred by the trade secret holder or unfair profits made by the infringer and, where appropriate, any moral prejudice caused to the trade secret holder. As an alternative, for example where, considering the intangible nature of trade secrets, it would be difficult to determine the amount of the actual prejudice suffered, the amount of the damages might be derived from elements such as the royalties or fees which would have been due had the infringer requested authorisation to use the trade secret in question. The aim of that alternative method is not to introduce an obligation to provide for punitive damages, but to ensure compensation based on an objective criterion while taking account of the expenses incurred by the trade secret holder, such as the costs of identification and research. This Directive should not prevent Member States from providing in their national law that the liability for damages of employees is restricted in cases where they have acted without intent.

(31) As a supplementary deterrent to future infringers and to contribute to the awareness of the public at large, it is useful to publicise decisions, including, where appropriate, through prominent advertising, in cases concerning the unlawful acquisition, use or disclosure of trade secrets, on the condition that such publication does not result in the disclosure of the trade secret or disproportionally affect the privacy and reputation of a natural person.

(32) The effectiveness of the measures, procedures and remedies available to trade secret holders could be undermined in the event of non-compliance with the relevant decisions adopted by the competent judicial authorities. For this reason, it is necessary to ensure that those authorities enjoy the appropriate powers of sanction.

(33) In order to facilitate the uniform application of the measures, procedures and remedies provided for in this Directive, it is appropriate to provide for systems of cooperation and the exchange of information as between Member States on the one hand, and between the Member States and the Commission on the other, in particular by creating a network of correspondents designated by Member States. In addition, in order to review whether those measures fulfil their intended objective, the Commission, assisted, as appropriate, by the European Union Intellectual Property Office, should examine the application of this Directive and the effectiveness of the national measures taken.

(34) This Directive respects the fundamental rights and observes the principles recognised in particular by the Charter, notably the right to respect for private and family life, the right to protection of personal data, the freedom of expression and information, the freedom to choose an occupation and right to engage in work, the freedom to conduct a business, the right to property, the right to good administration, and in particular the access to files, while respecting business secrecy, the right to an effective remedy and to a fair trial and the right of defence.

(35) It is important that the rights to respect for private and family life and to protection of personal data of any person whose personal data may be processed by the trade secret holder when taking steps to protect a trade secret, or of any person involved in legal proceedings concerning the unlawful acquisition, use or disclosure of trade secrets under this Directive, and whose personal data are processed, be respected. Directive 95/46/EC of the European Parliament and of the Council[10] governs the processing of personal data carried out in the Member States in the context of this Directive and under the supervision of the Member States' competent authorities, in particular the public independent authorities designated by the Member States. Thus, this Directive should not affect the rights and obligations laid down in Directive 95/46/EC, in particular the rights of the data subject to access his or her personal data being processed and to obtain the rectification, erasure or blocking of the data where it is incomplete or inaccurate and, where appropriate, the obligation to process sensitive data in accordance with Article 8(5) of Directive 95/46/EC.

(36) Since the objective of this Directive, namely to achieve a smooth-functioning internal market by means of the establishment of a sufficient and comparable level of redress across the internal market in the event of the unlawful acquisition, use or disclosure of a trade secret, cannot be sufficiently achieved by Member States but can rather, by reason of its scale and effects, be better achieved at Union level, the Union may adopt measures in accordance with the principle of subsidiarity as set out in Article 5 of the Treaty on European Union. In accordance with the principle of proportionality, as set out in that Article, this Directive does not go beyond what is necessary in order to achieve that objective.

(37) This Directive does not aim to establish harmonised rules for judicial cooperation, jurisdiction, the recognition and enforcement of judgments in civil and commercial matters, or deal with applicable law. Other Union instruments which govern such matters in general terms should, in principle, remain equally applicable to the field covered by this Directive.

(38) This Directive should not affect the application of competition law rules, in particular Articles 101 and 102 of the Treaty on the Functioning of the European Union ('TFEU'). The measures, procedures and remedies provided for in this Directive should not be used to restrict unduly competition in a manner contrary to the TFEU.

(39) This Directive should not affect the application of any other relevant law in other areas, including intellectual property rights and the law of contract. However, where the scope of application of Directive 2004/48/EC of the European Parliament and of the Council and the scope of this Directive[11] overlap, this Directive takes precedence as *lex specialis*.

(40) The European Data Protection Supervisor was consulted in accordance with Article 28(2) of Regulation (EC) No 45/2001 of the European Parliament and of the Council[12] and delivered an opinion on 12 March 2014,

NOTES

1 OJ C226, 16.7.2014, p 48.

2 Position of the European Parliament of 14 April 2016 (not yet published in the Official Journal) and decision of the Council of 27 May 2016.

3 Council Decision 94/800/EC of 22 December 1994 concerning the conclusion on behalf of the European Community, as regards matters within its competence, of the agreements reached in the Uruguay Round multilateral negotiations (1986–1994) (OJ L336, 23.12.1994, p 1).

4 Regulation (EC) No 1049/2001 of the European Parliament and of the Council of 30 May 2001 regarding public access to European Parliament, Council and Commission documents (OJ L145, 31.5.2001, p 43).

5 Regulation (EC) No 1367/2006 of the European Parliament and of the Council of 6 September 2006 on the application of the provisions of the Aarhus Convention on Access to Information, Public Participation in Decision-making and Access to Justice in Environmental Matters to Community institutions and bodies (OJ L264, 25.9.2006, p 13).

6 Directive 2003/4/EC of the European Parliament and of the Council of 28 January 2003 on public access to environmental information and repealing Council Directive 90/313/EEC (OJ L41, 14.2.2003, p 26).

7 Directive 2014/23/EU of the European Parliament and of the Council of 26 February 2014 on the award of concession contracts (OJ L94, 28.3.2014, p 1).

8 Directive 2014/24/EU of the European Parliament and of the Council of 26 February 2014 on public procurement and repealing Directive 2004/18/EC (OJ L94, 28.3.2014, p 65).

9 Directive 2014/25/EU of the European Parliament and of the Council of 26 February 2014 on procurement by entities operating in the water, energy, transport and postal services sectors and repealing Directive 2004/17/EC (OJ L94, 28.3.2014, p 243).

10 Directive 95/46/EC of the European Parliament and of the Council of 24 October 1995 on the protection of individuals with regard to the processing of personal data and on the free movement of such data (OJ L281, 23.11.1995, p 31).

11 Directive 2004/48/EC of the European Parliament and of the Council of 29 April 2004 on the enforcement of intellectual property rights (OJ L157, 30.4.2004, p 45).

12 Regulation (EC) No 45/2001 of the European Parliament and of the Council of 18 December 2000 on the protection of individuals with regard to the processing of personal data by the Community institutions and bodies and on the free movement of such data (OJ L8, 12.1.2001, p 1).

HAVE ADOPTED THIS DIRECTIVE:

CHAPTER I SUBJECT MATTER AND SCOPE

[3.660]
Article 1
Subject matter and scope

1. This Directive lays down rules on the protection against the unlawful acquisition, use and disclosure of trade secrets.

Member States may, in compliance with the provisions of the TFEU, provide for more far-reaching protection against the unlawful acquisition, use or disclosure of trade secrets than that required by this Directive, provided that compliance with Articles 3, 5, 6, Article 7(1), Article 8, the second subparagraph of Article 9(1), Article 9(3) and (4), Article 10(2), Articles 11, 13 and Article 15(3) is ensured.

2. This Directive shall not affect:

(a) the exercise of the right to freedom of expression and information as set out in the Charter, including respect for the freedom and pluralism of the media;

(b) the application of Union or national rules requiring trade secret holders to disclose, for reasons of public interest, information, including trade secrets, to the public or to administrative or judicial authorities for the performance of the duties of those authorities;

(c) the application of Union or national rules requiring or allowing Union institutions and bodies or national public authorities to disclose information submitted by businesses which those institutions, bodies or authorities hold pursuant to, and in compliance with, the obligations and prerogatives set out in Union or national law;

(d) the autonomy of social partners and their right to enter into collective agreements, in accordance with Union law and national laws and practices.

3. Nothing in this Directive shall be understood to offer any ground for restricting the mobility of employees. In particular, in relation to the exercise of such mobility, this Directive shall not offer any ground for:

(a) limiting employees' use of information that does not constitute a trade secret as defined in point (1) of Article 2;

(b) limiting employees' use of experience and skills honestly acquired in the normal course of their employment;

(c) imposing any additional restrictions on employees in their employment contracts other than restrictions imposed in accordance with Union or national law.

[3.661]
Article 2
Definitions

For the purposes of this Directive, the following definitions apply:

(1) 'trade secret' means information which meets all of the following requirements:

 (a) it is secret in the sense that it is not, as a body or in the precise configuration and assembly of its components, generally known among or readily accessible to persons within the circles that normally deal with the kind of information in question;

 (b) it has commercial value because it is secret;

 (c) it has been subject to reasonable steps under the circumstances, by the person lawfully in control of the information, to keep it secret;

(2) 'trade secret holder' means any natural or legal person lawfully controlling a trade secret;

(3) 'infringer' means any natural or legal person who has unlawfully acquired, used or disclosed a trade secret;

(4) 'infringing goods' means goods, the design, characteristics, functioning, production process or marketing of which significantly benefits from trade secrets unlawfully acquired, used or disclosed.

CHAPTER II ACQUISITION, USE AND DISCLOSURE OF TRADE SECRETS

[3.662]
Article 3
Lawful acquisition, use and disclosure of trade secrets

1. The acquisition of a trade secret shall be considered lawful when the trade secret is obtained by any of the following means:

(a) independent discovery or creation;

(b) observation, study, disassembly or testing of a product or object that has been made available to the public or that is lawfully in the possession of the acquirer of the information who is free from any legally valid duty to limit the acquisition of the trade secret;

(c) exercise of the right of workers or workers' representatives to information and consultation in accordance with Union law and national laws and practices;

(d) any other practice which, under the circumstances, is in conformity with honest commercial practices.

2. The acquisition, use or disclosure of a trade secret shall be considered lawful to the extent that such acquisition, use or disclosure is required or allowed by Union or national law.

[3.663]
Article 4
Unlawful acquisition, use and disclosure of trade secrets

1. Member States shall ensure that trade secret holders are entitled to apply for the measures, procedures and remedies provided for in this Directive in order to prevent, or obtain redress for, the unlawful acquisition, use or disclosure of their trade secret.

2. The acquisition of a trade secret without the consent of the trade secret holder shall be considered unlawful, whenever carried out by:

(a) unauthorised access to, appropriation of, or copying of any documents, objects, materials, substances or electronic files, lawfully under the control of the trade secret holder, containing the trade secret or from which the trade secret can be deduced;

(b) any other conduct which, under the circumstances, is considered contrary to honest commercial practices.

3. The use or disclosure of a trade secret shall be considered unlawful whenever carried out, without the consent of the trade secret holder, by a person who is found to meet any of the following conditions:

(a) having acquired the trade secret unlawfully;

(b) being in breach of a confidentiality agreement or any other duty not to disclose the trade secret;

(c) being in breach of a contractual or any other duty to limit the use of the trade secret.

4. The acquisition, use or disclosure of a trade secret shall also be considered unlawful whenever a person, at the time of the acquisition, use or disclosure, knew or ought, under the circumstances, to have known that the trade secret had been obtained directly or indirectly from another person who was using or disclosing the trade secret unlawfully within the meaning of paragraph 3.

5. The production, offering or placing on the market of infringing goods, or the importation, export or storage of infringing goods for those purposes, shall also be considered an unlawful use of a trade secret where the person carrying out such activities knew, or ought, under the circumstances, to have known that the trade secret was used unlawfully within the meaning of paragraph 3.

[3.664]
Article 5
Exceptions

Member States shall ensure that an application for the measures, procedures and remedies provided for in this Directive is dismissed where the alleged acquisition, use or disclosure of the trade secret was carried out in any of the following cases:

(a) for exercising the right to freedom of expression and information as set out in the Charter, including respect for the freedom and pluralism of the media;
(b) for revealing misconduct, wrongdoing or illegal activity, provided that the respondent acted for the purpose of protecting the general public interest;
(c) disclosure by workers to their representatives as part of the legitimate exercise by those representatives of their functions in accordance with Union or national law, provided that such disclosure was necessary for that exercise;
(d) for the purpose of protecting a legitimate interest recognised by Union or national law.

CHAPTER III MEASURES, PROCEDURES AND REMEDIES

SECTION 1 GENERAL PROVISIONS

[3.665]
Article 6
General obligation

1. Member States shall provide for the measures, procedures and remedies necessary to ensure the availability of civil redress against the unlawful acquisition, use and disclosure of trade secrets.
2. The measures, procedures and remedies referred to in paragraph 1 shall:
(a) be fair and equitable;
(b) not be unnecessarily complicated or costly, or entail unreasonable time-limits or unwarranted delays; and
(c) be effective and dissuasive.

[3.666]
Article 7
Proportionality and abuse of process

1. The measures, procedures and remedies provided for in this Directive shall be applied in a manner that:
(a) is proportionate;
(b) avoids the creation of barriers to legitimate trade in the internal market; and
(c) provides for safeguards against their abuse.
2. Member States shall ensure that competent judicial authorities may, upon the request of the respondent, apply appropriate measures as provided for in national law, where an application concerning the unlawful acquisition, use or disclosure of a trade secret is manifestly unfounded and the applicant is found to have initiated the legal proceedings abusively or in bad faith. Such measures may, as appropriate, include awarding damages to the respondent, imposing sanctions on the applicant or ordering the dissemination of information concerning a decision as referred to in Article 15.
Member States may provide that measures as referred to in the first subparagraph are dealt with in separate legal proceedings.

[3.667]
Article 8
Limitation period

1. Member States shall, in accordance with this Article, lay down rules on the limitation periods applicable to substantive claims and actions for the application of the measures, procedures and remedies provided for in this Directive.
The rules referred to in the first subparagraph shall determine when the limitation period begins to run, the duration of the limitation period and the circumstances under which the limitation period is interrupted or suspended.
2. The duration of the limitation period shall not exceed 6 years.

[3.668]
Article 9
Preservation of confidentiality of trade secrets in the course of legal proceedings

1. Member States shall ensure that the parties, their lawyers or other representatives, court officials, witnesses, experts and any other person participating in legal proceedings relating to the unlawful acquisition, use or disclosure of a trade secret, or who has access to documents which form part of those legal proceedings, are not permitted to use or disclose any trade secret or alleged trade secret which the competent judicial authorities have, in response to a duly reasoned application by an interested party, identified as confidential and of which they have become aware as a result of such participation or access. In that regard, Member States may also allow competent judicial authorities to act on their own initiative.
The obligation referred to in the first subparagraph shall remain in force after the legal proceedings have ended. However, such obligation shall cease to exist in any of the following circumstances:
(a) where the alleged trade secret is found, by a final decision, not to meet the requirements set out in point (1) of Article 2; or

(b) where over time, the information in question becomes generally known among or readily accessible to persons within the circles that normally deal with that kind of information.

2. Member States shall also ensure that the competent judicial authorities may, on a duly reasoned application by a party, take specific measures necessary to preserve the confidentiality of any trade secret or alleged trade secret used or referred to in the course of legal proceedings relating to the unlawful acquisition, use or disclosure of a trade secret. Member States may also allow competent judicial authorities to take such measures on their own initiative.

The measures referred to in the first subparagraph shall at least include the possibility:

(a) of restricting access to any document containing trade secrets or alleged trade secrets submitted by the parties or third parties, in whole or in part, to a limited number of persons;

(b) of restricting access to hearings, when trade secrets or alleged trade secrets may be disclosed, and the corresponding record or transcript of those hearings to a limited number of persons;

(c) of making available to any person other than those comprised in the limited number of persons referred to in points (a) and (b) a non-confidential version of any judicial decision, in which the passages containing trade secrets have been removed or redacted.

The number of persons referred to in points (a) and (b) of the second subparagraph shall be no greater than necessary in order to ensure compliance with the right of the parties to the legal proceedings to an effective remedy and to a fair trial, and shall include, at least, one natural person from each party and the respective lawyers or other representatives of those parties to the legal proceedings.

3. When deciding on the measures referred to in paragraph 2 and assessing their proportionality, the competent judicial authorities shall take into account the need to ensure the right to an effective remedy and to a fair trial, the legitimate interests of the parties and, where appropriate, of third parties, and any potential harm for either of the parties, and, where appropriate, for third parties, resulting from the granting or rejection of such measures.

4. Any processing of personal data pursuant to paragraphs 1, 2 or 3 shall be carried out in accordance with Directive 95/46/EC.

SECTION 2 PROVISIONAL AND PRECAUTIONARY MEASURES

[3.669]
Article 10
Provisional and precautionary measures

1. Member States shall ensure that the competent judicial authorities may, at the request of the trade secret holder, order any of the following provisional and precautionary measures against the alleged infringer:

(a) the cessation of or, as the case may be, the prohibition of the use or disclosure of the trade secret on a provisional basis;

(b) the prohibition of the production, offering, placing on the market or use of infringing goods, or the importation, export or storage of infringing goods for those purposes;

(c) the seizure or delivery up of the suspected infringing goods, including imported goods, so as to prevent their entry into, or circulation on, the market.

2. Member States shall ensure that the judicial authorities may, as an alternative to the measures referred to in paragraph 1, make the continuation of the alleged unlawful use of a trade secret subject to the lodging of guarantees intended to ensure the compensation of the trade secret holder. Disclosure of a trade secret in return for the lodging of guarantees shall not be allowed.

[3.670]
Article 11
Conditions of application and safeguards

1. Member States shall ensure that the competent judicial authorities have, in respect of the measures referred to in Article 10, the authority to require the applicant to provide evidence that may reasonably be considered available in order to satisfy themselves with a sufficient degree of certainty that:

(a) a trade secret exists;

(b) the applicant is the trade secret holder; and

(c) the trade secret has been acquired unlawfully, is being unlawfully used or disclosed, or unlawful acquisition, use or disclosure of the trade secret is imminent.

2. Member States shall ensure that in deciding on the granting or rejection of the application and assessing its proportionality, the competent judicial authorities shall be required to take into account the specific circumstances of the case, including, where appropriate:

(a) the value and other specific features of the trade secret;

(b) the measures taken to protect the trade secret;

(c) the conduct of the respondent in acquiring, using or disclosing the trade secret;

(d) the impact of the unlawful use or disclosure of the trade secret;

(e) the legitimate interests of the parties and the impact which the granting or rejection of the measures could have on the parties;

(f) the legitimate interests of third parties;

(g) the public interest; and

(h) the safeguard of fundamental rights.

3. Member States shall ensure that the measures referred to in Article 10 are revoked or otherwise cease to have effect, upon the request of the respondent, if:

(a) the applicant does not institute legal proceedings leading to a decision on the merits of the case before the competent judicial authority, within a reasonable period determined by the judicial authority ordering the measures where the law of a Member State so permits or, in the absence of such determination, within a period not exceeding 20 working days or 31 calendar days, whichever is the longer; or

(b) the information in question no longer meets the requirements of point (1) of Article 2, for reasons that cannot be attributed to the respondent.

4. Member States shall ensure that the competent judicial authorities may make the measures referred to in Article 10 subject to the lodging by the applicant of adequate security or an equivalent assurance intended to ensure compensation for any prejudice suffered by the respondent and, where appropriate, by any other person affected by the measures.

5. Where the measures referred to in Article 10 are revoked on the basis of point (a) of paragraph 3 of this Article, where they lapse due to any act or omission by the applicant, or where it is subsequently found that there has been no unlawful acquisition, use or disclosure of the trade secret or threat of such conduct, the competent judicial authorities shall have the authority to order the applicant, upon the request of the respondent or of an injured third party, to provide the respondent, or the injured third party, appropriate compensation for any injury caused by those measures.

Member States may provide that the request for compensation referred to in the first subparagraph is dealt with in separate legal proceedings.

SECTION 3 MEASURES RESULTING FROM A DECISION ON THE MERITS OF THE CASE

[3.671]
Article 12
Injunctions and corrective measures

1. Member States shall ensure that, where a judicial decision taken on the merits of the case finds that there has been unlawful acquisition, use or disclosure of a trade secret, the competent judicial authorities may, at the request of the applicant, order one or more of the following measures against the infringer:

(a) the cessation of or, as the case may be, the prohibition of the use or disclosure of the trade secret;

(b) the prohibition of the production, offering, placing on the market or use of infringing goods, or the importation, export or storage of infringing goods for those purposes;

(c) the adoption of the appropriate corrective measures with regard to the infringing goods;

(d) the destruction of all or part of any document, object, material, substance or electronic file containing or embodying the trade secret or, where appropriate, the delivery up to the applicant of all or part of those documents, objects, materials, substances or electronic files.

2. The corrective measures referred to in point (c) of paragraph 1 shall include:

(a) recall of the infringing goods from the market;

(b) depriving the infringing goods of their infringing quality;

(c) destruction of the infringing goods or, where appropriate, their withdrawal from the market, provided that the withdrawal does not undermine the protection of the trade secret in question.

3. Member States may provide that, when ordering the withdrawal of the infringing goods from the market, their competent judicial authorities may order, at the request of the trade secret holder, that the goods be delivered up to the holder or to charitable organisations.

4. The competent judicial authorities shall order that the measures referred to in points (c) and (d) of paragraph 1 be carried out at the expense of the infringer, unless there are particular reasons for not doing so. Those measures shall be without prejudice to any damages that may be due to the trade secret holder by reason of the unlawful acquisition, use or disclosure of the trade secret.

[3.672]
Article 13
Conditions of application, safeguards and alternative measures

1. Member States shall ensure that, in considering an application for the adoption of the injunctions and corrective measures provided for in Article 12 and assessing their proportionality, the competent judicial authorities shall be required to take into account the specific circumstances of the case, including, where appropriate:

(a) the value or other specific features of the trade secret;

(b) the measures taken to protect the trade secret;

(c) the conduct of the infringer in acquiring, using or disclosing the trade secret;

(d) the impact of the unlawful use or disclosure of the trade secret;

(e) the legitimate interests of the parties and the impact which the granting or rejection of the measures could have on the parties;

(f) the legitimate interests of third parties;

(g) the public interest; and

(h) the safeguard of fundamental rights.

Where the competent judicial authorities limit the duration of the measures referred to in points (a) and (b) of Article 12(1), such duration shall be sufficient to eliminate any commercial or economic advantage that the infringer could have derived from the unlawful acquisition, use or disclosure of the trade secret.

2. Member States shall ensure that the measures referred to in points (a) and (b) of Article 12(1) are revoked or otherwise cease to have effect, upon the request of the respondent, if the information in question no longer meets the requirements of point (1) of Article 2 for reasons that cannot be attributed directly or indirectly to the respondent.

3. Member States shall provide that, at the request of the person liable to be subject to the measures provided for in Article 12, the competent judicial authority may order pecuniary compensation to be paid to the injured party instead of applying those measures if all the following conditions are met:

(a) the person concerned at the time of use or disclosure neither knew nor ought, under the circumstances, to have known that the trade secret was obtained from another person who was using or disclosing the trade secret unlawfully;
(b) execution of the measures in question would cause that person disproportionate harm; and
(c) pecuniary compensation to the injured party appears reasonably satisfactory.

Where pecuniary compensation is ordered instead of the measures referred to in points (a) and (b) of Article 12(1), it shall not exceed the amount of royalties or fees which would have been due, had that person requested authorisation to use the trade secret in question, for the period of time for which use of the trade secret could have been prohibited.

[3.673]
Article 14
Damages

1. Member States shall ensure that the competent judicial authorities, upon the request of the injured party, order an infringer who knew or ought to have known that he, she or it was engaging in unlawful acquisition, use or disclosure of a trade secret, to pay the trade secret holder damages appropriate to the actual prejudice suffered as a result of the unlawful acquisition, use or disclosure of the trade secret.

Member States may limit the liability for damages of employees towards their employers for the unlawful acquisition, use or disclosure of a trade secret of the employer where they act without intent.

2. When setting the damages referred to in paragraph 1, the competent judicial authorities shall take into account all appropriate factors, such as the negative economic consequences, including lost profits, which the injured party has suffered, any unfair profits made by the infringer and, in appropriate cases, elements other than economic factors, such as the moral prejudice caused to the trade secret holder by the unlawful acquisition, use or disclosure of the trade secret.

Alternatively, the competent judicial authorities may, in appropriate cases, set the damages as a lump sum on the basis of elements such as, at a minimum, the amount of royalties or fees which would have been due had the infringer requested authorisation to use the trade secret in question.

[3.674]
Article 15
Publication of judicial decisions

1. Member States shall ensure that, in legal proceedings instituted for the unlawful acquisition, use or disclosure of a trade secret, the competent judicial authorities may order, at the request of the applicant and at the expense of the infringer, appropriate measures for the dissemination of the information concerning the decision, including publishing it in full or in part.

2. Any measure referred to in paragraph 1 of this Article shall preserve the confidentiality of trade secrets as provided for in Article 9.

3. In deciding whether to order a measure referred to in paragraph 1 and when assessing its proportionality, the competent judicial authorities shall take into account, where appropriate, the value of the trade secret, the conduct of the infringer in acquiring, using or disclosing the trade secret, the impact of the unlawful use or disclosure of the trade secret, and the likelihood of further unlawful use or disclosure of the trade secret by the infringer.

The competent judicial authorities shall also take into account whether the information on the infringer would be such as to allow a natural person to be identified and, if so, whether publication of that information would be justified, in particular in the light of the possible harm that such measure may cause to the privacy and reputation of the infringer.

CHAPTER IV SANCTIONS, REPORTING AND FINAL PROVISIONS

[3.675]
Article 16
Sanctions for non-compliance with this Directive

Member States shall ensure that the competent judicial authorities may impose sanctions on any person who fails or refuses to comply with any measure adopted pursuant to Articles 9, 10 and 12.

The sanctions provided for shall include the possibility of imposing recurring penalty payments in the event of non-compliance with a measure adopted pursuant to Articles 10 and 12.

The sanctions provided for shall be effective, proportionate and dissuasive.

[3.676]
Article 17
Exchange of information and correspondents

For the purpose of promoting cooperation, including the exchange of information, among Member States and between Member States and the Commission, each Member State shall designate one or more national correspondents for any question relating to the implementation of the measures provided for by this Directive. It shall communicate the details of the national correspondent or correspondents to the other Member States and the Commission.

[3.677]
Article 18
Reports

1. By 9 June 2021, the European Union Intellectual Property Office, in the context of the activities of the European Observatory on Infringements of Intellectual Property Rights, shall prepare an initial report on the litigation trends regarding the unlawful acquisition, use or disclosure of trade secrets pursuant to the application of this Directive.

2. By 9 June 2022, the Commission shall draw up an intermediate report on the application of this Directive, and shall submit it to the European Parliament and to the Council. That report shall take due account of the report referred to in paragraph 1.

The intermediate report shall examine, in particular, the possible effects of the application of this Directive on research and innovation, the mobility of employees and on the exercise of the right to freedom of expression and information.

3. By 9 June 2026, the Commission shall carry out an evaluation of the impact of this Directive and submit a report to the European Parliament and to the Council.

[3.678]
Article 19
Transposition

1. Member States shall bring into force the laws, regulations and administrative provisions necessary to comply with this Directive by 9 June 2018. They shall immediately communicate the text of those measures to the Commission.

When Member States adopt those measures, they shall contain a reference to this Directive or be accompanied by such a reference on the occasion of their official publication. Member States shall determine how such reference is to be made.

2. Member States shall communicate to the Commission the text of the main provisions of national law which they adopt in the field covered by this Directive.

[3.679]
Article 20
Entry into force

This Directive shall enter into force on the twentieth day following that of its publication in the *Official Journal of the European Union*.

[3.680]
Article 21
Addressees

This Directive is addressed to the Member States.

DIRECTIVE OF THE EUROPEAN PARLIAMENT AND OF THE COUNCIL

(2018/957/EU)

of 28 June 2018

amending Directive 96/71/EC concerning the posting of workers in the framework of the provision of services

(Text with EEA relevance)

[3.681]

NOTES

Date of publication in OJ: OJ L173, 9.7.2018, p 16.

THE EUROPEAN PARLIAMENT AND THE COUNCIL OF THE EUROPEAN UNION,

Having regard to the Treaty on the Functioning of the European Union, and in particular Article 53(1) and Article 62 thereof,

Having regard to the proposal from the European Commission,

After transmission of the draft legislative act to the national parliaments,

Having regard to the opinion of the European Economic and Social Committee,[1]

Having regard to the opinion of the Committee of the Regions,[2]

Acting in accordance with the ordinary legislative procedure,[3]

Whereas:

(1) The freedom of movement for workers, freedom of establishment and freedom to provide services are fundamental principles of the internal market enshrined in the Treaty on the Functioning of the European Union (TFEU). The implementation and enforcement of those principles are further developed by the Union and aim to guarantee a level playing field for businesses and respect for the rights of workers.

(2) The freedom to provide services includes the right of undertakings to provide services in the territory of another Member State and to post their own workers temporarily to the territory of that Member State for that purpose. In accordance with Article 56 TFEU, restrictions on the freedom to provide services within the Union are prohibited in respect of nationals of Member States who are established in a Member State other than that of the person for whom the services are intended.

(3) According to Article 3 of the Treaty on European Union, the Union is to promote social justice and protection. According to Article 9 TFEU, in defining and implementing its policies and activities, the Union is to take into account requirements linked to the promotion of a high level of employment, the guarantee of adequate social protection, the fight against social exclusion, and a high level of education, training and protection of human health.

(4) More than 20 years after its adoption, it has become necessary to assess whether Directive 96/71/EC of the European Parliament and of the Council [4]) still strikes the right balance between the need to promote the freedom to provide services and ensure a level playing field on the one hand and the need to protect the rights of posted workers on the other. To ensure that the rules are applied uniformly and to bring about genuine social convergence, alongside the revision of Directive 96/71/EC, priority should be given to the implementation and enforcement of Directive 2014/67/EU of the European Parliament and of the Council.[5]

(5) Sufficient and accurate statistical data in the area of posted workers is of utmost importance, in particular with regard to the number of posted workers in specific employment sectors and per Member State. The Member States and the Commission should collect and monitor such data.

(6) The principle of equal treatment and the prohibition of any discrimination on grounds of nationality have been enshrined in Union law since the founding Treaties. The principle of equal pay has been implemented through secondary law not only between women and men, but also between workers with fixed term contracts and comparable permanent workers, between part-time and full-time workers and between temporary agency workers and comparable workers of the user undertaking. Those principles include the prohibition of any measures which directly or indirectly discriminate on grounds of nationality. In applying those principles, the relevant case-law of the Court of Justice of the European Union is to be taken into consideration.

(7) The competent authorities and bodies, in accordance with national law and/or practice, should be able to verify whether the conditions of accommodation for posted workers directly or indirectly provided by the employer comply with the national rules in the Member State to whose territory the workers are posted (host Member State) that also apply to posted workers.

(8) Posted workers who are temporarily sent from their regular place of work in the host Member State to another place of work, should receive at least the same allowances or reimbursement of expenditure to cover travel, board and lodging expenses for workers away from home for professional reasons that apply to local workers in that Member State. The same should apply as regards the expenditure incurred by posted workers required to travel to and from their regular place of work in the host Member State. Double payment of travel, board and lodging expenses should be avoided.

(9) Posting is temporary in nature. Posted workers usually return to the Member State from which they were posted after completion of the work for which they were posted. However, in view of the long duration of some postings and in acknowledgment of the link between the labour market of the host Member State and the workers posted for such long periods, where posting lasts for periods longer than 12 months host Member States should ensure that undertakings which post workers to their territory guarantee those workers an additional set of terms and conditions of employment that are mandatorily applicable to workers in the Member State where the work is carried out. That period should be extended where the service provider submits a motivated notification.

(10) Ensuring greater protection for workers is necessary to safeguard the freedom to provide, in both the short and the long term, services on a fair basis, in particular by preventing abuse of the rights guaranteed by the Treaties. However, the rules ensuring such protection for workers cannot affect the right of undertakings posting workers to the territory of another Member State to invoke the freedom to provide services, including in cases where a posting exceeds 12 or, where applicable, 18 months. Any provision applicable to posted workers in the context of a posting exceeding 12 or, where applicable, 18 months must thus be compatible with that freedom. In accordance with settled case law, restrictions to the freedom to provide services are permissible only if they are justified by overriding reasons in the public interest and if they are proportionate and necessary.

(11) Where a posting exceeds 12 or, where applicable, 18 months, the additional set of terms and conditions of employment to be guaranteed by the undertaking posting workers to the territory of another Member State should also cover workers who are posted to replace other posted workers performing the same task at the same place, to ensure that such replacements are not used to circumvent the otherwise applicable rules.

(12) Directive 2008/104/EC of the European Parliament and of the Council[6] gives expression to the principle that the basic working and employment conditions applicable to temporary agency workers should be at least those which would apply to such workers if they were recruited by the user undertaking to occupy the same job. That principle should also apply to temporary agency workers posted to the territory of another Member State. Where that principle applies, the user undertaking should inform the temporary-work agency about the working conditions and remuneration it applies to its workers. Member States are able, under certain conditions to derogate from the principles of equal treatment and equal pay pursuant to Article 5(2) and (3) of Directive 2008/104/EC. Where such a derogation applies, the temporary-work agency has no need for the information about the user undertaking's working conditions and the information requirement should therefore not apply.

(13) Experience shows that workers who have been hired out by a temporary employment undertaking or placement agency to a user undertaking are sometimes sent to the territory of another Member State in the framework of the transnational provision of services. The protection of those workers should be ensured. Member States should ensure that the user undertaking informs the temporary employment undertaking or placement agency about the posted workers who are temporarily working in the territory of a Member State other than the Member State in which they normally work for the temporary employment undertaking or placement agency or for the user undertaking, in order to allow the employer to apply, as appropriate, the terms and conditions of employment that are more favourable to the posted worker.

(14) This Directive, in the same way as Directive 96/71/EC, should not prejudice the application of Regulations (EC) No 883/2004[7] and (EC) No 987/2009[8] of the European Parliament and of the Council.

(15) Because of the highly mobile nature of work in international road transport, the implementation of this Directive in that sector raises particular legal questions and difficulties, which are to be addressed, in the framework of the mobility package, through specific rules for road transport also reinforcing the combating of fraud and abuse.

(16) In a truly integrated and competitive internal market, undertakings compete on the basis of factors such as productivity, efficiency, and the education and skill level of the labour force, as well as the quality of their goods and services and the degree of innovation thereof.

(17) It is within Member States' competence to set rules on remuneration in accordance with national law and/or practice. The setting of wages is a matter for the Member States and the social partners alone. Particular care should be taken not to undermine national systems of wage setting or the freedom of the parties involved.

(18) When comparing the remuneration paid to a posted worker and the remuneration due in accordance with the national law and/or practice of the host Member State, the gross amount of remuneration should be taken into account. The total gross amounts of remuneration should be compared, rather than the individual constituent elements of remuneration which are rendered mandatory as provided for by this Directive. Nevertheless, in order to ensure transparency and to assist the competent authorities and bodies in carrying out checks and controls it is necessary that the constituent elements of remuneration can be identified in enough detail according to the national law and/or practice of the Member State from which the worker was posted. Unless the allowances specific to the posting concern expenditure actually incurred on account of the posting, such as expenditure on travel, board and lodging, they should be considered to be part of the remuneration and should be taken into account for the purposes of comparing the total gross amounts of remuneration.

(19) Allowances specific to posting often serve several purposes. Insofar as their purpose is the reimbursement of expenditure incurred on account of the posting, such as expenditure on travel, board and lodging, they should not be considered to be part of remuneration. It is for Member States, in accordance with their national law and/or practice, to set rules with regard to the reimbursement of such expenditure. The employer should reimburse posted workers for such expenditure in accordance with the national law and/or practice applicable to the employment relationship.

(20) In view of the relevance of allowances specific to posting, uncertainty as to which elements of such allowances are allocated to the reimbursement of expenditure incurred on account of the posting should be avoided. The entire allowance should be considered to be paid in reimbursement of expenditure unless the terms and conditions of employment resulting from the law, regulation or administrative provision, collective agreements, arbitration awards or contractual agreements that apply to the employment relationship determine which elements of the allowance are allocated to the reimbursement of expenditure incurred on account of the posting and which are part of remuneration.

(21) The constituent elements of remuneration and other terms and conditions of employment under national law or collective agreements as referred to in this Directive should be clear and transparent to all undertakings and posted workers. As transparency of, and access to, information are essential for legal certainty and law enforcement, it is, with regard to Article 5 of Directive 2014/67/EU, justified to extend Member States' obligation to publish the information on the terms and conditions of employment, on the single official national website, to the constituent elements of remuneration rendered mandatory as well as to the additional set of terms and conditions of employment applicable to postings exceeding 12 or, where applicable, 18 months under this Directive. Each Member State should ensure that the information provided on the single official national website is accurate and is updated on a regular basis. Any penalty imposed on an undertaking for non-compliance with the terms and conditions of employment to be ensured to posted workers should be proportionate, and the determination of the penalty should take into account, in particular, whether the information on the single official national website on the terms and conditions of employment was provided in accordance with Article 5 of Directive 2014/67/EU, respecting the autonomy of the social partners.

(22) Directive 2014/67/EU lays down a number of provisions to ensure that rules on the posting of workers are enforced and are respected by all undertakings. Article 4 of that Directive provides for factual elements that may be taken into account in the overall assessment of the specific situations in order to identify genuine posting situations and to prevent abuse and circumvention of the rules.

(23) Employers should, before the beginning of a posting, take appropriate measures to provide essential information to the worker about the terms and conditions of employment as regards the posting in accordance with Council Directive 91/533/EEC.[9]

(24) This Directive establishes a balanced framework with regard to the freedom to provide services and the protection of posted workers, which is non-discriminatory, transparent and proportionate while respecting the diversity of national industrial relations. This Directive does not prevent the application of terms and conditions of employment which are more favourable to posted workers.

(25) With a view to tackling abuses in subcontracting situations and in order to protect the rights of posted workers, Member States should take appropriate measures, in accordance with Article 12 of Directive 2014/67/EU, to ensure subcontracting liability.

(26) In order to ensure that Directive 96/71/EC is correctly applied, coordination between the Member States' competent authorities and/or bodies and cooperation at Union level on combating fraud relating to the posting of workers should be strengthened.

(27) In the context of combating fraud related to the posting of workers, the European Platform to enhance cooperation in tackling undeclared work (the 'Platform'), established by Decision (EU) 2016/344 of the European Parliament and the Council,[10] should, in accordance with its mandate, participate in the monitoring and the evaluation of cases of fraud, improve the implementation and efficiency of administrative cooperation between Member States, develop alert mechanisms and bring assistance and support to reinforced administrative cooperation and information exchanges between the competent authorities or bodies. In doing so, the Platform is to work in close cooperation with the Committee of Experts on Posting of Workers, established by Commission Decision 2009/17/EC.[11]

(28) The transnational nature of certain situations of fraud or abuses related to the posting of workers justifies concrete measures aiming to reinforce the transnational dimension of inspections, inquiries and exchanges of information between the competent authorities or bodies of the Member States concerned. To that end, in the framework of administrative cooperation provided for in Directives 96/71/EC and 2014/67/EU, in particular Article 7(4) of Directive 2014/67/EU, the competent authorities or bodies should have the necessary means for alerting on such situations and exchanging information aiming to prevent and combat fraud and abuses.

(29) In accordance with the Joint Political Declaration of 28 September 2011 of Member States and the Commission on explanatory documents,[12] Member States have undertaken to accompany, in justified cases, the notification of their transposition measures with one or more documents explaining the relationship between the components of a directive and the corresponding parts of national transposition instruments. With regard to this Directive, the legislator considers the transmission of such documents to be justified.

(30) Directive 96/71/EC should be amended accordingly,

NOTES

1 OJ C 75, 10.3.2017, p 81.

2 OJ C 185, 9.6.2017, p 75.

3 Position of the European Parliament of 29 May 2018 (not yet published in the Official Journal) and decision of the Council of 21 June 2018.

4 Directive 96/71/EC of the European Parliament and of the Council of 16 December 1996 concerning the posting of workers in the framework of the provision of services (OJ L18, 21.1.1997, p 1).

5 Directive 2014/67/EU of the European Parliament and of the Council of 15 May 2014 on the enforcement of Directive 96/71/EC concerning the posting of workers in the framework of the provision of services and amending Regulation (EU) No 1024/2012 on administrative cooperation through the Internal Market Information System ('the IMI Regulation') (OJ L159, 28.5.2014, p 11).

6 Directive 2008/104/EC of the European Parliament and of the Council of 19 November 2008 on temporary agency work (OJ L327, 5.12.2008, p 9).

7 Regulation (EC) No 883/2004 of the European Parliament and of the Council of 29 April 2004 on the coordination of social security systems (OJ L166, 30.4.2004, p 1).

8 Regulation (EC) No 987/2009 of the European Parliament and of the Council of 16 September 2009 laying down the procedure for implementing Regulation (EC) No 883/2004 on the coordination of social security systems (OJ L284, 30.10.2009, p 1).

9 Council Directive 91/533/EEC of 14 October 1991 on an employer's obligation to inform employees of the conditions applicable to the contract or employment relationship (OJ L288, 18.10.1991, p 32).

10 Decision (EU) 2016/344 of the European Parliament and of the Council of 9 March 2016 on establishing a European Platform to enhance cooperation in tackling undeclared work (OJ L65, 11.3.2016, p 12).

11 Commission Decision 2009/17/EC of 19 December 2008 setting up the Committee of Experts on Posting of Workers (OJ L8, 13.1.2009, p 26).

12 OJ C 369, 17.12.2011, p 14.

HAVE ADOPTED THIS DIRECTIVE:

Article 1 (*Amends European Parliament and Council Directive 96/71/EC at* **[3.176]**.)

[3.682]
Article 2
Review

1. The Commission shall review the application and implementation of this Directive. By 30 July 2023, the Commission shall submit a report on the application and implementation of this Directive to the European Parliament, the Council and the European Economic and Social Committee and propose, where appropriate, necessary amendments to this Directive and to Directive 96/71/EC.

2. The report referred to in paragraph 1 shall include an assessment of whether further measures to ensure a level playing field and protect workers are required:

(a) in the case of subcontracting;

(b) in the light of Article 3(3) of this Directive, taking into account the developments concerning the legislative act amending Directive 2006/22/EC of the European Parliament and of the Council[13] as regards enforcement requirements and laying down specific rules with respect to Directive 96/71/EC and Directive 2014/67/EU for posting drivers in the road transport sector.

NOTES

[1] Directive 2006/22/EC of the European Parliament and of the Council of 15 March 2006 on minimum conditions for the implementation of Council Regulations (EEC) No 3820/85 and (EEC) No 3821/85 concerning social legislation relating to road transport activities and repealing Council Directive 88/599/EEC (OJ L102, 11.4.2006, p 35).

[3.683]
Article 3
Transposition and application

1. Member States shall adopt and publish, by 30 July 2020, the laws, regulations and administrative provisions necessary to comply with this Directive. They shall immediately communicate the text of those measures to the Commission.

They shall apply those measures from 30 July 2020. Until that date, Directive 96/71/EC shall remain applicable in its wording prior to the amendments introduced by this Directive.

When Member States adopt those measures, they shall contain a reference to this Directive or shall be accompanied by such reference on the occasion of their official publication. The methods of making such reference shall be laid down by Member States.

2. Member States shall communicate to the Commission the text of the main measures of national law which they adopt in the field covered by this Directive.

3. This Directive shall apply to the road transport sector from the date of application of a legislative act amending Directive 2006/22/EC as regards enforcement requirements and laying down specific rules with respect to Directive 96/71/EC and Directive 2014/67/EU for posting drivers in the road transport sector.

[3.684]
Article 4
Entry into force

This Directive shall enter into force on the twentieth day following that of its publication in the Official Journal of the European Union.

[3.685]
Article 5
Addressees

This Directive is addressed to the Member States.

PART 4
STATUTORY CODES OF PRACTICE, ETC

A. ACAS

ACAS CODE OF PRACTICE 1
CODE OF PRACTICE ON DISCIPLINARY AND GRIEVANCE PROCEDURES (2015)

[4.1]

NOTES

This is the sixth version of the Code originally produced by ACAS in 1977, and reissued in 1998, 2000, 2004, and 2009.

This version was produced under the authority given to ACAS by TULR(C)A 1992, s 199 at **[1.515]** and approved by the Secretary of State and by Parliament in accordance with s 200(2) and (4) at **[1.516]** (see the Employment Code of Practice (Disciplinary and Grievance Procedures) Order 2015, SI 2015/649). It came into effect on 11 March 2015. For the legal status of the Code see s 207 of the 1992 Act at **[1.523]**. Note also that by s 207A of that Act at **[1.524]**, as inserted by s 2 of the Employment Act 2008, an employment tribunal may in the circumstances there provided increase or decrease any compensation awarded by up to 25% where there has been unreasonable failure to comply with any relevant provision of the Code.

The Code is reproduced here in full, but it should be noted that the Foreword does not form part of the Code for the purpose of the legal effects of the Code under ss 207 and 207A of the 1992 Act. The Guide issued by ACAS to amplify the Code is at **[4.6]** below.

See *Harvey* AII (7), (10).

CONTENTS

FOREWORD

[4.2]

The Acas statutory Code of Practice on discipline and grievance is set out at paragraphs 1 to 47 on the following pages. It provides basic practical guidance to employers, employees and their representatives and sets out principles for handling disciplinary and grievance situations in the workplace. The Code does not apply to dismissals due to redundancy or the non-renewal of fixed-term contracts on their expiry. Guidance on handling redundancies is contained in Acas' guide 'Handling small-scale redundancies – a step-by-step guide' and in its advisory booklet 'How to manage large-scale redundancies'.

The Code is issued under section 199 of the Trade Union and Labour Relations (Consolidation) Act 1992 and was laid before both Houses of Parliament on 16 January 2015. It comes into effect by order of the Secretary of State on 11 March 2015 and replaces the Code issued in 2009.

A failure to follow the Code does not, in itself, make a person or organisation liable to proceedings. However, employment tribunals will take the Code into account when considering relevant cases. Tribunals will also be able to adjust any awards made in relevant cases by up to 25 per cent for unreasonable failure to comply with any provision of the Code. This means that if the tribunal feels that an employer has unreasonably failed to follow the guidance set out in the Code they can increase any award they have made by up to 25 per cent. Conversely, if they feel an employee has unreasonably failed to follow the guidance set out in the Code they can reduce any award they have made by up to 25 per cent.

Employers and employees should always seek to resolve disciplinary and grievance issues in the workplace. Where this is not possible employers and employees should consider using an independent third party to help resolve the problem. The third party need not come from outside the organisation but could be an internal mediator, so long as they are not involved in the disciplinary or grievance issue. In some cases, an external mediator might be appropriate.

Many potential disciplinary or grievance issues can be resolved informally. A quiet word is often all that is required to resolve an issue. However, where an issue cannot be resolved informally then it may be pursued formally. This Code sets out the basic requirements of fairness that will be applicable in most cases; it is intended to provide the standard of reasonable behaviour in most instances.

Employers would be well advised to keep a written record of any disciplinary or grievances cases they deal with.

Organisations may wish to consider dealing with issues involving bullying, harassment or whistleblowing under a separate procedure.

More comprehensive advice and guidance on dealing with disciplinary and grievance situations is contained in the Acas booklet, 'Discipline and grievances at work: the Acas guide'. The booklet also contains sample disciplinary and grievance procedures. Copies of the guidance can be downloaded from the Acas website at www.acas.org.uk/discipline.

Unlike the Code employment tribunals are not required to have regard to the Acas guidance booklet. However, it provides more detailed advice and guidance that employers and employees will often find helpful both in general terms and in individual cases.

THE CODE OF PRACTICE

INTRODUCTION

[4.3]
1. This Code is designed to help employers, employees and their representatives deal with disciplinary and grievance situations in the workplace.

- Disciplinary situations include misconduct and/or poor performance. If employers have a separate capability procedure they may prefer to address performance issues under this procedure. If so, however, the basic principles of fairness set out in this Code should still be followed, albeit that they may need to be adapted.
- Grievances are concerns, problems or complaints that employees raise with their employers.

The Code does not apply to redundancy dismissals or the non-renewal of fixed term contracts on their expiry.

2. Fairness and transparency are promoted by developing and using rules and procedures for handling disciplinary and grievance situations. These should be set down in writing, be specific and clear. Employees and, where appropriate, their representatives should be involved in the development of rules and procedures. It is also important to help employees and managers understand what the rules and procedures are, where they can be found and how they are to be used.

3. Where some form of formal action is needed, what action is reasonable or justified will depend on all the circumstances of the particular case. Employment tribunals will take the size and resources of an employer into account when deciding on relevant cases and it may sometimes not be practicable for all employers to take all of the steps set out in this Code.

4. That said, whenever a disciplinary or grievance process is being followed it is important to deal with issues fairly. There are a number of elements to this:

- Employers and employees should raise and deal with issues **promptly** and should not unreasonably delay meetings, decisions or confirmation of those decisions.
- Employers and employees should act **consistently**.
- Employers should carry out any necessary **investigations**, to establish the facts of the case.
- Employers should **inform** employees of the basis of the problem and give them an opportunity to **put their case** in response before any decisions are made.
- Employers should allow employees to be **accompanied** at any formal disciplinary or grievance meeting.
- Employers should allow an employee to **appeal** against any formal decision made.

DISCIPLINE

KEYS TO HANDLING DISCIPLINARY ISSUES IN THE WORKPLACE

Establish the facts of each case

[4.4]
5. It is important to carry out necessary investigations of potential disciplinary matters without unreasonable delay to establish the facts of the case. In some cases this will require the holding of an investigatory meeting with the employee before proceeding to any disciplinary hearing. In others, the investigatory stage will be the collation of evidence by the employer for use at any disciplinary hearing.

6. In misconduct cases, where practicable, different people should carry out the investigation and disciplinary hearing.

7. If there is an investigatory meeting this should not by itself result in any disciplinary action. Although there is no statutory right for an employee to be accompanied at a formal investigatory meeting, such a right may be allowed under an employer's own procedure.

8. In cases where a period of suspension with pay is considered necessary, this period should be as brief as possible, should be kept under review and it should be made clear that this suspension is not considered a disciplinary action.

Inform the employee of the problem

9. If it is decided that there is a disciplinary case to answer, the employee should be notified of this in writing. This notification should contain sufficient information about the alleged misconduct or poor performance and its possible consequences to enable the employee to prepare to answer the case at a disciplinary meeting. It would normally be appropriate to provide copies of any written evidence, which may include any witness statements, with the notification.

10. The notification should also give details of the time and venue for the disciplinary meeting and advise the employee of their right to be accompanied at the meeting.

Hold a meeting with the employee to discuss the problem

11. The meeting should be held without unreasonable delay whilst allowing the employee reasonable time to prepare their case.

12. Employers and employees (and their companions) should make every effort to attend the meeting. At the meeting the employer should explain the complaint against the employee and go through the evidence that has been gathered. The employee should be allowed to set out their case and answer any allegations that have been made. The employee should also be given a reasonable opportunity to ask questions, present evidence and call relevant witnesses. They should also be given an opportunity to raise points about any information provided by witnesses. Where an employer or employee intends to call relevant witnesses they should give advance notice that they intend to do this.

Allow the employee to be accompanied at the meeting

13. Workers have a statutory right to be accompanied by a companion where the disciplinary meeting could result in:

- a formal warning being issued; or
- the taking of some other disciplinary action; or
- the confirmation of a warning or some other disciplinary action (appeal hearings).

14. The statutory right is to be accompanied by a fellow worker, a trade union representative, or an official employed by a trade union. A trade union representative who is not an employed official must have been certified by their union as being competent to accompany a worker. Employers must agree to a worker's request to be accompanied by any companion from one of these categories. Workers may also alter their choice of companion if they wish. As a matter of good practice, in making their choice workers should bear in mind the practicalities of the arrangements. For instance, a worker may choose to be accompanied by a companion who is suitable, willing and available on site rather than someone from a geographically remote location.

15. To exercise the statutory right to be accompanied workers must make a reasonable request. What is reasonable will depend on the circumstances of each individual case. A request to be accompanied does not have to be in writing or within a certain timeframe. However, a worker should provide enough time for the employer to deal with the companion's attendance at the meeting. Workers should also consider how they make their request so that it is clearly understood, for instance by letting the employer know in advance the name of the companion where possible and whether they are a fellow worker or trade union official or representative.

16. If a worker's chosen companion will not be available at the time proposed for the hearing by the employer, the employer must postpone the hearing to a time proposed by the worker provided that the alternative time is both reasonable and not more than five working days after the date originally proposed.

17. The companion should be allowed to address the hearing to put and sum up the worker's case, respond on behalf of the worker to any views expressed at the meeting and confer with the worker during the hearing. The companion does not, however, have the right to answer questions on the worker's behalf, address the hearing if the worker does not wish it or prevent the employer from explaining their case.

Decide on appropriate action

18. After the meeting decide whether or not disciplinary or any other action is justified and inform the employee accordingly in writing.

19. Where misconduct is confirmed or the employee is found to be performing unsatisfactorily it is usual to give the employee a written warning. A further act of misconduct or failure to improve performance within a set period would normally result in a final written warning.

20. If an employee's first misconduct or unsatisfactory performance is sufficiently serious, it may be appropriate to move directly to a final written warning. This might occur where the employee's actions have had, or are liable to have, a serious or harmful impact on the organisation.

21. A first or final written warning should set out the nature of the misconduct or poor performance and the change in behaviour or improvement in performance required (with timescale). The employee should be told how long the warning will remain current. The employee should be informed of the consequences of further misconduct, or failure to improve performance, within the set period following a final warning. For instance that it may result in dismissal or some other contractual penalty such as demotion or loss of seniority.

22. A decision to dismiss should only be taken by a manager who has the authority to do so. The employee should be informed as soon as possible of the reasons for the dismissal, the date on which the employment contract will end, the appropriate period of notice and their right of appeal.

23. Some acts, termed gross misconduct, are so serious in themselves or have such serious consequences that they may call for dismissal without notice for a first offence. But a fair disciplinary process should always be followed, before dismissing for gross misconduct.

24. Disciplinary rules should give examples of acts which the employer regards as acts of gross misconduct. These may vary according to the nature of the organisation and what it does, but might include things such as theft or fraud, physical violence, gross negligence or serious insubordination.

25. Where an employee is persistently unable or unwilling to attend a disciplinary meeting without good cause the employer should make a decision on the evidence available.

Provide employees with an opportunity to appeal

26. Where an employee feels that disciplinary action taken against them is wrong or unjust they should appeal against the decision. Appeals should be heard without unreasonable delay and ideally at an agreed time and place. Employees should let employers know the grounds for their appeal in writing.

27. The appeal should be dealt with impartially and wherever possible, by a manager who has not previously been involved in the case.

28. Workers have a statutory right to be accompanied at appeal hearings.

29. Employees should be informed in writing of the results of the appeal hearing as soon as possible.

Special cases

30. Where disciplinary action is being considered against an employee who is a trade union representative the normal disciplinary procedure should be followed. Depending on the circumstances, however, it is advisable to discuss the matter at an early stage with an official employed by the union, after obtaining the employee's agreement.

31. If an employee is charged with, or convicted of a criminal offence this is not normally in itself reason for disciplinary action. Consideration needs to be given to what effect the charge or conviction has on the employee's suitability to do the job and their relationship with their employer, work colleagues and customers.

GRIEVANCE

KEYS TO HANDLING GRIEVANCES IN THE WORKPLACE

Let the employer know the nature of the grievance

[4.5]
32. If it is not possible to resolve a grievance informally employees should raise the matter formally and without unreasonable delay with a manager who is not the subject of the grievance. This should be done in writing and should set out the nature of the grievance.

Hold a meeting with the employee to discuss the grievance

33. Employers should arrange for a formal meeting to be held without unreasonable delay after a grievance is received.

34. Employers, employees and their companions should make every effort to attend the meeting. Employees should be allowed to explain their grievance and how they think it should be resolved. Consideration should be given to adjourning the meeting for any investigation that may be necessary.

Allow the employee to be accompanied at the meeting

35. Workers have a statutory right to be accompanied by a companion at a grievance meeting which deals with a complaint about a duty owed by the employer to the worker. So this would apply where the complaint is, for example, that the employer is not honouring the worker's contract, or is in breach of legislation.

36. The statutory right is to be accompanied by a fellow worker, a trade union representative, or an official employed by a trade union. A trade union representative who is not an employed official must have been certified by their union as being competent to accompany a worker. Employers must agree to a worker's request to be accompanied by any companion from one of these categories. Workers may also alter their choice of companion if they wish. As a matter of good practice, in making their choice workers should bear in mind the practicalities of the arrangements. For instance, a worker may choose to be accompanied by a companion who is suitable, willing and available on site rather than someone from a geographically remote location.

37. To exercise the statutory right to be accompanied workers must make a reasonable request. What is reasonable will depend on the circumstances of each individual case. A request to be accompanied does not have to be in writing or within a certain time frame. However, a worker should provide enough time for the employer to deal with the companion's attendance at the meeting. Workers should also consider how they make their request so that it is clearly understood, for instance by letting the employer know in advance the name of the companion where possible and whether they are a fellow worker or trade union official or representative.

38. If a worker's chosen companion will not be available at the time proposed for the hearing by the employer, the employer must postpone the hearing to a time proposed by the worker provided that the alternative time is both reasonable and not more than five working days after the date originally proposed.

39. The companion should be allowed to address the hearing to put and sum up the worker's case, respond on behalf of the worker to any views expressed at the meeting and confer with the worker during the hearing. The companion does not however, have the right to answer questions on the worker's behalf, address the hearing if the worker does not wish it or prevent the employer from explaining their case.

Decide on appropriate action

40. Following the meeting decide on what action, if any, to take. Decisions should be communicated to the employee, in writing, without unreasonable delay and, where appropriate, should set out what action the employer intends to take to resolve the grievance. The employee should be informed that they can appeal if they are not content with the action taken.

Allow the employee to take the grievance further if not resolved

41. Where an employee feels that their grievance has not been satisfactorily resolved they should appeal. They should let their employer know the grounds for their appeal without unreasonable delay and in writing.

42. Appeals should be heard without unreasonable delay and at a time and place which should be notified to the employee in advance.

43. The appeal should be dealt with impartially and wherever possible by a manager who has not previously been involved in the case.

44. Workers have a statutory right to be accompanied at any such appeal hearing.

45. The outcome of the appeal should be communicated to the employee in writing without unreasonable delay.

Overlapping grievance and disciplinary cases

46. Where an employee raises a grievance during a disciplinary process the disciplinary process may be temporarily suspended in order to deal with the grievance. Where the grievance and disciplinary cases are related it may be appropriate to deal with both issues concurrently.

Collective grievances

47. The provisions of this code do not apply to grievances raised on behalf of two or more employees by a representative of a recognised trade union or other appropriate workplace representative. These grievances should be handled in accordance with the organisation's collective grievance process.

DISCIPLINE AND GRIEVANCES AT WORK THE ACAS GUIDE

February 2019

[4.6]

NOTES

This Guide was issued by ACAS to supplement the statutory guidance provided by the Code of Practice at **[4.1]** above. It was reissued in February 2019. It has no statutory force but provides detailed guidance as to the application of the Code of Practice; see further the notes to that Code, *ante*.

CONTENTS

INTRODUCTION

[4.7]
This guide provides good practice advice for dealing with discipline and grievances in the workplace. It complements the **Acas Code of Practice** on disciplinary and grievance procedures. Extracts from the Code of Practice are reproduced in boxes accompanied by further practical advice and guidance.

The Acas Code of Practice sets out principles for handling disciplinary and grievance situations in the workplace. This guide provides more detailed advice and guidance that employers and employees will often find helpful both in general terms and in individual cases.

Employment Tribunals and the Acas Code of Practice on Disciplinary and Grievance procedures
Employment tribunals are legally required to take the Acas Code of Practice into account when considering relevant cases. Tribunals are also be able to adjust any compensatory awards made in these cases by up to 25 per cent for unreasonable failure to comply with any provision of the Code. This means that if the tribunal feels that an employer has unreasonably failed to follow the guidance set out in the Code they can increase any award they have made by up to 25 per cent. Conversely, if they feel an employee has unreasonably failed to follow the guidance set out in the Code they can reduce any award they have made by up to 25 per cent. Employment tribunals are not required to have regard to guidance in this booklet that does not form part of the Code.

The law on unfair dismissal requires employers to act reasonably when dealing with disciplinary issues. What is classed as reasonable behaviour will depend on the circumstances of each case, and is ultimately a matter for employment tribunals to decide. However, the core principles are set out in the Acas Code of Practice.

Employers and employees should always seek to resolve disciplinary and grievance issues in the workplace. If discipline and grievance issues are settled at an early stage they are normally less time-consuming and less likely to damage working relationships.

Good employment relations practices – including for recruitment, induction training, communications and consultation – can prevent many discipline and grievance problems arising. Organisations are also more likely to have positive employment relationships if they make efforts to gain their employees' commitment through:

- showing them clear leadership and letting them know how they can contribute
- engaging them in their work and giving them the power to make some decisions themselves rather than trying to control and restrict them
- showing them respect and appreciation
- giving them ways to voice their views and concerns.

Acas provides comprehensive guidance on employment issues which you can download from our website, and information about suitable training. For further details see the Acas website www.acas.org.uk.

Handling discipline: an overview

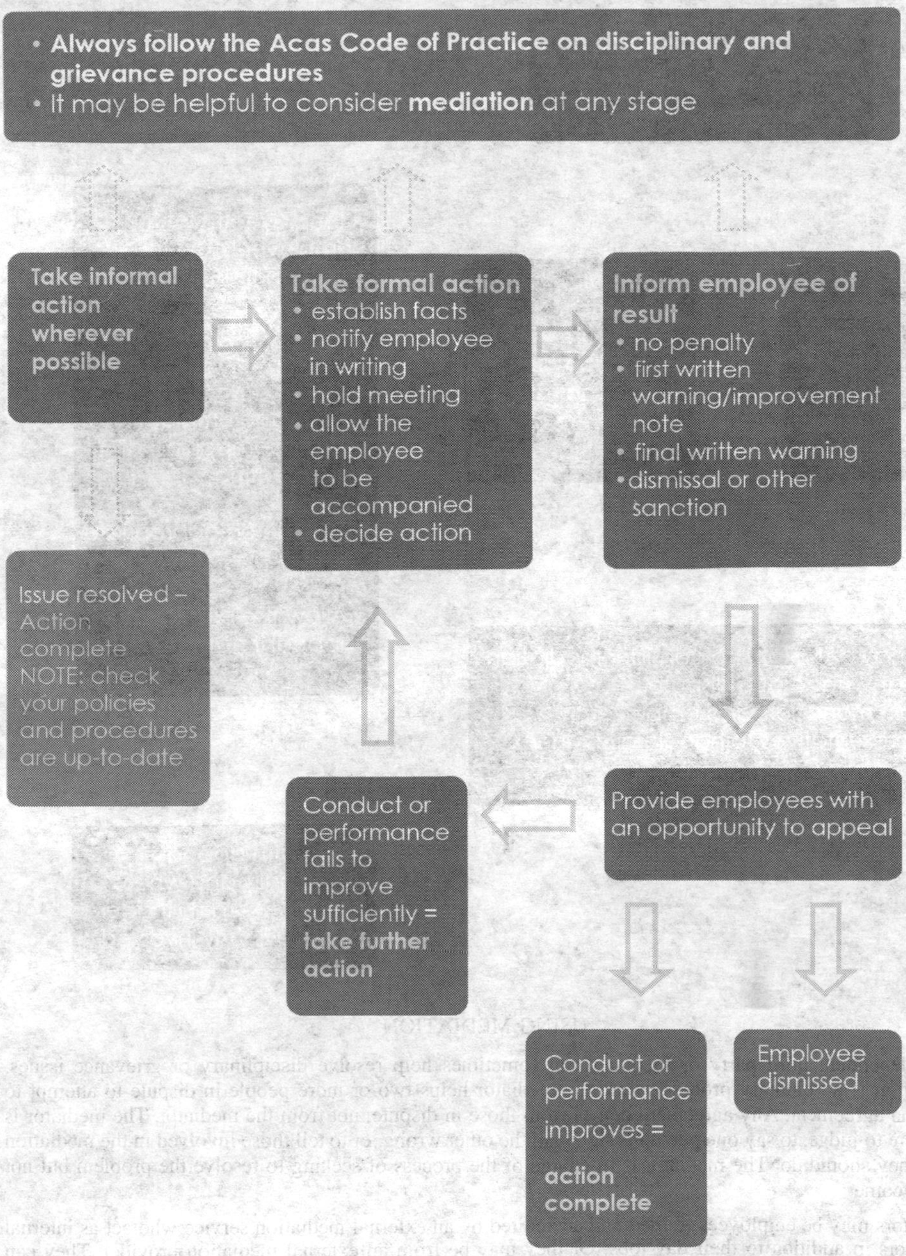
• Always follow the Acas Code of Practice on disciplinary and grievance procedures
• It may be helpful to consider mediation at any stage
Take informal action wherever possible
Take formal action
• establish facts
• notify employee in writing
• hold meeting
• allow the employee to be accompanied
• decide action
Inform employee of result
• no penalty
• first written warning/improvement note
• final written warning
• dismissal or other sanction
Issue resolved – Action complete NOTE: check your policies and procedures are up-to-date
Provide employees with an opportunity to appeal
Conduct or performance fails to improve sufficiently = take further action
Conduct or performance improves = action complete
Employee dismissed

Handling grievances: an overview

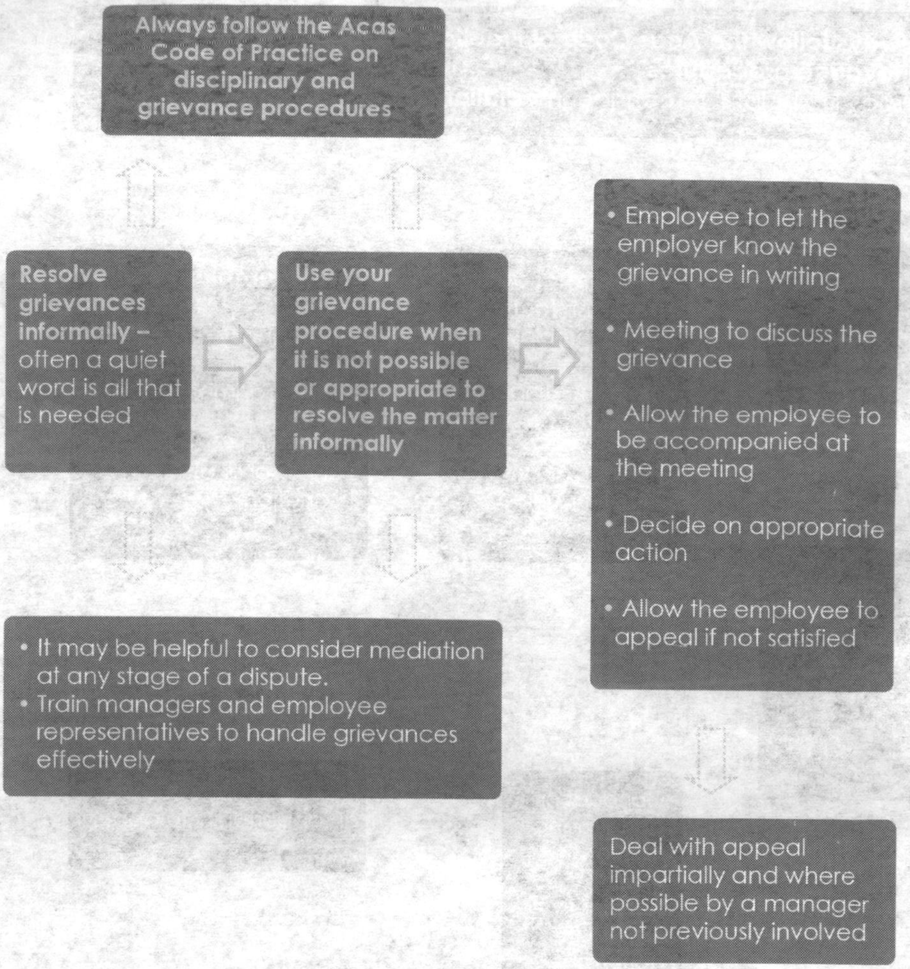

Always follow the Acas Code of Practice on disciplinary and grievance procedures
Resolve grievances informally – often a quiet word is all that is needed
Use your grievance procedure when it is not possible or appropriate to resolve the matter informally
• Employee to let the employer know the grievance in writing
• Meeting to discuss the grievance
• Allow the employee to be accompanied at the meeting
• Decide on appropriate action
• Allow the employee to appeal if not satisfied
• It may be helpful to consider mediation at any stage of a dispute.
• Train managers and employee representatives to handle grievances effectively
Deal with appeal impartially and where possible by a manager not previously involved

USING MEDIATION

An independent third party or mediator can sometimes help resolve disciplinary or grievance issues. Mediation is a voluntary process where the mediator helps two or more people in dispute to attempt to reach an agreement. Any agreement comes from those in dispute, not from the mediator. The mediator is not there to judge, to say one person is right and the other wrong, or to tell those involved in the mediation what they should do. The mediator is in charge of the process of seeking to resolve the problem but not the outcome.

Mediators may be employees trained and accredited by an external mediation service who act as internal mediators in addition to their day jobs. Or they may be from an external mediation provider. They can work individually or in pairs as co-mediators.

There are no hard-and-fast rules for when mediation is appropriate but it can be used:

- for conflict involving colleagues of a similar job or grade, or between a line manager and their staff
- at any stage in the conflict as long as any ongoing formal procedures are temporarily suspended, or where mediation is included as a stage in the procedures themselves
- to rebuild relationships after a formal dispute has been resolved
- to address a range of issues, including relationship breakdown, personality clashes, communication problems, bullying and harassment.

In some organisations mediation is written into formal discipline and grievance procedures as an optional stage. Where this is not the case, it is useful to be clear about whether the discipline and grievance procedure can be suspended if mediation is deemed to be an appropriate method of resolving the dispute.

Grievances most obviously lend themselves to the possibility of mediation. Managers may not always see it as appropriate to surrender their discretion in relation to disciplinary issues where they believe a point of principle is at stake, such as misconduct or poor performance. However, disciplinary and grievance issues can become blurred, and the employer may prefer to tackle the underlying relationship issues by means of mediation.

Cases unsuitable for mediation

Mediation may not be suitable if:

- used as a first resort – because people should be encouraged to speak to each other and talk to their manager before they seek a solution via mediation
- it is used by a manager to avoid their managerial responsibilities
- a decision about right or wrong is needed, for example where there is possible criminal activity
- the individual bringing a discrimination or harassment case wants it investigated
- the parties do not have the power to settle the issue
- one side is completely intransigent and using mediation will only raise unrealistic expectations of a positive outcome.

For more information about mediation see www.acas.org.uk/mediation and the Acas/CIPD guide *Mediation: an approach to resolving workplace issues* which can be downloaded from the website.

DISCIPLINE
KEYS TO HANDLING DISCIPLINARY PROBLEMS IN THE WORKPLACE

RESOLVE DISCIPLINE ISSUES INFORMALLY

[4.8]
Cases of minor misconduct or unsatisfactory performance are usually best dealt with informally. A quiet word is often all that is required to improve an employee's conduct or performance. In some cases additional training, coaching and advice may be what is needed. An informal approach may be particularly helpful in small firms, where problems can be resolved quickly and confidentially. There will be situations where matters are more serious or where an informal approach has been tried but is not working.

If informal action does not bring about an improvement, or the misconduct or unsatisfactory performance is considered too serious to be classed as minor, employers should provide employees with a clear signal of their dissatisfaction by taking formal action.

> ***Discipline in practice: Example 1***
>
> A valued and generally reliable employee is late for work on a number of occasions causing difficulty for other staff who have to provide cover.
>
> You talk to the employee on his own and he reveals that he has recently split up with his wife and he now has to take the children to school on the way to work. You agree a temporary adjustment to his start and finish times and he undertakes to make arrangements for 'school run' cover which solves the problem. You decide that formal disciplinary action is not appropriate.

How should it be done?

Talk to the employee in private. This should be a two-way discussion, aimed at discussing possible shortcomings in conduct or performance and encouraging improvement. Criticism should be constructive, with the emphasis being on finding ways for the employee to improve and for the improvement to be sustained.

Listen to whatever the employee has to say about the issue. It may become evident there is no problem – if so make this clear to the employee.

Where improvement is required make sure the employee understands what needs to be done, how their performance or conduct will be reviewed, and over what period. It may be useful to confirm in writing what has been decided.

Be careful that any informal action does not turn into formal disciplinary action, as this may unintentionally deny the employee certain rights, such as the right to be accompanied. If, during the discussion, it becomes obvious that the matter may be more serious, the meeting should be adjourned. The employee should be told that the matter will be continued under the formal disciplinary procedure.

Keep brief notes of any agreed informal action for reference purposes. There should be reviews of progress over specified periods.

Consider at any stage whether the use of an independent mediator may be helpful.

DEVELOP RULES AND PROCEDURES

[4.9]

> **Acas Code of Practice on disciplinary and grievance procedures Extract**
>
> Fairness and transparency are promoted by developing and using rules and procedures for handling disciplinary and grievance situations. These should be set down in writing, be specific and clear. Employees and, where appropriate, their representatives should be involved in the development of rules and procedures. It is also important to help employees and managers understand what the rules and procedures are, where they can be found and how they are to be used.

Rules and performance standards

Clear rules benefit employees and set standards of conduct. They also help employers to act fairly and consistently.

Employers should also set standards of performance so that employees know what is expected of them. This is usually done as part of an organisation's performance management which will involve agreeing objectives and reviewing performance on a regular basis.

What should rules cover?

Different organisations will have different requirements but rules often cover such matters as:

- timekeeping
- absence
- health and safety
- use of organisation facilities
- discrimination, bullying and harassment
- personal appearance
- the types of conduct that might be considered as 'gross misconduct'.

How should rules be drawn up and communicated?

Rules are likely to be more effective if they are accepted as reasonable by those covered by them and those who operate them. It is good practice to develop rules in consultation with employees (and their representatives where appropriate) and those who will have responsibility for applying them.

Unless there are reasons why different sets of rules apply to different groups they should apply to all employees at all levels in the organisation.

The rules should not discriminate on the grounds of age, disability, gender reassignment, marital or civil partnership status, pregnancy and maternity, race, religion or belief, sex, or sexual orientation.

Writing down the rules helps both managers and employees know what is expected of them. The rules should be made clear to employees. Ideally employees should be given their own printed copy of the rules or written information about how to access them. For example, on the organisation's intranet or in their personnel handbook. Employees are entitled to a written statement of employment particulars which must include a note about disciplinary rules and procedures. (Guidance on what the written statement must include is provided on www.acas.org.uk.)

In a small organisation, it may be sufficient for rules to be displayed in a prominent place. See Appendix 1 for a checklist on 'Disciplinary rules for small organisations'.

Clearly communicate the rules to everyone

Special attention should be paid to ensure that rules are understood by any employees without recent experience of working life (for instance young people new to the world of work, or those returning to work after a lengthy break), and by employees whose English or reading ability is limited, or who have a disability such as visual impairment.

Why have a disciplinary procedure?

A disciplinary procedure is the means by which rules are observed and standards are maintained.

The procedure should be used primarily to help and encourage employees to improve rather than just as a way of imposing punishment. It provides a method of dealing with any apparent shortcomings in conduct or performance and can help an employee to become effective again. The procedure should be fair, effective, and consistently applied.

Acas Code of Practice on disciplinary and grievance procedures Extract
Disciplinary situations include misconduct and/or poor performance. If employers have a separate capability procedure they may prefer to address performance issues under this procedure. If so, however, the basic principles of fairness set out in this Code should still be followed, albeit that they may need to be adapted.

What should disciplinary procedures contain?

When drawing up and applying procedures, employers should always bear in mind principles of fairness. For example, employees should be informed of the allegations against them, together with the supporting evidence, in advance of the meeting. Employees should be given the opportunity to challenge the allegations before decisions are reached and should be provided with a right to appeal. Good disciplinary procedures should:

- be in writing
- be non-discriminatory
- provide for matters to be dealt with speedily
- allow for information to be kept confidential
- tell employees what disciplinary action might be taken
- say what levels of management have the authority to take the various forms of disciplinary action
- require employees to be informed of the complaints against them and supporting evidence, before a disciplinary meeting
- give employees a chance to have their say before management reaches a decision
- provide for the right to be accompanied at disciplinary hearings
- provide that no employee is dismissed for a first breach of discipline, except in cases of gross misconduct

- require management to investigate fully before any disciplinary action is taken
- ensure that employees are given an explanation for any sanction and allow employees to appeal against a decision
- apply to all employees, irrespective of their length of service, status or say if there are different rules for different groups and ensure that:
  - any investigatory period of suspension is with pay, and specify how pay is to be calculated during this period. (If, exceptionally, suspension is to be without pay, this must be provided for in the contract of employment)
  - any suspension is brief, is never used as a sanction against the employee prior to a disciplinary meeting and decision, and the suspended employee is kept informed of progress
  - the employee will be heard in good faith and that there is no pre-judgement of the issue
  - where the facts are in dispute, no disciplinary penalty is imposed until the case has been carefully investigated, and there is a reasonably held belief that the employee committed the act in question.

Samples of disciplinary procedures are provided at Appendix 2 and may be adapted according to the requirements of the organisation.

Reviewing rules and procedures

Keep rules and procedures under review to make sure they are always relevant and effective. Address any shortcomings as they arise. Employees and their representatives should be consulted before new or additional rules are introduced.

Training

Good training helps managers achieve positive outcomes, reducing the need for any further disciplinary action. Those responsible for using and operating the disciplinary rules and procedures, including managers at all levels, should be trained for the task.

Ignoring or circumventing the procedures when dismissing an employee is likely to have a bearing on the outcome of any subsequent employment tribunal claim.

If the organisation recognises trade unions, or there is any other form of employee representation, it can be useful to undertake training on a joint basis –everyone then has the same understanding and has an opportunity to work through the procedure, clarifying any issues that might arise.

For information about suitable training see the Acas website www.acas.org.uk/training.

KEEPING WRITTEN RECORDS

What records should be kept?

[4.10]
The foreword to the Code of Practice advises employers to keep a written record of any disciplinary or grievances cases they deal with.

Records should include:
- the complaint against the employee
- the employee's defence
- findings made and actions taken
- the reason for actions taken
- whether an appeal was lodged
- the outcome of the appeal
- any grievances raised during the disciplinary procedure
- subsequent developments
- notes of any formal meetings.

Records should be treated as confidential and be kept no longer than necessary in accordance with the data protection principles set out in the Data Protection Act 2018. This Act also gives individuals the right to request and have access to certain personal data stored about them. See Appendix 5 for further information.

Copies of meeting records should be given to the employee including copies of any formal minutes that may have been taken. In certain circumstances (for example to protect a witness) the employer might withhold some information.

DEALING FAIRLY WITH FORMAL DISCIPLINARY ACTION

[4.11]

Acas Code of Practice on disciplinary and grievance procedures Extract

Where some form of formal action is needed, what action is reasonable or justified will depend on all the circumstances of the particular case. Employment tribunals will take the size and resources of an employer into account when deciding on relevant cases and it may sometimes not be practicable for all employers to take all of the steps set out in this Code.

That said, whenever a disciplinary or grievance process is being followed it is important to deal with issues fairly. There are a number of elements to this:

- Employers and employees should raise and deal with issues **promptly** and should not unreasonably delay meetings, decisions or confirmation of those decisions.

Acas Code of Practice on disciplinary and grievance procedures Extract	
•	Employers and employees should act **consistently**.
•	Employers should carry out any necessary **investigations**, to establish the facts of the case.
•	Employers should **inform** employees of the basis of the problem and give them an opportunity to **put their case** in response before any decisions are made.
•	Employers should allow employees to be **accompanied** at any formal disciplinary or grievance meeting.
•	Employers should allow an employee to **appeal** against any formal decision made.

The following pages give detailed guidance on handling formal disciplinary issues. Always bear in mind the need for fairness when following procedures taking account of the elements from the Acas Code of Practice reproduced above.

Dealing with absence is only one of any number of issues where disciplinary action may be considered. It can, however, raise particular problems and is dealt with separately at Appendix 4 – Dealing with absence.

A disciplinary process can be stressful for everyone involved. Sometimes a process may cause extreme distress or even impact on a person's mental health. Where there are signs of that happening to anyone involved in the process, employers should consider whether the process can be adjusted in some way, such as by allowing the individual to be accompanied at a disciplinary investigation meeting even where there is no formal right to be accompanied.

In some cases, it might be appropriate for an employer, with the agreement and involvement of the individual, to seek professional medical help or guidance as to how the disciplinary process can proceed fairly. If there are clear and repeated signs of distress, the employer should consider signposting the individual to an employee assistance programme, where one is available, or consider suggesting that the individual seeks advice from a GP. It is important to address this issue early to avoid it escalating.

If someone has an existing mental health condition which they have previously disclosed as a disability, the employer must make reasonable adjustments to the process.

ESTABLISHING THE FACTS

[4.12]

Acas Code of Practice on disciplinary and grievance procedures Extract
It is important to carry out necessary investigations of potential disciplinary matters without unreasonable delay to establish the facts of the case. In some cases this will require the holding of an investigatory meeting with the employee before proceeding to any disciplinary hearing. In others, the investigatory stage will be the collation of evidence by the employer for use at any disciplinary hearing.
In misconduct cases, where practicable, different people should carry out the investigation and disciplinary hearing.
If there is an investigatory meeting this should not by itself result in any disciplinary action. Although there is no statutory right for an employee to be accompanied at a formal [disciplinary] investigatory meeting, such a right may be allowed under an employer's own procedure.
In cases where a period of suspension with pay is considered necessary, this period should be as brief as possible, should be kept under review and it should be made clear that this suspension is not considered a disciplinary action.

Investigating cases

When investigating a disciplinary matter take care to deal with the employee in a fair and reasonable manner. The nature and extent of the investigations will depend on the seriousness of the matter and the more serious it is then the more thorough the investigation should be. It is important to keep an open mind and look for evidence which supports the employee's case as well as evidence against.

It is not always necessary to hold an investigatory meeting (often called a fact finding meeting). If a meeting is held, give the employee advance warning and time to prepare.

Any investigatory meeting should be conducted by a management representative and should be confined to establishing the facts of the case. It is important that disciplinary action is not considered at an investigatory meeting. If it becomes apparent that formal disciplinary action may be needed then this should be dealt with at a formal hearing at which the statutory right to be accompanied will apply. See also 'Use of external consultants'.

Further guidance on investigating disciplinary matters is available in the Acas guide on *Conducting Investigations in the Workplace* www.acas.org.uk/investigations.

Suspension

There may be instances where suspension with pay is necessary while investigations are carried out.

Employees must always receive their full pay and benefits during a period of suspension unless there is a clear contractual right for an employer to suspend without pay or benefits. Disciplinary procedures should specify how pay is to be calculated during any period of suspension.

Employers should seek advice if they are considering suspension without pay. A period of unpaid suspension is more likely to be viewed as a disciplinary sanction and could lead to accusations that the disciplinary procedure was not fair.

Suspension should be kept as brief as possible and should not exceed any maximum period which may be set out in the contract. If suspension is unreasonably prolonged it may then be open to the worker to take action for breach of contract, or in extreme cases to resign and claim constructive dismissal. Suspension should be reviewed regularly to decide whether it is still necessary and the suspended employee kept informed of progress.

Most disciplinary situations will not require suspension. It should only be considered exceptionally if there is a serious allegation of misconduct and:

- there are reasonable grounds to believe that the employee might seek to tamper with or destroy evidence, influence witnesses and/or sway an investigation into the disciplinary allegation
- working relationships have severely broken down to the point that there is a genuine risk to other employees, property, customers or other business interests if the employee remains in the workplace
- the employee is the subject of criminal proceedings which may affect whether they can do their job

Suspension can leave individuals feeling prejudged, demotivated and devalued. It should therefore only be used after very careful consideration. It should always be made clear that suspension is not an assumption of guilt and is not considered a disciplinary sanction.

Further guidance on suspension is available on the Acas website www.acas.org.uk/suspension

INFORMING THE EMPLOYEE

[4.13]

Acas Code of Practice on disciplinary and grievance procedures Extract

If it is decided that there is a disciplinary case to answer, the employee should be notified of this in writing. This notification should contain sufficient information about the alleged misconduct or poor performance and its possible consequences to enable the employee to prepare to answer the case at a disciplinary meeting.

It would normally be appropriate to provide copies of any written evidence, which may include any witness statements, with the notification. The notification should also give details of the time and venue for the disciplinary meeting and advise of the right to be accompanied at the meeting.

As well notifying the nature of the complaint and the right to be accompanied the employee should also be told about the procedure to be followed. A sample letter inviting an employee to a meeting is at Appendix 3.

HOLDING A DISCIPLINARY MEETING

[4.14]

Extract: Acas Code of Practice on disciplinary and grievance procedures

The meeting should be held without unreasonable delay whilst allowing the employee reasonable time to prepare their case.

Employers and employees (and their companions) should make every effort to attend the meeting. At the meeting the employer should explain the complaint against the employee and go through the evidence that has been gathered. The employee should be allowed to set out their case and answer any allegations that have been made. The employee should also be given a reasonable opportunity to ask questions, present evidence and call relevant witnesses. They should also be given an opportunity to raise points about any information provided by witnesses. Where an employer or employee intends to call relevant witnesses they should give advance notice that they intend to do this.

Preparing for the meeting

You should:

- ensure that all the relevant facts are available, such as disciplinary records and any other relevant documents (for instance absence or sickness records) and, where appropriate, written statements from witnesses
- where possible arrange for someone who is not involved in the case to take a note of the meeting and to act as a witness to what was said
- check if there are any special circumstances to be taken into account. For example, are there personal or other outside issues affecting performance or conduct?
- allow the employee time to prepare his or her case. Copies of any relevant papers and witness statements should be made available to the employee in advance
- be careful when dealing with evidence from a person who wishes to remain anonymous. In particular, take written statements that give details of time/place/dates as appropriate, seek corroborative evidence, check that the person's motives are genuine and assess the credibility and weight to be attached to their evidence

- consider what explanations may be offered by the employee, and if possible check them out beforehand
- if the employee concerned is a trade union representative discuss the case with a trade union full-time official after obtaining the employee's agreement. This is because the action may be seen as an attack on the union
- arrange a time for the meeting, which should be held as privately as possible, in a suitable room, and where there will be no interruptions. The employee may offer a reasonable alternative time, normally within five days of the original date, if their chosen companion cannot attend. You may also arrange another meeting if an employee fails to attend through circumstances outside their control, such as illness
- try and get a written statement from any witness from outside the organisation who is not prepared to or is unable to attend the meeting
- allow the employee to call witnesses or submit witness statements
- consider the provision of an interpreter or facilitator if there are understanding or language difficulties (perhaps a friend of the employee, or a co-employee). This person may need to attend in addition to the companion though ideally one person should carry out both roles
- make provision for any reasonable adjustments to accommodate the needs of a person with disabilities
- think about the structure of the meeting and make a list of points you will wish to cover.

What if an employee repeatedly fails to attend a meeting?

There may be occasions when an employee is repeatedly unable or unwilling to attend a meeting. This may be for various reasons, including genuine illness or a refusal to face up to the issue. Employers will need to consider all the facts and come to a reasonable decision on how to proceed. Considerations may include:

- any rules the organisation has for dealing with failure to attend disciplinary meetings
- the seriousness of the disciplinary issue under consideration
- the employee's disciplinary record (including current warnings), general work record, work experience, position and length of service
- medical opinion on whether the employee is fit to attend the meeting
- how similar cases in the past have been dealt with.

Where an employee continues to be unavailable to attend a meeting the employer may conclude that a decision will be made on the evidence available. The employee should be informed where this is to be the case. See also Appendix 4 'Dealing with absence'.

How should the disciplinary meeting be conducted?

Remember that the point of the meeting is to establish the facts, not catch people out. The meetings may not proceed in neat, orderly stages but it is good practice to:

- introduce those present to the employee and explain why they are there
- introduce and explain the role of the accompanying person if present
- explain that the purpose of the meeting is to consider whether disciplinary action should be taken in accordance with the organisation's disciplinary procedure
- explain how the meeting will be conducted.

Statement of the complaint

State precisely what the complaint is and outline the case briefly by going through the evidence that has been gathered. Ensure that the employee and his or her representative or accompanying person are allowed to see any statements made by witnesses and question them.

Employee's reply

Give the employee the opportunity to state their case and answer any allegations that have been made. They should be able to ask questions, present evidence and call witnesses. The accompanying person may also ask questions and should be able to confer privately with the employee. Listen carefully and be prepared to wait in silence for an answer as this can be a constructive way of encouraging the employee to be more forthcoming.

Establish whether the employee is prepared to accept that they may have done something wrong or are not performing to the required standard. Then agree the steps which should be taken to remedy the situation.

If it is not practical for witnesses to attend, consider proceeding if it is clear that their verbal evidence will not affect the substance of the complaint. Alternatively, consider an adjournment to allow questions to be put to a witness who cannot attend in person but who has submitted a witness statement.

General questioning and discussion

You should:

- use this stage to establish all the facts
- ask the employee if they have any explanation for the alleged misconduct or unsatisfactory performance, or if there are any special circumstances to be taken into account
- if it becomes clear during this stage that the employee has provided an adequate explanation or there is no real evidence to support the allegation, bring the proceedings to a close

- keep the approach formal and polite and encourage the employee to speak freely with a view to establishing the facts. A properly conducted disciplinary meeting should be a two-way process. Use questions to clarify the issues and to check that what has been said is understood. Ask open-ended questions, for example, 'what happened then?' to get the broad picture. Ask precise, closed questions requiring a yes/no answer only when specific information is needed
- do not get involved in arguments and do not make personal or humiliating remarks. Avoid physical contact or gestures which could be misinterpreted or misconstrued as judgemental.

If new facts emerge, it may be necessary to adjourn the meeting to investigate them and reconvene the meeting when this has been done.

Summing up

Summarise the main points of the discussion after questioning is completed. This allows all parties to be reminded of the nature of the offence, the arguments and evidence put forward and to ensure nothing is missed. Ask the employee if they have anything further to say. This should help to demonstrate to the employee that they have been treated reasonably.

Adjournment before decision

Adjourn before a decision is taken about whether a disciplinary penalty is appropriate. This allows time for reflection and proper consideration. It also allows for any further checking of any matters raised, particularly if there is any dispute over facts.

What problems may arise and how should they be handled?

Acas Code of Practice on disciplinary and grievance procedures Extract
Where an employee raises a grievance during a disciplinary process the disciplinary process may be temporarily suspended in order to deal with the grievance. Where the grievance and disciplinary cases are related, it may be appropriate to deal with both issues concurrently.

When an employee raises a grievance during the meeting it may sometimes be appropriate to consider stopping the meeting and suspending the disciplinary procedure – for example when:

- the grievance relates to a conflict of interest that the manager holding the disciplinary meeting is alleged to have
- bias is alleged in the conduct of the disciplinary meeting
- management have been selective in the evidence they have supplied to the manager holding the meeting
- there is possible discrimination.

It would not be appropriate to suspend the meeting where the employee makes an invalid point. For example if they mistakenly claim that they have the right to be legally represented or that a collectively agreed and applicable procedure does not apply to them because they are not a union member.

It is possible that the disciplinary meeting may not proceed smoothly – people may be upset or angry. If the employee becomes upset or distressed allow time for them to regain composure before continuing. If the distress is too great to continue then adjourn and reconvene at a later date – however, the issues should not be avoided. Clearly during the meeting there may be some 'letting off steam', and this can be helpful in finding out what has actually happened. However, abusive language or conduct should not be tolerated.

ALLOWING A WORKER TO BE ACCOMPANIED

[4.15]

<table>
<tr><th>Acas Code of Practice on disciplinary and grievance procedures Extract</th></tr>
<tr><td>Workers have a statutory right to be accompanied by a companion where the disciplinary meeting could result in:
• a formal warning being issued; or
• the taking of some other disciplinary action; or
• the confirmation of a warning or some other disciplinary action (appeal hearings).</td></tr>
</table>

Acas Code of Practice on disciplinary and grievance procedures Extract

The statutory right is to be accompanied by a fellow worker, a trade union representative, or an official employed by a trade union. A trade union representative who is not an employed official must have been certified by their union as being competent to accompany a worker. Employers must agree to a worker's request to be accompanied by any companion from one of these categories. Workers may also alter their choice of companion if they wish. As a matter of good practice, in making their choice workers should bear in mind the practicalities of the arrangements. For instance, a worker may choose to be accompanied by a companion who is suitable, willing and available on site rather than someone from a geographically remote location.

To exercise the statutory right to be accompanied workers must make a reasonable request. What is reasonable will depend on the circumstances of each individual case. A request to be accompanied does not have to be in writing or within a certain timeframe. However, a worker should provide enough time for the employer to deal with the companion's attendance at the meeting. Workers should also consider how they make their request so that it is clearly understood, for instance by letting the employer know in advance the name of the companion where possible and whether they are a fellow worker or trade union official or representative.

If a worker's chosen companion will not be available at the time proposed for the hearing by the employer, the employer must postpone the hearing to a time proposed by the worker provided that the alternative time is both reasonable and not more than five working days after the date originally proposed.

The companion should be allowed to address the hearing to put and sum up the workers case, respond on behalf of the worker to any views expressed at the meeting and confer with the worker during the hearing. The companion does not, however, have the right to answer questions on the worker's behalf, address the hearing if the worker does not wish it or prevent the employer from explaining their case.

What is the right to be accompanied?

Workers have a statutory right to be accompanied where they are required or invited by their employer to attend certain disciplinary meetings. The chosen companion may be a fellow worker, a trade union representative, or an official employed by a trade union. A trade union representative who is not an employed official must have been certified by their union as being competent to accompany a worker. Workers must make a reasonable request to their employer to be accompanied.

When does the right apply?

Workers have the right to be accompanied at disciplinary hearings that could result in:

- a formal warning being issued to a worker (ie a warning that will be placed on the worker's record)
- the taking of some other disciplinary action (such as suspension without pay, demotion or dismissal) or other action
- the confirmation of a warning or some other disciplinary action (such as an appeal hearing)

Informal discussions, counselling sessions or disciplinary investigatory meetings do not attract the right to be accompanied. Meetings to investigate a disciplinaryissue are not disciplinary hearings. If it becomes apparent that formal disciplinary action may be needed then this should be dealt with at a formal hearing at which the statutory right to be accompanied will apply.

What is a reasonable request?

Whether a request for a companion is reasonable will depend on the circumstances of the individual case and, ultimately, it is a matter for the courts and tribunals to decide if disputed. However, a worker should provide enough time for the employer to deal with the companion's attendance at the meeting.

Workers should also consider how they make their request so that it is clearly understood, for instance by letting the employer know in advance the name of the companion where possible and whether they are a fellow worker or trade union official or representative.

The companion

The companion may be:

- a fellow worker (ie another of the employer's workers)
- an official employed by a trade union
- a workplace trade union representative, as long as they have been reasonably certified in writing by their union as having experience of, or having received training in, acting as a worker's companion at disciplinary or grievance hearings. Certification may take the form of a card or letter.

Employers are free, but are not obliged, to allow workers to be accompanied by a companion who does not fall within the above categories. Some workers may have a contractual right to be accompanied by persons other than those listed above (for instance a professional support body, partner, spouse or legal representative).

Reasonable adjustment may be needed for a worker with a disability (and possibly for their companion if they are disabled). For example the provision of a support worker or advocate with knowledge of the disability and its effects.

Workers may ask an official from any trade union to accompany them at a disciplinary or grievance hearing, regardless of whether or not they are a member or the union is recognised.

Fellow workers or trade union officials do not have to accept a request to accompany a worker, and they should not be pressurised to do so.

Trade unions should ensure that their officials are trained in the role of acting as a worker's companion. Even when a trade union official has experience of acting in the role, there may still be a need for periodic refresher training. Employers should consider allowing time off for this training.

A worker who has agreed to accompany a colleague employed by the same employer is entitled to take a reasonable amount of paid time off to fulfil that responsibility. This should cover the hearing and it is also good practice to allow time for the companion to familiarise themselves with the case and confer with the worker before and after the hearing.

A lay trade union official is permitted to take a reasonable amount of paid time off to accompany a worker at a hearing, as long as the worker is employed by the same employer. In cases where a lay official agrees to accompany a worker employed by another organisation, time off is a matter for agreement by the parties concerned.

Applying the right

The employer should allow a companion to have a say about the date and time of a hearing. If the companion cannot attend on a proposed date, the law on the right of accompaniment provides that the worker has a right to suggest an alternative time and date so long as it is reasonable and it is not more than five working days after the original date.

Employers may, however, wish to allow more time than this for a re-arranged meeting, particularly in cases that might result in dismissal. An employer must always act fairly in order to avoid a finding of unfair dismissal. Where there is a request to postpone a hearing for more than five days because a trade union representative or other companion is not available, it may be fair to allow the postponement if it does not cause unreasonable delay. The employer should consider the facts and decide what is fair and reasonable in the circumstances.

Before the hearing takes place, the worker should tell the employer who they have chosen as a companion. In certain circumstances (for instance when the companion is an official of a non-recognised trade union) it can be helpful for the companion and employer to make contact before the hearing.

The companion must be allowed to address the hearing in order to:

- put the worker's case
- sum up the worker's case
- respond on the worker's behalf to any view expressed at the hearing.

The companion must also be allowed to confer with the worker during the hearing. It is good practice to allow the companion to participate as fully as possible in the hearing, including asking witnesses questions. The employer is, however, not legally required to permit the companion to answer questions on the worker's behalf, or to address the hearing if the worker does not wish it, or to prevent the employer from explaining their case.

Workers whose employers fail to comply with a reasonable request to be accompanied may present a complaint to an employment tribunal. Workers may also complain to a tribunal if employers fail to re-arrange a hearing to a reasonable date proposed by the worker when a companion cannot attend on the date originally proposed.

It is unlawful to disadvantage workers for using their right to be accompanied or for being companions. This could lead to a claim to an employment tribunal.

TAKING ACTION AFTER THE DISCIPLINARY MEETING

[4.16]

Acas Code of Practice on disciplinary and grievance procedures Extract

After the meeting decide whether or not disciplinary or any other action is justified and inform the employee accordingly in writing.

Where misconduct is confirmed or the employee is found to be performing unsatisfactorily it is usual to give the employee a written warning. A further act of misconduct or failure to improve performance within a set period would normally result in a final written warning.

If an employee's first misconduct or unsatisfactory performance is sufficiently serious, it may be appropriate to move directly to a final written warning. This might occur where the employee's actions have had, or are liable to have, a serious or harmful impact on the organisation.

A first or final written warning should set out the nature of the misconduct or poor performance and the change in behaviour or improvement in performance required (with timescale). The employee should be told how long the warning will remain current. The employee should be informed of the consequences of further misconduct, or failure to improve performance, within the set period following a final warning. For instance that it may result in dismissal or some other contractual penalty such as demotion or loss of seniority.

A decision to dismiss should only be taken by a manager who has the authority to do so. The employee should be informed as soon as possible of the reasons for the dismissal, the date on which the employment contract will end, the appropriate period of notice and their right of appeal.

Some acts, termed gross misconduct, are so serious in themselves or have such serious consequences that they may call for dismissal without notice for a first offence. But a fair disciplinary process, should always be followed, before dismissing for gross misconduct.

Acas Code of Practice on disciplinary and grievance procedures Extract

Disciplinary rules should give examples of acts which the employer regards as acts of gross misconduct. These may vary according to the nature of the organisation and what it does, but might include things such as theft or fraud, physical violence, gross negligence or serious insubordination.

Where an employee is persistently unable or unwilling to attend a disciplinary meeting without good cause the employer should make a decision on the evidence available.

What should be considered before deciding any disciplinary penalty?

When deciding whether a disciplinary penalty is appropriate and what form it should take, consideration should be given to:

- whether the rules of the organisation indicate what the likely penalty will be as a result of the particular misconduct
- the penalty imposed in similar cases in the past
- whether standards of other employees are acceptable, and that this employee is not being unfairly singled out
- the employee's disciplinary record (including current warnings), general work record, work experience, position and length of service
- any special circumstances which might make it appropriate to adjust the severity of the penalty
- whether the proposed penalty is reasonable in view of all the circumstances
- whether any training, additional support or adjustments to the work are necessary.

It should be clear what the normal organisational practice is for dealing with the kind of misconduct or unsatisfactory performance under consideration. This does not mean that similar offences will always call for the same disciplinary action: each case must be looked at on its own merits and any relevant circumstances taken into account. Such relevant circumstances may include health or domestic problems, provocation, justifiable ignorance of the rule or standard involved or inconsistent treatment in the past.

If guidance is needed on formal disciplinary action, seek advice, where possible, from someone who will not be involved in hearing any potential appeal. Call the Acas helpline on **0300 123 1100** (Open Monday – Friday 8am–6pm) to talk to one of our advisers.

Imposing the disciplinary penalty

First formal action – unsatisfactory performance

In cases of unsatisfactory performance an employee should be given an 'improvement note', setting out:

- the performance problem
- the improvement that is required
- the timescale for achieving this improvement
- a review date and
- any support, including any training, that the employer will provide to assist the employee.

The employee should be informed that the note represents the first stage of a formal procedure and is equivalent to a first written warning and that failure to improve could lead to a final written warning and, ultimately, dismissal. A copy of the note should be kept and used as the basis for monitoring and reviewing performance over a specified period (eg, six months).

If an employee's unsatisfactory performance – or its continuance – is sufficiently serious, for example because it is having, or is likely to have, a serious harmful effect on the organisation, it may be justifiable to move directly to a final written warning.

Discipline in practice: Example 2

A member of staff in accounts makes a number of mistakes on invoices to customers. You bring the mistakes to his attention, make sure he has had the right training and impress on him the need for accuracy but the mistakes continue. You invite the employee to a disciplinary meeting and inform him of his right to be accompanied by a colleague or employee representative. At the meeting the employee does not give a satisfactory explanation for the mistakes so you decide to issue an improvement note setting out: the problem, the improvement required, the timescale for improvement, the support available and a review date. You inform the employee that a failure to improve may lead to a final written warning.

First formal action – misconduct

In cases of misconduct, employees should be given a written warning setting out the nature of the misconduct and the change in behaviour required.

The warning should also inform the employee that a final written warning may be considered if there is further misconduct. A record of the warning should be kept, but it should be disregarded for disciplinary purposes after a specified period (eg, six months).

> ***Discipline in practice: Example 3***
>
> An employee in a small firm makes a series of mistakes in letters to one of your key customers promising impossible delivery dates. The customer is upset at your firm's failure to meet delivery dates and threatens to take his business elsewhere.
>
> You are the owner of the business and carry out an investigation and invite the employee to a disciplinary meeting. You inform her of her right to be accompanied by a colleague or employee representative.
>
> ***Example outcome of meeting***
>
> At the meeting the employee does not give a satisfactory explanation for the mistakes and admits that her training covered the importance of agreeing realistic delivery dates with her manager. During your investigation, her team leader and section manager told you they had stressed to the employee the importance of agreeing delivery dates with them before informing the customer. In view of the seriousness of the mistakes and the possible impact on the business, you issue the employee with a final written warning. You inform the employee that failure to improve will lead to dismissal and of her right to appeal.
>
> ***Example outcome of meeting in different circumstances***
>
> At the meeting, the employee reveals that her team leader would not let her attend training as the section was too busy. Subsequently the team leader was absent sick and the employee asked the section manager for help with setting delivery dates. The manager said he was too busy and told the employee to 'use her initiative'. Your other investigations support the employee's explanation. You inform the employee that you will not be taking disciplinary action and will make arrangements for her to be properly trained. You decide to carry out a review of general management standards on supervision and training.

Final written warning

If the employee has a current warning about conduct or performance then further misconduct or unsatisfactory performance (whichever is relevant) may warrant a final written warning. This may also be the case where 'first offence' misconduct is sufficiently serious, but would not justify dismissal. Such a warning should normally remain current for a specified period, for example, 12 months, and contain a statement that further misconduct or unsatisfactory performance may lead to dismissal.

Dismissal or other sanction

If the employee has received a final written warning, further misconduct or unsatisfactory performance may warrant dismissal. Alternatively the contract may allow for a different disciplinary penalty instead. Such a penalty may include disciplinary transfer, disciplinary suspension without pay (although see the considerations on suspension), demotion, loss of seniority or loss of increment. These sanctions may only be applied if allowed for in the employee's contract or with the employee's agreement.

Any penalty should be confirmed in writing, and the procedure and time limits for appeal set out clearly.

There may be occasions when, depending on the seriousness of the misconduct involved, it will be appropriate to consider dismissal without notice (see below).

Dismissal with notice

Employees should only be dismissed if, despite warnings, conduct or performance does not improve to the required level within the specified time period. Dismissal must be reasonable in all the circumstances of the case.

Unless the employee is being dismissed for reasons of gross misconduct, he or she should receive the appropriate period of notice or payment in lieu of notice.

Dismissal without notice

Employers should give all employees a clear indication of the type of misconduct which, in the light of the requirements of the employer's business, will warrant dismissal without the normal period of notice or pay in lieu of notice. So far as possible the types of offences which fall into this category of 'gross misconduct' should be clearly specified in the rules, although such a list cannot normally be exhaustive.

What is gross misconduct?

Gross misconduct is generally seen as misconduct serious enough to overturn the contract between the employer and the employee thus justifying summary dismissal. Acts which constitute gross misconduct must be very serious and are best determined by organisations in the light of their own particular circumstances. However, examples of gross misconduct might include:

- theft or fraud
- physical violence or bullying
- deliberate and serious damage to property

- serious misuse of an organisation's property or name
- deliberately accessing internet sites containing pornographic, offensive or obscene material
- serious insubordination
- unlawful discrimination or harassment
- bringing the organisation into serious disrepute
- serious incapability at work brought on by alcohol or illegal drugs
- causing loss, damage or injury through serious negligence
- a serious breach of health and safety rules
- a serious breach of confidence.

If an employer considers an employee guilty of gross misconduct and thus liable for summary dismissal, it is still important to follow a fair procedure as for any other disciplinary offence. This will include establishing the facts of the case before taking any action, holding a meeting with the employee and allowing the employee the right of appeal. It should be made clear to the employee that dismissal is a possibility.

A short period of suspension with full pay to help establish the facts or to allow tempers to cool may be helpful. However, such a period of suspension should only be imposed after careful consideration and should be kept under review. It should be made clear to the employee that the suspension is not a disciplinary action and does not involve any prejudgement.

Discipline in practice; Example 4

A member of your telephone sales team has been to lunch to celebrate success in an exam. He returns from lunch in a very merry mood, is slurring his speech and is evidently not fit to carry out his duties. You decide to send him home and invite him in writing to a disciplinary meeting setting out his alleged behaviour of gross misconduct for which he could be dismissed. Your letter includes information about his right to be accompanied by a colleague or employee representative.

At the meeting he admits he had too much to drink, is very apologetic and promises that such a thing will not happen again. He is one of your most valued members of staff and has an exemplary record over his 10 years service with you. You know that being unfit for work because of excessive alcohol is listed in your company rules as gross misconduct. In view of the circumstances and the employee's record, however, you decide not to dismiss him but give him a final written warning. You inform the employee of his right to appeal.

How should the employee be informed of the disciplinary decision?

Details of any disciplinary action should be given in writing to the employee as soon as the decision is made. See example letters at Appendix 3. A copy of the notification should be retained by the employer. The written notification should specify:

- the nature of the misconduct
- any period of time given for improvement and the improvement expected
- the disciplinary penalty and, where appropriate, how long it will last
- the likely consequences of further misconduct
- the timescale for lodging an appeal and how it should be made.

The organisation may wish to require the employee to acknowledge receipt of the written notification.

Written reasons for dismissal

Employees with two years' service or more have the right to request a 'written statement of reasons for dismissal'. Employers are required by law to comply within 14 days of the request being made, unless it is not reasonably practicable. It is good practice to give written reasons for all dismissals.

A woman who is dismissed during pregnancy or maternity or adoption leave is automatically entitled to the written statement without having to request it and irrespective of length of service.

The written statement can be used in evidence in any subsequent employment tribunal proceedings, for example, in relation to a complaint of unfair dismissal.

Time limits for warnings

Except in agreed special circumstances, any disciplinary action taken should be disregarded for disciplinary purposes after a specified period of satisfactory conduct or performance. This period should be established clearly when the disciplinary procedure is being drawn up. A decision to dismiss should not be based on an expired warning but the fact that there is an expired warning may explain why the employer does not substitute a lesser sanction.

Normal practice is for different types of warnings to remain in force for different periods. For example, a first written warning might be valid for up to six months while a final written warning may remain in force for 12 months (or more in exceptional circumstances). Warnings should cease to be 'live' following the specified period of satisfactory conduct.

There may be occasions where an employee's conduct is satisfactory throughout the period the warning is in force, only to lapse very soon thereafter. Where a pattern emerges and/or there is evidence of abuse, the employee's disciplinary record should be borne in mind in deciding how long any warning should last.

PROVIDE EMPLOYEES WITH AN OPPORTUNITY TO APPEAL

[4.17]

Acas Code of Practice on disciplinary and grievance procedures Extract

Where an employee feels that disciplinary action taken against them is wrong or unjust they should appeal against the decision. Appeals should be heard without unreasonable delay and ideally at an agreed time and place. Employees should let employers know the grounds for their appeal in writing.

The appeal should be dealt with impartially and wherever possible, by a manager who has not previously been involved in the case.

Workers have a statutory right to be accompanied at appeal hearings.

Employees should be informed in writing of the results of the appeal hearing as soon as possible.

The opportunity to appeal against a disciplinary decision is essential to natural justice, and appeals may be raised by employees on any number of grounds, for instance new evidence, undue severity or inconsistency of the penalty. The appeal may either be a review of the disciplinary sanction or a re-hearing depending on the grounds of the appeal.

An appeal must never be used as an opportunity to punish the employee for appealing the original decision, and it should not result in any increase in penalty as this may deter individuals from appealing.

What should an appeals procedure contain?

It should:

- specify a time-limit within which the appeal should be lodged (five working days is commonly felt appropriate although this may be extended in particular circumstances)
- provide for appeals to be dealt with speedily, particularly those involving suspension or dismissal
- wherever possible provide for the appeal to be heard by someone senior in authority to the person who took the disciplinary decision and, if possible, someone who was not involved in the original meeting or decision
- spell out what action may be taken by those hearing the appeal
- set out the right to be accompanied at any appeal meeting
- provide that the employee, or a companion if the employee so wishes, has an opportunity to comment on any new evidence arising during the appeal before any decision is taken.

Small organisations

In small organisations, even if there is no more senior manager available, another manager should, if possible, hear the appeal. If this is not possible consider whether the owner or, in the case of a charity, the board of trustees, should hear the appeal. Whoever hears the appeal should consider it impartially.

How should an appeal hearing be conducted? Before the appeal ensure that the individual knows when and where it is to be held, and of their statutory right to be accompanied. Hold the meeting in a place which will be free from interruptions. Make sure the relevant records and notes of the original meeting are available for all concerned. See sample letters at Appendix 3.

At the meeting

You should:

- introduce those present to each other, explaining their presence if necessary
- explain the purpose of the meeting, how it will be conducted, and the powers the person/people hearing the appeal have
- ask the employee why he or she is appealing
- pay particular attention to any new evidence that has been introduced, and ensure the employee has the opportunity to comment on it
- once the relevant issues have been thoroughly explored, summarise the facts and call an adjournment to consider the decision
- change a previous decision if it becomes apparent that it was not soundly based – such action does not undermine authority but rather makes clear the independent nature of the appeal. If the decision is overturned consider whether training for managers needs to be improved, if rules need clarification, or are if there other implications to be considered?
- inform the employee of the results of the appeal and the reasons for the decision and confirm it in writing. Make it clear, if this is the case, that this decision is final. See sample letters at Appendix 3.

DEALING WITH SPECIAL CASES

[4.18]

Acas Code of Practice on disciplinary and grievance procedures Extract

Where disciplinary action is being considered against an employee who is a trade union representative the normal disciplinary procedure should be followed. Depending on the circumstances, however, it is advisable to discuss the matter at an early stage with an official employed by the union, after obtaining the employee's agreement.

Acas Code of Practice on disciplinary and grievance procedures Extract
If an employee is charged with, or convicted of a criminal offence this is not normally in itself reason for disciplinary action. Consideration needs to be given to what effect the charge or conviction has on the employee's suitability to do the job and their relationship with their employer, work colleagues and customers.

Trade union officials

Although normal disciplinary standards apply to their conduct as employees, disciplinary action against a trade union representative can be construed as an attack on the union if not handled carefully (see Preparing for the meeting).

Criminal charges or convictions

An employee should not be dismissed or otherwise disciplined solely because he or she has been charged with or convicted of a criminal offence. The question to be asked in such cases is whether the employee's conduct or conviction merits action because of its employment implications.

Where it is thought the conduct warrants disciplinary action the following guidance should be borne in mind:

- the employer should investigate the facts as far as possible, come to a view about them and consider whether the conduct is sufficiently serious to warrant instituting the disciplinary procedure
- where the conduct requires prompt attention the employer need not await the outcome of the prosecution before taking fair and reasonable action
- where the police are called in they should not be asked to conduct any investigation on behalf of the employer, nor should they be present at any meeting or disciplinary meeting.

In some cases the nature of the alleged offence may not justify disciplinary action – for example, off-duty conduct which has no bearing on employment – but the employee may not be available for work because he or she is in custody or on remand. In these cases employers should decide whether, in the light of the needs of the organisation, the employee's job can be held open. Where a criminal conviction leads, for example, to the loss of a licence so that continued employment in a particular job would be illegal, employers should consider whether alternative work is appropriate and available.

Where an employee, charged with or convicted of a criminal offence, refuses or is unable to cooperate with the employer's disciplinary investigations and proceedings, this should not deter an employer from taking action. The employee should be advised in writing that unless further information is provided, a disciplinary decision will be taken on the basis of the information available and could result in dismissal.

Where there is little likelihood of an employee returning to employment, it may be argued that the contract of employment has been terminated through 'frustration'. In law, frustration occurs when, without the fault of either party, some event, which was not reasonably foreseeable at the time of the contract, renders future performance of the contract either impossible or something radically different from what was contemplated originally. This is normally accepted by the courts only where the frustrating event renders all performance of the employment contract clearly impossible. Legal advice should be sought if it is thought frustration of the employment contract has occurred. It is normally better for the employer to take disciplinary action.

An employee who has been charged with, or convicted of, a criminal offence may become unacceptable to colleagues, resulting in workforce pressure to dismiss or even threats of industrial action. Employers should bear in mind that they may have to justify the reasonableness of any decision to dismiss and that an employment tribunal will ignore threats of, and actual, industrial action when determining the fairness of a decision (Section 107, Employment Rights Act 1996). Employers should consider all relevant factors, not just disruption to production, before reaching a reasonable decision.

Use of external consultants

In some instances employers may wish to bring in external consultants to carry out an investigation. Employers will still be responsible for any inappropriate or discriminatory behaviour if the investigation is carried out by consultants. Make arrangements for the investigation to be overseen by a representative of management. Make sure that the consultants follow the organisation's disciplinary policies and procedures and deal with the case fairly in accordance with the Acas Code of Practice.

Employees to whom the full procedure is not immediately available

It may be sensible to arrange time off with pay so that employees who are in isolated locations or on shifts can attend a disciplinary meeting on the main site in normal working hours. Alternatively, if a number of witnesses need to attend it may be better to hold the disciplinary meeting on the nightshift or at the particular location.

GRIEVANCES
KEYS TO HANDLING GRIEVANCES IN THE WORKPLACE

RESOLVE GRIEVANCES INFORMALLY

[4.19]
In organisations where managers have an open policy for communication and consultation problems and concerns are often raised and settled as a matter of course.

Employees should aim to settle most grievances informally with their line manager. Many problems can be raised and settled during the course of everyday working relationships. This also allows for problems to be settled quickly.

In cases where the line manager is the subject of the grievance, individuals should be able to discuss their concerns with another manager or another appropriate person.

In some cases outside help such as an independent mediator can help resolve problems especially those involving working relationships.

DEVELOPING RULES AND PROCEDURES

[4.20]

Acas Code of Practice on disciplinary and grievance procedures Extract
Fairness and transparency are promoted by developing and using rules and procedures for handling disciplinary and grievance situations. These should be set down in writing, be specific and clear. Employees and, where appropriate, their representatives should be involved in the development of rules and procedures. It is also important to help employees and managers understand what the rules and procedures are, where they can be found and how they are to be used.

WHAT IS A GRIEVANCE AND WHY HAVE A PROCEDURE?

[4.21]

Acas Code of Practice on disciplinary and grievance procedures Extract
Grievances are concerns, problems or complaints that employees raise with their employers.

Anybody working in an organisation may, at some time, have problems or concerns about their work, working conditions or relationships with colleagues that they wish to talk about with management. They want the grievance to be addressed, and if possible, resolved. It is also clearly in management's interests to resolve problems before they can develop into major difficulties for all concerned.

Issues that may cause grievances include:

- terms and conditions of employment
- health and safety
- work relations
- bullying and harassment
- new working practices
- working environment
- organisational change
- discrimination.

Grievances may occur at all levels and the Acas Code of Practice, and this guidance, applies equally to management and employees.

A written procedure can help clarify the process and help to ensure that employees are aware of their rights such as to be accompanied at grievance meetings . Some organisations use, or may wish to use, external mediators to help resolve grievances. Where this is the case the procedure should explain how and when mediators may be used.

Employees might raise issues about matters not entirely within the control of the organisation, such as client or customer relationships (for instance where an employee is working on another employer's site). These should be treated in the same way as grievances within the organisation, with the employer/manager investigating as far as possible and taking action if required. The organisation should make it very clear to any third party that grievances are taken seriously and action will be taken to protect their employees.

Acas Code of Practice on disciplinary and grievance procedures Extract
The provisions of this Code do not apply to grievances raised on behalf of two or more employees by a representative of a recognised trade union or other appropriate workplace representative. These grievances should be handled in accordance with the organisation's collective grievance process.

Occasionally a collective grievance may arise where a number of people have the same grievance at the same time. If there is a grievance which applies to more than one person this should be resolved in accordance with the organisation's collective grievance process – where one exists.

Grievances about fellow employees

Employees may complain that they have been bullied, harassed or discriminated against by another employee or may complain about another employee's attitude, capability for the job or even personal habits or personal hygiene.

Employers must deal with these cases carefully. Conversations should be handled in a way that is sensitive to the circumstances and the needs of the individuals concerned. It is important not to make assumptions at the outset about the facts of the case.

Where a grievance about a fellow employee is raised informally, after listening to the employee who has made the complaint to understand their concern, the next step should generally be to talk privately to the person complained about. This may help clarify the situation and can help move things forward towards a resolution. Alternatively, if those involved are willing, an independent mediator may be able to help in some circumstances.

Employers should bear in mind that it is not only the individual who has raised the grievance who may be distressed, but also the person complained about. Care should be taken that any informal discussion with them remains non-judgmental. In particular, the discussion should not turn into a disciplinary hearing.

If a formal grievance about a fellow employee is raised, the guidance outlined below on handling formal grievances will apply.

Training for dealing with grievances

Management and employee representatives who may be involved in grievance matters should be trained for the task.

For handling informal grievances effectively, good line management skills are essential. Managers may benefit from training aimed at helping them become more confident and emotionally intelligent in dealing with people, as well as developing skills in handling difficult conversations.

Those who may be involved in handling formal grievances should be familiar with the employer's grievance procedure, and know how to conduct or represent at grievance hearings. Consideration might be given to training managers and employee representatives jointly on this. For information about suitable training go to www.acas.org.uk/training.

KEEPING WRITTEN RECORDS

What records should be kept?

[4.22]

The foreword to the Code of Practice advises employers to keep a written record of any disciplinary or grievances cases they deal with.

Records should include:

- the nature of the grievance
- what was decided and actions taken
- the reason for the actions
- whether an appeal was lodged
- the outcome of the appeal
- any subsequent developments.

Records should be treated as confidential and be kept no longer than necessary in accordance with the data protection principles set out in the Data Protection Act 2018. This Act also gives individuals the right to request and have access to certain personal data stored about them. See Appendix 5 for further information.

Copies of meeting records should be given to the employee including copies of any formal minutes that may have been taken. In certain circumstances (for example to protect a witness) the employer might withhold some information.

DEALING WITH FORMAL GRIEVANCES

[4.23]

Acas Code of Practice on disciplinary and grievance procedures Extract

Where some form of formal action is needed, what action is reasonable or justified will depend on all the circumstances of the particular case. Employment tribunals will take the size and resources of an employer into account when deciding on relevant cases and it may sometimes not be practicable for all employers to take all of the steps set out in this Code.

That said, whenever a disciplinary or grievance process is being followed it is important to deal with issues fairly. There are a number of elements to this:

- Employers and employees should raise and deal with issues **promptly** and should not unreasonably delay meetings, decisions or confirmation of those decisions.
- Employers and employees should act **consistently**.
- Employers should carry out any necessary **investigations**, to establish the facts of the case.
- Employers should **inform** employees of the basis of the problem and give them an opportunity to **put their case** in response before any decisions are made.
- Employers should allow employees to be **accompanied** at any formal disciplinary or grievance meeting.
- Employers should allow an employee to **appeal** against any formal decision made.

The following pages give detailed guidance on handling formal grievances. Always bear in mind the need for fairness when following procedures, taking account of the elements from the Acas Code of Practice reproduced above.

A grievance process can be stressful for everyone involved. Sometimes a process may cause extreme distress or even impact on a person's mental health. Where there are signs of that happening to anyone involved in the process, employers should consider whether the process can be adjusted in some way, such as by allowing the individual to be accompanied at a grievance meeting by a support worker or advocate from outside the organisation who has knowledge of the individual's mental health condition and its effects.

In some cases, it might be appropriate for an employer, with the agreement and involvement of the individual, to seek professional medical help or guidance as to how the grievance process can proceed fairly. If there are clear and repeated signs of distress, the employer should consider signposting the individual to an employee assistance programme, where one is available, or consider suggesting that the individual seeks advice from a GP. It is important to address this issue early to avoid it escalating.

If someone has an existing mental health condition which they have previously disclosed as a disability, the employer must make reasonable adjustments to the process.

LET THE EMPLOYER KNOW THE NATURE OF THE GRIEVANCE

[4.24]

Acas Code of Practice on disciplinary and grievance procedures Extract

If it is not possible to resolve a grievance informally employees should raise the matter formally and without unreasonable delay with a manager who is not the subject of the grievance. This should be done in writing and should set out the nature of the grievance.

Where a grievance is serious or an employee has attempted to raise a problem informally without success, the employee should raise it formally with management in writing.

Where employees have difficulty expressing themselves because of language or other difficulties they may like to seek help from trade union or other employee representatives or from colleagues.

When stating their grievance, employees should stick to the facts and avoid language which may be considered insulting or abusive.

Where the grievance is against the line manager the employee may approach another manager or raise the issue with their HR department if there is one. It is helpful if the grievance procedure sets out who the individual should approach in these circumstances.

In small firms run by an owner/ manager there will be no alternative manager to raise a grievance with. It is in the interests of such employers to make it clear that they will treat all grievances fairly and objectively even if the grievance is about something they have said or done.

HOLDING A GRIEVANCE MEETING

[4.25]

Acas Code of Practice on disciplinary and grievance procedures Extract

Employers should arrange for a formal meeting to be held without unreasonable delay after a grievance is received.

Employers, employees and their companions should make every effort to attend the meeting. Employees should be allowed to explain their grievance and how they think it should be resolved. Consideration should be given to adjourning the meeting for any investigation that may be necessary.

What is a grievance meeting?

In general terms a grievance meeting deals with any grievance raised by an employee. For the purposes of the legal right to be accompanied, a grievance meeting is defined as a meeting where an employer deals with a complaint about a 'duty owed by them to a worker'.

Preparing for the meeting

Managers should:

- arrange a meeting, ideally within five working days, in private where there will not be interruptions
- consider arranging for someone who is not involved in the case to take a note of the meeting and to act as a witness to what was said
- consider whether similar grievances have been raised before, how they have been resolved, and any follow-up action that has been necessary. This allows consistency of treatment
- consider arranging for an interpreter where the employee has difficulty speaking English
- consider whether any reasonable adjustments are necessary for a person who is disabled and/or their companion
- consider whether to offer independent mediation.

Conduct of the meeting

Managers should:

- remember that a grievance hearing is not the same as a disciplinary hearing, and is an occasion when discussion and dialogue may lead to an amicable solution
- make introductions as necessary
- remain impartial and objective at all times
- invite the employee to re-state their grievance and how they would like to see it resolved
- put care and thought into resolving grievances. They are not normally issues calling for snap decisions, and the employee may have been holding the grievance for a long time. Make allowances for any reasonable 'letting off steam' if the employee is under stress
- consider adjourning the meeting if it is necessary to investigate any new facts which arise

- sum up the main points
- tell the employee when they might reasonably expect a response if one cannot be made at the time, bearing in mind the time limits set out in the organisation's procedure. If there is a subsequent delay in the anticipated timescale for a response, for example due to the need to investigate matters, the employee should also be informed of this.

Be calm, fair and follow the procedure

In smaller organisations, grievances can sometimes be taken as personal criticism – employers should be careful to hear any grievance in a calm and objective manner, consider it impartially and be fair to the employee in seeking a resolution of the problem. Following the grievance procedure can make this easier.

Grievances in practice: an example

You are the owner of a small firm. An employee has been complaining that she is being given too much work and can't complete it in time. You have told the employee that her predecessor had no problem completing the same amount of work and that things will get easier with experience. The employee is not happy and puts her grievance to you in writing.

You invite the employee to a meeting to discuss the grievance and inform her of her right to be accompanied. At the meeting you discover that the employee is working on a different computer from her predecessor. The computer is slower and uses an old version of the software required to carry out the work. You agree to upgrade the software, provide training and to review progress in a month. You confirm what was agreed in writing and inform the employee of her right to an appeal meeting if she feels her grievance has not been satisfactorily resolved.

[4.26] ALLOWING A WORKER TO BE ACCOMPANIED AT THE GRIEVANCE MEETING

Acas Code of Practice on disciplinary and grievance procedures Extract

Workers have a statutory right to be accompanied by a companion at a grievance meeting which deals with a complaint about a duty owed by the employer to the worker. So this would apply where the complaint is, for example, that the employer is not honouring the worker's contract, or is in breach of legislation.

The statutory right is to be accompanied by a fellow worker, a trade union representative, or an official employed by a trade union. A trade union representative who is not an employed official must have been certified by their union as being competent to accompany a worker. Employers must agree to a worker's request to be accompanied by any companion from one of these categories. Workers may also alter their choice of companion if they wish. As a matter of good practice, in making their choice workers should bear in mind the practicalities of the arrangements. For instance, a worker may choose to be accompanied by a companion who is suitable, willing and available on site rather than someone from a geographically remote location.

To exercise the statutory right to be accompanied workers must make a reasonable request. What is reasonable will depend on the circumstances of each individual case. A request to be accompanied does not have to be in writing or within a certain timeframe. However, a worker should provide enough time for the employer to deal with the companion's attendance at the meeting. Workers should also consider how they make their request so that it is clearly understood, for instance by letting the employer know in advance the name of the companion where possible and whether they are a fellow worker or trade union official or representative.

If a worker's chosen companion will not be available at the time proposed for thehearing by the employer, the employer must postpone the hearing to a time proposed by the worker provided that the alternative time is both reasonable and not more than five working days after the date originally proposed.

The companion should be allowed to address the hearing to put and sum up the worker's case, respond on behalf of the worker to any views expressed at the meeting and confer with the worker during the hearing. The companion does not however have the right to answer questions on the workers behalf, address the hearing if the worker does not wish it or prevent the employer from explaining their case.

When do workers have the right to be accompanied?

A worker who raises a formal grievance about a duty owed to them by their employer has a right to be accompanied at a grievance hearing. This includes any meeting held with them to hear about, gather facts about, discuss, consider or resolve their grievance.

An employer's duties to a worker include the employer's legal and contractual obligations to the worker. In grievances raised about other types of issues the statutory right of accompaniment may not apply.

For instance, an individual is unlikely to have the statutory right to accompaniment at a meeting to consider a request for a pay rise, unless there is a specific contractual right to a pay increase, or their request raises an issue about an employer's legal obligations, such as payment of the National Minimum Wage or the law on equal pay.

Equally, as most employers will be under no duty to provide their workers with car parking facilities, usually there will be no statutory right to be accompanied at a meeting held to hear a grievance about such facilities. However, if a worker were disabled and needed a car to get to and from work, they would have a statutory right to a companion at a grievance meeting if their complaint about parking facilities concerned the employer's legal duties to the worker under the Equality Act 2010.

Similarly, as employers have a general duty of care to their workers under common law, a worker who raises a formal grievance about being bullied or harassed by a fellow worker will have the statutory right to a companion at a grievance hearing about the complaint.

Even where the statutory right to accompaniment does not apply, it is generally good practice to allow workers who raise a grievance to be accompanied at any formal grievance hearing.

The statutory right to accompaniment applies to the worker who has raised the grievance. However, it may be appropriate in some circumstances to allow other individuals to be accompanied at grievance hearings. For instance, where a formal grievance is raised about a fellow worker, such as a complaint about bullying or harassment, the person complained about should also be allowed to be accompanied, by a fellow employee or trade union representative of their choice, at grievance meetings that involve them. In such cases, the person complained about should also be allowed to see relevant evidence and copies of any witness statements, and given reasonable time to share these with their chosen companion, so that they can fairly prepare for the grievance meeting.

What is a reasonable request?

Whether a request for a companion is reasonable will depend on the circumstances of the individual case and, ultimately, it is a matter for the courts and tribunals to decide if disputed. However, a worker should provide enough time for the employer to deal with the companion's attendance at the meeting.

Workers should also consider how they make their request so that it is clearly understood, for instance by letting the employer know in advance the name of the companion where possible and whether they are a fellow worker or trade union official or representative.

The companion

The companion may be:

- a fellow worker (ie another of the employer's workers)
- an official employed by a trade union
- a workplace trade union representative, as long as they have been reasonably certified in writing by their union as having experience of, or having received training in, acting as a worker's companion at disciplinary or grievance hearings. Certification may take the form of a card or letter.

Employers are free, but are not obliged, to allow workers to be accompanied by a companion who does not fall within the above categories. Some workers may have a contractual right to be accompanied by persons other than those listed above (for instance a professional support body, partner, spouse or legal representative).

Reasonable adjustment may be needed for a worker with a disability (and possibly for their companion if they are disabled). For example the provision of a support worker or advocate with knowledge of the disability and its effects.

Workers may ask an official from any trade union to accompany them at a disciplinary or grievance hearing, regardless of whether or not they are a member or the union is recognised.

Fellow workers or trade union officials do not have to accept a request to accompany a worker, and they should not be pressurised to do so.

Trade unions should ensure that their officials are trained in the role of acting as a worker's companion. Even when a trade union official has experience of acting in the role, there may still be a need for periodic refresher training. Employers should consider allowing time off for this training.

A worker who has agreed to accompany a colleague employed by the same employer is entitled to take a reasonable amount of paid time off to fulfil that responsibility. This should cover the hearing and it is also good practice to allow time for the companion to familiarise themselves with the case and confer with the worker before and after the hearing.

A lay trade union official is permitted to take a reasonable amount of paid time off to accompany a worker at a hearing, as long as the worker is employed by the same employer. In cases where a lay official agrees to accompany a worker employed by another organisation, time off is a matter for agreement by the parties concerned.

Applying the right

The employer should allow a companion to have a say in the date and time of a hearing. If the companion cannot attend on a proposed date, the worker can suggest an alternative time and date so long as it is reasonable and it is not more than five working days after the original date.

Employers may, however, wish to allow more time than this for a re-arranged meeting, particularly where the grievance may be connected with a potential dismissal. For instance, a grievance raised by a worker who complains that an ongoing disciplinary process which may result in their dismissal is unfair in some way. An employer must always act fairly in order to avoid a finding of unfair dismissal. Where there is a request to postpone a grievance hearing for more than five days because a trade union representative or other companion is not available, it may be fair to allow the postponement if it does not cause unreasonable delay. The employer should consider the facts and decide what is fair and reasonable in the circumstances.

Before the hearing takes place, the worker should tell the employer who they have chosen as a companion. In certain circumstances (for instance when the companion is an official of a non-recognised trade union) it can be helpful for the companion and employer to make contact before the hearing.

The companion should be allowed to address the meeting in order to:

- put the worker's case
- sum up the worker's case
- respond on the worker's behalf to any view expressed at the hearing
- confer with the worker during the meeting.

The companion must also be allowed to confer with the worker during the hearing. It is good practice to allow the companion to participate as fully as possible in the hearing, including asking witnesses questions. The employer is, however, not legally required to permit the companion to answer questions on the worker's behalf, or to address the hearing if the worker does not wish it, or to prevent the employer from explaining their case.

Workers whose employers fail to comply with a reasonable request to be accompanied may present a complaint to an employment tribunal. Workers may also complain to a tribunal if employers fail to re-arrange a hearing to a reasonable date proposed by the worker when a companion cannot attend on the date originally proposed.

Employers should be careful not to disadvantage workers for using their right to be accompanied or for being companions, as this is against the law and could lead to a claim to an employment tribunal.

DECIDE ON APPROPRIATE ACTION

[4.27]

Acas Code of Practice on disciplinary and grievance procedures Extract
Following the meeting decide on what action, if any, to take. Decisions should be communicated to the employee, in writing, without unreasonable delay and, where appropriate, should set out what action the employer intends to take to resolve the grievance. The employee should be informed that they can appeal if they are not content with the action taken.

It is generally good practice to adjourn a meeting before a decision is taken about how to deal with an employee's grievance. This allows time for reflection and proper consideration. It also allows for any further checking of any matters raised.

Set out clearly in writing any action that is to be taken and the employee's right of appeal. Where an employee's grievance is not upheld make sure the reasons are carefully explained.

Bear in mind that actions taken to resolve a grievance may have an impact on other individuals. While confidentiality is of prime importance in handling any grievance, in some circumstances there may be other individuals who may need to know the outcome, or certain aspects of the outcome that will impact on them. For instance, in cases where the grievance was about a fellow employee, that individual should also be informed of any aspect of the decision that affects them and the reasons for it. In such cases, the employee who raised the grievance should be informed of who else will be told about the decision and what type of information they will be given.

If the grievance highlights any issues concerning policies, procedures or conduct (even if not sufficiently serious to merit separate disciplinary procedures) they should be addressed as soon as possible.

Ensure any action taken is monitored and reviewed, as appropriate, so that it deals effectively with the issues.

ALLOW THE EMPLOYEE TO TAKE THE GRIEVANCE FURTHER IF NOT RESOLVED

[4.28]

Acas Code of Practice on disciplinary and grievance procedures Extract
Where an employee feels that their grievance has not been satisfactorily resolved they should appeal. They should let their employer know the grounds for their appeal without unreasonable delay and in writing. Appeals should be heard without unreasonable delay and at a time and place which should be notified to the employee in advance. The appeal should be dealt with impartially and wherever possible by a manager who has not previously been involved in the case. Workers have a statutory right to be accompanied at any such appeal hearing. The outcome of the appeal should be communicated to the employee in writing without unreasonable delay.

Arranging an appeal

If an employee informs the employer that they are unhappy with the decision after a grievance meeting, the employer should arrange an appeal. As far as reasonably practicable the appeal should be dealt with by someone who was not involved in the original case and ideally with a more senior manager than the one who dealt with the original grievance.

In small organisations, even if there is no more senior manager available, another manager should, if possible, hear the appeal. If this is not possible consider whether the owner or, in the case of a charity, the board of trustees, should hear the appeal. Whoever hears the appeal should consider it impartially.

At the same time as inviting the employee to attend the appeal, the employer should remind them of their right to be accompanied at the appeal meeting.

The appeal meeting should be conducted in the same calm, impartial and fair manner as the initial grievance meeting.

As with the first meeting, the employer should write to the employee with a decision on their grievance as soon as possible. They should also tell the employee if the appeal meeting is the final stage of the grievance procedure.

Where the grievance is about a fellow employee, that individual should be informed both that the initial decision has been appealed and the anticipated timeframe for the appeal decision, and should be provided with support where necessary. Once a decision on the appeal has been made, that individual should then be informed of any aspect of the decision that affects them and the reasons for it.

As with the initial decision, the employee who raised the grievance should be told if anyone else will be informed about the appeal decision and the type of information they will be given.

Large organisations may wish to allow a further appeal to a higher level of management, such as a director. However, in smaller firms the first appeal will usually mark the end of the grievance procedure. A sample grievance procedure for small organisations is at Appendix 2.

Dealing with special cases

The foreword to the Code of Practice points out that organisations may wish to consider dealing with issues involving bullying, harassment or whistleblowing under a separate procedure.

For further advice about how to deal with bullying and harassment see the Acas advice leaflet Bullying and harassment at work: a guide for managers and employers available to download from the Acas website www.acas.org.uk/bullying.

Mediation may be particularly useful in these types of cases.

THE APPENDICES

APPENDIX 1
DISCIPLINARY RULES FOR SMALL ORGANISATIONS

CHECKLIST

[4.29]
As a minimum, rules should:

- be simple, clear and in writing
- be displayed prominently in the workplace
- be known and understood by all employees
- cover issues such as absences, timekeeping, health and safety and use of organisational facilities and equipment (add any other items relevant to your organisation)
- indicate examples of the type of conduct which will normally lead to disciplinary action other than dismissal – for instance lateness or unauthorised absence
- indicate examples of the type of conduct which will normally lead to dismissal without notice – examples may include working dangerously, stealing or fighting – although much will depend on the circumstances of each offence.

APPENDIX 2
SAMPLE DISCIPLINARY AND GRIEVANCE PROCEDURES

SAMPLE DISCIPLINARY PROCEDURE (ANY ORGANISATION)

1. Purpose and scope

[4.30]
This procedure is designed to help and encourage all employees to achieve and maintain standards of conduct, attendance and job performance. The company rules (a copy of which is displayed in the office) and this procedure apply to all employees. The aim is to ensure consistent and fair treatment for all in the organisation.

2. Principles

Informal action will be considered, where appropriate, to resolve problems.

No disciplinary action will be taken against an employee until the case has been fully investigated.

For formal action the employee will be advised of the nature of the complaint against him or her and will be given the opportunity to state his or her case before any decision is made at a disciplinary meeting.

Employees will be provided, where appropriate, with written copies of evidence and relevant witness statements in advance of a disciplinary meeting.

At all stages of the procedure the employee will have the right to be accompanied by a trade union representative, or work colleague.

No employee will be dismissed for a first breach of discipline except in the case of gross misconduct, when the penalty will be dismissal without notice or payment in lieu of notice.

An employee will have the right to appeal against any disciplinary action.

The procedure may be implemented at any stage if the employee's alleged misconduct warrants this.

3. The Procedure

First stage of formal procedure

This will normally be either:

- *an improvement note for unsatisfactory performance* if performance does not meet acceptable standards. This will set out the performance problem, the improvement that is required, the timescale, any help that may be given and the right of appeal. The individual will be advised that it constitutes the first stage of the formal procedure. A record of the improvement note will be kept for . . . months, but will then be considered spent – subject to achieving and sustaining satisfactory performance
- *a first warning for misconduct* if conduct does not meet acceptable standards. This will be in writing and set out the nature of the misconduct and the change in behaviour required and the right of appeal. The warning will also inform the employee that a final written warning may be considered if there is no sustained satisfactory improvement or change. A record of the warning will be kept, but it will be disregarded for disciplinary purposes after a specified period (eg, six months).

Final written warning

If the offence is sufficiently serious, or if there is further misconduct or a failure to improve performance during the currency of a prior warning, a final written warning may be given to the employee. This will give details of the complaint, the improvement required and the timescale. It will also warn that failure to improve may lead to dismissal (or some other action short of dismissal) and will refer to the right of appeal. A copy of this written warning will be kept by the supervisor but will be disregarded for disciplinary purposes after . . . months subject to achieving and sustaining satisfactory conduct or performance.

Dismissal or other sanction

If there is still further misconduct or failure to improve performance the final step in the procedure may be dismissal or some other action short of dismissal such as demotion or disciplinary suspension or transfer (as allowed in the contract of employment). Dismissal decisions can only be taken by the appropriate senior manager, and the employee will be provided in writing with reasons for dismissal, the date on which the employment will terminate, and the right of appeal.

If some sanction short of dismissal is imposed, the employee will receive details of the complaint, will be warned that dismissal could result if there is no satisfactory improvement, and will be advised of the right of appeal. A copy of the written warning will be kept by the supervisor but will be disregarded for disciplinary purposes after . . . months subject to achievement and sustainment of satisfactory conduct or performance.

Gross misconduct

The following list provides some examples of offences which are normally regarded as gross misconduct:

- theft or fraud
- physical violence or bullying
- deliberate and serious damage to property
- serious misuse of an organisation's property or name
- deliberately accessing internet sites containing pornographic, offensive or obscene material
- serious insubordination
- unlawful discrimination or harassment
- bringing the organisation into serious disrepute
- serious incapability at work brought on by alcohol or illegal drugs
- causing loss, damage or injury through serious negligence
- a serious breach of health and safety rules
- a serious breach of confidence.

If you are accused of an act of gross misconduct, you may be suspended from work on full pay, normally for no more than five working days, while the alleged offence is investigated. If, on completion of the investigation and the full disciplinary procedure, the organisation is satisfied that gross misconduct has occurred, the result will normally be summary dismissal without notice or payment in lieu of notice.

Appeals

An employee who wishes to appeal against a disciplinary decision must do so within five working days. The senior manager will hear all appeals and his/her decision is final. At the appeal any disciplinary penalty imposed will be reviewed.

SAMPLE DISCIPLINARY PROCEDURE (SMALL ORGANISATION)

1. Purpose and scope

The organisation's aim is to encourage improvement in individual conduct or performance. This procedure sets out the action which will be taken when disciplinary rules are breached.

2. Principles

(a) The procedure is designed to establish the facts quickly and to deal consistently with disciplinary issues. No disciplinary action will be taken until the matter has been fully investigated.

(b) At every stage employees will be informed in writing of what is alleged and have the opportunity to state their case at a disciplinary meeting and be represented or accompanied, if they wish, by a trade union representative or a work colleague.

(c) An employee has the right to appeal against any disciplinary penalty.

3. The Procedure

Stage 1 – first warning

If conduct or performance is unsatisfactory, the employee will be given a written warning or performance note. Such warnings will be recorded, but disregarded after . . . months of satisfactory service. The employee will also be informed that a final written warning may be considered if there is no sustained satisfactory improvement or change. (Where the first offence is sufficiently serious, for example because it is having, or is likely to have, a serious harmful effect on the organisation, it may be justifiable to move directly to a final written warning.)

Stage 2 – final written warning

If the offence is serious, or there is no improvement in standards, or if a further offence of a similar kind occurs, a final written warning will be given which will include the reason for the warning and a note that if no improvement results within . . . months, action at Stage 3 will be taken.

Stage 3 – dismissal or action short of dismissal

If the conduct or performance has failed to improve, the employee may suffer demotion, disciplinary transfer, loss of seniority (as allowed in the contract) or dismissal.

Gross misconduct

If, after investigation, it is confirmed that an employee has committed an offence of the following nature (the list is not exhaustive), the normal consequence will be dismissal without notice or payment in lieu of notice:

– theft, damage to property, fraud, incapacity for work due to being under the influence of alcohol or illegal drugs, physical violence, bullying and gross insubordination.

While the alleged gross misconduct is being investigated, the employee may be suspended, during which time he or she will be paid their normal pay rate. Any decision to dismiss will be taken by the employer only after full investigation.

Appeals

An employee who wishes to appeal against any disciplinary decision must do so to the named person in the organisation within five working days. The employer will hear the appeal and decide the case as impartially.

SAMPLE GRIEVANCE PROCEDURE (SMALL ORGANISATION)

Dealing with grievances informally

If you have a grievance or complaint to do with your work or the people you work with you should, wherever possible, start by talking it over with your manager. You may be able to agree a solution informally between you.

Formal grievance

If the matter is serious and/or you wish to raise the matter formally you should set out the grievance in writing to your manager. You should stick to the facts and avoid language that is insulting or abusive.

Where your grievance is against your manager and you feel unable to approach him or her you should talk to another manager or the owner.

Grievance hearing

Your manager will call you to a meeting, normally within five days, to discuss your grievance. You have the right to be accompanied by a colleague or trade union representative at this meeting if you make a reasonable request.

After the meeting the manager will give you a decision in writing, normally within 24 hours.

If it is necessary to gather further information before making a decision your manger will inform you of this and the likely timescale involved.

Appeal

If you are unhappy with your manager's decision and you wish to appeal you should let your manager know.

You will be invited to an appeal meeting, normally within five days, and your appeal will be heard by a more senior manager (or the company owner). You have the right to be accompanied by a colleague or trade union representative at this meeting if you make a reasonable request.

After the meeting the manager (or owner) will give you a decision, normally within 24 hours. The manager's (or owner's) decision is final.

APPENDIX 3
SAMPLE LETTERS

[4.31]

Contents

(1) NOTICE OF DISCIPLINARY MEETING

Date . . . .

Dear . . . .

I am writing to tell you that you are required to attend a disciplinary meeting on . . . . at . . . . am/pm which is to be held in . . . .

At this meeting the question of disciplinary action against you, in accordance with the Company Disciplinary Procedure, will be considered with regard to:

I enclose the following documents*:

The possible consequences arising from this meeting might be:

You are entitled, if you wish, to be accompanied by another work colleague or a trade union representative.

Yours sincerely

Signed Manager . . . .

Note:
* Delete if not applicable

(2) NOTICE OF WRITTEN WARNING OR FINAL WRITTEN WARNING

Date . . . .

Dear . . . .

You attended a disciplinary hearing on . . . . I am writing to inform you of your written warning/final written warning*.

This warning will be placed in your personal file but will be disregarded for disciplinary purposes after a period of . . . . months, provided your conduct improves/performance reaches a satisfactory level**.

a) The nature of the unsatisfactory conduct or performance was:

b) The conduct or performance improvement expected is:

c) The timescale within which the improvement is required is:

d) The likely consequence of further misconduct or insufficient improvement is:

Final written warning/dismissal

You have the right to appeal against this decision (in writing**) to . . . . within . . . . . . days of receiving this disciplinary decision.

Yours sincerely

Signed Manager . . . .

Note:
** The wording should be amended as appropriate*
*** Delete as appropriate*

(3) NOTICE OF APPEAL MEETING AGAINST WARNING

Date . . . .

Dear . . . .

You have appealed against the written warning/final written warning* confirmed to you in writing on . . . .

Your appeal will be heard by . . . . in . . . . on . . . . at . . . .

You are entitled to be accompanied by a work colleague or trade union representative.

The decision of this appeal hearing is final and there is no further right of review.

Yours sincerely

Signed Manager . . . .

Note:
** The wording should be amended as appropriate*

(4) NOTICE OF RESULT OF APPEAL AGAINST WARNING

Date . . . .

Dear . . . .

You appealed against the decision of the disciplinary hearing that you be given a . . . . warning/in accordance with the Company Disciplinary Procedure. The appeal hearing was held on . . . .

I am now writing to inform you of the decision taken by the Manager who conducted the appeal hearing, namely that the decision to . . . . stands*/the decision to . . . . be revoked* [specify if no disciplinary action is being taken or what the new disciplinary action is].

You have now exercised your right of appeal under the Company Disciplinary Procedure and this decision is final.

Yours sincerely

Signed Manager . . . .

Note:
** The wording should be amended as appropriate*

(5) LETTER TO BE SENT BY THE EMPLOYER TO ARRANGE A MEETING WHERE DISMISSAL OR ACTION SHORT OF DISMISSAL* IS BEING CONSIDERED

Date . . . .

Dear . . . .

I am writing to tell you that . . . . [insert organisation name] is considering dismissing OR taking disciplinary action [insert proposed action] against you.

This action is being considered with regard to the following circumstances: You are invited to attend a disciplinary meeting on . . . . at . . . . am/pm which is to be held in . . . . where this will be discussed.

You are entitled, if you wish, to be accompanied by another work colleague or your trade union representative.

Yours sincerely

Signed Manager . . . .

Note:
** Action other than a warning such as transfer or demotion*

(6) LETTER TO BE SENT BY THE EMPLOYER AFTER THE DISCIPLINARY MEETING ARRANGED IN LETTER 5

Date . . . .

Dear . . . .

On . . . . you were informed that . . . . [insert organisation name] was considering dismissing OR taking disciplinary action [insert proposed action] against you.

This was discussed in a meeting on . . . . At this meeting, it was decided that: [delete as applicable]

Your conduct/performance/etc was still unsatisfactory and that you be dismissed.

Your conduct/performance/etc was still unsatisfactory and that the following disciplinary action would be taken against you . . . .

No further action would be taken against you.

I am therefore writing to you to confirm the decision that you be dismissed and that your last day of service with the Company will be . . . .

The reasons for your dismissal are:

Or:

I am therefore writing to you to confirm the decision that disciplinary action will be taken against you. The action will be . . . . The reasons for this disciplinary action are:

You have the right of appeal against this decision. Please [write] to . . . . within . . . . days of receiving this disciplinary decision

Yours sincerely

Signed Manager . . . .

(7) NOTICE OF APPEAL MEETING AGAINST DISMISSAL/DISCIPLINARY ACTION*

Date . . . .

Dear . . . .

You have appealed against your dismissal/disciplinary action [delete as appropriate] on . . . . confirmed to you in writing on . . . .
Your appeal will be heard by . . . . in . . . . on . . . . at . . . .

You are entitled, if you wish, to be accompanied by another work colleague or a trade union representative.

The decision of this appeal meeting is final and there is no further right of review.

Yours sincerely

Signed Manager . . . .

Note:
** Action other than a warning such as transfer or demotion*

(8) NOTICE OF RESULT OF APPEAL AGAINST DISMISSAL/DISCIPLINARY ACTION*

Date . . . .

Dear . . . .

You appealed against the decision of the disciplinary hearing that you be dismissed/subject to disciplinary action [delete as appropriate].

The appeal meeting was held on . . . .

I am now writing to inform you of the decision taken by . . . .

[insert name of the manager] who conducted the appeal meeting, namely that the decision to . . . . stands/ the decision to . . . . be revoked [specify if no disciplinary action is being taken or what the new disciplinary action is].

You have now exercised your right of appeal under the Company Disciplinary Procedure and this decision is final.

Yours sincerely

Signed Manager . . . .

Note:
** Action other than a warning such as transfer or demotion*

(9) LETTER OF ENQUIRY REGARDING LIKELY CAUSE OF ABSENCE ADDRESSED TO A WORKER'S GENERAL PRACTITIONER

Date . . . .

Doctor's name . . . .

Address . . . .

PLEASE ACKNOWLEDGE RECEIPT OF THIS LETTER IF THERE IS LIKELY TO BE ANY DELAY IN REPLYING

Re . . . .

Name . . . .

Address . . . .

To administer Statutory Sick Pay, and the Company's sick pay scheme, and to plan the work in the department, it would be helpful to have a report on your patient, who works for our organisation.

His/her work as a . . . . has the following major features:

Management responsibility for
Seated/standing/mobile
Light/medium/heavy effort required
Day/shift/night work
Clerical/secretarial duties
Group I (private)/Group II (professional) driver
Other

The absence record for the past year is summarised as:

Total days lost
This month
Previous months

Attached is your patient's permission to enquire. He/she wishes/does not wish to have access to the report under the Access to Medical Reports Act 1988:

What is the likely date of return to work?

Will there be any disability at that time?

How long is it likely to last?

Are there any reasonable adjustments we could make to accommodate the disability?

Is there any underlying medical reason for this attendance record?

Is he/she likely to be able to render regular and efficient service in the future?

Is there any specific recommendation you wish to make about him/her which would help in finding him/her an alternative job, if that is necessary, and if there is an opportunity for redeployment (for instance no climbing ladders, no driving).

I would be grateful for an early reply and enclose a stamped addressed envelope. Please attach your account to the report (following the BMA guidance on fees).

Yours sincerely

Signed Name (BLOCK LETTERS) . . . .

Role in the company . . . .

Note:
Please amend/delete where necessary

APPENDIX 4
DEALING WITH ABSENCE

[4.32]
This appendix considers how to handle problems of absence and gives guidance about unauthorised short-term and long-term absences, and the failure to return from extended leave. More extensive advice on attendance management is available in the Acas advisory booklet *Managing attendance and employee turnover* available to purchase or download on the Acas website www.acas.org.uk.

A distinction should be made between absence on grounds of illness or injury and absence for no good reason which may call for disciplinary action. Where disciplinary action is called for, the normal disciplinary procedure should be used. Where the employee is absent because of illness or injury, the guidance in this Appendix should be followed.

Employers should be aware of the requirements of the Equality Act 2010 when making any decisions that affect someone who may be disabled as defined by the Act. (For further information see the Equality and Human Rights Commission website at www.equalityhumanrights.com.)

Records showing lateness and the duration of and reasons for all spells of absence should be kept to help monitor absence levels. These enable management to check levels of absence or lateness so that problems can be spotted and addressed at an early stage. (The Information Commissioner has produced a Code of Practice on employment records, available at www.ico.org.uk).

HOW SHOULD FREQUENT AND PERSISTENT SHORT-TERM ABSENCE BE HANDLED?

- unexpected absences should be investigated promptly and the employee asked for an explanation at a return-to-work interview
- if there are no acceptable reasons then the employer may wish to treat the matter as a conduct issue and deal with it under the disciplinary procedure
- where there is no medical certificate to support frequent short-term, self-certified, absences then the employee should be asked to see a doctor to establish whether treatment is necessary and whether the underlying reason for the absence is work-related. If no medical support is forthcoming the employer should consider whether to take action under the disciplinary procedure if the absence could be disability related the employer should consider what reasonable adjustments could be made in the workplace to help the employee (this might be something as simple as an adequate, ergonomic chair, or a power-assisted piece of equipment). Reasonable adjustment also means redeployment to a different type of work if necessary. (For further information see the Equality and Human Rights Commission website at www.equalityhumanrights.com.)
- if the absence is because of temporary problems relating to dependants, the employee may be entitled to have time off under the provisions of the Employment Rights Act 1996 relating to time off for dependants
- if the absence is because the employee has difficulty managing both work and home responsibilities then the employer should give serious consideration to more flexible ways of working. Employees have the right to request flexible working arrangements – including jobsharing, part-time working, flexi-time, working from home/ teleworking and school time contracts – and employers must have a good business reason for rejecting any application
- in all cases the employee should be told what improvement in attendance is expected and warned of the likely consequences if this does not happen
- if there is no improvement, the employee's length of service, performance, the likelihood of a change in attendance, the availability of suitable alternative work where appropriate, and the effect of past and future absences on the organisation should all be taken into account in deciding appropriate action.

In order to show both the employee concerned, and other employees, that absence is regarded as a serious matter and may result in dismissal, it is very important that persistent absence is dealt with promptly, firmly and consistently.

An examination of records will identify those employees who are frequently absent and may show an absence pattern.

HOW SHOULD LONGER-TERM ABSENCE THROUGH ILL HEALTH BE HANDLED?

Where absence is due to medically certificated illness, the issue becomes one of capability rather than conduct. Employers need to take a more sympathetic and considerate approach, particularly if the employee is disabled and where reasonable adjustments at the workplace might enable them to return to work.

There are certain steps an employer should take when considering the problem of long-term absence:

- employee and employer should keep in regular contact with each other
- the employee must be kept fully informed if there is any risk to employment
- if the employer wishes to contact the employee's doctor, he or she must notify the employee in writing that they intend to make such an application and they must secure the employee's consent in writing (Access to Medical Reports Act 1988). The employer must inform the individual that he or she has:
  - the right to withhold consent to the application being made
  - the right to state that he or she wishes to have access to the report. (The Access to Medical Reports Act 1988 also gives the individual the right to have access to the medical practitioner's report for up to six months after it was supplied)
  - rights concerning access to the report before (and/or after) it is supplied
  - the right to withhold consent to the report being supplied to the employer
  - the right to request amendments to the report
- where the employee states that he or she wishes to have access to the report, the employer must let the GP know this when making the application and at the same time let the employee know that the report has been requested
- the letter of enquiry reproduced in Appendix 3 – Sample letters, and approved by the British Medical Association, may be used, and the employee's permission to the enquiry should be attached to the letter
- the GP should return the report via the company doctor. If there is not one the employer should make it clear to the employee, when seeking permission to approach the GP, that the report will be sent direct to the employer. (Employers who wish to seek advice on securing the services of a company doctor should contact the Faculty of Occupational Medicine www.facoccmed.ac.uk)
- the employee must contact the GP within 21 days of the date of application to make arrangement to see the report. Otherwise the rights under the 1988 Act will be lost
- if the employee considers the report to be incorrect or misleading, the employee may make a written request to the GP to make appropriate amendments
- if the GP refuses, the employee has the right to ask the GP to attach a statement to the report reflecting the employee's view on any matters of disagreement
- the employee may withhold consent to the report being supplied to the employer
- on the basis of the GP's report the employer should consider whether alternative work is available
- the employer is not expected to create a special job for the employee concerned, nor to be a medical expert, but to take action on the basis of the medical evidence
- where there is a reasonable doubt about the nature of the illness or injury, the employee should be asked if he or she would agree to be examined by a doctor to be appointed by the organisation
- where an employee refuses to cooperate in providing medical evidence, or to undergo an independent medical examination, the employee should be told in writing that a decision will be taken on the basis of the information available and that it could result in dismissal
- where the employee is allergic to a product used in the workplace the employer should consider remedial action or a transfer to alternative work
- where the employee's job can no longer be held open, and no suitable alternative work is available, the employee should be informed of the likelihood of dismissal
- where dismissal action is taken the employee should be given the period of notice to which he or she is entitled by statute or contract and informed of any right of appeal.

Where an employee has been on long-term sick absence and there is little likelihood of he or she becoming fit enough to return, it may be argued that the contract of employment has been terminated through 'frustration'. However, the doctrine of frustration should not be relied on since the courts are generally reluctant to apply it where a procedure exists for termination of the contract. It is therefore better for the employer to take dismissal action after following proper procedures.

SPECIFIC HEALTH PROBLEMS

Consideration should be given to introducing measures to help employees, regardless of status or seniority, who are suffering from alcohol or drug abuse, or from stress. The aim should be to identify employees affected and encourage them to seek help and treatment. See the Acas advisory booklet *Health, work and wellbeing* available to purchase or download on the Acas website www.acas.org.uk Employers should consider whether it is appropriate to treat the problem as a medical rather than a disciplinary matter.

There is sometimes workforce pressure to dismiss an employee because of a medical condition, or even threats of industrial action. If such an employee is dismissed, then he or she may be able to claim unfair dismissal before an employment tribunal, or breach of contract. Employers should bear in mind that they may have to justify the reasonableness of any decision to dismiss and that an employment tribunal will ignore threats of, and actual, industrial action when determining the fairness of a decision (Section 107, Employment Rights Act 1996).

The Equality Act 2010 makes it unlawful for an employer of any size to treat a disabled person less favourably for a reason relating to their disability, without a justifiable reason. Employers are required to make a reasonable adjustment to working conditions or the workplace where that would help to accommodate a particular disabled person.

FAILURE TO RETURN FROM EXTENDED LEAVE ON THE AGREED DATE

Employers may have policies which allow employees extended leave of absence without pay, for example to visit relatives in their countries of origin, or relatives who have emigrated to other countries, or to nurse a sick relative. There is no general statutory right to such leave without pay, except to deal with an initial emergency relating to a dependant under the Employment Rights Act 1996.

Where a policy of extended leave is in operation, the following points should be borne in mind:

- the policy should apply to all employees, irrespective of their age, disability, gender reassignment, marital or civil partnership status, pregnancy and maternity, race, religion or belief, sex, or sexual orientation
- any conditions attaching to the granting of extended leave should be carefully explained to the employee, using interpreters if necessary, and the employee's signature should be obtained as an acknowledgement that he or she understands and accepts them
- employers should be aware that agreed extended leave can preserve continuity of employment, even when such leave is unpaid and other terms and conditions of employment are suspended for the duration of the leave
- if an employee fails to return on the agreed date, this should be approached in the same way as any other failure to abide by the rules and the circumstances should be investigated in the normal way, with disciplinary procedures being followed if appropriate
- care should be taken to ensure that foreign medical certificates are not treated in a discriminatory way: employees can fall ill while abroad just as they can fall ill in this country
- before deciding to dismiss an employee who overstays leave, the employee's experience, length of service, reliability record and any explanation given should all be taken into account
- failure to return from ordinary maternity leave does not of itself terminate the contract of employment. Employers should try and find out the reason for the failure and take action if necessary as in any other case of failing to return from leave (whether extended/additional maternity/paternity/adoption/parental leave; time off for dependants; or holiday leave).

An agreement that an employee should return to work on a particular date will not prevent a complaint of unfair dismissal to an employment tribunal if the employee is dismissed for failing to return as agreed. In all such cases, all the factors mentioned above and the need to act reasonably should be borne in mind before any dismissal action is taken.

APPENDIX 5
BASIC PRINCIPLES OF THE DATA PROTECTION ACT 2018 AND THE EQUALITY ACT 2010

THE DATA PROTECTION ACT 2018

[4.33]
The Data Protection Act provides a framework that controls how personal information is used by organisations, businesses or the government.

The Act works in two ways. Firstly, it states that anyone who processes personal information must comply with six principles, which make sure that the information is:

- used fairly, lawfully and transparently
- used for specified, explicit purposes
- used in a way that is adequate, relevant and limited to only what is necessary
- accurate and, where necessary, kept up to date
- kept for no longer than is necessary
- handled in a way that ensures appropriate security, including protection against unlawful or unauthorised processing, access, loss, destruction or damage

There is stronger legal protection for more sensitive information, such as:

- race
- ethnic background
- political opinions
- religious beliefs
- trade union membership
- genetics
- biometrics (where used for identification)
- health
- sex life or orientation

There are separate safeguards for personal data relating to criminal convictions and offences.

The second area covered by the Act provides individuals with important rights. These include the right to:

- be informed about how your data is being used
- access personal data
- have incorrect data updated
- have data erased
- stop or restrict the processing of your data
- data portability (allowing you to get and reuse your data for different services)
- object to how your data is processed in certain circumstances.

Should an individual or organisation feel they're being denied access to personal information they're entitled to, or feel their information has not been handled according to the six principles, they can contact the Information Commissioner's Office (ICO) for help on 0303 123 1113. Complaints are usually dealt with informally, but if this isn't possible, enforcement action can be taken.

The ICO provides comprehensive practical advice on how to comply with data protection law at www.ico.org.uk. In particular, the *Employment Practices Data Protection Code* deals with the impact of data protection laws on the employment relationship. It covers such issues as:

- **recruitment and selection** (job applications and pre-employment vetting)
- **employment records** (collecting, storing, disclosing and deleting records)
- **monitoring at work** (monitoring workers' use of telephones, the internet, e-mail systems and vehicles)
- **workers' health** (occupational health, medical testing, drug and genetic screening)

THE EQUALITY ACT 2010

The Equality Act gives disabled people some particular employment rights. A disabled person is defined in the Act as 'anyone with a physical or mental impairment which has a substantial and long-term adverse effect upon his or her ability to carry out normal day-to-day activities'.

However, disability does not necessarily affect someone's health, so insisting on a medical report purely on the basis of the disability may be unlawful discrimination. If your organisation believes that pre-employment health screening is necessary, you must make sure it is carried out in a non-discriminatory way. It is unlawful to ask health related questions before making a job offer (whether conditional or unconditional), except in order to:

- determine if a candidate can carry out a function which is essential to the job
- ask whether candidates need special arrangements for any part of the application process
- anonymously monitor whether candidates are disabled
- take positive action to assist disabled people
- check that a candidate has a disability where this is a genuine requirement of the job.

If a report from any individual's doctor is sought, then permission must be given by the individual, and they have the right to see the report (Access to Medical Reports Act 1988).

Discrimination means treating someone less favourably without a reasonable justification, and the Act requires that employers make reasonable adjustments if that will then remove the reason for the unfavourable treatment. An example of a reasonable adjustment could be the provision of a suitable computer keyboard to an operator who had difficulty through disability in using a conventional keyboard.

In relation to discipline and grievance procedures, employers must clearly ensure they do not discriminate in any area of practice which could lead to dismissal or any other detriment (for example warnings).

The Act also covers people who become disabled during the course of their employment, and this is particularly relevant to the absence handling section of this handbook. It is vital that the employer should discuss with the worker what their needs really are and what effect, if any, the disability may have on future work with the organisation. Any dismissal of a disabled employee for a reason relating to the disability would have to be justified, and the reason for it would have to be one which could not be removed or made less than substantial by any reasonable adjustment.

The Equality and Human Rights Commission provides information and advice about all aspects of the Equality Act 2010, as well as signposting specialist organisations where necessary. In addition, it can offer good practice advice on the employment of disabled people.

www.equalityhumanrights.com

Tel: England **0845 604 6610**, Scotland **0845 604 5510** and for Wales **0845 604 8810**

GLOSSARY

[4.34]

Capability: an employee's ability or qualification to do their job. Most often referred to in discipline cases where there is a lack of capability

Conduct: an employee's behaviour in the workplace

Disciplinary action: formal action against an employee: for example issuing a first written warning for misconduct or dismissing someone for gross misconduct

Disciplinary procedure: a procedure for organisations to follow to deal with cases of misconduct or unsatisfactory performance. It helps employers deal with discipline cases fairly and consistently

Employees: people who work for an employer under a contract of employment and who are entitled to all statutory employment rights. See also the glossary entry for "Workers" below

Grievance: a problem or concern that an employee has about their work, working conditions or relationships with colleagues or managers

Grievance procedure: a procedure for organisations to use to consider employees' grievances. It helps employers deal with grievances fairly and consistently

Gross misconduct: acts which are so serious as to justify possible dismissal. See example list in *Taking action after the disciplinary meeting*

Improvement note: in cases of unsatisfactory performance an employee should be given an improvement note setting out the performance problem, the improvement that is required, the timescale for achieving this improvement, a review date and any support the employer will provide to assist the employee

Natural justice: refers to the basic fundamental principles of fair treatment. These principles include the duty to give someone a fair hearing; the duty to ensure that the matter is decided by someone who is impartial; and the duty to allow an appeal against a decision

Reasonable adjustments: a way of preventing discrimination against disabled employees by making changes to ensure that they are not at a disadvantage. For example, providing a specialist keyboard may be a reasonable adjustment for a disabled employee unable to use a conventional keyboard

Sanction: a punishment imposed on an employee as a result of unsatisfactory performance or misconduct. Sanctions may include dismissal or actions short of dismissal such as loss of pay or demotion

Summary dismissal: dismissal without notice – usually only justifiable for gross misconduct. Summary is not necessarily the same as instant and incidents of gross misconduct should be investigated as part of a formal procedure

Workers: a term that includes employees and also other groups such as agency workers or anyone carrying out work who is not genuinely self-employed. Workers who are not employees often have flexible employment contracts that allow them to accept or reject any offer of work made to them, and have less statutory employment rights than employees.

FURTHER INFORMATION

[4.35]

Acas learning online

Acas offers free E-Learning on a wide range of topics including, Discipline & Grievance and Conflict Resolution. For more information go to www.acas.org.uk/elearning

Acas training

Acas offers a conducting investigations course that is carried out by experienced Acas staff who work with businesses every day.

Go to www.acas.org.uk/training for up-to-date information about our training and booking places on face-to-face courses.

Acas business solutions

Acas specialists can visit an organisation, diagnose issues in its workplace, and tailor training and support to address the challenges it faces. To find out more, see the Acas website page Business solutions www.acas.org.uk/businesssolutions

Related Acas guidance

- Acas Code of Practice on disciplinary and grievance procedures
- Managing absence at work
- Performance management
- Bullying and harassment at work: a guide for managers and employers
- Bullying and harassment at work: a guide for employees
- Guidance on discrimination is available at www.acas.org.uk/equality

Additional help

Employers may be able to seek assistance from groups where they are members. For example, if an employer is a member of the Confederation of British Industry or the Federation of Small Businesses, it could seek its help and guidance. If an employee is a trade union member, they can seek help and guidance from their trade union representative or equality representative.

KEEP UP-TO-DATE AND STAY INFORMED

[4.36]

Visit www.acas.org.uk for:

- Employment relations and employment law guidance – free to view, download or share
- Tools and resources including free-to-download templates, forms and checklists
- An introduction to other Acas services including mediation, conciliation, training, arbitration and the Acas Early Conciliation service
- Research and discussion papers on the UK workplace and employment practices
- Details of Acas training courses, conferences and events.

Sign up for the free Acas e-newsletter. The Acas email newsletter is a great way of keeping up to date with changes to employment law and to hear about events in your area. Find out more at:www.acas.org.uk/subscribe

The Acas Model Workplace. This engaging and interactive tool can help an employer diagnose employment relations issues in its workplace. The tool will work with you to identify areas of improvement you can consider, and will point toward the latest guidance and best practice: www.acas.org.uk/modelworkplace

Acas Helpline Online. Have a question? We have a database of frequently asked employment queries that has been developed to help both employees and employers. It is an automated system, designed to give you a straightforward answer to your employment questions, and also gives links to further advice and guidance on our website: www.acas.org.uk/helplineonline

Acas Helpline. Call the Acas Helpline for free and impartial advice. We can provide employers and employees with clear and confidential guidance about any kind of dispute or relationship issue in the workplace. You may want to know about employment rights and rules, best practice or may need advice about a dispute. Whatever it is, our team are on hand. Find out more: www.acas.org.uk/helpline

Look for us on:

Facebook https://www.facebook.com/acasorguk

LinkedIn http://linkd.in/cYJbuU

Twitter http://twitter.com/acasorguk

YouTube https://www.youtube.com/user/ac

ACAS CODE OF PRACTICE 2 DISCLOSURE OF INFORMATION TO TRADE UNIONS FOR COLLECTIVE BARGAINING PURPOSES (1998)

[4.37]

NOTES

This revised Code was issued on 28 October 1997, and was brought into force on 5 February 1998 by the Employment Protection Code of Practice (Disclosure of Information) Order 1998, SI 1998/45. It replaces the similarly named Code of 1977.

Authority: Trade Union and Labour Relations (Consolidation) Act 1992, s 201. For the legal status of this Code, see s 207 of the 1992 Act at **[1.523]**.

Text in bold type summarises statutory provisions on the disclosure of information, while practical guidance is set out in ordinary type. Notes are as in the Code.

See *Harvey* NI(a).

CONTENTS

INTRODUCTION

[4.38]

1. Under the Trade Union and Labour Relations (Consolidation) Act 1992 the Advisory, Conciliation and Arbitration Service (ACAS) may issue Codes of Practice containing such practical guidance as the Service thinks fit for the purpose of promoting the improvement of industrial relations. In particular, the Service has a duty to provide practical guidance on the information to be disclosed by employers to trade union representatives in accordance with sections 181 and 182 of that Act, for the purposes of collective bargaining.

2. The Act and the Code apply to employers operating in both the public and private sectors of industry. They do not apply to collective bargaining between employers' associations and trade unions, although the parties concerned may wish to follow the guidelines contained in the Code.

3. The information which employers may have a duty to disclose under section 181 is information which it would be in accordance with good industrial relations practice to disclose. In determining what would be in accordance with good industrial relations practice, regard is to be had to any relevant provisions of the Code. However, the Code imposes no legal obligations on an employer to disclose any specific item of information. Failure to observe the Code does not by itself render anyone liable to proceedings, but the Act requires any relevant provisions to be taken into account in proceedings before the Central Arbitration Committee.[1]

NOTES

[1] Trade Union and Labour Relations (Consolidation) Act 1992, sections 181(2)(b), 181(4) and 207(1) and (2).

This Code replaces the Code of Practice on Disclosure of Information to Trade Unions for Collective Bargaining Purposes, issued by the Service in 1977.

PROVISIONS OF THE ACT

[4.39]

4. The Act places a general duty on an employer who recognises an independent trade union to disclose, for the purposes of all stages of collective bargaining about matters, and in relation to

descriptions of workers, in respect of which the union is recognised by him, information requested by representatives of the union. The representative of the union is an official or other person authorised by the union to carry on such collective bargaining.

5. The information requested has to be in the employer's possession, or in the possession of any associated employer, and must relate to the employer's undertaking. The information to be disclosed is that without which a trade union representative would be impeded to a material extent in bargaining and which it would be in accordance with good industrial relations practice to disclose for the purpose of collective bargaining. In determining what is in accordance with good industrial relations practice, any relevant provisions of this Code are to be taken into account.

6. No employer is required to disclose any information which: would be against the interests of national security; would contravene a prohibition imposed by or under an enactment; was given to an employer in confidence, or was obtained by the employer in consequence of the confidence reposed in him by another person; relates to an individual unless he has consented to its disclosure; would cause substantial injury to the undertaking (or national interest in respect of Crown employment) for reasons other than its effect on collective bargaining; or was obtained for the purpose of any legal proceedings.

7. In providing information the employer is not required to produce original documents for inspection or copying. Nor is he required to compile or assemble information which would entail work or expenditure out of reasonable proportion to the value of the information in the conduct of collective bargaining. The union representative can request that the information be given in writing by the employer or be confirmed in writing. Similarly, an employer can ask the trade union representative to make the request for information in writing or confirm it in writing.

8. If the trade union considers that an employer has failed to disclose to its representatives information which he was required to disclose by section 181 of the Act, or to confirm such information in writing in accordance with that section, it may make a complaint to the Central Arbitration Committee. The Committee may ask the Advisory, Conciliation and Arbitration Service to conciliate. If conciliation does not lead to a settlement of the complaint, the Service shall inform the Committee accordingly who shall proceed to hear and determine the complaint. If the complaint is upheld by the Committee, it is required to specify the information that should have been disclosed or confirmed in writing, the date the employer failed to disclose, or confirm in writing, any of the information and a period of time within which the employer ought to disclose the information, or confirm it in writing. If the employer does not disclose the information, or confirm it in writing, within the specified time, the union (except in relation to Crown employment and Parliamentary staff) may present a further complaint to the Committee and may also present a claim for improved terms and conditions. If the further complaint is upheld by the Committee, an award, which would have effect as part of the contract of employment, may be made against the employer on the terms and conditions specified in the claim, or other terms and conditions which the Committee considers appropriate.

PROVIDING INFORMATION

[4.40]

9. The absence of relevant information about an employer's undertaking may to a material extent impede trade unions in collective bargaining, particularly if the information would influence the formulation, presentation or pursuance of a claim, or the conclusion of an agreement. The provision of relevant information in such circumstances would be in accordance with good industrial relations practice.

10. To determine what information will be relevant, negotiators should take account of the subject-matter of the negotiations and the issues raised during them; the level at which negotiations take place (department, plant, division, or company level); the size of the company; and the type of business the company is engaged in.

11. Collective bargaining within an undertaking can range from negotiations on specific matters arising daily at the workplace affecting particular sections of the workforce, to extensive periodic negotiations on terms and conditions of employment affecting the whole workforce in multi-plant companies. The relevant information and the depth, detail and form in which it could be presented to negotiators will vary accordingly. Consequently, it is not possible to compile a list of items that should be disclosed in all circumstances. Some examples of information relating to the undertaking which could be relevant in certain collective bargaining situations are given below:

(i) *Pay and benefits*: principles and structure of payment systems; job evaluation systems and grading criteria; earnings and hours analysed according to work-group, grade, plant, sex, out-workers and homeworkers, department or division, giving, where appropriate, distributions and make-up of pay showing any additions to basic rate or salary; total pay bill; details of fringe benefits and non-wage labour costs.

(ii) *Conditions of service*: policies on recruitment, redeployment, redundancy, training, equal opportunity, and promotion; appraisal systems; health, welfare and safety matters.

(iii) *Manpower*: numbers employed analysed according to grade, department, location, age and sex; labour turnover; absenteeism; overtime and short-time; manning standards; planned changes in work methods, materials, equipment or organisation; available manpower plans; investment plans.

(iv) *Performance*: productivity and efficiency data; savings from increased productivity and output, return on capital invested; sales and state of order book.

(v) *Financial*: cost structures; gross and net profits; sources of earnings; assets; liabilities; allocation of profits; details of government financial assistance; transfer prices; loans to parent or subsidiary companies and interest charged.

12. These examples are not intended to represent a check list of information that should be provided for all negotiations. Nor are they meant to be an exhaustive list of types of information as other items may be relevant in particular negotiations.

RESTRICTIONS ON THE DUTY TO DISCLOSE

[4.41]
13. Trade unions and employers should be aware of the restrictions on the general duty to disclose information for collective bargaining.[2]

14. Some examples of information which if disclosed in particular circumstances might cause substantial injury are: cost information on individual products; detailed analysis of proposed investment, marketing or pricing policies; and price quotas or the make-up of tender prices. Information which has to be made available publicly, for example under the Companies Acts, would not fall into this category.

15. Substantial injury may occur if, for example, certain customers would be lost to competitors, or suppliers would refuse to supply necessary materials, or the ability to raise funds to finance the company would be seriously impaired as a result of disclosing certain information. The burden of establishing a claim that disclosure of certain information would cause substantial injury lies with the employer.

NOTES

[2] Trade Union and Labour Relations (Consolidation) Act 1992, section 182. See paragraphs 6 and 7 of this Code.

TRADE UNIONS' RESPONSIBILITIES

[4.42]
16. Trade unions should identify and request the information they require for collective bargaining in advance of negotiations whenever practicable. Misunderstandings can be avoided, costs reduced, and time saved, if requests state as precisely as possible all the information required, and the reasons why the information is considered relevant. Requests should conform to an agreed procedure. A reasonable period of time should be allowed for employers to consider a request and to reply.

17. Trade unions should keep employers informed of the names of the representatives authorised to carry on collective bargaining on their behalf.

18. Where two or more trade unions are recognised by an employer for collective bargaining purposes they should co-ordinate their requests for information whenever possible.

19. Trade unions should review existing training programmes or establish new ones to ensure negotiators are equipped to understand and use information effectively.

EMPLOYERS' RESPONSIBILITIES[3]

[4.43]
20. Employers should aim to be as open and helpful as possible in meeting trade union requests for information. Where a request is refused, the reasons for the refusal should be explained as far as possible to the trade union representatives concerned and be capable of being substantiated should the matter be taken to the Central Arbitration Committee.

21. Information agreed as relevant to collective bargaining should be made available as soon as possible once a request for the information has been made by an authorised trade union representative. Employers should present information in a form and style which recipients can reasonably be expected to understand.

NOTES

[3] The Stock Exchange has drawn attention to the need for employers to consider any obligations which they may have under their Listing Agreement.

JOINT ARRANGEMENTS FOR DISCLOSURE OF INFORMATION

[4.44]
22. Employers and trade unions should endeavour to arrive at a joint understanding on how the provisions on the disclosure of information can be implemented most effectively. They should consider what information is likely to be required, what is available, and what could reasonably be made available. Consideration should also be given to the form in which the information will be presented, when it should be presented and to whom. In particular, the parties should endeavour to reach an understanding on what information could most appropriately be provided on a regular basis.

23. Procedures for resolving possible disputes concerning any issues associated with the disclosure of information should be agreed. Where possible such procedures should normally be related to any existing arrangements within the undertaking or industry and the complaint, conciliation and arbitration procedure described in the Act.[4]

NOTES

[4] Trade Union and Labour Relations (Consolidation) Act 1992, sections 183 to 185. See paragraph 8 of this Code.

ACAS CODE OF PRACTICE 3
TIME OFF FOR TRADE UNION DUTIES AND ACTIVITIES (INCLUDING GUIDANCE ON TIME OFF FOR UNION LEARNING REPRESENTATIVES) (2010)

[4.45]

NOTES

This Code was originally issued by ACAS under the Employment Protection Act 1975, s 6 (repealed) and was brought into effect on 1 April 1978 (by SI 1977/2076). The present Code is the fourth reissue. The statutory authority for the making of the Code and its revision is TULR(C)A 1992, s 199 at **[1.515]**, and its legal status is, as for the other ACAS Codes, as set out in s 207 at **[1.523]**. This Code came into effect on 1 January 2010 (see the Employment Protection Code of Practice (Time Off for Trade Union Duties and Activities) Order 2009, SI 2009/3223).

See *Harvey* NI(8).

CONTENTS

INTRODUCTION

[4.46]

1. Under section 199 of the Trade Union and Labour Relations (Consolidation) Act 1992 the Advisory, Conciliation and Arbitration Service (Acas) has a duty to provide practical guidance on the time off to be permitted by an employer:

(a) to a trade union official in accordance with section 168 of the Trade Union and Labour Relations (Consolidation) Act 1992; and

(b) to a trade union member in accordance with section 170 of the Trade Union and Labour Relations (Consolidation) Act 1992.

Section 199 of the Act, as amended by the Employment Act 2002, also provides for Acas to issue practical guidance on time off and training for Union Learning Representatives.

This Code, which replaces the Code of Practice issued by Acas in 2003, is intended to provide such guidance. Advice on the role and responsibilities of employee representatives is provided in two Acas Guides: *Trade union representation in the workplace: a guide to managing time off, training* and facilities and *Non-union representation in the workplace: a guide to managing time off, training and facilities*.

TERMINOLOGY

2. In this Code the term 'Trade union official', is replaced by 'union representative'. In practice there is often confusion between an 'official' and an 'officer' of a union and the term 'representative' is commonly used in practice. Section 119 of the Trade Union and Labour Relations (Consolidation) Act 1992 defines an official as '(a) an officer of the union or of a branch or section of the union, or (b) a person elected or appointed in accordance with the rules of the union to be a representative of its members or of some of them, and includes a person so elected or appointed who is an employee of the same employer as the members or one or more of the members whom he is to represent'. Section 181(1) of the same Act defines a 'representative', for the purposes of sections 181–185 of the Act, as 'an official or other person authorised by the union to carry on such collective bargaining'.

In this Code a union representative means an employee who has been elected or appointed in accordance with the rules of the independent union to be a representative of all or some of the union's members in the particular company or workplace, or agreed group of workplaces where the union is recognised for collective bargaining purposes. This is intended to equate with the legal term 'trade union official' for the purposes of this Code.

The term 'union full-time officer' in this Code means a trade union official who is employed by an independent trade union to represent members in workplaces, or groups of workplaces, where the union is recognised for collective bargaining purposes.

A Union Learning Representative is an employee who is a member of an independent trade union recognised by the employer who has been elected or appointed in accordance with the rules of the union to be a learning representative of the union at the workplace.

THE BACKGROUND

3. Union representatives have had a statutory right to reasonable paid time off from employment to carry out trade union duties and to undertake trade union training since the Employment Protection Act 1975.

Part 4 Statutory Codes of Practice

Union representatives and members were also given a statutory right to reasonable unpaid time off when taking part in trade union activities. Union duties must relate to matters covered by collective bargaining agreements between employers and trade unions and relate to the union representative's own employer, unless agreed otherwise in circumstances of multi-employer bargaining, and not, for example, to any associated employer. All the time off provisions were brought together in sections 168–170 of the Trade Union and Labour Relations (Consolidation) Act 1992. Section 43 of the Employment Act 2002 added a new right for Union Learning Representatives to take paid time off during working hours to undertake their duties and to undertake relevant training. The rights to time off for the purpose of carrying out trade union duties, and to take time off for training, were extended to union representatives engaged in duties related to redundancies under Section 188 of the amended 1992 Act and to duties relating to the Transfer of Undertakings (Protection of Employment) Regulations 2006.

GENERAL PURPOSE OF THE CODE

4. The general purpose of the statutory provisions and this Code of Practice is to aid and improve the effectiveness of relationships between employers and trade unions. Employers and unions have a joint responsibility to ensure that agreed arrangements work to mutual advantage by specifying how reasonable time off for union duties and activities and for training will work.

STRUCTURE OF THE CODE

5. Section 1 of this Code provides guidance on time off for trade union duties. Section 2 deals with time off for training of trade union representatives and offers guidance on sufficient training for Union Learning Representatives. Section 3 considers time off for trade union activities. In each case the amount and frequency of time off, and the purposes for which and any conditions subject to which time off may be taken, are to be those that are reasonable in all the circumstances. Section 4 describes the responsibilities which employers and trade unions share in considering reasonable time off. Section 5 notes the advantages of reaching formal agreements on time off. Section 6 deals with industrial action and Section 7 with methods of appeal.

6. The annex to this Code reproduces the relevant statutory provisions on time off. To help differentiate between these and practical guidance, the summary of statutory provisions relating to time off which appears in the main text of the Code is in **bold type**. Practical guidance is in ordinary type. While every effort has been made to ensure that the summary of the statutory provisions included in this Code is accurate, only the courts can interpret the law authoritatively.

STATUS OF THE CODE

7. The provisions of this Code are admissible in evidence in proceedings before an Employment Tribunal relating to time off for trade union duties and activities. Any provisions of the Code which appear to the Tribunal to be relevant shall be taken into account. However, failure to observe any provision of the Code does not of itself render a person liable to any proceedings.

SECTION 1
TIME OFF FOR TRADE UNION DUTIES

[4.47]

Union representatives undertake a variety of roles in collective bargaining and in working with management, communicating with union members, liaising with their trade union and in handling individual disciplinary and grievance matters on behalf of employees. There are positive benefits for employers, employees and for union members in encouraging the efficient performance of union representatives' work, for example in aiding the resolution of problems and conflicts at work. The role can be both demanding and complex. In order to perform effectively union representatives need to have reasonable paid time off from their normal job in appropriate circumstances.

ENTITLEMENT

8. Employees who are union representatives of an independent trade union recognised by their employer are to be permitted reasonable time off during working hours to carry out certain trade union duties.

9. Union representatives are entitled to time off where the duties are concerned with:

- **negotiations with the employer about matters which fall within section 178(2) of the Trade Union and Labour Relations (Consolidation) Act 1992 (TULR(C)A) and for which the union is recognised for the purposes of collective bargaining by the employer;**
- **any other functions on behalf of employees of the employer which are related to matters falling within section 178(2) TULR(C)A and which the employer has agreed the union may perform;**
- **the receipt of information from the employer and consultation by the employer under section 188 TULR(C)A, related to redundancy or under the Transfer of Undertakings (Protection of Employment) Regulations 2006 that applies to employees of the employer;**
- **negotiations with a view to entering into an agreement under regulation 9 of the Transfer of Undertakings (Protection of Employment) Regulations 2006 that applies to employees of the employer; or**
- **the performance on behalf of employees of the employer of functions related to or connected with the making of an agreement under regulation 9 of the Transfer of Undertakings (Protection or Employment) Regulations 2006.**

Matters falling within section 178(2) TULR(C)A are listed in the sub headings of paragraph 13 below.

10. The Safety Representatives and Safety Committees Regulations 1977 regulation 4(2)(a) requires that employers allow union health and safety representatives paid time, as is necessary, during working hours, to perform their functions.

Further advice on time off provisions for health and safety representatives is provided by the Health and Safety Executive in their approved Code and Guidance 'Consulting workers on health and safety'. This is not covered in this Acas Code.

11. An independent trade union is recognised by an employer when it is recognised to any extent for the purposes of collective bargaining. Where a trade union is not so recognised by an employer, employees have no statutory right to time off to undertake any duties except that of accompanying a worker at a disciplinary or grievance hearing (see para 20).

EXAMPLES OF TRADE UNION DUTIES

12. Subject to the recognition or other agreement, trade union representatives should be allowed to take reasonable time off for duties concerned with negotiations or, where their employer has agreed, for duties concerned with other functions related to or connected with the subjects of collective bargaining.

13. The subjects connected with collective bargaining may include one or more of the following:

(a) **terms and conditions of employment, or the physical conditions in which workers are required to work.** Examples could include:
- — pay
- — hours of work
- — holidays and holiday pay
- — sick pay arrangements
- — pensions
- — learning and training
- — equality and diversity
- — notice periods
- — the working environment
- — operation of digital equipment and other machinery;

(b) **engagement or non engagement, or termination or suspension of employment or the duties of employment, of one or more workers.** Examples could include:
- — recruitment and selection policies
- — human resource planning
- — redundancy and dismissal arrangements;

(c) **allocation of work or the duties of employment as between workers or groups of workers.** Examples could include:
- — job grading
- — job evaluation
- — job descriptions
- — flexible working practices
- — work-life balance;

(d) **matters of discipline.** Examples could include:
- — disciplinary procedures
- — arrangements for representing or accompanying employees at internal interviews
- — arrangements for appearing on behalf of trade union members, or as witnesses, before agreed outside appeal bodies or employment tribunals;

(e) **trade union membership or non membership.** Examples could include:
- — representational arrangements
- — any union involvement in the induction of new workers;

(f) **facilities for trade union representatives.** Examples could include any agreed arrangements for the provision of:
- — accommodation
- — equipment
- — names of new workers to the union;

(g) **machinery for negotiation or consultation and other procedures.** Examples could include arrangements for:
- — collective bargaining at the employer and/or multi-employer level
- — grievance procedures
- — joint consultation
- — communicating with members
- — communicating with other union representatives and union full-time officers concerned with collective bargaining with the employer.

14. The duties of a representative of a recognised trade union must be connected with or related to negotiations or the performance of functions both in time and subject matter. Reasonable time off may be sought, for example, to:
- — prepare for negotiations, including attending relevant meetings
- — inform members of progress and outcomes
- — prepare for meetings with the employer about matters for which the trade union has only representational rights.

15. Trade union duties will also be related to the receipt of information and consultation related to the handling of collective redundancies where an employer is proposing to dismiss as redundant 20 or more employees at one establishment within a period of 90 days, and where the Transfer of Undertakings (Protection of Employees) Regulations apply but also including the negotiations with a view to entering an agreement under regulation 9 of the Regulations (variation of contract in insolvency).

UNION LEARNING REPRESENTATIVES

16. Employees who are members of an independent trade union recognised by the employer can take reasonable time off to undertake the duties of a Union Learning Representative, provided that the union has given the employer notice in writing that the employee is a learning representative of the trade union and the training condition is met (see paras 28–33 for further information on the training condition). **The functions for which time off as a Union Learning Representative is allowed are:**

— **analysing learning or training needs**
— **providing information and advice about learning or training matters**
— **arranging learning or training**
— **promoting the value of learning or training**
— **consulting the employer about carrying on any such activities**
— **preparation to carry out any of the above activities**
— **undergoing relevant training.**

In practice, the roles and responsibilities of Union Learning Representatives will often vary by union and by workplace but must include one or more of these functions. In some cases it may be helpful if Union Learning Representatives attend meetings concerned with agreeing and promoting learning agreements. Employers may also see it in their interests to grant paid time off for these representatives to attend meetings with external partners concerned with the development and provision of workforce training.

Recognition needs to be given to the varying roles of Union Learning Representatives where the post holder also undertakes additional duties as a union representative.

17. Many employers have in place well established training and development programmes for their employees. Union Learning Representatives should liaise with their employers to ensure that their respective training activities complement one another and that the scope for duplication is minimised.

PAYMENT FOR TIME OFF FOR TRADE UNION DUTIES

18. An employer who permits union representatives time off for trade union duties must pay them for the time off taken. The employer must pay either the amount that the union representative would have earned had they worked during the time off taken or, where earnings vary with the work done, an amount calculated by reference to the average hourly earnings for the work they are employed to do.

The calculation of pay for the time taken for trade union duties should be undertaken with due regard to the type of payment system applying to the union representative including, as appropriate, shift premia, performance related pay, bonuses and commission earnings. Where pay is linked to the achievement of performance targets it may be necessary to adjust such targets to take account of the reduced time the representative has to achieve the desired performance.

19. There is no statutory requirement to pay for time off where the duty is carried out at a time when the union representative would not otherwise have been at work unless the union representative works flexible hours, such as night shift, but needs to perform representative duties during normal hours. Staff who work part time will be entitled to be paid if staff who work full time would be entitled to be paid. In all cases the amount of time off must be reasonable.

TIME OFF TO ACCOMPANY WORKERS AT DISCIPLINARY OR GRIEVANCE HEARINGS

20. Trade union representatives are statutorily entitled to take a reasonable amount of paid time off to accompany a worker at a disciplinary or grievance hearing so long as they have been certified by their union as being capable of acting as a worker's companion. The right to time off in these situations applies regardless of whether the certified person belongs to a recognised union or not although the worker being accompanied must be employed by the same employer. Time off for a union representative or a certified person to accompany a worker of another employer is a matter for voluntary agreement between the parties concerned.

SECTION 2
TRAINING OF UNION REPRESENTATIVES IN ASPECTS OF EMPLOYMENT RELATIONS AND EMPLOYEE DEVELOPMENT

[4.48]
Training is important for union representatives to enable them to carry out their duties effectively. Training should be available both to newly appointed and to more established union representatives. It is desirable, from time to time where resources permit it, for joint training and development activities between union representatives and managers to occur.

ENTITLEMENT

21. Employees who are union representatives of an independent trade union recognised by their employer are to be permitted reasonable time off during working hours to undergo training in aspects of industrial relations relevant to the carrying out of their trade union duties. These duties must be concerned with:

— **negotiations with the employer about matters which fall within section 178(2) TULR(C)A and for which the union is recognised to any extent for the purposes of collective bargaining by the employer; or**

— **any other functions on behalf of employees of the employer which are related to matters falling within section 178(2) TULR(C)A and which the employer has agreed the union may perform;**

— **matters associated with information and consultation concerning collective redundancy and the Transfer of Undertakings, and the negotiation of an agreement under Regulation 9 of the Transfer of Undertakings (Protection of Employees) Regulations.**

Matters falling within section 178(2) TULR(C)A are set out in paragraph 13 above.

22. The Safety Representatives and Safety Committees Regulations 1977 regulation 4(2)(b) requires that employers allow union health and safety representatives to undergo training in aspects of their functions that is 'reasonable in all the circumstances'.

Further advice on the training of health and safety representatives is provided by the Health and Safety Executive in their approved Code and Guidance 'Consulting workers on health and safety'. This is not covered in this Acas Code.

23. Employees who are Trade Union Learning Representatives are also permitted reasonable time off during working hours to undergo training relevant to their functions as a Union Learning Representative.

WHAT IS RELEVANT EMPLOYMENT RELATIONS TRAINING?

24. Training should be in aspects of employment relations relevant to the duties of a union representative. There is no one recommended syllabus for training as a union representative's duties will vary according to:

— the collective bargaining arrangements at the place of work, particularly the scope of the recognition or other agreement

— the structure of the union

— the role of the union representative

— the handling of proposed collective redundancies or the transfer of undertakings.

25. The training must also be approved by the Trades Union Congress or by the independent trade union of which the employee is a union representative.

26. Union representatives are more likely to carry out their duties effectively if they possess skills and knowledge relevant to their duties. In particular, employers should be prepared to consider releasing union representatives for initial training in basic representational skills as soon as possible after their election or appointment, bearing in mind that suitable courses may be infrequent. Reasonable time off could also be considered, for example:

— for training courses to develop the union representative's skills in representation, accompaniment, negotiation and consultation

— for further training particularly where the union representative has special responsibilities, for example in collective redundancy and transfer of undertakings circumstances

— for training courses to familiarise or update union representatives on issues reflecting the developing needs of the workforce they represent

— for training where there are proposals to change the structure and topics of negotiation about matters for which the union is recognised; or where significant changes in the organisation of work are being contemplated

— for training where legal change may affect the conduct of employment relations at the place of work and may require the reconsideration of existing agreements

— for training where a union representative undertakes the role of accompanying employees in grievance and disciplinary hearings.

27. E-learning tools, related to the role of union representatives, should be used where available and appropriate. However, their best use is as an additional learning aid rather than as a replacement to attendance at approved trade union and Trades Union Congress training courses. Time needs to be given during normal working hours for union representatives to take advantage of e-learning where it is available.

TRAINING FOR UNION LEARNING REPRESENTATIVES

28. Employees who are members of an independent trade union recognised by the employer are entitled to reasonable paid time off to undertake the functions of a Union Learning Representative. To qualify for paid time off the member must be sufficiently trained to carry out duties as a learning representative:

— **either at the time when their trade union gives notice to their employer in writing that they are a learning representative of the trade union**

— **or within six months of that date.**

29. In the latter case, the trade union is required to give the employer notice in writing that the employee will be undergoing such training and when the employee has done so to give the employer

notice of that fact. During the six month period in which he or she is undergoing this training, the Union Learning Representative must be allowed time off to perform their duties. It should be confirmed by the union in a letter that the training undertaken is sufficient to allow the Learning Representative to undertake their role and it is good practice for the union to give details of the training which has been completed and any previous training that has been taken into account. In the interests of good practice, the six month qualifying period may be extended, with agreement, to take into account any significant unforeseen circumstances such as prolonged absence from work due to ill health, pregnancy, bereavement or unavoidable delays in arranging an appropriate training course.

30. To satisfy this training requirement an employee will need to be able to demonstrate to their trade union that they have received sufficient training to enable them to operate competently in one or more of the following areas of activity relevant to their duties as a Union Learning Representative:

analysing learning or training needs;

— this could for example include understanding the different methods for identifying learning interests or needs, being able to effectively identify and record individual learning needs or being able to draw up a plan to meet identified learning requirements.

providing information and advice about learning or training matters;

— including, for example, the development of communication and interviewing skills
— knowledge of available opportunities, in order to be able to provide accurate information to members about learning opportunities within and outside the workplace
— the ability to signpost members to other sources of advice and guidance where additional support is needed, for example, basic skills tutors or fuller in depth professional career guidance.

arranging and supporting learning and training;

— for example, obtaining and providing information on learning opportunities including e-learning where available, supporting and encouraging members to access learning opportunities and helping to develop and improve local learning opportunities;
— promoting the value of learning and training;
— some examples of this activity could be, understanding current initiatives for the development of learning and skills in the workplace, promoting the value of learning to members and within trade union networks and structures, working with employers to meet the learning and skill needs of both individuals and the organisation, and appreciating the value of learning agreements and how they may be developed.

31. An employee could demonstrate to their trade union that they have received sufficient training to enable them to operate competently in one or more of these areas of activity by:

— completing a training course approved by the Trades Union Congress or by the independent trade union of which the employee is a Union Learning Representative, or by
— showing that they have previously gained the relevant expertise and experience to operate effectively as a learning representative.

In the latter case, previous experience and expertise gained in areas such as teaching, training, counselling, providing careers advice and guidance or human resource development, may well be relevant, as may periods of extensive on-the-job training and experience gained in shadowing an experienced Union Learning Representative.

32. Reasonable time off should also be considered for further training to help Union Learning Representatives develop their skills and competencies.

33. Although not required by law it is recognised that there would be clear advantages both to the individual and the organisation if training undertaken leads to a recognised qualification standard.

PAYMENT FOR TIME OFF FOR TRAINING

34. An employer who permits union representatives or Union Learning Representatives time off to attend relevant training, must pay them for the time off taken. The employer must pay either the amount that the union representative or the Union Learning Representative would have earned had they worked during the time off taken or, where earnings vary with the work done, an amount calculated by reference to the average hourly earnings for the work they are employed to do.

The calculation of pay for the time taken for training should be undertaken with due regard to the type of payment system applying to the union representative and Union Learning Representative including, as appropriate, shift premia, performance related pay, bonuses and commission earnings. Where pay is linked to the achievement of performance targets it may be necessary to adjust such targets to take account of the reduced time the representative has to achieve the desired performance.

35. There is no statutory requirement to pay for time off where training is undertaken at a time when the union representative or Union Learning Representative would not otherwise have been at work unless the union representative or Union Learning Representative works flexible hours, such as night shift, but needs to undertake training during normal hours. Staff who work part time will be entitled to be paid if staff who work full time would be entitled to be paid. In all cases, the amount of time off must be reasonable.

SECTION 3
TIME OFF FOR TRADE UNION ACTIVITIES

[4.49]

To operate effectively and democratically, trade unions need the active participation of members. It can also be very much in employers' interests that such participation is assured and help is given to promote effective communication between union representatives and members in the workplace.

ENTITLEMENT

36. An employee who is a member of an independent trade union recognised by the employer in respect of that description of employee is to be permitted reasonable time off during working hours to take part in any trade union activity. An employee who is a member of an independent and recognised trade union is also permitted to take reasonable time off during working hours for the purposes of accessing the services of a Union Learning Representative (provided those services are services for which the Union Learning Representative is entitled to time off).

WHAT ARE EXAMPLES OF TRADE UNION ACTIVITIES?

37. The activities of a trade union member can be, for example:

— attending workplace meetings to discuss and vote on the outcome of negotiations with the employer. Where relevant, and with the employer's agreement, this can include attending such workplace meetings at the employer's neighbouring locations.
— meeting full time officers to discuss issues relevant to the workplace
— voting in union elections
— having access to services provided by a Union Learning representative.

38. Where the member is acting as a representative of a recognised union, activities can be, for example, taking part in:

— branch, area or regional meetings of the union where the business of the union is under discussion
— meetings of official policy making bodies such as the executive committee or annual conference
— meetings with full time officers to discuss issues relevant to the workplace.

39. There is no right to time off for trade union activities which themselves consist of industrial action.

PAYMENT FOR TIME OFF FOR TRADE UNION ACTIVITIES

40. Paragraphs 18 and 19 set out the statutory entitlement to payment for time off to undertake trade union duties.

41. There is no statutory requirement that union members or representatives be paid for time off taken on trade union activities. Nevertheless employers may want to consider payment in certain circumstances, for example to ensure that workplace meetings are fully representative or to ensure that employees have access to services provided by Union Learning Representatives.

SECTION 4
THE RESPONSIBILITIES OF EMPLOYERS AND TRADE UNIONS

[4.50]

Employers, trade unions, union representatives and line managers should work together to ensure that time off provisions, including training, operate effectively and for mutual benefit. Union representatives need to be able to communicate with management, each other, their trade union and employees. To do so they need to be able to use appropriate communication media and other facilities.

GENERAL CONSIDERATIONS

42. The amount and frequency of time off should be reasonable in all the circumstances. Although the statutory provisions apply to all employers without exception as to size and type of business or service, trade unions should be aware of the wide variety of difficulties and operational requirements to be taken into account when seeking or agreeing arrangements for time off, for example:

— the size of the organisation and the number of workers
— the production process
— the need to maintain a service to the public
— the need for safety and security at all times.

43. Employers in turn should have in mind the difficulties for trade union representatives and members in ensuring effective representation and communications with, for example:

— shift workers
— part-time workers
— home workers
— teleworkers or workers not working in a fixed location
— those employed at dispersed locations
— workers with particular domestic commitments including those on leave for reasons of maternity, paternity or care responsibilities
— workers with special needs such as disabilities or language requirements.

44. For time off arrangements to work satisfactorily trade unions should:

— ensure that union representatives are aware of their role, responsibilities and functions
— inform management, in writing, as soon as possible of appointments or resignations of union representatives
— ensure that union representatives receive any appropriate written credentials promptly
— ensure that employers receive details of the functions of union representatives where they carry out special duties or functions.

45. Employers should ensure that, where necessary, work cover and/or work load reductions are provided when time off is required. This can include the allocation of duties to other employees, rearranging work to a different time or a reduction in workloads.

46. While there is no statutory right for facilities for union representatives, except for representatives engaged in duties related to collective redundancies and the Transfer of Undertakings, employers should, where practical, make available to union representatives the facilities necessary for them to perform their duties efficiently and communicate effectively with their members, colleague union representatives and full-time officers. Where resources permit the facilities should include:

— accommodation for meetings which could include provision for Union Learning Representatives and a union member(s) to meet to discuss relevant training matters
— access to a telephone and other communication media used or permitted in the workplace such as email, intranet and internet
— the use of noticeboards
— where the volume of the union representative's work justifies it, the use of dedicated office space
— confidential space where an employee involved in a grievance or disciplinary matter can meet their representative or to discuss other confidential matters
— access to members who work at a different location
— access to e-learning tools where computer facilities are available.

47. When using facilities provided by the employer for the purposes of communication with their members or their trade union, union representatives must comply with agreed procedures both in respect of the use of such facilities and also in respect of access to and use of company information. The agreed procedures will be either those agreed between the union and the employer as part of an agreement on time off (see section 6) or comply with general rules applied to all employees in the organisation. In particular, union representatives must respect and maintain the confidentiality of information they are given access to where, the disclosure would seriously harm the functioning of, or would be prejudicial to, the employer's business interests. The disclosure of information for collective bargaining purposes is covered by the Acas Code of Practice on that topic. Union representatives should understand that unauthorised publication risks damaging the employer's business, straining relations with the representative body concerned, possible breaches of individual contracts of employment and, in extreme cases such as unauthorised publication of price sensitive information, the commission of criminal offences.

48. Union representatives will have legitimate expectations that they and their members are entitled to communicate without intrusion in the form of monitoring by their employer. Rules concerning the confidentiality of communications involving union representatives should be agreed between the employer and the union. Guidance on this is set out in paragraphs 49 and 57 below.

49. Employers must respect the confidential and sensitive nature of communications between union representatives and their members and trade union. They should not normally carry out regular or random monitoring of union emails. Only in exceptional circumstances may employers require access to communications but such access should be subject to the general rules set out in statute and the Employment Practices Code issued by the Information Commissioner's Office. In the context of the Data Protection Act 1998 whether a person is a member of a trade union or not is defined as sensitive personal data. This also applies to data concerning individuals, for example communications concerned with possible or actual grievance and disciplinary issues. There are therefore very strict provisions on how such data can be used and monitored in compliance with the law.

REQUESTING TIME OFF

50. Trade union representatives and members requesting time off to pursue their duties or activities or to access the services of a Union Learning Representative should provide management, especially their line manager, with as much notice as practically possible concerning:

— the purpose of such time off, while preserving personal confidential information relating to individuals in grievance or disciplinary matters
— the intended location
— the timing and duration of time off required.

51. Union representatives should minimise business disruption by being prepared to be as flexible as possible in seeking time off in circumstances where the immediate or unexpected needs of the business make it difficult for colleagues or managers to provide cover for them in their absence. Equally employers should recognise the mutual obligation to allow union representatives to undertake their duties.

52. In addition, union representatives who request paid time off to undergo relevant training should:

— give at least a few weeks' notice to management of nominations for training courses
— provide details of the contents of the training course.

53. When deciding whether requests for paid time off should be granted, consideration would need to be given as to their reasonableness, for example to ensure adequate cover for safety or to safeguard the production process or the provision of service. Consideration should also be given to allowing Union Learning Representatives access to a room in which they can discuss training in a confidential manner with an employee. Similarly, managers and unions should seek to agree a mutually convenient time which minimises the effect on production or services. Where workplace meetings are requested, consideration should be given to holding them, for example:

— towards the end of a shift or the working week
— before or after a meal break.

54. For their part line managers should be familiar with the rights and duties of union representatives regarding time off. They should be encouraged to take reasonable steps as necessary in the planning and management of representatives' time off and the provision of cover or work load reduction, taking into account the legitimate needs of such union representatives to discharge their functions and receive training efficiently and effectively.

55. Employers need to consider each application for time off on its merits; they should also consider the reasonableness of the request in relation to agreed time off already taken or in prospect.

SECTION 5
AGREEMENTS ON TIME OFF

[4.51]

To take account of the wide variety of circumstances and problems which can arise, there can be positive advantages for employers and trade unions in establishing agreements on time off in ways that reflect their own situations. It should be borne in mind, however, that the absence of a formal agreement on time off does not in itself deny an individual any statutory entitlement. Nor does any agreement supersede statutory entitlement to time off.

56. A formal agreement can help to:

— provide clear guidelines against which applications for time off can be determined
— establish realistic expectations on the part of union representatives and managers
— avoid misunderstanding
— facilitate better planning
— ensure fair and reasonable treatment.

57. Agreements should specify:

— the amount of time off permitted recognising that this will vary according the fluctuations in demand on the union representatives' role
— the occasions on which time off can be taken including meetings with management, meetings with other union representatives, time needed to prepare for meetings, communicating with members and their trade union, time to undertake e-learning if appropriate and to attend approved training events
— in what circumstances time off will be paid
— arrangements for taking time off at short notice
— how pay is to be calculated
— to whom time off will be paid
— the facilities and equipment to be provided and limits to their use, if any
— arrangements for ensuring confidentiality of communications involving union representatives. These should include agreed rules on the use of data and the exceptional cases where monitoring may be necessary, for example in cases of suspected illegal use, specifying the circumstances where such monitoring may be undertaken and the means by which it is to be done, for example by company IT or security personnel
— the role of line managers in granting permission to legitimate requests for time off and, where appropriate and practical, ensuring that adequate cover or work load reductions are provided
— the procedure for requesting time off
— the procedure for resolving grievances about time off.

58. In addition, it would be sensible for agreements to make clear:

— arrangements for the appropriate payment to be made when time off relates in part to union duties and in part to union activities
— how and in what circumstances payment might be made to shift and part time employees undertaking trade union duties outside their normal working hours.

59. Agreements for time off and other facilities for union representation should be consistent with wider agreements which deal with such matters as constituencies, number of representatives and the election of officials.

60. The operation of time off agreements or arrangements should be jointly reviewed by the parties from time to time.

61. In smaller organisations, it might be thought more appropriate for employers and unions to reach understandings about how requests for time off are to be made; and more broadly to agree flexible arrangements which can accommodate their particular circumstances.

SECTION 6
INDUSTRIAL ACTION

[4.52]

62. Employers and unions have a responsibility to use agreed procedures to settle problems and avoid industrial action. Time off may therefore be permitted for this purpose particularly where there is a dispute. **There is no right to time off for trade union activities which themselves consist of industrial action.** However, where a union representative is not taking part in industrial action but represents members involved, normal arrangements for time off with pay for the union representatives should apply.

SECTION 7
RESOLVING DISPUTES

[4.53]

There is advantage in agreeing ways in which disputes concerning time off arrangements, including training and access to facilities, can be settled and any appropriate procedures to resolve disputes should be followed.

63. Every effort should be made to resolve any dispute or grievance in relation to time off work for union duties or activities. **Where the grievance remains unresolved, union representatives, Union Learning**

Representatives or members have a right to complain to an employment tribunal that their employer has failed to allow reasonable time off or, in the case of a Union Learning Representative or union representative, has failed to pay for all or part of the time off taken. Such complaints may be resolved by conciliation by Acas or through a compromise agreement and, if this is successful, no tribunal hearing will be necessary. Acas assistance may also be sought without the need for a formal complaint to a tribunal.

ANNEX

(The Annex sets out the law on time off for trade union duties and activities, ie, TULR(C)A 1992, ss 168, 168A, 169, 170, 178(1)–(3) and 173(1) and the definition of 'official' in s 119. The 1992 Act is set out at **[1.268]** *et seq.)*

ACAS CODE OF PRACTICE 4
SETTLEMENT AGREEMENTS
(under section 111A of the Employment Rights Act 1996) (2013)

[4.54]

NOTES

This is the fourth Code of Practice produced by ACAS, specifically to accompany the introduction by Enterprise and Regulatory Reform Act 2013 s 14 of protected conversations between employers and employees about terms of settlement for the termination of employment (the effect of s 14 is to add a new s 111A to the ERA 1996 at **[1.1029]**). The Code, which was made under TULR(C)A 1992 s 199 at **[1.515]**, was approved by the Secretary of State under TULR(C)A 1992 s 200 and brought into effect on 29 July 2013, the same date as the new s 111A came into force, by the Employment Code of Practice (Settlements) Order 2013, SI 2013/1665. The legal status of the Code, as of the other ACAS Codes, is as provided for by TULR(C)A 1992 s 207 at **[1.523]**. It remains for judicial determination whether this Code is also, as is the Discipline and Grievance Code, a 'relevant Code' within TULR(C)A 1992 s 207A, but it is suggested that it is; the definition of 'relevant Code' in s 207A(4) is a Code 'issued under this Chapter which relates exclusively or primarily to procedure for the resolution of disputes'. If this definition is held to cover the Settlements Code, an unreasonable failure by either employer or employee to comply with the Code may lead to an increase or decrease, as the case may be, in any compensation awarded to the employee, of up to 25%.

CONTENTS

FOREWORD

[4.55]

The Acas statutory Code of Practice set out in paragraphs 1 to 24 on the following pages is designed to help employers, employees and their representatives understand the implications of section 111A of the Employment Rights Act (ERA) 1996 for the negotiation of settlement agreements (formerly known as compromise agreements) before the termination of employment. In particular, it explains aspects of the confidentiality provisions associated with negotiations that take place to reach such agreements. The Code does not cover all aspects of settlement agreements. Further guidance on settlement agreements can be found in the Acas booklet 'Settlement Agreements: A Guide' which also offers more detailed guidance on the confidentiality provisions set out in section 111A.

The Code is issued under section 199 of the Trade Union and Labour Relations (Consolidation) Act 1992 and comes into effect by order of the Secretary of State on 29 July 2013. Failure to follow the Code does not, in itself, make a person or organisation liable to proceedings, nor will it lead to an adjustment in any compensation award made by an employment tribunal. However, employment tribunals will take the Code into account when considering relevant cases.

The discussions that take place in order to reach a settlement agreement in relation to an existing employment dispute can be, and often are, undertaken on a 'without prejudice' basis. This means that any statements made during a 'without prejudice' meeting or discussion cannot be used in a court or tribunal as evidence. This 'without prejudice' confidentiality does not, however, apply where there is no existing dispute between the parties. Section 111A of the ERA 1996 has therefore been introduced to allow greater flexibility in the use of confidential discussions as a means of ending the employment relationship. Section 111A, which will run alongside the 'without prejudice' principle, provides that even where no employment dispute exists, the parties may still offer and discuss a settlement agreement in the knowledge that their conversations cannot be used in any subsequent unfair dismissal claim. It is the confidentiality aspect of section 111A that is the specific focus of this Code.

Throughout this Code the word 'should' is used to indicate what Acas considers to be good employment practice, rather than legal requirements. The word 'must' is used to indicate where something is a legal requirement.

THE CODE OF PRACTICE

INTRODUCTION

[4.56]
1. This Code is designed to help employers, employees and their representatives understand the law relating to the negotiation of settlement agreements as set out in section 111A of the Employment Rights Act (ERA) 1996. In particular it gives guidance on the confidentiality provisions associated with negotiations about settlement agreements and on what constitutes improper behaviour when such negotiations are taking place.

2. Settlement agreements are only one way of handling potentially difficult employment situations. Problems in the workplace are best resolved in open conversations, including, where appropriate, through the use of performance management, or informal and formal disciplinary or grievance procedures.

WHAT ARE SETTLEMENT AGREEMENTS?

[4.57]
3. Settlement agreements are legally binding contracts which can be used to end the employment relationship on agreed terms. Their main feature is that they waive an individual's right to make a claim to a court or employment tribunal on the matters that are specifically covered in the agreement. Settlement agreements may be proposed prior to undertaking any other formal process. They usually include some form of payment to the employee by the employer and may also include a reference.

4. For a settlement agreement to be legally valid the following conditions must be met:

(a) The agreement must be in writing;
(b) The agreement must relate to a particular complaint or proceedings[1];
(c) The employee must have received advice from a relevant independent adviser[2] on the terms and effect of the proposed agreement and its effect on the employee's ability to pursue that complaint or proceedings before an employment tribunal;
(d) The independent adviser must have a current contract of insurance or professional indemnity insurance covering the risk of a claim by the employee in respect of loss arising from that advice;
(e) The agreement must identify the adviser;
(f) The agreement must state that the applicable statutory conditions regulating the settlement agreement have been satisfied.

5. Settlement agreements are voluntary. Parties do not have to agree them or enter into discussions about them if they do not wish to do so. Equally the parties do not have to accept the terms initially proposed to them. There can be a process of negotiation during which both sides make proposals and counter proposals until an agreement is reached, or both parties recognise that no agreement is possible.

NOTES

[1] Simply saying that the agreement is in 'full and final settlement of all claims' will not be sufficient to contract out of employment tribunal claims. To be legally binding for these purposes, a settlement agreement has to specifically state the claims that it is intended to cover.

[2] The independent adviser can be a qualified lawyer; a certified and authorised official, employee or member of an independent trade union; or a certified and authorised advice centre worker.

SETTLEMENT AGREEMENT DISCUSSIONS AND SECTION 111A OF THE ERA 1996

[4.58]
6. Section 111A of the ERA 1996 provides that offers to end the employment relationship on agreed terms (ie under a settlement agreement) can be made on a confidential basis which means that they cannot be used as evidence in an unfair dismissal claim to an employment tribunal. Under section 111A, such pre-termination negotiations can be treated as confidential even where there is no current employment dispute or where one or more of the parties is unaware that there is an employment problem. Section 111A can also apply to offers of a settlement agreement against the background of an existing dispute, although in such cases the 'without prejudice' principle can also apply.

7. There are, however, some exceptions to the application of section 111A. Claims that relate to an automatically unfair reason for dismissal such as whistleblowing, union membership or asserting a statutory right are not covered by the confidentiality provisions set out in section 111A. Neither are claims made on grounds other than unfair dismissal, such as claims of discrimination, harassment, victimisation or other behaviour prohibited by the Equalities Act 2010, or claims relating to breach of contract or wrongful dismissal. Throughout this Code there are a number of references to unfair dismissal. These references should be read in general as subject to the exceptions set out in this paragraph.

8. The confidentiality provisions of section 111A are, additionally, subject to there being no improper behaviour. Guidance on what constitutes improper behaviour is contained in paragraphs 17 and 18 of this Code. Where there is improper behaviour, anything said or done in pre-termination negotiations will only be inadmissible as evidence in claims to an employment tribunal to the extent that the tribunal considers it just. In some circumstances, for instance where unlawful discrimination occurs during a settlement discussion, this may itself form the basis of a claim to an employment tribunal.

9. Where there has been some improper behaviour for these purposes this does not mean that an employer will necessarily lose any subsequent unfair dismissal claim that is brought to an employment tribunal. Equally, the fact that an employer has not engaged in some improper behaviour does not mean that they will necessarily win any subsequent unfair dismissal claim brought against them.

10. Where the parties sign a valid settlement agreement, the employee will be unable to bring an employment tribunal claim about any type of claim which is listed in the agreement. Where a settlement agreement is not agreed, an employee may bring a subsequent claim to an employment tribunal but where this claim relates to an allegation of unfair dismissal the confidentiality provisions section 111A of the ERA 1996 will apply.

REACHING A SETTLEMENT AGREEMENT

[4.59]

11. Settlement agreements can be proposed by both employers and employees although they will normally be proposed by the employer. A settlement agreement proposal can be made at any stage of an employment relationship. How the proposal is made can vary depending on the circumstances. It may be helpful if any reasons for the proposal are given when the proposal is made. Whilst the initial proposal may be oral, one of the requirements for a settlement agreement to become legally binding is that the agreement must ultimately be put in writing (see paragraph 4).

12. Parties should be given a reasonable period of time to consider the proposed settlement agreement. What constitutes a reasonable period of time will depend on the circumstances of the case. As a general rule, a minimum period of ten calendar days should be allowed to consider the proposed formal written terms of a settlement agreement and to receive independent advice, unless the parties agree otherwise.

13. The parties may find it helpful to discuss proposals face-to-face and any such meeting should be at an agreed time and place. Whilst not a legal requirement, employers should allow employees to be accompanied at the meeting by a work colleague, trade union official or trade union representative. Allowing the individual to be accompanied is good practice and may help to progress settlement discussions.

14. Where a proposed settlement agreement based on the termination of the employment is accepted, the employee's employment can be terminated either with the required contractual notice or from the date specified in the agreement. The details of any payments due to the employee and their timing should be included in the agreement.

IMPROPER BEHAVIOUR

[4.60]

15. If a settlement agreement is being discussed as a means of settling an existing employment dispute, the negotiations between the parties can be carried out on a 'without prejudice' basis. 'Without prejudice' is a common law principle (ie non statutory) which prevents statements (written or oral), made in a genuine attempt to settle an existing dispute, from being put before a court or tribunal as evidence. This protection does not, however, apply where there has been fraud, undue influence or some other 'unambiguous impropriety' such as perjury or blackmail.

16. Section 111A of the ERA 1996 offers similar protection to the 'without prejudice' principle in that it provides that any offer made of a settlement agreement, or discussions held about it, cannot be used as evidence in any subsequent employment tribunal claim of unfair dismissal. Unlike 'without prejudice', however, it can apply where there is no existing employment dispute. The protection in section 111A will not apply where there is some improper behaviour in relation to the settlement agreement discussions or offer.

17. What constitutes improper behaviour is ultimately for a tribunal to decide on the facts and circumstances of each case. Improper behaviour will, however, include (but not be limited to) behaviour that would be regarded as 'unambiguous impropriety' under the 'without prejudice' principle.

18. The following list provides some examples of improper behaviour. The list is not exhaustive:

(a) All forms of harassment, bullying and intimidation, including through the use of offensive words or aggressive behaviour;

(b) Physical assault or the threat of physical assault and other criminal behaviour;

(c) All forms of victimisation;

(d) Discrimination because of age, sex, race, disability, sexual orientation, religion or belief, transgender, pregnancy and maternity and marriage or civil partnership;

(e) Putting undue pressure on a party. For instance:

- (i) Not giving the reasonable time for consideration set out in paragraph 12 of this Code;
- (ii) An employer saying before any form of disciplinary process has begun that if a settlement proposal is rejected then the employee will be dismissed;
- (iii) An employee threatening to undermine an organisation's public reputation if the organisation does not sign the agreement, unless the provisions of the Public Interest Disclosure Act 1998 apply.

19. The examples set out in paragraph 18 above are not intended to prevent, for instance, a party setting out in a neutral manner the reasons that have led to the proposed settlement agreement, or factually stating the likely alternatives if an agreement is not reached, including the possibility of starting a disciplinary process if relevant. These examples are not intended to be exhaustive.

20. In situations where there is no existing dispute between the parties, the 'without prejudice' principle cannot apply but section 111A can apply. In these circumstances the offer of, and discussions about, a settlement agreement will not be admissible in a tribunal (in an unfair dismissal case) so long as there has been no improper behaviour. Where an employment tribunal finds that there has been improper behaviour in such a case, any offer of a settlement agreement, or discussions relating to it, will only be inadmissible if, and in so far as, the employment tribunal considers it just.

21. Where there is an existing dispute between the parties, offers of a settlement agreement, and discussions about such an agreement, may be covered by both the 'without prejudice' principle and section 111A. The 'without prejudice' principle will apply unless there has been some 'unambiguous impropriety'. As the test of 'unambiguous impropriety' is a narrower test than that of improper behaviour, this means that pre-termination negotiations that take place in the context of an existing dispute will not be admissible in a subsequent unfair dismissal claim unless there has been some 'unambiguous impropriety'.

22. In court or tribunal proceedings other than unfair dismissal claims, such as discrimination claims, section 111A does not apply. In these cases, the 'without prejudice' principle can apply where there is an existing dispute at the time of the settlement offer and discussions, meaning that these will not be admissible in evidence unless there has been some 'unambiguous impropriety'.

WHAT IF A SETTLEMENT AGREEMENT CANNOT BE AGREED?

[4.61]

23. If a settlement agreement is rejected and the parties still wish to resolve the dispute or problem that led to the offer being made then some other form of resolution should be sought. Depending on the nature of the dispute or problem, resolution might be sought through a performance management, disciplinary or grievance process, whichever is appropriate. The parties cannot rely on the offer of a settlement agreement or any discussions about the agreement as being part of this process.

24. It is important that employers follow a fair process, as well as the other principles set out in the Acas discipline and grievance Code of Practice, because, if the employee is subsequently dismissed, failure to do so could constitute grounds for a claim of unfair dismissal.

ACAS CODE OF PRACTICE 5
HANDLING IN A REASONABLE MANNER REQUESTS TO WORK FLEXIBLY (2014)

[4.62]

NOTES

This Code was made under TULR(C)A 1992 s 199 at **[1.515]**, and was approved by the Secretary of State under TULR(C)A 1992 s 200. It came into effect on 30 June 2014 (see the Code of Practice (Handling in a Reasonable Manner Requests to Work Flexibly) Order 2014, SI 2014/1665). For the legal status and effect of the Code see s 207 of the 1992 Act at **[1.523]**.

See *Harvey* J(9).

CONTENTS

EXPLANATORY NOTE

[4.63]

Throughout this Code the word "should" is used to indicate what Acas considers to be good employment practice, rather than legal requirements. The word "must" is used to indicate where something is a legal requirement.

Further information for employees and employers with practical examples on making and managing requests for flexible working can be found in the good practice guide 'The right to apply for flexible working: an Acas guide'.

INTRODUCTION

[4.64]

1. Every employee has the statutory right to ask to work flexibly after 26 weeks employment service. An employee can only make a statutory request once in any 12 month period. This Code is intended to help employers deal with written requests made by employees to change their working hours or place of work under the statutory right in the Employment Rights Act 1996 to request flexible working.

2. The guidance in this Code, as well as helping employers, will also be taken into account by employment tribunals when considering relevant cases.

KEYS TO HANDLING REQUESTS IN A REASONABLE MANNER

THE REQUEST

[4.65]

3. A request from an employee under the Employment Rights Act 1996 and regulations made under it must be in writing and must include the following information:

- The date of their application, the change to working conditions they are seeking and when they would like the change to come into effect.
- What effect, if any, they think the requested change would have on you as the employer and how, in their opinion, any such effect might be dealt with.
- A statement that this is a statutory request and if and when they have made a previous application for flexible working.

You should make clear to your employees what information they need to include in a written request to work flexibly.

WHAT SHOULD YOU DO WITH A REQUEST?

[4.66]

4. Once you have received a written request, you must consider it. You should arrange to talk with your employee as soon as possible after receiving their written request. If you intend to approve the request then a meeting is not needed.

5. You should allow an employee to be accompanied by a work colleague for this and any appeal discussion and the employee should be informed about this prior to the discussion.

DISCUSS WITH EMPLOYEE

[4.67]

6. You should discuss the request with your employee. It will help you get a better idea of what changes they are looking for and how they might benefit your business and the employee.

7. Wherever possible the discussion should take place in a private place where what is said will not be overheard.

CONSIDER THE REQUEST

[4.68]

8. You should consider the request carefully looking at the benefits of the requested changes in working conditions for the employee and your business and weighing these against any adverse business impact of implementing the changes, see paragraph 11. In considering the request you must not discriminate unlawfully against the employee.

9. Once you have made your decision you must inform the employee of that decision as soon as possible. You should do this in writing as this can help avoid future confusion on what was decided.

10. If you accept the employee's request, or accept it with modifications, you should discuss with the employee how and when the changes might best be implemented.

11. If you reject the request it must be for one of the following business reasons as set out in the legislation:

- the burden of additional costs
- an inability to reorganise work amongst existing staff
- an inability to recruit additional staff
- a detrimental impact on quality
- a detrimental impact on performance
- detrimental effect on ability to meet customer demand
- insufficient work for the periods the employee proposes to work
- a planned structural change to your business.

12. If you reject the request you should allow your employee to appeal the decision. It can be helpful to allow an employee to speak with you about your decision as this may reveal new information or an omission in following a reasonable procedure when considering the application.

DEAL WITH REQUESTS PROMPTLY

[4.69]

13. The law requires that all requests, including any appeals, must be considered and decided on within a period of three months from first receipt, unless you agree to extend this period with the employee.

14. If you arrange a meeting to discuss the application including any appeal and the employee fails to attend both this and a rearranged meeting without a good reason, you can consider the request withdrawn. If you do so, you must inform the employee.

AGE DISCRIMINATION: KEY POINTS FOR THE WORKPLACE ACAS GUIDANCE

Febuary 2019

[4.70]

NOTES

This Guide was issued by ACAS. It has no formal statutory status but has been included here as a useful guide to a complex area of law impacting on a wide range of employment issues.

Throughout this Guide there are cross-references to other pages of the Guide. Those cross-references are to the Guide as published on the ACAS website. Footnotes are as in the original.

CONTENTS

ABOUT THIS GUIDE

[4.71]

This guide offers employers, managers, HR professionals, employees, employee/trade union representatives and job applicants:

- steps to take to prevent age discrimination happening in the workplace
- examples of how age discrimination might still occur, and
- how age discrimination should be dealt with if it does happen.

The guide encourages employers and employees to make their workplaces inclusive. For example, so staff feel they belong, no matter what their age, and are not disadvantaged or under-valued because of age.

While employers and employees can be liable for their own acts of discrimination, an employer will also be liable for an employee's actions unless it can show it took all reasonable steps to try to prevent them.

WHAT IS AGE DISCRIMINATION?

[4.72]

Age is one of nine features known as protected characteristics in the Equality Act 2010. Generally, an employee is protected against discrimination because of age. This includes protection against unfair treatment because a job applicant or employee is: a different age or in a different age group to another job applicant or employee; or thought to be a particular age; or associated with someone belonging to a particular age group.

WHAT IS A DIFFERENT AGE OR AGE GROUP?

Age discrimination is not always about an 'old person' being preferred over a 'young person' because of their age – or vice versa. The age difference might be small – for example, a few years between one person in their late 40s compared to another in their early 50s.

Or, for example, someone might feel they have been discriminated against because they are over 60. In another case, it might be because they are seen as middle-aged. Or, a 21-year-old might claim discrimination because they are being treated differently because of their age compared to their colleague who is 43.

No minimum length of employment by an employee, or any employment at all for a job applicant, is necessary to claim discrimination. It is unlawful from when a role is advertised through to the last day of employment and beyond, including job references. Whether a complaint amounts to unlawful age discrimination can ultimately rest with an employment tribunal or court.

Age discrimination, also commonly called ageism, is one of the most common forms of unfair treatment at work. The age gap at work can be 50 years or more.

The Equality Act does allow different treatment because of age in limited circumstances. See the section, **When different treatment because of age may be allowed**, further into this guide.

HOW AGE DISCRIMINATION MAY HAPPEN

[4.73]

There are four main types of discrimination under the Equality Act:

- Direct discrimination

- Indirect discrimination
- Harassment
- Victimisation.

Employers should be aware that successfully dealing with a discrimination complaint should not always be seen as the end of the matter. It is useful to think how any future instances might be prevented. This can include consulting with trade unions or employee representatives, if they are in the workplace, and organising equality training for managers and all staff. To find out more, see Acas guide **Prevent discrimination: support equality**.

DIRECT DISCRIMINATION

There are three different types. Direct discrimination is where someone is treated less favourably than others because of:

- their actual age – this is **ordinary direct discrimination.** This is the only type of direct discrimination which may be lawful in limited circumstances. For more information see **Where discrimination may be lawful**
- the age of someone else they are associated with, such as a member of their family or a colleague – this is **direct discrimination by association**
- the age they are thought to be, regardless of whether the perception is correct or not - this is **direct discrimination by perception**.

Direct discrimination in all three forms could, for example, involve a decision not to employ someone, make them redundant or turn them down for promotion because of age. In most circumstances it would be unlawful. Direct discrimination does not need to be intentional.

FOR EXAMPLE . . . ORDINARY DIRECT DISCRIMINATION

Manager Louise is looking to fill a role which will require the successful applicant to then complete difficult training. She instructs her HR manager to discount her team's younger members, presuming they will not want the hard work. She also tells HR to discount older members, thinking they will not adapt to the change. Instead she shortlists Bruce and Mikel, believing people in their mid-thirties are more likely to have the necessary blend of ambition and sense of responsibility. Her actions are likely to be discriminatory.

FOR EXAMPLE . . . DIRECT DISCRIMINATION BY ASSOCIATION

Senior manager Jurgen decides not to invite employee Sarah and her partner Claude to a business party because Claude is much older than her. Jurgen feels Claude would not fit in with the party mood. This is likely to be discriminatory.

FOR EXAMPLE . . . DIRECT DISCRIMINATION BY PERCEPTION

Siobhan is turned down for a supervisor's job because her bosses decide she does not look mature enough for the role. They think she looks about 20. In fact, she is 30. Her bosses' decision is likely to be discriminatory.

INDIRECT DISCRIMINATION

What is indirect discrimination?

It is usually less obvious than direct discrimination and is normally unintended. In law, it is where a 'provision, criterion or practice' involves all these four things:

(1) the 'provision, criterion or practice' is applied equally to a group of employees/job applicants, only some of whom share the protected characteristic – in this case, the same age or age group
(2) it has (or will have) the effect of putting those who share the protected characteristic at a particular disadvantage when compared to others of a different age or age group
(3) it puts, or would put, an employee/job applicant at that disadvantage, and
(4) the employer is unable to objectively justify it -what the law calls showing it to be a proportionate means of achieving a legitimate aim.

The Equality Act does not define a 'provision, criterion or practice'. However, the term is most likely to include an employer's policies, procedures, requirements, rules and arrangements, even if informal, and whether written down or not.

What an employee or job applicant must prove

If they are claiming indirect discrimination, they must show that the 'provision, criterion or practice' puts, or would put, other employees/job applicants of the same age or age group at a disproportionate disadvantage when compared to employees/job applicants not of that age or age group. The individual employee or job applicant must then show that they have been disadvantaged by the application of the provision, criterion or practice.

FOR EXAMPLE . . . INDIRECT DISCRIMINATION

City centre gym manager Esme tells employees she needs two more staff to work on reception. She adds that anyone interested needs to look 'fit and enthusiastic' as the gym is trying to encourage more young people to join. Her requirement may indirectly discriminate against older staff unless it can be objectively justified.

When is indirect discrimination allowed?

Unless the employer can show the provision, criterion or practice is proportionate, appropriate and necessary (this is objective justification and usually involves a business need) there will be indirect discrimination. What is 'proportionate' will vary from case to case. It can also depend on the size and resources of the business – for example, a large employer with many staff may find it easier to approve flexible working requests, which may come mostly from older staff, than a small firm with few staff. See the section, **Flexible working**, further into this guide.

If the employer can show objective justification, there is no indirect discrimination. See **Where discrimination may be lawful** in the section, When different treatment because of age may be allowed, further into this guide.

Employers should check their policies, practices and rules to see whether they may have a disproportionately adverse effect on job applicants and/or employees because of their age. Otherwise, they may inadvertently indirectly discriminate. Policies, practices and rules which were not discriminatory when introduced may become discriminatory over time, perhaps because of a change in the make-up of the workforce, law or work arrangements.

HARASSMENT

Harassment is defined as 'unwanted conduct' and must be related to a relevant protected characteristic – in this case, age. This might be because:

- of the employee's age, or
- the age they are thought to be, or
- the age of someone else they are associated with – for example, a partner who is much older than them - or
- ageism is common in their workplace.

The harassment must have the purpose or effect of violating a person's dignity or creating an intimidating, hostile, degrading, humiliating or offensive environment for them.

This can include bullying, nicknames, threats, intrusive or inappropriate questions and comments, excluding them (ignoring, not inviting them to meetings or events etc) or insults. It can be verbal, written or physical. Also, unwanted jokes and/or gossip which they find offensive can be harassment. To say the behaviour was not meant to be harassment or that the comments were 'banter' is no defence.

In cases of harassment, how the victim sees the unwanted conduct is more important than how the harasser sees it and their intent. Whether it is reasonable for the victim to feel the way they do is also taken into account.

Also, an employee can make a complaint of harassment where they are not on the receiving end of the conduct, but witness it and it has a negative impact on their dignity at work or working environment. The employee making a complaint of harassment in this situation would not need to be the same age, or in the same age group, as the colleague being harassed.

Managers should be careful not to let their own views influence a situation or dismiss a concern because they do not deem the behaviour offensive themselves. It is important to remember that if an employee feels strongly enough to raise a concern or make a complaint, the employer should take it seriously, and deal with it correctly.

For more general information on harassment, including protecting employees from harassment from customers and clients, see the companion guide, **Equality and discrimination: understand the basics**.

FOR EXAMPLE . . . HARASSMENT

Sixty-year-old Margaret feels humiliated and undermined at the store where she works because of her age. Despite her extensive experience in retailing and recently gaining a qualification as a visual merchandiser, her manager Darren regularly tells her in front of other staff that she is 'out of touch' and that the store needs 'fresh blood'. Darren's behaviour is likely to be harassment.

VICTIMISATION

Victimisation is when an employee suffers what the law terms a 'detriment' - something that causes disadvantage, damage, harm or loss because of:

- making an allegation of discrimination, and/or
- supporting a complaint of discrimination, and/or
- giving evidence relating to a complaint about discrimination, and/or
- raising a grievance concerning equality or discrimination, and/or

- doing anything else for the purposes of (or in connection with) the Equality Act, such as bringing an employment tribunal claim of discrimination.

Victimisation may also occur because an employee is suspected of doing one or more of these things, or because it is believed they may do so. A 'detriment', for example, might include the employee being labelled a 'troublemaker', being left out and ignored, being denied training or promotion, or being made redundant because they supported an age discrimination claim.

FOR EXAMPLE . . . VICTIMISATION

Manager Alan tells apprentice Reyansh he is happy with his progress and performance. Reyansh then feels confident enough to tell Alan that some of the older employees regularly make fun of him because of his age and play pranks such as leaving toys where he's working. Reyansh wants this to stop. Alan tells Reyansh to toughen up and that the firm has no time for complainers. Some weeks later Alan punishes Reyansh for complaining by cancelling his training course. This is likely to be victimisation.

An employee is protected under the Equality Act from victimisation if they make, or support, or are suspected of supporting, an allegation of discrimination in good faith – even if the information or evidence they give proves to be inaccurate. However, an employee is not protected if they give, or support, information or evidence maliciously.

WHERE AGE DISCRIMINATION MAY HAPPEN

[4.74]

Areas of employment where age discrimination may be most likely to occur include:

- recruitment
- training
- promotion
- pay and terms and conditions of employment
- performance management
- redundancy
- retirement
- dismissal
- flexible working.

RECRUITMENT

To avoid discrimination, employers when recruiting **should not** allow any bias or stereotypical thinking about age to influence their assessment or decision-making at any stage of the recruitment process. They **should** take these steps when -

Writing the essential documents

- be careful when writing an advertisement, job description and person specification for a vacancy. Generally avoid any suggestion that applicants should be in a particular age group. This includes wording and illustrations which could suggest bias – for example, a photograph showing a group of only young people.

Advertising the role

- generally, do not use wording suggesting that an applicant of a particular age would be best suited to the job. For example, do not ask for 'mature' applicants, as this suggests young applicants are not wanted
- use at least two different channels so as not to end up with applicants from too narrow an audience. So, generally, avoid solely using one kind of place or media - for example, advertising only on a website targeted at the young. An advert aimed at one age group suggests a discriminatory mind-set
- be careful, if spreading word of vacancies through existing staff. Relying only on 'word of mouth' is likely to extend any imbalance in the make-up of the workforce, particularly where it is mainly made up of people of the same age group. And it is likely to produce only a small pool of applicants.

Pinpointing skills, experience and qualifications for the job

- be clear on exactly what **skills** are needed for the post so managers are objective in assessing and selecting applicants. This should reduce the chances of ruling out an applicant because of their age
- be careful when saying what **experience** is needed for the role. Usually, it is better to set out the type or types of experience needed rather than ask for a number of years' experience
- only ask applicants for **qualifications** necessary for the role. Also, allow them the option to demonstrate in another way the knowledge and aptitudes required – for example, through equivalent qualifications, or skills and knowledge from work experience
- so don't insist on a specific qualification if not needed. The employer may need to be able to objectively justify asking for a specific qualification, including **a degree**,. This is because more people go to university now than, say, 30 years ago, so older people are less likely to have a degree. Also, avoid asking for 'recent graduates' – such a requirement is likely to be very difficult to objectively justify

- do not have an upper age limit for people to apply to be **apprentices** or **trainees**, as people are working for longer and now more likely to change their line of work. In law, apprentices must be aged 16 or over, but there must not be any other age limit for applicants. Neither must there be an age limit for management trainees. Also, see the section, Employing young people, further into this guide
- be careful making assessments or saying an applicant is overqualified for the job. This can indicate an opinion that they have too much experience or been working too long and that the employer is looking for someone younger. Also see the section, **Ageist language**, further into this guide.

Drafting the application form

- avoid asking for the applicant's **age or date of birth** on the form. Although it is not discriminatory to ask their age, if they do not get the job they may claim that the fact that the employer did ask is evidence of discrimination. On a separate **equality and diversity monitoring form**, the employer can ask for the applicant's age group. The monitoring form should be anonymous, confidential and not seen by anyone sifting applications, interviewing applicants or deciding who gets hired
- in very limited circumstances, an employer can specify that applicants must be a particular age. See **'Occupational requirements'** under the section, When different treatment because of age may be allowed, further into this guide
- ask for **details of education and training**, but only ask for dates if they are relevant to skills, knowledge and capabilities necessary for the role. Otherwise, asking for dates can be seen as a way to find out the applicant's age
- be careful in asking for **details of relevant skills, knowledge, capabilities and experience in previous employment**. Asking for dates on the form may suggest a way to find out the applicant's age. The employer would be better asking for recent information – say, details of relevant jobs, experience, skills and periods of unemployment in the last two years.

Using social media

- be aware that **checking an applicant's background** on social media, including their age, risks being discriminatory and may breach the General Data Protection Regulation (GDPR)
- **filtering tools** on websites to only target applicants based on their age are likely to be discriminatory
- be aware that while one social media network may be popular with one age group, it may be little used by another.

Interviewing

- generally, interviewers or others in the selection process should not be influenced by **an applicant's age if they give it**
- make sure **personal information** requested, either on the application form or in interview, is relevant to the job and/or administration of the recruitment
- interviewers should be trained to know how to **avoid asking discriminatory questions and making discriminatory assumptions, and how to ask questions correctly**. For example, interviewers should ask applicants about their management experience, not how they manage people older than themselves. And they should ask applicants to explain an example of when they adapted, rather than what they know about, for instance, a new piece of technology
- get interviewers on a panel to agree to constructively and subtlely **'call each other out'** if one or more of them stereotypes an applicant. See the section, **Risks of age stereotyping**, further into this guide
- those on the interview panel, and/or any other managers or staff involved, should take care when discussing which applicants should go on the shortlist. Talking informally and unguardedly is where discrimination may happen.

Seeking job references

- an employer should be aware that an applicant's referees should not give them a negative job reference because of the applicant's age, and the employer must not discriminate based on that information.

Offering the job

- select and appoint the best applicant – generally, an employer must not rule out the best applicant because of their age, how young or old they look, or the age of someone they are associated with. And it would be discriminatory to offer less attractive terms – for example, six months' probation instead of the usual three - because it is feared they would not fit in because of age.

Using a recruitment agency

- tell the agency it must comply with the Equality Act. Apart from in very limited circumstances of what the law calls an 'occupational requirement' or where the decision can be objectively justified, an employer must not suggest to the agency that it only wants applicants of a particular age. And apart from in these very limited circumstances, an agency must not follow such an instruction or, for example, decide itself to only put forward young applicants. Neither should it pass on the applicant's age to the employer. Both the agency and the employer can be liable for discriminatory acts. See the sections **Occupational requirements** and **Where discrimination may be lawful**, further into this guide

Also, an employer should tell an agency it prefers applicants of a range of ages where possible.

FOR EXAMPLE . . . RECRUITMENT DISCRIMINATION

A firm advertises for graduates who have achieved their degree in the last five years. This is likely to be discriminatory, as proving the business need for such a condition is likely to be difficult in most cases.

TRAINING

An employer **must not**:

- deny an employee training or development because of their age, perceived age, or because of the age of someone they are associated with. For more information regarding training, see the section, **Positive action**, further into this guide
- allow any bias, stereotypical thinking or assumptions about age to creep into decisions about who gets trained
- make assumptions about an employee's needs or ambitions based on their age, length of experience in a job, or length of time with the employer, or assume there is more value in training younger staff and no or little value in training older employees
- focus training for older workers only on their current role, or overlook older workers for opportunities for overall development, work experience, shadowing in other roles, or to move into a new or different role.

An employer **should not**:

- deny training to young employees because they do not have enough experience or are in low-paid roles.

An employer **should**:

- make sure all its employees, no matter what their age, are made aware of opportunities for training and personal development
- be aware that training should make under-performance less likely
- give support and encouragement to any older employees who are reluctant to discuss their training needs for fear they will be seen as underperformers or 'behind the times'
- use constructive and regular career/work-life discussions with all employees to identify training needs that benefit employees and the organisation
- be reasonable, flexible and considerate about when and where training takes place. For example, insisting on training outside of normal working hours, or that requires staying away from home for a few days or week, or long hours of travel, may discriminate against older employees if they are more likely to have caring responsibilities outside of work.

FOR EXAMPLE . . . TRAINING DISCRIMINATION

In carrying out job performance reviews with employees, manager Aleksander discusses career ambitions and opportunities for training with most staff. But he doesn't discuss them with staff over 55, as he thinks this a waste of time. His reasoning is that the over 55s are past their best and merely want to coast towards retirement. Aleksander's age-biased actions are likely to be discriminatory.

PROMOTION

An employer **must not** deny an employee promotion because of their age, perceived age, or because of the age of someone they are associated with. For example, it is likely to be discriminatory to:

- rule out a capable employee to take on extra responsibilities because they are considered to be too young for the new role
- discourage an employee with the necessary skills, knowledge and experience from applying for a more challenging job because of their age
- overlook inviting a colleague of a different age group to the rest of the team to regular socials – the gatherings are affecting decisions back at work about who gets development opportunities and promotion
- allow any bias or stereotypical thinking or assumptions about age to creep into decisions about who gets development opportunities or promotion.

An employer **should**:

- make sure job vacancies and promotion opportunities are publicised to all relevant staff, no matter what their age.

FOR EXAMPLE . . . PROMOTION DISCRIMINATION

Justine is excelling at her job, so applies for promotion. Her application is turned down because her employer is aware that away from work Justine has elderly parents. Her employer feels the promotion, on top of her responsibilities for her parents, would be too much for Justine. The employer made the decision without talking to her about its concerns or looking at and discussing any possible options, such as flexible working, that might have suggested a way forward for Justine. The employer's decision is likely to be discriminatory.

PAY AND TERMS AND CONDITIONS OF EMPLOYMENT

An employer **must not**:

- generally, have different terms and conditions of employment because of an employee's age, perceived age, or the age of someone they are associated with. This might, for example, include a bonus
  However, there are circumstances where different treatment because of age can or may be lawful. Examples include the National Minimum Wage and National Living Wage, redundancy pay, pay and job benefits linked to up to five years' length of service and, where the employer can objectively justify it, for more than five years' service. To find out more, see the section, **When different treatment because of age may be allowed**
- generally, allocate different work times, shift patterns or number of hours of work because of a job applicant or employee's age. There can be exceptions because of employee's flexible working requests approved by the employer. See the Flexible working section further into this guide.

FOR EXAMPLE . . . POTENTIAL PAY DISCRIMINATION

Sam, aged 50, and Mark, aged 35, work at the same firm and in the same role. While Sam is paid more than Mark based on his extra years of experience – 13 compared to Mark's five – Mark brings in more business. The firm would need to be able to objectively justify the difference in their pay, otherwise it is likely to be discriminatory.

PERFORMANCE MANAGEMENT

The appraisal

The manager doing an employee's appraisal **must:**

- make sure the appraisal is fair
- approach and conduct it without preconceptions or bias concerning age
- avoid raising or prompting a discussion about when the employee might retire, asking 'when are you planning to retire?', suggesting they retire or putting pressure on them to retire.

They **should:**

- treat relevant employees consistently when assessing their performance and setting future goals, no matter what their age. But they must make reasonable adjustments for employees with a disability. More information can be found at www.acas.org.uk/performance and in the **Impact of other protected characteristics** section further into this guide
- ask the employee, no matter what their age, about their work plans in the short-, medium- and long-terms, explaining the reason for asking is to help plan the workforce in shaping the business's future needs
- outline the employer's plans for the future.

They **should not**:

- ignore or overlook performance matters because the employee is younger or older than other staff.

WHAT A MANAGER SHOULD DO IF THE EMPLOYEE ASKS ABOUT RETIREMENT

Employees sometimes use an appraisal to say they've been thinking about options like full or partial retirement, a change in role or a development opportunity.

When an employee volunteers this information without being asked or prompted, managers can then start to discuss these future plans as part of the appraisal. Follow-up meetings will be needed to discuss and agree changes. But whatever the employee says about their future plans, employer and manager must not respond with discriminatory remarks or actions.

Some employers offer mid-career discussions with employees who request them. These, sometimes called 'mid-life MOTs', can help work out the best options for both employee and employer. To find out more, see the **Retirement** section in this guide or go to www.ageing-better.org.uk, www.unionlearn.org.uk/publications, www.acas.org.uk/retirement and www.youtube.com/watch?v=DgTq5NTKlHU

The employee **should**:

- approach their appraisal without preconceptions concerning age.

Managing under-performance

An employer **must**, regardless of the employee's age:

- ensure any dismissal of an employee for under-performance is based on relevant facts
- give an employee an adequate chance to reach and maintain an acceptable standard. Only if the employee fails to improve after reasonable steps have been taken to help them, can the employer consider dismissing them for under-performance
- use non-discriminatory language. Instead of saying 'I suppose there's no point in training you in the new system now you are nearing 60', say 'We are giving all staff the chance to learn the new system – would you like the training?'
- be consistent in the performance standards set for staff
- be consistent in managing absence from work because of illness. Do not assume older staff are more likely to be off work ill. See the **Age discrimination: top ten myths factsheet**.

An employer **should**, regardless of the employee's age:

- raise any performance problems with the employee as soon as possible, and **not** delay or wait until the employee's appraisal. This includes having a constructive conversation to explore reasons for the under-performance and finding out what the manager can do to help
- help the employee to try to improve through options such as coaching and/or training, making an agreed change to their role, or seeking the help of an occupational health adviser if the employee's health is affecting performance
- agree a way forward with the employee, setting clear targets for improvement and giving the employee a fair chance to improve
- give regular feedback to the employee, praising achievements and explaining how they can get better in any areas where they still need to improve.

TAKING CONSISTENT ACTION TO MANAGE PERFORMANCE

Like employees of all ages, each older worker has a different mix of physical and mental abilities, skills and experience. It's important to handle any under-performance by employees consistently no matter what their age. This includes giving them the same opportunities to improve and develop. Steps in managing an employee's under-performance should be in a workplace policy agreed between employer and any trade union/s or employee representatives. More information can be found at www.acas.org.uk/performance. Also see the section, **Retirement**, further into this guide.

FOR EXAMPLE . . . PERFORMANCE MANAGEMENT DISCRIMINATION

In a round of performance management reviews, Luciana sets targets for 29-year-old Haruki to improve in his role after poor results. Meanwhile, 63-year-old Joe in the same role has had similar poor results. However, Luciana decides to let that pass with Joe because she assumes he will be retiring soon. Haruki could claim discrimination because of his age.

REDUNDANCY

An employer **must**:

- make sure the need for redundancies is genuine and that the process for deciding who is made redundant fair. Decisions should be based on factors such as skills, work performance and abilities needed in the re-structured organisation.

An employer **must not:**

- base a decision on the age of an employee. However, there can be circumstances where what may appear a potentially discriminatory decision could be allowed. To find out more, see the section, **When different treatment because of age may be allowed**, further into this guide
- select staff for redundancy because they are part-time, as this is likely to involve discrimination, including against older employees
- pressurise older employees to opt for redundancy and/or retirement to help reduce the organisation's headcount
- select younger staff for redundancy instead of older, longer-serving staff to avoid higher redundancy pay-outs and maybe early pension pay-outs too, or because it thinks younger staff will find it easier to get another job.

An employer **should not**:

- select staff for redundancy solely or mainly based on 'last in, first out' because this is likely to discriminate against younger employees. However, there are circumstances where an employer may be able to objectively justify 'last in, first out' as part of redundancy selection criteria.

FOR EXAMPLE . . . REDUNDANCY DISCRIMINATION

Namono was made redundant after 18 years as an IT lecturer because she did not have recent experience working in a business. Before becoming a lecturer, Namono worked in computing in the private sector for 12 years, but this was not counted as 'recent' by her employer. This factor in selecting lecturers for redundancy is likely to have put the lecturers in Namono's age group at an unfair disadvantage and be discriminatory.

DECIDING REDUNDANCY PAYMENTS

Redundancy payments based on age are allowed under the statutory redundancy payments scheme and are capped at a maximum of 20 complete years of service with that employer. Alternatively, an employer may have its own redundancy payments scheme offering more money. Employers should be aware that a scheme not proportionately in line with the statutory scheme risks being discriminatory.

However, an employer's totally different scheme may be lawful if it can be objectively justified and pays all age groups more than the statutory scheme. Employers should also be aware that a scheme may be discriminatory if payments are capped for employees who are older employees. See **When different treatment because of age may be allowed**.

To find out about redundancy generally go to https://beta.acas.org.uk/manage-staff-redundancies

RETIREMENT

An employer **must not**:

- treat an employee detrimentally because they are thinking about retiring or could already take their work pension or State pension
- make the mistake of thinking it has the right to change an employee's employment contract once they take any pension.

THE EMPLOYEE'S RIGHT TO DECIDE WHEN TO RETIRE

Most employees now have the right to decide at what age they will retire. There is no legal 'standard' or 'default' retirement age. This ended in 2011. Also, an employee does not need to retire when they reach the State pension age. An employer can still set a retirement age if it meets legal requirements. This decision must meet the wider needs of society, such as giving young people the chance of employment or creating a workforce with a mix of age groups, as well as the organisation's business needs. However, the need to set a retirement age can be very difficult to prove. So, few employers do this apart from for some roles which are physically-demanding and/or involve public safety. To find out more, go to the section, **Where discrimination may be lawful**, further into this guide.

Whether or not an employee can take some or all of their pension when they retire will be determined by the pension scheme and Equality Act rules.

FOR EXAMPLE . . . RETIREMENT DISCRIMINATION

Clive, aged 66, has been clear with his employer that he would like to carry on working and developing at the firm where he's successfully built a new career in the last 15 years. However, the mood has changed with the arrival of a new manager, Michelle. He's now under the strong impression that she is trying to force him to retire. She regularly chips in remarks such as 'There's no point in training you to use the new software, Clive, you're 66 for goodness sake'. And 'You won't want a new role at your age, will you?' and 'You'll be retiring soon, I expect'. Michelle's behaviour is likely to be discriminatory.

DISMISSAL

An employer **must**:

- only ever dismiss an employee for a genuine reason and after a fair process.

An employer **must not**:

- apart from in very limited circumstances, dismiss an employee because of their age, including because they are thought to be too young or too old, or because of an ageist culture in the workplace. Neither must they be dismissed because of the age of someone they are associated with
- suggest that the employee should retire before or during a dismissal process
- use ageist language during a dismissal process
- base a dismissal on age, other than where lawful.

FOR EXAMPLE . . . DISMISSAL DISCRIMINATION

> Helen takes over the ownership and running of a hair and beauty salon. She then regularly picks on employee Ginette, aged 58, with comments such as 'she looks too old for the salon', 'she's putting off customers' and 'we need younger, prettier staff'. Finally, she dismisses Ginette claiming she's no longer the right kind of employee for the salon. This is likely to be discriminatory.

FLEXIBLE WORKING

An employer **must**:

- consider a flexible working request from an employee who has worked for it continuously for 26 weeks. It must agree to flexible working where it can accommodate the request, but can turn it down on business grounds defined in flexible working regulations. However, it must make sure it does not discriminate. To find out more, go to www.acas.org.uk/flexibleworking
- remember that changing or reducing work hours, going part-time, taking partial retirement or working from home can all be part of a flexible working request.

An employer **must not**:

- refuse a flexible working request from one employee because they feel another employee is more deserving because they are older, younger or have family care commitments. One way to manage requests is to consider them in the order they have been made.

An employer **should**:

- consider dropping the '26 weeks of service' eligibility requirement and allow job applicants and employees to request flexible working from day one of employment.

FOR EXAMPLE . . . FLEXIBLE WORKING DISCRIMINATION

> Sixty-year-old Liang asks manager Pablo if he could reduce his hours from full-time to four days a week in a year's time, so he can look after his grandson on the other day. Liang is hopeful because he knows some of the other staff, particularly the young mums, have flexible working arrangements such as jobshares and working from home. However, Liang's request is turned down without any discussion, with Pablo telling him: 'If you want to carry on working here, you've got to do a five-day week - final'. Liang believes Pablo is discriminating against him because of his age.

OTHER CONSIDERATIONS FOR EVERYONE

[4.75]

Employers, managers, HR personnel, employees and their employee or trade union representatives should make sure they also understand:

- age discrimination and where different treatment because of age may be allowed
- the risks of age stereotyping
- the importance of not using ageist language and not being biased in favour of or against particular age groups
- how the protected characteristic of age can interact with other protected characteristics, particularly sex and disability.

WHEN DIFFERENT TREATMENT BECAUSE OF AGE MAY BE ALLOWED

There are exceptions where different treatment because of age can or may be lawful including:

- where discrimination may be lawful
- occupational requirements
- positive action
- pay and extra job benefits linked to time with the employer
- National Minimum Wage and National Living Wage
- redundancy and redundancy pay
- pensions
- the Armed Forces
- employing people under 18.

Where discrimination may be lawful

Discrimination because of age is allowed where objectively justified:

- with ordinary direct discrimination, the employer must prove its action concerning the employee is 'a proportionate means of achieving a legitimate aim'
- with indirect discrimination, the employer must prove its 'provision, criterion or practice' affecting the employee and group of employees of that age or age group is 'a proportionate means of achieving a legitimate aim'.

WHAT IS A PROPORTIONATE MEANS OF ACHIEVING LEGITIMATE AIM?

> An employer must show both that:

• there is **a legitimate aim** such as a good business reason, but should note that cost alone is unlikely to be considered sufficient, and

• the actions are **proportionate, appropriate** and **necessary**.

To justify this sort of action, an employer must balance its business need against the discriminatory effect on affected employees. The more discriminatory the effect, the more difficult it will be to justify. Employers should explore ways to achieve their aims without discriminating, or without discriminating as much. If there are less discriminatory alternatives, they should be taken.

Proving a legitimate aim to an employment tribunal can be difficult.

If a claim of direct age discrimination goes before a tribunal, the employer would also have to show its legitimate aim would assist society in some way – for example, by helping young people get jobs or older people stay in work. However, in a case of indirect discrimination, an employer would not have to show any such wider benefit.

Occupational requirements

In very limited circumstances, it may be lawful for an employer to insist that employees or job applicants must be, or not be, a particular age or in a particular age group.

In law, this is known as an 'occupational requirement' and can provide the employer with a defence to a direct discrimination claim. But it is not enough for an employer to simply decide they would prefer, for example, not to employ someone because of their age.

An occupational requirement must be all of the following:

- crucial to the post, and not just one of several important factors, **and**
- relate to the nature of the job, **and**
- be 'a proportionate means of achieving a legitimate aim'. If there is any reasonable and less discriminatory way of achieving the same aim, it is unlikely the employer could claim an occupational requirement.

Occupational requirements should be reassessed every time a job is advertised because circumstances and needs can change.

Also, an employer should think carefully, and consider seeking legal advice, before claiming an occupational requirement because some can be **difficult to prove** to an employment tribunal.

EXAMPLES OF OCCUPATIONAL REQUIREMENTS

• to be 18 or over to serve alcohol

• to be between 18 and 60 to be a police officer because of the physical demands of the job

• to be between 18 and 60 to be a firefighter because of the physical demands of the job.

Positive action

An employer can take what the law calls 'positive action' if it can show reasonable evidence that job applicants and/or employees belonging to an age group:

- are at a disadvantage, and/or
- are in low numbers in the organisation, and/or
- have other needs because of their age.

Positive action must be proportionate and not discriminate against others. It does not mean giving applicants jobs or promotion solely because of their age. Actions may include training aimed at an age group or offering opportunities to use new skills to help them develop.

However, positive action can be used in a certain circumstance to decide who gets a vacancy where applicants are rated equally capable of doing the job. In this situation, the employer can select the applicant from the age group which it can show is under-represented in the organisation. An employer can only do this as a tie-breaker in deciding an individual vacancy. It would be discriminatory to give all applicants of an age group jobs, promotion or better terms and conditions because of their age.

For more on positive action, see the Acas guide, **Equality and discrimination: understand the basics**.

Pay and extra job benefits linked to time with the employer

An employer should usually base an employee's pay and any extra perks and benefits, such as private health insurance and additional holiday, on their job and skills, not how old they are. However:

- **For up to five years' service**, the law allows an employer to improve pay, perks and benefits because of length of service with the employer or working at a certain level with the employer (and may include any previous employment before transferring under the TUPE regulations)
- **For more than five years' service**, it may be discriminatory to increase pay and/or add perks and benefits as younger employees are more likely to have been with the employer for less time. However, an employer may be able to objectively justify rewarding more than five years' service if the business need is genuinely more important than any discriminatory effect it might have. There is more on 'objective justification' in the section, **Where discrimination may be lawful**, earlier in this guide

- **Insurance benefits** such as life insurance or health insurance can be stopped once an employee reaches the State pension age.

FOR EXAMPLE . . . LAWFUL PAY RISE LINKED TO TIME

Jen's employer gives all employees a pay increase after each year with the employer for up to five years on the basis that their growing experience enables them to do their job better.

National Minimum Wage and National Living Wage

The law allows different rates of minimum pay based on age up to 25 and applies even if people on different rates are doing the same job. The Government decided on this approach to make it easier for younger people to get work.

An employer can increase the amounts in each of the National Minimum Wage and National Living Wage pay scales, but the increases must go up using the same age bands.

For the current NMW and NLW rates, go to https://beta.acas.org.uk/national-minimum-wage-entitlement

Redundancy and redundancy pay

Redundancy: As mentioned in the earlier Redundancy section in this guide, there can be circumstances where a potentially discriminatory decision in selecting staff for redundancy could be allowed. For example, deciding to keep staff who have been with the company for longer, and making redundant staff with less time with the firm, is likely to discriminate against younger employees. However, the company could be allowed to do this if it can prove a good business reason. For instance, it might be that it is essential that the restructured company keeps its most experienced staff who are fully trained and skilled. To find out more about how to prove a good business reason, go to the earlier section, **Where discrimination may be lawful**.

Enhancing redundancy pay: As mentioned in the earlier Redundancy section in this guide, there can be circumstances where a potentially discriminatory decision in improving redundancy pay could be allowed. For example, basing the amount of redundancy pay on an employee's number of years with the employer is likely to encourage older employees to opt for redundancy and younger employees to stay with the employer. An employer could do this if it can prove a good business reason or reasons – maybe to reward long service and open up opportunities for new talent. Or, maybe, to encourage voluntary redundancies, avoid compulsory redundancies and give the restructuring of the organisation a positive feeling in moving forward. To find out more, go to the earlier section, **Where discrimination may be lawful**.

Capping redundancy pay: Usually, an employer should avoid a scheme which looks to cap redundancy pay for employees who it thinks might be nearing retirement. Before the ending of the standard retirement age of 65 in 2011, some employers had caps so long-serving older staff would only get a redundancy pay-out which matched what they would have earned had they stayed in work. But, with the end of the standard retirement age, it is now more difficult for an employer to justify fixed retirement ages, apart from in a few limited circumstances. Now, a long-serving employee is likely to argue that a cap on their redundancy pay because of their age is unlawful as they may well work long after what was once thought of as retirement age.

Pensions

An employer can offer an employee who has been part of its pension scheme since before October, 2006, an enhanced pension if they are being made redundant.

The law around age discrimination and pensions is extensive and complex. Employers and employees should seek legal advice and/or expert and independent financial guidance such as from the Pensions Advisory Service at www.pensionsadvisoryservice.org.uk/ or a regulated independent financial adviser – to find out more, go to the Financial Conduct Authority at www.fca.org.uk/

Armed Forces

Age discrimination law does not apply to the military in the army, navy and air force in the UK.

Employing people under 18

There are legal restrictions on employers offering work to young people, and taking them on, until they are 18. Find out more at www.acas.org.uk/employingyoungpeople

RISKS OF AGE STEREOTYPING

Employers and employees should avoid making assumptions about job applicants' and employees' capabilities and likely behaviours because of their age. Such guesswork can often be done without realising – this is known as unconscious bias. Whether intended or not, stereotyping can often lead to poor decision-making when recruiting, de-motivate existing staff, lead to reduced job performance and reduce trust among colleagues. Also, assumptions and uninformed decisions about job applicants or employees could lead to discrimination claims.

Myths about younger employees can include:

- they lack people skills because they are always on a mobile phone

- they are not team players.

Myths about older employees can include:

- their job performance will decline as they get older
- they will resist change.

HOW EMPLOYERS AND EMPLOYEES CAN AVOID AGE STEREOTYPING

Judge people on their job performance – not assumptions about them

Where possible, have different age groups in a team or project – shared goals can bring people together

Seek out and value different outlooks – they can come together to result in good ideas

Encourage the different age groups to swap ideas, knowledge and skills.

To find out more about unconscious bias, go to www.acas.org.uk/unconsciousbias

AGEIST LANGUAGE

Derogatory and abusive terms, and comments about an employee or job applicant are likely to be discriminatory if they are because of their:

- age
- perceived age (whether the perception is correct or not), and/or
- association with someone belonging to a particular age group.

They might include for example: a younger employee calling an older colleague 'Gramps' or 'old timer'; an older employee telling a young employee they are 'still wet behind the ears'; or an employer telling a job applicant 'you're not a good fit for our culture' or 'you're over-qualified' meaning 'you're too old' – here, the job applicant should challenge the employer to spell out what it means to see if the reasoning is justified or discriminatory.

In discrimination, how the recipient perceives words and actions matters more than the intention of the person delivering them.

The term 'banter' is often used when there is disparity between what was intended by one person and how it has been perceived by another. Employers should manage these situations with care. Sometimes a situation, where a 'joke', 'banter' or remark has caused offence or upset, can be dealt with by a manager having an informal discussion with an employee and explaining that they have caused offence, and to make sure they do not do it again. And in a situation where someone has used a word by mistake, or there has been a misunderstanding, or a comment has been made without thought, a manager may be able to handle it informally.

In other situations, where a term has been used on purpose and maliciously, or to embarrass and humiliate, the employer should look into the matter formally. There is more information about handling complaints in the companion guide, **Discrimination: what to do if it happens**, at www.acas.org.uk/equality

IMPACT OF OTHER PROTECTED CHARACTERISTICS

The protected characteristic of age can be affected by or interact with other protected characteristics. For example:

Sex: For a certain role, an employer may say the successful applicant will have to regularly work late and/or at weekends and/or travel abroad, and/or socialise after working hours. Unless the employer can give a good business reason or reasons, which are proportionate, appropriate and necessary, such requirements may be discriminatory because of age and/or sex. For example, this might be because older women are more likely to have family caring commitments outside of work and find it difficult to meet such demands.

Employers should be aware that older women are more likely to be treated unfairly because of their age than older men. As well as being overlooked for promotion and training, and full-time work because of a lack of flexible working, some older women are also being treated unfairly because of the **menopause**.

MANAGING THE MENOPAUSE AT WORK

The menopause is part of the natural ageing process for women, usually in their late forties or fifties. Employers should be aware of effects of the menopause including:

- insomnia, fatigue, mood swings and surges of feeling hot
- struggling to remember things, concentrate and focus at work
- taking longer to recover from illness.

Such effects can lead to an employee losing her confidence, and suffering from stress and anxiety. Many women who take time off work because of these effects do not tell their employers the real reasons for their absence.

> Employers and employees may find the menopause a difficult topic to discuss as it is a sensitive and personal matter. An employer should train managers and/or develop a policy to ensure an understanding in the organisation of how the menopause can affect women at work and what support might be appropriate. Such an approach may give an employee confidence to talk to their employer about any issues they have or support they feel they need. And it may prevent discrimination claims from female employees going through the menopause.
>
> There are more than three million women over 50 working in Britain. The impact of the menopause can vary from woman to woman.
>
> For guidance for union reps on supporting working women through the menopause, go to www.tuc.org.uk

For advice on sex discrimination, go to www.acas.org.uk/sexdiscrim

Disability: The risk of an employee developing a disability increases with age, particularly once over 50. A job applicant or employee must not be discriminated against:

- because they have a disability, and/or
- because of something linked to their disability – for example, it might be to do with being off work ill or difficulty coping with a certain task - and/or
- because they need 'reasonable adjustments' to remove or minimise their disadvantage at work caused by their disability – for example, this might be in applying for a job or to stay in work - or
- because they are thought to have a disability, or
- because they are associated with someone with a disability.

For advice on disability discrimination, go to www.acas.org.uk/disability

RAISING AND HANDLING COMPLAINTS

[4.76]

How an employee should raise a complaint of alleged discrimination, including the option of raising the matter with a trade union representative, and how the employer should handle it, are explained in companion guide **Discrimination: what to do if it happens**. Also, employers should be aware that after dealing successfully with a complaint of discrimination, there can be further steps. For example, it is useful to think of how any future instances might be prevented. Find out more in the companion guide, **Prevent discrimination: support equality**. Both guides are at www.acas.org.uk/equality

FURTHER INFORMATION

[4.77]

Acas learning online

Acas offers free e-learning. The Equality and diversity course gives: an overview of what equality and diversity mean; why they are important; putting the principles into practice in an organisation; and a test to gauge understanding of the key points. Go to www.acas.org.uk/elearning

Acas training

Our Equality and diversity training is carried out by experienced Acas staff who work with businesses every day. Training can be specially designed for smaller companies. Go to www.acas.org.uk/training for up-to-date information about our training and booking places on face-to-face courses. Also, Acas specialists can visit an organisation, diagnose issues in its workplace, and tailor training and support to address the challenges it faces. Find out more at www.acas.org.uk/businesssolutions

Acas guidance

Equality and discrimination: understand the basics, which includes the public sector equality duty

Prevent discrimination: support equality

Discrimination: what to do if it happens

Bullying and harassment at work

Flexible working

Recruiting staff

Redundancy

Age UK

Charity campaigning against ageism at work, at www.ageuk.org.uk/information-advice/work-learning/discrimination-rights/

Guidance on age-friendly recruitment at www.rec.uk.com/__data/assets/pdf_file/0013/215221/Age-Opportunity-4-page-A4-pledge-WEB.pdf

Business in the Community

Charity promoting responsible business, at https://age.bitc.org.uk/BusinessChampion

Centre for Ageing Better

Charitable foundation campaigning for more age-friendly workplaces, at www.ageing-better.org.uk/our-work/being-fulfilling-work

Equality Advisory Support Service

Government-funded service offering support to people with discrimination concerns, at the EASS helpline on 0808 800 0082 (Text phone: 0808 800 0084) or go to www.equalityadvisoryservice.com/

Equality and Human Rights Commission

Guidance on age discrimination in the workplace on www.equalityhumanrights.com/en/advice-and-guidance/age-discrimination

Employment Statutory Code of Practice on www.equalityhumanrights.com/codes

Government's Department for Work and Pensions

Report on managing a workforce when there will be more older staff, at https://assets.publishing.service.gov.uk/government/uploads/system/uploads/attachment_data/file/587654/fuller-working-lives-a-partnership-approach.pdf

Having a mid-life career conversation video, at www.youtube.com/watch?v=DgTq5NTKlHU

Trades Union Congress

To find out how a trade union representative should carry out a mid-life career conversation with an employee to help the employee make a case to their employer, go to www.unionlearn.org.uk/publications/valuing-skills-older-workers-how-do-mid-life-development-review

Additional help

Employers may be able to seek assistance from groups where they are members. For example, if an employer is a member of the Confederation of British Industry or the Federation of Small Businesses, it could seek its help and guidance. If an employee is a trade union member, they can seek help and guidance from their trade union representative or trade union equality representative.

KEEP UP-TO-DATE AND STAY INFORMED

[4.78]

Visit www.acas.org.uk for:

- free employment relations and employment law guidance
- tools and resources including free-to-download templates, forms and checklists
- an introduction to other Acas services including mediation, conciliation, training, arbitration and the Acas Early Conciliation service
- research and discussion papers on the UK workplace
- details of Acas training courses, conferences and events.

Sign up for the free Acas e-newsletter. The Acas email newsletter is a great way of keeping up to date with changes to employment law and to hear about events in your area. Find out more at: www.acas.org.uk/subscribe

Acas Helpline Online. Have a question? We have a database of frequently-asked employment queries that has been developed to help both employees and employers. It is an automated system designed to give you a straightforward answer to your employment questions, and also gives links to further advice and guidance on our website: www.acas.org.uk/helplineonline

Acas Helpline. Call the helpline for free and impartial advice on 0300 123 1100. We can provide employers and employees with clear and confidential guidance about any kind of dispute or relationship issue in the workplace. You may want to know about employment rights and rules, best practice or may need advice about a dispute. Whatever it is, our team are on hand. Find out more: www.acas.org.uk/helpline

Look for us on:

Facebook - https://www.facebook.com/acasorguk

LinkedIn - http://linkd.in/cYJbuU

Twitter - http://twitter.com/acasorguk

YouTube – https://www.youtube.com/user/acasorguk

B. HOME OFFICE

NOTES

The Codes of Practice in this section were previously issued by the Border & Immigration Agency.

CODE OF PRACTICE FOR EMPLOYERS AVOIDING UNLAWFUL DISCRIMINATION WHILE PREVENTING ILLEGAL WORKING MAY 2014

[4.79]

NOTES

This Code of Practice was issued by the Home Office. It is made under the authority of s 23 of the Immigration, Asylum and Nationality Act 2006; the Parliamentary authority for the Code is Immigration (Restrictions on Employment) (Codes of Practice and Amendment) Order 2014, SI 2014/1183, art 11 at **[2.1480]**. The Code came into force on 16 May 2014. Whilst the Code is issued under statutory powers, it does not carry any specific statutory status, and there is no formal requirement under the 2006 Act for any relevant body to take it into account. It replaces the previous Code issued by the Border & Immigration Agency in 2008, which applied where employment commenced on or after 29 February 2008. The previous Code continues to apply to any breach occurring before 16 May 2014 (see **[4.80]**). Notes are as in the original Code.

CONTENTS

1: INTRODUCTION

[4.80]

Employers have a duty to prevent illegal working in the UK by carrying out document checks on people before employing them to confirm they have a right to work here. Failing to conduct these checks is not itself a criminal offence, but if an employer only carries them out on people who they *believe* are not British citizens, for example, on the basis of their colour, or ethnic or national origins, they could find themselves accused of discrimination and it could be used as evidence against them in proceedings under the Equality Act 2010 or the Race Relations (Northern Ireland) Order 1997, as amended.

Anyone who believes that they have been discriminated against, either directly or indirectly, by an employer, a prospective employer or an employment agency, because of their race may bring a complaint before an Employment Tribunal, or an Industrial Tribunal in Northern Ireland. If the complaint is upheld, the Tribunal will normally order the payment of compensation, for which there is no upper limit.

This is why we recommend that you, as an employer, obtain a statutory excuse for **all** prospective workers as this will protect you from liability for a civil penalty if the person in question is an illegal worker, whilst also demonstrating consistent, transparent and non-discriminatory recruitment practices. Where the employee only has a limited entitlement to remain in the UK, these checks should be repeated as prescribed in the guidance and 'Code of practice on preventing illegal working: civil penalty scheme for employers' in order to retain the excuse. Further information on the right to work checks and the statutory excuse may be found at www.gov.uk/government/collections/employers-illegal-working-penalties.

It is important to remember that the population of the UK is ethnically diverse. Many people from ethnic minorities in this country are British citizens and many non-British citizens from black and minority ethnic communities are entitled to work here. You must not therefore *assume* that someone from an ethnic minority is an immigrant, or that someone born abroad or who speaks with a particular accent is not allowed to work in the UK.

We have issued this Code of practice for employers to strengthen the safeguards against unlawful discrimination when recruiting people.

FOR WHOM IS THIS CODE OF PRACTICE RELEVANT?

This Code of practice applies where employment commenced on or after 16 May 2014. It also applies where a repeat check on an existing worker is required to be carried out on or after 16 May 2014 to retain a statutory excuse.

All employers in England, Scotland, Wales and Northern Ireland must adhere to this Code. It also applies to certain organisations, such as employment businesses and employment and recruitment agencies (including on-line agencies). An employment agency or business practising unlawful discrimination may be liable, even if it is acting on the instructions of an employer, ie at the behest of one of its clients.

Whilst some smaller organisations may wish to adapt this guidance to suit their particular circumstances, it should be noted that no allowances can be made for smaller companies when considering their liability under the law. We recommend that smaller organisations ensure that their employment practices do not discriminate on any of the grounds set out in law and they follow the advice given in this Code.

HOW SHOULD THIS CODE OF PRACTICE BE USED?

This Code of practice has been issued under section 23(1) of the Immigration, Asylum and Nationality Act 2006. It sets out an employer's legal obligations under the Equality Act 2010 and the Race Relations (Northern Ireland) Order 1997, as amended. It provides practical guidance on how to avoid unlawful discrimination when complying with your duty as an employer to conduct right to work checks. It is not, however, intended to be a comprehensive statement of the law. This Code has been issued alongside guidance and the 'Code of practice on preventing illegal working: civil penalty scheme for employers'.

WHO SHOULD USE THIS CODE OF PRACTICE?

This is a statutory Code. This means it has been approved by the Secretary of State and laid before Parliament. The Code does not impose any legal duties on employers, nor is it an authoritative statement of the law; only the Courts and Employment Tribunals can provide that. However, this Code may be used as evidence in legal proceedings. Courts and Employment Tribunals may take account of any part of this Code which may be relevant to matters of discrimination.

Public authorities must also adhere to this Code. In addition, they are subject to the public sector equality duty which requires public authorities to have due regard to the need to:

(a) eliminate discrimination, harassment, victimisation and any other conduct that is prohibited by or under the 2010 Act;
(b) advance equality of opportunity between persons who share a relevant protected characteristic and persons who do not share it ('protected characteristic' is defined below); and
(c) foster good relations between persons who share a relevant protected characteristic and persons who do not share it.

REFERENCES IN THIS CODE

Throughout this Code of practice, the Equality Act 2010 is referred to as 'the 2010 Act', and the Race Relations (Northern Ireland) Order 1997, as amended, as 'the 1997 Order'.

When we refer to 'we' or us' in this Code we mean the Home Office. When we refer to 'you' and 'your' this means the employer.

2: YOUR DUTY UNDER THE LAW

[4.81]

It is unlawful to discriminate in employment practices because of race. In Great Britain under section 39 of the 2010 Act and in Northern Ireland under article 6 of the 1997 Order, you cannot discriminate against a potential or existing worker because of race (2010 Act) or on racial grounds (1997 Order). Race and racial grounds include colour, nationality and ethnic or national origins.

Race discrimination may be either **direct** or **indirect**.

DIRECT RACE DISCRIMINATION

Direct discrimination means treating a person less favourably because of race or on racial grounds, for example, by rejecting all job applicants who do not have British nationality or another specified nationality, or by refusing to consider any non-European job applicants. Treatment based on racial or national stereotypes can also constitute direct discrimination. Examples include:

- where the assumption is made that people from certain nationalities or ethnic groups cannot work as a team;
- where individuals are only recruited from one nationality or ethnic group;
- where all refugees are automatically rejected;
- where an employee with time-limited permission to be in the UK is given less favourable or more detrimental work than workers with unlimited leave; or
- where it is assumed that overseas qualifications and experience are inferior to those gained in the UK.

INDIRECT RACE DISCRIMINATION

Indirect discrimination occurs where a provision, criterion or practice, although applied equally to others, would put persons of a particular racial group at a particular disadvantage compared with other persons, unless the provision, criterion or practice is objectively justified by a legitimate aim. For example, to require that a person has been resident in the UK for over 5 years is likely to be indirectly discriminatory since some migrants will not have been resident in the UK for that period of time.

> It is unlawful to victimise a person because he or she has made or supported a complaint of race discrimination.
> It is also unlawful to instruct or induce another person to discriminate, or to publish an advertisement or notice that indicates an intention to discriminate.

UNLAWFUL RACE DISCRIMINATION

You must not discriminate because of race:

(a) in the arrangements you make to decide who should be offered employment; or

(b) as to the terms on which you offer to employ a person; or
(c) by refusing or deliberately failing to offer employment.

It is also unlawful for you to discriminate because of race against a worker:
(a) in the terms of employment provided; or
(b) in the way you make opportunities for training, promotion, transfer, facilities, services or other benefits available; or
(c) by refusing access to such opportunities, benefits, facilities or services; or
(d) by dismissing the worker or subjecting him to any other detriment.

You must also not subject a job applicant or worker to harassment under the terms of the 2010 Act. Harassment is unwanted conduct related to age, disability, gender reassignment, race, religion or belief, sex or sexual orientation that violates someone's dignity or creates an intimidating, hostile, degrading, humiliating or offensive environment for them. Harassment also includes unwanted conduct of a sexual nature which violates someone's dignity or creates an intimidating, hostile, degrading, humiliating or offensive environment for them.

It is also unlawful to segregate a worker from others on the basis of race.

Under the 2010 Act and the 1997 Order, discrimination committed by an **employee** in the course of their employment, is treated as having been committed by you as the employer, as well as by the individual employee, **whether or not you knew or approved the acts of discrimination**. You can avoid this liability if you can prove that you took all reasonable steps to prevent such discrimination, for example, by providing training to employees on how to apply checks in accordance with this Code. It might also be a reasonable step for an employer to have an equality policy in place and ensure that it is put into practice. A claim to an Employment Tribunal may be made against both you and the individual employee who is alleged to have discriminated.

OTHER DISCRIMINATION GROUNDS

The 2010 Act also prohibits discrimination in employment practices on the following grounds (which together with race are known as the 'protected characteristics' under the 2010 Act):

- age;
- disability;
- gender reassignment;
- marriage and civil partnership;
- pregnancy and maternity;
- religion or belief;
- sex; or
- sexual orientation.

Although this Code only addresses race discrimination, you should be mindful of these other forms of discrimination when applying the provisions of the Act. If, for example, people affected by religious discrimination are from a particular racial group, the discrimination might also amount to indirect race discrimination – for example, case law has established that Sikhs and Jews can be described as having an 'ethnic origin'. It should also be noted that in Northern Ireland, the 1997 Order also covers the Irish Traveller Community. The Fair Employment and Treatment (Northern Ireland) Order 1998, as amended, also makes it unlawful to discriminate on the grounds of religious belief and political opinion.

ACTION AGAINST YOU

Anyone who believes that they have been discriminated against, either directly or indirectly, by you, as an employer, a prospective employer or an employment agency, may issue a claim in an Employment Tribunal, or an Industrial Tribunal in Northern Ireland. If the claim is upheld, the Tribunal will normally order you to pay compensation, for which there is no upper limit.

The Equality and Human Rights Commission and the Northern Ireland Equality Commission can also take regulatory action against you if you publish a discriminatory advertisement, or instruct or induce another person to discriminate.

Where you are found to have committed an act of unlawful race discrimination, the Public Procurement Regulations 2006 provide that public authorities may disqualify your organisation from entering into public procurement contracts.

3: HOW YOU AVOID RACE DISCRIMINATION

[4.82]
As a matter of good employment practice, you should have clear written procedures for the recruitment and selection of all workers based on equal and fair treatment for all applicants. Copies of these procedures should be made available to all relevant staff.

All job selections should be on the basis of suitability for the post. You should ensure that no prospective job applicants are discouraged or excluded, either directly or indirectly, because of their personal appearance or accent. You should not make assumptions about a person's right to work or immigration status on the basis of their colour, nationality, ethnic or national origins, accent or the length of time they have been resident in the UK.

The best way to ensure that you do not discriminate is to treat all applicants fairly and in the same way at each stage of the recruitment process.

FAIR RECRUITMENT PRACTICES

If you provide information to prospective applicants or if you supply an application form, you could also include a reminder that the successful applicant, or short-listed applicants, will be required to produce original, acceptable documents.

You may ask applicants to provide the specified document(s) to obtain a statutory excuse at any stage **before** they start work. Depending on your recruitment processes, you may find it most convenient to request documents from all those called to a first interview, or just from those called to a second interview, or only from persons short-listed to fill the vacancy. Original documents should be checked before employment commences. **If you ask for documents from one applicant, you should make sure you ask for documents from all applicants being considered at that stage.**

Job applicants should not be treated less favourably if they produce acceptable documents showing a time-limited right to work in the UK. Once a person who has time-limited permission to stay in the UK has established their initial and on-going entitlement to work, they should not be treated less favourably during their employment, including the terms of their employment, opportunities for training, promotion or transfer, benefits, facilities or services, or by dismissing the worker or subjecting them to some other detriment, other than further right to work checks as prescribed in the guidance and 'Code of practice on preventing illegal working: civil penalty scheme for employers'.

You should only ask questions about an applicant's or worker's immigration status where it is necessary to determine whether their status imposes limitations on the number of hours they may work each week, the type of work they may carry out or on the length of time for which they are permitted to work.

If a person is not able to produce acceptable documents, you should not assume that they are living or working in the UK illegally. You should try to keep the job open for as long as possible in order to provide them with the opportunity to demonstrate their right to work, but you are not obliged to do so if you need to recruit someone urgently. **It is ultimately the decision of the employer whether or not to employ an individual.**

As a matter of good practice, you should monitor the diversity details of applications during the recruitment and selection process of job applicants. This will include the gender, disability status and the ethnic and national origins of applicants. This will help you to know whether you are reaching a wide range of potential job applicants. This information can then be used in reviewing recruitment procedures.

4: IF YOU NEED MORE INFORMATION

[4.83]

The Equality and Human Rights Commission (EHRC) and the Equality Commission for Northern Ireland provide further information on matters relating to the law on discrimination. Information and contact details are available at www.equalityhumanrights.com/ and www.equalityni.org.

The EHRC has produced a Statutory Code of Practice on Employment which contains detailed and practical guidance to help employers to comply with the Equality Act 2010, together with guidance and good practice for small businesses. These publications are available on its website.

Home Office guidance and the 'Code of practice on the prevention of illegal working: civil penalty scheme for employers' are available at: www.gov.uk/government/collections/employers-illegal-working-penalties.

Home Office advice for employers about complying with the law on preventing illegal migrant working is available from the Employers' Helpline on **0300 123 4699**. The Helpline is open Monday to Friday, between 9 am and 5 pm, except bank holidays.

CODE OF PRACTICE ON LABOUR MARKET ENFORCEMENT UNDERTAKINGS AND ORDERS (NOVEMBER 2016)

[4.84]

NOTES

This Code of Practice was made by the Home Office and the Department for Business, Energy & Industrial Strategy under s 25 of the Immigration Act 2016 at **[1.2051]** following Parliamentary approval. It was brought into force on 25 November 2016 by the Labour Market Enforcement (Code of Practice on Labour Market Enforcement Undertakings and Orders: Appointed Day) Regulations 2016, SI 2016/1044. By virtue of s 25(4) of the 2016 Act, an enforcing authority (within the meaning of that Act) must have regard to the current version of the Code in exercising its functions under ss 14–23 of the Act.

CONTENTS

1. REFERENCES IN THIS CODE

[4.85]

"**Enforcing Authorities**" is defined in section 14(5) of the Immigration Act 2016 ("the Act") and means the Employment Agency Standards Inspectorate (EAS), HMRC National Minimum Wage Enforcement (HMRC-NMW) and the Gangmasters and Labour Abuse Authority (GLAA).

"**Trigger offence**" is defined in section 14(4) of the Act and means an offence under the Employment Agencies (EA) Act 1973 (other than one under section 9(4)(b) of that Act), an offence under the National Minimum Wage (NMW) Act 1998 or an offence under the Gangmasters (Licensing) (G(L)) Act 2004 including secondary and inchoate offences.

"**Subject**" is defined in section 14(3) of the Act and means a person entering into an LME undertaking.

"**Respondent**" is defined in section 18(2) of the Act and means a person or business who is subject to an LME order.

2. INTRODUCTION

[4.86]

1. The Government has introduced measures in the Immigration Act 2016 ("the Act") to provide a more coherent framework for identifying and preventing abuses of labour market legislation, and to strengthen the enforcement response. This includes new powers to apply Labour Market Enforcement (LME) undertakings and orders, which are intended for more serious or persistent offenders where this type of intervention is judged appropriate to prevent further offending. Enforcing authorities will have regard to this Code when using the LME regime under the Act.

2. The new system of undertakings is designed to complement the existing powers already available to the enforcing authorities, and to be deployed where appropriate to prevent further labour market offences. These existing powers include:

- prosecution for offences under National Minimum Wage, Employment Agencies and Gangmaster Licensing legislation;[1]
- the imposition of civil penalties and "naming and shaming"[2] (for businesses which fail to comply with the National Minimum Wage Act);
- the imposition of prohibition orders preventing a person from carrying on an employment agency or employment business;
- the refusal or revocation of a licence to act as a gangmaster and
- lower level administrative measures such as warning letters.

3. Prosecution under existing legislation will remain available for the most serious offenders and enforcing authorities should consider on a case by case basis which sanction is most appropriate in the circumstances. The best response may be a combination of an existing civil or criminal penalty and an LME undertaking.

4. The introduction of the new LME undertakings and orders regime is integral to the Government's intention to introduce a broader and harder edge to enforcement of labour market offences where these are committed deliberately or recklessly and are not simply a consequence of a straightforward administrative error. The purpose of labour market legislation is to ensure there is a level playing field for legitimate competition between law-abiding businesses, in which workers are guaranteed the national living wage and are protected from exploitation. These objectives are undermined if these important legal protections are not upheld and enforced. Tackling non-compliant business supports growth by supporting legitimate businesses which treat their workers properly.

5. The new regime of LME undertakings and orders means that, for the first time, a prison sentence can ultimately result from some key labour market offences which currently only attract a civil penalty or criminal fine. A two year custodial penalty and/or unlimited fine is available where a business breaches an LME order which has been made by a court either following conviction for a trigger offence or on application from an enforcing authority following failure to enter into, or breach of, an LME undertaking. However, this is balanced by providing the employer with ample opportunity to make a sustained change to their behaviour to avert prosecution. The regime is designed to ensure that employers are no longer able to treat fines as acceptable business overheads.

6. The Government expects to see the enforcing authorities work together collaboratively to deliver the priorities in the annual strategy set out by the Director of Labour Market Enforcement (hereafter "the Director"), to share intelligence and to co-ordinate enforcement activity where the suspected offences in question engage the interests/responsibilities of more than one of the agencies. The authorities will have regard to the Director's strategy when taking decisions on their own caseloads. The Government expects the authorities to work collaboratively to determine which agency should lead in the context of a joint investigation and which enforcement tools would provide the most effective response to the offending behaviour and would be most likely to prevent it recurring.

7. The Government intends that the GLAA should be responsible for investigating the more serious cases of labour market abuse involving a modern slavery element or multiple offences across a range of specified legislation, working with the police and National Crime Agency (NCA) where appropriate. Although the list of labour market offences that the Director is working to prevent includes some Modern Slavery Act offences, these are too serious to be included within the scope of the undertakings and orders regime and they have maximum penalties which are far in excess of the two year custodial penalty for breach of an LME order.

WHAT IS THE PURPOSE OF THIS CODE?

8. This Code aims to ensure that LME undertakings and orders are applied in a consistent manner by the enforcing authorities. It is a statutory Code, issued under section 25 of the Immigration Act 2016. It has been approved by the Home Secretary and BEIS Secretary of State and laid before Parliament.

HOW SHOULD THIS CODE OF PRACTICE BE USED?

9. The Code sets out the factors to be considered by the enforcing authorities when using the LME regime. It also sets out how the enforcing authorities should work together. It should be read alongside the Director's strategy and complements existing joint working processes.

WHO SHOULD USE THIS CODE OF PRACTICE?

10. Enforcing authorities will have regard to this Code when using the LME regime under the Act. The Code does not impose any legal duties on employers, gangmasters, businesses or enforcing authorities, nor is it an authoritative statement of the law: only the courts can provide that. However, the Code may be used as evidence in legal proceedings and courts will take account of any part of the Code which may be relevant.

EXTENT

11. All trigger offences can trigger the use of an LME undertaking in Great Britain. Only NMW trigger offences can do so in Northern Ireland.

WHO CAN USE THE REGIME?

12. The EAS can seek an LME undertaking, apply for an LME order and investigate a breach of an LME order where the trigger offence is under the Employment Agencies Act 1973 (sections 14(5)(a) and 26(1) of the 2016 Act).

13. HMRC NMW can seek an LME undertaking, apply for an LME order and investigate a breach of an LME order where the trigger offence is under the National Minimum Wage Act 1998 (sections 14(5)(b) and 26(2) of the 2016 Act).

14. GLAA enforcement officers can seek an LME undertaking, apply for an LME order and investigate a breach of an LME order where the trigger offence is under the Gangmasters (Licensing) Act 2004 (sections 14(5)(c) and 26(3) of the 2016 Act).

15. Trained GLAA officers who have wider labour market enforcement powers can seek an LME undertaking, apply for an LME order and investigate a breach of an LME order where the trigger offence is under the Gangmasters (Licensing) Act 2004, the Employment Agencies Act 1973 or the National Minimum Wage Act 1998 (sections 14 and 26 of the 2016 Act).

NOTES

[1] Offences under section 31 of the NMW Act 1998 include failure to pay NMW and associated offences relating to record keeping and obstruction; Offences under the EA Act 1973 include failing to comply with a prohibition order, contravening regulations or the restriction on charging a work finding fee and associated offences relating to record keeping and obstruction; Offences under the G(L)A Act 2004 include acting as a gangmaster without a licence, entering into arrangements with an unlicensed gangmaster and associated offences relating to record keeping and obstruction.

[2] Naming and shaming is a function of BEIS

3. LME UNDERTAKINGS

CIRCUMSTANCES WHEN LME UNDERTAKINGS SHOULD BE CONSIDERED

[4.87]

16. An undertaking may be sought where an enforcing authority (see section 1) believes a trigger offence (see section 1) has been or is being committed and a measure in the undertaking is necessary to prevent further non-compliance. They are not designed to replace the use of current sanctions to punish breaches and seek redress and should be used alongside these (see chapter 4).

17. The following factors should be taken into account by the enforcing authority before seeking an undertaking from a business:

- the number of trigger offences that are believed to have been committed;
- if previous enforcement action has been taken;
- the number of workers affected by the offence;
- any harm, physical or otherwise, to workers;
- the amount of money due to workers;
- whether the breach believed to be have been committed was committed recklessly or intentionally, as opposed to by straightforward error, and if so;
- the level of recklessness by the business that led to the breach; and
- whether the enforcing authority believes that the breach was committed intentionally.

18. Enforcing authorities seeking an undertaking should consider whether they are prepared to take reasonable steps to monitor whether the recipient is adhering to it and to apply to the courts for an LME order in cases where the subject of an undertaking has failed to comply with its terms.

MEASURES IN AN LME UNDERTAKING OR ORDER

19. LME undertakings or orders may include prohibitions, restrictions or impose requirements on businesses, only if the measures do one or both of the following:

- prevent or reduce the risk of non-compliance with requirements in the enactment containing the trigger offence; or
- bring the existence of the undertaking, the circumstances in which it was given and any action taken (or not taken) to the attention of interested parties, or (in the case of action taken/not taken) to the attention of the enforcing authorities.

20. In addition, the measures in LME undertakings or orders must be just and reasonable; the undertaking or order must make clear how the measures address the trigger offence that the enforcing authority suspects has been committed and any risk of future non-compliance with the legislation which contains the trigger offence.

21. The Government expects the enforcing authorities to use their expertise and knowledge of the type of breach to choose the most appropriate measures to prevent future non-compliance in each case. Therefore this Code does not contain an exhaustive list of possible measures. Instead, the case study below provides illustrative examples.

CASE STUDY 1:

Measures match non-compliance
GLA - A short period of operating without a licence, where there is no exploitation of workers, or any identified non-compliance with labour market legislation including the GLA licensing standards, might result in a decision not to prosecute but to issue an undertaking that a person/business applies for a licence within a given period, does not continue to operate illegally during that time, and corrects any identified non-compliance before a licence is granted.

22. Where the trigger offence is a breach of the National Mimimum Wage Act 1988 and the £100 de minimis threshold for naming and shaming has not been reached, enforcing authorities should consider carefully whether it is appropriate for an undertaking to contain a measure requiring the subject to make interested parties aware of it. As the LME regime will be used against serious and persistent offenders, such a measure may still be appropriate on occasion where the subject is a persistent offender but the threshold has not been met in the individual case in question.

PROCESS FOR GIVING NOTICE OF AN UNDERTAKING

23. A notice seeking an undertaking may be given by the enforcing authority to a business. The undertaking cannot be imposed on the business: the business determines whether or not to give the undertaking. However, see below in relation to LME orders when a business does not give an undertaking.

24. A notice seeking the undertaking may be served in person, by post or electronically, (subject to the person specifying the electronic format and address), and can be served on an individual, a company officer or a partner, depending on the type of business. The notice must set out which offence the enforcing authority believes has been or is being committed, why the enforcing authority believes this to be the case, and will invite the person to give an undertaking to comply with any prohibitions, restrictions or requirements set by the enforcing authority (see 'Measures in an LME undertaking or order', above). The notice must set out how these measures prevent or reduce the risk of the particular non-compliance identified.

25. An undertaking can be given by an individual, a company or both.

NEGOTIATION PERIOD

26. A negotiation period of 14 days (or alternative period if the enforcing authority so proposes) will be triggered by service of the notice given to the business to provide an opportunity for them to propose alternative means of achieving compliance. If that alternative is not accepted by the enforcing authority (because the enforcing authority does not believe that it will achieve compliance to a similar degree or timescale) and the person does not agree to the measures in the original notice, the person is deemed to have refused to give an undertaking. In these circumstances, an enforcing body may apply to the courts for an LME order under section 19 of the Immigration Act 2016, or pursue alternative action under existing legal powers. Save in exceptional circumstances, an enforcing authority should always take one of these actions. This is to preserve the integrity of the LME undertakings regime and enable it to act as a deterrent.

DURATION

27. An undertaking takes effect when it is accepted by the enforcing authority unless a later date is specified in the undertaking. The duration is specified in the undertaking subject to a maximum of 2 years.

MONITORING COMPLIANCE

28. When an undertaking has been accepted, the enforcing authority should determine on a case by case basis how, and at what intervals, compliance with the measures should be monitored. This should be proportionate and in accordance with the Director's strategy. For example, if a business has used the services of an unlicensed gangmaster, an undertaking could require that business to notify the enforcing authority when new gangmasters are used. An initial visit could be made to check that the business was no longer using unlicensed gangmasters. The business would also be expected to register for the GLAA's active check service for all gangmasters that it used to ensure that it did not inadvertently use unlicensed gangmasters in the future. The undertaking could remain in place until the enforcing authority was satisfied that arrangements were in place to check that only licensed gangmasters were being used (subject to the two year maximum). A complaint from a worker might indicate the need for a follow up visit.

RELEASE

29. A business can be released from an undertaking by the enforcing authority and must be released where, in the judgement of the enforcing authority, compliance has been achieved and the compliance will be maintained without the measures in the undertaking being in place.

30. This will be the case either where the measures in the undertaking have been acted upon, or compliance has been achieved through measures other than that/those set out in the undertaking. It would, however, be appropriate for the enforcing authority to maintain the undertaking if it believed that, despite having complied on a particular occasion, the measures remained necessary to prevent future non-compliance. This requires the enforcing authority to form a view on the behaviour and response of the subject of the undertaking in the round.

31. If the practical measures contained in the undertaking have been taken by the business in question and compliance with the requirements of the legislation containing the trigger offence has still not been achieved, the enforcing authority should consider whether the original undertaking was inadequate, and whether the subject should be released from it. In these circumstances, the enforcing authority should consider whether, to secure compliance, a new undertaking should be sought containing different measures.

CASE STUDY 2:

Must be released as no further risk of trigger offence

- Enforcing authority seeks an undertaking with measure A
- Business gives undertaking on A but does B instead.
- Enforcing authority must release undertaking if compliance achieved using measure B, unless it believes it is necessary to leave measure A in place to prevent future non-compliance.

BREACHES OF LME UNDERTAKINGS

32. Save in exceptional circumstances, an enforcing authority should apply to a court for an LME order if it believes that an undertaking has been breached. The process is set out in the next chapter. This is to preserve the integrity of the LME undertakings regime and ensure that it acts as a suitably strong deterrent to prevent future offending.

4. LME ORDERS

LME ORDERS ON APPLICATION

[4.88]

33. An enforcing authority may apply to the court for an LME order where an undertaking has not been given within the negotiation period or where an undertaking has been breached. The standard of proof relating to the breach is the balance of probabilities. The higher criminal standard of proof will be applied if the respondent is prosecuted for breaching an LME order imposed by the court. This provides the business with a further opportunity to address non-compliance before facing a potential criminal sanction.

34. The relevant court is the magistrates' court in England and Wales, the sheriff court in Scotland or the court of summary jurisdiction in Northern Ireland, according to where the conduct constituting the trigger offence took place.

35. The scope of measures in an LME order mirrors that of the related undertaking, in that the measures must be just and reasonable. The enforcing authority will suggest measures when it applies to the court for an order, although a court is not obliged to include the measures suggested, or the measures contained in the undertaking. An LME order takes effect on the date specified in it by the court and has the same maximum duration as an undertaking (2 years). When an order is made, a court may release the respondent from a previous order made in the same jurisdiction or from an undertaking given in relation to the same trigger offence.

LME ORDERS FOLLOWING CONVICTION

36. A sentencing court may make an LME order where the respondent has been convicted of a trigger offence. Enforcing Authorities will wish to consider at the time of conviction whether to invite the court to make an LME order in addition to sentencing for the trigger offence.

VARIATION AND DISCHARGE

37. The respondent or the enforcing authority which applied for the order can apply to the court that made the order for it to be varied or discharged. Where the order was made following conviction, only the enforcing authority whose investigation led to the prosecution can apply.

BREACHES OF LME ORDERS

38. An offence is committed if the respondent fails to comply with an LME order.

39. The criminal standard of proof applies – i.e. that it is beyond reasonable doubt that the respondent has breached the LME order. The maximum penalty is 2 years' imprisonment and/or a fine on conviction on indictment and 12 months' imprisonment[3] (6 months in Northern Ireland) and/or a fine on summary conviction.

40. It is not necessary to wait until a new trigger offence is committed before prosecuting for breach of the LME order- it is enough that one of the measures in the order has not been complied with.

41. Bodies corporate, unincorporated associations and partnerships are liable to prosecution, as is an individual company officer where the offending conduct is attributable to their neglect or was committed with their consent or connivance.

NOTES

3 6 months in England and Wales pending commencement of section 154(1) of the Criminal Justice Act 2003.

5. HOW THE ENFORCEMENT REGIME OF LME UNDERTAKINGS AND ORDERS SITS ALONGSIDE EXISTING SANCTIONS ALREADY AVAILABLE TO ENFORCING AUTHORITIES

[4.89]

42. Undertakings may be used in parallel or as an alternative to existing powers available to enforcing authorities (as to which see paragraph 2). Enforcing authorities will determine the appropriate approach to adopt in each case based on their assessment of the best means of preventing or reducing the risk of further labour market offences being committed by the business in question. For example, an employment agency may have been fined for contravening the restriction on charging a work finding fee. If this is not a first offence or if the impact on workers is significant, EAS may consider it appropriate to seek an undertaking that the agency will not charge a work finding fee. This would prevent that agency treating the fine as an acceptable business overhead and charging the fee again within the validity of the undertaking. Individuals in the agency may ultimately face a custodial sentence (if it breaches the undertaking and a court makes an LME order) if it carries on contravening this restriction.

43. LME undertakings and orders are an additional tool in more serious and persistent cases, where the enforcing authority is of the view that existing civil sanctions will not prevent or stop the non-compliance and prosecution is not yet proportionate. For example, a previous civil penalty or other sanction may have already been given but the offending behaviour has continued or the business has resorted to a different type of non-compliance in order to maintain profits. The existence of an undertaking or order will ensure that there are consequences for businesses which treat a civil penalty or fine as an acceptable overhead and continue to mistreat workers.

44. The situation should be assessed on a case by case basis to ensure that the sanction is proportionate to the trigger offence. For example, although the primary objective of NMW enforcement is to recover money for the worker, and this may be achieved by a notice of underpayment, an undertaking may be appropriate alongside a notice in order to maintain compliance where there is a risk of further offending. An undertaking could also deal with any associated obstruction by requiring the employer to produce records within a specified timescale.

45. Although it is ultimately an operational decision for enforcing authorities whether or not to seek an undertaking, the LME regime has been designed to provide an additional tool against labour market exploitation and there is an expectation that it will be used where it is the best tool to prevent non-compliance. The Director may make recommendations in their annual strategy on the manner in which the LME undertaking and orders regime may best be used to target non-compliance. The regime will be reflected in the Government's NMW enforcement policy document,[4] EAS's enforcement policy statement[5] and the GLAA's enforcement statement on prosecution.[6]

46. It may be appropriate to use an LME undertaking for a first offence if the impact on workers is significant (especially if a prosecution is not yet being pursued) or a number of trigger offences are discovered simultaneously e.g. NMW underpayment combined with poor record keeping or obstruction. Relevant factors (as set out at paragraph 17 above) would include the extent of the underpayment, the number of workers affected and whether poor record keeping is intentional, reckless or the result of straightforward administrative error. An LME undertaking or order is designed to reduce the risk of future non-compliance and therefore complements existing sanctions which address past non-compliance. As stated above, the notice seeking the undertaking must set out how the particular measures prevent or reduce the risk of the particular non-compliance in question.

CASE STUDY 3:

Regime used alongside existing sanctions.

Employment agency fined for charging work finding fee. Persistent offender, so undertaking sought including measure requiring alteration to contract/registration form and no other fees to be charged without reference to the enforcing authority to ensure that they are legal, and not used to mask further non-compliance and hide recruitment fees

NOTES

4 https://www.gov.uk/government/publications/enforcing-national-minimum-wage-law

5 https://www.gov.uk/government/publications/employment-agency-standards-eas-inspectorate-enforcement-policy-statement

[6] http://www.gla.gov.uk/our-impact/how-we-inspect-and-prosecute/ - see prosecution

6. HOW THE ENFORCEMENT AUTHORITIES WILL WORK TOGETHER

[4.90]
47. All three enforcing authorities have the power to seek undertakings, apply for orders, and investigate the offence of breaching an LME order, where the trigger offence is in their own area (sections 14, 18 and 26 of the Immigration Act 2016 and see paragraphs 12–15 above).

48. In addition, the BEIS Secretary of State has made arrangements with the GLAA for certain officers who have been trained appropriately to act for the purposes of the National Minimum Wage Act 1998 and the Employment Agencies Act 1973 in England and Wales.

49. As the GLAA is the only enforcing authority whose remit covers all trigger offences, where trigger offences are committed under more than one area of legislation (see paragraphs 12–15 above), the GLAA is the only body which can co-ordinate activity and seek the undertaking/order. This is true even where there is no Gangmasters (Licensing) Act offence. HMRC NMW/EAS will continue to be involved/provide expert witness testimony on the following aspects in respect of their own legislation:

- framing measures in an undertaking;
- negotiating with the business during the 14 day period on any alternative proposals for securing compliance;
- monitoring compliance with undertakings or orders, including advising on whether a measure is still necessary to prevent non-compliance (a pre-requisite for undertakings);
- applications to the court for an order;
- variation of an order (either making an application or responding);
- responding to appeals against an order;
- prosecutions.

50. Enforcing authorities will work together closely to identify the appropriate response to non-compliance where more than one enforcing authority is involved. The Government's intention is that a business should only be subject to one undertaking at a time wherever possible.

TRANSPARENCY IN SUPPLY CHAINS ETC. A PRACTICAL GUIDE GUIDANCE ISSUED UNDER SECTION 54(9) OF THE MODERN SLAVERY ACT 2015 (2017)

[4.91]

NOTES

This Guidance was originally issued by the Home Office in October 2015, and was reissued in October 2017. It is made under the authority of s 54(9) of the Modern Slavery Act 2015 at **[1.1968]**. As formal guidance it has no statutory force and there are no sanctions for failure to follow the guidance, but it is reproduced here for its value as official guidance on how to discharge the statutory duties imposed by s 54. See also 'Modern slavery guidance for businesses' (March 2018) at: www.gov.uk/government/publications/transparency-in-supply-chains-a-practical-guide.

CONTENTS

HOME SECRETARY FOREWORD

[4.92]
Modern slavery is a heinous crime and tackling it is a top priority for this Government and for me personally as Home Secretary.

Businesses have a vital role to play. Modern slavery is a brutal way of maximising profits, by producing goods and services at ever lower costs with scant regard for the terrible impact this has on individuals. But my message is clear. Businesses must not be knowingly or unknowingly complicit in this horrendous and sickening crime.

This updated guidance, which explains how businesses should comply with the Modern Slavery Act, builds on our experience since the landmark Act was introduced in 2015. The Act requires all large businesses to produce an annual statement setting out the steps they have taken to prevent modern slavery in their business and supply chains. This refreshed guidance lays out our expectations for these statements, including more explanation of what best practice looks like.

Of course, these transparency statements on their own are not enough. The challenge for businesses is to take serious and effective steps to identify and root out contemporary slavery which can exist in any supply chain, in any industry. All businesses must be vigilant and aim to continuously improve.

The Prime Minister has described modern slavery as the great human rights issue of our time. It is simply not acceptable that anyone should be profiting, however indirectly, from this appalling abuse and exploitation. All businesses must take sustained and concerted action to ensure this is not the case.

We are committed to supporting businesses in this work and will keep this guidance under review. I would like to thank all of the organisations, businesses and trade bodies who have provided input to this guidance, as well as those businesses who are already leading the fight.

Together we will spot the signs of abuse, together we will help those who cannot help themselves and together, we will lead the way in defeating modern slavery.

Rt Hon Amber Rudd MP

Home Secretary

1. INTRODUCTION

[4.93]
The Transparency in Supply Chains provision in the Modern Slavery Act seeks to address the role of businesses in preventing modern slavery from occurring in their supply chains and organisations.

1.1 Modern slavery is a crime resulting in an abhorrent abuse of human rights. It is constituted in the Modern Slavery Act 2015 by the offences of 'slavery, servitude and forced or compulsory labour' and 'human trafficking'. A full definition of modern slavery is included at Annex A.

1.2 Many organisations are already taking action to promote ethical business practices and policies that protect workers from being abused and exploited in their own organisation and global supply chains.

1.3 However, there are still far too many people in the world being treated as commodities. There are also far too many organisations ignoring such abuses or who are knowingly responsible for policies and practices that result in workers being subjected to modern slavery in their operations.

1.4 The Government has introduced a provision in the Modern Slavery Act 2015 which requires certain businesses to produce a statement setting out the steps they have taken to ensure there is no modern slavery in their own business and their supply chains. If an organisation has taken no steps to do this, their statement should say so. The measure is designed to create a level playing field between those businesses, whose turnover is over a certain threshold, which act responsibly and those that need to change their policies and practices. However, the Government wants to encourage businesses to do more, not just because they are legally obliged to, but also because they recognise it is the right thing to do.

1.5 One key purpose of this measure is to prevent modern slavery in organisations and their supply chains. A means to achieve this is to increase transparency by ensuring the public, consumers, employees and investors know what steps an organisation is taking to tackle modern slavery. Those organisations already taking action can quickly and simply articulate the work already underway and planned. Organisations will need to build on what they are doing year on year. Their first statements may show how they are starting to act on the issue and their planned actions to investigate or collaborate with others to effect change.

1.6 This document sets out the basic requirements of the legislation, as well as advice on what can be included in a statement to give assurance to those scrutinising the statements.

This document provides guidance on how the Government expects organisations to develop a credible and accurate slavery and human trafficking statement each year and sets out what must be included in a statement.

1.7 A focus on tackling modern slavery not only protects vulnerable workers and helps prevent and remedy severe human rights violations, it can bring a number of business benefits too. These include:

- protecting and enhancing an organisation's reputation and brand;
- protecting and growing the organisation's customer base as more consumers seek out businesses with higher ethical standards;
- improved investor confidence;
- greater staff retention and loyalty based on values and respect; and
- developing more responsive, stable and innovative supply chains.

1.8 It is important for large organisations to be transparent and accountable, not just to investors but to other groups including employees, consumers and the public whose lives are affected by their business activity. Due diligence processes and reporting are essential management tools that improve risk identification and long-term social, environmental as well as financial performance.

1.9 Reporting requirements can drive better strategic understanding of the risks and impacts of an organisation's core activities in relation to the environment and human rights. The disclosure of these management tools allows investors to move capital towards more sustainable, responsible organisations and strengthen the long-term ethical sustainability of the financial system.

2. THE MODERN SLAVERY ACT 2015

[4.94]

Every organisation carrying on a business in the UK with a total annual turnover of £36m or more will be required to produce a slavery and human trafficking statement for each financial year of the organisation.

2.1 Section 54 of the Modern Slavery Act 2015 gives the Secretary of State the power to issue guidance. Section 54 is contained in Annex A.

2.2 The provision in the Act requires that any commercial organisation in any sector, which supplies goods or services, and carries on a business or part of a business in the UK, and is above a specified total turnover, must produce a slavery and human trafficking statement for each financial year of the organisation. For the purposes of this requirement, 'supply chain' has its everyday meaning. Regulations have set the total turnover threshold at £36m. The statement must set out what steps they have taken during the financial year to ensure that modern slavery is not occurring in their supply chains and in their own organisation. Further information on calculating the turnover of an organisation is contained in Chapter 3.

2.3 The Act specifically states that the statement must include 'the steps the organisation has taken during the financial year to ensure that slavery and human trafficking is not taking place in any of its supply chains, and in any part of its own business'. When the Act refers to ensuring that slavery and human trafficking is not taking part in any part of its supply chain, this does not mean that the organisation in question must guarantee that the entire supply chain is slavery free. Instead, it means an organisation must set out the steps it has taken in relation to any part of the supply chain (that is, it should capture all the actions it has taken).

2.4 The provision requires an organisation to be transparent about what is happening within its business. This means that if an organisation has taken no steps to ensure slavery and human trafficking is not taking place they must still publish a statement stating this to be the case.

2.5 The Government encourages all businesses to develop an appropriate and effective response to modern slavery. Businesses may choose to take further action over and above what is prescribed by the Act but this will be a decision for individual businesses themselves. The provision seeks to create a race to the top by encouraging businesses to be transparent about what they are doing, thus increasing competition to drive up standards.

FAILURE TO COMPLY

2.6 If a business fails to produce a slavery and human trafficking statement for a particular financial year the Secretary of State may seek an injunction through the High Court (or, in Scotland civil proceedings for specific performance of a statutory duty under section 45 of the Court of Session Act 1988) requiring the organisation to comply. If the organisation fails to comply with the injunction, they will be in contempt of a court order, which is punishable by an unlimited fine.

2.7 In practice failure to comply with the provision will mean the organisation has not produced a statement, published it on their website (where they have one) or has not set out the steps taken by the organisation in the relevant financial year. This can include setting out that it has taken no such steps, or is just beginning investigations. Whilst we would encourage clear, detailed and informative statements legal compliance does not turn on how well the statement is written or presented (provided that it sets out the steps taken or that no steps have in fact been taken).

2.8 We expect organisations to build on their statements year on year and for the statements to evolve and improve over time. However, a failure to comply with the provision, or a statement that an organisation has taken no steps, may damage the reputation of the business. It will be for consumers, investors and Non-Governmental Organisations to engage and/or apply pressure where they believe a business has not taken sufficient steps.

3. WHO IS REQUIRED TO COMPLY?

[4.95]

3.1 Any organisation in any part of a group structure will be required to comply with the provision and produce a statement if they:

- are a body corporate or a partnership (described as an "organisation" in this document), wherever incorporated;
- carry on a business, or part of a business, in the UK;
- supply goods or services; and
- have an annual turnover of £36m or more.

3.2 Total turnover is calculated as:

(a) the turnover of that organisation; and

(b) the turnover of any of its subsidiary undertakings (including those operating wholly outside the UK).

3.3 "Turnover" means the amount derived from the provision of goods and services falling within the ordinary activities of the commercial organisation or subsidiary undertaking, after deduction of—

(a) trade discounts;
(b) value added tax; and
(c) any other taxes based on the amounts so derived.

3.4 If any organisation in any part of a group structure meets these requirements, it is legally required to produce a statement. Where a parent and one or more subsidiaries in the same group are required to produce a statement, the parent may produce one statement that subsidiaries can use to meet this requirement (provided that the statement fully covers the steps that each of the organisations required to produce a statement have taken in the relevant financial year).

3.5 A 'commercial organisation' is defined at section 54(12) as a body corporate or partnership which carries on a business, or part of a business, in the UK wherever that organisation was incorporated or formed. The key concept here is that of an organisation which 'carries on a business'. The courts will be the final arbiter as to whether an organisation 'carries on a business' in the UK taking into account the particular facts in individual cases. However, the following paragraphs set out the Government's intention as to how this should work.

3.6 There are many ways in which a body corporate or a partnership in the UK can pursue business objectives. The Government expects that whether such a body or partnership can be said to be carrying on a business will be answered by applying a common sense approach. So long as the organisation in question is incorporated (by whatever means) or is a partnership, it does not matter if it pursues primarily charitable or educational aims or purely public functions. The organisation will be caught if it engages in commercial activities and has a total turnover of £36m – irrespective of the purpose for which profits are made.

3.7 As regards bodies incorporated, or partnerships formed, outside the United Kingdom, whether such bodies can properly be regarded as carrying on a business or part of a business 'in any part of the United Kingdom' will again be answered by applying a common sense approach.

3.8 However, we anticipate that applying a common sense approach will mean that organisations that do not have a demonstrable business presence in the United Kingdom will not be caught by the provision. Likewise, having a UK subsidiary will not, in itself, mean that a parent company is carrying on a business in the UK, since a subsidiary may act completely independently of its parent or other group companies.

FRANCHISE MODELS

3.9 Some organisations operate under a franchise model. Where the turnover of a franchiser is above the £36m threshold they will be required to produce a slavery and human trafficking statement. In determining the total turnover of a business operating a franchise model, only the turnover of the franchiser will be considered. The turnover of any franchisee using the franchiser's trademark and distributing goods or providing services will not be used in calculating the franchiser's turnover. However, franchisers who meet the turnover threshold may wish to consider the impact on their brand of the activities of franchisees in relation to modern slavery, and in so doing report on the steps taken to ensure the franchise as a whole is free from modern slavery.

3.10 Where the turnover of a franchisee is above the £36m threshold they will be required to produce a slavery and human trafficking statement in their own right.

PARENT AND SUBSIDIARY ORGANISATIONS

3.11 Each parent and subsidiary organisation (whether it is UK based or not) that meets the requirements set out in 3.1 above must produce a statement of the steps they have taken during the financial year to ensure slavery and human trafficking is not taking place in any part of its own business and in any of its supply chains. If a foreign subsidiary is part of the parent company's supply chain or own business, the parent company's statement should cover any actions taken in relation to that subsidiary to prevent modern slavery. Where a foreign parent is carrying on a business or part of a business in the UK, it will be required to produce a statement.

3.12 There is nothing to prevent a foreign subsidiary or parent from producing a statement, even if they are not legally obliged to do so. This provision is all about improving transparency to prevent slavery and forced labour occurring.

3.13 If a parent company is seen to be ignoring the behaviour of its non-UK subsidiaries, this may still reflect badly on the parent company. As such, seeking to cover non-UK subsidiaries in a parent company statement, or asking those non-UK subsidiaries to produce a statement themselves (if they are not legally required to do so already), would represent good practice and would demonstrate that the company is committed to preventing modern slavery. This is highly recommended, especially in cases where the non-UK subsidiary is in a high-risk industry or location.

SMALLER ORGANISATIONS

3.14 Organisations which do not meet the requirements in the Act, for example by having a turnover below £36m, can still choose to voluntarily produce a 'slavery and human trafficking statement'. Smaller organisations may be asked by those they are supplying goods or services to if they have a statement or policy setting out their approach to tackling modern slavery, especially if they are bidding for contracts with larger businesses above the threshold. Therefore, smaller organisations may find it helpful to voluntarily produce a statement as a means of managing these requests and providing a level of assurance to their customers. Even if the legislation does not apply, we would encourage all businesses to be open and transparent about their recruitment practices, policies and procedures in relation to modern slavery and to take steps that are consistent and proportionate with their sector, size and operational reach.

4. WRITING A SLAVERY AND HUMAN TRAFFICKING STATEMENT

[4.96]

4.1 The slavery and human trafficking statement will be a public-facing document. To aid transparency the statement should be written in simple language that is easily understood (the Plain English Campaign is well placed to assist with this – www.plainenglish.co.uk/). The statement can be succinct but cover all the relevant points and provide appropriate links to relevant publications, documents or policies for the organisation.

4.2 The Government has not been prescriptive about the layout or specific content of a slavery and human trafficking statement. It is up to organisations how they present information in the statement and how much detail they provide. However, organisations must include in the statement all the steps they have taken. The information presented in the statement will be determined by the organisation's sector, the complexity of its structure and supply chains, or the particular sectors and nations its suppliers are working in.

Top Tips

Keep the statement succinct but cover all the relevant points – if you can provide appropriate links to relevant publications, documents or policies for your organisation, do so.

Writing the statement in simple language will ensure that it is easily accessible to everyone.

The statement should be in English but may also be provided in other languages, relevant to the organisation's business and supply chains.

Specifying actions by specific country will help readers to understand the context of any actions or steps taken to minimise risks.

4.3 An organisation may already be undertaking procedures or have specific policies (such as CSR or Ethical Trade activities) that go some way to addressing the issue of modern slavery and may already be disclosing this in some form (for example, via a strategic statement as required under Chapter 4A of the Companies Act 2006). Therefore, it is not necessary for an organisation to start from scratch. Any relevant material used in other related reports may be used in an organisation's slavery and human trafficking statement. Statements should be true and refer to actual steps undertaken or begun.

4.4 It is not necessary for businesses to replicate the wording of an organisation's policies on every issue directly in the statement. Instead, a business may choose to support the narrative in the statement by providing relevant links to a particular document or policy that is publicly available and already published on the organisation's website.

Case study

ITP (the International Tourism Partnership), part of Business in the Community, is a non-profit member organisation which brings the hotel sector together to collaborate on social and environmental issues. Since 2010, the organisation has run a human trafficking working group to raise awareness, share best practice and develop practical solutions to tackle the risk of human trafficking and modern day slavery in the hotel industry. Children and adults may be trafficked via hotels for sexual exploitation and the volume of lower-skilled jobs in the industry can provide an opportunity for unscrupulous individuals and agencies to put people into forced or bonded labour. ITP also provides an interface for dialogue with specialist organisations working in this area. Outputs to date include a Position Statement, Know How Guide and Guidelines for Checking Recruitment Agencies. Fran Hughes, ITP Director, says; "Collaboration on this issue has accelerated learning and action on this key issue and helped the hotel industry work together to develop resources and responses. I would urge other sectors to come together to see how they may work together and with their stakeholders to advance activity to address trafficking and slavery risk."

To access ITP's resources, see:

tourismpartnership.org/human-trafficking/

5. THE STRUCTURE OF A STATEMENT

[4.97]

A statement must contain the steps an organisation has taken to prevent modern slavery in its supply chains and own business.

5.1 The Modern Slavery Act, does not dictate in precise detail what a statement must include or how it should be structured. It does, however, provide a non-exhaustive list of information that may be included.

5.2 A statement should aim to include information about:

(a) the organisation's structure, its business and its supply chains;
(b) its policies in relation to slavery and human trafficking;
(c) its due diligence processes in relation to slavery and human trafficking in its business and supply chains;
(d) the parts of its business and supply chains where there is a risk of slavery and human trafficking taking place, and the steps it has taken to assess and manage that risk;
(e) its effectiveness in ensuring that slavery and human trafficking is not taking place in its business or supply chains, measured against such performance indicators as it considers appropriate;
(f) the training and capacity building about slavery and human trafficking available to its staff.

5.3 The organisation should paint a detailed picture of all the steps it has taken to address and remedy modern slavery, and the effectiveness of all such steps.

5.4 **Annex E** provides information on the type of activity that could be included under each heading and why such information would be useful in a statement.

5.5 Organisations should be aware that their statement will be assessed by the public, investors, the media and other external parties. They will expect to see year-on-year improvements outlining practical progress on how they are tackling the risks and incidence of modern slavery in their operations and supply chains. Organisations are encouraged to be as open and transparent as possible, as this is likely to drive more honesty and collaboration between organisations in the knowledge that no single business can tackle the problem alone.

6. APPROVING A STATEMENT

[4.98]

The statement must be approved and signed by a director, member or partner of the organisation.

6.1 The Modern Slavery Act requires a slavery and human trafficking statement to be approved and signed by an appropriate senior person in the business. This ensures senior level accountability, leadership and responsibility for modern slavery and gives it the serious attention it deserves. An organisation's top management will be best placed to foster a culture in which modern slavery is not tolerated in any form. They need to lead and drive the measures required to address this problem throughout the business.

6.2 To effectively combat modern slavery, senior managers will need to ensure everyone in an organisation is alive to the risks of modern slavery. This is to ensure informed decisions are made in a timely way which mitigate and manage these risks, and to monitor the implementation of relevant policies. They will need to ensure credible evidence is used in identifying and reporting on human rights risks in supply chains, as well as to remedy workers and rectify problems where appropriate.

6.3 The person who is required to sign the statement depends on the type of organisation. For a body corporate (other than a limited liability partnership), the statement must be approved by the board of directors and signed by a director (or equivalent). Where this is the case, it is best practice for the director who signs the statement to also sit on the board that approved the statement. Where the organisation is a limited liability partnership it must be approved by the members and signed by a designated member. It is best practice for the statement to include the date on which the board or members approved the statement. For a limited partnership, registered under the Limited Partnerships Act 1907, a general partner must sign it and if the organisation is any other kind of partnership, a partner must sign it.

7. PUBLISHING A STATEMENT

[4.99]

The statement must be published on an organisation's website with a link in a prominent place on the homepage.

7.1 The Act requires each organisation to publish a slavery and human trafficking statement on their website and include a link in a prominent place on its homepage. The purpose of this measure is to increase transparency and it is vital that the statement can be easily accessible by anyone who wants to see it — the public, consumers, employees, NGOs or investors. For organisations with no website, a copy of the statement is to be provided to anyone who requests one in writing. The copy must be provided to the requestor within 30 days of the receipt of the request, where a statement has been produced and is available.

7.2 In some instances, where there is a complex organisational structure, an organisation may have more than one outward-facing website. For organisations where there is more than one website we recommend placing the statement on the most appropriate website relating to the organisation's business in the UK. Where there is more than one relevant website we recommend placing a copy of the statement or a link to the statement on each relevant website. This will increase transparency and ensure recognition for the efforts the business is making.

7.3 The Act is clear that the link must be in a prominent place on the home page itself. A prominent place may mean a modern slavery link that is directly visible on the home page or part of an obvious drop-down menu on that page. The link should be clearly marked so that the contents are apparent. We recommend a link such as 'Modern Slavery Act Transparency Statement'.

7.4 Organisations are legally required to publish a statement for each financial year of their organisation. Organisations should publish their statement as soon as possible after their financial year end. We expect this to be, at most, within six months of the organisation's financial year end. Organisations may wish to publish these statements at the same time as they publish other annual accounts.

7.5 Organisations should look to keep historic statements from previous years available online even when new statements are published. This will allow the public to compare statements between years and monitor the progress of the organisation over time.

7.6 Legally an organisation is required to complete a statement for each financial year (of that organisation) in which their turnover exceeds the specified threshold. However, we strongly recommend that businesses who produce a slavery and human trafficking statement in one financial year should continue to produce a statement in future years even if their turnover has fallen below the £36m threshold. Producing a regular annual statement will ensure organisations can build upon earlier statements and demonstrate to the public, consumers and investors that they are being transparent, not because they are required to do so but because they consider it important.

8. RESPONDING TO AN INCIDENT OF MODERN SLAVERY

[4.100]

Any incident of modern slavery should be dealt with appropriately and relevant remedies made available to potential victims.

8.1 Modern slavery is extremely prevalent across the globe. The ILO estimates that there are 21 million people in forced labour in the world today. It is important that businesses do not deny or try to ignore the problem. The Modern Slavery Act provisions are designed to encourage businesses to tackle slavery head on.

8.2 If a specific case of modern slavery is identified here in the UK, it should be reported to the police immediately on 101. If potential victims are in immediate danger the standard 999 emergency number should be used.

8.3 In the UK, mechanisms are in place to assist victims of slavery and human trafficking. If you identify a potential victim they can be referred to the National Referral Mechanism to be formally identified as a victim of modern slavery and offered Government-funded support. Referral for potential adult victims is by consent. Government-funded support is provided through a range of specialist providers across the UK. A list of the relevant organisations is provided at Annex F.

8.4 When training employees in the UK to identify the signs of modern slavery and to flag up potential issues, you should inform them about the Modern Slavery Helpline on 0800 0121 700. This will allow anyone who thinks they may have come across an instance of modern slavery, or indeed who may be a victim themselves, to call for more information and guidance on what to do next.

8.5 If modern slavery is identified or suspected abroad, then the response should be tailored to the local circumstances. In some cases the most appropriate response will be to engage with local NGOs, industry bodies, trade unions or other support organisations to attempt to remedy the situation. In other cases, it will be more appropriate to contact local Government and law enforcement bodies. Organisations must always consider which approach would produce the safest outcome for the potential victims but should always remember the economic influence and control which the organisation holds over those who may be committing these crimes.

8.6 If the local response seems inadequate and the local company seems unable to address coercion, threat, abuse and exploitation of workers, then the organisation should seek to give that company more support, guidance and incentives to tackle the issue. This could include working with at-risk suppliers to provide training, messages and business incentives or guidance to implement anti-slavery policies.

8.6 If, after receiving support, the supplier is not taking the issue seriously, the organisation ultimately could reconsider their commercial relationship with that supplier. These actions could then be included in the next statement produced.

8.7 Organisations can benefit from working collaboratively with others – such as industry bodies and multi-stakeholder organisations – to improve industry-wide labour standards and to advocate for improved laws and policies in sourcing countries, where appropriate. This could be more likely to achieve long-term change than working alone.

8.8 The Organisation for Economic Co-operation and Development (OECD) has produced detailed guidance for Multi-National Enterprises (MNEs) on responsible business conduct. Whilst not specifically focused on modern slavery, they provide principles and standards for responsible business conduct in areas such as employment and industrial relations and human rights which may help organisations when seeking to respond to or prevent modern slavery. The full guidelines can be accessed online here: mneguidelines.oecd.org/text/. There are other useful guides, such as Walk Free Business Guide business.walkfree.org and Verite, 2011 'Fair Trade Hiring Kit' www.verite.org/helpwanted/toolkit.

8.9 The Ethical Trading Initiative provides advice, support and training on these issues. The ETI Base Code is a globally recognised benchmark for businesses on ethical trade. www.ethicaltrade.org

ANNEX A
MODERN SLAVERY DEFINITION

[4.101]

Modern Slavery is a term used to encapsulate both offences in the Modern Slavery Act: slavery, servitude and forced or compulsory labour; and human trafficking. The offences are set out in section 1 and section 2 of the Act, which can be found at:

www.legislation.gov.uk/ukpga/2015/30/section/1/enacted

www.legislation.gov.uk/ukpga/2015/30/section/2/enacted

DEFINITION OF SLAVERY AND SERVITUDE

Slavery, in accordance with the 1926 Slavery Convention, is the status or condition of a person over whom all or any of the powers attaching to the right of ownership are exercised. Since legal 'ownership' of a person is not possible, the key element of slavery is the behaviour on the part of the offender as if he/ she did own the person, which deprives the victim of their freedom.

Servitude is the obligation to provide services that is imposed by the use of coercion and includes the obligation for a 'serf' to live on another person's property and the impossibility of changing his or her condition.

DEFINITION OF FORCED OR COMPULSORY LABOUR

Forced or compulsory labour is defined in international law by the ILO's Forced Labour Convention 29 and Protocol. It involves coercion, either direct threats of violence or more subtle forms of compulsion.

The key elements are that work or service is exacted from any person under the menace of any penalty and for which the person has not offered him/her self voluntarily.

DEFINITION OF HUMAN TRAFFICKING

An offence of human trafficking requires that a person arranges or facilitates the travel of another person with a view to that person being exploited. The offence can be committed even where the victim consents to the travel. This reflects the fact that a victim may be deceived by the promise of a better life or job or may be a child who is influenced to travel by an adult. In addition, the exploitation of the potential victim does not need to have taken place for the offence to be committed. It means that the arranging or facilitating of the movement of the individual was with a view to exploiting them for sexual exploitation or non-sexual exploitation. The meaning of exploitation is set out here: www.legislation.gov.uk/ukpga/2015/30/section/3/enacted.

DEFINITION OF CHILD LABOUR

Child labour is defined by international standards as children below 12 years working in any economic activities, those aged 12 – 14 engaged in more than light work, and all children engaged in the worst forms of child labour (ILO).

The term "child labour" is often defined as work that deprives children of their childhood, their potential and their dignity, and that is harmful to physical and mental development. Whether or not particular forms of "work" can be called "child labour" depends on the child's age, the type and hours of work performed, the conditions under which it is performed and the objectives pursued by individual countries.

Children can be particularly vulnerable to exploitation, but child labour will not always constitute modern slavery. It will still be necessary to determine whether, based on the facts of the case, the children in question are being exploited in such a way as to constitute slavery, servitude and forced or compulsory labour or human trafficking. For example, it is possible for children to undertake some 'light work' which would not necessarily constitute modern slavery. 'Light work' is defined by article 7 of ILO Convention No. 138.

Children do have particular vulnerabilities which should be considered when determining whether modern slavery is taking place. The Modern Slavery Act 2015 specifically recognises that it is not necessary for a child to have been forced, threatened or deceived into their situation for it to be defined as exploitation.

THE WORST FORMS OF CHILD LABOUR

The worst forms of child labour are very likely to constitute modern slavery.

The worst forms of child labour are defined by article 3 of ILO Convention No. 182 as:

(a) all forms of slavery or practices similar to slavery, such as the sale and trafficking of children, debt bondage and serfdom and forced or compulsory labour, including forced or compulsory recruitment of children for use in armed conflict;
(b) the use, procuring or offering of a child for prostitution, for the production of pornography or for pornographic performances;
(c) the use, procuring or offering of a child for illicit activities, in particular for the production and trafficking of drugs as defined in the relevant international treaties;
(d) work which, by its nature or the circumstances in which it is carried out, is likely to harm the health, safety or morals of children.

BEHAVIOUR CONSTITUTING MODERN SLAVERY

Identifying potential victims of modern slavery can be a challenge because the crime can manifest itself in many different ways. There is a spectrum of abuse and it is not always clear at what point, for example, poor working practices and lack of health and safety awareness seep into instances of human trafficking, slavery or forced labour in a work environment. However, businesses have a responsibility to ensure that workers are not being exploited, that they are safe and that relevant employment (include wage and work hour), health and safety and human rights laws and international standards are adhered to, including freedom of movement and communications.

There will be cases of exploitation that, whilst being poor labour conditions, nevertheless do not meet the threshold for modern slavery – for example, someone may choose to work for less than the national minimum wage, or in undesirable or unsafe conditions, perhaps for long work hours, without being forced or deceived. Such practices may not amount to modern slavery if the employee can leave freely and easily without threat to themselves or their family. Organisations do still nevertheless have a legal duty to drive out poor labour practices in their business, and a moral duty to influence and incentivise continuous improvements in supply chains.

ANNEX B
SECTION 54 – TRANSPARENCY IN SUPPLY CHAINS ETC

(*Section 54 of the Modern Slavery Act 2015 (omitted here for reasons of space) is set out in full at* **[1.1968]**.)

ANNEX C
EXAMPLE OF A GROUP STRUCTURE WITH A SUBSIDIARY BASED ABROAD

[4.102]
As set out in paragraph 3.1 an organisation must comply with section 54 of the Modern Slavery Act 2015 if they:

- are a body corporate (wherever incorporated) or a partnership;
- carry on a business, or part of a business, in the UK;
- supply goods or services; and
- have an annual turnover of £36m or more.

For simplicity, these are referred to below as the 'tests in the Act'. An organisation that meets all of the tests in the Act must publish a slavery and human trafficking statement.

An organisation's turnover is to be calculated as including the turnover of any of its subsidiaries, regardless of where those subsidiaries are based or carry on their business.

Whether a parent organisation's statement must include the steps taken in relation to its subsidiaries needs to be determined on a case-by-case basis.

A slavery and human trafficking statement is a statement of the steps the organisation has taken during the financial year to ensure slavery and human trafficking is not taking place

in any of its supply chains, and

in any part of its own business, or

a statement that the organisation has taken no such steps.

Therefore, a parent organisation which meets all the tests in the Act will have to include the steps taken in relation to its subsidiaries in its statement if, depending on the particular facts, the activities of the subsidiary in fact form part of the supply chain or business of the parent.

This will be the case even if the subsidiary in question does not meet all the tests in the Act (for example, if its turnover is below £36m). Of course, if the subsidiary meets all the tests in the Act in its own right, then it is required to produce a statement in its own right.

It will be for individual parent organisations to determine whether their subsidiaries in fact form a part of their own business or supply chain. The example below is given just for illustrative purposes to help explain the principles set out above.

EXAMPLE SCENARIO

Parent A	Meets all the tests in the act and is required to produce a statement
Subsidiary B	Meets all the tests in the act and is required to produce a statement
Subsidiary C	Meets all the tests in the act and is required to produce a statement
Subsidiary D	Does **not** meet all the tests in the act. It is a body corporate or partnership, it does supply goods or services, it does have a turnover above £36m, but it **does not** carry on a business or part of a business in the UK. It is based abroad and entirely operates abroad.

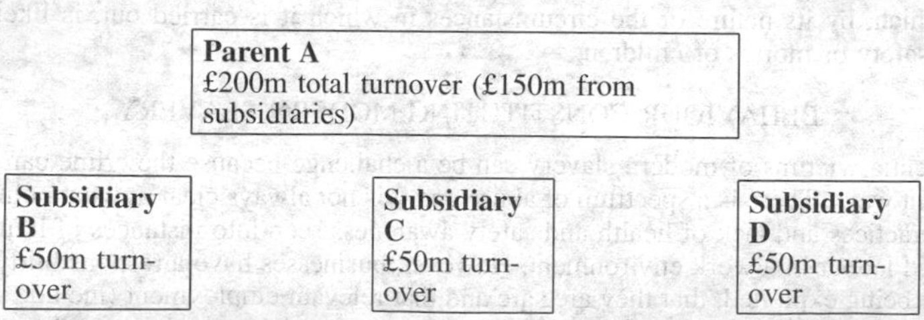

In this scenario parent A must produce a slavery and human trafficking statement setting out the steps it has taken to ensure that slavery and human trafficking is not taking place in its supply chains or own business. So must subsidiary B and subsidiary C. The three organisations can agree to produce a single statement that sets out that steps that each has taken. If not, parent A, subsidiary B and subsidiary C must produce separate slavery and human trafficking statements (although parent A's statement will need in any event to cover steps taken in relation to its subsidiaries in its statement if, depending on the particular facts, the activities of those subsidiaries in fact form part of the supply chain or business of the parent).

In relation to subsidiary D, there is no requirement for subsidiary D to prepare its own statement. However if, on the particular facts, the activities of subsidiary D form part of the supply chain or business of the parent, the parent's statement should include all steps taken in relation to subsidiary D).

If parent A determined that subsidiary D was neither a part of its own business nor a part of its supply chain, it could choose not to include steps taken in relation to subsidiary D in its statement. However, as set out in paragraph 3.13, including these steps would still represent good practice and would demonstrate that parent A is committed to preventing modern slavery. This is highly recommended, especially in cases where the non-UK subsidiary is in a high-risk industry or location.

ANNEX D
THE ACT IN THE CONTEXT OF OTHER REPORTING REQUIREMENTS

[4.103]
Many businesses are already required to undertake non-financial reporting on human rights.

The Government has set out a clear expectation in the National Action Plan on Implementing the UN Guiding Principles on Business and Human Rights. UK organisations should respect internationally recognised human rights wherever they operate and treat the risk of causing or contributing to gross human rights abuses as a legal compliance issue.[1]

The UN Guiding Principles (UNGPs) reporting framework is voluntary but sets out the ways in which businesses can meet their responsibilities with regard to human rights. The UNGPs are centred on three pillars: the duty of States to protect human rights; the responsibility of business to respect human rights; and the need for those affected by abuses to have access to effective remedy. In the UK, these rights are largely enforced by law and a law-abiding business is likely to be compliant with the responsibility to respect human rights within its own operations. However, the UNGPs are clear that the responsibility for businesses extends beyond their own staff and customers to include direct and indirect suppliers, wherever they are located.

Companies Act 2006 (Strategic Report and Directors' Report) Regulations 2013 also require UK quoted companies to report within its Strategic Report on human rights issues 'where necessary for an understanding of the development, performance or position of the company's business'. This includes any policies a business has in relation to these matters and the effectiveness of those policies. The wording in the Companies Act 2006 does not explicitly mention supply chains or modern slavery. It is left to the individual business to determine what policies are relevant and the level of detail required. However, the right to be free from forced labour, slavery and servitude is a fundamental human right under international law, including the European Convention on Human Rights and so may be a consideration in this reporting requirement.

The Financial Reporting Council has issued guidance on how to prepare the Strategic Report, including how to consider human rights related matters in the process of preparing the Strategic Report as a whole. Quoted companies obliged to prepare a Strategic Report, according to the Companies Act, who are also required to prepare a Slavery and Human Trafficking statement should ensure that it meets both requirements. Whilst a joint statement may be possible, it is envisioned most companies will opt for two separate statements.

In October 2014, the European Union adopted a Directive (2014/95/EU) which amended the EU Accounting Directive (2013/34/EU). This amending Directive requires large undertakings that are public interest entities (defined in the Accounting Directive, the definition including credit institutions, insurance undertakings and undertakings whose securities are traded on a regulated market in the EU) with an average number of 500 employees to prepare a 'non-financial statement' as part of their management report. The Directive was transposed into UK law on 19th December 2016 and applies to financial years commencing on, or after, 1st January 2017. The non-financial statement must provide information "to the extent necessary for an understanding of the undertaking's development, performance, position and impact of its activity, relating to, as a minimum, environmental, social and employee matters, respect for human rights, anti-corruption and bribery matters, including:

(a) a brief description of the undertaking's business model;
(b) a description of the policies pursued by the undertaking in relation to those matters, including due diligence processes implemented;
(c) the outcome of those policies;
(d) the principal risks related to those matters linked to the undertaking's operations including, where relevant and proportionate, its business relationships, products or services which are likely to cause adverse impacts in those areas, and how the undertaking manages those risks;
(e) non-financial key performance indicators relevant to the particular business."

Public interest entities that are parent undertakings of a large group exceeding on their balance sheet dates, on a consolidated basis, the criterion of the average number of 500 employees will be required to include in their consolidated management reports a consolidated non-financial statement containing this information.

Whilst there are differences, these new obligations are similar to the requirements for the Strategic Report contained in Chapter 4A of Part 15 of the Companies Act 2006.

Notably, there are similarities between the requirements of the Directive (set out at a) to e) above) and those areas we have set out in the Modern Slavery Act which businesses may include in a statement. This consistency across reporting requirements will ensure that businesses are well placed to comply with the transparency in supply chains measure and the wider non-financial requirements, once they are introduced.

It is likely that many businesses required to undertake non-financial reporting are already reporting on activities related to modern slavery. Businesses may demonstrate the activities and action they are taking in their slavery and human trafficking statement by drawing on existing relevant programmes of activity rather than creating new ones where that is appropriate.

Businesses may also be asked to respond to complaints received against them under the Organisation for Economic Co-operation and Development (OECD) Guidelines for Multinational Enterprises (MNEs). Whilst not specifically focused on modern slavery, the OECD Guidelines provide principles and standards for responsible business conduct in related areas such as employment and industrial relations and human rights. National Contact Points (NCPs) are set up by each country that adheres to the Guidelines and provide a platform for discussion and assistance to stakeholders to help find a resolution for issues arising from complaints of alleged non-observance of the Guidelines. NCPs focus on problem solving, offering good offices and facilitating access to consensual and non-adversarial procedures (e.g. conciliation or mediation). The UK Government expects businesses based or operating in the UK to engage with the UK NCP where complaints are made against them. The UK NCP is not a judicial body, however, and cannot deal with legal cases, e.g. contravention of the Act's modern slavery provisions. Such legal cases should be reported to the relevant authorities, see also Section 9 of these guidelines.

NOTES

1 The full National Action Plan is available online at https://www.gov.uk/government/publications/bhr-action-plan

ANNEX E
INFORMATION IN A SLAVERY AND HUMAN TRAFFICKING STATEMENT

ORGANISATIONAL STRUCTURE AND SUPPLY CHAINS

[4.104]

For businesses to produce an effective statement they will need to have a good understanding of their own supply chains in order to define the boundaries of the report and to support the identification of risk. Consumers, investors, campaigners and the public also need information about the business.

Information to disclose could include:

- the sector(s) the business operates in and whether any of its work is seasonal
- the organisational structure and group relationships
- the countries it sources its goods or services from including high risk countries where modern forms of slavery are prevalent.
- the make-up and complexity of the supply chains
- the businesses operating model
- relationships with suppliers and others, including trade unions and other bodies representing workers

Such information will allow people to consider the statement more effectively. A greater level of detail and explanation of efforts is likely to be more helpful, and perhaps prevent potential stakeholder misunderstanding. However, a huge amount of technical or legal information about a company structure may make the statement more inaccessible to many readers, so there is a balance to be struck here.

ORGANISATIONAL POLICIES

The establishment of effective policies and incentives shape the environment and set the tone of an organisation in assessing, preventing and mitigating the risk of and working to influence and remedy modern slavery in their supply chains and organisation. Clear organisational policies demonstrate an organisation's commitment to this issue and ensures that appropriate and coordinated action is taken throughout the business.

Tackling modern slavery does not necessarily require a standalone policy. It could simply be adapting, and/or clarifying how existing policies and practices, programmes and management systems already work to prevent modern slavery. These policies and approaches may need upgrading as the years pass, and as understanding of the issue and approaches to address it improve.

Case Study

A leading supermarket is collaborating with the Wilberforce Institute for the Study of Slavery and Emancipation (WISE) at Hull University. WISE is initially working with the supermarket through its fresh produce and horticulture supply chain to conduct a modern slavery risk assessment. This will involve in-depth supplier research and will draw on the Global Slavery Index at Hull University – the first comprehensive index of its kind estimating the number of people living in slavery or slavery like conditions in 162 countries.

The risk assessment will include:

- **a review of current ethical sourcing management systems, company policies and existing risk management tools;**
- **research into the challenges faced by suppliers at industry and country level for fresh produce and horticulture; and**
- **recommendations on areas for improvement in addressing modern slavery hotspots and risks with suppliers.**

The research goes beyond an audit based approach and will involve meetings with suppliers operating in high risk areas, suppliers developing good practice, local NGOs, relevant industry bodies and local authorities. The supermarket aims to understand existing challenges faced by suppliers locally and identify current initiatives to improve labour practices. This will provide them with information on the tools, policies and practices that are needed to support suppliers' sites to improve labour management systems and reduce the risk of modern slavery in the long term.

Policies supported by the board of directors and senior management that have the right incentives are likely to influence positive behaviour within the organisation. This may also externally influence suppliers and subcontractors particularly when assessment of risk in their operations is undertaken comprehensively.

If policies and practices are to have the desired effect they must be supported through effective communications and, where appropriate, training, resourcing and collaboration of effort by appropriately skilled personnel. Policies should be established and clearly communicated so that anti-slavery activity within a company and its supply chains becomes embedded as standard practice, which all staff are aware of and incentivised to partner on and support. It is up to each business how detailed they want to make their policy on modern slavery. However, some of the questions that an organisation might want to consider when drawing up a modern slavery policy could be:

- What minimum labour standards are expected of the business, its subsidiaries and suppliers, and how do these align to industry standards?
- Who in the business is responsible for a) ensuring efforts are made to investigate and remediate the risk of modern slavery in the business and/or supply chains, and b) ensuring that basic labour standards are met, and how are such leaders financially incentivised and resourced to do so?
- How does the business factor legal and fair full labour costs into production and sourcing costs to avoid the need for seemingly cheaper slave or bonded labour in operations or the supply chain?
- What is the company's policy where a supplier is found to have been involved in modern slavery?
- When entering into a contract with a new supplier or renewing contracts with existing suppliers what checks, assurances, investigations will the company conduct or accept?
- What support or guidance is available to business operations or suppliers willing to remediate situations of slavery or forced labour found?
- What due diligence will the company commit to conducting regarding its supply chains (see section below on due diligence)?
- What is the company policy to support whistle-blowing? What procedures are in place to facilitate reporting, including reporting by workers through helplines?
- What is the company's policy and approach to remediation for workers if and where cases of modern slavery and forced labour are found; and what measures are taken to protect them from further victimisation or vulnerability?

If an organisation is able to provide a clear policy on modern slavery, with clear rules in place about how the company will handle these sorts of issues, then the company should be able to take a consistent, sustainable and continuous improvement approach to tackling modern slavery. Clear policies should mean that all employees in the organisation and the organisation's suppliers know how to, and are resourced to prevent or identify exploitation. They should provide information about the first steps when modern slavery is identified and broadly how and with whom to partner (in and/or outside the business) in influencing remedy for workers (or ceasing of that business relationship in the worst cases).

Information to disclose could include:

- The process for policy development
- Policies that concern business relationships , for example, a Supplier Code of Conduct
- Recruitment policy
- Procurement policy and incentives to combat modern slavery
- Employee code of conduct
- Policies concerning access to remedy, compensation and justice for victims of modern slavery
- Polices that relate to staff training and increasing awareness of modern slavery

Over time, consistent training for all staff, with increasingly clear policies and approaches (backed by past industry case studies or what has worked previously), should help to ensure that modern slavery is targeted more effectively and persistently, regardless of staff turnover or changes in the supply chain.

Some policies and practices may be specific to an organisation's business model or the sector they are working in. For example, some sectors may make particularly frequent use of temporary workers sourced through an intermediary or employment agency. In this situation, they will not have a direct employment relationship with some of their workers, and so they may have specific policies in place to ensure that these particular relationships are managed in a way that mitigates any potential risk of modern slavery.

For example, organisations may have specific policies that require the business to only use specified reputable employment agencies to source labour or that they always seek specific information from the agency before accepting employees from that agency. It is important to note that the Modern Slavery Act requirements do not require any organisation to amend existing policies or to introduce new policies. If the organisation has any relevant policies they can be either referenced in the statement or copied directly into the statement itself.

Good practice

Examine internal business procedures to avoid making demands of suppliers or subcontractors that might lead them to violate human rights, including children's rights. These types of demands include insufficient or late payments, and late orders or high-pressure deadlines resulting from poor demand forecasting.

Ensure that zero tolerance for modern slavery and respect for human rights, including children's rights, are built into contracts and represented in dialogue, self-assessment, audits, training and capacity-building opportunities for suppliers, subcontractors, customers, and other business partners.

In some cases it may be beneficial to foster long-term relationships with suppliers, contractors and subcontractors.

Case Study

A prominent retailer's Ethical Trading Policy includes a detailed Ethical Trading Code of Conduct that contains, amongst other requirements, conditions whereby factories producing their goods must

ensure: employment is freely chosen, child labour shall not be used, and no harsh or inhumane treatment will occur. The Ethical Trading Policy also includes a Foreign Contract Worker Policy, specifically intended to protect workers who may be potentially vulnerable to the exploitation regrettably existent in certain flows of international contract labour. This Policy refers to international human rights norms and, in particular, factories are required to ensure all workers retain passports, ID Cards, bankcards and similar documents to facilitate their unhindered freedom of movement.

For all factories in all regions involved in the manufacture of products for or on behalf of the retailer, compliance with the Ethical Trading Policy, including the Ethical Trading Code of Conduct and the Foreign Contract Worker Policy, as well as all other local laws and relevant international standards, is a requirement of doing business with the retailer. Before the retailer places an order for production in a finished goods factory a social compliance audit (often unannounced) is carried out to assess the factory's compliance with the above Policies. It is only once the Ethical Trading Team is satisfied that the factory is committed to these standards for worker rights, that the factory can be approved.

To drive compliance further, a diverse programme of announced and unannounced follow-up audits, continuous improvement programmes, training programmes, and a confidential worker hotline services (in place especially in countries where there is high percentage of migrant workers) is overseen by the Ethical Trading team in respect of all factories involved in the production of the retailer's goods.

For suppliers that produce component parts of the goods such as fabric mills, dye houses, sundries and packaging factories, the retailer has commenced a programme of social and environmental audits, through an industry collaboration working group, where independent third parties are accredited to perform such audits. All audits (whether initial approval audits or on-going compliance audits) are conducted either by externally trained internal team members or by third party independent auditors, including NGO auditors. An integral part of the auditing process includes confidential interviewing of workers (in a manner protecting worker safety), which helps to understand any potential risks of bonded labour or other forced labour or slavery. By empowering workers and providing mechanisms for them to whistle blow through independent NGO worker hotlines, workers are able to contribute to the dialogue about the risks they face, communicate their priorities, and learn about their rights.

DUE DILIGENCE

The Modern Slavery Act also states that in producing a slavery and human trafficking statement a business may consider including information about its due diligence processes.

Many human rights breaches, including modern slavery, are not immediately apparent. In fact, some suppliers may even go to great lengths to hide the fact that they are using slave labour.

For example, some or all of their workers may be in forced or bonded labour (including coaching and pressuring workers to lie to auditors about their conditions being better than they are, and presenting fake records).

Human rights due diligence is also a key concept in the UN Guiding Principles on Business and Human Rights (UNGPs) The UNGPs specify that due diligence processes should 'include assessing actual and potential human rights impacts, integrating and acting upon the findings, tracking responses, and communicating how impacts are addressed.'[2]

For more detailed guidance on good practice with regards to due diligence organisations should refer directly to the UNGPs which are available online:

http://www.ohchr.org/Documents/Publications/GuidingPrinciplesBusinessHR_EN.pdf

The UNGPs have also been incorporated into the OECD Guidelines for Multinational Enterprises and the OECD is developing sector-based guidance as part of its "proactive agenda" to help businesses identify and respond to risks associated with particular products, regions, sectors or industries. For more information see http://mneguidelines.oecd.org/.

Human rights due diligence is related to corporate good governance. For many businesses due diligence, in relation to modern slavery, is likely to form part of a wider framework around ethical trade, corporate social responsibility and human rights and should form part of a wider human rights due diligence process where possible.

Human rights due diligence also requires consultation with stakeholders that are potentially or actually affected by a company's operations and supply chain, particularly vulnerable groups, such as children. This means bringing the voices of those vulnerable groups into this process so that a company can understand how the organisation affects their lives.

Due diligence procedures should be:

- proportionate to the identified modern slavery risk,
- the severity of the risk, and
- level of influence a business may have.
- informed by any broader risk assessments that have been conducted (see Risk Assessment section below).

Procedures may vary depending on the complexity of the relationships within an organisation and in their supply chains. For example:

(1) A business may have greater knowledge about their first-tier suppliers, and its stakeholders may expect it to make greater efforts at its first tier. However, they should also engage their lower tier suppliers where possible.

(2) Due-diligence includes on-going assessment of modern-slavery risks, and meeting changing expectations on industries to use their influence to encourage change where conditions of slavery may be persistent.

(3) Due-diligence includes the expectation that businesses will ensure integrity of their investigations. Some suppliers may go to great lengths to hide the fact that they are in some way involved in using forced labour. Audits and compliance-driven approaches are unlikely to identify or uncover hidden cases of slavery or trafficking. As such it is advisable that businesses seek to investigate working conditions with support from expert independent, third parties and civil society stakeholders, and hear from workers themselves about their working conditions.

Case Study

With the increased interest in retailer supply chains and the new Modern Slavery Act, one high street retailer took the decision to make their Social, Ethical & Environmental audit more robust. With advice from a third party who were administering their supplier assessment programme the retailer amended some of the existing questions in their audit questionnaire and added others. They have just completed testing of the new questionnaire and auditors have given very positive feedback, agreeing that it is a more robust audit.

Factories have been encouraged to improve accommodation where failings have been found, and issues with health & safety have been addressed. Instances have been found where conditions of employment have been unacceptable and factories have been asked to make changes and introduce better systems. Where factories have been unwilling or unable to make improvements they have been exited from the business. The main aim is to encourage continuous improvement in factories rather than simply 'failing' them and walking away. The retailer will be fully implementing the new questionnaire across all the sites for use shortly.

Due diligence in assessing modern slavery or human rights risk in operations or supply chains is not a legal requirement of the transparency provisions, however, it is good business practice and risk management and will enable both more effective reporting and, more importantly, more effective action to address modern slavery. A business already undertaking relevant due diligence to ensure that the products they purchase are of good sustainable quality and ethically sourced will be able to point to the work already underway in their slavery and human trafficking statement.

Information to consider as part of due diligence could include:

- Actions taken to understand the businesses operating context
- Details of risk management processes, including monitoring and evaluation measures
- Impact assessments undertaken
- Action plans to address and risk/actual instances of modern slavery and how actions have been prioritised
- Evidence of stakeholder engagement
- Business-level grievance mechanisms in place to address modern slavery
- Actions taken to embed respect for human rights and zero tolerance of modern slavery throughout the organisation

ASSESSING AND MANAGING RISK

If an organisation has properly assessed the nature and extent of its exposure to the risk of modern slavery, it will be more able to take targeted action to find it, to remedy it, and to prevent it occurring in the future.

Modern slavery risk assessments should be seen as part of an organisation's wider approach to risk management and could form part of more general risk assessments that are carried out for a variety of reasons.

It is important for businesses to adopt risk assessment policies and procedures that are proportionate to the organisation's size, structure, location of activities and supply chain(s), and nature of business(es).

Businesses firstly need to research and identify risks where they have operations or supply chain(s) and then prioritise those risks. Oversight of risk assessment or risk management frameworks is, in best practise, led by Directors or Partners so that issues found can be dealt with at the appropriate level.

Appropriate resources are needed to ensure that risk assessment strategies can be effective. This means that the assessments should be able to identify the risks and issues, properly assess their level of importance, and ensure that appropriate remedies are in place.

Identifying relevant information from internal and external sources will help businesses to undertake effective risk assessments and appropriate review of those risks. Particular business risks to consider in assessing and managing risks to workers include:

Country risks — exposure may be greater in global supply chains in countries where protection against breaches of human rights are limited, particularly with regard to rights of foreign contract workers to retain their own ID and papers, and/or where work arrangement by agents is common, etc.

Sector risks — there are different risks and levels of risk in different sectors. For example, the risks and arrangements which generate bonded labour situations for workers in the extractives sector may differ to those causes in manufacturing.

Transaction risks — banks or financial institutions may be involved in facilitating financing from or supporting cases of modern slavery and bonded labour in operations or supply chains or through money laundering.

Business partnership risks — Different supplier relationships and business partnerships will all carry different levels of risks. In some cases, existing long-term partnerships will involve less risk because the organisation will have a better knowledge of their partner's operations and policies. However, a new partnership or business relationship may be equally low risk as long as proper due diligence is conducted.

Organisations should then decide how identified risks can be investigated, and where issues are found, how they can best be remediated or mitigated through activities such as industry collaboration or improved purchasing practises internally. Training the Board, organisation's leadership, and employees to develop the skills and knowledge to understand and support risk prevention and remediation can greatly assist.

To ensure effectiveness, it is best practise to foster a culture that rewards the identification of risks and the effective mitigation and remedy of cases found. To be effective this should be part of a clear organisational ethos and performance management system which is promoted by senior management and company policy.

Businesses must be alive to the continuously changing nature of modern slavery. Whilst industry, NGOs, law enforcement and government may alone or together stop exploitation or workers in one area, without robust monitoring, communications, and incentives it can potentially arise in another part of operations or the supply chain, so constantly assessing and reviewing these risks is important.

Sharing risks with trusted partners such as representative bodies, industry associations and working groups to deepen understanding of macro issues and supporting improved government legislation where appropriate may also help sectors as a whole to prevent modern slavery, where it is possible to share this kind of information.

Case Study

Following negative media reports into the Thai fishing industry, in 2014, there was significant interest from the seafood industry and other stakeholders to collaborate on a way forward and so a number of stakeholders formed the Seafood Ethics Common Language Group.

The Seafood Ethics CLG is an example model of an integrated, interdisciplinary and collaborative approach to address ethical and social issues relating to responsible seafood production. The group convenes seafood stakeholders including major supermarket chains, smaller retailers, processors and suppliers throughout the whole supply chain, with government, NGOs, development organisations and charities in a 'safe' environment. The aim is to reach mutual consensus on issues which impact on the responsible sourcing of seafood – to facilitate a coherent and credible sector-wide response.

PERFORMANCE INDICATORS

Performance indicators are important in driving the performance of a business and shaping the way it operates. They can also affect how exposed the business is to the risk of modern slavery.

The direction and focus of particular performance incentives (such as that Sourcing Directors should buy the lowest cost products, that can be shipped in the fastest time) may influence and create a modern slavery risk if not managed carefully. This should be considered when improving internal management performance indicators and should be linked to the organisation's risk assessment.

Focusing on KPIs to increase production or shipment "turn-around" time speed, for example, may unintentionally increase pressure on those who are producing the goods on production lines. This could create environments where modern slavery (particularly in the shape of bonded labour) may become a way a supplier or production site tries to deal with unrealistic short time pressure and related expectations on their operations or supplying partnership.

KPIs could be used in a modern slavery statement in two ways. Firstly, businesses could choose to provide information on their existing KPIs and set out whether they have considered whether they make their business and supply chain vulnerable to modern slavery.

Secondly, this section of the statement could outline any additional KPIs which the company has introduced to measure the performance of any anti-slavery actions undertaken. If an initial risk assessment highlighted issues in a company's operations or supply chain, a KPI could be introduced to measure progress against reducing that risk, i.e. improving conditions for those people.

For example, a business could set targets for:

- training and capacity building of staff about modern slavery issues, measuring changes in awareness of risk; appropriate decision-making and swift action, as appropriate.;
- grievance procedures and whistle-blowing procedures for workers and employees if cases are suspected or found;
- visibility, leverage and oversight of suppliers in relevant goods and services supply chains

Whilst there is no requirement to introduce new KPIs, those companies that do will choose their own based on what is most effective and efficient for them.

Carefully designed KPIs could help a business to demonstrate as clearly as possible if they are making progress over time in preventing modern slavery in their business or supply chains.

Case Study

A sportswear manufacturer has taken a range of actions in relation to its supply chain which could be included in a slavery and human trafficking statement:

Supply chain verification – The company's policy is to evaluate potential contracted factories before they enter the supply chain to assess compliance with standards including country-related risk for issues including force labour, human trafficking and slavery. They use both internal and external third-party audits.

Direct suppliers' certification of materials – The company is working on mapping and understanding impacts further up the supply chain, to develop standards for upstream suppliers of contracted manufacturers.

Standards for compliance – If a contracted factory is found to violate laws or the manufacturer's standards, it is responsible for improving performance against a master action plan. If the factory fails to make progress against that plan, they are subject to review and sanctions, including potential termination.

TRAINING

Training is a fundamental way of raising awareness and ensuring that people understand the importance of a particular issue. It also helps people to understand what they need to do, and how to work together internally or externally if they encounter something that raises concerns. Training may be targeted at different groups of employees within a business, including leadership, or at different businesses within a supply chain, and the training itself could take a range of different forms. It may range from detailed training courses to broader awareness-raising programmes.

Training and development provide both the company as a whole and the individual employees with benefits that can make the cost and time a worthwhile investment. Such expense can be minimised where relevant training is undertaken alongside wider training, on similar issues. For modern slavery, this could be a module in a wider training programme for supply chain managers or for human resources managers dealing with recruitment and ongoing training. This may reference how all parts of the business influence purchasing practices which influence company or supply chain conditions, i.e. by merchandising and others demanding new products at unrealistically low prices (not taking into account proper wage rates) or shipped too fast.

Human rights can only be realised through an informed and continued demand by people for their protection. Human rights education promotes values, beliefs and attitudes that encourage all individuals to uphold their own rights and those of others, and can support employee pride in the ethical standards their employer strives for. It develops an understanding of everyone's common responsibility to make human rights a reality in each community.

Organisations should think about where training should be targeted to have the most effect. If those employees who might encounter victims directly are more aware of the indicators of modern slavery and of how to report suspected cases, and what actions they can expect the company to take, then they can raise flags, and help to root it out in a particular business or supply chain. Similarly, if a supply chain manager, procurement or product quality professional is trained and incentivised then they may be able to do a lot to prevent new modern slavery occurring in the supply chains they manage, and to assist its remediation for victims where it does exist. However, the training needs of these groups is likely to be very different so businesses will need to determine the most effective and efficient way to reach the most relevant groups in their business and supply chains.

NOTES

[2] UNGPs, p 17 [http://www.ohchr.org/Documents/Publications/GuidingPrinciplesBusinessHR_EN.pdf]

ANNEX F
UK MODERN SLAVERY ADULT VICTIM SUPPORT PROVIDERS

[4.105]

England and Wales

The Salvation Army 0300 303 8151

Scotland

Trafficking Awareness Raising Alliance (TARA) 0141 276 7724

Migrant Helpline 07837 937737 or 07789 791 110

Northern Ireland

Migrant Help 013 0420 3977 or 07766 668 781 (for male potential victims of human trafficking)

Women's Aid 028 9024 9041 (for female potential victims of human trafficking)

Modern Slavery Helpline

The NGO Unseen operates a UK-wide 24/7 Modern Slavery Helpline that victims, employers and members of the public who may encounter modern slavery can call for expert support and advice on 08000 121 700.

Case Study

Stronger Together
Tackling modern slavery in supply chains

Launched in October 2013, Stronger Together is a business led multi-stakeholder collaborative initiative to equip employers and recruiters with the practical knowledge and resources to tackle modern slavery in their business and supply chains.

Stronger together run two core workshops on 'Tackling Modern Slavery in UK Businesses' and 'Tackling Modern Slavery in Global Supply Chains' which are supplemented by a range of online e-learning training modules for UK and global businesses. Since its launch:

- **Free good practice toolkits and resources for business have been downloaded from www.** stronger2gether.org by over 6000 industry representatives.
- **Almost 3000 individuals from 1500 organisations have attended workshops and are taking the tackling slavery message back to around 800,000 workers.**
- **In a 2017 impact assessment: 96% of business respondents said that Stronger Together had increased their understanding of what modern slavery is; 87% that it has helped them to prepare how to manage potential situations of forced labour and 72% said that through engagement with Stronger Together, their senior management had made a commitment to tackle modern slavery in their business and supply chain.**
- **In partnership with the Chartered Institute of Building (CIOB) and international construction companies, a new construction industry programme was launched in 2017.**
- **In 2017, funded by the UK Home Office Modern Slavery Innovation Fund, in partnership with the Wine and Agricultural Ethical Trading Association (WIETA), a Stronger Together programme commenced to support businesses to tackle forced labour in the wine and fruit growing industries in South Africa.**

Stronger Together continues to develop its support for UK businesses, to deliver bespoke training solutions for international household brands and to expand globally by working collaboratively with local partners to introduce the programme into other countries and sectors.

ANNEX G
USEFUL INFORMATION AND RESOURCES

[4.106]

UK Government Modern Slavery Webpage www.gov.uk/government/collections/modern-slavery

Modern Slavery Act 2015 www.legislation.gov.uk/ukpga/2015/30/contents/enacted

The Modern Slavery Act 2015 (Transparency in Supply Chains) Regulations 2015 www.legislation.gov.uk/ukdsi/2015/9780111138847

Transparency in Supply Chains Consultation Document and Government Response www.gov.uk/government/consultations/modern-slavery-and-supply-chains

Anti-Slavery Commissioner www.antislaverycommissioner.co.uk/

Alliance 8.7 www.alliance87.org/

INTERNATIONAL GUIDELINES AND CONVENTIONS

UN Guiding Principles on Business and Human Rights (UNGPs) www.ohchr.org/Documents/Publications/GuidingPrinciplesBusinessHR_EN.pdf

UN Guiding Principles Reporting Framework www.ungpreporting.org/

Good Business: Implementing the UN Guiding Principles on Business and Human Rights (September 2013) and update (May 2016) www.gov.uk/government/publications/bhr-action-plan

Shift, Mapping the Provisions of the Modern Slavery Act against the Expectations of the UN Guiding Principles on Business and Human Rights www.shiftproject.org/resources/publications/mapping-modern-slavery-act-un-guiding-principles/

OECD, Guidelines for Multinational Enterprises http://mneguidelines.oecd.org/guidelines/

UN Global Compact www.unglobalcompact.org/

ILO Resources on Forced Labour, Human Trafficking and Slavery www.ilo.org/global/topics/forced-labour/lang--en/index.htm

ILO Resources on Child Labour www.ilo.org/global/topics/child-labour/lang--en/index.htm

The United Nations Convention on the Rights of the Child (UNCRC) www.ohchr.org/en/professionalinterest/pages/crc.aspx

UNICEF, The UN Global Compact and Save the Children, Children's Rights and Business Principles www.unicef.org/csr/12.htm

TOOLS, GUIDANCE AND RESOURCES

Walk Free Global Slavery Index www.globalslaveryindex.org/

U.S. Department of Labor: List of Goods Produced by Child Labor or Forced Labor www.dol.gov/ilab/reports/child-labor/list-of-goods/

CORE Coalition, Practical Guides http://corporate-responsibility.org/publications/practical-guides/

ETI Base Code Guidance: Modern Slavery www.ethicaltrade.org/resources/base-code-guidance-modern-slavery

ETI Base Code Guidance: Child Labour www.ethicaltrade.org/resources/base-code-guidance-child-labour

ETI Human Rights Due Diligence Framework www.ethicaltrade.org/resources/human-rights-due-diligence-framework

Verité eLearning on Supply Chain Accountability www.verite.org/research/elearning

Labour Exploitation Accountability Hub http://accountabilityhub.org/

Ergon Associates, Modern Slavery Statements – One Year On http://ergonassociates.net/publication/modern-slavery-statements-what-are-companies-reporting/

ETI and Hult International Business School, Corporate Leadership on Modern Slavery www.ashridge.org.uk/faculty-research/research/current-research/research-projects/corporate-leadership-on-modern-slavery/

Stronger Together http://stronger2gether.org/

International Tourism Partnership http://tourismpartnership.org/human-rights/

REPOSITORIES OF SLAVERY AND HUMAN TRAFFICKING STATEMENTS

Modern Slavery Registry https://www.modernslaveryregistry.org/

TISC Report https://tiscreport.org/

The Home Office would like to thank the following organisations for supporting the development of this guidance:

Amnesty International

Anti-Slavery International

Association of British Travel Agents

British Hospitality Association

British Retail Consortium

Burberry

Business in the Community

CAFOD

Children's Society

Confederation of British Industry

CORE coalition

ECPAT UK

Engineering Employers' Federation

Ethical Trading Initiative

Food and Drink Federation

FLEX

International Chamber of Commerce

International Tourism Partnership

KPMG

PWC

Rathbone Greenbank Investments

Shift Project

Stop the Traffik

Stronger Together / Alliance HR

The Society of Motor Manufacturers and Traders Limited

Unseen

Waitrose

Wilko

CODE OF PRACTICE ON PREVENTING ILLEGAL WORKING CIVIL PENALTY SCHEME FOR EMPLOYERS

January 2019

[4.107]

NOTES

This Code of Practice was issued by the Home Office. It is made under the authority of s 19 of the Immigration, Asylum and Nationality Act 2006; the Parliamentary authority for the Code is the Immigration (Restrictions on Employment) (Code of Practice and Miscellaneous Amendments) Order 2018, SI 2018/1340, art 4 at **[2.2110]**. The Code came into force on 28 January 2019. While the Code is issued under statutory powers, it does not carry any specific statutory status, and there is no formal requirement under the 2006 Act for any relevant body to take it into account. It replaces the previous Code issued in 2014, which itself replaced the Code issued by the Border & Immigration Agency in 2008. As to the continuing application of previous codes, see **[4.108]**). Notes are as in the original Code.

CONTENTS

1: INTRODUCTION

[4.108]

Illegal working often results in abusive and exploitative behaviour, the mistreatment of illegal migrant workers, tax evasion and illegal housing conditions. It can also undercut legitimate businesses and have an adverse impact on the employment of people who are in the UK lawfully.

As an employer, you have a responsibility to prevent illegal working in the UK by ensuring that your employees have the right to work here. The illegal working provisions of the Immigration, Asylum and Nationality Act 2006 ('the Act') came into force on 29 February 2008. Section 15 of the Act allows the Secretary of State to serve an employer with a notice requiring the payment of a penalty of a specified amount where they employ a person who is:

- subject to immigration control; and
- aged over 16; and
- not allowed to carry out the work in question because either they have not been granted leave to enter or remain in the UK or because their leave to enter or remain in the UK:
  - (i) is invalid;
  - (ii) has ceased to have effect (meaning it no longer applies) whether by reason of curtailment, revocation, cancellation, passage of time or otherwise; or
  - (iii) is subject to a condition preventing them from accepting the employment.

This Code of practice has been issued under section 19 of the Act to specify the factors to be considered by the Home Office in determining the amount of the civil penalty for employing an illegal worker. Separate guidance for employers sets out how to conduct right to work checks and how the Home Office administers the civil penalty scheme to prevent illegal working.

This Code updates the one issued in May 2014. It has been updated to reflect the Immigration (Restrictions on Employment) (Code of Practice and Miscellaneous Amendments) Order 2018, which provides that employers may establish a statutory excuse against liability for an illegal working civil penalty by conducting an online right to work check using the Home Office online right to work checking service.

FOR WHOM IS THIS CODE OF PRACTICE RELEVANT?

This Code applies:

(i) when calculating the penalty amount; in respect of any employment which commenced on or after 29 February 2008 where the breach of section 15 of the Act occurred on or after 28 January 2019; or

(ii) when determining liability; where an initial check on a potential employee, or a repeat check on an existing employee, is required on or after 28 January 2019 in order to establish or retain a statutory excuse.

When the employment commenced on or after 29 February 2008 and the breach occurred on or after 16 May 2014 and before 28 January 2019, the Code published in May 2014 applies.

When the employment commenced on or after 29 February 2008 and the breach occurred before 16 May 2014, the Code published in February 2008 applies.

This Code applies to employers who employ staff under a contract of employment (a contract of service or apprenticeship), whether express or implied and whether oral or in writing. It does not apply to those who undertake work for you who do not fall within these categories.

HOW SHOULD THIS CODE OF PRACTICE BE USED?

This Code has been issued under section 19 of the Act. It sets out the factors to be considered by the Home Office in determining the amount of the civil penalty.

This Code has been issued alongside guidance for employers setting out how to conduct right to work checks and how the Home Office administers the scheme, and a 'Code of practice on avoiding unlawful discrimination while preventing illegal working'. Please refer to this Code alongside these documents. They can be found at: www.gov.uk/government/collections/employers-illegal-working-penalties.

WHO SHOULD USE THIS CODE OF PRACTICE?

This is a statutory Code. This means that it has been approved by the Secretary of State and laid before Parliament. The Code does not impose any legal duties on employers, nor is it an authoritative statement of the law; only the Courts and Employment Tribunals can provide that. However, the Code may be used as evidence in legal proceedings and Courts and Employment Tribunals must take account of any part of the Code which may be relevant. Home Office officials will also have regard to this Code when administering illegal working civil penalties under the Act.

REFERENCES IN THIS CODE

'We' or 'us' in this Code mean the Home Office. References to 'you' and 'your' mean the employer.

'Days' means calendar days, i.e. including Saturdays, Sundays and bank holidays.

'Employee' means someone who is, or who will be, employed under a contract of employment (contract of service) or apprenticeship.

'Breach' or 'breaches' mean that section 15 of the Immigration, Asylum and Nationality Act 2006 has been contravened by employing someone who is:

- subject to immigration control; and
- aged over 16; and
- not allowed to carry out the work in question because either they have not been granted leave to enter or remain in the UK or because their leave to enter or remain in the UK:
  - (i) is invalid;
  - (ii) has ceased to have effect (meaning it no longer applies) whether by reason of curtailment, revocation, cancellation, passage of time or otherwise; or
  - (iii) is subject to a condition preventing them from accepting the employment.

'A current document' means a document that has not expired.

References to 'right to work checks' refer to prescribed manual document checks and prescribed online right to work checks.

'Home Office online right to work checking service' means the online system allowing employers to check whether a person is allowed to work in the United Kingdom and, if so, the nature of any restrictions on that person's right to do so. For the avoidance of doubt, this system is accessible for employers on the 'View a job applicant's right to work details' page on gov.uk. No other online portal relating to immigration status may be used instead for right to work checking purposes.

An 'online right to work check' means the response generated by the Home Office online right to work checking service in relation to a person.

'A civil penalty notice' means a notice given under section 15(2) of the Immigration, Asylum and Nationality Act 2006 that requires an employer to pay a penalty of a specified amount.

'Employment of illegal workers within the previous three years' means you have been issued with a civil penalty or warning notice in respect of a breach of the Act for one or more illegal workers which occurred within three years of the current breach, or you have committed an offence under section 21 of the Act during the same period.

2: AN OVERVIEW OF HOW THE CIVIL PENALTY WILL BE ADMINISTERED

[4.109]

The civil penalty scheme is designed to encourage you to comply with your duty as an employer to prevent illegal working by carrying out right to work checks. The civil penalty scheme is applied as the sanction for employing illegal workers in most cases. The civil penalties we impose are intended to be proportionate to the level of non-compliant behaviour and are therefore calculated on a sliding scale. Criminal sanctions may be applied in the most serious cases.

LIABILITY FOR A CIVIL PENALTY

If you are found employing an illegal worker we may issue you with a notice informing you that the details of your case are being referred to officials with responsibility for administering the civil penalty scheme, to consider your liability for a civil penalty for breaching section 15 of the Act.

This referral notice will inform you how your case will be considered and the possible decision outcomes. It will also specify the date on which the breach was encountered. If you receive this referral notice, you are advised to consult the separate guidance issued by the Home Office which sets out in more detail how the civil penalty scheme will be administered, including the various documents that you may receive and the deadlines that are relevant to each stage of the process.

The separate guidance will also set out how and when you may exercise your right to object to the Home Office and appeal to a court against a civil penalty. You may object and appeal on the following grounds:

- you are not liable to pay the penalty (for example, this could be because you are not the employer of the illegal worker(s) identified);
- you have a statutory excuse (this means you undertook a prescribed right to work check); or
- the level of penalty is too high (this means we have miscalculated the amount of your penalty by reference to the wrong scale or you have evidence that you have met specified mitigating criteria which we have not taken into account).

In the event that we visit your business premises and you are able to demonstrate to officials at this time that you have a statutory excuse in respect of the identified illegal workers, you will not be served with a referral notice in respect of these employees. Instead, you will be served with a notice indicating that no action will be taken in your case and it will be closed. It will not be taken into account in the event that you breach the Act in future.

FAST PAYMENT OPTION

We have a fast payment option which reduces the amount of your civil penalty by **30 per cent** if we receive payment **in full within 21 days** of the date of the civil penalty notice. The reduced penalty amount and the final date by which you must pay it will be clearly shown on your civil penalty notice.

If you object to your penalty before the deadline specified in your civil penalty notice, you will continue to be eligible for the fast payment option. If you are still required to pay a penalty following your objection, you will be given a fresh notice which specifies a new date by which you may pay your penalty at the lower amount.

If you have been found to be employing illegal workers within the previous three years, you are not eligible for this reduced payment after the first penalty notice or offence.

PAYMENT BY INSTALMENTS

We will consider the impact of the penalty on you insofar as you are unable to pay it in one lump sum. We may agree that you are able to pay your penalty by instalments over an agreed period of time, usually up to 24 months, and exceptionally up to 36 months. We will not reduce the penalty amount.

You must provide details of your ability to pay over the instalment plan period and why you cannot pay the penalty in full. This information should be supplied within 28 days of the civil penalty notice in order for your application to be considered. When we inform you of our decision, we will stipulate when the payment or payments are due. Your request to pay by instalments does not affect the time limits within which an objection or an appeal against the civil penalty must be brought.

In the event that you do not pay an instalment on the due date, debt recovery enforcement action will be taken.

A fast payment option may not be paid by instalments.

ENFORCEMENT AND OTHER CONSEQUENCES OF A CIVIL PENALTY

If you do not pay your penalty in full or by instalments, or object or appeal, by the specified due dates, we will commence enforcement action against you. This includes action in the civil court to recover the unpaid penalty. This action may have an adverse impact on your ability to act in the capacity of a director in a company.

If you are an employer who is subject to immigration control, you should also be aware that if you are liable for a civil penalty, this will be recorded on Home Office systems and may be taken into account when considering any future immigration application that you make.

If you are liable for a civil penalty, it could also affect your ability to sponsor migrants who come to the UK in the future, including those you wish to work for you under Tier 2 of the Points Based System, or to hold a Gangmaster licence.

The Act also provides, under section 21, a criminal sanction for use against employers who employ individuals they know or have reasonable cause to believe are working illegally. This Code does not cover this criminal offence.

3: DETERMINING LIABILITY AND CALCULATING THE PENALTY AMOUNT

[4.110]

When we consider your liability for a civil penalty, we will assess your case against published criteria contained in this Code. These are set out in the Consideration Framework below. It comprises three stages of consideration and explains how the level of breach is to be calculated.

Table1: Consideration Framework

<table>
<tr><td colspan="3">Stage 1: Determining liability</td></tr>
<tr><td rowspan="2">Liability:</td><td rowspan="2">Do you have a statutory excuse?</td><td>Yes: Issue a no action notice. Case is closed.</td></tr>
<tr><td>No: Proceed to Stage 2</td></tr>
<tr><td colspan="3">Stage 2: Determining the level of breach</td></tr>
<tr><td rowspan="2">Breach:</td><td rowspan="2">Have you been found to be employing illegal workers within the previous three years?</td><td>Yes: Proceed to Stage 3. Apply the Level 2 Civil Penalty Calculator</td></tr>
<tr><td>No: Proceed to Stage 3. Apply the Level 1 Civil Penalty Calculator</td></tr>
<tr><td colspan="3">Stage 3: Determining the penalty amount</td></tr>
<tr><td>Mitigating factor 1:</td><td>Have you already reported the suspected illegal worker to the Home Office and received a unique reference number?</td><td rowspan="3">Refer to the Civil Penalty Calculator (Table 2)</td></tr>
<tr><td>Mitigating factor 2:</td><td>Have you actively co-operated with the Home Office?</td></tr>
<tr><td>Mitigating factor 3: (This factor may be applied only where factors 1 and 2 have been met in relation to Level 1 penalties)</td><td>Do you have effective right to work checking practices in place and generally comply with your employer duties to prevent illegal working?</td></tr>
</table>

At **stage 3**, we determine the penalty amount. We do this by using the **Civil Penalty Calculator** (Table 2 below). This calculator sets out a sliding scale of penalty amounts **for each illegal worker.**

The actual penalty amount will depend on your history of compliance with right to work checks as an employer. It will be determined according to whether you qualify for reductions in the penalty amount by providing evidence that you have met the mitigating factors. Each case of illegal working is considered by officials on the basis of the information available, the Consideration Framework and the Civil Penalty Calculator.

Table 2: Civil Penalty Calculator

The Civil Penalty Calculator comprises two levels:

- The **Level 1** table should be used where you have **not** been found to be employing illegal workers within the previous three years. The starting point for the calculation of the civil penalty is £15,000 before reductions are applied.
- The **Level 2** table should be used where you have been found to be employing illegal workers within the previous three years. The starting point for the calculation of the civil penalty is £20,000 before reductions are applied.

Where a civil penalty notice has been cancelled following an objection or appeal and has not been replaced by a warning notice, it shall not be taken into account when calculating any subsequent penalty.

Level 1

Level 1: First breach							
→ **Starting maximum penalty amount £15,000**	**Mitigating factor 1:** Evidence of reporting suspected illegal workers? →		**Mitigating factor 2:** Evidence of active co-operation? →		→ **Ending minimum penalty amount £5,000***	**Mitigating factor 3:** Evidence of effective document checking practices together with mitigation for factors 1 and 2	
	If Yes→	Penalty decreased by **£5,000**	If Yes→	Penalty decreased by **£5,000**		If Yes→	**Action:** Issue a **warning notice**
	If No→	No penalty decrease **(£0)**	If No→	No penalty decrease **(£0)**		If No→	**Action:** Issue a **civil penalty notice** for the total value calculated in each case

* The ending minimum penalty amount may be reduced by 30% to £3,500 per illegal worker under our fast payment option.

Level 2

Level 2: Second or subsequent breach							
→ **Starting maximum penalty amount £20,000**	**Mitigating factor 1:** Evidence of reporting suspected illegal workers? →		**Mitigating factor 2:** Evidence of active co-operation? →		→ **Ending minimum penalty amount £10,000**	**Action** ↓	**Warning notice not available**
	If Yes→	Penalty decreased by **£5,000**	If Yes→	Penalty decreased by **£5,000**		**Issue a civil penalty notice** for the total value calculated in each case	
	If No→	No penalty decrease **(£0)**	If No→	No penalty decrease **(£0)**			

The fast payment option is not available where you have been found to be employing illegal workers within the previous three years.

DO YOU HAVE A STATUTORY EXCUSE?

In **stage 1** of our consideration we will determine if you have a statutory excuse against liability for a civil penalty. You will have a statutory excuse if you have correctly carried out the prescribed right to work checks before employment commences.

Where an employee has a time-limited right to work, and you have therefore established a **time-limited statutory excuse**, you are required to conduct repeat right to work checks to retain the excuse. Generally, this will be when the employee's permission to be in the UK and undertake the work in question expires, as evidenced by either the document (or combination of documents) produced or by the online right to work check.

It is your responsibility to demonstrate that you have complied with the requirements to establish and, where necessary, retain your statutory excuse.

You will **not** have a statutory excuse if:

- you cannot provide evidence of having conducted the prescribed right to work checks before the employment commenced;
- you have employed someone when it is reasonably apparent that they are not the holder of the document they present, or the person named and shown in the online right to work check (i.e. that person is an imposter);
- you have conducted a manual check and it is reasonably apparent that the document is false (the falsity would be considered to be 'reasonably apparent' if an individual who is untrained in the identification of false documents, examining it carefully, but briefly and without the use of technological aids, could reasonably be expected to realise that the document in question is not genuine);
- you have conducted an online check and it is reasonably apparent that the website you have used to do that check is not the official gov.uk Home Office online right to work checking service;
- you have attempted to conduct an online check but have not accessed the employer 'View a job applicant's right to work details' part of the service, you have only viewed information online that has been provided directly to the migrant;
- you have employed someone when it is clear from the right to work check that the person does not have valid permission to work in the UK or is subject to an immigration condition which prevents them from carrying out the work in question (i.e. you have employed a person with no right to work or a person in breach of their work restrictions or a person whose right to work has expired);
- you know you are employing a person who is not allowed to undertake the work regardless of whether you have carried out any document checks;
- your statutory excuse was time-limited and has expired; or
- in respect of a student who has a restricted right to work, you have not obtained and retained a copy of evidence setting out their term and vacation times covering the duration of their period of study in the UK.

If we are satisfied that you **have a statutory excuse** in respect of an illegal worker, you will not be liable for a civil penalty.

But if we consider that you **have not established a statutory excuse** in respect of an illegal worker we will consider the level of your civil penalty. Please see **stage 2** in the Consideration Framework.

HAVE YOU BEEN FOUND TO BE EMPLOYING AN ILLEGAL WORKER BEFORE?

During **stage 2** of our consideration process we will look at whether you have been found to be employing illegal workers within the previous three years. We will do this to determine the level of your breach, as this will be taken into account and a higher starting level of penalty will apply. We will then use **Level 2** of our **Civil Penalty Calculator** to determine the amount of your civil penalty.

If you **have not** received a civil penalty or warning notice or committed an offence under section 21 within this time period, we will use **Level 1** of our **Civil Penalty Calculator** to determine the amount of your penalty.

Multiple premises

A business with more than one premises which has been found to be employing illegal workers within the previous three years and where recruitment is devolved to each site, will not be subject to a penalty calculation using **Level 2** of the Civil Penalty Calculator if illegal workers are encountered at different sites, unless this can be attributed to a general failure in the business's centrally set recruitment practices.

Transfer of undertakings

Employers who acquire staff as a result of a Transfer of Undertakings (Protection of Employment) Regulations 2006 (TUPE) transfer are provided with a grace period of 60 days from the date of the transfer of the business to correctly carry out their first statutory right to work checks in respect of these acquired employees. There is no such grace period for any follow-up checks to retain the excuse, where applicable.

This 60-day grace period applies in <u>all</u> situations where the new employer acquires employees who are subject to a "relevant transfer",[1] even if the transferring business is subject to "terminal" insolvency proceedings falling within regulation 8(7) of the TUPE Regulations, such as cases involving compulsory liquidation.[2]

This means that in all circumstances where employees assigned to a business, or part of a business, that is the subject of a relevant transfer move with that work to a new employer, the new employer has 60 days from the date of the relevant transfer to carry out fresh right to work checks on those employees, even if regulation 8(7) applies.

By complying with prescribed right to work checks within this timescale, the transferee employer will acquire a statutory excuse against liability for a civil penalty in the event that illegal working is identified.

NOTES

1 as defined by Regulation 3 of the Transfer of Undertakings (Protection of Employment) Regulations 2006 (the "**TUPE Regulations**")

2 The employment protections set out in regulations 4 (continuation of employment) and 7 (protection from dismissal) of the TUPE Regulations are dis-applied in reg. 8(7) cases.

DO YOU HAVE MITIGATING EVIDENCE?

In **stage 3** of our consideration we will assess whether any of the published mitigating factors apply in your case when determining the amount of your penalty. Depending on the level of your breach, there are up to three mitigating factors which may be taken into account:

(1) Have you reported suspected illegal workers to us?

If you demonstrate that you have reported to us your suspicion about the right to work of one or more illegal workers who have been identified and received an acknowledgement in the form of a unique Home Office reference number, your penalty amount for each of these illegal workers will be reduced by £5,000. To qualify for this reduction you must have reported your suspicion about them to our Sponsorship and Employers' Helpline on 0300 123 5434 **before** we identify the illegal worker. This mitigating factor is taken into account for both **Level 1** and **Level 2** breaches.

(2) Have you actively co-operated with us?

If you demonstrate that you have actively co-operated with us when we investigate your compliance with the law, your penalty amount for each illegal worker will also be reduced by £5,000.

Active co-operation means:

- providing Home Office officials with access to your premises, recruitment and employment records and right to work checking systems when requested;
- responding promptly, honestly and accurately to questions asked during Immigration Enforcement visits and responding to any further requests for information by the deadline set;
- making yourself available to our officials during the course of our investigations if required; and
- fully and promptly disclosing any evidence you have which may assist us in our investigations.

This mitigating factor is taken into account for both **Level 1** and **Level 2** breaches.

(3) Do you have effective right to work checking practices in place?

If you demonstrate that you have effective recruitment practices in place **together with** evidence that you have reported your suspicion about the illegal worker(s) in question **and** actively co-operated with us, your penalty will be reduced to the minimum level of a **warning notice**. This will only apply if you have not been found to be employing illegal workers within the previous three years. A warning notice will be taken into account in determining the level of your penalty if you commit a subsequent breach of the Act within the following three years.

We will consider that you have effective right to work checking practices in place if you provide evidence of your general compliance with your responsibility to prevent illegal working. This includes:

- having robust document checking systems in place;
- thorough and consistent right to work checking processes;
- records of right to work checks for your staff; and
- a history of compliance with the requirements.

4: HOW TO CONDUCT A RIGHT TO WORK CHECK

[4.111]
Since 28 January 2019, employers have had the option to conduct either a manual right to work check or an online right to work check in order to establish a statutory excuse against a civil penalty in the event that an employee is found to be working illegally.

It will not be possible to conduct an online right to work check in all circumstances, as not all employees, or prospective employees, will have an immigration status that can be checked online at this stage. The Home Office online right to work checking service sets out what information and/or documentation you will need in order to access the service. In circumstances in which an online check is not possible in respect of an individual, you should conduct a manual right to work check.

When conducting follow-up checks required in respect of those whose right to work is time-limited, you may use either the manual right to work check or the online right to work check where applicable.

CONDUCTING A MANUAL RIGHT TO WORK CHECK

There are 3 basic steps to conducting a manual right to work check:

(1) Obtain original versions of one or more of the acceptable documents;

(2) Check the documents in the presence of the holder of the documents;[3] and

(3) Make copies of the documents, retain the copies and a record of the date on which the check is made.

NOTES

[3] The person must be present in person or via a live video link.

TABLE 3: 3-STEP CHECK

Step 1: Obtain→	**Step 2: Check→**	**Step 3: Copy**
You must **obtain** original acceptable documents.	You must **check** that they are genuine, that the person presenting them is the prospective employee or employee, the rightful holder and allowed to do the type of work you are offering.	You must make a clear copy of each document in a format which cannot later be altered, and retain the copy securely: electronically or in hardcopy. You must also make a contemporaneous record of the date on which you conducted your check. If this is recorded separately to the copy documents, it should also include a description of the documents checked
How: You must ask for and be given **original** documents from either **List A** or **List B** of acceptable documents.	**How:** You must check: 1) photographs and dates of birth are consistent across documents and with the person's appearance in order to detect impersonation; 2) expiry dates for leave have not passed; 3) any work restrictions to determine if they are allowed to do the type of work on offer (for **students** who have limited permission to work during term-times, you **must** also obtain, copy and retain details of their academic term and vacation times covering the duration of their period of study in the UK for which they will be employed); 4) the documents are genuine, have not been tampered with and belong to the holder; and 5) the reasons for any different names across documents (eg marriage certificate, divorce decree, deed poll). Supporting documents should also be photocopied and the copy retained.	**How:** You must copy and retain: 1) **Passports:** any page with the document expiry date, nationality, date of birth, signature, leave expiry date, biometric details and photograph, and any page containing information indicating the holder has an entitlement to enter or remain in the UK and undertake the work in question. 2) **All other documents:** the document in full, including both sides of a Biometric Residence Permit.

All copies of documents taken should be kept securely for the duration of the employee's employment and for two years afterwards.

LISTS OF ACCEPTABLE DOCUMENTS FOR RIGHT TO WORK CHECKS

The documents that are considered acceptable for demonstrating right to work in the UK are set out in two lists – **List A and List B**. These are shown in Tables 4 and 5 below.

List A contains the range of documents which may be accepted for checking purposes for a person who has a permanent right to work in the UK. If you follow the prescribed right to work checks you will establish a **continuous statutory excuse** for the duration of that person's employment with you.

List B contains the range of documents which may be accepted for checking purposes for a person who has a temporary right to work in the UK. If you follow the prescribed right to work checks, you will establish a **time-limited statutory excuse**. You will be required to carry out a follow-up check as set out below.

TABLE 4: LIST A – ACCEPTABLE DOCUMENTS TO ESTABLISH A CONTINUOUS STATUTORY EXCUSE

List A	
1.	A passport showing the holder, or a person named in the passport as the child of the holder, is a British citizen or a citizen of the UK and Colonies having the right of abode in the UK.
2.	A passport or national identity card showing the holder, or a person named in the passport as the child of the holder, is a national of a European Economic Area country or Switzerland.
3.	A Registration Certificate or Document Certifying Permanent Residence issued by the Home Office to a national of a European Economic Area country or Switzerland.
4.	A Permanent Residence Card issued by the Home Office to the family member of a national of a European Economic Area country or Switzerland.
5.	A **current** Biometric Immigration Document (Biometric Residence Permit) issued by the Home Office to the holder indicating that the person named is allowed to stay indefinitely in the UK, or has no time limit on their stay in the UK.
6.	A **current** passport endorsed to show that the holder is exempt from immigration control, is allowed to stay indefinitely in the UK, has the right of abode in the UK, or has no time limit on their stay in the UK.
7.	A **current** Immigration Status Document issued by the Home Office to the holder with an endorsement indicating that the named person is allowed to stay indefinitely in the UK, or has no time limit on their stay in the UK, **together with** an official document giving the person's permanent National Insurance number and their name issued by a Government agency or a previous employer.
8.	A birth or adoption certificate issued in the UK, **together with** an official document giving the person's permanent National Insurance number and their name issued by a Government agency or a previous employer.
9.	A birth or adoption certificate issued in the Channel Islands, the Isle of Man or Ireland, **together with** an official document giving the person's permanent National Insurance number and their name issued by a Government agency or a previous employer.
10.	A certificate of registration or naturalisation as a British citizen, **together with** an official document giving the person's permanent National Insurance number and their name issued by a Government agency or a previous employer.

TABLE 5: LIST B – ACCEPTABLE DOCUMENTS TO ESTABLISH A STATUTORY EXCUSE FOR A LIMITED PERIOD OF TIME

List B	
Group 1 – Documents where a time-limited statutory excuse lasts until the expiry date of leave	
1.	A **current** passport endorsed to show that the holder is allowed to stay in the UK and is currently allowed to do the type of work in question.
2.	A **current** Biometric Immigration Document (Biometric Residence Permit) issued by the Home Office to the holder which indicates that the named person can currently stay in the UK and is allowed to do the work in question.
3.	A **current** Residence Card (including an Accession Residence Card or a Derivative Residence Card) issued by the Home Office to a non-European Economic Area national who is a family member of a national of a European Economic Area country or Switzerland or who has a derivative right of residence.
4.	A **current** Immigration Status Document containing a photograph issued by the Home Office to the holder with a valid endorsement indicating that the named person may stay in the UK, and is allowed to do the type of work in question, **together with** an official document giving the person's permanent National Insurance number and their name issued by a Government agency or a previous employer.
Group 2 – Documents where a time-limited statutory excuse lasts for 6 months	

1.	A Certificate of Application issued by the Home Office under regulation 18(3) or 20(2) of the Immigration (European Economic Area) Regulations 2016 to a family member of a national of a European Economic Area country or Switzerland stating that the holder is permitted to take employment which is **less than 6 months** old **together with a Positive Verification Notice**[4] from the Home Office Employer Checking Service.
2.	An Application Registration Card issued by the Home Office stating that the holder is permitted to take the employment in question, **together with a Positive Verification Notice** from the Home Office Employer Checking Service.
3.	A **Positive Verification Notice** issued by the Home Office Employer Checking Service to the employer or prospective employer which indicates that the named person may stay in the UK and is permitted to do the work in question.

NOTES

[4] A 'Positive Verification Notice' is official correspondence from the Home Office Employer Checking Service which confirms that a named person has permission to undertake the work in question.

FOLLOW-UP RIGHT TO WORK CHECKS

If you conduct the prescribed right to work checks, you will establish a statutory excuse as follows:

In List A: your statutory excuse will be for the whole duration of your employee's employment with you because there are no restrictions on their permission to be in the UK. You do not have to repeat the right to work check.

In List B: your statutory excuse will be limited because your employee has restrictions on their permission to be in the UK and to do the work in question. In order to retain your excuse, you must undertake follow-up right to work checks as follows:

GROUP 1 DOCUMENTS:

- If your employee is able to produce a current document in this list, you should make a follow-up check using this document. Your time-limited statutory excuse will continue for as long as your employee has permission to be in the UK and do the work in question, as evidenced by the document, or combination of documents, your employee produced for the right to work check.
- If, however, at the point that permission expires, you are reasonably satisfied that your employee has an outstanding application or appeal to vary or extend their leave in the UK, your time-limited statutory excuse will continue from the expiry date of your employee's permission for a further period of up to 28 days. This is to enable you to verify whether the employee has permission to continue working for you.
- During this 28-day period you must contact the Employer Checking Service and receive a Positive Verification Notice confirming the employee continues to have the right to undertake the work in question.
- In the event that you receive a Positive Verification Notice your statutory excuse will last for a further six months from the date specified in your Notice. You will then need to make a further check upon its expiry.
- In the event that you receive a Negative Verification Notice, your statutory excuse will be terminated.

> An application or appeal must be made on or before a person's permission to be in the UK and do the work in question expires in order to be deemed 'in-time' and valid. In the event that you receive a Negative Verification Notice[5] from the Employer Checking Service stating that the employee does not have permission to undertake the work in question, you will not have a statutory excuse and you should no longer employ that person.

NOTES

[5] A 'Negative Verification Notice' is official correspondence from the Home Office Employer Checking Service which confirms that a named person does not have permission to undertake the work in question.

GROUP 2 DOCUMENTS:

- If your prospective employee or employee holds one of the documents in Group 2, or is unable to present an acceptable document because they have an outstanding application, appeal, or administrative review with the Home Office in respect of their leave, you must contact the Employer Checking Service and receive a Positive Verification Notice. Your time-limited statutory excuse will last for six months from the date specified in the Positive Verification Notice. You will then need to make a further check upon its expiry.

CONDUCTING AN ONLINE RIGHT TO WORK CHECK

With effect from 28 January 2019, you may choose to conduct an online right to work check to establish a statutory excuse against a civil penalty in the event of illegal working. You can do this by accessing the Home Office online right to work checking service. Not all employees, or prospective employees, will have an immigration status that can be checked online.

You must access the service using the employer page on gov.uk, entitled 'View a job applicant's right to work details' in order to obtain a statutory excuse. It is not sufficient to view the information provided to the employee, or prospective employee, when they view their profile using the migrant part of the Home Office online right to work checking service, and doing so will not provide you with a statutory excuse.

There are three basic steps to conducting an online right to work check:

(1) use the Home Office online right to work checking service (the 'View a job applicant's right to work details' page on gov.uk) in respect of an individual and only employ the person, or continue to employ an existing employee, if the online check confirms they are entitled to do the work in question;

(2) satisfy yourself that any photograph on the online right to work check is of the individual presenting themselves for work; and

(3) retain a clear copy of the response provided by the online right to work check (storing that response securely, electronically or in hardcopy) for the duration of employment and for two years afterwards.

If the online right to work check does not confirm that the individual has the right to work in the UK and to do the work in question, you will not have a statutory excuse from this check if you proceed to employ them. If you know, or have reasonable cause to believe that they do not have the right to work, and employ them anyway, you risk being found guilty of a criminal offence.

If you are unable to conduct an online check because the individual has an outstanding application, appeal, or administrative review with the Home Office in respect of their leave, you must contact the Employer Checking Service. A Positive Verification Notice from the Employer Checking Service will provide you with a statutory excuse for six months from the date specified in the Positive Verification Notice. You will then need to make a further check upon its expiry.

ADDITIONAL REQUIREMENT FOR STUDENTS

For students who have limited permission to work during term-times, you must also obtain, copy and retain details of their academic term and vacation times covering the duration of their period of study in the UK for which they will be employed.

FOLLOW-UP RIGHT TO WORK CHECKS

Conducting the online right to work check as prescribed above will provide you with a statutory excuse for the period for which the online right to work check confirmed that the person named in it is permitted to carry out the work in question. You must conduct the check before employment commences in order to have a statutory excuse.

Where an employee has a time-limited right to work, and you have therefore established a time-limited statutory excuse, you are required to do a follow-up right to work check at the point that permission is due to end in order to retain a statutory excuse.

C. EQUALITY & HUMAN RIGHTS COMMISSION

DISABILITY DISCRIMINATION ACT 1995 REVISED CODE OF PRACTICE: TRADE ORGANISATIONS, QUALIFICATIONS BODIES AND GENERAL QUALIFICATIONS BODIES (2008)

Equality and Human Rights Commission

[4.112]

NOTES

This Code was issued by the Equality and Human Rights Commission on 16 May 2008. The Code was approved by the Secretary of State and by Parliament in accordance with the Equality Act 2006, s 14 and came into effect on 23 June 2008 (see the Disability Discrimination Code of Practice (Trade Organisations, Qualifications Bodies and General Qualifications Bodies) (Commencement) Order 2008, SI 2008/1335). For the legal status of the Code see s 15(4) of the 2006 Act at **[1.1442]**.

It replaces the Disability Rights Commission Code of Practice: Trade Organisations and Qualifications Bodies 2004 which was revoked, as from 23 June 2008, subject to transitional provisions (see the Disability Discrimination Code of Practice (Trade Organisations and Qualifications Bodies) (Revocation) Order 2008, SI 2008/1336, for details). The original Code is available at: http://webarchive.nationalarchives.gov.uk/20070706000123/http://www.drc-gb.org/PDF/COPtrade_quals.pdf.

Note that the Disability Discrimination Act 1995 was repealed by the Equality Act 2010, s 211(2), Sch 27, Pt 1, as from 1 October 2010. Note, however, that this Code has not been replaced or updated since the repeal of the 1995 Act.

See *Harvey* L.

CONTENTS

1. INTRODUCTION

PURPOSE OF PART 2 AND CHAPTER 2A OF PART 4 OF THE ACT

[4.113]

1.1 The Disability Discrimination Act 1995 (the Act) brought in measures to prevent discrimination against disabled people. Part 2 of the Act is based on the principle that disabled people should not be discriminated against in employment or when seeking employment. Part 4 of the Act (as amended by the Special Education Needs and Disability Act 2002 and the Disability Discrimination Act 2005 and regulations made under both Acts) is based on similar principles that disabled people should not be discriminated against in accessing education opportunities or discriminated against during the course of their education in schools, colleges and universities. A person's prospects of gaining employment, or of progressing in or retaining employment, may be affected by his ability to become a member of a trade organisation or to take advantage of its membership services. A person's employment prospects may also be affected by his ability to obtain a general, professional or trade qualification.

1.2 It is for this reason that, in addition to imposing duties on employers which are intended to prevent discrimination against disabled people, Part 2 sets out a number of duties with which trade organisations and bodies which confer professional or trade qualifications must comply for the same purpose, and new provisions under Chapter 2A of Part 4 of the Act set out similar duties in respect of general qualifications bodies. The extension of Part 2 to cover qualifications bodies as from October 2004, and the extension of Part 4 to cover general qualification bodies as from September 2007, represents a change in the law.

PURPOSE OF THE CODE

1.3 This Code of Practice (the Code) gives practical guidance on how to prevent discrimination against disabled people by trade organisations, qualifications bodies and general qualifications bodies. It describes the duties on such organisations and bodies in this regard. The Code helps disabled people to understand the law and what they can do if they feel that they have been discriminated against. By encouraging good

Part 4 Statutory Codes of Practice

practice, the Code assists trade organisations, qualifications bodies and general qualifications bodies to avoid complaints being made against them and to work towards the elimination of discrimination against disabled people.

1.4 The Code also gives guidance on the law which is intended to help lawyers when advising their clients, and to assist courts and tribunals when interpreting new legal concepts. The Code explains the operation and effect of technical statutory provisions – some of which only came into force on October 2004 (for qualifications bodies) and September 2007 (for general qualifications bodies), and many of which have a complex legal effect. Because of this, the Code is necessarily comprehensive and detailed.

1.5 **[s 14 Equality Act 2006]** The Commission for Equality and Human Rights has prepared and issued this revised Code under the Equality Act 2006 on the basis of a request by the Lord Privy Seal. It applies to England, Wales and Scotland. A similar but separate Code applies to Northern Ireland.

1.6 As employers themselves, trade organisations, qualifications bodies and general qualifications bodies have duties under Part 2 in respect of disabled people whom they employ, or who apply to them for employment. However, these matters are not considered in the Code – which is concerned only with the duties of trade organisations, qualifications bodies and general qualifications bodies acting in their capacity as such. Guidance on the application of the Act to employers is given in a separate code of practice issued by the Disability Rights Commission (DRC) (see Appendix B for details). It is possible that a number of individuals, organisations and bodies may be involved at different stages in matters concerning the legal duties described within this Code, particularly in respect of general qualifications bodies, and the Code attempts to explain each party's responsibilities under these duties.

STATUS OF THE CODE

1.7 **[s 15(4) Equality Act 2006]** The Code does not impose legal obligations. Nor is it an authoritative statement of the law – that is a matter for the courts and tribunals. However, the Code can be used in evidence in legal proceedings under the Act. Courts and employment tribunals must take into account any part of the Code that appears to them relevant to any question arising in those proceedings. If trade organisations, qualifications bodies and general qualifications bodies follow the guidance in the Code, it may help to avoid an adverse decision by a court or tribunal in such proceedings.

HOW TO USE THE CODE

1.8 This chapter gives an introduction to the Code. Chapter 2 sets out some general guidance on how to avoid discrimination. Chapter 3 contains an overview of the relevant provisions of the Act, and those provisions are examined in more detail in subsequent chapters.

1.9 Chapter 4 details what is meant by discrimination and harassment, and Chapter 5 explains the duty to make reasonable adjustments for disabled people. Chapter 6 examines the relevance of justification under Part 2 and Chapter 2A of Part 4. Chapters 7, 8 and 9 focus on particular issues relating to discrimination by trade organisations, qualifications bodies and general qualifications bodies respectively. Chapters 8 and 9 provide further information about competence standards.

1.10 Chapter 10 looks at issues concerning adjustments to premises, and Chapter 11 deals with various other points and explains what happens if discrimination is alleged.

1.11 Appendix A gives more information on what is meant by 'disability' and by 'disabled person'. Separate statutory guidance relating to the definition of disability has been issued under the Act (see paragraph 3.6). Appendix B lists other sources of relevant information about matters referred to in the Code.

1.12 Each chapter of the Code should be viewed as part of an overall explanation of the relevant provisions of the Act and the regulations made under them. In order to understand the law properly it is necessary to read the Code as a whole. The Code should not be read too narrowly or literally. It is intended to explain the principles of the law, to illustrate how the Act might operate in certain situations and to provide general guidance on good practice. There are some questions which the Code cannot resolve and which must await the authoritative interpretation of the courts and tribunals. The Code is not intended to be a substitute for taking appropriate advice on the legal consequences of particular situations.

EXAMPLES IN THE CODE

1.13 Examples of good practice and how the Act is likely to work are given in boxes. They are intended simply to illustrate the principles and concepts used in the legislation and should be read in that light. The examples should not be treated as complete or authoritative statements of the law.

1.14 While the examples refer to particular situations, they should be understood more widely as demonstrating how the law is likely to be applied generally. They can often be used to test how the law might apply in similar circumstances involving different disabilities or situations. The examples attempt to use as many different varieties of disabilities and situations as possible to demonstrate the breadth and scope of the Act. Examples relating to men or women are given for realism and could, of course, apply to people of either gender.

REFERENCES IN THE CODE

1.15 References to the Act are shown in the margins. For example, s 1(1) means section 1(1) of the Act and Sch means Schedule to the Act. References to Part 2, 3 or 4 refer to the relevant Part of the Act. Where reference is made to regulations, the appropriate Statutory Instrument (SI) number is shown in the margin.

CHANGES TO THE LEGISLATION

1.16 The Code refers to the Disability Discrimination Act as of 1 October 2004 and as amended to September 2007. There may be changes to the Act or to other legislation, for example to the range of people who are considered to be disabled under the Act, which may have an effect on the duties explained in the Code. You will need to ensure that you keep up to date with any developments that affect the Act's provisions.

FURTHER INFORMATION

1.17 Copies of the Act and regulations made under it can be purchased from The Stationery Office (see Appendix B for contact details). Separate codes covering other aspects of the Act, and guidance relating to the definition of disability are also available from The Stationery Office.

2. HOW CAN DISCRIMINATION BE AVOIDED?

INTRODUCTION

[4.114]

2.1 There are various actions which trade organisations, qualifications bodies and general qualifications bodies can take in order to avoid discriminating against disabled people. By doing so, organisations and bodies are not only likely to minimise the incidence of expensive and time-consuming litigation, but will also improve their general performance and the quality of the services they provide.

2.2 In addition, these actions will assist organisations and bodies who are public authorities (including any organisation certain of whose functions are functions of a public nature) to comply with the disability equality duty. The duty requires all such public authorities when carrying out their functions to have due regard to the need to:

- promote equality of opportunity between disabled persons and other persons;
- eliminate discrimination that is unlawful under the Act;
- eliminate harassment of disabled persons that is related to their disabilities;
- promote positive attitudes towards disabled persons;
- encourage participation by disabled persons in public life; and
- take steps to take account of disabled persons' disabilities, even where that involves treating disabled persons more favourably than other persons.

2.3 To assist certain public authorities (including statutory regulators responsible for professional, trade and general qualifications in complying with the above duty – known as the general duty), regulations lay down certain steps which these authorities must take. These are known as the 'specific duties'. They include the obligation to produce a Disability Equality Scheme which, amongst other things, requires public authorities to set out the steps which they will take (the action plan) to comply with the general duty. The general and specific duties do not create any individual rights for disabled people, but the Equality and Human Rights Commission can enforce both the general and the specific duties, and a failure to comply with the general duties may result in actions in the High Court (in England and Wales) or the Court of Session (in Scotland) by way of judicial review proceedings.

2.4 This chapter sets out some guidance on ways to help ensure that disabled people are not discriminated against. It also addresses only some of the aspects of the disability equality duty. Organisations and bodies should refer to the **Statutory Codes of Practice: The Duty to Promote Disability Equality** (England and Wales) and (Scotland) for full details of the obligations which they must comply with in relation to the duty.

UNDERSTANDING THE SOCIAL DIMENSION OF DISABILITY

2.5 The concept of discrimination in the Act reflects an understanding that functional limitations arising from disabled people's impairments do not inevitably restrict their ability to participate fully in society. Rather than the limitations of an impairment it is often environmental factors (such as the structure of a building, or an organisation's practices) which unnecessarily lead to these social restrictions. This principle underpins the duty to make reasonable adjustments described in Chapter 5. Understanding this will assist trade organisations, qualifications bodies and general qualifications bodies to avoid discrimination. It is as important to consider which aspects of an organisation or body's activities create difficulties for a disabled person as it is to understand the particular nature of an individual's disability.

RECOGNISING THE DIVERSE NATURE OF DISABILITY

2.6 There are more than eight million disabled adults in our society. The nature and extent of their disabilities vary widely, as do their requirements for overcoming any difficulties they may face. If trade organisations, qualifications bodies and general qualifications bodies are to avoid discriminating, they need to understand this, and to be aware of the effects their decisions and actions – and those of their agents and employees – may have on disabled people. The evidence shows that many of the steps that can be taken to avoid discrimination cost little or nothing and are easy to implement.

AVOIDING MAKING ASSUMPTIONS

2.7 It is advisable to avoid making assumptions about disabled people. Impairments will often affect different people in different ways and their needs may be different as well. The following suggestions may help to avoid discrimination:

- Do not assume that because a person does not look disabled, he is not disabled.

- Do not assume that most disabled people use wheelchairs.
- Do not assume that all blind people read Braille or have guide dogs.
- Do not assume that all deaf people use sign language.
- Do not assume that disabled people have lesser abilities and career aspirations than non-disabled people.
- Do not assume that people with certain types of disability (such as mental health problems or epilepsy) present a health and safety risk.
- Do not assume that because you are unaware of any disabled members of an organisation there are none.
- Do not assume that because you are unaware of any disabled people who are engaged in a particular profession or trade there are none.

FINDING OUT ABOUT DISABLED PEOPLE'S NEEDS

2.8 As explained later in the Code (see paragraphs 5.14 and 8.22 for example), the Act requires trade organisations, qualifications bodies and general qualification bodies to think about ways of complying with their legal duties. Listening carefully to disabled people and finding out what they want will help organisations and bodies to meet their obligations by identifying the best way of meeting disabled people's needs. There is a better chance of reaching the best outcome if discussions are held with disabled people at an early stage.

2.9 Often, discussing with disabled people what is required to meet their needs will reassure a trade organisation, qualifications body or general qualifications body that suitable adjustments can be carried out cheaply and with very little inconvenience.

2.10 There are various ways in which the views of disabled people can be obtained. Many trade unions and professional bodies and general qualifications bodies may have established formal structures for seeking and representing the views of disabled people. These may take the form of an advisory committee, perhaps a sub-committee of the equal opportunities committee or national governing body. Some organisations have a standing national forum for disabled members as well as arranging periodic conferences. In addition, the specific duties regulations require prescribed public authorities to involve disabled people in the development of the Disability Equality Scheme.

SEEKING EXPERT ADVICE

2.11 It may be possible to avoid discrimination by using personal or in-house knowledge and expertise – particularly if information or views are obtained from the disabled person concerned. However, although the Act does not specifically require anyone to obtain expert advice about meeting the needs of disabled people, in practice it may sometimes be necessary to do so in order to comply with the principal duties set out in the Act. Expert advice might be especially useful if a person is newly disabled or if the effects of a person's disability become more marked. Local and national disability organisations in particular may be able to give useful advice about the needs of disabled people and steps that can be taken to meet those needs.

PLANNING AHEAD

2.12 The duties which the Act places on trade organisations, qualifications bodies and general qualifications bodies are owed to the individual disabled people with whom those organisations and bodies have dealings. There is no duty owed to disabled people in general. Nevertheless, it is likely to be cost effective for trade organisations and qualifications bodies to plan ahead. Considering the needs of a range of disabled people when planning for change (such as when planning a building refurbishment, a new IT system, or the design of a website) is likely to make it easier to implement adjustments for individuals when the need arises. In addition, the disability equality duty requires organisations and bodies that are public authorities to have due regard to the need to promote equality of opportunity – including the need to eliminate discrimination. This requirement may require public authorities to adopt a proactive approach, anticipating the needs of disabled people.

2.13 It is good practice for trade organisations, qualifications bodies and general qualifications bodies to check whether access audits have been carried out to identify any improvements which can be made to a building to make it more accessible. Access audits should be carried out by suitably qualified people, such as those listed in the National Register of Access Consultants (see Appendix B for details). Websites and intranet sites can also be reviewed to see how accessible they are to disabled people using access software.

> A trade organisation is re-fitting its premises including its facilities for members. The architects are asked to comply with British Standard 8300 to ensure that facilities such as the entrance, reception, meeting rooms, lecture theatre and toilets are accessible to a wide range of disabled visitors. BS8300 is a code of practice on the design of buildings and their approaches to meet the needs of disabled people (see Appendix B for details).

> A qualifications body is re-designing its website. In doing so it ensures that the new website is easy to read for people with a variety of access software; has the website checked for accessibility; and invites

disabled readers of the website to let the qualifications body know if they find any part of it inaccessible.

As part of the approval process for centres to deliver examinations and assessments for general qualifications, a general qualifications body asks a prospective centre to give details of the accessibility of its premises. Where there are concerns with the accessibility of the premises, the prospective centre is advised of the need to identify and make any improvements. The general qualifications body provides a leaflet with further information for centres on where to get advice and assistance in relation to access audits.

IMPLEMENTING ANTI-DISCRIMINATORY POLICIES AND PRACTICES

2.14 Trade organisations, qualifications bodies and general qualifications bodies are more likely to comply with their duties under the Act, and to avoid the risk of legal action being taken against them, if they implement anti-discriminatory policies and practices. These are often referred to as equality policies or diversity policies. Additionally, in the event that legal action is taken, trade organisations, qualifications bodies and general qualifications bodies may be asked to demonstrate to an employment tribunal or county/sheriff court that they have effective policies and procedures in place to minimise the risk of discrimination.

As part of the approval process for centres to deliver general qualifications, a general qualifications body advises centres that learners with disabilities should be accommodated in examination rooms that are appropriate to their needs. For example, a candidate with learning difficulties, who relies on the use of a prompter, is best accommodated in a room with few distractions, away from other candidates.

An inspector working on behalf of the general qualifications bodies visits a centre to ensure that the examinations are being carried out in accordance with relevant requirements. His checklist includes a check that any candidate with a disability has access to suitable accommodation. He reports to the general qualifications bodies any circumstances where unsuitable accommodation has been provided and they take up this issue with the centre.

RECOMMENDED STEPS FOR ALL TRADE ORGANISATIONS, QUALIFICATIONS BODIES AND GENERAL QUALIFICATIONS BODIES

2.15 Anti-discriminatory policies and practices will vary depending on the nature of the organisation (for example, on whether it is a trade organisation, qualifications body or general qualifications body and on the size and nature of its membership). However, it is advisable for all trade organisations, qualifications bodies and general qualifications bodies to take the following steps:

- Establish a policy which aims to prevent discrimination against disabled people and which is communicated to all employees and agents of the organisation or body.
- Provide disability awareness and equality training to all employees. In addition, train employees and agents so that they understand the organisation or body's policy on disability, their obligations under the Act and the practice of reasonable adjustments.
- Ensure that members and potential members of the organisation (or, in the case of a qualifications body and general qualifications body, people who wish to have a qualification conferred on them and people who already hold a qualification) are informed about the organisation or body's disability policy.
- Ensure that people within the organisation or body who have responsibility for liaising with members or applicants have more in-depth training about the organisation's duties under the Act.
- Inform all employees and agents that conduct which breaches the anti-discrimination policy will not be tolerated, and respond quickly and effectively to any such breaches.
- Monitor the implementation and effectiveness of such a policy.
- Address acts of disability discrimination by employees as part of disciplinary rules and procedures.
- Have complaints and grievance procedures which are easy for disabled people to use and which are designed to resolve issues effectively.
- Regularly review the effectiveness of reasonable adjustments made for disabled people in accordance with the Act, and act on the findings of those reviews.
- Keep clear records of decisions taken in respect of each of these matters.

ADDITIONAL RECOMMENDED STEPS FOR TRADE UNIONS

2.16 Trade unions are a particular kind of trade organisation. In addition to taking the general steps outlined in paragraph 2.15, it is advisable for trade unions to:

- Have (and inform local branches about) a central budget or 'access fund' to pay for adjustments for disabled members in circumstances where it would be too expensive for the adjustments to be funded by local branches.
- Ensure that union representatives understand the Act's provisions on employment and occupation so that they are able to support union members who encounter disability discrimination at work.
- Ensure that health and safety representatives have a proper understanding of the principles of risk assessment and reasonable adjustments, so that health and safety issues are not used to discriminate against disabled people in the workplace or when participating in union activities.

The above considerations apply just as much to unpaid union representatives in the workplace as to salaried employees of a union.

2.17 Trade unions should not enter into collective agreements containing terms which discriminate against disabled people (see paragraphs 11.14 to 11.16). In addition, European law encourages trade unions to enter into collective agreements at national and local level in respect of anti-discriminatory policies and practices. It is advisable for trade unions to monitor the effectiveness of any such agreements.

ADDITIONAL RECOMMENDED STEPS FOR QUALIFICATIONS BODIES

2.18 The general steps outlined in paragraph 2.15 are recommended for trade organisations and qualifications bodies alike. However, there are additional steps which it is advisable for qualifications bodies to take. These are to:

- Ensure that there are effective systems in place for disabled people to request reasonable adjustments for examinations or practical tests, so that qualifications bodies are in a position to respond quickly and effectively to individual requests for specific adjustments. This may involve establishing procedures with educational institutions to ensure that institutions request relevant information from their students and then pass this on to the qualifications bodies (see paragraph 8.23).
- Regularly review any competence standards which relate to particular professional or trade qualifications to ensure that they are framed in a way which does not unnecessarily exclude disabled people from being able to meet them. This will involve carefully scrutinising each competence standard to check that it is not discriminatory. Consideration should be given to whether each standard can be objectively justified. Disabled people who work in the relevant profession or trade could be consulted to learn from their experiences, and factors such as changes in technology, which can enable people to do jobs in different ways, should be taken into account.

Further advice about how to avoid discrimination in relation to competence standards is given at paragraph 8.41.

ADDITIONAL RECOMMENDED STEPS FOR GENERAL QUALIFICATIONS BODIES

2.19 The context within which general qualifications bodies operate is summarised in paragraph 3.30 and set out in more detail in Chapter 9. The general steps outlined in paragraph 2.15 are also recommended for general qualifications bodies. However, there are also additional steps specifically recommended for general qualifications bodies to take. These are to:

- Regularly review with their regulators the requirements for relevant general qualifications to ensure that they are framed in a way which does not unnecessarily exclude disabled people from being able to meet them. This will involve carefully scrutinising each requirement to check that it is not discriminatory. Consideration should be given to whether each requirement is objectively reasonable or, in the case of competence standards, legitimate and proportionate.
- Ensure that there are effective systems in place for disabled people to request reasonable adjustments for examinations or practical tests, so that general qualifications bodies are in a position to respond quickly and effectively to individual requests for specific adjustments. This may well involve establishing procedures for direct contact between disabled people, general qualifications bodies and educational institutions to ensure that all relevant information reaches the general qualifications bodies. In practice, most requests for adjustments may be received through educational institutions.
- Ensure that disabled people have effective recourse to the general qualifications bodies appeal procedures in respect of examinations and assessment results.

Further advice about how to avoid discrimination in relation to competence standards is given at paragraphs 9.57 to 9.82.

AUDITING POLICIES AND PROCEDURES

2.20 Although there is no duty under Part 2 (and Part 4 in respect of general qualifications bodies) to anticipate the needs of disabled people in general, it is a good idea for trade organisations and qualifications bodies to keep all their policies under review, and to consider the needs of such disabled people as part of this process. It is advisable for organisations and bodies to do this in addition to having a specific policy to prevent discrimination. In addition, the disability equality duty requires organisations and bodies that are public authorities to have due regard to the need to promote equality of opportunity – including the need to eliminate discrimination. This requirement may require public authorities to adopt a proactive approach, anticipating the needs of disabled people. Trade organisations and qualifications bodies are likely to have policies about matters such as:

- emergency evacuation procedures
- procurement of equipment, IT systems and websites
- information provision

- service standards for members.

> A trade organisation has a policy to ensure that all members are kept informed about the organisation's activities through a website. The policy states that the website should be accessible to disabled people, including those who use access software (such as speech synthesis).
>
> The website editor is given additional training in accessible website design.

> A trade organisation has a policy outlining the level of service that all members and potential members should receive. It includes standards of service for disabled members and potential members, such as provision of application forms in accessible formats.

> A new procurement policy requires a number of factors to be taken into account in procuring equipment and IT systems. These factors include cost and energy efficiency. It is good practice for such factors to include accessibility for disabled people as well.

> A trade union reviews its procedures for organising conferences to ensure that access for disabled members is taken into account at all stages.

2.21 Much of what is stated about auditing policies and procedures in paragraph 2.20 also applies to general qualifications bodies, apart from the fact that the relevant provisions of Chapter 2A of Part 4, and not Part 2, apply to general qualifications bodies. General qualifications bodies are particularly likely to have policies about matters such as:

- testing, assessment and examination arrangements
- adjustments to the testing, assessment and examination process
- standards for qualifications
- their relationship with those who are responsible for conducting examinations, testing and assessments (eg schools and colleges).

> A general qualifications body is updating its exam timetable. It ensures that the guidance to centres on timetabling refers to the flexibility available to candidates who may require adjustments to the timetable for a reason related to their impairment.

MONITORING

2.22 Monitoring of members or, in the case of qualifications bodies and general qualifications bodies, people applying for a qualification or people who hold qualifications, is an important way of determining whether anti-discrimination measures taken by an organisation or body are effective, and ensuring that disability equality is a reality. Information must be gathered sensitively, with appropriately worded questions, and confidentiality must be ensured. Knowing the proportion of disabled people and their status in respect of an organisation or body can help it determine where practices and policies need to be improved.

2.23 In addition, where applicable, the disability equality specific duties require public authorities to set out the following in their Disability Equality Schemes:

- arrangements for gathering information on the extent to which the services it provides and those other functions it performs take account of the needs of disabled persons.

2.24 It is important to understand that information gathering is not an end in itself but that the information obtained must be analysed and used as the basis for preparing disability action plans, and reviewing the effectiveness of those actions taken. The information gathered is in fact evidence of an authority's progress in relation to disability equality. For this reason the Disability Equality Scheme is also required to include a statement of the public authority's arrangements for making use of the information gathered in these ways and in particular its arrangements for reviewing on a regular basis the effectiveness of the action plan and preparing subsequent Disability Equality Schemes.

2.25 Information must be gathered sensitively, with appropriately worded questions, and confidentiality must be ensured.

2.26 Monitoring will be more effective if disabled people feel comfortable about disclosing information about their disabilities. This is more likely to be the case if the trade organisation, qualifications body or general qualifications body explains the purpose of the monitoring and if members and applicants believe that it genuinely supports equality for disabled people and is using the information gathered to create positive change.

By monitoring of its membership, a professional association becomes aware that disabled people are under-represented at fellowship level. The association uses this information to review its criteria for awarding fellowships, and carries out research into the barriers facing disabled people at senior levels of the profession.

A trade union becomes aware, through monitoring, that disabled people are under-represented as conference delegates. It uses this information to find out from disabled members how arrangements for conferences can be improved to enable fuller participation.

A general qualifications body monitors the numbers of disabled people who take their qualifications. The general qualifications body finds that disabled people are less likely to choose certain courses. It uses the information to involve disabled people to consider and review the accessibility of the syllabuses/specifications and the nature of the assessment of the qualifications in question.

2.27 Some organisations choose to monitor by broad type of disability to understand the barriers faced by people with different types of impairment.

A general qualifications body decides to monitor the numbers of issues raised by disabled people and groups representing disabled people. It finds that most of these issues relate to a particular examination paper which included materials that created an unnecessary barrier to assessment and one which was not required. It reviews the results of the candidates affected and then requires the subject team to check questions as they are written so that the problem can be avoided in future.

Through monitoring of people applying for and achieving registration, a qualifications body becomes aware that people with certain disabilities are significantly under-represented as applicants for, and holders of, a particular qualification. The qualifications body uses this information to review its competence standards to ensure that they do not present unnecessary barriers to disabled people.

2.28 Public authorities are required to put into effect arrangements for gathering information and making use of it. In their annual reporting on the disability equality duty, they must set out the results of the information gathering which they have carried out, detailing the evidence which has been obtained and the use to which it has been put – such as the actions which will be taken to address the issues raised by the evidence.

2.29 Gathering information on students is a different process to gathering information from individual disabled students about their reasonable adjustments requirements. The processes should be separate and it should be clear to students and applicants why the information is being collected.

PROMOTING EQUALITY

2.30 Organisations or bodies not subject to the disability equality duty may nevertheless have an important part to play in promoting equality of opportunity (and they may also find that they are required to do so in relation to contractual arrangements with public authorities). In order to enhance disabled people's opportunities for gaining, retaining and progressing in employment, trade organisations, qualifications bodies and general qualifications bodies need to consider equality of opportunity for disabled people from two perspectives. First, such organisations and bodies should ensure that disabled people have equal access to membership, and to the benefits of membership, or (as the case may be) to opportunities for gaining and retaining a general, professional or trade qualification. Secondly, it is good practice for a trade organisation, qualifications body or general qualifications body to seek to promote equality for disabled people within the trade, profession or employment/ education sector in which it operates.

A general qualifications body advises schools and colleges which can enter candidates for its qualifications about the variety of ways in which it delivers the course and its assessment in ways which meet the particular needs of disabled people with a variety of impairments.

A trade organisation in the tourism sector holds a conference in association with employers in that sector and disability organisations to promote opportunities for disabled people within the tourism industry.

A trade union representing people in the broadcasting trades ensures that its promotional literature and its website show positive images of disabled people carrying out a variety of jobs within this industry.

A qualifications body in the health sector promotes a scheme through which disabled people are encouraged to apply to train as health professionals.

2.31 Organisations and bodies should be ensuring that any marketing activity, such as advertising a course, which features students or prospective students positively represents disabled students within that. As well as contributing to the overall goal of equality of opportunity, promoting such attitudes will ensure that organisations and bodies demonstrate that they are aware of the needs of disabled people. This will, in turn, generate broader representation of disabled people in terms of the activities of organisations and bodies, and will also encourage participation of disabled people in their monitoring activities in particular. For organisations and bodies that are public authorities, one of the aspects of the disability equality duty, as outlined above, is the need to promote positive attitudes towards disabled people.

RESOLVING DISPUTES

2.32 Although the Act does not require trade organisations, qualifications bodies or general qualifications bodies to resolve disputes within the organisation or body, it is in the interests of such an organisation or body wherever possible to resolve problems as they arise. This should be done in a non-discriminatory way to comply with the requirements of the Act.

2.33 Grievance procedures can provide an open and fair way for concerns to be made known. Such procedures may be particularly appropriate for use by members of trade organisations, and can enable grievances to be resolved quickly before they become major problems. Use of the procedures may highlight areas in which the duty to make reasonable adjustments has not been observed, and can prevent misunderstandings leading to complaints to tribunals and courts.

2.34 Chapter 11 contains further information about grievance procedures and about resolving disputes under the Act.

3. DISCRIMINATION BY TRADE ORGANISATIONS, QUALIFICATIONS BODIES AND GENERAL QUALIFICATIONS BODIES – AN OVERVIEW

INTRODUCTION

[4.115]

3.1 This chapter gives an overview of those provisions of the Act which are relevant to trade organisations, qualifications bodies and general qualifications bodies. It explains who has rights and duties under those provisions and outlines what is made unlawful by them. Later chapters explain the provisions in greater detail.

WHO HAS RIGHTS UNDER THE ACT?

Disabled people

3.2 **[ss 1 and 2 and Sch 1 and 2]** The Act gives protection from discrimination to a 'disabled' person within the meaning of the Act. A disabled person is someone who has a physical or mental impairment which has an effect on his or her ability to carry out normal day-to-day activities. That effect must be:

- substantial (that is, more than minor or trivial), and
- adverse, and long term (that is, it has lasted or is likely to last for at least a year or for the rest of the life of the person affected).

3.3 Physical or mental impairment includes sensory impairment. Hidden impairments are also covered (for example, mental illness or mental health problems, learning disabilities, dyslexia, diabetes and epilepsy).

3.4 The definition of disability used in the Act is not the same as other definitions of disabled persons in other legislation that applies to education in schools and colleges – for example in relation to the special educational needs framework in England and Wales, or the Additional Support for Learning in Scotland. It is possible that some people may be covered by more than one definition, and others may be covered by only one of these definitions. In considering its duties under the Act, a trade organisation, qualifications body and general qualifications body should not use any definition of 'disabled person' which is narrower than that in the Act. If such an organisation or body is asked to make a disability-related adjustment, it may ask the person requesting it for evidence that the impairment is one which meets the definition of disability in the Act. It may be appropriate to do so where the disability is not obvious. However, it is not appropriate to ask for more information about the impairment than is necessary for this purpose. Nor should evidence of disability be asked for where it ought to be obvious that the Act will apply.

People who have had a disability in the past

3.5 People who have had a disability within the meaning of the Act (as set out in Appendix A) in the past are protected from discrimination even if they no longer have the disability.

More information about the meaning of disability

3.6 For a fuller understanding of the concept of disability under the Act, reference should be made to Appendix A. A government publication, *Guidance on matters to be taken into account in determining questions relating to the definition of disability*, provides additional help in understanding the concept of disability and in identifying who is a disabled person. Where relevant, the Guidance must be taken into account in any legal proceedings.

People who have been victimised

3.7 The Act also gives rights to people who have been victimised, whether or not they have a disability or have had one in the past (see paragraphs 4.31 to 4.34).

WHO HAS OBLIGATIONS UNDER THE ACT?

Trade organisations

3.8 **[s 13(4)]** The Act defines a trade organisation as an organisation of workers or of employers, or any other organisation whose members carry on a particular profession or trade for the purposes of which the organisation exists. Bodies like trade unions, employers' associations and chartered professional institutions are all trade organisations because they exist for the purposes of the profession or trade which their members carry on. Examples of trade organisations include the Law Society, the Royal College of Nursing, the Swimming Teachers' Association, the Society of Floristry, the British Computer Society, and the Institute of Carpenters. The Act applies to all trade organisations, no matter how many (or how few) members they may have.

Qualifications bodies

3.9 **[s 14A(5)]** The Act defines a qualifications body as an authority or body which can confer, renew or extend a professional or trade qualification. For this purpose a professional or trade qualification is an authorisation, qualification, recognition, registration, enrolment, approval or certification which is needed for, or which facilitates engagement in, a particular profession or trade. What this means in practice is considered in paragraphs 8.5 to 8.7. Qualifications bodies include examination boards, the General Medical Council, the Nursing and Midwifery Council, and the Driving Standards Agency. Other examples are City and Guilds, the Institute of the Motor Industry, the Hospitality Awarding Body and the Guild of Cleaners and Launderers.

3.10 **[s 14A(5)]** Nevertheless, certain bodies are not regarded as qualifications bodies for the purposes of Part 2, even though they may perform some of the functions mentioned in paragraph 3.9. These are listed in the Act. Broadly speaking, they comprise local education authorities in England and Wales, education authorities in Scotland, and other bodies having responsibility for schools and colleges. This is because discrimination by such bodies is the concern of Part 4 of the Act, which relates to discrimination in the provision of education. The DRC has issued two separate codes of practice giving guidance on the operation of Part 4 (see Appendix B for details).

3.11 Clearly, certain trade organisations (such as the Law Society) also confer professional or trade qualifications. Consequently, the same organisation or body can be both a trade organisation and a qualifications body. Where this is the case, the application of the Act's provisions depends upon the capacity in which the organisation or body is acting at the time in question. For example, if an alleged act of discrimination relates to conferring, renewing or extending a professional or trade qualification, the relevant provisions are those relating to discrimination by qualifications bodies – the fact that the body is also a trade organisation is irrelevant in this context.

General qualifications bodies

3.12 **[s 31AA(4) and (6) and Reg 2 and Sch of SI 2007/1764]** The Act defines a general qualifications body as an authority or body which can confer, renew or extend a relevant qualification, or authenticate a relevant qualification awarded by another person. For this purpose a relevant qualification is an authorisation, qualification, approval or certification which is listed in the regulations, and is one of the following qualifications:

- GCEs (General Certificate of Education)
- Advanced level (A and AS levels)
- VCEs (Vocational Certificate of Education)
- AEAs (Advanced Extension Awards)

- GCSEs (General Certificate of Secondary Education)
- Free standing Maths Qualifications
- Entry level qualifications
- Key Skills
- Certificates in Adult Literacy and Numeracy Entry Levels, Level 1, 2 and 3
- GNVQs (General National Vocational Qualifications)
- The National Qualifications framework in Scotland
- The Welsh Baccalaureate Qualification
- The International Baccalaureate.

[s 31AA(6)(i)–(iv)] In line with paragraph 3.10, under the Act certain bodies are deemed not to be general qualifications bodies. These include responsible bodies within the meaning of Chapters 1 and 2 of Part 4 of the Act (responsible bodies of schools and further and higher education institutions), local education authorities in England and Wales and education authorities in Scotland. **[s 31AA(5)]** A relevant general qualification cannot be a professional and trade qualification within the meaning given by s 14A(5) of the Act.

Employers and others to whom Part 2 applies

3.13 The primary focus of Part 2 is, of course, on the duties of employers to disabled people. As mentioned at paragraph 1.6, however, that is not the subject of this Code. Guidance on the application of the Act to employers (as well as its application to people and bodies concerned with certain occupations and to persons such as the trustees or managers of occupational pension schemes and the providers of group insurance services) is given in a separate code of practice issued by the DRC (see Appendix B for details). It has already been noted that, as employers themselves, trade organisations, qualifications bodies and general qualifications bodies have duties under Part 2 in respect of disabled people whom they employ, or who apply to them for employment. Those duties are governed by the employment provisions of the Act.

Education institutions to whom Chapter 2A of Part 4 applies

3.14 Part 4 of the Act is largely concerned with the duties of education providers ('responsible bodies'). However, this is also not the subject of this Code. Guidance on the application of the Act to education providers is given in two separate codes of practice issued by the DRC (see Appendix B for details).

WHAT DOES THE ACT SAY ABOUT DISCRIMINATION BY TRADE ORGANISATIONS, QUALIFICATIONS BODIES AND GENERAL QUALIFICATIONS BODIES?

Effect of the Act

3.15 The Act makes it unlawful for a trade organisation to **discriminate** against a disabled person in relation to membership of the organisation or access to membership benefits. The Act also makes it unlawful for a qualifications body and a general qualifications body to **discriminate** against a disabled person in relation to conferring professional or trade qualifications and relevant general qualifications respectively.

3.16 However, the Act does not prevent organisations or bodies from treating disabled people more favourably than those who are not disabled.

Forms of discrimination

3.17 The four forms of discrimination which are unlawful under Part 2 (and unlawful under Part 4 in relation to general qualifications bodies) are:

- direct discrimination (the meaning of which is explained at paragraphs 4.4 to 4.21)
- failure to comply with a duty to make reasonable adjustments (explained in Chapter 5)
- 'disability-related discrimination' (see paragraphs 4.25 to 4.30), and
- victimisation of a person (whether or not he is disabled) – what the Act says about victimisation is explained at paragraphs 4.31 to 4.34.

Discrimination by trade organisations

3.18 **[s 13(1)]** The Act says that it is unlawful for a trade organisation to discriminate against a disabled person:

- in the arrangements it makes for the purpose of determining who should be offered membership of the organisation, or
- in the terms on which it is prepared to admit him to membership, or
- by refusing to accept, or deliberately not accepting, his application for membership.

3.19 **[s 13(2)]** The Act also says that it is unlawful for a trade organisation to discriminate against a disabled member:

- in the way it affords the member access to any benefits or by refusing or deliberately omitting to afford access to them, or
- by depriving the member of membership, or varying the terms of his membership, or
- by subjecting the member to any other detriment.

What this means in practice is explained in Chapter 7.

3.20 It should be noted that the Act does not protect corporate members of trade organisations, even if a disabled person is a representative of a corporate member.

> A trade organisation in the building industry has both individual and corporate members. A disabled employee of a company which is a member of this trade organisation would not have protection from discrimination by the trade organisation under Part 2, whereas an individual member of the organisation would have such protection.

Discrimination by qualifications bodies

3.21 **[s 14A(1)]** In relation to conferring, renewing, or extending professional or trade qualifications (abbreviated to 'conferring'), the Act says that it is unlawful for a qualifications body to discriminate against a disabled person:

- in the arrangements it makes for the purpose of determining upon whom to confer a professional or trade qualification, or
- in the terms on which it is prepared to confer such a qualification, or
- by refusing or deliberately omitting to grant any application by him for a professional or trade qualification, or
- by withdrawing such a qualification from him or varying the terms on which he holds it.

What this means in practice is explained in Chapter 8.

Discrimination by general qualifications bodies

3.22 **[s 31AA(1)]** In relation to conferring, renewing, or extending a general qualification (collectively referred to in this code as 'conferring'), the Act says that it is unlawful for a general qualifications body to discriminate against a disabled person:

- in the arrangements it makes for the purpose of determining upon whom to confer a relevant general qualification, or
- in the terms on which it is prepared to confer such a qualification, or
- by refusing or deliberately omitting to grant any application by him for a relevant general qualification, or
- by withdrawing such a qualification from him or varying the terms on which he holds it.

What this means in practice is explained in Chapter 9.

WHAT ELSE IS UNLAWFUL UNDER THE RELEVANT PROVISIONS OF THE ACT?

Harassment

3.23 **[s 13(3) and s 14A(2) and s 31AA(2)]** In addition to what it says about discrimination, Part 2 (and Part 4) makes it unlawful for a trade organisation, qualifications body or general qualifications body to subject a disabled person to **harassment** for a reason which relates to his disability. What the Act says about harassment is explained in more detail at paragraphs 4.36 and 4.37. The Act treats disability-related harassment as a separate concept, and this is not one of the forms of discrimination.

Instructions and pressure to discriminate

3.24 **[s 16C and s 17B(1)]** It is also unlawful for a person who has authority or influence over another to instruct him, or put pressure on him, to act unlawfully under the provisions of Part 2 – this provision **does not** apply to general qualifications bodies. Where these duties apply they cover pressure to discriminate, whether applied directly to the person concerned, or indirectly but in a way in which he is likely to hear of it. However, the Act does not give individual disabled people the right to take legal action in respect of unlawful instructions or pressure to discriminate. Such action may only be taken by the Equality and Human Rights Commission (see paragraphs 11.26 to 11.28).

> A trade union is holding a conference. The conference organiser, who is a paid employee of the union working in the events department, instructs the branch representatives not to send any wheelchair users to the conference as the venue is not wheelchair accessible. This is likely to be unlawful as it is an instruction to discriminate.

Discriminatory advertisements

3.25 **[s 16B]** The Act does not prevent advertisements for membership of trade organisations, or for general, professional or trade qualifications from saying that applications from disabled people are welcome. However, in respect of trade organisations and qualifications bodies (but **not** in respect of general qualifications bodies) it does say that it is unlawful for those seeking members for an organisation (or seeking candidates for professional and trade qualifications) to publish an advertisement (or cause it to be published) which indicates, or might reasonably be understood to indicate:

- that the success of a person's application may depend to any extent on his not having any disability, or any particular disability, or
- that the person determining the application is reluctant to make reasonable adjustments.

3.26 This applies to every form of advertisement or notice, whether to the public or not. However, an advertisement may still be lawful even if it does indicate that having a particular disability will adversely affect an applicant's prospects of success. This will be the case where, for example, the particular circumstances are such that the trade organisation or qualifications body is entitled to take the effects of the disability into account when assessing the suitability of applicants.

> A qualifications body in the tourism industry advertises in a trade publication, inviting readers to apply to take a course leading to a qualification accredited by that body. The advertisement says that candidates 'must have excellent written and spoken English'. This would exclude people who used British Sign Language as their first language, or people who had dyslexia, and may be unlawful.

> However a qualifications body advertising a course in tree surgery, would not be discriminating by stipulating that candidates 'must not be afraid of heights', even if this would exclude people who had vertigo as a result of their disability.

3.27 It is good practice to consider carefully what information should be included in advertisements and where they should be placed.

3.28 **[s 17B(1)]** The Act does not give individual applicants for membership of trade organisations or applicants for professional or trade qualifications the right to take legal action in respect of discriminatory advertisements. Such action may only be taken by the Equality and Human Rights Commission (see paragraphs 11.26 to 11.28).

WHO IS LIABLE FOR UNLAWFUL ACTS?

Responsibility for the acts of others

3.29 **[s 58]** Trade organisations, qualifications bodies and general qualifications bodies who act through agents are liable for the actions of their agents done with the express or implied authority of the organisation or body in question – this can include the actions of unpaid union representatives in the workplace or education institutions (and/or their employees) in respect of exams and testing.

3.30 General qualifications bodies may directly provide, or contract with third parties to organise and to provide, examination and assessment facilities, and to undertake examinations and assessments that may result in conferring relevant general qualifications. In addition, statutory regulators may set criteria which general qualifications bodies use to determine examination and assessment objectives. Chapter 9 provides further information about the context in which general qualifications bodies operate and the duties that they have under the DDA.

> A person employed by an examination centre to invigilate an examination for a GCSE qualification refuses to allow a candidate with a severe disfigurement into the examination hall as he believes this candidate's disability would be off-putting for other candidates. This is likely to constitute unlawful direct disability discrimination. The invigilator in question is acting on behalf of the examination centre in relation to delivery of the examination and, therefore, he is likely to be acting as an agent of the general qualifications body who ultimately confer the GCSE qualification. The general qualifications body would be liable under the Act for the unlawful actions of the invigilator, who, together with the examination centre, would also be individually liable.

3.31 The Act also says that trade organisations, qualifications bodies and general qualifications bodies are responsible for the actions of their employees in the course of their employment. For example, a trade union is responsible for the actions of its salaried officials in the course of their employment.

3.32 However, in legal proceedings against a trade organisation, qualifications body or general qualifications body, based on the actions of an employee, it is a defence that the organisation or body took 'such steps as were reasonably practicable' to prevent such actions. It is not a defence simply to show that the action took place without the knowledge or approval of the organisation or body.

> A trade union has a disability policy which states that it will pay for sign language interpreters to interpret at branch meetings, should the need arise, from a central union fund. This policy, and the arrangements available for paying for sign language interpreters (and for other adjustments), is explained to all branch representatives and new members. In addition all branch representatives are required to undergo basic training in the policy. A deaf union member requests a sign language interpreter for a branch meeting, but the branch representative who has undergone this training says that this is not possible as there are insufficient funds in the branch to pay for this adjustment. In this case the union could demonstrate that it had taken 'such steps as were reasonably practicable' to prevent such actions and it is likely that it has not acted unlawfully. The branch representative, however, is

likely to be acting unlawfully (see paragraphs 3.29 and 3.30).

An Examiner working for a Scottish general qualifications body refuses to allow a pupil with a severe speech impediment to have extra time to answer in a French Speaking Test. The Examiner is employed by the general qualifications body so the body will be liable for the potentially discriminatory actions of the Examiner (in failing to make a reasonable adjustment), unless it could demonstrate that it had taken such steps as were reasonably practicable to prevent such actions (see paragraphs 3.29 and 3.30).

Aiding an unlawful act

3.33 [s 57] A person who knowingly helps another to do something made unlawful by the Act will be treated as having done the same kind of unlawful act. This means that, where a trade organisation, qualifications body or general qualifications body is liable for an unlawful act of its employee or agent, that employee or agent will be liable for aiding the unlawful act of the organisation or body.

3.34 Where an employee of a trade organisation, qualifications body or general qualifications body discriminates against or harasses a disabled person, it is the employing organisation or body which will be liable for that unlawful act – unless it can show that it took such steps as were reasonable to prevent the unlawful act in question. But the employee who committed the discrimination or harassment will be liable for aiding the unlawful act – and this will be the case even if the trade organisation, qualifications body or general qualifications body is able to show that it took reasonable steps to prevent the act.

In the last-but-one example, where the union has taken steps to ensure that disabled members can participate in branch meetings, it is likely that the branch representative would be acting unlawfully in aiding an unlawful act by the union, even though the union itself has avoided liability by taking reasonably practicable steps.

ENFORCING RIGHTS UNDER PART 2 OF THE ACT

3.35 **[s 17A]** Enforcement of rights under Part 2 takes place in the employment tribunals. More information about enforcement is given in Chapter 11.

ENFORCING RIGHTS UNDER PART 4 OF THE ACT (IN RESPECT OF GENERAL QUALIFICATIONS BODIES)

3.36 **[s 31ADA(4) and (5) and Reg 3 of SI 2007/2405]** Enforcement of rights under Part 4 in respect of general qualifications bodies takes place in the County Courts in England and Wales (or in the Sheriff Courts in Scotland). More information about enforcement is given in Chapter 11.

4. WHAT IS DISCRIMINATION AND HARASSMENT?

INTRODUCTION

[4.116]

4.1 The forms of discrimination by trade organisations, qualifications bodies and general qualifications bodies which the Act makes unlawful are:

- direct discrimination
- failure to comply with a duty to make reasonable adjustments
- disability-related discrimination, and victimisation.

4.2 This chapter describes these four forms of discrimination in more detail, and explains the differences between them. It explores, in particular, the distinction between direct discrimination and disability-related discrimination (see paragraphs 4.25 to 4.30, and 4.35). These two forms of discrimination both depend on the way in which the disabled person concerned is treated – both require the disabled person to have been treated less favourably than other people are (or would be) treated. However, whether such treatment amounts to one of these forms of discrimination or the other (and, indeed, whether the treatment is unlawful in the first place) depends on the circumstances in which it arose.

4.3 The chapter examines the four forms of discrimination in the order in which they are listed in paragraph 4.1. This is because less favourable treatment which does not amount to direct discrimination can sometimes be justified. (In contrast, neither direct discrimination nor a failure to comply with a duty to make a reasonable adjustment is justifiable. Victimisation cannot be justified either.) In deciding whether the treatment is justified, and therefore whether there has been disability-related discrimination, the Act requires the question of reasonable adjustments to be taken into account (see paragraphs 6.5 and 6.6 where this is explained in more detail). Consequently, although the chapter describes direct discrimination first, it touches on the subject of reasonable adjustments before moving on to disability-related discrimination. This chapter also explains what the Act means by 'harassment'.

WHAT DOES THE ACT MEAN BY 'DIRECT DISCRIMINATION'?

What does the Act say?

4.4 **[s 3A(5) and 31AB(8)]** The Act says that treatment of a disabled person by a trade organisation, qualifications body or general qualifications body amounts to direct discrimination if:

- it is on the ground of his disability
- the treatment is less favourable than the way in which a person not having that particular disability is (or would be) treated, and
- the relevant circumstances, including the abilities, of the person with whom the comparison is made are the same as, or not materially different from, those of the disabled person.

4.5 It follows that direct discrimination depends on treatment of a disabled person by a trade organisation, qualifications body or general qualifications body being on the ground of his disability. It also depends on a comparison of that treatment with the way in which the organisation or body treats (or would treat) an appropriate comparator. If, on the ground of his disability, the disabled person is treated less favourably than the comparator is (or would be) treated, the treatment amounts to direct discrimination.

When is direct discrimination likely to occur?

4.6 Treatment of a disabled person is 'on the ground of' his disability if it is caused by the fact that he is disabled or has the disability in question. In general, this means that treatment is on the ground of disability if a disabled person would not have received it but for his disability. However, disability does not have to be the only (or even the main) cause of the treatment complained of – provided that it is an effective cause, determined objectively from all the circumstances.

4.7 Consequently, if the less favourable treatment occurs because of generalised, or stereotypical, assumptions about the disability or its effects, it is likely to be direct discrimination. This is because a trade organisation, qualifications body or general qualifications body would not normally make such assumptions about a non-disabled person, but would instead consider his individual abilities.

> A trade union member who has a mental health condition – which her branch secretary is aware of – is refused admission to a meeting because the branch secretary wrongly assumes that she would seriously disrupt the meeting with loud interjections. The branch secretary has treated her less favourably than other members by refusing her entry to the meeting. The treatment was on the ground of the woman's disability (because assumptions would not have been made about a non-disabled person).

> A general qualifications body has a blanket policy not to allow candidates with epilepsy to take practical chemistry examinations. A candidate with epilepsy is refused the opportunity to take practical chemistry examinations. This is based on an assumption that all people with epilepsy present an unacceptable health and safety risk in this context. This amounts to direct discrimination.

> A general qualifications body has a practice of not allowing wheelchair users to undertake a GCSE qualification in Dance, because it has assumed all wheelchair users are not capable of undertaking this qualification, and it has operated this policy without considering the individual circumstances of each person. This amounts to direct discrimination.

4.8 In addition, less favourable treatment which is disability-specific, or which arises out of prejudice about disability (or about a particular type of disability), is also likely to amount to direct discrimination.

> An applicant for a professional hairdressing qualification is told that he would not be suitable for the qualification because he has a disability and thus the qualifications body refuses to confer the qualification upon him. This refusal is unrelated to any competence standard which is applied by the body when conferring the qualification, but arises instead from prejudice about the applicant's disability. This amounts to direct discrimination.

> A person with a severe visible disfigurement is not allowed to undertake a GNVQ in leisure and tourism because the body conferring this qualification believes this disability will prevent the person from

gaining employment in this sector. This amounts to direct discrimination.

A general qualifications body tells an applicant for a GCSE in biology that she should not take the course because she has HIV. This refusal arises from prejudice about the applicant's disability. This amounts to direct discrimination.

4.9 In some cases, an apparently neutral reason for less favourable treatment of a disabled person may, on investigation, turn out to be a pretext for direct discrimination.

A disabled member of a professional body wishes to represent the body publicly by giving a television interview but is told that only people who have been members for at least three years are permitted to do this. However, she discovers that another member, who is not disabled, has given a public presentation on behalf of the professional body even though he had only been a member for two years at the time. Although the reason given to the disabled member (that she had not been a member of the body for long enough to represent it publicly) appeared to be a neutral one, it would seem that the reason was actually a pretext for direct discrimination, and is therefore unlawful.

4.10 Direct discrimination will often occur where the trade organisation, qualifications body or general qualifications body is aware that the disabled person has a disability, and this is the reason for its treatment of him. Direct discrimination need not be conscious – people may hold prejudices that they do not admit, even to themselves. Thus, a person may behave in a discriminatory way while believing that he would never do so. Moreover, direct discrimination may sometimes occur even though the trade organisation, qualifications body or general qualifications body is unaware of a person's disability.

4.11 In situations such as those described in the above examples, it will often be readily apparent that the disabled person concerned has been treated less favourably on the ground of his disability. In other cases, however, this may be less obvious. Whether or not the basis for the treatment in question appears to be clear, a useful way of telling whether or not it is discriminatory (and of establishing what kind of discrimination it is), is to focus on the person with whom the disabled person should be compared. That person may be real or hypothetical (see paragraph 4.17).

Identifying comparators in respect of direct discrimination

4.12 In determining whether a disabled person has been treated less favourably in the context of direct discrimination, his treatment must be compared with that of an appropriate comparator. This must be someone who does not have the same disability. It could be a non-disabled person or a person with other disabilities.

4.13 It follows that, in the great majority of cases, some difference will exist between the circumstances (including the abilities) of the comparator and those of the disabled person – there is no need to find a comparator whose circumstances are the same as those of the disabled person in every respect. What matters is that the comparator's **relevant** circumstances (including his abilities) must be the same as, or not materially different from, those of the disabled person.

4.14 Once an appropriate comparator is identified, it is clear that the situations described in the examples at paragraph 4.7 amounts to direct discrimination:

In the example about the trade union member who is refused admission to a meeting because she has a mental health problem, there is direct discrimination because the woman was treated less favourably on the ground of her disability than an appropriate comparator (that is, a person who does not have a mental health problem but whose relevant circumstances (including abilities) are otherwise the same): such a person would not have been refused admission to the meeting in the same circumstances.

In the example about the general qualifications body with a blanket policy not allowing candidates with epilepsy to take practical chemistry examinations, there is direct discrimination because the candidate was treated less favourably on the ground of her disability than an appropriate comparator (that is, a person who does not have epilepsy but whose relevant circumstances (including abilities) are otherwise the same): such a person would not have been prevented from taking the assessment.

In the example about the general qualifications body with a blanket policy that does not allow wheelchair users to undertake a GCSE qualification in Dance, there is direct discrimination because a

> candidate who does not use a wheelchair with the same abilities as the candidate using a wheelchair would have been treated more favourably: such a person would have been allowed on to the course.

4.15 The examples of direct discrimination in paragraph 4.8 also become clearer when the appropriate comparator is identified:

> In the example about the applicant for a professional hairdressing qualification who is told that he would not be suitable for the qualification because he has a disability, there is direct discrimination because the man was treated less favourably on the ground of his disability than an appropriate comparator (that is, a person who does not have the same disability, but whose relevant abilities in respect of the qualification are the same): such a person would not have been treated in this way.

> In the example about the person with a severe visible disfigurement not being allowed to undertake a GNVQ in leisure and tourism, there is direct discrimination because the applicant with the severe disfigurement is treated less favourably than someone with the same abilities who does not have a severe disfigurement: such a person would have been allowed to undertake this course.

> In the example about the applicant for a GCSE in biology who is told she should not take the course because she has HIV, there is direct discrimination because the applicant was treated less favourably on the ground of her disability. An appropriate comparator would be a person who does not have the same disability, but whose relevant abilities in respect of the qualification are the same, and who was not treated in the same way.

4.16 The comparator used in relation to direct discrimination under the Act is the same as it is for other types of direct discrimination – such as direct sex discrimination. It is, however, made explicit in the Act that the comparator must have the same relevant abilities as the disabled person.

4.17 It may not be possible to identify an actual comparator whose relevant circumstances are the same as (or not materially different from) those of the disabled person in question. In such cases a hypothetical comparator may be used. Evidence which helps to establish how a hypothetical comparator would have been treated is likely to include details of how other people (not satisfying the statutory comparison test) were treated in circumstances which were broadly similar.

> In the example at paragraph 4.9, there is nobody who has represented the professional body in television interviews with whom the disabled person can be compared. Nevertheless, the treatment of the member who had only two years' membership but was able to give a public presentation on behalf of the body might be evidence of discrimination: it might be used as evidence that a hypothetical non-disabled member who wanted to participate in a television interview would not have been treated in the same way as the disabled member was treated.

4.18 It should be noted that the type of comparator described in the preceding paragraphs is only relevant to disability discrimination when assessing whether there has been **direct** discrimination. A different comparison falls to be made when assessing whether there has been a failure to comply with a duty to make reasonable adjustments (see paragraphs 5.2 and 5.3) or when considering disability-related discrimination (see paragraph 4.29).

Focusing on relevant circumstances

4.19 As stated in paragraph 4.13, direct discrimination only occurs where the **relevant** circumstances of the comparator, including his abilities, are the same as, or not materially different from, those of the disabled person himself. It is therefore important to focus on those circumstances which are, in fact, relevant to the matter to which the less favourable treatment relates. Although, in some cases, the effects of the disability may be relevant, the fact of the disability itself is not a relevant circumstance for these purposes. This is because the comparison must be with a person **not** having that particular disability.

> A woman who has a severe facial disfigurement applies for membership of a professional association in the tourism industry. Despite meeting the formal requirements for membership, she is told that her disability would not create a good impression and her application is rejected. The correct comparator in a claim for direct discrimination would be a person who does not have a facial disfigurement but who

meets the formal requirements for membership of the professional association

A pupil who has arthrogryposis (a muscular-skeletal condition) is credited with very high marks for a practical demonstration of swimming abilities. The general qualifications body queries the mark believing that there must have been an error. The correct comparator in a claim for direct discrimination would be a person who does not have this impairment, but whose abilities in respect of the swimming assessment are the same, or not materially different, from the person with arthrogryposis.

Relevance of reasonable adjustments to comparison

4.20 In making the comparison in respect of a claim of direct discrimination, the disabled person's abilities must be considered **as they in fact are**. In some cases, there will be particular reasonable adjustments which a trade organisation, qualifications body or general qualifications body was required by the Act to make, but in fact failed to make. It may be that those adjustments would have had an effect on the disabled person's relevant abilities. But in making the comparison, the disabled person's abilities should be considered as they **in fact** were, and not as they would or might have been had those adjustments been made. On the other hand, if adjustments have **in fact** been made which have had the effect of enhancing the disabled person's abilities, then it is those enhanced abilities which should be considered. The disabled person's abilities are being considered as they in fact are (and not as they might have been if the adjustments had not been made).

A disabled person has to sit an examination in order to obtain a relevant general qualification. Because of her disability she has difficulty writing, and asks to be allowed to type her answers or given extra time to complete the examination. The general qualifications body does not permit this (even though it would have been reasonable for it to do so) and, as a result, the woman is unable to complete the examination in time. This is not direct discrimination, as the comparator for the purposes of this claim is a non-disabled person who also fails to complete the examination in time. (But the woman would be likely to have good claims in respect of two other forms of discrimination – failure to make reasonable adjustments and disability-related discrimination – see paragraph 4.35.)

Can direct discrimination be justified?

4.21 **[s 3A(4) and s 31AB(7)]** Treatment of a disabled person which amounts to direct discrimination under the Act is unlawful. It can never be justified.

FAILURE TO MAKE REASONABLE ADJUSTMENTS – RELATIONSHIP TO DISCRIMINATION

4.22 For the reason given in paragraph 4.3, it may be necessary to consider whether a trade organisation, qualifications body or general qualifications body has failed to comply with a duty to make a reasonable adjustment in order to determine whether disability related discrimination has occurred.

4.23 **[s 3A(2) and s 31AB(2)]** Irrespective of its relevance to disability-related discrimination, however, a failure to comply with a duty to make a reasonable adjustment in respect of a disabled person amounts to discrimination in its own right. Such a failure is therefore unlawful. Chapter 5 explains the circumstances in which a trade organisation, qualifications body or general qualifications body has such a duty, and gives guidance as to what they need to do when the duty arises. Chapters 7, 8 and 9 also give further guidance on when an adjustment might be considered reasonable in relation to trade organisations, qualifications and general qualifications bodies respectively.

4.24 As with direct discrimination, the Act does not permit an organisation or body to justify a failure to comply with a duty to make a reasonable adjustment (see paragraphs 5.26 and 5.27).

WHAT IS DISABILITY-RELATED DISCRIMINATION?

What does the Act say?

4.25 **[s 3A(1) and s 31AB(1)]** The Act says that treatment of a disabled person by a trade organisation, qualifications body or general qualifications body amounts to discrimination if:

- it is for a reason related to his disability
- the treatment is less favourable than the way in which the trade organisation, qualifications body or general qualifications body treats (or would treat) others to whom that reason does not (or would not) apply, and
- the organisation or body cannot show that the treatment is justified.

4.26 Although the Act itself does not use the term 'disability-related discrimination', this expression is used in the Code when referring to treatment of a disabled person which:

- is unlawful because each of the conditions listed in paragraph 4.25 is satisfied, but
- does **not** amount to direct discrimination under the Act.

4.27 In general, direct discrimination occurs when the reason for the less favourable treatment in question is the disability, while disability-related discrimination occurs when the reason relates to the disability but is not the disability itself. The expression 'disability-related discrimination' therefore distinguishes less favourable treatment which amounts to direct discrimination from a wider class of less favourable treatment which, although not amounting to direct discrimination, is nevertheless unlawful.

When does disability-related discrimination occur?

4.28 In determining whether disability related discrimination has occurred, the treatment of the disabled person must be compared with that of a person **to whom the disability-related reason does not apply**. This contrasts with direct discrimination, which requires a comparison to be made with a person without the disability in question but whose relevant circumstances are the same. The comparator may be non-disabled or disabled – but the key point is that the disability-related reason for the less favourable treatment must not apply to him.

A trade union refuses to allow a disabled person, who has a severe back condition and has been unable to carry out branch activities for the past couple of months due to her disability, to go on a training course. The union says that anyone who had not been carrying out their branch activities for this amount of time would have been refused training. The disability related reason for the less favourable treatment is the fact that the woman has not been carrying out branch activities, and the correct comparator is a person to whom that reason does not apply – that is, someone who had been carrying out branch activities. Consequently, unless the trade union can show that the treatment is justified, it will amount to disability-related discrimination because the comparator would not have been refused the opportunity to go on the training course. However, the reason for the treatment is not the disability itself (it is only a matter related thereto, namely not carrying out branch activities). So there is no direct discrimination.

A general qualifications body has set a start time of 9am for pupils/students undertaking an examination and refuses to allow anyone to take this examination other than at this time. A disabled pupil who requires regular medical treatment (dialysis) at this time in the morning cannot attend the examination. Refusing to allow him to attend at a different time would constitute less favourable treatment for disability related reasons and would amount to disability-related discrimination unless the general qualifications body could justify the treatment. The reason for the treatment is not the disability itself, so there is no direct discrimination.

4.29 The relationship between a disabled person's disability and the treatment of him by the organisation or body in question must be judged objectively. The reason for any less favourable treatment may well relate to the disability even if the organisation or body does not have knowledge of the disability as such, or of whether its salient features are such that it meets the definition of disability in the Act. Less favourable treatment which is not itself direct discrimination will still be unlawful (subject to justification) if, in fact, the reason for it relates to the person's disability.

In the first example at paragraph 4.28, the trade union did not know that the reason why the woman had not been carrying out branch activities was disability-related. Nevertheless, its refusal to allow her to attend the training course is less favourable treatment for a disability-related reason, and would be unlawful unless it can be justified.

In the second example at paragraph 4.28, the general qualifications body did not know why (and didn't make any appropriate enquiries) as to why the pupil could not attend the examination at 9am and that the reason was disability related. Nevertheless, the refusal to allow the pupil to take the examination at another time is disability-related less favourable treatment and would be unlawful unless it can be justified.

4.30 The circumstances in which justification may be possible are explained in Chapter 6. However, it is worth noting that the possibility of justifying potential discrimination only arises at all when the form of discrimination being considered is disability-related discrimination, rather than direct discrimination or failure to make reasonable adjustments.

WHAT DOES THE ACT SAY ABOUT VICTIMISATION?

4.31 **[s 55(1) and (2)]** Victimisation is a special form of discrimination which is made unlawful by the Act. It is unlawful for one person to treat another ('the victim') less favourably than he treats or would treat other people in the same circumstances because the victim has:

- brought, or given evidence or information in connection with, proceedings under the Act (whether or not proceedings are later withdrawn)
- done anything else under the Act, or
- alleged someone has contravened the Act (whether or not the allegation is later dropped),

or because the person believes or suspects that the victim has done or intends to do any of these things.

> A member of a trade organisation brings a claim of discrimination against the organisation. He is accompanied to the hearing of the claim by a friend who is also a member of the organisation. This person is subsequently refused a place on a course run by the organisation because he accompanied the claimant to the hearing. This amounts to victimisation.

> A non-disabled pupil at a school supports his disabled colleague in respect of a complaint of disability discrimination made against a general qualifications body. Thereafter, because the general qualifications body in question has taken exception to this, they refuse to re-mark an examination paper that the non-disabled pupil has completed. This amounts to victimisation.

4.32 [s 55(4)] It is not victimisation to treat a person less favourably because that person has made an allegation which was false and not made in good faith.

4.33 However, the fact that a person has given evidence on behalf of an applicant in a claim which was unsuccessful does not, of itself, prove that his evidence was false or that it was not given in good faith.

4.34 [s 55(5)] Unlike the other forms of discrimination which are made unlawful by the Act, victimisation may be claimed by people who are not disabled as well as by those who are.

HOW DO THE DIFFERENT FORMS OF DISCRIMINATION COMPARE IN PRACTICE?

4.35 The way in which the different forms of discrimination which are unlawful under the Act may operate in practice can be demonstrated by the following series of examples.

> A disabled person who has multiple sclerosis applies to go to a union conference which lasts for one week. She mentions her disability on the booking form, but says that it would not affect her ability to attend. Nevertheless, the conference organiser wrongly assumes that the woman's disability will prevent her from participating at the conference and she is refused a place. This is direct discrimination.
>
> In the situation described above, the woman states on the booking form that she will have to miss one day of the conference in order to have hospital treatment in relation to her disability. Because full attendance is required of all conference participants, she is refused a place. This is not direct discrimination, as the reason for the refusal of a place was not the woman's disability, but the fact that she would not be able to attend the conference in full.
>
> However, the trade union has a duty to make reasonable adjustments. In order to prevent the disabled woman being substantially disadvantaged by the union's policy of only allowing people to attend the conference if they can attend it in full, it may be a reasonable adjustment for the union to waive this requirement. If so, the union will be unlawfully discriminating against the woman by refusing to do this.
>
> Although there is no direct discrimination, the union has still treated the woman less favourably for a reason relating to her disability (namely, the fact that she cannot attend the conference in full). This will be disability-related discrimination unless the union can show that it is justified – and the union will be unable to show this if it would have been reasonable for it to have waived the requirement for full attendance.
>
> Because of the way in which she has been treated, the woman makes a claim against the trade union under Part 2 of the Act. Some time later, however, she asks for union representation in relation to a grievance at work. Her request is rejected because she has previously made a claim against the union. This is victimisation.

> A disabled sixth form student is studying for an A level. Before the disabled student began studying, staff at the college met with him to discuss the reasonable adjustments that he would require in order to study there. However, the general qualifications body wrongly assumes that the student's disability will prevent his full participation in the A level course and it does not accept his entry onto the examination. This is likely to be direct discrimination.
>
> In the situation above the student mentions to the college that he will need a more flexible course programme, because his health condition means that he has to make regular hospital visits and he will not, therefore, be able to attend all lessons and hand all course work in on time. The college makes a request for varying the deadline (for the disabled student to hand in his coursework) to the general qualifications body conferring this qualification. The general qualifications body decides not to allow the student to have this flexibility because they require all coursework deadlines to be strictly adhered to and they subsequently refuse to confer the qualification because this student's coursework has been submitted after the deadline.
>
> The duty on the general qualifications body to make reasonable adjustments means that in order to prevent the disabled student from being substantially disadvantaged by this policy it may be reasonable

to waive the requirement that all coursework deadlines must be strictly adhered to. If the general qualifications body refuses to make the possible reasonable adjustments that could be made, it will be unlawfully discriminating.

Although there is no direct discrimination because the requirement to meet coursework deadlines applies equally to everyone, the general qualifications body has still treated him less favourably for a reason relating to his disability. This is because the refusal to confer the qualification is due to the fact that the disabled student could not hand his coursework in on time due to regular hospital appointments and this, in turn, is for reasons related to his disability. This will constitute unlawful disability-related discrimination, unless the general qualifications body can show that the treatment is justified. If it would be reasonable to allow flexibility in the deadlines for the submission of coursework, it would not be able to show that this requirement was justified.

Because of the way in which he has been treated, the student makes a claim of disability discrimination against the general qualifications body. A few years later, an application is made on his behalf to enter for a GCSE qualification that is administered by the same general qualifications body. His entry is denied because he has previously made a disability discrimination claim in good faith against the general qualifications body. This is victimisation.

WHAT DOES THE ACT SAY ABOUT HARASSMENT?

4.36 [s 3B(1) and s 31AC(1)] The Act says that harassment occurs where, for a reason which relates to a person's disability, another person engages in unwanted conduct which has the purpose or effect of:

- violating the disabled person's dignity, or
- creating an intimidating, hostile, degrading, humiliating or offensive environment for him.

4.37 [s 3B(2) and s 31AC(2)] If the conduct in question was engaged in with the intention that it should have either of these effects, then it amounts to harassment irrespective of its actual effect on the disabled person. In the absence of such intention, however, the conduct will only amount to harassment if it should reasonably be considered as having either of these effects. Regard must be had to all the circumstances in order to determine whether this is the case. Those circumstances include, in particular, the perception of the disabled person.

An assessor from a motor mechanics qualifications body is judging a number of practical tasks performed in the workplace by a trainee motor mechanic who has a speech impairment. The assessor imitates the mechanic's manner of speech and makes offensive remarks about him to the trainee's line manager. This is harassment, whether or not the disabled man was present when the comments were made, because they were made with the intention of humiliating him.

At an awards ceremony of a trade organisation, a member of the organisation makes a speech including derogatory remarks about people with schizophrenia. A woman with schizophrenia who is a member of the trade organisation and who is present in the audience complains about the speech but is told that the comments were made as a joke and that the speaker did not have any intention of causing offence. Nevertheless the experience of the woman is likely to amount to harassment because the comments made by the speaker could reasonably be considered as having either of the effects mentioned above.

A trade union member with HIV uses another member's mug at a union meeting. The other member then makes a point of being seen washing the mug with bleach, which is not something she would do if anyone else used her mug. She also makes offensive comments about having her mug used by someone with HIV. This is likely to amount to harassment.

A trade union branch representative circulates a joke about people with autism by email to branch members. A member with autism receives the email and finds the joke offensive. This is likely to amount to harassment.

During the course of an examination a teacher invigilating the examination – who is acting as an agent of the general qualifications body – makes a disabled candidate who is incontinent explain, in front of his colleagues and peers, why he needs to use the toilet. This is likely to amount to harassment.

> A general qualifications body offers resources and guidance for exam officers on exam administration. The materials suggest that candidates with dyslexia may be more likely to cheat and abuse the reasonable adjustments that they are offered. This is harassment, whether or not the disabled person was present when the written comments were made, because they were made with the intention of humiliating people with dyslexia.

WHAT DOES THE ACT SAY ABOUT STATUTORY OBLIGATIONS?

4.38 [s 59] Nothing is made unlawful by the Act if it is required by an express statutory obligation. However, it is only in cases where a statutory obligation is specific in its requirements, leaving a trade organisation, qualifications body or general qualifications body with no choice other than to act in a particular way that the provisions of the Act may be overridden. The provision in section 59 of the Act is thus of narrow application, and it is likely to permit disability discrimination only in rare circumstances.

WHAT EVIDENCE IS NEEDED TO PROVE THAT DISCRIMINATION OR HARASSMENT HAS OCCURRED?

4.39 A person who brings a claim for unlawful discrimination or harassment must show that discrimination or harassment has occurred. He must prove this on the balance of probabilities in order to succeed with a claim.

4.40 **[s 17A(1C), s 31ADA(2) and Reg 3 of SI 2007/2405]** However, in relation to trade organisations, qualifications bodies and general qualifications bodies, the Act says that, when such a claim is heard by a tribunal or court, the tribunal or court must uphold the claim if:

- the claimant/pursuer proves facts from which the tribunal or court could conclude in the absence of an adequate explanation that the person against whom the claim is made (the respondent or defendant/defender) has acted unlawfully, and
- the respondent/defendant/defender fails to prove that he did not act in that way.

> A disabled man with autism is the only trade union branch member in the workplace not to be sent an email inviting him to stand for election as a branch representative. Unless the union demonstrates a non-discriminatory reason for this omission, unlawful discrimination will be inferred in these circumstances.

4.41 Consequently, where a disabled person is able to prove on the balance of probabilities facts from which an inference of unlawful discrimination or harassment could be drawn, the burden of proof shifts to the respondent/defendant/defender, who must then show that it is more likely than not that its conduct was not unlawful. This principle applies to allegations in respect of all forms of discrimination, including victimisation, and to harassment. Its practical effect in relation to the three principal forms of disability discrimination can be summarised as follows:

- To prove an allegation of **direct discrimination**, a claimant/pursuer must prove facts from which it could be inferred in the absence of an adequate explanation that he has been treated less favourably on the ground of his disability than an appropriate comparator has been, or would be, treated. If the claimant/pursuer does this, the claim will succeed unless the respondent/defendant/defender can show that disability was not any part of the reason for the treatment in question.
- To prove an allegation that there has been a **failure to comply with a duty to make reasonable adjustments**, a claimant/pursuer must prove facts from which it could be inferred in the absence of an adequate explanation that such a duty has arisen, and that it has been breached. If the claimant/pursuer does this, the claim will succeed unless the respondent/defendant/defender can show that it did not fail to comply with its duty in this regard.
- To prove an allegation of **disability-related discrimination**, a claimant/ pursuer must prove facts from which it could be inferred in the absence of an adequate explanation that, for a reason relating to his disability, he has been treated less favourably than a person to whom that reason does not apply has been, or would be, treated. If the claimant/pursuer does this, the burden of proof shifts, and it is for the respondent/defendant/defender to show that the claimant has not received less favourable treatment for a disability related reason. Even if the respondent/defendant/defender cannot show this, however, the claim will not succeed if the respondent/defendant/defender shows that the treatment was justified.

4.42 [s 56] The Act provides a means by which a disabled person can seek evidence about whether he has been discriminated against, or subjected to harassment, under Part 2. However, no equivalent procedure exists in relation to Part 4 in respect of general qualifications bodies. Where such an opportunity to seek evidence arises under the Act, a person may do this by using a questionnaire to obtain further information from a person he thinks has acted unlawfully in relation to him (see paragraph 11.5). If there has been a failure to provide a satisfactory response to questions asked by the disabled person in this way, inferences may be drawn from that failure.

4.43 In addition, the fact that there has been a failure to comply with a relevant provision of the Code must be taken into account by a court or tribunal, where it considers it relevant, in determining whether there has been discrimination or harassment (see paragraph 1.7).

5. WHAT IS THE DUTY TO MAKE REASONABLE ADJUSTMENTS?

INTRODUCTION

[4.117]
5.1 One of the ways in which discrimination occurs under Part 2 or Part 4 of the Act is when a trade organisation, qualifications body or a general qualifications body fails to comply with a duty imposed on it to make 'reasonable adjustments' in relation to the disabled person. This chapter examines the circumstances in which a duty to make reasonable adjustments arises and outlines what a trade organisation, qualifications body or general qualifications body needs to do in order to discharge such a duty.

WHEN DOES THE DUTY TO MAKE REASONABLE ADJUSTMENTS ARISE?

5.2 **[s 14(1), s 14B(1), s 31AD(1) and (3)]** Subject to what is said in paragraph 5.7 about competence standards, the duty to make reasonable adjustments arises where a provision, criterion or practice applied by or on behalf of a trade organisation, qualifications body or general qualifications body, or any physical feature of premises which it occupies, places a disabled person at a substantial disadvantage compared with people who are not disabled. The trade organisation, qualifications body or general qualifications body has to take such steps as it is reasonable for it to have to take in all the circumstances to prevent that disadvantage – in other words it has to make a 'reasonable adjustment'. Where the duty arises, an organisation or body cannot justify a failure to make a reasonable adjustment.

> A trade organisation for hairdressers arranges a one-day training course in colouring techniques for its members. A disabled member wishes to attend this course, but the programme for the day does not allow him sufficient rest breaks. He would therefore be at a substantial disadvantage because of his disability. The trade organisation rearranges the programme for the day to include more breaks. This is likely to be a reasonable adjustment for it to make.

> A trade organisation for carpenters has an application form with several paragraphs in small print. A partially sighted carpenter cannot read the whole form and is therefore at a substantial disadvantage because he cannot fill it in correctly. The trade organisation provides him with an application form in large print. This is likely to be a reasonable adjustment for it to make.

> A qualifications body holds an awards ceremony at its headquarters. A newly qualified woman who uses a wheelchair wants to attend the ceremony but is at a substantial disadvantage because the stage where the awards are presented is only accessible by stairs. The qualifications body provides a ramp up to the stage. This is likely to be a reasonable adjustment for the qualifications body to make.

> A disabled woman who is unable to use public transport wishes to attend a trade fair in central London, organised by a trade organisation of which she is a member. There is very little parking in the area and the information brochure suggests that 'visitors to the trade fair are advised to come by public transport'. The woman asks the trade organisation if it can arrange a parking space and it does so. This is likely to be a reasonable adjustment for the trade organisation to make.

> A candidate for a general qualification with a visual impairment requests a range of reasonable adjustments to take a written test. In preparation for a test, the exams officer at the centre discusses with the candidate his requirements for the test in advance and then discusses these requirements with the general qualifications body. When he sits the paper, he is provided with a large print paper, additional time, a desk lamp and a rest break. These are likely to be reasonable adjustments.

> A general qualifications body allows a person with Chronic Fatigue Syndrome who, due to effects of her impairment, is unable to travel to an examination venue to take the examination (which is properly

invigilated by a teacher from her college) at her home. She is also granted extra time to undertake the examination. These are likely to be reasonable adjustments for the general qualifications body to make.

5.3 It does not matter if a disabled person cannot point to an actual non-disabled person compared with whom he is at a substantial disadvantage. The fact that a non-disabled person, or even another disabled person, would not be substantially disadvantaged by the provision, criterion or practice or by the physical feature in question is irrelevant. The duty is owed specifically to the individual disabled person.

WHICH DISABLED PEOPLE DOES THE DUTY PROTECT?

5.4 In order to avoid discrimination, it is prudent not to attempt to make a fine judgement as to whether a particular individual falls within the statutory definition of disability, but to focus instead on meeting the needs of each individual with whom a trade organisation, qualifications body or general qualifications body has dealings. However, the Act says that the duties are owed to the following people:

- **[s 14(2)]** disabled people who are members of trade organisations, or who are applicants, or potential applicants, for membership of such organisations, and
- **[s 14B(2)]** disabled people who are holders of professional or trade qualifications, or who are applicants, or potential applicants, for such qualifications.
- **[s 31AD(2) and (3)]** disabled people who are holders of general qualifications, or who are applicants, or potential applicants, for such qualifications.

5.5 The extent of the duty to make reasonable adjustments depends on the circumstances of the disabled person in question. For example, more extensive duties are owed to members of trade organisations and holders of professional or trade qualifications than to people who are merely thinking about applying. However, for general qualifications bodies more extensive duties are owed to people seeking to enter for relevant general qualifications and candidates taking examinations and assessments potentially leading to such qualifications, than to people who already hold such qualifications. More extensive duties are also owed to current members and qualification holders than to past members or to people who no longer hold a qualification. The extent to which trade organisations, qualifications bodies and general qualifications bodies have knowledge of relevant circumstances is also a factor. These issues are explained in more detail in Chapters 7, 8 and 9.

WHAT ARE 'PROVISIONS, CRITERIA AND PRACTICES'?

5.6 **[s 18D(2) and s 31AD(5)]** Provisions, criteria and practices include arrangements, for example for determining who to accept as a member of a trade organisation, or upon whom to confer a general, professional or trade qualification, as well as the rules of membership of an organisation. The duty to make reasonable adjustments applies, for example, to selection and interview procedures for trade organisations and to examination and assessment procedures used by qualifications bodies and general qualifications bodies. In addition, the duty applies to premises used for such procedures.

A trade union requires its members to be either employed or seeking employment in a specific sector. A woman with a spinal injury as a result of an accident is not in work or looking for work, because she is adjusting to her newly acquired disability, but nevertheless would like to remain a member of the union, as it would help her to maintain contact with the sector in which she worked prior to her accident. The union agrees that she can retain her membership. This is likely to be a reasonable adjustment for the trade union to make to a criterion (in this case a membership criterion).

A general qualifications body receives an application from a centre wishing to enter disabled candidates for an examination which, if successfully undertaken, will lead to a relevant general qualification. A candidate with a physical impairment affecting her ability to write cannot complete the written examination papers. The general qualifications body allows the centre to provide a scribe for this individual. This is likely to be a reasonable adjustment for the general qualifications body to make.

A general qualifications body regularly publishes a list of the approved access arrangements. In the light of comments from candidates, centres and organisations representing disabled people, it regularly reviews these arrangements to ensure that the criteria set out are fit for purpose. It also ensures that there are arrangements in place for requests for reasonable adjustments that are not covered in the guidance on access arrangements.

5.7 **[s 14B(1) and s 31AD(1) and (2) and s 31AB(9)]** It should be noted that, in relation to both qualifications bodies and general qualifications bodies, there is no duty to make any adjustment to a provision, criterion or practice of a kind which the Act defines as a 'competence standard'. What the Act says about competence standards is considered in more detail in respect of qualifications bodies in paragraphs 8.27 to 8.41 and in respect of general qualifications bodies in paragraphs 9.57 to 9.82.

WHAT IS A 'PHYSICAL FEATURE'?

5.8 [s 18D(2) and Reg 4 of SI 2007/1764] The Act says that the following are to be treated as a physical feature:

- any feature arising from the design or construction of a building on the premises occupied by the trade organisation, qualifications body
- or general qualifications body any feature on the premises of any approach to, exit from, or access to such a building
- any fixtures, fittings, furnishings, furniture, equipment or materials in or on the premises, and
- any other physical element or quality of any land comprised in the premises occupied by the trade organisation, qualifications body or general qualifications body.

All these features are covered, whether temporary or permanent. Considerations which need to be taken into account when making adjustments to premises are explained in Chapter 10.

> The design of a professional association's training facility makes it difficult for a person with a visual impairment to find his way around, as there are glass doors, glass panels and reflecting surfaces. That is a substantial disadvantage caused by the physical features of the professional association's premises.

5.9 Physical features will include steps, stairways, kerbs, exterior surfaces and paving, parking areas, building entrances and exits (including emergency escape routes), internal and external doors, gates, toilet and washing facilities, lighting and ventilation, lifts and escalators, floor coverings, signs, furniture, and temporary or movable items. This is not an exhaustive list.

WHAT DISADVANTAGES GIVE RISE TO THE DUTY?

5.10 The Act says that only substantial disadvantages give rise to the duty. Substantial disadvantages are those which are not minor or trivial. Whether or not such a disadvantage exists in a particular case is a question of fact. What matters is not that a provision, criterion or practice or a physical feature is capable of causing a substantial disadvantage to the disabled person in question, but that it actually has (or would have) this effect on him.

IS KNOWLEDGE OF THE DISABILITY A FACTOR?

5.11 [s 14(3) and s 14B(3) and s 31AD(4)] Although (as explained in paragraphs 4.10 and 4.29) less favourable treatment can occur even if a trade organisation, qualifications body or general qualifications body does not know that the person is disabled, the organisation or body only has a duty to make an adjustment if it knows, or could reasonably be expected to know, that the person has a disability and is likely to be placed at a substantial disadvantage. A trade organisation, qualifications body or general qualifications body must, however, do all it can reasonably be expected to do to find out whether this is the case. More information is given in Chapters 7, 8 and 9 about the relationship between the knowledge of a trade organisation, qualifications body or general qualifications body and its duties under the Act.

WHAT ADJUSTMENTS MIGHT HAVE TO BE MADE?

5.12 [s 18B(2)] Part 2 of the Act gives a number of examples of adjustments, or 'steps', which trade organisations and qualifications bodies may have to take, if it is reasonable for them to have to do so (see paragraphs 5.14 to 5.25). Many of these examples may also be relevant to general qualifications bodies and indicative of the type of adjustments that they may have to think about, even though no equivalent examples are listed in Chapter 2A of Part 4 of the Act. Any necessary adjustments should be implemented in a timely fashion, and it may also be necessary to make more than one adjustment. It is advisable for the appropriate body to agree any proposed adjustments with the disabled person in question before they are made. The Act does not give an exhaustive list of the steps which may have to be taken to discharge the duty. Not all of the steps listed in the Act are likely to be relevant to trade organisations and qualifications bodies. By the same token, steps other than those listed, or a combination of steps, will sometimes have to be taken. However, the steps in the Act which it is likely to be reasonable for trade organisations or qualifications bodies to have to take are:

- making adjustments to premises which they occupy

> A trade organisation or qualifications body might have to make structural or other physical changes such as: widening a doorway, providing a ramp or moving furniture for a wheelchair user; relocating light switches, door handles or shelves for someone who has difficulty in reaching; providing appropriate contrast in décor to help the safe mobility of a visually impaired person.

- giving, or arranging for, training or mentoring (whether for the disabled person or any other person)

> This could be training in the use of particular pieces of equipment which the disabled person uses while participating in activities as a benefit of their membership of the trade organisation, or training which any member can take part in but which needs altering for the disabled person because of their disability.

For example, all members might have the opportunity to be trained to use the trade organisation's library computer system but the trade organisation might have to provide longer or different training for a disabled person.

A trade union provides training for a branch in conducting meetings in a way that enables a deaf branch member to participate.

A disabled member of a professional association wishes to become a fellow of the organisation but has concerns about the requirement to pass an assessment – an oral presentation to fellows of the association with questions and answers – as she has a speech impairment. The professional association arranges for her to see a mentor (in this case a disabled fellow of the same organisation) to support her in achieving fellowship status.

- acquiring or modifying equipment

A trade organisation or qualifications body might have to arrange to provide, or consent to the provision of special equipment for a disabled person to enable him to take part in activities or benefit from services provided by the organisation or body. There is no requirement to provide or modify equipment for personal purposes unconnected with the person's dealings with the trade organisation or qualifications body, for example to provide a wheelchair if a person needs one in any event but does not have one.

- modifying instructions or reference manuals

The way instructions are normally given might need to be revised when telling a disabled person how to do a task. The format of instructions or reference manuals may need to be modified (eg produced in Braille or on audio tape) and instructions for people with learning disabilities may need to be conveyed orally with individual demonstration.

- modifying procedures for testing or assessment

This could involve ensuring that particular testing methods do not adversely affect particular disabled people. For example, a person with restricted manual dexterity might be disadvantaged by a hand written test and would need to have an alternative arrangement such as an oral test or to be permitted to use a computer with voice recognition software. More information about how the Act affects testing and examinations is set out in Chapters 8 and 9.

- providing a reader or interpreter

This could involve the provision of a sign language interpreter for meetings, talks or training; or could involve provision of a reader for a visually impaired person.

- providing supervision or other support

This could involve the provision of a support worker to enable a disabled person to participate in a conference, meeting, training session, interview, examination, assessment or social event; or extra support for a disabled trade union representative to enable that person to fulfil their role on an on going basis.

5.13 As mentioned above, it may be reasonable for a trade organisation, qualifications body or general qualifications body to take steps which are not given as examples in the Act. Such steps might include:

- arranging or consenting to a proper assessment of what reasonable adjustments may be required
- modifying the arrangements for meetings, and
- making adjustments to the way in which information is provided.

Further examples of the way in which reasonable adjustments work in practice are given in Chapters 7, 8 and 9.

WHEN IS IT 'REASONABLE' FOR A TRADE ORGANISATION, QUALIFICATIONS BODY OR GENERAL QUALIFICATIONS BODY TO HAVE TO MAKE ADJUSTMENTS?

5.14 Whether it is reasonable for a trade organisation, qualifications body or general qualifications body to make any particular adjustment will depend on a number of things, such as its cost and effectiveness. However, if an adjustment is one which it is reasonable to make, then the organisation or body must do so. Where a disabled person is placed at a substantial disadvantage by a provision, criterion or practice of the organisation or body, or by a physical feature of the premises it occupies, the organisation or body must consider whether any reasonable adjustments can be made to overcome that disadvantage. There is no onus on the disabled person to suggest what adjustments should be made but, where the disabled person does so, the organisation or body must consider whether such adjustments would help overcome the disadvantage, and whether they are reasonable.

5.15 Nevertheless, an organisation or body may not know enough about the disabled person to determine what adjustments are appropriate. It is therefore good practice to ask a disabled person whether he requires any adjustments to be made. It is also a good idea for a disabled person to make suggestions about adjustments which would be helpful. Schools and colleges may request information about the needs of disabled candidates and should seek their permission to pass this information on to the general qualifications body.

5.16 Effective and practicable adjustments for disabled people often involve little or no cost or disruption and are therefore very likely to be reasonable for a trade organisation, qualifications body or general qualifications body to have to make. Many adjustments do not involve making physical changes to premises. However, where such changes do need to be made, trade organisations, qualifications bodies and general qualifications bodies may need to take account of the considerations explained in Chapter 10, which deals with issues about making alterations to premises.

> A qualifications body allows a student to have extra time to take a written test because the student has dyslexia. This adjustment only involves the cost of paying an invigilator for the extra time in question, and is likely to be a reasonable one to make.

> A trade union member with a hearing impairment requests a seat at the front of the conference hall, so that she can lip read. This is likely to be a reasonable adjustment for the trade union to make and would involve no additional cost and no disruption to the union.

> A member of a professional association attending a meeting at that association asks for a mug half full of tea, rather than a china tea cup and saucer, because she has a hand tremor due to a neurological condition. This would involve very little cost or disruption to the professional association and is likely to be a reasonable adjustment to make.

5.17 **[SI 1999/3242]** If making a particular adjustment would increase the risks to the health and safety of any person (including the disabled person in question) then this is a relevant factor in deciding whether it is reasonable to make that adjustment. Suitable and sufficient risk assessments, such as those carried out for the purposes of the Management of Health and Safety at Work Regulations 999, should be used to help determine whether such risks are likely to arise.

5.18 **[s 18B(1)]** Part 2 of the Act lists a number of factors which may, in particular, have a bearing on whether it will be reasonable to have to make a particular adjustment. These factors make a useful checklist, particularly when considering more substantial adjustments. Many of these factors may also be relevant to general qualifications bodies when they consider reasonableness of adjustments, even though no equivalent factors are listed in Chapter 2A of Part 4 of the Act. The effectiveness and practicability of a particular adjustment might be considered first. If it is practicable and effective, the financial aspects might be looked at as a whole – the cost of the adjustment and resources available to fund it. Other factors might also have a bearing. The factors in the Act include the following:

The effectiveness of the step in preventing the disadvantage

5.19 It is unlikely to be reasonable to have to make an adjustment involving little benefit to the disabled person. However, such an adjustment may be one of several adjustments which, when looked at together, would be effective and, in that case, it is likely to be reasonable to have to make it.

> A candidate for a general qualification, who has a condition that causes fatigue (ME), makes enquiries with the exams centre as to what adjustments are available for her during examinations. One of the adjustments she needs is ensuring that non-fluorescent lighting is used in the exams hall. However, there is little benefit in having this or additional time on its own, but if these adjustments are provided

Part 4 Statutory Codes of Practice

together with a reader, the measures taken as a whole could be suitable to overcome the particular disadvantages that she experiences during examinations.

The practicability of the step

5.20 It is more likely to be reasonable to have to take a step which is easy to take than one which is difficult. In some circumstances it may be reasonable to have to take a step, even though it is difficult.

A trade organisation is asked by a woman with a severe allergy to many commonly found substances (such as latex) to ensure that a venue for a lecture is free of all these substances. This is likely to be an impractical step to take. However, it may instead be reasonable for the trade organisation to provide the woman with a video of the lecture.

A candidate for a GCSE qualification with a practical element requires treatment at a hospital during the exam period and asks to take the examination at the hospital. It would be impracticable to do this though, and it would also be impracticable to rearrange the timetabling of the exams, so the general qualifications body arranges for the candidate to sit the exams at a different centre nearer to the hospital.

The financial and other costs of the adjustment and the extent of any disruption caused

5.21 If an adjustment costs little or nothing and is not disruptive, it would be reasonable unless some other factor (such as practicability or effectiveness) made it unreasonable. It may, of course, be reasonable to have to make more expensive adjustments in some circumstances. The costs to be taken into account include those for staff and other resources. The significance of the cost of a step may depend in part on what the trade organisation, qualifications body or general qualifications body might otherwise spend in the circumstances. In assessing the likely costs of making an adjustment, the availability of external funding should be taken into account.

The extent of the financial or other resources available to the trade organisation, qualifications body or general qualifications body

5.22 It is more likely to be reasonable for a trade organisation, qualifications body or general qualifications body with substantial financial resources to have to make an adjustment with a significant cost, than for one with fewer resources. The resources in practice available to the organisation or body as a whole should be taken into account as well as other calls on those resources. It is good practice for organisations and bodies to have a specific budget for reasonable adjustments – but limitations on the size of any such budget will not affect the existence of the duties owed to disabled people. The reasonableness of an adjustment will depend not only on the resources in practice available for the adjustment but also on all other relevant factors (such as effectiveness and practicability).

A large professional association with 300,000 members and considerable funds would be expected to make more substantial changes to its premises, in order to make them accessible for a member, than would a small trade organisation with only fifty members and very limited funds.

A union branch is sending a disabled representative to a regional three-day conference. The disabled person, who has cerebral palsy, requires a support worker to accompany her to the conference. Although the cost of providing this support would be relatively high compared to the resources available to the branch, the cost is unlikely to be seen as unreasonably high when assessed against the overall funds of the union.

The availability of financial or other assistance to help make an adjustment

5.23 The availability of outside help may well be a relevant factor. This help may be financial or practical. Disability organisations may be able to provide further information or assistance.

5.24 A disabled person is not required to contribute to the cost of a reasonable adjustment. However, if a disabled person has a particular piece of special or adapted equipment which he is prepared to use, this might make it reasonable for a trade organisation, qualifications body or general qualifications body to have to take some other step (as well as allowing the use of the equipment).

A blind person wishes to go to an event organised by a trade organisation of which she is a member. She wishes to take notes at this event using a laptop computer. The trade organisation provides her with a table to put the computer on while she takes notes. This is likely to be a reasonable adjustment for the organisation to make.

The nature of the activities of the organisation or body, and the size of its undertaking

5.25 The size of an organisation or body's undertaking and the nature of its activities may be relevant in determining the reasonableness of a particular step.

CAN FAILURE TO MAKE A REASONABLE ADJUSTMENT EVER BE JUSTIFIED?

5.26 **[s 3A(2) and s 31AB(5)]** The Act does not permit a trade organisation, qualifications body or general qualifications body to justify a failure to comply with a duty to make a reasonable adjustment. For trade organisations this is a change in the law.

5.27 Clearly, however, an organisation or body will only breach such a duty if the adjustment in question is one which it is reasonable for it to have to make. So, where the duty applies, it is the question of 'reasonableness' which alone determines whether the adjustment has to be made.

A woman with severe back pain wishes to attend a trade union conference. The only adjustment she needs is for a space to be made available for her to set up a portable couch on which she can lie down during the conference proceedings. This is likely to be a reasonable adjustment for the trade union to make. It involves no cost and little disruption for the union. Nevertheless, the union does not allow this as it says 'nobody has ever needed this adjustment before and there may be health and safety implications'. The trade union will be acting unlawfully.

6. JUSTIFICATION

INTRODUCTION

[4.118]

6.1 Most conduct which is potentially unlawful under Part 2 of the Act and Part 4 of the Act (in respect of most post-16 education and general qualifications bodies) cannot be justified. Conduct which amounts to:

- direct discrimination
- failure to comply with a duty to make a reasonable adjustment
- victimisation
- harassment
- instructions or pressure to discriminate, or
- aiding an unlawful act

is unlawful irrespective of the reason or motive for it.

WHEN DOES THE ACT PERMIT JUSTIFICATION?

6.2 Paragraph 4.25 explains that one of the forms of discrimination which is unlawful under Part 2 and Chapter 2A of Part 4 is disability-related discrimination. However, the conduct of a trade organisation, qualifications body or a general qualifications body towards a disabled person does not amount to disability-related discrimination if it can be justified. This chapter explains the limited circumstances in which this may happen.

6.3 **[s 3A(3) and (4), s 31AB(3) and (7)]** Where less favourable treatment of a disabled person is capable of being justified (that is, where it is not direct discrimination), the Act says that it will, in fact, be justified if, but only if, the reason for the treatment is both material to the circumstances of the particular case and substantial. This is an objective test. 'Material' means that there must be a reasonably strong connection between the reason given for the treatment and the circumstances of the particular case. 'Substantial' means, in the context of justification, that the reason must carry real weight and be of substance.

Competence standards

6.4 **[s 14A(3) and s 31AB(4) and s 31AB(9)]** This general principle is subject to one exception – which relates to the application of a 'competence standard' to a disabled person by a qualifications body and general qualifications body. The Act says that less favourable treatment of a disabled person in this regard will be justified only if the qualifications body or general qualifications body can show that the standard is (or would be) applied equally to people who do not have the disabled person's disability, and that its application is a proportionate means of achieving a legitimate aim. What the Act says about competence standards is considered in more detail in paragraphs 8.27 to 8.4 and paragraphs 9.57 to 9.82.

Justification and reasonable adjustments

6.5 In certain circumstances, the existence of a material and substantial reason for less favourable treatment is not enough to justify that treatment. This is the case where a trade organisation, qualifications body or general qualifications body is also under a duty to make reasonable adjustments in relation to the disabled person but fails to comply with that duty.

6.6 **[s 3A(6) and s 31AB(5)]** In those circumstances, it is necessary to consider not only whether there is a material and substantial reason for the less favourable treatment, but also whether the treatment would still have been justified even if the organisation or body had complied with its duty to make reasonable adjustments. In effect, it is necessary to ask the question 'would a reasonable adjustment have made any difference?' If a reasonable adjustment would have made a difference to the reason that is being used to justify the treatment, then the less favourable treatment cannot be justified.

6.7 In relation to disability-related discrimination, the fact that a trade organisation, qualifications body or general qualifications body has failed to comply with a duty to make a reasonable adjustment means that the sequence of events for justifying disability-related less favourable treatment is as follows:

- The disabled person proves facts from which it could be inferred in the absence of an adequate explanation that:
  - (a) for a reason related to his disability, he has been treated less favourably than a person to whom that reason does not apply has been, or would be, treated, and
  - (b) a duty to make a reasonable adjustment has arisen in respect of him and the organisation or body has failed to comply with it.
- The trade organisation, qualifications body or general qualifications body will be found to have discriminated unless it proves that:
  - (a) the reason for the treatment is both material to the circumstances of the particular case and substantial, and
  - (b) the reason would still have applied if the reasonable adjustment had been made.

CAN HEALTH AND SAFETY CONCERNS JUSTIFY LESS FAVOURABLE TREATMENT?

6.8 Stereotypical assumptions about the health and safety implications of disability should be avoided, both in general terms and in relation to particular types of disability. Indeed, less favourable treatment which is based on such assumptions may itself amount to direct discrimination – which is incapable of justification (see paragraph 4.4). The fact that a person has a disability does not necessarily mean that he represents an additional risk to health and safety.

> A person with bi-polar affective disorder applies for registration as a health professional with a professional association. The association refuses to register her, simply on the basis that she has mentioned her disability on a health questionnaire. The association makes an assumption that her disability would present a health and safety risk, without making any attempt to find out whether or how it would present such a risk, or indeed whether she had made a recovery. This is likely to be direct discrimination and therefore likely to be unlawful.

> A young person with cerebral palsy is undertaking a Scottish Higher general qualification in chemistry. The general qualifications body refuses his application for entry for the general qualification because they assume that his cerebral palsy would present a health and safety risk, without making any attempt to find out whether there are, in fact, any health and safety risks. This is likely to be direct discrimination and, therefore, likely to be unlawful.

6.9 Genuine concerns about the health and safety of anybody (including a disabled person) may be relevant when seeking to establish that disability related less favourable treatment of a disabled person is justified. However, it is important to remember that health and safety legislation does not require the removal of all conceivable risk but that risk is properly appreciated, understood and managed. Further information can be obtained from the Health and Safety Executive (see Appendix B for details).

6.10 Paragraphs 6.11 to 6.15 examine the circumstances in which concerns about health and safety may justify less favourable treatment of a disabled person, and this is followed by a consideration of the relevance of medical information in this context. As noted in paragraph 6.4, however, the basis upon which a qualifications body may justify less favourable treatment of a disabled person in the application of a competence standard differs from that which usually applies under the Act. The following principles do not have the same relevance to justification in those circumstances, but regard should instead be had to paragraphs 8.35 to 8.40 (in respect of qualifications bodies) and paragraphs 9.67 to 9.73 (in respect of general qualifications bodies).

6.11 It is the trade organisation, qualifications body or general qualifications body which must decide what action to take, or to decide what advice to give an examination centre, in response to concerns about health and safety in relation to the examination. However, leaving aside the question of competence standards, it is prudent for a trade organisation, qualifications body or general qualifications body to have, or arrange for, a risk assessment to be carried out by a suitably qualified person in circumstances where it has reason to think that the effects of a person's disability may give rise to an issue about health and safety. This is because:

- If a trade organisation, qualifications body or general qualifications body treats a disabled person less favourably merely on the basis of generalised assumptions about the health and safety implications of having a disability, such treatment may itself amount to direct discrimination – which is incapable of justification.

> A qualifications body refuses to issue a certificate to operate heavy machinery to a man with epilepsy. No attempt is made to find out the actual circumstances of the individual through a risk assessment. The

qualifications body merely makes an assumption that it would be a health and safety risk to let someone with epilepsy operate heavy machinery. This is likely to be direct discrimination and therefore to be unlawful.

- Even where there is no direct discrimination, an organisation or body which treats a disabled person less favourably without having a suitable and sufficient risk assessment carried out is unlikely to be able to show that its concerns about health and safety justify the less favourable treatment.

6.12 Nevertheless, a trade organisation, qualifications body or general qualifications body should not subject a disabled person to a risk assessment if this is not merited by the particular circumstances of the case.

A man who has diabetes applies to go on a residential training course in accounting provided by a professional association of which he is a member. The man's condition is stable and he has successfully managed it for many years. Nevertheless, the association says that it has health and safety concerns; that it wants to undertake a risk assessment; and that it needs further medical evidence from the man's doctor. This is likely to be unlawful, as the circumstances of the case do not indicate that there would be any health and safety risk.

6.13 A risk assessment must be suitable and sufficient. It should identify the risks associated with a particular activity, taking account of any reasonable adjustments put in place for the disabled person, and should be specific for the individual carrying out a particular task. It is therefore unlikely that a trade organisation, qualifications body or general qualifications body which has a **general** policy of treating people with certain disabilities (such as epilepsy, diabetes or mental health problems) less favourably than other people will be able to justify doing so – even if that policy is in accordance with the advice of an occupational health adviser.

6.14 A 'blanket' policy of this nature will usually be unlawful. This is because it is likely to amount to direct discrimination (which cannot ever be justified) or to disability-related less favourable treatment which is not justifiable in the circumstances – ie disability-related discrimination.

A qualifications body for social care professionals has a policy of asking applicants for registration to fill out a health questionnaire. Any applicant who states that they have had treatment for a mental health problem is refused registration without any investigation into their individual circumstances. The qualifications body is applying a blanket policy, which is likely to amount to direct discrimination

A general qualifications body issues guidance that states that the qualification in ICT which they offer will be unsuitable to any candidate with a visual impairment and that people with visual impairments should not apply for the course. The general qualifications body is applying a blanket policy, which is likely to amount to direct discrimination.

6.15 Reasonable adjustments made by a trade organisation, qualifications body or general qualifications body may remove or reduce health and safety risks related to a person's disability. A suitable and sufficient assessment of such risks therefore needs to take account of the impact which making any reasonable adjustments would have. If a risk assessment is not conducted on this basis, then an organisation or body is unlikely to be able to show that its concerns about health and safety justify less favourable treatment of the disabled person.

CAN MEDICAL INFORMATION JUSTIFY LESS FAVOURABLE TREATMENT?

6.16 Consideration of medical information (such as a doctor's report or the answers to a medical questionnaire) is likely to form part of an assessment of health and safety risks. In most cases, however, having a disability does not adversely affect a person's general health. In other cases, its effect on a person's health may fluctuate. Although medical information about a disability may justify an adverse decision, it will not do so if there is no effect on the person's relevant skills and abilities (or if any effect is less than substantial), no matter how great the effects of the disability are in other ways. Indeed, less favourable treatment of a disabled person in a case where his disability has no effect on his relevant skills and abilities may well amount to direct discrimination – which is incapable of being justified.

6.17 In addition, where medical information is available, trade organisations, qualifications bodies and general qualifications bodies must weigh it up in the context of the relevant circumstances, and the capabilities of the individual. An organisation or body should also consider whether reasonable adjustments could be made in order to overcome any problems which may have been identified as a result of the medical information. It should not be taken for granted that the person who provides the medical information will be aware that trade organisations, qualifications bodies and general qualifications bodies have a duty to make reasonable adjustments, or what these adjustments might be. It is good practice, therefore, to ensure that medical advisers are made aware of these matters. Information provided by a medical adviser should only be relied on if the adviser has the appropriate knowledge and expertise.

6.18 In any event, although medical evidence may generally be considered as an 'expert contribution', it should not ordinarily be the sole factor influencing a decision by a trade organisation, qualifications body or general qualifications body. The views of the disabled person (about his/her own capabilities and possible adjustments) should also be sought. It may also be possible to seek help from disability organisations. Ultimately, it is for the trade organisation, qualifications body or general qualifications body – and not the medical adviser – to take decisions.

7. DISCRIMINATION BY TRADE ORGANISATIONS

INTRODUCTION

[4.119]

7.1 Chapter 3 explains what the Act means by 'trade organisation', and that the Act makes it unlawful for a trade organisation to discriminate against a disabled person who is a member of the organisation or an applicant for membership. Chapter 3 also explains that the Act says it is unlawful for a trade organisation to subject such a person to harassment, or to victimise any person – whether disabled or not.

7.2 This chapter looks at discrimination by trade organisations in more detail. In order to do so (and after considering an important point about the relationship of trade organisations to qualifications bodies), it is necessary to look at the different aspects of a trade organisation's functions, from those which relate to becoming a member of the organisation to those which concern the benefits of membership once achieved. It is also necessary to consider issues relating to the variation and withdrawal of membership.

TRADE ORGANISATIONS AS QUALIFICATIONS BODIES

7.3 It has already been noted (at paragraph 3.11) that some trade organisations confer professional or trade qualifications and that, as a consequence, such organisations can be subject to the Act's provisions about trade organisations or, depending upon the context, to those about qualifications bodies.

7.4 However, it should also be noted that membership of certain trade organisations (for example, the Institute of Linguists or the Chartered Institute of Personnel and Development) itself amounts to a professional or trade qualification for the reasons explained at paragraph 8.6. Where this is the case, decisions about granting, varying or withdrawing membership of the trade organisation will also be subject to the rules about conferring professional or trade qualifications. This fact is likely to be of particular significance where such decisions result from the application of a 'competence standard' (see paragraphs 8.27 to 8.41).

BECOMING A MEMBER

What does the Act say?

7.5 **[s 13(1)]** The Act says that it is unlawful for a trade organisation to discriminate against a disabled person:

- in the arrangements it makes for the purpose of determining who should be offered membership of the organisation

> A trade organisation asks a woman with a learning disability to take an additional test before allowing her membership, even though she already meets the entry criteria for that organisation. This is likely to be unlawful.

- in the terms on which it is prepared to admit him to membership

> A trade organisation for journalists asks a partially sighted woman to pay an extra fee for membership because of the cost of putting information onto audio tape. This is likely to be unlawful.

- by refusing to accept, or deliberately not accepting, his application for membership.

> A nursing organisation refuses to admit a woman with a history of mental health problems – without further enquiry. This is likely to be unlawful.

7.6 **[s 16B]** As explained at paragraphs 3.22 to 3.25, the Act also makes it unlawful in certain circumstances to publish a discriminatory advertisement for membership of a trade organisation.

What amounts to direct discrimination?

7.7 **[s 3A(5)]** A trade organisation may wish to differentiate between individuals when dealing with applications for membership of the organisation. However, in doing so, it should avoid discriminating against disabled applicants or potential applicants. As explained in Chapter 4, treating a disabled person in a different way from the way in which other people are (or would be) treated amounts to discrimination in certain circumstances. In particular, such treatment is unlawful if it amounts to direct discrimination under Part 2. As explained at paragraph 4.4, treatment of a disabled person amounts to direct discrimination if:

- it is on the ground of his disability
- the treatment is less favourable than the way in which a person not having that particular disability is (or would be) treated, and
- the relevant circumstances, including the abilities, of the person with whom the comparison is made are the same as, or not materially different from, those of the disabled person.

> A trade organisation refuses to let a woman who has schizophrenia become a member, even though the woman has shown that she has sufficient qualifications and experience to gain membership. This is likely to amount to direct discrimination, because she is being treated less favourably on the ground of her disability. The treatment is less favourable than the way in which someone who does not have schizophrenia would be treated; the relevant circumstances of the woman (in this case her qualifications and experience) are the same as those of other candidates who do not have schizophrenia.

What amounts to disability-related discrimination?

7.8 **[s 3A(1)]** Less favourable treatment of a disabled person may be unlawful under the Act even if it does not amount to direct discrimination. This will be the case if it amounts to disability-related discrimination instead. As explained at paragraph 4.25, this is less favourable treatment which is for a reason related to the person's disability. However, unlike treatment which amounts to direct discrimination (and which is therefore incapable of justification), a trade organisation's treatment of a disabled person does not amount to disability-related discrimination if the organisation can show that it is justified. The circumstances in which this may be possible are explained in Chapter 6.

7.9 In summary, less favourable treatment of a disabled person will be unlawful if it amounts either to direct discrimination or to disability related discrimination, and involves:

- a trade organisation's arrangements for selecting new members
- the terms on which membership is offered, or
- the rejection or non-acceptance of an application for membership.

When does the duty to make reasonable adjustments apply to applicants and potential applicants for membership?

7.10 **[s 14]** The duty of a trade organisation to make reasonable adjustments obviously applies in respect of its disabled members. However, the duty also applies in respect of any disabled person who is, or has notified the organisation that he may be, an applicant for membership.

> A disabled man, who is unable to write because of his disability, requests an electronic application form from a trade organisation so that he can fill it in on his computer. The organisation may have a duty to make this reasonable adjustment because it knows that this man is a potential applicant for membership.

7.11 **[s 14(3)]** The duty only applies in respect of a disabled person if the trade organisation knows that the person is, or may be, an applicant for membership. 'Knowledge', in this context, means that the organisation knows, or could reasonably be expected to know, about this. Likewise, the duty applies only if the organisation knows that the person has a disability which is likely to place him at a substantial disadvantage in comparison with people who are not disabled.

7.12 Where a trade organisation has knowledge that a person may be an applicant for membership, the duty to make reasonable adjustments applies to provisions, criteria or practices for determining to whom membership should be offered. However, reasonable adjustments to premises are only required in respect of existing members and actual applicants for membership of whom the organisation has knowledge.

7.13 Where it applies, the duty to make reasonable adjustments is likely to affect arrangements in relation to, for example, advertisements, application forms and interviews for membership of the organisation. This is not a complete list of everything which could be covered by the duty (and which would be relevant in connection with becoming a member of a trade organisation), but it is intended as an indication of the likely relevant areas.

> A man with a speech impairment applies for membership of a professional association. The association normally conducts a short interview for its potential members. Because the man has difficulty with verbal communication he asks if he can have the interview in the form of written questions and answers. This is likely to be a reasonable adjustment to the organisation's membership arrangements.

7.14 As explained in paragraphs 5.26 and 5.27, a trade organisation is never able to justify a failure to comply with a duty to make a reasonable adjustment under the Act.

MEMBERSHIP BENEFITS

What does the Act say?

7.15 **[s 13(2)]** The Act says that it is unlawful for a trade organisation to discriminate against a disabled person who is a member of the organisation:

- in the way it affords him access to any benefits or by refusing or deliberately omitting to afford him access to them, or
- by subjecting him to any other detriment.

> An employee of a trade organisation deliberately fails to invite a member with schizophrenia to an annual dinner, because she thinks that other members may be offended by this person's behaviour, even though she has never met the member and knows nothing about his behaviour. This is likely to be unlawful.

7.16 The Act does not define what a benefit is (although it does say that benefits include facilities and services). Whether something is a benefit will depend on all the relevant circumstances, including an organisation's rules and practices. However, the following are likely to amount to benefits: training facilities, welfare or insurance services, participation at meetings and other events and invitations to attend those events, information about the organisation's activities, and assistance to members in employers' disciplinary or dismissal procedures.

When does less favourable treatment in relation to membership benefits amount to discrimination?

7.17 **[s 3A]** A trade organisation needs to take care if it differentiates between members in relation to the provision of membership benefits. For example, if the organisation's treatment of a disabled member in this regard amounts to direct discrimination under the Act (see paragraph 7.7) it will be unlawful.

7.18 Even where it is not directly discriminatory, treatment of a disabled person will be unlawful if it amounts to disability-related discrimination (see paragraph 4.25).

When does the duty to make reasonable adjustments apply in respect of membership benefits?

7.19 **[s 14]** A trade organisation has a duty to make reasonable adjustments in respect of the way it makes benefits available to its members. It owes this duty to a disabled member of the organisation if it has knowledge of the fact that he has a disability and is likely to be placed at a substantial disadvantage in comparison with people who are not disabled. The duty is likely to apply, for example, in respect of the provision of the benefits mentioned in paragraph 7.16. Where the duty does apply, the trade organisation must take such steps as are reasonable to prevent the provision, criterion or practice, or the physical feature (as the case may be) from placing the disabled member at a substantial disadvantage.

> A trade union has a website through which it informs members about its services. A member with a learning disability requests that a summary of the information on the website is provided in a format that is easy for her to understand (Easy Read). This is likely to be a reasonable adjustment for the union to make.

> A trade organisation organises a trade fair. A blind member requests assistance at the trade fair to find his way around. This is likely to be a reasonable adjustment for the trade organisation to make.

> A deaf woman, who is a union member, has a problem at work which she wants to discuss in depth with a trade union representative. The trade union pays for and arranges a sign language interpreter for the meeting. This is likely to be a reasonable adjustment for the union to make.

7.20 For many members, the manner in which a trade organisation makes information available to them is likely to be an important issue. If this information is not provided in forms accessible to disabled people they are likely to be placed at a substantial disadvantage. However, recent technological developments have meant that it is increasingly practicable to produce material in alternative formats quickly and cheaply. Disability organisations and bodies like the Equality and Human Rights Commission are able to advise trade organisations about practicable methods of providing information in an accessible way. What is reasonable will depend on the individual circumstances of the case.

> A trade organisation provides a magazine for its members. A blind member of the organisation asks for the magazine to be sent to him electronically as an email attachment so that he can read it using access software on his home computer. This is likely to be a reasonable adjustment for the trade organisation to make.

7.21 In some cases a reasonable adjustment will not work without the co-operation of other members of the organisation. Members may therefore have an important role in helping to ensure that a reasonable adjustment is carried out in practice. Subject to considerations about confidentiality (explained at paragraphs 7.34 to 7.36), trade organisations must ensure that this happens. It is unlikely to be a valid defence to a claim under the Act that members were obstructive or unhelpful when the trade organisation tried to make reasonable adjustments. A trade organisation would at least need to be able to show that it took such behaviour seriously and dealt with it appropriately. Trade organisations will be more likely to be able to do this if they establish and implement the type of policies and practices described at paragraph 2.15 (and, in the case of trade unions, 2.16).

> A professional association organises a question and answer session with a panel of experts, to which it invites members. The event is organised at a venue with an induction loop to enable a deaf member who uses a hearing aid to participate. The Chair of the event reminds all contributors to speak in turn, and only when they are holding the microphone to enable everyone present to follow the proceedings. When a member persistently speaks out of turn, without the microphone, she is reminded that the organisation has a disability policy and that contributions will not be taken from her if she continues to ignore the rules laid down for the session which were designed to enable disabled people to participate.

VARIATION AND WITHDRAWAL OF MEMBERSHIP

What does the Act say?

7.22 **[s 13(2)]** The Act says that it is unlawful for a trade organisation to discriminate against a disabled person who is a member of the organisation:

- by depriving him of membership, or varying the terms on which he is a member, or
- by subjecting him to any other detriment.

> A man who is a member of a trade organisation becomes disabled after a spinal injury. His membership is withdrawn without any consideration or consultation with him about whether or how he can still meet the membership requirements. This is likely to be direct discrimination and therefore to be unlawful.

7.23 **[s 16A]** The Act also says that, where a disabled person's membership of a trade organisation has come to an end, it is still unlawful for the trade organisation:

- to discriminate against him by subjecting him to a detriment, or
- to subject him to harassment

if the discrimination or harassment arises out of his former membership of the organisation and is closely connected to it.

7.24 **[s 55]** It is also unlawful to victimise a person (whether or not he is disabled) after he has ceased to be a member of a trade organisation (see paragraphs 4.31 to 4.34).

When does less favourable treatment in relation to variation or withdrawal of membership amount to discrimination?

7.25 **[s 3A]** If a trade organisation varies the terms on which a disabled person is a member of the organisation, or withdraws his membership, it may be treating him less favourably than it treats other members. Depending upon the circumstances, the organisation may be discriminating against the disabled person by treating him in this way. For example, if the organisation's treatment of a disabled member amounts to direct discrimination under the Act (see paragraph 7.7) it will be unlawful.

7.26 Even where it does not amount to direct discrimination, treatment of a disabled person will be unlawful if it amounts to disability-related discrimination (see paragraph 4.25).

> A member of a trade union complains about another member who has Asperger's syndrome (a form of autism) after a conference, saying that the fellow member behaved in an inappropriate way whilst at the conference hotel. The man's behaviour was related to his disability but she was not aware of this at the time. The trade union disciplines the disabled man and his membership is withdrawn, even though the union knows about his disability. This is likely to be less favourable treatment for a disability-related reason and is therefore likely to be unlawful, unless the trade union can show that the treatment was justified.

When does the duty to make reasonable adjustments apply in respect of the variation or withdrawal of membership?

7.27 **[s 14]** The duty of a trade organisation to make reasonable adjustments for a member who it knows to have a disability extends to the way in which it operates grievance and disciplinary procedures, or procedures for the variation or withdrawal of membership. Where a provision, criterion or practice, or a physical feature, places a disabled member at a substantial disadvantage in this regard, the trade organisation must take such steps as are reasonable to prevent this.

> A disabled doctor has a meeting to discuss his continued membership of a professional association. The venue is changed to one that is accessible to the doctor, who has a mobility impairment. This is likely to be a reasonable adjustment for the association to make.

> A disabled woman has a grievance hearing at the offices of a trade union. She is provided with a car parking space at the venue because her disability makes it impossible for her to use public transport. This is likely to be a reasonable adjustment for the union to make, whether or not the grievance was related to her disability.

7.28 **[s 16A(4)–(6)]** A trade organisation's duty to make reasonable adjustments may also apply in respect of a former member who is a disabled person. This will be the case where:

- the disabled person is placed at a substantial disadvantage in comparison with other former members:
  - (a) by a provision, practice or criterion applied by the trade organisation to the disabled person in relation to any matter arising out of his former membership, or
  - (b) by a physical feature of premises occupied by the organisation, and the organisation either knows, or could reasonably be expected to know, that the former member in question has a disability and is likely to be affected in this way.

> A newly disabled person wishes to attend a conference of a trade organisation of which he is a former member. This conference is open to former members. He explains to the conference organisers that he is now partially sighted. They arrange for a guide to accompany him at the conference and produce conference papers in large print. These are likely to be reasonable adjustments for the trade organisation to make.

7.29 The former members with whom the position of the disabled person should be compared must be people who are not disabled, but who are former members of the same organisation. If it is not possible to identify an actual comparator for this purpose, then a hypothetical comparator may be used (see paragraph 4.17).

KNOWLEDGE OF DISABILITY

7.30 **[s 14(3)]** The point has been made a number of times in this chapter that a trade organisation only has a duty to make a reasonable adjustment if it knows, or could reasonably be expected to know, that a person is, or may be, an applicant for membership or has a disability and is likely to be placed at a substantial disadvantage in comparison with people who are not disabled. However, a trade organisation will be deemed to have that knowledge in certain circumstances.

Obtaining information

7.31 It is good practice for a trade organisation to invite its members to tell it about their disability-related needs. In any event, where information which should alert a trade organisation to the circumstances mentioned in paragraph 7.30 is available to it, or would be if it were reasonably alert, the organisation cannot simply ignore it. It is therefore in the interests of a trade organisation to be aware of the possibility that people it is dealing with may have a disability and to make reasonable enquiries if circumstances suggest this may be the case. It also means that it is a good idea for disabled people, if they wish to take full advantage of the provisions of the Act, to let trade organisations know of their disability and of substantial disadvantages at which they are likely to be placed. The earlier a trade organisation is told about a disability and its effects, the more likely it is to be able to make effective adjustments.

> A trade union has questions on its membership application form asking if the applicant is disabled or needs information in an accessible format (such as large print, Braille, tape or email). It also asks if the applicant has any additional disability-related needs.

> A professional association sends its members invitations to a conference. The invitation contains general details about access for disabled people, and the booking form asks about access requirements – such as whether delegate information is required in an accessible format, and whether delegates have any specific dietary requirements.

7.32 If a trade organisation's agent or employee (such as a trade union representative) knows, in that capacity, of a member's disability, the organisation will not usually be able to claim that it does not know of the disability. The same applies in respect of actual or potential applicants for membership of the organisation. Trade organisations therefore need to ensure that where information about disabled people may come through different channels, there is a means – suitably confidential – for bringing the information together, to make it easier for the organisation to fulfil its duties under the Act.

> A trade union member tells her branch secretary that she is unable to climb stairs due to her mobility impairment. The branch secretary arranges for the member to go on a training course organised by the union's education department. When the member arrives at the training session, she is unable to gain access to the building because of a flight of stairs. The union would be unable to claim that it did not know about the member's disability.

7.33 Information will not be imputed to a trade organisation if it is gained by a person providing services to members independently of the organisation. This is the case even if the organisation has arranged for those services to be provided.

> A trade organisation member uses a counselling Helpline which is independent of the organisation but which is provided as a benefit of membership. During his conversation with the counsellor the member discusses his worries about his worsening sight problem. The trade organisation itself should not be assumed to know about his need for the organisation's magazine to be in an accessible format, on the basis of this conversation.

Confidential information

7.34 The extent to which a trade organisation is entitled to let other members know about a fellow member's disability will depend partly on the terms of membership. An organisation could be discriminating against the member by revealing such information if it would not reveal similar information about another person for an equally legitimate purpose; or if the organisation revealed such information without consulting the individual, instead of adopting the usual practice of talking to a member before revealing personal information about him. Trade organisations also need to be aware that they have obligations under the Data Protection Act in respect of personal data.

> A member of a trade union wishes to go on a residential weekend conference, travelling there on a coach arranged by the union. The union member has to take dialysis equipment with her because she has had kidney failure. Another member needs to be informed, in order to help her load and unload the equipment. The disabled member gives her permission for another union member to be told that she is taking medical equipment with her, so that she can be helped with the equipment.

7.35 However, as noted at paragraph 7.21, sometimes a reasonable adjustment will not work without the co-operation of other members. In order to secure such co-operation, it may be necessary for a trade organisation to tell one or more of a disabled person's fellow members (in confidence) about a disability which is not obvious. Who it might be appropriate to tell will depend on the nature of the disability and the reason they need to know about it. In any event, a trade organisation must not disclose confidential details about a member without his consent. A disabled person's refusal to give such consent may impact upon the effectiveness of the adjustments which the trade organisation is able to make or its ability to make adjustments at all.

7.36 The Act does not prevent a disabled person keeping a disability confidential from a trade organisation. But this is likely to mean that unless the organisation could reasonably be expected to know about the person's disability anyway, it will not be under a duty to make a reasonable adjustment. If a disabled person expects a trade organisation to make a reasonable adjustment, he will need to provide the organisation – or someone acting on its behalf – with sufficient information to carry out that adjustment.

THE ROLE OF TRADE UNIONS

7.37 Trade unions are obvious examples of what the Act means by trade organisations. Representing the interests of their members in the workplace is one of the most important functions of trade unions, and so union representatives need to be familiar with the Act's provisions on employment and occupation. They need to be able to recognise potential claims under the Act and to know how to respond appropriately. Union representatives should also understand the need to make reasonable adjustments at branch meetings, for example, and that the reasonableness of the cost of making an adjustment should be assessed having regard to the union's overall resources, and to any access funds which may be available (see paragraphs 2.15 and 2.16).

7.38 It is important for trade unions to ensure that union representatives receive proper training on the Act and that they are aware of the DRC's code of practice on the Act's provisions on employment and occupation (see Appendix B). It is also advisable for trade unions to have arrangements in place so that appropriate cases are referred to the union's solicitors.

8. DISCRIMINATION BY QUALIFICATIONS BODIES

INTRODUCTION

[4.120]

8.1 Chapter 3 describes the meaning of 'qualifications body', and explains that it is unlawful for such a body to discriminate against a disabled person in relation to conferring professional or trade qualifications, or to subject him to harassment, or to victimise any person – whether disabled or not. This chapter does not concern the duties in respect of those bodies conferring of relevant general qualifications – these duties are considered further in Chapter 9.

8.2 This chapter looks at the provisions about qualifications bodies in more detail. It explains what the definition of 'professional or trade qualification' covers in practice. It considers when less favourable treatment of a disabled person by a qualifications body is unlawful, and when the duty to make reasonable adjustments arises. Finally, it examines the meaning and significance of 'competence standards'.

8.3 **[s 17A(1A)]** It should be noted that a disabled person is not permitted to bring a claim in an employment tribunal about alleged discrimination or harassment by a qualifications body if a statutory appeal is available in respect of the matter in question. For example, the Medical Act 1983 sets out specific mechanisms for appealing decisions of the General Medical Council or its committees regarding the registration of medical practitioners. A complaint to which these appeal mechanisms applied could not, therefore, be brought instead in an employment tribunal.

8.4 It should also be noted that the provisions of the Act which relate specifically to qualifications bodies' focus only on the functions of conferring professional or trade qualifications. The performance of other functions by such bodies may be subject to other provisions of the Act. For example, where a qualifications body is also a trade organisation, regard must also be had to what the Act says about trade organisations – and to Chapter 7 of the Code in particular.

WHAT IS A PROFESSIONAL OR TRADE QUALIFICATION?

8.5 **[s 14A(5)]** As noted at paragraph 3.9, the key feature of a qualifications body is that it confers professional or trade qualifications. The Act says that such a qualification is an authorisation, qualification, recognition, registration, enrolment, approval or certification which is needed for, or which facilitates engagement in, a particular profession or trade. Clearly, therefore, the expression includes those qualifications etc, which are conferred solely in anticipation of furthering a particular career. However, it is also capable of including more general qualifications if attaining them facilitates engagement in a particular profession or trade and if these general qualifications are not relevant general qualifications (see chapter 9 for further details). In order to decide whether a particular qualification is a professional or trade qualification for the purposes of the Act, it is necessary to address the following three questions:

- What is the profession or trade?
- What is the qualification?
- Does possession of that particular qualification make it easier to work in that particular profession or trade (rather than merely assisting general advancement in that or any other career)?

8.6 The word 'qualification' should not be interpreted narrowly – attaining a professional or trade qualification need not involve passing formal examinations or tests. In some cases, simply being a member of an organisation or body may amount to such a qualification if membership itself facilitates engagement in a particular profession or trade.

8.7 The following list (which is not intended to be exhaustive) gives examples of qualifications which would or could count as professional or trade qualifications under the Act provided that the criteria set out in paragraph 8.5 are met:

- Registration with the Nursing and Midwifery Council
- A certificate to practise as a solicitor issued by the Law Society
- Registration with the Council for Registered Gas Installers (CORGI)
- NVQs
- BTECs
- City and Guilds
- Scottish Vocational Qualifications
- HGV driving licences
- Membership, registration or fellowship of trade or professional bodies (eg Fellow of the Institute of Linguists).

8.8 In relation to certain professions or trades, educational institutions or other bodies may devise, run and examine their own courses, although approval for entry into the profession or trade is controlled by an external body. Because of the wide definition of 'professional or trade qualification', such external bodies are likely to be qualifications bodies if they perform any of the following functions:

- maintaining a register of people who are qualified to practice in the profession or trade
- conducting additional tests for people who have qualified, or who wish to qualify, into the profession or trade, such as basic skills tests or medical checks, or
- giving approval for a person's qualification to his course provider.

WHAT AMOUNTS TO DIRECT DISCRIMINATION?

8.9 **[s 14A(1)]** It is obvious that a qualifications body will differentiate between individuals when conferring, renewing or extending professional or trade qualifications. However, in doing so, it should avoid discriminating against disabled people – it is unlawful for a qualifications body to discriminate against a disabled person in respect of a number of matters which are specified in the Act (and listed in paragraph 3.19).

8.10 **[s 3A(5)]** As explained in Chapter 4, treating a disabled person in a different way from the way in which other people are (or would be) treated amounts to discrimination in certain circumstances. In particular, such treatment is unlawful if it amounts to direct discrimination under Part 2. As explained at paragraph 4.4, treatment of a disabled person amounts to direct discrimination if:

- it is on the ground of his disability
- the treatment is less favourable than the way in which a person not having that particular disability is (or would be) treated, and
- the relevant circumstances, including the abilities, of the person with whom the comparison is made are the same as, or not materially different from, those of the disabled person.

> A qualifications body recommends to a college of higher education that a man with a mobility impairment should not be allowed on to a social work course, as they wrongly assume that he may have difficulty visiting the homes of clients. This is likely to amount to direct discrimination.

WHAT AMOUNTS TO DISABILITY-RELATED DISCRIMINATION?

8.11 **[s 3A(1)]** Less favourable treatment of a disabled person may be unlawful under the Act even if it does not amount to direct discrimination. This will be the case if it amounts to disability-related discrimination instead. As explained at paragraph 4.25, this is less favourable treatment which is for a reason related to the person's disability. However, unlike treatment which amounts to direct discrimination (and which is therefore incapable of justification), a qualifications body's treatment of a disabled person does not amount to disability-related discrimination if the body can show that it is justified. The general circumstances in which this may be possible are explained in Chapter 6. However, special rules apply in respect of justification of less favourable treatment in the application of a competence standard (see paragraphs 8.35 to 8.40).

8.12 In summary, less favourable treatment of a disabled person will be unlawful if it amounts to either direct discrimination or disability related discrimination, and involves:

- the arrangements for determining upon whom to confer a professional or trade qualification
- the terms upon which a qualifications body confers, renews or extends such a qualification
- a refusal or deliberate omission by such a body to grant his application for a qualification, or
- the withdrawal of a qualification from him or a variation of the terms on which he holds it.

> A professional association which maintains a register of approved acupuncturists withdraws registration from a woman who, because of treatment for cancer, has not been able to work for a year. The association has a policy of withdrawing registration from anyone who has not practised for this length of time. The treatment of the woman is for a disability-related reason (her lack of recent practice is due to her disability). The treatment is less favourable than the way in which someone who had practised recently would have been treated. It would therefore amount to disability-related discrimination unless the association (acting as a qualifications body) can justify it.

8.13 **[s 16A]** The Act also says that, where a disabled person ceases to hold a professional or trade qualification, it is still unlawful for the qualifications body which conferred it:

- to discriminate against him by subjecting him to a detriment, or
- to subject him to harassment

if the discrimination or harassment arises out of his having formerly held the qualification and is closely connected to it.

8.14 It is also unlawful to victimise a person (whether or not he is disabled) after he has ceased to hold such a qualification (see paragraphs 4.31 to 4.34).

HOW DOES THE DUTY TO MAKE REASONABLE ADJUSTMENTS APPLY TO QUALIFICATIONS BODIES?

In respect of which disabled people is the duty owed?

8.15 **[s 14B(1)]** A qualifications body has a duty to make reasonable adjustments to the way it confers, renews or extends professional or trade qualifications (except in respect of competence standards). It owes this duty to a disabled person who holds a qualification conferred by it and to a disabled applicant or potential applicant for such a qualification.

8.16 **[s 14B(2)]** The duty extends to holders of a qualification conferred by the body and to applicants for such a qualification. However, in the case of a provision, criterion or practice for determining on whom a qualification is to be conferred, the duty only applies to a disabled person who has either applied for the qualification or has notified the body that he may apply.

8.17 **[s 14B(3)]** The duty only applies if the qualifications body knows, or could reasonably be expected to know, that the disabled person concerned is, or may be, an applicant for a professional or trade qualification. Likewise, the duty only applies if the body knows or should know that the person has a disability and is likely to be placed at a substantial disadvantage compared with people who are not disabled.

8.18 **[s 16A(4)–(6)]** The duty of a qualifications body to make reasonable adjustments may also extend to a disabled person who formerly held a professional or trade qualification. This is the case where a provision, practice or criterion, or a physical feature of premises occupied by the qualifications body, places the disabled person at a substantial disadvantage compared with others in the same position. The duty only applies, however, if the qualifications body knows, or could reasonably be expected to know, that the person concerned has a disability and is likely to be affected in this way.

8.19 The people with whom the position of the disabled person should be compared must be people who are not disabled, but who also formerly held the same professional or trade qualification conferred by the qualifications body in question. If it is not possible to identify an actual comparator for this purpose, then a hypothetical comparator may be used (see paragraph 4.17).

What is the effect of the duty?

8.20 Where it applies, the duty to make reasonable adjustments is likely to affect arrangements in relation to, for example, taking tests and examinations, and renewing qualifications where it is necessary to do so. However, there is no duty to make adjustments to competence standards applied to a disabled person by a qualifications body. Where the duty does apply, however, the qualifications body must take such steps as are reasonable to prevent the provision, criterion or practice, or the physical feature (as the case may be) from placing the disabled person in question at a substantial disadvantage.

> A woman with a mental health problem is informed that an oral examination for a diploma in interpreting and translation has been arranged for 8:30 am. The timing of the examination would substantially disadvantage the woman, because a side effect of her medication is extreme drowsiness for several hours after taking her morning dose – which prevents her from concentrating well. The qualifications body agrees to her request to take the examination later in the day.

> A man who lip-reads because of his hearing impairment is due to have a practical test as part of his beauty therapy course. The qualifications body instructs an assessor working on its behalf to face the man when she issues instructions during the assessment and to talk clearly.

> An advanced craft test for carpentry consists of a seven hour practical examination. A woman with arthritis who is only able to work part-time as a result of her disability wishes to take this test as two sessions of three and a half hours on two consecutive days. The qualifications body awarding the qualification allows the test to be taken in this way.

> A candidate for a written examination as part of a jewellery-making course has dyslexia. The qualifications body allows her extra time to sit the examination, and also permits the use of a reader and an amanuensis (someone to write on her behalf) as the candidate is not able to read and write well because of her dyslexia.

> A woman with a learning disability is allowed extra time by a qualifications body to take a written examination. This is likely to be a reasonable adjustment for the qualifications body to make, because the trade which the woman wants to enter would not require written work to be done in a short amount of time, so the ability to write quickly is not a competence standard.

> A disabled man asks for twice as much time for a test in shorthand because his disability makes it impossible for him to write quickly. This is unlikely to be a reasonable adjustment for the qualifications body to make, because speed is an essential element of the shorthand qualification – in other words, it is likely to be a competence standard, and thus the duty to make reasonable adjustments does not apply.

What are the practical implications of the duty?

8.21 Although there is no duty on a qualifications body to make a reasonable adjustment if it does not have the requisite knowledge (see paragraph 8.17), it will be deemed to have that knowledge in certain circumstances.

8.22 Where information is available which should alert a qualifications body to the circumstances mentioned in paragraph 8.17, or would be if it were reasonably alert, the body cannot simply ignore it. It is thus a good idea for disabled people, if they wish to take full advantage of the provisions of the Act, to let educational institutions and qualifications bodies know of their disability and of substantial disadvantages that are likely to arise. The earlier a qualifications body is told about a disability and its effects, the more likely it is to be able to make effective adjustments.

8.23 As mentioned at paragraph 2.15, it is also advisable for qualifications bodies to set up systems for working with educational institutions and other bodies with whom they work to ensure that qualifications bodies obtain the information they need to make adjustments for disabled students who are taking examinations or other assessments in order to obtain a professional or trade qualification. For example, such a system could comprise the following steps:

- Well in advance of the examination or assessment in question, the qualifications body asks educational institutions to seek information from candidates about whether they have disabilities which make reasonable adjustments necessary.
- Each educational institution requests this information from its students, together with their individual consent to inform the qualifications body. The information is then passed on to the qualifications body.
- Students may be given a contact at the qualifications body with whom they can discuss their requirements further.
- The qualifications body uses the information it obtains to decide what adjustments should be made. It then notifies educational institutions of its decision, and discusses with them how such adjustments will be implemented.

> A body which confers qualifications in accountancy asks a college for information about students who may require reasonable adjustments. The college seeks this information from its students. A student with cerebral palsy has difficulty writing, and therefore asks to be allowed to take the examinations using a computer. The colleges relays this request to the qualifications body, which gives its consent and liaises with the college to ensure that the college can provide him with appropriate facilities to take the examinations.

8.24 Educational institutions or other bodies often provide education, training or other services (such as facilities for taking examinations or assessments) which lead to the attainment of a professional or trade qualification, even though they do not themselves confer the qualification. Such institutions or bodies are likely to have separate duties under Part 3 or Part 4 in respect of the education, training or other services they provide. To ensure full compliance with the Act, it is advisable for such institutions or bodies to inform qualifications bodies at an early stage about an applicant's disability and its relevant implications – subject, of course, to obtaining the applicant's consent first.

8.25 In practice, the needs of a disabled person who is taking an examination, test or assessment can only be met fully if the educational institution or body and the qualifications body concerned work together to achieve an appropriate outcome.

> A partially sighted man requests a test paper in large print and a desk light. The qualifications body provides a large print test paper and liaises with the college where the man is sitting the test to ensure that it provides a desk light.

> A partially sighted man on another course has always had course information provided to him in large print by the college as a reasonable adjustment (under Chapter or 2 of Part 4 of the Act), and has used a desk light when taking internal tests as part of his course. With the man's consent, the college informs the qualifications body that the man needs an examination paper in large print for examinations set by the qualifications body. The college provides him with a desk light for such examinations.

8.26 The Act does not prevent a disabled person keeping a disability confidential from a qualifications body (although other legislation may require its disclosure – in relation to an application for a driving licence, for example). But this is likely to mean that unless the qualifications body could reasonably be expected to know about the person's disability anyway, it will not be under a duty to make a reasonable adjustment. If a disabled person expects a qualifications body to make a reasonable adjustment, he will need to provide it with sufficient information to carry out that adjustment.

WHAT DOES THE ACT SAY ABOUT COMPETENCE STANDARDS?

What is a competence standard?

8.27 **[s 14A(5)]** The Act says that a competence standard is an academic, medical, or other standard applied by or on behalf of a qualifications body for the purpose of determining whether or not a person has a particular level of competence or ability. So, for example, having a certain standard of eyesight is a competence standard required for a pilot's qualification. Having a certain level of knowledge of the UK taxation system is a competence standard for an accountancy qualification.

8.28 Qualifications bodies are likely to impose various requirements and conditions upon the conferment of a professional or trade qualification. However, any such requirement or condition only amounts to a competence standard if its purpose is to demonstrate a particular level of competence or ability. A requirement that a person has a particular level of knowledge of a subject, for example, or has the strength or ability to carry out a particular task or activity within a set period of time, would probably be a competence standard.

8.29 On the other hand, a condition that a person has, for example, a certain length of experience of doing something will not be a competence standard if it does not determine a particular level of competence or ability. The following are examples of requirements which are therefore unlikely to amount to competence standards:

- a requirement that a candidate must have at least ten years continuous experience (a person who has two periods of experience which total ten years may have equivalent ability and experience)
- a requirement that a candidate must complete twelve qualifying sessions (for qualification as a barrister)
- a requirement that a candidate must be currently professionally employed in a particular field.

8.30 Generally, there is a difference between a competence standard and the process by which attainment of the standard is determined. For example, the conferment of many qualifications is dependent upon passing an academic examination. Having the requisite level of knowledge to pass the examination is a competence standard. However, the examination itself (as opposed to performance in it) may not involve a competence standard – because the mechanical process of sitting the examination is unlikely to be relevant to the determination of a relevant competence or ability.

8.31 Sometimes, of course, the process of assessing whether a competence standard has been achieved is inextricably linked to the standard itself. The conferment of some qualifications is conditional upon having a practical skill or ability which must be demonstrated by completing a practical test. The ability to take the test may itself amount to a competence standard.

> An oral examination for a person training to be a Russian interpreter cannot be done in an alternative way, eg as a written examination, because the examination is to ascertain whether someone can speak Russian.

> A driving test for a heavy goods vehicle licence cannot be done solely as a written test because the purpose of the test is to ascertain whether someone can actually drive a heavy goods vehicle.

> A practical test in tree surgery cannot be taken on the ground because the test is to ascertain whether someone can actually cut the branches of trees, including the high branches.

What is the significance of this distinction?

8.32 Special rules apply in relation to the application of a competence standard to a disabled person by or on behalf of a qualifications body. The effect of the Act is that:

- there is no duty to make reasonable adjustments in respect of the application of a competence standard, and
- in the limited circumstances in which less favourable treatment of a disabled person in the application of such a standard may be justified, justification is assessed by reference to a special statutory test (see paragraph 8.36).

8.33 It follows that it is very important to ascertain whether a particular provision, criterion or practice of a qualifications body is a competence standard and, if so, whether the matter at issue concerns the application of that standard to the disabled person concerned. Although there is no duty to make reasonable adjustments in respect of the application of a competence standard, such a duty is likely to apply in respect of the process by which competence is assessed.

> A woman taking a written test for a qualification in office administration asks the relevant qualifications body for extra time for the test because she has dyslexia. This is likely to be a reasonable adjustment for the qualifications body to make. She also asks if she can leave out the questions asking her to write a business letter and to précis a document, because she feels these questions would substantially disadvantage her because of her dyslexia. The qualifications body would not have to make this adjustment because these questions are there to determine her competence at writing and précising, so are part of the competence standard being tested.

8.34 As noted in paragraphs 8.23 and 8.24, it is advisable for qualifications bodies and, where relevant, educational institutions to ensure that they have adequate information to assess their responsibilities to disabled people. Even though a qualifications body has no duty to alter a competence standard, it needs to obtain enough information about a person's disability to decide whether a reasonable adjustment should be made to some other aspect of the process by which it confers the qualification in question. A qualifications body must ascertain whether a person's disability impacts upon a competence standard in the first place. However, as noted at paragraph 8.31, there may be an overlap between a competence standard and any process by which an individual is assessed against that standard.

When can less favourable treatment be justified in relation to competence standards?

8.35 **[s 3A(4) applied by s 14A(4)]** Less favourable treatment of a disabled person can never be justified if it amounts to direct discrimination under Part 2 (see paragraph 8.10) – as where the treatment is based on generalised, or stereotypical, assumptions about the disability or its effects. This principle applies to the way that a disabled person is treated in the application of a competence standard in the same way that it applies to treatment of him in other respects.

8.36 [s 14A(3)] To the extent that it does not amount to direct discrimination, the Act says that, where the application of a competence standard to a disabled person amounts to less favourable treatment of him for a reason which relates to his disability, that treatment is justified if, but only if, the qualifications body can show that:

- the standard is (or would be) applied equally to people who do not have his particular disability, and
- its application is a proportionate means of achieving a legitimate aim.

A qualifications body refuses to grant a qualification to a man who fails a fitness test. This does not amount to direct discrimination because anyone, disabled or non-disabled, failing the fitness test would be treated in the same way. But it is less favourable treatment for a reason related to the man's disability. The treatment could be justified if the fitness test was applied equally to all candidates and the fitness test was a proportionate way of showing that the person was fit enough to carry out the essential requirements of the job to which the qualification relates.

In the above situation the qualifications body had not reviewed the fitness standards to see if they were proportionate to the requirements of the job. If it had done so, it would have found that the fitness standard demanded was much higher than many people actually working in that job could now achieve (even though these people achieved that standard at the time of qualification). The qualifications body would therefore be unlikely to be able to justify this competence standard.

8.37 The effect of these provisions is that, in the limited circumstances in which justification may be possible, less favourable treatment which is disability-related and which arises from the application of a competence standard is capable of justification on an objective basis. Justification does not depend on an individual assessment of the disabled person's circumstances, but depends instead on an assessment of the purpose and effect of the competence standard itself.

8.38 These special rules about justification are only relevant to the actual application of a competence standard. If a qualifications body applies a competence standard incorrectly, then it is not, in fact, applying the standard and these rules do not operate. Instead, the more usual test of justification operates (assuming, of course, that the incorrect application of the standard is not directly discriminatory, but that it is disability related less favourable treatment).

8.39 The application of a competence standard concerning a medical requirement may, depending on the circumstances, result in less favourable treatment of a disabled person. Medical requirements which are based on stereotypical assumptions about the health and safety implications of disability generally, or about particular types of disability, are likely to be directly discriminatory – less favourable treatment of a disabled person resulting from the application of such a requirement will therefore be unlawful.

A man studying to become a social care professional has epilepsy. His condition is controlled by medication and he has not had a seizure for two years. Nevertheless the relevant qualifications body prevents him from carrying on with his training for the qualification on health and safety grounds. It does this without first undertaking a risk assessment. This is likely to be unlawful.

8.40 Nevertheless, genuine concerns about health and safety may be relevant to the justification of a competence standard concerning a medical requirement. Assuming that it does not amount to direct discrimination, the application of such a requirement to a disabled person will be justified only if the body can show that the requirement applies (or would apply) equally to people who do not have that disability. It would also be necessary to show that the requirement serves a valid purpose and is a legitimate means of achieving that purpose. The qualifications body would have to provide cogent evidence that the standard is genuinely fundamental to the needs of the profession or trade in order to ensure the competence of practitioners.

How can qualifications bodies avoid discrimination in relation to competence standards?

8.41 If unlawful discrimination is to be avoided when the application of a competence standard results in less favourable treatment of a disabled person, the qualifications body concerned will have to show two things. First, it will have to show that the application of the standard does not amount to direct discrimination. Second, it will be necessary to show that the standard can be objectively justified. This is more likely to be possible where a qualifications body has considered the nature and effects of its competence standards in advance of an issue arising in practice. It would be advisable for qualifications bodies to review and evaluate competence standards. This process might involve:

- identifying the specific purpose of each competence standard which is applied, and examining the manner in which the standard achieves that purpose
- considering the impact which each competence standard may have on disabled people and, in the case of a standard which may have an adverse impact, asking whether the application of the standard is absolutely necessary
- reviewing the purpose and effect of each competence standard in the light of changing circumstances – such as developments in technology examining whether the purpose for which any competence standard is applied could be achieved in a way which does not have an adverse impact on disabled people, and
- documenting the manner in which these issues have been addressed, the conclusions which have been arrived at, and the reasons for those conclusions.

(Section 9 Discrimination by general qualifications bodies: outside the scope of this work.)

10. MAKING REASONABLE ADJUSTMENTS TO PREMISES – LEGAL CONSIDERATIONS

INTRODUCTION

[4.121]

10.1 In Chapter 5 it was explained that one of the situations in which there is a duty to make reasonable adjustments arises where a physical feature of premises occupied by a trade organisation, qualifications body or general qualifications body places a disabled person at a substantial disadvantage compared with people who are not disabled. In such circumstances the organisation or body must consider whether any reasonable steps can be taken to overcome that disadvantage. Making adjustments to premises may be a reasonable step to have to take. This chapter addresses the issues of how leases, building regulations and other statutory requirements affect the duty to make reasonable adjustments to premises.

10.2 The issues dealt with in this chapter largely concern the need to obtain consent to the making of reasonable adjustments where a trade organisation, qualifications body or general qualifications body occupies premises under a lease or other binding obligation. However, such organisations and bodies should remember that even where consent is not given for altering a physical feature, they still have a duty to consider taking other steps to overcome the disadvantage which the feature causes in respect of the disabled person.

WHAT ABOUT THE NEED TO OBTAIN STATUTORY CONSENT FOR SOME BUILDING CHANGES?

10.3 **[s 59]** A trade organisation, qualifications body or general qualifications body might have to obtain statutory consent before making adjustments involving changes to premises. Such consents include planning permission, building regulations approval or a building warrant in Scotland, listed building consent, scheduled monument consent and fire regulations approval. The Act does not override the need to obtain such consents.

10.4 Organisations and bodies should plan for and anticipate the need to obtain consent to make a particular adjustment. It might take time to obtain such consent, but it could be reasonable to make an interim or other adjustment – one that does not require consent – in the meantime.

> A trade organisation occupies premises with steps up to the main entrance. These premises have facilities for members, such as a conference room and a library. The trade organisation is not aware of any members who have a mobility impairment and does not do anything to make its premises more accessible. When a new member notifies the organisation that she walks with crutches and wishes to use the premises, the organisation tries to obtain statutory consent to install a ramp with a handrail. It takes several months to obtain such permission. Because it cannot make this adjustment in time, it decides to make a temporary adjustment – making an existing side entrance, without steps, available for the disabled member to use. If the trade organisation had anticipated that this need was very likely to arise (through carrying out an access audit, for example), it would have been able to make this adjustment sooner.

10.5 Where consent has been refused, there is likely to be a means of appeal. Whether or not the duty to take such steps as it is reasonable to take includes pursuing an appeal will depend on the circumstances of the case.

BUILDING REGULATIONS AND BUILDING DESIGN

10.6 **[SI 2000/2531]** The design and construction of a new building, or the material alteration of an existing one, must comply with Building Regulations. For buildings in England or Wales, Part M of the Building Regulations (access to and use of buildings) is intended to ensure that reasonable provision is made for people to gain access to and use buildings. A similar provision applies in Scotland under the Technical Standards for compliance with the Building Standards (Scotland) Regulations 990 and, from May 2005, under the Building (Scotland) Regulations 2004 and relevant functional standards and guidance in the associated Technical Handbooks.

10.7 Nevertheless, the fact that the design and construction of a building (or a physical feature of a building) which a trade organisation, qualifications body or general qualifications body occupies meets the requirements of the Building Regulations does not diminish its duty to make reasonable adjustments in respect of the building's physical features. In particular, it should be noted that the partial exemption from the duty to remove or alter physical features which applies to service providers under Part 3 of the Act does not apply to trade organisations, qualifications bodies under Part 2 of the Act or general qualifications bodies under Part 4 of the Act.

10.8 The Building Regulations building standards provide only a baseline standard of accessibility, which is not intended to address the specific needs of individual disabled people. It is therefore good practice for trade organisations, qualifications bodies and general qualifications bodies to carry out an assessment of the access needs of each disabled person with whom it has dealings, and to consider what alterations can be made to the features of its buildings in order to meet those needs. It is also good practice to anticipate the needs of disabled people when planning building or refurbishment works.

10.9 When assessing the access requirements of disabled people, it is likely to be helpful to refer to British Standard 8300:2001, **Design of buildings and their approaches to meet the needs of disabled people – Code of Practice**. Indeed, it is unlikely to be reasonable for a trade organisation, qualifications body or general qualifications body to have to make an adjustment to a physical feature of a building which it occupies if the design and construction of the physical features of the building is in accordance with BS8300. Further information about BS8300 can be found in Appendix B.

10.10 In addition, although less comprehensive than BS8300, guidance accompanying the Building Regulations (known as 'Approved Document M') sets out a number of 'provisions' as suggested ways in which the requirements of the Regulations might be met. It is unlikely to be reasonable for a trade organisation, qualifications body or general qualifications body to have to make an adjustment to a physical feature of a building which it occupies if that feature accords with the relevant provisions of the most up to date version of Approved Document M.

WHAT IF A BINDING OBLIGATION OTHER THAN A LEASE PREVENTS A BUILDING BEING ALTERED?

10.11 [s 18B(3) and Sch 4, Part 4, para 12] A trade organisation or qualifications body may be bound by the terms of an agreement or other legally binding obligation (for example, a mortgage, charge or restrictive covenant or, in Scotland, a real burden) under which it cannot alter the premises without someone else's consent. In these circumstances, the Part 2 of the Act provides that it is always reasonable for the organisation or body to have to request that consent, but that it is never reasonable for it to have to make an alteration before having obtained that consent. Under Chapter 2A of Part 4 of the Act, it may also be necessary for general qualifications bodies to obtain consent pursuant to a binding obligation and the Act does not override the need to obtain such consent.

WHAT HAPPENS IF A LEASE SAYS THAT CERTAIN CHANGES TO PREMISES CANNOT BE MADE?

10.12 [s 18A(2) and s 31ADB(2)] Special provisions apply where a trade organisation, qualifications body or general qualifications body occupies premises under a lease, the terms of which prevent it from making an alteration to the premises. In such circumstances, if the alteration is one which the organisation or body proposes to make in order to comply with a duty of reasonable adjustment, the Act overrides the terms of the lease so as to entitle it to make the alteration with the consent of its landlord ('the lessor'). In such a case the organisation or body must first write to the lessor asking for consent to make the alteration. The lessor cannot unreasonably withhold consent but may attach reasonable conditions to the consent.

10.13 [Sch 4, Part I, para 1 and Sch 4, Part 4, para 15] If a trade organisation, qualifications body or general qualifications body fails to make a written application to the lessor for consent to the alteration, it will not be able to rely upon the fact that the lease has a term preventing it from making alterations to the premises to defend its failure to make an alteration. In these circumstances, anything in the lease which prevents that alteration being made must be ignored in deciding whether it was reasonable for the organisation or body to have made the alteration.

WHAT HAPPENS IF THE LESSOR HAS A 'SUPERIOR' LESSOR?

10.14 The lessor may itself hold a lease the terms of which prevent it from consenting to the alteration without the consent of its landlord ('the superior lessor'). In such circumstances the effect of the superior lease is modified so as to require the lessee of that lease to apply in writing to its lessor (the 'superior lessor' in this context) if it wishes to consent to the alteration. As with the lessor of the trade organisation, qualifications body or general qualifications body, the superior lessor must not withhold such consent unreasonably but may attach reasonable conditions to the consent.

10.15 Where a superior lessor receives an application from its lessee, the provisions described in paragraphs 10.16 to 10.30 apply as if its lessee were the trade organisation, qualifications body or general qualifications body.

HOW DO ARRANGEMENTS FOR GAINING CONSENT WORK?

10.16 [SI 2004/153 and SI 2007/2405] Regulations made under the Act concerning trade organisations, qualifications bodies and general qualifications bodies govern the procedure for obtaining consent. These Regulations (the Disability Discrimination (Employment Field) (Leasehold Premises) Regulations 2004) and Disability Discrimination Act 1995 (Amendment etc) (General Qualifications Bodies) (Alternation of Premises and Enforcement) Regulations 2007 are commonly referred to in this chapter as the 'Leasehold Premises Regulations'. For the sake of clarity, references below to particular provisions in these regulations refer to the 2004 regulations and then the 2007 regulations.

10.17 **[Reg 4 and Reg 9]** In relation to trade organisations and qualifications bodies, the Leasehold Premises Regulations say that, once the application has been made, the lessor has 21 days, beginning with the day on which it receives the application, to reply in writing to the trade organisation, qualifications body (or the person who made the application on its behalf). If it fails to do so it is taken to have unreasonably withheld its consent to the alteration. However, where it is reasonable to do so, the lessor is permitted to take more than 21 days to reply to the request. Under the different duties applicable to general qualifications bodies, a lessor has 42 days to reply to an application for the lessor's consent made by a general qualifications body, beginning with the day on which it receives the application. However, the lessor has 21 days to make a written request for any plans and specifications that it is reasonable for him to require and which were not included within the general qualifications body's application.

10.18 If the lessor replies to a trade organisation or qualifications body's request by consenting to the application subject to obtaining the consent of another person (required under a superior lease or because of a binding obligation), but fails to seek the consent of the other person within 21 days of receiving the application (or such longer period as may be reasonable), it will also be taken to have withheld its consent. For general qualifications bodies, the relevant period for the lessor to seek the consent of another person is 42 days, and not 21 days, and the distinct duties applying to general qualifications bodies make no allowance for extending the period either for such longer period as may be reasonable, or at all.

10.19 The Leasehold Premises Regulations provide that a lessor will be treated as not having sought the consent of another person unless the lessor has applied in writing to the other person indicating that the occupier has asked for consent for an alteration in order to comply with a duty to make reasonable adjustments, and that the lessor has given its consent conditionally upon obtaining the other person's consent.

10.20 **[Reg 6 and Reg 11]** If the lessor replies refusing consent to the alteration, the trade organisation, qualifications body or general qualifications body must inform the disabled person of this, but has no further obligation to make the alteration (but see paragraph 10.2).

WHEN IS IT UNREASONABLE FOR A LESSOR TO WITHHOLD CONSENT?

10.21 Whether withholding consent will be reasonable or not will depend on the specific circumstances. For example, if a particular adjustment is likely to result in a substantial permanent reduction in the value of the lessor's interest in the premises, the lessor is likely to be acting reasonably in withholding consent. The lessor is also likely to be acting reasonably if it withholds consent because an adjustment would cause significant disruption or inconvenience to other tenants (for example, where the premises consist of multiple adjoining units).

> A particular adjustment helps make a public building more accessible generally and is therefore likely to benefit the landlord. It is likely to be unreasonable for consent to be withheld in these circumstances.

> A particular adjustment is likely to result in a substantial permanent reduction in the value of the landlord's interest in the premises. The landlord is likely to be acting reasonably in withholding consent.

> A particular adjustment would cause significant disruption or major inconvenience to other tenants (for example, where the premises consist of multiple adjoining units). The landlord is likely to be acting reasonably in withholding consent.

10.22 A trivial or arbitrary reason would almost certainly be unreasonable. Many reasonable adjustments to premises will not harm the lessor's interests and so it would generally be unreasonable to withhold consent for them.

10.23 **[Reg 5 and Reg 10]** The Leasehold Premises Regulations say that, provided the consent has been sought in the way required by the lease, it is unreasonable for a lessor to withhold consent in circumstances where the lease says that consent will be given to alterations of the kind for which consent has been sought.

10.24 **[Reg 6]** The Leasehold Premises Regulations concerning trade organisations and qualifications bodies only specifically provide that withholding consent will be reasonable where:

- there is a binding obligation requiring the consent of any person to the alteration
- the lessor has taken steps to seek consent, and
- consent has not been given or has been given subject to a condition making it reasonable for the lessor to withhold its consent.

It will also be reasonable for a lessor to withhold consent where it is bound by an agreement under which it would have to make a payment in order to give the consent, but which prevents it from recovering the cost from the trade organisation, qualifications body. **[Reg 11]** This particular requirement does not apply to an application for the lessor's consent made by a general qualifications body. In this specific context, a lessor may reasonably withhold consent where it does not know, and could not reasonably know, that the alteration is one that the general qualifications body proposes to make in order to comply with the duty to make reasonable adjustments.

WHAT CONDITIONS WOULD IT BE REASONABLE FOR A LESSOR TO MAKE WHEN GIVING CONSENT?

10.25 The Leasehold Premises Regulations set out some conditions which it is reasonable for a lessor to make. Depending on the circumstances of the case there may be other conditions which it would also be reasonable for a lessor to require a trade organisation, qualifications body or general qualifications body to make. Where a lessor imposes other conditions, their reasonableness may be challenged in the course of subsequent employment tribunal proceedings (where trade organisations and qualifications bodies are concerned) or county/sheriff court proceedings (where general qualifications bodies are concerned) – see paragraph 10.27.

10.26 **[Reg 7 and Reg 12]** The conditions set out in the Leasehold Premises Regulations as ones which a lessor may reasonably require a trade organisation, qualifications body or general qualifications body to meet are that it:

- obtains any necessary planning permission and other statutory consents
- submits plans and specifications for the lessor's approval (provided that such approval will not be unreasonably withheld) and thereafter carries out the work in accordance with them
- allows the lessor a reasonable opportunity to inspect the work after it is completed, or
- reimburses the lessor's reasonable costs incurred in connection with the giving of consent.

In the case of general qualifications bodies only, there is a further condition that the consent of another person required under a superior lease or binding obligation must be obtained. In addition, in a case where it would be reasonable for the lessor to withhold consent, the lessor may give such consent subject to a condition that the premises are reinstated to their original condition at the end of the lease. This condition does not apply to general qualifications bodies.

WHAT HAPPENS IF THE LESSOR REFUSES CONSENT OR ATTACHES CONDITIONS TO CONSENT?

10.27 **[Sch 4, Part I, para 2 and Sch 4, Part 4, para 17]** Where a disabled person brings legal proceedings against a trade organisation, qualifications body or general qualifications body under Part 2 or Part 4 – and those proceedings involve a failure to make an alteration to premises – he may ask the employment tribunal or County/Sheriff Court hearing the case to bring in the lessor as an additional party to the proceedings. The organisation or body may also make such a request. The tribunal or court will grant that request if it is made before the hearing of the case begins – save where the court can refuse the request if the court considers that another lessor should be brought into the proceedings. It may refuse the request if it is made after the hearing of the claim begins. The request will not be granted if it is made after the tribunal or court has determined the claim.

Reference to court

10.28 **[Sch 4, Part 4, para 16]** If a general qualifications body has written to the lessor for consent to make an alteration and the lessor has refused consent or has attached conditions to his consent, the general qualifications body or a disabled person who has an interest in the proposed alteration may refer the matter to a County Court or, in Scotland, the Sheriff Court. The court will decide whether the lessor's refusal or any of the conditions are unreasonable. If it decides that they are, it may make an appropriate declaration or authorise the general qualifications body to make the alteration under a court order (which may impose conditions on the general qualifications body). Where the general qualifications body occupies premises under a sub-lease or sub-tenancy, these provisions are modified to apply also to the general qualifications body's landlord.

10.29 Where the lessor has been made a party to the proceedings, the employment tribunal or County/Sheriff Court may determine whether the lessor has unreasonably refused consent to the alteration or has consented subject to unreasonable conditions. In either case, the tribunal or court can:

- make an appropriate declaration
- make an order authorising the organisation or body to make a specified alteration
- order the lessor to pay compensation to the disabled person.

10.30 The tribunal or court may require the organisation or body to comply with any conditions specified in the order. If the tribunal or court orders the lessor to pay compensation, it cannot also order the organisation or body to do so.

COMPARISON WITH THE PROCEDURE FOR OBTAINING CONSENT UNDER PART 3

10.31 There are similar provisions which govern the procedure by which a service provider may obtain consent to an alteration which it proposes to make in order to comply with a duty of reasonable adjustment under Part 3 of the Act. These procedures are broadly similar to procedures under Part 4 of the Act that apply to general qualifications bodies. However, it should be noted that the procedures for obtaining consent under Parts 2 and 3 respectively differ in certain ways. In particular:

- the periods within which the lessor must respond to an application for consent are not the same – under Part 3 (and in relation to Part 4 duties concerning general qualifications bodies) the relevant period is 42 days beginning with the day on which the application is received

- Under Part 3 (and in relation to Part 4 duties concerning general qualifications bodies) the lessor may require plans and specifications to be submitted **before** it decides whether to give consent.
- Under Part 3 (and in relation to Part 4 duties concerning general qualifications bodies) it is possible to make a freestanding reference to the court if the lessor has either refused consent or attached conditions to it. Under Part 2, the question of consent to alterations can only be considered by an employment tribunal in the course of a complaint of discrimination.

11. OTHER RELEVANT PROVISIONS

[4.122]

11.1 Additional provisions of the Act (and provisions of other legislation) are relevant to understanding the protection from discrimination afforded to disabled people in relation to trade organisations, qualifications bodies and general qualifications bodies. This chapter describes those provisions, and focuses in particular on the way in which disputes under the Act should be resolved. It should be noted at the outset that the duties imposed on trade organisations and qualifications bodies are contained in Part 2 of the Act (and are enforceable through employment tribunals), whereas the duties imposed on general qualifications bodies are contained in Chapter 2A of Part 4 of the Act (and are enforceable through the county courts in England and Wales and the sheriff courts in Scotland).

RESOLVING DISPUTES UNDER PART 2 OF THE ACT

11.2 Chapter 2 explained that, broadly speaking, the Act does not require the internal resolution of disputes by trade organisations and qualifications bodies, but that it is desirable for grievance procedures to be used where possible. Where grievance or disciplinary procedures exist, they must not discriminate against disabled people. Trade organisations and qualifications bodies may have to make reasonable adjustments to enable disabled people to use such procedures effectively, or to ensure that they do not place disabled people at a substantial disadvantage compared with others.

11.3 **[s 17A(1) and s 55 and Sch 3, para 3]** The Act says that a person who believes that someone has unlawfully discriminated against him (which includes victimising him or failing to make a reasonable adjustment) or has subjected him to harassment, may make an application to an employment tribunal. Such an application must normally be made within three months of the date when the incident complained about occurred.

11.4 **[s 17A(1A)]** This is subject to one proviso. In cases of alleged discrimination or harassment by a qualifications body, the Act says that no application may be made to an employment tribunal if a statutory appeal is available in respect of the matter in question.

11.5 Before making an application to an employment tribunal (or within 28 days of lodging it), a disabled person can request information relevant to his claim from the person against whom the claim is made. This is known as the 'questionnaire procedure'. There is a standard form of questionnaire (DL56) and accompanying booklet which explains how the procedure works (see Appendix B for details).

11.6 When an application to an employment tribunal has been made, a conciliation officer from the Advisory, Conciliation and Arbitration Service (ACAS) will try to promote settlement of the dispute without a tribunal hearing. However, if a hearing becomes necessary – and if the application is upheld – the tribunal may:

- **[s 7A(2)]** declare the rights of the disabled person (the applicant), and the other person (the respondent) in relation to the application
- order the respondent to pay the applicant compensation, and
- recommend that, within a specified time, the respondent takes reasonable action to prevent or reduce the adverse effect in question.

11.7 **[s 17A(4)]** The Act allows compensation for injury to feelings to be awarded whether or not other compensation is awarded.

11.8 **[s 17A(5)]** The Act also says that if a respondent fails, without reasonable justification, to comply with an employment tribunal's recommendation, the tribunal may:

- increase the amount of compensation to be paid, or
- order the respondent to pay compensation if it did not make such an order earlier.

11.9 Sources of information about how to make an application to an employment tribunal are listed in Appendix B.

OTHER PROVISIONS FOR PART 2 OF THE ACT

Anti-avoidance provisions

11.10 **[Sch 3A, Part 1]** Generally speaking, a disabled person cannot waive his rights (or the duties of a trade organisation or qualifications body) under the Act. The Act says that any term of a contract is 'void' (ie not valid) where:

- making the contract is unlawful under Part 2 because of the inclusion of the term
- the term is included in furtherance of an act which is
- itself unlawful under Part 2, or
- the term provides for the doing of an act which is unlawful under Part 2.

11.11 Trade organisations and qualifications bodies should not include in an agreement any provision intended to avoid obligations under the Act, or to prevent someone from fulfilling obligations. An agreement should not, therefore, be used to try to justify less favourable treatment or deem an adjustment unreasonable. Even parts of agreements which unintentionally have such an effect are unenforceable if they would restrict the working of Part 2. However, as explained in Chapter 10, special arrangements cover leases and other agreements which might restrict the making of adjustments to premises.

Compromise agreements

11.12 **[Sch 3A, Part 1]** The effect of the Act's provisions is also to make a contract term unenforceable if it would prevent anyone from making an application to an employment tribunal under Part 2, or a claim to a county/sheriff Court under Chapter 2A of Part 4, or would force them to discontinue such an application or claim (see paragraphs 11.3 and 11.24). There is a limited exception to this principle relating to settlement agreements concerning Part 2 claims which have either been brokered by an ACAS conciliation officer, or which are made in circumstances where the following conditions are satisfied:

- the disabled person has received advice from a relevant independent adviser about the terms and effects of the agreement, particularly its effect on his ability to apply to a tribunal
- the adviser has a contract of insurance or an indemnity provided for members of a profession or professional body, and
- the agreement is in writing, relates to the application, identifies the adviser and says that these conditions are satisfied.

[Sch 3A, Part 1] In this regard the Act defines the circumstances in which a person is a 'relevant independent adviser' for this purpose.

Variation of contracts

11.13 **[Sch 3A, para 3]** A disabled person interested in a contract which contains a term of the kind mentioned in paragraph 11.10 may apply to a county court or, in Scotland, a sheriff court, for an order removing or modifying that term.

Collective agreements and rules of undertakings

11.14 **[Sch 3A, Part 2]** There are also anti-avoidance provisions in the Act relating to the terms of collective agreements, and to rules made by trade organisations or qualifications bodies which apply to all or any of an organisation's members or prospective members, or (as the case may be), to all or any of the people on whom a body has conferred qualifications, or who are seeking qualifications from it.

11.15 The Act says that any such term or rule is void where:

- making the collective agreement is unlawful under Part 2 because of the inclusion of the term
- the term or rule is included in furtherance of an act which is itself unlawful under Part 2, or
- the term or rule provides for the doing of an act which is unlawful under Part 2.

11.16 It does not matter whether the collective agreement was entered into, or the rule was made, before or after these provisions became law – the term or rule in question can still be challenged under the Act. In addition, where these provisions apply, certain disabled people may ask an employment tribunal to make a declaration that a discriminatory term or rule is void if they believe that it may affect them in the future. The Act specifies which disabled people may make such an application.

RESOLVING DISPUTES UNDER CHAPTER 2A OF PART 4 OF THE ACT

Introduction

11.17 This part of the chapter explains what happens if someone makes a complaint against a general qualifications body, and what routes of redress exist. It also explains what action may be taken to put right any discrimination that is found to have taken place.

Resolving disputes

11.18 It is good practice (and a legal requirement under the Civil Procedure Rules in England and Wales) to attempt to resolve disputes without resorting to legal proceedings. Complainants may, therefore, want to raise complaints directly with general qualifications bodies before resorting to legal proceedings. Many general qualifications bodies will have complaints procedures which aid the speedy resolution of disputes.

11.19 General qualifications bodies must make reasonable adjustments to any internal complaints procedures to prevent a disabled person from being placed at a substantial disadvantage in comparison with people who are not disabled. Failure to do so will itself amount to a breach of the Act.

11.20 So, for example, it is likely to be a reasonable adjustment for a general qualifications body to allow a disabled person who has communication difficulties some assistance to make a written statement of a complaint he wishes to make (such as by providing him with assistance via a neutral party). Depending on the circumstances, it may be reasonable to allow a disabled person with learning disabilities to be accompanied to a meeting by a family member or friend, or to send written communications to a blind or visually impaired person in a format which is accessible to him.

11.21 Although, as stated above, it is good practice to try to resolve disputes internally wherever possible, there may be exceptional occasions where this will not be practical or appropriate.

CONCILIATION

Equality Act 2006

11.22 The Equality and Human Rights Commission is empowered by the Act to set up an independent conciliation service for disputes arising under Part 4 of the Act to promote the settlement of disputes without recourse to the courts, and has done so. Conciliation is made available locally around the country, and disputes may be referred to conciliation by the Equality and Human Rights Commission if both the complainant and the general qualifications body agree to this. The Equality and Human Rights Commission has no power to impose a settlement on either party.

11.23 Agreeing to participate in the conciliation process does not prevent a complainant from pursuing a case through the courts. The time limit for bringing an action in court is extended by three months if the conciliation process has been started within six months of a discriminatory act. No information disclosed to a conciliator during the conciliation process may be used in any subsequent court case without the permission of the person who disclosed it.

MAKING A CLAIM UNDER CHAPTER 2A OF PART 4 OF THE ACT

11.24 **[s 31ADA and SI 2007/2405]** The Act says that a person who believes that a general qualifications body has discriminated against him or has subjected him to harassment, may bring civil proceedings. Those proceedings take place in a County Court (in England and Wales) or the Sheriff Court (in Scotland). Similar proceedings may also be brought against a person who has aided someone else to commit an unlawful act. A claim must be lodged within six months of the alleged discrimination. Where there has been a continuing process of discrimination which takes place over a period of time, the six months begins at the date of the last discriminatory act. A court has the discretion to allow claims made outside of the six-month time limitation period to proceed, where they decide that it is just and equitable to do so.

11.25 If a complaint cannot be resolved and it is heard and determined by a court, the court may:

- declare the rights of the disabled person (the claimant in England and Wales and the pursuer in Scotland) and the other person (the defendant in England and Wales or the defender in Scotland) in relation to the claim (ie make a declaration of discrimination)
- order the defendant/defender to pay the claimant/pursuer compensation, including compensation for injury to feelings; and
- impose an injunction (in England and Wales) or specific implement or interdict (in Scotland) requiring a general qualifications body to take positive action or to prevent the general qualifications body from repeating any discriminatory act in the future.

Sources of information about how to make a claim to the courts are listed in Appendix B.

ENFORCEMENT OF CERTAIN PROVISIONS UNDER PART 2 OF THE ACT

11.26 In addition, the Equality and Human Rights Commission has a direct involvement in the enforcement of the provisions of Part 2 relating to:

- instructing or pressurising other people to act unlawfully (see paragraph 3.24), and
- discriminatory advertisements (see paragraphs 3.25 and 3.28).

11.27 **[s 25(2) Equality Act 2006]** Only the Equality and Human Rights Commission may bring proceedings in respect of these matters. Where it does so, the Equality and Human Rights Commission may seek:

- a declaration from an employment tribunal as to whether a contravention has occurred, and
- an injunction from a County Court (or, in Scotland, an order from a Sheriff Court) restraining further contraventions.

11.28 The Equality and Human Rights Commission may only apply for an injunction or order if it has first obtained a declaration from an employment tribunal that an unlawful act has occurred, and then only if it appears to the Equality and Human Rights Commission that a further unlawful act is likely to occur unless the person concerned is restrained.

(Appendix A (The meaning of disability) outside the scope of this work. Appendix B (Further information) omitted; see Useful addresses at **[5.120]***.)*

EQUALITY AND HUMAN RIGHTS COMMISSION: CODE OF PRACTICE ON EQUAL PAY (2011)

[4.123]

NOTES

This Code of Practice was prepared by the Equality and Human Rights Commission to accompany the Equality Act 2010. It replaces the Equal Opportunities Commission's *Code of Practice on Equal Pay*, issued in 2003.

The new Code was brought into effect on 6 April 2011 by the Equality Act 2010 Codes of Practice (Services, Public Functions and Associations, Employment and Equal Pay) Order 2011, SI 2011/857 and applies in relation to all matters occurring on or after that date. The former Equal Pay Code was revoked with effect immediately before the coming into force of the new Code, by the Former Equality Commissions' Codes of Practice (Employment, Equal Pay and Rights of Access for Disabled Persons) (Revocation) Order 2011, SI 2011/776. The old Code, which is no longer reproduced for reasons of space, continues to have effect in relation to matters occurring before the date of revocation (see SI 2011/776, art 3).

Note that the original Code contains references to sections and Schedules of the Equality Act 2010 (and other legislation) in the margin of the page, next to the paragraph to which they relate. These have been reproduced at the beginning of the paragraph in question in this Handbook (in bold and within square brackets). Note also that where there are more than two section (etc) references separated by a semi-colon, the second reference relates to a second (or subsequent) sentence within the paragraph in question.

See also, the Supplement to the Equal Pay Statutory Code of Practice which is available on the ECHR website at: www.equalityhumanrights.com/en/publication-download/equal-pay-statutory-code-practice. The Supplement does not form part of the statutory Code of Practice. It is intended to assist those using the Code by identifying developments in the law since the Code was approved.

Note also that the Code is reproduced here as per the original; ie, Part 1 begins at paragraph 23 even though the introduction ends with paragraph 24.

See *Harvey* K.

CONTENTS

INTRODUCTION

[4.124]

1. The Equality Act 2010 (the Act) gives women (and men) a right to equal pay for equal work. It replaces previous legislation, including the Equal Pay Act 1970 and the Sex Discrimination Act 1975, and the equality provisions in the Pensions Act 1995.

2. [Part 5 Chapter 3 Equality Act 2006] The provisions explained in this code are those set out in the Act under the heading 'Equality of terms'. They apply to pay and all the other terms of a person's contract of employment, but this code uses the language of 'equal pay' in the interests of both continuity and brevity.

POWERS OF THE COMMISSION

3. [ss 8, 9 & 10 Equality Act 2006] The Equality and Human Rights Commission (the Commission) was set up under the Equality Act 2006 to work towards the elimination of unlawful discrimination and promote equality and human rights.

[ss 16 & 20 Equality Act 2006] The Commission has powers to carry out inquiries, for example into the extent and causes of pay gaps in particular sectors or areas, and to conduct investigations of an employer it suspects of having unlawfully discriminatory pay practices.

The Commission uses its powers of investigation and inquiry strategically to promote equality and human rights, and to tackle entrenched discrimination and pay inequality.

4. [Schedule 2 Equality Act 2006] As part of an investigation or inquiry the Commission can require the employer to provide information about its policies or practices. This could include information about the pay of its employees. The employer cannot refuse to provide such information unless the Commission's request is unnecessary given the purpose of the inquiry or investigation or otherwise unreasonable.

It has previously used these powers to require companies in the financial services sector to provide data on pay gaps between men and women.[1]

5. [ss 31, 32 Equality Act 2006] The Commission has powers to assess and enforce compliance with the gender equality duty, including the duty to have due regard to the need to eliminate unlawful discrimination. It may also issue guidance.

6. [ss 28, 30 Equality Act 2006] The Commission may provide assistance to individuals taking legal action to enforce their right to equal pay, and may institute or intervene in legal proceedings to support an individual or help interpret and clarify the law.

NOTES

[1] Financial Services Inquiry, Sex Discrimination and Gender Pay Gap Report of the Equality and Human Rights Commission, September 2009.

PURPOSE OF THE EQUAL PAY PROVISIONS OF THE ACT

7. The full-time gender pay gap has narrowed since 1975 when equal pay legislation first came into force but there remains a gap of over 16 per cent between women's and men's pay.[2]

8. Historically, women have often been paid less than men for doing the same or equivalent work and this inequality has persisted in some areas.

9. The Act's provisions on equal pay and sex discrimination are intended to ensure that pay and other employment terms are determined without sex discrimination or bias.

10. There are sound business as well as legal reasons for implementing equal pay. Pay systems that are transparent and value the entire workforce send positive messages about an organisation's values and ways of working. Fair and non-discriminatory systems represent good management practice and contribute to the efficient achievement of business objectives by encouraging maximum productivity from all employees.

11. Although this code relates to equal pay between women and men, pay systems may be open to challenge on grounds of race, age or other protected characteristics under the Equality Act 2010.

NOTES

[2] There are several ways of measuring the pay gap. The figure quoted is the mean gender pay gap between full-time employees' earnings in the UK, based on the Office for National Statistics (ONS) Annual Survey of Hours and Earnings

2009. The hourly pay gap is bigger if women working part time are included.

PURPOSE OF THE CODE

12. The purpose of Part 1 of this code is to help employers, advisers, trade union representatives, human resources departments and others who need to understand and apply the law on equal pay, and to assist courts and tribunals when interpreting the law. Employees may also find it useful.

13. It is in everyone's interests to avoid litigation and Part 2 of the code – good equal pay practice – provides guidance on how to prevent or eliminate discriminatory pay practices and ensure that there are no unjustifiable pay inequalities.

14. The Equality and Human Rights Commission recommends that all employers regularly review and monitor their pay practices, although this is not a formal legal requirement. Involving trade unions or other employee representatives can help make pay systems more transparent. This code (Part 2) suggests that equal pay audits may be the most effective means of ensuring that a pay system delivers equal pay.

15. The Commission has extensive practical guidance available on its website to help employers to implement equal pay for women and men in their organisations.

STATUS OF THE CODE

16. This is a statutory code issued by the Commission under s 14 Equality Act 2006. It was approved by the Secretary of State and laid before Parliament on 27 July 2010. The code does not itself impose legal obligations. However it helps explain the legal obligations under the Equality Act 2010. Tribunals and courts considering an equal pay claim are obliged to take into account any part of the code that appears relevant to the proceedings. If employers and others who have obligations under the Act's equal pay provisions follow the guidance in the code, it may help to avoid an adverse decision by a tribunal or court in such proceedings.

17. This code applies to England, Scotland and Wales.

LARGE AND SMALL EMPLOYERS

18. The equal pay for equal work provisions of the Act apply to all employers regardless of size,[3] but the way employers discharge their obligation to avoid sex discrimination in pay may in practice vary according to the size of the organisation. Small employers are less likely to have a human resources team, and may have fewer written policies and more informal practices than large employers. They may also have less complex pay systems and may (though not necessarily) have narrower gender pay gaps.

NOTES

3 Except the reserve power in s 78 to require employers to report on their gender pay gap applies only to employers with 250 or more employees.

PUBLIC SECTOR EMPLOYERS

19. Employers in the public sector, and organisations in the private and voluntary sectors that exercise public functions, are subject to the gender equality duty in respect of those functions. They must have due regard to the need to eliminate discrimination and promote equality, and certain listed authorities have a particular duty in relation to reducing gender pay inequality.[4] This is explained in the Commission's Gender Equality Duty Code of Practice 2006.[5]

NOTES

4 Sex Discrimination Act (SDA) 1975 Public Authorities (Statutory Duties) Order 2006. Reg 2(5): 'A listed authority shall when formulating its objectives for the purposes of paragraph (4) consider the need to have objectives that address the causes of any differences between the pay of men and women that are related to their sex.'

5 The Equality Act 2010 contains a single public sector equality duty which will apply to all characteristics except marriage and civil partnership. However, at the time of issue of this code, this duty has not been commenced. The Gender Equality Duty Code of Practice 2006 has effect until replaced by any new public sector equality duty code.

MEN AND WOMEN

20. The equal pay provisions in the Equality Act 2010 apply to both men and women but to avoid repetition and for clarity, this code is written as though the claimant is a woman comparing her work and pay with those of a man, referred to as the male comparator.

USE OF THE WORDS 'EMPLOYER' AND 'EMPLOYEE'

21. The equal pay provisions of the Act apply to some people who are 'workers' but not employees in the legal sense – such as office-holders, police officers and those serving in the armed forces. In this code, these people are also referred to as 'employees' for convenience. Similarly, people who recruit or 'employ' these people are referred to as 'employers'.

REFERENCES IN THE CODE

22. In this Code, 'the Act' means the Equality Act 2010. References to particular sections (marked as 's.') and schedules of the Act are shown in the margins. Other legislation or regulations are also referenced in the margins.

FURTHER INFORMATION

23. Copies of the Act and regulations made under it can be purchased from The Stationery Office. Separate codes covering other aspects of the Act are also available from The Stationery Office. The text of all the Equality and Human Rights Commission's codes (including this Code) and guidance relating to the codes can also be downloaded free of charge from the Commission's website where Word and PDF versions are also available: www.equalityhumanrights.com

24. (*This paragraph contains contact details for the Equality and Human Right Commission and has been omitted. See the list of useful addresses at* **[5.120]**).

PART 1: EQUAL PAY LAW

OVERVIEW OF EQUAL PAY LAW

[4.125]
23. The principle that women and men are entitled to equal pay for doing equal work is embedded in British law and European Union law. Eliminating discrimination in pay is crucial to achieving gender equality and dignity for women.

24. Courts and tribunals will interpret equal pay law purposively because the legislation is grounded in European Union law, and in particular treaty provisions that have a broad social purpose.

British domestic law must conform to European Union law, which imposes specific obligations in respect of equal pay which can have direct effect. So, in considering equal pay claims under the Equality Act 2010, the British courts must take into account the relevant provisions of the Treaty,[6] relevant Directives and decisions of the Court of Justice of the European Union (formerly the European Court of Justice). If domestic law does not give full effect to these rulings then a woman may be able to rely on European Union law in British Courts.[7]

25. Pay is defined broadly under European Union law and includes pensions. Article 4 of the recast Equal Treatment Directive[8] requires that:

'For the same work or for work to which equal value is attributed, direct and indirect discrimination on grounds of sex with regard to all aspects and conditions of remuneration shall be eliminated.'

26. The equal pay provisions in the Act apply to all contractual terms not just those directly related to remuneration, such as holiday entitlement. This is why the Act calls them 'equality of terms'.

27. Although the law on equal pay may seem complicated its purpose is simple – to ensure that where women and men are doing equal work they should receive the same rewards for it.

NOTES

6 Article 157 of the Treaty of the Functioning of European Union; formerly Article 141 of the EC Treaty.

7 See for example *Levez v TH Jennings (Harlow Pools) Ltd (No 2)* [1999] IRLR 764 EAT.

8 The recast Equal Treatment Directive (No 2006/54/EC) on the implementation of the principle of equal opportunities and equal treatment of men and women in matters of employment and occupation consolidates a number of Directives on gender equality.

SEX EQUALITY CLAUSE

28. A woman doing equal work with a man in the same employment is entitled to equality in pay and other contractual terms, unless the employer can show that there is a material reason for the difference which does not discriminate on the basis of her sex.

29. **[s 66]** Where there is equal work, the Act implies a sex equality clause automatically into the woman's contract of employment, modifying it where necessary to ensure her pay and all other contractual terms are no less favourable than the man's.

30. Where a woman doing equal work shows that she is receiving less pay or other less favourable terms in her contract, or identifies a contract term from which her comparator benefits and she does not (for example he is entitled to a company car and she is not), the employer will have to show why this is. If the employer is unable to show that the difference is due to a material factor which has nothing to do with her sex, then the equality clause takes effect.

31. These equal pay provisions apply to all contractual terms including wages and salaries, non-discretionary bonuses, holiday pay, sick pay, overtime, shift payments, and occupational pension benefits, and to non-monetary terms such as leave entitlements or access to sports and social benefits.

32. **[s 70]** Other sex discrimination provisions apply to non-contractual pay and benefits such as purely discretionary bonuses, promotions, transfers and training and offers of employment or appointments to office.

Example: A female sales manager is entitled under her contract of employment to an annual bonus calculated by reference to a specified number of sales. She discovers that a male sales manager working for the same employer and in the same office receives a higher bonus under his contract for the same number of sales. She would bring her claim under the equality of terms (equal pay) provisions.

However, if the female sales manager is not paid a discretionary Christmas bonus that the male manager is paid, she could bring a claim under the sex discrimination at work provisions rather than an equal pay claim because it is not about a contractual term.

33. **[s 71]** Where an equality clause cannot operate, because for example the woman cannot identify an actual male comparator for an equal pay claim, but she has evidence of direct sex discrimination, she can bring a discrimination claim (see paragraph 61).

WHAT IS EQUAL WORK?

34. **[s 65(1)]** A woman can claim equal pay and other contract terms with a male comparator doing work that is:

- The same or broadly similar, provided that where there are any differences in the work these are not of practical importance (known as '**like work**')
- Different, but which is rated under the same job evaluation scheme as being work of equal value (known as '**work rated as equivalent**')
- Different, but of equal value in terms of factors such as effort, skill and decision-making (known as '**work of equal value**').

The comparator must be in the 'same employment' as the claimant, the meaning of which is explained at paragraph 51.

LIKE WORK

35. **[s 65(2), (3)]** There are two questions to ask when determining 'like work'.

The first question is whether the woman and her male comparator are employed on work that is the same or of a broadly similar nature. This involves a general consideration of the work and the knowledge and skills needed to do it.

If the woman shows that the work is broadly similar, the second question is whether any differences between her work and that done by her comparator are of practical importance having regard to:

- the frequency with which any differences occur in practice, and
- the nature and extent of those differences.

36. It is for the employer to show that there are differences of practical importance in the work actually performed. Differences such as additional duties, level of responsibility, skills, the time at which work is done, qualifications, training and physical effort could be of practical importance.

A difference in workload does not itself preclude a like work comparison, unless the increased workload represents a difference in responsibility or other difference of practical importance.

EXAMPLES OF 'LIKE WORK'

Like work comparisons that have succeeded, in the particular circumstances of the case, include:

- Male and female drivers where the men were more likely to work at weekends.[9]
- A woman cook preparing lunches for directors and a male chef cooking breakfast, lunch and tea for employees.[10]
- Male and female supermarket employees who perform similar tasks, requiring similar skill levels, although the men may lift heavier objects from time to time.
- Male and female laboratory assistants where the man spent some time on the shop floor.[11]

The differences were not found to be of practical importance in relation to their pay.

37. A detailed examination of the nature and extent of the differences and how often they arise in practice is required. A contractual obligation on a man to do additional duties is not sufficient, it is what happens in practice that counts.

Example: A woman working as a primary school administrator claimed equal pay with a male secondary school administrator. The courts found they were not doing like work. Although the work was broadly similar, the latter role carried greater financial and managerial responsibilities and was in a much larger school. The primary school administrator had more routine, term-time tasks while the secondary school administrator's work was year round and more strategic. These differences were considered to be of practical importance so the equal pay for like work claim failed.[12]

However where men but not women were obliged under their contracts to transfer to different duties and work compulsory overtime, this did not amount to a difference of practical importance because the flexibility was not used in practice.[13]

NOTES

[9] *Hatch v Wadham Stringer Commercials (Ashford) Ltd ET* Case No 40171/77.

[10] *Capper Pass Ltd v Allan* [1980] ICR 194 EAT.

[11] *Crook v Dexter Paints Ltd COET* 2089/166.

[12] *Morgan v Middlesborough Borough Council* 2005 EWCA Civ 1432.

[13] *Electrolux Ltd v Hutchinson and others* [1976] IRLR 410 EAT.

WORK RATED AS EQUIVALENT

38. **[s 65(4)]** woman's work is rated as equivalent to a man's if the employer's job evaluation study gives an equal value to their work in terms of the demands made on the workers, by reference to factors such as effort, skill and decision-making.

39. **[s 80(5)]** Job evaluation is a way of systematically assessing the relative value of different jobs. Work is rated as equivalent if the jobs have been assessed as scoring the same number of points and/or as falling within the same job evaluation grade. A small difference may or may not reflect a material difference in the value of the jobs, depending on the nature of the job evaluation exercise.

40. A job evaluation study will rate the demands made by jobs under headings such as skill, effort and decision-making. Because the focus is on the demands of the job rather than the nature of the job overall, jobs which may seem to be of a very different type may be rated as equivalent.

Example: The work of an occupational health nurse might be rated as equivalent to that of a production supervisor when components of the job such as skill, responsibility and effort are assessed by a valid job evaluation scheme.

41. To be valid, a job evaluation study must:

- encompass both the woman's job and her comparator's
- be thorough in its analysis and capable of impartial application[14]
- take into account factors connected only with the requirements of the job rather than the person doing the job (so for example how well someone is doing the job is not relevant), and
- be analytical in assessing the component parts of particular jobs, rather than their overall content on a 'whole job' basis.[15]

42. **[s 131(5) & (6)]** If a job evaluation study has assessed the woman's job as being of lower value than her male comparator's job, then an equal value claim will fail unless the Employment Tribunal has reasonable grounds for suspecting that the evaluation was tainted by discrimination or was in some other way unreliable.

43. **[s 65(5)]** Job evaluation studies must be non-discriminatory and not influenced by gender stereotyping or assumptions about women's and men's work. There has historically been a tendency to undervalue or overlook qualities inherent in work traditionally undertaken by women (for example, caring). A scheme which results in different points being allocated to jobs because it values certain demands of work traditionally undertaken by women differently from demands of work traditionally undertaken by men would be discriminatory. Such a scheme will not prevent a woman claiming that her work would be rated as equivalent to that of a male comparator if the sex-specific values were removed.

Example: A job evaluation study rated the jobs of female classroom teaching assistants and their better paid male physical education instructors as not equivalent. This was because the study had given more points to the physical effort involved in the men's jobs than it had to the intellectual and caring work involved in the jobs predominantly done by women. Because it uses a sex-biased points system, this job evaluation would not prevent the women succeeding in an equal pay claim.

44. **[s 65(4)(b)]** A woman's work can be treated as rated as equivalent if she can show that the work would have been assessed as being of equal value, had the evaluation not been itself discriminatory in setting different values for the demands being made of men and women.

45. A woman may also bring a claim of equal pay where her job is rated higher than that of a comparator under a job evaluation scheme but she is paid less. However, this will not entitle her, if an equality clause applies, to better terms than those her comparator has.[16]

Detailed guidance on designing, implementing and monitoring non-discriminatory job-evaluation schemes is available from the Commission's website. The Advisory, Conciliation and Arbitration Service (ACAS) and trade unions can also advise on job evaluation.

NOTES

14 *Eaton Ltd v Nuttall* 1977 ICR 272 EAT.

15 *Bromley v Quick* [1988] IRLR 249 CA.

16 *Evesham v North Hertfordshire Health Authority and another* [2000] ICR 612 CA.

WORK OF EQUAL VALUE

46. **[s 65(6)(a)]** A woman can claim equal pay with a man if she can show that her work is of equal value with his in terms of the demands made on her.

47. **[s 65(6)(b)]** This means that the jobs done by a woman and her comparator are different but can be regarded as being of equal worth, having regard to the nature of the work performed, the training or skills necessary to do the job, the conditions of work and the decision-making that is part of the role.

48. In some cases the jobs being compared may appear fairly equivalent (such as a female head of personnel and a male head of finance). More commonly, entirely different types of job (such as manual and administrative) can turn out to be of equal value when analysed in terms of the demands made on the employee.

Guidance on how to tell if jobs are of equal value is available from the Commission.

The Employment Tribunal Equal Value Rules of Procedure[17] apply to equal pay claims where a woman is claiming work of equal value.

49. A woman can claim equal pay using any or all of these methods of comparison. For example, a woman working as an office manager in a garage could claim 'like work' with a male office manager working alongside her and 'equal value' with a male garage mechanic.

NOTES

17 Employment Tribunals (Constitution and Rules of Procedure) Regulations 2004, Schedule 6.

WHO IS THE COMPARATOR?

50. [s 79] A woman can claim equal pay for equal work with a man or men in the same employment. It is for her to select the man or men with whom she wishes to be compared.

European Union law also allows a woman to compare herself to a man who is not in the same employment but where the difference in pay is attributable to 'a single source' which has the power to rectify the difference (see paragraph 57).

IN THE SAME EMPLOYMENT

51. [s 79] A woman can compare herself with a man employed:

- by the same or an associated employer at the same establishment or workplace, or
- by the same or an associated employer at a different establishment or workplace, provided that common terms and conditions apply either generally between employees or as between the woman and her comparator.

52. [s 79(9)] An associated employer means a company over which another company has control, or companies over which a third party has control (for example, the employer's parent company).

53. The definition of establishment is not restricted to a single physical location. For example, a woman may claim equal pay with a man doing equal work employed by the same council but working in a different geographic location.[18]

54. Where the woman and her comparator work at different establishments, she has to show that common terms and conditions apply. An example of common terms and conditions is where they are governed by the same collective agreement, but the concept is not limited to this type of arrangement.[19]

55. A woman can also compare herself with a comparator working at a different establishment if she can show that, had he been employed at the same establishment as her, he would have been working under the same common terms and conditions as those he and others in the comparator group are currently working under. The woman does not have to be working to the same common terms as him, and does not have to show that the comparator ever would, in reality, be employed at the same establishment as her.[20]

56. The Equality Act does not specify the geographical scope of the equal pay provisions but in most cases the woman and her male comparator will be based in Great Britain.

NOTES

18 *City of Edinburgh Council v Wilkinson and others*, EAT, 20/5/2010.

19 Per Lord Bridge in *Leverton*, relied on in *Barclays Bank plc v James* [1990] IRLR 90 EAT; *British Coal Corporation v Smith and others* [1996] ICR 515 HL; *South Tyneside Metropolitan Borough Council v Anderson* [2007] IRLR 715 CA.

20 *British Coal Corporation v Smith and others* [1996] ICR 515 HL.

COMPARING ACROSS EMPLOYERS: SINGLE SOURCE

57. Under European Union law differences in pay must be attributable to a single source which is capable of remedying an unlawful inequality. If this is different from the 'same employment' test in British domestic law, European Union law may be applied to produce a remedy. In practice, a woman and her comparator whose pay can be equalised by a single source are likely to be in the same employment.[21]

Example: A woman teacher can compare herself to a man employed by a different education authority where the difference in their pay is due to terms and conditions set by a national scheme and can be remedied by a national negotiating body.

NOTES

21 *Lawrence and others v Regent Office Care Ltd and others* [2003] ICR 1092 ECJ.

CHOICE OF COMPARATOR

58. A woman must select the man or men with whom she wishes to make a comparison, although she does not have to identify them by name at the outset.

The selected comparator could be representative of a group of workers or he could be the only person doing the particular type of work.

59. A woman can select more than one comparator and from her point of view this may be prudent. Multiple comparators may be necessary for a term-by-term comparison of a woman's contract. However, an Employment Tribunal can strike out a claim with a particular comparator, or could in exceptional cases require a claimant who unreasonably cites too many comparators to pay some costs.

60. [s 64(2)] The chosen comparator does not have to be working at the same time as the woman, so he may for example be her predecessor in the job.

61. [s 71] Where a woman has evidence of direct sex discrimination in relation to her contractual pay but there is no actual comparator doing equal work, so that a sex equality clause cannot operate, she can claim sex discrimination based on a hypothetical comparator.

Example: A woman's employer tells her that she would be paid more if she were a man. There are no men employed on equal work so she cannot claim equal pay using a comparator. However, she could claim direct sex discrimination as the less favourable treatment she has received is clearly based on her sex.

PART-TIME WORK AND EQUAL PAY

62. A pay practice that treats part-time workers less favourably than comparable full-time workers is likely to be indirectly discriminatory against women, as more women than men work part time. Unless an employer can objectively justify the pay differential or practice, it will be unlawful.

It is unlikely that an employer could justify a different basic hourly rate for full-time and part-time workers.

In most cases where a part-time worker is paid less (pro-rata) than a full-time worker, the Part-time Workers (Prevention of Less Favourable Treatment) Regulations would also apply.[22] These prohibit less favourable treatment of part-time workers (male or female) unless it can be objectively justified.

NOTES

[22] SI 2000/1551. Implementing the Part-time work Directive (97/81/EC).

EQUAL PAY AND OCCUPATIONAL PENSION SCHEMES

General

63. [Pensions Act 1995] Occupational pension schemes are also subject to the equal pay for equal work principle. Most occupational pension schemes are trust-based schemes where the scheme is legally separate from the employer and is administered by trustees, who are bound to implement equal treatment between women and men. The benefits will be in the form of pensions and lump sums.

Sex equality rule

64. [s 67(1), (2)] The sex equality rule operates to ensure that comparable women and men are treated equally in both access to and benefits of an occupational pension scheme. If an occupational pension scheme, or a term of it, is less favourable to a woman than it is to a male comparator, then the term is modified so that it is not less favourable.

65. The exclusion of part-time workers from an occupational pension scheme has been held to be indirectly discriminatory and unlawful.[23]

66. [s 67(3), (4)] Also, a discretion that is capable of being exercised in a way that would be less favourable to the woman than to her male comparator is modified so as to prevent the exercise of the discretion in that way.

67. [s 69(4)] However, if the trustees or managers of the scheme can show that the difference in treatment is because of a material factor which is not the difference in sex, then the sex equality rule will not apply to that difference.

68. The effect is that men and women are treated equally to comparable members of the opposite sex in relation both to the terms on which they are permitted to join the scheme and to the terms on which they are treated once they have become scheme members.

So a rule that provides for men and women to draw their benefits from the scheme at different ages, or on satisfying different conditions, is not consistent with the sex equality rule. The rule would be overridden to require benefits to be provided at the more favourable age or on the person satisfying the conditions applicable to either men or women.

69. [s 67(5) & (6)] The terms on which benefits are provided to dependants of members, and associated discretions, are also covered by the sex equality rule.

70. [s 67(7) & (8)] Where people of the same sex are treated differently according to their family, marital or civil partnership status, a woman must select a male comparator who has the same status. So if a scheme provides a particular benefit only to members who are married or in civil partnerships, a woman who is not married or in a civil partnership cannot choose as a comparator a man who is married or in a civil partnership for a claim in relation to that benefit.

71. [s 67(9)] A successful claim for access to an occupational pension scheme can result in the granting of retrospective access in respect of any period going back to 8 April 1976.

72. [s 67(10)] Equality in pension benefits can only be claimed for service from 17 May 1990.

73. [Schedule 7 Part 2] There is an exception to the sex equality rule that allows a difference in occupational pension contributions for women and men because of prescribed actuarial factors. For example, an employer may have to pay higher contributions for female than male employees because of their longer life expectancy.[24]

NOTES

[23] *Preston and others v Wolverhampton Healthcare NHS Trust and others (No 3)* [2004] ICR 993; *Bilka-Kaufhaus GmbH v Weber von Hartz* [1986] IRLR 317 ECJ.

[24] *Neath v Hugh Steeper Ltd* [1995] IRLR 91 ECJ.

DEFENCES TO AN EQUAL PAY CLAIM

74. The possible defences that an employer may raise in response to an equal pay claim are:

- the woman and her comparator are not doing equal work;
- the chosen comparator is not one allowed by law (for example he is not in the same employment);

- the difference in pay is genuinely due to a material factor, which is not related to the sex of the jobholders.

MATERIAL FACTOR DEFENCE

75. **[s 69]** Once a woman has shown that she is doing equal work with her male comparator, the equality clause will take effect unless her employer can prove that the difference in pay or other contractual terms is due to a material factor which does not itself discriminate against her either directly or indirectly because of her sex.

76. The employer must identify the factor(s) and prove[25]:

- it is the real reason for the difference in pay and not a sham or pretence
- it is causative of the difference in pay between the woman and her comparator
- it is material: that is, significant and relevant, and
- it does not involve direct or indirect sex discrimination.

Example: If an employer argues that it was necessary to pay the comparator more because of a skill shortage, they will have to provide evidence of actual difficulties in recruiting and retaining people to do the job being done by the higher-paid man. The employer will also need to monitor the discrepancy to ensure it is still justified.

77. Personal differences between the workers concerned such as experience and qualifications may be material factors.

Other examples of possible material factors are:

- geographical differences, for example London weighting
- unsocial hours, rotating shifts and night working.

78. Whether the defence is made out will depend on the specific circumstances in each case.

79. If the material factor accounts for only part of the variation in pay, the woman is entitled to a pay increase to the extent that the defence is not made out.[26]

80. To be a valid defence, the material factor must not be directly discriminatory and if it is indirectly discriminatory, the difference in terms must be justified.

81. For example, if an employer argues that the difference in pay is due to market forces, but gender segregation in the workforce means that women are still concentrated in lower paid jobs, this defence may be discriminatory. An employer cannot pay women less than men for equal work just because a competitor does so.[27]

82. **[s 69(1)(a)]** A material factor will be directly discriminatory where it is based on treating women and men differently because of their sex.

A directly discriminatory material factor cannot provide a defence to an equal pay claim, and it is not open to an employer to provide objective justification.

Example: Male maintenance workers in a bank were paid more than female administrators because the bank had always regarded and rewarded men as family breadwinners. This is directly discriminatory and cannot be justified.

83. Even if the employer can show that a material factor is not directly discriminatory, a woman claiming equal pay may be able to show that it is indirectly discriminatory.

84. **[s 69(2)]** Indirect discrimination arises where a pay system, policy or arrangement has a disproportionate adverse impact on women compared to their male comparators. If the employer cannot objectively justify it, the defence will not be made out.

85. Statistical analysis which demonstrates a difference in the terms offered to men and women doing equal work but where one job is predominantly carried out by one sex, is one way of showing disproportionate adverse impact but it is not the only way.

86. Where the disadvantaged group is predominately women, and the group of advantaged comparators is predominantly men, it will be difficult for the employer to prove an absence of sex discrimination.[28]

Example: Women employed as carers by a local authority, whose work was rated as equivalent to men employed as street cleaners and gardeners, were paid at a lower rate. The difference was due to a productivity bonus scheme which did not apply to carers, who were predominantly women. As the scheme had a disproportionately adverse effect on the women, the employer would have to provide objective justification for it. That is, they would need to prove that it is a proportionate means to achieve a legitimate end.[29]

87. **[s 69(1)(b)]** An employer can justify an indirectly discriminatory factor by showing that it is a proportionate means of achieving a legitimate aim.

Example: If an employer can show that the only way to ensure adequate staffing of unsocial hours shifts is to pay a shift premium, then even if there is evidence that more men than women work those shifts and receive the extra payments, the material factor defence may succeed.[30]

Example: A firm of accountants structures employees' pay on the basis of success in building client relationships. It uses as one of the key indicators of that success the number of functions attended out of hours. Due to childcare responsibilities, fewer women than men can participate in these functions and women's pay is much lower. The firm cannot show that attendance at these functions produces better client relationships or other business outcomes that warrant the pay premium, taking into account the disadvantage to women. It is unlikely in these circumstances to be able to justify the payment.

88. **[s 69(3)]** There is no list of aims that are accepted to be legitimate, and whether or not an employer's pay practice pursues a legitimate aim will depend on the facts and circumstances in a particular case. However, the Act does specify that, for the purpose of justifying reliance upon a material factor, the long-term objective of reducing inequality between men's and women's terms of work is always to be regarded as a legitimate aim.

The employer must be able to show that the measure was in fact adopted to reduce inequality.

89. Even where the aim is legitimate, the employer must be able to show that the means it adopts to achieve the aim is proportionate in the circumstances.

Example: A process to phase out historical disparity in pay and benefits between men and women, which involves a period of pay protection for men to cushion the impact on them of the new arrangements, has the long-term objective of reducing inequality between the sexes. This is a legitimate aim. However, the employer will have to prove on the facts of the case that the approach to achieving that aim is proportionate. It may be difficult to prove that protecting the men's higher pay for any length of time is a proportionate means of achieving the aim where the reason for the original pay disparity is sex discrimination.[31]

90. Where a material factor applies at a particular point in time but subsequently ceases to apply, it will no longer provide a defence to differences in contractual terms.[32]

Example: An employer recruits a new employee at a lower than normal rate of salary due to severe financial constraints at the time of recruitment. Later, the employer's financial position improves. Once the reason for the difference in pay ceases to exist the employer cannot continue to rely upon that factor to explain differences in pay or other contractual terms.

NOTES

25 *Glasgow City Council v Marshall* [2000] IRLR 272, HL.

26 *Enderby and Others v Frenchay Health Authority and Another* [1993] IRLR 591ECJ.

27 *Ratcliffe and others v North Yorkshire County Council* [1995] IRLR 439 HL. For information about gender segregation in the workforce and the undervaluing of women's work see, for example, the Women and Work Commission report Shaping a Fairer Future, 2006.

28 Lord Justice Pill in *Gibson and others v Sheffield City Council* [2010] IRLR 311 CA; *Enderby and Others v Frenchay Health Authority and Another* [1993] IRLR 591ECJ.

29 *Gibson and others v Sheffield City Council* [2010] IRLR 311 CA.

30 *Blackburn v Chief Constable of West Midlands Police* [2008] ICR 505 CA.

31 *Redcar and Cleveland Borough Council v Bainbridge & Others* [2008] EWCA Civ 885.

32 *Benveniste v University of Southampton* [1989] IRLR 123 CA.

PREGNANCY, MATERNITY LEAVE AND EQUAL PAY

91. **[s 73]** A woman should not receive lower pay or inferior contractual terms for a reason relating to her pregnancy and a maternity equality clause is implied into her contract to ensure this. There is no need to show equal work with a comparator in this situation.

92. **[ss 74, 74(10) & 18]** The maternity equality clause applies to:

- the calculation of contractual maternity-related pay
- bonus payments during maternity leave, and
- pay increases following maternity leave.

Maternity leave includes compulsory, ordinary and additional maternity leave.[33]

93. During maternity leave a woman's entitlement to receive her usual contractual remuneration (that is, salary or other benefits with a transferable cash value such as a car allowance or luncheon vouchers) stops unless her contract provides for maternity-related pay.[34]

94. **[s 74(6), (7)]** However she is entitled to any pay rise or contractual bonus payment awarded during her maternity leave period, or that would have been awarded had she not been on maternity leave.

95. **[s 74(9)]** Maternity-related pay means pay other than statutory maternity pay to which a woman is entitled as a result of being pregnant or being on maternity leave.[35]

96. **[s 74(3)]** Any pay increase a woman receives or would have received had she not been on maternity leave must be taken into account in the calculation of her maternity-related pay.

Example: Early in her maternity leave a woman receiving maternity-related pay becomes entitled to an increase in pay. If her terms of employment do not already provide for the increase to be reflected in her maternity-related pay, the employer must recalculate her maternity pay to take account of the pay increase.

97. **[s 74]** Similarly any pay or bonus related to time before the maternity leave starts, during compulsory maternity leave or after maternity leave ends must be paid without delay. So if a woman becomes entitled to a contractual bonus for work she undertook before she went on maternity leave, she should receive it when it would have been paid had she not been on maternity leave.

Example: A woman goes on maternity leave on 1 June. The contractual bonus for the year ending 30 April is payable on 1 July. Her employer says he will pay the bonus to her when she is back in a few months. The law requires the employer to pay the bonus on 1 July as it would if the woman was not on maternity leave. If this does not happen, she can claim equal pay relying on the maternity equality clause provisions.

98. **[s 74(8)]** On her return to work a woman should receive any pay increases which would have been paid to her had she not been on maternity leave.

99. **[s 76]** Unfavourable treatment because of pregnancy or maternity in relation to non-contractual pay and benefits is covered by the employment discrimination provisions in the Act.

Example: [s 18] A woman who has been approved for a promotion tells her employer that she is pregnant. The employer responds that he will not now promote her because she will be absent on maternity leave during a very busy period. This would be pregnancy discrimination at work and any claim would be brought by the woman under those provisions of the Equality Act.

However, if the same woman is promoted and her increased salary takes effect after the commencement of her maternity leave, her maternity-related pay will need to be recalculated to take account of the salary increase, and the salary increase will be payable to the woman on her return to work from maternity leave. If this does not happen, she can claim equal pay relying on the maternity equality clause provisions.

NOTES

[33] The statutory maternity leave scheme is set out in Part VIII of the Employment Rights Act 1996 (ERA) and in the Maternity and Parental Leave etc Regulations 1991 SI 1999/3312.

[34] *Gillespie and others v Northern Health and Social Services Board and others* 1996, ECJ. Note that the law on women's entitlement to full pay during their maternity leave may continue to evolve.

[35] Earnings-related Statutory Maternity Pay must also be recalculated to reflect a pay rise awarded to a woman after the end of the calculation period but before the end of her maternity leave. *Alabaster v Barclays Bank* [2005] ICR 1246. This is explained in the HMRC Employer Helpbook for Statutory Maternity Pay.

MATERNITY EQUALITY IN PENSION SCHEMES

100. **[s 75(1)–(6)]** An occupational pension scheme is treated as including a maternity equality rule if it does not have such a rule already. The effect of this is to ensure that a woman on paid maternity leave is treated as if she were at work for pension purposes.

101. **[s 75(9)]** The only time a woman on maternity leave may be treated differently is when she is on a period of unpaid additional maternity leave, when she is not entitled to accrue occupational pension benefits as of right.[36]

NOTES

[36] However, this is a developing area of domestic and EU law, so advice should be sought on whether pension accrual should be maintained throughout the entire maternity leave period.

PAY TRANSPARENCY

102. The Court of Justice of the European Union has held that pay systems that are not transparent are particularly at risk of being found to be discriminatory. Transparency means that pay and benefit systems should be capable of being understood by everyone (employers, workers and their trade unions). It should be clear to individuals how each element of their pay contributes to their total earnings in a pay period.

Where the pay structure is not transparent and a woman is able to show some indication of sex discrimination in her pay, the employer carries the burden of proving that the pay system does not discriminate.[37]

NOTES

[37] *Handels og Kontorfunktionaerernes Forbund i Danmark v Dansk Arbejdsgiverforening (acting for Danfoss)* [1989] IRLR 532, [1991] ICR 74.

DISCUSSING EQUAL PAY ISSUES WITH COLLEAGUES OR TRADE UNION REPRESENTATIVES

103. The Act introduces limits to the enforceability of what are often called 'gagging clauses' or 'secrecy clauses' that some employers use to restrict discussions about pay packages and differentials. Restricting use of these clauses is intended to promote openness and dialogue about pay and bring an end to opaque pay structures.

104. **[s 77]** Any term of a contract which prohibits or restricts a person from making a 'relevant pay disclosure' to anyone, including a trade union representative, or from seeking such a disclosure from a colleague, including a former colleague, is unenforceable.

105. Colleague is not defined in the Act but is likely to have similar scope to the definition of a comparator, as the intention is to protect the seeking of pay information for the purpose of identifying pay discrimination.

106. **[s 77(3)]** A relevant pay disclosure is one which is:

- about pay, and
- made for the purpose of finding out whether or to what extent there is a connection between pay and having (or not having) a protected characteristic.

107. The pay discussions that are protected in this way are those aimed at establishing whether or not there is pay discrimination. This provision is not confined to the protected characteristic of sex.

Example: A discussion between a woman and a man for the purpose of establishing whether the man is being paid more than the woman could involve a relevant pay disclosure. However, two male colleagues simply comparing their respective salaries are unlikely to be making a relevant pay disclosure, unless they are investigating pay disparities which may be linked to race or another protected characteristic.

108. Involvement in a relevant pay disclosure can include but is not limited to:

- asking a colleague to provide information about his/her pay and/or benefits
- providing information to a trade union representative about pay and/or benefits, and
- receiving information from a colleague about pay and/or benefits.

109. If an employer takes action against an employee for making or seeking to make such a disclosure, or for receiving information as a result of such a disclosure, the employee may claim victimisation.

Example: A female airline pilot believes she is underpaid compared with a male colleague. She asks him what he is paid, and he tells her. The airline takes disciplinary action against the man as a result. The man can bring a claim for victimisation against the employer for disciplining him.

Example: A female estate agent believes she may have received a smaller bonus than she should have. She asks her male colleagues what bonus payments they received. She then approaches her employer and complains about the discrepancy. She is reprimanded for discussing her pay and told she will not receive a bonus at all next year. She can claim victimisation, as well as making a discrimination or equal pay claim in respect of the bonus if she now has or can obtain sufficient evidence to do so.

Example: A male construction engineer employed by a road haulage company discloses information about his pay to a competitor company in breach of a confidentiality obligation. He would not be protected from disciplinary action, as the disclosure was unlikely to have been made for the purpose of finding out whether or to what extent there was pay discrimination in his workplace.

110. Guidance on protected pay discussions and disclosures is available on the Commission's website.

EQUAL PAY – OBTAINING INFORMATION

111. **[s 138]** A woman who believes she is not receiving equal pay can write to her employer asking for information that will help to establish whether this is the case and if so, the reasons for the pay difference.

112. A trade union equality representative or other trade union representative can assist in this process.

113. There is a procedure set out in the Act and there are forms prescribed by the accompanying Order that can be used by people to seek information. However, there is no restriction on the form or manner in which questions can be posed or answers given. A question or reply is admissible as evidence in Tribunal proceedings whether or not they are contained in the statutory question or reply form. So if similar questions are asked in a letter rather than using the form, that letter and any response that the employer provides can still be put before the Employment Tribunal for them to consider provided it is sent within the relevant time limits.

114. **[s 138(4) & (5)]** If the employer fails to answer the questions within eight weeks or answers in an evasive or equivocal way, an Employment Tribunal can draw an inference, including an inference that the employer is in breach of the equal pay provisions. Standard forms and guidance on their use are available on the Government Equalities Office website.

115. A woman can use the statutory question and reply process to request key information and in many cases an employer will be able to answer detailed questions in general terms, while still preserving the anonymity and confidentiality of other employees.

116. The statutory question and reply process cannot be used to require an employer to disclose an employee's personal details, unless an Employment Tribunal orders the employer to do so, or the employee concerned consents to such information being disclosed.

117. Guidance on using the Data Protection Act 1998 and Freedom of Information Act 2000 in employment discrimination cases, including equal pay, is available on the Commission's website.

118. The Information Commissioner also has helpful guidance ('When should salaries be disclosed?') on its website.

USING THE GRIEVANCE PROCEDURE

119. Before making a complaint to the Employment Tribunal about equal pay, a woman should consider trying to resolve the issue with her employer.

If informal resolution is not possible, a woman should lodge a formal written grievance.

120. It is not necessary for the woman to name her male comparator at the grievance stage.

121. The ACAS Code of Practice on disciplinary and grievance procedures includes guidance for employees and employers on raising and dealing with complaints about pay or contractual terms.

122. Employees may seek advice and help from employee or trade union representatives.

123. Employers and employees can also seek advice from an ACAS conciliator. ACAS advisors can provide guidance on implementing equal pay too. ACAS can be contacted at www.acas.org.uk.

124. **[s 207A Trade Union Labour Relations (Consolidation) Act 1992]** If Employment Tribunal proceedings are commenced and there has been an unreasonable failure by either party to adhere to the ACAS Code this could affect any compensation awarded.

125. The time limit for making a complaint to the Employment Tribunal is not extended to take account of the time taken to complete a grievance procedure.

126. It can be unclear whether a particular term or benefit is contractual or not and in this case a woman would be well advised to make a claim for both equal pay and sex discrimination.

127. When responding either to a grievance or to a statutory question form, employers need to:

- decide whether or not they agree that the woman and her comparator are doing equal work, and, if not, explain in what way the work is not equal
- consider the reasons for any difference in pay/benefits or other contractual terms and whether (if necessary) these can be objectively justified, and
- explain the reasons for the difference.

BURDEN OF PROOF

128. A woman claiming equal pay must prove facts from which an Employment Tribunal could decide that her employer has paid her less than a male comparator in the same employment doing equal work. It is then for her employer, if the claim is denied, to prove that the difference in pay and/or other terms is for a material reason other than sex. If the employer proves that there is a non-discriminatory material factor which has resulted in the difference in pay the woman's claim will fail.

129. If the woman asserts that the material factor is indirectly discriminatory it is for her to provide evidence of this, statistical or otherwise. The employer will then need to objectively justify the difference in terms (that is, prove that it is a proportionate means of achieving a legitimate aim).

EMPLOYMENT TRIBUNALS

130. **[s 131(5), (6) & (7)]** If an equal pay claim is made, the Employment Tribunal will assess the evidence about:

- the work done by the woman and her comparator
- the application and validity of the job evaluation study if the claim is for work rated as equivalent
- the value placed on the work (sometimes with the advice of an independent expert), in terms of the demands of the jobs if the claim is for work of equal value
- the pay and/or other contract terms of the woman and her comparator and how they are determined, and
- the reasons for the difference in pay and/or contract terms if the employer raises a material factor defence.

131. There are special Tribunal procedures for work of equal value claims.[38] These can be obtained from www.employmenttribunals.gov.uk

132. **[s 131]** Once a woman has lodged an equal pay claim, she can seek relevant information about pay and other contractual terms from her employer in a number of ways. These include:

- disclosure
- requests for additional information, and
- requests for written answers.

NOTES

[38] The Employment Tribunals (Equal Value) Rules of Procedure, Schedule 6 of the Employment Tribunals (Constitution and Rules of Procedure) Regulations 2004 (SI 2004/1861).

PROCEDURE

133. **[ss 127(1), (9) & 128]** A claim relating to a breach of an equality clause or rule is usually made to an Employment Tribunal. Where a claim is made to the civil court, the court may refer it to the tribunal which has more expertise in employment matters.

134. **[s 127(6)]** Members of the armed forces must make a service complaint before an Employment Tribunal can consider an equal pay or pensions claim from them, and cannot withdraw the service complaint if they wish the Employment Tribunal to hear their claim.

TIME LIMITS FOR EQUAL PAY CLAIMS

135. **[ss 129 & 123]** A complaint to an Employment Tribunal about equal pay must be made within six months of the end of what is known as the 'qualifying period'. In a 'standard case', this is six months from the last day of employment. This is different from sex discrimination claims for which the time limit is ordinarily three months from the last act of discrimination.

136. **[s 129(3)]** The date from which the six-month time limit starts to run is affected by the circumstances set out below.

137. **[s 130(3) & (10)]** In a stable work case (that is, where there have been breaks in what would otherwise have been continuous employment with the same employer), the six months would start to run from the date on which the stable employment relationship ended, not on the date a particular contract ended.

Whether it is a stable work case will depend on the facts.

For example, where a woman is on a series of contracts in what is essentially the same job (for example a teaching assistant on a series of annual contracts) or a progression within the same job (for example an administrative assistant who progresses to administrative officer), time will not start to run with the issue of a new contract.

Where a woman reduces her hours following a period of maternity leave and is issued with a new contract, this will not trigger the time limit as it is a stable employment relationship.

Example: Ms Smith had been continuously employed since 1980 by the local council as a cook in a residential home. In 2007, she wanted to reduce her hours of work. It was agreed to vary her contractual hours from 37 to 30 hours per week and reduce her days from five to four per week. She was issued with a letter headed 'Contract of employment' which stated that this superseded any previous contract. While this signed document did amount to a new contract, an uninterrupted succession of contracts is a stable employment relationship. She had done the same work for the same council over many years without any break in the work. The only variation made in the new contract was the reduction of working hours. Because Ms Smith had a stable employment relationship with the council the time limit would not be triggered until the end of this stable employment.

Example: Ms Auster was employed by her local council as a relief home carer from November 2000. In April 2009, she was appointed as a permanent home carer. With this change of status she became entitled to sick pay. Otherwise her terms of employment were unchanged. She signed a new contract stating that previous contracts were superseded. There was no gap or break in the continuity of her work for the council but because her status changed and some of her employment terms, a stable working relationship cannot necessarily be said to exist.[39]

138. A variation in terms and conditions will not start the six-month time limit running, providing the variation is not so significant as to amount to a termination of the previous contract.[40]

139. Where a woman is transferred to a new employer under the Transfer of Undertakings (Protection of Employment) Regulations 2006, and the equal pay claim relates to her employment with the transferor, if the liability for that claim passes under the Regulations, the equal pay claim must be lodged against the transferee within six months of the date of the transfer.

If the new employer, the transferee, fails to honour her pre-existing contractual right under the equality clause, she will have a separate claim against the transferee in respect of this breach. The six-month time limit for bringing that claim will not start to run until the end of her employment with the transferee.[41]

140. Example: Ms Jones worked for an NHS Trust as a domestic cleaner in a hospital. In January 2001, under a contracting-out arrangement, Ms Jones was transferred to the employment of a private cleaning company. She continued to work as before at the same hospital. In September 2006, she brought an equal pay claim against the cleaning company, relying on male comparators who had not transferred over to the company and were still employed by the NHS Trust. Ms Jones was paid £2 an hour less than men doing equal work for the Trust. Her claim relating to her employment with the Trust before the transfer is time-barred, as the six-month time limit ran from January 2001, the date of the transfer. The cleaning company, as transferee, is obliged to honour the equality clause, where it passes to them, and, if they fail to do so, she could bring a claim against them up to six months after the end of her employment with them.

141. [s 130(4)] Where the fact of the pay inequality was deliberately concealed and the woman could not reasonably have been expected to discover it, the time starts to run from the date she actually discovered or could reasonably have discovered the inequality. This is referred to as a concealment case.

142. [s 130(7)] Where the woman has an incapacity the time starts to run from the end of the incapacity.

[s 141(6)] 'Has an incapacity' in England and Wales means the woman has not attained the age of 18 or lacks capacity within the meaning of the Mental Capacity Act 2005.

[s 141(7)] In Scotland it means she has not attained the age of 16 or is incapable within the meaning of the Adults with Incapacity (Scotland) Act 2000.

143. [s 129(4)] Members of the armed forces have nine months from their last day of service to make their application to the Employment Tribunal provided that they raise a service complaint as mentioned at paragraph 134.

144. Civilians working with the armed forces are not governed by these rules and must make an application to an Employment Tribunal on the same basis as other people.

145. It is the claimant's responsibility to ensure their claim is made in time. Individuals and their representatives should be alert to the importance of observing these time limits, and err on the side of caution if there is any ambiguity or uncertainty about when time starts to run.

It should be noted that using an employer's grievance procedure does not extend the time limit for lodging a claim, nor does serving a statutory question and reply form.

NOTES

39 *Cumbria County Council v Dow (No 2)* [2009] IRLR 463, CA.

40 *Potter and others (appellants) v North Cumbria Acute Hospitals NHS Trust and others (respondents) (No 2)* [2009] IRLR 900, EAT.

41 *Sodexo Ltd v Gutridge* [2008] IRLR 752, CA.

EQUAL PAY AWARDS AND REMEDIES

146. [s 132] If an equal pay claim is heard by an Employment Tribunal and upheld, the Tribunal may:

- make a declaration as to the rights of the woman and/or her employer in relation to the claim brought. For example, a pay rise to the level of the comparator's pay (including any occupational pension rights) or the inclusion of any beneficial term not in the woman's contract, and
- order the employer to pay arrears of pay or damages to the person who has brought the claim.

147. A declaration may be made even if the Employment Tribunal decides not to award any compensation.

148. An Employment Tribunal cannot make an award for injury to feelings for breach of an equality clause.

149. [s 132(4)] In England and Wales, the Tribunal can award arrears of pay or damages going back not longer than six years before the date that proceedings were started in the Employment Tribunal.

This is extended to the day on which the breach first occurred where incapacity or concealment applies (see paragraphs 141 and 142).

[s 132(5)] In Scotland, the Employment Tribunal can award arrears of pay or damages going back not longer than five years from the date that proceedings were brought in the Employment Tribunal. This is extended to 20 years where the employee had a relevant incapacity or there was a fraud or error.

150. [Employment Tribunals (Interest on Awards in Discrimination Cases) Regulations 1996] As in other discrimination cases, equal pay awards can be made subject to interest. An award of arrears of pay will generally only attract interest for about half the arrears period. Interest will be calculated as simple interest accruing day to day in accordance with prescribed statutory rates.

151. [s 133] In cases involving occupational pension entitlements, an Employment Tribunal may make a declaration as to the rights of the parties concerned. The rules as to what compensation can be ordered or may be agreed are complicated so it is important to seek advice.

152. [s 133(8)] Where an Employment Tribunal makes a declaration about the terms on which a member of an occupational scheme must be treated, the employer must provide such resources to the scheme as are necessary to secure that person's rights without further contribution by her or any other members.

PROTECTION AGAINST VICTIMISATION

153. [s 27] It is unlawful for an employer to victimise a worker for bringing an equal pay or discrimination claim or for giving evidence about such a complaint.

Victimisation arises if a person is subjected to a detriment, because that person has done a protected act, or is believed to have done a protected act.

A protected act includes the following:
- bringing proceedings under the Act
- giving evidence or information in connection with such proceedings
- doing any other thing for the purposes of or in connection with the Act, and
- making an allegation that someone is in breach of the Act.

This means that protection from victimisation does not start only when a claim is filed with the Employment Tribunal. Protected acts can include any discussion or correspondence about the matter between the woman and her employer.

154. [s 77(4)] Workers who seek or make a relevant pay disclosure, or who receive information that is a relevant pay disclosure, are protected from victimisation. For explanation of what is a 'relevant pay disclosure' see paragraph 106.

155. There is no requirement for a comparator in a victimisation complaint.

156. In considering whether an act has caused detriment, the focus is on the effect on the alleged victim, rather than any intent or purpose on the part of the employer.

Example: A group of women employed by a local authority brought equal pay claims. Some of the women settled, the others proceeded with their claim. Shortly before the Tribunal hearing, the employer wrote to the latter group warning of the potential consequences of the case for the council's finances. The women experienced this as pressure to drop the case and were distressed by the letter. The House of Lords found that this did amount to victimisation.[42]

157. The protection against victimisation includes not only the woman bringing the claim, but also any person who assists her, for example, a comparator.

NOTES

[42] *Derbyshire and others v St Helens Metropolitan Borough Council* [2007] UKHL 16.

PART 2: GOOD EQUAL PAY PRACTICE

INTRODUCTION

[4.126]

158. Despite the implementation of equal pay and sex discrimination legislation in the 1970s, there is still a significant gender pay gap. It could take an estimated 20 years to close the gap without further corrective action. This section of the code of practice therefore provides information and guidance on steps that employers can take which go beyond compliance with legal requirements. These steps, taken in consultation with the workforce and trade union or other employee representatives, should help accelerate the achievement of substantive gender equality at work.

159. The financial loss to women arising out of unequal pay is well documented, but organisations also lose out by failing to properly value and reward the range of skills and experience that women bring to the workforce.

The most commonly recognised risk of failing to ensure that pay is determined without sex discrimination is the risk of time-consuming and costly litigation equal pay litigation. The direct costs to an organisation of a claim can include not only any eventual equal pay award to the woman or women bringing the claim but also the costs of time spent responding to the claim, and the costs of legal representation.

The indirect costs are harder to quantify, but could include lower productivity on the part of those employees who consider that they are not getting equal pay and on the part of managers whose time is taken up in dealing with staff dissatisfaction and other repercussions.

160. Tackling unequal pay can also increase efficiency and productivity by attracting the best employees, reducing staff turnover, increasing commitment, and reducing absenteeism. Pay is one of the key factors affecting motivation and relationships at work. It is therefore important to develop pay arrangements that are right for the organisation and that reward employees fairly. Providing equal pay for equal work is central to the concept of rewarding people fairly for what they do.

161. Employers should not discriminate on any protected ground in their pay arrangements. The information on good practice set out here focuses on eliminating gender pay inequalities, which are the subject of this code of practice. However, the methods used to identify and remedy unlawful gender pay discrimination can also be used to remedy unlawful pay discrimination on other grounds.

REVIEWING OR AUDITING PAY

162. Employers are responsible for providing equal pay for equal work and for ensuring that pay systems are transparent. Where a pay system lacks transparency the employer must be able to prove there is no sex discrimination behind a pay differential.[43]

Pay arrangements are often complicated and the features that can give rise to discrimination in pay are not always obvious. A structured pay system, based on sound, bias-free job evaluation, is more transparent and more likely to provide equal pay than a system that relies primarily on managerial discretion.

ACAS can advise on how to structure a pay system.

163. Most employers believe that they provide equal pay for equal work, irrespective of the sex of the job holders or whether they work full or part time. An equal pay audit is the most effective way of establishing whether an organisation is in fact providing equal pay.

Organisations subject to the gender equality duty must pay due regard to the need to eliminate sex discrimination in pay. Although conducting an equal pay audit is not mandatory, it demonstrates appropriate action to identify and eliminate gender pay discrimination.[44] It provides a risk assessment tool for pay structures.

The Commission recommends all employers carry out regular equal pay audits. A model for carrying out an equal pay audit is described below.

164. A number of common pay practices, listed below, pose risks in terms of potential non-compliance with an employer's legal obligations:

- Lack of transparency and unnecessary secrecy over grading and pay.
- Discretionary pay systems (for example, merit pay and performance-related pay) unless they are clearly structured and based on objective criteria.
- Different non-basic pay, terms and conditions for different groups of employees (for example, attendance allowances, overtime or unsocial hours payments).
- More than one grading and pay system within the organisation
- Long pay scales or ranges.
- Overlapping pay scales or ranges, where the maximum of the lower pay scale is higher than the minimum of the next higher scale, including 'broad-banded' structures where there are significant overlaps.
- Managerial discretion over starting salaries.
- Market-based pay systems or supplements not underpinned by job evaluation.
- Job evaluation systems which have been incorrectly implemented or not kept up to date.
- Pay protection policies.

There is detailed guidance on the Commission's website about the law and risk management in relation to these issues. In many cases, this will involve carrying out a few straightforward checks or reviewing a relevant policy.

165. Risks of equal pay challenges generally arise not out of any intention to discriminate, but through pay systems not being kept under review and up to date. ACAS provides basic advice on the various different types of pay systems and on job evaluation.

NOTES

[43] See Part 1 of the code, paragraph 102. The key legal authority for this is known as Danfoss, the full case name is *Handels og Kontorfunktionaerernes Forbund i Danmark v Dansk Arbejdsgiverforening (acting for Danfoss)* [1989] IRLR 532, [1991] ICR 74. See also *Barton v Investec Henderson Crosthwaite Securities Ltd* 2003 ICR 1205, EAT.

[44] See Gender Equality Code of Practice England and Wales, EOC 2006, paragraphs 3.40–3.52, which has effect until replaced by any new public sector equality duty code.

THE BENEFITS OF CONDUCTING AN EQUAL PAY AUDIT

166. The benefits to an organisation of carrying out an equal pay audit include:

- identifying, explaining and, where unjustifiable, eliminating pay inequalities
- having rational, fair and transparent pay arrangements
- demonstrating to employees and to potential employees a commitment to equality, and
- demonstrating the organisation's values to those it does business with.

167. An equal pay audit may be the most effective method of ensuring that a pay system is free from unlawful bias. An audit should include:

- comparing the pay of men and women doing equal work – ensuring that this considers work that is the same or broadly similar (like work), work rated as equivalent and work that can be shown to be of equal value or worth
- identifying and explaining any pay differences, and
- eliminating those pay inequalities that cannot be explained on non-discriminatory grounds.

168. A process that does not include these features cannot claim to be an equal pay audit. The Commission's extensive guidance for employers on conducting equal pay audits is available on its website.

169. An equal pay audit is not simply a data collection exercise. It entails a commitment to put right any unjustified pay inequalities. This means that the audit must have the involvement and support of managers who have the authority to deliver the necessary changes.

170. The validity of the audit and the success of subsequent action taken will be enhanced if the pay system is understood and accepted by the managers who operate the system, by the employees and by their unions. Employers should therefore aim to secure the involvement of employees and, where possible, trade union and other employee representatives, when carrying out an equal pay audit.

A MODEL FOR CARRYING OUT AN EQUAL PAY AUDIT

171. The Commission recommends a five-step equal pay audit model.

Step 1: Decide the scope of the audit and identify the information required.

Step 2: Determine where men and women are doing equal work.

Step 3: Collect and compare pay data to identify any significant pay inequalities between roles of equal value.

Step 4: Establish the causes of any significant pay inequalities and assess the reasons for them.

Step 5: Develop an equal pay action plan to remedy any direct or indirect pay discrimination.

The Commission's Equal Pay Resources and Audit Toolkit provides detailed guidance on how to conduct an audit.

STEP 1: DECIDE THE SCOPE OF THE AUDIT AND IDENTIFY THE INFORMATION REQUIRED

172. This is a particularly important aspect of the audit, especially if it is the first audit that an organisation has undertaken. It is worth investing time and thought at this stage. In scoping the audit, employers need to decide:

- Which employees are going to be included? It is advisable to include all employees who are deemed to be in the same employment or whose pay can be attributed to a single source (see paragraphs 51-57 of Part 1 of the code). If a comprehensive audit is not possible, or is deemed unnecessary, then a sample of roles may be audited but the basis for selecting the sample must be clear.
- What information will be needed and what tools are available? Employers will need to collect and compare two broad types of information about their employees: the jobs they do, and what they are paid (ensure that this information is collected about part-time as well as full-time workers):
  - All the various elements of their pay, including pensions and other benefits.
  - The sex of each employee; their job, grade or pay band.
- In addition, where there is gender pay inequality, it will be helpful to collect data on: qualifications related to the job; hours of work; length of service; any performance ratings and so on.

173. The Commission has produced guidance that explains an employer's legal obligations regarding data protection when carrying out an equal pay audit, which is available on its website.

174. The key tool for conducting pay audits is the Commission's equal pay audit kit and its five-step process. Guidelines on conducting equal pay audits have also been published by various bodies including Local Government Employers, and the Joint Negotiating Committee for Higher Education Staff, the TUC and individual trade unions. These contain useful additional sector specific advice.

175. The employer needs to consider carefully what resources are needed.

- Who should be involved in carrying out the audit? An equal pay audit requires different types of input from people with different perspectives, including those with knowledge and understanding of:
  - the organisation's pay and grading arrangements
  - any job evaluation system(s) in use
  - payroll and human resource information systems, and
  - key equality issues, such as occupational segregation and the systemic tendency to undervalue work done by women.
- When should the workforce be involved? Employers need to consider when to involve the trade unions or other employee representatives.
- Is expert advice needed? Employers may also wish to consider whether to bring in outside expertise. ACAS, the employment relations experts, offer practical, independent and impartial help to help bring pay systems up to date.

STEP 2: DETERMINE WHERE WOMEN AND MEN ARE DOING EQUAL WORK

176. In Step 2 an employer needs to check whether women and men are doing:

- like work – that is work that is the same or broadly similar, or

- work rated as equivalent under a valid job evaluation scheme, or
- work of broadly equal value or worth, considering factors such as effort, skill and decision-making.

These checks determine where women and men are doing equal work. They are the foundation of an equal pay audit.

Employers who do not have analytical job evaluation schemes designed with equal value in mind will need to find an alternative means of assessing whether men and women are doing equal work. The Commission's Equal Pay audit toolkit includes suggestions as to how this can be done.

Employers who do use analytical job evaluation schemes need to check that their scheme has been designed and implemented in such a way as not to discriminate on grounds of sex. The Commission's toolkit provides helpful guidance on this.

STEP 3: COLLECT AND COMPARE PAY DATA TO IDENTIFY ANY SIGNIFICANT PAY INEQUALITIES BETWEEN ROLES OF EQUAL VALUE

177. Once employers have determined which male and female employees are doing equal work, they need to collate and compare pay information to identify any significant inequalities by:

- calculating average basic pay and total earnings, and
- comparing access to and amounts received of each element of the pay package.

178. To ensure comparisons are consistent, when calculating average basic pay and average total earnings for men and women separately, employers should do this either on an hourly basis or on a full-time equivalent salary basis (grossing up or down for those who work fewer, or more, hours per week – excluding overtime - than the norm).

179. Employers then need to review the pay comparisons to identify any gender pay inequalities and decide if any are significant enough to warrant further investigation. It is advisable to record all the significant or patterned pay inequalities that have been identified. The Commission's toolkit gives detailed advice and guidance on collecting and comparing pay information and when pay gaps may be regarded as significant.

180. Modern software allows for speedy and in-depth investigation of pay inequalities on any protected ground and also provides an essential tool for equality impact assessments.

STEP 4: ESTABLISH THE CAUSES OF ANY SIGNIFICANT PAY INEQUALITIES AND ASSESS THE REASONS FOR THEM

181. In Step 4 employers need to:

- find out if there is a real, material reason for the difference in pay that has nothing to do with the sex of the jobholders, and
- examine their pay systems to find out which pay policies and practices may have caused or may be contributing to any gender pay inequalities.

182. Pay systems vary considerably. Pay systems that group jobs into pay grades or bands have traditionally treated jobs in the same grade or band as being of broadly equal value, either because they have been evaluated with similar scores under a job evaluation scheme, or because they are simply regarded as equivalent. However, recent years have seen a trend towards structures with fewer, broader grades or bands and greater use of performance pay and market factors.

A single broad band or grade may contain jobs or roles of significantly different value because it encompasses a wide range of job evaluation scores. This, combined with a wider use of other determinants of pay and more complex methods of pay progression, means employers should check all aspects of the pay system from a variety of standpoints: design, implementation, and differential impact on men and women.

183. The Commission has produced a series of checklists and guidance notes to help employers deal with the more common causes of unequal pay in the workplace (see paragraph 164).

STEP 5: DEVELOP AN EQUAL PAY ACTION PLAN TO REMEDY ANY DIRECT OR INDIRECT PAY DISCRIMINATION

184. Where the reason for the pay difference is connected with the employee's sex (or another protected ground), employers will need to remedy this and provide equal pay for current and future employees doing equal work.

If the pay differential arises from a factor that has an adverse impact on women, then it has to be objectively justified. For example, if an employee is entitled to a premium for working unsocial hours and fewer women than men can do this because of their caring responsibilities, it will be indirectly discriminatory and the employer will have to be able to prove it is justified. Further explanation of what this means is in Part 1 of the code (paragraph 83–89) and in other Commission guidance.

185. Employers who find no inequalities between men's and women's pay, or on other protected grounds, or who find pay differences for which there are genuinely non-discriminatory reasons, should nevertheless keep their pay systems under review by introducing regular monitoring undertaken jointly with trade unions. This will ensure that the pay system remains free of bias.

(List of contacts omitted; see the list of useful addresses at **[5.120]**.*)*

EQUALITY AND HUMAN RIGHTS COMMISSION: CODE OF PRACTICE ON EMPLOYMENT (2011)

[4.127]

NOTES

This Code of Practice was prepared by the Equality and Human Rights Commission to accompany the Equality Act 2010. It replaces Codes issued by the Equal Opportunities Commission in 1985 (*Code of Practice for the elimination of discrimination on the grounds of sex and marriage and the promotion of equality of opportunity in employment*), the Commission for Racial Equality in 2005 (*Code of Practice on racial equality in employment*), and the Disability Rights Commission in 2004 (*Employment and Occupation*), but not that on Equal Pay, which is the subject of a separate new Code (see **[4.123]**). The Employment Code covers all of the strands of employment discrimination covered by the Equality Act other than equal pay.

The new Code was brought into effect on 6 April 2011 by the Equality Act 2010 Codes of Practice (Services, Public Functions and Associations, Employment, and Equal Pay) Order 2011, SI 2011/857 and applies in relation to all matters occurring on or after that date. The former Codes, referred to above, were revoked with effect immediately before the coming into force of the new Code, by the Former Equality Commissions' Codes of Practice (Employment, Equal Pay and Rights of Access for Disabled Persons) (Revocation) Order 2011, SI 2011/776. The old Codes, which are no longer reproduced for reasons of space, continue to have effect in relation to matters occurring before the date of revocation (see SI 2011/776, art 3).

Note that the original Code contains references to sections and Schedules of the Equality Act 2010 (and other legislation) in the margin of the page, next to the paragraph to which they relate. These have been reproduced at the beginning of the paragraph in question in this Handbook (in bold and within square brackets). Note also that where there are more than two section (etc) references separated by a semi-colon, the second reference relates to a second (or subsequent) sentence within the paragraph in question.

See also, the Supplement to the Employment Pay Statutory Code of Practice which is available on the ECHR website at: www.equalityhumanrights.com/en/publication-download/employment-statutory-code-practice. The Supplement does not form part of the statutory Code of Practice. It is intended to assist those using the Code by identifying developments in the law since the Code was approved.

See *Harvey* L.

CONTENTS

CHAPTER 1 INTRODUCTION

PURPOSE OF THE EQUALITY ACT 2010

[4.128]

1.1 The Equality Act 2010 (the Act) consolidates and replaces most of the previous discrimination legislation for England, Scotland and Wales. The Act covers discrimination because of age, disability, gender reassignment, marriage and civil partnership, pregnancy and maternity, race, religion or belief, sex and sexual orientation. These categories are known in the Act as 'protected characteristics'.

1.2 An important purpose of the Act is to unify the legislation outlawing discrimination against people with different protected characteristics, where this is appropriate. There are, however, some significant differences and exceptions, which this Code explains.

1.3 As well as consolidating existing law, the Act makes discrimination unlawful in circumstances not covered previously. Discrimination in most areas of activity is now unlawful, subject to certain exceptions. These areas of activity include, for example: employment and other areas of work; education; housing; the provision of services, the exercise of public functions and membership of associations.

1.4 Different areas of activity are covered under different parts of the Act. Part 3 of the Act deals with discrimination in the provision of services and public functions. Part 4 deals with discrimination in the sale, letting, management and occupation of premises, including housing. Part 5 covers employment and other work-related situations. Part 6 covers education including schools, further education, higher education, and general qualifications bodies. Part 7 deals with discrimination by membership associations. An organisation may have duties under more than one area of the Act because, for example, it employs people and provides services to customers.

SCOPE OF THE CODE

1.5 This Code covers discrimination in employment and work-related activities under Part 5 of the Act. Part 5 is based on the principle that people with the protected characteristics set out in the Act should not be discriminated against in employment, when seeking employment, or when engaged in occupations or activities related to work.

1.6 In Part 5 of the Act, there are some provisions relating to equal pay between men and women. These provisions create an implied sex equality clause in employment contracts, in order to ensure equality in pay and other contractual terms for women and men doing equal work. Equal pay between men and women is covered in the Equal Pay Code published by the Equality and Human Rights Commission ('the Commission').

1.7 Part 5 also contains sections which make discrimination by trade organisations (including trade unions) and vocational qualifications bodies unlawful. Because the duties of qualifications bodies and trade organisations are different to the duties of employers, these will be covered by a separate Code.

1.8 This Code applies to England, Scotland and Wales.

PURPOSE OF THE CODE

1.9 The main purpose of this Code is to provide a detailed explanation of the Act. This will assist courts and tribunals when interpreting the law and help lawyers, advisers, trade union representatives, human resources departments and others who need to apply the law and understand its technical detail.

1.10 The Commission has also produced practical guidance for workers and employers which assumes no knowledge of the law and which may be more helpful and accessible for people who need an introduction to the Act. It can be obtained from the Commission, or downloaded from the Commission's website.

1.11 The Code, together with the practical guidance produced by the Commission will:

- help employers and others understand their responsibilities and avoid disputes in the workplace;
- help individuals to understand the law and what they can do if they believe they have been discriminated against;
- help lawyers and other advisers to advise their clients;
- give Employment Tribunals and courts clear guidance on good equal opportunities practice in employment; and
- ensure that anyone who is considering bringing legal proceedings under the Act, or attempting to negotiate equality in the workplace, understands the legislation and is aware of good practice in employment.

STATUS OF THE CODE

1.12 The Commission has prepared and issued this Code on the basis of its powers under the Equality Act 2006. It is a statutory Code. This means it has been approved by the Secretary of State and laid before Parliament.

1.13 The Code does not impose legal obligations. Nor is it an authoritative statement of the law; only the tribunals and the courts can provide such authority. However, the Code can be used in evidence in legal proceedings brought under the Act. Tribunals and courts must take into account any part of the Code that appears to them relevant to any questions arising in proceedings.

1.14 If employers and others who have duties under the Act follow the guidance in the Code, it may help them avoid an adverse decision by a tribunal or court.

ROLE OF THE EQUALITY AND HUMAN RIGHTS COMMISSION

1.15 The Commission was set up under the Equality Act 2006 to work towards the elimination of unlawful discrimination and promote equality and human rights.

1.16 In relation to equality, the Commission has duties to promote awareness and understanding and encourage good practice, as well as a power to provide advice and guidance on the law. It also has powers to enforce discrimination law in some circumstances.

HUMAN RIGHTS

1.17 Public authorities have a duty under the Human Rights Act 1998 (HRA) not to act incompatibly with rights under the European Convention for the Protection of Human Rights and Fundamental Freedoms (the Convention).

1.18 Courts and tribunals have a duty to interpret primary legislation (including the Equality Act 2010) and secondary legislation in a way that is compatible with the Convention rights, unless it is impossible to do so. This duty applies to courts and tribunals whether a public authority is involved in the case or not. So in any employment discrimination claim made under the Act, the court or tribunal must ensure that it interprets the Act compatibly with the Convention rights, where it can.

1.19 In practice, human rights issues in the workplace are likely to arise in relation to forced labour, privacy and data protection, freedom of expression and thought, trade union activity and harassment.

LARGE AND SMALL EMPLOYERS

1.20 While all employers have the same legal duties under the Act, the way that these duties are put into practice may be different. Small employers may have more informal practices, have fewer written policies, and may be more constrained by financial resources. This Code should be read with awareness that large and small employers may carry out their duties in different ways, but that no employer is exempt from these duties because of size.

HOW TO USE THE CODE

1.21 **Section 1** of the Code, comprising **Chapters 2 to 15**, gives a detailed explanation of the Act.

Chapter 2 explains the protected characteristics of age, disability, gender reassignment, marriage and civil partnership, pregnancy and maternity, race, religion or belief, sex and sexual orientation.

Chapters 3 to 9 cover different types of conduct that are prohibited under the Act. **Chapter 3** explains direct discrimination. **Chapter 4** deals with indirect discrimination as well as explaining the objective justification test. **Chapter 5** covers discrimination arising from disability and **Chapter 6** sets out the duty to make adjustments for disabled people. **Chapter 7** explains the provisions on harassment. **Chapter 8** deals with pregnancy and maternity discrimination. **Chapter 9** covers the remaining types of unlawful conduct: victimisation; instructing, causing or inducing discrimination; aiding contraventions of the Act; and gender reassignment discrimination (absence from work).

Chapter 10 explains the obligations and liabilities of the employer and the corresponding rights of workers. **Chapter 11** deals with the wider work relationships covered by Part 5 of the Act. **Chapter 12** sets out the legal provisions relating to positive action and how employers adopting positive action measures can ensure that such measures are lawful under the Act.

Chapter 13 explains occupational requirements and other exceptions related to work. **Chapter 14** covers pay and benefits including several specific exceptions to the work provisions of the Act. **Chapter 15** explains how the Act can be enforced by individuals or the Commission and gives an overview of alternatives to litigation.

Section 2, comprising **Chapters 16 to 19**, sets out recommended practice for employers, to help them comply with the Act and to achieve equality of opportunity and outcomes over the whole employment cycle. Public sector employers have specific obligations under the public sector equality duties and will find that this section helps them to meet these obligations.

Chapter 16 discusses how employers can avoid discrimination during the recruitment process. **Chapter 17** explains how discrimination can be avoided during employment and deals with issues such as working hours, accommodating workers' needs, training and development and disciplinary and grievance matters. **Chapter 18** discusses equality policies and implementation of such policies in the workplace. **Chapter 19** explains how discrimination can be avoided during termination of employment.

Additional information is appended at the end of the Code. **Appendix 1** gives further information on the definition of disability under the Act; **Appendix 2** provides information about diversity monitoring; and **Appendix 3** explains how leases and other legal obligations affect the duty to make reasonable adjustments to premises.

EXAMPLES IN THE CODE

1.22 Examples of good practice and how the Act is likely to work are included in the Code. They are intended simply to illustrate the principles and concepts used in the legislation and should be read in that light. The examples use different protected characteristics and work-related situations to demonstrate the breadth and scope of the Act.

USE OF THE WORDS 'EMPLOYER' AND 'WORKER'

1.23 The Act imposes obligations on people who are not necessarily employers in the legal sense – such as partners in firms, people recruiting their first worker, or people using contract workers. In this Code, these people are also referred to as 'employers' for convenience. The term 'employment' is also used to refer to these wider work-related relationships, except where it is specified that the provision in question does not apply to these wider relationships.

1.24 Similarly, the Code uses the term 'worker' to refer to people who are working for an 'employer', whether or not this is under a contract of employment with that 'employer'. These people include, for example, contract workers, police officers and office holders. The word 'workers' may also include job applicants, except where it is clear that the provision in question specifically excludes them. Where there is a reference to 'employees' in the Code, this indicates that only employees (within the strict meaning of the word) are affected by the particular provision.

REFERENCES IN THE CODE

1.25 In this Code, 'the Act' means the Equality Act 2010. References to particular Sections and Schedules of the Act are shown in the margins, abbreviated as 's' and 'Sch' respectively. Occasionally other legislation is also referenced in the margins.

CHANGES TO THE LAW

1.26 This Code refers to the provisions of the Equality Act 2010 that came into force on 1 October 2010. There may be subsequent changes to the Act or to other legislation which may have an effect on the duties explained in the Code.

1.27 The Act contains provisions on dual discrimination (also known as combined discrimination) and the new public sector equality duty. These provisions are not expected to come into force before April 2011. The government is considering how these provisions can be implemented in the best way for business and the public sector respectively.

1.28 Readers of this Code will therefore need to keep up to date with any developments that affect the Act's provisions and should be aware of the other Codes issued by the Commission. Further information can be obtained from the Commission (see below for contact details).

FURTHER INFORMATION

1.29 Copies of the Act and regulations made under it can be purchased from The Stationery Office. Separate codes covering other aspects of the Act are also available from The Stationery Office. The text of all the Equality and Human Rights Commission's codes (including this Code) and guidance relating to the codes can also be downloaded free of charge from the Commission's website where Word and PDF versions are also available: www.equalityhumanrights.com

1.30 *(Addresses and telephone numbers of the Equality and Human Right Commission have been omitted; see 'Useful Addresses' in Part 5 at* **[5.120]**.)

PART 1: CODE OF PRACTICE ON EMPLOYMENT

CHAPTER 2
PROTECTED CHARACTERISTICS

INTRODUCTION

[4.129]

2.1 This chapter outlines the characteristics which are protected under the Act and which are relevant to the areas covered by this Code.

2.2 The 'protected characteristics' are: age; disability; gender reassignment; marriage and civil partnership; pregnancy and maternity; race; religion or belief; sex; and sexual orientation.

AGE

What the Act says

2.3 [s 5(1)] Age is defined in the Act by reference to a person's age group. In relation to age, when the Act refers to people who share a protected characteristic, it means that they are in the same age group.

2.4 [s 5(2)] An age group can mean people of the same age or people of a range of ages. Age groups can be wide (for example, 'people under 50'; 'under 18s'). They can also be quite narrow (for example, 'people in their mid-40s'; 'people born in 1952'). Age groups may also be relative (for example, 'older than me' or 'older than us').

2.5 The meaning of certain age-related terms may differ according to the context. For example, whether someone is seen as 'youthful' can depend on their role: compare a youthful bartender with a youthful CEO. Age groups can also be linked to actual or assumed physical appearance, which may have little relationship with chronological age – for example, 'the grey workforce'.

2.6 There is some flexibility in the definition of a person's age group. For example, a 40 year old could be described as belonging to various age groups, including '40 year olds'; 'under 50s'; '35 to 45 year olds'; 'over 25s'; or 'middle-aged'. Similarly, a 16 year old could be seen as belonging to groups that include: 'children'; 'teenagers'; 'under 50s'; 'under 25s'; 'over 14s' or '16 year olds'.

Example: A female worker aged 25 could be viewed as sharing the protected characteristic of age with a number of different age groups. These might include '25 year olds'; 'the under 30s'; 'the over 20s'; and 'younger workers'.

Example: A man of 86 could be said to share the protected characteristic of age with the following age groups: '86 year olds'; 'over 80s'; 'over 65s'; 'pensioners'; 'senior citizens'; 'older people'; and 'the elderly'.

2.7 Where it is necessary to compare the situation of a person belonging to a particular age group with others, the Act does not specify the age group with which comparison should be made. It could be everyone outside the person's age group, but in many cases the choice of comparator age group will be more specific; this will often be led by the context and circumstances. (More detail on how to identify a comparator in direct discrimination cases is set out in paragraphs 3.22 to 3.31.)

Example: In the first example above, the 25 year old woman might compare herself to the 'over 25s', or 'over 35s', or 'older workers'. She could also compare herself to 'under 25s' or '18 year olds'.

DISABILITY

What the Act says

2.8 **[s 6, s 6(3)(b)]** Only a person who meets the Act's definition of disability has the protected characteristic of disability. When the Act refers to people who share a protected characteristic in relation to disability, it means they share the same disability.

2.9 [s 6(4)] In most circumstances, a person will have the protected characteristic of disability if they have had a disability in the past, even if they no longer have the disability.

2.10 People who currently have a disability are protected because of this characteristic against harassment and discrimination – including discrimination arising from disability (see Chapter 5) and a failure to comply with the duty to make reasonable adjustments (see Chapter 6). People who have had a disability in the past are also protected against harassment and discrimination (see paragraph 21.3).

2.11 Non-disabled people are protected against direct disability discrimination only where they are perceived to have a disability or are associated with a disabled person (see paragraphs 3.11 to 3.21). In some circumstances, a non-disabled person may be protected where they experience harassment (see Chapter 7) or some other unlawful act such as victimisation (see Chapter 9).

2.12 **[s 6(1)]** The Act says that a person has a disability if they have a physical or mental impairment which has a long-term and substantial adverse effect on their ability to carry out normal day-to-day activities. Physical or mental impairment includes sensory impairments such as those affecting sight or hearing.

2.13 **[Sch 1, para 3]** An impairment which consists of a severe disfigurement is treated as having a substantial adverse effect on the ability of the person concerned to carry out normal day-to-day activities.

2.14 **[Sch 1, para 2(1)]** Long-term means that the impairment has lasted or is likely to last for at least 12 months or for the rest of the affected person's life.

2.15 **[s 212(1)]** Substantial means more than minor or trivial.

2.16 **[Sch 1, para 5]** Where a person is taking measures to treat or correct an impairment (other than by using spectacles or contact lenses) and, but for those measures, the impairment would be likely to have a substantial adverse effect on the ability to carry out normal day to day activities, it is still to be treated as though it does have such an effect.

2.17 This means that 'hidden' impairments (for example, mental illness or mental health conditions, diabetes and epilepsy) may count as disabilities where they meet the definition in the Act.

2.18 **[Sch 1, para 6]** Cancer, HIV infection, and multiple sclerosis are deemed disabilities under the Act from the point of diagnosis. In some circumstances, people who have a sight impairment are automatically treated under the Act as being disabled.

2.19 **[Sch 1, paras 2(2) & 8]** Progressive conditions and those with fluctuating or recurring effects will amount to disabilities in certain circumstances.

2.20 For more on the concept of disability, see Appendix 1 to this Code. Guidance on matters to be taken into account in determining questions relating to the definition of disability is also available from the Office for Disability Issues:
www.officefordisability.gov.uk/docs/wor/new/ea-guide.pdf

GENDER REASSIGNMENT

What the Act says

2.21 [s 7(1)] The Act defines gender reassignment as a protected characteristic. People who are proposing to undergo, are undergoing, or have undergone a process (or part of a process) to reassign their sex by changing physiological or other attributes of sex have the protected characteristic of gender reassignment.

2.22 [s 7(2)] A reference to a transsexual person is a reference to a person who has the protected characteristic of gender reassignment.

2.23 Under the Act 'gender reassignment' is a personal process, that is, moving away from one's birth sex to the preferred gender, rather than a medical process.

2.24 The reassignment of a person's sex may be proposed but never gone through; the person may be in the process of reassigning their sex; or the process may have happened previously. It may include undergoing the medical gender reassignment treatments, but it does not require someone to undergo medical treatment in order to be protected.

Example: A person who was born physically female decides to spend the rest of his life as a man. He starts and continues to live as a man. He decides not to seek medical advice as he successfully passes as a man without the need for any medical intervention. He would be protected as someone who has the protected characteristic of gender reassignment.

2.25 The Act requires that a person should have at least proposed to undergo gender reassignment. It does not require such a proposal to be irrevocable. People who start the gender reassignment process but then decide to stop still have the protected characteristic of gender reassignment.

Example: A person born physically male lets her friends know that she intends to reassign her sex. She attends counselling sessions to start the process. However, she decides to go no further. She is protected under the law because she has undergone part of the process of reassigning her sex.

2.26 Protection is provided where, as part of the process of reassigning their sex, someone is driven by their gender identity to cross-dress, but not where someone chooses to cross-dress for some other reason.

2.27 In order to be protected under the Act, there is no requirement for a transsexual person to inform their employer of their gender reassignment status. However, if a worker is proposing to undergo gender reassignment or is still in the process of transitioning, they may want to discuss their needs with their employer so the employer can support them during the process.

Example: Before a formal dinner organised by his employer, a worker tells his colleagues that he intends to come to the event dressed as a woman 'for a laugh'. His manager tells him not to do this, as it would create a bad image of the company. Because the worker has no intention of undergoing gender reassignment, he would not have a claim for discrimination.

On the other hand, if the employer had said the same thing to a worker driven by their gender identity to cross-dress as a woman as part of the process of reassigning their sex, this could amount to direct discrimination because of gender reassignment.

2.28 Where an individual has been diagnosed as having 'Gender Dysphoria' or 'Gender Identity Disorder' and the condition has a substantial and long-term adverse impact on their ability to carry out normal day-to-day activities, they may also be protected under the disability discrimination provisions of the Act.

Gender recognition certificates

2.29 The Gender Recognition Act 2004 (GRA) provides that where a person holds a gender recognition certificate they must be treated according to their acquired gender (see the GRA for details on those who are covered by that Act; see also the Data Protection Act 1998 which deals with processing sensitive personal information).

2.30 Transsexual people should not be routinely asked to produce their gender recognition certificate as evidence of their legal gender. Such a request would compromise a transsexual person's right to privacy. If an employer requires proof of a person's legal gender, then their (new) birth certificate should be sufficient confirmation.

MARRIAGE AND CIVIL PARTNERSHIP

What the Act says

2.31 **[s 8(1)]** A person who is married or in a civil partnership has the protected characteristic of marriage and civil partnership.

2.32 Marriage will cover any formal union of a man and woman which is legally recognised in the UK as a marriage. A civil partnership refers to a registered civil partnership under the Civil Partnership Act 2004, including those registered outside the UK.

2.33 **[s 13(4)]** Only people who are married or in a civil partnership are protected against discrimination on this ground. The status of being unmarried or single is not protected. People who only intend to marry or form a civil partnership, or who have divorced or had their civil partnership dissolved, are not protected on this ground.

2.34 **[s 8(2)(b)]** People who are married or in a civil partnership share the same protected characteristic. For example, a married man and a woman in a civil partnership share the protected characteristic of marriage and civil partnership.

PREGNANCY AND MATERNITY

What the Act says

2.35 **[s 4; s 18(6)]** The Act lists pregnancy and maternity as a protected characteristic. It is unlawful for an employer to subject a woman to unfavourable treatment during the 'protected period' as defined by the Act. Pregnancy and maternity discrimination in the workplace is considered in detail in Chapter 8.

RACE

What the Act says

2.36 **[s 9(1)(a)–(c)]** The Act defines 'race' as including colour, nationality and ethnic or national origins.

2.37 **[s 9(2)]** A person has the protected characteristic of race if they fall within a particular racial group. A racial group can also be made up of two or more distinct racial groups. See paragraph 2.46 for the meaning of 'racial group'.

Nationality

2.38 Nationality (or citizenship) is the specific legal relationship between a person and a state through birth or naturalisation. It is distinct from national origins (see paragraph 2.43 below).

Ethnic origins

2.39 Everyone has an ethnic origin but the provisions of the Act only apply where a person belongs to an 'ethnic group' as defined by the courts. This means that the person must belong to an ethnic group which regards itself and is regarded by others as a distinct and separate community because of certain characteristics. These characteristics usually distinguish the group from the surrounding community.

2.40 There are two essential characteristics which an ethnic group must have: a long shared history and a cultural tradition of its own. In addition, an ethnic group may have one or more of the following characteristics: a common language; a common literature; a common religion; a common geographical origin; or being a minority; or an oppressed group.

2.41 An ethnic group or national group could include members new to the group, for example, a person who marries into the group. It is also possible for a person to leave an ethnic group.

2.42 The courts have confirmed that the following are protected ethnic groups: Sikhs, Jews, Romany Gypsies, Irish Travellers, Scottish Gypsies, and Scottish Travellers.

National origins

2.43 National origins must have identifiable elements, both historic and geographic, which at least at some point in time indicate the existence or previous existence of a nation. For example, as England and Scotland were once separate nations, the English and the Scots have separate national origins. National origins may include origins in a nation that no longer exists (for example, Czechoslovakia) or in a 'nation' that was never a nation state in the modern sense.

2.44 National origin is distinct from nationality. For example, people of Chinese national origin may be citizens of China but many are citizens of other countries.

2.45 A person's own national origin is not something that can be changed, though national origin can change through the generations.

Meaning of 'racial group'

2.46 [s 9(3)] A racial group is a group of people who have or share a colour, nationality or ethnic or national origins. For example, a racial group could be 'British' people. All racial groups are protected from unlawful discrimination under the Act.

2.47 A person may fall into more than one racial group. For example, a 'Nigerian' may be defined by colour, nationality or ethnic or national origin.

2.48 [s 9(4)] A racial group can be made up of two or more distinct racial groups. For example, a racial group could be 'black Britons' which would encompass those people who are both black and who are British citizens. Another racial group could be 'South Asian' which may include Indians, Pakistanis, Bangladeshis and Sri Lankans.

2.49 Racial groups can also be defined by exclusion, for example, those of 'non-British' nationality could form a single racial group.

RELIGION OR BELIEF

What the Act says

2.50 **[s 10(1) & (2)]** The protected characteristic of religion or belief includes any religion and any religious or philosophical belief. It also includes a lack of any such religion or belief.

2.51 For example, Christians are protected against discrimination because of their Christianity and non-Christians are protected against discrimination because they are not Christians, irrespective of any other religion or belief they may have or any lack of one.

2.52 The meaning of religion and belief in the Act is broad and is consistent with Article 9 of the European Convention on Human Rights (which guarantees freedom of thought, conscience and religion).

Meaning of religion

2.53 [s **10(1)**] 'Religion' means any religion and includes a lack of religion. The term 'religion' includes the more commonly recognised religions in the UK such as the Baha'i faith, Buddhism, Christianity, Hinduism, Islam, Jainism, Judaism, Rastafarianism, Sikhism and Zoroastrianism. It is for the courts to determine what constitutes a religion.

2.54 A religion need not be mainstream or well known to gain protection as a religion. However, it must have a clear structure and belief system. Denominations or sects within religions, such as Methodists within Christianity or Sunnis within Islam, may be considered a religion for the purposes of the Act.

Meaning of belief

2.55 [s **10(2)**] Belief means any religious or philosophical belief and includes a lack of belief.

2.56 'Religious belief' goes beyond beliefs about and adherence to a religion or its central articles of faith and may vary from person to person within the same religion.

2.57 A belief which is not a religious belief may be a philosophical belief. Examples of philosophical beliefs include Humanism and Atheism.

2.58 A belief need not include faith or worship of a God or Gods, but must affect how a person lives their life or perceives the world.

2.59 For a philosophical belief to be protected under the Act:

- it must be genuinely held;
- it must be a belief and not an opinion or viewpoint based on the present state of information available;
- it must be a belief as to a weighty and substantial aspect of human life and behaviour;
- it must attain a certain level of cogency, seriousness, cohesion and importance;
- it must be worthy of respect in a democratic society, not incompatible with human dignity and not conflict with the fundamental rights of others.

Example: A woman believes in a philosophy of racial superiority for a particular racial group. It is a belief around which she centres the important decisions in her life. This is not compatible with human dignity and conflicts with the fundamental rights of others. It would therefore not constitute a 'belief' for the purposes of the Act.

Manifestation of religion or belief

2.60 While people have an absolute right to hold a particular religion or belief under Article 9 of the European Convention on Human Rights, manifestation of that religion or belief is a qualified right which may in certain circumstances be limited. For example, it may need to be balanced against other Convention rights such as the right to respect for private and family life (Article 8) or the right to freedom of expression (Article 10).

2.61 Manifestations of a religion or belief could include treating certain days as days for worship or rest; following a certain dress code; following a particular diet; or carrying out or avoiding certain practices. There is not always a clear line between holding a religion or belief and the manifestation of that religion or belief. Placing limitations on a person's right to manifest their religion or belief may amount to unlawful discrimination; this would usually amount to indirect discrimination.

Example: An employer has a 'no headwear' policy for its staff. Unless this policy can be objectively justified, this will be indirect discrimination against Sikh men who wear the turban, Muslim women who wear a headscarf and observant Jewish men who wear a skullcap as manifestations of their religion.

SEX

What the Act says

2.62 **[ss 11(a) & (b), 212(1)]** Sex is a protected characteristic and refers to a male or female of any age. In relation to a group of people it refers to either men and/or boys, or women and/or girls.

2.63 A comparator for the purposes of showing sex discrimination will be a person of the opposite sex. Sex does not include gender reassignment (see paragraph 2.21) or sexual orientation (see paragraph 2.64).

SEXUAL ORIENTATION

What the Act says

2.64 **[s 12(1)]** Sexual orientation is a protected characteristic. It means a person's sexual orientation towards:

- persons of the same sex (that is, the person is a gay man or a lesbian);
- persons of the opposite sex (that is, the person is heterosexual); or
- persons of either sex (that is, the person is bisexual).

2.65 Sexual orientation relates to how people feel as well as their actions.

2.66 Sexual orientation discrimination includes discrimination because someone is of a particular sexual orientation, and it also covers discrimination connected with manifestations of that sexual orientation. These may include someone's appearance, the places they visit or the people they associate with.

2.67 **[s 12(2)]** When the Act refers to the protected characteristic of sexual orientation, it means the following:

- a reference to a person who has a particular protected characteristic is a reference to a person who is of a particular sexual orientation; and
- a reference to people who share a protected characteristic is a reference to people who are of the same sexual orientation.

2.68 Gender reassignment is a separate protected characteristic and unrelated to sexual orientation – despite a common misunderstanding that the two characteristics are related (see paragraph 2.21).

RESTRICTIONS ON PROTECTION UNDER THE ACT

2.69 For some protected characteristics, the Act does not provide protection in relation to all types of prohibited conduct.

- In relation to marriage and civil partnership, there is no protection from discrimination if a person is unmarried or single (see paragraph 2.33).
- For marriage and civil partnership, there is no protection from direct discrimination by association or perception (see paragraphs 3.18 and 3.21) or harassment (see paragraph 7.5). However, harassment related to civil partnership would amount to harassment related to sexual orientation.

- For pregnancy and maternity, there is no express protection from direct discrimination by association or perception (see paragraphs 3.18 and 3.21); indirect discrimination (see paragraph 4.1); or harassment (see paragraph 7.5). However, in these three situations, a worker may be protected under the sex discrimination provisions.
- Apart from discrimination by association or perception, protection from direct discrimination because of disability only applies to disabled people (see paragraph 3.35).
- Indirect disability discrimination and discrimination arising from disability only apply to disabled people (see Chapters 4 and 5).
- An employer is only under a duty to make reasonable adjustments for a disabled worker or an actual or potential disabled job applicant (see Chapter 6).

CHAPTER 3
DIRECT DISCRIMINATION

INTRODUCTION

[4.130]

3.1 This chapter explains what the Act says about direct discrimination in employment for all of the protected characteristics. It discusses how the requirement for a comparator may be met.

WHAT THE ACT SAYS

3.2 **[s 13(1)]** Direct discrimination occurs when a person treats another less favourably than they treat or would treat others because of a protected characteristic.

3.3 Direct discrimination is generally unlawful. However, it may be lawful in the following circumstances:

- **[s 13(2)]** where the protected characteristic is age, and the less favourable treatment can be justified as a proportionate means of achieving a legitimate aim (see paragraphs 3.36 to 3.41);
- **[s 13(3)]** in relation to the protected characteristic of disability, where a disabled person is treated more favourably than a non-disabled person (see paragraph 3.35);
- where the Act provides an express exception which permits directly discriminatory treatment that would otherwise be unlawful (see Chapters 12 to 14).

WHAT IS 'LESS FAVOURABLE' TREATMENT?

3.4 To decide whether an employer has treated a worker 'less favourably', a comparison must be made with how they have treated other workers or would have treated them in similar circumstances. If the employer's treatment of the worker puts the worker at a clear disadvantage compared with other workers, then it is more likely that the treatment will be less favourable: for example, where a job applicant is refused a job. Less favourable treatment could also involve being deprived of a choice or excluded from an opportunity.

Example: At a job interview, an applicant mentions she has a same sex partner. Although she is the most qualified candidate, the employer decides not to offer her the job. This decision treats her less favourably than the successful candidate, who is a heterosexual woman. If the less favourable treatment of the unsuccessful applicant is because of her sexual orientation, this would amount to direct discrimination.

3.5 The worker does not have to experience actual disadvantage (economic or otherwise) for the treatment to be less favourable. It is enough that the worker can reasonably say that they would have preferred not to be treated differently from the way the employer treated – or would have treated – another person.

Example: A female worker's appraisal duties are withdrawn while her male colleagues at the same grade continue to carry out appraisals. Although she was not demoted and did not suffer any financial disadvantage, she feels demeaned in the eyes of those she managed and in the eyes of her colleagues. The removal of her appraisal duties may be treating her less favourably than her male colleagues. If the less favourable treatment is because of her sex, this would amount to direct discrimination.

3.6 Under the Act, it is not possible for the employer to balance or eliminate less favourable treatment by offsetting it against more favourable treatment – for example, extra pay to make up for loss of job status.

Example: A saleswoman informs her employer that she intends to spend the rest of her life living as a man. As a result of this, she is demoted to a role without client contact. The employer increases her salary to make up for the loss of job status. Despite the increase in pay, the demotion will constitute less favourable treatment because of gender reassignment.

3.7 **[s 18]** For direct discrimination because of pregnancy and maternity, the test is whether the treatment is **unfavourable** rather than less favourable. There is no need for the woman to compare her treatment with that experienced by other workers (see Chapter 8).

Segregation

3.8 **[s 13(5)]** When the protected characteristic is race, deliberately segregating a worker or group of workers from others of a different race automatically amounts to less favourable treatment. There is no need to identify a comparator, because racial segregation is always discriminatory. But it must be a deliberate act or policy rather than a situation that has occurred inadvertently.

Example: A British marketing company which employs predominantly British staff recruits Polish nationals and seats them in a separate room nicknamed 'Little Poland'. The company argues that they have an unofficial policy of seating the Polish staff separately from British staff so that they can speak amongst themselves in their native language without disturbing the staff who speak English. This is segregation, as the company has a deliberate policy of separating staff because of race.

3.9 Segregation linked to other protected characteristics **may** be direct discrimination. However, it is necessary to show that it amounts to less favourable treatment.

SHARED PROTECTED CHARACTERISTICS

3.10 [**s 24(1)**] Direct discrimination can take place even though the employer and worker share the same protected characteristic giving rise to the less favourable treatment.

Example: A Muslim businessman decides not to recruit a Muslim woman as his personal assistant, even though she is the best qualified candidate. Instead he recruits a woman who has no particular religious or non-religious belief. He believes that this will create a better impression with clients and colleagues, who are mostly Christian or have no particular religious or non-religious belief. This could amount to direct discrimination because of religion or belief, even though the businessman shares the religion of the woman he has rejected.

'BECAUSE OF' A PROTECTED CHARACTERISTIC

3.11 'Because of' a protected characteristic has the same meaning as the phrase 'on grounds of' (a protected characteristic) in previous equality legislation. The new wording does not change the legal meaning of what amounts to direct discrimination. The characteristic needs to be a cause of the less favourable treatment, but does not need to be the only or even the main cause.

3.12 In some instances, the discriminatory basis of the treatment will be obvious from the treatment itself.

Example: If an employer were to state in a job advert 'Gypsies and Travellers need not apply', this could amount to direct discrimination because of race against a Gypsy or Traveller who might have been eligible to apply for the job but was deterred from doing so because of the statement in the advert. In this case, the discriminatory basis of the treatment is obvious from the treatment itself.

3.13 In other cases, the link between the protected characteristic and the treatment will be less clear and it will be necessary to look at why the employer treated the worker less favourably to determine whether this was because of a protected characteristic.

Example: During an interview, a job applicant informs the employer that he has multiple sclerosis. The applicant is unsuccessful and the employer offers the job to someone who does not have a disability. In this case, it will be necessary to look at why the employer did not offer the job to the unsuccessful applicant with multiple sclerosis to determine whether the less favourable treatment was because of his disability.

3.14 Direct discrimination is unlawful, no matter what the employer's motive or intention, and regardless of whether the less favourable treatment of the worker is conscious or unconscious. Employers may have prejudices that they do not even admit to themselves or may act out of good intentions – or simply be unaware that they are treating the worker differently because of a protected characteristic.

Example: An angling magazine produced by an all-male team does not recruit a female journalist. They are genuinely concerned that she would feel unhappy and uncomfortable in an all-male environment. Although they appear to be well-intentioned in their decision not to recruit her, this is likely to amount to direct sex discrimination.

3.15 Direct discrimination also includes less favourable treatment of a person based on a stereotype relating to a protected characteristic, whether or not the stereotype is accurate.

Example: An employer believes that someone's memory deteriorates with age. He assumes – wrongly – that a 60-year-old manager in his team can no longer be relied on to undertake her role competently. An opportunity for promotion arises, which he does not mention to the manager. The employer's conduct is influenced by a stereotyped view of the competence of 60 year olds. This is likely to amount to less favourable treatment because of age.

3.16 An employer cannot base their treatment on another criterion that is discriminatory – for example, where the treatment in question is based on a decision to follow a discriminatory external rule.

Example: A chemical company operates a voluntary redundancy scheme which provides enhanced terms to women aged 55 or older and men aged 60 or older. A woman of 56 is able to take advantage of the scheme and leave on enhanced terms but a man of 56 cannot do this. The company argues that their scheme is based on the original state pension age of 60 for women and 65 for men. The scheme discriminates because of sex against the male workers. The company cannot rely on an external policy which is itself discriminatory to excuse this discrimination, even though that external policy in this case may be lawful.

3.17 A worker experiencing less favourable treatment 'because of' a protected characteristic does not have to possess the characteristic themselves. For example, the person might be associated with someone who has the characteristic ('discrimination by association'); or the person might be wrongly perceived as having the characteristic ('discrimination by perception').

Discrimination by association

3.18 It is direct discrimination if an employer treats a worker less favourably because of the worker's association with another person who has a protected characteristic; however, this does not apply to marriage and civil partnership or pregnancy and maternity. In the case of pregnancy and maternity, a worker treated less favourably because of association with a pregnant woman, or a woman who has recently given birth, may have a claim for sex discrimination.

3.19 Discrimination by association can occur in various ways – for example, where the worker has a relationship of parent, son or daughter, partner, carer or friend of someone with a protected characteristic. The association with the other person need not be a permanent one.

Example: A lone father caring for a disabled son has to take time off work whenever his son is sick or has medical appointments. The employer appears to resent the fact that the worker needs to care for his son and eventually dismisses him. The dismissal may amount to direct disability discrimination against the worker by association with his son.

Example: A manager treats a worker (who is heterosexual) less favourably because she has been seen out with a person who is gay. This could be direct sexual orientation discrimination against the worker because of her association with this person.

3.20 Direct discrimination because of a protected characteristic could also occur if a worker is treated less favourably because they campaigned to help someone with a particular protected characteristic or refused to act in a way that would disadvantage a person or people who have (or whom the employer believes to have) the characteristic. The provisions of the Act on instructing, causing or inducing discrimination may also be relevant here (see paragraphs 9.16 to 9.24).

Example: An employer does not short-list an internal applicant for a job because the applicant – who is not disabled himself – has helped to set up an informal staff network for disabled workers. This could amount to less favourable treatment because of disability.

Discrimination by perception

3.21 It is also direct discrimination if an employer treats a worker less favourably because the employer mistakenly thinks that the worker has a protected characteristic. However, this does not apply to pregnancy and maternity or marriage and civil partnership.

Example: An employer rejects a job application form from a white woman whom he wrongly thinks is black, because the applicant has an African-sounding name. This would constitute direct race discrimination based on the employer's mistaken perception.

Example: A masculine-looking woman applies for a job as a sales representative. The sales manager thinks that she is transsexual because of her appearance and does not offer her the job, even though she performed the best at interview. The woman would have a claim for direct discrimination because of perceived gender reassignment, even though she is not in fact transsexual.

COMPARATORS

3.22 **[s 13(1)]** In most circumstances direct discrimination requires that the employer's treatment of the worker is less favourable than the way the employer treats, has treated or would treat another worker to whom the protected characteristic does not apply. This other person is referred to as a 'comparator'. However, no comparator is needed in cases of racial segregation (see paragraph 3.8) or pregnancy and maternity discrimination (see paragraph 3.7 and Chapter 8).

Who will be an appropriate comparator?

3.23 **[s 23(1)]** The Act says that, in comparing people for the purpose of direct discrimination, there must be no material difference between the circumstances relating to each case. However, it is not necessary for the circumstances of the two people (that is, the worker and the comparator) to be identical in every way; what matters is that the circumstances which are relevant to the treatment of the worker are the same or nearly the same for the worker and the comparator.

Example: When an employer has a vacancy for an IT supervisor, both the senior IT workers apply for promotion to the post. One of them is Scottish and the other is English. Both are of a similar age, have no disability, are male, heterosexual, and are non-practising Christians. However, the English worker has more experience than his Scottish counterpart. When the Scottish man is promoted, the English worker alleges direct race discrimination because of his national origin. In this case, the comparator's circumstances are sufficiently similar to enable a valid comparison to be made.

Example: The head office of a Japanese company seconds a limited number of staff from Japan to work for its UK subsidiary, alongside locally recruited UK staff. One of these local workers complains that his salary and benefits are lower than those of a secondee from Japan employed at the same grade. Although the two workers are working for the same company at the same grade, the circumstances of the Japanese secondee are materially different. He has been recruited in Japan, reports at least in part to the Japanese parent company, has a different career path and his salary and benefits reflect the fact that he is working abroad. For these reasons, he would not be a suitable comparator.

Hypothetical comparators

3.24 In practice it is not always possible to identify an actual person whose relevant circumstances are the same or not materially different, so the comparison will need to be made with a hypothetical comparator.

3.25 In some cases a person identified as an actual comparator turns out to have circumstances that are not materially the same. Nevertheless their treatment may help to construct a hypothetical comparator.

Example: A person who has undergone gender reassignment works in a restaurant. She makes a mistake on the till, resulting in a small financial loss to her employer, because of which she is dismissed. The situation has not arisen before, so there is no actual comparator. But six months earlier, the employer gave a written warning to another worker for taking home items of food without permission. That person's treatment might be used as evidence that the employer would not have dismissed a hypothetical worker who is not transsexual for making a till error.

3.26 Constructing a hypothetical comparator may involve considering elements of the treatment of several people whose circumstances are similar to those of the claimant, but not the same. Looking at these elements together, an Employment Tribunal may conclude that the claimant was less favourably treated than a hypothetical comparator would have been treated.

Example: An employer dismissed a worker at the end of her probation period because she had lied on one occasion. While accepting she had lied, the worker explained that this was because the employer had undermined her confidence and put her under pressure. In the absence of an actual comparator, the worker compared her treatment to two male comparators; one had behaved dishonestly but had not been dismissed, and the other had passed his probation in spite of his performance being undermined by unfair pressure from the employer. Elements of the treatment of these two comparators could allow a tribunal to construct a hypothetical comparator showing the worker had been treated less favourably because of sex.

3.27 Who could be a hypothetical comparator may also depend on the reason why the employer treated the claimant as they did. In many cases it may be more straightforward for the Employment Tribunal to establish the reason for the claimant's treatment first. This could include considering the employer's treatment of a person whose circumstances are not the same as the claimant's to shed light on the reason why that person was treated in the way they were. If the reason for the treatment is found to be because of a protected characteristic, a comparison with the treatment of hypothetical comparator(s) can then be made.

Example: After a dispute over an unreasonably harsh performance review carried out by his line manager, a worker of Somali origin was subjected to disciplinary proceedings by a second manager which he believes were inappropriate and unfair. He makes a claim for direct race discrimination. An Employment Tribunal might first of all look at the reason for the atypical conduct of the two managers, to establish whether it was because of race. If this is found to be the case, they would move on to consider whether the worker was treated less favourably than hypothetical comparator(s) would have been treated.

3.28 Another way of looking at this is to ask, 'But for the relevant protected characteristic, would the claimant have been treated in that way?'

Comparators in disability cases

3.29 **[s 23(2)(a)]** The comparator for direct disability discrimination is the same as for other types of direct discrimination. However, for disability, the relevant circumstances of the comparator and the disabled person, including their abilities, must not be materially different. An appropriate comparator will be a person who does not have the disabled person's impairment but who has the same abilities or skills as the disabled person (regardless of whether those abilities or skills arise from the disability itself).

3.30 It is important to focus on those circumstances which are, in fact, relevant to the less favourable treatment. Although in some cases, certain abilities may be the result of the disability itself, these may not be relevant circumstances for comparison purposes.

Example: A disabled man with arthritis who can type at 30 words per minute applies for an administrative job which includes typing, but is rejected on the grounds that his typing is too slow. The correct comparator in a claim for direct discrimination would be a person without arthritis who has the same typing speed with the same accuracy rate. In this case, the disabled man is unable to lift heavy weights, but this is not a requirement of the job he applied for. As it is not relevant to the circumstances, there is no need for him to identify a comparator who cannot lift heavy weights.

Comparators in sexual orientation cases

3.31 **[s 23(3)]** For sexual orientation, the Act says that the fact that one person is a civil partner while another is married is not a material difference between the circumstances relating to each case.

Example: A worker who is gay and in a civil partnership complains that he was refused promotion because of his sexual orientation. His married colleague is promoted instead. The fact that the worker is in a civil partnership and the colleague is married will not be a material difference in their circumstances, so he would be able to refer to his married colleague as a comparator in this case.

ADVERTISING AN INTENTION TO DISCRIMINATE

3.32 If an employer makes a statement in an advertisement that in offering employment they will treat applicants less favourably because of a protected characteristic, this would amount to direct discrimination. Only people who are eligible to apply for the job in question can make a claim for discrimination under the Act.

Example: A marketing company places an advert on its web site offering jobs to 'young graduates'. This could be construed as advertising an intention to discriminate because of age. An older graduate who is put off applying for the post, even though they are eligible to do so, could claim direct discrimination.

3.33 The question of whether an advertisement is discriminatory depends on whether a reasonable person would consider it to be so. An advertisement can include a notice or circular, whether to the public or not, in any publication, on radio, television or in cinemas, via the internet or at an exhibition.

Example: A dress manufacturing company places an advertisement in a local newspaper for a Turkish machinist. A reasonable person would probably view this as advertising an intention to discriminate because of race.

MARRIAGE AND CIVIL PARTNERSHIP

3.34 **[s 13(4); s 8(2)]** In relation to employment, if the protected characteristic is marriage and civil partnership, direct discrimination only covers less favourable treatment of a worker because the worker themselves is married or a civil partner. Single people and people in relationships outside of marriage or civil partnership (whether or not they are cohabiting), are not protected from direct discrimination because of their status.

Example: An employer offers 'death in service' benefits to the spouses and civil partners of their staff members. A worker who lives with her partner, but is not married to him, wants to nominate him for death in service benefits. She is told she cannot do this as she is not married. Because being a cohabitee is not a protected characteristic, she would be unable to make a claim for discrimination.

WHEN IS IT LAWFUL TO TREAT A PERSON MORE FAVOURABLY?

More favourable treatment of disabled people

3.35 **[s 13(3)]** In relation to disability discrimination, the Act only protects disabled people, so it is not discrimination to treat a disabled person more favourably than a non-disabled person.

Example: An employer with 60 staff has no disabled workers. When they advertise for a new office administrator, they guarantee all disabled applicants an interview for the post. This would not amount to direct discrimination because of disability.

Justifiable direct discrimination because of age

3.36 **[s 13(2)]** A different approach applies to the protected characteristic of age, because some age-based rules and practices are seen as justifiable. Less favourable treatment of a person because of their age is not direct discrimination if the employer can show the treatment is a proportionate means of achieving a legitimate aim. This is often called the 'objective justification test'.

3.37 In considering direct discrimination because of age, it is important to distinguish a rule or practice affecting workers in a particular age group from a neutral provision, criterion or practice applied equally to everyone that may give rise to indirect discrimination (see paragraph 4.6).

3.38 The objective justification test, which also applies to other areas of discrimination law, is explained in more detail in paragraphs 4.25 to 4.32.

3.39 The question of whether an age-based rule or practice is 'objectively justified' – that is, a proportionate means of achieving a legitimate aim – should be approached in two stages:

- First, is the aim of the rule or practice legal and non-discriminatory, and one that represents a real, objective consideration?
- Second, if the aim is legitimate, is the means of achieving it proportionate – that is, appropriate and necessary in all the circumstances?

3.40 The following is an illustration of an age-based rule that might well satisfy the objective justification test.

Example: A building company has a policy of not employing under-18s on its more hazardous building sites. The aim behind this policy is to protect young people from health and safety risks associated with their lack of experience and less developed physical strength. This aim is supported by accident statistics for younger workers on building sites and is likely to be a legitimate one. Imposing an age threshold of 18 would probably be a proportionate means of achieving the aim if this is supported by the evidence. Had the threshold been set at 25, the proportionality test would not necessarily have been met.

3.41 The following examples illustrate age-based rules that would probably fail the objective justification test.

Example: A haulage company introduces a blanket policy forcing its drivers to stop driving articulated lorries at 55, because statistical evidence suggests an increased risk of heart attacks over this age. The aim of public safety would be a legitimate one which is supported by evidence of risk. However, the company would have to show that its blanket ban was a proportionate means of achieving this objective. This might be difficult, as medical checks for individual drivers could offer a less discriminatory means of achieving the same aim.

Example: A fashion retailer rejects a middle-aged woman as a sales assistant on the grounds that she is 'too old' for the job. They tell her that they need to attract the young customer base at which their clothing is targeted. If this corresponds to a real business need on the part of the retailer, it could qualify as a legitimate aim. However, rejecting this middle-aged woman is unlikely to be a proportionate means of achieving this aim; a requirement for all sales assistants to have knowledge of the products and fashion awareness would be a less discriminatory means of making sure the aim is achieved.

Occupational requirements

3.42 **[Sch 9, para 1]** The Act creates a general exception to the prohibition on direct discrimination in employment for occupational requirements that are genuinely needed for the job. See Chapter 13 for details.

CHAPTER 4
INDIRECT DISCRIMINATION

INTRODUCTION

[4.131]

4.1 This chapter explains indirect discrimination and 'objective justification'. The latter concept applies to indirect discrimination, direct discrimination because of age, discrimination arising from disability and to some of the exceptions permitted by the Act.

4.2 Indirect discrimination applies to all the protected characteristics apart from pregnancy and maternity (although, in pregnancy and maternity situations, indirect sex discrimination may apply).

WHAT THE ACT SAYS

4.3 **[s 19(1) & (2)]** Indirect discrimination may occur when an employer applies an apparently neutral provision, criterion or practice which puts workers sharing a protected characteristic at a particular disadvantage.

4.4 **[s 19(2)]** For indirect discrimination to take place, four requirements must be met:

- the employer applies (or would apply) the provision, criterion or practice equally to everyone within the relevant group including a particular worker;
- the provision, criterion or practice puts, or would put, people who share the worker's protected characteristic at a particular disadvantage when compared with people who do not have that characteristic;
- the provision, criterion or practice puts, or would put, the worker at that disadvantage; and
- the employer cannot show that the provision, criterion or practice is a proportionate means of achieving a legitimate aim.

WHAT CONSTITUTES A PROVISION, CRITERION OR PRACTICE?

4.5 The first stage in establishing indirect discrimination is to identify the relevant provision, criterion or practice. The phrase 'provision, criterion or practice' is not defined by the Act but it should be construed widely so as to include, for example, any formal or informal policies, rules, practices, arrangements, criteria, conditions, prerequisites, qualifications or provisions. A provision, criterion or practice may also include decisions to do something in the future – such as a policy or criterion that has not yet been applied – as well as a 'one-off' or discretionary decision.

Example: A factory owner announces that from next month staff cannot wear their hair in dreadlocks, even if the locks are tied back. This is an example of a policy that has not yet been implemented but which still amounts to a provision, criterion or practice. The decision to introduce the policy could be indirectly discriminatory because of religion or belief, as it puts the employer's Rastafarian workers at a particular disadvantage. The employer must show that the provision, criterion or practice can be objectively justified.

Is the provision, criterion or practice a neutral one?

4.6 The provision, criterion or practice must be applied to everyone in the relevant group, whether or not they have the protected characteristic in question. On the face of it, the provision, criterion or practice must be neutral. If it is not neutral in this way, but expressly applies to people with a specific protected characteristic, it is likely to amount to direct discrimination.

Example: A bus company adopts a policy that all female drivers must re-sit their theory and practical tests every five years to retain their category D licence. Such a policy would amount to direct discrimination because of sex. In contrast, another bus company adopts a policy that drivers on two particular routes must re-sit the theory test. Although this provision is apparently neutral, it turns out that the drivers on these two routes are nearly all women. This could amount to indirect sex discrimination unless the policy can be objectively justified.

WHAT DOES 'WOULD PUT' MEAN?

4.7 **[s 19(2)(b)]** It is a requirement of the Act that the provision, criterion or practice puts **or would put** people who share the worker's protected characteristic at a particular disadvantage when compared with people who do not have that characteristic. The Act also requires that it puts **or would put** the particular worker at that disadvantage. This allows challenges to provisions, criteria or practices which have not yet been applied but which would have a discriminatory effect if they were.

4.8 **[s 19(2)(c)]** However, for a claim of indirect discrimination to succeed, the worker must show that they would experience a disadvantage if the provision, criterion or practice were applied to them.

Example: The contracts for senior buyers at a department store have a mobility clause requiring them to travel at short notice to any part of the world. A female senior buyer with young children considers that the mobility clause puts women at a disadvantage as they are more likely to be the carers of children and so less likely to be able to travel abroad at short notice. She may challenge the mobility clause even though she has not yet been asked to travel abroad at short notice.

By contrast, a female manager in customer services at the same store might agree that the mobility clause discriminates against women – but, as she is not a senior buyer, she cannot challenge the clause.

WHAT IS A DISADVANTAGE?

4.9 'Disadvantage' is not defined by the Act. It could include denial of an opportunity or choice, deterrence, rejection or exclusion. The courts have found that 'detriment', a similar concept, is something that a reasonable person would complain about – so an unjustified sense of grievance would not qualify. A disadvantage does not have to be quantifiable and the worker does not have to experience actual loss (economic or otherwise). It is enough that the worker can reasonably say that they would have preferred to be treated differently.

4.10 Sometimes, a provision, criterion or practice is intrinsically liable to disadvantage a group with a particular protected characteristic.

Example: At the end of the year, an employer decides to invite seasonal workers employed during the previous summer to claim a bonus within a 30 day time limit. By writing to these workers at their last known address, the employer is liable to disadvantage migrant workers. This is because these workers normally return to their home country during the winter months, and so they are unlikely to apply for the bonus within the specified period. This could amount to indirect race discrimination, unless the practice can be objectively justified.

4.11 In some situations, the link between the protected characteristic and the disadvantage might be obvious; for example, dress codes create a disadvantage for some workers with particular religious beliefs. In other situations it will be less obvious how people sharing a protected characteristic are put (or would be put) at a disadvantage, in which case statistics or personal testimony may help to demonstrate that a disadvantage exists.

Example: A hairdresser refuses to employ stylists who cover their hair, believing it is important for them to exhibit their flamboyant haircuts. It is clear that this criterion puts at a particular disadvantage both Muslim women and Sikh men who cover their hair. This may amount to indirect discrimination unless the criterion can be objectively justified.

Example: A consultancy firm reviews the use of psychometric tests in their recruitment procedures and discovers that men tend to score lower than women. If a man complains that the test is indirectly discriminatory, he would not need to explain the reason for the lower scores or how the lower scores are connected to his sex to show that men have been put at a disadvantage; it is sufficient for him to rely on the statistical information.

4.12 Statistics can provide an insight into the link between the provision, criterion or practice and the disadvantage that it causes. Statistics relating to the workplace in question can be obtained through the questions procedure (see paragraphs 15.5 to 15.10). It may also be possible to use national or regional statistics to throw light on the nature and extent of the particular disadvantage.

4.13 However, a statistical analysis may not always be appropriate or practicable, especially when there is inadequate or unreliable information, or the numbers of people are too small to allow for a statistically significant comparison. In this situation, the Employment Tribunal may find it helpful for an expert to provide evidence as to whether there is any disadvantage and, if so, the nature of it.

4.14 There are other cases where it may be useful to have evidence (including, if appropriate, from an expert) to help the Employment Tribunal to understand the nature of the protected characteristic or the behaviour of the group sharing the characteristic – for example, evidence about the principles of a particular religious belief.

Example: A Muslim man who works for a small manufacturing company wishes to undertake the Hajj. However, his employer only allows their staff to take annual leave during designated shutdown periods in August and December. The worker considers that he has been subjected to indirect religious discrimination. In assessing the case, the Employment Tribunal may benefit from expert evidence from a Muslim cleric or an expert in Islam on the timing of the Hajj and whether it is of significance.

THE COMPARATIVE APPROACH

4.15 **[s 19(2)(b); s 23(1)]** Once it is clear that there is a provision, criterion or practice which puts (or would put) people sharing a protected characteristic at a particular disadvantage, then the next stage is to consider a comparison between workers with the protected characteristic and those without it. The circumstances of the two groups must be sufficiently similar for a comparison to be made and there must be no material differences in circumstances.

4.16 It is important to be clear which protected characteristic is relevant. In relation to disability, this would not be disabled people as a whole but people with a particular disability – for example, with an equivalent level of visual impairment. For race, it could be all Africans or only Somalis, for example. For age, it is important to identify the age group that is disadvantaged by the provision, criterion or practice.

Example: If an employer were to advertise a position requiring at least five GCSEs at grades A to C without permitting any equivalent qualifications, this criterion would put at a particular disadvantage everyone born before 1971, as they are more likely to have taken O level examinations rather than GCSEs. This might be indirect age discrimination if the criterion could not be objectively justified.

The 'pool for comparison'

4.17 The people used in the comparative exercise are usually referred to as the 'pool for comparison'.

4.18 In general, the pool should consist of the group which the provision, criterion or practice affects (or would affect) either positively or negatively, while excluding workers who are not affected by it, either positively or negatively. In most situations, there is likely to be only one appropriate pool, but there may be circumstances where there is more than one. If this is the case, the Employment Tribunal will decide which of the pools to consider.

Example: A marketing company employs 45 women, 10 of whom are part-timers, and 55 men who all work full-time. One female receptionist works Mondays, Wednesdays and Thursdays. The annual leave policy requires that all workers take time off on public holidays, at least half of which fall on a Monday every year. The receptionist argues that the policy is indirectly discriminatory against women and that it puts her at a personal disadvantage because she has proportionately less control over when she can take her annual leave. The appropriate pool for comparison is all the workers affected by the annual leave policy. The pool is not all receptionists or all part-time workers, because the policy does not only affect these groups.

Making the comparison

4.19 Looking at the pool, a comparison must be made between the impact of the provision, criterion or practice on people **without** the relevant protected characteristic, and its impact on people **with** the protected characteristic.

4.20 The way that the comparison is carried out will depend on the circumstances, including the protected characteristic concerned. It may in some circumstances be necessary to carry out a formal comparative exercise using statistical evidence.

Carrying out a formal comparative exercise

4.21 If the Employment Tribunal is asked to undertake a formal comparative exercise to decide an indirect discrimination claim, it can do this in a number of ways. One established approach involves the Employment Tribunal asking these questions:

- What proportion of the pool has the particular protected characteristic?
- Within the pool, does the provision, criterion or practice affect workers without the protected characteristic?
- How many of these workers are (or would be) disadvantaged by it? How is this expressed as a proportion ('x')?
- Within the pool, how does the provision, criterion or practice affect people who share the protected characteristic?
- How many of these workers are (or would be) put at a disadvantage by it? How is this expressed as a proportion ('y')?

4.22 Using this approach, the Employment Tribunal will then compare (x) with (y). It can then decide whether the group with the protected characteristic experiences a 'particular disadvantage' in comparison with others. Whether a difference is significant will depend on the context, such as the size of the pool and the numbers behind the proportions. It is not necessary to show that the majority of those within the pool who share the protected characteristic are placed at a disadvantage.

Example: A single mother of two young children is forced to resign from her job as a train driver when she cannot comply with her employer's new shift system.

The shift system is a provision, criterion or practice which causes particular disadvantage to this single mother. In an indirect discrimination claim, an Employment Tribunal must carry out a comparative exercise to decide whether the shift system puts (or would put) workers who share her protected characteristic of sex at a particular disadvantage when compared with men.

The Employment Tribunal decides to use as a pool for comparison all the train drivers working for the same employer. There are 20 female train drivers, while 2,000 are men.

It is accepted as common knowledge that men are far less likely than women to be single parents with childcare responsibilities.

- Of the 2,000 male drivers, two are unable to comply with the new shift system. This is expressed as a proportion of 0.001
- Of the 20 female train drivers, five are unable to comply with the new shift system. This is expressed as a proportion of 0.25

It is clear that a higher proportion of female drivers (0.25) than male drivers (0.001) are unable to comply with the shift system.

Taking all this into account, the Employment Tribunal decides that female train drivers – in comparison to their male counterparts – are put at a particular disadvantage by the shift system.

IS THE WORKER CONCERNED PUT AT THAT DISADVANTAGE?

4.23 It is not enough that the provision, criterion or practice puts (or would put) at a particular disadvantage a group of people who share a protected characteristic. It must also have that effect (or be capable of having it) on the individual worker concerned. So it is not enough for a worker merely to establish that they are a member of the relevant group. They must also show they have personally suffered (or could suffer) the particular disadvantage as an individual.

Example: An airline operates a dress code which forbids workers in customer-facing roles from displaying any item of jewellery. A Sikh cabin steward complains that this policy indirectly discriminates against Sikhs by preventing them from wearing the Kara bracelet. However, because he no longer observes the Sikh articles of faith, the steward is not put at a particular disadvantage by this policy and could not bring a claim for indirect discrimination.

THE INTENTION BEHIND THE PROVISION, CRITERION OR PRACTICE IS IRRELEVANT

4.24 Indirect discrimination is unlawful, even where the discriminatory effect of the provision, criterion or practice is not intentional, unless it can be objectively justified. If an employer applies the provision,

Part 4 Statutory Codes of Practice

criterion or practice without the intention of discriminating against the worker, the Employment Tribunal may decide not to order a payment of compensation (see paragraph 15.44).

Example: An employer starts an induction session for new staff with an ice-breaker designed to introduce everyone in the room to the others. Each worker is required to provide a picture of themselves as a toddler. One worker is a transsexual woman who does not wish her colleagues to know that she was brought up as a boy. When she does not bring in her photo, the employer criticises her in front of the group for not joining in. It would be no defence that it did not occur to the employer that this worker may feel disadvantaged by the requirement to disclose such information.

WHEN CAN A PROVISION, CRITERION OR PRACTICE BE OBJECTIVELY JUSTIFIED?

4.25 **[s 19(2)(d)]** If the person applying a provision, criterion or practice can show that it is 'a proportionate means of achieving a legitimate aim', then it will not amount to indirect discrimination. This is often known as the 'objective justification' test. The test applies to other areas of discrimination law; for example, direct discrimination because of age (see paragraphs 3.36 to 3.41) and discrimination arising from disability (see Chapter 5).

4.26 If challenged in the Employment Tribunal, it is for the employer to justify the provision, criterion or practice. So it is up to the employer to produce evidence to support their assertion that it is justified. Generalisations will not be sufficient to provide justification. It is not necessary for that justification to have been fully set out at the time the provision, criterion or practice was applied. If challenged, the employer can set out the justification to the Employment Tribunal.

4.27 The question of whether the provision, criterion or practice is a proportionate means of achieving a legitimate aim should be approached in two stages:

- Is the aim of the provision, criterion or practice legal and non-discriminatory, and one that represents a real, objective consideration?
- If the aim is legitimate, is the means of achieving it proportionate – that is, appropriate and necessary in all the circumstances?

What is a legitimate aim?

4.28 The concept of 'legitimate aim' is taken from European Union (EU) law and relevant decisions of the Court of Justice of the European Union (CJEU) – formerly the European Court of Justice (ECJ). However, it is not defined by the Act. The aim of the provision, criterion or practice should be legal, should not be discriminatory in itself, and must represent a real, objective consideration. The health, welfare and safety of individuals may qualify as legitimate aims provided that risks are clearly specified and supported by evidence.

4.29 Although reasonable business needs and economic efficiency may be legitimate aims, an employer solely aiming to reduce costs cannot expect to satisfy the test. For example, the employer cannot simply argue that to discriminate is cheaper than avoiding discrimination.

Example: Solely as a cost-saving measure, an employer requires all staff to work a full day on Fridays, so that customer orders can all be processed on the same day of the week. The policy puts observant Jewish workers at a particular disadvantage in the winter months by preventing them from going home early to observe the Sabbath, and could amount to indirect discrimination unless it can be objectively justified. The single aim of reducing costs is not a legitimate one; the employer cannot just argue that to discriminate is cheaper than avoiding discrimination.

What is proportionate?

4.30 Even if the aim is a legitimate one, the means of achieving it must be proportionate. Deciding whether the means used to achieve the legitimate aim are proportionate involves a balancing exercise. An Employment Tribunal may wish to conduct a proper evaluation of the discriminatory effect of the provision, criterion or practice as against the employer's reasons for applying it, taking into account all the relevant facts.

4.31 Although not defined by the Act, the term 'proportionate' is taken from EU Directives and its meaning has been clarified by decisions of the CJEU (formerly the ECJ). EU law views treatment as proportionate if it is an 'appropriate and necessary' means of achieving a legitimate aim. But 'necessary' does not mean that the provision, criterion or practice is the only possible way of achieving the legitimate aim; it is sufficient that the same aim could not be achieved by less discriminatory means.

4.32 The greater financial cost of using a less discriminatory approach cannot, by itself, provide a justification for applying a particular provision, criterion or practice. Cost can only be taken into account as part of the employer's justification for the provision, criterion or practice if there are other good reasons for adopting it.

Example: A food manufacturer has a rule that beards are forbidden for people working on the factory floor. Unless it can be objectively justified, this rule may amount to indirect religion or belief discrimination against the Sikh and Muslim workers in the factory. If the aim of the rule is to meet food hygiene or health and safety requirements, this would be legitimate. However, the employer would need to show that the ban on beards is a proportionate means of achieving this aim. When considering whether the policy is justified, the Employment Tribunal is likely to examine closely the reasons given by the employer as to why they cannot fulfil the same food hygiene or health and safety obligations by less discriminatory means, for example by providing a beard mask or snood.

CHAPTER 5
DISCRIMINATION ARISING FROM DISABILITY

INTRODUCTION

[4.132]

5.1 This chapter explains the duty of employers not to treat disabled people unfavourably because of something connected with their disability. Protection from this type of discrimination, which is known as 'discrimination arising from disability', only applies to disabled people.

WHAT THE ACT SAYS

5.2 **[s 15]** The Act says that treatment of a disabled person amounts to discrimination where:

- an employer treats the disabled person unfavourably;
- this treatment is because of something arising in consequence of the disabled person's disability; and
- the employer cannot show that this treatment is a proportionate means of achieving a legitimate aim,

[s 15(2)] unless the employer does not know, and could not reasonably be expected to know, that the person has the disability.

How does it differ from direct discrimination?

5.3 Direct discrimination occurs when the employer treats someone less favourably because of disability itself (see Chapter 3). By contrast, in discrimination arising from disability, the question is whether the disabled person has been treated unfavourably because of something arising in consequence of their disability.

Example: An employer dismisses a worker because she has had three months' sick leave. The employer is aware that the worker has multiple sclerosis and most of her sick leave is disability-related. The employer's decision to dismiss is not because of the worker's disability itself. However, the worker has been treated unfavourably because of something arising in consequence of her disability (namely, the need to take a period of disability-related sick leave).

How does it differ from indirect discrimination?

5.4 Indirect discrimination occurs when a disabled person is (or would be) disadvantaged by an unjustifiable provision, criterion or practice applied to everyone, which puts (or would put) people sharing the disabled person's disability at a particular disadvantage compared to others, and puts (or would put) the disabled person at that disadvantage (see Chapter 4).

5.5 In contrast, discrimination arising from disability only requires the disabled person to show they have experienced unfavourable treatment because of something connected with their disability. If the employer can show that they did not know and could not reasonably have been expected to know that the disabled person had the disability, it will not be discrimination arising from disability (see paragraphs 5.13 to 5.19). However, as with indirect discrimination, the employer may avoid discrimination arising from disability if the treatment can be objectively justified as a proportionate means of achieving a legitimate aim (see paragraph 5.11)

Is a comparator required?

5.6 Both direct and indirect discrimination require a comparative exercise. But in considering discrimination arising from disability, there is no need to compare a disabled person's treatment with that of another person. It is only necessary to demonstrate that the unfavourable treatment is because of something arising in consequence of the disability.

Example: In considering whether the example of the disabled worker dismissed for disability-related sickness absence (see paragraph 5.3) amounts to discrimination arising from disability, it is irrelevant whether or not other workers would have been dismissed for having the same or similar length of absence. It is not necessary to compare the treatment of the disabled worker with that of her colleagues or any hypothetical comparator.

The decision to dismiss her will be discrimination arising from disability if the employer cannot objectively justify it.

WHAT IS 'UNFAVOURABLE TREATMENT'?

5.7 **[s 15(1)(a)]** For discrimination arising from disability to occur, a disabled person must have been treated 'unfavourably'. This means that he or she must have been put at a disadvantage. Often, the disadvantage will be obvious and it will be clear that the treatment has been unfavourable; for example, a person may have been refused a job, denied a work opportunity or dismissed from their employment. But sometimes unfavourable treatment may be less obvious. Even if an employer thinks that they are acting in the best interests of a disabled person, they may still treat that person unfavourably.

WHAT DOES 'SOMETHING ARISING IN CONSEQUENCE OF DISABILITY' MEAN?

5.8 **[s 15(1)(a)]** The unfavourable treatment must be because of something that arises in consequence of the disability. This means that there must be a connection between whatever led to the unfavourable treatment and the disability.

5.9 The consequences of a disability include anything which is the result, effect or outcome of a disabled person's disability. The consequences will be varied, and will depend on the individual effect upon a disabled person of their disability. Some consequences may be obvious, such as an inability to walk unaided or inability to use certain work equipment. Others may not be obvious, for example, having to follow a restricted diet.

Example: A woman is disciplined for losing her temper at work. However, this behaviour was out of character and is a result of severe pain caused by cancer, of which her employer is aware. The disciplinary action is unfavourable treatment. This treatment is because of something which arises in consequence of the worker's disability, namely her loss of temper. There is a connection between the 'something' (that is, the loss of temper) that led to the treatment and her disability. It will be discrimination arising from disability if the employer cannot objectively justify the decision to discipline the worker.

5.10 So long as the unfavourable treatment is because of something arising in consequence of the disability, it will be unlawful unless it can be objectively justified, or unless the employer did not know or could not reasonably have been expected to know that the person was disabled (see paragraph 5.13).

WHEN CAN DISCRIMINATION ARISING FROM DISABILITY BE JUSTIFIED?

5.11 **[s 15(1)(b)]** Unfavourable treatment will not amount to discrimination arising from disability if the employer can show that the treatment is a 'proportionate means of achieving a legitimate aim'. This 'objective justification' test is explained in detail in paragraphs 4.25 to 4.32.

5.12 It is for the employer to justify the treatment. They must produce evidence to support their assertion that it is justified and not rely on mere generalisations.

WHAT IF THE EMPLOYER DOES NOT KNOW THAT THE PERSON IS DISABLED?

5.13 **[s 15(2)]** If the employer can show that they:

- did not know that the disabled person had the disability in question; and
- could not reasonably have been expected to know that the disabled person had the disability,

then the unfavourable treatment does not amount to discrimination arising from disability.

5.14 It is not enough for the employer to show that they did not know that the disabled person had the disability. They must also show that they could not reasonably have been expected to know about it. Employers should consider whether a worker has a disability even where one has not been formally disclosed, as, for example, not all workers who meet the definition of disability may think of themselves as a 'disabled person'.

5.15 An employer must do all they can reasonably be expected to do to find out if a worker has a disability. What is reasonable will depend on the circumstances. This is an objective assessment. When making enquiries about disability, employers should consider issues of dignity and privacy and ensure that personal information is dealt with confidentially.

Example: A disabled man who has depression has been at a particular workplace for two years. He has a good attendance and performance record. In recent weeks, however, he has become emotional and upset at work for no apparent reason. He has also been repeatedly late for work and has made some mistakes in his work. The worker is disciplined without being given any opportunity to explain that his difficulties at work arise from a disability and that recently the effects of his depression have worsened.

The sudden deterioration in the worker's time-keeping and performance and the change in his behaviour at work should have alerted the employer to the possibility that these were connected to a disability. It is likely to be reasonable to expect the employer to explore with the worker the reason for these changes and whether the difficulties are because of something arising in consequence of a disability.

5.16 **[s 60]** However, employers should note that the Act imposes restrictions on the types of health or disability-related enquiries that can be made prior to making someone a job offer or including someone in a pool of successful candidates to be offered a job when one becomes available (see paragraphs 10.25 to 10.43).

When can an employer be assumed to know about disability?

5.17 If an employer's agent or employee (such as an occupational health adviser or a HR officer) knows, in that capacity, of a worker's or applicant's or potential applicant's disability, the employer will not usually be able to claim that they do not know of the disability, and that they cannot therefore have subjected a disabled person to discrimination arising from disability.

5.18 Therefore, where information about disabled people may come through different channels, employers need to ensure that there is a means – suitably confidential and subject to the disabled person's consent – for bringing that information together to make it easier for the employer to fulfil their duties under the Act.

Example: An occupational health (OH) adviser is engaged by a large employer to provide them with information about their workers' health. The OH adviser becomes aware of a worker's disability that is relevant to his work, and the worker consents to this information being disclosed to the employer. However, the OH adviser does not pass that information on to Human Resources or to the worker's line manager. As the OH adviser is acting as the employer's agent, it is not a defence for the employer to claim that they did not know about the worker's disability. This is because the information gained by the adviser on the employer's behalf is attributed to the employer.

5.19 Information will not be attributed ('imputed') to the employer if it is gained by a person providing services to workers independently of the employer. This is the case even if the employer has arranged for those services to be provided.

Example: An employer contracts with an agency to provide an independent counselling service to workers. The contract states that the counsellors are not acting on the employer's behalf while in the counselling role. Any information obtained by a counsellor during such counselling would not be attributed to the employer.

RELEVANCE OF REASONABLE ADJUSTMENTS

5.20 Employers can often prevent unfavourable treatment which would amount to discrimination arising from disability by taking prompt action to identify and implement reasonable adjustments (see Chapter 6).

5.21 If an employer has failed to make a reasonable adjustment which would have prevented or minimised the unfavourable treatment, it will be very difficult for them to show that the treatment was objectively justified.

5.22 Even where an employer has complied with a duty to make reasonable adjustments in relation to the disabled person, they may still subject a disabled person to unlawful discrimination arising from disability. This is likely to apply where, for example, the adjustment is unrelated to the particular treatment complained of.

Example: The employer in the example at paragraph 5.3 made a reasonable adjustment for the worker who has multiple sclerosis. They adjusted her working hours so that she started work at 9.30am instead of 9am.

However, this adjustment is not relevant to the unfavourable treatment – namely, her dismissal for disability-related sickness absence – which her claim concerns. And so, despite the fact that reasonable adjustments were made, there will still be discrimination arising from disability unless the treatment is justified.

CHAPTER 6
DUTY TO MAKE REASONABLE ADJUSTMENTS

INTRODUCTION

[4.133]

6.1 This chapter describes the principles and application of the duty to make reasonable adjustments for disabled people in employment.

6.2 The duty to make reasonable adjustments is a cornerstone of the Act and requires employers to take positive steps to ensure that disabled people can access and progress in employment. This goes beyond simply avoiding treating disabled workers, job applicants and potential job applicants unfavourably and means taking additional steps to which non-disabled workers and applicants are not entitled.

6.3 The duty to make reasonable adjustments applies to employers of all sizes, but the question of what is reasonable may vary according to the circumstances of the employer. Part 2 of the Code has more information about good practice in making reasonable adjustments in different work situations, such as in recruitment or during employment.

WHAT THE ACT SAYS

6.4 [s **21(2)**] Discrimination against a disabled person occurs where an employer fails to comply with a duty to make reasonable adjustments imposed on them in relation to that disabled person.

WHAT IS THE DUTY TO MAKE REASONABLE ADJUSTMENTS?

6.5 The duty to make reasonable adjustments comprises three requirements. Employers are required to take reasonable steps to:

- [s **20(3)**] Avoid the substantial disadvantage where a provision, criterion or practice applied by or on behalf of the employer puts a disabled person at a substantial disadvantage compared to those who are not disabled.
- [s **20(4)**] Remove or alter a physical feature or provide a reasonable means of avoiding such a feature where it puts a disabled person at a substantial disadvantage compared to those who are not disabled.
- [s **20(5)**] Provide an auxiliary aid (which includes an auxiliary service - see paragraph 6.13) where a disabled person would, but for the provision of that auxiliary aid, be put at a substantial disadvantage compared to those who are not disabled.

Accessible information

6.6 [s **20(6)**] The Act states that where the provision, criterion or practice or the need for an auxiliary aid relates to the provision of information, the steps which it is reasonable for the employer to take include steps to ensure that the information is provided in an accessible format; for example, providing letters, training materials or recruitment forms in Braille or on audio-tape.

Avoiding substantial disadvantages caused by physical features

6.7 [s **20(9)**] The Act says that avoiding a substantial disadvantage caused by a physical feature includes:

- removing the physical feature in question;
- altering it; or
- providing a reasonable means of avoiding it.

WHICH DISABLED PEOPLE DOES THE DUTY PROTECT?

6.8 **[Sch 8, paras 4 & 5]** The duty to make reasonable adjustments applies in recruitment and during all stages of employment, including dismissal. It may also apply after employment has ended. The duty relates to all disabled workers of an employer and to any disabled applicant for employment. The duty also applies in respect of any disabled person who has notified the employer that they may be an applicant for work.

6.9 In order to avoid discrimination, it would be sensible for employers not to attempt to make a fine judgment as to whether a particular individual falls within the statutory definition of disability, but to focus instead on meeting the needs of each worker and job applicant.

WHAT IS A PROVISION, CRITERION OR PRACTICE?

6.10 The phrase 'provision, criterion or practice' is not defined by the Act but should be construed widely so as to include, for example, any formal or informal policies, rules, practices, arrangements or qualifications including one-off decisions and actions (see also paragraph 4.5).

Example: An employer has a policy that designated car parking spaces are only offered to senior managers. A worker who is not a manager, but has a mobility impairment and needs to park very close to the office, is given a designated car parking space. This is likely to be a reasonable adjustment to the employer's car parking policy.

WHAT IS A 'PHYSICAL FEATURE'?

6.11 **[s 20(10), s 20(12)]** The Act says that the following are to be treated as a physical feature of the premises occupied by the employer:

- any feature of the design or construction of a building;
- any feature of an approach to, exit from or entrance to a building;
- a fixture or fitting, or furniture, furnishings, materials, equipment or other chattels (moveable property in Scotland) in or on the premises;
- any other physical element or quality of the premises.

All these features are covered, whether temporary or permanent.

6.12 Physical features will include steps, stairways, kerbs, exterior surfaces and paving, parking areas, building entrances and exits (including emergency escape routes), internal and external doors, gates, toilet and washing facilities, lighting and ventilation, lifts and escalators, floor coverings, signs, furniture and temporary or moveable items. This is not an exhaustive list.

Example: Clear glass doors at the end of a corridor in a particular workplace present a hazard for a visually impaired worker. This is a substantial disadvantage caused by the physical features of the workplace.

WHAT IS AN 'AUXILIARY AID'?

6.13 **[s 20(11)]** An auxiliary aid is something which provides support or assistance to a disabled person. It can include provision of a specialist piece of equipment such as an adapted keyboard or text to speech software. Auxiliary aids include auxiliary services; for example, provision of a sign language interpreter or a support worker for a disabled worker.

WHAT DISADVANTAGE GIVES RISE TO THE DUTY?

6.14 **[s 20(3), s 20(4), s 20(5)]** The duty to make adjustments arises where a provision, criterion, or practice, any physical feature of work premises or the absence of an auxiliary aid puts a disabled person at a substantial disadvantage compared with people who are not disabled.

6.15 **[s 212(1)]** The Act says that a substantial disadvantage is one which is more than minor or trivial. Whether such a disadvantage exists in a particular case is a question of fact, and is assessed on an objective basis.

6.16 **[s 23(1)]** The purpose of the comparison with people who are not disabled is to establish whether it is because of disability that a particular provision, criterion, practice or physical feature or the absence of an auxiliary aid disadvantages the disabled person in question. Accordingly – and unlike direct or indirect discrimination – under the duty to make adjustments there is no requirement to identify a comparator or comparator group whose circumstances are the same or nearly the same as the disabled person's.

WHAT IF THE EMPLOYER DOES NOT KNOW THAT A DISABLED PERSON IS AN ACTUAL OR POTENTIAL JOB APPLICANT?

6.17 **[Sch 8, para 20(1)(a)]** An employer only has a duty to make an adjustment if they know, or could reasonably be expected to know, that a disabled person is, or may be, an applicant for work.

6.18 There are restrictions on when health or disability-related enquiries can be made prior to making a job offer or including someone in a pool of people to be offered a job. However, questions are permitted to determine whether reasonable adjustments need to be made in relation to an assessment, such as an interview or other process designed to give an indication of a person's suitability for the work concerned. These provisions are explained in detail in paragraphs 10.25 to 10.43.

WHAT IF THE EMPLOYER DOES NOT KNOW THE WORKER IS DISABLED?

6.19 **[Sch 8, para 20(1)(b)]** For disabled workers already in employment, an employer only has a duty to make an adjustment if they know, or could reasonably be expected to know, that a worker has a disability and is, or is likely to be, placed at a substantial disadvantage. The employer must, however, do all they can reasonably be expected to do to find out whether this is the case. What is reasonable will depend on the circumstances. This is an objective assessment. When making enquiries about disability, employers should consider issues of dignity and privacy and ensure that personal information is dealt with confidentially.

Example: A worker who deals with customers by phone at a call centre has depression which sometimes causes her to cry at work. She has difficulty dealing with customer enquiries when the symptoms of her depression are severe. It is likely to be reasonable for the employer to discuss with the worker whether her crying is connected to a disability and whether a reasonable adjustment could be made to her working arrangements.

6.20 The Act does not prevent a disabled person keeping a disability confidential from an employer. But keeping a disability confidential is likely to mean that unless the employer could reasonably be expected to know about it anyway, the employer will not be under a duty to make a reasonable adjustment. If a disabled person expects an employer to make a reasonable adjustment, they will need to provide the employer – or someone acting on their behalf – with sufficient information to carry out that adjustment.

When can an employer be assumed to know about disability?

6.21 If an employer's agent or employee (such as an occupational health adviser, a HR officer or a recruitment agent) knows, in that capacity, of a worker's or applicant's or potential applicant's disability, the employer will not usually be able to claim that they do not know of the disability and that they therefore have no obligation to make a reasonable adjustment. Employers therefore need to ensure that where information about disabled people may come through different channels, there is a means – suitably confidential and subject to the disabled person's consent – for bringing that information together to make it easier for the employer to fulfil their duties under the Act.

Example: In the example in paragraph 5.18, if the employer's working arrangements put the worker at a substantial disadvantage because of the effects of his disability and he claims that a reasonable adjustment should have been made, it will not be a defence for the employer to claim that they were unaware of the worker's disability. Because the information gained by the OH adviser on the employer's behalf is assumed to be shared with the employer, the OH adviser's knowledge means that the employer's duty under the Act applies.

6.22 Information will not be 'imputed' or attributed to the employer if it is gained by a person providing services to employees independently of the employer. This is the case even if the employer has arranged for those services to be provided.

WHAT IS MEANT BY 'REASONABLE STEPS'?

6.23 The duty to make adjustments requires employers to take such steps as it is reasonable to have to take, in all the circumstances of the case, in order to make adjustments. The Act does not specify any particular factors that should be taken into account. What is a reasonable step for an employer to take will depend on all the circumstances of each individual case.

6.24 There is no onus on the disabled worker to suggest what adjustments should be made (although it is good practice for employers to ask). However, where the disabled person does so, the employer should consider whether such adjustments would help overcome the substantial disadvantage, and whether they are reasonable.

6.25 Effective and practicable adjustments for disabled workers often involve little or no cost or disruption and are therefore very likely to be reasonable for an employer to have to make. Even if an adjustment has a significant cost associated with it, it may still be cost-effective in overall terms – for example, compared with the costs of recruiting and training a new member of staff – and so may still be a reasonable adjustment to have to make.

6.26 **[Sch 21]** Many adjustments do not involve making physical changes to premises. However, where such changes need to be made and an employer occupies premises under a lease or other binding obligation, the employer may have to obtain consent to the making of reasonable adjustments. These provisions are explained in Appendix 3.

6.27 If making a particular adjustment would increase the risk to health and safety of any person (including the disabled worker in question) then this is a relevant factor in deciding whether it is reasonable to make that adjustment. Suitable and sufficient risk assessments should be used to help determine whether such risk is likely to arise.

6.28 The following are some of the factors which might be taken into account when deciding what is a reasonable step for an employer to have to take:

- whether taking any particular steps would be effective in preventing the substantial disadvantage;
- the practicability of the step;
- the financial and other costs of making the adjustment and the extent of any disruption caused;
- the extent of the employer's financial or other resources;
- the availability to the employer of financial or other assistance to help make an adjustment (such as advice through Access to Work); and
- the type and size of the employer.

6.29 Ultimately the test of the 'reasonableness' of any step an employer may have to take is an objective one and will depend on the circumstances of the case.

CAN FAILURE TO MAKE A REASONABLE ADJUSTMENT EVER BE JUSTIFIED?

6.30 The Act does not permit an employer to justify a failure to comply with a duty to make a reasonable adjustment. However, an employer will only breach such a duty if the adjustment in question is one which it is reasonable for the employer to have to make. So, where the duty applies, it is the question of 'reasonableness' which alone determines whether the adjustment has to be made.

WHAT HAPPENS IF THE DUTY IS NOT COMPLIED WITH?

6.31 **[s 21]** If an employer does not comply with the duty to make reasonable adjustments they will be committing an act of unlawful discrimination. A disabled worker will have the right to take a claim to the Employment Tribunal based on this.

REASONABLE ADJUSTMENTS IN PRACTICE

6.32 It is a good starting point for an employer to conduct a proper assessment, in consultation with the disabled person concerned, of what reasonable adjustments may be required. Any necessary adjustments should be implemented in a timely fashion, and it may also be necessary for an employer to make more than one adjustment. It is advisable to agree any proposed adjustments with the disabled worker in question before they are made.

6.33 Examples of steps it might be reasonable for employers to have to take include:

Making adjustments to premises

Example: An employer makes structural or other physical changes such as widening a doorway, providing a ramp or moving furniture for a wheelchair user.

Providing information in accessible formats

Example: The format of instructions and manuals might need to be modified for some disabled workers (for example, produced in Braille or on audio tape) and instructions for people with learning disabilities might need to be conveyed orally with individual demonstration or in Easy Read. Employers may also need to arrange for recruitment materials to be provided in alternative formats.

Allocating some of the disabled person's duties to another worker

Example: An employer reallocates minor or subsidiary duties to another worker as a disabled worker has difficulty doing them because of his disability. For example, the job involves occasionally going onto the open roof of a building but the employer transfers this work away from a worker whose disability involves severe vertigo.

Transferring the disabled worker to fill an existing vacancy

Example: An employer should consider whether a suitable alternative post is available for a worker who becomes disabled (or whose disability worsens), where no reasonable adjustment would enable the worker to continue doing the current job. Such a post might also involve retraining or other reasonable adjustments such as equipment for the new post or transfer to a position on a higher grade.

Altering the disabled worker's hours of work or training

Example: An employer allows a disabled person to work flexible hours to enable him to have additional breaks to overcome fatigue arising from his disability. It could also include permitting part-time working or different working hours to avoid the need to travel in the rush hour if this creates a problem related to an impairment. A phased return to work with a gradual build-up of hours might also be appropriate in some circumstances.

Assigning the disabled worker to a different place of work or training or arranging home working

Example: An employer relocates the workstation of a newly disabled worker (who now uses a wheelchair) from an inaccessible third floor office to an accessible one on the ground floor. It may be reasonable to move his place of work to other premises of the same employer if the first building is inaccessible. Allowing the worker to work from home might also be a reasonable adjustment for the employer to make.

Allowing the disabled worker to be absent during working or training hours for rehabilitation, assessment or treatment

Example: An employer allows a person who has become disabled more time off work than would be allowed to non-disabled workers to enable him to have rehabilitation training. A similar adjustment may be appropriate if a disability worsens or if a disabled person needs occasional treatment anyway.

Giving, or arranging for, training or mentoring (whether for the disabled person or any other worker)

This could be training in particular pieces of equipment which the disabled person uses, or an alteration to the standard workplace training to reflect the worker's particular disability.

Example: All workers are trained in the use of a particular machine but an employer provides slightly different or longer training for a worker with restricted hand or arm movements. An employer might also provide training in additional software for a visually impaired worker so that he can use a computer with speech output.

Acquiring or modifying equipment

Example: An employer might have to provide special equipment such as an adapted keyboard for someone with arthritis, a large screen for a visually impaired worker, or an adapted telephone for someone with a hearing impairment, or other modified equipment for disabled workers (such as longer handles on a machine).

There is no requirement to provide or modify equipment for personal purposes unconnected with a worker's job, such as providing a wheelchair if a person needs one in any event but does not have one. The disadvantages in such a case do not flow from the employer's arrangements or premises.

Modifying procedures for testing or assessment

Example: A worker with restricted manual dexterity would be disadvantaged by a written test, so the employer gives that person an oral test instead.

Providing a reader or interpreter

Example: An employer arranges for a colleague to read mail to a worker with a visual impairment at particular times during the working day. Alternatively, the employer might hire a reader.

Providing supervision or other support

Example: An employer provides a support worker or arranges help from a colleague, in appropriate circumstances, for someone whose disability leads to uncertainty or lack of confidence in unfamiliar situations, such as on a training course.

Allowing a disabled worker to take a period of disability leave

Example: A worker who has cancer needs to undergo treatment and rehabilitation. His employer allows a period of disability leave and permits him to return to his job at the end of this period.

Participating in supported employment schemes, such as Workstep

Example: A man applies for a job as an office assistant after several years of not working because of depression. He has been participating in a supported employment scheme where he saw the post advertised. He asks the employer to let him make private phone calls during the working day to a support worker at the scheme and the employer allows him to do so as a reasonable adjustment.

Employing a support worker to assist a disabled worker

Example: An adviser with a visual impairment is sometimes required to make home visits to clients. The employer employs a support worker to assist her on these visits.

Modifying disciplinary or grievance procedures for a disabled worker

Example: A worker with a learning disability is allowed to take a friend (who does not work with her) to act as an advocate at a meeting with her employer about a grievance. The employer also ensures that the meeting is conducted in a way that does not disadvantage or patronise the disabled worker.

Adjusting redundancy selection criteria for a disabled worker

Example: Because of his condition, a man with an autoimmune disease has taken several short periods of absence during the year. When his employer is taking the absences into account as a criterion for selecting people for redundancy, they discount these periods of disability-related absence.

Modifying performance-related pay arrangements for a disabled worker

Example: A disabled worker who is paid purely on her output needs frequent short additional breaks during her working day – something her employer agrees to as a reasonable adjustment. It may be a reasonable adjustment for her employer to pay her at an agreed rate (for example, her average hourly rate) for these breaks.

6.34 It may sometimes be necessary for an employer to take a combination of steps.

Example: A worker who is blind is given a new job with her employer in an unfamiliar part of the building. The employer:

- arranges facilities for her assistance dog in the new area;
- arranges for her new instructions to be in Braille; and
- provides disability equality training to all staff.

6.35 In some cases, a reasonable adjustment will not succeed without the co-operation of other workers. Colleagues as well as managers may therefore have an important role in helping ensure that a reasonable adjustment is carried out in practice. Subject to considerations about confidentiality, employers must ensure that this happens. It is unlikely to be a valid defence to a claim under the Act to argue that an adjustment was unreasonable because staff were obstructive or unhelpful when the employer tried to implement it. An employer would at least need to be able to show that they took such behaviour seriously and dealt with it appropriately. Employers will be more likely to be able to do this if they establish and implement the type of policies and practices described in Chapter 18.

Example: An employer ensures that a worker with autism has a structured working day as a reasonable adjustment. As part of this adjustment, it is the responsibility of the employer to ensure that other workers co-operate with this arrangement.

THE ACCESS TO WORK SCHEME

6.36 The Access to Work scheme may assist an employer to decide what steps to take. If financial assistance is available from the scheme, it may also make it reasonable for an employer to take certain steps which would otherwise be unreasonably expensive.

6.37 However, Access to Work does not diminish any of an employer's duties under the Act. In particular:

- The legal responsibility for making a reasonable adjustment remains with the employer – even where Access to Work is involved in the provision of advice or funding in relation to the adjustment.

- It is likely to be a reasonable step for the employer to help a disabled person in making an application for assistance from Access to Work and to provide on-going administrative support (by completing claim forms, for example).

6.38 It may be unreasonable for an employer to decide not to make an adjustment based on its cost before finding out whether financial assistance for the adjustment is available from Access to Work or another source.

6.39 More information about the Access to Work scheme is available from: www.direct.gov.uk/en/DisabledPeople/Employmentsupport/WorkSchemesAndProgrammes/DG_4000347

CHAPTER 7
HARASSMENT

INTRODUCTION

[4.134]
7.1 This chapter explains the Act's general test for harassment. It also explains the provisions on harassment related to a relevant protected characteristic, the provisions on sexual harassment, and less favourable treatment for rejecting or submitting to harassment.

7.2 Unlike direct discrimination, harassment does not require a comparative approach; it is not necessary for the worker to show that another person was, or would have been, treated more favourably. For an explanation of direct discrimination, please see Chapter 4.

WHAT THE ACT SAYS

7.3 The Act prohibits three types of harassment. These are:

- **[s 26(1)]** harassment related to a 'relevant protected characteristic';
- **[s 26(2)]** sexual harassment; and
- **[s 26(3)]** less favourable treatment of a worker because they submit to, or reject, sexual harassment or harassment related to sex or gender reassignment.

7.4 **[s 26(5)]** 'Relevant protected characteristics' are:

- Age
- Disability
- Gender Reassignment
- Race
- Religion or Belief
- Sex
- Sexual Orientation

7.5 Pregnancy and maternity and marriage and civil partnership are not protected directly under the harassment provisions. However, pregnancy and maternity harassment would amount to harassment related to sex, and harassment related to civil partnership would amount to harassment related to sexual orientation.

HARASSMENT RELATED TO A PROTECTED CHARACTERISTIC

7.6 **[s 26(1)]** This type of harassment of a worker occurs when a person engages in unwanted conduct which is related to a relevant protected characteristic and which has the purpose or the effect of:

- violating the worker's dignity; or
- creating an intimidating, hostile, degrading, humiliating or offensive environment for that worker.

7.7 Unwanted conduct covers a wide range of behaviour, including spoken or written words or abuse, imagery, graffiti, physical gestures, facial expressions, mimicry, jokes, pranks, acts affecting a person's surroundings or other physical behaviour.

7.8 The word 'unwanted' means essentially the same as 'unwelcome' or 'uninvited'. 'Unwanted' does not mean that express objection must be made to the conduct before it is deemed to be unwanted. A serious one-off incident can also amount to harassment.

Example: In front of her male colleagues, a female electrician is told by her supervisor that her work is below standard and that, as a woman, she will never be competent to carry it out. The supervisor goes on to suggest that she should instead stay at home to cook and clean for her husband. This could amount to harassment related to sex as such a statement would be self-evidently unwanted and the electrician would not have to object to it before it was deemed to be unlawful harassment.

'RELATED TO'

7.9 Unwanted conduct 'related to' a protected characteristic has a broad meaning in that the conduct does not have to be because of the protected characteristic. It includes the following situations:

a) Where conduct is related to the worker's own protected characteristic.

Example: If a worker with a hearing impairment is verbally abused because he wears a hearing aid, this could amount to harassment related to disability.

7.10 Protection from harassment also applies where a person is generally abusive to other workers but, in relation to a particular worker, the form of the unwanted conduct is determined by that worker's protected characteristic.

Example: During a training session attended by both male and female workers, a male trainer directs a number of remarks of a sexual nature to the group as a whole. A female worker finds the comments offensive and humiliating to her as a woman. She would be able to make a claim for harassment, even though the remarks were not specifically directed at her.

b) Where there is any connection with a protected characteristic.

Protection is provided because the conduct is dictated by a relevant protected characteristic, whether or not the worker has that characteristic themselves. This means that protection against unwanted conduct is provided where the worker does not have the relevant protected characteristic, including where the employer knows that the worker does not have the relevant characteristic. Connection with a protected characteristic may arise in several situations:

- The worker may be associated with someone who has a protected characteristic.

Example: A worker has a son with a severe disfigurement. His work colleagues make offensive remarks to him about his son's disability. The worker could have a claim for harassment related to disability.

- The worker may be wrongly perceived as having a particular protected characteristic.

Example: A Sikh worker wears a turban to work. His manager wrongly assumes he is Muslim and subjects him to Islamaphobic abuse. The worker could have a claim for harassment related to religion or belief because of his manager's perception of his religion.

- The worker is known not to have the protected characteristic but nevertheless is subjected to harassment related to that characteristic.

Example: A worker is subjected to homophobic banter and name calling, even though his colleagues know he is not gay. Because the form of the abuse relates to sexual orientation, this could amount to harassment related to sexual orientation.

- The unwanted conduct related to a protected characteristic is not directed at the particular worker but at another person or no one in particular.

Example: A manager racially abuses a black worker. As a result of the racial abuse, the black worker's white colleague is offended and could bring a claim of racial harassment.

- The unwanted conduct is related to the protected characteristic, but does not take place because of the protected characteristic.

Example: A female worker has a relationship with her male manager. On seeing her with another male colleague, the manager suspects she is having an affair. As a result, the manager makes her working life difficult by continually criticising her work in an offensive manner. The behaviour is not because of the sex of the female worker, but because of the suspected affair which is related to her sex. This could amount to harassment related to sex.

7.11 In all of the circumstances listed above, there is a connection with the protected characteristic and so the worker could bring a claim of harassment where the unwanted conduct creates for them any of the circumstances defined in paragraph 7.6

SEXUAL HARASSMENT

7.12 **[s 26(2)]** Sexual harassment occurs when a person engages in unwanted conduct as defined in paragraph 7.6 and which is of a sexual nature.

7.13 Conduct 'of a sexual nature' can cover verbal, non-verbal or physical conduct including unwelcome sexual advances, touching, forms of sexual assault, sexual jokes, displaying pornographic photographs or drawings or sending emails with material of a sexual nature.

LESS FAVOURABLE TREATMENT FOR REJECTING OR SUBMITTING TO UNWANTED CONDUCT

7.14 **[s 26(3)]** The third type of harassment occurs when a worker is treated less favourably by their employer because that worker submitted to, or rejected unwanted conduct of a sexual nature, or unwanted conduct which is related to sex or to gender reassignment, and the unwanted conduct creates for them any of the circumstances defined in paragraph 7.6.

Example: A shopkeeper propositions one of his shop assistants. She rejects his advances and then is turned down for a promotion which she believes she would have got if she had accepted her boss's advances. The shop assistant would have a claim for harassment.

7.15 **[s 26(3)(a)]** Under this type of harassment, the initial unwanted conduct may be committed by the person who treats the worker less favourably or by another person.

Example: A female worker is asked out by her team leader and she refuses. The team leader feels resentful and informs the Head of Division about the rejection. The Head of Division subsequently fails to give the female worker the promotion she applies for, even though she is the best candidate. She knows that the team leader and the Head of Division are good friends and believes that her refusal to go out with the team leader influenced the Head of Division's decision. She could have a claim of harassment over the Head of Division's actions.

'PURPOSE OR EFFECT'

7.16 For all three types of harassment, if the **purpose** of subjecting the worker to the conduct is to create any of the circumstances defined in paragraph 7.6, this will be sufficient to establish unlawful harassment. It will not be necessary to inquire into the effect of that conduct on that worker.

7.17 Regardless of the intended purpose, unwanted conduct will also amount to harassment if it has the **effect** of creating any of the circumstances defined in paragraph 7.6.

Example: Male members of staff download pornographic images on to their computers in an office where a woman works. She may make a claim for harassment if she is aware that the images are being downloaded and the effect of this is to create a hostile and humiliating environment for her. In this situation, it is irrelevant that the male members of staff did not have the purpose of upsetting the woman, and that they merely considered the downloading of images as 'having a laugh'.

7.18 In deciding whether conduct had that effect, each of the following must be taken into account:

(a) **[s 26(4)(a)]** The perception of the worker; that is, did they regard it as violating their dignity or creating an intimidating (etc) environment for them. This part of the test is a subjective question and depends on how the worker regards the treatment.

(b) **[s 26(4)(b)]** The other circumstances of the case; circumstances that may be relevant and therefore need to be taken into account can include the personal circumstances of the worker experiencing the conduct; for example, the worker's health, including mental health; mental capacity; cultural norms; or previous experience of harassment; and also the environment in which the conduct takes place.

(c) **[s 26(4)(c)]** Whether it is reasonable for the conduct to have that effect; this is an objective test. A tribunal is unlikely to find unwanted conduct has the effect, for example, of offending a worker if the tribunal considers the worker to be hypersensitive and that another person subjected to the same conduct would not have been offended.

7.19 Where the employer is a public authority, it may also be relevant in cases of alleged harassment whether the alleged perpetrator was exercising any of her/his Convention rights protected under the Human Rights Act 1998. For example, the right to freedom of thought, conscience and religion or freedom of speech of the alleged harasser will need to be taken into account when considering all relevant circumstances of the case.

LIABILITY OF EMPLOYERS FOR HARASSMENT BY THIRD PARTIES

7.20 Employers may be liable for harassment of their employees or job applicants by third parties – such as customers – who are not directly under their control. This is explained in paragraphs 10.19 to 10.24.

CHAPTER 8
PREGNANCY AND MATERNITY

INTRODUCTION

[4.135]

8.1 Specific provisions in the Act protect women from discrimination at work because of pregnancy or maternity leave. These apply during the protected period explained at paragraphs 8.9 to 8.13.

8.2 There is also a statutory regime setting out pregnant employees' rights to health and safety protection, time off for antenatal care, maternity leave and unfair dismissal protection.

8.3 European law, including the Pregnant Workers Directive (92/85/EEC) and the recast Equal Treatment Directive (2006/54/EC), gives women who are pregnant or on maternity leave protected status in employment. For example, Article 10 of the Pregnant Workers Directive prohibits the dismissal of pregnant workers and workers on maternity leave other than in exceptional circumstances not connected with their pregnancy or maternity leave.

WHAT THE ACT SAYS

8.4 **[s 18(1)–(4)]** It is unlawful discrimination to treat a woman unfavourably because of her pregnancy or a related illness, or because she is exercising, has exercised or is seeking or has sought to exercise her right to maternity leave.

8.5 In considering whether there has been pregnancy and maternity discrimination, the employer's motive or intention is not relevant, and neither are the consequences of pregnancy or maternity leave. Such discrimination cannot be justified.

8.6 The meaning of 'because of' is discussed in paragraph 3.11. However, unlike in cases of direct sex discrimination, there is no need to compare the way a pregnant worker is treated with the treatment of any other workers. If she is treated unfavourably by her employer because of her pregnancy or maternity leave, this is automatically discrimination.

8.7 **[s 18(7)]** Unfavourable treatment of a woman because of her pregnancy or maternity leave during 'the protected period' is unlawful pregnancy and maternity discrimination. This cannot be treated as direct sex discrimination (for which a comparator, actual or hypothetical, is required).

8.8 **[s 13(6)(b)]** In some cases, employers have to treat workers who are pregnant or have recently given birth more favourably than other workers. This is explained at paragraph 8.43. Men cannot make a claim for sex discrimination in relation to any special treatment given to a woman in connection with pregnancy or childbirth, such as maternity leave or additional sick leave.

THE PROTECTED PERIOD

8.9 **[s 18(6)]** The protected period starts when a woman becomes pregnant and continues until the end of her maternity leave, or until she returns to work if that is earlier (but see paragraphs 8.14 and 8.15 below).

8.10 The maternity leave scheme is set out in Part VIII of the Employment Rights Act 1996 (ERA) and the Maternity and Parental Leave (etc) Regulations 1999 (MPLR).

8.11 [s 213] The Act refers to the three kinds of maternity leave regulated by the ERA:

- Compulsory maternity leave – the minimum two-week period (four weeks for factory workers) immediately following childbirth when a woman must not work for her employer. All employees entitled to Ordinary Maternity Leave must take compulsory maternity leave.
- Ordinary maternity leave – all pregnant employees are entitled to 26 weeks ordinary maternity leave (which includes the compulsory leave period), provided they give proper notice.
- Additional maternity leave – all pregnant employees are entitled to a further 26 weeks maternity leave, provided they give proper notice.

8.12 There is no minimum period of qualifying service for ordinary and additional maternity leave but only employees are eligible to take it.

8.13 [s 18(6)] The protected period in relation to a woman's pregnancy ends either:

- if she is entitled to ordinary and additional maternity leave, at the end of the additional maternity leave period; or
- when she returns to work after giving birth, if that is earlier; or
- if she is not entitled to maternity leave, for example because she is not an employee, two weeks after the baby is born.

Unfavourable treatment outside the protected period

8.14 [s 18(7)] Outside the protected period, unfavourable treatment of a woman in employment because of her pregnancy would be considered as sex discrimination rather than pregnancy and maternity discrimination.

8.15 [s 18(5)] However, if a woman is treated unfavourably because of her pregnancy (or a related illness) after the end of the protected period, but due to a decision made during it, this is regarded as occurring during the protected period.

'PREGNANCY OF HERS'

8.16 [s 18(2)] For pregnancy and maternity discrimination, the unfavourable treatment must be because of the woman's own pregnancy. However, a worker treated less favourably because of association with a pregnant woman, or a woman who has recently given birth, may have a claim for sex discrimination.

KNOWLEDGE OF PREGNANCY

8.17 **[Reg 4 Maternity and Parental Leave etc Regulations 1999 (MPLR)]** There is no obligation on a job applicant or employee to inform the employer of her pregnancy until 15 weeks before the baby is due. However, telling the employer triggers the legal protection, including the employer's health and safety obligations.

8.18 Unfavourable treatment will only be unlawful if the employer is aware the woman is pregnant. The employer must know, believe or suspect that she is pregnant – whether this is by formal notification or through the grapevine.

NO NEED FOR COMPARISON

8.19 It is not necessary to show that the treatment was unfavourable compared with the treatment of a man, with that of a woman who is not pregnant or with any other worker. However, evidence of how others have been treated may be useful to help determine if the unfavourable treatment is in fact related to pregnancy or maternity leave.

Example: A company producing office furniture decides to exhibit at a trade fair. A pregnant member of the company's sales team, who had expected to be asked to attend the trade fair to staff the company's stall and talk to potential customers, is not invited. In demonstrating that, but for her pregnancy, she would have been invited, it would help her to show that other members of the company's sales team, either male or female but not pregnant, were invited to the trade fair.

NOT THE ONLY REASON

8.20 A woman's pregnancy or maternity leave does not have to be the only reason for her treatment, but it does have to be an important factor or effective cause.

Example: An employer dismisses an employee on maternity leave shortly before she is due to return to work because the locum covering her absence is regarded as a better performer. Had the employee not been absent on maternity leave she would not have been sacked. Her dismissal is therefore unlawful, even if performance was a factor in the employer's decision-making.

UNFAVOURABLE TREATMENT

8.21 An employer must not demote or dismiss a woman, or deny her training or promotion opportunities, because she is pregnant or on maternity leave. Nor must an employer take into account any period of pregnancy-related sickness absence when making a decision about her employment.

8.22 As examples only, it will amount to pregnancy and maternity discrimination to treat a woman unfavourably during the protected period for the following reasons:

- the fact that, because of her pregnancy, the woman will be temporarily unable to do the job for which she is specifically employed whether permanently or on a fixed-term contract;

- the pregnant woman is temporarily unable to work because to do so would be a breach of health and safety regulations;
- the costs to the business of covering her work;
- any absence due to pregnancy related illness;
- her inability to attend a disciplinary hearing due to morning sickness or other pregnancy-related conditions;
- performance issues due to morning sickness or other pregnancy-related conditions.

This is not an exhaustive list but indicates, by drawing on case law, the kinds of treatment that have been found to be unlawful.

8.23 The following are further examples of unlawful discrimination:

- failure to consult a woman on maternity leave about changes to her work or about possible redundancy;
- disciplining a woman for refusing to carry out tasks due to pregnancy related risks;
- assuming that a woman's work will become less important to her after childbirth and giving her less responsible or less interesting work as a result;
- depriving a woman of her right to an annual assessment of her performance because she was on maternity leave;
- excluding a pregnant woman from business trips.

OTHER EMPLOYMENT RIGHTS FOR PREGNANT WOMEN

8.24 **[s 99 & 47(c) ERA]** There are separate legal provisions in the ERA protecting employees from dismissal and other disadvantage (except relating to pay) where the reason or principal reason is related to pregnancy or maternity leave. These ERA rights can overlap with the discrimination provisions and if they are breached this may also constitute pregnancy and maternity discrimination.

Example: If an employer fails to consult a woman about threatened redundancy because she is absent on maternity leave, this will be unlawful discrimination.

8.25 **[MPLR, regs 10 & 20(1)(b)]** An employee who is made redundant while on statutory maternity leave is entitled to be offered any suitable alternative vacancy, in preference to other employees. If she is not offered it, she can claim automatically unfair dismissal.

8.26 **[MPLR, regs 18 & 18A]** A woman has a statutory right to return to the same job after ordinary maternity leave. After additional maternity leave, she has a right to return to the same job unless that is not reasonably practicable. If that is the case, she is entitled to be offered a suitable alternative job, on terms and conditions which are not less favourable than her original job. If a woman seeks to return on different terms where she does not have a specific contractual right to do so, a refusal could constitute direct discrimination because of sex, depending on the circumstances.

8.27 In addition, depending on the circumstances, refusing to allow a woman to return to work part-time could be indirect sex discrimination.

8.28 **[ERA 1996, Part 8A]** Parents of dependent children have a right to request flexible working set out in the ERA. This right entitles a woman returning from maternity leave to make a request to change her hours and if she does so, her employer must consider her request (see paragraphs 17.8 to 17.12).

8.29 **[MPLR, reg 12A]** An employee on statutory maternity or adoption leave may by agreement work for her employer for up to ten 'keeping in touch' (KIT) days without bringing the leave to an end. This can include training or attending staff meetings, for example.

HEALTH AND SAFETY AT WORK

8.30 **[Sch 22, para 2]** The Act permits differential treatment of women at work where it is necessary to comply with laws protecting the health and safety of women who are pregnant, who have recently given birth or are breastfeeding.

8.31 Steps taken to protect pregnant workers' health and safety should not result in them being treated unfavourably.

8.32 **[Pregnant Workers Directive, incl Annex II MHSW Regs; The Workplace (Health, Safety and Welfare) Regs 1992, reg 25(4)]** Employers have specific obligations to protect the health and safety of pregnant women and women who have recently given birth. Where a workplace includes women of childbearing age, and the work or workplace conditions are of a kind that could involve risk to a pregnant woman, a woman who has given birth within the previous six months or who is breastfeeding, or create a risk to her baby, the employer's general risk assessment must include an assessment of such risks. There is a non-exhaustive list of the working conditions, processes, and physical, chemical or biological agents that may pose a risk in Annexes I and II to the Pregnant Workers Directive.

8.33 **[MHSW Regs, reg 18]** In addition, where an employee has given notice in writing that she is pregnant, has given birth within the last six months, or is breastfeeding, the employer must consider the risks in relation to that individual and take action to avoid them. This may involve altering her working conditions or hours of work. For example, as a result of a risk assessment an employer may ensure that the worker takes extra breaks, refrains from lifting, or spends more time sitting rather than standing.

8.34 If it is not reasonable to do this, or it would not avoid the risk, the employer must suspend the woman from work for as long as is necessary to avoid the risk.

8.35 **[s 67 ERA 1996]** Before being suspended on maternity grounds, a woman is entitled to be offered suitable alternative work if it is available. If she unreasonably refuses an offer of alternative work, she will lose the statutory right to be paid during any period of maternity suspension.

8.36 The Health and Safety Executive produces guidance on New and Expectant Mothers at Work. This is available from:
www.hse.gov.uk/mothers/

PAY AND CONDITIONS DURING MATERNITY LEAVE

8.37 Employers are obliged to maintain a woman's benefits except contractual remuneration during both ordinary and additional maternity leave. Unless otherwise provided in her contract of employment, a woman does not have a legal right to continue receiving her full pay during maternity leave.

8.38 **[SMP (General) Regs (Amendment) 2005]** If a woman receives a pay rise between the start of the calculation period for Statutory Maternity Pay (SMP) and the end of her maternity leave, she is entitled to have her SMP recalculated and receive any extra SMP due. She may also, as a result of recalculation following such a pay rise, become eligible for SMP where previously she was not. Employers are reimbursed all or some of the cost of SMP.

Non-contractual payments during maternity leave

8.39 **[Sch 9, para 17(5)]** The Act has a specific exception relating to non-contractual payments to women on maternity leave. There is no obligation on an employer to extend to a woman on maternity leave any non-contractual benefit relating to pay, such as a discretionary bonus. For the purposes of this exception, 'pay' means a payment of money by way of wages or salary.

8.40 **[Sch 9, para 17(2)(a), (6)]** However, this exception does not apply to any maternity-related pay (whether statutory or contractual), to which a woman is entitled as a result of being pregnant or on maternity leave. Nor does it apply to any maternity-related pay arising from an increase that the woman would have received had she not been on maternity leave.

Example: A woman on maternity leave is receiving contractual maternity pay, which is worked out as a percentage of her salary. The date of her employer's annual review of staff pay falls while she is on maternity leave. All other staff are awarded a 2% pay rise with immediate effect. If the woman on maternity leave does not receive the increase, this would be unlawful discrimination. Her contractual maternity pay should be recalculated so that it is based on her salary plus the 2% increase given to all her colleagues. Any other benefits linked to salary should also be adjusted to take into account the pay rise. When she returns to work her normal pay must reflect the pay rise.

8.41 **[Sch 9, para 17(2)(b) & (c)]** Any non-contractual bonus relating to the period of compulsory maternity leave is not covered by the exception, so the employer would have to pay this. Neither does the exception apply to pay relating to times when a woman is not on maternity leave.

8.42 **[ss 72–76]** Further information on equal treatment and what may be unlawful discrimination in terms and conditions for pregnant women and women on maternity leave is set out in the Equal Pay Code.

SPECIAL TREATMENT IN CONNECTION WITH PREGNANCY AND CHILDBIRTH IS LAWFUL

8.43 **[s 13(6)(b)]** An employer does not discriminate against a man where it affords a woman 'special treatment' in connection with childbirth and pregnancy.

Example: A man who is given a warning for being repeatedly late to work in the mornings alleges that he has been treated less favourably than a pregnant woman who has also been repeatedly late for work, but who was not given a warning. The man cannot compare himself to the pregnant woman, because her lateness is related to her morning sickness. The correct comparator in his case would be a non-pregnant woman who was also late for work.

8.44 Treating a woman unfavourably because she is undergoing in vitro fertilisation (IVF) or other fertility treatment would not count as pregnancy and maternity discrimination. This is because a woman is not deemed pregnant until the fertilised ova have been implanted in her uterus. However, such unfavourable treatment could amount to sex discrimination (see paragraph 17.28).

Breastfeeding

8.45 There is no statutory right for workers to take time off to breastfeed. However, employers should try to accommodate women who wish to do so, bearing in mind the following:

- As explained above in paragraph 8.30, where risks to the health and safety of an employee who is breastfeeding have been identified in the employer's risk assessment, and where she has given written notice that she is breastfeeding, it may be reasonable for the employer to alter her working conditions or hours of work. If this is not reasonable or would not avoid the risks identified, the employer should suspend the employee from work for so long as is necessary to avoid the risks; as above, this is subject to the right to be offered alternative work if it is available.
- Employers have a duty to provide suitable workplace rest facilities for women at work who are breastfeeding mothers to use.
- A refusal to allow a woman to express milk or to adjust her working conditions to enable her to continue to breastfeed may amount to unlawful sex discrimination.

Example: An employer refused a request from a woman to return from maternity leave part-time to enable her to continue breastfeeding her child who suffered from eczema. The woman told her employer that her GP had advised that continued breastfeeding would benefit the child's medical condition. The employer refused the request without explanation. Unless the employer's refusal can be objectively justified, this is likely to be indirect sex discrimination.

CHAPTER 9
VICTIMISATION AND OTHER UNLAWFUL ACTS

INTRODUCTION

[4.136]
9.1 This chapter explains what the Act says about the unlawful acts of victimisation, instructing, causing or inducing discrimination, and aiding contraventions. It also sets out the provisions on gender reassignment discrimination (absence from work).

VICTIMISATION

What the Act says

9.2 [s **27(1)**] The Act prohibits victimisation. It is victimisation for an employer to subject a worker to a detriment because the worker has done a 'protected act' or because the employer believes that the worker has done or may do a protected act in the future.

9.3 [**s 27(2)(c) & (d)**] A worker need not have a particular protected characteristic in order to be protected against victimisation under the Act; to be unlawful, victimisation must be linked to a 'protected act' (see paragraph 9.5). Making an allegation or doing something related to the Act does not have to involve an explicit reference to the legislation.

Example: A non-disabled worker gives evidence on behalf of a disabled colleague at an Employment Tribunal hearing where disability discrimination is claimed. If the non-disabled worker is subsequently refused a promotion because of that action, they would have suffered victimisation in contravention of the Act.

9.4 Former workers are also protected from victimisation.

Example: A grocery shop worker resigns after making a sexual harassment complaint against the owner. Several weeks later, she tries to make a purchase at the shop but is refused service by the owner because of her complaint. This could amount to victimisation.

What is a 'protected act'?

9.5 A protected act is any of the following:
- [s **27(2)(a)**] bringing proceedings under the Act;
- [s **27(2)(b)**] giving evidence or information in connection with proceedings brought under the Act;
- [s **27(2)(c)**] doing anything which is related to the provisions of the Act;
- [s **27(2)(d)**] making an allegation (whether or not express) that another person has done something in breach of the Act; or
- [s **77(3)**] making or seeking a 'relevant pay disclosure' to or from a colleague (including a former colleague).

9.6 A 'relevant pay disclosure' is explained in paragraph 14.11 and in the Equal Pay Code.

9.7 Protected acts can occur in any field covered by the Act and in relation to any part of the Act. An employer must therefore not victimise a person who has done a protected act in relation to services, for example.

What is a 'detriment'?

9.8 'Detriment' in the context of victimisation is not defined by the Act and could take many forms. Generally, a detriment is anything which the individual concerned might reasonably consider changed their position for the worse or put them at a disadvantage. This could include being rejected for promotion, denied an opportunity to represent the organisation at external events, excluded from opportunities to train, or overlooked in the allocation of discretionary bonuses or performance-related awards.

Example: A senior manager hears a worker's grievance about harassment. He finds that the worker has been harassed and offers a formal apology and directs that the perpetrators of the harassment be disciplined and required to undertake diversity training. As a result, the senior manager is not put forward by his director to attend an important conference on behalf of the company. This is likely to amount to detriment.

9.9 A detriment might also include a threat made to the complainant which they take seriously and it is reasonable for them to take it seriously. There is no need to demonstrate physical or economic consequences. However, an unjustified sense of grievance alone would not be enough to establish detriment.

Example: An employer threatens to dismiss a staff member because he thinks she intends to support a colleague's sexual harassment claim. This threat could amount to victimisation, even though the employer has not actually taken any action to dismiss the staff member and may not really intend to do so.

9.10 Detrimental treatment amounts to victimisation if a 'protected act' is one of the reasons for the treatment, but it need not be the only reason.

What other factors are involved in proving that victimisation has occurred?

9.11 Victimisation does not require a comparator. The worker need only show that they have experienced a detriment because they have done a protected act or because the employer believes (rightly or wrongly) that they have done or intend to do a protected act.

9.12 There is no time limit within which victimisation must occur after a person has done a protected act. However, a complainant will need to show a link between the detriment and the protected act.

Example: In 2006, a trade union staff representative acted on behalf of a colleague in a claim of age discrimination. In 2009, he applies for a promotion but is rejected. He asks for his interview notes which make a reference to his loyalty to the company and in brackets were written the words 'tribunal case'. This could amount to victimisation despite the three-year gap between the protected act and the detriment.

9.13 [s 27(3)] A worker cannot claim victimisation where they have acted in bad faith, such as maliciously giving false evidence or information or making a false allegation of discrimination. Any such action would not be a protected act.

9.14 However, if a worker gives evidence, provides information or makes an allegation in good faith but it turns out that it is factually wrong, or provides information in relation to proceedings which are unsuccessful, they will still be protected from victimisation.

9.15 A worker is protected from victimisation by an employer or prospective employer where they do a protected act which is not in relation to employment. For example, a protected act may be linked to accessing goods, facilities and services provided by the employer.

INSTRUCTING, CAUSING OR INDUCING DISCRIMINATION

What the Act says

9.16 [s 111(1)] It is unlawful to instruct someone to discriminate against, harass or victimise another person because of a protected characteristic or to instruct a person to help another person to do an unlawful act. Such an instruction would be unlawful even if it is not acted on.

Example: A GP instructs his receptionist not to register anyone with an Asian name. The receptionist would have a claim against the GP if she experienced a detriment as a result of not following the instruction. A potential patient would also have a claim against the GP under the services provisions of the Act if she discovered the instruction had been given and was put off from applying to register.

9.17 [s 111(2), (3) & (8)] The Act also makes it unlawful to cause or induce, or to attempt to cause or induce, someone to discriminate against or harass a third person because of a protected characteristic or to victimise a third person because they have done a protected act.

9.18 [s 111(4)] An inducement may amount to no more than persuasion and need not involve a benefit or loss. Nor does the inducement have to be applied directly: it may be indirect. It is enough if it is applied in such a way that the other person is likely to come to know about the inducement.

Example: The managing partner of an accountancy firm is aware that the head of the administrative team is planning to engage a senior receptionist with a physical disability. The managing partner does not issue any direct instruction but suggests to the head of administration that to do this would reflect poorly on his judgement and so affect his future with the firm. This is likely to amount to causing or attempting to cause the head of administration to act unlawfully.

9.19 It is also unlawful for a person to instruct, cause or induce a person to commit an act of discrimination or harassment in the context of relationships which have come to an end (see paragraphs 10.57 to 10.62).

9.20 [s 111(1)–(3)] The Act also prohibits a person from causing or inducing someone to help another person to do an unlawful act (see paragraph 9.26 below).

9.21 [s 111(6)] It does not matter whether the person who is instructed, caused or induced to commit an unlawful act carries it out. This is because instructing, causing or inducing an unlawful act is in itself unlawful. However, if the person does commit the unlawful act, they may be liable. The person who instructed, caused or induced them to carry it out will also be liable for it.

When does the Act apply?

9.22 [s 111(7)] For the Act to apply, the relationship between the person giving the instruction, or causing or inducing the unlawful act, and the recipient must be one in which discrimination, harassment or victimisation is prohibited. This will include employment relationships, the provision of services and public functions, and other relationships governed by the Act.

Who is protected?

9.23 [s 111(5)] The Act provides a remedy for:

(a) the person to whom the causing, instruction or inducement is addressed; and

(b) the person who is subjected to the discrimination or harassment or victimisation if it is carried out,

provided that they suffer a detriment as a result.

Example: In the example in paragraph 9.18, if the head of administration were to experience a detriment as a result of the managing partner's actions, he would be entitled to a remedy against the managing partner. The disabled candidate is also entitled to a remedy if she suffers a detriment as a result of the managing partner's actions.

9.24 [s 111(5)(c)] In addition, the Equality and Human Rights Commission has the power to bring proceedings regardless of whether an individual has actually experienced a detriment.

AIDING CONTRAVENTIONS

What the Act says

9.25 **[s 112(1)]** The Act makes it unlawful knowingly to help someone discriminate against, harass or victimise another person. A person who helps another in this way will be treated as having done the act of discrimination, harassment or victimisation themselves. It is also unlawful to help a person to discriminate against or harass another person after a relationship covered by the Act has ended, where the discrimination or harassment arises from and is closely connected to the relationship.

9.26 **[s 112(1)]** The Act also makes it unlawful to help with an instruction to discriminate or with causing or inducing discrimination.

What does it mean to help someone commit an unlawful act?

9.27 'Help' should be given its ordinary meaning. It does not have the same meaning as to procure, induce or cause an unlawful act. The help given to someone to discriminate, harass or victimise a person will be unlawful even if it is not substantial or productive, so long as it is not negligible.

Example: A company manager wants to ensure that a job goes to a female candidate because he likes to be surrounded by women in the office. However the company's Human Resources (HR) department, in accordance with their equal opportunities policy, has ensured that the application forms contain no evidence of candidates' sex. The manager asks a clerical worker to look in the HR files and let him know the sex of each candidate, explaining that he wants to filter out the male candidates. It may be unlawful for the clerical worker to give the manager this help, even if the manager is unsuccessful in excluding the male candidates.

What does the helper need to know to be liable?

9.28 For the help to be unlawful, the person giving the help must know at the time they give the help that discrimination, harassment or victimisation is a probable outcome. But the helper does not have to intend that this outcome should result from the help.

Example: In the example above, the help will be unlawful unless the clerical worker fails to realise that an act of discrimination is a likely outcome of her actions. But she only needs to understand that discrimination is a likely outcome; she does not have to intend that discrimination should occur as a result of her help.

Reasonable reliance on another's statement

9.29 **[s 112(2), (3)]** If the helper is told that they are assisting with a lawful act and it is reasonable for them to rely on this statement, then the help they give will not be unlawful even if it transpires that it assisted with a contravention of the Act. It is a criminal offence to knowingly or recklessly make a false or misleading statement as to the lawfulness of an act.

Example: In the example above, the manager might tell the clerical worker that he has a responsibility as manager to balance the sexes in the workforce and the HR department is mistaken in its approach. If it is reasonable for the worker to believe this, she will escape liability for the discrimination. Whether it is reasonable to believe this depends on all the relevant circumstances, including the nature of the action and the relationship of the helper to the person seeking help to carry out an unlawful act.

If the manager tells the clerical worker that it is all right for her to get the information, either knowing that that is not true or simply not caring whether it is true or not, the manager will not only have civil liability under the Act for discrimination but will also commit a criminal offence.

9.30 'Reasonable' means having regard to all the circumstances, including the nature of the act and how obviously discriminatory it is, the authority of the person making the statement and the knowledge that the helper has or ought to have.

GENDER REASSIGNMENT DISCRIMINATION - ABSENCE FROM WORK

What the Act says

9.31 **[s 16(2)(a)]** If a transsexual worker is absent from work because of gender reassignment, it is unlawful to treat them less favourably than they would be treated if they were absent due to an illness or injury.

Example: A transsexual worker takes time off to attend a Gender Identity Clinic as part of the gender reassignment process. His employer cannot treat him less favourably than she would treat him for absence due to illness or injury, for example by paying him less than he would have received if he were off sick.

9.32 **[s 16(2)(b)]** It is also discrimination for an employer to treat a transsexual person less favourably for being absent because of gender reassignment, compared to how they would treat the same worker for being absent for a reason other than sickness or injury and it is unreasonable to treat them less favourably.

Example: A transsexual worker tells her boss that she intends to undergo gender reassignment and asks him if she can take an afternoon off as annual leave to attend counselling. The request is brusquely refused although there are sufficient staff members on duty that day to cover for her absence. This could amount to gender reassignment discrimination.

9.33 The Act does not define a minimum or maximum time which must be allowed for absence because of gender reassignment. It would be good practice for employers to discuss with transsexual staff how much time they will need to take off in relation to the gender reassignment process and accommodate those needs in accordance with their normal practice and procedures.

CHAPTER 10
OBLIGATIONS AND LIABILITIES UNDER THE ACT

INTRODUCTION

[4.137]

10.1 Part 5 of the Act sets out the prohibited conduct as it applies in the employment context. It introduces new forms of obligations on employers to protect job applicants and employees from harassment by third parties during the course of employment, and not to enquire about the disability or health of applicants during the recruitment process. Part 8 sets out the circumstances in which liability for breaches of the Act might be incurred and the defences available against allegations of breaches of the Act.

10.2 This chapter explains the obligations of employers to job applicants and employees; liability of employers, principals, employees and agents for breaches of the Act; and the statutory defences available. In addition, this chapter explains employers' obligations when entering into contracts and the territorial scope of the Act.

DEFINITION OF EMPLOYMENT

10.3 **[s 83]** The Act defines employment broadly and covers a wide category of relationships that constitute work. Employment is defined in the Act as:

(a) employment under a contract of employment, a contract of apprenticeship or a contract personally to do work;

(b) Crown employment;

(c) employment as a relevant member of the House of Commons staff; or

(d) employment as a relevant member of the House of Lords staff.

10.4 The definition of employment in the Act is wider than under many other employment law provisions. So, for example, it covers a wider group of workers than are covered by the unfair dismissal provisions in the Employment Rights Act 1996.

10.5 The fact that a contract of employment is illegal or performed in an illegal manner will not exclude an Employment Tribunal having jurisdiction to hear an employment-related discrimination claim. This will be so provided that the discrimination is not inextricably linked to illegal conduct (so as to make an award of compensation appear to condone that conduct).

Example: An employee is aware that her employer is not deducting income tax or National Insurance contributions from her wages which, in this particular situation, is illegal. She queries this but her employer tells her: 'It's the way we do business.' Subsequently, she is dismissed after her employer becomes aware that she is pregnant. She alleges that the reason for her dismissal was her pregnancy and claims discrimination because of her pregnancy. While she knew that her employer was not paying tax on her wages, she did not actively participate in her employer's illegal conduct. The illegal performance of the contract was in no way linked to her discrimination claim. In the circumstances, she may be able to pursue her claim, despite her knowledge of her employer's illegal conduct.

OBLIGATIONS OF EMPLOYERS TO JOB APPLICANTS AND EMPLOYEES

10.6 **[ss 39 & 40; s 83(4)]** An employer has obligations not to discriminate against, victimise or harass job applicants and employees. These obligations also apply to a person who is seeking to recruit employees even if they are not yet an employer.

Example: A man sets up a new gardening business and advertises for men to work as gardeners. A woman gardener applies for a job but is rejected because of her sex. She would be able to make a claim for direct discrimination even though the businessman is not yet an employer as he does not yet have any employees.

WHAT THE ACT SAYS ABOUT EMPLOYERS' OBLIGATIONS TO JOB APPLICANTS

10.7 **[s 39(1) & (3)]** Employers must not discriminate against or victimise job applicants in:

(a) the arrangements they make for deciding who should be offered employment;

(b) in the terms on which they offer employment; or

(c) by not offering employment to the applicant.

What are arrangements?

10.8 Arrangements refer to the policies, criteria and practices used in the recruitment process including the decision making process. 'Arrangements' for the purposes of the Act are not confined to those which an employer makes in deciding who should be offered a specific job. They also include arrangements for deciding who should be offered employment more generally. Arrangements include such things as advertisements for jobs, the application process and the interview stage.

What are terms on which employment is offered?

10.9 **[s 39(6)]** The terms on which an employer might offer employment include such things as pay, bonuses and other benefits. In respect of discrimination because of sex or pregnancy and maternity, a term of an offer of employment that relates to pay is treated as discriminatory where, if accepted by the employee, it would give rise to an equality clause or rule; or where the term does not give rise to an equality clause or rule but it nevertheless amounts to direct discrimination. For more information on sex equality and maternity clauses, please see the Equal Pay Code.

10.10 [s 60] Employers' obligations to job applicants extend to them not making enquiries about disability or health before the offer of a job is made. This is discussed at paragraph 10.25 below.

What the Act says about employers' obligations to employees

10.11 **[s 39(2) & (4)]** Employers must not discriminate against or victimise an employee:

(a) as to the terms of employment;

(b) in the way they make access to opportunities for promotion, transfer or training or for receiving any other benefit, facility or service;

(c) by dismissing the employee; or

(d) subjecting them to any other detriment.

Terms of employment

10.12 The terms of employment include such things as pay, working hours, bonuses, occupational pensions, sickness or maternity and paternity leave and pay. The Act has specific provisions on equality of contractual terms between women and men, which are explained in the Code of Practice on Equal Pay.

Dismissals

10.13 **[s 39(7) & (8)]** A dismissal for the purposes of the Act includes:

(a) direct termination of employment by the employer (with or without notice);

(b) **[s 39(7)(a) & (8)]** termination of employment through the expiry of a fixed term contract (including a period defined by reference to an event or circumstance) unless the contract is immediately renewed; and

(c) **[s 39(7)(b)]** constructive dismissal – that is, where because of the employer's conduct the employee treats the employment as having come to an immediate end by resigning (whether or not the employee gives notice).

10.14 An employee who is dismissed in breach of the Act does not have to complete a qualifying period of service to bring a claim in the Employment Tribunal.

Example: An employer decides not to confirm a transsexual employee's employment at the end of a six months probationary period because of his poor performance. The employee is consequently dismissed. Yet, at the same time, the employer extends by three months the probationary period of a non-transsexual employee who has also not been performing to standard. This could amount to direct discrimination because of gender reassignment, entitling the dismissed employee to bring a claim to the Employment Tribunal.

Discrimination and unfair dismissal

10.15 Unfair dismissal claims can generally only be brought by employees who have one year or more continuous employment – but many categories of 'automatically unfair' dismissal have no minimum service requirement. For example, where the principal reason for dismissal is related to a request for time off work for family reasons such as maternity or parental leave, there is no minimum qualifying service.

10.16 Provided that the employee had one year or more continuous employment at the date of termination, a dismissal that amounts to a breach of the Act will almost inevitably be an unfair dismissal as well. In such cases, a person can make a claim for unfair dismissal at the same time as a discrimination claim.

Example: An employee who has worked with his employer for five years provides a witness statement in support of a colleague who has raised a grievance about homophobic bullying at work. The employer rejects the grievance and a subsequent appeal. A few months later the employer needs to make redundancies. The employer selects the employee for redundancy because he is viewed as 'difficult' and not a 'team player' because of the support he gave to his colleague in the grievance. It is likely that the redundancy would amount to unlawful victimisation and also be an unfair dismissal.

Detriment

10.17 A detriment is anything which might cause an employee to change their position for the worse or put them at a disadvantage; for example, being excluded from opportunities to progress within their career. The concept of detriment is explained in paragraph 9.8.

Example: An employer does not allow a black male employee an opportunity to act up in a management post, even though he has demonstrated enthusiasm by attending relevant training courses and taking on additional work. He has also expressed an interest in progressing within the business. Instead the employer offers the acting up opportunity to an Asian woman because he perceives Asian people as more hard-working than black people. If the black worker were able to demonstrate that he was better qualified for the acting up position compared to his Asian colleague, he could claim discrimination because of race on the basis that he was subjected to a detriment.

EMPLOYERS' DUTY TO MAKE REASONABLE ADJUSTMENTS

10.18 **[s 39(5)]** Employers have a duty to make reasonable adjustments in the recruitment and selection process and during employment. Making reasonable adjustments in recruitment might mean providing and accepting information in accessible formats. During recruitment, making reasonable adjustments could entail amending employment policies and procedures to ensure disabled employees are not put at a substantial disadvantage compared to non-disabled employees. (See Chapter 6 for a detailed explanation of the duty to make reasonable adjustments, and Chapters 16 and 17 for information on what employers can do to comply with the law.)

Example: An employer's disciplinary policy provides that they will make reasonable adjustments for disabled employees in the disciplinary procedure. When the employer decides to take disciplinary action against an employee with a hearing impairment, they pay for a palantypist to enable the employee to discuss her case with her union representative and to attend all meetings and hearings pertaining to the disciplinary hearing.

HARASSMENT OF JOB APPLICANTS AND EMPLOYEES

10.19 **[s 40]** Employers have a duty not to harass job applicants or their employees. This duty extends to harassment by third parties of job applicants and employees in the course of employment. (Chapter 7 provides a detailed explanation of the provisions on harassment; see paragraph 10.20 below on harassment by third parties.)

Harassment by third parties

10.20 **[s 40(2) & (4)]** Employers may be liable for harassment of job applicants and employees by third parties. A third party is anyone who is not the employer or another employee. It refers to those over whom the employer does not have direct control, such as customers or clients. The duty on employers to prevent third party harassment arises where the employee or job applicant has been harassed by a third party on at least two previous occasions, and the employer is aware of the harassment but fails to take 'reasonably practical steps' to prevent harassment by a third party happening again.

Example: A Ghanaian shop assistant is upset because a customer has come into the shop on Monday and Tuesday and on each occasion has made racist comments to him. On each occasion the shop assistant complained to his manager about the remarks. If his manager does nothing to stop it happening again, the employer would be liable for any further racial harassment perpetrated against that shop assistant by any customer.

10.21 **[s 40(3)]** The employer will be liable for harassment by a third party whether or not it is committed by the same third party or another third party.

Example: An employer is aware that a female employee working in her bar has been sexually harassed on two separate occasions by different customers. The employer fails to take any action and the employee experiences further harassment by yet another customer. The employer is likely to be liable for the further act of harassment.

10.22 It may be difficult to determine whether an employee or job applicant has been subjected to third party harassment. Employers should not wait for harassment by a third party to have occurred on at least two occasions before taking action.

10.23 **[s 40(2)(b)]** Employers will be able to avoid liability for third party harassment of their employees if they can show they took reasonably practical steps to prevent it happening.

10.24 Depending on the size and resources of an employer, reasonably practical steps might include:

- having a policy on harassment;
- notifying third parties that harassment of employees is unlawful and will not be tolerated, for example by the display of a public notice;
- inclusion of a term in all contracts with third parties notifying them of the employer's policy on harassment and requiring them to adhere to it;
- encouraging employees to report any acts of harassment by third parties to enable the employer to support the employee and take appropriate action;
- taking action on every complaint of harassment by a third party.

PRE-EMPLOYMENT ENQUIRIES ABOUT DISABILITY AND HEALTH

10.25 **[s 60]** Except in the specific circumstances set out below, it is unlawful for an employer to ask **any** job applicant about their disability or health until the applicant has been offered a job (on a conditional or unconditional basis) or has been included in a pool of successful candidates to be offered a job when a position becomes available. This includes asking such a question as part of the application process or during an interview. Questions relating to previous sickness absence are questions that relate to disability or health.

10.26 It is also unlawful for an agent or employee of an employer to ask questions about disability or health. This means that an employer cannot refer an applicant to an occupational health practitioner or ask an applicant to fill in a questionnaire provided by an occupational health practitioner before the offer of a job is made (or before acceptance into a pool of successful applicants) except in the circumstances set out below.

10.27 This provision of the Act is designed to ensure that disabled applicants are assessed objectively for their ability to do the job in question, and that they are not rejected because of their disability. There are some limited exceptions to this general rule, which mean that there are specified situations where such questions would be lawful.

EXCEPTIONS TO THE GENERAL RULE PROHIBITING DISABILITY OR HEALTH-RELATED QUESTIONS

10.28 **[s 60(6) & (14)]** There are six situations when it will be lawful for an employer to ask questions related to disability or health.

Reasonable adjustment needed for the recruitment process

10.29 [s 60(6)(a)] It is lawful for an employer to ask questions relating to reasonable adjustments that would be needed for an assessment such as an interview or other process designed to assess a person's suitability for a job. This means in practice that any information on disability or health obtained by an employer for the purpose of making adjustments to recruitment arrangements should, as far as possible, be held separately. Also it should not form any part of the decision-making process about an offer of employment, whether or not conditional.

10.30 Questions about reasonable adjustments needed for the job itself should not be asked until after the offer of a job has been made (unless these questions relate to a function that is intrinsic to the job – see below at paragraph 10.36). When questions are asked about reasonable adjustments, it is good practice to make clear the purpose of asking the question.

Example: An application form states: 'Please contact us if you are disabled and need any adjustments for the interview'. This would be lawful under the Act.

10.31 [s 60(6)(a)] It is lawful to ask questions about disability or health that are needed to establish whether a person (whether disabled or not) can undertake an assessment as part of the recruitment process, including questions about reasonable adjustments for this purpose.

Example: An employer is recruiting play workers for an outdoor activity centre and wants to hold a practical test for applicants as part of the recruitment process. He asks a question about health in order to ensure that applicants who are not able to undertake the test (for example, because they have a particular mobility impairment or have an injury) are not required to take the test. This would be lawful under the Act.

Monitoring purposes

10.32 [s 60(6)(c)] Questions about disability and health can be asked for the purposes of monitoring the diversity of applicants. (For information on good practice on monitoring, see Chapter 18 and Appendix 2.)

Implementing positive action measures

10.33 [s 60(6)(d)] It is also lawful for an employer to ask if a person is disabled so they can benefit from any measures aimed at improving disabled people's employment rates. This could include the guaranteed interview scheme whereby any disabled person who meets the essential requirements of the job is offered an interview. When asking questions about, for example, eligibility for a guaranteed interview scheme, an employer should make clear that this is the purpose of the question (see Chapter 12).

Occupational requirements

10.34 [s 60(6)(e)] There would be a need to demonstrate an occupational requirement if a person with a particular impairment is required for a job. In such a situation, where an employer can demonstrate that a job has an occupational requirement for a person with a specific impairment, then the employer may ask about a person's health or disability to establish that the applicant has that impairment.

Example: An employer wants to recruit a Deafblind project worker who has personal experience of Deafblindness. This is an occupational requirement of the job and the job advert states that this is the case. It would be lawful under the Act for the employer to ask on the application form or at interview about the applicant's disability.

National security

10.35 [s 60(14)] Questions about disability or health can be asked where there is a requirement to vet applicants for the purposes of national security.

Function intrinsic to the job

10.36 [s 60(6)(b)] Apart from the situations explained above, an employer may only ask about disability or health (before the offer of a job is made or before the person is in a pool of candidates to be offered vacancies when they arise) where the question relates to a person's ability to carry out a function that is intrinsic to that job. As explained in paragraphs 16.5 to 16.9, only functions that can be justified as necessary to a job should be included in a job description. Where a disability or health-related question would determine whether a person can carry out this function with reasonable adjustments in place, then such a question is permitted.

Example: A construction company is recruiting scaffolders. It would be lawful under the Act to ask about disability or health on the application form or at interview if the questions related specifically to an applicant's ability to climb ladders and scaffolding to a significant height. The ability to climb ladders and scaffolding is intrinsic to the job.

10.37 Where a disabled applicant voluntarily discloses information about their disability or health, the employer must ensure that in responding to this disclosure they only ask further questions that are permitted, as explained above. So, for example, the employer may respond by asking further questions about reasonable adjustments that would be required to enable the person to carry out an intrinsic function of the job. The employer must not respond by asking questions about the applicant's disability or health that are irrelevant to the ability to carry out the intrinsic function.

Example: At a job interview for a research post, a disabled applicant volunteers the information that as a reasonable adjustment he will need to use voice activated computer software. The employer responds by asking: 'Why can't you use a keyboard? What's wrong with you?' This would be an unlawful disability-related question, because it does not relate to a requirement that is intrinsic to the job – that is, the ability to produce research reports and briefings, not the requirement to use a keyboard.

If the employer wishes to ask any questions arising from the person's disclosure of a disability they would need to confine them to the permitted circumstances, and this can be explained to the candidate. In this instance, this might include asking about the type of adjustment that might be required to enable him to prepare reports and briefings.

10.38 This exception to the general rule about pre-employment disability or health enquiries should be applied narrowly because, in practice, there will be very few situations where a question about a person's disability or health needs to be asked – as opposed to a question about a person's ability to do the job in question with reasonable adjustments in place.

DISABILITY AND HEALTH ENQUIRIES AFTER A JOB OFFER

10.39 Although job offers can be made conditional on satisfactory responses to pre-employment disability or health enquiries or satisfactory health checks, employers must ensure they do not discriminate against a disabled job applicant on the basis of any such response. For example, it will amount to direct discrimination to reject an applicant purely on the grounds that a health check reveals that they have a disability. Employers should also consider at the same time whether there are reasonable adjustments that should be made in relation to any disability disclosed by the enquiries or checks.

10.40 If an employer is not in a position to offer a job, but has accepted applicants into a pool of people to be offered a job when one becomes available, it is lawful for the employer to ask disability or health-related questions at that stage.

10.41 Where pre-employment health enquiries are made after an applicant has been conditionally offered a job subject to such enquiries, employers must not use the outcome of the enquiries to discriminate against the person to whom a job offer has been made.

Example: A woman is offered a job subject to a satisfactory completion of a health questionnaire. When completing this questionnaire the woman reveals that she has HIV infection. The employer then decides to withdraw the offer of the job because of this. This would amount to direct discrimination because of disability.

10.42 An employer can avoid discriminating against applicants to whom they have offered jobs subject to satisfactory health checks by ensuring that any health enquiries are relevant to the job in question and that reasonable adjustments are made for disabled applicants (see Chapter 6). It is particularly important that occupational health practitioners who are employees or agents of the employer understand the duty to make reasonable adjustments. If a disabled person is refused a job because of a negative assessment from an occupational health practitioner during which reasonable adjustments were not adequately considered, this could amount to unlawful discrimination if the refusal was because of disability.

Example: An employer requires all successful job applicants to complete a health questionnaire. The questionnaire asks irrelevant questions about mental health and in answering the questions an applicant declares a history of a mental health condition. If the employer then refused to confirm the offer of the job, the unsuccessful disabled applicant would be able to make a claim of direct discrimination because of disability.

10.43 It is good practice for employers and occupational health practitioners to focus on any reasonable adjustments needed even if there is doubt about whether the person falls within the Act's definition of disabled person. (See paragraphs 2.8 to 2.20 and Appendix 1 for further information about the definition of disability).

ARMED FORCES

10.44 **[Sch 9, para 4]** An employer's obligations do not apply to service in the armed forces in relation to the protected characteristics of age or disability (see paragraphs 13.21 to 13.23).

LIABILITY OF EMPLOYERS AND PRINCIPALS UNDER THE ACT

Employers

10.45 **[s 109(1) & (3)]** Employers will be liable for unlawful acts committed by their employees in the course of employment, whether or not they know about the acts of their employees.

10.46 The phrase 'in the course of employment' has a wide meaning: it includes acts in the workplace and may also extend to circumstances outside such as work-related social functions or business trips abroad. For example, an employer could be liable for an act of discrimination which took place during a social event organised by the employer, such as an after-work drinks party.

Example: A shopkeeper goes abroad for three months and leaves an employee in charge of the shop. This employee harasses a colleague with a learning disability, by constantly criticising how she does her work. The colleague leaves the job as a result of this unwanted conduct. This could amount to harassment related to disability and the shopkeeper could be responsible for the actions of his employee.

10.47 **[s 109(4)]** However, an employer will not be liable for unlawful acts committed by an employee if they can show that they took 'all reasonable steps' to prevent the employee acting unlawfully. It could be a reasonable step for an employer to have an equality policy in place and to ensure it is put into practice. It might also be a reasonable step for an employer to provide training on the Act to employees. (Part 2 of the Code provides detailed explanations of the types of action employers can take to comply with the Act.)

Principals

10.48 [s 109(2) & (3)] Principals are liable for unlawful acts committed by their agents while acting under the principal's authority. It does not matter whether the principal knows about or approves of the acts of their agents. An agent would be considered to be acting with the principal's authority if the principal consents (whether this consent is expressed or implied) to the agent acting on their behalf. Examples of agents include occupational health advisers engaged but not employed by the employer, or recruitment agencies.

Example: A firm of accountants engages a recruitment agency to find them a temporary receptionist. The agency only puts forward white candidates, even though there are suitably qualified black and minority ethnic candidates on their books. The firm could be liable for the actions of the agency even though they do not know about or approve of the agency's action.

10.49 [s 109(5)] The liability of employers and principals does not extend to criminal offences. The only exception to this is offences relating to disabled persons and transport under Part 12 of the Act.

How employers and principals can avoid liability

10.50 [s 109(4)]An employer will not be liable for unlawful acts committed by their employees where the employer has taken 'all reasonable steps' to prevent such acts.

Example: An employer ensures that all their workers are aware of their policy on harassment, and that harassment of workers related to any of the protected characteristics is unacceptable and will lead to disciplinary action. They also ensure that managers receive training in applying this policy. Following implementation of the policy, an employee makes anti-Semitic comments to a Jewish colleague, who is humiliated and offended by the comments. The employer then takes disciplinary action against the employee. In these circumstances the employer may avoid liability because their actions are likely to show that they took all reasonable steps to prevent the unlawful act.

10.51 An employer would be considered to have taken all reasonable steps if there were no further steps that they could have been expected to take. In deciding whether a step is reasonable, an employer should consider its likely effect and whether an alternative step could be more effective. However, a step does not have to be effective to be reasonable.

10.52 Reasonable steps might include:

- implementing an equality policy;
- ensuring workers are aware of the policy;
- providing equal opportunities training;
- reviewing the equality policy as appropriate; and
- dealing effectively with employee complaints.

More information on equality policies is set out in Chapter 18.

10.53 A principal will not be liable for unlawful discrimination carried out by its agents where the agent has acted without the authority of the principal, for example, by acting contrary to the principal's instructions not to discriminate.

Example: An hotel (the principal) uses an agency (the agent) to supply catering staff. The hotel management ensures that the agency is aware of the hotel's equality and diversity policy. Despite this, and without the hotel management's knowledge, the agency decides never to send for interview anyone whom they believe to be gay or lesbian. In this case, the agency has acted without the hotel's authority and the hotel would not, therefore, be liable for the unlawful discrimination by the agency.

Employers' and principals' liability for other unlawful acts

10.54 Employers and principals will be also liable for aiding, causing, instructing or inducing their employees or agents to commit an unlawful act. Employers and principals will also be liable for discrimination or harassment of former workers if the discrimination or harassment arises out of and is closely connected to a relationship covered by the Act which has ended (see paragraph 10.57 to 10.62 below).

LIABILITY OF EMPLOYEES AND AGENTS UNDER THE ACT

10.55 [s 110(1) & (2)] Employees and agents may be personally liable for breaches of the Act where the employer or principal is also liable. Employees may be liable for their actions where the employer is able to rely successfully on the 'reasonable steps' defence. An agent may be personally liable for unlawful acts committed under their principal's authority. The principal may avoid liability if they can show that the agent was not acting with their authority.

Example: A line manager fails to make reasonable adjustments for a machine operator with multiple sclerosis, even though the machine operator has made the line manager aware that he needs various adjustments. The line manager is not aware that she has acted unlawfully because she failed to attend equality and diversity training, provided by her employer. The line manager could be liable personally for her actions as her employer's action, in providing training, could be enough to meet the statutory defence.

10.56 [s 110(3)] However, if the employee or agent reasonably relies on a statement by the employer or principal that an act is not unlawful, then the employee or agent will not be liable.

Example: In the example above, the line manager has asked the company director if she needs to make these adjustments and the director has wrongly said, 'I don't think he's covered by the Equality Act because he isn't in a wheelchair, so don't bother.' In this situation, the line manager would not be liable, but the employer would be liable.

RELATIONSHIPS THAT HAVE ENDED

What the Act says

10.57 [s 108] The Act makes it unlawful for employers to discriminate against or harass employees after a relationship covered by the Act has ended. An employer will be liable for acts of discrimination or harassment arising out of the work relationship and which are 'closely connected to' it.

10.58 The expression 'closely connected to' is not defined in the Act but will be a matter of degree to be judged on a case-by-case basis.

Example: A worker who receives an inaccurate and negative job reference from her former employer because she is a lesbian could have a claim against her former employer for direct discrimination because of sexual orientation.

10.59 [s 108(3)] This protection will apply even if the relationship in question came to an end before this section came into force.

10.60 [s 108(4)] This protection includes a duty to make reasonable adjustments for disabled ex-employees who are placed at a substantial disadvantage when dealing with their former employer.

Example: A former worker has lifetime membership of a works social club but cannot access it due to a physical impairment. Once the former employer is made aware of the situation, they will need to consider making reasonable adjustments.

10.61 [s 108(3)] An employee will be able to enforce protection against discrimination or harassment as if they were still in the relationship which has ended.

10.62 If the conduct or treatment which an individual receives after a relationship has ended amounts to victimisation, this will be covered by the victimisation provisions (see paragraphs 9.2 to 9.15).

CONTRACTS

10.63 [s 142] The Act prevents employers from avoiding their responsibilities under the Act by seeking to enter into agreements which permit them to discriminate or commit other unlawful acts.

Unenforceable terms in contracts and other agreements

10.64 [s 142(1)] A term of a contract that promotes or provides for treatment that is prohibited by the Act is unenforceable. However, this will not prevent a person who is or would be disadvantaged by an unenforceable term from relying on it to get any benefit to which they are entitled.

10.65 [s 142(2) & (3)] In relation to disability only, these provisions on unenforceable terms apply to terms of non-contractual agreements pertaining to the provision of employment services, or group insurance arrangements for employees.

10.66 [s 142(1) & (4)] The Act also says that a term of a contract that attempts to exclude or limit the anti-discrimination provisions of the Act is unenforceable by a person in whose favour it would operate. However, this does not prevent the parties to a claim in the Employment Tribunal from entering into an agreement to settle the claim, provided the agreement is made with the assistance of Acas or is a 'qualifying compromise contract' (see also paragraph 15.13).

Removal or modification of unenforceable terms

10.67 [s 143] A person who has an interest in or is affected by an unenforceable term in a contract can apply to the county court (or sheriff court in Scotland) to have it modified or removed.

VOID OR UNENFORCEABLE TERMS IN COLLECTIVE AGREEMENTS AND RULES OF UNDERTAKINGS

10.68 [s 145] Any term of a collective agreement will be void insofar as it leads to conduct prohibited by the Act. A rule of an undertaking is unenforceable insofar as it also has that effect. A rule of an undertaking is a rule made by a trade organisation, qualifications body or employer which is applied respectively to members or prospective members, holders of relevant qualifications or those seeking them, and employees or prospective employees.

10.69 [s 146] Employees and prospective employees can apply to an Employment Tribunal for a declaration that a term is void or that a rule is unenforceable.

TERRITORIAL SCOPE

10.70 The employment provisions in the Act form part of the law of England, Scotland and Wales (Great Britain). The Act leaves it to Employment Tribunals to determine whether these provisions apply to the circumstances being considered, in line with domestic and European case law. This requires that protection be afforded when there is a sufficiently close link between the employment relationship and Great Britain.

10.71 Where an employee works physically wholly within Great Britain, this will be straightforward. Where an employee works partly or wholly outside Great Britain, in considering whether a sufficiently close link exists a tribunal may consider such matters as: where the employee lives and works, where the employer is established, what laws govern the employment relationship in other respects, where tax is paid, and other matters it considers appropriate.

10.72 The protection to be afforded to seafarers and employees who work on an offshore installation, for example an oil rig, a gas rig or a renewable energy installation, ship or hovercraft, will be set out in secondary legislation made under the Act.

CHAPTER 11
DISCRIMINATION IN WORK RELATIONSHIPS OTHER THAN EMPLOYMENT

INTRODUCTION

[4.138]

11.1 As explained in paragraph 1.22, the Act covers a variety of work relationships beyond employment. This Chapter explains the relevant provisions of Part 5 of the Act which focus specifically on these wider work-related provisions. In other respects, however, the employment provisions of the Act apply in the usual way.

DISCRIMINATION AGAINST CONTRACT WORKERS

What the Act says

11.2 [s 41] Contract workers are protected to a similar extent to employees against discrimination, harassment and victimisation. They are also entitled to have reasonable adjustments made to avoid being put to a substantial disadvantage compared with non-disabled people.

11.3 **[s 41(1) & (3)]** The Act says that it is unlawful for a 'principal' to discriminate against or victimise a contract worker:

- in the terms on which the principal allows the contract worker to work;
- by not allowing the contract worker to do or continue to do the work;
- in the way the principal affords the contract worker access to benefits in relation to contract work, or by failing to afford the contract worker access to such benefits; or
- by subjecting the contract worker to any other detriment.

11.4 **[s 41(2) & (4)]** The Act also says that it is unlawful for a principal to harass a contract worker and that the duty to make reasonable adjustments applies to a principal.

Example: A meat packing company uses agency workers who are engaged and supplied by an employment business to supplement its own workforce during times of peak demand. The employment business supplies the company with three agency workers, one of whom is gay. The owner of the company discovers this and asks the agency to replace him with someone who is not gay. By not allowing the gay man to continue to work at the meat packing plant, the company will be liable for discrimination as a 'principal'.

Who is a 'principal'?

11.5 [s **41(5)**] A 'principal', also known as an 'end-user', is a person who makes work available for an individual who is employed by another person and supplied by that other person under a contract to which the principal is a party (whether or not that other person is a party to it). The contract does not have to be in writing.

Example: A nurse is employed by a private health care company which sometimes uses an employment business to deploy staff to work in the NHS. The employment business arranges for the nurse to work at an NHS Trust. In this case the 'principal' is the NHS Trust.

Who is a contract worker?

11.6 [s **41(7)**] A contract worker is a person who is supplied to the principal and is employed by another person who is not the principal. The worker must work wholly or partly for the principal, even if they also work for their employer, but they do not need to be under the managerial power or control of the principal. Contract workers can include employees who are seconded to work for another company or organisation and employees of companies who have a contract for services with an employment business.

11.7 Agency workers engaged by an employment business may also be contract workers as long as they are employed by the employment business. An agency worker supplied to a principal to do work and paid by an employment business under a contract will also be protected. Self-employed workers who are not supplied through employment businesses are not contract workers but may still be covered by the Act (see paragraph 10.3).

Example: An individual owns X company of which he is the sole employee. He has a contract for services with an employment business whereby he has to personally do the work. The employment business supplies him to Y company. Although there is no contract between X and Y companies, the employee of X company would be a contract worker and would be protected under the Act.

Example: A self-employed person is supplied by an employment business to a company. The worker is racially and sexually harassed by an employee of the company. Because the worker is not employed, it is unlikely that she will be protected by the Act unless she is able to convince a tribunal that it is necessary for a contract to be implied between her and the end-user.

11.8 [s **41(5)(b)**] There is usually a contract directly between the end-user and supplier, but this is not always the case. Provided there is an unbroken chain of contracts between the individual and the end-user of their services, that end-user is a principal for the purposes of the Act and the individual is therefore a contract worker.

Example: A worker is employed by a perfume concession based in a department store, where the store profited from any sales he made and imposed rules on the way he should behave. In these circumstances, the worker could be a contract worker. The concession would be his employer and the store would be the principal. However, this would not apply if the store simply offered floor space to the concession, the concession paid a fixed fee to the store for the right to sell its own goods in its own way and for its own profit, and concession staff in no way worked for the store.

HOW DOES THE DUTY TO MAKE REASONABLE ADJUSTMENTS APPLY TO DISABLED CONTRACT WORKERS?

11.9 **[s 41(4)]** The duty to make reasonable adjustments applies to a principal as well as an employer. Therefore, in the case of a disabled contract worker, their employer and the principal to whom they are supplied may each be under a separate duty to make reasonable adjustments.

Example: A travel agency hires a clerical worker from an employment business to fulfil a three month contract to file travel invoices during the busy summer holiday period. The contract worker is a wheelchair user, and is quite capable of doing the job if a few minor, temporary changes are made to the arrangement of furniture in the office. It is likely to be reasonable for the travel agency to make these.

Employer's duty to make reasonable adjustments

11.10 **[Sch 8, para 5(1)]** A disabled contract worker's employer will have to make reasonable adjustments if the contract worker is substantially disadvantaged by their own provisions, criteria and practices, by a physical feature of the premises they occupy, or by the non-provision of an auxiliary aid (see Chapter 6).

11.11 **[Sch 8, para 5(2)–(5)]** The employer of a disabled contract worker is also under a duty to make reasonable adjustments where the contract worker is likely to be substantially disadvantaged by:

- a provision, criterion or practice applied by or on behalf of all or most of the principals to whom the contract worker is or might be supplied, and where the disadvantage is the same or similar in the case of each principal;
- a physical feature of the premises occupied by each of the principals to whom the contract worker is or might be supplied, and where the disadvantage is the same or similar in the case of each principal; or
- the non-provision of an auxiliary aid which would cause substantial disadvantage, and that disadvantage would be the same or similar in the case of all or most of the principals to whom the contract worker might be supplied.

Example: A blind secretary is employed by a temping agency which supplies her to other organisations for secretarial work. Her ability to access standard computer equipment places her at a substantial disadvantage at the offices of all or most of the principals to whom she might be supplied. The agency provides her with an adapted portable computer and Braille keyboard, by way of reasonable adjustments.

Principal's duty to make reasonable adjustments

11.12 **[Sch 8, para 6]** A principal has similar duties to make reasonable adjustments to those of a disabled contract worker's employer, but does not have to make any adjustment which the employer should make. So, in effect, the principal is responsible for any additional reasonable adjustments which are necessary solely because of its own provision, criterion or practice, the physical feature of the premises it occupies or to avoid the non-provision of or failure to provide an auxiliary aid.

Example: In the preceding example, a bank which hired the blind secretary may have to make reasonable adjustments which are necessary to ensure that the computer provided by the employment business is compatible with the system which the bank is already using.

11.13 In deciding whether any, and if so, what, adjustments would be reasonable for a principal to make, the period for which the disabled contract worker will work for the principal is important. It might not be reasonable for a principal to have to make certain adjustments if the worker will be with the principal for only a short time.

Example: An employment business enters into a contract with a firm of accountants to provide an assistant for two weeks to cover an unexpected absence. The employment business proposes a name. The person concerned finds it difficult, because of his disability, to travel during the rush hour and would like his working hours to be modified accordingly. It might not be reasonable for the firm to have to agree, given the short time in which to negotiate and implement the new hours.

11.14 It would be reasonable for a principal and the employer of a contract worker to co-operate with each other with regard to any steps taken by the other to assist the contract worker. It is good practice for the principal and the employer to discuss what adjustments should be made, and who should make them.

Example: The bank and the employment business in the example in paragraphs 11.12 above would need to co-operate with each other so that, for example, the employment business allows the bank to make any necessary adaptations to the equipment which the employment business provided to ensure its compatibility with the bank's existing systems.

DISCRIMINATION AGAINST POLICE OFFICERS

What the Act says

11.15 **[s 42(1) & (2); s 109]** The Act says that police officers and cadets are to be treated as employees of the chief officer (chief constable in Scotland) under whose direction and control they are serving, or of the 'responsible' authority. Police officers include special constables and those in private constabularies such as the British Transport Police. Police officers and police cadets have the same rights as employees under the Act and therefore have the same protection against discrimination, harassment and victimisation (see Chapter 10) under Part 5. The chief officer (chief constable in Scotland) or the responsible authority is liable for their unlawful acts against police officers, cadets and applicants for appointment. They are also vicariously liable for unlawful acts committed by one officer against another.

11.16 **[s 42(4) & (5)]**A constable serving with the Serious Organised Crime Agency (SOCA) or Scottish Police Services Authority (SPSA) is treated as employed by those agencies or authorities and is protected by the employment provisions of the Act.

11.17 **[s 42(6)]** A constable at the Scottish Crime and Drugs Enforcement Agency (SCDEA) is treated as employed by the Director General of SCDEA.

DISCRIMINATION AGAINST PARTNERS IN A FIRM AND MEMBERS OF LIMITED LIABILITY PARTNERSHIPS

11.18 The Act provides protection to partners and members of a limited liability partnership (LLP) and a person seeking to become a partner or member of a LLP, similar to that provided to workers and job applicants against an employer.

What the Act says

11.19 **[ss 44(1), (5), 45(1), (5)]** It is unlawful for a firm, proposed firm, LLP or proposed LLP to discriminate against or victimise a partner or member:

- in the arrangements they make to determine who should be offered the position of partner or member;
- in the terms on which they offer the person a position as partner or member; or
- by not offering the person a position as partner or member.

Example: An African Caribbean candidate with better qualifications than other applicants is not shortlisted for partnership with an accountancy firm. The firm is unable to provide an explanation for the failure to shortlist. This could amount to direct discrimination because of race.

11.20 **[ss 44(2), (6), 45(2), (6)]** Where the person is already a partner or a member of a LLP, it is unlawful to discriminate against or victimise that person:

- in the terms of partnership or membership;
- in the way it affords (or by not affording) the person who is a partner or member access to opportunities for promotion, transfer or training or for receiving any other benefits, facility or service;
- by expelling the person who is a partner or member; or
- by subjecting the person who is a partner or member to any other detriment.

Example: An LLP refuses a Muslim member access to its childcare scheme because all the other children who attend the scheme have Christian parents. This could amount to direct discrimination because of religion or belief.

11.21 **[s 44(4) & 45(4)]** It is also unlawful for a firm, proposed firm, LLP or proposed LLP to subject a partner or member or a person seeking to become a partner or member to harassment.

Example: A lesbian candidate who applies to become a partner is subjected to homophobic banter during her partnership interview. The banter is offensive and degrading of her sexual orientation and creates an offensive and degrading environment for her at interview. This would amount to harassment related to sexual orientation.

HOW DOES THE DUTY TO MAKE REASONABLE ADJUSTMENTS APPLY TO PARTNERS, AND MEMBERS OF AN LLP?

11.22 **[s 44(7) & 45(7)]** The duty to make reasonable adjustments for disabled partners and members applies to a firm, proposed firm, LLP and proposed LLP in the same way as it applies to an employer (see Chapters 6 and 10).

11.23 **[Sch 8, paras 7 & 8]** Where a firm or LLP is required to make adjustments for a disabled partner, disabled prospective partner, disabled member or disabled prospective member, the cost of making the adjustments must be borne by that firm or LLP. Provided that the disabled person is, or becomes, a partner or member, they may be required (because partners or members share the costs of the firm or LLP) to make a reasonable contribution towards this expense. In assessing the reasonableness of any such contribution (or level of such contribution), particular regard should be had to the proportion in which the disabled partner or member is entitled to share in the firm's or LLP's profits, the cost of the reasonable contribution and the size and administrative resources of the firm or LLP.

Example: A disabled person who uses a wheelchair as a result of a mobility impairment joins a firm of architects as a partner, receiving 20% of the firm's profits. He is asked to pay 20% towards the cost of a lift which must be installed so that he can work on the premises. This is likely to be reasonable.

DISCRIMINATION AGAINST BARRISTERS AND ADVOCATES

11.24 In England and Wales, barristers who are tenants and pupil barristers (including persons who apply for pupillage) have rights which are broadly similar to the rights of employees under the Act. Tenants include barristers who are permitted to work in chambers, door tenants and squatters (barristers who can practice from a set of chambers but who are not tenants).

What the Act says

11.25 **[s 47(1) & (4)]** It is unlawful for a barrister or a barrister's clerk to discriminate against or victimise a person applying for a tenancy or pupillage:

- in the arrangements made to determine to whom a tenancy or pupillage should be offered;
- in respect of any terms on which a tenancy or pupillage is offered; or
- by not offering a tenancy or pupillage to them.

Example: A barristers' chambers reject all CVs for pupillages from applicants who completed their law examinations over three years ago. This criterion tends to exclude older applicants and could amount to indirect age discrimination, unless it can be objectively justified.

11.26 **[s 47(3)]** A barrister or barrister's clerk must not in relation to a tenancy or pupillage harass a tenant or pupil or an applicant for a tenancy or pupillage.

Example: A male barrister pesters a female applicant for pupillage with repeated invitations to dinner and suggests that her application for pupillage would be viewed more favourably by the barristers' chambers if she accepted his invitation to dinner. This could amount to sexual harassment.

11.27 **[s 47(2) & (5)]** The Act also makes it unlawful for a barrister or barrister's clerk to discriminate against or victimise a tenant or pupil:

(a) in respect of the terms of their tenancy or pupillage;
(b) in the opportunities for training, or gaining experience, which are afforded or denied to them;
(c) in the benefits, facilities or services which are afforded or denied to them;
(d) by terminating their pupillage;
(e) by subjecting them to pressure to leave their chambers; or
(f) by subjecting them to any other detriment.

Example: On receiving a solicitor's instructions on behalf of a Christian client, a clerk puts forward a Christian barrister in his chambers in preference to a Hindu barrister. He does this because he thinks the Hindu barrister's religion would prevent him representing the Christian client properly. This could amount to direct discrimination because of religion or belief as the clerk's action could be a detriment to the Hindu barrister.

11.28 **[s 47(6)]** The Act also says it is unlawful for a person (for example, an instructing solicitor, firm of solicitors or client) in relation to instructing a barrister to discriminate against that barrister by subjecting them to a detriment, or harass or victimise that barrister. This includes the giving, withholding or termination of instructions.

Example: When a clerk puts forward a male barrister for a pregnancy discrimination case, the firm of solicitors representing the employer asks for a female barrister instead, because they consider the case would be represented better by a woman. This could amount to direct discrimination because of sex on the part of the firm of solicitors.

11.29 **[s 48]** The provisions applying to barristers and barristers' clerks, set out above, also apply to advocates, advocates' clerks, devils, members of stables and persons seeking to become devils or members of a stable in Scotland.

HOW DOES THE DUTY TO MAKE REASONABLE ADJUSTMENTS APPLY TO BARRISTERS AND CLERKS?

11.30 **[ss 47(7), 48(7)]** The duty to make reasonable adjustments applies to barristers and barristers' clerks (advocates' clerks in Scotland) in the same way as it applies to an employer (see Chapters 6 and 10).

Example: Barristers' clerks at a set of chambers routinely leave messages for barristers on scraps of paper. This practice is likely to disadvantage visually impaired members of chambers and may need to be altered for individual disabled tenants and pupils.

DISCRIMINATION AGAINST PERSONAL AND PUBLIC OFFICE HOLDERS

11.31 **[ss 49–52, Sch 6 paras (1) & (2)]** It is unlawful to discriminate against, victimise or harass office holders where they are not protected by other provisions (within Part 5) of the Act. Thus an office holder who is an employee will be protected by the provisions dealing with employment. Whilst an office holder may also be an employee, it is important to note that office holders do not hold their position as employees. An office holder's functions, rights and duties may be defined by the office they hold, instead of or in addition to a contract of employment.

11.32 The Act affords protection to those seeking to be appointed or those appointed to personal offices and public offices. Office holders include offices and posts such as directors, non-executive directors, company secretaries, positions on the board of non-departmental public bodies, some judicial positions and positions held by some ministers of religion.

What is a personal office?

11.33 **[s 49(1), (2) & (11)]** A personal office is an office or post to which a person is appointed to discharge a function personally under the direction of another person (who may be different from the person who makes the appointment) and is entitled to remuneration other than expenses or compensation for loss of income or benefits.

11.34 **[s 52(4)]** Where a personal office is also a public office it is to be treated as a public office only.

What is a public office?

11.35 **[s 50(1) & (2)]** A public office holder is a person who is appointed by a member of the executive or whose appointment is made on the recommendation of, or with the approval of, a member of the executive or either Houses of Parliament, the National Assembly for Wales, or the Scottish Parliament.

What the Act says

11.36 **[ss 49(3), (5) & 50(3), (5)]** It is unlawful for a person who has the power to make an appointment to a personal or public office to discriminate against or victimise a person:

- in the arrangements which are made for deciding to whom to offer the appointment;
- as to the terms on which the appointment is offered;
- by refusing to offer the person the appointment.

Example: A deaf woman who communicates using British Sign Language applies for appointment as a Chair of a public body. Without interviewing her, the public body making the appointments writes to her saying that she would not be suitable as good communication skills are a requirement. This could amount to discrimination because of disability.

11.37 **[ss 49(4) & 50(4)]** It is unlawful for a person who has the power to make an appointment to a personal or public office to harass a person who is seeking or being considered for appointment in relation to the office.

11.38 **[ss 49(6), (8) & 50(6), (9), (10)]** It is also unlawful for a 'relevant person' in relation to a personal office or public office to discriminate against or victimise an office holder:

- as to the terms of the appointment;
- in the opportunities which are afforded (or refused) for promotion, transfer, training or receiving any other benefit, facility or service;
- by terminating their appointment; or
- by subjecting the person to any other detriment.

11.39 **[ss 49(7) & 50(8)]** The Act also makes it unlawful for a relevant person to harass an appointed office holder in relation to that office.

11.40 **[s 52(6)]** A 'relevant person' is the person who has the power to act on the matter in respect of which unlawful conduct is alleged. Depending on the circumstances, this may be the person who can set the terms of appointment, afford access to an opportunity; terminate the appointment; subject an appointee to a detriment; or harass an appointee.

11.41 **[ss 49(9) & 50(11)]** The duty to make reasonable adjustments applies to those who can make an appointment to personal office and to public office and a 'relevant person' in relation to the needs of disabled office holders.

11.42 **[ss 49(12) & 50(12)]** In respect of sex or pregnancy and maternity discrimination, if an offer of appointment to an office has a term relating to pay that would give rise to an equality clause if it were accepted, this would be treated as discriminatory. If that is not the case, a term relating to pay will be discriminatory where the offer of the term constitutes direct discrimination.

Who can make appointments to a public office?

11.43 **[s 50(2)]** A member of the executive, for example a government Minister, or someone who makes an appointment on the recommendation of or subject to the approval of a member of the executive can make appointments to a public office.

11.44 **[s 50(7), (10); s 52(6)]** Where, in relation to a public office, an appointment is made on the recommendation or is subject to the approval of the House of Commons, the House of Lords, the National Assembly for Wales or the Scottish Parliament, it is unlawful for a relevant person to discriminate against or victimise an office holder in all respects as set out in paragraph 11.38, except by terminating the appointment. However, a relevant person does not include the House of Commons or the House of Lords, the National Assembly for Wales or the Scottish Parliament.

Example: A Secretary of State terminates the appointment of a Commissioner in a non-departmental public body because of the Commissioner's religious beliefs. This could amount to discrimination because of religion or belief.

Recommendations and approvals for the appointment to public offices

11.45 **[s 51(1) & (3)]** The Act says it is unlawful for a member of the executive or a 'relevant body' who has the power to make recommendations or give approval for an appointment, or a member of the executive, to discriminate or victimise a person:

- in the arrangements made for deciding who to recommend for appointment or to whose appointment to give approval;
- by not recommending that person for appointment or by not giving approval to the appointment;
- by making a negative recommendation for appointment.

11.46 **[s 51(2)]** It is unlawful for a member of the executive or 'relevant body' to harass a person seeking or being considered for a public office in relation to that office.

11.47 **[s 51(4)]** A 'relevant body' has a duty to make reasonable adjustments to avoid a disabled person being put at a substantial disadvantage compared to non-disabled people.

Example: A selection process is carried out to appoint a chair for a public health body. The best candidate for the appointment is a disabled person with a progressive condition who is not able to work full-time because of her disability. The person who approves the appointment should consider whether it would be a reasonable adjustment to approve the appointment of the disabled person on a job-share or part-time basis.

What is a 'relevant body'?

11.48 **[s 51(5)]** A relevant body is a body established by or in pursuance of an enactment or by a member of the executive, for example a non-departmental public body.

Example: A statutory commission which makes recommendations to the Minister for the appointment of its CEO would be a relevant body for the purpose of the Act.

Example: It could be direct discrimination for the government Minister responsible for approving the appointment of members of the BBC Trust to refuse to approve the appointment of a person because they are undergoing gender reassignment.

Personal and public offices that are excluded from the Act

11.49 **[Sch 6, para 2]** Political offices or posts are excluded from the definition of personal or public offices. Political offices and posts include offices of the House of Commons or House of Lords; the office of the leader of the opposition; the Chief or Assistant Opposition Whip; county council offices; an office of the Greater London Authority held by the Mayor of London; or assembly members of the Greater London Authority and offices of registered political parties.

11.50 Life peerages and any dignity or honour awarded by the Crown are also excluded from the definition of personal and public offices.

What the Act says about the termination of an office holder's post

11.51 **[s 52(7) & (8)]** The provisions on the termination of an office holder's office or post are the same as for termination of employment; that is, it applies to fixed term appointments which are not renewed on the expiration of the term of the appointment, and to termination of the appointment by an office holder because of the conduct of a relevant person.

QUALIFICATIONS BODIES AND TRADE ORGANISATIONS

11.52 **[ss 53 & 57]** Qualification bodies and trade organisations have the same obligations as employers in their capacity as employers. They also have separate obligations under the Act to members and prospective members and to those on whom they confer qualifications. The nature and effect of the obligations on qualification bodies and trade organisations will be set out in a separate Code of Practice.

EMPLOYMENT SERVICES

11.53 **[s 55]** The Act places obligations on employment service providers that are similar to those placed on employers. The definition of an employment service is set out in paragraph 11.59 below.

What the Act says

11.54 **[s 55(1) & (4)]** An employment service provider must not discriminate against or victimise a person in relation to the provision of an employment service:

- in the arrangements that it makes for selecting people to whom it provides, or offers to provide, the service;
- in the terms on which it offers to provide the service to that person;
- by not offering to provide the service to that person.

Example: An employment agency only offers its services to people with European Economic Area (EEA) passports or identity cards. This could be indirect race discrimination as it would put to a particular disadvantage non-European nationals who do not hold a European passport but have the right to live and work in the UK without immigration restrictions. It is unlikely that the policy could be objectively justified.

11.55 **[s 55(2) & (5)]** In addition, an employment service provider must not in relation to the provision of an employment service, discriminate against or victimise a person:

- as to the terms upon which it provides the service to that person;
- by not providing the service to that person;
- by terminating the provision of the service to that person; or
- by subjecting that person to a detriment.

Example: A headhunting company fails to put forward women for chief executive positions. It believes that women are less likely to succeed in these positions because they will leave to get married and start a family. This could amount to discrimination because of sex.

11.56 **[s 55(3)]** It is also unlawful for an employment service provider to harass, in relation to the provision of an employment service, those who seek to use or who use its services.

Example: An advisor for a careers guidance service is overheard by a transsexual client making offensive and humiliating comments to a colleague about her looks and how she is dressed. This could amount to harassment related to gender reassignment.

11.57 **[s 55(6)]** Under the Act, an employment service provider has a duty to make reasonable adjustments, except when providing a vocational service. The duty to make reasonable adjustments is an anticipatory duty.

Example: A woman who has dyslexia finds it difficult to fill in an employment agency's registration form. An employee of the agency helps her to fill it in. This could be a reasonable adjustment for the employer to make.

11.58 **[s 55(7)]** However, the anticipatory duty to make reasonable adjustments does not apply to vocational training (that is, training for work or work experience), where the duty is the same as in employment.

What are employment services?

11.59 'Employment service' includes:

- **[s 56(2)]** the provision of or making arrangements for the provision of vocational training, that is, training for employment and work experience;
- the provision of or making arrangements for the provision of vocational guidance, such as careers guidance;
- services for finding people employment, such as employment agencies and headhunters. It also includes the services provided by, for example, Jobcentre Plus, the Sector Skills Council and intermediary agencies that provide basic training and work experience opportunities such as the Adult Advancement and Careers Service and other schemes that assist people to find employment;
- services for supplying employers with people to do work, such as those provided by employment businesses.

11.60 **[s 56(8)]** The reference to training applies to facilities for training. Examples of the types of activities covered by these provisions include providing classes on CV writing and interviewing techniques, training in IT/keyboard skills, providing work placements and literacy and numeracy classes to help adults into work.

Which employment services are excluded?

11.61 **[s 56(4) & (5)]** The provision of employment services does not include training or guidance in schools or to students at universities or further and higher education institutions.

11.62 Those concerned with the provision of vocational services are subject to different obligations which are explained further in the code on Services, Public Functions and Associations under Part 3 of the Act (see Code on Services, Public Functions and Associations).

DISCRIMINATION AGAINST LOCAL AUTHORITY MEMBERS

11.63 **[s 58]** Local authority members carrying out their official duties are protected against unlawful discrimination, harassment and victimisation.

What the Act says

11.64 **[s 58(1) & (3)]** A local authority must not discriminate against or victimise a local authority member while they undertake official business:

(a) in the opportunities which are afforded (or refused) for training or receiving any other benefit; or
(b) by subjecting the local authority member to any other detriment.

Example: A councillor of Chinese origin sits on a local council's policy scrutiny committee. Officers of the council often send him papers for meetings late or not at all which means he is often unprepared for meetings and unable to make useful contributions. His colleagues, none of whom are Chinese, do not experience this problem. This could amount to direct discrimination against the councillor by the authority.

11.65 **[s 58(2)]** It is also unlawful for a local authority to harass a local authority member while they undertake official business.

Example: A councillor who is a Humanist regularly gets ridiculed about her beliefs by other councillors and council officers when attending council meetings. This could amount to harassment related to religion or belief.

11.66 **[s 58(4)]** It will not be a detriment if a local authority fails to elect, appoint or nominate a local authority member to an office, committee, sub-committee or body of the local authority.

Example: A local authority councillor who is a Christian fails to get appointed to a planning committee when another councillor who is an Atheist did get appointed. The Christian councillor would not have a claim under the Act.

11.67 **[s 58(6)]** Local authorities are also under a duty to make reasonable adjustments for disabled members of the local authority, who carry out official business, to avoid their being at a substantial disadvantage compared to non-disabled people.

Example: A local authority fails to provide documents for meetings in Braille for a councillor who is blind. As a result the councillor is unable to participate fully in Council business. By not making the documents available in Braille, the local authority would have failed to comply with its duty to make reasonable adjustments.

What is a local authority?

11.68 **[s 59(2)]** 'Local authority' refers to any of the twelve types of body listed in the Act. The government can by order change the list to add, amend or remove bodies which exercise functions that have been conferred on those covered by (a) to (l) of the list.

Who is a local authority member?

11.69 **[s 59(5)]** A local authority 'member' will usually mean an elected member of a local authority such as a councillor. In relation to the Greater London Authority, 'member' means the Mayor of London or a member of the London Assembly.

What is official business?

11.70 **[s 59(4)]** Official business is anything undertaken by a local authority member in their capacity as a member of:

(a) the local authority;
(b) a body to which the local authority member is appointed by their authority or by a group of local authorities, for example a planning committee; or
(c) any other public body.

CHAPTER 12
POSITIVE ACTION

INTRODUCTION

[4.139]
12.1 **[s 158]** The Act permits employers to take positive action measures to improve equality for people who share a protected characteristic. These optional measures can be used by employers, principals, partnerships, LLPs, barristers and advocates, those who make appointments to personal and public offices and employment service providers (the term 'employer' is used to refer to all those covered by the provisions).

12.2 As well as explaining the general positive action provisions in the Act, this chapter outlines the benefits of using these measures, describes the circumstances when positive action could be appropriate and illustrates the law with examples of approaches that employers might consider taking.

12.3 **[s 159]** The specific provisions on positive action in recruitment and promotion will not be in force when the Code is laid before Parliament and therefore are not covered in this Code.

DISTINGUISHING POSITIVE ACTION AND 'POSITIVE DISCRIMINATION'

12.4 Positive action is not the same as positive discrimination, which is unlawful. It may be helpful to consider the Act's positive action provisions within the continuum of actions to improve work opportunities for people who share a protected characteristic.

12.5 First, action taken to benefit those from one particular protected group that does not involve less favourable treatment of those from another protected group, or to eradicate discriminatory policies or practices, will normally be lawful. Examples might include placing a job advertisement in a magazine with a largely lesbian and gay readership as well as placing it in a national newspaper; or reviewing recruitment processes to ensure that they do not contain criteria that discriminate because of any protected characteristic. Such actions would not be classed as 'positive action'.

12.6 Second, there are actions that fall within the framework of the Act's positive action provisions, such as reserving places on a training course for a group sharing a protected characteristic. These actions are only lawful if they meet the statutory conditions for positive action measures and do not exceed the limitations set out in the Act.

Example: A large public sector employer monitors the composition of their workforce and identifies that there are large numbers of visible ethnic minority staff in junior grades and low numbers in management grades. In line with their equality policy, the employer considers the following action to address the low numbers of ethnic minority staff in senior grades:

- Reviewing their policies and practices to establish whether there might be discriminatory criteria which inhibit the progression of visible ethnic minorities;
- Discussing with representatives of the trade union and the black staff support group how the employer can improve opportunities for progression for the under-represented group;
- Devising a positive action programme for addressing under-representation of the target group, which is shared with all staff;
- Including within the programme shadowing and mentoring sessions with members of management for interested members of the target group. The programme also encourages the target group to take advantage of training opportunities such as training in management, which would improve their chances for promotion.

12.7 Third, there are actions – often referred to as 'positive discrimination' – which involve preferential treatment to benefit members of a disadvantaged or under-represented group who share a protected characteristic, in order to address inequality. However, these actions do not meet the statutory requirements for positive action, and will be unlawful unless a statutory exception applies (see Chapters 13 and 14).

Example: An LLP seeks to address the low participation of women partners by interviewing all women regardless of whether they meet the criteria for partnership. This would be positive discrimination and is unlawful.

12.8 It is important to note that it is not unlawful for an employer to treat a disabled person more favourably compared to a non-disabled person (see paragraph 3.35).

Voluntary nature of positive action

12.9 Positive action is optional, not a requirement. However, as a matter of good business practice, public and private sector employers may wish to take positive action measures to help alleviate disadvantage experienced in the labour market by groups sharing a protected characteristic; take action to increase their participation in the workforce where this is disproportionately low; or meet their particular needs relating to employment.

12.10 In addition, employers who use positive action measures may find this brings benefits to their own organisation or business. Benefits could include:

- a wider pool of talented, skilled and experienced people from which to recruit;
- a dynamic and challenging workforce able to respond to changes;
- a better understanding of foreign/global markets;
- a better understanding of the needs of a more diverse range of customers – both nationally and internationally.

WHAT THE ACT SAYS

12.11 Where an employer reasonably thinks that people who share a protected characteristic:
(a) **[s 158(1)(a)]** experience a disadvantage connected to that characteristic; or
(b) **[s 158(1)(b)]** have needs that are different from the needs of persons who do not share that characteristic; or
(c) **[s 158(1)(c)]** have disproportionately low participation in an activity compared to others who do not share that protected characteristic

the employer may take any action which is proportionate to meet the aims stated in the Act (the 'stated aims').

12.12 The 'stated aims' are:
(a) **[s 158(2)(a)]** enabling or encouraging persons who share the protected characteristic to overcome or minimise that disadvantage (referred to in this chapter as 'action to remedy disadvantage');
(b) **[s 158(2)(b)]** meeting those needs ('action to meet needs'); or
(c) **[s 158(2)(c)]** enabling or encouraging persons who share the protected characteristic to participate in that activity ('action to encourage participation in activities').

12.13 Action may be taken when any one or all of these conditions exist. Sometimes the conditions will overlap – for example, people sharing a protected characteristic may be at a disadvantage which may also give rise to a different need or may be reflected in their low level of participation in particular activities.

Example: National research shows that Bangladeshis have low rates of participation in the teaching profession. A local school governing body seeks to tackle this low participation by offering open days in schools to members of the Bangladeshi community who might be interested in teaching as a profession. This would be a form of positive action to encourage participation.

What does 'reasonably think' mean?

12.14 In order to take positive action, an employer must reasonably think that one of the above conditions applies; that is, disadvantage, different needs or disproportionately low participation. This means that some indication or evidence will be required to show that one of these statutory conditions applies. It does not, however, need to be sophisticated statistical data or research. It may simply involve an employer looking at the profiles of their workforce and/or making enquiries of other comparable employers in the area or sector. Additionally, it could involve looking at national data such as labour force surveys for a national or local picture of the work situation for particular groups who share a protected characteristic. A decision could be based on qualitative evidence, such as consultation with workers and trade unions.

12.15 More than one group with a particular protected characteristic may be targeted by an employer, provided that for each group the employer has an indication or evidence of disadvantage, different needs or disproportionately low participation.

ACTION TO REMEDY DISADVANTAGE

What is a disadvantage for these purposes?

12.16 'Disadvantage' is not defined in the Act. It may for example, include exclusion, rejection, lack of opportunity, lack of choice and barriers to accessing employment opportunities. Disadvantage may be obvious in relation to some issues such as legal, social or economic barriers or obstacles which make it difficult for people of a particular protected group to enter into or make progress in an occupation, a trade, a sector or workplace (see also paragraphs 4.9 to 4.14).

What action might be taken to overcome or minimise disadvantage?

12.17 **[s 158(2)(a)]** The Act enables action to be taken to overcome or minimise disadvantage experienced by people who share a protected characteristic. The Act does not limit the action that could be taken, provided it satisfies the statutory conditions and is a proportionate way of achieving the aim of overcoming a genuine disadvantage. Such action could include identifying through monitoring, consultation or a review of policies and practices any possible causes of the disadvantage and then:

- targeting advertising at specific disadvantaged groups, for example advertising jobs in media outlets which are likely to be accessed by the target group;
- making a statement in recruitment advertisements that the employer welcomes applications from the target group, for example 'older people are welcome to apply';
- providing opportunities exclusively to the target group to learn more about particular types of work opportunities with the employer, for example internships or open days;
- providing training opportunities in work areas or sectors for the target group, for example work placements.

Example: Research shows that women in Britain experience significant disadvantage in pursuing careers in engineering, as reflected in their low participation in the profession and their low status within it. Some of the key contributing factors are gender stereotyping in careers guidance and a lack of visible role models. A leading equalities organisation, in partnership with employers in the engineering sector, offers opportunities exclusively to girls and women to learn more about the career choices through a careers fair attended by women working in the profession.

ACTION TO MEET NEEDS

What are 'different' or 'particular' needs?

12.18 A group of people who share a particular protected characteristic have 'different needs' if, due to past or present discrimination or disadvantage or due to factors that especially apply to people who share that characteristic, they have needs that are different to those of other groups. This does not mean that the needs of a group have to be entirely unique from the needs of other groups to be considered 'different'. Needs may also be different because, disproportionately, compared to the needs of other groups, they are not being met or the need is of particular importance to that group.

Example: An employer's monitoring data on training shows that their workers over the age of 60 are more likely to request training in advanced IT skills compared to workers outside this age group. The employer could provide training sessions primarily targeted at this group of workers.

What action might be taken to meet those needs?

12.19 **[s 158(2)(b)]** The Act does not limit the action that employers can take to meet different needs, provided the action satisfies the statutory conditions and is a proportionate means of achieving the aim of meeting genuinely different needs. Such action could include:

- providing exclusive training to the target group specifically aimed at meeting particular needs, for example, English language classes for staff for whom English is a second language;
- the provision of support and mentoring, for example, to a member of staff who has undergone gender reassignment;
- the creation of a work-based support group for members of staff who share a protected characteristic who may have workplace experiences or needs that are different from those of staff who do not share that characteristic. (The Act's provisions on members associations might be relevant here: see the Code on services and public functions).

ACTION TO ENCOURAGE PARTICIPATION IN ACTIVITIES

What activities does this apply to?

12.20 This provision applies to participation in any activity where the participation of those who share a protected characteristic is disproportionately low; this can include employment and training. Action to increase participation might include making available training opportunities, open days or mentoring and shadowing schemes.

What does 'disproportionately low' mean?

12.21 **[s 158(1)(c)]** The Act says that action can only be taken where the employer reasonably thinks that participation in an activity by people sharing a particular protected characteristic is 'disproportionately low.' This means that the employer will need to have some reliable indication or evidence that participation is low compared with that of other groups or compared with the level of participation that could reasonably be expected for people from that protected group.

Example: An employer has two factories, one in Cornwall and one in London. Each factory employs 150 workers. The Cornish factory employs two workers from an ethnic minority background and the London factory employs 20 workers also from an ethnic minority background.

The ethnic minority population is 1% in Cornwall and 25% in London. In the Cornish factory the employer would not be able to meet the test of 'disproportionately low', since the number of its ethnic minority workers is not low in comparison to the size of the ethnic minority population in Cornwall. However, the London factory, despite employing significantly more ethnic minority workers, could show that the number of ethnic minority workers employed there was still disproportionately low in comparison with their proportion in the population of London overall.

12.22 Participation may be low compared with:

- the proportion of people with that protected characteristic nationally;

Example: A national labour force survey shows women are under-represented at board level in the financial services sector. An employer could take positive action to increase their representation in the sector.

- the proportion of people with that protected characteristic locally;

Example: An employer with a factory in Oldham employs 150 people but only one Asian worker. The employer may be able to show disproportionately low participation of Asian workers by looking at their workforce profile in comparison to the size of the Asian population in Oldham.

- the proportion of people with that protected characteristic in the workforce.

Example: A construction company's workforce monitoring data reveals low participation of women in their workforce. They collaborate with the sector skills council for the electro-technical, heating, ventilation, air conditioning, refrigeration and plumbing industries to provide information targeting women on apprenticeships in construction.

12.23 Employers will need to have some indication or evidence to show low participation. This might be by means of statistics or, where these are not available, by evidence based on monitoring, consultation or national surveys. For more information on evidence, see paragraph 12.14.

What action could be taken?

12.24 **[s 158(2)(c)]** The Act permits action to be taken to enable or encourage people who share the protected characteristic to participate in that activity. Provided that the action is a proportionate means of achieving the aim of enabling or encouraging participation, the Act does not limit what action could be taken. It could include:

- setting targets for increasing participation of the targeted group;
- providing bursaries to obtain qualifications in a profession such as journalism for members of the group whose participation in that profession might be disproportionately low;
- outreach work such as raising awareness of public appointments within the community;
- reserving places on training courses for people with the protected characteristic, for example, in management;
- targeted networking opportunities, for example, in banking;
- working with local schools and FE colleges, inviting students from groups whose participation in the workplace is disproportionately low to spend a day at the company;
- providing mentoring.

WHAT DOES 'PROPORTIONATE' MEAN?

12.25 **[s 158(2)]** To be lawful, any action which is taken under the positive action provisions must be a proportionate means of achieving one of the 'stated aims' described in paragraph 12.12 above.

12.26 'Proportionate' refers to the balancing of competing relevant factors. These factors will vary depending on the basis for the positive action – whether it is to overcome a disadvantage, meet different needs or address under-representation of a particular group. Other relevant factors will include the objective of the action taken, or to be taken, including the cost of the action.

12.27 The seriousness of the relevant disadvantage, the degree to which the need is different and the extent of the low participation in the particular activity will need to be balanced against the impact of the action on other protected groups, and the relative disadvantage, need or participation of these groups.

12.28 Organisations need to consider:

- Is the action an appropriate way to achieve the stated aim?
- If so, is the proposed action reasonably necessary to achieve the aim; that is, in all of the circumstances, would it be possible to achieve the aim as effectively by other actions that are less likely to result in less favourable treatment of others?

12.29 Paragraphs 4.30 to 4.32 provide a more detailed explanation of proportionality.

TIME-LIMITED POSITIVE ACTION

12.30 If positive action continues indefinitely, without any review, it may no longer be proportionate, as the action taken may have already remedied the situation which had been a precondition for positive action. This could make it unlawful to continue to take the action.

12.31 Therefore, when undertaking measures under the positive action provisions, it would be advisable for employers to indicate that they intend to take the action only so long as the relevant conditions apply, rather than indefinitely. During that period they should monitor the impact of their action and review progress towards their aim.

POSITIVE ACTION AND DISABILITY

12.32 **[s 13(3)]** As indicated above at paragraph 3.35, it is not unlawful direct disability discrimination to treat a disabled person more favourably than a non-disabled person. This means that an employer, if they wish, can for example restrict recruitment, training and promotion to disabled people and this will be lawful.

Example: An employer which has a policy of interviewing all disabled candidates who meet the minimum selection criteria for a job would not be acting unlawfully.

12.33 However, the positive action provisions may still be appropriate to achieve equality of opportunity between disabled people with different impairments. This means that an employer can implement positive action measures to overcome disadvantage, meet different needs or increase participation of people with one impairment but not those with other impairments.

POSITIVE ACTION AND THE PUBLIC SECTOR EQUALITY DUTIES

12.34 Public authorities which are subject to the public sector equality duties may wish to consider using positive action to help them comply with those duties.

IMPLEMENTING POSITIVE ACTION LAWFULLY

12.35 An employer does not have to take positive action but if they do, they will need to ensure they comply with the requirements of the Act to avoid unlawful discrimination. To establish whether there is any basis to implement a positive action programme, employers should collate evidence, for example through their monitoring data, and analyse that evidence to decide on the most appropriate course of action to take.

12.36 In considering positive action measures, employers might consider drawing up an action plan which:

- sets out evidence of the disadvantage, particular need and/or disproportionately low levels of participation, as appropriate, and an analysis of the causes;

- sets out specific outcomes which the employer is aiming to achieve;
- identifies possible action to achieve those outcomes;
- shows an assessment of the proportionality of proposed action;
- sets out the steps the employer decides to take to achieve these aims;
- sets out the measurable indicators of progress towards those aims, set against a timetable;
- explains how they will consult with relevant groups such as all staff, including staff support groups and members of the protected group for whom the programme is being established;
- specifies the time period for the programme;
- sets out periods for review of progress of the measures towards the aim to ensure it remains proportionate.

CHAPTER 13
OCCUPATIONAL REQUIREMENTS AND OTHER EXCEPTIONS RELATED TO WORK

INTRODUCTION

[4.140]
13.1 The Act contains a number of exceptions that permit discrimination that would otherwise be prohibited. Any exception to the prohibition on discrimination should generally be interpreted restrictively. Where an exception permits discrimination in relation to one protected characteristic, for example nationality, employers must ensure that they do not discriminate in relation to other protected characteristics.

13.2 This chapter explains occupational requirements and other exceptions related to work. There are other exceptions that apply to a particular characteristic, for example pregnancy and maternity, and these are dealt with in the relevant chapters throughout the code. Exceptions relating to pay and benefits are covered in Chapter 14.

OCCUPATIONAL REQUIREMENTS

13.3 **[Sch 9, para 1]** In certain circumstances, it is lawful for an employer to require a job applicant or worker to have a particular protected characteristic, provided certain statutory conditions are met.

13.4 The exception may also be used by a principal, a limited liability partnership (LLP), a firm or a person who has the power to appoint or remove office holders and a person who has the power to recommend an appointment to a public office.

What the Act says

13.5 **[Sch 9, para 1]** An employer may apply, in relation to work, a requirement to have a particular protected characteristic if the employer can show that having regard to the nature or context of the work:
- the requirement is an occupational requirement;
- the application of the requirement is a proportionate means of achieving a legitimate aim (see paragraphs 4.25 to 4.32); and
- the applicant or worker does not meet the requirement; or,
- except in the case of sex, the employer has reasonable grounds for not being satisfied that the applicant or worker meets the requirement.

13.6 **[Sch 9, para 1(3)]** In the case of gender reassignment and marriage and civil partnership, the requirement is not to be a transsexual person, married or a civil partner.

13.7 The requirement must not be a sham or pretext and there must be a link between the requirement and the job.

13.8 Examples of how the occupational requirement exception may be used include some jobs which require someone of a particular sex for reasons of privacy and decency or where personal services are being provided. For example, a unisex gym could rely on an occupational requirement to employ a changing room attendant of the same sex as the users of that room. Similarly, a women's refuge which lawfully provides services to women only can apply a requirement for all members of its staff to be women.

In what circumstances can an employer apply the occupational requirement exception?

13.9 **[Sch 9, para 1(2)]** In the case of an employer, firm, LLP or person with the power to appoint or remove an office holder, an occupational requirement may be applied in relation to:
- the arrangements made for deciding whom to offer employment or a position as a partner; or appoint as an office holder;
- an offer of employment, the position of partner or member or appointment of an office holder;
- the provision of access to opportunities for promotion, transfer, training; or
- except in relation to sex, dismissals, expulsions and terminations.

Example: A local council decides to set up a health project which would encourage older people from the Somali community to make more use of health services. The council wants to recruit a person of Somali origin for the post because it involves visiting elderly people in their homes and it is necessary for the post-holder to have a good knowledge of the culture and language of the potential clients. The council does not have a Somali worker already in post who could take on the new duties. They could rely on the occupational requirement exception to recruit a health worker of Somali origin.

13.10 It would be lawful for a principal (end-user) not to allow a contract worker to do work or, except in the case of sex, to continue to do work where the principal relies on the occupational requirement exception.

13.11 In the case of a person who has the power to recommend or approve the appointment of a public office holder, an occupational requirement may only be used in relation to:

- the arrangements that person makes for deciding whom to recommend or approve for appointment;
- not recommending or approving a person for appointment; or
- making a negative recommendation of a person for appointment.

OCCUPATIONAL REQUIREMENTS FOR THE PURPOSES OF AN ORGANISED RELIGION

What the Act says

13.12 **[Sch 9, para 2(1)]** The Act permits an employer (or a person who makes, recommends or approves appointments of office holders) to apply a requirement for a person to be of a particular sex or not to be a transsexual person, or a requirement relating to marriage, civil partnership or sexual orientation, if the employer can show that:

- the employment is for the purposes of an organised religion;
- the requirement is applied to comply with the doctrines of the religion (the 'compliance principle'); or
- because of the nature or context of the employment, the requirement is applied to avoid conflicting with the strongly held religious convictions of a significant number of the religion's followers (the 'non-conflict principle'); and
- the applicant or worker does not meet the requirement in question; or, except in the case of sex, the employer is not reasonably satisfied that the person meets it.

Example: An orthodox synagogue could apply a requirement for its rabbi to be a man.

Example: An evangelical church could require its ministers to be married or heterosexual if this enables the church to avoid a conflict with the strongly held religious convictions of its congregation.

13.13 The requirement must be a proportionate way of meeting the 'compliance' or 'non-conflict' principle. The occupational requirement exception should only be used for a limited number of posts, such as ministers of religion and a small number of posts outside the clergy including those which exist to promote or represent the religion.

When may the occupational requirement exception be applied for the purpose of an organised religion?

13.14 **[Sch 9, para 2(2)]** In relation to employment and personal or public offices, the occupational requirement exception may be used in:

- the arrangements made for deciding whom to offer employment or an appointment as an office holder;
- an offer of employment or an appointment to a personal or public office;
- the provision of access to opportunities for promotion, transfer or training; or
- except in the case of sex, the dismissal or termination of an appointment.

13.15 In the case of public offices for which a recommendation is needed for an appointment, the occupational requirement may be used in relation to:

- the arrangements made for deciding whom to recommend or approve for an appointment;
- not recommending or giving approval to an appointment; or
- making a negative recommendation for appointment.

Example: The trustees of a Mosque want to employ two youth workers, one who will provide guidance on the teachings of the Koran and the other purely to organise sporting activities not involving promoting or representing the religion. The trustees apply an occupational requirement for both workers to be heterosexual. It might be lawful to apply the occupational requirement exception to the first post but not the second post because the second post does not engage the 'compliance' or the 'non-conflict' principle.

OCCUPATIONAL REQUIREMENTS RELATING TO RELIGION OR BELIEF

What the Act says

13.16 **[Sch 9, para 3]** The Act says that where an employer has an ethos based on religion or belief, they are permitted to rely on the occupational requirement exception if they can show that, having regard to that ethos and the nature or context of the work:

- the requirement of having a particular religion or belief is an occupational requirement;
- the application of the requirement is a proportionate means of achieving a legitimate aim; and
- a person does not meet the requirement or the employer has reasonable grounds for not being satisfied that the person meets the requirement.

13.17 To rely on the exception, the employer must be able to show that their ethos is based on a religion or belief, for example, by referring to their founding constitution. An 'ethos' is the important character or spirit of the religion or belief. It may also be the underlying sentiment, conviction or outlook that informs the behaviours, customs, practices or attitudes of followers of the religion or belief.

13.18 The circumstances in which an employer with a religious or belief ethos may apply the exception are the same as those set out at paragraph 13.14.

Example: It could be a lawful use of the exception for a Humanist organisation which promotes Humanist philosophy and principles to apply an occupational requirement for their chief executive to be a Humanist.

WHAT CAN AN EMPLOYER DO TO ENSURE THEY APPLY THE OCCUPATIONAL REQUIREMENT EXCEPTION LAWFULLY?

13.19 A failure to comply with the statutory conditions described above could result in unlawful direct discrimination. Some of the issues that an employer may wish to consider when addressing the question of whether the application of an occupational requirement is proportionate to a legitimate aim are:

- Do any or all of the duties of the job need to be performed by a person with a particular characteristic?
- Could the employer use the skills of an existing worker with the required protected characteristic to do that aspect of the job?

13.20 Employers should not have a blanket policy of applying an occupational requirement exception, such as a policy that all staff of a certain grade should have a particular belief. They should also re-assess the job whenever it becomes vacant to ensure that the statutory conditions for applying the occupational requirement exception still apply.

OTHER WORK-RELATED EXCEPTIONS

ARMED FORCES

13.21 **[Sch 9, para 4]** The Act permits the armed forces to refuse a woman or a transsexual person employment or access to opportunities for promotion, transfer or training if this is a proportionate way of ensuring the combat effectiveness of the armed forces. This exception does not extend to dismissal or any other detriment.

13.22 The Act disapplies the provisions relating to age and disability to service in the armed forces and the provisions relating to disability to opportunities for work experience in the armed forces.

13.23 Non-service personnel are covered by the Act's provisions on employees (see Chapter 10).

EMPLOYMENT SERVICES

13.24 **[Sch 9, para 5]** The Act permits employment service providers, which include those providing vocational training, to restrict access to training or services to people with a protected characteristic if the training or services relate to work to which the occupational requirement exception has been applied.

13.25 The employment service provider can rely on this exception by showing that it reasonably relied on a statement from a person who could offer the work or training in question that having the particular protected characteristic was an occupational requirement. It is a criminal offence for such a person to make a statement of that kind which they know to be false or misleading.

DEFAULT RETIREMENT AGE

What the Act says

13.26 **[Sch 9, para 8]** Forcing someone to retire at a particular age is, on the face of it, age discrimination. However, the Act provides an exception for retirement; an employer is allowed to retire an employee at or over the age of 65, provided the dismissal satisfies all the legal tests for retirement, and provided the correct procedures are followed. This is known as the Default Retirement Age (DRA).

13.27 The DRA applies to 'relevant workers' only; that is:

- employees;
- those in Crown employment; and
- certain parliamentary staff.

13.28 The DRA retirement exception does not apply to any other type of worker, for example a partner, office holder, contract worker or police officer. Forced retirement of these workers is unlawful discrimination unless it can be objectively justified. The circumstances where retirement may be objectively justified are explained further in paragraphs 13.42 to 13.45.

The DRA and normal retirement age

13.29 The DRA means that employers, if they wish, can lawfully operate a 'normal retirement age' of 65 or above – that is, one which is the same as, or higher than, the DRA.

13.30 The 'normal retirement age' is the age at which employees in the same kind of position within an organisation are usually required to retire. It is not necessarily the same as the contractual retirement age, if in practice employees in that position retire at a different age.

Example: An employer has a contractual retirement age of 67, but regularly grants requests from employees to work beyond 67. However there is no consistency as to the age when employees then retire. In these circumstances, the employer's contractual retirement age of 67 would be treated as the normal retirement age.

Example: An employer has a contractual retirement age of 67 but normally grants requests to their senior managers to work until 70. In these circumstances, it is likely that 70 would be treated as the normal retirement age for senior managers.

13.31 Some employers do not operate any 'normal retirement age' for their employees. If this is the case, they can rely on the DRA of 65.

Example: An employer's employment contracts do not mention retirement and there is no fixed age at which employees retire. The employer can rely on the default retirement age of 65 if they wish to enforce a retirement.

13.32 Employers do not have to retire employees when they reach normal retirement age (or, if none applies, the DRA of 65). Indeed, there may be many good business reasons why an employer might benefit from retaining older employees in employment.

Statutory retirement procedure

13.33 Where an employer wants to retire an employee who has reached the DRA of 65 (or a normal retirement age of 65 or above), the employer must follow the retirement procedures that are set out in legislation. A dismissal that does not comply with these requirements may be unjustifiable age discrimination. In addition, the dismissal may not qualify as a 'retirement' and could be unfair.

13.34 [Employment Equality (Age) Regulations 2006 Sch 6] In summary, the statutory retirement procedure is as follows:

- The employer must give the employee six to 12 months' written notice of impending retirement and advise them of the 'right to request' that they continue working.
- Within three to six months of the intended retirement date, the employee may request in writing to be allowed to continue working indefinitely or for a stated period, quoting Schedule 6, paragraph 5 of the Employment Equality (Age) Regulations 2006.
- The employer has a duty to consider the written request within a reasonable period of receiving it by holding a meeting with the employee and giving written notice of their decision.
- If the request is refused or employment extended for a shorter period than requested, the employee has a right to appeal by giving written notice.
- The employer must consider any appeal by holding an appeal meeting as soon as is reasonably practicable and giving written notice of the appeal decision.

13.35 The dismissal will not amount to age discrimination provided that:

- the employee will be aged 65 or over at the intended date of retirement (or has reached the normal retirement age if this is higher);
- the employer has complied with the notice requirements and advised the employee of the right to request to continue working;
- the employee's contract is terminated on the intended date of retirement, as previously notified.

Example: An employer normally allows employees to continue working until age 70, but forces one employee to retire at age 65. That employee's dismissal will not qualify as retirement as the employee has been dismissed below the normal retirement age. It is likely to be both age discrimination and an unfair dismissal.

13.36 An employer who gives less than six months' notice of the date of retirement or the employee's right to request to continue working will be liable to pay compensation of up to eight weeks' pay.

13.37 However, even if full notice is not given, the employer might still be able to rely on the exception for retirement to escape liability for age discrimination. They would be expected to give the employee as much written notice as possible (and a minimum of 14 days) of the intended retirement date and of the right to request to continue to work. The employer would then have to comply with all other aspects of the statutory retirement procedure and show that the reason for dismissal is genuinely retirement.

Example: Because of inaccurate records, an employer only becomes aware that an employee is approaching her 65th birthday three months beforehand. The employer immediately issues her with written notice of intended retirement on her 65th birthday and informs her of the right to request to continue working. She does not pursue the request. Because the employer has given three months' notice and followed the correct procedure, this may qualify as a retirement dismissal. But as less than six months' notice was given, they would be liable for compensation of up to eight week's pay. The employer's safest course of action would be to give six months' notice from the date the error was discovered.

13.38 In certain cases, a dismissal may possibly qualify as a retirement but nonetheless be an unfair dismissal:

- where the employer has given the employee much less than six months' notice of the intended date of retirement; or
- where the employer has not followed the 'duty to consider' procedure under the statutory retirement rules.

Example: An employer gives an employee only a week's verbal notice that they intend to retire her on her 70th birthday, and fail to tell her of her right to request to continue working. In this case, because this is a serious breach of the legal requirements, retirement is unlikely to qualify as the reason for dismissal. The dismissal is likely to be unfair, as well as an act of unlawful age discrimination. Having breached the notice requirements, the employer would also be liable for compensation of up to eight weeks' pay.

Example: An employer without a normal retirement age forces an employee to retire at 67 on a month's notice. The employee's request to continue working is ignored. To decide whether the dismissal is a retirement, a tribunal would look at all the circumstances. It would probably find that the retirement was not the reason for the dismissal because the employer failed to consider the request to continue working. Even if the facts do not support a claim of age discrimination, the dismissal would be unfair because of the failure to follow the duty to consider procedure.

RETIREMENT FALLING OUTSIDE THE DRA EXCEPTION

13.39 The following types of retirement do not fall within the DRA exception and would therefore be unlawful age discrimination unless they can be objectively justified:

- the retirement, at any age, of someone who is not a 'relevant worker' (see paragraph 13.27);

- the retirement of a 'relevant worker' at a normal retirement age below 65.

Example: Partners in a law firm are required to retire from the partnership at 70. Partners are not 'relevant workers' for the purposes of the Act and so the retirement age of 70 would have to be objectively justified for it to be lawful.

Example: An airline company has a normal retirement age of 55 for their cabin attendants. As employees of the airline, the cabin attendants are 'relevant workers'. The airline would have to objectively justify the retirement age of 55 for it to be lawful.

13.40 Where there is no normal retirement age and an employee is forced to 'retire' before the age of 65, the reason for their dismissal cannot be retirement. It will be difficult for the employer to objectively justify the employee's dismissal; the dismissal is very likely to be unfair as well as being an act of unlawful age discrimination.

13.41 There are other circumstances where, due to a failure on the employer's part, dismissal of an employee over 65 will not qualify as retirement and is likely to be unfair dismissal and/or unjustifiable age discrimination (see paragraphs 3.36 to 3.41 above).

Objective justification

13.42 To avoid age discrimination, the Act requires employers to objectively justify any retirement that falls outside the DRA exception. This will apply to any normal retirement age below 65, and the forced retirement at any age of those who are not 'relevant workers'.

13.43 **[s 13(2)]** To objectively justify retirement in these circumstances, the employer must show that the retirement decision or policy is a proportionate means of achieving a legitimate aim. This concept is explained in more detail in paragraphs 4.25 to 4.32.

13.44 The first question is whether the aim behind the retirement decision is legitimate. Depending on the situation, the following are examples of aims that might be considered legitimate:

- to facilitate workforce planning, by providing a realistic long-term expectation as to when vacancies will arise;
- to provide sufficient opportunities for promotion, thereby ensuring staff retention at more junior levels.

However, the legitimacy of such aims would depend on all the circumstances of the case.

13.45 Even if the aim is a legitimate one, the second question is whether retiring someone at a particular age is a proportionate means of achieving that aim. In determining this, a balance must be struck between the discriminatory effect of the retirement and the employer's need to achieve the aim – taking into account all the relevant facts. If challenged in the Employment Tribunal, an employer would need to produce evidence supporting their decision.

Example: Partners in a small law firm are required to retire from the partnership at 65. The firm prides itself on its collegiate culture and has structured its partnership agreement to promote this. The fixed retirement age avoids the need to expel partners for performance management reasons, which the firm thinks would undermine the collegiate environment. While it is possible that fostering a collegiate environment may be a legitimate aim, the firm would need to show that compulsory retirement at 65 is a proportionate means of achieving it. For example, evidence would be needed to support the assumption that the performance of partners reduces when they reach the age of 65.

PROVISION OF SERVICES TO THE PUBLIC

13.46 **[Sch 9, para 19]** The Act says that an employer who provides services to the public is not liable for claims of discrimination or victimisation by an employee under Part 5 of the Act (the employment provisions) in relation to those services. Where a worker is discriminated against or victimised in relation to those services, their claim would be in the county court (or sheriff court in Scotland) under Part 3 of the Act relating to services and public functions.

Example: If an employee of a women's clothing retailer is denied the services of the retailer because she is a transsexual woman, her claim would be made under the services provisions of the Act. This means she should bring her claim in the county court.

13.47 However, where the service provided under the terms and conditions of employment differs from that provided to other employees, or is related to training, the worker can bring a claim in the Employment Tribunal under the employment provisions (Part 5).

Example: In the example above, the situation would be different if the same transsexual woman's employment contract provided her with a 20% discount on all clothes purchased from her employer, a discount not available to members of the public. If she tried to use the discount and was refused, then she would bring her claim in the Employment Tribunal under the employment provisions of the Act.

SUPPORTED EMPLOYMENT FOR DISABLED PEOPLE

13.48 **[s 193(3)]** The Act allows some charities to provide employment only to people who have the same disability or a disability of a prescribed description where this is to help disabled people gain employment.

STATUTORY AUTHORITY

13.49 **[Sch 22, para 1]** In relation to age, disability and religion or belief, it is not a contravention of the employment provisions in the Act to do anything that is required under another law. The exception also applies to a requirement or condition imposed pursuant to another law by a Minister of the Crown, a member of the Scottish Executive, the National Assembly for Wales or the Welsh Ministers, the First Minister for Wales or the Counsel General to the Welsh Assembly Government.

EDUCATIONAL APPOINTMENTS FOR RELIGIOUS INSTITUTIONS

13.50 **[Sch 22, para 3]** The Act allows schools and further and higher education institutions (FHEs) to reserve the posts of head teachers and principals for people of a particular religion and certain academic posts for women where the governing instrument provides for this. The exception for academic posts which are reserved for women only applies where the governing instrument was made before 16 January 1990.

13.51 **[Sch 22, para 3]** The Act also allows ordained priests to hold certain professorships where legislation or a university's governing instrument provides for this.

13.52 **[Sch 22, para 4]** Under the Act, faith schools are permitted to take into account religious considerations in employment matters relating to head-teachers and teachers, in accordance with the School Standards and Framework Act 1998. These considerations are different according to the category of school. Voluntary aided and independent faith schools have greater freedom than voluntary controlled and foundation schools. These exceptions only relate specifically to religion or belief – there is no scope in the Act for discrimination because of any other characteristic.

CROWN EMPLOYMENT

13.53 **[Sch 22, para 53]** The Act permits the Crown or a prescribed public body to restrict employment or the holding of a public office to people of a particular birth, nationality, descent or residence.

NATIONALITY DISCRIMINATION

13.54 **[Sch 23, para 1]** The Act permits direct nationality discrimination and indirect race discrimination on the basis of residency requirements where other laws, Ministerial arrangements or Ministerial conditions make provision for such discrimination. It does not matter whether the laws, instruments, arrangements or conditions were made before or after the Act was passed.

TRAINING FOR NON-EEA NATIONALS

13.55 **[Sch 23, para 4]** The Act permits an employer to employ or to contract non-EEA nationals who are not ordinarily resident in an EEA state, where the employment or contract is for the sole or main purpose of training them in skills, for example medical skills. The employer can only rely on the exception if they think that the person does not intend to exercise the skills gained as a result of the training in Great Britain. Where the training provider is the armed forces or the Secretary of State for Defence, the rules differ slightly.

NATIONAL SECURITY

13.56 **[s 192]** An employer does not contravene the Act only by doing something for the purpose of safeguarding national security and the action is proportionate for that purpose.

COMMUNAL ACCOMMODATION

13.57 **[Sch 23, para 3]** An employer does not breach the prohibition of sex discrimination or gender reassignment discrimination by doing anything in relation to admitting persons to communal accommodation or to providing any benefit, facility or service linked to the accommodation, if the criteria set out below are satisfied.

13.58 Communal accommodation is residential accommodation which includes dormitories or other shared sleeping accommodation which, for reasons of privacy, should be used only by persons of the same sex. It can also include shared sleeping accommodation for men and for women, ordinary sleeping accommodation and residential accommodation, all or part of which should be used only by persons of the same sex because of the nature of the sanitary facilities serving the accommodation.

13.59 A benefit, facility or service is linked to communal accommodation if it cannot properly and effectively be provided except for those using the accommodation. It can be refused only if the person can lawfully be refused use of the accommodation.

13.60 Where accommodation or a benefit, facility or service is refused to a worker, alternative arrangements must be made in each case where reasonable so as to compensate the person concerned.

Example: At a worksite, the only sleeping accommodation provided is communal accommodation occupied by men. A female worker wishes to attend a training course at the worksite but is refused permission because of the men-only accommodation. Her employer must make alternative arrangements to compensate her where reasonable; for example, by arranging alternative accommodation near the worksite or an alternative course.

13.61 Sex or gender reassignment discrimination in admitting people to communal accommodation is not permitted unless the accommodation is managed in a way which is as fair as possible to both women and men.

13.62 In excluding a person because of sex or gender reassignment, the employer must take account of:

- whether and how far it is reasonable to expect that the accommodation should be altered or extended or that further accommodation should be provided; and
- the relative frequency of demand or need for the accommodation by persons of each sex.

13.63 The Act permits a provider of communal accommodation to exclude people who are proposing to undergo, undergoing or who have undergone gender reassignment from this accommodation. However, to do so will only be lawful where the exclusion is a proportionate means of achieving a legitimate aim. This must be considered on a case-by-case basis; in each case, the provider of communal accommodation must assess whether it is appropriate and necessary to exclude the transsexual person.

CHAPTER 14
PAY AND BENEFITS

INTRODUCTION

[4.141]
14.1 This chapter looks at the implications of the Act for pay and employment benefits, including pensions. Employers must not discriminate directly or indirectly in setting rates of pay or offering benefits to workers. Likewise, they must avoid discrimination arising from disability and, in certain circumstances, may need to consider the duty to make reasonable adjustments to pay or to certain benefits that they provide. The Act also contains a number of specific provisions relating to pay and benefits, including certain exceptions to the general prohibition on discrimination in employment.

PAY

14.2 An employer must not discriminate in setting terms of employment relating to pay, or in awarding pay increases. Pay includes basic pay; non-discretionary bonuses; overtime rates and allowances; performance related benefits; severance and redundancy pay; access to pension schemes; benefits under pension schemes; hours of work; company cars; sick pay; and fringe benefits such as travel allowances.

14.3 Where workers work less than full time hours, employers should ensure that pay and benefits are in direct proportion to the hours worked. This will avoid the risk of the employer putting part-time workers who share a protected characteristic at a disadvantage that could amount to unjustifiable indirect discrimination or that could be unlawful under the Part Time Workers (Prevention of Less Favourable Treatment) Regulations 2000.

Exception for the national minimum wage

14.4 **[Sch 9, para 11]** However, there is an exception in the Act which allows employers to base their pay structures for young workers on the pay bands set out in the National Minimum Wage Regulations 1999.

14.5 These Regulations set minimum hourly wage rates, which are lower for younger workers aged 18 to 20, and lower again for those aged 16 and 17. Employers can use the rates of pay set out in the Regulations or may set pay rates that are higher, provided they are linked to the same age bands. However, the higher rates of pay need not be in proportion to the corresponding rates of the national minimum wage.

Example: A supermarket wants to pay a more attractive rate than the national minimum wage. Their pay scales must be based on the pay bands set out in the National Minimum Wage Regulations 1999. The supermarket opts for the following rates, which would be permissible under the Act:

- 16-17 years of age — 20p per hour more than the national minimum wage for workers in that age band;
- 18-20 years of age — 45p per hour more than the national minimum wage for workers in that age band; and
- 21 years of age or over — 70p per hour more than the national minimum wage for workers aged 21 or over.

14.6 Employed apprentices who are under the age of 19 or in the first year of their apprenticeship are entitled to the apprentice minimum wage which is lower than the ordinary national minimum wage. The apprentice minimum wage applies to all hours of work and training, including training off the job.

Performance related pay and bonuses

14.7 Where an employer operates a pay policy and/or bonus scheme with elements related to individual performance, they must ensure that the policy and/or scheme does not unlawfully discriminate against a worker because of a protected characteristic.

Example: A trade union equality representative obtains statistics which show that the best scores for appraisals are disproportionately awarded to white male workers. As a result, this group is more likely to receive an increase in pay and annual bonuses. The statistics suggest that the policy could be indirectly discriminatory, either through the criteria that have been selected, or the way that these criteria are applied.

14.8 If a worker has a disability which adversely affects their rate of output, the effect may be that they receive less under a performance related pay scheme than other workers. The employer must consider whether there are reasonable adjustments which would overcome this substantial disadvantage.

Example: A disabled man with arthritis works in telephone sales and is paid commission on the value of his sales. His impairment gets worse and he is advised to change his computer equipment. He takes some time to get used to the new equipment and, as a consequence, his sales fall. It is likely to be a reasonable adjustment for his employer to pay him a certain amount of additional commission for the period he needs to get used to the new equipment.

Equal pay

14.9 [s 64–66] The Act gives women and men the right to equal pay for equal work.

14.10 The provisions on equal pay operate by implying a sex equality clause into each contract of employment. This clause has the effect of modifying any term that is less favourable than for a comparator of the opposite sex. It also incorporates an equivalent term where the comparator benefits from a term not included in the worker's contract. These provisions are covered in more detail in the Equal Pay Code.

Pay secrecy clauses

14.11 [s 77] 'Pay secrecy clauses' or 'gagging clauses' are terms of employment which seek to prevent or restrict workers from discussing or disclosing their pay. Such terms are unenforceable in relation to a person making or seeking a 'relevant pay disclosure'. This is defined by the Act as a disclosure sought or made for the purpose of finding out whether – or to what extent – any pay differences are related to a protected characteristic.

14.12 The disclosure can be made to anyone (including a trade union representative), or requested from a colleague or former colleague. Any action taken by an employer against a worker who makes such a disclosure, or who receives information as a result, may amount to victimisation (see paragraphs 9.2 to 9.15).

Example: An African worker thinks he is underpaid compared to a white colleague and suspects that the difference is connected to race. The colleague reveals his salary, even though the contract of employment forbids this. If the employer takes disciplinary action against the white colleague as the result of this disclosure, this could amount to victimisation. But if he had disclosed pay information to the employer's competitor in breach of a confidentiality obligation, he would not be protected by the Act.

14.13 This provision is designed to improve pay transparency and relates to all protected characteristics. Further guidance in relation to the characteristic of sex can be found in the Equal Pay Code.

BENEFITS

14.14 Employment-related benefits might include canteens, meal vouchers, social clubs and other recreational activities, dedicated car parking spaces, discounts on products, bonuses, share options, hairdressing, clothes allowances, financial services, healthcare, medical assistance/insurance, transport to work, company car, education assistance, workplace nurseries, and rights to special leave. This is not an exhaustive list. Such benefits may be contractual or discretionary.

14.15 **[ss 13(1), 39(2)(b)]** Employers must ensure that they do not deny workers access to benefits because of a protected characteristic. Where denying access to a benefit or offering it on less favourable terms either:

- directly discriminates because of the protected characteristic of age, for example, by imposing an age restriction; or
- indirectly discriminates by putting a group of workers sharing a protected characteristic at a disadvantage when compared with other workers,

[ss 13(2), 19(2)(d)] the employer must be able to objectively justify the rule or practice as a proportionate means of achieving a legitimate aim.

14.16 But cost alone is not sufficient to objectively justify the discriminatory rule or practice. Financial cost may be taken into account only if there are other good reasons for denying or restricting access to the benefit. For more information about the application of the objective justification test, see paragraphs 4.25 to 4.32.

Example: An employer provides a company car to most of their sales staff, but not to those under 25 because of higher insurance costs. This amounts to direct discrimination because of age. The employer may not be able to objectively justify this policy by relying upon cost considerations alone.

14.17 In addition, where a disabled worker is put at a substantial disadvantage in the way that a particular benefit is provided, an employer must take reasonable steps to adjust the way the benefit is provided in order to avoid that disadvantage.

Example: An employer provides dedicated car parking spaces close to the workplace which are generally used by senior managers. A disabled worker finds it very difficult to get to and from the public car park further away. It is likely to be a reasonable adjustment for the employer to allocate one of the dedicated spaces to that worker.

14.18 Some benefits may continue after employment has ended. An employer's duties under the Act extend to its former workers in respect of such benefits.

Example: An employer provides a workplace nursery. Parents who leave their jobs with the employer are always offered the chance of keeping their nursery place until their child's fifth birthday – but this opportunity is not offered to a lesbian mother of a three year old. If this less favourable treatment is because of sexual orientation, it would amount to direct discrimination.

14.19 The Act also provides some specific exceptions to the general prohibition of discrimination in employment benefits, which are explained below. Exceptions relating to pregnancy and maternity are covered in Chapter 8 and in the Equal Pay Code.

Exception for service-related benefits

14.20 **[Sch 9, para 10(1)]** In many cases, employers require a certain length of service before increasing or awarding a benefit, such as pay increments, holiday entitlement, access to company cars or financial advice. On the face of it, such rules could amount to indirect age discrimination because older workers are more likely to have completed the length of service than younger workers. However, the Act provides a specific exception for benefits based on five years' service or less.

14.21 **[Sch 9, para 10(3)]** Length of service can be calculated by the employer in one of two ways:

(a) by the length of time that the person has been working for the employer at or above a particular level; or

(b) by the total length of time that person has been working for the employer.

14.22 Length of service may include employment by a predecessor employer under the Transfer of Undertakings (Protection of Employment) Regulations 2006.

Example: For junior office staff, an employer operates a five-point pay scale to reflect growing experience over the first five years of service. This would be permitted by the Act.

14.23 **[Sch 9, para 10(2)]** However, it may still be lawful for the employer to use length of service above five years to award or increase a benefit, provided they reasonably believe that this 'fulfils a business need'. Examples of a business need could include rewarding higher levels of experience, or encouraging loyalty, or increasing or maintaining the motivation of long-serving staff.

14.24 This test of 'fulfilling a business need' is less onerous than the general test for objective justification for indirect discrimination (see paragraph 14.15 above and paragraphs 4.25 to 4.32). However, an employer would still need evidence to support a reasonable belief that the length of service rule did fulfil a business need. This could include information the employer might have gathered through monitoring, staff attitude surveys or focus groups. An employer would be expected to take into account the interests of their workers and not be motivated simply by financial self-interest.

Example: An employer offers one additional day's holiday for every year of service up to a maximum of four years, to reward loyalty and experience. Although this may mean younger staff having fewer holidays than older workers, this approach is permitted by the Act. The same employer also provides free health insurance to all employees with over five years' service and will have to justify this by showing that it actually fulfils a business need – for example, by rewarding experience, encouraging loyalty or increasing staff motivation.

14.25 **[Sch 9, para 10(7)]** This exception does not apply to service-related termination payments or any other benefits which are provided only by virtue of the worker ceasing employment.

Exception for enhanced redundancy benefits

14.26 **[Sch 9, para 13(1)–(6)]** The Act also provides a specific exception for employers who want to make redundancy payments that are more generous than the statutory scheme. The exception allows an employer to use the formula of the statutory scheme to enhance redundancy payments. One of the following methods must be used:

- removing the statutory scheme's maximum ceiling on a week's pay so that an employee's actual weekly pay is used in the calculation;
- raising the statutory ceiling on a week's pay so that a higher amount of pay is used on the calculation; and/or
- multiplying the appropriate amount for each year of employment set out in the statutory formula by a figure of more than one.

Having done this, the employer may again multiply the total by a figure of one or more.

Example: An employer operates a redundancy scheme which provides enhanced redundancy payments based on employees' actual weekly pay, instead of the (lower) maximum set out in the statutory redundancy scheme. This is lawful under the Act.

Example: Using the statutory redundancy scheme formula and the scheme's maximum weekly wage, another employer calculates every employee's redundancy entitlement, then applies a multiple of two to the total. This is also lawful under the Act.

14.27 **[Sch 9, para 13(3)(b)–(d)]** The exception also allows an employer to make a redundancy payment to an employee who has taken voluntary redundancy or to an employee with less than two years continuous service, where no statutory redundancy payment is required. In such cases, an employer may make a payment equivalent to the statutory minimum, or an enhanced payment based on any of the above methods.

14.28 A redundancy payment will fall outside this exception if an employer's calculation is not based on the statutory scheme, or the method of enhancement differs from those set out in paragraph 14.26 above. As using length of service could amount to indirect age discrimination, the employer needs to show that calculating the redundancy payment in this way is justified as a proportionate means of achieving a legitimate aim. In this context, a legitimate aim might be to reward loyalty or to give larger financial payments to protect older employees because they may be more vulnerable in the job market.

14.29 For the means of achieving the aim to be proportionate, the employer would need to show that they had balanced the reasonable needs of the business against the discriminatory effects on the employees who do not stand to benefit. One factor would be the degree of difference between payments made to different groups of employees and whether that differential was reasonably necessary to achieve the stated aim.

Example: A company's redundancy scheme provides for one and a half weeks' actual pay for each year of employment for employees of all ages. Thus the scheme does not use the formula in the statutory scheme, which has different multipliers for employees under 22 and over 40. Although the company's scheme is less discriminatory because of age and more generous than the statutory scheme, it does not fit in with the calculations permitted by the exception. The company would have to show that their scheme was justified as a proportionate means of achieving a legitimate aim.

Exception relating to life assurance

14.30 [Sch 9, para 14] Some employers provide life assurance cover for their workers. If a worker retires early due to ill health, the employer may continue to provide life assurance cover. The Act provides an exception allowing an employer to stop providing cover when the worker reaches the age at which they would have retired had they not fallen ill. If there is no normal retirement age applicable to the worker's job, the employer can stop providing life assurance cover when the worker reaches 65.

Example: An employer operates a normal retirement age of 67. They provide life assurance cover to all workers up to this age. When one of their managers takes early retirement at 60 because of ill health, the employer continues her life assurance cover until she reaches 67. This is lawful.

Exception relating to child care benefits

14.31 [Sch 9, paras 15(1)–(2)] The Act creates an exception for benefits relating to the provision of childcare facilities that are restricted to children of a particular age group. It applies not only to natural parents, but also to others with parental responsibility for a child.

14.32 [Sch 9, para 15(3)] This exception also applies to actions taken to facilitate the provision of child care, including: the payment for some or all of the cost of the child care; helping a parent to find a suitable person to provide child care; and enabling a parent to spend more time providing care for the child or otherwise assisting the parent with respect to childcare they provide.

14.33 [Sch 9, para 15(4)] The exception covers benefits relating to the provision of care for children aged under 17.

Example: A sales assistant lives with his wife and seven year old stepdaughter, who attends an after school club run by the local authority. He receives childcare vouchers from his employer, but these are restricted to workers with children under 10. This restriction would be lawful. In this case, the sales assistant uses the vouchers to help pay for his stepdaughter's after school club.

Exception for benefits based on marital status

14.34 [Sch 9, para 18(2)] Benefits which are restricted on the basis of a worker's marital status are lawful under the Act, provided workers in a civil partnership have access to the same benefit. Workers who are not married or in a civil partnership can be excluded from such benefits.

Example: An employer gives an additional week's honeymoon leave to a woman who is getting married. Last year, her lesbian colleague who was celebrating a civil partnership was given only one extra day's leave to go on honeymoon. The difference in the treatment would not fall within the marital status exception.

14.35 [Sch 9, para 18(1)] There is also a limited exception for married workers only. This allows employers to provide a benefit exclusively for married workers, provided the benefit in question accrued before 5 December 2005 (the day on which section 1 of the Civil Partnership Act 2004 came into force) or where payment is in respect of periods of service before that date.

Exception for group insurance schemes

14.36 [Sch 9, para 20] Some employers offer their workers insurance-based benefits such as life assurance or accident cover under a group insurance policy. The Act allows employers to provide for differential payment of premiums or award of benefits based on sex, marital/civil partnership status, pregnancy and maternity or gender reassignment. However, the difference in treatment must be reasonable, and be done by reference to actuarial or other data from a source on which it is reasonable to rely.

14.37 [Sch 3, para 20] The Act also clarifies that it is the employer, not the insurer, who is responsible for making sure that provision of benefits under such group insurance schemes complies with the above exception.

Example: An employer arranges for an insurer to provide a group health insurance scheme to workers in their company. The insurer refuses to provide cover on the same terms to one of the workers because she is a transsexual person. The employer, who is responsible for any discrimination in the scheme, would only be acting lawfully if the difference in treatment is reasonable in all the circumstances, and done by reference to reliable actuarial or other data.

PENSIONS

Occupational pension schemes

14.38 Employers may provide benefits to current and former workers and their dependants through occupational pension schemes. The schemes are legally separate from the employers and are administered by trustees and managers. The benefits will be in the form of pensions and lump sums. Special provisions apply to such schemes because of their separate legal status and the nature of the benefits they provide.

14.39 [s 61(1) & (2)] An occupational pension scheme is treated as including a 'non-discrimination rule' by which a 'responsible person' must not discriminate against another person in carrying out any functions in relation to the scheme or harass or victimise another person in relation to the scheme.

14.40 [s 61(4)] A responsible person includes a trustee or manager of a scheme, the employer of members or potential members and a person who can make appointments to offices.

14.41 [s 61(3)] The provisions of an occupational pension scheme have effect subject to the non-discrimination rule. So, for example, if the rules of a scheme provide for a benefit which is less favourable for one member than another because of a protected characteristic, they must be read as though the less favourable provision did not apply.

14.42 There are a number of exceptions and limitations to the non-discrimination rule. The rule does not apply:

- [s 61(5)] to persons entitled to benefits awarded under a divorce settlement or on the ending of a civil partnership (although it does apply to the provision of information and the operation of the scheme's dispute resolution procedure in relation to such persons);
- [s 61(10)] in so far as an equality rule applies – or would apply if it were not for the exceptions described in part 2 of Schedule 7 (for more information on equality rules, please see the Equal Pay Code);
- [s 61(8)] to practices, actions or decisions of trustees or managers or employers relating to age specified by order of a Minister of the Crown, introduced under enabling powers in the Act.

14.43 It is expected that the exceptions relating to age will be based on those that previously applied under Schedule 2 to the Employment Equality (Age) Regulations 2006.

14.44 [s 61(11)] In addition to the requirement to comply with the non-discrimination rule, a responsible person is under a duty to make reasonable adjustments to any provision, criterion or practice relating to an occupational pension scheme which puts a disabled person at a substantial disadvantage in comparison with persons who are not disabled.

Example: The rules of an employer's final salary scheme provide that the maximum pension is based on the member's salary in the last year of work. Having worked full-time for 20 years, a worker becomes disabled and has to reduce her working hours two years before her pension age. The scheme's rules put her at a disadvantage as a result of her disability, because her pension will only be calculated on her part-time salary. The trustees decide to convert her part-time salary to its full-time equivalent and make a corresponding reduction in the period of her part-time employment which counts as pensionable. In this way, her full-time earnings will be taken into account. This is likely to be a reasonable adjustment to make.

14.45 [s 62(1) & (2)] The Act provides a mechanism for the trustees or managers of occupational pension schemes to make alterations to their schemes to ensure they reflect the non-discrimination rule. As most schemes already give trustees a power of alteration, the mechanism in the Act would only be required if a scheme does not have this. The mechanism would also be needed if the procedure for exercising the power is unduly complex or protracted or involves obtaining consents which cannot be obtained (or which can be obtained only with undue delay or difficulty).

14.46 [s 62(3) & (4)] Under this mechanism, the trustees or managers can make the necessary alterations by resolution. The alteration can have effect in relation to a period before the date of the resolution.

14.47 The rules on occupational pensions for women on maternity leave are covered in the Equal Pay Code.

Contributions to personal pension schemes

14.48 [s 61(8)] The enabling powers under the Act also allow exceptions to be introduced to the non-discrimination rule in respect of contributions to personal pension schemes or stakeholder pension schemes where the protected characteristic is age. As with exceptions for occupational pension schemes, it is expected that these exceptions will be based on those that previously applied under Schedule 2 to the Employment Equality (Age) Regulations 2006.

CHAPTER 15
ENFORCEMENT

INTRODUCTION

[4.142]

15.1 A worker who considers they have been affected by a breach of the Act has a right to seek redress through the Employment Tribunal (or, in the case of an occupational pension scheme, the county court or sheriff court in Scotland). Employment Tribunals can deal with the unlawful acts that are set out in Chapters 3 to 9. However, because litigation can be a costly and time-consuming exercise, employers should deal with complaints relating to a breach of the Act seriously and rigorously, with support from any recognised trade union, to avoid having recourse to the Employment Tribunal.

15.2 As explained in paragraph 1.22, the term 'employer' refers to all those who have duties in the areas covered by the Code. In this chapter, the term 'claimant' is used to refer to a worker who brings a claim under the Act and the term 'respondent' is used to refer to an employer against whom the claim is made.

15.3 This chapter gives an overview of enforcement by the Employment Tribunals of Part 5 of the Act. It is not intended to be a procedural guide to presenting a claim to an Employment Tribunal. The relevant procedures are set out in Schedule 1 to the Employment Tribunals (Constitution and Rules of Procedure) Regulations 2004.

15.4 This chapter covers the following:

- Obtaining information under the Act
- Settling complaints without recourse to a tribunal

- Jurisdiction for hearing complaints of discrimination related to work
- Time limits
- Burden of proof
- Remedies
- The Commission's enforcement powers
- National security.

THE PROCEDURE FOR OBTAINING INFORMATION

15.5 A worker who has a complaint under the Act should, as far as possible, seek to raise the complaint with the employer in the first instance. To avoid a claim proceeding to the Employment Tribunal, the employer should investigate thoroughly any allegations of a breach of the Act. This would enable the employer to determine whether there is any substance to the complaint and, if so, whether it can be resolved to the satisfaction of the parties.

15.6 **[s 138]** A worker who has a complaint under the Act may request information from their employer about the reason for the treatment which is the subject of the complaint. This is known as the procedure for obtaining information and it is additional to other means of obtaining information under the Employment Tribunal rules.

15.7 There are standard forms for asking and answering questions, as well as guidance which explains how the procedure works. However, standard forms do not have to be used to present questions or answers.

15.8 For the questions and any answers to be admissible in evidence, the questions should be sent to the employer before a claim is made to the Employment Tribunal, at the same time as the claim is made, or within 28 days of it being made; or if later, within the time specified by the tribunal.

15.9 **[s 138(3)]** The questions procedure is a way for workers to obtain information when they believe they have been subjected to conduct which is unlawful under the Act but do not have sufficient information to be sure. It could also assist the worker in their decision about how to proceed with the complaint. The questions and any answers are admissible in evidence in tribunal proceedings.

Example: A lesbian employee who suspects that she has been denied a promotion because of her sexual orientation could use the procedure to ask her employer about their decision not to promote her. This information could support her suspicion or resolve her concerns.

15.10 **[s 138(4); s 138(5)]** A respondent is not obliged to answer the questions. However, if they fail to answer within eight weeks (starting on the day the questions are received), or give equivocal or evasive replies, a tribunal may draw an inference from that, which could be an inference of discrimination. A tribunal must not draw an inference from a failure to answer questions if the answers might prejudice or reveal the reasons for bringing or not bringing criminal proceedings or in other circumstances specified in legislation.

SETTLING COMPLAINTS WITHOUT RECOURSE TO AN EMPLOYMENT TRIBUNAL

15.11 Nothing in the Act prevents the parties settling a claim or potential claim before it is decided by the Employment Tribunal (or the civil courts in the case of a claim relating to an occupational pension scheme). An agreement of this nature can include any terms the parties agree to and can cover compensation, future actions by the respondent, costs and other lawful matters.

Example: A worker raises a grievance with her employers alleging discrimination. The employer investigates this and accepts that there is substance to the complaint. The employer agrees to compensate the worker and undertakes to provide mandatory training for all staff to prevent such a complaint arising again.

15.12 Acas offers a conciliation service for parties in dispute, whether or not a claim has been made to an Employment Tribunal.

15.13 **[s 147]** A claim or potential claim to the Employment Tribunal can also be settled by way of a 'qualifying compromise contract'. Although contracts that seek to exclude or limit the application of the Act are normally unenforceable, this provision does not apply to a compromise contract, provided it fulfils certain conditions:

- the contract is in writing;
- the conditions in the contract are tailored to the circumstances of the claim;
- the claimant has received independent legal advice from a named person who is insured against the risk of a claim arising from that advice; and
- the named legal adviser is a qualified lawyer, a nominated trade union representative, an advice centre worker or another person specified by order under the Act.

JURISDICTION FOR HEARING COMPLAINTS OF DISCRIMINATION IN WORK CASES

15.14 **[s 120(1)]** An Employment Tribunal has jurisdiction to determine complaints related to work about a breach of the Act (that is, discrimination, harassment, victimisation, failure to make reasonable adjustments, breach of an equality clause or rule, instructing, causing or inducing and aiding unlawful acts).

15.15 **[s 120(2); s 120(3)]** An Employment Tribunal also has jurisdiction to determine an application relating to a non-discrimination rule of an occupational pension scheme (see paragraph 14.39). A responsible person (that is, the trustees or managers of an occupational pension scheme, the employer or a person who can make appointments to offices) can make an application to an Employment Tribunal for a declaration as to the rights of that person and a worker or member with whom they are in a dispute about the effect of a non-discrimination rule. An Employment Tribunal can also determine a question that relates to a non-discrimination rule which has been referred to it by a court.

15.16 **[s 120(5)]** Where proceedings relate to a breach of a non-discrimination rule of an occupational pension scheme, the employer is treated as a party to the proceedings and has the right to appear and be heard.

15.17 **[s 120(6)]** The Employment Tribunal's jurisdiction to determine proceedings that relate to a breach of a non-discrimination rule in an occupational pension scheme does not affect the jurisdiction of the High Court or county court, or (in Scotland) the Court of Session or the sheriff court, to also determine such proceedings.

15.18 **[s 121]** An Employment Tribunal will not have jurisdiction to hear a case from a member of the armed forces until a 'service complaint' has been made and not withdrawn (see paragraph 15.21).

15.19 **[s 60(2)]** The Employment Tribunal jurisdiction does not extend to complaints relating to disability or health enquiries under section 60(1) of the Act (see paragraphs 10.25 to 10.43). Only the Equality and Human Rights Commission can enforce a breach of the provisions relating to health or disability enquiries. Cases are brought in the county court in England and Wales or the sheriff court in Scotland. However, the Employment Tribunal will have jurisdiction to hear a complaint of discrimination where the worker is, for example, rejected for a job as a result of responding to a disability or health enquiry that is not permitted.

TIME LIMITS

15.20 **[s 123]** For work-related cases, an Employment Tribunal claim must be started within three months (less one day) of the alleged unlawful act. Where the unlawful act relates to an equality clause or rule different time limits apply; these are dealt with in the Equal Pay Code of Practice.

15.21 **[s 123(2)]** In the case of members of the armed forces, Employment Tribunal proceedings must be started within six months of the date of the alleged unlawful act. The time limit applies whether or not any service complaint has been determined. Civilians working for the armed forces are not governed by these rules and should make their application to an Employment Tribunal within the usual three months time limit.

15.22 **[s 123(1)(b)]** If proceedings are not brought within the prescribed period, the Employment Tribunal still has discretion to hear the proceedings, if it thinks it is just and equitable to do so (see paragraph 15.29 to 15.31 below).

When does the period for bringing the claim start?

15.23 **[s 123(1)(a)]** The Act says that the period for bringing a claim starts with the date of the unlawful act. Generally, this will be the date on which the alleged unlawful act occurred, or the date on which the worker becomes aware that an unlawful act occurred.

Example: A male worker applied for a promotion and was advised on 12 March 2011 that he was not successful. The successful candidate was a woman. He believes that he was better qualified for the promotion than his colleague and that he has been discriminated against because of his sex. He sent a questions form to his employer within two weeks of finding out about the promotion and the answers to the questions support his view. The worker must start proceedings by 11 June 2011.

15.24 **[s 123(3) & (4); s 123(4)(a)]** Sometimes, however, the unlawful act is an employer's failure to do something. The Act says that a failure to do a thing occurs when the person decides not to do it. In the absence of evidence to the contrary, an employer is treated as deciding not to do a thing when they do an act inconsistent with doing the thing.

15.25 **[s 123(4)(b)]** If the employer does not carry out an inconsistent act, they are treated as deciding not to do a thing on the expiry of the period in which they might reasonably have been expected to do the thing.

Example: A wheelchair-user asks her employer to install a ramp to enable her more easily to get over the kerb between the car park and the office entrance. The employer indicates that they will do so but no work at all is carried out. After a period in which it would have been reasonable for the employer to commission the work, even though the employer has not made a positive decision not to install a ramp, they may be treated as having made that decision.

15.26 **[s 123(3)(a)]** In addition, the Act recognises that where conduct extends over a period, it should be treated as being done at the end of that period for the purposes of calculating when the unlawful act occurred.

15.27 If an employer has a policy, rule, or practice (whether formal or informal) in accordance with which decisions are taken from time to time, this might amount to an 'act extended over a period'. So if an employer maintains an unlawful policy which results in a person being discriminated against on a continuing basis or on many occasions, the period for bringing a claim starts when the last act of discrimination occurred, or when the policy, rule or practice is removed.

Example: An employer operates a mortgage scheme for married couples only. A civil partner would be able to bring a claim to an Employment Tribunal at any time while the scheme continued to operate in favour of married couples. However, once the scheme ceased to operate in favour of married couples, the time limit for bringing proceedings would be within three months of that date.

15.28 For these purposes, a continuing state of affairs may constitute an act extended over a period. This means that even if the individual acts relied upon are done by different workers and are done at different places, they may be treated as a single act extending over a period. However, a single unlawful act which has continuing consequences will not extend the time period.

Example: A black worker is graded on lower pay than her Asian counterpart. The time period for starting proceedings is three months from the date the decision was taken to grade the workers or the date the worker discovered that she was being paid at a lower grade.

What happens if the claim is presented outside the correct time limit?

15.29 **[s 123(1)(b) & (2)(b)]** Where a claim is brought outside the time limits referred to above, an Employment Tribunal has discretion to hear the case if it considers it just and equitable to do so.

15.30 In exercising its discretion, a tribunal will consider the prejudice which each party would suffer as a result of the decision to extend the time limit. This means a tribunal will consider what impact hearing the case out of time would have on the respondent and the claimant.

15.31 When a tribunal considers whether to exercise its 'just and equitable' discretion, it will have regard to all the circumstances of the case including in particular:

- the length of and reasons for the delay;
- the extent to which the cogency of the evidence is likely to be affected;
- the extent to which the employer had cooperated with requests for information;
- the promptness with which the claimant bringing the claim acted once they knew of the facts giving rise to the claim;
- the steps taken by the claimant to obtain appropriate legal advice once they knew of the possibility of taking action.

BURDEN OF PROOF

15.32 **[s 136]** A claimant alleging that they have experienced an unlawful act must prove facts from which an Employment Tribunal could decide or draw an inference that such an act has occurred.

Example: A worker of Jain faith applies for promotion but is unsuccessful. Her colleague who is a Mormon successfully gets the promotion. The unsuccessful candidate obtains information using the questions procedure in the Act which shows that she was better qualified for the promotion than her Mormon colleague. The employer will have to explain to the tribunal why the Jain worker was not promoted and that religion or belief did not form any part of the decision.

15.33 An Employment Tribunal will hear all of the evidence from the claimant and the respondent before deciding whether the burden of proof has shifted to the respondent.

15.34 **[s 136(2) & (3)]** If a claimant has proved facts from which a tribunal could conclude that there has been an unlawful act, then the burden of proof shifts to the respondent. To successfully defend a claim, the respondent will have to prove, on the balance of probabilities, that they did not act unlawfully. If the respondent's explanation is inadequate or unsatisfactory, the tribunal must find that the act was unlawful.

15.35 Where the basic facts are not in dispute, an Employment Tribunal may simply consider whether the employer is able to prove, on the balance of probabilities, that they did not commit the unlawful act.

Example: A Jewish trainee solicitor complains that he has not been allowed to take annual leave to celebrate Jewish religious holidays and is able to compare himself to a Hindu trainee solicitor who has been allowed to take annual leave to celebrate Hindu religious holidays. If these facts are not in dispute, a tribunal may proceed directly to consideration of whether the law firm has shown that the treatment was not, in fact, an act of religious discrimination.

15.36 **[s 136(5)]** The above rules on burden of proof do not apply to proceedings following a breach of the Act which gives rise to a criminal offence.

REMEDIES FOR UNLAWFUL ACTS RELATING TO WORK

15.37 An Employment Tribunal may:

- **[s 124(2)(a)]** make a declaration as to the rights of the parties to the claim;
- **[s 124(2)(b)]** award compensation to the claimant for any loss suffered;
- **[s 124(2)(c)]** make an 'appropriate' recommendation, that is a recommendation that a respondent takes specified steps to obviate or reduce the adverse effect of any matter relating to the proceedings on the claimant and/or others who may be affected;
- **[s 139]** award interest on compensation;
- award costs (expenses in Scotland) if appropriate.

15.38 Information on remedies in equal pay claims is contained in the Equal Pay Code.

Declarations of unlawful acts

15.39 **[s 124(2)(a)]** An Employment Tribunal may make a declaration instead of or as well as making an award of compensation or a recommendation.

What compensation can an Employment Tribunal award?

15.40 **[ss 124(6) & 119]** An Employment Tribunal can award a claimant compensation for injury to feelings. An award for compensation may also include:

- past loss of earnings or other financial loss;
- future loss of earnings which may include stigma or 'career damage' losses for bringing a claim;
- personal injury (physical or psychological) caused by the discrimination or harassment;

- aggravated damages (England and Wales only) which are awarded when the respondent has behaved in a high-handed, malicious, insulting or oppressive manner; and
- punitive or exemplary damages (England and Wales only) which are awarded for oppressive, arbitrary or unconstitutional action by servants of the government or where the respondent's conduct has been calculated to make a profit greater than the compensation payable to the claimant.

15.41 Compensation for loss of earnings must be based on the actual loss to the claimant. The aim is, so far as possible by an award of money, to put the claimant in the position they would have been in if they had not suffered the unlawful act.

15.42 Generally, compensation must be directly attributable to the unlawful act. This may be straightforward where the loss is, for example, related to an unlawfully discriminatory dismissal. However, subsequent losses, including personal injury, may be difficult to assess.

15.43 A worker who is dismissed for a discriminatory reason is expected to take reasonable steps to mitigate their loss, for example by looking for new work or applying for state benefits. Failure to take reasonable steps to mitigate loss may reduce compensation awarded by a tribunal. However, it is for the respondent to show that the claimant did not mitigate their loss.

COMPENSATION FOR COMPLAINTS OF INDIRECT DISCRIMINATION

15.44 **[s 124(4) & (5)]** Where an Employment Tribunal makes a finding of indirect discrimination but is satisfied that the provision, criterion or practice was not applied with the intention of discriminating against the claimant, it must not make an award for compensation unless it first considers whether it would be more appropriate to dispose of the case by providing another remedy, such as a declaration or a recommendation. If the tribunal considers that another remedy is not appropriate in the circumstances, it may make an award of damages.

15.45 Indirect discrimination will be intentional where the respondent knew that certain consequences would follow from their actions and they wanted those consequences to follow. A motive, for example, of promoting business efficiency, does not mean that the act of indirect discrimination is unintentional.

EMPLOYMENT TRIBUNAL RECOMMENDATIONS

15.46 **[s 124(3)]** An Employment Tribunal can make an appropriate recommendation requiring the respondent within a specified period to take specific steps to reduce the negative impact of the unlawful act on the claimant or the wider workforce. The power to make a recommendation does not apply to equal pay claims.

15.47 A recommendation might, for example, require a respondent to take steps to implement a harassment policy more effectively; provide equal opportunities training for staff involved in promotion procedures; or introduce more transparent selection criteria in recruitment, transfer or promotion processes.

Example: An Employment Tribunal makes a finding that a respondent employer's probation policy has an indirect discriminatory impact on transsexual people generally and an individual transsexual worker specifically. The Employment Tribunal in addition to making a declaration to this effect makes a recommendation to the employer to review the policy and to take steps to remove the discriminatory provision.

15.48 Employment Tribunal recommendations often focus on processes (such as adoption of an equality policy or discontinuance of a practice or rule).

15.49 Whether a recommendation is made is a matter for the Employment Tribunal's discretion: the claimant does not have a right to have a tribunal recommend a course of action or process even if the tribunal makes a declaration of unlawful discrimination.

Making recommendations affecting the wider workforce

15.50 **[s 124(3)(b)]** As mentioned above, an Employment Tribunal can make recommendations which affect the wider workforce. A tribunal may consider making a wider recommendation if:

- the evidence in the case suggested that wider or structural issues were the cause of the discrimination and that they are likely to lead to further discrimination unless addressed; and
- it is commensurate (or 'proportionate') to the respondent's capacity to implement it.

15.51 A wider recommendation forms part of the Employment Tribunal decision in any particular case.

15.52 A recommendation is not contractually binding between the claimant and respondent (unless the parties make a separate agreement for the decision to have this effect).

What happens if a respondent fails to comply with a tribunal recommendation?

15.53 **[s 124(7)]** If a respondent fails to comply with an Employment Tribunal recommendation which related to the claimant, the tribunal may:

- increase the amount of any compensation awarded to that claimant; or
- order the respondent to pay compensation to the claimant if it did not make such an order earlier.

15.54 A failure to comply with a recommendation could also be adduced in evidence in any later cases against the same organisation.

REMEDIES IN RELATION TO OCCUPATIONAL PENSION SCHEMES

15.56 **[s 126]** If an Employment Tribunal finds that there has been discrimination in relation to:

(a) the terms on which persons become members of an occupational pension scheme; or

(b) the terms on which members are treated;

[s 126(2)] it may, in addition to the remedies it can make generally, declare that the person bringing the claim has a right to be admitted to the scheme or a right to membership without discrimination.

15.57 **[s 126(4)]** The Employment Tribunal's order may also set out the terms of admission or membership for that person. The order may apply to a period before it is made.

15.58 **[s 126(3)]** However, an Employment Tribunal may not make an order for compensation unless it is for injured feelings or for a failure by the recipient of an appropriate recommendation to comply with the recommendation. The tribunal cannot make an order for arrears of benefit.

THE COMMISSION'S POWERS TO ENFORCE BREACHES OF THE ACT

15.59 **[Equality Act (EA) 2006, s 24]** In addition to the rights given to the individual under the Act, the Commission has a power to apply to the court if it thinks that a person is likely to commit an unlawful act for an injunction (interdict in Scotland) to prohibit them from committing that act.

15.60 **[EA 2006, s 24A]** The Commission also has a power to enforce a breach of the prohibition on pre-employment health and disability enquiries (see paragraphs 10.25 to 10.43).

15.61 **[EA 2006, s 24A]** The Commission has power to take action even if no identifiable individual has been (or may be) affected by the unlawful act. It can take action in respect of arrangements which would, if they were applied to an individual, amount to an unlawful act; for example, to deal with the publication of an advertisement which suggests that an employer would discriminate (see Chapter 18 on recruitment). This power could also be used to challenge a provision, criterion or practice that indirectly discriminates, even if it has not yet put any particular person at a disadvantage.

15.62 **[EA 2006, s 20]** If the Commission suspects that an employer has committed an unlawful act, it can conduct an investigation. If it finds that the employer has done so, it can serve a notice requiring them to prepare an action plan to avoid repetition or continuation of that act or recommend that they take action for that purpose.

15.63 **[EA 2006, s 23]** The Commission may also, if it suspects that an employer is committing an unlawful act, enter into a binding agreement with the employer to avoid such contraventions.

15.64 **[EA 2006, s 28]** The Commission also has a power to assist a worker who is taking enforcement action against their employer.

NATIONAL SECURITY

15.65 **[s 192; Employment Tribunals Rules 2004 (rule 54)]** The Act includes an exception for acts for the purpose of safeguarding national security. Special rules apply in cases involving an assertion that national security is involved. The Employment Tribunal rules may allow the tribunal to exclude the claimant and/or their representative from all or part of the proceedings.

15.66 The claimant, and/or their representative who has been excluded, may make a statement to the tribunal before the exclusive part of the proceedings start. The Employment Tribunal may take steps to keep secret all or part of the reasons for its decision.

15.67 The Attorney General for England and Wales or the Advocate General for Scotland may appoint a special advocate to represent the interests of a claimant in the proceedings. However, that representative is not responsible to the claimant whose interest they are appointed to represent.

PART 2: CODE OF PRACTICE ON EMPLOYMENT

CHAPTER 16
AVOIDING DISCRIMINATION IN RECRUITMENT

INTRODUCTION

[4.143]

16.1 Ensuring fair recruitment processes can help employers avoid discrimination. While nothing in the Act prevents an employer from hiring the best person for the job, it is unlawful for an employer to discriminate in any of the arrangements made to fill a vacancy, in the terms of employment that are offered or in any decision to refuse someone a job (see Chapter 10). With certain limited exceptions, employers must not make recruitment decisions that are directly or indirectly discriminatory. As with other stages of employment, employers must also make reasonable adjustments for disabled candidates, where appropriate.

16.2 It is recognised that employers will have different recruitment processes in place depending on their size, resources, and the sector in which they operate. Whichever processes are used, applicants must be treated fairly and in accordance with the Act. This chapter examines the main issues arising in the recruitment of both external and internal applicants and explains the steps that should be taken to avoid unlawful conduct within each of the recruitment stages that are commonly used. It also makes some recommendations for good practice.

16.3 The Act's prohibition on pre-employment health and disability enquiries is covered more fully in Chapter 10.

DEFINING THE JOB

General principles

16.4 The inclusion of requirements in a job description or person specification which are unnecessary or seldom used is likely to lead to indirect discrimination. Employers who use job descriptions and person specifications should therefore review them each time they decide to fill a post. Reliance on an existing person specification or job description, may lead to discrimination if they contain discriminatory criteria.

Example: An employer uses a person specification for an accountant's post that states 'employees must be confident in dealing with external clients' when in fact the job in question does not involve liaising directly with external clients. This requirement is unnecessary and could lead to discrimination against disabled people who have difficulty interacting with others, such as some people with autism.

Job Descriptions

16.5 Job descriptions should accurately describe the job in question. Inclusion of tasks or duties that workers will not, in practice, need to perform has two pitfalls. It may discourage appropriately qualified people from applying because they cannot perform the particular task or fulfil the particular duty specified. It may also lead to discrimination claims if such people believe they have been unfairly denied an opportunity of applying.

16.6 Job titles should not show a predetermined bias for the recruitment of those with a particular characteristic. For example, 'shop girl' suggests a bias towards recruiting a younger woman, and 'office boy' suggests a bias towards recruiting a younger man.

16.7 Tasks and duties set out in the job description should be objectively justifiable as being necessary to that post. This is especially important for tasks and duties which some people may not be able to fulfil, or would be less likely to be able to fulfil, because of a protected characteristic. Similarly, the job description should not overstate a duty which is only an occasional or marginal one.

Example: A job description includes the duty: 'regular Sunday working'. In reality, there is only an occasional need to work on a Sunday. This overstated duty written into the job description puts off Christians who do not wish to work on a Sunday, and so could amount to indirect discrimination unless the requirement can be objectively justified.

16.8 Where there are different ways of performing a task, job descriptions should not specify how the task should be done. Instead, the job description should state what outcome needs to be achieved.

Example: A job description includes the task: 'Using MagicReport software to produce reports about customer complaints'. This particular software is not accessible to some disabled people who use voice-activated software. Discrimination could be avoided by describing the task as 'Producing reports about customer complaints'.

16.9 Job descriptions should not specify working hours or working patterns that are not necessary to the job in question. If a job could be done either part-time, full-time, or through job share arrangements, this should be stated in the job description. As well as avoiding discrimination, this approach can also widen the group of people who may choose to make an application.

Example: A job description for a manager states that the job is full-time. The employer has stated this because all managers are currently full-time and he has not considered whether this is an actual requirement for the role. The requirement to work full-time could put women at a disadvantage compared with men because more women than men work part-time or job share in order to accommodate childcare responsibilities. This requirement could amount to indirect discrimination unless it can be objectively justified.

Person specifications

16.10 Person specifications describe various criteria – including skills, knowledge, abilities, qualifications, experience and qualities – that are considered necessary or desirable for someone fulfilling the role set out in the job description. These criteria must not be discriminatory. Discrimination can be avoided by ensuring that any necessary or desirable criteria can be justified for that particular job.

16.11 Criteria that exclude people because of a protected characteristic may be directly discriminatory unless they are related to occupational requirements (see Chapter 13).

Example: Stating in a job description for a secretary that the person must be under 40 would amount to direct age discrimination against people over 40. In some circumstances, age criteria can be objectively justified, but in this case it is very unlikely.

16.12 Criteria that are less likely to be met by people with certain protected characteristics may amount to indirect discrimination if these criteria cannot be objectively justified.

Example: Asking for 'so many years' experience could amount to indirect discrimination because of age unless this provision can be objectively justified.

Example: A requirement for continuous experience could indirectly discriminate against women who have taken time out from work for reasons relating to maternity or childcare, unless the requirement can be objectively justified.

16.13 The person specification should not include criteria that are wholly irrelevant.

Example: A requirement that the applicant must be 'active and energetic' when the job is a sedentary one is an irrelevant criterion. This requirement could be discriminatory against some disabled people who may be less mobile.

16.14 Employers should ensure that criteria relating to skills or knowledge are not unnecessarily restrictive in specifying particular qualifications that are necessary or desirable. It is advisable to make reference to 'equivalent qualifications' or to 'equivalent levels of skill or knowledge' in order to avoid indirect discrimination against applicants sharing a particular protected characteristic if this group is less likely to have obtained the qualification. The level of qualification needed should not be overstated. Employers should avoid specifying qualifications that were not available a generation ago, such as GCSEs, without stating that equivalent qualifications are also acceptable.

Example: Requiring a UK-based qualification, when equivalent qualifications obtained abroad would also meet the requirement for that particular level of knowledge or skill, may lead to indirect discrimination because of race, if the requirement cannot be objectively justified.

16.15 As far as possible, all the criteria should be capable of being tested objectively. For example, attributes such as 'leadership' should be defined in terms of measurable skills or experience.

Health requirements in person specifications

16.16 The inclusion of health requirements can amount to direct discrimination against disabled people, where such requirements lead to a blanket exclusion of people with particular impairments and do not allow individual circumstances to be considered. Employers should also be aware that, except in specified circumstances, it is unlawful to ask questions about health or disability before the offer of a job is made or a person is placed in a pool of people to be offered a job (see paragraphs 10.25 to 10.43).

Example: A person specification states that applicants must have 'good health'. This criterion is too broad to relate to any specific requirement of the job and is therefore likely to amount to direct discrimination because of disability.

16.17 The inclusion of criteria that relate to health, physical fitness or disability, such as asking applicants to demonstrate a good sickness record, may amount to indirect discrimination against disabled people in particular, unless these criteria can be objectively justified by the requirements of the actual job in question.

16.18 Person specifications that include requirements relating to health, fitness or other physical attributes may discriminate not only against some disabled applicants, but also against applicants with other protected characteristics – unless the requirements can be objectively justified.

Example: A person specification includes a height requirement. This may indirectly discriminate as it would put at a disadvantaged women, some disabled people, and people from certain racial groups if it cannot be objectively justified for the job in question.

ADVERTISING A JOB

16.19 An employer must not discriminate in its arrangements for advertising jobs or by not advertising a job. Neither should they discriminate through the actual content of the job advertisement (see paragraphs 3.32 and 10.6).

Arrangements for advertising

16.20 The practice of recruitment on the basis of recommendations made by existing staff, rather than through advertising, can lead to discrimination. For example, where the workforce is drawn largely from one racial group, this practice can lead to continued exclusion of other racial groups. It is therefore important to advertise the role widely so that the employer can select staff from a wider and more diverse pool.

16.21 Before deciding only to advertise a vacancy internally, an employer should consider whether there is any good reason for doing so. If the workforce is made up of people with a particular protected characteristic, advertising internally will not help diversify the workforce. If there is internal advertising alone, this should be done openly so that everyone in the organisation is given the opportunity to apply.

16.22 Employers should also ensure that people absent from work (including women on maternity leave, those on long-term sick leave, and those working part-time or remotely) are informed of any jobs that become available so they can consider whether to apply. Failure to do so may amount to discrimination.

Content of job advertisements

16.23 Job advertisements should accurately reflect the requirements of the job, including the job description and person specification if the employer uses these. This will ensure that nobody will be unnecessarily deterred from applying or making an unsuccessful application even though they could in fact do the job.

16.24 Advertisements must not include any wording that suggests the employer may directly discriminate by asking for people with a certain protected characteristic, for example by advertising for a 'salesman' or a 'waitress' or saying that the applicant must be 'youthful'.

Example: An employer advertises for a 'waitress'. This suggests that the employer is discriminating against men. By using a gender neutral term such as 'waiting staff' or by using the term 'waiter or waitress', the employer could avoid a claim of discrimination based on this advert.

16.25 Advertisements must not include any wording that suggests the employer might indirectly discriminate. Wording should not, for example, suggest criteria that would disadvantage people of a particular sex, age, or any other protected characteristic unless the requirement can be objectively justified or an exception under the Act applies.

16.26 A job advertisement should not include wording that suggests that reasonable adjustments will not be made for disabled people, or that disabled people will be discriminated against, or that they should not bother to apply.

Example: An employer advertises for an office worker, stating, 'This job is not suitable for wheelchair users because the office is on the first floor'. The employer should state instead, 'Although our offices are on the first floor, we welcome applications from disabled people and are willing to make reasonable adjustments'.

When is it lawful to advertise for someone with a particular protected characteristic?

16.27 Where there is an occupational requirement for a person with a particular protected characteristic that meets the legal test under the Act, then it would be lawful to advertise for such a person; for example, if there is an occupational requirement for a woman (see paragraphs 13.2 to 13.15). Where the job has an occupational requirement, the advertisement should state this so that it is clear that there is no unlawful discrimination.

Example: An employer advertises for a female care worker. It is an occupational requirement for the worker to be female, because the job involves intimate care tasks, such as bathing and toileting women. The advert states: 'Permitted under Schedule 9, part 1 of the Equality Act 2010'.

16.28 An employer can lawfully advertise a job as only open to disabled applicants because of the asymmetrical nature of disability discrimination (see paragraph 3.35).

Example: A private nursery advertises for a disabled childcare assistant. This is lawful under the Act.

16.29 An employer may include statements in a job advertisement encouraging applications from under-represented groups, as a voluntary 'positive action' measure (see Chapter 12). An employer may also include statements about their equality policy or statements that all applications will be considered solely on merit.

Example: The vast majority of workers employed by a national retailer are under the age of 40. Consequently, people over the age of 40 are under-represented in the organisation. The retailer is looking to open new stores and needs to recruit more staff. It would be lawful under the Act for that retailer to place a job advert encouraging applications from all groups, especially applicants over the age of 40.

Recruitment through employment services, careers services or other agencies

16.30 When recruiting through recruitment agencies, job centres, career offices, schools or online agencies, an employer must not instruct them to discriminate, for example by suggesting that certain groups would – or would not be – preferred; or cause or induce them to discriminate (see paragraphs 9.16 to 9.24).

16.31 Any agencies involved in an employer's recruitment should be made aware of the employer's equality policy, as well as other relevant policies. They should also be given copies of the job descriptions and person specifications for posts they are helping the employer to fill.

APPLICATION PROCESS

General principles

16.32 An employer must not discriminate through the application process. A standardised process, whether this is through an application form or using CVs, will enable an employer to make an objective assessment of an applicant's ability to do the job and will assist an employer in demonstrating that they have has assessed applicants objectively. It will also enable applicants to compete on equal terms with each other. A standardised application process does not preclude reasonable adjustments for disabled people (see below).

Example: An application form asks applicants to provide 400 words stating how they meet the job description and person specification. Applicants are marked for each criterion they satisfy and short-listed on the basis of their marks. This is a standardised application process that enables the employer to show that they have assessed all applicants without discriminating.

Reasonable adjustments during the application process

16.33 An employer must make reasonable adjustments for disabled applicants during the application process and must provide and accept information in accessible formats, where this would be a reasonable adjustment.

16.34 Where written information is provided about a job, it is likely to be a reasonable adjustment for that employer to provide, on request, information in a format that is accessible to a disabled applicant (see paragraphs 6.6 and 6.33). Accessible formats could include email, Braille, Easy Read, large print, audio format, and data formats. A disabled applicant's requirements will depend upon their impairment and on other factors too. For example, many blind people do not read Braille and would prefer to receive information by email or in audio format.

16.35 Where an employer invites applications by completing and returning an application form, it is likely to be a reasonable adjustment for them to provide forms and accept applications in accessible formats. However, a disabled applicant might not have a right to submit an application in their preferred format (such as Braille) if they would not be substantially disadvantaged by submitting it in some other format (such as email) which the employer would find easier to access.

16.36 In employment, the duty to make reasonable adjustments is not anticipatory (see Chapter 6). For this reason, employers do not need to keep stocks of job information or application forms in accessible formats, unless they are aware that these formats will be in demand. However, employers are advised to prepare themselves in advance so they can create accessible format documents quickly, allowing a candidate using that format to have their application considered at the same time as other applicants. Otherwise, employers may need to make a further adjustment of allowing extra time for return of the form, if the applicant has been put at a substantial disadvantage by having less time to complete it.

16.37 Where applications are invited by completing and returning a form online, it is likely to be a reasonable adjustment for the form to be made accessible to disabled people. If on-line forms are not accessible to disabled people, the form should be provided in an alternative way.

16.38 Where an application is submitted in an accessible format, an employer must not discriminate against disabled applicants in the way that it deals with these applications.

Personal information requested as part of the application process

16.39 An employer can reduce the possibility of discrimination by ensuring that the section of the application form requesting personal information is detachable from the rest of the form or requested separately. It is good practice for this information to be withheld from the people who are short-listing or interviewing because it could allow them to find out about a person's protected characteristics (such as age or sex). However, where an applicant's protected characteristics are suggested by information in an application form or CV (for example, qualifications or work history) those who are short-listing or interviewing must not use it to discriminate against the applicant.

16.40 Where information for monitoring purposes is requested as part of an online application process, employers should find a way to separate the monitoring process from the application process. For example, a monitoring form could be sent out by email on receipt of a completed application form.

16.41 Any other questions on the main application form about protected characteristics should include a clear explanation as to why this information is needed, and an assurance that the information will be treated in strictest confidence. These questions should only be asked where they reflect occupational requirements for the post. Questions related to an occupational requirement should only seek as much information as is required to establish whether the candidate meets the requirement (see Chapter 13)

16.42 Applicants should not be asked to provide photographs, unless it is essential for selection purposes, for example for an acting job; or for security purposes, such as to confirm that a person who attends for an assessment or interview is the applicant.

SELECTION, ASSESSMENT AND INTERVIEW PROCESS

General principles

16.43 Arrangements for deciding to whom to offer employment include short-listing, selection tests, use of assessment centres and interviews. An employer must not discriminate in any of these arrangements and must make reasonable adjustments so that disabled people are not placed at a substantial disadvantage compared to non-disabled people (see Chapter 10). Basing selection decisions on stereotypical assumptions or prejudice is likely to amount to direct discrimination.

16.44 An employer should ensure that these processes are fair and objective and that decisions are consistent. Employers should also keep records that will allow them to justify each decision and the process by which it was reached and to respond to any complaints of discrimination. If the employer does not keep records of their decisions, in some circumstances, it could result in an Employment Tribunal drawing an adverse inference of discrimination.

16.45 In deciding exactly how long to keep records after a recruitment exercise, employers must balance their need to keep such records to justify selection decisions with their obligations under the Data Protection Act 1998 to keep personal data for no longer than is necessary.

16.46 The records that employers should keep include:

- any job advertisement, job description or person specification used in the recruitment process;
- the application forms or CVs, and any supporting documentation from every candidate applying for the job;
- records of discussions and decisions by an interviewer or members of the selection panel; for example, on marking standards or interview questions;
- notes taken by the interviewer or by each member of the panel during the interviews;
- each interview panel member's marks at each stage of the process; for example, on the application form, any selection tests and each interview question (where a formal marking system is used);
- all correspondence with the candidates.

16.47 An employer is more likely to make consistent and objective decisions if the same staff members are responsible for selection at all stages of the recruitment process for each vacancy. Staff involved in the selection process should receive training on the employer's equality policy (if there is one).

16.48 An employer should ensure that they do not put any applicant at a particular disadvantage in the arrangements they make for holding tests or interviews, or using assessment centres. For example, dates that coincide with religious festivals or tests that favour certain groups of applicants may lead to indirect discrimination, if they cannot be objectively justified.

Example: An all-day assessment that involves a social dinner may amount to indirect discrimination if the employer has not taken account of dietary needs relating to an applicant's religion – unless the arrangements can be objectively justified.

16.49 An employer is not required to make changes in anticipation of applications from disabled people in general – although it would be good practice to do so. It is only if the employer knows or could be reasonably expected to know that a particular disabled person is (or may be) applying, and that the person is likely to be substantially disadvantaged by the employer's premises or arrangements, that the employer must make reasonable adjustments. If an employer fails to ask about reasonable adjustments needed for the recruitment process, but could reasonably have been expected to know that a particular disabled applicant or possible applicant is likely to be disadvantaged compared to non-disabled people, they will still be under a duty to make a reasonable adjustment at the interview.

Short-listing

16.50 It is recommended that employers build the following guidelines for good practice into their selection procedures. By doing so, they will reduce the possibility of unlawful discrimination and avoid an adverse inference being made, should a tribunal claim be made by a rejected applicant.

- Wherever possible, more than one person should be involved in short-listing applicants, to reduce the chance of one individual's bias prejudicing an applicant's chances of being selected.
- The marking system, including the cut-off score for selection, should be agreed before the applications are assessed, and applied consistently to all applications.
- Where more than one person is involved in the selection, applications should be marked separately before a final mark is agreed between the people involved.
- Selection should be based only on information provided in the application form, CV or, in the case of internal applicants, any formal performance assessment reports.
- The weight given to each criterion in the person specification should not be changed during short-listing; for example, in order to include someone who would otherwise not be short-listed.

Guaranteed interviews for disabled applicants

16.51 Some employers operate a guaranteed interview scheme, under which a disabled candidate who wishes to use the scheme will be short-listed for interview automatically if they demonstrate that they meet the minimum criteria for getting the job. As explained above (paragraph 10.33), the Act permits questions to be asked at the application stage to identify disabled applicants who want to use this scheme.

Selection tests and assessment centres

16.52 Ability tests, personality questionnaires and other similar methods should only be used if they are well designed, properly administered and professionally validated and are a reliable method of predicting an applicant's performance in a particular job. If such a test leads to indirect discrimination or discrimination arising from disability, even if such discrimination is not intended and the reason for the discrimination is not understood, the test should not be used unless it can be objectively justified.

16.53 Where tests and assessment centres are used as part of the selection process, it is recommended that employers take account of the following guidelines:

- Tests should correspond to the job in question, and measure as closely as possible the appropriate levels of the skills and abilities included in the person specification.
- The Welsh Language Act 1993 puts Welsh and English on an equal basis in the delivery of public services in Wales and bilingual tests may need to be used for recruitment to some public sector jobs, where the ability to speak Welsh is essential or desirable.
- Where the purpose of a test is not to ascertain a person's level of proficiency in English (or Welsh in Wales), special care should be taken to make sure candidates whose first language is not English (or Welsh in Wales) understand the instructions. Tests that are fair for speakers of English (or Welsh) as a first language may present problems for people who are less proficient in the language.
- Deaf people whose first language is British Sign Language may be at a substantial disadvantage if a test is in English (or Welsh). An employer will need to consider what they should do to comply with the duty to make reasonable adjustments for such applicants.
- All candidates should take the same test unless there is a health and safety reason why the candidate cannot do so, for example because of pregnancy, or unless a reasonable adjustment is required (see below).
- Test papers, assessment notes and records of decisions should be kept on file (see paragraph 17.4).

16.54 Employers should make adjustments where a test or assessment would put a disabled applicant at a substantial disadvantage, if such adjustments would be reasonable (see Chapter 6). Examples of adjustments which may be reasonable include:

- providing written instructions in an accessible format;
- allowing a disabled person extra time to complete the test;
- permitting a disabled person the assistance of a reader or scribe during the test;
- allowing a disabled applicant to take an oral test in writing or a written test orally.

16.55 The extent to which such adjustments would be reasonable may depend on the nature of the disabled person's impairment, how closely the test is related to the job in question and what adjustments the employer would be reasonably required to make if the applicant were given the job.

16.56 However, employers would be well advised to seek professional advice in the light of individual circumstances before making adjustments to psychological or aptitude tests.

Interviews

16.57 An employer must not discriminate at the interview stage. In reality, this is the stage at which it is easiest to make judgements about an applicant based on instant, subjective and sometimes wholly irrelevant impressions. If decisions are based on prejudice and stereotypes and not based on factors relating to the job description or person specification, this could lead to unlawful discrimination. By conducting interviews strictly on the basis of the application form, the job description, the person specification, the agreed weight given to each criterion and the results of any selection tests, an employer will ensure that all applicants are assessed objectively, and solely on their ability to do the job satisfactorily.

16.58 Employers should try to be flexible about the arrangements made for interviews. For example, a woman with childcare responsibilities may have difficulties attending an early morning interview or a person practising a particular religion or belief may have difficulty attending on certain days or at certain times.

16.59 By the interview stage, an employer should already have asked whether reasonable adjustments are needed for the interview itself. This should have been covered on the application form or in the letter inviting a candidate for interview. However, it is still good practice for the interviewer to ask on the day if any adjustments are needed for the interview.

16.60 The practical effects of an employer's duties may be different if a person whom the employer previously did not know to be disabled (and it would not be reasonable to expect them to have known this) arrives for interview and is substantially disadvantaged because of the arrangements. The employer will be under a duty to make a reasonable adjustment from the time that they first learn of the disability and the disadvantage. However, the extent of the duty is less than might have been the case if they had known (or ought to have known) in advance about the disability and its effects.

16.61 An employer can reduce the possibility of unlawful discrimination by ensuring that staff involved in selection panels have had equality training and training about interviews, to help them:

- recognise when they are making stereotypical assumptions about people;
- apply a scoring method objectively;
- prepare questions based on the person specification and job description and the information in the application form; and
- avoid questions that are not relevant to the requirements of the job.

16.62 It is particularly important to avoid irrelevant interview questions that relate to protected characteristics, as this could lead to discrimination under the Act. These could include, for example, questions about childcare arrangements, living arrangements or plans to get married or to have children. Where such information is volunteered, selectors should take particular care not to allow themselves to be influenced by that information. A woman is under no obligation to declare her pregnancy in a recruitment process. If she volunteers that information, it should not be taken into account in deciding her suitability for the job.

16.63 Questions should not be asked, nor should assumptions be made, about whether someone would fit in with the existing workforce.

Example: At a job interview a woman is asked: 'You would be the only woman doing this job, and the men might make sexist jokes. How would you feel about this?' This question could amount to direct sex discrimination.

16.64 Except in particular circumstances, questions about disability or health must not be asked at the interview stage or at any other stage before the offer of a job (whether conditional or not) has been made, or where the person has been accepted into a pool of applicants to be offered a position when one becomes available. This is explained in paragraphs 10.25 to 10.43.

References

16.65 References should only be obtained, and circulated to members of the selection panel, after a selection decision has been reached. This can help ensure that the selection decision is based on objective criteria and is not influenced by other factors, such as potentially subjective judgments about a candidate by referees. Employers should send referees copies of the job description and person specification, requesting evidence of the candidate's ability to meet the specific requirements of the job. This is more likely to ensure that the reference focuses on information that is relevant to the job. Where a reference is subjective and negative, it is good practice to give the successful applicant an opportunity to comment on it.

Eligibility to work in the UK

16.66 Under the Immigration, Asylum and Nationality Act 2006, all employers (including small employers) are required to obtain information about a person's eligibility to work in the UK before employment begins. Many people from ethnic minorities in this country are British citizens or are otherwise entitled to work here. Employers should not make assumptions about a person's right to work in the UK based on race, colour or national origin, because all applicants should be treated equally under the Act.

16.67 Eligibility to work in the UK should be verified in the final stages of the selection process rather than at the application stage, to make sure the appointment is based on merit alone, and is not influenced by other factors. Depending on the employer's recruitment process, and the type of job being filled, candidates might be asked for the relevant documents when they are invited to an interview, or when an offer of employment is made. Employers can, in some circumstances, apply for work permits and should not exclude potentially suitable candidates from the selection process.

16.68 The UK Border Agency has published a code of practice for employers on how to avoid unlawful racial discrimination when complying with this requirement. Please see:

www.gov.uk/government/publications/right-to-work-checks-code-of-practice-on-avoiding-discrimination

JOB OFFERS

16.69 As stated at the beginning of this chapter, an employer must not discriminate against a person in the terms on which the person is offered employment.

Example: An employer offers a job but extends their usual probation period from three months to six months because the preferred candidate is a woman returning from maternity leave or a person with a disability. This would be discrimination in the terms on which the person is offered employment.

16.70 A refusal to recruit a woman because she is pregnant is unlawful even if she is unable to carry out the job for which she is to be employed. This will be the case even if the initial vacancy was to cover another woman on maternity leave. It is irrelevant that the woman failed to disclose that she was pregnant when she was recruited. A woman is not legally obliged to tell an employer during the recruitment process that she is pregnant because it is not a factor which can lawfully influence the employer's decision (see Chapter 8).

16.71 **[Sch 9, para 9]** Employers do not discriminate because of age by refusing to recruit someone who is older than 64 years and six months old or within six months of the normal retirement age where such normal retirement age is more than 65. This does not alter an existing employee's right to request to work beyond retirement age (see paragraphs 13.26 to 13.38).

Feedback to short-listed unsuccessful candidates

16.72 Having secured a preferred candidate, it is good practice for an employer to offer feedback to unsuccessful short-listed candidates if this is requested. By demonstrating objective reasons for the applicant's lack of success, based on the requirements of the job, an employer can minimise the risk of any claims for unlawful discrimination under the Act.

CHAPTER 17
AVOIDING DISCRIMINATION DURING EMPLOYMENT

INTRODUCTION

[4.144]

17.1 As explained in Chapter 10, the Act prohibits discrimination, victimisation and harassment at all stages and in all aspects of the employment relationship, including in workers' training and development. It also places employers under a duty to make reasonable adjustments for disabled workers. This chapter takes a closer look at the implications of the Act for a range of issues that are central to the relationship between employers and workers: working hours; sickness and absence; arranging leave from work; accommodating workers' needs; induction, training and development; disciplinary and grievance matters. Where appropriate, it also makes recommendations for good practice.

17.2 Many aspects of the employment relationship are governed by the contract of employment between the employer and the worker, which may be verbal or written. Practical day-to-day arrangements or custom and practice in the workplace are also important; in some cases, these features are communicated via written policies and procedures.

17.3 In many workplaces, a trade union is recognised by the employer for collective bargaining purposes. Where changes to policies and procedures are being considered, an employer should consult with a recognised trade union in the first instance. It is also good practice for employers to consult with trade union equality representatives as a first step towards understanding the diverse needs of workers. The role of trade unions in meeting the training and development needs of their members should also be recognised.

17.4 Where resources permit, employers are strongly advised to maintain proper written records of decisions taken in relation to individual workers, and the reasons for these decisions. Keeping written records will help employers reflect on the decisions they are taking and thus help avoid discrimination. In addition, written records will be invaluable if an employer has to defend a claim in the Employment Tribunal.

17.5 It is also useful for employers to monitor overall workplace figures on matters such as requests for flexible working, promotion, training and disciplinary procedures to see if there are significant disparities between groups of people sharing different protected characteristics. If disparities are found, employers should investigate the possible causes in each case and take steps to remove any barriers.

WORKING HOURS

17.6 Working hours are determined by agreement between the employer and the worker, subject to collective agreements negotiated by trade unions on behalf of workers. The Working Time Regulations 1998 set out certain legal requirements; for example, maximum average working hours per week, minimum rest breaks, daily and weekly rest periods and entitlement to annual leave. There are also special provisions for night workers.

17.7 Established working time agreements can be varied either simply by agreement between the employer and worker or following a statutory request for flexible working.

Flexible working

17.8 **[ERA 1996 ss 80F–80I]** There are statutory rules which give employees with caring responsibilities for children or specified adults the right to have a request for flexible working considered. The right is

Part 4 Statutory Codes of Practice

designed to give employees the opportunity to adopt working arrangements that help them to balance their commitments at work with their need to care for a child or an adult.

17.9 The statutory rules are set out in the Employment Rights Act 1996, and expanded in the Flexible Working (Procedural Requirements) Regulations 2002 and the Flexible Working (Eligibility, Complaints and Remedies) Regulations 2002. Under these rules, employees with caring responsibilities who have at least 26 weeks' continuous service are entitled to make a written request for flexible working; that is, to request changes to hours of work, times of work and the location of work. In practice this might mean:

- part-time working, term-time working or home working;
- adjusting start and finish times;
- adopting a particular shift pattern or extended hours on some days with time off on others.

17.10 Employers have a duty to consider a request for flexible working arrangements within specified timescales, and can refuse only on one of the business-related grounds set out in the statutory rules. The refusal must be in writing and include a sufficient explanation of the decision, based on correct facts. Employers who do not comply with these statutory procedures risk being taken to an Employment Tribunal and possibly having to pay compensation to the employee. For further details of the flexible working procedures, see:
www.direct.gov.uk/en/employment/employees/workinghoursandtimeoff/dg_10029491

17.11 It is also important to bear in mind that rigid working patterns may result in indirect discrimination unless they can be objectively justified. Although a flexible working request may legitimately be refused under the statutory rules, such a refusal may still be indirectly discriminatory if the employer is unable to show that the requirement to work certain hours is justified as a proportionate means of achieving a legitimate aim. For example:

- A requirement to work full-time hours may indirectly discriminate against women because they are more likely to have childcare responsibilities.
- A requirement to work full-time hours could indirectly discriminate against disabled people with certain conditions (such as ME). It could also amount to a failure to make reasonable adjustments.
- A requirement to work on certain days may indirectly discriminate against those with particular religious beliefs.

Example: An employee's contractual hours are 9am–3pm. Under the flexible working procedures, she has formally requested to work from 10am–4pm because of childcare needs. Her employer refuses, saying that to provide staff cover in the mornings would involve extra costs. This refusal would be compatible with the flexible working procedures, which do not require a refusal to be objectively justified. However, in some circumstances, this could amount to indirect sex discrimination. Where a refusal to permit certain working patterns would detrimentally affect a larger proportion of women than men, the employer must show that it is based on a legitimate aim, such as providing sufficient staff cover before 10am, and that refusing the request is a proportionate means of achieving that aim.

17.12 Employers should also be particularly mindful of their duty to make reasonable adjustments to working hours for disabled workers.

Example: A worker with a learning disability has a contract to work normal office hours (9am to 5.30pm in this particular office). He wishes to change these hours because the friend whom he needs to accompany him to work is no longer available before 9am. Allowing him to start later is likely to be a reasonable adjustment for that employer to make.

Rest breaks

17.13 Minimum rest break periods are set out in the Working Time Regulations 1998. Some employers operate a policy on rest breaks and lunch breaks that is more generous than the provisions of those Regulations.

17.14 In considering requests for additional or different breaks, employers should ensure that they do not discriminate because of any protected characteristic. In some circumstances, an employer's refusal to allow additional breaks or flexibility as to when they are taken might amount to indirect discrimination unless it can be objectively justified. When dealing with requests for additional breaks, an employer should consider whether it is possible to grant the request by allowing the person to work more flexible hours.

Example: An observant Muslim requests two additional 10-minute breaks every day to allow him to pray at work. The employer allows other workers to take additional smoking breaks of similar length. Refusing this request could amount to direct discrimination because of religion or belief. On the other hand, if the employer took a consistently strict approach to rest breaks, they could allow the prayer breaks on the understanding that the Muslim worker arrives at work 20 minutes earlier or makes up the time at the end of the day.

17.15 Allowing disabled workers to take additional rest breaks is one way that an employer can fulfil their duty to make reasonable adjustments.

Example: A worker has recently been diagnosed with diabetes. As a consequence of her medication and her new dietary requirements, she finds that she gets extremely tired at certain times during the working day. It is likely to be a reasonable adjustment to allow her to take additional rest breaks to control the effects of her impairment.

SICKNESS AND ABSENCE FROM WORK

17.16 Sickness and absence from work may be governed by contractual terms and conditions and/or may be the subject of non-contractual practices and procedures. Regardless of the nature of these policies, it is important to ensure that they are non-discriminatory in design, and applied to workers who are sick or absent for whatever reason without discrimination of any kind. This is particularly important when a policy has discretionary elements such as decisions about stopping sick pay or commencing attendance management procedures.

17.17 To avoid discrimination, sickness and absence procedures should include clear requirements about informing the employer of sickness and providing medical certificates. They should also specify the rate and the maximum period of payment for sick pay.

17.18 In order to defend any claims of discrimination, it is advisable for employers to maintain records of workers' absences. In relation to sick leave, this is a legal requirement under the Statutory Sick Pay (General) Regulations 1982. Particular care is needed to ensure that sensitive medical information about workers is kept confidential and handled in accordance with the Data Protection Act 1998.

17.19 When taking attendance management action against a worker, employers should ensure that they do not discriminate because of a protected characteristic. In particular, it will often be appropriate to manage disability, pregnancy and gender reassignment-related absences differently from other types of absence. Recording the reasons for absences should assist that process.

Disability-related absences

17.20 Employers are not automatically obliged to disregard all disability-related sickness absences, but they must disregard some or all of the absences by way of an adjustment if this is reasonable. If an employer takes action against a disabled worker for disability-related sickness absence, this may amount to discrimination arising from disability (see Chapter 5).

Example: During a six-month period, a man who has recently developed a long-term health condition has a number of short periods of absence from work as he learns to manage this condition. Ignoring these periods of disability-related absence is likely to be a reasonable adjustment for the employer to make. Disciplining this man because of these periods of absence will amount to discrimination arising from disability, if the employer cannot show that this is objectively justified.

17.21 Workers who are absent because of disability-related sickness must be paid no less than the contractual sick pay which is due for the period in question. Although there is no automatic obligation for an employer to extend contractual sick pay beyond the usual entitlement when a worker is absent due to disability-related sickness, an employer should consider whether it would be reasonable for them to do so.

17.22 However, if the reason for absence is due to an employer's delay in implementing a reasonable adjustment that would enable the worker to return to the workplace, maintaining full pay would be a further reasonable adjustment for the employer to make.

Example: A woman who has a visual impairment needs work documents to be enlarged. Her employer fails to make arrangements for a reasonable adjustment to provide her with these. As a result, she has a number of absences from work because of eyestrain. After she has received full sick pay for four months, the employer is considering a reduction to half-pay in line with its sickness policy. It is likely to be a reasonable adjustment to maintain full pay as her absence is caused by the employer's delay in making the original adjustment.

17.23 Disabled workers may sometimes require time out during the working day to attend medical appointments or receive treatment related to their disability. On occasions, it may be necessary for them to attend to access needs such as wheelchair maintenance or care of working dogs. If, for example, a worker needs to take a short period of time off each week over a period of several months it is likely to be reasonable to accommodate the time off.

17.24 However, if a worker needs to take off several days per week over a period of months it may not be reasonable for the employer to accommodate this. Whether or not it is reasonable will depend on the circumstances of both the employer and the worker.

Example: An employer allows a worker who has become disabled after a stroke to have time off for rehabilitation training. Although this is more time off than would be allowed to non-disabled workers, it is likely to be a reasonable adjustment. A similar adjustment may be reasonable if a disability gets worse or if a disabled worker needs occasional but regular long-term treatment.

Pregnancy-related absences

17.25 All pregnancy-related absences must be disregarded for the purposes of attendance management action. Workers who are absent for a pregnancy-related reason have no automatic right to full pay but should receive no less than the contractual sick pay that might be due for the period in question. However, employers have no obligation to extend contractual sick pay beyond what would usually be payable. Sickness absence associated with a miscarriage should be treated as pregnancy-related sickness. Pregnancy-related absence is covered in more detail in Chapter 8.

Example: A worker has been off work because of pregnancy complications since early in her pregnancy. Her employer has now dismissed her in accordance with the sickness policy which allows no more than 20 weeks' continuous absence. This policy is applied regardless of sex. The dismissal is unfavourable treatment because of her pregnancy and would be unlawful even if a man would be dismissed for a similar period of sickness absence, because the employer took into account the worker's pregnancy-related sickness absence in deciding to dismiss.

17.26 Pregnant employees are entitled to paid time off for antenatal care. Antenatal care can include medical examinations, relaxation and parenting classes.

Example: A pregnant employee has booked time off to attend a medical appointment related to her pregnancy. Her employer insists this time must be made up through flexi-time arrangements or her pay will be reduced to reflect the time off. This is unlawful: a pregnant employee is under no obligation to make up time taken off for antenatal appointments and an employer cannot refuse paid time off to attend such classes.

Absences related to gender reassignment

17.27 If a transsexual person is absent from work because they propose to undergo, are undergoing or have undergone gender reassignment, it is unlawful to treat them less favourably than they would be treated if they were absent due to illness or injury, or – if reasonable – than they would be treated for absence for other reasons (see paragraphs 9.31 to 9.33).

Example: A worker undergoing gender reassignment has to take some time off for medical appointments and also for surgery. The employer records all these absences for the purposes of their attendance management policy. However, when another worker breaks his leg skiing the employer disregards his absences because 'it wasn't really sickness and won't happen again'. This indicates that the treatment of the transsexual worker may amount to discrimination because the employer would have treated him more favourably if he had broken his leg than they treated him because of gender reassignment absences.

Absences related to in vitro fertilisation

17.28 There is no statutory entitlement to time off for in vitro fertilisation (IVF) or other fertility treatment. However, in responding to requests for time off from a woman undergoing IVF, an employer must not treat her less favourably than they treat, or would treat, a man in a similar situation as this could amount to sex discrimination. After a fertilised embryo has been implanted, a woman is legally pregnant and from that point is protected from unfavourable treatment because of her pregnancy, including pregnancy-related sickness. She would also be entitled to time off for antenatal care.

17.29 It is good practice for employers to treat sympathetically any request for time off for IVF or other fertility treatment, and consider adopting a procedure to cover this situation. This could include allowing women to take annual leave or unpaid leave when receiving treatment and designating a member of staff whom they can inform on a confidential basis that they are undergoing treatment.

Example: A female worker who is undergoing IVF treatment has to take time off sick because of its side effects. Her employer treats this as ordinary sickness absence and pays her contractual sick pay that is due to her. Had contractual sick pay been refused, this could amount to sex discrimination.

Example: Recently an employer agreed, as a one-off request, a week's annual leave for a male worker who wanted to undergo cosmetic dental surgery. Two months later, one of his female colleagues asks if she can take a week's annual leave to undergo IVF treatment. The employer refuses this request, even though the worker still has two weeks leave due to her. She may be able show that the employer's refusal to grant her request for annual leave for IVF treatment amounts to sex discrimination, by comparing her treatment to that of her male colleague.

Maternity, paternity, adoption and parental leave

17.30 When dealing with workers who request or take maternity, paternity, adoption or parental leave, employers should ensure that they do not discriminate against the worker because of a protected characteristic.

Example: A lesbian worker has asked her employer for parental leave. She and her partner adopted a child two years ago and she wants to be able to look after her child for part of the summer holidays. The worker made sure the time she has requested would not conflict with parental leave being taken by other workers. In exercising his discretion whether to grant parental leave, the woman's line manager refuses her request because he does not agree with same sex couples being allowed to adopt children. This is likely to be direct discrimination because of sexual orientation.

17.31 Detailed provisions dealing with maternity, paternity, adoption and parental leave and workers' rights during such leave are set out in other statutes and regulations; for example, the Employment Rights Act 1996, Maternity and Parental Leave etc Regulations 1999 (as amended), Paternity and Adoption Leave Regulations 2002 (as amended) and the Management of Health and Safety at Work Regulations 1999. For more information, please see Chapter 8.

Emergency leave

17.32 **[ERA 1996 s 57A]** Employees have a statutory right to take reasonable unpaid time off which is necessary to deal with immediate emergencies concerning dependants. Dependants include a spouse or civil partner or partner, a child or a parent, or a person living in the employee's household. In dealing with cases where emergency leave is required, employers should ensure that they do not discriminate.

Example: A worker receives a telephone call informing him that his civil partner has been involved in an accident. The worker has been recorded as next of kin on his civil partner's medical notes and is required at the hospital. The employer has a policy that only allows emergency leave to be taken where a spouse, child or parent is affected and refuses the worker's request for leave. This would amount to discrimination because of sexual orientation. It would also be a breach of the worker's statutory rights.

Annual leave

17.33 Annual leave policies and procedures must be applied without discrimination of any kind. It is particularly important for employers to avoid discrimination when dealing with competing requests for annual leave, or requests that relate to a worker's protected characteristic such as religion or belief.

17.34 The Working Time Regulations 1998 provide a minimum annual holiday entitlement of 5.6 weeks, which can include public and bank holidays; however, employers may offer workers more holiday than their minimum legal entitlement. The procedure in the Regulations for requesting annual leave and dealing with such requests may be replaced by agreement between the employer and worker. All policies and procedures for handling annual leave requests should be non-discriminatory in design and the employer must not refuse a request for annual leave because of a protected characteristic.

17.35 A policy leading to a refusal is also an application of a provision, criterion or practice. The policy could be indirectly discriminatory if it places the worker and people sharing the worker's characteristic at a particular disadvantage, unless the provision, criterion or practice is a proportionate means of achieving a legitimate aim.

17.36 A worker may request annual leave for a religious occasion or to visit family overseas. To avoid discrimination, employers should seek to accommodate the request – provided the worker has sufficient holiday due to them and it is reasonable for them to be absent from work during the period requested.

Example: An Australian worker requests three weeks' leave to visit his family in Australia. He works for a large employer, whose annual leave policy normally limits periods of annual leave to a maximum of two weeks at any one time. The two-week limit could be indirectly discriminatory because of nationality, unless it can be objectively justified. In this case, the employer has sufficient staff to cover the additional week's leave. They operate the annual leave policy flexibly, and agree to allow the worker to take three weeks' leave to visit his family.

17.37 Many religions or beliefs have special periods of religious observance, festivals or holidays. Employers should be aware that some of these occasions are aligned with lunar phases. As a result, dates can change from year to year and may not become clear until quite close to the actual day.

Example: Last year, a Sikh worker took annual leave on 1 and 2 March to celebrate Hola Mohalla. This year, he requests annual leave on 6th and 7th March to celebrate the same holiday. No other staff members in his department have requested leave on these dates. The employer refuses the request but says that the worker can take off the same days as he did last year. Festivals in Sikhism are based on the lunar calendar, so the dates on which they fall differ every year. It could be indirect discrimination for the employer to expect the worker to take annual leave on the same days every year, unless this can be objectively justified.

17.38 Employers who require everyone to take leave during an annual closedown should consider whether this creates a particular disadvantage for workers sharing a protected characteristic who need annual leave at other times, for example, during specific school holidays or religious festivals. This practice could amount to indirect discrimination, unless it can be objectively justified. Although the operational needs of the business may be a legitimate aim, employers must consider the needs of workers in assessing whether the closure is a proportionate means of achieving the aim (see paragraphs 4.25 to 4.32).

AVOIDING DISCRIMINATION – ACCOMMODATING WORKERS' NEEDS

Dress and business attire

17.39 Many employers enforce a dress code or uniform with the aim of ensuring that workers dress in a manner that is appropriate to the business or workplace or to meet health and safety requirements. However, dress codes – including rules about jewellery – may indirectly discriminate against workers sharing a protected characteristic. To avoid indirect discrimination, employers should make sure that any dress rules can be justified as a proportionate means of achieving a legitimate aim such as health and safety considerations.

17.40 It is good practice for employers to consult with workers as to how a dress code may impact on different religious or belief groups, and whether any exceptions should be allowed – for example, for religious jewellery.

Example: An employer introduces a 'no jewellery' policy in the workplace. This is not for health and safety reasons but because the employer does not like body piercings. A Sikh worker who wears a Kara bracelet as an integral part of her religion has complained about the rule. To avoid a claim of indirect discrimination, the employer should consider allowing an exception to this rule. A blanket ban on jewellery would probably not be considered a proportionate means of achieving a legitimate aim in these circumstances.

17.41 In some situations, a dress code could amount to direct discrimination because of a protected characteristic. It is not necessarily sex discrimination for a dress code to set out different requirements for men and women (for example, that men have to wear a collar and tie). However, it may be direct discrimination if a dress code requires a different overall standard of dress for men and for women; for example, requiring men to dress in a professional and business-like way but allowing women to wear more casual clothes. It could also be direct discrimination if the dress code is similar for both sexes but applied more strictly to men than women – or the other way round.

17.42 Where men are required to wear suits, it may be less favourable treatment to require women to wear skirts, if an equivalent level of smartness can be achieved by women wearing, for example, a trouser suit. If a male to female transsexual person is prevented from wearing a skirt where other women are permitted to do so, this could amount to direct discrimination because of gender reassignment.

Example: An employer's dress code requires men to wear shirts and ties and women to 'dress smartly'. The dress code is not enforced as strictly against women as against men. A male worker has been suspended for continually failing to wear a tie, while no action is taken against female colleagues for wearing T-shirts. This could amount to direct discrimination because of sex.

17.43 Employers should also be aware of the duty to make reasonable adjustments to a dress code in order to avoid placing disabled workers at a substantial disadvantage. For example, in some cases uniforms made of certain fabrics may cause a reaction in workers with particular skin conditions.

Language in the workplace

17.44 A language requirement for a job may be indirectly discriminatory unless it is necessary for the satisfactory performance of the job. For example, a requirement that a worker have excellent English skills may be indirectly discriminatory because of race; if a worker really only needs a good grasp of English, the requirement for excellent English may not be objectively justified. A requirement for good spoken English may be indirectly discriminatory against certain disabled people, for example, deaf people whose first language is British Sign Language. (See Chapter 4 for more information on indirect discrimination.)

Example: A superstore insists that all its workers have excellent spoken English. This might be a justifiable requirement for those in customer-facing roles. However, for workers based in the stock room, the requirement could be indirectly discriminatory in relation to race or disability as it is less likely to be objectively justified.

17.45 Under the Welsh Language Act 1993, public bodies providing services to the public in Wales must make their services available in Welsh as well as English. This operates as a statutory exception to the Equality Act, and allows a wide range of posts in public bodies in Wales (and some outside Wales) to require workers who can speak, write and read Welsh sufficiently well for the post in question. In some cases, Welsh language skills may be an essential requirement for appointment; in others, the worker may need to agree to learn the language to the required level within a reasonable period of time after appointment. On this issue, employers are recommended to seek advice from the Welsh Language Board.

Example: A local council in Wales requires all its newly recruited receptionists to speak Welsh or be willing to learn the language within a year of being employed. This requirement would be lawful under the Act.

17.46 In fulfilling the duty to make reasonable adjustments, employers may have to take steps to ensure that information is provided in accessible formats. This requirement is covered in more detail in paragraphs 6.6 and 6.33.

17.47 An employer might also wish to impose a requirement on workers to communicate in a common language – generally English. There is a clear business interest in having a common language in the workplace, to avoid misunderstandings, whether legal, financial or in relation to health and safety. It is also conducive to good working relations to avoid excluding workers from conversations that might concern them.

17.48 However, employers should make sure that any requirement involving the use of a particular language during or outside working hours, for example during work breaks, does not amount to unlawful discrimination. Blanket rules involving the use of a particular language may not be objectively justifiable as a proportionate means of achieving a legitimate aim. An employer who prohibits workers from talking casually to each other in a language they do not share with all colleagues, or uses occasions when this happens to trigger disciplinary or capability procedures or to impede workers' career progress, may be considered to be acting disproportionately.

17.49 English is generally the language of business in Britain and is likely to be the preferred means of communication in most workplaces, unless other languages are required for specific business reasons. There may be some circumstances where using a different language might be more practical for a line manager dealing with a particular group of workers with limited English language skills.

Example: A construction company employs a high number of Polish workers on one of its sites. The project manager of the site is also Polish and finds it more practical to speak Polish when giving instructions to those workers. However, the company should not advertise vacancies as being only open to Polish-speaking workers as the requirement is unlikely to be justified and could amount to indirect race discrimination.

17.50 Where the workforce includes people sharing a protected characteristic who experience disadvantage within the workplace because of limited English, employers could consider taking proportionate positive action measures to improve their communication skills. These measures might include providing:

- interpreting and translation facilities; for example, multilingual safety signs and notices, to make sure the workers in question understand health and safety requirements;
- English language classes to improve communication skills.

The provisions on positive action are explained in Chapter 12.

17.51 Inappropriate or derogatory language in the workplace could amount to harassment if it is related to a protected characteristic and is sufficiently serious. Workplace policies – if the employer has these in place – should emphasise that workers should not make inappropriate comments, jokes or use derogatory terms related to a protected characteristic (see Chapter 7 on harassment).

Example: A male worker has made a number of offensive remarks about a worker who is pregnant, such as 'women are only good for making babies'. The employer's equality policy makes it clear that inappropriate and offensive language, comments and jokes related to a protected characteristic can amount to harassment and may be treated as a disciplinary offence. The employer may bring disciplinary proceedings against the male worker for making offensive comments that relate to the pregnant worker's sex.

Understanding a worker's needs

17.52 The employer's duty to make reasonable adjustments continues throughout the disabled worker's employment (see Chapter 6). It is good practice for an employer to encourage disabled workers to discuss their disability so that any reasonable adjustments can be put in place. Disabled workers may be reluctant to disclose their impairment and the Act does not impose any obligation on them to do so. An employer can help overcome any concerns a disabled worker may have in this regard by explaining the reasons why information is being requested (that is, to consider reasonable adjustments). The employer should also reassure the worker that that information about disability is held confidentially.

Example: An office worker has symptomatic HIV and does not wish to tell his employer. His symptoms get worse and he finds it increasingly difficult to work the required number of hours in a week. At his annual appraisal, he raises this problem with his line manager and discloses his medical condition. As a result, a reasonable adjustment is made and his working hours are reduced to overcome the difficulty.

17.53 Sometimes a reasonable adjustment will not succeed without the co-operation of other workers. To secure such co-operation it may be necessary for the employer, with the disabled worker's consent, to tell their colleague(s) in confidence about a disability which is not obvious. This disclosure may be limited to the disabled person's line manager or it may be appropriate to involve other colleagues, depending on the circumstances.

17.54 However, an employer should obtain a worker's consent before revealing any information about their disability. Employers need to be aware that they have obligations under the Data Protection Act 1998 in respect of personal data.

Example: A factory worker with cancer tells her employer that she does not want colleagues to know of her condition. As an adjustment she needs extra time away from work to receive treatment and to rest. Neither her colleagues nor her line manager need to be told the precise reasons for the extra leave but the line manager will need to know that the adjustment is required in order to implement it effectively.

17.55 If a worker is undergoing gender reassignment, it is good practice for the employer to consult with them sensitively about their needs in the workplace and whether there are any reasonable and practical steps the employer can take to help the worker as they undergo their gender reassignment process. For further information on gender reassignment, please refer to paragraphs 2.21 to 2.30 and 9.31 to 9.33.

Example: A worker will soon be undergoing gender reassignment treatment and the employer has accepted that they want to continue working throughout the transition process. To avoid unresolved questions about which toilet facilities the worker should use, their uniform and communications with other members of staff, the employer should arrange to discuss the situation sympathetically with the worker. The discussion could cover setting a date for using different facilities and uniform; the timescale of the treatment; any impact this may have on the worker's job and adjustments that could be made; and how the worker would like to address the issue of their transition with colleagues.

17.56 Consultation will also help an employer understand the requirements of a worker's religion or belief, such as religious observances. This will help avoid embarrassment or difficulties for those who need to practice their religion or belief at the workplace.

Example: A large employer in an urban area is aware that their workers come from varied backgrounds. As part of their induction meeting, new workers are given the option of disclosing their religion or belief and of discussing whether there is anything the company can do to help them – such as allowing flexible breaks to accommodate prayer times. Workers do not have to disclose anything about their religion or belief if they do not want to. All information provided is kept confidential, unless the worker consents to its disclosure.

Quiet rooms

17.57 Some religions or beliefs require their followers to pray at specific times during the day. Workers may therefore request access to an appropriate quiet place (or prayer room) to undertake their religious observance.

17.58 The Act does not require employers to provide a quiet room. However, if a quiet place is available and allowing its use for prayer and contemplation does not cause problems for the business or for other workers, an employer with sufficient resources may be discriminating because of religion or belief by refusing such a request – especially if comparable facilities are provided for other reasons.

17.59 On the other hand, employers should be careful to avoid creating a disadvantage for workers who do not need a quiet room (for example, by converting the only rest room), as this might amount to indirect religion or belief discrimination. It would be good practice to consult with all workers before designating a room for prayer and contemplation and to discuss policies for using it, such as the wearing of shoes. If possible, employers may also wish to consider providing separate storage facilities for ceremonial objects.

Example: A large employer has one meeting room which is generally unused. There is also a separate rest room, and the employer has made provision for smokers by permitting them to use an open porch by the back entrance. A group of Muslim workers has asked the employer to convert the small meeting room into a quiet room. Refusing this request may amount to direct discrimination if the Muslim workers have been treated less favourably because of religion or belief, compared to non-Muslim workers.

Food and fasting

17.60 Some religions or beliefs have specific dietary requirements. If workers with such needs bring food into the workplace, they may need to store and heat it separately from other food. It is good practice for employers to consult their workforce on such issues and find a mutually acceptable way of accommodating such requirements.

Example: An orthodox Jewish worker in a small firm has a religious requirement that her food cannot come into direct contact with pork or indirect contact through items such as cloths or sponges. After discussion with staff, the employer allocates one shelf of a fridge for this worker's food, and separate cupboard space for the plates and cutlery that she uses. They also introduce a policy that any food brought into the workplace should be stored in sealed containers.

17.61 Some religions require extended periods of fasting. Although there is no requirement under the Act, employers may wish to consider how they can support workers through a fasting period. However, employers should take care to ensure that, in doing so, they do not place unreasonable extra burdens on other workers. As well as potentially causing conflict in the workplace, this could amount to less favourable treatment because of religion or belief and give rise to claims of discrimination.

Example: A Muslim teacher is fasting for Ramadan which is an integral part of her religion. The head teacher of the school, in consultation with the other teachers, has agreed to change the dinnertime rota so she does not have to supervise the dining hall during her fasting period. This adjustment to her duties does not amount to unfavourable treatment of non-Muslim staff members, so would not amount to direct discrimination.

Washing and changing facilities

17.62 An employer may require workers to change their clothing and/or shower for reasons of health and safety. Some religions or beliefs do not allow their adherents to undress or shower in the company of others. Insisting upon communal showers and changing facilities, even if segregated by sex, could constitute indirect discrimination as it may put at a particular disadvantage workers sharing a certain religion or belief whose requirement for modesty prevents them from changing their clothing in the presence of others, even others of the same sex. An employer would have to show that this provision, criterion or practice was objectively justified.

17.63 Some needs relating to religion or belief require no change to workplaces. For example, certain religions require people to wash before prayer, which can be done using normal washing facilities. It is good practice for employers to ensure that all workers understand the religion or belief-related observances of their colleagues, to avoid misunderstandings.

Breastfeeding

17.64 Although there is no legal right to take time off to breastfeed, wherever possible employers should try to accommodate workers who wish to do this. Breastfeeding at work is covered in more detail in Chapter 8.

LIABILITY FOR DISCRIMINATION OUTSIDE THE WORKPLACE

17.65 Employers are liable for prohibited conduct that takes place 'in the course of employment'. This may extend to discrimination and harassment occurring away from work premises or outside normal working hours where there is sufficient connection with work – for example, at team building days, social events to which all workers are invited, business trips or client events (see paragraph 10.46).

17.66 To avoid liability for discrimination and harassment outside the workplace, employers should consider taking steps such as: drafting disciplinary and equality policies that refer to acceptable behaviour outside the office; checking dietary requirements to ensure that all workers have appropriate food during work-related events; and making it clear to workers what is required of them to comply with acceptable standards of behaviour. Employers should also consider whether they need to make any reasonable adjustments to accommodate the needs of disabled workers.

Example: A worker aged 17 has a job in a telephone sales company. On Friday nights her team colleagues go to a local club to socialise. During this time they talk mainly about work-related issues. The team manager also buys drinks for the team member who has achieved the most sales that week. The worker cannot attend these events as the club has a strict 'over-18s only' policy; she feels excluded and undervalued. This treatment could amount to unjustifiable age discrimination. The manager should consider organising team social events somewhere that accepts under-18s.

INDUCTION, TRAINING AND DEVELOPMENT

Induction

17.67 It is important to make sure that induction procedures do not discriminate. Employers should ask themselves whether any changes are needed to remove the indirectly discriminatory effect of a provision, criterion or practice. They must also consider whether any reasonable adjustments are required to enable disabled workers to participate fully in any induction arrangements. In addition, employers may want to consider whether there are any proportionate positive action measures that would help remedy disadvantage experienced by workers sharing a protected characteristic (see also Chapter 12 on positive action).

Example: A worker with a hearing impairment is selected for a post as an engineer. He attends the induction course which consists of a video followed by a discussion. The video is not subtitled and thus the worker cannot participate fully in the induction. To avoid discrimination, the employer should have discussed with the worker what type of reasonable adjustment to the format of the induction training would enable him to participate.

Example: A worker with a learning disability finds it hard to assimilate the material in the employer's induction procedure at the same speed as a colleague who started on the same day. In relation to this worker's induction, it is likely to be a reasonable adjustment for the employer to provide more time, personal support and assistance, such as making available induction materials in Easy Read.

17.68 The induction process is also a good opportunity to make sure all new staff members are trained in the employer's equality policy and procedures. For more information on equality policies, see Chapter 18.

Training and development

17.69 Training and development opportunities, including training provided by a trade union to its members, should be made known to all relevant workers including those absent from the office for whatever reason (see paragraph 16.22 above).

Example: An employee who is on maternity leave asked to be kept updated about training opportunities, so her knowledge would be up to date when she returns to work. During her maternity leave, all other workers have been sent emails updating them on the latest training opportunities but she has not. Excluding this employee is unfavourable treatment and would amount to unlawful discrimination because of pregnancy and maternity.

17.70 However, it will not be appropriate for an employer to contact a worker who is absent for a disability-related reason if the employer has agreed to have limited contact.

17.71 To avoid discrimination, employers should ensure that managers and supervisors who select workers for training understand their legal responsibilities under the Act. It is advisable to monitor training applications and take-up by reference to protected characteristics, taking steps to deal with any significant disparities. Selection for training must be made without discrimination because of a protected characteristic.

Example: An employer has opened a new office overseas and is offering managers the chance of a six-month secondment at the new office to assist in the initial set up. They do not select any of the female managers with children who apply for the secondment, as they assume these women would miss their families and would not perform as well as other managers. This is likely to amount to direct discrimination because of sex.

17.72 Employers should be mindful of their duty to make reasonable adjustments in relation to training and development. For example, if a worker with a mobility impairment is expected to be attending a course, it is likely to be a reasonable adjustment for the employer to select a training venue with adequate disabled access. An employer may need to make training manuals, slides or other visual media accessible to a visually impaired worker (perhaps by providing Braille versions or having materials read out), or ensure that an induction loop is available for someone with a hearing impairment.

17.73 Employers should also consider whether opportunities for training are limited by any other potentially discriminatory factors. If food is provided at training events, employers should try to make sure that special dietary requirements are accommodated. If resources permit, training and development opportunities should be offered on a flexible basis, to accommodate those who work part-time, who have atypical working patterns or who cannot attend training on a particular day, for example, because of conflict with a religious festival or a medical appointment.

17.74 Any criteria used to select workers for training should also be regularly reviewed to make sure they do not discriminate.

Example: An employer offers team leading training for staff who wish to develop management skills. Staff must have been with the company for over seven years to apply for a place on this course. This could be indirectly discriminatory because of age, as older staff are likely to have longer service than younger staff. The employer would have to show that the age criterion is objectively justifiable.

17.75 As explained in Chapter 12, employers may want to consider taking positive action to remedy disadvantage, meet different needs or increase the participation of people who share a protected characteristic. Providing training opportunities for a group which is under-represented in the workforce might be one way of doing this. It is also lawful for employers to provide training for disabled workers, regardless of whether the criteria for positive action are met.

Example: A national education provider wishes to recruit science teachers for its chain of private colleges. It has evidence that almost all of its teachers are recently qualified and under 40. The provider decides to take positive action measures to increase the participation of older teachers. It undertakes a targeted recruitment drive to attract older teachers and recruits several teachers who are returning to teaching after working in industry for many years. In order to update their skills, the provider then offers them additional training on current curriculum and teaching practices.

17.76 Workers who have been absent (for example, on maternity or adoption leave, or for childcare or disability-related reasons) may need additional training on their return to work. It is good practice for employers to liaise with the worker either before or shortly after their return to work to consider whether any additional training is needed.

17.77 An employee on statutory maternity or adoption leave may by agreement work for her employer for up to 10 'keeping in touch' days (KIT days) without bringing the leave to an end; see paragraph 8.29.

Appraisals

17.78 An appraisal is an opportunity for a worker and their line manager to discuss the worker's performance and development. Appraisals usually review past behaviour and so provide an opportunity to reflect on recent performance. They also form an important part of a worker's continuing training and development programme.

17.79 The Act does not require employers to conduct appraisals, although it is good practice to do so if resources permit. Where a formal appraisal process is used, the starting point should be that employers take a consistent approach. In particular, they should ensure that in awarding marks for performance they do not discriminate against any worker because of a protected characteristic. This is especially important because low appraisal scores can have a negative impact on pay, bonuses, promotion and development opportunities.

Example: A woman with young children, who works part-time, is given the same performance targets as her full-time colleagues. She fails to meet the targets. When conducting her annual appraisal, her manager gives her a worse score than full-timers. Other part-time workers, who are mainly women, experience similar problems. This practice could amount to indirect sex discrimination; using identical targets regardless of working hours is unlikely to be objectively justified. This could also be considered as less favourable treatment of a part-time worker under the Part-Time Workers (Prevention of Less Favourable Treatment) Regulations 2000.

17.80 Employers should also be aware of the duty to make reasonable adjustments when discussing past performance. For example, they should consider whether performance would have been more effective had a reasonable adjustment been put in place, or introduced earlier. Appraisals may also provide an opportunity for workers to disclose a disability to their employer, and to discuss any adjustments that would be reasonable for the employer to make in future.

Example: An employer installed voice-activated software as a reasonable adjustment to accommodate the needs of a new manager with a visual impairment. The manager takes several weeks to familiarise herself with the software. After six months in post, the manager undergoes an appraisal. In assessing the manager's performance, it would be a reasonable adjustment for the employer to take account of the time the manager needed to become fully familiar with the software.

17.81 To avoid discrimination when conducting appraisals, employers are recommended to:

- make sure that performance is measured by transparent, objective and justifiable criteria using procedures that are consistently applied;
- check that, for all workers, performance is assessed against standards that are relevant to their role;
- ensure that line managers carrying out appraisals receive training and guidance on objective performance assessment and positive management styles; and
- monitor performance assessment results to ensure that any significant disparities in scores apparently linked to a protected characteristic are investigated, and steps taken to deal with possible causes.

PROMOTION AND TRANSFER

17.82 Issues and considerations that arise on recruitment (see Chapter 16) can arise again in respect of promoting or transferring existing workers to new roles. It is unlawful for employers to discriminate against, victimise or harass workers in the way they make opportunities for promotion or transfer available or by refusing or deliberately failing to make them available. An employer may need to make reasonable adjustments to the promotion or transfer process to ensure that disabled workers are not substantially disadvantaged by the process for promotion or transfer or by the way the process is applied.

17.83 Failure to inform workers of opportunities for promotion or transfer may be direct or indirect discrimination. To avoid discrimination, employers are advised to advertise all promotion and transfer opportunities widely throughout the organisation. This includes development or deputising opportunities or secondments that could lead to permanent promotion.

17.84 If an employer has an equal opportunities policy and/or recruitment policy and procedures, it would be good practice to ensure that these policies are followed when internal promotions or transfers are taking place. This can help ensure that that selection is based strictly on demonstrable merit. Unless a temporary promotion is absolutely necessary, employers should avoid bypassing the procedures they have adopted for recruiting other staff.

Example: An employer promotes a male worker to the position of section manager without advertising the vacancy internally. There are several women in the organisation who are qualified for the post and who could have applied if they had known about it. The decision not to advertise internally counts as a provision, criterion or practice and could amount to indirect discrimination: if challenged, the employer would need to be able to objectively justify their decision. Recruiting the man could also amount to direct discrimination, as one or more of the women could argue they have been treated less favourably because of their sex.

17.85 Employers should consider whether it is really necessary to restrict applications for promotion and other development opportunities to staff at a particular grade or level. This restriction would operate as a provision, criterion or practice and, unless it can be objectively justified, could indirectly discriminate by putting workers sharing a protected characteristic at a particular disadvantage.

17.86 Employers must also ensure that women on maternity leave are informed of any jobs that become available and must enable them to apply if they wish to do so. Failure to do so may be unfavourable treatment, and thus could amount to discrimination because of pregnancy and maternity (see also Chapter 8).

17.87 Arrangements for promoting workers or arranging transfers must not discriminate because of disability – either in the practical arrangements relating to selection for promotion or transfer, or in the arrangements for the job itself. It is also important for employers to consider whether there are any reasonable adjustments that should be made in relation to promotion or transfer.

Example: A woman with a disability resulting from a back injury is seeking a transfer to another department. A minor aspect of the role she is seeking is to assist with unloading the weekly delivery van.

She is unable to do this because of her disability. In assessing her suitability for transfer, the employer should consider whether reallocating this duty to someone else would be a reasonable adjustment to make.

17.88 Opportunities for promotion and transfer should be made available to all workers regardless of age. Different treatment because of age is only lawful if it can be objectively justified as a proportionate means of achieving a legitimate aim (see paragraphs 3.36 to 3.41).

Example: An employer decides to impose a maximum age of 60 for promotion to the position of technical manager, for which additional training is required. In deciding whether this age restriction is objectively justifiable, the time and costs of training for the post would be relevant, taking into account that an internal candidate would probably need less training than a new recruit. Average staff turnover across all groups should also be considered. The need for a reasonable period of employment before retirement might also be relevant – although employees' right to request to continue working beyond 65 should be factored in.

17.89 It would be good practice for employers to build the following guidelines into any policies and procedures they may have relating to promotion and career development:

- If posts are advertised internally and externally, the same selection procedures and criteria should apply to all candidates.
- If appropriate – especially with larger employers – selection decisions based on performance assessments should be endorsed by the organisation's human resources department.

17.90 Employers should not make assumptions about the suitability of existing workers for promotion or transfer.

Example: An employer makes an assumption that a particular woman is unsuitable for promotion because she appears to be of childbearing age and he assumes she might want to have children in the near future. This would amount to direct discrimination because of sex.

DISCIPLINARY AND GRIEVANCE MATTERS

17.91 It is good practice for employers (irrespective of their size) to have procedures for dealing with grievances and disciplinary hearings together with appeals against decisions under these procedures. Where procedures have been put in place, they should not discriminate against workers either in the way they are designed or how the employer implements them in practice. More information about disciplinary and grievance procedures, including a worker's right to be accompanied by a trade union representative or fellow worker, can be found on the Acas website: www.acas.org.uk/index.aspx?articleid=2174

17.92 An employer may in addition wish to introduce a separate policy designed specifically to deal with harassment. Such policies commonly aim to highlight and eradicate harassment whilst at the same time establishing a procedure for complaints, similar to a grievance procedure, with safeguards to deal with the sensitivities that allegations of harassment often bring.

Example: An employer has a procedure that allows a grievance relating to harassment to be raised with a designated experienced manager. This avoids the possibility of an allegation of harassment having to be raised with a line manager who may be the perpetrator of the harassment.

17.93 Employers should ensure that when conducting disciplinary and grievance procedures they do not discriminate against a worker because of a protected characteristic. For example, employers may need to make reasonable adjustments to procedures to ensure that they do not put disabled workers at a substantial disadvantage. Procedures might also need to be adapted to accommodate a worker at home on maternity leave.

Dealing with grievances

17.94 Employers must not discriminate in the way they respond to grievances. Where a grievance involves allegations of discrimination or harassment, it must be taken seriously and investigated promptly and not dismissed as 'over-sensitivity' on the part of the worker.

17.95 Wherever possible, it is good practice – as well as being in the interests of employers – to resolve grievances as they arise and before they become major problems. Grievance procedures can provide an open and fair way for complainants to make their concerns known, and for their grievances to be resolved quickly, without having to bring legal proceedings.

17.96 It is strongly recommended that employers properly investigate any complaints of discrimination. If a complaint is upheld against an individual co-worker or manager, the employer should consider taking disciplinary action against the perpetrator.

17.97 Whether or not the complaint of discrimination is upheld, raising it in good faith is a 'protected act' and if the worker is subject to any detriment because of having done so, this could amount to victimisation (see paragraphs 9.2 to 9.15).

Disciplinary procedures

17.98 Employers must not discriminate in the way they invoke or pursue a disciplinary process. A disciplinary process is a formal measure and should be followed fairly and consistently, regardless of the protected characteristics of any workers involved. Where a disciplinary process involves allegations of discrimination or harassment, the matter should be thoroughly investigated and the alleged perpetrator should be given a fair hearing.

17.99 If a complaint about discrimination leads to a disciplinary process where the complaint proves to be unfounded, employers must be careful not to subject the complainant (or any witness or informant) to any detriment for having raised the matter in good faith. Such actions qualify as 'protected acts' and detrimental treatment amounts to victimisation if a protected act is an effective cause of the treatment.

Avoiding disputes and conflicts

17.100 To help avoid disputes and conflicts with and between workers with different protected characteristics, employers should treat their workers with dignity and respect and ensure workers treat each other in the same way. If the principle of dignity and respect is embedded into the workplace culture, it can help prevent misunderstandings and behaviour that may lead to prohibited conduct. It is good practice to have a clear policy on 'dignity and respect in the workplace', setting out workers' rights and responsibilities to each other.

17.101 It is also good practice, and in the interests of both employers and their workers, to try to resolve workplace disputes so as to avoid litigation. Employers should have different mechanisms in place for managing disputes, such as mediation or conciliation. Where it is not possible to resolve a dispute using internal procedures, it may be better to seek outside help.

17.102 Employers will sometimes have to deal with complaints about prohibited conduct that arise between members of staff. They can avoid potential conflicts by noticing problems at an early stage and attempting to deal with them by, for example, talking to the people involved in a non-confrontational way. It is important to encourage good communication between workers and managers in order to understand the underlying reasons for potential conflicts. Employers should have effective procedures in place for dealing with grievances if informal methods of resolving the issue fail.

17.103 There may be situations where an employer should intervene to prevent a worker discriminating against another worker or against another person to whom that employer has a duty under the Act (such as a customer). In these circumstances, it may be necessary to take disciplinary action against the worker who discriminates.

CHAPTER 18
EQUALITY POLICIES AND PRACTICE IN THE WORKPLACE

INTRODUCTION

[4.145]

18.1 There is no formal statutory requirement in the Act for an employer to put in place an equality policy. However, a systematic approach to developing and maintaining good practice is the best way of showing that an organisation is taking its legal responsibilities seriously. To help employers and others meet their legal obligations, and avoid the risk of legal action being taken against them, it is recommended, as a matter of good practice, that they draw up an equality policy (also known as an equal opportunities policy or equality and diversity policy) and put this policy into practice.

18.2 This chapter describes why an employer should have an equality policy and how to plan, implement, monitor and review that policy.

WHY HAVE AN EQUALITY POLICY?

18.3 There are a number of reasons why employers should have an equality policy. For example:

- it can give job applicants and workers confidence that they will be treated with dignity and respect;
- it can set the minimum standards of behaviour expected of all workers and outline what workers and job applicants can expect from the employer;
- it is key to helping employers and others comply with their legal obligations;
- it can minimise the risk of legal action being taken against employers and workers; and/or
- if legal action is taken, employers may use the equality policy to demonstrate to an Employment Tribunal that they take discrimination seriously and have taken all reasonable steps to prevent discrimination.

18.4 Equality policies and practices are often drivers of good recruitment and retention practice. Information on these policies, as well as on equality worker network groups, on the organisation's website and/or in induction packs, send a very positive and inclusive signal encouraging people to apply to work for the organisation. This can indicate that the organisation seeks to encourage a diverse workforce and that, for example, applicants with any religion or belief and/or sexual orientation would be welcome in the organisation.

Example: For one organisation which is part of a multi-national corporation, being sensitive to local contexts is an important part of their operation. All their branches aim to reflect the local communities in which they operate in terms of their customers and their staff. In ethnically mixed areas, they aim to reflect this in the products they sell and in the mix of staff. This makes strong business sense since having a greater ethnic diversity of staff will attract more customers from that group.

PLANNING AN EQUALITY POLICY

18.5 It is essential that a written equality policy is backed by a clear programme of action for implementation and continual review. It is a process which consists of four key stages: planning, implementing, monitoring and reviewing the equality policy.

18.6 The content and details of equality policies and practices will vary according to the size, resources and needs of the employer. Some employers will require less formal structures but all employers should identify a time scale against which they aim to review progress and the achievement of their objectives.

18.7 A written equality policy should set out the employer's general approach to equality and diversity issues in the workplace. The policy should make clear that the employer intends to develop and apply procedures which do not discriminate because of any of the protected characteristics, and which provide equality of opportunity for all job applicants and workers.

Planning the content of equality policies

18.8 Most policies will include the following:
- a statement of the employer's commitment to equal opportunity for all job applicants and workers;
- what is and is not acceptable behaviour at work (also referring to conduct near the workplace and at work-related social functions where relevant);
- the rights and responsibilities of everyone to whom the policy applies, and procedures for dealing with any concerns and complaints;
- how the policy may apply to the employer's other policies and procedures;
- how the employer will deal with any breaches of policy;
- who is responsible for the policy; and
- how the policy will be implemented and details of monitoring and review procedures.

Example: An organisation informs new recruits that abuse and harassment are unacceptable and staff who make offensive, racist or homophobic comments are automatically subject to disciplinary proceedings.

18.9 It will help an employer avoid discrimination if the equality policy covers all aspects of employment including recruitment, terms and conditions of work, training and development, promotion, performance, grievance, discipline and treatment of workers when their contract ends. Areas of the employment relationship are covered in more detail in this Code and cross-references to the relevant chapters/sections are provided below:
- monitoring (see paragraph 18.23 and Appendix 2)
- recruitment (see Chapter 16)
- terms and conditions of work (see Chapter 17)
- pay and benefits (see Chapter 14)
- leave and flexible working arrangements (see Chapter 17)
- the availability of facilities, such as quiet/prayer rooms and meal options in staff canteens (see Chapter 17)
- pensions (see Chapter 14)
- dress codes (see Chapter 17)
- training and development (see Chapter 17)
- promotion and transfer (see Chapter 17)
- grievance and disciplinary issues (see Chapter 17)
- treatment of employees when their contract ends (see Chapter 9)
- health and safety (see Chapter 8 in relation to pregnancy and maternity)

Planning an equality policy – protected characteristics

18.10 It is recommended that adopting one equality policy covering all protected characteristics is the most practical approach. Where separate policies are developed, such as a separate race equality or sex equality policy, they should be consistent with each other and with an overall commitment to promoting equality of opportunity in employment.

IMPLEMENTING AN EQUALITY POLICY

18.11 An equality policy should be more than a statement of good intentions; there should also be plans for its implementation. The policy should be in writing and drawn up in consultation with workers and any recognised trade unions or other workplace representatives, including any equality representatives within the workforce.

18.12 Employers will be of different sizes and have different structures but it is advisable for all employers to take the following steps to implement an equality policy:
- audit existing policies and procedures;
- ensure the policy is promoted and communicated to all job applicants and workers and agents of the employer; and
- monitor and review the policy.

Promotion and communication of an equality policy

18.13 Employers should promote and publicise their equality policy as widely as possible and there are a number of ways in which this can be done. Promoting the policy is part of the process of effective implementation and will help an employer demonstrate that they have taken all reasonable steps to prevent discrimination.

18.14 Employers may use a number of methods of communication to promote their policy, including:
- email bulletins
- intranet and/or website
- induction packs
- team meetings
- office notice boards
- circulars, newsletters
- cascade systems

- training
- handbooks
- annual reports.

18.15 These methods of communication may not be appropriate in all cases. Some workers, for example those in customer-facing or shop floor roles, may not have regular access to computers. Alternative methods of communication, such as notice boards and regular staff meetings, should also be considered. Employers must also consider whether reasonable adjustments need to be made for disabled people so that they are able to access the information.

18.16 Promoting and communicating an equality policy should not be a one-off event. It is recommended that employers provide periodic reminders and updates to workers and others such as contractors and suppliers. Employers should also periodically review their advertising, recruitment and application materials and processes.

Responsibility for implementing an equality policy

18.17 The policy should have the explicit backing of people in senior positions such as the chair, owner, chief executive, or board of directors. Senior management should ensure that the policy is implemented, resourced, monitored and reviewed, and that there is regular reporting on its effectiveness.

Example: When a large company introduces a new equality policy, they might ask an external training company to run training sessions for all staff, or they might ask their human resources manager to deliver training to staff on this policy.

Example: A small employer introducing an equality policy asks the managing director to devote a team meeting to explaining the policy to her staff and discussing why it is important and how it will operate.

Implementing an equality policy – training

18.18 Employers should ensure that all workers and agents understand the equality policy, how it affects them and the plans for putting it into practice. The best way to achieve this is by providing regular training.

18.19 Some workers may need more specific training, depending on what they do within the organisation. For example, line managers and senior management should receive detailed training on how to manage equality and diversity issues in the workplace.

18.20 The training should be designed in consultation with workers, their workplace representatives and managers and by incorporating feedback from any previous training into future courses.

18.21 Employers should make sure in-house trainers are themselves trained before running courses for other workers. External trainers also need to be fully informed about the employer's policies, including their equality policy.

18.22 Training on the equality policy may include the following:

- an outline of the law covering all the protected characteristics and prohibited conduct;
- why the policy has been introduced and how it will be put into practice;
- what is and is not acceptable conduct in the workplace;
- the risk of condoning or seeming to approve inappropriate behaviour and personal liability;
- how prejudice can affect the way an employer functions and the impact that generalisations, stereotypes, bias or inappropriate language in day-to-day operations can have on people's chances of obtaining work, promotion, recognition and respect;
- the equality monitoring process (see paragraph 18.23 and Appendix 2).

Example: A large employer trains all their workers in the organisation's equality policy and the Equality Act. They also train all occupational health advisers with whom they work to ensure that the advisers have the necessary expertise about the Act and the organisation's equality policy.

MONITORING AND REVIEWING AN EQUALITY POLICY

18.23 Equality monitoring enables an employer to find out whether their equality policy is working. For example, monitoring may reveal that:

- applicants with a particular religion or belief are not selected for promotion;
- women are concentrated in certain jobs or departments;
- people from a particular ethnic group do not apply for employment or fewer apply than expected;
- older workers are not selected for training and development opportunities.

18.24 Equality monitoring is the process that employers use to collect, store and analyse data about the protected characteristics of job applicants and workers. Employers can use monitoring to:

- establish whether an equality policy is effective in practice;
- analyse the effect of other policies and practices on different groups;
- highlight possible inequalities and investigate their underlying causes;
- set targets and timetables for reducing disparities; and
- send a clear message to job applicants and workers that equality and diversity issues are taken seriously within the organisation.

Example: A large employer notices through monitoring that the organisation has been successful at retaining most groups of disabled people, but not people with mental health conditions. They act on this information by contacting a specialist organisation for advice about good practice in retaining people with mental health conditions.

Monitoring an equality policy – law and good practice

18.25 Public sector employers may find that monitoring assists them in carrying out their obligations under the public sector equality duty. For employers in the private sector, equality monitoring is not mandatory. However, it is recommended that all employers carry out equality monitoring. The methods used will depend on the size of the organisation and can be simple and informal. Smaller organisations may only need a simple method of collecting information about job applicants and workers. Larger organisations are likely to need more sophisticated procedures and computerised systems to capture the full picture across the whole of their organisation.

18.26 Monitoring will be more effective if workers (or job applicants) feel comfortable about disclosing personal information. This is more likely to be the case if the employer explains the purpose of the monitoring and if the workers or job applicants believe that the employer is using the information because they value the diversity of their workforce and want to use the information in a positive way.

18.27 Employers must take full account of the Data Protection Act 1998 (DPA) when they collect, store, analyse and publish data.

Monitoring an equality policy – key areas

18.28 Employers should monitor the key areas of the employment relationship including:

- recruitment and promotion
- pay and remuneration
- training
- appraisals
- grievances
- disciplinary action
- dismissals and other reasons for leaving

18.29 Employers who are carrying out equality monitoring will find it useful to compare progress over a period of time and against progress made by other employers in the same sector or industry.

Monitoring an equality policy – reporting back

18.30 It is important for employers to communicate on a regular basis to managers, workers and trade union representatives on the progress and achievement of objectives of the equality policy. Employers should also consider how the results of any monitoring activity can be communicated to the workforce. However, care should be taken to ensure that individuals are not identifiable from any reports.

Monitoring an equality policy – taking action

18.31 Taking action based on any findings revealed by the monitoring exercise is vital to ensure that an employer's equality policy is practically implemented. There are a number of steps employers can take, including:

- examine decision-making processes, for example recruitment and promotion;
- consider whether training or further guidelines are required on how to avoid discrimination;
- consider whether any positive action measures may be appropriate (see Chapter 12);
- work with network groups and trade union equality representatives to share information and advice;
- set targets on the basis of benchmarking data and develop an action plan.

REVIEWING AN EQUALITY POLICY AND OTHER EMPLOYMENT POLICIES

18.32 It is good practice for employers to keep both their equality policy and all other policies and procedures (such as those listed below) under regular review at least annually and to consider workers' needs as part of the process.

18.33 Policies which should be reviewed in light of an employer's equality policy might include:

- recruitment policies
- leave and flexible working arrangements
- retirement policies
- health and safety, for example, emergency evacuation procedures
- procurement of equipment, IT systems, software and websites
- pay and remuneration
- grievance policies, including harassment and bullying
- disciplinary procedure
- appraisal and performance-related pay systems
- sickness absence policies
- redundancy and redeployment policies
- training and development policies
- employee assistance schemes offering financial or emotional support

18.34 Part of the review process may entail employers taking positive action measures to alleviate disadvantage experienced by workers who share a protected characteristic, meet their particular needs, or increase their participation in relation to particular activities (see Chapter 12). Employers must also ensure they make reasonable adjustments where these are required by individual disabled workers. The review process can help employers to consider and anticipate the needs of disabled workers (see Chapter 6).

CHAPTER 19
TERMINATION OF EMPLOYMENT

INTRODUCTION

[4.146]

19.1 The employment relationship can come to an end in a variety of ways and in a range of situations. A worker may resign under normal circumstances, or resign in response to the employer's conduct and treat the resignation as a constructive dismissal. On the other hand, an employer may dismiss a worker, for example, for reasons of capability, conduct or redundancy. The Act makes it unlawful for an employer to discriminate against or victimise a worker by dismissing them (see paragraphs 10.11 and 10.13 to 10.16).

19.2 This chapter focuses on termination of employment by the employer, including in redundancy situations. It explains how to avoid discrimination in decisions to dismiss and in procedures for dismissal. The question of retirement is dealt with separately in paragraphs 13.26 to 13.45.

TERMINATING EMPLOYMENT

19.3 Those responsible for deciding whether or not a worker should be dismissed should understand their legal obligations under the Act. They should also be made aware of how the Act might apply to situations where dismissal is a possibility. Employers can help avoid discrimination if they have procedures in place for dealing with dismissals and apply these procedures consistently and fairly. In particular, employers should take steps to ensure the criteria they use for dismissal – especially in a redundancy situation – are not indirectly discriminatory (see paragraph 19.11 below).

19.4 It is also important that employers ensure they do not dismiss a worker with a protected characteristic for performance or behaviour which would be overlooked or condoned in others who do not share the characteristic.

Example: A Sikh worker is dismissed for failing to meet her set objectives, which form a part of her annual performance appraisal, in two consecutive years. However, no action is taken against a worker of the Baha'i faith, who has also failed to meet her objectives over the same period of time. This difference in treatment could amount to direct discrimination because of religion or belief.

19.5 Where an employer is considering dismissing a worker who is disabled, they should consider what reasonable adjustments need to be made to the dismissal process (see Chapter 6). In addition, the employer should consider whether the reason for dismissal is connected to or in consequence of the worker's disability. If it is, dismissing the worker will amount to discrimination arising from disability unless it can be objectively justified. In these circumstances, an employer should consider whether dismissal is an appropriate sanction to impose.

Example: A disabled worker periodically requires a limited amount of time off work to attend medical appointments related to the disability. The employer has an attendance management policy which results in potential warnings and ultimately dismissal if the worker's absence exceeds 20 days in any 12-month period. A combination of the worker's time off for disability-related medical appointments and general time off for sickness results in the worker consistently exceeding the 20 day limit by a few days. The worker receives a series of warnings and is eventually dismissed. This is likely to amount to disability discrimination.

19.6 Based on the facts in the example above, it is very likely to have been a reasonable adjustment for the employer to ignore the absences arising out of the worker's disability or increase the trigger points that would invoke the attendance policy. By making one or both of these adjustments, the employer could have avoided the possibility of claims for both a failure to make adjustments and discrimination arising from disability.

19.7 Employers must not discriminate against a transsexual worker when considering whether to dismiss the worker for absences or other conduct because of gender reassignment (see paragraphs 9.31 to 9.33). To avoid discrimination because of gender reassignment when considering the dismissal of a transsexual worker, employers should make provision within their disciplinary policy for dealing with such dismissals.

Example: A transsexual worker who experiences gender dysphoria and is considering gender reassignment takes time off from work because of his condition. The employer's attendance management policy provides that absence exceeding eight days or more in a 12-month rolling period will trigger the capability procedure. As the worker has had over eight days off, the employer invokes the procedure and consequently decides to dismiss him. However, over a previous 12-month rolling period, the worker was absent from work for more than eight days with various minor illnesses. The employer took no action against the worker because they viewed these absences as genuine. The dismissal could amount to an unlawful dismissal because of gender reassignment.

DISMISSAL FOR REASONS OF CAPABILITY AND CONDUCT

19.8 As noted in Chapter 17, employers must not discriminate against or victimise their workers in how they manage capability or conduct issues. To avoid discrimination in any disciplinary decision that leads to a dismissal (or could lead to a dismissal after a subsequent disciplinary matter), employers should have procedures in place for managing capability and conduct issues. They should apply these procedures fairly and in a non-discriminatory way.

Example: A white worker and a black worker are subjected to disciplinary action for fighting. The fight occurred because the black worker had made derogatory remarks about the white worker. The employer has no disciplinary policy and consequently does not investigate the matter. Instead, the employer decides to dismiss the white worker without notice and give the black worker a final written warning. This could amount to a discriminatory dismissal because of race. Had the employer had a disciplinary procedure in place and applied it fairly, they could have avoided a discriminatory outcome.

19.9 Where an employer is considering the dismissal of a disabled worker for a reason relating to that worker's capability or their conduct, they must consider whether any reasonable adjustments need to be made to the performance management or dismissal process which would help improve the performance of the worker or whether they could transfer the worker to a suitable alternative role.

How can discrimination be avoided in capability and conduct dismissals?

19.10 To avoid discrimination when terminating employment, an employer should, in particular:

- apply their procedures for managing capability or conduct fairly and consistently (or use Acas's Guide on Disciplinary and Grievance at Work, if the employer does not have their own procedure);
- ensure that any decision to dismiss is made by more than one individual, and on the advice of the human resources department (if the employer has one);
- keep written records of decisions and reasons to dismiss;
- monitor all dismissals by reference to protected characteristics (see paragraph 18.28 and Appendix 2); and
- encourage leavers to give feedback about their employment; this information could contribute to the monitoring process.

REDUNDANCY

19.11 A redundancy amounts to a dismissal and it is therefore unlawful for an employer to discriminate against or victimise a worker in a redundancy situation. Where an employer is planning dismissals because of redundancy, they should consult affected workers about ways of avoiding dismissals. They should also consult any recognised trade unions (and are required to consult with the unions if planning 20 or more redundancies in a 90-day period).

19.12 To avoid discrimination, an employer should, in consultation with any recognised trade union, adopt a selection matrix containing a number of separate selection criteria rather than just one selection criterion, to reduce the risk of any possible discriminatory impact.

19.13 Employers should ensure that the selection criteria are objective and do not discriminate directly or indirectly. Many of the selection criteria used in redundancy situations carry a risk of discrimination.

19.14 For example, 'last in, first out' may amount to indirect age discrimination against younger employees; indirect sex discrimination against women who may have shorter service due to time out for raising children; or indirect race discrimination where an employer might have only recently adopted policies that have had the effect of increasing the proportion of employees from ethnic minority backgrounds.

19.15 However, used as one criterion among many within a fair selection procedure, 'last in, first out' could be a proportionate means of achieving the legitimate aim of rewarding loyalty and creating a stable workforce. If it is the only or determinant selection criterion, or given disproportionate weight within the selection matrix, it could lead to discrimination.

Example: An employer wishing to make redundancies adopts a selection matrix which includes the following criteria: expertise/knowledge required for posts to be retained; disciplinary records; performance appraisals; attendance and length of service. Each person in the pool of employees who are potentially redundant is scored against each criterion from 1 to 4 points on a range of poor to excellent. There is provision in the matrix for deducting points for episodes of unauthorised absence in the prescribed period. Points are also added for length of service. Although length of service does have the potential to discriminate, in this redundancy selection process it is not obviously dominant or necessarily determinative of who will be selected for redundancy. In this context, length of service is likely to be an objectively justifiable criterion.

19.16 'Flexibility' – for example, willingness to relocate or to work unsocial hours, or ability to carry out a wide variety of tasks – may amount to discrimination because of (or arising from) disability or because of sex.

19.17 When setting criteria for redundancy selection, employers should consider whether any proposed criterion would adversely impact upon a disabled employee. If so, the employer will need to consider what reasonable adjustments will be necessary to avoid such discriminatory impact.

Example: A call centre re-tenders for a large contract and has to reduce its price to secure the work in the face of low-cost competition from overseas. The employer therefore decides that attendance records are a particularly important selection criterion for redundancy. This has the potential to disadvantage disabled employees who require additional time off for medical treatment. It is likely to be a reasonable adjustment to discount some disability-related sickness absence when assessing attendance as part of the redundancy selection exercise.

When should employers offer suitable alternative employment?

19.18 During a redundancy exercise, if alternative vacancies exist within the employer's organisation or with an associated employer, these should be offered to potentially redundant employees using criteria which do not unlawfully discriminate.

19.19 However, where there is a potentially redundant female employee on ordinary or additional maternity leave, she is entitled to be offered any suitable available vacancy with the employer, their successor or any associated employer. The offer must be of a new contract taking effect immediately on the ending of the worker's previous contract and must be such that:

- the work is suitable and appropriate for her to do; and
- the capacity, place of employment and other terms and conditions are not substantially less favourable than under the previous contract.

Example: A company decides to combine their head office and regional teams and create a 'centre of excellence' in Manchester. A new organisation structure is drawn up which involves a reduction in headcount. The company intends that all employees should have the opportunity to apply for posts in the new structure. Those unsuccessful at interview will be made redundant. At the time this is implemented, one of the existing members of the team is on ordinary maternity leave. As such, she has a priority right to be offered a suitable available vacancy in the new organisation without having to go through the competitive interview process.

APPENDICES

APPENDIX 1
THE MEANING OF DISABILITY

[4.147]
1. This Appendix is included to aid understanding about who is covered by the Act. Government guidance on determining questions relating to the definition of disability is also available from the Office of Disability Issues:
www.officefordisability.gov.uk/docs/wor/new/ea-guide.pdf

When is a person disabled?

2. A person has a disability if they have a physical or mental impairment, which has a substantial and long-term adverse effect on their ability to carry out normal day-to-day activities.

3. However, special rules apply to people with some conditions such as progressive conditions (see paragraph 19 of this Appendix) and some people are automatically deemed disabled for the purposes of the Act (see paragraph 18).

What about people who have recovered from a disability?

4. People who have had a disability within the definition are protected from discrimination even if they have since recovered, although those with past disabilities are not covered in relation to Part 12 (transport) and section 190 (improvements to let dwelling houses).

What does 'impairment' cover?

5. It covers physical or mental impairments. This includes sensory impairments, such as those affecting sight or hearing.

Are all mental impairments covered?

6. The term 'mental impairment' is intended to cover a wide range of impairments relating to mental functioning, including what are often known as learning disabilities.

What if a person has no medical diagnosis?

7. There is no need for a person to establish a medically diagnosed cause for their impairment. What it is important to consider is the effect of the impairment, not the cause.

What is a 'substantial' adverse effect?

8. **[s 212]** A substantial adverse effect is something which is more than a minor or trivial effect. The requirement that an effect must be substantial reflects the general understanding of disability as a limitation going beyond the normal differences in ability which might exist among people.

9. Account should also be taken of where a person avoids doing things which, for example, cause pain, fatigue or substantial social embarrassment; or because of a loss of energy and motivation.

10. An impairment may not directly prevent someone from carrying out one or more normal day-to-day activities, but it may still have a substantial adverse long-term effect on how they carry out those activities. For example, where an impairment causes pain or fatigue in performing normal day-to-day activities, the person may have the capacity to do something but suffer pain in doing so; or the impairment might make the activity more than usually fatiguing so that the person might not be able to repeat the task over a sustained period of time.

What is a 'long-term' effect?

11. A long-term effect of an impairment is one:

- which has lasted at least 12 months; or
- where the total period for which it lasts is likely to be at least 12 months; or
- which is likely to last for the rest of the life of the person affected.

12. Effects which are not long-term would therefore include loss of mobility due to a broken limb which is likely to heal within 12 months, and the effects of temporary infections, from which a person would be likely to recover within 12 months.

What if the effects come and go over a period of time?

13. If an impairment has had a substantial adverse effect on normal day-to-day activities but that effect ceases, the substantial effect is treated as continuing if it is likely to recur; that is, if it might well recur.

What are 'normal day-to-day activities'?

14. They are activities which are carried out by most men or women on a fairly regular and frequent basis. The term is not intended to include activities which are normal only for a particular person or group of people, such as playing a musical instrument, or participating in a sport to a professional standard, or performing a skilled or specialised task at work. However, someone who is affected in such a specialised way but is also affected in normal day-to-day activities would be covered by this part of the definition.

15. Day-to-day activities thus include – but are not limited to –activities such as walking, driving, using public transport, cooking, eating, lifting and carrying everyday objects, typing, writing (and taking exams), going to the toilet, talking, listening to conversations or music, reading, taking part in normal social interaction or forming social relationships, nourishing and caring for one's self. Normal day-to-day activities also encompass the activities which are relevant to working life.

What about treatment?

16. Someone with an impairment may be receiving medical or other treatment which alleviates or removes the effects (though not the impairment). In such cases, the treatment is ignored and the impairment is taken to have the effect it would have had without such treatment. This does not apply if substantial adverse effects are not likely to recur even if the treatment stops (that is, the impairment has been cured).

Does this include people who wear spectacles?

17. No. The sole exception to the rule about ignoring the effects of treatment is the wearing of spectacles or contact lenses. In this case, the effect while the person is wearing spectacles or contact lenses should be considered.

Are people who have disfigurements covered?

18. People with severe disfigurements are covered by the Act. They do not need to demonstrate that the impairment has a substantial adverse effect on their ability to carry out normal day-to-day activities. However, they do need to meet the long-term requirement.

Are there any other people who are automatically treated as disabled under the Act?

19. Anyone who has HIV, cancer or multiple sclerosis is automatically treated as disabled under the Act. In some circumstances, people who have a sight impairment are automatically treated as disabled under Regulations made under the Act.

What about people who know their condition is going to get worse over time?

20. Progressive conditions are conditions which are likely to change and develop over time. Where a person has a progressive condition they will be covered by the Act from the moment the condition leads to an impairment which has some effect on ability to carry out normal day-to-day activities, even though not a substantial effect, if that impairment might well have a substantial adverse effect on such ability in the future. This applies provided that the effect meets the long-term requirement of the definition.

APPENDIX 2
MONITORING – ADDITIONAL INFORMATION

WHAT TO MONITOR?

[4.148]

1. It is recommended that employers consider monitoring the list of areas below. This list is not exhaustive and an employer, depending on its size and resources, may wish to consider monitoring additional areas.

Recruitment

- Sources of applications for employment
- Applicants for employment
- Those who are successful or unsuccessful in the short-listing process
- Those who are successful or unsuccessful at test/assessment stage
- Those who are successful or unsuccessful at interview

During employment

- Workers in post

- Workers in post by type of job, location and grade
- Applicants for training
- Workers who receive training
- Applicants for promotion and transfer and success rates for each
- Time spent at a particular grade/level
- Workers who benefit or suffer detriment as a result of performance assessment procedures
- Workers involved in grievance procedures
- Workers who are the subject of disciplinary procedures

Termination of employment

- Workers who cease employment
- Dismissals for gross misconduct
- Dismissals for persistent misconduct
- Dismissals for poor performance
- Dismissals for sickness
- Redundancies
- Retirement
- Resignation
- Termination for other reasons

CONSIDERING CATEGORIES

2. It is recommended that employers ask job applicants and workers to select the group(s) they want to be associated with from a list of categories. The 2001/2011 census provides comprehensive data about the population in England, Scotland and Wales. This is supplemented by the Labour Force Survey and other survey statistics produced by the Office for National Statistics. Employers can therefore use categories which are compatible with the categories contained in these sources, for consistency.

3. Set out below are some of the issues to consider when monitoring particular protected characteristics. Please see the Commission's Non Statutory Guidance for further information.

Age

4. Monitoring age may not initially appear as controversial as some of the other protected characteristics.

The following age bands might provide a useful starting point for employers monitoring the age of job applicants and workers:

- 16–17
- 18–21
- 22–30
- 31–40
- 41–50
- 51–60
- 61–65
- 66–70
- 71+

Disability

5. Disclosing information about disability can be a particularly sensitive issue. Monitoring will be more effective if job applicants and workers feel comfortable about disclosing information about their disabilities. This is more likely to be the case if employers explain the purpose of monitoring and job applicants and workers believe that the employer genuinely values disabled people and is using the information gathered to create positive change. Asking questions about health or disability before the offer of a job is made or a person is placed in a pool of people to be offered a vacancy is not unlawful under the Act where the purpose of asking such questions is to monitor the diversity of applicants (see paragraphs 10.25 to 10.43).

Example: Through monitoring of candidates at the recruitment stage a company becomes aware that, although several disabled people applied for a post, none were short-listed for interview. On the basis of this information, they review the essential requirements for the post.

6. Some employers choose to monitor by broad type of disability to understand the barriers faced by people with different types of impairment.

Example: A large employer notices through monitoring that the organisation has been successful at retaining most groups of disabled people, but not people with mental health conditions. They act on this information by contacting a specialist organisation for advice about good practice in retaining people with mental health conditions.

Race

7. When employers gather data in relation to race, a decision should be made as to which ethnic categories to use. It is recommended that employers use the ethnic categories that were used in the 2001 census (or categories that match them very closely). If different categories are used, it may make it difficult to use the census data or other national surveys, such as the annual Labour Force Survey, as a benchmark (see also Chapter 18).

8. Subgroups are intended to provide greater choice to encourage people to respond. Sticking to broad headings may otherwise hide important differences between subgroups and the level of detail will provide employers with greater flexibility when analysing the data. Employers may wish to add extra categories to the recommended subcategories of ethnic categories. However, this should be considered carefully.

9. Employers should be aware that the way people classify themselves can change over time. It may therefore become necessary to change categories.

Religion and belief

10. Monitoring religion and belief may help employers understand workers' needs (for example, if they request leave for festivals) and ensure that staff turnover does not reflect a disproportionate number of people from specific religion or beliefs.

Sex

11. As well as the male and female categories, employers should consider whether to monitor for part-time working and for staff with caring responsibilities, including child-care, elder-care or care for a spouse or another family member. Both groups are predominantly women at a national level and are likely to be so for many employers as well.

Sexual orientation

12. Sexual orientation (and sexuality) may be considered to be a private issue. However, it is relevant in the workplace, particularly where discrimination and the application of equality policies, and other policies, are concerned. The way in which the question is asked is very important, particularly if employers are to ensure that the monitoring process does not create a further barrier.

13. The recommended way to ask job applicants and workers about their sexual orientation is outlined below:

What is your sexual orientation?

- Bisexual
- Gay man
- Gay woman/lesbian
- Heterosexual/straight
- Other
- Prefer not to say

14. Some employers, as an alternative, provide one option ('gay/lesbian') rather than the two options above, and then cross-reference the results of their data on gender in order to examine differences in experiences between gay men and gay woman.

15. It also acknowledges that some women identify themselves as gay rather than as lesbians. The option of 'other' provides an opportunity for staff to identify their sexual orientation in another way if the categories are not suitable.

16. Employers should note that transsexual or transgender status should not fall within the section on sexual orientation. It should instead have a section on its own (see paragraph 21 below).

17. In some monitoring exercises, for example, staff satisfaction surveys, it may be appropriate to ask a further question about how open an employee is about their sexual orientation:

If you are lesbian, gay or bisexual, are you open about your sexual orientation (Yes, Partially, No)

- At home
- With colleagues
- With your manager
- At work generally

The results from the above question may indicate wider organisational issues which need to be addressed.

Transgender status

18. Monitoring numbers of transsexual staff is a very sensitive area and opinion continues to be divided on this issue. While there is a need to protect an individual's right to privacy, without gathering some form of evidence, it may be difficult to monitor the impact of policies and procedures on transsexual people or employment patterns such as recruitment, training, promotion or leaving rates.

19. Because many transsexual people have had negative experiences in the workplace, many may be reluctant to disclose or may not trust their employers fully. (In order to obtain more reliable results, some employers have chosen to conduct monitoring through a neutral organisation under a guarantee of anonymity.)

20. If employers choose to monitor transsexual staff using their own systems, then privacy, confidentiality and anonymity should be paramount. For example, diversity statistics should not be linked to IT-based personnel records that indicate grade or job title, as the small number of transsexual workers in an organisation may be identified by these or other variables, compromising confidentiality.

21. Employers should note that it is important to recognise that transsexual people will usually identify as men or women, as well as transsexual people. In light of this, it is not appropriate to offer a choice between identifying as male, female or transsexual.

APPENDIX 3
MAKING REASONABLE ADJUSTMENTS TO WORK PREMISES – LEGAL CONSIDERATIONS

Introduction

[4.149]

1. In Chapter 6 it was explained that one of the situations in which a duty to make reasonable adjustments may arise is where a physical feature of premises occupied by an employer places a disabled worker at a substantial disadvantage compared with people who are not disabled. In such circumstances the employer must consider whether any reasonable steps can be taken to overcome that disadvantage. Making physical alterations to premises may be a reasonable step for an employer to have to take. This appendix addresses the issues of how leases and other legal obligations affect the duty to make reasonable adjustments to premises.

What happens if a binding obligation other than a lease prevents a building being altered?

2. An employer may be bound by the terms of an agreement or other legally binding obligation (for example, a mortgage, charge or restrictive covenant or, in Scotland, a feu disposition) under which they cannot alter the premises without someone else's consent.

3. **[Sch 21, para 2]** In these circumstances, the Act provides that it is always reasonable for the employer to have to request that consent, but that it is never reasonable for the employer to have to make an alteration before having obtained that consent.

What happens if a lease says that certain changes to premises cannot be made?

4. **[Sch 21, para 3]** Special provisions apply where an employer occupies premises under a lease, the terms of which prevent them from making an alteration to the premises.

5. In such circumstances, if the alteration is one which the employer proposes to make in order to comply with a duty of reasonable adjustment, the Act enables the lease to be read as if it provided:

- for the employer to make a written application to the landlord for that consent;
- for the landlord not to withhold the consent unreasonably;
- for the landlord to be able to give consent subject to reasonable conditions; and
- for the employer to make the alteration with the written consent of the landlord.

6. If the employer fails to make a written application to the landlord for consent to the alteration, the employer will not be able to rely upon the fact that the lease has a term preventing them from making alterations to the premises to defend their failure to make an alteration. In these circumstances, anything in the lease which prevents that alteration being made must be ignored in deciding whether it was reasonable for the employer to have made the alteration.

7. Whether withholding consent will be reasonable or not will depend on the specific circumstances.

8. For example, if a particular adjustment is likely to result in a substantial permanent reduction in the value of the landlord's interest in the premises, the landlord is likely to be acting reasonably in withholding consent. The landlord is also likely to be acting reasonably if it withholds consent because an adjustment would cause significant disruption or inconvenience to other tenants (for example, where the premises consist of multiple adjoining units).

9. A trivial or arbitrary reason would almost certainly be unreasonable. Many reasonable adjustments to premises will not harm the landlord's interests and so it would generally be unreasonable to withhold consent for them.

10. **[Sch 21, para 5]** In any legal proceedings on a claim involving a failure to make a reasonable adjustment, the disabled person concerned or the employer may ask the Employment Tribunal to direct that the landlord be made a party to the proceedings. The tribunal will grant that request if it is made before the hearing of the claim begins. It may refuse the request if it is made after the hearing of the claim begins. The request will not be granted if it is made after the tribunal has determined the claim.

11. Where the landlord has been made a party to the proceedings, the tribunal may determine whether the landlord has refused to consent to the alteration, or has consented subject to a condition, and in each case whether the refusal or condition was unreasonable.

12. If the tribunal finds that the refusal or condition is unreasonable it can:

- make an appropriate declaration;
- make an order authorising the employer to make a specified alteration (subject to any conditions); or
- order the landlord to pay compensation to the disabled person.

13. If the tribunal orders the landlord to pay compensation, it cannot also order the employer to do so.

What about the need to obtain statutory consent for some building changes?

14. An employer might have to obtain statutory consent before making adjustments involving changes to premises. Such consents include planning permission, Building Regulations approval (or a building warrant in Scotland), listed building consent, scheduled monument consent and fire regulations approval. The Act does not override the need to obtain such consents.

15. Employers should plan for and anticipate the need to obtain consent to make a particular adjustment. It might take time to obtain such consent, but it could be reasonable to make an interim or other adjustment – one that does not require consent – in the meantime.

16. Employers should remember that even where consent is not given for removing or altering a physical feature, they still have a duty to make all the adjustments that are reasonable to have to make to remove any substantial disadvantage faced by the disabled worker.

(Index and list of contacts omitted; see the list of useful addresses at **[5.120]**.*)*

D. DEPARTMENT FOR BUSINESS, ENERGY AND INDUSTRIAL STRATEGY

DEPARTMENT FOR BUSINESS INNOVATION & SKILLS WHISTLEBLOWING GUIDANCE FOR EMPLOYERS AND CODE OF PRACTICE MARCH 2015

[4.150]

NOTES

The Guidance and Code of Practice reproduced here have no formal statutory basis or authority. They are reproduced as helpful guidance for employers.

Note that the Department for Business Innovation & Skills is now the Department for Business, Energy and Industrial Strategy.

CONTENTS

WHAT IS WHISTLEBLOWING?

[4.151]

Whistleblowing is the term used when a worker passes on information concerning wrongdoing. In this guidance, we call that "making a disclosure" or "blowing the whistle". The wrongdoing will typically (although not necessarily) be something they have witnessed at work.

To be covered by whistleblowing law, a worker who makes a disclosure must reasonably believe two things. The first is that they are acting in the public interest. This means in particular that personal grievances and complaints are not usually covered by whistleblowing law.

The second thing that a worker must reasonably believe is that the disclosure tends to show past, present or likely future wrongdoing falling into one or more of the following categories:

- criminal offences (this may include, for example, types of financial impropriety such as fraud)
- failure to comply with an obligation set out in law
- miscarriages of justice
- endangering of someone's health and safety
- damage to the environment
- covering up wrongdoing in the above categories

Whistleblowing law is located in the Employment Rights Act 1996 (as amended by the Public Interest Disclosure Act 1998). It provides the right for a worker to take a case to an employment tribunal if they have been victimised at work or they have lost their job because they have 'blown the whistle'.

WHAT ARE AN EMPLOYER'S RESPONSIBILITIES IN REGARDS TO WHISTLEBLOWING?

[4.152]

As an employer it is good practice to create an open, transparent and safe working environment where workers feel able to speak up. Although the law does not require employers to have a whistleblowing policy in place, the existence of a whistleblowing policy shows an employer's commitment to listen to the concerns of workers. By having clear policies and procedures for dealing with whistleblowing, an organisation demonstrates that it welcomes information being brought to the attention of management. This is also demonstrated by the following:

Recognising workers are valuable ears and eyes: Workers are often the first people to witness any type of wrongdoing within an organisation. The information that workers may uncover could prevent wrongdoing, which may damage an organisation's reputation and/or performance, and could even save people from harm or death.

Getting the right culture: If an organisation hasn't created an open and supportive culture, the worker may not feel comfortable making a disclosure, for fear of the consequences. The two main barriers whistleblowers face are a fear of reprisal as a result of making a disclosure and that no action will be taken if they do make the decision to 'blow the whistle'. There have been a number of high profile cases, including evidence collated by the Mid-Staffordshire NHS Foundation Trust Public Inquiry[1], the Freedom to Speak Up Independent Review into creating an open and honest culture in the NHS[2]; and the Parliamentary Commission on Banking Standards[3] that confirm many workers are scared of speaking up about poor practice. Making sure your staff can approach management with important concerns is the most important step in creating an open culture. Employers should demonstrate, through visible leadership at all levels of the organisation, that they welcome and encourage workers to make disclosures.

Training and support: An organisation should implement training, mentoring, advice and other support systems to ensure workers can easily approach a range of people in the organisation.

Being able to respond: It is in the organisation's best interests to deal with a whistleblowing disclosure when it is first raised by a worker. This allows the organisation to investigate promptly, ask further questions of a worker and where applicable provide feedback. A policy should help explain the benefits of making a disclosure.

Better control: Organisations that embrace whistleblowing as an important source of information find that managers have better information to make decisions and control risk. Whistleblowers respond more positively when they feel that they are listened to.

Resolving the wrongdoing quickly: There are benefits for the organisation if a worker can make a disclosure internally rather than going to a third party. This way there is an opportunity to act promptly on the information and put right whatever wrongdoing is found.

NOTES

[1] http://www.midstaffspublicinquiry.com/

[2] https://freedomtospeakup.org.uk/the-report/

[3] http://www.publications.parliament.uk/pa/jt201213/jtselect/jtpcbs/98/98.pdf

COMMUNICATE POLICY AND PROCEDURE

[4.153]
Having a policy is a good first step to encourage workers to blow the whistle but each organisation needs to let its workers know about the policy and make sure they know how to make a disclosure. Some organisations choose to publicise their policy via their intranet or through a staff newsletter. If an organisation recognises a trade union it might develop a policy in consultation with them. It is a good idea for organisations to share the information with all staff regularly to make sure they are all reminded of the policy and procedures and to inform any newcomers. Providing training at all levels of an organisation on the effective implementation of whistleblowing arrangements will help to develop a supportive and open culture.

How? When someone blows the whistle an organisation should explain its procedures for making a disclosure and whether the whistleblower can expect to receive any feedback. Often a whistleblower expects to influence the action the organisation might take, or expects to make a judgement on whether an issue has been resolved – such expectations need to be managed.

Has the issue been resolved? It is for the organisation to be satisfied that the disclosure has been acted upon appropriately and that the issue has been resolved. There should be clear and prompt communications between the whistleblower and the organisation. It is best practice for organisations to provide feedback to whistleblowers, within the confines of their internal policies and procedures. Feedback is vital so that whistleblowers understand how their disclosure has been handled and dealt with. If a whistleblower is unhappy with the process or the outcome it will make them more likely to approach other individuals and organisations to 'blow the whistle', such as a "prescribed person".

DISCLOSURE OR GRIEVANCE?

[4.154]
Sometimes an employee believes they are blowing the whistle when, in fact, their complaint is a personal grievance. Workers who make a disclosure under an organisation's whistleblowing policy should believe that they are acting in the public interest. This means in particular that personal grievances and complaints are not usually covered by whistleblowing law. It is important that any policy, procedures and other communications make this clear.

An organisation may want to direct workers to the Government's guidance for whistleblowers to verify the position that a personal grievance is not generally regarded as a protected disclosure. Workers can also contact the Advisory, Conciliation and Arbitration Service (Acas) for guidance on whistleblowing and grievances. Useful information can be found at: www.acas.org.uk/grievances, add link to whistleblowing page

IS THERE A STANDARD WHISTLEBLOWING POLICY?

[4.155]
There is no one-size-fits-all whistleblowing policy as policies will vary depending on the size and nature of the organisation. Some organisations may choose to have a standalone policy whereas others may look to implement their policy into a code of ethics or may have 'local' whistleblowing procedures relevant to their specific business units.

A large organisation may have a policy where employees can contact their immediate manager or a specific team of individuals who are trained to handle whistleblowing disclosures. Smaller organisations may not have sufficient resources to do this.

Any whistleblowing policies or procedures should be clear, simple and easily understood.

Here are some tips about what a policy should include:

- An explanation of what whistleblowing is, particularly in relation to the organisation
- A clear explanation of the organisation's procedures for handling whistleblowing, which can be communicated through training
- A commitment to training workers at all levels of the organisation in relation to whistleblowing law and the organisation's policy
- A commitment to treat all disclosures consistently and fairly
- A commitment to take all reasonable steps to maintain the confidentiality of the whistleblower where it is requested (unless required by law to break that confidentiality)
- Clarification that any so-called 'gagging clauses' in settlement agreements do not prevent workers from making disclosures in the public interest
- An idea about what feedback a whistleblower might receive
- An explanation that anonymous whistleblowers will not ordinarily be able to receive feedback and that any action taken to look into a disclosure could be limited – anonymous whistleblowers may seek feedback through a telephone appointment or by using an anonymised email address
- A commitment to emphasise in a whistleblowing policy that victimisation of a whistleblower is not acceptable. Any instances of victimisation will be taken seriously and managed appropriately
- An idea of the time frame for handling any disclosures raised
- An idea of the time frame for handling any disclosures raised
- Clarification that the whistleblower does not need to provide evidence for the employer to look into the concerns raised
- Signpost to information and advice to those thinking of blowing the whistle, for example the guidance from the Government, Acas, Public Concern at Work or Trade Unions
- Information about blowing the whistle to the relevant prescribed person(s)

PROMOTING A POLICY AND MAKING SURE IT IS EASILY ACCESSIBLE

[4.156]
It's no good having a policy in place if no one knows about it. Actively promoting a policy shows the organisation is genuinely open to hearing concerns from its staff. Managers and leaders in the organisation can also promote a policy in the way they behave at work. Conduct and written policies will help to create an open culture, which will increase the likelihood of a worker speaking up about any wrongdoing they come across.

Written policies are not enough. Training should be provided to all staff on the key arrangements of the policy. Additional training should be provided to those with whistleblowing responsibilities, such as managers or designated contacts, so they are able to provide guidance confidently to workers. Managers should also lead by example and ensure they are committed to creating an open culture where disclosures are welcome. It is also a good idea to include handling whistleblowing disclosures as part of discipline and grievance training for managers and staff. Training should be offered at regular points to make sure it stays fresh in managers' minds and to capture any newcomers to the organisation.

Here are some ideas about how to promote a policy:

- Hold a staff session or in larger organisations require managers to hold smaller, consistent team meetings
- Make the policy accessible on the staff intranet
- Appoint a whistleblowers' champion to drive the commitment to valuing whistleblowing and protecting whistleblowers within the organisation
- Use promotional posters around the building
- Include the policy within induction packs for newcomers
- Set the policy out in staff handbooks and contracts

DECIDING HOW TO DEAL WITH THE WHISTLEBLOWING DISCLOSURE

[4.157]
Where a worker feels able to do so they may make a disclosure to their immediate manager who will be able to decide whether they can take forward the disclosure or whether it will require escalation. An organisation will need to equip managers with the knowledge and confidence to make these judgements. A whistleblowing policy and training can help with this.

Larger organisations may have a designated team who can be approached when workers make a disclosure. Although this may not be possible for smaller organisations, it is considered best practice that there is at least one senior member of staff as a point of contact for individuals who wish to blow the whistle. This is particularly helpful in cases where the immediate line management relationship is damaged or where the disclosure involves the manager. Alternatively, there are commercial providers who will manage a whistleblowing process on the employer's behalf.

DEALING WITH DISCLOSURES

[4.158]
Once a disclosure has been made it is good practice to hold a meeting with the whistleblower to gather all the information needed to understand the situation. In some cases a suitable conclusion may be reached

through an initial conversation with a manager. In more serious cases there may be a need for a formal investigation. It is for the organisation to decide what the most appropriate action to take is.

It is important to note that if an investigation concludes that the disclosure was untrue it does not automatically mean that it was raised maliciously by a worker.

When dealing with disclosures, it is good practice for managers to:

- Have a facility for anonymous reporting
- Treat all disclosures made seriously and consistently
- Provide support to the worker during what can be a difficult or anxious time with access to mentoring, advice and counselling
- Reassure the whistleblower that their disclosure will not affect their position at work
- Document whether the whistleblower has requested confidentiality
- Manage the expectations of the whistleblower in terms of what action and/or feedback they can expect as well clear timescales for providing updates
- Produce a summary of the meeting for record keeping purposes and provide a copy to the whistleblower
- Allow the worker to be accompanied by a trade union representative or colleague at any meeting about the disclosure, if they wish to do so
- Provide support services after a disclosure has been made such as mediation and dispute resolution, to help rebuild trust and relationships in the workplace

It will be useful to document any decisions or action taken following the making of a disclosure by a worker.

It is also good practice for organisations to:

- Record the number of whistleblowing disclosures they receive and their nature
- Maintain records of the date and content of feedback provided to whistleblowers
- Conduct regular surveys to ascertain the satisfaction of whistleblowers.

WHAT HAPPENS WHEN A WORKER BLOWS THE WHISTLE TO SOMEONE OTHER THAN THEIR EMPLOYER?

[4.159]
Ideally workers will feel able to make a disclosure to their organisation. Good policies and procedures for handling whistleblowing will help encourage this. However, there may be circumstances where they feel unable to. There are other ways, some of which are set out in law, that a worker may make a disclosure without losing their rights under whistleblowing law. One option for external disclosures of this type is prescribed persons. Prescribed persons are mainly regulators and professional bodies but include other persons and bodies such as MPs. The relevant prescribed person depends on the subject matter of the disclosure, for example a disclosure about wrongdoing in a care home could be made to the Care Quality Commission.

A complete list of prescribed persons can be found here. (https://www.gov.uk/government/publications/blowing-the-whistle-list-of-prescribed-people-and-bodies--2)

Prescribed persons have individual policies and procedures for handling concerns and complaints. Generally these will be accessible on their websites.

Alternatively, a worker might choose to approach the media with their concerns. If a worker goes to the media, they can expect in most cases to lose their whistleblowing law rights. It is only in exceptional circumstances that a worker can go to the media without losing their rights. They must reasonably believe that the information they disclose and any allegation contained in it are substantially true. They cannot be acting for personal gain. Unless the wrongdoing is exceptionally serious, if they have not already gone to their employer or a prescribed person, they must reasonably believe that their employer will subject them to "detriment" or conceal or destroy evidence if they do so. And even then, their choice to make the disclosure must be reasonable.

WHAT HAPPENS IF A WHISTLEBLOWER BELIEVES THEY HAVE BEEN UNFAIRLY TREATED?

[4.160]
If a whistleblower believes that they have been unfairly treated because they have blown the whistle they may decide to take their case to an employment tribunal. The process for this would involve attempted resolution through the Advisory, Conciliation and Arbitration Service (Acas) early conciliation service.

Information can be found at: www.acas.org.uk/conciliation and the Acas helpline can provide further advice.

The Acas helpline details are:

Telephone: 0300 123 1100

Textphone: 18001 030 0123 1100

Monday to Friday, 8am to 8pm

Saturday, 9am to 1pm

CONFIDENTIALITY

[4.161]
There may be good reasons why a worker wishes their identity to remain confidential. The law does not compel an organisation to protect the confidentiality of a whistleblower. However, it is considered best

practice to maintain that confidentiality, unless required by law to disclose it. Managers dealing with whistleblowing concerns should be briefed to ensure they understand how to handle the disclosure and protect personal information.

It will help to manage the expectations of whistleblowers if the risk that some colleagues may still speculate about who has raised the concern is explained to them.

Anonymous information will be just as important for organisations to act upon. Workers should be made aware that the ability of an organisation to ask follow up questions or provide feedback will be limited if the whistleblower cannot be contacted. It may be possible to overcome these challenges by using telephone appointments or through an anonymised email address.

Workers should be made aware that making a disclosure anonymously means it can be more difficult for them to qualify for protections as a whistleblower. This is because there would be no documentary evidence linking the worker to the disclosure for the employment tribunal to consider.

WHISTLEBLOWING CODE OF PRACTICE

[4.162]

It is important that employers encourage whistleblowing as a way to report wrongdoing and manage risks to the organisation. Employers also need to be well equipped for handling any such concerns raised by workers. It is considered best practice for an employer to:

- Have a whistleblowing policy or appropriate written procedures in place
- Ensure the whistleblowing policy or procedures are easily accessible to all workers
- Raise awareness of the policy or procedures through all available means such as staff engagement, intranet sites, and other marketing communications
- Provide training to all workers on how disclosures should be raised and how they will be acted upon
- Provide training to managers on how to deal with disclosures
- Create an understanding that all staff at all levels of the organisation should demonstrate that they support and encourage whistleblowing
- Confirm that any clauses in settlement agreements do not prevent workers from making disclosures in the public interest
- Ensure the organisation's whistleblowing policy or procedures clearly identify who can be approached by workers that want to raise a disclosure. Organisations should ensure a range of alternative persons who a whistleblower can approach in the event a worker feels unable to approach their manager. If your organisation works with a recognised union, a representative from that union could be an appropriate contact for a worker to approach
- Create an organisational culture where workers feel safe to raise a disclosure in the knowledge that they will not face any detriment from the organisation as a result of speaking up.
- Undertake that any detriment towards an individual who raises a disclosure is not acceptable
- Make a commitment that all disclosures raised will be dealt with appropriately, consistently, fairly and professionally
- Undertake to protect the identity of the worker raising a disclosure, unless required by law to reveal it and to offer support throughout with access to mentoring, advice and counselling
- Provide feedback to the worker who raised the disclosure where possible and appropriate subject to other legal requirements. Feedback should include an indication of timings for any actions or next steps

[illegible] that confidentiality [illegible] legal [illegible] how to [illegible] with the understanding of how to [illegible] information [illegible].

Anonymous [illegible] is not [illegible] organisations to act upon. Workers should [illegible] aware that it may be [illegible] difficult [illegible] with [illegible] possible to [illegible] without [illegible].

Workers should be [illegible]. This [illegible] employer [illegible].

[illegible]

E. HEALTH AND SAFETY EXECUTIVE

HEALTH AND SAFETY COMMISSION CODE OF PRACTICE: SAFETY REPRESENTATIVES AND SAFETY COMMITTEES (1978)

[4.163]

NOTES

This Code of Practice was issued under the Health and Safety at Work etc Act 1974, s 16 at **[1.44]**, and came into force on 1 October 1978. It has the legal effect indicated in that section. Minor amendments and corrections have been made to reflect changes to linked HSE guidance and revisions/revocations to other, related pieces of legislation. These have been incorporated below. For the Safety Representatives and Safety Committees Regulations 1977, SI 1977/500, see **[2.30]**.

The Health and Safety Commission was abolished and replaced by a new Health and Safety Executive, by the Legislative Reform (Health and Safety Executive) Order 2008, SI 2008/960, art 2. Para 8 of Sch 2 to the 2008 Order provides that codes of practice issued by the Commission under the Health and Safety at Work etc Act 1974, s 16, before 1 April 2008, have effect on or after that date as though they had been issued by the new Executive.

See *Harvey* NI(8)(c).

[4.164]

1. The Safety Representatives and Safety Committees Regulations 1977 concern safety representatives appointed in accordance with section 2(4) of the Health and Safety at Work etc Act 1974 (the 1974 Act) and cover:

(a) prescribed cases in which recognised trade unions may appoint safety representatives from amongst the employees;

(b) prescribed functions of safety representatives.

2. Section 2(6) of the Act requires employers to consult with safety representatives with a view to the making and maintenance of arrangements which will enable them and their employees to co-operate effectively in promoting and developing measures to ensure the health and safety at work of the employees, and in checking the effectiveness of such measures. Under section 2(4) safety representatives are required to represent the employees in those consultations.

3. This Code of Practice was approved by the Health and Safety Commission (now the Health and Safety Executive) with the consent of the Secretary of State for Employment. It relates to the requirements placed on safety representatives by section 2(4) of the Act and on employers by the Regulations and takes effect on the date the Regulations come into operation.

4. The employer, the recognised trade unions concerned and safety representatives should make full and proper use of the existing agreed industrial relations machinery to reach the degree of agreement necessary to achieve the purpose of the Regulations and in order to resolve any differences.

INTERPRETATION

5. In this Code:

(a) 'the 1974 Act' means the Health and Safety at Work etc Act 1974 and 'the Regulations' means the Safety Representatives and Safety Committees Regulations 1977 (SI 1977 No 500);

(b) words and expressions which are defined in the Act or in the Regulations have the same meaning in this Code unless the context requires otherwise.

FUNCTIONS OF SAFETY REPRESENTATIVES

6. In order to fulfil their functions under section 2(4) of the Act safety representatives should:

(a) take all reasonably practical steps to keep themselves informed of:

  (i) the legal requirements relating to the health and safety of people at work, particularly the group or groups of persons they directly represent;

  (ii) the particular hazards of the workplace and the measures deemed necessary to eliminate or minimise the risk deriving from these hazards;

  (iii) the health and safety policy of their employer and the organisation and arrangements for fulfilling that policy;

(b) encourage co-operation between the employer and their employees in promoting and developing essential measures to ensure the health and safety of employees and in checking the effectiveness of these measures;

(c) bring to the employer's notice (normally in writing) any unsafe or unhealthy conditions, working practices or unsatisfactory arrangements for welfare at work which come to their attention, whether on an inspection or day-to-day observation. The report does not imply that all other conditions and working practices are safe and healthy or that the welfare arrangements are satisfactory in all other respects.

7. Making a written report does not prevent bringing such matters to the attention of the employer or his representative by speaking to them directly in the first instance, particularly in situations where speedy remedial action is necessary. It will also be appropriate for minor matters to be handled through this sort of direct discussion without the need for a formal written approach.

INFORMATION TO BE PROVIDED BY EMPLOYERS

8. The Regulations require employers to make any information they are aware of available to safety representatives that is necessary for them to fulfil their functions. Such information should include:

(a) information about the plans and performance of their business and any changes proposed where they affect the health and safety at work of their employees;

(b) technical information about health and safety hazards and precautions needed to eliminate or minimise them, regarding machinery, plant, equipment, processes, systems of work and substances in use at work, including any relevant information provided by consultants or designers or by the manufacturer, importer or supplier of any article or substance used, or proposed to be used, at work by their employees;

(c) information the employer keeps relating to the occurrence of any accident, dangerous occurrence or notifiable industrial disease and any statistical records relating to such accidents, dangerous occurrences or cases of notifiable industrial disease;

(d) any other information specifically related to matters affecting the health and safety at work of their employees, including the results of any measurements taken by the employer or people acting on their behalf in the course of checking the effectiveness of their health and safety arrangements;

(e) information on articles or substances which an employer issues to homeworkers.

HEALTH AND SAFETY COMMISSION CODE OF PRACTICE: TIME OFF FOR THE TRAINING OF SAFETY REPRESENTATIVES (1978)

[4.165]

NOTES

This Code of Practice was issued under the Health and Safety at Work etc Act 1974, s 16, at **[1.44]**, and came into force on 1 October 1978. It has the legal effect indicated in that section. Minor amendments and corrections have been made to reflect changes to linked HSE guidance and revisions/revocations to other, related pieces of legislation. For the Safety Representatives and Safety Committees Regulations 1977, SI 1977/500, see **[2.30]**.

The Health and Safety Commission was abolished and replaced by a new Health and Safety Executive by the Legislative Reform (Health and Safety Executive) Order 2008, SI 2008/960, art 2. Para 8 of Sch 2 to the 2008 Order provides that codes of practice issued by the Commission under the Health and Safety at Work etc Act 1974, s 16, before 1 April 2008, have effect on or after that date as though they had been issued by the new Executive.

See *Harvey* NI(8)(c).

PREFACE

[4.166]

This document sets out a Code of Practice, which has been approved by the Health and Safety Commission, relating to the time off with pay which a safety representative is to be permitted to take during his working hours for the purpose of undergoing training approved by the TUC or by independent unions. It should be read in conjunction with the Safety Representatives and Safety Committees Regulations 1977, with particular reference to Regulation 4, which sets out the functions of a safety representative and the time off for training necessary to perform these functions.

The Advisory, Conciliation and Arbitration Service has also prepared a Code of Practice on Time Off for trade union duties and activities generally under Section 57 of the Employment Protection Act. However, this Code, approved by the Health and Safety Commission, is concerned with time off for training of safety representatives appointed under the Regulations.

Issues which may arise are covered by paragraph 3 of the Code of Practice on Safety Representatives approved by the Health and Safety Commission. The Schedule to the Regulations deals with the computation of pay for the time off allowed. Regulation 11 contains provisions as to reference of complaints to industrial tribunals about time off and the payment to be made.

To complement training approved by the TUC or by independent unions for safety representatives, an employer should make such arrangements as are necessary to provide training in the technical hazards of the workplace and relevant precautions on safe methods of work, and on his organisation and arrangements for health and safety.

CODE OF PRACTICE

1. The function of safety representatives appointed by recognised trade unions, as set out in section 2(4) of the 1974 Act, is to represent employees in consultations with employers about health and safety matters. Regulation 4(1) of the Safety Representatives and Safety Committees Regulations (SI 1977 No 500) prescribes other functions of safety representatives appointed under those Regulations.

2. Under regulation 4(2)(b) of those Regulations, the employer has a duty to permit those safety representatives such time off with pay during the employee's working hours as shall be necessary for the purpose of 'undergoing such training aspects of those functions as may be reasonable in all the circumstances'.

3. As soon as possible after their appointment, safety representatives should be permitted time off with pay to attend basic training facilities approved by the Trades Union Congress (TUC) or by the independent union or unions which appointed the safety representatives. Further training, similarly approved, should be undertaken where the safety representative has special responsibilities or where such training is necessary to meet changes in circumstances or relevant legislation.

4. With regard to the length of training required, this cannot be rigidly prescribed, but basic training should take into account the functions of safety representatives placed on them by the Regulations. In particular, basic training should provide an understanding of the role of safety representatives, of safety committees, and of trade unions' policies and practices in relation to:

(a) the legal requirements relating to the health and safety of those at work, particularly the group or class of people they directly represent;

(b) the nature and extent of workplace hazards, and the measures necessary to eliminate or minimise them;

(c) the health and safety policy of employers, and the organisation and arrangements for fulfilling those policies.

5. Additionally, safety representatives will need to acquire new skills in order to carry out their functions, including safety inspections, and in using basic sources of legal and official information and information provided by, or through, the employer on health and safety matters.

6. Trade unions are responsible for appointing safety representatives. When the trade union wishes a safety representative to receive training relevant to their function, it should inform management of the course it has approved and supply a copy of the syllabus, indicating its contents, if the employer asks for it. It should normally give at least a few weeks' notice of the safety representatives it has nominated to attend. The number of safety representatives attending training courses at any one time should be that which is reasonable in the circumstances, bearing in mind such factors as the availability of relevant courses and the employers' operational requirements. Unions and managers should endeavour to reach agreement on the appropriate numbers and arrangements and resolve any problems that may arise using the relevant agreed procedures.

F. INFORMATION COMMISSIONER

DATA PROTECTION: EMPLOYMENT PRACTICES CODE (2011)

[4.167]

NOTES

A consolidated Code of Practice was issued by the Information Commissioner in June 2005 to replace the four separate Parts originally issued between 2002 and 2004. In November 2011, a new version of the Code was published. The 2011 version is substantively the same as the 2005 version; the only differences being in formatting and updated website addresses etc. The Code was issued under the authority conferred by the Data Protection Act 1998, s 51(3)(b), which was repealed by the Data Protection Act 2018, s 211, Sch 19, Pt 1, para 44, as from 25 May 2018 (for transitional provisions, see Sch 20 to that Act at **[1.2232]**). It is understood that the Code is intended to continue to apply as a non-statutory guidance by the Information Commissioner's Office unless, and until, replaced by a new Code issued under the 2018 Act. The 1998 Act did not confer any specific legal status on the Code, and did not require either ministerial or Parliamentary approval. The Code came into effect on its issue by the Commissioner. The Supplementary Guidance referred to in the Code is not reproduced for reasons of space; it is available on the Commissioner's website (www.ico.org.uk).

Note that where the text of this Code originally cross-referred to a page number within the hardcopy version of the Code, the appropriate paragraph number has been substituted in its place.

CONTENTS

ABOUT THE CODE

OUR AIM:

[4.168]
This Code is intended to help employers comply with the Data Protection Act and to encourage them to adopt good practice. The Code aims to strike a balance between the legitimate expectations of workers that personal information about them will be handled properly and the legitimate interests of employers in deciding how best, within the law, to run their own businesses. It does not impose new legal obligations.

WHO IS THE CODE FOR?

The Employment Practices Data Protection Code deals with the impact of data protection laws on the employment relationship. It covers such issues as the obtaining of information about workers, the retention of records, access to records and disclosure of them. Not every aspect of the Code will be relevant to every organisation – this will vary according to size and the nature of its business. Some of the issues addressed may arise only rarely – particularly for small businesses. Here the Code is intended to serve as a reference document to be called on when necessary.

THE BENEFITS OF THE CODE

The Data Protection Act 1998 places responsibilities on any organisation to process personal information that it holds in a fair and proper way. Failure to do so can ultimately lead to a criminal offence being committed.

The effect of the Act on how an organisation processes information on its workers is generally straightforward. But in some areas it can be complex and difficult to understand, especially if your organisation has only limited experience of dealing with data protection issues. The Code therefore covers the points you need to check, and what action, if any, you may need to take. Following the Code should produce other benefits in terms of relationships with your workers, compliance with other legislation and efficiencies in storing and managing information.

Following the Code will:

- increase trust in the workplace – there will be transparency about information held on individuals, thus helping to create an open atmosphere where workers have trust and confidence in employment practices.
- encourage good housekeeping – following the Code encourages organisations to dispose of out-of-date information, freeing up both physical and computerised filing systems and making valuable information easier to find.
- protect organisations from legal action – adhering to the Code will help employers to protect themselves from challenges against their data protection practices.
- encourage workers to treat customers' personal data with respect – following the Code will create a general level of awareness of personal data issues, helping to ensure that information about customers is treated properly.
- help organisations to meet other legal requirements – the Code is intended to be consistent with other legislation such as the Human Rights Act 1998 and the Regulation of Investigatory Powers Act 2000 (RIPA).
- assist global businesses to adopt policies and practices which are consistent with similar legislation in other countries – the Code is produced in the light of EC Directive 95/46/EC and ought to be in line with data protection law in other European Union member states.
- help to prevent the illicit use of information by workers – informing them of the principles of data protection, and the consequences of not complying with the Act, should discourage them from misusing information held by the organisation.

WHAT IS THE LEGAL STATUS OF THE CODE?

The Code has been issued by the Information Commissioner under section 51 of the Data Protection Act. This requires him to promote the following of good practice, including compliance with the Act's requirements, by data controllers and empowers him, after consultation, to prepare Codes of Practice giving guidance on good practice.

The basic legal requirement on each employer is to comply with the Act itself. The Code is designed to help. It sets out the Information Commissioner's recommendations as to how the legal requirements of the Act can be met. Employers may have alternative ways of meeting these requirements but if they do nothing they risk breaking the law.

Any enforcement action would be based on a failure to meet the requirements of the Act itself. However, relevant parts of the Code are likely to be cited by the Commissioner in connection with any enforcement action that arises in relation to the processing of personal information in the employment context.

WHO DOES DATA PROTECTION COVER IN THE WORKPLACE?

The Code is concerned with information that employers might collect and keep on any individual who might wish to work, work, or have worked for them. In the Code the term 'worker' includes:

- applicants (successful and unsuccessful)
- former applicants (successful and unsuccessful)
- employees (current and former)
- agency staff (current and former)
- casual staff (current and former)
- contract staff (current and former)

Some of this Code will also apply to others in the workplace, such as volunteers and those on work experience placements.

WHAT INFORMATION IS COVERED BY THE CODE?

Information about individuals, that is kept by an organisation on computer in the employment context, will fall within the scope of the Data Protection Act and therefore, within the scope of this Code. However, information that is kept in simple manual files will often fall outside the Act. Where information falls outside the Act, this Code can do no more than offer advice on good information handling practice.

Personal information

The Code is concerned with 'personal information'. That is, information which:

- is about a living person and affects that person's privacy (whether in his/her personal or family life, business or professional capacity) in the sense that the information has the person as its focus or is otherwise biographical in nature, and
- identifies a person, whether by itself, or together with other information in the organisation's possession or that is likely to come into its possession.

This means that automated and computerised personal information kept about workers by employers is covered by the Act. It also covers personal information put on paper or microfiche and held in any 'relevant filing system'. In addition, information recorded with the intention that it will be put in a relevant filing system or held on computer is covered.

Only a well structured manual system will qualify as a relevant filing system. This means that the system must amount to more than a bundle of documents about each worker filed in date order. There must be some sort of system to guide a searcher to where specific information about a named worker can be found readily. This might take the form of topic dividers within individually named personnel files or name dividers within a file on a particular topic, such as 'Training Applications'.

Processing

The Act applies to personal information that is subject to 'processing'. For the purposes of the Act, the term 'processing' applies to a comprehensive range of activities. It includes the initial obtaining of personal information, the retention and use of it, access and disclosure and final disposal.

Examples of personal information **likely** to be covered by the Act include:

- details of a worker's salary and bank account held on an organisation's computer system
- an e-mail about an incident involving a named worker
- a supervisor's notebook containing information on a worker where there is an intention to put that information in that worker's computerised personnel file
- an individual worker's personnel file where the documents are filed in date order but there is an index to the documents at the front of the file
- an individual worker's personnel file where at least some of the documents are filed behind sub dividers with headings such as application details, leave record and performance reviews
- a set of leave cards where each worker has an individual card and the cards are kept in alphabetical order
- a set of completed application forms, filed in alphabetical order within a file of application forms for a particular vacancy.

Examples of information **unlikely** to be covered by the Act include:

- information on the entire workforce's salary structure, given by grade, where individuals are not named and are not identifiable
- a report on the comparative success of different recruitment campaigns where no details regarding individuals are held
- a report on the results of "exit interviews" where all responses are anonymised and where the results are impossible to trace back to individuals
- a personnel file that contains information about a named worker but where the information is simply filed in date order with nothing to guide a searcher to where specific information, such as the worker's leave entitlement, can be found.

SENSITIVE PERSONAL INFORMATION

What are sensitive data?

Sensitive data are information concerning an individual's:

- racial or ethnic origin
- political opinions
- religious beliefs or other beliefs of a similar nature
- trade union membership (within the meaning of the Trade Union and Labour Relations (Consolidation) Act 1992)
- physical or mental health or condition
- sexual life
- commission or alleged commission of any offence, or
- proceedings for any offence committed or alleged to have been committed, the disposal of such proceedings or the sentence of any court in such proceedings

Sensitive data processed by an employer might typically be about a worker's:

- physical or mental health
  - — as a part of sickness records revealed through monitoring e-mails sent by a worker to his or her manager or to an occupational health advisor
  - — obtained as part of a pre-employment medical questionnaire or examination.
  - — drug or alcohol test results
- criminal convictions
  - — to assess suitability for certain types of employment
- disabilities
  - — to facilitate adaptations in the workplace
  - — to ensure special needs are catered for at interview or selection testing
  - — in monitoring equality of opportunity
- racial origin
  - — to ensure that recruitment processes do not discriminate against particular racial groups
  - — to ensure equality of opportunity
- trade union membership
  - — to enable deduction of subscriptions from payroll
  - — revealed by internet access logs which show that a worker routinely accesses a particular trade union website.

The Act sets out a series of conditions, at least one of which has to apply before an employer can collect, store, use, disclose or otherwise process sensitive data.

See Supplementary Guidance page 72 which explains more about the conditions for processing sensitive data.

WHAT RESPONSIBILITIES DO WORKERS HAVE UNDER THE ACT?

Workers – as well as employers – have responsibilities for data protection under the Act. Line managers have responsibility for the type of personal information they collect and how they use it. No-one at any level should disclose personal information outside the organisation's procedures, or use personal information held on others for their own purposes. Anyone disclosing personal information without the authority of the organisation may commit a criminal offence, unless there is some other legal justification, for example under 'whistle-blowing' legislation.

Of course, applicants for jobs ought to provide accurate information and may breach other laws if they do not. However, the Act does not create any new legal obligation for them to do so.

Managing Data Protection (post) explains more about allocating responsibility.

PARTS OF THE CODE

The 'Employment Practices Code' starts with a section on managing data protection in employment practices. It is then split into four parts;

- **recruitment and selection** – is about job applications and pre-employment vetting
- **employment records** – is about collecting, storing, disclosing and deleting records
- **monitoring at work** – is about monitoring workers' use of telephones, the internet, e-mail systems and vehicles
- **workers' health** – is about occupational health, medical testing, drug and genetic screening.

Each part of the Code has been designed to stand alone. Which parts of the Code you choose to use will depend on the relevance to your organisation of each area covered.

THE GOOD PRACTICE RECOMMENDATIONS

Each part of the Code consists of a series of good practice recommendations. These good practice recommendations may be relevant to either large or small employers, but some of them address activities that are of a more specialist nature than others or may occur only rarely, particularly in a small business, These recommendations are most likely to be relevant to larger organisations. However, how far they are applicable and what is needed to achieve them will, of course, depend very much not just on size but also on the nature of each organisation.

SUPPLEMENTARY GUIDANCE

Supporting guidance, aimed mainly at those in larger organisations who are responsible for ensuring that employment policies and practices comply with data protection law, includes more detailed notes and examples. These notes and examples, do not form part of this Code.

MANAGING DATA PROTECTION

GOOD PRACTICE RECOMMENDATIONS – MANAGING DATA PROTECTION

[4.169]
Data protection compliance should be seen as an integral part of employment practice. It is important to develop a culture in which respect for private life, data protection, security and confidentiality of personal information is seen as the norm.

0.1 Identify the person within the organisation responsible for ensuring that employment policies and procedures comply with the Act and for ensuring that they continue to do so. Put in place a mechanism for checking that procedures are followed in practice.

Key points and possible actions

- The nature and size of the organisation will influence where responsibility should rest.
- Ensure the person responsible reads all relevant parts of the Code.
- Check employment policies and procedures, including unwritten practices, against the relevant parts of the Code.
- Eliminate areas of non-compliance.
- Inform those who need to know why certain procedures have changed.
- Introduce a mechanism for checking that procedures are followed in practice, for example, occasional audits and spot checks and/or a requirement for managers to sign a compliance statement.

0.2 Ensure that business areas and individual line managers who process information about workers understand their own responsibility for data protection compliance and if necessary amend their working practices in the light of this.

Key points and possible actions

- Prepare a briefing to departmental heads and line managers about their responsibilities.

0.3 Assess what personal information about workers is in existence and who is responsible for it.

Key points and possible actions

- Use the various parts of this Code as the framework to assess what personal information your organisation keeps and where responsibility for it lies.
- Remember that personal information may be held in different departments as well as within the personnel/human resource function.

0.4 Eliminate the collection of personal information that is irrelevant or excessive to the employment relationship. If sensitive data are collected ensure that a sensitive data condition is satisfied.

Key points and possible actions

- Consider each type of personal information that is held and decide whether any information could be deleted or not collected in the first place.
- Check that the collection and use of any sensitive personal data satisfies at least one of the sensitive data conditions.

See Supplementary Guidance page 72 which explains more about the conditions for processing sensitive data.

0.5 Ensure that all workers are aware how they can be criminally liable if they knowingly or recklessly disclose personal information outside their employer's policies and procedures. Make serious breaches of data protection rules a disciplinary matter.

Key points and possible actions

- Prepare a guide explaining to workers the consequences of their actions in this area.
- Make sure that the serious infringement of data protection rules is clearly indicated as a disciplinary matter.
- Ensure that the guide is brought to the attention of new workers.
- Ensure that workers can ask questions about the guide.

0.6 Ensure that your organisation has a valid notification in the register of data controllers that relates to the processing of personal information about workers, unless it is exempt from notification.

Key points and possible actions

- Consult the Data Protection Register website – www.ico.org.uk – to check the notification status of your organisation.
- Check whether your organisation is exempt from notification using the website.

- Check whether all your processing of information about workers is correctly described there – unless your organisation is exempt.
- Allocate responsibility for checking and updating this information on a regular basis, for example every 6 months.

0.7 Consult workers, and/or trade unions or other representatives, about the development and implementation of employment practices and procedures that involve the processing of personal information about workers.

Key points and possible actions

- Consultation is only mandatory under employment law, in limited circumstances and for larger employers but it should nevertheless help to ensure that processing of personal information is fair.
- When formulating new employment practices and procedures, assess the impact on collection and use of personal information.

PART 1: RECRUITMENT AND SELECTION

ABOUT PART 1 OF THE CODE

Data protection in recruitment and selection

[4.170]
The recruitment and selection process necessarily involves an employer in collecting and using information about workers. Much of this information is personal in nature and can affect a worker's privacy. The Act does not prevent an employer from carrying out an effective recruitment exercise but helps to strike a balance between the employer's needs and the applicant's right to respect for his or her private life.

What does this part of the Code cover?

This part of the Code covers all aspects of the recruitment and selection process from the advertising of vacancies through to the deletion of information on unsuccessful applicants. It does not though deal in detail with the collection and use of health information on job applicants. This is covered in Part 4. Nor does it deal in detail with the right of applicants to access to the information that an employer keeps about them. This is essentially no different from the right of access that a worker has once employed or engaged. This is covered in Part 2.

Some recommendations in the Code are only likely to be of relevance to those using sophisticated selection methods such as psychometric testing or to those employing workers with responsibilities that mean that special checks are justified, for example, criminal record checks on those working with children. For this reason some sub sections are likely to be of relevance mainly to larger or specialist organisations.

Verification and vetting

The terms "verification" and "vetting" are both used in this part of the Code. Verification covers the process of checking that details supplied by applicants (eg qualifications) are accurate and complete. Verification, therefore, is limited to checking of information that is sought in the application or supplied later in the recruitment process. As used here the term also includes the taking up of references provided by the applicant. Where an employer is justified in asking an applicant about any criminal convictions the Criminal Records Bureau provides a verification service covering certain, high risk areas of employment.

Vetting covers the employer actively making its own enquiries from third parties about an applicant's background and circumstances. It goes beyond the verification of details addressed above. As such it is particularly intrusive and should be confined to areas of special risk. It is for example used for some government workers who have regular access to highly classified information.

In some sectors vetting may be a necessary and accepted practice. Limited vetting may be a legal requirement for some jobs, for example, child care jobs under the Protection of Children Act 1999. The Department of Health has developed a Protection of Vulnerable Adults list which employers intending to recruit certain types of care workers are required to consult. Such vetting usually takes place through the Criminal Records Bureau.

See Supplementary Guidance, page 17 for background information on the Criminal Records Bureau.

GOOD PRACTICE RECOMMENDATIONS – PART 1

The parts of the Code in this section are:

1.1 Advertising

1.2 Applications

1.3 Verification

1.4 Short-listing

1.5 Interviews

1.6 Pre-employment vetting

1.7 Retention of recruitment records

1.1 Advertising

[4.171]

This sub-section covers any method used to notify potential applicants of job vacancies, using such media as notices, newspapers, radio, television and the internet.

1.1.1 Inform individuals responding to job advertisements of the name of the organisation to which they will be providing their information and how it will be used unless this is self-evident.

Key points and possible actions

- Ensure that the name of your organisation appears in all recruitment advertisements.
- Ensure that your organisation is named on the answerphone message which invites potential applicants to leave details.
- Ensure that your organisation is named on your website before personal information is collected on an online application form.
- To the extent that it is not self evident describe in the advertisement the purposes for which you may use personal information, for example, to market your organisations products and service.

1.1.2 Recruitment agencies, used on behalf of an employer, should identify themselves and explain how personal information they receive will be used and disclosed unless this is self-evident.

Key points and possible actions

- If you use a recruitment agency check that it identifies itself in any advertisement, and that it informs applicants if the information requested is to be used for any purpose of which the applicant is unlikely to be aware.

1.1.3 On receiving identifiable particulars of applicants from an agency ensure, as soon as you can, that the applicants are aware of the name of the organisation holding their information.

Key points and possible actions

- Inform the applicant as soon as you can of the employer's identity and of any uses that the employer might make of the information received that are not self-evident.

OR

- If the employer does not wish to be identified at an early stage in the recruitment process, ensure the agency only sends anonymised information about applicants. Ensure the employer is identified to individuals whose applications are to be pursued further.

1.2 Applications

[4.172]

This sub-section covers CVs sent 'on spec' as well as more formal responses to job advertisements.

1.2.1 State, on any application form, to whom the information is being provided and how it will be used if this is not self-evident.

Key points and possible actions

- Ensure the name of your organisation is stated on the application form.
- If information from the application form will be used for any other purpose than to recruit for a specific job or passed to anyone else, make sure that this purpose is stated on the application form.

1.2.2 Only seek personal information that is relevant to the recruitment decision to be made.

Key points and possible actions

- Determine whether all questions are relevant for all applicants.
- Consider customising application forms where posts justify the collection of more intrusive personal information.
- Remove or amend any questions which require the applicant to provide information extraneous to the recruitment decision.
- Remove questions that are only relevant to people your organisation goes on to employ (eg banking details) but are not relevant to unsuccessful applicants.

1.2.3 Only request information about an applicant's criminal convictions if and to the extent that the information can be justified in terms of the role offered. If this information is justified, make it clear that spent convictions do not have to be declared, unless the job being filled is covered by the Exceptions Order to the Rehabilitation of Offenders Act 1974.

Key points and possible actions

- Consider whether the collection of information about criminal convictions can be justified for each job for which it is sought.
- Check that it is stated that spent convictions do not have to be declared (unless the job is one covered by the Exceptions Order).
- In any case limit the collection of information to offences that have a direct bearing on suitability for the job in question.

See Supplementary Guidance, page 19 for more information on the Exceptions Order.

1.2.4 Explain the nature of and sources from which information might be obtained about the applicant in addition to the information supplied directly by the applicant.

Key points and possible actions

- Ensure there is a clear statement on the application form or surrounding documents, explaining what information will be sought and from whom.

1.2.5 If sensitive data are collected ensure a sensitive data condition is satisfied.

Key points and possible actions

- Assess whether the collection of sensitive data is relevant to the recruitment process.
- Remove any questions about sensitive data that do not have to be asked at the initial application stage.
- Ensure that the purpose of collecting any relevant sensitive data is explained on the application form or surrounding documentation.
- Ensure the purpose of collection satisfies one of the sensitive data conditions.
- If health information is to be collected, refer to Part 4 of the Code: Information About Workers' Health.

See Supplementary Guidance, page 72 which explains more about the conditions for processing sensitive data.

1.2.6 Provide a secure method for sending applications.

Key points and possible actions

- Ensure that a secure method of transmission is used for sending applications online. (Eg encryption-based software).
- Ensure that once electronic applications are received, they are saved in a directory or drive which has access limited to those involved in the recruitment process.
- Ensure that postal applications are given directly to the person or people processing the applications and that these are stored in a locked drawer.
- Ensure that faxed applications are given directly to the person or people processing the applications and that these are stored in a locked drawer.
- If applications are processed by line managers, make sure line managers are aware of how to gather and store applications.

1.3 Verification

[4.173]

1.3.1 Explain to applicants as early as is reasonably practicable in the recruitment process the nature of the verification process and the methods used to carry it out.

Key points and possible actions

- Ensure that information provided to applicants for example on an application form or associated documents explains what information will be verified and how, including in particular any external sources that will be used.
- Do not force applicants to use their subject access rights to obtain records from another organisation (ie by making such a requirement a condition of getting a job).

1.3.2 Where the need to protect the employer's business, customers, clients or others warrants the collection and verification of details of an applicant's criminal convictions use only a disclosure from the Criminal Records Bureau (CRB) or Disclosure Scotland for this verification.

Key points and possible actions

- Do not attempt to obtain information about criminal convictions by forcing an applicant to use his/her subject access right or from sources other than the CRB, Disclosure Scotland or the applicant.
- Confine the obtaining of a disclosure, as far as practicable, to an applicant it is intended to appoint. Avoid requiring all short-listed applicants to obtain a disclosure.
- Do not share with other employers the information obtained through a "disclosure".
- Abide by the CRB or Disclosure Scotland's Code of Practice in obtaining and handling disclosure information.

1.3.3 If it is necessary to secure the release of documents or information from another organisation or person, obtain a signed consent form from the applicant unless consent to their release has been indicated in some other way.

Key points and possible actions

- Ensure applicants provide signed consent if this is required to secure the release of documents to you from another organisation or person.
- Remember that if you mislead another person or organisation into giving you personal information about an applicant you may be committing a criminal offence.

1.3.4 Give the applicant an opportunity to make representations should any of the checks produce discrepancies.

Key points and possible actions

- Ensure that those staff who are involved in verification in your organisation are aware what to do should inconsistencies emerge between what the applicant said in the application and what your checks have discovered.
- Make sure that in this situation, staff inform the applicant and allow them the opportunity to provide an explanation of the inconsistencies.
- Ensure this feedback to the applicant is incorporated into any recruitment procedures.

1.4 Short-listing

[4.174]
1.4.1 Be consistent in the way personal information is used in the process of short-listing candidates for a particular position.

Key points and possible actions

- Check shortlist methods with sources of good practice such as the Equality and Human Rights Commission.

See Supplementary Guidance page 83 for contact details.

1.4.2 Inform applicants if an automated short-listing system will be used as the sole basis of making a decision. Make provisions to consider representations from applicants about this and to take these into account before making the final decision.

Key points and possible actions

- Ensure all the applicants are informed that an automated system is used as the sole basis of short-listing and of how to make representations against any adverse decision.
- Test and keep the results produced by the system under review to ensure they properly and fairly apply your short-listing criteria to all applicants.

1.4.3 Ensure that tests based on the interpretation of scientific evidence, such as psychological tests, are only used and interpreted by those who have received appropriate training.

Key points and possible actions

- Determine which such tests are used within your organisation.
- Ensure all tests are assessed by properly qualified persons.

1.5 Interviews

[4.175]
1.5.1 Ensure that personal information that is recorded and retained following interview can be justified as relevant to, and necessary for, the recruitment process itself, or for defending the process against challenge.

Key points and possible actions

- Ensure that all interviewers are aware that interviewees may have a right to request access to their interview notes.
- Ensure that all interviewers are given instructions on how to store interview notes.
- Make provisions for interview notes to be destroyed after a reasonable time, allowing the organisation to protect itself from any potential claims such as those for race or sex discrimination.
- Explain to interviewers or those in contact with applicants, how to deal with a request for access to interview notes.

1.6 Pre-employment vetting

[4.176]
1.6.1 Only use vetting where there are particular and significant risks involved to the employer, clients, customers or others, and where there is no less intrusive and reasonably practicable alternative.

Key points and possible actions

- Find out for which jobs, if any, pre-employment vetting takes place.
- Consider whether pre-employment vetting is justified for each of these jobs and whether the information could be obtained in a less intrusive way.
- Wherever practicable obtain relevant information directly from the applicant and, if necessary, verify it rather than undertake pre-employment vetting.
- Do not vet workers just because a customer for your products or services imposes a condition requiring you to do so, unless you can satisfy yourself that the condition is justified.

1.6.2 Only carry out pre-employment vetting on an applicant as at late a stage as is practicable in the recruitment process.

Key points and possible actions

- Ascertain at which point pre-employment vetting takes place and who is subject to it. Eliminate any comprehensive pre-employment vetting that takes place for all shortlisted applicants (only the people selected for the job should be submitted to comprehensive pre-employment vetting).

1.6.3 Make it clear early in the recruitment process that vetting will take place and how it will be conducted.

Key points and possible actions

- Provide information about any vetting that might take place on application forms or other recruitment material. This should explain the nature, extent and range of sources to be used to carry out the vetting.
- Make clear the extent to which you will release information about the applicant to the sources you use.

1.6.4 Only use vetting as a means of obtaining specific information, not as a means of general intelligence gathering. Ensure that the extent and nature of information sought is justified.

Key points and possible actions

- Ensure that there are clearly stated objectives in any vetting process.
- Consider the extent and nature of information that is sought against these objectives.
- Eliminate any vetting that consists of general intelligence-gathering. Ensure that it is clearly focused information that will have a significant bearing on the employment decision.

1.6.5 Only seek information from sources where it is likely that relevant information will be revealed. Only approach the applicant's family or close associates in exceptional cases.

Key points and possible actions

- Ensure that those who will seek the information are briefed about which sources to use, ensuring that those sources are likely to produce relevant information.
- Ensure that if family members or close associates are approached it can be justified by the special nature of the job.

1.6.6 Do not place reliance on information collected from possibly unreliable sources. Allow the applicant to make representations regarding information that will affect the decision to finally appoint.

Key points and possible actions

- Ensure that information that has been collected from a vetting process is evaluated in the light of the reliability of the sources.
- Ensure that no recruitment decision is made solely on the basis of information obtained from a source that may be unreliable.
- Ensure that if information received will lead to the applicant not being appointed, then this will be made known to the applicant.
- Put in place a mechanism for providing this feedback, allowing the applicant to respond and obliging those involved in the recruitment decision to take this response into account.

1.6.7 Where information is collected about a person other than the applicant that affects the other person's privacy, ensure so far as practicable that the other person is made aware of this.

Key points and possible actions

- Ensure that those conducting a vetting process are briefed to avoid discovering information about other people unnecessarily.
- Where substantial personal information has been collected about another person and is to be retained, ensure there is a process in place to inform the other person of this and of how the information will be used.

1.6.8 If it is necessary to secure the release of documents or information from a third party, obtain a signed consent from the applicant.

Key points and possible actions

- If you are asking a third party, such as a previous employer, to disclose confidential personal information to you the third party will need the applicant's permission before doing so.
- It may be easier for you to obtain this permission from the applicant and pass it on to the third party than for the third party to obtain permission directly.

1.7 Retention of recruitment records

[4.177]

1.7.1 Establish and adhere to retention periods for recruitment records that are based on a clear business need.

Key points and possible actions

- Assess who in your organisation retains recruitment records (eg are they held centrally, at departmental level or in the line).
- Ensure that no recruitment record is held beyond the statutory period in which a claim arising from the recruitment process may be brought unless there is a clear business reason for exceeding this period.
- Consider anonymising any recruitment information that is to be held longer than the period necessary for responding to claims.

1.7.2 Destroy information obtained by a vetting exercise as soon as possible, or in any case within 6 months. A record of the result of vetting or verification can be retained.

Key points and possible actions

- Check who in your organisation retains information from vetting. Ensure that vetting records are destroyed after 6 months. Manual records should be shredded and electronic files permanently deleted from the system.
- Inform those responsible for the destruction of this information that they may keep a record that vetting was carried out, the result and the recruitment decision taken.

1.7.3 Consider carefully which information contained on an application form is to be transferred to the worker's employment record. Do not retain information that has no bearing on the on-going employment relationship.

Key points and possible actions

- Check how information is transferred from recruitment records to employment records.
- Ensure those responsible for such transfers only move information relevant to on-going employment to employment files.

1.7.4 Delete information about criminal convictions collected in the course of the recruitment process once it has been verified through a Criminal Records Bureau disclosure unless, in exceptional circumstances, the information is clearly relevant to the on-going employment relationship.

Key points and possible actions

- Make sure it is only recorded whether a check has yielded a satisfactory or an unsatisfactory result. Delete other information.

1.7.5 If it is your practice to do so advise unsuccessful applicants that there is an intention to keep their names on file for future vacancies (if appropriate) and give them the opportunity to have their details removed from the file.

Key points and possible actions

- Ensure that application forms or surrounding documentation tell applicants that, should they be unsuccessful, their details will be kept on file unless they specifically request that this should not be the case.

1.7.6 Ensure that personal information received during the recruitment process are securely stored or are destroyed.

Key points and possible actions

- Assess who in your organisation presently processes recruitment information.
- Inform them that manual records should be kept securely, for example in a locked filing cabinet.
- Make sure that electronic files are kept securely, for example by using passwords and other technical security measures.

PART 2: EMPLOYMENT RECORDS

ABOUT PART 2 OF THE CODE

Data protection in employment records

[4.178]

Running a business necessarily involves keeping records about workers. Such records will contain information that is personal in nature and can affect a worker's privacy. The Act does not prevent an employer from collecting, maintaining and using records about workers but helps to strike a balance between the employer's need to keep records and the worker's right to respect for his or her private life. This part of the Code will assist employers not only to comply with the law but also to follow good records management practice.

What does this part of the code cover?

This part of the Code covers all aspects of the collection, holding and use of employment records from the initial obtaining of information once a worker has been employed or engaged through to the ultimate deletion of the former worker's record. It also deals with the rights of job applicants as well as workers to access to information the employer keeps about them. It does not though deal in detail with the collection and use of health information. This is covered in Part 4.

Some recommendations in the Code are only likely to be of relevance to those involved in particular activities such as marketing to their workers or to those who find themselves in particular situations such as a business merger or acquisition. For this reason some sub sections are likely to be of relevance mainly to larger organisations.

Sickness and injury records

For the purposes of this Code it is necessary to distinguish between records that include "sensitive data" and those that do not. The term 'sickness record' is therefore used to describe a record which contains details of the illness or condition responsible for a worker's absence. Similarly, an injury record is a record which contains details of the injury suffered. The term 'absence record' is used to describe a record that may give the reason for absence as 'sickness' or 'accident' but does not include any reference to specific medical conditions.

Many employers keep accident records. Such a record will only be an "injury record" if it includes details of the injury suffered by an identifiable worker.

Sickness and injury records include information about workers' physical or mental health. The holding of sickness or injury records will therefore involve the processing of sensitive personal data. This means one of the conditions for processing sensitive personal data must be satisfied.

Employers are advised as far as practicable to restrict their record keeping to absence records rather than sickness or injury records.

See Supplementary Guidance page 72 which explains more about the conditions for processing sensitive data.

Workers' access to information about themselves

Workers, like any other individuals, have a right to gain access to information that is kept about them. This right is known as subject access. The right applies, for example, to sickness records, disciplinary or training records, appraisal or performance review notes, e-mails, word-processed documents, e-mail logs, audit trails, information held in general personnel files and interview notes, whether held as computerised files, or as structured paper records. A fee of up to £10 can be charged by the employer for giving access.

Responding to a subject access request involves:

- telling the worker if the organisation keeps any personal information about him or her;
- giving the worker a description of the type of information the organisation keeps, the purposes it is used for and the types of organisations which it may be passed on to, if any;
- showing the worker all the information the organisation keeps about him or her, explaining any codes or other unintelligible terms used;
- providing this information in a hard copy or in readily readable, permanent electronic form unless providing it in that way would involve disproportionate effort or the worker agrees to receive it in some other way;
- providing the worker with any additional information the organisation has as to the source of the information kept about him or her.

There are a number of exemptions from the right of subject access which can be relevant in an employment context.

See Supplementary Guidance – Exemptions from the subject access right page 42 for details.

References

The provision of a reference about a worker from one party, such as a present employer, to another, such as a prospective employer, will generally involve the disclosure of personal data. In considering how the Act applies to such disclosure it is important to establish who the reference is being given by or on behalf of.

The Code therefore distinguishes between a reference given in a personal capacity and one given in a corporate capacity. A corporate reference is one given on behalf of the employer by one of its staff. Many employers have rules about who can give such a reference and what it can include. The employer remains legally responsible for compliance with the Data Protection Act.

A personal reference is one given by a member of staff in an individual capacity. It may refer to work done but it is not given on behalf of the employer. References that are given in a personal capacity do not, at least in data protection terms, incur a liability for the employer.

Under a specific exemption in the Act, a worker does not have the right to gain access to a confidential job reference from the organisation which has given it. However, once the reference is with the organisation to which it was sent then no such specific exemption from the right of access exists. That organisation is though entitled to take steps to protect the identity of third parties such as the author of the reference.

Disclosure requests

Employers regularly receive requests for information about individual workers that come from outside the employer's organisation. An employer has a responsibility to its workers to be cautious in responding to such requests. It risks a breach of the Act if it does not take sufficient care to ensure the interests of its workers are safeguarded. In some cases though the employer has no choice but to respond positively to a request for disclosure. This is where there is a legal obligation to disclose. It is not the Data Protection Act but other laws that create such obligations. Where they do so the Act does not stand in the way of disclosure.

In some other cases the employer will have a choice whether or not to disclose but provided sensitive data are not involved it is clear that the Act will not stand in the way of disclosure. This is where the circumstances of the disclosure are covered by one of the exemptions from the 'non-disclosure provisions' of the Act.

See Supplementary Guidance: Exemptions from non-disclosure page 43 for details.

GOOD PRACTICE RECOMMENDATIONS – PART 2

The parts of the Code referred to in this section are:

2.1 Collecting and keeping general records

[4.179]

2.1.1 Ensure that newly appointed workers are aware of the nature and source of any information stored about them, how it will be used and who it will be disclosed to.

Key points and possible actions

- It is not generally necessary to seek a worker's consent to keep employment records. It will usually be sufficient to ensure that the worker is aware that records are being kept and is given an explanation of the purposes they are kept for and the nature of any intended disclosures.
- It is only if sensitive data are collected that consent may be necessary.
- Decide on how best to inform new workers about how information about them will be held, used and disclosed.
- If your organisation has not done so previously, distribute this information to existing workers.
- In large organisations, randomly check with a sample of workers, that they did in fact receive this information. Rectify any communication gaps.

2.1.2 Inform new workers and remind existing workers about their rights under the Act, including their right of access to the information kept upon them.

Key points and possible actions

- Ensure that information given to new workers includes information about their rights under the Act.
- Set up a system to remind existing workers of their rights.

2.1.3 Ensure that there is a clear and foreseeable need for any information collected from workers and that the information collected actually meets that need.

Key points and possible actions

- Review all forms where information is requested from workers.
- Remove or amend any questions which require the worker to provide information extraneous to your needs.

2.1.4 Provide each worker with a copy of information that may be subject to change, eg personal details such as home address, annually or allow workers to view this on-line. Ask workers to check their records for accuracy and ensure any necessary amendments are made to bring records up-to-date.

Key points and possible actions

- Determine the different types of personal data kept about workers and whether they are likely to be subject to change.
- Decide whether data that change could easily be viewed electronically and make any changes to systems necessary to enable this.
- Ensure that the system restricts access to individuals' records so that each worker can only get access to his or her own record.
- If it is only possible for workers to view data manually, consider how this can best be done.
- Make provision to amend any details that are incorrect on individual workers' files.

2.1.5 Incorporate accuracy, consistency and validity checks into systems.

Key points and possible actions

- Review computerised systems to see if accuracy checks can be easily built in.

- Put in place arrangements to ensure that when systems are updated or new systems purchased they facilitate data protection compliance.
- Remember that legal responsibility for data protection compliance rests with users rather than suppliers of systems.

2.2 Security

[4.180]
2.2.1 Apply security standards that take account of the risks of unauthorised access to, accidental loss of, destruction of, or damage to employment records.

Key points and possible actions

- BS 7799: 1995 (Code of Practice for Information Security Management) provides guidance which, if followed, should address the main security risks.
- Obtain a copy of BS7799 if you do not have one already and compare its recommendations to your own existing procedures.
- Put in place measures to rectify any shortfalls, bearing in mind that not all controls will be relevant to all organisations.

2.2.2 Institute a system of secure cabinets, access controls and passwords to ensure that staff can only gain access to employment records where they have a legitimate business need to do so.

Key points and possible actions

- Review who in your organisation has access to employment records and determine whether it is necessary for everyone who currently has access to retain it.
- Remove access rights from those who have unnecessary or over-extensive access to personal information about others.
- Make sure manual files that hold personal information are securely held with locks and only those who should have access retain the key.
- In the case of computerised records, ensure that passwords or similar controls are set up to limit unauthorised access.

2.2.3 Use the audit trail capabilities of automated systems to track who accesses and amends personal information.

Key points and possible actions

- Check whether computerised systems that retain personal information currently have audit trail capabilities. If they do, check that the audit trail is enabled.
- If they do not, see if it would be possible to create audit trails of who accesses and amends personal information.
- If you have a system with audit trails, ensure that regular checks occur to detect unauthorised or suspicious use. Set up a procedure to investigate patterns of unusual or unauthorised access of personal information.

2.2.4 Take steps to ensure the reliability of staff that have access to workers' records.

Key points and possible actions

- Carry out background checks on staff that will have access to workers' records, for example by taking up references.
- Review the contracts of workers who deal with personal information to ensure they include confidentiality clauses concerning the unauthorised disclosure and use of personal information.
- Set up induction training for these staff that contains explanation about their responsibilities. Organise refresher training as and when necessary.

2.2.5 Ensure that if employment records are taken off-site, eg on laptop computers, this is controlled. Make sure only the necessary information is taken and there are security rules for staff to follow.

Key points and possible actions

- Formulate a procedure for taking laptop computers off-site (or review the existing procedure). Include points regarding the information that may be taken off-site, security of passwords and keeping the laptop in view or secured at all times.
- Inform all workers, including senior staff, of the procedure.

2.2.6 Take account of the risks of transmitting confidential worker information by fax or e-mail. Only transmit information between locations if a secure network or comparable arrangements are in place.

Key points and possible actions

- Check that your security policy properly addresses the risk of sending and receiving worker information by e-mail or fax and review the relevant procedures.
- Ensure that all managers use a secure system if workers' records are to be transmitted by fax.
- In the case of e-mail deploy some technical means of ensuring security, such as effective password protection and encryption.
- Advise all managers about permanently deleting e-mails that contain personal information about workers from their work-stations.

- Check whether deleted e-mails will still be kept on a server. Wherever possible ensure these too can be permanently deleted. In any case, restrict access to them.

2.3 Sickness and injury records

[4.181]
2.3.1 Where possible keep sickness and injury records separate from absence and accident records. Do not use sickness records for a particular purpose when records of absence could be used instead.

Key points and possible actions

- Review how sickness and accident records are currently kept.
- If necessary, change the way information on sickness and accidents is kept so that information on workers' health is not accessed when only information on absence or the circumstances of an accident at work is needed.
- Inform those accessing both sickness/injury and absence records of when it is and is not necessary to access the full sickness or injury records.

2.3.2 Ensure that the holding and use of sickness and injury records satisfies a sensitive data condition.

Key points and possible actions

- Check current practices on the use of sickness and injury records against the sensitive data conditions in the Code.
- Take any remedial action necessary including restricting the purposes for which records can be used and/or deleting records if no condition can be satisfied.
- Inform those handling sickness and injury records of any changes in procedures or practices.

See Supplementary Guidance page 72 which explains more about the sensitive data conditions.

2.3.3 Only disclose information from sickness or injury records about an identifiable worker's illness, medical condition or injury where there is a legal obligation to do so, where it is necessary for legal proceedings or where the worker has given explicit consent to the disclosure.

Key points and possible actions

- Ensure that all those who deal with workers' sickness or injury records are aware in which circumstances there may be a legal obligation to disclose.
- Ensure when appropriate, written consent is obtained from the worker.

2.3.4 Do not make the sickness, injury or absence records of individual workers available to other workers unless it is necessary for them to do their jobs.

Key points and possible actions

- Managers can be provided with information about those who work for them in so far as this is necessary for them to carry out their managerial roles.
- No 'league tables' of individual records should be published.
- Ensure that managers are aware of the sensitive nature of sickness and injury records.

2.4 Pension and insurance schemes

[4.182]
Pension or insurance-based schemes such as those offering private medical care are usually controlled by a third party but can be administered in-house. Some employers also insure their business against sickness by key workers. These recommendations are directed at employers who are party to such schemes rather than at insurance companies or pensions providers.

2.4.1 Do not access personal information required by a third party to administer a scheme, in order to use it for general employment purposes.

Key points and possible actions

- Identify and review schemes currently in operation in your business.
- Identify where information could possibly 'leak' from a scheme to be used for other employment purposes.
- Identify ways of stopping this occurring, for example by passing information in sealed envelopes.

2.4.2 Limit your exchange of information with a scheme provider to the minimum necessary for operation of the scheme bearing in mind the scheme's funding obligations.

Key points and possible actions

- Remember that if information on a worker's sickness, injury or other sensitive data is exchanged a sensitive data condition must be satisfied.
- Bear in mind that your funding of a scheme does not give you a right to receive information about individual scheme members beyond that necessary for the operation of the scheme.
- Review the exchange of information with any scheme providers.
- Identify and eliminate any personal information passed to you by the scheme provider that is not essential to the operation of the scheme.

2.4.3 Do not use information gained from the internal trustees or administrators of pension schemes for general employment purposes.

Key points and possible actions

- Inform trustees and administrators of their general data protection responsibilities. In particular make sure they know they must not use personal information acquired in their capacity as trustee or administrator in their capacity as employer.

2.4.4 If your business takes on the role of broker or your staff act as group secretary for a private medical insurance scheme, ensure that personal information gathered is kept to minimum, limit access to the information and do not use it for general employment purposes.

Key points and possible actions

- Consider carefully what information is actually needed to administer the scheme.
- Limit access to personal data arising from the administration of the scheme and ensure that information gathered in this context is not used for any other purposes.

2.4.5 Ensure that when a worker joins a health or insurance scheme it is made clear what, if any, information is passed between the scheme controller and the employer and how it will be used.

Key points and possible actions

- Assess the information given to workers when they join a health or insurance scheme.
- If no specific mention is made about the transfer of information, amend the documentation about the scheme accordingly.

2.5 Equal opportunities monitoring

[4.183]

2.5.1 Information about a worker's ethnic origin, disability, religion or sexual orientation is sensitive personal data. Ensure that equal opportunities monitoring of these characteristics satisfies a sensitive data condition.

Key points and possible actions

- Check your organisation's current equal opportunities monitoring against the sensitive data conditions in the Code.
- Make any necessary changes to the monitoring procedure to ensure that a sensitive data condition can always be satisfied.

See Supplementary Guidance page 72 for conditions to be satisfied.

2.5.2 Only use information that identifies individual workers where this is necessary to carry out meaningful equal opportunities monitoring. Where practicable, keep the information collected in an anonymised form.

Key points and possible actions

- Review current practices. Check whether any monitoring form gives the impression that information is anonymous, when in fact, it can be traced back to individuals.
- If identifiable information is held but it can be anonymised, do this.
- When there is no reasonable alternative but to be able to identify individuals, check whether the monitoring form states this and explains how the information is to be used.
- Ensure that identifiable information collected for equal opportunities monitoring is not used for any other purposes.
- Make any necessary changes to procedures and ensure that staff involved in monitoring understand why these changes have been made.

2.5.3 Ensure questions are designed so that the personal information collected through them is accurate and not excessive.

Key points and possible actions

- Check that questions allow people to identify themselves accurately. For example, in ethnic origin monitoring, do not limit the range of choices given so that workers are forced to make a choice that does not properly describe them.
- If you assign workers to categories ensure the record is clear that it is your assumption and not a matter of fact.

2.6 Marketing

[4.184]

2.6.1 Inform new workers if your organisation intends to use their personal information to deliver advertising or marketing messages to them. Give workers a clear opportunity to object (an 'opt-out') and respect any objections whenever received.

Key points and possible actions

- Review whether your business markets its, or anyone else's, products or services to current or former workers.
- Ensure that any new worker who will receive marketing information from your company has been informed that this will happen.

- Ensure that a clear procedure for 'opting-out' is made known to all workers.

2.6.2 Do not disclose workers' details to other organisations for their marketing unless individual workers have positively and freely indicated their agreement (an 'opt-in').

Key points and possible actions

- Review whether your business discloses workers' details. If so, put in place a procedure to ensure that a worker's details are not passed on until you have received a positive indication of agreement from him or her.

2.6.3 If you intend to use details of existing workers for marketing for the first time either in ways that were not explained when they first joined or that they would not expect, do not proceed until individual workers have positively and freely indicated their agreement (an 'opt-in').

Key points and possible actions

- When considering this type of campaign, construct an approval form to send to workers. Only direct material to those workers who have given a positive indication of agreement.
- Enclosing details of particular offers within a communication that workers will receive anyway, for example in a pay-slip, is acceptable as long as the offer includes an explanation of how to object.

2.7 Fraud detection

[4.185]
Public sector employers, in particular, use workers' records in the prevention and detection of fraud, for example, in order to check that they are not paying state benefits to those who by virtue of their employment are not entitled to receive them. Such exercises involve the electronic comparison of data sets held for different purposes in order to identify inconsistencies or discrepancies which may indicate fraud. This is known as data matching.

2.7.1 Consult workers, and/or trade unions or other representatives before starting a data matching exercise.

Key points and possible actions

- Inform trade unions and other workers' representatives of any proposed data matching exercise.
- Discuss how the plan will work in detail and take account of legitimate concerns raised before starting the exercise.

2.7.2 Inform new workers of the use of payroll or other information in fraud prevention exercises and remind them of this periodically.

Key points and possible actions

- Explain how fraud prevention exercises operate to new workers as part of information given about data protection.
- Set up regular reminders to workers on how the data matching exercise works – eg prior to the start of each new exercise.

2.7.3 Do not disclose worker information to other organisations for the prevention or detection of fraud unless:—

- you are required by law to make the disclosure, or
- you believe that failure to disclose, in a particular instance, is likely to prejudice the prevention or detection of crime, or
- the disclosure is provided for in workers' contracts of employment.

Key points and possible actions

- Ensure staff who would be approached by outside agencies for this type of information, understand the rules of disclosure.

2.8 Workers' access to information about themselves

[4.186]
Workers, like any other individuals, have a right to gain access to information that is kept about them. This right is known as subject access.

2.8.1 Establish a system that enables your organisation to recognise a subject access request and to locate all the information about a worker in order to be able to respond promptly and in any case within 40 calendar days of receiving a request.

Key points and possible actions

- Assess what personal information about workers is in existence and who is responsible for it (**See recommendation 0.3** ***ante***.)
- Ensure that the information is accessible.
- Establish who in the organisation is responsible for responding to subject access requests.
- Ensure that all workers who are likely to receive subject access requests can recognise them and know who to pass them to.
- Have a checklist in place listing all places where personal information might be held that should be checked.

- Use the checklist to gather all personal information in time to enable a response within 40 days.

2.8.2 Check the identity of anyone making a subject access request to ensure information is only given to the person entitled to it.

Key points and possible actions

- In smaller organisations where workers make access requests in person, identity checks may not be necessary, but in large organisations it should not simply be assumed all requests are genuine.
- Brief anyone responsible for responding to a subject access request on how to check the identity of the person making it.

2.8.3 Provide the worker with a hard copy of the information kept, making clear any codes used and the sources of the information.

Key points and possible actions

- In the checklist used to gather all personal information include a check to ensure that the information supplied is intelligible, that it includes sources and that if at all possible it is in hard copy form.
- Although a hard copy of the subject access information does not have to be provided if this would involve "disproportionate effort" some form of access to the information still has to be given.

2.8.4 Make a judgement as to what information it is reasonable to withhold concerning the identities of third parties.

Key points and possible actions

- Information released to a worker could include information that enables a third party such as another worker to be identified. The employer has to balance the worker's right to know against an expectation of privacy that the third party might have.
- You can use the guidance on Access when Information about Third Parties is involved on page 40 of the Supplementary Guidance to help you make the necessary judgement.
- Brief those handling subject access requests on how to make decisions concerning third party information.

2.8.5 Inform managers and other relevant people in the organisation of the nature of information that will be released to individuals who make subject access requests.

Key points and possible actions

- Managers should be made aware of the extent to which information relating to them might be released to workers.
- If managers and others are aware of the extent and nature of the information that an individual could gain access to it should encourage them to record only what is truly relevant and useful.

2.8.6 Ensure that on request, promptly and in any event within 40 calendar days, workers are provided with a statement of how any automated decision-making process, to which they are subject, is used, and how it works.

Key points and possible actions

- Determine whether your organisation has any automated systems which are used as the sole basis for decision-making, for example during short-listing.
- If so, document how the system works and the basis of its decisions.
- Make this information available to those who are responsible for responding to requests about the process and make sure that they are aware of the requirement to respond within 40 calendar days.

2.8.7 When purchasing a computerised system ensure that the system enables you to retrieve all the information relating to an individual worker without difficulty.

Key points and possible actions

- Ensure that the supplier of a system that you will use to take automated decisions about workers provides the information needed to enable you to respond fully to requests for information about how the system works.
- Put in place arrangements to ensure that when systems are updated or new systems purchased they facilitate responses to subject access requests.

2.9 References

[4.187]

The provision of a reference about a worker from one party, such as a present employer, to another, such as a prospective employer, will generally involve the disclosure of personal data. This sub section of the Code applies not only to references given to prospective employers, but also references given in other circumstances, for example character references given in connection with legal proceedings or financial references given in connection with a worker's application for a mortgage.

References Given:

2.9.1 Set out a clear company policy stating who can give corporate references, in what circumstances, and the policy that applies to the granting of access to them. Make anyone who is likely to become a referee aware of this policy.

Key points and possible actions

- Determine who is allowed to give corporate references, this may, for example, be done by grade. Check whether your organisation distinguishes between corporate and personal references. If not, consider doing so.
- Draw up a policy explaining how reference requests should be handled, outlining the types of information that can be provided and the extent to which workers are given access. Ensure the policy is brought to the attention of anyone who is likely to receive a reference request.

2.9.2 Do not provide confidential references about a worker unless you are sure that this is the worker's wish.

Key points and possible actions

- As part of the policy, include a requirement that all those giving corporate references must be satisfied that the worker wishes the reference to be provided.
- As part of an Exit Policy, include on file a record of whether the worker wishes references to be provided after he/she has left.

References received:

2.9.3 When responding to a request from a worker to see his or her own reference and the reference enables a third party to be identified, make a judgement as to what information it is reasonable to withhold.

Key points and possible actions

- You can use the guidance on Access when Information about Third Parties is Involved on page 40 of the Supplementary Guidance to help you make this judgement.
- Brief those responsible for responding to requests for access to references received on how to make decisions concerning third party information.

2.10 Disclosure requests

[4.188]

This is concerned with requests for information about individual workers that come from outside the employer's organisation.

2.10.1 Establish a disclosure policy to tell staff who are likely to receive requests for information about workers how to respond, and to where they should refer requests that fall outside the policy rules.

Key points and possible actions

- Distribute information, based on this Code, on how to handle disclosure requests and ensure that all those likely to handle such requests receive the information.
- Give examples of situations where a member of staff might need to refer a request to a higher authority within the organisation.
- Provide contact details of whom staff should contact, should they be unsure of how to deal with a disclosure request.

2.10.2 Ensure that disclosure decisions that are not covered by clear policy rules are only taken by staff who are familiar with the Act and this Code, and who are able to give the decision proper consideration.

Key points and possible actions

- Determine who will be responsible for dealing with disclosure requests not covered by the policy.
- Organise any necessary training for those who will take on this role.

2.10.3 Unless you are under a legal obligation to do so, only disclose information about a worker where you conclude that in all the circumstances it is right to do so.

Key points and possible actions

- In some cases you will be under a legal obligation to disclose. Where this is the case you have no choice but to disclose. The Act does not stand in your way provided that you disclose no more than you are obliged to.
- In some cases you will not be under an obligation to disclose but you will be able to rely on an exemption in the Act if you choose to do so. This is most likely to arise in the case of criminal or tax investigations or where legal action is involved.
- Where you can relay on an exemption in the Act you still need to take care with the disclosure of confidential or sensitive information.
- In other cases you could breach the Act if you disclose. Only disclose, if in all the circumstances you are satisfied that it is fair to do so. Bear in mind that the duty of fairness is owed primarily to the worker. Where possible seek and take account of the workers' views.
- Only disclose confidential information if the worker has clearly agreed or you are satisfied that despite the duty of confidence the worker's interest or the wider public interest justifies disclosure.
- Ensure that if you intend to disclose sensitive personal data a sensitive data condition is satisfied.

2.10.4 Where a disclosure is requested in an emergency, make a careful decision as to whether to disclose, considering the nature of the information being requested and the likely impact on the individual of not providing it.

Key points and possible actions

- Make sure staff who are likely to receive such requests know whether they can handle them themselves or if not, who to refer them to. If they handle them themselves make them aware of their responsibility to assess the nature of the emergency and determine whether the request could be submitted in writing.

2.10.5 Make staff aware that those seeking information sometimes use deception to gain access to it. Ensure that they check the legitimacy of any request and the identity and authority of the person making it.

Key points and possible actions

- As part of the disclosure policy, make it a requirement that staff check the identity of any person making a request, the authority of the individual concerned and the basis for the request.
- Ensure that when a request is made on the basis of a stated legal obligation, that it is received in writing, spelling out the legal obligation on which it is based. If the stated legal obligation is in doubt check it against the law.

2.10.6 Where the disclosure involves a transfer of information about a worker to a country outside the European Economic Area (EEA), ensure that there is a proper legal basis for making the transfer.

Key points and possible actions

- The Act restricts the transfer of personal information outside the EEA.
- Review the Information Commissioner's guidance at www.ico.org.uk, if you intend to pass workers' information outside the EEA.
- Keep a record of the legal basis on which you make the transfer.

2.10.7 Inform the worker before or as soon as is practicable after a request has been received that a non-regular disclosure is to be made, unless prevented by law from doing so, or unless this would constitute a "tip off" prejudicing a criminal or tax investigation.

Key points and possible actions

- For each non-regular disclosure, make a judgment as to whether the worker can be informed and whether a copy of the information can be provided to him or her. (A reminder of this could be placed in any system for handling non-regular disclosures.)
- In cases where the information can be provided to the worker do so as soon as possible.

2.10.8 Keep a record of non-regular disclosures. Regularly check and review this record to ensure that the requirements of the Act are being satisfied.

Key points and possible actions

- Set up a system for non-regular disclosures recording the details of the person who made the disclosure, the person who authorised it, the person requesting the disclosure, the reasons for the disclosure, the information disclosed and the date and time.
- Also set up a system to regularly check and review this record.

2.11 Publication and other disclosures

[4.189]

2.11.1 If publishing information about workers ensure that:

- there is a legal obligation to do so, or
- the information is clearly not intrusive, or
- the worker has consented to disclosure, or
- the information is in a form that does not identify individual workers.

Key points and possible actions

- An employer must balance the benefits of publishing information about workers with the reasonable expectations of its workers that their employer will respect the privacy of their personal information.
- Assess the current information published about named workers (eg in annual reports or on the website or in other publications) and the basis on which this takes place.
- Determine whether it is necessary to obtain consent from workers who are named and if so, set up an arrangement for obtaining consent from workers who are named in publications in the future.

2.11.2 Where information about workers is published on the basis of consent, ensure that when the worker gives consent he or she is made aware of the extent of information that will be published, how it will be published and the implications of this.

Key points and possible actions

- In any arrangement for obtaining consent for the publication of information on named workers, ensure that the worker is made aware of the full extent of any information to be published and where it is to be published. This is particularly important if information is to be published on the internet.

2.11.3 Personal information about workers should only be supplied to a trade union for its recruitment purposes if:

- the trade union is recognised by the employer,
- the information is limited to that necessary to enable a recruitment approach, and
- each worker has been previously told that this will happen and has been given a clear opportunity to object.

Key points and possible actions

- If your organisation has a recognised trade union that is requesting personal information about workers for a recruitment drive, inform all workers and give them an opportunity to object if they so wish.

2.11.4 Where staffing information is supplied to trade unions in the course of collective bargaining, ensure the information is such that individual workers cannot be identified.

Key points and possible actions

- Review your arrangements for the supply of information in connection with collective bargaining to ensure that in future all information on workers is supplied in an anonymised form.

2.12 Merger, acquisition, and business re-organisation

[4.190]
Business mergers and acquisitions will generally involve the disclosure of information about workers. This may take place during evaluation of assets and liabilities prior to the final merger or acquisition decision. Once a decision has been made disclosure is also likely to take place either in the run-up to or at the time of the actual merger or acquisition. A similar situation arises in business re-organisations that involve the transfer of workers' employment from one legal entity to another. This sub-section of the Code will be relevant to such situations.

2.12.1 Ensure, wherever practicable, that information handed over to another organisation in connection with a prospective acquisition, merger or business re-organisation is anonymised.

Key points and possible actions

- Ensure that in any merger or acquisition situation, those responsible for negotiation are aware of the Code, including its provisions on sensitive data.
- Assess any request for personal information from the other organisation. If at all possible, limit the information given to anonymised details.

2.12.2 Only hand over personal information prior to a final merger or acquisition decision after securing assurances that it will be used solely for the evaluation of assets and liabilities, it will be treated in confidence and will not be disclosed to other parties, and it will be destroyed or returned after use.

Key points and possible actions

- Remind those negotiating that they must receive strict assurances about how personal information will be used and what will happen to it should discussions end.
- Consider setting up a "data room" with accompanying rules of access.

2.12.3 Unless it is impractical to do so, tell workers if their employment records are to be disclosed to another organisation before an acquisition, merger or re-organisation takes place. If the acquisition, merger or re-organisation proceeds make sure workers are aware of the extent to which their records are to be transferred to the new employer.

Key points and possible actions

- In some circumstances "insider trading" or similar restrictions will apply. An example is where providing an explanation to workers would alert them to the possibility of a takeover of which they would otherwise be unaware and could thereby affect the price of a company's shares. The obligation to provide an explanation to workers is lifted in such circumstances.

2.12.4 Where a merger, acquisition or re-organisation involves a transfer of information about a worker to a country outside the European Economic Area (EEA) ensure that there is a proper basis for making the transfer.

Key points and possible actions

- Review the Information Commissioner's guidance at www.ico.org.uk: if you intend to pass workers' information outside the EEA.
- Check that there is a legal basis for the transfer that you intend to make.

2.12.5 New employers should ensure that the records they hold as a result of a merger, acquisition or re-organisation do not include excessive information, and are accurate and relevant.

Key points and possible actions

- Remember that a new employer's use of workers' information acquired as the result of a merger, acquisition or re-organisation is constrained by the expectations the workers will have from their former employer's use of information.
- When taking over an organisation assess what personal information you now hold as outlined in 0.3 and 0.4 (*ante*).

2.13 Discipline, grievance and dismissal

[4.191]
2.13.1 Remember that the Data Protection Act applies to personal information processed in relation to discipline, grievance and dismissal proceedings.

Key points and possible actions

- Assess your organisation's disciplinary procedures and grievance procedures. Consider whether they need to be amended in the light of the Code.
- Ensure that managers are aware that subject access rights apply even if responding to a request might impact on a disciplinary or grievance investigation or on forthcoming proceedings, unless responding would be likely to prejudice a criminal investigation.
- Ensure that those involved in investigating disciplinary matters or grievances are aware that they must not gather information by deception.
- Ensure that records used in the course of proceedings are of good enough quality to support any conclusion drawn from them.
- Ensure that all records are kept securely.
- Check that unsubstantiated allegations have been removed unless there are exceptional reasons for retaining some record.

2.13.2 Do not access or use information you keep about workers merely because it might have some relevance to a disciplinary or grievance investigation if access or use would be either:

- incompatible with the purpose(s) you obtained the information for, or
- disproportionate to the seriousness of the matter under investigation.

Key points and possible actions

- Make those in the organisation who are likely to carry out investigations aware that they do not have an unrestricted right of access to all information held about workers under investigation.
- Put in place a system to ensure that decisions on whether access is justified take into account the provisions of this Code and the Act.

2.13.3 Ensure that there are clear procedures on how "spent" disciplinary warnings are handled.

Key points and possible actions

- Determine what is meant by a "spent" warning in your organisation. Assess the disciplinary procedure and decide whether it needs to be amended to clarify what happens once a warning period has expired.
- Set up a diary system, either manual or computerised, to remove spent warnings from individual's records, if this is a requirement of your procedure.

2.13.4 Ensure that when employment is terminated the reason for this is accurately recorded, and that the record reflects properly what the worker has been told about the termination.

Key points and possible actions

- Ensure that if a worker has resigned, even if asked to do so, that this is recorded on his or her record, as "resigned" rather than "dismissed".

2.14 Outsourcing data processing

[4.192]
Frequently, organisations do not process all the information they hold on workers themselves but outsource this to other organisations. Such organisations are termed 'data processors' in the Data Protection Act.

2.14.1 Satisfy yourself that any data processor you choose adopts appropriate security measures both in terms of the technology it uses and how it is managed.

Key points and possible actions

- Check whether the data processor has in place appropriate security measures. Is it, for example, certified to BS7799?
- Check that the processor actually puts their security measures into practice.

2.14.2 Have in place a written contract with any data processor you choose that requires it to process personal information only on your instructions, and to maintain appropriate security.

Key points and possible actions

- If there is no contract, put one in place.
- Check that any contract you have with a data processor includes clauses ensuring proper data security measures.

2.14.3 Where the use of a data processor would involve a transfer of information about a worker to a country outside the European Economic Area (EEA), ensure that there is a proper basis for making the transfer.

Key points and possible actions

- Review the Information Commissioner guidelines at www.ico.org.uk: if you intend to pass workers' information outside the EEA.
- Check that there is a legal basis for the transfer that you intend to make.

2.15 Retention of records

[4.193]

See Part 1: Recruitment and Selection for specific recommendations on retention of recruitment records.

2.15.1 Establish and adhere to standard retention times for the various categories of information to be held on the records of workers and former workers. Base the retention times on business need taking into account relevant professional guidelines.

Key points and possible actions

- Remember that the Act does not override any statutory requirement to retain records, for example, in relation to income tax or certain aspects of health and safety.
- Only retain information on records that is still needed; eliminate personal information that is no longer of any relevance, once the employment relationship has ended.
- As far as possible set standard retention times for categories of information held in employment records. Consider basing these on a risk analysis approach.
- Assess who in your organisation retains employment records (**see 0.3** *ante*). Make sure no one retains information beyond the standard retention times unless there is a sound business reason for doing so.
- If possible, set up a computerised system which flags information retained for more than a certain time as due for review or deletion.

2.15.2 Anonymise any information about workers and former workers where practicable.

Key points and possible actions

- Where statistical information only is required, anonymised records should be sufficient.

2.15.3 If the holding of any information on criminal convictions of workers is justified, ensure that the information is deleted once the conviction is 'spent' under the Rehabilitation of Offenders Act.

Key points and possible actions

- Use a computerised or manual system to ensure spent convictions are deleted from the system.
- Identify if your organisation may be justified in making exceptions to this, for example, certain convictions held in connection with workers who work with children.

2.15.4 Ensure that records which are to be disposed of are securely and effectively destroyed.

Key points and possible actions

- Review arrangements for dealing with old records to ensure they are securely disposed of and advise anyone holding employment records of these arrangements for disposal.
- Do not assume that pressing the "delete" key on a computer based system necessarily removes a record completely from the system. Check that computer records that are to be deleted are in practice removed completely.
- Make sure that computer equipment that has held employment records is never sold on unless you are sure the records have been fully removed.

PART 3: MONITORING AT WORK

ABOUT PART 3 OF THE CODE

Data protection and monitoring at work

[4.194]

A number of the requirements of the Data Protection Act will come into play whenever an employer wishes to monitor workers. The Act does not prevent an employer from monitoring workers, but such monitoring must be done in a way which is consistent with the Act. Employers – especially in the public sector – must also bear in mind Article 8 of the European Convention on Human Rights which creates a right to respect for private and family life and for correspondence.

How does the Data Protection Act regulate monitoring?

Monitoring is a recognised component of the employment relationship. Most employers will make some checks on the quantity and quality of work produced by their workers. Workers will generally expect this. Many employers carry out monitoring to safeguard workers, as well as to protect their own interests or those of their customers. For example, monitoring may take place to ensure that those in hazardous environments are not being put at risk through the adoption of unsafe working practices. Monitoring arrangements may equally be part of the security mechanisms used to protect personal information. In other cases, for example in the context of some financial services, the employer may be under legal or regulatory obligations which it can only realistically fulfil if it undertakes some monitoring. However where monitoring goes beyond one individual simply watching another and involves the manual recording or any automated processing of personal information, it must be done in a way that is both lawful and fair to workers.

Monitoring may, to varying degrees, have an adverse impact on workers. It may intrude into their private lives, undermine respect for their correspondence or interfere with the relationship of mutual trust and confidence that should exist between them and their employer. The extent to which it does this may not always be immediately obvious. It is not always easy to draw a distinction between work-place and private information. For example monitoring e-mail messages from a worker to an occupational health advisor, or messages between workers and their trade union representatives, can give rise to concern.

In broad terms, what the Act requires is that any adverse impact on workers is justified by the benefits to the employer and others. This Code is designed to help employers determine when this might be the case.

What does this part of the Code cover?

This part of the Code applies where activities that are commonly referred to as "monitoring" are taking place or are planned. This means activities that set out to collect information about workers by keeping them under some form of observation, normally with a view to checking their performance or conduct. This could be done either directly, indirectly, perhaps by examining their work output, or by electronic means.

This part of Code is primarily directed at employers – especially larger organisations – using or planning some form of **systematic monitoring**. This is where the employer monitors all workers or particular groups of workers as a matter of routine, perhaps by using an electronic system to scan all e-mail messages or by installing monitoring devices in all company vehicles.

The Act still applies to **occasional monitoring**. This is where the employer introduces monitoring as a short term measure in response to a particular problem or need, for example by keeping a watch on the e-mails sent by a worker suspected of racial harassment or by installing a hidden camera when workers are suspected of drug dealing on the employer's premises.

This part of the Code deals with both types of monitoring, but it is likely to be of most relevance to employers involved in systematic monitoring, which will generally be larger organisations.

Examples of monitoring

There is no hard-and-fast definition of 'Monitoring' to which this part of the Code applies. Examples of activities addressed in this part of the Code include:

- gathering information through point of sale terminals, to check the efficiency of individual supermarket check-out operators
- recording the activities of workers by means of CCTV cameras, either so that the recordings can be viewed routinely to ensure that health and safety rules are being complied with, or so that they are available to check on workers in the event of a health and safety breach coming to light
- randomly opening up individual workers' e-mails or listening to their voice-mails to look for evidence of malpractice
- using automated checking software to collect information about workers, for example to find out whether particular workers are sending or receiving inappropriate e-mails
- examining logs of websites visited to check that individual workers are not downloading pornography
- keeping recordings of telephone calls made to or from a call centre, either to listen to as part of workers training, or simply to have a record to refer to in the event of a customer complaint about a worker
- systematically checking logs of telephone numbers called to detect use of premium-rate lines
- videoing workers outside the workplace, to collect evidence that they are not in fact sick
- obtaining information through credit reference agencies to check that workers are not in financial difficulties.

Outside this part of the Code

There are other activities that this part of the Code does not specifically address. Most employers will keep some business records that contain information about workers but are not collected primarily to keep a watch on their performance or conduct. An example could be records of customer transactions – including paper records, computer records or recordings of telephone calls. This part of the Code is **not** concerned with occasional access to records of this type in the course of an investigation into a specific problem, such as a complaint from a customer.

See Part 2: Employment Records, para 2.13, for guidance relating to grievance and disciplinary investigations.

Examples of activities not directly addressed in this part of the Code include;

- looking back through customer records in the event of a complaint, to check that the customer was given the correct advice
- checking a collection of e-mails sent by a particular worker which is stored as a record of transactions, in order to ensure the security of the system or to investigate an allegation of malpractice
- looking back through a log of telephone calls made that is kept for billing purposes, to establish whether a worker suspected of disclosing trade secrets has been contacting a competitor.

Impact assessments

The Data Protection Act does not prevent monitoring. Indeed in some cases monitoring might be necessary to satisfy its requirements. However, any adverse impact of monitoring on individuals must be justified by the benefits to the employer and others. We use the term "impact assessment" to describe the process of deciding whether this is the case.

In all but the most straightforward cases, employers are likely to find it helpful to carry out a formal or informal 'impact assessment' to decide if and how to carry out monitoring. This is the means by which employers can judge whether a monitoring arrangement is a proportionate response to the problem it seeks to address. This Code does not prejudge the outcome of the impact assessment. Each will necessarily depend on the particular circumstances of the employer. Nor does the Code attempt to set out for employers the benefits they might gain from monitoring. What it does do is assist employers in identifying and giving appropriate weight to the other factors they should take into account.

An impact assessment involves;

- identifying clearly the **purpose(s)** behind the monitoring arrangement and the benefits it is likely to deliver
- identifying any likely **adverse impact** of the monitoring arrangement
- considering **alternatives** to monitoring or different ways in which it might be carried out
- taking into account the **obligations** that arise from monitoring
- judging whether monitoring is **justified.**

Adverse impact

Identifying any likely adverse impact means taking into account the consequences of monitoring, not only for workers, but also for others who might be affected by it, such as customers. Consider:

- what intrusion, if any, will there be into the private lives of workers and others, or interference with their private e-mails, telephone calls or other correspondence? Bear in mind that the private lives of workers can, and usually will, extend into the workplace.
- to what extent will workers and others know when either they, or information about them, are being monitored and then be in a position to act to limit any intrusion or other adverse impact on themselves?
- whether information that is confidential, private or otherwise sensitive will be seen by those who do not have a business need to know, eg IT workers involved in monitoring e-mail content
- what impact, if any, will there be on the relationship of mutual trust and confidence that should exist between workers and their employer?
- what impact, if any, will there be on other legitimate relationships, eg between trades union members and their representatives?
- what impact, if any, will there be on individuals with professional obligations of confidentiality or secrecy, eg solicitors or doctors?
- whether the monitoring will be oppressive or demeaning.

Alternatives

Considering alternatives, or different methods of monitoring, means asking questions such as:

- can established or new methods of supervision, effective training and/or clear communication from managers, rather than electronic or other systemic monitoring, deliver acceptable results?
- can the investigation of specific incidents or problems be relied on, for example accessing stored e-mails to follow up an allegation of malpractice, rather than undertaking continuous monitoring?
- can monitoring be limited to workers about whom complaints have been received, or about whom there are other grounds to suspect of wrong-doing?
- can monitoring be targeted at areas of highest risk, eg can it be directed at a few individuals whose jobs mean they pose a particular risk to the business rather than at everyone?
- can monitoring be automated? If so, will it be less intrusive, eg does it mean that private information will be 'seen' only by a machine rather than by other workers?
- can spot-checks or audit be undertaken instead of using continuous monitoring? Remember though that continuous automated monitoring could be less intrusive than spot-check or audit that involves human intervention.

Obligations

Taking into account the obligations that arise from monitoring means considering such matters as:

- whether and how workers will be notified about the monitoring arrangements
- how information about workers collected through monitoring will be kept securely and handled in accordance with the Act.

See Part 2 – Employment Records, para 2.2, for more information on security requirements.

- the implications of the rights that individuals have to obtain a copy of information about them that has been collected through monitoring.

See Part 2 – Employment Records, para 2.8, which explains more about rights to access.

Is monitoring justified?

Making a conscious decision as to whether the current or proposed method of monitoring is justified involves;

- establishing the benefits of the method of monitoring

- considering any alternative method of monitoring
- weighing these benefits against any adverse impact
- placing particular emphasis on the need to be fair to individual workers
- ensuring, particularly where monitoring electronic communications is involved, that any intrusion is no more than absolutely necessary
- bearing in mind that significant intrusion into the private lives of individuals will not normally be justified unless the employer's business is at real risk of serious damage
- taking into account the results of consultation with trade unions or other representatives, if any, or with workers themselves.

See Supplementary Guidance page 57 for a chart to help assess the degree of intrusiveness involved in monitoring the content of various types of communication

Making an impact assessment need not be a complicated or onerous process. It will often be enough for an employer to make a simple mental evaluation of the risks faced by his or her business and to assess whether the carrying out of monitoring would reduce or eradicate those risks. In other cases the impact assessment will be more complicated, for example where an employer faces a number of different risks of varying degrees of seriousness. In such cases appropriate documentation would be advisable.

Is a worker's consent needed?

There are limitations as to how far consent can be relied on in the employment context to justify the processing of personal information. To be valid, for the purposes of the Data Protection Act, consent must be "freely given", which may not be the case in the employment environment. Once given, consent can be withdrawn. In any case, employers who can justify monitoring on the basis of an impact assessment will not generally need the consent of individual workers.

Are there special rules for electronic communications?

Electronic communications are broadly telephone calls, fax messages, e-mails and internet access. Monitoring can involve the 'interception' of such communications. The Regulation of Investigatory Powers Act, and the Lawful Business Practice Regulations made under it, set out when interception can take place despite the general rule that interception without consent is against the law. It should be remembered that – whilst the Regulations deal only with interception – the Data Protection Act is concerned more generally with the processing of personal information. Therefore when monitoring involves an interception which results in the recording of personal information an employer will need to satisfy both the Regulations and the requirements of the Data Protection Act.

See Supplementary Guidance page 58, for more details on The Lawful Business Practice Regulations.

GOOD PRACTICE RECOMMENDATIONS – PART 3

The parts of the Code in this section are:

3.1 The general approach to monitoring

3.2 Monitoring electronic communications

3.3 Video and audio monitoring

3.4 Covert monitoring

3.5 In-vehicle monitoring

3.6 Monitoring through information from third parties

3.1 The general approach to monitoring

[4.195]

Core Principles

- It will usually be intrusive to monitor your workers.
- Workers have legitimate expectations that they can keep their personal lives private and that they are also entitled to a degree of privacy in the work environment.
- If employers wish to monitor their workers, they should be clear about the purpose and satisfied that the particular monitoring arrangement is justified by real benefits that will be delivered.
- Workers should be aware of the nature, extent and reasons for any monitoring, unless (exceptionally) covert monitoring is justified.
- In any event, workers' awareness will influence their expectations.

3.1.1 Identify who within the organisation can authorise the monitoring of workers and ensure they are aware of the employer's responsibilities under the Act.

Key points and possible actions

- There are non-compliance risks if line mangers introduce monitoring arrangements without due authority.
- Those who monitor workers, or who can authorise such monitoring, should be briefed on the Act and this Code.

3.1.2 Before monitoring, identify clearly the purpose(s) behind the monitoring and the specific benefits it is likely to bring. Determine – preferably using an impact assessment – whether the likely benefits justify any adverse impact.

Key points and possible actions

- Identify the monitoring that currently takes place in your organisation.
- Identify any monitoring that you plan to implement.
- Consider conducting an impact assessment on either current or planned monitoring based on the guidance ante.

3.1.3 If monitoring is to be used to enforce the organisation's rules and standards make sure that the rules and standards are clearly set out in a policy which also refers to the nature and extent of any associated monitoring. Ensure workers are aware of the policy.

Key points and possible actions

- Identify which of your organisation's rules and standards are enforced partly or wholly through the use of monitoring.
- Ensure that these rules and standards are set out in policies that are clearly communicated to workers.

3.1.4 Tell workers what monitoring is taking place and why, and keep them aware of this, unless covert monitoring is justified.

Key points and possible actions

- Ensure that workers are aware of the nature and extent of any monitoring.
- Set up a system (for example by using the workers handbook or via an intranet) to ensure workers remain aware that monitoring is being conducted.
- Tell workers when significant changes are introduced.

3.1.5 If sensitive information is collected in the course of monitoring, ensure that a sensitive data condition is satisfied.

Key points and possible actions

- If monitoring workers' performance or conduct results in the collection of information on such matters as health, racial origin, trade union activities or sex life, check that at least one of the sensitive data conditions is met. See Supplementary Guidance page 72 which explains more about the conditions for processing sensitive data.

3.1.6 Keep to a minimum those who have access to personal information obtained through monitoring. Subject them to confidentiality and security requirements and ensure that they are properly trained where the nature of the information requires this.

Key points and possible actions

- Assess whether the organisation could reduce the number of staff involved in monitoring workers.
- Consider whether monitoring is more appropriately carried out by security or personnel functions rather than by line managers.
- Ensure that the training for workers who may come across personal information whilst monitoring makes them aware of data protection obligations.

3.1.7 Do not use personal information collected through monitoring for purposes other than those for which the monitoring was introduced unless:

(a) it is clearly in the individual's interest to do so; or
(b) it reveals activity that no employer could reasonably be expected to ignore.

Key points and possible actions

- Ensure that only senior management can authorise the use of personal information obtained through monitoring for new or different purposes.
- Ensure that they are familiar with the Act and the relevant parts of this Code.

3.1.8 If information gathered from monitoring might have an adverse impact on workers, present them with the information and allow them to make representations before taking action.

Key points and possible actions

- Equipment or systems malfunction can cause information collected through monitoring to be misleading or inaccurate. Information can also be misinterpreted or even deliberately falsified.
- Ensure that, within or alongside disciplinary or grievance procedures, workers can see, and if necessary explain or challenge, the results of any monitoring.

3.1.9 Ensure that the right of access of workers to information about them which is kept for, or obtained through, monitoring is not compromised. Monitoring systems must be capable of meeting this and other data protection requirements.

Key points and possible actions

- Assess whether monitoring systems collect information in a way that enables you to respond readily to access requests.
- If they do not, ensure that a mechanism that will allow you to do so is built into the system.
- Check that any electronic monitoring system, bought 'off-the-shelf', has the capability to enable you to meet access requests.

3.1.10 Do not monitor workers just because a customer for your products or services imposes a condition requiring you to do so, unless you can satisfy yourself that the condition is justified.

Key points and possible actions

- Monitoring is not justified simply because it is a condition of business. Such a condition cannot over-ride the employer's obligations to comply with the Act.
- Consider carrying out an impact assessment to assess whether meeting any external stipulation means that your organisation is in breach of the Act. If so, cease monitoring on this basis.

3.2 Monitoring electronic communications

[4.196]

This sub-section deals with the monitoring of telephone, fax, e-mail, voice-mail, internet access and other forms of electronic communication.

3.2.1 If you wish to monitor electronic communications, establish a policy on their use and communicate it to workers – see 'Policy for the use of electronic communications' below.

Key points and possible actions

- If your organisation does not have a policy on the use of electronic communications, decide whether you should establish one.
- Review any existing policy to ensure that it reflects data protection principles.
- Review any existing policies and actual practices to ensure that they are not out of line, eg whether private calls are banned in the policy but generally accepted in practice.
- Check that workers are aware of the policy and if not bring it to their attention.

Policy for the use of electronic communications

Employers should consider integrating the following data protection features into a policy for the use of electronic communications:

- Set out clearly to workers the circumstances in which they may or may not use the employer's telephone systems (including mobile phones), the e-mail system and internet access for private communications.
- Make clear the extent and type of private use that is allowed, for example restrictions on overseas phone calls or limits on the size and/or type of e-mail attachments that they can send or receive.
- In the case of internet access, specify clearly any restrictions on material that can be viewed or copied. A simple ban on 'offensive material' is unlikely to be sufficiently clear for people to know what is and is not allowed. Employers may wish to consider giving examples of the sort of material that is considered offensive, for example material containing racist terminology or nudity.
- Advise workers about the general need to exercise care, about any relevant rules, and about what personal information they are allowed to include in particular types of communication.
- Make clear what alternatives can be used, eg the confidentiality of communications with the company doctor can only be ensured if they are sent by internal post, rather than by e-mail, and are suitably marked.
- Lay down clear rules for private use of the employer's communication equipment when used from home or away from the workplace, eg the use of facilities that enable external dialling into company networks
- Explain the purposes for which any monitoring is conducted, the extent of the monitoring and the means used.
- Outline how the policy is enforced and penalties which exist for a breach of policy.

There may, of course, be other matters that an employer also wants to address in its policy.

3.2.2 Ensure that where monitoring involves the interception of a communication it is not outlawed by the Regulation of Investigatory Powers Act 2000.

Key points and possible actions

- Interception occurs when, in the course of its transmission, the contents of a communication are made available to someone other than the sender or intended recipient. It does not include access to stored e-mails that have been opened.
- The intended recipient may be the business, but it could be a specified individual.
- Check whether any interception is allowed under the Lawful Business Practice Regulations.
- Take any necessary action to bring such monitoring in line with RIPA and these Regulations.

See Supplementary Guidance page 58 for more information about the Lawful Business Practice Regulations.

3.2.3 Consider – preferably using an impact assessment – whether any monitoring of electronic communications can be limited to that necessary to ensure the security of the system and whether it can be automated.

Key points and possible actions

- Automated systems can be used to provide protection from intrusion, malicious code such as viruses and Trojans, and to prevent password misuse. Such systems may be less intrusive than monitoring of communications to or from workers.

3.2.4 If telephone calls or voice-mails are, or are likely to be, monitored, consider – preferably using an impact assessment – whether the benefits justify the adverse impact. If so, inform workers about the nature and extent of such monitoring.

Key points and possible actions

- If telephone calls or voice-mails are monitored, or will be monitored in the future, consider carrying out an impact assessment.
- If voice-mails need to be checked for business calls when workers are away, make sure they know this may happen and that it may be unavoidable that some personal messages are heard.
- In other cases, assess whether it is essential to monitor the content of calls and consider the use of itemised call records instead.
- Ensure that workers are aware of the nature and extent of telephone monitoring.

3.2.5 Ensure that those making calls to, or receiving calls from, workers are aware of any monitoring and the purpose behind it, unless this is obvious.

Key points and possible actions

- Consider the use of recorded messages, informing external callers that calls may be monitored.
- If this is not feasible, encourage workers to tell callers that their conversations may be monitored.

3.2.6 Ensure that workers are aware of the extent to which you receive information about the use of telephone lines in their homes, or mobile phones provided for their personal use, for which your business pays partly or fully. Do not make use of information about private calls for monitoring, unless they reveal activity that no employer could reasonably be expected to ignore.

Key points and possible actions

- Remember that expectations of privacy are likely to be significantly greater at home than in the workplace.
- If any workers using mobiles or home telephone lines, for which you pay, are currently subjected to monitoring ensure that they are aware of the nature and the reasons for monitoring.

3.2.7 If e-mails and/or internet access are, or are likely to be, monitored, consider, preferably using an impact assessment, whether the benefits justify the adverse impact. If so, inform workers about the nature and extent of all e-mail and internet access monitoring.

Key points and possible actions

- If e-mails and/or internet access are presently monitored, or will be monitored in the future, consider carrying out an impact assessment.
- Check that workers are aware of the nature and extent of e-mail and internet access monitoring.

3.2.8 Wherever possible avoid opening e-mails, especially ones that clearly show they are private or personal.

Key points and possible actions

- Ensure that e-mail monitoring is confined to address/heading unless it is essential for a valid and defined reason to examine content.
- Encourage workers to mark any personal e-mails as such and encourage them to tell those who write to them to do the same.
- If workers are allowed to access personal e-mail accounts from the workplace, such e-mails should only be monitored in exceptional circumstances.

3.2.9 Where practicable, and unless this is obvious, ensure that those sending e-mails to workers, as well as workers themselves, are aware of any monitoring and the purpose behind it.

Key points and possible actions

- It may be practicable – for example when soliciting e-mail job applications – to provide information about the nature and extent of monitoring.
- In some cases, those sending e-mails to a work-place address will be aware that monitoring takes place without the need for specific information.

3.2.10 If it is necessary to check the e-mail accounts of workers in their absence, make sure that they are aware that this will happen.

Key points and possible actions

- If e-mail accounts need to be checked in the absence of workers, make sure they know this will happen.
- Encourage the use of a marking system to help protect private or personal communications.
- Avoid, where possible, opening e-mails that clearly show they are private or personal communications.

3.2.11 Inform workers of the extent to which information about their internet access and e-mails is retained in the system and for how long.

Key points and possible actions

- Check whether workers are currently aware of the retention period of e-mail and internet usage.

- If it is not already in place, set up a system (eg displaying information online or in a communication pack) that informs workers of retention periods.

3.3. Video and audio monitoring

[4.197]

Some – though not all – of the data protection issues that arise when carrying out video monitoring in public places will arise in the workplace. Employers carrying out video monitoring of workers will therefore find the guidance in the Information Commissioner's CCTV Code useful. Audio monitoring means the recording of face-to-face conversations, not recording telephone calls.

See www.ico.org.uk and search for the CCTV Code of Practice.

3.3.1 If video or audio monitoring is (or is likely) to be used, consider – preferably using an impact assessment – whether the benefits justify the adverse impact.

Key points and possible actions

- Where possible, any video or audio monitoring should be targeted at areas of particular risk and confined to areas where expectations of privacy are low.
- Continuous video or audio monitoring of particular individuals is only likely to be justified in rare circumstances.

3.3.2 Give workers a clear notification that video or audio monitoring is being carried out and where and why it is being carried out.

Key points and possible actions

- Unless covert monitoring is justified, ensure that workers are informed of the extent and nature of any monitoring that is taking place and the reasons for it.

3.3.3 Ensure that people other than workers, such as visitors or customers, who may inadvertently be caught by monitoring, are made aware of its operation and why it is being carried out.

Key points and possible actions

- Ensure that there are adequate notices, or other means, to inform such people about the monitoring and its purpose(s).

3.4 Covert monitoring

[4.198]

Covert monitoring means monitoring carried out in a manner calculated to ensure those subject to it are unaware that it is taking place. This sub-section is largely directed at covert video or audio monitoring, but will also be relevant where electronic communications are monitored when workers would not expect it.

3.4.1 Senior management should normally authorise any covert monitoring. They should satisfy themselves that there are grounds for suspecting criminal activity or equivalent malpractice and that notifying individuals about the monitoring would prejudice its prevention or detection.

Key points and possible actions

- Covert monitoring should not normally be considered. It will be rare for covert monitoring of workers to be justified. It should therefore only be used in exceptional circumstances.

3.4.2 Ensure that any covert monitoring is strictly targeted at obtaining evidence within a set timeframe and that the covert monitoring does not continue after the investigation is complete.

Key points and possible actions

- Deploy covert monitoring only as part of a specific investigation and cease once the investigation has been completed.

3.4.3 Do not use covert audio or video monitoring in areas which workers would genuinely and reasonably expect to be private.

Key points and possible actions

- If embarking on covert monitoring with audio or video equipment, ensure that this is not used in places such as toilets or private offices.
- There may be exceptions to this in cases of suspicion of serious crime but there should be an intention to involve the police.

3.4.4 If a private investigator is employed to collect information on workers covertly make sure there is a contract in place that requires the private investigator to only collect information in a way that satisfies the employer's obligations under the Act.

Key points and possible actions

- Check any arrangements for employing private investigators to ensure your contracts with them impose requirements on the investigator to only collect and use information on workers in accordance with your instructions and to keep the information secure.

3.4.5 Ensure that information obtained through covert monitoring is used only for the prevention or detection of criminal activity or equivalent malpractice. Disregard and, where feasible, delete other information collected in the course of monitoring unless it reveals information that no employer could reasonably be expected to ignore.

Key points and possible actions

- In a covert monitoring exercise, limit the number of people involved in the investigation.
- Prior to the investigation, set up clear rules limiting the disclosure and access to information obtained.
- If information is revealed in the course of covert monitoring that is tangential to the original investigation, delete it from the records unless it concerns other criminal activity or equivalent malpractice.

3.5 In-vehicle monitoring

[4.199]

Devices can record or transmit information such as the location of a vehicle, the distance it has covered and information about the user's driving habits. Monitoring of vehicle movements, where the vehicle is allocated to a specific driver, and information about the performance of the vehicle can therefore be linked to a specific individual, will fall within the scope of the Data Protection Act.

3.5.1 If in-vehicle monitoring is or will be used, consider – preferably using an impact assessment – whether the benefits justify the adverse impact.

Key points and possible actions

- Where private use of a vehicle is allowed, monitoring its movements when used privately, without the freely given consent of the user, will rarely be justified.
- If the vehicle is for both private and business use, it ought to be possible to provide a 'privacy button' or similar arrangement to enable the monitoring to be disabled.
- Where an employer is under a legal obligation to monitor the use of vehicles, even if used privately, for example by fitting a tachograph to a lorry, then the legal obligation will take precedence.

3.5.2 Set out a policy that states what private use can be made of vehicles provided by, or on behalf of, the employer, and any conditions attached to use.

Key points and possible actions

- Make sure, either in the policy or separately, that details of the nature and extent of monitoring are set out.
- Check that workers using vehicles are aware of the policy.

3.6 Monitoring through information from third parties

[4.200]

Employers need to take special care when wishing to make use of information held by third parties, such as credit reference or electoral roll information. This section also applies to information held by employers in a non-employment capacity, such as when a bank monitors its workers' bank accounts. Where an employer wishes to obtain information about a worker's criminal convictions, a disclosure must be obtained via the Criminal Records Bureau.

See Part 1 – Recruitment and Selection, para 1.3.2, for more information about the Criminal Records Bureau.

3.6.1 Before undertaking any monitoring which uses information from third parties, ensure – preferably using an impact assessment – that the benefits justify the adverse impact.

Key points and possible actions

- A worker's financial circumstances should not be monitored unless there are firm grounds to conclude that financial difficulties would pose a significant risk to the employer.

3.6.2 Tell workers what information sources are to be used to carry out checks on them and why the checks are to be carried out.

Key points and possible actions

- Set up a system to tell workers the nature and extent of any monitoring which uses information from third parties. (This could be via a workers handbook, notice board or on-line.)
- Where a specific check is to be carried out, the workers should be directly informed, unless to do so would be likely to prejudice the prevention or detection of crime.

3.6.3 Ensure that, if workers are monitored through the use of information held by a credit reference agency, the agency is aware of the use to which the information is put. Do not use a facility provided to conduct credit checks on customers to monitor or vet workers.

Key points and possible actions

- If your organisation uses a credit reference agency to check customers, make sure this facility is not being used to monitor or vet workers. If such practices are in place, stop them immediately.

3.6.4 Take particular care with information about workers which you have as a result of a non-employment relationship with them.

Key points and possible actions

- Check whether your organisation routinely uses information about workers that has been obtained from them because they are also (or have been) your customers, clients or suppliers. If such practices are in place, stop them unless they are justified by a risk you face.

3.6.5 Ensure that workers carrying out monitoring which involves information from third parties are properly trained. Put in place rules preventing the disclosure or inappropriate use of information obtained through such monitoring.

Key points and possible actions

- Identify who may carry out monitoring using information from third parties.
- Assess whether the organisation could reduce the number of workers involved in this activity without compromising necessary monitoring.
- Set up instructions or training for workers involved in this monitoring, making them aware of the data protection principles involved.
- Consider placing confidentiality clauses in the contracts of relevant staff.

3.6.6 Do not retain all the information obtained through such monitoring. Simply record that a check has taken place and the result of this.

Key points and possible actions

- Review procedures on retaining information. Unless there is a legal or regulatory obligation, check that information is not normally retained for more than 6 months.

PART 4: INFORMATION ABOUT WORKERS' HEALTH

ABOUT PART 4 OF THE CODE

Data protection and information about workers' health

[4.201]
The Data Protection Act's sensitive data rules come into play whenever an employer wishes to process information about workers' health. These rules do not prevent the processing of such information but limit the circumstances in which it can take place. The processing must also be consistent with the other requirements of the Act. Employers, especially in the public sector, need to bear in mind Article 8 of the European Convention on Human Rights which creates a right to respect for private and family life.

What does this part of the Code cover?

This part of the Code addresses the collection and subsequent use of information about a worker's physical or mental health or condition. Collection will often be done by some form of medical examination or test, but may involve other means such as health questionnaires.

The issues addressed in this part of the Code will arise typically from the carrying out of medical examination and testing or from the operation of an occupational health scheme. This part of the Code is therefore most likely to be of relevance to larger organisations and those with specific health and safety obligations.

Examples of information about workers' health

This part of the Code applies to information such as:

- a questionnaire completed by workers to detect problems with their health
- information about a worker's disabilities or special needs
- the results of an eye-test taken by a worker using display screens
- records of blood tests carried out to ensure a worker has not been exposed to hazardous substances
- the results of a test carried out to check a worker's exposure to alcohol or drugs
- the results of genetic tests carried out on workers
- an assessment of fitness for work to determine entitlement to benefits or suitability for continued employment
- records of vaccination and immunisation status and history.

Outside the Code

The Data Protection Act only comes into play when personal information is or will be held electronically or recorded in a structured filing system. This will often be the case but sometimes it may not, for example where a line-manager enquires about a worker's health but does not keep, or intend to keep, any record of the conversation, or only keeps a note in a general notebook.

Where samples are taken, as might be the case with drug or alcohol testing, the Code only applies from the point at which samples yield personal information about a worker. This Code does not address consent for any physical intervention involved in taking a sample from a worker in the course of medical testing.

Sensitive data rules

Where information about workers' health is to be processed, one of the Act's sensitive data conditions must be satisfied. There are various conditions. Below we have listed the ones likely to be of most relevance to employers. Employers holding information about workers' health ought to be able to answer 'yes' to one or more of these questions:

- Is the processing necessary to enable the employer to meet its legal obligations, for example to ensure health and safety at work, or to comply with the requirement not to discriminate against workers on the grounds of sex, age, race or disability?
- Is the processing for medical purposes, eg the provision of care or treatment, and undertaken by a health professional or someone working under an equivalent duty of confidentiality, eg an occupational health doctor?
- Is the processing in connection with actual or prospective legal proceedings?
- Has the worker given consent explicitly to the processing of his or her medical information?

This is not an exhaustive list of all the conditions.

See Supplementary Guidance, page 72 for more information on these and other sensitive data conditions.

Relying on the worker's consent

There are limitations as to how far consent can be relied on as a basis for the processing of information about workers' health. To be valid, consent must be:

- **explicit.** This means the worker must have been told clearly what personal data are involved and have been properly informed about the use that will be made of them. The worker must have given a positive indication of agreement, eg a signature.
- **freely given.** This means the worker must have a real choice whether or not to consent and there must be no penalty imposed for refusing to give consent.

See Supplementary Guidance page 75 for further explanation of what this means in practice.

Impact assessments

Once a sensitive data condition is satisfied, an employer then needs to be clear that either:

- it is under a legal duty to process information about workers' health, eg the duty to monitor workers' possible exposure to hazardous materials under the Control of Substances Hazardous to Health Regulations 2002, or
- the benefits gained from processing information about workers' health justify the privacy intrusion or any other adverse impact on them. In other words, the collection and use of information about workers' health must be a proportionate response to a particular problem.

An 'impact assessment' is a useful tool for employers to use to help them to judge whether the second of the above options applies.

Particularly where medical testing is involved, employers are likely to find it helpful to carry out a formal or informal 'impact assessment' to decide how or whether to collect information about workers' health. This Code does not prejudge the outcome of the impact assessment. Each will necessarily depend on the particular circumstances of the employer. Nor does the Code attempt to set out for employers the benefits they might gain from holding information about workers' health. What it does do is assist employers in identifying and giving appropriate weight to the other factors they should take into account.

An impact assessment involves:

- identifying clearly the **purpose**(s) for which health information is to be collected and held and the benefits this is likely to deliver
- identifying any likely **adverse impact** of collecting and holding the information
- considering **alternatives** to collecting and holding such information
- taking into account the **obligations** that arise from collecting and holding health information
- judging whether collecting and holding health information is **justified**.

Purpose(s)

It is important that a realistic assessment is made of the extent to which the collection of health information will actually address the risks it is directed at. Decisions based on, for example, the effect of particular medical conditions on a worker's future employability or the effect of particular drugs on safety should be based on relevant and reputable scientific evidence.

Adverse impact

Identifying any likely adverse impact means taking into account the consequences of collecting and holding health information, not only for workers, but also for others who might be affected by it, such as a worker's family. Consider:

- how extensive will the intrusion into the private lives of workers and others be as a result of collecting information about their health?
- whether health information will be seen by those who do not have a business need to know, eg IT workers involved in maintaining electronic files about workers
- what impact, if any, will the collection of health information have on the relationship of mutual trust and confidence that should exist between workers and their employer?
- whether the collection of health information will be oppressive or demeaning.

Alternatives

Considering whether it is necessary to collect information about workers' health, and if so how to do this in the least intrusive manner, means asking questions such as:

- can health questionnaires rather than tests be used to obtain the information the employer requires?
- can changes in the workplace, for example eliminating exposure to a hazardous substance, remove the need to obtain information through testing?
- can medical testing be targeted at individuals who have exhibited behavioural problems that may be drink or drug related, rather than at all workers?
- can the collection of health information be confined to areas of highest risk, eg can it be directed at a few individuals the nature of whose jobs mean they pose a particular risk rather than at everyone?
- can medical testing be designed to reveal only a narrow range of information that is directly relevant to the purpose for which it is undertaken?
- can access to health information be limited so that it will only be seen by medically qualified staff or those working under specific confidentiality agreements?

Obligations

Taking into account the obligations that arise from collecting information about workers' health means considering such matters as:

- whether and how workers will be notified about the collection of their health information
- how information about workers' health will be kept securely and handled in accordance with the Act.

See Part 2 – Employment Records, para 2.2, for more information on security requirements.

- the implications of the rights that individuals have to obtain a copy of information that has been collected about their health.

See Part 2 – Employment Records, para 2.8, which explains more about rights to access.

Is health information justified?

Making a conscious decision as to whether the current or proposed collection and use of health information is justified involves:

- establishing the benefits the collection and use of health information will bring
- considering any alternative method of obtaining these benefits and/or the information needed
- weighing these benefits against the adverse impact
- placing particular emphasis on the need to be fair to individual workers
- ensuring that the intrusion is no more than absolutely necessary
- bearing in mind that health information can be particularly sensitive, that its obtaining can be particularly intrusive and that significant intrusion will not normally be justified unless the employer's business is at real risk of serious damage
- taking into account the results of consultation with trade unions or other representatives, if any, or with workers themselves.

Making an impact assessment need not be a complicated or onerous process. Even in the context of health information it may sometimes be enough for an employer to make a simple mental evaluation of the risks faced by his or her business and to assess whether the collection and use of information about workers' health would reduce or eradicate those risks or would bring particular benefits. In other cases the impact assessment will be more complicated, for example where an employer faces a number of different risks of varying degrees of seriousness. In such cases appropriate documentation would be advisable.

GOOD PRACTICE RECOMMENDATIONS – PART 4

The parts of the Code in this section are:

4.1 Information about workers' health: general considerations

4.2 Occupational health schemes

4.3 Information from medical examination and testing

4.4 Information from drug & alcohol testing

4.5 Information from genetic testing

Sickness and Injury records are dealt with in Part 2 of the Code. See para 2.3.

4.1 Information about workers' health: general considerations

Core Principles

- It will be intrusive and may be highly intrusive to obtain information about your workers' health.
- Workers have legitimate expectations that they can keep their personal health information private and that employers will respect their privacy.
- If employers wish to collect and hold information on their workers' health, they should be clear about the purpose and satisfied that this is justified by real benefits that will be delivered.
- One of the sensitive data conditions must be satisfied.
- Workers should be aware of the extent to which information about their health is held and the reasons for which it is held.

- Decisions on a worker's suitability for particular work are properly management decisions but the interpretation of medical information should be left to a suitably qualified health professional.

4.1.1 Identify who within the organisation can authorise or carry out the collection of information about workers' health on behalf of the organisation and ensure they are aware of their employer's responsibilities under the Act.

Key points and possible actions

- Those who handle information about workers' health, or who can authorise the collection of such information, should be briefed on the Act and this Code.
- There are non-compliance risks if those lacking proper authority and any necessary training introduce the collection of health information and in particular medical testing.
- Leave the interpretation of medical information to those who are qualified to do this.

4.1.2 If health information is to be collected ensure a sensitive data condition can be satisfied.

Key points and possible actions

- The collection and use of information about workers' health is against the law unless a sensitive data condition is satisfied.
- In general employers should only collect health information where this is necessary for the protection of health and safety, to prevent discrimination on the grounds of disability, to satisfy other legal obligations or if each worker affected has given his or her explicit consent.
- If consent is to be relied on, it must be freely given. That means a worker must be able to say 'no' without penalty and must be able to withdraw consent once given. Blanket consent obtained at the outset of employment cannot always be relied on.
- Consent should not be confined to the testing itself, it should also cover the subsequent recording, use and disclosure of the test results.

See Supplementary Guidance, page 72 which explains more about the conditions for processing sensitive data.

4.1.3 Identify clearly the purposes behind the collection of information about workers' health and the specific business benefits which it is likely to bring.

Key points and possible actions

- Identify the collection and use of information about workers' health that currently takes place in your organisation.
- Identify any collection or use of information about workers' health that you plan to implement.
- Consider conducting an impact assessment on current or planned collection and use of health information.

See above for information on how to carry out an impact assessment.

4.1.4 Protect information about workers' health with appropriate security measures. Ensure that wherever practicable only suitably qualified health professionals have access to medical details.

Key points and possible actions

- Managers should not have access to more information about a worker's health than is necessary for them to carry out their management responsibilities. As far as possible the information should be confined to that necessary to establish fitness to work, rather than consist of more general medical details.
- Safety representatives should be provided with anonymised information unless any workers concerned have consented to the provision of information in an identifiable form.
- Unless the general standard of information security in your organisation is sufficiently high, medical information about workers should be separated from other personnel information, for example by keeping it in a sealed envelope, or subject to additional access controls on an electronic system.
- Information about workers' health collected to run a pension or insurance scheme should not be available to the employer unless this is necessary for the employer's role in administering the scheme.

4.1.5 Do not collect more information about workers' health than is necessary for the purpose(s) behind its collection.

Key points and possible actions

- Review any health questionnaires to ensure that only information that is really needed is collected.
- If commissioning a medical report on a sick employee, seek information on the worker's fitness for continued employment rather than medical details.
- Do not ask workers to consent to the disclosure of their entire general practitioner record as a matter of expediency. Only seek the disclosure of the whole record, or substantial parts of it, where this is genuinely necessary.
- If seeking a report from a worker's general practitioner or other medical practitioner who has been responsible for the care of the worker, ensure that you meet the requirements of the Access to Medical Reports Act 1988. This includes obtaining the worker's consent to your application for a report.

4.2 Occupational health schemes

[4.203]

This sub-section gives good practice recommendations for employers with occupational health schemes. It does not provide detailed professional guidance to doctors, nurses and others involved in such schemes.

4.2.1 Ensure workers are aware of how information about their health will be used and who will have access to it.

Key points and possible actions

- Unless told otherwise workers are entitled to assume that information they give to a doctor, nurse or other health professional will be treated in confidence and not passed to others.
- Set out clearly to workers, preferably in writing, how information they supply in the context of an occupational health scheme will be used, who it might be made available to and why.

4.2.2 Do not compromise any confidentiality of communications between workers and health professionals in an occupational health service.

Key points and possible actions

- If workers are allowed to use telephone or e-mail for confidential communication with their occupational health service, do not compromise this confidentiality by monitoring the contents of these communications.

4.2.3 Act in a way that is consistent with the Guidance on Ethics for Occupational Physicians published by the Faculty of Occupational Medicine.

Key points and possible actions

- Although this is guidance for occupational physicians rather than employers, it should give you a clear understanding of the legal and ethical constraints that apply to the exchange of information when working with occupational health professionals.

4.3 Information from medical examination and testing

[4.204]

This sub-section gives good practice recommendations specific to the collection and handling of information derived from medical examination and testing. The general recommendations in section 4.1 should also be taken into account.

Employers should bear in mind that obtaining a worker's consent or satisfying another sensitive data condition is not, on its own, sufficient to ensure data protection compliance. There is still an obligation to ensure that information obtained through medical examination is relevant, is accurate, is up to date and is kept secure.

See Supplementary Guidance page 72 for more Information on the Sensitive Data Conditions.

4.3.1 Where information obtained from medical testing is used to enforce the organisation's rules and standards make sure that the rules and standards are clearly set out in a policy which workers are aware of.

Key points and possible actions

- Ensure workers understand these rules and standards.
- Set out the circumstances in which medical testing may take place, the nature of the testing, how information obtained through testing will be used, and the safeguards that are in place for the workers that are subject to it.

4.3.2 Only obtain information through medical examination or testing of applicants or other potential workers at an appropriate point in the recruitment process, ie where there is a likelihood of appointing them. You must also be satisfied that the testing is a necessary and justified measure to:

- Determine whether the potential worker is fit or likely to remain fit to carry out the job in question, or
- Meet any legal requirements for testing, or
- Determine the terms on which a potential worker is eligible to join a pension or insurance scheme.

Key points and possible actions

- Record the business purpose for which examination or testing is to be introduced and the sensitive data condition that can be satisfied.
- Consider less intrusive ways of meeting the objectives, for example using a health questionnaire as an alternative to a medical examination or as a means to select those required to undergo a full examination.
- Only carry out a pre-employment medical examination or medical testing where there is a real likelihood that the individual will be appointed.
- Make it clear early on in the recruitment process that individuals may be subjected to medical examination or testing once there is a likelihood that they will be appointed.

4.3.3 Only obtain information through a medical examination or medical testing of current workers if the testing is part of a occupational health and safety programme that workers have a free choice to participate in, or you are satisfied that it is a necessary and justified measure to:

- Prevent a significant risk to the health and safety of the worker, or others, or
- Determine a particular worker's fitness for carrying out his or her job, or
- Determine whether a worker is fit to return to work after a period of sickness absence, or when this might be the case, or
- Determine the worker's entitlement to health related benefits eg sick pay, or
- Prevent discrimination against workers on the grounds of disability or assess the need to make reasonable adjustments to the working environment, or
- Comply with other legal obligations.

Key points and possible actions

- Record the business purpose for which the programme of examination or testing of workers is to be introduced and the sensitive data condition that can be satisfied.
- Establish and document who will be tested, what precisely are they being tested for, the frequency of testing, and the consequences of a positive or negative test.
- Consider less intrusive ways of meeting the employer's objectives, for example collecting information via a health questionnaire either as a first stage or as an alternative to a medical examination.

4.3.4 Do not obtain a sample covertly or use an existing sample, test result or other information obtained through a medical examination for a purpose other than that for which it was originally obtained.

Key points and possible actions

- Be clear about the purpose(s) for which any testing is being carried out and communicate this to workers.
- The covert obtaining of bodily samples for testing is most unlikely ever to be justified.
- If there is a wish to carry out a different test on an existing sample, this can only be done if the worker has been told about it and has freely consented.

4.3.5 Permanently delete information obtained in the course of medical examination or testing that is not relevant for the purpose(s) for which the examination or testing is undertaken.

Key points and possible actions

- Health information that is excessive, irrelevant or out of date should not be retained by an employer.
- If the retention of medical information is necessary only for the operation of an occupational health service, it should be kept in a confidential occupational health file.

4.4 Information from drug and alcohol testing

[4.205]

This part of the Code gives good practice recommendations specific to the collection and handling of information derived from drug and alcohol testing. The recommendations in sub-sections 4.1 and 4.3 should also be taken into account.

4.4.1 Before obtaining information through drug or alcohol testing ensure that the benefits justify any adverse impact, unless the testing is required by law.

Key points and possible actions

- The collection of information through drug and alcohol testing is unlikely to be justified unless it is for health and safety reasons.
- Post-incident testing where there is a reasonable suspicion that drug or alcohol use is a factor is more likely to be justified than random testing.
- Given the intrusive nature of testing employers would be well advised to undertake and document an impact assessment.

See Part 4 above, at [4.201], for information about how to carry out an impact assessment.

4.4.2 Minimise the amount of personal information obtained through drug and alcohol testing.

Key points and possible actions

- Only use drug or alcohol testing where it provides significantly better evidence of impairment than other less intrusive means.
- Use the least intrusive forms of testing practicable to deliver the benefits to the business that the testing is intended to bring.
- Tell workers what drugs they are being tested for.
- Base any testing on reliable scientific evidence of the effect of particular substances on workers.
- Limit testing to those substances and the extent of exposure that will have a significant bearing on the purpose(s) for which the testing is conducted.

4.4.3 Ensure the criteria used for selecting workers for testing are justified, properly documented, adhered to and are communicated to workers.

Key points and possible actions

- It is unfair and deceptive to lead workers to believe that testing is being carried out randomly if, in fact, other criteria are being used.

- If random testing is to be used, ensure that it is carried out in a genuinely random way.
- If other criteria are used to trigger testing, for example suspicion that a worker's performance is impaired as a result of drug or alcohol use, the employer should ensure workers are aware of the true criteria that are used.

4.4.4 Confine the obtaining of information through random testing to those workers who are employed to work in safety critical activities.

Key points and possible actions

- Collecting personal information by testing all workers in a business will not be justified if in fact it is only workers engaged in particular activities that pose a risk.
- Even in safety-critical businesses such as public transport or heavy industry, workers in different jobs will pose different safety risks. Therefore collecting information through the random testing of all workers will rarely be justified.

4.4.5 Gather information through testing designed to ensure safety at work rather than to reveal the illegal use of substances in a worker's private life.

Key points and possible actions

- Very few employers will be justified in testing to detect illegal use rather than on safety grounds. Testing to detect illegal use may, exceptionally, be justified where illegal use would:
  - breach the worker's contract of employment, conditions of employment or disciplinary rules, and
  - cause serious damage to the employer's business, eg by substantially undermining public confidence in the integrity of a law enforcement agency.

4.4.6 Ensure that workers are fully aware that drug or alcohol testing is taking place, and of the possible consequences of being tested.

Key points and possible actions

- Explain your drug or alcohol policy in a staff handbook.
- Explain the consequences for workers of breaching the policy.
- Ensure workers are aware of the blood-alcohol level at which they may be disciplined when being tested for alcohol.
- Do not conduct testing on samples collected without the worker's knowledge.

4.4.7 Ensure that information is only obtained through drug and alcohol testing that is;

- of sufficient technical quality to support any decisions or opinions that are derived from it and,
- subject to rigorous integrity and quality control procedures and,
- conducted under the direction of, and positive test results interpreted by, a person who is suitably qualified and competent in the field of drug testing.

Key points and possible actions

- Use a professional service with qualified staff and that meets appropriate standards.
- Ensure workers have access to a duplicate of any sample taken to enable them to have it independently analysed as a check on the accuracy of the employer's results.
- Do not assume that the tests are infallible and be prepared to deal properly with disputes arising from their use.

4.5 Information from genetic testing

[4.206]

Genetic testing has the potential to provide employers with information predictive of the likely future general health of workers or with information about their genetic susceptibility to occupational diseases. Genetic testing is, though, still under development and in most cases has an uncertain predictive value. It is rarely, if ever, used in the employment context. The Human Genetics Commission advises that employers should not demand that an individual take a genetic test as a condition of employment. It should therefore only be introduced after very careful consideration, if at all. This sub-section supplements sub-sections 4.1 and 4.3.

4.5.1 Do not use genetic testing in an effort to obtain information that is predictive of a worker's future general health.

Key points and possible actions

- Obtaining information through genetic testing is too intrusive and the information's predictive value is insufficiently certain to be relied on to provide information about a worker's future health.

4.5.2 Do not insist that a worker discloses the results of a previous genetic test.

Key points and possible actions

- It is important that workers are not put off taking genetic tests that may be beneficial for their health care by the fear that they may have to disclose the results to a current or future employer.
- You can ask for information that is relevant to your health and safety or other legal duties but the provision of the information should be voluntary.

4.5.3 Only use genetic testing to obtain information where it is clear that a worker with a particular, detectable genetic condition is likely to pose a serious safety risk to others or where it is known that a specific working environment or practice might pose specific risks to workers with particular genetic variations.

Key points and possible actions

- Only seek information through genetic testing as a last resort, where:
  - it is not practicable to make changes to the working environment or practices so as to reduce risks to all workers and
  - it is the only reasonable method to obtain the required information.
- Inform the Human Genetics Commission of any proposals to use genetic testing for employment purposes.

4.5.4 If a genetic test is used to obtain information for employment purposes ensure that it is valid and is subject to assured levels of accuracy and reliability.

Key points and possible actions

- There should be scientific evidence that any genetic test is valid for the purpose for which it is used.
- Ensure the results of any test undertaken are always communicated to the person tested and professional advice is available.
- Ensure test results are carefully interpreted, taking account of how they might be affected by environmental conditions.

(*Contact details—omitted; see Useful addresses at* **[5.120]**.)

SUBJECT ACCESS CODE OF PRACTICE

Dealing with requests from individuals for personal information

(June 2017)

[4.207]

NOTES

This Code of Practice was originally issued by the Information Commissioner's Office (ICO) on 8 August 2013, under the powers conferred by Data Protection Act 1998 s 51, and came into effect on that date. It was subsequently reissued in June 2017. Note that the 1998 Act was repealed by the Data Protection Act 2018, s 211, Sch 19, Pt 1, para 44, as from 25 May 2018 (for transitional provisions, see Sch 20 to that Act at **[1.2232]**). It is understood that the Code is intended to continue to apply as a non-statutory guidance by the Information Commissioner's Office unless, and until, replaced by a new Code issued under the 2018 Act.

The Code has no formal legal status of the kind conferred on ACAS Codes, but will be taken into account as appropriate by the ICO in determining complaints to which it is relevant. The Code is also a useful guide to how to apply the Subject Access provisions of the 1998 Act. There was no requirement under the 1998 Act for Codes made by the ICO to be approved by a Minister or Parliament, hence the Code came into effect immediately on being issued by the ICO. The Code is reproduced in full here, except for Section 10, which is omitted. This deals with specific categories of case other than in the field of employment and is hence outside the scope of this work.

CONTENTS

1. ABOUT THIS CODE OF PRACTICE

PURPOSE OF THE CODE

[4.208]

This code of practice explains the rights of individuals to access their personal data. It also clarifies what you must do in this regard to comply with your duties as a data controller. These rights and duties are set out in sections 7-9A of the Data Protection Act 1998 (DPA) and are often referred to as 'the right of subject access', a phrase this code also uses. The code refers to a request made under section 7 of the DPA as a 'subject access request' (SAR).

The DPA's sixth data protection principle requires you to process personal data in accordance with the rights the Act gives to individuals. Subject access is one of those rights. The code is intended to help you provide subject access in accordance with the law and good practice. It aims to do this by explaining how to recognise a subject access request and by offering practical advice about how to deal with, and respond to, such a request. It provides guidance on the limited circumstances in which personal data is exempt from subject access. The code also explains how the right of subject access can be enforced when things go wrong.

WHO SHOULD USE THE CODE OF PRACTICE?

[4.209]
Any organisations that hold personal data should use the code to help them understand their obligations to provide subject access to that data, and to help them follow good practice when dealing with subject access requests. The good practice advice in the code will help all organisations – whether they are in the public, private or third sector. Although the practices that organisations adopt to respond to SARs are likely to differ, depending on their size and the nature of the personal data they hold, the underlying principles concerning subject access are the same in every case.

THE CODE'S STATUS

[4.210]
The Information Commissioner has issued this code of practice under section 51 of the DPA as part of her duty to promote good practice. The DPA says good practice includes, but is not limited to, compliance with the Act.

The code is the Information Commissioner's interpretation of what the DPA requires of organisations to comply with SARs. It gives advice on good practice, but compliance with our recommendations is not mandatory where they go beyond the strict requirements of the DPA. The code itself does not have the force of law, as it is the DPA that places legally enforceable obligations on organisations.

Organisations may find alternative ways of meeting the DPA's requirements and of adopting good practice. However, if they do nothing they risk breaking the law. The ICO cannot take enforcement action over a failure to adopt good practice or to act on the code's recommendations unless this itself breaches the DPA.

We have tried to distinguish our good practice recommendations from the DPA's legal requirements. We provide advice about taking a positive approach to subject access in chapter 3 and, where appropriate, we list at the end of subsequent chapters some likely indicators that an organisation is dealing well with subject access. However, there is inevitably an overlap between the DPA's requirements and good practice: although the DPA sets out the legal requirements, it provides no guidance on the practical measures that could be taken to comply with them. This code helps to plug that gap.

MORE INFORMATION

[4.211]
The code of practice is part of a series of guidance to help you as an organisation to fully understand your obligations under the DPA, as well as promoting good practice. You can find an overview of the DPA's main provisions in The ICO Guide to Data Protection.

The code is a guide to our general recommended approach, although decisions on individual cases will always be based on their particular circumstances.

If you need more information about this or any other aspect of data protection or freedom of information, please visit the ICO website: www.ico.org.uk

2. OVERVIEW OF SUBJECT ACCESS

WHAT IS SUBJECT ACCESS?

[4.212]
Enabling individuals to find out what personal data you hold about them, why you hold it and who you disclose it to is fundamental to good information-handling practice. The Data Protection Act 1998 (DPA) gives individuals the right to require you to do this.

This right, commonly known as subject access, is set out in section 7 of the DPA. Individuals may exercise the right by making a written 'subject access request' (SAR).

WHAT IS PERSONAL DATA?

[4.213]
For information to be personal data, it must *relate to* a living individual and allow that individual to be *identified* from it (either on its own or along with other information likely to come into the organisation's possession). See chapter 5 for more guidance about the meaning of personal data.

DOES A SAR HAVE TO BE IN A PARTICULAR FORMAT?

[4.214]
No. A SAR simply needs to be made in writing and, if you require payment of a fee for dealing with the request, to be accompanied by the fee. You may not insist on the use of a particular form for making a SAR, but making a form available may assist the requester to provide the information you need to deal with their request.

HOW MUCH IS THE FEE?

[4.215]
Unless a SAR relates to one of a small number of special categories of information, the maximum fee you can charge for dealing with it is £10. Different fee limits apply where the request concerns health or educational records or credit files (explained in chapter 10 'Special cases').

WHAT INFORMATION IS AN INDIVIDUAL ENTITLED TO?

[4.216]

Subject access is most often used by individuals who want to see a copy of the information an organisation holds about them. However, subject access goes further than this and an individual is entitled to be:

- told whether any personal data is being processed;
- given a description of the personal data, the reasons it is being processed, and whether it will be given to any other organisations or people;
- given a copy of the personal data; and
- given details of the source of the data (where this is available).

An individual can also request information about the reasoning behind any automated decisions taken about him or her, such as a computer-generated decision to grant or deny credit, or an assessment of performance at work (except where this information is a trade secret).

Subject access provides a right for the requester to see their own personal data, rather than a right to see copies of documents that contain their personal data. Often, the easiest way to provide the relevant information is to supply copies of original documents, but you are not obliged to do this.

WHAT IS THE TIME LIMIT FOR RESPONDING?

[4.217]

In most cases you must respond to a subject access request promptly and in any event within 40 calendar days of receiving it.

IS ANY INFORMATION EXEMPT FROM SUBJECT ACCESS?

[4.218]

Yes. Some types of personal data are exempt from the right of subject access and so cannot be obtained by making a SAR. Information may be exempt because of its nature or because of the effect its disclosure is likely to have. There are also some restrictions on disclosing information in response to a SAR – where this would involve disclosing information about another individual, for example. Chapter 9 provides more detail on exemptions from subject access.

3. TAKING A POSITIVE APPROACH TO SUBJECT ACCESS

[4.219]

Subject access is a fundamental right for individuals. But it is also an opportunity for you to improve your customer service and service delivery by responding to subject access requests (SARs) efficiently and transparently and by maximising the quality of the personal information you hold.

In our experience, most organisations want to help when an individual makes a SAR, whether that individual is their customer, an employee, or a stakeholder of some other kind. It makes good sense to help individuals exercise their information rights, rather than to hinder them. When things go wrong, complaints tend to follow. Many of the complaints we see could easily have been avoided by following the good practice advice in this code. In particular, if you clearly explain how individuals can request their personal information, what you need from them and what you will do in return – and if you keep to your word – you will probably avoid costly disputes and difficulties.

Adopting the good practice recommendations in this code will help you to:

- comply with your legal obligations under the Data Protection Act 1998 (DPA) – and show how you have done so;
- streamline your processes for dealing with SARs, saving you time and effort;
- increase levels of trust and confidence in your organisation by being open with individuals about the personal information you hold about them;
- retain your customers through better customer care;
- improve confidence in your information-handling practices;
- (if your organisation is in the public sector) improve the transparency of your activities in line with public policy requirements;
- enable customers, employees and others to verify that the information you hold about them is accurate, and to tell you if it is not; and
- improve your service delivery as a result.

An organisation that takes a positive approach to subject access might have the following indicators of good practice:

Training

All staff are trained to recognise a SAR as part of general data protection training. More detailed training on handling SARs is provided to relevant staff, dependent on job role.

Guidance

A dedicated data protection page is available for staff on the organisation's intranet with links to SAR policies and procedures.

Request handling staff

A specific person or central team is responsible for responding to requests. More than one member of staff is aware of how to process a SAR so there is resilience against absence.

In case requesters are dissatisfied with the initial response, arrangements are in place for a senior manager to review them.

Data protection experts

In a large organisation, there are data protection experts or 'information champions' to provide data protection expertise, including SAR advice, within departments where personal data is processed.

Monitoring compliance

Compliance with SARs is monitored and discussed at information governance steering group meetings, and management information is kept showing the number of SARs received. Details of any requests that have not been actioned within the statutory time limit are escalated to a suitably senior forum, so that any breach is tackled at a high level.

Additional indicators of good practice are given at the end of several subsequent chapters of the code. Not all of these indicators will be relevant to every organisation.

4. RECOGNISING A SUBJECT ACCESS REQUEST

WHAT IS A SUBJECT ACCESS REQUEST?

[4.220]
A subject access request (SAR) is simply a written request made by or on behalf of an individual for the information which he or she is entitled to ask for under section 7 of the Data Protection Act 1998 (DPA). The request does not have to be in any particular form. Nor does it have to include the words 'subject access' or make any reference to the DPA. Indeed, a request may be a valid SAR even if it refers to other legislation, such as the Freedom of Information Act (FOIA).

FORMAL REQUIREMENTS

[4.221]
A SAR must be made in writing. Standard forms can make it easier for you to recognise a subject access request and make it easier for the individual to include all the details you might need to locate the information they want. However, there is no legally prescribed request form. Nor can you require individuals to use your own in-house form to make a SAR. You may invite individuals to use your own request form, but you should make clear that this is not compulsory and you must not try to use this as a way of extending the 40-day time limit for responding.

An emailed or faxed request is as valid as one sent in hard copy. SARs might also be received via social media (see below) and possibly via third-party websites. You may not insist on the use of a particular means of delivery for a SAR, but if you have a preference (eg by email to a particular mailbox) it is good practice to state clearly what it is. This should encourage requesters to submit SARs by the means you find most convenient, but you must still respond to SARs sent to you by other means.

You should also note the following points when considering validity.

- You do not need to respond to a request made orally but, depending on the circumstances, it might be reasonable to do so (as long as you are satisfied about the person's identity), and it is good practice at least to explain to the individual how to make a valid request, rather than ignoring them.
- If a request does not mention the DPA specifically or even say that it is a subject access request, it is nevertheless valid and should be treated as such if it is clear that the individual is asking for their own personal data.
- Requesters do not have to tell you their reason for making the request or what they intend to do with the information requested, although it may help you to find the relevant information if they do explain the purpose of the request.
- A request is valid even if the individual has not sent it directly to the person who normally deals with such requests. So it is important to ensure that you and your colleagues can recognise a SAR and deal with it in accordance with your organisation's SAR process.

SUBJECT ACCESS REQUESTS AND SOCIAL MEDIA

[4.222]
Individuals may make a SAR using any Facebook page or Twitter account your organisation has, other social-media sites to which it subscribes, or possibly via third-party websites. This might not be the most effective way of delivering the request in a form you will be able to process quickly and easily, but there is nothing to prevent it in principle.

You should therefore assess the potential for SARs to be received via social-media channels and ensure that you take reasonable and proportionate steps to respond effectively to requests received in this way. However, as we explain in chapter 11, the Information Commissioner has discretion as to whether to take enforcement action and would not take it where it is clearly unreasonable.

You are entitled to satisfy yourself as to the identity of the person making the request. Because the requester must provide evidence of their identity and because you might require them to pay a fee, they will often have to supplement a SAR sent by social media with other forms of communication.

You may decline to use social media to supply information in response to a SAR if technological constraints make it impractical, or if information security considerations make it inappropriate to do so. In these circumstances you should ask for an alternative delivery address for the response.

REQUESTS MADE ON BEHALF OF OTHERS

[4.223]
The DPA does not prevent an individual making a subject access request via a third party. Often, this will be a solicitor acting on behalf of a client, but it could simply be that an individual wants someone else to act for them. In these cases, you need to be satisfied that the third party making the request is entitled to act on behalf of the individual, but it is the third party's responsibility to provide evidence of this entitlement. This might be a written authority to make the request or it might be a more general power of attorney.

If you think an individual may not understand what information would be disclosed to a third party who has made a SAR on their behalf, you may send the response directly to the individual rather than to the third party. The individual may then choose to share the information with the third party after having had a chance to review it.

In some cases an individual does not have the mental capacity to manage their own affairs. There are no specific statutory provisions enabling a third party to exercise subject access rights on such a person's behalf. But it is reasonable to assume that an attorney with authority to manage the individual's property and affairs, or a person appointed by the Court of Protection to make decisions about such matters, will have the appropriate authority.

REQUESTS FOR INFORMATION ABOUT CHILDREN

[4.224]
Even if a child is too young to understand the implications of subject access rights, data about them is still their personal data and does not belong to anyone else, such as a parent or guardian. So it is the child who has a right of access to the information held about them, even though in the case of young children these rights are likely to be exercised by those with parental responsibility for them.

Before responding to a SAR for information held about a child, you should consider whether the child is mature enough to understand their rights. If you are confident that the child can understand their rights, then you should respond to the child rather than the parent. What matters is that the child is able to understand (in broad terms) what it means to make a SAR and how to interpret the information they receive as a result of doing so. When considering borderline cases, you should take into account, among other things:

- where possible, the child's level of maturity and their ability to make decisions like this;
- the nature of the personal data;
- any court orders relating to parental access or responsibility that may apply;
- any duty of confidence owed to the child or young person;
- any consequences of allowing those with parental responsibility access to the child's or young person's information. This is particularly important if there have been allegations of abuse or ill treatment;
- any detriment to the child or young person if individuals with parental responsibility cannot access this information; and
- any views the child or young person has on whether their parents should have access to information about them.

In Scotland, the law presumes that a child aged 12 years or more has the capacity to make a SAR. The presumption does not apply in England and Wales or in Northern Ireland, but it does indicate an approach that will be reasonable in many cases. It does not follow that, just because a child has capacity to make a SAR, they also have capacity to consent to sharing their personal data with others – as they may still not fully understand the implications of doing so.

For more advice about data protection and children, see chapter 2 of our Personal information online code of practice.

There are separate rules about access to educational records – see chapter 10 'Special cases' for further guidance on this.

DEALING WITH FREEDOM OF INFORMATION REQUESTS FOR THE REQUESTER'S PERSONAL DATA

[4.225]

As mentioned above, a valid SAR may, at first sight, appear to be something else. It is not uncommon, for example, for the request to state that it is a freedom of information (FOI) request. If, in reality, it relates to the requester's personal data, you must treat it as a subject access request.

> **Example**
>
> A local authority receives a letter from a council tax payer requesting a copy of any information the authority holds about a dispute over his eligibility for a discount. The letter states it is a 'freedom of information request'. It is clear that the request concerns the individual's own personal data and the local authority should treat it as a subject access request.

You may be more likely to receive a SAR in the form of a freedom of information request if your organisation is a public authority for the purposes of FOIA or the Environmental Information Regulations 2004 (EIR). Whether or not the organisation is a public authority, however, you must deal with the request appropriately, and this will depend on whether it relates only to the requester's own personal data or to other information as well.

If it is clear that the requester is merely asking for their own personal data, but they have cited FOIA, you should do the following.

- Deal with the request as a SAR in the normal way. The requester does not need to make a new request. You may need to ask for payment of any necessary fee or ask the individual to verify their identity.
- If your organisation is a public authority, the requested personal data is, in fact, exempt from disclosure under FOIA or the EIR. Strictly speaking, you should issue a formal refusal notice saying so. In practice, however, we would not expect you to do this if you are dealing with the request as a SAR.
- It is good practice for public authorities to clarify within 20 working days (the time limit for responding to FOI requests) that the request is being dealt with as a SAR under the DPA, and that the 40-day time limit for responding applies.

If the request relates to information that cannot be requested by means of a SAR (eg it includes a request for non-personal information) then, if your organisation is a public authority, you should treat this as two requests: one for the requester's personal data made under the DPA; and another for the remaining, non-personal information made under FOIA. If any of the non-personal information is environmental, you should consider this as a request made under the EIR.

It is important to consider the requested information under the right legislation. This is because the test for disclosure under FOIA or the EIR is to the world at large – not just the requester. If personal data is mistakenly disclosed under FOIA or the EIR to the world at large, this could lead to a breach of the data protection principles.

For more information on dealing with FOI requests, please see the Guide to FOIA.

For more information on the exemption from FOIA for personal data, please see ICO guidance:

- Section 40: personal information
- Section 40: access to information held in complaint files
- Section 40: requests for personal data about public authority employees

For more about dealing with requests for environmental information, please see the Guide to EIR.

> An organisation that is alert to the need to deal with SARs effectively might have the following indicators of good practice:
>
> **Guidance**
>
> Guidance on making a SAR, along with a form, is made available on the organisation's website. The guidance:
>
> - makes it clear where the request should be sent to;
> - highlights the fee and explains the options for payment;
> - specifies the information that the requester will need to provide to confirm their identity;
> - mentions the 40-day period for responding to the request; and
> - gives details of a point of contact for any questions.
>
> While using a form is not mandatory, when it is used it helps to identify SARs. The form includes a 'for office use only' type section providing instructions to the receiver on what to do with the form, and space to record certain information to assist in processing the request (such as the date the form was received, whether ID has been checked and whether a fee has been paid).
>
> Guidance has been produced for staff to help them identify SARs. In particular, this has been directed at those members of staff who deal with personal data, such as staff in human resources. The guidance, which is available on the organisation's intranet, explains what staff should do if they receive a SAR and stresses the need to act promptly and refer it to the right team.
>
> **Training**

Data protection training includes a section on SARs and dealing with subject access. It also teaches staff about their own rights as data subjects (to put the training in context). There is a test at the end with a pass mark, and attendance is included as a performance objective for some staff.

Staff dealing with incoming correspondence, for example in the mailroom, are trained in how to recognise a SAR and to ensure that requests are delivered promptly to the relevant people.

If the organisation operates a shift-working system, the training is repeated at times that ensure all staff have the opportunity to attend.

5. RESPONDING TO A SUBJECT ACCESS REQUEST – GENERAL CONSIDERATIONS

SUBJECT ACCESS IS A RIGHT OF ACCESS TO THE PERSONAL DATA OF A PARTICULAR INDIVIDUAL

[4.226]
Under the right of subject access, an individual is entitled only to their own personal data, and not to information relating to other people (unless they are acting on behalf of that person). Before you can respond to a subject access request (SAR), you need to be able to decide whether information you hold is personal data and, if so, whose personal data it is.

The Data Protection Act 1998 (DPA) provides that, for information to be personal data, it must *relate to* a living individual and allow that individual to be *identified* from that information (either on its own or in conjunction with other information likely to come into the organisation's possession). The context in which information is held, and the way it is used, can have a bearing on whether it relates to an individual and therefore on whether it is the individual's personal data.

In most cases, it will be obvious whether the information being requested is personal data, but we have produced separate guidance (Determining what is personal data) to help you decide in cases where it is unclear.

The same information may be the personal data of two (or more) individuals. Additional rules apply where responding to a SAR may involve providing information that relates both to the individual making the request and to another individual. These rules are explained in chapter 7.

RESPONSIBILITY OF THE DATA CONTROLLER

[4.227]
If you determine the purpose for which and the manner in which the personal data in question is processed, then you (or your organisation) are/is the data controller in relation to that personal data and will be responsible for responding to the SAR. The DPA does not allow any extension to the 40-day time limit where you have to rely on a data processor to provide the information you need to respond.

Example

An employer is reviewing staffing and pay, which involves collecting information from and about a representative sample of staff. A third-party data processor is analysing the information.

The employer receives a SAR from a member of staff. To respond, the employer needs information held by the data processor. The employer is the data controller for this information and should instruct the data processor to retrieve any personal data that relates to the member of staff.

If you use a data processor, you need to make sure you have contractual arrangements in place to guarantee that SARs are dealt with properly, irrespective of whether they are sent to you or to the data processor.

The role of a data processor is explained in the ICO Guide to Data Protection.

INFORMATION MANAGEMENT SYSTEMS

[4.228]
You will find it difficult to deal with SARs effectively without adequate information management systems and procedures. Given that subject access has been a feature of data protection law since the 1980s, your information management systems should facilitate dealing with SARs. They should allow you to easily locate and extract personal data in response to subject access requests. Systems should be designed to allow for the redaction of third party data where this is deemed necessary. Not only should your systems have the technical capability to search for the information necessary to respond to a SAR, but they should also operate by reference to effective records management policies. For example, it is good practice to have a well-structured file plan and standard file-naming conventions for electronic documents, and for the retention and deletion of documents to be governed by a clear retention policy. If you are buying a new information management system, you should consider including requirements in the specification about searching and SARs.

TIME LIMITS

[4.229]
You must comply with a SAR 'promptly' and in any event within 40 days of the date on which the request is received or (if later) the day on which you receive:

- the fee (if any);
- any requested location information (see chapter 6); and
- any information requested to confirm the requester's identity (see below for further guidance).

The duty to comply promptly with a SAR clearly implies an obligation to act without unreasonable delay but, equally clearly, it does not oblige you to prioritise compliance over everything else. The 40-day long-stop period is generally accepted as striking the right balance in most cases between the rights of individuals to prompt access to their personal data and the need to accommodate the resource constraints of organisations to which SARs are made. Provided that you deal with the request in your normal course of business, without unreasonable delay, and within the 40-day period, you are likely to comply with the duty to comply promptly.

FEES AND COST LIMITS

[4.230]
You may charge a fee for dealing with a SAR. If you choose to do this, you need not comply with the request until you have received the fee. The maximum fee you can charge is normally £10 (including any card-handling or administration charges). There are different fee structures for organisations that hold health or education records (where the maximum fee is £50, depending on the circumstances – see chapter 10). These fees are not subject to VAT.

You need not comply with a request until you have received the fee, but you cannot ignore a request simply because the individual has not sent a fee. If a fee is payable but has not been sent with the request, you should contact the individual promptly and inform them that they need to pay.

Some organisations choose not to charge a fee. However, once you have started dealing with an individual's request without asking for a fee, it would be unfair to then demand a fee as a way of extending the period of time you have to respond to the request.

In many cases the fee you may charge for dealing with a SAR will not cover the administrative costs of doing so. You must comply with the request regardless of this fact.

There is one narrowly defined situation in which the likely cost of complying with a SAR is relevant in determining whether an organisation must comply. Where a request relates to 'unstructured personal data' (as defined in section 9A(1) of the DPA) held by a public authority, the authority is not required to comply with the request if it estimates that the cost of doing so would exceed either £450 or £600. The relevant limit depends on the identity of the public authority (see the Freedom of Information and Data Protection (Appropriate Limit and Fees) Regulations 2004).

MAKING REASONABLE ADJUSTMENTS FOR DISABLED PEOPLE

[4.231]
Some disabled people find it difficult to communicate in writing, and may therefore have difficulty making a SAR. You may have a legal duty to make reasonable adjustments for such a person if they wish to make a SAR. Reasonable adjustments could include treating a verbal request for information as though it were a valid SAR. If the request is complex, it would be good practice for you to document it in an accessible format and to send it to the disabled person to confirm the details of the request.

You might also have to respond in a particular format that is accessible to the disabled person, such as Braille, large print, email or audio formats. If an individual thinks you have failed to make a reasonable adjustment, they may make a claim under the applicable equality legislation. Information about making a claim is available from the Equality and Human Rights Commission or from the Equality Commission for Northern Ireland.

CONFIRMING THE REQUESTER'S IDENTITY

[4.232]
To avoid personal data about one individual being sent to another, either accidentally or as a result of deception, you need to be satisfied that you know the identity of the requester. You can ask for enough information to judge whether the person making the request is the individual to whom the personal data relates (or a person authorised to make a SAR on their behalf).

The key point is that you must be reasonable about what you ask for. You should not request a lot more information if the identity of the person making the request is obvious to you. This is particularly the case when you have an ongoing relationship with the individual.

Example

You have received a written SAR from a current employee. You know this employee personally and have even had a phone conversation with them about the request. Although your organisation's policy is to verify identity by asking for a copy of a utility bill, it would be unreasonable to do so in this case since you know the person making the request.

However, you should not assume that, on every occasion, the person making a request is who they say they are. In some cases, it is reasonable to ask the person making the request to verify their identity before sending them information.

Example

An online retailer receives a SAR by email from a customer. The customer has not used the site for some time and although the email address matches the company's records, the postal address given by the customer does not. In this situation, before responding to the request it would be reasonable to gather further information, which could be as simple as asking the customer to confirm other account details such as a customer reference number.

The means by which the SAR is delivered might affect your decision about whether you need to confirm the requester's identity. For example, if a request is made by means of an email account through which you have recently corresponded with the requester, you may feel it is safe to assume that the SAR has been made by the requester. On the other hand, if the request is made via a social networking website, it would be prudent to check it is a genuine request.

The level of checks you should make may depend on the possible harm and distress that inappropriate disclosure of the information could cause to the individual concerned.

Example

A GP practice receives a SAR from someone claiming to be a former patient. The name on the request matches a record held by the practice, but there is nothing else in the request to enable the practice to be confident that the requester is the patient to whom the record relates. In this situation, it would be reasonable for the practice to ask for more information before responding to the request. The potential risk to the former patient of sending their health records to the wrong person is such that the practice is right to be cautious. They could ask the requester to provide more information, such as a document providing evidence of date of birth or passport.

Before supplying any information in response to a SAR, you should also check that you have the requester's correct postal or email address (or both). If you are supplying information by fax (and we recommend that you do so only if the requester specifically asks you to), then you must ensure that you are sending it to the correct fax number.

WHERE A REQUESTER DIES BEFORE THE RESPONSE IS PROVIDED

[4.233]

As stated earlier, the definition of personal data covers "data which relate to a living individual". If a requester dies before a response is provided but the data controller received the SAR when the individual was living, it must provide the response to the individual's personal representatives. As a matter of good customer service we suggest that it would be advisable for data controllers who are aware that the data subject has died and who know the identity of the personal representative(s) to check with them if they in fact still wish to receive the information, before sending it.

DEALING WITH BULK REQUESTS

[4.234]

Depending on the size of your organisation and the nature of your business, you may from time to time receive several (and possibly many) SARs in a short period of time. In the financial services sector, for example, it is not uncommon for 'bulk' requests to be made by claims management companies on behalf of multiple individuals.

Each SAR within a bulk request must be considered individually and responded to appropriately. The Information Commissioner acknowledges the potential resource implications of this duty but recommends you bear in mind the following principles when dealing with high volumes of SARs:

- a SAR that is made as part of a bulk request has the same legal status as a SAR that is made individually;
- the purpose for which a SAR is made does not affect its validity, or your duty to respond to it;
- if the request is made by a third party on behalf of the individual concerned, you are entitled to satisfy yourself that the third party is authorised to make the request;
- you are also entitled to satisfy yourself as to the identity of the individual concerned;
- you must respond to the request even if you hold no information about the individual. Your response may obviously be very brief in such cases; and
- you should be prepared to respond to peaks in the volume of SARs you receive.

In considering a complaint about a SAR, the ICO will have regard to the volume of requests received by an organisation and the steps it has taken to ensure requests are dealt with appropriately even in the face of a high volume of similar requests. The organisation's size and resources are likely to be relevant factors. As we explain in chapter 11, the Information Commissioner has discretion as to whether to take enforcement action and would not take such action where it is clearly unreasonable to do so.

An organisation that responds effectively to SARs might have the following indicators of good practice:

Managing expectations

Guidance on the organisation's website mentions the 40-day time limit for responding to a SAR and each request is acknowledged with a letter or email informing the requester of the date by which a response must be provided. If there is a delay in dealing with the request for any reason, the organisation contacts the requester to explain the reason and the expected date for the response.

The response to a SAR includes an explanation of the searches that have been made to deal with the request and the information revealed by those searches. This helps the requester understand whether they have received all the information they are entitled to.

Logs and checklists

The organisation logs receipt of SARs and updates it to monitor progress as the SAR is processed. The log includes copies of information supplied in response to the SAR, together with copies of any material withheld and an explanation why.

A standard checklist is used to ensure consistency in identity verification procedures and fee collection, and to ensure that the necessary information is obtained from relevant departments across the organisation. The checklist forms a cover-sheet on the file for each SAR received.

Systems, technology and contracts

Reliable indexes, file contents pages, descriptions of documents and metadata and technical specifications for systems make it easier for those dealing with SARs to locate personal data, decide whose personal data it is and make decisions about its disclosure.

In a larger organisation, a dedicated IT system is used to process SARs. This enables the organisation effectively to manage and monitor requests received. The system records all correspondence, identity confirmation enquiries and fee payments. In addition it records details of the request, such as date received and date when response is due, and generates reports to monitor compliance.

Where a data processor is involved, the organisation ensures the data processor is aware of its obligations with regard to subject access before appointment. A clause specifying the organisation's requirements for SAR handling is included in the written contract.

6. FINDING AND RETRIEVING THE RELEVANT INFORMATION

EXTENT OF THE DUTY TO PROVIDE SUBJECT ACCESS

[4.235]

Dealing with a subject access request (SAR) may be challenging. This might be because of the nature of the request, because of the amount of personal data involved, or because of the way certain information is held. In this chapter we consider the extent of the right of subject access in relation to categories of information that may be difficult to access. We also explain what additional information you may require from the requester to help you find the data they want.

The DPA places a high expectation on you to provide information in response to a SAR. As explained in chapter 5, you should ensure that your information management systems are well-designed and maintained, so you can efficiently locate and extract information requested by the data subjects whose personal data you process, as well as redact third party data where it is deemed necessary.

You should be prepared to make extensive efforts to find and retrieve the requested information. Even so, you are not required to do things that would be unreasonable or disproportionate to the importance of providing subject access to the information. Any decision on these matters should reflect the fact that the right of subject access is fundamental to data protection.

The DPA deals with the situation where supplying the requester with information in permanent form is impossible or would involve disproportionate effort by means of an exception in section 8(2): see chapter 8 for details.

CLARIFYING THE REQUEST

[4.236]

Before responding to a SAR, you may ask the requester for information you reasonably need to find the personal data covered by the request. You need not comply with the SAR until you have received it. However, even if the relevant information is difficult to find and retrieve, it is not acceptable for you to delay responding to a SAR unless you reasonably require more information to help you find the data in question.

Example

A chain of supermarkets is dealing with a general SAR from a member of staff at one of its branches. The person dealing with the request is satisfied that the staff member has been sent all information held in personnel files and in files held by his line manager. However, he complains that not all information about him was included in the response.

The employer should not ignore this complaint, but it would be reasonable to ask him for more details. For example, some of the information may be in emails, and the employer could reasonably ask for the approximate dates when the emails were sent and who sent them, to help find what he wants.

It might also be useful for the employer to ask if the member of staff is seeking information that does not relate to his employment. For example, he may be seeking information that relates to a complaint he made as a customer of the supermarket.

You cannot require the requester to narrow the scope of their request, but merely to provide additional details that will help you locate the requested information. So, if a requester asks for 'all the information you hold' about them, they are entitled to do that. You may ask them to provide information about the context in which information about them may have been processed, and about the likely dates when processing occurred, if this will help you deal with the request.

As with a request that is sent without the required fee, you should not ignore a request simply because you need more information from the requester. You should not delay in asking for this, but should ensure the requester knows you need more information and should tell them what details you need. Provided you have done that, the 40-day period for responding to the request does not begin to run until you have received the appropriate fee and any additional information you need.

The type of information it might be reasonable for you to ask for includes, where personal data is held in electronic form, information as to the type of electronic data being sought (application form, letter, email etc) and roughly when the data was created. This may help you identify whether the information sought is likely to have been deleted or archived (either printed off and held in a manual data archive, or removed from your 'live' electronic data systems and held in an electronic archive).

ELECTRONIC RECORDS

[4.237]

In most cases, information stored in electronic form can easily be found and retrieved. However, as it is very difficult to truly erase all electronic records, it is arguable that a requester might be entitled to request access to personal data that you do not have ready access to – because you still hold the data and, with time and varying degrees of technical expertise, you could retrieve it.

You are likely to have removed information from your 'live' systems in a number of different ways. The information may have been:

- 'archived' to storage;
- copied to back-up files; or
- 'deleted'.

Archived information and back-up records

Generally speaking, information is archived because, although you wish to remove it from your live systems, you decide to retain a copy in case it is needed in the future.

You should have procedures in place to find and retrieve personal data that has been electronically archived or backed up. The process of accessing electronically archived or backed-up data may be more complicated than the process of accessing 'live' data. However, as you have decided to retain copies of the data for future reference, you will presumably be able to find the data, possibly with the aid of location information from the requester. So you will be required to provide such information in response to a SAR.

Electronic archive and back-up systems might not use such sophisticated search mechanisms as 'live' systems, and you may ask a requester to give you enough context about their request to enable you to make a targeted search. The requester's ability to provide it may significantly affect whether you can find what they want. Nevertheless, to the extent that your search mechanisms allow you to find archived or backed-up data for your own purposes, you should use the same effort to find information in order to respond to a SAR.

If a request relates specifically to back-up copies of information held on your 'live' systems, it is reasonable to consider whether there is any evidence that the back-up data differs materially from that which is held on the 'live' systems and which has been supplied to the requester. If there is no evidence that there is any material difference, the Information Commissioner would not seek to enforce the right of subject access in relation to the back-up records.

Deleted information

Information is 'deleted' when you try to permanently discard it and you have no intention of ever trying to access it again. The Information Commissioner's view is that, if you delete personal data held in electronic form by removing it (as far as possible) from your computer systems, the fact that expensive technical expertise might enable it to be recreated does not mean you must go to such efforts to respond to a SAR. The Commissioner would not seek to take enforcement action against an organisation that has failed to use extreme measures to recreate previously 'deleted' personal data held in electronic form. The Commissioner does not require organisations to expend time and effort reconstituting information that they have deleted as part of their general records management.

In coming to this view, the Information Commissioner has considered that the purpose of subject access is to enable individuals to find out what information is held about them, to check its accuracy and ensure it is up to date and, where information is incorrect, to request correction of the information or compensation if inaccuracies have caused them damage or distress. However, if you have deleted the information, you can no longer use it to make decisions affecting the individual. So any inaccuracies can have no effect as the information will no longer be accessed by you or anyone else.

For more information on deleted information, please see the ICO guidance on Deleting personal data.

Information contained in emails

The contents of emails stored on your computer systems are, of course, a form of electronic record to which the general principles above apply. For the avoidance of doubt, the contents of an email should not be regarded as deleted merely because it has been moved to a user's 'Deleted items' folder.

It may be particularly difficult to find information to which a SAR relates if it is contained in emails that have been archived and removed from your 'live' systems. Nevertheless, the right of subject access is not limited to the personal data which it would be easy for you to provide, and the disproportionate effort exception (see Chapter 8 for more detail) cannot be used to justify a blanket refusal of a SAR, as it requires you to do whatever is proportionate in the circumstances. You may, of course, ask the requester to give you some context that would help you find what they want.

Usually, once you have found the relevant emails, the cost of supplying a copy of the personal data within them is unlikely to be prohibitive.

Information stored on personal computer equipment

You are only obliged to provide personal data in response to a SAR if you are a data controller in respect of that data. In most cases, therefore, you do not have to supply personal data if it is stored on someone else's computer systems rather than your own (the obvious exception being where that person is a data processor (see chapter 5)). However, if the requester's personal data is stored on equipment belonging to your staff (such as smartphones or home computers) or in private email accounts, what is the position when you receive a SAR?

It is good practice to have a policy restricting the circumstances in which staff may hold information about customers, contacts, or other employees on their own devices or in private email accounts. Some organisations enable staff to access their systems remotely (eg via a secure website), but most are likely to prohibit the holding of personal data on equipment the organisation does not control. Nevertheless, if you do permit staff to hold personal data on their own devices, they may be processing that data on your behalf, in which case it would be within the scope of a SAR you receive. The purpose for which the information is held, and its context, is likely to be relevant in this regard. We would not expect you to instruct staff to search their private emails or personal devices in response to a SAR unless you have a good reason to believe they are holding relevant personal data.

For more advice about what you need to consider when permitting the use of personal devices to process personal data for which you are responsible, see our Bring your own device (BYOD) guidance.

As we explain in chapter 11, the Information Commissioner has discretion as to whether to take enforcement action where there has been a breach of the DPA. The Commissioner would not take such action where it is clearly unreasonable to do so.

OTHER RECORDS

[4.238]
If you hold information about the requester otherwise than in electronic form (eg in paper files or on microfiche records), you will need to decide whether it is covered by the right of subject access. You will need to make a similar decision if electronic records have been removed from your live systems and archived in non-electronic form.

Whether the information in such hard-copy records is personal data accessible via the right of subject access will depend primarily on whether the non-electronic records are held in a 'relevant filing system' and also on whether the requester has given you enough context to enable you to find it.

For further guidance on relevant filing systems, see The Guide to Data Protection and the guidance FAQs and answers about relevant filing systems on our website. Broadly speaking, however, we consider that a relevant filing system exists where information about individuals is held in a sufficiently systematic, structured way as to allow ready access to specific information about those individuals.

AMENDING DATA FOLLOWING RECEIPT OF A SAR

[4.239]
The DPA specifies that a SAR relates to the data held at the time the request was received. However, in many cases, routine use of the data may result in it being amended or even deleted while you are dealing with the request. So it would be reasonable for you to supply the information you hold when you send out a response, even if this is different to that held when you received the request.

However, it is not acceptable to amend or delete the data if you would not otherwise have done so. For organisations subject to the Freedom of Information Act (FOIA), it is an offence to make such an amendment with the intention of preventing its disclosure.

An organisation that is effective in finding and retrieving the information it needs to respond to a SAR might have the following indicators of good practice:

Seeking clarification

There is an optional standard form for making a SAR. The form invites the requester to give details of the specific information requested. Often, by narrowing the scope of the request (where feasible) you can avoid making unnecessary searches or sending the requester large amounts of information they do not want or expect.

As part of the SAR logging process, the clarity of the request is checked. If it is not immediately obvious what the request relates to or where the required personal information is located, the organisation contacts the requester by phone to seek clarification.

A check is also made to ensure that the organisation knows the address where it will send the response.

Asset registers

An information asset register is in place that states where and how personal data is stored. This helps speed up the process of locating the information required to respond to SARs. Information asset owners are in place and the register is regularly reviewed to ensure it is kept up to date.

Retention and deletion policies

There are documented retention and deletion policies relating to the personal information the organisation holds. Different retention periods apply to different classes of information, depending on the purpose for which it is held.

Monitoring

If the organisation receives a significant volume of SARs, appropriate governance structures are in place to ensure they are processed and responded to effectively. For example, the team responsible for dealing with SARs holds weekly meetings to discuss SARs' progress and to investigate any cases that appear to be facing delay.

7. DEALING WITH SUBJECT ACCESS REQUESTS INVOLVING OTHER PEOPLE'S INFORMATION

THE BASIC RULE

[4.240]
Responding to a subject access request (SAR) may involve providing information that relates both to the requester and another individual.

Example

An employee makes a request to her employer for a copy of her human resources file. The file contains information identifying managers and colleagues who have contributed to (or are discussed in) that file. This will require you to reconcile the requesting employee's right of access with the third parties' rights in respect of their own personal data.

The Data Protection Act 1998 (DPA) says you do not have to comply with a SAR if to do so would mean disclosing information about another individual who can be identified from that information, except where:

- the other individual has consented to the disclosure; or
- it is reasonable in all the circumstances to comply with the request without that individual's consent.

So, although you may sometimes be able to disclose information relating to a third party, you need to decide whether it is appropriate to do so in each case. This decision will involve balancing the data subject's right of access against the other individual's rights in respect of their own personal data. If the other person consents to you disclosing the information about them, it would be unreasonable not to do so. However, if there is no such consent, you must decide whether to disclose the information anyway.

You should make decisions about disclosing third-party information on a case-by-case basis. You must not apply a blanket policy of withholding it.

For the avoidance of doubt, you cannot refuse to provide subject access to personal data about an individual simply because you obtained that data from a third party. The rules about third-party information, described in this chapter, apply only to personal data that includes information about the individual who is the subject of the request and information about someone else.

THREE-STEP APPROACH TO DEALING WITH INFORMATION ABOUT THIRD PARTIES

[4.241]
To help you decide whether to disclose information relating to a third-party individual, it helps to follow the three-step process described below. The ICO guidance Access to information held in complaint files also gives more advice about this.

Step 1 – Does the request require the disclosure of information that identifies a third party?

You should consider whether it is possible to comply with the request without revealing information that relates to and identifies a third-party individual. In doing so, you should take into account the information you are disclosing **and** any information you reasonably believe the person making the request may have, or may get hold of, that would identify the third-party individual.

> **Example**
>
> In the previous example about a request for an employee's human resources file, even if a particular manager is only referred to by their job title it is likely they will still be identifiable based on information already known to the employee making the request.

As your obligation is to provide information rather than documents, you may delete names or edit documents if the third-party information does not form part of the requested information.

However, if it is impossible to separate the third-party information from that requested and still comply with the request, you need to take account of the following considerations.

Step 2 – Has the third-party individual consented?

In practice, the clearest basis for justifying the disclosure of third-party information in response to a SAR is that the third party has given their consent. It is therefore good practice to ask relevant third parties for consent to the disclosure of their personal data in response to a SAR.

However, you are not obliged to try to get consent and in some circumstances it will clearly be reasonable to disclose without trying to get consent, such as where the information concerned will be known to the requester anyway. Indeed it may not always be appropriate to try to get consent, for instance if to do so would inevitably involve a disclosure of personal data about the requester to the third party.

Step 3 – Would it be reasonable in all the circumstances to disclose without consent?

In practice, it may sometimes be difficult to get third-party consent, eg the third party might refuse consent or might be difficult to find. If so, you must consider whether it is 'reasonable in all the circumstances' to disclose the information about the third party anyway.

The DPA provides a non-exhaustive list of factors to be taken into account when making this decision. These include:

- any duty of confidentiality owed to the third-party individual;
- any steps you have taken to try to get the third-party individual's consent;
- whether the third-party individual is capable of giving consent; and
- any stated refusal of consent by the third-party individual.

CONFIDENTIALITY

[4.242]
Confidentiality is one of the factors you must take into account when deciding whether to disclose information about a third party without their consent. A duty of confidence arises where information that is not generally available to the public (that is, genuinely 'confidential' information) has been disclosed to you with the expectation it will remain confidential. This expectation might result from the relationship between the parties. For example, the following relationships would generally carry with them a duty of confidence in relation to information disclosed.

- Medical (doctor and patient)
- Employment (employer and employee)
- Legal (solicitor and client)
- Financial (bank and customer)
- Caring (counsellor and client)

However, you should not always assume confidentiality. For example, a duty of confidence does not arise merely because a letter is marked 'confidential' (although this marking may indicate an expectation of confidence). It may be that the information in such a letter is widely available elsewhere (and so does not have the 'necessary quality of confidence'), or there may be other factors, such as the public interest, which mean that an obligation of confidence does not arise.

In most cases where a duty of confidence does exist, it will usually be reasonable to withhold third-party information unless you have the third-party individual's consent to disclose it.

OTHER RELEVANT FACTORS

[4.243]
In addition to the factors listed in the DPA, the following points are likely to be relevant to a decision about whether it is reasonable to disclose information about a third party in response to a SAR.

- **Information generally known to the individual making the request.** If the third-party information has previously been provided to the individual making the request, is already known by them, or is generally available to the public, it will be more likely to be reasonable for you to disclose that information. It follows that third-party information relating to a member of staff (acting in the course of their duties), who is well known to the individual making the request through their previous dealings, would be more likely to be disclosed than information relating to an otherwise anonymous private individual.
- **Circumstances relating to the individual making the request.** The importance of the information to the requester is also a relevant factor. The need to preserve confidentiality for a third party must be weighed against the requester's right to access information about his or her life. Therefore, depending on the significance of the information to the requester, it may be appropriate to disclose it even where the third party has withheld consent.
- **Health, educational and social work records.** As explained in chapters 9 and 10, special rules govern subject access to health, educational and social-work records. In practice, these rules mean that relevant information about health, education or social work professionals (acting in their professional capacities) should usually be disclosed in response to a SAR.

RESPONDING TO THE REQUEST

[4.244]
Whether you decide to disclose information about a third party in response to a SAR or to withhold it, you will need to respond to the requester. If the third party has given their consent to disclosure of information about them or if you are satisfied that it is reasonable in all the circumstances to disclose it without consent, you should provide the information in the same way as any other information provided in response to the SAR.

If you have not got the consent of the third party and you are not satisfied that it would be reasonable in all the circumstances to disclose the third-party information, then you should withhold it. However, you are still obliged to communicate as much of the information requested as you can without disclosing the third-party individual's identity. Depending on the circumstances, it may be possible to provide some information, having edited or 'redacted' it to remove information that would identify the third-party individual.

You must be able to justify your decision to disclose or withhold information about a third party, so it is good practice to keep a record of what you decide, and why. For example, it would be sensible to note why you chose not to seek consent or why it was inappropriate to do so in the circumstances.

8. SUPPLYING INFORMATION TO THE REQUESTER

INFORMATION THAT MUST BE SUPPLIED

[4.245]
The focus of a subject access request (SAR) is usually the supply of a copy of the requester's personal data. In this chapter we consider a number of issues about supplying that information. However, you should remember that subject access entitles an individual to more than just a copy of their personal data. An individual is also entitled to be:

- told whether any personal data is being processed – so, if you hold no personal data about the requester, you must still respond to let them know this;
- given a description of the personal data, the reasons it is being processed, and whether it will be given to any other organisations or people; and
- given details of the source of the data (if known).

This information might be contained in the copy of the personal data you supply. To the extent it is not, however, you must remember to supply this information in addition to a copy of the personal data itself when responding to a SAR.

The right to a description of other organisations or people to whom personal information may be given is a right to this information in general terms; it is not a right to receive the names of those organisations or people.

The requester may also ask for an explanation of the reasoning behind any automated decisions taken about him or her, such as a computer-generated decision to grant or deny credit, or an assessment of performance at work (except where this information is a trade secret). You only need to provide this additional information if it has been specifically requested.

Before supplying any information in response to a SAR, you should check that you have the requester's correct postal or email address (or both). If you are supplying information by fax (and we recommend that you do so only if the requester specifically asks you to), then you must ensure you are sending it to the correct fax number.

DECIDING WHAT INFORMATION TO SUPPLY

[4.246]
Documents or files may contain a mixture of information that is the requester's personal data, personal data about other people and information that is not personal data at all. This means that sometimes you will need to consider each document within a file separately, and even the content of a particular document, to assess the information they contain.

It may be easier (and will be more helpful) to give a requester a mixture of all the personal data and ordinary information relevant to their request, rather than to look at every document in a file to decide whether or not it is their personal data. This approach is likely to be appropriate where none of the information is particularly sensitive or contentious or refers to third-party individuals.

FORM IN WHICH THE INFORMATION MUST BE SUPPLIED

[4.247]
Once you have located and retrieved the personal data that is relevant to the request, you must communicate it to the requester in intelligible form. In most cases, this information must be communicated to thc requester by supplying him or her with a copy of it in permanent form. You may comply with this requirement by supplying a photocopy or print-out of the relevant information.

But if the requester has made a SAR electronically, they will probably be content – and may even prefer – to receive the response electronically too. It is good practice to check their preference. If they agree to receive information in electronic form, you will comply with the DPA by sending it in that form.

Some requesters are starting to ask for certain personal data (such as their domestic energy consumption data) to be supplied to them in an 'open re-usable format', for example a CSV file. Offering the data in this format makes it far easier for the data to be used by the requester under their control in relation to other services. The Information Commissioner would encourage you to consider the feasibility of enabling requesters to receive their data in open re-usable formats, for appropriate datasets. Clearly, we recognise that the cost and practicality of doing so must be taken into account. Such an approach is consistent with the Government's 'Midata' project, which aims to allow people to view, access and use their personal and transaction data in a way that is portable and safe.

Subject access provides a right to see the information contained in personal data, rather than a right to see copies of the documents that include that information. You may therefore provide the information in the form of transcripts of relevant documents (or of sections of documents that contain the personal data), or by providing a print-out of the relevant information from your computer systems. Although the easiest way to provide the relevant information is often to supply copies of original documents, you are not obliged to do so.

EXPLAINING THE INFORMATION SUPPLIED

[4.248]
The DPA requires that the information you supply to the individual is in intelligible form. At its most basic, this means the information should be understandable by the average person. However, the DPA does not require you to ensure that the information is provided in a form that is intelligible to the particular individual making the request.

Example

An individual makes a request for their personal data. When preparing the response, you notice that a lot of it is in coded form. For example, attendance at a particular training session is logged as 'A', while non-attendance at a similar event is logged as 'M'. Also, some of the information is in the form of handwritten notes that are difficult to read. Without access to the organisation's key or index to explain this information, it would be impossible for anyone outside the organisation to understand. In this case, the Act requires you to explain the meaning of the coded information. However, although it would be good practice to do so, the Act does not require you to decipher the poorly written notes, since the meaning of 'intelligible form' does not extend to 'make legible'.

Example

You receive a SAR from someone whose English comprehension skills are quite poor. You send a response and they ask you to translate the information you sent them. The Act does not require you to do this since the information is in intelligible form, even if the person who receives it cannot understand all of it. However, it would be good practice for you to help them understand the information you hold about them.

Example

Your organisation is based in Wales and your language of business is Welsh, not English, which means the documents you hold are all in Welsh. You receive a SAR from someone who does not speak or understand Welsh. After receiving your response, they ask you to translate the information. The Act does not require you to do this since the information is in intelligible form, even if the person cannot understand it. However, it would be good practice for you to help them understand the information you hold about them. Of course there may also be a separate requirement for you to translate the information under Welsh-language legislation, but this falls outside the scope of the DPA.

SUPPLYING INFORMATION IN PERMANENT FORM – HOW THE 'DISPROPORTIONATE EFFORT' EXCEPTION APPLIES

[4.249]

There are two situations in which the obligation to supply the requester with a copy of the relevant information 'in permanent form' does not apply. The first is where the requester agrees to another arrangement, and the second is where the supply of such a copy is impossible or would involve disproportionate effort.

The 'disproportionate effort' exception is in section 8(2) of the DPA. The Court of Appeal has provided clarification as to its application in its 2017 judgments in the cases of Dawson-Damer[1] and Ittihadieh/Deer and Oxford University[2].

The DPA does not define 'disproportionate effort', but the court has explained that there is scope for assessing whether, in the circumstances of a particular case, complying with a request by supplying a copy of the requested information in permanent form would result in so much work or expense as to outweigh the requester's right of access to their personal data.

The court also made it clear that in assessing whether complying with a SAR would involve disproportionate effort under section 8(2)(a) you may take into account difficulties which occur throughout the process of complying with the request, including any difficulties you encounter in finding the requested information.

This approach accords with the concept of proportionality in EU law, on which the DPA is based. When responding to SARs, we expect you to evaluate the particular circumstances of each request, balancing any difficulties involved in complying with the request against the benefits the information might bring to the data subject, whilst bearing in mind the fundamental nature of the right of subject access.

In order to apply the exception, the burden of proof is on you as data controller to show that you have taken all reasonable steps to comply with the SAR, and that it would be disproportionate in all the circumstances of the case for you to take further steps.

We consider it good practice for you to engage with the applicant, having an open conversation about the information they require. This might help you to reduce the costs and effort that you would otherwise incur in searching for the information.

If we receive a complaint about your handling of a subject access request, we may take into account your readiness to engage with the applicant and balance this against the benefit and importance of the information to them, as well as taking into account their level of co-operation with you in the course of the handling of a request.

Even if you can show that supplying a copy of information in permanent form would involve disproportionate effort, you must still try to comply with the request in some other way, if the applicant agrees. This could form a useful part of your discussions with the applicant, in order to identify an alternative way of satisfying their request.

Example

An organisation has decided that to supply copies of an individual's records in permanent form would involve disproportionate effort. Rather than refuse the individual access, they speak to her and agree that it would be preferable if she visited their premises and viewed the original documents. They also agree that if there are documents she would like to take away with her, they can arrange to provide copies.

In addition, even if you do not have to supply a copy of the information in permanent form, the requester still has the right:

- to be informed whether you are processing their personal data; and
- if so, to be given a description of:
    - the personal data in question;
    - the purpose of the processing; and
    - the recipients or classes of recipients; and
- to be given information about the source of the personal data.

NOTES

1 *Dawson-Damer & Ors v Taylor Wessing LLP* [2017] EWCA Civ 74

2 *Ittihadieh v 5-11 Cheyne Gardens RTM Co Ltd & Ors*; *Deer v University of Oxford and University of Oxford v Deer*

DEALING WITH REPEATED OR UNREASONABLE REQUESTS

[4.250]

The DPA does not limit the number of SARs an individual can make to any organisation. However, it does allow some discretion when dealing with requests that are made at unreasonable intervals. The Act says you are not obliged to comply with an identical or similar request to one you have already dealt with, unless a reasonable interval has elapsed between the first request and any subsequent ones.

The DPA gives you some help in deciding whether requests are made at reasonable intervals. It says you should consider the following.

- The nature of the data – this could include considering whether it is particularly sensitive.
- The purposes of the processing – this could include whether the processing is likely to cause detriment (harm) to the requester.
- How often the data is altered – if information is unlikely to have changed between requests, you may decide that you need not respond to the same request twice.

Section 8(6) of the DPA states that the "information to be supplied pursuant to a request . . . .must be supplied by reference to the data in question at the time when the request is received . . . .". If there has been a previous request or requests, and the information has been added to or amended since then, when answering a SAR you are required to provide a full response to the request: not merely supply information that is new or has been amended since the last request.

However, in practice we would accept that you may attempt to negotiate with the requester to get them to restrict the scope of their SAR to the new or updated information; but if they insist upon a full response then you would need to supply all the information.

Example

A library receives a SAR from an individual who made a similar request one month earlier. The information relates to when the individual joined the library and the items borrowed. None of the information has changed since the previous request. With this in mind, along with the fact that the individual is unlikely to suffer any disadvantage if the library does not send any personal data in response, you need not comply with this request. However, it would be good practice to respond explaining why it has not provided the information again.

Example

A therapist who offers non-medical counselling receives a SAR from a client. She had responded to a similar request from the same client three weeks earlier. When considering whether the requests have been made at unreasonable intervals, the therapist should take into account the fact that the client has attended five sessions between requests, so there is a lot of new information in the file. She should respond to this request, and she could ask the client to agree that she only needs to send any 'new' information. But it would also be good practice to discuss with the client a different way of allowing the client access to the notes about the sessions.

If, for these reasons, you decide you are not obliged to provide the information requested, it is good practice to explain this to the requester. They may not realise, for example, that your records have not changed since their last request.

An organisation that has effective mechanisms in place for supplying information to requesters might have the following indicators of good practice.

Online and electronic formats

Where appropriate, customers are able to access their personal information free of charge by using a secure website. This is good customer service and is likely to reduce the number of SARs the organisation has to deal with.

If requested, personal information is supplied in a machine-readable and re-usable format.

Onsite viewing facilities

There are procedures in place for requesters to view the requested information on the premises if it is voluminous or may require further support or explanation or both.

Copy differentiation

SAR-response hard copies are stamped 'data subject copy' before release. This may help identify the source of any further disclosure of the information, should the need arise.

9. EXEMPTIONS

EXEMPTIONS AND RESTRICTIONS – GENERAL

[4.251]

The Data Protection Act 1998 (DPA) recognises that in some circumstances you might have a legitimate reason for not complying with a subject access request (SAR), so it provides a number of exemptions from the duty to do so. Where an exemption applies to the facts of a particular request, you may refuse to provide all or some of the information requested, depending on the circumstances. It is a matter for you to decide whether or not to use an exemption – the DPA does not oblige you to do so, so you are free to comply with a SAR even if you could use an exemption.

Certain restrictions (similar to exemptions) are also built into the DPA's subject access provisions. For example, there are restrictions on the disclosure of personal data about more than one individual in response to a SAR (see chapter 7).

This chapter of the code explains the operation of the main exemptions from the duty to provide subject access. Not all of the exemptions apply in the same way, and you should look at each exemption carefully to see how it applies in a particular SAR. Some exemptions apply because of the nature of the personal data in question, eg information contained in a confidential reference. Others apply because disclosure of the information would be likely to prejudice a particular function of the organisation to which the request is made. The DPA does not explain what is meant by 'likely to prejudice'. However, the Information Commissioner's view is that it requires there to be a substantial chance (rather than a mere risk) that complying with the SAR would noticeably damage the discharge of the function concerned.

If challenged, you must be prepared to defend to the Information Commissioner's Office or a court your decision to apply an exemption. It is therefore good practice to ensure that such a decision is taken at a suitably senior level in your organisation and that you document the reasons for it.

CONFIDENTIAL REFERENCES

[4.252]

From time to time you may give or receive references about an individual, eg in connection with their employment, or for educational purposes. Such references are often given 'in confidence', but that fact alone does not mean the personal data included in the reference is exempt from subject access.

The DPA distinguishes between references you give and references you receive.

References you give are exempt from subject access if you give them in confidence and for the purposes of an individual's education, training or employment or the provision of a service by them.

There is no such exemption for references you receive from a third party. If you receive a SAR relating to such a reference, you must apply the usual principles about subject access to decide whether to provide some or all of the information contained in the reference.

Example

Company A provides an employment reference for one of its employees to company B. If the employee makes a SAR to company A, the reference will be exempt from disclosure. If the employee makes the request to company B, the reference is not automatically exempt from disclosure and the usual subject access rules apply.

It may be difficult to disclose the whole of a reference to the individual it relates to without disclosing some personal data about the author of the reference – most obviously, their identity. If the reference was not provided in confidence, this difficulty should not prevent disclosure. However, if a question of confidentiality arises, you should contact the author to find out whether they object to the reference being disclosed and, if so, why.

Even if the provider of a reference objects to its disclosure in response to a SAR, you will need to supply the personal data it contains to the requester if it is reasonable to do so in all the circumstances. You will therefore need to weigh the referee's interest in having their comments treated confidentially against the requester's interest in seeing what has been said about them. Relevant considerations are likely to include:

- any clearly stated assurance of confidentiality given to the referee;
- any reasons the referee gives for withholding consent;
- the likely impact of the reference on the requester;
- the requester's interest in being able to satisfy himself or herself that the reference is truthful and accurate; and
- any risk that disclosure may pose to the referee.

For more advice about how to deal with SARs that include personal data about third parties, see chapter 7.

PUBLICLY AVAILABLE INFORMATION

[4.253]

If an enactment requires an organisation to make information available to the public, any personal data included in it is exempt from the right of subject access.

The exemption only applies to the information that the organisation is required to publish. If it holds additional personal data about an individual, the additional data is not exempt from the right of subject access even if the organisation publishes it.

CRIME AND TAXATION

[4.254]

Personal data processed for certain purposes related to crime and taxation is exempt from the right of subject access. These purposes are:

- the prevention or detection of crime;
- the capture or prosecution of offenders; and

- the assessment or collection of tax or duty.

Example

The police process an individual's personal data because they suspect him of involvement in a serious crime. If telling the individual they are processing his personal data for this purpose would be likely to prejudice the investigation (perhaps because he might abscond or destroy evidence), then the police do not need to do so.

However, the exemption applies, in any particular case, only to the extent that complying with a SAR would be likely to prejudice the crime and taxation purposes set out above. You need to judge whether or not this is likely in each case – you should not use the exemption to justify denying subject access to whole categories of personal data if for some individuals the crime and taxation purposes are unlikely to be prejudiced.

Example

A taxpayer makes a SAR to Her Majesty's Revenue and Customs (HMRC) for personal data they hold about him in relation to an ongoing investigation into possible tax evasion. If disclosing the information which HMRC have collected about the taxpayer would be likely to prejudice their investigation, eg because it would make it difficult for them to collect evidence, HMRC could refuse to grant subject access to the extent that doing so would be likely to prejudice their investigation.

If, however, the taxpayer does not make the request until some years later when the investigation (and any subsequent prosecution) has been completed, it is unlikely that complying with the SAR would prejudice the crime and taxation purposes – in which case HMRC would need to comply with it.

Nor would the exemption justify withholding all the personal data to which the request relates when only part of the personal data would be likely to prejudice those purposes.

Example

In the previous example about an ongoing investigation into possible tax evasion, HMRC would be entitled to refuse subject access to personal data that would be likely to prejudice their investigation. However, this would not justify a refusal to grant access to other personal data they hold about the taxpayer.

Personal data that:

- is processed for the purpose of discharging statutory functions; and
- consists of information obtained for this purpose from someone who held it for any of the crime and taxation purposes described above

is also exempt from the right of subject access to the extent that providing subject access to the personal data would be likely to prejudice any of the crime and taxation purposes. This prevents the right applying to personal data that is passed to statutory review bodies by law-enforcement agencies, and ensures that the exemption is not lost when the information is disclosed during a review.

Example

The Independent Police Complaints Commission (IPCC) begins an investigation into the conduct of a particular police force. Documents passed to the IPCC for the purposes of the investigation contain personal data about Mr A that the police force would not have been obliged to disclose to Mr A in response to a SAR – because doing so would be likely to prejudice its criminal investigation. If Mr A then makes a SAR to the IPCC, he has no greater right of access to the personal data in question.

Section 29(4) of the DPA provides an additional exemption from the right of subject access that is designed to prevent the right being used to force relevant authorities to disclose information about the operation of crime detection and anti-fraud systems, where such disclosure may undermine the operation of those systems.

MANAGEMENT INFORMATION

[4.255]

A further exemption applies to personal data that is processed for management forecasting or management planning. Such data is exempt from the right of subject access to the extent that complying with a SAR would be likely to prejudice the business or other activity of the organisation.

Example

The senior management of an organisation are planning a re-organisation. This is likely to involve making certain employees redundant, and this possibility is included in management plans. Before the plans are revealed to the workforce, an employee makes a SAR. In responding to that request, the organisation does not have to reveal its plans to make him redundant if doing so would be likely to prejudice the conduct of the business (perhaps by causing staff unrest in advance of an announcement of the management's plans).

NEGOTIATIONS WITH THE REQUESTER

[4.256]
Personal data that consists of a record of your intentions in negotiations with an individual is exempt from the right of subject access to the extent that complying with a SAR would be likely to prejudice the negotiations.

Example

An individual makes a claim to his insurance company. The claim is for compensation for personal injuries he sustained in an accident. The insurance company dispute the seriousness of the injuries and the amount of compensation they should pay. An internal paper sets out the company's position on these matters and indicates the maximum sum they would be willing to pay to avoid the claim going to court. If the individual makes a SAR to the insurance company, they would not have to send him the internal paper – because doing so would be likely to prejudice the negotiations to settle the claim.

REGULATORY ACTIVITY

[4.257]
Some organisations may use an exemption from subject access if they perform regulatory activities. The exemption is not available to all organisations, but only to those that have regulatory functions concerning the protection of the public or charities, or fair competition in business. Organisations that do have such functions may only apply the exemption to personal data processed for these core regulatory activities, and then only to the extent that granting subject access to the information concerned would be likely to prejudice the proper discharge of those functions.

For more detailed guidance on how this exemption applies, see ICO guidance on regulatory activity.

LEGAL ADVICE AND PROCEEDINGS

[4.258]
Personal data is also exempt from the right of subject access if it consists of information for which legal professional privilege (or its Scottish equivalent, 'confidentiality in communications') could be claimed in legal proceedings in any part of the UK.

The English law concept of legal professional privilege encompasses both 'legal advice' privilege and 'litigation' privilege. In broad terms, the former applies only to confidential communications between client and professional legal adviser, and the latter applies to confidential communications between client, professional legal adviser or a third party, but only where litigation is contemplated or in progress.

The Scottish law concept of confidentiality of communications provides protection both for communications relating to the obtaining or providing of legal advice and for communications made in connection with legal proceedings. Information that comprises confidential communications between client and professional legal adviser may be withheld under the legal privilege exemption in the same way that information attracting English law 'legal advice' privilege may be withheld. Similarly, the Scottish law doctrine that a litigant is not required to disclose material he has brought into existence for the purpose of preparing his case protects information that, under English law, would enjoy 'litigation' privilege.

Where legal professional privilege cannot be claimed, you may not refuse to supply information in response to a SAR simply because the information is requested in connection with actual or potential legal proceedings. The DPA contains no exemption for such information; indeed, it says the right of subject access overrides any other legal rule that limits disclosure. In addition, there is nothing in the Act that limits the purposes for which a SAR may be made, or which requires the requester to tell you what they want the information for.

It has been suggested that case law provides authority for organisations to refuse to comply with a SAR where the requester is contemplating or has already begun legal proceedings. The Information Commissioner does not accept this view. Whether or not the applicant has a 'collateral' purpose (ie other than seeking to check or correct their personal data) for making the SAR is not relevant.

However the court does have a wide discretion as to whether or not to order compliance with a SAR. Please see chapter 11 for more details.

Nevertheless, simply because a court may choose not to order the disclosure of an individual's personal data does not mean that, in the absence of a relevant exemption, the DPA does not require you to disclose it. It simply means that the individual may not be able to enlist the court's support to enforce his or her right.

SOCIAL WORK RECORDS

[4.259]
Special rules apply where providing subject access to information about social services and related

activities would be likely to prejudice the carrying out of social work by causing serious harm to the physical or mental health or condition of the requester or any other person. These rules are set out in the Data Protection (Subject Access Modification) (Social Work) Order 2000 (SI 2000/415). Their effect is to exempt personal data processed for these purposes from subject access to the extent that its disclosure would be likely to cause such harm.

A further exemption from subject access to social work records applies when a SAR is made by a third party who has a right to make the request on behalf of the individual, such as the parent of a child or someone appointed to manage the affairs of an individual who lacks capacity. In these circumstances, personal data is exempt from subject access if the individual has made clear they do not want it disclosed to that third party.

HEALTH AND EDUCATION RECORDS

[4.260]
The exemptions that may apply when a SAR relates to personal data included in health and education records are explained in chapter 10 of the code.

OTHER EXEMPTIONS

[4.261]
The exemptions mentioned in this chapter are those most likely to apply in practice. However, the DPA contains additional exemptions that may be relevant when dealing with a SAR. For more information about exemptions, see the ICO Guide to Data Protection.

An organisation that makes appropriate use of the exemptions in the DPA might have the following indicators of good practice:

Withholding or redacting information

If information is withheld in reliance on an exemption, the response explains, to the extent it can do so, the fact that information has been withheld and the reasons why. The explanation is given in plain English, and does more than simply specify that a particular exemption applies.

Information to be redacted is approved before source material is copied in a redacted form. It is then subject to at least one quality review by a manager to confirm that all data has been excluded appropriately. A copy of the disclosure bundle showing the redactions and the reasons behind them is retained for reference.

Once approved, redaction is either carried out manually using black marker which is then photocopied, or electronically using Adobe Acrobat or bespoke redaction software.

Ensuring consistency

Advice on applying the exemptions most likely to be relevant to the organisation's activities is included in SAR guidance for staff.

Quality assessments are carried out to ensure that exemptions are applied consistently.

10. SPECIAL CASES

(Outside the scope of this work.)

11. ENFORCING THE RIGHT OF SUBJECT ACCESS

THE INFORMATION COMMISSIONER'S ENFORCEMENT POWERS

[4.262]
Anyone who believes they are directly affected by the processing of personal data may ask the Information Commissioner's Office (ICO) to assess whether it is likely or unlikely that such processing complies with the Data Protection Act 1998 (DPA). This is called a compliance assessment.

If our assessment shows that it is likely that an organisation has failed to comply with the DPA (or is failing to do so), we may ask it to take steps to comply with the data protection principles. Where appropriate, the ICO may order the organisation to do so. However, the ICO has no power to award compensation to individuals – only the courts can do this.

The Information Commissioner may serve an enforcement notice if she is satisfied that an organisation has failed to comply with the subject access provisions. An enforcement notice may require an organisation to take specified steps to comply with its obligations in this regard. Failure to comply with an enforcement notice is a criminal offence. The Information Commissioner will not necessarily serve an enforcement notice simply because an organisation has failed to comply with the subject access provisions. Before serving a notice she has to consider whether the contravention has caused or is likely to cause any person damage or distress. She can serve a notice even though there has been no damage or distress but it must be reasonable, in all the circumstances, for her to do so. She will not require organisations to take unreasonable or disproportionate steps to comply with the law on subject access.

The Information Commissioner has a statutory power to impose a financial penalty on an organisation if she is satisfied that the organisation has committed a serious breach of the DPA that is likely to cause substantial damage or distress.

For more information about the Information Commissioner's enforcement powers, see the ICO Guide to Data Protection.

ENFORCEMENT BY COURT ORDER

[4.263]

If you fail to comply with a subject access request (SAR), the requester may apply for a court order requiring you to comply. It is a matter for the court to decide, in each particular case, whether to make such an order.

As stated in chapter 9, it is irrelevant whether or not the applicant has a 'collateral' purpose for making the SAR. The Court of Appeal[3] has said there is "nothing in the DPA or the Directive that limits the purpose for which a data subject may request his data".

Although the court will ordinarily exercise its discretion in favour of the data subject, it does have a wide discretion as to whether or not to order compliance with a SAR. There is a range of factors that the Court of Appeal suggested the court may wish to take into account, including:

- the nature and gravity of the data controller's breach of its s7 obligations;
- the general principle of proportionality;
- balancing the fundamental right of the individual right of subject access with the interests of the data controller;
- prejudice to the individual's rights;
- whether there is a more appropriate route to disclosure (note that this does not affect the obligation of the data controller to make disclosure in response to a SAR, but may have an impact on the use of the court's discretion); and
- where there is an abuse of process or a conflict of interest, this may influence the court not to make an order.

Nevertheless, as we explained in chapter 9, whether or not a court would be likely to grant an enforcement order has no bearing on your legal duty to comply with a SAR. You may only refuse to comply if a relevant exemption under the DPA applies in the particular circumstances of the request.

NOTES

[3] In Dawson-Damer, cited earlier

AWARDS OF COMPENSATION

[4.264]

If an individual suffers damage because you have breached the DPA – including, of course, by failing to comply with a SAR – they are entitled to claim compensation from you. This right can only be enforced through the courts. The DPA allows you to defend a claim for compensation on the basis that you took all reasonable care in the circumstances to avoid the breach, but it is likely to be difficult to establish this defence where you have failed to respond to a SAR within the prescribed time limit, or where you have not provided the requester with all the information to which they are entitled.

For more information about claims for compensation, see the ICO Guide to Data Protection.

FORCING AN INDIVIDUAL TO MAKE A SAR IS A CRIMINAL OFFENCE

[4.265]

It is a criminal offence, in certain circumstances and in relation to certain information, to require an individual to make a subject access request.

For more information on enforced subject access requests, please see Enforced subject access (section 56).

G. SECRETARY OF STATE

CODE OF PRACTICE: ACCESS AND UNFAIR PRACTICES DURING RECOGNITION AND DERECOGNITION BALLOTS (2005)

[4.266]

NOTES

This Code is issued under the power given to the Secretary of State by the Trade Union and Labour Relations (Consolidation) Act 1992, s 203 (at **[1.519]**), with the authority of Parliament. It came into effect on 1 October 2005 (see the Employment Code of Practice (Access and Unfair Practices during Recognition and Derecognition Ballots) Order 2005, SI 2005/2421). The statutory status of the Code is as stated in s 207 of the 1992 Act (at **[1.523]**).

This Code replaces the Code of Practice on Access to Workers during Recognition and Derecognition Ballots (2000). Notes are as in the original.

See *Harvey* NI(7).

CONTENTS

PREAMBLE

[4.267]

This document revises the Code of Practice on Access to Workers during Recognition and Derecognition Ballots, which came into effect on 6 June 2000. It also contains practical guidance on unfair practices during recognition and derecognition ballots, for which the law provides a separate power for the Secretary of State to issue a Code of Practice. These two Codes on access and unfair practices are therefore combined within this single document. For simplicity and ease of reference, the text refers to there being just one Code of Practice dealing with both topics.

This Code supersedes the Code of Practice on Access to Workers during Recognition and Derecognition Ballots, which came into effect on 6 June 2000. Pursuant to section 208(2) of the Trade Union and Labour Relations (Consolidation) Act 1992, that Code shall cease to have effect on the date on which this Code of Practice comes in force.

The legal framework within which this Code will operate is explained in its text. While every effort has been made to ensure that explanations included in the Code are accurate, only the courts can give authoritative interpretations of the law.

The Code's provisions apply equally to men and to women, but for simplicity the masculine pronoun is used throughout.

Unless the text specifies otherwise, (i) the term "union" should be read to mean "unions" in cases where two or more unions are seeking to be jointly recognised; (ii) the term "workplace" should be read to mean "workplaces" in cases where a recognition application covers more than one workplace; and (iii) the term "working day" should be read to mean any day other than a Saturday or a Sunday, Christmas Day or Good Friday, or a day which is a bank holiday.

Passages in this Code which appear in italics are extracts from, or re-statements of, provisions in primary legislation.

SECTION A
INTRODUCTION

BACKGROUND

[4.268]

1. Schedule A1 of the Trade Union and Labour Relations (Consolidation) Act 1992, inserted by the Employment Relations Act 1999 and subsequently amended by the Employment Relations Act 2004, sets out the statutory procedure for the recognition and derecognition of trade unions for the purpose of collective bargaining.

RECOGNITION

2. Where an employer and a trade union fail to reach agreement on recognition voluntarily, the statute provides for the union to apply to the Central Arbitration Committee (CAC) to decide whether it should be recognised for collective bargaining purposes. In certain cases, the CAC may award recognition, or dismiss the application, without a ballot. In other cases, the CAC will be obliged to hold a secret ballot

Part 4 Statutory Codes of Practice

of members of the bargaining unit to determine the issue. If a ballot takes place, the CAC will decide whether it should be held at the workplace, by post, or, if special factors make it appropriate, by a combination of the two methods. The ballot must be conducted by a qualified independent person appointed by the CAC.

3. Schedule A1 places various duties and obligations on parties during the period of a recognition ballot including the following:

(a) Paragraph 26(2) of Schedule A1 places a duty on the employer *to co-operate generally, in connection with the ballot, with the union and the independent person appointed to conduct the ballot;*

(b) Paragraph 26(3) of Schedule A1 places a duty on the employer to give a union applying for recognition *such access to the workers constituting the bargaining unit as is reasonable to enable the union to inform the workers of the object of the ballot and to seek their support and their opinions on the issues involved;*

(c) Paragraph 26(4A) of Schedule A1 places a duty on the employer *to refrain from making any offer to any or all of the workers constituting the bargaining unit which (i) has or is likely to have the effect of inducing any or all of them not to attend a relevant meeting between the union and the workers constituting the bargaining unit and (ii) is not reasonable in the circumstances.* A "relevant meeting" is defined as a meeting arranged in accordance with the duty to provide reasonable access to which the employer has agreed, or is required, to permit the worker to attend;

(d) Paragraph 26(4B) of Schedule A1 places a duty on the employer *to refrain from taking or threatening to take any action against a worker solely or mainly on the grounds that he attended or took part in any relevant meeting between the union and the workers in the bargaining unit, or on the grounds that he indicated his intention to attend or take part in such a meeting.* The definition of a "relevant meeting" is the same as at (c);

(e) *Paragraph 27A(1) of Schedule A1 places an obligation on both the employer and the union to refrain from using an unfair practice with a view to influencing the result of a recognition ballot. The unfair practices are defined by paragraph 27A(2) of Schedule A1.*

4. Section 203(1)(a) of the Trade Union and Labour Relations (Consolidation) Act 1992 gives a general power to the Secretary of State to issue Codes of Practice containing practical guidance for the purpose of promoting the improvement of industrial relations. Paragraphs 26(8) and 26(9) of Schedule A1 specify that this general power includes the particular power to issue a Code of Practice giving practical guidance about reasonable access during recognition ballots and about the employer's duty to refrain from making offers to workers not to attend access meetings. In addition, paragraph 27A(5) of Schedule A1 specifies that the general power includes the particular power to issue a Code of Practice about unfair practices for the purposes of paragraph 27A.

DERECOGNITION

5. The CAC can also call a derecognition ballot in cases where an employer, or his workers, are seeking to end recognition arrangements with a union. In general, the duties and obligations on the parties are the same in both recognition and derecognition ballots. Paragraph 118(3) of Schedule A1 contains identical wording to paragraph 26(3) of Schedule A1, placing a duty on the employer to give the recognised union reasonable access to the workers comprising the bargaining unit where the CAC is holding a ballot on derecognition. Similarly, paragraph 118(4A) places a duty on the employer to refrain from making offers to workers not to attend access meetings. And paragraph 119A(1) requires both the employer, the union and, in cases where workers are applying to derecognise the union, those workers to refrain from using an unfair practice during the period of a derecognition ballot. Paragraphs 118(8) and 119(9) and paragraph 119A(5) contain similar provisions to paragraphs 26(8) and 26(9) and 27A(5) enabling the Secretary of State to issue a Code of Practice giving practical guidance about reasonable access and unfair practices during derecognition ballots.

6. For simplicity, most examples and explanations in this Code relate to the case where the union is seeking recognition. However, the guidance contained in this Code applies equally to cases where the ballot is about recognition or derecognition.

GENERAL PURPOSE OF THE CODE

7. This Code covers two related issues: the union's access to workers during the period of recognition or derecognition ballots and the avoidance of unfair practices when campaigning during that period. As regards the first topic of **access**, this Code gives practical guidance about the issues which arise when an employer receives a request by a union to be granted access to his workers at their workplace and/or during their working time. Of course, the union does not need the employer's consent or assistance to arrange access outside the workplace and outside working hours – say, when hiring a public hall to hold a meeting or when using local newspapers and media to put across its case. The Code does not therefore deal with the issues that arise when arranging such access, though those parts of the Code which concern the conduct of parties when campaigning are relevant. This Code deals with the specific circumstances of access during the period of recognition or derecognition ballots. It does not provide guidance on access at other times.

8. Access can take many and varied forms depending largely on the type of workplace involved and the characteristics of the balloted workforce. The overall aim is to ensure that the union can reach the workers involved, but local circumstances will need to be taken into account when deciding what form the access should take. Each case should be looked at on the facts. This Code therefore aims to help the employer and the union arrive at agreed arrangements for access, which can take full account of the circumstances of each individual case.

9. The second purpose of this Code is to help parties avoid committing **unfair practices**. Recognition and derecognition ballots usually occur because the employer and the union cannot agree the way ahead. In some cases a party will wish to communicate its views to the workers concerned through active campaigning once the CAC has informed it that a ballot will be held. This Code aims to encourage reasonable and responsible behaviour by both the employer and the union when undertaking campaigning activity in this period. A failure to follow the Code's guidance on responsible behaviour may not necessarily mean that an unfair practice has occurred. However, responsible campaigning should help ensure that acrimony between the parties is avoided and it greatly reduces the risk that individual workers are exposed to intimidation, threat or other unfair practices when deciding which way to cast their vote. As regards the treatment of individuals, both parties should note that the law provides protections against dismissal or detriment for workers who campaign either for or against recognition. The Code does not cover campaigning activity which occurs before the CAC decides that a ballot should be held. However, parties are still advised to act responsibly when undertaking early campaigning and they may benefit by drawing on the guidance provided by this Code.

10. In order for a ballot to take place, the union must have satisfied the CAC that at least 10% of the proposed bargaining unit are already members of the union, and that a majority of the workers in the proposed bargaining unit would be likely to favour recognition. There is therefore a good chance that recognition will be granted to the union, and that a working relationship between the parties will have to be sustained after the ballot. This longer term perspective should encourage both the employer and the union to behave responsibly and in a co-operative spirit during the balloting period.

STRUCTURE OF THE CODE

11. This Code deals mainly with issues concerning access and unfair practices. These are distinct, though related, matters and all sections of the Code should therefore be read in conjunction. Sections B–D contain guidance on access, whilst Section E provides guidance on conduct to avoid committing an unfair practice. Finally, Section F provides guidance on the resolution of any disputes which might arise about the arrangement of access to the union or to the conduct of either the employer or the union when campaigning during the balloting period.

LEGAL STATUS OF THE CODE

12. *Under paragraphs 27 and 119 of Schedule A1, the CAC may order employers who are breaching their duty to allow reasonable access to take specified, reasonable steps to do so, and can award recognition without a ballot, or can refuse to award derecognition where applied for by the employer, if an employer fails to abide by its orders to remedy a breach. Paragraphs 27C–27F of Schedule A1 provide a number of actions which the CAC may take when it concludes that a party has committed an unfair practice during a recognition or derecognition ballot. For example, the CAC may order a further ballot and it may order a party to take specified actions to help remedy the effects of the unfair practice. In addition, the CAC may award recognition or derecognition (or dismiss an application for recognition or derecognition) where an unfair practice has involved the use of violence or the dismissal of a union official, or where the CAC has found that a party has committed a second unfair practice or failed to comply with a remedial order.*

13. *This Code itself imposes no legal obligations and failure to observe it does not in itself render anyone liable to proceedings. But section 207 of the Trade Union and Labour Relations (Consolidation) Act 1992 provides that any provisions of this Code are to be admissible in evidence and are to be taken into account in proceedings before any court, tribunal or the CAC where they consider them relevant.*

SECTION B
PREPARING FOR ACCESS

WHEN SHOULD PREPARATIONS FOR ACCESS BEGIN?

[4.269]

14. Preparations for access should begin as soon as possible. The CAC is required to give notice to the employer and the union that it intends to arrange for the holding of a ballot. There then follows a period of ten working days before the CAC proceeds with arrangements for the ballot. The parties should make full use of this notification period to prepare for access. The union should request an early meeting with the employer in this period to discuss access arrangements. The employer should agree to arrange the meeting on an early date and at a mutually convenient time. The employer and the union should ensure that the individual or individuals representing them at the meeting are expressly authorised by them to take all relevant decisions regarding access, or are authorised to make recommendations directly to those who take such decisions.

JOINT APPLICATIONS BY TWO OR MORE UNIONS

15. Where there is a joint application for recognition by two or more unions acting together, the unions should act jointly in preparing and implementing the access arrangements. Therefore, unless the employer and the unions agree otherwise, the unions should have common access arrangements. The amount of time needed for access would normally be the same for single or joint applications.

ESTABLISHING AN ACCESS AGREEMENT

16. It would be reasonable for the employer to want to give his prior permission before allowing a full time union official to enter his workplace and talk to his workers. In particular, the employer may have security and health and safety issues to consider. The parties should discuss practical arrangements for the union's activities at the workplace, in advance of the period of access actually beginning.

17. Consideration should be given to establishing an agreement, preferably in written form, on access arrangements. Such an agreement could include:

- the union's programme for where, when and how it will access the workers on site and/or during their working time; and
- a mechanism for resolving disagreements, if any arise, about implementing the agreed programme of access.

When discussions about access arrangements are taking place, parties should also seek to reach understandings about the standards of conduct expected of those individuals who campaign on their behalf (see paragraph 52 below for more guidance on this point).

18. In seeking to reach an agreement, the union should put its proposals for accessing the workers to the employer. The employer should not dismiss the proposals unless he considers the union's requirements to be unreasonable in the circumstances. If the employer rejects the proposals, he should offer alternative arrangements to the union at the earliest opportunity, preferably within three working days of receiving the union's initial proposals. In the course of this dialogue the union will need to reveal its plans for on-site access.

19. It is reasonable for the union to request information from the employer to help it formulate and refine its access proposals. In particular, the employer should disclose to the union information about his typical methods of communicating with his workforce and provide such other practical information as may be needed about, say, workplace premises or patterns of work. Where relevant to the union in framing its plans, the employer should also disclose information about his own plans to put across his views, directly or indirectly, to the workers about the recognition (or derecognition) of the union. The employer should not, however, disclose to the union the names or addresses (postal or e-mail) of the workers who will be balloted, unless the workers concerned have authorised the disclosure.

AMENDING THE ACCESS AGREEMENT

20. Every effort should be made to ensure access agreements are faithfully implemented. To avoid misunderstanding on the ground, the employer should seek to draw the attention of relevant managers to the agreement and the commitments to release workers to attend access meetings. Likewise, the union should take steps to ensure that the relevant union officials and representatives are made aware of the agreed arrangements. However, in some cases, the agreement may need to be changed if circumstances alter. For example, a union official selected to enter the workplace may be unexpectedly called away by his union on other urgent business. Likewise, the employer might wish to re-arrange an event if the selected meeting-room is unexpectedly and unavoidably needed for other important business purposes. If such circumstances arise, the union, or the employer if his situation changes, should notify the other party at the earliest opportunity that a change will need to be made to the agreed access arrangements, and offer alternative suggestions. The other party should generally accept the alternative arrangements, if they are of an equivalent nature to those already agreed.

RESOLVING DIFFERENCES ABOUT AGREEING ACCESS ARRANGEMENTS

21. Where the employer and the union fail to agree access arrangements voluntarily, either party, acting separately or together, may ask the Advisory, Conciliation and Arbitration Service (Acas) to conciliate. Given the limited time available, Acas will respond to the conciliation request as soon as possible, and preferably within one working day of receiving the request. Both parties should give all reasonable assistance to Acas to enable it to help the parties overcome their difficulties through conciliation.

22. Every effort should be made to resolve any procedural difficulties remaining, but, ultimately, where it remains deadlocked, the CAC may be asked to assist. The CAC could, in appropriate circumstances, consider delaying the arrangement of the ballot for a limited period to give extra time for the parties to settle their differences. However, where no agreement is forthcoming, the CAC may be asked to adjudicate and to make an order.

SECTION C
ACCESS IN OPERATION

WHAT IS THE ACCESS PERIOD?

[4.270]

23. *Following the notification period, and providing it does not receive a contrary request from the trade union, the CAC will be required to arrange the holding of the ballot. As soon as is reasonably practicable, the CAC must inform the parties of the fact that it is arranging the ballot, the name of the qualified independent person appointed to conduct the ballot, and the period within which the ballot must be conducted. The ballot must be held within 20 working days from the day after the appointment of the independent person, or longer if the CAC should so decide.*

24. The period of access will begin as soon as the parties have been informed of the arrangements for the ballot as in paragraph 23 above. The CAC will endeavour to inform both parties as soon as the independent person has been appointed. This may be achieved by a telephone call to both parties, followed by a letter of confirmation.

25. If the ballot is to be conducted by post, the period of access will come to an end on the closing date of the balloting period. If the ballot is to be conducted at the workplace, access will continue until the ballot has closed. However, where the ballot is to be conducted at the workplace, and where the union has already had adequate access opportunities, both the employer and the union should largely confine their activities during the actual hours of balloting to the encouragement of workers to vote. They should reduce or cease other campaigning activity at this time. For example, both the employer and the union should avoid scheduling large meetings at such times. This should ensure that the ballot is conducted in a calm and orderly fashion, with minimum disruption to the normal functioning of the workplace.

WHO MAY BE GRANTED ACCESS?

26. The access agreement should specify who should be given access to the workers who will be balloted. Employers should be prepared to give access to:

(a) individual union members employed by the employer, who are nominated by the union as the lead representative of their members at workplaces where the bargaining unit is situated;

(b) individual union members employed by the employer, who are nominated by the union as the lead representative of their members at other workplaces in the employer's business, provided that it is practicable for them to attend events at workplaces where the bargaining unit is situated. The costs of travelling from other workplaces should be met by the individuals or the union; and

(c) "full-time" union officials. (That is, individuals employed by the union, who are officials of the union within the meaning of the Sections 1 and 119 of the Trade Union and Labour Relations (Consolidation) Act 1992).

The number of union representatives entitled to gain access should be proportionate to the scale and nature of the activities or events organised within the agreed access programme.

WHERE WILL THE ACCESS TAKE PLACE?

27. Where practicable in the circumstances, a union should be granted access to the workers at their actual workplace. However, each case will depend largely on the type of workplace concerned, and the union will need to take account of the wide variety of circumstances and operational requirements that are likely to be involved. In particular, consideration will need to be given to the employer's responsibility for health and safety and security issues. In other words, access arrangements should reflect local circumstances and each case should be examined on the facts.

28. Where they are suitable for the purpose, the employer's typical methods of communicating with his workforce should be used as a benchmark for determining how the union should communicate with members of the same workforce during the access period. If the employer follows the custom and practice of holding large workforce meetings in, for example, a meeting room or a canteen, then the employer should make the same facilities available to the union. However, in cases where the workplace is more confined, and it is therefore the employer's custom and practice to hold only small meetings at the workplace, then the union will also be limited to holding similar small meetings at that workplace. In exceptional circumstances, due to the nature of the business or severe space limitations, access may need to be restricted to meetings away from the workplace premises, and the union will need to consider finding facilities off-site at its own expense unless it agrees otherwise with the employer. In these circumstances, the employer should give all reasonable assistance to the union in notifying the workers in advance of where and when such off-site events are to take place. Where such exceptional circumstances exist, it would normally be expected that the employer would not hold similar events at the workplace.

WHEN WILL THE ACCESS TAKE PLACE?

29. The union should ensure that disruption to the business is minimised, especially for small businesses which might find it more difficult to organise cover for absent workers. The union's access to the workers should usually take place during normal working hours but at times which minimise any possible disruption to the activities of the employer. This will ensure that the union is able to communicate with as large a number of the workers as possible. Again, the arrangements should reflect the circumstances of each individual case. Consideration should be given to holding events, particularly those involving a large proportion of the workers in the bargaining unit, during rest periods or towards the end of a shift. In deciding the timing of meetings and other events, the union and the employer should be guided by the employer's custom and practice when communicating with his workforce. If, due to exceptional circumstances, access must be arranged away from the workplace, it might be practicable to arrange events in work time if they are held nearby, within easy walking distance. Otherwise, off-site events should normally occur outside work time.

THE FREQUENCY AND DURATION OF UNION ACTIVITIES

30. The parties will need to establish agreed limits on the duration and frequency of the union's activities during the access period. Subject to the circumstances discussed in paragraphs 27–29 above, the employer should allow the union to hold one meeting of at least 30 minutes in duration for every 10 days of the access period, or part thereof, which all workers or a substantial proportion of them are given the opportunity to attend. In circumstances where the employer or others organise similar large-scale meetings in work time against the recognition application (or in favour of derecognition), then it would be reasonable for the union to hold additional meetings, if necessary, to ensure that in total it has the same number of large-scale meetings as the employer and his supporters.

31. Where they would be appropriate having regard to all the circumstances, union "surgeries" could be organised at the workplace during working hours at which each worker would have the opportunity, if they wish, to meet a union representative for fifteen minutes on an individual basis or in small groups of two or three. The circumstances would include whether there was a demand from the workforce for surgeries, whether the surgeries could be arranged off-site as effectively, whether the holding of surgeries would lead to an unacceptable increase in tension at the workplace and whether the employer, line managers or others use similar one-to-one or small meetings to put across the employer's case. The union should organise surgeries in a systematic way, ensuring that workers attend meetings at pre-determined times, thereby avoiding delays before workers are seen and ensuring that they promptly return to their work stations afterwards. Wherever practicable, the union should seek to arrange surgeries during periods of down-time such as rest or meal breaks. Where surgeries do not take place, the minimum time allowed for each larger scale meeting should be 45 minutes.

32. An employer should ensure that workers who attend a meeting or a "surgery" organised by the union with his agreement during work time, should be paid, in full, for the duration of their absence from work. The employer will not be expected to pay the worker if the meeting or surgery takes place when the worker would not otherwise have been at work, and would not have been receiving payment from the employer.

33. Where the union wishes one of the employer's workers within the meaning of paragraphs 26(a) and 26(b) above to conduct a surgery, the employer should normally give time off with pay to the worker concerned. The worker should ensure that he provides the employer with as much notice as possible, giving details about the timing and location of the surgery. Exceptionally, it may be reasonable for the employer to refuse time off. This will apply if unavoidable situations arise where there is no adequate cover for the worker's absence from the workplace and the production process, or the provision of a service cannot otherwise be maintained. Before refusing permission, the employer should discuss the matter with the union and the worker to explore alternative arrangements.

WHAT ABOUT WRITTEN COMMUNICATION?

34. The union may want to display written material at the place of work. Employers, where practicable, should provide a notice board for the union's use. This notice board should be in a prominent location in the workplace and the union should be able to display material, including references to off-site meetings, without interference from the employer. Often, an existing notice-board could be used for this purpose. The union should also be able to place additional material near to the noticeboard including, for example, copies of explanatory leaflets, which the workers may read or take away with them. If there are no union representatives within the meaning of paragraphs 26(a) and 26(b) above present at the workplace, the employer should allow access to a full time official of the union to display the material.

35. The union may also wish to make use of its web-site pages on the internet for campaigning purposes. An employer should allow his workers access to the union's material in the same way that he explicitly, or tacitly, allows his workers to down-load information in connection with activities not directly related to the performance of their job. If an employer generally disallows all such internet use, he should consider giving permission to one of his workers nominated by the union to down-load the material, and it would be this person's responsibility to disseminate it more widely among other workers.

36. A nominated union representative employed by the employer may also want to make use of internal electronic communication, such as electronic mail or intranets, for campaigning purposes. For example, he may want to remind workers of forthcoming union meetings or surgeries. The employer should allow the representative to make reasonable use of these systems if the employer explicitly, or tacitly, allows his workers to use them for matters which are not directly related to the performance of their job. In cases where such use is disallowed, it would still be reasonable for the representative to use them, if the employer uses such forms of communication to send to the workers information against the union's case. When sending messages in this capacity, the representative should make it clear that the advice comes from the union and not the employer.

WHAT ABOUT SMALL BUSINESSES?

37. Access arrangements for small businesses need not necessarily create difficulties. For example, it may be easier to arrange for a smaller number of workers to meet together. On the other hand, there may be difficulties providing cover for workers in smaller organisations, or in finding accommodation for meetings. In such cases, the employer and the union should try to reach an understanding about how access arrangements can be organised to ensure minimum disruption. Agreements may need to be flexible to accommodate any particular needs of the employer.

ARRANGEMENTS FOR NON-TYPICAL WORKERS

38. Many, or sometimes most, workers in a bargaining unit may not work full time in a standard Monday-Friday working week. Others might rarely visit the employer's premises. The employer should bear in mind the difficulties faced by unions in communicating with:

- shift workers
- part-time workers
- homeworkers
- a dispersed or peripatetic workforce
- those on maternity or parental leave
- those on sick leave.

39. The employer should be receptive to a union's suggestions for securing reasonable access to such "non-typical workers", and allow them, where practicable, to achieve a broadly equivalent level of access to those workers as to typical workers. It would be reasonable for the union to organise its meetings or surgery arrangements on a more flexible basis to cover shift workers or part-time workers. An employer should agree to the maximum flexibility of arrangements, where reasonable in the circumstances. This would not extend to an employer being obliged to meet the travel costs of his workers attending meetings arranged by the union.

40. In addition, the union will be able to make use of the independent person to distribute information to home addresses via the postal service. This will ensure that literature will be received by any workers who are not likely to attend the workplace during the access period, for example those on maternity or sick leave. The CAC will supply the name, address and telephone number of the independent person to both the union and the employer.

WHAT ABOUT JOINT EMPLOYER/UNION ACTIVITIES?

41. There may be scope for the union and the employer to undertake joint activities where they both put across their respective views about recognition or derecognition in a non-confrontational way. Such joint activities can be an efficient method of providing information, minimising business disruption and costs. For example, the parties may wish to consider:

- the arrangement of joint meetings with each party allocated a period of thirty minutes to address the workers; and
- the use of a joint notice-board where an equal amount of space is devoted to the employer and the union.

SECTION D
OTHER ACCESS ISSUES

OBSERVING AN ACCESS AGREEMENT

[4.271]

42. Both parties should ensure they keep to agreements about access arrangements. For example, if the parties agree to hold a meeting lasting 30 minutes in duration, every effort should be made to ensure that the meeting does not over-run its allocated time. Likewise, neither party should remove, or tamper, with material placed on a notice board by the other party, unless they are obliged to do so for legal reasons.

PRIVACY OF MEETINGS

43. Employers should respect the privacy of access meetings. *Paragraph 26(4D) of Schedule A1 of the Trade Union and Labour Relations (Consolidation) Act 1992 therefore provides that the employer or any representative of his must not attend an access meeting unless invited to do so. Likewise, the employer must not use the union's unwillingness to allow him or his representative to attend as a reason to refuse an access meeting unless it is reasonable to do so. The employer must not record or otherwise be informed of the proceedings of a meeting unless it is reasonable for him to do so.*

44. Supervisors or managers may attend an access meeting, even though they may be seen as representatives of the employer, provided they have been invited to attend by the union. In general, it should be expected that such workers would be invited by the union to attend access meetings where they fall within the bargaining unit and are therefore entitled to vote. However, there may be circumstances – for example, where the attendance of supervisors would deter other workers from expressing their opinions; or where managers are campaigning on behalf of the employer – where it is reasonable for the union not to invite them. In such circumstances, consideration should be given to arranging separate access meetings for the supervisors and managers concerned. In situations where they are not invited to attend meetings with other workers, supervisors or other managers should not insist on attending simply because they are part of the bargaining unit. To avoid uncertainty and the disruption of meetings, the union should consider in advance whether it wishes to exclude such individuals from meetings, taking steps where possible to inform the individuals concerned before the meeting occurs. The union should avoid issuing generalised or loosely drafted invitations to attend access meetings, if its intention is to prevent certain individuals from attending.

45. In small workplaces or in workplaces with no dedicated meeting rooms, it may be difficult to find suitable accommodation on site which can be set aside for the exclusive use of the union to hold a meeting. Achieving privacy in such circumstances may be difficult, but solutions might be found by holding meetings during lunch breaks or at other times when business would not be significantly affected if managers or other work colleagues were required to vacate the premises or meeting area in question. In extreme cases, for example where continuous working is necessary, privacy may be achieved only by holding meetings away from the workplace.

46. Many employers have security cameras or other recording equipment permanently positioned on site to monitor or record workplace activity. Most are installed for reasons of security, health and safety or quality control. Where such equipment is used, and could record meetings, the employer should inform the union accordingly unless key security considerations prevent such disclosure. The employer and the union should then discuss ways to ensure the privacy of meetings. It may be possible, for example, to turn off the equipment in question for the short period of meetings. Alternatively, the employer may wish to ensure that any transmissions from the surveillance equipment during the period of the meeting are not viewed live or recorded. The scope for such measures may be limited in rare cases where security or health and safety may be significantly and unavoidably jeopardised as a result.

47. The employer should not eavesdrop on access meetings or pressurise any of those attending to disclose what occurred at them. Generally, the employer should not seek to question attendees about the proceedings of meetings but, in exceptional cases of, say, alleged harassment or damage to property, there may be a need for the employer to investigate the conduct of meetings. However, it must be recognised that information often circulates quite widely within workplaces and the employer may therefore learn what took place even though he took no specific steps to discover what had occurred. In some cases, individual workers may disclose without prompting what took place at meetings in their ordinary exchanges with line managers or other work colleagues.

BEHAVING RESPONSIBLY

48. Both parties should endeavour to ensure that, wherever possible, potentially acrimonious situations are avoided. For access arrangements to work satisfactorily, the employer and the union should behave responsibly, and give due consideration to the requirements of the other party throughout the access period. For example, neither the union nor the employer should seek to disrupt or interfere with meetings being held by the other party. So, if the union is holding a meeting, the employer should avoid the scheduling of other conflicting meetings or events which would draw workers away from the union's meeting. Unless special factors apply, the employer should not offer inducements to workers not to attend access meetings. For example, where an access meeting is held towards the end of the working day, the employer should not tell workers that they could go home early if they do not attend the union's meeting. However, unforeseen events may arise – an urgent order, for example – where the employer may need to require workers not to attend an access meeting, paying them overtime, or some other additional payment or fringe benefit, for any extra work involved. The offer of additional pay for extra work in such circumstances is reasonable. Where such exceptional events occur, the employer should explain the position to the union as soon as practicable, and offer alternative but comparable access arrangements for the workers involved.

49. Where it is practicable to hold meetings or surgeries at the workplace, the employer should provide appropriate accommodation, fit for the purpose, which should include adequate heating and lighting, and arrangements to ensure that the meeting is held in private. In turn, the union should ensure that business costs and business disruption are minimised. Unions should be aware of the needs of the employer to maintain the production process, to maintain a level of service, and to ensure safety and security at all times.

SECTION E
RESPONSIBLE CAMPAIGNING AND UNFAIR PRACTICES

[4.272]

50. This Section of the Code provides guidance on those standards of behaviour which are likely to prevent undue influence or other unfair practices from occurring. In places, it also refers to behaviour which, if pursued, may constitute an unfair practice. However, given the range of possible behaviours involved, it is unrealistic for the Code to identify every circumstance which might give rise to undue influence or other unfair practice. In any event, as Section F discusses, it is the task of the Central Arbitration Committee to judge whether an unfair practice has been committed, basing its judgment on the particular facts of a case.

RESPONSIBLE CAMPAIGNING

51. Recognition and derecognition ballots concern important, and sometimes complex, issues. It may help those workers entitled to vote in these ballots to receive information from the employer and the union setting out their views on the implications of recognition and non-recognition. Parties are not required to undertake any campaigning activity during this period. Indeed, a party might choose to desist from campaigning altogether because it wishes to avoid unnecessary acrimony or because it sees an advantage in employment relations terms in leaving the issue to the workers to decide. This Code should not therefore be read as discouraging such behaviour. That said, there will be other cases where parties will wish to campaign and such activity can benefit the balloting process in helping the workers make informed decisions. But active campaigning needs to be responsible or it can lead to the use of unfair practices which distort the balloting process, increase workplace friction and can sour employment relations.

52. Campaigning can expose sharp divisions of opinion, and ill-judged activity can damage trust and long-term employment relations. Parties should therefore discuss with each other at an early stage how they would wish campaigning to be undertaken. This discussion could take place at the same time the parties seek to reach access agreements. There are advantages in parties exchanging information about their approach to campaigning, indicating for example those persons or organisations which are likely to undertake the activity on their behalf. Prior discussion should focus in particular on the standards of conduct expected of campaigners to minimise the risk of intimidation occurring. One way to structure such joint discussions might be for the parties to discuss how they think the guidance in this section of the Code could best be applied to their particular situation. Where they agree standards of conduct, parties should take steps to ensure that those who campaign on their behalf are fully aware of them.

WHAT ARE UNFAIR PRACTICES?

53. *Parties must refrain from using an unfair practice during recognition or derecognition ballots. A party uses an unfair practice if, with a view to influencing the result of the ballot, the party:*

(a) *offers to pay money or give money's worth to a worker entitled to vote in a ballot in return for the worker's agreement to vote in a particular way or to abstain from voting;*

(b) *makes an "outcome-specific" offer to a worker entitled to vote in a ballot. (An "outcome-specific" offer is an offer to pay money or give money's worth which is conditional on the issuing by the CAC of a declaration that the union is entitled to be recognised or is not entitled to be recognised, and such an offer is not conditional on anything which is done or occurs as a result of the declaration in question).* Thus, an offer by either a union (or an employer) to pay each worker £100, provided the ballot does (or does not) result in recognition would be categorised as an unfair practice. In contrast, an undertaking by a union to secure an increase of £1,000 in the annual pay of workers through the collective bargaining process following a vote for recognition would not be captured because the offer clearly depends on other circumstances – in this case, the negotiation of a collective agreement – which is contingent on recognition being awarded;

(c) *coerces or attempts to coerce a worker entitled to vote in a ballot to disclose whether he intends to vote or abstain from voting in the ballot, or how he intends to vote, or how he has voted, in the ballot;*
(d) *dismisses or threatens to dismiss a worker;*
(e) *takes or threatens to take disciplinary action against a worker;*
(f) *subjects or threatens to subject a worker to any other detriment by, for example, threatening to give a worker a lower performance mark or a worse promotional assessment if he supports recognition or non-recognition; or*
(g) *uses or attempts to use undue influence on a worker entitled to vote in a ballot.*[1]

54. The statute refers to the term "money's worth" when defining an unfair offer to a worker. The term covers the making of non-cash offers to workers. Such non-cash offers usually involve the provision of goods and services, for which workers would otherwise need to pay if they procured the goods or services for themselves. Most fringe benefits – say, a better company car, subsidised health insurance or free legal services – would normally fall into this category. In addition, offers to provide additional paid holiday or other paid leave are likely to constitute "money's worth". Of course, providing such "money's worth" for permissible reasons – for example, as a normal inducement to join a union or as a typical bonus for meeting a work target – would not be categorised as an unfair practice.

55. Unfair practices can involve the taking of disciplinary action against workers, where such disciplinary action has the purpose of influencing the result of the ballot. The period of ballots is relatively short and this lessens the scope for disciplinary matters to arise. However, it is worth noting that this unfair practice is not limited just to disciplinary action taken against workers entitled to vote in a ballot. It is possible that an unfair practice could be committed if, say, disciplinary action were taken against a union activist involved in the union's campaign who was not entitled to vote in the ballot. Equally, the employer is not prevented from taking any disciplinary action just because a ballot is occurring. There may be sound grounds for the employer to discipline a worker, which are totally unconnected with the ballot. Likewise, it is possible that a worker's campaigning activity – say, the use of threatening behaviour against other workers or the unauthorised use of work time for campaigning – may itself give rise to disciplinary action which would not constitute an unfair practice. When contemplating disciplinary action, the employer should in addition take note of the guidance provided in the *Acas Code of Practice on Disciplinary and Grievance Procedures*, especially its advice on the disciplining of union officials.

56. The statutory list of unfair practices highlights actions to bribe, pressurise or exert other undue influence on workers to vote in particular ways or not to vote at all. Such conduct, especially the exertion of undue influence, can take many forms. At one extreme, undue influence may take the obvious form of actual or threatened physical violence against workers. It may also take other, and more subtle, forms of behaviour to influence the outcome of the ballot. For example, the introduction of higher pay or better conditions in the ballot period may constitute undue influence if the ballot period is not the normal time for reviewing pay or if there is not some other pressing reason unconnected with the ballot for raising pay.

WHO SHOULD CAMPAIGN?

57. Transparency is an important feature of normal campaigning activity and reduces the risk that a worker might be unduly influenced through subterfuge or misrepresentation. So, those authorised by the employer or a union to campaign on their behalf should take steps to inform the workers involved that they are so authorised and are therefore acting under instruction or at the behest of the party involved. Where there is reason to believe that workers do not understand their role, supervisors and line managers who undertake such work on behalf of the employer should state that they are acting in that capacity when communicating campaign messages to the workforce. In similar circumstances, union members who act as officials of the union or who are otherwise authorised to represent the union in its campaigning work should also explain their role when speaking to other workers in their capacity as campaigners.

58. Sometimes, a party might employ or hire a paid consultant to assist its campaigning work. Such consultants are therefore acting as agents of the party involved. If their behaviour constitutes an unfair practice, then the party who hired their services is also committing an unfair practice where the party expressly or by implication authorised the behaviour. A failure by a party to repudiate and correct misconduct by a consultant can be taken as implying that such conduct is authorised. Parties should therefore monitor the activities of the consultants they hire. Where outside consultants are used by either party, and undertake active campaigning by speaking to the workforce, then they should inform the workers that they have been hired by that party. They should also take steps to inform the workers accurately about the general purpose of their engagement. Whilst there is no need to divulge commercial confidences or to detail the precise contractual remit, if a consultant has been hired to advance the case of the union or the employer in the campaign then that essential fact should be divulged to the workforce when the consultant is communicating with them. It follows that consultants should not present themselves as independent or impartial third parties when undertaking their campaigning work.

59. The employer and the union are usually responsible for the actions of those whom they authorise or hire to campaign on their behalf. They should therefore take steps to brief their representatives or agents accordingly in advance of undertaking such activity. The briefing should not be limited to just the messages or information which the union or employer wish to convey. It should also provide clear advice to representatives or agents on the behavioural standards expected of them and the need to avoid actions which could constitute an unfair practice.

60. The employer and the union should also dissociate themselves from material containing personal attacks or allegations which is circulated on an anonymous basis. The party whose case appears to be favoured by the anonymous material should usually repudiate it, informing all workers in the bargaining unit accordingly.

WHAT ARE THE MAIN FORMS OF CAMPAIGNING?

61. All campaigning involves communication with workers in the bargaining unit. Sometimes, that communication can take the form of face-to-face discussion with a worker or workers. Such encounters can perform useful functions as many workers may feel nervous about asking questions at mass meetings and small scale gatherings may encourage more open debate. Section C therefore refers to the option for unions to access the workforce by holding "surgeries" which individual workers or small groups of workers can attend if they wish. That said, the employer or the union must take particular care when handling one-to-one meetings or encounters with small groups, because a worker may feel more vulnerable in those situations and undue influence may arise if a worker feels threatened as a result. Workers should not normally be required to attend small meetings organised by either the employer or the union for campaigning purposes, and they should not be threatened with sanctions if they fail to attend. Workers who voluntarily attend should be informed that they are under no obligation to answer any direct questions which are put to them. In particular, they should not be required to disclose the way they have voted or their voting intentions.

62. Most small or one-to-one meetings occur at the place of work. But a party might also try to arrange similar encounters outside the workplace to canvass opinion by visiting a worker's home or by ringing a home telephone. When undertaking such activity, unions should note that neither the CAC nor the qualified independent person it employs to run the ballot will disclose to the union the names, addresses or telephone numbers of the workers involved. Whereas canvassing at a worker's home may be an acceptable practice, reflecting perhaps restricted access at work, considerable care needs to be taken by the party involved to avoid possible intimidation, however unintended, which could give rise to undue influence. Where practicable, a party should seek and obtain a worker's permission in advance before visiting him at home. In particular, the number of people visiting a worker's home to campaign or canvass, even where prior permission is obtained, should be limited to one or, perhaps, two people. If a worker does not wish to open or continue a discussion with the campaigners, then that wish must be completely respected. A failure to leave a worker's premises on request would almost certainly be seen as an intimidatory practice. Also, if a worker indicates he does not wish to be revisited at home, or rung again by telephone, then that wish should be respected.

63. The holding of one or two face-to-face meetings, either on site or off it, may not in itself be perceived as placing unwelcome pressure on the worker involved. Indeed, a worker might request further meetings himself to cover the issues fully or to follow up a discussion. However, the frequency of meetings, or frequent requests to attend meetings, can be perceived as potentially threatening by some workers. There may come a point where persistent approaches to workers will be construed as harassment. Parties must therefore be aware that the intensity of their campaigning activity can give rise to problems.

64. Campaigning can also be undertaken by circulating information by e-mails, videos or other mediums. There is nothing intrinsically wrong with communication of that nature. Indeed, because such communication does not require the physical presence of the campaigner, they may well be seen as having less potential to threaten the worker. That said, the content of such communications can still intimidate or threaten the voter, and care should therefore be taken to avoid such effects when drafting written communication or producing videos.

HOW SHOULD CAMPAIGNERS PUT ACROSS THEIR MESSAGE?

65. Campaigning is inherently a partisan activity. Each party is therefore unlikely to put across a completely balanced message to the workforce, and some overstatement or exaggeration may well occur. In general, workers will expect such behaviour and can deal with it. Also, by listening to both sides, they will be able to question and evaluate the material presented to them.

66. Campaigning should focus on the issues at stake. These will mostly concern the workplace, the performance of the union or the running of the employer's business. Sometimes, it will be legitimate to focus on the work behaviours and previous work histories of key individuals. For example, it may be pertinent to refer to the way a proprietor or a senior manager has responded to workplace grievances in the past or to the way a key union official has handled negotiations elsewhere. But campaigning about the personal lives of senior managers or union leaders usually adds nothing beneficial to the discussion of the issues and should be avoided. Personalised attacks and the denigration of individuals may also harm the long-term health of employment relations.

67. Parties, especially the employer, should take particular care if they discuss job losses or the relocation of business activity. Such statements can be seen as directly threatening the livelihoods of the workers involved, and can give rise to undue influence by implicitly threatening to harm the workers concerned. It is a fine line, therefore, to distinguish between fair comment about job prospects and intimidatory behaviour designed primarily to scare the workers to vote against recognition. In general, references to job prospects are more likely to constitute fair comment if they can be clearly linked to the future economic performance of the employer with or without union recognition, and are expressed in measured terms. Unsubstantiated assertions on this particularly sensitive issue should therefore be avoided. So, it might be fair comment to argue that the employer's business may run less successfully if recognition is awarded, and employment may be less secure as a result, because pay levels would rise or work would be organised less flexibly. On the other hand, statements that the employer will make redundancies or relocate simply because a union is recognised should be avoided.

68. Part of a party's normal campaigning is to engage with the arguments put forward by others. That can be helpful and can assist workers in understanding the issues at stake. Each party will therefore try to obtain the campaigning literature of the other party to enable them to discuss the points raised. This should not normally present a problem as literature tends to be widely available either on websites, notice boards or elsewhere. Indeed, parties may often find it mutually advantageous to exchange these materials.

69. Campaigning meetings should be treated as far as possible as private affairs, and there are legislative requirements covering the privacy of access meetings at work (see paragraphs 43–47 in Section D). Meetings or other campaigning activities which occur off-site are generally not covered by the access provisions, but the privacy of those gatherings should be respected. A party should not infiltrate meetings or use other covert methods to monitor another party's campaign. It is also likely to constitute an intimidatory practice for parties to photograph, record or otherwise place workers under surveillance without permission whilst they are undertaking campaigning or attending campaigning events off-site, unless such activity takes place at a location (for example, the entrance to a workplace) where surveillance equipment normally operates for other legitimate reasons. Parties should also not penalise workers, or threaten to penalise them, if they attend or take part in those off-site activities.

NOTES

[1] See paragraphs 27A(2) and 119A(2) of Schedule A1 of the Trade Union and Labour Relations (Consolidation) Act 1992.

SECTION F
RESOLVING DISPUTES

INTERVENTION BY THE CAC

Access

[4.273]

70. Disputes may arise between the parties during the access period about the failure to allow reasonable access or to implement access agreements. If these disputes cannot be resolved, the union may ask the CAC to decide whether the employer has failed to perform his statutory duties in relation to the ballot.

71. *If the CAC is satisfied that the employer has failed to perform one or more of his five duties:*

(a) *to co-operate generally with the union and the independent person on the ballot;*

(b) to give the union such access to the workers constituting the bargaining unit as is reasonable to inform them of the object of the ballot and to seek their support and opinions;

(c) *to provide the CAC with the names and home addresses of those workers;*

(d) to refrain from making any offer to any or all of the workers constituting the bargaining unit which (i) has or is likely to have the effect of inducing any or all of them not to attend any relevant meeting between the union and the workers constituting the bargaining unit and (ii) is not reasonable in the circumstances; and

(e) to refrain from taking or threatening to take any action against a worker solely or mainly on the grounds that he (i) attended or took part in any relevant meeting between the union and the workers constituting the bargaining unit, or (ii) indicated his intention to attend or take part in such a meeting.

and the ballot has not been held, the CAC may order the employer to take such steps to remedy the failure as the CAC considers reasonable, and within a time that the CAC considers reasonable. Where the CAC is asked to make an order very shortly before the end of the access period, it may be impracticable for the CAC to consider the request and for the employer and the union to remedy any failure in the short time before the ballot is held. In such circumstances, the CAC may extend the access period by ordering the ballot to be rescheduled for a later date to ensure that access is achieved.

72. *If the employer fails to comply with the CAC's order within the time specified, and the ballot has still not been held, the CAC may issue a declaration that the union is recognised, or that the union is not derecognised.*

73. It is the employer's duty to provide reasonable access, and complaints about a failure to provide such access can be made by unions only. However, in deciding whether the employer has complied with his duty to give the union access, the CAC may take into account all relevant circumstances. This may include the behaviour of the union. The CAC may therefore decide that the employer has complied with the duty in circumstances where, because the union has acted unreasonably, he denies the union access or refuses to implement agreed access arrangements.

UNFAIR PRACTICES

74. Complaints may also surface that a party has committed an unfair practice during the balloting period. Such complaints may be referred by the employer or the union to the CAC to adjudicate though any complaints must be made either before the ballot closes or on the first working day after that. Where time permits, it is a good practice for the parties to try to resolve them locally in the first instance.

75. The CAC must decide that a complaint is well-founded if the party complained against used an unfair practice and the CAC is satisfied that the practice changed or was likely to change, in the case of a worker entitled to vote in a ballot either (i) his intention to vote or to abstain from voting or (ii) his intention to vote in a particular way or (iii) how he voted.

76. *Where it considers a complaint is well-founded, the CAC must issue a declaration to that effect, and it may*

- *issue a remedial order to the party concerned to take such action as it specifies and within a timetable it specifies to mitigate the effect of the unfair practice, and /or*
- *give notice to the parties that it intends to hold a fresh secret ballot* (and thereby replace any which may have been contaminated by the unfair practice).

77. *Where a party either (i) fails to comply with a remedial order or (ii) has committed a second unfair practice in relation to the ballot (or a re-run ballot) or (iii) has committed an unfair practice involving* *the use of violence or the dismissal of a union official, the CAC may take other sanctions against that party. Where that party is the union, the CAC may declare that the union is not entitled to be recognised. Where that party is the employer, the CAC may declare that the union is entitled to be recognised.*[2]

MINOR DISPUTES

78. Some disputes about access may be minor by nature. For example, the employer may be aggrieved that an access meeting has over-run somewhat. Or a union might have cause to complain if it regards the meeting room provided by the employer as being too small to accommodate everyone in comfort. In such cases, both parties should avoid taking hasty action which might prejudice the implementation of other access arrangements. The union should generally avoid taking minor complaints about access to the CAC as a first course of action.

79. Instead, the parties should make every effort to resolve the dispute between themselves. They should make full use of any mechanism to resolve such disputes which they may have established in the access agreement, and consider the use of Acas's conciliation services. It would generally be a good practice if both the employer and the union nominated a person to act as their lead contact if disagreements or questions arose about the implementation of access arrangements.

80. The period of access will be limited in duration, given that the balloting period will normally be a maximum of 20 working days, and the parties should therefore ensure that disputes are swiftly resolved. The parties should endeavour to inform each other immediately if a dispute arises, and should seek to resolve any disputes as a matter of priority, preferably within one working day of their occurrence.

81. It is also a good practice to follow similar procedures in cases where there are complaints about a person's conduct whilst campaigning. For example, some complaints will be based on a misunderstanding which can be resolved quickly between the parties. And in cases where minor offence has been caused as a result of a careless or unintended remark, then the matter may be simply remedied by the issuing of an apology. Regular and early communication between the parties about the poor behaviour by individual campaigners may also ensure that senior figures on the union and employer sides can prevent repetitions of such behaviour and thereby ensure that unnecessary disputes are avoided.

82. It should be noted that a complaint to the CAC about an unfair practice is unlikely to succeed if it relates to minor aberrations in conduct because such matters are very unlikely to have influenced voting behaviours or intentions. So, for example, a campaigner's use of strong language or swearing (which, perhaps regrettably, is commonplace inside many workplaces and outside them as well) may not in itself constitute the basis for a well-founded complaint.

THE INDEPENDENT PERSON

83. The prime duties of the independent person are to ensure that:

- the names and addresses of the workers comprising the balloting constituency are accurate;
- the ballot is conducted properly and in secret; and
- the CAC is promptly informed of the ballot result.

It is not the function of the independent person to adjudicate disputes about access or unfair practices. That is the CAC's role. However, the independent person may have wide experience and knowledge of balloting arrangements in different settings. The parties might consider informing the independent person about their problems and draw on his experience to identify possible options to resolve their difficulties.

NOTES

[2] There are other sanctions which apply in the special case where a worker has applied to the CAC to derecognise a union.

GUIDANCE ON MATTERS TO BE TAKEN INTO ACCOUNT IN DETERMINING QUESTIONS RELATING TO THE DEFINITION OF DISABILITY (2011)

[4.274]

NOTES

This Guidance was issued by the Secretary of State under the Equality Act 2010, s 6(5) and was laid before Parliament on 10 February 2011. It was brought into effect on 1 May 2011 by the Equality Act 2010 (Guidance on the Definition of Disability) Appointed Day Order 2011, SI 2011/1159, art 2. Art 3 of the 2011 Order (transitional provisions) provides that the 2006 Guidance which it replaces (omitted from this edition) continues to have effect in relation to any proceedings arising from a complaint presented to an adjudicating body, whenever presented, alleging that a person has, before 1 May 2011, committed an act which is unlawful discrimination or harassment. For the legal status of the Guidance see the Equality Act 2010, Sch 1, para 12 at **[1.1771]**.

Notes are as in the original.

See *Harvey* L(2)(C)(2).

CONTENTS

STATUS AND PURPOSE OF THE GUIDANCE

[4.275]
This guidance is issued by the Secretary of State under section 6(5) of the Equality Act 2010. In this document, any reference to 'the Act' means the Equality Act 2010.

This guidance concerns the definition of disability in the Act. Section 6(5) of the Act enables a Minister of the Crown to issue guidance about matters to be taken into account in determining whether a person is a disabled person. The guidance gives illustrative examples.

This guidance does not impose any legal obligations in itself, nor is it an authoritative statement of the law. However, Schedule 1, Paragraph 12 to the Act requires that an adjudicating body[1] which is determining for any purpose of the Act whether a person is a disabled person, must take into account any aspect of this guidance which appears to it to be relevant.

This guidance applies to England, Wales and Scotland. Similar, but separate, guidance applies to Northern Ireland.

PART 1: INTRODUCTION

THE EQUALITY ACT 2010

[4.276]
1. The Equality Act 2010 prohibits discrimination against people with the protected characteristics that are specified in section 4 of the Act. Disability is one of the specified protected characteristics. Protection from discrimination for disabled people applies to disabled people in a range of circumstances, covering the provision of goods, facilities and services, the exercise of public functions, premises, work, education, and associations. Only those disabled people who are defined as disabled in accordance with section 6 of the Act, and the associated Schedules and regulations made under that section, will be entitled to the protection that the Act provides to disabled people. However, the Act also provides protection for non-disabled people who are subjected to direct discrimination or harassment because of their association with a disabled person or because they are wrongly perceived to be disabled.

USING THE GUIDANCE

2. This guidance is primarily designed for adjudicating bodies which determine cases brought under the Act. The definition of disability for the purposes of the Act is a legal definition and it is only adjudicating bodies which can determine whether a person meets that definition. However, the guidance is also likely to be of value to a range of people and organisations as an explanation of how the definition operates.

3. In the vast majority of cases there is unlikely to be any doubt whether or not a person has or has had a disability, but this guidance should prove helpful in cases where the matter is not entirely clear.

4. The Act generally defines a disabled person as a person with a disability. A person has a disability for the purposes of the Act if he or she has a physical or mental impairment and the impairment has a substantial and long-term adverse effect on his or her ability to carry out normal day-to-day activities. Therefore, the general definition of disability has a number of elements. The Guidance covers each of these elements in turn. Each section contains an explanation of the relevant provisions of the Act which supplement the basic definition. Guidance and illustrative examples are provided where relevant. **Those using this Guidance for the first time should read it all, as each part of the Guidance builds upon the part(s) preceding it.** It is important not to consider any individual element in isolation.

5. Throughout the guidance, descriptions of statutory provisions in the legislation are immediately preceded by bold text and followed by a reference to the relevant provision of the Act or to regulations made under the Act. References to sections of the Act are marked **'S'**; references to schedules are marked **'Sch'**; and references to paragraphs in schedules are marked **'Para'**.

OTHER REFERENCES TO 'DISABILITY'

6. The definition of disability set out in the Act and described in this guidance is the only definition relevant to determining whether someone is a disabled person for the purposes of the Act. References to 'disability' or to mental or physical impairments in the context of other legislation are not necessarily relevant but may assist adjudicating bodies when determining whether someone is a disabled person in accordance with the definition in this Act.

7. There is a range of services, concessions, schemes and financial benefits for which disabled people may qualify. These include, for example: local authority services for disabled people; the Blue Badge parking scheme; tax concessions for people who are blind; and disability-related social security benefits. However, each of these has its own individual eligibility criteria and qualification for any one of them does not automatically confer entitlement to protection under the Act, nor does entitlement to the protection of the Act confer eligibility for benefits, or concessions. Similarly, a child who has been identified as having special educational needs is not necessarily disabled for the purposes of the Act. However, having eligibility for such benefits may assist a person to demonstrate that they meet the definition in the Act.

8. In order to be protected by the Act, a person must have an impairment that meets the Act's definition of disability, or be able to establish that any less favourable treatment or harassment is because of another person's disability or because of a perceived disability.

PART 2: GUIDANCE ON MATTERS TO BE TAKEN INTO ACCOUNT IN DETERMINING QUESTIONS RELATING TO THE DEFINITION OF DISABILITY

SECTION A: THE DEFINITION

Main elements of the definition of disability

[4.277]

A1. The Act defines a disabled person as a person with a disability. A person has a disability for the purposes of the Act if he or she has a physical or mental impairment and the impairment has a substantial and long-term adverse effect on his or her ability to carry out normal day-to-day activities (**S 6(1)**).

A2. This means that, in general:

- the person must have an impairment that is either physical or mental (**see paragraphs A3 to A8**);
- the impairment must have adverse effects which are substantial (**see Section B**);
- the substantial adverse effects must be long-term (**see Section C**); and
- the long-term substantial adverse effects must be effects on normal day-to-day activities (**see Section D**).

This definition is subject to the provisions in **Schedule 1 (Sch 1)**.

All of the factors above must be considered when determining whether a person is disabled.

Meaning of 'impairment'

A3. The definition requires that the effects which a person may experience must arise from a physical or mental impairment. The term mental or physical impairment should be given its ordinary meaning. It is not necessary for the cause of the impairment to be established, nor does the impairment have to be the result of an illness. In many cases, there will be no dispute whether a person has an impairment. Any disagreement is more likely to be about whether the effects of the impairment are sufficient to fall within the definition and in particular whether they are long-term. Even so, it may sometimes be necessary to decide whether a person has an impairment so as to be able to deal with the issues about its effects.

A4. Whether a person is disabled for the purposes of the Act is generally determined by reference to the **effect** that an impairment has on that person's ability to carry out normal day-to-day activities. An exception to this is a person with severe disfigurement (**see paragraph B24**). It is not possible to provide an exhaustive list of conditions that qualify as impairments for the purposes of the Act. Any attempt to do so would inevitably become out of date as medical knowledge advanced.

A5. A disability can arise from a wide range of impairments which can be:

- sensory impairments, such as those affecting sight or hearing;
- impairments with fluctuating or recurring effects such as rheumatoid arthritis, myalgic encephalitis (ME), chronic fatigue syndrome (CFS), fibromyalgia, depression and epilepsy;
- progressive, such as motor neurone disease, muscular dystrophy, and forms of dementia;
- auto-immune conditions such as systemic lupus erythematosis (SLE);
- organ specific, including respiratory conditions, such as asthma, and cardiovascular diseases, including thrombosis, stroke and heart disease;
- developmental, such as autistic spectrum disorders (ASD), dyslexia and dyspraxia;
- learning disabilities;
- mental health conditions with symptoms such as anxiety, low mood, panic attacks, phobias, or unshared perceptions; eating disorders; bipolar affective disorders; obsessive compulsive disorders; personality disorders; post traumatic stress disorder, and some self-harming behaviour;
- mental illnesses, such as depression and schizophrenia;
- produced by injury to the body, including to the brain.

A6. It may not always be possible, nor is it necessary, to categorise a condition as either a physical or a mental impairment. The underlying cause of the impairment may be hard to establish. There may be adverse effects which are both physical and mental in nature. Furthermore, effects of a mainly physical nature may stem from an underlying mental impairment, and vice versa.

A7. It is not necessary to consider how an impairment is caused, even if the cause is a consequence of a condition which is excluded. For example, liver disease as a result of alcohol dependency would count as an impairment, although an addiction to alcohol itself is expressly excluded from the scope of the definition of disability in the Act. What it is important to consider is the effect of an impairment, not its cause — provided that it is not an excluded condition. (**See also paragraph A12 (exclusions from the**

definition).)

A woman is obese. Her obesity in itself is not an impairment, but it causes breathing and mobility difficulties which substantially adversely affect her ability to walk.

A man has a borderline moderate learning disability which has an adverse impact on his short-term memory and his levels of literacy and numeracy. For example, he cannot write any original material, as opposed to slowly copying existing text, and he cannot write his address from memory.

It is the effects of these impairments that need to be considered, rather than the underlying conditions themselves.

A8. It is important to remember that not all impairments are readily identifiable. While some impairments, particularly visible ones, are easy to identify, there are many which are not so immediately obvious, for example some mental health conditions and learning disabilities.

Persons with HIV infection, cancer and multiple sclerosis

A9. The Act states that a person who has cancer, HIV infection or multiple sclerosis (MS) is a disabled person. This means that the person is protected by the Act effectively from the point of diagnosis. **(Sch 1, Para 6). (See also paragraphs B18 to 23 (progressive conditions).)**

Persons deemed to be disabled

A10. The Act provides for certain people to be deemed to meet the definition of disability without having to show that they have an impairment that has (or is likely to have) a substantial and long-term adverse effect on the ability to carry out normal day-to-day activities. Regulations provide for a person who is certified as blind, severely sight impaired, sight impaired or partially sighted by a consultant ophthalmologist to be deemed to have a disability[2]. **(Sch 1, Para 7)**

A11. Anyone who has an impairment which is not covered by paragraphs A9 and A10 will need to meet the requirements of the definition as set out in paragraph A1 in order to demonstrate that he or she has a disability under the Act. **(But see paragraphs A16 to A17 for details of some people who are treated as having had a past disability.)**

Exclusions from the definition

A12. Certain conditions are not to be regarded as impairments for the purposes of the Act[3]. These are:

- addiction to, or dependency on, alcohol, nicotine, or any other substance (other than in consequence of the substance being medically prescribed);
- the condition known as seasonal allergic rhinitis (e.g. hayfever), except where it aggravates the effect of another condition;
- tendency to set fires;
- tendency to steal;
- tendency to physical or sexual abuse of other persons;
- exhibitionism;
- voyeurism.

A13. The exclusions apply where the tendency to set fires, tendency to steal, tendency to physical or sexual abuse of other persons, exhibitionism, or voyeurism constitute an impairment in themselves. The exclusions also apply where these tendencies arise as a consequence of, or a manifestation of, an impairment that constitutes a disability for the purposes of the Act. It is important to determine the basis for the alleged discrimination. If the alleged discrimination was a result of an excluded condition, the exclusion will apply. However, if the alleged discrimination was specifically related to the actual disability which gave rise to the excluded condition, the exclusion **will not** apply. Whether the exclusion applies will depend on all the facts of the individual case.

A young man has Attention Deficit Hyperactivity Disorder (ADHD) which manifests itself in a number of ways, including exhibitionism and an inability to concentrate. The disorder, as an impairment which has a substantial and long-term adverse effect on the young person's ability to carry out normal day-to-day activities, would be a disability for the purposes of the Act.

The young man is not entitled to the protection of the Act in relation to any discrimination he experiences as a consequence of his exhibitionism, because that is an excluded condition under the Act.

However, he would be protected in relation to any discrimination that he experiences in relation to the non-excluded effects of his condition, such as inability to concentrate. For example, he would be entitled to any reasonable adjustments that are required as a consequence of those effects.

A14. A person with an excluded condition may nevertheless be protected as a disabled person if he or she has an accompanying impairment which meets the requirements of the definition. For example, a person who is addicted to a substance such as alcohol may also have depression, or a physical impairment such as liver damage, arising from the alcohol addiction. While this person would not meet the definition simply on the basis of having an addiction, he or she may still meet the definition as a result of the effects of the depression or the liver damage.

A15. Disfigurements which consist of a tattoo (which has not been removed), non-medical body piercing, or something attached through such piercing, are to be treated as not having a substantial adverse effect on the person's ability to carry out normal day-to-day activities[4]. (**See also paragraphs B24 to B26.**)

People who have had a disability in the past

A16. The Act says that, except for the provisions in Part 12 (Transport[5]) and section 190 (improvements to let dwelling houses), the provisions of the Act also apply in relation to a person who previously has had a disability as defined in paragraphs **A1 and A2 (S 6(4) and Sch 1, Para 9).** This means that someone who is no longer disabled, but who met the requirements of the definition in the past, will still be covered by the Act. Also protected would be someone who continues to experience debilitating effects as a result of treatment for a past disability.

> **Four years ago, a woman experienced a mental illness that had a substantial and long-term adverse effect on her ability to carry out normal day-to-day activities, so it met the Act's definition of disability. She has experienced no recurrence of the condition, but if she is discriminated against because of her past mental illness she is still entitled to the protection afforded by the Act, as a person with a past disability.**

A17. A particular instance of someone who is treated under the Act as having had a disability in the past is someone whose name was on the register of disabled persons under provisions in the Disabled Persons (Employment) Act 1944[6] on both 12 January 1995 and 2 December 1996. The Disability Discrimination Act 1995 provided for such people to be treated as having had a disability in the past, and those provisions have been saved so that they still apply for the purposes of the Equality Act 2010.

SECTION B: SUBSTANTIAL

This section should not be read in isolation but must be considered together with sections A, C and D. Whether a person satisfies the definition of a disabled person for the purposes of the Act will depend upon the full circumstances of the case. That is, whether the adverse effect of the person's impairment on the carrying out of normal day-to-day activities is substantial and long term.

Meaning of 'substantial adverse effect'

[4.278]

B1. The requirement that an adverse effect on normal day-to-day activities should be a substantial one reflects the general understanding of disability as a limitation going beyond the normal differences in ability which may exist among people. A substantial effect is one that is more than a minor or trivial effect. This is stated in the **Act at S 212(1)**. This section looks in more detail at what 'substantial' means. **It should be read in conjunction with Section D which considers what is meant by 'normal day-to-day activities'.**

The time taken to carry out an activity

B2. The time taken by a person with an impairment to carry out a normal day-to-day activity should be considered when assessing whether the effect of that impairment is substantial. It should be compared with the time it might take a person who did not have the impairment to complete an activity.

> **A ten-year-old child has cerebral palsy. The effects include muscle stiffness, poor balance and unco-ordinated movements. The child is still able to do most things for himself, but he gets tired very easily and it is harder for him to accomplish tasks like eating and drinking, washing, and getting dressed. He has the ability to carry out everyday activities such as these, but everything takes much longer compared to a child of a similar age who does not have cerebral palsy. This amounts to a substantial adverse effect.**

The way in which an activity is carried out

B3. Another factor to be considered when assessing whether the effect of an impairment is substantial is the way in which a person with that impairment carries out a normal day-to-day activity. The comparison should be with the way that the person might be expected to carry out the activity compared with someone who does not have the impairment.

> **A person who has obsessive compulsive disorder (OCD) constantly checks and rechecks that electrical appliances are switched off and that the doors are locked when leaving home. A person**

without the disorder would not normally carry out these frequent checks. The need to constantly check and recheck has a substantial adverse effect.

Cumulative effects of an impairment

B4. An impairment might not have a substantial adverse effect on a person's ability to undertake a particular day-to-day activity in isolation. However, it is important to consider whether its effects on more than one activity, when taken together, could result in an overall substantial adverse effect.

B5. For example, a person whose impairment causes breathing difficulties may, as a result, experience minor effects on the ability to carry out a number of activities such as getting washed and dressed, going for a walk or travelling on public transport. But taken together, the cumulative result would amount to a substantial adverse effect on his or her ability to carry out these normal day-to-day activities.

A man with depression experiences a range of symptoms that include a loss of energy and motivation that makes even the simplest of tasks or decisions seem quite difficult. He finds it difficult to get up in the morning, get washed and dressed, and prepare breakfast. He is forgetful and cannot plan ahead. As a result he has often run out of food before he thinks of going shopping again. Household tasks are frequently left undone, or take much longer to complete than normal. Together, the effects amount to the impairment having a substantial adverse effect on carrying out normal day-to-day activities.

B6. A person may have more than one impairment, any one of which alone would not have a substantial effect. In such a case, account should be taken of whether the impairments together have a substantial effect overall on the person's ability to carry out normal day-to-day activities. For example, a minor impairment which affects physical co-ordination and an irreversible but minor injury to a leg which affects mobility, when taken together, might have a substantial effect on the person's ability to carry out certain normal day-to-day activities. The cumulative effect of more than one impairment should also be taken into account when determining whether the effect is long-term, **see Section C**.

A person has mild learning disability. This means that his assimilation of information is slightly slower than that of somebody without the impairment. He also has a mild speech impairment that slightly affects his ability to form certain words. Neither impairment on its own has a substantial adverse effect, but the effects of the impairments taken together have a substantial adverse effect on his ability to converse.

Effects of behaviour

B7. Account should be taken of how far a person can **reasonably** be expected to modify his or her behaviour, for example by use of a coping or avoidance strategy, to prevent or reduce the effects of an impairment on normal day-to-day activities. In some instances, a coping or avoidance strategy might alter the effects of the impairment to the extent that they are no longer substantial and the person would no longer meet the definition of disability. In other instances, even with the coping or avoidance strategy, there is still an adverse effect on the carrying out of normal day-to-day activities.

For example, a person who needs to avoid certain substances because of allergies may find the day-to-day activity of eating substantially affected. Account should be taken of the degree to which a person can reasonably be expected to behave in such a way that the impairment ceases to have a substantial adverse effect on his or her ability to carry out normal day-to-day activities. **(See also paragraph B12.)**

When considering modification of behaviour, it would be reasonable to expect a person who has chronic back pain to avoid extreme activities such as skiing. It would not be reasonable to expect the person to give up, or modify, more normal activities that might exacerbate the symptoms; such as shopping, or using public transport.

B8. Similarly, it would be reasonable to expect a person with a phobia to avoid extreme activities or situations that would aggravate their condition. It would not be reasonable to expect him or her to give up, or modify, normal activities that might exacerbate the symptoms.

A person with acrophobia (extreme fear of heights which can induce panic attacks) might reasonably be expected to avoid the top of extremely high buildings, such as the Eiffel Tower, but not to avoid all multi-storey buildings.

B9. Account should also be taken of where a person avoids doing things which, for example, cause pain, fatigue or substantial social embarrassment, or avoids doing things because of a loss of energy and motivation. It would **not** be reasonable to conclude that a person who employed an avoidance strategy was not a disabled person. In determining a question as to whether a person meets the definition of disability **it is important to consider the things that a person cannot do, or can only do with difficulty.**

> **In order to manage her mental health condition, a woman who experiences panic attacks finds that she can manage daily tasks, such as going to work, if she can avoid the stress of travelling in the rush hour.**
>
> **In determining whether she meets the definition of disability, consideration should be given to the extent to which it is reasonable to expect her to place such restrictions on her working and personal life.**

B10. In some cases, people have coping or avoidance strategies which cease to work in certain circumstances (for example, where someone who has dyslexia is placed under stress). If it is possible that a person's ability to manage the effects of an impairment will break down so that effects will sometimes still occur, this possibility must be taken into account when assessing the effects of the impairment.

(See also paragraphs B12 to B17 (effects of treatment), paragraphs C9 to C11 (likelihood of recurrence) and paragraph D22 (indirect effects).)

Effects of environment

B11. Environmental conditions may exacerbate or lessen the effect of an impairment. Factors such as temperature, humidity, lighting, the time of day or night, how tired the person is, or how much stress he or she is under, may have an impact on the effects. When assessing whether adverse effects of an impairment are substantial, the extent to which such environmental factors, individually or cumulatively, are likely to have an impact on the effects should, therefore, also be considered. The fact that an impairment may have a less substantial effect in certain environments does not necessarily prevent it having an overall substantial adverse effect on day-to-day activities. **(See also paragraphs C5 to C8, meaning of 'long-term' (recurring or fluctuating effects).)**

> **A woman has had rheumatoid arthritis for the last three years. The effect on her ability to carry out normal day-to-day activities fluctuates according to the weather conditions. The effects are particularly bad during autumn and winter months when the weather is cold and damp. Symptoms are mild during the summer months. It is necessary to consider the overall impact of the arthritis, and the extent to which it has a substantial adverse effect on her ability to carry out day-to-day activities such as walking, undertaking household tasks, and getting washed and dressed.**

Effects of treatment

B12. The Act provides that, where an impairment is subject to treatment or correction, the impairment is to be treated as having a substantial adverse effect if, but for the treatment or correction, the impairment is likely to have that effect. In this context, 'likely' should be interpreted as meaning 'could well happen'. The practical effect of this provision is that the impairment should be treated as having the effect that it would have without the measures in question **(Sch 1, Para 5(1)). The Act states** that the treatment or correction measures which are to be disregarded for these purposes include, in particular, medical treatment and the use of a prosthesis or other aid (**Sch 1, Para 5(2)**). In this context, medical treatments would include treatments such as counselling, the need to follow a particular diet, and therapies, in addition to treatments with drugs. (**See also paragraphs B7 and B16.**)

B13. This provision applies even if the measures result in the effects being completely under control or not at all apparent. Where treatment is continuing it may be having the effect of masking or ameliorating a disability so that it does not have a substantial adverse effect. If the final outcome of such treatment cannot be determined, or if it is known that removal of the medical treatment would result in either a relapse or a worsened condition, it would be reasonable to disregard the medical treatment in accordance with paragraph 5 of Schedule 1.

B14. For example, if a person with a hearing impairment wears a hearing aid the question as to whether his or her impairment has a substantial adverse effect is to be decided by reference to what the hearing level would be without the hearing aid. Similarly, in the case of someone with diabetes which is being controlled by medication or diet should be decided by reference to what the effects of the condition would be if he or she were not taking that medication or following the required diet.

> **A person with long-term depression is being treated by counselling. The effect of the treatment is to enable the person to undertake normal day-to-day activities, like shopping and going to work. If the effect of the treatment is disregarded, the person's impairment would have a substantial adverse effect on his ability to carry out normal day-to-day activities.**

B15. The Act states that this provision does not apply to sight impairments to the extent that they are capable of correction by spectacles or contact lenses. (**Sch 1, Para 5(3)**). In other words, the only effects on the ability to carry out normal day-to-day activities which are to be considered are those which remain when spectacles or contact lenses are used (or would remain if they were used). This does not include the use of devices to correct sight which are not spectacles or contact lenses.

B16. Account should be taken of where the effect of the continuing medical treatment is to create a permanent improvement rather than a temporary improvement. It is necessary to consider whether, as a consequence of the treatment, the impairment would cease to have a substantial adverse effect. For example, a person who develops pneumonia may be admitted to hospital for treatment including a course of antibiotics. This cures the impairment and no substantial effects remain. **(See also paragraph C11, regarding medical or other treatment that permanently reduces or removes the effects of an impairment.)**

B17. However, if a person receives treatment which cures a condition that would otherwise meet the definition of a disability, the person would be protected by the Act as a person who had a disability in the past. (**See paragraph A16.**)

Progressive conditions

B18. Progressive conditions, which are conditions that have effects which increase in severity over time, are subject to the special provisions set out in **Sch 1, Para 8.** These provisions provide that a person with a progressive condition is to be regarded as having an impairment which has a substantial adverse effect on his or her ability to carry out normal day-to-day activities **before** it actually has that effect.

B19. A person who has a progressive condition, will be treated as having an impairment which has a **substantial** adverse effect from the moment any impairment resulting from that condition first has some adverse effect on his or her ability to carry out normal day-to-day activities, provided that in the future the adverse effect is **likely** to become substantial. Medical prognosis of the likely impact of the condition will be the normal route to establishing protection under this provision. The effect need not be continuous and need not be substantial. (**See also paragraphs C5 to C8 on recurring or fluctuating effects**). The person will still need to show that the impairment meets the long-term condition of the definition. (**Sch 1, Para 2**)

B20. Examples of progressive conditions to which the special provisions apply include systemic lupus erythematosis (SLE), various types of dementia, and motor neurone disease. This list, however, is not exhaustive.

A young boy aged 8 has been experiencing muscle cramps and some weakness. The effects are quite minor at present, but he has been diagnosed as having muscular dystrophy. Eventually it is expected that the resulting muscle weakness will cause substantial adverse effects on his ability to walk, run and climb stairs. Although there is no substantial adverse effect at present, muscular dystrophy is a progressive condition, and this child will still be entitled to the protection of the Act under the special provisions in Sch 1, Para 8 of the Act if it can be shown that the effects are likely to become substantial.

A woman has been diagnosed with systemic lupus erythematosis (SLE) following complaints to her GP that she is experiencing mild aches and pains in her joints. She has also been feeling generally unwell, with some flu-like symptoms. The initial symptoms do not have a substantial adverse effect on her ability to carry out normal day-to-day activities. However, SLE is a progressive condition, with fluctuating effects. She has been advised that the condition may come and go over many years, and in the future the effects may become substantial, including severe joint pain, inflammation, stiffness, and skin rashes. Providing it can be shown that the effects are likely to become substantial, she will be covered by the special provisions relating to progressive conditions. She will also need to meet the 'long-term' condition of the definition in order to be protected by the Act.

B21. The Act provides for a person with one of the progressive conditions of cancer, HIV and multiple sclerosis to be a disabled person from the point at which they have that condition, so effectively from diagnosis. (**See paragraph A9.**)

B22. As set out in paragraph B19, in order for the special provisions covering progressive conditions to apply, there only needs to be **some** adverse effect on the person's ability to carry out normal day to day activities. It does not have to be a substantial adverse effect. If a person with a progressive condition is successfully treated (for example by surgery) so that there are no longer any adverse effects, the special provisions will not apply. However, if the treatment does not remove all adverse effects the provisions will still apply. In addition, where the treatment manages to treat the original condition but leads to other adverse effects the provisions may still apply.

A man has an operation to remove the colon because of progressing and uncontrollable ulcerative colitis. The operation results in his no longer experiencing adverse effects from the colitis. He

requires a colostomy, however, which means that his bowel actions can only be controlled by a sanitary appliance.

This requirement for an appliance substantially affects his ability to undertake a normal day-to-day activity and should be taken into account as an adverse effect arising from the original impairment.

B23. Whether the effects of any treatment can qualify for the purposes of **Sch 1, Para 8**, which provides that a person with a progressive condition is to be regarded as having an impairment that has a substantial adverse effect on his or her ability to carry out normal day-to-day activities, will depend on the circumstances of the individual case.

Severe disfigurements

B24. The Act provides that where an impairment consists of a severe disfigurement, it is to be treated as having a substantial adverse effect on the person's ability to carry out normal day-to-day activities. **There is no need to demonstrate such an effect (Sch 1, Para 3).**

A lady has significant scarring to her face as a result of a bonfire accident. The woman uses skin camouflage to cover the scars as she is very self conscious about her appearance. She avoids large crowds and bright lights including public transport and supermarkets and she does not socialise with people outside her family in case they notice the mark and ask her questions about it.

This amounts to a substantial adverse effect. However, the Act does not require her to show that her disfigurement has this effect because it provides for a severe disfigurement to be treated as having a substantial adverse effect on the person's ability to carry out normal day-to-day activities.

B25. Examples of disfigurements include scars, birthmarks, limb or postural deformation (including restricted bodily development), or diseases of the skin. Assessing severity will be mainly a matter of the degree of the disfigurement which may involve taking into account factors such as the nature, size, and prominence of the disfigurement. However, it may be necessary to take account of where the disfigurement in question is (e.g. on the back as opposed to the face).

B26. Regulations provide that a disfigurement which consists of a tattoo (which has not been removed) is not to be considered as a severe disfigurement. Also excluded is a piercing of the body for decorative purposes including anything attached through the piercing[7].

SECTION C: LONG-TERM

This section should not be read in isolation but must be considered together with sections A, C and D. Whether a person satisfies the definition of a disabled person for the purposes of the Act will depend upon the full circumstances of the case. That is, whether the adverse effect of the person's impairment on the carrying out of normal day-to-day activities is substantial and long term.

Meaning of 'long-term effects'

[4.279]

C1. The Act states that, for the purpose of deciding whether a person is disabled, a long-term effect of an impairment is one:

- which has lasted at least 12 months; or
- where the total period for which it lasts, from the time of the first onset, is likely to be at least 12 months; or
- which is likely to last for the rest of the life of the person affected (**Sch 1, Para 2**)

Special provisions apply when determining whether the effects of an impairment that has fluctuating or recurring effects are long-term. (**See paragraphs C5 to C11**). Also a person who is deemed to be a disabled person does not need to satisfy the long-term requirement. (**See paragraphs A9 to A10.**)

C2. The cumulative effect of related impairments should be taken into account when determining whether the person has experienced a long-term effect for the purposes of meeting the definition of a disabled person. The substantial adverse effect of an impairment which has developed from, or is likely to develop from, another impairment should be taken into account when determining whether the effect has lasted, or is likely to last at least twelve months, or for the rest of the life of the person affected.

A man experienced an anxiety disorder. This had a substantial adverse effect on his ability to make social contacts and to visit particular places. The disorder lasted for eight months and then developed into depression, which had the effect that he was no longer able to leave his home or go to work. The depression continued for five months. As the total period over which the adverse effects lasted was in excess of 12 months, the long-term element of the definition of disability was

met.

A person experiences, over a long period, adverse effects arising from two separate and unrelated conditions, for example a lung infection and a leg injury. These effects should not be aggregated.

Meaning of 'likely'

C3. The meaning of 'likely' is relevant when determining:

- whether an impairment has a long-term effect (**Sch 1, Para 2(1), see also paragraph C1)**;
- whether an impairment has a recurring effect (**Sch 1, Para 2(2), see also paragraphs C5 to C11)**;
- whether adverse effects of a progressive condition will become substantial (**Sch 1, Para 8, see also paragraphs B18 to B23)**; or
- how an impairment should be treated for the purposes of the Act when the effects of that impairment are controlled or corrected by treatment or behaviour (**Sch 1, Para 5(1), see also paragraphs B7 to B17**).

In these contexts, 'likely', should be interpreted as meaning that it could well happen.

C4. In assessing the likelihood of an effect lasting for 12 months, account should be taken of the circumstances at the time the alleged discrimination took place. Anything which occurs after that time will not be relevant in assessing this likelihood. Account should also be taken of both the typical length of such an effect on an individual, and any relevant factors specific to this individual (for example, general state of health or age).

Recurring or fluctuating effects

C5. The Act states that, if an impairment has had a substantial adverse effect on a person's ability to carry out normal day-to-day activities but that effect ceases, the substantial effect is treated as continuing if it is likely to recur. (In deciding whether a person has had a disability in the past, the question is whether a substantial adverse effect has in fact recurred.) Conditions with effects which recur only sporadically or for short periods can still qualify as impairments for the purposes of the Act, in respect of the meaning of 'long-term' (**Sch 1, Para 2(2), see also paragraphs C3 to C4 (meaning of likely).)**

C6. For example, a person with rheumatoid arthritis may experience substantial adverse effects for a few weeks after the first occurrence and then have a period of remission. **See also example at paragraph B11.** If the substantial adverse effects are likely to recur, they are to be treated as if they were continuing. If the effects are likely to recur beyond 12 months after the first occurrence, they are to be treated as long-term. Other impairments with effects which can recur beyond 12 months, or where effects can be sporadic, include Menieres Disease and epilepsy as well as mental health conditions such as schizophrenia, bipolar affective disorder, and certain types of depression, though this is not an exhaustive list. Some impairments with recurring or fluctuating effects may be less obvious in their impact on the individual concerned than is the case with other impairments where the effects are more constant.

A young man has bipolar affective disorder, a recurring form of depression. The first episode occurred in months one and two of a 13-month period. The second episode took place in month 13. This man will satisfy the requirements of the definition in respect of the meaning of long-term, because the adverse effects have recurred beyond 12 months after the first occurrence and are therefore treated as having continued for the whole period (in this case, a period of 13 months).

In contrast, a woman has two discrete episodes of depression within a ten-month period. In month one she loses her job and has a period of depression lasting six weeks. In month nine she experiences a bereavement and has a further episode of depression lasting eight weeks. Even though she has experienced two episodes of depression she will not be covered by the Act. This is because, as at this stage, the effects of her impairment have not yet lasted more than 12 months after the first occurrence, and there is no evidence that these episodes are part of an underlying condition of depression which is likely to recur beyond the 12-month period.

However, if there was evidence to show that the two episodes did arise from an underlying condition of depression, the effects of which are likely to recur beyond the 12-month period, she would satisfy the long term requirement.

C7. It is not necessary for the effect to be the same throughout the period which is being considered in relation to determining whether the 'long-term' element of the definition is met. A person may still satisfy the long-term element of the definition even if the effect is not the same throughout the period. It may change: for example activities which are initially very difficult may become possible to a much greater extent. The effect might even disappear temporarily. Or other effects on the ability to carry out normal day-to-day activities may develop and the initial effect may disappear altogether.

A person has Menières Disease. This results in his experiencing mild tinnitus at times, which does not adversely affect his ability to carry out normal day-to-day activities. However, it also causes temporary periods of significant hearing loss every few months. The hearing loss substantially and adversely affects his ability to conduct conversations or listen to the radio or television. Although his condition does not continually have this adverse effect, it satisfies the long-term requirement because it has substantial adverse effects that are likely to recur beyond 12 months after he developed the impairment.

C8. Regulations specifically exclude seasonal allergic rhinitis (e.g. hayfever) except where it aggravates the effects of an existing condition[8]. For example, this may occur in some cases of asthma. **(See also paragraphs A12 to A15 (exclusions).)**

Likelihood of recurrence

C9. Likelihood of recurrence should be considered taking all the circumstances of the case into account. This should include what the person could reasonably be expected to do to prevent the recurrence. For example, the person might reasonably be expected to take action which prevents the impairment from having such effects (e.g. avoiding substances to which he or she is allergic). This may be unreasonably difficult with some substances.

C10. In addition, it is possible that the way in which a person can control or cope with the effects of an impairment may not always be successful. For example, this may be because an avoidance routine is difficult to adhere to, or itself adversely affects the ability to carry out day-to-day activities, or because the person is in an unfamiliar environment. If there is an increased likelihood that the control will break down, it will be more likely that there will be a recurrence. That possibility should be taken into account when assessing the likelihood of a recurrence. **(See also paragraphs B7 to B10 (effects of behaviour), paragraph B11 (environmental effects); paragraphs B12 to B17 (effect of treatment); and paragraphs C3 to C4 (meaning of likely).)**

C11. If medical or other treatment is likely to permanently cure a condition and therefore remove the impairment, so that recurrence of its effects would then be unlikely even if there were no further treatment, this should be taken into consideration when looking at the likelihood of recurrence of those effects. However, if the treatment simply delays or prevents a recurrence, and a recurrence would be likely if the treatment stopped, as is the case with most medication, then the treatment is to be ignored and the effect is to be regarded as likely to recur.

Assessing whether a past disability was long-term

C12. The Act provides that a person who has had a disability within the definition is protected from some forms of discrimination even if he or she has since recovered or the effects have become less than substantial. In deciding whether a past condition was a disability, its effects count as long-term if they lasted 12 months or more after the first occurrence, or if a recurrence happened or continued until more than 12 months after the first occurrence (**S 6(4) and Sch 1, Para 2**). **For the forms of discrimination covered by this provision see paragraph A16.**

A person was diagnosed with a digestive condition that significantly restricted her ability to eat. She received medical treatment for the condition for over a year, but eventually required surgery which cured the condition. As the effects of the condition had lasted for over 12 months, and they had a substantial adverse effect on her ability to carry out a normal day-to-day activity, the condition met the Act's definition of a disability.

The woman is entitled to the protection of the Act as a person who has had a past disability.

SECTION D: NORMAL DAY-TO-DAY ACTIVITIES

This section should not be read in isolation but must be considered together with sections A, B and C. Whether a person satisfies the definition of a disabled person for the purposes of the Act will depend upon the full circumstances of the case. That is, whether the adverse effect of the person's impairment on the carrying out of normal day-to-day activities is substantial and long term.

[4.280]

D1. The Act looks at a person's impairment and whether it substantially and adversely affects the person's ability to carry out normal day-to-day activities.

Meaning of
'normal day-to-day activities'

D2. The Act does not define what is to be regarded as a 'normal day-to-day activity'. It is not possible to provide an exhaustive list of day-to-day activities, although guidance on this matter is given here and illustrative examples of when it would, and would not, be reasonable to regard an impairment as having a substantial adverse effect on the ability to carry out normal day-to-day activities are shown in the Appendix.

D3. In general, day-to-day activities are things people do on a regular or daily basis, and examples include shopping, reading and writing, having a conversation or using the telephone, watching television, getting washed and dressed, preparing and eating food, carrying out household tasks, walking and travelling by various forms of transport, and taking part in social activities. Normal day-to-day activities can include general work-related activities, and study and education-related activities, such as interacting with colleagues, following instructions, using a computer, driving, carrying out interviews, preparing written documents, and keeping to a timetable or a shift pattern.

A person works in a small retail store. His duties include maintaining stock in a stock room, dealing with customers and suppliers in person and by telephone, and closing the store at the end of the day. Each of these elements of the job would be regarded as a normal day-to-day activity, which could be adversely affected by an impairment.

D4. The term 'normal day-to-day activities' is not intended to include activities which are normal only for a particular person, or a small group of people. In deciding whether an activity is a normal day-to-day activity, account should be taken of how far it is carried out by people on a daily or frequent basis. In this context, 'normal' should be given its ordinary, everyday meaning.

D5. A normal day-to-day activity is not necessarily one that is carried out by a majority of people. For example, it is possible that some activities might be carried out only, or more predominantly, by people of a particular gender, such as breast-feeding or applying make-up, and cannot therefore be said to be normal for most people. They would nevertheless be considered to be normal day-to-day activities.

D6. Also, whether an activity is a normal day-to-day activity should not be determined by whether it is more normal for it to be carried out at a particular time of day. For example, getting out of bed and getting dressed are activities that are normally associated with the morning. They may be carried out much later in the day by workers who work night shifts, but they would still be considered to be normal day-to-day activities.

D7. In considering the ability of a child aged six or over to carry out a normal day-to-day activity, it is necessary to take account of the level of achievement which would be normal for a person of a similar age. **(See also Section E (Disabled children).)**

Specialised activities

D8. Where activities are themselves highly specialised or involve highly specialised levels of attainment, they would not be regarded as normal day-to-day activities for most people. In some instances work-related activities are so highly specialised that they would not be regarded as normal day-to-day activities.

A watch repairer carries out delicate work with highly specialised tools. He develops tenosynovitis. This restricts his ability to carry out delicate work though he is able to carry out activities such as general household repairs using more substantial tools.

Although the delicate work is a normal working activity for a person in his profession, it would not be regarded as a normal day-to-day activity for most people.

D9. The same is true of other specialised activities such as playing a musical instrument to a high standard of achievement; taking part in activities where very specific skills or level of ability are required; or playing a particular sport to a high level of ability, such as would be required for a professional footballer or athlete. Where activities involve highly specialised skills or levels of attainment, they would not be regarded as normal day-to-day activities for most people.

A woman plays the piano to a high standard, and often takes part in public performances. She has developed carpal tunnel syndrome in her wrists. This does not prevent her from playing the piano, but she cannot achieve such a high standard.

This restriction would not be an adverse effect on a normal day-to-day activity, because playing the piano to such a specialised level would not be normal for most people.

D10. However, many types of specialised work-related or other activities may still involve normal day-to-day activities which can be adversely affected by an impairment. For example they may involve normal activities such as: sitting down, standing up, walking, running, verbal interaction, writing, driving; using everyday objects such as a computer keyboard or a mobile phone, and lifting, or carrying everyday objects, such as a vacuum cleaner.

The work of the watch repairer referred to above also includes preparing invoices and counting and recording daily takings. These are normal day-to-day activities. The effects of his tenosynovitis increase in severity over time resulting in greater restriction of movement in his hands. As

a consequence he experiences substantial difficulties carrying out these normal day-to-day activities.

Adverse effects on the ability to carry out normal day-to-day activities

D11. This section provides guidance on what should be taken into account in deciding whether a person's ability to carry out normal day-to-day activities might be restricted by the effects of that person's impairment. The examples given are purely illustrative and **should not in any way be considered as a prescriptive or exhaustive list.**

D12. In the Appendix, examples are given of circumstances where it **would be reasonable** to regard the adverse effect on the ability to carry out a normal day-to-day activity as substantial. In addition, examples are given of circumstances where it would **not be reasonable** to regard the effect as substantial. In these examples, the effect described should be thought of as if it were the **only** effect of the impairment.

D13. The examples of what it would, and what it would not, be reasonable to regard as substantial adverse effects on normal day-to-day activities **are indicators and not tests.** They do not mean that if a person can do an activity listed then he or she does not experience any substantial adverse effects: the person may be affected in relation to other activities, and this instead may indicate a substantial effect. Alternatively, the person may be affected in a minor way in a number of different activities, and the cumulative effect could amount to a substantial adverse effect. (**See also paragraphs B4 to B6 (cumulative effects).)**

D14. The examples in this section describe the effect which would occur when the various factors described in Sections A, B and C have been allowed for, including for example disregarding the impact of medical or other treatment.

D15. Some of the examples in this section show how an adverse effect may arise from either a physical or a mental impairment. Where illustrations of both types of impairment have not been given, this does not mean that only one type of impairment could result in that particular effect. **Physical impairments can result in mental effects and mental impairments can have physical manifestations.**

- A person with a physical impairment may, because of pain or fatigue, experience difficulties in carrying out normal activities that involve mental processes.

A journalist has recurrent severe migraines which cause her significant pain. Owing to the pain, she has difficulty maintaining concentration on writing articles and meeting deadlines.

- A person with a mental impairment or learning disability may experience difficulty in carrying out normal day-to-day activities that involve physical activity.

A young man with severe anxiety and symptoms of agoraphobia is unable to go out more than a few times a month. This is because he fears being outside in open spaces and gets panic attacks which mean that he cannot remain in places like theatres and restaurants once they become crowded.

This has a substantial adverse effect on his ability to carry out normal day-to-day activities such as social activities.

A woman has Downs Syndrome and is only able to understand her familiar local bus route. This means that she is unable to travel unaccompanied on other routes, because she gets lost and cannot find her way home without assistance.

This has a substantial adverse effect on her ability to carry out the normal day-to-day activity of using public transport.

D16. Normal day-to-day activities also include activities that are required to maintain personal well-being or to ensure personal safety, or the safety of other people. Account should be taken of whether the effects of an impairment have an impact on whether the person is inclined to carry out or neglect basic functions such as eating, drinking, sleeping, keeping warm or personal hygiene; or to exhibit behaviour which puts the person or other people at risk.

A woman has had anorexia, an eating disorder, for two years and the effects of her impairment restrict her ability to carry out the normal day-to-day activity of eating.

A man has had paranoid schizophrenia for five years. One of the effects of this impairment is an inability to make proper judgements about activities that may result in a risk to his personal safety. For example, he will walk into roads without checking if cars are coming.

This has a substantial adverse effect on his ability to carry out the normal day-to-day activity of crossing the road safely.

D17. Some impairments may have an adverse impact on the ability of a person to carry out normal day-to-day communication activities. For example, they may adversely affect whether a person is able to speak clearly at a normal pace and rhythm and to understand someone else speaking normally in the person's native language. Some impairments can have an adverse effect on a person's ability to understand human non-factual information and non-verbal communication such as body language and facial expressions. Account should be taken of how such factors can have an adverse effect on normal day-to-day activities.

A six-year-old boy has verbal dyspraxia which adversely affects his ability to speak and make himself clear to other people, including his friends and teachers at school.

A woman has bipolar disorder. Her speech sometimes becomes over-excited and irrational, making it difficult for others to understand what she is saying.

A man has had a stammer since childhood. He does not stammer all the time, but his stammer, particularly in telephone calls, goes beyond the occasional lapses in fluency found in the speech of people who do not have the impairment. However, this effect can often be hidden by his avoidance strategies. He tries to avoid making or taking telephone calls where he believes he will stammer, or he does not speak as much during the calls. He sometimes tries to avoid stammering by substituting words, or by inserting extra words or phrases.

In these cases there are substantial adverse effects on the person's ability to carry out normal day-to-day communication activities.

A man has Asperger's syndrome, a form of autism. He finds it hard to understand non-verbal communications such as facial expressions, and non-factual communication such as jokes. He takes everything that is said very literally. He is given verbal instructions during office banter with his manager, but his ability to understand the instruction is impaired because he is unable to isolate the instruction from the social conversation.

This has a substantial adverse effect on his ability to carry out normal day-to-day communication.

D18. A person's impairment may have an adverse effect on day-to- day activities that require an ability to co-ordinate their movements, to carry everyday objects such as a kettle of water, a bag of shopping, a briefcase, or an overnight bag, or to use standard items of equipment.

A young man who has dyspraxia experiences a range of effects which include difficulty co-ordinating physical movements. He is frequently knocking over cups and bottles of drink and cannot combine two activities at the same time, such as walking while holding a plate of food upright, without spilling the food.

This has a substantial adverse effect on his ability to carry out normal day-to-day activities such as making a drink and eating.

A man with achondroplasia has unusually short stature, and arms which are disproportionate in size to the rest of his body. He has difficulty lifting everyday items like a vacuum cleaner, and he cannot reach a standard height sink or washbasin without a step to stand on.

This has a substantial adverse effect on his ability to carry out normal day-to-day activities, such as cleaning, washing up and washing his hands.

D19. A person's impairment may adversely affect the ability to carry out normal day-to-day activities that involve aspects such as remembering to do things, organising their thoughts, planning a course of action and carrying it out, taking in new knowledge, and understanding spoken or written information. This includes considering whether the person has cognitive difficulties or learns to do things significantly more slowly than a person who does not have an impairment.

A woman with bipolar affective disorder is easily distracted. This results in her frequently not being able to concentrate on performing an activity like making a sandwich or filling in a form without being constantly distracted from the task. Consequently, it takes her significantly longer than a person without the disorder to complete these types of task.

Therefore there is a substantial adverse effect on normal day-to-day activities.

Environmental effects

D20. Environmental conditions may have an impact on how an impairment affects a person's ability to carry out normal day-to-day activities. Consideration should be given to the level and nature of any environmental effect. Account should be taken of whether it is within such a range and of such a type that most people would be able to carry out an activity without an adverse effect. For example, whether background noise or lighting is of a type or level that would enable most people to hear or see adequately. **(See also paragraph B11.)**

A woman has tinnitus which makes it difficult for her to hear or understand normal conversations. She cannot hear and respond to what a supermarket checkout assistant is saying if the two people behind her in the queue are holding a conversation at the same time.

This has a substantial adverse effect on her ability to carry out the normal day-to-day activity of taking part in a conversation.

A man has retinitis pigmentosa (RP), a hereditary eye disorder which affects the retina. The man has difficulty seeing in poor light and experiences a marked reduction in his field of vision (referred to as tunnel vision). As a result he often bumps into furniture and doors when he is in an unfamiliar environment, and can only read when he is in a very well-lit area.

This has a substantial adverse effect on his ability to carry out normal day-to-day activities such as socialising in a cinema or lowly-lit restaurant.

D21. Consideration should be given to whether there may also be an adverse effect on the ability to carry out a normal day-to-day activity outside of that particular environment.

A man works in a factory where chemical fumes cause him to have breathing difficulties. He is diagnosed with occupational asthma. This has a substantial adverse effect while he is at work, because he is no longer able to work where he would be exposed to the fumes.

Even in a non-work situation he finds any general exertion difficult. This has some adverse effect on his ability to carry out a normal day-to-day activity like changing a bed.

Although the substantial effect is only apparent while he is at work, where he is exposed to fumes, the man is able to demonstrate that his impairment has an adverse effect on his ability to carry out normal day-to-day activities.

Indirect effects

D22. An impairment may not directly **prevent** someone from carrying out one or more normal day-to-day activities, but it may still have a substantial adverse effect on how the person carries out those activities. For example:

- pain or fatigue: where an impairment causes pain or fatigue, the person may have the ability to carry out a normal day-to-day activity, but may be restricted in the way that it is carried out because of experiencing pain in doing so. Or the impairment might make the activity more than usually fatiguing so that the person might not be able to repeat the task over a sustained period of time. **(See also paragraphs B7 to B10 (effects of behaviour))**;

A man with osteoarthritis experiences significant pain in his hands undertaking tasks such as using a keyboard at home or work, peeling vegetables, opening jars and writing.

The impairment substantially adversely affects the man's ability to carry out normal day-to-day activities.

A man has had chronic fatigue syndrome for several years. Although he has the physical capability to walk and to stand, he finds these very difficult to sustain for any length of time because he experiences overwhelming fatigue. As a consequence, he is restricted in his ability to take part in normal day-to-day activities such as travelling, so he avoids going out socially, and works from home several days a week.

Therefore there is a substantial adverse effect on normal day-to-day activities.

- medical advice: where a person has been advised by a medical practitioner or other health professional, as part of a treatment plan, to change, limit or refrain from a normal day-to-day activity on account of an impairment or only do it in a certain way or under certain conditions. **(See also paragraphs B12 to B17 (effects of treatment).)**

A woman who works as a teacher develops sciatic pain which is attributed to a prolapsed inter-vertebral disc. Despite physiotherapy and traction her pain became worse. As part of her treatment plan her doctor prescribes daily pain relief medication and advises her to avoid carrying moderately heavy items or standing for more than a few minutes at a time.

This has a substantial adverse effect on her carrying out a range of normal day-to-day activities such as shopping or standing to address her pupils for a whole lesson.

- frequency: some impairments may require the person to undertake certain activities, or functions at such frequent intervals that they adversely affect the ability to carry out normal day-to-day activities.

A young woman is a sales representative. She has developed colitis, an inflammatory bowel disease. The condition is a chronic one which is subject to periods of remission and flare-ups. During a flare-up she experiences severe abdominal pain and bouts of diarrhoea. This makes it very difficult for her to drive, including for the purposes of her job, as she must ensure she is always close to a lavatory.

This has a substantial adverse effect on her ability to carry out normal day-to-day activities.

Effect of treatment or correction measures

D23. Except as explained below, where a person is receiving treatment or correction measures for an impairment, the effect of the impairment on day-to-day activities is to be taken as that which the person would experience without the treatment or measures. **(See also paragraphs B12 to B17.)**

A man has a hearing impairment which has the effect that he cannot hold a conversation with another person even in a quiet environment. He has a hearing aid which overcomes that effect. However, it is the effect of the impairment without the hearing aid that needs to be considered.

In this case, the impairment has a substantial adverse effect on the day-to-day activity of holding a conversation.

D24. If a person's sight is corrected by spectacles or contact lenses, or could be corrected by them, what needs to be considered is any adverse effect that the visual impairment has on the ability to carry out normal day-to-day activities which remains while the person is wearing spectacles or lenses.

SECTION E: DISABLED CHILDREN

[4.281]

E1. The effects of impairments may not be apparent in babies and young children because they are too young to have developed the ability to carry out activities that are normal for older children and adults. Regulations provide that an impairment to a child under six years old is to be treated as having a substantial and long-term adverse effect on the ability of that child to carry out normal day-to-day activities where it would normally have a substantial and long-term adverse effect on the ability of a person aged six years or over to carry out normal day-to-day activities[9].

A six month old girl has an impairment that results in her having no movement in her legs. She is not yet at the stage of crawling or walking. So far the impairment does not have an apparent effect on her ability to move around. However, the impairment is to be treated as having a substantial and long-term adverse effect on her ability to carry out a normal day-to-day activity like going for a walk. This is because it would normally have such an adverse effect on the ability of a person aged six years or over to carry out normal day-to-day activities.

E2. Children aged six and older are subject to the normal requirements of the definition. That is, that they must have an impairment which has a substantial and long-term adverse effect on their ability to carry out normal day-to-day activities. However, in considering the ability of a child aged six or over to carry out a normal day-to-day activity, it is necessary to take account of the level of achievement which would be normal for a person of a similar age.

A six-year-old child has been diagnosed as having autism. He has difficulty communicating through speech and in recognising when someone is happy or sad. When going somewhere new or taking a different route he can become very anxious. Each of these factors amounts to a substantial adverse effect on his ability to carry out normal day-to-day activities, such as holding a conversation or enjoying a day trip, even for such a young child.

E3. Part 6 of the Act provides protection for disabled pupils and students by preventing discrimination against them at school or in post-16 education because of, or for a reason related to, their disability. A pupil or student must satisfy the definition of disability as described in this guidance in order to be protected by Part 6 of the Act. The duties for schools in the Act, including the duty for schools to make reasonable adjustments for disabled children, are designed to dovetail with duties under the Special Educational Needs (SEN) framework which are based on a separate definition of special educational needs. Further information on these duties can be found in the SEN Code of Practice and the Equality and Human Rights Commission's Codes of Practice for Education.

Examples of children in an educational setting where their impairment has a substantial and long-term adverse effect on the ability to carry out normal day-to-day activities:

A 10-year-old girl has a learning disability. She has a short attention span and has difficulty remembering facts from one day to the next. She can read only a few familiar words. Each of these factors has a substantial adverse effect on her ability to participate in learning activities.

A 14-year-old boy has been diagnosed as having attention deficit hyperactivity disorder (ADHD). He often finds it difficult to concentrate and skips from task to task forgetting instructions. Either of these factors has a substantial adverse effect on his ability to participate in class and join in team games in the playground.

A 12-year-old boy has cerebral palsy and has limited movement in his legs. This has a substantial adverse effect on his ability to move around the school and take part in physical sports activities.

SECTION F: DISABILITY AS A PARTICULAR PROTECTED CHARACTERISTIC OR AS A SHARED PROTECTED CHARACTERISTIC

[4.282]

F1. The Act provides protection from discrimination based on a range of protected characteristics and disability, as defined in the Act and related, is a protected characteristic.

F2. Certain provisions in the Act apply where a person has a "particular" protected characteristic. In the case of disability, **the Act states** that a reference to a person with a particular protected characteristic is a reference to a person who has a particular disability **(S 6(3))**.

A disabled man has a mobility impairment. This has a substantial and long-term adverse effect on his ability to carry out normal day-to-day activities like shopping and gardening. Therefore he is protected by the Act in general because he has the protected characteristic of disability.

However, for the purposes of the provisions of the Act that apply specifically to people with a particular protected characteristic, he would have the particular characteristic of being mobility impaired.

F3. Some provisions in the Act apply where persons share a protected characteristic. In the case of disability, **the Act states** that a reference to persons who share a particular characteristic is a reference to persons who have the same disability (**S 6(3)**).

For the purposes of the provisions that apply specifically to people who share a protected characteristic, the disabled man would share the protected characteristic with other people who have mobility impairments.

F4. This may be illustrated by reference to the following provisions in the Act.

- Schedule 9 paragraph 1 of the Act provides that it is not discrimination, under a range of work provisions, for it to be an occupational requirement that the job holder has a particular protected characteristic.

A charitable organisation that provides services to people with HIV and Aids has vacancies for counsellors for which being HIV positive is an occupational requirement.

It is not discriminatory for the organisation to only appoint people who have a particular protected characteristic which, in this instance, is having the particular disability of being HIV positive.

- Schedule 16 paragraph 1 relating to associations or clubs for people who have a single protected characteristic, apply where persons share a protected characteristic.

A group of people with hearing impairments form a private club that provides advice, support and recreational activities specifically for people who have that particular impairment.

For the purposes of the Act, a reference to people who share a protected characteristic would, in this instance, be to people who have hearing impairments.

APPENDIX

AN ILLUSTRATIVE AND NON-EXHAUSTIVE LIST OF FACTORS WHICH, IF THEY ARE EXPERIENCED BY A PERSON, **IT WOULD BE REASONABLE** TO REGARD AS HAVING A SUBSTANTIAL ADVERSE EFFECT ON NORMAL DAY-TO-DAY ACTIVITIES.

[4.283]

Whether a person satisfies the definition of a disabled person for the purposes of the Act will depend upon the full circumstances of the case. That is, whether the substantial adverse effect of the impairment on normal day-to-day activities is long term.

In the following examples, the effect described should be thought of as if it were the **only** effect of the impairment.

- Difficulty in getting dressed, for example, because of physical restrictions, a lack of understanding of the concept, or low motivation;
- Difficulty carrying out activities associated with toileting, or caused by frequent minor incontinence;
- Difficulty preparing a meal, for example, because of restricted ability to do things like open cans or packages, or because of an inability to understand and follow a simple recipe;
- Difficulty eating; for example, because of an inability to co-ordinate the use of a knife and fork, a need for assistance, or the effect of an eating disorder;
- Difficulty going out of doors unaccompanied, for example, because the person has a phobia, a physical restriction, or a learning disability;
- Difficulty waiting or queuing, for example, because of a lack of understanding of the concept, or because of pain or fatigue when standing for prolonged periods;
- Difficulty using transport; for example, because of physical restrictions, pain or fatigue, a frequent need for a lavatory or as a result of a mental impairment or learning disability;
- Difficulty in going up or down steps, stairs or gradients; for example, because movements are painful, fatiguing or restricted in some way;
- A total inability to walk, or an ability to walk only a short distance without difficulty; for example because of physical restrictions, pain or fatigue;
- Difficulty entering or staying in environments that the person perceives as strange or frightening;
- Behaviour which challenges people around the person, making it difficult for the person to be accepted in public places;
- Persistent difficulty crossing a road safely, for example, because of physical restrictions or a failure to understand and manage the risk;
- Persistent general low motivation or loss of interest in everyday activities;
- Difficulty accessing and moving around buildings; for example because of inability to open doors, grip handrails on steps or gradients, or an inability to follow directions;
- Difficulty operating a computer, for example, because of physical restrictions in using a keyboard, a visual impairment or a learning disability;
- Difficulty picking up and carrying objects of moderate weight, such as a bag of shopping or a small piece of luggage, with one hand;

- Inability to converse, or give instructions orally, in the person's native spoken language;
- Difficulty understanding or following simple verbal instructions;
- Difficulty hearing and understanding another person speaking clearly over the voice telephone (where the telephone is not affected by bad reception);
- Persistent and significant difficulty in reading or understanding written material where this is in the person's native written language, for example because of a mental impairment, or learning disability, or a visual impairment (except where that is corrected by glasses or contact lenses);
- Intermittent loss of consciousness;
- Frequent confused behaviour, intrusive thoughts, feelings of being controlled, or delusions;
- Persistently wanting to avoid people or significant difficulty taking part in normal social interaction or forming social relationships, for example because of a mental health condition or disorder;
- Persistent difficulty in recognising, or remembering the names of, familiar people such as family or friends;
- Persistent distractibility or difficulty concentrating;
- Compulsive activities or behaviour, or difficulty in adapting after a reasonable period to minor changes in a routine.

AN ILLUSTRATIVE AND NON-EXHAUSTIVE LIST OF FACTORS WHICH, IF THEY ARE EXPERIENCED BY A PERSON, **IT WOULD NOT BE REASONABLE** TO REGARD AS HAVING A SUBSTANTIAL ADVERSE EFFECT ON NORMAL DAY-TO-DAY ACTIVITIES.

Whether a person satisfies the definition of a disabled person for the purposes of the Act will depend upon the full circumstances of the case. That is, whether the substantial adverse effect of the impairment on normal day-to-day activities is long term.

- Inability to move heavy objects without assistance or a mechanical aid, such as moving a large suitcase or heavy piece of furniture without a trolley;
- Experiencing some discomfort as a result of travelling, for example by car or plane, for a journey lasting more than two hours;
- Experiencing some tiredness or minor discomfort as a result of walking unaided for a distance of about 1.5 kilometres or one mile;
- Minor problems with writing or spelling;
- Inability to reach typing speeds standardised for secretarial work;
- Inability to read very small or indistinct print without the aid of a magnifying glass;
- Inability to fill in a long, detailed, technical document, which is in the person's native language, without assistance;
- Inability to speak in front of an audience simply as a result of nervousness;
- Some shyness and timidity;
- Inability to articulate certain sounds due to a lisp;
- Inability to be understood because of having a strong accent;
- Inability to converse orally in a language which is not the speaker's native spoken language;
- Inability to hold a conversation in a very noisy place, such as a factory floor, a pop concert, sporting event or alongside a busy main road;
- Inability to sing in tune;
- Inability to distinguish a known person across a substantial distance (e.g. across the width of a football pitch);
- Occasionally forgetting the name of a familiar person, such as a colleague;
- Inability to concentrate on a task requiring application over several hours;
- Occasional apprehension about significant heights;
- A person consciously taking a higher than normal risk on their own initiative, such as persistently crossing a road when the signals are adverse, or driving fast on highways for own pleasure;
- Simple inability to distinguish between red and green, which is not accompanied by any other effect such as blurring of vision;
- Infrequent minor incontinence;
- Inability to undertake activities requiring delicate hand movements, such as threading a small needle or picking up a pin.

NOTES

1 Schedule 1, Para 12 defines an 'adjudicating body' as a court, tribunal, or a person (other than a court or tribunal) who may decide a claim relating to a contravention of Part 6 (education).

2 Regulation 7 of The Equality Act 2010 (Disability) Regulations 2010 (SI 2010/2128).

3 The Equality Act 2010 (Disability) Regulations 2010 (SI 2010/2128).

4 Provisions in The Equality Act 2010 (Disability) Regulations 2010 (SI 2010/2128).

5 Covering: taxis etc; public service vehicles and rail transport.

6 The Disability Discrimination Act 1995 (DDA) provided that any individual who was registered as a disabled person under the Disabled Persons (Employment) Act 1944 and whose name appeared on the register both on 12 January 1995 and 2 December 1996 was treated as having a disability for during the period of three years starting on 2 December 1996 (when the DDA employment provisions came into force). This applied regardless of whether the person met the DDA definition of a disabled person during that period. Following the end of the three-year transitional period, those persons who were treated by this provision as being disabled are now treated as having a disability in the past. **This provision is preserved for the purposes of the Equality Act 2010.**

7 See Note 3.

8 See Note 3.

[9] See Note 3.

CODE OF PRACTICE ON PICKETING (MARCH 2017)

[4.284]

NOTES

This Code was originally made under the Employment Act 1980, s 3 (as amended by the Employment Act 1988, s 18). See now the Trade Union and Labour Relations (Consolidation) Act 1992, ss 201, 202 at **[1.517]**, **[1.518]**.

This Code was made by the Secretary of State for Employment, and came into force on 1 May 1992 (see the Employment Code of Practice (Picketing) Order 1992, SI 1992/476). It has been revised to include references to the requirement to appoint a picket supervisor as a result of s 220A of the 1992 Act (which was inserted by the Trade Union Act 2016, s 10). The revised Code came into force on 1 March 2017 and applies only in relation to a trade union organising or encouraging members after that date to take part in picketing (in accordance with s 220A(1) of the 1992 Act); see the Code of Practice (Picketing) Order 2017, SI 2017/237. The 1992 Code replaced the previous Code issued in 1980. For the legal status of the Code, see now the Trade Union and Labour Relations (Consolidation) Act 1992, s 207 at **[1.523]**. The Code has passages which in the original published version are bold italics; this has been replicated here.

Notes are as in the Code.

See *Harvey* NII(11).

CONTENTS

PREAMBLE

[4.285]

The legal framework within which this Code operates is explained in the text. While every effort has been made to ensure that explanations included in the Code are accurate, only the courts can give authoritative interpretation of the law.

The Code's provisions apply equally to men and women, but for simplicity the masculine pronoun is used throughout. Wherever it appears in the Code, the word "court" is used to mean the High Court in England and Wales and the Court of Session in Scotland, but without prejudice to the Code's relevance to any proceedings before any other court.

Passages in this Code which are printed in ***bold italic type*** outline or re-state provisions in primary legislation.

This Code was made by the Secretary of State for Employment and came into force on 1 May 1992.[1] It has been revised to include references to the requirement to appoint a picket supervisor as a result of section 220A of the 1992 Act (which was inserted by section 10 of the Trade Union Act 2016).

The term "industrial tribunal" has been changed to "employment tribunal" throughout the Code in accordance with section 1 (industrial tribunals to be known as employment tribunals) of the Employment Rights (Dispute Resolution) Act 1998.

NOTES

[1] See the Employment Code of Practice (Picketing) Order 1992 SI 1992/476.

SECTION A
INTRODUCTION

[4.286]

1. The purpose of this Code is to provide practical guidance on picketing in trade disputes for those;

- contemplating, organising or taking part in a picket or activities associated with picketing, such as assemblies or demonstrations; and/or
- employers, workers or members of the general public who may be affected by a picket or any associated activities.

2. There is no legal "right to picket" as such, but attendance for the purpose of peaceful picketing has long been recognised to be a lawful activity. However, the law imposes certain limits on how, where, and for what purpose such picketing can be undertaken and also requires trade unions to appoint a picket supervisor during picketing and comply with certain requirements – see paragraphs 12 to 16 of this Code. These limits help to ensure proper protection for those may be affected by picketing - including those who wish to cross a picket line and go to work.

3. It is a **civil** wrong, actionable in the civil courts, to persuade someone to break his contract of employment, or to secure the breaking of a commercial contract. But the law exempts from this liability those acting in contemplation or furtherance of a trade dispute, including – in certain circumstances - pickets themselves.

4. This exemption is provided by means of special "statutory immunities" to prevent liability arising to such **civil law** proceedings. These immunities - which are explained in more detail in Section B of this Code - have the effect that trade unions and individuals can, in certain circumstances, organise or conduct a picket without fear of being successfully sued in the courts. However, this protection applies only to acts of inducing breach, or interference with the performance, of contracts, or threatening to do either of these things.

5. These "statutory immunities" afford no protection for a picket, anyone involved in activities associated with picketing, or anyone organising a picket who commits some other kind of civil wrong - such as trespass or nuisance.[2] Nor do they protect anyone - whether a picket, an employee who decides to take industrial action or to break his contract of employment because he is persuaded to do so by a picket, or anyone else - from the consequences which may follow if they choose to take industrial action or break their contracts of employment. These could include, for example, loss of wages, or other disciplinary action or dismissal from employment.

6. The **criminal** law applies to pickets just as it applies to everyone else. No picket, person involved in activities associated with picketing, or person organising a picket, has any exemption from the provisions of the criminal law as this applies, for example, to prevent obstruction, preserve public order, or regulate assemblies or demonstrations.

7. This Code outlines aspects of the law on picketing - although it is, of course for the courts and employment tribunals to interpret and apply the law in particular cases. Sections B and C, respectively, outline provisions of the civil and criminal law and, where relevant, give guidance on good practice. Section D describes the role of the police in enforcing the law. Sections E, F and G also give guidance on good practice in relation to the conduct of particular aspects of picketing and certain activities associated with picketing.

8. The Code itself imposes no legal obligations and failure to observe it does not by itself render anyone liable to proceedings. But statute law provides that any provisions of the Code are to be admissible in evidence and taken into account in proceedings before any court, employment tribunal or Central Arbitration Committee where they consider them relevant.

NOTES

[2] See the further explanation in paragraph 32 in Section B of the Code

SECTION B
PICKETING AND THE CIVIL LAW

[4.287]

9. The law sets out the basic rules which must be observed if picketing is to be carried out, or organised, lawfully. To keep to these rules, attendance for the purpose of picketing may only:

(i) ***be undertaken in contemplation or furtherance of a trade dispute;***

(ii) ***be carried out by a person attending at or near his own place of work; a trade union official, in addition to attending at or near his own place work, may also attend at or near the place of work of a member of his trade union whom he is accompanying on the picket line and whom he represents;***

(iii) ***Take place where a picket supervisor has been appointed in accordance with section 220A of the 1992 Act and the requirements at sections 220A (3) to (8) (see paragraph 12).***[3]

Furthermore, the only purpose involved must be peacefully to obtain or communicate information, or peacefully to persuade a person to work or not to work.

10. Picketing commonly involves persuading workers to break, or interfere with the performance of, their contracts of employment by not going into work. Picketing can also disrupt the business of the employer who is being picketed by interfering with the performance of commercial contract which the employer has with a customer or supplier. If pickets follow the rules outlined in paragraph 9, however, they may have the protection against civil proceedings afforded by the "statutory immunities". These rules, and immunities, are explained more fully in paragraphs 11 to 35 below.

IN CONTEMPLATION OR FURTHERANCE OF A TRADE DISPUTE

11. Picketing is lawful only if it is carried out in contemplation or furtherance of a "trade dispute". A "trade dispute" is defined in law so as to cover the matters which normally occasion disputes between employers and workers - such as terms and conditions of employment, the allocation of work, matters of discipline, trade union recognition.

APPOINTMENT OF PICKET SUPERVISOR UNDER SECTION 220A OF THE 1992 ACT

12. Where a trade union either organises the picketing or encourages its members to take part in picketing, the union must appoint a picket supervisor who is either a trade union official or other member of that union. Where more than one union is involved in the picketing, each union must appoint its own picket supervisor. The picket supervisor must be familiar with the provisions of this Code that deal with picketing[4] in order to be able to advise others on what constitutes 'peaceful' picketing. Peaceful picketing means that people involved in, or affected by, picketing activity can go about their business without fear of intimidation. Intimidatory behaviour by any individual may constitute a criminal offence and such a person will be treated in the same way as any member of the public who breaks the law. The picket supervisor has responsibility in relation to the pickets where the union has approved the picketing. Further information on the function of the picket supervisor is set out at Section F.

13. ***The picket supervisor must be present on the picket line or be readily contactable and able to attend at short notice.*** The term 'short notice' is not defined however the intention is that where the picket supervisor is not in attendance, they must be contactable in order to be able to return quickly so as to provide advice on peaceful picketing. Depending on the nature of the industrial dispute, it may be possible for a union to appoint a picket supervisor to supervise more than one picket line provided that they continue to be able to attend each picket line at short notice.

14. ***Either the union or the picket supervisor must take reasonable steps to inform the police of his name, contact details and the location of the picketing.*** This will mean contacting the police so that they have the necessary information. As the picket supervisor does not have to be on the picket line all of the time, this will enable the police to contact the picket supervisor should an issue arise which does not require police intervention but which could benefit from the picket supervisor's advice.

15. ***The union must provide the picket supervisor with a letter stating that the picketing is approved by the union.*** There is no legal requirement for the approval letter to contain the picket supervisor's personal details and the union should ensure that the letter does not breach Data Protection requirements. ***Only the employer involved in the trade dispute, or an individual acting on behalf of the employer, at whose workplace the picketing takes place, is entitled to see this letter.*** This provides confirmation that the union has approved the picketing activity. ***Where a request to see the letter has been made, the picket supervisor must show the letter as soon as reasonably practicable.*** This takes account of the possibility that the picket supervisor may be absent from the picket line. It may be good practice for the union or the picket supervisor to provide a copy of the letter with the employer in advance of the picket in any event.

16. ***When present, the supervisor must wear something that readily identifies him to both others and the picketers as being the supervisor*** to help others on the picket line or those seeking advice or further information. This could be achieved in a number of different ways, for example, by way of wearing a tabard, armband or a badge.

"SECONDARY" ACTION

17. ***The "statutory immunities" do not apply to protect a threat of, or a call for or other inducement of "secondary" industrial action. The law defines "secondary" action - which is sometimes referred to as "sympathy" or "solidarity" action - as that by workers whose employer is not a party to the trade dispute to which the action relates.***

18. However, a worker employed by a party to a trade dispute, picketing at his own place of work may try to persuade another worker, not employed by that employer to break, or interfere with the performance of, the second worker's contract of employment, and/or to interfere with the performance of a commercial contract. This could happen, for example, if a picket persuaded a lorry driver employed by another employer not to cross the picket line and deliver goods to be supplied, under a commercial contract, to the employer in dispute. Such an act by a picket would be an unlawful inducement to take secondary action unless provision was made to the contrary.

19. ***Accordingly, the law contains provisions which make it lawful for a peaceful picket, at the picket's own place of work, to seek to persuade workers other than those employed by the picket's own employer not to work, or not to work normally. To have such protection, the peaceful picketing must be done:***

(a) ***by a worker employed by the employer who is party to the dispute;***[5] ***or***

(b) ***by a trade union official whose attendance is lawful*** (see paragraphs 27 and 28 below).

20. Where an entrance or exit is used jointly by the workers of more than one employer, the workers who are not involved in the dispute to which a picket relates should not be interfered with by picketing activities. Particular care should be taken to ensure that picketing does not involve calls for a breach, or interference with the performance, of contracts by employees of the other employer(s) who are not involved in the dispute. Observing the principle will help avoid consequences which might otherwise be damaging and disruptive to good industrial relations.

ATTENDANCE AT OR NEAR A PICKET'S OWN PLACE OF WORK

21. ***It is lawful for a person to induce breach, or interference with the performance, of a contract in the course of attendance for the purpose of picketing only if he pickets at or near his own place of work.***

22. The expression "at or near his own place of work" is not further defined in statute law. The provisions mean that, except for those covered by paragraphs 27 and 28 below, lawful picketing must be limited to attendance at, or near, an entrance to or exit from the factory, site or office at which the picket works. Picketing should be confined to a location, or locations, as near as practicable to the place of work.

23. The law does not enable a picket to attend lawfully at an entrance to, or exit from, any place of work other than his own. This applies even, for example, if those working at the other place of work are employed by the same employer, or are covered by the same collective bargaining arrangements as the picket.

24. ***The law identifies two specific groups in respect of which particular arrangements apply. These groups are:***

- ***those (e.g. mobile workers) who work at more than one place; and***
- ***those for whom it is impracticable to picket at their own place of work because of its location.***

The law provides that it is lawful for such workers to picket those premises of their employer from which they work, or those from which their work is administered. In the case of lorry drivers, for example, this will usually mean, in practice, the premises of their employer from which their vehicles operate.

25. Special provisions also apply to people who are not in work, and who have lost their jobs for reasons connected with the dispute which has occasioned the picketing. This might arise, for example, where the dismissal of a group of employees has led directly to the organisation of a picket, or where an employer has dismissed employees because they refuse to work normally, and some or all of those dismissed then wish to set up a picket. ***In such cases the law provides that it is lawful for a worker to picket at his former place of work. This special arrangement ceases to apply, however, to any worker who subsequently takes a job at another place of work.***

26. The law does not protect anyone who pickets without permission on or inside any part of premises which are private property. The law will not, therefore protect pickets who trespass, or those who organise such trespass, from being sued in the civil courts.

TRADE UNION OFFICIALS

27. For the reasons described in Section F of this Code, it may be helpful to the orderly organisation and conduct of picketing for a trade union official[6] to be present on a picket line where his members are picketing. This person may or may not be the picket supervisor under section 220A of the 1992 Act. ***The law provides that it is lawful for a trade union official to picket at any place of work provided that:***

(i) ***he is accompanying members of his trade union who are picketing lawfully at or near their own place of work; and***

(ii) ***he personally represents those members.***

28. If these conditions are satisfied, then a trade union official has the same legal protection as other pickets who picket lawfully at or near their own place of work. ***However, the law provides that an official - whether a lay official or an employee of the union – is regarded for this purpose as representing only those members of his union whom he has been specifically*** appointed or elected to represent. An official cannot, therefore, claim that he represents a group of members simply because they belong to his trade union. He must represent and be responsible for them in the normal course of his trade union duties.

> For example, it is lawful for an official - such as shop steward - who represents members at a particular place of work to be present on a picket line where those members are picketing lawfully; for a branch official to be present only where members of his branch are lawfully picketing; for a regional official to be present only where members of his region are lawfully picketing; for a national official who represents a particular trade group or section within the union, to be present wherever members of that trade group or section are lawfully picketing; and for a national official such as a general secretary or president who represents the whole union to be present wherever any members of his union are picketing lawfully.

LAWFUL PURPOSES OF PICKETING

29. In no circumstances does a picket have power, under the law, to require other people to stop, or to compel them to listen or to do what he asks them to do. A person who decides to cross a picket line *must* be allowed to do so. ***In addition, the law provides a remedy for any union member who is disciplined by his union because he has crossed a picket line.***[7]

30. ***The only purposes of picketing declared lawful in statute are:***

- ***peacefully obtaining and communicating information: and***
- ***peacefully persuading a person to work or not to work.***

31. The law allows pickets to seek to explain their case to those entering or leaving the picketed premises, and/or to ask them not to enter or leave the premises where the dispute is taking place. This may be done by speaking to people, or it may involve the distribution of leaflets or the carrying of banners or placards putting the pickets' case. **In all cases, however, any such activity must be carried out *peacefully*.**

32. The law protects peaceful communication and persuasion. It does not give pickets, anyone organising or participating in any activity associated with picketing, or anyone organising a picket, protection against civil proceedings being brought against them for any conduct occurring during the picketing, or associated activity, which amounts to a separate civil wrong such as:

- unlawful threat or assault
- harassment (i.e. threatening or unreasonable behaviour causing fear or apprehension to those in the vicinity);
- obstruction of a path, road, entrance or exit to premises;
- interference (e.g. because of noise or crowds) in the rights of those neighbouring properties (i.e. private nuisance);
- trespassing on private property.

33. Both individual pickets, and anyone - including a union - organising a picket or associated activity, should be careful not to commit such civil wrongs. It is possible, for example, that material on placards carried by pickets - or, for that matter, by those involved in activities associated with picketing - could be defamatory or amount to a threat or harassment. Pickets will also have no legal protection if they do or say things, or make offensive gestures at people, which amount to unlawful threat or harassment. Section C of this Code explains that such actions may also give rise to prosecution under the criminal law.

34. Similarly, if the noise or other disturbance caused to residents of an area by pickets, or those associated with picketing activity, amounts to a civil wrong, those involved or responsible are not protected by the law from proceedings being brought against them.

35. Similar principles apply in respect of any breach of the criminal law by pickets, or their picket supervisor or organiser. As explained in Section C of this Code, a picket, or anyone involved in an associated activity, who threatens or intimidates someone, or obstructs an entrance to a workplace, or causes a breach of the peace, commits a criminal offence. Where pickets commit a criminal offence, then in many circumstances they will not be acting peacefully; consequently, any immunity under the civil law will be lost.

SEEKING REDRESS

36. An employer, a worker, or anyone else who is party to a contract which is, or may be, broken or interfered with by unlawful picketing has a civil law remedy. He may apply to the court for an order[8] preventing, or stopping, the unlawful picketing, or its organisation. Such a person may also claim damages from those responsible where activities of the unlawful picket have caused him loss. An order can be sought against the person - which could include a particular trade union or unions - on whose instructions or advice the unlawful picketing is taking place, or will take place.

37. In making an order, the court has authority to require a trade union which has acted unlawfully to take such steps as are considered necessary to ensure that there is no further call for, or other organisation of, unlawful picketing. An order may be granted by the court on an interim basis, pending a full hearing of the case.

38. If a court order is made, it can apply not only to the person or union named in the order, but to anyone else acting on his behalf or on his instructions. Thus an organiser of unlawful picketing cannot avoid liability, for example, merely by changing the people on the unlawful picket line from time to time.

39. Similarly, anyone who is wronged in any other way by a picket can seek an order from the court to get the unlawful act stopped or prevented, and/or for damages. Thus, for example, if picketing, or associated activities, give rise to unlawful disturbance to residents so affected can apply to the court for such an order and/or for damages. Such proceedings might be taken against individual pickets, or the person - including a union where applicable - responsible for the unlawful act.

40. If a court order is not obeyed, or is ignored, those who sought it can go back to court and ask to have those concerned declared in contempt of court. Anyone who is found to be in contempt of court may face heavy fines, or other penalties, which the court may consider appropriate. For example, a union may be deprived of its assets through sequestration, where the union's funds are placed in the control of a person appointed by the court who may, in particular, pay any fines or legal costs arising from the court proceedings. Similarly, if a person knows that such an order has been made against someone, or some union and yet aids and abets that person to disobey or ignore the order, he may also be found to be acting in contempt of court and liable to be punished by the court.

DETERMINING WHETHER A UNION IS RESPONSIBLE

41. Pickets will usually attend a place of work for the purpose of persuading others not to work, or not to work normally, and may thereby be inducing them to breach, or interfere with the performance of, contracts. The law lays down rules which determine whether a union will be held liable for any such acts of inducement which are unlawful.

42. ***The law provides that a union will be held responsible for such an unlawful act if it is done, authorised or endorsed by:***

(a) ***the union's principle executive committee, president, or general secretary;***

(b) ***any person given power under the union's own rules to so, authorise or endorse acts of the kind in question; or***

(c) ***any other committee of the union, or any official of the union[9] including those who are employed by the union, and those who are employed by the union, and those, like shop stewards, who are not.[10] A union will be held responsible for such an act by such a body or person regardless of any provisions to the contrary in its own rules, or anything in any other contract or rule of law.***

43. Pickets may, of course, commit civil wrongs other than inducing breach, or interference with the performance, of contracts. The question of whether a union will be held responsible for those wrongs will be determined according to common law principles of liability, rather than by reference to the rules described in paragraph 42 above.

THE NEED FOR A BALLOT

44. If what is done in the course of picketing amounts to a call for industrial action, and is an act for which the union is responsible in law, the union can only have the protection of statutory immunity if it has first held a properly-conducted secret ballot.

45. ***The law requires that entitlement to vote in such a ballot must be given to all the union's members who it is reasonable at the time of the ballot for the union to believe will be called upon to take part in, or continue with, the industrial action, and to no other member. In all ballots for industrial action, at least 50% of the trade union members entitled to vote must do so in order for the ballot to be valid. In addition, where the union reasonably believes that the majority of those entitled to vote in the ballot are***

normally engaged in the provision of a specified important public service the union must obtain the support of at least 40% of all **members entitled to vote in the ballot. In all cases, a simple majority (i.e. more than half) of the votes cast must be in favour of industrial action in order for it to go ahead.** These, and other requirements of the law in respect of such ballots, are restated in the statutory Code of Practice on Industrial Action Ballots and Notice to Employers.

NOTES

[3] Section 220A of the 1992 Act was inserted by section 10 of the Trade Union Act 2016.

[4] See section 220(3) of the 1992 Act.

[5] ***However, the peaceful picketing may be done by a worker who is not in employment but was last employed by the employer in dispute in certain circumstances*** – see paragraph 25

[6] ***The law defines an "official of the union" as a person who is an officer of the union (or of a branch or section of the union), or who, not being such an officer, is a person elected or appointed in accordance with the rules of the union to be representative of its members (or some of them), including any person so elected or appointed who is an employee of the same employer as the members, or one or more of the members, whom he is elected to represent.*** This could include, for example, a shop steward.

[7] ***A member disciplined for crossing a picket line is "unjustifiably disciplined"; the remedy for unjustifiable discipline is by complaint to an employment tribunal.*** (See also paragraphs 64 to 65 in Section F of this Code.)

[8] An injunction in England and Wales; an interdict in Scotland.

[9] See footnote to paragraph 27 for the relevant definition of "official". ***In this case, however, an act will also be taken to have been done by an "official of the union" if it was done (or authorised or endorsed) by a group of persons, or any member of a group, to which such an official belonged at the relevant time if the group's purposes included organising or co-ordinating industrial action.***

[10] ***However, if an act which is done (or authorised or endorsed) by a union committee or official is "effectively repudiated" by the union's principal executive committee, president or general secretary, the union will not be held responsible in law. In order to avoid liability in this way, the act concerned must be repudiated by any of these as soon as reasonably practicable after it has come to their knowledge. In addition, the union must, without delay***

(a) ***give written notice of the repudiation to the committee or official in question; and***

(b) ***do its best to give individual written notice of the fact and date of the repudiation to:***

(i) ***every member of the union who it has reason to believe is taking part - or might otherwise take part – in industrial action as a result of the act; and***

(ii) ***the employer of every such member.***

SECTION C
PICKETING AND THE CRIMINAL LAW

[4.288]

46. If a picket commits a criminal offence he is just as liable to be prosecuted as any other member of the public who breaks the law. The immunity provided under the civil law does not protect him in any way.

47. The criminal law protects the right of every person to go about his lawfully daily business free from interference by others. No one is under any obligation to stop when a picket asks him to do so, or, if he does stop, to comply with a request, for example, not to go into work. Everyone has the right, if he wishes to do so, to cross a picket line in order to go into his place of work or to deliver goods or collect goods. A picket may exercise peaceful persuasion, but if he goes beyond that and tries by means other than peaceful persuasion to deter another person from exercising those rights he may commit a criminal offence.

48. ***Among other matters, it is a criminal offence for pickets (as for others):***

- ***to use threatening, abusive or insulting words or behaviour, or disorderly behaviour within the sight or hearing of any person - whether a worker seeking to cross a picket line, an employer, an ordinary member of the public or the police - likely to be caused harassment, alarm or distress by such conduct;***
- ***to use threatening, abusive or insulting words or behaviour towards any person with intent to cause fear of violence or to provoke violence;***
- ***to use or threaten unlawful violence;***
- ***to obstruct the highway or the entrance to premises or to seek physically to bar the passage of vehicles or persons by lying down in the road, linking arms across or circling in the road, or jostling or physically restraining those entering or leaving the premises;***
- ***to be in possession of an offensive weapon;***
- ***intentionally or recklessly to damage property;***
- ***to engage in violent, disorderly or unruly behaviour or to take any action which is likely to lead to a breach of the peace;***
- ***to obstruct a police officer in the execution of his duty.***

49. A picket has no right under the law to require a vehicle to stop or to be stopped. The law allows him only to ask a driver to stop by words or signals. A picket may not physically obstruct a vehicle if the driver decides to drive on or, indeed in any other circumstances. A driver must - as on all other occasions - exercise due care and attention when approaching or driving past a picket line, and may not drive in such a manner as to give rise to a reasonably foreseeable risk of injury.

SECTION D
ROLE OF THE POLICE

[4.289]

50. It is not the function of the police to take a view of the merits of a particular trade dispute. They have a general duty to uphold the law and keep the peace, whether on the picket line or elsewhere. The law gives the police discretion to take whatever measures may reasonably be considered necessary to ensure that picketing remains peaceful and orderly.

51. The police have no responsibility for enforcing the civil law. An employer cannot require the police to help in identifying the pickets against whom he wishes to seek an order from the civil court. Nor is it the job of the police to enforce the terms of an order. Enforcement of an order on the application of a plaintiff is a matter for the court and its officer. The police may, however, decide to assist the officers of the court if they think there may be a breach of the peace.

52. As regards the criminal law the police have considerable discretionary powers to limit the number of pickets at any one place where they have reasonable cause to fear disorder.[11] The law does not impose a specific limit on the number of people who may picket at any one place; nor does this Code affect in any was the discretion of the police to limit the number of people on a particular picket line. It is for the police to decide, taking into account all the circumstances, whether the number of pickets at any particular place provides reasonable grounds for the belief that a breach of the peace is likely to occur. If a picket does not leave the picket line when asked to do so be the police, he is liable to be arrested for obstruction either of the highway or of a police officer in the execution of his duty if the obstruction is such as to cause, or be likely to cause, a breach of the peace.

NOTES

[11] In *Piddington v. Bates* (1960) the High Court upheld the decision of a police constable in the circumstances of that case to limit the number of pickets to two.

SECTION E
LIMITING NUMBERS OF PICKETS

[4.290]

53. Violence and disorder on the picket line is more likely to occur if there are excessive numbers of pickets. Wherever large numbers of people with strong feelings are involved there is a danger that the situation will get out of control, and that those concerned will run the risk of committing an offence, with consequent arrest and prosecution, or of committing a civil wrong which exposes them, or anyone organising them, to civil proceedings.

54. This is particularly so whenever people seek by sheer weight of numbers to stop others going into work or delivering or collecting goods. In such cases, what is intended is not peaceful persuasion, but obstruction or harassment - if not intimidation. Such a situation is often described as "mass picketing". In fact, it is not picketing in its lawful sense of an attempt at peaceful persuasion, and may well result in a breach of the peace or other criminal offences.

55. Moreover, anyone seeking to demonstrate support for those in dispute should keep well away from any picket line so as not to create a risk of a breach of the peace or other criminal being committed on that picket line. Just as with a picket itself, the numbers involved in any such demonstration should be conducted lawfully. ***Section 14 of the Public Order Act 1986 provides the police with the power to impose conditions (for example, as to numbers, location and duration) on public assemblies of 20 or more people where the assembly is likely to result in serious public disorder; or serious damage to property; or serious disruption to the life of the community; or if its purpose is to coerce.***

56. Large numbers on a picket line are also likely to give rise to fear and resentment amongst those seeking to cross that picket line, even where no criminal offence is committed. They exacerbate disputes and sour relations not only between management and employees but between the pickets and their fellow employees. Accordingly pickets and their organisers should ensure that in general the number of pickets does not exceed six at any entrance to, or exit from, a workplace; frequently a smaller number will be appropriate.

SECTION F
ORGANISATION OF PICKETING

[4.291]

57. Sections B and C of this Code outline aspects of the civil law and the criminal law, as they may apply to pickets, and to anyone, including a trade union, who organises a picket. While it is possible that a picket may be entirely "spontaneous", it is much more likely that it will be organised by an identifiable individual or group.

58. Paragraphs 41 to 43 in Section B of this Code describe how to identify whether a trade union is, in fact, responsible in terms of civil law liability, for certain acts. As explained in these paragraphs, the law means, for example, that if such an act takes place in the course of picketing, and if a trade union official has done, authorised or endorsed the act, then the official's union will be responsible in law unless the act is "effectively repudiated" by the union's national leadership.

FUNCTIONS OF THE PICKET SUPERVISOR OR ORGANISER

59. Pickets should not claim the authority and support of a union unless the union is prepared to accept the consequent responsibility. In particular, union authority and support should not be claimed by the pickets if the union has, in fact, repudiated calls to take industrial action made, or being made, in the course of the picketing.

60. Whether picketing is "official" (i.e. organised by a trade union) or "unofficial", the picket supervisor or the organiser (in the case of an unofficial picket) should maintain close contact with the police. Advance consultation with the police is always in the best interests of all concerned. In particular the picket supervisor or organiser and the pickets should seek directions from the police on the number of people who should be present on the picket line at any one time and on where they should stand in order to avoid obstructing the highway.

61. The other main functions of the picket supervisor and in the case of an unofficial picket, the organiser, is to ensure that:

- the pickets understand the law and are aware of the provisions of this Code,[12] and that the picketing is conducted peacefully and lawfully;
- badges or armbands, which authorised pickets should wear so that they are clearly identified, are distributed to such pickets and are worn while they are picketing;[13]
- workers from other places of work do not join the picket line, and that any offers of support on the picket line from outsiders are refused;
- the number of pickets at any entrance to, or exit from, a place of work is not so great as to give rise to fear and resentment amongst those seeking to cross that picket line (see paragraph 56 in Section E of this Code);
- close contact with his own union office (if any), and with the offices of other unions if they are involved in the picketing, is established and maintained;
- such special arrangements as may be necessary for essential supplies, services or operations (see paragraphs 66 to 68 in Section G of this Code) are understood and observed by the pickets.

CONSULTATION WITH OTHER TRADE UNIONS

62. Where several unions are involved in a dispute, they should consult each other about the organisation of any picketing. It is important that they should agree how the picketing is to be carried out, how many pickets there should be from each union, and who should have overall responsibility for organising them.

RIGHT TO CROSS PICKET LINES

63. Everyone has the right to decide for himself whether he will cross a picket line. Disciplinary action should not be taken or threatened by a union against a member on the grounds that he has crossed a picket line.

64. If a union disciplines any member for crossing a picket line, the member will have been "unjustifiably disciplined". In such a case, the individual can make a complaint to an employment tribunal. If the tribunal finds the complaint well-founded, it will make a declaration to that effect.

65. If the union has not lifted the penalty imposed on the member, or if it has not taken all necessary steps to reverse anything done on giving effect to the penalty, an application for compensation should be made to the Employment Appeal Tribunal (EAT). In any other case, the individual can apply to an employment tribunal for compensation. The EAT or tribunal will award whatever compensation it considers just and equitable in all the circumstances subject to a specified maximum amount. Where the application is made to the EAT, there will normally be a specified minimum award.

NOTES

[12] ***Under section 220A(3) the picket supervisor of an official picket is required to be familiar with the provisions of this Code which deal with picketing.***

[13] ***Under section 220A(8) of the 1992 Act the picket supervisor of an official picket will be required to wear something which makes them easily identifiable in this role.***

SECTION G
ESSENTIAL SUPPLIES, SERVICES AND OPERATIONS

[4.292]

66. Pickets, and anyone organising a picket should take very great care to ensure that their activities do not cause distress, hardship or inconvenience to members of the public who are not involved in the dispute. Particular care should be taken to ensure that the movement of essential goods and supplies, the carrying out of essential to the life of the community are not impeded, still less prevented.

67. The following list of essential supplies and services is provided as an illustration of the kind of activity which requires special protection to comply with the recommendations in paragraph 66 above. However, *the list is not intended to be comprehensive*. The supplies and services which may need to be protected in accordance with these recommendations could cover different activities in different circumstances. Subject to this caveat, "essential supplies, services and operations" include:

- the production, packaging, marketing and/or distribution of medical and pharmaceutical products;
- the provision of supplies and services essential to health and welfare institutions, e.g. hospitals, old peoples' homes;
- the provision of heating fuel for schools, residential institutions, medical institutions and private residential accommodation;
- the production and provision of other supplies for which there is a crucial need during a crisis in the interests of public health and safety (e.g. chlorine, lime and other agents for water purification; industrial and medical gases; sand and salt for road gritting purposes);
- activities necessary to the maintenance of plant and machinery;
- the proper care of livestock;
- necessary safety procedures (including such procedures as are necessary to maintain plant and machinery);

- the production, packaging, marketing and/or distribution of food and animal feeding stuffs;
- the operation of essential services, such as police, fire, ambulance, medical and nursing services, air safety, coastguard and air sea rescue services, and services provided by voluntary bodies (e.g. Red Cross and St. John's ambulances, meals on wheels, hospital car service), and mortuaries, burial and cremation services.

Arrangements to ensure these safeguards for essential supplies, services and operations should be agreed in advance between the pickets, or anyone organising the picket, and the employer, or employers, concerned

CODE OF PRACTICE: INDUSTRIAL ACTION BALLOTS AND NOTICE TO EMPLOYERS (MARCH 2017)

[4.293]

NOTES

This Code was issued under the power given to the Secretary of State by the Trade Union and Labour Relations (Consolidation) Act 1992, s 203 (at **[1.519]**), with the authority of Parliament. This Code revises and supersedes the Code of Practice on Industrial Action Ballots and Notice to Employers, which came into effect in September 2005 (see the Preamble *post*). It came into force on 1 March 2017 (see the Code of Practice (Industrial Action Ballots and Notice to Employers) Order 2017, SI 2017/233). The statutory status of the Code is as stated in s 207 of the 1992 Act (at **[1.523]**). Notes are as in the original. Text which in the original version is printed in bold italics is reproduced similarly here.

See *Harvey* NII(9).

CONTENTS

PREAMBLE

[4.294]

This document revises and supersedes the Code of Practice on Industrial Action Ballots and Notice to Employers [URN05/1462], which came into effect in September 2005. Pursuant to section 208(2) of the Trade Union and Labour Relations (Consolidation) Act 1992, that Code shall cease to have effect on the date on which this Code of Practice comes in force.

The legal framework for the operation of this Code is explained in Annex 1 and in its main text. While every effort has been made to ensure that explanations included in the Code are accurate, only the courts can give authoritative interpretations of the law.

The Code's provisions apply equally to men and to women, but for simplicity the masculine pronoun is used throughout. Wherever it appears in the Code the word "court" is used to mean the High Court in England and Wales and the Court of Session in Scotland, but without prejudice to the Code's relevance to any proceedings before any other court.

Passages in this Code which are printed in ***bold italic type*** outline or re-state provisions in primary legislation.

The Code has been revised to reflect the changes made by the Trade Union Act 2016.

SECTION A INTRODUCTION

[4.295]

1. This Code provides practical guidance to trade unions and employers to promote the improvement of industrial relations and good practice in the conduct of trade union industrial action ballots.

2. A union is legally responsible for organising industrial action only if it "authorises or endorses" the action. Authorisation would take place before the industrial action starts, and endorsement after it has previously started as unofficial action.[1]

3. Apart from certain small accidental failures that are unlikely to affect the result, a failure to satisfy the statutory requirements[2] relating to the ballot or giving employers notice of industrial action will give grounds for proceedings against a union by an employer, a customer or supplier of an employer, or an individual member of the public claiming that an effect or likely effect of the industrial action would be to prevent or delay the supply of goods or services to him or to reduce the quality of goods or services so supplied. With the exception of failures to comply with the requirements to give notice to employers, these will also give grounds for action by the union's members.

4. The Code does not deal with other matters which may affect a union's liability in respect of industrial action. For example, the law will give no protection against proceedings to a union which organises secondary action, intimidatory or violent picketing, industrial action which is not "in contemplation or furtherance of a trade dispute",[3] industrial action to establish or maintain any closed shop practice or in support of a worker dismissed while taking part in unofficial industrial action. Nor does it apply to union election ballots, ballots on union political funds or ballots on union recognition or derecognition arranged for by the Central Arbitration Committee under section 70A of and Schedule A1 to the Trade Union and Labour Relations (Consolidation) Act 1992 ("the 1992 Act").[4] These are subject to separate statutory requirements.

LEGAL STATUS

5. ***The Code itself imposes no legal obligations and failure to observe it does not by itself render anyone liable to proceedings. But section 207 of the 1992 Act provides that any provisions of the Code are to be admissible in evidence and are to be taken into account in proceedings before any court where it considers them relevant.***

NOTES

1 A note on trade union legal liability for the organisation of industrial action is set out in Annex 1 to this Code.

2 Set out in sections 226-232A and section 234A of the Trade Union and Labour Relations (Consolidation) Act1992 as amended by the Trade Union Reform and Employment Rights Act 1993, the Employment Relations Act 1999, the Employment Relations Act 2004 and the Trade Union Act 2016.

3 The term "trade dispute" is defined in section 244 of the 1992 Act.

4 Inserted by the Employment Relations Act 1999

SECTION B
WHETHER A BALLOT IS APPROPRIATE

OBSERVING PROCEDURAL AGREEMENTS

[4.296]

6. An industrial action ballot should not take place until any agreed procedures, whether formal or otherwise, which might lead to the resolution of a dispute without the need for industrial action have been completed and consideration has been given to resolving the dispute by other means, including seeking assistance from Acas.[5] A union should hold a ballot on industrial action only if it is contemplating the organisation of industrial action.

BALLOTING BY MORE THAN ONE UNION

7. Where more than one union decides that it wishes to ballot members working for the same employer in connection with the same dispute, the arrangements for the different ballots should be co-ordinated so that, as far as practicable, they are held at the same time and the results are announced simultaneously.

NOTES

5 Acas can provide assistance after the ballot stage as well. Parties should therefore consider using its services at other times during the course of a dispute to avoid industrial action altogether or to bring that action to an end through a negotiated resolution of the issues at dispute.

SECTION C
PREPARING FOR AN INDUSTRIAL ACTION BALLOT

ARRANGING FOR INDEPENDENT SCRUTINY OF THE BALLOT

[4.297]

8. For a ballot where more than 50 members are given entitlement to vote (see paragraph 21 below), under sections 226B and 226C of the 1992 Act the union must appoint a qualified person as the scrutineer of the ballot.[6] For a person to be qualified for appointment as scrutineer of an industrial action ballot, he must be among those specified in an order made by the Secretary of State[7] and the union must not have grounds for believing that he will carry out the functions which the law requires other than competently or that his independence in relation to the union might reasonably be called into question.

9. ***The scrutineer's terms of appointment[8] must require him to take such steps as appear appropriate to him for the purpose of enabling him to make a report to the union as soon as reasonably practicable after the date of the ballot (i.e. the last day on which votes may be cast, if they maybe cast on more than one day), and in any event not later than four weeks[9] after that date.***

10. ***The union must ensure that the scrutineer carries out the functions required to be part of his terms of appointment, and that there is no interference with this from the union, or any of its members, officials or employees. In accordance with section 226(B)(4) the union shall comply with all reasonable requests made by the scrutineer for the purpose of carrying out those functions.***

11. It may be desirable to appoint the scrutineer before steps are taken to satisfy any of the other requirements of the law to make it easier for the scrutineer to satisfy himself whether what is done conforms to the legal requirements.

12. In some circumstances, it may help ensure adequate standards for the conduct of the ballot or simplify the balloting process if a union gives the scrutineer additional tasks to carry out on the union's behalf, such as:

- supervising the production and distribution of voting papers;

- being the person to whom the voting papers are returned by those voting in the ballot; and
- retaining custody of all returned voting papers for a set period after the ballot.

13. Although the scrutiny requirement does not apply to ballots where 50[10] or fewer members are entitled to vote, a union may want to consider whether the appointment of a scrutineer would still be of benefit in enabling it to demonstrate compliance with the statutory requirements more easily.

PROVIDING BALLOT NOTICE TO EMPLOYERS

14. ***Under section 226A of the 1992 Act the union must take such steps as are reasonably necessary to ensure that any employer who it is reasonable for the union to believe will be the employer of any of its members who will be given entitlement to vote receives written notice of the ballot not later than the seventh day before the intended opening day of the ballot (i.e. the first day on which a voting paper is sent to any person entitled to vote).***

That notice must:

- ***state that the union intends to hold the ballot;***
- ***specify the date which the union reasonably believes will be the opening day of the ballot; and***
- ***contain either:***
  - (a) ***a list of the categories of employee to which the employees concerned belong, a list of the workplaces at which they work and figures (together with an explanation of how they were arrived at) showing the total number of employees concerned, the number of them in each of the categories listed and the number of them that work at each of the workplaces listed; or***
  - (b) ***where some or all of the employees concerned are employees from whose wages the employer makes deductions representing payments to the union, a practice commonly known as "checkoff" or "DOCAS",[11] other alternatives apply. In such circumstances, the notice must contain either:***
    - (i) ***those same lists, figures and explanations as set out in (a); or***
    - (ii) ***such information as will enable the employer to readily deduce the total number of employees concerned, the categories of employee to which they belong, the number of employees concerned in each of those categories, the workplaces at which the employees concerned work and the number of them at each of these workplaces.***

Where only some of the employees concerned pay their union contributions by the "check off", the union's notice may include both types of information. That is, the lists, figures and explanations should be provided for those who do not pay their subscriptions through the checkoff whilst information relating to checkoff payments may suffice for those who do.

The "employees concerned" are those whom the union reasonably believes will be entitled to vote in the ballot.

The lists and figures or information supplied should be as accurate as is reasonably practicable in the light of the information in the union's possession at the time when it complied with subsection 226A(1)(a). Information is "in the union's possession" provided it is held for union purposes in a document (either in electronic or other form) and provided it is in the possession or under the control of an officer or employee of the union. Dependent on the precise status of the individuals concerned, information held by shop stewards or other lay representatives would probably not qualify for these purposes as being "in the union's possession".

But a notice will not fail to satisfy the requirements simply because it does not name any employees.

15. There are many ways to categorise a group of employees. When deciding which categories it should list in the notice, the union should consider choosing a categorisation which relates to the nature of the employees' work. For example, the appropriate categorisation might be based on the occupation, grade or pay band of the employees involved. The decision might also be informed by the categorisations of the employees typically used by the employer in his dealings with the union. The availability of data to the union is also a legitimate factor in determining the union's choice.

16. When providing an explanation of how the figures in the written notice were arrived at, unions should consider describing the sources of the data used (for example, membership lists held centrally or information held at regional offices, or data collected from surveys or other sources). It is not reasonable to expect union records to be perfectly accurate and to contain detailed information on all members. Where the union's data are known to be incomplete or to contain other inaccuracies, it is a desirable practice for unions to describe in the notices the main deficiencies. In some cases, the figures will be estimates based on assumptions and the notice should therefore describe the main assumptions used when making estimates.

17. To reduce the risk of legal action, the union should allow sufficient time for delivery, use a suitable means of transmission (such as first class post, courier, fax, email or hand delivery) and consider obtaining confirmation that the employer has received the notice, by using recorded delivery or otherwise.

18. It may also reduce the risk of litigation for a union to check that an employer accepts that the information provided complies with the requirements of section 226A(2)(c) of the 1992 Act. Similarly, it would be in the interests of good industrial relations for an employer who believes the notice he has received does not contain sufficient information to comply with the statutory requirements to raise that with the union promptly before pursuing the matter in the court.

PROVIDING SAMPLE VOTING PAPER(S) TO EMPLOYERS

19. ***The union must take such steps as are reasonably necessary to ensure that any employer who it is reasonable for the union to believe will be the employer of any of its members who will be given entitlement to vote receives a sample voting paper (and a sample of any variant of that voting paper) not later than the third day before the opening day of the ballot. Where more than one employer's workers are being balloted, it is sufficient to send each employer only the voting paper or papers which will be sent to his employees.***

20. If the sample voting paper is available in time, the union may wish to include it with the notice of intention to ballot. As with the ballot notice, the risk of non-compliance can be reduced by allowing enough time, using appropriate means of transmission and, possibly, by obtaining confirmation of receipt.

ESTABLISHING ENTITLEMENT TO VOTE (THE "BALLOTING CONSTITUENCY")

21. ***Under section 227 of the 1992 Act entitlement to vote in the ballot must be given to all the union's members who it is reasonable at the time of the ballot for the union to believe will be induced by the union (whether that inducement will be successful or not) to take part in or continue with the industrial action, and to no other members.***[12]

22. ***The validity of the ballot will not however be affected if the union subsequently induces members to take part in or continue with industrial action who at the time of the ballot:***

- ***were not members or***
- ***were members but who it was not reasonable to expect would be induced to take action (for example because they changed jobs after the ballot).***

23. ***It should also be noted that under section 232B of the 1992 Act accidental failures to comply with the requirements on:***

- ***in particular, who is given entitlement to vote;***
- ***the dispatch of voting papers;***
- ***giving members the opportunity to vote conveniently by post, and***
- ***balloting merchant seamen employed in a ship at sea or outside Great Britain at some time during the voting period***

will be disregarded if, taken together, they are on a scale unlikely to affect the ballot's result.

24. In order to reduce the likelihood of dispute the union may wish to invite an opinion from the relevant employer that its conclusion on entitlement to vote complies with the requirements of section 226A(2)(c) of the 1992 Act. Similarly, where an employer believes the entitlement to vote has not been accurately determined in order to comply with statutory requirements, it would be in the interests of good industrial relations to raise that with the union promptly before pursuing the matter in court.

BALLOT THRESHOLDS FOR INDUSTRIAL ACTION

25. ***Section 226(2) of the 1992 Act sets minimum thresholds of a 50% turnout in all industrial action ballots, and for a 40% level of support in favour of industrial action where the majority of those entitled to vote are normally engaged in the provision of a specified important public service unless at that time the union reasonably believes this not to be the case. In all cases, a simple majority (i.e. more than half) of the votes cast must be in favour of industrial action in order for it to go ahead.***

50% Turnout threshold in all ballots for industrial action

26. ***In all ballots for industrial action, at least 50% of the trade union members entitled to vote must do so in order for the ballot to be valid.***

40% Support threshold in ballots for industrial action in important public services

27. ***In addition, where the majority of those entitled to vote in the ballot are normally engaged in the provision of a specified important public service the union must obtain the support of at least 40% of all members entitled to vote in the ballot unless at that time the union reasonably believes this not to be the case. The "important public services" are specified in regulations***[13] ***and may only fall within any of the following categories:***

- ***health services;***
- ***fire services;***
- ***transport services;***
- ***the education of those under the age of 17;***
- ***decommissioning of nuclear installations and management of radioactive waste and spent fuel; and***
- ***border security.***

These regulations are accompanied by separate non-statutory guidance.[14]

28. The 40% threshold will not apply where the union reasonably believes that a majority of those who are entitled to vote are workers are not normally engaged in the provision of important public services.

BALLOTING MEMBERS AT MORE THAN ONE WORKPLACE

29. ***Where the members of a union with different workplaces are to be balloted, a separate ballot will be necessary for each workplace unless one of the conditions set out below is met. Where separate ballots are held, it will be unlawful for the union to organise industrial action at any such workplace where the thresholds set out in paras 25-28 were not met at that workplace (see paragraph 35 below).***

(If an employee works at or from a single set of premises, his workplace is those premises. If not, it is the premises with which his employment has the closest connection.)

30. In summary, the conditions for holding a single ballot for more than one workplace are:

- ***at each of the workplaces covered by the single ballot there is at least one member of the union affected[15] by the dispute; or***
- ***entitlement to vote in the single ballot is given, and limited, to all of a union's members who, according to the union's reasonable belief, are employed in a particular occupation or occupations by one employer or any of a number of employers with whom the union is in dispute; or***
- *entitlement to vote in the single ballot is given, and limited, to all of a union's members who are employed by a particular employer or any of a number of employers with whom the union is in dispute.*

Where a single ballot across a number of workplaces is held in accordance with the legal requirements relating to thresholds under section 226, it is lawful for the union to organise industrial action at any such workplace. It is possible for a union to hold more than one ballot on a dispute at a single workplace. If the conditions above are met, some or all of those ballots may also cover members in other workplaces.

THE BALLOTING METHOD

31. ***Votes must be recorded by the individual voter marking a voting paper. Voting papers must be sent out by post and members must be enabled conveniently to return them by post at no direct expense to themselves.***[16] In practice, this means that those properly entitled to vote should be supplied with pre-paid reply envelopes in which to return the voting paper.

32. The period between sending out voting papers (i.e. the opening day of the ballot) and the date by which completed voting papers should be returned should be long enough for the voting papers to be distributed and returned and for the members concerned to consider their vote. The appropriate period may vary according to such factors as the geographical dispersion of the workforce, their familiarity or otherwise with the issues in the dispute, the class of post used and whether the ballot is being held at a time of year when members are more than usually likely to be away from home or the workplace, for example during the summer holidays. Generally, seven days should be the minimum period where voting papers are sent out and returned by first class post and fourteen days where second class post is used, although – very exceptionally – shorter periods may be possible for ballots with very small, concentrated constituencies who can be expected to be familiar with the terms of the dispute.

33. In order to reduce the likelihood of dispute over whether or not sufficient time has been allowed, the union may wish to consider obtaining one or more certificates of posting to confirm the date when voting papers were actually put into the post, and the number sent out.

VOTING PAPERS

34. ***Section 229 of the 1992 Act states that the voting paper must:***

- ***where applicable, state the name of the independent scrutineer;***
- ***clearly specify the address to which, and the date by which, it is to be returned;***
- ***be marked with a number, which is one of series of consecutive numbers used to give a different number to each voting paper;***
- ***include a summary of the matter or matters in issue in the trade dispute to which the proposed industrial action relates;***
- ***make clear whether voters are being asked if they are prepared to take part in, or to continue to take part in, industrial action which consists of a strike, or in industrial action short of a strike, which for this purpose includes overtime bans and call-out bans;***
- ***where it contains a question about taking part in industrial action short of a strike, specify the types of industrial action (either in the question itself or elsewhere on the voting paper);***
- ***indicate the period or periods within which the industrial action or each type of industrial action is expected to take place; and***
- ***specify the person or persons (and/or class or classes of person/s) who the union intends to have authority to make the first call for industrial action to which the ballot relates, in the event of a vote in favour of industrial action.***[17]

35. While the question (or questions) maybe framed in different ways, the voter must be asked to say by answering "Yes" or "No" whether he is willing to take part in or continue with the industrial action. If the union has not decided whether the industrial action would consist of a strike or action short of a strike (including overtime bans or call-out bans), separate questions in respect of each type of action must appear on the voting paper. If there is a question about industrial action short of a strike the types of industrial action short of a strike must be specified either in the question itself or elsewhere on the voting paper.

36. The relevant required question (or questions) should be simply expressed. Neither they, nor anything else which appears on the voting paper, should be presented in such a way as to encourage a voter to answer one way rather than another as a result of that presentation. It is not in general good practice for the union to include additional questions on the voting paper (for example, asking if voters agree with the union's opinion on the merits of the dispute or are prepared to "support" industrial action), but if it chooses to do so they should be clearly separate from the required question(s).

37. The following words must appear on every voting paper:

"If you take part in a strike or other industrial action, you may be in breach of your contract of employment. However, if you are dismissed for taking part in strike or other industrial action which

is called officially and is otherwise lawful, the dismissal will be unfair if it takes place fewer than twelve weeks after you started taking part in the action, and depending on the circumstances may be unfair if it takes place later."

This statement must not be qualified or commented upon by anything else on the voting paper.

38. An example voting paper containing the information required by law and other useful information is set out in Annex 2 to this Code. Factual information as indicated would appear in the square brackets and either or both questions could be used as appropriate.

PRINTING AND DISTRIBUTION OF THE VOTING PAPERS

39. The union will wish to ensure that arrangements for producing and distributing voting papers will prevent mistakes which might invalidate the ballot. If in doubt, the independent scrutineer may be able to provide useful advice.

40. If there is no independent scrutineer, or if a union decides that it cannot follow the advice offered by the scrutineer, it should consider:

- printing the voting papers on a security background to prevent duplication;
- whether the arrangements proposed for printing (or otherwise producing) the voting papers, and for their distribution to those entitled to vote in the ballot, offer all concerned sufficient assurance of security.

COMMUNICATION WITH MEMBERS

41. A union should give relevant information to its members entitled to vote in the ballot, including (so far as practicable):

- the background to the ballot and the issues to which the dispute relates;
- any considerations in respect of turnout or size of the majority vote in the ballot that will be taken into account in deciding whether to call for industrial action;
- the possible consequences for workers if they take industrial action; and
- likely timing of industrial action.

In doing so, the union should ensure that any information it gives to members in connection with the ballot is accurate and not misleading.

NOTES

6 Where separate workplace ballots are required, the scrutiny procedures must be followed in respect of each separate ballot if the number of members given entitlement to vote aggregated across all of the ballots is more than 50.

7 In broad terms, the current order (SI 1993 No. 1909) covers practising solicitors, qualified accountants and named bodies.

8 Section 226B(1)(a).

9 Section 226B(1)(b).

10 Section 226C.

11 Deductions of contributions at source.

12 ***The union may choose whether or not to give a vote to any "overseas member", ie any member (other than a merchant seaman or offshore worker) who is outside Great Britain for the whole of the voting period. However, members who may be called upon to take part in or continue with the industrial action, and will be in Northern Ireland for the whole of the voting period, must be given entitlement to vote in a ballot where: (i) the ballot is a workplace ballot at their workplace in Great Britain; or (ii) they work in Northern Ireland but it is intended that they should be called upon to take part in the industrial action alongside their counterparts in Britain, and the ballot is a general ballot covering places of work in both Northern Ireland and Great Britain.***

13 http://www.legislation.gov.uk/uksi/2017/132/contents/made
http://www.legislation.gov.uk/uksi/2017/133/contents/made
http://www.legislation.gov.uk/uksi/2017/134/contents/made
http://www.legislation.gov.uk/uksi/2017/135/contents/made
http://www.legislation.gov.uk/uksi/2017/136/contents/made

14 https://www.gov.uk/government/publications/important-public-services-regulations-2017-guidance-on-the-regulations

15 Section 228A(5) of the 1992 Act defines for this purpose which members are affected by a dispute.

16 ***There is a limited exception for the balloting of union members who are merchant seamen, where the union reasonably believes that they will be employed in a ship at sea (or outside Great Britain) at some time in the period during which votes may be cast and that it will be convenient for them to vote while on the ship or where the ship is. So far as reasonably practicable, the union must ensure that, in these circumstances, those members get a voting paper while on board ship (or at the place where the ship is located), and an opportunity to vote on board ship (or at that place).*** The recommendations in this Code should be applied to such ballots, however, save to the extent that they are irrelevant because the dispatch of voting papers is not by post.

17 Where a person who has not been specified on the voting paper calls industrial action before it is first called by a specified person, then – in order to be certain that the ballot will give protection against legal proceedings – the union should if possible ensure that the call by the unspecified person is effectively repudiated.

SECTION D
HOLDING AN INDUSTRIAL ACTION BALLOT

[4.298]
42. ***In an industrial action ballot:***

- ***every person entitled to vote must be allowed to do so without interference from, or constraint imposed by, the union or any of its members, officials or employees;***
- ***as far as reasonably practicable, every person entitled to vote must be:***
  - ***sent a voting paper by post to his home address, or another address which he has asked the union (in writing) to treat as his postal address;***
  - ***given a convenient opportunity to vote by post; and***
  - ***allowed to do so without incurring any direct cost to himself (see also paragraph 31); and***
- ***as far as reasonably practicable, the ballot must be conducted in such a way as to ensure that those voting do so in secret.***

CHECKS ON NUMBER OF VOTING PAPERS FOR RETURN

43. In order to reduce the risk of failures to satisfy the statutory requirements and invalidating the ballot, the union should establish an appropriate checking system so that:

- no-one properly entitled to vote is accidentally disenfranchised, for example through the use of an out of date or otherwise inaccurate membership list; and
- votes from anyone not properly entitled to vote are excluded.

The independent scrutineer may provide advice on this.

ENSURING SECRECY OF VOTING

44. Any list of those entitled to vote should be compiled, and the voting papers themselves handled, so as to preserve the anonymity of the voter so far as this is consistent with the proper conduct of the ballot.

45. Steps should be taken to ensure that a voter's anonymity is preserved when a voting paper is returned. This means, for example, that:

- envelopes in which voting papers are to be posted should have no distinguishing marks from which the identity of the voter could be established; and
- the procedures for counting voting papers should not prejudice the statutory requirement for secret voting.

SECTION E
FOLLOWING AN INDUSTRIAL ACTION BALLOT

[4.299]

46. ***The union must:***

- ***ensure that the votes given in an industrial action ballot are fairly and accurately counted;***
- ***observe its obligations in connection with the notification of details of the result of an industrial action ballot to all those entitled to vote in the ballot and their employers; and***
- ***provide a copy of the scrutineer's report on the ballot to anyone entitled to receive it.***

An inaccuracy in the counting of the votes is to be disregarded if it is both accidental and on a scale which could not affect the result of the ballot. Whether an accidental inaccuracy meets this test in practice will depend on the closeness of the ballot result.

COUNTING VOTES ACCURATELY AND FAIRLY

47. Where the union itself is conducting the ballot, it may wish to apply some or all of the following procedures to secure that the statutory requirements have been complied with:

- ensuring all unused or unissued voting papers are retained only for so long as is necessary after the time allowed for voting has passed to allow the necessary information for checking the number of voting papers issued and used to be prepared, and that a record is kept of such voting papers when they are destroyed;
- rejection of completed voting papers received after the official close of voting or the time set for receipt of voting papers;
- settlement well in advance of the actual ballot of the organisational arrangements for conducting the count of votes cast, and making available equipment or facilities needed in the conduct of the count to those concerned;
- storage of all voting papers received at the counting location under secure conditions from when they arrive until they are counted;
- setting clear criteria to enable those counting the votes to decide which voting papers are to be rejected as "spoiled", and designating someone who is neither directly affected by the dispute to which the ballot relates nor a union official who regularly represents any of those entitled to vote in the ballot to adjudicate on any borderline cases;
- locking and securing the counting room during the period during which votes are to be counted whenever counting staff are not actually at work; and
- storage of voting papers, once counted, under secure conditions (i.e. so that they cannot be tampered within any way and are available for checking if necessary) for at least 6months after the ballot.

The union may wish to consider putting the counting exercise as a whole into the hands of the independent scrutineer.

ANNOUNCING DETAILS OF THE RESULT OF A BALLOT

48. ***Under section 231 and 231A of the 1992 Act a union must, as soon as reasonably practicable after holding an industrial action ballot, take steps to inform all those entitled to vote,[18] and their employer(s), of:***

- *the number of individuals entitled to vote in the ballot;*
- *the number of votes cast in the ballot;*
- *the number of individuals answering "Yes" to the required question (or each question);*
- *the number of individuals answering "No" to the required question (or each question);*
- *the number of spoiled or otherwise invalid voting papers returned;*
- *whether or not the number of votes cast in the ballot is at least 50% of the number of individuals who were entitled to vote in the ballot, and*
- *in important public services,[19] whether or not the number of individuals answering "yes" to the question (or each question) is at least 40% of the number of individuals entitled to vote in the ballot.*

Where separate workplace ballots are required (see paragraphs 29 and 30 above), these details must be notified separately for each such workplace to those entitled to vote there.

49. To help ensure that its result can be notified as required, the union may wish to consider, for example:

- designating a "Returning Officer" for the centralised count of votes cast in the ballot (or separate "Returning Officers" for counts conducted at different locations) to whom the results will be notified in the form required prior to their announcement;
- organising the counting of votes in such a way that the information required to satisfy the relevant statutory requirements can be easily obtained after the counting process is over;
- using its own journals, local communications news-sheets, company or union branch
- noticeboards to publicise the details of the ballot result to its members; and
- checking with relevant employers that the ballot result details notified to them have arrived.

50. ***Before giving the 14-day (or seven days where agreed between the employer and the union)[20] notice to employers of intended industrial action, the union must have taken the required steps to notify the relevant employer(s) of the ballot result details. In accordance with section 234A(1), where the employees of more than one employer have been balloted, a failure to provide the required ballot result details to a particular employer or employers will mean that if the union organises industrial action by the workers of that employer or those employers it will not have the support of a ballot. In cases where it is lawful to hold a single ballot across the workplaces of several or many employers (see paragraph 30 above), the "ballot result" refers to the result aggregated across all the employers and workplaces involved.***

51. ***If the inducement of industrial action to which the ballot relates is to be capable of being protected by the law, it will cease to be so regarded at the end of the period, beginning with the date of the ballot:[21] of six months or, of such longer duration not exceeding nine months, as agreed by the union and the members' employer. (To reduce the risk of misunderstanding, both parties may find it helpful for such agreements to be in writing.) If a ballot results in a "Yes" vote for both a strike and action short of a strike and action short of a strike is induced and starts to take place within the relevant period, the ballot would also continue to protect strike action subsequently, and vice versa.***

52. ***A union may be allowed to make its call for industrial action more than six months after the date of the ballot only if either (a) the employer and union agree on an extension, for example to enable talks to continue, of up to nine months after the date of the ballot or, (b) an injunction granted by a court or an undertaking given by the union to the court prohibits the union from calling for industrial action during some part, or the whole, of the six months following the date of the ballot, and the injunction subsequently lapses or is set aside or the union is released from its undertaking.***

53. ***In the latter case, a union may forthwith apply to the court for an order which, if granted, would provide that the period during which the prohibition had effect would not count towards the six month period for which ballots are normally effective. However, if the court believes that the result of a ballot no longer represents the views of union members, or that something has happened or is likely to happen which would result in union members voting against taking, or continuing with, action if there were a fresh ballot, it may not make such an order. In any case, a ballot can never be effective if industrial action takes place more than six (or nine if agreed between the union and the employer) months after the date of the ballot.***

OBTAINING, AND PROVIDING COPIES OF, THE SCRUTINEER'S REPORT

54. ***Where more than 50 members are given entitlement to vote, a union must appoint an independent scrutineer, whose terms of appointment must include the production of a report on the conduct of the ballot. This report must be produced as soon as reasonably practicable after the date of the ballot, and in any event not later than four weeks after that date.***

55. ***The union must provide a copy of the scrutineer's report to any union member who was entitled to vote in the ballot, or any employer of such a member, who requests one within six months of the date of the ballot, see section 231B(2). The copy must be supplied as soon as reasonably practicable and free of charge (or on payment of a reasonable fee specified by the union).***

56. In order to reduce the risk of challenge to a ballot's compliance with the statutory requirements, a union may wish to delay any call for industrial action, following a ballot, until it has obtained the scrutineer's report on the ballot.

IF THE UNION DECIDES TO AUTHORISE OR ENDORSE INDUSTRIAL ACTION

57. ***In accordance with section 234A if the union decides to authorise or endorse industrial action following a ballot, it must take such steps as are reasonably necessary to ensure that any employer who it is reasonable for the union to believe employs workers who will be, or have been, called upon to take***

part in the action receives no less than 14 days, or seven days if so agreed by the union and the employer, before the day specified in the notice as the date on which workers are intended to begin to take part in continuous action or as the first date on which they are intended to take part in discontinuous action a written notice from the union which:

- ***is given by any officer, official or committee of the union for whose act of inducing industrial action the union is responsible in law (an indication of whom this might cover is given in Annex 1 to this Code);***
- ***specifies: (i) whether the union intends the action to be "continuous"***
- ***or "discontinuous";[22] and (ii) the date on which any of the affected employees are intended to begin to take part in the action (where it is continuous action), or all the dates on which any of them are intended to take part (where it is discontinuous action);***
- ***states that it is a notice given for the purposes of section 234A of the 1992 Act; and***
- ***contains either***
  - (a) ***a list of the categories of employee to which the affected employees belong, a list of the workplaces at which they work and figures (together with an explanation of how they were arrived at) showing the total number of affected employees, the number of them in each of the categories listed and the number of them that work at each of the workplaces listed; or***
  - (b) ***where some or all of the employees are employees from whose wages the employer makes deductions representing payments to the union, a practice commonly known as "checkoff" or "DOCAS", other alternatives apply. In such circumstances the notice must contain either:***
    - (i) ***those same lists, figures and explanations as set out in (a); or***
    - (ii) ***such information as will enable the employer to readily deduce the total number of affected employees, the categories of employee to which they belong, the number of employees concerned in each of those categories, the workplaces at which the affected employees work and the number of them at each of these workplaces.***

Where only some of the affected employees pay their union contributions by the "check off", the union's notice may include both types of information. That is, the lists, figures and explanations should be provided for those who do not pay their subscriptions through the checkoff whilst information relating to checkoff payments may suffice for those who do.

The "affected employees" are those whom the union reasonably believes will be induced by the union or have been so induced to take part in or continue to take part in the industrial action.

The lists and figures or information supplied should be as accurate as is reasonably practicable in the light of the information in the union's possession at the time when it complied with subsection 234A(1). Information is "in the union's possession" if it is held for union purposes in a document (either in electronic or other form) and it is in the possession or under the control of an officer or employee of the union. Dependent on the precise status of the individuals concerned, information held by shop stewards or other lay representatives would probably not qualify for these purposes as being "in the union's possession".

But a notice will not fail to satisfy the requirements simply because it does not name any employees.

Changes in the union's intentions, for example as to the dates on which action is to be taken, require further notices to be given accordingly.

58. With the exception of the requirements relating to continuous and discontinuous action and to the need to give further notices in the event of changes in the union's intentions, the statutory requirements applying to notice of industrial action are for the most part the same as those applying to notice of industrial action ballots and the guidance in paragraphs 15-18 will be of relevance, taking account of the different circumstances.

59. ***In accordance with section 234A(7) where continuous industrial action is suspended, for example for further negotiations between the employer and union, the union must normally give the employer a further notice as in paragraphs 57 and 58 above before resuming the action. There is an exception to this requirement to give further notice, however, where the union agrees with the employer that the industrial action will cease to be authorised or endorsed with effect from a date specified in the agreement but may be authorised or endorsed again on or after another date specified in the agreement and the union:***

- ***ceases to authorise or endorse the action with effect from the specified date; and***
- ***subsequently re-authorises or re-endorses the action from a date on or after the originally specified date or such later date as may be agreed with the employer.***

For this exception to apply, the resumed industrial action must be of the same kind as covered in the original notice. That will not be so if, for example, the later action is taken by different or additional descriptions of workers. In order to avoid misunderstanding, both parties may find it helpful for such agreements to be in writing.

SEEKING UNION MEMBERS' VIEWS AFTER A UNION HAS AUTHORISED OR ENDORSED INDUSTRIAL ACTION

60. There is no statutory obligation on a union to ballot, or otherwise consult, its members before it decides to call off industrial action. However, if a union decides to seek its members' views about continuing with industrial action, it may wish to apply the same standards to the process of seeking their views as are set out in this Code.

NOTES

18 ***If overseas members of a trade union have been given entitlement to vote in an industrial action ballot the detailed information about its result need not be sent to them, but the information supplied to non-overseas members in accordance with the statutory requirements must distinguish between votes cast, individuals voting, and spoiled ballot papers to show which details relate to overseas, and which to non-overseas, members. (For these purposes members in Northern Ireland given entitlement to vote do not count as "overseas" members.)***

19 Important public services are specified in
http://www.legislation.gov.uk/uksi/2017/132/contents/made
http://www.legislation.gov.uk/uksi/2017/133/contents/made
http://www.legislation.gov.uk/uksi/2017/134/contents/made
http://www.legislation.gov.uk/uksi/2017/135/contents/made
http://www.legislation.gov.uk/uksi/2017/136/contents/made

20 Section 234A of the 1992 Act.

21 Section 246 defines "date of the ballot" to be the date that the ballot closes. Where a ballot allows votes to be cast on more than one day, the last day will be considered the "date of the ballot".

22 ***For these purposes, industrial action is "discontinuous" if it is to involve action other than on all the days when action might be taken by those concerned.*** An indefinite strike would, therefore, be "continuous"; an overtime ban might be "continuous" or "discontinuous", depending on whether the ban applied to overtime working on all the days on which overtime would otherwise be worked or to overtime working on only some of those days.

ANNEX 1
TRADE UNION LIABILITY

[4.300]

1. ***Section 20 of the Trade Union and Labour Relations (Consolidation) Act 1992 ("the 1992 Act") lays down when a union is to be held responsible for the act of inducing, or threatening, a breach or interference with a contract in circumstances where there is no immunity. The union will be held liable for any such act which is done, authorised or endorsed by:***

- ***its Executive Committee, General Secretary, President;***
- ***any person given power under the union's rules to do, authorise or endorse acts of the kind in question; or***
- ***any committee or official of the union (whether employed by it or not).***

A union will be held responsible for such an act by such a body or person regardless of any term or condition to the contrary in its own rules, or in any other contractual provision or rule of law.

2. ***For these purposes:***

- ***a "committee of the union" is any group of persons constituted in accordance with the rules of the union;***
- ***an "official of the union" is any person who is an officer of the union or of a branch or section of the union or any person who is elected or appointed in accordance with the union's own rules to be a representative of its members, including any person so elected or appointed who is an employee of the same employer as the members, or one or more of the members, he is elected to represent (e.g. a shop steward); and***
- ***an act will be treated to have be end one (or authorised or endorsed) by an official if it was so done (or authorised or endorsed) by a group of persons, or any member of a group, to which an official belonged at the relevant time if the group's purposes included organising or co-ordinating industrial action.***

3. ***A union will not be held liable for such an act of any of its committees or officials, however, if its Executive Committee, President or General Secretary repudiates the act as soon as reasonably practicable after it has come to the attention of any of them, and the union takes the steps which the law requires to make that repudiation effective. But the union will not be considered to have "effectively repudiated" an act if the Executive Committee, President or General Secretary subsequently behave in a manner which is inconsistent with the repudiation.***

4. The fact that a union is responsible for organising industrial action to which immunity does not apply does not prevent legal action also being taken against the individual organisers of that action.

"IMMUNITY"

5. A trade union which organises (i.e. authorises or endorses) industrial action without satisfying the requirements of section 226 (for balloting on industrial action), or 234A (for notice to employers of official industrial action), of the 1992 Act will have no "immunity". Without immunity the trade union will be at risk of legal action by (i) an employer (and/or a customer or supplier of such an employer) who suffers (or may suffer) damage as a consequence of the trade union's unlawful inducement to his workers to break or interfere with the performance of contracts; and/or (ii) any individual who is(or is likely to be) deprived of goods or services because of the industrial action. Such legal proceedings might result in a court order requiring the trade union not to proceed with, and/or desist from, the unlawful inducement of its members to take part or continue with the action, and that no member does anything after the order is made as a result of unlawful inducement prior to the making of the order.

6. Under section 62 of the 1992 Act, a member of a trade union who claims that members of the union, including himself, are likely to be or have been induced by the union to take industrial action which does not have the support of a ballot may apply to the court for an order, which may require the trade union to take steps to ensure that there is no, or no further, unlawful inducement to members to take part or continue to take part in the action, and that no member does anything after the order is made as a result of unlawful inducement prior to the making of the order.

CONTEMPT AND OTHER PROCEEDINGS

7. If a court order issued following legal proceedings as described in paragraphs 5 and 6 above is not obeyed, anyone who sought it can go back to court and ask that those concerned be declared in contempt of court. A union found in contempt of court may face heavy fines, or other penalties which the court may consider appropriate.

8. In addition, any member of the union may have grounds for legal action against the union's trustees if they have caused or permitted the unlawful application of union funds or property.

ANNEX 2
EXAMPLE OF VOTING PAPER FOR BALLOT ON TAKING INDUSTRIAL ACTION

[4.301]

(To note - provided the legal requirements as to the content of the voting paper are met, its layout can be amended)

[VOTING PAPER NUMBER]

[NAME OF THE TRADE UNION]

The union must provide a *[SUMMARY OF THE MATTER OR MATTERS IN ISSUE IN THE TRADE DISPUTE TO WHICH THE PROPOSED INDUSTRIAL ACTION RELATES*]

The union must *[INDICATE THE PERIOD OR PERIODS WITHIN WHICH THE INDUSTRIAL ACTION, OR EACH TYPE OF INDUSTRIAL ACTION, IS EXPECTED TO TAKE PLACE]*

ARE YOU PREPARED TO TAKE PART IN INDUSTRIAL ACTION CONSISTING OF A STRIKE?[23]

YES ☐ NO ☐

ARE YOU PREPARED TO TAKE PART IN INDUSTRIAL ACTION SHORT OF A STRIKE [the union must *EITHER SPECIFY THE TYPE OR TYPES OF INDUSTRIAL ACTION HERE OR ELSEWHERE ON THE VOTING PAPER] (which for this purpose is defined to include overtime and call-out bans)?*[23]

YES ☐ NO ☐

Your union intends the following to have authority to make the call for industrial action to which this ballot relates:

[DETAILS OF RELEVANT PERSON, PERSONS, AND/OR CLASS OR CLASSES OF PERSONS]

If your vote is to count, this voting paper must be returned to *[FULL ADDRESS OF LOCATION TO WHICH THE VOTING PAPER IS TO BE RETURNED] by [FULL DATE AND TIME AS APPROPRIATE]*. Please use the enclosed pre-paid envelope provided for this purpose.

The independent scrutineer for this ballot is *[DETAILS OF RELEVANT PERSON]*.

The law requires your union to ensure that your vote is accurately and fairly counted and that you are able to vote without interference from the union or any of its members, officials or employees and, so far as is reasonably practicable, in secret.

If you take part in a strike or other industrial action, you may be in breach of your contract of employment. However, if you are dismissed for taking part in a strike or other industrial action which is called officially and is otherwise lawful, the dismissal be unfair if it takes place fewer than twelve weeks after you started taking part in the action, and depending on the circumstances may be unfair if it takes place later.

INFORMATION TO BE GIVEN TO EMPLOYERS

The following paragraphs of the Code deal with requirements to provide information to employers:

	Paragraph
Ballot notice	14-18
Sample voting papers	19-20
Results of the ballot	48-50
Scrutineer's report on the conduct of the ballot	55
Notice of intention to authorise or endorse industrial action or resume suspended industrial action	57-58

NOTES

[23] Either question or both should be included as appropriate

H. CODES MADE BY THE BODIES REPLACED BY THE EHRC

COMMISSION FOR RACIAL EQUALITY: CODE OF PRACTICE ON THE DUTY TO PROMOTE RACE EQUALITY (2002)

[4.302]

NOTES

This Code was issued by the Commission for Racial Equality under the Race Relations Act 1976, s 71C (as inserted by the Race Relations (Amendment) Act 2000 and repealed as noted below). Following Parliamentary approval, the Code was brought into effect by the Race Relations Act 1976 (General Statutory Duty: Code of Practice) Order 2002 (SI 2002/1435) with effect from 30 May 2002.

The statutory provision under which this Code was made was repealed by the Equality Act 2006, ss 40, 91, Sch 3, paras 21, 30, Sch 4; however the Code is continued in force by s 42(3) of the 2006 Act (see **[1.1464]**).

Much of the Code relates to the application of the general statutory duty to the provision of public services and, in particular, education; Section 4 (in Part II) and much of Section 6 (in Part III) have been omitted as outside the scope of this work. The bodies subject to the general statutory duty are listed in Appendix 1 (omitted for reasons of space). Similarly, Appendix 2 (Bodies required to publish a race equality scheme) which reproduces Sch 1 to the Race Relations Act 1976 (Statutory Duties) Order 2001, SI 2001/3458, is omitted for reasons of space. Appendix 3 is included; it lists the bodies subject to the duty to undertake ethnic monitoring of employees, comprising the bodies listed in Sch 1 to the Race Relations Act 1976 (now repealed) *other than* those listed in Sch 3 to the 2001 Order. Appendices 4 and 6 are omitted as outside the scope of this work; Appendix 5, which lists those bodies within Sch 1A to the Act which are Scottish public authorities, is also omitted.

The equivalent Code for Scotland 'The Duty to Promote Race Equality in Scotland' (2003) (applicable to those bodies subject to the authority of the Scottish Parliament) is omitted for reasons of space.

The statutory duties imposed by the Race Relations Act 1976 have been replaced by a general statutory duty in relation to equal treatment under the Equality Act 2010, s 149, and it was originally intended that this Code (and its equivalent for the gender equality duty) would be replaced by a new Code under s 149 of the 2010 Act. However, the Equality and Human Rights Commission subsequently announced that the Secretary of State is unlikely to approve a new statutory code, and that the new Guidance would be issued on a non-statutory basis. The new Guidance on the equality duty for England, Wales and Scotland is on the EHRC website at:
www.equalityhumanrights.com/en/advice-and-guidance/public-sector-equality-duty-guidance.

CONTENTS

GLOSSARY

[4.303]
In this Code, the words below have the meanings shown beneath them.

action plan

a practical and realistic plan, with an agreed timetable, showing how an authority is planning to meet its duties.

assessing impact

a systematic way of finding out whether a policy (or proposed policy) affects different racial groups differently. This may include obtaining and analysing data, and consulting people, including staff, on the policy.

complementary

this refers to the fact that the three parts of the general duty support each other and may, in practice, overlap. However, they are different, and public authorities should consider each one individually.

consultation

asking for views on policies or services from staff, colleagues, service-users, or the general public. Different circumstances call for different types of consultation. For example, consultation includes meetings, focus groups, reference groups, citizens' juries, surveys, and questionnaires.

direct discrimination

treating one person less favourably than another on racial grounds (see [below]). Direct discrimination is unlawful under the Race Relations Act.

disciplinary procedures

the arrangements and procedures used to discipline staff. These may include informal and formal disciplinary measures.

duty to promote race equality

the general duty, unless the context suggests otherwise.

ethnic monitoring

the process you use to collect, store and analyse data about people's ethnic backgrounds.

focus groups, reference groups and citizens' juries

various forms of face-to-face consultation with members of the public, service-users, or others.

formal investigation

an investigation by the CRE under sections 49–52 of the Race Relations Act. The investigation can be either a "named person" investigation or a general investigation.

- A "named person" investigation can be carried out if the CRE suspects that an organisation is discriminating on racial grounds. The CRE can ask the organisation for documents and information. If the CRE is satisfied that unlawful discrimination has taken place, or is taking place, the CRE can issue a "non-discrimination notice".
- A general investigation can be carried out, without suspicion of discrimination, to examine practice within an area of activity. At the end of the investigation, the CRE can make recommendations.

functions

the full range of a public authority's duties and powers.

further and higher education institution

the governing body of an institution in the further and higher education sectors (as defined in sections 91(3) and 91(5) of the Further and Higher Education Act).

general duty

the duty as given in section 71(1) of the Race Relations Act (see chapter 3, paragraph 3.1).

grievance procedures

arrangements or procedures for dealing with grievances, such as complaints about bullying, harassment or discrimination; or appeals against decisions on promotion or appraisal marks.

indirect racial discrimination

occurs when a rule or condition which is applied equally to everyone—

- can be met by a considerably smaller proportion of people from a particular racial group;
- is to the disadvantage of that group; and

- cannot be justified on non-racial grounds.

All three conditions must apply.

judicial review

a claim to the High Court or the Scottish Court of Sessions asking the court to review the way a public authority or certain other bodies made a decision. The court will not decide the merits of the decision, only whether it is legal. The court can ask the authority to reconsider the matter.

monitoring

the process of collecting, analysing and evaluating information, to measure performance, progress or change.

non-devolved authorities

public authorities in Scotland whose functions and powers remain the responsibility of the Westminster Parliament rather than the Scottish Parliament.

obligatory

this refers to the fact that public authorities are legally bound to meet the general duty, and must make race equality a central part of their functions.

orders

ministerial directions to apply the law, or to change the way it applies.

performance assessment procedures

formal and informal staff appraisals that are likely to affect career development, pay and benefits.

policies

the formal and informal decisions about how a public authority carries out its duties and uses its powers.

positive action

action permitted by the Race Relations Act that allows a person to—

- provide facilities to meet the special needs of people from particular racial groups in relation to their training, education or welfare (section 35); and
- target job training at people from racial groups that are under-represented in a particular area of work, or encourage them to apply for such work (sections 37 and 38).

promoting race equality

public authorities should have "due regard to the need", in carrying out their functions, to—

- tackle unlawful racial discrimination;
- promote equality of opportunity; and
- promote good relations between people from different racial groups.

proportionate

this refers to the fact that the weight given to race equality should be proportionate to its relevance to a particular function. This approach may mean giving greater consideration and resources to functions or policies that have most effect on the public, or on the authority's employees.

public appointments

appointments to the boards of public bodies. These are bodies that have a role in the processes of national government, but operate at arm's length from government.

public authority

a body named, defined or described in schedule 1A to the Race Relations Act or, depending on the context, a body named, defined or described in one of the schedules to the Race Relations Act 1976 (Statutory Duties) Order 2001.

public functions

functions that affect, or are likely to affect, the public or a section of the public. While only the courts can decide this, public functions would normally not include internal management or contractual matters such as employing staff; purchasing goods, works or services; or buying or selling premises. This term is used to refer to those authorities that are bound by the duties only in relation to their public functions (for example professional representative organisations, such as the Royal College of Surgeons, or broadcasting authorities).

public procurement

the contractual or other arrangements that a public authority makes to obtain goods, works or services from an outside organisation.

publish

making publicly available; for example by producing a written document for distribution.

race equality policy

a written statement of an educational establishment's policy on race equality, which is put into practice and monitored.

race equality scheme

a timetabled and realistic plan, setting out an authority's arrangements for meeting the general and specific duties.

Race Relations Act

the Race Relations Act 1976, as amended by the Race Relations (Amendment) Act 2000.

racial group

a group of people defined by their race, colour, nationality (including citizenship), ethnic or national origins.

racial grounds

reasons of race, colour, nationality (including citizenship), ethnic or national origins.

relevance

this refers to the fact that race equality will be more relevant to some public functions than others. Relevance is about how far a function or policy affects people, as members of the public, and as employees of the authority.

schedule

an appendix to legislation, such as schedule 1A to the Race Relations Act. This schedule lists the public authorities to which the general duty applies.

school

the governing body of an educational establishment maintained by local education authorities in England and Wales, or of a city technology college, a city college for technology of the arts, or a city academy.

Scottish public authority

a public authority whose functions can only be carried out in, or in relation to, Scotland.

specific duty

a duty imposed by the Race Relations Act 1976 (Statutory Duties) Order 2001.

statutory code of practice

a document such as this one, which offers practical guidance on the law, has been approved by Parliament, and is admissible in evidence in a court of law.

statutory duties

duties, either general or specific, which an authority is legally bound to meet.

training

a wide range of career development opportunities, which could include informal in-house training as well as more formal courses.

victimisation

punishing or treating someone unfairly because they have made a complaint of racial discrimination, or are thought to have done so; or because they have supported someone else who has made a complaint of racial discrimination. Victimisation is defined as unlawful discrimination under the Race Relations Act.

PART I
PROMOTING RACE EQUALITY IN ALL LISTED PUBLIC AUTHORITIES

1—INTRODUCTION

[4.304]

1.1 The Race Relations Act (see the glossary) places a general duty on a wide range of public authorities to promote race equality. This duty means that authorities (listed in appendix 1 of this code) must have due regard to the need to—

(a) eliminate unlawful racial discrimination;
(b) promote equality of opportunity; and
(c) promote good relations between people of different racial groups.

1.2. Most public authorities are bound by this duty. Many of them provide major public services, such as education or health. Some of them (for example professional representative organisations, such as the Royal College of Surgeons, or broadcasting authorities) are bound by this duty only so far as their public functions (see the glossary) are concerned.

1.3. The duty aims to make the promotion of race equality central to the way public authorities work. Promoting race equality will improve the way public services are delivered for everyone. In most cases, these authorities should be able to use their existing arrangements – such as those for policy making – to meet the duty's requirements. This should help to avoid any unnecessary or duplicated work.

Benefits of the duty

1.4. The duty will help public authorities to make steady progress in achieving race equality. In relation to policy development and service delivery, the duty will—

(a) encourage policy makers to be more aware of possible problems;
(b) contribute to more informed decision making;
(c) make sure that policies are properly targeted;
(d) improve the authority's ability to deliver suitable and accessible services that meet varied needs;
(e) encourage greater openness about policy making;
(f) increase confidence in public services, especially among ethnic minority communities;
(g) help to develop good practice; and
(h) help to avoid claims of unlawful racial discrimination.

1.5. The duty of public authorities to promote race equality in *employment* will—

(a) help to make the authority's workforce more representative of the communities it serves;
(b) attract able staff;
(c) avoid losing or undervaluing able staff;
(d) improve staff morale and productivity;
(e) improve the way staff are managed;
(f) help to develop good practice; and
(g) help to avoid claims of unlawful racial discrimination.

Purpose of the Code

1.6. Public authorities can decide how they will meet their duty to promote race equality. The Race Relations Act gives the CRE the power to issue codes of practice, with the approval of Parliament.

1.7. This code offers practical guidance to public authorities on how to meet their duty to promote race equality. It includes guidance on both the general duty (see 1.1) and specific duties imposed by the Home Secretary. The code's aim is to help public authorities to adopt good practice and to eliminate racial discrimination. The code should also help the public understand what public authorities have to do, and the role that the public can play.

1.8. The specific duties imposed by order of the Home Secretary came into effect on **3 December 2001**. Public authorities bound by these duties (see appendices 2, 3 and 4) were required to have properly timetabled and realistic plans for meeting these duties in place by **31 May 2002**.

1.9. This code applies to public authorities in England and Wales (see appendix 1) and to "non-devolved" public authorities in Scotland (see the glossary and appendix 1). Chapter 6 of this code applies only to the governing bodies of educational institutions in England and Wales. The Code of Practice for Scotland will apply to devolved public authorities in Scotland (see the glossary).

Nature of the Code

1.10. This code of practice is a "statutory" code. This means that it has been approved by Parliament. It also means that the code is admissible in evidence in any legal action, and a court or tribunal should take the code's recommendations into account. On its own, the code does not place any legal obligations on public authorities. It is not a complete statement of the law, as only the courts can give this. If a public authority does not follow the code's guidance, it may need to be able to show how it has otherwise met its legal obligations under the general duty and any specific duties.

How to use this Code

1.11. The code is divided into five parts, seven chapters and six appendices.

(a) Part I (chapters 2 and 3) applies to all listed public authorities, including schools, and further and higher education institutions.

(b) Part II (chapters 4 and 5) deals with promoting race equality in certain public authorities other than educational institutions.

(c) Part III (chapter 6) deals with promoting race equality in educational institutions.

(d) Part IV (chapter 7) deals with the CRE's role, including enforcing this code.

(e) Part V (appendices 1 to 6) lists the public authorities that are bound by the general duty (appendix 1), the public authorities that are required to publish a race equality scheme (appendix 2), the public authorities bound by the employment duty (appendix 3), the public authorities bound by the duties for educational institutions (appendix 4), Scottish public authorities (appendix 5), and other guidance published by the CRE (appendix 6).

2—THE LEGAL FRAMEWORK

[4.305]

2.1. The Race Relations Act (see the glossary) defines direct and indirect discrimination, and victimisation (see the glossary for each of these terms). It outlaws racial discrimination in employment, training, education, housing, public appointments, and the provision of goods, facilities and services. The Race Relations (Amendment) Act 2000 came into force on 2 April 2001 and since then the Race Relations Act (the Act) has covered all the functions of public authorities (with just a few exceptions).

2.2. Section 71(1) of the Act places a general duty on listed public authorities (see appendix 1). The Act also gives the Home Secretary power to make orders placing specific duties on all or some of these authorities (section 71(2)). Scottish ministers have a similar power over Scottish public authorities (section 71B(1); see the glossary). Under the Race Relations Act 1976 (Statutory Duties) Order 2001, the specific duties discussed in this code came into force on **3 December 2001**.

2.3. The Act gives the CRE enforcement powers over the specific duties imposed by the Home Secretary and Scottish ministers. The Act also gives the CRE power to issue codes of practice containing practical guidance on how public authorities can meet the general duty (see chapter 3) and specific duties (see chapters 4, 5 and 6). This is a statutory code, issued for this purpose.

The general duty to promote race equality

2.4. This general duty applies to all public authorities listed in schedule 1A to the Act (see appendix 1). The duty's aim is to make the promotion of race equality central to the work of the listed public authorities.

Specific duties to promote race equality

2.5. Specific duties have been placed on some public authorities responsible for delivering important public services. The duties involve making arrangements that will help these authorities to meet the general duty to promote race equality.

(a) The public authorities listed in appendix 2 must prepare and publish a race equality scheme. This scheme should set out the "functions" or "policies" (see the glossary for both terms) that are relevant to meeting the general duty, and the arrangements that will help to meet the duty in the areas of policy and service delivery (see chapter 4).

(b) The public authorities listed in appendix 3 must monitor their employment procedures and practice (see chapter 5). Some of these authorities have to produce a race equality scheme. They may find it useful to include the arrangements they make to meet their employment duties in their race equality schemes.

(c) The educational institutions listed in appendix 4 have to prepare a race equality policy and put in place arrangements for meeting their specific duties on policy and employment (see chapter 6).

2.6. Public authorities that introduce effective arrangements, as required under the specific duties, should be able to show that they are meeting the general duty to promote race equality. Taking action to promote race equality should give authorities the evidence they need to show that they are meeting the general duty.

2.7. Chapters 4, 5, and 6 give guidance on the specific duties.

Liability under the Race Relations Act

2.8. Public authorities are responsible for meeting their general and specific duties. Within each public authority, this responsibility will rest with the groups or individuals who are liable (legally responsible) for the authority's acts or failure to act.

Private or voluntary organisations carrying out a public authority's functions

2.9. When a public authority has a contract or other agreement with a private company or voluntary organisation to carry out any of its functions (see the glossary), and the duty to promote race equality applies to those functions, the public authority remains responsible for meeting the general duty and any specific duties that apply to those functions. The authority should therefore consider the arrangements it will need. If the authority's race equality duties are relevant to the functions it is contracting out, it may be appropriate to incorporate those duties among the performance requirements for delivery of the service. For example, a contractor could be required to monitor service users by their racial group, to make sure the authority is meeting its duties. This would not involve requirements concerning the contractor's internal practices. Whatever action the authority takes, it must be consistent with the policy and legal framework for public procurement.

2.10. In addition to specifications for the general duty and any specific duties, public authorities may promote race equality by encouraging contractors to draw up policies that will help them (contractors) to avoid unlawful discrimination, and promote equality of opportunity. Such encouragement should only be within a voluntary framework, once contracts have been awarded, rather than by making specific criteria or conditions part of the selection process. Public authorities should bear in mind that the general duty does not override other laws or regulations on public procurement. In particular, as above, whatever action the authority takes must be consistent with the policy and legal framework for public procurement.

Partnership

2.11. Public authorities should take account of their general duty to promote race equality – and any specific duties – when they work with other public, private or voluntary organisations. There is no similar obligation on private or voluntary-sector partners.

2.12. Public authorities that are involved in partnership work with other public authorities, or with private or voluntary-sector organisations, are still responsible for meeting their general duty to promote race equality, and any specific duties.

2.13. In practice, this will mean that a public authority working within a partnership will need to seek agreement from its partners to arrangements for planning, funding and managing joint work that will allow it to meet its statutory race equality duties. Public authorities should reflect their partnership work in their race equality schemes.

Inspecting and auditing public authorities

2.14. Agencies that audit or inspect public authorities are bound by the duty to promote race equality. These agencies need to consider how the duty fits with their inspection or audit obligations. In most cases, inspection and audit bodies should be able to use their existing inspection arrangements to promote race equality.

3—THE GENERAL DUTY

[4.306]

3.1 This chapter explains what public authorities can do to meet the general duty to promote race equality. The duty is set out in section 71(1) of the Race Relations Act (the Act) and it applies to every public authority listed in schedule 1A to the Act (see appendix 1 of this code). Section 71(1) says—

(1) Every body or other person specified in Schedule 1A or of a description falling within that Schedule shall, in carrying out its functions, have due regard to the need

- (a) to eliminate unlawful racial discrimination; and
- (b) to promote equality of opportunity and good relations between persons of different racial groups.*

* For immigration and nationality functions, the general duty does not include the words "equality of opportunity and" (section 71A(1)).

Guiding principles

3.2. Four principles should govern public authorities' efforts to meet their duty to promote race equality.

(a) Promoting race equality is obligatory for all public authorities listed in schedule 1A to the Act (see appendix 1).

(b) Public authorities must meet the duty to promote race equality in all relevant functions.

(c) The weight given to race equality should be proportionate to its relevance.

(d) The elements of the duty are complementary (which means they are all necessary to meet the whole duty).

"Obligatory"

3.3. Public authorities listed in schedule 1A to the Act must make race equality a central part of their functions (such as planning, policy making, service delivery, regulation, inspection, enforcement, and employment). The general duty does not tell public authorities how to do their work, but it expects them to assess whether race equality is relevant to their functions. If it is, the authority should do everything it can to meet the general duty. The duty should underpin all policy and practice, and it should encourage improvement. It is not necessarily a new responsibility for the authority, just a more effective way of doing what it already does.

"Relevant"

3.4. Race equality will be more relevant to some functions than others. Relevance is about how much a function affects people, as members of the public or as employees of the authority. For example, a local authority may decide that race equality is more relevant to raising educational standards than to its work on highway maintenance. Public authorities should therefore assess whether, and how, race equality is relevant to each of their functions. A public authority may decide that the general duty does not apply to some of its functions; for example those that are purely technical, such as traffic control or weather forecasting.

"Proportionate"

3.5. Under section 71(1) of the Act, public authorities are expected to have "due regard" to the three parts of the duty to promote race equality (see 1.1). This means that the weight given to race equality should be proportionate to its relevance to a particular function. In practice, this approach may mean giving greater consideration and resources to functions or policies that have most effect on the public, or on the authority's employees. The authority's concern should be to ask whether particular policies could affect different racial groups in different ways, and whether the policies will promote good race relations.

3.6. "Due regard" does not mean that race equality is less important when the ethnic minority population is small. It is also not acceptable for a public authority to claim that it does not have enough resources to meet the duty. This is because meeting the general duty is a statutory requirement. In practice, this means that public authorities should draw on work they already do to promote race equality, and build on it, using their existing administrative systems and processes and adjusting their plans and priorities, where necessary.

3.7. The general duty is a continuing duty. What a public authority has to do to meet it may change over time as its functions or policies change, or as the communities it serves change.

"Complementary"

3.8. The general duty has three parts—

(a) eliminating unlawful racial discrimination;

(b) promoting equality of opportunity; and

(c) promoting good relations between people of different racial groups.

3.9. These three parts support each other. And, in practice, they may overlap (for example, promoting equality of opportunity may also eliminate or prevent unlawful racial discrimination, *and* promote good race relations). However, it is important to remember that the three parts are different, and that achieving one of them may not lead to achieving all three. For example, a new equal opportunities policy that is not clearly explained when it is introduced may improve equality of opportunity, but it may also damage race relations and create resentment if staff do not understand how it benefits everyone.

3.10. Public authorities should consider and deal with all three parts of the general duty.

How to meet the general duty

3.11. Public authorities should consider the following four steps to meet the general duty.

(a) Identify which of their functions and policies are relevant to the duty, or, in other words, affect most people.

(b) Put the functions and policies in order of priority, based on how relevant they are to race equality.

(c) Assess whether the way these 'relevant' functions and policies are being carried out meets the three parts of the duty.

(d) Consider whether any changes need to be made to meet the duty, and make the changes.

Identifying relevant functions

3.12. To identify relevant functions, a public authority will find it useful, first, to make a list of all its functions, including employment. It should then assess how relevant each function is to each part of the general duty. As shown in paragraph 3.4, some functions may, by their nature, have little or no relevance.

3.13. A public authority should consider setting priorities, and giving priority to those functions that are most relevant to race equality.

Assessing impact and considering change

3.14. To assess the impact its functions and policies have on race equality, the authority may find it useful to draw up a clear statement of the aims of each function or policy. It should then consider whether it has information about how different racial groups are affected by the function or policy, as employees or users (or possible users) of services. The authority should also consider whether its functions and policies are promoting good race relations. The authority could get this information from various sources; for example previous research, records of complaints, surveys, or local meetings. These methods should help public authorities to assess which of their services are used by which racial groups, or what people think of their services, and whether they are being provided fairly to people from different racial groups. This kind of evidence should help public authorities to decide what they might need to do to meet all three parts of the general duty.

3.15. Public authorities may also need to consider adapting their existing information systems, so that they can provide information about different racial groups and show what progress the authority is making on race equality.

3.16. To assess the effects of a policy, or the way a function is being carried out, public authorities could ask themselves the following questions.

(a) Could the policy or the way the function is carried out have an adverse impact on equality of opportunity for some racial groups? In other words, does it put some racial groups at a disadvantage?

(b) Could the policy or the way the function is carried out have an adverse impact on relations between different racial groups?

(c) Is the adverse impact, if any, unavoidable? Could it be considered to be unlawful racial discrimination? Can it be justified by the aims and importance of the policy or function? Are there other ways in which the authority's aims can be achieved without causing an adverse impact on some racial groups?

(d) Could the adverse impact be reduced by taking particular measures?

(e) Is further research or consultation necessary? Would this research be proportionate to the importance of the policy or function? Is it likely to lead to a different outcome?

3.17. If the assessment suggests that the policy, or the way the function is carried out, should be modified, the authority should do this to meet the general duty.

PART II
PROMOTING RACE EQUALITY IN LISTED PUBLIC AUTHORITIES OTHER THAN EDUCATIONAL INSTITUTIONS

4—SPECIFIC DUTIES: POLICY AND SERVICE DELIVERY

(*Outside the scope of this work.*)

5—SPECIFIC DUTIES: EMPLOYMENT

[4.307]
5.1. The specific duty on employment applies to most of the public authorities bound by the general duty (see appendix 3). Schools and further and higher education institutions are not bound by the employment duty, as they have separate employment responsibilities (see chapter 6). A few, mainly advisory, agencies are also not bound by the employment duty.

5.2. Articles 5(1), 5(2), and 5(3) of the Race Relations Act 1976 (Statutory Duties) Order 2001 say the following—

5

(1) A person to which this article applies shall,
- (a) before 31st May 2002, have in place arrangements for fulfilling, as soon as is reasonably practicable, its duties under paragraph (2); and
- (b) fulfil those duties in accordance with such arrangements.

(2) It shall be the duty of such a person to monitor, by reference to the racial groups to which they belong,
- (a) the numbers of—
  - (i) staff in post, and
  - (ii) applicants for employment, training and promotion, from each such group, and
- (b) where that person has 150 or more full-time staff, the numbers of staff from each such group who—
  - (i) receive training;
  - (ii) benefit or suffer detriment as a result of its performance assessment procedures;
  - (iii) are involved in grievance procedures;
  - (iv) are the subject of disciplinary procedures; or
  - (v) cease employment with that person.

(3) Such a person shall publish annually the results of its monitoring under paragraph (2).

5.3. Public authorities that have to produce race equality schemes may find it useful to include their arrangements for meeting their employment duty in their race equality schemes.

5.4. The specific duties on employment are designed to provide a framework for measuring progress in equality of opportunity in public-sector employment. The specific duties are also aimed at providing monitoring information to guide initiatives that could lead to a more representative public-sector workforce. For example, these initiatives could include setting recruitment targets for under-represented racial groups, or targeting management development courses at racial groups that are under-represented at certain levels. The specific duties on employment set minimum standards. Other issues may also be relevant for good employment practice. This will depend on local circumstances.

5.5. Ethnic monitoring (see the glossary) is central to providing a clear picture of what is happening during the authority's employment cycle – from applying for a job and joining the authority to leaving it. Monitoring helps to measure overall progress and to show whether the authority's equal opportunities policies are effective. Monitoring is the essential tool to assess progress – or lack of it – in removing barriers to equality of opportunity in the public services.

5.6. It is important that the authority explains to applicants and existing staff why they are monitoring employment. People will normally only have to give information about their racial group voluntarily, and the authority should explain the conditions of the Data Protection Act 1998 (about processing this information) to them.

5.7. Wherever possible, the authority should build monitoring information into the information systems it already uses. The authority may be able to publish its monitoring results each year through its existing reporting systems. In its published results, the authority should explain how it is dealing with trends or problems highlighted by its monitoring. The authority may also find it useful to combine and analyse ethnic monitoring data with other data; for example on sex and disability.

5.8. To help meet the specific duty on employment, public authorities should—
(a) collect ethnic monitoring data; and
(b) publish the results of the monitoring each year.

5.9. To check that they are meeting the general duty, public authorities may want to—
(a) analyse the data to find any patterns of inequality; and

(b) take whatever steps are needed to remove barriers and promote equality of opportunity.

5.10. If the monitoring shows that current employment policies, procedures and practice are leading to unlawful racial discrimination, the authority should take steps to end the discrimination. As a first step, the authority should examine each of its procedures closely to find out where and how discrimination might be happening, and then consider what changes to introduce.

5.11. On the other hand, the monitoring may show that current policies, procedures and practice have an adverse impact on equality of opportunity or good race relations (even though they are not causing unlawful discrimination). If this is the case, the authority should consider changing its policies or procedures so that they still meet the same aims, but do not harm equality of opportunity or race relations.

Positive action

5.12. If monitoring reveals that some racial groups are under-represented in the workforce, the authority could consider using "positive action" (see the glossary). This allows employers and others to target their job training and recruitment efforts at those groups that are under-represented in a particular area of work. However, positive action does not allow discrimination when deciding who will be offered a job.

Ethnic categories and the 2001 census

5.13. Public authorities are encouraged to use the same ethnic classification system as the one used in the 2001 census. Some authorities already have systems in place. If an authority chooses to collect more detailed information, it should make sure that the categories are the same as, or similar to, those used in the 2001 census. Any extra ethnic categories it adds to reflect its particular circumstances should fit in with the 2001 census categories.

5.14. Public authorities should make realistic and timetabled plans to adapt their ethnic monitoring systems to meet the specific duties.

5.15. The 2001 census used different ethnic classifications for England and Wales, and Scotland.

PART III
PROMOTING RACE EQUALITY IN EDUCATIONAL INSTITUTIONS

6—SPECIFIC DUTIES: EDUCATIONAL INSTITUTIONS

Introduction

[4.308]

6.1. This part of the code is written mainly for education providers. They are as follows.

(a) The governing bodies of maintained schools (see the glossary) and other educational institutions maintained by a local education authority (LEA) – in other words, all community, foundation and voluntary schools, and special schools maintained by the LEA.

(b) The governing bodies of City Technology Colleges, City Colleges for Technology or the Arts, and City Academies.

(c) The governing bodies of further education institutions (see the glossary).

(d) The governing bodies of higher education institutions (see the glossary).

6.2. Schools and further and higher education institutions must all meet the general duty. Chapter 3 explains what they need to do to meet the duty. The Home Secretary has also placed specific duties on schools (see 6.7–6.22), and on further and higher education institutions (see 6.23–6.44), to help them to meet the general duty.

6.3. The specific duties on employment, described in chapter 5, do not apply directly to schools. The main responsibility for monitoring employment rests with LEAs. All schools are expected to give their LEA ethnic monitoring data on their staff from their regular returns, so that the LEA can meet the duty.

6.4. Further and higher education institutions have other employment duties, which are described in paragraphs 6.39 to 6.41. As well as these duties, further and higher education institutions will have to give bodies such as the higher education funding councils (see 6.45–6.48 for details of the specific duties placed on these bodies), monitoring information about their teaching staff.

6.5. The aim of the general duty is to make race equality central to the way public authorities carry out their functions (see the glossary). Promoting race equality should be a central part of all policy development, service delivery and employment practice.

6.6–6.22. (*Outside the scope of this work.*)

Further and higher education institutions

6.23–6.34. (*Outside the scope of this work.*)

Monitoring admission, recruitment and progress

6.35. Under the duty, further and higher education institutions must monitor, by racial group, student admission and progress, and staff recruitment and career progress (see 6.23).

6.36. Monitoring involves collecting information to measure an institution's performance and effectiveness. The results may suggest how the institution can improve.

6.37. The institution should monitor all stages of the student admissions process, from applications to outcomes. To help interpret the information, the institution might also consider monitoring other areas that could have an adverse impact on students from some racial groups, such as—

(a) choice of subject;
(b) home or international status; and
(c) selection methods.

6.38. The institution should monitor all students' achievements and progress. To help interpret the information, the institution might also consider monitoring other areas that could have an adverse impact on students from some racial groups, such as—
(a) student numbers, transfers and drop-outs;
(b) different methods of assessing students;
(c) work placements;
(d) the results of programmes targeted at people from specific racial groups; and
(e) bullying and racial harassment.

6.39. The institution should monitor all activities that relate to staff recruitment and selection, and to career development and opportunities for promotion. It might consider monitoring for each department as well as the whole institution. This is likely to include—
(a) selecting and training panel members;
(b) applications and appointments;
(c) success rates for the different selection methods;
(d) permanent, temporary or fixed-term appointments; and
(e) home or international status (for institutions that recruit internationally).

6.40. The institution should identify areas where career progress could be affected and monitor those. They might include—
(a) staff, by their grade and type of post;
(b) staff, by their length of service;
(c) staff training and development, including applications and selection, if appropriate;
(d) the results of training and career-development programmes or strategies that target staff from particular racial groups;
(e) staff appraisals; and
(f) staff promotion, including recruitment methods and criteria for choosing candidates.

6.41. The institution will find it useful to assess its monitoring information regularly. This will allow it to evaluate the progress it is making in meeting its race equality targets and aims. These assessments will help the institution to—
(a) highlight any differences between staff and students from different racial groups;
(b) ask why these differences exist;
(c) review how effective its current targets and aims are;
(d) decide what more it can do to improve the performance of students from different racial groups (including positive action as allowed in section 35 of the Race Relations Act; see the glossary) and to improve the recruitment and progression of staff from different racial groups (again including positive action as allowed in sections 37 and 38 of the Race Relations Act; see the glossary); and
(e) decide what further action it may need to take to meet the three parts of the general duty.

6.42–6.44. (*Outside the scope of this work.*)

Employment duties of bodies with specific responsibilities for education

6.45. Local education authorities (LEAs) have a duty to monitor by racial group, for all the maintained schools in their area, the following—
(a) staff in post; and
(b) applicants for employment, training and promotion;
(c) for schools with 150 or more full-time staff, or equivalent, the number of staff—
(i) receiving training;
(ii) benefiting, or suffering a detriment, as a result of performance assessment procedures;
(iii) involved in grievance procedures;
(iv) subject to disciplinary procedures; and
(v) ending employment with these schools.

6.46. LEAs have a duty to take reasonably practicable steps to publish, each year, the results of this monitoring.

6.47. The Department for Education and Skills has a duty to—
(a) monitor, by racial group, the number of teaching staff from each racial group at all maintained schools;
(b) take reasonably practicable steps to use information provided by LEAs for that purpose; and
(c) take reasonably practicable steps to publish, each year, the results of this monitoring.

6.48. The Learning and Skills Council for England, the Higher Education Funding Councils for England and Wales, and the National Council for Education and Training for Wales have a duty to—
(a) monitor, by racial group, the number of teaching staff at all the establishments for which they are responsible; and
(b) take reasonably practicable steps to publish, each year, the results of this monitoring.

PART IV
ROLE OF THE COMMISSION FOR RACIAL EQUALITY

7—ROLE OF THE COMMISSION FOR RACIAL EQUALITY

[4.309]
7.1. The Commission for Racial Equality (CRE) was set up under the Race Relations Act as an

independent statutory agency. The CRE reports every year to the Home Secretary, but it is not formally part of the Home Office. The duties of the CRE, as set out in the Act, are to—

(a) work towards eliminating discrimination;
(b) promote equality of opportunity and good relations between persons of different racial groups; and
(c) review the workings of the Act.

7.2. The CRE has both promotional and enforcement powers, and both apply to its work on the duty to promote race equality. This chapter explains how the CRE will use both these powers to help promote race equality.

Partnership

Helping public authorities to meet their duty

7.3. The CRE will—

(a) give practical advice;
(b) work with main parts of the public sector, including the inspectorates, to develop good practice; and
(c) monitor and spread good practice.

Providing practical guidance

7.4. The CRE has issued non-statutory supplementary guides to this code, for public authorities, schools and further and higher education institutions (see appendix 6).

7.5. The CRE will continue to work with public authorities to help them to meet their general and specific duties.

Developing and monitoring good practice

7.6. The CRE works with public authorities to develop and share good practice in a number of ways, for example by—

(a) sharing and demonstrating good practice;
(b) supporting training;
(c) giving information and advice;
(d) updating guidance and publishing other material;
(e) promoting good practice; and
(f) identifying poor practice.

Enforcement

7.7. The CRE is committed to using the full range of its enforcement powers appropriately. The CRE has a new power under the Act to enforce the specific duties to promote race equality.

The general duty

7.8. If a public authority does not meet the general duty, its actions (or failure to act) can be challenged by a claim to the High Court for judicial review (see the glossary). A claim for judicial review can be made by a person or group of people with an interest in the matter, or by the CRE.

Specific duties

7.9. If a public authority does not meet any of its specific duties, it could face enforcement action by the CRE under section 71D of the Race Relations Act.

7.10. If the CRE is satisfied that a public authority has failed (or is failing) to meet any of its specific duties, the CRE can serve a "compliance notice" on that authority. This notice will state that the authority must meet its duty and tell the CRE, within 28 days, what it has done, or is doing, to meet its duty.

7.11. In the compliance notice, the CRE can also ask the authority to give it written information showing that it has met its duty. The notice will state the time by which the CRE should receive the information. The CRE cannot ask for more information than a public authority would have to provide during High Court proceedings in England, or in the Scottish Court of Session.

7.12. If, three months after a compliance notice has been served, the CRE considers that the authority has still not met one or more of its specific duties referred to in the notice, the CRE can apply to the county court (in England) or sheriff court (in Scotland) for an order to obey the notice.

7.13. If the compliance notice says that the authority must provide information, and it has not done so within the given time – or the CRE believes that the authority will not provide the information – the CRE can apply to the county court (in England) or sheriff court (in Scotland) for an order saying that the authority must provide the relevant information.

7.14. The county court or sheriff court may grant the order in the terms that the CRE applied for, or in more limited terms. If the court makes an order and the authority does not keep to it, the authority may be found in contempt of court.

Unlawful discrimination

7.15. The Act gives individuals the right to take legal action against unlawful racial discrimination. The Act also gives the CRE the power to take legal action against certain acts of unlawful discrimination. This power includes the power to carry out formal investigations (see the glossary).

CRE codes of practice

7.16. This and other statutory codes of practice that the CRE issues under the Act are admissible in evidence in court. A court will be expected to take the code of practice into account if it seems relevant to any matter the court is ruling on. Public authorities do not have to follow the guidance in this code of practice. However, they are expected to meet the general duty and any specific duties by which they are bound.

(Appendix 1 (Public authorities bound by the general duty), Appendix 2 (Public authorities required to publish a race equality scheme) omitted: see the introductory notes to this Code.)

APPENDIX 3
PUBLIC AUTHORITIES BOUND BY THE EMPLOYMENT DUTY

MINISTERS OF THE CROWN AND GOVERNMENT DEPARTMENTS

[4.310]
(1) A Minister of the Crown or government department

(2) Sub-paragraph (1) does not include the Security Service, the Intelligence Service or the Government Communications Headquarters

SCOTTISH ADMINISTRATION

(1) An office-holder in the Scottish Administration (within the meaning given by section 126(7)(a) of the Scotland Act 1998)

(2) Members of the staff of the Scottish Administration (within the meaning given by section 126(7)(b) of that Act)

NATIONAL ASSEMBLY FOR WALES

(1) The National Assembly for Wales

(2) An Assembly subsidiary as defined by section 99(4) of the Government of Wales Act 1998

ARMED FORCES

Any of the naval, military or air forces of the Crown

NATIONAL HEALTH SERVICE: ENGLAND AND WALES

A health authority established under section 8 of the National Health Service Act 1977

A National Health Service trust established under section 5 of the National Health Service and Community Care Act 1990

A primary care trust established under section 16A of that Act

A special health authority established under section 11 of that Act

LOCAL GOVERNMENT

A body corporate established pursuant to an order under section 67 of the Local Government Act 1985 (transfer of functions to successors of residuary bodies, etc)

A body corporate established pursuant to an order under section 22 of the Local Government Act 1992 (residuary bodies)

The Broads Authority established by section 1 of the Norfolk and Suffolk Broads Act 1988

Any charter trustees constituted under section 246 of that Act

The Common Council of the City of London in its capacity as a local authority or port health authority

The Council of the Isles of Scilly

A fire authority constituted by a combination scheme under section 5 or 6 of the Fire Services Act 1947

The Greater London Authority

An internal drainage board which is continued in being by virtue of section 1 of the Land Drainage Act 1991

A joint authority established under Part IV of the Local Government Act 1985 (fire services, civil defence and transport)

A joint authority established under section 21 of the Local Government Act 1992

A joint board which is continued in being by virtue of section 263(1) of that Act

A joint committee constituted in accordance with section 102(1)(b) of the Local Government Act 1972

A joint planning board constituted for an area in Wales outside a National Park by an order under section 2(1B) of the Town and Country Planning Act 1990

A local authority (within the meaning of the Local Government Act 1972), namely
(a) in England, a county council, a London borough council, a district council;
(b) in Wales, a county council, a county borough council

A local probation board established under section 4 of the Criminal Justice and Court Services Act 2000

The London Development Agency

The London Fire and Emergency Planning Authority

A magistrates' courts committee established under section 27 of the Justices of the Peace Act 1997

A national park authority established by an order under section 63 of the Environment Act 1995

A passenger transport executive for a passenger transport area (within the meaning of Part II of the Transport Act 1968)

A port health authority constituted by an order under section 2 of the Public Health (Control of Disease) Act 1984

A regional development agency established under the Regional Development Agencies Act 1998 (other than the London Development Agency)

The Sub-Treasurer of the Inner Temple or the Under-Treasurer of the Middle Temple, in his capacity as a local authority

Transport for London

A waste disposal authority established by virtue of an order under section 10(1) of the Local Government Act 1985

EDUCATION

The Adult Learning Inspectorate

The British Educational Communication and Technology Agency

The Construction Industry Training Board

The Engineering Construction Industry Training Board

The General Teaching Council for Scotland

The General Teaching Council for Wales

The Higher Education Funding Council for England

The Higher Education Funding Council for Wales

The Learning and Skills Council for England

The managers of a grant-aided school (within the meaning of section 135 of the Education (Scotland) Act 1980)

The National Council for Education and Training for Wales

The Qualifications and Curriculum Authority

The Qualifications, Curriculum and Assessment Authority for Wales

The Student Loans Company

The Teacher Training Agency

HOUSING BODIES

A housing action trust established under Part III of the Housing Act 1988

The Housing Corporation

POLICE

The British Transport Police

A chief constable of a police force maintained under section 2 of the Police Act 1996

The Chief Constable for the Ministry of Defence Police appointed by the Secretary of State under section 1(3) of the Ministry of Defence Police Act 1987

The Commissioner of Police for the City of London

The Commissioner of Police of the Metropolis

The Common Council of the City of London in its capacity as a police authority

The Metropolitan Police Authority established under section 5B of the Police Act 1996

A police authority established under section 3 of the Police Act 1996

The Police Complaints Authority

The Police Information Technology Organisation

A selection panel for independent members of police authorities

The Service Authority for the National Crime Squad

The Service Authority for the National Criminal Intelligence Service

HEALTH

The Commission for Health Improvement

The Council for Professions Supplementary to Medicine, in respect of its public functions

The Dental Practice Board

The English National Board for Nursing, Midwifery and Health Visiting
The Human Fertilisation and Embryology Authority
The Joint Committee on Postgraduate Training for General Practice
The National Biological Standards Board
The Public Health Laboratory Service Board
The Royal College of Anaesthetists, in respect of its public functions
The Royal College of General Practitioners, in respect of its public functions
The Royal College of Midwives, in respect of its public functions
The Royal College of Nursing, in respect of its public functions
The Royal College of Obstetricians and Gynaecologists, in respect of its public functions
The Royal College of Ophthalmologists, in respect of its public functions
The Royal College of Paediatrics and Child Health, in respect of its public functions
The Royal College of Pathologists, in respect of its public functions
The Royal College of Physicians, in respect of its public functions
The Royal College of Psychiatrists, in respect of its public functions
The Royal College of Radiologists, in respect of its public functions
The Royal College of Speech and Language Therapists, in respect of its public functions
The Royal College of Surgeons of England, in respect of its public functions
The Specialist Training Authority of the Medical Royal Colleges
The Welsh National Board for Nursing, Midwifery and Health Visiting

LIBRARIES, MUSEUMS AND ARTS

The Arts Council of England
The Arts Council of Wales
The British Library
The British Museum
The British Tourist Authority
The Commission for Architecture and the Built Environment
The Countryside Council for Wales The Design Council
English Nature
The English Tourist Board
The Film Council
The Geffrye Museum
The Historic Buildings and Monuments Commission for England
The Historic Royal Palaces Trust
The Horniman Museum
The Imperial War Museum
The Library and Information Services Council (Wales)
The Millennium Commission
The Museum of London
The Museum of Science and Industry in Manchester
The National Endowment for Science, Technology and the Arts
The National Gallery
The National Heritage Memorial Fund
The National Library of Wales
The National Lottery Charities Board
The National Maritime Museum
National Museums and Galleries on Merseyside
National Museums and Galleries of Wales
The National Portrait Gallery
The Natural History Museum
The Registrar of Public Lending Right Resource: The Council for Museums, Archives and Libraries
The Royal Armouries
The Royal Botanic Gardens, Kew
The Royal Commission on Ancient and Historical Monuments of Wales

The Royal Commission on Historical Manuscripts
The Science Museum
Sir John Soane's Museum
Sport England
The Sports Council for Wales
The Tate Gallery
The UK Sports Council
The Victoria and Albert Museum
The Wales Tourist Board
The Wallace Collection

PUBLIC CORPORATIONS AND NATIONALISED INDUSTRIES

The Bank of England, in respect of its public functions
The British Broadcasting Corporation, in respect of its public functions
The Broadcasting Standards Commission, in respect of its public functions
The Channel Four Television Corporation, in respect of its public functions
The Civil Aviation Authority
The Coal Authority
The Covent Garden Market Authority
A Customer Service Committee maintained under section 28 of the Water Industry Act 1991
The Independent Television Commission, in respect of its public functions
The Radio Authority, in respect of its public functions
Sianel Pedwar Cymru (Welsh Fourth Channel Authority), in respect of its public functions
The United Kingdom Atomic Energy Authority, in respect of its public functions

REGULATORY, AUDIT AND INSPECTION

The Advisory, Conciliation and Arbitration Service (ACAS)
The Association of Authorised Public Accountants
The Association of Certified Chartered Accountants
The Association of Child Psychotherapy
The Audit Commission for Local Authorities and the National Health Service in England and Wales
The British Hallmarking Council
The British Standards Institute
The Chartered Institute of Patent Agents, in respect of its public functions
The Council for Licensed Conveyancers, in respect of its public functions
The Engineering Council
The Financial Services Authority
The General Chiropractic Council
The General Council of the Bar of England and Wales, in respect of its public functions
The General Dental Council
The General Medical Council
The General Optical Council
The General Osteopathic Council
The General Social Care Council
The Insolvency Practitioners Association
The Institute of Chartered Accountants in England and Wales
The Institute of Legal Executives, in respect of its public functions
The Institute of Trade Mark Attorneys
The Law Society of England and Wales, in respect of its public functions
Her Majesty's Magistrates' Courts Service Inspectorate
The Master of the Court of the Faculties of the Archbishop of Canterbury, in respect of its public functions
The National Audit Office
The Royal Pharmaceutical Society of Great Britain, in respect of its statutory functions and the regulation of the pharmacy profession
The United Kingdom Central Council for Nursing, Midwifery and Health Visiting, in respect of its public functions

RESEARCH

The Alcohol Education and Research Council
The Apple and Pear Research Council
The Biotechnology and Biological Sciences Research Council
The Council for the Central Laboratory of the Research Councils
The Economic and Social Research Council
The Engineering and Physical Sciences Research Council
The Fire Service Research and Training Trust
The Horticultural Development Council
The Medical Research Council
The Natural Environment Research Council
The Particle Physics and Astronomy Research Council

OTHER BODIES, ETC

A board of visitors established under section 6(2) of the Prison Act 1952
The Britain-Russia Centre
The British Association for Central and Eastern Europe
The British Council
The British Potato Council
The British Waterways Board
The British Wool Marketing Board
The Children and Family Court Advisory and Support Service
The Commission for Racial Equality
The Community Development Foundation
The Criminal Injuries Compensation Authority
The Disability Rights Commission
The Electoral Commission
English Partnerships
The Environment Agency
The Equal Opportunities Commission
Food From Britain
The Gaming Board for Great Britain
The Gas and Electricity Consumer Council
The Great Britain-China Centre
The Health and Safety Commission
The Health and Safety Executive
The Home-Grown Cereals Authority
The Horserace Betting Levy Board
The Horserace Totalisator Board
The Information Commissioner
Investors in People UK
The Joint Nature Conservation Committee
The Legal Services Commission
The Local Government Commission for England
The Marshall Aid Commemoration Commission
The Meat and Livestock Commission
The Milk Development Council
The National Consumer Council
The National Forest Company
The National Radiological Protection Board
The New Opportunities Fund
The Northern Lighthouse Board
The Oil and Pipelines Agency
The Sea Fish Industry Authority

The Strategic Rail Authority

The Trinity House Lighthouse Service

A visiting committee appointed under section 152 of the Immigration and Asylum Act 1999 for an immigration detention centre

The Welsh Development Agency

The Welsh Language Board

The Westminster Foundation for Democracy

The Wine Standards Board of the Vintners' Company

The Youth Justice Board for England and Wales.

(Appendix 4 (Public authorities bound by the duties for educational institutions), Appendix 5 (Scottish public authorities), Appendix 6 (Other guidance published by the CRE) omitted: see the introductory notes to this Code.)

EQUAL OPPORTUNITIES COMMISSION: GENDER EQUALITY DUTY CODE OF PRACTICE ENGLAND AND WALES (2007)

[4.311]

NOTES

This Code of Practice was issued by the Equal Opportunities Commission under the Sex Discrimination Act 1975, s 76E(1) (repealed as noted below), and was brought into effect, on 6 April 2007, by the Sex Discrimination Code of Practice (Public Authorities) (Duty to Promote Equality) (Appointed Day) Order 2007, SI 2007/741.

The statutory provision under which this Code was made was repealed by the Equality Act 2006, ss 40, 91, Sch 3, paras 6, 16, Sch 4, however the Code is continued in force by s 42(3) of the 2006 Act (see **[1.1464]**); its legal effect is provided for by s 15(4) of the 2006 Act at **[1.1442]**.

The statutory duties imposed by the Sex Discrimination Act 1975 have been replaced by a general statutory duty in relation to equal treatment under the Equality Act 2010, s 149, and it was originally intended that this Code would be replaced by a new Code under s 149 of the 2010 Act. However, the Equality and Human Rights Commission subsequently announced that the Secretary of State is unlikely to approve a new statutory code, and that the new Guidance would be issued on a non-statutory basis. The new Guidance on the equality duty for England, Wales and Scotland is on the EHRC website at: www.equalityhumanrights.com/en/advice-and-guidance/public-sector-equality-duty-guidance.

Only those parts of the Code of particular relevance to employment law are reproduced. The following are omitted: Foreword; paras 2.53–2.61; paras 3.57–3.74; Chapters 4–6; Appendices C–G.

The equivalent Code for Scotland ('Gender Equality Duty Code of Practice for Scotland') is omitted for reasons of space. It applies to those bodies subject to the authority of the Scottish Parliament.

CONTENTS

CHAPTER 1: OVERVIEW OF THE GENDER EQUALITY DUTY

WHAT THIS CODE IS AND HOW TO USE IT

[4.312]

1.1. This Code of Practice (the Code) gives practical guidance to public authorities on how to meet the legal requirements of the gender equality duty. The Equal Opportunities Commission (EOC) has prepared and issued this Code under the Sex Discrimination Act 1975, as amended by the Equality Act 2006. The Code is expected to come into effect on April 6 2007.

1.2. Those parts of the Code which deal with the general gender equality duty in section 76A of the Sex Discrimination Act 1975 apply (subject to the exceptions set out in Appendix B) to all public authorities in England and Wales and to reserved functions of public authorities in Scotland. A similar but separate code applies to Scotland. Those parts of the Code (primarily Chapter 3) which deal with the specific duties imposed by the Sex Discrimination Act 1975 (Public Authorities) (Statutory Duties) Order 2006 (the Order) apply only to the public authorities listed in the Schedule to that Order. This does not include authorities all of whose functions are public functions in relation to Wales.

1.3. This Code of Practice is a 'statutory' code and has been laid before Parliament before taking effect. This means that the Code is admissible in evidence in any legal action under the Sex Discrimination Act 1975 or the Equal Pay Act 1970, in criminal or civil proceedings before any court or tribunal.

1.4. A court or tribunal must take into account any part of the Code that appears to them to be relevant to any question arising in the proceedings. This includes the question of whether public authorities have breached the law. A tribunal or court may draw an adverse inference that a breach of the law has occurred if a public authority has failed to follow relevant provisions in the Code. If a public authority does not follow the Code's provisions, it will need to show how it has otherwise met its legal obligations under the general duty and any specific duties.

1.5. On its own, the Code does not impose any legal obligations on public authorities. The Code is not a complete statement of the law – only the courts can give this.

1.6. References to the Sex Discrimination Act 1975 (SDA), the Equal Pay Act 1970 (EqPA) and the Equality Act 2006 are shown in the margins.

1.7. Where examples are used, they are intended to illustrate the ways in which different types of public authorities can comply with the duty. They should be read in that light, and not as authoritative statements of the law. Where examples are taken from the voluntary sector, they are intended to illustrate gender equality issues and possible means of addressing them, not to imply that those bodies are covered by the gender duty.

1.8. The EOC will be issuing non-statutory guidance to supplement this Code, to cover particular parts of the public sector, aspects of the duty such as gender impact assessment and how the duty applies to procurement.

WHAT IS THE GENDER EQUALITY DUTY?

1.9. The Equality Act 2006 amends the SDA to place a statutory duty on all public authorities, when carrying out their functions, to have due regard to the need:

- to eliminate unlawful discrimination and harassment
- to promote equality of opportunity between men and women.

1.10. This is known as the 'general duty' and will come into effect on 6 April 2007.

1.11. The duty applies to all public authorities in respect of all of their functions (with limited exceptions described in Appendix B). This means it applies to policy-making, service provision, employment matters, and in relation to enforcement or any statutory discretion and decision-making. It also applies to a public authority in relation to services and functions which are contracted out. In addition, it applies to private and voluntary bodies which are carrying out public functions, but only in respect of those functions. For examples of the kind of public authorities which are covered, see Appendix A.

1.12. Public authorities are expected to have 'due regard' to the need to eliminate unlawful discrimination and harassment and promote equality of opportunity between men and women in all of their functions. Due regard comprises two linked elements: proportionality and relevance. The weight which public authorities give to gender equality should therefore be proportionate to its relevance to a particular function. The greater the relevance of a function to gender equality, the greater regard which should be paid to it. For more detail on due regard and the component parts of the duty, see Chapter 2, paragraphs 2.1–2.16 and 2.21–2.32.

1.13. As part of the duty, public authorities are required to have due regard to the need to eliminate unlawful discrimination and harassment in employment and vocational training (including further and higher education), for people who intend to undergo, are undergoing or have undergone gender reassignment. For the purposes of this Code, the expression 'transsexual people' is used to refer to the people who are covered by those provisions. For more detail, see Chapter 2, paragraphs 2.17–2.20.

1.14. To support progress in delivering the general duty, there is also a series of 'specific duties' which apply to listed public authorities as laid out in the Order in Appendix C. The Order sets out steps those authorities must take to help them meet the general duty.

1.15. Those specific duties, in brief, are:

- **To prepare and publish a gender equality scheme**, showing how it will meet its general and specific duties and setting out its gender equality objectives.
- In formulating its overall objectives, **to consider the need to include objectives to address the causes of any gender pay gap.**
- **To gather and use information** on how the public authority's policies and practices affect gender equality in the workforce and in the delivery of services.
- **To consult stakeholders (ie employees, service users and others, including trade unions) and take account of relevant information** in order to determine its gender equality objectives.
- **To assess the impact of its current and proposed policies and practices** on gender equality.
- **To implement the actions set out in its scheme** within three years, unless it is unreasonable or impracticable to do so.
- **To report** against the scheme every year and **review** the scheme at least every three years.

1.16. The first scheme must be published by 30 April 2007. For more detail on these specific duties and how to meet them, see Chapter 3.

1.17. This document contains guidance on how to meet both the general and the specific duties in Chapters 2 and 3. Even if a public authority is not subject to the specific duties (such as public authorities operating solely in Wales), it will still be expected to provide clear evidence of meeting the general duty. The specific duties laid out in Chapter 3 can act as a framework to assist authorities in complying with the general duty.

WHY HAS THE GENDER EQUALITY DUTY BEEN INTRODUCED?

1.18. The gender equality duty aims to make gender equality central to the way that public authorities work, in order to create:

- better-informed decision-making and policy development
- a clearer understanding of the needs of service users
- better-quality services which meet varied needs
- more effective targeting of policy and resources
- better results and greater confidence in public services
- a more effective use of talent in the workforce.

1.19. The duty is intended to address the fact that, despite 30 years of individual legal rights to sex equality, there is still widespread discrimination – sometimes intentional, sometimes unintentional – and persistent gender inequality. Policies and practices that seem neutral can have a significantly different effect on women and on men, often contributing to greater gender inequality and poor policy outcomes. Individual legal rights have not been enough by themselves to change this.

1.20. The duty is intended to improve this situation, both for men and for women, for boys and for girls. Gender roles and relationships structure men's and women's lives. Women are frequently disadvantaged by policies and practices that do not recognise their greater caring responsibilities, the different pattern of their working lives, their more limited access to resources and their greater vulnerability to domestic violence and sexual assault. Men are also disadvantaged by workplace cultures that do not support their family or childcare responsibilities, by family services that assume they have little or no role in parenting, or by health services which do not recognise their different needs. Both sexes suffer from stereotyping of their roles and needs. The duty should help the public sector, and those working with it, to identify and respond to stereotyping, sex discrimination and sexism, resulting in improvements for all.

1.21. The duty requires public authorities to identify and tackle discrimination, to prevent harassment, and to ensure that their work promotes equality of opportunity between men and women. It is a form of legally enforceable 'gender mainstreaming' – building gender equality into the core business thinking and processes of an organisation. It is different from previous sex equality legislation in two crucial respects:

- public authorities have to be proactive in eliminating discrimination and harassment, rather than waiting for individuals to take cases against them.
- public authorities have to be proactive in promoting equality of opportunity, and not just avoiding discrimination.

OUTCOMES – THE CHANGES TO WHICH THE GENDER EQUALITY DUTY SHOULD LEAD

1.22. The aim of the duty is not to establish processes but to make visible and faster progress towards gender equality. Indicators of progress might include:

- Service-users notice that services are more accessible and better tailored to their needs, and service outcomes by gender begin to improve.
- Women and men are making greater use of services that their sex had previously under-used.
- Service-users with caring responsibilities are receiving appropriate support, such as better pushchair access on public transport and crèche facilities for trainees.
- Fathers receive greater support for their childcare responsibilities from public services and employers.
- Girls have higher aspirations for their future careers.
- Women and men from all groups feel effectively engaged in decision and policy-making around issues that have a direct effect on them.
- Women and men are represented at all levels of the workforce and in all areas of work.
- Harassment and sexual harassment of staff, service users and others is dealt with promptly and systematically, according to agreed procedures, and tolerance of harassment drops within the organisation as a whole.
- The reported level of discrimination experienced by pregnant staff and staff returning from maternity leave reduces significantly and is eventually eliminated.
- The gap between women and men's pay narrows and is eventually eliminated.
- Employees with caring responsibilities are receiving greater support from the public authority, including flexible and part-time working opportunities at all levels of work.
- Transsexual people feel supported and valued as staff and potential staff.
- Barriers to the recruitment and retention of transsexual staff have been identified and removed.
- Employees are aware of the gender equality duty, understand how it will affect their work, and have the skills to implement the duty in their work.
- Gender equality issues, and their budgetary implications, are considered at the beginning of policy-making.
- It is easy to find a wide variety of data and information to assess effectively how certain actions will affect women and men.

HOW THE GENDER EQUALITY DUTY FITS INTO THE BROADER EQUALITY PICTURE

1.23. Women and men, including transsexual women and men, will experience different forms of disadvantage depending on their age, ethnicity, religion or belief, sexual orientation, marital or civil partnership status, and whether or not they have a disability. In order to understand and address questions of gender equality under the duty, public authorities may need to consider that complexity and whether particular groups of women or men are experiencing particular disadvantages.

> Only 47% of disabled women are in employment, compared with 53% of disabled men. Of the disabled women in employment, only 52% work full-time. This compares with an employment rate of 75% for

non-disabled women and 86% for non-disabled men. (EOC Facts about women and men in Great Britain 2005)

1.24. The gender equality duty is similar to the existing duties on race and disability equality and all three have the same spirit and intention behind them, requiring public authorities to take action to tackle discrimination, to prevent harassment, and to ensure that their work promotes equality of opportunity across all their functions. The gender equality duty has fewer requirements to set up processes than the race duty, however, in order to ensure that public authorities focus on the achievement of outcomes.

1.25. The gender equality scheme, which is a requirement for listed public authorities under the specific duties, can be published as part of an overall equality scheme, covering the requirements of all three duties. There are, however, slight differences in the requirements of the three duties. Public authorities which choose to take the overall equality scheme approach must ensure that they clearly meet the requirements of the gender equality duty, including specific objectives on gender equality. The scheme should show clearly and specifically which elements of the overall equality scheme refer to gender equality.

WHICH ORGANISATIONS HAVE TO TAKE ACTION ON THE GENERAL DUTY?

S76A Sex Discrimination Act (margin note)

1.26. The general duty applies to all functions of every public authority (bar the exceptions listed in Appendix B). The definition of a public authority is 'any person who has functions of a public nature'. Despite a slight difference in the wording, this is the same approach as the definition of public authorities covered by the Disability Discrimination Act 2005 and the Human Rights Act 1998.

1.27. Because the duty is based on this definition, public authorities covered by the general gender duty are not individually listed. The duty would apply to all of the authorities listed in Schedule 1A to the amended Race Relations Act 1976. Further details on the definition of a public authority are contained in Appendix A.

1.28. The gender duty can also apply directly to certain private or voluntary sector bodies when they are carrying out public functions (the private functions of such bodies being excluded). Further details of who is affected by this are contained in Appendix A.

WHICH PUBLIC AUTHORITIES HAVE TO TAKE ACTION ON THE SPECIFIC DUTIES?

1.29. To find out whether a public authority is covered, check the list at Appendix D. The list will be subject to periodic updating by Government, the relevant order being available on the Stationery Office website.

HOW WILL THE GENDER EQUALITY DUTY BE ENFORCED?

1.30. The general duty is enforceable by judicial review. Any person or body affected by a failure to comply with the general duty by a public authority may take action through judicial review proceedings.

S32 Equality Act (margin note)

1.31. From late 2007, the Commission for Equality and Human Rights (CEHR) will have the power to conduct formal assessments and to issue compliance notices in connection with a breach of the general duty which will be enforceable in the courts.

S76D SDA (margin note)

1.32. The CEHR and EOC will have the power to issue compliance notices in respect of the specific duties. For more detail see Chapter 4.

1.33. In addition it is likely that relevant inspection bodies will require evidence of compliance with the general and specific duties.

FUTURE CHANGES IN THE LEGISLATION

1.34. There may be changes in the future to the sex equality legislation which will affect the definition of unlawful discrimination and harassment under the duty. Public authorities will need to ensure that they keep up-to-date with any developments which affect the duties explained in this Code. Relevant information will be publicised by the EOC on the gender duty section of their website, and will be available from the CEHR in the future. This Code will remain in force after the dissolution of the EOC, however, until the CEHR updates it.

WHERE TO OBTAIN FURTHER INFORMATION NOW AND IN THE FUTURE

1.35. Copies of the Sex Discrimination Act, the Equal Pay Act, the Equality Act and the orders or regulations made under them can be obtained from the Stationery Office. The text of this Code and of the Equal Pay Code of Practice can be downloaded free of charge from the EOC's website on www.eoc.org.uk. There is also supporting guidance available on the EOC website.

1.36. Free information on the duty is available through the EOC Helpline on 0845 601 5901 or by email on info@eoc.org.uk.

1.37. The Equality Act also provides for the dissolution of the EOC and the passing of its functions to the CEHR. This is currently expected to happen in late 2007. Once this transition has occurred, promotion and enforcement of the gender equality duty will pass to the CEHR.

CHAPTER 2: HOW TO MEET THE GENERAL DUTY

INTRODUCTION

[4.313]

2.1. All public authorities and private and voluntary bodies carrying out public functions on behalf of a public authority are subject to the general duty, and this Chapter explains how to meet it.

2.2. All public authorities are legally required, when exercising their functions, to have due regard to the need:

- to eliminate discrimination and harassment that is unlawful under the Sex Discrimination Act 1975 (SDA) and discrimination that is unlawful under the Equal Pay Act 1970 (EqPA)
- to promote equality of opportunity between men and women.

2.3. This means that the duty is not a negative or passive one, but requires public authorities to adopt a proactive approach to meeting the duty. When the EOC (and subsequently the CEHR) and public sector inspectorates are monitoring and evaluating compliance with this duty, they will be looking for evidence of action and positive change. Without such evidence, it will be difficult to establish that the authority is meeting the gender equality duty.

2.4. Smaller public authorities will have fewer resources and this will affect the steps which they take to ensure compliance with the general duty.

HOW THE DIFFERENT PARTS OF THE DUTY WORK TOGETHER

2.5. As stated above the general duty has three parts:

- eliminating unlawful discrimination
- eliminating harassment
- promoting equality of opportunity between men and women

2.6. These three parts support each other, and in practice may overlap. For example, promoting equality of opportunity may also eliminate or prevent unlawful discrimination and harassment. It is important to remember, however, that the three parts are different, and that achieving on one may not lead to achieving all three. Public authorities should consider and deal with all three parts of the gender duty.

UNLAWFUL DISCRIMINATION

2.7. Unlawful discrimination includes discrimination as defined by the SDA, and discrimination that is unlawful under the EqPA. Public authorities are legally required to have due regard to the need to eliminate both forms of discrimination.

2.8. In the SDA, unlawful discrimination is defined as:

- direct and indirect discrimination on grounds of sex
- discrimination on the grounds of pregnancy and maternity leave
- discrimination on the grounds of gender reassignment
- direct and indirect discrimination against married persons and civil partners
- victimisation
- harassment and sexual harassment.

Further details of the above definitions and where they apply can be found in Appendix E.

In the employment field, the SDA prohibits discrimination in non-contractual pay and benefits, such as discretionary bonuses. Sex discrimination related to contractual pay and benefits is dealt with under the EqPA.

2.9. The EqPA (read in the light of article 141 of the Treaty of Rome) gives an individual a right to the same contractual pay and benefits as a person of the opposite sex in the same employment, or where the source of the pay is the same, where the man and the woman are doing:

- the same or broadly similar work
- work which has been rated as equivalent under an analytical job evaluation study
- work that is of equal value (work of equal value is where the work done is different but considered to be of equal value or worth in terms of demands such as effort, skill and decision-making).

A public authority can pay a man more than a woman (or vice versa) in such circumstances if there is a genuine and material factor for doing so which is not attributable to direct or indirect sex discrimination.

HARASSMENT AND SEXUAL HARASSMENT

2.10. Harassment and sexual harassment are unlawful under the SDA and the duty requires public authorities to have due regard to the need to eliminate them. The duty to have due regard to the need to promote equality of opportunity between men and women is also relevant to ensuring that harassment is prevented before it occurs.

2.11. Different legal definitions apply, depending on whether the harassment occurs in:

- employment and related fields, vocational training (including further and higher education) and in the exercise of public functions; or
- schools, the provision of goods, facilities or services, or in the disposal or management of premises.

Appendix E explains the definitions of harassment. Paragraphs 2.69–2.77 provide information on how to meet the duty to have due regard to the need to eliminate harassment.

THE PROMOTION OF EQUALITY OF OPPORTUNITY BETWEEN MEN AND WOMEN

2.12. The term 'sex' is used to describe biological differences between women and men. The term 'gender' refers to the wider social roles and relationships which structure men's and women's lives. Gender inequality exists in all aspects of society and refers to lasting and embedded patterns of advantage and disadvantage.

2.13. The duty on public authorities to have due regard to the need to promote equality of opportunity between men and women is a new aspect of the SDA. In order to achieve actual equality of opportunity, it is necessary to recognise that in certain circumstances women and men, because of their sex or gender roles, are not in the same position. In some circumstances it may therefore be appropriate for public authorities to treat women and men differently, if that action is aimed at overcoming previous disadvantage.

2.14. For example, where one sex is under-represented in particular work, a public authority could promote equality of opportunity by taking positive action to encourage members of the under-represented sex to apply for such work, or to provide training to equip the under-represented sex for such work. It would not, however, be lawful to discriminate in favour of one sex in the actual appointments procedure. See Chapter 6 for more detail.

2.15. As another example, women make up the substantial majority of victims of domestic violence and rape. It would not be appropriate, therefore, for a local council to seek to fund refuge services on a numerically equal basis for men and for women. The promotion of equal opportunities between men and women requires public authorities to recognise that the two groups are not starting from an equal footing and identical treatment would not be appropriate.

2.16. In some instances, promoting equality of opportunity may require separate provision to be offered, as an alternative approach to improve take-up of services by the under-represented sex, where this is permitted under the SDA. An example of this might be to encourage men to increase their low take-up of primary health care services. For more detail, see Chapter 6 on single-sex activities.

THE GENDER EQUALITY DUTY AND GENDER REASSIGNMENT

2.17. The gender equality duty requires public authorities to have due regard to the need to eliminate unlawful discrimination and harassment against transsexual people in the fields of employment and vocational training (including further and higher education). This section gives further details on issues relating to the gender duty and gender reassignment.

S2A SDA (margin note)

2.18. The SDA provides that people who intend to undergo, are undergoing or have undergone gender reassignment are protected against discrimination and harassment in the fields of employment and related areas and in vocational training (including further and higher education). This means that public authorities must have due regard to the need to eliminate unlawful discrimination and harassment in those fields against transsexual people when discharging their gender duty.

2.19. The scope of legal protection against discrimination on grounds of gender reassignment will be extended in the SDA, by 21 December 2007, by the implementation of the Goods and Services Directive 2004/113. As a matter of domestic law, as a consequence, by that date (or the date of implementation if earlier), public authorities will be under a duty to have due regard to the need to eliminate unlawful discrimination and harassment on grounds of gender reassignment in the provision of goods and services.

2.20. Public authorities may wish to take the need to have due regard to the need to eliminate gender reassignment discrimination and harassment into account when discharging their gender equality duty in relation to the provision of goods and services, before they are required to do so following the implementation of the Goods and Services Directive.

WHAT DOES THE GENERAL DUTY MEAN? DUE REGARD, PROPORTIONALITY AND RELEVANCE

S76A SDA (margin note)

2.21. Public authorities will be expected to have due regard to the need to eliminate unlawful discrimination and harassment and promote equality of opportunity between women and men in relation to all their functions and to provide evidence that they have done so. This includes their core functions of policy development, service design and delivery, decision-making and employment, the exercise of statutory discretion, enforcement and any services and functions which have been contracted out. For details on contracted-out services see Chapter 5 on procurement.

2.22. Having due regard means that the weight given to the need to promote gender equality is **proportionate** to its **relevance** to a particular function. In practice, this principle will mean public authorities should prioritise action to address the most significant gender inequalities within their remit, and take actions which are likely to deliver the best gender equality outcomes. This is likely to mean focusing on functions or policies that have most effect on the public, or on the authority's employees, or on a section of the public or on a section of the authority's employees. The authority should ask whether particular functions could affect women and men in different ways, and whether functions can be carried out in a way which promotes equality of opportunity between men and women.

2.23. The general duty applies to public authorities whatever their size, but the way in which it is implemented should be appropriate to the size of the authority and its functions. For example, a primary school may wish to train its staff in gender equality in order to meet the duty, but does not have sufficient budget to meet this training need alongside other competing needs. It decides to meet the duty by arranging gender equality training for the head teacher, who then runs a feedback session for staff and governors at the next in-service training day. This could be a proportionate means of meeting the duty.

2.24. Gender equality will be more relevant to some functions than others. Relevance is about how much a function affects people's gender equality, as members of the public or as employees of the authority. For example, a school may decide that gender equality is more relevant to the way that it designs its teaching methods than to its building maintenance work. Public authorities should therefore assess whether, and how, gender equality is relevant to each of their functions. A public authority may decide that little or no action is required to discharge the gender equality duty in some of its services, for example those which are purely technical, such as traffic control or weather forecasting. Gender equality will always be relevant, however, to the employment side of any of a public authority's functions.

2.25. The requirement for proportionality and relevance should not be interpreted, however, as a simple question of the numbers of people affected. Public authorities should also take into account the seriousness or extent of the discrimination, harassment or gender inequality, even if the number of people affected is small. This would often be the case where, for example, transsexual people were affected, as their numbers would be likely to be small but the seriousness or extent of discrimination and harassment might be significant.

2.26. Where changing a function or proposed policy would lead to significant benefits to the gender equality of men and women, (or, in employment and vocational training – including further and higher education – for transsexual men and women), public authorities should give greater weight to the case for change and take steps accordingly.

2.27. For example, a Regional Development Agency has a target of increasing employment rates in a particular district. When developing this policy, it discovers that women are less economically active than men in that district but the employment services and training opportunities which they are providing are not being accessed by women, because of lack of childcare support. They decide to adjust their policy and resource allocations to provide childcare advice and support.

2.28. It will not be acceptable for a public authority to claim that it does not have enough resources to meet the duty. This is because meeting the general duty is a statutory requirement. Existing resources may therefore need to be reprioritised to meet the duty. In practice this may mean that public authorities will use their existing administrative systems and processes, adjusting their plans and priorities where necessary.

2.29. The general duty does not only require authorities to have due regard to gender equality when making decisions about the future. It also requires them to take action to tackle the ongoing consequences of decisions made in the past which failed to give due regard to gender equality. This will entail identifying and addressing any significant inequalities resulting from policies currently in place.

2.30. For example, previous organisational policy may have given training allowances to full-time staff but not to part-time staff, resulting in more men than women taking up the benefit and improving their qualifications. The public authority may need to consider what action it can take to redress this balance, in order to meet the duty.

2.31. Public authorities are not likely to be able to take action to improve all of their functions in a single cycle, for example during the three year life of a gender equality scheme. They have, however, a continuing duty which requires them to prioritise for review functions with the most relevance to gender equality. Consulting male and female employees and service users will be helpful to this process of prioritisation and review, and is a legal requirement under the specific duties.

2.32. The technique of impact assessment, discussed in detail in Chapter 3, is designed to assist authorities in ensuring that they have due regard to gender equality in all their decisions and functions.

HOW TO MEET THE GENERAL DUTY

2.33. The steps which will assist a public authority to comply with the duty are as follows:

- gathering and analysing information
- consulting stakeholders
- carrying out impact assessments
- prioritising and implementing gender equality objectives
- reporting and reviewing.

These steps are covered in more detail in Chapter 3. Although they are a legal requirement for listed public authorities, they can also assist those authorities which are only covered by the general duty.

2.34. Other important mechanisms for successful compliance with the duty include:

- accountability and leadership
- mainstreaming the duty into core functions
- ensuring implementation through clear staff roles
- staff expertise and training.

ACCOUNTABILITY AND LEADERSHIP

2.35. Public authorities are responsible for meeting their general and specific duties. Within each public authority, this responsibility will rest with the groups or individuals who are liable (legally responsible) for the authority's acts or failure to act.

2.36. As well as being legally liable for meeting the duty, these individuals and senior staff have an important leadership role to play in ensuring the success of the duty. As a matter of good practice, it is recommended that all such individuals should be briefed on their responsibilities under the duty and given regular reports on progress. They should be encouraged to build the duty into strategic planning, keynote speeches and organisational development work, so that a consistent message is given to staff and stakeholders that gender equality is integral to the core business of the authority.

2.37. Senior management will be responsible for ensuring that the necessary resources and expertise to meet the duty are made available within the organisation.

MAINSTREAMING THE DUTY INTO THE CORE FUNCTIONS OF A PUBLIC AUTHORITY

2.38. The duty requires public authorities to have due regard to the need to eliminate unlawful discrimination and harassment and to promote equality of opportunity in all their functions. This includes the high-level functions of a public authority such as business planning, budget allocation, annual reporting and organisational development. These will be particularly important in ensuring that the duty is mainstreamed into the day-to-day workings of the public authority, is not marginalised, and results in changes in the most relevant areas of the authority's work.

2.39. Reflecting the duty in the mainstream business plan will also have practical benefits, through bringing together the planning processes of the public authority as a whole with those required under the duty. Having clear gender equality objectives in the organisational business plan, and reporting against them in the annual report could also improve staff ownership, and transparency and accountability to stakeholders.

ENSURING IMPLEMENTATION THROUGH CLEAR STAFF ROLES

2.40. It is recommended as a matter of good practice that a senior member of staff should be given strategic responsibility for ensuring the duty is implemented. In larger authorities, they will need to work with a group of colleagues from policy development, service delivery, employment and, where contracted-out services form a part of the authority's functions, procurement staff. This working group may also be working on the wider equality agenda, including the race and disability duties, but will need to pay specific attention to meeting gender equality goals. The working group will need to develop and drive forward a specific action plan, which allows for effective monitoring and review of progress.

2.41. Smaller authorities will also need to ensure one person is given responsibility for ensuring the duty is implemented, that all functions of the authority are appropriately dealt with, and that there is an action plan.

2.42. Many larger authorities employ specialist equality staff to steer the process of implementing equality; smaller ones may make it part of a person's responsibilities. It is recommended that specialist equality posts should be located in a strategic part of the public authority such as policy, performance management, planning or strategy. The human resources function will have to play a crucial role in the employment aspects but is not best placed to lead overall, as the duty requires due regard in all functions of a public authority, including service delivery and policy-making.

2.43. Wherever they are situated, equality staff or lead individuals cannot be expected to bear all responsibility for the successful implementation of the duty. That will require ownership, action and culture change across the organisation as a whole. Designating a senior person with significant strategic or management responsibilities, supported by designated key staff, should contribute to change across the organisation.

2.44. Reporting on progress to senior management team meetings should help increase their understanding that gender equality can and should be a core part of their business and of their policy development and service delivery objectives, not just a marginal issue or a small part of human resources work.

STAFF EXPERTISE AND TRAINING

2.45. In addition to any specialist equality staff, it will also be necessary to build the skills and understanding of relevant staff within the public authority, for example policy and service managers, procurement staff, and human resource managers. Where an authority is subject to the specific duties, relevant staff throughout the organisation will have to have the skills to collect and analyse gender data, to ensure that stakeholders are consulted effectively and to undertake gender impact assessments. These skills will also be useful for authorities which are subject to the general duty only. In some specialist areas, such as understanding the needs of transsexual people, public authorities may wish to obtain external assistance.

2.46. It is recommended that all relevant staff in the public authority should have some understanding of the duty, its meaning for their work and the authority's priority goals in gender equality. This can be achieved by staff briefing, and where relevant, training programmes, and by building goals and targets relevant to the duty into individual personal development plans across the organisation. It can also be supported by recognising progress in achieving gender equality when rewarding individual and team performance.

SUCCESS FACTORS IN GENDER MAINSTREAMING

2.47. When planning for implementation of the duty, and reviewing progress, public authorities may wish to consider the factors commonly associated with successful gender mainstreaming in organisations:

- ongoing top-level commitment and willingness to commit resources to achieving gender equality
- developing a shared understanding of the problem, and a shared vision of what gender equality would look like for the authority, which links directly to organisational objectives

- board-level leadership and accountability (with engagement of elected representatives where applicable)
- senior management support and accountability
- specialist staff to steer the process and support staff capacity
- good systems for disaggregating new and existing data by gender
- developing staff understanding of gender equality and skills in analysing the gender impact of policy
- involving staff, service users, unions and voluntary sector organisations
- building gender equality standards and objectives into routine organisational procedures such as policy and budget approval documentation, organisational and departmental targets and objectives, and individual job descriptions, objectives and appraisals.

2.48. These processes are needed to make the duty work, but they are not an end in themselves. The purpose of the duty is to eliminate unlawful discrimination and harassment and promote equality of opportunity between women and men. Ultimately, the key to the success of the duty is achieving culture change in public authorities, a process which will take time and commitment. An authority which makes the effort to meet the needs of women and of men will see the benefits, however, through delivering better quality services and having a more productive workforce.

MEETING THE GENDER EQUALITY DUTY IN POLICY DEVELOPMENT

2.49. To meet the duty effectively, public authorities must ensure that they have due regard to the need to eliminate unlawful discrimination and harassment against either women or men, (and, in employment and vocational training – including further and higher education – against transsexual men and women) and that their policies are not maintaining or leading to gender inequality. To assist public authorities to do this, it is recommended that they should:

- collect evidence on the impact of core policies on women and men
- when new policies are being developed, assess their likely consequences for women and men
- alter or amend proposed policies so that they have due regard to the need to promote gender equality and eliminate unlawful discrimination and harassment
- resource the above changes appropriately.

2.50. Conducting impact assessments on policies is a useful way of demonstrating that public authorities have had due regard to the need to eliminate unlawful discrimination and harassment and to promote equality of opportunity when developing policy. It is also a legal requirement if a public authority is subject to the specific duties. Even for those public authorities which are not, however, it can be a useful tool for meeting the duty. For more detail on conducting gender impact assessments, see Chapter 3.

2.51. The best way to find out if a policy is likely to have a negative or a positive impact on gender equality is to:

- find out if research or data already exist, and if so, analyse and apply it
- take action to develop relevant information if it does not exist
- ask and involve external and internal stakeholders, such as women's and men's voluntary sector groups, service user and consumer groups, trade unions and employee or staff networks.

2.52. Going through this process brings significant benefits to the effectiveness of policymaking. Developing a good base of evidence about differences in the impact of policies on women and men will avoid resources being misdirected and potentially wasted.

Women's current and future entitlement to pensions is significantly lower than men's. The DWP produced a report 'Women and Pensions – The Evidence' that specifically investigated the gender differences in pension provision between men and women. It showed that only 24% of recently retired women were entitled to a full Basic State Pension in their own right. Even when looking at working-age women, 2.2 million women are not building up rights to even the Basic State Pension.

Women's greater likelihood of undertaking unpaid parenting and caring commitments, and the subsequent impact on their ability to engage in paid employment, were identified as the key causes of the gender differences.

The subsequent DWP White Paper 'Security in retirement: towards a new pensions system' put forward several changes to the recognition of unpaid caring work within the state pension system that will mean for the first time paid work and unpaid care will be equally recognised within the state pension system.

This will benefit not just women, but also the increasing number of men undertaking unpaid care and help produce a pensions system that fully reflects working lives both now and in the future.

2.53–2.61. (*Outside the scope of this work.*)

MEETING THE GENDER EQUALITY DUTY IN EMPLOYMENT

2.62. To meet the gender equality duty as an employer, a public authority will need to ensure that it has due regard to the need to eliminate unlawful discrimination and harassment in its employment practices and actively promotes gender equality within its workforce. This includes discrimination and harassment of transsexual people on grounds of their gender reassignment.

2.63. In practice this will involve a cyclical process of: data collection, analysis of data, developing an action plan, implementing the plan and monitoring the outcomes to inform further action. It is recommended that the public authority involves the workforce in the process and agrees a timescale over which it will take action. Doing this will not only enable that authority to meet its obligations under the duty, but will also improve its ability to recruit and retain staff and improve service delivery. For more detail on data collection, see Chapter 3.

2.64. The following issues are usually the most common ones to be considered when a public authority is deciding employment priorities for action:

- ensuring fair recruitment processes
- avoiding concentration of women and men into particular areas of work and addressing it where it already exists ('occupational segregation')
- promoting and managing flexible working
- ensuring high-level part-time work and supporting part-time workers
- managing leave for parents and carers
- managing pregnancy and return from maternity leave
- eliminating harassment including sexual harassment
- eliminating discrimination against, and harassment of, transsexual staff and potential staff
- grievance and disciplinary procedures
- redundancy
- retirement
- equal pay
- work-based training opportunities.

London Underground has targeted women in its recruitment of train drivers as part of a strategy that identified the lack of gender balance in the workforce as a central factor affecting its ability to move from being an asset-based organisation to a customer-focused organisation. In an 18-month campaign, it increased the number of female tube drivers from 75 to 167. It broadened its recruitment advertising by placing an advertisement in Cosmopolitan magazine, which produced 6,000 applications. The strategy also tackled ongoing workplace issues that were discouraging women:

— sexual harassment and a culture that was unwelcoming to women
— the lack of adequate physical facilities such as women's toilets and showers and difficulties accessing the facilities that did exist
— inflexibility in working time and rostering

A central feature of the work was the implementation of a Managing Equality and Diversity competence programme, which was rolled out to all managers, the introduction of a managing diversity competence statement and the development of personal diversity goals and measures for managers.

IDS Diversity at Work No 4, October 2004

TRANSSEXUAL EMPLOYEES AND POTENTIAL EMPLOYEES

2.65. Discrimination on the grounds of sex includes discrimination on the grounds of gender reassignment in employment and vocational training (including further and higher education). Public authorities should review all employment policies and procedures to ensure that they adequately cover transsexual employees – especially those dealing with recruitment, confidentiality, harassment, access to training and development, occupational pensions and insurance.

2.66. It is important to remember that the legal obligation to prevent discrimination against transsexual people in employment and vocational training (including further and higher education) covers not only those who have undergone gender reassignment in the past but also those who intend to undergo gender reassignment and those who are undergoing it.

MEETING THE GENDER EQUALITY DUTY FOR EQUAL PAY

2.67. Public authorities are required to comply with the EqPA. The requirement to have due regard to the need to eliminate unlawful discrimination includes discrimination that is unlawful under the EqPA.

2.68. The right of an individual under the EqPA is set out in paragraph 2.9 above. 'Like work' means work which is the same or broadly similar. Work rated as equivalent means work that has been rated using a non-discriminatory job evaluation scheme as equivalent. Work of equal value is where the work done is different but considered to be of equal value or worth in terms of demands such as effort, skill and decision-making. More detail on this can be found in the Code of Practice on Equal Pay and the EOC website, at www.eoc.org.uk

A public sector organisation based in Wales, with over five hundred staff undertook an equal pay review (EPR). Just under half the workforce was female. Part-time work was fairly common and this group was slightly more likely to be female than male. Prior to the review, the organisation had a fairly complicated pay structure which was felt to have too many grades for the number of staff. There were also several people outside of the pay structure. The organisation began a pay and grading exercise in 1999 and this eventually evolved into a full EPR. There was significant union involvement throughout the process and members of each staff grade were also involved in the working group. The working group used consultants to help them draft the job evaluation system and set up the EPR. The review was thorough and included data on every aspect of recruitment, pay and progression. The review found that

> women were earning 81% of men's basic hourly wages, but only 71% once additional allowances were taken into account. Since action was taken, the pay gap has reduced to 13% for total pay – ie women are now earning 87% of men's total hourly pay.
>
> Equal Pay Reviews in Practice, IES for EOC 2005

MEETING THE DUTY TO ELIMINATE HARASSMENT

2.69. Having due regard to the need to eliminate harassment, including sexual harassment, is a legal requirement under the general duty. The duty to have due regard to the need to promote equality of opportunity between men and women is also relevant here as this may help eliminate harassment. A public authority should consider the steps it needs to take to ensure that harassment is prevented across all its activities before it occurs.

2.70. In order to discharge this duty, it is recommended that public authorities develop and regularly review a clear policy for preventing and tackling harassment across all of its functions where relevant. This would include, for example:

- in employment, education and service delivery
- in relation to those not traditionally thought of as receiving a service, such as those who are subject to state powers, for example prisoners or asylum seekers
- in regulatory and enforcement functions
- in management of premises.

2.71. It is recommended that public authorities actively promote the policy to ensure that everyone is aware of and understands it. It is also recommended that public authorities provide training so that their managers and staff are equipped to deal with instances of harassment should they occur.

2.72. Public authorities should also adopt and communicate complaints and investigations procedures for dealing both formally and informally (as appropriate) with harassment, in a supportive manner. In the employment context, it is recommended that procedures for investigating harassment complaints should be linked to grievance and disciplinary procedures and should conform to the accepted standards for disciplinary action in the Acas Code of Practice on Disciplinary and Grievance Procedures.

2.73. Public authorities will need to determine the effectiveness of their policy and procedures. They can do this by monitoring the number of complaints of harassment and their outcome, and by reviewing policies and procedures periodically to ensure they are working effectively and that those who have made complaints are not victimised.

2.74. Where complaints of harassment are upheld, there should be a consistent and proportionate relationship between the severity of the harassment and the penalty imposed on the harasser. In the case of harassment by an employee, this may include disciplinary action and, in severe cases, dismissal. In the case of harassment by service users, tenants, pupils etc, public authorities should ensure that they deal with complaints of harassment by male and female employees consistently to avoid any direct discrimination. Appropriate action may involve warnings as to the consequences of repeated acts of harassment and, in serious cases, the withdrawal of services or the withdrawal of normal services.

2.75. 'Sexual Harassment: Guidance for Managers and Supervisors' explains how to prevent harassment taking place and how to handle complaints. It is available, along with other information and guidance on harassment, on the EOC website www.eoc.org.uk

2.76. A public authority is liable for any acts of harassment carried out by its employees in the course of their employment, or by any other person over whom the public authority has direct control and therefore for whose conduct it could reasonably be held responsible. This is the case, in most circumstances, even where those acts are carried out without either the knowledge or approval of the public authority. Public authorities will have a defence to claims of harassment which has been committed by their employees or agents if they have taken such prior measures as are reasonably practicable to prevent harassment taking place.

2.77. The harassment provisions in the employment and vocational training sections of the SDA do not expressly extend to harassment of employees by someone who is not under the direct control of the employer. An employee who has been subjected to serious harassment, however, which the employer could have prevented but did not, may be entitled to resign and claim constructive unfair dismissal.

CHAPTER 3: HOW TO MEET THE SPECIFIC DUTIES

INTRODUCTION

[4.314]

3.1. All the public authorities listed in Appendix D are subject to the specific duties described in this chapter. Further orders may be made by government from time to time to update the list of authorities.

3.2. The duties set out a framework to assist listed public authorities in planning, delivering and evaluating action to meet the general duty and to report on those activities. At the heart of this framework is the Gender Equality Scheme (the scheme), which is explained below. When developing and implementing the scheme, however, public authorities should bear in mind the scheme is a means of meeting the three elements of the general duty, not an end in itself. When public authorities are being assessed on whether or not they have met the duty, the existence of the scheme will not in itself be enough. They will have to demonstrate what action they have taken and the outcomes they have achieved.

3.3. The duties apply to all listed authorities whatever their size, but the way in which they are implemented should be appropriate to the size of the authority and its functions. A large NHS trust, for example, may have the capacity to undertake a significant change project to implement the duty. A small school, while still obliged to implement the specific duties, will do so on a scale appropriate to its size and resources.

WHAT DO THE SPECIFIC DUTIES REQUIRE PUBLIC AUTHORITIES TO DO?

3.4. The full text of the specific duties Order is set out at Appendix C, but in summary it provides that the public authority should:

- **prepare and publish a Gender Equality Scheme** showing how it intends to fulfil the general and specific duties and setting out its gender equality objectives
- **in preparing a scheme:**
  - **consult employees, service users and others** (including trade unions)
  - **take into account any information it has gathered or considers relevant** as to how its policies and practices affect gender equality in the workplace and in the delivery of its services
  - in formulating its overall gender equality objectives, **consider the need to have objectives to address the causes of any gender pay gap**
- **ensure that the scheme sets out the actions** the authority has taken or intends to take to—
  - gather information on the effect of its policies and practices on men and women, in employment, services and performance of its functions
  - use the information to review the implementation of the scheme objectives
  - assess the impact of its current and future policies and practices on gender equality
  - consult relevant employees, service users and others (including trade unions)
  - ensure implementation of the scheme objectives
- **implement the scheme and their actions for gathering and using information** within three years of publication of the scheme, unless it is unreasonable or impracticable to do so
- **review and revise the scheme** at least every three years
- **report on progress annually**.

3.5. All listed public authorities must publish their schemes no later than 30 April 2007.

3.6. All listed public authorities are required to comply with the same specific duties. This contrasts with the specific duties under the Race Relations Act 1976 (as amended), which have different requirements for different sectors, and the specific duties under the Disability Discrimination Act 1995 (as amended) which have different requirements in relation to information gathering.

PREPARING AND PUBLISHING A GENDER EQUALITY SCHEME

3.7. In order to prepare a scheme identifying gender equality objectives, and setting out the actions it intends to carry out to achieve them, each public authority will have to develop an understanding of the major gender equality issues in its functions. This should be based on a good evidence base and developed through consultation with stakeholders, and the specific duties set out these elements of the process as a legal requirement. Public authorities are then required to commit to a set of priority objectives, selected according to the principles of proportionality and relevance. Public authorities have discretion to decide those priorities themselves, but the priorities which they select should reflect the evidence. The general duty requires public authorities to focus on the issues within their remit which have the greatest importance and impact on gender equality.

3.8. The scheme should be published in a readily accessible format, for example, in a clearly signposted part of the public authority's website. It can be published as part of another published document or within a number of other published documents, for example within the business plan of a public authority or within a general equality scheme. Public authorities will have to ensure, however, that the individual elements of the scheme are easily identifiable, in order to show evidence of meeting the gender duty. This is also recommended in order to assure accountability to stakeholders.

WHAT SHOULD BE IN A GENDER EQUALITY SCHEME AND ACTION PLAN?

3.9. The gender equality scheme is legally required to contain the public authority's overall objectives for meeting the duty (see paragraphs 3.34–3.39) including any pay objectives (paragraphs 3.40–3.52). To demonstrate that the public authority is meeting the duty in full, it is recommended that the scheme should also contain a rationale for the choice of those objectives, based on:

- an overview of the remit and functions of the authority, including functions carried out through partnership and procurement
- the major findings of the information-gathering exercise
- the major findings of the consultation exercise.

3.10. Schemes are legally required to contain information on how the public authority will take action to:

- collect information (paras 3.12–3.23)
- use this information, and any other relevant information, to meet the general and specific duties
- use the information to review the effectiveness of its implementation of the duty and to prepare subsequent schemes (paras 3.22–3.23)
- assess the impact on gender equality of its existing and new policies and practices (paras 3.57–3.74)
- consult relevant employees, service users and others (including trade unions) (paras 3.24–3.33)
- achieve fulfilment of the objectives (paras 3.75–3.78)

3.11. Although not a formal legal requirement, evidence of effective practice which could usefully be included in the scheme might be:

- evidence of commitment from senior leaders
- evidence of the link to the authority's priorities and business plans
- the identification of individuals with clear responsibilities for taking action on the scheme or elements of the scheme
- the allocation of specific budgets, for example, for consultation or information gathering
- measurable and time bound indicators of progress towards the objectives
- measures to strengthen the capacity of the authority to meet the duty
- separate action plans for individual identifiable departments
- details of how impact assessment will be incorporated into the authority's decision-making process
- details of how the public authority will ensure the duty is met in procurement and partnerships.

GATHERING AND USING INFORMATION

3.12. In order to understand which of its functions have the greatest relevance to gender equality, a public authority will need to gather and use information on how women and men are affected by its activities. A public authority may already have this information, disaggregated by gender. This information will have a crucial role in helping the public authority to determine its gender equality priorities, conduct effective gender impact assessments of policies and practices, and monitor progress towards its gender equality objectives. Information can be both quantitative and qualitative, and from a variety of sources.

3.13. The specific duties require each listed public authority to gather information on the effect of its policies and practices on men and women, and in particular:

- the extent to which they promote equality between male and female staff
- the extent to which the services it provides and the functions it performs take account of the needs of women and men.

3.14. Policies and practices are very broad terms, and cover every aspect of a public authority's activities and functions.

3.15. The specific duties also require the public authority to take into account any other information which it considers relevant. This might include, for example, the national level gender equality policies and documents which relate to their business – for example, Public Service Agreements, national policy frameworks in their sector, or existing research which indicates the major gender issues in their area of work.

3.16. In order to meet the gender equality duty, public authorities will have to set up systems, or adapt existing systems, to ensure they obtain and monitor the relevant information. In many cases this should involve disaggregating existing information; in some cases this may require the collection of new information. Information should be collected on the gender profile of service users, on staff, and on any other people, such as tenants, who may be affected by decision-making and policy functions.

3.17. Information may also need to be collected to compare the profile of potential staff or service users with actual staff or service users. For example, to analyse the gender aspects of an employment scheme, a public authority would have to compare the percentage of women in the scheme with the pool of economically inactive or unemployed women relative to men.

3.18. Setting up these systems or adapting existing systems may be a significant task initially, in order to develop the evidence base for the initial scheme. It will, however, have major benefits in improving the performance management of the organisation overall. It is recommended that public authorities ensure their systems allow them to cross-reference information by ethnicity, disability, age and other categories, so that there is evidence of any issues for different groups of women and men.

3.19. Public authorities which do not already have data might look at collecting information in the following areas:

- gender differences in service use – needs, expectations, barriers, satisfaction rates, outcomes
- balance of women and men in key decision-making bodies, including public appointments
- the gender profile of their staff, including analysis of patterns for part-time staff and those with caring responsibilities
- the extent and causes of the gender pay gap in the authority for full-time and part-time staff – including data on pay systems, the impact of caring responsibilities and occupational segregation (see paras 3.40–3.56)
- the prevalence of harassment and sexual harassment of staff and service users, the number of formal complaints and the outcome of complaints
- return rates of women on maternity leave and whether they are returning to jobs at the same level of responsibility and pay
- issues and barriers affecting transsexual staff and potential staff.

3.20. Quantitative monitoring is likely to be difficult in relation to transsexual staff or job applicants because of very low numbers and privacy concerns. Staff and job applicants should be told why the information is being collected and what it will be used for and be assured of confidentiality and genuine anonymity. They should also be told that they are under no obligation to give such information. Further advice can be sought from Acas and transsexual groups.

3.21. Quantitative data can be supplemented by qualitative information from consultation with stakeholders, including voluntary sector groups and trade unions, and from focus groups or other sources.

3.22. The duty is not just about collecting information, however, but analysing and using it, so that public authorities know where they are being successful and where they need to take action. For example, information may indicate that very few men are accessing flexible working policies, relative to the proportion of women staff who do so, so a public authority may want to take steps to support more men to work on a flexible basis.

3.23. Once enough information has been collected to give a picture of gender equality priorities across the public authority, priority indicators in key areas should be identified for annual monitoring to allow the public authority to meet the specific duty to review progress.

> Using data to develop the Women's Offending Reduction Programme – Home Office
>
> Women make up 6% of the prison population and just one in five of known offenders[1] and are therefore often forgotten in debates around criminal justice policy. However, between 1992 and 2002 the male prison population increased by 50%, while the female prison population increased by 173%.[2] 71% of women sentenced to prison in 2002 received a sentence of less than 12 months.[3] 55% of women in prison have at least one child under 16.[4] In 1993 there was one female suicide in custody, in 2003 there were 14.[5] Half of women in prison have experienced domestic violence compared with 25% of the female population.[6] Women are twice as likely as men to have received help for mental or emotional problems in the twelve months prior to custody and more likely to have a serious mental illness.[7]
>
> The Women's Offending Reduction Programme seeks to co-ordinate work across government departments and agencies to ensure that policies, services, programmes and other interventions respond more appropriately to the particular needs and characteristics of women offenders. A number of government departments, agencies and organisations are 'stakeholders' in the Programme. By ensuring the delivery of a co-ordinated multi-agency response to women's offending, the Programme seeks to tackle the variety of factors which can affect why women offend, including poor housing, mental health problems, substance misuse, abuse, child care, education and employment.
>
> By gathering data on the patterns and trends in women's offending, sentencing and the characteristics of women offenders, they are better able to identify issues and to track the progress of their work. The ultimate measure of success of the Programme will be a reduction in offending by women and fewer women held in custody.

NOTES

1 www.homeoffice.gov.uk/rds/pdfs2/s95women03

2 www.homeoffice.gov.uk/rds/pdfs2/s95women03

3 www.homeoffice.gov.uk/rds/pdfs2/s95women03

4 Social Exclusion Unit Report (July 2002): Reducing Re-offending by Ex-prisoners.

5 www.homeoffice.gov.uk/rds/pdfs2/s95women03

6 Home Office & Prison Service, *Abuse, Interventions and Women in Prison: A Literature Review* (London, Home Office, 2003).

7 Department of Health, *Mainstreaming Gender and Women's Mental Health* (London, Department of Health, 2003).

CONSULTATION

3.24. The specific duties require listed public authorities to consult stakeholders when preparing a scheme. The requirement is to consult employees, service users and others (including trade unions) who appear to the authority to have an interest in the way the authority carries out its functions.

3.25. In addition, the scheme itself must include an outline of the actions which the authority intends to take or has taken in order to consult.

3.26. By consulting stakeholders, public authorities will be able to:

- build up a better picture of the most important gender issues in their work
- gather evidence to use in determining priorities and in the gender impact assessment process
- get feedback on their initial draft objectives
- develop greater ownership and understanding of their gender equality objectives
- improve accountability to their staff, service users and the general public.

3.27. Consultation will be especially important where one sex is under-represented in the formal decision-making processes of the public authority.

3.28. Using the information gathered during consultation will also be beneficial in conducting impact assessments, gathering evidence and monitoring progress. Public authorities may choose to consult stakeholders again at any relevant stages of the implementation or review process, although there is no legal requirement to do so.

3.29. The extent of consultation should be appropriate to the size, remit and resources of the authority and there is no prescribed means of carrying it out. Public authorities are free to adapt their existing processes of public consultation. It is important to remember, however, that the duty is to consult on gender equality. Women and men (and, where appropriate, girls and boys) should both be consulted, but public authorities will have to ensure that the consultation process gives adequate attention to issues of gender equality, and any questions are structured in such a way as to bring out any potential differences in views between women and men, or between groups of women and men.

3.30. It is also important that women and men are enabled to participate fully in a consultation process, in order to get a full picture of their concerns. Some women may be less likely to attend, or to speak out at a traditional public meeting if they do not feel sufficiently confident, if their community discourages women taking up public roles, or if there are language barriers.

3.31. Where one sex has been under-represented or disadvantaged in a policy area, service or employment issue, public authorities may need to make special efforts to encourage participation. For example, women have rarely been involved in decision-making on regeneration. Similarly, men may not have been previously included in discussions on childcare services. There may also be particular barriers to participation where a minority group has experienced multiple disadvantages, for example, on the grounds of ethnicity and sexual orientation. Public authorities may wish to consult such groups in a single-sex or group-specific environment.

3.32. It is recommended that consultation on employment issues with the transsexual community is conducted separately, although they should also be actively encouraged to participate in mainstream consultation processes.

3.33. Voluntary sector organisations, such as women's groups and men's groups, are likely to be useful sources of information through consultation. Public authorities should bear in mind, however, that such organisations may have limited capacity and resources and may need support to develop their capacity to engage with the process.

> Overcoming consultation fatigue
>
> One problem that has been faced in the implementation of positive equality duties in Northern Ireland is 'consultation fatigue', with community and voluntary groups being overloaded with lengthy consultation documents. In its review of the implementation of the duties, the Equality Commission for Northern Ireland (ECNI) stated that there was "consensus that blanket mail shots to everyone on a public authority's consultation list are rarely appropriate and should not be routinely advocated".
>
> One means of tackling 'consultation fatigue' is to ensure that consultation is 'joined-up' within organisations, so that there can be one consultation exercise on related policies with affected groups. The ECNI has also recommended that "a number of public authorities should consolidate consultation exercises where possible on the same, or similar, policies". Health authorities in Northern Ireland undertake a region-wide equality impact assessment (EQIA) timetable so that each policy area is subject to equality impact assessment by all health authorities at the same time. This joined-up approach enables one consultation exercise for each EQIA.

PRIORITISING AND SETTING GENDER EQUALITY OBJECTIVES

3.34. The purpose of producing the scheme is to bring about change. It is therefore important that public authorities focus on achieving outcomes – specific identifiable improvements in policies, in the way services and functions are delivered and in the gender equality outcomes for employees. Focussing on outcomes rather than processes will be of benefit to smaller public authorities, which may not necessarily have the resources to undertake large-scale processes.

3.35. The specific duties require listed public authorities to ensure that their schemes set out overall objectives that the authority has identified for meeting the duty.

3.36. The duty does not prescribe which objectives should be chosen and it is up to the authority to select the priorities for action, in consultation with service users and employees, and taking into account all relevant information.

3.37. In deciding priorities for action, public authorities will also need to consider the resource implications – a major deep-seated inequality may take significant staff and cash resource to correct. It may be, however, that it is so clearly a significant gender inequality issue that not to address it could lay the public authority open to enforcement action by the EOC or CEHR.

3.38. The priorities are intended to cover a three-year period. It will clearly not be possible to address and resolve all issues of gender inequality in that 3 year period, but the requirement to have due regard means that public authorities are expected to begin to address the most significant problems.

3.39. Appropriate weight must be given to the three elements of the duty, as set out in Chapter 2, across all of the authority's functions. In determining priorities, therefore, public authorities must review questions of harassment, discrimination and the promotion of gender equality across employment, service provision, public functions and any other functions. In addition, they must take into account services and functions that are contracted out.

OBJECTIVES TO ADDRESS THE GENDER PAY GAP

3.40. The general duty includes a requirement to have due regard to the need to eliminate discrimination that is unlawful under the EqPA. The specific duties require listed public authorities, when setting their overall objectives, to 'consider the need to have objectives that address the causes of any differences between the pay of men and women that are related to their sex'.

3.41. These requirements, taken together with the specific duty to collect and make use of information on gender equality in the workforce and the duty to assess the impact of policies and practices, mean that listed public authorities have to undertake a process of determining whether their policies and practices are contributing to the causes of the gender pay gap. This should be done in consultation with employees and others, including trade unions.

3.42. The gender pay gap is determined by calculating women's overall average pay as a percentage of men's. The main factors which contribute to this gap are:

- discrimination, including pay discrimination (which is often inadvertent, but nonetheless unlawful)
- the impact of women's disproportionate share of caring responsibilities (which often results in women undertaking part-time work which is often poorly paid and often restricts career continuity and progression)

- the concentration of women in particular occupations ('occupational segregation'), usually characterised by lower levels of pay than in those numerically dominated by men.

3.43. The first step for a public authority considering the need for pay objectives should be to gather information to ascertain if there is a gender pay gap in its workforce. If there is, the authority should gather the information needed to identify the main cause or causes of that gap. These steps will enable it to give proper consideration to whether pay objectives are needed, and help it identify the causes those objectives may need to address. The size of the pay gap and the relative significance of each of the three causes will vary between different public authorities.

3.44. If a public authority fails to demonstrate that it has adequately collected and analysed information to establish whether or not there is a gender pay gap in its workforce, or fails to take action if there is a problem, it risks non-compliance with the duty, and subsequent enforcement action. Public authorities that do not set their own pay systems will still be expected to gather information and take appropriate action on any causes of the gender pay gap within their organisation which remain within their control.

3.45. Public authorities must be able to demonstrate that they have considered the need to have objectives that address the gender pay gap. For this reason, if a public authority does not include such objectives it should give reasons for that decision in its scheme. This might include providing evidence that there is no gender pay gap within its workforce, or within any wider group of women and men who are affected by its functions as an organisation, or that the alternative objectives which it has chosen have greater significance for gender equality. Public authorities should bear in mind, however, that pay discrimination is unlawful, and the general duty requires them to have due regard to the need to eliminate unlawful discrimination.

PAY DISCRIMINATION

3.46. In order to fulfil the general duty to have due regard to the need to eliminate discrimination that is unlawful under the EqPA, a public authority must be able to demonstrate that it has considered the need to take action on pay discrimination.

3.47. The gender equality duty does not require public authorities to undertake equal pay reviews. No specific course of action is prescribed to tackle pay discrimination. The statutory Code of Practice on Equal Pay recommends, however, that the most effective way of establishing whether a public authority's pay policies and pay systems are discriminatory is to undertake an equal pay review.

The fundamental components of an equal pay review are:

- comparing the pay of women and men doing equal work. Here employers need to check for one or more of the following: like work; work rated as equivalent; work of equal value – these checks are the foundation of an equal pay review
- identifying any equal pay gaps, including by differences between part-time and full-time workers' pay
- eliminating those pay gaps that cannot satisfactorily be explained on grounds other than sex.

The Code of Practice on Equal Pay and supporting toolkits are the recommended tools for undertaking this process. These can be found at www.eoc.org.uk

3.48. A public authority that has undertaken a pay review, containing the elements described above, in the preceding four years may not need to repeat it, unless it has undergone significant changes to its workforce, as it should already have evidence of the situation in its organisation and should be taking action.

3.49. Public authorities may also choose to collect pay information across a selected sample of their staff, for example administrators, manual workers, or departments or units such as IT or physiotherapy, to see if women and men carrying out the same jobs or jobs of equal value are receiving equal pay. Given the requirement to consult, any such approach should be discussed with the relevant trade union. Sampling may indicate a problem which suggests the need to proceed to a full pay review.

3.50. If a public authority decides not to undertake a full pay review, it may be appropriate for it to carry out a screening process, for example, to address areas known to pose a high risk of pay discrimination. These will include:

- starting salaries: checking whether women and men who have been recruited to the same jobs or jobs of equal value are being appointed on the same starting salary and whether any patterns are related to sex-based factors
- progression: whether unjustifiably long pay scales are inadvertently discriminating against women (who may be less likely to have continuous service)
- bonus payments: whether bonuses are paid, or higher bonuses are paid, in jobs where men predominate.

3.51. Many public authorities, such as schools, do not set their own pay systems. They are legally liable, however, under the EqPA, for the implementation of those pay systems. Some are likely to find the screening of high-risk factors, as set out above, which they, as employers, have control over, particularly useful in complying with the duty. Schools should ensure that decisions made within the school, which have an impact on an individual's pay (such as the allocation of Teaching and Learning Responsibility payments) are free of discrimination. Where a public authority does not set its own pay system, any pay review of that system would often be more appropriately carried out at a higher level (for example Local Education Authorities for schools).

3.52. Where public authorities do not set their own pay systems, but an authority becomes aware that there are elements in that system which are causing, or risk causing, pay discrimination, it is recommended that the public authority should alert the relevant pay body. The remit of pay review bodies in Great Britain includes a requirement to seek to ensure non-discriminatory pay systems, and to develop systems that support diversity.

CARING RESPONSIBILITIES AND OCCUPATIONAL SEGREGATION

3.53. Public authorities should also gather evidence on the impact of caring responsibilities on their workforces. Based on that evidence and on consultation with employees and trade unions, they should consider whether it is appropriate to set objectives to address any relevant issues. Women are significantly more likely than men to work part-time, often because of childcare and other caring responsibilities. Part-time work in Britain is characterised by particularly low rates of hourly pay and reduced access to promotion and development opportunities. In addition, lack of availability of suitable childcare restricts women's employment choices. Support to female and male employees with childcare responsibilities, through providing more flexible working and training opportunities or childcare provision or subsidy, will also contribute to the promotion of equality of opportunity between women and men.

3.54. Public authorities should also collect evidence on the extent of occupational segregation in their workforces. Based on that evidence and on consultation with employees and trade unions, they should consider whether it is appropriate to set objectives to address it. Employers who have strongly segregated workforces may be at higher risk of having equal pay claims taken against them. In a highly segregated workforce it can be easy for pay arrangements to evolve in which women are paid less than men when they are doing work of equal value, giving rise to equal pay tribunal claims.

3.55. Public authorities can check which issues are relevant to any gender pay gap in their organisation by:

- monitoring where women and men work in their organisation, what hours they work and at what grade. This will map any segregation by seniority and by types of work and will alert public authorities to the possible impact of caring responsibilities.
- using any annual staff monitoring exercise to ask staff if they have caring responsibilities, and whether this is for children or for older people.

CLOSING THE GENDER PAY GAP WITHIN THE WIDER REMIT OF A PUBLIC AUTHORITY

3.56. In addition to its functions as an employer, a public authority may have functions which have the potential to address the gender pay gap in a wider policy sense. This would be the case, for example, for a Regional Development Agency, a Learning and Skills Council or a local authority in its education functions. If this is the case, the public authority should also be considering whether it can address the causes of the gender pay gap within that wider remit where appropriate. This might include reviewing the high-level policy priorities of the authority overall, for example setting regional economic objectives that address the under-utilisation of the skills of part-time women workers. It might also include specific measures such as improving school careers advice so that boys and girls consider a wider range of career options, training women to fill areas of skills shortage in traditionally male-dominated areas and vice versa, or providing childcare support for male and female students in vocational training.

3.57–3.74. (*Outside the scope of this work.*)

IMPLEMENTING THE SCHEME

3.75. Listed public authorities are expected, within the three year period, to implement:

- their actions for gathering and using information
- the objectives in their scheme.

3.76. If a public authority does not comply with any specific duty imposed by the Order, including implementing the elements indicated above, the EOC or CEHR may issue a compliance notice (see Chapter 4 for further information about enforcement).

3.77. The public authority will not be under an obligation to implement their actions for gathering or using information or to implement the scheme objectives if, in all the circumstances of the case, it would be unreasonable or impracticable for it to do so. The words 'unreasonable' and 'impracticable' are intended to relate to particular and unforeseen circumstances. For example:

- where there are particular difficulties with implementing objectives in the scheme but these difficulties could not have been foreseen, then it is likely to be unreasonable to have to implement them
- where costs associated with an action unexpectedly escalate so as to be out of proportion to the duty, then it is unlikely to be practicable to implement the duty.

3.78. It is important, however, that public authorities consider other solutions where it is not reasonable or practicable for them to carry out a particular part of the scheme. Once barriers to equality have been identified, an authority will need to address them, considering alternative methods of overcoming them if those proposed originally are not practicable or reasonable.

ANNUAL REPORTS

3.79. Listed public authorities must take such steps as are reasonably practicable to publish annually a report, summarising the actions they have taken to implement their scheme objectives. This report can be published as a separate document or within another published document, for example, the public authority's main annual report.

REVIEWING AND REVISING THE SCHEME

3.80. Listed public authorities have an obligation to review and revise the scheme every three years. It is recommended that this should involve a review of progress to date and of the appropriateness of the previous scheme objectives, with a view to continuous improvement in the implementation of the duty. Evidence for this process would include the information gathered to date, the results of impact assessments, and any feedback from stakeholders on the effectiveness of the preceding scheme.

3.81. In preparing the new scheme, public authorities are required to collect and make use of information, and to consult stakeholders as before. Stakeholders can also usefully be involved in the review of the previous scheme, although this is not a legal requirement.

(*Chapters 4, 5, 6 omitted: outside the scope of this work.*)

APPENDIX A: WHAT IS THE DEFINITION OF A PUBLIC AUTHORITY FOR THE PURPOSES OF THE GENERAL DUTY?

[4.315]
For the purposes of the gender duty, public authorities are bodies whose functions are those of a public nature. The most obvious examples of this are government departments, local authorities, the police and the armed forces. They will generally possess special powers, be democratically accountable, be publicly funded in whole or in part, be under an obligation to act only in the public interest and have a statutory constitution. These bodies are sometimes referred to as 'pure public authorities'. The gender duty will therefore apply for example to:

- Ministers, government departments and executive agencies (such as the Home Office and its executive agencies, including the Prison Service, and the Immigration and Nationality Directorate).
- The National Assembly for Wales.
- Army, Navy and Air Forces of the Crown (subject to a limited exception relating to work with the Government Communications Headquarters).
- Local government including local authorities, fire authorities, local probation boards, regional development agencies, magistrates courts committees, passenger transport executives and licensing boards.
- Governing bodies of further and higher education institutions, colleges and universities.
- Governing bodies of educational establishments maintained by local education authorities (including schools).
- The National Health Service including NHS Trusts, Health Authorities and primary care trusts, Local Health Boards (Wales).
- Police, including Chief Officers of Police, police authorities and the Independent Police Complaints Commission.
- Inspection and audit agencies such as the National Audit Office, Wales Audit Office, Audit Commissions, Her Majesty's Inspectorate of Constabulary (HMIC), the Healthcare Commission, the Health and Safety Executive.
- Some publicly-funded cultural bodies or institutions such as Sports Councils and Big Lottery Fund.
- Other bodies such as the Criminal Injuries Compensation Authority, the Crown Prosecution Service, Courts and tribunals (though not for judicial acts), Prison Boards of Visitors, the Children and Family Court Advisory and Support Service, the Community Development Foundation, Visiting Committees for Immigration Detention Centres, the Youth Justice Board for England and Wales, the Sentencing Advisory Panel.

This is not an exhaustive list.

Equivalent public authorities in Scotland are also covered by the general duty. Further detail is provided in the Scottish Code of Practice.

PRIVATE BODIES CARRYING OUT PUBLIC FUNCTIONS

The Equality Act 2006 is designed to ensure that a wide number of authorities are subject to the gender duty in relation to the performance of public functions. 'Public authority' therefore includes any person who has functions of a public nature. This will include private bodies or voluntary organisations who are carrying out public functions on behalf of a public authority. An organisation will be exercising a public function where it is in effect exercising a function which would otherwise be exercised by the state – and where individuals have to rely upon that person for the exercise of that function. These bodies are sometimes referred to as 'functional public bodies'. Whether or not an organisation is exercising a function of a public nature will ultimately be a matter for the courts. As the law presently stands, a private body may be held to be performing public functions and thus subject to the gender equality duty in relation to those functions if:

- it is publicly funded
- it is exercising powers of a public nature directly assigned to it by statute; or
- it is taking the place of central or local government
- it is providing a public service
- its structures and work are closely linked with the delegating or contracting-out state body
- there is a close relationship between the private body and any public authority.

Additional factors which may be relevant in determining whether or not a body is carrying out a function of a public nature include:

- the extent to which the private body is supervised by a state regulatory body
- the fact of supervision by a state regulatory body.

For example, the following bodies are likely to be deemed to be performing 'functions of a public nature' in relation to their public functions, and therefore subject to the gender equality duty in relation to those functions:

- the privatised utilities

- private security firms managing contracted-out prisons
- GPs when providing services under contract to a Primary Care Trust.

In relation to a particular act, a person is not a public authority if the nature of the act is private (for example, a private company running a prison will not be covered by the duty in relation to its private activities such as providing security guards for supermarkets).

A pure public authority contracting out services will always remain subject to the duty. It is possible that a 'pure' public authority which is subject to the duty could also be contracting out services to a 'functional' public authority (ie a private organisation providing a service of a public nature). In this case, both bodies will be subject to the duty in their own right. If there is a breach of the general duty, the legal responsibility for this could rest, depending on the circumstances, with either body. Actual responsibility would depend on the act which is the subject of the complaint, who was responsible for it and who was in breach of the general duty in respect of it. For example, a private prison might close down its childcare facilities for use by visitors, contrary to the terms of its contract with the Home Office. Whilst both the prison and the Home Office could be challenged in judicial review proceedings, the likelihood is that the Home Office would establish they had discharged their duty if they had included a requirement for childcare facilities in the contractual specifications. The private prison would be more likely to have difficulty in establishing that it had discharged the duty.

It is recommended that those authorities who may be carrying out functions of a public nature, but who are unsure whether they fall within the definition of a 'public authority' should safeguard their position by ensuring that they comply with the general duty in relation to those functions. It may also be advisable to seek legal advice on whether or not the gender equality duty applies in such a situation.

APPENDIX B: PUBLIC BODIES AND FUNCTIONS WHICH ARE EXEMPT FROM THE GENDER DUTY

[4.316]

S76A(3) SDA 1975

The Act currently exempts the following public authorities from the gender duty:

- both Houses of Parliament
- the Scottish Parliament
- the General Synod of the Church of England
- the Security Service
- the Secret Intelligence Service
- the Government Communications Headquarters
- a part of the armed forces of the Crown which is, in accordance with a requirement of the Secretary of State, assisting the Government Communications Headquarters, or
- a person specified by order of the Secretary of State.

S76A(4) SDA 1975

In addition there are certain functions of public authorities which the Act excludes from being subject to the duty. The general duty does not apply to the exercise of:

- a function in connection with proceedings in the House of Commons or the House of Lords
- a function in connection with proceedings in the Scottish Parliament (other than a function of the Scottish Parliamentary Corporate Body)
- a judicial function (whether in connection with a court or tribunal)
- a function exercised on behalf of or on the instructions of a person exercising a judicial function (whether in connection with a court or a tribunal)
- a function specified by order of the Secretary of State.

(*Appendices C–G omitted: outside the scope of this work.*)

I. CABINET OFFICE

CODE OF PRACTICE ON THE ENGLISH LANGUAGE REQUIREMENTS FOR PUBLIC SECTOR WORKERS

Part 7 of the Immigration Act 2016 (November 2016)

[4.317]

NOTES

This Code of Practice was issued by the Minister for the Cabinet Office and Paymaster General under the Immigration Act 2016, s 80(1). Under s 77(1) of 2016 Act, a public authority must ensure that each person who works for the public authority in a customer-facing role speaks fluent English. Under section 77(2) of that Act, in determining how to comply with this duty a public authority must have regard to the Code of Practice issued under s 80(1). This Code was brought into force on 22 December 2016 by the Code of Practice (English Language Requirements for Public Sector Workers) Regulations 2016, SI 2016/1157. Notes are as in the original version.

CONTENTS

FOREWORD

[4.318]

The quality of public services in the UK is amongst the finest in the world and everyone in society wants our public services in the UK to be accessible and delivered to the highest standards possible.

To serve the public it is vital that those working in public-facing roles can communicate in English, or in Wales, English or Welsh, fluently; be it with patients in hospitals, with students in schools, or with members of the public receiving local authority services.

Part 7 of the Immigration Act 2016 delivers on our manifesto commitment to help ensure the safe and high quality delivery of public services by ensuring that they are provided to an appropriate standard of fluency in English, or in Wales, English or Welsh.

This Code supports public authorities to meet their obligations under Part 7 of the Immigration Act 2016. The Code sets out considerations public authorities will need to take into account when deciding how to comply with this new legal duty, without creating more red tape in the recruitment of public sector staff. The intention is clear: a common sense approach to meeting the public's reasonable expectation to be able to communicate in English, or in Wales, English or Welsh, when accessing public services.

This Code should be simple to comply with: nothing is required of anyone already fluent in English. The aim is to bring standards up to the best.

Part 7 of the Immigration Act 2016 is in force from 21st November and so relevant employers need to ensure that they comply with the duty set out in the legislation from that date. This Code is to be issued on 29th November 2016 and then promptly brought into force by Regulations under the Act.

Rt Hon Ben Gummer MP

Minister for the Cabinet Office and Paymaster General

USING THE CODE OF PRACTICE

STATUS OF THE CODE

[4.319]

The relevant Minister is required to issue a Code under Part 7 of the Immigration Act 2016 for the purposes of section 80 of that Act. It is a statutory Code. This means it has been prepared by the relevant Minister and s/he has laid a draft of it before Parliament. The Code contains practical guidance on the standards and practices expected of public authorities when complying with their legal duty under the Act.

This Code is not intended to prescribe the process for every type of public-facing[1] role and it is not a definitive statement of the law. However, it provides principles and examples which public authorities can consider when fulfilling their legal duties and obligations.

TO WHOM THIS CODE APPLIES

This Code is aimed at public authorities defined in Part 7 of the Immigration Act 2016. It aims to assist public authorities in meeting their statutory duty under Part 7 of the Immigration Act 2016.

HOW TO USE THE CODE

Public authorities must have regard to this Code when fulfilling their statutory duty under Part 7 of the Immigration Act 2016. Further references to that duty in this Code will be to the "fluency duty". The Code aims to provide assistance to public authorities to determine the necessary standard of spoken English (or English or Welsh in Wales) to be met by their public-facing staff, the appropriate complaints procedure to follow should a member of the public consider that the required standard has not been met and the appropriate forms of remedial action which may be taken if a member of staff falls below the standard required.

Although all staff in public-facing roles will be required to speak English (or Welsh) to the necessary standard, the fluency duty does not require public authorities to ensure that their public-facing staff speak only in English or Welsh to communicate with members of the public. Public authorities are free to provide guidance to their public-facing staff that they may where appropriate, make use of any language skills they have to communicate with citizens who speak other languages.

This Code is made up of five sections:

- **Section 1** defines the scope of the Code.
- **Section 2** explains the appropriate ways in which public authorities can set a standard of spoken English (or Welsh) for public-facing roles.
- **Section 3** provides options for remedial action where staff do not meet the necessary standard of spoken English (or Welsh).
- **Section 4** outlines the complaints procedure that must be followed in respect of complaints raised by a member of the public under the fluency duty.
- **Section 5** provides guidance on compliance with other legal obligations.

Examples in the Code

Examples included in this Code are intended simply to illustrate the principles and concepts used in the legislation and should be read in that light.

Territorial Extent

The Code applies to all public authorities who are subject to the fluency duty. This is all public authorities in England and in relation to Scotland, Wales and Northern Ireland public authorities exercising functions relating to non-devolved matters.

Non-devolved matters means:

- reserved matters in Scotland, as defined by the Scotland Act 1998;
- matters which are outside the legislative competence of the National Assembly for Wales, as defined by the Government of Wales Act 2006; and
- excepted matters in Northern Ireland, as defined by the Northern Ireland Act 1998.

In Scotland, Wales and Northern Ireland certain public authorities will hold a dual function and deal with both devolved and non-devolved matters. Public authorities must comply with the fluency duty and take the Code of Practice into account in respect of all staff in public-facing roles dealing with relevant non-devolved functions, such as equality and standards officers.

Public authorities exercising functions in Wales must ensure that someone working for them in a public-facing role dealing with non-devolved matters speaks fluent English or Welsh and comply also with the requirements of language schemes under the Welsh Language Act 1993 and/or the standards stipulated by the Welsh Language (Wales) Measure 2011.

NOTES

[1] In this Code, a public sector worker is determined to be 'public-facing' if as a regular and intrinsic part of their role, they are required to speak to members of the public in English, or in Wales in English or Welsh. This is described in Part 7 of the Act as a 'customer-facing role' and defined in section 77(7) of the Act.

SECTION 1: INTRODUCTION

SCOPE OF THE CODE

Public Authorities

[4.320]

1.1. This Code applies to all public authorities defined in section 78 of the Immigration Act 2016, as bodies which carry out functions of a public nature. This includes central government departments, non-departmental public bodies, councils and other local government bodies, NHS bodies, state-funded schools, the police and the armed forces, and public corporations.

1.2. This Code does not apply to the security and intelligence agencies or the Government Communications Headquarters.

1.3. If bodies are uncertain as to whether they carry out functions of a public nature the following factors should be considered:

- **undertaking the responsibilities of central or local government** - the extent to which the organisation has assumed responsibility for the function in question;
- **public Perception** - the nature and extent of the public perception as to whether the function in question is public rather than private;

- **exercising statutory powers** - the nature and extent of any statutory power or duty in relation to the function in question, or whether the function involves or may involve the use of statutory powers;
- **publicly funded** - the extent to which the state makes payment for the function in question.

1.4. The duty will not initially apply to voluntary sector or private sector providers of public services. However, Part 7 of the Immigration Act 2016 gives a power to extend the duty to these sectors at a later date.

Workers

1.5. Public authorities are subject to the fluency duty and should have regard to the guidance in this Code in relation to all of their staff who work in public-facing roles including permanent and fixed-term employees, apprentices, self-employed contractors, agency temps, police officers and service personnel.[1]

1.6. For a public sector worker whose first language is a signed language and who is in a public-facing role, the fluency duty will be met by the provision of a sign language interpreter who speaks English or Welsh to the necessary standard of fluency for that role.

1.7. The fluency duty does not extend to workers employed directly by a private or voluntary sector provider of a public service, or whose work is carried out mainly or wholly outside the UK.

Members of the Public

1.8. 'Members of the public' should be given its usual dictionary meaning as members of the general population. Public authorities may use other terminology to describe a person using, interacting or receiving a service such as customer, patient or client.

Public-facing Roles

1.9. Members of staff who, as a regular and intrinsic part of their role, are required to speak to members of the public in English or Welsh are considered as working in a public-facing role. Public-facing roles would include, but are not limited to the following illustrative examples:

- ***A work coach directly employed by the Department of Work and Pensions*** *would be viewed as operating in a public-facing role, as s/he will have face-to-face discussions with members of the public who are accessing the service on a daily basis.*
- ***A local government employee working in customer service****, receiving calls and fielding queries from members of the public would be viewed as operating in a public-facing role, as they will have regular telephone and face-to-face conversations with the public.*
- ***A teaching assistant*** *required to communicate with pupils to support their learning, would be viewed as operating in a public-facing role.*

1.10. As shown in these examples, both face-to-face and telephone conversations bring a role within the scope of the fluency duty. The degree of interaction with the public needs to be regular and planned to be an intrinsic part of the job role, as defined in a job description or in clear occupational goals.

1.11. Members of staff who occasionally speak to the public as they carry out their duties are not considered to be working in public-facing roles as discussions with the public are not a regular or intrinsic part of their role. Such roles would be outside the scope of the duty and would include but are not limited to the following illustrative examples:

- ***A local authority employed street cleaner*** *would not be viewed as working in a public-facing role as their main duties do not require regular interaction with members of the public.*
- ***A clerical officer*** *or* ***IT user technician*** *providing internal support within an organisation would not be viewed as working in a public-facing role as they are not required to communicate with members of the public over the telephone or face-to-face on a regular basis.*

1.12. When determining whether a role is public-facing or not, employers should consider the following aspects of the work involved:

- is there a business need for interaction with the public;
- what is the frequency and form of this interaction;
- what is the level of service quality and responsiveness expected by the public;
- what is the proportion of the role which would require spoken interaction with members of the public;
- what is the nature of the role; and
- is English or Welsh language the primary language required for the role?

1.13. For example, taking these considerations into account, the fluency duty is unlikely to apply to members of staff whose role involves performing content or editorial functions for a public service broadcaster, such as journalists, programme-making roles or broadcast output. The nature of these roles may require interaction with members of the public, but the extent, frequency and form of interaction with the public either face-to-face or by telephone is likely to be limited and thus not an intrinsic part for the effective performance of the role.

SECTION 2: SETTING A STANDARD

[4.321]

2.1. This section of the Code is about setting the necessary standard of fluent English or Welsh required for a public-facing role in a public authority to which this Code applies.

2.2. Public authorities must ensure that members of staff in such roles, whatever their nationality or origins, are able to speak fluent English or Welsh. This means that they must have a command of spoken

English or Welsh which is sufficient to enable the effective performance of their role. The fluency duty applies in respect of existing staff as well as to new recruits.

DECIDING ON THE STANDARD

2.3. Setting the necessary standard of English or Welsh spoken language proficiency will depend on the type of public-facing role. Each public authority must carefully consider the nature and extent of the spoken communication which is necessary for effective performance. The following factors may be relevant when considering the standard required:

- the frequency of spoken interaction;
- the topic of spoken interaction;
- whether the communication is likely to include technical, profession-specific or specialist vocabulary;
- the typical duration of spoken interaction;
- whether the communication is repeated in or supplemented by, written material provided to members of the public; and
- the significance of the spoken interaction for service delivery.

2.4. Some public-facing roles of public authorities are already subject to a language standard. It is not anticipated that public authorities will need to impose a higher standard in fulfilling the fluency duty than already required for such roles. For example:

- Teachers in local authority maintained schools must be appraised annually against the Teachers Standards. One of the Standards states that teachers must:

  "Demonstrate an understanding of and take responsibility for promoting high standards of literacy, articulacy and the correct use of standard English, whatever the teacher's specialist subject."
- The General Medical Council core guidance, Good Medical Practice (2013) states:

  "All doctors who practise medicine in the UK must have the necessary knowledge of English language to provide a good standard of practice and care in the UK."

2.5. A standard specification of English speaking ability could include:

"An ability to fulfil all spoken aspects of the role with confidence through the medium of English or (in public functions in Wales) Welsh."

2.6. The level of fluency required must however be matched to the demands of the role in question to ensure a proportionate approach to the fluency duty.

Level of Language Proficiency

2.7. Employers must satisfy themselves that an individual has the necessary level of fluency appropriate for the role they will be undertaking, whether an existing or a potential new member of staff.

2.8. Fluency relates to a person's language proficiency and their ability to speak with confidence and accuracy, using accurate sentence structures and vocabulary. In the context of a public-facing role, a person should be able to choose the right kind of vocabulary for the situation at hand without a great deal of hesitation. They should listen to the member of the public and understand their needs. They should tailor their approach to each conversation appropriate to the member of the public, responding clearly with fine shades of meaning, even in complex situations. The Common European Framework of Reference for Languages (CEFR) provides a useful descriptor of fluency levels, a summary extract is referenced at 2.18 below.

2.9. Public authorities may consider using descriptors to explain to candidates the necessary level of fluency required for the role when recruiting, such as:

The ability to converse at ease with members of the public and provide advice in accurate spoken English is essential for the post.

2.10. The Welsh Language Commissioner's guidance for workplace assessments describes spoken fluent Welsh as:

'able to conduct a conversation and answer questions, for an extended period of time where necessary.'

2.11. Fluency does not relate to regional or international accents, dialects, speech impediments or the tone of conversations.

Language Qualifications and Tests

2.12. Where a particular standard of spoken language ability has been legitimately set as an essential requirement for the role, applicants may need to be assessed on their English or Welsh-speaking ability, either through a formal test or as part of the interview process as commonly used to assess communicative competence. However, it is not envisaged that existing members of staff will all need to be tested. Where staff or job applicants are clearly fluent to the necessary standard for the role in question, no further action is necessary.

2.13. Public authorities should be prepared to accept a range of evidence of spoken English or Welsh language ability. There are a number of ways a member of staff or job applicant could demonstrate their fluency, including, but not limited to:

- competently answering interview questions in English or Welsh;
- possessing a relevant qualification for the role attained as part of education in the UK or fully taught in English or Welsh by a recognised institution abroad;[2] or

- passing an English or Welsh spoken language competency test or possessing a relevant spoken English or Welsh qualification at CEFR Level B1 or above, taught in English or Welsh by a recognised institution abroad (and from September 2017 this includes Welsh second language GCSE).[3]

2.14. When the fluency duty is met by the provision of a sign language interpreter, the interpreter should be registered with the National Registers of Communication Professionals working with Deaf and Deaf blind People (NRCPD). Registration will satisfy employers that the level of language proficiency will be met, as NRCPD Registrants will be highly skilled in a signed language like BSL, ISL or ASL and hold a second language that can be another signed language or a spoken language. One of those languages must be native to the UK and Ireland. If it is impossible, after a determined effort, to engage an NRCPD Registrant, employers must make sure the communication and language professional holds at least the qualification(s) required for NRCPD registration.[4]

2.15. Public authorities can, but are not required to, specify a minimum spoken English or Welsh qualification if they determine this is appropriate for a public-facing role. The specified level must not be below the CEFR Level B1. A British General Qualification may denote a particular standard of language ability but it would not be acceptable evidence as a qualification of spoken fluency, because spoken English is not part of the overall assessment of British qualifications. Although some elements of spoken English will be assessed as part of GCSE English from 2017[5] onwards, this is still not a generally recognised spoken language qualification or test.

2.16. The UK National Academic Recognition Information Centre[6] (UK NARIC) provides information and advice about how qualifications and skills from overseas compare to the UK Regulated Qualification Framework including English language tests. Applicants may provide a letter of comparability from UK NARIC for public authorities to use in the selection process.

2.17. The Common European Framework of Reference for Languages[7] (CEFR) was put together by the Council of Europe as a way of standardising the levels of language tests and qualifications across national and regional languages. It provides a good reference point for authorities by describing the levels of spoken interaction and fluency, with a wide-range of available information and guidance for setting standards. It is very widely used internationally and language exams are often mapped to the CEFR Levels.

2.18. The table below provides a useful summary extracted from the CEFR levels[8] of fluency:

CEFR Certificate	Description	Linguistic Fluency
B1	Threshold or intermediate	• Can exploit a wide range of simple language flexibly to express much of what he/she wants. • Can keep going comprehensibly, even though pausing for grammatical and lexical planning and repair is very evident, especially in longer stretches of free production.
B2	Vantage or upper intermediate	• Can adjust to the changes of direction, style and emphasis normally found in conversation. • Can produce stretches of language with a fairly even tempo; although he/she can be hesitant as he or she searches for patterns and expressions, there are few noticeably long pauses.
C1	Effective operational proficiency or advanced	• Can express him/herself fluently and spontaneously, almost effortlessly. Only a conceptually difficult subject can hinder a natural, smooth flow of language.
C2	Mastery or proficiency	• Can express him/herself spontaneously at length with a natural conversational flow, avoiding or backtracking around any difficulty so smoothly that the person with whom they are conversing is hardly aware of it.

2.19. There are a range of external assessment tools available to determine English language competency. English language courses and tests examples include, but are not limited to:

- International Speaking and Listening (IESOL) Diploma: City and Guilds
- International English Language Testing System (IELTS): Cambridge English Language Assessment
- EIKEN test in Practical English Proficiency: The Society for Testing English Proficiency (STEP)
- Europass – self assessment language passport: Council of Europe.

2.20. Some workforce groups are already subject to specific language standards that require assessment or qualifications and these are likely to be sufficient evidence of the necessary standard to fulfil the fluency duty for their role:

Health

Many of the statutory health regulatory bodies have adopted the use of IELTS to assess workers for the health care setting. The overall IELTS English language test score of 7.0 has been set, this is the equivalent of C1 of the Common European Framework for Reference of Languages.

2.21. The Home Office sets language requirements as a condition of granting immigration status in some cases. Individuals from outside the EEA who make an immigration application may need to provide evidence that they have passed an appropriate language test listed by the Home Office.[9] Whilst these are not tailored to employment, public authorities may wish to have regard to such tests when determining whether an individual meets the required standard for a particular public-facing role. However, employers will need to satisfy themselves independently that members of staff or prospective employees have the necessary level of fluency for the role.

POLICIES AND PRACTICES

2.22. Each public sector organisation will need to review HR policies and practices to ensure that they reflect the fluency duty as well as comply with existing legislation. In order to fulfil the fluency duty public authorities should consider if it is appropriate to:

- make all public-facing members of staff aware of this new duty and explain the possible actions which may be taken if their proficiency in spoken English or Welsh is found to be insufficient;
- ensure existing selection and appointment practices facilitate compliance with the fluency duty and inform those responsible for evaluating candidates of the spoken language requirements for the role in question in each case;
- stipulate in contracts of employment the standard of fluent English or Welsh required for the role;
- ensure that their recruitment processes do not contravene the Equality Act 2010; all job applicants must be treated in the same way at each stage of their recruitment process (save for any reasonable adjustments required for disabled applicants);
- make clear in adverts and job descriptions the necessary standard of spoken English or Welsh required for the sufficient performance of the public-facing role;
- ensure consistency when advertising for similar types of public-facing roles; and
- ensure those responsible for evaluating candidates understand the spoken language requirements for the role. Interview panel members should be provided with an objective method of evaluating candidates against clear criteria set out in the role specification.

2.23. Public authorities in Wales should be mindful that their selection and appointment policies and practices will also need to comply with the Welsh Language Act 1993 and/or the Welsh Language (Wales) Measure 2011.

Agency workers

2.24. Agency staff are engaged to work for public authorities under the terms of a contract between the public authority and an employment agency. For public-facing roles the instructions of public authorities to employment agencies should include reference to the standard of spoken English or Welsh required, which will help ensure that the employment agency only supplies candidates who meet the necessary standard. This can be integrated into the service level agreement.

2.25. The selection of agency workers can be undertaken under pressure of time and without the degree of formal assessment applied to the recruitment of employees. However, public authorities must ensure that included in the selection process for agency workers is a specific assessment of their ability to speak English or Welsh to the necessary standard required for the public-facing role. No higher or lower standard of spoken English or Welsh should be applied to agency workers than to employees of the public authority working in an equivalent role.

NOTES

2 Recognised institutions:https://www.gov.uk/check-a-university-is-officially-recognised/overview

3 http://qualificationswales.org/news/update-gcses/?lang=en

4 http://www.nrcpd.org.uk/training

5 https://www.gov.uk/government/uploads/system/uploads/attachment_data/file/432097/2015-06-04-assessment-of-spoken-language-in-the-new-gcse-english-language.pdf

6 https://www.naric.org.uk/naric/

7 http://www.coe.int/lang-cefr

8 http://www.coe.int/t/dg4/education/elp/elp-reg/Source/Key_reference/Overview_CEFRscales_EN.pdf

9 https://www.gov.uk/government/publications/guidance-on-applying-for-uk-visa-approved-english-language-tests

SECTION 3: REMEDIAL ACTION

[4.322]

3.1. This section of the Code explains the actions which may be taken by a public authority where a person who works in a public-facing role does not meet the necessary standard of spoken English or Welsh. This may become apparent because of a complaint received from a member of the public or as a result of performance management.

3.2. It is the responsibility of the public authority to implement measures to support members of staff in public-facing roles who are found to not demonstrate the necessary standard of spoken English or Welsh fluency.

TRAINING

3.3. Public authorities should consider providing training or re-training to support their staff to meet the requirements of the fluency duty. Suitable training courses or qualifications determined by the organisation must reflect the necessary standard of fluent English or Welsh required. The interventions must give the member of staff the opportunity to meet the necessary standard within a reasonable period. Where appropriate, public authorities should meet the cost of training and enable members of staff to undertake training during their working hours. Staff already clearly fluent should not need training however, managers may consider supporting those who have themselves identified learning needs, as part of regular learning and development practices.

3.4. Public authorities in Wales are already required to comply with any standards specified in accordance with the Welsh Language (Wales) Measure 2011 in planning for and training its workforce. It is therefore likely that such authorities will already have provisions in place to support staff to meet the necessary standard of fluent Welsh required for any public-facing role.

3.5. Public authorities should consider individual learning and development needs to determine which aspects of spoken communicative competence needs to be addressed and the nature of any training should, if possible, be agreed with the member of staff.

3.6. There are many resources and means of providing training and support for employees to develop their spoken language proficiency to the necessary level, such as:

- listening to language podcasts;
- mobile language applications;
- providing an internal mentor or coach;
- online resources:
  - communities – supports interaction and practice of language through conversation, study and social exchange with others;
  - self-study and tutoring – these often offer individual study plans and access to interactive study material and support from qualified teachers;
  - courses and vocabulary training – there are many free courses and on-line resources available, for example from the British Council[10] or the BBC;
- interactive language programmes; and
- more traditional language classes are available in a number of community venues and educational institutions.

3.7. One of the best ways to improve language skills is to converse with native speakers. One-to-one support with someone who understands the context of the role is likely to help individuals currently operating in the workplace more than a generic English or Welsh language class.

RE-DEPLOYMENT

3.8 If the member of staff does not meet the necessary standard of spoken English or Welsh fluency, adjustments to their role may also be considered, such as reducing the frequency of communications with the public or supplementing communications with written material for the public. Consideration could also be given to moving or job swapping the individual to a non-public-facing role.

DISMISSAL

3.9. Public authorities must ensure that fair and consistent policies are in place in respect of the fluency duty and that these are effectively communicated to staff and managers.

3.10. Members of staff must be given a reasonable opportunity to meet the necessary standard of spoken English or Welsh fluency. As a last resort, the public authority could consider dismissing the individual on the basis that they are not capable of fulfilling their duties, for example if:

- a member of staff has unreasonably refused to undertake training aimed to bring them up to the necessary standard for their role; or
- a member of staff has not been able to attain the standard of fluent English or Welsh required for the role within a reasonable amount of time, after reasonable training opportunities have been provided; or
- no other suitable post without public-facing duties can be made available for that individual.

3.11. Prior to the dismissal of an employee, a public authority must ensure that the situation has been investigated fully in accordance with its capability and disciplinary procedures. All other usual policies and procedures should be followed to give the employee the opportunity to explain their position and provide mitigation, including an opportunity for the employee to appeal against a disciplinary decision. Public authorities should only consider dismissal after considering all reasonable alternatives and where appropriate, take legal advice.

3.12. During this process public authorities should adhere to the Advisory, Conciliation and Arbitration Service Code of Practice on Disciplinary and Grievance Procedures[11] as appropriate.

AGENCY WORKERS AND SELF-EMPLOYED CONTRACTORS

3.13. Agency workers are not employed by a public authority and the terms on which they are engaged depend on the contract between the employment agency and the public authority and their own arrangements with the employment agency. If an individual agency worker is unable to meet the necessary standard of spoken English or Welsh fluency, a public authority can consider terminating the agreement with the employment agency for their engagement in accordance with the terms of the contract between the employment agency and public authority.

3.14. Self-employed contractors work for public authorities in accordance with the terms of a services contract. The terms of the contract will determine the steps which a public authority can reasonably take should the individual fail to meet the necessary standard of spoken English or Welsh fluency required for a public-facing role.

NOTES

10 http://learnenglish.britishcouncil.org/en/

11 http://www.acas.org.uk/media/pdf/f/m/Acas-Code-of-Practice-1-on-disciplinary-and-grievance-procedures.pdf

SECTION 4: COMPLAINTS PROCEDURE

[4.323]

4.1. This section of the Code is about the procedure a public authority should follow should there be a complaint regarding an alleged breach of the fluency duty.

COMPLAINT HANDLING

4.2. A public authority must operate a complaints procedure so that if a member of the public feels that a public-facing public authority worker has insufficient proficiency in spoken English or Welsh for the performance of their role they can make a formal complaint to the public authority which is then investigated and a response provided.

What is a complaint?

4.3. For the purposes of the fluency duty, a legitimate complaint is one about the standard of spoken English or Welsh of a public sector member of staff in a public-facing role. It will be made by a member of the public or someone acting on his or her behalf complaining that the authority has not met the fluency duty.

4.4. A complaint about a public sector member of staff's accent, dialect, manner or tone of communication, origin or nationality would not be considered a legitimate complaint about the fluency duty. Public authorities should make this clear in the terms of their complaints policy.

4.5. Public authorities are not obliged by this Code of Practice to respond to complaints that are vexatious, oppressive, threatening or abusive. These words should be given their usual dictionary meaning and should be seen as those complaints which are without foundation and/or which are intended to result in harsh or wrongful treatment of the person who is the subject of the complaint. In these types of circumstances a complaint should not be taken forward by the public authority

Providing effective means for the public to make complaints

4.6. Knowing how to complain and what will happen when a complaint is made is essential to confidence in public services. The public needs information about the complaints system: who can make a complaint, how they go about it and what complaints come within the scope of the fluency duty.

4.7. Public authorities are responsible for dealing with such complaints and must therefore:

- establish an appropriate complaints procedure, using existing channels where appropriate;
- update their complaints procedure as necessary;
- provide first and second line managers and supervisors with an appropriate level of training and support to enable them to deal with complaints confidently and professionally;
- adequately publicise and signpost the complaints procedure;
- ensure appropriate reasonable adjustments are in place so that all members of the public are able to make a complaint;
- ensure that complaints are dealt with in line with the Data Protection Act 1998;
- ensure that all legitimate complaints are treated seriously;
- ensure complaints are progressed and complainants receive a response efficiently and in a timely manner. Some complaints may take longer to resolve than others and the likely timescale should be made clear; and
- ensure the complainant or their representative are made aware of any escalation route in relation to the decision on the complaint, for example to an ombudsman service. Escalation routes across the public sector will vary however, if a public authority does not comply with the fluency duty, its failure to comply can also be challenged through an application to the High Court for judicial review.

4.8. Following the receipt of a legitimate complaint, public authorities must assess its merits against the necessary standard of spoken English or Welsh fluency required for the role in question. This should be undertaken through an objective assessment against clear criteria set out in the role specification or against the level of fluency descriptors relevant to the role in question. The table above at 2.17 in Section 2, provides a useful summary extracted from the CEFR levels[12] of fluency.

4.9. If the complaint is upheld, a public authority must consider what steps can be taken to meet the fluency duty. Steps may include specific training, retraining or assessment, re-deployment or dismissal. Public authorities should refer to Section 3 of this Code of Practice and ensure they take account of the:

- nature of the complaint;
- information received from the complainant or their representative; and
- complainant's expectations of an outcome.

4.10. Members of staff who are the subject of a complaint should be notified of the complaint and the action being taken in relation to it. They should be given the opportunity, as soon as practicable, to give their own account of the facts leading to the complaint. The complaints procedure should make it clear to prospective complainants that this will take place following a legitimate complaint. Public authorities must also ensure:

- that staff who are the subject of a complaint are kept fully informed at each stage of the complaints process; and
- that complaints are dealt with efficiently and brought to a timely conclusion.

4.11. Public authorities have a duty of care toward their members of staff and should consider their wellbeing, being mindful of the potential impact complaints may have. They should consider providing staff with appropriate support to ensure that they are protected from vexatious complaints and not subjected to unnecessary fluency testing.

4.12. Public authorities in Wales must also ensure their complaints practices and procedures meet the requirements of any schemes under the Welsh Language Act 1993 and any relevant standards specified under the Welsh Language (Wales) Measure 2011 relating to complaints.

Complaints data

4.13. As standard practice, a record should be kept of all complaints. If authorities publish their complaints data, they should include any complaints that fall under the fluency duty. At the time of publishing this guidance, the fluency duty does not require public authorities to publish complaints data.

4.14. Public authorities in Wales subject to the Welsh Language (Wales) Measure 2011 must also ensure they comply with standards relating to a body keeping records. This also requires authorities to keep a copy of any written complaints that they receive that relates to the Welsh language, whether or not that complaint relates to the standards with which they are under a duty to comply.

NOTES

[12] http://www.coe.int/t/dg4/education/elp/elp-reg/Source/Key_reference/Overview_CEFRscales_EN.pdf

SECTION 5: COMPLIANCE

[4.324]

5.1. This section of the Code is about how a public authority should comply with its other legal obligations as well as complying with the fluency duty.

OBLIGATIONS UNDER THE EQUALITY ACT

5.2. Public authorities must take into account their obligations under the Equality Act 2010 when considering their duty to ensure that each person in a public-facing role speaks fluent English or Welsh. The processes and methods used to determine whether a person has a command of spoken English or Welsh for effective performance in the role must be fair and transparent.

5.3. It is unlawful to discriminate directly or indirectly against a person on grounds of race. Public authorities should ensure that people from particular nationalities or ethnic backgrounds, in a recruitment process or whilst at work, are treated in the same way as people from an English or Welsh ethnic background. When a public authority considers a complaint in relation to the fluency duty it should reject any complaint which relates to the public-facing worker's race, nationality, ethnic origin or disability.

5.4. Public authorities have a duty towards disabled members of staff under the Equality Act 2010 to provide such adjustments as are reasonable to remove a disadvantage caused by the application of a particular provision, criterion or practice. For a public sector worker whose first language is a signed language, the fluency duty will be met by the provision of a sign language interpreter who speaks English or Welsh to the necessary standard of fluency for that role.

5.5. The public sector equality duty (PSED) came into force in England, Scotland and Wales in 2011. The PSED is set out at Section 149 of the Equality Act 2010. It requires that those public authorities in scope must, when exercising their functions, have "due regard" to the need to:

- eliminate discrimination, harassment, victimisation and any other conduct that is prohibited under the Equality Act 2010;
- advance equality of opportunity between persons who share a relevant protected characteristic and persons who do not share it; and
- foster good relations between persons who share a relevant protected characteristic and persons who do not share it.

OTHER LEGAL OBLIGATIONS

5.6. In Wales, the Welsh language should be treated no less favourably than the English language. The Welsh Language (Wales) Measure 2011 sets a new legal context for the Welsh language. This creates a legislative framework for enforcing duties on persons operating in Wales with regard to the Welsh language.

5.7. Although the fluency duty and the Welsh Language (Wales) Measure 2011 are different in their application and policy intent, relevant public authorities in Wales should consider obligations required under the Welsh Language (Wales) Measure 2011 when deciding how to comply with the fluency duty.

5.8. Many of the public authorities subject to the standards of the Welsh Language (Wales) Measure 2011 currently operate Welsh Language Schemes under the Welsh Language Act 1993. Each public authority will still be obliged to comply with its Welsh Language Scheme, as approved under the Welsh Language Act 1993, until such a time as that public authority becomes subject to standards under the Welsh Language (Wales) Measure 2011.

5.9. Public authorities may have specific legal duties towards members of the public, for example under the Medical Act 1983, which will inform the decision as to the standard of spoken English or Welsh required for particular public-facing roles.

5.10. Additionally, as referred to in paragraph 2.4 above, a certain standard of fluency in English or Welsh can be required as an entry requirement for some roles, or stipulated by the regulatory body of certain professionals. This will inform the decision as to the standard of spoken English or Welsh required for particular public-facing roles: it is not anticipated that public authorities will impose any higher standard in fulfilling the fluency duty than are already required for such roles.

J. EMPLOYMENT TRIBUNALS

EMPLOYMENT TRIBUNALS
PRINCIPLES FOR COMPENSATING PENSION LOSS
(FOURTH EDITION: AUGUST 2017)

NOTES

This document was prepared by a working group of Employment Judges (see Appendix 5 below at **[4.337]** for details) and is intended as guidance for employment tribunals and for parties appearing in tribunal proceedings. It has no formal statutory status but its use is supported by Guidance issued jointly by the Presidents of Employment Tribunals for England and Wales and Scotland (see **[5.88]**) to which Employment tribunals must have regard.

CONTENTS

FOREWORD

[4.325]

Over recent years, it had become clear that the guidance contained in the third edition of the booklet on *Compensation for Loss of Pension Rights*, published in 2003 and last revised in 2004, was no longer reliable for calculating pension loss in Employment Tribunal cases. Following the decision of the Court of Appeal in *Griffin v. Plymouth Hospital NHS Trust* [2015] ICR 347 in September 2014, the guidance was withdrawn in 2015. That has left a considerable gap in the guidance available to parties and to Employment Tribunals in cases where the measurement of quite significant sums of money by way of pensions loss compensation assumes great importance.

A working group of Employment Judges has worked hard to produce a fourth edition containing guidance for tribunals and parties. The fourth edition is presented in this document, entitled *Employment Tribunals: Principles for Compensating Pension Loss* (and now referred to as the "Principles"). This is an impressive document that stands as tribute to the endeavours of the judicial working group and the input of many public consultees. It has been written and published with little expenditure of public money and with the benefit of invaluable *pro bono* contributions from experts drawn from several disciplines.

It is one of the hallmarks of the tribunal system that it is intended to be accessible, with proceedings handled fairly, quickly and efficiently. The work of the Employment Judges, and those who have assisted them, is a valuable contribution when it comes to turning that aspiration into a practical reality.

Whether the Principles accurately capture the legal essentials of this complex area of compensation law, and whether their application to real-life cases will withstand their first contact with the appellate courts, I must expressly reserve my position. Nevertheless, I pay tribute to the quality of the work undertaken and I commend the Principles to litigants and practitioners in the Employment Tribunal as a mechanism for compensating pension loss.

The Rt Hon Sir Ernest Ryder

Senior President of Tribunals

10 August 2017

INTRODUCTION

[4.326]

The President of Employment Tribunals for England and Wales and the President of Employment Tribunals for Scotland have issued short Presidential Guidance confirming the approach that Employment Tribunals will take when calculating the amount of compensation that claimants should receive in respect of their pension loss[1]. That approach will involve applying the principles set out in this further, and more detailed, document. This document is the fourth edition of its kind, having evolved from guidance first published in 1990. It is to be referred to as the "Principles". It is publicly available. It does not have statutory force. It does not set out legal advice or financial advice.

The Principles have been prepared by a working group of judges appointed by the two Presidents[2], following a process of public consultation carried out in 2016[3]. They constitute a wholesale replacement of the revised third edition of the booklet *Compensation for Loss of Pension Rights: Employment Tribunals*, which was last updated in 2004 and withdrawn in 2015[4]. Self-evidently, the third edition took no account of many significant changes to the pensions landscape in the intervening years.

The Principles have been guided by five concepts:

- ***Justice***
  When a person is dismissed, they usually suffer financial loss. If a tribunal decides that a dismissal is unlawful, it can award compensation for that loss. The financial loss incurred by a dismissed claimant may include pension loss. By "pension loss", we mean simply this: the person receives a smaller pension in retirement than they would have done if they had not been unlawfully dismissed. It is a type of future loss. It is a matter of justice that, in appropriate cases, pension loss should be compensated.
- ***Simplicity***
  In many cases, pension loss will be a modest amount and straightforward to calculate. In some cases, it may be for a large amount and difficult to calculate. The difficulty in calculation is caused by several factors. First, a person's pension arrangements can be complex. Second, there are many issues that a tribunal cannot predict with certainty. These include the length of time a person would have remained in work until retirement, the length of their life in retirement when they receive their reduced pension and how their career might have developed but for the dismissal. Precision in such cases is impossible to achieve. The tribunal's task is like trying to hit a moving target. Recognising this, the approach to calculating pension loss should, in most of the cases before the tribunal, be as simple as possible while remaining consistent with the need to achieve a just result. More complex approaches should only be adopted where unavoidable. This is more likely to be the case where, for example, defined benefit schemes and longer periods of unemployment after dismissal are involved.
- ***Proportionality***
  In complex cases, greater accuracy in calculating pension loss comes at a cost. The more accuracy that is required, the greater the need for expert evidence from a person such as an actuary. As a matter of proportionality, the parties should only bear the costs associated with obtaining expert evidence, and be subject to the associated delay, where it is justified by the pension loss at stake. This is more likely to be the case where the statutory cap on the compensatory award for unfair dismissal does not apply.
- ***Pragmatism***
  Previous editions benefited from input from the Government Actuary's Department ("GAD"). This led to a series of bespoke tables and multipliers, unique to the Employment Tribunals. The optimum solution is to have new tables and multipliers, updated to the present day. Unfortunately, no funding has been made available to support GAD's further involvement. It follows that the optimum solution is not feasible. The Principles have instead adopted a pragmatic alternative for complex cases, which is to use – albeit with some modifications – the Ogden Tables.
- *Flexibility*
  The absence of bespoke tables and multipliers has the advantage that the Principles can be quickly updated to accommodate decisions of the higher courts about how pension loss should be valued and further changes in the pensions landscape and to various tax thresholds.

The members of the working group consider that the concepts set out above reflect the overriding objective, set out at Rule 2 of the Employment Tribunals Rules of Procedure 2013, to deal with cases fairly and justly. Dealing with a case fairly and justly includes, so far as practicable: (a) ensuring that the parties are on an equal footing; (b) dealing with cases in ways which are proportionate to the complexity and importance of the issues; (c) avoiding unnecessary formality and seeking flexibility in the proceedings; (d) avoiding delay, so far as compatible with proper consideration of the issues; and (e) saving expense.

To avoid the unwieldy and cumbersome use of multiple pronouns for a claimant (he/she and his/her), we have chosen to use the plural pronoun (they, their) throughout.

NOTES

1 See https://www.judiciary.gov.uk/publications/employment-rules-and-legislation-practice-directions (for England and Wales) and https://www.judiciary.gov.uk/publications/directions-for-employment-tribunals-scotland (for Scotland).

2 A list of working group members is set out at Appendix 5.

3 The consultation period lasted from 30 March 2016 to 20 May 2016. The consultation paper and the response are available here: https://www.judiciary.gov.uk/publications/compensation-for-loss-of-pension-rights-in-employment-tribunals

4 The revised third edition is still available to download at this link, along with confirmation of its withdrawal: https://www.gov.uk/government/publications/compensation-for-loss-of-pension-rights-employment-tribunals-third-edition

CHAPTER 1: UNDERSTANDING THE PROBLEM

[4.327]

1.1 In the Principles, we use the phrase "unlawful dismissal" to describe three scenarios. Each scenario gives rise to different approaches to the calculation of loss and, therefore, the calculation of pension loss:

(a) Wrongful dismissal. This occurs where an employer terminates an employee's contract of employment in breach of the terms of that contract[5]. It usually means that the employer has not given the employee the required notice to bring the contract to an end. Where a claimant has succeeded in a claim for wrongful dismissal, they are entitled to be put back in the position they would have been in if the contract had been performed lawfully (i.e. if the proper notice had been given). In pension terms, that would mean an award of damages for the pension loss that relates to the notice period.

(b) Unfair dismissal. This occurs where a tribunal decides that an employer's decision to dismiss is unfair[6]. The tribunal may order a respondent to pay a claimant two types of statutory award: a "basic award" and a "compensatory award". The compensatory award is defined as the amount "the tribunal considers just and equitable in all the circumstances, having regard to the loss sustained by the complainant in consequence of the dismissal in so far as that loss is attributable to action taken by the employer"[7]. This can include loss of benefits such as pension rights[8]. In what we might call "standard" unfair dismissal cases, the maximum compensatory award is the lower of a monetary cap (which, from 6 April 2017, stands at £80,541) and 52 weeks' pay[9]. To the extent that a claimant's loss (including pension loss) exceeds this monetary cap, it is not recoverable. There are categories of unfair dismissal where this monetary cap does not apply[10] and, in such cases, it may be possible to recover substantial amounts of pension loss.

(c) Discriminatory dismissal. This occurs where a tribunal concludes that an employer's decision to dismiss was because of a protected characteristic such as sex, race, age or disability[11]. The tribunal's approach to compensating discrimination corresponds to the damages that, in England and Wales, a County Court can award in respect of a successful claim in tort or, in Scotland, that a sheriff can award in proceedings for reparation[12]. That means the tribunal must attempt to identify a sum of money that puts the claimant back in the position they would have been in but for the unlawful conduct. For our purposes, the task facing the tribunal is to ascertain the pension position that the claimant would have been in if the unlawful discrimination had not occurred and then seek, as best as can be done with an award of money, to restore the claimant to that position[13]. In discrimination cases, there is no monetary cap[14].

1.2 A tribunal may conclude that a dismissal is unlawful in one, two or three of the above scenarios[15]. Each of these three scenarios includes a so-called "express" dismissal (which happens when the employer dismisses the employee) and a so-called "constructive" dismissal (which happens when the employee resigns in response to the employer's unlawful conduct). For the sake of simplicity, these Principles use the phrase "unlawful dismissal" to cover all such scenarios. The Principles also use the word "compensation" as a convenient shorthand for damages for breach of contract, the compensatory award for unfair dismissal and tortious-equivalent damages for discrimination.

1.3 When assessing compensation for a claimant's pension loss, difficulties arise because the claimant has not lost money, as such, at the time of dismissal; their loss is experienced in the future, during retirement, in the form of a reduced pension. The approach the tribunal should take to compensating that pension loss depends on the type of pension scheme operated by the employer. In many cases, a reasonable assessment of such loss can be made by adding up the pension contributions that the employer would have made if the dismissal had not occurred. This is known as the "contributions method". It is simple to apply. In other cases, the tribunal must try to work out the reduction in the value of a defined benefit pension. As we shall see, that is not so simple.

1.4 Previous editions of this document received judicial approval for making this task easier, but the third edition was no longer fit for purpose. There had been many changes in the pensions landscape since its last revision in 2004. To name just a few: changes to state pension age; a new state pension system; reduced earnings growth; widespread closure of final salary schemes; the advent of auto-enrolment; and the introduction of complex rules for taxation of pension benefits. These changes meant that the assumptions underlying the tables and multipliers in the third edition were no longer safe. Tribunals often speak of "old job facts" and "new job facts" when calculating compensation for future loss[16]. The changes in the pensions landscape in recent years have altered both.

1.5 As noted in the introduction, no funding has been made available to support GAD's involvement in drawing up new tables and multipliers that better reflect the current – and more complex – pensions landscape. The working group's members are not actuaries and they do not have the expertise to undertake this task themselves.

1.6 Based on their combined experience as practitioners and judges, the members of the working group have observed some typical behaviour patterns around pension loss:

(a) Many claimants, particularly those who are not represented, do not seek compensation for pension loss at all, even though they may be entitled to it. They will often focus on lost salary and overlook other benefits such as the employer's contributions to a pension scheme in which they were enrolled.

(b) Even when claimants do seek compensation for their pension loss, it is often poorly expressed or vague. Many schedules of loss, for example, frequently say that pension loss is "to be confirmed"[17]. This makes it difficult for the parties to have a sensible discussion about the possible settlement of their dispute.

(c) Many settlements occur between the liability hearing (the point at which the parties learn that a claimant has won their case) and the remedy hearing (the point at which the parties learn the amount of compensation that the respondent is ordered to pay the claimant). Parties frequently reach agreement on remedy once they know the outcome of the liability hearing or once they are in possession of certain information about matters such as pension rights.

1.7 What causes these patterns of behaviour? It may be ignorance about the occupational pension arrangements that applied in an employment relationship or even ignorance about pensions in general. For others, the cause may be a "fear factor" in dealing with pensions, perhaps due to concerns about complexity. For representatives, there may be a concern that it is not cost-effective to look at pension loss in detail until it is known whether a claimant's claim has succeeded.

1.8 The working group wishes to confront these concerns. To that end, the Principles must serve multiple purposes. They need to assist parties in understanding the developing pensions landscape, how pension loss arises following an unlawful dismissal and how it might be compensated; they must encourage early exchanges of information that make clear whether a particular case is one that might involve significant pension loss, they should steer parties towards settlement where appropriate; they must ensure that parties invest time and expense in calculating pension loss only where it is proportionate to do so; they must describe approaches for calculating loss where expert actuarial advice is not available or affordable; and they need to achieve all this without input from GAD. We have aimed for simplicity of expression, aided by several examples. Regrettably, however, it has been impossible to avoid using pensions and tax jargon, especially in more complex scenarios.

1.9 All of us, whether judges or parties, should not lose sight of the artificiality of this exercise. Any calculation of future loss is based on a series of imponderables. All complex pension calculations, even those involving actuarial assumptions, start from a series of estimates and then apply a formula to produce a final figure. That figure may descend to pounds and pence, and look satisfyingly precise, but it is only an extension of the original estimates. Bespoke tables and multipliers appeal because the admirable precision of the awards for pension loss they produce projects a veneer of accuracy. But it is a veneer nonetheless; the precise figures mask the broad brush that produced them.

1.10 We set out below a summary of the main points in these Principles.

(a) The Principles provide a framework for establishing the age at which a claimant will retire from the workforce where that is relevant to the calculation of their compensation. In broad terms, we adopt the approach that, where a claimant has not accrued significant occupational pension rights, the tribunal will assume retirement at state pension age. By contrast, if a claimant has accrued significant occupational pension rights in a scheme with a normal retirement age (and entitlement to an unreduced pension) below state pension age, the tribunal will assume retirement at the scheme's normal retirement age. The tribunal will decide, based on the facts of each case, what level of accrued benefits is "significant" for this purpose. This approach can be displaced by evidence from the parties.

(b) The Principles explain the difference between gross income and net income, which is relevant when assessing both loss of earnings (and how this is affected by the tax relief on pension contributions and the types of pensions tax that might be applied) and loss of pension rights. The Principles explain how awards of compensation are grossed up in accordance with the so-called Gourley principle.

(c) The Principles explain the operation of the new state pension system introduced in April 2016. They provide a framework for calculating loss of state pension rights under this new system. It involves use of the Ogden Tables in the small number of cases where such an award may be appropriate.

(d) Insofar as loss of occupational pension rights are concerned, the Principles identify a category of "simple" cases. In such cases, the tribunal will exclusively use the contributions method to assess a claimant's net pension loss. This method requires the tribunal to aggregate the contributions that, but for the dismissal, the employer would have made to the claimant's pension scheme during the period of loss that has been identified. This approach will invariably be adopted in cases where the claimant's lost pension rights relate to a defined contribution scheme, including a scheme into which the claimant was automatically enrolled. It will also be adopted in some cases where the lost pension rights relate to a defined benefit scheme; for example, those cases where the period of loss relates to a relatively short period or where the application of the monetary cap on compensation or a very large withdrawal factor means it will be disproportionate to engage in complex analysis.

(e) The Principles identify a category of "complex" cases. These are cases for which the contributions method is not suited. In general, a case will be a "complex" one if the claimant's lost pension rights derive from a defined benefit scheme (including both final salary schemes and Career Average Revalued Earnings schemes) and the loss relates to a longer period. "Complex" cases include, but are not limited to, career loss cases. Such cases will benefit from a more tailored approach to case management. For example, liability issues and remedy issues will be considered at separate hearings.

(f) The Principles describe a "seven steps" model by which loss will be ascertained in these "complex" cases. The model incorporates the Ogden Tables (with a bespoke age-related modification). The outcome will be imprecise but ought still to be just. Alternatively, the parties may call expert actuarial evidence, with the tribunal's preference being for a jointly-instructed expert. There is also scope for a blended approach, with expert evidence on a limited number of points rather than the overall assessment of loss.

(g) In some "complex" cases, it may also be appropriate for the remedy hearing to proceed in two stages. At the first stage, the tribunal would decide the more straightforward (non-pension) aspects of the compensation and issue a judgment to that effect. It would also make findings of fact on those matters that, in consultation with the parties, were thought relevant to calculating pension loss in the circumstances of the individual case. The parties would then be given a time-limited opportunity to agree the value of pension loss. In the absence of agreement, pension loss would be decided at the second stage and set out in a further judgment. The underlying idea is that the parties are encouraged to agree the amount of pension loss (with the benefit of the tribunal's findings of fact where appropriate) and only bear the cost of expert actuarial evidence where it is proportionate to do so in view of the compensation at stake.

(h) Finally, to give the parties as much assistance as possible, the Principles contain links to useful websites, either throughout the text or in footnotes. There are also substantial appendices. Appendix 1 summarises the benefits of the main public sector defined benefit pension schemes. Appendix 2 contains "at a glance" extracts from the Ogden Tables. Appendix 3contains numerous examples of the Principles in operation.

1.11 The Principles do not have the force of law. They are not rigid rules. If the parties wish to advance arguments for using their own calculations, rather than following the recommended approaches, the tribunal will consider them[18].

1.12 The members of the working group will meet periodically to review and update the fourth edition and to ensure that revisions take account of future changes to the pensions landscape and decisions of appellate courts. Weblinks will be checked to ensure that they remain live. Future revisions will also reflect changes to the Ogden Tables. As time passes, the number of examples that are available may also increase.

1.13 If readers wish to suggest further examples that should be provided in a future edition, if they wish to suggest improvements to the Principles or if they identify any errors in the text or examples requiring correction, they should email details to pensionprinciples@ejudiciary.net. This email account will be monitored by a member of the administrative staff of the office of the President of Employment Tribunals for England & Wales. It should not be used for correspondence about individual cases or to seek advice about the application of the Principles to such cases.

NOTES

5 The tribunal has jurisdiction to decide a complaint of wrongful dismissal by virtue of Article 3 of the Employment Tribunals Extension of Jurisdiction (England and Wales) Order 1994 and Article 3 of the Employment Tribunals Extension of Jurisdiction (Scotland) Order 1994.

6 That is, unfair within the statutory scheme that is mostly set out at Part X of the Employment Rights Act 1996 ("ERA").

7 Section 123(1) ERA.

8 Section 123(2)(b) ERA.

9 Section 124(1ZA) ERA (and see also paragraph 2.25).

10 See Section 124(1A) ERA. One example is where the tribunal decides that the reason for the dismissal is that the claimant made a protected disclosure (Section 103A ERA).

11 The list of protected characteristics is at Section 4 of the Equality Act 2010 ("EqA").

12 Sections 119(2)(a), 119(3)(a), 124(2)(b) and 124(6) EqA.

13 *Livingstone v. Rawyards Coal Co* [1880] 5 App Cas 25 and *Ministry of Defence v. Cannock & others* [1994] ICR 918.

14 Following the ECJ's decision in *Marshall v. Southampton and South West Hampshire Area Health Authority (No.2)* [1993] IRLR 445.

15 Where a dismissal is both unfair and discriminatory, the more favourable scheme for compensation should apply (*D'Souza v. London Borough of Lambeth* [1997] IRLR 677). Compensation for discrimination is more favourable for several reasons: there is no monetary cap; it is not subject to the Employment Protection (Recoupment of Benefits) Regulations 1996; it attracts interest; and it includes compensation for injury to feelings.

16 The phrases "old job facts" and "new job facts" were used by the EAT in *Kingston Upon Hull City Council v. Dunnachie (no.3)* [2003] IRLR 843. "Old job facts" include whether the claimant would have remained in their old job anyway and, if so, for how long, whether they would have been promoted and whether their pay and pension benefits would have remained stable. "New job facts" concern whether the claimant would be likely to obtain a new job and, if so, what sort of job, by what sort of date and with what level of pay and pension benefits.

17 This approach is often criticised by respondents, sometimes fairly, for displaying a lack of effort by claimants' representatives. However, it can be an understandable position for claimants' representatives to adopt, because respondents will possess more knowledge than claimants about applicable occupational pension arrangements.

18 As was the case with previous editions; see, for example, *Port of Tilbury (London) Limited v. Birch* [2005] IRLR 92.

CHAPTER 2: SOME PRELIMINARY ISSUES

[4.328]

2.1 Before examining how pension loss should be assessed, there are some preliminary points about both pensions and tax to consider. We start with the most basic question of all.

WHAT IS A PENSION?

2.2 A pension is best understood as a regular income that a person receives in retirement. There are three main types of pension arrangement in the UK: state, personal and occupational. They operate in parallel; some individuals in retirement receive all three. An individual will receive only one state pension but may receive money from several different personal or occupational pensions.

2.3 In short:

(a) The state pension is income that is paid by the state to an individual who receives that income in their capacity as a citizen. At its simplest, individuals qualify for a state pension upon reaching state pension age (see below) and having paid National Insurance ("NI") contributions for sufficient years during their working life.

(b) A personal pension, in contrast, is more like a traditional savings vehicle. Individuals pay money into a pension scheme, often described as a pension "pot" or "fund". There may be a gap of many years, perhaps decades, between when the contributions are made and when the benefits are received. A private provider, chosen by the individual, invests the pot or fund with a view to increasing its value over time. Later in life those individuals can use the money thereby accumulated to purchase an "annuity", which is a financial product giving a retirement income for the remainder of a person's life, and which they receive in their capacity as a consumer. That is why this type of scheme has often been referred to as a "money purchase" scheme. Recent reforms provide more flexibility over the use that can be made of the fund.

(c) An occupational pension, which is sometimes called a workplace pension, is a benefit an employer provides as part of an individual's overall remuneration package and which is a form of deferred pay. Such pensions typically take contributions from the individual, the employer and (through tax relief) the state. These contributions should not be confused with the NI contributions underpinning the state pension.

2.4 There are two main types of occupational pension scheme to consider:

(a) Defined contribution (or "DC") schemes. In such a scheme, a private provider, usually chosen by the employer, invests the pot or fund with a view to increasing it. The usual situation is that both the employer and the employee have contributed defined amounts to the pot or fund, expressed as percentages of salary. The amount of the resulting pension will depend on the performance of that pot or fund and the size of the annuity it can purchase. It operates rather like a personal pension and it is "money purchase" in nature.

(b) Defined benefit (or "DB") schemes. In such schemes, the pension benefits are defined in advance and thereby guaranteed regardless of the performance of any underlying fund. Until quite recently, DB schemes were commonly "final salary" schemes. Increasingly, they are Career Average Revalued Earnings (or "ARE") schemes. We explain the difference later. For employees whose earnings quickly reach a plateau, membership of a CaRe scheme may well provide better benefits; for others, such as those who anticipate promotion later in their career, the benefits will be less generous.

Some schemes are hybrid in nature. For example, an employer may have closed a DB scheme to new employees but created for them a DC section within the same scheme.

2.5 DB schemes and DC schemes differ greatly in how risk is allocated. In a DB scheme, the employer who has guaranteed the defined benefit faces the risks associated with an employee's life expectancy, inflation and investment performance. In a DC scheme, those risks are faced by the employee, and this creates uncertainty about the level of income that can be expected in retirement.

2.6 There will also usually be an option upon retirement to "commute" part of the pension income. This means that some of the future income element of the pension is sacrificed in exchange for an immediate lump sum, which is usually tax-free.

WHAT IS PENSION LOSS?

2.7 A claimant may, after an unlawful dismissal, receive a smaller pension in retirement than they would have done if they had not been dismissed. That shortfall in their pension is what we mean by pension loss.

2.8 The tribunal will generally consider two types of pension loss:

(a) Loss of state pension rights
It is possible that a claimant's dismissal results in a reduced state pension in a manner that merits an award of compensation. This is because the state pension system is rooted in an individual's NI record, which is itself linked to employment history.

(b) Loss of occupational pension rights
An occupational pension provides a benefit to an individual in their capacity as an employee; losing that employment, and losing that benefit, causes loss.

2.9 What about personal pensions, the other arrangement we mentioned above? These are usually independent of employment relationships. It may be true that, following dismissal, a person can no longer afford to put money into a personal pension; but it may also be true that they can no longer afford mortgage payments or household bills. A tribunal will make an award that compensates a claimant for their underlying loss of income from employment, rather than for the loss of items on which that income was formerly spent. It will be a matter for a successful claimant to decide how to spend the compensation. A tribunal will only need to consider making an award of compensation for loss of personal pension benefits where the employer had agreed to make contributions to such a scheme. The approach will be the same as when compensating a claimant for loss of an employer's contributions to a DC pension scheme. We provide an example at Appendix 3 (see Christopher).

2.10 These Principles focus on compensating claimants for the loss of state pension rights and the loss of occupational pension rights (for both DC and DB schemes). That said, it may be helpful if we make some points about the way tribunals calculate compensation for loss of earnings.

LOSS OF EARNINGS

2.11 When awarding compensation to a claimant, it is common for the award to cover past loss of earnings and future loss of earnings. Taking each in turn:

(a) Past loss of earnings relates to income lost between the date of the dismissal and the date of the tribunal hearing. It is straightforward to calculate because the tribunal will have heard evidence about what happened between the dismissal and the hearing and so can make findings of fact about that period.

(b) Future loss of earnings relates to income lost from the date of the tribunal hearing until a terminal date in the future. It may be a date when the claimant's notice period would have expired or when they would have lost their job anyway. It may be a date when it is thought that they will have mitigated their loss by finding a new job for the same pay. In a few cases, it may even be the date on which, but for the dismissal, they would have retired; this last category includes what is sometimes known as a "career loss" case.

Where a tribunal makes an award for future loss of earnings, it will be calculated separately to its award for past loss of earnings.

2.12 A tribunal has the power to award interest on the compensation payable to a claimant – but only in discrimination cases[19]. This recognises the fact that the claimant has had to wait before receiving compensation for their past loss of earnings and it provides for additional compensation in respect of that delay. Self-evidently, interest is not awarded on future loss[20]. Pension loss is a form of future loss; it is a loss experienced in retirement. It follows that no interest is awarded on compensation for loss of pension rights[21].

2.13 Although pension loss is a type of future loss, it will sometimes go hand in hand with loss of earnings. By way of example, take a case where the tribunal decides that a person would have lost their job anyway, but for a different reason, within a period of three months. At a remedy hearing, the tribunal therefore awards three months' past loss of earnings. The tribunal also decides to award pension loss to the claimant using the "contributions method" (this approach is explained later, in **Chapter 4**), by aggregating the pension contributions the employer would have made to its DC scheme during the same period of three months.

2.14 Sometimes pension loss will not go hand in hand with loss of earnings. Take, for example, a case where the claimant was dismissed from a job which had a generous DB final salary pension scheme. The tribunal decides that the claimant will find another job within the next six months which pays the same salary as they received before but with much less valuable pension benefits – perhaps the minimum rights under the auto-enrolment regime. The claimant's loss of earnings lasted six months, but the loss of pension rights relates to a longer period. It may even continue until the claimant's retirement.

2.15 That said, the tribunal will not apply different standards of causation to a claimant's loss of earnings and their loss of pension rights. A claimant's pension benefits, it must be remembered, are merely part of the overall remuneration package. The tribunal will be alert to the possibility that a future rise in salary in new employment is sufficient to offset both loss of earnings and loss of pension rights arising from dismissal from the old employment[22].

2.16 We have already noted that a claimant's intended date of retirement is relevant to the assessment of their future loss of earnings. For example, a claimant may already be close to state pension age. Or the tribunal may conclude that a claimant will never work again (the so-called "career loss" case). In both cases, the tribunal will need to decide the likely age at which, but for their dismissal, the claimant would have retired: before state pension age, at state pension age or after state pension age? We return to this point when discussing the state pension in **Chapter 3**.

NET PAY, NOT GROSS PAY

2.17 It should be emphasised that awards for loss of earnings, whether in the past or in the future, are based on net pay[23]. In this context, "net pay" is what is left from gross pay after income tax and Class 1 (employee) NI contributions have been deducted. We shall briefly explain both.

2.18 For the tax year 2017-2018, the income tax bands, for most people living in England, Wales or Northern Ireland, are:

- A personal allowance of £11,500 – no income tax is paid on earnings up to £11,500;
- On the next slice of £33,500 (which is usually earnings between £11,500 and £45,000), basic rate tax is paid at 20%;
- On the next slice of £105,000 (which is usually earnings between £45,000 and £150,000), higher rate tax is paid at 40%; and
- On income over £150,000, additional rate tax is paid at 45%.

This is subject to any restriction of the personal allowance, discussed at paragraphs 2.20 and 2.21 below. Details on past income tax rates are available here: https://www.gov.uk/government/publications/rates-and-allowances-income-tax.

2.19 The situation is slightly different in Scotland, where income tax is partially devolved. For the tax year 2017-2018, the Scottish Government retained a higher rate threshold of £43,000. This means that, for taxpayers in Scotland, basic rate income tax applies at 20% to earnings on the next slice of £31,500 (which is usually between £11,500 and £43,000) while higher rate tax applies at 40% to earnings on the next slice of £107,000 (which is usually between £43,000 and £150,000). Additional rate tax is not affected. This is also subject to restriction of the personal allowance. Further details on Scottish income tax are available here: https://www.gov.uk/scottish-rate-income-tax/how-it-works

2.20 This situation is more complicated for higher earners. An individual's tax-free personal allowance of £11,500 goes down by £1 for every £2 that their "adjusted net income" exceeds £100,000. Confusingly, "adjusted net income" (which is an HMRC phrase) does not, in this context, mean "net of income tax". It means total gross earnings less certain tax reliefs, which include donations made to charities through Gift Aid and employee pension contributions (those on which no tax relief has been given or those on which only tax relief at the basic rate has been given).

2.21 By way of example, consider an individual earning a gross annual salary of £125,000 who, in the current tax year, has paid employee pension contributions of £9,000 and Gift Aid donations totalling £2,000. This individual's adjusted net income will be £114,000 (which is £125,000 less £9,000 less £2,000). For every £2 that the figure of £114,000 exceeds £100,000, this individual's personal allowance reduces by £1. With an excess of £14,000, this means that their personal allowance has reduced by £7,000 to £4,500. In turn, this means that they will pay basic rate tax at 20% on earnings on the next slice of £33,500[24] between £4,500 and £38,000, while the higher rate tax band is expanded to earnings between £38,000 and £150,000. Additional rate tax is not affected. The effect of restriction of the personal allowance, in other words, is to increase the slice of an individual's earnings upon which they pay tax at

40%. As the examples in Appendix 3 demonstrate, this will have an impact when grossing up significant awards of compensation, which (as we shall see) are taxed as income in the year of receipt.

2.22 In addition, employees pay Class 1 NI contributions. NI is calculated on gross earnings (which, in this context, means earnings before income tax and before pension contributions) between lower and upper limits:

- No Class 1 NI contributions are paid on weekly earnings below £113 a week (equivalent to £5,876 a year);
- No Class 1 NI contributions are paid on weekly earnings between £113 and £157 a week (equivalent to between £5,876 and £8,164 a year) (this threshold, as we shall see, is relevant to the number of qualifying years for state pension purposes);
- Class 1 NI contributions are paid at 12% on weekly earnings between £157 and £866 a week (equivalent to between £8,164 and £45,000 a year); and
- Class 1 NI contributions are paid at 2% on weekly earnings over £866 a week (equivalent to over £45,000 a year).

Further details on NI contributions are available here: https://www.gov.uk/government/publications/rates-and-allowances-national-insurance-contributions/rates-and-allowances-national-insurance-contributions

2.23 A word of caution: the ET1 claim form distinguishes between "pay before tax" (i.e. gross pay) and "normal take-home pay". In this context, "normal take-home pay" is not necessarily the same as gross pay less income tax and NI contributions. It means pay after all deductions. These may include the claimant's own contributions to a workplace pension, their savings made to a workplace savings scheme or money that they are paying under an attachment of earnings order. These deductions are the claimant's own money, and the claimant loses that money when dismissed. The parties and the tribunal need to be vigilant, to ensure that the right figure for net pay is used when calculating loss of earnings.

2.24 In most cases, the proper amount of net pay needed to calculate loss of earnings (and the amount of any deductions) is revealed by a claimant's payslips, both in respect of their old job and any new job obtained since dismissal. If payslips are not available, an online calculator developed by HMRC can provide a good estimate of net pay. It may be appropriate to use it where there is no other source of information: https://www.gov.uk/estimate-income-tax

2.25 When working out gross pay and net pay, the tribunal and the parties must take care to avoid confusion with the statutory concept of a "week's pay" as set out in the ERA[25]. This concept applies in many contexts. For example, when subject to a monetary cap (presently £489), a "week's pay" is relevant to the calculation of the basic award for unfair dismissal, statutory redundancy pay and awards for failure to provide a statement of employment particulars[26]. When it is not subject to a monetary cap, it is relevant to matters such as the calculation of notice pay for periods of statutory minimum notice, protective awards and the upper limit on the compensatory award for unfair dismissal[27]. While it is correct that a "week's pay" is assessed before deducting income tax and employee NI contributions, the EAT has confirmed that it also includes the employer's pension contributions[28]. For this purpose, there is no distinction to be drawn between contributions to a DC scheme and contributions to a DB scheme. Self-evidently, this increases the potential value of an award for unfair dismissal in cases where the monetary cap operates.

2.26 Importantly, the principle that loss of earnings is compensated on a net basis also applies to loss of pension rights. Just as the tribunal looks to compensate a claimant for the difference between the net amount they earned in the job from which they were dismissed and the net amount they are now earning, subject to the normal rules of causation, so the tribunal looks to compensate a claimant for the difference between the net pension benefits they would have received, but for their dismissal, and the net pension benefits they will now receive.

TAX RELIEF ON PENSION CONTRIBUTIONS

2.27 Almost all pension schemes are registered for tax. This means, among other matters, that employee contributions paid to the scheme attract tax relief. The mechanism for tax relief is relevant to understanding pension loss. It can also be relevant when working out a claimant's correct net pay for loss of earnings calculations. It requires a brief explanation.

2.28 Consider the situation of an employee who pays basic rate income tax at 20%. The contributions they make to their occupational pension attract tax relief at 20% in this way: for every 80 pence saved to the scheme, the state contributes 20 pence. If the employer takes those contributions out of their pay before deducting income tax at source, which is what usually happens, the tax relief is obtained automatically. This means that the "gross pay" figure appearing on their P60, which is the amount on which income tax is paid, will be less than their gross annual salary. The difference exists because their gross pay has been reduced to reflect their contributions to their pension scheme: the reduction in their taxable income is the mechanism by which tax relief on those contributions has been bestowed[29].

2.29 For an employee paying higher rate income tax at 40%, the effect is more generous: for every 60 pence paid in contributions to a pension scheme, the state contributes 40 pence. The same applies at additional rate income tax: for every 55 pence paid in contributions to a pension scheme, the state contributes 45 pence. If the employer takes those contributions out of their pay before deducting income tax at source, the only tax relief that is obtained automatically is at the basic rate of 20%. A higher rate taxpayer would claim tax relief on the extra 20% (and an additional rate taxpayer would claim tax relief on the extra 25%) through their self-assessment tax return.

2.30 Since April 2006, however, an individual may only claim tax relief on contributions within a set "Annual Allowance" ("AA"). The AA is currently £40,000. It applies to all tax-registered pension arrangements that an individual has in total, not to each separately. In this context, the figure of £40,000 is not the maximum amount of tax relief available, but the maximum amount of payments into a pension scheme that an individual can make that attract tax relief. Put another way, higher rate and additional rate taxpayers obtain more generous tax relief from the state on pension savings up to £40,000 in a tax year, but then pay tax on their pensions savings that exceed £40,000 in a tax year.

2.31 There is a further complication for higher earners. Since April 2016, the AA has been reduced ("tapered") for those who meet two conditions. The first condition is that their "threshold income" (which is their income excluding any pension contributions) exceeds £110,000 during the tax year. The second condition is that their "adjusted income" (which, in this context, means their income plus the pension contributions that they and their employer have both made) exceeds £150,000 during the tax year. For such individuals, every £2 of excess income over £150,000 reduces their AA by £1. This up to a maximum reduction of £30,000 to the AA. It follows that an individual earning an adjusted income of £210,000 or more will have a reduced AA of £10,000.

Further details are available here:https://www.gov.uk/government/publications/rates-and-allowances-pension-schemes/pension-schemes-rates

2.32 If the AA of £40,000 (or such lower tapered amount as may apply) is exceeded, the individual pays tax on the balance at their marginal rate through self-assessment, just as if it were additional income. The effect is to reduce the individual's net pay further. This tax – known as the AA charge – is therefore relevant when calculating a high earner's loss of earnings based on net pay. (In some cases, the occupational pension scheme meets the charge each year and recovers it from the scheme member, further down the line, by way of reduced pension benefits. This is discussed further below; as we shall see, its application requires care in respect of DB schemes.)

2.33 To be clear: there is no limit on the maximum amount of contributions that a person can make to a pension scheme that is tax-registered but, if they exceed the AA, tax is levied on the excess.

2.34 It should be noted that, for those who do not pay income tax due to low income, tax relief is still available at the present basic rate level of 20% on the first £2,880 paid into the pension (which has the effect of topping it up to £3,600).

2.35 In addition to the AA, there is a personal "Lifetime Allowance" ("LTA") for all pension savings that a person makes into a registered scheme, which was also introduced in April 2006. Again, it applies to all an individual's tax-registered pension arrangements, not to each separately. Although individuals can have pension savings that exceed the LTA (presently £1m), the excess is subject to a tax charge. Unlike the AA, this is not a charge imposed on an individual's earnings; it is a charge imposed at the point of retirement and on their pension income and/or lump sum, which therefore reduces the net value of their benefits. We will look at this in more detail in **CHAPTER 5**, in the context of DB schemes.

GROSSING UP: THE GOURLEY PRINCIPLE

2.36 We now return to the point that compensation for loss of earnings and compensation for loss of pension rights are both awarded on a net basis. The tribunal must take care, when identifying an award of compensation, that its approach to tax does not put the claimant in either a better or a worse financial position than if the dismissal had not occurred. This is the so-called Gourley principle[30].

2.37 Assume, by way of illustration, that an employer wrongfully dismisses an employee by failing to give them three months' notice of the termination of their employment. Let us also assume that, during their notice period, if they had worked it, the claimant would have been entitled to receive a gross salary of £5,000. If the tribunal had ordered the employer to pay the claimant the sum of £5,000, as past loss of earnings, it would have placed them in a better position than if the contract had been performed. This is because, if the employee had received pay during notice, they would probably have been liable to tax and NI contributions – reducing it to, say, £3,500. The Gourley principle requires the tribunal to award net loss of £3,500. Put another way, a gross sum has been reduced to a net sum to make sure that the claimant is not put in a better position.

2.38 Where a tribunal awards more than £30,000 in compensation for an unlawful dismissal, income tax is generally charged on the excess over £30,000[31]. The compensation is taxed in the year that it is received by the claimant. It is declared by means of self-assessment (the claimant has left employment, so it cannot be paid by the usual method of PAYE deductions). Here, the Gourley principle requires the tribunal to increase the amount awarded to make sure that, when this income tax is paid, the claimant does not end up in a worse position. This is known as "grossing up". (NI contributions are not levied on compensation. Compensation is grossed up to offset the income tax – and only the income tax – that is payable in the year of receipt.)

2.39 Grossing up is done as follows. The tribunal starts by calculating the loss on a net basis. As described above, this is done by identifying the true net pay in the old job and comparing it, where necessary, to the true net pay in any new job; and the same is done regarding the net pension benefits the claimant will now receive compared to the net pension benefits their old job would have delivered but for the dismissal. Having arrived at a net figure, the tribunal then deducts any part of the £30,000 exempt slice that remains available. It then increases the resulting figure by the amount of tax that will be charged and adds that increased figure to the award of compensation. Interest is calculated separately where compensation is being awarded for discrimination, but pension loss does not attract interest; see paragraph 2.12.

2.40 The amount of tax charged will depend on the individual circumstances of the claimant. For some claimants, it will mean that their compensation is grossed up at a single marginal rate; for others, it may mean grossing up using a blend of different rates as each separate tax band is exhausted[32]. We provide examples at Appendix 3 (see Ashok). In some cases, where it is cost-effective to do so and the parties desire greater precision, it may be appropriate to seek assistance from an accountant. This might be appropriate where, for example, the tribunal must take account of the restriction of the personal allowance or there are complex aspects of a claimant's income from new employment.

2.41 The AA and the LTA have no impact on the grossing up calculation. This is because they do not result in any tax charge on compensation that the tribunal has awarded, which is taxed as income. More particularly:

(a) The AA charge will only be relevant to the tribunal's calculations for loss of earnings if the charge is paid at the time. This is because it will have the effect of reducing net pay.

(b) The AA charge will only be relevant to the tribunal's calculations for loss of pension rights if it is paid by the scheme and repaid at the point of retirement. This is because it will have the effect of reducing net pension benefits.

(c) The LTA charge will only be relevant to the tribunal's calculations for loss of pension rights because, if imposed, it will have the effect of reducing net pension benefits, in the manner explained in more detail in the section on DB schemes. It will not affect net pay.

2.42 The Employment Judge and non-legal members are not themselves accountants. When it comes to working out a claimant's net pay in their old job and any new job (for the loss of earnings element) and their net pension benefits (for the loss of pension rights element), the "broad brush" is often applied. Although precision is impossible, the summary set out in this Chapter will hopefully improve accuracy.

2.43 We turn next to the state pension system and our approach to cases where a claimant, through dismissal, loses state pension benefits.

NOTES

19 See the Employment Tribunals (Interest on Awards etc) Regulations 1996 (as amended). Since 29 July 2013, the rate of interest has been 8% (aligned with Section 17 of the Judgments Act 1838). For past loss of earnings, interest is awarded from the mid-point date between the act of discrimination (in our context, this will usually be the dismissal) and the date of the hearing when the compensation figure is calculated. For awards for injury to feelings, interest is awarded for the whole of the period from the act of discrimination to the date of the hearing. No interest is awarded outside of discrimination cases (e.g. unfair dismissal). This type of interest should not be confused with the interest that accrues on an unpaid judgment, which is governed by the Employment Tribunals (Interest) Order 1990.

20 As confirmed by Regulation 5 of the Employment Tribunals (Interest on Awards etc) Regulations 1996 (as amended).

21 See *Ministry of Defence v. Cannock & others* [1994] IRLR 509, para 113.

22 By way of example, see *Aegon UK Corporate Services Ltd v. Roberts* [2010] ICR 596 CA.

23 We are referring here to loss of earnings that form part of the compensatory award for unfair dismissal, an award of compensation for a discriminatory dismissal and/or damages for wrongful dismissal. Some awards, however, are made gross, such as unpaid wages awarded under Section 24(1) ERA or unpaid holiday pay awarded under Regulation 30(1)(b) of the Working Time Regulations 1998; in such cases, a claimant is responsible for any income tax or employee NI contributions that may be due on the sum awarded.

24 In Scotland, on the next slice of £31,500.

25 See Chapter II (Sections 220 to 229) of the ERA. The "week's pay" rules of the ERA will not necessarily apply to the calculation of statutory holiday pay under Regulation 13 of the Working Time Regulations 1998 for employees with normal working hours; further comment is outside the scope of these Principles.

26 See Sections 119, 162 and 227(1) ERA and Section 38(6) of the Employment Act 2002.

27 See Sections 88, 89 and 124(1ZA)(b) ERA and Section 190(2) of the Trade Union and Labour Relations (Consolidation) Act 1992.

28 *University of Sunderland v. Drossou* (EAT/0341/16). In so deciding, the EAT rejected established practice to the contrary (for example, *Payne v. Port of London Authority* (ET/155560/89)).

29 Therefore, care must be taken when using a claimant's P60 as the basis for making findings of fact about their rate of pay – it may not accurately reflect their gross annual salary.

30 From *British Transport Commission v. Gourley* [1955] UKHL 4.

31 See Sections 401 and 403 of the Income Tax (Earnings and Pensions) Act 2003 ("ITEPA") and *Shove v. Downs Surgical Limited* [1984] 1 All ER 7. There are certain exceptions to the charge, which are outside the scope of these Principles.

32 See, by way of illustration, *Yorkshire Housing Ltd v. Cuerden* (EAT/0397/09) and *P A Finlay & Co Ltd v. Finlay* (EAT/0260/14, EAT/0062/16 & EAT/0117/16).

CHAPTER 3: THE STATE PENSION SYSTEM

[4.329]

3.1 Modern governments of all colours have sought, through state pension policy, to address the problem of relative poverty in old age. The policy approach has been influenced by the assumptions made about why people experience poverty in retirement. For example:

(a) If it is thought that people experience poverty in retirement because they have not saved enough during their working lives, in consequence of poor planning and a lack of self-control, there will be pressure on public policy to tend towards state intervention in the form of compulsory saving.

(b) If it is thought that people experience poverty in retirement because of lifelong low incomes or factors outside of their control, there will be pressure on public policy to tend instead towards state intervention in the form of income support for pensioners.

3.2 Over the years, public policy has experimented with carrots and sticks to varying degrees. All governments have faced the difficult task of reconciling the prohibitive cost of universal coverage with the perceived disincentives of means testing. Policy has also shifted because of improved health in old age and increased life expectancy. At various times, public policy has also reflected contemporary assumptions about gender and marriage.

3.3 The state pension in the UK has existed since the Old Age Pensions Act 1908. This provided for payment of a means-tested amount to women and men who had reached the age of 70. That age was seen, at the time, as advanced: few expected to reach it; even fewer expected to go beyond it.

3.4 A more recognisably modern state pension system developed with the implementation of the 1942 Beveridge Report. This resulted in the system of social insurance known as the basic state pension, embodied in the National Insurance Act 1946. The age of receipt for this pension was 65 for men and 60 for women.

3.5 The essential idea since 1946 has been to provide income in retirement to those individuals who have paid sufficient NI contributions during their working lives. With its roots in such contributions, the state pension system has had to consider ways of addressing the difficulties faced by those who experience long-term unemployment (for example through ill health) or who have taken time out of paid employment for other reasons (such as childcare). However, the contributory nature of the state pension system can be misleading: over time, the link has weakened between NI contributions and the state benefits they were originally intended to fund. Nowadays, governments tend to set NI rates according to their overall budgetary needs. The various benefits paid to pensioners depend less on the number of years in which they made NI contributions and hardly at all on the precise amount of NI contributions they paid: those of pension age can now take advantage of a mixture of pensioner benefits that are universal (e.g. the winter fuel payment) and means-tested.

3.6 The state pension system has recently been the subject of significant reform. A new state pension ("nSP") was launched on 6 April 2016. The nSP is paid to people reaching state pension age on or after that date. For reasons that will be explained shortly, these people are men born on or after 6 April 1951 and women born on or after 6 April 1953 – and they are likely to form the vast majority of claimants to the tribunal. The nSP is based on a person's NI record. There is a new minimum qualifying period: 35 qualifying years are needed to get the full amount of nSP. However, most people will have made, or been credited with, NI contributions before 6 April 2016, and these will be taken into account when the nSP is calculated. There are also provisions dealing with those who were "contracted out" for a period before 2016.

3.7 These points are best explained by reference to the history of the state pension system.

THE BASIC STATE PENSION (1946–2016)

3.8 Until April 2016, we talked of the basic state pension ("BSP"). The BSP was payable to an individual who had reached state pension age and who had paid a minimum number of NI contributions. The amount paid depended on the number of qualifying years during an individual's working life that he or she had been credited with accrual to the BSP. A "qualifying year" for this purpose was any year in which the individual earned more than a specified amount.

3.9 A full BSP was paid to those who had accrued a set number of qualifying years. That set number of years has varied over time. For a while, it was 44 years (for men born before 6 April 1945) and 39 years (for women born before 6 April 1950). Later, these figures were reduced to 30 years. They are now at 35 years, following the Pensions Act 2014 (applicable to men born on or after 6 April 1951 and women born on or after 6 April 1953).

3.10 Those people who had accrued fewer than the maximum number of qualifying years received their BSP on a *pro rata* basis. It was possible, in certain circumstances, to fill in the gaps in a NI record by making voluntary (Class 3) NI contributions. A BSP based on an individual's past contributions was known as a Category A pension. Any individual not entitled to a full BSP based on their own NI contributions record might also have been entitled to a supplementary pension based on the record of a partner, which was known as a Category B pension.

3.11 For the financial year 2016-17, the full amount of the weekly BSP was £119.30; for the financial year 2017-18, it is £122.30. (It seems odd to give a figure for BSP in 2016-17 and 2017-18, given its abolition on 6 April 2016, but this is needed for comparison purposes with the nSP, as will be explained.) It was possible to increase BSP by delaying the point of receipt past state pension age, known as "extra state pension". A supplement was also payable upon reaching the age of 80.

DETOUR: THE STATE PENSION AGE

3.12 As noted above, from its inception the state pension age was 65 for men and 60 for women. It remained so until April 2010. It was modified to reflect two changes in the political consensus. The first was the view that women and men should be treated equally. The second was the view that increases in life expectancy should be accompanied by an increase in the length of a working life.

3.13 Only men born on or before 5 December 1953 retain a state pension age of 65 and only women born on or before 5 April 1950 retain a state pension age of 60. The Pensions Act 1995 provided that, between April 2010 and March 2020, the state pension age for women would increase by one month every month (tapered by date of birth) until the state pension age for women reached 65, the same as for men. The Pensions Act 2011 accelerated the process of equalisation. It will now be achieved by November 2018 (in respect of women born on or after 5 December 1953).

3.14 From December 2018, the identical state pension age for both women and men will increase steadily. The rate of increase has, however, been modified. The Pensions Act 2007 aimed to increase it to

66 by 2024-26, to 67 by 2034-36 and to 68 by 2044-46. The Pensions Act 2014 accelerated this change. Women and men born between 6 December 1953 and 5 October 1954 will now have a tapered state pension age falling somewhere between 65 and 66. Those born between 6 October 1954 and 5 April 1960 will have a state pension age of 66. It then tapers again: those born between 6 April 1960 and 5 March 1961 will have a tapered state pension age falling somewhere between 66 and 67.

3.15 Until recently, the intention was that those born between 6 March 1961 and 5 April 1977 would have a state pension age of 67 and that the increase in state pension to 68 would not proceed until 2044-46 (i.e. for those born on or after 5 April 1977). However, on 23 March 2017, the Independent Reviewer of the State Pension Age (John Cridland CBE) produced his final report[33]. His review had been tasked with considering how the state pension system should be funded in the years to come and how to ensure fairness within and between different generations. The final report recommended that the increase in state pension age to 68 should be brought forward to 2037-39 (i.e. for those born after 5 April 1970, with tapering) with no further changes until 2047[34] On 19 July 2017, the Government confirmed it would accept this recommendation[35]. This will require Parliamentary approval. The Government proposes that the next state pension age review will be conducted by July 2023. The Principles will be revised in the light of further changes.

3.16 In the meantime, a state pension calculator is available here: https://www.gov.uk/state-pension-age The calculator will no doubt be amended to incorporate the accelerated arrival of a state pension age of 68 once it becomes law[36].

WHY THE STATE PENSION AGE IS IMPORTANT

3.17 The state pension age is important in the field of occupational pensions for two reasons. The first reason is that many pension schemes align the age from which a scheme member can claim an unreduced occupational pension — known as their "normal retirement age" or "scheme retirement age" — with their state pension age. Some schemes, still available for those who were insulated from recent pension reforms, may provide for a younger age at which an unreduced pension is available, such as 60 or 65[37].

3.18 The second reason is that it can be important when assessing the appropriate terminal date for a claimant's future lost earnings. As noted at paragraph 2.11(b), the terminal date is when the claimant's lost earnings cease or, if they do not cease, when it is no longer appropriate for the employer to compensate them. This date may not be in the distant future. For example, the tribunal may conclude that a claimant will obtain alternative employment within six months or a year. Or the tribunal may conclude that a claimant would have lost their employment, for a different but fair reason, within a short period. In many cases, the tribunal will not be concerned with the date a person intends to retire. However, there are cases where a person's intended date of retirement is relevant to the assessment of future loss of earnings. For example, a claimant may already be close to state pension age. Or the tribunal may be dealing with a "career loss" case. In both situations, as mentioned at paragraph 2.16, the tribunal needs to decide the age at which, but for their dismissal, the claimant would have retired: <u>before</u> state pension age, <u>at</u> state pension age or <u>after</u> state pension age? This is one of the "old job facts" to which we referred earlier.

3.19 A related scenario, more common today than it used to be, is for the tribunal to conclude that a claimant will find work again within a reasonable period but in a job with less generous pension benefits. This may be experienced by a claimant who, in mitigating their loss, moves from public sector to private sector employment. This will result in a period of future pension loss that is much longer than the period of future loss of earnings (unless the diminution in pension benefits is offset by an increase in salary). In such a case, the tribunal must still decide the claimant's likely date of retirement. This is one of the "new job facts" to which we referred earlier.

3.20 In general, the tribunal will proceed as follows:

(a) If the claimant has not accrued significant occupational pension rights, the tribunal will assume retirement at state pension age;

(b) If the claimant has accrued significant occupational pension rights in a scheme with a normal retirement age (and an entitlement to an unreduced pension) below state pension age, the tribunal will assume retirement at the scheme's normal retirement age; and

(c) If the claimant has accrued benefits in more than one occupational pension scheme, the tribunal will assume retirement at the age at which the bulk of those benefits can be taken on an unreduced basis.

This approach provides a clear terminal date for future loss of earnings that should be simple to understand and easy to apply in most cases. It will be for the tribunal to decide, based on the facts of each case, what level of accrued benefits is "significant" for this purpose.

3.21 This is not, however, intended to operate as a concrete principle. It can be displaced by evidence from the parties. For example, a claimant may persuade the tribunal that they would have wished to work beyond state pension age, resulting in a longer period of loss of earnings; it is, after all, increasingly common for people to work past their state pension age. If the tribunal has already found a claimant to be a credible and reliable witness, it may even be enough for them simply to declare "it was my intention to work until 70". In some cases, a respondent may contend that the claimant would have retired before reaching their state pension age (or even before reaching their scheme pension age), thereby shortening the period of future loss of earnings. The tribunal will weigh up the evidence, and hear submissions from the parties, before deciding the point. We provide examples in Appendix 3 (see Janet, Derek and Peter).

3.22 When awarding loss of earnings beyond state pension age, there are two further points for the tribunal and the parties to bear in mind. First, employees who work beyond state pension age continue to pay income tax on their earnings but they no longer pay NI contributions[38]. Second, they will be entitled to draw upon their state pension while continuing to earn (although some may choose to delay receipt, resulting in higher nSP payments later[39]). In calculating loss of earnings beyond state pension age, therefore, the tribunal should note that a claimant's net pay will increase (because of the absence of NI contributions) and that there should be no deduction for receipt of nSP.

THE ADDITIONAL STATE PENSION (1961–2016)

3.23 Putting back the age at which the state pension is received has not been the only mechanism by which, over the years, governments have sought to maintain a sustainable state pension system. Another mechanism, which lasted for 55 years until its abolition in 2016, was the additional state pension. This resulted from public pressure, which began to build in the late 1950s, to introduce a method of supplementing the basic state pension through an earnings-related "top-up". A top-up was considered necessary because, in the 1950s, occupational pension schemes were rare.

3.24 This top-up system has varied in structure and gone by different names over the years:

(a) The first top-up scheme was introduced in 1961. Known as the Graduated Retirement Benefit ("GRB"), it operated until 1975. Few such individuals who participated in the GRB will still be in the labour market. It introduced the idea that further NI contributions could result in a "graduated" increase in the pension through the accumulation of "units". An individual could accumulate a maximum number of units during employment in this way: 86 units for men and 72 units for women. Each unit was translated into a weekly pension supplement. Individuals who accrued GRB between 1961 and 1975 still retain it; the value of each unit was set each financial year and, for the 2017-18 financial year, stands at a modest 13.43 pence. Thus, for 2017-18, the income supplements available to pensioners in receipt of maximum GRB are £11.55 a week for men (86 × 0.1343) and £9.67 a week for women (72 × 0.1343).

(b) The second top-up scheme, known as the State Earnings-Related Pension Scheme ("SERPS"), operated between 1978 and 2002. It was a response to the growth in occupational pension schemes during the 1970s. In essence, employees would receive a SERPS pension representing 20-25% of their earnings above a "lower earnings limit" (about the same as the weekly basic state pension) and subject to a cap at the "upper earnings limit". The resulting pension income would be calculated at retirement in accordance with complex formulae.

(c) The third and final iteration of the concept of an earnings-related top-up was the State Second Pension ("S2P"). It was introduced by the Child Support, Pensions and Social Security Act 2000 and came into force in April 2002. Whereas SERPS had been of particular value to employees in middle-income brackets, the policy rationale behind S2P was redistributive: to focus on those on low incomes or unable to work because of their caring responsibilities. By introducing three new bands between the lower earnings limit and the upper earnings limit, the effect was to skew the accrual of benefits to those on lower incomes: those in the lowest band, for example, accrued benefits at twice the rate they would have done under SERPS.

3.25 Until April 2016, many individuals, depending on their date of retirement, would have received additional state pension income derived from a combination of GRB, SERPS and/or S2P. As time passed the recipients of GRB in retirement became fewer and fewer, but many people still expected top-up benefits under SERPS and S2P. However, S2P was abolished in April 2016 with the advent of the nSP.

CONTRACTING OUT OF THE ADDITIONAL STATE PENSION (1961–2016)

3.26 During the years when the state pension incorporated an earnings- related top-up element, it was open to individuals to "contract out" of it. To be clear: it has never been possible for individuals to contract out of the basic state pension, just the additional state pension. Individuals could give up all or part of their additional state pension and opt instead to receive extra pension benefits from their occupational pension or from their personal pension.

3.27 The rules governing contracting out have changed over time:

(a) In relation to the GRB (1961–1975), the decision about contracting out was left to the employer. An employer could contract its employees out of part of the benefit if it operated an occupational pension scheme that paid out sums at least as good as the top-up benefits payable under the GRB. A decision to contract out did not entirely remove the employee's entitlement to an additional state pension; it simply reduced the maximum number of GRB units that could be accrued: 48 for men and 40 for women.

(b) In relation to SERPS, the choice to contract out was one for the employee. Initially (1978–1988), individuals were only permitted to contract out of SERPS if the employer operated a DB scheme. In return for contracting out, the employee and the employer paid NI contributions at a reduced rate. Latterly (1988–2002), individuals could also contract out of SERPS if the employer operated a DC scheme. The mechanism was straightforward: some of the NI contributions paid by the employer and the employee would be diverted, in the form of age-related rebates, into a money-purchase scheme operated by a private provider. Reflecting the consensus and economic outlook of the time, it was believed that the amounts thereby invested would ultimately yield a better return — and purchase a better annuity — than could be provided by remaining "contracted in" to the additional state pension. For a long time, there were separate rules about the investment of the so-called "protected rights" deriving from NI rebates. These rules were eventually abolished and such sums became an ordinary part of the investments made in individual or group personal pensions.

(c) In relation to S2P (2002–2016), the method for contracting out was essentially the same as the method for contracting out of SERPS: a system of age-related rebates of NI contributions. However, the ability to contract out of S2P through an employer's DC scheme came to an end in

April 2012; the process had become increasingly complex and the rebate levels were seen as less attractive. After April 2012, it was only possible to contract out of S2P through an employer's DB scheme; again, this was in the form of reduced NI contributions.

3.28 All contracting out options ceased on 6 April 2016 with the abolition of S2P and the advent of the nSP.

THE NSP (APRIL 2016 ONWARDS)

3.29 Recognising that the method of providing an additional state pension had become ever more complex, plans were set out in the Pensions Act 2007 to make S2P a simple flat-rate pension by some point in the 2030s. This would be achieved through annual earnings growth while keeping the various thresholds unchanged. The idea was that the ever-loosening link to an earnings-related element would make contracting out less and less attractive, and it would wither on the vine.

3.30 In an important development, the Pensions Act 2014 accelerated that process. The decision was taken to abolish both the BSP and S2P and to replace them, from 6 April 2016, with a single-tier state pension, which we are calling the nSP. Because the UK had not achieved equalisation of state pension ages by the time nSP was introduced on 6 April 2016, it applies to men and women at different ages: to men born on or after 6 April 1951 and to women born on or after 6 April 1953. A tribunal will only rarely be dealing with claimants born before those dates.

3.31 The nSP is a universal benefit. It is also a simpler benefit: people now know from a younger age how much they are likely to get, which the Government believes will provide a more solid platform for planning for retirement. By returning to a flat-rate system with no earnings-related element, the state pension system will have come full circle to the system that existed before 1961.

3.32 For 2017-18, the full amount of the nSP is £159.55 a week. Had it not been abolished, the full amount of the BSP would now be £122.30 a week and topped up (save to the extent a person had contracted out) by amounts derived from the GRB, SERPS and/or S2P.

3.33 The nSP is easiest to explain by reference to people who enter the job market after 6 April 2016 and so have no NI record before that date. Such people would need at least ten qualifying years to get some state pension and 35 qualifying years to get the full amount. A qualifying year, as noted above, is a tax year during which a person has made, or been credited with, NI contributions on earnings over a minimum amount (which, for 2017-18, is £5,876.) From April 2016, each qualifying year on a person's NI record adds 1/35th of the full amount of the nSP. Put another way, a person would get around £4.56 (i.e. £159.55 divided by 35) a week for each qualifying year, up to a maximum of £159.55 at the 2017/18 rate[40].

3.34 Of course, tribunals will mainly deal with claimants whose working lives started before 6 April 2016. These individuals will have made, or been credited with, NI contributions before the nSP was introduced. These NI contributions will be accounted for in essentially the same way when the nSP is calculated, although complicated by periods of contracting out.

3.35 This makes it easier for individuals to calculate the starting amount of their nSP. The Department for Work and Pensions (DWP) has assessed all employees currently in the workforce to determine their starting amount of nSP. Take, for example, a female aged 49 who experienced some periods of time when not making NI contributions (perhaps due to childcare) but, by 6 April 2017, had 21 qualifying years on her NI record. That person can calculate the current starting amount of her nSP easily. As at 6 April 2017, she has accrued 21/35ths of the current weekly rate of £159.55, which would be £95.73 a week. She also knows that she must fit in a further 14 qualifying years before reaching her state pension age of 67 to ensure that she gets the full nSP.

3.36 A person's starting amount of nSP will be compared with the amount of BSP (and additional state pension) that the person would have received under the old rules, and the higher of these two amounts will be paid.

3.37 What about those people who, for a period before 6 April 2016, were contracted out? The best answer to this question was given in evidence to the House of Commons Work and Pensions Committee on 25 November 2015, when the former Pensions Minister Sir Steven Webb explained the choice faced by policy-makers when deciding how to treat contracted out benefits[41]:

> **We had a real dilemma. Millions of [us] . . . have paid less NI than our neighbours [because] we have been contracted out. Our employer paid less; we paid less, and a deal was done that the scheme would replace part of the state benefit. That was the deal. The question is: we get to 2016 and there is no contracting out, there is just one pension, one bit of the system, so what do you do with the past contractors-out?**
>
> **There are two extremes. One is you forget contracting out ever happened, which would be beautiful, simple and clear; I would have loved it. But it would have cost billions because all of us would have suddenly got full state pensions, not reduced ones, and it would have been grossly unfair on our next-door neighbours, who never contracted out, who paid more NI than we did and still got the same pension. So we could not afford to do it and it would not have been fair.**
>
> **The other extreme would have been to remember contracting out forever, to say, "Right, you spent one year, once, contracted out. We will remember that forever". So my daughter starts work and does a year contracted out before we abolish it. In 50 years' time she retires, goes on getting a pension, God willing, for another 20 or 30 years, and in 70 years' time we are still deducting for contracting out. That would have been ridiculous.**
>
> **What did we do? We did a compromise. We said: "In 2016, we will once adjust for past contracting out and make a one-off deduction. That is fair. But then, post-2016, we will allow you**

to burn off that deduction by subsequent work and contributions." That is why in 2016-17 not many people get the flat rate, because people have not had time to burn it off. But by the end of this Parliament [i.e. 2020], the majority of new pensioners get the flat rate. So within four or five years, we are already in a situation where the majority are getting the flat rate. I would love it to have been far, far quicker – that would have been great – but there was no money to spend.

3.38 The DWP will not know the precise amount of extra benefits that individuals will receive from their occupational or personal pensions because of an historic decision to contract out for a period. It will depend on the rules of the scheme or the performance of the pension fund. Instead, the DWP will estimate the amount. This estimate is called the "Contracted Out Pension Equivalent" (or "COPE"). A person who was contracted out for only a year would have a small COPE. A person who was contracted out for longer would have a larger COPE. The COPE is then deducted from the starting amount of nSP.

3.39 Some individuals will have time, before they reach state pension age, to accrue more qualifying years, which — to use Sir Steven Webb's description — will "burn off" the COPE deduction and result in a full nSP (subject always to the nSP being capped at 35 qualifying years). Some individuals, such as those reaching state pension age in the near future, will not have time to "burn off" the COPE deduction and so will receive less than full nSP.

3.40 People can check their nSP entitlement by using the online "Government Gateway"[42]. It shows the estimated weekly amount of nSP as at the date of the enquiry (based on a person's existing NI record) and the predicted amount of nSP if there is time, before reaching state pension age, to accrue further qualifying years. It also shows the estimated COPE deduction based on prior periods of contracting out.

3.41 The government of the day sets the uprating policy that will apply to the nSP. At present, this is the so-called "triple lock" system[43]. Under this system, nSP increases by the higher of (a) price inflation (measured by CPI), (b) average earnings growth or (c) 2.5%. In the tax year 2017-18, the 2.5% increase applied; as a result, the full amount of nSP rose to £159.55 per week and the full amount of BSP, for comparison purposes, rose to £122.30 per week.

LOSS OF STATE PENSION: ISSUES FOR THE EMPLOYMENT TRIBUNAL

3.42 Dismissal interrupts an individual's NI record. In most cases, however, it will not interrupt it for long enough to result in a loss of nSP benefits. This is because it will rarely stop a person from going on to accrue the 35 qualifying years needed to receive the full amount of nSP. A current school leaver may have a working life of over 50 years. The period of unemployment following dismissal is, in most cases, unlikely to be so long that nSP benefits are thereby reduced. It follows that a tribunal is unlikely, in most cases, to make an award for loss of nSP. An example of a decision to make no award is given in Appendix 3 (see Jessica).

3.43 Nonetheless, in some cases, dismissal will reduce nSP benefits: a person will fail to reach 35 qualifying years (or will accrue fewer years) than, but for the dismissal, they would have done. The dismissal may also reduce the prospects that they "burn off" any applicable COPE deduction arising from a previous period of contracting out. This will be a loss they experience for the reminder of their life in retirement. One such case might be a claimant, with a pre-existing gap in their NI record resulting from periods of absence from the labour market (such as for childcare reasons), who has been dismissed by their employer at an age where there is insufficient time to accrue more qualifying years. Another example is a career-loss case, where the tribunal is persuaded to award compensation on the assumption that the claimant will never work again — and so never accrue another qualifying year[44].

3.44 It will be for a claimant to show that they are entitled to compensation for loss of nSP benefits. In the first instance, they should obtain a statement of the starting amount of their nSP at current rates. The easiest way to obtain this information is to use the Government Gateway; this requires the claimant to set up a Gateway account and it also presupposes that they can access digital services. If that is not feasible, a claimant can instead complete a BR19 application form to obtain a postal statement of their nSP benefits; alternatively, they can obtain details by telephoning the Government's Future Pension Centre[45].

3.45 Such a claimant would need to persuade the tribunal that, because of the dismissal, they will accrue fewer qualifying years and that they have insufficient time or prospects of making good the resulting gap in their NI record. The basis for calculating loss of nSP benefits is straightforward in principle, if not in application: each qualifying year lost equates to a reduction in nSP of 1/35th, and that loss repeats for each year of retirement in which nSP is received. The annual loss must be converted into a one-off capital sum that can be awarded as compensation.

3.46 A lot of guesswork is needed to reach a capital sum. There are many unknowns. One unknown is the amount by which the nSP is uprated each year (which itself depends on the sustainability of the triple lock). Another unknown is the length of a claimant's life in retirement (although life expectancy calculators are available, including one produced by the Office for National Statistics[46]). Precision is impossible.

3.47 The members of the working group consider that the safest approach is to apply the Ogden Tables. They are explained elsewhere in these Principles. An example of their application to the calculation of loss of state pension is given in Appendix 3 (see Arthur). The sums involved are not trivial: for a 63-year old male whose dismissal results in the loss of three qualifying years, the example produces an award of over £16,000.

3.48 The working group does not propose that there should be adjustments for age or contingencies other than mortality when making an award for loss of state pension rights using the Ogden Tables; those contingencies relate mainly to future employment, not to retirement. That said, if the parties consider that the Ogden Tables approach is inappropriate in an individual case, or that certain adjustments should be made for other contingencies when making an award for loss of state pension rights, they will be free to make their arguments to the tribunal.

3.49 We noted above that, just as loss of earnings are assessed on a net basis, so is loss of pension income. The nSP is treated as earned income for income tax purposes, so that, in principle, income tax is payable on it. However, the maximum amount of the nSP, at 2017-18 rates, is £8,296.60. For most people, the personal allowance remains available to them in retirement; it is currently set at £11,500. The reality for most people, then, is that no income tax will be charged on nSP income. That is why the Government pays the nSP gross; for most people, the gross amount and the net amount are the same.

3.50 Similarly, when the tribunal awards a claimant a figure of compensation for their loss of state pension rights, it can be assumed that those nSP benefits, while calculated gross, are being assessed on a net basis. Moreover, because a claimant is receiving that sum now, as part of an overall award of compensation, it should still be grossed up to the extent that the overall award exceeds £30,000. The parties will free to make their arguments to the tribunal if they consider that the circumstances of a particular case require a different approach to grossing up[47].

NOTES

33 Available here: https://www.gov.uk/government/publications/state-pension-age-independent-review-final-report

34 See paragraph 4.2.2 of the final report.

35 Department for Work and Pensions, State Pension Age Review, available here: https://www.gov.uk/government/uploads/system/uploads/attachment_data/file/630065/state-pension-age-review-final-report.pdf

36 Further details here: https://www.gov.uk/government/news/proposed-new-timetable-for-state-pension-age-increases

37 The government's reforms to public sector DB pension schemes generally provided relief for members who were, at a particular date, within ten years of reaching the scheme's retirement age. The effect of the relief was to enable such individuals to remain members of the unreformed DB scheme (so that, for example, all their pension benefits retained the link to final salary) rather than become members of the new DB scheme (so that, for example, their benefits would accrue on a CARE basis). The situation has been made more complex by two factors. First, many members will have accrued benefits in the unreformed scheme before joining the new scheme (so that, for example, some of their benefits are linked to final salary and some are not). Second, there was transitional relief for members who were more than ten years away (but no more than 13½ years) from the scheme's normal retirement age: the effect was to delay, on a sliding scale, the date at which they joined the reformed scheme. Further details are provided in Appendix 1.

38 Further details here: https://www.gov.uk/tax-national-insurance-after-state-pension-age/overview. This concerns Class 1 employee NI contributions. The self-employed who continue working beyond state pension age must still pay Class 2 and 4 NI contributions. Also, employer NI contributions continue to be payable in respect of employees who work beyond state pension age; see https://www.gov.uk/employee-reaches-state-pension-age.

39 nSP increases by 1% for every 9 weeks of deferral (about 5.8% for every full year of deferral). Further details are here: https://www.gov.uk/deferring-state-pension/how-it-works.

40 It is not possible to accrue part years. A person either does, or does not, satisfy the test for a qualifying year. Consequently, when calculating a person's nSP, the denominator will always be 35 and the numerator will always be a whole number between 10 and 35.

41 Oral evidence to the Work and Pensions Committee on 25 November 2015: http://data.parliament.uk/writtenevidence/committeeevidence.svc/evidencedocument/work-and-pensions-committee/understanding-the-new-state-pension/oral/25270.html

42 The link to the Government Gateway is here: https://www.gov.uk/government-gateway. The Gateway is a website used to register for online government services. It enables people to communicate and transact with the Government from a single point of entry. The online services available include child maintenance, driver licensing, income tax self-assessment, tax credits, money claims and, for our purposes, state pension details. The separate link for state pension details is here: https://www.gov.uk/check-state-pension.

43 In March 2017, the final report of the Independent Reviewer of State Pension Age, John Cridland CBE, recommended that the triple lock should be abandoned. However, by virtue of the confidence and supply agreement reached between the Conservative Party and the DUP and published in June 2017, the triple lock will be retained in the current Parliament; see https://www.gov.uk/government/publications/conservative-and-dup-agreement-and-uk-government-financial-support-for-northern-ireland. CPI is the measure of inflation used in the triple lock; it is examined further when CARE schemes are discussed in Chapter 5.

44 It will still be open to a person to make voluntary NI contributions to accrue further qualifying years, perhaps doing so from compensation they receive, just as they may choose to invest some of their compensation in a private pension plan.

45 The BR1 application form can be collected from a Post Office or downloaded from here: https://www.gov.uk/government/publications/application-for-a-state-pension-statement. Details for the Future Pension Centre are here: https://www.gov.uk/future-pension-centre

46 http://visual.ons.gov.uk/how-long-will-my-pension-need-to-last/

47 For example, in some cases it might be appropriate to add in state pension income at Steps 1 and 2 of the "seven steps" model, described in **Chapter 5**, to gain a more accurate picture of net pension loss in a complex DB case. As will become clear, however, that would usually mean that state pension loss would be assessed by reference to an Ogden multiplier that has been subjected to a two-year age adjustment.

CHAPTER 4: OCCUPATIONAL PENSIONS – DEFINED CONTRIBUTION SCHEMES

INTRODUCTION

[4.330]

4.1 We next consider the issues that arise when compensating a claimant for loss of pension rights arising after dismissal from employment with benefits under a DC scheme. DC schemes are cheaper for employers to operate because they only promise to pay a defined amount into the scheme now, the present cost of which can easily be ascertained. They do not promise to pay a retired employee a defined amount in the future. The present cost of a future benefit is more difficult to ascertain, based as it must be upon a series of imponderables relating to life expectancy, investment returns, length of service and future rates of pay.

4.2 In a DC scheme, the cost to the employer is mainly limited to the total cost of contributions it makes into a pension pot for each employee. The administrative aspects, such as management charges, need not concern us. The employee's contributions into the scheme are sometimes called "member contributions" (where the word "member" relates to their status as a "member" of the occupational pension scheme).

4.3 DC schemes are typically of two types:

(a) In a trust-based scheme, the employer establishes a board of trustees to administer the scheme. They will be responsible for monitoring the performance of the underlying fund and ensuring that it complies with legislative requirements. Such a scheme might be "branded" with the employer's name. There will be ongoing legal and accounting costs involved with keeping records up to date and reporting to members.

(b) In a contract-based scheme, an independent provider (such as an insurance company or building society) is appointed to run the scheme. The employer is responsible for ensuring that the appropriate contributions are made, including in respect of employee contributions deducted from payroll, but the provider handles most of the administration. They are sometimes seen as cheaper alternatives because they can be bought "off the shelf".

4.4 There are certain tax advantages in registering a DC scheme for tax – and most schemes are registered for tax. For example, contributions paid to the scheme attract tax relief; investment returns during the life of the fund are largely free from income tax and capital gains tax; and, on retirement, part of the employee's benefits can be taken as a tax-free lump sum (traditionally up to 25% of the value of the fund). The tribunal will assume it is dealing with a tax-registered scheme in the absence of any evidence to the contrary.

4.5 The aim of the trustees or the independent provider will be to invest the pot or fund of contributions with a view to increasing it. The amount of the resulting pension will self-evidently depend on the performance of that pot or fund. Like personal pensions, a bigger fund will support the purchase of a bigger annuity and a bigger tax-free lump sum. Indeed, one of the few differences between an orthodox DC scheme organised by an employer and a purely personal pension scheme is that in the former case the individual, who benefits from being a member of a larger group, can expect to pay a lower administration charge.

"PENSION FREEDOMS"

4.6 A personal pension fund, or occupational DC pension fund, may be used to purchase an annuity. How do annuities work? As a rough idea, take an individual retiring at the age of 65 with a personal pension pot valued at £133,333. Suppose they take a cash-free lump sum of £33,333 (25% of the overall value) and the remaining £100,000 is available to purchase an annuity. At current rates a sum of £100,000 would buy a 65-year old a no-frills annuity (i.e. an annual pension income) of about £5,300. (Annuity rates have fallen: in 2008, it would have been closer to £7,500.) The annuity would reduce further if an individual wanted to retire early and/or build in guaranteed future increases and/or make a portion of the annuity available to their spouse upon death. So, for example, if an individual wanted to retire at age 60 with an income that increased by 3% a year, including 50% joint life cover, £100,000 would presently buy an annuity of about £2,750.

4.7 Given the low level of annuity rates, the legal compulsion to purchase an annuity was the subject of debate. Some criticised it as poor value for money; others defended it as a necessary mechanism for protecting people from themselves (to reduce the risk that they would exhaust the pension pot too quickly). Ultimately this debate was a political one about how much people could or should be trusted to spend their savings.

4.8 An attempt to resolve that debate came with the Pension Schemes Act 2015. It introduced in stages, between 2015 and 2016, one of the more important pension reforms of recent years: the so-called "pension freedoms". These allow individuals to access their full pension pots from age 55 (although the age rises for those born later). Crucially, individuals are no longer compelled to purchase an annuity, although there are tax consequences of exercising the pension freedoms. In April 2015, the Government launched the "Pension Wise" service, in partnership with the Pensions Advisory Service and Citizens Advice, to provide free and impartial advice to people with a DC pension approaching retirement and considering exercising the freedoms[48].

4.9 Those freedoms will have no impact upon the calculation of pension loss in tribunal cases. We are not concerned with how people spend their pension savings, but how the employer contributes to the cost of accruing them. It is the disappearance of the employer's contributions to the DC scheme, following an unlawful dismissal, which leads to loss that the tribunal can compensate.

AUTO-ENROLMENT

4.10 We noted above that some successful claimants forget to claim pension loss entirely and focus instead on their salary loss. This may reflect the fact that, for many years, it was not compulsory for an employer to set up a pension scheme. This landscape has changed in recent years, and continues to change, as the UK moves towards a system in which the law encourages private pension provision through employment even if it does not go so far as to compel it.

4.11 The Welfare Reform and Pensions Act 1999 was a previous attempt to encourage private pension provision. It introduced "stakeholder" pension schemes to the UK in April 2001. Certain employers were required to provide access to a designated stakeholder scheme to their employees. The designated scheme would be a DC scheme set up with certain conditions such as a cap on administration charges and flexibility for stopping and starting contributions. However, there was no compulsion on employees to join such schemes and no compulsion on employers to make contributions to them. Stakeholder schemes had little impact on the work of the tribunals in calculating pension loss and limited effect on encouraging lower earners to improve private pension provision. The system was repealed in October 2012.

4.12 Following the recommendations of the Turner Report[49], the Pensions Act 2008 introduced a new approach, by which most workers would be enrolled automatically (known as "auto-enrolment") into a qualifying pension scheme. The Government has set up a vehicle for that purpose: the National Employment Savings Trust (or "NEST"). NEST is a trust-based not-for-profit DC scheme with low administration charges; we refer in chapter 5 to a useful online calculator on the NEST website. Other pension vehicles operated by private providers are available and employers are also free to set up their own schemes (or use existing ones), so long as they satisfy certain minimum requirements. The idea is for individual employees to have portable personal accounts.

4.13 The auto-enrolment scheme for employees formally commenced in October 2012 and will be implemented fully by February 2018. This new regime has had a long gestation and the hope is that it will provide the architecture for occupational pension provision for many years to come.

4.14 The auto-enrolment scheme can be summarised as follows:

(a) Since October 2012, employers have been required to assess their workforces and enrol eligible workers into an occupational pension. Under the new regime, crucially, workers must no longer make a conscious decision to join such a scheme but instead must make a conscious decision to leave it. The underlying policy idea is that the tendency of some individuals towards inertia on financial matters will encourage them to make pension savings.

(b) The extended period of implementation started with the largest employers and will end with the smallest. It was originally intended to be three years, but has been lengthened twice. As matters stand the implementation period will last 5½ years with the last employers finally joining in February 2018. The Pensions Regulator writes to employers to give them 18 months' notice of their staging date for compliance with the regime. By way of overview:

- Employers with more than 250 workers were assigned their staging dates first, falling between October 2012 and February 2014;
- Employers with between 50 and 249 workers were assigned staging dates between April 2014 and April 2015;
- Employers with fewer than 50 workers have been assigned staging dates between June 2015 and April 2017; and
- New employers set up between April 2012 and September 2017 have been assigned staging dates between May 2017 and February 2018.

(c) As matters stand, most of the respondents seen in the tribunal will either have an existing DC or DB occupational pension scheme or will already have enrolled workers automatically into a DC scheme. This will be true of all employers by February 2018. Any employer that breaches its obligations will be subject to compliance and penalty notices issued by the Pensions Regulator[50].

(d) However, not all workers must be auto-enrolled. There are detailed rules about the circumstances in which an individual worker qualifies as an eligible "jobholder" (which is the term used by the new regime). Given that many workers today have atypical working arrangements, it is expected that employers must make continuous assessments of the auto-enrolment eligibility status of their individual workers, such as those on "zero-hours" arrangements. In general terms, the conditions for auto-enrolment are that a worker ordinarily works in Great Britain under a contract, is aged between 22 and their state pension age and is paid "qualifying earnings" by an employer (taking account of bonuses, overtime, maternity pay etc). The gross annual "earnings trigger" for auto-enrolment is £10,000. Once triggered, contributions are paid upon earnings that fall within a qualifying earnings band; this is reviewed annually and, for the 2017-18 tax year, runs from £5,876 to £45,000[51].

(e) The basic requirements for such a scheme include mandatory minimum pension contributions by both employer and jobholder. In other words, the element of compulsion is not in respect of jobholder membership of such schemes but in respect of employer and jobholder contribution to such schemes. By way of overview:

- Until April 2018, the jobholder makes a mandatory minimum contribution of 1% of pensionable pay, while the employer must make a matching contribution of 1% (i.e. a total of 2%).
- Between April 2018 and April 2019, the jobholder makes a mandatory minimum contribution of 3% of pensionable pay, while the employer must contribute 2% (i.e. a total of 5%).
- After April 2019, the jobholder makes a mandatory minimum contribution of 5% of pensionable pay, while the employer must contribute 3% (i.e. a total of 8%).

(f) These contributions must continue until the worker opts out, leaves employment or reaches the age of 75, whichever is the sooner[52].

4.15 Because of tax relief, the employee's actual contributions will be slightly lower: if tax relief is given at the present basic rate of 20% on an employee contribution of 1%, the effective contribution rate is in fact 0.8%. Similarly, for 3% the effective contribution rate will be 2.4% and for 5% the effective contribution rate will be 4%.

4.16 It is hoped that opt-out rates will not increase as employee contribution rates increase. The eligibility criteria for jobholders are drafted broadly enough to increase the chances of the regime achieving wide coverage. Each month the Pensions Regulator publishes a report detailing how many employers have submitted a declaration of compliance and summarising how many workers are involved[53]. For example, by the end of July 2017, nearly 700,000 employers had confirmed compliance. This covers about 26.2m workers. Of these, about 8.3m workers counted as eligible jobholders who were auto-enrolled, while about 10.2m were already active members of their employer's scheme on the relevant staging date. The cross-party House of Commons Work and Pensions Committee has described this as a "tremendous success"[54].

SIMPLE DC CASES: ISSUES FOR THE EMPLOYMENT TRIBUNAL

4.17 Where a successful claimant has, through dismissal, lost the benefit of membership of a DC scheme, it is usually straightforward to calculate the resulting net loss of pension that is attributable to the employer and which flows from its unlawful conduct. The basis for calculation will be the employer's contributions for whatever period of loss the tribunal has identified. This is known as the "contributions method".

4.18 The contributions method is a "broad brush" approach. The precise level of future pension loss a claimant will experience in retirement because of dismissal from a job with DC pension benefits is, as at the date of the hearing, very difficult to predict. The fund associated with that pension might, in the future, perform well. It might perform poorly. A process of aggregating the employer's pension contributions for the appropriate period of loss is felt to be a tolerably accurate assessment of the pension loss that, after income tax, a claimant will experience in retirement. It is worth emphasising that, despite appearances to the contrary, an award of pension contributions for a past period is not an award of past loss; it is an award designed to capture future net loss of pension income.

4.19 This approach does not extend to the loss of the employee's own contributions: those contributions are deducted from their salary and they are still free to make contributions of the same amount to a personal pension from whatever sum the tribunal awards in respect of salary loss. It is true that the successful claimant may face higher administration charges when no longer a member of a DC scheme, but these charges are often difficult to identify and calculate and would likely be relatively small. For this reason, they can, in most cases, be ignored. If a claimant feels strongly about the point, they will need to adduce evidence of this element of loss and seek to persuade the tribunal, on normal principles, that it is attributable to their dismissal and appropriate for compensation.

4.20 Some occupational schemes permit employees to make additional voluntary contributions (or "AVCs"). Where AVCs to a DC scheme are entirely employee-funded, they can be ignored for the same reason as normal employee contributions. It is feasible, however, that the employer might have provided some form of contribution towards the employee's AVCs; in that case, the loss of that employer contribution should be brought into account when assessing the claimant's pension loss.

4.21 So, in cases where a claimant has incurred occupational pension loss following their unlawful dismissal from employment in which they were a member of a DC scheme (which, for this purposes, includes a scheme into which they were auto-enrolled), compensation will be assessed using the contributions method. Examples are given in Appendix 3 (see Bethan, Christopher, Diane, Edward and Fatima). This will be subject to normal principles about the terminal date for such loss, questions of contributory fault, the application of the statutory cap and so on. The tribunal will use standard case management orders to establish the employee's pensionable pay and the employer's rate of contribution to any DC scheme it operates. It ought to be easy to obtain this information. Even if the employer does not provide the information, it should be apparent from payslips or from previous pension statements.

4.22 There is one proviso to this approach: short service refunds. Those who leave an occupational DC scheme before they have been in it for two years may have the option of a refund of their own contributions, leaving them with no pension for that period. The effect is to treat them as if they had never been a member of that scheme. The "may" is for this reason: since 1 October 2015, members of DC schemes have no longer been entitled to short service refunds if they leave employment (or opt out) with less than two years of qualifying service. This change only applies to individuals who became members of an occupational DC scheme on or after 1 October 2015 (or those who re-joined after having already taken a refund or transferred out); short service refunds are still available to those who joined before that date. Also, regardless of this change, those with less than 30 day' service are still able to request a short service refund. The return of contributions does not, in and of itself, compensate a claimant for the pension benefits that they would have received but for the unlawful dismissal, or for the lost benefit of the employer's pension contributions. The point is that, when compensation is assessed overall, the claimant must give credit for any contributions that have been refunded.

4.23 Because the employer's pension contributions are not treated as part of a claimant's wages, they will not, in an unfair dismissal case, be subject to recoupment[55]. Pension loss must therefore be calculated separately.

4.24 The longer the period of loss, the greater the care that must be taken to ensure that the employer's pension contributions reflect possible future pay rises in the old job. An example is given at Appendix 3 (see Diane).

4.25 As noted above, the tribunal will not apply different standards of causation to a claimant's loss of earnings and their loss of pension benefits. This is because a claimant's pension benefits are merely part of an overall remuneration package. The tribunal must be alert to the possibility that a future rise in salary in new employment is sufficient to offset both pension loss and earnings loss arising from dismissal from the old employment.

4.26 If the respondent takes no part in the proceedings and the claimant has failed to adduce any evidence (e.g. from payslips or pension statements) as to the percentage rate of contributions that the old employer made to a DC scheme, what should the tribunal do? In that scenario, the tribunal should check that the claimant's earnings in the old job exceeded the lower level of the qualifying earnings band. If they did not, and there was no reasonable prospect of them doing so had dismissal not occurred, there will be no pension loss. If they did, the tribunal will assume, in the absence of any basis on which to infer the contrary, that the respondent's contribution rate was at the minimum level required by auto-enrolment. An example is given at Appendix 3 (see Edward). If the claimant's earnings exceeded the upper level of the qualifying earnings band, the contributions should only be incurred on earnings within the band.

4.27 The tribunal will not need to look at annual pay figures for this purpose. The website of the Pensions Regulator helpfully sets out the qualifying earnings band for pay periods of one week, two weeks, four weeks, one month and one quarter[56].

4.28 Auto-enrolment provides that contributions could, in principle, continue until a person's 75th birthday. They may therefore constitute an element of loss that continues beyond state pension age (for those claimants who persuade the tribunal that they would continue working beyond that age).

4.29 Auto-enrolment benefits may be a "new job fact"[57]. When giving credit for earnings received through mitigation of future loss, the tribunal should consider a hypothetical future employer's duty to pay mandatory minimum pension contributions. It can be left to the good sense of the tribunal, with its knowledge of local labour market conditions and having heard evidence from the parties, to decide whether this is appropriate. The tribunal might decide, having regard to the type of work for which the claimant is likely to apply when mitigating their loss, that a hypothetical new employer might pay more than mandatory minimum contributions that are required for auto-enrolment, and take this into account by a deduction from the loss awarded; or the tribunal may decide that the minimum contributions required by auto-enrolment are appropriate, and deduct accordingly; or it may decide to make no deductions at all, for example on the basis that the claimant would not exceed the lower level of qualifying earnings in the new employment. If the tribunal chooses mandatory minimum employer contributions under auto-enrolment, it will need to bear in mind their increase to 2% of pensionable pay (from 6 April 2018) and 3% of pensionable pay (from 6 April 2019). An example is given at Appendix 3 (see Fatima).

4.30 It is possible that the tribunal is persuaded that a claimant will experience a lengthy or career-long earnings loss from employment which had DC scheme benefits. For such a case, we make the following observations:

(a) Although it will depend on the circumstances, the simplest way to assess loss of DC pension rights in such a case may be to increase the level of the claimant's net earnings in the old job by the percentage of earnings the employer contributed to the DC scheme (and, if there is a new job, doing the same to earnings from the new job) and to use the Ogden Tables to calculate net loss of earnings using this adjusted multiplicand.

(b) This approach has the advantage of simplicity. It is also consistent with paragraph 30 of the explanatory notes to the Ogden Tables. However, an adjustment may be needed to ensure that recoupment is applied correctly and, in a discrimination case, to reflect the fact that no interest is awarded on pension loss.

(c) It bears repeating that, in such a scenario, the claimant is not being compensated for their pension loss by receiving the employer's pension contributions personally, since those contributions are not the measure of their loss. Instead, the contributions method works by identifying a broad-brush one-off sum that compensates the claimant for the net shortfall in their future pension income.

(d) Just as with loss of earnings, it may be appropriate to factor in the possibility of future promotion (whereby an increase in salary would be accompanied by an increase in the amount – albeit not the percentage – contributed to the DC scheme by the employer) as well as adjustments for contingencies other than mortality.

(e) In respect of highly-paid claimants, care must be taken, when using this methodology, to identify the correct level of net earnings to which such contributions are added. There may an AA charge or a restriction of the personal allowance, either of which will reduce net pay. The net pay set out in the claimant's payslips will be the best guide (subject to our points at paragraphs 2.23 and 2.24).

(f) Such cases will be rare. Significant loss of pension rights is more likely to arise where DB pension benefits are concerned. These Principles discuss the Ogden Tables in more detail in Chapter 5. As with DB cases, it will be open to the parties to obtain expert evidence, such as from an actuary, to achieve greater precision in calculating DC pension loss than the method suggested above.

4.31 By way of reminder, grossing up of compensation may be required.

NOTES

48 Pension Wise unveiled: https://www.gov.uk/government/news/pension-wise-unveiled. The Pension Wise website is at https://www.pensionwise.gov.uk. A free appointment is available to those aged 50 or over.

49 The first report of the Pensions Commission ("Challenges and Choices", 2004) is at https://www.webarchive.org.uk/wayback/archive/20070802120000/http:/www.pensionscommission.org.uk/publications/2004/annrep/fullreport.pdf. The second report of the Pensions Commission ("A New Pension Settlement for the Twenty-First Century", 2005) is at http://webarchive.nationalarchives.gov.uk/+/http:/www.dwp.gov.uk/publications/dwp/2005/pensionscommreport/main-report.pdf.

50 Details are here: http://www.thepensionsregulator.gov.uk/en/employers/what-happens-if-i-dont-comply.aspx. An employer can challenge such a notice, first by applying to the Pensions Regulator for a review (http://www.thepensionsregulator.gov.uk/en/employers/apply-for-a-review.aspx) and then by means of an appeal to the General Regulatory Chamber of the First-tier Tribunal (https://www.gov.uk/guidance/appeal-against-a-pensions-regulator-fine).

51 Details available from the website of the Pensions Regulator: http://www.thepensionsregulator.gov.uk/automatic-enrolment-earnings-threshold.aspx

52 The Pensions Regulator has provided an employer contribution calculator here: http://www.workplacepensions.gov.uk/employee/employer-contribution-calculator/

53 http://www.thepensionsregulator.gov.uk/docs/automatic-enrolment-declaration-of-compliance-monthly-report.pdf

54 See Summary (page 3) of Eleventh Report of Session 2015-16 (May 2016), at https://www.publications.parliament.uk/pa/cm201516/cmselect/cmworpen/579/579.pdf.

55 Under the Employment Protection (Recoupment of Benefits) Regulations 1996.

56 http://www.thepensionsregulator.gov.uk/automatic-enrolment-earnings-threshold.aspx

57 See *Kingston Upon Hull City Council v. Dunnachie (no.3)* [2003] IRLR 843.

CHAPTER 5: OCCUPATIONAL PENSIONS – DEFINED BENEFIT SCHEMES

[4.331]

5.1 We turn next to the issues that arise when compensating a claimant for loss of pension rights arising after dismissal from employment with benefits under a DB scheme. In a DB scheme, the pension benefit is guaranteed regardless of the performance of any underlying pot or fund. DB schemes have often been thought synonymous with final salary schemes. That is understandable since, for many years, DB schemes were usually structured around delivering retirement benefits based on final salary. More recently, however, CARE designs have emerged.

5.2 A profound change in the occupational pensions landscape of the last decade has been the widespread closure of DB schemes in the private sector, at first to new entrants and then to existing members. This has been accompanied by a shift in the public sector from final salary designs to CARE designs. Corroboration of this can be found in the Pensions Trends series that was produced by the Office for National Statistics until 2013 (and, until January 2016, took the form of a periodically updated "pensions compendium")[58] and in the "Purple Book" issued annually by the Pensions Regulator and the Pension Protection Fund[59]. The Purple Book sets out data on the decreasing number of open schemes (where members join a DB section and accrue benefits), the increasing number of those schemes that are closed to new members (in which existing members continue to accrue benefits) or are closed to future accruals (where existing members can no longer accrue new years of service) and those schemes that are being wound up.

FUNDED AND UNFUNDED SCHEMES

5.3 DB schemes are sometimes described as being funded or unfunded (or non-funded). What is the difference? In a funded scheme, the employer sets aside money to meet the predicted cost of the benefits when they fall due. This money is usually called the "employer contribution". The amount of money the employer sets aside is, in turn, based on actuarial advice about the minimum level of ongoing funding required to pay future benefits. This used to be known as the "minimum funding requirement" (or "MFR") but, since the Pensions Act 2004, it has been replaced by a "statutory funding objective". Of the few remaining DB schemes in the private sector based around final salary benefits, most are funded. The associated pension funds can be huge.

5.4 The funding for such schemes does not come solely from the employer's contributions. Most schemes levy a charge on employee members who pay their own contributions; so-called "non-contributory final salary pension schemes" are rare indeed today. As with DC schemes, these can be called "employee contributions" or "member contributions". As more schemes struggle to produce a surplus, attempts can be made to increase employee contributions.

5.5 The third edition of the guidance for calculating pension loss in tribunals estimated that the cost to an employer of operating a final salary scheme was typically 15% of pensionable pay (or 20% of pensionable pay for a non-contributory scheme). This estimate was based on assumptions about investment returns at the time and, today, such percentage figures would probably be higher. The third edition also discussed the "holidays" an employer might take from making pension contributions. Nowadays it is not pension scheme surpluses that are in the news, but deficits. Indeed, there have been examples of employers becoming insolvent while its pension scheme was in deficit, resulting in unexpected hardship and a failure to meet the "pension promise". In a response to this, the Pensions Act 2004 set up the Pension Protection Fund with effect from April 2006[60]. This can provide compensation to affected individuals. It is funded by a levy on those employers operating similar schemes.

5.6 In an unfunded scheme, the employer does not set aside any assets but instead simply pays the benefits as and when they fall due. Indeed, by that definition, the UK state pension system is also an unfunded scheme: benefits are paid out as and when due, and are funded from the public purse. It is now rare to find an unfunded DB pension scheme outside of the public sector. The pension schemes for the NHS, teachers and civil servants are all unfunded and operated centrally (the schemes for police officers and firefighters are unfunded but operated locally). By contrast, the local government scheme is a funded scheme, with assets currently valued at £217 billion[61]. Appendix 1 provides a summary of the benefits available under these schemes.

5.7 Even unfunded schemes have a notional level of employer contributions (alongside the employee's contributions) so that the promised benefits can be met. These figures can be obtained upon inquiries being made of either the employer or the trustees of the pension scheme.

ANCILLARY BENEFITS OF DB SCHEMES

5.8 As Appendix 1 illustrates, some public sector DB pension schemes are more generous than others. For example, some of these schemes allow members to take an unreduced ("unabated") pension at a younger age than the age at which they would receive a state pension (although they would still have to wait until state pension age to receive their nSP); an example is police officers. Other schemes have aligned their retirement ages to the later of 65 or state pension age. Members can still elect to leave earlier with a pension, subject to the scheme's rules, but the amount of their pension is then actuarially reduced to reflect the longer period of receipt[62]. These schemes also have different accrual rates.

5.9 Some DB schemes include a range of other ancillary benefits including pensions for survivors (widows, widowers and dependants), ill health or redundancy (including early retirement with unreduced pensions or "added years" of service) and payments for death in service[63].

5.10 If scheme members leave employment other than for retirement (e.g. they have been dismissed and do not qualify for early retirement), their pension will be deferred in the usual way until they reach the age at which it comes into payment.

FINAL SALARY SCHEMES

5.11 The third edition proceeded on the assumption that the DB scheme the tribunal would typically examine when assessing pension loss would be a final salary scheme. That is no longer a safe assumption. As already noted, there has been a widespread move in the public sector to CARE schemes; this affects future benefit accrual for all employees save those with the benefit of provisions protecting those closest to retirement. That said, the steady decline of final salary schemes across the board does not mean that they can be ignored when assessing pension loss. Some of the claimants before the tribunal will have accrued a substantial period of membership in a final salary scheme before being moved into a CARE scheme. Those accrued final salary rights remain valuable: they will still lead to a final salary pension for the period of membership of the final salary scheme and may also benefit from future pay enhancements[64].

5.12 So, it is still necessary for tribunals and parties to understand how final salary pension schemes operate[65]. At their simplest, they provide for an income in retirement and for a lump sum (or for the opportunity to exchange some of the pension income for a lump sum). More particularly:

(a) The pension income is calculated using accrual of fractions of pensionable pay. In a sixtieths scheme, for example, one-sixtieth of the full-time equivalent of pensionable pay at retirement will be multiplied by the total number of years in employment. This will then provide a pension income up to a typical maximum of two-thirds of final salary after 40 years' service. In eightieths schemes, the typical maximum is half of pensionable pay after 40 years' service. Parttime employees accrue service on a slower, pro rata, basis. (Some final salary schemes also permit employees to pay AVCs, with the effect of purchasing "added years" of scheme membership.)

(b) The lump sum benefit is usually one of two types:

- Some schemes (usually eightieths) provide for a lump sum <u>in addition to</u> the pension income. In such cases the lump sum accrues in the same way as pension income. Broadly speaking, in an eightieths scheme, the pension income accrues at an effective rate of 1/80 (or 1.25% of pensionable pay) for each year of pensionable service. If the lump sum represents three times an employee's pension income, it will accrue at the rate of 3/80 (or 3.75% of pensionable pay) for each year of service.
- Other schemes (usually sixtieths) only provide for a lump sum in return for a sacrifice of some of the pension income, through a process called "commutation". A typical rate of exchange is for £1 of annual pension income to be converted into a £12 one-off lump sum payment. This 1:12 conversion rate may vary between schemes. It will also be subject to HMRC rules and limits and the rules of the pension scheme.

So, although the accrual rate in most public sector DB schemes has often varied between sixtieths and eightieths, the overall value of benefits has broadly been the same because the latter invariably provides for a lump sum in addition to the pension income whereas the former only provides for a lump sum through commutation.

CARE SCHEMES

5.13 A small number of final salary pension schemes remain in operation in the private sector but, apart from in respect of accrued rights or those benefitting from protection who maintain future accrual rights, they are effectively extinct in the public sector. In their place are CARE schemes.

5.14 When it took office in 2010, the Coalition Government's desire to achieve savings across the public sector was well known. The cost of funding the provision of pensions to public sector workers had risen steadily in recent years, principally because of increased life expectancy. It was thought that, unless public sector pension schemes were reformed, they would become unaffordable. The Coalition Government commissioned a report on the subject from Lord Hutton. The Hutton Commission published its final report in March 2011[66]. Its key recommendations were as follows:

(a) Final salary designs would be replaced by CARE designs. In other words, pension benefits would no longer be linked to final pensionable pay but to the pensionable pay averaged over the time a person spent as a scheme member. To calculate the "career average" for this purpose, each year's pay would be uprated for inflation, then all such "slices" would be aggregated and the overall total then divided by the number of years of scheme membership. (Final salary schemes benefit those promoted later in their career. CARE schemes, by contrast, often benefit those with consistent incomes throughout their career; this is because, as Appendix 1 illustrates, they often have better accrual rates.)

(b) Existing members would move to new schemes for future accruals, while maintaining the link to final salary for calculating the value of the pension rights they had accrued up to that point.
(c) Normal pension age would be aligned with the state pension age and, accordingly, increase over time with it (save for the police, firefighters and armed services, where the age of entitlement to an unreduced pension would only rise as far as 60).
(d) There would be a cost ceiling for the schemes, limiting employer contributions to a percentage of pensionable pay. To keep costs under control, automatic stabilisers (such as increases to employee contributions or reductions in benefits) would be built in, and would be imposed if agreement could not be reached.

5.15 The Government accepted these recommendations and, in so doing, set out its "preferred scheme design" for reform. The design was set out in a Treasury Command Paper published in November 2011[67]. It formed the basis for negotiations with trade unions about individual schemes across the public sector. Its main features included the following:
(a) Public sector schemes would remain DB schemes, but based on a CARE design rather than a final salary design;
(b) Retirement benefits accrued prior to the implementation of the reforms would, as Lord Hutton recommended, remain linked to the final salary at the date when retirement benefits were taken;
(c) There would be an accrual rate of sixtieths, equivalent to 1.66% (as Appendix 1 shows, however, some unions have negotiated better accrual rates);
(d) The "banked slices" would be revalued in line with CPI (although some schemes revalue at a rate that tracks CPI)[68]; and
(e) Lump sums would be available through commutation only, whereby £1 of annual pension income could be converted to a £12 one-off lump sum payment, subject to HMRC rules and limits.

5.16 The Principal Civil Service Pension Scheme (PCSPS) offers a useful illustration. As Appendix 1 shows, the new version of the PCSPS (known as "Alpha") has adopted an accrual rate of 1:43.1. This can be expressed as 2.32%. It is obviously superior to the rate of sixtieths (or 1.66%) set out in the preferred scheme design. In broad terms, prior to the recent pension reforms, the pension schemes for civil servants were as follows:
(a) About 60% were in the "Classic" PCSPS: a final salary scheme, with member contributions of 1.5%, an accrual rate of 1/80ths (1.25%), a maximum pension of 45/80ths, a lump sum of three times the pension income, and entitlement to an unabated pension at age 60. It closed to new members in 2002.
(b) About 25% were in the "Premium" PCSPS: a final salary scheme, with member contributions of 3.5%, an accrual rate of 1/60ths (1.66%), a maximum pension of 45/60ths, no lump sum (but 1:12 commutation), and entitlement to an unabated pension at age 60. It closed to new members in 2007.
(c) About 15% were in the "Nuvos" PCSPS: a CARE scheme, with member contributions of 3.5%, an accrual rate of 1/43.5 (2.3%), a maximum pension of 75% of final pensionable pay, no lump sum (but 1:12 commutation), and entitlement to an unabated pension at age 65. It closed on 31 March 2015.

5.17 The "Alpha" version of PCSPS opened on 1 April 2015. It incorporates CARE, higher member contributions, an accrual rate of 1/43.1 (2.32%), no lump sum (but 1:12 commutation) and entitlement to an unabated pension at the later of 65 or state pension age. On a gross annual salary of £30,000, 1/43.1 represents a "slice" of about £696 in pension income; which is set aside and "banked" each year, then revalued at the point of retirement by reference to CPI. As noted above, those civil servants who remain on static incomes throughout their career will do better under a CARE scheme than a final salary scheme, because of the better accrual rate. Those civil servants benefitting from promotions and pay rises in the later parts of their career do less well.

5.18 It is still possible to pay AVCs into a CARE scheme, and (subject to the annual allowance) they will attract tax relief. In CARE schemes the AVC element will usually operate as a money-purchase supplement, i.e. it will be a DC "add on" to a predominantly Db scheme. Under the current pension freedoms, a member would be entitled to draw down from an AVC pot from the age of 55.

5.19 As this summary demonstrates, a proper assessment of substantial loss of CARE pension benefits must consider the lost "slices" of pensionable pay that, but for the unlawful dismissal, the claimant would continue to have "banked" (see the example of Gaynor at Appendix 3). The prospect of future promotion remains important, but will be less financially valuable. This is because accrued pension rights in a final salary scheme are, by definition, the only rights that will be pegged to final salary at retirement. Accrued rights in a CARE scheme are pegged to the salary in the year that they accrued.

BACK TO TAX

5.20 At CHAPTER 2 of these Principles, we examined the Annual Allowance (AA) and the Lifetime Allowance (LTA). They are also relevant to DB schemes, almost all of which are tax-registered. Some high-earning claimants appearing in the tribunal will be affected by the AA and LTA in complex ways, which we will now explain.

5.21 The mechanism for assessing whether an individual's public sector pension pot is likely to exceed the LTA is as follows: take the annual pension income at the date of retirement, without any commutation, and multiply it by a factor of 20. If the scheme provided for an additional lump sum without commutation, this should be added separately. By way of example, consider Jane, a highly paid civil servant who retired in May 2016, when (thanks to protection) she was still a member of the "Classic" PCSPS. We will assume that she retired on a final salary of £130,000 after 45 years' service. Her pension at that time would be 45/80ths of £130,000, i.e. £67,500. Multiplied by 20, the deemed value of her pension pot would be

£1,350,000. Her separate tax-free lump sum would be three times £67,500, which is £202,500, which should be added. For LTA purposes, then, her pension pot would be valued at £1,350,000 plus £202,500, which is £1,552,000. (This would need to be added to the value of any private pension pot that she had accumulated; for the sake of simplicity, we shall assume that there is none.) The LTA is currently set at £1m, so the deemed value of Jane's retirement benefits would exceed it by £552,000.

5.22 The LTA charge would involve tax being levied on Jane's benefits as follows: there would be a one-off charge of 55% of the amount of the excess that she took as a lump sum and an annual charge based on 25% of the amount of the excess that is taken as pension income (in a DB scheme, the 25% figure is divided by 20 and the annual pension income reduced by that twentieth). Subject to scheme rules, it might be possible to choose whether and in what proportion the tax penalty is borne by the lump sum and/or the pension income. So, Jane might choose to pay 55% of her lump sum of £202,500 in tax (being £111,375); and this would deal with £202,500 of the £552,000 excess. The remaining £349,500 would then be taxed at 25% (being £87,375), such that 1/20th of that amount (i.e. £4,368.75) would be taken from her annual pension income each year in addition to ordinary income tax. Alternatively, Jane could take her entire lump sum tax-free and pay all the excess as tax on her pension income. In that case, all the £552,000 would be taxed at 25% (i.e. £138,000) and 1/20th of that amount (i.e. £6,900) would be taken from her annual pension income in addition to ordinary income tax. Depending on her circumstances, a combination of income tax and the 25% charge may mean that a 55% charge on the lump sum would result in a lower overall tax charge. Jane would need to take financial advice as to how best to meet the charge.

5.23 It is proposed that the LTA will be indexed annually in line with CPI from 6 April 2018.

5.24 We described earlier how the AA represents the ceiling up to which — but not beyond — the state will grant tax relief on pension savings. In tax- registered DC schemes, it is straightforward to identify the level of an individual's own contributions. The more generous benefits available in DB pension schemes, however, attract a different regime for calculating the amount of pension savings for tax purposes: put simply, there is a deemed increase in the value of a person's DB pension benefits over the course of a tax year. This figure results from the application of a factor of 16 (which was increased in April 2011 from a factor of 10) to the increase in the value of the pension income (and any separate lump sum) between two input dates. There is scope for rolling over unused AA from previous tax years.

5.25 To explain its operation, we return to Jane; this time, let us assume that she has not yet retired, but is still in employment as a civil servant. She is still in receipt of a gross annual salary of £130,000. However, because she is now younger, we will assume that she was moved into the "Alpha" scheme in April 2015. She pays member contributions of 8.05%, which are equivalent to £10,465. This accrual rate means that, this year, she will "bank" a CARE slice of 1/43.1 × £130,000, which is £3,016.24. The figure of £3,016.24 is then multiplied by 16. This produces a figure of £48,259.84, which we round down to £48,259. This figure of £48,259 represents the deemed increase in the value of Jane's pension pot for that year; put another way, it is the amount by which her pot is deemed to have grown to deliver the promised retirement benefits. Crucially, it is much higher than her actual member contributions of £10,465.

5.26 Although Jane's gross annual salary is £130,000, her adjusted income for AA purposes is £167,794. Where does this figure come from? It is the result of this piece of arithmetic: her gross annual salary of £130,000, less her member contributions of £10,465, plus the deemed increase in value of her pension pot of £48,259.

5.27 As we noted above in Chapter 2, the AA is tapered where a person's adjusted income falls between £150,000 and £210,000. The tax impact on Jane is then as follows: her adjusted income of £167,794 exceeds £150,000 by £17,794. Every £2 of that excess reduces Jane's AA by £1. Half of £17,794 is £8,897; it follows, then, that an excess of £17,794 reduces her AA by £8,897. Jane's AA during the 2017/18 financial year will be £40,000 less £8,897, which is £31,103. The deemed increase in the value of Jane's pension pot of £48,259 exceeds her tapered AA of £31,103 by £17,156.

5.28 Jane adjusted net income for personal allowance purposes is £130,000 less her pension contributions of £10,465, which is £119,535 (reducing her personal allowance by £9,767.50 to £1,732.50). But she will still not reach the additional tax rate. Accordingly, she will pay tax on the sum of £17,156 at the rate of 40%. That will mean that she faces a tax liability of 40% of £17,156, which is £6,862[69].

5.29 There are two options for Jane in paying this: either she can declare it at the end of the tax year, through her self-assessment, or she can ask the pension scheme to pay it for her. If she chooses the second option, known as "Scheme Pays", the scheme will recover the tax from her for that year, and each subsequent year that it paid it for her, when she later retires, together with adjustments for interest levied in the meantime. The is achieved through a corresponding reduction in Jane's pension benefits, using complex actuarial formulae. This will reduce Jane's net pension benefits (and, if she were dismissed, her net pension loss).

SIMPLE DB CASES: ISSUES FOR THE EMPLOYMENT TRIBUNAL

5.30 Where the period of loss to be compensated is relatively short, a tolerably accurate assessment of the net value of lost DB pension benefits can be done using the contributions method. As with using that method in DC cases, it is enough to aggregate the employer's pension contributions for all relevant pay periods covered by the award of compensation (without recoupment). There are several points, however, needing emphasis.

5.31 Just as with DC schemes, members of contributory DB schemes may be entitled to a refund of their contributions if they leave with less than two years' qualifying service; this will be subject to the scheme's rules. A claimant who has chosen a refund of their contributions must give credit for them when compensation is assessed.

5.32 The first type of DB case we consider appropriate for the contributions method is where the tribunal decides that the claimant's dismissal would have been very likely to occur within a relatively short period, bringing an end to their loss of earnings and loss of DB pension rights. For example:

(a) A tribunal finds that a dismissal for redundancy was procedurally unfair but that a fair process, which might have taken longer, would almost certainly have led to the same outcome. In other words, the dismissal would still have occurred, but it would have only been delayed[70]. An illustration is given at Appendix 3 (see George).

(b) Another example is a procedurally unfair dismissal for gross misconduct that would still have occurred at a later point if a proper procedure had been followed.

Such scenarios are perhaps rare, but they provide a terminal point for all losses which, even for a claimant who was formerly in a DB scheme, point towards use of the contributions method. They represent what we might call, later in this chapter, a very high "withdrawal factor". However, if the tribunal is satisfied that there is a significant element of ongoing DB pension loss, the contributions method is unlikely to be appropriate. The contributions method is a better choice where, for example, the reduction under the *"Polkey"* principle, or because of contributory fault, is high.

5.33 These Principles do not set in stone the period of loss that would be short enough to merit use of the contributions method in a DB case, since much will depend on the facts. As a rule of thumb, six months would very likely be a short period; twelve months would probably still be short; 18 months and above would probably not be short. As always, the parties will be free to make their arguments to the tribunal[71].

5.34 Another scenario involving loss of both earnings and pension rights on a short-term basis is where a claimant mitigates their loss fully by obtaining alternative employment in a role with equivalent DB benefits (replacing like with like) or a role where the total remuneration, even with a less generous pension, exceeds the salary and pensions package of the old job. An example is given at Appendix 3 (see Fiona). Again, if a tribunal is persuaded that the pension loss is truly short-lived, the contributions method is appropriate. Such scenarios may be rare: even where the claimant finds employment with DB scheme benefits, the tribunal should be alert to a change in their value (for example, if the claimant had DB benefits in the old job that were linked to final salary at retirement, whereas in the new job they accrue on a CARE basis).

5.35 The application of the statutory cap on the compensatory award for unfair dismissal may sometimes mean that it is disproportionate to engage in a complex analysis of pension loss. For example, a high award for pension loss will be greatly reduced upon application of the statutory cap of 52 weeks' pay[72]. It will be open to the tribunal to treat the application of the statutory cap as a reason to adopt the contributions method in respect of DB pension loss. For example, if the cap is nearly exceeded by loss of earnings alone, carrying out complex pension loss calculations will waste the tribunal's time and the parties' costs. (We recognise that the parties may not know whether the statutory cap will apply until the outcome of the liability hearing, which is why we recommend that the remedy hearing is parked in cases that may require a complex pension calculation. This is explained further in **CHAPTER 6**.)

5.36 Where the contributions method is considered suitable, the tribunal must ascertain the rate of the employer's contribution to the DB scheme:

(a) In a funded scheme, it should be easy to establish the standard level of the employer's contributions. The standard level should be the usual percentage contributions as opposed to any periodic increase (to cover a deficit) or decrease (to benefit from a surplus).

(b) In an unfunded scheme, the contribution rate is the notional level of contributions required from the employer to deliver the benefits. The tribunal will apply those figures, as percentages of the gross annual salary previously enjoyed by the claimant, to the relevant period of loss that resulted from the dismissal. An example is at Appendix 3 (see Fiona).

The reports and accounts of the scheme may help determine the true rate of employer contributions relative to the claimant's age and gender and, if available, they may be used as a way of producing a fairer figure[73]. If the DB pension scheme provided ancillary benefits such as a pension for a surviving partner, the parties should be careful to identify the value of any separate contributions by the employer (actual or notional) which fund that benefit. The tribunal will manage the proceedings to assist the parties in obtaining these figures.

5.37 Where a claimant has found other paid employment, it will be appropriate for the tribunal — as part of the process of examining mitigation of loss — to take account of any pension contributions made by their new employer during the period of loss, for example those arising from auto-enrolment. Again, there is an example at Appendix 3 (see Hannah).

5.38 This method does not stop the parties from agreeing, in an appropriate case, that the best way to compensate a claimant would be to augment their benefits in the former employer's DB scheme by means of a credit for additional service. This would likely require the trustees' consent as well as additional payments from the former employer to that scheme.

5.39 The third edition had a section on calculating the loss of enhancement of final salary pension rights that accrued before dismissal, as part of what it called the simplified approach. A multiplier was selected by reference to the claimant's gender, their age at dismissal, whether they were in a public sector or private sector pension scheme and their retirement age. This multiplier would then be applied to the amount of the claimant's deferred annual pension to provide them with a further compensatory sum, additional to the aggregate value of the employer's contributions for the relevant period of loss. The further award was designed, in broad terms, to compensate the claimant for the fact that the final salary pension rights they had accrued in the past would, after their dismissal, no longer benefit from future increases in pay. This further award reflected two assumptions:

(a) The first assumption was that earnings growth would outstrip growth in the pension income derived from a final salary scheme. The most populous final salary schemes now exist in the public sector and, after several years of public sector pay restraint, this assumption is no longer valid (or, at least, is less valid than once it was)[74].

(b) The second assumption was that the employer against which the claimant's claim had succeeded would continue to operate a final salary scheme. That assumption is no longer valid. CARE designs have largely replaced final salary designs in respect of future pensionable service. If a claimant were dismissed from employment carrying CARE benefits, the "slices" of earnings that would have been "banked" in the past would not benefit from future increases in pay resulting from a promotion that, but for the dismissal, they may have achieved. Each slice would only be revalued in line with CPI (or, in some cases, a system that tracks CPI).

Without the involvement of GAD, the working group has been unable to produce replacement multipliers reflecting these changing assumptions. We have borne in mind that these multipliers would only ever be used in simple DB cases for which the contributions method was appropriate. In most cases, especially following the emergence of CARE schemes, the multipliers would be so small that they can safely be ignored. It is unlikely that expert evidence in such a case would be proportionate.

5.40 There are two scenarios, however, where accrued DB pension benefits would benefit from future increases in pay:

(a) The first is a case where a claimant was, because of their age, able to remain in the final salary scheme and continue to accrue benefits linked to final salary. In the public sector, this is usually those within ten years of their normal retirement age at a specified date, with some transitional protection for those who, at the same date, were between ten and 13½ years from normal retirement age.

(b) The second is a case where a claimant had accrued benefits in a final salary scheme before they were removed from the old scheme and transferred to a new scheme based on CARE principles, and where those benefits remain pegged to final salary at retirement (not the final salary at the date of exit from the old scheme). This is true of all reformed DB schemes in the public sector.

If the period of loss is long enough that the loss of enhancement of final salary pension rights is more than negligible, perhaps because the period of loss includes a time at which the claimant might have been promoted, the contributions method is less likely to be appropriate. This would probably be a complex DB case, to which we now turn. Compensation for the loss of enhancement of accrued pension rights is built in to the approach we recommend for a complex DB case.

COMPLEX DB CASES: ISSUES FOR THE EMPLOYMENT TRIBUNAL

5.41 Many cases featuring a loss of DB pension rights will not be suitable for the contributions method. We call these "complex" cases. They are those cases where the period of loss cannot be categorised as short or which, for some other reason, involve a potentially significant quantifiable loss; a bright-line rule that fits all cases is impossible. Calculating pension loss in a complex DB case will involve choosing one of two approaches (or, sometimes, a blend of these two approaches). The first involves use of the Ogden Tables. The second involves expert evidence, typically from an actuary. We start by explaining the Ogden Tables.

AN INTRODUCTION TO THE OGDEN TABLES

5.42 These Principles referred earlier to the Ogden Tables in the context of calculating loss of state pension rights and calculating career-long loss of earnings that include a career-long loss of employer contributions to a DC scheme. Their formal title is "Actuarial Tables with Explanatory Notes for Use in Personal Injury and Fatal Accident Cases". They are named after Sir Michael Ogden QC, who chaired the working group that originally produced them in the early 1980s. They are admissible in evidence in civil proceedings; see Section 10 of the Civil Evidence Act 1995. In 2011, a working group chaired by Robin de Wilde QC produced the most recent (seventh) edition. At the time of publication, it was hoped that an eighth edition would follow in 2012. It is still awaited.

The full Tables are available here: https://www.gov.uk/government/publications/ogden-tables-actuarial-compensation-tables-for-injury-and-death.

5.43 The information in the Ogden Tables is provided in two sections:

(a) The tables themselves are produced by GAD. They act as an aid to assessing the lump sum that will compensate for a continuing financial loss caused by personal injury or a fatal accident. Put simply, they help courts produce a single one-off sum that, while not capable of perfect accuracy, represents the present capital value of future loss. The idea is that the one-off sum should fully compensate the claimant, who spends it responsibly and invests it in a risk-averse fashion, such that it is exhausted by the time the period of loss comes to an end (which may be at a defined point in future, like a specific age, or at the end of their life).

(b) The explanatory notes are produced by a working group. They provide commentary on how the multipliers should be used. They are divided into five sections. The most relevant parts of the notes for our purposes are found at Section A ("General") and Section B ("Contingences Other Than Mortality").

5.44 The courts have available to them an alternative to producing a one-off lump sum, which is to make a Periodical Payments Order (PPO). Under a PPO, compensation is paid to a claimant at regular intervals; it is often viewed as a more effective mechanism for compensating claimants. In the personal injury field, the effect of a PPO is to transfer mortality and investment risk from the claimant to the insurer (although the claimant then takes on the risk of the insurer defaulting at some time in the future when a payment is due). PPOs are not available in the Employment Tribunal[75]. Our task, instead, is to identify a one-off capital lump sum that properly compensates a claimant who has been unlawfully dismissed.

5.45 The explanatory notes to the tables make clear that if, for some reason, the facts of a case do not correspond with the assumptions on which one of the Ogden Tables is based, an appropriate allowance can be made for this difference. The notes also acknowledge that, in some cases, the assistance of an actuary should be sought. These Principles make the same acknowledgement; the approach using expert actuarial evidence is discussed below.

5.46 In trying to capture a single figure representing the present capital value of future loss, the Ogden Tables use a system of multiplicands and multipliers. In broad terms:

(a) The multiplicand is the present-day value of the future loss. Where it is an ongoing recurrent loss, which is usually the case with loss of earnings and loss of pension, it will be the present-day value of one year's loss. Because loss of earnings and loss of pension are assessed net of tax, it will be the present-day value of one year's net loss. By way of example, if a claimant's career-long income loss is thought to comprise, at today's value, a net loss of £30,000 for each of the next ten years, the multiplicand will be £30,000. If their recurrent net pension loss is, at today's value, £1,000 for each year spent in retirement, the multiplicand will be £1,000.

(b) The multiplier is a figure derived from the relevant Ogden Table. It takes account of the predicted length of a working life (or the length of time a person will live in retirement). The Ogden Tables are derived from mortality data produced periodically by the Office for National Statistics. The current edition is based on the ONS's 2008-based projections of future mortality rates. It relates to the whole UK population. The multiplier differs with the rate of investment return (what is known as the "discount rate") to which we turn next.

5.47 Whether dealing with loss of earnings or loss of pension, the multiplier chosen must reflect the appropriate rate of return on investments. The current edition of the Ogden Tables provides multipliers in columns that range from minus 2% to plus 3%. These represent various rates of return if the one-off lump sum were to be invested. In the case of *Wells v. Wells* [1999] 1 AC 345, the House of Lords decided that the discount rate applied to compensation should be based on the yields on index-linked government stock (ILGS). This reflects the likelihood that an injured claimant would adopt a risk-averse approach to the investment of their award, so that it would be exhausted at the end of the period which was being compensated and not before.

5.48 The discount rate is fixed by the Lord Chancellor under Section 1 of the Damages Act 1996. When the Damages (Personal Injury) Order 2001 came into force, the rate was set at 2.5%. This reflected the expectation of the time that, once invested in ILGS, a lump sum award of damages would yield annual growth of 2.5%. A corresponding discount of 2.5% would minimise the chances of a claimant being over-compensated.

5.49 The rates of return on ILGS have fallen consistently in recent years. By the time the current edition of the Ogden Tables was released in 2011, its editor was already describing the discount rate of 2.5% as long out of date. The Lord Chancellor confirmed that the discount rate would be reconsidered and, following a consultation period, a panel of experts was convened to advise on any change. On 27 February 2017, the Lord Chancellor announced that the discount rate would be reduced to minus 0.75% with effect from 20 March 2017[76]. This rate reflects the prevailing assumption that, in the current economic climate, a lump sum invested in ILGS will lose money: a negative discount rate increases the amount of compensation to offset that loss. An interim set of Ogden Tables has now been produced (available at the link at paragraph 5.42 above), with a new range of multipliers incorporating a discount rate of minus 0.75%. "At a glance" versions of the Tables are also at Appendix 2, which extract all the relevant columns using that discount rate.

5.50 When applying the Ogden Tables to both loss of earnings and loss of pension, the tribunal will mirror the Lord Chancellor's discount rate of minus 0.75% (and will track future changes to the rate). The EAT has confirmed that it is good practice for the tribunal to apply the same discount rate as the courts[77] and the courts themselves are applying it consistently when making lump sum awards[78].

USING THE OGDEN TABLES IN THE EMPLOYMENT TRIBUNAL

5.51 Save in exceptional cases, the tribunal will only be examining two types of loss to which the Ogden Tables relate.

5.52 The first type is loss of earnings:

(a) Lost earnings are assessed up to a specific point in the future, measured by reference to the age of the claimant at five-yearly intervals: 50, 55, 60, 65, 70 or 75. In other words, insofar as lost earnings are concerned, the Ogden Tables are chiefly aimed at career-long losses ending between the ages of 50 and 75.

(b) The approach is as follows. A multiplier is selected from Tables 3 to 14 depending upon the claimant's gender and the pension age to which their loss of earnings is to be assessed. (When dealing with variable future losses, it may be necessary to apportion the selected multiplier in the manner described at paragraph 23 of the explanatory notes to the Ogden Tables.) On the vertical axis of the selected table, the multiplier reflects the claimant's age at the date of the hearing at which their loss of earnings is to be assessed. On the horizontal axis, the multiplier reflects the discount rate; as explained above, the tribunal will use the minus 0.75% column. If the claimant's loss of earnings end at an age between the five-yearly intervals provided (e.g. at the age of 62), a process called "interpolation" finds a more accurate multiplier. Paragraphs 13 and 14 of the explanatory notes explain how interpolation is done. It appears complex, but the tribunal and the parties only need to follow the steps set out in the explanatory notes and enter numbers at the appropriate points. At Appendix 2, there are further tables that have already done the interpolation calculations for pension ages of 66, 67, 68 and 69 — these are reproduced with the kind permission of the Professional Negligence Bar Association.

(c) The selected multiplier may then be adjusted further by applying discounts set out at four tables (Tables A to D), to be found at Section B of the explanatory notes. These further tables address three other contingencies besides mortality (which is already built in to the multiplier), which are considered relevant when calculating compensation for personal injury. They are: employment status (i.e. whether a person was employed at the time of the accident); disability status (whether a person had a pre-existing disability[79] at the time of the accident); and educational attainment (measured by reference to degree equivalent or higher, GCSE/A level and below GCSE). If adjustments are made for these contingencies, the resulting sum will reflect an improved estimate of the proportion of time that the claimant would, but for the accident, have spent in employment. In other words, they take account of other factors that influence how a person's working life might have panned out if they had not been injured. The EAT has emphasised that it would not be right, in loss of earnings cases, to use multipliers taken from the main tables without considering other contingencies which those tables do not reflect[80].

(d) There are further contingencies that the Ogden Tables, in their current edition, do not cover, which may be relevant to cases before the tribunal: occupation or industrial sector, geographical region, the possibility that the claimant would have taken time out from work to care for children or other dependants, as well as risks like redundancy. Self-evidently, as generalised tables, they also take no account of risks that are pertinent or unique to the claimant being compensated or the employer for whom they worked.

(e) These Principles deal with ongoing loss of pension, not career-long loss of earnings. Nonetheless, we emphasise that, when awarding career-long loss of earnings, it will usually be appropriate for the tribunal to make an adjustment for contingencies besides mortality. Ultimately, this will be a matter for evidence and submissions.

(f) It is always helpful to bear in mind the words of Elias LJ in *Wardle v. Crédit Agricole Corporate and Investment Bank*[81]:

> **In the normal case, if a tribunal assesses that the employee is likely to get an equivalent job by a specific date, that will encompass the possibility that he might be lucky and secure the job earlier, in which case he will receive more in compensation than his actual loss, or he might be unlucky and find the job later than predicted, in which case he will receive less than his actual loss. The tribunal's best estimate ought in principle to provide the appropriate compensation. The various outcomes are factored into the conclusion. In practice the speculative nature of the exercise means that the tribunal's prediction will rarely be accurate. But it is the best solution which the law, seeking finality at the point where the court awards compensation, can provide.**

5.53 The second type is loss of pension:

(a) Pension loss is assessed from a specific age at which the claimant would have retired, at the same five-yearly intervals (50, 55, 60, 65, 70 or 75), and which continues for the remainder of the claimant's life in retirement.

(b) The process is like the one described above. A multiplier is selected from Tables 15 to 26 depending on the claimant's gender and retirement age. Experience suggests that the tables most likely to require use by the tribunal are those dealing with loss of pension commencing at the ages of 60, 65 and 70 (Tables 19 to 24). On the vertical axis of the selected table, the multiplier again reflects the claimant's age at the date of the hearing at which their loss of pension is to be assessed. On the horizontal axis, the multiplier reflects the discount rate; and, again, the tribunal will use the minus 0.75% column.

(c) The calculation of pension loss that varies across different periods carries an additional complexity, which is the need to apportion the selected multiplier with the help of a further multiplier from Ogden Table 28. An example of apportioning the multiplier when an award is made for variable pension loss is at Appendix 3 (see Rosa).

(d) To identify a multiplier for retirement at (say) age 68, it is necessary to locate a mid-point though interpolation. We again remind readers of the tables at Appendix 2 that already deal with retirement ages of 66, 67, 68 and 69, and which reduce the need for interpolation. We have included interpolation examples at Appendix 3; see Tom (for a retirement age of 63) and Gaynor (for a retirement age of 64). We have also included an example of calculating pension loss from an age below 50 by estimating the multiplier (see Rosa).

(e) As noted above, the Ogden Tables are derived from 2008 mortality data relating to the UK population at large. When calculating loss of occupational pension rights, however, we are dealing with a narrower cohort of individuals: those who have been members of occupational pension schemes and expect to enjoy the associated benefits when retired. It is generally accepted that the wealthier retirements enjoyed by such individuals correlate with increased life expectancy. If we were to apply the Ogden Tables without any adjustment for this factor, claimants would be under-compensated.

(f) Having sounded out actuarial opinion about the appropriateness of using the Ogden Tables, the working group recommends making an allowance for the expected higher life expectancy of members of occupational pension schemes, compared to the average for the UK population at large. This is done by reducing the age of the claimant by two years when selecting the multiplier.

The assumed age of retirement should also be reduced by two years; this ensures that the period up to retirement age is not changed and that what is being altered is the length of the claimant's life in retirement. We provide several examples of this adjustment at Appendix 3 (see Tom, Gaynor, Ahmed and Rosa).

(g) This general approach is subject to the right of either party to contend that the adjustment for future mortality should be greater or less. Appendix 3 includes an example of a case where the tribunal might decline to make the age adjustment (see Katarzyna).

(h) The explanatory notes to the Ogden Tables make clear that the tables at Section B (dealing with contingencies other than mortality) do not apply to loss of pension rights. The notes suggest that, if an adjustment is made to one, it may be appropriate to adjust the other. However, we do not recommend using the tables at Section B when considering pension loss. This is for several reasons:

- The Section B tables are designed for cases dealing with loss of earnings before retirement age. The relationship between these factors and loss of pension is opaque. The explanatory notes to the Ogden Tables are vague as to what adjustment is needed for pension loss as opposed to loss of earnings (saying only "some reduction would often be appropriate").
- The Section B tables have not been updated since the discount rate was lowered to minus 0.75%.
- The Section B tables do not cover the sort of contingencies that may be relevant to tribunal cases, like occupation, industrial sector, geographical region, future care responsibilities or future redundancy risks.

(i) We propose an alternative approach: to apply what previous editions called a "withdrawal factor". This factor caters for other contingencies that arise in the case, and which may affect how long employment would have continued but for the unlawful dismissal (i.e. whether the claimant would have "withdrawn" from the pension scheme, for different reasons, at a future date). It is conceptually similar to a "*Polkey*" analysis, in that the tribunal engages in some speculation about what the future — indeed, a hypothetical future — may have held. The contingencies could arise from the claimant's personal situation; for example, ill health, caring responsibilities or family circumstances. Equally, they might be factors affecting the respondent, such as the overall viability of the business, its plans for restructuring or the extent to which its workers tend to remain for full careers (e.g. police officers). Put another way, the possibility that the claimant would have left the respondent's employment (and its DB pension scheme) for other reasons can be allowed for by making one or more adjustments during the quantification process after assessing the "old job facts". We provide examples at Appendix 3 (see Ahmed, Rosa and Katarzyna).

(j) That said, a huge discount for withdrawal would suggest that DB pension loss could be better assessed by the contributions method. As Underhill LJ said in *Griffin v. Plymouth Hospital NHS Trust*[82]:

> **In such a case [the claimant] would have suffered, perhaps only a year or two later, precisely the same kind of loss as is being claimed for in the proceedings; and it is more appropriate simply to award lost contributions up to that date, as per the simplified approach, rather than embarking on the exercise of valuing rights on retirement which would almost certainly never have accrued and then applying a massive "finger-in-the-air" discount. The question is whether the uncertainties that would have to be reflected in such a discount are so great that they undermine the point of assessing the hypothetical whole-career loss in the first place. Whether that is so in any particular case is a matter for the judgment of the tribunal.**

(k) The Ogden Tables also assist when calculating the loss of a tax-free pension lump sum. In most cases, we should make clear, lump sum calculations can safely be ignored. This is because most DB schemes in the public sector (whether using a final salary or CARE design) only provide for a lump sum through commutation of part of the pension income. In such cases, the loss can adequately be assessed using the pension income in the presumed absence of commutation. For those who have accrued benefits in a scheme that provided for a separate tax-free lump sum (such as the older final salary schemes based on eightieths), a further calculation is necessary. Because the lump sum is invariably a multiple of the gross pension income, the lost lump sum will simply be the same multiple of the lost gross pension income. Once we have that figure, we turn to Table 27 of the Ogden Tables, so that the sum can be adjusted at the discount rate at minus 0.75% for the "term certain" reflecting its early receipt. We provide examples at Appendix 3 (see Tom and Rosa).

THE SEVEN STEPS MODEL

5.54 Bringing the above comments together, the working group's members have identified seven steps that the tribunal and the parties should follow when calculating loss of DB pension rights using the Ogden Tables.

5.55 ***Step 1: Identify what the claimant's net pension income would have been at their retirement age if the dismissal had not occurred.***

(a) The starting point is to contact the employer's pension department or the administrators of its pension scheme. They should be able to provide gross figures confirming not just the claimant's current projected pension income at retirement (i.e. what their pension income will be following their dismissal) but also what their pension income would have been, at today's rates, if they had continued to work until retirement and not been dismissed. In a career-loss case, this will be the claimant's retirement age – and the claimant may already have this figure from a recent pension statement[83]. If not, the tribunal would expect the respondent to take responsibility for obtaining these figures. In a case that may require a complex DB calculation, the tribunal will use its case management powers to direct early provision of this information.

(b) Paragraph 3.20 above is relevant for cases where the tribunal must decide the age at which, but for the dismissal, the claimant would have retired.

(c) The employer or scheme administrators might also be willing to provide a further statement of the claimant's projected pension benefits based on a hypothetical scenario. Such a scenario might include the claimant's promotion at a future date. If the claimant had accrued service in a DB scheme with a final salary design, this would enhance the value of their accrued benefits as assessed at Step 1. This is the mechanism by which the complex approach can produce compensation for the loss of enhancement of accrued pension rights (see paragraphs 5.39 and 5.40 above).

(d) If a pension statement cannot be provided, it may be possible for the parties to establish a tolerably accurate figure at Step 1 through deduction. This is easier when dealing with a pension scheme with a final salary design (see the example of Tom in Appendix 3). It is trickier when dealing with a pension scheme with a CARE design (see the example of Gaynor in Appendix 3). The tribunal is not equipped to predict the compound impact of annual CPI revaluation of all the slices of earnings — not just those banked before dismissal but also those that would continue to be banked if dismissal had not occurred. If a party wishes to aim for greater precision, they will need to obtain estimates from the scheme administrators or instruct an expert. If they do neither then, in the interests of simplicity, the tribunal will ignore the impact of CPI revaluation.

(e) Once in possession of a gross figure for pension income, the tribunal should, as part of Step 1, take account of any withdrawal factors that may apply. The analysis is like the one done when applying the "*Polkey*" principle; the tribunal considers the "old job facts" and engages in a degree of speculation about what the future may have held. For example, without applying any withdrawal factor and based entirely on a pension statement, a tribunal might decide that, if a claimant had not been dismissed but worked through until retirement for the same employer, their gross annual pension income would have been £8,000. However, the tribunal might decide that there was a 25% chance that the respondent would become insolvent within the next five years or that the claimant would have been made redundant. It might decide that the claimant's service to retirement would have included a reduction to part-time working because of caring for an elderly parent. After taking account of such factors (usually expressed as percentage reductions), the tribunal might decide that a fairer, albeit broad-brush, assessment is that the claimant's gross annual pension income at retirement would, but for the dismissal, have been £5,000. Example are given at Appendix 3 (see Ahmed, Katarzyna and Rosa).

(f) As can be seen, the parties may disagree about the claimant's retirement age and promotion prospects and the withdrawal factors that might apply. These are the sorts of matters on which a tribunal might make rulings at a first-stage remedy hearing (a concept we examine in **CHAPTER 6**) before performing detailed calculations. They can offer a platform for the parties to reach agreement on pension loss while keeping down their legal costs.

(g) Finally, any gross figure must be converted to a net figure. This can be done by using the HMRC online calculator, which provides a workable estimate of take-home pay[84]. It has been used on several occasions in the examples at Appendix 3.

5.56 ***Step 2: Identify what the claimant's net pension income will be at their retirement age in the light of their dismissal.***

(a) The tribunal and the parties should have this figure, at least in part, as a result of their enquiries at Step 1. The claimant may already have received an updated statement of projected pension benefits to reflect the fact that, after the termination of their employment, they will accrue no more pensionable service. Otherwise, the employer's pension department or the administrators of its pension scheme should be able to provide gross figures confirming the claimant's projected annual pension income at retirement in the light of their dismissal.

(b) If the tribunal decides that, because of the dismissal, the claimant will never work again, it will be enough to convert this figure into a projected net annual pension income and then proceed to Step 3.

(c) However, cases where a tribunal concludes that a claimant will never work again are rare. A more common outcome is that the claimant mitigates their loss by finding alternative work by the time of the remedy hearing (perhaps on reduced pay) or that the tribunal concludes that the claimant will find alternative work by a specific date in the future. This is the sort of analysis in which the words of Elias LJ in the *Wardle* case, quoted at paragraph 5.52(f) above, are especially pertinent. In such circumstances, the tribunal is required to decide the amount by which this actual or anticipated new job affects the claimant's future loss, both in terms of earnings and pension. As we have emphasised before in these Principles, the tribunal and the parties must be alive to the possibility that a future rise in salary in the new employment might be sufficient to offset both the loss of earnings and the loss of pension caused by the dismissal. If it is thought this will occur in the not-too-distant future, it could point towards use of the contributions method.

(d) If the new employment has DB pension benefits (and experience suggests this happens more rarely nowadays), the basis on which those benefits accrue must be established. The new benefits will not necessarily replace like with like. Take a situation where the old employer's pension scheme was based on a final salary design but the new employer's pension scheme is based on a CARE design. For some claimants on static incomes throughout their career, a CARE scheme may deliver better benefits (because of the better accrual rate), even to the extent of meaning no pension loss and reduced earnings loss. For other claimants, such as those with a good chance of experiencing promotions throughout their careers and the accompanying increases in their pensionable pay, a CARE scheme may deliver inferior benefits, because those promotions will have no impact on the value of their accrued benefits. To assist the tribunal, the claimant should obtain a statement of projected pension benefits from the new employer's DB scheme. (We repeat the point made above that, in the interests of simplicity, the tribunal will ignore the impact of annual CPI revaluation on banked slices in a CARE scheme; if a party wishes to aim for greater precision, they will need to obtain more accurate figures from the pension scheme administrators or instruct an expert.)

(e) If the new employment has DC pension benefits (and experience suggests this is more often the case), we still need an estimate of the pension income that the scheme will deliver; if we simply take account of pension contributions the new employer pays into the DC scheme, we will not be comparing like with like[85]. The preferred solution would be for the administrators of the new scheme to provide a statement of projected pension benefits at today's value. Statements are issued annually and include assumptions about likely investment performance. The Pension Wise website, to which we have already referred in the context of "pension freedoms" (see paragraph 4.8 above), can assist individuals in understanding their pension statement[86].

(f) If, for some reason, a statement is not available, there is an alternative: the website for the NEST service (see paragraph 4.12) provides a simple and helpful online calculator[87]. The information required by the calculator to produce an estimate of gross pension income from a DC scheme is: date of birth; gender; intended age of retirement; the rate of both employee contributions and employer contributions to the scheme; and the claimant's gross annual salary. The figure produced by the NEST calculator should be treated with caution; the further away that a person is from their retirement age, the less likely that the figure it produces will be accurate. However, it can provide a workable estimate of pension income – especially for older claimants – that, in the absence of a statement of benefits or expert input, may be thought better than nothing and a rational way to proceed. Its use is shown in examples in Appendix 3 (see Tom, Katarzyna and Rosa). It may also provide the parties with a way to carry out their own broad-brush evaluation of pension loss prior to instructing an expert and which provides a platform for settlement.

(g) When assessing the pension benefits that the new employment delivers (or that the anticipated employment will deliver), a similar analysis to the one conducted at Step 1 should be adopted. This may mean looking at the "new job facts", such as the claimant's promotion prospects in the new employment or considering what withdrawal factor (usually expressed as a percentage reduction) might apply to membership of a new pension scheme. Speculation is inevitable. Much will depend on the tribunal's assessment of the facts and its knowledge of the local labour market.

(h) The claimant may give evidence that, because of their dismissal, they will delay their retirement; deprived of the benefits of the old employer's DB scheme, they assert that they can no longer afford to retire at the normal retirement age under the scheme and now must work until, or beyond, state pension age. In such a case, it may be appropriate to assess their loss of earnings for a longer period and for their loss of pension to commence at a later age or to apply an apportioned multiplier to variable periods of loss.

(i) When using the NEST calculator to assess loss in a case where a claimant was dismissed from employment with DB benefits and has found (or is expected to find) employment with inferior DC benefits, it may assist to work through different scenarios (including the claimant's subsequent promotion or their withdrawal from the new scheme) to arrive at a workable figure at Step 2.

(j) Once again, the parties may disagree about many aspects of the claimant's case, such as their retirement age, promotion prospects and the withdrawal factors that might apply in relation to any new employment. And, once again, these are the sorts of matters on which a tribunal might make rulings at a first-stage remedy hearing before carrying out detailed calculations. As before, they can offer a platform for the parties to reach agreement on pension loss while keeping down their legal costs.

(k) Finally, any gross figure must be converted to a net figure. As before, this can be done by using the HMRC online calculator, which provides a workable estimate of take-home pay[88].

5.57 *Step 3: Deduct the result of Step 2 from the result of Step 1, which produces a figure for net annual loss of pension benefits.*

(a) This should be a straightforward piece of arithmetic. The result is our multiplicand.

(b) In case it is necessary to carry out a separate lump sum calculation (see Step 6), keep a note of the difference between the gross figure produced at Step 1 and the gross figure produced at Step 2.

5.58 *Step 4: Identify the period over which that net annual loss is to be awarded, using the Ogden Tables to identify the multiplier.*

(a) We explained above that, to reflect the improved mortality of those in occupational pension schemes, we recommend a two-year age adjustment. Take a female claimant, aged 57 at the date of the remedy hearing, and who, the tribunal decides, had intended to retire at the age of 67 from the employment from which she was unlawfully dismissed. Without the adjustment, and with a discount rate of minus 0.75%, the multiplier in her case would be 26.35. The adjustment requires that, purely for the purposes of calculating her loss of pension income[89], we treat her as being aged 55 at the date of the remedy hearing and with an intended retirement age of 65. This produces a multiplier of 28.82.

(b) In Appendix 2, we have provided "at a glance" tables for pension loss from retirement ages of 50, 55, 60, 65, 66, 67, 68, 69, 70 and 75. If, after the two-year adjustment, a different retirement age is required, such as 63, interpolation will be required. Examples of interpolation are provided at Appendix 3 (see Tom and Gaynor).

(c) In the personal injury field, adjustments are made to the multiplier to reflect the various contingencies of the case besides mortality. As we have noted, we recommend that tribunals focus on the withdrawal factor, which adjusts the multiplicand. Another reason to be wary about preferring a single adjustment to the multiplier over adjustments to the multiplicand is that the former effectively results in a uniform withdrawal factor applied to both the old job and the new job. That said, if a party prefers the approach of adjusting the multiplier instead of the multiplicand, they will be free to make their arguments to the tribunal.

5.59 ***Step 5: Multiply the multiplicand by the multiplier, which produces the present capital value of that loss.***

Once again, this should be a simple piece of arithmetic.

5.60 ***Step 6: Check the lump sum position and perform a separate calculation if required.***

(a) Most public sector DB schemes do not provide for a tax-free lump sum other than by commuting the pension income, subject to the scheme's rules and HMRC limits. It follows that, in most complex DB cases, the figure produced at Step 5 above will cover the pension loss (albeit in the presumed absence of commutation); no further compensation will be appropriate.

(b) However, let us imagine that a claimant was a member of a pension scheme that did provide for separate entitlement to a lump sum, such as some of the older public sector DB schemes with a final salary design based on an eightieths accrual rate. Although these schemes have long since closed to new members or to further accruals, the tribunal may encounter claimants who have accrued past benefits in such schemes (and which are still pegged to final salary at retirement). Examples include the "Classic" version of the PCSPS and the 1995 NHS scheme; see Appendix 1.

(c) It is straightforward to calculate the loss of lump sum in such cases. As noted above, the lump sum accrues in the same way as pension income. In an eightieths scheme, the pension income accrues at an effective rate of 1/80 for each year of pensionable service; and, because the lump sum is a multiple of three times an employee's pension income, it accrues at the rate of 3/80 for each year of pensionable service. In such a case, rather than work from first principles, it would be enough simply to take the gross figure from Step 3 above (see paragraph 5.57(b)) and multiply it by three. The resulting figure is then added to the figure produced at Step 5. This calculation has been performed in the examples of Tom and Rosa at Appendix 3.

5.61 ***Step 7: Taking account of the other sums awarded by the tribunal, gross up the compensation awarded.***

(a) Finally, the tribunal must gross up the award of compensation in accordance with the Gourley principle. The approach to adopt has been described elsewhere in these Principles and in examples at Appendix 3. Not all elements of the compensation will need to be grossed up — just those that are treated as taxable income under Sections 401 and 403 ITEPA[90]. The process of grossing up can lead to complications; we have tried to keep matters as simple as possible in Appendix 3, but there will be cases where the input of an accountant would be desirable.

(b) The parties and the tribunal would need to bear in mind that the lump sum would have been a tax-free benefit in the claimant's hands. It will now form part of an award of compensation that will be subject to income tax to the extent that it exceeds £30,000. It must therefore also be grossed up.

(c) Although some commentary in these Principles on the calculation of loss of earnings has been inevitable, we have generally kept away from broader principles for the assessment of remedy in a successful case. Guidance on the order of deductions can be found in the Court of Appeal's decision in *Digital Equipment Company Ltd v. Clements* [1998] ICR 258. Tribunals should be wary of making the same deduction twice. If, for example, the tribunal has already taken account of *Polkey*-type considerations when assessing loss of pension benefits (in the context of applying a withdrawal factor, as a percentage reduction), it would not be appropriate to make a further *Polkey* deduction to the final figure that includes loss of pension. It may only be appropriate to apply such a deduction to the loss of earnings element.

THE EXPERT EVIDENCE APPROACH

5.62 The main reason why parties may prefer to use the Ogden Tables is that it will be cheaper than instructing an expert.

5.63 There may be cases, however, where the amount of pension loss at stake is such that the parties are prepared to incur the cost of instructing an expert. Indeed, once armed with the tribunal's findings of fact, the parties may wish to outsource the entire calculation process to an expert. Alternatively, they may prefer a blended approach, by which the expert provides evidence on one or more constituent parts of the calculation to help the tribunal achieve greater precision in its award. Such evidence could focus on these (non-exhaustive) factors:

(a) Adjustments to the quantification process, taking account of:
- More recent mortality data;
- More relevant mortality data (e.g. based on geographical area or occupational sector);
- More precise withdrawal factors (e.g. based on geographical area or industrial/occupational sector);
- A claimant's education and/or training history; and
- A claimant's health.

(b) The future performance of the pension fund under consideration. A more accurate assessment of pension loss might be achieved with better information about matters such as the solvency prospects of a DB scheme or the investment performance of a DC scheme.

(c) The impact of future compound CPI revaluation on the slices of earnings that a claimant has already banked in a CARE scheme and on the further slices of earnings which, but for their dismissal, they would continue to have banked.

(d) The impact of the tax charging regime associated with the LTA and the AA, when establishing the figures at Step 1 and Step 2. If the value of pension benefits exceeds the LTA, a tax charge will apply and have the effect of reducing net pension benefits (as explained at paragraph 5.22 above). If the deemed increase in the value of pension benefits exceeds an individual's AA, a tax charge will also apply (see paragraph 5.29 above). If the "Scheme Pays" option has been chosen, it will reduce the value of net pension income.

(e) Complexities in establishing the true level of net earnings (caused, for example, by an election to pay the AA charge when it falls due or by a restriction of the personal allowance).

(f) Complexities in the grossing up calculation.

Whereas evidence on items (a) to (c) above might typically come from an actuary, evidence on items (d) to (f) might come from an accountant.

5.64 In addition, actuarial evidence is not necessarily limited to complex DB cases. There are certain scenarios where an expert might give evidence in a simple case, although it may not be cost-effective. For example, in a simple DB case, an actuarial expert might give evidence on whether the claimant's age and health justify the application of a multiplier (and, if so, of what value) to the aggregate value of the employer's notional contributions to an unfunded DB scheme. Expert evidence might also assist in a case involving lengthy or career-long loss of earnings from employment which had DC scheme benefits; see paragraph 4.30 above.

5.65 In a case where expert evidence is considered appropriate, the tribunal, in consultation with the parties, would make directions. The strongly preferred approach would be for a jointly instructed expert. The parties would be encouraged to agree the basis for funding such evidence.

5.66 In the absence of agreement, prescription is unwise, since so much will depend on the circumstances of the case. Just as with expert medical evidence sometimes used in determining whether a claimant meets the statutory definition of a disabled person, situations vary. For example, if a respondent wishes to instruct an expert to argue that the tribunal should apply a discount rate above minus 0.75%, which goes against the recommended approach of these Principles, it is highly unlikely that the tribunal will order the claimant to contribute to the costs incurred. Conversely, if a claimant wishes to instruct an expert to argue that the tribunal should apply a discount rate below minus 0.75%, it is highly unlikely that the tribunal will order the respondent to contribute to the costs incurred. If both parties would welcome limited input from an expert on more recent general mortality data, or mortality data that was relevant to the claimant's occupation, or the impact of the LTA charge on pension income, or the impact of repaying the amount of the AA charge absorbed by the scheme under a "Scheme Pays" mechanism, the tribunal may be more inclined to order a party to contribute an appropriate amount to the cost. We recognise that expert evidence can be expensive and that many parties, but most especially claimants, will find it unaffordable. The claimant's ability to contribute towards the cost of expert evidence could be assisted by an interim award of compensation made at the first-stage remedy hearing. The parties will be free to make their arguments to the tribunal.

5.67 Where a joint expert has been instructed, the intention would be for the tribunal to adopt their recommended approach unless there was a very good reason to do otherwise. If the expert was not jointly instructed or if the expert's views were disputed by one of the parties, the tribunal would have to hear argument on the point and reach its own decision on the amount to award for pension loss.

5.68 If the parties were unable or unwilling to fund expert evidence, the tribunal would have to do its best with the available material, using the broader brush of the Ogden Tables. This would produce a figure which, while less precise, should still be just and proportionate.

COMPENSATING FOR THE LOSS OF ANCILLARY BENEFITS IN DB SCHEMES

5.69 At paragraph 5.9 of these Principles, we mentioned the ancillary benefits bestowed by some DB pension schemes. It may be appropriate to award compensation for the loss of those benefits. The most significant is likely to be death-in-service benefit; it is a real loss that a claimant suffers even though it is the surviving dependants who stand to benefit financially[91].

Other benefits deriving from membership of such schemes, like survivor pensions payable to partners and dependants, are subject to further contingencies after dismissal involving the survival of those dependants. We observe that they are speculative and difficult to value as a one-off capital sum, but that is not intended to deter the parties from presenting their arguments to the tribunal.

5.70 In many DB schemes, death-in-service benefit is often two or three times salary. Other provisions may apply (such as a multiple of pensionable pay, or a multiple of pension income, perhaps less lump sums that may be payable under other arrangements). The usual approach to valuing a lost benefit of this nature is to identify the cost of securing equivalent insurance on the open market[92].

5.71 While there is a wide range of information in the public domain regarding the cost of pension annuities, the same does not hold good for life cover; brokers and life companies will generally not provide information save in the context of specific individual requirements. An example is provided in Appendix 3 (see Adrian). The intention is that the example is not too remote from actual cost, but an indicator of the approach to adopt rather than a set of data on which reliance can be placed.

5.72 One of the examples in Appendix 3 deals with early retirement on the grounds of poor health (see Rosa).

NOTES

58 Although still available at this link: https://www.ons.gov.uk/economy/investmentspensionsandtrusts/compendium/pensiontrends/2014-11-28

59 Available here: http://www.pensionprotectionfund.org.uk/Pages/ThePurpleBook.aspx

60 Further details at http://www.pensionprotectionfund.org.uk.

61 According to the LGPS annual report 2016: http://www.lgpsboard.org/index.php/schemedata/scheme-annual-report. The LGPS includes over 13,000 employers and 5.3m members.

62 The amount of actuarial reduction will vary from scheme to scheme but, by way of illustration, a person typically faces a reduction of around 5% in pension income for each year of early receipt.

63 Some of these will be so-called "Beckmann rights" which may transfer with employees under the Transfer of Undertakings (Protection of Employment) Regulations 2006. Such rights are outside the scope of these Principles, but see the CJEU's judgments in *Beckmann v. Dynamco Whicheloe Macfarlane Ltd* [2002] IRLR 578 and *Martin v. South Bank University* [2004] IRLR 74 ECJ and the High Court's judgment in *The Procter & Gamble Company v. Svenska Cellulosa Aktiebolaget SCA & another* [2012] IRLR 733.

64 Sometimes, when DB schemes are closed to future accruals on a final salary basis, the link to final salary at retirement is also broken; instead, the link is to the final salary at the point at which the move to a CARE scheme occurred. However, for all the public sector DB pension schemes summarised in Appendix 1, the link to final salary at retirement is retained in respect of accrued rights.

65 The words "final" and "salary" can both mislead. As for "final", it may in fact not be the salary paid on the final day of work before retirement. Other formulae are used, such as the best salary paid over 12 consecutive months in the three years prior to retirement or the highest average of any three consecutive salaries paid in the last ten years. As for "salary", pensionable pay may differ from salary. For example, the BBC has decided to cap at 1% the part of a pay rise that would be used to calculate pensionable pay in the final salary sections of its own DB scheme; this was held to be lawful in *Bradbury v. BBC* [2017] EWCA Civ 1144.

66 The final report of the Independent Public Service Pensions Commission is available here: https://www.gov.uk/government/uploads/system/uploads/attachment_data/file/207720/hutton_final_100311.pdf

67 Entitled "Public Service Pensions: Good Pensions That Last", it is available here: https://www.gov.uk/government/uploads/system/uploads/attachment_data/file/205837/Public_Service_Pensions_-_good_pensions_that_last._Command_paper.pdf

68 The main measure of UK inflation used to be the Retail Prices Index (RPI). In 2003, the main measure of inflation changed to the Consumer Prices Index (CPI). CPI is usually described by reference to a large shopping basket containing all the goods and services bought by UK households. It is calculated differently to RPI (applying a geometric rather than arithmetic mean to the basket of goods) and it does not include owner-occupier housing costs such as mortgages and council tax. The contents of the basket of goods is reviewed regularly to ensure that it is properly representative of people's spending patterns. There has been litigation around attempts by pension scheme trustees to change pension revaluation from RPI to CPI (seen by some as less generous), which usually revolves around the wording of the scheme rules. Insofar as public sector DB schemes are concerned, the Court of Appeal held that the switch from RPI to CPI in 2011 was lawful; see *R (FDA and others) v Secretary of State for Work and Pensions and another* [2012] EWCA Civ 332. On 21 March 2017, the main measure of UK inflation changed again; this time, to CPIH (CPI + Housing). CPIH is the CPI amended to include owner-occupier housing costs (see the ONS announcement here https://www.ons.gov.uk/news/statementsandletters/statementonfutureofconsumerpriceinflationstatisticsintheuk). The move is not without controversy; some contend that CPIH is less generous than CPI because of the way housing costs are valued. As at the date of publication of the fourth edition of the Principles, there has been no announcement that public sector DB pension schemes will move to a system of indexation and revaluation based on CPIH. If this happens, it will be noted in future revisions of these Principles. Those researching historic CPI increases will find these links helpful: https://www.gov.uk/government/collections/public-service-pensions-increases and https://www.ons.gov.uk/economy/inflationandpriceindices/datasets/consumerpriceinflation

69 Jane might have had unused AA from previous tax years, which she could carry forward to reduce her tax charge. Note that pension input periods may vary and may not necessarily align with the tax year.

70 See, on this point, the Court of Appeal's judgment in *O'Donoghue v. Redcar & Cleveland Borough Council* [2001] IRLR 615, as applied in *Zebrowski v. Concentric Birmingham Ltd* (EAT/0245/16). The case of *Abbotts & Standley v. Wesson-Glynwed Steels Ltd* [1982] IRLR 51 provides an early example of this principle in operation a redundancy context.

71 In *Network Rail Infrastructure Ltd v. Booth* (EAT/0071/06), the EAT said this: "it would be a mistake for tribunals to take the view that they were obliged to adopt a substantial loss approach if the period of loss was for more than two years" (our emphasis).

72 Although tribunals and parties should bear in mind that, applying the EAT's judgment in *University of Sunderland v. Drossou* (EAT/0341/16), a week's pay includes the employer's pension contributions. This will increase the level at which the cap operates, especially where the claimant was a member of a DB pension scheme.

73 Appendix 7 of the revised third edition provided a table of multipliers to apply to the contribution rates to DB pension schemes to reflect the age and gender of the claimant. Without GAD involvement, we have been unable to produce a similar table. The parties are free to make submissions on the point, and use expert evidence, if they consider that the application of the contributions method in a simple DB case requires use of similar multipliers.

74 See the House of Commons Library briefing paper "Public Sector Pay" (29 June 2017), at http://researchbriefings.parliament.uk/ResearchBriefing/Summary/CBP-8037. At page 3: "The experience of earnings growth across both the public and private sector is very broad and there are a substantial number of workers who see large rises or falls in pay each year. Nevertheless, since 2012 pay increases have been more positively skewed in the private sector than in the public sector."

75 A point that the working group emphasised in its response to the Ministry of Justice's consultation (available at https://consult.justice.gov.uk/digital-communications/personal-injury-discount-rate/supporting_documents/discountrateconsultationpaper.pdf) on how the personal injury discount rate should be set in future. The consultation ended on 11 May 2017 and, as at the date of publication of these Principles, the Government's response is awaited.

[76] The Lord Chancellor's statement of reasons for the decision can be found here: https://www.gov.uk/government/uploads/system/uploads/attachment_data/file/594972/discount-rate-statement-of-reasons.pdf

[77] See *Benchmark Dental Laboratories Group Ltd v. Perfitt* (EAT/0304/04), para 20.

[78] See, for example, *Marsh v. Ministry of Justice* [2017] EWHC 1040 (QB), paras 222-228.

[79] The Ogden Tables adopt a slightly different definition of disability for this purpose. It sets out three elements, all of which must be satisfied. The second of these is the definition in the EqA with which employment law practitioners will be familiar.

[80] *Abbey National plc v. Chagger* [2009] IRLR 86, para 114.

[81] [2011] ICR 1290 (at paragraph 52).

[82] [2015] ICR 347.

[83] Statements are issued annually; see https://www.pensionsadvisoryservice.org.uk/pension-problems/avoiding-problems/what-you-have-the-right-to-ask-your-scheme.

[84] https://www.gov.uk/estimate-income-tax. Where appropriate, it is important to state that a person is (or is assumed to be) over state pension age, so that no deduction for NI contributions is made.

[85] In taking this approach, we have been mindful of the points made by the EAT in *Network Rail Infrastructure Ltd v. Booth* EAT/0071/06 (paras 14 and 15) and by the Court of Appeal in *Griffin v. Plymouth Hospital NHS Trust* [2015] ICR 347 (para 64).

[86] https://www.pensionwise.gov.uk.

[87] http://www.nestpensions.org.uk. The NEST online pension calculator is at: https://www.nestpensions.org.uk/schemeweb/NestPublicWeb/faces/public/BE/pages/pensionCalculationPublicArea.xhtml. Users should disable the assumption that 25% of the fund is taken as a tax-free lump sum; this will ensure that like is compared with like. Also, when dealing with a tranche of loss that does not start until the future (e.g. the tribunal decides that a claimant will be out of work for, say, three years, and will then start a job with DC benefits), a corresponding adjustment must be made to the date of birth and date of retirement.

[88] https://www.gov.uk/estimate-income-tax. Where appropriate, it is important to state that a person is (or is assumed to be) over state pension age, so that no deduction for NI contributions is made.

[89] Not her state pension loss, her lump sum loss or her loss of earnings.

[90] The taxation of compensation for injury to feelings is a developing area, which is outside the scope of these Principles. In short, the Upper Tribunal (Tax and Chancery Chamber) held in *Moorthy v. HMRC* [2016] IRLR 258 that compensation for injury to feelings will be taxable under Section 401 ITEPA (to the extent that compensation exceeds £30,000) if the discrimination was connected with the termination of employment. By contrast, the EAT (whose decisions bind the Employment Tribunal) has decided that compensation for injury to feelings falls under "injury" in Section 406 ITEPA and is therefore entirety exempt from tax; see *Orthet Ltd v. Vince-Cain* [2005] ICR 324 and *Timothy James Consulting Ltd v. Wilton* [2015] ICR 764. Compensation for injury to feelings in connection with pre-termination discrimination remains exempt by either analysis. The *Moorthy* case is currently due to come before the Court of Appeal in February 2018. In the meantime, the draft Finance Bill 2017 proposes an amendment to Section 406 ITEPA (with effect from 6 April 2018) to provide that "injury" does not include injury to feelings.

[91] As confirmed by the Court of Appeal in *Fox v. British Airways plc* [2013] ICR 1257.

[92] Although the case of *Fox v. British Airways plc* justified a different approach. The claimant in that case had died soon after dismissal and so he was unable put alternative life insurance cover in place. His estate was entitled to be put in the position that the claimant would have been in if he had not been unlawfully dismissed. In those circumstances, it was virtually certain that he would still have been in employment at the date of death and his beneficiaries would have become entitled to be paid out in full under the death-in-service benefit. It followed that his loss should be calculated as the whole amount of the lost benefit.

CHAPTER 6: CASE MANAGEMENT

[4.332]

6.1 With the assistance of the parties, the tribunal will seek to identify at an early stage those cases with a realistic prospect of a significant award for pension loss. In England and Wales, a question on the tribunal's standard case management agenda form[93] will invite the parties to specify the type of pension scheme in which the claimant accrued benefits prior to their dismissal (i.e. whether DC or DB). Some cases will obviously raise the prospect of a complex approach: dismissals of civil servants, teachers, nurses, medics, academics, firefighters and so on. Appendix 1 will assist in such cases.

6.2 In such cases, the tribunal will be more likely to list a hearing on liability first and "park" issues of remedy. There is no point the parties incurring significant time and cost associated with preparing detailed calculations of pension loss (including the possibility of instructing an expert) until it is known if, and to what extent, the claimant's claim has succeeded; this includes, for example, whether the statutory cap will apply. The liability stage should ideally include findings about reductions for *Polkey* and/or contributory fault, since they have a bearing on whether it is appropriate to categorise a case as simple (and therefore suited to the contributions method) or as complex (and therefore suited to use of the Ogden Tables or use of expert evidence)[94].

6.3 The tribunal will discourage professionally represented claimants from using the phrase "to be confirmed" in schedules of loss when setting out pension loss. The tribunal and the parties need to know as early as possible the sort of case with which they are dealing. This is part of the overriding objective; it helps the tribunal manage the case in a way that saves expense, retains flexibility and is proportionate to its complexity. Early consideration of these Principles will enable those preparing schedules of loss for claimants to provide a workable estimate of the pension loss claimed at an early stage of the proceedings (even if the details can wait). Similarly, they should enable respondents to produce a counter-schedule. With a clearer sense of their respective positions, the parties are better equipped to achieve settlement.

6.4 Even in cases where either or both parties are not legally represented, there is scope for the tribunal, through interventionist case management methods, to assist the parties in understanding what is required of them.

6.5 To assist in that process, the parties will be directed to disclose to one another documents and information relevant to pension loss, much of which will be in the hands of the respondent. Examples include:

(a) Pension scheme rules (for the old job and any new job obtained). If the details we have provided in Appendix 1 are insufficient in the circumstances of the case, information required might include:
- The rate of employee contributions (preferably expressed as a percentage of salary);
- The rate of employer contributions (preferably expressed as a percentage of salary) — and, in an unfunded DB scheme, the notional level of employer contributions (and, possibly, also the reports and accounts of the scheme, which may be needed to determine the true standard rate of employer contributions);
- Details of any ancillary benefits of the scheme, such as death-in-service benefit;
- Normal retirement age under the scheme, i.e. the age at which an individual can retire with an unreduced pension;
- In a DC scheme or a funded DB scheme, the current value of the invested funds;
- In a DB scheme, whether the claimant has accrued benefits in part of the scheme that has now closed to future accruals (and, if so, the way in which those benefits accrued, e.g. by reference to final salary and accrual rate);
- In a DB scheme, whether future accruals are based on a final salary, CARE or other design; and
- In a DB scheme, whether there is any separate entitlement to a lump sum (not just through commutation of pension income);

(b) A statement of the claimant's projected benefits in their old job in the light of their dismissal and (ideally) a statement of projected benefits if dismissal had not occurred on in certain other scenarios that may help quantify the impact of various withdrawal factors;

(c) In respect of any new job obtained by the claimant, a statement of their projected benefits;

(d) The claimant's payslips from their old job, setting out deductions from pay and corroborating, if necessary, the percentage amount of their contributions to the old job's pension scheme; and

(e) As above, but for the claimant's new job.

6.6 If the claimant succeeds at the liability stage, and there is a realistic prospect of a significant award for pension loss, the tribunal can then allocate dates for a two-stage remedy hearing. Ideally this would be done as part of a case management discussion with the parties following the liability hearing, so that the parties understand what is required of them. Failing that, there should be a preliminary hearing, probably by telephone, to set out orders and directions such as an updated schedule (and counter-schedule) of loss, disclosure of further evidence if required, preparation and exchange of witness evidence and so on.

6.7 The purpose of the first-stage remedy hearing would be to enable the tribunal to do three things:

(a) First, to issue a judgment on non-pension compensation (the basic award for unfair dismissal, a sum for loss of statutory rights, awards for injury to feelings, holiday pay and the like);

(b) Second, to rule on as many areas as possible that are relevant to calculating pension loss, without descending into precise figures. This may include the age at which the claimant would have retired but for their dismissal, their future promotion prospects and what adjustments should be applied to reflect various withdrawal factors relevant to the old job and the new job; and

(c) Third, to hear submissions on whether the Ogden approach or the expert evidence approach (or a blend of the two) will be adopted.

At Appendix 3, we have given examples of how this approach would be followed in three hypothetical cases (Ahmed, Katarzyna and Rosa).

6.8 In many cases, it will be appropriate for the tribunal to give the parties a time-limited opportunity to agree a figure for pension loss. The period for this purpose would be agreed between the parties and the tribunal. If the parties did agree a figure for pension loss, there would be no need for a second-stage remedy hearing. The tribunal could issue a supplementary judgment on remedy by consent under Rule 64 of its Rules of Procedure. If the parties did not agree a figure for pension loss, the second-stage remedy hearing would go ahead. In most cases, the "seven steps" model would then produce a suitable figure and the tribunal would issue judgment accordingly. In cases where the tribunal had approved the use of expert evidence, it would adopt the joint expert's recommended approach unless there was a very good reason to do otherwise. If the parties have each instructed an expert, the tribunal will simply have to decide whose figures to adopt after hearing submissions.

6.9 The parties would be consulted throughout. The underlying idea is that they are given every encouragement to agree a figure for pension loss (with the benefit of the tribunal's findings of fact where appropriate) and that they bear the cost of obtaining expert evidence only where it is proportionate to do so in view of the potential compensation at stake.

6.10 If the circumstances justified it, it might be possible for the tribunal to offer Judicial Mediation or Judicial Assessment.

NOTES

93 Available here: https://www.judiciary.gov.uk/wp-content/uploads/2013/08/presidential-guidance-general-case-management-20170406-3.2.pdf

94 For further guidance on the clarity needed when proceeding with a split hearing on liability and remedy, see the comments

of Elias LJ at paras 67 to 70 of *Salford Royal NHS Foundation Trust v. Roldan* [2010] ICR 1457.

APPENDIX 1: SUMMARY OF MAIN PUBLIC SECTOR DEFINED BENEFIT PENSION SCHEMES

INTRODUCTION

[4.333]
Complex cases will mostly involve DB pension schemes and many of those will be public sector schemes. This appendix therefore provides a summary of the principal terms of the main public sector defined benefit pension schemes. The differing provisions applying in England and Wales and in Scotland have been set out where relevant.

This summary is intended to assist parties and the tribunal by providing core information in relation to each scheme. It should be viewed as a "starting point" in the assessment of pension loss. It will be the responsibility of any party wishing to depart from this to provide supporting evidence.

By way of background, each of the main areas of the public sector operates a DB pension scheme for employees working in that area. The main schemes relate to civil service, local government, NHS, education, firefighting and police. Historically, these schemes operated on a final salary basis, involving an accrual rate of either sixtieths or eightieths and with the ability to commute part of the eventual pension for a lump sum. These schemes have now switched the basis of accrual from final salary to CARE. In local government in England and Wales (not in Scotland), the change took place on 1 April 2014; in all other public sector DB schemes the change took place on 1 April 2015.

Broadly, the schemes maintained the existing final salary basis of accrual for members who, at a specified date, were within ten years of normal retirement age (and applied the change on a tapered basis for members approximately ten and 13½ years from normal retirement age). The change to CARE was implemented immediately in respect of future service only for members more than 13½ years from normal retirement age. For example, where the scheme's normal retirement age was 65, the tapering occurred in respect of those individuals aged between 51½ and 55 as at 1 April 2012. The effect of tapering was to delay their entry into the new scheme[95]. Where the normal retirement age was younger (for example, in respect of service as a police officer or firefighter), the tapering occurred at a younger age. In some cases, therefore, the tribunal must be alert to the possibility that a claimant's pension rights prior to dismissal accrued in both a final salary scheme and a CARE scheme; and it will need to be alert to the possibility that, if the dismissal had not occurred, a claimant benefiting from tapering may not have moved into the new CARE scheme for some time.

The summary below provides details of the main features of the current CARE scheme in each case together with the main features of the relevant DB scheme prior to the change in the basis of accrual. It should be noted that, in all cases, there were even earlier iterations of the DB arrangements and claimants may have retained entitlement to benefits under those earlier iterations. Details of some of them have been included in this summary but others have not (such as local government service prior to the 2008 scheme and NHS service prior to the 1995 scheme). Where the summary does not provide such information and it is relevant to the calculation of pension loss, information should be obtained from the administrators of the relevant scheme.

Employer contribution rates have not been specified in this summary. This is because they vary from scheme to scheme (in the case of the local government scheme, they also vary from employer to employer within the scheme). By way of illustration, employer contribution rates currently range from a low of 14.38% in the NHS scheme to a high of 27.9% in relation to certain members of the PCSPS. The employer contribution rate will be relevant in those DB cases where the contributions method for calculating pension loss is appropriate and for working out the value of a "week's pay"[96].

CIVIL SERVICE

The Principal Civil Service Pension Scheme ("PCSPS") was created under the Superannuation Act 1972. It has been modified on several occasions. It is comprised of several separate sections; each section provides benefits on a different basis depending on the point at which a member joined the scheme.

The current scheme, operating on a CARE basis, was established under the Public Service Pensions Act 2013 and comprises what is referred to as the "Alpha" section. The PCSPS had already changed to accrual on a CARE basis from 2007, in what is referred to as the "Nuvos" section. Prior to that that, two defined benefit sections were in operation: the "Classic" scheme from 1972, and the "Premium" scheme from 2002. While the earlier sections are closed to new members, existing members may continue to accrued benefits under them.

Up to date information about the scheme can be obtained here: http://www.civilservicepensionscheme.org.uk

	"Classic" PCSPS	"Premium" PCSPS	"Nuvos" PCSPS	"Alpha" PCSPS
Benefit basis	Final salary (1/80th) with additional lump sum	Final salary (1/60th)	Career average. 2.3% of pensionable earnings each year, revalued in line with CPI.	Career average. 2.32% (1/43.1) of pensionable earnings each year, revalued in line with CPI.

Part 4 Statutory Codes of Practice

	"Classic" PCSPS	"Premium" PCSPS	"Nuvos" PCSPS	"Alpha" PCSPS
Member contributions	1.5%	3.5%	3.5%	Based on member's pensionable pay at rates applicable to the band into which the member's salary falls, starting at 4.6% of pensionable salary and rising to 8.05% for the highest paid employees.
Normal retirement age	60	60	65	The later of age 65 or state pension age
Retirement benefits	A pension based on 1/80th of final salary, accrued for each year of pensionable service. Additional lump sum based on 3/80th of final salary, accrued for each year of pensionable service.	A pension based on 1/60th of final salary, accrued for each year of pensionable service. Optional commutation of pensionto receive lump sum (at rate of 1:12).	A pension based on accrual of career-average pension of 2.3% for each year of pensionable service revalued at CPI. A maximum lump sum of 25% of the total value of pension benefits. Optional commutation of pension to receive lump sum (at rate of 1:12).	A pension based on accrual of career-average pension of 2.32% for each year of pensionable service revalued at CPI. A maximum lump sum of 25% of the total value of pension benefits. Optional commutation of pension to receive lump sum (at rate of 1:12).
Death benefits	2 x pensionable pay	3 x pensionable pay	The higher of: (a) 2 x the member's final pay, less any lump sum payments payable under PCSPS arrangements; or (b) 5 x the pension built up, less any payments already made from PCSPS arrangements.	The higher of: (a) 2 x the member's final pay, less any lump sum payments payable under PCSPS arrangements; or (b) 5 x the pension built up, less any payments already made from PCSPS arrangements.
Ill-health benefits	Single tier with enhancements based on length of service	*Lower tier*. To qualify, the member must be considered permanently incapable of doing their own job. *Higher tier*. To qualify, the member must be considered permanently incapable of working in any kind of employment.	*Lower tier*. To qualify, the member must be considered permanently incapable of doing their own job, or another similar role. The amount of pension will be the member's total Nuvos pension built up to date. *Higher tier*. To qualify, the member must be considered permanently incapable of working in any kind of employment. The amount of pension will be the lower tier pension plus an increased Nuvos pension.	*Lower tier*. To qualify, the member must be considered permanently incapable of doing their own job, or another similar role. The amount of pension will be the member's total Alpha pension built up to date. *Upper tier*. To qualify, the member must be considered permanently incapable of working in any kind of employment. The amount of pension will be the lower tier pension plus an increased Alpha pension.

LOCAL GOVERNMENT

The Local Government Pension Scheme ("LGPS") is governed by regulations, currently the Local Government Pension Scheme Regulations 2013. Up to date information can be obtained from the LGPS member site here: https://www.lgpsmember.org

This website includes further detail on variances such as the "Rule of 85".

	2008 LGPS	2014 LGPS
Benefit basis	Final salary (1/60th)	Career average. 2.04% (1/49th) of pensionable earnings each year, revalued in line with CPI
Member contributions	Tiered contributions based on salary bands, rising from 5.5% to 7.5%.	Tiered contributions based on salary bands, rising from 5.5% to 12.5%.
Normal retirement age	65	The later of age 65 or state pension age
Retirement benefits	A pension based on 1/60th accrual for each year of pensionable service. Optional commutation of pension for increased lump sum at rate of 1:12.	A pension based on accrual of career-average pension of 2.04% per year of pensionable service revalued at CPI. Optional commutation of pension for increased lump sum at rate of 1:12.
Death benefits	3 × pensionable pay	3 × pensionable pay
Ill-health benefits	*Tier 1.* Immediate payment with service enhanced to normal pension age (65). *Tier 2.* Immediate payment with 25% service enhancement to normal pension age. *Tier 3.* Temporary payment of pension for up to three years.	*Tier 1.* Immediate payment with service enhanced to normal pension age. *Tier 2.* Immediate payment with 25% service enhancement to normal pension age. *Tier 3.* Temporary payment of pension for up to three years.

Scottish Local Government Pension Scheme

The Scottish Local Government Pension schemes tend to be administered locally and there are some regional variations but, in general, the benefits of current schemes are in line with the schemes in England and Wales. The accrual rate is 1/49th, revalued in line with CPI. Up to date information can be obtained from http://scotlgps2015.org.

HEALTH SERVICE

The National Health Service Pension Scheme ("NHSPS") is governed by regulations, currently the National Health Pension Scheme Regulations 2015. The Scheme operates with some differences between different categories of staff, but the main provisions are set out below. More detailed, and up to date, information about the scheme can be obtained from: https://www.nhsbsa.nhs.uk/nhs-pensions

	NHSPS 1995 Section	NHSPS 2008 Section	2015 NHSPS
Benefit basis	Final salary (1/80th) Additional lump sum of 3 × pension and further option to exchange part of pension for more cash.	Final salary (1/60th) Option to exchange part of pension for cash up to 25% of capital value.	Career average. 1.85% (1/54th) of pensionable earnings each year, revalued in line with CPI plus 1.5%.
Member contributions	Tiered contributions based on salary bands, rising from 5% to 8.5%.	Tiered contributions based on salary bands, rising from 5% to 8.5%.	Tiered contributions based on salary bands, rising from 5% to 14.5%.
Normal retirement age	65 (lower ages apply for individuals undertaking particular roles, such as those with Mental Health Officer status)	65 (lower ages apply for individuals undertaking particular roles, such as those with Mental Health Officer status)	The later of age 65 or state pension age
Retirement benefits	A pension based on 1/80th accrual for each year of pensionable service. Additional lump sum of 3 × pension.	A pension based on 1/60th accrual for each year of pensionable service. Optional commutation of pension for increased lump sum at rate of 1:12.	A pension based on accrual of career-average pension of 1/54th per year of pensionable service revalued at CPI plus 1.5%. Optional commutation of pension for increased lump sum at rate of 1:12.

	NHSPS 1995 Section	NHSPS 2008 Section	2015 NHSPS
Death benefits	2 × pensionable pay	2 × pensionable pay	The higher of: The higher of: (a) 2 x relevant earnings; or (b) 2 x revalued pensionable earnings for the scheme year at the highest revalued pensionable earnings.
Ill-health benefits	Two-tier benefit payable after two years' service.	Two-tier benefit payable after two years' service.	Two-tier benefit payable after two years' service.

NHS pensions in Scotland

In Scotland, health service pensions are administered by the Scottish Public Pensions Agency (SPPA). Up to date information on pensions can be obtained from their website at www.sppa.gov.uk. The pensions provided under the old (2008) NHS scheme were similar to those in England and Wales. The 2015 scheme is also similar save that whilst the accrual rate is the same at 1/54th, the revaluation measure is CPI plus 1.25%.

EDUCATION

The Teachers' Pension Scheme ("TPS") is governed by regulations, currently the Teachers' Pensions Regulations 2010. Up to date information about the scheme can be found at: https://www.teacherspensions.co.uk.

	2007 scheme	2015 scheme
Benefit basis	Final salary (1/60th)	Career average. 1.75% (1/57th) of pensionable earnings each year, revalued in line with CPI.
Member contributions	6.4% of salary	Tiered contributions based on salary bands, rising from 7.4% to 11.7%.
Normal retirement age	65	The later of age 65 or state pension age.
Retirement benefits	A pension based on 1/60th accrual for each year of pensionable service. Optional commutation of pension for increased lump sum at rate of 1:12.	A pension based on accrual of career-average pension of 1/57th per year of pensionable service revalued at CPI. Optional commutation of pension for increased lump sum at rate of 1:12.
Death benefits	3 × final salary	3 × average pensionable pay
Ill-health benefits	Two-tier benefit	Two-tier benefit

Education in Scotland

The Scottish Teachers' Superannuation Scheme is administered by the SPPA. Up to date information can be obtained from their website www.sppa.gov.uk

	2007 scheme	2015 scheme
Benefit basis	Final salary (1/60th) (best consecutive three years revalued salary from last ten years)	Career average. 1.75% (1/57th) of pensionable earnings each year, revalued in line with CPI plus 1.6%.
Member contributions	Tiered	Tiered contributions based on salary bands, rising from 7.4% to 11.9%.
Normal retirement age	65	The later of age 65 or state pension age
Retirement benefits	A pension based on 1/60th accrual for each year of pensionable service. Optional commutation of pension for increased lump sum.	A pension based on accrual of career-average pension of 1/57th per year of pensionable service revalued at CPI +1.6%. Optional commutation of pension for increased lump sum at rate of 1:12.
Death benefits	3 × final salary	3 × average pensionable pay
Ill-health benefits	Two-tier benefit	Two-tier benefit

FIRE SERVICE

Responsibility for firefighters' pension schemes is devolved. This means that there are separate statutory provisions applicable in England and in Wales. These are the Firefighters' Pension Scheme (England) and the Firefighters' Pension Scheme (Wales), operating under the Firefighters' Pension Scheme (England)

Regulations 2014 and the Firefighters' Pension Scheme (Wales) Regulations 2015 respectively. These replaced the previous schemes: the Firefighters' Pension Scheme 1992 (which operated across both England and Wales), and the Firefighters' Pension Scheme 2006 (which operated in England only) and the Firefighters' Pension Wales Scheme 2007 (which operated in Wales only). The prior schemes continue in operation for those who remain eligible.

Up to date information about the scheme can be found at: https://www.yourpensionservice.org.uk/firefighters

	2006 FPS	2015 FPS
Benefit basis	Final salary (1/60th) ("fast accrual" in 1992 Scheme)	Career average. 1.675% (1/59.7) in England and 1.629% (1/61.4) in Wales of pensionable earnings each year, revalued in line with CPI
Member contributions	8.5% of salary	Tiered contributions based on salary bands, between 10.5% (increasing to 11% from 1 April 2018) and 14.5%.
Normal retirement age	60 (55 in 1992 Scheme)	60
Retirement benefits	A pension based on 1/60th accrual for each year of pensionable service. (The 1992 Scheme operated on a "fast accrual" basis of 1/60th for each of the first 20 years of service and 2/60ths for each subsequent year up to a maximum of 40/60ths.) Optional commutation of pension for increased lump sum at rate of 1:12 (1:20.8 in the 1992 Scheme).	A pension based on accrual of career-average pension of 1.675% (1/59.7) in England and 1.629% (1/61.4) in Wales per year of pensionable service revalued at CPI. Optional commutation of pension for increased lump sum at rate of 1:12.
Death benefits	3 × final salary (3 × final salary in 1992 Scheme)	3 × final pay
Ill-health benefits	Two-tier benefit	Two-tier benefit

Firefighters' Pension Scheme (Scotland)

In Scotland, there were two pre-existing pension schemes known as the Firefighters' Pension Scheme (FPS) and the New Firefighters Pension Scheme introduced in 2006 (NFPS). Retained and volunteer firefighters could not be members of FPS but could be members of the NFPS. The benefits of both schemes were similar to that of "Old FPS".

A new firefighters pension scheme known as the Scottish Firefighters Pension Scheme 2015 was introduced in 2015 with transitional protections similar to England and Wales. The terms of this scheme are similar to the 2015 scheme for England and Wales, save that the accrual rate in Scotland is 1.623% (1/61.6) of pensionable earnings in each year revalued in line with CPI.

POLICE SERVICE

Whilst pension schemes have been in existence for police officers since 1890, the modern structure of the Police Pension Scheme was set out in 1987. Revisions to that structure were made in 2006, before the current CARE structure was put in place by the Police Pensions Regulations 2015. Up to date information about the scheme can be found at: http://www.yourpensionservice.org.uk/police

	1987 Scheme	2006 Scheme	2015 Scheme
Benefit basis	Final salary (1/60th) – "fast accrual"	Final salary (1/70th) with additional lump sum	Career average. 1.808% (1/55.3) of pensionable earnings each year, revalued in line with CPI
Member contributions	Tiered contributions based on salary bands, ranging from 14.25% to 15.05%.	Tiered contributions based on salary bands, ranging from 11% to 12.75%.	Tiered contributions based on salary bands, ranging from 12.44% to 13.78%.
Normal retirement age	55 – 60 depending on rank, or 50 after 25 years' service	55	60

Retirement benefits	A pension based on "fast accrual" of 1/60th for each of the first 20 years of service and 2/60ths for each subsequent year up to a maximum of 40/60ths. Optional commutation of pension for increased lump sum at a rate of approximately 1:20.	A pension based on 1/70th accrual for each year of pensionable service. Additional lump sum of 4 × annual pension.	A pension based on accrual of career-average pension of 1/55.3 per year of pensionable service revalued at CPI. Optional commutation of pension for increased lump sum at rate of 1:12.
Death benefits	2 × pensionable pay	3 × pensionable pay	3 × final pay
Ill-health benefits	Single-tier benefit	Two-tier benefit	Two-tier benefit

Police Pension Scheme (Scotland)

In Scotland, the 1987 and 2006 schemes operate in a similar way to the equivalent schemes in England and Wales. The 2015 scheme is also similar save that the accrual rate in Scotland is 1.783% (1/56.1) of pensionable earnings each year revalued in line with CPI plus 1.25%.

NOTES

95 In the Local Government Pension Scheme, this is known as the "underpin".

96 See paragraph 2.25 above.

APPENDIX 2: OGDEN TABLES (AT A GLANCE)

[4.334]

This appendix provides "at a glance" extracts from the Ogden Tables, using a discount rate of minus 0.75%.

The Ogden Tables are prepared by the Government Actuary's Department. The tables in this appendix for retirement ages 66 to 69 are reproduced with kind permission of the Professional Negligence Bar Association.

MINUS 0.75% DISCOUNT RATE (MALE)

Age now	Losses for life	Loss of earnings						Loss of pension					
		⇨50	⇨55	⇨60	⇨65	⇨70	⇨75	50⇨	55⇨	60⇨	65⇨	70⇨	75⇨
	1	**3**	**5**	**7**	**9**	**11**	**13**	**15**	**17**	**19**	**21**	**23**	**25**
0	128.73							68.85	61.71	54.40	46.96	39.47	32.00
1	127.21							68.46	61.34	54.05	46.64	39.16	31.73
2	125.07							67.74	60.68	53.44	46.08	38.67	31.30
3	122.92							67.02	60.01	52.83	45.53	38.18	30.87
4	120.79							66.30	59.34	52.22	44.98	37.69	30.45
5	118.67							65.59	58.68	51.62	44.43	37.21	30.03
6	116.57							64.88	58.03	51.02	43.89	36.73	29.61
7	114.49							64.18	57.38	50.42	43.36	36.25	29.20
8	112.42							63.48	56.74	49.84	42.83	35.78	28.79
9	110.36							62.79	56.10	49.25	42.30	35.32	28.39
10	108.32							62.10	55.46	48.67	41.78	34.86	27.99
11	106.29							61.42	54.84	48.10	41.26	34.40	27.60
12	104.29							60.75	54.22	47.54	40.76	33.95	27.21
13	102.30							60.09	53.61	46.98	40.25	33.50	26.83
14	100.33							59.44	53.00	46.43	39.76	33.07	26.45
15	98.38							58.79	52.41	45.88	39.27	32.64	26.08
16	96.45	38.30	44.63	51.11	57.67	64.24	70.74	58.15	51.82	45.35	38.79	32.21	25.71
17	94.55	37.02	43.31	49.73	56.23	62.76	69.20	57.53	51.24	44.82	38.31	31.79	25.35
18	92.66	35.75	41.99	48.36	54.82	61.28	67.67	56.91	50.67	44.30	37.85	31.38	24.99
19	90.80	34.50	40.69	47.01	53.41	59.83	66.16	56.30	50.11	43.79	37.39	30.98	24.65
20	88.96	33.25	39.40	45.67	52.02	58.38	64.66	55.71	49.57	43.29	36.94	30.58	24.31
21	87.14	32.02	38.12	44.34	50.64	56.95	63.17	55.12	49.02	42.80	36.50	30.19	23.97
22	85.33	30.79	36.84	43.02	49.27	55.53	61.69	54.54	48.48	42.31	36.05	29.80	23.63
23	83.53	29.57	35.58	41.71	47.92	54.12	60.23	53.96	47.95	41.82	35.61	29.41	23.30
24	81.75	28.37	34.33	40.41	46.57	52.72	58.77	53.38	47.42	41.34	35.18	29.03	22.97
25	79.99	27.17	33.09	39.12	45.23	51.33	57.33	52.82	46.90	40.86	34.76	28.65	22.65
26	78.25	25.98	31.85	37.85	43.91	49.96	55.91	52.27	46.39	40.40	34.34	28.29	22.34

Age now	Losses for life	Loss of earnings						Loss of pension					
		⇨50	⇨55	⇨60	⇨65	⇨70	⇨75	50⇨	55⇨	60⇨	65⇨	70⇨	75⇨
	1	**3**	**5**	**7**	**9**	**11**	**13**	**15**	**17**	**19**	**21**	**23**	**25**
27	76.52	24.80	30.63	36.58	42.59	48.60	54.49	51.73	45.89	39.95	33.93	27.93	22.03
28	74.81	23.63	29.42	35.32	41.29	47.24	53.09	51.18	45.39	39.49	33.52	27.57	21.72
29	73.11	22.47	28.21	34.07	39.99	45.90	51.69	50.64	44.89	39.03	33.11	27.21	21.41
30	71.43	21.31	27.02	32.84	38.71	44.57	50.31	50.11	44.41	38.59	32.72	26.86	21.11
31	69.77	20.17	25.84	31.61	37.44	43.25	48.95	49.60	43.93	38.16	32.33	26.52	20.82
32	68.14	19.04	24.67	30.40	36.19	41.95	47.60	49.10	43.48	37.74	31.96	26.19	20.54
33	66.54	17.92	23.51	29.20	34.94	40.67	46.27	48.62	43.03	37.34	31.59	25.87	20.27
34	64.94	16.80	22.36	28.01	33.71	39.39	44.95	48.14	42.59	36.93	31.23	25.55	20.00
35	63.36	15.70	21.21	26.83	32.49	38.12	43.63	47.66	42.15	36.53	30.87	25.24	19.73
36	61.80	14.60	20.08	25.65	31.28	36.87	42.33	47.19	41.72	36.14	30.52	24.93	19.46
37	60.25	13.51	18.95	24.49	30.07	35.62	41.05	46.73	41.29	35.75	30.17	24.62	19.20
38	58.71	12.43	17.84	23.34	28.88	34.39	39.76	46.28	40.87	35.37	29.83	24.32	18.94
39	57.18	11.36	16.73	22.19	27.69	33.16	38.49	45.82	40.45	34.99	29.48	24.02	18.68
40	55.66	10.29	15.63	21.05	26.52	31.94	37.23	45.37	40.04	34.61	29.15	23.72	18.43
41	54.16	9.23	14.53	19.92	25.35	30.73	35.98	44.94	39.63	34.24	28.82	23.43	18.18
42	52.68	8.18	13.45	18.80	24.19	29.54	34.74	44.51	39.24	33.88	28.49	23.15	17.94
43	51.22	7.13	12.37	17.69	23.04	28.35	33.52	44.09	38.85	33.53	28.18	22.87	17.70
44	49.77	6.10	11.30	16.59	21.91	27.18	32.30	43.68	38.47	33.18	27.87	22.60	17.47
45	48.34	5.06	10.24	15.49	20.78	26.01	31.10	43.28	38.10	32.85	27.56	22.33	17.24
46	46.92	4.04	9.19	14.41	19.66	24.86	29.91	42.88	37.74	32.51	27.26	22.06	17.01
47	45.52	3.02	8.14	13.33	18.55	23.72	28.73	42.50	37.38	32.19	26.97	21.81	16.79
48	44.14	2.01	7.10	12.27	17.45	22.58	27.56	42.13	37.04	31.87	26.69	21.56	16.58
49	42.78	1.00	6.07	11.21	16.37	21.46	26.41	41.78	36.71	31.57	26.41	21.31	16.37
50	41.44		5.05	10.16	15.29	20.36	25.27	41.44	36.39	31.28	26.15	21.08	16.17
51	40.12		4.03	9.12	14.22	19.26	24.14		36.09	31.00	25.90	20.86	15.98
52	38.82		3.01	8.08	13.17	18.18	23.03		35.81	30.74	25.66	20.64	15.80
53	37.55		2.01	7.06	12.12	17.11	21.93		35.55	30.49	25.43	20.44	15.62
54	36.30		1.00	6.04	11.08	16.05	20.85		35.30	30.26	25.22	20.25	15.45

Age now	Losses for life	Loss of earnings						Loss of pension					
		⇨50	⇨55	⇨60	⇨65	⇨70	⇨75	50⇨	55⇨	60⇨	65⇨	70⇨	75⇨
	1	**3**	**5**	**7**	**9**	**11**	**13**	**15**	**17**	**19**	**21**	**23**	**25**
55	35.07			5.02	10.05	15.00	19.78		35.07	30.05	25.02	20.07	15.30
56	33.87			4.01	9.03	13.96	18.72			29.86	24.84	19.91	15.15
57	32.69			3.01	8.01	12.93	17.67			29.68	24.68	19.76	15.02
58	31.52			2.00	7.00	11.91	16.63			29.51	24.52	19.61	14.88
59	30.35			1.00	5.99	10.89	15.60			29.35	24.36	19.47	14.75
60	29.19				4.98	9.87	14.57			29.19	24.21	19.32	14.62
61	28.05				3.98	8.87	13.55				24.06	19.18	14.50
62	26.92				2.99	7.87	12.55				23.94	19.05	14.38
63	25.82				1.99	6.88	11.55				23.83	18.94	14.27
64	24.74				1.00	5.90	10.57				23.74	18.85	14.17
65	23.70					4.92	9.60				23.70	18.78	14.10
66	22.68					3.94	8.64					18.74	14.04
67	21.69					2.96	7.68					18.73	14.01
68	20.73					1.98	6.73					18.75	14.00
69	19.78					0.99	5.78					18.79	14.00
70	18.85						4.83					18.85	14.02
71	17.92						3.88						14.04
72	17.00						2.93						14.07
73	16.07						1.96						14.11
74	15.15						0.99						14.16
75	14.22												14.22
76	13.32												
77	12.44												
78	11.58												
79	10.77												
80	9.99												
81	9.27												
82	8.61												

Age now	Losses for life	Loss of earnings						Loss of pension					
		⇨50	⇨55	⇨60	⇨65	⇨70	⇨75	50⇨	55⇨	60⇨	65⇨	70⇨	75⇨
	1	**3**	**5**	**7**	**9**	**11**	**13**	**15**	**17**	**19**	**21**	**23**	**25**
83	7.99												
84	7.42												
85	6.89												
86	6.38												
87	5.90												
88	5.44												
89	5.00												
90	4.59												
91	4.21												
92	3.85												
93	3.52												
94	3.22												
95	2.96												
96	2.74												
97	2.55												
98	2.37												
99	2.21												
100	2.06												

MINUS 0.75% DISCOUNT RATE (FEMALE)

Age	Losses for life	Loss of earnings						Loss of pension					
		50⇨	55⇨	60⇨	65⇨	70⇨	75⇨	⇨50	⇨55	⇨60	⇨65	⇨70	⇨75
	2	**4**	**6**	**9**	**10**	**12**	**14**	**16**	**18**	**20**	**22**	**24**	**26**
0	135.52							75.34	68.08	60.62	52.96	45.17	37.29
1	133.87							74.89	67.66	60.22	52.59	44.82	36.97
2	131.69							74.13	66.95	59.57	52.00	44.29	36.51
3	129.52							73.38	66.25	58.93	51.42	43.77	36.05
4	127.36							72.63	65.56	58.29	50.83	43.25	35.60

Age	Losses for life	Loss of earnings						Loss of pension					
		50⇨	55⇨	60⇨	65⇨	70⇨	75⇨	⇨50	⇨55	⇨60	⇨65	⇨70	⇨75
	2	**4**	**6**	**9**	**10**	**12**	**14**	**16**	**18**	**20**	**22**	**24**	**26**
5	125.21							71.88	64.87	57.65	50.26	42.73	35.14
6	123.07							71.14	64.18	57.02	49.69	42.22	34.70
7	120.96							70.41	63.50	56.40	49.12	41.72	34.25
8	118.85							69.68	62.83	55.78	48.56	41.21	33.81
9	116.77							68.96	62.16	55.16	48.00	40.72	33.38
10	114.70							68.25	61.50	54.56	47.45	40.23	32.95
11	112.65							67.54	60.84	53.96	46.91	39.74	32.53
12	110.62							66.84	60.20	53.36	46.37	39.26	32.11
13	108.60							66.15	59.55	52.77	45.83	38.78	31.69
14	106.60							65.47	58.92	52.19	45.31	38.32	31.28
15	104.62							64.79	58.29	51.62	44.79	37.85	30.88
16	102.65	38.53	44.98	51.60	58.38	65.26	72.17	64.12	57.67	51.05	44.27	37.39	30.48
17	100.71	37.25	43.65	50.22	56.94	63.77	70.62	63.46	57.06	50.49	43.76	36.94	30.08
18	98.78	35.98	42.33	48.85	55.52	62.29	69.09	62.80	56.45	49.93	43.26	36.49	29.69
19	96.88	34.72	41.02	47.49	54.11	60.82	67.56	62.16	55.86	49.39	42.77	36.05	29.31
20	94.99	33.46	39.72	46.14	52.71	59.37	66.05	61.53	55.27	48.85	42.28	35.62	28.94
21	93.12	32.22	38.43	44.80	51.32	57.92	64.55	60.90	54.69	48.32	41.80	35.20	28.57
22	91.26	30.99	37.15	43.47	49.93	56.49	63.06	60.27	54.11	47.79	41.33	34.77	28.20
23	89.41	29.76	35.87	42.15	48.56	55.06	61.58	59.65	53.54	47.26	40.85	34.35	27.83
24	87.58	28.54	34.61	40.84	47.20	53.65	60.12	59.03	52.97	46.74	40.37	33.93	27.46
25	85.76	27.34	33.36	39.54	45.85	52.25	58.66	58.43	52.40	46.22	39.91	33.51	27.10
26	83.97	26.14	32.12	38.25	44.52	50.86	57.22	57.83	51.85	45.72	39.45	33.11	26.75
27	82.19	24.95	30.89	36.97	43.19	49.48	55.78	57.24	51.30	45.22	39.00	32.71	26.40
28	80.42	23.78	29.66	35.70	41.87	48.11	54.36	56.65	50.76	44.72	38.55	32.31	26.06
29	78.68	22.61	28.45	34.45	40.56	46.76	52.96	56.07	50.23	44.23	38.11	31.92	25.72
30	76.95	21.45	27.25	33.20	39.27	45.41	51.56	55.50	49.70	43.75	37.68	31.53	25.39
31	75.24	20.30	26.05	31.96	37.98	44.08	50.17	54.94	49.18	43.28	37.25	31.16	25.06
32	73.54	19.15	24.87	30.73	36.71	42.76	48.80	54.39	48.67	42.81	36.83	30.78	24.74

Age	Losses for life	Loss of earnings						Loss of pension					
		50⇨	55⇨	60⇨	65⇨	70⇨	75⇨	⇨50	⇨55	⇨60	⇨65	⇨70	⇨75
	2	**4**	**6**	**9**	**10**	**12**	**14**	**16**	**18**	**20**	**22**	**24**	**26**
33	71.86	18.02	23.69	29.51	35.45	41.44	47.44	53.84	48.17	42.35	36.42	30.42	24.42
34	70.20	16.90	22.53	28.30	34.19	40.14	46.09	53.30	47.67	41.89	36.00	30.05	24.11
35	68.54	15.78	21.37	27.10	32.95	38.85	44.75	52.76	47.17	41.44	35.60	29.69	23.79
36	66.91	14.67	20.22	25.91	31.71	37.57	43.42	52.24	46.68	40.99	35.19	29.34	23.49
37	65.29	13.57	19.09	24.73	30.49	36.30	42.10	51.72	46.20	40.56	34.80	28.99	23.19
38	63.69	12.48	17.96	23.56	29.28	35.05	40.80	51.20	45.73	40.12	34.41	28.64	22.89
39	62.10	11.40	16.84	22.40	28.07	33.80	39.50	50.70	45.26	39.70	34.02	28.30	22.59
40	60.52	10.33	15.72	21.25	26.88	32.56	38.22	50.19	44.80	39.27	33.64	27.96	22.30
41	58.96	9.26	14.62	20.11	25.70	31.33	36.95	49.70	44.34	38.86	33.27	27.63	22.02
42	57.42	8.20	13.53	18.98	24.52	30.12	35.69	49.22	43.90	38.45	32.90	27.31	21.74
43	55.90	7.15	12.44	17.85	23.36	28.91	34.44	48.74	43.46	38.05	32.54	26.99	21.46
44	54.39	6.11	11.36	16.74	22.20	27.72	33.20	48.28	43.03	37.65	32.18	26.67	21.19
45	52.90	5.08	10.29	15.63	21.06	26.53	31.97	47.82	42.61	37.27	31.84	26.37	20.93
46	51.42	4.05	9.23	14.53	19.93	25.36	30.76	47.38	42.19	36.89	31.50	26.06	20.67
47	49.96	3.03	8.18	13.45	18.80	24.20	29.56	46.94	41.79	36.52	31.16	25.77	20.41
48	48.53	2.01	7.13	12.37	17.69	23.05	28.37	46.52	41.40	36.16	30.84	25.48	20.16
49	47.11	1.00	6.09	11.30	16.59	21.91	27.19	46.11	41.02	35.81	30.52	25.20	19.92
50	45.71		5.06	10.24	15.50	20.78	26.03	45.71	40.65	35.47	30.22	24.93	19.69
51	44.33		4.04	9.19	14.41	19.67	24.88		40.29	35.14	29.92	24.66	19.46
52	42.97		3.02	8.14	13.34	18.56	23.73		39.94	34.82	29.63	24.40	19.23
53	41.62		2.01	7.10	12.27	17.46	22.61		39.61	34.52	29.35	24.15	19.01
54	40.29		1.00	6.07	11.22	16.38	21.49		39.29	34.22	29.08	23.91	18.80
55	38.99			5.05	10.17	15.30	20.38		38.99	33.94	28.82	23.68	18.60
56	37.70			4.03	9.12	14.24	19.29			33.67	28.57	23.46	18.41
57	36.43			3.01	8.09	13.18	18.20			33.41	28.34	23.25	18.23
58	35.17			2.01	7.06	12.13	17.13			33.16	28.11	23.04	18.04
59	33.92			1.00	6.04	11.08	16.06			32.92	27.88	22.84	17.86
60	32.68				5.02	10.05	15.00			32.68	27.66	22.63	17.68

Age	Losses for life	Loss of earnings						Loss of pension					
		50⇨	55⇨	60⇨	65⇨	70⇨	75⇨	⇨50	⇨55	⇨60	⇨65	⇨70	⇨75
	2	**4**	**6**	**9**	**10**	**12**	**14**	**16**	**18**	**20**	**22**	**24**	**26**
61	31.45				4.01	9.02	13.95				27.44	22.43	17.50
62	30.24				3.00	8.00	12.91				27.24	22.24	17.33
63	29.04				2.00	6.98	11.88				27.04	22.06	17.16
64	27.88				1.00	5.98	10.86				26.88	21.90	17.01
65	26.74					4.98	9.85				26.74	21.76	16.88
66	25.63					3.98	8.86					21.65	16.77
67	24.55					2.99	7.87					21.56	16.68
68	23.49					1.99	6.88					21.50	16.61
69	22.45					1.00	5.90					21.45	16.55
70	21.41						4.92					21.41	16.49
71	20.39						3.94						16.44
72	19.35						2.96						16.39
73	18.31						1.98						16.33
74	17.27						0.99						16.28
75	16.23												16.23
76	15.20												
77	14.19												
78	13.21												
79	12.27												
80	11.39												
81	10.56												
82	9.78												
83	9.06												
84	8.39												
85	7.76												
86	7.16												
87	6.59												
88	6.05												

Age	Losses for life	Loss of earnings						Loss of pension					
		50⇨	55⇨	60⇨	65⇨	70⇨	75⇨	⇨50	⇨55	⇨60	⇨65	⇨70	⇨75
	2	4	6	9	10	12	14	16	18	20	22	24	26
89	5.53												
90	5.05												
91	4.60												
92	4.18												
93	3.81												
94	3.48												
95	3.20												
96	2.96												
97	2.75												
98	2.56												
99	2.38												
100	2.21												

MINUS 0.75% DISCOUNT (MALE) FOR RETIREMENT AGES 66 TO 69

	Loss of earnings to age ...				Loss of pension from age ...			
	66	67	68	69	66	67	68	69
16	58.97	60.27	61.59	62.91	37.53	36.24	34.93	33.58
17	57.52	58.82	60.13	61.44	37.07	35.79	34.49	33.15
18	56.09	57.38	58.68	59.98	36.61	35.35	34.06	32.73
19	54.68	55.95	57.24	58.53	36.16	34.91	33.63	32.32
20	53.27	54.54	55.81	57.10	35.72	34.47	33.20	31.91
21	51.89	53.14	54.40	55.67	35.28	34.04	32.78	31.50
22	50.51	51.75	53.00	54.26	34.85	33.63	32.37	31.10
23	49.14	50.37	51.61	52.86	34.43	33.21	31.97	30.70
24	47.78	49.00	50.23	51.47	34.00	32.80	31.57	30.31
25	46.43	47.65	48.87	50.10	33.59	32.40	31.18	29.93
26	45.10	46.30	47.51	48.73	33.18	31.99	30.79	29.55
27	43.78	44.97	46.17	47.38	32.78	31.60	30.40	29.18

	Loss of earnings to age ...				Loss of pension from age ...			
	66	**67**	**68**	**69**	**66**	**67**	**68**	**69**
28	42.46	43.64	44.83	46.03	32.38	31.21	30.02	28.80
29	41.16	42.34	43.51	44.70	31.99	30.84	29.65	28.44
30	39.87	41.04	42.21	43.38	31.60	30.46	29.29	28.08
31	38.59	39.75	40.91	42.08	31.22	30.09	28.93	27.74
32	37.33	38.48	39.63	40.79	30.85	29.72	28.58	27.40
33	36.07	37.21	38.36	39.51	30.49	29.37	28.23	27.07
34	34.83	35.96	37.10	38.24	30.14	29.02	27.89	26.73
35	33.60	34.72	35.85	36.98	29.79	28.68	27.56	26.41
36	32.38	33.49	34.61	35.74	29.44	28.35	27.23	26.09
37	31.17	32.27	33.38	34.50	29.10	28.01	26.90	25.77
38	29.97	31.06	32.16	33.27	28.77	27.68	26.58	25.46
39	28.77	29.86	30.95	32.05	28.43	27.36	26.27	25.15
40	27.59	28.67	29.75	30.84	28.11	27.04	25.96	24.85
41	26.42	27.49	28.56	29.64	27.78	26.73	25.65	24.55
42	25.25	26.31	27.38	28.46	27.47	26.42	25.35	24.26
43	24.10	25.15	26.21	27.28	27.15	26.11	25.06	23.97
44	22.95	24.00	25.05	26.11	26.85	25.82	24.76	23.69
45	21.82	22.86	23.91	24.96	26.56	25.53	24.48	23.41
46	20.69	21.73	22.77	23.81	26.26	25.24	24.20	23.14
47	19.58	20.61	21.64	22.68	25.98	24.97	23.93	22.88
48	18.48	19.50	20.53	21.55	25.70	24.70	23.67	22.62
49	17.39	18.40	19.42	20.44	25.44	24.44	23.42	22.38
50	16.30	17.32	18.33	19.34	25.18	24.19	23.17	22.14
51	15.23	16.24	17.25	18.25	24.93	23.95	22.94	21.91
52	14.17	15.17	16.18	17.18	24.70	23.72	22.71	21.69
53	13.12	14.12	15.12	16.11	24.48	23.50	22.50	21.48
54	12.08	13.07	14.07	15.06	24.27	23.30	22.30	21.29
55	11.04	12.03	13.02	14.01	24.07	23.10	22.12	21.11
56	10.01	11.00	11.99	12.98	23.88	22.92	21.94	20.94

	Loss of earnings to age ...				Loss of pension from age ...			
	66	67	68	69	66	67	68	69
57	8.99	9.98	10.96	11.95	23.71	22.74	21.77	20.77
58	7.98	8.96	9.94	10.93	23.55	22.58	21.60	20.62
59	6.97	7.95	8.93	9.91	23.40	22.43	21.45	20.46
60	5.97	6.95	7.93	8.90	23.26	22.29	21.30	20.31
61	4.97	5.95	6.93	7.90	23.12	22.16	21.17	20.18
62	3.97	4.96	5.93	6.90	23.00	22.04	21.05	20.06
63	2.98	3.97	4.94	5.91	22.90	21.94	20.95	19.95
64	1.99	2.98	3.96	4.93	22.81	21.85	20.87	19.87
65	1.00	1.99	2.97	3.95	22.75	21.80	20.81	19.81
66		1.00	1.99	2.97	18.96	21.76	20.78	19.77
67			1.00	1.98		14.22	20.77	19.76
68				0.99			9.48	19.78
69								4.74

MINUS 0.75% DISCOUNT (FEMALE) FOR RETIREMENT AGES 66 TO 69

	Loss of earnings				Loss of pension			
	⇨ 66	⇨ 67	⇨ 68	⇨ 69	⇨ 66	⇨ 67	⇨ 68	⇨ 69
16	59.74	61.10	62.48	63.86	42.95	41.61	40.23	38.83
17	58.29	59.64	61.01	62.38	42.46	41.12	39.76	38.36
18	56.85	58.20	59.55	60.91	41.97	40.64	39.29	37.91
19	55.43	56.76	58.10	59.46	41.48	40.17	38.83	37.46
20	54.02	55.34	56.67	58.01	41.00	39.70	38.37	37.01
21	52.61	53.92	55.25	56.58	40.53	39.23	37.91	36.57
22	51.22	52.52	53.83	55.16	40.07	38.78	37.46	36.13
23	49.84	51.13	52.43	53.74	39.60	38.33	37.02	35.70
24	48.47	49.75	51.04	52.34	39.14	37.88	36.59	35.27
25	47.11	48.38	49.66	50.95	38.68	37.43	36.15	34.85
26	45.77	47.03	48.29	49.57	38.23	36.99	35.72	34.43
27	44.43	45.68	46.94	48.20	37.79	36.56	35.30	34.02

	Loss of earnings				Loss of pension			
	⇨ 66	⇨ 67	⇨ 68	⇨ 69	⇨ 66	⇨ 67	⇨ 68	⇨ 69
28	43.10	44.34	45.59	46.85	37.36	36.13	34.88	33.61
29	41.79	43.02	44.25	45.50	36.93	35.71	34.47	33.21
30	40.48	41.70	42.93	44.17	36.50	35.30	34.07	32.82
31	39.19	40.40	41.62	42.84	36.08	34.89	33.67	32.43
32	37.90	39.10	40.31	41.53	35.67	34.48	33.28	32.04
33	36.63	37.82	39.02	40.23	35.26	34.08	32.89	31.66
34	35.37	36.55	37.74	38.94	34.86	33.69	32.50	31.29
35	34.11	35.29	36.47	37.66	34.46	33.31	32.12	30.92
36	32.87	34.03	35.21	36.39	34.07	32.92	31.75	30.56
37	31.64	32.79	33.96	35.13	33.68	32.54	31.38	30.20
38	30.42	31.56	32.72	33.88	33.30	32.17	31.02	29.84
39	29.20	30.34	31.49	32.64	32.92	31.80	30.66	29.49
40	28.00	29.13	30.27	31.41	32.55	31.44	30.30	29.14
41	26.81	27.93	29.06	30.19	32.19	31.08	29.95	28.80
42	25.63	26.74	27.86	28.98	31.83	30.73	29.61	28.47
43	24.46	25.56	26.67	27.79	31.47	30.39	29.28	28.14
44	23.30	24.39	25.49	26.60	31.13	30.05	28.95	27.82
45	22.15	23.23	24.33	25.43	30.79	29.71	28.62	27.50
46	21.01	22.09	23.17	24.26	30.46	29.39	28.30	27.19
47	19.88	20.95	22.03	23.11	30.13	29.07	28.00	26.89
48	18.76	19.82	20.89	21.97	29.81	28.76	27.69	26.60
49	17.65	18.71	19.77	20.84	29.50	28.46	27.40	26.31
50	16.55	17.60	18.66	19.72	29.20	28.16	27.11	26.03
51	15.46	16.50	17.56	18.61	28.91	27.88	26.83	25.76
52	14.38	15.42	16.46	17.51	28.63	27.60	26.56	25.49
53	13.31	14.34	15.38	16.42	28.35	27.34	26.30	25.24
54	12.24	13.27	14.31	15.34	28.09	27.08	26.05	24.99
55	11.19	12.21	13.24	14.27	27.83	26.83	25.80	24.75
56	10.14	11.16	12.19	13.21	27.58	26.58	25.56	24.53

	Loss of earnings				Loss of pension			
	⇨ 66	⇨ 67	⇨ 68	⇨ 69	⇨ 66	⇨ 67	⇨ 68	⇨ 69
57	9.10	10.12	11.14	12.16	27.35	26.35	25.33	24.30
58	8.07	9.08	10.10	11.11	27.12	26.12	25.11	24.09
59	7.05	8.05	9.06	10.07	26.90	25.90	24.89	23.87
60	6.03	7.03	8.03	9.04	26.69	25.69	24.68	23.66
61	5.01	6.01	7.02	8.02	26.48	25.49	24.48	23.46
62	4.00	5.00	6.00	7.00	26.28	25.30	24.29	23.27
63	3.00	4.00	5.00	5.99	26.10	25.13	24.12	23.10
64	2.00	3.00	3.99	4.99	25.94	24.97	23.97	22.94
65	1.00	2.00	2.99	3.99	25.79	24.83	23.83	22.81
66		1.00	2.00	2.99	25.67	24.71	23.72	22.70
67			1.00	1.99		24.61	23.62	22.61
68				1.00			23.54	22.54
69								22.48

TABLE 27: DISCOUNTING FACTORS FOR TERM CERTAIN (MINUS 0.75%)

TABLE 28: MULTIPLIERS FOR PECUNIARY LOSS FOR TERM CERTAIN (MINUS 0.75%)

Years	Table 27	Table 28
0.5	1.0038	0.501
1	1.0076	1.004
1.5	1.0114	1.509
2	1.0152	2.015
2.5	1.0190	2.524
3	1.0228	3.034
3.5	1.0267	3.547
4	1.0306	4.061
4.5	1.0345	4.577
5	1.0384	5.095
6	1.0462	6.138
7	1.0541	7.188
8	1.0621	8.246
9	1.0701	9.312
10	1.0782	10.386
11	1.0863	11.468
12	1.0945	12.559
13	1.1028	13.657
14	1.1112	14.764
15	1.1195	15.880
16	1.1280	17.004
17	1.1365	18.136
18	1.1451	19.277
19	1.1538	20.426
20	1.1625	21.584
21	1.1713	22.751
22	1.1801	23.927
23	1.1890	25.111
24	1.1980	26.305
25	1.2071	27.507
26	1.2162	28.719
27	1.2254	29.94
28	1.2347	31.170
29	1.2440	32.409
30	1.2534	33.658
31	1.2629	34.916
32	1.2724	36.184
33	1.2820	37.461
34	1.2917	38.748
35	1.3015	40.044
36	1.3113	41.351
37	1.3212	42.667
38	1.3312	43.993
39	1.3413	45.329
40	1.3514	46.676
41	1.3616	48.032
42	1.3719	49.399
43	1.3823	50.776
44	1.3927	52.163

Years	Table 27	Table 28
45	1.4032	53.561
46	1.4138	54.970
47	1.4245	56.389
48	1.4353	57.819
49	1.4461	59.260
50	1.4570	60.711
51	1.4681	62.174
52	1.4792	63.647
53	1.4903	65.132
54	1.5016	66.628
55	1.5129	68.135
56	1.5244	69.654
57	1.5359	71.184
58	1.5475	72.726
59	1.5592	74.279
60	1.5710	75.844
61	1.5828	77.421
62	1.5948	79.010
63	1.6069	80.611
64	1.6190	82.224
65	1.6312	83.849
66	1.6436	85.486
67	1.6560	87.136
68	1.6685	88.798
69	1.6811	90.473
70	1.6938	92.160
71	1.7066	93.860
72	1.7195	95.574
73	1.7325	97.299
74	1.7456	99.039
75	1.7588	100.791
76	1.7721	102.556
77	1.7855	104.335
78	1.7990	106.127
79	1.8125	107.933
80	1.8262	109.752

APPENDIX 3: EXAMPLES

[4.335]

This appendix provides examples of points discussed in the Principles. In all cases, it is assumed that the claimants have succeeded in their claims: the tribunal has decided that they were unlawfully dismissed.

The examples are not intended to set out rigid approaches to the brief facts on which they are based. They are illustrative only. They are not intended, for example, to offer views on what the correct award for loss of statutory rights should be. The examples have a narrative rather than arithmetic presentation.

Any readers who would like to see examples of other scenarios, or to offer such examples, are welcome to send details to pensionprinciples@ejudiciary.net.

1. GROSSING UP

These examples relate to paragraphs 2.39 and 2.40 of the Principles. They apply the income tax rates in England and Wales, not Scotland.

The formula for grossing up is:

$$\frac{x}{(100-r)} \times 100 = y$$

Where: x is the award before grossing up;

y is the award after grossing up; and

r is the rate of income tax.

Ashok — grossing up at higher rate

Ashok was unfairly dismissed from a job paying him a gross annual salary of £50,000. The tribunal awards Ashok a basic award of £5,000 and a compensatory award of £38,400, calculated as set out below. The compensatory award includes an award for loss of DC pension rights, which has been calculated using the contributions method (by which the tribunal has aggregated the employer's pension contributions at 15% of gross salary corresponding to the period of loss).

The expression "contributions to hearing" is used, but this is a convenient shorthand in cases where the contributions method is used. It is not intended to mislead about the nature of pension loss, which is always a form of future loss, which is why it attracts no interest. The contributions method, it should be emphasised, does not compensate for the loss of the employer's contributions themselves; instead, it is the mechanism by which the loss of pension income in retirement, after deduction of tax, is assessed.

The unfair dismissal award comprises the following:

Basic award		£5,000
Compensatory award		
• Loss of statutory rights	£450	
• Net loss of earnings to hearing	£8,000	
• Net pension loss (contributions to hearing)	£1,200	
• Net loss of future earnings	£25,000	
• Net pension loss (future contributions)	£3,750	
Total compensatory award (net)		£38,400
Total of basic and compensatory award		£43,400

The total award exceeds £30,000 by £13,400 (the basic award counts against the £30,000 exempt slice). This is the sum that must be grossed up.

We will assume that, in the tax year in which Ashok is due to receive the award, his earnings from his new job have already exhausted his personal allowance of £11,500 and the entire 20% basic rate band. The tribunal's grossing up calculation will therefore be at a single marginal rate of 40%.

The calculation is as follows:

- £13,400/60 × 100 = £23,333
- The tax element is £23,333 less £13,400, which is £8,933
- The sum of £8,933 is added to the compensatory award
- The compensatory award is now £38,400 plus £8,933, which is £47,333

So, after grossing up, the tribunal awards Ashok a basic award of £5,000 and a compensatory award of £47,333.

Ashok — grossing up at basic rate

The facts are as above but, this time, Ashok's gross earnings in the tax year of receipt are only £5,000. This means that he has only used some of his personal allowance of £11,500 and none of the 20% basic rate band. The process of grossing up would then look like this:

- Ashok's taxable earnings of £5,000 means that £6,500 of his personal allowance is available
- This reduces the taxable sum to £6,900 (which is simply £13,400 less £6,500)
- The sum of £6,900 is taxed at 20%
- £6,900/80 × 100 = £8,625
- The tax element is £8,625 less £6,900, which is £1,725
- The sum of £1,725 is added to the compensatory award
- The compensatory award is now £38,400 plus £1,725, which is £40,125

So, after grossing up, the tribunal awards Ashok a basic award of £5,000 and a compensatory award of £40,125.

Ashok — grossing up at differential rates

Now, we assume that Ashok was unfairly dismissed from a job paying him a gross annual salary of £100,000 and that, this time, his earnings in the tax year in which the award of compensation is to be received are £27,000. The tribunal has decided that Ashok was dismissed for making a protected disclosure, so the statutory cap does not apply. The compensatory award includes an award for lost DC pension rights, calculated using the simple method of aggregating employer pension contributions at 10% of gross salary corresponding to the period of loss.

The tribunal calculates Ashok's compensation as a basic award of £5,000 and a compensatory award of £88,500. The award comprises the following:

Basic award		£5,000
Compensatory award		

• Loss of statutory rights	£500	
• Net loss of earnings to hearing	£35,000	
• Net pension loss (contributions to hearing)	£3,500	
• Net loss of future earnings	£45,000	
• Net pension loss (future contributions)	£4,500	
Total compensatory award (net)		£88,500
Total of basic and compensatory award		£93,500

The total award exceeds £30,000 by £63,500. This is the sum that must be grossed up. The process of grossing up would look like this:

- Ashok's new job will pay him taxable income of £27,000
- After deduction of the personal allowance of £11,500, this leaves £15,500 of the income from his new job to be taxed at the basic rate
- Save where the personal allowance has been restricted, the basic rate applies to the next slice of £33,500 (earnings between £11,500 to £45,000)
- If Ashok's new job uses up £15,500 of this slice, it leaves £18,000 to apply to the taxable award of compensation
- If £18,000 of the taxable award of compensation (£63,500) is taxed at the basic rate, the remaining £45,500 will be taxed at the higher rate

Basic rate (20%): £18,000/80 × 100 = £22,500

Tax element is £22,500 less £18,000, which is £4,500

Higher rate (40%): £45,500/60 × 100 = £75,833

Tax element is £75,833 less £45,500, which is £30,333

Total tax to be added: £4,500 + £30,333 = £34,833

- The sum of £34,833 is added to the compensatory award
- The compensatory award is now £88,500 plus £34,833, which is £123,333

So, after grossing up, the tribunal awards Ashok a basic award of £5,000 and a compensatory award of £123,333.

In some of the complex DB examples, we address the position where the size of the tribunal's taxable award is such that it leads to restriction of the personal allowance, which will affect the grossing up calculation (see Tom) and, in respect of increased tax paid on any new job secured by the claimant, merit a further award of compensation (see Ahmed and Katarzyna).

2. RETIREMENT AGE

These examples relate to paragraph 3.21 of the Principles.

To identify a terminal date for a claimant's loss of income from employment, a tribunal may need to decide whether they would have retired before, at or after state pension age. It should be remembered that a person's state pension age varies in accordance with their date of birth and (at least until November 2018) their gender.

Janet — award of loss of earnings beyond state pension age

Janet is aged 64. She has a tapered state pension age between 65 and 66. She was recently dismissed from employment as a cleaner after ten years with a local company. In her evidence, she states that she has worked almost all her adult life, supporting two children and then a disabled husband who recently died; she says that her grandchildren no longer want regular involvement with her and that she liked the bustle of work and the fact that it took her out of herself. She has been unable to find work in the eight months since her dismissal and she does not think she will ever find paid employment again. She says that she had intended to work until age 70 and then perhaps work part-time thereafter.

The tribunal may decide that Janet is likely to find similar work quickly and draw an end to her future loss, perhaps within a further six months. Alternatively, it may decide that she will face insurmountable barriers to finding new work. Let us assume that the tribunal is persuaded to award loss of earnings until the point at which Janet intended to retire. It must therefore decide the age at which she would have retired had it not been for her unlawful dismissal. If the tribunal found Janet to be a reliable and credible witness generally, it may accept her evidence that she intended to work until age 70. In the interests of simplicity and given the level of speculation involved, the tribunal may decide not to award further loss based on part-time work beyond that date.

It should be remembered that, in calculating loss of earnings beyond Janet's state pension age, her net income must be assumed to have gone up. This is because she would have ceased paying Class 1 employee NI contributions upon reaching state pension age. Also, the tribunal should make no deduction for receipt of nSP. This is because Janet is entitled to receive nSP from state pension age, regardless of whether she is in work.

Derek — award of loss of earnings until state pension age

Derek is aged 64. He has a tapered state pension age between 65 and 66. He was recently dismissed from employment as a shop assistant. In his evidence, he says nothing about when he intended to retire but did mention how he had shortly been hoping to spend more time with friends and grandchildren and his dismissal means that he does not look forward to this as much. In the absence of much more to go on, the tribunal decides that Derek would have retired in any event from his job upon reaching state pension age. It therefore awards no loss of earnings beyond then.

Peter — award of loss of earnings until retirement before state pension age

In most cases, a tribunal will not be awarding loss of earnings until state pension age, simply because it can safely be assumed that a claimant will manage successfully to mitigate their loss long before then. This example is directed instead at a situation where the tribunal accepts that a claimant will not work again before retirement, but draws an end to that loss before they reach their state pension age.

Peter is aged 61. He was recently dismissed from employment as a school janitor. His state pension age is 66. However, if he had not been dismissed, he would have been entitled to an unreduced Local Government pension from the age of 65. This is because he was a member of the cohort that were insulated from recent pension reforms based on his proximity to scheme retirement age. In the absence of any evidence suggesting he would have worked beyond 65, the tribunal concludes that Peter's loss of income will cease from the date.

3. LOSS OF STATE PENSION

These examples relate to paragraphs 3.42 to 3.50 of the Principles.

Jessica — no award of compensation for loss of state pension

Jessica is aged 43. She was unemployed for a year after leaving College at the age of 19. She then inherited some money and spent a year travelling. She returned to the UK and found a job in retail, which she performed for seven years. After spending six years at home raising two children, she qualified as a teaching assistant. Her unlawful dismissal from her job as a teaching assistant is what brought her to the tribunal.

Jessica has checked the Government Online service and this confirms that, as at the date of her dismissal, she had accrued 16 qualifying years towards her nSP. Her state pension age under current rules is 67 (although the Government proposes to increase it to 68). That means she has 24 years (and probably 25) in which to accrue the 19 further qualifying years she needs for the full amount of nSP. For the tribunal to be persuaded that Jessica this dismissal would cause a loss of state pension rights, it would have to be persuaded that she would be out of work for at least five (and probably six) years. After hearing evidence, the tribunal decides that Jessica would mitigate her loss by finding other work within 15 months. It therefore awards her no compensation for loss of state pension.

Arthur — award of compensation for loss of state pension

This example involves use of the Ogden Tables.

Arthur is dismissed from his job as a security guard at the age of 63 years. The tribunal decides on the evidence it hears that he would have stayed in the same job until he reached his state pension age of 66, retired at that age and then not worked beyond it. However, as at the date of his dismissal, due to prior periods of unemployment and sickness, Arthur had only accrued 32 qualifying years. His nSP, at present rates, is 32/35ths of £159.55, which is £145.87. Arthur persuades the tribunal that he will not find work again before reaching state pension age. The tribunal therefore concludes that, in addition to loss of earnings and loss of occupational pension rights, his dismissal has resulted in the loss of three qualifying years. In other words, Arthur's nSP is £13.68 per week (i.e. 3/35ths × £159.55) below the amount that it would have been but for the fact he was unlawfully dismissed. At present values, this amounts to a loss of £711.36 for each year of his retirement during which he receives nSP.

There are numerous unknown factors at play when trying to convert this into a capital sum. The figure of £711.36 is based on 2017/18 rates, and (by current government policy, at least) will benefit from the triple lock until Arthur reaches state pension age in three years' time; and it will likely continue to increase for at least some of the years when it is received. Also, no-one knows how long Arthur will live in retirement. It is safer to address these unknown factors by applying an Ogden Table multiplier to our multiplicand of £711.36. There is no need to "net down" this figure because it is assumed that Arthur will not pay tax on his state pension.

The current edition of the Ogden Tables only sets out retirement ages at five-yearly intervals. However, Appendix 2 of these Principles contains a bespoke table of multipliers for retirement ages between 66 and 69 at the discount rate of minus 0.75%. For an individual male aged 63, in respect of pension loss commencing from the age of 66, the multiplier is 22.90. The tribunal decides that no adjustment factors are necessary because it is dealing with pension loss arising from only three years out of the workforce.

Arthur's loss of state pension rights is therefore: 22.9 × £711.36 = £16,290.14.

4. SIMPLE DC CASES

These examples relate to paragraphs 4.17 to 4.30 of the Principles.

The expression "loss to hearing" is sometimes used, but this is a convenient shorthand in cases where the contributions method is used. It is not intended to mislead about the nature of pension loss, which is always a form of future loss, which is why it attracts no interest. The contributions method, it should be emphasised, does not compensate for the loss of the employer's contributions themselves; instead, it is the mechanism by which the loss of pension income in retirement, after deduction of tax, is assessed.

Bethan — contributions method — short period of loss

Bethan succeeds in a complaint of wrongful dismissal. She has a contractual notice period of three months. She remained unemployed for this period, making reasonable but ultimately unsuccessful attempts to mitigate her loss. She had received a gross annual salary of £40,000. Her employer contributed 6% of her salary into its DC pension scheme on her behalf.

The award of compensation to Bethan in respect of the net pension loss arising from her wrongful dismissal will be as follows:

6% x £40,000 x 0.25 (3 months)	£600.00

This will be payable in addition to three months' net salary and the loss of any contractual benefits.

Christopher — contributions method — personal pension case

This examples also relates to paragraph 2.9 of these Principles.

Christopher succeeds in a complaint of unfair dismissal. He had been employed on a gross annual salary of £25,000 and his employer paid contributions of 3% into his personal pension scheme. He remains unemployed at the date of the hearing, which takes place nine months after his dismissal. The tribunal decides that he will remain unemployed for a further six months, at which point he will obtain a job at an equivalent salary and with the same level of employer pension contributions.

The award of compensation to Christopher in respect of the net pension loss arising from his unfair dismissal will be as follows:

Loss to hearing:	3% × £25,000 × 0.75 (9 months)	£562.50
Future loss:	3% × £25,000 × 0.5 (6 months)	£375.00
Total:		£937.50

Diane — contributions method — lost future pay rise

Diane succeeds in a complaint of unfair dismissal. The hearing takes place six months after her dismissal. The tribunal decides that it will take her a further nine months to obtain an alternative position with equivalent benefits. She was employed at a salary of £30,000 per annum, but the tribunal is satisfied from the evidence it hears that that her salary would have increased to £35,000 three months after the hearing. Her employer contributed 5% of her salary into its DC pension scheme.

The award of compensation to Diane in respect of the net pension loss arising from her unfair dismissal will be as follows:

Loss to hearing:	5% x £30,000 x 0.5 (6 months)		£750.00
Future loss:	5% x £30,000 x 0.25 (3 months)	£375.00	
	5% x £35,000 x 0.5 (6 months)	£875.00	
Total future loss:			£1,250.00
Total:			£2,000.00

Edward — Rule 21 judgment — assumption of auto-enrolment

A tribunal issues a Rule 21 liability judgment in favour of Edward, following his employer's failure to file an ET3 response to his complaint of unfair dismissal. Edward was earning a gross annual salary of £20,000. The tribunal arranges a separate remedy hearing, at which Edward tells the tribunal that his employer started a pension scheme a short while ago, but he is unclear as to the type of scheme or the level of employer contribution. He is also unable to provide any documentary evidence, having not kept his payslips.

Edward obtained an alternative job at an equivalent salary six months after dismissal, with the hearing taking place shortly after that. His new employment is with an employer whose auto-enrolment staging date has passed and it is paying only the minimum employer contribution.

In the absence of any clear evidence, the tribunal concludes that Edward had, in his old job, been enrolled into a scheme which complied with the auto-enrolment rules and into which his employer was paying the minimum level of contributions. The compensation the tribunal awards to Edward in respect of his net pension loss will therefore be as follows:

1% x £20.000 x 0.5 (6 months)	£100.00

Furthermore, as Edward's new employer is paying the same contribution rate as his old employer, no further loss arises.

Note that, in this example, Edward's earnings in the old and new jobs exceed the lower level of the qualifying earnings band, hence his auto-enrolment rights.

Fatima — contributions method — changing rate of employer contributions under auto-enrolment

Fatima was dismissed on 6 July 2017. She had been employed on a gross annual salary of £25,000 and a member of her employer's DC pension scheme into which her employer was paying contributions of 3%

of her salary. Fatima finds an alternative job on 6 January 2018; it pays her the same salary, but her new employer only operates an auto-enrolment pension scheme into which it pays the minimum employer contributions (1% up to 5 April 2018, 2% from 6 April 2018 to 5 April 2019, and 3% from then on). Fatima's claim for unfair dismissal is heard on 6 April 2018; she is successful. The tribunal notes that, within 12 months, her new employer will be paying the same level of pension contribution rate as her old employer. The tribunal's award in respect of the net pension loss arising from Fatima's unfair dismissal therefore ends 12 months after the hearing:

Loss to hearing:		
3% × £25,000 × 0.5 (6 months)	£375.00	
2% (3% - 1 %) × £25,000 × 0.25 (3 months)	£125.00	
Total loss to hearing:		£500.00
Future loss: 1 % (3% – 2%) × £25,000 × 1 (12 months)		£250.00
Total:		£750.00

Note that, in this example, Fatima's earnings in her new job exceed the lower level of the qualifying earnings band, hence her auto-enrolment rights.

5. SIMPLE DB CASES

These examples relate to paragraphs 6.30 to 6.40 of the Principles.

They are examples of the types of case where the tribunal can properly decide to use the contributions method, even though dismissal was from employment with DB scheme benefits.

George — contributions method — short period of loss (Polkey)

George is made compulsorily redundant by his public sector employer, having come last in an exercise in which he and others were scored against selection criteria. He had been earning a gross annual salary of £35,000 and was in his employer's DB pension scheme. He succeeds in his complaint of unfair dismissal. The tribunal decides that his employer consulted inadequately about those criteria. The tribunal also decides that adequate consultation would have made no difference to the selection criteria ultimately adopted by the employer; it would simply have delayed George's dismissal (as he would still have come bottom) by the period of one month that such consultation would have lasted.

George's basic award for unfair dismissal is zero, as he has already received a statutory redundancy payment from his employer (see Section 122(4)(b) ERA). As for his compensatory award, the tribunal assesses it on this basis: a sum for one month's loss of net earnings and a sum for loss of net pension benefits corresponding to the same period. As for the pension loss, the evidence before the tribunal is that the employer's average contribution rate to that scheme was 17.5%. No further information is available as to whether George's age or gender suggest a different contribution rate. The award of compensation to George in respect of the net pension loss arising from his unfair dismissal will therefore be as follows:

17.5% x £35,000 x 1/12 (one month)	£510.42

Note that it is possible that the compensatory award might be reduced further by reference to any redundancy pay that George's employer paid him over and above his entitlement to statutory redundancy pay; see Section 123(7) ERA.

Hannah — contributions method — short period of loss (closure of DB scheme)

Hannah is unfairly dismissed, having been a member of a DB pension scheme. She was earning a gross annual salary of £28,000 with her former employer and its contribution rate in respect of future service at the time of her dismissal was 14.5%. However, the evidence before the tribunal at the hearing is that the employer closed its scheme to further accrual six months after Hannah's dismissal and replaced it with a DC scheme into which it now pays 6% employer contributions. Nine months after her dismissal, but still prior to the hearing, Hannah found a replacement job at the same salary. Her new employer is also paying employer contributions at the rate of 6% into its DC pension scheme.

Given the short period of loss, the tribunal decides that the appropriate basis for assessing Hannah's pension loss is to use the contributions method.

The award of compensation in respect of the net pension loss arising from her unfair dismissal will therefore be as follows:

14.5% × £28,000 × 0.5 (6 months)	£2,030.00
6% × £28,000 × 0.25 (3 months)	£420.00
Total:	£2,450.00

If Hannah's new job came with only auto-enrolment pension rights, the tribunal might consider that the pension loss would extend beyond the date she started her new job even though her loss of earnings would have ceased then. Using the contributions method, her ongoing loss of pension rights would be 3% (i.e. 6% less 3%) of her salary. The tribunal would need to decide how long this loss would continue.

Fiona — contributions method — full mitigation

Fiona qualified as a teacher in Scotland. She started as a mathematics teacher at the age of 21 but she was dismissed in circumstances that the tribunal decides involved direct racial discrimination and racial harassment. She is now aged 25. Before her dismissal, she earned a gross annual salary of £34,000 and was a member of the Scottish Teachers' Superannuation Scheme, which is unfunded. The tribunal is informed that she paid employee pensions contributions of 8.7% of her gross pay. The parties have provided no further information about pension rights, apart from Fiona's representative who has provided a printout from the scheme's website; this shows that the rate of contribution paid by employers into this scheme is currently 17.2%.

Since being dismissed, Fiona has left teaching and, with her mathematics degree, she has obtained a job in financial services. Her starting salary was £45,000 and she has already done extremely well. By the time of the remedy hearing, her gross annual salary is £80,000 and she is in line to receive a bonus of an equivalent sum. She was unemployed for a period of three months before obtaining this higher paid employment. She has stated that she will never return to teaching.

The tribunal awards Fiona £20,000 for the injury to her feelings and three months' loss of net earnings (having taken care to add back in her own pension contribution rate of 8.7%, to identify the true level of her net pay). Regarding net pension loss, the tribunal decides that, although Fiona was in a DB pension scheme, it is appropriate to calculate her loss using the contributions method. The tribunal accepts the website page as a reliable source of evidence for the employer's contribution rate. The calculation is as follows:

£34,000 x 17.2% x 0.25 (3 months)	£1,462.00

6. COMPLEX DB CASES

These examples relate to paragraph 5.51 onwards of the Principles (especially the seven steps model at paragraphs 5.54 to 5.61).

These are examples where the parties have declined to provide expert actuarial evidence on any element of the pension loss calculation or expert accounting evidence on grossing up.

Tom — career loss — final salary scheme — interpolation — no withdrawal factor — mitigation in job with auto-enrolment

Tom was dismissed from a public sector job in Swansea, after 30 years' service, at the age of 55. He was unfairly dismissed for making a protected disclosure, so the statutory cap does not apply. The job from which he was dismissed, a quite senior managerial role, paid him a gross annual salary of £40,000. He was a member of a final salary scheme based on an accrual rate of sixtieths.

The tribunal decides that, but for his unlawful dismissal, Tom would have carried on working until retirement at age 65 (the age at which he could take an unreduced occupational pension) — he would not have waited until his state pension age of 67. By that point, he would have completed 40 years' service. The tribunal also decides that Tom would have been promoted at the age of 61 to the next management grade, with a higher gross annual salary of £50,000.

Our focus will be on calculating Tom's award for pension loss rather than his award for loss of earnings.

Step 1: Identify what Tom's net pension income would have been at his appropriate retirement age if the dismissal had not occurred.

A statement of Tom's pension benefits, obtained from the administrators of the scheme, confirms that the present-day value of his annual pension income at the date of dismissal is 30/60ths of £40,000, which is £20,000. This could, in any event, have been inferred from what we already know about the benefits of the scheme. However, Tom would have been promoted to a position with a salary of £50,000 after ten years of further service. But for his dismissal, then, the present-day value of Tom's gross pension income at retirement would have been 40/60ths of £50,000, which is £33,333. Using the HMRC online calculator which estimates take-home pay, the net value of a pension income of £33,333 is **£28,970**.

The tribunal decides that no withdrawal factor is appropriate. This is because Tom's employment was highly stable; his employer faced no risk of insolvency; he had no dependants for whom he might assume caring responsibilities in the future; he was in good health; and there was no prospect of him moving to fresh pastures.

Step 2: Identify what Tom's net pension benefits will be at his retirement age, given that he has been dismissed.

The present-day gross value of Tom's annual pension income at the date of his, is 30/60ths of £40,000, which is £20,000. The HMRC online calculator confirms that the net value of a pension income of £20,000 is about £18,300.

The tribunal decides that Tom will find another job within two years of dismissal. Based on its knowledge of the local labour market, the tribunal decides that it will be a job in retail management; it will be less well paid, with poor promotion prospects and with auto-enrolment into a DC pension scheme. To keep our example simple, we will add that the tribunal assumes that Tom will remain in this new job without resigning or being dismissed and that he will still choose to retire at the age of 65 once he has accessed his public sector pension.

The tribunal decides to use the NEST calculator to approximate the pension income Tom would receive, at today's value, if he were to spend eight years between the ages of 57 and 65 receiving a gross annual salary of £25,000 in a job where the employer makes post-April 2019 minimum contribution levels under the auto-enrolment regime. The NEST calculator tells us that, if Tom declined to choose a lump sum (so that we compare like with like), his gross annual pension income from that job would be £880. If this sum had been added to his gross pension income from the old job, it would have increased his gross annual pension income to £20,880. Using the HMRC online calculator, his net annual pension income would increase to **£19,005** a year.

Step 3: Deduct the result of Step 2 from the result of Step 1, which produces a figure for net annual loss of pension benefits.

£28,970 less £19,005 is **£9,965.**

In other words, following his unlawful dismissal, Tom's net annual pension income has reduced by £9,965. This is our multiplicand.

(Note that £9,965 is the net shortfall in Tom's pension income. His gross shortfall would be £33,333 less £20,880, which is £12,453. We may need this figure later, when looking at the lump sum position.)

Step 4: Identify the period over which that net annual loss is to be awarded, using the Ogden Tables to identify the multiplier.

To adjust for the improved mortality of those in occupational pension schemes, the tribunal now makes the two-year age adjustment, purely for the purposes of calculating Tom's occupational pension loss. We therefore assume that he is 53, not 55. We make a corresponding adjustment to the age at which he retires, which is now 63.

This presents us with an opportunity to demonstrate interpolation, and here we follow the guidance at paragraphs 13 and 14 of the explanatory notes to the Ogden Tables:

(1) Tom's adjusted retirement age ('R') for the purposes of the Ogden Tables is 63. The lower age ('A') for which a table is provided is 60 (Table 19). The higher age ('B') for which a table is provided is 65 (Table 21).

(2) Next, we determine how many years must be subtracted from Tom's adjusted retirement age of 63 to get to A (the answer is three years) and we subtract that period from his adjusted age of 53. This means treating Arthur as being three years younger than 53, i.e. 50.

(3) We then look up this reduced age in Ogden Table 19 at the discount rate of minus 0.75%, which produces a multiplier of 31.28 ('M').

(4) Next, we determine how many years must be added to Tom's adjusted retirement age of 63 to get to B (the answer is two years) and we add that period to his adjusted age of 53. This means treating Tom as being 55.

(5) We then look up this increased age in Ogden Table 21 at the discount rate of minus 0.75%, which produces a multiplier of 25.02 ('N').

(6) The interpolation calculation is:

$$\frac{(B-R)\times M+(R-A)\times N}{[(B-R)+(R-A)]}$$

or

$$\frac{(65-63)\times 31.28+(63-60)\times 25.02}{[(65-63)+(63-60)]}$$

or

$$\frac{137.62}{5}$$

This yields a final calculation of 137.62 ÷ 5 which, in turn, produces the required multiplier of 27.524 (which we will round down to 27.52).

The tribunal therefore chooses an interpolated multiplier of 27.52.

Step 5: Multiply the multiplicand by the multiplier, which produces the present capital value of that loss.

In Tom's case, this is the following arithmetic calculation: 27.52 × £9,965 = £274,236.80

(If Tom's age had not been adjusted in the manner we have recommended, this calculation would have been 25.02 × £9,965 = £249,324.30.)

Step 6: Check the lump sum position and perform a separate calculation if required.

This is a sixtieths scheme, with a lump sum available via commutation only on a 1:12 basis. Tom has no entitlement to a separate tax-free lump sum; the figure at Step 5 above covers it and no further compensation is appropriate.

What if Tom had been entitled under the terms of his pension to a separate tax-free lump sum, calculated at three times his gross pension income? The loss would be three times the gross shortfall in his pension caused by his unlawful dismissal. Three times £12,453 is £37,359. Tom would be receiving this money now as compensation, instead of waiting to receive it at the age of 65. He is aged 55 at the date of the remedy hearing so, put another way, he would receive the shortfall in his lump sum ten years early. This takes us to Table 27. At a discount rate of minus 0.75%, we apply a multiplier of 1.0782, increasing the amount awarded from £37,359 to £40,280.47. In awarding this sum to Tom, the parties and the tribunal would need to bear in mind that it would have been a tax-free benefit in his hands. It will now form part of an award of compensation that will be subject to income tax to the extent that it exceeds £30,000, and so it must be grossed up in accordance with usual principles to ensure that Tom is properly compensated.

However, we shall continue with our original assumption that no further compensation for loss of a lump sum is appropriate in Tom's case.

Step 7: Taking account of the other sums awarded by the tribunal, gross up the compensation awarded.

In Tom's case, we have not itemised the other elements of his award of compensation, which would have included additional sums attracting tax such as compensation for loss of earnings. However, for illustrative purposes, we will imagine that the total sum awarded to Tom, incorporating the sum of £274,236.80 for loss of pension rights, is £400,000. We will ignore injury to feelings.

We must deduct the tax-exempt element of £30,000 from the figure of £400,000; this reduces the amount we must gross up to £370,000. A taxable award of this size will reduce Tom's personal allowance of £11,500 to zero, with the effect that the basic rate tax band now runs from £0 to £33,500 and the higher rate tax band now runs from £33,500 to £150,000. This will leave £220,000 to be taxed at the additional rate. The calculation is done in the tax year of receipt, which we will take to be 2017/18. Let us also assume that Tom has no other taxable income in the tax year of receipt. The grossing up calculation will be as follows:

Basic rate (20%): £33,500/80 × 100 = £41,875

Tax element is £41,875 less £33,500, which is £8,375

Higher rate (40%): £116,500/60 × 100 = £194,167

Tax element is £194,167 less £116,500, which is £77,667

Additional rate (45%): £220,000/55 × 100 = £400,000

Tax element is £400,000 less £220,000, which is £180,000

Total tax to be added: £8,375 + £77,667 + £180,000 = £266,042

The overall award will therefore be £400,000 plus £266,042, which is £666,042.

Note on withdrawal factor

At Step 1 of the above examples, the tribunal applied no withdrawal factor. However, these scenarios might have justified a percentage reduction to the multiplicand:

- The evidence shows that Tom's elderly parents require care. It might be appropriate to make an adjustment on the basis that he would have retired early to look after them.
- Tom is now assumed to have been dismissed by a private sector employer. The evidence shows his employer was struggling financially, with fixed charges over its premises and a poor order book from fewer customers. It might be appropriate to make an adjustment on the basis of the chance that it would close its final salary pension scheme to future accruals in the next five years.
- The evidence shows that Tom's employer was planning to restructure the business by selling off the part in which he worked. Bearing in mind that TUPE does not protect pension rights, it might be appropriate to make an adjustment on the basis that Tom would transfer to an employer that offered a much less generous pension such as that provided for by auto-enrolment.

These sorts of assessments are common in tribunals: they are not scientific and are necessarily speculative. The parties must be prepared to bring evidence about, and make submissions on, these points at a remedy hearing dealing with pension loss, so that the tribunal can issue a reasoned judgment on them.

Gaynor — career loss — CARE scheme — interpolation — CPI revaluation considered — no withdrawal factor

This example will illustrate how banked slices of earnings are accrued and revalued in a CARE scheme and also the difficulty of predicting the value of accrued benefits in the absence of details about CPI revaluation. It also shows the application of the seven steps model in a CARE scheme context. It relates to paragraphs 5.19 and 5.55(d) of the Principles.

Gaynor was born on 31 March 1956. She is a Band 3 nurse on a gross annual salary of £20,000, at the top of her pay scale and neither seeking nor expecting promotion. Her annual pay increases in recent years have been 1%. She has been a member of the 2015 section of the NHS pension scheme (a CARE scheme) since 1 April 2015, which has an accrual rate of 1/54. She is dismissed on 31 March 2018, at the age of 62, after three years of membership of that scheme. In recent years, her annual pay increases have been capped at 1%. The tribunal decides that, if Gaynor had not been dismissed, she would have continued working until reaching state pension age on 31 March 2022 (in her case, 66), resulting in four more years of membership of the 2015 scheme. The statutory cap on compensation for unfair dismissal does not apply. We assume that she remains 62 at the date of the remedy hearing.

For the purposes of this example, we will assume that Gaynor had no accrued service in the 1995 or 2008 sections of the NHS scheme (both final salary designs). We also ignore the fact that, if she had been a longer serving employee, she would have been insulated from recent pension reforms by virtue of being within ten years of normal retirement age as at 1 April 2012.

Step 1: Identify what Gaynor's net pension income would have been at her retirement age if the dismissal had not occurred.

We would expect this figure to be produced by the pension scheme administrators.

However, it provides an opportunity to explain how CARE revaluation works. For the purposes of this example, we have estimated CPI at 0.3% for year 1 (2015–16), 0.7% for year 2 (2016–17) and 2.6% for year 3 (2017–18). In accordance with the rules of the 2015 section of the NHS pension scheme, revaluation tracks CPI at 1.5% over these rates, producing uprating figures of 1.8% for year 1 (2015–16), 2.2% for year 2 (2016–17) and 4.1% for year 3 (201718). Revaluation is compound. It works like this:

Year	**Pensionable salary (1% growth)**	**Banked slice**	**Revaluation**		
			Y1 1.8%	**Y2 2.2%**	**Y3 4.1%**
2015-16	20,000	370.37	377.04	385.34	401.14
2016-17	20,200	374.07		382.30	397.98
2017-18	20,402	377.81			393.30
Total					**1,192.42**

Pausing there, we note that, following dismissal (and before commutation), Gaynor's gross pension income will be £1,192.42. We can also observe that the uprating of her pension has been at a higher rate than her 1% wage growth, which explains why the revalued banked slice for 2015-16 (£401.14) is higher than the non-revalued banked slice for 2017-18 (£393.30).

Gaynor's future loss until 2022, measured for the purposes of Step 1, must assume that she has not been dismissed. Working out her pension entitlement under the CARE scheme in this hypothetical scenario of four more years of scheme membership is difficult. Even if the tribunal were to assume that her annual pay increases in future would continue to be limited to 1%, the future rates of CPI over the next four years are unknown. This will affect the revaluation of the slices of her earnings that, but for the dismissal, she would have banked over the next four years and the further revaluation of her historic banked slices, as this table shows:

Year	Pensionable salary (1% growth)	Banked slice	Revaluation						
			Y1 1.8%	Y2 2.2%	Y3 4.1%	Y4	Y5	Y6	Y7
2015-16	20,000	370.37	377.04	385.34	401.14	?	?	?	?
2016-17	20,200	374.07		382.30	397.98	?	?	?	?
2017-18	20,402	377.81			393.30	?	?	?	?
2018-19	20,606	381.59				?	?	?	?
2019-20	20,812	385.41					?	?	?
2020-21	21,020	389.26						?	?
2021-22	21,230	393.15							?
Total									?

In the absence of a statement of projected benefits from the scheme's administrators (based on an assumption of working until state pension age) or expert evidence, the tribunal is not equipped to predict the compound impact of future CPI rates. As a result, if the parties do not provide this information, the tribunal will ignore CPI revaluation. In such a scenario, the tribunal would use the four banked slices of £381.59, £385.41, £389.26 and £393.15 for 2018-22 to produce additional pension income of £1,549.41. The slices banked for 201518 would retain the total value of £1,192.42.

We recognise that this is likely to be less than Gaynor's true entitlement. It serves to emphasise the difficulties in obtaining precision without expert input and how important it is to ensure that the tribunal has the proper information from those who administer the pension scheme. The tribunal will use its case management powers to maximise the prospects of its production but, ultimately, it needs a mechanism for calculation if this information is not forthcoming.

As matters stand, total gross income at Step 1 would be £1,192.42 plus £1,549.41, which is £2,741.83. We will assume, for the sake of simplicity, that the tribunal declines to apply a withdrawal factor; it accepts that Gaynor would have worked through to retirement if she had not been dismissed.

This pension income would be within Gaynor's personal allowance. There is no need to "net it down".

Step 2: Identify what Gaynor's net pension income will be at her retirement age in the light of her dismissal.

We already have this figure: £1,192.42. Again, there is no need to net it down. For the sake of simplicity, we will assume that the tribunal decides that Gaynor will not work again until reaching her state pension age, despite her best efforts to mitigate her loss.

Step 3: Deduct the result of Step 2 from the result of Step 1, which produces a figure for net annual loss of pension benefits.

The difference is £1,549.41. That is our multiplicand.

Step 4: Identify the period over which that net annual loss is to be awarded, using the Ogden Tables to identify the multiplier.

The tribunal proceeds with the usual approach of adjusting Gaynor's age so that she is treated as being 60, not 62, at the date of the hearing. Her loss of pension now runs from 64, not 66. To identify the correct multiplier, the tribunal must use interpolation.

The interpolation calculation is:

$$\frac{(B-R)\times M+(R-A)\times N}{[(B-R)+(R-A)]}$$

or

$$\frac{(65-64)\times 32.68+(64-60)\times 27.66}{[(65-64)+(64-60)]}$$

or

$$\frac{143.32}{5}$$

This yields a final calculation of 143.32 ÷ 5 which, in turn, produces the required interpolated multiplier of 28.664. We will round this down to 28.66.

Step 5: Multiply the multiplicand by the multiplier, which produces the present capital value of that loss.

28.66 × £1,549.41 = **£44,406.09**. This is the capital value of Gaynor's pension loss.

Step 6: Check the lump sum position and perform a separate calculation if required.

No separate calculation is required.

Step 7: Taking account of the other sums awarded by the tribunal, gross up the compensation awarded.

We will ignore this step for now. Instead, we ask: what if the contributions method had been adopted for a period of four years of future loss? The employer contribution rate to the NHS 2015 scheme is 14.38%. As the calculation below shows, that would have produced an award for pension loss of only £12,031.45. It is considerably below the award produced by the complex approach, suggesting its use was justified in this case.

2018-19	£20,606 × 14.38%	£2,963.14
2019-20	£20,812 × 14.38%	£2,992.76
2020-21	£21,020 × 14.38%	£3,022.68
2021-22	£21,230 × 14.38%	£3,052.87
Total		**£12,031.45**

Ahmed — blend of final salary and CARE pension rights — mitigation of loss — withdrawal factor — includes loss of earnings

In this example, gross figures for annual salary have been converted into net figures for annual salary using the HMRC online calculator referred to in the Principles (https://www.gov.uk/estimate-income-tax), inputting the default income tax code. Salary and pensionable pay are treated as equivalent.

Ahmed was born on 1 May 1967. He started a job in local government in Leeds aged 25 in May 1992. He was a member of the "old" Local Government Pension Scheme (LGPS) for 22 years between 1992 and 2014. It had a final salary design. For the purposes of this illustration, we shall assume the benefits accrued during these 22 years were in the 2008 section of the LGPS, which are summarised in Appendix 1. On 1 April 2014, shortly before he turned 48, Ahmed moved to the "new" 2014 LGPS. This has a CARE design. A member of the 2014 LGPS becomes entitled to an unreduced pension at their state pension age. In Ahmed's case, that will be 67. He reaches that age on 1 May 2034.

Ahmed resigned on 1 May 2017, after 25 years' service, when aged 50. At the time of his resignation he performed a service delivery management role. As at the date of his constructive dismissal, he was on a gross annual salary of £40,000. After deductions for income tax and NI contributions, this amounts to net pay of £30,481.

At a preliminary hearing by telephone, dealing with case management, the tribunal notes that Ahmed was in a public sector DB scheme. It decides to list a hearing that, at this stage, deals with liability only. Orders are nonetheless made for the disclosure of pension-related information, so that the parties can prepare more informed schedules and counter-schedules of loss.

In a reserved judgment following the liability-only hearing, the tribunal decides that Ahmed's resignation was a constructive unfair dismissal, following 12 months of racist bullying by colleagues and a failure by senior managers to support him and treat his grievance seriously. Ahmed also succeeds in a complaint of harassment related to race and a complaint that his constructive dismissal was an act of direct race discrimination. Having consulted the parties, the tribunal lists a first-stage remedy hearing. At this hearing, the tribunal will determine some of his non-pension losses and make findings on those matters that will assist the parties in calculating his pension loss for themselves and thereby promote settlement.

The first-stage remedy hearing is held on 1 May 2018, when Ahmed is 51. He gives evidence that he found no alternative work for a period of 12 months, but has just secured new employment as a manager in the NHS on a gross annual salary of £37,000. After deductions for income tax and NI contributions, this amounts to net pay of £28,441. The tribunal decides that, during the period from 1 May 2017 to 1 May 2018, Ahmed made reasonable efforts to mitigate his loss and so this loss should be compensated in full. In his new job, Ahmed has joined the 2015 section of the NHS pension scheme. This also has a CARE design. The retirement age for that scheme, once again, is his state pension age of 67. The tribunal finds that, whether we are speaking of the old LGPS job or the new NHS job, Ahmed would have wished to retire at the age of 67.

The tribunal decides that, if Ahmed not been constructively dismissed, he would have wanted to remain in his local government job and that he would have been promoted to a role earning a gross annual salary of £45,000 gross (or £33,881 net) with effect from 1 May 2019. The tribunal decides that he would have stayed in that role until the age of 57 (on 1 May 2024), but had only a 50% chance of completing the next ten years to retirement at 67 (on 1 May 2034); this is because of the impact of attempts to reduce the number of mid-level managers through IT reform and digitalisation of local government services. Having heard evidence about the structure of NHS management roles and Ahmed's renewed vigour to further his career, the tribunal decides that he will be promoted in his new job to a role paying a gross annual salary of £42,000 (£31,841 net) on 1 May 2020 and then further promoted to a role paying a gross annual salary of £45,000 (£33,881 net) on 1 May 2024. The tribunal notes that the process of IT reform and digitalisation is proceeding apace in the NHS. It therefore decides that Ahmed has a 75% chance of staying in the new job until 1 May 2020, but then a 50% chance of making it to 1 May 2024 and only a 20% chance of staying until retirement on 1 May 2034.

The percentage chances identified above represent the application of various Polkey/withdrawal factors based on the evidence given to the tribunal (which we have not described in detail) and submissions from the parties. The tribunal decides to treat it as a complex DB case because Ahmed will continue to experience a potentially substantial and quantifiable pension loss.

At the end of the first-stage remedy hearing, the tribunal issues a judgment in respect of part of the remedy. This is in the sum of £29,710.50:

Basic award for unfair dismissal: 24.5 × 489*	£11,980.50	
Compensatory award for unfair dismissal:		
Loss of statutory rights only	£450.00	
Total award for unfair dismissal:		£12,430.50
Compensation for discrimination:		
Injury to feelings	£16,000.00	
Interest thereon (May 2017 to May 2018) at 8%	£1,280.00	
Total award for injury to feelings		£17,280.00
Total:		**£29,710.50**

* On the assumption, for the purposes of this example, that this is the cap on a week's pay that applies at the time — but it will have increased by then.

The tribunal decides not to award any sum for past loss of earnings at this stage, as it does not yet know what impact this will have on grossing up. It also decides that the award for injury to feelings is exempt from income tax (applying *Orthet Ltd v. Vince-Cain* and *Timothy James Consulting Ltd v. Wilton* — see paragraph 5.61(a) of the Principles).

Having consulted the parties, the tribunal gives Ahmed and his former local government employer 21 days to agree a figure for loss of earnings and loss of pension and, in the absence of agreement, to inform the tribunal if they wish to instruct an expert to assist in calculating his lost pension. However, the parties do not reach agreement. They also decide against instructing an expert. They return to the tribunal for a second-stage remedy hearing for these figures to be judicially determined (and, in the case of pension loss, by applying the seven steps model).

After hearing submissions from the parties, the tribunal approaches the supplemental points of remedy as set out below.

Past loss of earnings

1 May 2017 to May 2018	£30,481.00 **	
Interest thereon from mid-point date at 8%	£1,219.24	
Total		£31,700.24

** Ahmed's past loss of earnings are subject to recoupment.

Part 4 Statutory Codes of Practice

Future loss of earnings

1 May 2018 to 1 May 2019		
Lost from old job	£30,481.00	
Earned from new job	£28,441.00	
Difference (one year)		£2,040.00
1 May 2019 to 1 May 2020		
Lost from old job	£33,881.00	
Earned from new job	£28,441.00	
Difference (one year)	£5,440.00	
1 May 2020 to 1 May 2024		
Lost from old job	£33,881.00	
Earned from new job	£31,841.00	
Difference (four years × £2,040)		£8,160.00

To keep the illustration simple, we have not applied *Polkey* to adjust the above sums to reflect the withdrawal factors of 75%, 50% and 20%. The tribunal would no doubt decide whether to do so after submissions from the parties. However, we think it is worth providing one example of how an Ogden multiplier is used in a loss of earnings context. Let us assume that the tribunal does not adjust the figures for loss of earnings in the immediate two-year period (from 1 May 2018 to 1 May 2020), but decides to adjust the last figure (from 1 May 2020 to 1 May 2024) using an Ogden multiplier; this is because it is loss arising between two and six years in the future (when Ahmed will be aged between 53 and 57) and would ordinarily raise an issue about accelerated receipt. In fact, what the example shows is that a negative discount rate (close to zero), for loss in the mid-term, makes little overall difference to the award. The tribunal looks at the "at a glance" table in Appendix 2, dealing with loss of earnings for men using the minus 0.75% discount rate. Ahmed is 51 at the date of the remedy hearing. Taking a broad-brush approach, the tribunal decides that it is compensating him for loss of earnings from the age of 55. The multiplier is 4.03. Having regard to the modest amount involved and the fact that it has already addressed some contingencies besides mortality through use of *Polkey*/withdrawal factors, the tribunal declines to make any further adjustment to the multiplier. When applied to the multiplicand of £2,040, it produces a slightly amended figure for loss for the final period (from 1 May 2020 to 1 May 2024) of £8,221.20. This difference is about £60; that is all.

The tribunal makes no award for loss of earnings after 1 May 2024 because Ahmed's projected net annual earnings, at today's value, will be the same: £33,881.00.

In respect of loss of earnings, therefore, the tribunal's award is for the sum of £31,700.24 for past loss and the sum of £15,701.20 for future loss (subject to grossing up — see below). The latter figure is derived from £2,040 + £5,440 + £8,221.20.

Pension loss

In respect of pension loss, the tribunal follows the seven steps model.

Step 1: Identify what Ahmed's net pension income would have been at his retirement age if the dismissal had not occurred.

The tribunal must take account of rights Ahmed has already accrued in the LGPS (both on a final salary and CARE basis) and the additional rights he would have accrued (on a CARE basis) if he had not been dismissed.

A statement from the pension scheme administrators is obtained, from which the tribunal can reach the following conclusions:

- Ahmed's accrued rights in the old LGPS scheme will produce a gross annual pension income of 22/60ths of his final salary. Because the tribunal found that Ahmed would have been earning £45,000 within two years of his resignation, his pension income would be 22/60 × £45,000, which, to today's value, is £16,500 per annum.
- Prior to his constructive dismissal, Ahmed had three years of membership of the CARE scheme as well. The accrual rate is 1/49th (or 2.04%) for each year of scheme membership. His gross annual salary at the time was £40,000 per annum, which means that he "banks" £816 per year. The pension statement has already taken account of CPI revaluation and informs us that the present-day value of these three banked slices is a gross pension income of £2,600.
- That means, but for the dismissal, Ahmed's accrued rights prior to dismissal would have produced a gross pension income of £16,500 plus £2,600.

If Ahmed had remained in local government employment until reaching state pension age on 1 May 2034, he would have continued to accrue 1/49th of his salary on a CARE basis for each further year of service: a total of 17 more slices to bank. This would have resulted in further accrual of pension income as follows (some of these figures have been rounded):

- Two years (1 May 2017 to 1 May 2019): 2 × 1/49 × £40,000 = £1,632
- Five years (1 May 2019 to 1 May 2024): 5 × 1/49 × £45,000 = £4,592
- Ten years (1 May 2024 to 1 May 2034): 10 £ 1/49 × £45,000 = £9,184

This last figure is subject to a withdrawal factor of 50% because of the finding that Ahmed had a 50% chance of staying in the LGPS until retirement. This means that the additional annual pension he would have derived from the final ten years is halved from £9,184 to £4,592.

The additional pension per annum from prospective service which Ahmed lost because of his constructive dismissal is therefore assessed as £1,632 + £4,592+ £4,592 = £10,816. Without expert evidence, the tribunal ignores the impact of post-2018 CPI revaluation on the three banked slices prior to the constructive dismissal and the 17 banked slices after dismissal.

In summary, if Ahmed had not been dismissed, his total gross pension income at retirement would have been £16,500 (accrued final salary) + £2,600 (accrued CARE) + £10,816 (prospective CARE), which is £29,916. (For the sake of simplicity, we have not included his nSP entitlement in this calculation. While it would increase the accuracy of calculating the overall net value of his pension benefits — both occupational and state — it must be borne in mind that we do not apply the age-related adjustment to the Ogden multiplier when compensating for loss of state pension.)

We use the HMRC calculator, taking care to confirm that Ahmed is now over state pension age so that NI contributions are ignored, using a default tax code. This produces a net pension income of **£26,234**.

Step 2: Identify what Ahmed's net pension income will be at his retirement age in the light of his dismissal.

Ahmed experiences a substantial loss because his 22 years of accrued benefits in the LGPS final salary scheme are now pegged to gross annual salary at dismissal (£40,000) and not the gross annual salary he would have received if dismissal had not occurred and he had been promoted (£45,000). Those accrued rights are now worth 22/60 × £40,000, which is £14,667. The present-day value of his three banked slices in the CARE scheme is a gross pension income of £2,600. His accrued LGPS rights at dismissal will now produce a gross pension income of £14,667 plus £2,600, which is £17,267.

There are other pension rights to consider at Step 2, deriving from Ahmed's partially successful mitigation of loss through obtaining employment in the NHS. In the 2015 section of the NHS scheme, he gets an annual pension income based on 1/54th of pensionable earnings for each year of scheme membership, subject to the withdrawal factors explained above. The tribunal calculates Ahmed's NHS pension rights at age 67 as follows:

1 May 2018 to 1 May 2020: 2 × 1/54 × £37,000 = £1,370	
Reduction by 25% due to withdrawal factor	£1,027.50
1 May 2020 to 1 May 2024: 4 × 1/54 × £42,000 = £3,111	
Reduction by 50% due to withdrawal factor	£1,555.50
1 May 2024 to 1 May 2034: 10 × 1/54 × £45,000 = £8,333	
Reduction by 80% due to withdrawal factor	£1,666.67

So, absent CPI revaluation, Ahmed's gross pension income from his NHS job will be £4,249.67.

Added together with his accrued LGPS pension, Ahmed's total gross pension income will be £21,516.67. For the sake of simplicity, we have not included his nSP in this calculation.

Using the HMRC calculator, while taking care to confirm that Ahmed is now over state pension age so that NI contributions are ignored, this equates to a rounded down net pension income of **£19,515**.

Step 3: Deduct the result of Step 2 from the result of Step 1, which produces a figure for net annual loss of pension benefits.

£26,234 less £19,514 is **£6,719**. That is our multiplicand.

Step 4: Identify the period over which that net annual loss is to be awarded, using the Ogden Tables to identify the multiplier.

The tribunal makes the two-year age adjustment: Ahmed is deemed to be two years younger (49 instead of 51), with a retirement age two years earlier (65 instead of 67). Our "at a glance" extracts from the Ogden Tables at Appendix 2 show that the correct multiplier is 26.41. The tribunal does not adjust the multiplier further on the basis that the withdrawal factors already deal adequately with non-mortality contingencies.

Step 5: Multiply the multiplicand by the multiplier, which produces the present capital value of that loss.

26.41 × £6,719 = **£177,448.79**.

Step 6: Check the lump sum position and perform a separate calculation if required.

No separate calculation is required. Both the 2014 LGPS scheme and the 2015 NHS scheme require the employee to commute some annual pension income to secure a lump sum. There are no lump sum rights on top of the annual pension. Because the tribunal has worked with uncommuted figures, it can safely ignore lump sum compensation.

Step 7: Taking account of the other sums awarded by the tribunal, gross up the compensation awarded.

The tribunal's total award before grossing up is as follows:

Unfair dismissal		
Basic award	£11,980.50	
Compensatory award (loss of statutory rights)	£450.00	
Total award for unfair dismissal:		£12,430.50
Compensation for discrimination		
Injury to feelings	£16,000.00	
Interest thereon	£1,280.00	
Total award for injury to feelings		£17,280.00
Past loss of earnings		
1 May 2017 to 1 May 2018	£30,481.00	
Interest thereon	£1,219.24	
Total		£31,700.24
Future loss of earnings		£15,701.20
Pension loss		£177,448.79
Total		£254,560.73

As noted above, the tribunal follows EAT authority and decides that its award for injury to feelings (and interest thereon) of £17,280 is not chargeable to tax. £30,000 of the remainder is exempt as a termination payment. That means that the balance of £207,280.73 will be taxed as income in the 2018/19 tax year. (For the purposes of this illustration, we assume that the tax bands for 2018/19 are as they stand in 2017/18.)

Information about Ahmed's circumstances shows that in that tax year he will also have taxable income from his new NHS job of £37,000. His total taxable income in the year will be £207,280.73 plus £37,000, which is £244,280.73. With income at that level, he will lose all his personal allowance. His NHS salary of £37,000 will take up the whole basic rate band (now running from £0 to £33,500). The balance of his NHS salary will then use up £3,500 of the higher rate tax band (now running from £33,500 to £150,000); this means that the remaining part of the higher rate tax band left will be £150,000 less £33,500 less £3,500, i.e. £113,000. The remainder of £94,280.73 will be taxed at the additional rate of 45%.

The sum of £207,280.73 must therefore be grossed up as follows:

Higher rate (40%): £113,000/60 × 100 = £188,333.33

Tax element is £188,333.33 less £113,000, which is £75,333.33

Additional rate (45%): £94,280.73/55 × 100 = £171,419.50

Tax element is £171,419.50 less £94,280.73, which is £77,138.77

Total tax to be added: £75,333.33 + £77,138.77 = £152,472.10

The effect of receiving this compensation also means that Ahmed has to pay more tax on his NHS salary than would otherwise have been the case. Before, he would have had the entire personal allowance of £11,500 and he would only have paid basic rate tax at 20% on the balance of £25,500, which was £5,100. Now, he will pay basic rate tax at 20% on £33,500 (i.e. £6,700) and higher rate tax on £3,500 (i.e. £1,400), which is a total of £8,100. Put another way, by receiving compensation for unlawful discrimination, Ahmed has had to pay £4,000 more tax in his new job. The tribunal decides it would be appropriate to add this sum to the overall award.

The grand total of the tribunal's award is therefore as follows:

Total as above	£254,560.73
Add tax due on £207,281.73	£152,472.10
Add further tax due on NHS job:	£4,000.00
Total after grossing-up:	**£411,032.83**
Less amount already awarded at first-stage:	£29,710.50
Balance outstanding:	**£381,322.33**

Accordingly, in a supplemental judgment, the tribunal awards Ahmed a further sum of £381,322.33.

Katarzyna — no age adjustment made — withdrawal factor — use of NEST calculator — includes loss of earnings

In this example, gross figures for annual salary have been converted into net figures for annual salary using the HMRC online calculator referred to in the Principles (https://www.gov.uk/estimate-income-tax), inputting the default income tax code. Salary and pensionable pay are treated as equivalent.

Katarzyna was born on 1 February 1983. She is now aged 34. On 1 February 2008, at the age of 25, she commenced work with an NHS hospital in England as a specialist clinical technician. She has always worked part-time, at 25 hours a week, which represents 66.66% (or 2/3rds) of a full-time (37½-hour) equivalent working week. She was paid at Band 6. This meant a pay range of between £26,000 and £35,000 for a 37½-hour week and between £17,333 and £23,333 for a 25-hour week. The net equivalents (after deductions for income tax and NI contributions) are between £20,961 and £27,081 for a 37½-hour week and between £15,068 and £19,148 for a 25-hour week. A few years ago, Katarzyna was diagnosed with lupus. She is a disabled person within the meaning of the Equality Act 2010.

Katarzyna resigned on 1 February 2017, after nine years' service, because of a failure by hospital management to comply with the duty to make reasonable adjustments for her disability. As at the date of her resignation, her gross annual salary was £20,000 (which nets down to £16,881) — the full-time equivalent was £30,000. At this point, she had accrued seven years of service in the 2008 section of the NHS pension scheme (final salary design, 1/60ths accrual, with a normal retirement age of 65) and two years of service in the 2015 section of the NHS pension scheme (CARE design, 1/54ths accrual, with a normal retirement age that aligns with state pension age). Her state pension age is 68, which she reaches on 1 February 2051.

At a preliminary hearing by telephone, dealing with case management, the tribunal notes that Katarzyna was in a public sector DB scheme. It decides to list a hearing that, at this stage, deals with liability only. Orders are nonetheless made for the disclosure of pension-related information, so that the parties can prepare more informed schedules and counter-schedules of loss.

The liability hearing is held on 19 to 22 September 2017. The tribunal decides that Katarzyna was constructively dismissed, which was both unfair and an act of disability discrimination. No statutory cap applies. Having consulted the parties, the tribunal lists a first-stage remedy hearing. At this hearing, the tribunal will determine some of her non-pension losses and make findings on those matters that will assist the parties in calculating her pension loss for themselves and thereby promote settlement.

The first-stage remedy hearing takes place on 6 December 2017. The tribunal makes the following findings:

- Katarzyna is unlikely to find other employment in her technical specialism. There are no alternative medical specialist employers in her local area, to which she is tied by family responsibilities.
- For the same reason, it is unlikely that, but for the dismissal, she would have changed employer. The need for adjustments to accommodate her disability added to her reluctance to change jobs. But for her dismissal, she would have wished to remain in work until 68, when she reached her state pension age; this is because she would have worked until the age when she could draw the bulk of her pension benefits without reduction.
- The technical nature of her NHS work limited Katarzyna's opportunity for career progression. She would have reached the top of her pay band in two years' time (2019) and have remained in that role until retirement: a final salary, at today's rates, of £23,333 for a 25-hour working week (or £35,000 for a full-time employee).
- Because of medical advances in the use of artificial intelligence to assist in making diagnostic assessments, the tribunal is reluctant to conclude that Katarzyna's job would have remained open to her until 2051. It recognises that there may have been further training opportunities for her and the chance to diversify in her technical specialism, but decides there is a 20% risk that her job might disappear. Also, although she successfully manages her symptoms, the tribunal also decides that there is a 30% chance that Katarzyna might lose her job through a medical incapability procedure. Applying a broad brush, it concludes that there is therefore only a 50% chance she would have remained in employment until reaching state pension age. We have not set out the evidence heard by the tribunal that was the basis for this conclusion; it is illustrative only.
- Since her constructive dismissal, Katarzyna has found no paid work at all. However, she has just started an NVQ with a placement as a volunteer to gain experience. The tribunal finds that this represents reasonable steps to mitigate her loss. The award for past loss of earnings is therefore a year's net pay. This is a figure of £16,881, which will be subject to recoupment.
- It is anticipated that, a year after her dismissal, Katarzyna will find work on similar hours with a gross annual salary of £12,000 (the net equivalent is £11,441). It is also anticipated that she will progress through promotion in such a new role, reaching her former pay grade within 12 years of her dismissal. Her loss of earnings will therefore be extinguished after 12 years. However, she is unlikely to find employment with another DB scheme. Any new job is far more likely to be in the private sector with auto-enrolled DC scheme benefits.

At the end of the first-stage remedy hearing, the tribunal issues a judgment in respect of part of the remedy. This is in the sum of £15,651:

Basic award for unfair dismissal: 9 × 489	£4,401.00
Compensatory award for unfair dismissal:	
Loss of statutory rights only	£450.00

Total award for unfair dismissal:		£4,851.00
Compensation for discrimination:		
Injury to feelings	£10,000.00	
Interest thereon (Feb 2017 to Feb 2018) at 8%	£800.00	
Total award for injury to feelings		£10,800.00
Total:		**£15,651.00**

The tribunal decides not to award any sum for past loss of earnings at this stage, as it does not yet know what impact this will have on grossing up. It also decides that the award for injury to feelings is exempt from income tax (applying *Orthet Ltd v. Vince-Cain* and *Timothy James Consulting Ltd v. Wilton* – see paragraph 5.61(a) of the Principles).

Having consulted the parties, the tribunal gives Katarzyna and her former NHS employer 21 days to agree a figure for loss of earnings and loss of pension and, in the absence of agreement, to inform the tribunal if they wish to instruct an expert to assist in calculating her lost pension. However, the parties do not reach agreement. They also decide against instructing an expert. They return to the tribunal for a second-stage remedy hearing for these figures to be judicially determined (and, in the case of pension loss, by applying the seven steps model).

After hearing submissions from the parties, the tribunal approaches the supplemental points of remedy as set out below.

Past loss of earnings

1 February 2017 to1 February 2018	£16,881.00 *	
Interest thereon (from midpoint)	£675.24	
Total		£17,556.24

* Katarzyna's past loss of earnings are subject to recoupment.

Future loss of earnings

For the purposes of this example, we will assume that the tribunal calculates 11 years of future net lost earnings (taking account of pay progression) as being, at today's value, £195,000. After deducting the income Katarzyna will receive through mitigating her loss (£160,000), the tribunal awards her the sum of £35,000 for net loss of earnings. The tribunal applies the Ogden Tables and (for reasons of simplicity) we shall simply assume this increases the sum for future net loss of earnings to £37,000.

Pension loss

In respect of pension loss, the tribunal follows the seven steps model.

Step 1: Identify what Katarzyna's net pension income would have been at her retirement age if the dismissal had not occurred.

The tribunal must take account of the rights Katarzyna has already accrued in the NHS scheme (both on a final salary basis in the 2008 section and on a CARE basis in the 2015 section) and the additional rights she would have accrued (on a CARE basis in the 2015 section) if she had not been dismissed.

A statement from the pension scheme administrators is obtained, from which the tribunal can reach the following conclusions:

- Katarzyna's accrued rights in the 2008 scheme can be calculated using either her part-time final salary (7/60 × her part-time final salary) or her full-time final salary (2/3 × 7/60 × her full-time final salary); the result will be the same. If she had not been dismissed, her part-time final salary, at today's value, would have been £23,333. So, her accrued final salary rights are 7/60 × £23,333, which is £2,722 (rounded down).
- Prior to her constructive dismissal, Katarzyna had two years of membership of the 2015 scheme as well. The CARE accrual rate is 1/54th (or 1.85%) for each year of scheme membership. Her gross annual salary at the time of dismissal was £20,000, so she would have "banked" a gross pension income of £370 (rounded down) for that year. The pension statement has already taken account of CPI revaluation and informs us that the present-day value of these two banked slices is a gross pension income of £770.

That means, but for the dismissal, Katarzyna's accrued rights prior to dismissal would have produced a gross pension income of £2,722 plus £770.

Katarzyna was 34 when she resigned. If she had remained in her NHS job until she reached state pension age of 68 on 1 February 2051, she would have continued to accrue 1/54th of her salary on a CARE basis for each further year of service: a total of 34 more slices to bank. From 2018, she would have been at the top of her pay scale. This would have resulted in further accrual of pension income as follows (these figures have been rounded):

Two years (1 February 2017 to 1 February 2019): 2 × 1/54 × £20,000 = £741

32 years (1 February 2019 to 1 February 2051): 32 × 1/54 × £23,333 = £13,828

Without expert evidence, the tribunal ignores the impact of post-2017 CPI revaluation on the two banked slices prior to the constructive dismissal and the 32 banked slices after dismissal. This last figure is subject to a withdrawal factor of 50% because of the earlier finding that Katarzyna had a 50% chance of staying with the NHS until retirement. This means that the additional annual pension she would have derived from this period is halved from £13,828 to £6,914.

The additional pension per annum from prospective service which Katarzyna lost because of her constructive dismissal is therefore £741 plus £6,914, which is £7,655.

In summary, if Katarzyna had not been dismissed, her total gross pension income at retirement would have been £2,722 (accrued final salary) + £770 (accrued CARE) + £7,655 (prospective CARE), which is **£11,147**. (For the sake of simplicity, we have not included her nSP entitlement in this calculation.)

The figure of £11,147 is beneath Katarzyna's personal allowance, so the gross sum and the net sum are the same.

Step 2: Identify what Katarzyna's net pension income will be at her retirement age in the light of her dismissal.

The statement from the pension scheme administrators confirms that Katarzyna's accrued rights in the 2008 section of the NHS scheme must now be calculated using her part-time final salary at dismissal, which is £20,000. Her accrued final salary rights are: 7/60 × £20,000. At present values, that is £2,333 (rounded down). We already have the present-day value of her two banked slices, which is a gross pension income of £770. Following her dismissal, Katarzyna's accrued rights from her NHS job will produce a gross pension income of £2,333 plus £770, which is £3,103.

The tribunal has assumed that Katarzyna will find paid employment from February 2018 after a year out of work. This new job, the tribunal decides, will only carry minimum auto-enrolment rights in a DC pension scheme. The tribunal notes that the minimum contribution levels required by auto-enrolment vary until April 2019 and then stabilise at 5% employee contributions and 3% employer contributions from April 2019. Taking a broad-brush approach to the profile of Katarzyna's gross income over the next 12 years, until her loss of earnings are extinguished, the tribunal decides to use these figures:

- Gross annual salary Feb 2017 to Feb 2018: nil
- Gross annual salary Feb 2018 to Feb 2019: £12,000
- Gross annual salary Feb 2019 to Feb 2029 (assumed average): £17,000
- Gross annual salary Feb 2029 to Feb 2051 (assumed average): £23,333

The tribunal calculates that this equates to an average salary, at today's value, of £21,070 over 33 years. It decides, in the interests of simplicity, to use the contribution rates that apply from April 2019. In the absence of any expert evidence, and having consulted the parties, the tribunal uses the NEST calculator to assess what pension this arrangement might generate at today's value. It takes care, when entering details, to adjust Katarzyna's date of birth so that she is treated as now starting 33 years' membership of an auto-enrolled pension with minimum contributions and an intention to take that pension at the age of 68. The option for a lump sum is declined, so that we compare like with like. The NEST calculator predicts a gross annual pension income from the age of 68 of £4,630. With nothing better to go on, the tribunal adopts this figure.

The tribunal also decides, in the interests of consistency, to apply a withdrawal factor of 30% to reflect the chance that Katarzyna might lose her job through a medical incapability procedure. That reduces the figure to £3,241.

In summary, the tribunal decides that, having been dismissed, Katarzyna's gross annual pension income will be £3,103 plus £3,241, which is **£6,344**.

The figure of £6,344 is, once again, beneath Katarzyna's personal allowance, so the gross sum and the net sum are the same.

Step 3: Deduct the result of Step 2 from the result of Step 1, which produces a figure for net annual loss of pension benefits.

£11,147 less £6,344 is **£4,803**. That is our multiplicand.

Step 4: Identify the period over which that net annual loss is to be awarded, using the Ogden Tables to identify the multiplier.

The tribunal has heard medical evidence about the impact of Katarzyna's condition on her life expectancy. It declines to make the two-year adjustment to her age. (A reminder: this example is for illustrative purposes only.) For the purposes of identifying the Ogden multiplier, she remains 34 at the date of the hearing with loss of pension from age 68. Our "at a glance" extracts from the Ogden Tables at Appendix 2 show that the correct multiplier is 27.89.

Step 5: Multiply the multiplicand by the multiplier, which produces the present capital value of that loss.

27.89 × £4,803 = **£133,955.67**.

Step 6: Check the lump sum position and perform a separate calculation if required.

No separate calculation is required. Both the 2008 and 2015 sections of the NHS scheme require the employee to commute some annual pension income to secure a lump sum. There are no lump sum rights on top of the annual pension. Because the tribunal has used uncommuted figures, it can safely ignore lump sum compensation.

Step 7: Taking account of the other sums awarded by the tribunal, gross up the compensation awarded.

The tribunal's total award before grossing up is as follows:

Unfair dismissal		
Basic award	£4,401.00	
Compensatory award (loss of statutory rights)	£450.00	
Total award for unfair dismissal:		£4,851.00
Compensation for discrimination		
Injury to feelings	£10,000.00	
Interest thereon	£800.00	
Total award for injury to feelings		£10,800.00
Past loss of earnings		
1 February 2017 to 1 February 2018	£16,881.00	
Interest thereon (from midpoint)	£675.24	
Total		£17,556.24
Future loss of earnings		£37,000.00
Pension loss		£133,955.67
Total		£204,162.91

The tribunal follows EAT authority and decides that its award for injury to feelings (and interest thereon) of £10,800 is not chargeable to tax. £30,000 of the remainder is exempt as a termination payment. That means that the balance of £163,362.91 will be taxed as income in the 2017/18 tax year. Katarzyna's only other taxable income in 2017/18 is two months in February and March 2018, when the tribunal assumes she will be earning a gross annual salary of £12,000 (or £1,000 for each month). Her total income in this tax year – including the taxable award of compensation – will mean that she has no personal allowance. Her new job will take up £2,000 of the basic rate tax band (now running from £0 to £33,500), leaving £31,500 of it available. The whole higher rate tax band will be available, from £33,500 to £150,000, which will apply to £116,500 of the award. So far, this accounts for £148,000 of the taxable award of compensation (£31,500 plus £116,500). There is £15,362.91 remaining, which will be taxed at the additional rate.

Basic rate (20%): £31,500/80 × 100 = £39,375

Tax element is £39,375 less £31,500, which is £7,875

Higher rate (40%): £116,500/60 × 100 = £194,166.67

Tax element is £194,166.67 less £116,500, which is £77,666.67

Additional rate (45%): £15,362.91/55 × 100 = £27,932.56

Tax element is £27,932.56 less £15,272.91, which is £12,659.65

Total tax to be added: £7,875 + £77,666.67 + £12,659.65 = £98,201.32

The effect of receiving this compensation also means that Katarzyna must pay more tax on the income from her new job than would otherwise have been the case. Before, she would have had the entire personal allowance of £11,500 available. Now, she will pay basic rate tax at 20% on £2,000 (i.e. £400). Put another way, by receiving compensation for unlawful discrimination, she has had to pay £400 more tax in her new job than would otherwise have been the case. The tribunal decides it would be appropriate to add this sum to the overall award.

The grand total of the tribunal's award is therefore as follows:

Total as above	£204,072.91
Add tax due on £163,272.91	£98,201.32
Add further tax due on new job:	£400.00
Total after grossing-up:	**£302,674.23**
Less amount already awarded at first-stage:	£15,651.00
Balance outstanding:	**£287,023.23**

Accordingly, in a supplemental judgment, the tribunal awards Katarzyna a further sum of £287,023.23.

Rosa – loss of pension rights that vary with period — apportionment of multiplier — pension loss from early age — withdrawal factors — enhancement on grounds of ill-health — use of NEST calculator — loss of lump sum

In this example, gross figures for annual salary have been converted into net figures for annual salary using the HMRC online calculator referred to in the Principles (https://www.gov.uk/estimate-income-tax), inputting the default income tax code. Salary and pensionable pay are treated as equivalent. The main purpose of this example is to illustrate how the Ogden multiplier must be apportioned for variable periods of pension loss.

Rosa was born on 1 July 1981. She commenced employment with a major retail bank in London at the age of 25. The bank operated a DB pension scheme, which Rosa joined. The scheme provides for 1/80th of final salary for each year of service, up to a maximum of 40/80ths after 40 years' service, with a separate entitlement to a tax-free lump sum of three times the annual pension income (it was not necessary to commute the pension income to receive the lump sum). The scheme had a normal retirement age of 55, meaning that employees could retire from that age with an unreduced pension. The scheme also had ill-health benefits: someone who left the job on health grounds because they were unable to work would have 5/80ths added to their pensionable service.

Rosa was dismissed in January 2017, shortly after she told her employer she was pregnant. She was aged 35 at her dismissal and had just completed ten years' service. Rosa's normal retirement age under the DB scheme was 55, which she will reach on 1 July 2036. Her state pension age is 68, which she will reach on 1 July 2049. At the date of her dismissal, Rosa was paid a gross annual salary of £30,000. This was the top of her pay grade. After deductions for income tax and NI contributions, this amounts to net pay of £23,681 (this would be relevant when calculating loss of earnings).

At a preliminary hearing by telephone, dealing with case management, the tribunal notes that Rosa was in a private sector DB scheme. It therefore decides to list a hearing that, at this stage, deals with liability only. Orders are nonetheless made for the disclosure of pension-related information, so that the parties can prepare more informed schedules and counter-schedules of loss.

At the liability hearing in May 2017, Rosa succeeds in showing that her dismissal was unfair and an act of pregnancy discrimination. No statutory cap applies. Having consulted the parties, the tribunal lists a first-stage remedy hearing. At this hearing, the tribunal will determine some of her non-pension losses and make findings on those matters that will assist the parties in calculating her pension loss for themselves and thereby promote settlement.

The first-stage hearing is held on 1 October 2017, when Rosa is 36. The tribunal makes the following findings.

- Rosa was at the top of the relevant pay scale and further rises would have been cost of living only, if anything. The tribunal did not consider she would ever be promoted from her existing grade.
- Rosa's baby was born on 30 June 2017. She had been planning to take maternity leave of 12 months before returning to work on 1 July 2018, initially on a part-time basis (50%). She and her partner Sue had no plans for any more children.
- Sue is employed by the same bank, but in a much more senior role. A month before the first-stage remedy hearing, Sue was offered a new role setting up a branch of the bank in New York. It was a five-year contract from July 2019 to the end of June 2024. Rosa has decided to accompany her. Sue's remuneration package is eye-wateringly high. If Rosa had still been employed by the bank, she could not have transferred there too. However, the bank has a scheme under which employees can take up to five years as a career break. They must resign but have a conditional right to return to their old job, or the nearest equivalent, on the same terms and conditions (including membership of the pension scheme). The tribunal decides that, but for the dismissal, Rosa would have stayed with the bank for the rest of her career. It also concludes that she would have moved with Sue to New York even if she had not been dismissed, taking the five-year career break, then returning to work full-time.
- Medical evidence shows that Rosa has a degenerative condition. The condition is likely to render her incapable of working beyond the age of 50. The tribunal concludes that she would have ended up taking ill-health retirement. The condition does not, however, affect her life expectancy.
- Rosa will not get a job with pension rights in New York. When she comes back to the UK in 2024, the tribunal considers it very unlikely she will get employment with a pension above and beyond that provided for by the auto-enrolment regime: probably a private sector role in administration, in which she will earn more than the qualifying amount for auto-enrolment purposes (the tribunal's estimate is a gross annual salary of £25,000).

Having consulted the parties, the tribunal gives Rosa and the bank 21 days to agree a figure for loss of earnings and loss of pension and, in the absence of agreement, to inform the tribunal if they wish to instruct an expert to assist in calculating his lost pension. However, the parties do not reach agreement. They also decide against instructing an expert. They return to the tribunal for a second-stage remedy hearing for these figures to be judicially determined (and, in the case of pension loss, by applying the seven steps model).

The following calculation deals only with loss of pension rights.

Step 1: Identify what Rosa's net pension income would have been at her retirement age if the dismissal had not occurred.

A statement from the pension scheme administrators is obtained, from which the tribunal can draw several conclusions. At the time of her dismissal, Rosa had worked for the bank for ten years and had therefore

Part 4 Statutory Codes of Practice

accrued 10/80ths of her final salary. On the face of it she had a further 20 years of service to go until reaching 55, the normal retirement age under the scheme. This would have meant an annual pension of 30/80ths of final salary. The tribunal ignores cost of living rises on the basis that they are cancelled out by inflation so, at face value, if she had not been dismissed, the present-day value of Rosa's bank pension would have been 30/80 × £30,000, which is £11,250.

However, the tribunal makes several adjustments, to reflect the prospects of withdrawal from the pension scheme. It goes through it period by period:

- For the period from January 2017 to June 2018 (18 months), the tribunal accepts that, if Rosa had not been dismissed, she would have carried on working (or been on maternity leave) until 1 July 2018. This would have added 1.5/80ths to her pensionable service.
- For the period from July 2018 to June 2019 (one year), Rosa would have been working part-time. Under the DB scheme rules, this would have counted pro rata. This would have added 0.5/80ths to her pensionable service.
- For the period from July 2019 to June 2024 (five years), Rosa would have been on a career break with Sue in New York. No pension rights would have accrued in this period.
- Thereafter, Rosa would have been back in the UK and returned to full-time work with the bank. She could, in principle, have worked until reaching the age of 55 in July 2036 and then taken an unreduced pension. However, the tribunal decides that the likelier outcome is that she have worked for the bank between July 2024 to June 2031 (seven years), having wanted to go back to her old job. Because of her medical position, she would have retired early, at the age of 50, in July 2031. The tribunal therefore adjusts the loss in this period by limiting it to 7 years (7/80ths), but adding 5/80ths for the ill-health retirement enhancement. That makes 12/80ths.
- The tribunal also decides, having heard evidence on the future of retail banking and increased automation, that there is only a 50% chance that Rosa's type of job will still be needed in 2024. The loss of 12/80ths for this final period is therefore reduced by 50% to 6/80ths.

This means that the calculation of pension loss at Step 1 is as follows:

- Accrued rights at dismissal: 10 × 1/80 × £30,000
- Dismissal to end of maternity leave: 1.5 × 1/80 × £30,000
- Return from maternity leave: 0.5 × 1/80
- Career break: Nil
- Return from career break and early retirement: 6 × 1/80 × £30,000

Rosa's gross annual pension at retirement from age 50:

18 × 1/80 × £30,000 = £6,750

The figure of £6,750 is beneath Rosa's personal allowance, so the gross sum and the net sum are the same.

(In the interests of simplicity, the tribunal ignores Rosa's nSP entitlement, which would take it over her personal allowance (at today's rates) and require a small amount of "netting down". While including nSP would increase the accuracy of calculating the overall net value of Rosa's pension benefits — both occupational and state — it must be borne in mind that we do not apply the age-related adjustment to the Ogden multiplier when compensating for loss of state pension.)

Step 2: Identify what Rosa's net pension income will be at her retirement age in the light of her dismissal.

There are three different periods to consider:

(1) The first period is for when Rosa is between 50 and 55. Her actual pension benefits at age 50 will be nil, because there will be no pension entitlement from the bank or from any other job.

(2) The second period is for when Rosa is between 55 and 68, during which she can receive her deferred bank pension of £3,750 per annum.

(3) The third period is for when Rosa is 68 and above. As noted above, the tribunal has decided that, in 2024 at the age of 43, Rosa will find full time employment with auto-enrolment DC pension rights. In this hypothetical scenario, requiring a degree of speculation, the tribunal predicts a job paying (at today's value) a gross annual salary of £25,000. The tribunal's approach to withdrawal at Step 2 mirrors its approach at Step 1: it decides that Rosa will be unable to work in this new role beyond age 50. The auto-enrolment pension would not provide for any early retirement with enhanced benefits. It also decides that Rosa would wait until the age of 68 before accessing the additional pension generated by this job. Applying the Principles, the tribunal notes that this new role would involve employer contributions of 3% (£750) and employee contributions of 5% (£1,250). The NEST calculator estimates that, without taking 25% of the fund as a tax-free lump sum, seven years of these contributions would lead to a gross pension income, at today's value, of £1,280 from her state pension age of 68.

These figures are below Rosa's personal allowance, so do not need to be "netted down".

Step 3: Deduct the result of Step 2 from the result of Step 1, which produces a figure for net annual loss of pension benefits.

In Rosa's case, there are three multiplicands from three different ages:

(1) For the five years between ages 50 and 55, Rosa's net pension income from the bank would (but for the dismissal) have been £6,750. As it is, she will have no pension in this period. For this period, the multiplicand is £6,750.

(2) For the 13 years between the ages of 55 and 68, the multiplicand changes. Rosa's bank pension of £3,750 will now be in payment. Her annual loss for this period — the multiplicand — is £6,750 less £3,750, which is £3,000.

(3) From the age of 68 (when she decides to take her auto-enrolled pension) until the day she dies, Rosa's annual loss reduces to £6,750 less £3,750 less £1,280. The multiplicand for this period is £1,720.

Step 4: Identify the period over which that net annual loss is to be awarded, using the Ogden Tables to identify the multiplier.

A simplistic approach would be to say that Rosa will lose five lots of £6,750 for period (1), 13 lots of £3,000 for period (2) and whatever number of lots of £1,720 until she dies for period (3). The Ogden Tables will inform and improve these multipliers and take account of the negative discount rate.

At the date of the hearing, Rosa is 36. Her degenerative condition does not adjust her life expectancy. The tribunal proceeds with the usual approach of adjusting her age so that she is treated as being 34 at the hearing, with the three periods of loss now being:

(1) The five years between ages 48 and 53 (loss from age 48);
(2) The 13 years between ages 53 and 66 (loss from age 53); and
(3) Her loss from age 66.

But her loss itself starts (or, rather, is now deemed to start) at the age of 48.

Neither the full Ogden Tables nor the "at a glance" extracts in Appendix 2 provide a multiplier for loss of pension for a woman aged 48. The tribunal has no expert actuarial evidence available to work out what the multiplier from age 48 should be. However, looking at the pattern of multipliers at the minus 0.75% discount rate, and having heard submissions from the parties, the tribunal's best estimate is a multiplier of 55.

It would be wrong for the tribunal to apply the multiplier of 55 to each multiplicand separately. It would have the effect of compensating Rosa for the loss of £6,750 per annum for the rest of her life (when that loss will last for only five years) and for the loss of £3,000 per annum for the rest of her life (when it will only last for 13 years). Instead, the tribunal needs to adjust the multiplier of 55 using the "apportionment method" described at paragraph 22 of the explanatory notes to the Ogden Tables.

We must start with Table 2 of the Ogden Tables. This provides multipliers for pecuniary loss for life for females. A 34-year old has a life expectancy of a further 55.69 years (using the column for a discount rate of 0% gives the actual life expectancy). In other words, we can infer from Ogden Table 2 that Rosa will live to the age of 89.69. This means that, if Rosa draws her bank pension from the (deemed) age of 48, she will be drawing it for 41.69 years. That is the assumed period of her pension loss in retirement, even though she experiences that loss at different levels across three periods.

Next, we turn to Table 28. This is the table dealing with multipliers for pecuniary loss for a term certain. We need to find a multiplier for a term certain of 41.69 years. Table 28 tells us that, for a term certain of 41 years, the multiplier is 48.032, and that, for a term certain of 42 years, the multiplier is 49.399. The tribunal decides that a suitable midway multiplier for a term certain of 41.69 years is 48.98.

However, this multiplier of 48.98 needs to be split, so that each segment of the three periods of loss is represented by a figure. This is done as follows:

- The first five years of loss (between the deemed ages of 48 and 53) is represented by a multiplier for a term certain of five years, which is 5.095.
- To get the multiplier for the next 13 years of loss (between the deemed ages of 53 and 66), we need to identify the multiplier for a term certain of 18 years (which is 19.277) and subtract the multiplier for a term certain of five years (which is 5.095). This gives us a multiplier of 14.182.
- To get the multiplier for the final 23.69 years of loss (between the deemed ages of 66 and 89.69), we need to identify the multiplier for a term certain of 41.69 years (which, as we have already established, is 48.98) and subtract the multiplier for a term certain of 18 years (which is 19.277). This gives us a multiplier of 29.703.

Each of those smaller segmented multipliers can be shown as a percentage or fraction of the whole; so, for the first five years, the segmented multiplier of 5.095 is 10.4% of the figure of 48.98; for the next 13 years, the segmented multiplier of 14.182 is 28.96% of the figure of 48.98; and, for the final period of 23.69 years, the segmented multiplier of 29.703 is 60.64% of the figure of 48.98.

The tribunal's "best estimate" multiplier of 55 can now be split up in identical proportions to the way in which the Table 28 multiplier has been treated above. So: the first five-year period is now represented by a multiplier of 5.72 (which is calculated by taking 10.4% of 55); the next 13 years is now represented by a multiplier of 15.93 (which is calculated by taking 28.96% of 55); and the final period of 23.69 years is now represented by a multiplier of 33.35 (which is calculated by taking 60.64% of 55).

The tribunal does not discount those multipliers further, being content that contingencies other than mortality are adequately covered by the withdrawal factors considered at Steps 1 and 2.

Step 5: Multiply the multiplicand by the multiplier, which produces the present capital value of that loss.

The multiplicand for each segment of life in retirement past the deemed age of 48 is now multiplied by the appropriate segmented multiplier to calculate the lost pension income for each period. The total of those losses represents the full sum of lost pension income.

(1)	Deemed ages 48 to 53 (five years): £6,750 × 5.72	£38,610.00
(2)	Deemed aged 53 to 66 (13 years): £3,000 × 15.93	£47,790.00
(3)	Deemed ages 66 to 89.69 (23.69 years): £1,720 × 33.35	£57,362.00
Total		**£143,762.00**

Rosa's net loss of pension income is therefore £143,762.

Step 6: Check the lump sum position and perform a separate calculation if required.

Here, we revert to Rosa's true age. The two-year age adjustment has no application to lump sums which, by their nature, are received once and do not depend on longevity in retirement.

As matters stand, Rosa's lump sum at age 55 will be three times her gross annual pension income: 3 × £3,750 = £11,250. As noted above, to ensure that we are comparing like with like, we will assume that Rosa does not opt to take 25% of the pension fund she built up from auto-enrolment as a tax-free lump sum.

If there had been no dismissal (and allowing for the withdrawal factors discussed above), Rosa's gross pension income would have been £6,750, and her lump sum would have been three times that amount, which is £20,250. Rosa would have received that lump sum at the age of 50 when taking early retirement on the grounds of ill-health.

It follows that Rosa's dismissal has caused a £9,000 shortfall in her lump sum and has also deprived her of the opportunity to invest £20,250 over the five-year period between ages 50 and 55.

Dealing first with the £9,000 shortfall. Rosa will receive her compensation from the tribunal at the age of 36, which is earlier receipt by 14 years than if dismissal had not occurred. Using Ogden Table 27, the tribunal selects a multiplier of 1.1112. That increases the sum awarded to £10,000.80 (a negative discount rate assumes that money invested will shrink, not grow, and so its application will increase the overall sum).

As for the lost opportunity to invest £20,250 over five years, the tribunal bears in mind the negative discount rate and an assumption of investment in ILGS; it concludes that Rosa has only lost the opportunity to invest that sum and watch it shrink. That is no loss at all. The tribunal declines to make any further award.

The total award for Rosa's net pension income, therefore, is:

£143,762 + £10,000.80 = **£153,762.80**

Step 7: Taking account of the other sums awarded by the tribunal, gross up the compensation awarded.

No calculations are shown for this step, because we have not set out Rosa's loss of earnings.

7. LOSS OF DEATH-IN-SERVICE BENEFIT

This example relates to paragraphs 5.68 to 5.70 of the Principles.

Adrian — DB scheme — loss of death-in-service benefit

Adrian, aged 45 at dismissal and a smoker, has been unlawfully dismissed from employment that included membership of a DB pension scheme. The scheme provided for a death-in-service benefit of twice his annual salary (which was £100,000). Adrian has lost this benefit in consequence of his dismissal.

Having heard evidence, the tribunal decides that Adrian would have continued in employment until the age of 70. Consequently, if Adrian wishes to purchase level term insurance, this would be over a 25-year term. At this stage, he has made enquiries about taking out life insurance that would pay out £200,000 in the event of his death before age 70. There may be other specific factors in relation to his lifestyle which may render cover more expensive but, leaving it at his cigarette consumption, a wide range of total cost of policies can be found online. They vary from discount brokers at the cheaper end of the market, advisory brokers in the middle range and direct purchase from insurers and banks at the expensive end. The total cost of premiums over the life of the policy varied from £13,000 to £20,000.

The policy premium would normally be paid by monthly instalments. There will therefore be an element of advance payment discount to be deducted from the total of the monthly premiums. It may also be possible to tailor the policy to provide for an increasing lump sum to keep step with projected rising earning levels. It is an area where the parties might seek some expert input.

APPENDIX 4: GLOSSARY OF ACRONYMS

[4.336]

AA	Annual Allowance
AVC	Additional Voluntary Contributions
BSP	Basic State Pension
CARE	Career Average Revalued Earnings
COPE	Contracted Out Pension Equivalent
CPI	Consumer Price Index
DB	Defined Benefit
DC	Defined Contribution
DWP	Department for Work and Pensions
EAT	Employment Appeal Tribunal
EqA	Equality Act 2010
ERA	Employment Rights Act 1996
GAD	Government Actuary's Department
GRB	Graduated Retirement Benefit
HMRC	Her Majesty's Revenue and Customs
ILGS	Index-linked Government Stock
ITEPA	Income Tax (Earnings and Pensions) Act 2003
LGPS	Local Government Pension Scheme
LTA	Lifetime Allowance
MFR	Minimum Funding Requirement (now, Statutory Funding Objective)
NEST	National Employment Savings Trust
NI	National Insurance
nSP	New State Pension
ONS	Office for National Statistics
P60	End-of-year certificate of income tax and NI paid
PCSPS	Principal Civil Service Pension Scheme
PPO	Periodical Payments Order
S2P	State Second Pension
SERPS	State Earnings-related Pension Scheme
SFO	Statutory Funding Objective
SPPA	Scottish Public Pensions Agency

APPENDIX 5: LIST OF WORKING GROUP MEMBERS

[4.337]
Elizabeth Potter

Regional Employment Judge, London Central (chair)

Barry Clarke

Regional Employment Judge, Wales

Peter Hildebrand

Regional Employment Judge, London South

Susan Walker

Vice-President of Employment Tribunals, Scotland

Pauline Hughes

Salaried Employment Judge, Midlands West

David Franey

Salaried Employment Judge, North West England

Ian McFatridge

Salaried Employment Judge, Scotland

Sarah Goodman

Salaried Employment Judge, London Central

Stephen Jenkins

Solicitor, fee paid Employment Judge, South East England

FORMER MEMBERS

Tudor Garnon

Salaried Employment Judge, North East England

Colin Goodier

Salaried Employment Judge, Midlands West (retired)

Michael Zuke

Salaried Employment Judge, London South (retired)

PART 5
MISCELLANEOUS MATERIALS

A. INTERNATIONAL LAW MATERIALS

INTERNATIONAL LABOUR ORGANISATION CONVENTION (NO 87) ON FREEDOM OF ASSOCIATION AND PROTECTION OF THE RIGHT TO ORGANISE (1948)

NOTES

This Convention was adopted on 9 July 1948 and came into force on 4 July 1950. It was ratified by the UK on 27 June 1949.

PART I FREEDOM OF ASSOCIATION

[5.1]

Article 1

Each Member of the International Labour Organisation for which this Convention is in force undertakes to give effect to the following provisions.

Article 2

Workers and employers, without distinction whatsoever, shall have the right to establish and, subject only to the rules of the organisation concerned, to join organisations of their own choosing without previous authorisation.

Article 3

1. Workers' and employers' organisations shall have the right to draw up their constitutions and rules, to elect their representatives in full freedom, to organise their administration and activities and to formulate their programmes.
2. The public authorities shall refrain from any interference which would restrict this right or impede the lawful exercise thereof.

Article 4

Workers' and employers' organisations shall not be liable to be dissolved or suspended by administrative authority.

Article 5

Workers' and employers' organisations shall have the right to establish and join federations and confederations and any such organisation, federation or confederation shall have the right to affiliate with international organisations of workers and employers.

Article 6

The provisions of Articles 2, 3 and 4 hereof apply to federations and confederations of workers' and employers' organisations.

Article 7

The acquisition of legal personality by workers' and employers' organisations, federations and confederations shall not be made subject to conditions of such a character as to restrict the application of the provisions of Articles 2, 3 and 4 hereof.

Article 8

1. In exercising the rights provided for in this Convention workers and employers and their respective organisations, like other persons or organised collectivities, shall respect the law of the land.
2. The law of the land shall not be such as to impair, nor shall it be so applied as to impair, the guarantees provided for in this Convention.

Article 9

1. The extent to which the guarantees provided for in this Convention shall apply to the armed forces and the police shall be determined by national laws or regulations.
2. In accordance with the principle set forth in paragraph 8 of Article 19 of the Constitution of the International Labour Organisation the ratification of this Convention by any Member shall not be deemed to affect any existing law, award, custom or agreement in virtue of which members of the armed forces or the police enjoy any right guaranteed by this Convention.

Article 10
In this Convention the term 'organisation' means any organisation of workers or of employers for furthering and defending the interests of workers or of employers.

PART II PROTECTION OF THE RIGHT TO ORGANISE

[5.2]
Article 11
Each Member of the International Labour Organisation for which this Convention is in force undertakes to take all necessary and appropriate measures to ensure that workers and employers may exercise freely the right to organise.

PART III MISCELLANEOUS PROVISIONS

[5.3]
Article 12
1. In respect of the territories referred to in Article 35 of the Constitution of the International Labour Organisation as amended by the Constitution of the International Labour Organisation Instrument of Amendment 1946, other than the territories referred to in paragraphs 4 and 5 of the said article as so amended, each Member of the Organisation which ratifies this Convention shall communicate to the Director-General of the International Labour Office with or as soon as possible after its ratification a declaration stating:
   (a) the territories in respect of which it undertakes that the provisions of the Convention shall be applied without modification;
   (b) the territories in respect of which it undertakes that the provisions of the Convention shall be applied subject to modifications, together with details of the said modifications;
   (c) the territories in respect of which the Convention is inapplicable and in such cases the grounds on which it is inapplicable;
   (d) the territories in respect of which it reserves its decision.
2. The undertakings referred to in subparagraphs (a) and (b) of paragraph 1 of this Article shall be deemed to be an integral part of the ratification and shall have the force of ratification.
3. Any Member may at any time by a subsequent declaration cancel in whole or in part any reservations made in its original declaration in virtue of subparagraphs (b), (c) or (d) of paragraph 1 of this Article.
4. Any Member may, at any time at which the Convention is subject to denunciation in accordance with the provisions of Article 16, communicate to the Director-General a declaration modifying in any other respect the terms of any former declaration and stating the present position in respect of such territories as it may specify.

Article 13
1. Where the subject-matter of this Convention is within the self-governing powers of any non-metropolitan territory, the Member responsible for the international relations of that territory may, in agreement with the government of the territory, communicate to the Director-General of the International Labour Office a declaration accepting on behalf of the territory the obligations of this Convention.
2. A declaration accepting the obligations of this Convention may be communicated to the Director-General of the International Labour Office:
   (a) by two or more Members of the Organisation in respect of any territory which is under their joint authority; or
   (b) by any international authority responsible for the administration of any territory, in virtue of the Charter of the United Nations or otherwise, in respect of any such territory.
3. Declarations communicated to the Director-General of the International Labour Office in accordance with the preceding paragraphs of this Article shall indicate whether the provisions of the Convention will be applied in the territory concerned without modification or subject to modifications; when the declaration indicates that the provisions of the Convention will be applied subject to modifications it shall give details of the said modifications.
4. The Member, Members or international authority concerned may at any time by a subsequent declaration renounce in whole or in part the right to have recourse to any modification indicated in any former declaration.
5. The Member, Members or international authority concerned may, at any time at which this Convention is subject to denunciation in accordance with the provisions of Article 16, communicate to the Director-General a declaration modifying in any other respect the terms of any former declaration and stating the present position in respect of the application of the Convention.

PART IV FINAL PROVISIONS

[5.4]
Article 14
The formal ratifications of this Convention shall be communicated to the Director-General of the International Labour Office for registration.

Article 15
1. This Convention shall be binding only upon those Members of the International Labour Organisation whose ratifications have been registered with the Director-General.

2. It shall come into force twelve months after the date on which the ratifications of two Members have been registered with the Director-General.
3. Thereafter, this Convention shall come into force for any Member twelve months after the date on which its ratification has been registered.

Article 16
1. A Member which has ratified this Convention may denounce it after the expiration of ten years from the date on which the Convention first comes into force, by an act communicated to the Director-General of the International Labour Office for registration. Such denunciation shall not take effect until one year after the date on which it is registered.
2. Each Member which has ratified this Convention and which does not, within the year following the expiration of the period of ten years mentioned in the preceding paragraph, exercise the right of denunciation provided for in this article, will be bound for another period of ten years and, thereafter, may denounce this Convention at the expiration of each period of ten years under the terms provided for in this article.

Article 17
1. The Director-General of the International Labour Office shall notify all Members of the International Labour Organisation of the registration of all ratifications, declarations and denunciations communicated to him by the Members of the Organisation.
2. When notifying the Members of the Organisation of the registration of the second ratification communicated to him, the Director-General shall draw the attention of the Members of the Organisation to the date upon which the Convention will come into force.

Article 18
The Director-General of the International Labour Office shall communicate to the Secretary-General of the United Nations for registration in accordance with Article 102 of the Charter of the United Nations full particulars of all ratifications, declarations and acts of denunciation registered by him in accordance with the provisions of the preceding articles.

Article 19
At such times as it may consider necessary the Governing Body of the International Labour Office shall present to the General Conference a report on the working of this Convention and shall examine the desirability of placing on the agenda of the Conference the question of its revision in whole or in part.

Article 20
1. Should the Conference adopt a new Convention revising this Convention in whole or in part, then, unless the new Convention otherwise provides:
(a) the ratification by a Member of the new revising Convention shall ipso jure involve the immediate denunciation of this Convention, notwithstanding the provisions of Article 16 above, if and when the new revising Convention shall have come into force;
(b) as from the date when the new revising Convention comes into force this Convention shall cease to be open to ratification by the Members.
2. This Convention shall in any case remain in force in its actual form and content for those Members which have ratified it but have not ratified the revising Convention.

Article 21
The English and French versions of the text of this Convention are equally authoritative.

INTERNATIONAL LABOUR ORGANISATION CONVENTION (NO 98) ON THE RIGHT TO ORGANISE AND COLLECTIVE BARGAINING (1949)

NOTES
This Convention was adopted on 1 July 1949 and came into force on 18 July 1951. It was ratified by the UK on 30 June 1950.

[5.5]
Article 1
1. Workers shall enjoy adequate protection against acts of anti-union discrimination in respect of their employment.
2. Such protection shall apply more particularly in respect of acts calculated to:
(a) Make the employment of a worker subject to the condition that he shall not join a union or shall relinquish trade union membership

(b) Cause the dismissal of or otherwise prejudice a worker by reason of union membership or because of participation in union activities outside working hours or, with the consent of the employer, within working hours.

Article 2

1. Workers' and employers' organisations shall enjoy adequate protection against any acts of interference by each other or each others' agents or members in their establishment functioning or administration.

2. In particular, acts which are designed to promote the establishment of workers' organisations under the domination of employers or employers' organisations, or to support workers' organisations by financial or other means, with the object of placing such organisations under the control of employers or employers' organisations, shall be deemed to constitute acts of interference within the meaning of this article.

Article 3

Machinery appropriate to national conditions shall be established, where necessary, for the purpose of ensuring respect for the right to organise as defined in the preceding articles.

Article 4

Measures appropriate to national conditions shall be taken where necessary, to encourage and promote the full development and utilisation of machinery for voluntary negotiation between employers or employers' organisations and workers' organisations, with a view to the regulation of terms and conditions of employment by means of collective agreements.

Article 5

1. The extent to which the guarantees provided for in this Convention shall apply to the armed forces and the police shall be determined by national laws or regulations.

2. In accordance with the principle set forth in paragraph 8 of Article 19 of the Constitution of the International Labour Organisation the ratification of this Convention by any Member shall not be deemed to affect any existing law, award, custom or agreement in virtue of which members of the armed forces or the police enjoy any right guaranteed by this Convention.

Article 6

This Convention does not deal with the position of public servants engaged in the administration of the State, nor shall it be construed as prejudicing their rights or status in any way.

Article 7

The formal ratifications of this Convention shall be communicated to the Director-General of the International Labour Office for registration.

Article 8

1. This Convention shall be binding only upon those Members of the International Labour Organisation whose ratifications have been registered with the Director-General.

2. It shall come into force twelve months after the date on which the ratifications of two Members have been registered with the Director-General.

3. Thereafter, this Convention shall come into force for any Member twelve months after the date on which its ratification has been registered.

Article 9

1. Declarations communicated to the Director-General of the International Labour Office in accordance with paragraph 2 of Article 35 of the Constitution of the International Labour Organisation shall indicate—

(a) the territories in respect of which the Member concerned undertakes that the provisions of the Convention shall be applied without modification;

(b) the territories in respect of which it undertakes that the provisions of the Convention shall be applied subject to modifications, together with details of the said modifications;

(c) the territories in respect of which the Convention is inapplicable and in such cases the grounds on which it is inapplicable;

(d) the territories in respect of which it reserves its decision pending further consideration of the position.

2. The undertakings referred to in subparagraphs (a) and (b) of paragraph 1 of this Article shall be deemed to be an integral part of the ratification and shall have the force of ratification.

3. Any Member may at any time by a subsequent declaration cancel in whole or in part any reservation made in its original declaration in virtue of subparagraph (b), (c) or (d) of paragraph 1 of this Article.

4. Any Member may, at any time at which the Convention is subject to denunciation in accordance with the provisions of Article 11, communicate to the Director-General a declaration modifying in any other respect the terms of any former declaration and stating the present position in respect of such territories as it may specify.

Article 10

1. Declarations communicated to the Director-General of the International Labour Office in accordance with paragraph 4 or 5 of Article 35 of the Constitution of the International Labour Organisation shall indicate whether the provisions of the Convention will be applied in the territory concerned without modification or subject to modifications; when the declaration indicates that the provisions of the Convention will be applied subject to modifications, it shall give details of the said modifications.
2. The Member, Members or international authority concerned may at any time by a subsequent declaration renounce in whole or in part the right to have recourse to any modification indicated in any former declaration.
3. The Member, Members or international authority concerned may, at any time at which this Convention is subject to denunciation in accordance with the provisions of Article 11, communicate to the Director-General a declaration modifying in any other respect the terms of any former declaration and stating the present position in respect of the application of the Convention.

Article 11

1. A Member which has ratified this Convention may denounce it after the expiration of ten years from the date on which the Convention first comes into force, by an act communicated to the Director-General of the International Labour Office for registration. Such denunciation shall not take effect until one year after the date on which it is registered.
2. Each Member which has ratified this Convention and which does not, within the year following the expiration of the period of ten years mentioned in the preceding paragraph, exercise the right of denunciation provided for in this article, will be bound for another period of ten years and, thereafter, may denounce this Convention at the expiration of each period of ten years under the terms provided for in this Article.

Article 12

1. The Director-General of the International Labour Office shall notify all Members of the International Labour Organisation of the registration of all ratifications, declarations and denunciations communicated to him by the Members of the Organisation.
2. When notifying the Members of the Organisation of the registration of the second ratification communicated to him, the Director-General shall draw the attention of the Members of the Organisation to the date upon which the Convention will come into force.

Article 13

The Director-General of the International Labour Office shall communicate to the Secretary-General of the United Nations for registration in accordance with Article 102 of the Charter of the United Nations full particulars of all ratifications, declarations and acts of denunciation registered by him in accordance with the provisions of the preceding articles.

Article 14

At such times as it may consider necessary the Governing Body of the International Labour Office shall present to the General Conference a report on the working of this Convention and shall examine the desirability of placing on the agenda of the Conference the question of its revision in whole or in part.

Article 15

1. Should the Conference adopt a new Convention revising this Convention in whole or in part, then, unless the new Convention otherwise provides,
   (a) the ratification by a Member of the new revising Convention shall ipso jure involve the immediate denunciation of this Convention, notwithstanding the provisions of Article 11 above, if and when the new revising Convention shall have come into force;
   (b) as from the date when the new revising Convention comes into force, this Convention shall cease to be open to ratification by the Members.
2. This Convention shall in any case remain in force in its actual form and content for those Members which have ratified it but have not ratified the revising Convention.

Article 16

The English and French versions of the text of this Convention are equally authoritative.

EUROPEAN CONVENTION FOR THE PROTECTION OF HUMAN RIGHTS AND FUNDAMENTAL FREEDOMS (1950) (NOTE)

[5.6]

NOTES

Signed 4 November 1950; in force September 1953.

The European Convention is given domestic legal status by the Human Rights Act 1998. Sch 1 to that Act at **[1.1241]** et seq sets out the operative provisions of the Convention relevant to this work, except for Article 13, which provides that everyone whose Convention rights and freedoms are violated shall have an effective remedy before a national authority notwithstanding that the violation has been committed by persons acting in an official capacity.

INTERNATIONAL LABOUR ORGANISATION CONVENTION (NO 132) CONCERNING ANNUAL HOLIDAYS WITH PAY (REVISED), (1970)

NOTES

This Convention was adopted on 24 June 1970 and came into force on 30 June 1973. As of 15 May 2019, this Convention has not been ratified by the UK.

[5.7]

Article 1

The provisions of this Convention, in so far as they are not otherwise made effective by means of collective agreements, arbitration awards, court decisions, statutory wage fixing machinery, or in such other manner consistent with national practice as may be appropriate under national conditions, shall be given effect by national laws or regulations.

Article 2

1. This Convention applies to all employed persons, with the exception of seafarers.
2. In so far as necessary, measures may be taken by the competent authority or through the appropriate machinery in a country, after consultation with the organisations of employers and workers concerned, where such exist, to exclude from the application of this Convention limited categories of employed persons in respect of whose employment special problems of a substantial nature, relating to enforcement or to legislative or constitutional matters, arise.
3. Each Member which ratifies this Convention shall list in the first report on the application of the Convention submitted under Article 22 of the Constitution of the International Labour Organisation any categories which may have been excluded in pursuance of paragraph 2 of this Article, giving the reasons for such exclusion, and shall state in subsequent reports the position of its law and practice in respect of the categories excluded, and the extent to which effect has been given or is proposed to be given to the Convention in respect of such categories.

Article 3

1. Every person to whom this Convention applies shall be entitled to an annual paid holiday of a specified minimum length.
2. Each Member which ratifies this Convention shall specify the length of the holiday in a declaration appended to its ratification.
3. The holiday shall in no case be less than three working weeks for one year of service.
4. Each Member which has ratified this Convention may subsequently notify the Director-General of the International Labour Office, by a further declaration, that it specifies a holiday longer than that specified at the time of ratification.

Article 4

1. A person whose length of service in any year is less than that required for the full entitlement prescribed in the preceding Article shall be entitled in respect of that year to a holiday with pay proportionate to his length of service during that year.
2. The expression ***year*** in paragraph 1 of this Article shall mean the calendar year or any other period of the same length determined by the competent authority or through the appropriate machinery in the country concerned.

Article 5

1. A minimum period of service may be required for entitlement to any annual holiday with pay.
2. The length of any such qualifying period shall be determined by the competent authority or through the appropriate machinery in the country concerned but shall not exceed six months.
3. The manner in which length of service is calculated for the purpose of holiday entitlement shall be determined by the competent authority or through the appropriate machinery in each country.
4. Under conditions to be determined by the competent authority or through the appropriate machinery in each country, absence from work for such reasons beyond the control of the employed person concerned as illness, injury or maternity shall be counted as part of the period of service.

Article 6

1. Public and customary holidays, whether or not they fall during the annual holiday, shall not be counted as part of the minimum annual holiday with pay prescribed in Article 3, paragraph 3, of this Convention.
2. Under conditions to be determined by the competent authority or through the appropriate machinery in each country, periods of incapacity for work resulting from sickness or injury may not be counted as part of the minimum annual holiday with pay prescribed in Article 3, paragraph 3, of this Convention.

Article 7

1. Every person taking the holiday envisaged in this Convention shall receive in respect of the full period of that holiday at least his normal or average remuneration (including the cash equivalent of any part of that remuneration which is paid in kind and which is not a permanent benefit continuing whether or not the person concerned is on holiday), calculated in a manner to be determined by the competent authority or through the appropriate machinery in each country.
2. The amounts due in pursuance of paragraph 1 of this Article shall be paid to the person concerned in advance of the holiday, unless otherwise provided in an agreement applicable to him and the employer.

Article 8

1. The division of the annual holiday with pay into parts may be authorised by the competent authority or through the appropriate machinery in each country.
2. Unless otherwise provided in an agreement applicable to the employer and the employed person concerned, and on condition that the length of service of the person concerned entitles him to such a period, one of the parts shall consist of at least two uninterrupted working weeks.

Article 9

1. The uninterrupted part of the annual holiday with pay referred to in Article 8, paragraph 2, of this Convention shall be granted and taken no later than one year, and the remainder of the annual holiday with pay no later than eighteen months, from the end of the year in respect of which the holiday entitlement has arisen.
2. Any part of the annual holiday which exceeds a stated minimum may be postponed, with the consent of the employed person concerned, beyond the period specified in paragraph 1 of this Article and up to a further specified time limit.
3. The minimum and the time limit referred to in paragraph 2 of this Article shall be determined by the competent authority after consultation with the organisations of employers and workers concerned, or through collective bargaining, or in such other manner consistent with national practice as may be appropriate under national conditions.

Article 10

1. The time at which the holiday is to be taken shall, unless it is fixed by regulation, collective agreement, arbitration award or other means consistent with national practice, be determined by the employer after consultation with the employed person concerned or his representatives.
2. In fixing the time at which the holiday is to be taken, work requirements and the opportunities for rest and relaxation available to the employed person shall be taken into account.

Article 11

An employed person who has completed a minimum period of service corresponding to that which may be required under Article 5, paragraph 1, of this Convention shall receive, upon termination of employment, a holiday with pay proportionate to the length of service for which he has not received such a holiday, or compensation in lieu thereof, or the equivalent holiday credit.

Article 12

Agreements to relinquish the right to the minimum annual holiday with pay prescribed in Article 3, paragraph 3, of this Convention or to forgo such a holiday, for compensation or otherwise, shall, as appropriate to national conditions, be null and void or be prohibited.

Article 13

Special rules may be laid down by the competent authority or through the appropriate machinery in each country in respect of cases in which the employed person engages, during the holiday, in a gainful activity conflicting with the purpose of the holiday.

Article 14

Effective measures appropriate to the manner in which effect is given to the provisions of this Convention shall be taken to ensure the proper application and enforcement of regulations or provisions concerning holidays with pay, by means of adequate inspection or otherwise.

Article 15

1. Each Member may accept the obligations of this Convention separately—
   (a) in respect of employed persons in economic sectors other than agriculture;
   (b) in respect of employed persons in agriculture.
2. Each Member shall specify in its ratification whether it accepts the obligations of the Convention in respect of the persons covered by subparagraph (a) of paragraph 1 of this Article, in respect of the persons covered by subparagraph (b) of paragraph 1 of this Article, or in respect of both.
3. Each Member which has on ratification accepted the obligations of this Convention only in respect either of the persons covered by subparagraph (a) of paragraph 1 of this Article or of the persons covered by subparagraph (b) of paragraph 1 of this Article may subsequently notify the Director-General of the International Labour Office that it accepts the obligations of the Convention in respect of all persons to whom this Convention applies.

Article 16

This Convention revises the Holidays with Pay Convention, 1936, and the Holidays with Pay (Agriculture) Convention, 1952, on the following terms:

(a) acceptance of the obligations of this Convention in respect of employed persons in economic sectors other than agriculture by a Member which is a party to the Holidays with Pay Convention, 1936, shall ipso jure involve the immediate denunciation of that Convention;

(b) acceptance of the obligations of this Convention in respect of employed persons in agriculture by a Member which is a party to the Holidays with Pay (Agriculture) Convention, 1952, shall ipso jure involve the immediate denunciation of that Convention;

(c) the coming into force of this Convention shall not close the Holidays with Pay (Agriculture) Convention, 1952, to further ratification.

Article 17

The formal ratifications of this Convention shall be communicated to the Director-General of the International Labour Office for registration.

Article 18

1. This Convention shall be binding only upon those Members of the International Labour Organisation whose ratifications have been registered with the Director-General.
2. It shall come into force twelve months after the date on which the ratifications of two Members have been registered with the Director-General.
3. Thereafter, this Convention shall come into force for any Member twelve months after the date on which its ratifications has been registered.

Article 19

1. A Member which has ratified this Convention may denounce it after the expiration of ten years from the date on which the Convention first comes into force, by an act communicated to the Director-General of the International Labour Office for registration. Such denunciation shall not take effect until one year after the date on which it is registered.
2. Each Member which has ratified this Convention and which does not, within the year following the expiration of the period of ten years mentioned in the preceding paragraph, exercise the right of denunciation provided for in this Article, will be bound for another period of ten years and, thereafter, may denounce this Convention at the expiration of each period of ten years under the terms provided for in this Article.

Article 20

1. The Director-General of the International Labour Office shall notify all Members of the International Labour Organisation of the registration of all ratifications and denunciations communicated to him by the Members of the Organisation.
2. When notifying the Members of the Organisation of the registration of the second ratification communicated to him, the Director-General shall draw the attention of the Members of the Organisation to the date upon which the Convention will come into force.

Article 21

The Director-General of the International Labour Office shall communicate to the Secretary-General of the United Nations for registration in accordance with Article 102 of the Charter of the United Nations full particulars of all ratifications and acts of denunciation registered by him in accordance with the provisions of the preceding Articles.

Article 22

At such times as it may consider necessary the Governing Body of the International Labour Office shall present to the General Conference a report on the working of this Convention and shall examine the desirability of placing on the agenda of the Conference the question of its revision in whole or in part.

Article 23

1. Should the Conference adopt a new Convention revising this Convention in whole or in part, then, unless the new Convention otherwise provides:

(a) the ratification by a Member of the new revising Convention shall ipso jure involve the immediate denunciation of this Convention, notwithstanding the provisions of Article 19 above, if and when the new revising Convention shall have come into force;

(b) as from the date when the new revising Convention comes into force this Convention shall cease to be open to ratification by the Members.

2. This Convention shall in any case remain in force in its actual form and content for those Members which have ratified it but have not ratified the revising Convention.

Article 24

The English and French versions of the text of this Convention are equally authoritative.

INTERNATIONAL LABOUR ORGANISATION CONVENTION (NO 135) CONCERNING PROTECTION AND FACILITIES TO BE AFFORDED TO WORKERS' REPRESENTATIVES IN THE UNDERTAKING (1971)

NOTES

This Convention was adopted on 23 June 1971 and came into force on 30 June 1973. It was ratified by the UK on 15 March 1973.

[5.8]

Article 1

Workers' representatives in the undertaking shall enjoy effective protection against any act prejudicial to them, including dismissal, based on their status or activities as a workers' representative or on union membership or participation in union activities, in so far as they act in conformity with existing laws or collective agreements or other jointly agreed arrangements.

Article 2

1. Such facilities in the undertaking shall be afforded to workers' representatives as may be appropriate in order to enable them to carry out their functions promptly and efficiently.
2. In this connection account shall be taken of the characteristics of the industrial relations system of the country and the needs, size and capabilities of the undertaking concerned.
3. The granting of such facilities shall not impair the efficient operation of the undertaking concerned.

Article 3

For the purpose of this Convention the term ***workers' representatives*** means persons who are recognised as such under national law or practice, whether they are—

(a) trade union representatives, namely, representatives designated or elected by trade unions or by members of such unions; or

(b) elected representatives, namely, representatives who are freely elected by the workers of the undertaking in accordance with provisions of national laws or regulations or of collective agreements and whose functions do not include activities which are recognised as the exclusive prerogative of trade unions in the country concerned.

Article 4

National laws or regulations, collective agreements, arbitration awards or court decisions may determine the type or types of workers' representatives which shall be entitled to the protection and facilities provided for in this Convention.

Article 5

Where there exist in the same undertaking both trade union representatives and elected representatives, appropriate measures shall be taken, wherever necessary, to ensure that the existence of elected representatives is not used to undermine the position of the trade unions concerned or their representatives and to encourage co-operation on all relevant matters between the elected representatives and the trade unions concerned and their representatives.

Article 6

Effect may be given to this Convention through national laws or regulations or collective agreements, or in any other manner consistent with national practice.

Article 7

The formal ratifications of this Convention shall be communicated to the Director-General of the International Labour Office for registration.

Article 8

1. This Convention shall be binding only upon those Members of the International Labour Organisation whose ratifications have been registered with the Director-General.
2. It shall come into force twelve months after the date on which the ratifications of two Members have been registered with the Director-General.
3. Thereafter, this Convention shall come into force for any Member twelve months after the date on which its ratification has been registered.

Article 9

1. A Member which has ratified this Convention may denounce it after the expiration of ten years from the date on which the Convention first comes into force, by an act communicated to the Director-General of the International Labour Office for registration. Such denunciation shall not take effect until one year after the date on which it is registered.
2. Each Member which has ratified this Convention and which does not, within the year following the expiration of the period of ten years mentioned in the preceding paragraph, exercise the right of denunciation provided for in this Article, will be bound for another period of ten years and, thereafter, may denounce this Convention at the expiration of each period of ten years under the terms provided for in this Article.

Article 10

1. The Director-General of the International Labour Office shall notify all Members of the International Labour Organisation of the registration of all ratifications and denunciations communicated to him by the Members of the Organisation.
2. When notifying the Members of the Organisation of the registration of the second ratification communicated to him, the Director-General shall draw the attention of the Members of the Organisation to the date upon which the Convention will come into force.

Article 11

The Director-General of the International Labour Office shall communicate to the Secretary-General of the United Nations for registration in accordance with Article 102 of the Charter of the United Nations full particulars of all ratifications and acts of denunciation registered by him in accordance with the provisions of the preceding Articles.

Article 12

At such times as it may consider necessary the Governing Body of the International Labour Office shall present to the General Conference a report on the working of this Convention and shall examine the desirability of placing on the agenda of the Conference the question of its revision in whole or in part.

Article 13

1. Should the Conference adopt a new Convention revising this Convention in whole or in part, then, unless the new Convention otherwise provides:
   (a) the ratification by a Member of the new revising Convention shall ipso jure involve the immediate denunciation of this Convention, notwithstanding the provisions of Article 9 above, if and when the new revising Convention shall have come into force;
   (b) as from the date when the new revising Convention comes into force this Convention shall cease to be open to ratification by the Members.
2. This Convention shall in any case remain in force in its actual form and content for those Members which have ratified it but have not ratified the revising Convention.

Article 14

The English and French versions of the text of this Convention are equally authoritative.

INTERNATIONAL LABOUR ORGANISATION CONVENTION (NO 154) CONCERNING THE PROMOTION OF COLLECTIVE BARGAINING (1981)

NOTES

This Convention was adopted on 19 June 1981 and came into force on 11 August 1983. As of 15 May 2019, this Convention has not been ratified by the UK.

PART I. SCOPE AND DEFINITIONS

[5.9]

Article 1

1. This Convention applies to all branches of economic activity.
2. The extent to which the guarantees provided for in this Convention apply to the armed forces and the police may be determined by national laws or regulations or national practice.
3. As regards the public service, special modalities of application of this Convention may be fixed by national laws or regulations or national practice.

Article 2

For the purpose of this Convention the term ***collective bargaining*** extends to all negotiations which take place between an employer, a group of employers or one or more employers' organisations, on the one hand, and one or more workers' organisations, on the other, for—

(a) determining working conditions and terms of employment; and/or
(b) regulating relations between employers and workers; and/or
(c) regulating relations between employers or their organisations and a workers' organisation or workers' organisations.

Article 3

1. Where national law or practice recognises the existence of workers' representatives as defined in Article 3, subparagraph (b), of the Workers' Representatives Convention, 1971, national law or practice may determine the extent to which the term ***collective bargaining*** shall also extend, for the purpose of this Convention, to negotiations with these representatives.
2. Where, in pursuance of paragraph 1 of this Article, the term ***collective bargaining*** also includes negotiations with the workers' representatives referred to in that paragraph, appropriate measures shall be taken, wherever necessary, to ensure that the existence of these representatives is not used to undermine the position of the workers' organisations concerned.

PART II. METHODS OF APPLICATION

[5.10]
Article 4

The provisions of this Convention shall, in so far as they are not otherwise made effective by means of collective agreements, arbitration awards or in such other manner as may be consistent with national practice, be given effect by national laws or regulations.

PART III. PROMOTION OF COLLECTIVE BARGAINING

[5.11]
Article 5

1. Measures adapted to national conditions shall be taken to promote collective bargaining.
2. The aims of the measures referred to in paragraph 1 of this Article shall be the following:
(a) collective bargaining should be made possible for all employers and all groups of workers in the branches of activity covered by this Convention;
(b) collective bargaining should be progressively extended to all matters covered by subparagraphs (a), (b) and (c) of Article 2 of this Convention;
(c) the establishment of rules of procedure agreed between employers' and workers' organisations should be encouraged;
(d) collective bargaining should not be hampered by the absence of rules governing the procedure to be used or by the inadequacy or inappropriateness of such rules;
(e) bodies and procedures for the settlement of labour disputes should be so conceived as to contribute to the promotion of collective bargaining.

Article 6

The provisions of this Convention do not preclude the operation of industrial relations systems in which collective bargaining takes place within the framework of conciliation and/or arbitration machinery or institutions, in which machinery or institutions the parties to the collective bargaining process voluntarily participate.

Article 7

Measures taken by public authorities to encourage and promote the development of collective bargaining shall be the subject of prior consultation and, whenever possible, agreement between public authorities and employers' and workers' organisations.

Article 8

The measures taken with a view to promoting collective bargaining shall not be so conceived or applied as to hamper the freedom of collective bargaining.

PART IV. FINAL PROVISIONS

[5.12]
Article 9

This Convention does not revise any existing Convention or Recommendation.

Article 10

The formal ratifications of this Convention shall be communicated to the Director-General of the International Labour Office for registration.

Article 11

1. This Convention shall be binding only upon those Members of the International Labour Organisation whose ratifications have been registered with the Director-General.
2. It shall come into force twelve months after the date on which the ratifications of two Members have been registered with the Director-General.

3. Thereafter, this Convention shall come into force for any Member twelve months after the date on which its ratification has been registered.

Article 12
1. A Member which has ratified this Convention may denounce it after the expiration of ten years from the date on which the Convention first comes into force, by an act communicated to the Director-General of the International Labour Office for registration. Such denunciation shall not take effect until one year after the date on which it is registered.
2. Each Member which has ratified this Convention and which does not, within the year following the expiration of the period of ten years mentioned in the preceding paragraph, exercise the right of denunciation provided for in this Article, will be bound for another period of ten years and, thereafter, may denounce this Convention at the expiration of each period of ten years under the terms provided for in this Article.

Article 13
1. The Director-General of the International Labour Office shall notify all Members of the International Labour Organisation of the registration of all ratifications and denunciations communicated to him by the Members of the Organisation.
2. When notifying the Members of the Organisation of the registration of the second ratification communicated to him, the Director-General shall draw the attention of the Members of the Organisation to the date upon which the Convention will come into force.

Article 14
The Director-General of the International Labour Office shall communicate to the Secretary-General of the United Nations for registration in accordance with Article 102 of the Charter of the United Nations full particulars of all ratifications and acts of denunciation registered by him in accordance with the provisions of the preceding Articles.

Article 15
At such times as it may consider necessary the Governing Body of the International Labour Office shall present to the General Conference a report on the working of this Convention and shall examine the desirability of placing on the agenda of the Conference the question of its revision in whole or in part.

Article 16
1. Should the Conference adopt a new Convention revising this Convention in whole or in part, then, unless the new Convention otherwise provides:
   (a) the ratification by a Member of the new revising Convention shall ipso jure involve the immediate denunciation of this Convention, notwithstanding the provisions of Article 12 above, if and when the new revising Convention shall have come into force;
   (b) as from the date when the new revising Convention comes into force this Convention shall cease to be open to ratification by the Members.
2. This Convention shall in any case remain in force in its actual form and content for those Members which have ratified it but have not ratified the revising Convention.

Article 17
The English and French versions of the text of this Convention are equally authoritative.

INTERNATIONAL LABOUR ORGANISATION CONVENTION (NO 158) CONCERNING TERMINATION OF EMPLOYMENT AT THE INITIATIVE OF THE EMPLOYER (1982)

NOTES

This Convention was adopted on 22 June 1982 and came into force on 23 November 1985. As of 15 May 2019, this Convention has not been ratified by the UK.

PART I. METHODS OF IMPLEMENTATION, SCOPE AND DEFINITIONS

[5.13]
Article 1
The provisions of this Convention shall, in so far as they are not otherwise made effective by means of collective agreements, arbitration awards or court decisions or in such other manner as may be consistent with national practice, be given effect by laws or regulations.

Article 2
1. This Convention applies to all branches of economic activity and to all employed persons.

2. A Member may exclude the following categories of employed persons from all or some of the provisions of this Convention:

(a) workers engaged under a contract of employment for a specified period of time or a specified task;

(b) workers serving a period of probation or a qualifying period of employment, determined in advance and of reasonable duration;

(c) workers engaged on a casual basis for a short period.

3. Adequate safeguards shall be provided against recourse to contracts of employment for a specified period of time the aim of which is to avoid the protection resulting from this Convention.

4. In so far as necessary, measures may be taken by the competent authority or through the appropriate machinery in a country, after consultation with the organisations of employers and workers concerned, where such exist, to exclude from the application of this Convention or certain provisions thereof categories of employed persons whose terms and conditions of employment are governed by special arrangements which as a whole provide protection that is at least equivalent to the protection afforded under the Convention.

5. In so far as necessary, measures may be taken by the competent authority or through the appropriate machinery in a country, after consultation with the organisations of employers and workers concerned, where such exist, to exclude from the application of this Convention or certain provisions thereof other limited categories of employed persons in respect of which special problems of a substantial nature arise in the light of the particular conditions of employment of the workers concerned or the size or nature of the undertaking that employs them.

6. Each Member which ratifies this Convention shall list in the first report on the application of the Convention submitted under Article 22 of the Constitution of the International Labour Organisation any categories which may have been excluded in pursuance of paragraphs 4 and 5 of this Article, giving the reasons for such exclusion, and shall state in subsequent reports the position of its law and practice regarding the categories excluded, and the extent to which effect has been given or is proposed to be given to the Convention in respect of such categories.

Article 3

For the purpose of this Convention the terms ***termination*** and ***termination of employment*** mean termination of employment at the initiative of the employer.

PART II. STANDARD'S OF GENERAL APPLICATION

DIVISION A. JUSTIFICATION FOR TERMINATION

[5.14]

Article 4

The employment of a worker shall not be terminated unless there is a valid reason for such termination connected with the capacity or conduct of the worker or based on the operational requirements of the undertaking, establishment or service.

Article 5

The following, inter alia, shall not constitute valid reasons for termination:

(a) union membership or participation in union activities outside working hours or, with the consent of the employer, within working hours;

(b) seeking office as, or acting or having acted in the capacity of, a workers' representative;

(c) the filing of a complaint or the participation in proceedings against an employer involving alleged violation of laws or regulations or recourse to competent administrative authorities;

(d) race, colour, sex, marital status, family responsibilities, pregnancy, religion, political opinion, national extraction or social origin;

(e) absence from work during maternity leave.

Article 6

1. Temporary absence from work because of illness or injury shall not constitute a valid reason for termination.

2. The definition of what constitutes temporary absence from work, the extent to which medical certification shall be required and possible limitations to the application of paragraph 1 of this Article shall be determined in accordance with the methods of implementation referred to in Article 1 of this Convention.

DIVISION B. PROCEDURE PRIOR TO OR AT THE TIME OF TERMINATION

Article 7

The employment of a worker shall not be terminated for reasons related to the worker's conduct or performance before he is provided an opportunity to defend himself against the allegations made, unless the employer cannot reasonably be expected to provide this opportunity.

DIVISION C. PROCEDURE OF APPEAL AGAINST TERMINATION

Article 8

1. A worker who considers that his employment has been unjustifiably terminated shall be entitled to appeal against that termination to an impartial body, such as a court, labour tribunal, arbitration committee or arbitrator.
2. Where termination has been authorised by a competent authority the application of paragraph 1 of this Article may be varied according to national law and practice.
3. A worker may be deemed to have waived his right to appeal against the termination of his employment if he has not exercised that right within a reasonable period of time after termination.

Article 9

1. The bodies referred to in Article 8 of this Convention shall be empowered to examine the reasons given for the termination and the other circumstances relating to the case and to render a decision on whether the termination was justified.
2. In order for the worker not to have to bear alone the burden of proving that the termination was not justified, the methods of implementation referred to in Article 1 of this Convention shall provide for one or the other or both of the following possibilities:
   (a) the burden of proving the existence of a valid reason for the termination as defined in Article 4 of this Convention shall rest on the employer;
   (b) the bodies referred to in Article 8 of this Convention shall be empowered to reach a conclusion on the reason for the termination having regard to the evidence provided by the parties and according to procedures provided for by national law and practice.
3. In cases of termination stated to be for reasons based on the operational requirements of the undertaking, establishment or service, the bodies referred to in Article 8 of this Convention shall be empowered to determine whether the termination was indeed for these reasons, but the extent to which they shall also be empowered to decide whether these reasons are sufficient to justify that termination shall be determined by the methods of implementation referred to in Article 1 of this Convention.

Article 10

If the bodies referred to in Article 8 of this Convention find that termination is unjustified and if they are not empowered or do not find it practicable, in accordance with national law and practice, to declare the termination invalid and/or order or propose reinstatement of the worker, they shall be empowered to order payment of adequate compensation or such other relief as may be deemed appropriate.

DIVISION D. PERIOD OF NOTICE

Article 11

A worker whose employment is to be terminated shall be entitled to a reasonable period of notice or compensation in lieu thereof, unless he is guilty of serious misconduct, that is, misconduct of such a nature that it would be unreasonable to require the employer to continue his employment during the notice period.

DIVISION E. SEVERANCE ALLOWANCE AND OTHER INCOME PROTECTION

Article 12

1. A worker whose employment has been terminated shall be entitled, in accordance with national law and practice, to-
   (a) a severance allowance or other separation benefits, the amount of which shall be based inter alia on length of service and the level of wages, and paid directly by the employer or by a fund constituted by employers' contributions; or
   (b) benefits from unemployment insurance or assistance or other forms of social security, such as old-age or invalidity benefits, under the normal conditions to which such benefits are subject; or
   (c) a combination of such allowance and benefits.
2. A worker who does not fulfil the qualifying conditions for unemployment insurance or assistance under a scheme of general scope need not be paid any allowance or benefit referred to in paragraph 1, subparagraph (a), of this Article solely because he is not receiving an unemployment benefit under paragraph 1, subparagraph (b).
3. Provision may be made by the methods of implementation referred to in Article 1 of this Convention for loss of entitlement to the allowance or benefits referred to in paragraph 1, subparagraph (a), of this Article in the event of termination for serious misconduct.

PART III. SUPPLEMENTARY PROVISIONS CONCERNING TERMINATIONS OF EMPLOYMENT FOR ECONOMIC, TECHNOLOGICAL, STRUCTURAL OR SIMILAR REASONS

DIVISION A. CONSULTATION OF WORKERS' REPRESENTATIVES

[5.15]
Article 13

1. When the employer contemplates terminations for reasons of an economic, technological, structural or similar nature, the employer shall:
   (a) provide the workers' representatives concerned in good time with relevant information including the reasons for the terminations contemplated, the number and categories of workers likely to be affected and the period over which the terminations are intended to be carried out;
   (b) give, in accordance with national law and practice, the workers' representatives concerned, as early as possible, an opportunity for consultation on measures to be taken to avert or to minimise the terminations and measures to mitigate the adverse effects of any terminations on the workers concerned such as finding alternative employment.
2. The applicability of paragraph 1 of this Article may be limited by the methods of implementation referred to in Article 1 of this Convention to cases in which the number of workers whose termination of employment is contemplated is at least a specified number or percentage of the workforce.
3. For the purposes of this Article the term ***the workers' representatives concerned*** means the workers' representatives recognised as such by national law or practice, in conformity with the Workers' Representatives Convention, 1971.

DIVISION B. NOTIFICATION TO THE COMPETENT AUTHORITY

Article 14

1. When the employer contemplates terminations for reasons of an economic, technological, structural or similar nature, he shall notify, in accordance with national law and practice, the competent authority thereof as early as possible, giving relevant information, including a written statement of the reasons for the terminations, the number and categories of workers likely to be affected and the period over which the terminations are intended to be carried out.
2. National laws or regulations may limit the applicability of paragraph 1 of this Article to cases in which the number of workers whose termination of employment is contemplated is at least a specified number or percentage of the workforce.
3. The employer shall notify the competent authority of the terminations referred to in paragraph 1 of this Article a minimum period of time before carrying out the terminations, such period to be specified by national laws or regulations.

PART IV. FINAL PROVISIONS

[5.16]
Article 15

The formal ratifications of this Convention shall be communicated to the Director-General of the International Labour Office for registration.

Article 16

1. This Convention shall be binding only upon those Members of the International Labour Organisation whose ratifications have been registered with the Director-General.
2. It shall come into force twelve months after the date on which the ratifications of two Members have been registered with the Director-General.
3. Thereafter, this Convention shall come into force for any Member twelve months after the date on which its ratification has been registered.

Article 17

1. A Member which has ratified this Convention may denounce it after the expiration of ten years from the date on which the Convention first comes into force, by an act communicated to the Director-General of the International Labour Office for registration. Such denunciation shall not take effect until one year after the date on which it is registered.
2. Each Member which has ratified this Convention and which does not, within the year following the expiration of the period of ten years mentioned in the preceding paragraph, exercise the right of denunciation provided for in this Article, will be bound for another period of ten years and, thereafter, may denounce this Convention at the expiration of each period of ten years under the terms provided for in this Article.

Article 18

1. The Director-General of the International Labour Office shall notify all Members of the International Labour Organisation of the registration of all ratifications and denunciations communicated to him by the Members of the Organisation.

2. When notifying the Members of the Organisation of the registration of the second ratification communicated to him, the Director-General shall draw the attention of the Members of the Organisation to the date upon which the Convention will come into force.

Article 19

The Director-General of the International Labour Office shall communicate to the Secretary-General of the United Nations for registration in accordance with article 102 of the Charter of the United Nations full particulars of all ratifications and acts of denunciation registered by him in accordance with the provisions of the preceding Articles.

Article 20

At such times as it may consider necessary the Governing Body of the International Labour Office shall present to the General Conference a report on the working of this Convention and shall examine the desirability of placing on the agenda of the Conference the question of its revision in whole or in part.

Article 21

1. Should the Conference adopt a new Convention revising this Convention in whole or in part, then, unless the new Convention otherwise provides-

- (a) the ratification by a Member of the new revising Convention shall ipso jure involve the immediate denunciation of this Convention, notwithstanding the provisions of Article 17 above, if and when the new revising Convention shall have come into force;
- (b) as from the date when the new revising Convention comes into force this Convention shall cease to be open to ratification by the Members.

2. This Convention shall in any case remain in force in its actual form and content for those Members which have ratified it but have not ratified the revising Convention.

Article 22

The English and French versions of the text of this Convention are equally authoritative.

INTERNATIONAL LABOUR ORGANISATION CONVENTION (NO 175) CONCERNING PART-TIME WORK (1994)

NOTES

This Convention was adopted on 24 June 1994 and came into force on 28 February 1998. As of 15 May 2019, this Convention has not been ratified by the UK.

[5.17]

Article 1

For the purposes of this Convention:

- (a) the term ***part-time worker*** means an employed person whose normal hours of work are less than those of comparable full-time workers;
- (b) the normal hours of work referred to in subparagraph (a) may be calculated weekly or on average over a given period of employment;
- (c) the term ***comparable full-time worker*** refers to a full-time worker who:
  - (i) has the same type of employment relationship;
  - (ii) is engaged in the same or a similar type of work or occupation; and
  - (iii) is employed in the same establishment or, when there is no comparable full-time worker in that establishment, in the same enterprise or, when there is no comparable full-time worker in that enterprise, in the same branch of activity, as the part-time worker concerned;
- (d) full-time workers affected by partial unemployment, that is by a collective and temporary reduction in their normal hours of work for economic, technical or structural reasons, are not considered to be part-time workers.

Article 2

This Convention does not affect more favourable provisions applicable to part-time workers under other international labour Conventions.

Article 3

1. This Convention applies to all part-time workers, it being understood that a Member may, after consulting the representative organisations of employers and workers concerned, exclude wholly or partly from its scope particular categories of workers or of establishments when its application to them would raise particular problems of a substantial nature.

2. Each Member having ratified this Convention which avails itself of the possibility afforded in the preceding paragraph shall, in its reports on the application of the Convention under article 22 of the Constitution of the International Labour Organisation, indicate any particular category of workers or of establishments thus excluded and the reasons why this exclusion was or is still judged necessary.

Article 4

Measures shall be taken to ensure that part-time workers receive the same protection as that accorded to comparable full-time workers in respect of:

(a) the right to organize, the right to bargain collectively and the right to act as workers' representatives;

(b) occupational safety and health;

(c) discrimination in employment and occupation.

Article 5

Measures appropriate to national law and practice shall be taken to ensure that part-time workers do not, solely because they work part time, receive a basic wage which, calculated proportionately on an hourly, performance-related, or piece-rate basis, is lower than the basic wage of comparable full-time workers, calculated according to the same method.

Article 6

Statutory social security schemes which are based on occupational activity shall be adapted so that part-time workers enjoy conditions equivalent to those of comparable full-time workers; these conditions may be determined in proportion to hours of work, contributions or earnings, or through other methods consistent with national law and practice.

Article 7

Measures shall be taken to ensure that part-time workers receive conditions equivalent to those of comparable full-time workers in the fields of:

(a) maternity protection;

(b) termination of employment;

(c) paid annual leave and paid public holidays; and

(d) sick leave,

it being understood that pecuniary entitlements may be determined in proportion to hours of work or earnings.

Article 8

1. Part-time workers whose hours of work or earnings are below specified thresholds may be excluded by a Member:

(a) from the scope of any of the statutory social security schemes referred to in Article 6, except in regard to employment injury benefits;

(b) from the scope of any of the measures taken in the fields covered by Article 7, except in regard to maternity protection measures other than those provided under statutory social security schemes.

2. The thresholds referred to in paragraph 1 shall be sufficiently low as not to exclude an unduly large percentage of part-time workers.

3. A Member which avails itself of the possibility provided for in paragraph 1 above shall:

(a) periodically review the thresholds in force;

(b) in its reports on the application of the Convention under article 22 of the Constitution of the International Labour Organisation, indicate the thresholds in force, the reasons therefor and whether consideration is being given to the progressive extension of protection to the workers excluded.

4. The most representative organisations of employers and workers shall be consulted on the establishment, review and revision of the thresholds referred to in this Article.

Article 9

1. Measures shall be taken to facilitate access to productive and freely chosen part-time work which meets the needs of both employers and workers, provided that the protection referred to in Articles 4 to 7 is ensured.

2. These measures shall include:

(a) the review of laws and regulations that may prevent or discourage recourse to or acceptance of part-time work;

(b) the use of employment services, where they exist, to identify and publicize possibilities for part-time work in their information and placement activities;

(c) special attention, in employment policies, to the needs and preferences of specific groups such as the unemployed, workers with family responsibilities, older workers, workers with disabilities and workers undergoing education or training.

3. These measures may also include research and dissemination of information on the degree to which part-time work responds to the economic and social aims of employers and workers.

Article 10
Where appropriate, measures shall be taken to ensure that transfer from full-time to part-time work or vice versa is voluntary, in accordance with national law and practice.

Article 11
The provisions of this Convention shall be implemented by laws or regulations, except in so far as effect is given to them by means of collective agreements or in any other manner consistent with national practice. The most representative organisations of employers and workers shall be consulted before any such laws or regulations are adopted.

Article 12
The formal ratifications of this Convention shall be communicated to the Director-General of the International Labour Office for registration.

Article 13
1. This Convention shall be binding only upon those Members of the International Labour Organisation whose ratifications have been registered with the Director-General.
2. It shall come into force 12 months after the date on which the ratifications of two Members have been registered with the Director-General.
3. Thereafter, this Convention shall come into force for any Member 12 months after the date on which its ratification has been registered.

Article 14
1. A Member which has ratified this Convention may denounce it after the expiration of ten years from the date on which the Convention first comes into force, by an act communicated to the Director-General of the International Labour Office for registration. Such denunciation shall not take effect until one year after the date on which it is registered.
2. Each Member which has ratified this Convention and which does not, within the year following the expiration of the period of ten years mentioned in the preceding paragraph, exercise the right of denunciation provided for in this Article, will be bound for another period of ten years and, thereafter, may denounce this Convention at the expiration of each period of ten years under the terms provided for in this Article.

Article 15
1. The Director-General of the International Labour Office shall notify all Members of the International Labour Organisation of the registration of all ratifications and denunciations communicated to him by the Members of the Organisation.
2. When notifying the Members of the Organisation of the registration of the second ratification communicated to him, the Director-General shall draw the attention of the Members of the Organisation to the date upon which the Convention will come into force.

Article 16
The Director-General of the International Labour Office shall communicate to the Secretary-General of the United Nations for registration in accordance with Article 102 of the Charter of the United Nations full particulars of all ratifications and acts of denunciations registered by him in accordance with the provisions of the preceding Articles.

Article 17
At such times as it may consider necessary, the Governing Body of the International Labour Office shall present to the General Conference a report on the working of this Convention and shall examine the desirability of placing on the agenda of the Conference the question of its revision in whole or in part.

Article 18
1. Should the Conference adopt a new Convention revising this Convention in whole or in part, then, unless the new Convention otherwise provides–
   (a) the ratification by a Member of the new revising Convention shall ipso jure involve the immediate denunciation of this Convention, notwithstanding the provisions of Article 14 above, if and when the new revising Convention shall have come into force;
   (b) as from the date when the new revising Convention comes into force this Convention shall cease to be open to ratification by the Members.
2. This Convention shall in any case remain in force in its actual form and content for those Members which have ratified it but have not ratified the revising Convention.

Article 19
The English and French versions of the text of this Convention are equally authoritative.

EUROPEAN SOCIAL CHARTER (1996)

(Revised)

Strasbourg, 3.V.1996

NOTES

The revised European Social Charter was adopted by the Council of Ministers of the Council of Europe on 3 May 1996 and came into force on 1 July 1999. It was signed by the United Kingdom on 7 November 1997 but, as at 15 May 2019, had not been ratified (although the UK did ratify the original 1961 Charter on 11 July 1962). For provisions as to commencement see Art K at **[5.24]**.

[5.18]

PREAMBLE

The governments signatory hereto, being members of the Council of Europe,

Considering that the aim of the Council of Europe is the achievement of greater unity between its members for the purpose of safeguarding and realising the ideals and principles which are their common heritage and of facilitating their economic and social progress, in particular by the maintenance and further realisation of human rights and fundamental freedoms;

Considering that in the European Convention for the Protection of Human Rights and Fundamental Freedoms signed at Rome on 4 November 1950, and the Protocols thereto, the member States of the Council of Europe agreed to secure to their populations the civil and political rights and freedoms therein specified;

Considering that in the European Social Charter opened for signature in Turin on 18 October 1961 and the Protocols thereto, the member States of the Council of Europe agreed to secure to their populations the social rights specified therein in order to improve their standard of living and their social well-being;

Recalling that the Ministerial Conference on Human Rights held in Rome on 5 November 1990 stressed the need, on the one hand, to preserve the indivisible nature of all human rights, be they civil, political, economic, social or cultural and, on the other hand, to give the European Social Charter fresh impetus;

Resolved, as was decided during the Ministerial Conference held in Turin on 21 and 22 October 1991, to update and adapt the substantive contents of the Charter in order to take account in particular of the fundamental social changes which have occurred since the text was adopted;

Recognising the advantage of embodying in a Revised Charter, designed progressively to take the place of the European Social Charter, the rights guaranteed by the Charter as amended, the rights guaranteed by the Additional Protocol of 1988 and to add new rights,

Have agreed as follows—

PART I

[5.19]

The Parties accept as the aim of their policy, to be pursued by all appropriate means both national and international in character, the attainment of conditions in which the following rights and principles may be effectively realised—

1. Everyone shall have the opportunity to earn his living in an occupation freely entered upon.
2. All workers have the right to just conditions of work.
3. All workers have the right to safe and healthy working conditions.
4. All workers have the right to a fair remuneration sufficient for a decent standard of living for themselves and their families.
5. All workers and employers have the right to freedom of association in national or international organisations for the protection of their economic and social interests.
6. All workers and employers have the right to bargain collectively.
7. Children and young persons have the right to a special protection against the physical and moral hazards to which they are exposed.
8. Employed women, in case of maternity, have the right to a special protection.
9. Everyone has the right to appropriate facilities for vocational guidance with a view to helping him choose an occupation suited to his personal aptitude and interests.
10. Everyone has the right to appropriate facilities for vocational training.
11. Everyone has the right to benefit from any measures enabling him to enjoy the highest possible standard of health attainable.
12. All workers and their dependents have the right to social security.
13. Anyone without adequate resources has the right to social and medical assistance.
14. Everyone has the right to benefit from social welfare services.
15. Disabled persons have the right to independence, social integration and participation in the life of the community.
16. The family as a fundamental unit of society has the right to appropriate social, legal and economic protection to ensure its full development.
17. Children and young persons have the right to appropriate social, legal and economic protection.
18. The nationals of any one of the Parties have the right to engage in any gainful occupation in the territory of any one of the others on a footing of equality with the nationals of the latter, subject to restrictions based on cogent economic or social reasons.

19. Migrant workers who are nationals of a Party and their families have the right to protection and assistance in the territory of any other Party.
20. All workers have the right to equal opportunities and equal treatment in matters of employment and occupation without discrimination on the grounds of sex.
21. Workers have the right to be informed and to be consulted within the undertaking.
22. Workers have the right to take part in the determination and improvement of the working conditions and working environment in the undertaking.
23. Every elderly person has the right to social protection.
24. All workers have the right to protection in cases of termination of employment.
25. All workers have the right to protection of their claims in the event of the insolvency of their employer.
26. All workers have the right to dignity at work.
27. All persons with family responsibilities and who are engaged or wish to engage in employment have a right to do so without being subject to discrimination and as far as possible without conflict between their employment and family responsibilities.
28. Workers' representatives in undertakings have the right to protection against acts prejudicial to them and should be afforded appropriate facilities to carry out their functions.
29. All workers have the right to be informed and consulted in collective redundancy procedures.
30. Everyone has the right to protection against poverty and social exclusion.
31. Everyone has the right to housing.

PART II

[5.20]
The Parties undertake, as provided for in Part III, to consider themselves bound by the obligations laid down in the following articles and paragraphs.

Article 1
The right to work
With a view to ensuring the effective exercise of the right to work, the Parties undertake—

1. to accept as one of their primary aims and responsibilities the achievement and maintenance of as high and stable a level of employment as possible, with a view to the attainment of full employment;
2. to protect effectively the right of the worker to earn his living in an occupation freely entered upon;
3. to establish or maintain free employment services for all workers;
4. to provide or promote appropriate vocational guidance, training and rehabilitation.

Article 2
The right to just conditions of work
With a view to ensuring the effective exercise of the right to just conditions of work, the Parties undertake—

1. to provide for reasonable daily and weekly working hours, the working week to be progressively reduced to the extent that the increase of productivity and other relevant factors permit;
2. to provide for public holidays with pay;
3. to provide for a minimum of four weeks' annual holiday with pay;
4. to eliminate risks in inherently dangerous or unhealthy occupations, and where it has not yet been possible to eliminate or reduce sufficiently these risks, to provide for either a reduction of working hours or additional paid holidays for workers engaged in such occupations;
5. to ensure a weekly rest period which shall, as far as possible, coincide with the day recognised by tradition or custom in the country or region concerned as a day of rest;
6. to ensure that workers are informed in written form, as soon as possible, and in any event not later than two months after the date of commencing their employment, of the essential aspects of the contract or employment relationship;
7. to ensure that workers performing night work benefit from measures which take account of the special nature of the work.

Article 3
The right to safe and healthy working conditions
With a view to ensuring the effective exercise of the right to safe and healthy working conditions, the Parties undertake, in consultation with employers' and workers' organisations—

1. to formulate, implement and periodically review a coherent national policy on occupational safety, occupational health and the working environment. The primary aim of this policy shall be to improve occupational safety and health and to prevent accidents and injury to health arising out of, linked with or occurring in the course of work, particularly by minimising the causes of hazards inherent in the working environment;
2. to issue safety and health regulations;
3. to provide for the enforcement of such regulations by measures of supervision;
4. to promote the progressive development of occupational health services for all workers with essentially preventive and advisory functions.

Article 4
The right to a fair remuneration

With a view to ensuring the effective exercise of the right to a fair remuneration, the Parties undertake—

1. to recognise the right of workers to a remuneration such as will give them and their families a decent standard of living;
2. to recognise the right of workers to an increased rate of remuneration for overtime work, subject to exceptions in particular cases;
3. to recognise the right of men and women workers to equal pay for work of equal value;
4. to recognise the right of all workers to a reasonable period of notice for termination of employment;
5. to permit deductions from wages only under conditions and to the extent prescribed by national laws or regulations or fixed by collective agreements or arbitration awards.

The exercise of these rights shall be achieved by freely concluded collective agreements, by statutory wage-fixing machinery, or by other means appropriate to national conditions.

Article 5
The right to organise

With a view to ensuring or promoting the freedom of workers and employers to form local, national or international organisations for the protection of their economic and social interests and to join those organisations, the Parties undertake that national law shall not be such as to impair, nor shall it be so applied as to impair, this freedom. The extent to which the guarantees provided for in this article shall apply to the police shall be determined by national laws or regulations. The principle governing the application to the members of the armed forces of these guarantees and the extent to which they shall apply to persons in this category shall equally be determined by national laws or regulations.

Article 6
The right to bargain collectively

With a view to ensuring the effective exercise of the right to bargain collectively, the Parties undertake—

1. to promote joint consultation between workers and employers;
2. to promote, where necessary and appropriate, machinery for voluntary negotiations between employers or employers' organisations and workers' organisations, with a view to the regulation of terms and conditions of employment by means of collective agreements;
3. to promote the establishment and use of appropriate machinery for conciliation and voluntary arbitration for the settlement of labour disputes;

and recognise—

4. the right of workers and employers to collective action in cases of conflicts of interest, including the right to strike, subject to obligations that might arise out of collective agreements previously entered into.

Article 7
The right of children and young persons to protection

With a view to ensuring the effective exercise of the right of children and young persons to protection, the Parties undertake—

1. to provide that the minimum age of admission to employment shall be 15 years, subject to exceptions for children employed in prescribed light work without harm to their health, morals or education;
2. to provide that the minimum age of admission to employment shall be 18 years with respect to prescribed occupations regarded as dangerous or unhealthy;
3. to provide that persons who are still subject to compulsory education shall not be employed in such work as would deprive them of the full benefit of their education;
4. to provide that the working hours of persons under 18 years of age shall be limited in accordance with the needs of their development, and particularly with their need for vocational training;
5. to recognise the right of young workers and apprentices to a fair wage or other appropriate allowances;
6. to provide that the time spent by young persons in vocational training during the normal working hours with the consent of the employer shall be treated as forming part of the working day;
7. to provide that employed persons of under 18 years of age shall be entitled to a minimum of four weeks' annual holiday with pay;
8. to provide that persons under 18 years of age shall not be employed in night work with the exception of certain occupations provided for by national laws or regulations;
9. to provide that persons under 18 years of age employed in occupations prescribed by national laws or regulations shall be subject to regular medical control;
10. to ensure special protection against physical and moral dangers to which children and young persons are exposed, and particularly against those resulting directly or indirectly from their work.

Article 8
The right of employed women to protection of maternity
With a view to ensuring the effective exercise of the right of employed women to the protection of maternity, the Parties undertake—

1. to provide either by paid leave, by adequate social security benefits or by benefits from public funds for employed women to take leave before and after childbirth up to a total of at least fourteen weeks;
2. to consider it as unlawful for an employer to give a woman notice of dismissal during the period from the time she notifies her employer that she is pregnant until the end of her maternity leave, or to give her notice of dismissal at such a time that the notice would expire during such a period;
3. to provide that mothers who are nursing their infants shall be entitled to sufficient time off for this purpose;
4. to regulate the employment in night work of pregnant women, women who have recently given birth and women nursing their infants;
5. to prohibit the employment of pregnant women, women who have recently given birth or who are nursing their infants in underground mining and all other work which is unsuitable by reason of its dangerous, unhealthy or arduous nature and to take appropriate measures to protect the employment rights of these women.

Article 9
The right to vocational guidance
With a view to ensuring the effective exercise of the right to vocational guidance, the Parties undertake to provide or promote, as necessary, a service which will assist all persons, including the handicapped, to solve problems related to occupational choice and progress, with due regard to the individual's characteristics and their relation to occupational opportunity: this assistance should be available free of charge, both to young persons, including schoolchildren, and to adults.

Article 10
The right to vocational training
With a view to ensuring the effective exercise of the right to vocational training, the Parties undertake—

1. to provide or promote, as necessary, the technical and vocational training of all persons, including the handicapped, in consultation with employers' and workers' organisations, and to grant facilities for access to higher technical and university education, based solely on individual aptitude;
2. to provide or promote a system of apprenticeship and other systematic arrangements for training young boys and girls in their various employments;
3. to provide or promote, as necessary—
   (a) adequate and readily available training facilities for adult workers;
   (b) special facilities for the retraining of adult workers needed as a result of technological development or new trends in employment;
4. to provide or promote, as necessary, special measures for the retraining and reintegration of the long-term unemployed;
5. to encourage the full utilisation of the facilities provided by appropriate measures such as—
   (a) reducing or abolishing any fees or charges;
   (b) granting financial assistance in appropriate cases;
   (c) including in the normal working hours time spent on supplementary training taken by the worker, at the request of his employer, during employment;
   (d) ensuring, through adequate supervision, in consultation with the employers' and workers' organisations, the efficiency of apprenticeship and other training arrangements for young workers, and the adequate protection of young workers generally.

Article 11
The right to protection of health
With a view to ensuring the effective exercise of the right to protection of health, the Parties undertake, either directly or in co-operation with public or private organisations, to take appropriate measures designed *inter alia*—

1. to remove as far as possible the causes of ill-health;
2. to provide advisory and educational facilities for the promotion of health and the encouragement of individual responsibility in matters of health;
3. to prevent as far as possible epidemic, endemic and other diseases, as well as accidents.

Article 12
The right to social security
With a view to ensuring the effective exercise of the right to social security, the Parties undertake—

1. to establish or maintain a system of social security;
2. to maintain the social security system at a satisfactory level at least equal to that necessary for the ratification of the European Code of Social Security;
3. to endeavour to raise progressively the system of social security to a higher level;
4. to take steps, by the conclusion of appropriate bilateral and multilateral agreements or by other means, and subject to the conditions laid down in such agreements, in order to ensure—

(a) equal treatment with their own nationals of the nationals of other Parties in respect of social security rights, including the retention of benefits arising out of social security legislation, whatever movements the persons protected may undertake between the territories of the Parties;

(b) the granting, maintenance and resumption of social security rights by such means as the accumulation of insurance or employment periods completed under the legislation of each of the Parties.

Article 13
The right to social and medical assistance

With a view to ensuring the effective exercise of the right to social and medical assistance, the Parties undertake—

1. to ensure that any person who is without adequate resources and who is unable to secure such resources either by his own efforts or from other sources, in particular by benefits under a social security scheme, be granted adequate assistance, and, in case of sickness, the care necessitated by his condition;
2. to ensure that persons receiving such assistance shall not, for that reason, suffer from a diminution of their political or social rights;
3. to provide that everyone may receive by appropriate public or private services such advice and personal help as may be required to prevent, to remove, or to alleviate personal or family want;
4. to apply the provisions referred to in paragraphs 1, 2 and 3 of this article on an equal footing with their nationals to nationals of other Parties lawfully within their territories, in accordance with their obligations under the European Convention on Social and Medical Assistance, signed at Paris on 11 December 1953.

Article 14
The right to benefit from social welfare services

With a view to ensuring the effective exercise of the right to benefit from social welfare services, the Parties undertake—

1. to promote or provide services which, by using methods of social work, would contribute to the welfare and development of both individuals and groups in the community, and to their adjustment to the social environment;
2. to encourage the participation of individuals and voluntary or other organisations in the establishment and maintenance of such services.

Article 15
The right of persons with disabilities to independence, social integration and participation in the life of the community

With a view to ensuring to persons with disabilities, irrespective of age and the nature and origin of their disabilities, the effective exercise of the right to independence, social integration and participation in the life of the community, the Parties undertake, in particular—

1. to take the necessary measures to provide persons with disabilities with guidance, education and vocational training in the framework of general schemes wherever possible or, where this is not possible, through specialised bodies, public or private;
2. to promote their access to employment through all measures tending to encourage employers to hire and keep in employment persons with disabilities in the ordinary working environment and to adjust the working conditions to the needs of the disabled or, where this is not possible by reason of the disability, by arranging for or creating sheltered employment according to the level of disability. In certain cases, such measures may require recourse to specialised placement and support services;
3. to promote their full social integration and participation in the life of the community in particular through measures, including technical aids, aiming to overcome barriers to communication and mobility and enabling access to transport, housing, cultural activities and leisure.

Article 16
The right of the family to social, legal and economic protection

With a view to ensuring the necessary conditions for the full development of the family, which is a fundamental unit of society, the Parties undertake to promote the economic, legal and social protection of family life by such means as social and family benefits, fiscal arrangements, provision of family housing, benefits for the newly married and other appropriate means.

Article 17
The right of children and young persons to social, legal and economic protection

With a view to ensuring the effective exercise of the right of children and young persons to grow up in an environment which encourages the full development of their personality and of their physical and mental capacities, the Parties undertake, either directly or in co-operation with public and private organisations, to take all appropriate and necessary measures designed—

(a) to ensure that children and young persons, taking account of the rights and duties of their parents, have the care, the assistance, the education and the training they need, in particular by providing for the establishment or maintenance of institutions and services sufficient and adequate for this purpose;

(b) to protect children and young persons against negligence, violence or exploitation;

(c) to provide protection and special aid from the state for children and young persons temporarily or definitively deprived of their family's support;

to provide to children and young persons a free primary and secondary education as well as to encourage regular attendance at schools.

Article 18

The right to engage in a gainful occupation in the territory of other Parties

With a view to ensuring the effective exercise of the right to engage in a gainful occupation in the territory of any other Party, the Parties undertake—

1. to apply existing regulations in a spirit of liberality;
2. to simplify existing formalities and to reduce or abolish chancery dues and other charges payable by foreign workers or their employers;
3. to liberalise, individually or collectively, regulations governing the employment of foreign workers;

and recognise—

4. the right of their nationals to leave the country to engage in a gainful occupation in the territories of the other Parties.

Article 19

The right of migrant workers and their families to protection and assistance

With a view to ensuring the effective exercise of the right of migrant workers and their families to protection and assistance in the territory of any other Party, the Parties undertake—

1. to maintain or to satisfy themselves that there are maintained adequate and free services to assist such workers, particularly in obtaining accurate information, and to take all appropriate steps, so far as national laws and regulations permit, against misleading propaganda relating to emigration and immigration;
2. to adopt appropriate measures within their own jurisdiction to facilitate the departure, journey and reception of such workers and their families, and to provide, within their own jurisdiction, appropriate services for health, medical attention and good hygienic conditions during the journey;
3. to promote co-operation, as appropriate, between social services, public and private, in emigration and immigration countries;
4. to secure for such workers lawfully within their territories, insofar as such matters are regulated by law or regulations or are subject to the control of administrative authorities, treatment not less favourable than that of their own nationals in respect of the following matters—
   (a) remuneration and other employment and working conditions;
   (b) membership of trade unions and enjoyment of the benefits of collective bargaining;
   (c) accommodation;
5. to secure for such workers lawfully within their territories treatment not less favourable than that of their own nationals with regard to employment taxes, dues or contributions payable in respect of employed persons;
6. to facilitate as far as possible the reunion of the family of a foreign worker permitted to establish himself in the territory;
7. to secure for such workers lawfully within their territories treatment not less favourable than that of their own nationals in respect of legal proceedings relating to matters referred to in this article;
8. to secure that such workers lawfully residing within their territories are not expelled unless they endanger national security or offend against public interest or morality;
9. to permit, within legal limits, the transfer of such parts of the earnings and savings of such workers as they may desire;
10. to extend the protection and assistance provided for in this article to self-employed migrants insofar as such measures apply;
11. to promote and facilitate the teaching of the national language of the receiving state or, if there are several, one of these languages, to migrant workers and members of their families;
12. to promote and facilitate, as far as practicable, the teaching of the migrant worker's mother tongue to the children of the migrant worker.

Article 20

The right to equal opportunities and equal treatment in matters of employment and occupation without discrimination on the grounds of sex

With a view to ensuring the effective exercise of the right to equal opportunities and equal treatment in matters of employment and occupation without discrimination on the grounds of sex, the Parties undertake to recognise that right and to take appropriate measures to ensure or promote its application in the following fields—

(a) access to employment, protection against dismissal and occupational reintegration;

(b) vocational guidance, training, retraining and rehabilitation;

(c) terms of employment and working conditions, including remuneration;
(d) career development, including promotion.

Article 21
The right to information and consultation
With a view to ensuring the effective exercise of the right of workers to be informed and consulted within the undertaking, the Parties undertake to adopt or encourage measures enabling workers or their representatives, in accordance with national legislation and practice—
(a) to be informed regularly or at the appropriate time and in a comprehensible way about the economic and financial situation of the undertaking employing them, on the understanding that the disclosure of certain information which could be prejudicial to the undertaking may be refused or subject to confidentiality; and
(b) to be consulted in good time on proposed decisions which could substantially affect the interests of workers, particularly on those decisions which could have an important impact on the employment situation in the undertaking.

Article 22
The right to take part in the determination and improvement of the working conditions and working environment
With a view to ensuring the effective exercise of the right of workers to take part in the determination and improvement of the working conditions and working environment in the undertaking, the Parties undertake to adopt or encourage measures enabling workers or their representatives, in accordance with national legislation and practice, to contribute—
(a) to the determination and the improvement of the working conditions, work organisation and working environment;
(b) to the protection of health and safety within the undertaking;
(c) to the organisation of social and socio-cultural services and facilities within the undertaking;
(d) to the supervision of the observance of regulations on these matters.

Article 23
The right of elderly persons to social protection
With a view to ensuring the effective exercise of the right of elderly persons to social protection, the Parties undertake to adopt or encourage, either directly or in co-operation with public or private organisations, appropriate measures designed in particular—
to enable elderly persons to remain full members of society for as long as possible, by means of—
(a) adequate resources enabling them to lead a decent life and play an active part in public, social and cultural life;
(b) provision of information about services and facilities available for elderly persons and their opportunities to make use of them;
to enable elderly persons to choose their life-style freely and to lead independent lives in their familiar surroundings for as long as they wish and are able, by means of—
(a) provision of housing suited to their needs and their state of health or of adequate support for adapting their housing;
(b) the health care and the services necessitated by their state;
to guarantee elderly persons living in institutions appropriate support, while respecting their privacy, and participation in decisions concerning living conditions in the institution.

Article 24
The right to protection in cases of termination of employment
With a view to ensuring the effective exercise of the right of workers to protection in cases of termination of employment, the Parties undertake to recognise—
(a) the right of all workers not to have their employment terminated without valid reasons for such termination connected with their capacity or conduct or based on the operational requirements of the undertaking, establishment or service;
(b) the right of workers whose employment is terminated without a valid reason to adequate compensation or other appropriate relief.
To this end the Parties undertake to ensure that a worker who considers that his employment has been terminated without a valid reason shall have the right to appeal to an impartial body.

Article 25
The right of workers to the protection of their claims in the event of the insolvency of their employer
With a view to ensuring the effective exercise of the right of workers to the protection of their claims in the event of the insolvency of their employer, the Parties undertake to provide that workers' claims arising from contracts of employment or employment relationships be guaranteed by a guarantee institution or by any other effective form of protection.

Article 26
The right to dignity at work
With a view to ensuring the effective exercise of the right of all workers to protection of their dignity at work, the Parties undertake, in consultation with employers' and workers' organisations—
1. to promote awareness, information and prevention of sexual harassment in the workplace or in relation to work and to take all appropriate measures to protect workers from such conduct;
2. to promote awareness, information and prevention of recurrent reprehensible or distinctly negative and offensive actions directed against individual workers in the workplace or in relation to work and to take all appropriate measures to protect workers from such conduct.

Article 27
The right of workers with family responsibilities to equal opportunities and equal treatment
With a view to ensuring the exercise of the right to equality of opportunity and treatment for men and women workers with family responsibilities and between such workers and other workers, the Parties undertake—
1. to take appropriate measures—
   (a) to enable workers with family responsibilities to enter and remain in employment, as well as to re-enter employment after an absence due to those responsibilities, including measures in the field of vocational guidance and training;
   (b) to take account of their needs in terms of conditions of employment and social security;
   (c) to develop or promote services, public or private, in particular child daycare services and other childcare arrangements;
2. to provide a possibility for either parent to obtain, during a period after maternity leave, parental leave to take care of a child, the duration and conditions of which should be determined by national legislation, collective agreements or practice;
3. to ensure that family responsibilities shall not, as such, constitute a valid reason for termination of employment.

Article 28
The right of workers' representatives to protection in the undertaking and facilities to be accorded to them
With a view to ensuring the effective exercise of the right of workers' representatives to carry out their functions, the Parties undertake to ensure that in the undertaking—
(a) they enjoy effective protection against acts prejudicial to them, including dismissal, based on their status or activities as workers' representatives within the undertaking;
(b) they are afforded such facilities as may be appropriate in order to enable them to carry out their functions promptly and efficiently, account being taken of the industrial relations system of the country and the needs, size and capabilities of the undertaking concerned.

Article 29
The right to information and consultation in collective redundancy procedures
With a view to ensuring the effective exercise of the right of workers to be informed and consulted in situations of collective redundancies, the Parties undertake to ensure that employers shall inform and consult workers' representatives, in good time prior to such collective redundancies, on ways and means of avoiding collective redundancies or limiting their occurrence and mitigating their consequences, for example by recourse to accompanying social measures aimed, in particular, at aid for the redeployment or retraining of the workers concerned.

Article 30
The right to protection against poverty and social exclusion
With a view to ensuring the effective exercise of the right to protection against poverty and social exclusion, the Parties undertake—
(a) to take measures within the framework of an overall and co-ordinated approach to promote the effective access of persons who live or risk living in a situation of social exclusion or poverty, as well as their families, to, in particular, employment, housing, training, education, culture and social and medical assistance;
(b) to review these measures with a view to their adaptation if necessary.

Article 31
The right to housing
With a view to ensuring the effective exercise of the right to housing, the Parties undertake to take measures designed—
1. to promote access to housing of an adequate standard;
2. to prevent and reduce homelessness with a view to its gradual elimination;
3. to make the price of housing accessible to those without adequate resources.

PART III

[5.21]
Article A
Undertakings

1. Subject to the provisions of Article B below, each of the Parties undertakes—
   (a) to consider Part I of this Charter as a declaration of the aims which it will pursue by all appropriate means, as stated in the introductory paragraph of that part;
   (b) to consider itself bound by at least six of the following nine articles of Part II of this Charter: Articles 1, 5, 6, 7, 12, 13, 16, 19 and 20;
   (c) to consider itself bound by an additional number of articles or numbered paragraphs of Part II of the Charter which it may select, provided that the total number of articles or numbered paragraphs by which it is bound is not less than sixteen articles or sixty-three numbered paragraphs.
2. The articles or paragraphs selected in accordance with sub-paragraphs b and c of paragraph 1 of this article shall be notified to the Secretary General of the Council of Europe at the time when the instrument of ratification, acceptance or approval is deposited.
3. Any Party may, at a later date, declare by notification addressed to the Secretary General that it considers itself bound by any articles or any numbered paragraphs of Part II of the Charter which it has not already accepted under the terms of paragraph 1 of this article. Such undertakings subsequently given shall be deemed to be an integral part of the ratification, acceptance or approval and shall have the same effect as from the first day of the month following the expiration of a period of one month after the date of the notification.
4. Each Party shall maintain a system of labour inspection appropriate to national conditions.

Article B
Links with the European Social Charter and the 1988 Additional Protocol

No Contracting Party to the European Social Charter or Party to the Additional Protocol of 5 May 1988 may ratify, accept or approve this Charter without considering itself bound by at least the provisions corresponding to the provisions of the European Social Charter and, where appropriate, of the Additional Protocol, to which it was bound.

Acceptance of the obligations of any provision of this Charter shall, from the date of entry into force of those obligations for the Party concerned, result in the corresponding provision of the European Social Charter and, where appropriate, of its Additional Protocol of 1988 ceasing to apply to the Party concerned in the event of that Party being bound by the first of those instruments or by both instruments.

PART IV

[5.22]
Article C
Supervision of the implementation of the undertakings contained in this Charter

The implementation of the legal obligations contained in this Charter shall be submitted to the same supervision as the European Social Charter.

Article D
Collective complaints

1. The provisions of the Additional Protocol to the European Social Charter providing for a system of collective complaints shall apply to the undertakings given in this Charter for the States which have ratified the said Protocol.
2. Any State which is not bound by the Additional Protocol to the European Social Charter providing for a system of collective complaints may when depositing its instrument of ratification, acceptance or approval of this Charter or at any time thereafter, declare by notification addressed to the Secretary General of the Council of Europe, that it accepts the supervision of its obligations under this Charter following the procedure provided for in the said Protocol.

PART V

[5.23]
Article E
Non-discrimination

The enjoyment of the rights set forth in this Charter shall be secured without discrimination on any ground such as race, colour, sex, language, religion, political or other opinion, national extraction or social origin, health, association with a national minority, birth or other status.

Article F
Derogations in time of war or public emergency

1. In time of war or other public emergency threatening the life of the nation any Party may take measures derogating from its obligations under this Charter to the extent strictly required by the exigencies of the situation, provided that such measures are not inconsistent with its other obligations under international law.

2. Any Party which has availed itself of this right of derogation shall, within a reasonable lapse of time, keep the Secretary General of the Council of Europe fully informed of the measures taken and of the reasons therefor. It shall likewise inform the Secretary General when such measures have ceased to operate and the provisions of the Charter which it has accepted are again being fully executed.

Article G
Restrictions

1. The rights and principles set forth in Part I when effectively realised, and their effective exercise as provided for in Part II, shall not be subject to any restrictions or limitations not specified in those parts, except such as are prescribed by law and are necessary in a democratic society for the protection of the rights and freedoms of others or for the protection of public interest, national security, public health, or morals.

2. The restrictions permitted under this Charter to the rights and obligations set forth herein shall not be applied for any purpose other than that for which they have been prescribed.

Article H
Relations between the Charter and domestic law or international agreements

The provisions of this Charter shall not prejudice the provisions of domestic law or of any bilateral or multilateral treaties, conventions or agreements which are already in force, or may come into force, under which more favourable treatment would be accorded to the persons protected.

Article I
Implementation of the undertakings given

1. Without prejudice to the methods of implementation foreseen in these articles the relevant provisions of Articles 1 to 31 of Part II of this Charter shall be implemented by—
   (a) laws or regulations;
   (b) agreements between employers or employers' organisations and workers' organisations;
   (c) a combination of those two methods;
   (d) other appropriate means.

2. Compliance with the undertakings deriving from the provisions of paragraphs 1, 2, 3, 4, 5 and 7 of Article 2, paragraphs 4, 6 and 7 of Article 7, paragraphs 1, 2, 3 and 5 of Article 10 and Articles 21 and 22 of Part II of this Charter shall be regarded as effective if the provisions are applied, in accordance with paragraph 1 of this article, to the great majority of the workers concerned.

Article J
Amendments

1. Any amendment to Parts I and II of this Charter with the purpose of extending the rights guaranteed in this Charter as well as any amendment to Parts III to VI, proposed by a Party or by the Governmental Committee, shall be communicated to the Secretary General of the Council of Europe and forwarded by the Secretary General to the Parties to this Charter.

2. Any amendment proposed in accordance with the provisions of the preceding paragraph shall be examined by the Governmental Committee which shall submit the text adopted to the Committee of Ministers for approval after consultation with the Parliamentary Assembly. After its approval by the Committee of Ministers this text shall be forwarded to the Parties for acceptance.

3. Any amendment to Part I and to Part II of this Charter shall enter into force, in respect of those Parties which have accepted it, on the first day of the month following the expiration of a period of one month after the date on which three Parties have informed the Secretary General that they have accepted it.

In respect of any Party which subsequently accepts it, the amendment shall enter into force on the first day of the month following the expiration of a period of one month after the date on which that Party has informed the Secretary General of its acceptance.

4. Any amendment to Parts III to VI of this Charter shall enter into force on the first day of the month following the expiration of a period of one month after the date on which all Parties have informed the Secretary General that they have accepted it.

PART VI

[5.24]

Article K
Signature, ratification and entry into force

1. This Charter shall be open for signature by the member States of the Council of Europe. It shall be subject to ratification, acceptance or approval. Instruments of ratification, acceptance or approval shall be deposited with the Secretary General of the Council of Europe.

2. This Charter shall enter into force on the first day of the month following the expiration of a period of one month after the date on which three member States of the Council of Europe have expressed their consent to be bound by this Charter in accordance with the preceding paragraph.

3. In respect of any member State which subsequently expresses its consent to be bound by this Charter, it shall enter into force on the first day of the month following the expiration of a period of one month after the date of the deposit of the instrument of ratification, acceptance or approval.

Article L
Territorial application

1. This Charter shall apply to the metropolitan territory of each Party. Each signatory may, at the time of signature or of the deposit of its instrument of ratification, acceptance or approval, specify, by declaration addressed to the Secretary General of the Council of Europe, the territory which shall be considered to be its metropolitan territory for this purpose.

2. Any signatory may, at the time of signature or of the deposit of its instrument of ratification, acceptance or approval, or at any time thereafter, declare by notification addressed to the Secretary General of the Council of Europe, that the Charter shall extend in whole or in part to a non-metropolitan territory or territories specified in the said declaration for whose international relations it is responsible or for which it assumes international responsibility. It shall specify in the declaration the articles or paragraphs of Part II of the Charter which it accepts as binding in respect of the territories named in the declaration.

3. The Charter shall extend its application to the territory or territories named in the aforesaid declaration as from the first day of the month following the expiration of a period of one month after the date of receipt of the notification of such declaration by the Secretary General.

4. Any Party may declare at a later date by notification addressed to the Secretary General of the Council of Europe that, in respect of one or more of the territories to which the Charter has been applied in accordance with paragraph 2 of this article, it accepts as binding any articles or any numbered paragraphs which it has not already accepted in respect of that territory or territories. Such undertakings subsequently given shall be deemed to be an integral part of the original declaration in respect of the territory concerned, and shall have the same effect as from the first day of the month following the expiration of a period of one month after the date of receipt of such notification by the Secretary General.

Article M
Denunciation

1. Any Party may denounce this Charter only at the end of a period of five years from the date on which the Charter entered into force for it, or at the end of any subsequent period of two years, and in either case after giving six months' notice to the Secretary General of the Council of Europe who shall inform the other Parties accordingly.

2. Any Party may, in accordance with the provisions set out in the preceding paragraph, denounce any article or paragraph of Part II of the Charter accepted by it provided that the number of articles or paragraphs by which this Party is bound shall never be less than sixteen in the former case and sixty-three in the latter and that this number of articles or paragraphs shall continue to include the articles selected by the Party among those to which special reference is made in Article A, paragraph 1, sub-paragraph b.

3. Any Party may denounce the present Charter or any of the articles or paragraphs of Part II of the Charter under the conditions specified in paragraph 1 of this article in respect of any territory to which the said Charter is applicable, by virtue of a declaration made in accordance with paragraph 2 of Article L.

Article N
Appendix

The appendix to this Charter shall form an integral part of it.

Article O
Notifications

The Secretary General of the Council of Europe shall notify the member States of the Council and the Director General of the International Labour Office of—

(a) any signature;
(b) the deposit of any instrument of ratification, acceptance or approval;
(c) any date of entry into force of this Charter in accordance with Article K;
(d) any declaration made in application of Articles A, paragraphs 2 and 3, D, paragraphs 1 and 2, F, paragraph 2, L, paragraphs 1, 2, 3 and 4;
(e) any amendment in accordance with Article J;
(f) any denunciation in accordance with Article M;
(g) any other act, notification or communication relating to this Charter.

In witness whereof, the undersigned, being duly authorised thereto, have signed this revised Charter.

Done at Strasbourg, this 3rd day of May 1996, in English and French, both texts being equally authentic, in a single copy which shall be deposited in the archives of the Council of Europe. The Secretary General of the Council of Europe shall transmit certified copies to each member State of the Council of Europe and to the Director General of the International Labour Office.

APPENDIX TO THE REVISED EUROPEAN SOCIAL CHARTER

SCOPE OF THE REVISED EUROPEAN SOCIAL CHARTER IN TERMS OF PERSONS PROTECTED

[5.25]

1. Without prejudice to Article 12, paragraph 4, and Article 13, paragraph 4, the persons covered by Articles 1 to 17 and 20 to 31 include foreigners only in so far as they are nationals of other Parties lawfully resident or working regularly within the territory of the Party concerned, subject to the understanding that these articles are to be interpreted in the light of the provisions of Articles 18 and 19.

This interpretation would not prejudice the extension of similar facilities to other persons by any of the Parties.

2. Each Party will grant to refugees as defined in the Convention relating to the Status of Refugees, signed in Geneva on 28 July 1951 and in the Protocol of 31 January 1967, and lawfully staying in its territory, treatment as favourable as possible, and in any case not less favourable than under the obligations accepted by the Party under the said convention and under any other existing international instruments applicable to those refugees.

3. Each Party will grant to stateless persons as defined in the Convention on the Status of Stateless Persons done in New York on 28 September 1954 and lawfully staying in its territory, treatment as favourable as possible and in any case not less favourable than under the obligations accepted by the Party under the said instrument and under any other existing international instruments applicable to those stateless persons.

PART I, PARAGRAPH 18, AND PART II, ARTICLE 18, PARAGRAPH 1

It is understood that these provisions are not concerned with the question of entry into the territories of the Parties and do not prejudice the provisions of the European Convention on Establishment, signed in Paris on 13 December 1955.

PART II

Article 1, paragraph 2
This provision shall not be interpreted as prohibiting or authorising any union security clause or practice.

Article 2, paragraph 6
Parties may provide that this provision shall not apply—
(a) to workers having a contract or employment relationship with a total duration not exceeding one month and/or with a working week not exceeding eight hours;
(b) where the contract or employment relationship is of a casual and/or specific nature, provided, in these cases, that its non-application is justified by objective considerations.

Article 3, paragraph 4
It is understood that for the purposes of this provision the functions, organisation and conditions of operation of these services shall be determined by national laws or regulations, collective agreements or other means appropriate to national conditions.

Article 4, paragraph 4
This provision shall be so understood as not to prohibit immediate dismissal for any serious offence.

Article 4, paragraph 5
It is understood that a Party may give the undertaking required in this paragraph if the great majority of workers are not permitted to suffer deductions from wages either by law or through collective agreements or arbitration awards, the exceptions being those persons not so covered.

Article 6, paragraph 4
It is understood that each Party may, insofar as it is concerned, regulate the exercise of the right to strike by law, provided that any further restriction that this might place on the right can be justified under the terms of Article G.

Article 7, paragraph 2
This provision does not prevent Parties from providing in their legislation that young persons not having reached the minimum age laid down may perform work in so far as it is absolutely necessary for their vocational training where such work is carried out in accordance with conditions prescribed by the competent authority and measures are taken to protect the health and safety of these young persons.

Article 7, paragraph 8
It is understood that a Party may give the undertaking required in this paragraph if it fulfils the spirit of the undertaking by providing by law that the great majority of persons under eighteen years of age shall not be employed in night work.

Article 8, paragraph 2
This provision shall not be interpreted as laying down an absolute prohibition. Exceptions could be made, for instance, in the following cases—
(a) if an employed woman has been guilty of misconduct which justifies breaking off the employment relationship;
(b) if the undertaking concerned ceases to operate;
(c) if the period prescribed in the employment contract has expired.

Article 12, paragraph 4

The words "and subject to the conditions laid down in such agreements" in the introduction to this paragraph are taken to imply *inter alia* that with regard to benefits which are available independently of any insurance contribution, a Party may require the completion of a prescribed period of residence before granting such benefits to nationals of other Parties.

Article 13, paragraph 4

Governments not Parties to the European Convention on Social and Medical Assistance may ratify the Charter in respect of this paragraph provided that they grant to nationals of other Parties a treatment which is in conformity with the provisions of the said convention.

Article 16

It is understood that the protection afforded in this provision covers single-parent families.

Article 17

It is understood that this provision covers all persons below the age of 18 years, unless under the law applicable to the child majority is attained earlier, without prejudice to the other specific provisions provided by the Charter, particularly Article 7.

This does not imply an obligation to provide compulsory education up to the above-mentioned age.

Article 19, paragraph 6

For the purpose of applying this provision, the term "family of a foreign worker" is understood to mean at least the worker's spouse and unmarried children, as long as the latter are considered to be minors by the receiving State and are dependent on the migrant worker.

Article 20

1. It is understood that social security matters, as well as other provisions relating to unemployment benefit, old age benefit and survivor's benefit, may be excluded from the scope of this article.
2. Provisions concerning the protection of women, particularly as regards pregnancy, confinement and the post-natal period, shall not be deemed to be discrimination as referred to in this article.
3. This article shall not prevent the adoption of specific measures aimed at removing *de facto* inequalities.
4. Occupational activities which, by reason of their nature or the context in which they are carried out, can be entrusted only to persons of a particular sex may be excluded from the scope of this article or some of its provisions. This provision is not to be interpreted as requiring the Parties to embody in laws or regulations a list of occupations which, by reason of their nature or the context in which they are carried out, may be reserved to persons of a particular sex.

Articles 21 and 22

1. For the purpose of the application of these articles, the term "workers' representatives" means persons who are recognised as such under national legislation or practice.
2. The terms "national legislation and practice" embrace as the case may be, in addition to laws and regulations, collective agreements, other agreements between employers and workers' representatives, customs as well as relevant case law.
3. For the purpose of the application of these articles, the term "undertaking" is understood as referring to a set of tangible and intangible components, with or without legal personality, formed to produce goods or provide services for financial gain and with power to determine its own market policy.
4. It is understood that religious communities and their institutions may be excluded from the application of these articles, even if these institutions are "undertakings" within the meaning of paragraph 3. Establishments pursuing activities which are inspired by certain ideals or guided by certain moral concepts, ideals and concepts which are protected by national legislation, may be excluded from the application of these articles to such an extent as is necessary to protect the orientation of the undertaking.
5. It is understood that where in a state the rights set out in these articles are exercised in the various establishments of the undertaking, the Party concerned is to be considered as fulfilling the obligations deriving from these provisions.
6. The Parties may exclude from the field of application of these articles, those undertakings employing less than a certain number of workers, to be determined by national legislation or practice.

Article 22

1. This provision affects neither the powers and obligations of states as regards the adoption of health and safety regulations for workplaces, nor the powers and responsibilities of the bodies in charge of monitoring their application.
2. The terms "social and socio-cultural services and facilities" are understood as referring to the social and/or cultural facilities for workers provided by some undertakings such as welfare assistance, sports fields, rooms for nursing mothers, libraries, children's holiday camps, etc.

Article 23, paragraph 1
For the purpose of the application of this paragraph, the term "for as long as possible" refers to the elderly person's physical, psychological and intellectual capacities.

Article 24
1. It is understood that for the purposes of this article the terms "termination of employment" and "terminated" mean termination of employment at the initiative of the employer.
2. It is understood that this article covers all workers but that a Party may exclude from some or all of its protection the following categories of employed persons—
 (a) workers engaged under a contract of employment for a specified period of time or a specified task;
 (b) workers undergoing a period of probation or a qualifying period of employment, provided that this is determined in advance and is of a reasonable duration;
 (c) workers engaged on a casual basis for a short period.
3. For the purpose of this article the following, in particular, shall not constitute valid reasons for termination of employment—
 (a) trade union membership or participation in union activities outside working hours, or, with the consent of the employer, within working hours;
 (b) seeking office as, acting or having acted in the capacity of a workers' representative;
 (c) the filing of a complaint or the participation in proceedings against an employer involving alleged violation of laws or regulations or recourse to competent administrative authorities;
 (d) race, colour, sex, marital status, family responsibilities, pregnancy, religion, political opinion, national extraction or social origin;
 (e) maternity or parental leave;
 (f) temporary absence from work due to illness or injury.
4. It is understood that compensation or other appropriate relief in case of termination of employment without valid reasons shall be determined by national laws or regulations, collective agreements or other means appropriate to national conditions.

Article 25
1. It is understood that the competent national authority may, by way of exemption and after consulting organisations of employers and workers, exclude certain categories of workers from the protection provided in this provision by reason of the special nature of their employment relationship.
2. It is understood that the definition of the term "insolvency" must be determined by national law and practice.
3. The workers' claims covered by this provision shall include at least—
 (a) the workers' claims for wages relating to a prescribed period, which shall not be less than three months under a privilege system and eight weeks under a guarantee system, prior to the insolvency or to the termination of employment;
 (b) the workers' claims for holiday pay due as a result of work performed during the year in which the insolvency or the termination of employment occurred;
 (c) the workers' claims for amounts due in respect of other types of paid absence relating to a prescribed period, which shall not be less than three months under a privilege system and eight weeks under a guarantee system, prior to the insolvency or the termination of the employment.
4. National laws or regulations may limit the protection of workers' claims to a prescribed amount, which shall be of a socially acceptable level.

Article 26
It is understood that this article does not require that legislation be enacted by the Parties.
 It is understood that paragraph 2 does not cover sexual harassment.

Article 27
It is understood that this article applies to men and women workers with family responsibilities in relation to their dependent children as well as in relation to other members of their immediate family who clearly need their care or support where such responsibilities restrict their possibilities of preparing for, entering, participating in or advancing in economic activity. The terms "dependent children" and "other members of their immediate family who clearly need their care and support" mean persons defined as such by the national legislation of the Party concerned.

Articles 28 and 29
For the purpose of the application of this article, the term "workers' representatives" means persons who are recognised as such under national legislation or practice.

PART III

It is understood that the Charter contains legal obligations of an international character, the application of which is submitted solely to the supervision provided for in Part IV thereof.

Article A, paragraph 1
It is understood that the numbered paragraphs may include articles consisting of only one paragraph.

Article B, paragraph 2

For the purpose of paragraph 2 of Article B, the provisions of the revised Charter correspond to the provisions of the Charter with the same article or paragraph number with the exception of—

(a) Article 3, paragraph 2, of the revised Charter which corresponds to Article 3, paragraphs 1 and 3, of the Charter;
(b) Article 3, paragraph 3, of the revised Charter which corresponds to Article 3, paragraphs 2 and 3, of the Charter;
(c) Article 10, paragraph 5, of the revised Charter which corresponds to Article 10, paragraph 4, of the Charter;
(d) Article 17, paragraph 1, of the revised Charter which corresponds to Article 17 of the Charter.

PART V

Article E

A differential treatment based on an objective and reasonable justification shall not be deemed discriminatory.

Article F

The terms "in time of war or other public emergency" shall be so understood as to cover also the *threat* of war.

Article I

It is understood that workers excluded in accordance with the appendix to Articles 21 and 22 are not taken into account in establishing the number of workers concerned.

Article J

The term "amendment" shall be extended so as to cover also the addition of new articles to the Charter.

INTERNATIONAL LABOUR ORGANISATION CONVENTION (NO 183) CONCERNING THE REVISION OF THE MATERNITY PROTECTION CONVENTION (REVISED), (2000)

NOTES

This Convention was adopted on 15 June 2000 and came into force on 7 February 2002. As of 15 May 2019, this Convention has not been ratified by the UK.

SCOPE

[5.26]

Article 1

For the purposes of this Convention, the term ***woman*** applies to any female person without discrimination whatsoever and the term ***child*** applies to any child without discrimination whatsoever.

Article 2

1. This Convention applies to all employed women, including those in atypical forms of dependent work.
2. However, each Member which ratifies this Convention may, after consulting the representative organisations of employers and workers concerned, exclude wholly or partly from the scope of the Convention limited categories of workers when its application to them would raise special problems of a substantial nature.
3. Each Member which avails itself of the possibility afforded in the preceding paragraph shall, in its first report on the application of the Convention under article 22 of the Constitution of the International Labour Organisation, list the categories of workers thus excluded and the reasons for their exclusion. In its subsequent reports, the Member shall describe the measures taken with a view to progressively extending the provisions of the Convention to these categories.

HEALTH PROTECTION

Article 3

Each Member shall, after consulting the representative organisations of employers and workers, adopt appropriate measures to ensure that pregnant or breastfeeding women are not obliged to perform work which has been determined by the competent authority to be prejudicial to the health of the mother or the child, or where an assessment has established a significant risk to the mother's health or that of her child.

MATERNITY LEAVE

Article 4

1. On production of a medical certificate or other appropriate certification, as determined by national law and practice, stating the presumed date of childbirth, a woman to whom this Convention applies shall be entitled to a period of maternity leave of not less than 14 weeks.
2. The length of the period of leave referred to above shall be specified by each Member in a declaration accompanying its ratification of this Convention.
3. Each Member may subsequently deposit with the Director-General of the International Labour Office a further declaration extending the period of maternity leave.
4. With due regard to the protection of the health of the mother and that of the child, maternity leave shall include a period of six weeks' compulsory leave after childbirth, unless otherwise agreed at the national level by the government and the representative organisations of employers and workers.
5. The prenatal portion of maternity leave shall be extended by any period elapsing between the presumed date of childbirth and the actual date of childbirth, without reduction in any compulsory portion of postnatal leave.

LEAVE IN CASE OF ILLNESS OR COMPLICATIONS

Article 5

On production of a medical certificate, leave shall be provided before or after the maternity leave period in the case of illness, complications or risk of complications arising out of pregnancy or childbirth. The nature and the maximum duration of such leave may be specified in accordance with national law and practice.

BENEFITS

Article 6

1. Cash benefits shall be provided, in accordance with national laws and regulations, or in any other manner consistent with national practice, to women who are absent from work on leave referred to in Articles 4 or 5.
2. Cash benefits shall be at a level which ensures that the woman can maintain herself and her child in proper conditions of health and with a suitable standard of living.
3. Where, under national law or practice, cash benefits paid with respect to leave referred to in Article 4 are based on previous earnings, the amount of such benefits shall not be less than two-thirds of the woman's previous earnings or of such of those earnings as are taken into account for the purpose of computing benefits.
4. Where, under national law or practice, other methods are used to determine the cash benefits paid with respect to leave referred to in Article 4, the amount of such benefits shall be comparable to the amount resulting on average from the application of the preceding paragraph.
5. Each Member shall ensure that the conditions to qualify for cash benefits can be satisfied by a large majority of the women to whom this Convention applies.
6. Where a woman does not meet the conditions to qualify for cash benefits under national laws and regulations or in any other manner consistent with national practice, she shall be entitled to adequate benefits out of social assistance funds, subject to the means test required for such assistance.
7. Medical benefits shall be provided for the woman and her child in accordance with national laws and regulations or in any other manner consistent with national practice. Medical benefits shall include prenatal, childbirth and postnatal care, as well as hospitalization care when necessary.
8. In order to protect the situation of women in the labour market, benefits in respect of the leave referred to in Articles 4 and 5 shall be provided through compulsory social insurance or public funds, or in a manner determined by national law and practice. An employer shall not be individually liable for the direct cost of any such monetary benefit to a woman employed by him or her without that employer's specific agreement except where:
   (a) such is provided for in national law or practice in a member State prior to the date of adoption of this Convention by the International Labour Conference; or
   (b) it is subsequently agreed at the national level by the government and the representative organisations of employers and workers.

Article 7

1. A Member whose economy and social security system are insufficiently developed shall be deemed to be in compliance with Article 6, paragraphs 3 and 4, if cash benefits are provided at a rate no lower than a rate payable for sickness or temporary disability in accordance with national laws and regulations.
2. A Member which avails itself of the possibility afforded in the preceding paragraph shall, in its first report on the application of this Convention under article 22 of the Constitution of the International Labour Organisation, explain the reasons therefor and indicate the rate at which cash benefits are provided. In its subsequent reports, the Member shall describe the measures taken with a view to progressively raising the rate of benefits.

EMPLOYMENT PROTECTION AND NON-DISCRIMINATION

Article 8

1. It shall be unlawful for an employer to terminate the employment of a woman during her pregnancy or absence on leave referred to in Articles 4 or 5 or during a period following her return to work to be prescribed by national laws or regulations, except on grounds unrelated to the pregnancy or birth of the child and its consequences or nursing. The burden of proving that the reasons for dismissal are unrelated to pregnancy or childbirth and its consequences or nursing shall rest on the employer.
2. A woman is guaranteed the right to return to the same position or an equivalent position paid at the same rate at the end of her maternity leave.

Article 9

1. Each Member shall adopt appropriate measures to ensure that maternity does not constitute a source of discrimination in employment, including - notwithstanding Article 2, paragraph 1 - access to employment.
2. Measures referred to in the preceding paragraph shall include a prohibition from requiring a test for pregnancy or a certificate of such a test when a woman is applying for employment, except where required by national laws or regulations in respect of work that is:
   (a) prohibited or restricted for pregnant or nursing women under national laws or regulations; or
   (b) where there is a recognized or significant risk to the health of the woman and child.

BREASTFEEDING MOTHERS

Article 10

1. A woman shall be provided with the right to one or more daily breaks or a daily reduction of hours of work to breastfeed her child.
2. The period during which nursing breaks or the reduction of daily hours of work are allowed, their number, the duration of nursing breaks and the procedures for the reduction of daily hours of work shall be determined by national law and practice. These breaks or the reduction of daily hours of work shall be counted as working time and remunerated accordingly.

PERIODIC REVIEW

Article 11

Each Member shall examine periodically, in consultation with the representative organisations of employers and workers, the appropriateness of extending the period of leave referred to in Article 4 or of increasing the amount or the rate of the cash benefits referred to in Article 6.

IMPLEMENTATION

Article 12

This Convention shall be implemented by means of laws or regulations, except in so far as effect is given to it by other means such as collective agreements, arbitration awards, court decisions, or in any other manner consistent with national practice.

FINAL PROVISIONS

Article 13

This Convention revises the Maternity Protection Convention (Revised), 1952.

Article 14

The formal ratifications of this Convention shall be communicated to the Director-General of the International Labour Office for registration.

Article 15

1. This Convention shall be binding only upon those Members of the International Labour Organisation whose ratifications have been registered with the Director-General of the International Labour Office.
2. It shall come into force 12 months after the date on which the ratifications of two Members have been registered with the Director-General.
3. Thereafter, this Convention shall come into force for any Member 12 months after the date on which its ratification has been registered.

Article 16

1. A Member which has ratified this Convention may denounce it after the expiration of ten years from the date on which the Convention first comes into force, by an act communicated to the Director-General of the International Labour Office for registration. Such denunciation shall not take effect until one year after the date on which it is registered.

2. Each Member which has ratified this Convention and which does not, within the year following the expiration of the period of ten years mentioned in the preceding paragraph, exercise the right of denunciation provided for in this Article, will be bound for another period of ten years and, thereafter, may denounce this Convention at the expiration of each period of ten years under the terms provided for in this Article.

Article 17

1. The Director-General of the International Labour Office shall notify all Members of the International Labour Organisation of the registration of all ratifications and acts of denunciation communicated by the Members of the Organisation.
2. When notifying the Members of the Organisation of the registration of the second ratification, the Director-General shall draw the attention of the Members of the Organisation to the date upon which the Convention shall come into force.

Article 18

The Director-General of the International Labour Office shall communicate to the Secretary-General of the United Nations, for registration in accordance with article 102 of the Charter of the United Nations, full particulars of all ratifications and acts of denunciation registered by the Director-General in accordance with the provisions of the preceding Articles.

Article 19

At such times as it may consider necessary, the Governing Body of the International Labour Office shall present to the General Conference a report on the working of this Convention and shall examine the desirability of placing on the agenda of the Conference the question of its revision in whole or in part.

Article 20

1. Should the Conference adopt a new Convention revising this Convention in whole or in part, then, unless the new Convention otherwise provides:
   (a) the ratification by a Member of the new revising Convention shall ipso jure involve the immediate denunciation of this Convention, notwithstanding the provisions of Article 16 above, if and when the new revising Convention shall have come into force;
   (b) as from the date when the new revising Convention comes into force, this Convention shall cease to be open to ratification by the Members.
2. This Convention shall in any case remain in force in its actual form and content for those Members which have ratified it but have not ratified the revising Convention.

Article 21

The English and French versions of the text of this Convention are equally authoritative.

UNITED NATIONS CONVENTION ON THE RIGHTS OF PERSONS WITH DISABILITIES

[13 December 2006]

[5.27]

NOTES

In accordance with Article 45(1) *post*, this Treaty entered into force on 3 May 2008 following ratification by the twentieth party. The UK ratified the Convention on 8 June 2009 and, in accordance with Article 45(2), the Treaty entered into force for the UK on 8 July 2009. The UK has entered a reservation in relation to Article 27 stating that "The United Kingdom accepts the provisions of the Convention, subject to the understanding that none of its obligations relating to equal treatment in employment and occupation, shall apply to the admission into or service in any of the naval, military or air forces of the Crown.". (Other reservations made by the UK relate to aspects of the Convention outside the scope of this work.)

The European Communities (Definition of Treaties) (United Nations Convention on the Rights of Persons with Disabilities) Order 2009, SI 2009/1181 declares that the Convention is to be one of the European Union Treaties.

Arts 7–11, 13–25, 29–43, 47–49, which are outside the scope of this work, are omitted.

The Optional Protocol (which relates to the competence of the UN Committee on the Rights of Persons with Disabilities to receive communications from persons alleging violations of the Convention) is omitted for reasons of space; it was also ratified by the UK, on 7 August 2009, but is not within the scope of the designation in SI 2009/1181. The Optional Protocol is available at: www.un.org/disabilities/documents/convention/convoptprot-e.pdf.

PREAMBLE

THE STATES PARTIES TO THE PRESENT CONVENTION,

(a) Recalling the principles proclaimed in the Charter of the United Nations[1] which recognize the inherent dignity and worth and the equal and inalienable rights of all members of the human family as the foundation of freedom, justice and peace in the world,

(b) Recognizing that the United Nations, in the Universal Declaration of Human Rights and in the International Covenants on Human Rights, has proclaimed and agreed that everyone is entitled to all the rights and freedoms set forth therein, without distinction of any kind,

(c) Reaffirming the universality, indivisibility, interdependence and interrelatedness of all human rights and fundamental freedoms and the need for persons with disabilities to be guaranteed their full enjoyment without discrimination,

(d) Recalling the International Covenant on Economic, Social and Cultural Rights,[2] the International Covenant on Civil and Political Rights,[3] the International Convention on the Elimination of All Forms of Racial Discrimination,[4] the Convention on the Elimination of All Forms of Discrimination against Women,[5] the Convention against Torture and Other Cruel, Inhuman or Degrading Treatment or Punishment,[6] the Convention on the Rights of the Child,[7] and the International Convention on the Protection of the Rights of All Migrant Workers and Members of Their Families,

(e) Recognizing that disability is an evolving concept and that disability results from the interaction between persons with impairments and attitudinal and environmental barriers that hinders their full and effective participation in society on an equal basis with others,

(f) Recognizing the importance of the principles and policy guidelines contained in the World Programme of Action concerning Disabled Persons and in the Standard Rules on the Equalization of Opportunities for Persons with Disabilities in influencing the promotion, formulation and evaluation of the policies, plans, programmes and actions at the national, regional and international levels to further equalize opportunities for persons with disabilities,

(g) Emphasizing the importance of mainstreaming disability issues as an integral part of relevant strategies of sustainable development,

(h) Recognizing also that discrimination against any person on the basis of disability is a violation of the inherent dignity and worth of the human person,

(i) Recognizing further the diversity of persons with disabilities,

(j) Recognizing the need to promote and protect the human rights of all persons with disabilities, including those who require more intensive support,

(k) Concerned that, despite these various instruments and undertakings, persons with disabilities continue to face barriers in their participation as equal members of society and violations of their human rights in all parts of the world,

(l) Recognizing the importance of international cooperation for improving the living conditions of persons with disabilities in every country, particularly in developing countries,

(m) Recognizing the valued existing and potential contributions made by persons with disabilities to the overall well-being and diversity of their communities, and that the promotion of the full enjoyment by persons with disabilities of their human rights and fundamental freedoms and of full participation by persons with disabilities will result in their enhanced sense of belonging and in significant advances in the human, social and economic development of society and the eradication of poverty,

(n) Recognizing the importance for persons with disabilities of their individual autonomy and independence, including the freedom to make their own choices,

(o) Considering that persons with disabilities should have the opportunity to be actively involved in decision-making processes about policies and programmes, including those directly concerning them,

(p) Concerned about the difficult conditions faced by persons with disabilities who are subject to multiple or aggravated forms of discrimination on the basis of race, colour, sex, language, religion, political or other opinion, national, ethnic, indigenous or social origin, property, birth, age or other status,

(q) Recognizing that women and girls with disabilities are often at greater risk, both within and outside the home, of violence, injury or abuse, neglect or negligent treatment, maltreatment or exploitation,

(r) Recognizing that children with disabilities should have full enjoyment of all human rights and fundamental freedoms on an equal basis with other children, and recalling obligations to that end undertaken by States Parties to the Convention on the Rights of the Child,

(s) Emphasizing the need to incorporate a gender perspective in all efforts to promote the full enjoyment of human rights and fundamental freedoms by persons with disabilities,

(t) Highlighting the fact that the majority of persons with disabilities live in conditions of poverty, and in this regard recognizing the critical need to address the negative impact of poverty on persons with disabilities,

(u) Bearing in mind that conditions of peace and security based on full respect for the purposes and principles contained in the Charter of the United Nations and observance of applicable human rights instruments are indispensable for the full protection of persons with disabilities, in particular during armed conflicts and foreign occupation,

(v) Recognizing the importance of accessibility to the physical, social, economic and cultural environment, to health and education and to information and communication, in enabling persons with disabilities to fully enjoy all human rights and fundamental freedoms,

(w) Realizing that the individual, having duties to other individuals and to the community to which he or she belongs, is under a responsibility to strive for the promotion and observance of the rights recognized in the International Bill of Human Rights,

(x) Convinced that the family is the natural and fundamental group unit of society and is entitled to protection by society and the State, and that persons with disabilities and their family members should receive the necessary protection and assistance to enable families to contribute towards the full and equal enjoyment of the rights of persons with disabilities,

(y) Convinced that a comprehensive and integral international convention to promote and protect the rights and dignity of persons with disabilities will make a significant contribution to redressing the profound social disadvantage of persons with disabilities and promote their participation in the civil, political, economic, social and cultural spheres with equal opportunities, in both developing and developed countries,

NOTES

1 Treaty Series No 67 (1946) Cmd 7015

2 Treaty Series No 6 (1977) Cmnd 6702

3 Treaty Series No 6 (1977) Cm 6702

4 Treaty Series No 77 (1969) Cmnd 4108

5 Treaty Series No 2 (1989) Cm 643

6 Treaty Series No 107 (1991) Cm 1775

7 Treaty Series No 44 (1992) Cm 1976

HAVE AGREED AS FOLLOWS:

Article 1
Purpose

The purpose of the present Convention is to promote, protect and ensure the full and equal enjoyment of all human rights and fundamental freedoms by all persons with disabilities, and to promote respect for their inherent dignity. Persons with disabilities include those who have long-term physical, mental, intellectual or sensory impairments which in interaction with various barriers may hinder their full and effective participation in society on an equal basis with others.

Article 2
Definitions

For the purposes of the present Convention:

"Communication" includes languages, display of text, Braille, tactile communication, large print, accessible multimedia as well as written, audio, plain language, human-reader and augmentative and alternative modes, means and formats of communication, including accessible information and communication technology;

"Language" includes spoken and signed languages and other forms of non-spoken languages;

"Discrimination on the basis of disability" means any distinction, exclusion or restriction on the basis of disability which has the purpose or effect of impairing or nullifying the recognition, enjoyment or exercise, on an equal basis with others, of all human rights and fundamental freedoms in the political, economic, social, cultural, civil or any other field. It includes all forms of discrimination, including denial of reasonable accommodation;

"Reasonable accommodation" means necessary and appropriate modification and adjustments not imposing a disproportionate or undue burden, where needed in a particular case, to ensure to persons with disabilities the enjoyment or exercise on an equal basis with others of all human rights and fundamental freedoms;

"Universal design" means the design of products, environments, programmes and services to be usable by all people, to the greatest extent possible, without the need for adaptation or specialized design. "Universal design" shall not exclude assistive devices for particular groups of persons with disabilities where this is needed.

Article 3
General Principles

The principles of the present Convention shall be:

(a) Respect for inherent dignity, individual autonomy including the freedom to make one's own choices, and independence of persons;
(b) Non-discrimination;
(c) Full and effective participation and inclusion in society;
(d) Respect for difference and acceptance of persons with disabilities as part of human diversity and humanity;
(e) Equality of opportunity;
(f) Accessibility;
(g) Equality between men and women;
(h) Respect for the evolving capacities of children with disabilities and respect for the right of children with disabilities to preserve their identities.

Article 4
General Obligations

1. States Parties undertake to ensure and promote the full realization of all human rights and fundamental freedoms for all persons with disabilities without discrimination of any kind on the basis of disability. To this end, States Parties undertake:

(a) To adopt all appropriate legislative, administrative and other measures for the implementation of the rights recognized in the present Convention;
(b) To take all appropriate measures, including legislation, to modify or abolish existing laws, regulations, customs and practices that constitute discrimination against persons with disabilities;
(c) To take into account the protection and promotion of the human rights of persons with disabilities in all policies and programmes;
(d) To refrain from engaging in any act or practice that is inconsistent with the present Convention and to ensure that public authorities and institutions act in conformity with the present Convention;
(e) To take all appropriate measures to eliminate discrimination on the basis of disability by any person, organisation or private enterprise;
(f) To undertake or promote research and development of universally designed goods, services, equipment and facilities, as defined in article 2 of the present Convention, which should require the minimum possible adaptation and the least cost to meet the specific needs of a person with disabilities, to promote their availability and use, and to promote universal design in the development of standards and guidelines;
(g) To undertake or promote research and development of, and to promote the availability and use of new technologies, including information and communications technologies, mobility aids, devices and assistive technologies, suitable for persons with disabilities, giving priority to technologies at an affordable cost;
(h) To provide accessible information to persons with disabilities about mobility aids, devices and assistive technologies, including new technologies, as well as other forms of assistance, support services and facilities;
(i) To promote the training of professionals and staff working with persons with disabilities in the rights recognized in the present Convention so as to better provide the assistance and services guaranteed by those rights.

2. With regard to economic, social and cultural rights, each State Party undertakes to take measures to the maximum of its available resources and, where needed, within the framework of international cooperation, with a view to achieving progressively the full realization of these rights, without prejudice to those obligations contained in the present Convention that are immediately applicable according to international law.

3. In the development and implementation of legislation and policies to implement the present Convention, and in other decision-making processes concerning issues relating to persons with disabilities, States Parties shall closely consult with and actively involve persons with disabilities, including children with disabilities, through their representative organisations.

4. Nothing in the present Convention shall affect any provisions which are more conducive to the realization of the rights of persons with disabilities and which may be contained in the law of a State Party or international law in force for that State. There shall be no restriction upon or derogation from any

of the human rights and fundamental freedoms recognized or existing in any State Party to the present Convention pursuant to law, conventions, regulation or custom on the pretext that the present Convention does not recognize such rights or freedoms or that it recognizes them to a lesser extent.

5. The provisions of the present Convention shall extend to all parts of federal States without any limitations or exceptions.

Article 5
Equality and Non-discrimination

1. States Parties recognize that all persons are equal before and under the law and are entitled without any discrimination to the equal protection and equal benefit of the law.
2. States Parties shall prohibit all discrimination on the basis of disability and guarantee to persons with disabilities equal and effective legal protection against discrimination on all grounds.
3. In order to promote equality and eliminate discrimination, States Parties shall take all appropriate steps to ensure that reasonable accommodation is provided.
4. Specific measures which are necessary to accelerate or achieve de facto equality of persons with disabilities shall not be considered discrimination under the terms of the present Convention.

Article 6
Women with Disabilities

1. States Parties recognize that women and girls with disabilities are subject to multiple discrimination, and in this regard shall take measures to ensure the full and equal enjoyment by them of all human rights and fundamental freedoms.
2. States Parties shall take all appropriate measures to ensure the full development, advancement and empowerment of women, for the purpose of guaranteeing them the exercise and enjoyment of the human rights and fundamental freedoms set out in the present Convention.

Article 12
Equal Recognition before the Law

1. States Parties reaffirm that persons with disabilities have the right to recognition everywhere as persons before the law.
2. States Parties shall recognize that persons with disabilities enjoy legal capacity on an equal basis with others in all aspects of life.
3. States Parties shall take appropriate measures to provide access by persons with disabilities to the support they may require in exercising their legal capacity.
4. States Parties shall ensure that all measures that relate to the exercise of legal capacity provide for appropriate and effective safeguards to prevent abuse in accordance with international human rights law. Such safeguards shall ensure that measures relating to the exercise of legal capacity respect the rights, will and preferences of the person, are free of conflict of interest and undue influence, are proportional and tailored to the person's circumstances, apply for the shortest time possible and are subject to regular review by a competent, independent and impartial authority or judicial body. The safeguards shall be proportional to the degree to which such measures affect the person's rights and interests.
5. Subject to the provisions of this article, States Parties shall take all appropriate and effective measures to ensure the equal right of persons with disabilities to own or inherit property, to control their own financial affairs and to have equal access to bank loans, mortgages and other forms of financial credit, and shall ensure that persons with disabilities are not arbitrarily deprived of their property.

Article 26
Habilitation and Rehabilitation

1. States Parties shall take effective and appropriate measures, including through peer support, to enable persons with disabilities to attain and maintain maximum independence, full physical, mental, social and vocational ability, and full inclusion and participation in all aspects of life. To that end, States Parties shall organize, strengthen and extend comprehensive habilitation and rehabilitation services and programmes, particularly in the areas of health, employment, education and social services, in such a way that these services and programmes:
   (a) Begin at the earliest possible stage, and are based on the multi-disciplinary assessment of individual needs and strengths;
   (b) Support participation and inclusion in the community and all aspects of society, are voluntary, and are available to persons with disabilities as close as possible to their own communities, including in rural areas.
2. States Parties shall promote the development of initial and continuing training for professionals and staff working in habilitation and rehabilitation services.
3. States Parties shall promote the availability, knowledge and use of assistive devices and technologies, designed for persons with disabilities, as they relate to habilitation and rehabilitation.

Article 27
Work and Employment

1. States Parties recognize the right of persons with disabilities to work, on an equal basis with others; this includes the right to the opportunity to gain a living by work freely chosen or accepted in a labour market and work environment that is open, inclusive and accessible to persons with disabilities. States

Parties shall safeguard and promote the realization of the right to work, including for those who acquire a disability during the course of employment, by taking appropriate steps, including through legislation, to, inter alia:

(a) Prohibit discrimination on the basis of disability with regard to all matters concerning all forms of employment, including conditions of recruitment, hiring and employment, continuance of employment, career advancement and safe and healthy working conditions;

(b) Protect the rights of persons with disabilities, on an equal basis with others, to just and favourable conditions of work, including equal opportunities and equal remuneration for work of equal value, safe and healthy working conditions, including protection from harassment, and the redress of grievances;

(c) Ensure that persons with disabilities are able to exercise their labour and trade union rights on an equal basis with others;

(d) Enable persons with disabilities to have effective access to general technical and vocational guidance programmes, placement services and vocational and continuing training;

(e) Promote employment opportunities and career advancement for persons with disabilities in the labour market, as well as assistance in finding, obtaining, maintaining and returning to employment;

(f) Promote opportunities for self-employment, entrepreneurship, the development of cooperatives and starting one's own business;

(g) Employ persons with disabilities in the public sector;

(h) Promote the employment of persons with disabilities in the private sector through appropriate policies and measures, which may include affirmative action programmes, incentives and other measures;

(i) Ensure that reasonable accommodation is provided to persons with disabilities in the workplace;

(j) Promote the acquisition by persons with disabilities of work experience in the open labour market;

(k) Promote vocational and professional rehabilitation, job retention and return-to-work programmes for persons with disabilities.

2. States Parties shall ensure that persons with disabilities are not held in slavery or in servitude, and are protected, on an equal basis with others, from forced or compulsory labour.

Article 28
Adequate Standard of Living and Social Protection

1. States Parties recognize the right of persons with disabilities to an adequate standard of living for themselves and their families, including adequate food, clothing and housing, and to the continuous improvement of living conditions, and shall take appropriate steps to safeguard and promote the realization of this right without discrimination on the basis of disability.

2. States Parties recognize the right of persons with disabilities to social protection and to the enjoyment of that right without discrimination on the basis of disability, and shall take appropriate steps to safeguard and promote the realization of this right, including measures:

(a) To ensure equal access by persons with disabilities to clean water services, and to ensure access to appropriate and affordable services, devices and other assistance for disability-related needs;

(b) To ensure access by persons with disabilities, in particular women and girls with disabilities and older persons with disabilities, to social protection programmes and poverty reduction programmes;

(c) To ensure access by persons with disabilities and their families living in situations of poverty to assistance from the State with disability related expenses, including adequate training, counselling, financial assistance and respite care;

(d) To ensure access by persons with disabilities to public housing programmes;

(e) To ensure equal access by persons with disabilities to retirement benefits and programmes.

Article 44
Regional Integration Organisations

1. "Regional integration organisation" shall mean an organisation constituted by sovereign States of a given region, to which its member States have transferred competence in respect of matters governed by the present Convention. Such organisations shall declare, in their instruments of formal confirmation or accession, the extent of their competence with respect to matters governed by the present Convention. Subsequently, they shall inform the depositary of any substantial modification in the extent of their competence.

2. References to "States Parties" in the present Convention shall apply to such organisations within the limits of their competence.

3. For the purposes of article 45, paragraph 1, and article 47, paragraphs 2 and 3, of the present Convention, any instrument deposited by a regional integration organisation shall not be counted.

4. Regional integration organisations, in matters within their competence, may exercise their right to vote in the Conference of States Parties, with a number of votes equal to the number of their member States that are Parties to the present Convention. Such an organisation shall not exercise its right to vote if any of its member States exercises its right, and vice versa.

Article 45
Entry into Force

1. The present Convention shall enter into force on the thirtieth day after the deposit of the twentieth instrument of ratification or accession.

2. For each State or regional integration organisation ratifying, formally confirming or acceding to the present Convention after the deposit of the twentieth such instrument, the Convention shall enter into force on the thirtieth day after the deposit of its own such instrument.

Article 46
Reservations

1. Reservations incompatible with the object and purpose of the present Convention shall not be permitted.

2. Reservations may be withdrawn at any time

Article 50
Authentic Texts

The Arabic, Chinese, English, French, Russian and Spanish texts of the present Convention shall be equally authentic.

IN WITNESS THEREOF the undersigned plenipotentiaries, being duly authorized thereto by their respective Governments, have signed the present Convention.

B. EMPLOYMENT TRIBUNAL & EAT PRACTICE DIRECTIONS & PRACTICE STATEMENTS, ETC

1. EAT PRACTICE DIRECTIONS

PRACTICE DIRECTION (EMPLOYMENT APPEAL TRIBUNAL – PROCEDURE) 2018

[5.28]

NOTES

Commencement: 19 December 2018 (see para 1.1).

CONTENTS

1 INTRODUCTION AND OBJECTIVE

[5.29]

1.1 This Practice Direction ("PD") supersedes all previous Practice Directions. It comes into force on Wednesday 19 December 2018.

1.2 The following statutory provisions apply to the way appeals are handled at the Employment Appeal Tribunal ("the EAT"), whenever those appeals were begun:

a) Employment Tribunals Act 1996 (as amended) ("ETA 1996");
b) Employment Appeal Tribunal Rules 1993 (SI 1993/2854) (as amended) ("the Rules").

1.3 Where the Rules do not otherwise provide, the following procedure will apply to all appeals to the EAT.

1.4 By s30(3) of the ETA 1996 the Employment Appeal Tribunal ("the EAT") has power, subject to the Rules, to regulate its own procedure. In so doing, the EAT regards itself as subject in all its actions to the duties imposed by Rule 2A. It will seek to apply the overriding objective when it exercises any power given to it by the Rules or interprets any Rule.

1.5 The overriding objective of this PD is to enable the EAT to deal with cases justly. Dealing with a case justly includes, so far as is practicable:

1.5.1 ensuring that the parties are on an equal footing;
1.5.2 dealing with the case in ways which are proportionate to the importance and complexity of the issues;

1.5.3 ensuring that it is dealt with expeditiously and fairly;
1.5.4 saving expense.

1.6 Dealing with a case justly also includes safeguarding the resources of the EAT so that each case gets its fair share of available time, but no more.

1.7 The parties are required to help the EAT to further the overriding objective.

1.8 Where it is appropriate to the EAT's jurisdiction, procedure, unrestricted rights of representation and restricted costs regime, the EAT is guided by the Civil Procedure Rules. So, for example:

1.8.1 for the purpose of serving a valid Notice of Appeal under Rule 3 and paragraph 3 below, when an Employment Tribunal decision is sent to parties on, for example, a Wednesday, that day does not count when calculating time limits, and the Notice of Appeal must arrive at the EAT before, or by 4pm on, the Wednesday 6 weeks (i.e. 42 days) later.
1.8.2 When a date is given for serving of a document or for doing some other act, the complete document must be received by the EAT or the relevant party by 4pm on that date. Any document received after 4pm will be deemed to be lodged on the next working day.
1.8.3 Except as provided in 1.8.4 below, all days count, but if a time limit expires on a day when the central office of the EAT, or the EAT office in Edinburgh (as appropriate), is closed, it is extended to the next working day.
1.8.4 Where the time limit is 5 days (e.g. an appeal against a Registrar's order or direction), Saturdays, Sundays, Christmas Day, Good Friday and Bank Holidays do not count. For example an appeal against an order made on a Wednesday must arrive at the EAT on or before the following Wednesday.

1.9 The provisions of this PD are subject to any specific directions which the EAT makes in any particular case. Otherwise, the directions set out below must be complied with in all appeals from Employment Tribunals. In national security appeals, and appeals from the Certification Officer and the Central Arbitration Committee, the Rules set out the separate procedures to be followed and the EAT will normally give specific directions.

1.10 In this PD any reference to the date of an order shall mean the date stamped upon the relevant order by the EAT ("the seal date").

1.11 The parties can expect the EAT normally to have read the documents (or the documents indicated in any essential reading list if permission is granted under paragraph 7.4 below for an enlarged appeal bundle) in advance of any hearing.

2 BASIS OF APPEAL

[5.30]
2.1 Since the ETA 1996 provides that appeal lies only on a "question of law", the parties must expect any decision of fact made by an Employment Tribunal, Certification Officer or Central Arbitration Committee to be decisive.

2.2 It is not an error of law for a Tribunal, judge, CO or CAC to reach a decision which one party to the case thinks should have been differently made. The appeal is not a rehearing of the case. The Employment Tribunal must be shown to have made an error of law.

2.3 If a party is in any doubt about whether a point is one of law or not, legal advice should be sought where it is at all possible to do so. The EAT cannot and does not give legal advice to any party.

3 INSTITUTION OF APPEAL: WHAT SHOULD BE IN A NOTICE OF APPEAL

[5.31]
3.1 A Notice of Appeal and accompanying documents may be delivered to the EAT by any method, such as email, fax, post, courier, or hand-delivery. The Notice of Appeal must be, or be substantially, in accordance with Form 1 (in the amended form annexed to this Practice Direction) or Forms 1A or 2 of the Schedule to the Rules. It must identify the date of the judgment, decision or order being appealed. Copies of the judgment, decision or order appealed against must be attached by the Appellant. In addition the Appellant must provide copies of the Employment Tribunal's written reasons, together with a copy of the claim (the form ET1 and any attached grounds) and the response (the form ET3 and any attached grounds), or if not, a written explanation for the omission of the reasons, ET1 and ET3 must be given. It must include a postal address at or through which the Appellant can be contacted, and may also include an email address if the Appellant wishes the EAT to communicate by email. A Notice of Appeal without such documentation will not be validly presented.

3.2 If the Appellant has made an application to the Employment Tribunal for a reconsideration of its judgment or decision, a copy of that application should accompany the Notice of Appeal together with the judgment and written reasons of the Employment Tribunal in respect of that reconsideration application, or a statement, if such be the case, that a judgment is awaited.

3.3 If any of these documents cannot be included, a written explanation must be given. The Appellant should also attach (where they are relevant to the appeal) copies of any orders (including case management orders) made by the Employment Tribunal, CO or CAC.

3.4 Where written reasons of the Employment Tribunal are not attached to the Notice of Appeal, either (as set out in the written explanation) because a request for written reasons has been refused by the Employment Tribunal or for some other reason, an Appellant must, when presenting the Notice of Appeal, apply in writing to the EAT to exercise its discretion to hear the appeal without written reasons or to exercise its power to request written reasons from the Employment Tribunal, setting out the full grounds of that application.

3.5 The Notice of Appeal must clearly identify the point(s) of law which form(s) the ground(s) of appeal from the judgment, decision or order of the Employment Tribunal to the EAT. It should also state the order which the Appellant will ask the EAT to make at the hearing.

3.6 Notices of appeal should set out the grounds relied on in numbered paragraphs, in line with the forms set out in the Rules 1993, Rule 3 and Schedule.

3.7 A point of law should be easy to identify in a few words. Whatever the paragraph numbering of the surrounding text is, the grounds of appeal themselves:

3.7.1 should begin with the heading "Numbered Grounds" and be numbered consecutively, starting at (1);

3.7.2 each be headed by a brief description – underlined or in bold or both – of the points of law relied on (e.g. "Misinterpreted Section XX of the Equality Act 2010"; "Reached a decision on a point which had not been argued"; etc) followed only by what is needed to enable a Judge of the EAT to understand the point and identify what the error of law(s) is/are said to be;

3.7.3 should (except in the case of appeals alleging either perversity or bias) usually occupy in total no more than 2 sides of A4 paper – a well-directed notice of appeal is usually more persuasive than a long one, and in general, the more points raised the more it suggests that none is a good one;

3.7.4 in the case of appeals alleging either perversity or bias, or both, should comply with paragraph 3.10 (perversity) or paragraph 12 (bias) of this Practice Direction;

3.7.5 should not include any quotation from either the Tribunal judgment under appeal (which can and will be read by the EAT) or any authority (though if it is important and relevant to refer to an authority, the reference should allow it to be identified, and the relevant page and paragraph number should be stated);

3.7.6 should not contain any footnote, nor incorporate any other document.

3.8 If introductory or further explanatory text is necessary in addition to the grounds themselves, it should in most appeals be short, and should avoid making a complaint about the judgment of the Tribunal which is not made as one of the numbered grounds. Notices of Appeal are not meant to be skeleton arguments and should not set out detailed argument unless this is essential for understanding.

3.9 If it appears to the Judge or Registrar that a Notice of Appeal gives insufficient grounds of, or lacks clarity in identifying, a point of law, or fails to comply with these Directions, the Judge or Registrar may send it back to be resubmitted, or a preliminary hearing may be directed for the Appellant alone to attend, to persuade the EAT there is reasonable ground for the appeal. Any expense, inconvenience and delay caused by this is the Appellant's sole responsibility. In some cases, the failure may be regarded as unreasonable conduct of litigation and expose the Appellant to a risk of costs.

3.10 Perversity Appeals: an Appellant may not state as a ground of appeal simply words to the effect that "the judgment or order was contrary to the evidence", or that "there was no evidence to support the judgment or order", or that "the judgment or order was one which no reasonable Tribunal could have reached and was perverse" unless the Notice of Appeal also sets out full particulars of the matters relied on in support of those general grounds.

3.11 Where it appears that the Notice of Appeal or any part of it (a) discloses no reasonable grounds for bringing the appeal, or (b) is an abuse of the Employment Appeal Tribunal's process or is otherwise likely to obstruct the just disposal of proceedings, Rules 3(7)-(10) give a judge or the Registrar power to decide that no further action shall be taken on the appeal. The Rules specify the rights of the Appellant and the procedure to be followed. The Appellant can request an oral hearing before a judge to reconsider the decision, unless the judge or Registrar has made an order under Rule3(7ZA), in which case the decision may be appealed to the Court of Appeal (Court of Session in Scotland).

3.12 A party cannot "reserve a right" to amend, alter or add, to a Notice of Appeal or a Respondent's Answer. No party has the right to amend any Notice of Appeal or Answer without the prior permission of the EAT. Any application for permission to amend must be made as soon as practicable and must be accompanied by a draft of the amended Notice of Appeal or amended Answer which makes clear the precise amendments for which permission is sought.

3.13 Where an application is made for permission to institute or continue relevant proceedings by a person who has been made the subject of a Restriction of Proceedings Order pursuant to s33 of ETA 1996, that application will be considered on paper by a judge, who may make an order granting, refusing or otherwise dealing with such application on paper.

4 TIME FOR INSTITUTING APPEALS

[5.32]

4.1 The time within which an appeal must be instituted depends on whether the appeal is against a judgment or against an order, direction or decision of the Employment Tribunal. In either case, time limits are strictly applied.

4.2 If the appeal is against an order, direction or decision, the appeal must be instituted within 42 days of the date of the order, direction or decision. The EAT will treat a Tribunal's refusal to make an order or decision as itself constituting an order, direction or decision. The date of an order, direction or decision is the date when the order, direction or decision was sent to the parties, which is normally recorded on or in the order, direction or decision.

4.3 If the appeal is against a Judgment, the appeal must be instituted within 42 days from the date on which the written record of the Judgment was sent to the parties. However in four situations the time for appealing against a Judgment will be 42 days from the date when written reasons for the Judgment were sent to the parties. This will be the case if (and only if) (i) written reasons were requested orally at the hearing before the Tribunal or (ii) written reasons were requested in writing within 14 days of the date on which the written record of the judgment was sent to the parties or (iii) the Tribunal itself reserved its reasons and gave them subsequently in writing or (iv) where a request to the Tribunal for written reasons is made out of time (and granted). The date of the written record of the Judgment and of the written reasons for the Judgment is the date when they are sent to the parties, which is normally recorded on or in the written record and the written reasons.

4.4 The time limit referred to in paragraphs 4.1 to 4.3 above applies even though the question of remedy and assessment of compensation by the Employment Tribunal has been adjourned or has not been dealt with and even though an application has been made to the Employment Tribunal for a reconsideration.

4.5 An application for an extension of time for appealing cannot be considered until a Notice of Appeal in accordance with paragraph 3 above has been presented to the EAT.

4.6 Any application for an extension of time for appealing must be made as an interim application to the Registrar, who will normally determine the application after inviting and considering written representations from each side. An interim appeal lies from the Registrar's decision to a judge. Such an appeal must be notified to the EAT within 5 working days of the date when the Registrar's decision was sent to the parties: this means that where, for example, the Registrar's decision is sent to the parties on a Wednesday, any appeal against it must be received no later than 4pm on the following Wednesday [See paragraph 1.8.2 above].

4.7 In determining whether to extend the time for appealing, particular attention will be paid to whether any good excuse for the delay has been shown and to the guidance contained in the decisions of the EAT and the Court of Appeal, as summarised in cases such as *United Arab Emirates v Abdelghafar* [1995] ICR 65, *Aziz v Bethnal Green City Challenge Co Ltd* [2000] IRLR 111, *Jurkowska v HLMAD Ltd* [2008] ICR 841 and *Muschett v London Borough of Hounslow* [2009] ICR 424. These, and other, case reports may be accessed without charge at www.bailii.org.

4.8 It is not usually a good reason for late presentation of a Notice of Appeal that (a) an application for litigation support from public funds has been made, but not yet determined; or that support is being sought from, but has not yet been provided by, some other body, such as a trade union, employers' association or the Equality and Human Rights Commission; (b) the Appellant was waiting for the result of an application for reconsideration; (c) negotiations between the parties were occurring.

4.9 In any case of doubt or difficulty, a Notice of Appeal should be presented in time and an application made to the Registrar for directions.

5 INTERIM APPLICATIONS

[5.33]

5.1 Interim applications should be made in writing (no particular form is required) and will initially be referred to the Registrar who (after considering the parties' submissions) may deal with the case or refer it to a judge. The judge may deal with it without a hearing (known as "on the papers") if he or she considers an oral hearing is not necessary, or refer it to a full EAT hearing. Parties are encouraged to make any such applications at a Preliminary Hearing ("PH") if one is ordered.

5.2 Unless otherwise ordered, any application for an extension of time will be considered and determined as though it were an interim application to the Registrar, who will normally determine the application after inviting and considering written representations from each side.

5.3 An interim appeal lies from the Registrar's decision to a judge. Such an appeal must be notified to the EAT within five days of the date when the Registrar's decision was sent to the parties.

6 THE RIGHT TO INSPECT CERTAIN DOCUMENTS AND TO TAKE COPIES

[5.34]

6.1 Any document presented to the Central Office of the EAT in London or in the EAT office in Edinburgh in any proceedings before the EAT shall be stamped with the seal of the EAT showing the date (and time, if received after 4pm) on which the document was presented.

6.2 Particulars of the date of delivery at the London or Edinburgh EAT office of any document for filing or presentation together with the time, if received after 4pm, the date of the document and the title of the appeal of which the document forms part of the record shall be entered in the list of registered cases kept in London and in Edinburgh or in the file which forms part of the list of registered cases.

6.3 Any person shall be entitled to inspect by requesting a copy of any of the following documents filed or presented to the London or Edinburgh EAT office, namely:

6.3.1 any Notice of Appeal or Respondent's Answer or any copy thereof;
6.3.2 any judgment or order given or made in court or any copy of such judgment or order.

6.4 Any other document may be inspected only with the permission of the EAT, which may be granted for proper reason on an application, following consultation with any other affected party, and subject to conditions as appropriate.

6.5 A copying charge per page will be payable for those documents mentioned in paragraphs 6.3 and 6.4 above.

6.6 Nothing in this Direction shall be taken as preventing any party to an appeal from inspecting and requesting a copy of any document filed or presented to the EAT office in London or Edinburgh before the commencement of the appeal, but made with a view to its commencement.

7 PAPERS FOR USE AT THE HEARING

[5.35]

7.1 The Appellant is responsible for preparing and lodging bundles of papers for use at any hearing, however a represented Respondent may be willing to take this responsibility from an unrepresented Appellant. Paragraphs 7.3 below lists the documents required for the core bundle, but all parties should agree what additional documents are to be included. Failure by the Appellant to comply with orders or directions to lodge bundles in time may result in an appeal being adjourned with costs sanctions, or struck out for non-compliance.

7.2 The bundle must include only those exhibits (productions in Scotland) and documents used before the Employment Tribunal which are considered to be necessary for the appeal. It is the duty of the parties or their advisers to ensure that only those documents are included which are (a) relevant to the point(s) of law raised in the appeal and (b) likely to be referred to at the hearing. It is also the responsibility of parties to retain copies of all documents and correspondence, including hearing bundles, sent to EAT. Bundles (see paragraph 7.4 below) used at one EAT hearing will not be retained by the EAT for a subsequent hearing.

7.3 The documents that are required to be included in the core bundle should be numbered by item, then paginated continuously and indexed, in the following order:

7.3.1 Judgment, decision or order appealed from and written reasons
7.3.2 Sealed Notice of Appeal
7.3.3 Respondent's Answer if a Full Hearing ("FH"), Respondent's Submissions if any for a PH
7.3.4 ET1 claim (and any Additional Information or Written Answers)
7.3.5 ET3 response (and any Additional Information or Written Answers)
7.3.6 Questionnaire and Replies, if any (discrimination and equal pay cases)
7.3.7 Relevant orders, judgments and written reasons of the Employment Tribunal
7.3.8 Relevant orders and judgments of the EAT
7.3.9 Affidavits and Employment Tribunal comments (where ordered)
7.3.10 Any documents agreed or ordered (subject to paragraph 7.4 below).

7.4 Other documents necessary for and relevant to the appeal, which were referred to at the Employment Tribunal may follow in the core or a supplementary bundle, if the total pages additional to the documents set out in paragraphs 7.3 - 7.3.9 do not exceed 50. No bundle containing more than 50 such additional pages should be agreed or lodged without the permission of the Registrar or order of a judge which will not be granted without the provision of an essential reading list as soon as practicable thereafter. If permitted or ordered, further pages should follow, with consecutive pagination, in an additional bundle or bundles if appropriate.

7.5 All documents must be legible and unmarked.

7.6 For PH cases (see paragraph 10.9 below), Appeals from Registrar's Order, Rule 3(10) hearings, Rule 6(16) hearings, or Appointments for Directions: the Appellant (or party whose cross-appeal or application it is) must prepare and present two copies (four copies if the judge has directed a sitting with lay members) of the bundle as soon as possible after service of the Notice of Appeal and no later than 28 days prior to the date fixed for the hearing, unless otherwise directed.

7.7 For FH cases (see paragraph 10.21 below): the parties must co-operate in agreeing a bundle of papers for the hearing. By no later than 28 days prior to the date fixed for the hearing, unless otherwise directed, the Appellant is responsible for ensuring that two copies (four copies if the judge has directed a sitting with lay members) of a bundle agreed by the parties is presented to the EAT.

7.8 For Fast Track FH cases: the bundles should be presented as soon as possible and (unless the hearing date is within seven days) in any event within seven days after the parties have been notified that the case is expedited.

7.9 In the event of disagreement between the parties or difficulty in preparing the bundles, the Registrar may give appropriate directions, whether on application in writing (on notice) by one or more of the parties or his/her own initiative.

7.10 In general the EAT will not accept documents or communications on the basis that they are to be confidential to the EAT and are not to be disclosed to another party. All documents presented by one party are presumed to be disclosable to the other(s), and the parties must expect that to be the case in the absence of a direction or order made by a judge on application by a party to the contrary effect.

8 EVIDENCE BEFORE THE EMPLOYMENT TRIBUNAL

[5.36]

8.1 An Appellant who considers that a point of law raised in the Notice of Appeal cannot be argued without reference to evidence given (or not given) at the Employment Tribunal, the nature or substance of which does not, or does not sufficiently, appear from the written reasons, must ordinarily submit an application with the Notice of Appeal. The application is for the nature of such evidence (or lack of it) to be admitted, or if necessary for the relevant parts of the employment judge's notes of evidence to be produced. If such application is not so made, then it should be made:

8.1.1 if a PH is ordered, in the skeleton argument or written submissions presented prior to such PH; or
8.1.2 if the case is listed for FH without a PH, then within 14 days of the seal date of the order so providing.

Any such application by a Respondent to an appeal, must, if not made earlier, accompany the Respondent's Answer.

8.2 The application must explain why such a matter is considered necessary in order to argue the point of law raised in the Notice of Appeal or Respondent's Answer. The application must identify:

8.2.1 the issue(s) in the Notice of Appeal or Respondent's Answer to which the material is relevant;
8.2.2 the names of the witnesses whose evidence is considered relevant, alternatively the nature of the evidence the absence of which is considered relevant;
8.2.3 (if applicable) the part of the hearing when the evidence was given;
8.2.4 the gist of the evidence (or absence of evidence) alleged to be relevant; and
8.2.5 (if the party has a record of the evidence), saying so and by whom and when it was made, or producing an extract from a witness statement given in writing at the hearing.

8.3 The application will be considered on the papers, or if appropriate at a PH, by the Registrar or a judge. The Registrar or a judge may give directions for written representations (if they have not already been lodged), or may determine the application, but will ordinarily make an order requiring the party who seeks to raise such a matter to give notice to the other party (or parties) to the appeal/cross-appeal. The notice will require the other party (or parties) to co-operate in agreeing, within 21 days (unless a shorter period is ordered), a statement or note of the relevant evidence, alternatively a statement that there was no such evidence. All parties are required to use their best endeavours to agree such a statement or note.

8.4 In the absence of such agreement within 21 days (or such shorter period as may be ordered) of the requirement, any party may make an application within seven days thereafter to the EAT, for directions. The party must enclose all relevant correspondence and give notice to the other parties. The directions may include: the resolution of the disagreement on the papers or at a hearing; the administration by one party to the others of, or a request to the employment judge to provide, information; or, if the EAT is satisfied that such notes are necessary, a request that the employment judge produce his/her notes of evidence either in whole or in part.

8.5 If the EAT requests any documents from the employment judge, it will supply copies to the parties upon receipt.

8.6 A note of evidence is not to be produced or supplied to the parties to enable the parties to embark on a "fishing expedition" to establish grounds or additional grounds of appeal or because they have not kept their own notes of the evidence. If an application for such a note is found by the EAT to have been unreasonably made or if there is unreasonable lack of co-operation in agreeing a relevant note or statement, the party behaving unreasonably is at risk of being ordered to pay costs.

9 FRESH EVIDENCE AND NEW POINTS OF LAW

[5.37]

9.1 Usually the EAT will not consider evidence which was not placed before the Employment Tribunal unless and until an application has first been made to the Employment Tribunal against whose judgment the appeal is brought for that Tribunal to reconsider its judgment. Where such an application has been made, it is likely that unless a judge of the EAT dismisses the appeal as having no reasonable prospect of success the judge will stay (or sist) any further action on that appeal until the result of the reconsideration is known. The Employment Tribunal as the fact-finding body, which has heard relevant witnesses, is the appropriate forum to consider "fresh evidence" and in particular the extent to which (if at all) it would or might have made a difference to its conclusions. When deciding if an Employment Tribunal erred in law when deciding on an application to reconsider an earlier decision, the EAT will have regard to any evidence placed before the Employment Tribunal in relation to the application to reconsider.

9.2 Subject to paragraph 9.1, where an application is made by a party to an appeal to put in, at the hearing of the appeal, any document which was not before the Employment Tribunal, and which has not been agreed in writing by the other parties, the application and a copy of the document(s) sought to be admitted should be presented to the EAT with the Notice of Appeal or the Respondent's Answer, as appropriate. The application and copy should be served on the other parties. The same principle applies to any oral evidence not given at the Employment Tribunal which is sought to be adduced on the appeal. The application to consider Fresh Evidence must explain what that evidence is, and how it came to light. Generally, a witness statement detailing this should be filed with the EAT and served on the other parties when the application is made.

9.3 In exercising its discretion to admit any fresh evidence, the EAT will only admit the evidence (in accordance with the principles set out in *Ladd v Marshall* [1954] 1WLR 1489 and having regard to the overriding objective), if all of the following apply:

9.3.1 the evidence could not have been obtained with reasonable diligence for use at the Employment Tribunal hearing; and
9.3.2 it is relevant and would probably have had an important influence on the hearing; and
9.3.3 it is apparently credible.

Accordingly the evidence and representations in support of the application must address these principles.

9.4 A party wishing to resist the application must, within 14 days of its being sent, submit any representations in response to the EAT and other parties.

9.5 The application will be considered by the Registrar or a judge on the papers (or, if appropriate, at a PH) who may stay (or sist) the appeal in accordance with paragraph 9.1, determine the issue or give directions for a hearing or may seek comments from the employment judge. A copy of any comments received from the employment judge will be sent to all parties.

9.6 If a Respondent intends to contend at the FH that the Appellant has raised a point which was not argued below, the Respondent shall say so:

9.6.1 if a PH has been ordered, in writing to the EAT and all parties, within 14 days of receiving the Notice of Appeal;

9.6.2 if the case is listed for a FH without a PH, in a Respondent's Answer.

In the event of dispute the employment judge should be asked for his/her comments as to whether a particular legal argument was deployed.

10 THE SIFT OF APPEALS: CASE TRACKS AND DIRECTIONS

[5.38]

10.1 Once a Notice of Appeal has been received, properly instituted within time (and compliant with these Directions), it will be sifted by a judge or the Registrar who will consider the Notice of Appeal to determine:

(a) whether it discloses any reasonable ground for bringing an appeal; (see further paragraph 10.5 below);

(b) if so, whether the whole or only part of the grounds of appeal should be argued before a Full Hearing;

(c) if not, whether the appeal is wholly without merit (in which case there is no right for the Appellant to an oral hearing before a judge at the EAT, though this does not remove any right to appeal to the Court of Appeal);

10.1.1 The EAT will deal with applications in order, and parties must not expect their appeal to take precedence over any other unless there are truly exceptional circumstances.

10.1.2 The EAT may, where necessary, seek additional information from either party.

10.2 If the Notice of Appeal does or might disclose a reasonable ground or grounds, the judge considering it on the sift will determine the most effective case management of the appeal. This will be to allocate the relevant ground(s) of appeal for further consideration on paper having directed the Respondent to lodge a written response to the proposed appeal; or at a Preliminary Hearing (PH): or for determination at a Full Hearing (FH), and in any case to give appropriate directions.

10.3 The judge or Registrar may also stay (or sist in Scotland) the appeal for a period, normally 21 days, pending the making or the conclusion of an application by the Appellant to the Employment Tribunal for a reconsideration (if necessary out of time) or pending the response by the Employment Tribunal to an invitation from the judge or Registrar to clarify, supplement or give its written reasons.

10.4 Paragraphs 10.1 to 10.3 apply equally to a Respondent's cross-appeal which will be sifted and case managed in the same way as a Notice of Appeal.

10.5 An appeal or cross-appeal will not be treated as showing any reasonable ground for bringing the appeal if it is an abuse of the process or otherwise likely to obstruct the just disposal of the matters in issue between the parties.

10.6 Reasons will be sent and within 28 days the Appellant (or Respondent in the case of a cross-appeal) may request an oral hearing (known as a "Rule 3(10) hearing" or "Rule 6(16) hearing") before a judge unless the judge determining the sift has ruled that the appeal is wholly without merit.

10.7 At a Rule 3(10) or 6(16) hearing the judge may confirm the earlier decision or order that the appeal proceeds in whole or in part to a PH or FH, giving appropriate directions. These directions may permit an amendment to be made to the grounds of appeal. Such a proposed amendment should be made available in writing at the hearing wherever practicable, and will not take effect unless the judge has approved it. The Amended Grounds of Appeal are to be drafted as explained in paragraph 13.6 below.

10.8 A hearing under Rule 3(10) or 6(16), including judgment and any directions, will normally last not more than one hour including time for oral judgment to be given.

PRELIMINARY HEARINGS (PHS)

10.9 The purpose of a PH is to determine whether any of the grounds in the Notice of Appeal or cross-appeal raise a point of law which gives:

10.9.1 reasonable grounds to appeal i.e. a reasonable prospect of success at a FH; or

10.9.2 that for some other compelling reason the appeal should be heard e.g. that the Appellant seeks a declaration of incompatibility under the Human Rights Act 1998; or to argue that a decision binding on the EAT should be considered by a higher court.

10.10 Prior to the PH there will be automatic directions. These include sending the Notice of Appeal to the Respondent(s) to the appeal and/or cross-appeal to the Appellant. The direction may order but in any event will enable the opposing party to present and serve, within 14 days of the seal date of the order (unless otherwise directed), concise written submissions in response to the appeal, dedicated to showing that there is no reasonable prospect of success for all or any grounds of any appeal. Those submissions will be considered at the PH.

10.11 If the Respondent to the appeal intends to serve a cross-appeal this must be accompanied by written Notice to that effect which must be presented and served within 28 days of service of the Notice of Appeal. The Respondent to the appeal must make clear whether it is intended to advance the cross-appeal:

10.11.1 in any event (an unconditional cross-appeal); or

10.11.2 only if the Appellant succeeds (a conditional cross-appeal).

Any cross-appeal will be sifted and case managed in accordance with paragraphs 10.1 to 10.3 above.

10.12 All parties will be notified of the date fixed for the PH. In the normal case, unless ordered otherwise, only the Appellant and/or a representative should attend to make submissions to the EAT on the issue whether the Notice of Appeal raises any reasonable ground for bringing an appeal. A Respondent pursuing a cross-appeal to be considered at a PH should attend to make similar submissions. The opposing party will not normally be permitted to take part save where the judge considers it desirable that either should do so. Any written submissions as referred to in paragraph 10.10 above will be considered at the PH.

10.13 If the relevant party does not attend, the appeal or cross-appeal may nevertheless be dealt with as above on written submissions, and be dismissed wholly or in part or allowed to proceed.

10.14 The PH, including judgment and directions, will normally last no more than one hour. Arguments should be carefully planned so that this time is not exceeded; if it is, the Appeal Tribunal may impose a guillotine on further argument, in order to ensure that the case does not take a share of the Appeal Tribunal's resources which is disproportionate to that taken by other appeals yet to be heard.

10.15 The same procedure will be applied to cross-appeals as to appeals. If satisfied that the appeal (and/or the cross-appeal) should be heard at a FH on all or some of the grounds of appeal, the EAT will give directions relating to, for example, a time estimate, any application for fresh evidence, a procedure in respect of matters of evidence before the Employment Tribunal not sufficiently appearing from the written reasons, the exchange and lodging of skeleton arguments and an Appellant's Chronology, and bundles of documents and authorities.

10.16 Permission to amend a Notice of Appeal (or cross-appeal) may be granted at a PH:

10.16.1 If the proposed amendment is produced at the hearing, then, if such amendment has not previously been notified to the other parties, and the appeal (or cross-appeal) might not have been permitted to proceed but for the amendment, the opposing party (or parties) will have the opportunity to apply on notice to vary or discharge the permission to proceed, and for consequential directions as to the hearing or disposal of the appeal or cross-appeal.

10.16.2 A draft amendment should wherever practicable be made available at the PH or on the same day unless otherwise directed.

10.17 If not satisfied that the appeal, or any particular ground of it, should go forward to a FH, the EAT at the PH will dismiss the appeal, wholly or in part, and give a judgment setting out the reasons for doing so.

10.18 If an appeal is permitted to go forward to an FH on all grounds, a reasoned judgment will not normally be given.

10.19 Parties who become aware that a similar point is raised in other proceedings at an Employment Tribunal or the EAT are encouraged to co-operate in bringing this to the attention of the Registrar so that consideration can be given to the most expedient way of dealing with the cases, in particular to the possibility of having two or more appeals heard together.

10.20 If an appeal is permitted to go forward to an FH, a listing category will be assigned i.e.:

P (recommended to be heard in the President's list);

A (complex, and raising point(s) of law of public importance);

B (any other cases).

The President reserves the discretion to alter any relevant category as circumstances require.

FULL HEARINGS (FHS)

10.21 If a judge or the Registrar decides to list the case for an FH s/he will consider appropriate directions, relating for example to amendment, further information, a procedure in respect of matters of evidence at the Employment Tribunal not sufficiently appearing from the written reasons, allegations of bias, apparent bias or improper conduct, provisions for skeleton arguments, Appellant's Chronology and bundles of documents and of authorities, time estimates and listing category (as set out in paragraph 10.20 above).

10.22 The EAT aims to hear FH cases in the order in which they are received. However, there are times when it is expedient to hear an appeal as soon as it can be fitted into the list. Appeals thus fast-tracked, at the discretion of a judge or the Registrar, will normally fall into the following cases:

- 10.22.1 appeals where the parties have made a reasoned case on the merits for an expedited hearing;
- 10.22.2 appeals against interim orders or decisions of an Employment Tribunal, particularly those which involve the taking of a step in the proceedings within a specified period, for example adjournments, further information, amendments, disclosure, witness orders;
- 10.22.3 appeals on the outcome of which other applications to the Employment Tribunal or the EAT or the civil courts depend;
- 10.22.4 appeals in which a reference to the European Court of Justice (ECJ), or a declaration of incompatibility under the Human Rights Act 1998, is sought;
- 10.22.5 appeals involving reinstatement, re-engagement, or interim relief.

10.23 Category B cases estimated to take two hours or less may also be fast-tracked.

11 RESPONDENT'S ANSWER AND DIRECTIONS

[5.39]

11.1 The EAT will send the Notice of Appeal, with any amendments which have been permitted, and any submissions or skeleton argument lodged by the Appellant, to all parties who are Respondents to the appeal. Within 28 days of the seal date of the order (unless otherwise directed), the Respondent must present to the EAT and serve on the other parties a Respondent's Answer, including any cross-appeal if one is to be pursued. If it contains a cross-appeal the Appellant must present and serve a Reply. In both cases, the opposing party must state how it would wish the EAT to deal with the appeal if the Appellant or cross-appellant succeeds: see paragraph 3.5 above.

11.2 A Respondent's Answer should address the contentions set out in the Grounds of Appeal. A Respondent to an appeal is not obliged to respond in their answer to any additional contentions made in any text which accompanies the Notice of Appeal.

11.3 A Respondent may rely solely, or partly, on the Employment Tribunal's reasons to answer the appeal. They need not repeat those reasons in their Answer, but should shortly state any additional legal reasoning on which they wish to rely.

11.4 A Respondent to the appeal who wishes to resist the appeal and/or to cross-appeal, but who has not delivered a Respondent's Answer as directed by the Registrar, or otherwise ordered, may be barred from taking part in the appeal unless permission is granted to serve an Answer out of time.

11.5 After presentation and service of the Respondent's Answer and of any Reply to a cross-appeal, the Registrar may, where necessary, invite applications from the parties in writing, on notice to all other parties, for directions, and may give any appropriate directions on the papers or may fix a day when the parties should attend on an Appointment for Directions.

11.6 A judge may at any time, upon consideration of the papers or at a hearing, make an order requiring or recommending consideration by the parties or any of them of compromise, conciliation, mediation or, in particular, reference to ACAS.

12 COMPLAINTS ABOUT THE CONDUCT OF THE EMPLOYMENT TRIBUNAL HEARING OR BIAS

[5.40]

12.1 An Appellant who intends to complain about the conduct of the Employment Tribunal (for example bias, apparent bias or improper conduct by the employment judge, any lay members or any material procedural irregularity at the hearing) must include in the Notice of Appeal full particulars of each complaint made.

12.2 An appeal which is wholly or in part based on such a complaint will be sifted by a judge or the Registrar as set out in paragraph 10.1 above. The judge or Registrar may postpone a decision on the sift, and direct that the Appellant or a representative provide an affidavit or statement setting out full particulars of all allegations of bias or misconduct relied upon, and/or may enquire of the party making the complaint whether it is intended to proceed with it and may draw attention to paragraph 12.6 below.

12.3 If a decision is taken at the sift to proceed further with the appeal, the EAT may take the following steps prior to any hearing within a time-limit set out in the relevant order:

12.3.1 require the Appellant or a representative to provide, if not already provided, an affidavit or statement as set out in paragraph 12.2 above;

12.3.2 require any party to give an affidavit or to obtain a witness statement from any person who has represented any of the parties at the Tribunal hearing, and any other person present at the Tribunal hearing or a relevant part of it, giving their account of the events set out in the affidavit of the Appellant or the Appellant's representative. For this purpose, the EAT will provide copies of any affidavits received from or on behalf of the Appellant to any other person from whom an account is sought;

12.3.3 seek comments, upon all affidavits or witness statements received, from the employment judge of the Employment Tribunal from which the appeal is brought and may seek such comments from any lay members of the Tribunal. For this purpose, copies of all relevant documents will be provided by the EAT to the employment judge and, if appropriate, the lay members; such documents will include any affidavits and witness statements received, the Notice of Appeal and other relevant documents;

12.3.4 the EAT will on receipt supply to the parties copies of all affidavits, statements and comments received.

12.4 A Respondent who intends to make such a complaint must include such particulars as set out in paragraphs 12.1 and 12.2 above:

12.4.1 in the Respondent's Answer

12.4.2 or in the cross-appeal referred to in paragraph 10.6 above, or,

12.4.3 where a PH is ordered in the absence of a cross-appeal, in written submissions, as referred to in paragraph 10.10 above.

A similar procedure will then be followed as in paragraph 12.3 above.

12.5 In every case raising bias which is permitted to proceed to a FH the parties must agree (or the EAT may give appropriate directions, ordinarily on the papers after notice to the Appellant and Respondent) as to the procedure to be adopted at, and material to be provided to, the FH; including, the names of witnesses required to attend to give evidence and be cross-examined. If agreement cannot be reached, an application for directions can be made to the Registrar.

12.6 Parties should note the following:

12.6.1 The EAT will not permit complaints of the kind mentioned above to be raised or developed at the hearing of the appeal unless this procedure has been followed.

12.6.2 The EAT recognises that employment judges and Employment Tribunals are themselves obliged to observe the overriding objective and are given wide powers and duties of case management (see Employment Tribunal (Constitution and Rules of Procedure) Regulations 2013 (SI 2013/1237)), so appeals in respect of conduct of Employment Tribunals which is in exercise of those powers and duties, are the less likely to succeed.

12.6.3 Unsuccessful pursuit of an allegation of bias or improper conduct, particularly in respect of case management decisions, may put the party raising it at risk of an order for costs against them.

13 CASE MANAGEMENT

[5.41]

13.1 Consistent with the overriding objective, the EAT will seek to give directions for case management so that the appeal can be dealt with quickly, or better considered, and in the most effective and just way.

13.2 Applications and directions for case management will usually be dealt with on the papers at the sift stage by a judge, or by the Registrar with an appeal to a judge.

13.3 Any party seeking directions must serve a copy on all parties.

13.4 Directions may be given at any stage, before or after the registration of a Notice of Appeal. An order made will contain a time for compliance, which must be observed or be the subject of an application by any party to vary or discharge it, or to seek an extension of time. Otherwise, failure to comply with an order in time or at all may result in the EAT exercising its power under Rule 26 to strike out the appeal, cross-appeal or Respondent's Answer, to debar the party from taking any further part in the proceedings or to make any other order it thinks fit, including an award of costs. The power to strike out an appeal, cross-appeal or answer to an appeal will not be exercised without the party subject to it being sent notification that the power may be exercised: but a notice stating that "unless . . . (a particular step is taken by a certain time) . . . the appeal (or a specified part of it) will be struck out" is sufficient notification for this purpose, and if the step is not taken before the time specified has elapsed the consequential strike-out will occur automatically.

13.5 Any application to vary or discharge an order, or to seek an extension of time, must be presented to the EAT and served on the other parties within the time fixed for compliance. Such other parties must, if opposing the application and within 14 days (or such shorter period as may be ordered) of receiving it, submit their representations to the EAT and the other parties.

13.6 An application to amend a Notice of Appeal or Respondent's Answer must include the text of the original document with any changes clearly marked and identifiable, for example with deletions struck through in red and the text of the amendment either written or underlined in red. Any subsequent amendments will have to be in a different identifiable colour. Where provided from a computer print-out, the deleted wording should be struck through, and new wording put in italics. Where re-amendment is made, the new wording must be in bold italics or a distinctive and easily readable font.

14 LISTING OF APPEALS

[5.42]

14.1 **Estimate of Length of Hearing:** All parties are required to ensure that the estimates of length of hearing (allowing for the fact that the parties can expect the EAT to have pre-read the papers and for deliberation and the giving of a judgment) are accurate when first given. This is of particular importance in any case in which it is directed that lay members should sit. Lay members of the EAT are part-time members. They attend when available on pre-arranged dates. They do not sit for continuous periods. Consequently appeals which run beyond their estimated length have to be adjourned part-heard (often with substantial delay) until a day on which the judge and members are all available again. Any change in such estimate, or disagreement with an estimate made by the EAT on a sift or at a PH, is to be notified immediately to the EAT.

14.2 The estimate should include time for judgment to be considered and delivered orally on the day of hearing.

14.3 If the EAT concludes that the hearing is likely to exceed the estimate, or if for other reasons the hearing may not be concluded within the time available, it may seek to avoid such adjournment by placing the parties under appropriate time limits in order to complete the presentation of the submissions within the estimated or available time.

14.4 A judge may at any time during any hearing, and with a view to achieving the overriding objective (including ensuring that the appeal finishes within its allocated time) require submissions to take place in whatever order the judge considers appropriate, and within whatever time limit seems fit. It will not be a legitimate objection that different time limits are prescribed for different parties: where this happens, it will be with a view to ensuring overall fairness.

14.5 The EAT will normally consult the parties on dates, and will accommodate reasonable requests if practicable, but is not bound to do so. Once the date is fixed, the appeal will be set down in the list. A party finding that the date which has been fixed causes serious difficulties may apply to the EAT for it to be changed, having first notified all other parties entitled to appear on the date, of their application and the reasons for it.

14.6 Parties receiving such an application must, as soon as possible and within seven days, notify the EAT of their views.

14.7 In addition to this fixed date procedure, a list ("the warned list") may be drawn up. Cases will be placed in such warned list at the discretion of the EAT or may be so placed by the direction of a judge or the Registrar. These will ordinarily be short cases, or cases where expedition has been ordered. Parties or their representatives will be notified that their case has been included in this list, and as much notice as possible will be given of the intention to list a case for hearing, when representations by way of objection from the parties will be considered by the EAT and if necessary on appeal to the Registrar or a judge. The parties may apply on notice to all other parties for a fixed date for hearing.

14.8 Other cases may be put in the list by the EAT with the consent of the parties at shorter notice: for example, where other cases have been settled or withdrawn or where it appears that they will take less time than originally estimated. Parties who wish their cases to be taken as soon as possible and at short notice should notify the EAT. Representations by way of objection may be made by the parties to the EAT and if necessary by appeal to a judge or the Registrar.

14.9 Each week an up-to-date list for the following week will be prepared, including any changes which have been made, in particular specifying cases which by then have been given fixed dates. The list appears on the EAT website.

15 SKELETON ARGUMENTS

[5.43]

15.1 Paragraphs 15.2 to 15.14 of the Practice Direction do not apply to an appeal heard in Scotland, unless otherwise directed in relation to that appeal by the EAT.

15.2 Skeleton arguments must be provided by all parties in all hearings, unless the EAT is notified by a party or representative in writing that the Notice of Appeal or Respondent's Answer or relevant application contains the full argument, or the EAT otherwise directs in a particular case. It is the practice of the EAT for all the members to read the papers in advance. A well-structured skeleton argument helps the EAT and the parties to focus on the point(s) of law required to be decided and so makes the oral hearing more effective.

15.3 The skeleton argument should be concise. It should identify the paragraphs of the judgment appealed where an error or point of law is said to arise; and the argument should correspond to the numbered grounds set out in the Notice of Appeal. It should identify and summarise the point(s) of law, the steps in the legal argument and the statutory provisions and case law to be relied on, identifying these by name, page and paragraph and stating the legal principle for which legislation or case law is cited. It is not, however, the purpose of the skeleton argument to set out a full written argument and it should be as short as the nature of the case permits. The mere fact that the judgment under appeal is lengthy does not mean that the skeleton argument should be lengthy.

15.4 The skeleton argument should be self-contained: though it may give references for relevant legal authorities, it should not incorporate arguments set out in other documents by adopting them.

15.5 Where possible the skeleton argument should be in print, rather than handwritten, using A4 paper, 12 point typescript, arranged in consecutively numbered paragraphs each separated from the other by a double space, and in a standard readable font.

15.6 The parties should be referred to by name or as they appeared at the Employment Tribunal i.e. Claimant (C) and Respondent (R).

15.7 The skeleton argument should state the form of order which the party will ask the EAT to make at the hearing: for example, in the case of an Appellant, whether the EAT will be asked to remit the whole or part of the case to the same or to a different Employment Tribunal, or whether the EAT will be asked to substitute a different decision for that of the Employment Tribunal.

15.8 The Appellant's skeleton argument must unless dispensed with by direction of the Registrar or a judge be accompanied by a Chronology of events relevant to the appeal which, if possible, should be agreed by the parties. That will normally be taken as an uncontroversial document, unless corrected by another party or the EAT. It is good practice to give references to paragraphs in the ET Judgment or pages in the EAT bundle.

15.9 Unless impracticable, the skeleton argument should be prepared using the pagination in the index to the appeal bundle. In a case where a note of the evidence at the Employment Tribunal has been produced, the skeleton argument should identify the parts of the record to which that party wishes to refer.

15.10 Represented parties should give the instructions necessary for their representative to comply with this procedure within the time limits.

15.11 The fact that conciliation or settlement negotiations are in progress in relation to the appeal does not excuse delay in lodging and exchanging skeleton arguments.

15.12 A skeleton argument may be lodged by the Appellant with the Notice of Appeal or by the Respondent with the Respondent's Answer.

15.13 Skeleton arguments must (if not already so lodged):

15.13.1 be lodged at the EAT not less than 14 days (unless otherwise ordered) before the date fixed for the hearing; or, if the hearing is fixed at less than 14 days notice, as soon as possible after the hearing date has been notified, and unless otherwise directed be provided to the other party (or parties);

15.13.2 in cases that are either fast-tracked or in the warned list, be lodged at the EAT and exchanged between the parties as soon as possible and (unless the hearing date is less than seven days later) in any event within seven days after the parties have been notified that the case is expedited or in the warned list.

15.14 Failure to comply with the requirement to lodge skeleton arguments in time or at all may lead to postponement of an appeal or dismissal for non-compliance with the PD pursuant to Rule 26, and to an award of costs. The party in default may also be required to attend before the EAT to explain their failure. It will always mean that:

(a) the defaulting party must immediately despatch any delayed skeleton argument to the EAT by hand or by fax, or by email to londoneat@justice.gov.uk or, as appropriate, edinburgheat@justice.gov.uk; and

(b) unless notified by the EAT to the contrary, the defaulting party must bring to the hearing sufficient copies (a minimum of 4, or 6 if the judge is sitting with Lay Members) of the skeleton argument. The EAT staff will not be responsible for printing or copying skeleton arguments on the day of the hearing.

See section 16.7 below for the similar provisions which apply for authorities.

15.15 Scotland: Skeleton Arguments Skeleton arguments are considered particularly helpful to the EAT. Subject to any direction specific to a particular case, parties are at liberty to present a skeleton argument to the EAT. If they do so, however, they must serve a copy on every other party at the same time as presenting it to the EAT; and since the purpose is to indicate to the EAT in advance of a hearing how the argument is to be developed, in enough time for the judge (and members, if any) to consider it before the hearing, it should be presented at least 7 days prior to the day appointed for the hearing. Any skeleton argument presented later than that may not be read, and the party presenting it will lose the advantage of it. A party is entitled to present a skeleton argument even if the opposing party does not choose to do so.

16 AUTHORITIES

GENERAL

[5.44]
16.1 It is undesirable for parties to cite the same case from different sets of reports. The parties should, if practicable, agree which report will be used at the hearing. Where the Employment Tribunal has cited from a report it may be convenient to cite from the same report.

16.2 The parties must co-operate in agreeing a list of authorities.

16.3 It is the responsibility of a party wishing to cite any authority to provide photocopies for the use of each member of the Tribunal and photocopies or at least a list for the other parties. All authorities should be indexed and incorporated in an agreed bundle.

16.4 For those parties who are represented, best practice is to use photo or online copies of formal reports, such as the ICR's or IRLR's rather than those available from other on-line sources. These reports have head notes and are more useful to the Court than other electronic copies of the same case. The reports should be presented in a bundle, in chronological order, because that assists the Court in seeing how the law has developed. Relevant passages on which a party intends to rely should be sidelined and/or highlighted clearly.

16.5 Some familiar authorities are so frequently cited to the Appeal Tribunal that sufficient copies of those authorities for any hearing are maintained at the EAT in every court. This avoids unnecessary work for the parties, and overuse of paper and copying resources. A list of such cases will be maintained on the website of the Appeal Tribunal, and any case on the list should not be photocopied. It may be relied on if necessary in argument before the Appeal Tribunal (which may refer to the maintained copy), and if so it will be sufficient for the party relying upon it to identify the principle contended for, or said to be inapplicable, by reference to the paragraph number(s) of the report.

16.6 The Practice Direction in respect of civil appeals in England and Wales issued by the Lord Chief Justice and Heads of Division on 23rd. March 2012 applies to appeals to the EAT in England and Wales, subject only to necessary adaptations. It directs that in cases to which it relates reference should be made to no more than 10 authorities unless the scale of the appeal warrants more extensive citation. The same general principle applies to the Employment Appeal Tribunal in both Scotland and England/Wales. Authorities should set out legal principle, rather than be merely illustrative of an application of it. Parties must be prepared to justify more extensive citation of authority.

16.7 If a requirement for additional authorities is identified close to the date of the hearing (e.g. if the skeleton argument has been lodged late, see paragraph 15.14 above) the party wishing to refer to such authorities must (unless notified by the EAT to the contrary) bring to the hearing sufficient copies of any authority not contained in the "familiar authorities" bundle. A minimum of 4 copies (6 if the judge is sitting with Lay Members) will be required. EAT staff will not supply copies of authorities on the day of the hearing.

PH CASES

16.8 If it is thought necessary to cite any authority at a PH, appeal against Registrar's Order, Rule 3(10) or 6(16) hearing or Appointment for Directions, two copies should be provided for the EAT (four copies if a judge is sitting with members) no less than 10 days before the hearing, unless otherwise ordered: and additional copies for any other parties notified. All authorities should be bundled, indexed and incorporated in one bundle as set out above.

16.9 The parties are reminded that the Employment Appeal Tribunal will expect them to identify authorities which stand in opposition to their case on the question of law raised in the appeal, just as much as those which favour it.

17 DISPOSAL OF APPEALS BY CONSENT

[5.45]
17.1 An Appellant who wishes to abandon or withdraw an appeal should notify the other parties and the EAT immediately. If a settlement is reached, the parties should inform the EAT as soon as possible. The Appellant should submit to the EAT a letter signed by or on behalf of the Appellant and by or on behalf of the Respondent, asking the EAT for permission to withdraw the appeal and to make a consent order in the form of an attached draft signed by or for both parties dismissing the appeal, together with any other agreed order sought.

17.2 If the other parties do not agree to the proposed order the EAT should be informed. Written submissions should be lodged at the EAT and served on the parties. Any outstanding issue may be determined on the papers by the EAT, particularly if it relates to costs, but the EAT may fix an oral hearing to determine the outstanding matters in dispute between the parties.

17.3 If the parties reach an agreement that the appeal should be allowed by consent, and that an order made by the Employment Tribunal should be reversed or varied or the matter remitted to the Employment Tribunal on the ground that the decision contains an error of law, it is usually necessary for the matter to be heard by the EAT to determine whether there is a good reason for making the proposed order. On notification by the parties, the EAT will decide whether the appeal can be dealt with on the papers or by a hearing at which one or more parties or their representatives should attend to argue the case for allowing the appeal and making the order that the parties wish the EAT to make.

17.5 If the application for permission to withdraw an appeal is made close to the hearing date the EAT may require the attendance of the Appellant and/or a representative to explain the reasons for delay in making a decision not to pursue the appeal.

18 APPELLANT'S FAILURE TO PRESENT A RESPONSE

[5.46]
18.1 If the Appellant in an appeal did not present a response (ET3) to the Employment Tribunal and did not apply to the Employment Tribunal for an extension of time for doing so, or applied for such an extension and was refused, the Notice of Appeal must include particulars directed to the following issues, namely whether:

18.1.1 there is a good excuse for failing to present a response (ET3) and (if that be the case) for failing to apply for such an extension of time; and

18.1.2 there is a reasonably arguable defence to the claim (ET1).

18.2 In order to satisfy the EAT on these issues, the Appellant must in addition to the Notice of Appeal, present a witness statement explaining in detail the circumstances in which there has been a failure to serve a response (ET3) in time or apply for such an extension of time, the reason for that failure and the facts and matters relied upon for contesting the claim (ET1) on the merits. There should be exhibited to the witness statement all relevant documents and a completed draft response (ET3).

19 HEARINGS

HEARINGS BEFORE JUDGE AND ONE LAY MEMBER

[5.47]
19.1 Where consent is to be obtained from the parties pursuant to s28(4) of the ETA 1996 to an appeal commencing or continuing to be heard by a judge together with only one lay member, the parties must, prior to the commencement or continuation of such hearing before a two-member court, themselves or by their representatives, each sign a form containing the name of the one member remaining, and stating whether the member is a person falling within s28(6)(a) or (b) of the ETA 1996.

VIDEO AND TELEPHONE HEARINGS

19.2 Facilities can exceptionally be arranged for the purpose of holding short PHs or short Appointments for Directions by telephone link, upon the application (in writing) of an Appellant or Respondent who, or whose representative, has a relevant disability (supported by appropriate medical evidence). An application for a telephone hearing will be determined by a judge or the Registrar, and must be made well in advance of the intended hearing date, so that arrangements may be made. Video conferencing facilities are not currently available at the EAT's premises. Where a hearing by video link is considered necessary and proportionate in a particular case and having regard to all the circumstances, arrangements may be made for such a hearing to take place at an alternative location.

RECORDING OF HEARINGS

19.3 Hearings will not normally be recorded, except for the giving of any judgment. Parties are reminded that they are NOT permitted to make any video or audio recording nor take any photograph of the proceedings except with the express prior consent of the judge at the hearing, for which good reason must be shown, and that it is a contempt of court to do so, the penalties for which include fines and imprisonment.

20 HANDING DOWN OF JUDGMENTS

ENGLAND AND WALES

[5.48]

20.1 When the EAT reserves judgment to a later date, the parties will be notified of the date when it is ready to be handed down. It is not generally necessary for a party or representative to attend.

20.2 The judgment will be pronounced without being read aloud, by the judge who presided or by another judge, on behalf of the EAT. The judge may deal with any application or may refer it to the judge and/or the Tribunal who heard the appeal, whether to deal with on the papers or at a further oral hearing on notice. Applications for permission to appeal should be made pursuant to paragraph 24 below. Applications for costs should be made pursuant to paragraph 21.2 below.

20.3 Transcripts of unreserved judgments at a PH, appeals against Registrar's Orders, Appointment for Directions and Rule 3(10) or 6(16) hearings will not (save as below) be produced and provided to the parties:

20.3.1 Where an appeal, or any ground of appeal, is dismissed in the presence of the Appellant, no transcript of the judgment is produced unless, within 14 days of the seal date of the order, either party applies to the EAT for a transcript, or the EAT of its own initiative directs that a judgment be transcribed (in circumstances such as those set out in paragraph 20.4.2 below).

20.3.2 Where an appeal or any ground of appeal is dismissed in the absence of the Appellant, a transcript will be supplied to the Appellant.

20.3.3 Where an appeal is allowed to go forward to a PH or an FH, reasons will usually be given by the judge for permitting the appeal to go forward. In general a written note of the judge's reasons will be provided to all parties to the appeal.

20.4 Transcripts of unreserved judgments at an FH: where judgment is delivered at the hearing, no transcript will be produced and provided to the parties unless:

20.4.1 either party applies for it to the EAT within 14 days of that hearing;

20.4.2 the EAT of its own initiative directs that the judgment be transcribed, e.g. where it is considered that a point of general importance arises or that the matter is to be remitted to, or otherwise continued before, the Employment Tribunal; or

20.4.3 a party is not present at the hearing of the appeal.

20.5 Where judgment at either a PH or an FH is reserved, and later handed down in writing, a copy is provided to all parties, and to recognised law reporters. It will at the discretion of the judge be provided in advance on suitable undertakings as to confidentiality for the purpose of correcting any obvious errors of transcription or expression: the reasoning is not open to revision unless a review (see Rule 33) is applied for and granted. The parties may apply in advance of the handing down in respect of costs, or permission to appeal, and unless it is otherwise directed that application will normally be dealt with on paper without an oral hearing.

SCOTLAND

20.6 Judgments are often reserved in Scotland and will be handed down as soon as practicable thereafter on a provisional basis to both parties who will thereafter have a period of 14 days to make any representations with regard to expenses, leave to appeal or any other relevant matter. At the expiry of that period or after such representations have been dealt with, whichever shall be the later, an order will be issued to conform to the original judgment.

EAT WEBSITE

20.7 All FH judgments which are transcribed or handed down will be posted on the EAT website. Any other judgment may be posted on the EAT website if so directed by the Registrar or a Judge.

21 COSTS (REFERRED TO AS EXPENSES IN SCOTLAND)

[5.49]

21.1 In this PD "costs" includes legal costs, expenses, allowances paid by the Secretary of State and payment in respect of time spent in preparing a case. Such costs may relate to interim applications or hearings or to a PH or FH.

21.2 An application for costs must be made either during or at the end of a relevant hearing, or in writing to the Registrar within 14 days of the seal date of the relevant order of the EAT or, in the case of a reserved judgment, as provided for in paragraph 21.4 below, copied to all parties.

21.3 The party seeking the order must state the legal ground and facts on which the application is based and, by a schedule or otherwise, show how the costs have been incurred. If the application is made in respect of only part of the proceedings, particulars must be given showing how the costs have been incurred on that specific part. If the party against whom the order is sought wishes the EAT to have regard to means and/or an alleged inability to pay, a witness statement giving particulars and exhibiting any documents must be served on the other party (or parties) and presented to the EAT. Further directions may need to be given by the EAT in such cases.

21.4 Such application may be resolved by the EAT on the papers, provided that the opportunity has been given for representations in writing by all relevant parties, or the EAT may refer the matter for an oral hearing, and may assess the costs either on the papers or at an oral hearing, or refer the matter for detailed assessment.

21.5 Wasted Costs: An application for a wasted costs order must be made in writing, setting out the nature of the case upon which the application is based and the best particulars of the costs sought to be recovered. Such application must be presented to the EAT and served upon the party (or parties) who will pay the costs/expenses if the application succeeds. Further directions may need to be given by the EAT in such cases.

21.6 Where the EAT makes any costs order by decision on the papers it shall provide written reasons for so doing. If such order is made at a hearing, then written reasons will be provided if a request is made at the hearing or within 21 days of the seal date of the costs order. The Registrar shall send a copy of the written reasons to all the parties to the proceedings.

22 REMISSION OF CASES TO THE EMPLOYMENT TRIBUNAL

[5.50]
22.1 Where the EAT makes an order remitting the case or part of it to an Employment Tribunal for further or re-hearing, the parties must immediately raise any uncertainty as to the precise scope of the remission, for it is this which defines the jurisdiction of the Employment Tribunal on the remitted issues. The scope of the remission will be recorded in the Order following the hearing. It is the obligation of each party to ensure that the scope as there set out corresponds with their understanding and to raise any question without delay if it appears not to do so.

22.2 If at a later hearing before an Employment Tribunal an issue arises as to the scope of remission, the Tribunal may invite the EAT to give whatever clarification is thought necessary, and if given this will be conclusive.

23 REVIEW

[5.51]
23.1 Where an application is made for a review of a judgment or order of the EAT, it will normally be considered by the judge or judge and lay members who heard the appeal in respect of which the review is sought, who may exercise any power of case management as seems appropriate. If the original judgment or order was made by the judge together with lay members, then the judge may, pursuant to Rule 33, consider and refuse such application for review on the papers. If the judge does not refuse the application, he or she may make any relevant further order, but will not grant the application without notice to the opposing party and reference to the lay members, for consideration with them, either on paper or in open court. A request to review a judgment or order of the EAT must be made within 14 days of the seal date of the order, or must include an application, for an extension of time, with reasons, copied to all parties.

24 APPEALS FROM THE EAT

APPEALS HEARD IN ENGLAND AND WALES

[5.52]
24.1 An application to the EAT for permission to appeal to the Court of Appeal must be made (unless the EAT otherwise orders) at the hearing or when a reserved judgment is handed down or in writing within seven days thereafter as provided in paragraph 20.5 above. If not made then, or if refused, or unless the EAT otherwise orders, any such application must be made to the Court of Appeal within 21 days of the sealed order. An application for an extension of time for permission to appeal may be entertained by the EAT where a case is made out to the satisfaction of a judge or Registrar that there is a need to delay until after a transcript is received (expedited if appropriate) or for other good reason. Applications for an extension of time for permission to appeal should however normally be made to the Court of Appeal.

24.2 The party seeking permission must state the point of law to be advanced and the grounds.

APPEALS HEARD IN SCOTLAND

24.3 An application to the EAT for permission to appeal to the Court of Session must be made within 42 days of the date of the hearing where judgment is delivered at that hearing: if judgment is reserved, within 42 days of the date the transcript was sent to parties.

24.4 The party seeking permission must state the point of law to be advanced and the grounds.

LEAPFROG APPEALS TO THE SUPREME COURT

24.5 Section 37A of the Employment Tribunals Act 1996 (as amended) permits the grant of a certificate by the EAT for an appeal from the EAT directly to the Supreme Court in cases where the appeal involves a point of law of general public importance and satisfies the conditions set out at subsection (4) or (5) and the EAT is satisfied that a sufficient case for an appeal to the Supreme Court is made out to justify an application under section 37B.

24.6 An application to the EAT for permission to pursue a 'leapfrog' appeal to the Supreme Court must be made at the hearing or when a reserved judgment is handed down or in writing within seven days thereafter. An application for an extension of time for permission to pursue a 'leapfrog' appeal may be entertained by the EAT where a case is made out to the satisfaction of a judge or the registrar that there is a need to delay until after a transcript is received (expedited where appropriate) or for other good reason.

24.7 The party seeking permission must state the point of law to be advanced and the grounds, and must identify how and in what way the conditions for a 'leapfrog' appeal are met.

25 CONCILIATION

[5.53]

25.1 Pursuant to Rule 36 and the overriding objective, the EAT encourages alternative dispute resolution.

25.2 In all cases the parties should, and when so directed must, consider conciliation of their appeals. The Registrar or a judge may at any stage make such a direction and require the parties to report on steps taken, but not the substance, to effect a conciliated settlement with the assistance of an ACAS officer notified by ACAS to the EAT.

The Honourable Mrs Justice Simler DBE President

Dated: 19 December 2018

NOTICE OF APPEAL FROM DECISION OF EMPLOYMENT TRIBUNAL

[5.54]

1. The appellant is (*name and address of appellant*).

2. Any communication relating to this appeal may be sent to the appellant at (*appellant's address for service, including telephone number if any*).

3. The appellant appeals from (*here give particulars of the judgment, decision or order of the employment tribunal from which the appeal is brought including the location of the employment tribunal and the date*).

4. The parties to the proceedings before the employment tribunal, other than the appellant, were (*names and addresses of other parties to the proceedings resulting in judgment, decision or order appealed from*).

5. Copies of—

(a) the written record of the employment tribunal's judgment, decision or order and the written reasons of the employment tribunal;
(b) the claim (ET1);
(c) the response (ET3); and/or (*where relevant*)
(d) an explanation as to why any of these documents are not included; are attached to this notice.

6. If the appellant has made an application to the employment tribunal for a review of its judgment or decision, copies of—

(a) the review application;
(b) the judgment;
(c) the written reasons of the employment tribunal in respect of that review application; and/or
(d) a statement by or on behalf of the appellant, if such be the case, that a judgment is awaited;

are attached to this Notice. If any of these documents exist but cannot be included, then a written explanation must be given.

7. The grounds upon which this appeal is brought are that the employment tribunal erred in law in that (*here set out in paragraphs the various grounds of appeal*).

Date: . . . . Signed: . . . .

NB. The details entered on your Notice of Appeal must be legible and suitable for photocopying or electronic scanning. The use of black ink or typescript is recommended.

The Ministry of Justice and HM Courts and Tribunals Service processes personal information about you in the context of tribunal proceedings. For details of the standards we follow when processing your data, please visit the following address https://www.gov.uk/government/organisations/hm-courts-and-tribunalsservice/about/personal-information-charter *To receive a paper copy of this privacy notice, please call 0300 123 1024/ Textphone 18001 0300 123 1024. If calling from Scotland, please call 0300 790 6234 Textphone 18001 0300 790 6234.*

2. EAT PRACTICE STATEMENTS

EMPLOYMENT APPEAL TRIBUNAL PRACTICE STATEMENT (2005)

[5.55]

NOTES

This is a Practice Statement handed down by the President of the Employment Appeal Tribunal on 3 February 2005.

1. The attention of litigants and practitioners in the Employment Appeal Tribunal is expressly drawn to the wording and effect of Rules 3(1)(b) and 3(3) of the Employment Appeal Tribunal Rules (1993) (as amended). As is quite clear from the terms of paragraph 2.1 of the Employment Appeal Tribunal Practice Direction 2004 handed down on 9 December 2004, a Notice of Appeal without the specified documentation will not be validly lodged. The documentation required to accompany the Notice of Appeal in order for it to be valid now includes a copy of the Claim (ET1) and the Response (ET3) in the Employment Tribunal proceedings appealed from, if such be available to the appellant, and in any event if such not be available for whatever reason then a written explanation as to why they are not provided. Paragraph 2.1 of the Practice Direction makes this entirely clear:

> "2.1 . . . Copies of the judgment, decision or order appealed against and of the Employment Tribunal's written reasons, together with a copy of the Claim (ET1) and the Response (ET3) must be attached, or if not, a written explanation must be given. A Notice of Appeal without such documentation will not be validly lodged."

2. The reported decision of the Employment Appeal Tribunal in ***Kanapathiar v London Borough of Harrow*** [2003] IRLR 571 made quite clear that the effect of failure to lodge documents required by the Rules with the Notice of Appeal within the time limit specified for lodging of a Notice of Appeal would mean that the Notice of Appeal had not been validly lodged in time. The same now applies to the additional documents required by the amended Rule, namely the Claim and the Response.

3. It is apparent that both practitioners and litigants in person are not complying with the new Rules and Practice Direction, and not appreciating the consequences of their non-compliance. Between 2 and 26 January 2005, 20 Notices of Appeal were received by the Employment Appeal Tribunal and returned as invalid (compared with 4 during the similar period in 2004). Of those 20 Notices of Appeal, 7 would have been invalid in any event under the old Rules. 13 however were only invalid because they were neither accompanied by the Claim nor the Response nor by any explanation as to their absence or unavailability. If the Notices of Appeal are relodged well within the very generous 42-day time limit, there may still be time for the missing documents to be supplied and the time limit to be complied with. If however, as is very often the case, such Notices of Appeal are delivered either at, or only immediately before, the expiry of the time limit, the absence of the relevant documents is, even if speedily pointed out by the Employment Appeal Tribunal, likely to lead to the Notice of Appeal being out of time.

4. Of the 20 Notices of Appeal which were invalidly lodged during the period above referred to, only 10 were lodged by litigants in person and 10 by solicitors or other representatives: and it is plain that the latter ought certainly to have known of the requirements, although, given the wide publication both of the Rules and the Practice Direction, together with the guidance given by the Employment Tribunals, both at the Tribunal and sent with their judgments, there can be no excuse for litigants in person either.

5. The reason for this Statement in open court is to re-emphasise these requirements and the consequence of failure to comply with them, namely that an appeal not lodged within the 42 days validly constituted, ie accompanied by the required documents, will be out of time, and extensions of time are only exceptionally granted (see paragraph 3.7 of the Practice Direction).

6. From the date of this Practice Statement, ignorance or misunderstanding of the requirements as to service of the documents required to make a Notice of Appeal within the 42 days valid will not be accepted by the Registrar as an excuse.

The Hon Mr Justice Burton
President of the Employment Appeal Tribunal
3 February 2005

EMPLOYMENT APPEAL TRIBUNAL PRACTICE STATEMENT: NOTICES OF APPEAL AND SKELETON ARGUMENTS (2015)

[5.56]

NOTES

INTRODUCTION

1. Too many notices of appeal are simply too long. If a Notice of Appeal is too long, focus on what really matters can easily be lost. Justice then suffers. A change of culture is needed.

2. Parties should realise that short, well-directed notices of appeal are usually more persuasive than long ones. The more points an appeal raises, the more it suggests that none is a very good one.

WHAT GROUNDS IN A NOTICE OF APPEAL SHOULD LOOK LIKE

3. Notices of appeal should be set out in numbered paragraphs, in line with the forms set out in the EAT Rules 1993, rule 3 and Schedule. The grounds are contained within the notice.

4. There is no right to appeal except on a point of law. A point of law should be easy to identify in a few words. Whatever the paragraph numbering of the surrounding text is, the grounds of appeal themselves:

(a) should begin with the heading "Numbered Grounds" and be numbered consecutively, starting at (1);

(b) each be headed by a brief description – underlined or in bold or both – of the point of law relied on (eg, "Misinterpreted Section XX of the Equality Act 2010"; "Reached a decision on a point which had not been argued"; etc.) followed only by what is needed to enable a Judge of the EAT to understand the point;

(c) should (except in the case of appeals alleging either perversity or bias) usually occupy in total no more than 2 sides of A4 paper;

(d) in the case of appeals alleging either perversity or bias, or both, should comply with paragraph 3.8 (perversity) or paragraph 13 (bias) of the EAT Practice Direction 2013;

(e) should not include any quotation from either the Tribunal judgment under appeal (which can and will be read by the EAT) or any authority (though if it is important and relevant to refer to an authority, the reference should allow it to be identified, and the relevant page and paragraph number should be stated);

(f) should not contain any footnote, nor incorporate any other document.

5. If introductory, or further explanatory, text is considered desirable in addition to the grounds themselves, it should in most appeals be short, and should avoid making a complaint about the judgment of the Tribunal which is not made as one of the numbered grounds. Notices of Appeal are not meant to be skeleton arguments though it is permissible for enough to be said to persuade a judge at the EAT who considers the appeal on paper that it shows a reasonable ground for appealing.

RESPONDENT'S ANSWER

6. A Respondent to an appeal is not obliged to respond in any answer to contentions made in any text which accompanies the notice of Appeal. Unless it has additional reasons to add, it is enough simply to say it relies on the Reasons of the Tribunal. Additional reasons to support the Decision, if any, should be stated shortly.

WHAT WILL HAPPEN IF NOTICES OF APPEAL DO NOT FOLLOW THESE DIRECTIONS?

7.

(a) A judge may send them back to be shortened and resubmitted. Any delay caused by this will be regarded as that party's responsibility (though will not itself result in the appeal being ruled to be out of time).

(b) A preliminary hearing may be directed, for the Appellant alone to attend, to persuade the EAT there is reasonable ground for the appeal. Any expense, inconvenience and delay caused by this is the Appellant's sole responsibility.

(c) In some cases, the failure may be regarded as unreasonable conduct of litigation and expose the Appellant to a risk of costs.

WHY IS THIS PRACTICE STATEMENT NEEDED?

8. An appeal which is too long risks losing focus. There are other consequences too. Too long a Notice of Appeal invites too lengthy a Respondent's answer. This in turn can add to the length of hearings. This takes up time, to the disadvantage of the parties and to other cases which are also entitled to be heard in good time. It costs money where at least one party pays to be represented, not only in the additional length of a hearing, but because longer Notices and Answers may be thought by those who prepare them to justify higher charges.

9. It is particularly unfair for litigants in person to have to try to work out from a mass of material what appeal point is really being made, when it could be simply and clearly stated.

10. The judges of the EAT consider that Notices of Appeal have become longer and longer in recent times, and less helpful as a result.

11. Other senior courts have found the same, and taken similar steps e.g. the Commercial Court (*Tchenguiz v Grant Thornton* [2015] EWHC 405) and Court of Appeal (*Standard Bank PLC v Via Mat International Ltd* [2013] EWCA Civ 490), and this has been echoed in the EAT (e.g. in *Salmon v Castlebeck Care (Teesdale) Ltd* [2014] UKEAT/0304/14 (10th Dec 2014)).

SKELETON ARGUMENTS

12. Skeleton arguments are not expected to be full written arguments, but instead are intended to provide the framework within which oral submissions will be made, and should be as short as the nature of the case permits. In particular they should not be lengthy just because the judgment under appeal is lengthy.

13. They should refer to the decision or judgment under appeal, identifying the paragraphs of the judgment where an error of law may be detected or point of law arise; and the argument should correspond to the numbered grounds set out in the Notice of Appeal.

14. It is often helpful to include citations to relevant legislation and authorities (i.e. case law) which are critical to the argument, though it is sufficient to identify these by adequate reference. As well as giving the reference, there should be a concise statement of what the legislation relevantly provides, and the legal principle for which a case is being cited.

15. The argument should be self-contained: though it may give references for relevant legal authorities, it should not incorporate arguments set out in other documents by adopting them.

Mr. Justice Langstaff
President EAT.
13 May 2015

EMPLOYMENT APPEAL TRIBUNAL PRACTICE IN RELATION TO FAMILIAR AUTHORITIES (2016)

[5.57]

NOTES

This Practice Statement was reissued on 17 March 2016. It is an amended version of the Practice Statement originally issued in 2012. In particular, a new paragraph 19 has beenadded to the Familiar Authorities Bundle and subsequent paragraphs were renumbered accordingly. It is reproduced here as so amended.

Certain key authorities (important court cases) have in the past been frequently included in the Bundles of Authorities prepared by parties for hearings at the EAT and regularly cited to the Appeal Tribunal.

As explained in the EAT President's **Practice Statement** of 17 April 2012 the Appeal Tribunal has adopted a new arrangement in relation to those frequently cited cases:

"A number of familiar authorities are so frequently cited to the Appeal Tribunal that sufficient copies of those authorities for any hearing will be maintained at the Tribunal in every court. This will avoid unnecessary work for the parties, and avoid overuse of paper and copying resources.
A list of such cases will be maintained on the website of the Appeal Tribunal, and any case on the list should not be photocopied. It may be relied on if necessary in argument before the Appeal Tribunal (which may refer to the maintained copy), and if so it will be sufficient for the party relying upon it to identify the principle contended for, or said to be inapplicable, by reference to the paragraph number(s) of the report."

Pursuant to that Statement, each EAT courtroom (in London and Edinburgh) is now supplied with sufficient copies of a *Bundle of Familiar Authorities* for use by each member of any Appeal Tribunal which is sitting.

The **Contents List** of those Bundles is attached.

Parties and their advisers should check the Contents List before assembling their own Bundles of Authorities and the cases shown in the Contents List should not be included in parties' bundles for hearings taking place from 25 June 2012 onwards.

Two particular points should be noted:

(1) the cases included in the Contents List are kept under review and the Appeal Tribunal expects to revise the Contents List from time to time. Parties and their advisers should always check this webpage for the current version before assembling their own bundles: and
(2) the cases included appear in the form of report available at the time of assembly of the bundles. Where cases have been reported in more than one source, a report has been selected which reflects paragraph 6 of the Practice Direction issued by the Lord Chief Justice on 23 March 2012 addressing Citation of Authorities.

Familiar Authorities Bundle—Contents

Amendment *(notice of appeal – whether to grant)*

1. Khudados v Leggate [2005] ICR 1013, EAT
2. Readman v Devon Primary Care Trust [2011] UKEAT 0116/11, EAT

Bias *(allegations – EAT procedure)*

3. Facey v Midas Retail Security [2001] ICR 287, EAT

Bias *(test for)*

4. Porter v Magill [2002] 2 AC 357, HL

Deciding a case on ground not argued

5. Chapman v Simon [1994] IRLR 124, CA

Error of law *(jurisdiction of EAT)*

6. British Telecommunications plc v Sheridan [1990] IRLR 27, CA
7. Brent London Borough Council v Fuller [2011] ICR 806, CA

New points of law *(taken for first time at the EAT)*

8. Kumchyk v Derby City Council [1978] ICR 1116, EAT
9. Jones v Governing Body of Burdett Coutts School [1999] ICR 38, CA
10. Glennie v Independent Magazines (UK) Ltd [1999] IRLR 719, CA
11. Secretary of State for Health v Rance [2007] IRLR 665, EAT

New points *(taken for first time during an employment tribunal hearing)*

12. Ladbrokes Racing Ltd v Traynor UKEATS 0067/06, EAT

Perversity

13. Yeboah v Crofton [2002] IRLR 634, CA

Polkey

14. Polkey v AE Dayton Services Ltd [1988] 1 AC 344, HL

Reasons *(duty to give)*

15. Meek v City of Birmingham District Council [1987] IRLR 250, CA
16. English v Emery Reimbold & Strick Ltd [2002] 1 WLR 2409, CA
17. Greenwood v NWF Retail [2011] ICR 896, EAT

Reasons *(EAT power to ask for further reasons)*

18. Barke v SEETEC Business Technology Centre Ltd [2005] IRLR 633, CA

Remission *(whether obliged to remit)*

19. Jafri v Lincoln College [2014] ICR 920, CA

Remission *(whether to the same or differently-constituted Tribunal)*

20. Sinclair Roche & Temperley v Heard [2004] IRLR 763, EAT

Time Limits *(whether to grant an extension of time for appealing)*

21. United Arab Emirates v Abdelghafar [1995] ICR 65, EAT
22. Aziz v Bethnal Green City Challenge Co Ltd [2000] IRLR 111, CA
23. Jurkowska v HLMAD Ltd [2008] ICR 841, CA
24. Muschett v London Borough of Hounslow [2009] ICR 424, EAT

Striking-out *(exercise of employment tribunal's powers)*

25. Tayside Public Transport Co Ltd v Reilly [2012] CSIH 46, CS

3. EMPLOYMENT TRIBUNALS ENGLAND AND WALES: PRESIDENTIAL PRACTICE DIRECTIONS

NOTES

Practice Directions in this section are issued under the authority of Regulation 11 of the Employment Tribunals (Constitution & Rules of Procedure) Regulations 2013 at **[2.1333]**.

EMPLOYMENT TRIBUNALS (ENGLAND & WALES) DIRECTION OF THE PRESIDENT IN THE MATTER OF CLAIMS BROUGHT IN EMPLOYMENT TRIBUNALS (ENGLAND AND WALES) IN RESPECT OF THE CALCULATION OF UNPAID HOLIDAY PAY (2015)

[5.58]

NOTES

This PD was issued in March 2015 to replace the one issued in December 2014. An accompanying note was also published in March 2015 explaining the reasons for the revocation of the December 2014 PD. See www.judiciary.gov.uk/announcements/revocation-of-directions-related-to-holiday-pay/.

HAVING REGARD TO the European Union Working Time Directive (No 2003/88);

AND having regard to the decisions of the Court of Justice of the European Union in *British Airways plc v Williams* [2012] ICR 847 and in *British Gas Trading Ltd v Lock* [2014] ICR 813;

AND having regard to the decision of the Employment Appeal Tribunal in *Bear Scotland Ltd and others v Fulton and others*; *Hertel (UK) Ltd v Woods and others*; and *Amex Group Ltd and others* (4 November 2014);

AND having regard to regulations 13, 13A and 30 of the Working Time Regulations 1998;

AND having regard to Part II and Part XIV (Chapters II and III) of the Employment Rights Act 1996;

AND having regard to the Employment Tribunals (Constitution and Rules of Procedure) Regulations 2013 and the Employment Tribunals Rules of Procedure, as set out in Schedule 1 of the Regulations;

AND having regard to the decisions of the Employment Appeal Tribunal in *Okugade v Shaw Trust* (EAT 0172/05) and in *Prakash v Wolverhampton City Council* (EAT 0140/06)

THEN

ACTING in accordance with my powers under regulations 7 and 11 of the Employment Tribunals (Constitution and Rules of Procedure) Regulations 2013 and under rules 2 and 29 of the Employment Tribunals Rules of Procedure

IT IS ORDERED THAT

1. A claimant or group of claimants who have previously presented a claim or claims in respect of a complaint of alleged non-payment of holiday pay may, if so advised, apply to amend the claim or claims so presented in order to add a further complaint or complaints of alleged non-payment of holiday pay that have accrued or arisen after the presentation of the original claim and which could not have been included in the original claim or claims.

2. They may do so, if so advised, instead of presenting a new claim to the Tribunal.

3. Any such application shall identify clearly the original claim that is sought to be amended by case number, claimant(s) and respondent(s). It shall also set out the amended particulars of the claim to include the additional dates or periods of alleged non-payment of holiday pay and the basis of the complaint.

4. Any such application shall be copied to the respondent(s) by the claimant(s) at the same time as making the application. The claimant(s) shall invite the respondent(s) to provide any written comments upon the application to the Tribunal within 7 days.

5. After that period of 7 days the application to amend will then be considered by a judge in accordance with the usual principles for the amendment of a claim. In the event that the claim affected is stayed at the time of the application, the stay will be lifted temporarily to allow for such consideration. Accordingly, parties should make such representations in connection with the application as they see fit at this stage.

6. An Employment Judge, if the interests of justice so require, may permit a claim to be amended even if the application to amend does not comply with the terms of this direction but in such a case the application must explain the reason for non compliance and why, nonetheless, it would be in the interests of justice to allow the amendment.

7. Any party or representative wishing to make representations for the further conduct of such claims should do so upon application to the President.

8. A copy of this Direction shall be sent to ACAS and to all known interested parties, and shall be

published on the Judiciary website: www.judiciary.gov.uk/publications/directions-employment-tribunals-england-wales/

9. The Direction of the President dated 11 December 2014 "In the matter of claims brought in Employment Tribunals (England and Wales) in respect of the calculation of unpaid holiday pay" is hereby revoked.

Judge Brian Doyle
President
Dated: 27 March 2015

EMPLOYMENT TRIBUNALS (ENGLAND & WALES) PRESIDENTIAL PRACTICE DIRECTION – ADDRESSES FOR SERVING DOCUMENTS IN SPECIAL CASES (2017)

[5.59]

NOTES

Commencement: 19 October 2017 (see para 1).

1. This Presidential Practice Direction, which sets out the addresses for serving in the special cases, is made in accordance with provisions of Regulation 11 of the Employment Tribunals (Constitution and Rules of Procedure) Regulations 2013 ("the Rules"). The Practice Direction has effect on and from 19th October 2017.

2. Rule 88 of the Schedule 1 of the Rule is in the following terms:-

"Special Cases

Rule 88 – Addresses for serving the Secretary of State, the Law Officers and the Counsel General to the Welsh Assembly Government, in cases where they are not parties, shall be issued by Practice Direction."

DIRECTION

3. For the purpose of Rule 88 the relevant addresses which are to be used when sending a notice or document in such special cases are set out in the schedule attached hereto.

Brian Doyle

President, Employment Tribunals (England and Wales)

Dated: 19th October 2017

SCHEDULE

Office	Address
Redundancy Payments Service (UK)	Secretary of State for Business, Energy and Industrial Strategy Employment Tribunal Section PO Box 16684 Birmingham B2 2EF RPS.ET@insolvency.gsi.gov.uk
Secretary of State for Business, Energy, and Industrial Strategy (BEIS)	Secretary of State for BEIS 1 Victoria Street London SW1H 0ET
Attorney General's Office (England)	Attorney General's Office 5-8 The Sanctuary London SW1P 3JS
Counsel General for Wales	Counsel General for Wales Welsh Government Cathays Park Cardiff CF10 3NQ
Advocate General for Scotland	Director and Solicitor to the Advocate General Victoria Quay Edinburgh EH6 6QQ
Lord Advocate (Scotland)	Lord Advocate 25 Chambers Street Edinburgh EH1 1LA

EMPLOYMENT TRIBUNALS (ENGLAND & WALES) PRESIDENTIAL PRACTICE DIRECTION – PRESENTATION OF CLAIMS (2017)

[5.60]

NOTES

Commencement: 26 July 2017 (see para 1).

1. This Presidential Practice Direction, which sets out the methods by which a completed form may be presented, is made in accordance with the provisions of Regulation 11 of the Employment Tribunals (Constitution & Rules Procedure) Regulations 2013. The Practice Direction has effect on and from 26 July 2017.

2. Rule 8 (1) of Schedule 1 of the Employment Tribunals (Constitution and Rules of Procedure) Regulations 2013 ("the Rules") is in the following terms:

"Presenting the claim

8.—(1)A claim shall be started by presenting a completed claim form (using a prescribed form) in accordance with any practice direction made under regulation 11 which supplements this rule."

3. For the purpose of this Presidential Practice Direction "claims" are defined by Rule 1 of the Rules as any proceedings before an Employment Tribunal making a complaint. A "complaint" is also clarified as anything that is referred to as a claim, complaint, reference, application or appeal in any enactment which confers jurisdiction on the Tribunal.

4. Methods of starting a claim

A completed claim form may be presented to an Employment Tribunal in England & Wales:

Online by using the online form submission service provided by Her Majesty's Courts and Tribunals Service, accessible at www.employmenttribunals.service.gov.uk;

By post to: **Employment Tribunal Central Office (England & Wales), PO Box 10218, Leicester, LE1 8EG**.

A claim may also be presented in person to an Employment Tribunal Office listed in the Schedule to this Practice Direction (and exceptionally by email to such an Office only during the period 26 July 2017 to 31 July 2017 inclusive and not otherwise).

5. The Presidential Practice Direction dated 14 December 2016 is hereby revoked.

Judge Brian Doyle

President, Employment Tribunals (England and Wales)

Dated: 2 November 2017

SCHEDULE

Region	***Address***
London Central	Victory House 30-34 Kingsway London WC2B 6EX
London East	2nd Floor Anchorage House 2 Clove Crescent London E14 2BE
London South	Montague Court 101 London Road West Croydon CR0 2RF
Midlands West	13th Floor Centre City Tower 7 Hill Street Birmingham B5 4UU
Midlands East	Nottingham Justice Centre Carrington Street Nottingham NG2 1EE

Region	***Address***
North East	4th Floor City Exchange 11 Albion Street Leeds LS1 5ES 2nd Floor, Kings Court Earl Grey Way Royal Quays North Shields Tyne & Wear NE29 6AR
North West	Alexandra House 14-22 The Parsonage Manchester M3 2JA
South East	3rd Floor Radius House 51 Clarendon Road Watford Hertfordshire WD17 1HP Employment Tribunals Cambridge County Court & Family Court 197 East Road Cambridge CB1 1BA
South West	Bristol Civil and Family Justice Centre 2 Redcliff Street Bristol BS1 6GR
Wales	Wales Employment Tribunal 3rd Floor Cardiff and Vale Magistrates Court Fitzalan Place Cardiff CF24 0RZ

4. EMPLOYMENT TRIBUNALS (ENGLAND AND WALES): PRESIDENTIAL GUIDANCE

NOTES

Guidance in this section is issued under the authority of Rule 7 of the Employment Tribunals Rules of Procedure 2013 at **[2.1344]**.

EMPLOYMENT TRIBUNALS (ENGLAND & WALES) PRESIDENTIAL GUIDANCE – RULE 21 JUDGMENT (2013)

[5.61]

NOTES

The Guidance is issued on the Fourth day of December 2013 under the provisions of Rule 7 of the first schedule to Employment Tribunals (Constitution and Rules of Procedure) Regulation 2013 ("the Rules").

Note:

Whilst the Tribunals in England and Wales must have regard to such Guidance they will not be bound by it.

Background:

1. Rule 21 of the Rules provides that where the time limit provided for under Rule 16 has expired and no response has been presented or any response received has been rejected, and no application for a reconsideration is outstanding or where the Respondent has stated that no part of the claim is contested, then an Employment Judge will consider whether on the available material, a determination can properly be made of the claim or part of it, issue a Judgment and make detailed provisions to that effect.

2. In applying the provisions of that Rule the procedure that will normally apply is as set out below.

Action by Parties:

1. Unless there are exceptional circumstances no action is required nor provided for by the Rules.

2. If there are exceptional circumstances then the party who believes such to exist must notify the Tribunal in writing immediately.

3. It is of benefit for all concerned for documentation sent to the Tribunal which will be considered by the Employment Judge, and in particular the claim form and any response form submitted, to provide sufficient detail for appropriate consideration to be made by an Employment Judge in accordance with this Rule.

Action by the Employment Judge:

1. The Employment Judge will review all the material that is then available. This will normally consist of the claim form and any response form that has been validly submitted and any other supplementary documents.

2. They will consider whether the matter requires more information. If so, they will cause a letter to be written to the party/ies specifying the further information that is required.

3. If no such information is required, or once such information has been received then the Employment Judge will consider whether it is appropriate to:-

(a) issue a Judgment in full for all claims and remedy; or
(b) issue a Judgment in full for all liability issues and hold a hearing for remedy or request further details of remedy matters; or
(c) issue a Judgment in part for one or more of the items claimed, together with any remedy issues arising; or
(d) issue a Judgment in part for one or more of the items claimed but not remedy issues and hold a hearing for remedy or request further details of remedy matters; or
(e) consider any of the combinations of Judgment for liability matters or remedy matters which they consider appropriate on the facts available to them at the time of consideration; and
(f) arrange for a hearing to be held for any part of the claim that has not had a judgment issued or for any remedy matters remaining outstanding as a result of such judgment having been issued and make appropriate case management orders.

4. If such a hearing is to be held then the Respondent will be entitled to receive notice

(a) of any hearings and decisions but entitlement to participate in the hearing will be limited as provided by Rule 21(3); and
(b) the hearing that will be held ordinarily will be a hearing as provided for under Rule 57.

5. If a judgment is issued it will be copied to all parties as soon as possible thereafter and notice sent of any hearing if an Employment Judge has considered it appropriate for such a hearing to take place.

6. Judgment will be issued as provided for under paragraph 3 above where an Employment Judge is satisfied that they have sufficient information properly so do to. For example, an Employment Judge will

examine whether the claim is clearly stated and whether there are any matters which might affect whether the Tribunal has jurisdiction to hear the claim. The Employment Judge will consider all detail contained in the written matters before them; consider any obligation or burden on either of the parties in relation to proving such matters; the calculations that have been provided (if any) by the claimant; any case management orders that have previously been made; and any response. If the Employment Judge has any reasonable doubt as to the whole or any part of such matters contained in the claim then the claim will be listed for hearing. The provisions of Rules 57-59 will apply.

7. Any party who wish to ask for reconsideration of such a decision must make such application in accordance with the provision of Rules 70-72.

8. Any party who considers lodging an appeal against such a judgment must comply with the Rules of the Employment Appeal Tribunal.

4th December 2013
David J Latham
President

EMPLOYMENT TRIBUNALS (ENGLAND & WALES) PRESIDENTIAL GUIDANCE – SEEKING A POSTPONEMENT OF A HEARING (2013)

[5.62]

NOTES

The Guidance is issued on the Fourth day of December 2013 under the provisions of Rule 7 of the first schedule to the Employment Tribunals (Constitution and Rules of Procedure) Regulation 2013 ("the Rules").

Note:

Whilst the Tribunals in England and Wales must have regard to such Guidance they will not be bound by it.

Background:

1. Rule 29 of the Rules permits an Employment Judge to make Case Management Orders. That includes the power to order that a hearing be postponed.

2. In applying the provisions of that Rule the procedure that will normally apply is as set out below.

Action by Parties:

1.

1.1 Whilst any application for a postponement can be made either at the hearing or in advance of the hearing it should ordinarily be made in writing to the Employment Tribunal office dealing with the case. That application should state.

1.2 The reason why it is made; and

1.3 Why it is considered that it would be in accordance with the overriding objective to grant the postponement

2. Where a party applies in writing, they shall notify the other parties that any objections to the application should be sent to the Tribunal as soon as possible. Here the expression "the party" is referring to all parties in the case.

3. All relevant documents relevant to the application should be provided.

4. If any of the requirements set out above are not complied with the application will ordinarily not be considered unless there are exceptional circumstances. If however the matters as set out above are not complied with then an explanation as to why it has not been so complied with and the exceptional circumstances should be given.

5. The party wishing to make the application for postponement of hearing should wherever possible try to discuss the proposal either directly with the other parties or through their representatives. If that discussion has taken place then the detail should also be provided to the Tribunal. If the other parties are in agreement that also should be indicated in the application to the Tribunal.

6. Where the hearing concerned has been fixed with agreement by the parties that matter will be taken into account by the Employment Judge considering the application.

7. Set out below are some specific examples of additional information that would be of assistance depending on the nature and the basis upon which the application for postponement is made.

Examples

1. When a party or witness is unable for medical reasons to attend a hearing. All medical certificates and supporting medical evidence should be provided in addition to an explanation of the nature of the health condition concerned. Where medical evidence is supplied it should include a statement from the medical

practitioner that in their opinion the applicant is unfit to attend the hearing, the prognosis of the condition and an indication of when that state of affairs may cease

2. Where parties and witnesses are not available this should be notified to the Tribunal as soon as possible stating the details of the witness or party concerned; what attempts have been made to make alternative arrangements; the reason for the unavailability and in the case of a witness the relevance of their evidence. Any supporting documents should also be provided.

3. Similar information should be provided where a representative has become unavailable or a newly appointed representative is unavailable.

4. If a representative has withdrawn from acting details should be given as to when this has happened and whether alternative representation has been or is being sought.

5. Where there is an outstanding appeal to the Employment Appeal Tribunal or other Appellate Court full details of the dates of the appeal and the matters being appealed should provided.

6. Where there are other court proceedings, be they civil or criminal, details should be given as to when these proceedings were commenced; what they entail; and how it is said that they will affect the Employment Tribunal case or how the Employment Tribunal case will be said to affect those other proceedings.

7. Where the basis of the application is the late disclosure of information or documents or the failure so to disclose then details of the documents or information concerned should be given; how they are relevant to the issues in the case; the terms of any Orders that already have been made by the Tribunal or requests made by the parties for such information or documents; and the response of the other party concerned.

Action by the Employment Judge

1. Where the appropriate information has been supplied then the Employment Judge will deal with the matter as soon as applicable. If the information has not been supplied any application may become the subject of further enquiry from the Employment Judge for relevant information which will have the effect of delaying the consideration of the application.

2. Once all the relevant information is available to the Employment Judge he/she will take into account all matters and information now available to them and consider whether to grant or refuse the postponement. The decision however remains in the discretion of the Employment Judge concerned.

3. The decision of the Employment Judge will be notified to all parties as speedily as possible after the decision has been made.

4th December 2013
David J Latham
President

EMPLOYMENT TRIBUNALS (ENGLAND & WALES) PRESIDENTIAL GUIDANCE – GENERAL CASE MANAGEMENT (2018)

[5.63]

NOTES

This is a reissue of the Guidance first issued in March 2014, which has been amended to remove references to fees following the abolition of fees in July 2017. See paragraph 1 below.

CONTENTS

1. This Presidential Guidance was first issued in England & Wales on 13 March 2014 under the provisions of Rule 7 of the First Schedule to the Employment Tribunals (Constitution and Rules of Procedure) Regulation 2013 ("the Rules"). It is now amended and reissued on 22 January 2018 to take account of the decision of the UK Supreme Court in *R (on the application of UNISON) v Lord Chancellor*

[2017] UKSC 51 so as to remove all relevant and related references to Employment Tribunal fees. The opportunity has also been taken to make other editorial amendments.

NOTE

2. Whilst the Employment Tribunals in England & Wales must have regard to such Presidential Guidance, they will not be bound by it and they have the discretion available to them as set out in the Rules as to how to apply the various case management provisions.

3. This Presidential Guidance in relation to General Case Management matters does not supersede or alter any other Presidential Guidance.[1]

NOTES

[1] Practice Directions and Presidential Guidance in general may be found at: https://www.judiciary.gov.uk/publications/employment-rules-and-legislation-practice-directions/.

BACKGROUND

[5.64]

4. The overriding objective set out in Rule 2 applies.

5. Rule 29 of the Rules permits a Tribunal to make Case Management Orders. The particular powers subsequently identified in the Rules do not restrict the general power contained in Rule 29.

6. Any Case Management Order may vary, suspend or set aside any earlier Case Management Order where that is necessary in the interests of justice. In particular, this may be necessary where a party affected by the earlier Order did not have a reasonable opportunity to make representations before it was made.

7. Rule 30 specifies details of how an application for a Case Management Order is made generally. Rules 31, 32, 34, 35, 36 and 37 deal with specific instances where Case Management Orders may be made.

8. Rule 38 deals specifically with the situation where Unless Orders can be made.

9. Rule 39 deals with the provision relating to Deposit Orders.

10. The Rules generally contain other Case Management provisions: for example, Rule 45 in relation to timetabling.

11. In applying the provisions of the Rules this Presidential Guidance attempts to set out the procedure, processes and considerations that will normally apply in the circumstances specified below.

ACTION BY PARTIES

[5.65]

12. While any application for a Case Management Order can be made at the hearing or in advance of the hearing, it should ordinarily be made in writing to the Employment Tribunal office dealing with the case or at a Preliminary Hearing which is dealing with Case Management issues.

13. Any such application should be made as early as possible.

14. Where the hearing concerned has been fixed – especially with the agreement of the parties – that will be taken into account by the Employment Judge considering the application.

15. The application should state the reason why it is made. It should state why it is considered to be in accordance with the overriding objective to make the Case Management Order applied for. Where a party applies in writing, they should notify the other parties (or other representatives, if they have them) that any objections should be sent to the Tribunal as soon as possible.

16. All relevant documents should be provided with the application.

17. If the parties are in agreement, that should also be indicated in the application to the Tribunal.

EXAMPLES OF CASE MANAGEMENT

[5.66]

18. These are examples of case management situations:

- amendment of claim and response
- adding or removing parties
- disclosure of documents
- preparation of hearing bundles
- witnesses and witness orders
- preparation and exchange of witness statements
- disability issues
- timetabling
- remedies
- costs
- concluding a case without a hearing

Further Guidance Notes on these matters are appended to this Presidential Guidance.

19. Where the parties' circumstances or contact details have changed, such changes should be notified to the Employment Tribunal office and to the other parties immediately.

ACTION BY THE EMPLOYMENT JUDGE

[5.67]
20. Where the appropriate information has been supplied, an Employment Judge will deal with the matter as soon as practicable. If any information has not been supplied, an Employment Judge may request further relevant information, which will have the effect of delaying consideration of the application.

21. The decision of the Employment Judge will be notified to all parties as soon as practicable after the decision has been made

22. Orders are important. Non-compliance with them may lead to sanctions. Therefore, if a party is having difficulty in complying with such an Order, they should discuss it with the other parties and then apply to the Tribunal to vary the Order.

AGENDA FOR PRELIMINARY HEARING

[5.68]
23. In preparation for a Preliminary Hearing concerned with Case Management matters, the Tribunal will often send out an agenda to the parties in advance of such a Preliminary Hearing. The agenda should be completed in advance of that Preliminary Hearing and returned to the Tribunal. If possible it should be agreed by the parties. A copy of the current form of agenda can be found at: https://www.judiciary.gov.uk/publications/employment-rules-and-legislation-practice-directions/.

ALTERNATIVE DISPUTE RESOLUTION

[5.69]
24. There is separate Presidential Guidance in respect of alternative dispute resolution (ADR) and, in particular, judicial assessments and judicial mediation at: https://www.judiciary.gov.uk/publications/employment-rules-and-legislation-practice-directions/.

Judge Brian Doyle

President

22 January 2018

Guidance Note 1: Amendment of the Claim and Response Including Adding and Removing Parties

Amendment

[5.70]
1. Amendment means changing the terms of the claim or response. This note concentrates on amendments to the claim. The Employment Tribunal can allow amendments, but it will generally only do so after careful consideration and taking into account the views of the other parties. In some cases a hearing may be necessary to decide whether to allow an amendment.

2. Generally speaking, minor amendments cause no difficulties. Sometimes the amendment is to give more detail. There may have been a typographical error or a date may be incorrect. The Tribunal will normally grant leave to amend without further investigation in these circumstances.

3. More substantial amendments can cause problems. Regard must be had to all the circumstances, in particular any injustice or hardship which would result from the amendment or a refusal to make it. If necessary, leave to amend can be made conditional on the payment of costs by the claimant if the other party has been put to expense as a result of a defect in the claim form.

4. In deciding whether to grant an application to amend, the Tribunal must carry out a careful balancing exercise of all of the relevant factors, having regard to the interests of justice and the relative hardship that will be caused to the parties by granting or refusing the amendment.

5. Relevant factors would include:

5.1 The amendment to be made. Applications can vary from the correction of clerical and typing errors to the addition of facts, the addition or substitution of labels for facts already described, and the making of entirely new factual allegations which change the basis of the existing claim. The Tribunal must decide whether the amendment applied for is a minor matter or a substantial alteration, describing a new complaint.

5.2 Time limits. If a new complaint or cause of action is intended by way of amendment, the Tribunal must consider whether that complaint is out of time and, if so, whether the time limit should be extended. Once the amendment has been allowed, and time taken into account, then that matter has been decided and can only be challenged on appeal. An application for leave to amend when there is a time issue should be dealt with at a preliminary hearing to address a preliminary issue. This allows all parties to attend, to make representations and possibly even to give evidence.

5.3 The timing and manner of the application. An application can be made at any time, as can an amendment even after Judgment has been promulgated. Allowing an application is an exercise of a judicial discretion. A party will need to show why the application was not made earlier and why it is being made at that time. An example which may justify a late application is the discovery of new facts or information from disclosure of documents.

6. The Tribunal draws a distinction between amendments as follows:

6.1 those that seek to add or to substitute a new claim arising out of the same facts as the original claim; and

6.2 those that add a new claim entirely unconnected with the original claim.

7. In deciding whether the proposed amendment is within the scope of an existing claim or whether it constitutes an entirely new claim, the entirety of the claim form must be considered.

Re-labelling

8. Labelling is the term used for the type of claim in relation to a set of facts (for example, "unfair dismissal"). Usually, mislabelling does not prevent the re-labelled claim being introduced by amendment. Seeking to change the nature of the claim may seem significant, but very often all that is happening is a change of label. For instance, a claimant may describe his or her claim as for a redundancy payment when, in reality, he or she may be claiming that they were unfairly dismissed.

9. If the claim form includes facts from which such a claim can be identified, the Tribunal as a rule adopts a flexible approach and grants amendments that only change the nature of the remedy claimed. There is a fine distinction between raising a claim which is linked to an existing claim and raising a new claim for the first time. In the leading case, the claimant tried to introduce an automatically unfair dismissal claim on the specific ground of his trade union activity in addition to the ordinary unfair dismissal claim in his claim form. The appeal court refused the amendment because the facts originally described could not support the new claim. Furthermore, there would be a risk of hardship to the employer by increased costs if the claimant was allowed to proceed with this new claim.

10. While there may be a flexibility of approach to applications to re-label facts already set out, there are limits. Claimants must set out the specific acts complained of, as Tribunals are only able to adjudicate on specific complaints. A general complaint in the claim form will not suffice. Further, an employer is entitled to know the claim it has to meet.

Time Limits

11. The Tribunal will give careful consideration in the following contexts:

11.1 The fact that the relevant time limit for presenting the new claim has expired will not exclude the discretion to allow the amendment. In one case, a Tribunal allowed the amendment of a claim form complaining of race discrimination to include a complaint of unfair dismissal. The appeal court upheld the Tribunal's decision, although the time limit for unfair dismissal had expired. The facts in the claim form were sufficient to found both complaints. The amendment would neither prejudice the respondent nor cause it any injustice.

11.2 It will not always be just to allow an amendment even where no new facts are pleaded. The Tribunal must balance the injustice and hardship of allowing the amendment against the injustice and hardship of refusing it. Where for instance a claimant fails to provide a clear statement of a proposed amendment when given the opportunity through case management orders to do so, an application at the hearing may be refused because of the hardship that would accrue to the respondent.

Seeking to add new ground of complaint

12. The Tribunal looks for a link between the facts described in the claim form and the proposed amendment. If there is no such link, the claimant will be bringing an entirely new cause of action.

13. In this case, the Tribunal **must consider** whether the new claim is in time.

14. The Tribunal will take into account the tests for extending time limits:

14.1 the "just and equitable" formula in discrimination claims;

14.2 the "not reasonably practicable" formula in most other claims;

14.3 the specific time limits in redundancy claims;

14.4 the special time limits in equal pay claims.

Adding a new party

15. The Tribunal may of its own initiative, or on the application of a party, or a person wishing to become a party, add any other person as a party by adding them or substituting them for another party. This can be done if it appears that there are issues between that person and any of the existing parties falling within the jurisdiction of the Tribunal and which it is in the interests of justice to have determined in the proceedings.

Adding or removing parties

16. These are some of the circumstances which give rise to addition of parties:

16.1 Where the claimant does not know, possibly by reason of a business transfer situation, who is the correct employer to be made respondent to the claim.

16.2 Where individual respondents, other than the employer, are named in discrimination cases on the grounds that they have discriminated against the claimant and an award is sought against them.

16.3 Where the respondent is a club or an unincorporated association and it is necessary to join members of the governing body.

16.4 Where it is necessary in order to decide a claim which involves a challenge to a decision of the relevant Secretary of State. The Secretary of State is responsible by statute for certain sums of money in different insolvency situations. The Tribunal decides if a refusal to pay is correct, provided conditions are met in relation to timing.

17. Asking to add a party is an application to amend the claim. The Tribunal will have to consider the type of amendment sought. The amendment may deal with a clerical error, add factual details to existing allegations, or add new labels to facts already set out in the claim. The amendment may, if allowed, make new factual allegations which change or add to an existing claim. The considerations set out above in relation to amendments generally apply to these applications.

18. When you apply to add a party you should do so promptly. You should set out clearly in your application the name and address of the party you wish to add and why you say they are liable for something you have claimed. You should further explain when you knew of the need to add the party and what action you have taken since that date.

19. The Tribunal may also remove any party apparently wrongly included. A party who has been added to the proceedings should apply promptly after the proceedings are served on them if they wish to be removed.

20. A party can also be removed from the proceedings if the Claimant has settled with them or no longer wishes to proceed against them.

21. The Tribunal may permit any person to participate in proceedings on such terms as may be specified in respect of any matter in which that person has a legitimate interest. This could involve where they will be liable for any remedy awarded, as well as other situations where the findings made may directly affect them.

Guidance Note 2: Disclosure of Documents and Preparing Hearing Bundles

[5.71]

1. The Employment Tribunal often requires the parties to co-operate to prepare a set of documents for the hearing. Even if no formal order is made, the Tribunal prefers that documentary evidence is presented in one easily accessible set of documents (often known as "the hearing bundle") with everyone involved in the hearing having an identical copy.

Why have an agreed set of documents?

2. Early disclosure of documents helps the parties to see clearly what the issues are. It helps them to prepare their witness statements and their arguments. There is no point in withholding evidence until the hearing. This only causes delay and adds to the costs. It may put you at risk of having your case struck out.

3. Agreeing a set of documents means that all parties agree which documents are relevant and the Tribunal will need to see. It does not mean they agree with what the documents contain or mean.

4. It avoids problems at a hearing when a party produces a document which the other party has not seen before. This is unfair and may lead to the hearing being delayed or adjourned. This is costly to all concerned and may result in the offending party paying the costs of the adjournment.

5. An agreed set of documents – rather than each party bringing their own set of documents to the hearing – prevents uncertainty and delay at the hearing.

What is the disclosure of documents?

6. Disclosure is the process of showing the other party (or parties) all the documents you have which are relevant to the issues the Tribunal has to decide. Although it is a formal process, it is not a hostile process. It requires co-operation in order to ensure that the case is ready for hearing.

7. Relevant documents may include documents which record events in the employment history: for example, a letter of appointment, statement of particulars or contract of employment; notes of a significant meeting, such as a disciplinary interview; a resignation or dismissal letter; or material such as emails, text messages and social media content (Facebook, Twitter, Instagram, etc). The claimant may have documents to disclose which relate to looking for and finding alternative work.

8. Any relevant document in your possession (or which you have the power to obtain) which is or may be relevant to the issues must be disclosed. This includes documents which may harm your case as well as those which may help it. To conceal or withhold a relevant document is a serious matter.

9. A party is usually not required to disclose a copy of a "privileged" document: for example, something created in connection with the preparation of a party's Tribunal case (such as notes of interviews with witnesses); correspondence between a party and their lawyers; correspondence between parties marked "without prejudice"; or part of discussions initiated on a "without prejudice" basis with a view to settlement of the matters in issue; or records of exchanges with ACAS.

How and when does disclosure take place?

10. The process should start and be completed as soon as possible. A formal order for disclosure of documents usually states the latest date by which the process must be completed.

11. In most cases, the respondent (usually the employer) has most or all of the relevant documents. This often makes it sensible for the respondent to take the lead in disclosure. Each party prepares a list of all relevant documents they hold and sends it as soon as possible to the other party.

12. Sometimes the parties meet and inspect each other's documents. More commonly, they agree to exchange photocopies of their documents in the case, which should be "clean" copies (that is, unmarked by later notes or comments, unless those notes or comments are themselves evidence).

How is the hearing bundle produced?

13. The parties then co-operate to agree the documents to go in the hearing bundle. The hearing bundle should contain only the documents that are to be mentioned in witness statements or to be the subject of cross-examination at the hearing, and which are relevant to the issues in the proceedings. If there is a dispute about what documents to include, the disputed documents should be put in a separate section or folder, and this should be referred to the Tribunal at the start of the hearing.

14. One party then prepares the hearing bundles. This is often the respondent because it is more likely to have the necessary resources. Whoever is responsible for preparing the hearing bundles prepares the documents in a proper order (usually chronological), numbers each page (this is called "pagination") and makes sufficient sets of photocopies, which are stapled together, tagged or put into a ring binder.

15. Each party should have at least 1 copy. The Tribunal will need 5 copies for a full Tribunal panel or 3 copies if the Employment Judge is to sit alone. That is 1 copy for the witness table, 1 for each member of the Tribunal and 1 to be shown to the public or media, where appropriate. The copies for the Tribunal must be brought to the hearing. They should not be sent to the Tribunal in advance, unless requested.

Are the documents confidential?

16. All documents and witness statements exchanged in the case are to be used only for the hearing. Unless the Tribunal orders otherwise, they must only be shown to a party and that party's adviser/representative or a witness (insofar as is necessary). The documents must not be used for any purpose other than the conduct of the case.

17. Because it is a public hearing, the Tribunal will enable persons (including the press and media) present at the hearing to view documents referred to in evidence before it (unless it orders otherwise).

Guidance Note 3: Witnesses and Witness Statements

Witnesses

[5.72]
1. The parties should consider who they need to give evidence in support of their case at the Employment Tribunal hearing.

2. As part of the Case Management of the proceedings, the Tribunal will need to know how many witnesses are to be called, so that the required length of the hearing can be properly allocated and, if necessary, timetabled. The identity of the witnesses and the relevance of their evidence to the issues will also often be important.

3. Rule 43 provides that where a witness is called to give oral evidence, any witness statement of that person shall stand as that witness's evidence in chief unless the Tribunal orders otherwise. Witnesses are required to give their oral evidence on oath or affirmation.

4. The Tribunal may exclude from the hearing any person who is to appear as a witness in the proceedings, until such time as that person gives evidence, if it considers it in the interests of justice to do so. This is not the usual practice of the Employment Tribunal in England & Wales.

Witness orders

5. The Tribunal may order any person in Great Britain to attend a hearing to give evidence, produce documents or produce information (Rule 32).

6. If a party believes that a person has relevant information or evidence to give, but that they might not attend the hearing voluntarily, that party can apply to the Tribunal for a witness order. A witness order requires the witness to attend the hearing. It can also be useful where the witness is willing to attend, but their employer will not release them to attend.

7. An application for a witness order may be made at a hearing or by an application in writing to the Tribunal. In order that the Tribunal can send the witness order to the witness in good time before the hearing, it is important to make any application as early as possible. A witness order might be refused if the attendance of the witness cannot be ensured in time.

8. The application will need to give the name and address of the witness; a summary of the evidence it is believed they will give (or a copy of their witness statement, if there is one); and an explanation as to why a witness order is necessary to secure their attendance.

9. Exceptionally, an application for a witness order does not have to be copied to the other parties, unless the Tribunal considers that it is in the interests of justice to do otherwise. If the Tribunal grants a witness order, the other parties will then be informed that a witness order has been made and who the witness is, unless there is a good reason not to do so.

Witness statements

10. The Tribunal often orders witness statements to be prepared and exchanged. Even if no formal order is made, the Tribunal generally prefers evidence to be presented by means of written statements.

These are normally read in advance by the Tribunal so that they stand as the evidence in chief (that is, the main evidence of the witness before questions are put in cross-examination) without being read out loud by the witness.

Why prepare witness statements?

11. It helps to write down what you have to say in evidence. You often remember much more and feel more comfortable when giving evidence having done so.

12. Early exchange of witness statements enables the parties to know the case they have to meet and what the issues are going to be. All the relevant evidence will come out at the hearing. There is nothing to gain (and much to lose) by withholding it until then.

13. Preparation of witness statements helps the Tribunal to identify the issues and to ensure that the case is completed in the time allowed.

14. A witness statement should be prepared for each witness who is to give evidence. This includes the claimant (and the respondent where he or she is an individual).

How should a witness statement be set out and what should it contain?

15. It is easier for everyone if the statement is typewritten or word-processed (although a clear and legible handwritten statement is acceptable) with each page numbered.

16. The witness statement should be in a logical order (ideally, chronological) and contain numbered paragraphs. It should cover all the issues in the case. It should set out fully what the witness has to tell the Tribunal about their involvement in the matter, usually in date order.

17. The statement should be as full as possible because the Tribunal might not allow the witness to add to it, unless there are exceptional circumstances and the additional evidence is obviously relevant.

18. When completed, it is good practice for the statement to be signed, particularly if the witness is unavailable to attend the hearing. The Employment Tribunal Rules of Procedure do not require a witness statement to contain a "statement of truth" (such as "This statement is true to the best of my knowledge and belief" or "I believe the facts in this statement to be true") at the end. There is no objection to a witness statement that does or does not contain such a statement of truth.

19. A copy of any witness statements should be provided to the other party. You should bring 5 copies with you to the hearing if there is a full Tribunal panel and 3 copies if the Employment Judge is to sit alone. That is 1 copy for the witness table, 1 for each member of the Tribunal and 1 to be shown to the public and media, where appropriate.

20. If you realise that your statement has left out something relevant when you receive the other party's statements, you should make a supplementary statement and send it immediately to the other party. You do not need to comment on or respond to every point in the other side's statements or repeat what you said originally.

How should a witness statement be exchanged?

21. When the witness statements are ready, a copy should usually be sent to the other side, whether or not their statements have been received or are ready to be exchanged.

22. Exchange of witness statements at the same time is the norm, but it is not always appropriate. In some cases, it makes sense for the claimant's witness statement to be sent first. The respondent will then know exactly what case has to be answered. This avoids irrelevant statements being taken from witnesses who are not needed. In other cases, however, it may make sense for the respondent's statements to be sent first. Any particular directions made by the Tribunal must be followed.

23. Unless there is a different date fixed, the exchange of witness statements should be completed by no later than 2 weeks before the hearing.

Inspection of witness statements

24. Rule 44 provides that any witness statement, which stands as evidence in chief, shall be available for inspection during the course of the hearing by members of the public (that includes the media) attending the hearing. That is, unless the Tribunal decides that all or any part of the statement is not to be admitted as evidence. In that case, the statement or that part of it shall not be available for inspection.

25. There are exceptions to this rule where the Tribunal has made an order protecting the privacy of a witness or restricting the disclosure of documents (rule 50) or in national security proceedings (rule 94).

Guidance Note 4: Disability

[5.73]

1. The terms "disabled", "disabled person" and "disability" are words in common use. In disability discrimination cases in Employment Tribunals these terms have a particular meaning set out in section 6 of the Equality Act 2010 (and Schedule 1 to that Act) and regulations made under those provisions.

2. Reference should be made to those statutory provisions and to those regulations, as well as to the statutory *Guidance on matters to be taken into account in determining questions relating to the definition of disability* (2011) issued by the Secretary of State. That *Guidance* is available at: https://www.equalityhumanrights.com/en/publication-download/equality-act-2010-guidance-matters-be-taken-account-determining-questions.

Evidence of disability

3. A claimant who relies upon the protected characteristic of disability may be able to provide much of the information required without medical reports. A claimant may be able to describe their impairment and its effects on their ability to carry out normal day to day activities.

4. Sometimes medical evidence may be required. For instance, where there is a dispute about whether the claimant has a particular disability or whether an impairment is under effective control by medication or treatment.

5. The question then to be answered is what effects the impairment would have if the medication was withdrawn. Once more, a claimant may be able to describe the effects themselves, but respondents frequently ask for some medical evidence in support.

6. Claimants must expect to have to agree to the disclosure of relevant medical records or occupational health records.

7. Few people would be happy to disclose all of their medical records or for disclosure to be given to too many people. Employment Judges are used to such difficulties. They will often limit the documents to be disclosed and the people to whom disclosure should be made. Disclosure is generally for use only in the proceedings and not for sharing with third parties.

8. Even after a claimant's description of their impairment and disclosure of relevant documents in support, respondents may dispute that the claimant is disabled. If that happens the intervention of an Employment Judge may be necessary.

9. The following possibilities might arise, although there might be others:

9.1 That the claimant has to agree to undergo medical examination by a doctor or specialist chosen and paid for by the respondent.

9.2 That the claimant agrees to provide further medical evidence at their own expense.

9.3 That the claimant and the respondent may agree to get a report jointly. That would involve sharing the decision as to who to appoint, the instructions to be given and the cost of any report. This may be the most effective course, but neither party may in the end be bound by the findings of the report, even if they agree to this course of action.

10. It can be expensive to obtain medical evidence. Limited financial assistance may be available. Whether it is granted is a matter which only a member of the administrative staff of Her Majesty's Courts & Tribunals Service can decide. Any application for such assistance should be made to the manager of the relevant Employment Tribunal office.

11. Care should be taken to decide whether a medical report is necessary at all. For instance, if a claimant has epilepsy which is well-controlled by medication, then medical evidence may be unnecessary for a Tribunal to consider what effect would follow if the medication was not taken.

12. Claimants must remember that they have the burden of proving that they are disabled. They may be satisfied that they can do this, perhaps with the assistance of the records of their General Practitioner, their medical consultant and their own evidence.

Reasonable adjustments to the Tribunal hearing or procedure

13. If the disability of a party, representative, witness or other person might affect their participation in the Tribunal hearing or procedure, an application should be made to the Tribunal as soon as possible so that the Tribunal can consider what reasonable adjustments might be made.

Guidance Note 5: Timetabling

[5.74]
1. The overriding objective in Rule 2 of the Employment Tribunals Rules of Procedure means that each case should have its fair share of available time, but no more. Otherwise other cases would be unjustly delayed. Each party must also have a fair share of the time allowed for the hearing of their case.

What is timetabling?

2. Each party has a duty to conduct the case so that wherever possible the Tribunal can complete the case within the time allowed. Failing to do that may mean a delay of many weeks before the case can return for further hearing. It also means that other cases waiting to be heard might be delayed.

3. To avoid the risk of this happening the Tribunal sometimes divides up the total time allowed for a hearing into smaller blocks of time to be allowed for each part of the hearing. This is called "timetabling". It is necessary in particularly long or complicated hearings or sometimes where a party has no experience of conducting hearings.

4. Timetabling is permitted by Rule 45. It provides that a Tribunal may impose limits on the time that a party may take in presenting evidence, questioning witnesses or making submissions. The Tribunal may then prevent the party from proceeding beyond any time so allotted.

How and when is timetabling done?

5. Employment Judges estimate the amount of time to be allowed for a hearing based on all the information they have when the hearing is listed. In straightforward cases that might be when the claim first comes in or when the response arrives. In complex cases it is often done at a preliminary hearing as part of case management.

6. For very short cases it is rare for a formal timetable to be issued. Nevertheless, even for a hearing of one day it might be helpful for the judge and the parties to agree at the beginning of the hearing roughly how long they expect each of the various stages to take. For longer or more complex hearings a timetable is often decided in consultation with the parties at a preliminary hearing or at the start of the hearing itself.

7. Fairness does not always mean that the hearing time must be divided equally between the parties or each witness.

8. For example, the party giving evidence first – in unfair dismissal cases this is usually the employer, but in discrimination cases this is often the employee – will often have to explain the relevance of the documents referred to in the witness statements, which requires time. Also some witnesses might have to give evidence about many separate incidents, whereas others perhaps just one short conversation. If an interpreter is required extra time has to be allowed. The Tribunal will take these things into account when estimating how long the evidence and examination of each witness should take.

9. The Tribunal will set the timetable using its own experience, but the Employment Judge will often ask for the parties' views on how long each stage of the hearing might take.

10. The stages involved in a typical hearing are as follows:

10.1 At the start of the hearing, if this has not already been done, the Tribunal should make sure that everybody understands the questions the Tribunal has to answer. This is about identifying the issues that are to be decided. The Tribunal will also check that everyone has copies of all of the documents, etc.

10.2 Often the Tribunal will then read the witness statements and any pages in the agreed bundle of documents to which they refer.

10.3 Each witness is then questioned on their own statement. This is called "cross-examination". The Tribunal may also ask questions of the witnesses. A specific time may be allocated for questions in respect of each witness and for the witness to clarify any points that have arisen from those questions (this is called "re-examination").

10.4 When the evidence is finished, each party is entitled to make "submissions". This means that they may summarise the important evidence in their case and may highlight any weak parts of the other side's case. They may also refer the Tribunal to any legal authorities (statutory provisions or previous case law) which might be relevant. Although each party has the right to make submissions, they are not obliged to do so. Again, the Tribunal might timetable the amount of time for submissions.

10.5 After submissions, the Tribunal will reach its decision. Sometimes it needs to "retire" or "adjourn" (which simply means to leave the hearing room) in order to consider everything that has been said. The length of time it needs to do this might just be a few minutes or an hour in a simple, straightforward case. It may be days or weeks in a very long or complex case, in which instance the parties will usually be sent away with an indication of when a decision might be expected.

10.6 The Tribunal will then tell the parties what has been decided and why. This is referred to as "delivering judgment". This might be done orally – that is, by telling the parties the decision in their presence in the hearing room. If the decision has been made later (a "reserved decision"), then it may be sent to the parties in writing.

10.7 After delivering judgment, the Tribunal will, if the claim succeeds, hear evidence about the claimant's loss. The parties may then make submissions on what award is necessary. The Tribunal may then have to retire or to adjourn again to decide on remedy. It will then deliver its judgment on remedy either orally or reserve it and send it later in writing.

10.8 Lastly, the Tribunal might have to consider orders in respect of any costs matters. Orders for costs are not the norm. The Tribunal will then give judgment with reasons on those matters, again either orally or in writing.

11. If a party believes that the time estimate for the whole or any part of the hearing is wrong, the Tribunal will expect them to say so as soon as possible. Waiting till the day before the hearing or the start of it to ask for extra time is not helpful. It can save time to try to agree a more accurate estimate and then to ask the Tribunal to change the timetable.

What can a party do to assist the Tribunal to keep to the timetable?

12. It is helpful for each party to make a list, for their own use, of the questions to be asked of the witnesses about each of the issues in the case. It is also useful to decide which of the questions are the most important, so that if time is running out the really important questions can be asked, even if others have to be abandoned.

13. Being able to find and quote the page number of the relevant documents in the bundle can save a lot of time. Asking questions using words the witness will understand, so that less time is wasted having to explain what is being asked, also saves time. A series of short, precise questions is generally better than one long, complicated one. They take less time to ask and to answer, and are easier for the witness and the Tribunal to understand and for everyone to take a note of.

14. There is nothing to be gained by asking the same question several times or to argue with the witness. That will just waste the time allowed. The purpose of asking questions is not to try to make the witness agree with the questioner, but to show the Tribunal which side's evidence is more likely to be accurate. If necessary, the Tribunal can be reminded in submissions at the end of the case that, for example, the witness would not answer a question or gave an answer which was not believable or which was not consistent with a document in the bundle, etc. An explanation of why your evidence is more reliable can be given at that stage.

What if the time allowed is exceeded?

15. The parties must try to conclude their questioning of each witness, and their submissions, within the time limit allocated. Usually the Employment Judge will remind a party of how long they have left when time is nearly up. If a party does not finish in time, they run the risk that the Tribunal may stop their questioning of that witness (which is sometimes called "guillotining" the evidence). This is not a step the Tribunal likes to take. Sometimes it is necessary, especially if one side takes so long that they might prevent the other side from having a fair opportunity to ask their own questions.

16. If later witnesses take less time than expected, it might be possible to "re-call" the witness who did not have enough time, if the Tribunal agrees.

Guidance Note 6: Remedy

What is remedy?

[5.75]

1. After an Employment Tribunal has decided whether the claimant's claim succeeds it will consider how the successful party should be compensated. This part of the judgment is called "Remedy". Sometimes it is done immediately after the merits or liability judgment, but in long or complex cases it may be adjourned to another day.

2. The Tribunal has different powers for each different type of claim. It must calculate loss and order an appropriate remedy for each part of a successful claim. Accurate and often detailed information from both parties is needed to make correct calculations and to issue a judgment which is fair to all. Sometimes the Tribunal can only estimate the loss: for example, for how long a party may be out of work.

Different types of remedy

3. For some claims the only remedy is to order the employer/respondent to pay a sum of money: for example, wages due, holiday pay and notice pay.

4. For unfair dismissal the Tribunal may:

4.1 Order the employer to "reinstate" the dismissed employee. This is to put them back in their old job, as if they had not been dismissed; or to "re-engage" them, which is to employ them in a suitable but different job. In each case the Tribunal may order payment of lost earnings, etc.

4.2 If those orders are not sought by the claimant or are not practicable, the Tribunal may order the employer to pay compensation. This is calculated in two parts:

- a "Basic Award", which is calculated in a similar way to a statutory redundancy payment; and
- a "Compensatory Award", which is intended to compensate the employee for the financial loss suffered.

5. In claims of unlawful discrimination, the Tribunal may:

5.1 make a declaration setting out the parties' rights; and/or

5.2 order compensation to be paid by the employer and/or fellow workers who have committed discriminatory acts. If the employer can show that it has taken all reasonable steps to prevent employees from committing such acts (called the "statutory defence"), the only award which can be made is against the fellow worker, not the employer; and/or

5.3 make a recommendation, such as for the claimant's colleagues or managers to be given training to ensure that discrimination does not happen again.

Mitigation

6. All persons who have been subjected to wrongdoing are expected to do their best, within reasonable bounds, to limit the effects on them. If the Tribunal concludes that a claimant has not done so, it must reduce the compensation so that a fair sum is payable.

7. The Tribunal will expect evidence to be provided by claimants about their attempts to obtain suitable alternative work and about any earnings from alternative employment.

8. The Tribunal will expect respondents, who consider that the claimant has not tried hard enough, to provide evidence about other jobs which the claimant could have applied for.

Statement of remedy

10. The Tribunal will usually order the claimant to make a calculation showing how each amount claimed has been worked out. For example: x weeks' pay at £y per week. Sometimes this is called a "Schedule of loss" or a "Statement of remedy".

11. Tribunals are expected to calculate remedy for each different type of loss – sometimes called "Heads of loss" or "Heads of damage". Therefore the statement should show how much is claimed under each head.

12. 12. If the claimant has received State benefits, he or she should also specify the type of benefit, the dates of receipt, the amount received and the claimant's national insurance number. (See also "Recoupment" below).

13. Typical heads of loss include;

- wages due

notice (where no notice or inadequate notice was given)
day pay
redundancy payment
in settle...
should be upd...

...eads of loss will typically include:
...es (which are ra...
...nly when the ac... discrimination is the cause of the claimant
...ent to be prod... ...ly in the proceedings, as it can help
...diation and wi... ...ssing the length of the hearing. It

16. In an unfair dismissal claim, ... a proper procedure (such as the ACAS Code ... subsequent ... dismissed, ... employer has not followed ... v AE Dayton Services Limited and ... will follow the ... in the case of Polkey ... procedure had been followed, the claimant ... might still have ... whether, if a fair ... later time. This question is often referred to as the "Polkey" question ... at all, or at some

17. There are also cases where the dismissal may be procedurally ... conduct has contributed to the position they now find themselves in. This is ... employee's own ... "contributory conduct".

18. Where either or both of these are relevant, the Tribunal will reduce the ... appropriate percentage in each case. This means that there may be two reductions ... awarded by an been really serious misconduct, could be as high as 100%, so that nothing would be payable. ... where there has

19. Generally the Tribunal will decide these issues at the same time as it reaches its decision on the merits of the claim. Sometimes this will be done at a separate remedy hearing. The Tribunal will usually explain at the start of the hearing which of those options it will follow. If it does not, then the parties should ask for clarification of when they are expected to give evidence and to make submissions on these matters.

Injury to Feelings

20. In discrimination cases and some other detriment claims, Tribunals may award a sum of money to compensate for injury to feelings. When they do so, they must fix fair, reasonable and just compensation in the particular circumstances of the case. The Tribunal will bear in mind that compensation is designed to compensate the injured party rather than to punish the guilty one. It will also remind itself that awards should bear some relationship to those made by the courts for personal injury.

21. The Tribunal will follow guidelines first given in the case of Vento v Chief Constable of West Yorkshire Police and in subsequent cases. These guidelines are referred to as the "Vento guidelines" or the "Vento bands". The President of Employment Tribunals will issue from time to time separate guidance on the present value of the Vento bands or guidelines.

22. The Tribunal will expect claimants to explain in their statement of remedy which Vento band they consider their case falls in. They will also expect both parties to make submissions on this during the remedy part of the hearing.

Information needed to calculate remedy

23. This varies in each case dependent on what is being claimed. Each party should look for any relevant information which could help the Tribunal with any necessary calculations in their case. They should provide copies of this information to each other and include those copies in the hearing bundle.

24. Thhe types of information that could be relevant include:

- the contract of employment or statement of terms & conditions with the old employer
- the date the claimant started work with that employer
- details of any pension scheme and pension contributions
- pay slips for the last 13 weeks in the old employment
- any other document showing the claimant's gross pay and net pay
- proof of any payments actually made by the old employer, such as a redundancy payment or payment in lieu of notice
- any document recording the day the claimant last actually worked
- any document explaining how many days and hours per week the claimant worked
- any document explaining how overtime was paid
- any document recording when the holiday year started
- any document recording when holiday has been taken in that year and what has been paid for those days
- any documents setting out the terms of the old employer's pension scheme
- any documents showing the claimant's attempts to find new or other work
- contract of employment and payslips for any new job with a new employer
- documents such as bank statements, if losses for bank charges are claimed
- medical reports or "Fit notes" if unable to work since dismissal

- any documents showing that jobs were or are available in the locality for which the cl[illegible] have applied.

25. The witness statements should tell the Tribunal which parts of these documents are import[illegible] why. Providing enough information to the Tribunal at an early stage could help to promote a settle[illegible] and so avoid a hearing.

Is all lo[illegible]warded?

26. For claims such as unpaid wages, holiday and notice pay the Tribunal will o[illegible] between what should have been paid and what [illegible] actually been paid. Wages and h[illegible] calculated gross, but pay in lieu of notice [illegible] ordered has been calculated net of tax and [illegible] judgment should specify whether each p[illegible]

27. In the case of unfair dismissal there [illegible] several limits (called statut[illegible]

Grossing up

28. The rules on when tax is pa[illegible] on awards made by [illegible] When it is clear that the claimant [illegible] paid [illegible] to pay tax on [illegible] figure, calculated so that tax is [illegible] represents the loss. This ca[illegible]

29. There are two separate situations where interest is relevant.

30. First, when a Tribunal calculates compensation for discrimination, it is obliged to consider awarding interest. If it decides to do so it calculates interest from the date of the act of discrimination up to the date of the calculation. The exception is for interest on lost wages, where the calculation is made from the middle of that period (that is simpler than calculating interest separately on each missing wage, but leads to a roughly similar result). The Tribunal will then include that interest in the award made.

31. In addition, interest is payable on awards for all claims if they are not paid when due. A note accompanying the Tribunal's judgment will explain how interest has been calculated. In respect of all claims presented on or after 29 July 2013 interest is calculated from the day after the day upon which the written judgment was sent to the parties, unless payment is actually made within the first 14 days, in which case no interest is payable.

32. The Employment Tribunal plays no part in enforcing payment of the award it makes. That is done by the civil courts, who issue separate guidance on how to enforce payments.

Recoupment

33. For some claims, such as unfair dismissal, if the claimant has received certain State benefits the Tribunal is obliged to ensure that the employer responsible for causing the loss of earnings reimburses the State for the benefits paid. In those cases the Tribunal will order only part of the award to be paid to the claimant straightaway, with the rest set aside until the respondent is told by the State how much the benefits were. The respondent then pays that money to the State and anything left over to the claimant.

34. This is called "recoupment". The Tribunal should set out in the judgment whether or not recoupment applies, and if it does, how much of the award is set aside for recoupment purposes. If either party is in any doubt about recoupment, they should ask the Tribunal to explain how it affects them.

Costs

35. See the separate guidance on "Costs".

Pensions loss

36. The President of Employment Tribunals has issued separated guidance and principles on the calculation of pensions loss. See:

https://www.judiciary.gov.uk/wp-content/uploads/2013/08/presidential-guidance-pension-loss-20170810.pdf

https://www.judiciary.gov.uk/wp-content/uploads/2015/03/principles-for-compensating-pension-loss-20170810.pdf.

Guidance Note 7: Costs

[5.76]

1. The basic principle is that Employment Tribunals do not order one party to pay the costs which the other party has incurred in bringing or defending a claim. However, there are a number of important exceptions to the basic principle, as explained below.

What are costs?

2. "Costs" means some or all of the legal and professional fees, charges, payments or expenses incurred by a party in connection with the Tribunal case. It includes the expenses incurred by a party or witness in attending a hearing.

What orders for payment of costs can be made?

3. There are three different types of payment orders: costs orders; preparation time orders (sometimes referred to as PTOs); and wasted costs orders. These specific terms have the following meanings.

4. A costs order generally means that a party is ordered to pay some or all of the costs paid by the other party to its legal representatives (barristers and solicitors) or to its lay representative. No more than the hourly rate of a preparation time order can be claimed for a lay representative. Separately, costs orders can be made for the expenses reasonably and proportionately incurred by a party or witness in attending a hearing.

5. Preparation time orders are for payment in respect of the amount of time spent working on the case by a non-represented party, including its employees or advisers, but not the time spent at any final hearing.

6. Wasted costs orders are for payment of costs incurred by a party as a result of any improper, unreasonable or negligent act or failure to act by a representative or for costs incurred after such act where it would be unreasonable to expect the party to bear them. They require payment by a representative to any party, including the party represented by the payer.

When may orders for costs and preparation time be made?

7. Apart from costs orders for the attendance of witnesses or parties at hearings, a party cannot have both a costs order and a preparation time order made in its favour in the same proceedings. So it is often sensible for a Tribunal in the course of the proceedings (for example, at a preliminary hearing) to decide only that an order for payment will be made, but to leave to the end of the case the decision about which type of order and for how much.

8. Orders for payment of costs or for preparation time may be made on application by a party, a witness (in respect of their expenses) or on the Tribunal's initiative up to 28 days after the end of the case. If judgment on the claims is given at a hearing, it will usually be sensible to make any application for costs or PTOs then, in order to avoid delay and the additional cost of getting everyone back for another hearing.

9. The circumstances when payment orders may be made are as follows.

10. If an employer in unfair dismissal proceedings requires an adjournment to obtain evidence about the possibility of re-employment, the Tribunal must order the employer to pay the costs of the adjournment provided:

- the claimant notified the desire to be re-employed at least 7 days before the hearing;
- the employer cannot prove a special reason why it should not pay.

11. A party may be ordered to pay costs or preparation time to the other party, without any particular fault or blame being shown, where:

- the paying party has breached an order or practice direction; or
- an adjournment or postponement is granted at the request of or due to the conduct of the paying party.

12. A party may be ordered to pay costs in the form of the expenses incurred or to be incurred by a witness attending a hearing, without any particular fault or blame being shown. The order may be in favour of or against the party who called the witness. It may be made on the application of a party, the witness or at the Tribunal's own initiative. It may be payable to a party or to the witness.

13. A party may be ordered to pay costs or preparation time to the other party where the Tribunal considers that:

- a party has acted vexatiously, abusively, disruptively or otherwise unreasonably in bringing or defending the proceedings or in its conduct of the proceedings; or
- the claim or response had no reasonable prospect of success.

14. The circumstances described at paragraph 13 require a Tribunal to consider first whether the criteria for an order are met. Each case will turn on its own facts. Examples from decided cases include that it could be unreasonable where a party has based the claim or defence on something which is untrue. That is not the same as something which they have simply failed to prove. Nor does it mean something they reasonably misunderstood. Abusive or disruptive conduct would include insulting the other party or its representative or sending numerous unnecessary emails.

15. If the criteria are met, the Tribunal is at the threshold for making an order. It will decide whether it is appropriate to order payment. It will consider any information it has about the means of the party from whom payment is sought, the extent of any abusive or unreasonable conduct, and any factors which see[m] to indicate that the party which is out-of-pocket should be reimbursed. For example, sometim[es] ... clear that a party never intended to defend on the merits (that is, for example, wh... unfairly dismissed), but pretended that it was doing so until the last minu[te] ... his or her lawyer more, before conceding what was really always obvious ...

When may a wasted costs order be made?

16. A Tribunal may consider making a wasted costs order of its own initia[tive] ... any party, provided the circumstances described at paragraph 6 above are esta[blished] ... event. When it happens, usually a party will seek costs from the other party an[d] ... costs from that party's representative. The representative from whom payme[nt] ... notice and so is the party – because they may need separate representation at ...

Amount of costs, preparation time and wasted costs orders

17. Broadly speaking, costs orders are for the amount of legal or professional fees and related expenses reasonably incurred, based on factors like the significance of the case, the complexity of the facts and the experience of the lawyers who conducted the litigation for the receiving party.

18. In addition to costs for witness expenses, the Tribunal may order any party to pay costs as follows:

18.1 up to £20,000, by forming a broad-brush assessment of the amounts involved; or working from a schedule of legal costs; or, more frequently and in respect of lower amounts, just the fee for the barrister at the hearing (for example);

18.2 calculated by a detailed assessment in the County Court or by the Tribunal up to an unlimited amount;

18.3 in any amount agreed between the parties.

19. Preparation time orders are calculated at the rate of £33 per hour (until April 2014, when the rate increases by £1 as at every April) for every hour which the receiving party reasonably and proportionately spent preparing for litigation. This requires the Tribunal to bear in mind matters such as the complexity of the proceedings, the number of witnesses and the extent of documents.

20. Wasted costs orders are calculated like costs orders: the amount wasted by the blameworthy (as described at paragraph 6 above) conduct of the representative.

21. When considering the amount of an order, information about a person's ability to pay may be considered. The Tribunal may make a substantial order even where a person has no means of payment. Examples of relevant information are: the person's earnings, savings, other sources of income, debts, bills and necessary monthly outgoings.

Guidance Note 8: Concluding Cases Without a Hearing

[5.77]

1. A claim or response which has been accepted may be disposed of by the Employment Tribunal at any point in any number of stages before the final hearing. This note sets out most of the situations generally encountered and refers you to the relevant rules.

Rejection at presentation stage

2. A claim may be rejected by an Employment Judge at the time of presentation under Rule 12 where there are certain substantive defects. A claimant may have a right to make representations and attend a hearing before this occurs.[2]

3. The claimant may apply for reconsideration of that rejection by an Employment Judge within 14 days on the grounds that it is wrong or that the defect can be rectified. Unless the claimant asks for a hearing, the issue is decided on paper by the Employment Judge. If there is a hearing, only the claimant attends.

NOTES

2 The guidance in paragraphs 2 and 3 are subject to the decision of the Employment Appeal Tribunal in *Trustees of the William Jones's Schools Foundation v Parry* [2016] ICR 1140 which has put the scope and validity of rule 12 in doubt.

Failure to respond and Rule 21 judgment

4. If no response to the claim is received from the respondent within the prescribed time, the Tribunal considers whether a judgment can be issued under Rule 21 on the available material. An Employment Judge may seek further information from the claimant or order a hearing. The respondent will receive notice of the hearing, but will only be allowed to participate in the hearing to the extent permitted by the judge.

Notice under Rule 26 after response received

5. If a response to the claim from the respondent is accepted, the Tribunal conducts an initial consideration of the claim form and response form under Rule 26. If the Employment Judge considers that the Tribunal has no jurisdiction to hear the claim, or that the claim or the response has no reasonable prospect of success, notice will be sent to the parties setting out the judge's view and the reasons for it. The judge will order that the claim or response (or any part of it) shall be dismissed on a date specified unless the claimant or respondent (as the case might be) has before that date written to explain why that should not happen.

6. If no representations are received then the claim or response or the relevant part will be dismissed. If representations are received, they will be considered by an Employment Judge, who will either permit the laim or response to proceed or fix a hearing for the purposes of deciding whether it should be permitted do so. Such a hearing may consider other matters in relation to preparing the case for hearing.

Preparation for the final hearing

Employment Judge directs the case is to proceed to final hearing, orders will normally be made 29 to prepare for the hearing which is listed. These may include disclosure of documents and witness statements. Failure to comply with these orders may lead to sanctions as set out

Striking out under Rule 37

8. Under rule 37 the Tribunal may strike out all or part of a claim or response on a number of grounds at any stage of the proceedings, either on its own initiative, or on the application of a party. These include that it is scandalous or vexatious or has no reasonable prospect of success, or the manner in which the proceedings have been conducted has been scandalous, unreasonable or vexatious.

9. Non-compliance with the rules or orders of the Tribunal is also a ground for striking out, as is the fact that the claim or response is not being actively pursued.

10. The fact that it is no longer possible to have a fair hearing is also ground for striking out. In some cases the progress of the claim to hearing is delayed over a lengthy period. Ill health may be a reason why this happens. This means that the evidence becomes more distant from the events in the case. Eventually a point may be reached where a fair hearing is no longer possible.

11. Before a strike out on any of these grounds a party will be given a reasonable opportunity to make representations in writing or request a hearing. The Tribunal does not use these powers lightly. It will often hold a preliminary hearing before taking this action.

12. In exercising these powers the Tribunal follows the overriding objective in seeking to deal with cases justly and expeditiously and in proportion to the matters in dispute. In some cases parties apply for strike out of their opponent at every perceived breach of the rules. This is not a satisfactory method of managing a case. Such applications are rarely successful. The outcome is often further orders by the Tribunal to ensure the case is ready for the hearing.

13. It follows that before a claim or response is struck out you will receive a notice explaining what is being considered and what you should do. If you oppose the proposed action you should write explaining why and seeking a hearing if you require one.

Unless orders under Rule 38

14. The Tribunal may, in order to secure compliance with an order for preparation of the case, make an "unless order" under rule 38. This is an order that will specify that, if it is not complied with, the claim or response or part of it shall be dismissed without further order. The party may apply, within 14 days of the date that the "unless order" was sent, to have the order set aside or for time for compliance to be extended. If the party does not comply with the order then the case is struck out without further order. A party may also apply after the strike out for the claim or response to be reinstated.

Deposit orders under Rule 39

15. The Tribunal has power under Rule 39 to order that a deposit be paid on the ground that a specific allegation or argument has little reasonable prospect of success. If such an order is made the deposit must be paid in the time specified as a condition of continuing to advance the allegation or argument. If the party fails to pay the deposit by the date specified, the allegation to which the deposit relates is struck out.

Withdrawal under Rule 51

16. When a claimant withdraws the claim it comes to an end. The Tribunal must issue a dismissal judgment under Rule 52, unless for some reason this is inappropriate. Often the settlement of a claim includes an agreement that the claimant withdraws the claim and that a dismissal judgment is made.

Compromise agreements and ACAS

17. Section 203 of the Employment Rights Act 1996 and section 144 of the Equality Act 2010 restrict any contracting out of the provisions of these two Acts. Claims can be settled using an ACAS conciliator to produce a COT3 agreement or, where legal advice is available to the claimant, a compromise or settlement agreement.

Conclusion

18. In the absence of one of the outcomes outlined above the case will be determined at a final hearing following consideration of the evidence and law by a Tribunal.

EMPLOYMENT TRIBUNALS (ENGLAND & WALES) PRESIDENTIAL GUIDANCE RULE 3 – ALTERNATIVE DISPUTE RESOLUTION

[5.78]

NOTES

1. This Presidential Guidance is issued on 22 January 2018 under the provisions of Rule 7 of the First Schedule to the Employment Tribunals (Constitution and Rules of Procedure) Regulations 2013 ("the Employment Tribunals Rules of Procedure").

2. It replaces Presidential Guidance on Judicial Assessments first issued on 3 October 2016 and it incorporates an up-dated Guidance Note on Judicial Mediation that was first issued on 13 March 2014 as part of Presidential Guidance on General Case Management.

3. The Employment Tribunals in England and Wales must have regard to such Presidential Guidance, but they shall not be bound by it.

4. Rule 2 of the Employment Tribunals Rules of Procedure provides that the overriding objective of the Rules is to enable Employment Tribunals to deal with cases fairly and justly.

5. Dealing with a case fairly and justly includes, so far as practicable —

- ensuring that the parties are on an equal footing;
- dealing with cases in ways which are proportionate to the complexity and importance of the issues;
- avoiding unnecessary formality and seeking flexibility in the proceedings;
- avoiding delay, so far as compatible with proper consideration of the issues; and
- saving expense.

6. A Tribunal shall seek to give effect to the overriding objective in interpreting, or exercising any power given to it by, the Rules. The parties and their representatives shall assist the Tribunal to further the overriding objective and in particular shall co-operate generally with each other and with the Tribunal.

7. Rule 3 of the Employment Tribunals Rules of Procedure provides that a Tribunal shall wherever practicable and appropriate encourage the use by the parties of the services of ACAS, judicial or other mediation, ***or other means of resolving their disputes by agreement.***

8. Having regard to Rule 2 and Rule 3, this Presidential Guidance reproduces a Protocol for an Employment Judge conducting a Judicial Assessment of a claim and a response as part of a preliminary hearing (case management) held under Rule 53(1)(a) of the Employment Tribunals Rules of Procedure. The Protocol on Judicial Assessments is appended to this Presidential Guidance (together with some Questions and Answers for the parties). It provides a formal framework for the preliminary consideration of the claim and response with the parties that is already often an important part of a preliminary hearing (case management) in defining the issues to be determined at a final hearing. It is not anticipated that it will lead to longer preliminary hearings or to an increase in the number of preliminary hearings conducted by electronic communications under Rule 46. It will be particularly helpful, but not exclusively so, where a party to a claim is not professionally represented at the preliminary hearing (case management).

9. Having regard to Rule 2 and Rule 3, this Presidential Guidance also reproduces the Explanatory Note to the parties in respect of Judicial Mediation.

Judge Brian Doyle

President

Employment Tribunals (England & Wales)

22 January 2018

APPENDIX 1: PROTOCOL FOR JUDICIAL ASSESSMENT

INTRODUCTION

[5.79]

1. This protocol sets out the basis on which the Employment Tribunals will offer to parties the facility of Judicial Assessment of their cases.

THE AIMS AND PURPOSE OF JUDICIAL ASSESSMENT

2. Judicial Assessment is an impartial and confidential assessment by an Employment Judge, at an early stage in the proceedings, of the strengths, weaknesses and risks of the parties' respective claims, allegations and contentions.

3. The statutory basis for the offer is Rule 3 of the Employment Tribunals Rules of Procedure 2013, which provides that "A Tribunal shall wherever practicable and appropriate encourage the use by the parties of the services of ACAS, judicial or other mediation, or other means of resolving their disputes by agreement."

4. Although the purpose of Judicial Assessment is to encourage parties to resolve their dispute by agreement, it is not envisaged that settlement discussions will necessarily occur during the Judicial Assessment itself.

5. Employment Tribunal proceedings are costly of parties' time and resources. They are stressful for parties and witnesses. Almost every case entails risks for both parties.

6. An early assessment of the case by an Employment Judge may assist the parties in identifying what the case is really about, what is at stake, and may clarify and narrow the issues and encourage settlement. This may lead to resolution of the case by agreement between the parties before positions become entrenched and costs excessive, or may shorten and simplify the scope of hearings.

7. This reflects the overriding objective of the Employment Tribunals to deal with cases justly, speedily and cost-effectively (Rule 2). Judicial Assessment is particularly valuable in view of the lack of information and advice available to parties in Employment Tribunal cases, many of whom are unrepresented.

IDENTIFICATION OF SUITABLE CASES

8. Judicial Assessment will generally be offered at the first case management hearing in the proceedings. It will take place after the issues have been clarified and formal case management orders have been made in the first part of the case management hearing.

9. Most cases of any complexity which are listed for a case management hearing on service of proceedings will be suitable for Judicial Assessment. However, the following (non-exclusive) factors may render the case unsuitable for an offer of Judicial Assessment:

- there are multiple claimants not all of whom request Judicial Assessment
- a party is insolvent
- High Court or other proceedings exist or are intimated.

INITIAL FORMALITIES

10. Written information about Judicial Assessment will be available to parties in all cases listed for an initial case management hearing.

11. The parties are encouraged to inform the Tribunal in advance of the case management hearing that they wish to have Judicial Assessment in their case. This will enable the Employment Judge to prepare for the process and to make sure that sufficient time is available on the day. However, even if the parties have made no request in advance, the Employment Judge, in suitable cases, may offer Judicial Assessment during the case management hearing.

12. Judicial Assessment will almost invariably take place at the initial case management hearing. This reflects the need for it to happen at an early stage in the proceedings. It will not generally be offered later in the proceedings.

13. If Judicial Assessment is expected to take place, the case management hearing may be listed in person rather than by telephone conference call if it is envisaged that the necessary in-depth discussion could not take place in a telephone conference call. However, the Employment Judge will have the discretion to conduct a Judicial Assessment by telephone or other electronic communication means in appropriate cases. Sufficient time will be allocated to the case management hearing (generally up to two hours, depending always on the nature of the case).

14. It is a requirement for Judicial Assessment that the parties freely consent to it. Whilst the Employment Judge will explain the advantages of Judicial Assessment, no pressure should ever be placed on any party to agree to it.

15. The information provided to the parties in advance will make clear that Judicial Assessment is strictly confidential. This will be repeated by the Employment Judge before the Judicial Assessment takes place.

16. Although anything said in the Judicial Assessment might be used in subsequent "without prejudice" discussions between the parties, or in a Judicial Mediation, the views expressed by the Employment Judge are non-attributable and must be kept strictly confidential. They must not be disclosed to third parties, other than advisers, as having been expressed by the Employment Judge, or attributed or identified as the views of the Employment Judge in subsequent proceedings, including the final hearing. Unless the parties agree to these conditions, Judicial Assessment will not take place.

THE CONDUCT OF THE JUDICIAL ASSESSMENT

17. Judicial Assessment involves evaluating the strength of the parties' cases. Employment Judges will use their skill and experience in doing this, whilst remaining wholly impartial. Whilst recognising that evidence will not have been heard, Employment Judges may, when appropriate, give indications about the possible outcome of the case.

18. Judicial Assessment is not the same as Judicial Mediation. An outcome of Judicial Assessment may be that a case is listed for Judicial Mediation. Judicial Assessment is indicative in nature and will involve a practical assessment of the case by the Employment Judge. Judicial Mediation is usually facilitative, but can be indicative or evaluative; has the aim of assisting the parties to achieve a resolution of the issues between them without giving any indication of prospects of success; and is usually allocated a full day of the Employment Tribunal's time.

19. It is possible that the Judicial Assessment process will lead to immediate settlement negotiations between the parties. This is not the primary purpose of Judicial Assessment, but will be encouraged if it occurs, and time will be made available for it.

20. The Judicial Assessment must only be conducted after the issues between the parties have been fully clarified and case management orders made in the usual way at the case management hearing. The Judicial Assessment is not a way of avoiding the discipline of a properly conducted case management hearing and indeed is dependent upon the process.

21. If the parties consent, the Employment Judge may then give an assessment of the liability and/or remedy aspects of the case. It will be made clear that the assessment is provisional and that the Employment Tribunal hearing the case may come to a different view. In conducting the assessment the Employment Judge must make it clear that they are assessing the case on the state of the allegations and not evaluating the evidence, which has not been heard or seen, and assessing provisionally the risks as to liability and, typically, brackets of likely compensation on remedy. The Employment Judge will encourage parties to approach the process with an open mind and to be prepared to enter into the assessment pragmatically and to be receptive and to listen to the Employment Judge's views.

22. The Judicial Assessment will be conducted with a view to assisting eventual settlement of all or part of the claim. If the parties express the wish to enter into immediate settlement negotiations, this may be encouraged, but care must be taken to make sure that unrepresented parties have time to think and to consider any offer, and are advised that if an offer is made, they should take time to reflect upon it.

23. Judicial Assessment of parties' cases must be provisionally and guardedly expressed because no evidence will have been heard. Employment Judges must recognise that parties may not fully understand the distinction between a provisional indication and the eventual result of the case.

24. The Employment Judge may make their own notes of the Judicial Assessment. These will not be placed on the case file and the parties will be informed that such notes are kept only as the Employment Judge's record and will not be distributed to them or to any third parties.

25. The Employment Judge who conducted the Judicial Assessment will normally not then be involved in any part of the proceedings which may entail final determination of the parties' rights (except that they may conduct any subsequent Judicial Mediation). This is to encourage full and frank assessment of the claim and ensure public trust in the confidentiality and impartiality of the evaluation. This does not preclude involvement in day to day case management of the proceedings, including, in particular, case management hearings.

ACTION FOLLOWING THE JUDICIAL ASSESSMENT

26. In some cases, a settlement may be reached at the Judicial Assessment. Any settlement will be recorded by one of the following means:

- ACAS COT3;
- Formal settlement agreement between the parties;
- Consent judgment by the Tribunal;
- Conditional withdrawal and dismissal of the claim upon payment within an agreed period.

27. More usually, the parties will wish to consider their positions following the Judicial Assessment. If the parties agree, a Judicial Mediation may be listed. Otherwise the Employment Judge will remind the parties of the availability of the conciliation services of ACAS.

APPENDIX 2: JUDICIAL ASSESSMENT QUESTIONS AND ANSWERS FOR THE PARTIES

Not every case is suitable for Judicial Assessment. It is in the discretion of the Employment Judge whether to offer Judicial Assessment.

WHAT IS JUDICIAL ASSESSMENT?

Judicial Assessment is a service offered by the Employment Tribunals to assess the strengths, weaknesses and risks of the parties' respective claims, allegations and contentions on liability and remedy, at an early stage on an impartial and confidential basis. If all parties and the Employment Judge agree, the Judicial Assessment will take place at the end of the private case management hearing. The service is optional and the Employment Judge cannot decide anything about your case at a Judicial Assessment.

WHY MIGHT I WANT TO CONSIDER TAKING PART IN A JUDICIAL ASSESSMENT?

Judicial Assessment may save time and expense if it leads to a settlement. The first part of your case management hearing will clarify the issues between the parties and set a timetable to ensure that the case is ready for a full hearing. This involves a great deal of work over the coming weeks and months (organising documents and witness statements and having other evidence ready such as medical reports). Preparation for a hearing is expensive and time consuming for all parties. The Employment Judge will normally arrange a full hearing, which may be in several months' time. It may involve several days or weeks in Tribunal depending on the complexity of the case. Judicial Assessment may lead to an early settlement of the proceedings.

HOW IS THE JUDICIAL ASSESSMENT DIFFERENT FROM THE FIRST PART OF THE PRIVATE PRELIMINARY HEARING?

Judicial Assessment is strictly confidential and will involve the Judge giving a provisional assessment of the case.

WHAT DOES "CONFIDENTIAL" MEAN?

The parties cannot give details of the assessment to anyone other than their advisers. Although anything said in the Judicial Assessment might be used in subsequent "without prejudice" discussions between the parties or in a Judicial Mediation, the views expressed by the Employment Judge are non-attributable and must be kept strictly confidential. They must not be disclosed to third parties, other than advisers, as having been expressed by the Employment Judge, or attributed or identified as the views of the Employment Judge in subsequent proceedings, including the final full merits hearing. Unless the parties agree to these conditions, Judicial Assessment will not take place. The Judge's notes will be kept separate from the case file and if the case proceeds to a full hearing the Tribunal will not see those notes.

WHAT DOES "WITHOUT PREJUDICE" MEAN?

Anything said during the Judicial Assessment may not be referred to in correspondence or at subsequent hearings. Such statements are inadmissible evidence. They include offers of settlement and what is said leading up to and to explain such offers. They are made with view to settling the case and are without prejudice to the parties' position at a full merits hearing. They include anything said by the Employment Judge during the Judicial Assessment.

WHAT IS AN ASSESSMENT?

The Employment Judge in the Judicial Assessment may express a provisional view on the strengths and weaknesses of parts of the case without having heard any evidence, but by considering the law and what parties say about their cases. The Employment Judge will use his or her skill and experience in the assessment, while remaining wholly impartial. The assessment may identify possible ranges of compensation for remedy if liability is established. The purpose of the provisional assessment is to help the parties to resolve their differences by way of settlement. The eventual outcome at the hearing may be different from the Employment Judge's assessment. An assessment is not legal advice nor does it relieve a party from the need to take legal advice.

WILL THE JUDGE ALWAYS OFFER A JUDICIAL ASSESSMENT?

There is no presumption that an Employment Judge will offer a Judicial Assessment. The Employment Judge will take into account the time available and matters that might mean settlement is difficult or impossible. These might include where a party is insolvent or bankrupt, other proceedings exist or the parties indicate an intention to commence other proceedings, or the parties express a view that the case cannot be settled.

IS THERE ANY FEE PAYABLE FOR A JUDICIAL ASSESSMENT?

No.

WHAT DO I HAVE TO DO IF I WANT A JUDICIAL ASSESSMENT?

You should indicate your interest in the box on the case management agenda for the case management hearing and bring it to the case management hearing or send it in advance to the Tribunal. A Judicial Assessment will only take place if all parties agree.

HOW CAN A CASE SETTLE AT A JUDICIAL ASSESSMENT?

There are four ways in which this can happen:

- ACAS may be contacted to produce a conciliated settlement (normally recorded by way of an ACAS COT3 agreement).
- There may be a formal settlement agreement between the parties (often called a compromise agreement).
- There may be a consent judgment by the Employment Judge.
- There may be conditional withdrawal and dismissal of the claim upon payment within an agreed period.

WHAT IF THE CASE DOES NOT SETTLE AT A JUDICIAL ASSESSMENT?

The case will proceed as ordered at the case management hearing. The Employment Judge will not normally be involved in any part of the proceedings which may entail a final determination of the parties' rights, but the Employment Judge may conduct any subsequent judicial mediation and is not precluded from day to day case management, including any further case management hearing. It is still open to the parties to agree to Judicial Mediation, if offered. The services of ACAS are available to the parties at any time.

APPENDIX 3: JUDICIAL MEDIATION – AN EXPLANATION FOR THE PARTIES

INTRODUCTION TO JUDICIAL MEDIATION

[5.80]

1. It is often better for everyone involved to settle their legal dispute by agreement rather than by going through a possibly stressful, risky, expensive and time-consuming hearing. The process of judicial mediation is one method for achieving settlement. It is entirely voluntary and it is private. It no longer incurs a fee.

2. Judicial mediation has several potential advantages over a hearing. The parties remain in control of their own agreement, rather than having the Tribunal impose outcomes. The parties may include practical solutions which would not be open to the Tribunal at a hearing (for example, an agreed reference, an apology and/or confidentiality). The parties might agree to consider and settle other litigation or disputes between them, even if not within the Tribunal's jurisdiction. It provides a certain, speedier outcome which cannot be appealed.

IS YOUR CASE SUITABLE FOR MEDIATION?

3. Cases with complaints under any jurisdiction are potentially suitable for mediation, although it is not likely to be cost-effective – and therefore not available - in short cases. A working guide is that the hearing has been listed for at least three days. Discrimination complaints and those where a claimant is still employed by the respondent may be particularly suitable. Multiple respondents may diminish suitability. Particular features in an individual case may make mediation desirable. Mediation will not be offered unless both parties actively want it. Even if both are willing, mediation may not be offered. The decision whether or not to offer judicial mediation is made by the Regional Employment Judge (or his or her nominated judge).

HOW IS YOUR CASE IDENTIFIED AS SUITABLE?

4. At a preliminary hearing an Employment Judge may ask you if you consider your case suitable for mediation. If both parties are keen to enter mediation the judge will refer the file to the Regional Employment Judge, who will decide whether the case may qualify for an offer of judicial mediation. This may include consideration of how reasonably the litigation is being conducted. An up-to-date schedule of loss or statement of remedy will assist the Regional Employment Judge.

TELEPHONE PRELIMINARY HEARING

5. If satisfied, the Regional Employment Judge will hold a preliminary hearing with the parties (or their representatives) by telephone. It is likely that judicial mediation will be offered in this hearing if both parties persuade the Regional Employment Judge that it has a high prospect of success. This means, in large part, that they must demonstrate a real willingness to compromise.

6. Where judicial mediation is offered and accepted by both parties, the Regional Employment Judge will list a date for the mediation, usually within the next three weeks, and make any necessary orders and directions. The Regional Employment Judge will need to know that decision-makers with authority to make decisions *on the* day will be at the mediation in person, so parties should be able to provide names and job titles during the telephone hearing.

WHAT HAPPENS IN JUDICIAL MEDIATION?

7. The parties to a judicial mediation come to the Tribunal hearing centre for what is listed as a private preliminary hearing. They receive the assistance of a judge trained in mediation for a day, very occasionally two days. The judge will not make decisions for the parties, impose solutions, give advice or hear evidence. However, if requested and subject to mutual agreement, the judge may give an indication as to the strength of a particular point. The judge will help the parties to reach their own solution by managing the process in a fair and constructive manner, making sure that they understand what is going on and helping them to focus on areas of agreement and common interest.

8. The mediation day starts relatively early. On arrival, the parties are provided with separate consultation rooms which they may occupy for the duration of the mediation. At 9.30 a.m. the parties are invited to meet the judge and each other around a table in a private room. The judge will outline what the parties should expect to happen and remind them of the vital confidentiality of the mediation process. The judge will emphasise that if the mediation fails, no mention may be made of it *at all* in the further stages of the case or at any hearing. The judge who conducts the mediation will not hear the case if the mediation fails. The parties need not contribute anything at this initial meeting: but they do have an opportunity to ask questions if they are at all unclear about what is to happen.

9. Occasionally one party may not wish to meet the other in this way. Although the initial meeting is intended as a helpful part of the process, it is not compulsory. If a party has concerns about the meeting, they should tell the Tribunal clerk at the start of the day.

10. After the round-table meeting, the parties withdraw to their own rooms. The judge then visits the parties in their separate rooms. The judge will seek to understand what each side wishes to achieve and, sometimes, to manage their expectations. The judge will use that understanding to help the parties move to a position where they have reached a solution which they both agree.

11. If lawyers are involved, they will often be able to record the agreement in writing. So it is likely to be useful if they bring laptops with internet access, memory sticks and template compromise agreements.

12. After the initial meeting, the parties need not meet up again, but often do if they (perhaps more realistically, their lawyers) wish to discuss matters directly or at the end when agreement is reached.

13. When agreement is reached the judge and/or the parties will usually contact ACAS, which is independent of the judiciary. To this end, the parties are requested to bring the name and contact details of their ACAS conciliation officer, having notified the officer in advance of the mediation date. The ACAS officer may be sent any written agreement and/or a telephone conference call may be set up to speak to the officer to establish that there is a binding legal agreement. It is advisable for any draft settlement agreement to be copied to the other party in advance of the judicial mediation.

14. A successful mediation is one which concludes with a signed agreement. The hearing will then be vacated and the dispute will be over.

5. EMPLOYMENT TRIBUNALS (SCOTLAND): PRESIDENTIAL PRACTICE DIRECTIONS

NOTES

The first three Practice Directions in this section (one of which has since been revoked) were issued under the authority of reg 13 of the Employment Tribunals (Constitution and Rules of Procedure) Regulations 2004 (revoked). The 2013 and subsequent Practice Directions are issued under the authority of reg 11 of the Employment Tribunals (Constitution and Rules of Procedure) Regulations 2013 at **[2.1333]**.

EMPLOYMENT TRIBUNALS (SCOTLAND) PRACTICE DIRECTION NO 1 (2006)

[5.81]

NOTES

In consequence of the power given to me under Regulation 13 of the Employment Tribunals (Constitution and Rules of Procedure) Regulations 2004 I make the following Practice Direction:—

INTIMATION OF LIST OF DOCUMENTS 14 DAYS BEFORE A HEARING

When a party is legally represented their representative will intimate a list of the documents to be relied upon at any Hearing on the merits of the claim to the other party (or parties) or their representative (if represented) not later than 14 days before any such Hearing.

COLIN M MILNE
President of Employment Tribunals, Scotland
14 December 2006

NOTES

Many cases before the Employment Tribunal are subject to extensive case management by the judiciary, an element of which may involve orders being made regarding the identification and disclosure of documents. There is currently less opportunity to undertake in-depth case management of cases that might be regarded as more straightforward. Nevertheless, in keeping with one of the principal objectives identified in the Report of the Employment Tribunal System Taskforce, it is generally agreed that there is merit in each side having as much notice of the other side's case as possible in advance of the Hearing. The Rules of Procedure generally assist this objective but users have expressed concern about the lack of direction regarding the lodging of documents. There is no provision in the rules requiring the lodging of documents within a certain time span. It is not uncommon for a party to wait until the day of the Hearing to reveal the documents upon which they intend to rely to the other party (or parties, as the case may be). That on occasion leads to delay as the implications of that documentation are considered by the other side. Following extensive consultation with Scottish users, I have agreed to make a Practice Direction requiring parties who are legally represented to provide a list of the documents they are going to rely upon to the other party/parties no later than 14 days before a Hearing on the merits of the case. It is expected that this list will be sufficiently detailed to enable the other party/parties to understand the nature of each of the documents which is to be produced. However, this direction is without prejudice to the right of any Employment Tribunal Chairman to impose a more onerous direction in respect of the provision of information about documents to be relied upon at any Hearing.

Consideration was given to the idea of actually requiring copies of the documents themselves to be provided to the other party/parties at least 14 days before the Hearing but that was considered to place too heavy a cost burden on parties, given the number of cases which settle in the 14 day period before the Hearing. Requiring a simple list however should at least put the other side on notice as to the documents which are going to be relied upon, thereby minimising the risk of delay arising from last minute surprises.

With regard to the general need for Employment Tribunals to be accessible to all users, it was felt unduly onerous to apply this Practice Direction to parties who are not legally represented. The imposition of a requirement, as here, which applies only to those who are legally represented finds a parallel in the provisions of the Rules themselves (see, for example, the obligations imposed when a party is legally represented under Rule 11).

NOTES

This Practice Direction applies to Scotland only.

EMPLOYMENT TRIBUNALS (SCOTLAND) PRACTICE DIRECTION NO 2 (2006)

[5.82]

NOTES

In consequence of the power given to me under Regulation 13 of the Employment Tribunals (Constitution and Rules of Procedure) Regulations 2004 I make the following Practice Direction:—

SIST FOR MEDIATION

Where both (or, as the case may be, all) parties to a claim agree that it should be sisted for mediation a Chairman of Employment Tribunals shall sist it for that purpose. The Chairman shall nevertheless review the need for that sist within such timescale as he or she thinks necessary having regard to the interests of justice.

COLIN M MILNE
President of Employment Tribunals, Scotland
14 December 2006

NOTES

The sole purpose of this Practice Direction is to focus parties' minds on mediation as an option for the resolution of employment disputes. The role of Acas in providing a conciliation service is well known and highly valued but in certain circumstances Acas may also provide mediation. In recent times an employment dispute meditation service has also become more widely available from other providers. However, while mediation is on the increase in employment cases there is some evidence to suggest that not all parties are aware of this as an option which might be utilised.

While the direction directs that, where parties agree, a Chairman will sist the case, it must be borne in mind that Chairmen still have to consider the overriding objective, which involves taking account of what is in the interests of justice overall. It is therefore appropriate that any sist granted to allow for mediation to take place should be kept under regular review. The timing and circumstances of the review process are a matter for judicial discretion in each individual case in light of the interests of justice in that case.

This Practice Direction in relation to mediation clearly envisages what might be described as external mediation. It is without prejudice to the pilot being carried out in England and Wales (which pilot has not been extended to Scotland) in relation to judicial mediation.

NOTES

This Practice Direction applies to Scotland only.

EMPLOYMENT TRIBUNALS (SCOTLAND) PRACTICE DIRECTION NO 3 (2006) (NOTE)

[5.83]

NOTES

This Practice Direction was revoked by the President of Employment Tribunals (Scotland) on 10 February 2014 under the powers conferred by the Employment Tribunals (Constitution and Rules of Procedure) Regulations 2013, SI 2013/1237, reg 11 at **[2.1333]**.

EMPLOYMENT TRIBUNALS (SCOTLAND) PRESIDENTIAL PRACTICE DIRECTION — ADDRESSES FOR SERVING DOCUMENTS IN SPECIAL CASES (2013)

[5.84]

NOTES

Commencement: 17 December 2013 (see para 1).

1. This Presidential Practice Direction, which sets out the addresses for service of documents in special cases, is made in accordance with the provisions of Regulation 11 of the Employment Tribunals (Constitution and Rules of Procedure) Regulations 2013. The Practice Direction has effect on and from 17th of December 2013.

2. Rule 88 of the Employment Tribunals Rules of Procedure (as set out in Schedule 1 of the Employment Tribunals (Constitution and Rules of Procedure Regulations 2013) is in the following terms:

'Special cases

88 – Addresses for serving the Secretary of State, the Law Officers, and the Counsel General to the Welsh Assembly Government, in cases where they are not parties, shall be issued by practice direction.'

DIRECTION

3. For the purposes of Rule 88 the relevant addresses which are to be used when sending a notice or document in such special cases are set out in the schedule attached hereto.

Shona Simon
President, Employment Tribunals (Scotland)
Dated: 17th December 2013

Schedule

Office	Address
Redundancy Payments Service (UK)	Redundancy Payments Service (UK) ET Section PO Box 16684 Birmingham B2 2EF RPS.ET@insolvency.gsi.gov.uk
Secretary of State (BIS)	Department for Business, Innovation and Skills 1 Victoria Street London SW1H 0ET
Attorney General's Office (England)	Attorney General's Office 20 Victoria Street London SW1H 0NF
Counsel General for Wales	Counsel General for Wales Welsh Government Cathays Park Cardiff CF10 3NQ
Advocate General for Scotland	Director and Solicitor to the Advocate General Victoria Quay Edinburgh EH6 6QQ
Lord Advocate (Scotland)	Lord Advocate 25 Chambers Street Edinburgh EH1 1LA

NOTES

The addresses of the Secretary of State and the Attorney General's Office in this Schedule are, as of 15 May 2019, incorrect. See the addresses in the Schedule to the 2017 English equivalent of this Practice Direction at **[5.59]**.

EMPLOYMENT TRIBUNALS (SCOTLAND) DIRECTION OF THE PRESIDENT IN THE MATTER OF CLAIMS BROUGHT IN EMPLOYMENT TRIBUNALS (SCOTLAND) IN RESPECT OF THE CALCULATION OF UNPAID HOLIDAY PAY (2015)

[5.85]

NOTES

This PD was issued in March 2015 to replace the one issued in December 2014. An accompanying note was also published in March 2015 explaining the reasons for the revocation of the December 2014 PD. See www.judiciary.gov.uk/wp-content/uploads/2015/03/Accompanying-Note-explaining-changes-made-to-holiday-pay-direction-dated-11-December-2014-_2_.pdf.

HAVING REGARD TO the European Union Working Time Directive (No 2003/88);

AND having regard to the decisions of the Court of Justice of the European Union in *British Airways plc v Williams* [2012] ICR 847 and in *British Gas Trading Ltd v Lock* [2014] ICR 813;

AND having regard to the decision of the Employment Appeal Tribunal in *Bear Scotland Ltd and others v Fulton and others*; *Hertel (UK) Ltd v Woods and others*; and *Amex Group Ltd and others* (4 November 2014);

AND having regard to regulations 13, 13A and 30 of the Working Time Regulations 1998;

AND having regard to Part II and Part XIV (Chapters II and III) of the Employment Rights Act 1996;

AND having regard to the Employment Tribunals (Constitution and Rules of Procedure) Regulations 2013 and the Employment Tribunals Rules of Procedure, as set out in Schedule 1 of the Regulations;

AND having regard to the decisions of the Employment Appeal Tribunal in *Okugade v Shaw Trust* (EAT 0172/05) and in *Prakash v Wolverhampton City Council* (EAT 0140/06)

THEN

ACTING in accordance with my powers under regulations 7 and 11 of the Employment Tribunals (Constitution and Rules of Procedure) Regulations 2013 and under rules 2 and 29 of the Employment Tribunals Rules of Procedure

IT IS ORDERED THAT

1. A claimant or group of claimants who have previously presented a claim or claims in respect of a complaint of alleged non-payment of holiday pay may, if so advised, apply to amend the claim or claims so presented in order to add a further complaint or complaints of alleged non-payment of holiday pay that have accrued or arisen after the presentation of the original claim and which could not have been included in the original claim or claims.

2. They may do so, if so advised, instead of presenting a new claim to the Tribunal.

3. Any such application shall identify clearly the original claim that is sought to be amended by case number, claimant(s) and respondent(s). It shall also set out the amended particulars of the claim to include the additional dates or periods of alleged non-payment of holiday pay and the basis of the complaint.

4. Any such application shall be copied to the respondent(s) by the claimant(s) at the same time as making the application. The claimant(s) shall invite the respondent(s) to provide any written comments upon the application to the Tribunal within 7 days.

5. After that period of 7 days the application to amend will then be considered by a judge in accordance with the usual principles for the amendment of a claim. In the event that the claim affected is sisted at the time of the application, the sist will be recalled to allow for such consideration. Accordingly, parties should make such representations in connection with the application as they see fit at this stage.

6. An Employment Judge, if the interests of justice so require, may permit a claim to be amended even if the application to amend does not comply with the terms of this direction but in such a case the application must explain the reason for non compliance and why, nonetheless, it would be in the interests of justice to allow the amendment.

7. Any party or representative wishing to make representations for the further conduct of such claims should do so upon application to the President.

8. A copy of this Direction shall be sent to ACAS and to all known interested parties, and shall be published at www.judiciary.gov.uk/publications/directions-for-employment-tribunals-scotland.

9. The Direction of the President dated 11 December 2014 "In the matter of claims brought in Employment Tribunals (Scotland) in respect of the calculation of unpaid holiday pay" is hereby revoked.

Judge Shona Simon
President
Dated: 27 March 2015

EMPLOYMENT TRIBUNALS (SCOTLAND) PRESIDENTIAL PRACTICE DIRECTION – PRESENTATION OF CLAIMS (2017)

[5.86]

NOTES

1. Rule 8 (1) of the Employment Tribunals Rules of Procedure (as set out in Schedule 1 of the Employment Tribunals (Constitution and Rules of Procedure Regulations 2013) is in the following terms:

> "**Presenting the claim**
>
> **8.**—(1)A claim shall be started by presenting a completed claim form (using a prescribed form) in accordance with any practice direction made under regulation 11 which supplements this rule."

2. This Presidential Practice Direction, which sets out the methods by which a completed claim form may be presented, is made in accordance with the powers set out in Regulation 11 of the Employment Tribunals (Constitution and Rules of Procedure) Regulations 2013. The Practice Direction has effect on and from 26 July 2017.

METHODS OF PRESENTING A COMPLETED CLAIM FORM

3. A completed claim form may be presented to an Employment Tribunal in Scotland:

(1) Online by using the online form submission service provided by Her Majesty's Courts and Tribunals Service, accessible at www.employmenttribunals.service.gov.uk;

(2) By post to **Employment Tribunals Central Office (Scotland), PO Box 27105, GLASGOW, G2 9JR**.

(3) **Only** during the period 26 July 2017 to 31 July 2017 inclusive, **and not otherwise** by email to GlasgowET@hmcts.gsi.gov.uk.

(4) By hand to an Employment Tribunal Office listed in the schedule to this Practice Direction.

4. The Presidential Practice Direction dated 14 December 2016 is hereby revoked.

Shona Simon

President, Employment Tribunals (Scotland)

Dated: 2 November 2017

SCHEDULE

Office	***Address***
Aberdeen	Employment Tribunals Ground Floor AB1 48 Huntly Street Aberdeen AB10 1SH Telephone: 01224 593137
Dundee	Ground Floor Block C Caledonian House Greenmarket Dundee DD1 4QB Telephone: 01382 221578
Edinburgh	54-56 Melville Street Edinburgh EH37HF Telephone: 0131 226 5584
Glasgow	Eagle Building 215 Bothwell Street Glasgow G2 7TS Telephone: 0141 204 0730

6. EMPLOYMENT TRIBUNALS (SCOTLAND): PRESIDENTIAL GUIDANCE

NOTES

Guidance in this section is issued under the authority of Rule 7 of the Employment Tribunals Rules of Procedure 2013 at [2.1344].

EMPLOYMENT TRIBUNALS (SCOTLAND) PRESIDENTIAL GUIDANCE ON SEEKING THE POSTPONEMENT OF A HEARING (2014)

[5.87]

NOTES

This Guidance is issued in accordance with the Rule 7 of the Employment Tribunals Rules of Procedure ("the Rules"). The Rules are set out in Schedule 1 of the Employment Tribunals (Constitution and Rules of Procedure) Regulations 2013.

Employment Judges and Employment Tribunals are expected to have regard to this Guidance but are not bound by it.

This Guidance has effect from 1 February 2014.

1. Power to grant a postponement

Rule 29 of the Rules allows an Employment Judge to make case management orders. That includes the power to order that a hearing should be postponed.

2. Purpose of Guidance and the relevance of the overriding objective

2.1 The purpose of this Guidance is to provide parties with information about the practice of Employment Tribunals in Scotland in connection with requests (known legally as "applications") for postponement of a hearing and what Employment Judges will normally expect of parties who make such an application. Parties can proceed on the basis that the information set out below is sought because it will normally be relevant and taken into account in the decision making process although a range of other factors, which will vary depending on the circumstances of the case, are also likely to be relevant.

2.2 The **overriding objective** of the tribunal is to deal with cases fairly and justly. If a party wishes a hearing to be postponed for any reason the Employment Judge who considers the request will have to be satisfied that it is in accordance with the overriding objective to order that the hearing be postponed.

3. How a request should be made and the information it should contain

3.1 While an application for a postponement may have to be made at the start of the hearing itself, that is unusual. Most applications of this type are made in advance of the hearing. What follows deals with postponement requests which are made before the start of the hearing when the party making the request is not actually present in the tribunal hearing centre. Any reference below to the "other party" is to be taken as referring to all other parties, where there is more than one other party in the case.

3.2 An application for a postponement should be made in writing as soon as it becomes clear that it is going to be necessary to make a request of this type. The application should be sent to the Employment Tribunal Office dealing with the case and should state:

(i) the reason why it is made; and

(ii) why it is considered that it would be in accordance with the overriding objective to grant the postponement

3.3 If possible supporting documents (see below for examples) should be provided at the time the request is made. The request (with supporting documents) should also be copied to the other party (or representative if there is one) who should be told that any objections to the application should be sent to the tribunal as soon as possible. When the application is sent to the tribunal the party making it should make it clear that the other party has been sent a copy and told of the right to object. If the request has not been copied to the other party, **it will not be considered, except in exceptional circumstances**. If a request is made which has not been copied to the other party then an explanation should be provided as to why that has not happened.

3.4 If the party applying for the postponement is legally represented then, unless it is not possible to do so, the application should be discussed with the other party/representative before it is made with a view to finding out:

- Whether the other party objects to the hearing being postponed;
- The earliest date(s) possible at which the hearing could proceed if the postponement was granted.

If this information is provided at the time the application is made it will mean that the request can be dealt with more quickly by the Employment Judge than might otherwise be the case.

4. Specific situations which may arise

The following Guidance deals with common situations that arise where a party may make an application for a postponement. It is not an exhaustive list.

4.1 Ill health

If the request is made because of the ill health of a party or a witness, the request should be accompanied by medical evidence (normally a medical certificate and a letter/document from the treating G.P. or hospital doctor) that confirms:

- The nature of the health condition concerned and
- **Importantly, that the doctor considers in his or her professional opinion that s/he is unfit to attend the hearing and the basis of this conclusion.** This is important as the fact that a person has a medical condition does not necessarily mean s/he cannot attend a hearing.

If possible, the medical evidence should also indicate **when it is expected that the person *will* be fit to attend**.

An Employment Judge must be satisfied on the evidence that it is just to grant a postponement: s/he may ask for additional evidence in a particular case. Parties may wish to note that a medical certificate to the effect that a person is not fit to attend a hearing is not conclusive evidence of that fact.

The request for a postponement should be made as soon as it becomes apparent that the person will be unfit to attend. If the illness develops suddenly and so close to the start of the hearing that it is not possible to obtain the medical evidence before requesting a postponement, the request should be made at once with an undertaking to provide the necessary medical information within 7 days.

If the person who has become ill is a witness (rather than a party) the request should explain why the evidence of this witness is relevant and important in the context of the issues which will require to be decided by the Employment Tribunal.

4.2 A party or witness is not available

The application for a postponement should be made as soon as it becomes clear that there is a difficulty and should:

- state why the person is not available;
- state when the difficulty first came to light;
- state, in the case of a witness, why his/her evidence is considered to be relevant and important to the case;
- if the hearing is scheduled to last for more than one day, state whether a change in the normal order in which evidence is heard might deal with the problem and
- include any supporting evidence available. For example, if a person is not available because s/he will be on holiday or abroad for some other reason then written confirmation of the travel booking should be provided. If the person is not available because s/he is required to attend a hospital appointment then written evidence of that appointment should be provided.

It should be noted that one of the factors which an Employment Judge will take into account is whether parties were consulted about the dates of the hearing in advance of it being fixed and, if so, whether the alternative commitment (e.g. the holiday) was known about at the time the date consultation took place or was booked after parties were informed of the date of the hearing. Generally parties are expected to give a tribunal hearing priority over most other matters.

4.3 A representative is not available

The application for a postponement should be made as soon as possible and should:

- state when the difficulty first came to light;
- explain why it is considered that any alternative commitment should take precedence over the Employment Tribunal hearing;
- if there was consultation on the date to be fixed for any alternative commitment, state when that took place relative to parties being informed of the date of the Employment Tribunal hearing and
- if there is more than one qualified representative in the firm, explain why it is not possible for someone else in the firm to appear at the hearing.

It should be noted that one of the factors which an Employment Judge will take into account is whether parties were consulted about the dates of the hearing in advance of it being fixed and, if so, whether any alternative commitment was known about at that time.

While the tribunal will normally seek to accommodate the availability of a representative within reason, there may come a point where the overriding objective requires that the hearing go ahead even if this means that the party has to find another representative.

4.4 A representative has withdrawn

If a representative has withdrawn from acting, the application for a postponement should state:

- when that happened and
- whether the party affected intends to seek alternative representation and, if so, what steps have been taken to obtain such representation and when it is anticipated that a new representative will be appointed.

4.5 Outstanding appeals to the EAT

If a party seeks a postponement of a hearing because there is an outstanding appeal from an earlier decision, the party making the application for the postponement should give the date the appeal is to be heard, if known, and also say why it is considered that the hearing cannot take place until the appeal is heard.

4.6 Related criminal proceedings

If there is a risk that evidence will be heard in the Employment Tribunal that overlaps with related criminal proceedings, the tribunal case will be delayed until the criminal proceedings have been concluded to avoid prejudice to the person involved in the criminal proceedings. This may be a party or another witness.

An application to postpone a hearing for this reason should include:
- the nature of the criminal proceedings and the connection between those proceedings and the issues which will be considered by the Employment Tribunal;
- the date of any hearing fixed in the criminal proceedings;
- the name and address of the police officer or procurator fiscal dealing with the case and
- a crime reference number if available.

4.7 Related civil court proceedings

An application to postpone a hearing on the basis that there are related civil proceedings ongoing should include:
- the nature of the proceedings which are said to be related to the Employment Tribunal proceedings and why it is said that the Employment Tribunal hearing needs to be postponed;
- when the court proceedings were commenced and when they are expected to be concluded and
- an explanation as to why it is said that the civil court proceedings should be progressed ahead of the Employment Tribunal proceedings.

4.8 Late disclosure of documents or information

If this is the reason for the application for a postponement, the request should set out:
- the nature of the evidence that has been disclosed;
- when it was disclosed and
- why it is said that the hearing cannot proceed as a result.

If the evidence has been disclosed as a result of a request from the party seeking the postponement then the date when the information was first requested should also be stated.

4.9 Failure to disclose documents or information

If this is the reason for the application for a postponement, the request should set out:
- what documents or other information have been sought but not provided;
- when the request for the documents or other information was first made and the dates of any subsequent requests;
- the relevance of the documents or information sought to the issues before the tribunal and
- the dates of any tribunal orders which are believed to have been breached by the failure to disclose.

5. What the Employment Judge will do

Compliance with this Guidance does not guarantee that a request for a postponement will be granted. The information referred to above will be taken into account by an Employment Judge when making a decision about whether to grant or refuse the postponement but the decision remains a matter of discretion for the judge concerned. S/he will take account of all relevant circumstances in the individual case (including the timing of the request) and may ask for more information than is set out above.

The President has no power to overturn or interfere with any decision made by an Employment Judge in connection with an application for a postponement.

Signed: Shona M W Simon
Date: 16 January 2014
President

7. EMPLOYMENT TRIBUNALS: JOINT PRESIDENTIAL GUIDANCE

PRESIDENTIAL GUIDANCE EMPLOYMENT TRIBUNALS: PRINCIPLES FOR COMPENSATING PENSION LOSS (2017)

[5.88]

NOTES

This Presidential Guidance is issued by the President of Employment Tribunals (England and Wales) and the President of Employment Tribunals (Scotland) in accordance with Rule 7 of the Employment Tribunals Rules of Procedure, which are set out in the Schedule 1 of the Employment Tribunals (Constitution and Rules of Procedure) Regulations 2013.

As such, Employment Tribunals must have regard to this Guidance although they are not bound by it.

This Guidance has effect from 10 August 2017.

BACKGROUND

It had become clear that the guidance contained in the third edition of the booklet on Compensation for Loss of Pension Rights, published in 2003 and last revised in 2004, was no longer reliable for calculating pension loss in Employment Tribunal cases. The guidance was withdrawn in 2015.

A working group of Employment Judges was tasked by the President of Employment Tribunals (England and Wales) and the President of Employment Tribunals (Scotland) to produce a fourth edition containing guidance for tribunals and parties. The fourth edition is presented in a separate document entitled "Employment Tribunals: Principles for Compensating Pension Loss" (referred to as the "Principles"). It is available at these locations:

— https://www.judiciary.gov.uk/publications/employment-rules-and-legislation-practice-directions (for England and Wales)

— https://www.judiciary.gov.uk/publications/directions-for-employment-tribunals-scotland (for Scotland)

The Principles will be revised from time to time with the agreement of the Presidents. It is important that parties and tribunals ensure that they are referring to the latest version of the Principles when calculating pension loss.

THE PRINCIPLES: KEY CONCEPTS

The Principles are guided by five concepts: justice; simplicity; proportionality; pragmatism; and flexibility. More particularly:

(1) The Principles provide a framework for establishing the age at which a claimant will retire from the workforce where that is relevant to the calculation of their compensation. In broad terms, where a claimant has not accrued significant occupational pension rights, the tribunal will assume retirement at state pension age. By contrast, if a claimant has accrued significant occupational pension rights in a scheme with a normal retirement age (and entitlement to an unreduced pension) below state pension age, the tribunal will assume retirement at the scheme's normal retirement age. The tribunal will normally decide, based on the facts of each case, what level of accrued benefits is "significant" for this purpose. This approach can be displaced by evidence from the parties.

(2) The Principles explain the difference between gross income and net income, which is relevant when assessing both loss of earnings (and how this is affected by the tax relief on pension contributions and the types of pensions tax that might be applied) and loss of pension rights. The Principles also explain how awards of compensation are grossed up in accordance with the so-called "Gourley principle".

(3) The Principles explain the operation of the new state pension system that launched in April 2016. They provide a framework for calculating loss of state pension rights under this new system. It involves use of the Ogden Tables in the small number of cases where such an award may be appropriate.

(4) Insofar as loss of occupational pension rights are concerned, the Principles identify a category of "simple" cases. In such cases, the tribunal will exclusively use the contributions method to assess a claimant's net pension loss. This method requires the tribunal to aggregate the contributions that, but for the dismissal, the employer would have made to the claimant's pension scheme during the period of loss that has been identified. This approach will invariably be adopted in cases where the claimant's lost pension rights relate to a defined contribution scheme, including a scheme into which the claimant was automatically enrolled. It will also be adopted in some cases where the lost pension rights relate to a defined benefit scheme; for example, those cases where the period of loss relates to a relatively short period or where the application of the monetary cap on compensation or a very large withdrawal factor means that it will be disproportionate to engage in complex analysis.

(5) The Principles identify a category of "complex" cases. These are cases for which the contributions method is not suited. In general, a case will be a "complex" one if the claimant's lost pension rights derive from a defined benefit scheme (including final salary schemes and CARE schemes) and the

loss relates to a longer period. "Complex" cases include, but are not limited to, career loss cases. Such cases will benefit from a more tailored approach to case management. For example, liability issues and remedy issues will be considered at separate hearings.

(6) The Principles describe a "seven steps" model by which loss will be ascertained in these "complex" cases. The model incorporates the Ogden Tables (with a bespoke age-related modification). The outcome will be imprecise but ought still to be just. Alternatively, the parties may call expert actuarial evidence, with the tribunal's preference being for a jointly-instructed expert. There is also scope for a blended approach, with expert evidence on a limited number of points rather than the overall assessment of loss.

(7) In some "complex" cases, it may also be appropriate for the remedy hearing to proceed in two stages. At the first stage, the tribunal would decide the more straightforward (non-pension) aspects of the compensation and issue a judgment to that effect. It would also make findings of fact on those matters that, in consultation with the parties, were thought relevant to calculating pension loss in the circumstances of the individual case. The parties would then be given a time-limited opportunity to agree the value of pension loss. In the absence of agreement, pension loss would be decided at the second stage and set out in a further judgment. The underlying idea is that the parties are encouraged to agree the amount of pension loss (with the benefit of the tribunal's findings of fact where appropriate) and only bear the cost of expert actuarial evidence where it is proportionate to do so in view of the compensation at stake.

(8) Finally, to give the parties as much assistance as possible, the Principles contain links to useful websites, either throughout the text or in footnotes. There are also substantial appendices. Appendix 1 summarises the benefits of the main public sector defined benefit pension schemes. Appendix 2 contains "at a glance" extracts from the Ogden Tables. Appendix 3 contains numerous examples of the Principles in operation.

(9) The Principles do not have the force of law. They are not rigid rules. If the parties wish to advance arguments for using their own calculations, rather than following the Principles, the tribunal will consider them.

The Presidents expect that Employment Tribunals will have regard to the Principles when calculating compensation for pension loss.

Judge Brian Doyle

President, Employment Tribunals

(England and Wales)

10 August 2017

Judge Shona Simon

President, Employment Tribunals

(Scotland)

10 August 2017

PRESIDENTIAL GUIDANCE: VENTO BANDS (2017)

Employment Tribunal awards for injury to feelings and psychiatric injury following *De Souza v Vinci Construction (UK) Ltd* [2017] EWCA Civ 879

[5.89]

NOTES

1. An Employment Tribunal may order a respondent to pay compensation to a claimant[1] if the Tribunal finds that there has been a contravention of a relevant provision of the Equality Act 2010 in respect of which it has jurisdiction.[2] The amount of compensation which may be awarded corresponds to the amount which could be awarded by a county court in England & Wales or a sheriff in Scotland.[3] An award of compensation may include compensation for injured feelings (whether or not it includes compensation on any other basis).[4] An injury to feelings award might also be appropriate in certain claims of unlawful detriment.

2. In *Vento v Chief Constable of West Yorkshire Police (No. 2)* [2002] EWCA Civ 1871, [2003] IRLR 102, [2003] ICR 318 the Court of Appeal in England & Wales identified three broad bands of compensation for injury to feelings awards, as distinct from compensation awards for psychiatric or similar personal injury. The lower band of £500 to £5,000 applied in less serious cases. The middle band of £5,000 to £15,000 applied in serious cases that did not merit an award in the upper band. The upper band of between £15,000 and £25,000 applied in the most serious cases (with the most exceptional cases capable of exceeding £25,000).

3. In *Da'Bell v NSPCC* (2009) UKEAT/0227/09, [2010] IRLR 19 the Employment Appeal Tribunal revisited the bands and uprated them for inflation. The lower band was raised to between £600 and £6,000; the middle band was raised to between £6,000 and £18,000; and the upper band was raised to between £18,000 and £30,000.

4. The Employment Appeal Tribunal has subsequently stated that the bands and awards for injury to feelings can be adjusted by individual Employment Tribunals where there is cogent evidence of the rate of change in the value of money: *AA Solicitors Ltd v Majid* (2016) UKEAT/0217/15. See also *Bullimore v Pothecary Witham Weld* (2010) UKEAT/0189/10, [2011] IRLR 18 at para 31. However, the bands themselves have not been uprated in general since the decision in *Da'Bell* in 2009.

5. In a separate development in *Simmons v Castle* [2012] EWCA Civ 1039 and 1288, [2013] 1 WLR 1239 the Court of Appeal in England & Wales declared that with effect from 1 April 2013 the proper level of general damages in all civil claims for pain and suffering, loss of amenity, physical inconvenience and discomfort, social discredit or mental distress would be 10% higher than previously. This followed upon changes to the rules governing the recovery of costs in personal injury litigation in the civil courts in England & Wales.

6. In *De Souza v Vinci Construction (UK) Ltd* [2017] EWCA Civ 879 the Court of Appeal has ruled that the 10% uplift provided for in *Simmons v Castle* should also apply to Employment Tribunal awards of compensation for injury to feelings and psychiatric injury in England and Wales. The Court expressly recognised (see footnote 3) that it was not for it "to consider the position as regards Scotland." However, account has now been taken of the position in that jurisdiction by the Scottish President before formulating this Guidance.[5]

7. So far as awards for psychiatric injury are concerned, the Court of Appeal in *De Souza* observed that the Judicial College *Guidelines for the Assessment of General Damages in Personal Injury Cases* now incorporated the 10% uplift provided for in *Simmons v Castle*. If an Employment Tribunal relied upon the Judicial College *Guidelines* in making an award for psychiatric injury then that award would comply with *Simmons v Castle* and *De Souza v Vinci Construction (UK) Ltd*.

8. The Court of Appeal in *De Souza* invited the President of Employment Tribunals in England & Wales to issue fresh guidance which adjusted the *Vento* figures for inflation and so as to incorporate the *Simmons v Castle* uplift. In light of that invitation the Scottish President decided that it was also appropriate that consideration be given to the matter in that jurisdiction.

9. Following consultation with Employment Tribunal stakeholders and users, we have decided to address the issues arising by using our power to issue Presidential Guidance under rule 7 of Employment Tribunal Rules of Procedure.[6] The Presidents may publish guidance for England and Wales and for Scotland, respectively, as to matters of practice and as to how the powers conferred by the Rules may be exercised. Any such guidance shall be published by the Presidents in an appropriate manner to bring it to the attention of claimants, respondents and their advisers. Tribunals must have regard to any such guidance, but they shall not be bound by it.

10. Subject to what is said in paragraph 12, in respect of claims presented on or after 11 September 2017, and taking account of *Simmons v Castle* and *De Souza v Vinci Construction (UK) Ltd*, the Vento bands shall be as follows: a **lower band of £800 to £8,400** (less serious cases); a **middle band of £8,400 to £25,200** (cases that do not merit an award in the upper band); and an **upper band of £25,200 to £42,000** (the most serious cases), with the most **exceptional cases capable of exceeding £42,000**.

11. Subject to what is said in paragraph 12, in respect of claims presented before 11 September 2017, an Employment Tribunal may uprate the bands for inflation by applying the formula x divided by y (178.5) multiplied by z and where x is the relevant boundary of the relevant band in the original *Vento* decision and z is the appropriate value from the RPI All Items Index for the month and year closest to the date of presentation of the claim (and, where the claim falls for consideration after 1 April 2013, then applying the *Simmons v Castle* 10% uplift).

12. So far as claims determined by an Employment Tribunal in Scotland are concerned, if an Employment Tribunal determines that the *Simmons v Castle* 10% uplift does not apply then it should adjust the approach and figures set out above accordingly, but in so doing it should set out its reasons for reaching the conclusion that the uplift does not apply in Scotland.

Judge Shona Simon, President (Scotland)

Judge Brian Doyle, President (England & Wales)

5 September 2017

NOTES

1 Equality Act 2010 section 124(2)(b).

2 Equality Act 2010 section 124(1) cross-referring to section 120(1) and relating to a contravention of Part 5 (work) or a contravention of sections 108, 111 or 112 that relate to Part 5.

3 Equality Act 2010 section 124(6) cross-referring to section 119.

4 Equality Act 2010 section 119(4).

5 The Scottish President's reasons for issuing Presidential Guidance in the same terms as that issued in England and Wales are set out in an Appendix to the document recording responses to the Presidents' consultation that preceded this Presidential Guidance. See: https://www.judiciary.gov.uk/wp-content/uploads/2017/07/vento-consultation-response-20170904.pdf

6 Employment Tribunals (Constitution and Rules of Procedure) Regulations 2013, SI 2013/1237, reg 13(1) and Sch 1.

PRESIDENTIAL GUIDANCE: MAKING A STATUTORY APPEAL FALLING WITHIN THE JURISDICTION OF THE EMPLOYMENT TRIBUNAL (2017)

[5.90]

NOTES

This guidance is issued in accordance with Rule 7 of the Employment Tribunals Rules of Procedure ("the Rules"). The Rules are set out in Schedule 1 of the Employment Tribunals (Constitution and Rules of Procedure) Regulations 2013.

Employment Judges and Employment Tribunals are expected to have regard to this guidance but are not bound by it.

Both Presidents issued separate, identical guidance on this topic which had effect from 23rd June 2014, but we have concluded it is appropriate to issue this amended Guidance in a single document on a joint basis. Our original Guidance is now amended to remove references to Employment Tribunal Fees following the decision of the Supreme Court in *R (on the application of UNISON) v Lord Chancellor* (2017) UKSC 51 and to include guidance on making a statutory appeal under section 37G of the Employment Tribunals Act 1996 (financial penalties for failure to pay sums ordered to be paid or settlement sums).

1. THE JURISDICTION OF EMPLOYMENT TRIBUNALS TO HEAR APPEALS

Employment Tribunals have jurisdiction to hear appeals against:-

- An assessment to levy imposed under section 11 of the Industrial Training Act 1982;
- An Improvement Notice issued under section 21 of the Health and Safety at Work etc Act 1974 and a Prohibition Notice issued under section 22 of the same Act;
- An unlawful act notice issued by the Commission for Equality and Human Rights under section 21 of the Equality Act 2006;
- A notice of underpayment issued under section 19 of the National Minimum Wage Act 1998; and
- A financial penalty notice issued by an enforcement officer under section 37F of the Employment Tribunals Act 1996.

2. THE POSITION REGARDING HOW AN APPEAL MAY BE SUBMITTED

2.1 Regulation 12 of the Employment Tribunals (Constitution and Rules of Procedure) Regulations 2013 makes it clear that it is not necessary to use a prescribed claim form (ET1) in connection with proceedings in which the tribunal will be exercising its appellate jurisdiction.

2.2 There are no other legal provisions which make it necessary, when making any of the appeals listed at paragraph 1 above, to submit the appeal on any particular type of form.

3. THE PROVISION OF INFORMATION TO ASSIST THE TRIBUNAL

3.1 To enable the tribunal to deal with an appeal expeditiously and fairly certain information needs to be provided by the appellant. We have concluded that it would be of assistance to the tribunal and appellants if a form is made available, for completion by the appellant, in respect of each type of appeal identified at paragraph 1.

3.2 Accordingly, forms have been prepared by the Employment Tribunals for use by appellants if they so wish, when submitting appeals. These forms are attached as Appendices 1, 2, 3, 4 and 5.

3.3 The forms have been drafted to ensure that an appellant, who properly completes the form, will normally have provided all of the relevant information needed at the outset of an appeal to assist the tribunal in dealing with it expeditiously and fairly.

3.4 A form may be subject to minor amendments from time to time without the need to issue fresh Presidential Guidance. The latest version of any such amended form will be that available on the internet at the relevant time. Appellants and their advisers or representatives should always check that they are using the latest version of any particular form appended to the Presidential Guidance.

4. GUIDANCE TO APPELLANTS

While an appellant is not legally required to use the relevant form, we commend the forms for use as a helpful tool which, by their nature, will guide an appellant in connection with the information which an Employment Judge will need to know when considering the basis of the appeal, and which the administration will need in order to serve the appeal on the respondent.

Judge Shona Simon, President (Scotland)

Judge Brian Doyle, President (England & Wales)

11 September 2017

APPENDICES
NOTICE OF APPEAL AGAINST TRAINING LEVY ASSESSMENT

[5.91]

For official use only	
Tribunal Office	
Case number	
Date received	

INDUSTRIAL TRAINING ACT 1982
NOTICE OF APPEAL AGAINST AN ASSESSMENT TO A LEVY

Before completing this form you should note that the power of the Employment Tribunal in appeals against levy assessments is limited to considering whether the levy has been properly calculated and whether the appellant business falls within the scope of the Levy Order. The tribunal has no power to grant an extension of time for payment of the levy and the financial implications for the appellant of the assessment to levy are not a valid ground of appeal.

You must complete all questions marked with an '*'

1.1 Appellant Details*

Name of Appellant	

[5.92]
Address*

Number or Name	
Street	
Town/City	
County	
Post Code	

Telephone Number	
Fax Number	
Email address	

2.1 If a representative is acting for you please give their details below:

(Note that all correspondence will be sent to your representative)

Name	

2.2 Address

Number or Name	
Street	
Town/City	
County	
Post Code	

Telephone No		Fax No	

Email address	

3.1 Details of Training Board which made the assessment to a levy*

Name of Training Board	

3.2 Address*

Number or Name	
Street	
Town/City	
County	
Post Code	

4. Information about the assessment

Date of Issue		Assessment Number	

5. Grounds of Appeal*

The grounds of appeal are as follows:

Signature	
**Capacity/Authority	
Date	

**Note: If the notice is signed on behalf of the appellant, the signatory must state in what capacity or what authority he/she signs.

Once the form has been signed it should be sent to the appropriate Central Office where claims are first processed. The addresses of the Central Offices are:

Employment Tribunals Central Office (England and Wales)

PO Box 10218

Leicester

LE1 8EG

Or

Employment Tribunals Central Office (Scotland)

PO Box 27105

Glasgow

G2 9JR

NOTICE OF APPEAL ON HEALTH AND SAFETY MATTERS

[5.93]

For official use only	
Tribunal Office	
Case number	
Date received	

APPEAL TO AN EMPLOYMENT TRIBUNAL AGAINST AN IMPROVEMENT OR PROHIBITION NOTICE ISSUED UNDER THE HEALTH AND SAFETY AT WORK ETC ACT 1974

You must complete all questions marked with an '*'

1.1 Please give the name of the appellant*

Name	

1.2 Address*

Number or Name	
Street	
Town/City	
County	
Post Code	

Telephone Number	
Fax Number	
Email address	

2.1 If a representative is acting for you please give their details below:

(Note that all correspondence will be sent to your representative)

Name	

2.2 Address

Number or Name	
Street	
Town/City	
County	
Post Code	

Telephone No		Fax No	

Email address	

3. 3. Information about the notice under appeal

3.1 3.1 What type of Notice is it?

Prohibition		Improvement	

3.2 Please give the address of the premises or place to which the Notice applies (if applicable)

Number or Name	
Street	
Town/City	
County	
Post Code	

Telephone No	

Date of the Notice		Serial Number of Notice	

4.1 Please give the name of the Inspector who served the Notice*

Name	

4.2 Address*

Number or Name	
Street	
Town/City	
County	
Post Code	

5. Which requirement(s) or direction(s) in the Notice do you want to appeal against?*

6 **Please give full details of your grounds for this appeal**

Signature		Name	

Date		Telephone No	

Position (if in company organisation)	

Once the form has been signed it should be sent to the appropriate Central Office where claims are first processed. The addresses of the Central Offices are:

Employment Tribunals Central Office (England and Wales)

PO Box 10218

Leicester

LE1 8EG

Or

Employment Tribunals Central Office (Scotland)

PO Box 27105

Glasgow

G2 9JR

NOTICE OF APPEAL AGAINST AN UNLAWFUL ACT NOTICE

[5.94]

For official use only	
Tribunal Office	
Case number	
Date received	

APPEAL TO AN EMPLOYMENT TRIBUNAL AGAINST AN UNLAWFUL ACT NOTICE ISSUED BY THE COMMISSION FOR EQUALITY AND HUMAN RIGHTS

You must complete all questions marked with an '*'

1.1 Please give the name of the appellant*

Name	

1.2 Address*

Number or Name	
Street	
Town/City	
County	
Post Code	

Telephone Number	

Fax Number	
Email address	

2.1 If a representative is acting for you please give their details below:

(Note that all correspondence will be sent to your representative)

Name	

2.2 Address

Number or Name	
Street	
Town/City	
County	
Post Code	

Telephone No		Fax No	

Email address	

3. Information about the notice

3.1 Date of issue

3.2 What unlawful act does the notice specify has been committed?

3.3 What provisions of the Equality Act do EHRC say make that act unlawful?

3.4 Does the notice require the preparation of an action plan for the purpose of avoiding the repetition or continuation of the unlawful act?

Yes		No	

3.5 Does the notice recommend action to be taken for the purpose of avoiding the repetition or continuation of the unlawful act?

Yes		No	

4. What are the grounds of appeal?

That the unlawful act specified in the notice has not been committed	
That the requirement to prepare an action plan is unreasonable	

5. What remedy is being sought?

To annul the notice	
To vary the notice	
To annul the requirement	
To vary the requirement	

6. Please give full details of your grounds for this appeal. If you are seeking a variation of the notice or requirements please explain what variation is being asked for.

Signature		Name	

Date	

Position (if in company organisation)	

Once the form has been signed it should be sent to the appropriate Central Office where claims are first processed. The addresses of the Central Offices are:

Employment Tribunals Central Office (England and Wales)
PO Box 10218
Leicester
LE1 8EG

Or

Employment Tribunals Central Office (Scotland)
PO Box 27105
Glasgow
G2 9JR

NOTICE OF APPEAL AGAINST NMW ENFORCEMENT NOTICE

[5.95]

For official use only	
Tribunal Office	
Case number	
Date received	

APPEAL TO AN EMPLOYMENT TRIBUNAL AGAINST A NOTICE OF UNDERPAYMENT ISSUED UNDER THE NATIONAL MINIMUM WAGE ACT

You must complete all questions marked with an '*'

1.1 Please give the name of the appellant *

Trading Name	

1.2 Address*

Number or Name	
Street	
Town/City	
County	
Post Code	

Telephone Number	
Fax Number	
Email address	

2.1 If a representative is acting for you please give their details below:

(Note that all correspondence will be sent to your representative)

Name	

2.2 Address

Number or Name	
Street	
Town/City	
County	
Post Code	

Telephone No		Fax No	

Email address	

3. Information about the notice

3.1 Please give the names and/or descriptions of the workers to whom the notice relates (continue on a separate sheet of paper if necessary)

Name	Description

Date of the Notice		Serial Number of Notice	

4. Respondent details (please see note below)*

Name	

4.1 4.1 Address*

Number or Name	
Street	
Town/City	
County	
Post Code	

5. Reason(s) for your appeal

Please tick one or more boxes to indicate the grounds upon which you are appealing the issue of the Notice of Underpayment (the "Notice"), including a Notice which has replaced one which was withdrawn.

1. The decision to serve the Notice was incorrect because no arrears were owed to any worker named in the Notice		
2. The requirement imposed by the Notice to pay arrears to a specific worker (or workers) was incorrect because(tick one or both bullet points):		
	• the amount specified in the Notice as the sum due to the worker (or workers) is incorrect • no arrears were owed to the worker (or workers) in respect of any pay reference period specified in the Notice	

3. The requirement imposed by the Notice to pay a penalty was incorrect because (tick one or both boxes):		
	• directions made by the Secretary of State prevent the imposition of a penalty • the amount of the penalty has been incorrectly calculated	
4. The requirement imposed by the Notice relates to a worker who was not included in the original Notice		

6. Please give full details of your grounds for this appeal*

7. Signature of Appellant

Signature		Name	
Date		Telephone No	
Position (if in company organisation)			

Note:

For employers based in England and Wales the respondent should be named as:

Commissioners for Revenue and Customs

HMRC Solicitors Office Commercial & Employment Team (NMW)

Bush House South

West Wing

London WC2B 4RD

For employers based in Scotland the respondent should be named as:

Commissioners for Revenue & Customs

HMRC Division Office of the Solicitor to the Advocate General

Area G

Victoria Quay

Edinburgh EH6 6QQ

Once the form has been signed it should be sent to the appropriate Central Office where claims are first processed. The addresses of the Central Offices are:

Employment Tribunals Central Office (England and Wales)

PO Box 10218

Leicester

LE1 8EG

Or

Employment Tribunals Central Office (Scotland)

PO Box 27105

Glasgow
G2 9JR

NOTICE OF APPEAL AGAINST A FINACIAL PENALTY

[5.96]

For official use only	
Tribunal Office	
Case number	
Date received	

APPEAL TO AN EMPLOYMENT TRIBUNAL AGAINST A FINANCIAL PENALTY NOTICE ISSUED UNDER SECTION 37F OF THE EMPLOYMENT TRIBUNALS ACT 1996

You must complete all questions marked with an asterisk (*)

1.1 Please give the name of the appellant*

Name	

1.2 Address*

Number or Name	
Street	
Town/City	
County	
Post Code	

Telephone Number	
Fax Number	
Email address	

2.1 If a representative is acting for you please give their details below:

(Note that all correspondence will be sent to your representative)

Name	

2.2 Address of representative

Number or Name	
Street	
Town/City	
County	
Post Code	

Telephone Number	
Fax Number	
Email address	

3. Information about the penalty notice being appealed against

Note that it is helpful to provide to the Tribunal now a copy of:

- the penalty notice
- any previous warning notice
- any relevant Employment Tribunal judgment to which the notice relates
- any relevant settlement document to which the notice relates

3.1 Is a copy of the penalty notice attached to this appeal?*

Yes	No

3.2 If not, please provide the following details of the penalty notice*

Name of enforcement officer who issued the penalty notice	
Address of enforcement officer	

Date of issue of penalty notice	
Date of issue of any previous warning notice	
The amount of the financial penalty required to be paid to the Secretary of State	
The period within which the penalty must be paid	
Any other relevant information:	

4. Grounds of appeal

4.1 What are you appealing against?*

The penalty notice	Yes / No
The amount of the penalty	Yes / No

4.2 An appeal may be made on one or more of the following grounds. Identify the ground(s) relied upon:*

The grounds stated in the penalty notice were incorrect	Yes / No
It was unreasonable for the enforcement officer to have given the notice	Yes / No
The calculation of an amount stated in the penalty notice was incorrect	Yes / No

4.3 Please give full details of your grounds of appeal:

4.4 If the appeal is allowed, what outcome do you seek?

Cancel the penalty notice	Yes / No
Substitute the correct amount for the amount stated in the penalty notice	Yes / No

Signature	
Name	
Date	
Telephone number	
Position (if in company or organisation)	

Once the form has been signed it should be sent to the appropriate Central Office where claims are first processed. The addresses of the Central Offices are:

Employment Tribunals Central Office (England & Wales)

PO Box 10218

Leicester

LE1 8EG

OR

Employment Tribunals Central Office (Scotland)

PO Box 27105

Glasgow

G2 9JR

C. FORMS FOR EMPLOYMENT TRIBUNAL CLAIMS

ACAS: EARLY CONCILIATION NOTIFICATION FORM

[5.99]

NOTES

The form reproduced here is the version available on the ACAS website (www.acas.org.uk/earlyconciliation), for electronic submission. A hard copy version for postal submission is obtainable from ACAS by calling 0300 123 11 22. An explanatory leaflet is also available on the ACAS website.

acas

Early Conciliation Notification Form

Early Conciliation Support: 0300 123 1122

Early Conciliation Form - for idividuals intending to bring a claim to an Employment Tribunal

Fields marked with an asterisk (*) must be completed.

Section A: About you and your claim

Please read the important information on the Individual Claimants page (opens in a new tab), then tick here to confirm your understanding of it ☐

1. Your name and contact details

Title [Please Select...]

If you do not wish to supply a title please select "Other".

* First name(s) [ ]

* Surname or family name [ ]

* Search by postcode [ ]

If you don't have a postcode or cannot find your address, please select the button to the right

* Your address (line 1) [ ]

Your address (line 2) [ ]

* Town/City [ ]

County [ ]

Postcode [ ]

Main contact no [ ]

If you do not wish to supply a contact number please enter "None".

Alternative contact no

Email address

Confirm email address

2. Your representative details

Having a representative is optional, you are **not** required to appoint one to submit a notification.

You only need to fill in this section if you have appointed a person to act on your behalf (a representative). A representative might be a legal rep, a trade union official, a relative, friend, etc.... Please do not give the name of a representative unless they have agreed to act for you. Do not give the name of a person or organisation who is only giving you advice on filling in this form.

If you appoint a representative we will deal directly with them, not with you.

Representative contact name

If you know the name of the person representing you, give it here. If you don't know it, leave this section blank.

Representative organisation name

Give the full name of the representative's organisation (for example, a trade union, a firm of solicitors, the Citizens Advice Bureau, or other organisation)

Address line 1

This field is limited to 100 characters

If your representative's address is long please click here for advice

Address line 2

This field is limited to 50 characters

If your representative's address is long please click here for advice

Town/City

County

Postcode

Main contact no

Alternative contact no

Email address

Confirm email address

3. The relevant employer, person or organisation

Please note, we will always contact you before we contact your employer

* Employer name [ ]

This field is limited to 100 characters

If the employer name you want to enter is longer than this please enter just the first word of the name in the field above and type the name in full into the box in Section B below.

* Employer address line 1 [ ]

This field is limited to 100 characters

If the employer address is long please click here for advice

Employer address line 2 [ ]

This field is limited to 100 characters

If the employer address is long please click here for advice

* Town/City [ ]

County [ ]

Postcode [ ]

Telephone no [ ]

If you do not wish to supply a contact number please enter "None".

4. Your employment

What date did you start work for above employer? [ ]

If applicable, on what date did your employment finish? [ ]

What job did you or do you do for your employer? [ ]

On what date did the event that you intend to make a claim about take place? [ ]

Do you know if anyone else is also making a claim about this? ○ Yes ○ No

Section B: How should we get in touch with you?

When we receive your form we will contact you, or your representative where you have named one, using the telephone number you have given us. If you, or your representative, have different accessibility needs please let us know here. [ ]

Number of characters remaining including spaces: 200

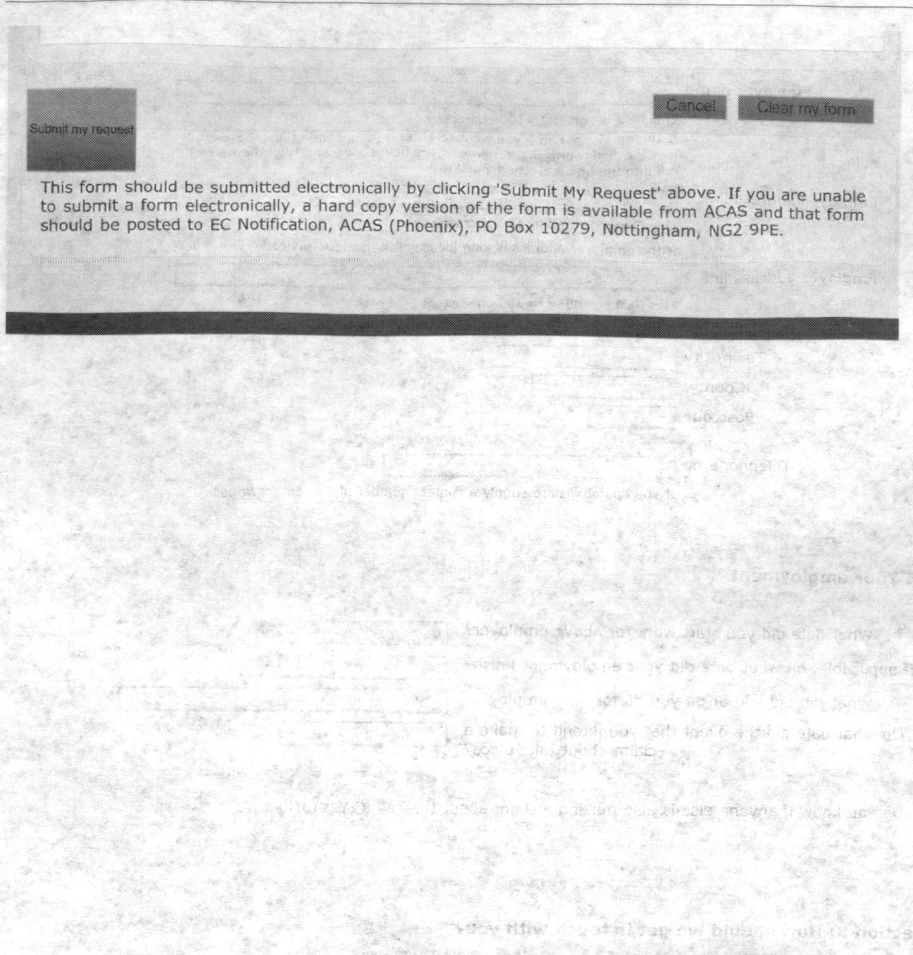

Submit my request

Cancel Clear my form

This form should be submitted electronically by clicking 'Submit My Request' above. If you are unable to submit a form electronically, a hard copy version of the form is available from ACAS and that form should be posted to EC Notification, ACAS (Phoenix), PO Box 10279, Nottingham, NG2 9PE.

CLAIM TO AN EMPLOYMENT TRIBUNAL (ET1)

[5.100]

NOTES

The following Forms ET1 and ET3 are the current versions prescribed by HM Courts and Tribunals Service for the submission of a paper copy. The forms may also be completed and submitted electronically via the employment tribunals website at www.gov.uk/employment-tribunals.

Employment Tribunal

Claim form

Official Use Only			
Tribunal office			
Case number		Date received	

You must complete all questions marked with an "*"

1 Your details

1.1 Title ☐ Mr ☐ Mrs ☐ Miss ☐ Ms

1.2* First name (or names)

1.3* Surname or family name

1.4 Date of birth __ __ / __ __ / __ __ __ __ Are you? ☐ Male ☐ Female

1.5* Address
Number or name
Street
Town/City
County
Postcode

1.6 Phone number
Where we can contact you during the day

1.7 Mobile number (if different)

1.8 How would you prefer us to contact you? (Please tick only one box) ☐ Email ☐ Post ☐ Fax Whatever your preference please note that some documents cannot be sent electronically

1.9 Email address

1.10 Fax number

2 Respondent's details (that is the employer, person or organisation against whom you are making a claim)

2.1* Give the name of your employer or the person or organisation you are claiming against (If you need to you can add more respondents at 2.5)

2.2* Address
Number or name
Street
Town/City
County
Postcode

Phone number

ET1 - Claim form (05.19)

2.3* Do you have an Acas early conciliation certificate number? ☐ Yes ☐ No

Nearly everyone should have this number before they fill in a claim form. You can find it on your Acas certificate. For help and advice, call Acas on 0300 123 1100 or visit www.acas.org.uk

If Yes, please give the Acas early conciliation certificate number.

If No, why don't you have this number?

☐ Another person I'm making the claim with has an Acas early conciliation certificate number

☐ Acas doesn't have the power to conciliate on some or all of my claim

☐ My employer has already been in touch with Acas

☐ My claim consists only of a complaint of unfair dismissal which contains an application for interim relief. (See guidance)

2.4 If you worked at a different address from the one you have given at 2.2 please give the full address

Address

Number or name

Street

Town/City

County

Postcode

Phone number

2.5 If there are other respondents please tick this box and put their names and addresses here. ☐

(If there is not enough room here for the names of all the additional respondents then you can add any others at Section 13.)

Respondent 2

Name

Address

Number or name

Street

Town/City

County

Postcode

Phone number

2.6 Do you have an Acas early conciliation certificate number? ☐ Yes ☐ No

Nearly everyone should have this number before they fill in a claim form. You can find it on your Acas certificate. For help and advice, call Acas on 0300 123 1100 or visit www.acas.org.uk

If Yes, please give the Acas early conciliation certificate number.

If No, why don't you have this number?

☐ Another person I'm making the claim with has an Acas early conciliation certificate number

☐ Acas doesn't have the power to conciliate on some or all of my claim

☐ My employer has already been in touch with Acas

☐ My claim consists only of a complaint of unfair dismissal which contains an application for interim relief. (See guidance)

Respondent 3

2.7 Name

Address

Number or name

Street

Town/City

County

Postcode

Phone number

2.8 Do you have an Acas early conciliation certificate number? ☐ Yes ☐ No

Nearly everyone should have this number before they fill in a claim form. You can find it on your Acas certificate. For help and advice, call Acas on 0300 123 1100 or visit www.Acas.org.uk

If Yes, please give the Acas early conciliation certificate number

If No, why don't you have this number?

☐ Another person I'm making the claim with has an Acas early conciliation certificate number

☐ Acas doesn't have the power to conciliate on some or all of my claim

☐ My employer has already been in touch with Acas

☐ My claim consists only of a complaint of unfair dismissal which contains an application for interim relief. (See guidance)

3 Multiple cases

3.1 Are you aware that your claim is one of a number of claims against the same employer arising from the same, or similar, circumstances?

☐ Yes ☐ No

If Yes, and you know the names of any other claimants, add them here. This will allow us to link your claim to other related claims.

4 Cases where the respondent was not your employer

4.1 If you were not employed by any of the respondents you have named but are making a claim for some reason connected to employment (for example, relating to a job application which you made or against a trade union, qualifying body or the like) please state the type of claim you are making here. (You will get the chance to provide details later):

Now go to Section 8

5 Employment details

If you are or were employed please give the following information, if possible.

5.1 When did your employment start?

Is your employment continuing? ☐ Yes ☐ No

If your employment has ended, when did it end?

If your employment has not ended, are you in a period of notice and, if so, when will that end?

5.2 Please say what job you do or did.

6 Earnings and benefits

6.1 How many hours on average do, or did you work each week in the job this claim is about? ☐ hours each week

6.2 How much are, or were you paid?

Pay before tax £ ☐ Weekly ☐ Monthly

Normal take-home pay (Incl. overtime, commission, bonuses etc.) £ ☐ Weekly ☐ Monthly

6.3 If your employment has ended, did you work (or were you paid for) a period of notice? ☐ Yes ☐ No

If Yes, how many weeks, or months' notice did you work, or were you paid for? ☐ weeks ☐ months

6.4 Were you in your employer's pension scheme? ☐ Yes ☐ No

6.5 If you received any other benefits, e.g. company car, medical insurance, etc, from your employer, please give details.

7 If your employment with the respondent has ended, what has happened since?

7.1 Have you got another job? ☐ Yes ☐ No

If No, please **go to section 8**

7.2 Please say when you started (or will start) work.

7.3 Please say how much you are now earning (or will earn). £

8 Type and details of claim

8.1* Please indicate the type of claim you are making by ticking one or more of the boxes below.

- ☐ I was unfairly dismissed (including constructive dismissal)
- ☐ I was discriminated against on the grounds of:
  - ☐ age
  - ☐ race
  - ☐ gender reassignment
  - ☐ disability
  - ☐ pregnancy or maternity
  - ☐ marriage or civil partnership
  - ☐ sexual orientation
  - ☐ sex (including equal pay)
  - ☐ religion or belief
- ☐ I am claiming a redundancy payment
- ☐ I am owed
  - ☐ notice pay
  - ☐ holiday pay
  - ☐ arrears of pay
  - ☐ other payments
- ☐ I am making another type of claim which the Employment Tribunal can deal with.

(Please state the nature of the claim. Examples are provided in the Guidance.)

8.2* Please set out the background and details of your claim in the space below.

The details of your claim should include **the date(s) when the event(s) you are complaining about happened.** Please use the blank sheet at the end of the form if needed.

9 What do you want if your claim is successful?

9.1 Please tick the relevant box(es) to say what you want if your claim is successful:

- ☐ If claiming unfair dismissal, to get your old job back and compensation (reinstatement)
- ☐ If claiming unfair dismissal, to get another job with the same employer or associated employer and compensation (re-engagement)
- ☐ Compensation only
- ☐ If claiming discrimination, a recommendation (see Guidance).

9.2 What compensation or remedy are you seeking?

If you are claiming financial compensation please give as much detail as you can about how much you are claiming and how you have calculated this sum. (Please note any figure stated below will be viewed as helpful information but it will not restrict what you can claim and you will be permitted to revise the sum claimed later. See the Guidance for further information about how you can calculate compensation). **If you are seeking any other remedy from the Tribunal which you have not already identified please also state this below.**

10 Information to regulators in protected disclosure cases

10.1 If your claim consists of, or includes, a claim that you are making a protected disclosure under the Employment Rights Act 1996 (otherwise known as a 'whistleblowing' claim), please tick the box if you want a copy of this form, or information from it, to be forwarded on your behalf to a relevant regulator (known as a 'prescribed person' under the relevant legislation) by tribunal staff. (See Guidance). ☐

11 Your representative

If someone has agreed to represent you, please fill in the following. We will in future only contact your representative and not you.

11.1 Name of representative

11.2 Name of organisation

11.3 Address

Number or name

Street

Town/City

County

Postcode

11.4 DX number (If known)

11.5 Phone number

11.6 Mobile number (If different)

11.7 Their reference for correspondence

11.8 Email address

11.9 How would you prefer us to communicate with them? (Please tick only one box) ☐ Email ☐ Post ☐ Fax

11.10 Fax number

12 Disability

12.1 Do you have a disability? ☐ Yes ☐ No

If Yes, it would help us if you could say what this disability is and tell us what assistance, if any, you will need as your claim progresses through the system, including for any hearings that maybe held at tribunal premises.

13 Details of additional respondents

Section 2.4 allows you to list up to three respondents. If there are any more respondents please provide their details here

Respondent 4

Name

Address

Number or name

Street

Town/City

County

Postcode

Phone number

Do you have an Acas early conciliation certificate number? ☐ Yes ☐ No

Nearly everyone should have this number before they fill in a claim form. You can find it on your Acas certificate. For help and advice, call Acas on 0300 123 1100 or visit www.acas.org.uk

If Yes, please give the Acas early conciliation certificate number.

If No, why don't you have this number?

☐ Another person I'm making the claim with has an Acas early conciliation certificate number

☐ Acas doesn't have the power to conciliate on some or all of my claim

☐ My employer has already been in touch with Acas

☐ My claim consists only of a complaint of unfair dismissal which contains an application for interim relief. (See guidance)

Respondent 5

Name

Address
Number or name

Street

Town/City

County

Postcode

Phone number

Do you have an Acas early conciliation certificate number? ☐ Yes ☐ No

Nearly everyone should have this number before they fill in a claim form. You can find it on your Acas certificate. For help and advice, call Acas on 0300 123 1100 or visit www.acas.org.uk

If Yes, please give the Acas early conciliation certificate number.

If No, why don't you have this number?

- ☐ Another person I'm making the claim with has an Acas early conciliation certificate number
- ☐ Acas doesn't have the power to conciliate on some or all of my claim
- ☐ My employer has already been in touch with Acas
- ☐ My claim consists only of a complaint of unfair dismissal which contains an application for interim relief. (See guidance)

14 Final check

Please re-read the form and check you have entered all the relevant information.
Once you are satisfied, please tick this box. ☐

General Data Protection Regulations

The Ministry of Justice and HM Courts and Tribunals Service processes personal information about you in the context of tribunal proceedings.

For details of the standards we follow when processing your data, please visit the following address https://www.gov.uk/government/organisations/hm-courts-and-tribunals-service/about/personal-information-charter.

To receive a paper copy of this privacy notice, please call our Customer Contact Centre:

England and Wales: 0300 123 1024

Welsh speakers: 0300 303 5176

Scotland: 0300 790 6234

Textphone: 18001 0300 123 1024 (England and Wales)

Textphone: 18001 0300 790 6234 (Scotland)

Please note: a copy of the claim form or response and other tribunal related correspondence may be copied to the other party and Acas for the purpose of tribunal proceedings or to reach settlement of the claim.

15 Additional information

You can provide additional information about your claim in this section.

If you're part of a group claim, give the Acas early conciliation certificate numbers for other people in your group. If they don't have numbers, tell us why.

HM Courts & Tribunals Service

Diversity Monitoring Questionnaire

It is important to us that everyone who has contact with HM Courts & Tribunals Service, receives equal treatment. We need to find out whether our policies are effective and to take steps to ensure the impact of future policies can be fully assessed to try to avoid any adverse impacts on any particular groups of people. That is why we are asking you to complete the following questionnaire, which will be used to provide us with the relevant statistical information.

Your answers will be treated in strict confidence.

Thank you in advance for your co-operation.

Claim type

Please confirm the type of claim that you are bringing to the employment tribunal. This will help us in analysing the other information provided in this form.

(a) ☐ Unfair dismissal or constructive dismissal
(b) ☐ Discrimination
(c) ☐ Redundancy payment
(d) ☐ Other payments you are owed
(e) ☐ Other complaints

Sex

What is your sex?

(a) ☐ Female
(b) ☐ Male
(c) ☐ Prefer not to say

Age group

Which age group are you in?

(a) ☐ Under 25
(b) ☐ 25-34
(c) ☐ 35-44
(d) ☐ 45-54
(e) ☐ 55-64
(f) ☐ 65 and over
(g) ☐ Prefer not to say

Ethnicity

What is your ethnic group?

White

(a) ☐ English / Welsh / Scottish / Northern Irish / British
(b) ☐ Irish
(c) ☐ Gypsy or Irish Traveller
(d) ☐ Any other White background

Mixed / multiple ethnic groups

(e) ☐ White and Black Caribbean
(f) ☐ White and Black African
(g) ☐ White and Asian
(h) ☐ Any other Mixed / multiple ethnic background

Asian / Asian British

(i) ☐ Indian
(j) ☐ Pakistani
(k) ☐ Bangladeshi
(l) ☐ Chinese
(m) ☐ Any other Asian background

Black / African / Caribbean / Black British

(n) ☐ African
(o) ☐ Caribbean
(p) ☐ Any other Black / African / Caribbean background

Other ethnic group

(q) ☐ Arab
(r) ☐ Any other ethnic group

(s) ☐ Prefer not to say

Disability

The Equality Act 2010 defines a disabled person as 'Someone who has a physical or mental impairment and the impairment has a substantial and long-term adverse effect on his or her ability to carry out normal day-to-day activities'.

Conditions covered may include, for example, severe depression, dyslexia, epilepsy and arthritis.

Do you have any physical or mental health conditions or illnesses lasting or expected to last for 12 months or more?

(a) ☐ Yes
(b) ☐ No
(c) ☐ Prefer not to say

Marriage and Civil Partnership

Are you?

(a) ☐ Single, that is, never married and never registered in a same-sex civil partnership
(b) ☐ Married
(c) ☐ Separated, but still legally married
(d) ☐ Divorced
(e) ☐ Widowed
(f) ☐ In a registered same-sex civil partnership
(g) ☐ Separated, but still legally in a same-sex civil partnership
(h) ☐ Formerly in a same-sex civil partnership which is now legally dissolved
(i) ☐ Surviving partner from a same-sex civil partnership
(j) ☐ Prefer not to say

Religion and belief

What is your religion?

(a) ☐ No religion
(b) ☐ Christian (including Church of England, Catholic, Protestant and all other Christian denominations)
(c) ☐ Buddhist
(d) ☐ Hindu
(e) ☐ Jewish
(f) ☐ Muslim
(g) ☐ Sikh
(h) ☐ Any other religion (please describe)

(i) ☐ Prefer not to say

Caring responsibilites

Do you have any caring responsibilities, (for example; children, elderly relatives, partners etc.)?

(a) ☐ Yes
(b) ☐ No
(c) ☐ Prefer not to say

Sexual identity

Which of the options below best describes how you think of yourself?

(a) ☐ Heterosexual/Straight
(b) ☐ Gay /Lesbian
(c) ☐ Bisexual
(d) ☐ Other
(e) ☐ Prefer not to say

Gender identity

Please describe your gender identity?

(a) ☐ Male (including female-to-male trans men)
(b) ☐ Female (including male-to-female trans women)
(c) ☐ Prefer not to say

Is your gender identity different to the sex you were assumed to be at birth?

(f) ☐ Yes
(g) ☐ No
(h) ☐ Prefer not to say

Pregnancy and maternity

Were you pregnant when the issue you are making a claim about took place?

(a) ☐ Yes
(b) ☐ No
(c) ☐ Prefer not to say

Thank you for taking the time to complete this questionnaire.

Employment Tribunals check list

Please check the following:

1. Read the form to make sure the information given is correct and truthful, and that you have not left out any information which you feel may be relevant to you or your client.
2. Do not attach a covering letter to your form. If you have any further relevant information please enter it in the 'Additional Information' space provided in the form.
3. Send the completed form to the relevant office address.
4. Keep a copy of your form posted to us.

If your claim has been submitted on-line or posted you should receive confirmation of receipt from the office dealing with your claim within five working days. If you have not heard from them within five days, please contact that office directly. If the deadline for submitting the claim is closer than five days you should check that it has been received before the time limit expires.

You have opted to print and post your form. We would like to remind you that forms submitted online are processed much faster than ones posted to us. If you want to submit your claim online please go to www.gov.uk/employment-tribunals/make-a-claim

A list of our office's contact details can be found at the hearing centre page of our website at – www.gov.uk/guidance/employment-tribunal-offices-and-venues; if you are still unsure about which office to contact please call our Employment Tribunal Customer Contact Centre (Mon – Fri, 9am – 5pm) they can also provide general procedural information about the Employment Tribunals.

Customer Contact Centre:

England and Wales: 0300 123 1024

Welsh speakers: 0300 303 5176

Scotland: 0300 790 6234

Textphone: 18001 0300 123 1024 (England and Wales)

Textphone: 18001 0300 790 6234 (Scotland)

RESPONSE TO AN EMPLOYMENT TRIBUNAL CLAIM (ET3)

[5.101]

NOTES

See the notes to Form ET1 at **[5.100]**.

Employment Tribunal

Response form

Case number	
Date Submission Received	Additional information supplied as RTF file

You must complete all questions marked with an "*"

1 Claimant's name

1.1 Claimant's name

2 Respondent's details

2.1* Name of individual, company or organisation

2.2 Name of contact

2.3* Address

Number or name

Street

Town/City

County

Postcode

DX number (If known)

2.4 Phone number
Where we can contact you during the day

Mobile number (If different)

2.5 How would you prefer us to contact you? (Please tick only one box) ☐ Email ☐ Post ☐ Fax Whatever your preference please note that some documents cannot be sent electronically

2.6 Email address

Fax number

2.7 How many people does this organisation employ in Great Britain?

2.8 Does this organisation have more than one site in Great Britain? ☐ Yes ☐ No

2.9 If Yes, how many people are employed at the place where the claimant worked?

3 Acas Early Conciliation details

3.1 Do you agree with the details given by the claimant about early conciliation with Acas? ☐ Yes ☐ No

If No, please explain why, for example, has the claimant given the correct Acas early conciliation certificate number or do you disagree that the claimant is exempt from early conciliation, if so why?

4 Employment details

4.1 Are the dates of employment given by the claimant correct? ☐ Yes ☐ No

If Yes, please **go to question 4.2**

If No, please give the dates and say why you disagree with the dates given by the claimant

When their employment started

When their employment ended or will end

I disagree with the dates for the following reasons

4.2 Is their employment continuing? ☐ Yes ☐ No

4.3 Is the claimant's description of their job or job title correct? ☐ Yes ☐ No

If Yes, please **go to Section 5**

If No, please give the details you believe to be correct

5 Earnings and benefits

5.1 Are the claimant's hours of work correct? ☐ Yes ☐ No

If No, please enter the details you believe to be correct. ______ hours each week

5.2 Are the earnings details given by the claimant correct? ☐ Yes ☐ No

If Yes, please **go to question 5.3**

If No, please give the details you believe to be correct below

Pay before tax (Incl. overtime, commission, bonuses etc.) £ ______ ☐ Weekly ☐ Monthly

Normal take-home pay (Incl. overtime, commission, bonuses etc.) £ ______ ☐ Weekly ☐ Monthly

5.3 Is the information given by the claimant correct about being paid for, or working a period of notice? ☐ Yes ☐ No

If Yes, please **go to question 5.4**

If No, please give the details you believe to be correct below. If you gave them no notice or didn't pay them instead of letting them work their notice, please explain what happened and why.

5.4 Are the details about pension and other benefits e.g. company car, medical insurance, etc. given by the claimant correct? ☐ Yes ☐ No

If Yes, please **go to Section 6**

If No, please give the details you believe to be correct.

6 Response

6.1* Do you defend the claim? ☐ Yes ☐ No

If No, please **go to Section 7**

If Yes, please set out the facts which you rely on to defend the claim.
(See Guidance - If needed, please use the blank sheet at the end of this form.)

7 Employer's Contract Claim

7.1 Only available in limited circumstances where the claimant has made a contract claim. (See Guidance)

7.2 If you wish to make an Employer's Contract Claim in response to the claimant's claim, please tick this box and complete question 7.3 ☐

7.3 Please set out the background and details of your claim below, which should include all important dates
(see Guidance for more information on what details should be included)

8 Your representative

If someone has agreed to represent you, please fill in the following. We will in future only contact your representative and not you.

8.1 Name of representative

8.2 Name of organisation

8.3 Address

Number or name

Street

Town/City

County

Postcode

8.4 DX number (If known)

8.5 Phone number

8.6 Mobile phone

8.7 Their reference for correspondence

8.8 How would you prefer us to communicate with them? (Please tick only one box) ☐ Email ☐ Post ☐ Fax

8.9 Email address

8.10 Fax number

9 Disability

9.1 Do you have a disability? ☐ Yes ☐ No

If Yes, it would help us if you could say what this disability is and tell us what assistance, if any, you will need as the claim progresses through the system, including for any hearings that maybe held at tribunal premises.

Please re-read the form and check you have entered all the relevant information.
Once you are satisfied, please tick this box. ☐

Employment Tribunals check list and cover sheet

Please check the following:

1. Read the form to make sure the information given is correct and truthful, and that you have not left out any information which you feel may be relevant to you or your client.
2. Do not attach a covering letter to your form. If you have any further relevant information please enter it in the 'Additional Information' space provided in the form.
3. Send the completed form to the relevant office address.
4. Keep a copy of your form posted to us.

Once your response has been received, you should receive confirmation from the office dealing with the claim within five working days. If you have not heard from them within five days, please contact that office directly. If the deadline for submitting the response is closer than five days you should check that it has been received before the time limit expires.

You have opted to print and post your form. We would like to remind you that forms submitted on-line are processed much faster than ones posted to us. If you want to submit your response online please go to www.gov.uk/being-taken-to-employment-tribunal-by-employee.

A list of our office's contact details can be found at the hearing centre page of our website at – www.gov.uk/guidance/employment-tribunal-offices-and-venues; if you are still unsure about which office to contact please call our Customer Contact Centre - see details below

General Data Protection Regulations

The Ministry of Justice and HM Courts and Tribunals Service processes personal information about you in the context of tribunal proceedings.

For details of the standards we follow when processing your data, please visit the following address https://www.gov.uk/government/organisations/hm-courts-and-tribunals-service/about/personal-information-charter.

To receive a paper copy of this privacy notice, please call our Customer Contact Centre - see details below

Please note: a copy of the claim form or response and other tribunal related correspondence may be copied to the other party and Acas for the purpose of tribunal proceedings or to reach settlement of the claim.

Customer Contact Centre

England and Wales: 0300 123 1024
Welsh speakers only: 0300 303 5176
Scotland: 0300 790 6234

Textphone: 18001 0300 123 1024 (England and Wales)
Textphone: 18001 0300 790 6234 (Scotland)

(Mon - Fri, 9am -5pm), they can also provide general procedural information about the Employment Tribunals.

AGENDA FOR CASE MANAGEMENT AT PRELIMINARY HEARING (ENGLAND & WALES)

COMPLETED BY: CLAIMANT/RESPONDENT
RULES 29–40, 53 AND 56 EMPLOYMENT TRIBUNALS RULES OF PROCEDURE 2013

[5.102]

NOTES

This Agenda is the version used by employment tribunals in England and Wales. For the equivalent documents used in Scotland, see **[5.103]** and **[5.104]**. This Agenda is also available in Welsh.

The form reproduced here is the version available at www.judiciary.uk/publications/employment-rules-and-legislation-practice-directions/. A version of this document is also available in Welsh (not printed here for reasons of space).

It will help the efficient management of the case if you complete this agenda, as far as applies and send it to every other party and the Tribunal to arrive no later than 2 days before the preliminary hearing (PH). A completed agreed agenda is particularly helpful.

1. PARTIES

1.1	Are the names of the parties correct? Is the respondent a legal entity? If not what is the correct name?	
1.2	Should any person be joined or dismissed as a respondent? If yes, why?	

2. THE CLAIM AND RESPONSE

2.1	What are the complaints (claims) are brought? If any are withdrawn, say so.	
2.2	Is there any application to amend the claim or response? If yes, write out what you want it to say. Any amendment should be resolved at the PH, not later.	
2.3	Has any necessary additional information been requested? If not set out a limited, focussed request and explain why the information is necessary. If requested, can the relevant information be provided for the PH? If so, please do.	

3. REMEDY

3.1	If successful, what does the claimant seek? This means e.g. compensation or reinstatement where possible etc.	
3.2	What is the financial value of the monetary parts of the remedy? All parties are encouraged to be realistic.	
3.3	Has a schedule of loss been prepared? If so, please provide a copy.	
3.4	Has the Claimant started new work? If yes, when?	
3.5	In cases involving dismissal, please confirm whether the claimant was a member of an occupational pension scheme. If so, was it a defined benefit scheme or a defined contribution scheme?	

4. THE ISSUES

4.1	What are the issues or questions for the Tribunal to decide? It is usually sensible to set this out under the title of the complaints.	
4.2	Are there any preliminary issues which should be decided before the final hearing? If yes, what preliminary issues? Can they be added to this preliminary hearing? If not, why not?	

5. PRELIMINARY HEARINGS

5.1	Is a further preliminary hearing needed for case management? NB This should be exceptional. If so, for what agenda items? For how long? On what date?	
5.2	Is a further substantive preliminary hearing required to decide any of the Issues at 4.1? If so, for which Issues? How long is needed? Possible dates?	

6. DOCUMENTS AND EXPERT EVIDENCE

6.1	Have lists of documents been exchanged? If not, date/s for exchange of lists	
6.2	Have documents copy documents been exchanged? If not, date/s for exchange of copies? • for any further preliminary hearing • for the Hearing	
6.3	Who will be responsible for preparing • index of documents? • the hearing bundles? Date for completion of this task and sending copy to other side?	
6.4	Is this a case in which medical evidence is required? Why? Dates for • disclosure of medical records • agreeing any joint expert • agreeing any joint instructions • instructing any joint expert • any medical examination • producing any report • asking questions of any expert • making any concessions	

7. WITNESSES

7.1	How many witnesses will each party call? Who are those witnesses? Why are they needed?	

7.2	Should witness statements be exchanged on the same date or provided sequentially? Dates for exchange: For further preliminary hearing For the final hearing	

8. THE HEARING(S)

8.1	Time estimate for final hearing with intended time table Is a separate hearing needed for remedy?	
8.2	Dates to avoid (with reasons) or to list Any dates prelisted by the Tribunal	

9. OTHER PREPARATION

9.1	Should there be admissions and/or any agreed facts If so by what date/s?	
9.2	Should there be a cast list? From whom and when?	
9.3	Should there be a chronology? From whom and when?	
9.4	Are there special requirements for any hearing? (e.g. interpreter, hearing loop, evidence by video, hearing party in private under rule 50) If yes give reasons	

10. JUDICIAL ASSESSMENT/JUDICIAL MEDIATION

10.1	Is this a case that might be suitable for judicial assessment?	
10.2	Are the parties interested and do they consent to judicial assessment?	
10.3	Is this a case that might be suitable for judicial mediation?	
10.4	Are the parties interested in the possibility of judicial mediation?	
10.5	JUDICIAL USE ONLY	If relevant, Judge to consider whether criteria for judicial assessment/judicial mediation apply and then raise with the parties and record response. If appropriate, conduct JA and/or list for judicial mediation subject to liaison as appropriate with listing and the REJ.

11. ANY OTHER MATTERS

AGENDA FOR PRELIMINARY HEARING (SCOTLAND) (TO BE COMPLETED BY THE CLAIMANT)

[5.103]

NOTES

This Agenda is the version used by employment tribunals in Scotland. For the equivalent documents used in England and Wales, see **[5.102]**.

This document sets out the agenda for the preliminary hearing ("PH") that is to take place in your case. **You should complete this document as far as possible and as relevant to your case and send a completed copy to the respondent and the tribunal at least 21 days before the PH.** The respondent will be asked to complete a similar form and send a copy to you and to the tribunal at least 7 days before the PH. This timetable has been fixed so that the respondent can use information provided by you to identify areas of agreement and disagreement. The accompanying guidance is designed to assist you in completing this document.

Your answers and those of the respondent will form the basis of the discussion at the PH. They do not form part of the claim or response at this stage. Following discussion, some of your answers may be accepted as further details of your claim.

If you do not have a legal representative, it is recognised that you may find it difficult to complete some parts of this document but it is important that you answer as many of the questions as far as you can. You will have an opportunity to discuss your answers with the Employment Judge at the PH. However the Judge cannot give legal advice.

CASE NUMBER:

1. PARTIES

1.1	Is the name of the respondent correct?	
1.2	Are you aware of any other similar claims that should be considered with this claim? If so, please list the case number(s) and parties and give brief reasons why.	

2. DETAILS OF THE CLAIM

You may wish to take some advice before completing this section. This could be a solicitor, your trade union, your local Citizens Advice Bureau or other organisation. Information is also available from ACAS (www.acas.org.uk) and the Equality and Human Rights Commission (www.equalityhumanrights.com)

2.1	We think you are making a complaint under the Equality Act 2010. Is that right? If you answer "no", proceed to 2.2 If you answer "yes", the Employment Judge will want to discuss with you the kind of complaint you are making. This needs to be clearly identified before the case can proceed to a Hearing. It is helpful if you can answer the following questions – the sections refer to the Equality Act: Do you complain of : • direct discrimination (section 13) • indirect discrimination (section 19) • harassment (section 26) • victimisation (section 27) • discrimination arising from disability (section 15) • failure to make reasonable adjustments for your disability (section 20) (Tick all which apply) **Please also complete the appropriate schedule(s) for your complaint. These are at the end of this agenda.**	
2.2	We think you are making a complaint that you have been dismissed or otherwise disadvantaged because you have made a protected disclosure (often called whistle blowing). Is that right? If you answer "yes", please answer questions 2.3 to 2.6. If you answer "no", please go to 2.7	

2.3	What is the disclosure that you say you have made, when was this made and to whom?	
2.4	Do you say that the information disclosed tends to show any of the following: (a) That a criminal offence has been, is being or is likely to be committed? If so, what? (b) That a person has failed, is failing or is likely to fail to comply with any legal obligation? If so, what? (c) That a miscarriage of justice has occurred, is occurring or is likely to occur? If so, what? (d) That the health or safety of an individual has been is being or is likely to be endangered? If so, how? (e) That the environment has been, is being or is likely to be damaged? If so, how? That information tending to show any matter in a-e has been or is likely to be concealed? If so, which and by whom?	
2.5	Why do you say that the making of each disclosure has been in the public interest;	
2.6	What is the disadvantage you say you have suffered as a result of making each disclosure (include the date(s) of such treatment and the person(s) responsible)?	
2.7	Do you make any other complaints, such as unfair dismissal, failure to pay notice or holiday pay? If so , please set out here the nature of the other complaint(s) being made and, if you can, the legal provisions upon which you rely	
2.8	Having considered matters further, do you wish to withdraw any part of your claim at this stage?	
2.9	Do you wish to be provided with any additional information from the respondent? If so, what and why is this relevant to your claim?	

3. REMEDY

3.1	If successful, what do you seek by way of remedy?	
3.2	If you seek financial compensation, what do you consider to be the value of the claim?	
3.3	How did you calculate that sum and do you have any documents to support your claim (such as payslips)?	
3.4	In cases involving dismissal, please confirm whether you were a member of an occupational pension scheme. If so, was it a defined benefit scheme or a defined contribution scheme?	

4. THE ISSUES

You do not have to complete this section if you do not have a legal representative.

4.1	What are the issues that you consider the tribunal will have to determine? (an agreed draft list is particularly helpful and may be attached to this document)	

5 DOCUMENTS AND EXPERT EVIDENCE

5.1	By what date will you be ready to provide the respondent with a copy of the documents you will be referring to at the final hearing?	
5.2	Who do you propose should be responsible for preparing the joint sets of documents for the final hearing?	
5.3	Is this a case in which medical or other expert evidence is required? If so, do you consider that it would be helpful to instruct a joint expert report in respect of these matters?	

6. WITNESSES

6.1	How many witnesses will you call? Who are those witnesses and what will they give evidence about? Please explain why the evidence of each one is relevant to your claim.	
6.2	Are any witness orders required? Who for?	
6.3	Do you have any comments on whether or not this is an appropriate case for the use of witness statements?	

7. THE HEARING

7.1	How long do you estimate it will take to hear your side of the case?	
7.2	Timetable of witnesses – set out here the order of the witnesses you will call and how long you expect each will take to give evidence (not including time answering questions from the respondent)	
7.3	Are there any dates that need to be avoided in the listing period?	

8 JUDICIAL MEDIATION

8.1	Are you interested in the possibility of judicial mediation?	

9. PRIVACY

9.1	Do you think that the Judge should consider making an order to prevent or restrict the public disclosure of any aspect of the case? If so, please say why	

10 ARE THERE ANY OTHER MATTERS YOU WISH TO DISCUSS AT THE PH?

We intend to send a copy of this completed form to your named conciliator at ACAS.

Please tick here if you do not wish us to do so ()

SCHEDULE 1

The Equality Act 2010 makes it unlawful to discriminate because of certain "protected characteristics". These are age; disability; gender reassignment; marriage and civil partnership; pregnancy and maternity; race; religion or belief; sex; and sexual orientation.

If you are making any complaint under the Equality Act, please answer the questions in this Schedule. If your claim (or part of it) relates to disability, please also complete Schedule 2 in respect of that part of your claim.

If you are claiming in respect of more than one protected characteristic (e.g. sex and race) please set out your claim in respect of each separately. If you are not claiming unlawful discrimination under the Equality Act, do not complete this Schedule or Schedule 2.

You may find it helpful to take some advice before completing this schedule. This could be a solicitor, your trade union, local Citizens Advice Bureau or other organisation. Information is also available from ACAS (www.acas.org.uk) or the Equality and Human Rights Commission (www.equalityhumanrights.com)

S.1 If you have made a claim for discrimination because of race, what is the specific racial group that you rely on?
S.2 If you have made a claim for discrimination because of age, what is the age group that you rely on? (this may be a particular age or a range of ages)
S.3 If you have made a claim for discrimination because of religion or belief, what is the specific "religion or religious or philosophical belief" that you rely on?
S.4 If you complain about **direct discrimination**: (i) What is the less favourable treatment which you say you have suffered, (include the date or dates of this treatment and the person or persons responsible.) (ii) Why do you consider this treatment to have been because a protected characteristic?
S.5 If you complain about **indirect discrimination**: (i) What is the 'provision, criterion or practice', which you say the respondent has applied to you? (ii) When do you say that 'provision, criterion or practice' was applied to you? (iii) What is the particular disadvantage you say that people who share your protected characteristic would have been put at when compared to other people because of that protected characteristic? (iv) Were you at this particular disadvantage due to having the protected characteristic?
S.7 If you complain about **harassment**: (i) Give brief details of all instances of the 'unwanted conduct' that you complain of including, in each case, the date (s) and the person(s) responsible. (ii) Why do you consider that the conduct was related to a protected characteristic? (iii) Do you say that this conduct had the purpose or effect of violating your dignity? If so, how? (iv) Do you say that this conduct had the purpose or effect of 'creating an intimidating, hostile, degrading, humiliating or offensive environment" for you? If so, why? (v) Do you say that this conduct was of a sexual nature or related to sex (as in gender)? If so why?
S.8 If you complain about **victimisation**: (f) Which of the protected acts described in section 27(2) of the Equality Act have you carried out? (g) What is the disadvantage you say that you have suffered as a result of doing that protected act (include the date or dates of the treatment and the person or persons responsible.) (h) Why do you consider that this was because you had done a protected act?

SCHEDULE 2 (DISABILITY)

If you complain of disability discrimination, please complete this Schedule 2 as well as Schedule 1.

You may find it helpful to take some advice before completing this section. This could be a solicitor, trade union, your local CAB or other voluntary organisation. Information is also available from ACAS (www.acas.org.uk) or the Equality and Human Rights Commission (www.equalityhumanrights.com)

D.1 What physical or mental impairment do you consider affects you?
D.2 Please explain in what way this impairment has a substantial and long-term adverse effect on your ability to carry out normal day-to-day activities?
D.3 Do you have medical evidence to support what you say in D.1 and D.2? If so, please provide details here.
D.4 Do you say that the respondent knew or could reasonably be expected to know that you had a disability at the time you say you were discriminated against? If so, why?
D.5 If you complain about discrimination **arising from disability**, in what way do you say that the respondent treated you "unfavourably because of something arising as a consequence of your disability"?
If you consider there was an unfulfilled duty on the part of the respondents to make reasonable adjustments, please answer D.6 to D.10. If this is not part of your claim, do not answer these questions. **D.6** Do you complain that: (i) A provision, criterion or practice applied by or on behalf of the respondent placed you at a substantial disadvantage in comparison with people who are not disabled? If so, what is the provision, criterion or practice? (ii) A physical feature of premises occupied by the respondent placed you at a substantial disadvantage in comparison with people who are not disabled? If so, what is this physical feature? (iii) You were placed at a substantial disadvantage in comparison with people who are not disabled because you were not provided with an auxiliary aid? If so what is the nature of this aid.
D.7 What is the substantial disadvantage at which you say you were placed?
D.8 Do you say that the respondent knew or could reasonably be expected to know that you were likely to be placed at the substantial disadvantage?
D.9 What are the steps which you say it would have been reasonable for the respondent to take?
D.10 In what way would those steps have prevented the substantial disadvantage which you believe has arisen?

AGENDA FOR PRELIMINARY HEARING (SCOTLAND) (TO BE COMPLETED BY THE RESPONDENT)

[5.104]

NOTES

This Agenda is the version used by employment tribunals in Scotland. For the equivalent documents used in England and Wales, see **[5.102]**.

A preliminary hearing ("PH") is to take place in a case in which you have been named as a respondent. The purpose of the PH is to conduct a preliminary consideration of the claim and make case management orders. This document sets out to gather information which will allow that discussion to be as useful as possible. You should complete this document, as far as possible and as relevant to the case. The accompanying Guidance has been prepared to assist you. The claimant has a different version of this document and should send a completed copy of that to you and to the Tribunal at least 21 days before the PH.

You should send a completed copy of your document to the claimant and the tribunal at least 7 days before the PH. This timetable has been fixed so that you can use information provided by the claimant to identify areas of agreement and disagreement.

Please read the claimant's answers carefully before completing your document. If (for whatever reason) you have not received the claimant's completed document, you should nevertheless submit this document completed as fully as circumstances permit. Your answers and those of the claimant will form the basis of the discussion at the PH. They do not form part of the claim or response at this stage. Following discussion, some of your answers may be accepted as further details of your response.

If you do not have a legal representative, it is recognised that you may find it difficult to complete some parts of this document but it is important that you answer as many of the questions as far as you can. You will have an opportunity to discuss your answers with the Employment Judge at the PH. However the Judge cannot give legal advice.

CASE NUMBER:

1. PARTIES

R1.1	Is the respondent's name correct?	
R1.2	Should any other person be added as a respondent?	
R1.3	Should any named respondent be dismissed from the proceedings?	
R1.4	Are there any other claims that should be considered with this claim? If so, please list the case number(s) and parties and give brief reasons why.	

2. DETAILS OF THE RESPONSE

If the claimant has completed Schedule 2, s/he is claiming disability discrimination under the Equality Act 2010 and you should complete all the questions in this section. If the claimant has not completed Schedule 2, but has completed Schedule 1 proceed to question R2.5.

R2.1	Do you accept that the claimant was a disabled person in terms of the Act at the time of the alleged discrimination?	
R2.2	If so, do you accept that you knew or should have known that the claimant was a disabled person at the time of the alleged discrimination?	
R2.3	If the claimant is claiming that you failed to make a reasonable adjustment, do you accept that the provision, criterion or practice, physical feature or failure to provide an auxiliary aid identified by the claimant (D.6 of Schedule 2), put the claimant at a substantial disadvantage because of his/her disability?	
R2.4	If so, do you accept that you knew or should have known of that disadvantage at the time it is alleged there was a failure to make reasonable adjustments?	

R2.5	If the claimant claims indirect discrimination, do you accept that the provision, criterion or practice identified in S.5 of Schedule 1 was applied by you to the claimant?	
R2.6	Do you accept that the claimant made a protected disclosure in terms of s43A of the Employment Rights Act 1996?	
R2.7	Are there any further matters that you can concede at this stage?	
R2.8	Do you wish to request any additional information about the claim? If so, what?	

3. REMEDY

R3.1	Do you require any further information about the remedy that the claimant is seeking?	

4. THE ISSUES

You do not have to complete this section if you are not legally represented.

R4.1	What are the issues that you consider the tribunal will have to decide to deal with this case? (an agreed draft list is particularly helpful and may be attached to this document)	
R4.2	Are there any preliminary issues or jurisdictional issues? If so, what are they? Is a further preliminary hearing required?	

5. DOCUMENTS AND EXPERT EVIDENCE

R5.1	By what date will you be ready to provide the claimant with a copy of the documents you will be referring to at the final hearing?	
R5.2	Who do you propose should be responsible for preparing the joint set of productions?	
R5.3	Is this a case in which medical or other expert evidence is required? If so, do you consider that it would be helpful to instruct a joint expert report in respect of these matters?	

6 WITNESSES

R6.1	How many witnesses will you call? Who are those witnesses and what is the relevance of their evidence?	
R6.2	Are any witness orders required? Who for?	
R6.3	Do you have any comments on whether or not this is an appropriate case for the use of witness statements?	

7. THE HEARING

R7.1	How long do you estimate it will take to hear your side of the case?	
R7.2	Timetable of witnesses – set out here the order of the witnesses you will call and how long you expect each will take to give evidence (not including being questioned by the claimant)	
R7.3	Are there any dates that need to be avoided in the listing period?	

8. JUDICIAL MEDIATION

R8.1	Are you interested in the possibility of judicial mediation?	

9. PRIVACY

9.1	Do you think that the Judge should consider making an order to prevent or restrict the public disclosure of any aspect of the case? If so, please say why	

10 ARE THERE ANY OTHER MATTERS YOU WISH TO DISCUSS AT THE PH?

We intend to send a copy of this completed form to your named conciliator at ACAS.
Please tick here if you do not wish us to do so ( )

D. CABINET OFFICE AND GOVERNMENT EQUALITIES OFFICE MATERIALS

PRINCIPLES OF GOOD EMPLOYMENT PRACTICE

A statement of principles that reflect good employment practice for Government, Contracting Authorities and Suppliers (2010)

[5.105]

NOTES

This Statement of Principles of Good Employment Practice is the replacement for the Code of Practice on Workforce matters in Public Sector Employment Contracts, colloquially referred to as the 'Two-tier Code', which had been issued by the Cabinet Office in 2005, and was withdrawn with immediate effect on 13 December 2010. The Code had no statutory basis, and its revocation therefore required no legislation. However, notes issued by the Cabinet Office in the statement announcing the withdrawal of the Code make it clear that provisions in contracts which have applied the Code continue to apply, unless the terms applying the Code are removed by renegotiation; in such an event, the changes in the contractor's obligations will only apply to future new entrants to its workforce. However, when contracts are re-competed, resulting in a new contract, the Code will not apply to the new contract. Revocation is also stated not to affect obligations under TUPE or the application of statutory equality duties.

The Coalition Government has committed to opening up government procurement and reducing costs. It has also set itself the aspiration that 25% of government contracts should be awarded to small and medium-sized businesses.

Government understands that value for money means securing the best mix of quality and effectiveness for the least outlay. This applies to the whole lifetime of goods or services from purchase through to disposal.

In support of its aspirations, Government has developed a statement of principles of good employment practice that will form part of good practice literature and be shared with contracting authorities and suppliers.[1]

NOTES

[1] This set of principles is voluntary and sits outside of the formal procurement decision making process, but will be disseminated to suppliers and commissioners

Government wants:

- employers of all sizes and from all sectors to have the freedom and flexibility to motivate and reward their workforce, to meet business needs.
- public, private, voluntary and community organisations to learn from each other and share best practice in the spirit of continuous improvement.
- employers to be aware of the best practice that fosters employee engagement, access to skills and development whilst securing quality outcomes in the provision of public services.

Six principles

This document is a statement of principles that reflect good employment practice. These principles are supported by Government and are voluntary.

1. Government as a good client

i. Through its commissioning, procurement standards and processes, central Government should encourage contracting authorities and suppliers to promote good workforce practices in the delivery of public services. Government will ensure that the workforce practices of the supplier are considered throughout the procurement process, where appropriate.

ii. Government will use outcome-based commissioning wherever possible; this is instead of prescribing how services are to be delivered. Using outcome-based commissioning will encourage more innovative approaches to the delivery of public services.

2. Training and skills

i. In letting and managing public contracts, the procurement process of contracting organisations will recognise the importance of basic skills such as literacy, numeracy and spoken English where these skills are relevant. These skills are often required in the delivery of public services, and enable the workforce to provide better quality services, particularly those in customer facing roles.

ii. Suppliers will be able to demonstrate that staff have appropriate training, qualifications and access to continuing professional development as befits their role; and that staff are supported to develop their skills and grow their experience in line with any future roles that maybe expected of them.

iii. Where there is a recognised trade union, suppliers will consult on workforce training and development issues.

3. A commitment to fair and reasonable terms and conditions

i. Where a supplier employs new entrants that sit alongside former public sector workers, new entrants should have fair and reasonable pay, terms and conditions. Suppliers should consult with their recognised trade unions on the terms and conditions to be offered to new entrants.

4. Equality

i. Contracting organisations will ensure that supplier policies and processes are entirely consistent with the responsibilities they have as employers under the Equality Act 2010. Government will ensure it delegates relevant legal obligations when suppliers are carrying out public functions.

ii. Government expects that suppliers will be able to demonstrate how working practices support their responsibilities as good employers.

5. Dispute resolution

i. All suppliers delivering public services should have regard to good industrial relations practice on dispute resolution. This includes treating employees fairly and ensuring compliance with the law on trade union membership.

ii. Suppliers will ensure that where there is a dispute, employees are aware of and have access to clear processes for dispute resolution. Government expects suppliers to consider the services of ACAS[2] as an option that is explored when disputes have not been resolved by internal support systems and processes.

iii. Where an employee has a right to be represented by a trade union, the employer will work with the employee and recognised trade union representative in resolving any dispute.

NOTES

[2] ACAS is the Advisory, Conciliation and Arbitration Service. ACAS provides free, confidential and impartial advice on a wide range of employment and industrial relations issues

6. Employee engagement

*i. The themes identified in **Drive for Change**[3] place leadership, the design and delivery of service improvements, communications and a framework for staff engagement as vital components in ensuring and enhancing employee engagement.*

*ii. The **MacLeod Review**[4] on employee engagement cited evidence of a positive correlation between an engaged workforce and improving performance. Building on the findings of the review, Government will encourage contractors to develop effective staff engagement strategies that enable people to be the best they can be at work.*

iii. Government recognises the premise that engagement between employee, employer and a recognised trade union where appropriate can be a key to unlocking productivity and creating a motivated workforce that feels respected, involved, heard, is well led and valued by those they work for and with.

NOTES

[3] Drive for Change is a practical tool for staff engagement in service improvement. The Drive for Change initiative was developed and supported by Cabinet Office and the Trades Union Congress and is currently in the process of being refreshed.

[4] The MacLeod Review was commissioned by the Department for Business, Innovation and Skills to take an in-depth look at employee engagement and to report on the potential benefits for organisations and employees.

Review

The impact of these principles on employment practice will be reviewed by the Public Services Forum in January 2012. The Forum will assess how the principles contribute to good employment practices in the delivery of contracted out services.

STAFF TRANSFERS IN THE PUBLIC SECTOR

Statement of Practice
January 2000 (Revised December 2013)

[5.106]

NOTES

This Statement of Practice was issued in January 2000 by the Cabinet Office. It has no statutory basis or force, but represents the policy which Government departments are required to follow and provides guidance for the rest of the public service, as to the application of the principles of TUPE in the contracting out or market testing of public service activities. The Statement was reissued in November 2007 with detailed revisions to reflect legislative changes (principally but not only the revision of the TUPE Regulations in 2006). It was further revised in December 2013 to make reference to the new arrangements for the HM Treasury "Fair Deal" policy. It is reproduced here, in full, in its revised form.

GUIDING PRINCIPLES

- The Government is committed to ensuring that the public sector is a good employer and model contractor and client. The people employed in the public sector, directly and indirectly, are its biggest asset and critical in developing modern, high quality, efficient, responsive, customer focused and environmentally friendly public services.
- The Government's approach to modernising public services is a pragmatic one, based on finding the best supplier who can deliver quality services and value for money for the taxpayer. This involves some services or functions being provided by, or in partnership with, the private or voluntary sector, or restructured and organised in a new way within the public sector. The involvement, commitment and motivation of staff are vital for achieving smooth and seamless transition during such organisational change.
- Public Private Partnerships and the process of modernisation through organisational change in the public sector will be best achieved by clarity and certainty about the treatment of staff involved. The Government is committed to ensuring that staff involved in all such transfers are treated fairly and consistently and their rights respected. This will encourage a co-operative, partnership approach to the modernisation of the public sector with consequential benefits for all citizens.

INTRODUCTION

1. In order to meet these guiding principles the Government believes that there must be a clear and consistent policy for the treatment of staff, founded upon the provisions of the Transfer of Undertaking (Protection of Employment) Regulations 2006 (TUPE), which replace the Transfer of Undertaking (Protection of Employment) Regulations 1981. This Statement of Practice[1] sets out the framework that the Government expects all public sector organisations to work within to achieve this aim (see paragraph 6 for the coverage of this Statement).

2. TUPE implements the 2001 European Council Acquired Rights Directive. In broad terms, TUPE protects employees' terms and conditions (except certain occupational pension arrangements) when the business or service in which they work is transferred from one employer to another. Employment with the new employer is treated as continuous from the date of the employee's start with the first employer. Terms and conditions cannot be changed where the operative reason for the change is the transfer although changes for other reasons may be negotiated, subject to certain conditions.

3. The Government takes a positive attitude towards TUPE, regarding it as an important aspect of employment rights legislation with the potential to promote a co-operative, partnership approach towards business restructuring and change in the public sector.

4. The Government's strategy in revising this legislation is based on the principle that it must be made to work effectively for all those whose interests depend upon it. This mirrors the Government's approach to employment relations issues generally.

5. In the area of Public Private Partnerships and change in the public sector, the consultations that the Government has undertaken and the representations which have been made, have showed a strong consensus between private sector employers, the voluntary sector, employee representatives and public sector organisations for the application of TUPE to situations where a service or function is contracted out, then retendered, brought back into the public sector, transferred within the public sector, or restructured and organised in a new way in a different part of the public sector. In any event, the TUPE Regulations 2006 have expanded the previous definition of what constitutes a transfer. It is accepted that there will still be some genuinely exceptional circumstances where TUPE will not apply but it is anticipated that there will be fewer than under the 1981 Regulations. Attempts to orchestrate a non-TUPE situation in other circumstances should not be tolerated. The policy in this Statement of Practice is therefore based on the following principles:

- contracting-out exercises with the private sector and voluntary organisations and transfers between different parts of the public sector, will be conducted on the basis that staff will transfer and TUPE should apply, unless there are genuinely exceptional reasons not to do so.
- this includes second and subsequent round contracts that result in a new contractor and where a function is brought back into a public sector organisation where, in both cases, when the contract was first awarded staff transferred from the public sector;
- in circumstances where TUPE does not apply in strict legal terms to certain types of transfer between different parts of the public sector, the principles of TUPE should be followed (where possible using legislation to effect the transfer) and the staff involved should be treated no less favourably than had the Regulations applied; and
- there should be appropriate arrangements to protect occupational pensions, redundancy and severance terms of staff in all these types of transfer. The Annex provides links to the relevant HM Treasury's policy guidance on the arrangements to be put into place for compulsory transfers out of the public sector:

(i) "Fair Deal for staff pensions: staff transfers from central government" issued October 2013; which sets out the revised policy on staff pensions (originally announced by the Chief Secretary to the Treasury on 4 July 2012) that must be followed by Central Government Departments and Agencies, and which Ministers expect to be adopted by other public sector employers where Fair Deal applies;

(ii) Statement of Practice on Staff Transfers from Central Government "A fair deal for Staff Pensions" which sets out the original Fair Deal policy on staff pensions announced by the Chief Secretary on 14 June 1999, which may still be relevant in certain circumstances, and which, where relevant, Ministers expect to be adopted by other public sector employers; and

(iii) "Fair deal for Staff Pensions: Procurement of Bulk Transfer Agreements and related issues", which supplemented the original Fair Deal policy (set out in (ii) above).

NOTES

1 Further copies of this Statement can be obtained from Phillip Jones tel. 020 7271 6355 or by email to Phillip.Jones@cabinet-office.gsi.gov.uk

COVERAGE

6. This Statement of Practice sets out a framework to be followed by public sector organisations to implement the Government's policy on the treatment of staff transfers where the public sector is the employer when contracting out or the client in a subsequent retendering situation. It applies directly to central government departments and agencies and to the NHS. The Government expects other public sector organisations to follow this Statement of Practice. Local government is subject to some different considerations particularly the current restrictions in legislation contained in Parts I and II of the Local Government Act 1988. However abolition of CCT from January 2000 and proposals to modify Section 17 of the 1988 Act, as part of the introduction of Best Value, will remove in part obstacles to local authorities following this Statement of Practice. However, in doing so, they must have regard to the need to comply with their best value duties. The Personnel and Human Resources panel of the Local Government Association support the principles set out in this Statement of Practice and have encouraged their adoption by individual local authorities.

7. The Statement of Practice covers the following types of situation that may involve transfers of staff:

- Public Private Partnerships (e.g. following Better Quality Service reviews). This includes contracting-out; market testing; PFI; privatisation and other outsourcing and contracting exercises, (paragraph 10-16);
- Second and subsequent generation contracting where, when the contract was first awarded, staff transferred from the public sector, (paragraph 12);
- Reorganisations and transfers from one part of the public sector to another, (paragraphs 17–20); and
- Reorganisations and transfers within the civil service (where TUPE cannot apply because there is no change in employer but TUPE principles should be followed), (paragraphs 21 and 22).

8. This Statement deals only with the policy framework for the treatment of staff involved in such transfers. It does not offer policy advice or guidance on:

- assessing the options for a particular service or function;
- project appraisal or procurement (except on the application of TUPE);
- managing a contracting exercise;
- how to discharge the obligations when TUPE applies or not; or
- how to secure appropriate pension provision, redundancy or severance terms.

Nor does it remove the need to seek legal advice in each individual case.

9. Detailed guidance on these aspects is provided separately, often tailored for different parts of the public sector to reflect their different needs, and for different types of Public Private Partnership.

TRANSFERS AS A RESULT OF PUBLIC PRIVATE PARTNERSHIPS

10. This section of the Statement deals with the policy that should be adopted for the transfer of staff from the public sector to a private sector employer or a voluntary sector body. This will be as a result of a Public Private Partnership where a service or function currently performed by the public sector will in future be carried out by a private sector organisation. This may, for example, be a result of a PFI initiative, strategic contracting out or market testing exercises. All will involve some sort of contracting exercise where the public sector organisation (not necessarily the one in which the staff are employed) is the contracting authority.

11. In such transfers the application of TUPE will always be a matter of law based on the individual circumstances of the particular transfer. However, the policy adopted in defining the terms of the contracting exercise can help ensure that staff should be protected by TUPE and that all parties have a clear understanding that TUPE should apply and will be followed. In such transfers, therefore, the public sector contracting authority should, except in genuinely exceptional circumstances (see paragraph 14), ensure that:

- at the earliest appropriate stage in the contracting exercise, it states that staff are to transfer and this should normally have the effect of causing TUPE to apply, although legal advice should always be taken to confirm the applicability of TUPE in individual cases;
- at the earliest appropriate stage staff and recognised unions (or, if none, other independent staff representatives) are informed in writing of the intention that staff will transfer (and where possible when the transfer will take place) and that TUPE should apply;
- potential bidders are then invited to tender, drawing their attention in the Invitation to Tender letter to the intention that staff will transfer and TUPE should apply. The public sector contracting authority should also be aware of the new requirement in the 2006 TUPE Regulations in relation to notification of employee liability information, and legal advice should be taken as necessary. Potential bidders should also be advised that they can, if they wish, submit bids on the basis that staff do not transfer and TUPE does not apply, but that these will only be accepted if they fall within the genuinely exceptional circumstances i.e. unless the bid falls within one of the exceptions at paragraph 14 it must comply with the condition that staff transfer and TUPE should apply;

- the contracting exercise is then operated on the basis that the intention is that staff will transfer and TUPE should apply. Public sector contracting authorities should however consider all bids received. If a tenderer considers that staff should not transfer, they should be asked to give their reasons for this. Tenderers should be reminded if they do not consider that staff should transfer and the contract does not fall within the exceptions in paragraph 14, the contracting authority reserves the right not to accept the tender;
- in a very few cases bids made on the basis staff will not transfer and TUPE not apply will fall within the genuinely exceptional circumstances set out in paragraph 14 and cause the authority to accept the bid. The costs of redeploying staff and redundancies costs to the public sector employer must be taken into account when assessing such a bid. In all other cases the bid should not be accepted as it will not conform to the contracting authority's view that staff should transfer and TUPE apply; and
- where there is then a contractual requirement that staff should transfer, the requirements of TUPE should be scrupulously followed by the public sector contracting authority who should also ensure that it is satisfied that bidders' proposals fully meet the requirements of TUPE.

SECOND AND SUBSEQUENT TRANSFERS

12. This part of the Statement also extends to the retendering of contracts where, when the contract was first awarded staff transferred from the public sector (irrespective of whether TUPE applied at the time). Where a public contracting authority retenders such a contract then, except in exceptional circumstances (and where the incumbent contractor is successful), TUPE should apply and staff working on the contract should usually transfer. Views should be sought from the current contractor as to whether, from their point of view, there are any exceptional circumstances why staff should not transfer (by reference to paragraph 14). The retendering exercise should then be conducted as described above in paragraph 11.

TRANSFER OF SERVICES OR FUNCTIONS BACK INTO THE PUBLIC SECTOR

13. There may also be circumstances that require a function contracted-out to a private sector contractor or voluntary sector body to be brought back into the public sector on the termination of the contract. If, when the contract was first awarded staff transferred from the public sector (irrespective of whether TUPE applied at the time), then the public sector organisation should ensure that staff working on the contract transfer (and TUPE should therefore apply) into its organisation unless there are genuinely exceptional reasons not to do so. Views should be sought from the current contractor as to whether, from their point of view, there are any exceptional circumstances why staff should not transfer (by reference to paragraph 14). For transfers into the Civil Service, where TUPE applies, then the recruitment provisions of the Civil Service Order in Council and Civil Service Commissioners Recruitment Code are not relevant.[2] The Civil Service Nationality rules, which are statutorily based, will continue to apply.

NOTES

[2] Civil Service Management Code.

EXCEPTIONS

14. There may be a small number of cases where the policy set out in paragraphs 11–13 may not be followed and TUPE may not apply. There must be genuinely exceptional reasons why this should be the case. Circumstances that may qualify for such exceptions are, broadly:

- where a contract is for the provision of both goods and services, but the provision of services is ancillary in purpose to the provision of the goods; or
- where the activity for which the public sector organisation is contracting is essentially new or a one off project; or
- where services or goods are essentially a commodity bought 'off the shelf' and no grouping of staff are specifically and permanently assigned to a common task.

15. Where a public sector organisation believes such genuinely exceptional circumstances exist then it should be prepared to justify this, and the departure from the Government's policy (paras 11–13), publicly, if challenged. In central Government, the agreement of the relevant departmental Ministers may need to be obtained before such an exception is made.

16. In such exceptional cases where staff do not transfer and TUPE does not apply, the public sector organisation should, in the case of first generation contracts, seek to identify as soon as possible with the contractor any staff that will be taken on voluntarily by the contractor,[3] and then, where possible, to redeploy those members of staff remaining within the public sector organisation (the costs of such redeployments and possible resulting redundancy payments must be taken into account when evaluating the bid).

NOTES

[3] Public Sector organisations should be aware that the transfer of a major part of the workforce, in terms of numbers or skills, may cause TUPE to apply.

TRANSFERS AND REORGANISATIONS WITHIN THE PUBLIC SECTOR

17. TUPE can apply to the transfers of a function from one part of the public sector to another where there is a change of employer. This, for example, can include:[4]

- Transfers between local government and Civil Service Departments and Agencies
- Transfers between local government and NDPBs

- Transfers between local government and the NHS
- Transfers between the NHS and Civil Service Departments and Agencies
- Transfers between the NHS and NDPBs
- Transfers between NDPBs and Civil Service Departments and Agencies

18. The application of TUPE will, again, always be a matter of law based on the individual circumstances of the particular transfer. The amended Acquired Rights Directive directly legislates the *Henke* judgement of the European Court of Justice that: an administrative reorganisation of public administrative authorities or the transfer of administrative functions is not a transfer and, therefore, as a matter of law, does not fall within the Directive. This provision in the Directive has been incorporated into the 2006 TUPE Regulations at 3(5). Case law[5] suggests that it excludes from the legislation's application only a relatively limited range of situations involving the transfer of entities pursuing non-economic objectives within the public sector. Nevertheless the issue has still to be tested fully in the tribunals and courts. The *Henke* exception has been thought to apply where: the reason for a transfer is only because there is a change of geographical boundaries and the type of public sector body carrying out the function does not change (eg the transfer of administrative staff as a result of changes to police authority boundaries); or where the main function is a judicial, quasi-judicial or quasi-judicial regulatory function (eg the creation of the Financial Services Authority) and incapable of being performed other than by a public sector authority. Officeholders who are not workers are also excluded from the scope of the Directive.

19. However, transfers at the instigation and under the control of central Government will usually be effected through legislation, in particular those involving Officeholders. Provision can then be made for staff to transfer on TUPE terms, irrespective of whether the transfer is excluded from the scope of the Directive implemented by TUPE. Departments must therefore ensure that legislation effecting transfers of functions between public sector bodies makes provision for staff to transfer and on a basis that follows the principles of TUPE along with appropriate arrangements to protect occupational pension, redundancy and severance terms.

20. Section 38 of the Employment Relations Act also includes a power that can be used to apply the requirements of TUPE specifically to transfers outside the scope of the Directive e.g. Transfer of Undertakings (Protection of Employment) (Rent Officer Service) Regulations 1999 (SI 2511/1999). BIS should be consulted about any proposal to exercise this power. Where, for whatever reason, this power or other legislation is not used there will be no legal requirement or obligation in such cases for staff to transfer to another part of the public sector where the function is to be performed (as to attempt to compel them would, in effect, constitute a unilateral change in their employment contract by imposing a change of employer). In such cases, as a matter of policy, public sector bodies should ensure that the principles underpinning TUPE are followed, so staff are offered the opportunity to transfer on terms that are, overall, no less favourable than had TUPE applied. They should also ensure that appropriate pension provision and redundancy and severance terms are applied. Staff who choose not to transfer should, where possible, be redeployed within the transferring public sector organisation.

NOTES

4 This list is not exhaustive.

5 *Mayeur v Association Promotion de l'Information Messine*: C-175/99 2000 IRLR 783, ECJ and *Collino v Telecom Italia SpA*: C-343/98 2000 IRLR 788, ECJ. These cases limit the application of the Henke exception to cases involving simply a re-organisation of public administrative structures or the transfer of administrative functions between public administrative authorities.

TRANSFERS AND REORGANISATIONS WITHIN THE CIVIL SERVICE

21. Reorganisation and transfers between central Government departments and agencies (i.e. within the Civil Service) do not involve a change in employer and TUPE therefore cannot apply.

However, terms and conditions of employment do vary between different departments and many of the considerations addressed in the Statement for other types of transfer may also apply.

22. As a matter of policy, therefore, such reorganisations and transfers between central Government departments will be conducted on the basis that:

- as a general rule, when functions are transferred from one department to another staff will be transferred with the work;
- departments should, however, make every effort to provide an opportunity for those who wish to stay with or return to their original department to do so, having regard to ensuring consistent treatment of staff affected and the needs of the work;
- departments should ensure that wherever possible the principles of TUPE are followed. The existing terms and conditions of staff cannot be changed unilaterally, over time, the receiving department may aim to move, through negotiation with staff, towards fuller alignment of the terms of transferred staff to those of the main body of staff.
- staff and their recognised unions are informed at the earliest appropriate stage of the reorganisation and transfer.

ANNEX

HM Treasury Guidance:

1. Fair Deal for staff pensions: staff transfer from central government (October 2013): www.gov.uk/government/uploads/system/uploads/attachment_data/file/246933/PU1571_Fair_Deal_for_staf_pensions.pdf

2. Fair Deal for staff pensions: procurement of bulk transfer agreements and related issues (June 2004) www.gov.uk/government/uploads/system/uploads/attachment_data/file/81340/pensions_bta_guidance_290604.pdf

3. Staff Transfers from Central Government: A Fair Deal for Staff Pensions (June 1999) www.gov.uk/government/uploads/system/uploads/attachment_data/file/81339/staff_transfers_145.pdf

CABINET OFFICE GUIDANCE ON SETTLEMENT AGREEMENTS, SPECIAL SEVERANCE PAYMENTS AND CONFIDENTIALITY CLAUSES ON TERMINATION OF EMPLOYMENT

(1 February 2015)

[5.107]

NOTES

CABINET OFFICE GUIDANCE ON THE USE OF SETTLEMENT AGREEMENTS, SPECIAL SEVERANCE PAYMENTS AND CONFIDENTIALITY CLAUSES ON TERMINATION OF EMPLOYMENT

1. This guidance covers the use of settlement agreements (formerly known as compromise agreements) to terminate employment and the associated use of confidentiality clauses and special severance payments.

2. This guidance explains the principles and process to be followed when considering the use of settlement agreements when terminating employment. It aligns with both HM Treasury guidance on **Managing Public Money**[1] and the **ACAS Code of Practice: Settlement Agreements.**[2]

3. This guidance applies to all Civil Service organisations and their ALBs[3], and includes all cases where public money is being spent on civil servants or non-civil servants employed by government departments or Arms Length Bodies (ALBs).

4. This guidance includes cases where agreements are reached without a statutory settlement agreement being used, for example following involvement by the Advisory, Conciliation and Arbitration Service (ACAS) in resolving the dispute, known as 'COT3 agreements' Departments should always use this guidance in conjunction with HM Treasury guidance on special severance cases and ensure they seek appropriate legal advice for each individual case.

5. This guidance applies to all confidentiality clauses regardless of whether these are linked to termination of employment.

NOTES

1 Managing Public Money: available at https://www.gov.uk/government/publications/managing-public-money

2 http://www.acas.org.uk/media/pdf/j/8/Acas-Code-of-Practice-on-Settlement-Agreements.pdf

3 These include Ministerial Departments, Non-Ministerial Departments, Executive Agencies, Crown Non-Departmental Bodies and Non-Departmental Public Bodies (NDPBs).

SETTLEMENT AGREEMENTS

6. A settlement agreement may be used in connection with the termination of employment following legal advice and where there is mutual agreement that this would be in the best interests of both the employee and employer. Settlement agreements are entirely voluntary and parties do not have to enter into discussions about them or agree to them if they do not wish to do so.

7. A settlement agreement should not be used in the following circumstances:

- to avoid taking appropriate performance/attendance management or disciplinary action. Separate policies and procedures exist to address poor performance or attendance;
- to cover up individual or organisational failure;
- to prevent an employee from speaking out - for example, to mask malpractice;
- to terminate a person's employment because they have made a protected disclosure under the Employment Rights Act 1996 (often known as "whistle blowing").

SPECIAL SEVERANCE PAYMENTS

8. A special severance payment is a payment made to the employee outside their statutory or contractual entitlement upon termination of their employment contract. Special severance payments are expected to be rare and exceptional. If a Department is considering making a special severance payment, they must take legal advice and be able to demonstrate that any payment is in the public interest and provides value for money for the Exchequer. Any payment may be open to public scrutiny, including by the National Audit Office and the Committee of Public Accounts.

9. Accounting Officers are responsible for ensuring that any special severance payment demonstrates value for money and that expenditure is used 'efficiently, economically and effectively.' They must set out clear governance routes, delegation authority and responsibilities that apply to special severance payments in the Department and any ALBs.

10. Accounting Officers are also responsible for ensuring that HM Treasury approval is obtained in all cases prior to the Department offering any payment, either orally or in writing. Departments must submit a full business case to HM Treasury to demonstrate that any special severance payment provides value for money for the Exchequer.

CONFIDENTIALITY CLAUSES

11. A confidentiality clause should only be used when necessary and not be included in settlement agreements as a matter of course. Departments should always consider whether each part of a confidentiality clause is required in a particular case, and take legal advice on the use of any confidentiality clause and the agreement as a whole. These principles apply whenever confidentiality clauses are used, even where they are not linked to termination of employment.

12. Confidentiality clauses should not seek to stifle or discourage staff from raising concerns with a regulatory or other statutory body about wrongdoing or poor practice in the Department, or give the impression that they affect the protection provided to an employee who acts as a "whistleblower" under the **Public Interest Disclosure Act 1998** (PIDA).

13. Employees who disclose information about matters such as wrongdoing or poor practice in their current or former workplace are protected under PIDA, subject to set conditions which are given in the Employment Rights Act 1996. This means that confidentiality clauses cannot and should not prevent the proper disclosure of matters of public interest.

14. If a confidentiality clause is to be used, departments must expressly remind the individual of their rights under the PIDA. Standard wording for the relevant subclauses of a confidentiality clause is attached at **Annex A**.

15. Departments should always seek legal advice on the appropriate use of confidentiality clauses. Confidentiality clauses must not override the obligation on departments to disclose appropriate details in relation to a department's essential business needs or those of Government. For example: for departmental and government management processes; where required by law; where required by a parliamentary committee; or under government guidance on the publication of information. Such clauses will therefore need to include suitable exceptions to allow for publication in appropriate circumstances, and the suggested wording in **Annex A** covers this.

APPROVALS PROCESS

16.From 1 February 2015, Departments must seek the prior approval of their Minister and then of the Minister for the Cabinet Office for the use of confidentiality clauses in settlement agreements which meet any of the following criteria:

(a) involves any member of the Senior Civil Service;
(b) is high visibility or is likely to be contentious (at any grade);
(c) has a proposed payment of £100,000 or more (at any grade);
(d) has a confidentiality clause that deviates, in respect of whistle blowing or protected disclosures, from the standard wording attached at Annex A (at any grade); or
(e) where a decision to dismiss an employee based on disciplinary, performance or attendance issues has been overturned on appeal, but the employer wishes to terminate the employment contract (at any grade).

17. From 1 February 2015 Accounting Officers must seek the prior approval of the Department's Minister for any case involving a member of the delegated grades that includes a confidentiality clause of any kind.

REPORTING TO CABINET OFFICE

18. From 1 January 2015 departments and their ALBs are required to report to the Minister for the Cabinet Office on a quarterly basis any special severance payment made in connection with the termination of employment. These returns will enable Cabinet Office to provide assurance on whether the use of special severance payments across the Civil Service is both proportionate and appropriate, including the use of any confidentiality clauses alongside such payments.

19. Civil Service-wide data on special severance payments will be published annually by the Cabinet Office.

ANNEX A: CONFIDENTIALITY CLAUSE STANDARD WORDING

Confidentiality clauses should not be included in settlement agreements as a matter of course. Departments should always consider whether each part of a confidentiality clause is required in a particular case, and take legal advice on how the below subclauses fit into the confidentiality clause and the agreement as a whole.

Sub-clause regarding employee's undertaking to keep the agreement confidential

In consideration of the sum of [£] (which shall be subject to statutory deductions), the Employee undertakes to the Employer:

to keep the existence, negotiation and terms of this agreement confidential except to the Employee's professional advisers, immediate family or where required by law. The Employee agrees to procure that the Employee's professional advisers and immediate family comply with the terms of this agreement as if they were a party to this agreement. In the case of the Employee's Trade Union representatives, the fact of and terms of this agreement can only be disclosed to the extent required by the union rules so long as those rules only require disclosure to union officials or advisors and not to the wider union membership.

Sub-clause relating to the whistleblowers' rights

For the avoidance of doubt, s43J of the Employment Rights Act 1996 applies in relation to protected disclosures as defined by s43A of that Act, i.e. nothing in this agreement can prevent the making of a protected disclosure (commonly known as "whistleblowing") in accordance with that Act.

Sub-clause containing exceptions to employer's undertaking to keep the agreement confidential

The Employer undertakes to the Employee to keep the existence, negotiation and terms of this agreement confidential, except for the purposes of essential management, accounting and audit processes or where required by law, by Parliament or by the Government Financial Reporting Manual and/or the Civil Service Guidance on Settlement Agreements.

ANNEX B: SCOPE OF GUIDANCE

This guidance applies to all Civil Service organisations and their ALBs. All other Public Sector organisations are not in scope, for example the NHS, further education colleges, broadcasters, the police, the Armed Forces, universities and academies and site licence companies. You should consult your Accounting Officer if you are unsure if this guidance applies to you.

This guidance does not cover payments which may be made in connection with the termination of employment under the Civil Service Compensation Scheme.[4] It also does not cover the use of settlement agreements where the employee remains in employment, such as those relating to employee grievances. In these circumstances, departments should ensure they are following relevant departmental policy and ACAS guidance.

An employee does not have a right to a settlement agreement and agreeing one is at the discretion of the employer.

At all times, civil servants remain bound by confidentiality obligations which form part of their terms of employment, including the **Official Secrets Act**.[5] These obligations will cover confidential information to which the employee has had access during the employment, such as client files. For legal and practical reasons it may also be appropriate to confirm these obligations in a confidentiality clause in the settlement agreement.

NOTES

4 http://www.civilservice.gov.uk/pensions/latest-news/compensation-scheme

5 www.legislation.gov.uk/ukpga/1989/6/contents

ANNEX C: GLOSSARY OF TERMS

Settlement agreement: Settlement agreements are legally binding contracts, used either to settle statutory disputes or claims, or disputes or claims under an individual employment contract. The agreement, which should be used only in exceptional circumstances, sets out the terms agreed by an employer and employee which settle the dispute and, where relevant, the terms on which the contract of employment will be terminated.

Special severance payment: A special severance payment is a payment made to the employee outside their statutory or contractual entitlement upon termination of their employment contract. It may be paid where an employee is dismissed or agrees the termination of their contract in a settlement agreement. It may also be paid in order to settle current legal proceedings such as an Employment Tribunal claim. In some cases an employee may also receive a payment under the Civil Service Compensation Scheme or under the terms of their contract of employment (for example, arrears of pay, accrued holiday pay, pay in lieu of notice etc.) or under a Tribunal or Court order.

Confidentiality clause: A confidentiality clause can include various elements. One element may be a requirement on the employee or employer, or both, to keep the existence, negotiation and terms of the settlement agreement confidential. In some cases confidentiality clauses may also include wording which precludes one or both parties from making derogatory comments about the other after the employment has ended.

GOVERNMENT EQUALITIES OFFICE: THE RECRUITMENT AND RETENTION OF TRANSGENDER STAFF GUIDANCE FOR EMPLOYERS (NOVEMBER 2015)

[5.108]

NOTES

DOCUMENT PURPOSE

This guide, which is specifically aimed at employers, is designed to help them recruit and retain transgender employees. It is also a useful guide for the managers of trans staff and for trans staff themselves.

The document addresses the recruitment and retention of transgender staff from an operational and strategic perspective. We include practical advice, suggestions and ideas, based on the expertise and experience of our contributors (below).

By following this guidance employers will be better equipped to create a more inclusive culture for all staff.

(*List of acknowledgements to employers who helped with the production of this Guidance is omitted.*)

CREATING A TRANSGENDER-FRIENDLY WORKPLACE: A GUIDE FOR EMPLOYERS

INTRODUCTION

[5.109]
For the majority of people their innate sense of being male or female - their gender identity - matches their birth sex and they do not have any questions over their gender identity. However, there are a small number of people whose gender identity does not match the gender they were assigned at birth. These are transgender people. Many will undergo the process of aligning their life and physical identity to match their gender identity, and this is called transitioning.

Individuals will always view themselves and their experience in a unique way, and will have personal preferences in terms of the language that their employers use, but we use the umbrella term "transgender" in this guidance, which includes non-binary.

People can change gender without any medical intervention. Medical processes are not essential to transitioning. Some people choose not to, or cannot, undergo a medical process but are still trans.

This guidance is designed to provide employers with advice on the recruitment and retention of trans employees and potential employees.

Those employers who understand the business and service benefits of a diverse and engaged workforce will recognise the need to respond to the differing needs of all their staff. They will understand the importance of affording everyone dignity and of making people feel included so that each individual adds value and can fulfil their potential without fear of discrimination.

However, there is sometimes a lack of awareness and understanding in relation to gender identity which sometimes results in employers failing to support staff effectively; often they lack the knowledge and the confidence to do so. Because only a small proportion of the population is trans, employers may never have needed to consider these issues.

The recruitment and retention of trans employees in the workforce need not be a complex process for employers.

Employers need only exercise a good approach to business practices. This guide provides some additional practical advice and clarification about how the law applies in England, Wales and Scotland.

To support employers to be trans-friendly, this practical guide is for:
- anyone in an organisation who wants to build their awareness and knowledge of trans issues; and
- it may be of specific interest to strategic and operational managers, directors, recruiters, human resource teams, trade unions, staff support networks and staff.

We hope that this guide enables employers to respond fully and confidently to specific issues that impact on trans people, be they employees or potential employees.

THE BUSINESS CASE

[5.110]
We are all different. Our different backgrounds, experience and perspectives mean we think about issues in different ways, see new solutions and opportunities to improve. The opportunity to think differently means we can do things differently.

These diverse skills are important for employers in all sectors; for private sector employers seeking commercial advantage and for public sector employers who need to deliver the best possible service to citizens.

We know that there is a wealth of research to show that workplaces that are more inclusive are also more productive.

When people feel valued by their employer for the contribution they can make to the organisation as an individual, regardless of their personal (or protected) characteristics, they are more likely to:
- Feel engaged and enthusiastic;
- Go the extra mile and expend discretionary effort;
- Have better attendance;
- Be a better team member;
- Stay longer and offer loyalty; and
- Talk about their employer in positive terms.

> "My employer treated me as an individual, they listened and provided support. Although they didn't always get everything right, I know that they tried hard and as a result benefit hugely from having an extremely loyal employee."

If barriers exist to the recruitment and retention of transgender staff, employers miss out on this potential. We know that trans people often leave their jobs before transitioning and often take lower paid jobs when they return to the workplace, often because of the possible discrimination they imagine they will face if they stay in their place of work. This can result in a loss of expertise and investment for their original employer. A more inclusive environment would retain the skills and expertise of that employee.

RECRUITMENT

[5.111]
It is in an employer's interest to secure the best possible applicants in order to gain or retain competitive advantage or be able to offer the best possible service. We know that significant barriers exist for trans people seeking employment but there are various steps that employers can take to:

- Be thought of as a "good employer" within the trans community;
- Attract applications from suitably qualified trans job seekers;
- Ensure that the recruitment processes do not present barriers to trans applicants; and
- Ensure that recruiting managers respond to, and assess trans candidates appropriately.

WEBSITE AND BRAND

[5.112]
Most job seekers will check the website of prospective employers to get a picture of what it would be like to work there, so you may wish to consider how you present yourself as a diverse employer in order to attract the widest pool of applicants. Statements about values and culture are really important but these need to be backed up with activities and plans, and this is true for all groups. Examples include:

- Show how you understand the business/service benefits of having an inclusive and diverse workforce.
- Include a statement about your values.
- Be aware that LGB (lesbian, gay, bisexual) issues are not necessarily the same as trans issues.
- Talk about challenging transphobia as well as homophobia and biphobia,
- Make your inclusion plans and HR policies accessible, including any trans policy you may have.
- Encourage your networks to write about what they are doing.
- Mention the wider partnerships you might have with other organisations - including trans-related charities.
- Give people the confidence to consider you as a prospective employer.

APPLICATION PROCESS

[5.113]
There are a small number of issues that are relevant to trans applicants which represent minor, but important, amendments to standard application processes.

Application forms

It can help to be flexible to let people identify their gender as they choose so where organisations ask for titles, you may want to provide 'other' as an option.

For some people providing previous names may be problematic, so ensure that where you do need information, it is asked for in a sensitive way and that it is stored and treated in a secure manner.

Security and vetting

Certain jobs require security vetting, for example the requirement for a Disclosure and Barring Service (DBS) check. This must be disclosed to candidates at an early stage of the process with signposts to further information. There is a confidential DBS process specifically for trans applicants, who should contact the DBS sensitive applications line on 0151 676 1452 or email sensitive@dbs.gsi.gov.uk for further advice about completing the form.

Genuine Occupational Requirements

Very occasionally, there may be genuine occupational factors that legitimately restrict applicants. This is known as a 'Genuine Occupational Requirement' (GOR).

Very careful consideration should be given before applying a GOR. Such restrictions are rare and, if wrongly applied, unlawful. The Equality and Human Rights Commission (EHRC) provides advice for employers on the use of GORs (under occupational requirements in the Employment Statutory Code of Practice).

Equality monitoring forms

Equality monitoring is a very important part of a recruitment process because it tells employers whether they are attracting a diverse range of applicants. It also shows whether there are any issues within the process that are preventing certain groups from progressing through the selection process to appointment, or from advancing through the organisation on promotion.

It is usual practice to gather monitoring information such as ethnicity, faith and sexual orientation and it is possible to also collect information on gender identity.

Employers will have standards and practices in relation to the management of the information of these forms that typically involve an anonymous submission, unconnected with the application form/CV, which is stored separately for analysis and reporting and not available to short-listers or the interview panel.

Monitoring forms could explain why the range of questions are being asked, how the information will be used and stored, the standards of confidentiality that apply and the fact that completion of the form is discretionary. It must be clear that if candidates decide not to complete the monitoring form, this will not have any impact on their application for the job.

By asking appropriate questions about gender identity and trans status on these forms, employers can send a signal that they are serious about equality, diversity and inclusion. Although the "T" is often included with LGB in relation to networks, employers should ask about gender identity in a separate question from one about sexual orientation.

For example, employers could ask, 'Please tick here if your gender is different from the sex you were assigned at birth'. This can enable trans people who have a clear male or female identity to choose male or female, but also let you know they are transgender. This is likely to need a little supporting explanation. It is also good practice to include an option of 'prefer not to say'.

Employers should recognise that collecting certain data will present some risk in relation to confidentiality. It may be possible to identify trans individuals within a very small workforce, for example if the data shows that one person in a workforce of 20 is trans. As with all personal information, employers should treat this information sensitively and securely.

Human resources (HR)

Employers may wish to ensure that HR (or any part of the organisation that may have a need) has sufficient knowledge and awareness of transgender issues and could also consider, where appropriate, identifying a point of contact in HR for any potential trans applicants, should they wish to make contact. This arrangement would be beneficial to both applicant and employer:

- The applicant gets access to someone who knows how to deal with specific issues (such as the names on documentation not matching up); and
- The employer has the reassurance that they are minimising any barriers to high quality candidates and, also, that their systems will not contravene the legal requirements in relation to disclosing someone's trans status inappropriately.

Smaller organisations could seek support from external specialists such as those listed at the end of this guidance.

The interview/selection process

The principles of good recruitment practice apply at interview. Recruiting managers could receive training and ongoing refresher training on best practice, the employer's recruitment and equality policies and the law. Managers also need to be able to "sell the benefits" of the job in terms of the support that is available to all staff through an inclusive culture and networks, for example.

Candidates may not wish to disclose their trans status at interview and it is not a question that should be asked, any more than questions about race or religion should be asked. It is best not to assume someone's gender simply by their appearance.

In some circumstances, candidates may advise a recruitment panel that it is their intention to transition. In such circumstances recruiting managers could:

- Thank the candidate for their openness;
- Explain that if appointed the employer will support the individual; and
- Remain focussed on the purpose of the interview, i.e. does this person have the skills and experience for the job.

> "At the end of my interview, I was asked if I had any questions or wanted to add anything. I plucked up my courage and told the panel that I intended to transition very soon. The chair of the panel's jaw dropped, he looked at the HR rep and said, "One for you, HR", but immediately recovered himself and said, "I don't care if you are a man or a woman (he included a range of other characteristics to make his point). All I care is that you can do the job". He got there in the end although it would have been better if his response had been well informed and more professional."

Job offers and documentation

All offers of employment involve identity and documentation checks. Sometimes, the names on a trans person's documentation (such as passport, driver's licence, utility bills or qualification certificates) do not tally. Ideally, trans candidates should have access to a nominated person in HR who is knowledgeable and available to deal with the documentation sensitively. This will involve retaining only what is needed, ensuring that the data is held securely and that there is no informal sharing of this information as this could be unlawful.

Induction

Once the trans person commences work, the lead should be taken from the individual about whether their trans status is discussed. Reference should be made to the requirements of relevant policy (such as dignity at work).

The new starter may be happy for *particular* colleagues to know they are trans but not others. Even if someone appears to open up about their trans status, it must always be their decision about who to share this information with. Revealing someone is trans ("outing" them), could place them at risk of discrimination, and violate their right to privacy. It may also be an offence under the Gender Recognition Act 2004 that carries a potential fine.

RETENTION

[5.114]
Businesses and organisations need to retain their skilled and experienced staff. They need to see the return on the investment of recruitment and training and be able to maximise the positive impact of the employee's experience, abilities, professionalism and creativity.

If people are unhappy, feel marginalised or experience discrimination, there is a risk of grievances or complaints or even that the organisation may lose a valued employee.

Effective retention strategies address these avoidable costs to the organisation.

This section of the guidance covers organisational strategy and retention advice relating to individual issues that managers will need to consider.

Retention - individual issues

This section addresses the retention of people who are considering or planning transition, are transitioning or have transitioned.

Managers need to listen and agree the approach that suits the business and the trans individual. Although this section addresses a series of practical issues and approaches, no two situations are the same.

Before transitioning – making a plan

Because of the general lack of awareness in relation to gender identity issues in the workplace, it can be an extremely difficult step for someone to approach their manager to tell them that they are planning to transition. Often individuals do not know what the manager's response will be or how the organisation or business would deal with the news.

These concerns can be offset if the employer has an inclusive approach and a culture that values difference. However, the key issues for managers at this early stage are:

- Listen, show support, discuss levels of confidentiality, agree to seek advice and agree to work in partnership. The process should be led by the individual as much as possible.
- Take advice from the HR, inclusion and diversity team or one of the organisations listed at the end of this guidance.
- Understand that individuals could have a range of experiences or objectives. Some people prefer as few people as possible to know about their transition and decide to discuss this with their manager but require no further action. Others may be planning a medical intervention and others may prefer transition that does not involve any medical intervention or surgery. The key thing is that managers need to adopt an approach that meets the needs of the employee.
- Agree with the member of staff what steps need to be taken before, during and after their transition. Some people refer to this as developing an agreement or an action plan. A suggested template for such a plan is at page 26 of this guidance.
- A series of review meetings should be scheduled, at an agreed frequency as part of any action plan, and at any significant stage of the process (fortnightly/monthly).
- The plan should be updated and developed, not fixed.
- There should be an agreement about where the plan or any meeting notes are kept and who has access.

A trusting and open relationship between the trans employee and the manager and HR is really important. This should involve joint problem-solving (such as anticipating and planning for any problems), confidentiality, reliability (doing what you say you are going to do) and empathy (providing support).

"When I first became the Store Manager where Paul worked, he was living as a male, transitioning from female. I decided not to approach Paul about it, but to wait for a while to see if he wanted to talk to me about it. As he was one the supervisors reporting to me, I developed a good relationship with him after a few weeks, and talked at length with him about his development potential and supporting his progression. At this point he asked to talk to me. He confided in me his situation, and was really open about what he was going through. He explained that although he really did want to progress, that there was only a certain amount of things he could deal with and he felt it would be too much for him.

"I agreed to support him by keeping him in a department he was confident in, and of course allowing for him to attend appointments. He had a very supportive manager, and had built a great relationship with the all-male team in his department, which was also important to him. Paul asked me not to treat him specially, but to just be aware of his situation, and to try to understand. He was really open and willing to answer questions, which encouraged me outside of work to research as much as I could about his situation.

"Over the following nine months, Paul needed support from us all at the store. He needed supporting when his appointments at the gender clinic were postponed or cancelled. We supported him when he first started getting his hormone injections, which caused him physical pain and discomfort. He had highs and lows. If things got too much for him, especially in his customer-facing role, we allowed him time away from the shop floor. He didn't get special treatment; he just got some additional support and understanding from all of us.

> "When I arrived at the store he was using the First Aid room for his locker, as the previous management was unsure of what to do. I knew he should be in the male locker room, and shortly after him completing the period of living as a male for two years, we moved him into the male changing rooms, and dealt swiftly with the two colleagues that complained about it. I specifically didn't treat Paul any differently, but I did respond to his individual needs. I also became super-sensitive to any language or behaviour from the rest of the store team, and ensured that he was always referred to appropriately. It was the small things that mattered, that all added up to a culture of support."

There are a series of practical considerations, (some of which have legal implications) that managers should address:

- **Dates and timescales** – when key changes will take place and how they fit with any relevant work deadlines. These key changes will vary depending on the individual but could include name, documentation, physical changes or short term or permanent role changes. Practical issues relating to the availability of key people to support the process, shift patterns etc. could be considered.

> "We decided to tell people during the period between Boxing Day and the New Year, as it was a quiet time for the business, yet almost everyone in my team would be in work."

- **Records and systems** – what needs to be changed, when this will happen, what will happen to "old" records? This includes photographs/biographies etc. on company websites through to historical information on personal records (such as a reference to a previous period of maternity leave for a transgender man). Payroll and National Insurance details may also need to be adjusted so it is essential that where other people in the organisation need to be aware, this is within an informed context.
- **Communication with colleagues** – managers should encourage the individual to describe what they think will be best for them. This could be a verbal communication at team meetings or on a 1:1 basis, the trans person could be present or absent, it could be an electronic communication. The person may not be ready to tell anyone else at the early stages and if that is the case, this should be respected. Every situation is different but the communication needs to provide some general awareness-raising and also address issues specific to the individual. Colleagues need to be able to ask questions and managers must set a tone of absolute inclusion and respect. This communication will need to be practical and address important issues such as how to address the trans colleague (new name, correct pronoun), how to support the colleague, how to deal with questions that may come from outside the team without breaching confidentiality etc.

> "The HR manager told my supervisor in a private meeting in which I was not present. My supervisor was very sympathetic and, together, the three of us developed a plan for telling colleagues.
>
> I spoke to a senior manager who said she would be willing to tell my colleagues. I prepared a document that she would read out. I said that it would be better for me not to be present at the meeting, but be available in the building to answer any immediate questions."

- **Use of facilities** – a trans person should be free to select the facilities appropriate to the gender in which they present. For example, when a trans person starts to live in their acquired gender role on a full time basis they should be afforded the right to use the facilities appropriate to the acquired gender role. Employers should avoid discriminating against anyone with the protected characteristic of 'gender reassignment'. Where employers already offer gender-neutral toilets and changing facilities, the risk of creating a barrier for transgender people is alleviated.
- **Absences from work** – there may be absences for medical reasons and other appointments associated with the transition process which should be recorded, but not used in relation to any absence management process i.e. they should be regarded as a short-term reasonable adjustment.
- **Short-term job change** – may be appropriate in some cases. This can only be in agreement with the trans employee and employer.
- **Pensions and insurance** – financial services organisations will have systems in place to manage data stored about trans contributors. When dealing with other agencies, care should be taken to ensure information is only shared on a "need to know" basis with those responsible for records/policies.
- **Communication with customers/clients** – the need for this will vary depending on the employer's business. Include your employee in considering how best to communicate the information. This may need to include a plan to deal with media interest.
- **Respect and try to accommodate requests for anonymity** – if it is wanted. Transitioning can be a difficult process and trans colleagues may not want any attention, preferring relocation for example. Any change like this must be led by the trans employee working with their employer.

Managers need to take their lead from the trans employee in relation to the frequency and type of support that is provided during and after transition. There are some general points that should be considered:

Bullying

Any instances of harassment or bullying should be treated with the same degree of seriousness as other instances of bullying in the organisation. Employers should be aware that subtle bullying, such as excluding people from distribution lists, or persistent use of the wrong pronoun (she, he) can be very undermining and must be identified and addressed.

Questions

Never let natural curiosity about trans issues override sensitivity and respect. If staff have questions, direct them to reputable resources e.g. guidance and websites such as those listed at the end of this guidance.

Anonymity and checking details

Ideally, employers should maintain a complete list of all the systems (electronic and paper) that hold personal data or references to any individual employee. This could range from HR systems through to stand alone roster systems; they could be centralised systems or remote databases. It is essential that trans employees are not "outed" due to old data emerging from such a system.

Someone must take responsibility for checking that agreements in relation to information and records have been fulfilled. Double check the online and paper records, website etc.

> "I have heard horror stories of an old HR system producing a report that showed a period of maternity leave eight years ago for a trans man (which effectively 'outed' him) and a trans colleague getting locked out of the IT system but the help desk could only re-set the access with the person's previous details including their pre transition name. No one had made all the proper system checks."

Networks

Employees' networks are often referred to as "LGBT" networks. Sometimes the "T" (transgender) is added without any real thought as to what this means in practice, so employers should ensure that networks are adequately equipped to support trans people.

Strong networks are an indicator of a supportive employer and in reality offer a really practical support system where colleagues can seek help, offer help and avoid isolation. Most large employers with networks have an LGBT (lesbian, gay, bisexual, and trans) network. These groups are run by members of staff, for members of staff with the support of the employer.

Maintain contact

At some point, the trans employee may no longer want or need specific support from their manager in relation to their gender reassignment. Communications will revert to the usual management interventions. It is important that managers do not make any assumptions about this and should agree when employer support around the transition is complete. Some colleagues may want a longer period of support and may request different support at different times of their transition, such as counselling. Managers should be aware that sometimes transition results in personal or family relationships breaking down temporarily or permanently and the workplace can offer a place of stability during difficult times.

> "We talked regularly, I met with an appointed HR Manager, initially every week, then fortnightly and then monthly over a period of a year. Having a HR manager as a point of contact served to illustrate [my employer's] commitment to getting it right and also meant decisions and any issues raised could be dealt with or made immediately."

Post transition

When people complete their transition, some people may consider this part of their history that has now been resolved. In such cases, they will simply describe themselves as a man or woman, and so should their employer.

> "I transitioned three jobs ago and the transition feels like ancient history to me. I am in a sought-after profession and my experience is that employers just treat me as any other employee . . . but one they really need to retain for my expertise."

References

When asked for a reference for a trans person, the usual principles of fairness and accuracy apply. If asked for a reference from someone who has transitioned since leaving your employment, it is advisable to make direct contact with the ex-employee to discuss the reference. Clearly the content of the reference in terms of capabilities, experience etc. will be the same but care must be taken around the use of pronouns and names.

RETENTION - STRATEGIC ISSUES

[5.115]
There are organisation-wide cultural factors that will aid retention and also a series of practical interventions.

For all of these groups, there are some important cultural factors that will aid retention.

Culture, values and awareness

Employers that actively promote a culture of dignity and respect are more likely to successfully recruit and retain trans staff. This would involve being explicit about inclusion and the behaviour and approaches that go with an inclusive approach. The values and culture could be supported by clear policy statements and procedures (where appropriate) which are linked to business objectives. People need to understand the business/service benefits of an inclusive approach.

Leadership

Clear and consistent leadership is central to helping everyone respond to transition in a positive and supportive way. This can relate to:

- employment culture (value and respect for all individuals);
- management standards (addressing problems as they arise); and
- communication processes (balancing openness with confidentiality as appropriate).

> "With a largely male and heterosexual workforce, coming out as trans after almost ten years working with these people was always going to be a challenge. The nature of the work means the crews form close-knit bonds very quickly, and these are rarely broken.
>
> As a member of the management team I was aware of this culture as was my employer. The key for my employer was to ensure that my transition was managed from the very beginning from a position of equality, intolerance of discrimination and bullying and to provide support to me as an individual and as an educator to staff who had never come across trans issues. They needed to show strong leadership from HR to ensure all department managers understood what transition meant, they needed to provide information to staff and more importantly ensure they understood the information and they needed to make sure their policies and procedures were up to date, trans-inclusive and fit for purpose. For me though, the key way they showed leadership was they listened. They listened to me, to staff and colleagues who simply didn't understand nor had any experience, to the trade unions and they listened to medical advice.
>
> By doing all this they were able to portray good leadership, that this was something important, to get right and to allow me to get on with my job."

Learning and development

Inclusion, diversity and equality and human rights training for all staff establishes the organisation's culture, setting and maintaining standards and allowing all staff to be themselves at work. In addition, managers should be supported in their roles through effective management development programmes.

Employee assistance programmes (EAP)

These contracted-out services generally offer 24-hour telephone support to employees on a wide range of issues including counselling support. Employers may consider checking the trans-friendly credentials of their EAP.

Role models

A diverse workforce will generally be a more comfortable environment for minority staff groups including trans colleagues. Trans employees generally will not want to be the centre of attention; however, sometimes colleagues are happy to be seen as role models in order to give others confidence about transition at work.

Mentors

Mentoring is a relationship in which a more experienced colleague uses their greater knowledge and understanding of the work or workplace to support the development of a more junior or inexperienced member of staff. Mentoring relationships work best where there is a learning opportunity for both parties. This is particularly productive when used to encourage inclusive working practices; for example, where a senior leader mentors a more junior colleague, where both individuals or just one individual is trans. Reverse mentoring (where a more junior colleague mentors a senior leader) can also be effective in encouraging sharing and learning across generations and/or between role levels.

Champions

Some organisations identify "champions" of particular protected characteristics from amongst the senior management team. This role helps to develop awareness amongst the wider staff group, in order to develop a more inclusive working environment.

LEGAL FRAMEWORK

The Equality Act

[5.116]
The Equality Act 2010 consolidated and replaced existing equality law including the Sex Discrimination

Act 1975 with a single Act. The Equality Act 2010 provides protection from discrimination in respect of people who have what the Act describes as the protected characteristic of gender reassignment. It states:

> A person has the protected characteristic of gender reassignment if the person is proposing to undergo, is undergoing or has undergone a process (or part of a process) for the purpose of reassigning the person's sex by changing physiological or other attributes of sex.
>
> A reference to a transsexual person is a reference to a person who has the protected characteristic of gender reassignment.

The Act defines nine "protected characteristics" which are age, disability, marriage and civil partnership, pregnancy and maternity, race and ethnicity, religion or belief, sex, sexual orientation and gender reassignment. The Act provides protection from discrimination in relation to these protected characteristics in a range of areas including the provision of services and employment.

No employment decision (for example, relating to recruitment, promotion, pay and benefits, training, discipline and dismissal including redundancy) based on one of these characteristics is likely to be lawful (with a few minor exceptions).

This means that the same balance that managers apply to decisions relating to gender or disability for example, must also be applied in decisions relating to the recruitment and employment of staff who possess the characteristic of 'gender reassignment'.

The legislation makes clear that it is not necessary for people to have any medical diagnosis or treatment to gain gender reassignment protection; it is a *personal* process of moving from one's birth gender to the preferred gender.

Employers can be held responsible for the actions of their staff under the Act (even if it is without the employers' knowledge or approval). Employees are also individually responsible for their own discriminatory actions.

Practical steps to limit the risk of discrimination are included elsewhere in this guidance and managers should carefully consider learning and development options for their staff.

The Act provides protection from discrimination in the following circumstances (these case studies are trans-specific - where someone possesses the characteristic of gender reassignment or is perceived to possess the characteristic – but the principles apply to all nine protected characteristics).

Direct discrimination

This means treating someone with a protected characteristic less favourably than other employees.

> **Example:**
>
> The best applicant for a vacancy has the protected characteristic of gender reassignment and is not offered the job because the recruiting manager does not feel comfortable about working with trans people. This is direct discrimination because of gender reassignment.

Direct discrimination by association

This means treating someone less favourably than other employees because of their association with someone who has the characteristic of gender reassignment.

> **Example:**
>
> When someone is excluded from work activities because they have a transgender spouse, this is direct discrimination by association.

Direct discrimination by perception

This means treating someone less favourably than other employees because of a perception of gender reassignment.

Example:

Where someone is refused a job because they are perceived to be transgender even though they are not, this is direct discrimination by perception.

Indirect discrimination

This can occur where there is a policy, practice or procedure that applies to all workers, but particularly disadvantages a particular protected group such as people who intend to undergo, are undergoing or have undergone gender reassignment.

> **Example:**
>
> If people have to comply with a policy or procedure that forces individuals to disclose that they have undergone gender reassignment, this is an example of indirect discrimination – such as in some circumstances, needing to provide an original birth certificate.

Harassment

This can occur when unwanted conduct related to gender reassignment has the purpose or effect of violating a person's dignity or creating an intimidating, hostile, degrading, humiliating or offensive environment for that person.

Victimisation

This is the unfair treatment of an employee who has made or supported a complaint about gender reassignment discrimination.

Example:

When someone is ostracised by colleagues having given evidence in a grievance case where a trans colleague has been bullied. This could be victimisation due to gender reassignment.

Also, section 16 of the Equality Act has specific provision to protect the right of trans employees to have time off work for reasons relating to their gender reassignment. An employer will be discriminating against the trans person if they would treat another person who is absent from work due to illness or injury more favourably.

The Equality Act 2010 does not apply to Northern Ireland. Gender reassignment protection in employment was introduced by the Sex Discrimination (Gender Reassignment) Regulations (Northern Ireland) 1999.

Public sector duties

The Equality Act 2010 requires that public bodies have due regard to eliminate discrimination, harassment, victimisation and any other conduct prohibited under the Act (including discrimination by association or perception), to advance equality of opportunity between persons who share a protected characteristic and those who do not, and to foster good relations between persons who share a protected characteristic and those who do not.

Service providers

Separate guidance is available in relation to the provision of services. However, employers have a duty to take reasonable steps to protect their trans staff from harassment.

The Gender Recognition Act 2004 (GRA)

This legislation allows trans people (aged over 18) to change their legal gender. The Act gives trans people the right to obtain a new birth certificate, affording them recognition of their acquired gender in law for all purposes.

However, whether or not a person has a Gender Recognition Certificate (GRC) should have no bearing on their employment or employment protections, apart from providing an extra layer of privacy. Employers should treat people in accordance with their gender identity, whether or not they have a GRC and should not ask trans staff if they have one.

The Act requires applicants to satisfy the Gender Recognition Panel (a judicial body of lawyers and doctors) that:

- they have or have had gender dysphoria;
- they have lived in the acquired gender for two years prior to the application; and
- they intend to live permanently in the acquired gender.

Following a successful application, a trans person will be recognised as being a person of their acquired gender with all the legal implications which flow from this.

The Act also includes important measures to protect privacy. The Act makes it a criminal offence for a person who has acquired protected information (information which relates to a person's application for a GRC or information which identifies a person with a GRC as transgender) in an official capacity (such as through a recruiting process) to disclose the information to any other person. The offence does not apply if the individual has agreed to the disclosure of such information or in certain prescribed circumstances (such as disclosure being for the purpose of preventing or investigating crime). Section 22 of the GRA sets out the circumstances under which such information may be disclosed lawfully.

Not all trans people apply for a GRC. There may be a number of reasons for this including health, personal and family reasons.

Employment rights do not depend on whether a person has a GRC. Employers should not ask for a person's GRC and it should never be a pre-condition for transitioning at work.

Exceptions to normal recruitment practice

Very rarely, it is an occupational requirement of a role is that it is done by someone of a particular sex. This is called a Genuine Occupational Requirement. In order to claim this, the employer must show that applying the requirement is a proportionate means of achieving a legitimate aim.

Other legislation

The wide range of other legislative provision which relates to gender identity includes:

- Pensions Act 1995

- Employment Rights Act 1996
- Protection from Harassment Act 1997
- Human Rights Act 1998
- Data Protection Act 1998
- Civil Partnership Act 2004
- Marriage (Same Sex Couples) Act 2013.

GLOSSARY

[5.117]

Terms and language regarding transgender people and transgender issues are evolving rapidly and many terms may mean different things to different people. The definitions given here are common, but not universal, understandings of these terms.

Acquired gender

The law uses the phrase 'acquired gender' to refer to the gender in which a transgender person lives and presents to the world. This is not the gender that they were assigned at birth, but it is the gender in which they should be treated.

Cross-dresser

Someone who wears the clothes usually expected to be worn by someone of the 'opposite' gender. Other terms include 'transvestite' (now becoming a dated term and disliked by some) and 'dual role'. A cross-dresser is unlikely to have a full-time identity as a member of their cross-dressed gender and typically does not seek medical intervention.

Gender binary

A binary system allows only two things or states – for example, on/off. In terms of gender, it refers to the either/or categories of male/female that do not allow for, or recognise, other experiences of gender.

Gender dysphoria

Transgender people who seek medical intervention are typically diagnosed with 'gender dysphoria' as a first step. Gender dysphoria describes the sense of a strong, persistent discomfort or distress caused by the dissonance between a person's self-identified gender and the gender they were assigned at birth.

Gender identity

A person's sense of self as a man, woman, non-binary person or other sense of gender. A person's gender identity is typically expected to follow directly from the sex they were assigned at birth (based on physical attributes), but this is not always the case.

Gender reassignment

The process of changing or transitioning from one gender to another.

Gender Recognition Certificate (GRC)

A certificate issued under the Gender Recognition Act[1] which enables trans people to be legally recognised in their acquired gender.

Mis-gendering

You mis-gender someone when you refer to them using a word, especially a pronoun or a form of address, that does not correctly reflect the gender with which they identify.

Non-binary person

Someone who does not subscribe to the customary binary approach to gender, and who may regard themselves as neither male nor female, or both male and female, or take another approach to gender entirely.

Real life experience (RLE)

Sometimes called the Real-Life Test (RLT), this is a period of time in which trans individuals live full-time in their preferred gender role. The purpose of the RLE is to confirm that the person can function in their preferred gender successfully in society, as well as to confirm that they are sure they want to live in their preferred gender for the rest of their life. A documented RLE is a requirement of some doctors before prescribing hormone replacement therapy, and a requirement of most surgeons before performing gender reassignment surgery.

Transgender (or trans) person

A broad, inclusive term referring to anyone whose personal experience of gender extends beyond the typical experiences of those of their assigned sex. Amongst others, transsexual people, non-binary people and cross-dressers may all consider themselves transgender people.

Transsexual person

This term is most closely associated with the legally protected characteristic of 'gender reassignment'. A transsexual person may be a person assigned female at birth who has transitioned or is transitioning to live as a man, or a person assigned male at birth who has transitioned or is transitioning to live as a woman. The law does not require a person to undergo a medical procedure to be recognised as a transsexual person. Once a transsexual person has acquired a GRC, they should generally be treated entirely as in their acquired gender.

Transgender man

A transgender man is a female-to-male transgender person who was assigned female at birth but has a male gender identity.

Transgender woman

A transgender woman is a male-to-female transgender person who was assigned male at birth but has a female gender identity.

Transition

Taking the journey from your assigned gender to the one you know yourself to be. This may refer to social transition (changing name, clothes etc), medical transition (hormones and/or surgery) or both.

NOTES

1 GOV.UK website: Applying for a Gender Recognition Certificate

ACTION PLAN TEMPLATE

[5.118]

This type of template is a useful starting point to develop a plan. Questions and points to consider:

Who needs to know?

	Who will tell them?	When?	Date completed
HR Business Partner			
Senior Manager			
Line Manager (if not main point of contact)			
Others (please specify)			

Planning the future

Your new name (in full, if known)	
Your role	
Name of line manager	
Medical advisor (name/contact details)	

Telling colleagues/friends and people you work with/external partners

- Who will tell colleagues/partners?
- Will you be there?
- When will this take place?
- Where will this take place?
- What information will be provided?

Getting ready for your first day back

- When will this be?
- Change of role?
- Are you ready?
- Is your wardrobe/uniform ready?
- Are colleagues ready?
- Additional support for you and/or loved ones?
- Any media concerns?

Changing everything into your new identity

	Who will do this?	When?	Date completed
Name badge			
Business cards			
Website 'About Us' section			
IT systems			
Voicemail			
Intranet address entry			
Work-based social media			
Union membership			
Pensions scheme			

	Who will do this?	When?	Date completed
Uniform stores data			
Certificates/awards			

Medical appointments and absences

Reason	Dates

Details of meetings

Date	Comments	Actions	Date of next meeting

USEFUL SOURCES OF INFORMATION AND ADVICE

[5.119]

www.inclusiveemployers.co.uk The UK's leading inclusion and diversity experts, working with employers to create inclusive workplaces.

www.scottishtrans.org The Scottish Transgender Alliance works to improve gender identity and gender reassignment equality, rights and inclusion in Scotland.

http://genderedintelligence.co.uk/ Gendered Intelligence work predominantly with the transgender community and those who impact on transgender lives. They particularly specialise in supporting young transgender people aged 11-25.

www.gires.org.uk Gender Identity Research and Education Society provides information for trans people, their families and the professionals who care for them.

www.depend.org.uk Offering free, confidential advice, information and support to all family members, spouses, partners and friends of transsexual people in the UK.

www.gendertrust.org.uk The Gender Trust supports all those affected by gender identity issues.

www.clareproject.org.uk The Clare Project is a self-supporting group based in Brighton and Hove open to anyone wishing to explore issues around gender identity.

http://www.ntpa.org.uk/ The National Trans Police Association exists primarily to provide support to serving and retired Police Officers, Police Staff and Special Constables with any gender identity issue.

gender-matters.org.uk Wolverhampton based, Gender Matters provides a comprehensive programme of practical support, counselling, advice and information.

www.equalityhumanrights.com The Equality and Human Rights Commission seeks to identify and tackle areas where there is still unfair discrimination or where human rights are not being respected and to act as a catalyst for change. The EHRC also provide statutory guidance on the Equality Act for employers, which can be found here: http://www.equalityhumanrights.com/private-and-public-sector-guidance

www.blgbt.org Supports the LGBT community in Birmingham.

www.northernconcord.org.uk Northern Concord is a Manchester based transvestite, transgendered and transsexual support and social group.

www.translondon.org.uk TransLondon is a discussion/support group for all members of the trans community, whatever their gender identity.

www.gayadvicedarlington.co.uk Offers free, confidential support, advice and drop in sessions to trans people at a full time LGBT centre.

www.transgenderwales.bravepages.com Supports transgendered people in Wales.

www.transgenderni.com Supports transgendered people in Northern Ireland.

Government Equalities Office (GEO)

GEO is responsible for equality strategy and legislation across government.

www.gov.uk/geo

Department for Business, Innovation and Skills (BIS)

BIS is the department for economic growth. The department invests in skills and education to promote trade, boost innovation and help people to start and grow a business. BIS also protects consumers and reduces the impact of regulation.

www.gov.uk/bis

Equality and Advisory Support Service (EASS)

EASS has a helpline that advises and assists individuals on issues relating to equality and human rights, across England, Scotland and Wales.

www.equalityadvisoryservice.com/

British Chambers of Commerce (BCC)

BCC is the national voice of local business and serves business members across the UK. The BCC is a voice for the interests of business, delivers services that help business grow, and is the private sector source of advice and support for international trade.

http://www.britishchambers.org.uk/

E. USEFUL ADDRESSES

USEFUL ADDRESSES

NOTES

Note: if an email address is not supplied in the information below then, generally, a contact form is available on the website of the body concerned.

[5.120]

1. ADVISORY, CONCILIATION AND ARBITRATION SERVICE

NOTES

Further information is available on the ACAS website at www.acas.org.uk.

ACAS Helpline	Tel: 0300 123 1100
	Text Relay service: 18001 0300 123 1100
	Acas training and business solutions customer services team: 0300 123 1150
Head Office	Euston Tower, 286 Euston Road, London, NW1 3JJ
Regional offices (no telephone numbers or email addresses are given on the ACAS website)	
London	Euston Tower, 286 Euston Road, London, NW1 3JJ
East of England	Forest Heath District Council Offices, College Heath Road, Mildenhall, Suffolk IP28 7EY
East Midlands	Apex Court, City Link, Nottingham, NG2 4LA
West Midlands	Victoria Square House, Victoria Square, Birmingham, B2 4AJ
North West	3rd Floor, Piccadilly Gate, Store Street, Manchester, M1 2WD
North East	Newcastle Civic Centre, Barras Bridge, Newcastle upon Tyne, NE1 8QH
Scotland	151 West George Street, Glasgow G2 2JJ
South West	Temple Quay House, 2 The Square, Bristol, BS1 6DG
South East	Civic Offices, 1st Floor, Harlington Way, Fleet, Hampshire, GU51 4AE
Wales	Companies House, Crown Way, Cardiff, CF14 3UZ
Yorkshire & Humber	The Cube, 123 Albion Street, Leeds, LS2 8ER
Early Conciliation website:	ec.acas.org.uk
Early Conciliation support:	Tel: 0300 123 1122
Address for sending in Early Conciliation forms:	EC Notification, ACAS (Phoenix), PO Box 10279, Nottingham, NG2 9PE. Also via www.acas.org.uk/earlyconciliation.

2. ADVOCATE

(*formerly the BAR PRO BONO UNIT*)
The National Pro Bono Centre, 48 Chancery Lane, London, WC2A 1JF
Tel: 020 7092 3960 (Mon, Weds, Fri,10.15am–12.45pm)
DX 188 London Chancery Lane
Email: enquiries@weareadvocate.org.uk
Website: www.weareadvocate.org.uk

3. BAR COUNCIL

289–293 High Holborn, London, WC1V 7HZ
Tel: 020 7242 0082 Fax: 020 7831 9217
DX 240 LDE
Email: ContactUs@BarCouncil.org.uk
Website: www.barcouncil.org.uk

4. BRITISH PSYCHOLOGICAL SOCIETY

St Andrews House, 48 Princess Road East, Leicester, LE1 7DR
Tel: 0116 254 9568 Fax: 0116 227 1314
Email: enquiries@bps.org.uk
Website: www.bps.org.uk

5. CENTRAL ARBITRATION COMMITTEE
Fleetbank House, 2–6 Salisbury Square, London, EC4Y 8JX
Tel: 0330 109 3610
Email: enquiries@cac.gov.uk
Website: www.gov.uk/government/organisations/central-arbitration-committee

6. CHARTERED INSTITUTE OF PERSONNEL AND DEVELOPMENT
151 The Broadway, Wimbledon, London, SW19 1JQ
Tel: 020 8612 6200
Central London Office: Fourth Floor, 46 Grosvenor Gardens, London SW1W 0EB
Tel: 020 7259 8030
Website: www.cipd.co.uk

7. CERTIFICATION OFFICER
Lower Ground Floor, Fleetbank House, 2–6 Salisbury Square, London, EC4Y 8JX
Tel: 0330 109 3602
Email: info@certoffice.org
Website: www.gov.uk/government/organisations/certification-officer

8. CITIZENS ADVICE
Head Office: 3rd Floor North, 200 Aldersgate Steet, London, EC1A 4HD
Tel: 03000 231 231 (admin only no advice available on this number)
National Advice Line (England): 03444 111 444
Website: www.citizensadvice.org.uk
Contact details for regional offices and local advice bureaux are available on the website.
Wales
Citizens Advice Cymru, Cardiff Field Office: 4th Floor, Trafalgar House, 5 Fitsalan Place, Cardiff, CF24 0ED.
Adviceline, Wales: 03444 77 20 20

9. CITIZENS ADVICE SCOTLAND
Spectrum House, 2 Powderhall Road, Edinburgh EH7 4GB
Tel: 0131 550 1000 Fax: 0131 550 1001
Citizens Advice Direct: 0808 800 9060
Email: info@cas.org.uk
Website: www.cas.org.uk
Contact details for local advice bureaux are available on the website.

10. DEPARTMENT FOR BUSINESS, ENERGY & INDUSTRIAL STRATEGY (BEIS) EMPLOYMENT MATTERS
General enquiries
1 Victoria Street, London, SW1H 0ET
Tel: 020 7215 5000
Email: enquiries@beis.gov.uk
Website: www.gov.uk/government/organisations/department-for-business-energy-and-industrial-strategy

11. DISCLOSURE AND BARRING SERVICE
(*formerly the CRIMINAL RECORDS BUREAU*)
The Criminal Records Bureau has been replaced by the Disclosure and Barring Service
DBS customer services, PO Box 3961, Royal Wootton Bassett, SN4 4HF
Telephone: 0300 0200 190 Minicom: 0300 0200 192
Email: customerservices@dbs.gov.uk
DBS certificate disputes: PO Box 165, Liverpool, L69 3JD
DBS sensitive applications: Sensitive applications team, Customer services, PO Box 165, Liverpool, L69 3JD
Email: sensitive@dbs.gov.uk
Website: www.gov.uk/government/organisations/disclosure-and-barring-service

12. DISCLOSURE SCOTLAND
PO Box 250, Glasgow, G51 1YU
Tel: 03000 2000 40 Fax: 03000 2000 50
Email: info@disclosurescotland.gov.uk
Website: www.mygov.scot/organisations/disclosure-scotland/

13. EMPLOYMENT APPEAL TRIBUNAL
England & Wales
5th Floor, Rolls Building, 7 Rolls Buildings, Fetter Lane, London EC4A 1NL
Tel: 020 7273 1041 Fax: 01264 785 028
Email: londoneat@justice.gov.uk
Website: www.gov.uk/courts-tribunals/employment-appeal-tribunal

Scotland
George House, 126 George Street, Edinburgh EH2 4HH
Tel: 0131 225 3963 Fax: 01264 785 030
Email: edinburgheat@justice.gov.uk

14. EMPLOYMENT LAWYERS ASSOCIATION

PO Box 1609, High Wycombe HP11 9NG
Tel: 01895 256972
Website: www.elaweb.org.uk

15. EMPLOYMENT TRIBUNALS

NOTE: the Employment Tribunals Service has, since 1 April 2011, been part of the HM Courts and Tribunals Service, an executive agency of the Ministry of Justice. This section contains the contact details for employment tribunals. Location and contact details for hearing centres not listed below (and not permanently staffed) may be obtained at www.gov.uk/guidance/employment-tribunal-offices-and-venues.

The information below is as it appeared on the Employment Tribunals website on 15 May 2019; users are advised to check before contacting local offices listed below as showing an email address ending '@hmcts.gsi.gov.uk' whether this has changed to '@justice.gov.uk'.

Employment Tribunals Service
England & Wales
Employment Tribunal Customer Contact Centre, PO Box 10218, Leicester, LE1 8EG
Tel: 0300 123 1024 Textphone: 18001 0300 123 1024
Scotland
Employment Tribunal Customer Contact Centre, PO Box 27105, Glasgow, G2 9JR
Tel: 0300 790 6234 Textphone: 18001 0300 790 6234
Website: www.gov.uk/employment-tribunals

Postal addresses for claim forms and applications for fee remission

Employment Tribunal Central Office (England and Wales) PO Box 10218, Leicester, LE1 8EG

Employment Tribunals Central Office Scotland, PO Box 27105, Glasgow, G2 9JR

Employment Tribunals Offices in England, Wales and Scotland

Note: in addition to the venues listed below, the Employment Tribunal may hold sittings at the following venues: Brighton, Burnley, Carmarthen, Dumfries, Fort William, Havant, Haverfordwest, Kirkwall, Lerwick, Lochmaddy, Mold, Pontypridd, Portree, Prestatyn, Stornaway, Taunton, Truro, Wrexham. Details of locations are provided to the parties if a case is allocated to nay of these locations.

Aberdeen **Office and hearing venue**
Ground floor, AB1, 48 Huntly Street, Aberdeen, AB10 1SH
Tel: 01224 593137 Fax: 0870 761 7766 DX AB77 Aberdeen
Email: aberdeenet@hmcts.gsi.gov.uk

Ashford **Hearing venue only**
1st Floor, Ashford House, County Square Shopping Centre, Ashford, Kent, TN23 1YB
Contact the London South Office (*for details see below*)

Birmingham See Midlands, West.

Boston **Hearing venue only**
55 Norfolk Street, Boston, PE21 6PE
Contact the Midlands East Office (*for details see below*)

Bristol **Office and hearing venue**
Bristol Civil and Family Justice Centre
2 Redcliff Street, Bristol, BS1 6GR
Tel: 0117 929 8261 Fax: 0870 739 4009
Email: bristolet@hmcts.gsi.gov.uk

Bury St Edmunds **Hearing venue only**
Triton House, St Andrews Street North, Bury St Edmunds, Suffolk, IP33 1TR
Contact the Watford Office (*for details see below*)

Cambridge **Hearing venue only**
197 East Road
Cambridge
CB1 1BA
Contact the Watford Office (*for details see below*).

Cardiff **Office and hearing venue**
Fitzalan Place, Cardiff, South Wales, CF24 0RZ
Tel: 029 2067 8100 Fax: 0870 761 7635 DX 743942 Cardiff 38
Email: cardiffet@justice.gov.uk

Carlisle **Hearing venue only**
Rickergate, Carlisle, Cumbria, CA3 8QH
Contact the Manchester Office (*for details see below*)

Dundee **Office and hearing venue**
Ground Floor, Caledonian House, Greenmarket, Dundee, DD1 4QB
Tel: 01382 221 578 Fax: 01382 227 136 DX DD51 Dundee
Email: dundeeet@justice.gov.uk

Edinburgh **Office and hearing venue**
54–56 Melville Street, Edinburgh, EH3 7HF
(Correspondence address: Eagle Building, 215 Bothwell Street, Glasgow, G2 7TS)
Tel: 0131 226 5584 Fax: 0131 220 6847 DX ED147 Edinburgh
Email: edinburghet@justice.gov.uk

Exeter **Hearing venue only**
2nd Floor, Keble House, Southernhay Gardens, Exeter, EX1 1NT
Contact the Bristol Office (*for details see above*)

Glasgow **Office and hearing venue**
Eagle Building, 215 Bothwell Street, Glasgow, G2 7TS
Tel: 0141 204 0730 Fax: 01264 785 177 DX 580003 Glasgow 17
Email: glasgowet@justice.gov.uk

Inverness **Hearing venue only**
2nd Floor, 2 Baron Taylor Street, Inverness, IV1 1QL
Contact the Glasgow Office (*for details see above*)

Leeds **Office and hearing venue**
4th Floor, City Exchange, 11 Albion Street, Leeds, LS1 5ES
Tel: 0113 245 9741 Fax: 0113 242 8843 DX 742940 Leeds 75
Email: leedset@hmcts.gsi.gov.uk

Leicester **Hearing venue only**
Kings Court, 5a New Walk, Leicester, LE1 6TE
Contact the Midlands East Office (*for details see below*)

Lincoln **Hearing venue only**
The Court House, 358 High Street, Lincoln, LN5 7QA
Contact the Midlands East Office (*for details see below*)

Liverpool **Hearing venue only**
35 Vernon Street, Liverpool L2 2BX
Liverpool Civil and Family Court Hearing Centre
Contact the Manchester Office (*for details see below*)

London Central **Office and hearing venue**
Victory House, 30–34 Kingsway, London, WC2B 6EX
Tel: 020 7273 8603 Fax: 01264 785 100 DX 141420 Bloomsbury
Email: londoncentralet@hmcts.gsi.gov.uk

London, East **Office and hearing venue**
2nd Floor, Import Building, 2 Clove Crescent, London, E14 2BE
Tel: 020 7538 6161 Fax: 0870 0324 0200
Email: eastlondon@justice.gov.uk

London, South **Office and hearing venue**
Montague Court, 101 London Road, West Croydon, CR0 2RF
Tel: 020 8667 9131 Fax: 0870 324 0174 DX 155061 Croydon 39
Email: londonsouthet@justice.gov.uk

Manchester **Office and hearing venue**
Alexandra House, 14–22 The Parsonage, Manchester M3, 2JA
Tel: 0161 833 6100 Fax: 0870 739 4433 DX 743570 Manchester 66
Email: manchesteret@justice.gov.uk

Midlands, East
Office only:
Carrington Street, Nottingham, NG2 1EE
Tel: 0115 947 5701 Fax: 01264 785 076 DX 719030 Nottingham 32
Email: midlandseastet@justice.gov.uk
Hearing venue
50 Carrington Street, Nottingham NG1 7FG

Midlands, West **Office and hearing venue**
Centre City Tower, 13th Floor, 5–7 Hill Street, Birmingham, B5 4UU
Tel: 0121 600 7780 Fax: 01264 347 999
Email: midlandswestet@justice.gov.uk

Newcastle **Office and hearing venue**
Kings Court, Earl Grey Way, Royal Quay, North Shields, Tyne and Wear, NE29 6AR
Tel: 0191 260 6900 Fax: 0870 739 4206 DX 65137 North Shields 2
Email: newcastleet@hmcts.gsi.gov.uk

Norwich **Hearing venue only**
Bishopgate, Norwich, Norfolk, NR3 1UP
Contact the Watford Office (*for details see above*)

Reading **Hearing venue only**
2nd Floor, 30–31 Friar Street, Reading, RG1 1DX
Contact the Watford Office (*see below for details*).

Sheffield **Hearing venue only**
The Law Courts, 50 West Bar, Sheffield, S3 8PH
Contact the Leeds Office (*see above for details*).

Southampton **Hearing venue only**
Southampton Courthouse, 100 The Avenue, Southampton, Hampshire, SO17 1EY
Contact the Bristol office (*see above for details*).

Teesside **Hearing venue only**
Teesside Magistrates' Court and Family Court Hearing Centre
Victoria Square, Middlesbrough, Cleveland, TS1 2AS
Contact the Newcastle Office (*see above for details*).

Telford **Hearing venue only**
Telford Justice Centre
Telford Square, Malinsgate, Telford, Shropshire, TF3 4HX
Contact the Midlands West Office (*see above for details*).

Watford **Office and hearing venue**
3rd Floor, Radius House, 51 Clarendon Road, Watford, WD17 1HP
Tel: 01923 281 750 Fax: 0870 324 0174 DX 155650 Watford 3
Email: watfordet@justice.gov.uk

Public Register of ET judgments

England & Wales
Judgment Register, Triton House, St Andrew Street (N), Bury St Edmunds, IP33 1TR
Tel: 01284 762171 DX 310501 Bury St Edmunds 10

Scotland
Central Office of Employment Tribunals (Scotland), Eagle Building, 215 Bothwell Street, Glasgow, G2 7TS
Tel: 0141 204 0730 Fax: 0141 204 0732
Email: glasgowet@justice.gov.uk

All judgments of employment tribunals are now published on the gov.uk website at www.gov.uk/employment-tribunal-decisions, and at www.bailii.org/ (which has a more useful search facility). Contact the addresses above for copies of decisions promulgated before February 2017.

President of Employment Tribunals

England & Wales
Victory House, 30–34 Kingsway, London, WC2B 6EX

Scotland
Eagle Building, 215 Bothwell Street, Glasgow, G2 7TS

16. EQUALITY AND HUMAN RIGHTS COMMISSION

NOTE: successor to the Equal Opportunities Commission, the Commission for Racial Equality, and the Disability Rights Commission.

Website: www.equalityhumanrights.com

Equality Advisory Support Service (EASS) (*formerly the Equality and Human Rights Commission Helpline*)

Tel: 0808 800 0082
Textphone: 0808 800 0084
Website: www.equalityadvisoryservice.com
Post: FREEPOST EASS HELPLINE FPN6521

Equality and Human Rights Commission Offices in England, Wales and Scotland

London
Fleetbank House, 2–6 Salisbury Square, London EC4Y 8JX
Tel: 0207 832 7800 Fax: 020 7832 7801

Manchester
Arndale House, The Arndale Centre, Manchester, M4 3AQ
Tel: 0161 829 8100 Fax: 0161 829 8110

Cardiff
Block 1, Spur D, Government Buildings, St Agnes Rd, Gabalfa, Cardiff CF14 4YJ
Tel: 02920 447710 Fax: 02920 447712
Email: wales@equalityhumanrights.com

Glasgow
151 West George Street, Glasgow G2 2JJ
Tel: 0141 228 5910
Email: scotland@equalityhumanrights.com

17. FREE REPRESENTATION UNIT
London Office
5th Floor Kingsbourne House, 229–231 High Holborn, London, WC1V 7DA
Tel: 020 7611 9555
Nottingham Office
Nottingham Law School Legal Advice Clinic, Chaucer Building, Chaucer Street, Nottingham, NG1 5LP
Tel: 0115 848 4262
nls.legaladvicecentre@ntu.ac.uk
Website: www.thefru.org.uk

18. HEALTH AND SAFETY EXECUTIVE
HSE Head Office
Redgrave Court, Merton Road, Bootle, Merseyside, L20 7HS
Tel: 0151 951 4000; 0300 003 1747 (advisory team); 0345 300 9923 (incident reporting)
Website: www.hse.gov.uk
For details of London & regional offices and specialist divisions see www.hse.gov.uk/contact/maps/index.htm

19. INFORMATION COMMISSIONER
Information Commissioner's Office
Wycliffe House, Water Lane, Wilmslow, Cheshire, SK9 5AF
Helpline: 0303 123 1113 (or 01625 545745)
Textphone: 01625 545860
Email (First contact team): casework@ico.org.uk
Website: www.ico.org.uk

Scotland
Information Commissioner's Office
45 Melville Street, Edinburgh, EH3 7HL
Tel: 0303 123 1115
Email: scotland@ico.org.uk

Wales
Information Commissioner's Office
2nd Floor, Churchill House, Churchill Way, Cardiff, CF10 2HH
Tel: 0330 414 6421
Email: wales@ico.org.uk

20. THE LAW SOCIETY
Website: www.lawsociety.org.uk
England
The Law Society's Hall, 113 Chancery Lane, London, WC2A 1PL
Tel: 020 7242 1222
Fax: 020 7831 0344
DX 56 London Chancery Lane

Wales
The Law Society, Wales Office, Capital Tower, Greyfriars Road, Cardiff, CF10 3AG
Tel: 029 2064 5254
Fax: 29 2022 5944
DX 33080 Cardiff
Email: wales@lawsociety.org.uk

21. LAW SOCIETY OF SCOTLAND
Atria One, 144 Morrison St, Edinburgh, EH3 8EX
Tel: 0131 226 7411 Fax: 0131 225 2934
Textphone: 0131 476 8359
DX ED 1, Edinburgh
Email: lawscot@lawscot.org.uk
Website: www.lawscot.org.uk

22. PENSIONS OMBUDSMAN
10 South Colonnade, Canary Wharf E14 4PU
Tel: 0800 917 4487
Email: enquiries@pensions-ombudsman.org.uk

Website: www.pensions-ombudsman.org.uk

23. PENSIONS REGULATOR
Website: www.thepensionsregulator.gov.uk
Pension scheme regulation enquiries
Napier House, Trafalgar Square, Brighton, BN1 4DW
Tel: 0345 600 0707
Email: customersupport@tpr.gov.uk

Automatic enrolment enquiries
PO Box 16871, Birmingham, B23 3LG
Tel: 0345 600 1011
Email: customersupport@autoenrol.tpr.gov.uk

Levy, scheme return or exchange enquiries
Napier House, Trafalgar Place, Brighton, BN1 4DW
Tel: 0345 600 5666
Email: exchange@tpr.gov.uk

24. TPAS (THE PENSIONS ADVISORY SERVICE)
The Pensions Advisory Service, 11 Belgrave Road, London, SW1V 1RB
Tel: 0800 011 3797
Website: www.pensionsadvisoryservice.org.uk

25. TSO (THE STATIONERY OFFICE)
For general order and customer service enquiries:
Tel: 0333 202 5070
Email: customer.services@tso.co.uk
Website: www.tsoshop.co.uk

26. TRADES UNION CONGRESS
Congress House, Great Russell Street, London, WC1B 3LS
Tel: 020 7636 4030
Email: info@tuc.org.uk
Website: www.tuc.org.uk

27. UK VISAS AND IMMIGRATION
NOTE: The UK Border Agency (UKBA) has been replaced by UK Visas and Immigration (UKVI) and the Border Force.
Lunar House, 40 Wellesley Road, Croydon, CR9 2BY
Tel: 0870 606 7766; 0870 241 0645; 0300 123 2241
Email: ukbanationalityenquiries@ukba.gsi.gov.uk
Website: www.gov.uk/government/organisations/uk-visas-and-immigration

Index

A

B

I

U